The Classic Series

The Classic
French Dictionary

FRENCH-ENGLISH
and
ENGLISH-FRENCH

Revised with Preface by
ANTONIO J. PROVOST
Officer d 'Académie

Diplomé de 1 'Enseignement Supérieur (University of Dijon) Head
Modern Languages Department at University of Notre Dame.

FOLLETT PUBLISHING COMPANY
CHICAGO   ILLINOIS
1962

PREFACE

The student who is without a sufficiently comprehensive dictionary of the language which he is seeking to acquire, is, indeed, in no better position than the workman without proper tools. The better the artisan the better the tools he requires.

The reason for this work is found in the demand of the better students for a dictionary which they can use as an efficient vade mecum. It is not too bulky to be carried along with ordinary class books, and so it can be used at any time and place. And the time to make use of any book to the best advantage is when the question arises and the mind is in a receptive mood for an answer.

Within this portable volume the student will find not only all the words for which he will look, but he will especially benefit by a very complete list of word groups showing idiomatic uses, following the direct translation of the given word. The use of this work will help one avoid the difficulty of the student whose French teacher, in the city of Paris, returned to him a lengthy written exercise without a single correction appearing on it. When the teacher was asked whether no grammatical error could be detected in the exercise, he was obliged to qualify his negative answer by the words: "—but it is not French."

A thorough examination of this dictionary will indicate that every effort has been made to compile a work which will include, within proper limits, all words admitted by the French Academy to the present time.

In addition, many words that may be considered obsolete have been retained in order to help the student who will find such words in the older writings. And because he must know current usage when translating from English to French, those obsolete words are prefixed with the following sign: ⊙

Supplementing the two general vocabularies will be found five valuable appendices. Those on French pronunciation, Irregular and Defective Verbs, and Nouns of Double Gender will give exceptional aid.

Nothing has been spared by the publishers to make the book both attractive and of easy access. The index will instantly give one the proper letter, and the bold faced type will facilitate the finding of the word.

In making the present revision of the Classic French Dictionary, we have been careful to benefit by the suggestions found in the latest and the best English as well as French dictionaries, and have endeavored to associate the two languages in such manner as to give a concise and adequate understanding of the genius of each.

While we are not so presumptuous as to promise a perfect book, we are nevertheless confident of presenting a product that will be appreciated for its practical qualities.

University of Notre Dame
May 1, 1927

Antonio J. Provost
Officier d'Académie.

ON FRENCH PRONUNCIATION.

NOTE.—The rules given below must be considered as general. Some are subject to more or less exceptions, which, for the sake of brevity, have not been mentioned, but they will all be found clearly and fully noticed in their respective places.

ALPHABET.

French Alphabet.	Old French Pronunciation.	Approximate English Pronunciation.	Modern French Pronunciation.	Approximate English Pronunciation.
A a	a	ah	a	ah
B b	bé	bay	be	bu-t
C c	cé	say	ce	su-m
D d	dé	day	de	du-ll
E e	é	a	e	u-p
F f	èff	eff	fe	fu-n
G g	jé	zhay	ge	zhu-t
H h	ash	ash	he	hu-g
I i	i	ee	i	ee-l
J j	ji	zhee	je	zhu-g
K k	k	kah	ke	cu-t
L l	èl	el	le	lu-ck
M m	èmm	em	me	mu-d
N n	ènn	en	ne	nu-t
O o	o	o	o	o-ld
P p	pé	pay	pe	pu-n
Q q	qu	ku	ke	cu-rl
R r	èr	air	re	ru-st
S s	èss	ess	se	su-n
T t	té	tay	te	tu-b
U u	u	u	u	u
V v	vé	vay	ve	vu-lgar
X x	iks	eeks	kse	ksu
Y y	i grec	ee grèk	y	y-ore
Z z	zed	zed	ze	zu

FRENCH SOUNDS.

The Simple, or Vowel sounds, in the French language, are as follows:

French.		English.		French.
a sounded like	a	in *bat*, exemplified by		*mal*.
â	...	a	...*bar* ...	*âge*.
e	...	u	...*sun* ...	{ *me*. { *je*.
è	...	e	...*met* ...	*père*.
é	...	ai	...*air* ...	*été*.
ê	...	e	...*there* ...	*tête*.

French.		English.		French.
i sounded like	i	in *pin* exemplified by		*pique*.
î	...	ie	...*field* ...	*gîte*.
o	...	o	...*rob* ...	*mol*.
ô	...	o	...*no* ...	*môle*.
u no equivalent in English...				*suc*.
û	...	...	...	*sûre*.
eû sounded like	e	in *her* (but longer and deeper.)		*jeûne*.
ou	...	oo	...*root* ...	*goutte*.
où	...	oo	...*noose* ...	*voûte*.
an no equivalent in English				*tan*.
in	...	...	...	*fin*.
on	...	...	...	*bon*.
un	...	...	...	*brun*.

Y, when alone, or when preceded or followed by a consonant, is pronounced like an *i*; except in *pays, poysan, paysage*. When placed between two vowels, it performs the office of two *i's*, and is always preceded by *a, e, o*, or *u*. When preceded by *a* or *e*, it unites its first *i* with this vowel, and sounds *è*, as in *rayon*, which is pronounced *rè-ion*; when preceded by *o*, its first *i* is sounded in conjunction with *o*, like *wa* in the English word *wag*, as in *joyeux*, which is pronounced *joa-ieû*; and when preceded by *u*, its own two *i's* preserve their natural sound, as in *appuyer*, which is pronounced *appui-ié*.

A is long in the termination *aille*, except in *médaille, je travaille, détaille, émaille, baille* (I give.) It is also long in *ation*, as, *nation, admiration, oblation*; pronounce, therefore, *paille, limaille, canaille, nation, admiration, oblation*, &c.

In the terminations of the imperfect of the subjunctive of verbs of the first conjugation, the *a* is always short; as, *que je parlasse, que je donnasse*.

DIPHTHONGS.

The number of French Diphthongs is differently stated by different grammarians. The following table of them is perhaps the most exact:—

eoi	exemplified in	*villageois.*
ia	... ...	*verbiage.*
iai	... ...	*biais.*
ié	... ...	*marié.*
iè	... ...	*fièvre.*
oe	... ...	*moelle.*
oi	... ...	*loi.*
oin	... ...	*soin.*
ouai	... ...	*ouais.*
ouin	... ...	*baragouin.*
io	... ...	*idiot.*
ien	... ...	*bien.*
ian	... ...	*confiant.*
iau	... ...	*miauler.*
ient	... ...	*patient.*
ieu	... ...	*lieu.*
ion	... ...	*pion.*
iou	... ...	*chiourme.*
oua	... ...	*loua.*
ouan	... ...	*louange.*
oue	... ...	*ouest.*
oui	... ...	*Louis.*
ua	... ...	*nuage.*
ue	... ...	*manuel.*
ui	... ...	*lui.*
uin	... ...	*juin.*

The final *é, i,* and *u,* become longer when they are followed by the unaccented *e,* which is always mute, as in *tirée, finie, vue.*

It must, however, be observed, that the diphthong *iè* does not sound in *fièvre* as it does in *bière*; for the *r* has the property of opening every vowel that precedes it, except the *a.* It must therefore be pronounced more open in *bière* than in *fièvre.* For the same reason, *eu, i, o, u,* are more open in *beurre, fuir, aurore,* and *mur,* than in *jeune, fini, mot, but.* The *a,* however, becomes also very broad when the *r* is doubled, as in *barre, bizarre.*

COMPOUND VOWELS.

The compound vowels are: *ai, ay, ei, ey, er, ez, ed, egs, es, et, au, eau, eu, œu, uei, oi, oy, oe, oê,* and *ou.*

Ai, ay, ei, ey are pronounced *è* when initial or final, when preceding a mute syllable, and silent or sounded final consonants and vowels: *e.g., aime, air, je parlais, je danserais, il finirait, elles vendraient, étai, laie, aynet, reine, Sidney, Paraguay.*

In the past tense and in the future of verbs, however, *ai* final is sounded *é*: *je dansai, je sortirai;* also when initial before any but a mute syllable: *aimable, aisance;* and when medial before *é,* or *er*: *traité, baiser.*

When *i* is preceded by *é,* both are sounded separately: *ré-itéré.*

Er, ez, ed, sound like *é*: *papier, assez, pied, il s'assied.*

Egs is sounded *è;* it is only found in one word, viz., *legs,* a legacy.

Es, et, are sounded *è*: *les, mes, des, ces, tu es, volet, sujet.*

The conjunction *et,* is sounded *é;* and its final *t* is *never* pronounced.

Est (is) is sounded *è;* and its final *t* is *always* pronounced with the word which follows when the latter begins with a vowel; *il est à Paris* should, for instance, be sounded as if spelled: *il è ta Paris.*

Au, eau, are sounded like *o*: *autre, mauvais, bateau.*

When *au* is preceded by *é,* both are sounded separately: *flé-au, ypré-au.*

Eu, œu, uei, are sounded like *e* in *her*: *seul, heure, orgueil, cueillir*; but *eû* and *eu* when final, are sounded longer and deeper: *jeûne, jeûner, feu, jeu.*

When *u* is preceded by *é,* both are sounded separately: *ré-ussir, ré-ussite.*

In the past participle, the past indicative and the imperfect subjunctive of *avoir* (to have) *eu* is sounded like a French *u.*

Oi, oy, oe, oê, are sounded as *wa* in *wag: loi, poire, joie, joyeux, loyal, moelle, poêle.*

In *fouet, fouetter,* as well as in *couenne, couenneux, couennouse, oue* is sounded like *oi* (see § above).

Ou is sounded as *oo* in *root: pour, fou, vous, toux.*

Oin, ouin, are a combination of the sound *ou* (§ above), and the nasal sound *in.*

NASAL SOUNDS.

The nasal syllables are: *aim, ain, am, an, aon; ean, eim, ein, em, en, eon, eun; im, in; om, on; um, un; ym.*

Am, an, ean, are pronounced like *an,* without exception; as *ambition, vendant, songeant. Em* and *en* are also pronounced like *an,* as in *emploi, empire, envie;* but not always. In words derived from foreign languages, they are pronounced like *ème, ène;* as *Jerusalem, hymen.* In words terminating in *en* or *ein,* and in their derivatives, *en* is pronounced like *in*: as *mien, Chrétien, Chrétienté;* and inthe verbs *tenir, venir,* and their derivatives, *en* is sounded like *in;* as *tiens, viens.*

In *femme, em* is pronounced like *am.*

The preceding examples must therefore be pronounced like *anbition, vandant; anploi, anpire, anvie; Jérusalème, hymène; mi-in, Chréti-in, Chréti-inté; ti-in, vi-in; famme.*

Im, in, aim, ain, ein, are all pronounced like *in.* The *i,* however, keeps its natural sound in words taken from foreign languages, as in *Sélim, Éphraim,* which are pronounced as if the *m* were followed by a silent *e;* in all words in which *in* is followed by a vowel; as *in-animé, in-octavo, in-odore, in-humain;* and in the beginning of words commencing with *imm* and *inn.*

Om, on, are pronounced like *on;* as in *pont, tombe; complet, donjon. Automne* is pronounced *ôtonn.*

Aen, aon, ean are sounded *an* in the following words: *Caen, Laon, taon, faon, paon, Jean.*

Eon is sounded *on* when following *g: mangeons, plongeon.*

Um, un, eun, are pronounced like *un;* as in *parfum, importun, à jeun.*

Un is, however, sounded *on* in a few words of foreign origin: *punch, de profundis.*

Um is pronounced like *ome* in words of Latin origin, as *duumvir, triumvir; factum, factotum.*

No nasal pronunciation occurs before a vowel, or a double consonant: *âme, anonyme, vaine, annotation, peine, une; parfume, cretonne, pomme.*

CONSONANTS.

B has the same sound as in English; as *bal,* ball. It is pronounced in the middle and at the end of words.

C has the sound of *k* before *a, o, u, l, n, r,* except when it has a cedilla under it, in which case it is pronounced like *s,* as *reçu.* It is also pronounced like *s* before *e, i,* and *y. Ch* has the sound of *sh,* except when it is followed by a consonant, in which case it is pronounced like *k;* as in *chronologie.*

D has the same sound as in English. It is sounded in the middle of words, as in *adverbe.* When it is final, and carried to the following word, it sounds like *t,* as in *grand homme,* which is pronounced *gran-tomme.*

F is pronounced like the same letter in English, as in *fleur,* flower. It is sounded at the end of words: but in *neuf* it is pronounced like *v* when followed by a word beginning with a vowel or *h* mute,

as in *neuf enfants,* which words are pronounced *neu-van-fan.*

G has the hard sound of *g* in the English word *go,* before *a, o, u, l, m, r,* as in *gomme, gris;* gum, gray. But it has always the soft sound of *s* as in *pleasure* before *e, i, y,* as in *génie, gîte.*

When combined with *n* in the middle of words, it has a liquid sound, somewhat similar to that of *ni* in the English word onion, as *régner, saigner, agneau, compagnon,* &c. Every word in which this sound occurs is preceded by a star (*) throughout this work. Whenever *gn* is not liquid, it sounds as in the English word ignorant.

H is sounded with a guttural impulse, when aspirated, as in *héros,* hero. When mute, it has no use but that of showing the etymology of the word, as in *honneur,* honour. It is always silent after *t,* as in *méthode, arithmétique,* which are pronounced *métod, a-rit-mé-tik.* The aspirated *h* is marked throughout this work with a dagger (†).

J has always the sound of *s* in *pleasure,* and is subject to no irregularity.

K has always a hard sound, as in the English word *king,* and is subject to no irregularity.

L has two sounds. The first is precisely the same as *l* in the English word lily. The second is liquid. The liquid *l,* whether double or single, is always preceded by *i.* It is similar to the sound of the last *i* in William.

It is to be remarked, that *i,* followed by *l* or *ll,* and preceded by another vowel, is always silent in pronunciation; it only serves to indicate the liquid sound of the *l,* as in *paille, soleil, patrouille,* which ought to be pronounced *pá-i, solé-i, patrou-i.* But when *i* is not preceded by another vowel, as in *fille,* it retains its natural sound, and serves at the same time to indicate the liquid sound of *l.* And here in *fille,* pronounced *fi-i,* we find both the *i* natural, and the *i* which stands for *ll.*

Whenever *i* begins a word, as in *illusion,* the *l*'s are never liquid. The liquid *l* is marked throughout this work with a star (*).

M has the sound of the same letter in English, as in *monnaie,* money.

N is sounded like the same letter in English, as in *nègre,* negro.

P has the sound of the same letter in English, as in *peine,* pain. When combined with *h,* it has the sound of *f,* as in *philosophe,* philosopher.

Q has the hard sound of *k*, as in the English word *quaker*. Whether initial or medial, *q* is always followed by *u*, which is not sounded except in a few words that are noticed in the course of this work.

R has the same sound as in English, but is articulated much more strongly, as in *rivière*, river. It is always sounded at the end of words, when preceded by the vowels, *a, i, o, u*. In substantives, adjectives, and verbs ending in *er*, it is silent, unless it is followed by a word beginning with a vowel or *h* mute, as in *dernier ouvrage*, which is pronounced *dernié-rouvraj*.

S has two sounds. The first is hissing, as in the English word *sister* ; the second is soft, as in the English word *please*. It has uniformly the hissing sound at the beginning of words, and the soft between two vowels. Both sounds occur in *saison*. It preserves its hissing sound in compound words, as in *parasol, vraisemblable* ; and when it happens to be sounded at the end of words, as in *Pallas, Brutus, vis.* ..

When *s* final is joined to the following word, it is always articulated like *z*, as in *dans un cas important*, which must be pronounced *dän-zun-kä-zin-por-tän*.

T has two sounds ; one hard, as in the English word *tutor*, and the other like the hissing *s*, as in *sister*. Both occur in *situation*, which is pronounced *si-tuä-sion*. It has the hissing sound before *i*, connected with some other following vowel or vowels, as in *patience, factieux*, which are pronounced *pasian-s, fak-sieü*.

When *t*, however, is immediately preceded by *s*, it preserves the hard sound, as in *bastion, question*, which are pronounced *bas-tion, kès-tion*.

In the imperfect indicative and subjunctive of verbs, as *nous partions, vous partiez ; que nous sortions, que vous sortiez*, the *t* is always sounded hard.

V has the same sound as in English, and is subject to no irregularity.

X has generally the sound of *ks*, as in *sexe, boxer ;* sex, to box. In all words beginning with *x* or *ex*, followed by a vowel, it has the sound of *gz*, as in *Xavier, exil*, which are pronounced *gza-vié, èg-zil*. When final, it is joined to the following word, and sounds like *z*, as in *beaux yeux, dix hommes*, which are pronounced *bô-zieü, di-zom*. X has the sound of *ss* in *Auxerre, Auxonne* and *Bruxelles*

Z has the sound of *z* in *zone*.

FINAL CONSONANTS.

The final consonants that are sounded are *b, c, f, k, l, m, q, r*.

The final consonants that are not sounded in words which stand alone, or terminate a sentence, are, *d, g, h, n, p, r* (in the termination *er* only), *s, t, x, z*.

J and *v* are never final.

Some of those final consonants that are not sounded are subject to many irregularities when followed by words beginning with a vowel or *h* mute.

D is pronounced like *t* when joined to the following word, as in *quand il parle*, which must be pronounced *kän-til parle*.

G is pronounced like *k*, as in *sang impur*, which is pronounced *sän-kin-pur*.

H has no power whatever.

P is only pronounced in *Alep, cap, Gap, cep, jalap ;* and in *beaucoup, trop*, when those two words come before a vowel. In *cep de vigne*, the *p* is silent.

R, preceded by *e*, is frequently silent in conversation before a vowel, but it must always be sounded in poetry, unless it terminates the verse.

S, before a vowel, sounds like *z*, as in *nous avons eu*, which must be pronounced *nou-zavôn-zu*. S is sounded in *aloès, bibus, blocus, chorus, choléra-morbus, dervis, florès, gratis, jadis, laps, maïs, mars, orémus, ours, rébus, relaps, Reims, Rubens, sinus, en sus, vasistas*, etc. It is silent in *Jésus-Christ*, but sounded in *le Christ*.

T is generally pronounced before a vowel, except when it is preceded by a sounded consonant, as in *effort étonnant*. pronounced *é-for-éto-nan ;* in *quatre-vingt-un* it is not pronounced, but it is sounded in *vingt et un*. In all plural nouns, and in the conjunction *et ;* also before a vowel in *fort*, adjective, it is silent, but it is sounded in *fort*, adverb. Final *t* is also sounded in *brut, circonspect, déficit, distinct, dot, mat, exact, fat, granit, gratuit, infect, intact, net, rapt, subit, succinct, tact, toast, transit, zénith*, etc. It is not heard in *Jésus-Christ*, though it is sounded in *le Christ*.

X is invariably pronounced like *z* when connected with the following word.

Z, which is frequently silent in conversation, even before a vowel, is subject to no irregularity when connected with the following word.

TABLE OF IRREGULAR AND DEFECTIVE VERBS.

The Imperfect of the Indicative, the Conditional, the Imperative, and the Imperfect of the Subjunctive, are wanting in this Table. These four tenses are formed as follows :—

The imperfect of the indicative is regularly formed from the present participle by changing *ant* into *ais*, as : *parl-ant, je parl-ais ; finiss-ant, je finiss-ais*, &c.

The conditional has always the same root as the future ; so that the first person of the future being known, it is easy to form the conditional, as : *je parlerai, je parlerai-s ; je finirai, je finirai-s.*

The imperative is always regularly formed from the present of the indicative, by suppressing the pronouns, as: *je parle*, imperative, *parle ;* except in the verbs *avoir, être*, and *savoir*. The third person singular and plural of the imperative are always the same as in the present of the subjunctive, and belong to that tense.

The imperfect of the subjunctive is always regularly formed from the preterit indicative, by adding *se*, etc., to the second person singular, as: *tu parlas, que je parlas-se ; tu finis, que je finis-se ; tu reçus, que je reçus-se ; tu vendis, que je vendis-se.*

FIRST CONJUGATION.

Infinitive.	Present participle.	Past participle.	Present.	Indicative Preterit.	Future.	Subjunctive Present.	English.
Aller	allant	allé	je vais, allons vas, allez va, vont	j'allai	j'irai	aille, allions ailles, alliez aille, aillent	to go.
Envoyer	envoyant	envoyé	j'envoie, envoyons envoies, envoyez envoie, envoient	j'envoyai	j'enverrai	envoie, envoyions envoies, envoyiez envoie, envoient	to send.

SECOND CONJUGATION.

Infinitive.	Present participle.	Past participle.	Present.	Indicative Preterit.	Future.	Subjunctive Present.	English.
Acquérir	acquérant	acquis	j'acquiers, acquérons acquiers, acquérez acquiert, acquièrent	j'acquis	j'acquerrai	acquière, acquérions acquières, acquériez acquière, acquièrent	to acquire.
Assaillir	assaillant	assailli	j'assaille, assaillons assailles, assaillez assaille, assaillent	j'assaillis	j'assaillirai	assaille, assaillions assailles, assailliez assaille, assaillent	to assault.
Avenir[1]	avenant	avenu	il avient	il avint	il aviendra	qu'il avienne	to happen.
Bouillir[2]	bouillant	bouilli	je bous, bouillons bous, bouillez bout, bouillent	je bouillis	je bouillirai	bouille, bouillions bouilles, bouilliez bouille, bouillent	to boil.
Courir	courant	couru	je cours, courons cours, courez court, courent	je courus	je courrai	coure, courions coures, couriez coure, courent	to run.
Cueillir	cueillant	cueilli	je cueille, cueillons cueilles, cueillez cueille, cueillent	je cueillis	je cueillerai	cueille, cueillions cueilles, cueilliez cueille, cueillent	to gather.

---

[1] *Advenir* is more often used.

[2] The verb *faire* is generally used to conjugate this verb ; as, *faire bouillir*, &c.

SECOND CONJUGATION.

Infinitive.	Present participle.	Past participle.	Present.	Indicative Preterit.	Future.	Subjunctive Present.	English.
Défaillir[1]		défailli	nous défaillons vous défaillez ils défaillent	je défaillis ils défaillirent			to faint
Dormir	dormant	dormi	je dors, dormons dors, dormez dort, dorment	je dormis	je dormirai	dorme, dormions dormes, dormiez dorme, dorment	to sleep.
Ébouillir		ébouilli					to boil away.
Faillir[2]	faillant	failli	je faux, faillons faux, faillez faut, faillent	je faillis	je faudrai		to fail.
Férir[3]		féru					to strike.
Fleurir	fleurissant florissant	fleuri	je fleuris, fleurissons fleuris, fleurissez fleurit, fleurissent	je fleuris	je fleurirai	fleurisse, fleurissions fleurisses, fleurissiez fleurisse, fleurissent	to flourish, to prosper.
Fuir	fuyant	fui	je fuis, fuyons fuis, fuyez fuit, fuient	je fuis	je fuirai	fuie, fuyions fuies, fuyiez fuie, fuient	to flee.
Gésir[4]	gisant		gisons gisez gît, gisent				to lie.
Mésavenir			il mésavient	il mésavint		qu'il mésavienne	to succeed ill.
Mourir	mourant	mort	je meurs, mourons meurs, mourez meurt, meurent	je mourus	je mourrai	meure, mourions meures, mouriez meure, meurent	to die.
Ouïr[5]		ouï	j'ois, oyons ois, oyez oit, oient	j'ouïs	j'oirai		to hear.
Ouvrir	ouvrant	ouvert	j'ouvre, ouvrons ouvres, ouvrez ouvre, ouvrent	j'ouvris	j'ouvrirai	ouvre, ouvrions ouvres, ouvriez ouvre, ouvrent	to open.
Quérir[6]							to fetch.
Saillir[7]	saillant	sailli	il saille ils saillent		il saillera ils sailleront	qu'il saille qu'ils saillent	to project.
Sentir	sentant	senti	je sens, sentons sens, sentez sent, sentent	je sentis	je sentirai	sente, sentions sentes, sentiez sente, sentent	to feel, smell.
Servir	servant	servi	je sers, servons sers, servez sert, servent	je servis	je servirai	serve, servions serves, serviez serve, servent	to serve.
Sortir[8]	sortissant	sorti	il sortit ils sortissent		il sortira ils sortiront	qu'il sortisse qu'ils sortissent	to obtain.
Surgir[9]			il surgit ils surgissent	il surgit	il surgira		to land, to arise.
Tenir	tenant	tenu	je tiens, tenons tiens, tenez tient, tiennent	je tins	je tiendrai	tienne, tenions tiennes, teniez tienne, tiennent	to hold.
Vêtir	vêtant	vêtu	je vêts, vêtons vêts, vêtez vêt, vêtent	je vêtis	je vêtirai	vête, vêtions vêtes, vêtiez vête, vêtent	to clothe.

THIRD CONJUGATION.

Infinitive.	Present participle.	Past participle.	Present.	Indicative Preterit.	Future.	Subjunctive Present.	English.
Apparoir[10]			il appert				to appear.
Asseoir	asseyant	assis	j'assieds, asseyons assieds, asseyez assied, asseient	j'assis	j'assiérai or j'asseoirai	asseie, asseyions asseies, asseyiez asseie, asseient	to set.

---

1 The imperfect of the indicative, *je défaillais*, is used.
2 This verb is seldom used but in the preterit, the compound tenses, and in the infinitive after another verb.
3 The infinitive is only used in the phrase, *sans coup férir*, without striking a blow.
4 The imperfect of the indicative, *je gisais*, &c., is used.

5 This verb is seldom used but in the infinitive present, and in the compound tenses.
6 Used only in familiar conversation, and in the infinitive after *aller*, *venir*, *envoyer*.
7 Used only in the third persons. When it means " to gush." it is conjugated like *finir*.
8 Used as a law term only.
9 Seldom used but in the infinitive.
10 Used as a law term only.

THIRD CONJUGATION.

Infinitives.	Present participle.	Past participle.	Present.	Indicative. Preterit.	Future.	Subjunctive Present.	English.
Avoir	ayant	eu	j'ai, avons as, avez a, ont	j'eus	j'aurai	aie, ayons aies, ayez ait, aient	to have.
Choir		chu					to fall.
Comparoir[1]							to appear.
Déchoir[2]		déchu	je déchois, déchoyons déchois, déchoyez déchoit, déchoient	je déchus	je décherrai	déchoie, déchoyions déchoies. déchoyiez déchoie, déchoient	to fall, lose.
Démouvoir							to make one desist.
Échoir[3]	échéant	échu	il échoit or il échet	il échut	il écherra	échoie	to fall due, to expire.
Falloir[4]		fallu	il faut	il fallut	il faudra	qu'il faille	to be necessary.
Mouvoir	mouvant	mu	je meus, mouvons meus, mouvez meut, meuvent	je mus	je mouvrai	meuve, mouvions meuves, mouviez meuve, meuvent	to move.
Pleuvoir	pleuvant	plu	il pleut	il plut	il pleuvra	qu'il pleuve	to rain.
Pourvoir	pourvoyant	pourvu	je pourvois, pourvoyons pourvois, pourvoyez pourvoit, pourvoient	je pourvus	je pourvoirai	pourvoie, pourvoyions pourvoies, pourvoyiez pourvoie, pourvoient	to provide.
Pouvoir	pouvant	pu	[5] je puis, pouvons peux, pouvez peut, peuvent	je pus	je pourrai	puisse, puissions puisses, puissiez puisse, puissent	to be able.
Prévaloir	prévalant	prévalu	je prévaux, prévalons prévaux, prévalez prévaut, prévalent	je prévalus	je prévaudrai	prévale, prévalions prévales, prévaliez prévale, prévalent	to prevail.
Prévoir	prévoyant	prévu	je prévois, prévoyons prévois, prévoyez prévoit, prévoient	je prévis	je prévoirai	prévoie, prévoyions prévoies, prévoyiez prévoie, prévoient	to foresee.
Promouvoir[6]		promu					to promote.
Ravoir[7]							to recover, to have again.
Savoir[8]	sachant	su	je sais, savons sais, savez sait, savent	je sus	je saurai	sache, sachions saches, sachiez sache, sachent	to know.
Seoir[9]	seyant		il sied ils siéent		il siéra ils siéront	qu'il siée qu'ils siéent	to become, to befit.
Seoir[10]	séant	sis					to sit, situate.
Surseoir	sursoyant	sursis	je sursois, sursoyons sursois, sursoyez sursoit, sursoient	je sursis	je surseoirai	sursoie, sursoyions sursoies, sursoyiez sursoie, sursoient	to put off, to suspend.
Valoir[11]	valant	valu	je vaux, valons vaux, valez vaut, valent	je valus	je vaudrai	vaille, valions vailles, valiez vaille, vaillent	to be worth.
Voir	voyant	vu	je vois, voyons vois, voyez voit, voient	je vis	je verrai	voie, voyions voies, voyiez voie, voient	to see.
Vouloir[12]	voulant	voulu	je veux, voulons veux, voulez veut, veulent	je voulus	je voudrai	veuille, voulions veuilles, vouliez veuille, veuillent	to be willing.

1 Used as a law term only.
2 Imperfect of the indicative, je déchoyais, &c.
3 Used generally in the third person only.
4 Il fallait is used. No imperative.
5 Je peux is also used.
6 Only used in the infinitive, in the compound tenses, and in the imperfect of the subjunctive.
7 Used in the infinitive only.
8 Imperative: sache, sachons, sachez. Je ne sache

pas is sometimes used in the first person of the indicative present. The imperfect of the indicative is je savais, &c.
9 Used in the third person only. No compound tenses.
10 Used in the two participles only.
11 No imperative.
12 The second person plural of the imperative is veuillez, please to.

FOURTH CONJUGATION.

Infinitive.	Present participle.	Past participle.	Present.	Indicative Preterit.	Future.	Subjunctive Present.	English.
Absoudre	absolvant	absous, m. absoute, f.	j'absous, absolvons absous, absolvez absout, absolvent		j'absoudrai	absolve, absolvions absolves, absolviez absolve, absolvent	to absolve.
Abstraire	abstrayant	abstrait	j'abstrais, abstrayons abstrais, abstrayez abstrait, abstraient		j'abstrairai	abstraie, abstrayions abstraies, abstrayiez abstraie, abstraient	to abstract.
Accroire[1]							to make one believe.
Battre	battant	battu	je bats, battons bats, battez bat, battent	je battis	je battrai	batte, battions battes, battiez batte, battent	to beat.
Boire	buvant	bu	je bois, buvons bois, buvez boit, boivent	je bus	je boirai	boive, buvions boives, buviez boive, boivent	to drink.
Braire			il brait ils braient		il braira ils braï ront		to bray.
Bruire[2]	bruyant						to roar, to rustle.
Circoncire	circoncisant	circoncis	je circoncis, circoncisons circoncis, circoncisez circoncit, circoncisent	je circoncis	je circoncirai	circoncise, circoncisions circoncises, circoncisiez circoncise, circoncisent	to circumcise.
Clore[3]		clos	je clos clos clôt		je clorai		to close.
Conclure	concluant	conclu	je conclus, concluons conclus, concluez conclut, concluent	je conclus	je conclurai	conclue, concluions conclues, concluiez conclue, concluent	to conclude.
Confire	confisant	confit	je confis, confisons confis, confisez confit, confisent	je confis	je confirai	confise, confisions confises, confisiez confise, confisent	to pickle, preserve.
Coudre	cousant	cousu	je couds, cousons couds, cousez coud, cousent	je cousis	je coudrai	couse, cousions couses, cousiez couse, cousent	to sew.
Croire	croyant	cru	je crois, croyons crois, croyez croit, croient	je crus	je croirai	croie, croyions croies, croyiez croie, croient	to believe.
Croître	croissant	crû	je crois, croissons crois, croissez croit, croissent	je crûs	je croîtrai	croisse, croissions croisses, croissiez croisse, croissent	to grow.
Déconfire		déconfit					to discomfit.
Dire	disant	dit	je dis, disons dis, dites dit, disent	je dis	je dirai	dise, disions dises, disiez dise, disent	to say.
Éclore		éclos	il éclôt ils éclosent		il éclora ils écloront	qu'il éclose qu'ils éclosent	to hatch, to blow.
Écrire	écrivant	écrit	j'écris, écrivons écris, écrivez écrit, écrivent	j'écrivis	j'écrirai	écrive, écrivions écrives, écriviez écrive, écrivent	to write.
s'Emboire[4]		embu					to imbibe.
s'Ensuivre	ensuivant	ensuivi	il s'ensuit ils s'ensuivent	il s'ensuivit ils s'ensuivirent	il s'ensuivra ils s'ensuivront	qu'il s'ensuive qu'ils s'ensuivent	to follow, to result.
s'Eprendre		épris					to be smitten.
Être	étant	été	je suis, sommes es, êtes est, sont	je fus	je serai	sois, soyons sois, soyez soit, soient	to be.

---

[1] Used only in the infinitive, and always with the verb *faire*.
[2] Imperfect of the indicative *il bruyait, ils bruyaient.*

[3] Used in all the compound tenses.
[4] Used in painting.

FOURTH CONJUGATION.

Infinitive.	Present participle.	Past participle.	Present.	Indicative Preterit.	Future.	Subjunctive Present.	English.
Faire	faisant	fait	je fais, faisons fais, faites fait, font	je fis	je ferai	fasse, fassions fasses, fassiez fasse, fassent	to make, to do.
Forfaire[1]		forfait					to forfeit, to trespass.
Frire[2]		frit	fris fris frit		je frirai		to fry.
Joindre	joignant	joint	je joins, joignons joins, joignez joint, joignent	je joignis	je joindrai	joigne, joignions joignes, joigniez joigne, joignent	to join.
Lire	lisant	lu	je lis, lisons lis, lisez lit, lisent	je lus	je lirai	lise, lisions lises, lisiez lise, lisent	to read.
Luire	luisant	lui	je luis, luisons luis, luisez luit, luisent		je luirai	luise, luisions luises, luisiez luise, luisent	to shine.
Malfaire							to do mischief.
Maudire	maudissant	maudit	je maudis, maudissons maudis, maudissez maudit, maudissent	je maudis	je maudirai	maudisse, maudissions maudisses, maudissiez maudisse, maudissent	to curse.
Médire	médisant	médit	je médis, médisons médis, médisez médit, médisent	je médis	je médirai	médise, médisions médises, médisiez médise, médisent	to slander.
Méfaire		méfait					to misdo.
Mettre	mettant	mis	je mets, mettons mets, mettez met, mettent	je mis	je mettrai	mette, mettions mettes, mettiez mette, mettent	to put.
Moudre	moulant	moulu	je mouds, moulons mouds, moulez moud, moulent	je moulus	je moudrai	moule, moulions moules, mouliez moule, moulent	to grind.
Naître	naissant	né	je nais, naissons nais, naissez naît, naissent	je naquis	je naîtrai	naisse, naissions naisses, naissiez naisse, naissent	to be born.
Nuire	nuisant	nui	je nuis, nuisons nuis, nuisez nuit, nuisent	je nuisis	je nuirai	nuise, nuisions nuises, nuisiez nuise, nuisent	to hurt, to injure.
Paître	paissant	pu	je pais, paissons pais, paissez paît, paissent		je paîtrai	paisse, paissions paisses, paissiez paisse, paissent	to graze.
Paraître	paraissant	paru	je parais, paraissons parais, paraissez paraît, paraissent	je parus	je paraîtrai	paraisse, paraissions paraisses, paraissiez paraisse, paraissent	to appear.
Plaire	plaisant	plu	je plais, plaisons plais, plaisez plaît, plaisent	je plus	je plairai	plaise, plaisions plaises, plaisiez plaise, plaisent	to please.
Poindre			il point		il poindra		to dawn; to sting.
Prendre	prenant	pris	je prends, prenons prends, prenez prend, prennent	je pris	je prendrai	prenne, prenions prennes, preniez prenne, prennent	to take.
Réduire	réduisant	réduit	je réduis, réduisons réduis, réduisez réduit, réduisent	je réduisis	je réduirai	réduise, réduisions réduises, réduisiez réduise, réduisent	to reduce.
Repaître	repaissant	repu	je repais, repaissons repais, repaissez repaît, repaissent	je repus	je repaîtrai	repaisse, repaissions repaisses, repaissiez repaisse, repaissent	to feed.
Résoudre	résolvant	résolu résous	je résous, résolvons résous, résolvez résout, résolvent	je résolus	je résoudrai	résolve, résolvions résolves, résolviez résolve, résolvent	to resolve.

---

1 Used only in the infinitive and compound tenses. | 2 The verb *faire* is used to supply the persons and tenses that are wanting: as, *nous faisons frire*, &c.

FOURTH CONJUGATION.

Infinitive.	Present participle.	Past participle.	Present.	Indicative Preterit.	Future.	Subjunctive Present.	English
Rire	riant	ri	je ris, rions ris, riez rit, rient	je ris	je rirai	rie, riions ries, riiez rie, rient	to laugh.
Rompre	rompant	rompu	je romps, rompons romps, rompez rompt, rompent	je rompis	je romprai	rompe, rompions rompes, rompiez rompe, rompent	to break.
Sourdre			il sourd ils sourdent				to issue; to arise.
Suffire	suffisant	suffi	je suffis, suffisons suffis, suffisez suflit, suffisent	je suffis	je suffirai	suffise, suffisions suffises, suffisiez suffise, suffisent	to suffice.
Suivre	suivant	suivi	je suis, suivons suis, suivez suit, suivent	je suivis	je suivrai	suive, suivions suives, suiviez suive, suivent	to follow.
Traire	trayant	trait	je trais, trayons trais, trayez trait, traient		je trairai	traie, trayions traies, trayiez traie, traient	to milk.
Vaincre	vainquant	vaincu	je vaincs, vainquons vaincs, vainquez vainc, vainquent	je vainquis	je vaincrai	vainque, vainquions vainques, vainquiez vainque, vainquent	to conquer.
Vivre	vivant	vécu	je vis, vivons vis, vivez vit, vivent	je vécus	je vivrai	vive, vivions vives, viviez vive, vivent	to live.

LIST OF IRREGULAR AND DEFECTIVE VERBS, CONJUGATED AFTER THE VERBS IN THE FOREGOING TABLE.

FIRST CONJUGATION.

CONJUGATED		LIKE
Renvoyer............to send back		....envoyer.
s'En aller............to go away		........aller.

SECOND CONJUGATION.

Conquérir............to conquer	⎫	
Reconquérir............to reconquer	⎬ ...acquérir.	
Requérir............to request		
s'Enquérir............to inquire	⎭	

Tressaillir............to start up .....assaillir.

Rebouillir............to boil again ..... bouillir.

Accourir............to hasten to	⎫	
Concourir............ to concur		
Discourir............to talk about	⎬ ....courir.	
Encourir............to incur		
Parcourir............to run over		
Recourir............to have recourse		
Secourir............to succour	⎭	

Accueillir............to welcome	⎫	
Recueillir............to gather	⎬ ... cueillir.	
se Recueillir........to collect one's [self	⎭	

Endormir............to lull asleep	⎫	
s'Endormir............to fall asleep	⎬ ..... dormir.	
Rendormir...to lull to sleep again		
se Rendormir..to fall asleep again	⎭	

s'Enfuir............to run away ....fuir.

Couvrir............to cover	⎫	
Découvrir............to uncover		
Entr'ouvrir.........to open a little	⎬ ....ouvrir.	
Mésoffrir............to underbid		
Offrir............to offer		
Recouvrir............to cover again		
Rouvrir............to open again		
Souffrir............to suffer	⎭	

Consentir............to agree	⎫	
Départir............to distribute		
se Départir....to desist, to swerve		
Démentir............to belie		
Mentir............to lie		
Partir............to set out		
Pressentir............to foresee	⎬ ....sentir.	
Repartir............to set off again		
se Repentir............to repent		
Ressentir............to feel		
se Ressentir............to feel		
Ressortir............to go out again		
Sortir............to go out	⎭	

Desservir........to clear a table, to [do an ill office	⎬ ....servir.	
se Servir ....to make use		

CONJUGATED ... LIKE

s'Abstenir............to abstain	⎫	
Appartenir............to belong to		
Circonvenir............to circumvent		
Contenir............to contain		
se Contenir:............to refrain		
Contrévenir............to infringe		
Convenir............to suit, to agree		
Déprévenir.to divest of prejudice		
Devenir............to become		
Disconvenir............ to deny		
Entretenir .. ..to entertain		
s'Entretenir ....to discourse with		
Intervenir............to intervene		
Maintenir............to maintain	⎬ ...... tenir.	
Obtenir............to obtain		
Parvenir............to arrive		
Prévenir............to prepossess, to [forewarn		
Provenir............to proceed from		
Redevenir............to become again		
Retenir............to retain		
se Retenir............to forbear		
Revenir............to come back		
se Ressouvenir........to remember		
se Souvenir............to recollect		
Soutenir............to maintain		
Subvenir............to provide for		
Survenir............ .....to befall		
Venir ....to come	⎭	

Dévêtir............ .. ...to undress	⎫	
se Dévêtir......to divest one's self	⎬ ...... vêtir.	
Revêtir............to clothe. to dress		
se Vêtir............to clothe one's self	⎭	

THIRD CONJUGATION.

s'Asseoir............to sit down	⎫	
Rasseoir.......to place down again	⎬ ... asseoir.	
se Rasseoir.......to sit down again	⎭	

Rechoir............to fall again ...... choir.

Émouvoir......to move, to stir up	⎬ mouvoir.	
s'Émouvoir.........to be moved, to [be concerned		

Dépourvoir............to deprive pourvoir.

Équivaloir........to be equivalent	⎫	
Revaloir....to return like for like	⎬ prévaloir.	
se Prévaloir....to take advantage	⎭	

Messeoir ....to be unbecoming ...... seoir.

Entrevoir....to have a glimpse of	⎫	
s'Entrevoir....to see each other	⎬ .... voir.	
Revoir............to see again	⎭	

FOURTH CONJUGATION.

Dissoudre.....to dissolve, to melt absoudre.

FOURTH CONJUGATION.

CONJUGATED	LIKE	CONJUGATED	LIKE
Abattre ....to pull down s'Abattre ....to fall down se Battre..................to fight Combattre......to fight, to combat Debattre..............to debate se Débattre ....to struggle s'Ébattre....to take one's pleasure Embattre......to lay the tire of a [wheel] Rabattre...to abate, to bring down se Rabattre................to turn off Rebattre..............to beat again	} battre.	Enjoindre......... ....to enjoin Épreindre ....to squeeze out Éteindre ....to extinguish Étreindre ....to tie close Feindre............................tofeign Geindre..........to whine, to moan Oindre ....to anoint Peindre.......... ....to paint Plaindre..........................topity se Plaindre...............to complain Ratteindre........to overtake again Rejoindre.................to join again Repeindre...........to paint again Restreindre...........to restrain, to [confine] Teindre...............to dye, to colour	} joindre.
Reboire...............to drink again	boire.		
Déclore....................to unclose Enclore....................to enclose Forclore....................to foreclose	} clore.	Élire..............to elect, to choose Prélire ....to read over previously Réélire...................to elect again Relire....................to read again	} lire.
Exclure ....to exclude Reclure ....to shut up	} conclure.	Reluire...........to glitter, to shine Entre-luire..........to shine a little	} luire.
Découdre ....to unsew Recoudre..............to sew again	} coudre.	Contredire.............to contradict Dédire...........to disown, to unsay se Dédire........to recant, to retract Interdire...to interdict, to forbid Prédire....to foretell, to predict	} médire.
Mécroire..................to disbelieve	croire.		
Accroître..................to increase Décroître..................to decrease Recroître........to grow again Surcroître................to grow out	} croître.	Admettre..................to admit Commettre................to commit Compromettre...........to compro-[mise, to expose] se Compromettre ..... to compro-[mise one's self] Démettre...................to dislocate se Démettre...............to resign Émettre.......to issue, to set forth s'Entremettre...........to interpose, [to meddle] Omettre..........................to omit Permettre......to permit, to allow Promettre...............to promise Remettre...........to replace, to set [again] Soumettre...to submit, to subdue Transmettre....... ......totransmit	} mettre.
Redire ....to say again	dire.		
Circonscrire.........to circumscribe Décrire ....to describe Inscrire ....to inscribé s'Inscrire.......to enter one's name Prescrire ....to prescribe se Prescrire......to be lost by limi-[tation (law)] Proscrire...to proscribe, to outlaw Récrire..................to write again Souscrire ....to subscribe Transcrire ....to transcribe	} écrire.	Émoudre.......to whet, to sharpen Remoudre....to grind over again Rémoudre..........to sharpen again	} moudre.
Contrefaire...to imitate, to mimic Défaire ....to undo se Défaire....................to get rid Parfaire ....to perfect Redéfaire..............to undo again Refaire...................to make again se Refaire..................to recover Satisfaire...................to satisfy Surfaire..............to ask too much	} faire.	Renaître......to revive, to be born [again]	} naître.
Refrire....................to fry again	frire.	Apparaître..................to appear Comparaître................to appear Connaître..............to know, to be [acquainted with] Disparaître............todisappear Méconnaître..........to disown, not [to know] se Méconnaître......to forget one's [self] Reconnaître.........to recognise, to [acknowledge] Reparaître..........to appear again	} paraître.
Adjoindre....................to adjoin Astreindre ....to subject s'Astreindre...to confine one's self Atteindre...to overtake, to reach Aveindre....................to take out Ceindre......to gird, to encompass Conjoindre ....to conjoin Contraindre.............to constrain Craindre........to fear, to be afraid Déjoindre....................to disjoin Dépeindre................to describe Déteindre.................to discolour Disjoindre................to disjoin Empreindre ....to imprint Enceindre....................to enclose Enfreindre ....to transgress, to [infringe]	} joindre.	Complaire.............to humour, to [please] se Complaire...............to delight Déplaire ....to displease	} plai.

FOURTH CONJUGATION.

CONJUGATED	LIKE	CONJUGATED	LIKE
se Déplaire.........to be displeased [with]	} ....plaire.	Produire......to produce, to bring [forth]	} ...réduire.
Taire.....to conceal, to keep secret		Reconduire........to conduct again	
se Taire.......... . to remain silent		Reconstruire ....to build again	
		Recuire........to bake again, to do [again]	
Apprendre .....to learn, to hear of	} .... prendre.	Renduire ....to plaster anew	
Comprendre ....to understand, [to include]		Reproduire ....to reproduce	
Déprendre.......to loosen, to dis-[engage]		Séduire ....to seduce, to bribe	
Désapprendre.. ....to unlearn		Traduire .... to translate	
Entreprendre.........to undertake			
se Méprendre........... to mistake		se Repaitre ......to thirst after, to [delight in]	} ...repaitre.
Rapprendre...........to learn again			
Reprendre.........to take again, to [chide]		se Rire de.................to laugh at	} ....rire.
se Reprendre........to correct one's [self]		Sourire.........................to smile	
Surprendre............to surprise, to [astonish]		Corrompre.................to corrupt	} ...rompre.
		Interrompre ....to interrupt	
Conduire.........to conduct, to lead	} .....réduire.	Poursuivre......to pursue, to pro-[secute]	} ... suivre.
Construire...... ....to construct, to [build]			
Cuire.................to cook, to bake		Abstraire ....to abstract	} .... traire.
Décuire........to thin (syrups, &c.)		Distraire......to distract, to divert	
Déconstruire..... to take to pieces		Extraire ....to extract	
Déduire........... .... to deduct		Retraire ....to redeem an estate	
Détruire........ ....to destroy		Rentraire.................to fine-draw	
se Détruire........to kill one's self, [to decay]		Soustraire ....to subtract, to [deduct]	
Éconduire..............to bow out, to [refuse]		se Soustraire ....to avoid, to [escape]	
Enduire......to plaster, to do over			
Induire.......................to induce		Convaincre ....to convince	...vaincre.
Instruire............. ....to instruct			
Introduire...............to introduce		Revivre.......................to revive	} ...... vivre.
		Survivre......to survive, to outlive	

LIST OF THE NOUNS OF DOUBLE GENDER EXISTING IN THE FRENCH LANGUAGE.

Aide	*m.*, a male assistant.	**Cornette**	*m.*, cornet, ensign-bearer (cavalry).
	f., a female assistant; aid, help, succour.		*f.*, cornet, mob-cap; (milit.) colours of a company of cavalry; cornetcy; (nav.) broad pendant.
Aigle	*m.*, male eagle.	**Couple**	*m.*, a married pair, husband and wife.
	f., she-eagle; standard, eagle.		*f.*, a brace, two.
Ange	*m.*, angel; (artil.) chain-shot, bar-shot; angel-shot; (ich.) angel-fish.*	**Cravate**	*m.*, Croatian horse; ⊙ trooper of light cavalry regiments which bore the same name.
	f., not used.		*f.*, cravat, neck-tie, neckcloth.
Apologé-	*m.*, Tertullian's treatise in defence of the early Christians.	**Crêpe**	*m.*, crape.
tique	*f.*, apologetics, a part of theology.		*f.*, pancake.
	m., wood-louse.	**Critique**	*m.*, a critic.
Armadille	*f.*, armadilla, Spanish fleet to defend Spain's possessions in the New World; Spanish frigate belonging to this fleet.		*f.*, criticism.
		Décime	*m.*, copper coin worth 10 centimes, the tenth part of a franc; a war-tax.
Asclépiade	*m.*, (ancient poet.) asclepiad.		*f.*, tithe formerly levied on ecclesiastical revenues; *pl.*, tax paid formerly to the king by the holders of benefices.
	f., (bot.) asclepias, swallow-wort.		
Aune	*m.*, alder tree.	**Dentale**	*m.*, (conch.) dentalium, dental, tooth-shell.
	f., obsolete French measure = one ell.		*f.*, dental, dental consonant.
Barbe	*m.*, Barbary horse.	**Ébène***	*m., not used.*
	f., beard.		*f.*, ebony, ebon; (fig.) black colour.
Barde	*m.*, a bard, Celtic poet.	**Écho**	*m.*, echo.
	f., a thin slice, a rasher of bacon.		*f.*, Echo (nymph).
Basque	*m.*, Biscayan; Basque (nation and language).	**Élève**	*m.*, male pupil, school-boy.
	f., flap, skirt, tail, of a coat, or any other garment.		*f.*, female pupil, school-girl, breeding of horses, cattle, & .
Bourgogne	*m.*, Burgundy (wine).	**Enseigne**	*m.*, ensign, standard-bearer.
	f., Burgundy (province).		*f.*, sign-board.
Brie	*m.*, Brie (cheese).	**Éphémère**	*m.*, (ent.) ephemera, ephemeran, day-fly, May-fly.
	f., Brie (province); rolling-pin.		*f.*, spider-wort, *tradescantia virginica.*
Bulbe	*m.*, (anat.) bulb.		
	f.,† (bot.) bulb.	**Espace**	*m.*, space, distance, interval.
Câpre‡	*m.*, ⊙ pirate; privateer; piratical ship.		*f.*, (print.) space, metallic plate to separate words.
	f., (bot.) caper.	**Exemple**	*m.*, example.
Carpe	*m.*, wrist.		*f.*, writing-copy.
	f., (ich.) carp.	**Faune**	*m.*, faun (myth.).
Cartouche	*m.*, (arch.) cartouch, modillion.		*f.*, fauna.
	f., cartridge for small fire-arms.	**Faux**	*m.*, forgery; falsehood.
Champagne	*m.*, Champagne (wine).		*f.*, scythe.
	f., Champagne (province).	**Finale**	*m.*, (mus.) finale.
Chorée	*m.*, choreus, choree, trochee.		*f.*, (gram.) final letter or syllable.
	f., (med.) chorea, St. Vitus' dance.	**Flasque**	*m.*, cheek (of a gun-carriage).
Claque	*m.*, opera hat.		*f.*, powder-flask, powder-horn; (nav.) whelp (of the capstan); board (of bellows).
	f., flap, slap, smack; (thea.) claque, paid clappers.		
Cloaque	*m.*, sink, receptacle of filth; filthy, dirty place; filthy person; (anat.) cloaca.	**Follicule**	*m.*, (anat., bot.) follicle.
			f.,† small sheet of paper; (pharm.) pod of senna.
	f., (Rom. antiq.) common sewer.	**Forêt‡**	*m.*, drill (to bore holes).
Coche	*m.*, barge for the conveyance of travellers, track-boat; coach.		*f.*, forest.
	f., sow, she-pig; notch, nick, indentation.		
Contumace	*m.*, a man guilty of contumacy (jur.).		
	f., contumacy.		

Foudre
m., (st. e.) thunder-bolt, lightning; (paint., sculpt.) thunder-bolt, Jupiter's attribute; (fig.) irresistible eloquence; great general, orator, hero; divine anger, vengeance; fulmination of excommunication, &c.; artillery, mines, war; (poet.) catastrophe, destruction. A tun (cask).
f., thunder-bolt, lightning; (fig.) divine anger, vengeance; fulmination of excommunication, &c.; superior eloquence; artillery, mines, &c.

Fourbe
m., knave.
f., deceit, craftiness.

Garde
m., a guard, a keeper.
f., guarding, guard; watching; keeping.

Garde-robe
m., lady's apron.
f., wardrobe; (bot.) artemisia.

Geste
m., gesture, actions. movement; pl., ⊙great deeds of generals, princes, &c.
f., poem in old French.

Givre
m., hoar frost, rime.
f., (her.) snake, serpent.

Grave
m., (phys.) body, heavy body; (lit.) grave style; (mus.) flat; wine made at Grave (France).
f., shore, beach (Newfoundland); pl., gravelly and clayey soil in the department of Gironde (France).

Greffe
m., record-office of a court of justice.
f., graft.

Guide
m., a guide.
f., rein.

Havane
m., Havannah (cigar).
f., Havannah (town).

Hymne
m., ode, hymn.
f., hymn (church).

Inde
m., indigo, indigo blue; logwood.
f., India.

Interligne
m., space between printed or written lines; space between the lines of the stave (mus.).
f., (print.) lead, metallic plate to separate lines.

Jujube
m., the extract of jujube (fruit).
f.,* jujube (fruit).

Laque
m., lacker, lacquer.
f., lac, lake, gum-lake.

Lepte
m., (ent.) leptus, wheal-worm, harvest-bug.
f. (bot.) a triphyllous plant of the order celastraceæ.

Lévite
m., Levite.
f., surtout, overcoat.

Liquide
m., a liquid.
f., (gram.) liquid, liquid consonant.

Litre
m., litre, French measure of capacity, less than a quart.
f., band of black cloth bearing the coat of arms of a deceased person, and hung in church at his funeral.

Livre
m., book.
f., pound (weight, money).

Loutre
m., ⊙a hat, a muff, &c., made of otter-skin or hair.
f., otter.

* The French Academy gives to *jujube* (fruit) the feminine gender; but it is contrary to general present usage.

Maheutre
m., (French hist.) Protestant soldier.
f., a sleeve that was formerly worn and did not reach further than the elbow.

Manche
m., handle of a tool, a knife, &c.
f., sleeve; the English Channel.

Manœuvre
m., day-labourer; bricklayer's journeyman; (fig.) bungler; crafty person.
f., (milit. nav.) manœuvre; running rigging, cordages of a ship.

Marengo
m., Oxford gray (colour).
f., (cook.) marengo (sauce for fowl).

Maroufle
m., ragamuffin, lout, rascallion, clodhopper.
f., (paint.) lining-paste.

Martyre
m., martyrdom.
f., a female martyr.

Masque
m., mask.
f., ⊙ ugly woman, ugly girl.

Mémoire
m., memorandum; memoir; bill (of large amount).
f., the memory.

Merci
m., thanks.
f., mercy, grace, benevolence, favour.

Mestre de Camp
m., ⊙colonel; general.
f., ⊙the 1st company of a regiment.

Minime
m., minim, Franciscan monk.
f., ⊙(mus.) minim.

Mode
m., mood, mode; method.
f., fashion.

Môle
m., mole, pier, jetty.
f., (med.) mole.

Mort
m., a dead man.
f., death.

Moufle*
m., (chem.) muffle.
f., (mec.) tackle (assemblage of pulleys; fingerless glove.

Moule
m., mould, matrix to cast lead, iron, &c.
f., (ich.) mussel.

Mousse
m., cabin-boy, apprentice sailor.
f., moss; froth; foam.

Nielle
m., niello.
f., blight, smut; (bot.) rose campion.

Noël
m., Christmas; Christmas carol.
f., *la Noël* (ellipsis for *la fête de Noël*), Christmas-day.

Œuvre
m., the philosopher's stone; (arch.) walls; the whole of the works of an engraver, painter, or composer of music; argentiferous lead; (jur.) summons to one who builds upon another man's ground.
f., work, deed, action; work of the hand; handiwork; (jewel.) bezel; (nav.) hull of a ship; the works of a writer.

Office
m., divine service; duty; officet; employment; formulary of prayers. Saint- —: holy-office, Inquisition.
f., servant's hall; pantry.

Ombre‡
m., (ich.) umbra, chromis, corvo; umber, grayling, char; (card game) ombre.
f., shade, shadow; spirit, ghost.

* French mechanicians give to this noun, in the sense of *tackle*, the masculine gender.

† This word has never in French the meaning of *room, apartment*, for the transaction of business.

‡ *Ombre*, card game, is also spelt *hombre*.

Once .... { *m.*, mountain-cat, catamount. / *f.*, ounce (weight); jaguar, ounce.

Orphiques... { *m..* Orpheus' poems ; Pythagoreans. votaries of Orpheus. / *f.*, orgies, feast in honour of Bacchus.

Page .... { *m.*, page, young male servant. / *f.*, page of a book, &c.

Paillasse ... { *m.*, clown, merry-andrew. / *f.*, straw-bed, straw-bed ticking.

Palme ..... { *m.*, palm ; hand (measures). / *f.*, palm ; palm-branch ; (bot.) palm-tree ; pattern of cashmere shawls ; (sculpt., arch.) palm ; (her.) palm ; (bot.) Cuban reed ; (nav.) a kind of East Indian ship with two masts.

Pantomime { *m.*, pantomimist, pantomime. / *f.*, dumb-show, pantomime.

Pâque* ...... { *m.*, Easter (Christian religion). / *f.*, Passover, Easter (Jewish religion).

Parallèle ... { *m..* comparison ; (geog.) parallel of latitude. / *f.*, (geom.) parallel line ; (fort.) trench, trenches.

Part .... { *m.*, (jur.) new-born child, infant; birth. / *f.*, share, portion, part ; concern, interest, part ; side.

Peau-rouge { *m.*, American Indian, Red-skin. / *f.*, (no hyphen) any one's skin when it is red, or redder than usual.

Pendule...... { *m.*, pendulum. / *f.*, time-piece. .

Période ...... { *m.*, highest point, acme, height. / *f.*, period, epoch.

Personne ... { *m.*, (pron.) nobody, anybody. / *f.*, (noun) a person.

Physique ... { *m.*, a person's constitution, body. / *f.*, natural philosophy.

Pique......... { *m..* spade (cards). / *f.*, pike (weapon); tiff, pique, quarrel.

Pivoine ...... { *m.*, (orni.) bull-finch. / *f.*, (bot.) peony, piony.

Plane .... { *m.*, (bot.) plane-tree ; inside surface of scissors blades. / *f.*, joiner's plane ; spoke-shave, drawing-knife ; (ich.) plaice.

Platine ...... { *m.*, (metal.) platinum. / *f.*, lock (of small fire-arms); metallic plate.

Podagre ... { *m.*, a podagrical man, *i.e.* one having the gout in his feet. / *f.*, podagra, gout in the feet.

Poêle .... { *m.*, pall ; stove. / *f.*, frying-pan.

Polacre *or* Polaque { *m.*, ⊙ Polish cavalry. / *f.*, (nav.) polacca, polacre.

Politique ... { *m.*, politician. / *f.*, politics ; policy.

Ponte .... { *m.*, punter (gambling). / *f.*, laying of eggs.

Poste .... { *m.*, post, situation. / *f.*, post. mail, post-office ; buckshot.

Poulpe ...... { *m.*, (mol.) poulp, octopus. / *f.*, pulp ; pap.

* *Pâque*, or *Pâques*, Christian religion. is often used in the plural, and is then feminine. *Pâque*, Jewish religion, is always feminine, and never used in the plural.

Pourpre...... { *m..* purple (colour); (her.) purpure; (chem.) purple ; (med.) purples. / *f.*, purple, colouring matter extracted from *buccinum lapillus ;* stuff, fabric dyed in purple ; (fig.) vivid red colour; sovereign dignity. cardinal's dignity.

Prétexte ... { *m.*, pretence, pretext. / *f.*, (Rom. antiq.) prætexta.

Primevère { *m.*, ⊙ spring season. / *f.*, (bot.) primrose, cowslip, oxlip

Pupille ...... { *m.*, a male ward. / *f.*, a female ward ; pupil of the eye.

Pyrrhique... { *m.*, pyrrhic (poet.). / *f.*, pyrrhic, military dance.

Quadrille ... { *m.*, quadrille (card game); quadrille, a dance ; (mus.) quadrille. / *f.*, troup of horse in a tournament.

Queux ...... { *m.*, ⊙ cook. / *f.*, whetting-stone, hone.

Réciproque { *m.*, like, like for like, tit for tat. / *f.*, (log.) converse.

Régale ... ..{ *m..* organ stop imitating the human voice ; regal (musical instrument). / *f.*, the king's right to receive the revenue of a vacant bishoprie.

Réglisse...... { *m..* *du réglisse* (popular ellipsis for *du jus de réglisse*) extract of liquorice, Spanish juice. / *f.*, (bot.) liquorice. licorice ; liquorice root.

Relâche...... { *m.*, (thea.) non-performance. / *f.*, (nav.) putting into port.

Remise ...... { *m.*, coach let on hire, livery-coach. / *f.*, coach-house ; (com.) remittance.

Rencontre { *m.*, (her.) rencounter. / *f.*, encounter, rencounter. accidental meeting ; accident, chance, collision ; meeting ; accidental fight ; opportunity, occurrence, case ; juncture.

Rhingrave { *m.*, count of the Rhine. / *f.*, ⊙ knee-breeches. .

Rossinante { *m.*, Rosinante, Don Quixote's horse. / *f.*, Rosinante, a sorry horse. a jade.

Sagittaire ... { *m.*, (astron.) Sagittarius. / *f.*, (bot.) arrow-head, adder's tongue.

Satyre ...... { *m.*, (myth.) satyr. / *f.*, (Grec. antiq.) satyric tragedy.

Scolastique { *m..* scholastic. school-man. / *f.*, scholasticism.

Scolie......... { *m.*, (geom.) scholium. / *f.*, scholium. annotation ; (Grec. antiq.) table-song.

Scytale ...... { *m.*, (zool.) a species of very venomous snakes. / *f.*, (antiq.) staff used in Sparta as a cypher to write secret dispatches.

Serpentaire { *m..* (astron.) Serpentarius ; (orni.) secretary-bird. snake-eater. / *f.*, (bot.) dragon's-wort.

Solde .... { *m..* balance of an account. / *f.*, soldier's pay.

Somme ...... { *m.*, nap. slumbers. doze. sleep. / *f.*, a sum of money ; total ; load, burden.

Souris .... { *m.*, smile.
{ *f.*, mouse.

Statère* ...... { *m.*, (antiq.) stater. (coin).
{ *f.*, (antiq.) staters, Roman balance.

Statuaire ... { *m.*, a sculptor.
{ *f.*. the art of making statues, statuary.

Stipe .... { *m.*, (bot.) stipe; caudex.
{ *f.*, (bot.) stipa, feather-grass;
{ ⊙a tax on leases.

Superbe ...... { *m.*, proud, haughty man.
{ *f.*. arrogance, haughtiness, vainglory.

Technique { *m.*. (arts) material execution. technicalities.
{ *f.*, technics.

Teneur ...... { *m.*, keeper, accountant; *teneur de livres;* book-keeper.
{ *f.*. text, terms, purport, tenor. contents, of writings.

Terre-neuve { *m.*. Newfoundland dog.
{ *f.*, Newfoundland.

Tirelire ...... { *m.*, ⊙song, earoi of the lark.
{ *f.*, money-box.

Tonique ...... { *m.*, (med.) tonic.
{ *f.*, (mus.) tonic, key-note, key.

Tour .... { *m.*, turn; tour; lathe; trick.
{ *f.*, tower.

Triomphe ... { *m.*, triumph.
{ *f.*. triumph (card game).

Trochée ...... { *m.*, (poet.) trochee.
{ *f.*. (agri.) brushwood.

Trompette { *m.*. trumpeter.
{ *f.*. trumpet.

Trouble ...... { *m.*. confusion, disorder, disturbance; dispute, quarrel: *pl.*, troubles, broils, commotions.
{ *f.*, hoop-net (for fishing).

Vague ...... { *m.*, space, emptiness; vagueness; looseness; uncertainty.
{ *f.*, sea-wave, billow.

Vapeur ...... { *m.*, steamer, steam-boat
{ *f.*, steam; vapour.

Vase .... { *m.*, vase.
{ *f.*, mud, slime, mire.

Vigogne ... { *m.*, hat made of vicugna wool.
{ *f.*, (zool.) vicugna.

Voile .... { *m.*, veil.
{ *f.*. sail.

Vulnéraire { *m.*, (pharm.) vulnerary.
{ *f.*, (bot.) kidney-vetch, woundwort.

* When it means a coin, it is also spelt *stater.*

SUPPLEMENT

Caustique ... { *m.*, (med.) caustic.
{ *f.*, (geom., phys.) caustic curve.

Cinquième { *m.*, the fifth part; pupil in the 5th form in public schools.
{ *f.*, 5th form in public schools.

Cistophore { *m.*, (antiq.) Asiatic coin marked with a cist.
{ *f.*, (antiq.) a female cist bearer in the feasts of Ceres and Bacchus

Connétable { *m.*, High-Constable.
{ *f.*, High-Constable's wife.

Cosaque ... { *m.*, Cossack.
{ *f.*, Cossack dance.

Cosmétique { *m.*, cosmetic.
{ *f.*, the art of using cosmetics.

Cotte .... { *m.*, (ich.) bull-head, miller's-thumb.
{ *f.*, ⊙ petticoat — *d'armes*; coat of arms. — *de mailles*; coat of mail. -- *morte*; property left by a deceased monk.

Custode ...... { *m.*, warden.
{ *f.*, cloth to cover the pyx in which the Host is kept; curtain of the high altar; ⊙ curtain.

Didactique { *m.*, didactic language, didactic style.
{ *f.*, the art of teaching.

Dixième ... { *m.*, the tenth part; a tax.
{ *f.*, (mus.) tenth.

Fin .... { *m.*, sharp, astute man; gist, main point; (metal.) pure metal.
{ *f.*, end, termination; aim, object, view, design, intention.

Grêle ...... { *m.*, nut-coal.
{ *f.*, hail; (med.) chalazion, granulo, hailstone.

Guérilla ... { *m.*, guerilla-soldier.
{ *f.*, guerilla, small army of irregulars.

Louche ...... { *m.*, ambiguity; equivocalness; underhand dealing.
{ *f.*, soup-ladle.

Mobile ...... { *m.*, mover, spring, motive power; motive; soldier in the *garde mobile*.
{ *f.*, the *garde mobile*, a French infantry corps no longer in existence.

Mulle .... { *m.*, (ich.) mullet.
{ *f.*, ⊙ rennet, prepared membrane of the calf's stomach.

Myope ...... { *m.*, myope, short-sighted man; (ent.) conops.
{ *f.*, myope, short-sighted female.

Mystique ... { *m.*, mystic (man).
{ *f.*, mystic (female); the study of spirituality.

Néphrétique { *m.*, (med.) nephritic; man affected with nephritis.
{ *f.*, nephritic, renal colic.

Quadruple { *m.*, quadruple, fourfold; (Spanish coin) doubloo
{ *f.*, Spanish gold coin worth about £3 8s.

Quatrième { *m.*, fourth; 4th floor; pupil of the 4th form in public schools.
{ *f.*, 4th form in public schools; (piquet) quart.

Réclame ... { *m.*, (hawking) cry, sign to bring back a hawk to the lure or to the fist.
{ *f.*, (print) catch-word; primer; editorial advertisement in newspapers; (c. rel.) part of the response recited in the versicle (thea.) cue.

Romaïque ... { *m.*, Romaic, modern Greek language.
{ *f.*, the Greek national dance.

Sarde .... { *m.*, a native of Sardia.
{ *f.*, (ich.) whale; scombe; sardan; Brazilian sardine or pilchard.

Septième ... { *m.*, seventh, seventh part; seventh day.
{ *f.*, (piquet) septième; (mus.) seventh.

Silène .... { *m.*, (myth.) Silenus; Satyr, attendant of Bacchus; (ent.) a South European butterfly.
{ *f.*, (bot.) catch-fly.

Sixième ...... { *m.*, sixth, sixth part; sixth day; pupil of the 6th form in public schools.
{ *f.*, (piquet) seizième; 6th form in public schools.

Topique ...... { *m.*, (rhet., med.) toric.
{ *f.*, (rhet.) the art of finding topics or arguments.

Troisième ... { *m.*, third; third floor; pupil of the 3rd form in public schools.
{ *f.*, 3rd form in public schools.

Trolle ...... { *m.*, globe-flower, trollius.
{ *f.*, (hunt.) trolling.

EXPLANATION OF THE SIGNS USED IN THIS WORK.

* Represents the liquid sounds of *gn*, *l*, or *ll*.

† Signifies that the *h* is aspirated.

— Indicates the repetition of the same word.

(—) Indicates the plural of foreign and compound nouns when it is like the singular.

(—*s*) Indicates the plural of foreign nouns when it is formed by adding *s*.

When the plural of foreign and compound nouns is formed by changing the final letter or letters, the whole plural form is given. Thus, *e.g.*, (*Lazaroni*), plural of *Lazarone* ; (— -*amiraux*), plural of *vice-amiral*.

(—*s* —*s*), or (—*s* —*x*), or (—*x* —*s*), or (—*x* —*s*) Indicate the plural of compound nouns when it is formed by adding *s* or *x* to each component.

(—*s* —) or (—*x* —) Indicate the plural of compound nouns when it is formed by adding *s* or *x* to the first component only.

(— —*s*) or (— —*x*) Indicate the plural of compound nouns when it is formed by adding *s* or *x* to the second component only.

(*n.s.*) Indicates foreign and compound nouns not used in the singular.

(*n.p.*) Indicates foreign and compound nouns not used in the plural.

Before final letters, points out the masculine termination, which is to be changed in the feminine; as, *acti-f*, *-ve*. actif, active; *act-eur*. *-rice*. acteur, actrice ; *honteu-x*, *-se*, honteux, honteuse.

The long sound of the vowels is designated by a horizontal mark over the vowel, thus: ā, ē, ī, ō, ū.

The short sound of the vowels is designated by a curved mark. thus : ă, ĕ, ĭ, ŏ, ŭ. This mark seldom occurs but over the unaccented *e*. When there is no mark over the other vowels, they may be considered as natural ; that is, as neither long nor short.

Words in parentheses serve to complete the sense of those words that precede or follow them ; or they refer to the object with which they are connected, or indicate the art, trade. profession, &c., to which they relate. They are given in English and in French.

Those words of which the pronunciation is quite irregular are noticed in full ; but those that are only partly irregular are noticed in their irregularities only. Therefore, such words as *chiromancie*, *archétype*, *équateur*, which are irregular in one syllable only, are noticed in that syllable alone ; as, *ki-*, *-kĕ-*, *-koua-*.

As none but French spelling can give a correct idea of French pronunciation, it is used throughout this dictionary, with the exception of *ch*, which is rendered by *sh*, so that it may not be mistaken for *k* ; of *ou*, which is expressed by *oo* ; and of *oi*, which is represented by *oa*.

⊙ Indicates obsolete words. When found in the middle of lines, it indicates that the French word is obsolete in the meaning before which it is placed.

ABBREVIATIONS USED IN THIS WORK.

a., active, *actif.*
ab., abbreviation, *abréviation.*
Acad., Academy, *Académie.*
adj., adjective, *adjectif.*
adject.. adjectively, *adjectivement.*
adv., adverb, *adverbe.*
agri., agriculture, *agriculture.*
alch.. alchymy, *alchimie.*
alg., algebra, *algèbre.*
anat., anatomy, *anatomie.*
antiq., antiquity, *antiquité.*
arch.. architecture, *architecture.*
arith., arithmetic. *arithmétique.*
art., article, *article.*
artil.. artillery, *artillerie.*
astrol., astrology, *astrologie.*
astron.. astronomy, *astronomie.*
auxil., auxiliary, *auxiliaire.*
bookbind., bookbinding, *reliure.*
bot., botany, *botanique.*
b. s., bad sense, *mauvaise part.*
carp., carpentry, *charpenterie.*
chem., chemistry, *chimie.*
coin., coining, *monnayage.*
com., commerce, *commerce.*
conch., conchology, *conchologie.*
conj., conjunction, *conjonction.*
cook.. cookery, *cuisine.*
c. rel.. catholic religion, *religion catholique.*
dy., dying, *teinture.*
ecc.. ecclesiastical, *ecclésiastique.*
engr.. engraving, *gravure.*
ent.. entomology. *entomologie.*
exc.. exclamation, *exclamation.*
f., feminine, *féminin.*
fam., familiar, *familier.*
fenc.. fencing, *escrime.*
fig., figuratively, *au figuré.*
fin., finance. *finances.*
fort., fortification, *fortification.*
foss., fossils, *fossiles.*
gard., gardening, *jardinage.*
geog., geography, *géographie.*
geol., geology, *géologie.*
geom.. geometry, *géométrie.*
gold.. goldsmith's work. *orfèvrerie.*
gram.. grammar, *grammaire.*
her., heraldry, *blason.*
hist.. history, *histoire.*
horl.. horology, *horlogerie.*
hort.. horticulture, *horticulture.*
hunt.. hunting, *chasse.*
hydr., hydraulics, *hydraulique.*
ich., ichthyology, *ichtyologie.*
imp., impersonal, *impersonnel.*
indecl.. indeclinable. *invariable.*
int., interjection, *interjection.*
iron.. ironically, *ironiquement.*
jest.. jestingly, *par plaisanterie.*

jur., jurisprudence, *jurisprudence.*
l. ex., low expression, *terme bas.*
lit., literature, *littérature.*
log., logic, *logique.*
l. u., little used, *peu usité.*
m., masculine. *masculin.*
mam., mammalogy, *mammalogie.*
man., manege, *manège.*
manu., manufacture, *manufactures.*
mas., masonry, *maçonnerie.*
math., mathematics, *mathématiques.*
mec., mechanics, *mécanique.*
med., medicine, *médecine.*
metal., metallurgy, *métallurgie.*
milit., military art, *art militaire.*
min., mineralogy, *minéralogie.*
mol., mollusk, *mollusque.*
mus., music, *musique.*
myth., mythology, *mythologie.*
n., noun-substantive, *nom substantif.*
nav., navy, *marine.*
opt., optics, *optique.*
orni., ornithology, *ornithologie.*
paint., painting, *peinture.*
part., participle, *participe.*
pers., person, *personne.*
persp., perspective, *perspective.*
pharm., pharmacy, *pharmacie.*
philos., philosophy, *philosophie.*
phys., natural philosophy (physics), *physique.*
pl., plural, *pluriel.*
poet., poetry, *poésie.*
pol., politics, *politique.*
pop., popular, *populaire.*
prep., preposition, *préposition.*
print., printing, *imprimerie.*
pron., pronoun, *pronom.*
prov., proverbially, *proverbialement.*
r., reflected, *réfléchi.*
rel., religion, *religion.*
rhet.. rhetoric, *rhétorique.*
sculpt., sculpture, *sculpture.*
sing., singular, *singulier.*
st. e., elevated style, *style soutenu.*
subst., substantively, *substantivement.*
surg., surgery, *chirurgie.*
tech., technology, *technologie.*
thea., theatre, *théâtre.*
theol., theology, *théologie.*
triv., trivial, *trivial.*
v., verb, *verbe.*
v. a., verb active, *verbe actif.*
vet., veterinary art, *art vétérinaire.*
v. imp., verb impersonal, *verbe impersonnel.*
v. n., verb neuter, *verbe neutre.*
v. r., verb reflected, *verbe réfléchi.*
V., vide, *voir.*
zool., zoology, *zoologie.*

GENERAL FRENCH-ENGLISH DICTIONARY.

a

a, *n.m.,* the first letter of the alphabet, a. *Panse d'a ;* oval of an a. *Il ne sait ni a ni b ;* he does not know *a* from *b. Il n'a pas fait une panse d'a ;* he has not done a letter, a stroke.

a. (ab.)*; Altesse;* Highness.

aa. (ab.)*, Altesses;* Highnesses.

a., at the beginning of French words, often comes from the privative *a* of the Greeks, and denotes privation; as, *atonie,* debility; *acéphale,* acephalous.

à, *prep.,* denotes the end or term of the action of the verb, and indicates the person or thing this action tends to. *Aller à Paris ;* to go to Paris. *Parler à quelqu'un ;* to speak to some one.

à denotes extraction, separation. *Ôter une bague à quelqu'un ;* to take a ring from one. *Se soustraire aux poursuites de la justice ;* to absecond.

à denotes property, possession. *Cette montre est à mon frère ;* this watch is my brother's. *Il a un style, une manière, à lui ;* he has a style, a manner, of his own. *Cette ferme appartient à mon père ;* that farm belongs to my father.

à denotes period, time. *Au lever du soleil ;* at sunrise. *A l'aube du jour ;* at daybreak. *Arriver à temps ;* to arrive in time. *A mon retour ;* on my return.

à indicates what stops on the surface, or penetrates beyond it. *Il a une bague au doigt ;* he has a ring on his finger. *Blessé à l'épaule ;* wounded in the shoulder.

à establishes the relative distance between things and persons. *A portée de canon ;* within cannon-shot. *Il demeure à vingt lieues d'ici ;* he lives twenty leagues off. *De vous à moi ;* between you and me. *De Paris à Rouen ;* from Paris to Rouen.

à points out whatever furnishes an inference or ground for conjecture. *A l'œuvre on connaît l'ouvrier ;* the workman is known by his work.

à denotes succession, gradation, order. *Petit à petit ;* little by little. *Un à un ;* one by one. *Traduire mot à mot ;* to translate word for word.

à is used in speaking of goods sold or bought by weight, measure, or quantity. *Vendre du vin à la bouteille ;* to sell wine by the bottle. *Vendre de la viande à la livre ;* to sell meat by the pound.

à denotes value, price. *Dîner à trois francs par tête ;* to dine at three francs a head.

à denotes conformity, manner. *S'habiller à la Française ;* to dress after the French fashion. *A l'instar de la capitale ;* after the manner of the capital. *A mon avis ;* in my opinion. *Aller à pied, à cheval ;* to go on foot, to ride on horseback. *Marcher à reculons ;* to walk backward.

aba

à, between two nouns, makes the second serve to denote the species or quality of the first. *Canne à sucre ;* sugar-cane. *Vache à lait ;* milch-cow.

à, between two numeral adjectives, signifies between, or about. *Un homme de quarante à cinquante ans ;* a man between forty and fifty. *Il y a quatre à cinq lieues ;* it is about four or five leagues distant. Remark.—The French say *quatre à cinq lieues,* because leagues are things which may be divided into fractions; but, in speaking of things which cannot be divided, *ou* must be used: *Quatre ou cinq personnes ;* four or five persons.

à, before an infinitive, commonly denotes what is proper to be done. *Un avis à suivre ;* an opinion worth following. *Un homme à récompenser ou à pendre ;* a man that deserves to be rewarded or hanged.

à, used in speaking of vehicles, signifies *and. Une voiture à quatre chevaux, à grandes guides ;* a carriage and four.

a. has.

Ⓒ**abacus,** (-kuss), *n.m.,* abacus.

abaisse, *n.f.,* the under-crust of pastry.

abaissé,-e, *part.,* lowered, brought low; dejected; diminished, flattened. *Le pal est —* (her.)*;* the pale is abased.

abaissement (-bèss-man), *n.m.,* lowering, falling, abatement, depression; humiliation, abasement; (surg.) couching. *L'— des eaux ;* the abatement of the waters. *Opération de la cataracte par —;* couching.

abaisser, *v.a.,* to let down, let fall, to lower; to bring low down; to diminish, to reduce; (gard.) to lop out, to debase, to cry down; to humble; to roll (paste—*pâte*); (surg.) to couch. *— un pont-levis ;* to let down a drawbridge. *— la voix ;* to lower the voice. *Dieu abaisse les superbes ;* God humbles the proud. *Abaisser une cataracte ;* to couch a cataract.

s'abaisser, *v.r.,* to fall, to decrease, to subside, to abate, to decline; to humble one's self, to stoop. *S' — à le prier ;* to stoop so low as to entreat him.

abaisseur, *n.m.,* (anat.) depressor.

abaisseur, *adj.,* (anat.) depriment. *Muscle —;* depriment muscle.

abajoue, *n.f.,* (mam.) cheek-pouch; gill, gills.

Ⓒ**abaliénation,** *n.f.,* abalienation.

abalourdir, *v.a.,* (fam.) to make dull and stupid.

abandon, *n.m.,* forsaking, relinquishment, surrender; leaving things at random : abandonment, the being forsaken, forlornness, destitution, ease, unconstraint. *Avoir un — séduisant ;*

1

to have seductive manners. *Se livrer avec* — *à* ; to luxuriate in.

à l'abandon, *adv.*, at random, in confusion, **at** sixes and sevens. *Laisser ses enfants à l'* — ; to neglect one's children. *Un champ qui est à l'* — ; a field left to run wild.

abandonnataire, *n.m.f.*, (jur.) releasee.

abandonné, -e, *part.*, abandoned, forsaken, given over. *Un malade abandonné* ; a patient given up.

abandonné, -e, *adj.*, abandoned, lost to decency, shameless, graceless, profligate.

abandonné, *n.m.*, **-e**, *n.f.*, profligate, rake; lewd, wicked, abandoned person.

abandonnement (-do-n-mān), *n.m.*, abandonment, abandoning, forsaking; desertion, the being forsaken; the giving up one's effects; leaving, quitting; dissoluteness, debauchery.

abandonner, *v.a.*, to abandon, to quit, to leave, to desert, to forsake; to give up. to give over; to leave one the disposal of; to deliver up; to let loose, let go. *Il abandonna le pays* ; he left the country. — *une cause* ; to give up a cause. — *ses prétentions* ; to give up one's claims. *Mes forces m'abandonnent* ; my strength fails me. — *une corde* ; to let go a rope. — *la partie* ; to give it up.

s'abandonner, *v.r.*, to give one's self up, to addict one's self, to give way to; to indulge in, to commit one's self to ; to prostitute one's self ; to be easy in one's manners. *S'* — *à la colère, au plaisir, au hasard* ; to give way to anger, to indulge in pleasure, to trust to fortune.

⊙**abannation** (-ba-na-), *n.f.*, (jur.) abannition, exile for a year or two.

abaptiste (-ba-tist), *adj.*, (surg.) abaptiston.

abaque, *n.m.*, (arch. antiq.) abacus, plinth, the uppermost part of the capital of a column ; raised table.

abarticulation, *n.f.*, (anat.) abarticulation, diarthrosis.

abasourdir, *v.a.*, (fam.) to stun, to dumbfound, to astound ; to stupify.

abatage, *n.m.*, cutting down, felling ; clearance (of a forest—*d'une forêt*) ; (nav.) heaving down ; careening ; slaughtering (of animals—*des animaux*).

abâtardir, *v.a.*, to render degenerate ; to debase, to corrupt, to spoil, to mar, to adulterate. *La servitude abâtardit le courage* ; slavery debases courage. *Un homme abâtardi* ; a degenerate man.

s'abâtardir, *v.r.*, to degenerate, to grow worse.

abâtardissement(-mān),*n.m.*, degeneracy.

abat-chauvée, *s.f.* (n.p.), flock-wool.

abatée, *n.f.*, (nav.) casting ; falling off to leeward. *Faire son* — ; to cast ; to fall off.

abat-faim (-fin), *n.m.* (—), large joint of meat.

abat-foin, *n.m.*, (—) opening above the rack to put the hay through.

abatis, *n.m.*, houses, walls, trees, thrown down ; the killing of game ; giblets (of poultry —*de volaille*) ; garbage ; stones hewn down in a quarry ; raw hides. *Abatis en ragoût* ; stewed giblets.

abat-jour, *n.m.*, (—) (arch.) sky-light, trunk-light ; shade for a lamp ; window-blind ; (bot.) open.ng.

⊙**abattant**, *n.m.*, the shutter of a sky-light in a shop; flap (of a counter—*d'un comptoir*).

abattement (-mān),*n.m.*, faintness, low state, weakness, prostration ; dejection, despondency, low spirits ; (her.) abatement. *Tomber dans l'* — ; to become low-spirited. *Jeter dans l'* — ; to deject. *Qui jette dans l'* — ; depressive.

abatteur, *n.m.*, one that pulls, beats, throws or casts down. *C'est un grand* — *de bois* ; he is a great braggart.

⊙**abattis**, *n.m.* V. **abatis**.

abattoir, *n.m.*, slaughter-house.

abattre, *v.a.*, to throw down, to hurl down ; to pull down ; to beat, batter down ; to bring down ; to fell, to cut down, to hew down, to cut off ; to knock down ; to blow down ; to lay (the dust—*la poussière*) ; to let down ; to soak (skins —*peaux*) ; to couch (the cataract—*la cataracte*) ; to waste (strength—*les forces*) ; to dispirit ; to dishearten ; to unman ; to cast down, to depress ; to humble. *Le vent abattra le blé* ; the wind will throw the corn down. — *un rideau* ; to let a curtain down. *Abattez votre robe* ; pull your gown down. — *les cuirs* ; to skin dead animals. — *les peaux* ; to soak the skins. — *un vaisseau pour le caréner* ; to heave a ship down, to careen a ship. *Un vaisseau dur à* — ; a stiff ship. —*un mat* (nav.) ; to carry away a mast. *La moindre chose l'abat* ; the least thing unmans him. *Elle a l'air bien abattu* ; she looks very much dejected. — *l'orgueil de quelqu'un* ; to humble any one's pride.

abattre. *v.n.*, to lay down one's cards (at play—*au jeu*) ; (nav.) to fall off to leeward, to cast. *Le vaisseau s'abat* ; the ship drives to leeward.

s'abattre, *v.r.*, to fall, tumble down ; to stoop, to abate ; to be cast down, dejected ; to break down (of horses—*des chevaux*) ; to burst (of a storm—*d'un orage*) ; to despond. *Le vent s'abat* ; the wind falls. *La chaleur s'abat* ; the heat abates. *Un orage terrible va s'abattre sur nous* ; a dreadful storm is about to burst upon us.

abattu, -e. *adj.*, pulled, broken, cast down ; depressed, dejected ; humbled, crest-fallen. *Je me sens tout—* ; I am quite out of spirits. *Un visage* — ; a woe-begone countenance.

abattures, *n.f. pl.*, (hunt.) abature ; foiling (of a stag—*du cerf*).

abat-vent, *n.m.*, (—) penthouse (of a steeple—*d'un clocher*) ; pentice.

abat-voix, *n.m.*, (—) sounding-board (of a pulpit—*d'une chaire*).

abbatial (-cial), **-e**,*adj.*, abbatial, abbatical.

abbaye (abéi), *n.f.*, monastery, abbey. *Administration d'une* — ; abbacy.

abbé, *n.m.*, abbe, abbot.

abbesse, *n.f.*, abbess. *Dignité, fonctions d'abbé, d'abbesse* ; abbotship.

abc, *n.m.*, a,b,c, alphabet, primer ; a.b.c. book. *Apprendre son* — ; to learn one's letters. *Etre à l'—de* ; to be at the a, b, c, of. *Renvoyer quelqu'un à l'* — ; to use one like an ignorant person.

abcéder, *v.n.*, to form into an abscess, to apostemate.

abcès, *n.m.*, abscess, aposteme. *Former, vider, un—* ; to form, to take the matter out of, an abscess.

abcisse, *n.f.* V. **abscisse**.

abdication, *n.f.*, abdication ; (jur.) disinheritance of a son during his father's life-time ; abandoning (property—*propriété*). *Faire* — ; to abdicate.

abdiquer, *v.a.*, to abdicate.

abdomen (-mè-n), *n.m.*, abdomen.

abdominal, -e, *adj.*, abdominal.

abducteur, *adj.*, (anat.) abducent.

abducteur, *n.m.*, abductor.

abduction, *n.f.* (anat. and log.), abduction.

abécédaire, *adj.*, abecedary, of the a, b, c. *Ouvrage* —; child's first-book.

abécédaire, *n.m.*, alphabet, primer.

abecquer, *v.a.*, to feed a bird.

abée, *n.f.*, mill-dam.

***abeille**, *n.f.*, bee. — *bourdon* ; humble bee, — *domestique* ; hive bee. — *mère* ; queen bee, — *ouvrière* ; working bee. *Ruche d'* — *s* ; bee-hive. *Éleveur d'* — ; bee-master. *Carillonner les* — *s* ; to ring bees.

abéquer. V. **abecquer**.

aberration, *n.f.*, aberration ; (sciences)

aberration. — *de réfrangibilité;* Newtonian aberration. *Cercle d'*—; crown of aberration.

abêtir, *v.a.,* to stupify; to stultify.

abêtir, *v.n.,* **s'abêtir,** *v.r.,* to grow stupid.

ab hoc et ab hac, *adv.,* at random.

abhorrer, *v.a.,* to abhor, detest.

s'abhorrer, *v.r.,* to abominate one's self.

abime, *n.m.,* unfathomable depth, abyss, hell; a thing most abstruse or obscure; dipping-mould (for candles—*pour chandelles*); (her.) the middle of the shield.

abimé, -e, *part.,* swallowed up, ingulfed, destroyed. — *de dettes;* over head and ears in debt.

abimer, *v.a.,* to overthrow, to ingulf, to swallow up; to destroy entirely, to cut up, to cast, throw into an abyss; to spoil, to injure.

abimer, *v.n.,* to be destroyed, to be swallowed up, to sink; to perish.

s'abimer, *v.r.,* to fall into an abyss, to sink; to ruin, to undo one's self; to be spoiled.

ab intestat, *adv.,* abintestate. *Succession* —; intestate's estate.

ab irato, *adv.,* in an angry fit. *Parler, agir,* —; to speak, to act, under the influence of anger.

abject, -e (-jèkt), *adj.,* abject, base, mean, low, vile, despicable.

abjection, *n.f.,* abjection, baseness; humiliation; vileness, meanness.

abjuration, *n.f.,* solemn renunciation, abjuration.

abjurer, *v.a.,* to abjure, to deny, to forswear. — *une opinion;* to give up an opinion.

ablactation, *n.f.,* (med.) ablactation.

ablaquéation, *n.f.,* (gard.) ablaqueation.

ablatif, *n.m.,* (gram.) ablative.

ablation, *n.f.,* (surg.) ablation.

ablativo, (triv.) *adv.,* in confusion; higgledy-piggledy.

able, *n.m.,* or **ablette,** *n.f.,* ablet, bleak, whitebait.

ablégat, *n.m.,* ablegate.

⊙**ablégation,** *n.f.,* ablegation.

ablepsie, *n.f.,* (med.) ablepsy.

ableret, *n.m.,* (fishing—*pêche*) hoop-net, purse-net.

⊙**abluant, -e,** *adj.,* (med.) abluent, cleansing.

⊙**abluer,** *v.a.,* to revive old writing, to wash with gall-nut.

ablution, *n.f.,* ablution, washing, purification. *Faire ses*—*s;* to perform one's ablutions.

abnégation, *n.f.,* abnegation, renunciation, sacrifice. — *de soi-même;* self-denial. *Faire* — *de;* to renounce.

aboi, *n.m.,* barking, baying.

aboiement or **aboiment** (-boa-mān), *n.m.,* barking, baying.

abois, *n.m. pl.,* despairing condition, last shift, distress. *Aux*— at bay, hard up. *Mettre aux* —; to keep at bay.

abolir, *v.a.,* to abolish, to repeal, to annul. — *un impôt;* to take off a tax.

s'abolir, *v.r.,* to fall into disuse, to become obsolete.

abolissable, *adj.,* abolishable.

abolissement (-mān), *n.m.,* abolishment.

abolition, *n.f.,* abolition; royal pardon.

abolitionniste, *n.m.,* abolitionist.

abominable, *adj.,* abominable, execrable.

abominablement, *adv.,* abominably.

abomination, *n.f.,* abomination, detestation. *Avoir en* —; to abominate. *Être en* — ; to be detested.

abondamment (-da-mān), *adv.,* abundantly.

abondance, *n.f.,* abundance, plenty, copiousness, plentifulness; multitude, affluence; richness (of language—*de langage*); weak wine-and-water (in schools—*dans les pensions*). *Corne*

d'—; horn of plenty, cornucopia. — *de biens;* opulence. *Vivre, être, dans l'*—; to live in plenty.

Parler avec —; to speak fluently. *Écrire, parler, d'*—; to write, to speak, extempore. — *de biens ne nuit pas;* store is no sore.

abondant, -e, *adj.,* abounding, plentiful, copious; fruitful, exuberant, teeming, voluble, diffusive. *Une langue* — *e;* a copious language.

abonder, *v.n.,* to abound in or with, to be full of; to overflow. *Il abonde dans votre sens;* he supports your opinion. — *dans son sens;* to be wedded to one's own opinion.

⊙**abonné, -e,** *part.,* valued, estimated.

abonné, *n.m.,* **-e,** *n.f.,* subscriber (to periodicals, theatres, &c.—*aux journaux, théâtres, &c.*).

abonnement (mān), *n.m.,* subscription (to periodicals, theatres, &c.—*aux journaux, théâtres, &c.*); agreement. *Les*—*s sont suspendus pour ce soir* (of places of amusement—*de lieux de plaisir*); season-tickets not available this evening.

abonner, *v.a.,* to subscribe for.

s'abonner, *v.r.,* to subscribe; to compound for. *On s'abonne à;* subscriptions are received at.

⊙**abonnir,** *v.a.,* to better, to mend, to improve.

⊙**abonnir,** *v.n.,* **s'abonnir,** *v.r.,* to mend, to grow better.

⊙**abonnissement** (nis-mān), *n.m.* (fam.), improvement, amelioration.

abord, *n.m.,* landing; arrival; access; admittance, approach; attack, onset. *Avoir l'* —*facile;* to be easy of access. *De prime abord;* at first.

à bord, *adv.,* aboard, on board.

d'abord, *adv.,* first, at first, at first sight. *Tout d'abord, au premier abord, dès l'abord;* at first, from the very first. *Dès l'abord, j'ai senti que je devais . . .* I felt, from the very first, that I ought . . .

abordable, *adj.,* accessible, accostable, of easy access.

abordage, *n.m.,* (nav.) boarding; fouling. *Aller à l'*—; to board a ship.

aborder, *v.n.,* to arrive at; to land.

aborder, *v.a.,* to come near, to come to, to come up with; to board, to run foul of (a ship—*un vaisseau*); to accost; to broach, handle (a subject—*un sujet*). — *un vaisseau ennemi;* to board an enemy's ship. — *par accident;* to run foul of.

s'aborder, *v.r.,* to run foul of each other; to come up with another.

aborigène, *adj.,* first, original, aboriginal.

aborigènes, *n.m. pl.,* aborigines.

abornement, *n.m.,* the placing of boundaries, landmarks, &c., to designate the limits of fields, estates, &c.

aborner, *v.a.,* to place boundaries, landmarks, &c., designating the limits of fields, estates, &c.

aborti-f, -ve, *adj.,* abortive.

abot, *n.m.,* log (for tying to horses' fore feet — *pour entraver les pieds de devant des chevaux*).

abouchement (-boosh-mān), *n.m.,* interview, conference, parley; (anat.) anastomosis.

aboucher, *v.a.,* to bring together, to confer.

s'aboucher, *v.r.,* to have an interview; to confer with; (anat.) to inosculate.

about, *n.m.,* (carp.) end.

abouté, -e, *adj.,* placed end to end.

aboutement (-boot-mān), *n.m.,* (carp.) but, abutment.

abouter, *v.a.,* to join end to end.

aboutir, *v.n.,* to join; to border upon; to meet; (surg.) to burst; to come to, to tend to; to end in. *N'* — *à rien;* to come to nothing. *Ce champ aboutit à un marais;* this field borders upon a fen. *Faire* — *un abcès;* to bring an abscess to a head. *S'aboutir* (gard.); to bud, be covered with buds.

aboutissant, -e, *adj.,* bordering upon.

aboutissants (rarely used without the word *tenants*), *n.m. pl.*, limits of a thing; abuttal; particulars; connexions. *Je n'aime pas les tenants et — de cet homme;* I do not like the set by which that man is surrounded. *Savoir les tenants et — d'une affaire;* to know all about a thing.

aboutissement (-măn), *n.m.*, eking piece (tailoring—*terme de tailleur*); (surg.) the drawing to a head.

ab ovo. *adv.*, from the beginning.

aboyant, -e, *adj.*, barking.

aboyer, *v.n.*, to bark, to bay, to yelp; to dun. *Il aboie après tout le monde;* he snarls at everybody. *— après quelque chose:* to long for, covet, a thing. *— à la lune;* to bark when one cannot bite.

aboyeur, *n.m.*, barker; snarler; dun; linkman (at the door of a theatre—*à la porte des théâtres*); (orni.) greenshank. *Ce journaliste n'est qu'un —;* this journalist is nothing but a snarler.

abracadabra, *n.m.*, abracadabra.

abrasion. *n.f.*, (med.) abrasion, excoriation.

abraxas, *n.m.*, abracadabra.

abrégé, -e, *adj.*, short, summary.

abrégé, *n.m.*, abridgment, compendium, epitome, abstract, summary. *En —;* compendiously, briefly. *Réduire en —;* to epitomize.

abréger, *v.a.*, to abridge, to shorten, to epitomize; to abbreviate, to cut down, to cut short. *Pour —;* to be brief.

abreuver, *v.a.*, to water, to give drink to; to make drink; to soak, to drench; to fill; (paint.) to prepare, to prime; to soak (wood—*du bois*).

s'abreuver de. *v.r.*, (of animals—*des animaux*) to go to water; to drink plentifully.

abreuvoir, *n.m.*, watering-place, horsepond; (mas.) abreuvoir. *— à mouches* (burlesque style—*style burlesque*); a large wound on the head or face.

abréviateur, *n.m.*, abbreviator, abridger.

abréviati-f, -ve, *adj.*, abbreviatory.

abréviation, *n.f.*, abbreviation, contraction.

abri, *n.m.*, shelter, cover. *Être sous l' — d'un bois;* to be sheltered by a wood. *Sans —;* homeless. *Donner un — à;* to shelter. *A l'—;* sheltered, under cover. *Être à l' —;* to be under shelter. *Être à l' — du vent;* to be sheltered from the wind. *A l' — de la persécution;* safe from persecution. *Mettre à l'—;* to shelter, screen.

abricot, *n.m.*, apricot.

abricoté, *n.m.*, candied apricot.

abricotier, *n.m.*, apricot-tree.

abrier, *v.a.*, (nav.) to becalm; to belee.

abriter. *v.a.*, to shelter, to shield, to screen, (nav.) to becalm.

abrité, -e, *adj.*, (gard.) sheltered.

s'abriter, *v.r.*, to shelter one's self; to take shelter; to assist. *Abritez-vous mutuellement;* mutually assist each other.

abrivent, *n.m.*, (gard.) matting, screen; shelter; sentry-box; hut.

abrogation, *n.f.*, abrogation, repeal; annulment.

abroger, *v.a.*, to abrogate, to repeal.

s'abroger, *v.r.*, to fall into disuse, to grow obsolete.

abrouti, -e, *adj.*, nipped, browsed.

abroutissement (-măn), *n.m.*, damage done to trees by cattle browsing.

abrupt, -e, *adj.*, rugged; (bot.) abrupt.

abruption, *n.f.*, abruption; (surg.) rupture, fracture.

ex abrupto, *adv.*, suddenly, bluntly, off-hand.

abrutir, *v.a.*, to stupify, to besot, to brutalize.

s'abrutir, *v.r.*, to become stupid, to be besotted, to get brutalized.

abrutissant, -e, *adj.*, brutalizing; stupifying.

abrutissement. (-măn), *n.m.*, brutishness stupor.

abrutisseur, *n.m.*, brutalizer; stupifying

abscisse, *n.f.*, (geom.) abscissa.

absence. *n.f.*, absence. *— d'esprit;* absence of mind. *Avoir des — s d'esprit;* to have fits of absence. *Remarquer l'— de;* to miss.

absent, -e. *adj.*, absent, out of the way, missing; wanting; (of the mind — *de l'esprit*) wandering.

absent. *n.m.*, one absent, absentee. *Les — s ont toujours tort;* the absent are always in the wrong.

s'absenter, *v.r.*, to be absent; to keep out of the way.

absentéisme. *n.m.*, absenteeism.

abside. *n.f.*, (arch. and rel.) apsis.

absinthe, *n.f.*, absinthium; wormwood; bitters.

absinthé, -e, *adj.*, absinthiated.

absolu. *n.m.*, absolute, existing independent of any other cause.

absolu,-e, *adj.*, absolute; arbitrary, despotical, unlimited; peremptory; magisterial; positive, unconditional.

absolument, *adv.*, absolutely, arbitrarily, peremptorily; positively, indispensably. *Il refusa —;* he gave a flat denial.

absolution, *n.f.*, absolution; acquittal. *Sans avoir reçu l'—;* unabsolved.

absolutisme, *n.m.*, absolutism.

absolutiste, *n.m.f.*, partisan of absolute power.

absolutoire, *adj.*, absolutory.

absorbable, *adj.*, absorbable.

absorbant, -e, *adj.*, absorptive, absorbent.

⊙absorbant, *n.m.*, absorbent.

absorbé, -e, *part.*, absorbed, drowned, rapt. *Il est — dans l'étude;* he is absorbed in study.

absorbement, *n.m.*, absorption (of mind—*d'esprit*).

absorber. *v.a.*, to absorb, to swallow up, to drown; to consume, to waste; to engross, to occupy entirely; to take up.

s'absorber, *v.r.* to be absorbed.

absorption. *n.f.*, absorption.

absoudre (absolvant, absous), *v.a.*, to absolve, to acquit, to bring in not guilty, to clear; to give absolution.

absou-s, -te, *part.*, acquitted, absolved, discharged.

absoute. *n.f.*, (c. rel.) general absolution.

abstème, *adj.*, abstemious.

abstème, *n.m.f.*, one who abstains from wine.

s'abstenir. *v.r.*, to abstain, to refrain, to forbear, to forego. *S'—de vin;* to abstain from wine.

abstention, *n.f.*, abstention; retirement of a judge from a trial.

abstergent. -e, *adj.*, (med.) cleansing; abstersive; abstergent.

abstergent, *n.m.*, (med.) abstergent.

absterger, *v.a.*, to absterge; to cleanse.

abstersi-f, -ve, *adj.*, (med.) abstersive, cleansing.

abstersion, *n.f.*, (surg.) abstersion.

abstinence, *n.f.*, abstinence, temperance, sobriety.

abstinent, -e, *adj.*, abstemious, sober.

abstracti-f, -ve, *adj.*, abstractive.

abstraction, *n.f.*, absence of mind, abstraction. *Avoir des — s;* to have fits of absence. *Par —;* abstractedly.

abstractivement (-man), *adv.*, abstractly, separately.

abstraire (abstrayant, abstrait), *v.a.*, to draw from, to separate, to abstract.

abstrait, -e, *adj.*, abstract; abstruse; inattentive, absent (in mind—*en esprit*).

abstraitement (-trèt-mān), *adv.*, abstractedly, separately

abstrus, -e, *adj.*, abstruse, intricate, difficult; dark, obscure, recondite.

absurde, *adj.*, absurd, nonsensical, foolish, irrational, preposterous. *Réduire une opinion à l'—;* to show the absurdity of an opinion *Tomber dans l'—;* to fall into the absurd.

absurdement, *adv.*, absurdly, nonsensically.

absurdité, *n.f.*, absurdity, nonsense, preposterousness, foolishness.

abus, *n.m.*, abuse, misuse (of a thing—*des choses*); grievance; error. *Réformer, corriger, les abus;* to redress grievances.

abuser, *v.n.*, to abuse, to impose on, to misuse, to use ill, to make a bad use of, to misemploy. *Vous abusez de ma patience,* you wear out my patience.

abuser, *v.a.*, to cheat, to deceive, to delude, to gull.

s'abuser. *v.r.*, to mistake, to be mistaken.

abuseur, *n.m.*, (l.u.), cheat, deceiver, impostor.

abusi-f,-ve. *adj.*, abusive, improper, against right use.

abusivement (-mān), *adv.*, abusively, improperly.

abuter, *v.a.*, to throw for first go; *v.n.*, (shipbuilding—*construction de vaisseaux*) to abut.

abyme. *n.m.*, V. abime.

acabit. *n.m.*, quality (of fruits, vegetables—*des fruits, légumes*); quality (of persons—*des personnes*). *Cet homme est d'un bon —;* he is a good sort of fellow. *Ce sont des du même acabit;* they are all tarred with the same brush.

acacia. *n.m.*, acacia; gum-tree.

académicien (-si-in), *s.m.*, academician; academic (of Plato's school—*de l'école de Platon*).

académie, *n.f.*, academy, society of learned men; academy (division of the University of France — *une des divisions de l'Université de France*); academy (Plato's—*de Platon*); university; riding-school; pupils, school; gaming-house; (paint.) academical figure.

académique. *adj.*, belonging to an academy, academical, *Système* —; academism.

académiquement (-mik-mān), *adv.*, academically.

académiser, *v.n.*, to paint from a model.

académiste. *s.m.*, academist, pupil (of a riding school—*d'une école d'équitation*).

acagnarder, *v.a.*, (fam.) to accustom to sloth.

s'acagnarder, *v.r.*, to grow slothful, to lead an idle life; to become besotted.

acajou. *n.m.*, mahogany.

acanthe, *n.f.*, acanthus, bear's-foot.

acare or **acarus.** *n.m*, acarus, itch animalcule.

acariâtre. *adj.*, crabbed, cross-grained, waspish, shrewish.

acariens, *n.m. pl.*, (ent.) arachnidans.

acatalecte, acatalectique, *n.m. and adj.*, acatalectic.

acatalepsie, *n.f.*, (med.) acatalepsy.

acataleptique. *adj.*, acataleptic.

acaule, *adj.*, (bot.) acaulous.

accablant, -e, *adj.*, grievous, oppressive, insufferable, overwhelming; annoying.

accablé, -e, *adj.*, dejected, depressed. *Être —;* to be extremely low-spirited.

accablement, *n.m.*, heaviness, grief, dejection of spirits, oppression, discouragement. *Être dans l'—;* to be in the greatest dejection.

accabler, *v.a.*, to crush, to bear down, to overwhelm; to throw, to weigh, to press down; to overload; to overpower; to afflict, to deject, to depress, to overwhelm; to load with, to heap on.

accalmie. *n.f.*,(nav.) lull.

accaparement (-mān), *n.m.*, monopoly. engrossment. forestalling.

accaparer. *v.a.*, to engross, to monopolize, to forestall; to swallow up.

accapareu-r. *n.m.*, **-se,** *n.f.*, monopolist, engrosser, forestaller.

accastillage. *n.m.*, the space occupied by the forecastle and quarter-deck.

accastiller. *v.a.*, to provide a ship with a fore and a hind-castle.

accastillé. -e, *adj.*, (of a ship—*d'un vaisseau*) having a fore and a hind-castle.

accéder. *v.n.*, to accede, to agree to.

accélérat-eur. -rice. *adj.*, accelerative.

accélération, *n.f.*, acceleration; hastening, dispatch.

accéléré, -e. *adj.*, accelerated, quickened. *Au pas —;* in quick time.

accélérer, *v.a.*, to accelerate, to quicken; to despatch, to forward, to hasten.

accenser or **acenser,** *v.a.*, to lease, to let, to rent.

accent. *n.m.*, stress of the voice, accent; pronunciation; emphasis. — *aigu, circonflexe, grave:* acute, circumflex, grave, accent. — *nasillard;* twang. — *très-fortement prononcé;* broad accent. *Sans —;* unaccented. *Prêtes l'oreille à mes — s:* hearken to my strain.

accentuation, *n.f.*, accentuation.

accentué. -e. *adj.*, accented, accentuated.

accentuer. *v.a.*, to accent, to accentuate.

acceptable. *adj.*, acceptable, worth accepting.

acceptant. *n.m.*, (jur.) a person who accepts.

acceptation, *n.f.*, acceptance.

accepter. *v.a.*, to accept, to receive. *Qui vaut la peine d'être accepté:* worth accepting

accepteur, *n.m.*, (com.) acceptor.

acceptilation, *n.f*, acceptilation

acception, *n.f.*, respect, regard; (of words—*des mots*) sense, meaning, acceptation. — *de personnes;* respect to persons.

accès, *n.m.*, access, approach, admittance; attack, fit (of fever, madness, &c.—*de fièvre, de folie, &c.*). *Par —;* by fits and starts.

accessibilité, *n.f.*, accessibility

accessible. *adj.*, accessible, approachable, easy to come at.

accession, *n.f.*, access, entry; accession; adhesion.

accessit, (-sit), *n.m*, the second best, the first after the prizeman (in academies. schools, &c.—*dans les écoles, les pensions, les collèges, &c.*).

accessoire. *adj.*, accessory, additional.

accessoire. *n.m.*, accessory; (paint.) accessory; (thea.) property. *Fournisseur d'—s;* property-man.

accessoirement. *adv.*, accessorily.

accident, *n.m.*, accident, incident, casualty; (paint.) accident; (med.) symptom; (mus.) incidental; irregularity (in ground—*de terrain*). *Par—;* accidentally.

accidenté. -e. *adj.*, rough, uneven, unequal, broken (of ground—*de terrain*).

accidentel. -le, *adj.*, accidental, adventitious, incidental; fortuitous, eventual, casual.

accidentellement (-mān), *adv.*, accidentally, by chance.

accipitres, *n.m. pl.*, accipiters.

accipitrin, -e, *adj.*, accipitrine.

accise. *n.f.*, inland duty, excise. *Préposé à l'—:* exciseman.

acclamation, *n.f.*, acclamation, shout, cheering, huzza. *Saluer par des —s;* to cheer.

acclamer, *v.a.*, to acclaim, to applaud.

acclimatation, *n.f.*, acclimation, acclimatization.

acclimater. *v.a.*, to acclimatize, to accustom to a climate

*s'***acclimater**, *v.r.*, to become accustomed to a new climate.

accointance, *n.f.*, (fam. and b.s.) acquaintance, commerce.

*s'***accointer**, *v.r*, to become intimately acquainted with any one.

⊙**accoisement**, *n.m.*, appeasement.

⊙**accoiser**, *v.a.*, to appease; *s'—*, *v.r.*, to become appeased; to end.

accolade. *n.f.*, embrace; accolade; (cook.—mus.—print.) brace; a crooked line. brace. — *brisée* (print.); half-brace. *Une—de lapereaux;* a brace of rabbits. *Donner l'— à:* to embrace. to dub a knight.

accolage. *n.m.*, act of tying the vine to its prop

accolé. *-e*, *part.*, (her.) joined together.

accolement. *n.m.*, joining, uniting; union.

accoler, *v.a.*, to hug, to embrace; to place side by side; to couple; (hort.) to prop, to tie up.

accolure. *n.f.*, (agri.) a band of straw, osier.

accommodable, *adj.*, that may be settled, accommodable.

accommodage, *n.m.*, the dressing of meat, cooking; hair-dressing.

accommodant. *-e*, *adj.*, accommodating, complying, courteous.

accommodé. *-e*, *part.*, fitted up, adjusted; (cook.) dressed. *Étrangement —;* In a nice mess.

accommodement (-mån), *n.m.*, accommodation; agreement, composition; settlement; reconciliation; way, medium. *Un homme d' —;* a man easy to deal with. *En venir à un —,* to come to terms.

accommoder, *v.a.*, to adapt, to accommodate, to fit, to make up; to mend, to improve; to reconcile, to conciliate; to adjust; to be convenient; to dress, to trim; to cook; to treat, to serve out; to thrash; to let one have, to sell *Ceci vous accommodera-t-il!* will this suit you?

*s'***accommoder**. *v.r.*, to agree. to come to terms; to accommodate one's self. to suit; to make free with; to be pleased with, to put up with. *— à tout;* to put up with anything. *— de tout;* to be pleased with everything.

*****accompagnage**, *n.m.*, the woof of a stuff worked with gold and silk.

*****accompagnat-eur**. *n.m.*,**-rice** *n.f.*, (mus) accompanist.

*****accompagnement** (-mån), *n.m.*, accompanying; attendance, retinue; accompaniment, accessory, appendix. *— de quatuor;* accompaniment for stringed instruments *— d'harmonie;* accompaniment for wind instruments. *— à grand orchestre;* full accompaniment.

*****accompagner**, *v.a.*, to accompany, to wait on, to attend; to be of the retinue, to follow; to match, to suit with; to add, to back; to be the accompanist. *J'ai eu l'honneur de l'— chez elle:* I had the honour of seeing her home.

*s'***accompagner**, *v.r.*, to be accompanied; to accompany one's self (with an instrument—*d'un instrument*).

accompli, *-e*, *adj.*, accomplished, finished, fulfilled; complete; faultless, perfect. *Une beauté — e:* a perfect beauty.

accomplir. *v.a.*, to accomplish, to effect; to finish, to complete; to fulfil, to make good. *— sa promesse:* to perform one's promise.

*s'***accomplir**. *v.r.*, to be accomplished, to be performed.

accomplissement (-mån), *n.m.*, accomplishment, fulfilment; completion, execution, observance.

accon. *n.m.*, small lighter

accoquiner. *V.* **acoquiner**.

accord, *s.m.*, agreement, bargain, contract, convention, settlement, stipulation; consent, concurrence; good understanding, unity; (mus.) accord, chord; (paint.) harmony, accord *Étre d' —; demeurer d' —; tomber d' —;* to agree, to be agreed. *D' —;* granted, done *D'un commun —,* by common consent. *Étre d' —;* (mus.) to be in tune. *Tenir l' —;* to keep in tune.

accordable. *adj.*, grantable, that may be granted; (mus) tunable; (of men—*des hommes*) reconcilable

*****accordailles**, *n.f. pl.*, (pop.) the ceremony of signing the articles of marriage

accordant. *-e*, *adj.*, (mus) accordant; tunable. harmonious.

accorde! *int.* (nav) now! (order given to rowers to pull together—*ordre donné aux rameurs de ramer ensemble*).

accordé. *n.m.*, *-e*. *n.f.*, bridegroom, bride (after the marriage-articles are signed—*après la signature du contrat*), one who is betrothed

accordéon. *n.m.*, accordion.

accorder. *v.a.*, to grant, to allow, to accord, to give, to allot, to bestow, to concede; to admit, to give up; to make friends, to reconcile; (gram.) to make agree; (mus.) to tune, to string *— mal;* to mistune. *Accordez vos flûtes;* agree in between you

*s'***accorder**. *v.r.*, to agree, to suit, to be suited, to accord, to correspond; to square; to join, to concur. *S'— du prix,* to agree upon the price. *Il ne s'accorde pas avec lui-même;* he is inconsistent with himself.

accordeu-r, *n.m.*,**-se**. *n.f.*, tuner (of instruments—*d'instruments*). *Clef d' —;* tuning-hammer.

accordoir, *n.m.*, tuning-hammer.

accore, *n.f.*, (nav.) shore, prop, stanchion.

accorer, *v.a.*, (nav) to shore up, to prop, to stay.

accorné, *-e*. *adj.*, (her.) horned.

accort. *-e*. *adj.*, flexible, complying, courteous, affable.

accortise. *n.f.*, complaisance, affability.

accostable (l.u.), *adj.*, accostable, easy of access *Il n' est pas —;* he is not approachable.

accoste. *n.m.*, (nav.) order to bring alongside.

accoster, *v.a.*, to accost, to make up to, to come or go up to one; (nav.) to come alongside.

*s'***accoster de**. *v.r.*, to keep company with, to make acquaintance with.

accotar, *n.m.* *V.* **accotoir**

accotement, *n.m.*, (engineering—*terme d'ingénieur*), driftway.

accoter, *v.a.*, to prop up, to support, to bear up, to lean

*s'***accoter**, *v.r.*, to lean on anything, to support one's side.

accotoir, *n.m.*, prop, leaning-stock, stanchion; (nav.) filling piece.

accouchée. *n.f.*, a woman in child-bed, lying-in woman.

accouchement (-koosh-mån), *n.m.*, childbed; delivery, confinement; obstetrics; midwifery. *Hôpital des —s;* lying-in-hospital. *Faire un —:* to deliver a woman.

accoucher, *v.n.*, to lie in, to be brought to bed. to be delivered. *— avant terme;* to miscarry. *Accouchez donc* (fam.) come, out with it!

accoucher. *v.a.*, to deliver a woman.

accoucheur, *n.m.*, man-midwife, accoucheur.

accoucheuse. *n.f.*, a midwife.

*s'***accouder**. *v.r.*, to lean on one's elbow.

accoudoir, *n.m.*, anything to lean the elbow upon.

accouer, *v.a.*, to tie the halter of the first horse to the tail of the second, and so on; to wound a stag in the shoulder, to hamstring him.

accoulins, *n.m. pl.*, alluvion; clay for making bricks.

accouple, *n.f.*, leash, brace.

accouplement, *s.m.*, coupling, pairing, joining or yoking together; copulation.

accoupler, *v.a.*, to couple; to tack or join together; to yoke; to match, to pair. — *des bœufs;* to yoke oxen.

s'accoupler, *v.r.*, to couple, to copulate; to pair.

accourcir, *v.a.*, to shorten, to make shorter, to abridge.

s'accourcir, *v.a.*, to shorten, to grow shorter, to decrease.

accourcissement (-màn), *n.m.*, shortening, diminution.

accourir, *v.n.*, to run to, to hasten, to flock together.

accourcie. *n.f.*, short cut; a passage formed in a ship's hold, to go fore and aft.

accoutré.-e, *part*, accoutred, dressed.

accoutrement, *n.m.*, (jest. or iron.) garb, dress, gear.

accoutrer, *v.a.*, (jest. or iron.) to dress out.

s'accoutrer, *v.r.*, to dress one's self out ridiculously.

ⓈⒶ**accoutumance,** *n.f.*, habit, custom.

accoutumé, -e, *adj*, accustomed, habitual, used to. *A l'—;* as usual, customarily.

accoutumer, *v.a.*, to accustom, to use, to habituate; to inure.

accoutumer, *v.n* , to use, to be wont.

s'accoutumer, *v.r.*, to accustom, to use, to inure, one's self.

ⓈⒶ**accouvé, -e,** (fam.) *adj.*, brooding over (the fire, &c.—*au coin du feu, &c.*).

accréditer, *v.a.*, to accredit; to give reputation, credit, sanction to; to bring into vogue, to procure esteem.

s'accréditer, *v.r.*, to get a name or reputation, to get into credit; to ingratiate one's self.

accrétion. *n.f.* (med.) accretion.

accroc (-krò), *n.m.*, impediment, hinderance; rent *Faire un — à;* to rend.

Ⓢ**accroche.** *n.f*, hinderance, obstacle.

accroche-cœur, *n.m.*, (—) (curl —*coiffure*) heart-breaker.

accrochement, *n.m.*, locking of two carriages together.

accrocher, *v.a.*, to hang up or upon, to hook; to catch, to tear; to get, to pick up; to lock, to get locked with; to grapple (a ship—*unvaisseau*). *Il lui à accroché de l'argent;* he has done him out of some money.

s'accrocher, *v.r.*, to catch in; to hang on; to lay hold of.

accroire, *v.a.*, to believe. *Faire — à;* to make believe. *En faire — à quelqu'un;* to impose upon one. *S'en faire —;* to be self-conceited.

accroissement, *n.m.*, increase, growth, enlargement.

accroître, *v.a*, to increase, to enlarge, to amplify, *to* augment.

accroître, *v.n.*, to increase, to augment.

s'accroître, *v.r.*, to increase, to grow; to be augmented or advanced.

accroupi.-e. *adj.*, squat, cowering.

s'accroupir, *v.r.*, to sit down upon the hams or heels, to squat.

accroupissement (-màn), *n.m.*, cowering, squatting.

accru, *n.m.*, sprig produced by roots.

accrue, *n.f.*, increase of land caused by the retiring of waters; encroachment by trees on adjoining land.

Ⓢ***accueil** (-keu), *n.m.*, reception, welcome; (com.) protection, honour (of bills—*de billets,*

lettres de change). *Faire —;* to receive kindly. *Recevoir bon —* (com.); to meet due honour, protection.

*accueillir (-keu-), *v.a.*, to receive, to make welcome, to entertain; to overtake; to assail; (com.) to honour; to protect. *Être bien accueilli;* to be received with a hearty welcome. *La tempête nous accueillit;* we were overtaken by a storm.

accul. *n.m.*, place that has no egress; blind alley; small bay, cove; (hunt.) terrier, lodge, hole; breeching (of a cannon—*d'un canon*)

acculer, *v.a.*, to bring one to a stand; to drive one into a corner; to drive one into a place from which he cannot escape; (hunt.) to run home.

accumulat-eur, *n.m.*, **-rice,** *n.f.*, accumulator.

accumulation, *n.f.*, accumulation.

accumuler, *v.a.*, to accumulate, to heap up, to store, to amass. — *crime sur crime;* to add one crime to another.

s'accumuler, *v.r.*, to accumulate, to increase.

accusable, *adj.*, accusable, impeachable, chargeable.

accusat-eur, *n.m.*, **-rice,** *n.f.*, accuser, indicter, impeacher.

accusatif, *n.m.*, (gram.) accusative case. *A l'—;* in the accusative.

accusation. *n.f.*, accusation, indictment, impeachment, charge; complaint; prosecution. *Chef d' —;* count of an indictment. *Mise en —;* arraignment. *Intenter une —;* to prefer an indictment. *Mettre en —;* to impeach. *Prononcer la mise en —;* to find a true bill.

accusatoire, *adj.*, accusatory.

accusé, *n.m.*, **-e,** *n.f.*, person accused, prisoner, culprit. — *de réception* (com.); acknowledgment.

accuser, *v.a.*, to accuse of, to charge with; to indict, to arraign, to impeach; to reproach, to tax; to blame, to accuse; to dispute the validity of a deed; to mention, to give notice. —*réception d'une lettre;* to acknowledge the reception of a letter.

s'accuser, *v.r.*, to accuse one's self.

acéphale, *adj.*, acephalous, without a head.

acéphales, *n.m. pl.*, acephala.

acérain, -e, *adj.*, relating to steel.

acerbe, *adj.*, sour, sharp, acerb; harsh, bitter.

acerbité, *n.f.*, acerbity, harshness; bitterness.

acéré, -e, *adj*, steely, steeled; sharp, keen, sharp-edged; acerose.

acérer, *v.a.*, to steel.

Ⓢ**acéreu-x, -se,** *adj.*, acerose, needle-shaped.

acescence, *n.f.*, acescency.

acescent, -e, *adj.*, acescent.

acétabule, *n.m.*, acetabulum.

acétate, *n.m.*, acetate.

acéteu-x, -se, *adj.*, acetous.

acétique, *adj.*, acetic.

achalandage, *n.m.*, customers of a shop; good will and fixtures.

achalandé, -e, *part.*, that has customers. *Boutique bien —e;* a well-frequented shop.

achalander, *v.a.*, to get custom, to procure customers, to procure custom to.

s'achalander, *v.r.*, to get or draw customers.

acharné, -e, *adj*, fleshed; rabid; infuriated; implacable; desperate; intense. *Un combat —;* a desperate fight. *Une haine — e;* an implacable hatred.

acharnement, *n.m.*, tenacity; rancour, blind fury; stubbornness, ill-nature; obstinacy, desperation. *Avec —;* unmercifully. *C'est de l'—;* this is bare fury.

acharner, *v.a.*, to flesh; to rouse, to madden; to embitter, to envenom.

s'acharner, *v.r.*, to be intent, bent, set upon; to set one's heart upon; to be infuriated,

implacable. *Il s'acharne à l'étude ;* his heart is set upon study.

⊙**achars,** *n.m. pl.,* Indian pickle.

achat, *n.m.,* purchase, purchasing, buying ; bargain.

ache. *n.f.,* (bot.) smallage.

acheminement (ash-mi-n-màn), *n.m.,* step ; preparatory measure.

acheminer (ash-mi-né), *v.a.,* to forward, to send on.

*s'***acheminer.** *v.r.,* to set out or forward, to take one's way ; to begin one's journey ; to get on.

acheter (ash-té), *v.a.,* to buy, to purchase. — *cher ou bon marché :* to buy dear or cheap. —*en bloc ;* to buy in a lump. —*chat en poche ;* to buy a pig in a poke.

acheteur (ash-teur), *n.m.,* buyer, purchaser, bidder.

achevé, -e, *part.,* finished, perfect, exquisite ; absolute ; right-down, arrant. *Beauté — e ;* a perfect beauty. *Sot —.* downright ass.

achèvement (shèv-màn), *n.m.,* completion, finishing.

achever (ash-vé), *v.a.,* to finish, to put the finishing hand to ; to close, to end, to conclude, to terminate, to perfect, to consummate ; to despatch. — *de boire ;* to drink up. *Achevez !* out with it !

achillée, *n.f.,* (bot.) milfoil.

achit, *n.m.,* wild vine.

achoppement (-shop-màn),*n.m.,* stumbling, impediment. *Pierre d'—;* stumbling-block.

achopper, *v.n.,* to stumble, to knock one's self against anything ; (fig.) to fail.

achromatique (-kro-), *adj.,* achromatic.

achromatisme (-kro-), *n.m.,* (opt.) achromatism.

⊙**achronique,** (-kro-) *adj.* V. **acronyque.**

aciculaire, *adj.,* acicular.

acide. *n.m.,* acid.

acide, *adj.,* acid, sour, tart, sharp.

acidifier, *v.a.,* to acidify.

acidité, *n.f.,* acidity, sourness, sharpness, tartness.

acidule, *adj.,* of the nature of acids,acidulous.

acidulé, -e, *adj.,* acidulated.

aciduler, *v.a.,* to acidulate.

acier, *n.m.,* steel. — *fondu ;* cast steel. — *indien, wootz ;* wootz. — *poule, de cémentation ;* blistered steel. *Articles d'—;* steel wares. *Bijouterie d'—;* polished steel wares. *Fil d'—;* steel wire.

aciérage, *n.m.,* (metal.) the hardening of copper.

aciération, *n.f.,* the converting of iron into steel.

aciérer, *v.a.,* to convert into steel, to steel.

aciérie, *n.f.,* steel manufactory.

acineux, -se, *adj.,* acinose, acinous.

aciniforme, *adj.,* aciniform.

acmé, *n.m.,* (med.) acme.

acolyte, *n.m.,* acolothist, acolyte ; companion.

acompte, *n.m.,* instalment, partial payment.

acon, *n.m.* V. **accon.**

aconit (-nit), *n.m.,* aconite, wolf's-bane. — *tue-chien :* dog's-bane.

acoquinant, -e, *adj.,* (fam.) alluring, engaging, captivating.

acoquiner. *v.a.,* (fam.) to allure, to bewitch, to captivate.

*s'***acoquiner.** *v.r.,* (fam.) to be bewitched, to be greatly attached. *Il s'acoquine auprès de cette femme :* he is bewitched with that woman.

acotylédone, *adj.,* (of plants—*des plantes*), acotyledonous.

à-coup, *n.m.* (— — *s*), jerk.

acoustique. *n.f.* (*n.p.*), acoustics.

acoustique, *adj.,* acoustic. *Cordon —,*

speaking-pipe. *Cornet —;* ear-trumpet. *Voûte —;* whispering dome, gallery.

acquéreur, *n.m.,* buyer, purchaser.

acquérir (acquérant, acquis), *v.a.,* to acquire, to purchase, to buy, to obtain ; to get, to achieve, to attain, to gain.

*s'***acquérir,** *v.r.,* to get, to be gotten, to be acquired, obtained, or purchased.

acquêt. *n.m.,* (jur.) common property of two married people.

acquiescement (-màn), *n.m.,* acquiescence, compliance, consent, willingness.

acquiescer, *v.n.,* to acquiesce, to agree, to assent, to yield, to comply.

acquis, *part.* of Acquérir.

acquis, -e, *adj.,* acquired ; (med.) adventitious.

acquis, *n.m.,* acquired knowledge, acquirements.

acquisition. *n.f.,* acquisition, getting, acquiring, attaining, purchase. *Contrat d' —;* deed of purchase.

acquit, *n.m.,* discharge, receipt ; lead (at billiards—*au billard*). *Par manière d' —;* for form's sake. *Jouer à l'—;* to play who shall pay for the whole. *Pour acquit* (on bills—*sur billets, factures, &c.*); paid. *Donner — de;* to give a receipt for. *Mettre son— à :* to put " paid " on, to receipt.

acquit-à-caution, *n.m.,* (—*s* —) (customs) permit.

⊙**acquit-patent,** *n.m.,* (—*s* —*s*) royal decree granting the remission of a debt.

acquittement (-màn). *n.m.,* payment, clearing off, liquidation ; acquittal.

acquitter, *v.a.,* to pay, to pay off, to clear, to quit ; to receipt ; to acquit, to discharge.

*s'***acquitter,** *v.r.,* to fulfil, to perform ; to pay off one's debts.

acre, *n.f.,* acre.

âcre, *adj.,* sharp, sour, tart, acrimonious ; bitter, biting ; acrid.

âcreté, *n.f.,* acrity, sharpness, sourness, tartness, acrimony.

acrimonie, *n.f.,* acrimony, sharpness, keenness.

acrimonieu-x, -se, *adj.,* acrimonious, sharp.

acrobate, *n.m.f.,* rope-dancer.

acronyque, *adj.,* acronic, acronical, acronycal.

acropole. *n.f.,* acropolis.

acrostiche, *n.m.,* acrostic.

acrotère, *n.m.,* (arch.) acroterium, blocking course ; (nav.) cape, headland.

acte. *n.m.,* act ; deed ; indenture, instrument ; document ; charter ; *pl.,* records, public registers, rolls. — *faux ;* forged deed. *Les — s des apôtres ;* the acts of the apostles. *Expédition d'un —;* copy of a deed. *Donner — de;* to deliver an official certificate of. *Rédiger un —;* to draw up a document.

act-eur, *n.m.,* **-rice.** *n.f.,* actor ; actress ; player.

actif, *n.m.* (*n.p.*), assets, (pl.) ; (gram.) active voice. *Actif et passif;* assets and debts.

acti-f, -ve, *adj.,* active ; real, actual ; quick, nimble, brisk, agile, stirring, busy, energetic. *Dettes actives;* assets.

action, *n.f.,* action, act, agency, operation, virtue, motion ; deed, feat, performance ; gesture, posture ; engagement, battle ; suit, plea ; share, stock. — *cessible* (com.) ; transferable share. — *nominative;* personal share. *Promesse d'—s;* scrip. *Détenteur de promesse d'—s;* scrip-holder. *Titre d'une —;* document of a share. *Par —s;* joint-stock. — *d'éclat;* splendid achievement. — *s de banque;* bank stock. *Hausse, baisse, des — s;* rise, fall, of shares. *Action de grâces;* thanksgiving. *En —;* in motion. *Entrer en —;* to begin operations. *Intenter une — à quelqu'un ;* to bring an

action against any one. *Mettre en* —, to carry into action, to carry out.

actionnaire, *n.m.*, shareholder, stockholder.

actionner, *v.a.*, to bring an action, to sue at law.

activement (-màn), *adv.*, actively, vigorously.

activer, *v.a.*, to press, to hasten, to forward.

activité, *n.f.*, action, activity; nimbleness, expedition, employment. *En* —; in activity, in active service.

actualisation, *n.f.*, actualness.

actualiser, *v.a.*, to actualize.

actualité, *n.f.*, actuality.

actuel, **-le**, *adj.*, actual, real; present.

actuellement (-èl-màn), *adv.*, now, at this very time.

acuité, *n.f.*, (mus.) acuteness.

acuminé, **-e**, *adj.*, (bot.) acuminated.

acuponcture, *n.f.*, (surg.) acupuncture.

acutangle, *adj.*, acute-angled.

acutangulé, **-e**, *adj.*, (bot.) acute-angled.

adage, *n.m.*, adage, proverb; saying.

adagio, *n.m.*, (—*s*) (mus.) adagio.

adagio, *adv.*, (mus.) adagio, slowly.

adamantin, **-e**, *adj.*, adamantine.

adaptation, *n.f.*, adaptation.

adapter, *v.a.*, to apply, to adapt, to suit; to fit. **s'adapter**, *v.r.*, to apply, fit, suit. *Qui peut* —; which is adaptable.

addition (ad-di-), *n.f.*, addition; accession; bill, reckoning; (print.) marginal note. — *composée*, compound addition. — *en hache* (print.); interlineary matter. *Faire l'addition de*; to add, sum up.

additionnel, **-le**, *adj.*, additional.

additionner, *v.a.*, to add, to cast up.

adducteur, *n.m.*, (anat.) adductor.

adducteur, *adj.*, (anat.) adducent.

adduction, *n.f.*, (anat.) adduction.

ademption, *n.f.*, (jur.) revocation of a legacy.

adepte, *n.m.*, adept.

adéquat, **-e**, (-kouat), *adj.*, (philos.) complete, entire, adequate.

adhérence, *n.f.*, adhesion; adherence, attachment.

adhérent, **-e**, *adj.*, adherent, sticking to.

adhérent, *n.m.*, adherer, follower, favourer.

adhérer, *v.n.*, to adhere, to be adherent, to cling, to hold, to cleave, to stick; to adhere to, to approve

adhési-f, **-ve**, *adj.*, adhesive.

adhésion, *n.f.*, adhesion, adherence; compliance.

ad hoc, *adv.*, to that effect or purpose.

ad hominem, *adv.*, personal, direct; argument —; *argumentum ad hominem*.

⊙**ad honores**, *adv.*, honorary.

adiante, *n.m.*, (bot.) adiantum, maiden-hair.

adieu, *adv.*, adieu, farewell, good-bye. *Dire* —; to bid adieu. *Sans* —; without bidding you adieu. —*va !* (nav.) about ship!

adieu, *n.m.*, farewell, parting, leave. *Faire ses* — *x*; to take one's leave.

adipeu-x, **-se**, *adj.*, adipous, adipose, fat.

adipocire, *n.f.*, adipocere.

adirer, *v.a.*, (jur.) to mislay, to lose.

adition, *n.f.*, (jur.) acceptance of an inheritance

adjacent, **-e**, *adj.*, adjacent, bordering upon, contiguous.

adjectif, *n.m.*, (gram.) adjective.

adjecti-f, **-ve**, *adj.*, (gram.) adjectival.

adjectivement (-màn), *adv.*, adjectively.

adjoindre, *v.a.*, to adjoin, to associate, to give as an assistant.

adjoint, *n.m.*, adjunct, associate, colleague, assistant, deputy. *Maire* —; deputy mayor.

adjonction, *n.f.*, adjunction.

adjudant, *n.m.*, adjutant. *Fonctions d'* — adjutancy.

adjudicataire, *n.m.f.*, purchaser; contractor.

adjudicataire, *adj.*, purchasing; contracting.

adjudicat-eur, *n.m.*, **-rice**, *n.f.*, awarder.

adjudicati-f, **-ve**, *adj.*, (jur.) adjudging.

adjudication, *n.f.*, adjudication; auction; contract. *Par* —; by contract. *Mettre en* —; to contract for.

adjuger, *v.a.*, to adjudge, to adjudicate, to award. *Adjugé !* (at auctions—*aux enchères*) gone ! **s'adjuger**, *v.r.*, to appropriate to one's own use.

adjuration, *n.f.*, adjuration.

adjurer, *v.a.*, to adjure; to conjure, to call upon.

adjuvant, *n.m.*, (med.) adjuvant.

ad libitum (-tom.), *adv.*, ad libitum.

admettre, *v.a.*, to admit, to receive; to allow, to approve of, to suppose; to give admittance, to take in; to let in, to suffer to come into, to let enter.

adminicule, *n.m.*, (jur.) presumptive proof.

administra-teur, *n.m.*, **-trice**, *n.f.*, administrator, administratrix, manager, trustee, governor; guardian (of the poor—*des pauvres*).

administrati-f, **-ve**, *adj.*, administrative.

administration, *n.f.*, administration, management, government, conduct. *Mauvaise* —; maladministration.

administrativement, *adv.*, administratively.

administré, *n.m.*, **-e**, *n.f.*, person under one's administration.

administrer, *v.a.*, to administer, to manage, to officiate, to govern; to minister, to dispense; (jur.) to finish, find. *Droit d'* —; letters of administration. —*des témoins*; to find witnesses. **s'administrer**, *v.r.*, to administer to one's self; to be managed, to be administered.

admirable, *adj.*, admirable.

admirablement, *adv.*, admirably.

admirat-eur, *n.m.*, **-rice**, *n.f.*, admirer, praiser.

admirati-f, **-ve**, *adj.*, of admiration or exclamation.

admiration, *n.f.*, admiration, wonder, marvel. *Point d'* —; note of exclamation. *Avoir de l'* — *pour*, *Être dans l'* —; to admire. *Saisir d'* —; to strike with admiration.

admirer, *v.a.*, to admire, to wonder at.

admissibilité, *n.f.*, admissibility.

admissible, *adj.*, allowable, admissible.

admission, *n.f.*, admission, admittance, reception.

admonestation, *n.f.*, admonishment, admonition.

admonester, *v.a.*, (jur.) to admonish. to warn, to reprimand.

admonit-eur, *n.m.*, **-rice**, *n.f.*, adviser.

admonition, *n.f.*, admonition, advice, exhortation; reprimand.

adolescence, *n.f.*, adolescence.

adolescent, *n.m.*, **-e**, *n.f.*, lad; lass.

adolescent, **-e**, *adj.*, adolescent.

adonien, **-ne** (-in, -è-n), *adj.*, (poet.) adonic.

adonique. *V.* adonien.

adonis (-nis), *n.m.*, Adonis, beau; (bot.) adonis, pheasant's-eye.

adoniser, *v.a.*, to deck out, to make fine. **s'adoniser**, *v.r.*, to dizen one's self.

adonner, *v.n.*, (nav.) to veer. **s'adonner**, *v.r.*, to give, to apply, to devote, to addict one's self, to give one's mind (to a thing —*à quelque chose*), to follow, to take to a thing. *S'* — *au vin*, to addict one's self to drinking.

adoptable, *adj.*, that can be adopted.

adoptant, *n.m.*, adopter.
adopté, *n.m.*, **-e**, *n f.*, adoptive son, daughter, heir, &c.
adopter, *v.a.*, to adopt; to embrace, to espouse, to give into.
adopti-f, -ve, *adj.*, adoptive, by adoption. *Enfant* —: adoptive child. *Père* —; foster-father.
adoption, *n.f.*, adoption.
adorable, *adj.*, adorable, charming.
adorat-eur, *n.m.*, **-rice**, *n.f.*, adorer, worshipper; great admirer.
adoration, *n.f.*, adoration, worshipping; worship; admiration, respect, reverence.
adorer, *v.a.*, to adore, to worship; to have a passionate love for.
ados, *n.m.*, (gard.) shelving-bed, border against a wall.
adossé, -e, *adj.*, back to back.
adossement, *n.m.*, the state of a thing being supported by another, backing.
adosser, *v.a.*, to set or lean one's back against a thing, to put back to back. *S'— contre un mur;* to lean one's back against a wall.
adouber, *v.n.*, (chess—*aux échecs*) to adjust a piece; (nav.) to mend, to repair.
adoucir, *v.a.*, to soften, to mitigate, to sweeten; to modify, to compose, to calm, to soothe; to smooth, to render bland; to ease, to allay, to relieve, to cool, to pacify; to tame. *Rien ne peut — son chagrin;* nothing can mitigate his sorrow. — *un esprit irrité;* to pacify an exasperated mind.
s'adoucir, *v.r.*, to grow sweet, soft, mild; to be assuaged, mitigated; to relent.
adoucissant, *n.m.*, emollient, mollifier.
adoucissant, -e, *adj.*, softening, emollient.
adoucissement (-män), *n.m.*, sweetening, softening, mollifying; assuaging, appeasing; ease, mitigation, alleviation, relief, consolation.
adoucisseur, *n.m.*, glass-polisher.
adoué, -e, *adj.*, (hunt.) coupled, paired.
ad patres (-èss), to kingdom come. *Aller* —; to go to one's fathers.
adrachne (-rakn), *n.m.*, strawberry-tree. *V.* **arbousier.**
adragante, *adj.*, tragacanth.
adragant, *n.m.*, tragacanth.
ad rem, *adv.*, pertinently. *Répondre* —; to answer pertinently.
adresse, *n.f.*, speech; direction, address; skill, dexterity, expertness, cleverness, ingenuity; shrewdness, cunning. *Être à l'* — *de;* to be directed to. *Faire tenir à son* —; to forward to its destination. *Tour d'*—; legerdemain. *Avoir l'adresse de;* to be artful enough to.
adresser, *v.a.*, to direct, to address. — *mal;* to misdirect (letters, *&c.*—*lettres, &c.*).
s'adresser, *v.r.*, to be directed; to address one's self, to apply, to make application. — *ici;* apply within. *Vous vous adressez mal;* you mistake your man.
adroit, -e, *adj.*, dexterous, ingenious, clever, skilful; handy, neat; cunning, shrewd, artful.
adroitement (-droat-män), *adv.*, adroitly, skilfully, artfully, cleverly, happily; smartly, handily.
adula-teur, *n.m.*, **-trice**, *n.f.*, adulator, flatterer, fawner, sycophant; parasite.
adula-teur, -trice, *adj.*, adulatory, parasitical.
adulation, *n.f.*, adulation, sycophancy.
aduler, *v.a.*, to fawn upon, to cringe to, to flatter.
adulte, *adj.*, adult, grown-up.
adulte, *n.m.f.*, adult.
adultération, *n.f.*, (pharm.) adulteration.
adultère, *n f.*, adulteress.
adultère, *n.m.*, adulterer; adultery, crim. con.

adultère, *adj.*, adulterous; adulterate. *Femme* —; adulteress.
adultérer, *v.a.*, (phar.) to adulterate.
adultérin, *n.m.*, **-e**, *n.f.*, adulterine child.
adultérin. -e, *adj.*, adulterine.
aduste, *adj.*, (med.) adust.
adustion, *n.f.*, (med.) adustion, burning.
advenant, *part.*, in case, in the event of. — *le décès;* in the event of the death.
advenir, *v.n.*, to occur, happen. *Advienne que pourra;* happen what may. *V.* **avenir.**
adventice, *adj.*, adventitious.
adventi-f, -ve, *adj.*, adventive, casual.
adverbe, *n.m.*, (gram.) adverb.
adverbial. -e, *adj.*, adverbial.
adverbialement (-män), *adv.*, adverbially.
adverbialité, *n.f.*, being an adverb.
adversaire, *n.m.*, adversary, opponent, antagonist, opposer.
adversati-f, -ve, *adj.*, (gram.) adversative.
adverse, *adj.*, adverse, opposite. *Avocat* —; counsel on the opposite side.
adversité, *n.f.*, adversity, affliction.
adynamie, *n.f.*, (med.) adynamy, debility.
adynamique, *adj.*, adynamic.
aérage, *n.m.*, renewal of air, airing. *Puits d'* —; air-shaft.
aéré, -e, *adj.*, aired, airy.
aérer, *v.a.*, to air, to renew the air; (chem.) to aerate.
aérien. -ne (-in,-è-n), *adj.*, aerial.
aérifère, *adj.*, aerial.
aériforme, *adj.*, aeriform.
aérodynamique, *n.f.* (*n.p.*), aero-dynamics, *pl.*
aérographie, *n.f.*, aerography.
aérolithe, *n.m.*, aerolite, aerolith.
aérologie, *n.f.*, aerology.
aéromancie, *n.f.*, aeromancy.
aéromètre, *n.m.*, aerometer.
aérométrie, *n.f.*, aerometry.
aéronaute, *n.m.f.*, aeronaut. *Art, science de l'* —; aeronautics.
aérophobie, *n.f.*, aerophobia.
aérostat, *n.m.*, aerostat; air-balloon.
aérostation, *n.f.*, aerostation.
aérostatique, *adj.*, aerostatic.
aétite, *n.f.*, aetites, eagle-stone.
affabilité, *n.f.*, affability, affableness, kindness.
affable, *adj.*, affable, courteous, of easy manners.
affablement, *adv.*, affably, courteously.
affabulation, *n.f.*, the moral of a fable.
affadir, *v.a.*, to make unsavoury or insipid, to flatten; to be nauseous, to cloy, to satiate.
s'affadir, *v.r.*, to become insipid.
affadissement (-män), *n.m.*, cloying, insipidity.
affaiblir, *v.a.*, to enfeeble, to weaken, to debilitate; to impair; to debase (coins—*monnaies*).
affaiblir, *v.n.*, to grow weak, to weaken, to droop.
s'affaiblir, *v.r.*, to grow weak, to be impaired; to abate.
affaiblissant, -e, *adj.*, weakening, enfeebling.
affaiblissement (-män), *n.m.*, weakening, enfeebling, impairment, diminution of strength; allaying, abatement; debasement (of coins—*des monnaies*).
affaire, *n.f.*, thing, affair, matter; business, concern, job, employ; dealing; trouble, scrape, quarrel; action, case, lawsuit; fight, skirmish, battle; need, occasion, want; work, transaction. *Belle* —; fine thing, pretty mess. — *s courantes;* current business. — *de rien;* trifling

affair. — *d'intérêt*; money matter. *Bien, mal, dans ses* —; in good, bad, circumstances. *Homme d'*—*s*; man of business, agent, steward, middle-man. *Relation d'* —*s*; mercantile connexion. *Dans les* —*s*; in business. *En* —; engaged in business. *Pour* —; on business. *Aller à ses* —*s*: to go to one's business. *S'attirer une* —; to get into a scrape. *Avoir* —*à*; to have some business with. *Avoir bien des* —*s*; to be much employed. *Avoir des* —*s pardessus la tête*; to be over head and ears in business. *Céder ses* —*s*; to give up business. *Être à ses* —*s*; to attend to business. *Éviter les* —*s*; to keep clear of scrapes. *Faire des* —*s*; to do business. *Faire l'* — *de quelqu'un*; to answer some one's purpose, turn. *Faire son* —*à quelqu'un*; to settle any one's business, do the job for him. *Faire de grandes*—*s*; to carry on an extensive business. *Ne faire rien à l'* —; to be nothing to the purpose. *Mettre quelqu'un dans les* —*s*; to set any one up in business, to apprentice any one to a business. *Se retirer des* —*s*; to retire from business. *Sortir d'une* — *avec honneur*; to come off honourably. *Tirer d'* —; to extricate, to help out. *Se tirer d'* —; to get out of trouble. *Vaquer aux* — *s*, to attend to business. *Vider une* —; to settle an affair. *C'est, ce n'est pas, une* —; it is no, it is an, easy matter. *Je ferai son* —; I have what you want. *Je ferai son* —; I will do for him. *C'est mon* —; leave that to me. *J'en fais mon* —: I take that upon myself. *Ce ne sont pas là mes* —*s*; that is none of my business. *Au point où en sont les* — *s*; as affairs are. *Son*—*est bonne*; he is in for it. *Son*—*est faite*; he is done for.

affairé, -e. *adj.*, full of business, busy *Faire l'*—; to play the man of business.

affaissement (-män), *n.m.*, depression, sinking, subsiding, giving way, weakness, weighing down.

affaisser, *v.a.*, to cause to sink, to weigh down, to press down, to bear down, to weaken.

s'affaisser, *v.r.*, to sink (with too much weight—*par un trop grand poids*), to give way.

affaiter. *v.a.*, (falconry—*fauconnerie*); to reclaim and train (hawks—*faucons*).

affaler, *v.a.*, (nav.) to overhaul (a rope—*une corde*); to embay, drive upon a lee-shore.

s'affaler, *v.r.*, (nav.) to slide down; to be driven upon a lee-shore.

affamé, -e. *adj.*, famished, hungry, starving, craving; greedy of; eager for.

affamer. *v.a.*, to famish, to starve.

affection, *n.f.*, affectation; (jur.) mortgage, charge.

affecté, -e, *adj.*, affected; destined; (alg.) affected.

affecter, *v a.*, to affect; to appropriate, to destine.

s'affecter, *v.r.*, to be affected ȹ to be moved.

affecti-f, -ve. *adj.*, affective.

affection, *n.f.*, affection, love, attachment, liking, inclination, partiality; (med.) affection. *Témoignage d'* —; token of affection. *Par* —; out of affection. *Prendre quelqu'un en* —; to become attached, to take a fancy, to any one. — *nerveuse*; nervous affection.

affectionné, -e, *adj.*, affectionate.

affectionner, *v.a.*, to love, to have an affection for, to fancy, to be fond of, to like; to take an interest in.

s'affectionner, *v.r.*, to apply one's self to a thing with delight, to attach one's self to, to delight in.

affectueusement (-män), *adv.*, affectionately, fondly, friendly, heartily.

affectueu-x, -se, *adj.*, affectionate, warm-hearted.

afférent, -e. *adj.*, (jur.) indivisible. *Portion* —*e*: share of indivisible property.

affermer, *v.a.*, to farm or let out by lease; to take a lease of; to rent.

affermir, *v.a.*, to strengthen, to give strength to; to make firm or strong; to fasten; to harden, to make hard or firm; to confirm, to establish, to fix firmly.

s'affermir. *v.r.*, to become strong, firm or fast; to grow hard; to fortify one's self, to become established.

affermissement (-män), *n.m.*, strengthening, settling, consolidation, establishment, stay, support, prop.

affété, -e, *adj.*, affected, full of affectation, prim, finical; canting. *Mine* —*e*; affected looks. *Manières* —*es*; affected manners.

afféterie, *n.f.*, affectation, affectedness; primness; affected, formal ways; cant. *Les* — *s d'une coquette*; the finicalness of a coquette.

affichage, *n.m.*, the posting up of placards, bills, &c., bill-sticking, placarding.

affiche, *n.f.*, placard, bill, hand-bill. *Poser une* —; to post up a placard.

afficher, *v.a.*, to post up; to publish, to proclaim, to divulge. *Défense d'* —; stick no bills. **s'afficher**, *v.r.*, to set up for; to expose one's self. *Cette femme s'affiche*; that woman observes no decency.

afficheur, *n.m.*, bill-sticker.

affidé, *n.m.*,-e, *n.f.*, confederate, trusty, confidential agent.

affidé, -e, *adj.*, trusty, trustworthy.

affilage, *n.m.*, whetting, sharpening, grinding, setting.

affilé,-e, *adj.*, sharp; nimble (of the tongue —*de la langue*).

affiler, *v.a.*, to set, to put an edge on, to sharpen.

affiliation. *n.f.*, affiliation, association.

affilier, *v.a.*, to receive, to affiliate, to admit.

s'affilier, *v.r.*, to get affiliated, admitted.

affiloir. *n.m.*, hone.

affinage, *n.m.*, affinage, refining (of metals, sugar—*des métaux, du sucre*).

affiner, *v.a.*, to fine, to refine; to try.

s'affiner, *v.r.*, to be refined; to be fined, tried.

affinerie, (-rî), (metal.) *n.f.*, finery.

affineur, *n.m.*, finer; (metal.) refiner.

affinité, *n.f.*, affinity, alliance; congeniality. *Avoir de l'* — *avec*; to be congenial to.

affinoir, *n.m.*, hatchel.

affiquet, *n.m.*, a knitting-sheath; —*s*, *pl.* gewgaws, knick-knacks.

affirmati-f, -ve, *adj.*, affirmative; positive.

affirmation, *n.f.*, affirmation, assertion; (log.) predication; affidavit, oath.

affirmative, *n.f.*, affirmative. *Prendre l'*— *pour ou contre*; to decide for or against.

affirmativement, (-män), *adv.*, affirmatively, positively.

affirmer, *v.a.*, to affirm, to avouch, to assert, to assure; to confirm with an oath; (log.) to predicate.

affixe, *n.m.*, affix.

affleuré, -e. *adj.*, level; (arch.) flush.

affleurement. *n.m.*, levelling; making flush; (mining—*mines*), crop out.

affleurer, *v.a.*, to make even, to level; (arch.) to make flush; (ship-building—*construction de vaisseaux*); to fay; (mining—*mines*); to crop out.

afflicti-f, -ve. *adj.*, (jur.) that affects the person (of punishments—*de condamnations*).

affliction, *n.f.*, affliction, grief, trouble, anguish, sorrow, tribulation; trial, vexation.

affligé, -e, *adj.*, afflicted, grieved, dejected, disconsolate. — *d'une maladie*; labouring under a disease.

affligeant, -e, (-jän, -t), *adj.*, afflicting, afflictive, distressing, grievous, woeful.

affliger, *v.a.*, to afflict, to grieve, to vex, to trouble, to cast down ; to mortify.

s'affliger, *v.r.*, to grieve, to be concerned ; to be afflicted, troubled, cast down, sorrowful ; to fret.

affluence. *n.f.*, a flowing together ; affluence, abundance, multitude, crowd.

. **affluent, -e**, *adj.*, (of rivers—*rivières*) falling into, running into.

affluent, *n.m.*, confluence ; tributary stream.

affluer, *v.a.*, to fall, to run, to flow into ; to abound ; to resort, to flock, to come in great numbers ; (med.) to flow, to rush.

afflux, *n.m.*, (med.) afflux, affluxion.

affolé, -e. *adj.*, (nav.) erroneous, defective (of the magnetic needle—*de l'aiguille aimantée*). *Une boussole —e ;* a compass that is not true.

affoler, *v.a.*, to make extemely fond, to make one dote upon ; to madden.

affouage. *n.m.*, the right of cutting wood.

affouillement, *n.m.*, undermining, washing away.

affouiller, *v.a.*, (arch.) to undermine ; to wash away.

affourche, *n.f.*, (nav.) small bower. *Ancre d' — :* small bower-anchor.

affourché -e, *part.*, astraddle, astride, moored.

affourcher, *v.n.* and *a.*, s' — *v.r.*, (nav.) to moor across, to moor by the head or by the head and stern.

affranchi, *n.m.*, **-e**, *n.f.*, freed man ; freed woman.

affranchi. -e, *part.*, freed ; post-paid.

affranchir, *v.a.*, to set free, to free, to enfranchise, to give liberty ; to make free ; to absolve ; to exempt, to discharge ; to deliver ; to pay the carriage of ; to prepay.

s'affranchir, *v.r.*, to rid one's self of, to free oneself. to get free, to shake off, to break through.

affranchissement (-shis-män), *n.m.*, enfranchisement, manumission ; exemption, discharge ; delivery, deliverance ; payment of postage (of a letter—*d'une lettre*) ; payment of carriage (of a parcel—*d'un paquet*). *Timbre d' — ;* postage-stamp.

affre, *n.f.*, dread. *Les — s de la mort ;* the terrors of death.

affrètement (-män), *n.m.*, chartering, freighting.

affréter, *v.a.*, (nav.) to charter, to freight.

affréteur. *n.m.*, charterer, freighter.

affreusement (-män), *adv.*, frightfully, horribly, dreadfully.

affreu-x, -se, *adj.*, frightful, hideous, horrible, fearful, ghastly, horrid.

affriander, *v.a.*, to accustom, use, bring up, to dainties ; to allure, to entice.

affriolement (-män), *n.m.*, (fam.) act of alluring, enticing.

affrioler, *v.a.*, (fam.) to allure, to entice, to draw by enticement.

affront, *n.m.*, affront, outrage, insult ; disgrace, shame, reproach. *Recevoir un — sanglant ;* to receive an outrageous affront. *Boire, avaler, un — ;* to pocket an affront.

affronté, -e, *adj.*, (her.) affrontee.

affronter, *v.a.*, to affront, to face ; to cheat, to take in.

affronterie, *n.f.*, braving, daring, affronting.

affronteu-r, *n.m.*, **-se**, *n.f.*, affronter.

affublement. *n.m.*, grotesque make up (of dress—*d'habillement*).

affubler, *v.a.*, to wrap up, (b.s.) to dress out, up, to muffle up. *S— d'un manteau ;* to muffle one's self up in a cloak.

s'affubler, *v.r.*, to dress ridiculously. *— de quelqu'un :* to be wrapped up in any one.

affusion, *n.f.*, (phar.) affusion.

affût. *n.m*, gun-carriage ; watch. *Être à l'— ;* to be upon the watch.

affutage, *n.m.*. the mounting of a piece of ordnance ; a set of tools, implements ; sharpening (of tools—*d'outils*) ; the dressing (of a hat).

affûter, *v.a.*, to mount (a cannon—*un canon*) ; to stock (with tools—*d'outils*) ; to set or sharpen (tools, pencils—*outils, crayons*).

affutiau, (-tio), *n.m.*, trifle, bauble, knick-knack.

afin, *conj.*, to, in order to ; that ; so that.

à fortiori. *V.* **fortiori**.

africain, *n.m.*, **-e**, *n.f.*, African.

africain, -e. *adj.*, African.

aga, *n.m.*, a Turkish officer, aga.

agaçant, -e, *adj.*, inciting, alluring, enticing.

agace, *n.f.*, magpie.

agacé, -e, *part.*, set on edge. *Avoir les dents —es ;* to have one's teeth set on edge.

agacement (-män), *n.m.*, setting on edge ; irritation. *—des nerfs ;* irritation of the nerves.

agacer, *v.a.*, to incite, to provoke, to egg on, to spur on, to entice, to allure ; to set on edge, to irritate.

agacerie, *n.f.*, allurement, incitement. *Faire des — s à quelqu'un ;* to set one's cap at any one.

agame, *adj.*, (bot.) agamous.

agami, *n.m.*, (orni.) agami, gold-breasted trumpeter.

agape. *n.f.*, agape, love-feast.

agapètes, *n.m.* and *f. pl.*, agapetæ.

agaric, *n.m.*, (bot.) agaric. — *champêtre ;* field agaric, mushroom. — *femelle ;* female agaric. — *de chêne ;* touch-wood.

agasse, *n.f.* *V.* **agace**.

agate, *n.f.*, agate (stone—*pierre*) ; agate (burnisher—*brunissoir*).

agavé, *n.m.*, (bot.) agave, American aloe.

âge, *n.m.*, age ; years ; generation, century. *Bas —;* infancy. *Jeune — ;* childhood. *Moyen —,* middle ages. — *mûr ;* mature age. — *tendre ;* early age. *Vieil — ;* old age. — *viril ;* manhood. — *d'airain ;* brazen age. — *d'argent ;* silver age. — *de fer ;* iron age. — *d'or ;* golden age. — *de raison ;* age of discretion. *Doyen d'— ;* the oldest. *Fleur de l' — ;* prime of life. *Avant l'— ;* before one's time. *D'— en — ;* from age to age, from generation to generation. *D'un certain —;* elderly. *Entre deux — s ;* of middle age. *Être d'— à ;* to be of an age to. *Être bien pour son — ;* to wear well, to bear one's years well. *Être sur l' — ;* to be growing old. *Honoré par l' — ;* time-honoured. *Paraître son — ;* to look one's age. *Tirer sur l' — ;* to be elderly.

âgé, -e. *adj.*, aged, in years, elderly. —*de vingt ans ;* twenty years old. *Un peu — ;* somewhat old.

agence, *n.f.*, agency, business ; agency. *Bureau d' — ;* agency office.

agencement (-jäns-män), *n.m.*, the placing appropriately, arrangement ; (arch.) order, composition ; (paint.) disposition.

agencer, *v.a.*, to arrange, dispose, to fit up, to adjust.

s'agencer, *v.r.*, to dress up, to trim one's self.

agenda (-jin-da), *n.m.*, (—s) memorandum-book.

*agenouiller, *v.a.*, to make kneel down

*s'agenouiller. *v.r.*, to kneel down.

* **agenouilloir**, *n.m.*, hassock.

agent, *n.m.*, agent ; middleman ; transactor. — *comptable ;* accountant, (nav.) purser. — *d'affaires ;* agent, man of business. — *monétaire ;* circulating medium. —*de change ;* stock-broker

agglomération, *n.f.*, agglomeration.

agglomérer, *v.a.*, to agglomerate.

s'agglomérer, *v.r.*, to agglomerate.

agglutinant, -e *adj.*, agglutinant.
agglutinati-f. -ve, *adj.*, agglutinative.
agglutination, *n.f.*, agglutination.
agglutiner, *v.a.*, to agglutinate, to unite.
s'agglutiner, *v.r.*, to agglutinate, to cohere.
aggravant, -e, *adj.*, (jur.) aggravating.
aggravation. *n.f.*, aggravation (addition).
— *de peine;* increase of punishment.
aggrave, *n.m.*, (canon law—*loi canon*)
menace of excommunication, after three admonitions.
aggraver, *v.a.*, to aggravate, to augment, to
make worse.
s'aggraver, *v.r.*, to increase, to be aggravated.
aggrégat. aggrégation. aggréger. *V.*
agrégat, agrégation. agréger.
agile, *adj.*, agile, quick, nimble, active,
lightfooted.
agilement (-mān), *adv.*, nimbly, with agility, quickly.
agilité, *n.f.*, agility, nimbleness, activity,
quickness, lightness.
agio, *n.m.*, agio.
agiotage, *n.m.*, stock-jobbing; jobbing.
Faire l'—; to deal in the stocks
agioter. *v.n.*, to be a stock-jobber; to gamble
in the funds, to job.
agioteur, *n.m.*, stock-jobber, jobber.
agir, *v.n.*, to act, to do; to operate, to have
an influence; to negotiate, to manage a business; to sue, to prosecute; to behave; to work.
Faire —; to set going. *Agir de concert avec*
quelqu'un; to go hand in hand with one. *Il agit*
en ami; he acts like a friend. *Agir mal envers;*
to use ill. *Agir d'après;* to act on, after. *C'est*
mal agir; that is behaving ill.
s'agir, *v.r.*, to be in question; to be the
matter. *Il s'agit;* the question is, the point in
question is. *De quoi s'agit-il?* what is the
matter? *Il ne s'agit pas de cela;* that is not the
question. *Il s'agit de votre vie;* your life is at
stake. *Il s'agit bien de;* I, they, we, have something else to think of.
agissant, -e, *adj.*, active, stirring, busy;
efficacious, effectual.
agitateur, *n.m.*, agitator.
agitation. *n.f.*, agitation; tossing, jolting,
shaking; trouble, emotion, disturbance; uneasiness.
agiter, *v.a.*, to agitate, to put in motion, to
move; to shake, to heave, to jolt; to swing; to
disturb, to disquiet, to torment, to debate, to
dispute.
s'agiter, *v.r.*, to be agitated or in movement;
to get rough; to be restless, disturbed, uneasy;
to stir, writhe, wag, struggle; to be debated.
S— *dans l'eau;* to flounder about in the water.
agglomération, &c. *V.* **agglomération.**
aglutinant, &c. *V.* **agglutinant,** &c.
agnat. *n.m.*, agnate.
agnation. *n.f.*, agnation.
agnatique. *adj.*, agnatic.
*agneau, *n.m.*, lamb. —*femelle;* ewe. *Laine*
d'—; lamb's wool. *Peau d'*—; lamb-skin.
⊙***agnel,** *n.m.*, an old French golden coin,
agnel.
*agneler, *v.n.*, to lamb, to ewe; to bring
forth lambs, to yean.
*agnelet, *n.m.*, lamb-kin. house-lamb.
*agneline, *adj., f.*, of a lamb. *Laine* —;
lamb's-wool.
*agnès, (-ess), *n.f.*, a young raw girl, simpleton.
agnus, *or* **agnus-Dei,** *n.m.*, (—), (c. rel.)
Agnus-Dei.
agnus-castus. *n.m.*, (—), (bot.) chaste-tree.
agon. *n.m.*, (antiq.) agon, agonism.
agonie *n.f.*, agony, the pangs of death :

grief, trouble, anguish. *Être à l'*—; to be at the
point of death.
agonir, *v.a.*, (pop.) to insult grossly, to pull
to pieces.
agonisant, -e, *n.* and *adj.*, a dying person;
dying, in a dying condition.
agoniser, *v.n.*, to be at the point of death.
agonistique, *n.f.*, (antiq.) agonistics.
⊙**agonothète,** *n.m.*, agonothete.
agora, *n.f.*, (—s) (from Gr. 'Αγορà) market-
place, public place.
agouti. *n.m.*, (mam.) agouti.
agrafe, *n.f.*, hook, clasp, hasp; (arch.) cramp-
iron; sculptured ornament. — *et porte;* hook
and eye.
agrafer. *v.a.*, to hook, to clasp, to fasten
with a clasp.
s'agrafer, *v.r.*, to hook, to clasp, to cling, to
lay hold on.
agraire. *adj.*, agrarian.
agrandir, *v.a.*, to make greater; to enlarge;
to augment; to lengthen, to widen; to raise, to
promote, to advance; to amplify, to exaggerate;
to give dignity to. — *ses prétentions;* to raise
one's pretensions. *Le génie agrandit les héros;*
genius exalts heroes.
s'agrandir, *v.r.*, to become greater, larger;
to widen, to grow long or longer; to enlarge
one's estate.
agrandissement (-mān), *n.m.*, enlargement, aggrandizement; the making greater,
larger, bigger; lengthening, widening, increase; advancement, preferment, exaltation,
dignifying.
agravant, &c. *V.* **aggravant.** &c.
agréable, *adj.*, agreeable, desirable, pleasant, pleasing, comfortable, gladsome, grateful.
— *au goût;* palatable. *Feu* —; comfortable fire.
Avoir pour —; to allow, permit. *Faire l'*—*auprès*
d'une femme; to act the gallant to a lady.
agréablement. *adv.*, agreeably, pleasantly,
comfortably, gratefully.
agréé, *n.m.*, solicitor, attorney, in the tribu-
nals of commerce.
agréer. *v.a.*, to accept, to receive kindly; to
like, to relish; to approve, to allow; ⊙ to rig.
(*V.* **gréer.**) — *un vaisseau;* to rig, to equip a
ship.
agréer. *v.n.*, to be liked, to like, to please, to
be agreeable. *Cela ne m'agrée pas;* I don't like
that.
⊙**agréeur,** *n.m. V.* **gréeur.**
agrégat, *n.m.*, aggregate.
agrégati-f, -ve. *adj.*, aggregative.
agrégation, *n.f.*, aggregate; aggregation;
admission (into a society—*dans une société*);
examination for the degree of fellow; fellowship; aggregate body, assemblage. *Concours*
d'—; examination for a fellowship.
agrégé, *n.m.*, fellow (of the university);
supernumerary professor.
agrégé, -e. *adj.*, aggregate; (bot.) clustered.
agréger, *v.a.*, to aggregate, to receive, to
admit into a society, to associate.
agrément, *n.m.*, liking, approbation, consent; accomplishment; agreeableness; pleasingness; pleasure, charm; gracefulness; ornament,
embellishment; advantage, amusement, comfort; (mus.) grace. *Arts d'*—; accomplishments.
De grands —*s;* great comfort.
agréner. *v.a.*, to pump water out of a boat.
agrès, *n.m. pl.*, rigging (of a ship—*d'un*
vaisseau).
agresseur. *n.m.*, aggressor.
agressi-f, -ve. *adj.*, aggressive.
agression. *n.f.*, aggression.
agreste. *adj.*, agrestic, wild, rustic; ill-bred,
clownish. unmannerly.
agricole, *adj.*, agricultural.
agriculteur, *n.m.*, agricultor, husbandman.

agriculture, *n.f.*, agriculture, husbandry, tillage.

s'agriffer, *v.r.*, to cling to with claws, to lay hold of.

agripaume, *n.f.*, (bot.) mother-wort.

agripper, *v.a.*, (pop.) to gripe, to snatch up.

s'agripper, *v.r.*, (pop.) to lay hold of, to cling to.

agronome, *n.m.*, agriculturist.

agronomie, *n.f.*, agronomy.

agronomique, *adj.*, agricultural.

agrostemme, *n.m.*, (bot.) agrostemma. — *des jardins;* rose-campion.

agrostide, *n.f.*, (bot.) bent-grass.

agrouper, *v.a.*, to group.

aguerri. -e. (-ghè-) *part.*, used to war; disciplined. *Soldats mal — s;* raw soldiers.

aguerrir (-ghè-), *v.a.*, to train up in, to inure to the hardships of war, to discipline, to accustom to war; to accustom, to inure, to use.

s'aguerrir, *v.r.*, to grow warlike or martial; to use one's self to a thing, to be inured.

aguets (-ghè-), *n.m. pl.*, watch, watching. *Être aux —, se tenir aux —;* to lie in wait, to be upon the watch.

agueustie, (-gheus-tî), *n.f.*, (med.) loss of taste.

ah, *int.*, ah! hah! oh!

ahan, *n.m.*, great bodily exertion, effort. *Suer d' —;* to perform hard work, to toil and moil.

ahaner, *v.n.*, to have much difficulty in performing work.

aheurtement, *n.m.*, stubbornness, obstinacy.

s'aheurter, *v.r.*, to maintain a thing obstinately, to be stiff or obstinate in a thing, to stick to it, to persist in it. — *à une opinion;* to be wedded to an opinion.

ahi, *int.* V. **aie.**

ahurir, *v.a.*, to amaze, to astound, to strike all of a heap.

ahurissement, *n.m.*, bewilderment, confusion, perplexity.

ai, *n.m.*, (mam.) sloth.

aide, *n.f.*, aid, help, relief, assistance, succour, support; chapel of ease; (man.) aid, coaxing; aid (tax—*impôt*); female assistant. *A l' —!* help! *A l' — de;* with the help of. *Dieu vous soit en —;* God help you. *Ainsi Dieu vous soit en —;* so help you God.

aide, *n.m.*, helper, assistant, mate, help, coadjutor. — *major* (— *s* — *s*); assistant surgeon. — *chirurgien* (— *s* — *s*); surgeon's mate. — *de cuisine* (— *s de* —); under cook. — *de camp* (— *s de* —); aid-de-camp.

aider, *v.a.*, to aid, to help, to relieve, to assist, to succour. — *à descendre, à surmonter, à relever;* to help down, over, up.

aider, *v.n.*, to aid, to help, to assist. — *à la lettre;* to add to the matter. — *au succès;* to contribute to the success.

s'aider, *v.r.*, to help one another, to use, to make use of; to bestir one's self; to help one's self. *On s'aide de ce qu'on a;* people make use of what they have. — *l'un l'autre;* to help one another.

aides, *n.f. pl.*, (man.) aids.

aie, *int.*, ay! oh! ah! oh dear!

aïeul, *n.m.*, grandfather, grandsire.

aïeule, *n.f.*, grandmother, grandam.

aïeux, *n.m. pl.*, forefathers, ancestors.

aigle, *n.m.*, eagle; star (noted person—*personne de marque*); reading-desk (in churches — *dans les églises*); (astron.) Aquila, Eagle. *A vol d' —;* eagle-winged. *Aux yeux d' —;* eagle-eyed.

aigle, *n.f.*, she-eagle; (her.) eagle; eagle (standard of the Romans—*étendard des Romains*).

aiglette, *n.f.* V. **aiglon.**

aiglon, *n.m.*, eaglet, a young eagle; (her.) eaglet.

aigre, *n.m.*, sourness; rawness; sharpness; mustiness.

aigre, *adj.*, sour, tart, sharp, bitter; crabbed; ill-natured; rough, harsh; eager, brittle; shrill; musty. *Voix —;* harsh, shrill voice. *Paroles — s;* sharp words.

aigre-dou-x. -ce. *adj.*, bitterish, sourish.

aigrefin, *n.m.*, sharper.

aigrelet. -te, *adj.*, sourish, somewhat sour.

aigrement, *adv.*, acrimoniously, sourly, sharply, bitterly, roughly, harshly.

aigremoine, *n.f.*, (bot.) agrimony, liver-wort.

aigremore, *n.m.*, aigremore.

aigret. -te, *adj.*, sourish, somewhat sour.

aigrette, *n.f.*, egret, aigret; aigrette, tuft, or plume (of feathers, diamonds, &c.—*de plumes, diamants, &c.*); (bot.) egret; (milit.) tuft; horn (of the owl—*du hibou*); crest (of the peacock—*du paon*).

aigretté. -e, *adj.*, with an egret.

aigreur, *n.f.*, sourness, sharpness, tartness, harshness, bitterness; surliness; ill-nature, grudge, spite; *pl.*, (med.) acidity of stomach; (engrav.) harsh strokes, hatches made too hard.

aigrir, *v.a.*, to make sour or sharp, to sour, to turn sour; to irritate, to imbitter, to make worse; to incense, to provoke; to make ill-humoured. *Sa disgrâce lui a aigri l'esprit;* his disgrace has soured his temper.

s'aigrir, *v.r.*, to turn sour, to grow sour or sharp; to grow worse, to be exasperated. *Son mal s'aigrit;* his disease gets worse.

aigu. -ë, *adj.*, pointed, that has a sharp point; sharp, keen, acute, piercing. *Son —;* sharp, shrill sound. *Douleur —ë;* acute pain. *Faire un son —;* to shrill.

aiguade (-gad), *n.f.*, (nav.) fresh water; watering-place. *Faire —;* to take in fresh water.

aiguail (-ga-), *n.m.*, (hunt.) dew-drop.

aiguayer (-gay-), *v.a.*, to water (a horse—*un cheval*); to rinse (clothes—*du linge*).

aigue-marine (egg-), *n.f.*, (— *s* — *s*), aqua-marina, beryl.

aiguière (-ghièr), *n.f.*, ewer.

aiguiérée (-ghié-), *n.f.*, ewer-full.

*****aiguillade**, *n.f.*, goad.

*****aiguillage**, *n.m.*, (railways) the shifting of the points.

*****aiguillat**, *n.m.*, (ich.) dog-fish.

*****aiguille**, *n.f.*, needle; hand (of a dial, or watch—*d'horloges, de montres, &c.*); cock (balance); spindle (of a compass—*d'une boussole*); spire (of a steeple—*d'un clocher*); (ich.) horn-fish, needle-fish; (railways) point. — *d'emballeur;* packing-needle. — *à tricoter;* knitting-needle. — *à reprises;* darning-needle. — *s à contre-poids;* self-acting points (railways). *Trou d'une —;* eye of a needle. *Ouvrage à l' —,* needle-work. — *aimantée;* magnetic needle. *Disputer sur la pointe d'une —;* to quarrel about straws. *Enfiler une —;* to thread a needle.

*****aiguillée**, *n.f.*, needleful.

*****aiguiller**, *v.a.*, (surg.) to couch (a cataract —*la cataracte*); (railways) to shift the points for the passage of a train from one line to another.

*****aiguilletage**, *n.m.*, (nav.) seizing.

*****aiguilleter**, *v.a.*, (nav.) to trap, to seize, to mouse. — *les canons;* to lash the guns.

aiguilletier, *n.m.*, tagger.

*****aiguillette**, *n.f.*, aiglet, point; shoulder-knot; slice (of flesh, skin—*de viande, de peau*); (nav.) knittle, tricing-line. *Le ferret de l' —;* the tag of a point.

aiguilleur, *n.m.*, (railways) pointsman.

*****aiguillier**, *n.m.*, needle-case. V. **étui.**

*****aiguillier**, *n.m.*, needle-maker.

*aiguillière, n.f., net for catching horn-fish; needle-maker.

*aiguillon, n.m., goad, spur, incentive, incitement, encouragement, stimulus, motive; sting (of insects, serpents—d'insectes, de serpents); (bot.) prickle, stimulus. Briser l'— de; to disarm of a sting.

*aiguillonner, v.a., to goad,to prick; to incite, to spur on, to stimulate.

*aiguillots, n.m. pl., (nav.) pintles.

aiguisé, -e, part., whetted, sharpened. Une croix aiguisée; (her.) a pointed cross.

aiguisement (-mǎn), n.m., whetting, sharpening.

aiguiser, v.a., to whet, to sharpen, to make sharp; to set an edge on; to point. — l'appétit; to sharpen the appetite. — une épigramme; to give point to an epigram. — ses couteaux; to prepare for battle. — ses dents; to prepare one's self to eat heartily. Pierre à —; hone.

aiguiseur, n.m., knife-grinder.

*ail, n.m., (ails), (aulx) (ō), garlic. — stérile; eschalot. Une tête d'—, une gousse d'—; a clove of garlic.

ailante, n.m., (bot.) ailanthus.

aile, n.f., wing, pinion; van, fan; wing (of an army, building—d'une armée, d'un bâtiment); aisle (of churches—d'église); fly (horol.); rung (of ships—de vaisseaux). Avoir les —s rapides; to be swift-winged. A tire d'—; at a single flight. En avoir dans l'—; to be different to what one was, to be in love. Il en a dans l'—; there is a screw loose. Frapper à l'—; to wing. Couper le bout de l'—; to pinion. Être sur l'—; to be on the wing. Battre des —s; to clap the wings. Trémousser des —s; to flutter. Rogner les —s à quelqu'un; to clip one's wings. Voler de ses propres —s; to be able to do without the help of others; to stand on one's own legs. Vouloir voler sans avoir des —s; to undertake a thing beyond one's strength. Ne battre plus que d'une —; to have lost one's strength, credit. Tirer de l'—; to make wing. — de moulin; wind-sail of a wind-mill. ☉ —; ale.

ailé, -e, adj., winged.

aileron, n.m., small wing; pinion; fin (of some fish—de quelques poissons); float-board (of a water-wheel—des roues à eau); (arch.) scroll.

ailette, n.f., side-lining of a shoe; small wing (of a building—d'un bâtiment).

*aillade, n.f., garlic sauce.

*ailleurs, adv., elsewhere, somewhere else. D'—; from another reason, cause, principle; on another account; besides, moreover, in other respects.

aimable, adj., amiable, lovely, agreeable, worthy to be loved. Un caractère —; a sweet temper.

aimablement, adv., in an amiable manner, amiably.

aimant, -e, adj., loving, affectionate.

aimant, n.m., loadstone, magnet. La déclinaison de l'—; the variation of the compass.

aimanté, -e, adj., magnetic.

aimanter, v.a., to rub or touch with a loadstone.

☉aimantin, -e, adj., magnetical.

aimé, -e, adj., loved, beloved.

aimer, v.a., to love, to be fond of, to have a passion for; to be in love with; to like, to be fond of, to fancy, to have a fancy for, to admire, to delight in, to have an inclination for. Il aime à monter à cheval; he delights in riding. Il aime sa personne; he loves his dear self. Aimez qu'on vous conseille, et non pas qu'on vous loue; love to be advised, not to be praised. — mieux; to prefer, to like better. — passionnément; to be passionately fond of. — à l'idolâtrie; to idolize.

Se faire —; to endear one's self. Qui aime bien, châtie bien; he chasteneth that loveth well. Qui m'aime aime mon chien; love me, love my dog.

s'aimer, v.r., to love one's self. S'— les uns les autres; to love one another.

aimez-moi, n.f., marsh scorpion-grass.

ain, n.m., woollen thread; (cloth-manufacturing—manufacture du drap) the number of threads contained in a given space.

aine, n.f., the groin.

aîné, n.m., -e, n.f., elder, senior.

aîné, -e, adj., eldest, elder, the eldest son or daughter; senior.

aînesse, n.f., primogeniture. Droit d'—; birthright, primogenitureship.

☉ains, conj., but.

ainsi, adv., thus, so, in this, that, manner. Je suis — fait; that's my temper. Le monde est —; such is the world. — du reste; and so forth. Il en est — des autres passions; thus it is with the other passions. — soit-il; amen; so be it. — va le monde; so the world goes.

ainsi, conj., thus, therefore, so that. — que, tout — que; as, as well as, even as, in the same manner as. Cela s'est passé — que je vous l'ai dit; that happened in the manner I have told you.

air, n.m., air; look, appearance, countenance, deportment; aspect; (mus.) tune; (chem., man., paint., sculp.) air. — abattu; downcast look. — chagrin; sour look. — éveillé; sharp look. — farouche; forbidding look. Faire des châteaux en l'—; to build castles in the air. Un coup d'—; a cold. Prendre l'—; to take the air. Donner de l'— à une chambre; to let the air into, to ventilate, a room. Chasser l'— renfermé; to let out the confined air. En plein —; in the open air. Se tenir entre deux —s; to be in a draught. Il ne fait point d'—; there is not the least breath of wind. Être en l'—; to be in a flutter. Paroles en l'—; silly words. Parler en l'—; to talk idly. Il forme des desseins en l'—; he forms extravagant designs. Il a tiré son coup en l'—; he has miscarried. Prendre l'— du bureau; to go and see how matters stand. Faire prendre l'—; to give an airing to. Les gens du bel —; people of high life. Un homme de méchant —; an ill-looking man. Un homme du grand —; a man who makes a great figure. Avoir l'— à; to have a mind to. Avoir l'— de; to look like. Avoir l'— bien portant; to look well. Lancer en l'—; to toss (of horned cattle—des bêtes à cornes). Avoir l'— bon, l'— mauvais; to look good-natured, ill-natured. Prendre un — riant; to put on a smiling countenance. Rempli d'— vicié; filled with foul air. Cela a l'— grand; that looks grand. Elle n'a pas l'— spirituel; she doesn't look sprightly. Elle a l'— bien étourdi; she looks very giddy. Il n'a pas l'— content; he doesn't seem pleased. Prendre des —s, se donner des —s; to take airs, to carry it high. Prendre des —s de bel esprit; to set up for a wit. Un — de famille; a family likeness. Air de tête (paint.); the attitude of the head. Un — gai, triste; a gay, dull, tune. Faire un — sur des paroles; to set words to music. Jouer un — rapide; to play a flourish. Ce cheval va à tout —; this horse has all his paces.

airain, n.m., brass. L'âge d'—; the brazen age. Avoir un front d'—; to have a brazen face, to blush at nothing. Avoir des entrailles d'—; to have a heart of stone.

aire, n.f.; area, barn-floor, threshing-floor; aerie (of a bird of prey—des oiseaux de proie). L'aire d'un bâtiment (arch.); the area of a building. — de plancher; superficies of a floor. L'— d'un triangle (geom.); the area or inside of a triangle. Une — de vent (nav.); a point of the compass.

airée, n.f., the lot of wheat, &c., lying on a barn-floor.

airelle, *n.f.*, whortle-berry, cow-berry.

airer, *v.n.*, to make its aerie or nest (of birds of prey—*des oiseaux de proie*).

ais (è), *n.m.*, board, shelf, plank; (print.) wetting-board; butcher's block.

aisance, *n.f.*, ease, freedom, easiness; the comforts or conveniences of life; — *s. pl.*, water-closet. *Il fait tout avec —*; he does everything with ease. *Avoir de l'— dans les manières;* to have an easy deportment. *Être dans l'—;* to be in easy circumstances. *Cabinet d'—s, lieux d'—s;* water-closet. *Fosse d'—s;* cess-pool.

aise, *n.f.*, gladness, joy, content; ease, comfort, conveniency. *A l'—;* easily; comfortable. *Se pâmer d'—;* to be overjoyed. *Tressaillir d'—;* to leap for joy. *Elle ne se sent pas d'—;* she is ready to jump out of her skin for joy. *Être à son —;* to be well off. *Mettre quelqu'un à son —;* to make one easy, to reassure any one. *Vous en parlez bien à votre —;* it is easy for you to say so. *N'en prendre qu'à son —;* to do but what pleases one, to take it easy. *Se sentir mal à l'—;* to feel uncomfortable. *Aimer ses —s;* to love one's ease. *On n'a pas toutes ses —s en ce monde;* we cannot have all we wish in this world.

aise, *adj.*, glad, joyful, well pleased. *Je suis bien — de vous voir;* I am very glad to see you.

aisé, **-e**, *adj.*, easy, convenient, commodious; in easy circumstances. *Cela est — à dire;* it is an easy thing to say so. *Un homme — à vivre;* an easy good-natured man. *Des souliers —s;* comfortable shoes. *Un air —;* an easy deportment. *Un style—;* a free, clear, easy style. *Il est fort —;* he is in very easy circumstances.

aisément, *adv.*, easily, readily, commodiously, freely, comfortably.

aisselle, *n.f.*, arm-pit; (anat., bot.) axil, axilla.

aitiologie. *V.* **étiologie.**

ajonc, *n.m.*, furze; thorn-broom.

ajournement, *n.m.*, adjournment; (jur.) summons.

ajourner, *v.a.*, to adjourn, to put off; (jur.) to summon.

ajourner,*v.n.*, *s'ajourner*,*v.r.*,to adjourn; to be adjourned.

ajoutage, *n.m.*, piece joined on.

ajouter, *v.a.*, to add, to join, to put to, to tag, to subjoin, to supply, to interpolate. *Ce passage a été ajouté à ce livre;* this passage is an interpolation. —*foi à quelque chose;* to give credit to a thing.

ajoutoir. *V.* **ajoutage, ajutage.**

ajustage, *n.m.*, adjusting, or giving the legal weight to a coin.

ajusté, **-e**, *part.*, adjusted, fitted, accommodated, dressed. *Un style bien —;* a very elaborate style. *Vous voilà bien —!* you are in a fine pickle.

ajustement, *n.m.*, adjustment, adjusting, fitting, regulation, settlement; laying out; attire, garb, apparel, dress, garment; accommodation, agreement, reconciliation. *L'— d'un poids;* the adjusting a weight. *L'— d'une machine;* the regulating a machine. *Elle n'est pas belle, elle a besoin d'—;* she is not handsome, she needs dress.

ajuster, *v.a.*, to adjust, to regulate, to square, to size, to tally; to aim, to take aim at, to aim at; to fit, to adapt, to set in order, to accommodate; to trim, to bedeck, to dress. —*un lièvre;* to take aim at a hare. —*de nouveau;* to recompose. —*ses cheveux;* to put one's hair in order. —*deux personnes;* to reconcile two people, to make them agree. —*un différend;* to reconcile a difference. *Ajustez vos flûtes;* prepare your measures. *On l'a bien ajusté;* they have given it him well. — *des passages d'un livre;* to make passages of a book agree.

s'ajuster, *v.r.*, to prepare one's self, to get one's self ready; to dress, to deck, one's self

out; to agree, to take measures, to concert together.

ajusteur, *n.m.*, weigher at the mint.

ajustoir, *n.m.*, a pair of scales (used in the mint—*employé à l'hôtel des monnaies*).

ajutage, ajutoir, *n.m.*, adjutage, a tube or pipe (for water-works—*pour ouvrages hydrauliques*).

alambic, *n.m.*, alembic, still. *Faire passer par l'—;* to distil, to draw by distillation. *Passer par l'—;* to undergo a careful examination.

alambiqué, **-e**, *part.*, far-fetched, too subtle, too refined. *Cette pensée est trop —e;* that thought is too refined.

alambiquer, *v.a.*, to puzzle, to refine too much upon. *S'— l'esprit sur quelque chose;* to beat, puzzle one's brains about a thing, to pore over it.

alanguir (-ghir), *v.a.*, to enfeeble, to make languid.

s'alanguir, *v.r.*, to languish, to flag, to become languid.

alarguer (-ghé), *v.n.*, (nav.) to bear away, to put to sea, to sheer off.

alarmant, **-e**, *adj.*, alarming, dreadful.

alarme, *n.f.*, alarm; sudden fear, fright. *Sonner l'—, donner l'—;* to sound, to give the alarm. *Cloche d'—;* alarm-bell. *Fausse —;* false alarm. *Donner des —;* to give uneasiness to. *Porter l'— dans;* to alarm. *L'— est au camp;* they are in a great fright.

alarmer, *v.a.*, to alarm, to give an alarm, to startle.

s'alarmer, *v.r.*, to take alarm, to be alarmed. *Ne vous alarmez point;* don't frighten yourself.

alarmiste, *n.m.f.*, alarmist.

alaterne,*n.m.*,species of buck-thorn; alatern.

albâtre, *n.m.*, alabaster.

albatros, *n.m.*, (orni.) albatross.

alberge, *n.f.*, a small forward peach.

albergier, *n.m.*, an alberge-tree.

albigeois, *n.m.*, Albigens.

albinos, *n.m.*, albino.

albion, *n.f.*, Albion (England).

albran. *V.* **halbran.**

albuginé, **-e**, *adj.*, (anat.) albugineous.

albugineu-x, **-se**, *adj.*, (anat.) albugineous, whitish.

albugo, *n.m.*, (med.) albugo.

album, (-bom), *n.m.*, album, scrap-book.

albumine, *n.f.*, albumen, white (of an egg —*d'œuf*).

albumineu-x, **-se**, *adj.*, albuminous.

alcade, *n.m.*, Spanish alcaid, alcade.

alcaïque, *adj.*, alcaic. *Vers —s;* alcaic verses.

alcalescence, *n.f.*, alkalescency.

alcalescent, **-e**, *adj.*, alkalescent.

alcali, *n.m.*, alkali.

alcalimètre, *n.m.*, alkalimeter.

alcalin, **-e**, *adj.*, alkaline.

alcalisation, *n.*, alkalization.

alcaliser, *v.a.*, (chem.) to alkalize.

alcaloïde, *n.m.*, (chem.) alkaloid.

alcantara, *n.m.*, a Spanish military order.

alcarazas, *n.m.*, water-cooler.

alcée, *n.f.*, holly-hock.

alchimie, *n.f.*, alchymy.

***alchimille**, *n.f.*, (bot.) lady's mantle

alchimique, *adj.*, alchymical.

alchimiste, *n.m.*, alchymist.

alcool, *n.m.*, alcohol.

alcoolique, *adj.*, alcoholic.

alcoolisation, *n.f.*, alcoholization.

alcooliser, *v.a.*, to alcoholize.

alcoolisme, *n.m.*, (med.) alcoholism, a peculiar morbid state produced by the excessive use of spirits.

alcoran, *n.m.*, Koran.

alcóve, *n.f.*, alcove, recess.
alcyon, *n.m.*, halcyon.
alcyonien, -ne, (-in,-è-n), halcyon.
aldébaran, *n.m.*, (astron.) Aldebaran.
alderman, *n.m.*, alderman.
aléatoire, *adj.*, (jur.) eventual.
alène, *n.f.*, awl. *Feuilles en —;* acuminated leaves.
alénier, *n.m.*, awl-maker.
alentir, *s'alentir*. *V.* **ralentir** and **se ralentir.**
alénois, *n.m.*, common-garden cress.
alentour, *adv.*, about, around, round about. *Les bois d':* — the neighbouring woods.
alentours, *n.m. pl.*, the neighbouring grounds; environs, neighbourhood; persons about, around one.
alépine, *n.f.*, bombazine.
alérion, *n.m.*, (her.) eaglet without beak or feet.
alerte, *n.f.*, alarm, warning.
alerte, *adj.*, alert, vigilant, watchful; active, stirring, quick, sprightly, brisk, lively, agile.
alerte, *int.*, take care, be quick; up!
alésage, *n.m.*, (tech.) boring, drilling.
aléser, *v.a.*, (tech.) to hammer planchets; to bore. — *un canon;* to bore a cannon.
alésoir, *n.m.*, borer (instrument).
alevin (-vin), *n.m.*, fry (fish—*poisson*).
alevinage, *n.m.*, small fry (fish—*poisson*).
aleviner (-né), *v.a.*, to stock with fry.
alevinier (-nié), *n.m.*, a small pond wherein fish are kept for breeding.
alexandrien, -ne, *adj.*, Alexandrian.
alexandrin, *n.m.*, (poet.) alexandrine.
alexandrin, -e, *adj.*, alexandrine.
alezan (zăn), *n.m.*, chesnut-horse.
alezan,'-e (zăn,-za-n), *adj.*, chesnut.
alèze, *n.f.*, sheet (placed under sick persons —*mis sous un malade*).
alfa, *n.m.*, (bot.) an African plant.
alfange, *n.f.*, phalanx, battalion (Chinese, Tartar—*chinois, tartare*). *V.* **cimeterre.**
algalie, *n.f.*, (surg.) catheter.
alganon, *n.m.*, a chain for galley-slaves.
algarade, *n.f.*, (fam.) insult, affront; rating, blowing up. *Faire une —;* to insult, to rate, one; to blow any one up.
algèbre, *n.f.*, algebra.
algébrique, *adj.*, algebraical.
algébriquement, *adv.*, algebraically.
algébriste, *n.m.*, algebraist.
algide, *adj.*, (med.) cold as ice, algid.
algor, *n.m.*, (med.) algor.
algorithme, *n.m.*, algorithm.
alguazil (-goua-zil), (—*s*) *n.m.*, alguazil.
algue, *n.f.*, alga, sea-weed, sea-wrack grass.
alibi, *n.m.*, (—*s*) (jur.) alibi.
alibiforain, *n.m.* (fam. l.u.), irrelevant, rambling answer; evasion, shuffling, prevarication.
alibile, *adj.*, (med.) alible.
aliboron, *n.m.*, a self-conceited fellow. *Maître —;* ass.
aliboufier, *n.m.*, a fragrant resin, storax.
alidade, *n.f.*, alidade, the index of any surveying instrument, such as a quadrant, sextant, &c.
aliénable. *adj.*, alienable.
aliénataire, *n.m.*, alienee.
aliénat-eur, *n.m.*, **-rice**, *n.f.*, alienator.
aliénation, *n.f.*, a legal conveyance of property to another, alienation; alienation (of the mind—*d'esprit*). — *d'esprit, mentale;* mental derangement, madness.
aliéné, -e, *n.*, lunatic, maniac. *Hospice pour les — s;* lunatic asylum. *Maison d' — s;* madhouse.

aliéné, -e, *adj.*, (of property—*de propriété*) alienated, transferred to another; (affections) estranged, withdrawn; (of the mind—*de l'esprit*) deranged, mad.
aliéner, *v.a.*, to alienate, to give away, to part with, to make over, to deliver up the possession or right of. — *les affections, les cœurs, les esprits;* to alienate, to estrange, to disaffect, to lose the affection. *Il a aliéné les esprits;* he has disaffected all minds. — *l'esprit à quelqu'un;* to drive one mad.
***aligné, -e**, *part.*, laid out by a line; that stands in a right line.
***alignement**, *n.m.*, laying out by a line; line; (milit.) dressing; (print.) ranging. *Cette maison sort de l';* that house stands out of the row. *Rentrer dans l' —;* to fall into line. *Prendre l' —;* to trace the line of. — *!* (milit.) dress!
***aligner**, *v.a.*, to lay out by a line; to square; to put in a straight line; (milit.) to dress; (print.) to range. — *des troupes;* to form troops in a line. — *ses phases;* to square one's sentences.
s'aligner, *v.r.*, (milit.) to dress; (pop.) to have a set to, to fight.
aliment, *n.m.*, food, aliment, nourishment, meat, nutriment, nutrition; fuel; (jur.) allowance.
aliments, *n.m. pl.*, (jur.) alimony, maintenance.
alimentaire, *adj.*, alimentary; alimental. *Pension —;* alimony, maintenance. *Régime —;* diet.
alimentation, *n.f.*, alimentation; feeding.
alimenter, *v.a.*, to feed, to nourish; to maintain; to supply with what is necessary, to furnish; to fuel. *Le marché ne fournit pas de quoi — la ville;* the market does not furnish what is necessary for the supply of the town.
alimenteu-x, -se, *adj.*, (med.) nutritive, alimentary; alimental.
alinéa, *n.m.* (—*s*), new paragraph, break.
aliquante, *adj.*, (math.) aliquant.
aliquote, *adj.*, (math.) aliquot.
alise, *n.f.*, the berry of the service-tree, beam-berry.
alisier, *n.m.*, service-tree, beam-tree.
alité, -e, *part.*, bedridden, bedrid.
aliter, *v.a.*, to make one keep one's bed.
s'aliter, *v.r.*, to keep one's bed, to be bedridden.
alizari, *n.m.*, madder-root.
alizé, *adj.*, (nav.) *Vents —s;* trade-winds.
alize, *n.f. V.* **alise.**
alizier, *n.m. V.* **alisier.**
alkali, &c. *V.* **alcali**, &c.
alkékenge, *n.m.*, winter-cherry.
alkermès (-èss), *n.m.*, alkermes.
allah, (al-la), *n.m.*, (the Arabic name of the Supreme Being—*nom arabe de l'Être suprême*) Alla, Allah.
allaitement (-lèt-măn), *n.m.*, lactation, suckling.
allaiter, *v.a.*, to suckle, to give suck, to nurse.
allant, *n.m.*, goer. *Allants et venants;* comers and goers.
allant, -e, *adj.*, stirring, bustling, fond of going about.
allantoïde, *n.f.*, (anat.) allantois.
allèchement, *n.m.*, allurement, enticement, bait.
allécher, *v.a.*, to allure, to entice.
allée, *n.f.*, going; passage, entry, alley; lane; walk. *Une — couverte;* a shady walk. *Faire des —s et venues;* to go in and out, to and fro.
allégation (al-lé-), *n.f.*, citation, quotation, allegation.
allège, *n.f.*, lighter, tender; (arch.) window basement, sill of the window.

allégeance (al-lé-jan-s), n.f., (l.u.) allegiance. *Serment d'—;* oath of allegiance.

allégeance, n.f., alleviation, relief.

allégement (al-léj-mān), n.m., alleviation, ease, relief.

alléger (al-lé-jé), v.a., to ease, to disburden, to lighten, to unload (a boat—*un bateau*); to alleviate, to soften, to relieve, to assuage pain or grief; (nav.) to buoy up.

allégir, v.a., to lighten, to reduce.

allégorie (al-lé-), n.f., allegory. *Par—;* allegorically.

allégorique (al-lé-), adj., allegoric, allegorical.

allégoriquement (-mān), adv., allegorically.

allégoriser (al-lé-), v.a., to allegorize.

allégoriseur (al-lé-), n.m., allegorizer.

allégoriste (al-lé-), n.m., allegorist.

allègre (al-lègr), adj., brisk, nimble, sprightly, jolly, cheerful.

allègrement, adv., joyfully, merrily, joyously.

allégresse, n.f., mirth, cheerfulness, gladness, joy, gaiety, sprightliness, alacrity, jovialness, glee, joyfulness. *Cris d'—;* shouts, huzzas.

allégretto (al-lé-grèt-to), adv. and n.m., (—s) (mus.) allegretto.

allégro (al-lé-) adv. and n.m., (—s) (mus.) allegro.

alléguer (-al-lé-ghé), v.a., to allege; to quote, to bring in, to cite, to plead, to produce, to advance, to urge.

alléluia, n.m., hallelujah; (bot.) wood-sorrel.

allemand, **-e** (-mān, -d-), adj., German. *Une querelle d' —;* a groundless quarrel.

allemand, n.m., -e, n.f., German.

allemande, n.f., allemande, a dance.

aller, n.m., going, course of time, run; (nav.) outward voyage. *— et retour;* voyage out and in. *Au long —;* in the long run. *Avoir l' — pour le venir;* to lose one's labour. *Au pis —;* at the worst. *C'est votre pis —;* it's your last shift.

aller (allant, allé), v.n., to go, to be going; to move, to be in motion or movement; to burn; to depart, to repair, to resort; to reach, to come, to lead, to end; to do; to be; to go forward, to go on; to succeed; to amount; to act; to proceed; to go about; to tend, to aim; to arrive; to lay; to stake, to play; to go to the water-closet; to work; to chance; to fit, to become, to be matched; to sail. *— au marché;* to go to market. *Allez en paix;* depart in peace. *Allez au diable;* go to the devil. *— croissant;* to go on increasing. *La carte va à dix francs;* the bill amounts to ten francs. *Faire —;* to make go, to set going. *— à pied;* to go on foot. *— à cheval;* to go on horseback, to ride. *— en voiture;* to ride in a carriage, to drive. *— au pas;* to walk, to pace. *— au trot;* to trot. *— au galop;* to gallop. *— au petit galop;* to canter. *— son train;* to keep on, to take one's own course. *— bon train;* to go on at a good round pace, to get on well. *— à tâtons;* to grope along. *— au-devant de quelqu'un, à la rencontre de quelqu'un;* to go and meet one. *— çà et là;* to ramble about. *Ne faire qu' — et venir;* to do nothing but run backwards and forwards. *Je ne ferai qu'— et venir;* I will not stay; I shall be back again directly. *Ma montre ne va pas;* my watch does not go. *Va vite;* go quickly. *Allant à —;* (nav.) bound to. *Cela vous va;* that suits you. *Allons donc;* come then; nonsense! *Allez, va;* be gone; be off. *Ils vont venir;* they will come presently. *— se promener;* to go for a walk. *Allez vous promener;* go about your business. *La rivière va serpentant;* the river runs winding about. *— aux informations;* to make inquiries. *— aux voix;* to put to the vote. *— aux provisions;* to go to market. *Ce vase va au feu;* this jug stands the fire.

— de pair; to be equal. *— de pair à compagnon avec quelqu'un;* to be cheek by jowl with one. *Ce chemin va à l'église;* this way leads to the church. *La montagne va jusqu'aux nues;* the mountain reaches to the clouds. *— de mal en pis;* to grow worse and worse. *Comment va la santé?* how are you in health? *Comment cela va-t-il?* how are you? *Sa santé va de mieux en mieux;* his health is better and better. *Comment allez-vous?* how are you getting on? *Tout va bien;* all is well. *Cet homme ira loin dans les sciences;* that man will distinguish himself in the sciences. *Le feu ne va pas bien;* the fire does not burn well. *Nos affaires vont mal;* our affairs are in a sad state. *Le commerce ne va plus;* trade is at a stand. *Cela ne va pas mal;* things are in a fair way. *Votre habit vous va mal;* your coat doesn't fit you. *Ces deux couleurs-là vont bien ensemble;* those two colours are well matched together. *Il y va de bonne foi;* he acts sincerely. *— rondement;* to act candidly. *Tous mes désirs vont là;* all my wishes tend that way. *C'est un adroit qui va à ses fins;* he is a cunning fellow, he pushes his point. *— à la gloire;* to aim at glory. *Est-ce ainsi que vous y allez?* is this your way? *Tudieu, comme vous y allez;* egad! you go on at a fine rate. *De combien allez-vous?* how much do you stake? *Va pour du vin!* (fam.) well, let us have some wine. *Ce malade laisse tout — sous lui;* everything runs through this sick man. *Allons, mes amis, courage;* come, my friends, cheer up, take courage. *Allez, n'avez-vous point de honte?* fie, are you not ashamed? *Allez, je veux m'employer pour vous;* take heart, I'll rest myself for you. *Voyez où j'en serais, si elle allait croire cela;* see what a situation I should be in, if she should chance to believe that. *— toujours;* to keep on, (b.s.) to rattle, blunder, on. *Allez toujours;* go on. *Se laisser aller;* to yield, to give way, to abandon one's self to a thing. *Se laisser — à la tentation;* to yield to temptation. *Se laisser — à la douleur;* to give one's self up to grief. *Laisser —;* to release, to let go. *Quand il devrait y — de tout mon bien;* though my whole fortune were at stake. *Songez qu'il y va de votre honneur;* reflect that your honour is concerned in it. *Il y allait de la vie;* life was at stake. *Quand il irait de ma vie;* although my life were at stake. *Il en va, il en ira;* it is, it will be. *Il en va de cette affaire-là comme de l'autre;* it is with that affair as with the other. *Où va le navire?* (nav.) where are you bound to? *— son chemin;* to pursue one's design. *Il ira son chemin;* he will make his way. *Je m'en vais vous dire;* I'll tell you what. *Faire en — tout le monde;* to drive everybody away. *Faire en — des taches;* to take out stains. *Tous chemins vont à Rome;* there are more ways than one to Heaven. *Cela va tout seul;* there is no difficulty in the thing. *Cela ne va pas;* that wont do; it's no go. *Cela va sans dire;* that goes without saying; of course. *Cela ira;* that will do; we shall succeed. *Cela n'ira pas loin;* that will not last long. *Cela n'ira pas plus loin;* it shall go no further. *Tout s'en est allé en fumée;* all is come to nothing. *N'y va pas — de main morte;* to go to it both tooth and nail.

s'en aller, v.r., to go away, to set out, to go out, to march off, to depart, to take one's self off; to run, to scamper, away; to retire; to run out; to boil over, to dwindle away; to evaporate; to die, to wear out; to sneak off. *Va-t'en; allez-vous-en;* go away; be off with you! *Il faut que tout le monde s'en aille;* everybody must go away. *Allons-nous-en;* let us go. *Ils s'en vont;* they are going away. *Mon habit s'en va;* my coat is wearing out. *Il s'en va;* he is dying. *Qui va là?* who goes there?

alleu, n.m., allodium. *Franc- — (—s—s);* a freehold.

alliacé, -e, *adj.*, (bot.) alliaceous.

alliage, *n.m.*, alloyage, alloy, mixture; (arith.) alligation. *Sans* —*;* pure, without alloy. — *pour caractères d'imprimerie;* type-metal.

alliaire, *n.f.*, hedge-garlic.

alliance, *n.f.*, alliance, marriage, match; confederacy; union; blending; wedding-ring; covenant.

allié, *n.m.*, **-e,** *n.f.*, ally; relation (by marriage—*par mariage*).

allié, -e, *part.*, allied, related (by marriage —*par mariage*); akin, kindred. *Les rois alliés;* the confederate kings.

allier, *v.a.*, to mix; to combine, to unite; to match, to marry; to join, to unite, to ally, to reconcile. — *l'or avec l'argent;* to alloy gold with silver.

s'allier, *v.r.*, to be incorporated or mixed; to match, to enter into a confederacy; to unite; to suit; to combine (of metals—*des métaux*).

allier, *n.m.*, partridge-net.

⊙**alliez,** *n.m.*, (bot.) tare. *V.* **ivraie.**

alligator, *n.m.*, the American crocodile, alligator.

allitération (al-li-), *n.f.*, alliteration.

allobroge (al-lo-), *n.m.*, clown, lout.

allocation (al-lo-), *n.f.*, allocation, allowance.

allocution (al-lo-), *n.f.*, allocution, address, speech, harangue.

allodial, -e (al-lo-), *adj.*, allodial. *Terres —es* freehold lands, freeholds.

allodialité (al-lo-), *n.f.*, free-tenure.

allonge, *n.f.*, a piece of stuff to eke out anything; leaf (of a table—*de table*); rider (of a bill —*d'un billet, lettre de change, &c.*); (nav.) futtock.

allongé, -e, *part.*, lengthened, elongated.

allongement (-măn), *n.m.*, lengthening, stretching out, elongation, delaying.

allonger, *v.a.*, to lengthen, to elongate, to piece, to eke out; to stretch out; to wire-draw; to delay, to protract; (fenc.) to allonge.

s'allonger, *v.r.*, to stretch out, to lengthen, to grow longer, to stretch.

allouable, *adj.*, allowable, that may be granted.

allouer, *v.a.*, to allow, to grant, to pass in an account.

alluchon, *n.m.*, cog, catch, tooth (of a wheel—*d'une roue*).

allumer, *v.a.*, to light, to kindle, to set in a flame or on fire, to inflame. — *le feu;* to kindle the fire. — *une chandelle;* to light a candle. — *la guerre;* to kindle war.

s'allumer, *v.r.*, to be lighted, to light, to kindle, to catch or take fire, to be inflamed; to brighten up. *Ce bois a bien de la peine à s'—;* this wood won't kindle.

allumette, *n.f.*, match (for procuring fire). — *chimique;* lucifer-match.

allumeur, *n.m.*, lighter, lamp-lighter.

allure, *n.f.*, gait, pace, way of walking; conduct, behaviour, way of proceeding; turn; *pl.*, intrigues. *Je le connais à son —;* I know him by his gait. *Je connais les —s de cet homme;* I know that man's way of dealing.

allusion (al-lu-), *n.f.*, allusion, hint. *Faire — à quelque chose;* to allude to something. *Faire une — peu voilée;* to give a broad hint.

alluvial, -e, *adj.*, alluvious.

alluvien, -ne, (-in,-è-n), *adj.* *V.* **alluvial.**

alluvion (al-lu-), *n.f.*, alluvion.

almageste, *n.m.*, almagest.

almanach (-nă), *n.m.*, almanac, calendar. — *du commerce;* commercial directory. *Composer des —s;* to indulge in idle dreams.

aloès (-èss), *n.m.*, aloe; the juice of the aloe, aloes.

aloétique, *adj.*, aloetical.

aloi, *n.m.*, alloy, standard; quality (of persons). *Argent de bon —;* good money. *Homme de bas —;* man of mean birth.

⊙**aloïque,** *adj.*, aloetic.

alonge, &c. *V.* **allonge,** &c.

alopécie, *n.f.*, (med.) alopecy, fox-evil.

alors, *adv.*, then, at that time. *D'—;* of that time. — *comme —;* we shall know what to do, all in good time.

alose, *n.f.*, (ich.) shad, alose.

alouchier, *n.m.*, (bot.) white beam tree.

alouette, *n.f.*, (orni.) lark. — *huppée;* tuftell lark. — *des champs;* sky-lark. — *lulu;* wood-lark. — *des prés;* tit-lark. *Il attend que les —s lui tombent toutes rôties dans le bec;* he expects a fortun? to drop into his mouth. *Pied d'—;* (bot.) lark's heel, larkspur.

alourdir, *v.a.*, to make dull, heavy, stupid. *Je suis tout alourdi;* my head is quite heavy.

alourdissement, *n.m.*, heaviness, dulness (of mind—*d'esprit*).

aloyage, *n.m.*, alloying, mixture.

aloyau, *n.m.*, sirloin of beef.

aloyer, *v.a.*, to alloy gold and silver.

alpaca, *n.m.*, alpaca, llama.

alpaga, *n.m.*, alpaca (stuff—*étoffe*).

alpestre, *adj.*, alpine.

alpha, *n.m.*, beginning; alpha.

alphabet, *n.m.*, alphabet.

alphabétique, *adj.*, alphabetical. *Par ordre —;* alphabetically. *Répertoire —;* alphabetical index.

alphabétiquement (-măn), *adv.*, alphabetically.

alpin, -e, *adj.*, growing on high mountains, alpine.

alpiou, *n.m.*, *Faire un —;* to stake double.

alpiste, *n.m.*, canary-grass.

alsine, *n.f.* *V.* **morgeline.**

altaïque, *adj.*, altaic, altaian.

alte, *n.f.* *V.* **halte.**

altérable, *adj.*, corruptible, alterable.

altérant, *n.m.*, (med.) alterative.

altérant, -e, *adj.*, that causes thirst; (med.) alterative.

altérati-f, -ve, *adj.*, (med.) alterative.

altération, *n.f.*, deterioration, corruption; adulteration, debasing; weakening, impairing, alteration, misrepresentation; excessive thirst. *L'— de sa voix;* the faltering of his voice. *Tous les excès causent de l'— dans la santé;* all excesses impair the health.

altercas, *n.m.* *V.* **altercation.**

altercation, *n.f.*, altercation, contest, wrangle, dispute.

altéré, -e, *part.*, altered, adulterated; thirsty, dry, adry. — *de gloire;* greedy of glory. — *de sang;* blood-thirsty.

alter ego, *n.m.* (*n.p.*), alter ego. *C'est mon —;* he is my other self.

altérer, *v.a.*, to alter, to change, to impair; to adulterate, to weaken; to mis-state, to distort; to debase; to cause thirst. *Le soleil altère les couleurs;* the sun makes colours fade. — *la viande;* to taint meat. — *le caractère;* to spoil the temper. — *l'amitié;* to weaken friendship. — *la monnaie;* to debase the coin. *Cette sauce aux anchois m'a fort altéré;* that anchovy sauce has made me very dry.

s'altérer, *v.r.*, to be impaired or altered; to taint, to spoil. *Le vin s'altère à l'air;* wine spoils in the air. *Sa santé commence à s'—;* his health begins to be impaired.

altérer, *v.n.*, to excite thirst, make thirsty.

alternance, *n.f.*, alternation.

alternat, *n.m.*, alternateness; alternacy.

alternati-f, -ve, *adj.*, alternate, alternative.

alternative, *n.f.*, alternative, choice, option. *Je vous donne l'—;* I put it to your choice.

alternativement (-man), *adv.*, alternately; alternatively.

alterne, *adj.*, alternate

alterné, **-e**, *adj.*, (her.) alternate (quarters--*quartiers*).

alterner, *v.n.*, to alternate, to succeed each other alternately.

alterquer, *v.n.*, to altercate, to dispute.

altesse, *n.f.*, highness. *Son --; royale*; his, her. royal highness.

althæa, *n.f.*, (bot.) marsh-mallow.

alti-er, **-ère**, *adj.*, haughty, proud, arrogant, lordly, lofty, elate, stately. *Mine altière*; haughty look.

altimètre, *n.m.*, altimeter. *V.* **hypsomètre**.

altitude, *n.f.*, altitude.

alto, *n.m.*, (--s) (mus.) tenor violin.

alude, *n.f.*, coloured sheep-skin.

aludel, *n.m.*, (chem.) aludel, earthen subliming pot

alumelle, *n.f.*, long and thin knife or swordblade; (nav.) handspike-hole; sheathing.

alumine, *n.f.*, alumina.

aluminé, **-e**, *adj.*, alumish.

alumineux, **-se**, *adj.*, aluminous.

aluminière. *V.* **alunière**.

aluminium, *n.m.*, (n.p.), aluminum, aluminium.

alun, *n.m.*, alum.

alunage, *n.m.*, (dy.) steeping in alum.

alunation, *n.f.*, (chem.) alum-making.

aluner, *v.a.*, to steep in alum-water.

alunière, *n.f.*, alum-pit.

alvéolaire, *adj.*, alveolar.

alvéole, *n.m.*, alveolus, cell (in a honey-comb --*d'un rayon de miel*); socket. *Les --s des dents*; the alveoli of the teeth.

alvin, **-e**, *adj.*, (med.) alvine.

alysson, *n.m.*, **alysse**, *n.f.*, madwort.

amabilité, *n.f.*, loveliness; kindness; amiableness.

amadis, *n.m.*, tight sleeve.

amadou, *n.m.*, German tinder; touch-wood; pyrotechnical sponge.

amadouer, *v.a.*, to coax, to wheedle, to cajole, to flatter.

amadouvier, *n.m.*, agaric, touch-wood.

amaigrir, *v.a.*, to make lean, meagre, or thin, to emaciate; (arch.) to thin. *C'est cela qui l'amaigrit*; it is that which makes him grow thin.

amaigrir, *v.n.*, to fall away, to grow lean or thin; (arch.) to shrink.

s'amaigrir, *v.r.*, to grow thin, to fall away.

amaigrissement (-gris-mān), *n.m.*, emaciation; growing lean, falling away, tabefaction.

amalgamation, *n.f.*, amalgamation.

amalgame, *n.m.*, amalgam; medley, mixture, amalgamation.

amalgamer, *v.a.*, to amalgamate, to combine, to blend.

s'amalgamer, *v.r.*, to amalgamate; to blend together.

amande, *n.f.*, almond, kernel; nucleus. -- *amère, douce*; bitter, sweet, almond. --*s lissées*; sugar-plums. --*s à la praline*; burnt almonds. -- *d'amazone*; Brazil-nut. *Huile d'--s douces*; oil of sweet almonds.

amandé, *n.m.*; amygdalate; milk of almonds.

amandier, *n.m.*, almond-tree.

amant, *n.m.*, **-e**, *n.f.*, lover. wooer. suitor; sweetheart. mistress; votary, spark, gallant, paramour.

amarante, *n.f.*, amaranth, purple flowergentle, cock's-comb, prince's feather.

amarante, *adj.*, amaranthine, amaranth-coloured.

amarinage, *n.m.*, action of manning a ship taken from the enemy, manning a prize.

amariner, *v.a.*, to man (a prize--*une prise*); to inure to sea.

amarrage, *n.m.*, (nav.) anchoring, seizure. *Ligne d'--*; lasher.

amarre, *n.f.*, (nav.) cable, rope, hawser, seizing.

amarrer, *v.a.*, (nav.) to moor, to belay, to make fast, to lash, to tie, to seize.

amaryllis (-ril-lis), *n.f.*, amaryllis, lily-asphodel.

amas, *n.m.*, mass, heap, pile, collection, hoard, store, accumulation, cluster; *congerïes*. *Un -- de peuple*; a great mob. *-- de sable*; heap of sand.

amasser, *v.a.*, to heap up, to hoard up, to lay up, to treasure up, to gather up, to get together, to accumulate, to rake together; to assemble, to congregate, to put together, to cluster. *-- de l'argent*; to hoard up money. *L'avare ne se plaît qu'à --*; the miser's whole delight is in hoarding up money.

s'amasser, *v.r.*, to gather, to get together, to accumulate, to be collected, to crowd.

amassette, *n.f.*, small palette-knife.

amatelotage (-mat-lo-), *n.m.*, (nav.) messmating.

amateloter (-mat-lo-), *v.a.*, (nav.) to class (the crew--*l'équipage*).

amateur, *n.m.*, lover, admirer; amateur, virtuoso. *-- des beaux-arts*; lover of the fine arts. *-- de la nouveauté*; fond of novelty.

amatir, *v.a.*, (gold--*l'or*) to deaden; (coin.) to blanch the planchets.

amaurose, *n.f.*, (med.) amaurosis.

amazone, *n.f.*, amazon, riding-habit.

ambages, *n.f. pl.*, ambages, idle circumlocution.

ambassade, *n.f.*, embassy, embassade; ambassador's house.

ambassadeur, *n.m.*, ambassador; messenger, envoy.

ambassadrice, *n.f.*, ambassadress.

ambe, *n.m.*, two numbers taken and winning at a lottery.

ambesas (anb-zâs), *n.m.*, ambs-ace, two aces.

ambi, *n.m.*, (surg.) ambe, ambi.

ambiant, **-e**, *adj.*, ambient, surrounding.

ambidextérité, *n.f.*, double dealing; ambidexterity.

ambidextre, *adj.*, ambidexterous.

ambigu, *n.m.*, ambigu.

ambigu, **-ë**, *adj.*, ambiguous, equivocal.

ambiguïté, *n.f.*, ambiguity. *Parler sans --*; to speak plainly.

ambigument, *adv.*, ambiguously.

ambitieusement (-mān), *adv.*, ambitiously.

ambitieu-x, **-se**, *adj.*, ambitious.

ambition, *n.f.*, ambition.

ambitionner, *v.a.*, to desire earnestly, to be ambitious of.

amble, *n.m.*, amble, pace. *Aller l'--*; to amble. *Être franc d'--*; to amble freely. *Ce cheval a l'-- doux*; that horse ambles easy.

ambler, *v.n.*, to amble, to pace.

ambon, *n.m.*, ambo, rood-loft.

ambre, *n.m.*, amber. *-- gris*; ambergris. *Il est fin comme l'--*; he is a shrewd fellow.

ambré, **-e**, *adj.*, amber-coloured.

ambrer, *v.a.*, to perfume with amber.

ambrette, *n.f.*, amber-seed.

ambroisie, *n.f.*, ambrosia. *D'--*; ambrosial.

ambrosien, **-ne**(-in,-ène), *adj.*, pertaining to St. Ambrose: Ambrosian.

ambulance, *n.f.*, field-hospital. *Chirurgien d'--*: field-surgeon.

ambulant, **-e**, *adj.*, ambulatory, ambulant; itinerant, strolling. *Marchand --*; itinerant dealer. *Comédiens --s*; strolling players. *Érési-*

pêle —; flying erysipelas. *Mener une vie* —*e;* to stroll, be upon the tramp.

ambulatoire, *adj.*, ambulatory, movable, itinerant.

âme, *n.f.*, soul; mind; conscience; ghost, spirit, sentiment; person, people; motto; chamber (of a gun—*d'un canon, d'un canon de fusil*); small wood (in faggots—*dans les fagots*); (sculp.) a rough figure of clay; the model made use of to form a mould; (mus.) sounding-post. *Les faculités de l'* —; the faculties of the mind. *Grandeur d'* —; magnanimity. *Du fond de l'* —; from the bottom of the soul. *Dieu veuille avoir son* —; God rest his soul. *Avoir la mort dans l'* —; to be sick at heart. *Il n'y a pas* — *qui vive ici;* there is not a living creature here. *Je le veux de toute mon* —; I consent to it with all my soul. *Sans* —; spiritless. *La vérité est l'* — *de l'histoire;* truth is the life of history. *La bonne foi est l'* — *du commerce;* honesty is the very soul of trade. *Il n'y a point l'* — *dans sa déclamation;* his delivery is spiritless. *Il est l'*—*damnée du ministre;* he is the minister's tool. *Rendre l'* —; to give up the ghost. *Il a l'* — *bourrelée;* his conscience is filled with remorse. *Cet homme n'a point d'* —; that man has no spirit. *Il n'y a pas une* — *vivante dans cette maison;* there is not a living soul in that house.

⊙**amé, -e**, *adj.*, well-beloved.

amélioration, *n.f.*, amelioration, improvement, mending. *Susceptible d'* —; improvable.

améliorer, *v.a.*, to ameliorate, to improve, to meliorate, to better, to cultivate, to mend.

s'améliorer, *v.r.*, to mend, to improve.

amen (amè-n), *n.m.*, amen.

aménagement (-naj-màn), *n.m.*, management of a forest.

aménager, *v.a.*, to regulate the felling, replanting, and preserving of a wood or forest. — *un arbre;* to cut up a tree.

amendable, *adj.*, improvable, mendable.

amende, *n.f.*, fine, penalty, forfeit, ransom. *Mettre à l'* —; to fine. *Faire* — *honorable;* to make an apology.

amendé, -e, *part.*, amended, mended, reclaimed.

amendement (-màn), *n.m.*, amendment, mending, bettering, improvement. — *d'une terre;* improvement of a piece of ground. *La loi a passé sans* —; the bill passed without amendment.

amender, *v.a.*, to mend, to better, to correct, to improve, to manure.

amender, *v.n.*, to grow better, to improve.

s'amender, *v.r.*, to amend, to grow better, to reform; to mend.

amener, *v.a.*, to bring; to bring in, to bring up, to bring over, to bring about, to bring round, to bring on; to lead; to fetch, to introduce; to prevail upon, to induce; to throw (of dice—*des dés*); (nav.) to haul down, lower, strike. *Je l'ai amené où je voulais;* I have brought him to the terms I wanted. *Il a amené cette affaire à bien;* he has brought the matter to bear. — *des maladies;* to bring on diseases. — *des modes;* to bring in fashions. — *quelqu'un à faire une chose;* to induce any one to do a thing. — *son pavillon:* to lower her flag. *Amène!* (nav.) amain, strike! *N'amenez jamais la conversation sur la politique;* never introduce politics into conversation.

aménité, *n.f.*, amenity, pleasantness.

amentacées, *n.f. pl.*, (bot.) amentaceous plants.

amenuiser, *v.a.*, to make thin, to make smaller; to lessen.

am-er (amè-r), **-ère**, *adj.*, bitter, sad, painful, grievous; harsh, biting, galling, briny. *Principe* —; (chem.) bitter principle. *Rendre* —: to imbitter. *Cela est d'un goût* —: that tastes bitter. *Avoir la bouche* -*ère;* to have a bitter taste in the mouth. *Des plaintes* -*ères;* bitter complaints. *Une raillerie* -*ère;* cutting raillery.

amer (amè-r), *n.m.*, bitterness, gall (of some animals and fish—*d'animaux et de poissons*); —*s* (med.) bitters.

amèrement (-màn), *adv.*, bitterly, grievously.

américain, *n.m.*, **-e**, *n.f.*, American.

américain, -e, *adj.*, American.

américaine, *n.f.*, (print.) script.

amers, *n.m. pl.*, (nav.) seamarks, landmarks.

amertume, *n.f.*, bitterness, acerbity; grief; gall, venom.

améthyste, *n.f.*, amethyst.

améthystin, -e, *adj.*, amethystine.

ameublement, *n.m.*, furniture, household goods, set of furniture.

ameublir, *v.a.*, (agri.) to make lighter.

ameublissement (-màn), *n.m.*, (agri.) the making lighter.

amelonner, *v.a.*, to stack hay, corn, &c.

ameuter, *v.a.*, to train dogs to hunt together; to stir up.

s'ameuter, *v.r.*, to gather in a mob to riot; to mutiny.

ami, *n.m.*, **-e**, *n.f.*, friend. *Bon* —, *véritable* —; good, true, friend. — *de table;* table companion. *Bonne* — *e;* sweetheart. *C'est un de mes vieux* —*s;* he is an old crony of mine. *Traiter quelqu'un en* —; to use one like a friend. *Être* — *de;* to be the companion of, to be friendly to. *Les bons comptes font les bons* —*s;* short reckonings make long friends. *M'*—*e* (for *mon amie*)! my dear, my duck! *Mon* —! my dear!

ami, -e, *adj.*, friendly; kind; (paint.) friendly.

amiable, *adj.*, amiable, kind, friendly, courteous, amicable.

à l'amiable, *adv.*, amicably, private (of sales—*de ventes*). *Terminer un différend à l'* —; to make up a difference amicably. *Vente à l'* —; sale by private contract.

amiablement, *adv.*, amicably, in a friendly manner.

amiante, *n.m.*, amianthus, mountain-flax, earth-flax.

amical, -e, *adj.*, amicable, friendly, kind.

amicalement (-màn), *adv.*, amicably, kindly, in a friendly manner.

amict (a-mi), *n.m.*, amice.

amidon, *n.m.*, starch; fecula.

amidonner, *v.a.*, to starch.

amidonnerie (-do-n-rî), *n.f.*, starch manufactory.

amidonnier, *n.m.*, starch-maker.

⊙**amigdale**, *n.f.* *V.* **amygdale.**

amincir, *v.a.*, to make thinner, smaller; to lessen.

s'amincir, *v.r.*, to become thinner.

amincissement (-màn), *n.m.*, thinning, thinness.

amiral, *n.m.*, admiral; admiral (ship—*vaisseau*); (conch.) admiral. *Grand* —; high-admiral. *Vice* —; vice-admiral. *Contre* —; rear-admiral. *Vaisseau* —: admiral's ship.

amiralat, *n.m.*, admiralship.

amirale, *n.f.*, admiral's wife.

amirauté, *n.f.*, admiralship; admiralty.

amitié, *n.f.*, friendship, amity; affection, good-will; favour, kindness; pleasure; *pl.*, kind regards, compliments. *Avoir de l'* — *pour;* to entertain friendship for. *Être sur un pied d'* — *avec:* to be on friendly terms with. *Faites-moi l'* — *de lui en parler;* do me the kindness to mention it to him. *Par* —; out of friendship. *Prendre quelqu'un en* —; to take a liking to one. *L'*—*des couleurs;* the suitableness of colours.

Il m'a fait des —; he made very much of me.
Faites-lui mes —: remember me kindly to him.

amman, *n.m.,* amman, a judge who has cognizance of civil causes, in Switzerland.

ammi, *n.m.,* (bot.) bishop's-wort.

ammon, *n.m.,* ammonite.

ammonia-c. -que. *adj.,* ammoniac. *Sel —:* sal ammoniac. *Gomme — que;* gum ammoniac. *Gaz —;* ammoniac gas.

ammoniacal. *adj.,* ammoniacal.

ammoniaque, *n.m.f.,* ammonia.

ammonite, *n.f.,* (foss.) serpent-stone.

amnios, *n.m.* (*n.p.*), (anat.) amnion, amnios.

amnistie (am-nis-ti), *n.f.,* amnesty.

amnistié (am-nis-tié), *n.m., -e, n.f.,* person pardoned by amnesty. *Les —s rentrèrent dans leur pays;* those included in the amnesty returned to their country.

amnistier (am-nis-tié), *v.a.,* to pardon by amnesty.

amodiateur, *n.m.,* tenant of land, lessee, farmer.

amodiation, *n.f.,* leasing, letting out to farm.

amodier, *v.a.,* to farm out an estate; to rent an estate.

amoindrir, *v.a.,* to lessen, to make less.

amoindrir, *v.n.,* to lessen, to grow less, to decrease.

s'amoindrir, *v.r.,* to lessen, to grow less.

amoindrissement (-màn), *n.m.,* lessening, decrease, abating, diminution.

amollir, *v.a.,* to mollify, to soften, to mellow; to enervate, to effeminate, to unman.

s'amollir, *v.r.,* to soften, to grow tender, to grow soft; to grow effeminate or weak.

amollissant, -e, *adj.,* enervating, effeminating, softening.

amollissement (-màn), *n.m.,* softening, enervation, abatement.

. amome, *n.m.,* amomum. *— à grappes;* cardamom-tree.

amonceler, *v.a.,* to heap up, to lay in a heap, to fill up.

s'amonceler, *v.r.,* to gather; to be filled up; to accumulate. *Les nuages s'amoncellent;* the clouds are gathering.

amoncellement (-sèl-màn), *n.m.,* heaping up, accumulation.

amont, *adv.,* up the river, above. *Vent d' —;* (nav.) easterly wind. *Aller en —;* to go up. *En — du pont;* above bridge.

amorce, *n.f.,* bait; priming; tinder, train; allurement, attraction, enticement, decoy, charm. *Douce —, dangereuse —;* sweet, dangerous attraction. *Trompeuses —s;* deceitful baits. *Sans brûler une —;* without firing a shot.

amorcer, *v.a.,* to bait; to prime; to allure, to entice, to decoy, to draw in. *— un hameçon;* to bait a hook. *— une arme à feu;* to prime a gun.

amorçoir, *n.m.,* boasting tool. *V.* **ébauchoir.**

amoroso, *adv.,* (mus.) amoroso.

amorphe. *adj.,* amorphous.

amortir, *v.a.,* to deaden, allay, moderate; to weaken ; to break (a fall—*une chute*); (fin.) to sink ; to redeem (land, stock—*terre, fonds publics*); to pay off; to cool (passions); (jur.) to amortize; (paint.) to flatten; to buy up. *— un coup, le bruit;* to deaden a blow, the sound. *— une pension;* to redeem a pension. *— des dettes ;* to pay off debts. *—la fièvre;* to allay the fever. *Son chapeau amortit le coup;* his hat deadened the blow.

s'amortir, *v.r.,* to be quenched, deadened ; to slacken; to be paid off; to be bought up; to grow weak.

amortissable, *adj.,* (fin.) that can be redeemed, paid off.

amortissement (-màn), *n.m.,* redeening, buying up; liquidation; sinking; redemption; amortization: (arch.) the uppermost part of a building, top, pediment, finishing. *Caisse d'—;* sinking-fund office. *Fonds d' —:* sinking-fund (capital).

amour, *n.m.,* love, lovingness. *L'Amour;* (myth.) Cupid. *Beau comme l'Amour;* a very Adonis. *— -propre,* self-love. *Lacs d'—;* love-knot. *Faire l' — à une fille:* to make love to a girl. *Se marier par —:* to marry for love. *Mourir d'—;* to be lovesick. *Avoir de l' — pour;* to be in love with. *En —:* (of animals— *des animaux*) in heat. *Filer le parfait —:* to love long and timidly. *Pour l' — de Dieu;* for God's sake. *Je voudrais pour l' — de vous que cela fût;* I wish it were so for your sake. *C'est un vrai remède d'—;* she is a perfect fright. *La terre est en —;* the land is ripe for vegetation. *Cette montre est un véritable —:* that is a love of a watch. *Quel — d'enfant!* what a love of a child !

amours, *n.f. pl.,* one's love, flame, amours; delight. *Ses premières —;* his first love. *Les —;* (myth.) the Loves. *De folles —;* foolish love. *Les tableaux sont ses —;* pictures are his delight. *Froides mains, chaudes —;* cold hand, warm heart.

amouracher, *v.a.,* to make fall in love.

amouraché. -e, *part.,* (fam.) smitten.

s'amouracher, *v.a.,* (fam.) to become enamoured of.

amourette, *n.f.,* intrigue, ove, love-affair; amour. *— s de veau;* calf's marrow.

amoureusement (-euz-màn), *adv.,* amorously, lovingly ; tenderly, softly.

amoureu-x, -se, *adj.,* in love, enamoured, amorous; loving. *Il est — de cette femme;* he is in love with that woman. *Regards —;* looks full of love. *Devenir —;* to fall in love. *Être — des onze mille vierges;* to be a universal lover.

amoureu-x, -se, *n.f.,* lover, wooer, sweetheart, spark; (thea.) actor, actress, who performs lovers' parts.

amovibilité, *n.f.,* revocableness, liability to removal.

amovible, *adj.,* removable, revocable. *Emploi —;* revocable appointment, office held during pleasure.

amphibie, *n.m.,* amphibian ; (pers.) jack of all trades; man of two different trades.

amphibie, *adj.,* amphibious.

amphibologie, *n.f.,* amphibology.

amphibologique, *adj.,* amphibological, ambiguous.

amphibologiquement (-jik-màn), *adv.,* amphibologically, ambiguously.

amphibraque, *n.m.,* (poet.) amphibrach.

amphictyonide, *adj. Ville —;* a town having the right of sending a deputy to the Amphictyonic council.

amphictyonie, *n.f.,* right which the principal cities of Greece possessed of sending a deputy to the Amphictyonic council.

amphictyonique, *adj.,* Amphictyonic.

amphictyons (-ti-ón), *n.m. pl.,* Amphictyons.

ampligouri, *n.m.,* ludicrous poem or speech; rigmarole, unintelligible rhapsody.

amphigourique, *adj.,* ludicrous, nonsensical, burlesque.

amphigouriquement (-rik-màn), *adv.,* nonsensically, rhapsodically.

amphimacre, *n.m.,* (poet.) amphimacer.

amphisciens (-si-in), *n.m. pl.,* (geog.) amphiscii.

amphithéâtral, -e, *adj.,* amphitheatral; amphitheatrical.

amphithéâtre, *n.m.,* amphitheatre; first gallery ; dissecting-room.

amphitryon, *n.m.*, (myth.) Amphitryon; host, master of the feast.

amphore. *n.f.*, amphora.

ample. *adj.*, ample, of great compass; large, vast; spacious, roomy, wide, broad; copious, diffuse.

amplement. *adv.*, amply, fully; largely, plentifully, broadly, extensively, diffusively.

ampleur, *n.f.*, amplitude, largeness, wideness. *Il n'a pas assez d'—*; it is too scanty.

ampliati-f, **-ve**, *adj.*, (of the Pope's briets and bulls) additional.

ampliation, *n.f.*, the duplicate (of an acquittance, or any writing—*de quittance ou d'aucun autre écrit*). *Pour —*; a true copy.

⊙**amplier**, *v.a.*, (jur.) to prolong, to put off, to defer.

amplificateur. *n.m.*, (b.s.) amplifier.

amplification, *n.f.*, amplification.

amplifier, *v.a.*, to amplify, to enlarge, to enrich, to enlarge upon; to expatiate upon.

amplitude, *n.f.*, (astron., geol.) amplitude.

ampoule, *n.f.*, blister on the hands or feet; (med., bot.) ampulla. *La sainte —*; ampulla (for holy oil—*pour le Saint Chrême*). *Faire venir des —s*; to blister.

ampoulé, **-e**, *adj.*, tumid, high-flown, swelling, bombastic, turgid. *Un style —*, *des vers —; s;* high-flown style, bombastic verses.

ampouler, *v.a.*, (metal.) to blister.

ampouler, *v.n.*, to blister.

ampoulette, *n.f.*, (nav.) clock; glass.

amputation, *n.f.*, amputation. *Faire une —;* to perform an amputation.

amputé, *n.m.*, **-e**, *n.f.*, one who has had a limb amputated.

amputer, *v.a.*, to amputate, to cut off.

amulette, *n.f.*, amulet.

amure, *n.f.*, (nav.) tack of a sail. *Première — de misaine;* fore-tack. *Grande —;* main-tack.

amurer, *v.a.*, (nav.) to haul or bring aboard the tack of a sail. *Amure la grande voile!* aboard main tack!

amusable, *adj.*, capable of being amused.

amusant, **-e**, *adj.*, amusing, diverting, entertaining, amusive.

amusement (-mãn), *n.m.*, amusement, pastime, entertainment, sport, diversion; sham, trick, mere put off; fooling, trifling. *Pas tant d' —;* less trifling.

amuser, *v.a.*, to amuse, to divert; to entertain, to recreate, to solace, to beguile; to put one off with fair words and promises; to trifle with; to stop, to detain; to deceive. *Ne m'amusez pas;* don't detain me. *— le tapis;* to talk the time away, to be long in coming to the point. *— l'ennemi;* to deceive the enemy.

s'amuser, *v.r.*, to amuse one's self, to busy one's self, to disport, to sport, to tarry, to stay, to trifle, to stand trifling. *S' — de quelqu'un;* to trifle with one. *Ne vous amusez pas en chemin;* don't loiter on the way. *S' — à des bagatelles;* to mind nothing but trifles. *S' — à la moutarde;* to stand trifling.

amusette, *n.f.*, amusement, trifling, child's play.

amuseur, *n.m.*, amuser.

amusoire, *n.f.*, something amusing.

amygdale. *n.f.*, (anat.) almond, tonsil.

amygdaloïde. *n.f.*, amygdaloid.

amylacé, **-e**, *adj.*, amylaceous.

an. *n.m.*, year, twelvemonth. *Le jour de l' —;* new year's day. *L' — bissextile;* leap year. *Bon —, mal —;* one year with another. *Au bout d'un —;* twelve months after that. *L' — de notre Seigneur;* the, in the, year of our Lord. *L' — du monde;* the, in the, year of the world. *Il y a un —;* a year ago. *Nouvel —;* new year. *L' — passé;* last year. *Tous les —s;* every year, yearly. *Tous*

les deux —s; every other year. *Elle a quinze —s,* she is fifteen. *Une fois, deux fois, l' —;* once, twice, a year. *Bon jour, bon —;* a happy new year to you. *Bout de l' —, service du bout de l' —;* service celebrated in the Romish church, for the repose of a person's soul, twelve months after death.

ana, *n.m.*, (—) termination, denoting a collection of sayings, ana; (phar.) ana, āā *or* ā.

anabaptisme (-ba-tism), *n.m.*, anabaptism.

anabaptiste (-ba-tist), *n.m.*, anabaptist.

anacarde. *n.m.*, anacardium, cashew-nut.

anacardier, *n.m.*, anacardium, cashew-tree.

anachorète (-ko-), *n.m.*, anachoret, anchorite, hermit.

anachronisme (-kro-), *n.m.*, anachronism.

anacoluthe, *n.f.*, (gram.) anacoluthon.

anacréontique, *adj.*, anacreontic.

anagallis. *V.* **mouron**.

anagnoste, *n.m.*, (antiq.) a slave who, among the Romans, read during the meals.

anagogique, *adj.*, (theol.) anagogical, mystical.

anagrammatique, *adj.*, anagrammatical.

anagrammatiser, *v.a.*, to anagrammatize.

anagrammatiste, *n.m.*, anagrammatist.

anagramme, *n.f.*, anagram.

anagyris (-ris), *n.m.*, bean-trefoil.

analectes, *n.m. pl.*, (phil.) analects.

analemme, *n.m.*, (astron.) analemma.

analeptique, *adj.*, (med.) analeptic.

analeptique, *n.m.*, (med.) analeptic.

analogie, *n.f.*, analogy.

analogique, *adj.*, analogous, analogical.

analogiquement (-jik-mãn), *adv.*, analogically.

analogisme, *n.m.*, analogism.

analogue (-log), *adj.*, analogous.

analyse, *n.f.*, analysis; outline; parsing. *Faire l' — de l'eau;* to analyze water. *Faire l' — d'un passage;* (gram.) to parse a passage. *En dernière analyse*, after all is said and done; the upshot of it is.

analyser, *v.a.*, to analyze. *— une fleur;* to dissect a flower.

analyste, *n.m.*, analyzer, analyst.

analytique, *adj.*, analytical.

analytique, *n.f.*, analytics.

analytiquement (-tik-mãn), *adv.*, analytically.

anamorphose, *n.f.*, (persp.) anamorphosis.

ananas (-nâ), *n.m.*, ananas, pine-apple. *Champ d' —;* pinery.

anapeste, *n.m.*, (poet.) anapæst.

anapestique, *adj.*, anapæstic.

anaphore, *n.f.*, (rhet.) anaphora.

anaphrodisiaque, *adj.*, (pharm.) antaphrodisiac, anti-aphrodisiac.

anaphrodite, *adj.*, (med.) impotent.

anarchie, *n.f.*, anarchy.

anarchique, *adj.*, anarchical.

anarchiser, *v.a.*, to throw into anarchy.

anarchiste, *n.m.f.*, anarchist.

anarrhique, *n.m.*, wolf-fish. *— loup;* ravenous wolf-fish.

anasarque, *n.f.*, anasarca, dropsy of the skin.

anastomose. *n.f.*, (anat.) anastomosis.

s'anastomoser, *v.r.*, to anastomose.

anastrophe, *n.f.*, (gram.) anastrophe.

anathématiser, *v.a.*, to anathematize.

anathème, *n.m.*, anathema; reprobation. *Frapper d' —;* to anathematize. *— maranatha; anathema, maranatha.

anathème, *adj.*, anathematized.

anatife, *n.m.*, barnacle.

anatocisme. *n.m.*, anatocism (interest upon interest—*intérêt des intérêts*).

anatomie. *n.f.*, anatomy, dissection; subject (body under dissection—*cadavre en dissection*); methodical analysis (of a book—*d'un livre*). — *comparée*; comparative anatomy.

anatomique. *adj.*, anatomical.

anatomiquement (-măn), *adv.*, anatomically.

anatomiser. *v.a.*, to anatomize. — *un livre*; to dissect a book.

anatomiste. *n.m.*, anatomist.

ancêtres. *n.m. pl.*, ancestors, forefathers. *De ses —*; ancestral.

anche. *n.f.*, reed (of a hautboy or other wind instruments—*d'un hautbois et autres instruments à vent*). — *d' orgue*; reed-stop of an organ.

anché, -e. *adj.*, (her.) curved.

anchilops (-ki-), *n.m.*, (med.) anchilops.

anchois. *n.m.*, anchovy.

anchoité, -e. *adj.*, pickled like anchovies.

ancien, -ne (-si-in, si-è-n), *adj.*, ancient, old; senior; of old times, of ancient standing; former. *Une — ne coutume*; an old custom. *L' — et le Nouveau Testament*; the Old and New Testament.

ancien. *n.m.*, senior; ancient; elder; old codger. *Les ouvrages des — s*; the works of the ancients. *Les — s d'une église*; the elders. *L' —*; Old Nick.

anciennement (-è-n-măn), *adv.*, anciently, formerly; of yore, of old; in former times.

ancienneté. (-è-n-té), *n.f.*, ancientness, primitiveness; seniority, priority of reception. *De toute —*; from the earliest times.

ancile. *n.m.*, (antiq.) sacred buckler.

ancolie. *n.f.*, (bot.) columbine.

ancone. *n.m.*, (anat.) ancon.

ancrage. *n.m.*, anchor-ground; anchorage.

ancre. *n.f.*, anchor; (arch.) brace, an *s*. *L' — de flot*; the flood anchor. *L' — de jusant*; the ebb anchor. *L' — de large*; the sea anchor. *Maîtresse —*; the sheet anchor. *— de rechange*; spare anchor. *La seconde —*; the best bower anchor. *L' — d'affourche*; the small bower anchor. *L' — de touée*; the stream anchor. *— de miséricorde, de salut*; sheet anchor. *— surjalée*; foul anchor. *Chasser sur ses — s*; to drag the anchors. *Empenneler une —*; to back an anchor. *Caponner l' —*; to cat the anchor. *Traverser l' —*; to fish the anchor. *Gouverner sur son —*; to steer the ship to her anchor. *Étre à l' —*; to ride at anchor. *Fatiguer à l' —*; to ride hard. *Ne pas fatiguer à l' —*; to ride easy. *Jeter l' —*; to cast anchor. *Brider l' —*; to shoe the anchor. *Lever l' —*; to unmoor, to weigh anchor. *Mettre l' — à poste*; to stow the anchor. *Jeter sa dernière —*; (fig.) to make a last effort.

⊙**ancrer**. *v.n.*, to anchor, to come to anchor. *V.* **mouiller**.

s'ancrer. *v.r.*, to settle one's self, to get a footing in a place.

ancrure. *n.f.*, small fold made in cloth while shearing it, crease; (arch.) iron prop.

andabate. *n.m.*, (antiq.) gladiator who fought blindfolded.

andain. *n.m.*, (agr.) swath.

andanté. *adv.*, (mus.) andante.

andante. *n.m.*, (—*s*) (mus.) an air to be played or sung andante.

⊙**andelle**, *n.f.*, beech-wood.

***andouille**. *n.f.*, (of pigs—*de porcs*) chitterlings; twist (of tobacco—*de tabac*).

***andouiller**. *n.m.*, antler. *Les premiers — s*; the brow-antlers. *Sur — s*; bez-antlers.

***andouillette**. *n.f.*, forced-meat ball.

androgyne. *n.m.*, androgynus, hermaphrodite.

androgyne. *adj.*, androgynal, androgynous.

androïde, *n.m.*, android, automaton.

andromède. *n.f.*, (astron.) Andromeda.

andropogon, *n.m.*, (bot.) camel's hay.

âne. *n.m.*, ass, jackass, donkey; blockhead, ignorant fool, idiot; vice (instrument). *Fait en dos d' —*; (arch.) made with a shelving ridge. *Coq-à-l' — (—)*; cock-and-bull story. *Promenade à —*; donkey-ride. *Pont aux — s*; ass's bridge. *C'est le pont aux — s*; every fool knows that. *A laver la tête d'un —, on perd _a lessive*; there is no washing a blackamoor white. *Faute d'un point, Martin perdit son —*; a miss is as good as a mile. *Il ne sera jamais qu'un —*; he will be an ass as long as he l_ves. *Conte de peau d' —*; child's story. *On ne sa_rait faire boire un — qui n'a pas soif*; you may take a horse to water, but you cannot make him drink. *Têtu comme un —*; as stubborn as a mule. *Sérieux comme un — qu'on étrille*; as grave as a judge. *Tête d' —*; ass's head; (ich.) bull-head, miller's-thumb, cottus; (bot.) a kind of centaury.

anéantir, *v.a.*, to annihilate, to put out of existence, to destroy; to reduce to nothing, to prostrate, to thunderstrike.

s'anéantir, *v.r.*, to be annihilated or destroyed, to come to nothing; to cease to be.

anéantissement (-măn), *n.m.*, annihilation, annihilating; abjection, humiliation; prostration, depression; destruction, destroying, ruin, overthrow.

anecdote, *n.f.*, anecdote.

anecdotier (-tié), *n.m.*, relater of anecdotes.

anecdotique, *adj.*, anecdotical. *Recueil —*; collection of anecdotes.

ânée. *n.f.*, as much as an ass can carry.

anémie, *n.f.*, (med.) anæmia.

anémique, *adj.*, suffering with anæmia.

anémographie, *n.f.*, anemography.

anémomètre, *n.m.*, anemometer.

anémone, *n.f.*, anemone, wind-flower.

anémoscope, *n.m.*, anemoscope, weather-cock.

ânerie, *n.f.*, gross ignorance; stupidity; gross blunder.

ânesse, *n.f.*, she-ass. *Lait d' —*; ass's milk.

anesthésie, *n.f.*, (med.) anæsthesia.

anesthésique, *adj.*, anæsthetic.

aneth, *n.m.*, (bot.) dill.

anévrismal, -e, *adj.*, aneurismal.

anévrisme, *n.m.*, aneurism.

anfractueu-x, -se, *adj.*, anfractuous.

anfractuosité, *n.f.*, anfractuousness, anfracture.

⊙**angar**, *n.m.* *V.* **hangar**.

ange, *n.m.*, a spirit, angel; (artil.) chain-shot, cross-bar shot; angel-shot; (ich.) angel-fish, skate, squatina. — *déchu*; fallen angel. — *tutélaire*; guardian angel. *Rire aux — s*; to be in a laughing fit. *Être aux — s*; to be in a transport of joy.

angélique, *adj.*, angelical.

angélique, *n.f.*, angelica.

angéliquement (-lik-măn), *adv.*, angelically.

angelot (anj-lo), *n.m.*, angelot (a small, rich sort of cheese made in Normandy).

angélus (ân-), *n.m.*, (n.p.) (c.rel.) Angelus.

angine, *n.f.*, (med.) angina, quinsy, sore throat. — *couenneuse*; diphtheria.

angineu-x, -se, *adj.*, (med.) attended with angina.

angiographie, *n.f.*, angiography.

angiologie, *n.f.*, angiology.

angiosperme, *adj.*, (bot.) angiospermous.

angiospermie, *n.f.*, (bot.) angiosperm.

angiotomie, *n.f.*, angiotomy.

anglais, -e, *adj.*, English; British. *La langue —e*; the English tongue.

anglais, *n.m.*, English, Englishman.

anglaise, *n.f.*, English girl, woman; anglaise (dance—*danse*); upholsterer's thread *or* silk lace.

anglaiser, *v.a.*, to dock a horse's tail.

angle, *n.m.*, angle, corner, turning. —*aigu;* acute angle. —*droit;* right angle. —*rectiligne;* rectilinear angle. —*flanqué, rentrant, saillant;* flanked, re-entering, salient angle. *A — s saillants;* sharp-cornered. *A —droit;* rectangular. —*facial;* (anat.) facial angle.

anglet, *n.m.*, (arch.) indenture, channel.

angleu-x, -se, *adj.*, (bot.) imbedded in angular cavities. *Une noix—se;* a walnut difficult to pick out of its shell.

anglican, -e, *adj.*, Anglican, English. *L'Église —e;* the Church of England.

anglican, *n.m.*, -e, *n.f.*, Anglican; member of the Church of England.

anglicisme, *n.m.*, anglicism.

anglomane, *n.* and *adj.*, mad after the English and their manners.

anglomanie, *n.f.*, anglomania.

angoisse, *n.f.*, anguish, pang; great distress; affliction, tribulation. *Les —s de la mort;* the pangs of death. *Poire d'—;* choke-pear, gag. *Avaler des poires d'—;* to go through hardships.

⊙**angola**. *V.* **angora**.

angon, *n.m.*, (antiq.) javelin; (fishing. —*pêche*) shell-fish hook.

angora, *n.m.*, Angora-cat.

angora, *adj.*, of Angora.

angousse, *n.f.*, (bot.) hell-weed, dodder.

anguichure (-ghi-shur), *n.f.*, huntsman's horn-belt.

***anguillade** (-ghi-), *n.f.*, lash (with a whip, eel-skin, &c.—*de fouet, de peau d'anguille, &c.*).

***anguille** (-ghi-), *n.f.*, eel; fly the garter (boy's game—*jeu de garçons*); bilge-ways, launching-ways (square bed of timber placed under a vessel's bilge to support her while launching—*appareil de support pour lancer un vaisseau*). — *de mer;* conger. —*plat-bec;* grig. *Écorcher l'—par la queue;* to begin a thing at the wrong end. *Il y a quelque — sous roche;* there is a snake in the grass.

angulaire, *adj.*, angular, cornered. *Pierre —;* corner-stone.

angulé, -e, *adj.*, angular, angulated.

anguleu-x, -se, *adj.*, angulous; (bot.) angular.

angusticlave, *n.m.*, (antiq.) angusticlave.

anhydre, *adj.*, (chem.) anhydrous.

anicroche, *n.f.*, obstacle; impediment, slight difficulty.

âni-er, *n.m.*, -**ère**, *n.f.*, ass-driver.

anil, *n.m.*, (bot.) anil. *V.* **indigo**.

aniline, *n.f.*, aniline.

anille, *n.f. V.* **annille**.

animadversion, *n.f.*, animadversion, reproof, reprimand.

animal, *n.m.*, animal, beast; brute, ass, booby, sot, dolt. *Un ennuyeux —;* a bore. *Un vilain —;* a nasty brute.

animal, -e, *adj.*, animal; sensual, carnal (in Scripture language—*Écriture Sainte*). *Règne —;* the animal kingdom.

animalcule, *n.m.*, animalcule.

animalisation, *n.f.*, animalization.

s'animaliser, *v.r.*, to become animalized.

animalité, *n.f.*, animality.

animation, *n.f.*, animation.

animé, -e, *part.*, animated, incensed; enlivened, spirited, gay, sprightly.

animé, *n.f.*, a resin, anime.

⊙**animelles**, *n.f. pl.*, (cook.) lamb's-fry.

animer, *v.a.*, to animate, to give life; to quicken; to hearten, to stir up, to excite, to urge on, to embolden, to rouse; to provoke, to exasperate. — *la conversation;* to enliven the

conversation. — *le teint;* to heighten the complexion. — *les yeux, les regards;* to give fire to the eyes, to give animation to the looks. — *d'ardeur;* to fill with ardour. — *au combat;* to excite to combat. *D'une manière propre à —;* animatingly.

s'animer, *v.r.*, to become animated, to be encouraged, to take courage, to cheer up; to chafe, to take fire, to be angry.

animosité, *n.f.*, animosity; ill-will, spite, rancour, spleen, animus. *Il a de l'—, il est porté d'—, contre moi;* he has a spite against me.

anis, *n.m.*, anise; aniseed. — *de Verdun;* candied aniseed. — *de la Chine or étoilé;* Indian anise. *Graine d'—;* aniseed.

aniser, *v.a.*, to strew over with aniseed, to mix with aniseed.

anisette, *n.f.*, aniseed cordial.

ankylose, *n.f.*, (med.) anchylosis.

ankyloser, *v.a.*, to produce anchylosis. *S'—*, *v.r.*, to become anchylosed.

annal, -e (a-n-nal), *adj.*, (jur.) that lasts but one year.

annales (a-n-nal), *n.f. pl.*, annals.

annaliste (a-n-na-), *n.m.*, annalist.

annate, *n.f.*, annats, first-fruits of a living.

anneau, *n.m.*, ring; link (of a chain—*d'une chaine*); ringlet (of hair—*de cheveux*); (nav.) mooring-ring. *L' — de Saturne;* (astron.) Saturn's ring.

année, *n.f.*, year, twelvemonth. —*bissextile;* leap-year. *L'— qui vient, l'— prochaine;* next year. *D'— en —;* from year to year. —*lunaire, solaire;* lunar, solar year. *Une bonne —;* a plentiful year. *Ses belles —s;* the prime of life. *Cette terre vaut tant. — commune, moyenne;* that land yields so much one year with another. *Une — dans l'autre;* one year with another. —*s subséquentes;* after-life. *Plein d'—;* full of years.

annelé, -e, *adj.*, ring-streaked, having rings; in ringlets; annulated.

anneler, *v.a.*, to curl the hair (locks or ringlets—*boucles*). — *une cavale;* to ring a mare.

annelet, *n.m.*, ringlet, a small ring; (arch.) annulet.

annélides, *n.m. pl.*, (zool.) annelides.

annelure, *n.f.*, crisping of the hair.

annexe (a-n-nèks), *n.f.*, annex; appendant; schedule, rider; parochial chapel; chapel of ease.

annexer (a-n-nèk-sé), *v.a.*, to annex, to add to.

annexion (a-n-nèk-sion), *n.f.*, annexment, annexation.

annihilation (a-n-ni-), *n.f.*, annihilation.

annihiler (a-n-ni-), *v.a.*, to annihilate, to destroy.

annille, *n.f.*, (her.) anille, fer de mouline, millrind; (tech.) cramping-iron.

anniversaire, *adj.*, anniversary.

anniversaire, *n.m.*, anniversary. — *de sa naissance;* birthday.

annomination, *n.f.*, annomination.

loi **annonaire**, *adj.*, (antiq.) a Roman law to prevent the price of provisions from rising.

annonce, *n.f.*, announcement, publication, notification; advertisement; banns of matrimony. *Faiseur d'—s;* puffer. *Faire une —;* to advertise.

annoncer, *v.a.*, to announce, to tell, to declare, to inform, to proclaim, to advertise; to usher in; to publish, to give out, to preach, to set forth; to foretell, to forebode; to augur, to show, to promise. *Faites vous —;* send in your name. *Cela ne nous annonce rien de bon;* that promises us no good.

s'annoncer, *v.r.*, to present one's self.

annonceur, *n.m.*, the actor who gives out the next play.

annonciade, *n.f.*, annunciade (name of several military and religious orders—*nom de plusieurs ordres religieux et militaires*).

annonciation, *n.f.*, Annunciation; Lady-day.

annotateur, *n.m.*, annotator.

annotation. *n.f.*, annotation; inventory of goods attached or distrained.

annoter (a-n-no-), *v.a.*, to make an inventory of goods attached or distrained; to annotate.

annuaire (a-n-nu-èr), *n.m.*, annual.

annuel, *n.m.*, (c. rel.) a mass celebrated every day for a year, for a deceased person.

annuel, **-le** (a-n-nu-èl), *adj.*, annual, yearly.

annuellement (a-n-nu-èl-màn), *adv.*, annually, yearly.

annuité (a-n-nu-), *n.f.*, annuity.

annulable (a-n-nu-), *adj.*, defeasible; reversible.

annulaire (a-n-nu-), *adj.*, annulary. *Le doigt —*; the ring finger.

annulation, *n.f.*, annulling; (jur.) abatement.

annuler, *v.a.*, to annul, to make void, to repeal, to cancel, to abolish, to set aside, to quash.

anobli, **-e**, *part.*, newly raised to the peerage.

anobli, *n.m.*, newly-created nobleman.

anoblir, *v.a.*, to raise to the peerage.

anoblissement (-màn), *n.m.*, nobilitation.

anodin, **-e**, *adj.*, (med.) anodyne, paregoric. *Remèdes —s; anodynes.*

anomal, **-e**, *adj.*, anomalous.

anomalie, *n.f.*, anomaly.

anomalistique, *adj.*, (astron.) anomalistical. *Année —; anomalistical, periodical, year.*

anomie, *n.f.*, (conch.) anomia, bowl-shell, beaked-cockle.

ânon, *n.m.*, ass's foal, young ass.

ânonnement (-màn), *n.m.*, stuttering, stammering.

ânonner, *v.n.*, to falter, to stutter, to stammer.

ânonner, *v.a.*, to stammer, blunder through (a lesson, reading, &c.—*en répétant une leçon, en lisant, &c.*).

anonymat, *n.m.*, the quality of being anonymous.

anonyme, *adj.*, anonymous, nameless; joint-stock.

anonyme, *n.m.f.*, anonymous person. *Garder l'—; to keep anonymous.*

anorexie, *n.f.*, (med.) anorexy.

anormal, *adj.*, abnormal.

anse, *n.f.*, the handle (of a pot, basket, &c. —*d'un pot, d'une écuelle, d'un panier, &c.*); creek, little bay, cove. *Qui a des —s; ansated. Faire danser l'— du panier; (of a servant—d'une bonne) to pocket something on everything purchased. L'— du panier vaut beaucoup à cette cuisinière, that cook makes a good deal by her perquisites. Faire le pot à deux —s; to set one's arms a-kimbo.*

anse. *V.* **hanse**.

anséatique, *adj. V.* **hanséatique**.

anspect, *n.m.*, (nav.) handspike.

antagonisme, *n.m.*, antagonism.

antagoniste, *n.m.*, antagonist, adversary; opponent; competitor, rival; (anat.) antagonist.

antagoniste, *adj.*, antagonist. *Les muscles —s; the antagonist muscles.*

⊙**antan**, *n.m.*, last year.

antanaclase, *n.f.*, antanaclasis.

antarctique, *adj.*, antarctic.

antarès (-ès), *n.m.*, (astron.) Antares.

ante, *n.f.*, (antiq. arch.) anta, ante.

antécédemment (-da-màn), *adv.*, antecedently, previously, before.

antécédent. *n.m.*, antecedent; precedent; *pl.*, previous conduct. *Avoir de bons —s; to be known for a person of previous good character.*

antécédent, *adj.*, antecedent, preceding, foregoing, previous.

⊙**antécesseur**, *n.m.*, a professor of law in a university.

antéchrist (-kri), *n.m.*, antechrist.

antéciens (-si-in), *n.m. pl.*, antecians.

antédiluvien, **-ne** (-in, -è-n-), *adj.*, antediluvian.

antéfixe, *n.f.*, (antiq. arch.) antefixæ.

antenne (-tè-n), *n.f.*, (nav.) lateen sail-yard; (ent.) *pl.*, horns, feelers.

antépénultième, *adj.*, antepenultimate.

antépénultième, *n.f.*, antepenult.

antérieur, **-e**, *adj.*, anterior, going before,. antecedent, prior, previous; former; frontal. *La partie —e de la tête; the fore part of the head.*

antérieurement (-màn), *adv.*, previously.

antériorité, *n.f.*, anteriority.

antes, *n.f. pl.*, (arch.) antæ, pilasters.

anthelminthique, *adj.*, (med.) anthelmintic.

anthère, *n.f.*, (bot.) anther, tip.

anthologie, *n.f.*, anthology.

anthracite, *n.m.*, anthracite; coal-stone.

anthrax (-traks), *n.m.*, (med.) anthrax.

anthropographie, *n.f.*, anthropography.

anthropologie, *n.f.*, anthropology.

anthropologique, *adj.*, anthropological.

anthropomorphe, *adj.*, anthropomorphous.

anthropomorphisme, *n.m.*, anthropomorphism.

anthropomorphite, *n.m.*, anthropomorphite.

anthropophage, *adj.*, anthropophagous.

anthropophage, *n.m.f.*, anthropophagus, cannibal, man-eater.

anthropophagie, *n.f.*, anthropophagy, cannibalism.

anthyllide, *n.f.*, (bot.) kidney-vetch, Jupiter's beard.

anti (prefix from Greek, ἀντὶ), anti, against, opposite, contrary; (prefix from Latin, *ante*) before.

antiapoplectique, *adj.*, antapoplectic, anti-apoplectic.

antibiblique, *adj.*, unscriptural.

antichambre, *n.f.*, antechamber, anteroom, lobby, hall. *Propos d'—; servant's gossip. Faire —; to dance attendance.*

antichrèse (-krèz), *n.f.*, (jur.) pledge; mortgage.

antichrétien, **-ne** (-ti-in, -ti-è-n-), *adj.*, antichristian.

antichristianisme, *n.m.*, antichristianity, antichristianism.

anticipation, *n.f.*, anticipation, forestalling; encroachment, invasion. *Par —; anticipatory, beforehand.*

anticipé. **-e**, *part. adj.*, anticipated. *Joie —e; foretaste of joy. Connaissance —e; foreknowledge. Une vieillesse —e; a premature old age.*

anticiper, *v.a.*, to anticipate, to take up beforehand or before the time, to forestall. *— sur les droits de quelqu'un; to encroach upon another's rights. — sur ses revenus; to spend one's income beforehand.*

anticœur, *n.m.*, anticor (inflammation in a horse's throat—*inflammation de la gorge chez le cheval*).

antidartreu-x, **-se**, *adj.*, (med.) antiherpetic.

antidate. *n.f.*, antedate, antedating.

antidater *v.a.*, to antedate.

antidotaire, *n.m.*, antidotary, a book containing a collection of antidotes.

antidote, *n.m.*, antidote, counter-poison.

antienne (-ti-è-n), *n.f.*, anthem. *Annoncer une mauvaise —;* to announce a disagreeable piece of news. *Chanter toujours la même —;* to be always repeating the same thing.

antiépileptique, *adj.*, antiepileptic.

antiépiscopal, **-e**, *adj.*, antiepiscopal.

antiévangélique, *adj.*, antievangelical.

antifébrile, *n.m.*, antifebrile.

antigorium (-riom), *n.m.*, coarse enamel, glazing.

antilaiteu-x, **-se**, *adj.* and *n.m.*, antilactic.

antilogie, *n.f.*, antilogy.

antiloïmique, *adj.*, (med.) antiloimic.

antilope, *n.f.*, antelope, gazelle.

antimoine, *n.m.*, antimony.

antimonarchique, *adj.*, antimonarchical.

antimonial. **-e**, *adj.*, antimonial.

antimonial, *n.m.*, antimonial.

antimonié, **-e**, *adj.*, antimonial.

antinational, **-e**, *adj.*, antinational.

antinomie, *n.f.*, antinomy, contradiction.

antipape, *n.m.*, antipope.

antiparalytique, *n.m.*, antiparalytic.

antipathie, *n.f.*, antipathy, repugnance. *Avoir de l' —;* to have an antipathy.

antipathique, *adj.*, antipathetical, repugnant. *Cette chose m'est profondément —;* I have a great antipathy for that thing.

antipéristaltique, *adj.*, antiperistaltic.

antipéristase, *n.f.*, antiperistasis.

antipestilentiel. **-le**, *adj.*, antipestilential.

antiphilosophique, *adj.*, antiphilosophical.

antiphlogistique, *adj.*, antiphlogistic.

antiphone, *n.m.*, antiphon.

antiphonier or **antiphonaire**, *n.m.*, antiphonary.

antiphrase, *n.f.*, antiphrasis.

⊙**antipodal**, **-e**, *adj.*, antipodal, antipodean.

antipode, *n.m.*, antipode.

antipsorique, *adj.*, antipsoric.

antipsorique, *n.m.*, antipsoric.

antiptose. *n.f.*, (gram.) antiptosis.

antiputride, *adj.*, antiseptic.

*****antiquaille**, *n.f.*, old piece of antiquity ; old stuff ; old rubbish ; an old coquette. *Ce n'est qu'une —;* she is but an antiquated jilt.

antiquaire, *n.m.*, antiquary.

antique, *adj.*, antique, ancient, old.

antique, *n.f.*, antique. *A l'—;* *adv.*, after the old fashion.

antiquer, *v.a.*, (book-bind.), to adorn the edges of books with little figures, &c.

antiquité, *n.f.*, antiquity, ancientness, old times ; piece of antiquity. *Les héros de l'—;* the heroes of former ages. *De toute—;* from the remotest times.

antisciens (-si-in), *n.m. pl.*, antiscii.

antisocial. **-e**, *adj.*, anti-social.

antiscorbutique, *adj.*, antiscorbutical.

antiscorbutique, *n.m.*, antiscorbutic.

antiseptique. *n.m.*, (med.) antiseptic.

antispase. *n.f.*, (med.) antispasis.

antispasmodique, *n.m.*, antispasmodic.

antispaste, *n.m.*, antispast, antispatus.

antispastique, *adj.*, antispastic.

antistrophe. *n.f.*, antistrophe.

antisyphilitique, *adj.*, antisyphilitic.

antithèse, *n.f.*, antithesis.

antithétique, *adj.*, antithetic.

antitrinitaire, *n.m.*, antitrinitarian, unitarian.

⊙**antitype**. *n.m.*, antitype, symbol.

antivénérien, **-ne**, (-in, -è-n), *adj.*, antivenereal.

antoiser, *v.a.*, to heap up dung, to make a dunghill.

antonomase, *n.f.*, antonomasia.

antre, *n.m.*, cave, den, natural grotto, cavern.

antrustions, *n.m. pl.*, (antiq.) German volunteers.

s'anuiter, *v.r.*, to be benighted, to stay till it is night.

anus. *n.m.*, (anat., bot.) anus.

anxiété (ank-si-), *n.f.*, anxiety, sorrow, anguish.

anxieu-x, **-se**; (ank-, si-), *adj.*, (med.) anxious.

aoriste (-o-rist), *n.m.*, (gram.) aorist.

aorte, *n.f.*, (anat.) norta.

aortique, *adj.*, aortal.

août (où), *n.m.*, August. *La mi-coût;* the middle of August. *Faire l'—;* to make harvest.

aoûté, **-e**, *adj.*, ripened by the heat of August.

aoûter (a-ou-té), *v.a.*, to ripen.

aoûteron (ou-tron), *n.m.*, (l. u.) reaper.

a.p., (com.) abbreviation of the words *à protester;* to be protested.

apagogie, *n.f.*, apagogy.

apaisement, *n.m.*, appeasement.

apaiser, *v.a.*, to appease, to soothe, to pacify, to calm, to quiet, to alleviate; to assuage, to allay, to quench, to mitigate. *— un enfant qui crie;* to quiet a squalling child. *— une révolte;* to quash a rebellion. *— les flots;* to calm the waves.

s'apaiser, *v.r.*, to be appeased, stilled, assuaged, &c.; to allay one's passion, to grow quiet, calm; to abate, subside. *Sa colère s'est apaisée;* his anger is allayed. *L'orage s'est apaisé;* the storm has subsided. *Le vent s'est apaisé;* the wind has abated.

apalachine, *n.f.*, (bot.) emetic holly.

apalanche, *n.f.*, (bot.) winter-berry.

apanage, *n.m.*, appanage; lot. *Les infirmités sont l' — de la nature humaine;* infirmities are the lot of human nature.

apanager, *v.a.*, to settle an appanage upon any one.

apanagiste, *adj.*, having an appanage.

apanagiste, *n.m.*, one who has an appanage.

apanthropie, *n.f.*, apanthropy.

à part. *V.* **part**.

aparté, *adv.*, aside.

aparté, *n.m.*, words spoken aside; separate group in an assembly.

apathie, *n.f.*, apathy, indolence.

apathique. *adj.*, apathetic.

apepsie, *n.f.*, (med.) bad digestion, apepsy.

apercevable, *adj.*, perceivable, perceptible.

apercevance, *n.f.*, the power of perceiving.

apercevoir, *v.a.*, to perceive, to discover, to discern, to notice; to remark, to observe.

s'apercevoir, *v.r.*, to perceive, to remark; to see, to be aware of; to find out, to discover; to take notice. *Ne pas s'—;* to overlook.

aperçu, *n.m.*, sketch, rapid view, glance; idea, hint; estimate at first sight, rough estimate.

apériti-f. **-ve**. *adj.*, aperient, opening.

apétale, *adj.*, (bot.) apetalous.

apetissement, *n.m.* **V. rapetissement**.&c.

apetisser, *v.a.*, to make smaller; *v.n.*, to diminish, to become smaller.

à peu près, *n.m.*, approximation, approach, approaching.

aphélie, *n.f.*, (astron.) aphelion.

aphérèse, *n.f.*, (gram.) apheresis.

aphone, *adj.*, suffering from aphonia, voiceless.

aphonie, *n.f.*, aphony, loss of speech.

aphorisme, *n.m.*, aphorism.
aphoristique, *adj.*, aphoristic.
aphrodisiaque, *adj.*, aphrodisiacal.
aphrodisiasme. *n.f.*, (med.) aphrodisia.
aphrodite, *n.f.*, aphrodita, sea-mouse.
aphte, *n.m.*, vesicle in the mouth; *pl* thrush. aphtæ.
aphylle, *adj.*, (bot.) aphyllous, leafless.
api, *n.m.*, small red apple, api. *Avoir un visage de pomme d'—;* (prov.) to have cheeks like biffin apples.
à pic, *adv.*, perpendicularly; (nav.) apeak. *L'ancre est —;* the anchor is apeak. *Virer —;* to heave short.
apiculture, *n.f.*, bee culture, bee-keeping.
apiquer, *v.a.*, (nav.) to top.
apitoyer. *v.a.*, to move one to pity.
s'apitoyer, *v.r.*, to pity. *Elle s'est apitoyée sur votre sort;* she pitied your fate.
aplaigner or **aplaner**, *v.a.*, to raise the nap (with teasels or burs, in manufacturing cloth—*au moyen de chardons dans la manufacture des draps*).
aplanir, *v.a.*, to smooth, to level, to make even, smooth, to unrumple; to plane; to make easy, to remove, to clear up. *— le chemin;* to level the road. *— les difficultés;* to clear up difficulties.
s'aplanir, *v.r.*, to grow easy, smooth, &c.
aplanissement (-mân), *n.m.*, smoothing, levelling, making smooth or even; smoothness, levelness, evenness.
aplatir, *v.a.*, to flatten, to make, strike flat, to flat.
s'aplatir, *v.r.*, to become flat, to be flattened.
aplatissement (-mân), *n.m.*, flattening, making flat, flatness; oblateness.
aplatisseur, *n.m.*, flatter.
aplatissoire, *n.f.*, flatter (tool).
aplomb, *n.m.*, equilibrium, perpendicularity, plumb; assurance, self-command, self-possession. *Ce mur tient bien son —;* this wall keeps plumb very well.
d'aplomb, *adv.*, perpendicularly, plumb. *Cette ligne tombe d'—;* that line falls plumb. *Être d'—;* to stand plumb.
aplysie, *n.f.*, sea-hare.
apocalypse, *n.f.*, Apocalypse, revelation; obscure thing. *C'est un vrai style d'—;* it is a perfectly obscure style. *Cheval d'—;* (prov. and pop.) sorry horse.
apocalyptique, *adj.*, apocalyptical.
apoco, *n.m.*, fool, ninny.
apocope, *n.f.*, (gram.) apocope, elision, suppression of a letter (as in *Grand'mère*).
apocrisiaire, *n.m.*, nuncio. apocrisiary.
apocryphe, *adj.*, apocryphal.
apocyn, *n.m.*, (bot.) apocynum, apocynom. *- gobe-mouches;* dog-bane.
apode, *adj.*, apodal, having no feet, footless.
apode, *n.m.*, apode.
apodictique, *adj.*, apodictical, evident.
apogée, *n.m.*, apogee.
apogée. *adj.*, at its apogee. *La lune est.—;* the moon is at her apogee.
apographe, *n.m.*, apograph, transcript, copy.
apologétique. *adj.*, by way of apology, apologetical, exculpatory.
apologétique, *n.m.*, Tertullian's treatise in defence of the early Christians; *n.f.*, apologetics, a part of theology.
apologie, *n.f.*, apology, vindication, excuse, justification. *Faire son —;* to apologize for.
apologiste, *n.m.*, apologist.
apologue (-log), *n.m.*, apologue.
aponévrose, *n.f.*, (anat.) aponeurosis.
aponévrotique, *adj.*, (anat.) aponeurotic.

apophlegmatique, *adj.*, (med.) apophlegmatic.
apophlegmatique, *n.m.*, (med.) apophlegmatic.
apophtegme,*n.m.*,apophthegm, apothegm
apophyge, *n.f.*, (arch.) apophyge, the spring of a column.
apophyse, *n.f.*, (anat.) process of a bone. apophysis.
apoplectique, *adj.*, apoplectical; apoplectic.
apoplectique. *n.m.*, apoplectic.
apoplexie, *n.f.*, apoplexy. *— foudroyante:* instantaneously fatal apoplexy. *— congestive;* serous apoplexy. *Attaque d'—:* apoplectic stroke. *Être attaqué, frappé, d'—;* to be struck with apoplexy. *Tomber en.—;* to fall down in a fit of apoplexy.
apostasie, *n.f.*, apostasy.
apostasier, *v.n.*, to apostatize.
apostat, *adj.*, apostate.
apostat, *n.m.*, apostate.
Ⓒ**apostème**. *n.m.*, aposteme. *V.* **apostume**.
aposter, *v.a.*, (b.s.) to secrete, place in ambush (witnesses, assassins—*des témoins*, &c.).
à posteriori, *adv.*, a posteriori.
Ⓒ*apostillateur*,*n.m.*,(jur.), annotator, commentator.
apostille, *n.f.*, marginal note, postscript; recommendatory note to urge or back a petition, &c.
apostiller, *v.a.*, to write notes; put a postscript to; to write a recommendation on a petition. *Il a apostillé ma pétition;* he has backed my petition with his recommendation.
apostolat, *n.m.*, apostleship.
apostolique, *adj.*, apostolic; papal; apostolical. *Nonce —;* the pope's nuncio.
apostoliquement (-mân), *adv.*, apostolically.
apostrophe, *n.f.*, apostrophe; address; reproach.
apostropher, *v.a.*, to apostrophize, to address, to fall foul (upon one—*quelqu'un*).
Ⓒ**apostume**, *n.m.*, (med.) aposteme, aposte-ma.
Ⓒ**apostumer**, *v.n.*, (med.) to apostemate.
apothéose, *n.f.*, apotheosis, deification.
apothicaire, *n.m.* (l.u.), apothecary. *Faire de son corps une boutique d'—;* to be always physicking one's self. *Un mémoire d'—;* a exorbitant bill.
apothicairerie (-kèr-rî). *n.f.* (l.u.), pharmacy; apothecary's shop; dispensary.
apotome, *n.m.*, (math.) apotome.
apôtre, *n.m.*, apostle. *Faire le bon —;* to play the saint.
apozème, *n.m.*, (med.)'apozem, decoction.
apparaître, *v.n.*, to come, to be in sight, to appear. *Un ange iui apparut en songe;* an angel appeared to him in a dream.
apparat, *n.m.*, formal preparations; ostentation, affectation, parade, show; compendious dictionary, alphabetical table, syllabus. *Un discours d'—;* a studied speech.
apparaux, *n.m.* *pl.*, (nav.) the sails. the rigging, the tackle, yards, guns, &c., of a ship.
appareil, *n.m.*, formal preparation, solemnity, magnificence; train, equipage, attendance; apparatus; (surg.) dressing (of wounds *—de blessures*); (arch.) dressing; (nav.) purchase. *— de guerre;* warlike preparations. *Mettre le premier —;* to give a wound its first dressing. *Une assise de haut —;* a layer of large stones.
appareillage, *n.m.*, (nav.) act of getting under sail.
appareillement, *n.m.*, yoking, pairing. *L'— des bœufs;* the yoking of oxen.

*appareiller, *v.a.,* to match; (arch.) to dress.

*s'appareiller, *v.r.,* to join one's self to; to pair. to mess with.

*appareiller, *v.n.,* (nav.) to weigh, to get under sail.

*appareilleur. *n.m.,* (mas.) dresser.

*appareilleuse, *n.f.,* procuress.

apparemment (-ra-män), *adv.,* apparently.

apparence. *n.f.,* appearance, outside show, seeming; likelihood, probability; sign, semblance. *En* — ; seemingly, apparently. *Pour les* —s ; for show. *Avoir une belle* — ; to look well. *Donner tout aux* —s; to go altogether by outward appearances. *Sauver les* —s; to save appearances.

apparent. -e, *adj.,* apparent, plain, obvious, manifest, evident; remarkable, chief, eminent, considerable.

apparenté, -e, *adj.,* related, descended. *Il est bien* — ; he is well descended. *Il est mal* — ; he is of mean descent.

apparenter, *v.a.,* (l.u.) to ally, to give relations by marriage.

s'apparenter, *v.r.,* to ally one's self (by marriage).

apparesser, *v.a.,* (l.u.) to make heavy and dull.

s'apparesser, *v.r.,* to grow dull, heavy, lazy.

appariement, or **apparîment,** *n.m.,* pairing, matching; coupling, mating.

apparier, *v.a.,* to pair, to sort, to match. — *des chevaux, des gants ;* to match horses, gloves.

s'apparier, *v.r.,* to couple, to pair.

appariteur, *n.m.,* apparitor, bedel (in universities—*dans les universités*); beadle.

apparition, *n.f.,* apparition, appearance, appearing. — *d'anges ;* a vision of angels.

apparoir. *v.n.,* to appear, to be evident. *Comme il appert ;* as it appears.

appartement, *n.m.,* apartments, lodgings, *Pièce d'un* — ; room, apartment.

appartenance, *n.f.,* appurtenance.

appartenant, -e, *adj.,* belonging, appertaining.

appartenir, *v.n.,* to belong, to appertain; to relate, to concern; to be incident, to be related.

s'appartenir, *v.r.,* to be master of one's own actions, to be free.

il **appartient** (-ti-in), *v. imp.,* it becomes; it is meet, fit; it is the duty, business. *Ainsi qu'il appartiendra ;* as they shall see cause. *A tous ceux qu'il appartiendra ;* to all those whom it may concern.

appas, *n.m. pl.,* charms, attractions; allurements.

appât, *n.m.,* bait; allurement, enticement.

appâter, *v.a.,* to bait, to allure; to feed; to make an infant or an invalid eat.

appaumé, *adj.,* (her.) apaume.

appauvrir, *v.a.,* to impoverish; to make poor, to beggar.

s'appauvrir, *v.r.,* to grow poor, to become impoverished.

appauvrissement (-män), *n.m.,* impoverishment.

appeau, *n.m.,* bird-call; decoy-bird.

appel, *n.m.,* appeal, appealing; calling over; levy (recruiting—*recrutement*); call (on shareholders—*aux actionnaires*); roll-call, muster; ruffle (of a drum—*du tambour*); (jur.) call. *Acte d'* — ; writ of appeal. — *nominal ;* (parliament —*parlement*) call of the House. *Officier d'* — ; muster-master. *Interjeter* — ; to lodge an appeal. *Faire l'* — ; to call over the names, the muster-roll. *Manquer à l'* — ; to be absent. *Passer l'* — ; to pass muster. *Répondre à l'* — ; to answer to one's name.

appelant, -e (-län, -t), *adj.,* appellant.

appelant, *n.m.,* **-e,** *n.f.,* decoy-bird; (jur.) appellant.

appelé. -e. *part..* called. *Beaucoup d'appelés et peu d'élus;* many are called, but few are chosen.

appeler. *v.a.,* to call, to name, to appeal; to chuck (of cocks—*des coqs*); to term; to call over; to give a call, to call to; to invoke; to send for; to invite; to summon; to call for, to call on (cause); to challenge. *Comment appelez-vous cela?* what do you call that ? — *et rappeler ;* to call over and over, again and again. — *en duel;* to call out. — *un médecin ;* to call in a physician.

appeler, *v.n.,* to appeal, to chuck (of cocks —*des coqs*); to caterwaul (of cats—*des chats*). *En* — ; (jur.) to appeal. *J'en appelle à votre honneur ;* I appeal to your honour.

s'appeler. *v.r..* to be called, to call one's self. *Comment s'appelle cet homme-là ?* what is that man's name ?

appellatif (pèl-la-), *adj.,* (gram.) appellative.

appellation (pèl-la-), *n.f.,* appealing, calling, naming, appellation.

appendice (-pin-), *n.m.,* appendix, appendage; process (natural sciences).

appendre, *v.a.,* to hang up.

appentis, *n.m.,* shed, penthouse.

il **appert,** *o.imp. V.* **apparoir.**

⊙appartement. *adv.,* openly.

appesantir, *v.a.,* to make heavy, to weigh down; to impair, to dull, to make dull.

s'appesantir, *v.r.,* to grow heavy and dull, to be weighed down, to lie heavy; to dwell, expatiate on.

appesantissement (-män), *n.m.,* heaviness, dulness.

appétence (ap-pé-), *n.f.,* appetence, appetency.

appéter, *v.a.,* to desire, to crave for.

appétibilité, *n.f.,* appetibility, desire.

appétible. *adj.,* appetible, desirable.

appétissant, -e, *adj.,* relishing, that provokes the appetite, tempting; delicious, desirable.

appétit, *n.m.,* appetite; stomach. *De bon* — ; heartily. — *de cheval;* ravenous appetite. *Bon* —*je vous souhaite ;* I wish you a good appetite. *Avoir de l'* — ; to have an appetite. *Être sans* — ; to have no appetite. *L'* — *vient en mangeant ;* eating brings on a good appetite. *Il n'est chère que d'* — ; hunger is the best sauce. *Demeurer sur son* — ; to check one's appetite, inclination. — *de femme grosse ;* whimsical appetite.

appétiti-f, -ve, *adj.,* appetitive.

appétition. *n.f.,* appetition.

⊙ s'appiétrir. *v.a.,* to become deteriorated (of merchandise—*de marchandise*).

applaudir, *v.n. a.,* to applaud, to clap, to clap the hands, to cheer; to praise, to commend, to approve. — *aux acteurs ;* to applaud the actors. *Tout le monde lui applaudit;* everybody gives him applause. *Applaudi de tout le monde ;* applauded by everybody.

s'applaudir, *v.r.,* to applaud one's self for, to glory in (a thing—*de quelque chose*); to congratulate one's self, to rejoice. *Il s'applaudit lui-même;* he admires himself.

applaudissement (-män), *n.m.,* applause, public praise; plaudits, cheering. *Donner des* —s; to applaud. *Salve d'*—s; round of applause, of cheering.

applaudisseur, *n.m.,* (b.s.) applauder.

applicable, *adj.,* applicable, apposite.

application. *n.f.,* application, employment (of a sum of money—*d'argent*); attention, diligence, sedulousness: (gold.) charging. *Avec* —; sedulously. *Sans* — *déterminée;* unappropriated.

applique, *n.f.,* (gold.) charging.

appliqué, -e, *adj.*, intent, sedulous.

appliquer, *v.a.*, to apply, to stick; to award (judgment—*jugement*); to employ (money—*argent*); to put, to set, to lay one thing to another, to bring close; to adapt, to fit; to apply to. to appropriate; to bestow on. — *des ventouses*, to cup. — *mal à propos :* to misapply.

s'appliquer, *v.r.*, to apply a thing to one's self. to take it for one's self; to apply one's self. to fall to, to set to, to take to, to labour at, to make it one's study; to stick.

appoint. *n.m.*, change, odd money; appoint. *Net* —; appoint. *Par net* —; perappoint. *Faire l'* —; to pay the difference.

Ⓔ**appointé**, *n.m.*, sub-corporal.

appointements (-män), *n.m.*, *pl.*, salary.

appointer, *v.a.*, to put, to give a salary to; to punish (in the army—*terme militaire*); to sew strips of cloth, &c., on anything that is rolled up (as a mattress, cloth—*matelas, tissus*, &c.), in order to keep it compact. *Commis appointé ;* salaried clerk

apport, *n.m.*, documents deposited; personal property; share (brought by a partner into a firm—*d'un associé*).

apporter, *v.a.*, to bring; to bring forward; to cause, to procure, to occasion; to use, to cite, to quote, to allege; to adduce, to produce. — *des difficultés;* to raise difficulties. — *de la précaution;* to use precaution. — *de bonnes raisons;* to adduce good reasons.

apposer, *v.a.*, to set, to put, to insert, to affix.

apposition. *n.f.*, setting, putting, inserting; affixing; accretion; (gram.) apposition. *Croître par* —; to grow by accretion.

appréciable. *adj.*, appreciable.

appréciat-eur, *n.m.*, **-rice**, *n.f.*, valuer, esteemer, rater.

appréciati-f, -ve, *adj.*, denoting the value.

appréciation, *n.f.*, appreciation, rating, valuation, estimation.

apprécier, *v.a.*, to value, to rate, to estimate; to appreciate, to esteem.

appréhender, *v.a.*, to apprehend, to be apprehensive of, to fear; to arrest, to take up. — *au corps;* to arrest.

appréhensible, *adj.*, apprehensible.

appréhensi-f, -ve, *adj.*, timid.

appréhension, *n.f.*, apprehension; fear, dread. *Avoir des* —*s ;* to be under apprehension.

apprendre, *v.a.*, to learn, to be informed of ; to hear of; to teach; to tell, to inform of. — *par cœur ;* to learn by heart. — *des nouvelles ;* to hear of news. *Je l'ai appris de bonne part ;* I have it from a good source. *Il m'a appris l'algèbre;* he taught me algebra. *Faire —un métier à un enfant ;* to put a child to a trade. *Je lui apprendrai qui je suis;* I will let him know who I am.

apprenti, *n.m.*, **-e**, *n.f.*, apprentice ; novice, tyro. *Obliger un* —; to bind an apprentice.

apprenti, -e, *adj.*, apprenticed, articled.

apprentissage, *n.m.*, apprenticeship. *Être en* —; to be an apprentice. *Faire son* —; to serve one's apprenticeship. *Mettre en* —; to apprentice. to article. *Brevet d'* —; apprentice's indentures. *Il a fini son* —; he is out of his time.

apprêt, *n.m.*, preparation, preparative; cooking, (manu.) dressing; painting on glass; stiffness, affectation. *Faire de grands* —*s ;* to make great preparations. *Sans* —; unstudied.

apprêtage, *n.m.*, (manu.) dressing; finishing.

apprêté, -e, *part.*, prepared, dressed; studied. *Des manières apprêtées;* affected manners.

apprêter, *v.a.*, to prepare, to get ready; to cook; (manu.) to dress; to afford matter for. — *un chapeau;* to dress a hat. — *à dîner;* to prepare dinner. — *à rire;* to afford matter for laughter.

s'apprêter. *v.r.*, to prepare one's self. to make one's self ready; to be in course of preparation.

apprêteur. *n.m.*, painter upon glass.

apprêteu-r, *n.m.*, **-se**, *n.f.* (manu.) dresser.

appris, -e, *part.*, learned, taught. *Bien* —*:* well-bred. *Mal* —, ill-bred. *Un mal* —; an ill-bred or an unmannerly fellow.

apprivoisement (-voaz-män), *n.m.*, taming.

apprivoiser, *v.a.*, to tame (animals—*animaux*); to make sociable (persons—*personnes*); (hunt.) to reclaim.

s'apprivoiser, *v.r.*, to be tamed, to grow tame (of animals—*des animaux*); to become sociable (of persons—*des personnes*).

approbat-eur, *n.m.*, **-rice**, *n.f.*, approver.

approbat-eur, -rice, *adj.*, approving, commending.

approbati-f, -ve, *adj.*, approving. *Geste* —; nod of approbation.

approbation, *n.f.*, approbation, consent; approval. *Incliner la tête en signe d'* —; to nod.

approbativement (-män), *adv.*, approvingly, with approbation.

approchant, -e, *adj.*, (fam.) something like; like; near allied, near akin.

approchant, *prep.*, (l.u. fam.) near, about. *Il a reçu dix mille francs* —; he received about ten thousand francs.

approche, *n.f.*, approach; coming; (print.) space, closing up. *Lunette d'* —; spy-glass. *Greffe en* —; graft by approach.

approcher, *v.a.*, to bring. put, or draw near; to bring, put, or draw close; to have access (to one—*auprès de quelqu'un*). *Approchez la table du feu;* draw the table near the fire.

approcher, *v.n.*, to approach, to draw nigh or near, to come near; to be something like. *Il me fit — de lui ;* he made me come near him. — *du but;* to come near the mark. *Ceci n'en approche pas;* this does not come near it.

s'approcher, *v.r.*, to approach, to draw near, to come near, to advance. *Approchez-vous du feu;* draw near the fire.

approfondir, *v.a.*, to deepen, to make deeper; to examine thoroughly; to search, dive, into. — *une question;* to sift, to dive to the bottom of, a question.

approfondissement, *n.m.*, deepening, sinking lower.

appropriation, *n.f.*, appropriation; (jur.) conversion.

approprier, *v.a.*, to appropriate, to accommodate, to adapt, to fit, to suit; to clean, to make neat. — *une chambre;* to make a room tidy. — *son langage aux circonstances;* to adapt one's language to circumstances.

s'approprier, *v.r.*, to appropriate a thing to one's self. to convert to one's own use.

approuver, *v.a.*, to approve, to approve of, to consent to; to ratify, to authorize; to pass (accounts—*comptes*).

approvisionnement (-zio-n-män), *n.m.*, victualling; supply. *Vaisseau d'* —; (nav.) victualler.

approvisionner, *v.a.*, to supply with necessaries; to victual.

s'approvisionner. *v.r.*, to supply one's self; to lay, take. in a supply.

approvisionneur. *n.m.*, victualler.

approximati-f, -ve, *adj.*, approximative.

approximation, *n.f.*, approximation. *Détermination par* —; (math.) approximation.

Méthode des —s successives; method of approaches.

approximativement (-män), *adv.,* by approximation.

⊙**approximer.** *v.a.,* to approximate.

appui, *n.m.,* prop, stay, support, leaningstock; help, protection ; buttress; sill (of windows—*de fenêtres*) ; rail (of stairs—*d'escaliers*) ; (man.) appui; (mec.) fulcrum. *A hauteur d'—;* breast-high. *Point d'—;* point of support. *A l'— de;* in support of. *Sans —;* unsupported, friendless. *Il est l'— des malheureux;* he is the support of the unfortunate. *Ce cheval a l'— bon;* that horse has a good appui.

appui-main. *n.m.,* (—*s* —) painter's maulstick.

appuyer. *v.a.,* to prop up, to stay, to support, to second ; to hold up, to sustain; to set upon; to lean upon; to ground, to found; to back, to stand by; to favour, to countenance; to protect; to enforce. to strengthen. *— une maison contre un coteau;* to build a house against a hill. *— le coude sur la table;* to lean one's elbow upon the table. *Son droit est appuyé sur de bons titres;* his claim is founded on just titles. *Il m'a promis d'— mon placet;* he has promised to back my petition. *— les chiens;* to urge on the hounds.

appuyer. *v.n.,* to bear upon, to lean; to rest; to lay a stress on; to dwell upon; to insist upon, to urge. *— sur un mot;* to lay a stress on a word. *— sur un passage;* to dwell upon a passage. *— sur la droite, la gauche;* to turn towards the right, the left. *Ce cheval appuie sur le mors;* that horse hangs down his head.

s'appuyer. *v.r.,* to lean, to lean upon ; to lie, to rest, to recline upon; to confide in, to rely upon, to depend upon, to trust to; to lay a stress on, to dwell upon. *Appuyez-vous sur moi;* lean upon me. *— sur un roseau;* (fig.) to trust to a rotten plank.

âpre. *adj.,* rough, harsh ; tart, sharp; hard, rugged, uneven ; biting, cutting, bitter; severe, crabbed, peevish ; violent; greedy, eager. *Chemin — et raboteux;* rough, rugged way. *— au gain;* greedy of gain. *— au ieu;* eager of play. *— à se venger;* eager for revenge. *— à la curée;* eager for prey (of animals—*des animaux*) ; greedy of gain (of persons—*des personnes*).

âprèle. *n.f.,* (bot.) horse-tail.

âprement, *adv.,* harshly, sharply, roughly, rigorously ; severely ; peevishly. crabbedly ; gruffly ; violently ; eagerly, greedily.

après, *prep.,* after, next to ; about ; next. *Sa maison vient — la vôtre;* his house is next to yours. *Il est toujours — moi;* he is always after me. always teasing, persecuting, me. *Être — quelque chose;* to be about something. *On est —; it is being done. On attend — votre consentement;* your consent is waited for. *Attendre — quelqu'un;* to wait for any one. *Soupirer — quelque chose;* to long for anything. *Ne pas attendre — quelqu'un;* not to need, to be able to do without any one. *— cela, il faut tirer l'échelle;* after that, nothing can be better. *— coup;* too late. *Crier — quelqu'un;* to scold anybody. *Tout le monde crie — lui;* everybody cries out against him. *Ci—;* hereafter, in the sequel. *— qui;* after which. *D'—;* after, from, according to. *Peindre d'— nature;* to paint from nature. *— tout;* after all.

après, *adv.,* afterwards, after; abou* (doing —*à faire*) ; go on; what next, what then ? *Vous arrivâtes malade; —?* you arrived ill ; and what then ?

après que. *conj.,* after, when. *— que vous aurez fait;* after you have done. *— que je l'eus vu;* when I had seen him.

après-demain, *adv.,* the day after tomorrow.

après-dînée, *n.f.,* (— —*s*) **après-dîné,** *n.m..* (— —*s*) after dinner, afternoon.

après-diner, *n.m.,* (— —*s*) after dinner, afternoon.

après-midi, *n.m.f.,* (—) afternoon.

après-soupée, *n.f.,* (— —*s*) **après-soupé,** *n.m..* (— —*s*) between supper and bed-time; the evening.

après-souper, *n.m.,* (— —*s*) between supper and bedtime, evening.

âpreté, *n.f.,* harshness, tartness, sharpness; roughness, ruggedness ; acrimony, asperity; violence, fierceness, severity; eagerness; greediness.

à priori. *V.* **priori.**

à propos, *adj., adv.; à-propos,* *n.m. V.* **propos.**

apside, *n.f.,* (astron.) apsis, (*plur.,* apsides, apses).

apte, *adj.,* apt, fit, proper, qualified.

aptère, *n.m.,* apteral.

aptère, *adj.,* apteral.

aptitude, *n.f.,* aptitude, aptness, disposition ; readiness, inclination, taste.

apurement (-män), *n.m.,* auditing one's accounts.

apurer, *v.a.,* to audit one's accounts.

apyre, *adj.,* apyrous.

apyrexie, *n.f.,* (med.) apyrexy.

aquarelle (-koua-), *n.f.,* painting in watercolours, aquarelle.

aquarium, *n.m.,* (—*s*) aquarium.

aqua-tinta (—), *or* **aquatinte** (-koua-), (—*s*) *n.f..* aquatinta, aquatint.

aquatique (-koua-), *adj.,* aquatic, watery.

aqueduc, *n.m.,* water-pipe, aqueduct, conduit. *Petit —;* culvert.

aqueu-x, -se, *adj.,* aqueous, watery, waterish.

aquilin, *adj.,* aquiline, curving, hooked, prominent.

aquilon, *n.m.,* north-wind, northerly wind.

⊙**aquilonaire,** *adj.,* northern, boreal.

aquosité (-kouo-), *n.f.,* aqueousness, wateriness.

ara, *n.m.,* (orni.) macaw.

arabe, *n.m.,* Arabian (person—*personne*) ; miser, a Shylock; Arabic (language—*langue*).

arabe, *adj.,* Arabic, Arabian.

arabesque, *adj.,* arabesque (seldom used in the singular).

arabesque, *n.f.,* arabesque (seldom used in the singular).

arabique, *adj.,* Arabian, Arabic.

arable, *adj.,* arable, tillable.

arachide, *n.f.,* earth-nut.

arachnide (-rak-), *n.m.,* arachnidan.

arachnoïde (-rak-no-id), *n.f.,* (anat.) arachnoid, arachnoid tunic.

arachnoïde, *adj.,* (anat.) arachnoid ; cobwebbed.

arack *or* **rack,** *n.m.,* a spirituous liquor; arack.

*****araignée,** *n.f.,* spider; (mining—*mines militaires*) araignee, arraign ; (nav.) crow-foot. *Toile d'—;* cobweb, spider-work. *— de mer;* weaver. *Pattes d'—;* spider's legs, scrawling hand (writing—*écriture*). *Ôter les —s;* to sweep the cobwebs away. *J'en ai horreur comme d'une —;* (fam.) I hate it as I do sin.

araméen, -ne. *adj.,* aramean.

aramer, *v.a.,* to stretch cloth upon tenters, to tenter.

aranéeu-x, -se. *adj.,* cobwebbed.

arase, *n.f., Pierres d'—,* levelling course (mas.).

arasement (-män), *n.m.,* levelling, making even.

araser, *v.a.,* to level (a wall, a building &c.—*un mur, un bâtiment, &c.*); to make even.

arases, *n.f., pl.*, levelling course (mas.).

aratoire, *adj.*, aratory. *Instruments —s; Implements* of husbandry.

arbalète, *n.f.*, arbalist, cross-bow. — *à jalet;* a stone-bow.

⊙**arbaléter**, *v.a.*, (arch.) to stay, to bear or shore up with pieces of timber.

arbalétrier, *n.m.*, cross-bowman, archer. —*s*; principal rafters (carp.); (orni.) swift (*cypselus apus*).

arbitrage, *n.m.*, arbitrage, arbitration, arbitrament, umpirage.

arbitraire, *adj.*, arbitrary, optional.

arbitrairement (-mān), *adv.*, arbitrarily.

arbitral, -e, *adj.*, by arbitration.

arbitralement (-mān), *adv.*, by arbitration.

arbitrateur, *n.m.*, arbitrator, arbiter.

arbitration, *n.f.*, decision, award.

arbitre, *n.m.*, will; arbiter, arbitrator, umpire, referee; master, sovereign disposer. *Libre —;* free will.

arbitrer, *v.a.*, to arbitrate, to decree, to regulate, to award.

arboré, -e, *adj.*, (bot.) arboreous.

arborer, *v.a.*, to put up, to hoist; to set up for, to proclaim. — *un pavillon;* to hoist a flag.

arborescence, *n.f.*, arborescence.

arboriculteur, *n.m.*, arboriculturist.

arboriculture, *n.f.*, arboriculture.

arborisation, *n.f.*, arborization.

arborisé, -e, *adj.*, arborised. *Pierres —es;* arborized stones.

arbouse, *n.f.*, arbute-berry, wilding.

arbousier, *n.m.*, arbute, strawberry-tree.

arbre, *n.m.*, tree; beam; piece of timber; (tech.) arbor, cylinder, shaft, spindle; (nav.) mast (in the Mediterranean—*dans la Méditerranée*). *Jeune —;* sapling. —*fruitier;* fruit-tree. — *en espalier;* wall-tree. — *sur pied;* standing tree. — *en buisson;* bush. — *de haute futaie;* forest-tree. —*de plein vent;* standard. —*nain;* dwarf-tree. *Grand —;* shaft. — *de couche;* horizontal shaft. — *moteur;* main shaft. — *vertical;* upright shaft. — *de diane,* or *philosophique* (chem.); arbor dianæ. — *déshonoré;* tree lopped of its top or side branches. — *chablis;* tree blown down. *Arbre généalogique;* genealogical tree. — *à cire;* myrica. — *de mestre;* mainmast. — *de trinquet;* foremast. *Se tenir au gros de l'—;* to adhere to what is ancient. *Tel —, tel fruit;* such as the tree is, such is the fruit. *Faire l'— fourchu;* to walk on one's two hands, with one's legs in the air. *L'— ne tombe pas du premier coup;* (prov.) Rome was not built in a day.

arbrisseau, *n.m.*, tree; young tree; small tree; underwood; shrub.

arbuste, *n.m.*, shrub; bush.

arc (ark), *n.m.*, bow, long-bow; (arch.) arch; (geom.) arc, arch; (astron.) arc; (nav.) cambering. *Tirer de l'—;* to draw the bow. *Corde de l'—;* bow-string. *A portée d'—;* within bowshot. *Avoir plusieurs cordes à son —;* to have more than one string to one's bow. — *en plein cintre;* semi-circular arch. — *de-biais;* sloping arch. — *en décharge;* arch of discharge. — *doubleau* (—*s* —*x*); massive rib, chief arch of a vault. — *de triomphe;* triumphal arch. — *diurne;* (astron.) diurnal arc. *Bander, détendre, l'—,* to bend, to unbend, the bow.

arc-boutant (ar-boo-tān), *n.m.*, (—*s* —*s*) arc-boutant, abutment, arched buttress; prop, shore, supporter; stretcher; ringleader, supporter, chief man in any business; (nav.) spar, boom. —*s d'un train de carrosse;* rods that serve to keep the mainbraces of a coach in place. — *de misaine;* foresail boom. *Grand —* (nav.); mainsail boom.

arc-bouter, *v.a.*, to prop, to support, to buttress.

arcade, *n.f.*, arcade; (anat.) arch.

arcane, *n.m.*, (chem.) arcanum.

arcanson, *n.m.*, colophony, black resin, rosin.

arcasse, *n.f.*, (nav.) buttock of a ship, sternframe.

arc-doubleau, *n.m.*, (—*s* —*x*) groin (of vaults—*d'arches*).

arceau, *n.m.*, arch, small arch, vault.

arc-en-ciel (ar-kan-si-èl), *n m.*, (—*s* —) rainbow, iris.

archaïque, *adj.*, archaical.

archaïsme (-ka-ism), *n.m.*, archaism.

archal, *n.m.*, *Fil d'—;* iron wire.

archange (-kanj), *n.m.*, archangel.

arche, *n.f.*, arch; ark. *L'— sainte, l'— du Seigneur;* the ark of the Lord. *L'— de Noé;* Noah's ark. *L'— d'alliance;* the ark of the covenant. *C'est l'— du Seigneur;* it is forbidden ground. *Pont à plusieurs —s;* bridge of several arches. *Être hors de l'—;* to be excluded from the church. *Cour des Arches;* Arches-Court.

archée, *n.f.*, principle of life, archeus.

archelet, *n.m.*, drill-bow.

archéologie (-ké-), *n.f.*, archeology.

archéologique (-ké-), *adj.*, archeological.

archéologue (ar-ké-o-log), *n.m.*, archeologist.

archer, *n.m.*, archer, bowman; ⊙policeman, constable.

⊙**archerot**, *n.m.*, little archer, Cupid.

archet, *n.m.*, bow, fiddle-stick; upper part of a cradle; turner's poll or bow; drill-bow; bow-hand (mus.).

archétype (-ké-), *n.m.*, archetype.

archétype (-ké-), *adj.*, archetypal.

archevêché, *n.m.*, archbishopric; the archbishop's residence.

archevêque, *n.m.*, archbishop.

archi, prefix from Gr. ἄρχειν, arch.

archichancelier, *n.m.*, archchancellor.

archidiaconat, *n.m.*, archdeaconship; archdeaconry.

archidiaconé, *n.m.*, archdeaconry.

archidiacre, *n.m.*, archdeacon.

archiduc, *n.m.*, archduke.

archiduché, *n.m.*, archdukedom, archduchy.

archiduchesse, *n.f.*, archduchess.

archiépiscopal, -e (-ki-), *adj.*, archiepiscopal.

archiépiscopat (-ki-), *n.m.*, archiepiscopacy.

archiluth, *n.m.*, archlute.

archimandritat, *n.m.*, the living of an archmandrite; abbey.

archimandrite, *n.m.*, archmandrite.

archinoble, *adj.*, (iron.) most noble.

archipel, *n.m.*, archipelago.

archipompe, or **arche-de-pompe**, *n.f.*, (—*s* —), (nav.) well, well-pump.

archipresbytéral, *adj.*, appertaining to an archpresbyter.

archipresbytérat, *n.m.*, archpresbyter.

archiprêtre, *n.m.*, archpriest, archpresbyter.

archiprêtré, *n.m.*, archpresbytery.

architecte, *n.m.*, architect; master-builder.

architectonique, *adj.*, architectonic.

architectonique, *n.f.*, architectonics.

architectonographe, *n.m.*, architectonographer.

architectonographie, *n.f.*, architectonography.

architectural, -e, *adj.*, architectural.

architecture, *n.f.*, architecture.

architrave, *n.f.*, (arch.) architrave.

architriclin, *n.m.*, (antiq.) steward; (fam. and jest.) head-man.

archives, *n.f. pl.*, archives, records; record-office.

archiviste, *n.m.*, archivist, keeper of the records.

archivolte, *n.f.*, (arch.) archivolt.

archontat (-kon-ta), *n.m.*, archonship.

archonte (-kont), *n.m.*, archon.

archure, *n.f.*, casing, woodwork round the millstones of a flour-mill.

arcot, *n.m.*, scoria, dross of brass.

arçon, *n.m.*, saddle-bow; bow (tool—*outil*). *Perdre les* —*s*; to be thrown out of the saddle; to be at a loss. *Vider les* —*s*; to be thrown from one's horse. *Être ferme dans les* —*s*; to sit firm on horseback; to be true to one's principles. *Se remettre dans les* —*s*; to recover one's stirrups. *Pistolets d'*—; horse-pistols.

⊙**arctier** (-tié), *n.m.*, bow-maker. — *fléchier*; bow and arrow maker.

arctique, *adj.*, arctic, north.

arcturus, *n.m.*, (astron.) Arcturus.

ardélion, *n.m.*, (l. u.) a busybody.

ardemment (-da-män), *adv.*, ardently, intensely, eagerly, passionately, vehemently, spiritedly, fervently, hotly.

ardent, **-e**, *adj.*, hot, burning, fiery, glowing; scorching; ardent, vehement, violent; strenuous, spirited, mettlesome; zealous; hasty, passionate; sanguine, fervent, earnest; greedy; red (of the hair—*cheveux*); (nav.) griping. *Charbon* —; burning-coal. *Chapelle* —*e*; the room where a dead person lies in state, with lighted tapers round the corpse. *Chambre* —*e* (French history); ardent-chamber. *Verre* —; burning-glass.

ardent, *n.m.*, ignis fatuus, will-o'-the-wisp.

⊙**arder** *or* **ardre**. *V.* **brûler.**

ardeur, *n.f.*, ardour, heat, burning heat; ardency, warmth, fervency; vividness, intensity; eagerness, fieriness, spirit, spiritedness, mettle, fervour; earnestness, forwardness, strenuousness; passion. *Cheval plein d'*—; high-mettled horse. *Avec* —; spiritedly.

*****ardillon**, *n.m.*, tongue (of a buckle—*d'une boucle*).

ardoise, *n.f.*, slate. *Carrière d'*—; slate-quarry. *Crayon d'*—; slate-pencil. *Couvreur en* —; slater. *Couvrir d'*—; to slate.

ardoisé, **-e**, *adj.*, slate-coloured.

ardoiser, *v.a.*, to slate.

ardoisier, *n.m.*, owner of, workman in, a slate-quarry.

ardoisi-er, **-ère**, *adj.*, slaty.

ardoisière, *n.f.*, slate-quarry.

⊙**ardre**. *V.* **brûler.**

ardu, **-e**, *adj.*, arduous, hard, difficult.

are, *n.m.*, are, 119·6046 square yards.

arec, *n.m.*, (bot.) areca.

aréfaction, *n.f.*, arefaction.

arénacé, **-e**, *adj.*, arenaceous.

arénation, *n.f.*, arenation.

arène, *n.f.*, sand; arena; cock-pit.

aréneu-x, **-se**, *adj.*, sandy, arenous.

aréole, *n.f.*, (anat., med.) areola.

aréomètre, *n.m.*, areometer.

aréométrie, *n.f.*, areometry.

aréopage, *n.m.*, areopagus.

aréopagite, *n.m.*, areopagite.

aréostyle, *n.m.*, (arch.) aræostyle.

aréotectonique, *n.f.*, areotechtonics (military architecture).

⊙**aréotique**, *n.m.*, (med.) areotic.

aréquier, *n.m.*, (bot.) cabbage palm.

arête, *n.f.*, fish-bone; skeleton of a fish; (bot.) awn, beard, prickle; (arch.) arris; (nav.) quoin; (geom.) corner, edge; (geog.) foot; (metal.) angle or edge; ridge of a sword-blade. — *de poisson*; (arch.) herring-bone work. *À vive* —; (carp.) sharp-edged.

arêtier (-tié), *n.m.*, (arch.) hip.

arêtière, *n.f.*, layers of mortar used in slating.

argala, *n.m.*, (orni.) hurgil.

argali, *n.m.*, (mam.) argali.

arganeau, *n.m.*, (nav.) ring-bolt, anchoring.

argémone, *n.f.*, argemone, thorny Mexican poppy.

argent, *n.m.*, silver; money, coin, cash; (her.) argent; pearl. — *vierge*; virgin silver. *Lingot d'*—; silver bullion. — *en feuilles, battu;* silver-leaf. — *vif* (l.u.), vif-argent (n.p.); quicksilver. *Vaisselle d'*—; plate, silver-plate. — *blanc*; silver money. — *comptant*; ready money. — *monnayé*; coined money. — *d'Allemagne*; German silver. — *doré*; silver-gilt. — *amati*; deadened silver. — *en caisse*; cash in hand, money put by. — *dormant*; unemployed money. — *mignon*; money put by for superfluous expenses. — *rouge*; silver glance. *Un* — *fou*; no ends of money. *Bourreau d'*—; spendthrift. *Pigne d'*—; pena silver. *À pomme d'*—; silver-headed. *À tête d'*—; silver-eyed. *Au croissant d'*—; (her.) argent-horned. *D'*—; silvery; (her.) argent. *En avoir pour son* —; to have one's money's worth. *Avoir le temps et l'*—; to have all one can wish. *Être brouillé avec l'*— comptant; never to have any ready money. *Être cousu d'*—, avoir de l'*— *à gogo*; to be rolling in riches. *Être court d'*—; to be short of money. *Jeter son* — *par la fenêtre*; to throw one's money away. *Homme d'*—; mercenary man. *Lâcher de l'*—; to come down with one's money. *Payer* — *sec, bas,* — *sur table*; to pay down, in ready money. *Manger son* —; to squander one's fortune away. — *comptant porte médecine*; money is a cure for all sores. *Faire rentrer de l'*—; to call in money. *Rapporter de l'*—; to bring in money. *Toucher de l'*—; to receive money. *Trouver de l'*—; to raise money. *Y aller bon jeu, bon* —; to be in earnest, to act frankly. *J'ai toujours l'*— *à la main*; I am always laying money out. *Payer* — *comptant*; to pay ready money. *Placer de l'*—; to put money out. *Prendre quelque chose pour* — *comptant*; to take anything for gospel. *Faire* — *de tout*; to turn everything into money. *C'est de l'*— *en barre*; it is as good as ready money. — *fait tout*; money makes the mare go. *Point d'*—, point de Suisse; no penny, no paternoster.

⊙**argental**, **-e**, *adj.*, pertaining to silver.

argenté, *adj.*, plated, silvered over; silvery, silver, snowy.

argenter, *v.a.*, to silver over, to plate, to do over with silver.

argenterie (-jan-tri), *n.f.*, plate, silver-plate.

argenteur, *n.m.*, plater, silverer.

argenteu-x, **-se**, *adj.*, (pop., l.u.) moneyed.

⊙**argentier**, *n.m.*, steward; silversmith.

argentifère, *adj.*, argentiferous.

argentin, **-e**, *adj.*, silvery, argentine; silvery-toned (paint.) silvery.

argentine, *adj.*, (geog.) argentine.

argentine, *n.f.*, argentine, silver-weed; wild tansy; (ich.) argentina, silver-fish.

argenture, *n.f.*, silver-plating.

argilacé, **-e**, *adj.*, clayey, argillaceous.

argile, *n.f.*, clay, potter's clay, argil. — *à porcelaine*; China-clay.

argileu-x, **-se**, *adj.*, clayey, clayish, argillous.

argilière, *n.f.*, clay-pit.

argilifère, *adj.*, argilliferous.

argilolithe, *n.m.*, clay-stone.

argo, *n.m.*, (astr.) Argo.

2

argonaute, *n.m.*, argonaut; conch. argonauta; (moll.) nautilus.

argonautes, *n.m. pl.*, Argonauts.

argot, *n.m.*, cant, professional slang; slang; (gard.) the stub of a branch, above an eye or bud.

argoter, *v.a.*, to cut the stub of a tree above the eye.

argousin, *n.m.*, convict-keeper.

argue (arg), *n.f.*, (tech.) draw-bench, drawroom (for wire-drawing—*pour tréfiler*).

arguer, *v.a.*, (jur.) to accuse.

arguer, *v.n.*, to argue; to conclude, to infer; to urge.

argument, *n.m.*, argument, reasoning; conjecture; evidence, proof, reason; theme, subject. — *en forme*; argument in form. *Faire un* —; to propose an argument.

argumentant, *n.m.*, arguer.

argumentateur, *n.m.*, arguer, disputer.

argumentation, *n.f.*, argumentation, arguing, reasoning.

argumenter, *v.n.*, to argue.

argus, *n.m.*, (myth.) Argus; (ent., orn.) argus.

argutie (-ci), *n.f.*, quibble.

argyraspides, *n.m. pl.*, (antiq.) the name of a picked body of the army of Alexander, thus named from their having a silvered shield.

arianisme, *n.m.*, arianism.

aride, *adj.*, arid, dry, sterile. *Une terre* —; a barren ground.

aridité, *n.f.*, aridity, dryness; barrenness, unfruitfulness.

arien, -ne (-in, -èn), *adj.*, Arian.

arien, *n.m.*, **-ne**, *n.f.*, Arian.

ariette, *n.f.*, arietta.

⊙**arigot**, *n.m.*, a kind of fife. *V.* **larigot.**

****arille**, *n.f.*, (bot.) seed-coat, mace, aril.

aristarque, *n.m.*, Aristarchus; hypercritic.

aristocrate, *adj.*, aristocratic.

aristocrate, *n.m.f.*, aristocrat.

aristocratie, *n.f.*, aristocracy.

aristocratique. *adj.*, aristocratic.

aristocratiquement (-mān), *adv.*, aristocratically.

aristoloche, *n.f.*, aristolochia, birth-wort, hard-wort.

aristotélicien, -ne (-in, -è-n), *adj.*, Aristotelian.

aristotélicien, *n.m.*, Aristotelian.

aristotélisme, *n.m.*, Aristotelianism, Aristotelian philosophy.

arithméticien (-in), *n.m.*, arithmetician.

arithmétique, *n.f.*, arithmetic; accounts.

arithmétique, *adj.*, arithmetical.

arithmétiquement (-mān), *adv.*, arithmetically.

arithmomancie, *n.f.*, arithmomancy.

arizarum (-rom), *n.m.*, (bot.) friar's cowl.

arlequin, *n.m.*, harlequin, merry-andrew; (orni.) spotted red-shank.

arlequinade, *n.f.*, harlequinade.

****armadille**, *n.f.*, armadilla.

****armadille**, *n.m.*, (ent.) wood-louse.

armand, *n.m.*, arman, drench (for sick horses—*pour chevaux malades*).

armateur, *n.m.*, a merchant that fits out a ship of war or a trading vessel; owner of a privateer; shipowner; captain of a privateer.

armature, *n.f.*, (arch., tech.) iron braces.

arme, *n.f.*, arm, weapon; (bot.) weapon. (her.) —*s*; arms, coat of arms, hatchment; troops; warfare; fencing. —*s blanches*; sidearms (the sabre, sword, bayonet). —*s fausses, à enquerre*; (her.) irregular arms. —*s parlantes*; (her.) allusive heraldry. *Jaque d'*—*s*; coat of arms. *A* —*s parlantes*; (her.) exemplary. *Assaut d'*—*s*; assault of arms.

— *de trait*; missile weapon. *Faisceau d'*—*s*; pile of arms. *Pas d'*—*s*; passage of arms. *Une salle d'*—*s*; a fencing school; armoury. *Un maître d'*—*s*; a fencing-master. *Faire des* —*s, tirer des* —*s*; to fence. *Avoir les* —*s belles*; to fence gracefully. *Né pour les* —*s*; born to be a soldier. *Quitter les* —*s*; to leave the army. *Faire ses premières* —*s*; to make one's first campaign. *Un fait d'*—*s*; a warlike feat or exploit. *Héraut d'*—*s*; herald at arms. *Homme d'*—*s*; man at arms. *Place d'*—*s*; place of arms. *Port d'*—*s*; carrying arms; gun license. *En venir aux* —*s*; to begin the war. *Porter les* —*s*; to be a soldier. *Aux* —*s!* to arms! *Prendre les* —*s*; to take up arms. *Demeurer sous les* —*s*; to continue under arms. *Rendre les* —*s*; to lay down arms. *Faire passer par les* —*s*; to shoot, put to the sword. *Suspension d'*—*s*; cessation of hostilities. *Les supports des* —*s*; (her.) supporters. — *au bras!* (milit.) support arms! *Haut les* —*s!* lodge arms! *Portez* —*s!* shoulder arms! *Présentez* —*s!* present arms! *Reposez vos* —*s!* ground arms! *Par la force des* —*s*; by force of arms. *Prendre les* —*s contre*; to take up arms against. *Sans* —*s*; unarmed. *Les* —*s sont journalières*; (prov.) one must expect losses sometimes.

armé, -e, *part.*, armed, equipped; (her.) armed. — *de toutes pièces*; armed from top to toe. *A main* —*e*; by force of arms.

armée, *n.f.*, army; forces, troops; fleet (from 15 to 27 ships—*de 15 à 27 vaisseaux*); host; bevy. *La grande* —; Napoleon's army. — *de mer et de terre*; sea and land forces. *Corps d'*—; main body of troops. — *permanente*; standing army. *Fournisseur de l'*—; army-contractor. *Entrer dans l'*—; to enter the army.

armeline, *n.f.*, ermine (skin—*fourrure*).

armement, *n.m.*, armament; arming, raising of forces; warlike preparations; accoutrements.

arménien, -ne (-in, -èn), *adj.*, Armenian.

arménien, *n.m.*, **-ne**, *n.f.*, Armenian.

arménienne, *n.f.*, Armenian stone.

armer, *v.a.*, to arm, to furnish with arms; to provoke; to rouse; to excite; to cock (a gun, &c.—*un fusil, &c.*); to fortify; to heel (cocks—*des coqs*); (nav.) to equip, to fit out; (nav.) to man (a pump—*une pompe*); to strengthen, to bind; (phys.) to arm. — *une poutre de bandes de fer*; to strengthen a beam with iron bands —*un aimant*; to arm a loadstone. — *les avirons*; (nav.) to ship the oars.

s'armer, *v.r.*, to arm one's self, to take up arms, to put on one's arms; to fortify, to protect, to secure, one's self against a thing; to summon up. *S'*— *de la prière*; to fortify one's self with prayer. — *de tout son courage*; to summon up all one's courage. *S'*— *de patience*; to be patient.

armet, *n.m.*, (ant.) helmet, head-piece.

armillaire (-mil-lèr), *adj.*, (astron.) armillary. *Sphère* —; armillary sphere.

armilles, *n.f. pl.*, (arch.) annulets.

arminianisme, *n.m.*, Arminianism.

arminien, -ne (-in, -èn), *adj.*, Arminian.

armistice, *n.m.*, armistice, truce.

armoire, *n.f.*, closet; cupboard; press.

armoiries, *n.f. pl.*, (her.) coat of arms, arms, armorial bearings, hatchment. —*fausses, à enquerre*; irregular arms.

armoise, *n.f.*, artemisia. —*commune*; mugwort.

armoisin, *n.m.*, sarcenet.

armon, *n.m.*, fetchel (of a coach).

armorial, *n.m.*, book of heraldry.

armoricain, *n.m.*, armoric (language—*langue*).

armorier, *v.a.*, to set, put, paint, a coat of arms upon anything.

armorique, *n.f.*, Armorica.

armoriste, *n.m.*, armourist, herald.

armure, *n.f.*, armour; (phys.) armour; (nav.) fish (of a mast, yard—*d'un mât, d'une vergue*). — *de tête*; head-piece. — *à l'épreuve*; armour in proof. *Revêtir son* —; to buckle on one's armour. —*de la clef*; (mus.) signature.

armurier, *n.m.*, armourer, gunsmith.

arnica, *or* **arnique**, *n.f.*, (bot.) arnica.

arnicine, *n.f.*, (chem.) extract of arnica.

arnotto, *n.m.*, (bot.) arnotto. *V.* **roucou.**

aromate, *n.m.*, aromatic.

aromatique, *adj.*, aromatical, fragrant, spicy.

aromatisation, *n.f.*, aromatization.

aromatiser, *v.a.*, to aromatize.

aromatite, *n.f.*, aromatite.

arome, *n.m.*, flavour, aroma.

aronde, *n.f.*, swallow-fish. *Queue d'*—; (carp.) dove-tail. *Assembler en queue d'*—; to dove-tail.

arondelle, *n.f.*, a kind of fishing-tackle. — *de mer*; any small vessel; a brigantine, pinnace, &c.

arpailleur, *n.m.*, gold-searcher. *V.* **orpailleur.**

arpège, *n.m.*, (mus.) arpeggio.

arpéger, *v.n.*, (mus.) to perform arpeggios.

arpent, *n.m.*, a measure of from one acre to one acre and a half.

arpentage, *n.m.*, land-measuring; survey.

arpenter, *v.a.*, to survey, to measure lands; to walk at a great pace.

arpenteur, *n.m.*, land-surveyor.

arpenteuse, *n.f.*, (ent.) citigrade spider.

arqué, -e, *part.*, bent, crooked; arched; (arch.) forticate.

arquebusade, *n.f.*, arquebusade. *Eau d'*—; arquebusade-water.

arquebuse, *n.f.*, arquebuse.

arquebuser, *v.a.*, to shoot with an arquebuse.

arquebuserie (-buz-ri), *n.f.*, the business of a gunsmith.

arquebusier, *n.m.*, arquebusier, musketeer; gunsmith.

arquer, *v.a. and n.*, to bend, to curve, to arch, to make crooked.

arrachement (-rash-măn), *n.m.*, tearing up, away, pulling up or out, rooting up or out, clearing away; (arch.) toothing.

d'arrache-pied, *adv.*, without intermission, incessantly.

arracher, *v.a.*, to force from, out of, away from, off; to pull away; to drag, to draw, to lug away; to extort; to snatch from; to extract (teeth—*dents*); to wring (tears—*larmes*); to tear out, down; to wrest; to grub up. — *de mauvaises herbes*; to grub up weeds. — *un secret à quelqu'un*; to get a secret from one.

s'arracher, *v.r.*, to tear; to tear away, off; to get away; to break away. *S'arracher les cheveux*; to tear one's hair.

arracheur, *n.m.*, drawer. — *de dents*; tooth-drawer. — *de cors*; corn-cutter. *Il ment comme un — de dents*; he lies like a scoundrel.

arracheuse, *n.f.*, (hat-making—*chapellerie*) workwoman who pulls the long hair from beaver-skins.

arrachis, *n.m.*, (woods and forests—*bois et forêts*) fraudulent rooting up of young trees.

arraisonner, *v.a.*, to argue with any one. — *un vaisseau*; (nav.) to inquire whence a ship comes, or whither she is bound.

arrangé, -e, *part.*, arranged; affected.

arrangement, *n.m.*, arrangement, disposing, setting in order, laying out; cooking up; trimming (lamps—*lampes*); accommodating; order, regularity, composure; method, proper arrangement or disposition; economy;

composition; *pl.*, terms; measures. *Entrer en* —; to compound. *J'ai pris des —s avec eux pour le paiement*; I have come to terms with them about the payment.

arranger, *v.a.*, to set in order, to arrange, to do up; to rank, to range, to dispose, to class; to accommodate, to make up, to compromise, to conciliate, to compose; to suit, to agree with; to settle, to wind up; to cook up; to trim (lamps—*lampes*); to ill-treat; to blow up (any one—*quelqu'un*); to fit up (a house—*une maison*); to do up, to dress out. — *un jardin*; to do up a garden. — *quelque chose*; to contrive something. — *ses affaires*; to settle one's affairs. *Il l'a arrangé de la belle manière*; he gave it him well. *Comme vous voilà arrangé!* what a state your clothes are in! what a figure you are! *Arrangez tout cela*; set all those things in order. *Cela m'arrange*; that suits me. *Cela ne m'arrange pas*; that does not suit me.

s'arranger, *v.r.*, to put, place, one's self; to settle; to set to rights; to be placed, arranged; to arrange, to make arrangements; to set one's house in order; to compound; to be all right; to contrive; to make shift, to put up (with). *Cela s'arrangera*; that will be all right. *Il s'est très bien arrangé*; he has made his house very comfortable. *Qu'il s'arrange comme il voudra*; let him do as he likes. *Arrangez-vous*; do as best you can. *Ou vous disiez la vérité hier, ou vous la niez aujourd'hui, arrangez-vous*; either you spoke the truth yesterday, or you deny it to-day; decide; be consistent. *Je m'en arrange*; I make shift with it.

arrentement (măn), *n.m.*, (l.u.) renting; letting out.

arrenter, *v.a.*, (l.u.) to rent, to let out.

arrérager, *v.n.*, to get in arrears.

arrérages, *n.m. pl.*, arrears. *Mandat d'— de rentes*; dividend warrant. *Laisser courir ses —*; to let one's arrears run on.

arrestation, *n.f.*, arrest; custody. *Être en état d'—*; to be in custody. *Mettre quelqu'un en —*; to arrest any one. *Opérer l'— d'une bande de voleurs*; to capture a gang of thieves.

arrêt, *n.m.*, decree; decision, award, judgment; sentence; attachment (of both persons and goods—*des personnes et des choses*); arrest of one's person; stopping (of a horse—*d'un cheval*); (horl.) stop-work; (tech.) rest, stop, stay. — *de mort*; sentence of death. — *par défaut*; judgment by default. *Chien d'—*; setting-dog. *Robinet d'—*; stop-cock. *Maison d'—*; jail. *Mandat d'—*; warrant. — *s forcés, simples;* (milit.) close, open, arrest. *Aux —s* (milit.) under arrest. *Mettre aux —s* (milit.) to put under arrest. *Lever les —s;* (milit.) to release from arrest. *Prononcer un* —; to pronounce judgment, to pass sentence. *Mettre la lance en* —; to couch the lance.

arrêté, *n.m.*, agreement, resolution; order (of the police, &c.—*de police, &c.*). — *de compte;* (com.) account agreed upon.

arrêté, -e, *part.*, stopped; hired, agreed for; decreed, agreed on, resolved on; arrested; fastened. *Avoir des idées —es*; to have fixed ideas. *Il n'a pas l'esprit bien —*; he is not over intelligent. *Dessein —*; settled design.

arrête-bœuf, *n.m.*, (—) (bot.) cammoc, rest-harrow.

arrête-nef, *n.m.*, (—) (ich.) sucking-fish.

arrête-porte, *n.m.*, (—) anything to keep a door open.

arrêter, *v.a.*, to arrest, to stop, to stay; to make fast, to fasten; to delay, to detain, to keep back; to give over; to put an end to; to

suppress: to fix the attention of : to apprehend. to take into custody; to seize. to distrain: to hinder. to impede; to check. to curb: to stanch: to alleviate : to throw out of gear (machinery —machine); to hire. to engage: to secure : to resolve upon. to agree; to conclude. to decree: to settle (an account—un compte); to pin ; to scotch. — un point en cousant : to fasten a stitch. — ses yeux sur ; to fix one's eyes on. — un courrier ; to delay a courier. — un volet; to fasten a shutter. Ses créanciers l'ont fait — : his creditors have had him arrested. Qu'a-t-on arrêté dans cette assemblée? what has been resolved on in that meeting? — un marché ; to conclude a bargain. — un domestique, une chambre; to hire a servant, a room. — une place à la diligence ; to secure a place in the diligence.

arrêter, v.n., to stand still, to stop, to make a stay ; to stop to bait (horses—chevaux).

s'arrêter, v.r., to stop, to pause. to rest; to stand still, to halt; to tarry, to loiter; to stop; to remain ; to lag; to forbear ; to give over, to suspend ; to leave off; to be concluded (of bargains—marchés); to desist; to resolve upon ; to draw up (of carriages—voitures) ; to be allayed (of pain—douleurs); to be thrown out of gear (of machinery—machines); to be fastened, to be pinned down. Ma montre s'arrête; my watch stops. Il s'arrête, la mémoire lui manque; he is at a stand, his memory fails him. Il ne faut pas s'arrêter à ce qu'il dit; one must not mind what he says. Vous vous arrêtez à des bagatelles ; you stop at trifles.

arrêtiste, n.m., compiler of decrees.

⊙**arrhement**, n.m., the giving of earnest money.

arrher, v.a., to give earnest for a thing.

arrhes (âr), n.f. pl., earnest, earnest-money. Donner des — ; to give earnest.

arrière, n.m., back part; (nav.) stern. D'— ; (nav.) aft. En — ! back ! En — ; (nav.) abaft. En — ; in arrears. En — de ; behind. Surveillant de l'— ; (nav.) after-guard. Se ranger de l'— ; (nav.) to veer. Tomber de l'— ; (nav.) to fall astern.

arrière, adv., behind (of time and place—temps et lieux); (nav.) aft, abaft. Droit —; right abaft. Avoir vent — ; to go before the wind.

arrière, int., away ! avaunt !

arriéré, -e, adj., in arrears ; behindhand.

arriéré, n.m., arrears. Liquider l'— ; to pay up arrears. Il a beaucoup d'— dans sa correspondance ; he is very much behindhand in his correspondence.

arrière-ban, n.m., (— —s) arriere-ban.

arrière-bec, n.m., (— —s) (arch.) starling, breakwater.

arrière-bouche, n.f., (— —s), (anat.) swallow of the throat, pharynx.

arrière-boutique, n.f., (— —s) back shop.

⊙**arrière-change**, n.m., (— —s) interest upon interest, compound interest.

arrière-corps, n.m., (—) (arch) recess.

arrière-cour, n.f., (— —s) back yard.

arrière-dos, n.m., (—) (arch.) altar-screen, reredos.

arrière-essaim, n.m., (— —s) after-swarm.

⊙**arrière-faix**, n.m., (—) (surg.) after-birth.

arrière-fermier, n.m., (— —s) under-farmer, under-tenant.

arrière-fief, n.m., (— —s) arriere-fee or fief.

arrière-fleur, n.f., (— —s) second blossom.

arrière-garant, n.m., (— —s) (jur.) the bail of a bail.

arrière-garde, n.f., (— —s) rear-guard.

arrière-goût, n.m.. (— —s) after-taste.

arrière-main, n.m., (— —s) back stroke; hind-quarters (of a horse—du cheval).

arrière-neveu, n.m.. (— —x) great-nephew. Les —x; the latest posterity.

arrière-pensée, n.f., (— —s) mental reservation.

arrière-petit-fils, n.m., (— —s —) great-grand-son.

arrière-petite-fille, n.f., (— —s —s) great-grand-daughter.

arrière-plan, n.m., (— —s) (paint.) back-ground.

arrière-point, n.m.. (— —s) back-stitch.

arrière-pointeuse, n.f., (— —s) back-stitcher.

arriérer, v.a., to defer, to put off; to throw behindhand.

s'arriérer, v.r., to stay behind; to be in arrears (of payment—de payement).

arrière-saison, n.f.. (— —s) autumn. the latter end of autumn. L'— de la vie; old age.

arrière-train, n.m.. (— —s) after-carriage.

arrière-vassal, n.m., (— vassaux) rear-vassal.

arrière-voussure, n.f., (— —s) back-arch.

arrimage, n.m., (nav.) stowage; trim of the hold.

arrimer, v.a., (nav.) to stow away; to trim the hold.

arrimeur, n.m., man who stows the hold.

arriser, v.a., (nav.) to frap.

arrivage, n.m., (nav.) arrival.

arrivée, n.f.. arrival, coming advent; (nav.) falling off. À l'— de ; on the arrival of. Aussitôt son — ; immediately after her arrival.

arriver, v.n., to come to land; to bear down; to arrive at; to approach, to be coming ; to happen, to chance ; (nav.) to bear up, to bear down. to veer; to come to pass; to occur; to attain, to reach. — à l'âge de ; to attain the age of. Le navire arrive de ce côté; the ship is coming this way. La voiture arriva; the coach arrived. La nuit arriva; night came on. Un accident lui est arrivé; an accident has happened to him. Il arrivait à grands pas; he was approaching with rapid strides. — à bon port; to come safe home. to land. — à ses fins, à son but; to compass one's ends. Il arrive tous les jours que, &c.; it happens every day that, &c. Il lui est arrivé de dire, he happened to say. D'où il est arrivé que; whence it came to pass that. S'il arrive que vous ayez besoin de moi; if you chance to want me. Quel malheur en peut-il arriver; what mischief can it produce? Quoi qu'il en arrive; come what may. Qu'en arrivera-t-il? what will be the consequence? Cela ne m'arrivera plus ; I will never do so again. Un malheur n'arrive jamais seul. one misfortune never comes alone. Arrivez! (fam.) come on! come in ! Arrive qui plante; (prov.) happen what may.

arrobe, n.f., Spanish weight, arroba.

arroche, n.f., (bot.) orach, goose-foot; mountain spinach.

arrogamment (-ga-mân), adv., arrogantly, haughtily, insolently.

arrogance, n.f., arrogance; haughtiness; superciliousness.

arrogant, -e, adj., arrogant. haughty, supercilious.

s'arroger, v.r., to arrogate to one's self.

⊙**arroi**, n.m., array, equipage. Être en mauvais — : to be in a sad pickle.

arrondi, -e, part., rounded, made round; full. Un visage — ; a full face.

arrondir, v.a.. to make a thing round. to round; to aggrandize; (paint.) to round off; (nav.) to double (a cape—un cap). — une période; to round a period. — un cheval; (man.) to round a horse. — *une île;* (nav.) to sail round an island.

s'arrondir, *v.r.*, to round, to get round ; to increase one's estate.

arrondissement (-mån), *n.m.*, rounding, making round ; roundness ; district, circuit ; ward (of a town—*d'une ville*).

arrosage, *n.m.*, irrigation ; watering.

arrosement (a-rôz-mån), *n.m.*, watering, sprinkling, besprinkling; (cook.) basting ; paying all round (at play—*au jeu*).

arroser, *v.a.*, to water, to irrigate, to besprinkle, to wet; to bedew ; to soak; to bathe (with tears—*de larmes*); (cook.) to baste; to distribute money. — *des créanciers;* to pay one's creditors a trifle. *Arrosez ces gens-là ;* keep in with those people (by giving them trifling presents—*en leur faisant de petits présents*).

arrosoir, *n.m.*, watering-pot.

arrowroot, *n.m.* (*n.p.*) arrow-root.

arrugie, *n.f.*, (mining—*mines*) drain.

ars, *n.m. pl.* (vet.) vein of the fore leg; limb. *Saigner un cheval des quatre —;* to bleed a horse in the four legs.

arsenal, *n.m.*, arsenal. — *de marine;* dockyard.

arséniate, *n.m.*, arseniate.

arséniaté, *adj.*, combined with arseniate.

arsenic, *n.m.*, arsenic.

arsenical, *-e*, *adj.*, arsenical.

arsénieux, *adj.*, arsenious.

arsénique, *adj.*, (chem.) arsenic.

arsénite, *n.m.*, arsenite.

arsis, *n.f.*, (gram., mus.) arsis.

art, *n.m.*, art. *Les termes de l' —;* technical terms. *L' — militaire;* military art. *Les —s libéraux;* the liberal arts. *Les beaux- —s;* the fine arts. —*s manufacturiers;* arts and manufactures. — *angélique;* (hist.) angelic art. —*s d'agrément;* accomplishments. *Bachelier ès —s;* bachelor of arts. *Maître ès —s;* master of arts. *Ouvrage d' —;* work of art. *Maîtres de l' —;* the connoisseurs, the learned. *Il a l' — de réussir dans tout ce qu'il entreprend;* he has the art of succeeding in all his undertakings. *L' — perfectionne la nature;* art improves nature.

artère, *n.f.*, artery. *Piquer une —;* to open an artery.

artériel, *-le*, *adj.*, arterial. *Tunique —le;* tunic of an artery.

artériole, *n.f.*, (anat.) small artery.

artériologie, *n.f.*, arteriology.

artériotomie, *n.f.*, arteriotomy.

artérite, *n.f.*, inflammation of the arteries.

artésien, *-ne* (-in, -è-n), *adj.*, artesian. *Puits —;* artesian well.

arthralgie, *n.f.*, arthritis.

arthrite, *n.f.*, (med.) arthritis.

arthritique, *adj.*, arthritic.

arthrodie, *n.f.*, (anat.) arthrodia.

arthrose, *n.f.*, arthrosis.

artichaut, *n.m.*, artichoke. —*s;* spikes on a fence or gate.

article, *n.m.*, article, head ; paragraph ; matter, thing, subject ; point; (gram.) article; (anat.) articulation; (bot.) article. — *défini, indéfini;* (gram.) definite, indefinite article. *C'est un autre —;* that's another thing. *Ce n'est pas un — de foi;* it is not worthy of credit. *Nous reviendrons sur cet —;* we shall resume this subject. *C'est un — à part;* that is a separate article. *A l' — de la mort;* at the point of death. *Faire l' —;* to puff one's goods.

articulaire, *adj.*, (med.) articular.

articulation, *n.f.*, articulation, joint; (bot., anat.) joint, articulation; (jur.) allegation.

articulé, *-e*, *part.*, articulate; articulated, jointed, vertebrated. *D'une manière —e;* articularly.

articulément, *adv.*, articulately.

articuler, *v.a.*, to articulate, to pronounce; to enumerate; to set forth.

s'articuler, *v.r.*, to be articulated or jointed, to joint.

articuler, *v.n.*, to articulate.

artifice, *n.m.*, art ; contrivance ; slyness, cunning, craft, deceit; trick, stratagem ; shuffle. *Caisse d' —;* (nav.) powder-chest. *Un feu d' —;* fireworks. *Tirer un feu d' —;* to let off fireworks.

artificiel, *-le*, *adj.*, artificial.

artificiellement (-mån), *adv.*, artificially.

artificier, *n.m.*, fire-worker, pyrotechnist.

artificieusement (-eûz-man), *adv.*, cunningly, craftily, artfully, slily.

artificieu-x, *-se*, *adj.*, artful, cunning, crafty; shuffling, sly.

☞***artillé***, *-e*, *adj.*, (nav.) mounted with cannon.

*****artillerie**, *n.f.*, artillery, ordnance. *Une pièce d' —;* a piece of ordnance. *Grosse —;* heavy artillery. — *légère;* light artillery. — *de campagne;* field artillery. — *de siège;* battering artillery. — *à pied;* foot artillery. — *à cheval;* horse artillery. *Parc d' —;* park of artillery. *Train d' —;* train of artillery. *Comité d' —;* board of ordnance. *Directeur de l' —;* master of the ordnance.

*****artilleur**, *n.m.*, artillery-man.

artimon, *n.m.*, (nav.) mizzen. *Mât d' —;* mizzenmast. *Perroquet d' —;* mizzen top-mast.

artisan, *n.m.*, artisan, handicraftsman, operative, artificer, mechanic, craftsman ; author, contriver.

artison, *n.m.*, (ent.) wood-fretter.

artisonné, *adj.*, worm-eaten.

artiste, *n.m.f.*, artist, player, performer.

artistement, *adv.*, in an artistic manner ; skilfully.

artistique, *adj.*, artist-like ; artistic.

arum, (-rom), *n.m.*, (bot.) arum, wake-robin.

aruspice, *n.m.*, aruspex, diviner, soothsayer.

aruspicine, *n.f.*, (antiq.) aruspicy.

arvales, *n.m. pl.*, (antiq.) a college of twelve priests among the Romans.

aryen, *-ne*, *adj.*, Aryan.

aryténoïde, *adj.*, (anat.) arytænoid.

as (âss), *n.m.*, ace (at cards, dice—*aux cartes, aux dés*); as (Roman weight—*poids romain*).

asaret, *n.m.*, (bot.) asarum.

asarum (-rom), *n.m.*, asarabacca, asarum.

asbeste, *n.m.*, asbestus.

ascaride, *n.m.*, (ent.) ascaris.

ascendant, *n.m.*, ascendant ; ascendency, influence; power, predominancy, ancestor. *Avoir de l' — sur;* to have influence over. —*s et descendants;* ancestors and descendants.

ascendant, *-e*, *adj.*, ascending, ascendant.

ascension, *n.f.*, ascent; up-stroke (of machinery—*des machines*); ascension; ascending, rising ; Ascension-day, Holy Thursday. *Jour de l' —;* Holy Thursday.

ascensionnel, *-le*, *adj.*, ascensional.

ascète, *n.m.* and *f.*, ascetic, anchoret ; monk.

ascétique, *adj.*, ascetic, rigid, severe.

ascétique, *n.m.*, ascetic.

ascétisme, *n.m.*, ascetism.

asciens (-as-si-în), *n.m. pl.*, (geog.) Ascii.

ascite, *n.f.*, ascites, common dropsy.

ascitique, *adj.*, dropsical, ascitic.

asclépiade, *n.m.*, (poet.), asclepiad.

asclépiade, *adj.*, (poet.) formed of asclepiads.

asclépiade, *n.f.*, or **asclépias**, *n.m.*, (bot.) asclepias, swallow-wort.

asiarcat, *n.m.*, dignity of an asiarch.

asiarque, *n.m.*, (hist.) asiarch.

asiatique, *adj.*, Asiatic.

asile, *n.m.*, asylum, refuge, place of refuge, shelter, sanctuary; harbour, retreat. *Salle d'—*; infant school. *Servir d'—*; to shelter. *Sans —*; shelterless, homeless.

asile, *n.m.*, wasp-fly.

asine, *adj. f.* (l.u.). *Bête —*; ass; blockhead.

aspect, *n.m.*, aspect, sight; look, countenance; phase, point of view. *— du ciel*; (astrol.) decumbiture.

asperge, *n.f.*, head of asparagus. *Botte d'—s*; bundle of asparagus.

asperger, *v.a.*, to sprinkle, to besprinkle.

aspergerie, *n.f.*, asparagus-bed or ground.

aspergès (-jèss), *n.m.*, aspergillus, holy-water sprinkler; time of sprinkling the holy-water. *Je suis arrivé à l'—*; I entered the church as the priest was sprinkling the people with holy-water.

aspérité, *n.f.*, asperity, roughness; harshness; unevenness.

aspersion, *n.f.*, aspersion, sprinkling, besprinkling.

aspersoir, *n.m.*, holy-water brush.

aspérule, *n.f.*, (bot.) wood-ruff.

asphalte, *n.m.*, asphalt, asphaltum.

asphaltique *or* **asphaltite**, *adj.*, asphaltic, bituminous. *Le lac —*; the asphaltic lake, the Dead Sea.

asphodèle, *n.m.*, (bot.) asphodel, king's-spear.

asphyxiant, *adj.*, which can produce asphyxia.

asphyxie, *n.f.*, (med.) asphyxy, suffocation, suspension of animation.

asphyxié, *n.m.*, -e, *n.f.*, a person in a state of asphyxy.

asphyxier, *v.a.*, to bring about, to occasion asphyxy, to suffocate. *Le gaz les asphyxia*; the gas suffocated them.

s'asphyxier, *v.r.*, to destroy one's self by suffocation.

aspic, *n.m.*, aspic; asp; (bot.) aspic; spikenard; lavender-spike; (cook.) cold meat or fish with jelly.

aspirant, -e, *adj.*, suction, sucking (of pumps—*pompes*).

aspirant, *n.m.*, -e, *n.f.*, candidate, suitor, aspirant; midshipman. *— au doctorat*; candidate for a doctor's degree. *— de marine*; midshipman.

aspirateur, *n.m.*, (of air pumps—*de pompes à air*), exhauster.

aspiration, *n.f.*, inhaling, inspiration; (gram.) aspiration, breathing; (of pumps—*de pompes*) exhaustion, suction; aspiration, longing after, fervent desire. *Tuyau d'—*; exhausting pipe.

aspiré, -e, *adj.*, aspirate; (hydr.) exhausted.

aspirée, *n.f.*, (gram.) aspirate.

aspirer, *v.a.*, to inspire; to inhale; to draw in; to suck in; (gram.) to aspirate; (hydr.) to exhaust.

aspirer, *v.n.*, to aspire, to covet, to aim at. *— aux honneurs*; to thirst after honours.

s'aspirer, *v.r.*, to suck; to be aspirated.

aspre, *n.m.*, asper, a Turkish coin.

assa, *n.f.* (n.p.), concrete gum, asa, assa.

assa dulcis, *n.f.* (n.p.), asa-dulcis, benzoin.

assa fœtida, *n.f.*, (phar.) assafœtida.

assagir, *v.a.*, to make wise, to impart wisdom.

*****assaillant**, *n.m.*, aggressor; assailant, besieger.

assaillant, -e, *adj.*, aggressive.

*****assaillir**, *v.a.*, to assault, to assail, to attack; to surprise, to come upon.

assainir, *v.a.*, to make, to render, wholesome.

assainissement (-mĕn), *n.m.*, rendering wholesome; salubrity, wholesomeness.

assaisonnement (-zo-n-mãn), *n.m.*, condiment, seasoning.

assaisonner, *v.a.*, to season, to dress, to spice; to give a relish to; to make palatable; to set off in an agreeable manner.

assaisonneu-r, *n.m.*, -se, *n.f.*, seasoner.

assassin, *n.m.*, assassin, murderer, murderess; ruffian. *A l'—!* murder!

assassin, -e, *adj.*, killing, murdering, murderous.

assassinant, -e, *adj.*, exceedingly tiresome, boring; killing, murdering.

assassinat, *n.m.*, assassination, wilful murder, homicide; act of a ruffian, murder.

assassinateur, *n.m.*, person that causes another to assassinate; assassin, murderer.

assassiner, *v.a.*, to assassinate, to murder, to make away with; to beat in a ruffianly manner; to bore, to tease, to plague one to death.

assaut, *n.m.*, assault, storm, onset, onslaught; attack, shock; fencing-match, assault. *Donner l'—* à *une place*; to storm a place. *Emporter une ville d'—*; to carry a town by storm. *Faire — d'esprit*; to make a trial of wit. *Faire — de*; to vie with each other in.

assécher, *v.a.*, to drain (mine).

assemblage, *n.m.*, assemblage, collection, union; (print.) gathering; (nav.) tabling; (carp.) bond, scarf.

assemblé, -e, *part.*, assembled, united, joined.

assemblée, *n.f.*, assembly, meeting, company, party; convocation; congregation (of churches—*d'églises*); meeting of hunters. *Se réunir en — publique*; to meet in public assembly. *L'— se tient*; the assembly is held.

assembler, *v.a.*, to collect, to gather; to get, bring, put or lay, together; to assemble, to convoke, to call together; (print.) to gather; (carp.) to trim, to scarf.

s'assembler, *v.r.*, to assemble, to meet; to come, to get or gather, together; to congregate, to muster. *Qui se ressemble s'assemble*; birds of a feather flock together.

assembleu-r, *n.m.*, -se, *n.f.*, gatherer, collector.

assener, *v.a.*, to strike, to deal (a blow — *un coup*). *Il lui assena un coup de poing*; he struck him a violent blow with his fist.

assentiment, *n.m.*, assent.

assentir, *v.n.*, to agree to, to assent.

asseoir (-soâr), (asseyant, assis), *v.a.*, to seat; to set or put in a chair; to set, to lay, to fix; to establish, to rest, to ground; to pitch; to lay, to settle; to train (a horse—*un cheval*). *— les fondements d'une maison*; to lay the foundation of a house. *— une rente*; to settle an annuity. *— un camp*; to pitch a camp. *Faire — quelqu'un à sa table*; to admit any one to one's table.

s'asseoir, *v.r.*, to sit, to sit down; to be seated. *Asseyez-vous*; sit down.

assermenté, -e, *part.*, sworn.

assermenter, *v.a.*, to swear in. *— un fonctionnaire public*; to swear in a public functionary.

asserti-f, **-ve**, *adj.*, assertive.

assertion, *n.f.*, assertion.

asservir, *v.a.*, to enslave, to reduce to servitude; to subject; to enslave, to enthral; to bring under subjection; to master, to subdue, to conquer.

asservissant, *adj.*, enslaving, subjecting, submitting.

asservissement (-mãn), *n.m.*, subjection, enthralment, bondage, servitude, slavery.

assesseur, *n.m.*, assessor (judge—*juge*).

assez, *adv.*, enough, sufficiently; pretty, rather. *J'en ai —;* I have had enough of it. *Vous avez — fait;* you have done enough. *Cela est — bien;* that is pretty well. *Cette femme est — jolie;* this woman is rather pretty. *Cela paraît — vraisemblable;* that appears likely enough. *— et plus qu'il ne faut;* enough and more than enough. *C'est —, en voilà —;* enough, that will do. *— disputé;* enough of discussion. *— parlé;* enough of words. *C'est — loin;* it is a good step off. *On ne saurait avoir — de soin de sa santé;* one cannot take too much care of one's health. *Cela est — de mon goût;* I like it well enough. *Suis-je — malheureux!* could I be more unfortunate !

assidu, -e, *adj.*, assiduous, punctual; diligent, sedulous, attentive.

assiduité, *n.f.*, assiduity, application, diligence, sedulousness.

assidûment, *adv.*, assiduously, constantly, sedulously, diligently, punctually.

assiégé, *n.m.*, besieged. *Les —s firent une sortie;* the besieged made a sally.

assiégeant, -e, *adj.*, besieging.

assiégeant, *n.m.*, besieger.

assiéger, *v.a.*, to besiege, to lay siege to ; to surround ; to beset. *Ses créanciers l'assiègent;* his creditors beset him.

assiente, *or* **assiento**, *n.m.*, assiento (slave company—*compagnie espagnole pour l'importation des esclaves.* La compagnie de l'—; the assiento company).

assiette, *n.f.*, plate; seat, situation, sitting, posture ; tone, state of the mind ; temper, condition of one's mind ; assessment (of taxes—*des impôts);* (nav.) trim; (man.) seat; (arch.) site. *—s blanches;* clean plates. *Une — à soupe;* a soup plate. *— d'argent;* a silver plate. *L'— d'une église;* the site of a church. *L'— d'un bâtiment;* the situation of a building. *Cela n'est pas dans son —;* that is not steady. *Il n'est pas dans son —;* he is out of humour, out of his sphere, not at his ease. *Faire l'— de;* to assess. *Piquer l'—;* to sponge. *Piqueur d'—;* sponger. *L'— d'une rente;* the fund of an annuity. *— d'un vaisseau;* trim of a ship.

assiettée, *n.f.*, a plateful.

*****assignable**, *adj.*, assignable.

⊙***assignant**, *n.m. V.* **demandeur.**

*****assignat**, *n.m.*, assignat (French paper money).

*****assignation**, *n.f.*, summons, subpœna, writ; appointment, rendezvous, assignation; assignment; transfer; (com.) check. *Donner une — à quelqu'un;* to have a writ out against any one. *Signifier une — à quelqu'un;* to serve a writ upon any one. *Faire une — de;* to make an assignment of.

*****assigné**, -e, *part.*, summoned.

*****assigné**, *n.m.*, -e, *n.f.*, defendant. *V.* **défendeur.**

*****assigner**, *v.a.*, to summon, to subpœna ; to assign ; to appoint, to allow, to allot. *Obtenir permission d'— quelqu'un;* to take out a writ against any one.

assimilable, *adj.*, assimilable.

assimilation, *n.f.*, assimilation.

assimiler, *v.a.*, to assimilate, to liken, to compare. *S'— à quelqu'un;* to compare one's self to any one.

assis, -e, *part.*, seated. *Restez —;* keep your seat. *Voter par — et levé;* to give one's vote by rising or by remaining seated.

assise, *n.f.*, (arch.) a course; (geol.) layer, stratum.

assises, *n.f. pl.*, assizes, session. *Cour d'—;* court of assizes. *Tenir les —;* to hold the assizes. *Cet homme tient ses — dans la maison;* this man is the oracle of the house.

assistance, *n.f.*, assistance, help, aid ; relief, comfort ; audience, company, by-standers ; congregation (in a church —*à l'église).*

assistant, *n.m.*, -e, *n.f.*, assistant (of religious orders—*dans les ordres religieux) ;* person present; by-stander. *Il prit tous les —s à témoin;* he took as witnesses all those that were present.

assistant, -e, *adj.*, assistant, helper, adjutor.

assister, *v.n.*, to be at, to be present at, to attend, to stand by.

assister, *v.a.*, to assist, to help; to succour; to aid, to support; to attend. *— les pauvres;* to relieve the poor. *—ses amis de son crédit;* to help one's friends with one's interest. *Dieu vous assiste.* God help you !

association, *n.f.*, association, partnership, society; combination. *Contrat d'—;* deed of partnership. *— illégale;* conspiracy. *— de secours mutuels;* friendly benefit society. *Faire une — avec quelqu'un;* to enter into partnership with any one.

associé, *n.m.*, -e, *n.f.*, associate; fellow; member; companion; partner. *— bailleur de fonds,* — *commanditaire;* sleeping partner.

associer, *v.a.*, to associate, to admit or receive as a partner; to take into partnership; to divide or share something with any one.

s'associer, *v.r.*, to enter, to get into partnership with one; to associate one's self with, to join, to be joined or connected with; to make any one a party to.

assolement (-măn), *n.m.*, (agri.) varied succession of crops.

assoler, *v.a.*, (agri.) to vary the crops.

assombrir, *v.a.*, to darken, to make gloomy; *s'—*, *v.r.*, to become dark, gloomy ; to darken.

assommant, -e, *adj.*, wearisome, tiresome, boring. *Cet homme est —;* this man is a great bore.

assommer, *v.a.*, to beat to death, to knock on the head; to beat unmercifully; to overpower; to overwhelm, to bear down; to pester, to bore; to grieve, to oppress; to plague to death. *— à coups de bâton;* to beat to death with a stick. *La chaleur m'assomme;* the heat overpowers me.

s'assommer, *v.r.*, to kill one's self, to be overwhelmed, to overburden one's self. *Vous vous assommez à force de travail;* you are killing yourself by too much labour.

assommeur, *n.m.*, slaughterer, feller (of oxen—*de bestiaux).*

assommoir, *n.m.*, trap; loaded bludgeon.

assompti-f, -ve, *adj.*, assumptive.

assomption, *n.f.*, assumption; (rel.) Assumption.

assonah, *n.m.*, sonna (book of the Mahometan creed—*livre de la foi mahométane).* *V.* **sonna.**

assonance, *n.f.*, assonance.

assonant, -e, *adj.*, assonant.

assorti, -e, *part.*, stocked, furnished; matched; sorted; paired; suitable. *Il n'y a point de marchand mieux —;* no shop-keeper is better stocked. *Un mariage bien —;* a very suitable match.

assortiment, *n.m.*, set; assortment, match; sorting.

assortir, *v.a.*, to sort, to match, to pair, to stock, to furnish. *Mal —;* to mis-match. *—des couleurs;* to match colours. *— une boutique;* to stock a shop.

assortir, *v.n.*, to match, to sort with, to suit.

s'assortir, *v.r.*, to match, to agree, to suit; to be a match, to be suitable.

assortissant, -e, *adj.*, suitable, becoming.

assoté, -e, *adj.*, infatuated, extremely fond, doting on.

assoter, *v.a.*, (fam. and iron.) to befool, to

s'infatuate; to besot. *S —;* to be foolishly fond of.

assoupir, *v.a.,* to make drowsy, heavy, dull; to lull, to assuage, to allay; to deaden; to suppress, to stifle, to still, to quiet, to hush, to hush up.

s'assoupir. *v.r.,* to grow drowsy, dull, heavy, sleepy; to fall asleep; to doze; to be assuaged, to be weakened; to be appeased.

assoupissant, -e, *adj.,* drowsy, sleepy, soporiferous, soporific. *Discours —;* soporiferous speech.

assoupissement (-män), *n.m.,* drowsiness, sleepiness, heaviness; carelessness, sloth, negligence, supineness; (med.) coma.

assouplir, *v.a.,* to make supple, to render flexible; (man.) to break. *— un cheval;* to break a horse. *— une étoffe;* to make a stuff soft.

s'assouplir, *v.r.,* to become supple.

assourdir, *v.a.,* to deafen, to make deaf; to stun; to muffle (a bell, an oar—*une cloche, une rame*); (paint.) to darken.

s'assourdir, *v.r.,* to grow deaf.

assourdissant, *adj.,* deafening.

assouvir, *v.a.,* to glut, to satiate, to cloy, to surfeit, to gratify. *— ses passions;* to glut one's passions. *— sa faim;* to satiate one's hunger.

s'assouvir, *v.r.,* to be satiated, glutted, surfeited, cloyed, gratified.

assouvissement (-män), *n.m.,* glutting, cloying, satiating.

assujettir, *or* **assujétir,** *v.a.,* to subdue, to enthral, to bring under, into, subjection; to subject, to tie down; to oblige; to fix, to fasten, to wedge in. *— ses passions;* to master one's passions. *S— à quelque chose;* to tie one's self down to a thing.

s'assujettir, *v.r.,* to subject one's self.

assujettissant, -e, *adj.,* that requires a great deal of attendance.

assujettissement (-män), *n.m.,* subjection, enthralment; constraint.

assumer, *v,n.,* to take upon one's self, to assume.

assurance, *n.f.,* assurance, certainty, certitude; security, safety; pledge, assurance; trust, confidence; protestation, promise; insurance; boldness, confidence, hardihood. *— exagérée;* (com.) over insurance. *— insuffisante;* under insurance. *—maritime;* marine insurance. *—contre l'incendie;* fire insurance. *— sur risques ordinaires;* common insurance. *— sur la vie;* life insurance. *Bureau d'—;* insurance-office. *Courtier d'—;* insurance broker. *Police d'—;* policy of insurance. *Avec —;* safely. *Il est en lieu d'—;* he is in a safe place. *Donnez-moi des —s;* give me a security. *Prenez ma montre pour —;* take my watch as a security. *Il met son —en Dieu;* he puts his trust in God. *Il parle avec —;* he speaks boldly. *Prenez de l'—;* put on a little assurance. *Il n'y a pas d'— à prendre en vous;* there is no reliance to be placed in you.

assure, *n.f.,* woof, texture.

assuré, -e, *adj.,* sure, safe, secure; certain; bold, confident; impudent; trusty; insured. *Une retraite —e;* a safe retreat. *Sa perte est —e;* his ruin is infallible.

assuré, *n.m.,* **-e,** *n.f.,* person insured.

assurément, *adv.,* assuredly, surely, to be sure; doubtless; certainly, sure enough. *Oui, —;* yes, doubtless. *— non;* certainly not.

assurer, *v.a.,* to assure; (a person of a thing —*une personne de quelque chose*), to assert, to affirm, to promise; to secure, to make sure of; to guarantee; to inspire with confidence; to fix firmly; to fasten; to insure, to underwrite; (man.) to accustom to the bit. *Il a assuré son argent;* he has made sure of his money. *— la bouche d'un cheval;* to accustom a horse to bear the bit. *— une maison contre l'incendie;* to in-

sure a house in the fire office. *— pour l'aller;* (com.) to insure out. *— pour le retour;* to insure home.

s'assurer, *v.r.,* to secure, to make sure of; to ascertain; to be confident of; to satisfy one's self; to be assured, to be sure; to be persuaded, to be convinced. *— de quelqu'un;* to secure any one, to engage him. *S— d'un poste;* to take possession of a position.

assureur, *n.m.,* underwriter; insurer, assurer.

assyrien, -ne, *adj.,* Assyrian.

astéisme. *n.m.,* (rhet.) asteism, irony.

astelle, *n.f.,* (surg.) splint, bolster.

attelle.

aster, *n.m.,* (bot.) star-wort.

astérie, *n.f.,* asteria, cat's eye; star-stone; star-fish.

astérisme, *n.m.,* (astron.) asterism.

astérisque, *n.m.,* asterisk.

astéroïde, *n.m.,* asteroid.

asthénie, *n.f.,* (med.) depression of vital power, asthenia.

asthmatique (as-ma-tik), *adj.,* asthmatical.

asthme (as-m), *n.m.,* asthma.

astic, *n.m.,* glazing-stick.

asticot, *n.m.,* gentle, maggot.

asticoter, *v.a.,* to plague; to tease, to vex. *Il est toujours à m'—;* he is always plaguing me.

astracan, *n.m.,* a kind of fur coming from Astrakhan.

astragale, *n.m.,* (arch., bot.) astragal; (anat.) astragalus, talus, ankle-bone; (gilding, paint.) fillet; milk-vetch, wild liquorice.

astral, -e, *adj.,* astral, starry.

astre, *n.m.,* star, fixed star. *—s errants;* wandering stars. *Cette femme est belle comme un —;* this woman is as beautiful as an angel.

astrée, *n.f.,* (astron.) Astrea; (zool.) astrea.

astreindre (astreignant, astreint), *v.a.,* to force, to compel; to subject; to bind down, to oblige.

s'astreindre, *v.r.,* to confine one's self, to tie one's self down, to any thing.

astriction, *n.f.,* (med.) astriction.

astringence, *n.f.,* astringency.

astringent, -e, *adj.,* astringent.

astringent, *n.m.,* astringent.

astroïte, *n.f.,* astroit.

astrolabe, *n.m.,* (astron.) astrolabe, Jacob's staff.

astrolâtre, *n.m.,* star-worshipper.

astrolâtrie, *n.f.,* astrolatry.

astrolâtrique. *adj.,* star-worshipping.

astrologie, *n.f.,* astrology.

astrologique, *adj.,* astrological.

astrologue (-log), *n.m.,* astrologer.

astronome, *n.m.,* astronomer.

astronomie, *n.f.,* astronomy.

astronomique, *adj.,* astronomical, astronomic.

astronomiquement (-män), *adv.,* astronomically.

astuce, *n.f.,* craft, guile, wile, cunning.

astucieusement, *adv.,* craftily, cunningly.

astucieu-x, se, *adj.,* crafty, wily.

asyle. *V.* asile.

asymétrie, *n.f.,* asymmetry.

asymptote, *n.f.,* (geom.) asymptote.

asymptotique, *adj.,* asymptotical.

asyndète, *n.m.,* (rhet.) asyndeton.

ataraxie, *n.f.,* ataraxy.

ataxie, *n.f.,* (med.) ataxy.

ataxique, *adj.,* (med.) ataxic, irregular.

atelier, *n.m.,* workshop, manufactory; study; studio; office; shed; gang (workmen—*ouvriers*). *Chef d'—;* foreman. *Tout l'— m'a quitté;* all the workmen have left me.

atellanes, *n.f.pl.,* (hist.) atellans.

atermoiement or **atermoîment**, *n.m.*, delay of payment; composition.

atermoyer, *v.a.*, to put off; to delay a payment.

s'atermoyer, *v.r.*, to compound with one's creditors.

athée, *n.m.*, atheist.

athée, *adj.*, atheistical, atheistic.

athéisme, *n.m.*, atheism.

athénée, *n.m.*, athenæum.

athénien, **-ne**, (-ni-in, -ni-è-n), *adj.*, Athenian.

athénien, *n.m.*, **-ne**, *n.f.*, Athenian.

athérome, *n.m.*, (med.) atheroma.

athlète, *n.m.*, athlete; champion. *Un vrai —;* a strong, lusty fellow.

athlétique, *n.f.*, wrestling.

athlétique, *adj.*, athletic, athletical.

☉**atinter**, *v.a.*, to adorn with affectation; *s'—*, *v.r.*, to adorn one's self with affectation.

atlante, *n.m.*, (arch.) atlantis.

atlantides, *n.f. pl.* (astron.) Atlantides.

atlantique, *adj.*, Atlantic. *L'Océan —;* the Atlantic Ocean.

atlantique, *n.f.*, Atlantic.

atlas, *n.m.*, atlas; (anat.) atlas.

atmosphère, *n.f.*, atmosphere.

atmosphérique, *adj.*, atmospherical, atmospheric.

atome, *n.m.*, atom; corpuscle.

atomique, *adj.*, atomical, atomic.

atomisme, *n.m.*, atomism, atomicism.

atomiste, *n.m.*, atomist.

atomistique, *adj.*, atomical. *Théorie —;* atomic theory.

atonie, *n.f.*, (med.) atony, debility.

atonique, *adj.*, (med.) atonic, debilitated.

atour, *n.m.*, woman's attire, ornament, dress. *Dame d'—;* lady of the bedchamber. *Être dans ses plus beaux —;* to be dressed in all one's finery. [Generally used in the plural.]

☉**atourner**, *v.a.*, to attire, to trick out, to dress out, to bedizen.

atout. *n m.*, a trump; trump-card. *Jouer —;* to play trumps.

atrabilaire, *adj.*, atrabilarious; bilious; full of, troubled with, melancholy. *C'est un homme —;* he is a melancholy man.

atrabilaire, *n.m.*, splenetic.

atrabile, *n f.*, (med) black bile, hypochondria.

âtre, *n.m.*, fire-place, hearth, floor (of ovens —*de fours*).

atroce, *adj.*, atrocious, grievous, cruel, flagitious.

atrocement (-mān), *adv.*, atrociously.

atrocité, *n.f.*, atrociousness, heinousness, grievousness; atrocity.

atrophie, *n.f.*, (med.) atrophy.

atrophié, **-e**, *adj.*, wasted, withered, atrophied.

atrophier, *v.a.*, to produce atrophy; *s'—*, *v.r.*, to waste away.

attaballe, *n.m.*, attabal (Turkish music—*musique turque*).

attablé, **-e**, *part.*, seated at table.

attabler, *v.a.*, to set to table.

s'attabler. *v.r.*, to sit down to, to take one's place at, table.

attachant, **-e**, *adj.*, engaging, interesting, attractive.

attache. *n.f.*, string, cord, strap, leash (for dogs—*de chien*); band (of wood, iron, &c.—*de bois, de fer, &c.*); tie, fastening, rivet; attachment, inclination; consent; (anat.) attachment. *Mettre un chien à l'—;* to tie a dog up. *Prendre des chevaux à l'—;* to take in horses. *Vivre sans —;* to live free.

☖**attaché**, **-e**, *part.*, fastened, fixed, attached;

tied, bound; intent on, bent on. *— à son opinion;* wedded to one's own opinion.

attaché. *n.m.*, attaché (of an embassy—*d'ambassade*).

attachement (-tash-măn), *n.m.*, attachment; affection; inclination; eagerness, constant application; (arch.) *pl.*, memoranda of work done. *— à l'étude,* fondness for study.

attacher, *v.a.*, to fasten, to make fast, to attach, to fix, to stick, to tack; to connect, to join; to apply to, to affix; to suspend, to hang; to hook, to link, to chain; to engage, to bind, to endear; to interest, to make attentive, to occupy. *— avec une épingle;* to pin. *— avec une courroie;* to strap. *— avec un crochet;* to hook. *— avec de la colle de pâte;* to paste. *— avec de la colle forte;* to glue. *C'est ce qui m'attache à vous;* this binds me to you. *— du prix à quelque chose;* to set a value upon something. *— de l'importance à quelque chose;* to attach importance to something.

s'attacher, *v.r.*, to take hold, to hold to, to fasten on; to cling; to cleave, to stick, to keep close, to adhere; to be attached, to have an affection for, to interest one's self in; to apply one's self to; to gain over. *La poix s'attache aux doigts;* pitch sticks to the fingers. *Ils s'attachèrent l'un à l'autre;* they became attached to each other. *Le chien s'attache à son maître;* the dog attaches himself to his master. *S'— à son devoir;* to give one's mind to the fulfilment of one's duty.

attaquable, *adj.*, assailable; that may be attacked; of doubtful validity.

attaquant, *n.m.*; assailant, aggressor.

attaque, *n.f.*, attack, onset; assault; approach; insult, reproach, aggression; fit, touch. *Il a eu une — de goutte;* he has had a fit of the gout.

attaqué, **-e**, *part.*, attacked, assaulted, set upon; provoked, urged. *— d'une maladie;* afflicted with a disease.

attaquer, *v.a.*, to attack, to assail, to assault, or set upon one, to come upon; to sue; (man.) to spur; to impugn; to contest the validity of a document; to begin; to provoke; (nav.) to near an island, a cape, the coast. *— quelqu'un de paroles;* to fall foul upon one with words. *L'— sur sa naissance;* to reproach him with his birth. *— quelqu'un de conversation;* to begin a conversation with any one. *Bien attaqué, bien défendu;* a Roland for an Oliver. *Il attaque bien la note;* (mus.) he makes the note tell distinctly. *Il attaque bien la corde;* he makes the string tell.

s'attaquer, *v.r.*, to challenge, to defy, to set upon; to find fault with; to fall foul of one; to fall upon, to encounter one. *Il s'est attaqué à son maître;* he has encountered one who is more than his match.

☉**attarder**, *v.a.*, to delay. *V.* **retarder**.

s'attarder, *v.r.*, to be belated.

atteindre (atteignant, atteint), *v.a.*, to touch, to strike, to hit; to reach, to attain; to affect; to arrive at, to come to; to come up to, to overtake, to catch, to join; to equal. *Il n'a pas atteint le but;* he has not hit the mark *La balle l'atteignit au front;* the ball struck him in the forehead. *— son maître;* to equal one's master. *— l'âge de;* to attain the age of. *Ce danger ne saurait m'—;* this danger cannot reach me. *Nous atteindrons le village avant la nuit;* we shall reach the village before night. *— l'ennemi;* to come up with the enemy. *Il a beau courir, je l'atteindrai;* it is in vain for him to run, I shall overtake him. *Être atteint de;* to be attacked with.

atteindre, *v.n.*, to reach, to come at, to touch; to attain, to compass. *Je ne saurais y—;*

I cannot reach it. — *au but;* to hit the mark. — *à la perfection;* to attain to perfection.

atteint, -e, *part.,* hit, struck; attacked, affected, reached. — *d'un crime;* arraigned for a crime.

atteinte, *n.f.,* blow, stroke, touch; attack, fit (of disease—*de maladie*); injury, damage, harm, wrong; reach; outrage; (man.) attaint. *Les —s du froid;* the approaches of cold. *Une légère — de goutte;* a slight touch of the gout. *Sa santé n'a jamais reçu d'—;* his health has never received any injury. *Porter — à;* to injure, to impair, to commit an offence against. *Subir une —;* to receive a blow, an injury. *Je suis hors de ses —s;* I am out of his reach.

attelage (-laj), *n.m.,* team, yoke (of horses, oxen, &c.—*de chevaux, de bœufs, &c.*).

atteler (-lé), *v.a.,* to put horses to; to yoke. *Dites au cocher qu'il attelle;* tell the coachman to put the horses to.

attelle, *n.f.,* haum; (surg.) splint.

attenant, -e (-nàn, -t), *adj.,* next, contiguous, adjoining. *Il loge dans la maison —e;* he lodges next door.

☉**attenant,** *prep.,* next to, close by.

en **attendant,** *adv.,* in the meantime, in the interim, meanwhile. *Lisez — —;* read in the meantime.

en **attendant que,** *conj.,* till, until. *Jouons — —qu'il vienne;* let us play till he comes.

attendants, *n.m. pl.,* the name of a sect who maintain that there is no true church in the world.

attendre, *v.a.,* to wait for, to stay for, to tarry for; to look forward to; to expect; to look for; to await, to attend, to be reserved for. *la mort;* to await death. *Le dîner nous attend;* the dinner is waiting for us. *Nous l'attendons à dîner;* we expect him to dinner. *Je l'attends à tout moment;* I expect him every minute. *C'est où je l'attends;* there I shall have him. *Attendez-moi sous l'orme;* you may wait for me till doomsday. *Voilà le sort qui vous attend;* this is the fate reserved for you. *Attendez!* stay! hold! *Je suis las d'—;* I am tired of waiting. *Attendons encore un peu;* let us wait a little longer. *Qu'il attende;* let him wait. *Tout vient à point à qui sait —;* patience brings all things about. *Il attend que son fils revienne;* he is waiting till his son returns. *Attendez jusqu'à demain;* wait till to-morrow. *Je n'attends plus qu'après cela;* I only wait for that.

*s'***attendre,** *v.r.,* to rely upon, to count upon; to trust, to trust to; to expect, to look forward to, to anticipate; to reckon upon. *Se faire —;* to keep people waiting. *Il ne faut pas s'— à cela;* we must not rely upon that. *Je m'y attends;* I expect it. *Je ne m'attendais pas à cela;* I did not expect that. *Attendez-vous-y!* I wish you may get it!

attendri, -e, *part.,* moved, affected, touched.

attendrir, *v.a.,* to make tender, to soften; to touch; to move, to affect. *Cela attendrit la viande;* that makes meat tender. *Ses larmes m'ont attendri le cœur;* his tears have softened my heart.

*s'***attendrir,** *v.r.,* to grow tender; to be moved, to melt, to pity, to relent, to soften. *S'— sur le sort de quelqu'un;* to be moved at the fate of any one.

attendrissant, -e, *adj.,* moving, affecting.

attendrissement (-màn), *n.m.,* compassion, feeling; emotion, sensibility; relenting, tenderness.

attendu, *prep.,* considering, on account of, in consideration of. — *que;* seeing that, as, whereas, in or for as much as.

attentat, *n.m.,* attempt at crime; crime; attempt; criminal attempt; outrage. — *à la pudeur;* outrage on decency. — *contre la vie de;*

attempt upon the life of. — *contre les lois;* outrage upon the laws.

attentatoire, *adj.,* (jur.) that attempts.

attente, *n.f.,* expectation, waiting; hope, expectation. *Remplir, tromper, l'—;* to come up to, to deceive, expectation. *Pierre d'—;* (arch.) toothing; (fig.) stepping-stone. *Être dans l'— de;* to be in the expectation of. *Ligature d'—;* (surg.) temporary ligature.

attenter, *v.n.,* to attempt, to make an attempt. — *à la vie de quelqu'un;* to make an attempt upon any one's life. — *contre la liberté publique;* to make an attempt against public liberty. — *à ses jours;* to lay violent hands upon one's self.

attenti-f, -ve, *adj.,* attentive, heedful, mindful; studious; diligent, careful. *Être — à;* to look after, to see to. *Être — à un discours;* to be attentive to a discourse. *Être — à son livre;* to be intent upon one's book.

attention, *n.f.,* attention, attentiveness, care; heedfulness, mindfulness, carefulness, vigilance; regard, respect, consideration. *Faute d'—;* inadvertently. *Force d'—;* intentness. *Avec —;* attentively. *Manque d'—;* heedlessness. *Faire une chose avec —;* to do a thing with care. *Faire — à;* to mind. — *au commandement!* (milit.) attention! *Je faisais peu — à ses discours;* I paid little attention to his discourses. *N'y faites pas —!* do not name it! *Regarder avec —;* to look fixedly. *Prêtez-y —;* pay attention to it. *Cela mérite —;* that deserves notice. *S'attirer l'— du public;* to attract the notice of the public. *Plein d'—;* regardful. *Sans —;* reckless. *Il a eu l'— de m'avertir;* he was so good as to warn me. *Il a pour moi de grandes —s;* he has a great regard for me.

attentionné, -e, *adj.,* attentive.

attentivement (-màn), *adv.,* attentively, carefully.

attenu, *part.* (of ☉*atenir*), next, contiguous, adjoining.

atténuant, -e, *adj.,* attenuant; (jur.) palliating, extenuating.

atténuant, *n.m.,* (med.) attenuant.

atténuation, *n.f.,* attenuation, weakness; extenuation, mitigation, palliation.

atténué, -e, *adj.,* attenuated, wasted, emaciated, palliated; tapering.

atténuer, *v.a.,* to attenuate, to weaken, to make thin, to impair (one's strength—*les forces*); to extenuate, to mitigate, to palliate. — *ue crime;* to palliate a crime.

atterrage, *n.m.,* (nav.) landing, landfall.

atterrant, -e, *adj.,* astounding, startling, overwhelming.

atterrer, *v.a.,* to throw or strike down, to bring to the ground; to overthrow; to destroy, to demolish, to ruin; to subvert; to deject, to cast down; to astound, to overwhelm.

atterrer, *v.n.,* (nav.) to make land.

atterrir, *v.n.,* (nav.) to land, to make land.

atterrissage, *n.m.,* landing, making land.

atterrissement (-èr-ris-màn), *n.m.,* alluvion, accretion, alluvium.

attestation, *n.f.,* attestation, certificate, voucher.

attester, *v.a.,* to attest, to certify; to avouch, to witness, to swear, to testify; to call, to take to witness. *J'en atteste le ciel; j'en atteste les dieux;* heaven be witness; witness ye gods.

atticisme, *n.m.,* Atticism.

atticiste, *n.m.,* Atticist.

attiédir, *v.n.,* to make lukewarm, to cool. *Le temps attiédira leur zèle;* time will cool their ardour.

*s'***attiédir,** *v.r.,* to cool, to grow cool, become cool.

attiédissement (-màn), *n.m.,* lukewarmñess; abatement. *L'— de l'amitié;* the lukewarmness of friendship.

attifer, *v.a.,* to dress out; to bedizen.

s'attifer, *v.r.,* to dress one's self out, to bedizen one's self.

Ⓗ**attifet,** *n.m.,* woman's head-gear.

attique (at-tik), *adj.,* Attic, (arch.) attic. *Goût —;* Attic taste. *Sel —;* Attic salt, Attic wit.

attique, *n.m.,* Attic; (arch.) attic, attic story.

attiquement, *adv.,* (gram.) after the Attic dialect.

*attirail, *n.m* sing., apparatus, implements, utensils, tire, gear, furniture, tackle ; baggage, train, equipage, paraphernalia. *L'— d'une imprimerie;* the materials and implements of a printing-office. *L'— d'une cuisine;* kitchen apparatus and utensils.

attirant, -e, *adj.,* attractive, alluring, enticing.

attirer, *v.a.,* to attract, to draw; to incite; to bring over, to win over, to gain over; to lure, to wheedle, to entice. *L'aimant attire le fer;* the loadstone attracts iron. *— par des caresses;* to wheedle over by caresses. *— l'ennemi dans une embuscade;* to draw the enemy into an ambuscade. *— les yeux, les regards de tout le monde;* to attract the eyes of all the world. *Un malheur en attire un autre;* one misfortune seldom comes alone.

s'attirer, *v.r.,* to draw down upon one, to draw *or* bring upon one's self; to incur, to run into, to get into, to attract; to win, to gain, to get. *— l'attention du public;* to attract the notice of the public. *— des affaires;* to get one's self into scrapes.

attiser, *v.a.,* to make up (the fire—*du feu*), to stir up; to poke.

attiseur, *n.m.,* a meddlesome person who likes to cause quarrels and discord.

attisoir *or* **attisonnoir,** *n.m.,* (in foundries—*fonderies*), poker.

attitrer, *v.a.,* (seldom used but in the *past participle*) to appoint; to bribe. *Juges attitrés;* appointed judges. *Marchand attitré;* the shopkeeper one usually deals with. *Témoins attitrés;* bribed witnesses.

attitude. *n.f.,* attitude, (paint) posture.

attouchement (-toosh-mān), *n.m.,* touch, feeling, contact.

attract-eur, -rice, *adj.,* attractile.

attracti-f, -ve. *adj.,* attractive.

attraction, *n.f.,* attraction. *--Newtonienne;* attraction of gravitation.

attraire, *v.a.,* to allure, to entice.

attrait, *n.m.,* allurement, attraction, charm; (rel.) comfort. *La beauté est un puissant —;* beauty is a powerful charm. *Une fille pleine d'—s;* a girl full of charms.

attrape, *n.f.,* bite, trick, take-in. *—!* you are caught!

attrape-lourdaud, *n.m.* (—, *or —* —s), clap-trap; catch-penny.

attrape-mouche, *n.m.* (—, *or* — —s), fly-trap.

attrape-nigaud, *n.m.* (—, *or* — —s), take-in, fool-trap.

attrape-parterre, *n.m.* (—, *or* — —s), (l.u.) clap-trap for the pit, clap-trap.

attraper, *v.a.,* to entrap, to ensnare, to trap; to take in, to catch; to overreach; to cheat, to trick; to overtake; to get, to secure; to receive; to compass; to take, to surprise; to hit, to reach; to seize. *— un renard dans un piège;* to entrap a fox. *Prenez garde à vous, il vous attrapera;* look to yourself, he'll take you in. *Il en a attrapé de plus fins que vous;* he has ensnared more cunning people than you are. *Tâcher d'—;* to scramble for. *Il a attrapé un*

bon bénéfice; he has got a good living. *— un rhume;* to catch a cold. *— un coup;* to get a blow. *— quelqu'un sur le fait;* to catch one in the act. *La pierre l'a attrapé à la tempe;* the stone has hit him on the temple. *— le sens, la pensée, d'un auteur;* to catch the sense, to hit upon the meaning of an author. *— un caractère;* to hit a character. *— la ressemblance;* to hit off the likeness.

s'attraper, *v.r.,* to be caught; (man.) to clip.

attrapeu-r, *n.m.,* **-se,** *n.f.,* deceiver, deluder, cheat.

attrapoire, *n.f.,* trap, pit-fall, snare; wile, trick.

attrayant, -e, *adj.,* attractive, inviting, winning, engaging, charming. *Beauté manière,—e;* alluring beauty, winning manner.

attribuer, *v.a.,* to attach, to annex; to attribute, to ascribe, to impute (a thing to one —*quelque chose à quelqu'un*) ; to assign, to confer. *— des privilèges à une charge;* to annex privileges to an office.

s'attribuer, *v.r.,* to assume, to take upon one's self, to arrogate to one's self; to claim. *Il s'attribue de grands droits;* he claims extensive rights.

attribut, *n.m.,* attribute; (log.) predicate, attribute; symbol, emblem.

attributi-f. -ve, *adj.,* attributive.

attribution, *n.f.,* conferring; privilege, prerogative; *pl.,* powers; province, department. *Dans mes —s;* in my department (office).

attristant, -e, *adj.,* sad, sorrowful, melancholy, grievous.

attrister, *v.a.,* to grieve, to make sad, to afflict, to trouble, to cast down. *Cette nouvelle l'attriste;* that piece of news grieves him.

s'attrister, *v.r.,* to grieve, to yield to sorrow ; to be sad, to become sorrowful.

attrition, *n.f.,* (theol.) attrition; (phys.) attrition, friction.

attroupement (-troop-mān), *n.m.,* riotous assemblage, mob, rabble.

attrouper, *v.a.,* to assemble, to gather together. *Il attroupa toute la canaille;* he gathered all the rabble together.

s'attrouper, *v.r.,* to flock together, to gather in crowds, to get together tumultuously.

au, contraction of *à le,* to the. *Céder au torrent;* to give way to the torrent.

aubade, *n.f.,* morning serenade; reproof, insult, lecture. *Il en a eu l'—;* he was reproved for it.

Ⓗ**aubain,** *n.m.,* alien, foreigner.

aubaine, *n.f.,* (jur.) aubaine, escheat, escheatage; windfall.

aube, *n.f.,* the dawn; alb (priest's garment —*vêtement ecclésiastique*); (hydr.) flat board; float; paddle-board (of steamers—*de bateaux à vapeur*). *L'— du jour;* the break of day. *—s de moulin;* flat-boards of a mill. *Roue à —s;* paddle-wheel.

aubépine. *n.f.,* hawthorn, whitethorn.

aubère, *adj.,* (man.) flea-bitten grey. *Cheval —;* flea-bitten grey horse.

auberge. *n.f.,* inn, public-house.

aubergine, *n.f. V.* **mélongène.**

aubergiste, *n.m.,* innkeeper, publican, landlord, host.

auberon, *n.m.,* catch (of a lock—*de serrure*).

auberonnière, *n.f.,* clasp (of a lock—*de serrure*).

*aube-vigne, *n.f.,* (bot.) virgin's-bower.

aubier, *n.m.,* (bot.) sap-wood, alburnum. [This word is sometimes, but incorrectly, used for *obier,* guelder-rose.]

aubifoin, *n.m.,* (bot.) bluebottle.

aubin, *n.m.,* (man.) canter, hand-gallop.

aubiner, *v.n.,* (man.) to canter.

aubour, *n.m.,* (bot.) laburnum.

aucun, -e, *uaj.*, any; (negation) none, no one; not any; no. *Je ne connais — de vos juges;* I know none of your judges. *— ne le dira;* no one will say so. *Je doute qu'— de vous le fasse;* I doubt whether any of you will do it. *Il n'y a — de ses sujets qui ne mourût pour lui;* there is not one of his subjects who would not die for him. *De tous ceux qui se disaient mes amis, — m'a-t-il secouru?* did any of all those who called themselves my friends assist me? *Je vous le cède sans bénéfice —;* I let you have it without any profit whatever. *Il n'a fait —es dispositions;* he has made no arrangements. *Il a obtenu ce qu'il demandait sans —s frais;* he has obtained his request without any expense.

aucunement (-mān), *adv.*, in no wise, not at all, not in the least. *Je ne le connais —;* I do not know him at all. *—, Monsieur;* not in the least, Sir.

audace, *n.f.*, audacity, insolence, assurance, daring, boldness. *Avec —;* insolently. *Payer d'—;* to brazen it out.

audacieusement (-eûz-mān), *adv.*, audaciously, daringly, boldly.

audacieu-x, -se, *adj.*, audacious, daring; impudent, insolent; presumptuous, bold; high-spirited, enterprising. *Génie —;* daring genius. *Entreprise —se;* bold enterprise.

☉**au deçà** (ô-dsa), *prep.* V. **deçà**.

au delà (ô-dla), *prep.*, on the other side, beyond. V. **delà**.

audience. *n.f.*, audience, auditory; court, sitting, the judges who hear causes; hall (where causes are heard—*salle d'audience*). *Jour d'—;* court day. *Ouvrir l'—;* to open the court. *— publique;* open court. *— à huis clos;* a sitting with closed doors. *En pleine —;* in open court. *L'— est levée;* the court has broken up. *On le mit hors de l'—;* he was turned out of the court.

audiencier, *adj. m.* *Huissier —;* crier of a court.

audiencier, *n.m.*, usher, crier of a court.

auditeur, *n.m.*, auditor, auditress, hearer; auditor (of accounts—*de comptes*).

auditi-f, -ve. *adj.*, auditory. *Conduit — externe;* cavity of the ear.

audition. *n.f.*, (jur.) hearing, audit, auditing. *L'— des témoins;* the hearing of the witnesses.

auditoire, *n.m.*, congregation (in a church —*à l'église*); audience (theatre, &c.); auditory.

auge. *n.f.*, trough; a plasterer's hod; spout (of a water-mill—*de moulin à eau*). *— à goudron* (nav.) tar-bucket.

augée. *n.f.*, hodful, troughful.

augelot (ôj-lo), *n.m.*, little ditch in which vines are planted; small trough (used by salt-boilers—*employés par les sauniers*).

auger, *v.a.*, (tech.) to hollow out.

auget, *n.m.*, seed-box, drawer (of a bird-cage —*de cage*); spout (of a mill-hopper—*d'une trémie*); small trough; bucket (of a water-wheel —*de roue hydraulique*).

augment, *n.m.*, (gram.) augment; (med.) increase.

augmentateur, *n.m.*, augmenter.

augmentati-f, -ve, *adj.*, (gram.) augmentative.

augmentation, *n.f.*, augmentation, increase, enlargement, addition; (com.) rise.

augmenté, -e, *part.*, augmented, increased. *Un livre revu, corrigé et —;* a book revised, corrected, and augmented.

augmenter, *v.a.*, to augment, to increase, to enlarge; to add to, to raise the salary of; (com.) to raise. *Il a augmenté sa maison;* he has enlarged his house. *— le prix;* to raise the price. *Je vais — mon commis;* I am about to increase my clerk's salary.

augmenter, *v.n.*, to augment, to increase, to grow, to multiply. *Il augmente en biens;* he increases in wealth.

s'augmenter, *v.r.*, to increase, to enlarge.

augural, -e, *adj.*, augural.

augure, *n.m.*, augury; omen, token; augur, soothsayer. *Un bon, un mauvais —;* a good, bad omen. *De mauvais —;* ominous, ill-boding. *Funeste —;* ill-boding omen. *Un oiseau de mauvais —;* a bird of ill-omen; an ominous person.

augurer, *v.a.*, to augur; to conjecture, to surmise. *Qu'en pouvez-vous —?* what can you augur from it? *Je n'en augure rien de bon;* I augur nothing good from it.

auguste. *adj.*, august, sacred, venerable.

auguste, *n.m.*, (antiq.) Augustus.

augustement, *adv.*, (l.u.) in an august manner.

augustin, *n.m.*, Austin friar. *Saint —;* (print.) English.

aujourd'hui, *adv.*, to-day, this day; nowadays, now, at present. *D'— en huit;* this day week. *D'— en quinze;* this day fortnight. *Dès —;* from this day, henceforth. *— il y a huit, quinze, jours;* it is a week, a fortnight, ago. *La mode d'—;* the present fashion. *Les hommes d'—;* the men of the present day. *Ce n'est pas d'— que nous nous connaissons;* we are no new acquaintance.

aulique, *adj.*, aulic.

aulique, *n.f.*, thesis (for a doctor's degree in divinity—*pour le doctorat en théologie*).

aulnaie, aulne, aulnée. V. **aunaie, aune, aunée**.

auloffée, *n.f.*, (nav.) luff.

aulx (ô), *pl.* of **ail**.

aumône, *n.f.*, alms, alms-giving, charity. *Faire l'—;* to give alms. *Demander l'—;* to beg. *Vivre d'—;* to live upon alms. *Être réduit à l'—;* to be reduced to beggary.

☉**aumônée**, *n.f.*, sum given to hospitals.

☉**aumôner**, *v.a.*, to pay a fine to the poor.

aumônerie, *n.f.*, almonry.

aumônier, *n.m.*, almoner, chaplain, ordinary.

aumônière, *n.f.*, alms-box, alms-purse; almoner (nun—*nonne*).

aumôni-er, -ère, *adj.*, charitable, loving to give alms.

aumusse *or* **aumuce**, *n.f.*, amess (fur cap worn by officials in Roman churches).

aunage, *n.m.*, aluage, ell-measure; measuring.

aunaie, *n.f.*, an alder-plot, grove of alders.

☉**aune**, *n.f.*, ell. *Acheter à l'—;* to buy by the ell. *Mesurer les autres à son —;* to measure another man's corn by one's own bushel. *Les hommes ne se mesurent pas à l'—;* one must not judge of a man's merit by his stature. *Il sait ce qu'en vaut l'—;* he knows it to his cost, by experience. *En avoir tout du long de l'—;* to get it well.

aune, *n.m.*, alder-tree.

aunée *or* **aulnée**, *n.f.*, (bot.) elecampane.

auner, *v.a.*, to measure.

auneur, *n.m.*, alnager, measurer.

auparavant, *adv.*, before, first; heretofore, precedently; ere now. *Longtemps —;* a long time before.

auprès, *prep.*, near, by; close to; close by; near to; with, in, over; to, in comparison with. *Sa maison est — de la mienne;* his house is close by mine. *Être — d'un seigneur;* to live with a nobleman. *Excusez-le — de son père;* excuse him to his father. *Il cherche à me nuire — de vous;* he endeavours to hurt me in your opinion. *N'être pas bien — de quelqu'un;* to be under any-body's displeasure. *Elle peut tout — de lui;* she can do anything with him. *Votre mal n'est rien*

—du sien; your distress is nothing to his. *Vivre* —*de ses parents;* to live with one's parents.

auprès, *adv.*. by, hard by. close to.

aurate, *n.m.*, (chem.) aurate.

auréole, *n.f.*. glory, halo; (paint.) aureola; (anat.) areola. *Son front brillait d'une sainte* —; a lambent glory played around his head.

auriculaire. *adj.*, auricular. *Témoin* —; ear-witness. *Le doigt* —; the little finger. —, *n.m.*. the little finger.

auricule, *n.f.*. auricle, external ear; (bot.) bear's ear, auricula.

auriculé. -e, *adj.*, (bot.) auriculate.

aurifère, *adj.*. auriferous.

aurillard. *V.* **orillard**.

aurique, *adj.*, shoulder-of-mutton shaped. *Voiles* —*s;* shoulder-of-mutton sails.

aurochs (oroks), *n.m.*, (mam.) urus, wild bull.

aurone, *n.f.*, abrotanum, southern-wood.

aurore, *n.f.*,dawn, morning, morn, morning-dawn, day-spring; East; gold colour; (myth., astron.) Aurora. *A l'*—; before dawn. *L'— commençait à paraître*, the morning began to dawn. *L'— aux doigts de roses;* rosy-fingered morn. *Du couchant à l'—;* from west to east. — *boréale;* aurora borealis. *L'— de la vie;* the dawn of life.

auscultation, *n.f.*, (med.) auscultation.

ausculter, *v.a.*, (med.) to auscultate.

auspice, *n.m.*, auspice, omen, presage. *Heureux* —*s;* a good omen.

auspicine, *n.f.*, (antiq.) aruspicy, auguration.

aussi, *adv.*, too, also, likewise; besides, therefore, moreover; accordingly; so; as much; as. *Vous le voulez, et moi* —; you will have it so, and I too. *Donnez-m'en* —; give me some too. *Il est — sage que vaillant;* he is as prudent as courageous. *Il est — sot que son ami;* he is as much a fool as his friend.

aussi, *conj.*, therefore, but then. *Ces dentelles sont belles, —coûtent-elles beaucoup;* these laces are fine, but then they are dear. —*bien* for, and the more so as; as well. *Je ne veux point y aller, — bien est-il trop tard;* I won't go thither, for it is too late. *Je n'ai que faire de l'en prier, — bien ne m'écouterait-il pas;* it would be in vain for me to entreat him, the more so as he would not listen to me. *Je sais cela — bien que vous;* I know that as well as you. *Le fanatisme religieux est ennemi des arts — bien que de la philosophie;* religious fanaticism is inimical to the arts as well as to philosophy.

aussière or **haussière**, *n.f.*, (nav.) hawser, small cable.

aussitôt, *adv.*. immediately, directly,forthwith. — *après votre départ;* immediately after your departure. — *dit.* — *fait;* no sooner said than done. — *que;* as soon as. whenever. — *qu'il viendra;* as soon as he comes.

auster (os-tèr), *n.m.*., auster, south-wind.

austère, *adj.*, austere. severe, stern, grave; harsh, sharp (to the taste—*au goût*).

austèrement (-män), *adv.*, austerely, severely, rigidly.

austérité, *n.f.*, austerity; severity, sternness; strictness.

austral. -e, *adj.*. austral.

autan, *n.m.*, (poet.) auster, blast.

autant. *adv.*, as much, as many; so much, so many; as far. *Ce vase contient — que l'autre;* this vase contains as much as the other. *Il y avait — d'hommes que de femmes;* there were as many men as women. *Travaillez — que vous pourrez;* work as much as you can. *Je suis — que vous;* I am as good as you. *Je l'ai vendu tout —;* I sold it for quite as much. *Une fois —;* as much again. — *que jamais;* as much as ever. — *l'esclavage me répugne, — la liberté m'effraie;* liberty alarms as much as slavery is repugnant ,t to me. — *de têtes,* — *d'opinions:* so many minds. *Cela est fini, ou — vaut:* that is as good as done. — *en emporte le vent:* all that is idle talk. *Boire d'—;* to drink a great deal. *A la charge d'—;* on condition of a return. — *ne pas y aller du tout;* as well not go at all. — *que;* as, as far as. — *que j'en puis juger:* as far as I can conjecture.

d'autant mieux or **d'autant plus**, *adverb. phrase,* the more so, so much the more so, the rather. *Je l'estime d'autant plus qu'il est pauvre,* I esteem him the more because he is poor. *Je l'en aime d'autant mieux;* I love her all the more for it.

d'autant moins, *adverb. phrase,* the less, so much the less. *Il en est d'autant moins à craindre;* he is all the less to be feared.

d'autant que, *conj.*,seeing, more especially as.

autel, *n.m*, altar; (astron.) ara. *Le Sacrement de l'—;* the host; the holy Sacrament, Eucharist. *Les —s;* religion. *Grand, maître,* — high altar. *Nappe d'—;* altar cloth. *Tableau d'—;* altar-piece. *Il mérite qu'on lui élève des —s;* he deserves the greatest honours.

auteur, *n.m. and f.*, author, authoress; inventor, maker, cause, contriver, framer; writer; perpetrator; achiever; artist, engraver, composer, sculptor; owner. *Dieu est l'— de toutes choses;* God is the author of all things. *L'— d'un projet;* the framer of a project *L'— d'une découverte;* the author of a discovery. *L'— d'un procédé,* the inventor of a process. *C'est elle qui est l'— de ce livre;* she is the author of that book. *Se faire —;* to turn author. *Droit d'—;* copy-right.

authenticité, *n.f.*, authenticity, genuineness.

authentique, *adj.*, original; authentic, genuine.

authentique, *n.f.*, authentics, Justinian's authentics.

authentiquement (-män), *adv.*, authentically.

authentiquer, *v.a.*, (jur.) to sign and seal (by a judge—*par un juge*).

autobiographe, *n.m.*, autobiographer.

autobiographie, *n.f.*, autobiography.

autocéphale, *n.m.*, name given by the Greeks to the Bishops who were not under the jurisdiction of the Patriarch.

autochtone (-tok-to-n), *n.m. and adj.*, (antiq.) autochthon.

autocrate. *n.m.*, autocrat.

autocratie (-cî), *n.f.*, autocracy.

autocratrice, *n.f.*, autocratrix, autocratrice.

autodafé, *n.m.*, (—s) auto-da-fe.

autographe, *n.m.*, autograph.

autographe, *adj.*, autographic, autographical.

autographie, *n.f.*, autography.

autographier, *v.a.*, to autograph.

autographique, *adj.*, autographic.

automate. *n.m.*, automaton.

automatique, *adj.*. automatic. automatical.

automnal. -e (-tom-nal), *adj.*, autumnal. [Has no masc. pl.]

automne (-to-n), *n.m.*, autumn; fall of the leaf; fall.

automot-eur, -rice, *adj.*, self-acting, self-moving.

autonome, *adj.*, autonomous.

autonomie, *n.f.*, autonomy.

autopsie, *n.f.*, post-mortem examination; autopsy.

autorisation, *n.f.*, authorization; authority; license (of a preacher—*d'un prédicateur*); warrant; consent.

autoriser, *v.a.*, to authorize, to empower; to allow by authority, to legalize, to license, to warrant.

s'autoriser, *v.r.*, to get or gain authority, to be authorized.

autorité, *n.f.*, authority, legal power, rule, sway; credit, power, interest, weight, consideration. *L'— des magistrats, des lois;* the authority of the magistrates, of the laws. *Avoir de l'— sur;* to have power with. *Être en —;* to be invested with authority. *Il l'a fait de son — privée;* he did it from his own private authority. *Alléguer, apporter des —s;* to quote or cite authorities. *Faire—;* to be an authority.

autour, *n.m.*, goshawk.

autour, *prep.*, about; round; around. *— de sa personne;* about his person. *— du bras;* round the arm.

autour, *adv.*, about, round, round about. *Il regardait tout —;* he looked about. *Ici —;* hereabouts.

autourserie, *n.f.*, art of training goshawks.

autoursier, *n.m.*, one that trains goshawks.

autre, *adj.*, other, different, else, second, another. *L'— jour;* the other day. *Une —fois;* another time. *Tout —;* quite different. *Aucun —;* no one else. *Vous —s;* you. *Encore un —;* another, one more. *Il le regarde comme un — lui-même;* he looks upon him as a second self.

autre, *pron.*, another, other, else. *Nul — n'y aurait consenti;* nobody else would have consented to it. *Un — le fera;* another will do it. *Tout — l'aurait fait;* any other would have done it. *Les uns se plaisent à une chose, les —s à une —;* some delight in one thing and some in another. *Un petit nombre d'—s;* a few others. *L'un l'—;* one another, each other. *L'un et l'—;* both. *L'un ou l'—;* either. *Ni l'un ni l'—;* neither. *L'un et l'— vous ont obligé;* both have obliged you. *Les uns et les —;* all. *Ni l'un ni l'— ne valent rien;* both are good for nothing. *A l'un ou à l'—;* to either. *Ni pour l'un ni pour l'—;* for neither. *On les a payés l'un et l'—;* both have been paid. *A l'envi l'un de l'—;* in emulation of one another. *Entre —s;* among other people or among other things. *De côté et d'—;* up and down. *De part et d'—;* on both sides, on all sides. *C'est un — homme;* he is no more the same man. *Il ne fait — chose que jouer;* he does nothing but play. *C'est — chose;* it is quite another thing. *Nous —s Français, nous mangeons beaucoup de pain;* we French folk eat a great deal of bread. *Causer de choses et d'—s;* to talk of different things. *Il dit d'une façon et il fait d'une —;* he says one thing and does another. *L'un vaut l'—;* one is as good as the other. *Comme dit l'—;* as somebody says; as the saying is. *Il n'en fait point d'—s;* he does nothing else than are his pranks. *L'un dans l'—, l'un portant l'—;* one with another; on an average. *Il en sait bien d'—s;* he knows a trick worth two of that. *J'en ai vu bien d'—s;* I have seen many stranger things than that. *A d'—s!* pshaw! I know better, you must not tell that to me.

autrefois, *adv.*, formerly, in former times; of old.

autrement, *adv.*, otherwise; after another manner, another way; else; or else. *Faisons —;* let us go another way to work. *Entrez, — je fermerai la porte;* come in, or else I'll shut the door. *C'est un homme qui n'est pas — riche;* he is a man who is not over rich.

autrichien, -ne (-in,-è'n), *adj.*, Austrian.

autrichien, *n.m.*, **-ne**, *n.f.*, Austrian.

autruche, *n.f.*, (orni.) ostrich. *Avoir un estomac d'—;* to have the stomach of an ostrich; to eat like a farmer.

autrui, *n.m.*, *pron.*, others, other people. *Dépendre d'—;* to depend on others. *Faire à —*

ce que nous voudrions qu'on nous fît; to do by others as we would be done by. *Le bien d'—;* another's property.

auvent, *n.m.*, shed, penthouse.

auvernat, *n.m.*, Orléans wine.

aux (*pl.* of au), *art.*, to the. *V.* **à.**

auxèse, *n.f.*, (rhet.) auxesis.

auxiliaire, *adj.*, auxiliary, subsidiary. *Verbe —;* auxiliary verb.

auxiliaire, *n.m.*, auxiliary; helper, assistant.

s'avachir, *v.r.*, to flag; to grow fat and flabby; to get out of shape, to run down at heel.

aval, *n.m.*, down, downwards, down the river. *Le vent vient d'—;* the wind comes up the river. *En — de;* below. *Vent d'—;* westerly wind.

aval, *n.m.*, (com.) guaranty.

avalaison, *n.f.*, flood, torrent; (nav.) a long-continued west or northwest wind.

avalanche, *n.f.*, avalanche.

avalasse, *n.f.* *V.* **avalaison.**

avalé, -e, *part.*, flagging, hanging down; sunk, fallen in.

avaler, *v.a.*, to swallow, to swallow down; to let down; to endure, to pocket (affront); to lower (things into a cellar—*quelque chose dans une cave*); to drink, to toss off; (gard.) to lop. *— gloutonnement;* to gulp down. *— un affront;* to pocket an injury. *Il ne fait que tordre et —;* it is but one twist, and down it goes. *— la lanterne;* to let the lantern down. *— du vin dans une cave;* to let wine down into a cellar. *— une branche;* to lop off a branch close to the trunk.

avaler, *v.n.*, to go down, drop down, the river with the stream.

s'avaler, *v.r.*, to flag, to hang down; to fall down or in; to be swallowed.

avalette, *n.f.*, a sort of float (used in angling. *—employé à la péche*).

avaleur, *n.m.*, one that swallows up. *— de pois gris;* a great glutton. *— de charrettes ferrées;* a braggadocio.

avaloire, *n.f.*, a large throat or swallow; (saddlery—*pièce de harnais*) breeching; (hat making—*chapellerie*) stamper. *Quelle —!* what a greedy gut!

avançage, *n.m.*, coach stand.

avance, *n.f.*, advance, start, distance in advance; projection, prominence; advance-money; first step, offer. *Il a quatre lieues d'— sur moi;* he is four leagues ahead of me. *Faire une —de mille écus;* to advance a thousand crowns. *Faire les —s d'une entreprise;* to advance the funds for an enterprise. *Faire des —s;* to make advances to. *Prendre l'—;* to get the start. *D'—;* beforehand. *Payer d'—;* to pay beforehand. *Prévenir d'—;* to warn beforehand.

avancé, -e, *part.*, advanced; forward, early; late (of the hour—*de l'heure*). *Un homme — en âge;* an elderly man. *Un jeune homme fort —;* a very forward youth. *Les arbres sont —s;* the trees are forward. *La nuit est bien —e;* it is very late in the night. *Je n'en suis pas plus —;* I am not a bit the better off for it. *Viande —c;* meat which is getting bad.

avancée, *n.f.*, (milit.) advance guard.

avancement (-mān), *n.m.*, progress, advancement; improvement; preferment, promotion, rise.

avancer, *v.a.*, to advance, to bring, to put forward; to hold out, to stretch out, to set forward; to bring nearer; to hasten; to forward; to pay beforehand; to lay out or down; to assert, to bring forth, to hold forth; to promote, to put on (a clock—*une montre, une pendule, &c.*); to broach (opinion); to give (a chair—*une chaise*). *Avancez la table;* push the table forward. *— le pied;* to put one's foot forward.

Faire —, to push, to push on. *Cela a avancé sa mort*, that has hastened his death. — *l'horloge*, to put the clock forward. — *le dîner ;* to hasten dinner. — *un ouvrage :* to forward a piece of work. *Il lui a avancé de l'argent*, he has advanced him some money. — *les intérêts de quelqu'un ;* to promote any one's interests. *Pouvez-vous prouver ce que vous avancez ?* can you prove your assertion? *On l'a avancé :* he has been promoted.

avancer, *v.n.*, to advance, to get on, to proceed, to march on, to move forward, to keep on, to go too fast; to come out ; to jut out; to lean over, to bear out; to encroach ; to improve, to make some progress; to thrive ; to rise. *Avancez-donc !* come on! *L'horloge avance ;* the clock is too fast. *Cette maison avance trop sur la rue;* that house juts out too much into the street. — *en âge ;* to advance in age. *Faire — une voiture :* to call a coach.

*s'*avancer, *v.r.*, to advance, to go on, to move forward ; to stand forth; to draw near, to come up ; to get on, to improve; to get preferred, to be successful; to go far ; to jut out, to project. *Il s'avance vers nous ;* he is making up to us. *Cet ambassadeur s'est trop avancé :* that ambassador has gone too far. *Le temps s'avance ;* time advances. — *à cheval;* to ride up. — *en voiture;* to drive up. — *à la voile ;* to sail up. — *en courant ;* to run up.

avanceur, *n.m.*, gold-wire drawer.

avanie, *n.f.*, insult, affront, outrage.

avant. *n.m.*, (nav.) prow, head, bow of a ship. *De l'*— *à l'arriere :* from stem to stern. *Aller de l'*— *:* to have head-way. *Gagner l'*— *de ;* to get ahead of.

avant, *prep.*, (of time and order—*d'ordre et de temps*) before. *J'ai vu cela* — *vous ;* I have seen that before you. — *toutes choses*, above all things. — *tout ;* first of all, before all.

avant, *adv.*, far, deep, forward, far advanced. *D'*— *;* before. *En* — *!* forward! on! *En* — *de;* before, in front of. *Mettre en* — *;* to bring forward. *N'allez pas si* — *;* don't go so far. *Creuser fort* — *dans la terre,* to dig very deep in the ground. *Plus* — *;* further, deeper. *Bien* — *dans l'hiver ;* when the winter is far advanced. *Nous étions bien* — *en mer ;* we had got a great way to sea.

avant que, *conj.*, before. — *qu'il soit un an ;* before a year.

avantage, *n.m.*, advantage, vantage-ground; benefit, interest; behalf, behoof ; (nav.) weather-gauge; (man.) whip-hand; odds (at play—*au jeu*). *Avoir l'*— *sur ;* to have the advantage over. *Avoir l'*— *; to gain, to prevail. *On lui a fait tous les* —*s possibles :* they gave him all possible advantages. *Quel* — *vous en revient-il ?* what benefit do you reap by it ? *On peut dire ceci à son* — *;* this may be said in his behalf. *Nos troupes ont eu l'*— *;* our troops have had the best of it. *Tirer* — *de tout :* to take advantage of everything. *J'ai perdu, vous avez l'*—*:* I have lost, you have the better of the game. *S'habiller à son* — *;* to dress to the best advantage.

avantager, *v.a.*, to give or allow an advantage ; to bestow an advantage on ; to favour. *La nature l'avait avantagé de beaucoup de qualités précieuses :* nature had endowed him with many inestimable qualities.

avantageusement (-mān), *adv.*, advantageously; usefully ; beneficially; highly. *S'habiller* — *;* to dress to the best advantage. *Parler* — *de quelqu'un ;* to speak highly of one. *Il parle trop* — *de ses actions :* he speaks with too much ostentation of his own actions.

avantageu-x, -se, *adj.*, advantageous, profitable, beneficial; conceited, presuming; overbearing. *Conditions* —*ses ;* advantageous terms.

Un air — *:* a conceited air. *Un ton* —, a confident, assuming, tone. *C'est un homme* — *;* he is a conceited fellow.

avant-bec, *n.m.* (— —s), (arch.) starling of a bridge, pier.

avant-bras, *n.m.* (—), fore-arm.

avant-corps, *n.m.* (—), (arch.) fore-part.

avant-cour, *n.f.* (— —s), fore-court.

avant-coureur, *n.m.* (— —s), van-courier, forerunner ; harbinger.

avant-courri-er, *n.m.*, -ère, *n.f.* (— —s), forerunner, harbinger.

avant-derni-er, **-ère**, *adj.* and *n.* (— —s), the last but one. *L'*—*e syllabe ;* the penultima.

avant-faire-droit, *n.m.* (—), preventive injunction.

avant-fossé, *n.m.* (— —s), (fortif.) advance-fosse.

avant-garde, *n.f.* (— —s), vanguard; (nav.) van.

avant-goût, *n.m.* (— —s), foretaste.

avant-hier (ti-ère), *adv.*, the day before yesterday.

avant-jour, *n.m.* (*n.p.*), morning-twilight.

avant-main, *n.m.* (— —s), (man.) forehand of a horse ; (tennis) fore-hand stroke.

⊙**avant-midi**, *n.m.* (—), forenoon.

avant-mur, *n.m.* (— —s), outward wall.

avant-pêche, *n.f.* (— —s), white nutmeg peach.

avant-pied, *n.m.* (— —s), vamp, upper-leather of a boot.

⊙**avant-plancher**, *n.m.* (— —s), false ceiling.

avant-poignet, *n.m.* (— —s), fore-wrist.

avant-port, *n.m.* (— —s), (nav.) outer port.

avant-portail, *n.m.* (— —s), fore-portal.

avant-poste, *n.m.* (— —s), (milit.) outpost.

avant-propos. *n.m.* (—), preface, preamble ; introduction, exordium.

avant-quart, *n.m.* (— —s), (horl.) warning.

avant-scène, *n.f.* (— —s), front of the stage ; events preceding the opening of a drama ; proscenium.

avant-toit, *n.m.* (— —s), fore-roof, projecting roof, eaves.

avant-train, *n.m.* (— —s), fore-carriage.

*avant-veille, *n.f.* (— —s), two days before.

avare, *adj.*, avaricious, miserly, covetous; stingy, close-fisted, sparing ; penurious, niggard. *Étre* — *de ses louanges ;* to be sparing of one's praise.

avare, *n.m.*, miser, niggard ; pinch-penny.

avarement, *adv.*, avariciously.

avarice, *n.f.*, avarice, avariciousness, covetousness ; stinginess. *Par* — *;* from avarice.

avaricieu-x, -se, *adj.*, (l.u.) avaricious, covetous ; stingy.

avarie, *n.f.*, damage (done in conveying goods—*pendant le transport de marchandises*) ; (com.) damage. —*s communes;* (com.) general average. *Menues* —*s;* small averages. —*s simples ;* ordinary damage. *Sans* — *;* undamaged. *Causer une* —, to damage. *Régler les* —*s ;* to state the averages.

avarié, -e, *adj.*, damaged.

avarier, *v.a.*, to damage.

avaste, *int.*, (nav.) avast, stop, stay.

à vau-l'eau, *adv.*, with the stream. *Toutes ses entreprises sont allées* — *;* all his undertakings are come to nought. *A vau-de-route ;* in flight.

avé, *n.m.* (—), ave. — *Maria ;* ave Maria.

avec, *prep.*, with, together with ; among. *Venez* — *moi ;* come along with me. — *dessein ;* designedly. — *tout cela ;* for all that, nevertheless. *Il a pris mon manteau, et s'en est* allé —; he has taken my cloak, and has gone away with it. *Discerner le bien d'— le mal ;* to discern good from evil.

avecque, *prep.,* obsolete spelling of (*orthographe vieillie de*) **avec,** with.

aveindre (aveignant, aveint), *v.a.,* to take out, to fetch out.

aveine. *n.f.* V. **avoine.**

avelanède, *n.f.,* acorn-cup.

aveline, *n.f.,* filbert.

avelinier, *n.m.,* filbert-tree.

avénage, *n.m.,* avenage.

avenant, *part.* V. **advenant.**

avenant, -e. *adj.,* well-looking, prepossessing, pleasing, taking. *Un homme fort — ;* a very good-looking man. *Physionomie —e ;* pleasing look. *Manières —es,* prepossessing manners.

*à l'***avenant,** *adv.,* appropriate; in keeping with. *Le dessert fut à l'— du repas ;* the dessert answered to the repast.

avénement (-mân), *n.m.,* coming, accession, succession, advent, advancement. *L'— du roi à la couronne ;* the king's accession to the crown. *L'— du Messie ;* the coming of the Messiah.

avenir, *n.m.,* the future, futurity, existence, future welfare, hopes, prospects; (jur.) *venire facias. À l'— ;* in future. *On ne peut répondre de l'— ;* one cannot answer for the future. *J'assure un — à mes enfants ;* I secure an existence for my children. *Cet homme n'a aucun — ;* that man has no prospects.

avenir. *v.n.,* to chance, to happen, to come to pass. *Quoi qu'il avienne ;* whatever be the consequence. *Le cas avenant ;* the case occurring.

*à-***venir,** *n.m.* (—), (jur.) summons to an attorney to appear before the Court for his client.

avent, *n.m.,* advent.

aventure, *n.f.,* adventure. *À l'— ;* at a venture, at random. *Une plaisante — ;* a droll adventure. *Une triste — ;* a sad adventure. *Grosse — ;* (com.) bottomry. *Dire la bonne — ;* to tell people's fortune. *Se faire dire sa bonne — ;* to have one's fortune told. *Une diseuse de bonne — ;* a fortune-teller. *Tenter l'— ;* to make a trial, to try one's luck. *Mal d'— ;* whitlow. *D'—, par — :* by chance, perchance.

aventuré, -e, *part.,* hazardous, hazarded.

aventurer, *v.a.,* to venture, to put to the venture, to risk.

*s'***aventurer,** *v.r.,* to venture, to take one's chance, to hazard.

aventureu-x, -se. *adj.,* venturous, venturesome, adventurous. *Une vie —e ;* a life full of adventures.

aventuri-er, *n.m.,* **-ère,** *n.f.,* adventurer, adventuress.

aventurine, *n.f.,* avanturine.

avenu, -e. *part.,* come to pass, happened. *Acte nul et non — ;* act that is null and void.

avenue, *n.f.,* avenue, walk.

avéré, -e, *part.,* averred, established by evidence.

avérer, *v.a.,* to aver, to prove the truth of.

avéron, *n.m.,* wild oats.

à verse, *adv.,* fast (of rain). *Il pleut — ;* it rains very fast; it pours.

averse, *n.f.,* shower of rain.

aversion. *n.f.,* aversion, hate, hatred; antipathy, dislike. *Avoir de l'— pour quelque chose :* to have an aversion for a thing. *Prendre quelqu'un en — ;* to take an aversion to one. *C'est ma bête d'— ;* it is a perfect eyesore for me.

averti, -e, *part.,* warned, informed.

avertin, *n.m.,* (med.) insanity ; raving maniac ; (vet.) turn-sick.

avertir, *v.a.,* to warn, to caution ; to inform of, to acquaint with, to give notice of, to admonish. *— quelqu'un d'un danger ;* to warn any one of a danger. *— quelqu'un de son salut ;* (fig.) to give any one a wholesome piece of advice.

avertissement (-mân), *n.m.,* information, advice, (b.s.) warning, caution ; notification ; advertisement (of books—*de livres*); (b.s.) admonition.

avertisseur, *n.m.,* monitor; (thea.) call-boy.

aveu, *n.m.,* avowal, confession, acknowledgment ; approbation. *Homme sans — ;* vagrant. *Faire l'— de ;* to confess.

aveugle, *adj.,* blind, sightless ; deluded ; implicit. *— de naissance ;* born blind. *Obéissance — ;* implicit obedience. *Changer son cheval borgne contre un — ;* to change from bad to worse. *La fortune est — ;* fortune is blind.

aveugle, *n.m.f.,* blind person. *Un — y mordrait :* a blind man would see it. *C'est un — qui en conduit un autre ;* it is the blind leading the blind. *Crier comme un — qui a perdu son bâton ;* to cry out before one is hurt.

aveuglement, *n.m.,* blindness.

aveuglément, *adv.,* blindly, rashly, implicitly.

aveugler, *v.a.,* to blind, to make blind ; to put out the eyes, to take away the sight ; to dazzle ; to obscure ; (nav.) to fother. *La passion aveugle l'entendement ;* passion obscures the understanding. *— une voie d'eau ;* (nav.) to fother a leak. *La trop grande lumière aveugle ;* too much light dazzles the eyes.

*s'***aveugler,** *v.r.,* to blind one's self, to shut one's eyes, to be blinded.

*à l'***aveuglette,** *adv.,* (fam.) groping. *Aller — ;* to go groping along, blindly, rashly.

avicule, *n.f.* (mol.). V. **aronde.**

avide, *adj.,* greedy, eager, desirous ; voracious ; covetous, rapacious. *Un homme — ;* a covetous man. *— d'honneurs ;* eager after honours.

avidement (-mân), *adv.,* greedily, eagerly, voraciously, covetously.

avidité, *n.f.,* avidity, greediness, eagerness, covetousness.

avilir, *v.a.,* to debase, to demean, to disgrace, to vilify ; to disparage, to depreciate, to lower.

*s'***avilir,** *v.r.,* to undervalue one's self, to grow contemptible, to be disgraced.

avilissant, -e, *adj.,* debasing, disgraceful, humiliating.

avilissement (-mân), *n.m.,* degradation, debasement, contempt, vileness. *Tomber dans l'— ;* to fall into contempt.

aviné, -e, *part.,* seasoned with wine. *Il est — ; c'est un corps — ;* he is a regular tippler.

aviner, *v.a.,* to season with wine.

aviron, *n.m.,* (nav.) oar. *— à couple ;* scull. *Aviron***nerie,** *n.f.,* oar-maker's shed. **aviron***nier,* *n.m.,* oar-maker.

avis, *n.m.,* opinion, sentiment, mind, judgment ; advice, counsel, deliberation, admonition ; notice, notification ; warning, caution ; account, information, intelligence, news ; motion ; vote ; advertisement (in books—*dans les livres*). *À mon — ;* in my opinion. *Les — sont partagés ;* they are divided in their opinions. *Je suis d'— que vous lui écriviez ;* I am of opinion that you write to him. *Je ne suis pas d'— d'y aller ;* I am not for going thither. *Direson — ;* to tell one's mind. *Je profiterai de l'— que vous me donnez :* I shall avail myself of the caution you have given me. *— au lecteur ;* advertisement to the reader ; a word to the wise. *J'ai changé d'— ;* I have altered my mind. *On a reçu — de Paris ;* we are advised from Paris. *Lettre d'—;* letter of advice. *Faute d'—;* for want of advice. *Sous—;* with advice. *Suivant l'—de;* as per advice. *Donner à quelqu'un un—de quelque chose;* to advise any one of anything. *Ne m'écris plus jusqu'à nouvel—;* write no more till you hear further. *Ouvrir un—;* to broach an opinion. *Être d'—;* to opine. *Prendre les—;* to take the opinion. *Aller aux—;* to put to the vote. *Donner un—assez clair à quelqu'un;* to give a pretty broad hint to any one.

avisé, -e, adj., wary, discreet, prudent, cautious, advised, circumspect. *Mal—;* ill advised. *Il est fort—;* he is a very discreet man.

aviser, v.a., to apprise; to perceive; to espy; (com.) to advise.

aviser, v.n., to consider, to see, to think upon. *Avisez-y bien;* consider it well. *Vous y aviserez;* you will look to it.

s'aviser, v.r., to think of, to consider, to take it into one's head; to bethink one's self. *Il ne s'avise de rien;* he thinks of nothing. *Il s'avisa de;* he took it into his head to. *Il n'y a sottise dont il ne s'avise;* there is no folly he does not commit. *Il s'avisa d'un bon expédient;* he bethought himself of a good expedient.

aviso, n.m., (nav.) advice-boat.

***avitaillement,** n.m., (nav., milit.) victualling; stores.

***avitailler,** v.a., to victual, to furnish with victuals, to store. *—un vaisseau;* to victual a ship.

⊙***avitailleur,** n.m., army or navy contractor.

avivage, n.m., first laying of tin-foil on glass; washing of dyed cotton to heighten the colour.

aviver, v.a., to polish, to burnish, to brighten.

avives, n.f. pl., (vet.) vives.

avivoir, n.m., polisher, burnisher (tool—outil).

avocasser. v.n., to be a pettifogger.

avocasserie, n.f., pettifoggery.

avocat, n.m., counsellor, barrister, advocate. *—de causes perdues.—de Pilate,—de balle,—à tort;* briefless barrister. *—consultant;* chamber-counsel. *—principal;* leading barrister. *—général;* attorney-general.

avocate, n.f., female advocate; defender, intercessor.

avocette, n.f., (orni.) avoset.

avoine, n.f., oats; *—s,* oats still standing. *D'—;* oaten. *Farine d'—;* oatmeal. *Balle d'—;* oat-chaff.

avoinerie, n.f., oat-field.

avoir (ayant, eu), v.a., to have; to get; to be; to be worth; to be the matter with; to have on. *—pour agréable;* to like. *—honte;* to be ashamed. *—raison;* to be right. *—tort;* to be wrong. *—peur;* to be afraid. *—faim;* to be hungry. *—soif;* to be thirsty. *Vous n'avez qu'à dire;* you need only say the word. *Qu'est-ce que vous avez?* what ails you? what is the matter with you? *Faire—;* to procure for. *Il aura le prix;* he will get the prize. *Quel âge avez-vous?* how old are you? *Il a quarante ans;* he is forty. *J'ai à vous parler;* I must speak to you. *Il avait un habit bleu;* he had a blue coat. *En—;* to meet with disappointment, to catch it. *Il en a;* he has caught it. *En a-t-il!* what a lot he has! *Y—;* there to be, to be the matter. *Il ne saurait y—de différence;* there can be no difference. *Il y avait bien des tulipes dans son jardin;* there were a great many tulips in his garden. *Il y aurait une armée;* there would be an army. *Il y en a de noirs;* there are some black ones. *C'est une femme comme il n'y en a point;* she has not her like. *Il y a plus;* nay, more. *Il y en a encore;* there is still some left. *Il y a de quoi vous amuser;* you will find amusement enough. *Il n'y a pas de quoi;* don't name it; there is no offence. *Je suis venu ici il y a deux mois;* I came here two months

ago. *Il y a un an qu'il est mort;* he has been dead a year. *Il y a deux mois que je suis ici;* I have been here two months. *Il y a une heure que nous écrivons;* we have been writing an hour. *Combien y a-t-il de Paris à Londres?* how far is it from Paris to London? *Il y eut cent hommes tués, et deux cents de blessés;* there were a hundred men killed, and two hundred wounded.

avoir, n.m., possessions, substance, property, what one is worth; (com.) credit, creditor. creditor-side. *Voilà tout mon—;* this is all I have.

avoir du poids, n.m., (n.p.) avoirdupois. (English weight—*poids anglais.*)

avoisinant, -e, adj., neighbouring, near, close by.

avoisiné, part., to have neighbours. *Être bien—;* to have good neighbours.

⊙**avoisinement** (-mãn), n.m., nearness, proximity.

avoisiner, v.a., to border upon, to be situated near.

avorté, -e, adj., abortive; (bot.) abortive.

avortement, n.m., abortion, miscarriage.

avorter, v.n., to bring forth young ones before the time; to miscarry; to slip; to prove abortive; not to ripen. *Faire—;* to cause abortion. *Ce dessein avorta;* that design proved abortive. *Faire—les desseins de quelqu'un;* to baffle one's designs.

avorton, n.m., abortion; abortive child.

avouable, adj., avowable.

avoué, n.m., attorney; solicitor. *Une étude d'—;* an attorney's office.

avouer, v.a., to confess, to avow; to own, to acknowledge, to grant, to allow; to approve. *Il a avoué le fait;* he has confessed the fact. *Il avoue l'avoir fait;* he confesses having done it. *S'—vaincu;* to own one's self vanquished. *J'étais, je l'avoue, un peu confus;* I was rather confused, I allow. *—un enfant;* to acknowledge a child. *J'avouerai tout ce qu'il fera;* I will approve of all he does.

avoyer, n.m., avoyer (chief magistrate in Switzerland—*premier magistrat en Suisse*).

***avril,** n.m., April. *Un poisson d'—;* an April-fool. *Donner un poisson d'—à quelqu'un;* to make any one an April-fool. *Recevoir un poisson d'—;* to be made an April-fool.

avron, n.m., (bot.) wild oats.

avuer, v.a., (hunt.) to mark down, to mark in.

avulsion, n.f., avulsion.

axe, n.m., axis; axle, axle-tree; (artil.) trunnion. *—tournant;* axle-tree. *—de vis;* screw-arbor.

axifuge, adj., centrifugal. V. **centrifuge.**

axillaire (ak-sil-lèr), adj., (anat., bot.) axillar, axillary. *Fleurs—s;* axillary flowers.

axiome, n.m., axiom.

axiomètre, n.m., (nav.) tell-tale.

axonge, n.f., (phar.) hog's lard.

ayan, n.m. (—s), ayan, superior Turkish official.

ayant cause, n.m. (—s—), (jur.) assign.

ayant droit, n.m. (—s—), (jur.) party concerned.

aynet, n.m., skewer (for herrings—*à harengs*).

azalée, n.f., (bot.) azalea.

azédarac, n.m., azedarach, bead-tree.

azerole, n.f., (bot.) azerole.

azerolier, n.m., azarole-tree.

⊙**azime,** adj. V. **azyme.**

azimut (-mut), n.m., (astron.) azimuth.

azimutal, -e, adj., azimuthal.

azotate, n.m., (chem.) nitrate.

azote, n.m., (chem.) azote.

azote, adj., azotic.

azoté, adj., azotized, nitrogenized.

azotique, adj., azotic, nitric.

azur, *n.m.*, azure, blue; sky-colour. — *de Hollande;* Dutch blue.

azuré, -e, *adj.*, azure, sky-coloured. *La voûte —e;* the azure skies.

azurer, *v.a.*, to paint azure colour.

azurin, -e, *adj.*. azure.

azyme, *adj.*, azymous, unleavened.

azyme, *n.m.*, azym, unleavened bread. *Fête des —s;* feast of unleavened bread.

azymite, *n.m.*, Azymite.

B

b, *n.m.*, the second letter of the alphabet, *b. Être marqué au —;* to be either one-eyed, hunchbacked, or lame. (Borgne, bossu, boiteux.) *Ne parler que par b ou par f;* never to speak without swearing.

baba, *n.m.*, bun.

babel, *n.f.*, Babel. *Tour de —;* tower of Babel. *C'est une vraie tour de —, c'est une —;* it is a perfect tower of Babel.

babeurre, *n.m.*, butter-milk.

babiche, *n.f.*, lapdog.

babichon, *n.m.*, lapdog.

*babil, *n.m.*, chattering, prate, talk, gabbling, tattle, prattle. *Il nous étourdit par son —;* he stuns us with his chattering.

*babillage, *n.m.*, chit-chat, tittle-tattle, babbling, twaddle.

*babillard, *n.m.*, **-e,** *n.f.*, babbler, tattler; blab, blabber; (orni.) nettle-creeper. *C'est un franc —;* he is a regular babbler. *Une grande —e; a* great tattler. *Ne vous fiez pas à cet homme-là, c'est un —;* don't trust that man, he is a great blab.

*babillard, -e, *adj.*, babbling, talkative, chattering.

*babillement, *n.m.*, talkativeness, loquacity, garrulity.

*babiller, *v.n.*, to prate, to tattle, to gossip.

babine, *n.f.*, lip (of animals—*des animaux*); chop. *Il s'en lèche les —s;* he is smacking his chops at, after, it.

babiole, *n.f.*, bauble, gewgaw, toy, knick-knack, plaything, trifle, trinket.

bâbord, *n.m.*, (nav.) larboard.

bâbord, *adv.*, larboard; aport.

bâbordais, *n.m.*, (nav.), larboard-watch.

babouche, *n.f.*, Turkish slipper.

babouin, *n.m.*, baboon, monkey (person — *personne*). *Faire baiser le — à quelqu'un;* to make one truckle.

babouine, *n.f.*, little fool, little hussy; lip. *V.* **babine.**

babouiner, *v.n.*, (fam.) to play the buffoon.

bac, *n.m.*, ferry, ferry-boat.

baccalauréat, *n.m.*, bachelorship, the degree of bachelor.

bacchanal (-ka-), *n.m.*, racket, uproar. *Faire —;* to make a racket.

bacchanale (-ka-), *n.f.*, noisy drinking-bout, revel; *pl.*, bacchanals, bacchanalia.

⊙**bacchanaliser** (-ka-), *v.n.*, to revel, to riot.

bacchante (-kant), *n.f.*, bacchante, priestess of Bacchus; termagant.

baccharis (-ka-ris), *n.f.*, baccharis, ploughman's spikenard.

baccifère, *adj.*, that produces berries, bacciferous.

bacha, *n.m.*, bashaw, a title of honour in Turkey.

bâche, *n.f.*, cart tilt; hot-bed frame; tank, cistern; awning (of a waggon—*d'une charrette, &c.*).

⊙**bachelette,** *n.f.*, young girl, maid, lass, damsel.

bachelier, *n.m.*, bachelor of a university; knight bachelor.

bâcher, *v.a.*, to tilt (a cart—*une charrette*).

bachique, *adj.*, bacchic, jovial, drunken.

bachon, *n.m.*, wooden pail.

bachot, *n.m.*, wherry, small ferry-boat.

bachotage, *n.m.*, ferry-man's business.

bachoteur, *n.m.*, ferry-man.

bacile, *n.m.*, (bot.) sea-fennel.

bacillaire, *n.m.*, pyramidal feldspar, scapolite.

bâclage, *n.m.*, line of boats (in a port—*dans un port*).

bâclé, -e, *part.*, barred. *C'est une affaire —e;* (fam.) that affair is settled.

bâcler, *v.a.*, to bar or chain, to fasten (a door, a window, a boat—*une porte, une fenêtre, un bateau*); to do hastily, to patch up; to hurry over.

badaud, *n.m.*, **-e,** *n.f.*, ninny, booby; gazer; cockney.

badaudage, *n.m.*, cockneyism.

badauder, *v.n.*, to stand gaping in the air.

badauderie, *n.f.*, foolery, silliness, simplicity.

baderne, *n.f.*, (nav.) dolphin, paunch.

badian, *n.m.*, or **badiane,** *n.f.*, aniseed-tree.

badigeon (-jon), *n.m.*, badigeon, stone-colour.

badigeonnage (-jo-naj), *n.m.*, painting stone-colour.

badigeonner (-jo-né), *v.a.*, to paint with stone-colour.

badigeonneur (-jo-neur), *n.m.*, white-washer.

badin, -e, *adj.* and *n.*, waggish, jocular, playful, roguish; sportive. *Il a l'humeur —e;* he is of a sportive humour. *Air —;* playful air. *Style —;* playful style. *C'est un vrai —;* he is a regular banterer.

badinage, *n.m.*, sport, play, jest; foolery, playfulness, jocularity. *Ceci n'est point un —; this* is no foolery. *Il se prête volontiers au —;* he has no objection to a little foolery. *Finissez votre —;* have done with your fooling. *Ce n'est pour lui qu'un —;* it is mere child's play for him.

badine, *n.f.*, switch; *pl.*, small tongs.

badiner, *v.n.*, to trifle, to dally, to play, to toy, to sport; to wave about. *Il ne badine pas;* he is not joking. *En badinant;* roguishly. *La dentelle est trop tendue, il faut qu'elle badine un peu;* the lace is too tight, it must wave about a little.

badinerie, *n.f.*, silly stuff, foolery, trifling.

bafouer, *v.a.*, to scout, to scoff at, to baffle. *On l'a bafoué;* he was scouted. *Il s'est fait —; he* got scoffed at.

bâfre, *n.f.*, (pop.) guttling, blow out.

bâfrer, *v.n.*, (l. ex.) to guttle, to eat greedily, to have a blow out.

bâfreu-r, *n.m.*, **-se,** *n.f.*, (l. ex.) guttler, one who loves guttling.

bagace. *V.* **bagasse.** .

bagage, *n.m.*, luggage, baggage. *Nous avons laissé notre — en arrière;* we have left our luggage behind. *Plier —;* to pack off. *Il a plié —;* he has taken his last journey (died—*mort*).

bagarre, *n.f.*, squabble, scuffle, fray. *Se trouver dans une —;* to get into a fray. *Se tirer d'une —;* to get out of a scuffle.

bagasse, *n.f.*, bagasse, cane trash; hussy, drab, slut.

bagatelle, *n.f.*, bauble, trash, trinket, trifle, nonsense. *Table de —;* bagatelle table. *Il ne s'amuse qu'à des —s;* he has no pleasure but in trifles. *S'amuser à une —;* to stand trifling. *Bagatelle!* nonsense!

*bagne, n.m., bagnio (prison).

☉***bagnolette**, n.f., a head-dress (for ladies —de dames).

bague (bag), n.f., ring. — gravée en cachet; seal-ring. —s et joyaux, jewels and ornaments. Course de —; running at the ring. Jeu de —; roundabout.

baguenaude (bag-nôd), n.f., bladder-nut.

baguenauder (bag-nô-).v.n.,to mind trifles, to trifle time away, to stand trifling.

baguenaudier (bag-nô), n.m., bladder-nut-tree, bastard senna tree; trifler; ring-puzzle.

baguer (ba-ghé), v.a., to baste, to stitch.

bagues, n.f. pl., (l.u.) luggage.

baguette (ba-ghèt), n.f., switch, rod, ramrod, drum-stick, small stick, wand; pl., (milit.) gauntlet; (arch.) baguet. Ce cheval obéit à la —; that horse obeys the switch. — à gant; glovestick. —s de tambour; drum-sticks. Coup de —; beat of the drum. — de fusée volante; stick of a rocket. — d'or; golden stick. — d'huissier; usher's rod. — divinatoire; conjuror's wand. Commander à la —; to command magisterially. Passer par les —s; to run the gauntlet.

baguier (ba-ghié), n.m., casket for rings.

bah, int., pooh, pshaw.

bahut, n.m., trunk, chest.

bahutier, n.m., trunk-maker.

bai, -e, adj., bay. Un cheval —; a bay-horse. — châtain; of a chesnut colour. — miroité; dapple bay.

baie, n.f., bay, gulf, road; (arch.) bay; (bot.) berry; ☉humbug, trick. Donner une — à quelqu'un; to humbug one.

*baigné, -e, part., bathed, weltering; (geog.) washed. On l'a trouvé — dans son sang; he was found weltering in his blood. Des yeux —s de larmes; eyes bathed in tears. Être — de sueur; to be suffused in sweat.

*baigner, v.a., to bathe, to give a bath, to wash. Faire — les chevaux; to wash horses.

se **baigner**, v.r., to bathe, to wash; to welter (in blood—dans le sang). Se — dans le sang; to delight in blood.

*baigner, v.n., to soak; to be steeped.

*baigneu-r, n.m., -se, n.f., bather; bathkeeper.

☉***baignoir**, n.m., bathing-place.

*baignoire, n.f., bathing-tub; bath; corner box (thea.).

*bail, n.m., (baux) lease. — à ferme; lease of ground. — à long terme; long lease. Donner à —; to lease. Passer un —; to draw up a lease. Rompre, résilier, un —; to break, to throw up, a lease. Cela n'est pas de mon —; I did not agree for that.

baile, n.m., formerly the name given to the Venetian Ambassador to the Porte.

*baille, n.f., (nav.) half tub. — de sonde; bucket to hold the plummet and line on deck ready for sounding.

*bâillement, n.m., yawning, yawn; (gram.; l.u.) hiatus.

*bâiller, v.n., to yawn; to gape; to open (fissures); to be on the jar (of doors—portes). On bâille souvent en voyant bâiller les autres; we often yawn at seeing others yawn. Bâiller de sommeil; to yawn with drowsiness.

☉***bailler**, v.a., to give, to deliver. — à ferme; to let, to lease, to farm out. Vous me la baillez belle; you are humbugging me.

*baillet, adj., (of horses—chevaux) light red.

☉***bailleul**, n.m., bone-setter. V. **rebouteur**.

*bâill-eur, n.m., -euse, n.f., yawner; gaper. Un bon — en fait bâiller deux; yawning is catching.

bâill-eur, n.m., -eresse, n.f., one who leases, lessor. Un — de fonds; a money-lender, sleeping partner.

*bailli, n.m., bailiff.

*bailliage, n.m., bailiwick.

*bailliag-er, -ère, adj., pertaining to, peculiar to, a bailiwick.

*baillive, n.f., bailiff's wife.

*bâillon, n.m., gag.

*bâillonner, v.a., to stop the mouth, to gag; to wedge up (a door—une porte).

bain, n.m., bath; bathing-tub; pl., baths, bathing establishment, bathing place, bathing room, waters. — de mer; salt water bath. — à domicile; bath at home. — de siège; sitting bath. — de vapeur; vapour bath. — de pieds; foot bath. — de sable; sand bath. — chaud, froid; warm, cold bath. La chambre de —; the bath room. L'ordre du —; the Order of the Bath.

bain-marie, n.m., (chem.) water-bath; warming anything in a vessel immersed in boiling water.

baïonnette, n.f., bayonet. Mettre la — au bout du fusil; to fix bayonets. —s au canon! fix bayonets! Croiser la —; to cross bayonets. Charger à la —; to charge with bayonets. Enlever un poste à la —; to carry a post at the point of the bayonet.

baïoque, n.f., small Papal coin worth about a halfpenny.

baïram or **beiram**, n.m., Bairam (name of two Mahometan festivals—nom de deux fêtes mahométanes).

☉**baisemain**, n.m., vassalage; kissing (of hands—de mains); pl., compliments, respects, commendations.

baisement, n.m., kissing (of the Pope's feet —des pieds du pape); (geom.) osculation.

baiser, v.a., to kiss. — sur la bouche; to kiss the lips. — les mains d'une femme; to kiss a lady's hands.

baiser, n.m., kiss, salute. Un — de Judas; a treacherous kiss.

baiseu-r, n.m., -se, n.f., kisser.

baisoter, v.a., to be always kissing.

baisse, n.f., fall, abatement, diminution in value. En —; (com.) on the decline. Jouer à la —; to bear, to speculate on a fall. Subir une —; to suffer a decline.

baissé, -e, part., down, let down, lowered. Il marchait les yeux —s; he walked with downcast eyes. Se retirer tête —e; to sneak away. Donner tête —e dans le péril; to plunge headlong into danger.

baisser, v.a., to let down, to lower, to bring down, to hang down; to droop; (nav.) to lower, to strike. Elle baissa son voile; she let down her veil. — le rideau; to drop the curtain. — la visière d'un casque; to lower the beaver of a helmet. — le drapeau; to lower the colours. — pavillon; to strike one's flag; to knock under to one. — les yeux; to cast one's eyes down. — la tête; to hold, hang, down, to droop one's head.

baisser, v.n., to lower, to wear, to break, to fail, to decay; to go down; to ebb; to be on the decline, on the wane; to flag, to droop; to fall. Le jour baisse; the day wears apace. Ce vieillard baisse; this old man is breaking. Sa vue commence à —; his sight begins to fail. Il baisse à vue d'œil; he decays visibly. Son génie baisse; his genius is on the decline. Ce malade baisse; the patient droops. Les actions baissent; there is a fall in the shares. Les fonds baissent; the funds fall.

se **baisser**, v.r., to stoop; to bow down, to be lowered.

baissier, n.m., bear, stock-jobber, speculator on a fall.

baissière, n.f., what remains at the bottom of a cask of wine, &c.

baisure, n.f., kissing-crust.

☉**bajoire**, n.f., double-faced coin.

bajoue, n.f., hog's cheek.

bajoyer, n.m., lateral wall of a canal-lock.

bal, n.m., ball. — masqué; masquerade. — paré; dress-ball. — bourgeois; private ball. —champêtre; country ball. Donner le — à quelqu'un; to make one dance for it. Fermer un —; to break up a ball.

baladin, n.m., -e, n.f., mountebank, juggler, buffoon.

baladinage, n.m., merry-andrew's witticism.

balafre, n.f., gash, slash; scar.

balafrer, v.a., to gash, to slash.

balai, n.m., broom, brush, besom. — de jonc; carpet-broom. — de crin; hair-broom. — de plume; duster. — à laver; mop. Manche à —; broom-stick. Donner un coup de —; to sweep up. Rôtir le —; to play one's pranks, to lead a fast life. — du ciel; (nav.) north-east wind.

balais, adj., balass. Un rubis —; a balass ruby.

balance, n.f., balance, scales, pair of scales; balance (of an account—de compte); balance-sheet; (astron.) Libra. — romaine; steelyard. Trait de la —; turn of the scale. — juste; good scales. Arrêter une —; to agree a balance. Réaliser une —; to withdraw a balance. Faire pencher la —; to turn the scale. Mettre en —; to balance. Ses droits peuvent-ils entrer en — avec les miens? can his claims be weighed in the same scale with mine? Être en — ; to be irresolute. Cela tient l'esprit en —; that makes one irresolute.

balancé, n.m., (dance—danse) setting to one's partner.

balancelle, n.f., (nav.) felucca.

balancement (-män), n.m., rocking, see-saw, fluctuation.

balancer, v.a., to balance; to swing, to wave, to weigh, to counterbalance, to rock. to square (accounts—des comptes). — un javelot; to poise a javelin. Se —; to swing. Cette femme se balance trop en marchant; that woman swings too much in her walk. Un oiseau qui se balance dans l'air; a bird hovering in the air. — les avantages et les inconvénients; to weigh the advantages and disadvantages. — les pertes par le gain; to balance the loss by the profit. Ses vertus balancent tous ses vices; his virtues counterbalance all his vices. — la victoire; to keep the victory in doubt. — un compte; to balance an account.

balancer, v.n., to balance, to hesitate, to be in suspense, to waver, to fluctuate, to demur. Il balança s'il accepterait la place qu'on lui offrait; he hesitated whether he should accept the situation offered him. Il y a consenti sans —; he consented to it without hesitating. Il n'y a pas à —; there is no room for hesitating.

se balancer, v.r., to swing, to rock; (in walking—en marchant) to waddle; to balance; to be counterbalanced.

balancier, n.m., scale-maker; pendulum, balance; (coin.) coining-engine; balancing-pole. Le — d'une horloge; the pendulum of a clock. Le — d'un tourne-broche; the flyer of a roasting jack. Le — d'une machine à vapeur; the beam of a steam-engine. Le — transversal d'une machine à vapeur; cross-beam of an engine.

balancine, n.f., (nav.) lift.

balançoire, n.f., see-saw; swing.

balandran or **balandras**, n.m., great-coat, cloak for foul weather.

balane, n.m., (conch.) acorn-shell.

balauste, n.f., balaustine, wild pomegranate.

balaustier, n.m., wild pomegranate-tree.

balayage, n.m., sweeping.

balayer, v.a., to sweep. Sa robe balaie la terre; her gown sweeps the ground. Le vent balaie la plaine; the wind sweeps the plain.

balayeu-r, n.m., -se, n.f., scavenger, sweeper.

balayures, n.f. pl., sweepings. — de mer; sea-weed washed on shore.

balbutiement (-si-män), n.m., stuttering. stammering.

balbutier (-cié), v.a. and n., to lisp, to stammer. Un enfant qui commence à —; a child beginning to lisp. La confusion le fit rougir et —; confusion made him blush and stammer. Elle balbutia quelques mots; she lisped a few words. — un compliment; to stammer out a compliment.

balbuzard, n.m., bald-buzzard, fishing eagle.

balcon, n.m., balcony.

baldaquin, n.m., baldachin; (arch.) canopy.

bâle, **bale**, or **balle**, n.f., (bot.) glume, chaff, husk.

baleine, n.f., whale. Barbe de —; whalebone. Huile de —; whale oil. La pêche de la —; the whale fishery. Blanc de —; spermaceti.

baleiné, -e, adj., with whalebone. Un corset —; whalebone stays. Un col —; a whalebone collar.

baleineau, n.m., young whale.

baleinier, n.m., adj., whaler. Un navire —; a whale-ship.

baleinière, n.f., whaler's boat.

balénas, n.m., pizzle of a whale.

baleston, n.m., (nav.) sprit.

⊙**balèvre**, n.f., under lip; (arch.) jutting or projection of one stone beyond another.

bali, n.m. V. pali.

balisage, n.m., (nav.) establishing of buoys, of beacons.

balise, n.f., (nav.) sea-mark, buoy, beacon; (bot.) the fruit of the shot.

baliser, v.a., (nav.) to buoy, to erect beacons.

baliseur, n.m., water-bailiff.

balisier, n.m., (bot.) shot, American reed.

baliste, n.f., war machine, ballista; (ich.) balistes.

balistique, n.f., ballistics.

balivage, n.m., staddling.

baliveau, n.m., staddle.

baliverne, n.f., nonsense, humbug, stuff. Il vous conte des —s; he talks nonsense to you.

baliverner, v.n., to trifle, to talk idly, to fiddle-faddle.

ballade, n.f., ballad.

ballage, n.m., (metal) balling.

ballant, adj., waving, swinging. Il marche les bras —s; he swings his arms in walking.

ballast, n.m., (railways) ballasting.

balle, n.f., ball; bullet, shot; husk of rice; bale, pack; (print.) ball. A vous la —; it is your turn. Jouer à la —; to play at ball. Prendre la — à la volée; to hit the ball in the air. Prendre la — au bond; to take the ball at the rebound; to improve the opportunity. Enfants de la —; children following the business of their father. Renvoyer la —; to return the ball, to give tit for tat. Fusil chargé à —; a musket loaded with ball. —s ramées; chain-shot. — morte; spent shot. — au camp; rounders (boy's game—jeu de garçons). Marchandise de —; goods of no value. V. bale.

⊙**baller**, v.n., to hop, to skip, to dance.

ballet, n.m., ballet.

ballon, n.m., balloon; football. Faire une ascension en —; to make an ascent in a balloon.

ballonné, -e, adj., distended, swollen.

ballonnement (-män), n.m., (med.) swelling.

ballonnier, n.m., football-maker.

ballot, n.m., bale, package. *Voilà votre —;* that will suit you exactly.

ballote, n.f., (bot.) horehound, marrubium.

ballotin, n.m., small parcel, packet.

ballottade, n.f., (man.) ballotade.

ballottage, n.m., balloting.

⊙**ballotte**, n.f., ballot. *V.* **boule**.

ballottement (-män), n.m., shaking.

ballotter, v.a., to toss, to toss about; to bandy (a tennis-ball—*la balle, à la paume*); to debate; to ballot. *— quelqu'un;* to toss one from pillar to post.

ballotter, v.n.. to shake. *Cette porte ballotte;* that door shakes.

balourd, n.m., -e, n.f., numskull, dunce.

balourd, -e, adj.. dull,heavy, thick-headed.

balourdise, n.f., stupidity, heaviness, doltishness; stupid thing.

balsamier, n.m. *V.* **baumier**.

balsamine (-za-), n.f., balsamine.

balsamique (-za-), adj., balsamic, balsamical.

balsamite (-za-). *V.* **tanaisie**.

balustrade, n.f., balustrade.

balustre, n.m., a baluster.

balustrer, v.a., to ornament with a baluster.

balzan, adj., (man.) trammelled, cross-trammelled.

balzane, n.f., (man.) whitefoot, white spot, blaze.

bambin, n.m., baby, brat, bantling.

bambochade, n.f., (paint.) scene, sketch of low life.

bamboche, n.f., (pop.) puppet; shrimp (person—*personne*); drinking bout, spree; young bamboo, bamboo-cane. *Faire une —;* to have a spree. *Faire des —s;* to lead a disorderly life.

bambocheu-r, n.m., -se, n.f., (pop.) libertine.

bambou, n.m., bamboo-cane, bamboo.

ban, n.m., ban; public proclamation; ban (of matrimony—*de mariage*); banishment. *Dispense de —s;* marriage license. *Mettre au —;* to send to Coventry. *Rompre son —;* to break one's ban.

banal, -e, adj., belonging to a manor, common; common-place; mercenary. *Expression —e;* vulgar, common-place expression.

⊙**banalité**, n.f., (feud. law) socome (privilege of the lord of a manor—*privilège seigneurial*); a common-place, a trite expression.

banane, n.f., banana.

bananier, n.m., banana-tree.

banc (ban), n.m., bench, seat; pew; reef, shoal, bank; bed. *Un — à dos;* a bench with a back. *Un — de gazon;* a turf seat. *— d'église;* church seat, pew. *— de l'œuvre;* churchwardens' pew. *Il est encore sur les —s;* he is still at college. *Échouer sur un — de sable;* to run aground on a sand bank. *Un — de corail;* a coral reef. *Un — de harengs;* a shoal of herrings. *Un — d'huîtres;* a bed of oysters. *— de pierre;* layer, bed, of stone.

bancal, -e, adj., bandy-legged.

⊙**bancelle**, n.f., long narrow form, seat.

banche, n.f., clay and sand bank under water.

banco, adj., banco (a term used in exchange business—*terme de banque*); one staking against many (gambling expression—*terme de jeu*).

bancroche, adj., (fam.) bandy-legged, rickety.

bandage, n.m., (surg.) bandage; employment of bandages; belt; truss; tire (of wheels —*de roues*); hoop. *— herniaire;* truss. *Délier un —; -*to undo a bandage.

bandagiste, n.m., truss-maker.

bandana, n.m., bandana, bandanna.

bande, n.f., band, belt, strip; company; gang; set of people, crew; flight; troop; (her.) bend; (arch.) fascia. string; (anat.) tract. *— de papier;* a slip of paper. *La — d'une selle;* the side bar of a saddle. *La — d'un billard;* the cushion of a billiard-table. *Une — de voleurs;* a gang of thieves. *Une — de musiciens;* a company of musicians. *Une — joyeuse;* a set of merry people. *Ces oiseaux vont par —s;* those birds go in flights. *Faire — à part;* to keep apart. *Donner à la —;* (nav.) to heel. *Demi-—;* parliament-heel of a ship.

bandé, -e, part., (her.) bendy.

bandeau, n.m., headband, fillet, frontlet, bandage; veil, mist; (arch.) string-course. *Avoir un — sur les yeux;* to be blindfolded.

bandelette, n.f., little band, string, fillet; (surg.) fascia; (arch.) bandelet.

bander, v.a., to bind up; to tighten, to bend; to bandy (at tennis—*à la paume*); (arch.) to lay the stones of an arch. *— une plaie;* to bind up a wound. *Se — la tête;* to bind up one's head. *Se — les yeux;* to blindfold one's self.

bander, v.n., to be stretched, tight, taut.

⊙se **bander**, v.r., to oppose, to resist.

bandereau (ban-dro), n.m., trumpet-string.

banderole (ban-drol), n.f., bandrol, streamer, small flag; shoulder-belt.

bandière, n.f., (milit.) front. *Front de —;* line of battle in front of a camp. ⊙Banner, flag.

bandit, n.m., vagrant, vagabond, bandit.

⊙**bandoulier**, n.m., highwayman; mountaineer.

bandoulière, n.f., shoulder-belt, bandoleer. *Porter la —;* to be a game-keeper.

bandure, n.f., (bot.) bandura.

bang, n.m., (bot.) bangue.

banian, n.m., Banian (idolater in India—*idolâtre indien*).

banlieue, n.f., outskirts (of a town—*d'une ville*).

bannatte or **bannasse**, n.f., tallow sieve or strainer.

banne, n.f., awning, tilt; hamper (of boats —*de bateaux*).

banneau, n.m., small hamper, fruit basket.

banner, v.a., to cover with a tilt.

banneret (-rè), adj., having the charge of the banner, banneret. *Chevalier —;* knight banneret.

banneton, n.m., (fishing—*pêche*) cauf.

bannette, n.f., small hamper.

banni, -e, part., banished, outlawed.

bannière, n.f., banner, standard, flag. *Se ranger sous la — de quelqu'un;* to side with one. *Aller au-devant de quelqu'un avec la croix et la —;* to give one a handsome reception.

bannir, v.a., to banish, to expel, to dismiss. *— un ingrat de sa mémoire;* to banish an ingrate from one's memory.

bannissable, adj., deserving banishment.

bannissement (-män) n.m., banishment.

banque, n.f., bank, banking-business; (print. office—*imprimerie*) wages. *Carnet de —;* bank book. *Mandat de la —;* bank-post-bill. *— succursale;* branch bank. *— particulière;* private bank. *Compte de —;* bank account. *Assignation de —;* bank-transfer. *Mettre à la —;* to put in the bank. *Faire la —;* to be a banker. *Action de la —;* bank-stock. *Billet de — de cinq livres;* a five pound bank note. *Avoir un compte en —;* to have an account open at the bank. *Faire sauter la —;* to break the bank.

banqueroute (ban-kroot), n.f., bankruptcy. *— frauduleuse;* fraudulent bankruptcy. *Faire*

—; to be bankrupt. *Faire — à quelqu'un;* not to keep one's word with any one. *Faire — à l'honneur;* to forfeit one's honour.

banqueroutier, *n.m.,* **-ère,** *n.f.,* bankrupt.

banquet, *n.m.,* banquet, feast.

banqueter, *v.n.,* to banquet, to feast.

banquette, *n.f.,* bench; (fort.) banquette; outside (of a coach—*d'une diligence*); footway (of a road—*d'une route*). *Jouer devant les —s;* (theat.) to play to empty benches.

banquier, *n.m.,* money-agent, banker.

banquise, *n.f.,* ice-berg.

bans, *n.m, pl.,* (hunt.) litter for dogs.

bantam, *n.m.,* bantam.

banvin, *n.m.,* (feudal law—*loi féodale*) right which the lord had alone to sell wine in his parish, during an appointed time.

baobab, *n.m.,* (bot.) baobab.

baptême (ba-têm). *n.m.,* Baptism, christening. *Nom de —;* Christian name. *Extrait de —;* certificate of baptism. *Recevoir le —;* to be baptized. *Tenir un enfant sur les fonts de —;* to stand godfather or godmother to a child. *Le — du tropique;* the ceremony of crossing the line, ducking at sea.

baptiser (ba-ti-zé), *v.a.,* to baptize, to christen. *— des cloches;* to consecrate bells. *— un vaisseau;* to give a ship her name. *— quelqu'un;* to give one a nickname. *C'est un enfant bien difficile à —;* it is no easy task.

baptismal. -e, (ba-tis-mal), *adj.,* baptismal.

baptistaire (ba-tis-tèr), *adj.,* of baptism. *Registre —;* parish register. *Extrait —;* certificate of baptism.

baptiste (ba-tist), *n.m.,* baptist; *Saint Jean —;* John the Baptist.

baptistère (ba-tis-tèr), *n.m.,* baptistery.

baquet, *n.m.,* tub, trough.

bar, *n.m.,* (ich.) umbrina.

baragouin, *n.m.,* gibberish. *Je ne comprends pas son —;* I don't understand his gibberish.

baragouinage, *n.m.,* gibberish; rigmarole.

baragouiner, *v.n.,* to talk gibberish; to gabble. *Comme ces étrangers baragouinent;* how these foreigners gabble.

baragouiner, *v.a.,* to sputter out. *— un discours;* to sputter out a speech. *— une langue;* to mangle a language.

baragouineu-r, *n.m.,* **-se,** *n.f.,* jabberer.

baraque, *n.f.,* barrack, hut; shed, hovel.

baraquement, *n.m.,* (milit.) hutting.

baraquer, *v.a.,* to make barracks; to hut.

se baraquer, *v.r.,* (milit.) to make huts.

baraterie, *n.f.,* (nav.) barratry.

baratte, *n.f.,* churn.

baratter, *v.a.,* to churn.

barbacane, *n.f.,* (fort.) barbacan; outlet.

⊙**barbacole,** *n.m.,* pedagogue, schoolmaster.

barbare, *adj.,* savage, merciless, barbarous, rude; barbarian. *C'est un peuple —;* they are a barbarous people. *Des mœurs rudes et —s;* rude and barbarous manners.

barbare, *n.m.,* barbarian.

barbarement (-män), *adv.,* barbarously.

barbaresque, *adj.,* of Barbary.

barbarie, *n.f.,* barbarity, rudeness, savageness. *Commettre une —;* to commit a piece of barbarity. *— de langage, de style;* barbarity of language, of style.

barbarisme, *n.m.,* (gram.) barbarism.

barbe, *n.f.,* beard; whiskers (of cats, dogs, &c.—*de chats, de chiens, &c.*); (vet.) barbel; lappet (of caps—*de bonnets*); (arts) rough edge; beard (of corn, barley, &c.—*de blé, &c.*); gills (of cocks—*de coqs*); wattle (of fish—*de poisson*). *Jours de —;* shaving days. *— bleue;* blue beard. *Sainte —;* (nav.) gun-room. *Jeune —;* beardless boy. *Vieille —;* old man. *Se faire la —;* to shave one's self. *Se faire faire la —;* to get one's self shaved. *Je le lui dirai à sa —;* I'll tell

it to his face. *Faire la — à quelqu'un;* to abuse one. *Rire dans sa —;* to laugh in one's sleeve. *La — d'une plume;* the feather of a quill. *Mouiller en —;* (nav.) to come with two anchors ahead. *— d'une coiffe;* pinner. *— -de-bouc;* (bot.) goat's beard, tragopogon. *— -de-Jupiter;* Jupiter's beard. *— -de-chèvre;* meadow sweet. *— -de-moine;* dodder. *— -de-capucin;* bleached dandelion.

barbe. *n.m.,* barb, Barbary horse.

barbé, -e, *adj.,* (her.) barbed, bearded; (bot.) barbated.

barbeau, *n.m.,* (ich.) barbel; (bot.) blue-bottle.

barbelé, -e. *adj.,* bearded, barbed. *Flèche —e;* bearded arrow.

barbet, *n.m.,* **-te,** *n.f.,* water spaniel. *Ce va bien à l'eau;* that spaniel takes water well. *Être crotté comme un —;* to be as dirty as can be.

barbette, *n.f.,* (milit.) barbette. *Tirer en —;* to fire in barbe, in barbette.

barbeyer, *v.a.,* (nav.) to shiver.

barbiche, *n.f.,* a tuft of beard under and on the chin.

barbichon, *n.m.,* shaggy spaniel puppy.

barbier, *n.m.,* barber, shaver.

barbifier, *v.a.,* (fam.) to shave. *Se faire —;* to get shaved. *Sé —,* *v.r.,* to shave one's self.

*****barbillon,** *n.m.,* a little barbel; gills (of a cock—*du coq*); wattle (of a fish, a turkey—*des poissons, du dindon*).

*****barbillons,** *n.m. pl.,* (vet.) barbles.

barbon, *n.m.,* graybeard, dotard; (bot.) sweet rush. *— odorant;* lemon grass.

barbote, *n.f.,* (ich.) eel-pout, loach, groundling.

barboter, *v.n.,* to dabble; (nav.) to shiver. *Des canes qui barbotent dans une mare;* ducks dabbling in a puddle.

barboteur, *n.m.,* tame duck.

barboteuse, *n.f.,* (l. ex.) dirty drab; street-walker.

barbotine, *n.f.,* (bot.) wormseed; the dried buds of artemisia.

*****barbouillage,** *n.m.,* daub, daubing; scrawl; rigmarole.

*****barbouillé, -e,** *part.,* daubed, besmeared.

*****barbouiller,** *v.a.,* to daub, to besmear; to soil, to dirty, to blot; to scrawl, to scribble; to slur; to stammer, to sputter out; to mumble; to stumble, to flounder; to bungle. *Il lui a barbouillé le visage;* he has besmeared his face for him. *On l'a tout barbouillé d'encre;* they have daubed him all over with ink. *— un plancher;* to daub a floor. *Il n'écrit pas, il barbouille;* he does not write, he scrawls. *Il ne peint pas, il barbouille;* he does not paint, he daubs. *— un compliment;* to stammer out a compliment. *— Qu'est-ce qu'il barbouille?* what is he mumbling? *— un récit;* to make a bungle of a story. *— une feuille;* (print.) to slur a sheet.

*****se barbouiller,** *v.r.,* to besmear, to harm one's self.

*****barbouilleur,** *n.m.,* dauber, scribbler; mumbler, babbler.

barbu, -e, *adj.,* bearded; (bot.) barbate, bearded.

barbu, *n.m.,* (orni.) barbet.

barbue, *n.f.,* (ich.) brill.

⊙**barcade,** *n.f.,* embarkation of horses.

barcarolle, *n.f.,* barcarolle.

⊙**barce** or **berche,** *n.f.,* a small cannon.

barcelonnette, *n.f.,* child's cradle.

bard, *n.m.,* hand-barrow.

bardane, *n.f.,* (bot.) bur, burdock.

barde. *n.f.,* barb (iron-armour for horses—*armure pour les chevaux*); thin, broad slice of bacon.

barde, *n.m.*, bard, poet.

bardé, -e, *part.*, barded; covered with a thin, broad slice of bacon, larded. *Un cheval — et caparaçonné;* a horse barded and caparisoned. *Chapon —;* larded capon.

bardeau, *n.m.*, shingle (board—*ais*); (bot.) mealy-tree; (print.) fount-case.

bardelle, *n.f.*, bardelle. a kind of saddle.

barder, *v.a.*, to cover a fowl with a thin, broad slice of bacon, to lard; to barb a horse; to remove stones, wood, &c., on a handbarrow.

bardeur, *n.m.*, day-labourer (who carries the handbarrow—*employé à brouetter*).

bardis. *n.m.*, (nav.) water-board, partition in the hold.

bardit, *n.m.*, (antiq.) war song of the ancient Germans.

bardot. *n.m.*, small mule; drudge.

barège, *n.m.*, barege.

barème, *n.m.*, ready reckoner.

baret, *n.m.*, roaring of an elephant.

bareter, *v.n.*, to roar like an elephant.

barge, *n.f.*, (orni.) godwit; (nav.) a barge.

barguette (-ghèt), *n.f.*, small barge.

*****barguignage** (-ghi-gnaj), *n.m.*, (fam.) hesitating, haggling, wavering.

*****barguigner** (-ghi-gné), *v.n.*, to be irresolute, to haggle, to waver.

*****barguigneu-r**, *n.m.*, **-se**, *n.f.*, haggler.

barigel, *n.m.*. chief of the archers in Rome and other towns of Italy.

baril (-ri), *n.m.*, barrel, cask.

*****barille**. *n.f.*, barilla.

*****barillet**, *n.m.*, rundlet; bow; barrel of a watch.

bariolage, *n.m.*, variegation, odd medley of colours.

barioler, *v.a.*, to streak with several colours, to variegate.

bariquaut, *n.m. V.* **barriquaut**.

baritel, *n.m.*, winding engine. *— à chevaux;* horse-whim, whim-gin.

barlong, -ue, *adj.*, longer on one side than on the other.

barnabite, *n.m.*, monk. barnabite.

barnache, *n.f.*, (orni.) barnacle.

baromètre, *n.m.*, barometer, weather-glass. *Le — est au beau temps;* the barometer is at fair.

barométrique. *adj.*, barometrical.

baron, *n.m.*, baron.

baronnage, *n.m.*, baronage.

baronne, *n.f.*, baroness.

baronnet, *n.m.*, baronet. *Chevalier —;* knight baronet.

baronnial, -e, *adj.*. baronial.

baronnie, *n.f.*, barony.

baroque, *adj.*, rough, irregular, uncouth, odd, singular, strange.

barque, *n.f.*, bark, boat, craft; barge. *— de pêcheur;* fishing boat. *Conduire la —;* to steer the boat. *Il conduit bien sa —;* he is getting on very well. *Il sait bien conduire sa —;* he knows how to conduct his self. *Patron de —;* barge-master.

barquée. *n.f*, boatful of any goods or stores.

barquerolle, *n.f.*, small barge used on the Adriatic Sea.

barrage. *n.m.*. toll-bar; barrier; dam; weir.

barrager, *n.m.*. toll-gatherer.

barras. *n.m. V.* **galipot**.

barre. *n.f.*. bar (of metal or wood—*de métal ou de bois*); cross-bar; railing; bolt; division; lever, crow; dash; (nav.) helm, tiller, bar; stripe; (mus.) bar; bar (of courts of judicature, public assemblies—*des tribunaux, des assemblées publiques*). *Avoir —s sur quelqu'un;* to have the advantage over any one. *Jouer aux —s;* to play at base (a game—*jeu de garçons*). *— sous le vent!* (nav.) helm alee! (man.) *—s.* bars.

barré, *part. V.* **dent**.

barreau, *n.m.*.. bar (for closing—*de clôture*); bar (place reserved for barristers—*place réservée aux avocats*); lawyers, counsellors; splat (of chairs—*de chaises*). *Fréquenter le —;* to attend the courts. *Suivre le —;* to be a barrister.

barrer, *v.a.*, to bar; to bar up; to fence up; to obstruct; to stop up; to cancel; to dash over; to cross off; (her.) to bar; (vet.) to knit fast (a vein—*une veine*).

barrette, *n.f.*, man's cap; cardinal's cap.

barricade, *n.f.*, barricade.

barricader, *v.a.*, to barricade.

barrière, *n.f.*, rail, bar, barrier, stile; starting post.

barriquaut, *n.m.*, keg.

barrique, *n.f.*, large barrel or cask, hogshead.

barrot, *n.m.*, (nav.) beam.

barroté, -e, *adj.*, (of a vessel—*d'un vaisseau*) full to the beams.

barroter, *v.a.*, (nav.) to load. *— un vaisseau;* to load a vessel up to the beams.

barrotin, *n.m.*, (nav.) lodge (put across the deck beam—*placé entre les baux du pont*).

bartavelle, *n.f.*, red partridge.

baryte, *n.f.*, baryta.

baryton, *n.m.*, (mus.) barytone; (Greek gram.) barytone.

bas, -se, *adj.*, not high, low; shallow; vile, mean, despicable; abject, sordid; low, lower; inferior. *La marée est —se;* it is low water. *—se mer;* low water. *Une rivière —se;* a shallow river. *Les eaux sont —ses chez lui;* he is at a low ebb. *Faire des actions —ses;* to do low things. *Des sentiments —;* mean sentiments. *Une —se flatterie;* mean flattery. *Avoir l'âme —se;* to have a sordid soul. *Le — peuple;* the mob. the common people. *Parler d'un ton —;* to speak with a low voice. *Avoir le cœur haut et la fortune —se;* to have more spirit than fortune. *Avoir la vue —se;* to be short-sighted. *Une messe —se;* a low mass. *— étage;* lower story. *Une —se-fosse;* a dungeon. *Ce — monde;* this lower world. *Les Pays-Bas;* the Netherlands. *Le Bas-Rhin;* the Lower Rhine. *La Basse-Saxe;* Lower Saxony. *Les — officiers;* the inferior officers. *J'ai acheté cela à — prix;* I bought that at a very low price. *Les —ses cartes;* the small cards. *—se naissance;* mean birth. *Le — bout d'une chose;* the lower end of a thing. *La —se latinité;* low Latin. *Faire prendre à quelqu'un un ton plus —;* to make any one lower his tone.

bas, *n.m.*.. lower part; bottom; foot (of a thing—*de quelque chose*); small (of the leg—*de la jambe*). *Le — du visage;* the lower part of the face. *Le — de l'escalier;* the foot of the stairs. *Il y a du haut et du — dans la vie;* there are ups and downs in life. *Être au —;* to be low (of liquids in casks—*de liquides en tonneaux*). *Sa voix est belle dans le —;* (mus.) his voice is excellent in the lower notes.

bas, *adv.*. down. low. *A —!* down with. *A — le tyran!* down with the tyrant! *A — les ministres!* down with the ministers! *Au plus —;* at the very lowest. *Bien —;* very low. *En —;* below, down stairs. *Être à —;* to be ruined. *Être — percé;* to be short of. to be run aground for. money. *Chapeaux —!* hats off! *Jeter —;* to throw down. *Ici —;* here below. *Là —;* over there, over the way. yonder. *Le malade est encore bien —;* the patient is still dangerously ill. *Mettre —;* (of animals—*des animaux*) to bring forth. to whelp. to foal. to cub. to lamb. to pup, to kitten; to lay down; to take off. *Parler —;* to speak low. *Regarder, traiter, quelqu'un du haut en —;*

to look at, to treat, any one contemptuously. *Tenir —;* to keep in submission, to keep under.

bas, *n.m.,* stocking. *— bleu;* blue-stocking (literary woman—*femme auteur*). *— à côtes, à jour;* ribbed, open-worked, stocking. *— de laine, de soie;* woollen, silk, stocking. *Cela vous va comme un — de soie;* it fits you like a glove.

basalte, *n.m.,* a species of black marble; basalt.

basaltique, *adj.,* basaltic.

basane, *n.f.,* sheep-leather.

basané, -e, *adj.,* tawny, sun-burnt, swarthy.

bas-bord, *n.m.* (*n.p.*), (nav.). *V.* **bâbord.**

bascule, *n.f.,* see-saw; weighing-machine; plyer (of a draw-bridge—*d'un pont-levis*); reciprocating motion; rocker (of cradles—*de berceaux*); lever. *Chaise à —;* rocking-chair. *Faire la —;* to see-saw.

basculer, *v.n.,* to see-saw, to tip off (to fall —*tomber*).

bas-dessus, *n.m.* (—), (mus.) low treble.

base, *n.f.,* base, basis, bottom, foundation; ground-work, ground-plot; fort, stock; radix (of logarithms). *De la — au sommet;* from top to bottom. *La — d'un système;* the basis of a system. *— des fondations;* (engineering— *terme d'ingenieur*) footing.

baselle, *n.f.,* (bot.) basella.

baser, *v.a.,* to found, to fix, to base, to ground.

se baser, *v.r.,* to be fixed; to be grounded; to be founded.

bas-fond, *n.m.* (— —*s*), flat; (nav.) shoal, shallow, shallow water.

basilaire, *adj.,* (anat.) basilar.

basilic, *n.m.,* (bot.) basil, sweet basil; (erpetology) basilisk, cockatrice.

basilicon or **basilicum,** *n.m.,* ointment, basilicon.

basilique, *n.f.,* (anat., arch.) basilic, basilica.

basilique, *adj.,* (anat.) basilical.

basiliques, *n.f. pl.,* Basilic Constitutions.

basin, *n.m.,* dimity.

basique, *adj.,* (chem.) basic.

bas-métier, *n.m.* (— —*s*), (manu.) hand-frame.

○**basoche,** *n.f.,* basoche (company and jurisdiction of lawyers—*gens de robe*).

basque, *n.m.f.,* Biscayan; Basque (nation and language—*nation et langue*).

basque, *n.f.,* flap, skirt, tail, of a garment. *Être toujours pendu à la — de quelqu'un;* to be always after one.

basquine, *n.f.,* upper petticoat worn by Spanish women.

bas-relief, *n.m.* (— —*s*), (sculpt.) basso-relievo, bas-relief.

basse, *n.f.,* (mus.) bass, bass-string. *— continue;* thorough-bass. *Contre- —;* double-bass.

basse, *n.f.,* (nav.) shallow, flat, shoal, ridge of rocks, sand-bank, breaker.

basse-contre, *n.f.* (—*s* —), (mus.) bass-counter, lower tenor.

basse-cour, *n.f.* (—*s* —*s*), inner court, poultry-yard.

basse-étoffe, *n.f.* (*n.p.*), mixture of lead and pewter.

basse-fosse, *n.f.* (—*s* —*s*), dungeon.

basse-marche, *n.f.* (*n.p.*), treadle (for weaving—*pour tisserand*).

bassement, (bâs-mân), *adv.,* meanly, pitifully, poorly, despicably, vilely. *Se conduire —;* to conduct one's self meanly. *Louer —;* to flatter fawningly. *Il s'exprime;* he expresses himself vulgarly. *Penser —;* to have ignoble ideas.

bassesse, *n.f.,* baseness, meanness, vileness, littleness, villany, servileness; mean,

sordid, action. *Avec —;* meanly. *Faire une —;* to do a base action.

basset, *n.m.,* (mam.) terrier; turnspit.

basset, -te. *n.* and *adj.,* of low stature.

***basse-taille,** *n.f.* (—*s* —*s*), (mus.) bass; (sculpt.) bas-relief. *V.* **baryton** and **bas-relief.**

bassette, *n.f.,* basset (game at cards—*jeu de cartes*).

basse-voile, *n.f.* (—*s* —*s*), (nav.) lower sail of a ship.

bassin, *n.m.,* basin; pond; (anat.) pelvis; scale (balance); (nav.) -dock. *Droit de —;* dock-due. *Le — d'un port,* the basin of a harbour; wet dock. *Les —s d'une balance,* the scales of a balance. *Cracher au —;* (fig.) to contribute. *Mettre dans le —;* (nav.) to dock.

bassine, *n.f.,* deep, wide pan.

bassiner, *v.a.,* to warm (a bed—*un lit*); to bathe (with warm lotions—*avec une lotion chaude*), to foment, to steep; to water.

bassinet, *n.m.,* pan, fire-pan (of fire-arms— *d'armes à feu*); (bot.) crowfoot; (anat.) calyx.

bassinoire, *n.f.,* warming-pan.

bassiot, *n.m.,* small wooden tub (used by brandy distillers—*employé par les distillateurs*).

basson, *n.m.,* (mus.) bassoon; bassoonist.

○**bastant, -e,** *adj.,* sufficient.

baste, *n.m.,* basto (cards—*terme de jeu de cartes*).

○**baster,** *v.n.,* to suffice. Only employed in, *Baste pour cela;* well, so be it. *Baste!* pooh! nonsense!

○**basterne,** *n.f.,* basterna (ancient French chariot—*ancien char français*).

bastide, *n.f.,* country-house (in the south of France—*dans le midi de la France*).

***bastille,** *n.f.,* Bastile; fortress.

***bastillé, -e,** *adj.,* (her.) having inverted battlements.

bastingage, *n.m.,* (nav.) barricading a ship, netting.

bastingue (-ghe), *n.f.,* quarter-netting.

bastinguer, *v.a.,* (nav.) to barricade.

se bastinguer (-ghé), *v.r.,* (nav.) to barricade, to put up the netting.

bastion, *n.m.,* bastion.

bastionné, -e, (-tio-né) *adj.,* having bastions.

bastonnade, *n.f.,* bastinade, bastinado, drubbing.

bastringue (-ghe). *n.m.,* public-house ball.

bastude, *n.f.,* fishing-net (used in Southern France—*employé dans le midi de la France*).

bas-ventre, *n.m.* (— —*s*), lower part of the abdomen.

○**bat** (bate), *n.m.,* tail of a fish.

bât (bâ), *n.m.,* pack-saddle. *Un cheval de —;* a pack-horse; stupid person. *Vous ne savez pas où le — le blesse;* you know not where the shoe pinches him.

bataclan, *n.m.,* confusion; rattle; crowd.

***bataille,** *n.f.,* battle, fight, engagement; battle array; beggar-my-neighbour (game at cards—*jeu de cartes*). *— rangée;* pitched battle. *Ranger une armée en —;* to draw up an army in battle-array. *Cheval de —;* war-horse. *Livrer —;* to give battle. *Livrer — pour quelqu'un;* to take up the cudgels for any one. *C'est son cheval de —;* it is his sheet-anchor; stronghold.

***batailler,** *v.n.,* to battle, to fight; to struggle hard.

***batailleur, -se,** *adj.,* disputatious.

***bataillon,** *n.m.,* battalion; squadron; (fig.) great number, regiment; *pl.,* army. *Chef de —;* major.

bâtard, -e, *adj.,* bastard, base-born, illegitimate, spurious; mongrel; inclined (of writ

ing—*écriture*). *Chien* —; mongrel. *Fruits*
—*s;* bastard fruit. *Porte* —*e;* house-door.

bâtard, *n.m.*, -**e**, *n.f.*, bastard, natural child.

batardeau, *n.m.*, coffer-dam.

batardière, *n.f.*, slip of a grafted tree.

bâtardise, *n.f.*, bastardy, spuriousness.

⊙**batate** (bot.). *V.* **patate**.

batavique, *adj. V.* **larme**.

batayole, *n.f.*, (nav.) stanchion.

bâté, -e, *part.*, saddled with a pack. *Il n'y
a point d'âne plus mal — que celui du commun;*
public affairs are generally taken less care of
than private ones.

bateau, *n.m.*, boat, barge, bark; frame of a
coach. — *à vapeur;* steamer, steamboat. —
d'agrément; pleasure-boat. — *non ponté;* open
boat. — *pêcheur;* fishing-boat. — *délesteur;*
ballast-boat, lighter. *Porter* —; (of rivers—
des rivières) to be navigable. *Pont de* —*x;*
bridge of boats.

batelage (-laj), *n.m.*, juggling, juggler's
trick. legerdemain ; boating.

batelée (-lée), *n.f.*, boat-load, boatful of
people ; crowd, flock.

batelet (-lè), *n.m.*, a little boat.

bateleu-r, *n.m.*, -**se**, *n.f.*, juggler, buffoon,
mountebank, merry-andrew, vaulter, rope-
dancer.

batelier, *n.m.*, waterman, ferryman, boatman.

batelière, *n.f.*, woman who rows a boat.

bâter, *v.a.*, to load with a pack-saddle.

bâti, *n.m.*, basting (of coats and dresses—
d'habits et de robes).

bâti, -e, *part.*, built. *Un homme bien* —; a
well-built man.

bâtier (-tié), *n.m.*, pack-saddle maker.

batifolage, *n.m.*, romping.

batifoler, *v.n.*, to play, to romp.

batifoleur, *n.m.*, (i.u.) romp.

bâtiment, *n.m.*, building, pile, structure,
edifice, ship, vessel. — *marchand;* merchant,
ship. — *parlementaire;* (nav.) flag of truce.
Emplacement d'un —; ground-plot of a building. — *qui menace ruine;* building ready to
fall.

bâtir, *v.a.*, to build, to raise, to erect, to
rear up; to found; to trump up, to tack, to
baste (linen, cloth—*étoffes*). *C'est — en l'air;*
it is building castles in the air. — *sur le
devant* (triv.); to grow bulky.

bâtisse, *n.f.*, building, construction (in
masonry).

bâtisseur, *n.m.*, (b.s.) builder, one that
loves building; wretched builder.

batiste, *n.f.*, cambric. — *de coton;* imitation muslin. — *de France;* French muslin.

bâton, *n.m.*, stick, staff, cudgel, cane, walking-staff, perch, truncheon ; straight stroke
(writing—*écriture*). — *de canelle;* roll of cinnamon. — *de commandement;* staff of command. — *de pavillon;* flag-staff. *Donner des
coups de* — *à quelqu'un;* to cudgel any one. *Il
l'a menacé du* —; he threatened to cane him.
— *à deux bouts;* quarter-staff. *Tour du* —; by-
profit. *Faire une chose à* —*s rompus;* to do a
thing by fits and starts. *Aller à cheval sur un*
—; to ride on a stick. *Faire mourir sous le* —;
to beat to death. *Jeter des* —*s dans les roues;*
(fig.) to throw bars into one's way, to raise obstacles. *Sauter le* —; to do anything in spite
of one's self.

bâtonnat, *n.m.*, the presidentship of the
order of French advocates.

bâtonner, *v.a.*, to cudgel, to cane, to bastinade; to cross out.

bâtonnet, *n.m.*, cat, tip-cat (boys' game—
jeu de garçons).

bâtonnier, *n.m.*, staff-bearer; president of
the order of French advocates.

bâtonniste, *n.m.*, cudgel-player.

batraciens (-si-in), *n.m. pl.*, (erpetology),
batracians.

battage, *n.m.*, threshing (grain); striking
(metal).

battant, *n.m.*, clapper (of bells—*de cloche*);
leaf (of a table or door—*d'une table, d'une
porte*); fly (of a flag—*de drapeau*).

battant, *adj.*, at work; beating, pelting;
(nav.) ready for battle (of a ship—*d'un vaisseau*). *Porte* —*e;* swing-door. *Tout* —*neuf;*
span new. *Mener quelqu'un tambour* —; to
carry it with a high hand over any one. *Par
une pluie* —*e;* in a pelting rain.

battant-l'œil, *n.m.* (—), woman's cap (for
dishabille—*déshabillé*).

batte, *n.f.*, wooden sabre; beater; washing-
board; (gard.) turf-beetle. — *à beurre;* churn-
staff

battellement (-mân), *n.m.*, house-eaves.

battement (-mân), *n.m.*, clapping (of hands
—*de mains*); stamping (of feet—*de pieds*); flap-
ping (of wings—*d'ailes*); beating (of the heart
—*de cœur*); shuffling (of cards—*de cartes*);
(horl.) beat.

batterie (-rî), *n.f.*, fight; battery; scuffle;
lock (of fire-arms—*d'armes à feu*); beating (of
the drum—*de tambour*); broadside (of a ship—
d'un vaisseau). *Dresser une* —; to erect a battery. — *de cuisine;* kitchen utensils. — *électrique;* electric battery.

batteur, *n.m.*, beater. — *d'or;* goldbeater.
— *en grange;* (agri.) thrasher. — *de pavé;*
rambler, vagabond.

batteuse, *n.f.*, (agri.) thrashing-machine.

battoir, *n.m.*, beetle (of washerwomen—
de blanchisseuse); battledore, racket.

battologie, *n.f.*, tautology.

battologique, *adj.*, tautological.

battre, *v.a.*, to beat, to strike, to bang, to
thrash, to whip (a horse—*un cheval*); to shuffle
(cards—*les cartes*); to gammon; to flag (of a
sail against a mast—*d'une voile contre un mât*).
(agri.) — *en grange;* to thrash. — *un noyer;*
to thrash a walnut-tree. — *du beurre;* to churn
milk. — *monnaie;* to coin money; (fig.) to
raise money. — *le fusil;* to strike a light. —
en retraite; to beat a retreat. — *quelqu'un de
ses propres armes;* to foil a man with his own
weapons. — *la mesure;* to beat time. — *les
cartes;* to shuffle the cards. — *le pavé;* to
ramble about. — *la semelle;* to beat the hoof,
to be upon the tramp. — *le bois;* to beat the
wood for game.

se battre, *v.r.*, to fight, to combat, to scuffle.
Se — à qui aura quelque chose; to scramble
for.

battre, *v.n.*, to beat, to pant, to throb; to
be loose (of a horse-shoe—*d'un fer de cheval*).
Le pouls lui bat; his pulse beats. *Le cœur me
bat;* my heart beats. *Le fer de ce cheval bat;*
the shoe of that horse is loose. — *des mains;*
to applaud. — *de l'aile;* to flutter. — *froid à
quelqu'un;* to give any one the cold shoulder.

battu, -e, *part.*, beaten.

battue, *n.f.*, (hunt.) battue.

batture, *n.f.*, gold-lacquering; *pl.*, (nav.)
flats, shallows.

bau, *n.m.*, (nav.) beam. *Demi —;* half-
beam. *Maître —;* midship-beam.

baud, *n.m.*, stag-hound.

baudet, *n.m.*, ass; sawyer's trestle; stupid
ass.

baudir, *v.a.*, (hunt.) to excite the dogs with
the horn and voice.

baudrier, *n.m.*, baldrick, shoulder-belt, belt.

baudroie, *n.f.*, (ich.) sea-devil, frog-fish.

baudruche, *n.f.*, gold-beater's skin.

bauge, *n.f.*, lair of a wild boar; dirty lodgings; (mas.) pugging-mortar.

baume, *n.m.*, balm; balsam; balm-mint. *Je n'ai pas de foi dans son —;* I have no faith in his talk, promises.

baumier, *n.m.*, balm-tree.

bauque *or* **bauge**, *n.f.*, grass-wrack.

banquière, *n.f.*, (nav.) clamp.

bavard, -e, *adj.*, prating, talkative, loquacious.

bavard, *n.m.*, -e, *n.f.*, prater, blab.

bavardage, *n.m.*, babbling, prattling, garrulity.

bavarder, *v.n.*, to babble, to prattle, to blab, to jabber.

bavarderie, *n.f.*, babbling, prating, garrulity.

bavardin, -e (l.u.). *V.* **bavard**.

bavardiner, *v.n.*, (l.u.) to talk; to prate, to prattle.

bavardise, *n.f.*, (l.u.) babbling, prating.

bavaroise, *n.f.*, bavaroise (an infusion of tea and capillaire—*breuvage*).

bave, *n.f.*, drivel, slaver; foam; slime.

baver, *v.n.*, to drivel, to slabber, to slaver.

bavette, *n.f.*, bib, slabbering-bib. *Tailler des —s;* to gossip.

baveu-x, -se, *adj.*, drivelling, slabbering.

baveu-x, *n.m.*, -se, *n.f.*, driveller.

baveuse, *n.f.*, (ich.) blenny.

bavoché, -e, *part.*, (engr.) uneven.

bavocher, *v.a.*, (engr.) to render uneven.

bavochure, *n.f.*, unevenness.

bavolet, *n.m.*, rustic head-gear.

bavure, *n.f.*, seam (in moulding—*moulage*); blister (on pipes—*tuyaux*).

bayadère, *n.f.*, Bayadère (dancing-girl in the East Indies—*danseuse indienne*). ·

bayart, *n.m.*, hand-barrow.

baye. *V.* **baie**.

⊕**bayer**, *v.n.*, tó gape, to hanker after. — *après les richesses;* to hanker after riches. — *aux corneilles;* to stand gaping in the air.

⊕**bayeu-r**, *n.m.*, -se, *n.f.*, gaper.

bayonnette. *V.* **baionnette**.

bazar, *n.m.*, bazaar.

bazat, *n.m.*, Jerusalem cotton, bazat.

bdollium (-om), *n.m.*, gum resin from the East Indies.

béant, -e, *adj.*, gaping, wide open. *Gouffre —;* open pit. *Bouche —e;* gaping mouth.

béat, *n.m.*, -e. *n.f.*, devout person; (b.s.) sanctimonious individual.

béat, -e, *adj.*, (b.s.) sanctimonious.

béatification, *n.f.*, beatification.

béatifier, *v.a.*, to beatify.

béatifique, *adj.*, beatifical, blissful.

*****béatilles**, *n.f. pl.*, tit-bits, dainty bits.

béatitude. *n.f.*, beatitude, blessedness.

beau *or* **bel, -le**, *adj.* [*Bel* before nouns in the singular beginning with a vowel or *h* mute], beautiful, fine, lovely, handsome; fair; smart, spruce; glorious; lofty, noble; seemly, becoming. *Un beau temps;* fine weather. *Une belle journée;* a fine day. *C'est un beau parleur;* he is a fine-spoken man. *Se faire beau;* to make one's self smart. *Comme vous voilà beau aujourd'hui!* how spruce you are to-day! *Une belle femme;* a handsome woman. *De beaux traits;* handsome features. *Un beau teint;* a fair complexion. *Le beau sexe;* the fair sex. *Le temps se met au beau;* the weather is getting fine. *A beau jeu, beau retour;* one good turn deserves another. *Donner beau jeu à quelqu'un;* to give one good cards, to give one fair play. *Avoir beau jeu;* to have good cards, to have fair play. *Prendre sa belle;* to

seize the opportunity. *Faire un beau coup;* to make a lucky hit. *Une belle âme;* a lofty soul. *Il fait beau à se promener aujourd'hui;* it is fine weather for walking to-day. *Il en fait de belles;* he is doing some pretty foolish things; he is going on at a fine rate, acting wildly. *Il m'en a compté de belles;* he told me a lot of lies. *Il m'en a compté de belles sur votre compte;* he abused you right and left to me. *Belle demande!* a fine thing indeed to ask! *Il l'a échappé belle;* he has had a narrow escape of it. *Charles le Bel;* (of France) Charles the Fair. *Philippe le Bel;* (of France) Philip the Fair. *Philippe le Beau;* (of Spain) Philip the Handsome. *Le beau monde;* the fashionable world. *Mourir de sa belle mort;* to die a natural death. *Au beau milieu;* right in the middle. *La belle plume fait le bel oiseau;* fine feathers make fine birds. *Quel beau temps!* what fine weather!

beau, bel, belle, *adv.*, *De plus belle;* with renewed ardour, more than ever. *Tout beau;* gently, not so quick. *Avoir beau faire;* to try in vain. *J'ai beau faire;* it is in vain that I try. *Avoir beau dire;* to speak in vain. *J'ai beau dire;* it is useless for me to speak. *Bel et bien;* entirely, quite, altogether.

beau, *n.m.*, **belle**, *n.f.*, beauty; beau, belle; charmer.

beaucoup, *adv.*, many, much; a great many, a great deal; deeply; considerably; far. *Avoir — d'argent;* to have much money. *Avoir — d'enfants;* to have many children. *Il a — de patience;* he has a great deal of patience. *A — près;* by a great deal; near. *Il n'est pas à — près aussi riche qu'un tel;* he is not near so rich as so-and-so. *Il s'intéresse — à votre affaire;* he is deeply interested in your case. *De —;* by far. *Vous l'emportez de — sur lui;* you are far superior to him. *Vous le surpassez de —;* you are far beyond him. *Il s'en faut de —;* is very far from. *Il s'en faut de — que son ouvrage soit achevé;* his work is very far from being finished. *A — moins;* for much less.

beau-fils. *n.m.* (*— x —*), son-in-law.

beau-frère, *n.m.* (*—x —s*), brother-in-law.

beau-partir, *n.m.* (*u.p.*). (man.) *— de la main;* swift start of a horse that continues its fleetness, in a straight line, till it stops.

beau-père, *n.m.* (*—x —s*), father-in-law.

beaupré, *n.m.*, (nav.) bowsprit.

beau-semblant, *n.m.* (*— x—s*), pretence, feint.

beauté, *n.f.*, beauty; fineness, comeliness, prettiness, loveliness, elegance, agreeableness, neatness. *Tache de —;* beauty-spot. *Être dans toute sa —;* to be in one's prime, at the height of one's beauty. *Conserver sa —;* to preserve, to keep up, one's beauty. *Les —s d'une langue;* the beauties of a language.

bec, *n.m.*, beak; bill, nib, rostrum; burner; snout; spout; socket. *Le — de certains poissons;* the snout of some fishes. *Le — d'une aiguière;* the spout of an ewer. *Le — d'une plume;* the nib of a pen. *— de lampe;* socket of a lamp. *— de gaz;* gas-burner. *— d'une ancre;* bill of an anchor. *—de-lièvre* (*—s —*); hare-lip. *Blanc —* (*—s —s*); greenhorn; youngster. *—en-ciseaux* (*—s —*); (orni.) cut-water. *Coups de —;* pecking. *Donner des coups de —;* to peck. *Percer à coups de —;* to peck through. *Coup de —;* wipe, taunt. *Tour de —;* kiss, buss. *Causer — à —;* to have a private chat. *Avoir le — bien effilé;* to have one's tongue well hung. *Elle n'a que le —;* she is all tongue. *Avoir le — gelé;* to be tongue-tied. *Avoir — et ongles;* to have teeth and nails. *Faire le — à quelqu'un;* to give one his cue. *Tenir quelqu'un le — dans l'eau;* to amuse one, to keep one off and on by false promises. *S'humecter le —;* to wet one's whistle. *Se prendre de — avec quelqu'un;* to have a quarrel with any one. *Mener quelqu'un par le —;* to lead any one by the nose.

bécabunga, *or* **beccabunga,** *n.m.,* (bot.) beccabunga, brook-lime.

*bec-à-cuiller, *n.m.* (*—s —*), (orni.) spoonbill.

bécard *or* **beccard,** *n.m.,* female salmon.

bécarre, *n.m.* and *adj.,* (mus.) natural.

bécasse, *n.f.,* woodcock; idiot. *Brider la —;* to cozen one. *C'est une —;* she is a goose.

bécasseau, *n.m.,* young woodcock; dunlin, sand-piper.

bécassine, *n.f.,* (orni.) snipe. *Tirer la —;* to disguise one's skill at play, in order to take any one in.

bec-courbé, *n.m.* (*—s —s*). *V.* **avocette.**

bec-croisé, *n.m.* (*—s —s*), (orni.) crossbill.

bec-d'âne (bé-dâ-n), *n.m.* (*—s —*), mortisechisel.

bec-de-corbin, *n.m.* (*—s —*), bill-head; (nav.) ripping-iron.

bec-de-grue, *n.m.* (*—s —*), crane's bill, stork-bill.

bec-de-lièvre, *n.m.* (*—s —*), harelip; harelipped person.

becfigue, *n.m.,* (orni.) fig-pecker.

bec-fin, *n.m.* (*—s —s*), (orni.) warbler; (*pl.*) the group of warblers.

béchamel, *n.f.,* (cook.) cream-sauce.

bécharu, *n.m.,* (orni.) flamingo.

bêche, *n.f.,* grafting-tool; spade.

bêcher, *v.a.,* to dig, to break the ground with a spade.

béchique, *adj.,* (med.) bechic.

bec-jaune (*—s —s*). *V.* **béjaune.**

becqué, *adj.,* (her.) beaked.

becquée *or* **béquée,** *n.f.,* a billful. *Donner la — à un oiseau;* to feed a bird.

becqueter *or* **béqueter,** *v.a.,* to peck. *se* **becqueter** *or* **béqueter,** *v.r.,* to peck one another; to beak; to bill.

bécune, *n.f.,* (ich.) trumpet-fish, seasnipe.

bedaine, *n.f.,* (jest.) paunch. *Remplir, farcir sa —;* to stuff one's belly.

bédane, *n.m.,* mortise-chisel.

bedeau, *n.m.,* beadle.

bédégar, *n.m.,* (phar.) bedeguar.

bedon, *n.m.,* tabret, drum; barrel-bellied person.

bédouin, *n.m.* and *adj.,* Bedouin.

bée, *adj.,* (of casks—*de tonneaux*); open at one end.

bée, *n.f.,* mill-dam. *V.* **abée.**

béer. *V.* **bayer.**

beffroi, *n.m.,* belfry; watch-tower; steeple; alarm-bell. *Le — sonne;* the alarm-bell is ringing.

bégaiement *or* **bégayement** (-ghê-mān), *n.m.,* stammering, faltering.

bégayer, *v.n.,* to stammer; to lisp; to falter.

bégayer. *v.a.,* to stammer out, to stutter, to lisp (of babies—*des petits enfants*).

bégu, *-ë,* *adj.,* (of a horse—*du cheval*) that does not mark age.

bègue (bèg), *adj.,* stammering. *Il est —;* he stammers in his speech.

bègue, *n.m.f.,* stammerer.

bégueule (-gheul), *n.f.,* prudish, haughty woman; proud minx.

bégueule, *adj.,* prudish.

bégueulerie (-gheul-ri), *n.f.,* prudery, affected austerity.

béguin (-ghin), *n.m.,* biggin, child's linen cap.

béguin, *n.m.,* beguin, beghard; **-e,** *n.f.,* beguine; (b.s.) affectedly devout person.

béguinage (-ghi-), *n.m.,* convent of beguins; affected devotion.

bégum (-gom), *n.f.,* begum (Indian title—*titre indien*).

béhémoth, *n.m.,* behemoth, hippopotamus.

béhen (-hène), *n.m.,* (bot.) behen.

beige, *adj.,* (of wool—*de la laine*); natural.

beige, *n.f.,* unbleached serge.

*beignet, *n.m.,* fritter.

beïram. *V.* **baïram.**

béjaune, *n.m.,* (falconry), eyas, nias; ninny; blunder, silliness, mistake. *Montrer à quelqu'un son —;* to show any one his ignorance. *Payer son —;* to pay one's footing.

bel, *adj.,* *m.* *V.* **beau.**

bélandre, *n.f.,* (nav.) bilander.

bêlant, -e, *adj.,* bleating.

bêlement (-mān), *n.m.,* bleating of sheep.

bélemnite, *n.f.,* (foss.) belemnite.

bêler, *v.n.,* to bleat. *Brebis qui bêle perd sa goulée;* (prov.) one must not talk too much at table.

belette, *n.f.,* weasel, fitchet.

belge, *n.m.f.* and *adj.,* Belgian.

belgique, *adj.,* Belgic.

belic, belif, *or* **bellif,** *n.m.,* (her.) gules.

bélier, *n.m.,* ram; battering-ram; Aries(one of the signs of the zodiac—*signe du zodiaque*).

belière, *n.f.,* ring (of the clapper of a bell — *d'un battant de cloche*).

bélître, *n.m.,* rascal, scoundrel, ragamuffin.

belladone, *n.f.,* bella-dona, deadly nightshade.

bellâtre, *n.m.,* insipid beauty.

belle, *n.f.* *V.* **beau.**

belle, *adj.* *V.* **beau.**

belle-dame, *n.f.,* (*—s —s*). *V.* **arroche.**

belle-de-jour, *n.f.* (*—s —*), convolvulus, yellow day-lily.

belle-de-nuit, *n.f.* (*—s —*), marvel of Peru.

belle-d'un-jour, *n.f.* (*—s —*), (bot.) yellow day-lily.

belle-fille, *n.f.* (*—s —s*), daughter-in-law; step-daughter.

bellement (-mān), (l.u.) *adv.,* softly.

belle-mère, *n.f.* (*—s —s*), mother-in-law; step-mother.

belles-lettres, *n.f. pl.* (*n. s.*), polite literature, belles-lettres.

belle-sœur, *n.f.* (*—s —s*), sister-in-law; step-sister.

belligérant, -e (bèl-li-), *n.* and *adj.,* belligerent, engaged in war.

belliqueu-x, -se (bèl-li-), *adj.,* warlike, martial, valiant.

bellissime, *adj.,* (l.u.) extremely fine, most fine.

bellot, -te, *adj.,* pretty, neat.

beluge, *n.m.,* (ich.) beluga.

belvéder (-dère), *or* **belvédère,** *n.m.,* turret, terrace, belvidere.

belzébuth, *n.m.,* (mus.) Beelzebub.

bémol, *n.m.,* (mus.) flat, bemol.

bémol. *adj.,* flat.

bémoliser, *v.a.,* (mus.) to mark with a flat.

ben (bène), *n.m.,* (bot., pharm.) ben; ben-nut. *Noix de —;* ben-nut, oil-nut.

bénarde, *n.f.,* mortise dead-lock.

bénédicité, *n.m.,* grace (before a meal—*avant un repas*); blessing; benediction. *Dites le —;* say grace.

bénédictin, n.m., -e, n.f., Benedictine.
bénédictin, -e, adj., Benedictine.
bénédiction, n.f., consecration, benediction, blessing, benison. La — d'une église; the consecration of a church. Pays de —; country of plenty. Maison de —; house of piety. Combler de —s; to load with blessings. Donner la —; to bless.
bénéfice, n.m., benefice, living; benefit, advantage, profit; privilege. À —; (com.) at a premium. — brut; gross profit. — net; net profit. — à charge d'âmes; a living with care of souls. Il faut prendre le — avec les charges; we must take it for better or worse. Avoir une représentation à —; (theat.) to take a benefit.
⊙**bénéficence**, n.f., beneficence, favour.
bénéficiaire, adj., Héritier —; heir liable to no debts above the value of the assets.
bénéficiaire, n.m.f., heir liable to no debts above the value of the assets; (thea.) person who takes a benefit.
bénéficial, -e, adj., beneficiary.
bénéficier, n.m., beneficed clergyman possessed of a living or church-preferment, incumbent.
bénéficier, v.a., to extract metal from its ore.
bénéficier, v.n., (com.) to get, to gain, to profit by.
benêt, n. and adj. m., booby, fool; silly, simple.
⊙**bénévole**, adj., gentle, kind, kindly. Lecteur —; kind, gentle, reader.
⊙**bénévolement** (-mān), adv., out of good will.
bengali (bin-), n.m., Bengalee; (orni.) bengalee.
bengali, -e, adj., Bengalee.
béni, -e, part., blessed, praised. V. **bénit**.
*bénignement, adv., benignly, kindly, graciously.
*bénignité, n.f., benignity, graciousness, kindness.
*béni-n, -gne, adj., benign, kind, gentle, good-natured, placid; (med.) mild.
bénir, v.a., to bless, to praise; to bless, to wish well; to hallow; to consecrate. Dieu vous bénisse; God bless you.
bénit, -e, part., hallowed, consecrated. Du pain —; consecrated bread. De l'eau —e; holy-water. Eau —e de cour; empty promises.
bénitier (-tié), n.m., holy-water basin; fount.
benjamin (bin-), n.m., favourite, youngest child.
benjoin (bin-), n.m., benjamin, benzoin, asa-dulcis.
benoîte, n.f., (bot.) herb-bennet, avens.
benzine, n.f., benzine.
benzoate (bin-), n.m., (chem.) benzoate.
benzoïque (bin-), adj., (chem.) benzoic.
*béquillard, n.m., (pop.) person that uses crutches; cripple.
*béquille, n.f., crutch, crutch-stick; (agri.) spud.
*béquiller, v.n., to walk on crutches.
*béquiller, v.a., (gard.) to dig weeds up with a spud.
ber (bère), n.m., (nav.) cradle.
berbère, n.m. and f., Berber, (nation and language—nation et langue).
berberis, n.m., (bot.) barberry.
*bercail, n.m., (n.p.) sheepfold. Ramener une brebis au —; to bring back a lost sheep to the fold.
berce, n.f., (bot.) cow-parsnip.
berceau, n.m., cradle; place of one's infancy; arbour, bower; (arch.) vault; (nav.) cradle.

bercelle, n.f., pincers (used by enamellers—pour émailleurs).
bercelonnette, n.f. V. **barcelonnette**.
bercer, v.a., to rock, to lull asleep; to lull, to amuse, to feed with hope; to delude, to flatter. se **bercer**, v.r., to delude one's self. Il se berce de vaines espérances; he deludes himself with vain hopes. Le diable le berce; he is always uneasy.
berceuse, n.f., female who rocks a cradle, rocker.
béret, n.m., head-dress.
bergame, n.f., coarse hangings.
bergamotte, n.f., odoriferous citron; bergamot (pear—poire); little box for holding sweet-meats.
berge, n.f., steep bank of a river.
berger, n.m., shepherd; swain, lover. L'heure du —; the happy, favourable, moment.
bergère, n.f., shepherdess; nymph, lass; easy-chair.
bergerette, n.f., little shepherdess, country lass.
bergerie, n.f., sheepfold, pen; pl., pastorals.
bergeronnette, n.f., little shepherd girl; (orni.) dish-washer.
béril, n.m. V. **béryl**.
berle, n.f., smallage, water-parsnip.
berline, n.f., a coach, berlin.
berlingot, n.m., chariot resembling a berlin.
berloque or **bre'oque**, n.f., (milit.) dinner-drum, breakfast-drum.
berlue, n.f., dimness of sight, dazzling. Avoir la —; to be dim-sighted; (fig.) to be blind.
berme, n.f., (fort.) berme.
bermudienne (-di-è-n.), n.f., (bot.) bermudiana.
⊙**bernable**, adj., deserving to be laughed at.
bernacle, n.f. V. **barnacle**.
bernardin, n.m., -e, n.f., bernardine (monk, nun—moine, nonne).
berne, n.f., tossing in a blanket; banter. En —; (nav.) awaft. Mettre le pavillon en —; to set up the flag.
bernement, n.m. V. **berne**.
berner, v.a., to toss in a blanket; to ridicule, to make a fool of, to deride, to laugh at.
berneur, n.m., one that tosses another in a blanket; sneerer.
bernique, int., (pop.) not at all; not a bit of it, not in the least. Je croyais le trouver encore chez lui, mais —! I thought to find him still in the house, but the bird had flown!
berniquet, n.m., (pop.) bran-basket. Only used in the expressions: Être au —; to be reduced to beggary. Mettre quelqu'un au —; to reduce anyone to beggary.
bernous, n.m., bernous. hooded cloak.
berret, n.m. V. **béret**.
béryl, n.m., beryl.
besace, n.f., wallet. Être à la —; to be reduced to beggary. Mettre à la —; to bring one to beggary.
besacier, n.m., one who carries a wallet, a beggar.
besaigre, adj., (of wine—du vin) sourish, tartish. Tourner au —; to turn sour.
besant, n.m., (her.) bezant; (antiq.) byzant.
besas, beset, n.m., (trictrac.) ambsace.
besi, n.m., a species of pear.
besicles, n.f. pl., spectacles; barnacles.
bésigue, n.m., besique (a card game—jeu de cartes).
*besogne, n.f., work, business, labour. Abattre de la —; to get through a great deal of work. Mettre la main à la —; to go to work. Mettre quelqu'un à la —; to set one to work. Vous avez fait là une belle —; you have made a fine piece of

work of it. *Aimer — faite ;* to hate work. *S'endormir sur la — ;* to be slack about one's work. *Tailler de la — à quelqu'un ;* to cut out work for, to give trouble to, any one.

⊙***besogner**, *v.n.*, to work, to labour ; to do one's business.

*besogneu-x, -se, *adj.*, necessitous, needy.

besoin, *n.m.*, need, want, occasion ; distress, necessity, requirement. *Avoir — de quelque chose ;* to want something. *Je n'en ai pas — ;* I have no occasion for it. *J'en ai plus — que vous ;* I want it more than you do. *J'ai — d'aller en tel endroit ;* I must go to such a place. *Il est dans le — ;* he is in distress. *N'avoir — de rien ;* to want nothing. *Au — ;* at a pinch, in case of need. *Il l'a assisté dans le — ;* he was a friend to him in his distress. *Autant qu'il est — ;* as much as is needful. *Il n'est pas — de, il n'est pas — que ;* it is not necessary to, there is no occasion for. *Pour subvenir à ses —s ;* to supply one's wants.

besson, -ne, *adj.*, twin.

bestiaire, *n.m.*, (antiq.) one condemned to fight with wild beasts, bestiarius ; collection of fables.

bestial, -e, *adj.;* beastly, bestial, brutish.

bestialement (-män), *adv.*, bestially, brutally, like a beast.

bestialité (-tia-), *n.f.*, bestiality.

bestiasse (-tias), *n.f.*, dolt, simpleton.

bestiaux (-tiô), *n.m.* (plural of **bétail**), cattle.

bestiole (-tiol), *n.f.*, (l.u.) little animal ; poor fool.

béta, *n.m.*, blockhead, loggerhead, tom-fool. *C'est un gros — ;* he is a stupid fellow.

*bétail, *n.m.,* (bestiaux) cattle. *Gros—;* great cattle. *Menu — ;* small cattle.

bête, *n.f.*, beast, brute, dumb creature, beast ; fool, blockhead, stupid creature, tom-fool ; beast (game at cards—*jeu de cartes*). — *à laine ;* sheep. — *à cornes ;* horned beast. — *de somme ;* beast of burden. — *brute ;* brute beast. — *de la Vierge ;* lady-bird. *Une bonne — ;* a good-natured fool. *C'est une maligne — ;* he is a spiteful animal. *C'est ma — noire ;* he, she, it, is my aversion. *Faire la — ;* to play the fool, to stand in one's own light. *Remonter sur sa — ;* to get on one's legs again. *Morte la —, mort le venin ;* dead dogs don't bite.

bête, *adj.*, silly, stupid, foolish, nonsensical. *Cet homme-là est bien — ;* he is a very stupid fellow. *Pas si — ;* not such a fool.

bétel, *n.m.*, (bot.) betel, pepper.

bêtement (-män), *adv.*, like a fool, foolishly, stupidly.

bêtise, *n.f.*, silliness, stupidity, tom-foolery, silly thing. *C'est sa — qui l'a perdu ;* it was his stupidity which lost him. *Il a fait une— ;* he did a stupid thing. *Quelle —!* how stupid ! *Il a dit une — ;* he said a silly thing. *Il ne dit que des —s ;* he talks nothing but nonsense. *C'est de la — ;* it's all nonsense.

bétoine, *n.f.*, (bot.) betony.

béton, *n.m.*, a kind of mortar, beton.

bette, *n.f.*, (bot.) beet.

betterave (-rav), *n.f.*, beet, beet-root. *Du sucre de — ;* beet-root sugar.

bétyle, *n.f.*, (myth.) a kind of stone bearing certain mark, and worshipped as an idol ; also used for the making of idols. (Gr. βαίτυλος.)

beuglement, *n.m.*, the bellowing, lowing (of oxen and cows—*des bœufs et des vaches*).

beugler, *v.n.*, to bellow, to low. *Il se mit à — ;* he began to roar like a bull.

beurre, *n.m.*, butter. *—frais;* fresh butter. *—fondu;* melted butter. *Pot de — ;* jar of butter. *Pot à — ;* butter-jar. *— noir;* brown butter. *Avoir les yeux pochés au — noir;* to have

one's eyes black and blue. *Promettre plus de — que de pain ;* to promise more than one will or can perform.

beurré, *n.m.*, butter-pear.

beurrée, *n.f.*, slice of bread and butter.

beurrer, *v.a.*, to butter.

beurrerie (beur-ri) *n.f.*, butter-dairy.

beurrier, *n.m.*, butter-dish.

beurri-er, *n.m.*, **-ère**, *n.f.*, butter-man, butter-woman. *Il n'est bon que pour la beurrière ;* (of a book—*d'un livre*) it is only fit for the cheesemonger's shop.

bévue, *n.f.*, blunder, oversight, mistake. *Une lourde — ;* a gross blunder. *Une — grossière ;* an egregious mistake. *Faiseur de —s ;* blunderer.

bey, *n.m.*, bey.

bezet, *n.m.* V. **besas.**

bézoard, *n.m.*, (phar.) bezoar.

bezole, *n.m.*, (ich.) bezola.

b-fa-si, (mus.) B ; (vocal mus.) si.

biais, *n.m.*, slope ; slant, sloping, askew ; way, manner, shift. *Couper une étoffe de — ;* to cut a stuff slanting. *Prendre une affaire du bon, du mauvais — ;* to go the right, the wrong, way to work. *User de — ;* (b.s.) to use shifts.

biaisement (-män), *n.m.*, sloping, slanting, shift, evasion.

biaiser, *v.n.*, to slope, to slant, to lean ; to use shifts, evasions. *C'est un homme qui biaise ;* he is a shuffler.

biaiseur, *n.m.*, shuffler, shifter.

biangulaire, *adj.*, biangulated.

bibelot, *n.m.*, bauble, trinket, object of virtu.

biberon, *n.m.*, bibber, toper, tippler, pot-companion ; the lip of a cruet ; sucking bottle. *Élever un enfant au — ;* to bring up a child by the hand.

biberonne, *n.f.*, tippler, toper.

bible, *n.f.*, Bible.

bibliographe, *n.m.*, bibliographer.

bibliographie, *n.f.*, bibliography.

bibliographique, *adj.*, bibliographical.

bibliolithe, *n.f.*, bibliolite.

bibliomane, *n.m.*, bibliomaniac.

bibliomanie, *n.f.*, bibliomania.

bibliophile, *n.m.*, lover of books.

bibliopole, *n.m.*, bibliopole, bibliopolist.

bibliothécaire, *n.m.*, librarian, library-keeper.

bibliothèque, *n.f.*, library ; book-case, book-shelves. *C'est une — vivante ;* he is a walking library.

biblique, *adj.*, biblical.

bibliste, *n.m.*, biblist.

bibus, *n.m.*, trifle. *Des raisons de— ;* paltry reasons.

bicarbonate, *n.m.*, (chem.) bicarbonate.

biceps, (-sèps), *n.m.*, (anat.) biceps.

⊙**bicêtre**, *n.m.*, a mad-house near Paris ; misfortune, disgrace.

biche, *n.f.*, hind ; roe.

⊙**bichet**, *n.m.*, ancient measure for corn, of about 24 lb.

bichette, *n.f.*, little dear, love (child—*enfant*).

bichon, *n.m.*, **-ne**, *n.f.*, lap-dog ; comforter ; little dear, love (child—*enfant*).

bichonner, *v.a.*, to curl (the hair—*les cheveux*). *Se — ;* to curl one's hair.

biconcave, *adj.*, concavo-concave.

bicoque, *n.f.*, little paltry town ; hut, hovel.

bicorne, *adj.*, bicornous, two-horned.

bicornu, -e, *adj.*, irregular ; (bot.) having two horns, dichotomous.

bicuspidé, -e,*adj.*, (bot.) having two points, bicuspid.

bidenté, -e, *adj.*, bidental.

bidet, *n.m.*, pony, nag ; bidet (bath—*meuble*).

bidon, *n.m.,* can; bidon.

bief (bié), or **biez** (bié), *n.m.,* (of water-mills
—*moulins à eau*) mill-course, mill-race; reach
(canals).

bielle, *n.f.,* crank. — *de parallélogramme;*
motion-rod.

bien (bi-in), *n.m.,* good, benefit, welfare, well-
being, blessing; gift; boon, mercy; endowment;
estate; property; *pl.,* good things; goods;
chattels. *Le souverain —;* the sovereign good.
Les —s de la terre; the good things of the earth.
Faire du — à quelqu'un; to do one good. *Rendre
le — pour le mal;* to render good for evil. *Cela
ne fait ni — ni mal:* that does neither good nor
harm. *Cela fait du —;* that does one good.
Dire du — de quelqu'un; to speak well of one.
Grand —vous fasse; much good may it do you.
Un homme de —; an honest, virtuous man.
Les gens de —; good men. *En tout — et tout
honneur;* with honourable intentions. — *clair
et liquide;* unencumbered estate. — *embarrassé;*
encumbered estate. — *engagé, hypothéqué;*
mortgaged estate. *Avoir du —;* to have a fortune or an estate. *Avoir du — mal acquis;* to
have an ill-gotten fortune. *Dépenser, manger
son —;* to spend one's fortune. *Le — public;*
public weal. *La santé est le — le plus précieux;*
health is the most precious of blessings.

bien (bi-in), *adv.,* well; right; proper, properly; finely, in a fine plight, pickle, mess;
comfortable; well off; on good terms; in favour;
good-looking; much; certainly; truly; indeed;
quite; full; completely; formally; clearly;
expressly; very; far; very much; very well;
many; great many; a great deal. *Il se conduit —;* he behaves well. *Il se porte —;* he is
well. *Il parle — français;* he speaks French
well. *Il joue — de cet instrument;* he plays well
on that instrument. *Assez —;* pretty well.
Fort —; very well. *Passablement —;* tolerably
well. *Ils sont fort — ensemble;* they are on very
good terms with each other. *On est fort — ici;*
this is a very comfortable place. *Cette femme
est —;* that woman is good-looking. *Cette jeune
personne se tient —;* that young lady has a good
carriage. — *trouvé;* cleverly thought of. *C'est
—;* that's right. *Tout va —;* all's right. *Je
me trouve — de ce nouveau régime;* I am all the
better for this new regimen. *Il est — dans ses
affaires;* he is well to do in the world. *Nous
voilà —;* we are in a fine mess. *Voilà — du
bruit pour un rien;* here is a mighty deal of
noise about nothing. — *des hommes;* many
men. *Il y avait — du monde;* there were many
people. *Il est déjà — loin;* he is very far off by
this time. *Vous êtes — bon;* you are very kind.
— *mieux;* far better. *Il a été — attrapé;* he has
been finely caught. *Il a été — battu;* he has
been soundly beaten. *Je suis — las de tout ce
monde;* I am heartily tired of all these people.
Il y a — dix lieues d'ici; it is full ten leagues
off. *Je l'ai — pensé;* I thought so. *Je vous
l'avais — dit;* I told you so. *Il y a — là de quoi
plaisanter!* a fine matter truly for joking! *Auriez-
vous — l'assurance de le nier?* would you really
have the assurance to deny it? *C'est être —
prompt;* this is being rather hasty. *Je le savais
—, je m'en doutais —;* I knew as much, I
suspected as much. — *lui a pris de;* he was
right to. *Je le veux —;* I have no objection.
Voulez-vous — me donner son adresse? would you
be so good as to give me his direction? *Regardez-
moi —;* look at me steadfastly.

bien-aime, -e. *adj.* (— —s), beloved, well-
beloved, darling, dear, lief.

bien-aimé, *n.m.,* **-e,** *n.f.* (— —s), well-
beloved.

bien-dire, *n.m.,* (*n.p.*) (fam.) fine speaking.
Le bienfaire vaut mieux que le —; to act well is
better than to talk well.

bien-disant, -e, *adj.* (— —s). well-spoken.

bien-être, *n.m.,* (*n.p.*) well-being. comfort-
ableness; comforts. *Tout le monde cherche son
—;* every one looks after his own comfort.

bienfaisance, *n.f.,* beneficence. bounty,
munificence.

bienfaisant, -e, *adj.,* beneficent, kind, gracious, bountiful. munificent.

bienfait, *n.m.,* good turn, good office. kindness. benefit, favour, pleasure, courtesy. *Combler
de —s;* to load with favours. *On oublie plus tôt
les —s que les injures;* services are sooner forgotten than injuries. *Un — n'est jamais perdu;*
a kindness is never thrown away.

bienfait-eur, *n.m.,* **-rice,** *n.f.,* benefactor,
benefactress.

bien-fonds, *n.m.* (—s —), landed property.

bienheureu-x, -se, *adj.,* happy, blest, blissful; blessed.

bien-jugé, *n.m.,* (*n.p.*) (jur.) correct judgment.

biennal. -e (bi-èn-nal), *adj.,* biennial.

bien que, *conj.,* though, although. *Bien qu'il
le sache, il n'en parle pas;* although he knows
it, he says nothing about it. *Si —;* so that.

bienséance, *n.f.,* decency, decorum, regard,
seemliness; conveniency; manners. *Garder
la —, les —s;* to keep within the bounds of
decorum, of good breeding.

bienséant, -e, *adj.,* decent, becoming, fitting, seemly, beseeming, decorous, fit.

⊙**bien-tenant,** *n.m.,* **-e,** *n.f.* (— —s), (jur.)
person in possession.

bientôt, *adv.,* soon, ere long. shortly. *Je
reviendrai —;* I shall soon be back.

*****bienveillance,** *n.f.,* benevolence, good-will,
protection, favour, friendliness, kindness. *Un
sourire de —;* a smile of benevolence. *Gagner
la — de quelqu'un;* to win any one's good will.

*****bienveillant, -e,** *adj.,* benevolent, kind,
friendly.

bienvenir, *v.n.,* to cause one's self to be
welcomed. Only used in the expression: *Se
faire — de;* to ingratiate one's self with.

bienvenu, -e (bi-in-vnu), *adj.,* welcome.
C'est un homme qui est — partout; he is welcome
everywhere. *Soyez le —;* you are very welcome.

bienvenue, *n.f.,* welcome. *Payer sa —;* to
pay one's welcome, entrance or initiation.

⊙**bienvoulu, -e,** *adj.,* beloved, loved.

bière, *n.f.,* beer. *Petite —;* small beer.
Débit de —; beer-shop. *Ce n'est pas de la petite
—;* it is no joke.

bière, *n.f.,* coffin, bier.

⊙**bièvre,** *n.m.,* beaver, castor.

biez, *n.m.* **V. bief.**

biffer, *v.a.,* to cancel, to strike off; to scratch,
to blot out.

bifide, *adj.,* (bot.) bifid.

bifiore, *adj.,* (bot.) biflorous.

bifolié, -e, *adj.,* (bot.) two-leaved.

bifteck, *n.m.,* beefsteak. *Faux —;* rump-
steak.

bifurcation, *n.f.,* bifurcation.

bifurqué, -e, *adj.,* bifurcated, forked.

se bifurquer, *v.r.,* to be forked, bifurcated.

bigame, *adj.,* guilty of bigamy.

bigame, *n.m.,* bigamist.

bigamie, *n.f.,* bigamy.

bigarade. *n.f.,* Seville orange.

bigaradier, *n.m.,* Seville orange-tree.

bigarré, -e, *adj.,* (b.s.) party-coloured, motley, streaked.

bigarreau, *n.m.,* bigarreau (cherry—*cerise*).

bigarreautier, *n.m.,* bigarreautier, cherry-
tree.

bigarrer, *v.a.,* to chequer, to streak, to
make motley, party colour.

bigarrure, *n.f.,* medley, mixture.

bigéminé, -e, *adj.,* bigeminate.

bigle, *adj.*, (l.u.) squint-eyed

bigler, *v.n.*, (l.u.) to squint.

⊙**bigne**, *n.f.*, a tumour on the forehead, produced by a blow.

*****bignonic**, *n.f.*, trumpet-flower.

bigorne, *n.f.*, beaked anvil, bickern.

bigorneau, *n.m.*, periwinkle.

bigot, *n.m.*, -**e**, *n.f.*, bigot; devotee; hypocrite.

bigot, -**e**, *adj.*, bigoted.

bigoterie (-trî), *n.f.*, bigotry. *Donner dans la* — ; to turn bigot.

bigotisme, *n.m.*, bigotry.

bigourneau. *V.* **bigorneau**.

bigue (big), *n.f.*, (nav.) sheers.

bihoreau, *n.m.*, night-heron.

bijon, *n.m.*, (l.u.). *V.* **térébenthine**.

bijou, *n.m.*, jewel, trinket. *Cet enfant est son* — ; that child is his darling. *Venez, mon* — ; come, dear.

bijouterie (-trî), *n.f.*, jewellery.

bijouti-er, *n.m.*, -**ère**, *n.f.*, jeweller.

bijugué, -**e** (-ghé), *adj.*, bijugous.

bilabié, -**e**, *adj.*, (bot.) bilablate.

bilan, *n.m.*, (com.) balance-sheet; schedule. *Déposer son* — ; to file one's schedule.

bilatéral, -**e**, *adj.*, bilateral; (jur.) reciprocal.

bilboquet, *n.m.*, cup and ball; curling-pipe. *C'est un véritable* — ; he is a giddy-headed fellow.

bile, *n.f.*, bile, gall; choler, anger, spleen. *Echauffer la* — *à quelqu'un;* to provoke any one's anger. *Décharger sa* — ; to vent one's anger.

biliaire, *adj.*, (med.) bilious.

bilieu-x, -**se**, *adj.*, bilious; choleric, passionate, angry. *Au teint* — ; bilious looking.

bilingue, *adj.*, double-tongued, bilinguous.

bill, *n.m.* (—*s*), (English parliament—*parlement anglais*) bill, projet de loi.

*****billard**, *n.m.*, billiards; billiard-table; billiard-room.

*****billarder**, *v.n.*, to strike a ball twice; to strike the two balls together.

*****bille**. *n.f.*, billiard-ball; marble taw (to play with—*jouet*); a log (of wood—*de bois*). *Faire une* — ; to hole a ball.

*****billebaude**, *n.f.*, hurly-burly, confusion. *A la* — ; in confusion.

*****billet**, *n.m.*, note, letter: bill, hand-bill; label; promissory note; billet (for quartering soldiers—*de logement pour soldats*); note of hand; circular letter. — *à vue, à ordre;* bill payable at sight, to order. — *payable à présentation;* bill payable on demand. — *de complaisance;* accommodation bill. — *véreux;* unsafe bill. — *échu;* bill due. *Faire les fonds d'un* — ; to provide for a bill. *J'en ai fait mon* — ; I gave my note for it. — *de banque;* bank-note. — *doux;* love-letter. — *d'entrée;* entrance-ticket. — *blanc;* a blank.

*****billeté**, -**e**, *adj.*, ticketed; labelled; (her.) billeted.

*****billeter**, *v.a.*, to ticket. to label; to billet.

*****billette**, *n.f.*, notice to pay toll; (her.) billet.

*****billevesée**, *n.f.*, idle story, foolish trash, crotchet.

billion, *n.m.*, one thousand millions.

*****billon**, *n.m.*, base coin; place where base coin is received (to be melted—*pour être fondu*); (agri.) ridge. *Monnaie de* — ; copper money.

*****billonnage**, *n.m.*, debasing the coin; throwing up of land into ridges.

⊙*****billonnement** (bi-lo-n-màn), *n.m.*, debasing coin.

⊙*****billonner**, *v.a.*, to debase coin, to circulate debased coin.

⊙*****billonneur**, *n.m.*, debaser, utterer of debased coin.

*****billot**, *n.m.*, block, log; clog (for animals—*pour les animaux*).

bilobé, -**e**, *adj.*, (bot.) bilobate.

biloculaire, *adj.*, (bot.) bilocular.

bimane, *n.m.* and *adj.*, (zool.) creature having two hands; bimane, bimanous.

bimbelot (bin-blo), *n.m.*, plaything, toy.

bimbeloterie (bin-blo-trî), *n.f.*, playthings, toy trade.

bimbelotier (bin-blo-), *n.m.*, toyman.

binage, *n.m.*, ploughing, digging, the ground over again; celebrating mass twice on the same day.

binaire, *adj.*, binary.

binard, *n.m.*, four-wheeled waggon, truck.

biné, -**e**, *adj.*, binated.

biner, *v.a.*, (agri.) to dig again, to dress a second time.

biner, *v.n.*, to say mass twice in one day.

binet, *n.m.*, save-all. *Faire* — ; to be miserly.

binocle, *n.m.*, double eye-glass; binocle.

binoculaire, *adj.*, binocular.

binôme, *n.m.*, (alg.) binomial.

biographe, *n.m.*, biographer.

biographie, *n.f.*, biography.

biographique, *adj.*, biographical.

biologie, *n.f.*, biology.

biologique, *adj.*, biological.

bipédal, -**e**, *adj.*, bipedal.

bipède, *n.m.*, biped. — *antérieur;* (man.) fore limbs of a horse. — *postérieur;* hind limbs of a horse.

bipède, *adj.*, two-legged, bipedal.

bipinné, -**e**, *adj.*, (bot.) bipennated.

biquadratique (-koua-), *adj.*, (alg.) of the fourth degree, biquadratic.

bique, *n.f.*, she-goat.

biquet, *n.m.*, kid; scales to weigh gold.

birème, *n.f.*, bireme.

biribi, *n.m.*, biribi (a game of chance—*jeu de hasard*); back lining (of a shoe—*de soulier*).

birloir, *n.m.*, window-sash holder.

bis (bi), -**e**, *adj.*, brown; tawny, swarthy. *Du pain* — ; brown bread.

bis (biss), *int.*, twice; encore. *Crier* — ; to encore.

bisaïeul, *n.m.*, great-grandfather.

bisaïeule, *n.f.*, great-grandmother.

bisannuel, -**le**, *adj.*, (bot.) biennial.

*****bisbille**, *n.f.*, quarrel, bickering, jangling.

biscaïen (i-in), *n.m.*, ⊙long-barrelled musket; grapeshot ball.

biscaïen, -**ne**, *adj.*, long-barrelled (of guns —*fusils*).

bischof or **bishof**, *n.m.*, bishop (liquor).

biscornu, -**e**, *adj.*, outlandish, odd, queer.

biscotin, *n.m.*, sweet biscuit.

biscuit, *n.m.*, biscuit, sea-bread; hard kind of brick; semi-vitrified porcelain. *S'embarquer sans* — ; to engage in an undertaking without having the things necessary to succeed. — *à la cuiller;* Savoy biscuit.

bise, *n.f.*, north wind.

biseau, *n.m.*, (cook.) kissing-crust; bevelling; basil; (carp.) feather edge; (print.) side-stick.

biseauter, *v.a.*, to bend the corner of cards to cheat in gambling. *Cartes biseautées;* corner-bend cards.

biser, *v.n.*, to degenerate, to grow brown (of seeds—*graines*).

biser, *v.a.*, (dy.) to dye a stuff over again.

biset, *n.m.*, rock-dove; coarse grey cloth; national guard on duty in private clothes.

bisette, *n.f.*, footing (a kind of narrow lace —*dentelle étroite*).

bismuth, *n.m.*, bismuth, tin-glass.

bison, *n.m.*, (mam.) bison.

bisonne. *n.f.*, grey cloth used for lining.

bisquain.*n.m.*.sheep's skin with the wool on.

bisque. *n.f.*, (cook.) bisk, cullis; odds (at tennis—*au jeu de paume*). *Avoir quinze et — sur la partie;* to have the odds in one's favour.

bisquer, *v.n.*, (fam.) to be vexed, to be in a pet.

bissac. *n.m.*, wallet.

bissection, *n.f.*, (geom.) bisection.

bisser. *v.a.*, to encore.

bissexe, *adj.*, bisexous, bisexual.

bissexte, *n.m.*, bissextile.

bissextil, -e, *adj.*, bissextile. *Année —e;* leap-year.

bissexuel, -le, *adj.*, (bot.) bisexous, bisexual.

bissus (-sus), *n.m.* V. **byssus**.

⊙**bistoquet**, *n.m.*, billiard-mace.

bistorte, *n.f.*, (bot.) bistort, snake-weed.

bistouri, *n.m.*, (surg.) bistoury.

bistourné, -e, *adj.*, twisted, crooked.

bistourner, *v.a.*, to twist.

bistre, *n.m.*, (paint.) bistre.

bistré, -e, *adj.*, colour of bistre; swarthy, dusky, tawny. *Teint —;* swarthy complexion.

bistreu-x, -se, *adj.*, of bistre.

biterné, -e, *adj.*, (bot.) biternate.

bitord, *n.m.*, (nav.) twine, spun-yarn.

bitte, *n.f.*, (nav.) bit.

bitter, *v.a.*, (nav.) to bit.

bitton. *n.m.*, (nav.) timber-head.

bitume, *n.m.*, bitumen.

bituminer, *v.a.*, to bituminate.

bitumineu-x, -se, *adj.*, bituminous.

bivalve, *adj.*, bivalvular.

bivalve, *n.m.*, bivalve.

bivouac *or* **bivac**. *n.m.*, bivouac.

bivouaquer *or* **bivaquer**, *v.n.*, to bivouac.

bizarre, *adj.*, odd, fantastical, singular, strange, whimsical, extravagant. *Un homme —;* an odd sort of a man.

bizarre, *n.m.* V. **bizarrerie**.

bizarrement, *adv.*, oddly, fantastically, whimsically.

bizarrerie (-rar-rî), *n.f.*, caprice, extravagance, whim, singularity, oddness, fantasticalness.

⊙**blade**, *n.f.*, tobacco-box.

blafard, -e, *adj.*, palish, dull, wan. *Lumière —e;* wan-light.

blague (blag), *n.f.*, tobacco-pouch; (pop.) fudge, humbug; hoax.

blaguer (-ghé), *v.a.* and *n.*, (pop.) to hoax, to humbug; to draw the long bow.

blagueur (-gheur), *n.m.*, (pop.) hoaxer, humbug.

blaireau, *n.m.*, badger, pig-badger.

blâmable, *adj.*, blameable, faulty, culpable.

blâme, *n.m.*, blame, reproach, obloquy, disapprobation, reprehension. *Action digne de —;* blameable action. *Déverser du — sur;* to cast blame on. *Éviter le —;* to avoid being blamed. *Donner le — à quelqu'un;* to blame one. *Rejeter le — sur;* to throw the blame on. *Tout le — en tombe sur lui;* all the blame falls upon him.

blâmer, *v.a.*, to blame, to censure, to disapprove, to find fault with. *On ne saurait le —;* he cannot be blamed.

blanc, -he (blan, blansh), *adj.*, white; clean; hoar; (print.) open (of type—*caractère d'imprimerie*); blank (of verses—*vers, poésie*). *— comme neige;* as white as snow. *Gelée —he;* hoar frost. *Vers —s;* blank verse. *C'est bonnet —, et — bonnet;* there are six of one and half a dozen of the other. *Rouge soir et — matin, c'est la journée du pèlerin;* evening red and morning grey are two sure signs of a very fine day. *Du linge —;* clean linen.

blanc, *n.m.*, white, blank. *— -seing;* blank signature. *Le — de l'œil;* the white of the eye.

— d'Espagne: whiting. *— de baleine;* spermaceti. *— de céruse;* ceruse. *— de plomb;* white lead. *— de chaux:* whitewash. *— de volaille;* breast of a fowl. *De but en —;* bluntly. *Il y a autant de différence de l'un à l'autre que du — au noir;* they are as different as black is from white. *Ligne de —;* (print.) white line. *Tirage en —;* (print.) working the white paper. *Tirer en —;* (print.) to work the white paper. *En —;* left blank.

blanc-bec. *n.m.* (*—s —s*), beardless youth, youngster; (b.s.) greenhorn.

****blanchaille**, *n.f.*, fry, small fish.

blanchâtre. *adj.*, whitish, somewhat white.

blanche, *n.f.*, minim (in music—*musique*).

blanchement (blaush-mân), *adv.*, (l.u.) cleanly.

blancher, *n.m.*, tanner (of small skins—*petites peaux*).

blancherie, *n.f.* V. **blanchisserie**.

blanchet, *n.m.*, strainer; (print.) blanket.

blancheur, *n.f.*, whiteness; hoariness.

blanchiment, *n.m.*, bleaching, blanching, washing. *Le — de l'argent;* the washing of silver. *Mettre des chandelles au —;* to bleach candles.

blanchir, *v.a.*, to whiten, to make white; to whitewash; to wash, to bleach, to make clean; to blanch; to boil off, to scald (fruits, greens—*légumes*); (print.) to white over; to plane, to rough down. *— un plafond;* to whitewash a ceiling. *— des toiles;* to bleach linen. *— les flans;* (coin.) to blanch planchets. *— du linge;* to wash linen. *On me blanchit;* they find me in washing. *On blanchit aujourd'hui chez nous;* this is washing-day with us. *— un ais;* to plane a board.

blanchir, *v.n.*, to whiten, to grow white, to foam. *Il commence à —;* he begins to grow grey-haired. *Tête de fou ne blanchit jamais;* a fool's head is never grey.

se **blanchir**, *v.r.*, to whiten, to wash.

blanchissage, *n.m.*, washing.

blanchissant, -e, *adj.*, that whitens, grows white, foaming.

blanchisserie (shis-rî), *n.f.*, bleaching-house.

blanchisseur. *n.m.*, washerman, bleacher.

blanchisseuse, *n.f.*, washerwoman, laundress. *— de fin;* clear-starcher.

blanc-manger, *n.m.*, (*—s —s*) (cook.) blanc-mange.

blanc-seing, *n.m.*, (*—s —s*) signature in blank.

blanque. *n.f.*, private lottery.

blanquette, *n.f.*, blanket (pear—*poire*); blanquette (wine—*vin*); ragout with white sauce; chasselas doré (a kind of grape—*raisin*); (ich.) white-bait.

blaque, *n.f.* V. **blague**.

blaser, *v.a.*, to blunt; to pall; to cloy, sicken. *Il est blasé sur les plaisirs;* he is cloyed with pleasure. *Il est blasé sur tout;* he is sick of everything.

se **blaser**, *v.r.*, to be palled, surfeited, to ruin one's constitution.

blason, *n.m.*, heraldry, blazon, blazonry; coat of arms.

blasonner, *v.a.*, to blazon; to explain, armorial bearings; to paint armorial bearings; (fam.) to criticize, to traduce, to blacken.

blasphémat-eur, *n.m.*, **-rice**, *n.f.*, blasphemer.

blasphématoire, *adj.*, blasphemous.

blasphème, *n.m.*, blasphemy.

blasphémer, *v.n.*, to blaspheme.

blasphémer, *v.n.*, to blaspheme, to curse.

blatier, *n.m.*, corn-chandler, dealer in corn.

blatte, *n.f.*, (ent.) mill-moth. *— d'Amérique;* cockroach. V. **cafard**.

blaude. *n.f. V.* **blouse.**

blé. *n.m.*. wheat, corn ; grain. — *-froment :* wheat. — *-seigle ;* rye. *Grands —s,* wheat and rye. *Petits —s ;* oats, barley. — *méteil ;* wheat and rye. — *de Turquie :* Indian corn. — *noir.* — *sarrasin :* buckwheat. — *barbu ;* stiff wheat. *Du — en herbe ;* corn in the blade. *Serrer du — ;* to house corn. *Manger son — en herbe ;* to spend one's money before one has it. *Facteur en — ;* corn-factor. *Halle au — :* corn exchange.

bleime, *n.f.,* (vet.) bleyme.

blême. *adj.,* sallow, pale, pallid, wan.

blêmir, *v.n.,* to grow pale.

biende, *n.f.,* (min.) mock ore.

biennie (blè-ni), *n.f.,* (ich.) blenny.

blennorrhée (blèn-no-rée), *n.f.,* blennor-rhœa, gleet.

blésement, *n.m.,* lisping.

bléser, *v.n.,* to lisp.

blessant, -e, *adj.,* offensive, shocking.

blessé, -e, *part.,* wounded, hurt, diseased.

blesser, *v.a.,* to wound, to cut, to hurt, to pinch, to offend, to grate, to fret, to wring, to gall. *Cela me blesse ;* that hurts me. *Mes souliers me blessent ;* my shoes pinch me. *Cette phrase blesse l'oreille ;* that sentence grates upon the ear. — *la vue ;* to offend the eye. — *les oreilles chastes ;* to offend chaste ears. — *l'honneur de quelqu'un ;* to wound one's honour. — *les convenances ;* to offend against propriety. *se* **blesser,** *v.r.,* to hurt or cut one's self ; to take offence.

blessure, *n.f.,* wound, cut, hurt. *Les —s faites à l'honneur ;* the wounds inflicted upon one's honour. *Gratification pour — ;* (milit.) smart-money.

blet, -te, *adj.,* (fruit) soft. *Poire blette ;* soft pear.

blète *or* **blette,** *n.f.,* (bot.) blite, strawberry-spinach ; kind of amaranth, flower-gentle.

bleu, -e, *adj.* (—s), blue. *Avoir les yeux —s ;* to be blue-eyed. *Cordon — ;* knight of the Holy Ghost ; first-rate cook. *Conte — ;* tale of a tub. *Il m'a battu tout — ;* he has beaten me black and blue.

bleu, *n.m.* (—s), blue, blueness. — *de Prusse ;* Prussian blue. — *d'azur ;* smalt. — *de cobalt ;* cobalt blue. — *de ciel ;* sky blue.

bleuâtre, *adj.,* bluish, somewhat blue.

bleuet, *n.m. V.* **bluet.**

bleuette, *n.f. V.* **bluette.**

bleuir, *v.a.,* to make blue, to blue.

blindage, *n.m.,* sheeting ; (milit.) poling.

blinder, *v.a.,* to sheet ; (milit.) to cover with blinds.

blindes, *n.f. pl.,* (fort.) blinds.

bloc, *n.m.,* lump, bulk ; block, log ; stocks. *Acheter en — ;* to buy in a lump. *Un — de marbre ;* a block of marble.

blocage, *n.m.,* rubbish.

blocage, *n.m.,* (print.) turned letter, turning.

*****blocaille,** *n.f.,* (mas.) rubble-stone ; pebble-work.

blockhaus (blok-hôs), *n.m.* (—), blockhouse.

blocus, *n.m.* (—), (milit.) investment ; (nav.) blockade.

blond, -e, *adj.,* flaxen, fair, light. *Des cheveux —s ;* light hair. *Un homme — ;* a fair man. *Il est délicat et — ;* he is a dainty spark, difficult to please.

blond, *n.m.,* **-e.** *n.f.,* fair, light colour ; fair person. — *ardent ;* sandy colour. *Courtiser la brune et la —e ;* to make love to a number of women.

blonde, *n.f.,* blond, blond-lace.

blondier, *n.m.,* blond-lace maker.

blondin, *n.m.,* **-e,** *n.f.,* a fair-complexioned person ; spark. *Un beau — ;* a fine young spark.

⊙ **blondir,** *v.n.,* to grow light or fair.

⊙ **blondissant, -e** *adj..* yellowish, golden.

bloqué, *n.m.,* ball holed with strength (at billiards—*au billard*).

bloquer, *v.a.,* to blockade ; to blockade, to fill up (cavities in walls with mortar, &c.—*cavités de murs, &c,* avec *du mortier, des pierres, &c.*) ; (print.) to turn ; to hole a ball with strength (billiards—*billard*).

se **blottir,** *v.r.,* to squat, to cower, to lie close to the ground.

blouse. *n.f.,* pocket (of a billiard table—*de billard*) ; smock-frock ; blouse ; pinafore.

blouser, *v.a.,* to hole (at billiards—*au billard*) ; to cheat. *Il m'a blousé ;* he has cheated me.

se **blouser,** *v.r..* to hole one's own ball (at billiards—*au billard*) ; to mistake, to be in the wrong box.

bluet, *n.m.,* (bot.) bluebottle ; (orni.) blue-bird.

bluette, *n.f.,* spark, flake of fire ; (lit.) light production of wit.

blutage, *n.m.,* bolting, sifting (of flour—*de la farine*).

bluteau *or* **blutoir,** *n.m.,* bolter (for flour—*à farine*).

bluter, *v.a.,* to bolt, to sift (meal—*farine*).

bluterie (-tri), *n.f.,* bolting-room.

boa, *n.m.* (—s), (erpetology) boa ; fur tippet.

bobèche, *n.f.,* sconce ; socket (of a candlestick—*de chandelier*).

bobine, *n.f.,* bobbin ; spool.

bobiner, *v.a.,* to wind on a bobbin, to spool.

bobineuse, *n.f.,* winder.

bobo, *n.m.,* (infantine—*expression enfantine*) little hurt. *Avoir — ;* to have a slight ailment.

bocage, *n.m.,* grove, coppice.

bocag-er, -ère, *adj.,* of groves, rural.

bocal, *n.m.,* short-necked bottle ; glass bowl ; large phial ; mouth-piece (of wind instruments—*d'instruments à vent*).

bocard, *n.m.,* (metal.) stamper, stamping-mill.

bocardage, *n.m.,* (metal.) crushing, pounding, stamping.

bocarder, *v.a.,* (metal.) to stamp, to pound.

bock, *n.m.,* name, used in French coffee-houses, of a measure of beer ; = 1¼ pints English nearly.

bodi-uche. *V.* **baudruche.**

bœur, *n.m.,* ox, bull ; beef (flesh—*viande morte*). *Troupeau de —s ;* drove of oxen. *Accoupler, découpler, les —s ;* to yoke, to unyoke, the oxen. *Du — à la mode ;* a-la-mode beef. *Un — ;* a dull-pated fellow. *Mettre la charrue devant les —s ;* to put the cart before the horse.

bœufs (beû), *n.m. pl.,* oxen.

boghei (-gay), *n.m.* (—s), light gig.

bogue (bog), *n.f.,* husk (of chestnuts—*de marrons*).

bohé *or* **bohea,** *n.* and *adj.m.,* (*n.p.*), bohea. *Thé — ;* bohea tea.

bohême, *n.m.f.,* **bohémien,** *n.m.,* **-ne,** *n.f.,* gipsy.

boiard, *n.m. V.* **boyard.**

boire (buvant, bu), *v.a.,* to drink, to imbibe ; to absorb ; to pocket (affront). — *un affront ;* to pocket an affront. — *le calice jusqu'à la lie ;* to drain the cup to the dregs. *Qui fait la folie la boit ;* as you brew, so you must drink.

boire, *v.n.,* to drink, to tipple ; to blot, to be puckered (of needle-work—*coutures, &c.*). — *à la ronde ;* to put the glass about. — *à la santé de quelqu'un ;* to drink one's health. *C'est un homme qui boit ;* the man loves drinking. — *à longs traits ;* to drink long draughts. — *sec :* to drink hard, neat. — *comme un trou :* to drink

3

like a fish. *A* —; some drink. *Ce papier boit;* this paper blots.

boire. *n.m.,* drink. drinking. *Le* — *et le manger;* eating and drinking. *Elle lui apprête son* — *et son manger;* she prepares his repasts for him.

bois, *n.m.,* wood. forest; timber; horns (of a deer—*de cerfs, daims, &c.*); cross (of Christ—*du Christ*); bedstead; stock (of a gun—*de fusil*); staff (of a lance—*de lance*). *Un* — *de haute futaie;* a wood of lofty trees. *Un* — *taillis;* a copse. — *mort sur pied;* dead wood. *Mort*—; wood of little value. such as hawthorn, bramble, &c. *La lisière d'un* —; the skirt of a wood. *La faim chasse le loup du* —; hunger will break through stone walls. — *puant;* bean trefoil. — *de rose;* rose-wood. — *de gaïac;* lignum vitæ. — *de Sainte-Lucie;* Mahaleb. — *de palissandre;* violet ebony. — *sur pied;* standing wood. — *d'équarrissage;* square timber. — *en grume;* round timber. *Le fil du* —; the grain of the wood. — *de sciage;* sawn timber. — *de refend;* cleft timber. —*chablis;* wind-fallen wood. — *de charpente;* timber, straight timber. — *de charronnage;* wheel-wrights' timber. — *de construction pour la marine;* ship timber. — *de chauffage;* firewood. — *flotté;* floated wood. — *d'araignée;* crow-foot. *Faire du* —; to get wood. *Une voie de* —; a load of wood. *Un train de* —; a float of wood. *Il ne sait plus de quel* — *faire flèche;* he knows no longer what shift to make. *Je sais de quel* — *il se chauffe;* I know what metal he is made of. *Il est du* — *dont on fait les flûtes;* he will chime in with anything. *Trouver visage de* —; to find the door shut. *Un* — *de lit;* a bedstead.

boisage, *n.m.,* wood-work.

boisé, -e, *adj.,* woody, abounding with wood, wooded. *Pays* —; country abounding with woods. *Chambre* —*e;* wainscoted room.

boisement, *n.m.,* planting land with trees.

boiser, *v.a.,* to put wood-work to.

boiserie (boaz-ri), *n.f.,* wainscot, wainscoting.

boiseu-x, -se, *adj.,* woody, ligneous.

boisseau, *n.m.,* bushel.

boisselée (boas-lée), *n.f.,* a bushelful.

boisselier, *n.m.,* white cooper, bushel maker.

boissellerie (boa-sèl-ri), *n.f.,* white cooperage, bushel-making.

boisson, *n.f.,* drink, beverage, drinking, drunkenness. *Être adonné à la* —; to be addicted to drinking. *Être pris de* —; to be intoxicated.

⊙**boite,** *n.f.,* ripeness, maturity of wine.

boîte, *n.f.,* box; case (of a watch, a rudder —*de montre, de gouvernail*). — *de montre;* watchcase. — *à poudre;* powder-box. — *à thé;* teacaddy. — *aux lettres;* letter-box.

boîte, *n.f.,* foot-soreness (of cattle—*des bestiaux*).

boitement (boat-mān), *n.m.,* halting, limping.

boiter, *v.n.,* to be lame, to walk lame, to limp, to halt, to hobble. — *d'un pied;* to walk lame of one foot. *En boitant;* limpingly.

boiterie (boa-tri), *n.f.,* (vet.) halting.

boiteu-x, -se, *n.* and *adj.,* lame person; lame, halt, hobbling; limping. *Le Diable* —; the Devil on two sticks.

boîtier, *n.m.,* surgeon's box of instruments.

bol, *n.m.,* a large pill, bolus; (min.) bole; bowl, basin, finger-glass. *Un* — *de punch;* a bowl of punch.

bolaire, *adj.,* (min.) bolary.

bolet, *n.m.,* (bot.) boletus.

bolide, *n.m.,* (astron.) bolis.

bollandistes, *n.m. pl.,* the name given to the Antwerp Jesuits who wrote the Lives of the Saints, and of which Bollandus was the chief writer.

bolus, *n.m. V.* **bol.**

bombance, *n.f.,* feasting. junketing. *Faire* —; to feast.

bombarde, *n.f.,* bomb-ketch, bomb-vessel; (mus.) bombardo.

bombardement, *n.m.,* bombardment.

bombarder, *v.a.,* to bombard.

bombardier, *n.m.,* bombarder.

⊙**bombasin,** *n.m.,* bombazine.

bombe, *n.f.,* bomb-shell. *La* — *a crevé en l'air;* the bomb has burst in the air. *Voûte à l'épreuve de la* —; bomb-proof vault.

bombé, -e, *adj.,* arched; barrelled; convex.

bombement (-mān), *n.m.,* swelling, bulging out, convexity.

bomber, *v.a.,* to cause anything to bulge, to jut, to swell out.

bomber, *v.n.* to bulge, to jut out.

bomberie (bon-bri), *n.f.,* shell-foundry, bomb-foundry.

bombeur, *n.m.,* maker of convex glasses.

bombyx, *n.m.,* (ent.) bombyx, silkworm.

bomerie (bôm-ri), *n.f.,* (com.) bottomry.

bon, -ne, *adj.,* good, kind; favourable; fine, convenient, advantageous, profitable, proper; solvent; full; silly, foolish; wholesome; easy, good-natured. *Bon* —! good! *C'est* —; that's right. *De* — *pain;* good bread. *De* —*ne viande;* good meat. *De* —*nes nouvelles;* good news. *Cela ne présage rien de* —; that bodes no good. *En* — *état;* sound. —*ne foi;* plain dealing, uprightness. —*sens;* sensibleness. *Faire* —*ne chère;* to live luxuriously. *À* — *appétit il ne faut point de sauce;* a good appetite needs no sauce. *Un homme* —; a good man. *Un* — *homme;* a simple old man, old codger, old buffer. *Vous êtes trop* —; you are too kind. *C'est une* —*ne personne;* she is a good creature. — *à prendre;* worth taking. — *à boire;* good to drink. *À quoi* — *tant de peines?* what is the use of so much trouble? —*ne nourriture;* wholesome food. *Voilà ce qu'il y a de* —; that's one comfort. *Prendre quelque chose en* —*ne part;* to take a thing well. *Ce qui est* — *à prendre est* — *à rendre;* it is always worth our while to accept what we may give up when anything better offers. *C'est une* —*ne tête;* he has a good head-piece. *Il a un fort* — *revenu;* he has a very good income. —*jour,* —*ne œuvre;* the better the day, the better the deed. *De* —*ne heure;* early. *Il est encore de* —*ne heure;* it is still early. — *temps;* pastime, diversion, pleasure. *Se donner du* — *temps;* to divert one's self. *Trouver* —; to approve, to like. *Sentir* —; to have a good smell. *Tenir* —; to hold out. *Il ne fait pas* — *avoir affaire à lui;* it is dangerous meddling with him. *La lui garder* —*ne;* to owe one a grudge. *Faire quelque chose de* —*ne grâce;* to do a thing with a good grace. *Être homme à* —*nes fortunes;* to be successful with the fair sex. *Il y va de* —*ne foi;* he deals sincerely. *Si* — *vous semble;* if you think proper. *Il est* — *là!* excellent indeed! *De* — *cœur;* heartily. *De* —*né foi;* sincerely. *La faire courte et* —*ne;* to have a short but merry life. *Que vous êtes* —! how silly you are! *Tout de* —; in earnest.

bon, *n.m.,* good quality, what is good in a thing; the best, the fun of a thing; voucher, check, bond. *Il a cela de* — *qu'il ne ment jamais;* he has this good quality, that he never tells a lie. *Le* — *de l'histoire;* the cream of the story.

bon, *int.,* well, good, right. —, *je suis content de cela;* well, I like that.

bonace, *n.f.,* (nav.) calm, smooth sea.

bonasse, *adj.*, simple, easy ; silly.

bonbon, *n.m.*, bonbon, sweetmeat, comfit.

bonbonnière, *n.f.*, sugar-plum box ; neat little house.

bon-chrétien (-kré-), *n.m.*, (—*s* —*s*), kind of pear.

bond, *n.m.*, bound, skip, gambol, caper, capering. *Faire un* —; to make a bound. *Second* —; rebound. *Prendre la balle au* —; to catch the ball at the bound; to seize time by the forelock. *Il m'a fait faux* —; he has given me the slip. *Il s'élança d'un* — *par dessus la muraille*; he cleared the wail at a bound. *Aller par* —*s*; to skip about. *Il ne va que par sauts et par* —*s*, he only goes by fits and starts.

bonde, *n.f.*, sluice ; bung, bung-hole (of a cask—*d'un tonneau*).

bonder, *v.a.*, (nav.) to lade full.

bondir, *v.n.*, to bounce, to bound, to rebound ; to caper, to skip, to frisk. *Il bondissait de rage*; he bounded with rage. *Cela fait* — *le cœur*; that makes one's heart leap.

bondissant, -e, *adj.*, bounding, skipping, frisking.

bondissement (-mǎn), *n.m.*, bouncing, bounding, skipping, frisking.

bondon, *n.m.*, bung; bunghole.

bondonner, *v.a.*, to bung, to stop with a bung, to close up.

bondonnière, *n.f.*, bung-borer.

bonduc, *n.m.*, (bot.) bezoar.

bon-henri, *n.m.* (—), (bot.) all-good.

bonheur (bo-neur), *n.m.*, happiness, prosperity, felicity, welfare, blessing, good fortune, good luck, fortunate event. *Envier le* — *d'autrui*; to envy another's prosperity. *Le* — *de l'État*; the welfare of the state. *Faire le* — *de quelqu'un*; to make one happy. *Avoir du* —; to be lucky. *Être en* —; to be fortunate. *Par* —; luckily. *Porter* —; to bring good luck.

bonhomie (bo-no-mi), *n.f.*, good nature, easy humour, simplicity, credulity.

bonhomme (bo-nom), *n.m.*, (bonshommes) simple, good-natured man; old codger. *Vieux* —; old fellow, old buffer. *Petit* —; little fellow.

⊙**bonhommeau**, *n.m.* *V.* **bonhomme**.

boni, *n.m.* (—*s*), (fin.) bonus.

bonification, *n.f.*, amelioration, improvement ; (com.) allowance.

bonifier, *v.a.*, to better, to improve, to ameliorate ; to make up, to make good.

bonite, *n.f.*, (ich.) bonito.

bonjour, *n.m.*, good morning, good day. *Je vous souhaite le* —; I wish you good morning.

bonne, *n.f.*, nursery-maid ; lady's-maid. — *pour tout faire*; servant of all work.

bonneau, *n.m.*, (nav.) buoy of an anchor.

bonne-dame, *n.f.*, (—*s* —*s*). *V.* **arroche**.

bonnement (bo-n-mǎn), *adv.*, plainly, simply.

bonnet, *n.m.*, cap. — *de laine*; woollen cap. — *de nuit*; night-cap. *Gros* —; big wig, person of importance. *Opiner du* —; to adopt the opinion of another; to vote blindly. *Triste comme un* — *de nuit*; as dull as ditch water. *Porter la main au* —; to take one's cap off, to touch one's hat. *Avoir la tête près du* —; to be hot-headed. *Ce sont deux têtes dans un* —; they are hand and glove together. *C'est* — *blanc et blanc* —; there are six of one, and half a dozen of the other.

bonnetade, *n.f.*, capping, half-capping (jest).

⊙**bonneter**, *v.a.*, to cap, to doff one's hat (jest); to cringe.

bonneterie (bo-n-tri), *n.f.*, hosiery business.

bonneteur, *n.m.*, (l.u.) cringer, cringeling ; sharper.

bonnetier (bo-n-tié), *n.m.*, hosier.

bonnette, *n.f.*, (fort.) bonnet; (nav.) studding sail.

bonne-voglie, *n.m.* (—), volunteer rower in a galley.

bonsoir, *n.m.*, good evening. — *et bonne nuit!* a good night's rest to you !

bonté, *n.f.*, goodness, excellence, kindness, good-heartedness, favour. *Abuser de la* — *de quelqu'un*; to take advantage of one's goodness. *Des actes de* —; acts of kindness. *Avoir la* — *de*; to be so good as.

bonze, *n.m.*, bonze (Boodhist priest—*prêtre bouddhiste*).

⊙**boquillon*, *n.m.*, woodman, feller of wood.

boracique, *adj.* *V.* **borique**.

borax (-raks), *n.m.*, borax.

borborygme, *n.m.*, (med.) borborygm.

bord, *n.m.*, shore ; bank, strand, side, margin ; brink, edge, brim, skirt; rim, border, extremity ; hem, edging, lace; (nav.) board; (nav.) broadside; (nav.) tack. *Le* — *de la mer*; the seashore. *Le* — *d'une rivière*; the bank of a river. *Le* — *d'un précipice*; the brink of a precipice. *Le* — *d'une table*; the edge of a table. *Le* — *d'un chapeau*; the rim of a hat. *Le* — *d'un bateau*; the side of a boat. *Le—d'une robe*; the skirt of a gown. *J'ai son nom sur le* — *des lèvres*; I have his name at my tongue's end. *J'allai à son* —; I went aboard his ship. *Coucher à* —; to sleep on board a ship. *Tourner, changer, virer, de* —; to tack about, to veer. *Faire un* —; (nav.) to make a board. *Courir même* — *que l'ennemi*; to stand on the same tack with the enemy. — *au large*; standing off shore. — *à* —; alongside.

bordage, *n.m.*, (nav.) planking, flat, plank, poling.

bordé, *n.m.*, hem, edging, bordering.

bordeaux, *n.m.*, claret, Bordeaux wine.

bordée, *n.f.*, (nav.) broadside; volley; stretch, tack. *Lâcher une* —; to fire a broadside. *Une* — *d'injures*; a shower of abuse. *Courir des* —*s*; to tack about.

bordel, *n.m.*, (l.ex.) brothel.

bordelais, -e, *adj.*, of Bordeaux.

bordelais, *n.m.*, -e, *n.f.*, native of Bordeaux.

bordement, *n.m.*, edge.

border, *v.a.*, to edge, to hem, to bind, to lace, to border ; (nav.) to gather (the sheets—*les voiles*); to plank; to lay (a deck—*un pont*); to tuck up (bed-clothes—*les couvertures*); to line (a road, &c.—*une route*, &c.). *Les soldats bordent la côte*; soldiers line the coast. — *les côtés d'un vaisseau*; to plank a ship. — *les ponts*; to lay a ship's decks. — *une écoute*; to tally a sheet.

bordereau, *n.m.*, (com.) account, memorandum.

bordi-er, -ère, *adj.*, (nav.) lap-sided.

bordier, *n.m.*, lap-sided ship.

bordigue (-dig), *n.f.*, crawl (for taking fish —*filet à pêcher*).

bordure, *n.f.*, frame, edge, edging ; border, curb ; (nav.) flat.

boré, *n.m.*, (chem.) boron.

boréal, -e, *adj.*, boreal, northern.

borée, *n.m.*, Boreas, North-wind.

*borgne, *n.* and *adj.*, one-eyed person; blind of one eye; one-eyed; dark, obscure, paltry. *Changer son cheval* — *contre un aveugle*; to change for the worse. *Au royaume des aveugles les* —*s sont rois*; in the kingdom of the blind, one-eyed people are kings.

*borgnesse, *n.f.*, (pop.) one-eyed woman.

borique, *adj.*, (chem.) boracic.

bornage, *n.m.*, settling bounds ; boundaries.

borne, *n.f.*, landmark ; boundary, limit, confine ; bounds ; mile-stone, spur-post. *Passer les* —*s de la raison*; to go beyond the bounds of reason. *Mettre des* —*s à son ambition*; to set bounds to one's ambition. *Cela passe toutes les*

—*s*; that is going beyond all bounds. — *mi-liaire*; mile-stone.

borné, -e, *part.*, bounded, limited, confined; narrow, mean, small; shallow. *Esprit fort —*; narrow mind.

borne-fontaine, *n.f.* (—*s* —*s*), water-post.

borner, *v.a.*, to set land-marks; to bound, to set bounds to, to limit, to circumscribe, to restrict, to terminate, to confine. — *son ambition*; to set bounds to one's ambition.

se borner, *v.r.*, to keep within bounds. *Il faut — à cela*; we must be content with that.

bornous (-noos), *n.m.*, bournous (Arabian cloak—*manteau arabe*).

bornoyer, *v.a.*, to place, to set marks in (for plantations, foundations—*pour plantations, fondations, &c.*).

bornoyer, *v.a.*, to look over a surface with one eye (to see that it is even—*pour s'assurer qu'elle est plane*).

bosan, *n.m.*, bosan (Turkish beverage—*breuvage turc*).

bosel, *n.m.*, (arch.) torus.

bosphore, *n.m.*, Bosphorus.

bosquet, *n.m.*, grove, thicket.

bossage, *n.m.*, (arch.) bossage, embossment.

bosse, *n.f.*, hunch, hump; bump; bruise; knob, protuberance, lump; bunch; boss; embossment; (sculp.) relievo, relief, embossment; (paint.) bust; boss (at tennis—*au jeu de paume*). *Ne demander que plaie et —*; to think of nothing but mischief. *Ouvrage relevé en —*; embossed piece of work. *Ouvrage de demi —*; figure in half-relief. *Donner dans la —*; to fall into the snare, to be duped, to be caught. *Travailler en —*; to emboss.

bosselage (bos-laj), *n.m.*, embossing.

bosselé, -e, *adj.*, bruised (metal); (bot.) bunched; embossed.

bosseler (bos-le), *v.a.*, to dent; to emboss.

bosselure (bos-lur), *n.f.*, embossment.

bosseman (bos-män), *n.m.*, (nav.) boatswain's mate.

bosser, *v.a.*, (nav.) to stopper.

bossette, *n.f.*, (arch., man.) boss.

bossoir, *n.m.*, (nav.) cat-head.

bossu, -e, *n.* and *adj.*, hunchback; hunch-backed, humpbacked, crook-backed.

bossuer, *v.a.*, to bruise, to dent, to batter.

se bossuer, *v.r.*, to get bruised, dented.

bostangi, *n.m.* (—*s*), soldier of the Turkish militia.

boston, *n.m.*, boston (game at cards—*jeu de cartes*).

bostrychite (-kit), *n.f.*, (min.) bostrychite.

bot, *adj.*, club-footed. *Pied —*; (subst.) club-foot. *C'est un pied —*; he is club-footed.

bot, *n.m.*, Dutch-boat.

botanique, *n.f.*, botany.

botanique, *adj.*, botanical.

botaniste, *n.m.*, botanist.

botargue, *n.f.* *V.* Boutargue.

botte, *n.f.*, boot (man's only—*d'homme*); Wellington boot; bunch, bundle, truss; (fenc.) pass thrust; step of a coach; cask; clod of dirt or snow; wine vessel, butt. —*s à genouillère*; jack-boots. —*s à l'écuyère*; Hessian boots. *Souliers —s*; Blucher boots. —*s retroussées*, —*s à revers*; top-boots. —*s de sept lieues*; ogre's boots. —*s fines*; dress boots. *Tirant de —*; boot-strap. *Tige de —*; boot-leg. *Tire- —*; boot-jack. *Mettre du foin dans ses —*; to feather one's nest. *À propos de —s*; for nothing. *Graisser ses —*; to prepare for kingdom come. *Décrotter, cirer, des —s*; to clean, to polish, boots. *Une, —d'asperges*; a bundle of asparagus. *Une — de foin*; a truss of hay. *Porter une —à quelqu'un*; (fenc.) to make a pass at one. *Parer une —*; to parry a pass. *Il lui a porté une vilaine —*; he served him a very scurvy trick.

botté, -e, *adj.*, booted, that has boots on.

bottelage (bo-tlaj), *n.m.*, tying up in bundles (hay or straw—*du foin ou de la paille*).

botteler (bo-tlé), *v.a.*, to put up in bundles (hay or straw—*du foin ou de la paille*).

botteleur (bo-tleur), *n.m.*, (agri.) binder.

botter, *v.a.*, to make, to supply any one with, boots; to boot anybody. *Ce bottier botte bien, mal*; this bootmaker makes boots well, badly.

se botter, *v.r.*, to put one's boots on; to get one's shoes clogged with dirt; to ball (of horses—*chevaux*); (milit.) to boot. *Cet homme se botte bien, mal*; this man wears well made, badly made, boots.

bottier, *n.m.*, bootmaker, shoemaker.

bottine, *n.f.*, half-boot; lady's boot.

boubie, *n.f.*, (orni.) booby, gannet.

bouc, *n.m.*, he-goat; goat-skin. — *émissaire*; scape-goat.

boucage, *n.m.*, (bot.) burnet saxifrage.

boucan, *n.m.*, a place to dry-smoke in.

boucaner, *v.a.*, to smoke (meat—*viande*). — *des cuirs*; to smoke hides.

boucaner, *v.n.*, to hunt wild bulls for their hides.

boucanier, *n.m.*, buccaneer, bucanier; free-booter; buccaneer's musket.

boucaro, *n.m.*, boucaro, red clay.

boucassin, *n.m.*, lining, cotton stuff for lining.

boucaut, *n.m.*, cask (for dry goods—*pour marchandises sèches*); hogshead.

bouche, *n.f.*, mouth; lips; tongue; muzzle (of a cannon—*de canon*); voice; victuals; eating, living; cooks (of a sovereign—*d'un roi, &c.*); mouth (of canals, rivers—*de canaux, rivières, &c.*). *Dépense de —*; expenses for eating. *Munitions de —*; provisions. — *à —*; face to face. — *béante*; open-mouthed. *De —*; by word of mouth. *Être sur sa —*; to be given to gluttony. *Que l'imposture ne souille point votre —*; let not falsehood sully your lips. — *close*; keep it to yourself; mum! *Il dit cela de —, mais le cœur n'y touche*; he says one thing and thinks another. *Fermer la — à quelqu'un*; to stop any one's mouth. *Il dit tout ce qui lui vient à la —*; he says whatever comes uppermost. *Faire la petite —*; to be difficult to please. *Elle n'en fait point la fine —*; she does not mince it. *Faire la — en cœur*; to screw up one's mouth. *Cela rend la — amère*; that leaves a bitter taste in the mouth. *Garder une chose pour la bonne —*; to keep a tit-bit till the last. *Cela fait venir l'eau à la —*; that makes one's mouth water. *Prendre sur sa —*; to stint one's belly. *Selon ta bourse, gouverne ta —*; you must cut your coat according to your cloth. *Il arrive bien des choses entre la — et le morceau*; there is many a slip between the cup and the lip. *Cheval qui a bonne —*; hard-feeding horse. *Un cheval qui n'a ni — ni éperon*; a horse that obeys neither bridle nor spur. *Un homme fort en —*; a man that out-talks everybody.

bouchée, *n.f.*, mouthful. *Ne faire qu'une — de quelqu'un*; to make but a mouthful of any one, to beat any one with ease.

boucher, *v.a.*, to stop, stuff, choke up, to obstruct. — *une bouteille*; to cork a bottle. — *un tonneau*; to bung a barrel. — *la vue d'un voisin*; to obstruct a neighbour's view. *Se — les oreilles*; to stop one's ears. *Se — le nez*; to hold one's nose. — *un trou*; to stop a gap, to pay a debt.

boucher, *n.m.*, butcher. — *en gros*; carcass-butcher.

bouchère, *n.f.*, a butcher's wife, woman keeping a butcher's shop.

boucherie (boo-shri), *n.f.*, shambles, butchery, market; slaughter, carnage, massacre.

bouc...c-trou. *n.m.* (— —*s*), a stop-gap.

bouchoir, *n.m.*, stopper (of an oven—*d'un four*).

bouchon.,*n.m.*,cork,stopper; ⊙darling; wisp (of straw, &c.—*de paille, &c.*); packet (of linen —*de linge*); public-house. *Frotter un cheval avec un — de paille;* to rub down a horse with a wisp of straw. — *de cabaret;* tavern-bush. *Mon petit* ⊙ — ; my little darling.

bouchonner, *v.a.*, to rub down (a horse with a wisp of straw—*un cheval avec un bouchon de paille*).

bouchonnier, *n.m.*, corkcutter.

boucle, *n.f.*, buckle; ring; curl, ringlet, lock; (arch.) knocker; (nav.) staple, ring. *Des —s d'oreilles;* ear-rings. *Mettre une perruque en —s;* to curl a wig.

bouclé, -e, *part.*, buckled, curled. *Cheveux —s;* curled hair.

boucler, *v.a.*, to buckle; to put a ring to; to curl (hair—*les cheveux*).

se **boucler,** *v.r.*, to curl one's hair.

boucler, *v.n.*, to curl.

bouclier. *n.m.*, buckler, shield; defence, protection; (ich.) lump-fish.

boucon, *n.m.*, (l.ex.) poisoned drink or dish.

bouddhique, *adj.*, Buddhistic.

bouddhisme. *n.m.*, Buddhism.

bouddhiste, *n.m.* and *f.*, Buddhist.

bouder, *v.n.*, to pout, to look sour; to pout at; not to be able to play (dominoes); (hort.) to be stunted.

se **bouder,** *v.r.*, to be sulky with, to be cool, towards each other.

bouderie (bou-dri), *n.f.*, pouting; sulkiness.

boudeu-r, -se, *adj.*, sulky.

boudeu-r. *n.m.*, **-se,** *n.f.*, person who sulks.

boudin, *n.m.*, pudding; (nav.) pudding; (arch.) torus; saddle-bag, cloak-bag; spring (of a coach—*d'une voiture*); long curl.

boudinage, *n.m.*, twisting of cotton thread, roving.

boudine, *n.f.*, (glass-making—*manufacture du verre*) bunt, knot.

boudineu-r, *n.m.*, **-se,** *n.f.*, rover (of cotton thread).

boudini-er, *n.m.*, **-ère,** *n.f.*, pudding-maker.

boudinoir, *n.m.*, roving-machine.

boudoir, *n.m.*, boudoir, lady's private room.

boue, *n.f.*, dirt, mire, mud; sediment (of ink —*de l'encre*). *Être tout couvert de —;* to be dirty all over. *Je n'en fais pas plus de cas que de la — de mes souliers;* I don't value it more than the dirt of my shoes. *Une âme de —;* a dirty soul. *Tirer quelqu'un de la —;* to raise one from the dunghill. *Traîner quelqu'un dans la —;* to load one with abuse.

bouée, *n.f.*, (nav.) buoy. — *de sauvetage;* life-buoy.

boueur, *n.m.*, scavenger, dustman, street-orderly.

boueu-x, -se, *adj.*, dirty, miry; muddy; foul. *Chemin —;* dirty road. *Écriture —se;* thick writing.

bouffant, -e. *adj.*, puffed.

⊙**bouffante,** *n.f.*, hoop, farthingale.

bouffarde. *n.f.*, (pop.) weed (pipe). *Téter sa —;* to do one's weed, to blow one's cloud.

bouffe. *n.m.*, buffoon; *pl.*, Italian opera (at Paris). *Aller aux —s;* to go to the Italian opera.

bouffée. *n.f.*, puff, gust, blast, whiff; fit. *Une — de vent;* a puff of wind. *Une — de fumée;* a puff of smoke. *Une — de fièvre;* a short attack of fever. *Par —s;* by fits and starts.

bouffer, *v.n.*, to puff, to swell.

bouffer, *v.a.*, to blow (meat—*terme de boucher*).

bouffette, *n.f.*, bow (ribbon); ear-knot.

bouffi, -e, *adj.*, puffed up, swollen. *Des joues*

—*es;* puffed cheeks. — *d'orgueil;* puffed up with pride.

bouffir, *v.a.*, to puff up, to swell, to bloat.

bouffissure, *n.f.*, swelling, puffing up; turgidness, bombast.

bouffon, *n.m.*, buffoon, jester, merry-andrew, jack-pudding, droll. *Un mauvais —;* a sorry jester. *Faire le —;* to play the buffoon.

bouffon, -ne, *adj.*, jocose, facetious, comical.

bouffonner. *v.n.*, to be jocose, full of jests; to play the buffoon.

bouffonnerie (fo-n-ri), *n.f.*, buffoonery, drollery, jesting.

bouge, *n.m.*, little closet, hole, wretched lodging, bulge of a cask.

bougeoir (-joar), *n.m.*, flat candlestick, chamber-candlestick; taper-stand.

bouger, *v.n.*, to stir, to budge, to wag. *Il ne bouge de cette maison;* he is always at that house.

⊙**bougette,** *n.f.*, budget (bag); pouch.

bougie, *n.f.*, wax-candle, wax-light; (surg.) bougie.

bougier, *v.a.*, to wax.

bougonner, *v.n.*, to grumble, to mum.

bougran, *n.m.*, buckram.

***bouillabaisse,** *n.f.*, Provencal fish-soup with garlic, &c.

***bouillant, -e.** *adj.*, boiling, boiling-hot, scalding-hot, piping-hot; hot, fiery, hasty, eager, fierce, hot-headed. *Jeunesse —e;* fiery youth. — *de colère;* boiling with anger. — *d'impatience;* burning with impatience.

***bouille,** *n.f.*, fishing pole.

***bouiller,** *v.a.*, to stir the water with a pole.

***bouillerie,** *n.f.*, boilery.

***bouilleur,** *n.m.*, boiler-tube (of a steam-engine—*de machine à vapeur*).

***bouilli,** *n.m.*, boiled beef, bouilli.

***bouillie,** *n.f.*, pap (for infants—*pour les petits enfants*); pulp (to make paper—*pour faire le papier*). *Faire de la — pour les chats;* to have trouble for nothing.

***bouillir,** *v.n.*, to boil; to simmer. *Faire — à demi;* to parboil. *Il faut d'impatience;* he boils with impatience. *Cela sert à faire — la marmite;* that helps to make the pot boil.

***bouillir,** *v.a.*, to boil. Only used in the popular and figurative expression: — *du lait à quelqu'un;* to say something very pleasant to somebody.

***bouilloire,** *n.f.*, boiler, kettle.

***bouillon,** *n.m.*, broth; bubble, ripple, bubbling; ebullition, transport; puff (of a lady's dress—*de robe*). — *en tablette;* portable broth. — *de poulet;* chicken broth. — *de veau;* veal-broth. — *coupé;* broth diluted with water. *Prendre un —;* to take some broth. *Boire un —;* to swallow a mouthful (in bathing—*en nageant, en se baignant*); to meet with a loss. — *pointu;* clyster. *L'eau sort de la roche à gros —s;* the water comes gushing out of the rock. *Le sang sortait à gros —s;* the blood gushed out abundantly. *Un — d'eau;* a bubbling fountain.

***bouillon-blanc,** *n.m.* (—*s* —*s*), mullen, cow's-lung-wort.

***bouillonnant, -e,** *adj.*, bubbling; gurgling.

***bouillonnement** (-io-n-màn), *n.m.*, bubbling up, spouting or gushing out; ebullition.

***bouillonner,** *v.n.*, to bubble, to gush out, to boil, to boil over.

bouillonner, *v.a.*, to put puffs to. — *une robe;* to put puffs to a dress.

***bouillotte,** *n.f.* *V.* **bouilloire.**

***bouillotte.** *n.f.*, bouillotte (game at cards played by five persons—*jeu de cartes*).

bouin, *n.m.*, (dy.) head of silk.

bouis, *n.m.*, glazing-stick.

boujaron, *n.m.*, about half a gill.

boulaie. *n.f.*, (l.u.) birch plantation.

boulang-er, *n.m.*, **-ère**, *n.f.*, baker; baker's wife.

boulanger, *v.a.*, to make bread. *Du pain bien boulangé;* well-made bread.

boulanger, *v.n.*, to bake.

boulangerie (-lan-jrî), *n.f.*, baking, bakers' business; bakehouse.

boule, *n.f.*, bowl, ball, pate, sconce. *Il est rond comme une —;* he is as round as a ball. *Un jeu de —;* a bowling-green. *Jouer à la —;* to play at bowls. *Avoir la —;* to play first. *Boule-de-neige (—s —);* (bot.) snow-ball. ☉*À la — vue;* in haste, carelessly. — (for voting—*de vote*), ballot.

bouleau, *n.m.*, birch, birch-tree.

bouledogue, *n.m.*, bull-dog.

boulet, *n.m.*, bullet, ball; fetlock-joint (of a horse—*du cheval*); (man.) boulet. *Un — de canon;* a cannon-ball. *Un coup de —;* a cannon-shot. — *rouge;* red-hot ball. *Condamner au —;* (milit.) to condemn to drag a cannon-ball. *Tirer à —s rouges sur quelqu'un;* to load one with abuse.

bouleté, **-e**, *adj.*, (vet.) boulet (of the fore-legs only—*des jambes de devant seulement*). *V.* **juché**.

boulette, *n.f.*, forced-meat ball; pellet, blunder. *Faire des —s;* to commit blunders.

bouleux, *n.m.*, thick-set horse; heavy hack; drudge. *Un bon —;* a plodding man, a drudge.

boulevard, *or* **boulevart** (bool-var), *n.m.*, bulwark, rampart; boulevard.

bouleversement (bool-vers-măn), *n.m.*, destruction; overthrow; overthrowing; over-turning; commotion.

bouleverser (bool-vèr-), *v.a.*, to overthrow; to throw down, to subvert; to agitate, to trouble, to throw into commotion; to upset; to unsettle, to unhinge. *Cela m'a tout bouleversé;* it has quite unhinged me.

☉*à la* **boule vue**, *adv. V.* **boule**.

boulier, *n.m.*, bag-net (fishing—*péche*).

boulimie, *n.f.*, (med.) bulimy.

boulimique, *adj.*, bulimic.

boulin, *n.m.*, pigeon-hole; (mas.) pigeon-cove; putlog. *Trous de —;* scaffolding-holes.

bouline, *n.f.*, (nav.) bowline, gauntlet. *Aller à la —;* to go near the wind; to tack about. *Courir la —;* to run the gauntlet.

bouliner, *v.n.*, to go with a side-wind.

bouliner, *v.a.*, to haul windward. —*une voile;* to haul a sail to the windward.

boulingrin, *n.m.*, bowling-green, grass-plot.

boulinier, *n.m.*, (nav.) *Un bon —;* a ship that goes well with a side-wind.

bouloir, *n.m.*, (mas.) larry.

boulon, *n.m.*, bolt, great iron pin.

boulonner, *v.a.*, to pin, to fasten with iron pins, to bolt.

☉**bouque**, *n.f.*, channel, strait, canal, passage; mouth of a river.

☉**bouquer**, *v.a.*, and *n.*, to kiss forcibly, to compel (a child *or* a monkey—*un enfant ou un singe*) to kiss some object; to compel, to force.

bouquet, *n.m.*, bunch, cluster, tuft; nosegay; bouquet; birthday ode, sonnet; birthday present; flavour (of wine—*du vin*). *Un — de plumes;* a plume of feathers. *Un — de pierreries;* a sprig of jewels. *Un — de bois;* a cluster of trees. *Fleur qui vient en —s;* flower that grows in bunches. — *de fusées;* bunch of rockets. *Réserver une chose pour le —;* to keep a thing for the last.

bouquetier (book-tié), *n.m.*, flower-vase.

bouquetière, *n.f.*, flower-girl.

bouquetin, *n.m.*, wild goat.

bouquin, *n.m.*, old he-goat; buck-hare; old book.

bouquiner, *v.n.*, to buck, to couple (of hares—*lièvres*); to hunt after, to read, old books.

bouquinerie, (-ki-n-rî), *n.f.*, old-book trade.

bouquineur, *n.m.*, lover of old books.

bouquiniste, *n.m.*, dealer in old books.

bouracan, *n.m.*, a sort of camlet, barracan.

bouracanier, *n.m.*, barracan maker.

bourbe, *n.f.*, mire, mud, dirt.

bourbeux, **-se**, *adj.*, miry, muddy, sloughy.

bourbier, *n.m.*, slough, puddle, mire, mud; lurch, plunge, scrape, danger. *Il s'est mis dans le —;* he has got himself into a scrape.

*bourbillon**, *n.m.*, core (of an abscess—*d'un abcès*).

bourcette. *V.* **mâche**.

bourdaine, *or* **bourgène**, *n.f.*, black alder.

bourdalou, *n.m.*, hat-band; sort of chamber-pot.

bourde, *n.f.*, fib, sham, humbug, lie. *Donner une — à quelqu'un;* to tell any one a fib.

bourder, *v.n.*, to fib, to sham, to humbug.

bourdeur, *n.m.*, fibber, shammer.

*bourdillon**, *n.m.*, stave-wood (for casks —*pour tonneaux*).

bourdon, *n.m.*, drone; pilgrim's staff; great bell; (mus.) drone; humble-bee; great bell (print.) out, omission.

bourdonnant, **-e**, *adj.*, humming, buzzing.

bourdonnement (-măn), *n.m.*, buzz, buzzing; hum, humming; murmur; tinkling noise.

bourdonner, *v.n.*, to buzz, to hum; to murmur.

bourdonner, *v.a.*, to hum; to bore; te pester.

bourdonnet, *n.m.*, (surg.) dossil.

bourdonneur, *n.m.*, humming-bird, colibri.

bourg, *n.m.*, country-town, market-town.

bourgade, *n.f.*, small market-town, straggling village.

bourgène, *n.f. V.* **bourdaine**.

bourgeois, *n.m.*, **-e**, *n.f.*, (-joâ, -joaz), burgess, citizen, townsman, commoner; master, mistress, owner of a merchant-ship; contractor. *Un bon —;* a substantial citizen. *Un petit —;* an humble, a mean, citizen.

bourgeois, **-e**, *adj.*, belonging to, or becoming, a citizen, citizenlike; private; plain; common. *Famille —e;* good creditable family. *Avoir l'air —, les manières —es;* to have the carriage, manners of a citizen.

bourgeoisement (joaz-măn), *adv.*, citizen-like.

bourgeoisie (-joa-zî), *n.f.*, freedom of the city; citizenship, citizens. *Avoir le droit de—;* to be free of a city.

bourgeon (boor-jon), *n.m.*, bud, gem, shoot; pimple.

bourgeonnant, **-e**, *adj.*, budding.

bourgeonné, **-e**, *part.*, budded, pimpled. *Avoir le nez —;* to have a nose covered with pimples.

bourgeonnement (-jo-n-măn), *n.m.*, budding-time.

bourgeonner (-jo-né), *v.n.*, to bud, to shoot, to put forth young shoots.

bourgeonnier (-jo-nié), *n.m.*, (orni.) bullfinch.

bourgmestre, *n.m.*, burgomaster.

*bourgogne**, *n.m.*, Burgundy wine.

bourguépine (-ghé-), *n.f.*, (bot.) purging thorn.

*bourguignon**, **-ne** (-ghi-), *n.* and *adj.*, Burgundian, of Burgundy.

bourlet, *n.m. V.* **bourrelet**.

bournous, *V.* **bornous**.

bourrache, *n.f.*, (bot.) borage.

bourrade, *n.f.*, blow with the butt-end of a gun; (hunt.) snapping.

bourras, *n.m. V.* **bure**.

bourrasque, *n.f.*, squall; relapse; new attack (of a disease—*des maladie*); vexation; caprice; fit of anger, of ill-humour.

bourre, *n.f.*, hair (of animals—*des animaux*); stuff, trash; flock (of wool—*de laine*); floss (of silk—*de soie*); wad (of fire-arms—*d'armes à feu*); kind of down (on the buds of certain trees—*sur les bourgeons de certains arbres*). *Lit de* —; flock-bed.

bourreau, *n.m.*, hangman, executioner; tormentor, cruel man, butcher. *Un — d'argent*; a spendthrift.

bourrée, *n.f.*, brushwood; small fagot; boree (dance).

bourreler (boŏr-), *v.a.*, to torment, to sting; to torture, to rack.

bourrelet or **bourlet**, *n.m.*, pad; cushion with a hole in the middle; swelling (about the loins—*aux reins*); kind of padded cap worn by children.

bourrelier (boor-), *n.m.*, harness-maker, for beasts of burden.

⊙**bourrelle**, *n.f.*, the hangman's wife.

bourrellerie (boo-rèl-11), *n.f.*, business of a harness-maker.

bourrer, *v.a.*, to ram; to thrash; to abuse; to stuff, to wad; to cram with food; ⊙ to nonplus; (hunt.) to snap.

se **bourrer**, *v.r.*, to cram one's self with food; to abuse each other.

bourrer, *v.n.*, (of horses—*des chevaux*) to bolt.

bourriche, *n.f.*, game-basket.

bourrique, *n.f.*, she-ass; ignorant, stupid person.

bourriquet, *n.m.*, ass's colt; hand-barrow; windlass; mason's horse.

bourroir, *n.m.*, tamping-bar.

bourru, **-e**, *adj.*, cross, morose, peevish, crabbed, moody, wayward, surly, snappish; unfermented.

bourse, *n.f.*, purse; hair-bag; purse-net; saddle-bag; scholarship; foundation; (anat.) sac; (bot.) wrapper; (surg.) suspensory bandage; (com.) exchange. *Coupeur de —*; cut-throat. *Avoir la —*; to keep the money. *Faire — commune*; to live in common. *Faire — à part*; to keep one's own money. *La — ou la vie!* your money or your life! *Aller à la —*; to go to the Exchange, to go on 'Change.

bourses, *n.f. pl.*, scrotum.

boursette, *n.f.*, small purse.

boursicaut, *n.m.*, small purse; small sum.

boursier, *n.m.*, purse-maker; foundation scholar; exhibitioner (at the universities—*terme d'université*).

*****boursiller**, *v.n.*, to club together, to contribute something towards any expense.

bourson, *n.m.*, fob, little pocket.

boursouflage, *n.m.*, turgidness, bombast.

boursouflé, **-e**, *adj.*, bloated; bombastic, inflated, turgid. *Style —*; turgid style.

boursoufler, *v.a.*, to bloat, to make turgid, to puff up.

boursouflure, *n.f.*, bloatedness (of countenance—*du visage*); turgidness (style).

bousage, *n.m.*, dunging.

bousard, or **bouzard**, *n.m.*, deer's dung.

bousculement (boos-kul-măn), *n.m.*, jostling, justling, hustling.

bousculer, (boos-) *v.a.*, to turn upside down, to throw into disorder; to jostle, to justle, to squeeze.

bouse, (booz), *n.f.*, cow-dung.

*****bousillage**, *n.m.*, mud-wall; mud-walling; bungling piece of work.

*****bousiller**, *v.a.*, to make a mud-wall; to bungle, to botch.

*****bousilleu-r**, *n.m.*, **-se**, *n.f.*, mud-wall builder; bungler, botcher.

bousin, *n.m.*, the soft crust of freestone; (l.ex.) noise, clamour.

boussole, *n.f.*, sea compass, compass; mariner's needle; guide, direction.

boustrophédon, *n.m.*, (antiq.) boustrophedon (manner of writing alternately from the right to the left, and from the left to the right —*manière d'écrire alternativement de droite à gauche, et de gauche à droite sans discontinuer la ligne*).

bout, *n.m.*, end; tip; bit; nipple; muzzle, ferrule; fag-end. *Le — des doigts;* the finger-ends. *Savoir une chose sur le — des doigts;* to have a thing at one's finger-ends, to know it perfectly. *Brûler la chandelle par les deux —s;* to burn the candle at both ends, to be a bad manager. *Le bas —;* the lower end. *Le — de la langue;* the tip of the tongue. *Le — de la mamelle;* the nipple of the breast. *—s de manches;* false sleeves. *—s d'aile;* pinions. *Bâton à deux —s;* quarter staff. *Au — d'une heure de conversation;* when we had conversed together an hour. *Tenir le haut —;* to get the upper hand. *Se tenir sur le — des pieds;* to stand on tip-toe. *Patience, nous ne sommes pas au —;* have patience, we have not done yet. *Tirer un coup de pistolet à — portant;* to fire off a pistol close to a person or thing. *Rire du — des dents;* to laugh the wrong side of one's mouth. *Un — de ruban;* a bit of riband. *Un — de chandelle;* a piece of candle. *Mettre la patience de quelqu'un à —;* to exhaust one's patience. *Pousser quelqu'un à —;* to nonplus any one; to drive any one to extremities. *Venir à — de;* to succeed. *On ne saurait venir à — de cet enfant;* this child cannot be managed. *À tout — de champ;* at every turn. *Au — du compte;* after all; upon the whole. *D'un — à l' autre;* from beginning to end. *— -rimé.* V. **bout-rimé**.

boutade, *n.f.*, (boo-) whim, fit, start, caprice, frolic, freak. *Par —;* by fits and starts.

boutant, *adj.*, (arch.) supporting. *Arc —;* buttress.

boutargue or **botargue**, *n.f.*, botargo.

bout-dehors. (—s —) V. **boute-hors**.

bouté, **-e**, *adj.*, (măn.) straight-legged. *Cheval —;* straight-legged horse.

boute-en-train, *n.m.* (—), stallion kept with mares; bird that teaches others the notes; merry companion that gives others the cue; life and soul of the company.

boutefeu, *n.m.* (artil.) linstock; incendiary, firebrand.

boute-hors, *n.m.* (—), a game long out of use; (nav.) boom; good command of words. *Jouer au —;* to try to oust one another.

*****bouteille**, *n.f.*, bottle; bottleful; bubble; bottle case. *Boucher une —;* to cork a bottle. *Déboucher une —;* to uncork a bottle. *Mise en —;* bottling. *Faire sauter le bouchon d'une —;* to crack a bottle (instead of uncorking it). *N'avoir rien vu que par le trou d'une —;* to know nothing of the world.

⊙*****bouteiller**. V. **boutillier**.

*****bouteilles**, *n.f. pl.*, (nav.) round house.

⊙**bouter**, *v.a.*, to put.

⊙**bouter**, *v.n.*, (of wine—*du vin*) to become ropy.

bouterolle (boo-trol), *n.f.*, chape (of a scabbard—*d'un fourreau de sabre, &c.*).

boute-selle, *n.m.* (— —s), (milit.) signal to saddle. *Sonner le —;* to sound the signal to saddle.

⊙**boute-tout-cuire**, *n.m.* (—), (fam.) a spendall, glutton.

bouteuse, *n.f.*, pin-sticker.

⊙*****boutillier**, *n.m.*, cup-bearer.

boutique, *n.f.*, shop; merchandise of a

shop; tools; implements; well for fish. *Garçon de* —; shop-boy. *Demoiselle de* —; shop-girl. *Cela vient de votre* —; that is your doing. *— bien fournie;* a well-stocked shop. *Il a vendu toute sa* —; he has left off business.

boutiqu-ier (boo-), *n.m.*, **-ière**, *n.f.*, tradesman; shopkeeper.

boutis, *n.m.*, (hunt.) rooting-place (of a wild boar, &c.—*du sanglier, &c.*).

boutisse (boo-)*, n.f.*, (mas.) header.

boutoir, *n.m.*, snout of a wild boar; buttress; parer; currier's knife. *Coup de* —; rough answer; disagreeable proposal.

bouton, *n.m.*, button; stud; bud; nipple; pimple; gem; knob; sight (of a gun—*de fusil*); (chem.) button. *— à queue;* shank button. — *d'or;* butter-cup. *Le — d'une serrure;* the knob, button of a lock. *Serrer le — à quelqu'un;* to be urgent upon one.

boutonné, -e, *part.*, buttoned, pimpled. *Nez* —; nose full of red pimples. *C'est un homme* —; he is very reserved.

boutonnement (-mān), *n.m.*, budding; buttoning.

boutonner, *v.a.*, to button.

se boutonner, *v.r.*, to button one's coat.

boutonner, *v.n.*, to bud, to button.

boutonnerie (boo-to-n-rî), *n.f.*, button-trade.

⊙**boutonnet**, *n.m.*, little bud, button, gem.

boutonnier, *n.m.*, button-maker.

boutonnière, *n.f.*, button-hole.

bout-rimé, *n.m.*, poetry made on given rhymes; (*—s —s*) rhymes given to be formed into verse.

bouts-rimeur, *n.m.* (— —*s*), person who fills up given rhymes.

*****bout-saigneux**, *n.m.* (—*s* —), scrag end (of a neck of mutton, &c.—*d'un cou de mouton, &c.*).

bouture, *n.f.*, (hort.) slip; cutting.

⊙**bouvard**, *n.m.*, hammer formerly used in coining.

bouveau, *n.m.*, young bullock.

bouverie (boo-vrî), *n.m.*, ox-stall.

bouvet, *n.m.*, joiner's grooving-plane.

bouvi-er, *n.m.*, **-ere**, *n.f.*, cowherd, drover, ox-drover.

*****bouvillon**, *n.m.*, young bullock. steer.

| *****bouvreuil**, *n.m.*, (boo-) bullfinch.

bovine, *adj.*, bovine.

boxe, *n.f.*, boxing (fight—*combat*).

boxer, *v.n.*, to box.

se boxer, *v.r.*, to box.

boxeur, *n.m.*, boxer. *Combat de —s;* boxing match.

boyard, *n.m.*, boyard (Russian nobleman—*noble russe*).

boyau, *n.m.*, bowel, gut; (hort.) branch; hose, pipe. *Corde à* —; catgut. *— de tranchée;* branch of a trench (fort.). *Racler le —;* to scrape (the violin—*le violon*).

boyauderie, *n.f.*, place where the entrails of animals are cleaned and prepared; gut-work.

boyaudier, *n.m.*, gutspinner.

brabançon, -ne, *adj.*, pertaining to Brabant. Brabantine.

bracelet (bra-slè), *n.m.*, armlet. bracelet.

brachial, -e (-ki-), *adj.*, (anat.) brachial.

brachygraphie (-ki-), *n.f.*, brachygraphy.

brachylogie (-ki-), *n.f.*, (rhet.) brachylogy.

braconnage, *n.m.*, poaching.

braconner, *v.n.*, to poach, to steal game.

braconnier, *n.m.*, poacher.

bractée, *n.f.*, (bot.) bract, bractea.

bractéifère, *adj.*, (bot.) bracteate.

bractélé, -e, *adj.*, *V.* **bractéifère.**

brague (brag), *n.f.*, (nav.) breeching. *— de canon;* breeching of a cannon.

braguette, *n.f.*, *V.* **brayette.**

brahmane, *n.m.*, Bramin, Brahmin, Brachman.

brahmanique, *adj.*, pertaining to the Bramins, Braminic.

brahmanisme, *n.m.*, Braminism.

brai, *n.m.*, resin.

braie, *n.f.*, ⊙child's clout; (nav.) coat; *pl.*, breeches. trousers. *S'en tirer les —s nettes;* to get off unharmed, clear.

*****braillard**, *n.m.*, **-e**, *n.f.*, bawler, brawler, squaller.

*****braillard, -e**, *adj.*, brawling, squalling.

*****brailler**, *v.n.*, to bawl, to be noisy.

brailleu-r, -se, *adj.* and *n.* *V.* **braillard.**

braiment, *n.m.*, braying of an ass.

braire, *v.n.*, to bray.

braise, *n.f.*, live coal; embers; burning coal. *Il l'a donné chaud comme* —; he blurted it out all at once.

braiser, *v.a.*, (cook.) to bake.

braisier, *n.m.*, brazier.

braisière, *n.f.*, oven.

brame. *V.* **brahmane.**

bramement, *n.m.*, (hunt.) belling.

bramer, *v.n.*, (of stags only—*du cerf seulement*) to bell.

bramin or **bramine**, *n.m.* *V.* **brahmane.**

⊙**bran**, *n.m.*, excrement. *— de son;* coarse bran; saw dust.

bran ! *int.*, (l.ex.) *— de lui !* a fig for him !

brancard, *n.m.*, sedan, litter, hand-barrow; shaft (of a cart, &c.—*d'une charrette, &c.*).

brancardier, *n.m.*, (milit.) sick-bearer, litter-bearer.

branchage, *n.m.*, branches, boughs.

branche, *n.f.*, branch, bough, stick, arm; pinwire; part, division; (arch.) branch; side (of a ladder—*d'une échelle*); branch (of a family —*d'une famille*); (bot.) grain. *A —s;* branched, branchy. *Sauter de — en —;* to go from one thing to another. *Jeune* —; twig. *—s gourmandes;* proud wood. *S'accrocher à toutes les —s;* to try every possible means, whether fair or foul. *Les —s d'une science;* the branches of a science.

⊙**brancher**, *v.a.*, to hang on a tree.

brancher, *v.n.*, (hunt.) to perch, to roost.

branche-ursine, or **branc-ursine**, *n.f.* (—), (bot.) brank-ursine.

branchial, -e, *adj.*, (ich.) of the gills. *Opercule* —; gill-cover.

branchier, *adj. m.*, that flies from branch to branch.

branchies (-shî), *n.f. pl.*, fish-gills.

branchiostège (-shee-), *adj.*, (ich.) branchiostegous.

branchu, -e, *adj.*, full of branches, ramous.

brandade, *n.f.*, manner of cooking cod

brande, *n.f.*, heath.

brandebourg, *n.m.*, gimp. *À —s;* frogged.

⊙**brandevin**, *n.m.*, wine-brandy.

*****brandillement**, *n.m.*, tossing, swinging.

*****brandiller**, *v.a.*, to swing, to shake to and fro.

*****se brandiller**, *v.r.*, to swing.

*****brandilloire**, *n.f.*, swing. see-saw; (agri.) swing-plough.

brandir, *v.a.*, to brandish, to swing; (carp.) to pin.

brandon, *n.m.*, wisp of straw lighted; fire-brand, flake of fire. *— de discorde;* cause of discord.

brandonner, *v.a.*, to place brands in to mark the seizure of a field.

branlant, -e, *adj.*, shaking, wagging, tottering. *Un château* —; anything ready to fall.

branle, *n.m.*, jogging, push, swing, tossing, motion, shaking; sort of dance, brawl; hammock : (nav.) hammock. *Étre en —;* to be in motion. *Donner le —;* to set going. *Mener le —;* to lead the dance.

branle-bas, *n.m.* (—), (nav.) clearing. *Faire le —;* to clear the decks. *— !* up all hammocks !

branlement (bran-mān), *n.m.,* jogging; motion ; swinging.

branle-queue, *n.m.* (—), (orni.) wag-tail ; dish-washer.

branler, *v.a.,* to jog, to wag, to move, to shake, to brandish.

se **branler**, *v.r.,* to move.

branler, *v.n.,* to shake, to jog, to totter, to rock ; to stir, to move, to wag : to give ground. *— dans le manche;* to shake in the handle, to be unsteady, irresolute. *Tout ce qui branle ne tombe pas;* everything that shakes doesn't fall.

branloire, *n.f.,* see-saw ; swing.

braque, *n.m.,* brach-hound ; a hare-brained fellow.

⊙**braquemart**, *n.m.,* cutlass.

braquement (brak-mān), *n.m.,* pointing of a piece of ordnance.

braquer, *v.a.,* to set, to turn, to level, to point. *— un canon;* to level a cannon. *— une lunette;* to point a telescope.

bras, *n.m.,* arm ; power; sconce (candelabrum *—candélabre*); arm (of anchors, capstans, levers, seats—*d'ancres, de cabestans, de leviers, de sièges*); brace (of yards—*de vergues*); handle ; shaft (of litters—*de litières*); (mec.) side rod ; arm (of a horse—*du cheval*); claw (of a crawfish—*de l'écrevisse*). *Étre blessé au —;* to be wounded in the arm. *Il a le — en écharpe;* he has his arm in a sling. *Recevoir quelqu'un à — ouverts;* to receive one with open arms. *Demeurer les — croisés;* to stand with folded arms. *À pleins —;* by armfuls. *Un — de mer;* an arm of the sea. *À force de —;* by strength of arms. *Ne vivre que de ses —;* to live by the labour of one's hands. *Avoir quelqu'un sur les —;* to have one to maintain. *Avoir de grandes affaires sur les —;* to have great concerns in hand. *J'ai sur les — un puissant ennemi;* I have to do with a powerful enemy. *Les — m'en sont tombés;* I stood amazed at it. *Se jeter entre les — de quelqu'un;* to fly to any one for protection. *Tendre les — à quelqu'un;* to offer one's aid to one. *Moulin à —;* handmill. *Les — de la mort;* the jaws of death. *À tour de —;* with all one's might. *À — -le- corps;* in one's arms. *Saisir quelqu'un à — -le- corps;* to seize any one round the body. *— dessus — dessous;* arm in arm.

braser, *v.a.,* to braze, to solder.

brasier, *n.m.,* quick clear fire; brazier (pan for coals—*réchaud*).

*****brasillement** (-mān), *n.m.,* (nav.) glittering, glancing, sparkling of the sea.

*****brasiller**, *v.a.,* to sparkle (of the sea—*de la mer*).

brasque, *n.f.,* brasque (cement made of clay and charcoal dust—*ciment fait d'argile et de poussière de charbon*).

brasquer, *v.a.,* to cover with brasque.

brassage, *n.m.,* stirring up; (coin.) mixing.

brassard, *n.m.,* brace (armour—*armure*); armulet.

brasse, *n.f.,* (nav.) fathom, six feet. *Pain de —;* a twenty or twenty-five pound loaf.

brassée, *n.f.,* armful.

brasser, *v.a.,* to brew ; to stir ; to hatch, to work, to plot.

brasserie, *n.f.,* brewery, brewhouse.

brasseur, *n.m.,* *-se*, *n.f.,* brewer; brewer's wife.

brasseyage, *n.m.,* (nav.) quarter (of a yard).

brassiage, *n.m.,* (nav.) fathoming depth (of the sea—*de la mer*).

brassières, *n.f. pl.,* bodice for infants; restraint. *Étre en —;* to be under restraint. [This word is often used in the singular.]

brassin, *n.m.,* brewing tub; brewing (quantity brewed—*quantité brassée*); boiling (soapmaking—*manufacture du savon*).

brassoir, *n.m.,* (metal.) stirring-stick.

brasure, *n.f.,* brazing, soldering.

bravache, *n.m.,* bully, swaggerer, hector.

bravade, *n.f.,* bravado, hectoring.

brave, *adj.,* brave, gallant, true; smart, fine, spruce; honest; good, kind. *— capitaine;* gallant captain. *Il est — comme l'épée qu'il porte;* he is as true as steel. *Il n'est — qu'en paroles;* he is brave as far as words go. *Un homme —; a* brave man. *Vous voilà bien — aujourd'hui;* how smart you are to-day. *C'est un — homme;* he is an honest, worthy, fellow.

brave, *n.m.,* brave, courageous, man ; (b.s.) ruffian, bully. *Faux —;* blustering bully. *Faire le —;* to play the bully. *— à trois poils;* man of real courage, right down plucky, regular game.

bravement (-mān), *adv.,* bravely, stoutly, valiantly, manfully ; skilfully, finely.

braver, *v.a.,* to defy, to set at defiance, to bid defiance, to dare, to beard, to face, to brave. *— les autorités;* to bid the authorities defiance. *— la mort;* to face death.

braverie (vri), *n.f.,* finery, fine clothes.

bravo, *n.m.* (bravi), bravo, hired assassin.

bravo! *adv.,* bravo! well done! *—*, *n.m.* (*-s*), applause.

bravoure, *n.f.,* bravery, courage, manhood, gallantry ; (mus.) bravura. *Il a fait preuve de —;* he has given proofs of courage.

brayer (bra-ié), *n.m.,* (surg.) truss, bandage.

brayer (brè-ié), *v.a.,* (nav.) to pay over.

brayette (bra-iète), *n.f.,* flap (of trousers—*de pantalons*); (bot.) common primrose.

brayon (bra-ion), *n.m.,* trap (for fetid animals —*à bêtes puantes*).

break (brèke), *n.m.* (*— s*), break (carriage—*voiture*).

bréant *or* **bruant**, *n.m.,* (orni.) bunting, yellow-hammer.

brebis, *n.f.,* ewe; sheep; *pl.,* flock. *— égarée;* stray sheep. *Troupeau de —;* flock of sheep. *Une — galeuse;* a black sheep. *Mener paître les —;* to lead the sheep to pasture. *Il ne faut qu'une — galeuse pour gâter tout un troupeau;* one scabbed sheep will taint a whole flock. *Qui se fait —, le loup le mange;* daub yourself with honey, and you'll never want flies. *À — tondue, Dieu mesure le vent;* God tempers the wind to the shorn lamb. *Faire un repas de —;* to eat a dry meal.

brèche, *n.f.,* breach, flaw, rupture, hiatus, notch, gap. *Battre en —;* to batter in, to breach. *Monter à la —;* to mount the breach. *La — d'un couteau;* the notch of a knife. *Faire — à un pâté;* to make a gap in a pie. *C'est une — à l'honneur;* it is a breach of honour.

brèche, *n.f.,* (min.) breccia.

brèche-dent, *adj.* (—), that has lost a front tooth or two.

brèche-dent, *n.m.f.* (—), person with a front tooth out.

brechet, *n.m.,* breast-bone, brisket.

bredi-breda, *adv.,* (fam.) hastily.

bredindin, *n.m.,* (nav.) garnet.

brédissure, *n.f.,* (med.) locked jaw.

*****bredouillage**, *n.m.,* jabber, sputtering.

*****bredouille**, *n.f.,* (trictrac) lurch. *Jouer —;* to play lurches. *Sortir —;* to go away as one came.

*****bredouillement**, *n.m.,* stuttering, stammering, faltering.

3*

*bredouiller, *v.n.*, to stammer, stutter, to falter.

*brodouilleu-r, *n.m.*, **-se**, *n.f.*, stammerer, stutterer.

br-ef, -ève, *adj.*, brief, short, compact, succinct. *Une réponse brève;* a brief reply. *Avoir le parler —;* to be a man of few words.

bref, *adv.*, in a few words. —; in short, to be short.

bref, *n.m.*, brief (pope's pastoral letter—*pastorale du pape*); church calendar.

brège, *n.f.*, salmon net.

bregin, *n.m.*, fish-net with narrow meshes.

*bréhaigne, *adj.*, (of animals—*des animaux*) barren, sterile.

*bréhaigne, *n.f.*, (pop.) barren, sterile woman.

brelan, *n.m.*, brelan (game at cards—*jeu de cartes*); three cards of the same; gaming-house. *Tenir —;* to keep a gaming-house.

brelander, *v.n.*, to game, to be a gamester.

brelandi-er, *n.m.*, **-ère**, *n.f.*, gamester, gambler.

brelle, *n.f.*, raft, float of wood.

breloque, *n.f.*, bauble, gewgaw, toy, trinket.

⊙**breloquet**, *n.f.*, trinkets tied together.

breluche, *n.f.*, cotton and woollen stuff, drugget.

brème, *n.f.*, (ich.) bream.

breneu-x, -se, *adj.*, (l.ex.) dirty.

brequin, *n.m.*, wimble, bit of a wimble.

brésil, *n.m.*, Brazil-wood.

*brésiller, *v.a.*, to break into small pieces, to cut small; to dye with Brazil-wood.

*brésillet, *n.m.*, Brazil or Jamaica-wood.

bresto, *n.f.*, the catching of small birds with bird-lime.

*brétailler, *v.n.*, (b.s.) to tilt, to be fond of fighting.

*brétailleur, *n.m.*, (b.s.) bruiser, bully.

bretaudé, -e, *adj.*, crop-eared.

bretauder, *v.a.*, to crop badly (animals—*animaux*).

bretelle, *n.f.*, strap; braces. *En avoir jusqu'aux —s;* to be over head and ears in trouble.

breton, -ne, *adj.*, of Brittany.

breton, *n.m.*, **-ne**, *n.f.*, native of Brittany.

brette, *n.f.*, (jest.) long sword.

bretté, -e, *adj.*, notched, indented, jagged, toothed like a saw.

bretteler, *v.a.*, (arch.) to indent.

bretter, *v.a.*, (arch.) to indent.

bretteur, *n.m.*, bully, hector.

bretture, *n.f.*, teeth, notches (in tools—*des outils*).

*breuil, *n.m.*, enclosed copse, thicket.

breuvage, *n.m.*, beverage, potion, draught, liquor, drink; (vet.) drench.

brève, *n.f.*, short syllable; (mus.) short note.

brevet, *n.m.*, warrant, brevet; (milit.) commission; patent; licence (of printers—*d'imprimeurs*). — *d'apprentissage;* indentures of apprenticeship.

breveté, -e, (brèv-), *part.*, patented.

breveté, *n.m.*, **-e**, *n.f.*, patentee.

breveter, (brèv-), *v.a.*, to patent; to license.

bréviaire, *n.m.*, breviary.

brévité, *n.f.*, (gram.) shortness (of syllables —*de syllabes*).

bribe, *n.f.*, great lump of bread; *pl.*, scraps, fragments of meat; odd ends.

bric-à-brac, *n.m.* (—), odds and ends; old stores. *Marchand de —;* dealer in old iron, old pictures, old stores.

brick, *n.m.*, (nav.) brig.

bricole, *n.f.*, breast-collar of a horse; rebound of a ball (at tennis—*à la paume*); back stroke (at billiards—*au billard*); strap; (nav.)

uneasy rolling of a ship. *De —;* indirectly, unfairly.

bricoler, *v.n.*, (billiards, tennis—*au billard, à la paume*) to hit a back stroke.

bride, *n.f.*, bridle, reins, check, curb; string (of a woman's cap, bonnet—*d'un bonnet ou chapeau*); loop (for a button—*d'un bouton*); (surg.) frenum. *Mettre la — à un cheval;* to put a bridle upon a horse. *Tenir la — haute à un cheval;* to keep a tight rein. *Lui tenir la — courte;* to shorten the rein. *Lâcher la —;* to slacken the rein. *Courir à toute —, à — abattue;* to run full speed. *Tourner —;* to turn back. *Tenir quelqu'un en —;* to curb any one. *Lâcher la — à ses passions;* to gratify one's passions.

bridé, -e, *part.*, bridled. *Oison —;* silly creature.

brider, *v.a.*, to bridle, to put on a bridle; to tie fast, to fasten; to restrain, to curb, to keep under; to oblige. — *l'ancre;* (nav.) to shoe the anchor. — *ses désirs;* to curb one's desires. — *la bécasse;* to make a noodle of any one.

bridon, *n.m.*, snaffle-bridle.

brie, *n.f.*, rolling-pin.

bri-ef, -ève, *adj.*, short, brief.

brièvement (-èv-män), *adv.*, briefly, succinctly, in short. *Expliquez-moi cela —;* explain it to me briefly.

brièveté (èv-té), *n.f.*, brevity, shortness, briefness, conciseness, succinctness. *La — de la vie;* the brevity of human life.

brigade, *n.f.*, (milit.) brigade; gang (of workmen—*d'ouvriers*).

brigadier, *n.m.*, corporal (in the cavalry—*de cavalerie*); (nav.) bowman.

brigand, *n.m.*, brigand, highwayman, robber; embezzler, thief.

brigandage, *n.m.*, robbery, depredation.

brigandeau, *n.m.*, paltry cheat (of lawyers, &c.—*gens de loi*); pettifogging knave.

brigander, *v.n.*, to rob.

brigandine, *n.f.*, coat of mail.

brigantin, *n.m.*, brigantine, brig.

brigantine, *n.f.*, small vessel used in the Mediterranean.

*brignole, *n.f.*, French plum.

brigue (brig), *n.f.*, intrigue to get preferred, canvassing by indirect means; cabal, faction.

briguer (-ghé), *v.a.*, to canvass by indirect means, to solicit, to seek, to court, to put in for.

brigueur (-gheur), *n.m.*, canvasser, solicitor.

*brillamment (-män), *adv.*, brilliantly, in a brilliant manner.

*brillant, -e, *adj.*, brilliant, shining, sparkling, glittering, bright, showy, gleamy, effulgent, radiant. *Une carrière —e;* a brilliant career. *Esprit —;* sparkling wit. *Humeur —e et enjouée;* brisk and lively humour. — *s appas, charmes —s;* dazzling charms. *Pensée —e;* brilliant thought. *Affaire —;* (milit.) famous action.

*brillant, *n.m.*, brilliancy, brightness, splendour, radiancy, refulgence, resplendency, lustre; brilliant (diamond—*diamant*).

*brillanté, -e, *adj.*, cut into a brilliant.

*brillanter, *v.a.*, to cut into a brilliant.

*briller, *v.n.*, to shine, to glitter, to sparkle, to glisten, to be bright, sparkling; to play, to blaze, to dawn, to lighten, to flourish, to gleam, to glare. *Le soleil brille;* the sun shines. *Les étoiles brillent;* the stars glitter. *Ses yeux brillent d'un vif éclat;* a dazzling lustre sparkles in her eyes.

brimbale, *n.f.*, brake, handle of a pump.

brimbaler, *v.a.*, (fam., l.u.) to ring. — *les cloches;* to ring the bells.

brimborion, *n.m.*, bauble, gewgaw, toy, knick-knack.

brin. *n.m.,* blade, slip, slender stalk; sprig, shoot; bit, jot. *Un — de romarin;* a sprig of rosemary. *Un beau — de bois;* a fine straight piece of timber. *Un beau — d'homme;* a tall well-set youth. *Un — de paille;* a straw. *Un — de fil;* a bit of thread. *Il n'y en a —;* there is none at all.

brinde, *n.f.,* health, toast. *Porter des —s;* to drink toasts. *Être dans les —s;* to be drunk, tipsy.

*****brindille.** *n.f.,* sprig, twig.

bringuebale, *n.f. V.* **brimbale.**

brioche, *n.f.,* sort of cake; mistake, blunder. *Si le peuple n'a pas de pain, qu'il mange des —s;* if the people have no bread, let them eat curry.

brion, *n.m.,* (bot.) tree-moss.

*****briquaillons,** *n.m. pl.,* brickbats, old pieces of bricks.

brique, *n.f.,* brick.

briquet, *n.m.,* a steel (for striking a light—*pour allumer de l'amadou*); short sabre. *Battre le —;* to strike a light. *— pneumatique;* fire syringe. *Pierre à —;* flint.

briquetage (brik-taj), *n.m.,* brick-work; imitation brick-work.

briqueté (brik-), *part.,* bricked; brick-like.

briqueter (brik-), *v.a.,* to brick; to imitate brick-work.

briqueterie (brik-trî), *n.f.,* brick-field, brick-making.

briqueteur (brik-teur), *n.m.,* bricklayer.

briquetier (brik-tié), *n.m.,* brickmaker.

briquette, *n.f.,* small brick-like mass of coal and peat mixed together and hardened, which serves as fuel.

bris, *n.m.,* (jur.) breaking open (of doors, &c.—*portes, &c.*); breaking prison; wreck.

brisant, *n.m.,* breaker; breakwater.

*****briscambille.** *n.f. V.* **brusquembille.**

brise, *n.f.,* breeze. *— carabinée;* stiff gale.

brisé, -e, *part.,* broken to pieces; harassed, fatigued; folding; (her.) rompu. *Lit —;* folding-bed. *Chaise —e;* folding-chair. *Porte —e;* folding-door.

⊙**brise-cou.** *n.m.* (—). break-neck pace; (man.) rough-rider. *V.* **casse-cou.**

brise-eau, *n.m.* (—), (of harbour—*de ports*) breakwater.

brisée, *n.f.,* fan-joint (of umbrellas—*de parapluies*).

brisées, *n.f. pl.,* boughs cast in the road; boughs cut off; footsteps, wake. *Marcher sur les — de quelqu'un;* to follow in any one's footsteps. *Aller sur les — de quelqu'un;* to walk in any one's shoes. *Reprendre ses —;* to retrace one's steps.

brise-glace, *n.m.* (—, or — —s), starling (of a bridge—*d'un pont*).

brise-lames, *n.m.* (—), (of harbours—*de ports*) breakwater.

brisement (briz-mān), *n.m.,* breaking (of the heart, of the waves—*du cœur, des vagues*); contrition.

brise-pierre, *n.m.* (—), (surg.) lithotriptor.

briser, *v.a.,* to break to pieces, to beat to pieces; to flaw, to burst, to crack, to knock off, to shatter, to shiver, to snap, to crush, to crash; to bruise. *Être brisé;* to feel sore all over.

briser, *v.n.,* (nav.) to break, to dash, to split. *Le vaisseau alla — contre un écueil;* the ship was dashed to pieces against a rock. *Brisons-là;* let us say no more about it.

se **briser,** *v.r.,* to break, to be broken to pieces; to fold up.

brise-raison, *n.m.* (—), wrong-headed person.

brise-scellé. *n.m.* (— —s), (l.u.) seal-breaker.

brise-tout, *n.m.* (—), person that breaks everything.

briseur, *n.m.,* (l.u.) one who breaks anything. *— d'images;* image-breaker.

briseuse. *n.f.,* breaker (of things—*des choses*); breaker-engine.

brise-vent, *n.m.* (—, or — —s), (gard.) screen.

brisis. *n.m.,* (arch.) angle at the junction of the curb and roof.

brisoir, *n.m.,* brake (for flax—*à lin*).

brisque. *n.f.,* a card game; trump (at "brisque").

brisure, *n.f.,* part broken, fold; (her.) rebatement.

britannique, *adj.,* British. Britannic. *Les Iles —s;* the British islands.

broc (brô.), *n.m.,* large jug; spit. *De bric et de —;* anyhow; by hook or by crook. *Manger de la viande de — en bouche;* to have one's meat hot from the spit. [When this word is used in the sense of *spit,* its final *c* is sounded.]

brocantage, *n.m.,* dealing in second-hand goods, broker's business.

brocanter, *v.n.,* to deal in second-hand goods.

brocanteu-r, *n.m.,* **-se,** *n.f.,* a dealer in second-hand goods; broker.

brocard, *n.m.,* taunt, rub; joke, scoff.

brocarder, *v.a.,* to give a rub, to taunt, to jest upon, to jeer.

brocardeu-r, *n.m.,* **-se,** *n.f.,* scoffer, jeerer.

brocart, *n.m.,* brocade.

brocatelle, *n.f.,* brocatel; (min.) brocate.

brochage, *n.m.,* stitching (books—*de livres*).

brochant, *part.,* (her.) bronchant.

broche, *n.f.,* spit; needle to knit with; spindle; spigot, peg (of casks—*de tonneaux*); gudgeon (of locks—*de serrures*); tusk (of wild boars—*du sanglier*); spindle, iron-pin. *Mettre la viande à la —;* to spit the meat.

broché, -e, *adj.,* stitched (books—*livres*); embossed (linen—*linge*); figured (stuffs—*étoffes*).

brochée, *n.f.,* what is on the spit; rod full of candles.

brocher, *v.a.,* to stitch (a book—*livres*); to figure (stuffs—*étoffes*); to emboss (linen—*linge*); to knit (stockings—*bas*); to stitch (a nail into a horse's foot—*un clou dans le pied d'un cheval*); to do things in a hurry, to dispatch.

brochet, *n.m.,* pike, jack.

brocheter (brosh-té), *v.a.,* (cook.) to skewer.

brocheton (brosh-ton), *n.m.,* small pike, pickerel.

brochette, *n.f.,* little skewer; meat (roasted on skewers—*rôti à la brochette*); pin. *Élever des oiseaux à la —;* to feed birds by hand. *Enfant élevé à la —;* child brought up with great care.

brocheu-r, *n.m.,* **-se,** *n.f.,* knitter; bookstitcher.

brochoir, *n.m.,* smith's shoeing-hammer.

brochure, *n.f.,* stitching; book stitched and covered with a wrapper; pamphlet.

brocoli. *n.m.,* brocoli.

brodé, -e. *part.,* embroidered.

brodequin (brod-kin), *n.m.,* buskin, sock; half-boot, laced-boot (generally of women and children—*de femmes et d'enfants*).

broder, *v.a.,* to embroider; to adorn, to embellish a story, to exaggerate.

broderie (bro-drî), *n.f.,* embroidery; flourishing, embellishment, exaggeration.

brodeu-r, *n.m.,* **-se,** *n.f.,* embroiderer.

broie, *n.f.,* brake (for hemp—*à chanvre*).

broiement (broa-mān), *n.m.,* grinding, powdering, pounding, pulverization.

brome. *n.m.,* (chem.) brome.

bromure, *n.m.,* (chem.) bromide.

bronchade. *n.f.,* stumbling, tripping (of animals—*d'animaux*).

bronchement (bronsh-mān), *n.m.*, (l.u.) *V.* **bronchade.**

broncher, *v.n.*, to stumble, to trip, to reel; to blunder, to falter, to fail, to flinch. *Il n'y a si bon cheval qui ne bronche;* it is a good horse that never stumbles.

bronches, *n.f. pl.*, (anat.) bronchi, bronchia.

bronchies, *n.f. pl. V.* **branchies.**

bronchique, *adj.*, (anat.) bronchial.

bronchite, *n.f.*, (med.) bronchitis.

bronchotomie (-ko-), *n.f.*, (surg.) bronchotomy.

bronze, *n.m.*, bronze; iron (insensibility). *Un cœur de —;* a heart of iron.

bronzer, *v.a.*, to bronze, to paint in bronze colour; to tan (face). *— un canon de fusil;* to bronze the barrel of a musket. *Bronzé par le hâle;* sunburnt, tanned by the sun.

broquart, *n.m.*, (hunt.) brocket.

broquette, *n.f.*, tin tack, small nail; tintacks.

⊙**brossailles.** *V.* **broussailles.**

brosse, *n.f.*, brush; painter's brush. *— à dents;* tooth-brush.

brossée, *n.f.*, (fam.) brushing; drubbing, thrashing.

brosser, *v.a.*, to brush, to rub with a brush. *se* **brosser**, *v.r.*, to brush one's self.

brosser, *v.n.*, to run through woods or bushes; to scour.

brosserie (bros-rî), *n.f.*, brushmaking business; brush manufactory.

brosseur, *n.m.*, (milit.) an officer's servant.

brossier, *n.m.*, brushmaker; brusher.

brou, *n.m.*, shell (of walnuts, almonds—*de noix, d'amandes*).

brouée, *n.f.*, fog, mist, blight.

brouet, *n.m.*, thin broth. *— noir;* black broth (of the Spartans—*des Lacédémoniens*).

brouette, *n.f.*, wheelbarrow; brouette, sort of sedan chair.

brouetter, *v.a.*, to wheel in a barrow.

brouetteur, *n.m.*, he that draws a brouette.

brouettier, *n.m.*, wheelbarrow man.

brouhaha, *n.m.*, uproar, hurly-burly.

*brouillamini, *n.m.*, confusion; thing that has neither head nor tail; disorder.

*brouillard, *n.m.*, fog, mist, haze, damp; (com.) waste-book. *Un — épais;* a dense fog. *Je n'y vois que du —;* I see nothing but mist.

*brouillard, *adj.*, blotting. *Du papier —;* blotting paper.

*brouillasser, *v. imp.*, to drizzle. *Il brouillasse;* it drizzles.

*brouille, *n.f.*, quarrelling, disagreement, discord; pique.

*brouillé, -e, *part.*, jumbled, at variance. *Des œufs —s;* buttered eggs. *Nous sommes —s;* we have fallen out.

*brouillement, *n.m.*, mixing together, jumbling.

*brouiller, *v.a.*, to throw into confusion, to mix together, to blend, to stir up, to shake, to jumble, to shuffle, to confound; to set at variance; to embroil, to confuse; to puzzle. *deux personnes l'une avec l'autre;* to set two people at variance. *Vous me brouillez;* you put me out.

se **brouiller**, *v.r.*, to be out, to put one's self out, to confound one's self; to fall out with one. *Le temps se brouille;* the weather begins to be overcast.

*brouiller, *v.n.*, to blunder, to mar.

*brouillerie (broo-), *n.f.*, misunderstanding, disagreement, coolness, variance.

*brouillon, *n.m.*, rough draft, foul copy.

*brouillon, *n.m.*, -**ne**, *n.f.*, blunderer, marall, mar-plot.

*brouillon, -ne, *adj.*, mischief-making; blundering.

brouir, *v.a.*, to blight, to burn up, to parch (of the sun—*du soleil*).

brouissure, *n.f.*, blight.

*broussailles, *n.f. pl.*, bushes, brushwood.

broussin, *n.m.*, excrescence from a tree.

brout, *n.m.*, browse.

broutant, -e, *adj.*, browsing.

brouter, *v.a.*, to browse. *L'herbe sera bien courte s'il ne trouve de quoi —;* the grass must be very short, if he cannot get a bite.

brouter, *v.n.*, to browse.

broutilles, *n.f. pl.*, small branches (for making faggots—*pour faire des fagots*); trinkets, knick-knacks.

broyer, *v.a.*, to grind, to pound, to beat small, to bray, to bruise; to break (hemp—*le chanvre*). *— l'encre;* (print.) to bray the ink.

broyeur, *n.m.*, grinder, pounder, hemp or flax-breaker.

⊙**broyon**, *n.m.*, brayer (for printer's ink—*à encre d'imprimeur*).

bru, *n.f.*, daughter-in-law.

bruant, *n.m.*, (orni.) yellow-hammer.

brucelles, *n.f.*, (bot.) brownwort; *pl.*, tweezers.

*brugnon, *n.m.*, nectarine.

bruine, *n.f.*, small drizzling rain.

bruiner, *v.imp.*, to drizzle.

bruire, *v.n.*, to rustle, to rattle; (of the wind, &c.—*du vent, &c.*) to roar.

bruissement (-mān), *n.m.*, rustling noise, rattling, roaring; noise in one's ears; whistling (of the wind—*du vent*).

bruit, *n.m.*, noise, bustle, din, racket, creaking, knocking, sound, clamour, buzz; quarrel, dispute; fame, name, reputation; report, talk; rumour. *— d'une arme à feu;* report of a firearm. *Faire un — sourd;* to rumble, to hum. *Au — des cloches; du canon;* at the ringing of bells, the firing of guns. *On le fit entrer sans —;* he was let in noiselessly. *Cet événement fait du —;* that affair is making a great noise. *Ils ont eu du — ensemble;* they came to high words. *Il s'est répandu un —;* a rumour was spread. *Un faux —;* a false report. *Il court un —;* it is reported.

brûlable, *adj.*, (l.u.) that can be burnt.

brûlant, -e, *adj.*, burning, scorching, hot, burning hot, torrid; eager, earnest, ardent.

brûlé, *n.m.*, burning. *Cela sent le —;* that smells of burning.

brûlé, -e, *part.*, burnt.

brûle-gueule, *n.m.* (—), short pipe.

brûlement (-mān), *n.m.*, a burning, setting on fire.

à **brûle-pourpoint**, *adv.*, (of shooting with a gun *or* pistol) close to; unreservedly; (of arguments) irrefutable. *Un argument —;* an irrefutable argument.

brûler, *v.a.*, to burn, to consume by fire, to cauterize; to parch, to scorch, to blast, to sear, to swelter. *— de fond en comble;* to burn to the ground. *— la cervelle à quelqu'un;* to blow any one's brains out. *Son style brûle le papier;* his style is full of fire. *— de l'encens devant quelqu'un;* to flatter excessively. *— une étape;* to pass a halting-place without stopping.

brûler, *v.n.*, to burn, to be on fire; to be all in a flame. *Les mains lui brûlent;* his hands burn. *— de colère, d'amour;* to be inflamed with anger, with love. *Je brûle de vous revoir;* I am impatient to see you again. *— d'un feu lent;* to be consumed by degrees.

se **brûler**, *v.r.*, to burn one's self, to be burnt, to scorch. *Venir se — à la chandelle;* to burn one's wings in the candle. *— la cervelle;* to blow one's brains out.

brûlerie, *n.f.,* (l.u.) distillery (for brandy—*d'eau-de-vie*).

brûle-tout, *n.m.* (—), save all.

brûleur, *n.m.,* incendiary, firer, one who sets houses on fire. *Il est fait comme un — de maisons;* he looks like a blackguard.

brûlot, *n.m.,* fire-ship; firebrand, incendiary.

brûlure, *n.f.,* burn, scald, scalding.

brumaire, *n.m.,* Brumaire, second month of the calendar of the first French republic, from Oct. 25th to Nov. 21st.

brumal, -e, *adj.,* (l.u.) brumal, winterly.

brume, *n.f.,* fog, haze.

brumeu-x, -se, *adj.,* foggy, hazy.

brun, e, *adj.,* brown, dark, dun, dusk; melancholy, sad. *Il commence à faire —;* it begins to be dusk.

brun, *n.m.,* brown; dark person. *— châtain;* chesnut brown. *— clair;* light brown. *— foncé;* dun-coloured.

brunâtre, *adj.,* brownish.

brune, *n.f.,* dusk (of the evening—*du soir*); dark woman, dark girl.

brunelle, *n.f.,* (bot.) self-heal.

brunet, -te, *adj.,* brownish.

brunette, *n.f.,* dark woman, dark girl; ☉love ballad.

bruni, *n.m.,* (tech.) burnish.

brunir, *v.a.,* to brown, to make brown, to darken; to burnish.

se brunir, *v.r.,* to turn dark or brown.

brunir, *v.n.,* to turn brown.

brunissage, *n.m.,* burnishing.

brunisseu-r, *n.m.,* **-se,** *n.f.,* one who burnishes, burnisher.

brunissoir, *n.m.,* burnisher (tool—*outil*).

brunissure, *n.f.,* burnishing; browning.

brusque, *adj.,* blunt, abrupt, rough, gruff, sturdy; sudden, unexpected.

*****brusquembille,** *n.f.,* game at cards.

brusquement, *adv.,* bluntly, abruptly, roughly, hastily, gruffly, sturdily.

brusquer, *v.a.,* to offend; to be short, blunt, sharp, with one. *Il brusque tout le monde;* he is blunt with everybody. *— une chose;* to do a thing in haste. *— l'aventure;* to decide at once.

. **brusquerie,** *n.m.,* bluntness; abruptness, roughness.

brut (brut), **-e,** *adj.,* rough, raw, unpolished, unhewn, coarse, unfashioned; clownish, awkward; rude, ill-bred. *Diamant —;* rough diamond. *Sucre —;* brown sugar. *Bête —e;* (fam.) brute beast. *Produit —;* gross produce (of a farm—*d'une ferme*); gross returns.

brut (brut), *adv.,* (com.) gross.

brutal, -e, *adj.,* brutal, brutish, surly, bearish, churlish, cynical.

brutal, *n.m.,* brute (person—*personne*).

brutalement (-tal-măn), *adv.,* brutally, brutishly, rudely, churlishly.

brutaliser, *v.a.,* to bully; to use one brutally.

brutalité, *n.f.,* brutality, brutishness; outrageous language; brutal passion. *Dire des —s à quelqu'un;* to abuse one in a brutal manner.

brute, *n.f.,* brute, beast; brutal person.

bruyamment (bru-ia-măn), *adv.,* noisily, clamorously.

bruyant,-e,(bru-iăn;-te),*adj.,*noisy,blustering, clamorous, clattering, loud, open-mouthed.

bruyère(bru-ièr),*n.f.,* heath; sweet-heather. *Coq de —;* grouse.

bryon, *n.m.* V. **brion.**

bryone, *n.f.,* (bot.) bryony.

buanderie (-drî), *n.f.,* wash-house, washing house.

buandi-er, *n.m.,* **-ère,** *n.f.,* bleacher; washerman, washerwoman.

bubale, *n.m.,* a species of buffalo.

bube, *n.f.,* pimple.

bubon, *n.m.,* (med.) bubo.

bubonocèle, *n.m.,* (med.) bubonocele.

bucarde, *n.m.,* (conch.) heart-shell.

buccal, -e, *adj.,* buccal.

buccin (buk-sin), *n.m.,* (conch.) whelk.

buccinateur, *n.m.,* (anat.) buccinator.

bucentaure, *n.m.,* Bucentaur.

bucéphale, *n.m.,* Bucephalus (Alexander's horse—*le cheval d'Alexandre*).

bûche, *n.f.,* billet, chump of wood, log; dull-pated fellow, blockhead. *— de charbon de terre;* lump of coal.

bûcher, *n.m.,* wood-house; funeral-pile, pyre.

bûcher, *v.a.,* (carp.) to rough-hew; to cut out a piece in order to replace it by another.

bûcheron, (bûsh-ron), *n.m.,* woodcutter.

bûchette, *n.f.,* stick of dry-wood, fallen wood.

bucoliaste, *n.m.,* bucolic, writer of bucolics.

bucolique, *n.f.,* bucolic.

bucolique, *adj.,* bucolic.

bucoliques, *n.f.pl.,*Virgil's bucolics; things of no value, odds and ends.

budget, *n.m.,* budget. *Le — de l'État;* the state budget. *Le — de la marine;* the navy budget. *Le — de la guerre;* the war budget. *Le — d'un ménage;* household expenses.

budgétaire, *adj.,* pertaining, relating, to the budget.

buée, *n.f.,* ☉lye, washing in lye; steam, reek.

buffet, *n.m.,* cupboard, sideboard; service (of plate, &c.—*de table*). *— d'orgues;* organ-case.

buffle, *n.m.,* buffalo; buff-leather; buff. *Un vrai —;* a dull-pated fellow.

buffleterie (-flè-trî), *n.f.,* belts, straps, &c., of a soldier.

buffletin, *n.m.,* young buffalo.

bufonite, *n.f.,* (foss.) bufonite.

bugle, *n.f.,* (bot.) bugle.

buglosse, *n.f.,* (bot.) bugloss.

bugrane, *n.f.,* (bot.) rest-barrow.

☉**buire,** *n.f.,* a vessel for liquors.

buis, *n.m.,* box; box-tree, box-wood. *— piquant;* butcher's broom.

buissaie, *n.f.,* grove of box-trees.

buisson, *n.m.,* bush, thicket. *-- ardent;* (bot.) evergreen thorn; (scriptures—*écriture sainte*) burning bush.

buissonner, *v.n.,* (bot.) to bush.

buissonneu-x, -se, *adj.,* bushy, woody.

buissonni-er, -ère, *adj.* Only used in the expressions: *Lapins buissonniers;* thicket-rabbits. *Faire l'école buissonnière;* to play truant.

bulbe, *n.f.,* (bot.) bulb.

bulbe, *n.m.,* (anat.) bulb.

bulbeu-x, -se, *adj.,* bulbous.

bulbifère, *adj.,* (bot.) bulbiferous.

bullaire (-lèr), *n.m.,* collection of popes' bulls.

bulle, *n.f.,* bubble; (med.) bubble, blister; (metal.) bead. *— d'eau;* water-bubble. *— d'air;* air-bubble.

bulle, *n.f.,* pope's bull. *La — d'or;* the golden bull.

bulle, *adj.,* whity-brown (of paper). *Papier —;* whity-brown paper.

☉**bullé, -e,** *adj.,* authentic; by pope's bull.

bulletin, *n.m.,* vote; (milit.) bulletin; bulletin (official report—*rapport officiel*).

bunium, *n.m.,* earth-nut; ☉g-nut.

buphthalme, *n.m.,* (bot.) ox-eye.

buplèvre, *n.m.,* (bot.) hare's-ear. *— à feuilles rondes;* thorough-wax.

bupreste, *n.m.,* (ent.) burn-cow.

buraliste, *n.m.,* office-keeper.

burat, *n.m.,* drugget.

buratine, *n.f.,* poplin made of silk and wool.

bure, *n.f.,* drugget; (min.) shaft, pit-hole.

bureau, *n.m.,* bureau, desk; office; board (in a court of judicature—*dans les tribunaux*); committee; court (personages). — *de tabac;* tobacconist's shop. *Chef de* —; head clerk. *Déposer sur le* —; (parliament—*parlement*) to lay upon the table. *Payer à — ouvert;* (com.) to pay on demand.

⊙**bureau,** *n.m.,* drugget.

bureaucrate, *n.m.,* bureaucrat, clerk in a public office.

bureaucratie, *n.f.,* bureaucracy.

burette, *n.f.,* cruet; vase.

burgau, *n.m.,* **burgaudine,** *n.f.,* burgau; burgau mother of pearl.

burgrave, *n.m.,* Burgrave.

burgraviat, *n.m.,* Burgraviate.

burin, *n.m.,* graver, graving-tool; (fig.) pen.

buriner, *v.a.,* to engrave.

burlesque, *adj.,* burlesque, merry, comical, jocose, jocular, ludicrous. *Vers —s;* doggerel verses.

burlesque, *n.m.,* burlesque.

burlesquement, *adv.,* comically, ludicrously, in a jocose way.

burnous, *n.m.* *V.* **bornous** and **bournous.**

bursal, -o, *adj.,* concerning the raisers of an extraordinary tax.

busard, *n.m.,* (orni.) buzzard.

busc, *n.m.,* busk (of stays—*de corsets*); mitre (of locks on canals—*d'écluses*).

buse, *n.f.,* (orni.) buzzard; blockhead.

busqué, *part.,* busked; curve, curved, arched.

busquer, *v.a.,* to put a busk in.

se **busquer,** *v.r.,* to wear a busk.

⊙**busquière,** *n.f.,* place for a busk.

⊙**bussard,** *n.m.,* a measure of capacity of 268 litres.

busserole, *n.f.,* (bot.) bear's whortle-berry.

buste, *n.m.,* (sculpt.) bust; head and shoulders. *Portrait en* —; half-length portrait.

but, *n.m.,* mark; object, end, aim, purpose, design, view; goal. *Viser au* —; to aim at the mark. *Le — de ses désirs;* the object of his desires. *Se proposer un* —; to have an object in view. *Arriver le premier au* —; to be the first to reach the goal. — *à* —; without any odds, upon a par. *Jouer — à* —; to play even. *De — en blanc;* bluntly, without any preamble.

butant, *adj.* *V.* **boutant.**

bute, *n.f.,* farrier's butteris.

butée, *n.f.,* (arch.) abutment-pier. *V.* **buttée.**

⊙**buter,** *v.n.,* to hit the mark; to stumble; to aim at. *Ce cheval bute à chaque pas;* that horse stumbles at every step.

buter, *v.a.,* (gard.) to earth up; (arch.) to prop up. — *un mur;* to prop a wall with a buttress. — *un arbre;* to heap up earth round the root of a tree. — *du céleri;* to earth up celery.

se **buter,** *v.r.,* to be resolved or fixed; to contradict, to oppose.

⊙**butière,** *adj.,* said formerly of a kind of arquebuse.

butin, *n.m.,* booty, pillage, spoils gained from the enemy, capture, plunder.

butiner, *v.n.,* to spoil, to pillage, to plunder, to get a booty.

butiner, *v.a.,* (fig.) to pilfer.

butome, *n.m.,* (bot.) flowering rush; watergladiole.

butor, *n.m.,* (orni.) bittern; stupid man, dull fellow.

butorde, *n.f.,* booby (woman); blockhead.

butte, *n.f.,* rising ground, knell. *Être en — à;* to be exposed to.

buttée, *n.f.,* abutment of a bridge. *V.* **butée.**

butter, *v.a.,* (gard.) to earth up.

butter, *v.n.,* to stumble (of horses—*les chevaux*). *V.* **buter.**

butyreu-x, -se, *adj.,* butyrous; buttery.

buvable, *adj.,* drinkable, fit to drink.

buvant, -e, *adj.,* (l.u.) drinking.

buvard, *n.m.,* blotting-case.

buvetier (buv-tié), *n.m.,* keeper of a tavern.

buvette, *n.f.,* refreshment-room.

buveu-r, *n.m.,* **-se,** *n.f.,* drinker; drunkard, toper.

buvoter, *v.n.,* to sip, to tipple.

bysse, *n.m.* *V.* **byssus.**

byssus, *n.m.,* (bot, antiq.) byssus.

byzantin, -e, *adj.,* Byzantine.

C

c, *n.m.,* the third letter of the alphabet, c.

c., (ab.) (com.) *compte;* account.

c' (contraction of *ce,* and used only before the verb *être*), this, it.

çà, *adv.,* here. — *et là;* this way and that way; here and there, up and down, to and fro.

çà, *int.,* now. — *voyons!* now, let us see! *Or — commencez!* come, begin!

ça, *pron.,* (for cela) that. *Donnez-moi* —; give me that. *Comme* —; like that; so. *Comment vous portez-vous? comme* —; how do you do? so-so.

cabalant, -e, *adj.,* caballing. *Secte —e;* cabailing sect.

cabale, *n.f.,* cabal; cabala.

cabaler, *v.n.,* to cabal, to intrigue.

cabaleur, *n.m.,* caballer, intriguer.

cabaliste, *n.m.,* cabalist.

cabalistique, *adj.,* cabalistic.

caban, *n.m.,* thick woollen cloak with a hood.

cabanage, *n.m.,* camp (of American Indians —*d'Indiens américains*).

cabane, *n.f.,* cot, hut, shed, cabin, cottage; flat-bottomed boat on the Loire.

cabaner, *v.r.,* (nav.) to turn a boat keel upwards (on shore—*sur le rivage*).

cabaner, *v.n.,* (nav.) to capsize.

cabanon, *n.m.,* cell (prison).

cabaret, *n.m.,* wine-shop, tavern; tea-service; (bot.) asarum. *Pilier de* —; tavern haunter, tippler. — *borgne;* pot-house. *Un — de porcelaine;* a set of china tea-things.

cabareti-er, *n.m.,* **-ère,** *n.f.,* publican, tavern-keeper.

cabas, *n.m.,* basket; cottage bonnet; wicker-workcarriage, rumbling-carriage.

⊙**cabasset,** *n.m.,* helmet.

cabéliau, *n.m.,* (ich.) keeling.

cabestan, *n.m.,* capstan, capstern, hand-winch. *Grand* —; main capstern. — *volant;* crab. *Envoyer un homme au* —; to send a man to the capstern (to be punished—*par punition*).

***cabillaud,** *n.m.,* (ich.) cod (live cod—*morue en vie*).

cabine, *n.f.,* (nav.) cabin.

cabinet, *n.m.,* closet, study, cabinet; practice (of a professional man—*d'un avocat, &c.*); summer-house; office (of an attorney, a barrister—*d'un avoué, d'un avocat*); cabinet, cabinet-council. — *de lecture;* reading-room. — *de toilette;* dressing-room. — *de bains;* bath-room. — *d'aisance;* water-closet. *Affaires de* —; chamber practice (of lawyers—*d'avocats, &c.*).

câble, *n.m.,* cable. *Filer du* —; to pay away, to veer more cable; (fig.) to spin out the time. — *de remorque;* tow-cable. *Bitter le* —; to bit the cable. *Maître* —; sheet-cable. — *d'affourche;* small bower-cable. — *de touées;* stream-cable.

câblé. *n.m.*, thick cord.

câblé, -e, *adj.*, (arch.) cabled.

câbleau or câblot, *n.m.*, cablet, small cable; mooring-rope, painter.

câbler, *v.a.*, to twist threads into a cord; to make ropes or cables.

cabliau, *n.m.* V. cabillaud.

caboche, *n.f.*, pate, noddle; head-piece, hobnail. *Grosse* —; logger-head. *Être bonne* —; to have a good head-piece.

cabochon, *n.m.*, polished, uncut, precious stone.

cabochon. *adj.*, (of precious stones—*pierres précieuses*) polished only.

cabosse, *n.f.*, cacao pod.

cabot, *n.m.*, (ich.) bull-head. V. chabot.

cabotage, *n.m.*, coasting, coasting-trade. *Vaisseau de* —; coasting-vessel.

caboter, *v.n.*, to sail near a coast, to coast.

caboteur, *n.m.*, one who sails near the shore, coaster.

cabotier, *n.m.*, coasting-vessel.

cabotin, *n.m.*, (b.s.) strolling player.

se cabrer, *v.r.*, to rise or stand upon the two hind feet, to prance, to rear; to fly into a passion; to be refractory. *Faire — un cheval;* to make a horse rear.

cabrer, *v.a.*, to provoke one, to make one fly into a passion.

cabri, *n.m.*, kid.

cabriole. *n.f.*, caper; (man.) cabriole.

cabrioler, *v.n.*, to caper, to cut capers.

cabriolet, *n.m.*, cabriolet, cab. — *à pompe;* curricle. *Place de* —; cab-stand.

cabrioleur, *n.m.*, caperer.

cabus, *adj.*, (of cabbages—*chou*) headed.

caca, *n.m.*, child's excrement. *Faire* —; to do one's excrement.

cacade, *n.f.*, (l.u., l. ex.) evacuation; mistake, failure.

cacao, *n.m.*, cacao, chocolate-nut.

cacaotier or cacaoyer, *n.m.*, cacao-tree.

cacaoyère, *n.f.*, cacao-plantation.

cacatois, *n.m.*, (nav.) royal, mast-top.

cacatois or kakatoès, *n.m.*, (orni.) cockatoo.

caccaber, *v.n.*, to cry (of partridges—*perdrix*).

cachalot, *n.m.*, cachalot; spermaceti-whale.

cache, *n.f.*, hiding-place.

caché, -e, *part.*, hid, hidden. *Ressorts* —s; hidden, secret springs. *N'avoir rien de — pour quelqu'un;* to keep nothing secret from one. *Un esprit* —; a close character. *Jeu* —; under-hand game.

cache-cache, *n.m.* (*n.p.*), hide and seek (play—*jeu*).

cachectique (shek-), *adj.*, (med.) cachetic.

cache-entrée, *n.m.* (—, or — —s), drop (of a key-hole—*d'un trou de serrure*).

cachement (kash-mǎn), *n.m.*, (l.u.) concealing, hiding.

cachemire, *n.m.*, cashmere.

cache-nez, *n.m.*, (woollen neck-tie) comforter.

*cache-peigne, *n.m.* (—, or — —s), tresses that cover the comb (in a lady's hair—*dans les coiffures de dames*).

cacher, *v.a.*, to hide, to secrete, to conceal, to abscond. *Cachez votre jeu;* hide your cards. — *son jeu;* to hide, to mask, one's play. — *son nom, son âge;* to conceal one's name, one's age. — *sa vie;* to lead a secluded life.

se cacher, *v.r.*, to hide, to secrete one's self; to lurk; to abscond.

cachet, *n.m.*, seal (of private individuals—*de particuliers*); stamp; ticket. *Lettre de* —; lettre-de-cachet, a private letter of state or warrant of imprisonment without accusation or

trial. — *de chiffres, d'armes;* seal with a cipher, with a coat of arms. — *volant:* flying seal. *Courir le* —; to give private lessons in town. *Son style a un — particulier;* his style bears a particular stamp.

cacheté, -e, *part.*, sealed. *Soumissions —es;* sealed tenders.

cacheter (kash-té), *v.a.*, to seal, to seal up. *Cire à* —; sealing-wax. *Pain à* —; wafer.

cachette, *n.f.*, hiding-place. *En* —; secretly, by stealth.

cachexie (-shè-ksi), *n.f.*. (med.) cachexy.

cachot, *n.m.*, dungeon; (milit.) black hole.

cachotte, *n.f.*, tobacco-pipe without a heel.

cachotterie (-sho-tri), *n.f.*, mysterious ways, secret practice (with respect to trifling things—*pour des bagatelles*).

cachotti-er, *n.m.*, -ère, *n.f.*, one who makes mysteries about trifles.

cachou, *n.m.*, cashoo.

cacique, *n.m.*, cazic (Indian chief—*chef indien*).

cacis. V. cassis.

cacochyme (-shim), *adj.*, (med.) cacochymic.

cacochymie (-shi-), *n.f.*, (med.) cacochymy.

cacoèthe, *adj.*, (med.) (ulcers) malignant, incurable.

cacographie, *n.f.*, cacography.

cacolet, *n.m.*, (milit.) a saddle supporting a seat on each side for the removal of the wounded.

cacologie, *n.f.*, cacology.

cacophonie, *n.f.*, cacophony.

cacotrophie, *n.f.*, (med.) cacotrophy.

caotier or cactus, *n.m.*, (bot.) torch-thistle, cactus.

cadastral, -e, *adj.*, referring to the register of lands.

cadastro, *n.m.*, register of the survey of lands.

cadastrer, *v.a.*, to survey.

cadavéreu-x, -se, *adj.*, cadaverous, wan, ghastly.

cadavérique, *adj.*, (anat.) of a dead body.

cadavre, *n.m.*, corpse, dead body. *C'est un — ambulant;* he is a walking ghost.

cadeau, *n.m.*, present, gift. *Faire — de;* to make a present of.

cadédis (-diss), *int.*, zounds.

cadenas, (-nä), *n.m.*, padlock; clasp (of bracelets, &c.) — *à secret;* secret padlock. *En-fermer sous* —; to padlock.

cadenasser, *v.a.*, to padlock; to clasp (bracelets. &c.).

cadence, *n.f.*, time (in dancing—*de danse*); (mus.) quivering, shake; (man., harmony) cadence. *Aller en* —; to keep time.

cadencé, -e, *part.*, cadenced, numbered, harmonious.

cadencer, *v.a.*, to cadence, to harmonize; (mus.) to time, to shake, to trill.

cadène, *n.f.*, (l.u.) chain for galley slaves.

cadenette (-nett), *n.f.*, hair-cue (tress of hair worn below the rest—*tresse plus basse que les autres*).

cadet, -te, *adj.*, younger, eldest but one (of brothers and sisters, of branches of families); junior (of those one is with—*de ceux avec qui l'on se trouve*).

cadet, *n.m.*, (milit.) cadet; younger brother; youngest son; junior (of those one is with—*de ceux avec qui l'on est*); (fam.) young fellow. *C'est un jeune — de haut appétit;* he is an extravagant young gentleman.

cadette, *n.f.*, younger sister, younger daughter; paving stone; long billiard cue.

cadi, *n.m.*, cadi, a judge among the Turks.

cadis, *n.m.*, caddis, sort of woollen serge.

cadisé, *n.m.*, kind of drugget.

cadmie, *n.f.*, (chem. metal.) oxide of zinc.

cadmium, *n.m.*, cadmium.
cadogan, *n.m.* *V.* **catogan.**
cadole, *n.f.*, latch, little bolt.
cadran, *n.m.*, dial-plate, dial.
cadrat, *n.m.*, (print.) quadrat. — *creux* ; quotation.
cadratin, *n.m.*, (print.) M quadrat. *Demi* — ; N quadrat.
cadrature, *n.f.*, (horl.) movement ; dial-work.
cadre, *n.m.*, frame (for a picture, &c.—*de tableau*, &c.); (nav. milit.), list of officers; frame-work; limits. *Être sur les* — ; (nav.) to be on the sick list.
cadrer, *v.n.*, to agree, to square with, to tally.
cadu-c, -que, *adj.*, decrepit; decayed, crazy; lapsed (of legacies—*de legs*); (bot.) caducous. *Âge* — ; decrepit old age. *Devenir* — ; to decay. *Legs* — ; legacy that lapsed (for want of a claimant, or that cannot be paid for want of effects, &c.). *Le mal* — ; the falling sickness, epilepsy.
caducée, *n.m.*, caduceus, Mercury's wand ; tipstaff (of the king at arms and heralds—*du roi d'armes et des hérauts*).
caducité, *n.f.*, caducity ; decay.
cæcum, (sékom) *n.m.*, (anat.) cœcum.
cafard, -e, *adj.*, hypocrite ; canting.
cafard, *n.m.*, -e, *n.f.*, canter, hypocrite ; tell-tale ; —, *n.m.*, (ent.) cockroach. *V.* **blatte.**
cafarderie, *n.f.*, cant, hypocrisy, false devotion.
cafardise, *n.f.*, (l.u.) piece of hypocrisy, cant.
café, *n.m.*, coffee; coffee-house; coffee(berry). *Tasse de* — ; cup of coffee. *Rôtir, moudre, prendre, du* — ; to roast, to grind, to drink, coffeé. — *au lait* ; coffee with milk. — *à la crème* ; coffee with cream.
caféier, *n.m.* *V.* **cafier.**
caféière, *n.f.*, coffee plantation.
cafetan, or **caftan**, *n.m.*, caftan (Turkish garment—*vêtement turc*).
cafetier, *n.m.*, coffee-house keeper.
cafetière, *n.f.*, coffee-pot.
cafier or **caféier**, *n.m.*, coffee-tree.
cafre, *n.m.f.*, Caffre.
cage, *n.f.*, cage (for fowls—*pour les poules*) ; (tech.) frame ; casing, housing. *Mettre un homme en* — ; to put a man in the cage (prison). *La belle* — *ne nourrit pas l'oiseau* ; all is not gold that glitters.
cagée, *n.f.*, cage-full.
__cagnard, -e__ *adj.*, lazy, skulking, slothful.
__cagnard__, *n.m.*, -e, *n.f.*, lazy-bones, skulker. *C'est un* — ; he is a lazy-bones.
__cagnarder__, *v.n.*, to lead a lazy life.
__cagnardise__, *n.f.*, laziness, slothfulness, idleness.
__cagne__, *n.f.*, (l.u.) slut.
__cagneu-x, -se__, *adj.*, knock-kneed, splay-footed.
cagot, -e, *adj.*, (fam.) bigoted, hypocritical.
cagot, *n.m.*, -e, *n.f.*, (fam.) bigot.
cagoterie, *n.f.*, (fam.) affected devotion, hypocrisy, bigotry.
cagotisme, *n.m.*, (fam.) bigotry, false devotion.
cagoule, *n.f.*, a monk's cowl.
cague, *n.f.*, Dutch sloop.
cahier, *n.m.*, paper-book ; copy-book ; quarter of a quire of paper ; book (manuscript) ; sheet. — *des charges* ; conditions at which any public work is to be contracted for.
cahin-caha, *adv.*, (fam.) so-so, lamely, poorly.
cahot, *n.m.*, jerk ; jolt of a coach.
cahotage, *n.m.*, jolting, jerking.

cahotant, -e, *adj.*, rough, jolting.
cahoter, *v.n.*, to jolt.
cahoter, *v.a.*, to jolt, to jog, to jerk.
cahute, *n.f.*, hut, crib, hovel ; (nav.) small cabin.
caïc or **caïque**, *n.m.*, yawl, long-boat.
caïche, *n.f.*, (nav.) ketch.
caïd, *n.m.* (—*s*), military chief, governor of a town, among the Arabs.
caïeu, *n.m.*, (hort.) sucker, off-shoot.
__caille__, *n.f.*, (orni.) quail.
__caillé__. *n.m.*, curdled milk, curds.
__caillebot__, *n.m.*, wayfaring-tree.
__caillebotis__, *n.m.*, (nav.) gratings of the hatches.
__caillebotté, -e__ *part.*, curdled.
__caillebotte__, *n.f.*, mass of curds (of milk—*lait*).
__caillebotter__, *v.n.*, to curdle.
__caille-lait__, *n.m.* (—), (bot.) cheese-rennet.
__caillement__, *n.m.*, curdling, coagulating.
__cailler__, *v.a.*, to curdle, to clot, to turn to curds.
__se cailler__, *v.r.*, to coagulate, to turn to curds.
__cailletage__, *n.m.*, gossipping, idle talk.
__cailleteau__, *n.m.*, young quail.
__cailletot__, *n.m.*, young turbot.
__caillette__, *n.f.*, rennet ; gossip ; silly gossipping marr or woman.
__caillot__, *n.m.*, clot of blood ; lump of clotted blood ; (med.) coagulum.
__caillotis__, *n.m.*, kelp (calcined ashes of sea-weed—*cendres calcinées d'herbes marines*).
__caillot-rosat__, *n.m.* (—*s* —*s*), a kind of pear.
__caillou__, *n.m.*, flint, flint-stone, pebble.
__cailloutage__, *n.m.*, pebble work, flint-ware.
__caillouter__, *v.a.*, to macadamize.
__caillouteu-x, -se__, *adj.*, pebbly, flinty.
__cailloutis__, *n.m.*, metal (of roads — *pour les routes*) ; broken flint.
caïmacan, *n.m.*, caimacan (a Turkish officer —*officier turc*).
caïman, *n.m.*, American crocodile, caiman.
caïmand. *V.* **quémand.**
caïmander. *V.* **quémander.**
caïmandeu-r, -se. *V.* **quémandeur.**
caïque, *n.m.* *V.* **caïc.**
caisse, *n.f.*, case, box, chest, trunk ; coffer ; till ; cash-room, counting-house ; cylinder (of a drum—*d'un tambour*); (anat.) drum (of the ear —*de l'oreille*); body (of a coach—*d'une voiture*); pay-office. — *de médicaments* ; medicine chest. — *militaire* ; military chest. *La* — *du régiment* ; the regimental chest. *Avoir tant d'argent en* — ; to have so much money in the coffer. *Les* —*s de l'État* ; the coffers of the state. *Livre de* — ; cash-book. *Tenir la* — ; to keep the cash. — *des pensions* ; pension fund. —*d'amortissement* ; sinking fund. — *d'épargne* ; savings-bank. — *d'escompte* ; discounting bank. *Grande* — ; big drum. *Battre la* — ; to beat the drum. *Bander la* — ; to brace the drum. — *catoptrique* ; catoptrical cistula. *Tenir la* — ; to act as cashier.
caissier, *n.m.*, cash-keeper, cashier.
caisson, *n.m.*, (milit.) covered waggon, caisson, chest ; (nav.) locker ; (arch.) coffer ; compartment ceiling ; (artil.) limber. *Les* —*s des vivres* ; the provision waggons. — *à poudre* ; powder-chest.
cajoler, *v.a.*, to cajole, to coax, to wheedle.
cajolerie, *n.f.*, cajolery, coaxing, wheedling.
cajoleu-r, *n.m.*, -se, *n.f.*, cajoler, coaxer, wheedler.
cal, *n.m.*, callus, callosity ; (med.) callus.
calade, *n.f.*, (man.) calade.
calaison, *n.f.*, load water line.
calambour, *n.m.*, calambac.

calamendrier, *n.m.,* (bot.) common wall-germander.

calament, *n.m.,* (min. bot.) calamint.

calaminaire, *adj.,* (l.u.) belonging to calamine.

calamine, *n.f.,* (min.) calamine.

calamite, *n.f.,* (min.) calamite.

calamité, *n.f.,* calamity.

calamiteu-x, -se, *adj.,* distressful, calamitous.

calandrage, *n.m.,* calendering, hot-pressing.

calandre, *n.f.,* (ent.) weevil; machine used to press cloths, calender; (orni.) calandra.

calandrer, *v.a.,* to calender, to press, to smooth.

calandreur, *n.m.,* one who calenders cloth, calenderer.

calangue, *n.f.,* (nav.) small cove.

calao, *n.m.,* (orni.) horn-bill.

calatrava, *n.m.,* a Spanish military order.

calcaire, *adj.,* calcareous.

calcaire, *n.m.,* limestone.

calcanéum (-om), *n.m.,* (anat.) calcaneum, os calcis, heel-bone.

calcédoine, *n.f.,* (min.) chalcedony.

calcédonieu-x, -se, *adj.,* chalcedonic.

calcin, *n.m.,* calcined glass.

calcinable, *adj.,* calcinable.

calcination, *n.f.,* calcination.

calciner, *v.a.,* to calcine.

se **calciner,** *v.r.,* to calcine.

calcis, *n.m.,* (orni.) night-hawk.

calcite. *V.* **chalcite.**

calcium (-om), *n.m.,* calcium.

calcographie, *n.f.,* calcography.

calcul, *n.m.,* calculation, ciphering, computation, reckoning, counting, estimate; (med.) calculus; stone in the bladder. — *différentiel* ; differential calculus. — *approximatif* ; rough calculation. *Il apprend le* — ; he learns ciphering.

calculable, *adj.,* that may be calculated, calculable.

calculant, -e, *adj.,* calculating, reckoning.

calculateur, *adj.,* calculating. *Esprit* — ; calculating head.

calculateur, *n.m.,* calculator.

calculatoire, *adj.,* belonging to calculation.

calculer, *v.a.,* to calculate, to compute, to reckon, to estimate.

calculeu-x, -se, *adj.,* (med.) calculous.

calculeu-x, *n.m.,* **-se,** *n.f.,* person affected with calculus.

cale, *n.f.,* (nav.) hold (of a ship—*de vaisseau*); wedge, prop.; keel-hauling (punishment—*punition*); (tech.) block. — *de construction* ; stocks. — *de magasin, d'un quai* ; slip. *Donner la* — *à un matelot* ; to give a sailor a ducking. — *sèche* ; dry ducking.

calebasse, *n.f.,* (bot.) calabash; gourd, bottle-gourd calabash.

calebassier, *n.m.,* calabash tree.

calèche, *n.f.,* calash, open carriage; cover for the head.

caleçon, *n.m.,* drawers, pair of drawers.

caleçonnier, *n.m.,* one who makes drawers.

caléfacteur, *n.m.,* cooking apparatus.

caléfaction, *n.f.,* calefaction, heating.

calédonien, -ne, *n.* and *adj.,* Caledonian.

calembour, *n.m.,* pun.

calembouriste, *n.m.,* a punster.

calembredaine, *n.f.,* fib, fetch, quibble, subterfuge.

calencar, *n.m.,* a kind of Indian chintz.

calender (-dèr), *n.m.,* monk (Turkish, Persian—*turc, persan*).

calendes, *n.f.pl.,* (antiq.) calends; convoca-tion of the country clergy. *Renvoyer aux* — *grecques* ; to put off till doomsday.

calendrier, *n.m.,* calendar, almanac. *Vieux* — ; the old calendar (old style—*vieux style*). *Nouveau* —, — *grégorien* ; the new, the Gregorian calendar, (new style—*nouveau style*).

calenture, *n.f.,* (med.) calenture.

calepin, *n.m.,* note-book, scrap-book.

caler, *v.a.,* (nav.) to lower, to strike ; to support, to wedge up. — *les voiles* ; to strike sail. *Cale tout !* let go amain ! — *la voile* ; to yield, to buckle to.

caler, *v.n.,* to have more or less draught, to sink. *Ce navire cale trop* ; that ship sinks too much.

calfait, *n.m.,* (nav.) calking iron.

calfat, *n.m.,* (nav.) calker.

calfatage, *n.m.,* (nav.) calking.

calfater, *v.a.,* (nav.) to calk.

calfatin, *n.m.,* (nav.) calker's help-mate.

calfeutrage, *n.m.,* stopping of chinks.

calfeutrer, *v.a.,* to stop the chinks of a door or window.

se **calfeutrer,** *v.r.,* to stop up the chinks.

calibre, *n.m.,* caliber, calibre, bore (of a gun—*d'armes à feu*); caliber, calibre, size (of a bullet—*d'une balle, d'un boulet*); diameter of a body ; kind, sort, stamp ; caliber, calibre.

calibrer, *v.a.,* to give, to take, the caliber.

calice, *n.m.,* chalice, communion-cup; (bot.) calyx, flower-cup. *Boire le* — *jusqu'à la lie* ; to drink the cup to the dregs. *Boire, avaler, le* — ; to swallow the pill.

calicinal, -e, *adj.,* (bot.) calycinal, calycine.

calicot, *n.m.,* calico ; counter-jumper.

califat, *n.m.,* califate, caliphate, kalifate.

calife, *n.m.,* calif, caliph, kalif.

à **califourchon,** *adv.,* astraddle, with legs across anything.

califourchon, *n.m.,* hobby. *C'est son* — ; it is his hobby.

câlin, *n.m.,* **-e,** *n.f.,* wheedler, cajoler. *C'est une petite* —*e* ; she is a little wheedling creature.

câlin, -e, *adj.,* wheedling, cajoling. *Cet homme a l'air* — ; that man has a wheedling look with him.

câliner, *v.a.,* to fondle, to cajole, to wheedle.

se **câliner,** *v.r.,* to be lazy, to idle, to give one's self up to indolence, to nurse one's self.

câlinerie, *n.f.,* wheedling, cajolery.

caliorne, *n.f.,* (nav.) winding-tackle.

calleu-x, -se, *adj.,* callous, hard.

calligraphe, *n.m.,* caligraphist, good penman.

calligraphie, *n.f.,* caligraphy, calligraphy, penmanship.

calligraphique, *adj.,* caligraphic.

callosité (kal-lo-), *n.f.,* callousness; callosity.

calmande, *n.f.,* calamanco ; woollen stuff ; (ich.) whiff.

calmant, *n.m.,* (med.) composing draught ; anodyne.

calmant, -e, *adj.,* anodyne, calming.

calmar, *n.m.,* ⊙ pen-case; (ich.) calamary.

calme, *adj.,* still, quiet, free from motion, calm ; dispassionate ; (com.) dull.

calme, *n.m.,* stillness, calmness, tranquillity, quiet, calm. — *plat* ; (nav.) dead calm. *Le* — *des nuits* ; the calm of the nights.

se **calmer,** *v.r.,* to become calm, to calm one's self; to get appeased, to blow over. *Calmez-vous* ; be composed.

calmer, *v.a.,* to still, to quiet, to appease, to allay, to pacify, to calm ; to soothe.

calmer, *v.n.,* (nav.) to lull, to fall. *Le vent calme* ; the wind lulls.

calmie, *n.f.*, (nav.) lull.
calomel *or* **calomélas**, *n.m.*, calomel.
calomniat-eur, *n.m.*, **-rice**, *n.f.*, calumniator, slanderer.
calomnie, *n.f.*, calumny, slander.
calomnier, *v.a.*, to calumniate.
calomnieusement (-eûz-măn), *adv.*, calumniously. slanderously.
calomnieu-x, **-se**, *adj.*, calumnious, slanderous.
ⓒ**calomniographe**, *n.m.*, writer of calumny.
calonière, *n.f.*, (pop.) pop-gun. *V.* **canonnière**.
calorifère, *n.m.*, hot-air stove.
calorimètre, *n.m.*, calorimeter.
calorifique, *adj.*, calorific.
calorique, *n.m.*, caloric.
calotte, *n.f.*, calotte, calote (of priests--*de prêtre*); cap (man's—*d'homme*); (surg.) headpiece; (anat.) pan (of the brain—*du crâne*); (arch.) calotte; box on the ears. *La — rouge d'un cardinal*; the red calotte of a cardinal. *Donner des -s à*; to box any one's ears.
calotter, *v.a.*, to box the ears of.
calottier, *n.m.*, calotte-maker; cap-maker.
caloyer, *n.m.*, caloyer, Greek monk of the order of Saint Basil.
calque, *n.m.*, counter-drawing; imitation copy.
calquer, *v.a.*, to counter-draw, to trace; to copy, to imitate closely. *— à la pointe*; to trace with a point. *— à la vitre*; to counter-draw on glass.
calquoir *n.m.*, tracing-point.
calumet, *n.m.*, pipe, calumet.
calus (-luss), *n.m.*, callus; callousness; calosity; (med.) callus.
calvaire, *n.m.*, mount Calvary; calvary; large crucifix placed on a mound on a road.
calvanier, *n.m.*, (agri.) day-labourer.
calville, *n.m.*, calville (apple—*pomme*).
calvinien, **-ne**, (i-in, i-è-n), *adj.*, pertaining to Calvin, Calvinistic.
calvinisme, *n.m.*, Calvinism.
calviniste, *n.m.*, Calvinist.
calviniste, *adj.*, Calvinistic.
calvitie (-sĭ), *n.f.*, baldness.
camaïeu, *n.m.*, cameo; (paint.) camaieu; cameo brooch; monotonous play.
***camail**, *n.m.* (—s), hood, capuchin, cardinal (garment—*vêtement*); bishop's purple ornament worn over the rochet.
camaldule, *n.m.*, monk of the Order of Saint Benedict founded at Camaldoli, in Tuscany, by Saint Romuald.
camarade, *n.m.f.*, comrade, fellow, mate; female companion; playmate, play-fellow; fellow-labourer; fellow-servant. *— de collège*; college companion. *— de classe*; school-fellow. *— de lit*; bed-fellow. *— de voyage*; fellow-traveller. *— de malheur*; fellow-sufferer. *— de chambre*; chum.
camaraderie, *n.f.*, companionship, intimacy; coterie.
camard, **-e**, *adj.*, flat-nosed; flat.
camard, *n.m.*, **-e**, *n.f.*, flat-nosed person. *La —e* (pop.); death.
***camarilla**, *n.f.*, camarilla, a coterie influential at a court.
camarine, *n.f.*, (bot.) crow-berry.
cambiste, *n.m.*, cambist.
cambouis, *n.m.*, coom, cart-grease.
cambre, *n.f.*, cambering.
cambré, **-e**, *part.*, bent, cambering, having a fall (in the back—*chute du dos*). *Pont de navire —*; cambering deck.
cambrer, *v.a.*, to bend. *— la forme d'un soulier*; to give the bend to a last.

se **cambrer**, *v.r.*, to camber; to take a sweep.
***cambrillon**, *n.m.*, stiffener (of a shoe—*de soulier*).
cambrure, *n.f.*, bend, flexure, incurvation.
cambuse, *n.f.*, (nav.) store-room.
cambusier, *n.m.*, (nav.) steward's mate.
came, *n.f.*, (conch.) chama; heart-cockle; (tech.) peg-cam; cog. *V.* **chame**.
camée, *n.m.*, a cameo.
camélée, *n.f.*, (bot.) widow-wail.
caméléon, *n.m.*, chameleon; (astron.) chameleon.
caméléopard, *n.m.*, cameleopard.
camélia, *n.m.*, (bot.) camelia.
cameline, *n.f.*, (bot.) camelina, gold of pleasure.
camelot (-lô), *n.m.*, camlet.
camelote (-lott), *n.f.*, worthless merchandise, trash, stuff; bosh.
camelotine, *n.f.*, a sort of camlet.
camérier, *n.m.*, chamberlain (of the pope or of a cardinal—*du pape, d'un cardinal*).
camériste, *n.f.*, maid of honour (in Spain—*en Espagne*).
camerlingat, *n.m.*, camerlingate (at Rome—*à Rome*).
camerlingue, *n.m.*, camerlingo (officer of the Roman court—*officier de la cour de Rome*).
camion, *n.m.*, minikin-pin; little cart; truck.
camionnage, *n.m.*, carting (in a dray—*sur un camion*).
camionneur, *n.m.*, dray-man.
camisade, *n.f.*, (milit.) an attack at night camisade.
camisard, *n.m.*, Camisard (French Calvinist of the Cevennes in the reign of Louis XIV.—*calviniste des Cévennes sous Louis XIV*).
camisole, *n.f.*, short night-dress. *— de force*; strait waistcoat.
***camomille**, *n.f.*, camomile.
camouflet, *n.m.*, smoke of burning paper blown into any one's face; affront; rap over the knuckles.
camp (kăn), *n.m.*, camp; combat. *Lever le —*; to break up the camp. *Prendre le —*; to pack off. *Aide de —*; aide-de-camp.
***campagnard**, **-e**, *adj.*, rustic, of the country.
***campagnard**, *n.m.*, **-e**, *n.f.*, countryman; clown. *C'est une —e*; she is a hoiden.
***campagne**, *n.f.*, country fields; seat, estate, country-house; field, campaign; (nav.) voyage, cruise. *Gens de la —*; peasantry. *Comédiens de —*; strolling players. *En plaine —*; in the open fields. *Battre la —*; to scour the country; to wander; to be delirious; (fig.) to blunder, to bungle. *Les armées sont en —*; the armies have taken the field. *Pièces de —*; field pieces. *Faire une —*; to make a campaign. *Ouvrir la —*; to open the campaign. *Cet officier a fait vingt —*; that officer has served twenty campaigns. *Mettre ses amis en —*; to set one's friends to work. *— de croisière*; cruising voyage. *Être à la —*; to be in the country. *Être en —*; to be out (not at home—*dehors*).
***campagnol**, *n.m.*, field-mouse.
campane, *n.f.*, (arch.) bell; (sculp.) ornament with fringe and tassels.
campanelle *or* **campanette**, *n.f.*, bell-flower, Canterbury-bell.
campanile, *n.m.*, (arch.) campanile.
ⓒ**campanini**, *n.m.*, Carrara marble.
campanule, *n.f.*, campanula, bell-flower. *— gantelée*; throat-wort. *— raiponce*; rampion bell-flower. *— à feuilles rondes*; hare-bell.
campanulé, **-e**, *adj.*, campanulate, bell-shaped.
campé, **-e**, *part.*, encamped.

campêche, *n.m.*, (bot.) campeachy wood, logwood, blood-wood.

campement (känp-män), *n.m.*, (milit.) encampment, encamping ; camp detachment. *Matériel de* — ; camping apparatus. *Effets de* — ; camping baggage.

camper, *v.n.*, to encamp, to pitch tents. *Faire* — *son armée ;* to encamp one's army.

camper, *v.a.*, to encamp. — *là quelqu'un ;* to leave one in the lurch.

se **camper**, *v.r.*, to set, to clap one's self down. *Il se campa dans un fauteuil ;* he sat himself down in an arm-chair.

ⓞ**camphorata**, *n.f.* *V.* **camphrée.**

camphre, *n.m.*, camphor.

camphré, **-e**, *adj.*, camphorate, camphorated.

camphrée, *n.f.*, camphorosma.

camphrier, *n.m.*, (bot.) camphor-tree.

campine, *n.m.*, fine fat pullet.

campos, *n.m.*, play-day, holiday, relaxation. *Les écoliers demandent* — ; the boys ask for a holiday. *Prendre* — ; to take a holiday.

camus, **-e**, *adj.*, flat-nosed ; disappointed. *Un vilain* — ; an ugly flat-nosed fellow.

***canaille**, *n.f.*, rabble, riff-raff, mob ; scum ; scoundrel ; noisy children, brats. *Hors d'ici,* —*!* begone, you scoundrel ! *Vile* — ; miserable scum. *Ces* —*s de domestiques ;* these rascally servants !

canal, *n.m.*, canal, pipe ; conduit, duct ; drain ; tube ; spout ; watercourse (of water-mills —*de moulins à eau) ;* channel, bed, strait ; (arch.) fluting, means. *Creuser un* — ; to dig a canal. *Ce pays est tout coupé de canaux ;* that country is quite intersected with canals. — *latéral,* — *de dérivation ;* lateral drain. — *de cheminée ;* chimney-flue. — *d'irrigation ;* trench for irrigation. — *thoracique ;* thoracic duct. — *de larmier ;* (arch.) channel of a coping. *Il est le* — *de toutes les grâces ;* all favours come through his channel.

canaliculé, **-e**, *adj.*, (bot.) channelled, furrowed.

canalisation, *n.f.*, establishment of canals, communication by canals.

canaliser, *v.a.*, to establish canals, to intersect with canals.

canamelle, *n.f.*, (bot.) sugar-cane ; reed.

canapé, *n.m.*, sofa, couch.

ⓞ**canapsa**, *n.m.*, artisan's knapsack ; person who carries a knapsack.

canard, *n.m.*, drake, duck ; hoax ; water-spaniel. — *privé ;* tame duck. — *ordinaire ;* mallard. *Donner des* —*s à ;* to hoax.

canard, **-e**, *adj.*, for ducks. *Bâtiment* — ; vessel that pitches. *Chien* — ; water-spaniel for duck-shooting.

canardeau, *n.m.*, young duck.

canarder, *v.a.*, to shoot at one from a sheltered position.

canarder, *v.n.*, (nav.) to pitch (of a ship— *d'un vaisseau) ;* (mus.) to imitate the cry of the duck.

ⓞ**canardier**, *n.m.*, wild-duck shooter.

canardière, *n.f.*, place for catching wild-ducks ; loop-hole (to shoot through—*pour tirer) ;* duck-gun ; duck-yard.

canari, *n.m.*, canary, canary-bird.

cancan, *n.m.*, tittle-tattle ; scandal ; tale-bearing ; noise ; indecent dance. *Faire des* —*s ;* to tittle-tattle, to invent scandalous stories.

cancaner, *v.n.*, to tattle, to invent scandalous stories ; to dance the cancan.

cancani-er, *n.m.*, **-ère**, *n.f.*, lover of tittle-tattle.

ⓞ**cancel**, *n.m.*, chancel ; place where the great seal was kept.

canceller, *v.a.*, (l.u.) to cancel.

cancer (-sèr), *n.m.*, (med., astron.) cancer.

cancéreu-x, **-se**, *adj.*, (med.) cancerous.

cancre, *n.m.*, crab, crab-fish ; miser ; dunce (at schools—*dans les pensions, &c).* *Un vilain* — ; a miserly hunks.

cancrelat, *n.m.*, cockroach.

candélabre, *n.m.*, candelabrum, sconce.

candeur, *n.f.*, openness of heart, frankness, candour.

candi, *n.m.*, sugar-candy, candy.

candi, **-e**, *adj.*, candied.

candidat, *n.m.*, candidate.

candidature, *n.f.*, candidateship.

candide, *adj.*, fair, open, frank, candid.

candidement (-män), *adv.*, openly, frankly, candidly.

se **candir**, *v.r.*, to candy. *Faire* — ; to candy.

cane, *n.f.*, the female duck.

canéficier, *n.m.*, cassia. *V.* **casse.**

canepetière, *n.f.*, (orni.) lesser bustard.

canéphore, *n.f.*, (antiq.) canaphore.

canepin (ka-n-pin), *n.m.*, lamb's skin (for women's gloves—*pour gants de femme).*

canescent, **-e**, *adj.*, (bot.) canescent.

caneton (ka-n-ton), *n.m.*, young duck, duck-ling.

canette, *n.f.*, small duck, young duck ; (her.) duck without legs ; a measure for beer.

canevas (ka-n-vä), *n.m.*, canvas ; sail-cloth ; sketch, rough draught ; (mus.) canvass. *Tracer son* — ; to prepare one's ground-work. *Faire un* — *sur un air ;* to make the canvass of an air.

canezou, *n.m.*, woman's jacket.

ⓞ**cangrène**, *n.f.* *V.* **gangrène.**

cangue, *n.f.*, a kind of pillory used in China.

caniche, *n.m.*, poodle-dog, water-spaniel.

caniculaire, *adj.*, canicular. *Les jours* —*s ;* the dog-days.

canicule, *n.f.*, dog-days ; (astron.) canicule, dog-star.

canif, *n.m.*, penknife.

canin, **-e**, *adj.*, pertaining to dogs, canine. *Les dents* —*es sont à côté des incisives,* the canine teeth are close to the incisors.

caniveau, *n.m.*, (arch.) kennel-stone.

cannage, *n.m.*, (l.u.) a measuring by the cane.

cannaie, *n.f.*, cane-brake, cane-field.

canne, *n.f.*, walking-stick ; long measure ; cane, reed ; glassblower's pipe. — *à sucre ;* sugar-cane. — *à épée ;* sword-stick. — *à vent ;* air-gun.

canneberge (-bèrj), *n.f.*, cranberry, moor-berry.

cannelas (-lä), *n.m.*, cinnamon, candied cinnamon.

canneler, *v.a.*, to flute, to channel.

cannelle, *n.f.*, cinnamon bark. — *blanche ;* canella.

cannelle *or* **cannette**, *n.f.*, spigot ; tap, cock.

cannelier, *n.m.*, cinnamon-tree.

cannelon (ka-n-lon), *n.m.*, channelled mould for ices.

cannelure, *n.f.*, channelling, fluting. —*à côtes ;* fluting with intervals. — *avec rudentures ;* fluting enriched with cables. — *à vive arête ;* fluting without intervals. —*s plates ;* square fluting.

cannequin, *n.m.*, sort of cotton stuff.

***cannetille**, *n.f.*, wire-ribbon.

cannibale (can-ni-bal), *n.m.*, man-eater, cannibal.

cannibalisme, *n.m.*, cannibalism ; ferocity.

canon, *n.m.*, cannon, gun ; barrel (of a gun, of a quill—*d'un fusil, d'une plume) ;* (ecc.) canon law, rule ; catalogue of saints ; (mus.) canon ; (print.) canon ; (man.) canon-bit ; leg (of trousers—*de pantalon) ;* pipe. *L'âme d'un* — ; the chamber of a cannon. *La lumière, la culasse, le recul, d'un* — ; the touch-hole, the breech, the recoil, of a cannon. *L'affût d'un* — ; a gun-car-

riage. *Enclouer un* —; to spike a cannon. *Une pièce de* —; a piece of ordnance. *Gros* —; (print.) canon. *Petit* —; (print.) two-line English. — *de dix livres* ; ten-pounder. *Un coup de* —; a cannon-shot. *De la poudre à* —; gunpowder. *Être à portée de* —; to be within cannon-shot. *Être hors de portée de* —; to be beyond the range of cannon. — *de retraite* ; (milit.) gun-fire; (nav.) stern-chase. — *démarré* ; cannon drawn in to be charged. — *moindre* ; cannon whose bore is not proportioned to the thickness of the metal. — *renforcé* ; cannon whose breech is thicker than its bore. *Amarrer un homme sur un* —; to tie a man to a gun (a punishment—punition). — *d'un soufflet* ; pipe of a pair of bellows. — *de gouttière* ; spout of a gutter. *Les* —*s d'un concile* ; the canons of a council. *École de droit* —; school of canon law. — *des Écritures* ; the sacred canon. *Le* — *de la messe* ; the canon of the mass. — *enluminé* ; illuminated canon.

canonial, -e, *adj.,* canonical.
canonicat, *n.m.,* canonry, canonship, prebend.
canonicité, *n.f.,* canonicalness.
canonique, *adj.,* canonical.
canoniquement (-măn), *adv.,* canonically.
canonisation, *n.f.,* canonization.
canoniser, *v.a.,* to canonize.
canoniste, *n.m.,* canonist.
canonnade, *n.f.,* cannonading, cannonade.
canonnage, *n.m.,* gunnery.
canonner, *v.a.,* to attack with heavy artillery, to cannonade.
se canonner, *v.r.,* to cannonade.
canonnier, *n.m.,* gunner.
canonnière, *n.f., adj.,* ⊙ loop-hole (in a wall, to shoot through—*embrasure dans un mur*) ; tent; tilt; drain-hole ; pop-gun. —, or *chaloupe* — (nav.) ; gun-boat.
canot, *n.m.,* ship's-boat, cutter, yawl. — *de sauvetage* ; life-boat.
canotier, *n.m.,* rower ; boat-keeper ; bargeman.
cantabile (-lé), *n.m.,* (mus.) cantabile.
cantal, *n.m.,* cantal (sort of cheese—*fromage*).
cantalabre, *n.m.,* door-case, casing.
cantaloup, *n.m.,* cantaloup (melon).
cantate, *n.f.,* (mus.) cantata.
*cantatille, *n.f.,* cantatilla.
cantatrice, *n.f.,* eminent female professional singer.
cantharide, *n.f.,* (ent.) cantharis, Spanish fly ; (pharm.) (*pl.*) cantharides.
canthus, *n.m.,* (anat.) canthus, angle of the eye.
cantilène, *n.f.,* (mus.) cantilena.
cantine, *n.f.,* bottle-case ; (milit.) canteen.
cantini-er, *n.m.,* -**ère,** *n.f.,* sutler, canteenwoman.
cantique, *n.m.,* song, canticle.
canton, *n.m.,* (of a country—*district d'un pays*) canton ; (her.) canton.
cantonade, *n.f.,* (theat.) wing. *Parler à la* —; to speak to a person who is at the wing, behind the scenes.
cantonal, -e, *adj.,* cantonal.
cantonné, -e, *adj.,* (arch., her.) milit.) cantoned.
cantonnement (to-n-măn), *n.m.,* (milit.), cantonment.
cantonner, *v.a.,* (milit.) to canton.
se cantonner, *v.r.,* to canton, to fortify one's self.
cantonner, *v.a.,* (milit.) to be cantoned.
cantonnier, *n.m.,* one employed to keep the roads in a state of repair, road-labourer.
cantonnière, *n.f.,* valance.
canule, *n.f.,* clyster-pipe ; faucet, quill.

canzone, *n.f.,* (mus.) canzone.
caolin, *n.m.* V. **kaolin.**
caoutchouc, *n.m.,* caoutchouc, India-rubber ; (bot.) gum-tree.
cap, *n.m.,* cape, headland, point, promontory, foreland ; (nav.) head. *Doubler un* —; to double a cape. *Où est le* —? (nav.) how is the head? *Avoir le* — *au large*; to stand off. *Gouverne où tu as le* —! steer as you go! *De pied en* —; from top to toe.
capable, *adj.,* able, fit, capable. *Seriez-vous* —*d'une telle action!* would you be capable of such an action? *Il est* — *de vous desservir*; he is capable of doing you an ill office. *Il est* — *de tout*; he is capable of any thing. *C'est un homme* —; he is a clever man. *Avoir l'air* —; to wear a conceited air. *Faire le* —; to play the man of capacity.
capablement, *adv.,* (l.u.) learnedly, skilfully.
capacité, *n.f.,* extent, capaciousness ; ability, capacity. *Manquer de* —; to want capacity. *Juger de la* — *d'un homme par ses ouvrages*; to judge of a man's capacity by his works.
caparaçon, *n.m.,* caparison.
caparaçonner, *v.a.,* to caparison (a horse —*un cheval*).
cape, *n.f.,* cloak with a hood ; riding-hood ; cape ; (nav.) try-sail. *Rire sous* —; to laugh in one's sleeve. *N'avoir que la* — *et l'épée* ; to have nothing but one's nobility. *Être à la* —; (nav.) to try. *À la* —! hull to !
capéer, *v.n.,* (nav.) to tie.
capelan, *n.m.,* poor beggarly priest ; (ich.) capelan.
capelet, *n.m.,* (vet.) capped hock.
⊙**capeline,** *n.f.,* woman's broad-brimmed hat.
capendu, *n.m.,* capender (apple—*pomme*).
caperon. V. **capron.**
capharnaüm, *n.m.,* (—*s*), (fig. fam.) a place in which things are in confusion and disorder.
capillaire (-pil-lèr), *adj.,* capillary.
capillaire, *n.m.,* (anat.) capillary ; (bot.) maiden's-hair ; Venus's-hair. *Sirop de* —; capillaire.
capillarité, *n.f.,* (phys.) capillarity, capillary attraction or repulsion.
capilotade, *n.f.,* hash, ragout made of hashed meat ; thrashing, drubbing ; slandering. *Mettre quelqu'un en* —; to thrash anyone soundly ; to slander anyone unsparingly.
capitaine, *n.m.,* captain. — *d'infanterie* ; captain of foot. — *de cavalerie* ; captain of horse. — *de vaisseau* ; post-captain. — *au long cours* ; captain of a trading vessel going to foreign parts. — *de pavillon* ; flag-captain. — *d'armes* ; master-at-arms.
capitainerie, *n.f.,* captaincy.
capital, -e, *adj.,* capital, main, chief, leading. *Les sept péchés capitaux* ; the seven capital sins. *Peine* —*e* ; capital punishment.
capital, *n.m.,* capital ; principal ; stock. *Mettre un* — *à fonds perdu* ; to sink a capital. *Rembourser le* —; to reimburse the principal.
capitale, *n.f.,* capital, chief city ; capital letter.
capitalisation, *n.f.,* capitalizing of money.
capitaliser, *v.a.* and *n.,* to capitalize money.
capitaliste, *n.m.,* capitalist, moneyed man.
capitan, *n.m.,* braggadocio, swaggerer, hector.
capitane, *n.f.,* (nav.) admiral's galley.
capitan-pacha, *n.m.* (—*s* —*s*), Turkish admiral.
capitation, *n.f.,* capitation-tax, poll-tax.
capiteu-x, -se, *adj.,* heady. *Bière* —*se* ; strong beer.

capitole, *n.m.*, Capitol (of Rome, of the United States—*de Rome, des Etats-unis*).
capitolin, *adj.*, capitoline.
capiton, *n.m.*, (com.) cappadine.
capitonner, *v.a.*, to pad (arm-chairs, carriages, &c.—*fauteuils, voitures, &c.*).
⊙**capitoul**, *n.m.*, capitoul (alderman, town-councillor at Toulouse).
⊙**capitoulat**, *n.m.*, capitoulship.
capitulaire, *adj.*, capitulary.
capitulaire, *n.m.*, capitular, capitulary.
capitulairement (lèr-mān), *adv.*, capitularly.
capitulant, *adj.*, capitulary.
capitulant, *n.m.*, capitular, capitulary.
capitulation, *n.f.*, capitulation; accommodation. *On en vint à bout par —; matters were managed by an accommodation. — de conscience;* a compromise with conscience.
capitule, *n.m.*, capitule (part of the Liturgy —*partie de la Liturgie*).
capituler, *v.n.*, to surrender by treaty to an enemy; to compound, to capitulate. — *avec sa conscience;* to compound with one's conscience.
caplan, (ich.). *V.* **capelan.**
capon, *n.m.*, mean fellow, sneak; cheat, coward; (nav.) cat-tackle. *Poulie de —;* cat-block.
caponner, *v.n.*, to trick, to cheat; to be cowardly, to hang back.
caponner, *v.a.*, (nav.) to cat (the anchor—*l'ancre*).
caponnière, *n.f.*, (fort.) covered lodgment.
caporal, *n.m.*, corporal.
capot, *n.m.*, (nav.) hood (of ladders—*d'échelles*).
capot, *adj.*, capot (at cards—*au piquet*); silly. *Faire —;* to capot, to win all the tricks. *Être —;* to look foolish; to be balked. *Faire —;* (nav.) to capsize, to upset.
capote, *n.f.*, large cloak with a hood; soldier's great-coat; capuchin, hood, mantle.
capraire, *n.f.*, (bot.) goat-weed, capraria.
⊙**capre**, *n.m.*, corsair; a sailor on board a corsair.
câpre, *n.f.*, (bot.) caper.
capricant, *adj.*, (med.) hard, unequal (of the pulse—*du pouls*).
caprice, *n.m.*, caprice, whim, humour, freak; fit, flight, sally; (mus.) caprice. *Les —s de la mode;* the caprice of fashion. *Les —s de la fortune;* the fickleness of fortune.
capricieusement (-mān), *adv.*, capriciously, fantastically, whimsically.
capricieu-x, -se, *adj.*, capricious, freakish.
capricorne, *n.m.*, (astron.) Capricorn; (ent.) capricorn-beetle.
câprier, *n.m.*, (bot.) caper-bush.
caprification, *n.f.*, caprification.
caprifiguier (-ghié), *n.m.*, wild fig-tree.
capripède, *n.m.*, one who has feet like those of a goat; satyr.
capron or **caperon**, *n.m.*, the hautboy-strawberry.
capronier, *n.m.*, the hautboy-strawberry plant.
capselle, *n.f.*, (bot.) casweed; shepherd's pouch.
capsulaire, *adj.*, (bot.) capsular; (anat.) capsular.
capsule, *n.f.*, (bot.) capsule, pod; (anat.) capsula; cap (of fire-arms—*pour armes à feu*).
⊙**captal**, *n.m.*, chief.
captateur, *n.m.*, (jur.) inveigler; one who uses undue influence.
captation, *n.f.*, inveigling, captation.
captatoire, *adj.*, which inveigles.
capter, *v.a.*, to court, to coax. — *la bienveillance de quelqu'un;* to curry the favour of any

one. — *les suffrages;* to bribe, to curry, suffrages.
captieusement (-sieûz-mān), *adv.*, captiously, insidiously, cunningly, deceitfully.
captieu-x, -se, (-cieu-), *adj.*, captious, insidious.
capti-f, -ve, *adj.*, captive.
capti-f, *n.m.*, **-ve**, *n.f.*, captive.
captiver, *v.a.*, to captivate, to enslave; to bring under. — *l'attention;* to captivate attention. *La beauté qui le captive;* the beauty that enslaves him. — *la bienveillance;* to win one's favour.
se **captiver**, *v.r.*, (l.u.) to brook restraint.
captivité, *n.f.*, captivity, bondage. *Racheter de —;* to ransom from captivity.
capture, *n.f.*, capture.
capturer, *v.a.*, to capture; to apprehend, to arrest.
capuce, *n.f.*, or **capuchon**, *n.m.*, hood, cowl (of a monk's cloak—*de l'habillement des moines*); (bot.) cowl, hood.
capuchonné, -e, *adj.*, hooded.
capuchonner, *v.n.*, (man.) to arch a horse's neck.
capucin, *n.m.*, **-e**, *n.f.*, capuchin friar, capuchin nun.
capucinade, *n.f.*, stupid sermon.
capucine, *n.f.*, (bot.) nasturtium; (nav.) standard; band (of a soldier's musket—*du fusil de munition*).
capucinière, *n.f.*, (b.s.) capuchin friary.
capulet, *n.m.*, a hood worn by women in the Pyrenees.
caput-mortuum, *n.m.*, (chem.) caput-mortuum; worthless remains.
caquage, *n.m.*, dressing and curing of herrings; barrelling (of powder—*de poudre à tirer*).
caque, *n.f.*, keg, barrel. *La — sent toujours le hareng;* what is bred in the bone will never come out of the flesh.
caquer, *v.a.*, to cure (herrings—*harengs*); to barrel (herrings, gunpowder—*harengs, poudre à tirer*).
caquet, *n.m.*, cackle (of geese, &c.—*d'oies, &c.*); tittle-tattle, idle talk. *Avoir bien du —;* to be a chatter-box. *Rabattre, rabaisser, le — à quelqu'un;* to snub one's pride. — *bon bec;* dame prattler.
caquetage (kak-taj), *n.m.*, tattling, cackling.
caquète, *n.f.*, carp-tub.
caqueter (kak-té), *v.n.*, to cackle, to chatter, to babble.
caqueterie (kak-tri), *n.f.*, babbling, prattling.
caqueteu-r, *n.m.*, **-se**, *n.f.*, prattler, tattler, idle prater, talkative gossip.
caqueur, *n.m.*, herring-curer.
car, *conj.*, for, because, as.
carabé, *n.m.*, yellow, amber.
carabin, *n.m.*, ⊙skirmisher; one who tries his chance at a game; saw-bones (medical student—*étudiant en médecine*).
carabinade, *n.f.*, (l.u.) a medical student's trick.
carabine, *n.f.*, carabine, carbine, rifle.
carabiné, -e, *adj.*, (nav.) stiff (of the wind —*du vent*).
⊙**carabiner**, *v.n.*, to skirmish.
carabiner, *v.a.*, to rifle a gun-barrel.
carabinier, *n.m.*, carabineer.
⊙**caraco**, *n.m.*, woman's dress.
caracole, *n.f.*, (man.) caracole.
caracoler, *v.n.*, to caracole.
caracouler, *v.n.*, to coo. *V.* **roucouler.**
caractère, *n.m.*, character, letter, type, print; hand-writing; stamp, badge, mark, dignity, temper, humour, spirit, expression; digit; charm, spell. — *lisible;* legible print, *Beaux*

—s ; fine type. *Le — d'un auteur ;* the stamp of an author. *Un homme d'un bon — ;* a good natured man. *Ne pas démentir son — ;* not to belie one's character. *Il est sorti de son — ;* he lost his tem_er. *Avoir, montrer, du — ;* to have, to show, spirit. *C'est un homme à — ;* he is a spirited man.

caractériser, *v.a.,* to characterize.

caractéristique, *adj.,* characteristic.

caractéristique, *n.f.,* (gram., math.) characteristic ; (logarithms) index.

carafe, *n.f.,* decanter, flagon, water-bottle, carafe.

carafon. *n.m.,* cooler ; small decanter (quarter of a bottle *—quart de bouteille*).

*caragne, *n.f.,* aromatic resin, caranna.

caraïte, *n.m.,* caraïte (sectary among the Jews—*sectaire juif*).

carambolage, *n.m.,* (billiards) cannon.

caramboler, *v.n.,* (billiards) to cannon.

caramel, *n.m.,* burnt sugar, caramel.

carapace, *n.f.,* turtle-shell, carapace.

carapat, *n.m.,* oil of palma Christi.

caraque, *n.f.,* carack (Portuguese Indiaman *—navire portugais*).

carat, *n.m.,* (gold.) carat ; small diamonds sold by weight.

caratch, *n.m.* (n.p.), tribute paid to the Sultan by Christians.

caravane, *n.f.,* caravan, convoy. *Marcher en — ;* to walk in a band. *Faire ses —s ;* to run a career of folly and dissipation.

caravanier, *n.m.,* leader of caravan.

*caravansérail, *n.m.,* a caravansary, kind of inn in the East.

caravanséraskier, *n.m.,* keeper of a caravansary.

caravelle, *n.f.,* caravel (Portuguese, Turkish ship—*navire turc, portugais*).

carbatine, *n.f.,* green hide.

carbazotique, *adj.* (chem.), carbazotic.

carbonarisme, *n.m.,* carbonarism.

carbonaro, *n.m.,* carbonaro.

carbonate, *n.m.* (chem.), carbonate.

☉**carboncle.** *V.* escarboucle ; furoncle ; rubis.

carbone, *n.m.,* (chem.) carbon.

carboné, -e, *adj.,* carbonated.

carboneu-x, -se, *adj.,* (chem.) carboneous.

carbonique, *adj.,* carbonic.

carbonisation, *n.f.,* carbonization.

carboniser, *v.a.,* to carbonize.

carbonnade, *n.f.,* (cook.) carbonade.

carbure, *n.m.,* (chem.) carburet.

carburé, -e, *adj.,* (chem.) carburetted.

carcan, *n.m.,* an iron collar ; carcan (pillory *—piloris*) ; carcanet (collar of jewels—*collier de pierreries*).

carcasse, *n.f.,* carcass ; (arch.) shell ; body.

carcinomateu-x, -se, *adj.,* (med.) carcinomatous.

carcinome, *n.m.,* (med.) carcinoma.

cardage, *n.m.,* act of carding, carding.

cardamine, *n.f.,* (bot.) land-cress, lady's smock.

cardamome. *n.m.,* (bot.) cardamom.

cardasse. *n.f.,* (bot.) nopal.

carde, *n.f.,* chard (stalk in the leaves of some plants—*côte des feuilles de certaines plantes*) ; card (instrument for combing wool or flax—*sorte de peigne pour la laine et le lin*) ; carding machine.

cardée, *n.f.,* as much wool as is combed at one time.

carde-poirée, *n.f.* (bot.) chard of beet.

carder. *v.a.,* to card, to comb wool, flax, &c.

cardère, *n.f.,* (bot.) teasel.

carderie, *n.f.,* carding-house ; card-manufactory.

cardeu-r, *n.m.,* **-se,** *n.f.,* carder, wool-comber.

cardiaire, *adj.,* (zool.) *Ver — ;* a parasite living in the heart. (bot.) *V.* **cardère ;** **chardon à foulon.**

cardialgie, *n.f.,* cardialgy, heartburn.

cardialgie, *n.f.,* treatise on the different parts of the heart.

cardiaque, *n.m.,* (med.) cardiac.

cardiaque, *adj.,* (med., anat.) cardiac.

cardier, *n.m.,* card-maker.

cardinal, *adj.,* cardinal, chief.

cardinal, *n.m.,* cardinal ; (orni.) cardinal.

cardinalat, *n.m.,* the dignity of a cardinal, cardinalship.

cardinale, *n.f.,* (bot.) cardinal flower.

cardine, *n.f.,* (ich.) flat-fish, whiff.

cardon, *n.m.,* (bot.) cardoon.

cardonnette, *n.f.* *V.* **chardonnette.**

carême, *n.m.,* lent. *Faire le — ;* to keep lent. *Provisions de — ;* fish and vegetables. *Cela vient comme marée en — ;* that comes in the very nick of time. *Face de — ;* pale-face, wan-face.

carême-prenant, *n.m.* (*—s —s*), carnival time ; Shrove Tuesday : masker ; one dressed like a merry-andrew.

carénage, *n.m.,* careening.

carence, *n.f.,* (jur.) absence of assets, insolvency. *Procès-verbal de — ;* declaration of insolvency.

carène, *n.f.,* (nav.) keel ; bottom, careen ; (bot.) keel. *Demi — ;* (nav.) parliament-heel.

caréné, -e, *adj.,* (bot.) keeled, carinated.

caréner, *v.a.,* (nav.) to careen.

caressant, -e, *adj.,* caressing ; fawning.

caresse, *n.f.,* caress, endearment. *Faire des —s ;* to fawn. *Il ne faut pas se fier aux —s de la fortune ;* we must not trust the smiles of fortune.

caressé, -e, *part.,* caressed. *Les tableaux de plusieurs peintres flamands sont très —s ;* the pictures of several of the Flemish painters have a peculiar richness and mellowness of finish.

caresser, *v.a.,* to caress, to stroke ; to fawn upon, to make much of. *— l'orgueil de quelqu'un ;* to pamper one's pride. *— une chimère ;* to cherish, to hug, a visionary scheme.

caret, *n.m.,* ropemaker's reel ; (erpetology) tortoise. *Fil de — ;* rope-yarn.

carex (-rèks), *n.m.,* (bot.) carex.

cargaison, *n.f.,* lading of a ship, cargo.

cargue (karg), *n.f.,* (nav.) brail.

carguer (-ghé), *v.a.,* (nav.) to brail, to clue up. *— une voile ;* to clue up a sail.

cargueur (-gheur), *n.m.,* (nav.) reefer ; top-block.

cariatide, *n.f.,* (arch.) caryatide.

caribou, *n.m.,* (mam.) cariboo.

caricature. *n.f.,* caricature.

caricaturer, *v.a.,* to caricature, to ridicule.

caricaturiste, *n.m.,* caricaturist.

carie, *n.f.,* brown rust ; fire-blast ; (med.) caries.

carier, *v.a.,* to make carious, to rot.

se carier, *v.r.,* to grow carious, rotten. *Dent cariée ;* carious tooth.

*carillon, *n.m.,* chime, peal ; musical bells, chimes ; clutter, racket. *A double — ;* soundly, heartily. *Le — des verres ;* the jingling of glasses.

*carillonnement, *n.m.,* chiming.

*carillonner, *v.n.,* to chime.

*carillonneur, *n.m.,* chimer.

☉**caristade,** *n.f.,* alms, charity.

carlin, *n.m.,* carlin (Italian silver coin *— monnaie d'argent italienne*) ; pug-dog.

carline. *n.f.,* (bot.) carline-thistle.

carlingue (-linghe), *n.f.*, (nav.) carline, carling. — *de cabestan ;* step.

carliste, *n.m.f.*, Carlist (partisan of Charles).

carliste, *adj.*, Carlist.

carlovingien, **-ne** (-in, -ê-n), *n.* and *adj.*, Carlovingian ; of Charlemagne.

*carmagnole. *n.f.*, carmagnole (jacket — *jaquette*) ; carmagnole (revolutionary song and dance—*chanson et danse révolutionnaires*).

carmagnole, *n.m.*, carmagnole (violent Jacobin).

carme, *n.m* , carmelite friar. —*s déchaussés ;* barefooted carmelites. *Eau des* —*s ;* carmelite water.

carme. *n.m.*, (trick-track) two fours.

carmeline, *n.f.*, carmeline wool.

carmélite, *n.f.*, a carmelite nun.

carmin, *n.m.*, carmine.

carminati-f, **-ve**, *adj.*, (med.) carminative.

carminati-f, *n.m.*, (med.) carminative.

carnage, *n.m.*, carnage, slaughter.

carnassi-er, **-ère**. *adj.*, carnivorous.

carnassier, *n.m.*, feline animal ; flesh-eater.

carnassière, *n.f.*, game-bag, shooting-bag.

carnation, *n.f.*, carnation, natural flesh-colour.

carnaval, *n.m.*, a carnival.

carne, *n.f.*, corner, edge (of a table, &c.).

carné, **-e**, *adj.*, of a carnation colour.

carnet, *n.m.*, note-book, memorandum-book. — *d'échéances ;* bill-book.

carnier, *n.m.* V. **carnassière**.

carnification, *n.f.* (med.) carnification.

se **carnifier**, *v.r.*, (med.) to carnify.

carnivore, *adj.*, carnivorous.

carnosité. *n.f.*, carnosity.

*carogne, *n.f.*, (l. ex.) hag, jade, impudent slut.

carolus (-lus), *n.m.*, carolus (an old French coin—*ancienne monnaie française*).

caronade, *n.f.*, (artil.) carronade.

caroncule, *n.f.*, (anat., bot.) caruncle.

carotide, *adj.*, (anat.) carotid.

carotide, *n.f.*, (anat.) carotid.

carotidien, *adj. m.*, (anat.) carotid. *Canal* —*; ì* carotid canal.

carotique, *adj.*, (med.) comatose.

carotte, *n.f.*, carrot. — *de tabac ;* roll of tobacco.

carotter, *v.n.*, to venture but little at play, to play low.

carotti-er, *n.m.*, **-ère**, *n.f.* (triv.). V. **carotteur**.

carotteu-r, *n.m.*, **-se**, *n.f.*, one who plays low.

caroube *or* **carouge**, *n.f.*, (bot.) carob-bean.

caroubier, *n.m.*, carob-tree, St. John's bread tree.

carpe, *n.f.*, (Ich.) carp. *Saut de* — *;* somerset. *Elle fait la* — *pâmée*, she falls into a sham swoon.

carpe, *n.m.*, (anat.) wrist.

carpeau, *n.m*, small carp, caught in the Rhône and Saône.

carpien, **-ne** (-in, ê-n), *adj.*, (anat) carpal.

*carpillon, *n.m* , (ich.) young carp ; very small carp.

carquois, *n.m.*, quiver. *Il a vidé son* —*;* he has shot all his bolts.

carrare, *n.m.*, carrara marble

carre, *n.f.*, back and shoulders (of any one—*d'un homme*) ; crown (of a hat—*de chapeau*). *La* — *d'un chapeau ;* the crown of a hat. *La* — *d'un habit ;* the part of a coat from the waist upwards *La* — *d'un soulier ;* the crown or toe of a shoe. *Un homme d'une bonne* — *;* a broad-shouldered man *Lame à trois* —*s ;* three-edged sword.

carré, *n.m.*, square ; landing-place, floor ; printing demy (of paper—*papier*). *Un* — *de tulipes ;* a square bed of tulips. *Un* — *d'eau ;*

a square sheet of water. — *de toilette ;* dressing-case

carré, **-e**, *adj.*, square, quadratic ; demy (of paper—*papier*) ; (rhet.) flowing *Période* —*e* (rhet.) ; flowing period. *Partie* —*e ;* party of two men and two women.

carreau, *n.m* , (med.) t ibes mesenterica.

carreau, *n m.*, square, square tile or brick ; small flag-stone ; ground, floor ; pane (of glass —*de verre*) ; cushion, hassock ; tailor's goose ; diamond (at cards—*aux cartes*) ; (gard.) bed, square ; (arch.) stretcher ; rubber (file—*lime*) ; square-headed arrow, cross-arrow. *Brochet* —*;* very large pike. *Tomber sur le* — *;* to fall ou the floor. *Coucher sur le* —*;* to sleep on the floor *Jeter quelqu'un sur le* — *;* to lay one sprawling upon the ground. *Rester sur le* —*; ì* to be killed on the spot *Étoffes à* —*x ;* stuffs with square stripes. *C'est un valet de* — *;* he is a contemptible fellow.

carrefour, *n.m.*, cross-way or street, place where several ways or streets meet. *Les* —*s d'une ville ;* the public places of a town. — *des auteurs ;* Grub-street.

carrelage, *n.m.*, pavement, paving with tiles, bricks, &c.

carreler, *v.a.*, to pave a floor with square tiles, bricks, stones ; to cobble.

carrelet, *n.m.*, (ich.) flounder ; square net ; shoemaker's awl.

carrelette, *n.f.*, flat file.

carreleur, *n.m.*, workman that paves floors with tiles ; tramping cobbler.

carrelier, *n m.*, a tile-maker.

carrelure, *n.f.*, new-soling of shoes.

carrément, *adv.*, squarely. *Couper* —*; ì* to cut square. *Tracer un plan* —*;* to draw a plan square.

carrer, *v.a.*, to square.

se **carrer**, *v.r.*, to strut. — *dans son fauteuil ;* to sit proudly. —*;* to double one's stake (at *bouillotte*—a card game).

carrick, *n m.*, box-coat.

carrier, *n.m.*, a quarry-man.

carrière, *n.f*, race-ground, course, &c. ; career, race ; course ; scope ; quarry *Le bout de la* —*;* the goal. *Parcourir la* —*;* to run round, to run over the course. *Donner* — *à son esprit ;* to give one's wit ample scope. *Se donner* —*;* to indulge one's fancy, &c. *La* — *des armes ;* the career of arms. — *de marbre ;* marble quarry.

carriole, *n.f.*, covered cart, jaunting car

carrossable, *adj.*, (of roads—*des routes*) practicable for carriages. *Route* — *;* carriage road.

carrosse, *n.m.*, four-wheeled carriage, coach. — *de remise ;* livery-coach. — *de louage ;* hackney-coach. *Mener un* — *;* to drive a carriage. *Aller en* — *;* to ride in a coach.

carrossée, *n.f.*, a coachful

carrossier, *n.m.*, coachmaker ; coach-horse.

carrousel, *n m.*, tournament, carousal.

⊙**carrousse**, *n.f.*, carouse. *Faire* — *; ì* carouse, to drink hard.

carrure, *n.f.*, breadth of the shoulders.

cartahu, *n.m.*, (nav) whip. *Poulie de* —*;* single block.

⊙**cartayer**, *v.n.*, to avoid the two ruts of a road (in driving—*en conduisant une voiture*).

carte, *n.f.*, pasteboard ; card ; ticket ; bill ; bill of fare ; account. *Un jeu de* —*s.* a pack of cards *Les basses* —*s ;* the small cards. —*t préparées ;* marked cards. *Donner les* —*s , tè* deal. *Faire des tours de* — *;* to play tricks with cards. *Mettre aux* —*s ;* to pay the card-money. *Château de* —*s ;* ginger-bread house. *Brouiller les* —*s ;* to sow dissension. *Voir le dessous des* —*s ;* to be in the secret *Avoir* — *blanche ;* to have full power. *Tirer les* —*s ;* to tell fortunes with the cards. — *de géographie*; map, chart. *Faire la — d'un pays*; to map a country. — *topographique*; topographical chart. — *marine*; sea-chart. *Perdre la —*; to lose one's wits. *Dîner à la —*; to dine by the bill of fare.

cartel, *n.m.*, challenge, cartel; dial-case, clock; (milit., nav.) cartel.

carterie, *n.f.*, card-making, card-factory.

carteron, *n.m. V.* **quarteron**.

cartésianisme, *n.m.*, Cartesian philosophy.

cartésien, **-ne** (-in, -è-n), *adj.*, Cartesian.

carthaginois, **-e**, *n.* and *adj.*, Carthaginian.

carthame, *n.m.*, (bot.) carthamus.

cartier, *n.m.*, playing-card maker.

cartilage, *n.m.*, (anat.) cartilage, gristle.

cartilagineu-x, **-se**, *adj.*, cartilaginous, gristly.

cartisane, *n.f.*, thread (for lace—*à dentelle*). *Dentelle à —*; vellum-lace.

cartomancie, *n.f.*, cartomancy.

cartomancien, *n.m.*, **-ne**, *n.f.*, one who attempts to tell the fortunes of people by means of combinations of cards.

carton, *n.m.*, pasteboard; (paint.) cartoon; band-box; case; hat-box; bonnet-box; (print.) four-page cancel. — *lissé*; glazed pasteboard. *Les —s de Raphaël*; the cartoons of Raphael. — *de dessins*; portfolio of drawings.

cartonnage, *n.m.*, (book-bind.) boarding.

cartonné, **-e**, *adj.*, (book-bind.) in boards.

cartonner, *v.a.*, to board a book, to put a book in boards.

cartonnerie, *n.f.*, pasteboard manufactory.

cartonneu-r, *n.m.*, **-se**, *n.f.*, binder who boards books.

cartonnier, *n.m.*, pasteboard-maker, seller.

carton-pierre, *n.m.*, (n.p.), statuary pasteboard.

cartouche, *n.m.*, (arch.) cartouch, modillion.

cartouche, *n.f.*, cartouch (of cannon—*pour canon*); cartridge (of fire-arms—*pour fusils, &c.*); ☉furlough; discharge.

cartouchier, *n.m.*, (nav.) cartridge-box.

cartouchière, *n.f.*, cartridge-box.

cartulaire, *n.m.*, cartulary.

carus, *n.m.*, (med.) deep coma.

carvi, *n.m.*, (bot.) caraway; caraway-seed.

caryatide. *V.* **cariatide**.

caryophyllée. *adj.,f.*,(bot.) caryophylleous.

caryophyllées, *n.f. pl.*, caryophyllæ.

caryophylloïde, *n.f.*, caryophilloid.

cas, *n.m.*, case, event, esteem, value; (jur., math., gram., med.) case. *Un — pendable*; a hanging matter. *Un — imprévu*; an unforeseen case. *Au —, en — que cela soit*; in case that should turn out. *Auquel —*; in which case. *Le —échéant*, should such be the case. *En tel —, en pareil —*; in such a case, in a similar case. *C'est le — de parler*; it is the time for speaking. *Faire grand — de quelqu'un*; to have a great esteem for any one. *Faire peu de —*; to make light of, to slight. *En tout —*; at all events, however. *En — de besoin*; in case of need.

☉**cas**, **-se**, *adj.*, cracked, broken (of the voice—*de la voix*). *Voix —se*; hoarse voice.

casani-er, **-ère**. *n.* and *adj.*, domestic person; domestic, retired, fond of remaining at home.

casaque, *n.f.*, great coat, cassock. *Tourner —*, to change sides.

casaquin, *n.m.*, short gown. *On lui a donné sur le —*; they have trimmed his jacket for him.

cascade, *n.f.*, cascade, water-fall. *Un discours plein de —s*; an unconnected discourse.

cascarille, *n.f.*, cascarilla.

cascatelle, *n.f.*, cascade (of Tivoli).

case, *n.f.*, division; dwelling-place, mean house, hut; box (for animals—*pour les animaux*);

pigeon-hole; point (backgammon—*trictrac*); (nav.) berth. *Le patron de la —* (triv.); master of the house.

casé, **-e**, *part.*, placed. *Le voilà —*; he is settled.

caséeu-x, **-se**, *adj.*, caseous.

casemate, (kaz-mat), *n.f.*, (fort.) casemate.

casematé, **-e**, *adj.*, furnished with a casemate.

caser, *v.n.*, (backgammon—*trictrac*) to make a point.

caser, *v.a.*, to place, to find a place, situation.

se **caser**, *v.r.*, to take up one's abode, one's quarters, to get settled.

caserne, *n.f.*, barracks.

casernement, *n.m.*, lodging troops in barracks.

caserner, *v.a.*, to put in barracks. — *des troupes*; to lodge soldiers in barracks.

caserner, *v.n.*, to be in barracks.

casier, *n.m.*, set of pigeon holes of a bureau.

*casilleux, adj., m., (of glass—du verre) brittle.

casimir, *n.m.*, kerseymere cloth.

casino, *n.m.*, casino, club.

casoar, *n.m.*, (orni.) cassowary.

casque, *n.m.*, helmet, casque, head-piece; (bot.) hood; (her.) helmet, casque; (conch.) helmet-shell.

casquette, *n.f.*, cap (of a man or boy).

☉**cassade**, *n.f.*, sham, flam; lie, fib, cheat.

cassage, *n.m.*, the act of breaking.

*cassaille, *n.f.*, the breaking up (of a piece of ground—*d'un terrain*).

cassant, **-e**, *adj.*, brittle, apt to break.

cassation, *n.f.*, cassation, annulment, repeal, quashing. *Se pourvoir en —*; to sue for a writ of error. *Cour de —*; the highest court; of appeal in France.

cassave. *n.f.*, cassava.

casse, *n.f.*, (bot.) cassia; (print.) case; (com.) breakage; (milit.) cashiering. — *aromatique*; bastard cinnamon. *Cet officier mérite la —*; that officer deserves to be broken. *Haut de —*; (print.) upper-case. *Bas de —*; (print.) lower-case. *Apprendre la —*; to learn the boxes.

casseau, *n.m.*, (print.) half-case.

casse-cou, *n.m.* (—, *or* — —*s*), break-neck; (man.) rough-rider.

casse-lunette, *n.m.* (—, *or* — —*s*), (bot.) eye-breaker.

casse-motte, *n.m.* (—, *or* — —*s*), (agri.) clod-breaker.

casse-noisette, *n.m.* (—, *or* — —*s*), nut-crackers.

casse-noix, *n.m.* (—), nut-crackers; (orni.) nut-hatch.

casser, *v.a.*, to break; to crack; to cashier; to waste; to wear out; to annul; to rescind; to shiver (a mast—*un mât*). *Qui casse les verres les paie*; he that breaks the glasses must pay the damage. — *un jugement*; to reverse a judgment. *Cassé de vieillesse*; worn out with old age. *Voix cassée*; broken voice.

se **casser**, *v.r.*, to break; to break down; to wear out; to snap. *Se — la tête*; to break one's head; to puzzle one's brains. *Se — le cou*; to break one's neck. *Se — la jambe*; to break one's leg.

casser, *v.n.*, to break.

casserole, *n.f.*, saucepan.

casse-tête, *n.m.* (—), tomahawk; puzzle-brain; heady wine; din. *Quel —!* what a din!

cassetin, *n.m.*, (print.) box.

cassette, *n.f.*, casket; cash-box. *La — du roi*; the King's privy purse.

casseu-r, *n.m.*, **-se**, *n.f.*, one who breaks

many things through awkwardness. *C'est un grand — de raquettes ;* he is a stout fellow. *Un — d'assiettes ;* a quarrelsome fellow.

cassier, *n.m.*, cassia-tree.

cassine, *n.f.*, little country-box ; (milit.) small, isolated house, in the country, that can be occupied and defended as a post.

cassiopée, (-pē-), (astron.) Cassiopeia.

cassis (kâ-sis), *n.m.*, black currant ; black currant-tree ; black-currant ratafia (liquor).

cassolette, *n.f.*, perfuming pan ; pleasant, fragrant smell ; (b.s.) stench, odour. *Quelle —! what a perfume !*

casson, *n.m.*, pieces of broken plate-glass ; lump sugar in masses.

cassonade, *n.f.*, moist sugar.

cassure, *n.f.*, broken place ; break ; breaking.

***castagnette**, *n.f.*, castanet.

caste. *n.f.*, caste.

⊙**castel**. *n.m.*, castle.

***castillan**, **-e**, *n.* and *adj.*, Castilian.

⊙***castille**, *n.f.*, altercation, contention, strife.

castine, *n.f.*, (metal.) flux.

castor, *n.m.*, (mam.) castor, beaver ; beaver hat.

castoréum (-om), *n.m.*, (phar.) castoreum

castorine. *n.f.*, castorine.

castramétation, *n.f.*, castrametation.

castrat, *n.m.*, castrato.

castration, *n.f.*, castration.

casualité, *n.f.*, (l.u.) casualty, casualness, fortuitousness.

casuel, **-le**, *adj.*, casual ; precarious.

casuel, *n.m.*, perquisites. *Le — d'une cure ;* surplice fees.

casuellement (-mān), *adv.*, casually, accidentally, by chance.

casuiste, *n.m.*, casuist.

catachrèse (-krèz), *n.f.*, (rhet.) catachresis.

cataclysme, *n.m.*, cataclysm, deluge, overflowing, great inundation.

catacois. *V.* cacatois.

catacombes, *n.f. pl.*, catacombs.

catacoustique, *n.f.*, catacoustics.

catadioptrique, *n.f.*, catadioptrics.

catadioptrique, *adj.*, catadioptrical.

⊙**catadoupe**, *or* **catadupe**, *n.f.*, catadupa, cataract, waterfall.

catafalque, *n.m.*, catafalco.

cataire, *adj.*, of a cat, cat-like. *Frémissement —* (med.) ; thrill, purring tremor, of. the heart.

cataire, *n.f.*, (bot.) catmint, catnip.

catalan. **-e**, *n.* and *adj.* Catalonian.

catalecte, *or* **catalectique**, *adj.*, (poet.) catalectic.

catalectes, *n.m. pl.*, (lit.) catalectics.

catalepsie, *n.f.*, catalepsy.

cataleptique, *adj.*, cataleptic.

catalogue, (-log), *n.m.*, list, enumeration, catalogue.

cataloguer (-ghé), *v.a.*, to catalogue.

catalpa. *n.m.*, (bot.) catalpa.

cataplasme, *n.m.*, cataplasm, poultice.

catapuce, *n.f.*, (bot.) caper-spurge.

catapulte, *n.f.*, (antiq.) catapult.

catoracte. *n.f.*, cataract ; (religious style —écriture sainte) windows of heaven ; (med.) cataract.

cataracté. **-e**, *adj.*, (med.) afflicted with a cataract.

se **cataracter**, *v.r.*, to have an incipient cataract.

catarrhal, **-e**. *adj.*, (med.) catarrhal.

catarrhe, *n.m.*, catarrh, a cold.

catarrheu-x. **-se**, *adj.*, (med.) liable to catarrh, catarrhous.

catastrophe, *n.f.*, catastrophe.

catéchiser, *v.a.*, to catechise ; to reason with ; to give one his cue.

catéchisme, *n.m.*, catechism. *Faire le — à quelqu'un ;* to give one his cue.

catéchiste. *n.m.*, catechist.

catéchuménat (-ku-), *n.m.*, the state of a catechumen.

catéchumène (-ku-), *n.m.f.*, catechumen.

catégorie, *n.f.*, category, predicament.

catégorique, *adj.*, categorical, proper, explicit.

catégoriquement (-rik-mān), *adv.*, categorically, to the purpose.

⊙**caterve**, *n.f.*, troop, band.

cathartine, *n.f.*, cathartine.

cathartique, *n.m.* and *adj.*, cathartic. purgative.

cathédrale, *n.* and *adj. f.*, cathedral ; cathedral church.

cathédrant, *n.m.*, president (over a thesis —d'une thèse).

cathérétique. *adj.*, (pharm.) caustic.

cathéter (-tèr). *n.m.*, (surg.) catheter.

cathétérisme, *n.m.*, (surg.) catheterism.

catholicisme, *n.m.*, Catholicism.

catholicité, *n.f.*, Catholicism ; Catholic countries.

catholicon, *n.m.*, (phar.) catholicon.

catholique, *adj.*, Catholic, moral. *Cela n'est pas — ;* that is not orthodox.

catholique, *n.m.f.*, Catholic. *Un — d gros grains ;* a lax Catholic.

catholiquement (-mān), *adv.*, in a catholic way.

cati, *n.m.*, pressing, gloss, lustre.

cati, *adj.*, pressed.

en **catimini**, *adv.*, slily, stealthily.

catin, *n.f.*, (l.ex.) harlot.

catir, *v.a.*, to give a gloss to. *— à chaud ; to hot-press. — à froid ;* to cold-press.

catissage, *n.m.*, glossing, giving a lustre.

catisseur, *n.m.*, presser.

catodon. *n.m.*, catodan, a species of whale.

catogan, *or* **cadogan**, *n.m.*, club of hair.

catoptrique, *n.f.*, catoptrics.

catoptromancie, *n.f.*, catoptromancy.

caucasique, *adj.*, (geog.) Caucasian.

cauchemar (kosh-mar), *n.m.*, nightmare. *Il donne le — ;* he tires one to death.

caucher, *n.m.*, vellum-mould (in gold-beating—terme de batteur d'or).

cauchois, **-e**, *adj.*, of Caux.

caudataire, *n.m.*, the train-bearer to a cardinal.

caudé, **-e**, *adj.*; (her.) having a tail ; caudated.

⊙**caudebec** (-bek), *n.m.*, woollen French hat.

caudex (kô-dèks), *n.m.*, stem of a tree.

caudicule, *n.f.*, (bot.) caudicle.

caudines, *adj.f.pl.*, caudine.

caulicoles, *n.f.pl.*, (arch.) caulicole.

caulinaire, *adj.*, (bot.) cauline.

cauris, *n.m.*, cowry.

causal. **-e**, *adj.*, causal.

causalité, *n.f.*, causality.

causant, **-e**, *adj.*, chatting, talkative.

causati-f, **-ve**. *adj.*, (gram.) causative.

causation, *n.f.*, causation.

causativement, *adv.*, causatively.

cause, *n.f.*, cause ; grounds, motive ; subject. *Déterminer, assigner, la —d'un phénomène ;* to determine, to assign, the cause of a phenomenon. *—s éloignées ;* remote causes. *Prendre fait et — pour quelqu'un :* to espouse one's cause. *— appelée, remise ;* cause called in court, put off. *— embrouillée, douteuse ;* intricate, doubtful cause. *Donner gain de — ;* to give it up. *Avoir — gagnée ;* to carry the cause. *Être hors de — ;* to have nothing more to do with a law-suit. *Être con-*

damné sans connaissance de — ; to be cast without a hearing. *Ses héritiers ou ayants —* ; his heirs or assigns. *Un avocat sans —* ; a briefless barrister. *Parler avec connaissance de —* ; to speak from a knowledge of the case. *Vous êtes — de mon bonheur* ; you are the cause of my happiness. *Être la — innocente, involontaire d'un accident* ; to be the harmless, involuntary cause of an accident. *Il ne le fera pas, et pour —* ; he won't do it, and for a very good reason. *A ces —s* ; (jur.) these reasons moving us thereunto. *A — de* ; for the sake of, on account of, because of, for. *A — de quoi ?* why ? wherefore ? for what reason ? *A — que* ; because.

causer, v.a., to cause, to be the cause of, to occasion, to give.

causer, v.n., to chat, to talk, to prate. *— de choses et d'autres* ; to talk of one thing and another. *— de la pluie et du beau temps* ; to talk about the weather. *— littérature, voyages* ; to talk about literature, travels.

causerie (köz-ri), n.f., prattling, chatting, gossiping.

causette, n.f., chit-chat.

causeu-r, -se, adj., talkative.

causeu-r, n.m., **-se,** n.f., talker, tattler.

causeuse. n.f., small sofa.

causticité, n.f., causticity.

caustique, adj., biting, cutting, caustic.

caustique, n.m., caustic.

caustique, n.f., (geom., phys.) caustic curve.

caustiquement, adv., caustically.

cautèle, n.f., cunning, craft ; precaution.

cauteleusement (kôt-leûz-măn), adv., craftily, slily.

cauteleu-x, -se (kôt-leû), adj., cunning, crafty.

cautère, n.m., (med.) issue, cautery. *Panser un —* ; to dress a cautery. *Pois à —* ; issue peas.

cautérétique. *V.* **cathérétique.**

cautérisation, n.f., cauterization.

cautériser, v.a., to cauterize, to sear, to burn.

caution, n.f., surety, security, bail, pledge. *— légale* ; common bail. *— solvable* ; special bail. *Un homme sujet à —* ; a man not to be trusted.

cautionné, -e, part., bailed.

cautionnement (kô-sio-n-măn), n.m., bailing, bail, giving security ; security.

cautionner, v.a., to bail one, to be bound for one ; to guarantee.

cavage, n.m., charge for storing in a cellar, cellarage.

cavalcade, n.f., ride, cavalcade.

cavalcadour, n.m., riding-master, equerry, gentleman of the horse.

cavale, n.f., mare.

cavalerie (ka-val-rî), n.f., cavalry.

cavalier, n.m., horseman ; rider, cavalier ; trooper ; gentleman ; (dancing—*danse*) partner ; knight (at chess—*aux échecs*) ; (fort.) cavalier ; (man.) rider ; (mec.) spoil-bank. *Servir de — à une dame* ; to escort a lady.

cavali-er, -ère, adj., cavalier, free, proud, haughty.

cavalièrement (-măn), adv., cavalierly, bluntly.

cavatine, n.f., (mus.) cavatina.

cave, n.f., cellar ; boot (of a coach—*d'une voiture*) ; case of bottles, cellaret ; (cards—*aux cartes*) poor, stock. *Rat de —* ; twisted taper. *Rats de —* ; excisemen.

cave, adj., hollow. *Œil —* ; hollow eye. *Lune —* ; lunar month of 29 days.

caveau, n.m., small cellar ; vault (in a church—*dans une église*).

cavecé, -e, adj., with a black head (of a roan horse or mare—*d'un cheval rouan*). *Cheval rouan — de noir* ; roan horse with a black head.

caveçon, n.m., (man.) cavezon. *Il a besoin de —* ; he wants a curb.

cavée, n.f., (hunt.) hollow way.

caver, v.a., to hollow, to make hollow, to dig under ; to stake (at play—*au jeu*). *— au plus fort* ; to play deep ; to carry things to extremes.

se caver, v.r., to become hollow ; (at play—*au jeu*) to stake.

caverne, n.f., cavern ; den.

caverneu-x, -se, adj., hollow, sepulchral (of the voice—*de la voix*) ; (anat.) cavernous, spongy. *Voix —se* ; hollow voice.

cavet, n.m., (arch.) cavetto.

caviar, n.m., (cook.) caviar.

cavillation (-vil-la-), n.f., sophistry.

caviste, n.m., cellarer, cellarist.

cavité, n.f., cavity.

ce, cet, m., **cette,** f., **ces,** pl., demonst. adj., this, these ; that, those. *Ce livre* ; this or that book. *Ce héros* ; this or that hero. *Cet arbre* ; this or that tree. *Cet homme* ; this or that man. *Cette femme* ; this or that woman. *Ces livres* ; these or those books. *Ce livre-ci* ; this book. *Ce livre-là* ; that book.

ce, demonst. pron., he, she, it ; they. *J'aime votre frère, c'est un bon ami* ; I love your brother, he is a good friend. *Lisez Racine et Boileau, ce sont de grands poètes* ; read Racine and Boileau, they are great poets.

ce (for *cela*), it, that ; he, she, they. *C'est fait* ; it is done. *C'est fort bien fait* ; that's very well done. *C'est fait de moi* ; I am lost. *C'en est fait* ; it is all over. *C'est bien fait à lui* ; he is very right. *Et ce, pour cause* ; and this for a good reason. *Je lui ai dit telle chose, et ce pour le persuader de le faire* ; I told him such a thing, and it was to persuade him to do it. *Qui est-ce ?* who is he ? *Qui était-ce ?* who was it ? *Qui sera-ce ?* who will it be ? *Qui est-ce qui arrive là ?* who is arriving there ? *Est-ce moi ?* is it I ? *Est-ce lui ?* is it he ? *Est-ce nous qu'il menace ?* is it to us his threats are directed ? *Est-ce eux que vous prétendez soumettre ?* is it to them you pretend to give laws ? *Sont-ce les Anglais ?* is it the English ? *C'est vous qu'on demande* ; it is you who are wanted. *Ce sont eux que j'ai vus* ; it is they I have seen. *Sont-ce là les dames que vous attendiez ?* are these the ladies you expected ? *Oui, ce sont elles* ; yes, they are. *C'était eux, ce furent eux, ce sera nous, ce sera vous autres, ce sera eux ; ce serait eux* ; it was they, &c. *Qu'est-ce ?* what is that ? *Qu'est-ce que je vois là-bas ?* what do I see yonder ? *Sont-ce là vos raisons ?* are those your reasons ? *Est-ce là votre carrosse ?* is that your coach ? *Oui, ce l'est* ; yes, it is. *Sont-ce là vos chevaux ?* are these your horses ? *Oui, ce les sont* ; yes, they are. *Quel jour est-ce aujourd'hui ?* what day is this ? *C'est jeudi* ; it is Thursday. *Quand sera-ce ?* when will it be ? *Ce sera pour demain* ; it will be for to-morrow.

ce qui, que, dont, à quoi ; that, which, what, of what, to what. *Je ne sais ce que nous deviendrons* ; I do not know what will become of us. *Ce qui se passe* ; what happens. *Ce que je vous dis* ; what I tell you. *Faites ce dont je vous ai parlé* ; do what I told you of. *Ce qui réussit est toujours approuvé* ; what meets with success always meets with approbation. *C'est ce que je disais* ; it is what I said. *Ce que j'ai vu de beau* ; the fine things I saw. *Tout ce qu'on fait de mauvais* ; all the mischief that is done.

ce qui, ce que, serve for two verbs, the latter of which, when *ce* begins the sentence, is governed by *ce* : if the latter verb is *être*, followed by *que* or *de*, *ce* must be repeated before it.

Ce que je crains, c'est d'être surpris; what I fear is to be surprised. *Ce qu'il demande, c'est une pension:* what he asks for is a pension. [But ce cannot be repeated when *être* is followed by an adjective.] *Ce qu'on vous a dit est vrai;* what you have been told is true. *Ce qu'on vous a dit, ce sont des contes;* what you have been told is a mere story. *C'était un grand capitaine que César;* Cæsar was a great captain. *C'est une sorte de honte que d'être malheureux;* it is a kind of shame to be unfortunate. *Sont-ce les richesses qui vous rendront heureux?* can riches make you happy? *C'est moi qu'on veut perdre;* I am the man they wish to ruin. *C'est à vous que je parle;* it is to you I speak. *C'est d'elle que je parle;* it is of her that I speak. *C'est là que je les attends;* there I shall have them. *C'est un bonheur que d'avoir échappé;* it is good luck to have escaped. *C'était à vous de parler;* you ought to have spoken. *Si c'était à refaire;* if it were to be done again. *C'est à qui parlera;* they speak in emulation of one another. *C'était à qui s'enfuirait;* they ran away as for a wager. *Ce serait pour moi un grand plaisir;* it would give me great pleasure. *Ce n'est pas qu'il la craigne, mais il aime la paix;* not that he fears her, but he loves peace. *Ces malheureux ne savent ce que c'est que la vertu;* these wretches know not what virtue is. *C'est-à-dire;* that is to say. *Ce n'est pas à dire que;* it does not follow that. *C'est pourquoi;* therefore, wherefore, for which reason.

céans, *adv.,* within, here within, in this house, home. Seldom used but in the expressions: *Maître de —;* master of the house. *Il dînera —:* he will dine at home.

ceci, *demonstrative pronoun,* this. *Que veut dire —?* what does this mean? *C'est —, c'est cela;* it is first one thing and then another.

cécité, *n.f.,* blindness, cecity. *Frapper de —;* to strike blind.

cédant, *n.m.,* **-e,** *n.f.,* (jur.) grantor; assignor, transferrer.

cédant, -e, *adj.,* that assigns, transfers; that grants.

céder, *v.a.,* to give, to give up, to yield. to transfer; to sell. to part with, to make over. *— le pas à quelqu'un;* to give precedence to any one. *— le haut du pavé;* to give the wall.

céder, *v.n.,* to give way, to give; to submit; to give in. *Il faut —;* we must submit. *— à son penchant;* to give way to one's propensity. *Je lui cède en tout;* I give in to him in everything.

*cédille, *n.f.,* (gram.) cedilla.

cédrat, *n.m.,* (bot.) (tree—*arbre*) cedrate, lemon-tree; (fruit) lemon.

cédratier, *n.m.,* (bot.) cedrate, lemon-tree.

cèdre, *n.m.,* cedar; cedar of Lebanon.

cédrie, *n.f.,* cedria.

cédule, *n.f.,* (jur.) cedule, note of hand.

ceindre, (ceignant, ceint), *v.a.,* to enclose, to encompass, to surround, to bind; to fence; to gird on, to encircle. *Une corde lui ceignait les reins;* his loins were girt with a cord. *— le diadème;* to put on the diadem.

se ceindre, *v.r.,* to bind round one; to encircle one's brow with any thing.

ceintrage, *n.m.,* (nav.) frapping.

ceintrer, *v.a.,* (nav.) to frap. *— un vaisseau;* to frap a ship. *Le vaisseau ceintre son câble;* the ship bears upon the cable.

ceinture, *n.f.,* sash, girdle, belt; waist-band, waist-ribbon; the waist; enclosure, circle; (arch.) cincture (of a column—*d'une colonne*), moulding; (nav.) swifter. *Bonne renommée vaut mieux que — dorée:* a good name is better than riches. *— de deuil:* funeral hangings.

ceinturé, -e, *adj.,* confined; wearing a sash.

ceinturier, *n.m.,* girdle-maker, belt-maker.

ceinturon, *n.m.,* belt, sword-belt.

cela, *demonstrative pronoun;* that. *— est vrai;* that is true. *Comment —? how so?* *C'est —;* that's it. *N'est-ce que —! is that all?* *Comme —;* so so. *Il est comme —;* it is his way, it is just like him.

céladon, *adj. m.,* sea-green (colour). *Ruban —;* sea-green riband.

céladon, *n.m.,* sea-green (colour); sentimental lover; beau.

célébrant, *n.m.,* officiating priest at mass.

célébration, *n.f.,* solemn performance, celebration.

célèbre, *adj.,* celebrated, famous.

célébrer, *v.a.,* to praise, to extol, to sing, to solemnize; to celebrate, to record.

célébrité, *n.f.,* celebrity; fame; ⊙solemnity.

celer, *or* **céler,** *v.a.,* to conceal, to keep close or secret, to keep, to secrete. *Se faire —:* to send word to a visitor that one is out, although being at home.

céleri (sèl-ri), *n.m.,* celery. *Botte de —;* bundle of celery.

célérité, *n.f.,* celerity, rapidity, dispatch.

céleste, *adj.,* celestial, heavenly. *Bleu —;* sky-blue. *La colère —;* the anger of heaven.

célestin, *n.m.,* celestin (monk—*moine*).

céliaque, *adj.,* (anat.) cœliac.

célibat, *n.m.,* celibacy, single life; single state. *Femme, homme, dans le —;* single woman, single man.

célibataire, *n.m.,* single man, bachelor.

celle, *demonstrative pronoun;* she, that. *V.* **celui.**

⊙**celle,** *n.f.,* cell (of a hermit—*d'hermite*).

cellér-ier, *n.m.,* **-ière,** *n.f.,* cellarer.

cellier, *n.m.,* cellar, store-room.

cellulaire, *adj.,* cellular.

cellule, *n.f.,* cell, partition; cell (in a honeycomb—*d'un rayon de miel*).

celluleu-x, -se, *adj.,* cellular.

célozie, *n.f.,* (bot.) cock's comb; coxcomb.

celte, *n.m.,* Celt.

celtique, *adj.,* Celtic. *La langue —;* the Celtic language.

celtique, *n.m.,* Celtic language.

celui, *m.,* **celle,** *f.,* **ceux, celles,** *pl.,* *demonstrative pronouns,* he, him; she, her, they, them; that, those. *Vous avez puni celui qui ne la méritait pas, et récompensé celle qui était coupable;* you have punished him who did not deserve it, and rewarded her who was in the wrong. *Ceux qui ont vécu avant nous;* those who lived before us.

celui-ci, celle-ci, *sing.,* **ceux-ci, celles-ci,** *pl. demonstrative pronouns;* this, these.

celui-là, celle-là, *sing.,* **ceux-là, celles-là,** *pl.,* *demonstrative pronouns;* that, those. *Aimez-vous mieux celui-ci?* do you like this best? *Celui-là n'est pas si beau;* that is not so fine. *Celui-ci est meilleur que celui-là;* this is better than that. [*Celui-ci* relates to an object near the speaker; *celui-là,* to an object distant from him; or after two nouns already expressed, *celui-ci* refers to the last, *celui-là* to the first mentioned.]

cément, *n.m.,* cement.

cémentation, *n.f.,* cementation.

cémentatoire, *adj.,* cementatory.

cémenter, *v.a.,* to cement.

cénacle, *n.m.,* (antiq.) guest-chamber (where the Lord's supper was taken—*endroit où eut lieu la Cène de N. S.*).

cendre, *n.f.,* ashes; embers; cinder; dust, ashes (of the dead—*des morts*). *C'est un feu qui couve sous la —:* it is a fire burning under the ashes. *La —, les —s des morts;* the ashes of the dead.

cendres, *n.f. pl.,* ashes. *— ardentes;* live embers. *— qui couvent;* mouldering ashes. *Le mercredi des —;* Ash-Wednesday. *Mettre en*

—; to lay in ashes. *Renaître de ses —;* to rise from one's ashes.

cendré, -e, *adj.,* ashy. *Gris —;* ashy gray. pale gray.

cendrée, *n.f.,* small shot.

cendreu-x, -se, *adj.,* ashy, full of, covered with, ashes.

cendrier, *n.m.,* ash-pan ; ash-hole

*cendrille, *n.f.,* (orni.) tomtit.

cène, *n.f.,* the Lord's supper, communion. *Participer à la sainte —;* to partake of the Lord's supper.

cenelle, *n.f.,* (bot.) haw.

cénobite, *n.m.,* cenobite, monk.

cénobitique, *adj.,* cenobitical.

cénotaphe, *n.m.,* cenotaph.

cens (sans), *n.m.,* cense, quit-rent ; census.

cense, *n.f.,* (local expression) farm.

censé, -e, *adj.,* accounted, deemed, reputed, supposed.

censeur, *n.m.,* censor ; censurer ; critic ; proctor (of universities—*d'universités*).

censier, *adj.,* of quit-rent.

censi-er, *n.m.,* **-ère,** *n.f.,* farmer; rent-roll.

censitaire, *n.m.,* copyholder.

censive, *n.f.,* quit-rent. manor.

censorial, -e, *adj.,* relating to the censorship of theatres, &c.

censuel, -le, *adj.,* pertaining to quit-rent.

censurable, *adj.,* censurable.

censure, *n.f.,* censorship; censure, criticism ; reproof ; ecclesiastical censure ; the censors.

censurer, *v.a.,* to find fault with ; to blame, to censure, to condemn.

cent, *adj.,* hundred, cent. *— un ans ;* one hundred and one years. *Cinq pour — ;* five per cent. [*Cent* takes the sign of the plural, if preceded and multiplied, but not followed, by a number: *trois cents; trois cent cinquante.*]

centaine, *n.f.,* a hundred ; thread that ties up a skein. *V.* **sentène.**

centaure, *n.m.,* (myth., astron.) centaur.

centaurée, *n.f.,* (bot.) centaury.

centenaire, *adj.,* centenary, a hundred years old, of a hundred years' standing.

centenaire, *n.m.f.,* person of a hundred years of age, centenarian.

centenier, *n.m.,* (biblical expression—*expression biblique*) centurion.

centésimal, -e, *adj.,* centesimal.

centiare, *n.m.,* the hundredth part of an are (square yard 1.1960).

centième, *adj.,* hundredth.

centième, *n.m.,* the hundredth part.

centigrade, *adj.,* centigrade.

centigramme, *n.m.,* the hundredth part of a gram (grain 0.1543).

centilitre, *n.m.,* the hundredth part of a litre (cubic inch 0.61028).

centime, *n.m.,* the hundredth part of a franc (penny 0.10).

centimètre, *n.m.,* the hundredth part of a meter (inch 0.39371).

centinode, *n.f.,* centinody, knot-grass.

centon, *n.m.,* (lit.) cento.

central, -e, *adj.,* central.

centralisation, *n.f.,* centralization.

centraliser, *v.a.,* to centralize.

centre, *n.m.,* centre, middle. *Chaque chose tend à son —;* everything tends to its centre. *Être dans son —;* to be in one's element.

centrifuge, *adj.,* centrifugal.

centripète, *adj.,* centripetal.

centrisque, *n.m.,* (ich.) centriscus, trumpet-fish.

cent-suisse, *n.m.,* one of the hundred that formed the body-guard to the king of France. *Les —s :* the hundred Swiss guards.

centumvir, *n.m.,* centumvir.

centumviral, -e, *adj.,* centumviral.

centumvirat, *n.m.,* centumvirate.

centuple, *n.m.,* centuple, hundred-fold.

centuple, *adj.,* a hundred-fold.

centupler, *v.a.,* to augment a hundred-fold, to centuple.

centuriateur, *n.m.,* (ecc. lit.) centuriator.

centurie, *n.f.,* (antiq., ecc.) century; hundred (territorial division).

centurion, *n.m.,* centurion.

cep, *n.m.,* vine-stock.

cépage, *n.m.,* vines. *Les —s de la Bourgogne ;* the vines of Burgundy.

cèpe, *n.m.,* (bot.) esculent boletus.

cépée, *n.f.,* (agri.) tuft of shoots from the same stump; (hunt.) a wood of one or two years' growth.

cependant, *adv.,* in the mean time, in the mean while; however, nevertheless; yet.

cependant, *conj.,* yet, and yet.

céphalalgie, *n.f.,* cephalalgy, headache.

céphalée, *n.f.,* (med.) headache.

céphalique, *adj.,* (med.) cephalic.

céphée, *n.m.,* (astron.) Cepheus.

céramique, *adj.,* ceramic, fictile.

céramique, *n.f.,* fictile art, moulding.

céraste, *n.m.,* cerastes, horned viper.

cérat, *n.m.,* cerate.

cerbère, *n.m.,* (myth.) Cerberus.

cerceau, *n.m.,* hoop, ring; hoop-net: pinion-quill. *Faire courir un —;* to trundle a hoop.

cercelle, *n.f.,* water-fowl, teal.

cerclage, *n.m.,* hooping (of casks, &c.—*de tonneaux, &c.*).

cercle, *n.m.,* circle, sphere, round, ring, orb, hoop; club, company; binding-hoop. *Un quart de — :* a quadrant. *Un demi-cercle :* a semicircle. *Décrire, former, un —;* to describe, to form, a circle.

cercler, *v.a.,* to bind with hoops, to hoop.

cerclier, *n.m.,* hoop-maker.

*cercueil (-keu-), *n.m.,* coffin; (fig.) grave. *— de bois;* shell. *Mettre au —;* to bring to the grave.

céréale, *adj.,* cereal.

céréales, *n.f. pl.,* corn grain, corn crops, cerealia. *Commerce des —;* corn-trade.

cérébral, -e, *adj.,* cerebral, brain. *Fièvre —e, brain fever.*

cérébrite, *n.f.,* (med.) inflammation of the brain.

cérémonial, *n.m.,* ceremonial ; ceremony, ceremonies.

cérémonie, *n.f.,* ceremony ; (biblical style —*style biblique*) ceremonial. *Visite de —;* formal visit. *Faire des —s;* to stand upon ceremonies.

cérémonieu-x, -se, *adj.,* ceremonious, formal, precise.

cérès, *n.f.,* (myth., astron.) Ceres.

cerf (sèr), *n.m.,* stag, hart, deer. *— commun;* red-deer. *Un bois de —;* the horns of a stag. *Corne de —;* hartshorn.

*cerfeuil, *n.m.,* (bot.) chervil.

cerf-volant (sèrvo-), *n.m.,* (—s —s) (ent.) stag-beetle, bull-fly ; kite, paper-kite.

cerisaie, *n.f.,* cherry-orchard.

cerise, *n.f.,* cherry.

cerisier, *n.m.,* (bot.) cherry-tree.

cerne, *n.m.,* (bot.) ring.

cerneau, *n.m.,* kernel of a green walnut; green walnut.

cerner, *v.a.,* to cut round (a tree—*un arbre*); to surround, to encompass, to hem in: to take the kernel out of green walnuts : (arch.) to gird; (milit.) to invest. *Des yeux cernés ;* eyes with a dark circle round them.

cérocome, *n.m.,* (ent.) cerocoma.

céroxyle, *n.m.,* (bot.) wax-palm, wax-tree.

certain, -e, *adj.,* certain, sure, positive. undoubted; resolved, fixed, determined; some. *C'est un homme d'un — mérite*; he is a man of some merit. *À —es époques de l'année*; at certain periods of the year. *Dans —s cas*; in certain cases. *Un — personnage*; a certain personage.

certain, *n.m.*, certainty; certain; (exchange language—*terme de bourse, de commerce*) certain price. *Il ne faut pas quitter le — pour l'incertain*; we must not quit a certainty for an uncertainty.

certainement (-män), *adv.*, certainly, assuredly, without fail, indeed, surely, infallibly.

certes, *adv.*, indeed, certainly.

certificat, *n.m.*, certificate, testimonial. *— de vie*; certificate of existence.

certificateur, *n.m.*, (jur.) certifier, voucher.

certification, *n.f.*, certifying.

certifier, *v.a.*, to certify, to testify, to aver, to guarantee the solvability of a surety. *— une caution*; to guarantee that bail is valid.

certitude, *n.f.*, certitude, certainty.

cérumen (mè-n), *n.m.*, cerumen, ear-wax.

cérumineu-x, -se, *adj.*, waxy, ceruminous.

céruse, *n.f.*, ceruse, white lead.

cervaison, *n.f.*, (hunt.) stag-season.

cerveau, *n.m.*, brain; mind; intelligence. *Rhume de —*; cold in the head. *— brûlé*; disordered brain. *Avoir le — creux*; to be crack-brained. *Être pris du cerveau*; to have a cold in one's head.

cervelas, *n.m.*, cervelas, Bologna sausage.

cervelet, *n.m.*, (anat.) cerebellum.

cervelle, *n.f.*, brains; head; mind; pith (of palm-trees—*du palmier*). *Se brûler la —*; to blow one's brains out. *Cela lui tourne la —*; that turns his head. *Se creuser la —*; to puzzle one's brains.

cervical, -e, *adj.*, (anat.) cervical.

cervier. *V.* **loup-cervier**.

cervoise, *n.f.*, a sort of beer made of grain and herbs.

césar, *n.m.*, Cæsar.

césarienne (-è-n), *adj.f.*, Cesarean. *Opération —*; Cesarean operation.

cessant, -e, *adj.*, ceasing. *Toute affaire —e*; to the suspension of all other business.

cessation, *n.f.*, cessation, suspension, intermission, discontinuance.

cesse, *n.f.*, ceasing, intermission. *Parler sans —*; to talk for ever. [The article is never used with this noun.]

cesser, *v.n.*, to cease, to leave off, to forbear, to discontinue, to give over, to be at an end, to have done, to intermit, to end. *Il ne cesse de pleurer*; he never leaves off crying.

cesser, *v.a.*, to cease, to leave off; to intermit; to break off. *— ses payements*; (com.) to stop payment.

cessible, *adj.*, (jur., com.) transferable, assignable.

cession, *n.f.*, transfer; assignment (of property—*de propriété*); yielding up, relinquishment; surrender.

cessionnaire, *n.m.*, grantee; assignee, transferee.

ceste, *n.m.*, (antiq., myth.) cestus, gauntlet; whirl-bat.

césure, *n.f.*, cesura.

cet. cette. *V.* **ce**.

cétacé, -e, *adj.*, cetaceous.

cétacé, *n.m.*, cetaceous animal.

cétérac, *n.m.*, (bot.) ceterach.

cétine, *n.f.*, pure spermaceti, cetine.

cétoine, *n.f.*, (ent.) floral-beetle.

chabler, *v.a.*, to fasten a cable to a piece of timber; to lash, to fasten a cable.

chableur, *n.m.*, water-bailiff.

chablis, *n.m.*, wind-fallen wood; chablis (white wine—*vin blanc*).

chaboisseau, *n.m.*, sea-scorpion.

chabot, *n.m.*, (ich.) miller's-thumb, bull-head.

chabraque, *n.f.* *V.* **schabraque**.

chacal, *n.m.*, jackal.

chaconne, *n.f.*, chacone.

chacun, -e, *pron.*, every one, each. *— veut être heureux*; every body wishes to be happy. *— en parle*; every body speaks of it. *Rendre à —ce qui lui appartient*; to return every body his own. *— vit à sa guise*; every one lives as he likes. *— le sien, n'est pas trop*; every one his own. *— a sa marotte*; every man has his hobby. *— pour soi*; every one for himself. *— each in his turn. Qu'on s'en retourne— chez soi*; let every one return to his own house. *Ils s'en retournèrent — chez eux*; each of them returned to his own home. *Vous danserez — à votre tour*; you will dance each in your turn. *Ils auront — leur part*; each of them will have his share. *Donnez c — sa part*; give every one his share. *Tous les membres ont voté. — selon ses instructions*; every member voted according to his instructions.

⊙**chacunière**, *n.m.*, one's own house.

chafouin, -e, *adj.*, sorry, mean-looking, pitiful.

chafouin, *n.m.*, -**e**, *n.f.*, pitiful object; poor wretch.

chagrin, *n.m.*, sorrow, grief, vexation, trouble, concern, regret; fretfulness, peevishness, chagrin; shagreen (leather—*cuir*).

chagrin, -e, *adj.*, gloomy, melancholy, sad, dull, fretful, peevish, waspish, discontented, sullen, cross, morose.

chagrinant, -e, *adj.*, sorrowful, sad; vexatious, troublesome.

⊙**chagrinement** (-män), *adv.*, sorrowfully; peevishly.

chagriner, *v.a.*, to render gloomy, to grieve, to vex, to afflict, to cross, to trouble, to perplex, to disquiet; to shagreen (skins—*peaux*).

se **chagriner**, *v.r.*, to fret, to vex one's self, to grieve, to take on.

chagrinier, *n.m.*, shagreen-maker.

chai, *n.m.*, wine and spirit warehouse on the ground floor.

chaîne, *n.f.*, chain, shackle, cord; galleys, chain of galley-slaves; belting-course (for walls —*de murs*); bonds, bondage; drag-chain (of canals—*de canaux*); warp (weaving—*tissage*); (land-surveying—*arpentage*) chain, Gunter's chain; (dancing—*danse*); right and left. *Charger quelqu'un de —s*; to load one with fetters. *— de montagnes*; long ridge of mountains. *La — des idées*; the chain of ideas. *Attacher avec des —s*; to chain up. *Tendre des —s*; to lay chains across. *À la —*; chained up.

chaînetier (shên-tié), *n.m.*, chain-maker.

chaînette, *n.f.*, little chain; (arch.) catenarian arch.

chaînon, *n.m.*, link.

chair, *n.f.*, flesh, meat; skin (of a person—*de personne*); *pl.*, (paint.) flesh. *—vire*; quick flesh. *— morte*; dead skin. *— ferme, molle*; firm. soft, flesh. *—s baveuses*; (med.) proud flesh. *— blanche*; white meat. *— noire*; game. *— de poule*; goose-flesh. (med.) *cutis anseris. J'en ai la — de poule*; I shudder at it, it makes my flesh crawl. *Un morceau de —*; a piece of meat. *La — d'un poisson*; the fleshy part of a fish. *Couleur de —*; flesh-colour. *L'aiguillon de la —*; the thorn in the flesh. *Convoitises de la —*; the lusts of the flesh. *Le Verbe s'est fait —*; the Word was made flesh. *La résurrection de la —*; the resurrection of the body. *Pester entre* cuir et — ; to be dissatisfied without daring to say so.

chaire, n.f., pulpit; professorship; desk (in churches—à l'église); bishop's throne, Monter en — ; to mount the pulpit. —apostolique; apostolic see. — curule; curule chair. — de droit; professorship of law.

chaise, n.f., chair, seat ;(carp.) timber-work. frame; curb; chaise (carriage—voiture). — à dos; chair with a back. — de paille; straw-bottomed chair. — percée; close-stool. — brisée; folding chair. — à deux chevaux; chaise and pair. — à bascule; rocking-chair. — à porteurs; sedan-chair.

chaisier, n.m., chair-maker.

chako, n.m. V. shako.

chaland, n.m., -e, n.f., customer.

chaland, n.m., (nav.) lighter, barge.

chalandeau, n.m., lighterman, bargeman.

⊙**chalandise,** n.f., custom.

chalastique (ka-), adj., (med.) chalastic.

chalcédoine. V. **calcédoine.**

chalcite (kalsit), n.m., (chem.) chalcite.

chalcographe (kal-), n.m., chalcographer, engraver on brass.

chalcographie (kal-), n.f., chalcography, engraving on brass; engraving establishment; printing-office (of the pope—du pape).

chaldaïque (kal-), adj., Chaldaic.

chaldéen,-ne(-in,-è-n),adj. V. **chaldaïque.**

chaldéen, n.m., -ne, n.f., Chaldean.

chaldéen, n.m., Chaldaic, Chaldean (language—langue).

châle, n.m., shawl.

châlet, n.m., cheese-house, Swiss cottage.

chaleur, n.f., heat, hotness; fervency. zeal, ardour; warmth; (phys.) caloric. Il fait une grande —; it is very hot weather. Son style manque de —; his style wants energy. Sentir de la —; to feel warm.

chaleureu-x, -se, adj., warm, ardent.

châlit, n.m., bedstead.

⊙**chaloir,** v. imp., to care for. Il ne m'en chaut; I don't care for it.

chalon, n.m., drag, drag-net.

chaloupe, n.f., (nav.) ship's boat, long boat. — canonnière; gun-boat.

chalumeau, n.m., stalk of corn; straw; pipe, reed; blow-pipe; shawm.

chalut, n.m., fishing drag-net.

chalybé, -e (ka-), adj., chalybeate.

⊙**cham or chan** (kan), n.m., Cham (prince of Tartary). V. **kan.**

chamade, n.f., (milit.) parley, chamade.

*****chamailler,** v.n., to bicker, to squabble, to wrangle.

***se chamailler,** v.r., to squabble, to wrangle.

*****chamaillis,** n.m., fray, squabble, uproar, wrangle.

chamarrer, v.a., to lace, to trim with lace, to bedizen; to load with ridicule.

chamarrure, n.f., trimming, lacing, bedizening.

⊙**chambellage,** n.m., duty paid to the lord of a manor upon every change of tenant.

chambellan (-bel-län), h.m., chamberlain.

chambourin, n.m., strass.

chambranle, n.m., (carp.) chambranle; casing of a chimney, door-case, window-case. — de cheminée; mantel-shelf.

chambre, n.f., chamber, room; lodging, apartment; house (of parliament—parlement); (metal.) bead, chaplet; (opt.) camera, chamber; (artil.) chamber; (nav.) cabin; honey-comb (of cannon—des canons). — ardente; ardent chamber (history of France). — claire; light-room; (opt.) camera lucida. — haute; House of Lords. — à coucher; bed-chamber. — garnie; furnished lodging. Femme de —; chamber-maid. Robe de —; morning-gown. Garder la —; to keep one's room. Convoquer les —s; to convoke parliament. Avoir des —s à louer dans la tête; to be rather cracked, to be a visionary. Arrêter, louer, une —; to hire a room. Faire une —; to do (clean) a room.

chambré, -e, adj., (of fire-arms—des armes à feu) chambered, provided with a powder-chamber; honey-combed (of cannon—de canons).

chambrée, n.f., persons sleeping in one room; (thea.) house; mess (of soldiers—de soldats).

chambrelan, n.m., (pop., l.u.) workman who works in his own room; tenant occupying only one room.

⊙**chambrer,** v.n., to lodge together in the same room.

se **chambrer,** v.r., to become honey-combed (of cannon—des canons).

chambrer, v.a., to keep one confined either by force or art; to take one aside in a company; to chamber, to make a powder-chamber in, a fire-arm.

chambrette, n.f., little room.

⊙**chambrier,** n.m., chamberlain.

chambrière, n.f., chamber-maid; (man.) horse-whip.

chame, or came, n.f., (conch.) chama; muscle, heart-cockle.

chameau, n.m., camel.

chamelier, n.m., camel-driver.

chamelle, n.f., female camel.

chamelon (sham-lon), n.m., young camel.

chamois, n.m., chamois, shamoy, wild goat; shammy; shammy-leather.

chamoiser, v.a., to shamoy,

se **chamoiser,** v.r., to be shamoyed.

chamoiserie, n.f.,shamoy-factory; shamoy-leather.

chamoiseur, n.m., shamoy-dresser.

champ (shän), n.m., field, piece of ground; career; opportunity; matter, theme, subject; compass, space; (her.) field. À tout bout de —; every moment. À travers —s; over hedge and ditch. — de bataille; field of battle. — clos; lists (for combat). Sur-le —; at once, immediately. Battre aux —s; (milit.) to beat a salute. Donner la clef des —s; to give any one his liberty. Être aux —s; to be in the country; to be angry. Courir les —s; to run about the country. Prendre la clef des —s; to take to one's heels; to bolt. Avoir le — libre; to have a clear stage.

*****champagne,** n.m., champagne. — frappé; iced champagne. — mousseux; sparkling champagne. — non mousseux; still champagne.

champart, n.m., (feudality—féodalité) field-rent paid in kind to the lord.

champarter, v.a., (feudality—féodalité) to exercise the right of levying field-rent in kind.

champarteur, n.m., (feudality—féodalité) bailiff charged to collect field-rent in kind.

⊙**champeaux,** n.m. pl., grass-fields.

⊙**champenois,** n.m., -e, n.f., native of Champagne.

champenois, -e, adj., of Champagne.

champêtre, adj., rural, country-like, sylvan. Garde —; keeper (of a wood, park, &c.—d'un bois, d'un parc, &c.).

*****champignon,** n.m., mushroom, toadstool; thief (in a candle—à la mèche d'une chandelle); proud flesh; (arch.) cap.

*****champignonnière,** n.f., mushroom-bed.

champion, n.m., champion, chieftain; combatant.

chance, n.f., hazard (at dice—aux dés); chance, luck, good luck, good fortune; risk. Courir la —; to run the risk. Être en —; to be lucky. Souhaiter bonne — à quelqu'un; to wish any one good luck.

⊙**chancel**. *n.m.*, cancel.

chancelant, -e. *adj.*, staggering, tottering. unsettled; unsteady, wavering.

chanceler, *v.n.*. to stagger, to totter, to falter, to waver, to be unsteady.

chancelier, *n.m.*, chancellor. *Grand* —; high chancellor.

chancelière. *n.f.*, chancellor's wife; carriage-boot (for keeping the feet warm—*pour tenir les pieds chauds*).

chancellement (-măn), *n.m.*, reeling, tottering. staggering.

chancellerie (-sèl-rî), *n.f.*, chancellor's house, chancellor's office. *Grande* —; office of the great seal. *Petite* —; office of the privy seal.

chanceu-x, -se, *adj.*, lucky, fortunate; uncertain.

⊙**chancir**, *v.n*., to grow musty, mouldy (of eatables—*de comestibles*).

⊙**chancissure**, *n.f.*, mustiness, mouldiness (of eatables—*de comestibles*).

chancre, *n.m.*, (agri., bot., vet.) canker; (med.) chancre.

chancreu-x, -se, *adj.*, cancerous, cankered; (med.) chancrous.

chandeleur (shand-lĕur), *n.f.*, Candlemas.

chandelier, *n.m.*, candlestick; chandler, tallowchandler; (nav.) crotch. — *à manche*; flat candlestick. *Être le* — ; to be in a conspicuous situation.

chandelière, *n.f.*, tallow-chandler(woman).

chandelle, *n.f.*, candle. tallow-candle; light. *Allumer la* —; to light the candle. *Moucher la* —; to snuff the candle. *Éteindre la* —; to put out the candle. *Souffl. la* —; to blow out the candle. *Travailler à la* —; to work by candle-light. *Brûler la* — *par les deux bouts*; to burn the candle at both ends. *Le jeu n'en vaut pas la* —; it is not worth one's while. *S'en aller comme une* —; to go off like the snuff of a candle. *Voir trente-six* —*s*; to be stunned; to see the stars by daylight.

chanfrein, *n.m.*, forehead (of a horse—*du cheval*); chanfrin (armour for a horse's head—*armure de tête du cheval*); (arch.) chamfer, chamfret; (zool.) chaffron.

chanfreiner, *v.a.*, (arch.) to chamfer, to rabbet; (carp.) to cant, to edge.

change. *n.m.*, exchange (barter—*échange*); (com.) exchange; money-change; agio; (fig.) wrong scent. *Lettres de* —; letters of exchange. *Agent de* —; stock-broker. — *commun*; average exchange. — *direct*; direct exchange. — *extérieur*; foreign exchange. — *du jour*; current exchange. *Commerce de* —; exchange business. *Cote de* —; current exchange. *Fausse lettre de* —; forged bill. *Lettre de* — *sur l'étranger*; foreign bill of exchange. *Pair de* —; par of exchange. *Première de* —; first of exchange. *Seconde de* —; second of exchange. *Seule de* —; sole of exchange. *Au* — *de*; at the rate of exchange of. *Bureau de* — *de monnaie*; exchange-office. *Donner le* — *à quelqu'un*; to put any one on the wrong scent. *Rendre le* — *à quelqu'un*; to give a Roland for an Oliver. *Tirer une lettre de* — *sur quelqu'un*; to draw a bill on any one.

changeant, -e (-jăn, -t), *adj.*, changeable, fickle, unsteady, variable, inconstant, unstable, unsettled (of the weather—*du temps*).

changement (shanj-măn), *n.m.*, change, alteration, changing, variation, mutation; (jur.) amendment. *Amener un* —; to bring about a change.

changeoter (-jo-té), *v.n.*, (fam., l.u.) to change often.

changer, *v.a.*, to change, to exchange; to alter, to turn, to commute, to convert, to transform.

se **changer**. *v.r.*, to be changed, converted; to alter. to change.

changer, *v.n.*, to change, to alter. — *de logis, de demeure*; to shift one's quarters, to remove. — *d'avis*; to alter one's mind. — *de chemise*; to change one's shirt.

changeur, *n.m.*, money-changer.

chanoine, *n.m.*, canon.

chanoinesse, *n.f.*, canoness.

⊙**chanoinie**, *n.f.*, canonry, canonship.

chanson, *n.f.*, song, ditty; idle story, stuff, trash. *Refrain d'une* —; chorus of a song. *C'est toujours la même* —; it is the same thing over and over again. *Voilà bien une autre* —; that is another story altogether. —*s que tout cela!* all idle stories! —*s!* humbug, stuff!

chansonner, *v.a.*, (b.s.) to make songs against any one; to lampoon.

chansonnette, *n.f.*, little song, ditty.

chansonnier, *n.m.*, ballad-writer; song-book.

chansonnière, *n.f.*, song-writer (woman).

chant, *n.m.*, singing, strain, song; air; lay, ditty, melody; canto, book. *Plain* —; plain chant, canto fermo. *Le* — *du coq*; the crowing of the cock.

chantable, *adj.*, that may be sung, worth singing.

chantage, *n.m.*, extortion of hush-money.

chantant, -e, *adj.*, tunable, easily sung, easy to be set to music.

chanteau, *n.m.*, piece (cut off a larger piece —*détaché d'une pièce plus grande*).

chantepleure (shant-pleur), *n.f.*, funnel with a rose; gully-hole.

chanter, *v.n.*, to sing, to chant; to chirp, to warble, to crow; (fam.) to say too much. *Ce criminel a chanté à la question*; (fam.) that prisoner let the cat out of the bag. — *juste*, *agréablement, passablement*; to sing true, agreeably, tolerably. — *faux*; to sing out of tune. — *à livre ouvert*; to sing at sight. *C'est comme si vous chantiez*; it is as if you were talking to the wind. *L'alouette chante*: the lark carols. *Le coq chante*: the cock crows. *La cigale chante*; the grasshopper chirps.

chanter, *v.a.*, to sing, to chant; to extol, to praise; to celebrate; to warble; to talk, to tell, stuff. *Que me chantez-vous là?* what stuff are you telling me now?

chanterelle (shăn-trèl), *n.f.*, first string of a violin, &c.; decoy-bird; musical-bottle.

chanteu-r, -se, *adj.*, singing (of birds—*des oiseaux*).

chanteur, *n.m.*, singer, vocalist; singing-bird. — *des rues*; ballad-singer.

chanteuse, *n.f.*, singer, vocalist, chantress.

chantier (-tié), *n.m.*, timber-merchant's wood-yard; stone-yard; dock-yard; stand,block, stocks; shop, shed. *L'ouvrage est sur le* —; the work is begun.

***chantignole**, *n.f.*, (carp.) wooden block.

chantonner, *v.n.*, to hum, to hum a tune.

chantonner, *v.a.*, to hum (of a person—*des personnes*).

⊙**chantonnerie** (to-n-rî), *n.f.*, humming, drawling.

chantournage, *n.m.*, cutting in profile.

chantourné, *n.m.*, head-piece of a bedstead.

chantourner, *v.a.*, to cut in profile.

chantre, *n.m.*, singer, singing-man, chanter; precentor, lay-clerk (in churches—*à l'église*); songster, songstress (of birds—*d'oiseaux*). *Les* —*s des bois*; the feathered songsters.

chantrerie, *n.f.*, chantership.

chanvre, *n.m.*, hemp.

chanvrier, *n.m.*, hemp-dresser, dealer in hemp.

chanvrière, *n.f.*, hemp-field.

chaos (kaŏ), *n.m.*, chaos, confusion.

chaotique, adj., chaotic.

chape, n.f., cope (church garment—*vêtement d'église*); (arch.) cope. *Disputer de la —
à l'évêque*; to dispute about what does not
concern one.

chapeau, n.m., hat; bonnet; wreath of
flowers (for a bride—*pour une fiancée*); (carp.)
hand-piece; (bot.) cap; pileus (of a mushroom
—*d'un champignon*). — *à grand bord*: broad-
brimmed hat. — *à petit bord*: narrow-brimmed
hat. — *d'évêque*; (bot.) barrenwort. —*chinois*;
(milit. mus.) Chinese bells. — *de paille d'Italie*;
Leghorn bonnet. *La carre d'un —*; the crown
of a hat. *Mettre son —*; to put on one's hat.
Ôter son —; to take off one's hat. —*x bas!* hats
off. — *de paille*; straw bonnet. — *de velours*;
velvet bonnet. *Le bord, la passe, la forme
d'un —*; the border, the front, the shape of a
bonnet. — *de fleurs*; garland of flowers.
Frère —; assistant-brother (monk—*moine*).
Enfoncer son —; to pull one's hat over one's
eyes; to screw up one's courage.

⊙**chape-chute**, n.f., wind-fall, lucky hit.

⊙**chape-chuter**, v.n., to make a slight noise.

chapelain (shap-lin), n.m., chaplain. ·

chapeler (sha-plé), v.a., to rasp (bread—
du pain).

chapelet (cha-plè), n.m., chaplet, rosary,
beads, bead-roll; (man., arch.) chaplet; bead
(in brandy—*sur l'eau-de-vie*). *Dire son —*; to tell
one's beads. *Défiler son —*; to repeat the bead-
roll; to empty one's budget.

chapelier, n.m., hatter, hat manufacturer.

chapelière, n.f., seller of hats; hatter's
wife.

chapelle, n.f., chapel; church plate. *Faire
—*; (nav.) to broach to. *Maître de —*; precentor. — *ardente*; place where a dead person
lies in state.

chapellenie (sha-pèl-ni), n.f., chaplainship,
chaplaincy.

chapellerie (sha-pèl-ri), n.f., hat-making;
hat-trade.

chapelure (sha-plur), n.f., raspings (of
bread—*de pain*).

chaperon (sha-pron), n.m., chaperon, hood;
shoulder-knot; chaperon (an aged companion—
compagne âgée); coping of a wall; holster-cap.

chaperonner, v.a., to cope a wall; to
chaperon (a young girl—*une jeune fille*); to hood
(a hawk—*un faucon*).

chapier, n.m., priest with a cope.

chapiteau, n.m., (arch.) capital; crest; top
(of a press, mirror, &c.—*d'une armoire, d'une glace,
&c.*); head of a still; cap (of a fusee—*de fusée*).

chapitre, n.m., chapter (of a book, of
knights, of a cathedral—*d'un livre, de chevaliers,
d'une cathédrale*); chapter; chapter-house; subject, matter of discourse, head. *En voilà assez
sur ce —*; that is quite enough upon this head.
Avoir voix au —; to have interest at the board.
Passons sur ce —; let us waive that subject.

chapitrer, v.a., to reprimand, to rebuke, to
lecture any one.

chapon, n.m., capon; piece of bread boiled
in the soup; crust of bread rubbed with garlic. *Le vol du —*; certain extent of ground
about a country-seat. *Avoir les mains faites en
— rôti*; to have crooked fingers; to be light-
fingered.

chaponneau, n.m., (l.u.) young capon.

chaponner, v.a., to capon.

chaponnière, n.f., stew-pan (for dressing
capons—*pour chapons*).

chaque, adj., each, every. — *pays a ses coutumes*: every country has its customs. *A —
jour suffit sa peine*; sufficient for the day is the
evil thereof.

char, n.m., car, chariot. —*funèbre*; hearse.

— *à bancs*; wagonette, pleasure car. — *de
triomphe*; triumphal car.

charabia, n.m., gibberish, gabble.

charade, n.f., charade.

charançon, n.m., small beetle, weevil.

charançonné, -e, adj., (of corn) attacked
by the weevils.

charbon, n.m., coal; embers; charcoal; carbuncle; (agri.) black rust; (med.) anthrax.
— *allumé*; lighted coal. — *de terre*; coal.
Être sur les —s; to be upon thorns.

charbonnage, n.m., (l.u.) coal-mine, coal-
pit.

charbonnée, n.f., short rib of beef.

charbonner, v.a., to char; to black with
coal; to besmut.

se **charbonner**, v.r., to be charred.

charbonnerie (-bo-n-ri), n.f., coal-store;
the Carbonari association.

charbonneu-x,-se, adj., (med.) carbuncled.

charbonnier, n.m., coal-seller, coal-man;
coal-shed, coal-hole; (ich.) coal-fish; (nav.) collier. *Le — est maître dans sa maison*; a man's
house is his castle.

charbonnière, n.f., place where charcoal
is made; coal-seller; coal-man's wife; (orni.)
titmouse.

*****charbouiller**, v.a., (agri.) to blight.

charbucle, n.f., (agri.) blight (of corn—*du
blé*).

charcuter, v.a., to chop up (meat—*de la
viande*); to hack, to mangle.

charcuterie (-ku-tri), n.f., pork-butcher's
meat; pork-butcher's business.

charcuti-er, n.m., **-ère**, n.f., (-tié, -ti-èr),
pork-butcher.

chardon, n.m., thistle; spike (on a wall—*sur
un mur*). — *aux ânes*; cotton-thistle. — *à
foulon*; teasel. — *étoilé*; star-thistle.

chardonneret (-do-n-rè), n.m., (orni.) goldfinch.

chardonnette or **cardonnette**, n.f.,
prickly artichoke.

chardonnière, n.f., land covered with
thistles.

charge, n.f., load, lading; freight, pack;
tax, expense; burden, clog; charge; accusation,
imputation, indictment; post, place, office,
employment; order, command, commission;
custody, care; charge, onset; charge (of a gun
—*d'une arme à feu*); (vet., paint., &c.) charge;
exaggeration, caricature. *Femme de —*; housekeeper. *Être à — à quelqu'un*; to be a burden
upon any one. *Il faut prendre le bénéfice avec
les —s*; we must take the good with the bad.
Faire une —; (milit.) to charge. *Se démettre de
sa —*; to resign one's place. *On a donné trop
de — à ce mur*; this wall has been overloaded.
Sonner la —; to sound the charge. *Revenir à
la —*; to make a new attempt. *A la — de, ·à
la — que*; upon condition that, provided that.

chargé, -e, part., loaded, burdened; (print.)
foul (of proofs—*des épreuves*). *Dés —s*; loaded
dice. *Le temps est —*; the weather is overcast.
— *d'affaires*; chargé d'affaires.

chargeant,-e (-jân,-t), adj., clogging, heavy.

chargement, n.m., cargo, lading; freight;
bill of lading; shipment.

charger, v.a., to load, to saddle, to lade, to
freight, to charge; to burden, to clog, to over-
burthen, to encumber; to impute, to lay a
thing to one's charge; to charge with, to command, to give a thing in charge, to trust with;
to charge, to fall upon, to make an onset on;
to load (a gun—*une arme à feu*); to fill (pipe);
to set down; to lay on; (paint.) to overcharge,
to exaggerate. *Il les chargea vigoureusement*;
he attacked them briskly — *un fusil*; to

load a gun. — *toutes les voiles;* to clap on all the sails.

se **charger,** *v.r.,* to take charge, to charge one's self; to become overcast (of the weather —*du temps*); to burden one's self, to saddle one's self.

charger, *v.n.,* to load; to exaggerate, to lay it on.

chargeur, *n.m.,* loader; (nav.) gunner.

⊙**charier.** *V.* **charrier.**

chariot, *n.m.,*waggon, cart, wain. (astron.) *Le grand* —; Charles' wain. *Le petit* —; Ursa Minor.

charitable, *adj.,* charitable.

charitablement, *adv.,* charitably.

charité, *n.f.,* charity, love, benevolence. *Faire la* —; to give alms. *Demander la* —; to beg. — *bien ordonnée commence par soi-même;* charity begins at home.

charivari, *n.m.,* rough music, hubbub, clatter, rout, noise.

charivariser, *v.a.,* to give the rough music.

charivariseur, charivarieur, *or* **charivariste,** *n.m.,* one who gives the rough music.

charlatan, *n.m.,* mountebank, quack, charlatan, empiric, wheedler.

charlatane, *n.f.,* wheedler.

charlataner, *v.a.,* to gull, to wheedle, to cajole.

charlatanerie, *n.f.,* quackery, charlatanery, juggling.

charlatanesque, *adj.,* quackish.

charlatanisme, *n.m.,* quackery, charlatanism, charlatanry.

charlotte, *n.f.,* (cook.) charlotte.

charmant, -e, *adj.,* charming, delightful, agreeable.

charme, *n.m.,* charm, spell, enchantment; attraction, delight; (bot.) horn-beam, yoke-elm.

charmer, *v.a.,* to charm, to enchant, to bewitch, to fascinate; to captivate, to please, to delight. *Je suis charmé de vous voir;* I am delighted to see you.

charmeur, *n.m.,* (l.u.) charmer, enchanter.

charmeuse, *n.f.,* (l.u.) bewitching woman, enchantress.

charmille, *n.f.,* horn-beam, yoke-elm; hedge of yoke-elm trees.

charmoie, *n.f.,* grove of horn-beam or yoke-elm trees.

charnage, *n.m.,* (pop.) time during which the Roman Catholic Church allows the eating of flesh.

charnel, -le, *adj.,* carnal, sensual.

charnellement (-män), *adv.,* carnally.

charneu-x, -se, *adj.,* fleshy, carneous.

charnier, *n.m.,* charnel-house; ⊙larder.

charnière, *n.f.,* hinge.

charnu, -e, *adj.,* fleshy, plump; brawny, carneous.

charnure, *n.f.,* flesh, skin.

charogne, *n.f.,* carrion.

charpente, *n.f.,* timber-work, carpenter's work; frame, frame-work. *Bois de* —; timber.

charpenter, *v.a.,* to square timber; to hack, to mangle.

charpenterie (-pän-tri), *n.f.,* carpentry; carpenter's work, carpenter's trade; timberwork; timber-yard (of dock-yards—*d'arsenal*).

charpentier (-tié), *n.m.,* carpenter; (whalefishery—*pêche de la baleine*) whale-cutter.

charpi, *n.m.,* cooper's block.

charpie, *n.f.,* lint.

charrée, *n.f.,* buck-ashes.

charretée (shar-tée), *n.f.,* cart-load.

charretier (shar-tié), *n.m.,* carman, carter. waggoner; plough-boy, ploughman; (astron.) charioteer.

charreti-er, -ère, *adj.,* passable for carts.

&c. (of roads—*routes*). *Chemin* —; cart-road. *Voie* —*ère;* track (space between the two wheels of a cart—*espace entre les deux roues des charrettes*).

charrette, *n.f.,* cart. — *à bras;* hand-cart. — *à ressorts;* spring-cart. *Train de* —; skeletoncart.

charriage, *n.m.,* cartage.

charrier, *v.a.,* to cart, to bring in a cart; to drift; (med.) to be loaded with.

charrier, *v.n.,* to drift ice. *La rivière charrie;* the river is filled with floating pieces of ice. — *droit;* to behave one's self well.

charrier, *n.m.,* bucking-cloth.

charroi, *n.m.,* carting, waggonage.

charron, *n.m.,* wheel-wright.

charronnage, *n.m.,* wheel-wright's work.

charroyer, *v.a.,* to cart (heavy things—*des choses de grand poids*).

charrue, *n.f.,* plough. *Mettre la* — *devant les bœufs;* to put the cart before the horses. *Passer la* — *sur;* to plough.

charte, *n.f.,* charter. *La grande* —; Magna Charta.

charte partie, *n.f.* (—*s* — *s*), (com.) charterparty.

chartographe, *n.m.,* chartographer.

chartographique, *adj.,* chartographic.

chartographie, *n.f.,* chartography; mapping.

charton, *or* **charreton,** *n.m.,* carter, coachman.

⊙**chartre,** *n.f.,* charter (old document— *ancien titre*).

⊙**chartre,** *n.f.,* prison; consumption. *Tenir quelqu'un en* — *privée;* to keep any one a prisoner (in a private house—*dans une maison particulière*).

chartreuse, *n.f.,* Carthusian convent; Carthusian nun; isolated country-house; (cook.) mixed vegetables.

chartreux, *n.m.,* Carthusian friar, cat of a blueish gray.

chartrier, *n.m.,* charter-house; charterroom, place where the charters of a convent are kept; keeper of charters.

charybde, *n.m.,* Charybdis. *Tomber de* — *en Scylla;* to fall from the frying-pan into the fire.

chas, *n.m.,* eye (of a needle—*d'aiguille*); weaver's starch.

châsse, *n.f.,* reliquary; shrine; frame; handle (of lancets—*de lancettes*); cheek (of a balance—*de balances*).

chassé, *n.m.,* chasse, a step in dancing.

chasse, *n.f.,* chase, hunt, hunting, chasing, pursuit; game; (mus.) chasse; play (of machinery—*de machines*). — *à courre;* coursing, hunting. — *au tir;* shooting. — *au vol;* — *aux oiseaux;* fowling. — *aux flambeaux;* bat-fowling. *Un garde*— —; a gamekeeper. *Prendre* — (nav.); to sheer off. *Donner* —; to pursue. *Soutenir* —; to maintain a running fight.

chasse-avant, *n.m.,* (—), overseer, foreman.

chasse-chien, *n.m.,* (—, *or* — —*s*), beadle employed to drive away dogs.

chasse-coquin, *n.m.,* (—, *or* — —*s*), beggardriver.

chasse-cousin, *n.m.,* (—, *or* — —*s*), paltry, bad wine (anything fitted to drive away poor relations, importunate persons, &c.—*tout ce qui peut éloigner les parasites*).

chassé-croisé, *n.m.,* (—*s* —*s*), (dancing— *danse*) chassé-croisé; (fig.) a change of office, situation, &c., between several persons.

chasse-ennui, *n.m.,* (—), that which drives away care and sorrow.

chasselas (shas-la), *n.m.,* grapes, chasselas.

chasse-marée, *n.m.,* (—), fish-cart; driver of a fish-cart; lugger.

4

chasse-mouches, *n.m.* (—), fly-flap; fly-net (for horses—*pour chevaux*).

chasse-mulet, *n.m.* (—, *or* —*s*), miller's man.

chasse-pierres, *n.m.* (—), (railways) guard-irons, cow-catcher.

*****chasse-poignée**, *n.m.* (—, *or* — —*s*), cutler's tool, driver.

chassepot, *n.m.*, name of the rifle in use in the French army until 1871.

chasser, *v.a.*, to hunt, to chase, to pursue; **to give the first beating** (to gold—*à l'or*); to turn out, to expel; to drive, to drive forward. — *un clou;* to drive in a nail. — *un domestique;* to turn away, to discharge, a servant. *Qui deux choses chasse, ni l'une ni l'autre ne prend;* (prov.) between two stools one falls to the ground. — *le mauvais air;* to let out the bad air. — *les mauvaises pensées;* to discard bad thoughts. — *la terre* (nav.); to approach, to reconnoitre, the coast.

chasser, *v.n.*, to shoot; to hunt; to roll along easily; to drive (of clouds—*des nuages*); (print.) to drive out. — *au fusil;* to shoot. *aux perdrix;* to shoot partridges. — *aux lions;* to hunt lions. — *sur son ancre* (nav.); to drag the anchor. — *à courre;* to hunt, to course. — *au faucon;* to hawk. — *de race* (prov.); to be a chip of the old block. — *aux blancs moineaux;* to lose one's time in running after impossibilities.

chasseresse (shas-rès), *n.f.*, huntress.

chasse-roue, *n.m.* (—, *or* — —*s*), spur-post; guard-iron.

chasseu-r, *n.m.*, **-se**, *n.f.*, hunter, sportsman; huntsman, gamekeeper; chasseur (footman—*laquais*); light infantry soldier; ship that chases another. —*s à cheval;* (milit.) light horse.

chassie, *n.f.*, gum of the eye; (med.) gowl.

chassieu-x, **-se**, *adj.*, blear-eyed.

châssis, *n.m.*, (print.) chase; window-sash frame. *Fenêtre à —;* sash-window. — *dormant;* the fixed part of a window-frame. — *de jardin;* garden-frame.

chassoir, *n.m.*, cooper's tool, driver; (tech.) drift.

chaste, *adj.*, chaste, continent, honest, modest, pure, virtuous; style, neat, correct, terse. *Cela blesse les oreilles —s;* that offends chaste ears.

chastement, *adv.*, chastely, honestly, purely, virtuously.

chasteté, *n.f.*, chastity, chasteness, continence, purity.

chasuble, *n.f.*, chasuble.

chasublier, *n.m.*, a maker of chasubles.

chat, *n.m.*, **-te**, *n.f.*, cat; searcher (to examine cannons—*pour l'examen de l'âme des canons*); brittle slate; (nav.) cat, cat-ship. *Petit —;* kitten. *Herbe aux —;* cat's-mint. — *musqué;* civet, musk-cat. — *cervier;* lynx. — *bon aux souris;* good mouser. — *à neuf queues;* cat-o'nine-tails. *Votre chatte est pleine;* your cat is with kitten. *A bon — bon rat;* set a thief to catch a thief. — *échaudé craint l'eau froide;* a burnt child dreads the fire. *La nuit tous les —s sont gris;* all cats are gray in the dark. *Il n'y a pas là de quoi fouetter un —;* it is a mere trifle. *N'éveillez pas le — qui dort;* when sorrow is asleep, wake it not. *Acheter — en poche;* to buy a pig in a poke. *Se servir de la patte du — pour tirer les marrons du feu;* to make a cat's-paw of any one. *Il n'y a pas un —;* there is not a soul there. *Œil-de-chat;* cat's-eye, snap-dragon. *Patte-de—;* ground-ivy. *Pied-de—;* cat's-foot, cat-hoof, tune-hoof. *Sabbat de—, musique de—;* caterwauling. *Mon petit —;* (term of endearment—*terme d'affection*) my dear, my darling. *A bon — bon rat;* tit for

tat, diamond cut diamond. *Appeler un — un —;* to call a spade a spade, not to mince matters. *Avoir un — dans la gorge;* to have something the matter with one's throat (of singers—*de chanteurs*). *Quand les —s n'y sont pas, les souris dansent sous la table,* or, *absent le —, les souris dansent;* (prov.) when the cat's away the mice will play. *Bailler le — par les pattes;* to bell the cat. *Ces gens vivent comme chien et —;* these people live like cat and dog. *Emporter le —;* to go away without saying good bye to any one, without paying one's reckoning.

*****châtaigne**, *n.f.*, chestnut. — *amère;* horse-chestnut. — *d'eau;* water-caltrops.

*****châtaigneraie**, *n.f.*, grove of chestnut-trees.

*****châtaignier**, *n.m.*, chestnut-tree.

châtain, *adj.*, chestnut, nut-brown, auburn. — *clair;* light auburn.

chataire, *n.f.* V. **cataire**.

château, *n.m.*, castle, fort, citadel; country-seat, mansion, palace. — *fort;* fortress. *Faire des —x en Espagne;* to build castles in the air. — *de carte;* paste-board house. — *d'eau;* water-works.

châtelain (shâ-tlin), *n.m.*, **-e**, *n.f.* and *adj.*, lord, lady, of a manor, castellan.

châtelé, **-e**, *adj.*, (her.) turreted.

⊙**châtelet** (shâ-tlè), *n.m.*, little castle; a former prison at Paris.

⊙**châtellenie**, *n.f.*, castellany, castle-ward.

⊙**chatepeleuse**, *n.f.*, curculio, weevil.

chat-huant (sha-uân), *n.m.* (—*s* —*s*), owl, screech-owl, horn-owl.

châtiable, *adj.*, chastisable, punishable.

châtier (-tié), *v.a.*, to chastise, to correct, to punish, to scourge, to flog; (c. rel.) to chasten. *Qui aime bien, châtie bien;* spare the rod and spoil the child. — *une pièce de vers;* to polish a piece of poetry.

chatière (-ti-èr), *n.f.*, cat's hole; cat-trap.

châtiment, *n.m.*, chastisement, correction, punishment, castigation; (c. rel.) chastening.

chatoiement, *or*, **chatoîment**, *n.m.*, chatoyment, play of colours.

chaton, *n.m.*, kitten; bezel (of a ring—*de bague*); outward husk or cup of the nut; (bot.) catkin, cat's-tail.

*****chatouillement**, *n.m.*, tickling; titillation.

*****chatouiller**, *v.a.*, to tickle, to titillate; to please; to flatter; to touch a horse lightly with the spur.

se **chatouiller**, *v.r.*, to tickle one's self; to excite one's self (to gaiety, good humour—*à la gaîté, à la bonne humeur*).

*****chatouilleu-x**, **-se**, *adj.*, ticklish, delicate, nice; touchy.

chatoyant, **-e**, *adj.*, chatoyant, shot (of colours—*des couleurs*).

chatoyer, *v.n.*, to be chatoyant; to play (of colours—*des couleurs*).

chat-pard, *n.m.* (—*s* —*s*), mountain-cat.

châtré, *n.m.*, eunuch. *Voix de —;* shrill voice.

châtré, **-e**, *adj.*, emasculate, castrated.

châtrer, *v.a.*, to castrate; to expurgate; to take away the honey and wax from a bee-hive (with an instrument made on purpose —*avec un instrument fait exprès*); to lop, prune; to take away part of the felly of a wheel; (vet.) to geld. — *une truie;* to spay a sow. — *des cotrets;* to take some sticks from faggots of wood. — *les tiges de tabac;* to top tobacco-plants.

se **châtrer**, *v.r.*, to castrate one's self; to be mutilated (in speaking of works mutilated by the censors—*d'ouvrages mutilés par la censure*).

C'est ainsi que se châtrent les écrits; It is in this manner that books are mutilated.

châtreur, *n.m.*, gelder.

chatte, *n.f.*, she-cat. *V.* **chat**.

chattée, *n.f.*, litter of kittens.

chattemite, *n.f.*, one that looks demure.

chatter, *v.n.*, to kitten.

chatterie, *n.f.*, (fam.) sweetmeats; hypo-critical caresses.

chaud, -e, *adj.*, hot, warm, burning; fervent, fervid, fierce; zealous, eager; hasty, hot-headed, passionate; proud (of animals—*d'animaux*). *Cavale —e*; mare ready to take the horse. *Fièvre —e*; violent fever. *Pleurer à —es larmes*; to cry bitterly. *Tomber de fièvre en — mal*; to fall out of the frying-pan into the fire. *Avoir la tête—e*; to be passionate. *Tout —*; quite hot. *Il faut battre le fer pendant qu'il est —*; (prov.) strike while the iron is hot; make hay while the sun shines. *Cet ouvrage est tout —*; this work is quite new. *Ne trouver rien de trop — ni de trop froid*; to wish to have everything. *La donner bien —e*; to excite unnecessarily great alarm. *Être — de vin* (fam.); to be a little sprung. *L'action fut —e* (milit.); the engagement was warm. *Manger —, boire —*; to eat, drink, warm things.

chaud, *n.m.*, heat, warmth. *Il fait —*; it is hot. *Il fait grand —*; it is very hot. *Avoir —*; to be hot. *Souffrir le — et le froid*; to endure heat and cold. *Cela ne fait ni — ni froid*; that is immaterial, of no importance. *Souffler le — et le froid*; to blow hot and cold in the same breath. *Cela ne lui fait ni — ni froid*; that is quite indifferent to him.

chaud, *adv.*, hot, warm.

chaude, *n.f.*, (metal.) heating. *Battre la —*; to beat ingots out into thin plates whilst the metal is hot. *À la —*; in the first heat of passion, on the spur of the moment.

○**chaudeau**, *n.m.*, caudle.

chaudement (shô-män), *adv.*, warmly; briskly, quickly, eagerly, fiercely, hotly.

chaudier, *v.n.*, (hunt.) (of bitches—*des chiennes*) to be proud; to couple.

chaudière, *n.f.*, copper, large kettle; boiler (of a steam-engine—*de machine à vapeur*).

chaudret, or **chauderet**, *n.m.*, (gold-beating—*terme de batteur d'or*) mould of about one thousand leaves.

chaudron, *n.m.*, large kettle, boiler, cal-dron.

chaudronnée, *n.f.*, caldronful.

chaudronnerie, *n.f.*, coppersmith's trade, copper wares, brazier's wares.

chaudronni-er, *n.m.*, **-ère**, *n.f.*, brazier, copper-smith. *— de campagne*; a tinker.

chauffage, *n.m.*, fuel, firewood, firing; right of cutting firewood; (nav.) breaming.

chauffe, *n.f.*, (metal.) furnace.

chauffe-assiettes, *n.m.* (—), plate-warmer.

chauffe-chemise, *n.m.* (—, or — —s), or **chauffe-linge**, *n.m.* (—), clothes-horse, linen-warmer.

chauffe-cire, *n.m.* (—), chafe-wax.

chauffe-lit, *n.m.* (—, or — —s), bed-warmer.

chauffe-pieds, *n.m.* (—), foot-warmer.

chauffer, *v.a.*, to heat, to warm; to excite. *— un vaisseau*; (nav.) to bream a ship. *— un poste*; (milit.) to keep up a sharp fire on a post. *— quelqu'un*; to attack any one with ridicule. *se chauffer*, *v.r.*, to warm one's self. *Ne pas — du même bois*; not to be of the same way of thinking. *Savoir de quel bois on se chauffe*; to know of what metal any one is made.

chauffer, *v.n.*, to be heating, to grow warm; (of a steam engine—*de machine à vapeur*) to get up her steam. *Ce n'est pas pour vous que le four chauffe*; there is nothing for you.

chaufferette (shô-frèt), *n.f.*, foot-warmer; chafing-dish.

chaufferie, *n.f.*, chafery.

chauffeur, *n.m.*, fireman, stoker; bellows-blower (of a forge—*d'une forge*).

chauffoir, *n.m.*, warming-place; warm cloth (for a sick person—*pour un malade*); heater.

chauffure, *n.f.*, burning (of iron or steel till it scales—*du fer ou de l'acier jusqu'à ce qu'il s'écaille*).

chaufour, *n.m.*, lime-kiln.

chaufournier, *n.m.*, lime-burner.

chaulage, *n.m.*, (agri.) liming.

chauler, *v.a.*, to lime; to steep wheat in lime-water previous to sowing it.

chaulier, *n.m.*, lime-burner.

chaumage, *n.m.*, cutting of stubble; time at which stubble is cut.

chaume, *n.m.*, stubble; stubble-field; thatch; (bot.) culm, haulm. *Être né sous le —*; to be born in a cottage. *Couvreur en —*; thatcher. *Couvrir de —*; to thatch. *Plein de —*; stubbly.

chaumer, *v.a.* and *n.*, to cut stubble.

chaumière, *n.f.*, thatched house, cottage, cot.

chaumine, *n.f.*, small cottage.

chaussant, -e, *adj.*, (l.u.) (of stockings—*de bas*) easy to put on.

chausse, *n.f.*, stocking, hose; shoulder-knot (worn by members of the French univer-sities—*portée par les membres des universités françaises*); straining-bag, filter. *— d'aisances*; waste-pipe of a water-closet.

chaussé, -e, *part.*, shod. *Bien —*; wearing shoes that fit well; nicely booted.

chaussée, *n.f.*, causey, causeway; bank, highway. *Au rez de —*; even with the ground. *J'habite le rez-de-chaussée*; I live on the ground-floor.

chausse-pied, *n.m.* (— —s), shoeing-horn, shoe-horn.

chausser, *v.a.*, to put on (shoes, boots, stockings—*souliers, bottes, bas*); to make shoes; to get firmly fixed in one's head; to suit; (man.) to put one's feet too forward in the stirrups. *— le cothurne*; to put on the buskin; to write in an inflated style. *— le brodequin*; to put on the sock; to compose; to act comedy. *Les cordonniers sont les plus mal chaussés*; nobody is worse shod than the shoemaker's wife. *— des arbres*; to raise the earth round the root of trees. *— une opinion*; to be wedded to an opinion. *Cet homme n'est pas aisé à chausser*; (fam. and fig.) that man is not easily persuaded. *se chausser*, *v.r.*, to put on one's shoes, boots, stockings; to become strongly wedded to an opinion.

chausser, *v.n.*, to make boots or shoes, to wear shoes. *Ils chaussent au même point*; they are of the same kidney or stamp.

chausses, *n.f. pl.*, breeches, small-clothes, trowsers. *— à tuyaux d'orgue*; trunk hose. *Ne pas avoir de —*; to be very poor. *Avoir la clef de ses —*; to be past whipping. *Laisser ses — quelque part*; to leave one's bones somewhere, to die. *Tirer ses —*; to scamper away. *Elle porte les —*; she wears the breeches.

chaussetier (shôs-tié), *n.m.*, hosier.

chausse-trape, *n.f.* (— —s), (milit.) cal-trop; snare, trap; (bot.) star-thistle.

chaussette, *n.f.*, sock; under stocking.

chausson, *n.m.*, sock; under-stocking; pump; light shoe (worn when playing rackets, fencing, &c.—*qu'on porte à la salle d'armes, et à divers jeux*); list-shoe; puff paste.

chaussure, *n.f.*, hose, stockings, shoes, slippers, boots, pumps. *Il a trouvé — à son*

pied; he has found what he wanted; he has met with his match.

chauve, *adj.*, bald, baldpated.

chauve-souris, *n.f.* (— *s* —), bat, flitter-mouse.

⊙**chauveté** (shôv-té), *n.f.*, baldness, calvity.

chauvinisme, *n.m.*, chauvinism.

chauvir, *v.n.*, to prick up the ears (of horses, asses, mules—*chevaux, ânes, mulets*).

chaux, *n.f.*, lime; limestone; (chem.) calx, lime. — *éteinte*; slaked lime. — *vive*; quick-lime. *Pierre à* —; limestone. *Donner un blanc de* — (mas.); to give a coat of whitewash. *Être fait à* — *et à ciment*; to be well and thoroughly done.

chavayer, *n.m.*, (bot.) lady's-bedstraw.

chavirer, *v.n.*, to capsize, to upset.

chavirer, *v.a.*, to turn upside down; to turn inside out.

chebec, *n.m.*, (nav.) xebeck.

chef, *n.m.*, chief, head, commander. conductor, master, principal, ringleader; fag-end (of a piece of linen—*d'une pièce de toile*); (nav.) end of a cable; (med.) tail of a bandage. *En* —; in chief. — *de famille*; head of a house. — *de cuisine*; master-cook. — *d'accusation*; count. *Faire quelque chose de son* —; to do a thing of one's own accord, without consulting any body.

chef-d'œuvre (shè-deuvr), *n.m.* (— *s* —), trial piece; master-piece; chef-d'œuvre.

⊙**chefecier**. *V.* **chevecier.**

chef-lieu, *n.m.* (— *s* —*x*), chief residence; head-quarters, chief-town; county-town.

chégros, *n.m.*, shoemaker's thread or end, cobbler's-ends.

cheik *or* **scheik**, *n.m.*, sheik.

chéiroptère (ké-). *V.* **chiroptère.**

chélidoine (ké-), *n.f.*, (bot.) celandine, swallow-wort.

chélone (ké-), *n.f.*, (bot.) chelone, snake-head, shell-flower.

chélonée (ké-), *n.f.*, sea-tortoise.

chélonite (ké-), *n.f.*, chelonite.

⊙*se* **chêmer**, *v.r.*, to fall away, to waste, to pine.

chemin, *n.m.*, way, road, path, track; means; course; (nav.) way; (railways) line, road. *Grand* —; highway, high-road. *Voleur de grand* —; highwayman. — *passant*; much frequented thoroughfare. —*s vicinaux*; village roads. — *de traverse*; cross-road. — *détourné*; out of the way road. — *de fer*; railway, railroad. — *de fer à rail plat*; tramroad. — *de service* (railways); attendant path. *Embranchement de* — *de fer*; branch railway. *Le* — *de l'hôpital*; the way to the workhouse. — *couvert* (fort.); covered way, corridor. — *de halage*; towing-path. *À mi*—; half-way. —*faisant*; going along. *Le* — *des écoliers*; the longest way. *Se mettre en* —; to begin a journey. *Rebrousser* —; to go back. *Être toujours par voie et par* —; to be always gadding about. *Aller toujours son* —; to pursue one's point. *Passer votre* —; go your way. *Tout* — *mène à Rome*; there are more ways to heaven than one. *Ce jeune homme fera son* —; this young man will make his way. — *de Saint-Jacques* (astron.); milky-way

cheminée, *n.f.*, chimney; fire-place; mantel-shelf; nipple (of a percussion gun—*d'un fusil à percussion*). *Tuyau de* —; chimney-flue. *Ramoneur de* —; chimney-sweep. *Corps de* —; chimney-stack. *Il faut faire une croix à la* —; we must chalk that up. *Se chauffer à la* — *du roi René*; to warm one's self in the sun.

cheminement, *n.m.*, (milit.) progress (of siege operations towards a besieged town—*d'opérations de siège vers une ville assiégée*).

cheminer, *v.n.*, to walk, to go; to be well connected (of things—*des choses*). *Ce poème*

chemine bien; the various parts of this poem are well connected.

chemise, *n.f.*, shirt, shift, chemise; (fort., mas.) chemise; coat (of a mould—*d'un moule*); wrapper, cover, envelop; case. — *blanche*; clean shirt. — *de nuit*; bed-gown. — *de mailles*; coat of mail. *Vendre jusqu'à sa* —; to sell the shirt off one's back. *La peau est plus proche que la* —; near is my shirt, but nearer is my skin.

chemisette, *n.f.*, light under-waistcoat; shirt-front; chemisette. *Corps de* —; habit-shirt.

chemisi-er, *n.m.*, -**ère**, *n.f.*, shirt-maker.

chênaie, *n.f.*, grove of oaks.

chenal, *n.m.*, channel (of harbours, &c.—*de ports, &c.*); (geog.) track; gutter (of roofs—*de toits*).

chenaler, *v.n.*, (nav.) to sail in a channel.

chenapan, *n.m.*, (pop.) vagabond, good for nothing wretch, scamp, blackguard.

chêne, *n.m.*, (bot.) oak. *De* —; oaken. — *vert*; evergreen-oak.

chêneau, *n.m.*, young oak.

chéneau, *n.m.*, gutter (of roofs—*de toits*).

chenet, *n.m.*, andiron, fire-dog.

chênette, *n.f.*, (bot.) germander. — *amère*; wall germander.

chènevière, *n.f.*, hemp-field.

chènevis (shèn-vi), *n.m.*, hemp-seed.

chènevotte, *n.f.*, boon (of hemp—*de chanvre*).

chènevotter, *v.n.*, (agri.) to shoot weak wood.

chenil (-ni), *n.m.*, dog-kennel; dirty hovel; kennel of hounds.

****chenille**, *n.f.*, caterpillar, worm; kind of silk cord; kind of dressing-gown; evil doer; bore (troublesome person—*importun*). — *velue*; hairy caterpillar. — *rase*; naked caterpillar. *Laid comme une* —; as ugly as a toad.

****chenillette**, *n.f.*, (bot.) caterpillar.

chénopode (ké-), *n.m.*, (bot.) all-good.

chenu, -**e**, *adj.*, hoary, hoar; gray-headed.

cheptel (shè-tèl), *n.m.*, (jur.) leaso of cattle for half the profit; cattle leased out. — *de fer* (jur.); obligation by a tenant to leave to his landlord, at the end of the lease, the same value in cattle as he received on entering.

chèque, *n.m.*, check (banking—*terme de banque*).

ch-er, -**ère**, *adj.*, dear, beloved; dear, costly. *Rendre* —; to endear. *Il fait* — *vivre à Paris*; living is dear in Paris.

cher, *adv.*, dear. *Acheté, payé* —; dear bought. *Je le lui ferai payer plus* — *qu'au marché*; I will make him pay dearly for it.

cher., *ab.* for Chevalier.

chercher, *v.a.*, to seek, to look for, to search, to be in quest of; to endeavour, to attempt, to try. *Que cherchez-vous?* what are you looking for? *Aller* —; to go and bring, to go and fetch, to go for. *Je viendrai vous* —; I will come for you. *J'ai envoyé mon fils* — *sa sœur*; I have sent my son to fetch his sister. *Envoyer* —; to send for. *Il est allé* — *son cheval*, he is gone to fetch his horse. *Allez me* — *la lettre*; go and bring me the letter. — *noise, querelle*; to pick a quarrel. — *quelqu'un par mer et par terre*; to look for one high and low. — *des yeux*; to look for. — *midi à quatorze heures*; to seek for difficulties where there are none; (prov.) to look for a knot in a bulrush. *Le bien cherche le bien*; the more a man has, the more he obtains; deep calls to deep.

chercheu-r, *n.m.*, -**se**, *n.f.*, seeker, searcher. — *de franches lippées*; spunger.

chère, *n.f.*, cheer, entertainment, fare; reception. *Bonne* —; junketing. *Homme de bonne* —; a man who likes good living. *Fair*

œonne — ; to live high. *Faire maigre* — ; to live poorly. *Ne savoir quelle* — *faire à quelqu'un ;* not to know how to welcome any one enough.

chèrement, *adv.*, dearly, tenderly ; dear, at a high price.

chéri. -e, *part.*, beloved, cherished.

chérif. *n.m.* (—*s*), cherif (Arabian prince).

chérir, *v.a.*, to love dearly, to cherish ; to hug.

chérissable, *adj.*, deserving, worthy of affection, worthy of being cherished.

chersonèse (kèr-), *n.f.*, (ancient geography —*géographie ancienne*), peninsula.

cherté, *n.f.*, dearness, high price.

chérubin, *n.m.*, cherub.

chervis, *n.m.*, (bot.) skirret.

chéti-f. -ve, *adj.*, lean, thin, pitiful, piteous, puny ; sorry, bad, mean, wretched.

chétivement (-tiv-màn), *adv.*, meanly, pitifully, sorrily, penuriously ; leanly.

cheval, *n.m.*, horse, nag ; horse-flesh ; (astron.) horse. — *de frise ; cheval de frise. — fondu ;* saddle my nag (game—*jeu*). — *marin ;* sea-horse. — *de rivière ;* river-horse. *Fer à* — ; horse-shoe. — *gris pommelé, truité, aubère, rouan, poil de souris, isabelle, soupe au lait ;* dapple-grey, trout-coloured, fleabitten-grey, roan, mouse-coloured, light dun, cream-coloured. horse. *Petit* — ; nag, pony. — *de parade, de bataille ;* prancer, charger. — *de selle, de chasse, de trait ;* saddle-horse, hunter, draught-horse. — *de brancard, de main, à deux mains ;* shaft-horse, led-horse, saddle and shaft-horse. — *de bât ;* pack-horse ; lout, looby, booby. — *de course, d'amble ;* race-horse, nag. — *de Barbarie* or *Barbe ;* barb. — *entier ;* — *hongre ;* entire horse, stone-horse ; gelding. — *à bascule ;* rocking-horse. — *simulé ;* (fowling—*chasse à l'affût*) stalking-horse. — *de bois ;* (milit.) horse (for punishment—*punition*). — *de charrue, de labour ;* plough-horse. — *de conduite ;* led horse. — *de gauche ;* near-side horse. — *de louage ;* horse for hire, livery horse. — *à une main ;* horse for riding or driving only. — *à deux mains, à deux fins, à toutes mains ;* horse for riding and driving. — *sous la main ;* off-side horse. — *de race, de pur sang ;* blood-horse. — *au vert ;* grass-horse. — *qui a beaucoup d'action ;* high stepper. *Chevaux de frise ;* (milit.) chevaux de frise. *Case, wagon, pour les chevaux ;* horse-box. *Chair de* — ; horse-flesh. *L'art de monter à* — ; horsemanship. *Aller à* — ; to ride. *A* — *!* to horse! *Être à* — ; to be on horseback. *Être à* — *sur un bâton ;* to ride a stick. *Il est le* — *de bât ;* he is the drudge. *Travail de* — ; hard work. *Brider son* — *par la queue ;* to begin at the wrong end. *Parler à* — ; to speak magisterially. *Être mal à* — ; to be at an ill pass. *Monter sur ses grands chevaux ;* to ride a high horse. *À* — *donné il ne faut point regarder à la bride ;* one must not look a gift horse in the mouth. *Il n'est si bon* — *qui ne bronche ;* 'tis a good horse that never stumbles. *Huile de* — ; horse-grease.

chevalement, *n.m.*, (arch.) prop, stay, shore.

chevaler, *v.a.*, to prop, to shore up.

chevaler, *v.n.*, to run about, to run up and down.

chevaleresque. a *lj.*, chivalrous, knightly.

chevalerie, *n.f.*, knighthood, chivalry. — *errante ;* knight-errantry.

chevalet, *n.m.*, wooden horse (instrument of torture) ; bridge (of a stringed instrument—*d'instrument à cordes*) ; easel ; the gallows of a printing-press, stay of the frisket ; horse for scraping hides on ; sawing-trestle or horse ; buttress, prop, shore ; clothes-horse ; cross-beam (of a dormer window—*d'une fenêtre en mansarde*) ;

pyrotechnist's horse or rack ; (nav.) roller (to pass the cables from one place to another—*pour changer les câbles de place*). *Tableau de* — ; (paint.) easel-piece.

chevalier, *n.m.*, knight ; cavalier ; knight (at chess—*aux échecs*) ; (orni.) sandpiper. *Armer quelqu'un* — ; to dub one a knight. — *d'honneur ;* the first gentleman-usher to the queen or to a princess. *Le* — *du guet ;* formerly the captain of the night watch at Paris. — *de l'arquebuse ;* one of the artillery-company. — *errant ;* knight-errant. — *d'industrie ;* one that lives by his wits, sharper. — *de la coupe ;* tavern-knight. *Se faire le* — *de quelqu'un ;* to take one's part warmly. — *de Saint-Louis ;* knight of St. Louis. — *de la légion d'honneur ;* knight of the legion of honour. — *rouge ;* (orni.) red-shank.

chevalière, *n.f.*, knight's lady ; lady invested with an order of knighthood.

chevaline, *adj.*, of the horse kind.

chevalis, *n.m.*, passage made with boats when a river is low.

①chevance, *n.f.*, goods and chattels, substance.

chevauchage, *n.m.*, (print.) riding.

chevauchant. -e, *adj.*, (bot.) equitant.

①chevauchée, *n.f.*, circuit, progress ; the distance that a beast of burden can traverse in a certain given time.

chevauchement (-vôsh-màn), *n.m.*, (of bones—*des os*) riding of one part over another.

chevaucher, *v.n.*, to ride ; (nav.) to ride, to be fayed upon ; (carp.) to overlap ; (print. and surg.) to ride. — *le vent, v.a. ;* to fly into the wind.

①à chevauchons, *adv.*, astraddle.

chevau-léger, *n.m.*, light-horseman. — *s ;* light cavalry.

chevêche, *n.f.*, white owl, owlet, church owl.

chevecier, *n.m.*, dean (in certain churches —*dans certaines églises*) ; the person who takes care of the tapers.

chevelé. -e, *adj.* (her.) of the hair when it is of an enamel different from that of the head.

cheveline (shèv-), *n.f.*, coral club-top.

chevelu. -e, (shèv-), *adj.*, long-haired, hairy ; (bot.) fibrous. *Comète* — *e ;* haired comet. *Cuir* — ; scalp.

chevelu, *n.m.*, (bot.) chevelure ; beard of the root.

chevelure (shèv-), *n.f.*, hair, head of hair ; beams. *La* — *de Bérénice ;* (constellation) Berenice's hair.

chever, *v.a.*, (gold.) to hollow (the underside of a precious stone in order to soften its colour—*le dessous d'une pierre précieuse pour en adoucir la couleur*).

chevet, *n.m.*, pillow ; bolster ; the head (of a bed—*d'un lit*) ; bedside ; (nav.) cushion. bag. *Droit de* — ; sort of fee or present. *Le* — *d'une église ;* apsis of a church. *Trouver quelqu'un sous son* — ; to dream of any one.

chevêtre, *n.m.*, halter ; (carp.) binding-joist ; (surg.) bandage to support the lower jaw.

cheveu, *n.m.*, hair. *Les* —*x ;* the hair of the head. —*x de Vénus ;* (bot.) maiden-hair. *Tresse de* —*x ;* plait of hair. —*x roux ;* sandy hair. —*x d'ébène ;* raven locks. —*x épars ;* scattered locks. —*x postiches ;* false hair. *Je désire me faire couper les* —*x ;* I want to have my hair cut. *Raser les* —*x ;* to shave the head. *Se prendre aux* —*x ;* to take one another by the hair. *Cela fait dresser les* —*x ;* that makes one's hair stand on end. *Prendre l'occasion aux* —*x ;* to take time by the forelock.

*chevillage, *n.m.*, pegging, bolting.

*cheville, *n.f.*, peg, pin ; bolt ; plug ; botch, stop-gap ; (poet.) line or word of necessity ; (nav.) iron bolt ; branch (of a deer's head—*d'un bois de daim*). *Trouver à chaque trou une* — ; to find a peg for every hole. — *ouvrière ;* pole-bolt of a coach ; principal agent, mainspring of a party, of an affair. *La* — *du pied ;* the ankle-bone. — *à goujon;* common bolt. — *à goupille;* forelock bolt. — *à bouche et à croc ;* bolt with a ring and hook. — *à tête de diamant ;* square-headed bolt. — *à pointe perdue;* short drove-bolt. — *d'affût ;* gun-carriage bolt. — *à cosse ;* fender-bolt.

*chevillé, **-e**, *adj.*, (her.) branched.

*cheviller, *v.a.*, to peg or pin, to fasten with a peg ; (dy.) to wring. *Des vers chevillés ;* botched verses. *Il a l'âme chevillée dans le corps :* he has nine lives.

*chevillette, *n.f.*, key or peg (of a bookbinder's sewing press—*de presse de relieur*).

*chevillon, *n.m.*, turner's peg.

*chevillot, *n.m.*, (nav.) toggel, belaying-pin.

*chevillure, *n.f.*, branches of a deer's head.

chèvre, *n.f.*, she-goat, nanny-goat ; (mec.) crab, gin ; (astron.) capella. *Enter en pied de* — ; to graft slopeways. *Barbe-de-* — ; (bot.) jew's beard. — *à musc ;* musk goat, Thibet musk. *Avoir la* —, *prendre la* — ; to be very irritable. *Ménager la* — *et le chou ;* to run with the hare and hold with the hounds.

chevreau, *n.m.*, kid ; kid (skin—*peau*).

*chèvrefeuille, *n.m.*, honeysuckle. — *des bois :* woodbine, woodbind.

chèvre-pied, or **chèvre-pieds**, *adj.*, (of satyrs) goat-footed.

chevrette, *n.f.*, roe, doe ; shrimp, prawn ; syrup-pot ; little andiron or fire dog.

*chevreuil, *n.m.*, roebuck, roe-deer.

chevri-er, *n.m.*, **-ère**, *n.f.*, goat-herd.

*chevrillard, *n.m.*, young roebuck, fawn of a roe.

chevron, *n.m.*, rafter; stripe (on a soldier's sleeve—*sur la manche d'un soldat*) ; (nav.) scantling, long wedge ; (her.) chevron. — *de long pan ;* long rafter. —*s de croupe ;* hips. —*s cintrés ;* arched rafters. —*s de remplage ;* joists. *Mettre les* —*s à la batterie ;* to apply the wedges to the trucks.

chevronné, **-e**, *adj.*, (her.) chevroned.

chevrotage, *n.m.*, goat-fee.

chevrotain, *n.m.*, chevrotain.

chevrotant, **-e**, *adj.*, quivering, tremulous (of the voice—*de la voix*).

chevrotement (-mān), *n.m.*, tremulous motion, trembling of the voice.

chevroter, *v.n.*, to kid ; to sing or speak in a tremulous voice.

chevrotin, *n.m.*, kid leather.

chevrotine, *n.f.*, buck-shot.

chez (shé), *prep.*, at, to, in, one's house ; at the home of ; at, to, the native place of ; in, with ; among. *J'ai été* — *vous ;* I have been at your house. *Chacun est maître* — *soi ;* every man is master in his own house. *Je viens de* — *vous ;* I come from your house. *J'ai passé par* — *vous ;* I called at your house in passing. *Je viens de* — *ma mère ;* I come from my mother's. *C'est* — *lui une habitude ;* it is with him a habit. *Avoir un* — *soi ;* to have a home of one's own.

chiaoux, *n.m.*, Turkish officer, messenger.

chiasse, *n.f.*, dross, scum ; dung (of flies and worms—*de mouches et de vers*).

chibouque, *n.f.*, chibook (Turkish pipe).

chic, *n.m.*, tact. effect, knack (paint.). *Il a du* — ; (fam.) he is a dab hand.

chicambaut, *n.m.*, (nav.) bumkin, luff-block.

chicane, *n.f.*, cavil, evasion, quibble ; chicanery, pettifogging, cavilling, quibbling ; the quirks of law ; wrangling. *Gens de* — ; petti-foggers. *Chercher* — *à quelqu'un ;* to pick a quarrel with one.

chicaner, *v.n.*, to chicane, to cavil, to quibble, to use tricks, fetches at law ; to use quirks, shifts ; to wrangle, to perplex. — *le vent ;* (nav.) to lie too near the wind, to hug the wind.

chicanerie (shi-), *n.f.*, chicanery ; quibbling, cavilling.

chicaneu-r, *n.m.*, **-se**, *n.f.*, and *adj.*, chicaner, caviller, pettifogger, wrangler ; litigious, cavilling.

chicani-er, *n.m.*, **-ère**, *n.f.*, and *adj.*, wrangler, chicaner ; cavilling, wrangling.

chiche, *adj.*, niggardly, penurious, stingy, scurvy, shabby, scanty, sordid, sparing, parsimonious, niggard. *Pois* — *s ;* chick-peas, dwarf-peas.

chichement (shish-mān), *adv.*, niggardly, penuriously, stingily, parsimoniously.

chicheté, *n.f.*, niggardliness, covetousness, penuriousness.

chicon, *n.m.*, coss-lettuce ; heart (of a lettuce—*de laitue*).

chicoracé, **-e**, *adj.*, endive-like, chicoraceous.

chicoracée, *n.f.*, (bot.) chicoraceous plant.

chicorée, *n.f.*, succory, endive, chicory.

chicot, *n.m.*, small broken piece of wood ; stump (of teeth—*des dents*) ; stub, stump (of trees—*des arbres*). — *du Canada ;* bonduc.

chicoter, *v.n.*, (pop.) to wrangle, to trifle, to dispute about nothing.

chicotin, *n.m.*, orpine, rosewort, rose-root, livelong ; juice of bitter apple. *Amer comme* — ; as bitter as gall.

chie-en-lit, *n.m.*, (—) merry-andrew, jack-pudding.

chien, *n.m.*, **-ne**, *n.f.*, (-in, -è-n), dog, bitch ; cock (of a gun or pistol—*des armes à feu*). — *babillard* (hunt.) ; liar. — *caniche ;* poodle dog ; poodle ; water-dog. — *volant ;* tailless bat. *Grand* — ; dog-star. — *de pure race ;* true-bred dog. — *métis ;* half-bred dog ; mongrel. *Cette chienne est pleine ;* that bitch is with pup. — *d'arrêt ;* pointer. — *couchant ;* setter ; toad-eater ; lick-spittle. — *courant ;* beagle. — *turc ;* Barbary, Turkish dog. — *d'attache ;* ban-dog. — *de basse-cour ;* house-dog. — *de berger ;* shepherd's dog. — *de boucher ;* mastiff. — *de ferme ;* house-dog. — *marin ;* — *de mer* (ich.) ; dog-fish, hound-fish. — *de race ;* thorough-bred dog. — *pour le renard ;* fox-hound. — *pour le sanglier ;* boar-hound. — *du grand Saint-Bernard ;* Alpine mastiff. — *de Terre-neuve ;* Newfoundland dog. — *terrier ;* terrier. *Une meute de* —*s ;* a pack of hounds. *Un petit* —, *un jeune* — ; a puppy, a whelp. — *de demoiselle ;* lap-dog. *Chasser au* — *d'arrêt ;* to set. *Donner, lâcher les* —*s ;* to let loose, cast off, the dogs. *Jeter sa langue aux* —*s ;* to give it up (of a riddle, &c.—*énigmes, &c.*). *C'est Saint Roch et son* — ; like Darby and Joan. *Hâler les* —*s ;* to set on the dogs. *Rompre les* —*s ;* to call off the dogs. *Battre le* — *devant le lion ;* to correct one that is not culpable in the presence of a superior who is so. *Être comme un* — *à l'attache ;* to be like a galley-slave. *Faire le* — *couchant ;* to creep and crouch. *Mener une vie de* — ; to live like a dog. *Bons* —*s chassent de race ;* like father, like son. *Entre* — *et loup ;* in the dusk of the evening. *Ils s'accordent comme* — *et chat ;* they agree like cat and dog. *Leurs* —*s ne chassent pas ensemble ;* they don't agree together. *Qui m'aime, aime mon* — ; love me, love my dog. *Tout* — *qui aboie ne mord pas ;* barking dogs seldom bite. — *hargneux a toujours l'oreille déchirée ;* quarrelsome curs have dirty coats.

chien de mer, or **chien marin**. *n.m.*, (ich.) dog-fish, hound-fish.

chiendent, *n.m.*, dog's-grass, quitch-grass, couch-grass. — *fossile;* amianthus.

chiennée, *n.f.*, a litter of pups.

chienner (shiè-), *v.n.*, to whelp, to pup.

chiffe, *n.f.*, poor stuff; rags.

chiffon. *n.m.*, rag; trinket, frippery. *Mon petit* — ; you little darling (in speaking to an infant—*parlant à un petit enfant*).

chiffonnage, *n.m.*, (paint.) rumpled, wrinkled. drapery; a rumpling.

chiffonne, *adj. f.*, (gard.) puny, useless. *Branche* —; puny, stunted, branch.

chiffonner, *v.a.*, to rumple, to wrinkle, to crumple, to tumble, to ruffle.

chiffonni-er, *n.m.*, **-ère**, *n.f.*, rag-picker.

chiffonni-er. *n.m.*, or **-ère**, *n.f.*, chiffonier (furniture—*meuble*).

chiffre, *n.m.*, figure, number; total amount; cipher; flourish of letters, monogram; digit. — *périodique;* (arith.) figure of the recurring period. *Écrire en* — ; to write in cipher.

chiffrer, *v.n.*, to cipher, to write in cipher.

chiffrer. *v.a.*, to cipher; to figure (the bass of a piece of music—*la basse d'un morceau de musique*).

chiffreur, *n.m.*, reckoner.

*****chignon**. *n.m.*, nape (of the neck—*du cou*); hair twisted behind.

chimère, *n.f.*, (myth.) chimera; chimera, idle fancy, vain imagination; (conch., ich.) chimera.

chimérique, *adj.*, chimerical, visionary, fantastical.

chimériquement, *adv.*, chimerically.

chimie, *n.f.*, chemistry.

chimique, *adj.*, chemical.

chimiste, *n.m.*, chemist.

chimpanzé, *n.m.*, (zool.) chimpanzee.

china, *n.m.*, (bot.) china-root. *V.* **squine**.

chinchilla, *n.m.*, (mam.) chinchilla.

chiner, *v.a.*, (manu.) to colour, to dye.

chinois, -e. *n.* and *adj.*, Chinese.

chinoiserie, *n.f.*, Chinese ornaments (for chimney-pieces—*de cheminée*).

chiourme. *n.f.*, formerly, all the convicts on a galley; in modern use, all the convicts in a bagnio.

chiper, *v.a.*, to pilfer, to crib, to prig.

chipie, *n.f.*, affected, peevish woman.

chipoter. *v.n.*, to dally, to trifle, to dispute about trifles.

chipoti-er, *n.m.*, **-ère**, *n.f.*, trifler, dallier, shuffler.

chique, *n.f.*, quid of tobacco; (ent.) chegre, chegoe, chigre; marble (to play with—*jouet*).

chiquenaude (shik-nôd), *n.f.*, fillip.

⊙**chiquenauder**, *v.a.*, to fillip.

chiquer. *v.n.*, to chew tobacco ; to eat heartily ; (paint.) to execute skilfully.

chiquet, *n.m.*, driblet. *Un — de vin;* a drop of wine. — *à* — ; bit by bit.

chiragre (ki-), *n.f.*, chiragra.

⊙**chirimoya**, *n.f.*, custard-apple.

chirographaire (ki-), *adj.*,of a debt proved by a written document.

chirologie (ki-), *n.f.* chirology.

chiromancie (ki-), *n.f.*, chiromancy.

chiromancien (ki-), *n.m.*, chiromancer.

chirone. *n.f.*, (bot.) centaury.

chiroptère (ki-), *n.m.*, (mam.) cheiropter, bat.

chirurgical, -e, *adj.*, surgical.

chirurgie, *n.f.*, surgery.

chirurgien (-in), *n.m.*, surgeon. *Aide —* (—*s —s*); assistant surgeon

chirurgique, *adj.*, surgical.

chiste (kist), *n.m.*, (surg.) cyst. .

chiure. *n.f.*, fly-blow. *Marqué de —s de mouches;* fly-bitten. *Faire des —s de mouches sur;* to fly-blow.

chlamyde (kla-), *n.f.*, chlamys.

chlorate (klo-), *n.m.*, (chem.) chlorate.

chlore (klor), *n.m.*, (chem.) chlorine; (bot.) yellow-wort.

chloré. -e (klo-), *adj.*, chloruretted.

chlorhydrate (klo-), *n.m.*, (chem.) hydrochlorate.

chlorhydrique (klo-), *adj.*,(chem.) hydrochloric, muriatic.

chloride (klo-), *n.m.*, (chem.) a combination of chlorine with a simple substance, chloride.

chlorique (klo-). *adj.*, (chem.) chloric.

chloroforme (klo-), *n.m.*, chloroform.'

chloroformer, *v.a.*, to administer chloroform.

chloromètre (klo-), *n.m.*, chlorometer.

chlorométrie (klo-), *n.f.*, chlorometry.

chlorose (klo-rôz), *n.f.*, (med.) chlorosis, green sickness.

chlorotique (klo-), *adj.*, chlorotic, affected with chlorosis.

chlorure (klo-). *n m.*, chloride.

choc, *n.m.*, shock, clashing; encounter; brunt; collision, disaster, blow. *Soutenir le* —; to stand the shock.

chocolat, *n.m.*, chocolate. *Bâton de* —; stick of chocolate.

chocolati-er, *n m.*, **-ère**, *n.f.*, chocolatemaker; chocolate-dealer.

chocolatière (-ti-èr), *n.f.*, chocolate-pot.

chœur (keur), *n.m.*, choir, chorus. *Enfant de* —; singing boy (in churches—*dans les églises*). *Chanter en* — ; to sing in chorus.

choir (chu), *v.n.*, to fall.

choisir. *v.a.*, to choose, to make choice of; to pitch upon, to pick out; to nominate; to single out, to select. *Il n'y a point à* —; there is no choice left.

choix (shoâ), *n.m.*, choice, choosing, option, selection. *Par* —; from choice. *Sans* —; indifferently. *Avoir le → forcé;* to have Hobson's choice.

cholagogue (ko-la-gog), *n.m.*, (med.) cholagogue.

cholédoque. *adj.*, (anat.) biliary, hepatic. *Canal* —; hepatic duct.

choléra-morbus (ko-), *n.m.* (*n.p.*), choleramorbus. *Faux* —; cholerine.

cholérine (ko-), *n.f.*, cholerine

cholérique, *n.m., f.*, and *adj.*, (med.) person affected with cholera; referring, belonging to cholera; choleric, bilious.

choliambe (ko-), *n.m.*, choliambic verse.

chômable, *adj.*, that ought to be kept as a holiday.

chômage, *n.m.*, stoppage; respite. *Le — d'un moulin;* the standing still of a mill.

chômer, *v.a.*, to abstain from work on a particular day, to rest. *C'est un saint qu'on ne chôme pas;* he is a disgraced person.

chômer, *v.n.*, to want work, to stand still for want of work; (agri.) to lie fallow. *Il chôme de besogne;* he is out of work. — *de quelque chose;* to stand in need of a thing.

*****chondrille** (kon-), *n.f.*, (bot.) gum-succory; wall-lettuce.

chondrologie, *n.f.*, chondrology.

chope, *n.f.*, large beer-glass.

⊙**chopine**. *n.f.*, chopin (a measure nearly equal to an English pint).

chopiner, *v.n.*, to tipple, to drink little and often.

chopper. *v.n.*, to stumble, to trip up.

choquant, -e, *adj.*, rude, offensive; shocking.

choquer, *v.a.*, to shock, to strike, to dash against, to clash with; to offend, to give offence, to shock, to disgust, to displease, to grate upon ; (nav.) to surge.

se **choquer**, *v.r.*, to take offence ; to come into contact with.

choquer, *v.n.*, to strike glasses; to be offensive; to hurt any one's feelings; to be shocking.

choraïque (ko-), *adj.*, choraïc.

choral (ko-), *adj.*, choral. — *n.m.*, chant.

chorée (ko-), *n.m.*, (poet.) choreus

chorée (ko-), *n.f.*, chorea, St. Vitus' dance.

chorège (ko-), *n.m.*, (antiq.) choragus.

chorégraphe (ko-), *n.m.*, one conversant with choregraphy.

chorégraphie (ko-), *n.f.*, choregraphy.

chorégraphique (ko-), *adj.*, choregraphical.

chorévêque (ko-), *n.m.*, chorepiscopus.

choriambe (ko-ri-änb), *n.m.*, (poet.) choriambus.

chorion, *n.m.*, (anat.) chorion.

choriste (ko-), *n.m.*, chorister (of a church— *d'église*); chorus singer (thea.).

chorographie (ko-), *n.f.*, chorography.

chorographique (ko-), *adj.*, chorographical.

choroïde (ko-), *n.f.*, *adj*, (anat.) choroïd.

chorus (ko-rûss), *n.m.*, chorus. *Faire —*; to sing the chorus, to quire ; to chime in ; to applaud, to approve

chose, *n.f.*, thing; matter, business, affair, deed ; reality, action ; (jur.) chattels. —*s* (jur.); chose. *Ce n'est pas grand —*; 'tis no great thing. *Quelque — de beau*; something fine. *Peu de —*; a mere trifle, nothing. *La — publique*; the commonwealth, common weal. *Être tout — *(pop.); to be out of sorts. *C'est tout autre —*; that is quite another thing. *—s de la mer* (nav.); wreck, or whatever is floating at sea; flotage, flotsam (jur.).

chou, *n.m.*, cabbage; colewort; puff-paste; kale; darling, dear (of persons—*personnes*). *— cabus*; headed-cabbage. *— marin*; sea-cole-wort, sea-cabbage. *— pommé*; white-headed cabbage. *— non pommé*; bore-cole, brown-cole. *Filet à —*; cabbage-net. *Rejet de —*; cabbage-sprout. *Pomme de —*; cabbage-head. *Tige, trognon, de —*; cabbage-stalk. *— crépu*; Scotch kale. *— de Milan*; savoy. *—x verts, jeunes —x,* sprouts. *—x blancs*; white-heart cabbages *—x brocolis*; broccoli. *Aller au travers des choux*; to go hand over head. *— pour —*; 'tis all one. *Il en fait ses —x gras*; he feathers his nest with it. *Il s'entend à cela comme à ramer des —x*; he knows nothing about it. *Sauver, ménager, la chèvre et le —*, to provide against two inconveniences at once. *Aller planter ses —x*; to retire to one's country-seat. *Mon petit —*; my little darling. *— oléifère*; colza. *— de chien*; dog's-cabbage. *— palmiste (—x —s)*; cabbage-tree. *— navet (—x —s)*; rape-cole-wort. *— rave (—x —s)*; turnip-cabbage. *— !*; *— là ! — -pille !* (hunt.) at it ! go to it !

chouan, *n.m.*, brown owl ; royalist insurgent during the French Revolution ; a seed of the Levant.

chouanisme, *n.m.*, the politics of the Chouans, chouanism.

chouanner *v.n.*, to carry on war in the manner of the Chouans.

chouannerie, *n.f.*, the party of the Chouans.

chouant. *n.m.*, a sort of owl.

choucas. *n.m.*, or **chouchette**, *n.f.*, jack-daw.

choucroute, *n.f.*, sour-krout, sour-crout, sauer-kraut.

chouette, *n.f.*, screech-owl. *Faire la —* (piquet) ; to play alone against two.

chou-fleur. *n.m.* (*—x —s*), cauliflower.

***chou-pille**. *n.m.* (—), setting-dog which, in beating the field, will not go far from its master.

chouquet, *n.m.* . (nav.) block, moor's-head, cap of the mast-head.

chou-rave, *n.m.* (*—x —s*), turnip-cabbage.

choyer, *v.a.*, to take great care of, to be fond of, to pamper, to fondle, to make much of, to cocker-up.

se **choyer**, *v.r.*, to pamper one's self.

chrématologie (kré-), *n.f.*, (l.u.) chrematology.

chrématologique (kré-), *adj.*, chrematological.

chrême (krêm), *n.m.*, chrism, holy oil.

chrémeau (kré-), *n m*, chrism-cloth.

chrestomathie (krès-to-ma-ci), *n.f.*, chrestomathy.

chrétien, -ne (kré-ti-in,-ti-è-n), *n.* and *a.lj*, Christian.

chrétiennement (kré-tièn-män), *adv.*, Christianly, Christian-like.

chrétienté (kré-ti-in-té), *n.f.*, Christendom. *Marcher sur la —*; (fam.) to wear shoes and stockings in holes.

⊙**chrie** (kri), *n.f.*, (rhet.) short, concise, but lively and eloquent narration.

chrismal (kri-), *n.m.*, chrysmatory.

chrismation, *n.f.*, chrismation.

le **christ** (krist), *n.m.*, Christ. *Jésus Christ* (jé-zu-kri) ; Jesus Christ. [*Christ* without *Jésus* is never used in French without *le*.]

christe (krist), *n.f.*, (bot.) crithmum, samphire, sea-fennel. *— marine*; crithmum, samphire, sea-fennel.

christianiser (kris-), *v.a.*, to Christianize

christianisme (kris-tia-njsm), *n.m.*, Christianity.

christiaque (kris-tiak), *adj.*, Christian

chromate (kro-), *n m*.. (chem.) chromate.

chromatique (kro-), *adj.*, (chem. and mus.) chromatic.

chromatique, *n.m.*, (mus., paint) chromatics.

chromatiquement, *adv.*, (mus.) chromatically.

chrome (krôm), *n.m*, chromium.

chromique, *adj.*, (chem.) chromic.

chromolithographie, *n.f.*, chromo-lithography.

chronicité (kro-), *n.f.*, (med.) chronicity.

chronique (kro-), *n.f.*, chronicle, history. *— scandaleuse*; slander, scandalous reports.

chronique, *adj.*, (med.) chronic.

chroniqueur (kro-), *n.m.*, chronicler.

chronogramme (kro-), *n.m.*, chronogram.

chronographe (kro-), *n.m.*, chronographer.

chronographie (kro-), *n.f.*, chronography.

chronologie (kro-), *n.f.*, chronology.

chronologique (kro-), *adj.*, chronological.

chronologiste (kro-), *n.m.*, chronologer.

⊙**chronologue** (kro-), *n.m.*, chronologer.

chronomètre (kro-), *n.m.*, chronometer.

chrysalide (kri-), *n.m.*, aurelia, chrysalis, nympha ; pupa ; pupe ; grub.

chrysanthème (kri-), *n.m.*, chrysanthemum ; ox-eye daisy ; marigold.

chrysite (kri-), *n.f.*, chrysite, touch-stone.

chrysobate (kri-), *n.f.*, chrysobates.

chrysobéril (kri-), *n.m.*, chrysober.

chrysocale (kri-), *n.m.*, an alloy of copper and zinc, resembling gold ; pinchbeck.

chrysocolle (kri-), *n.f.*, chrysocolla, borax.

chrysocome (kri-), *n.f.*, (bot.) chrysocoma, goldylocks.

chrysogonum (kri-), *n.m.*, moth-mullein ; red turnip.

chrysolithe (kri-), *n.f.*, chrysolite.

chrysophris (kri-),*n.m.*, (ich.) gilt-head.

chrysoprase (kri-), *n.f.*, chrysoprase.

☉**chrysulée** (kri-), (chem.) *n.f.*, chrysulea, aqua regia.

chu, -e, *part.*, (of choir) fallen.

☉**chucheter**, *v.n.*, to whisper; (of sparrows—*des moineaux*) to twitter.

chuchotement, *n.m.*, whispering, whisper.

chuchoter, *v.n.* and *a.*, to whisper.

chuchoterie (sho-trî), *n.f.*, whispering.

chuchoteu-r *n.m.*, **-se**, *n.f.*, whisperer.

chut (shut), *int.*, hush !

chute, *n.f.*, fall, tumble; decline; falling, overthrow, lapse, downfall, descension, decay; catastrophe, disaster; failure, miscarriage. — *d'eau;* waterfall, cataract. *La — du jour;* the close of day. *La — d'une période:* the cadence of a period. — *d'une voile*, (nav.) depth of a sail; drop (of the principal square sails—*des grandes voiles carrées*). — *de courants;* setting of the tides.

chuter, *v.n.*, (thea.) to fail, to be damned.

chyle, *n.m.*, chyle.

chyleu-x, -se, *adj.*, chylous.

chylifère, *adj.*, (anat.) chyliferous.

chylification, *n.f.*, chylifaction, chylification.

chylose, *n.f.*, chylification.

chyme, *n.m.*, chyme.

chymification, *n.f.*, chymification.

ci, *adv.*, here. *Celui — est meilleur que celui-là;* this is better than that. *Cet homme— —;* this man. — *-dessus,* — *-devant;* above, before, heretofore. *Par— —, par-là;* here and there, up and down; off and on. — *-après;* hereafter. — *-dessous;* below. — *-contre;* opposite. *Entre*☉ — *et demain;* between this time and to-morrow. *Entre*☉ — *et là;* between this and then. (French Revolution) *Un — -devant noble, un — -devant;* a nobleman. *Les — -devant nobles, les — -devant;* the nobility, the aristocracy.

cibagé, *n.m.*, a sort of pine of India, cibage.

cible, *n.f.*, mark to be shot at, target.

ciboire, *n.m*, a sacred vase, pyx; (arch.) ciborium, canopy.

ciboule, *n.f.*, scallion, green onion; eschalot.

ciboulette, *n.f.*, (bot.) chive. *V.* **civette**.

cicatrice, *n.f.*, scar, seam.

cicatricule, *n.f.*, cicatricula, eye or thread (of an egg—*d'un œuf*); small scar.

cicatrisant, -e, *adj.*, cicatrizing.

cicatriser, *v.a.*, to mark with a scar, to scar; to cicatrize; to close, bind up.

se **cicatriser**, *v.r.*, to be cicatrized, to skin over, to heal up.

ciccus, *n.m.*, a species of grasshopper; a species of wild-goose; ciccus.

cicéro, *n.m*, (print.) pica. — *gros œil;* pica. — *petit œil;* small pica.

cicérole, *n.f.*, chick-pea.

cicérone, *n.m.*, cicerone.

cicéronien, -ne (-in, -è-n), *adj.*, Ciceronian.

cicindèle, *n.f.*, cicindela.

☉**cicisbée**. *V.* **sigisbée**.

ciclamor, *n.m*. *V.* **orle**.

cicutaire, *n.f.*, cicuta, water-hemlock.

cid (sid), *n.m.*, cid (chief, commander—*chef*).

cidre, *n.m.*, cider. *Gros —;* strong cider. — *paré;* old cider. — *piquant;* rough cider.

cie, (ab.) Co. (for Company).

ciel (sièl), *n.m.* (cieux), heavens, the heavens, the firmament, the sky; paradise. *Grâces au —;* thanks be to heaven, to God. *C'est un coup du —;* it is a judgment of heaven. *O — !* O heavens! *Du —;* heavenly. *Arc-en-— (-s —);* rainbow. *Remuer — et terre;* to leave no stone unturned.

ciel, *n.m.* (ciels), tester of a bed; (c.rel.) the canopy which is carried over the host; sky (paint.); the roof of a quarry; air, climate. *Un beau —;* a fine climate. *L'Italie est sous un des plus beaux —s de l'Europe:* Italy has one of the finest climates in Europe.

cierge. *n.m.*, wax-taper, wax-light. — *du Pérou;* torch-thistle. — *pascal* Easter cierge. — *s d'eau:* water-jets (placed in a row—*sur la même ligne*).

ciergier, *n.m.*, wax-chandler.

cigale, *n.f.*, cicada, grasshopper. — *de rivière:* water-grasshopper. — *de mer;* shrimp.

cigare, *n.m.*, cigar or segar; Cuba tobacco.

cigarette, *n.f.*, small cigar, cigarette.

*****cigogne**, *n.f.*, (orni.) stork. — *à sac;* hurgil. *Bec de —;* (bot.) crane's-bill. *Conte à la —, conte de la —;* nonsensical and improbable story.

*****cigogneau**, *n.m.*, (fam.) a young stork.

ciguë (si-gû), *n.f.*, hemlock. — *vireuse*, — *d'eau;* water-hemlock, cow-bane.

cil. *n.m*, eye-lash; (bot.) lash, hair.

ciliaire, *adj.*, ciliary.

cilice, *n.m.*, hair-cloth.

cilié, -e, *adj.*, (bot.) ciliated, lashed.

*****cillement**, *n.m.*, twinkle, winking.

*****ciller**, *v.a.*, to wink, to twinkle; (hawking—*fauconnerie*) to seel.

☉*****ciller**, *v.n.*, to wink; (man.) to have white hairs over the eyes.

*****cillo**, *n.m.*, (med.) a person who winks incessantly, winker.

cimaise, *n.f.*, cyma, ogee.

cimbalaire, *n.f.*, *V.* **cymbalaire**.

cime, *n.f.*, top, summit (of a mountain, tree, &c.); peak; (bot.) cyme, summit. *En —;* (bot.) cymose.

ciment, *n.m.*, cement.

cimenter, *v.a.*, to cement; to confirm, to strengthen.

cimentier (-tié), *n.m.*, (tech.) cement-maker.

cimeterre (sim-tèr), *n.m.*, cimiter, falchion.

cimetière (sim-tièr), *n.m.*, churchyard, burying-ground, cemetery.

cimier, *n.m.*, buttock of beef; crest of a head-piece; apex. — *de cerf;* haunch of venison.

cimolée, *n.f.*, cimolite; cimolian earth; cutler's dust.

cimolée or **cimolie**, *adj. f.*, cimolian.

cinabre, *n.m.*, cinnabar.

cinchonine, *n.f.*, cinchonia, cinchonine.

cincle, *n.m.*, (orni.) water-ouzel.

cinéraire, *adj.*, cinerary.

cinéraire, *n.f.*, (bot.) cineraria.

cinération, *n.f.*, cineration.

cinglage, *n.m.*, ☉run of a ship in twenty-four hours; (metal.) shingling.

cingler, *v.n.*, to sail before the wind.

cingler, *v.a.*, to lash; (metal) to shingle.

cinglerie, *n.f.*, shingling-house.

cinnamome, *n.m.*, cinnamomum.

cinq (sink), *adj.*, five.

cinq, *n.m.*, a five; cinque (at certain games —*à certains jeux*).

cinquantaine, *n.f.*, fifty; half a hundred.

cinquante, *adj.*, fifty.

☉**cinquantenier**, *n.m.*, captain of fifty men.

cinquantième (-ti-èm), *adj.*, fiftieth.

cinquantième, *n.m.*, fiftieth part.

cinquième, *adj.*, fifth.

cinquième, *n.m.*, fifth part; pupil on the fifth form; — *n.f.*, the fifth form in colleges and public schools.

cinquièmement, *adv.*, fifthly.

cintre, *n.m.*, semi-circle; centre; (carp.) centre-bit. *Cette cave est en —;* that cellar is

built arch-wise. — *surbaissé;* elliptical arch.

À plein —; semi-circular.

cintrer, *v.a.,* to arch, to build in the form of an arch, to curve.

cioutat, *n.m.,* cioutat (a kind of grape—*sorte de raisin*).

cipaye, *n.m.,* sepoy.

cipolin, *n.m.,* cipollino, cipolin marble.

cippe, *n.m.,* cippus.

cirage, *n.m.,* the act of waxing; waxing; blacking (for shoes, &c.); (paint.) cameo with a yellow ground.

circée, *n.f.,* (bot.) enchanter's nightshade.

circompolaire, *adj.,* circumpolar.

circoncire, *v.a.,* to circumcise.

circoncis, *n.m.,* one that is circumcised.

circonciseur, *n.m.,* circumciser.

circoncision, *n.f.,* circumcision.

circonférence, *n.f.,* circumference.

circonflexe, *n.m.* and *adj.,* circumflex accent; circumflex.

circonlocution, *n.f.,* circumlocution.

circonscription, *n.f.,* circumscription.

circonscrire, *v.a.,* to circumscribe, to encircle, to stint.

circonspect, -e (-pé, -pèkt), *adj.,* circumspect, wary, heedful, discreet, cautious.

circonspection, *n.f.,* circumspection, wariness, heedfulness. *Avec —;* heedfully.

circonstance, *n.f.,* circumstance. — *aggravante;* aggravation. *De —;* prepared for the circumstance. *Des —s;* circumstantial. *Dans les —s critiques;* upon emergent occasions.

circonstancier, *v.a.,* to state circumstantially; to tell, to describe the circumstances of.

circonvallation (-val-la-), *n.f.,* circumvallation.

circonvenir, *v.a.,* to circumvent, to overreach.

circonvention, *n.f.,* circumvention, overreaching. *User de —;* to circumvent.

circonvoisin, -e, *adj.,* circumjacent, neighbouring, adjoining.

circonvolution, *n.f.,* circumvolution.

circuit, *n.m.,* circuit; round-about road; circumlocution.

circulaire, *adj.,* circular, round.

circulaire, *n.f.,* circular.

circulairement (-lèr-mǎn), *adv.,* circularly.

circulant, -e, *adj.,* circulating.

circulation, *n.f.,* circulation; currency; traffic. *Mettre en —;* to issue (money—*monnaie*).

circulatoire, *adj.,* circulatory, circulating.

circuler, *v.n.,* to circulate; to pass from hand to hand; to spread.

circumnavigateur (-kom-), *n.m.,* circumnavigator.

circumnavigation (-kom-), *n.f.,* circumnavigation.

cire, *n.f.,* wax; bees'-wax; wax-candle; seal. *— à cacheter;* sealing-wax. *Pain de —;* cake of wax.

cirer, *v.a.,* to wax; to black (boots).

cirier, *n.m.,* wax-chandler; wax-maker; (bot.) candle-berry, wax-tree.

ciroène, *n.m.,* (pharm.) a wax and wine tonic plaster.

ciron, *n.m.,* (ent.) flesh-worm.

cirque, *n.m.,* circus.

cirre, *n.m.,* (bot.) tendril; cirrus.

cirrou-x, -se, *adj.,* ending in a cirrus.

cirsakas, *n.m.* *V.* sirsacas.

cirse, *n.m.,* (bot.) horse-thistle. — *des champs;* way-thistle, field-thistle.

cirsion, *n.f.,* (bot.) cirsium, gentle-thistle.

cirsocèle, *n.f.,* (med.) cirsocele.

cirure, *n.f.,* prepared wax (for varnishing —*pour vernir*)

*cisailler, *v.a.,* (coin.) to mark, to clip.

*cisailles, *n.f. pl.,* (coin.) clippings or shearings of metals; shears.

cisalpin, -e, *adj.,* Cisalpine.

ciseau, *n.m.,* chisel. — *d'orfèvre;* graver.

ciseaux, *n.m.. pl.,* scissors. — *de jardinier;* shears. — *de tailleur;* shears. — *boutonnés* (surg.); probe-scissors. — *mousses* (surg.); blunt-pointed scissors.

ciseler (siz-lé), *v.a.,* to chase, to carve, to emboss.

ciselet (siz-lè), *n.m.,* graver; chasing-tool.

ciseleur (siz-leur), *n.m.,* chaser; carver; sculptor.

ciselure (siz-lur), *n.f.,* chasing, sculpture, carving; chased work, carved work, sculpturing.

cisoires, *n.f.,* bench-shears.

cissite, *n.f.,* aetites, eagle-stone.

cissoïdal, -e, *adj.,* cissoid.

cissoïde, *n.f.,* (geom.) cissoid.

ciste, *n.m.,* (antiq.) basket; (arch.) cist; (bot.) cistus, rock-rose.

cistophore, *n.f.,* (antiq.) cistophora; canephora.

cistophore, *n.m.,* (antiq.) cistophorus.

citadelle, *n.f.,* citadel.

citadin, *n.m.,* **-e,** *n.f.,* citizen, burgess; (b.s.) cit.

citadine, *n.f.,* hackney-coach.

citateur, *n.m.,* quoter; book containing a collection of quotations.

citation, *n.f.,* citation, quotation, quoting; summons. *Se faire délivrer une —;* to take out a summons. *Lancer une —* (jur.); to issue a summons.

cité, *n.f.,* city; town; city (most ancient part of a town—*la plus ancienne partie d'une ville*). *La céleste —;* the heavenly city. *Droits de —;* the rights of a citizen; freedom (of a city—*d'une ville*).

citer, *v.a.,* to cite, to quote; to name; to summon; to subpœna.

citérieur, -e, *adj.,* citerior, hither.

citerne, *n.f.,* cistern.

citerneau, *n.m.,* small cistern.

cithare, *n.f.,* (antiq.) cithara.

citli, *n.m.,* tapeti, Brazilian rabbit.

citole, *n.m.,* a musical instrument, dulcimer.

citoyen, *n.m.,* **-ne,** *n.f.* (-in, -èn), citizen, inhabitant, freeman of a city.

citragon, *n.m.,* balm-mint.

citrate, *n.m.,* (chem.) citrate.

citrin, -e, *adj.,* citrine, lemon-coloured, pale yellow.

citrique, *adj.,* citric.

citron, *n.m.,* citron, lemon; lime; lemon-colour; —, *adj.,* lemon-coloured.

citronnat, *n.m.,* candied lemon-peel; sugar-plum with lemon-peel in it.

citronné, -e, *adj.,* that has the taste or flavour of lemon.

citronnelle, *n.f.,* balm-mint, garden-mint, citron-water.

citronnier, *n.m.,* lemon-tree; citron-tree.

*citrouille, *n.f.,* pumpion, pumpkin, gourd.

civade, *n.f.,* a kind of beard-fish.

civadière, *n.f.,* (nav.) sprit-sail.

cive or **civette,** *n.f.,* (bot.) chive.

civet, *n.m.,* stewed or jugged hare.

civette, *n.f.,* (mam.) civet-cat; civet; (bot.) chive.

civière, *n.f.,* hand-barrow; litter.

civil, -e, *adj.,* relating to the community in general; civil, courteous, well-bred, gallant. *Requête —e;* bill of review. *Partie —e;* the prosecutor suing for damages in a criminal prosecution.

civilement (-mǎn), *adv.*, civilly; courteously, politely. *Mort* —; dead in law.

civilisable, *adj.*, that can be civilized, civilizable.

civilisat-eur, -rice. *adj.*, civilizing.

civilisation, *n.f.*, civilization.

civiliser, *v.a.*, to civilize; (jur.) to civilize a criminal process.

se **civiliser**, *v.r.*, to become civilized.

civilité, *n.f.*, civility, good manners, good breeding, politeness, courtesy, manners; compliments, courteousness. *La — puérile et honnête :* the title of an old child's book of politeness. *Il n'a pas lu la — puérile et honnête;* he never learned politeness. *Mes —s à Monsieur votre frère ;* my compliments to your brother. *Il est de la —, il est de — ;* it is but common civility.

civique, *adj.*, civic.

civisme, *n.m.*, civism.

clabaud. *n.m.*, (hunt.) liar; (b.s.) babbler.

clabaudage, *n.m.*, barking, baying; clamour, bawling.

clabauder, *v.n.*, to bark often and without cause ; to clamour, to bawl.

clabauderie (-bo-drĭ), *n.f.*, clamour, bawling.

clabaudeu-r, *n.m.*, **-se**, *n.f.*, bawler, a bawling man or woman.

claie, *n.f.*, wattle, hurdle ; (of a sieve —*d'un tamis*) screen. *Passer à la — ;* to screen.

clair, -e, *adj.*, clear, bright, relucent, shining, luminous ; light, lightsome, light-coloured ; transparent ; pure, limpid ; thin; plain, manifest, evident, intelligible, visible. *Étoffe —e ;* thin, flimsy stuff. *Lait —;* whey.

clair, *n.m.*, light, clearness ; (paint.) light. *Il fait — de lune;* it is moonlight. *Vin tiré au — ;* racked wine.

clair, *adv.*, clearly, plain, plainly. *Parler — et net ;* to speak out.

clairçage, *n.m.*, decolouring (of sugar—*du sucre*).

clairçer, *v.a.*, to decolour (sugar—*sucre*).

claire, *n.f.*, burnt bones, *or* phosphate of lime, employed in cupellation ; sugar-boiler.

clairée, *n.f.*, clarified sugar.

clairement (klĕr-mǎn), *adv.*, clearly, plainly, distinctly, evidently, intelligibly.

clairet, *adj.*, (of wines—*vins*) pale, pale-coloured.

clairet, *n.m.*, precious stone that is too pale ; pale wine ; clairet (an infusion of wine, honey, sugar, and aromatic plants—*infusion de vin, de miel, de sucre et d'aromates*).

clairette, *n.f.*, a kind of grape.

claire-voie, *n.f.* (—*s* —*s*), opening in the wall of a park ; (nav.) sky-light. *À —;* in open work. *Semer à —;* to sow thin.

clairière, *n.f.*, glade (in a forest—*de forêt*) ; a thin part (in linen—*dans le linge*).

clair-obscur, *n.m.* (—*s* —*s*), (paint.) chiaro-oscuro, clare-obscure.

clairon, *n.m.*, clarion ; (nav.) clear spot in a cloudy sky.

clairsemé, -e, *adj.*, thin, thinly sown, scarce.

clairvoyance, *n.f.*, sharpness, acuteness ; clear-sightedness ; clairvoyance.

clairvoyant, -e, *adj.*, clear-sighted, discerning, perspicacious, sharp, acute ; clairvoyant.

clameur, *n.f.*, clamour, outcry.

clan, *n.m.*, clan. *Chef de — :* chieftain of a clan. *Membre d'un — ;* clansman.

clandestin, -e, *adj.*, clandestine, secret, underhand.

clandestine, *n.f.*, (bot.) motherwort.

clandestinement (-ti-n-mǎn), *adv.*, clandestinely, privately, underhand.

clandestinité. *n.f.*, clandestineness.

clape. *n.f.*, (mec.) sluice.

clapet, *n.m.*, valve, clapper, clack.

clapier, *n.m.*, wild rabbit's burrow ; hutch (for tame rabbits—*pour lapins domestiques*).

se **clapir**, *v.r.*, (of rabbits—*lapins*) to hide one's self in a hole, to squat.

clapotage, *n.m.*, rippling, chopping (of the sea—*de la mer*).

clapoter, *v.n.*, to ripple, to chop (of the sea —*de la mer*).

clapoteu-x, -se, *adj.*, rippling ; (nav.) sugar-loaf (of the sea—*de la mer*).

clapotis, *n.m. V.* **clapotage**.

clappement (klap-mǎn), *n.m.*, clacking (of the tongue against the palate—*de la langue contre le palais*.)

clapper, *v.n.*, to clack (of the tongue—*la langue*).

claque, *n.f.*, flap, slap, smack ; claque, paid clappers at theatres ; *pl.*, clogs, galoches.

claque, *n.m.*, opera hat.

claquedent, *n.m.*,(l.u.) poor wretch, beggar, shivering with cold (in contempt—*par mépris*) ; confounded chatterer ; boaster, braggart.

claquement (klak-mǎn), *n.m.*, clapping ; snapping (of the fingers—*des doigts*) ; cracking (of whips—*de fouets*) ; chattering (of the teeth—*des dents*).

claquemurer, *v.a.*, to immure, to coop up.

se **claquemurer**, *v.r.*, to shut one's self up.

*****claque-oreille**, *n.m.* (——*s*), (pop.) flapped hat.

claquer, *v.n.*, to snap, crack ; to clap, to smack, to clack. *Faire —;* to crack (a whip—*un fouet*), to snap (one's fingers—*les doigts*), to smack (one's tongue—*la langue*). — *des mains;* to clap hands. — *des dents;* to chatter with one's teeth. (fig.) *Faire — son fouet;* to boast.

claquer, *v.a.*, to slap, to smack ; (fig.) to applaud.

claquet, *n.m.*, mill-clapper.

claquette, *n.f.*, clapper.

claqueur, *n.m.*, clapper.

clarification, *n.f.*, clarification, clarifying.

clarificatoire, *adj.*, clarifying.

clarifier, *v.a.*, to clarify, to purify.

se **clarifier**, *v.r.*, to clarify, to get clarified.

clarine, *n.f.*, little bell (attached to the neck of cattle—*pour les bestiaux*).

clarinette, *n.f.*, (mus.) clarinet, clarionet.

clarté, *n.f.*, light, splendour, clearness, transparency, brightness ; perspicuity.

classe, *n.f.*, class, order, rank ; tribe ; form (in a grammar-school—*dans les écoles*) ; schoolroom, school-time ; *pl.*, school-days. *En —;* in school. *Basses —s ;* junior classes. *Hautes —s, —s supérieures;* upper classes (of schools—*dans les écoles*). *Il a fait toutes ses —s;* he has gone through all the forms. *L'ouverture des —s;* the opening of the schools. *Hautes —s :* higher classes (of society—*de la société*).

classement (klas-mǎn), *n.m.*, classing, classification.

classer. *v.a.*, to class.

classicisme, *n.m.*, classicism.

classification, *n.f.*, classification.

classifier, *v.a.*, to classify.

classique, *adj.*, classic, academical ; standard (of authors, books—*de livres*).

classique, *n.m.*, classic.

clatir, *v.n.*, (hunt.) to blab (of dogs—*des chiens*).

claude, *n.m.* and *adj.*, (fam.) simpleton, doit : doltish ; silly.

claudication. *n.f.*, claudication, lameness, limping.

claudicant, -e, *adj.*, lame, limping.

clause, *n.f.*, clause, condition,

claustral, -e, *adj.*, claustral; monastical.
clavaire, *n.f.,* (bot.) club-top.
clavé, -e, *adj.*, (bot.) club-like.
claveau, *n.m.,* rot, scab (of the sheep—*des moutons*); (arch.) key-stone.
clavecin (klav-sin), *n.m.,* harpsichord.
⊙**claveciniste,** *n m.,* harpsichord-player.
clavelé, -e, *adj.*, (vet.) that has the rot.
clavelée, *n.f.,* rot, scab (of the sheep—*des moutons*).
clavette, *n.f.,* (tech.) collar; key.
clavicule, *n.f.,* clavicle, collar-bone.
claviculé, -e, *adj.*, (zool.) having a collar-bone.
clavier, *n.m.,* key-board, key-frame; key-ring.
claviforme, *adj.*, (bot.) clavate, club-shaped.
claymore. *n.f.,* claymore.
clayon. *n.m.,* stand (for cheese, preserves, &c.—*pour fromages, &c.*).
clayonnage. *n.m.,* wicker; basket-work.
clef (klé), *n.f.,* key; plug (of cocks—*de robinets*); (arch.) crown; fid (of masts—*de mâts*); (nav.) hitch. *Un trousseau de —s ;* a bunch of keys. — *de voute;* key-stone of a vault. *Fermer une porte à —;* to lock a door. *La grammaire est la — des sciences;* grammar is the key of the sciences. *Mettre la — sur la fosse ;* to relinquish an inheritance. *La — est à la porte;* the key is in the door. —(mus.); clef.
clématite. *n.f.,* (bot.) clematis, climber.
clémence. *n.f.,* clemency, mercy.
clément, -e, *adj.*, clement, merciful.
clémentines. *n.f. pl.,* Clementines (the constitutions of Clement the Fifth.
clenche, *or* **clenchette,** *n.f.,* thumb-lift of a latch. — (mus.); clef.
clephte, *n.m.,* free Greek mountaineer.
clepsydre, *n.f.,* clepsydra.
clerc (klèr), *n.m.,* clerk, clergyman ; scholar. *Petit —;* junior clerk; *maître —;* head-clerk (of lawyers—*de gens de loi*). *Pas de —;* blunder. *Ce n'est pas un grand —;* he is no conjuror.
clergé. *n.m.,* clergy.
⊙**clergeon** (-jon). *n.m.,* junior clerk (of attorneys. notaries—*de gens de loi*).
⊙**clergie.** *n.f.,* clergy. learning, scholarship. *Bénéfice de —;* benefit of clergy.
clérical, -e, *adj.*, clerical.
cléricalement (-kal-mān), *adv.,* clerically.
cléricature, *n.f.,* clerkship; ministry, holy orders.
cléristère. *n.m.,* (arch.) clear story.
clichage, *n.m.,* stereotyping. stereotype.
cliché. *n.m.,* stereotype plate.
clicher, *v.a.,* to stereotype.
clicheur, *n.m.,* stereotyper.
clic-clac, *n.m.,* click-clack, crack (the sharp sound of a whip—*bruit sec du fouet*).
client. *n.m.,* **-e,** *n.f.,* dependant ; client (of lawyers—*de gens de loi*); patient (of physicians—*de médecins*); customer (of tradesmen—*de commerçants*).
clientèle. *n.f.,* clients; practice (of physicians—*de médecins*); (Rom. antiq.) protection, patronage, dependents ; business ; custom (of tradesmen—*de marchands*); connexion. *Se faire une —;* to form a connexion.
clifoire. *n.f.,* squirt (toy—*jouet*).
*****clignement,** *n.m.,* winking, blinking.
⊙*****cligne-musette.** *n.f.,* (n.p.) hide and seek.
*****cligner,** *v.a.,* to blink, to wink (the eyes—*les yeux*).
*****clignotant. -e,** *adj.*, winking, blinking.
*****clignotement** (kli-gnot-mān), *n.m.,* winking, twinkling, blinking.
*****clignoter,** *v.n.,* to wink, to twinkle, to blink.
climat. *n.m.,* climate, clime.
climatérique, *adj.*, climateric.

climatérique. *n.f.,* climateric. *La grande —;* the great climateric.
climax (-maks), *n.m ,* (l.u.) (rhet.) climax.
clin. *n.m.,* wink (of an eye—*d'œil*). *Faire un — d'œil à quelqu'un ;* to wink to any one. *En un — d'œil;* in the twinkling of an eye.
*****clincaille, clincaillerie, clincaillier.** *V* **quincaille, quincaillerie, quincaillier.**
clinique, *adj ,* clinic, clinical.
clinique, *n.f.,* clinical surgery, clinical medicine.
clinquant, *n.m.,* tinsel; glitter; foil.
cliquart, *n.m.,* a sort of Portland-stone.
clique. *n.f.,* gang, party, clan ; clique.
cliquet, *n.m ,* click ; catch (to prevent a wheel turning the wrong way—*pour empêcher une roue de tourner dans un certain sens*)
cliqueter (klik-té), *v.n.,* to clack, to click.
cliquetis (klik-ti), *n.m.,* clanking of arms, rattling, jingle.
cliquette (kli-kèt), *n.f.,* snappers.
clisse, *n.f.,* wicker mat; (surg.) splint.
clissé, -e. *adj.*, enclosed in wicker. *Bouteille —e ;* bottle enclosed in wicker.
clitoris (-rî), *n.m.,* (anat.) clitoris.
clivage, *n.m.,* (min.) cleavage.
cliver, *v.a.,* to cleave (diamonds—*diamants*).
cloaque, *n.m.,* sink; receptacle of filth ; filthy person; (anat.) cloaca.
cloaque, *n.f.,* (antiq.) common sewer, drain.
cloche, *n f.,* bell ; blister (on the hands, feet —*aux mains, aux pieds*); cover, dish-cover ; (cook.) stew-pan ; (gard.) bell-glass, hand-glass ; (chem. phys.) receiver — *de plongeur ;* diving-bell. *Tinter les —s ;* to toll the bells.
clochement (klosh-mān), *n.m.,* hobbling, halting.
cloche-pied, *n.m.* (n.p.), hopping on one leg. *A —;* upon one foot, hopping. *Aller à —;* to hop.
clocher, *n.m.,* steeple, belfry ; parish. *Course au —;* steeple-chase.
clocher, *v.n.,* to halt, to limp, to hobble. — *du pied droit;* to limp with the right foot. *Raisonnement qui cloche ;* lame argument.
clocher, *v.a.,* (gard.) to cover with a glass-bell.
clocheton. *n.m.,* little steeple, bell-turret.
clochette, *n.f.,* small bell, hand-bell ; (bot.) bell-flower.
cloison. *n.f.,* partition (of boards or masonry — *de bois ou de maçonnerie*); (anat., bot.) partition.
cloisonnage, *n.m.,* partition-work.
cloisonné, -e, *adj.*, (bot.) valved ; (conch.) chambered.
cloître, *n.m.,* cloister.
cloîtré, -e. *adj.*, cloistered (of a person—*des personnes*).
cloîtrer. *v.a.,* to shut up in a cloister, to cloister, to immure.
cloîtrier, *n.m.,* cloisteral monk.
clopin-clopant, *adv.,* limpingly.
clopiner, *v.n.,* to limp, to halt.
cloporte, *n.m.,* (ent.) multiped, woodlouse.
cloque. *n.f.,* (agri.) brown rust.
clore. *v.a.,* to enclose, to fence, to shut in ; to end, to finish, to conclude ; to close (accounts, discussions, a session—*comptes ; discussions ; sessions*).
clore, *v.n.,* to close, to shut.
clos, -e, *part.,* closed, tight, shut. *A huis —;* with closed doors. *Bouche —e ;* hush for that. *Champ —;* lists. *Ce sont lettres —es ;* that's a secret.
clos, *n.m.,* close, enclosure, field.
closeau, *n.m.,* peasant's garden enclosed by hedges.

closerie, *n.f.*, small close.

clossement, *n.m* V. **gloussement**.

closser, *v.n.* V. **glousser**.

clôture, *n.f.*, enclosure, fence; seclusion (of nuns—*de nonnes*); closing, close. *Mettre une* —; to enclose.

clôturer, *v.a.*, (jur., parliament) to close.

clou, *n.m.*, nail; stud (with a large head —*à grosse tête*); (med.) furuncle, boil; clove. — *à crochet*; tenter-hook. —*s à vis*; clincher-nails. *Enfoncer un* —; to drive a nail. *River le* — *à quelqu'un*; to clinch any one's argument.

clouer, *v.a.*, to nail; to fix; to detain, to confine.

se **clouer**, *v.r.*, to apply one's self; to be nailed (of a thing—*des choses*).

clouter, *v.a.*, to adorn with studs, to stud.

clouterie (-trî), *n.f.*, nail manufactory, nail-trade.

cloutier(-tié), *n.m.*, nail-maker, nail-dealer.

cloutière, *n.f.*, anvil for making nails.

clovisse, *n.m.*, (conch.) winkle.

cloyère, *n.f.*, oyster-basket.

club, *n.m.*, club, assembly.

clubiste, *n.m.*, member of a club.

clysoir, *n.m.*, clyster-pipe.

clystère, *n.m.*, injection, clyster, enema.

clystériser, *v.a.*, (jest.) to give clysters.

cnique (knik), *n.m.*, (bot.) horse-thistle.

co (prefix used in composition, signifying *with, conjointly*), co.

coaccusé, *n.m.*, **-e**, *n.f.*, fellow-prisoner.

coacquéreur, *n.m.*, co-purchaser, co-buyer; joint buyer.

coacti-f, **-ve**, *adj.*, coactive, coercive.

coaction, *n.f.*, coaction.

coadjut-eur, *n.m.*, **-trice**, *n.f.*, coadjutor, coadjutrix.

coadjutorerie (-torî), *n.f.*, coadjutorship.

coadné, **-e**, *adj.*, (bot.) joined.

coadunation, *n.f.*, coadunition.

coagulant, **-e**, *adj.*, coagulative.

coagulation, *n.f.*, coagulation, congealing.

coaguler, *v.a.*, to coagulate, to congeal.

se **coaguler**, *v.r.*, to coagulate, to congeal.

coagulum (-lom), *n.m.*, (chem.) coagulum.

coalescence, *n.f.*, coalescence.

coalescent, **-e**, *adj.*, coalescent.

se **coaliser**, *v.r.*, to coalesce.

coalition, *n.f.*, coalition.

⊙ **coalitionner**, *v.a.*, to form a coalition.

coassement (ko-as-män), *n.m.*, croaking (of frogs—*des grenouilles*).

coasser, *v.n.*, to croak (of frogs—*des grenouilles*).

coassocié, *n.m.*, (com.) co-partner.

coati, *n.m.*, (mam.) coati.

cobæa, *n.m.*, (bot.) cobæa.

cobaye, *n.m.*, guinea-pig.

cobalt, *n.m.*, (min.) cobalt.

cobelligérant, **-e**, *adj.*, cobelligerent.

cobit, *n.m.*, (ich.) cobitis, loach.

cobourgeois, *n.m.*, co-partner in a ship.

cobra-capello, *n.m.*, (—), cobra de capello, hooded-snake, spectacle-snake.

coca, *n.m.*, (bot.) coca, erythroxylon coca.

*****cocagne**, *n.f.*, the land of plenty, of milk and honey. ⊙ *Donner une* —; to give a feast to the people. *Mât de* —; greasy pole. *Pays de* —; country where things are to be had for the asking.

cocarde, *n.f.*, cockade.

cocasse, *adj.*, (pop.) odd, laughable, ridiculous.

cocatrix, *n.m.*, cockatrice.

coccinelle, *n.f.*, (ent.) lady-bird, lady-cow.

coccoloba, *n.m.* (—), (bot.) grape-tree.

cocoyx (kok-sis), *n.m.*, (anat.) coccyx.

coche, *n.m.*, barge; coach. — *d'eau*; barge (for travelling—*pour voyageurs*). *Manquer le* —; to let slip the opportunity.

coche, *n.f.*, notch; sow, she-pig. *Faire une* —; to notch.

*****cochenillage**, *n.m.*, cochineal.

*****cochenille** (kosh-). *n.f.*, cochineal.

*****cocheniller**, *v.a.*, to dye with cochineal.

*****cochenillier**, *n.m.*, cochineal-fig.

cocher, *n.m.*, coachman; (astron.) Auriga — *de fiacre, de cabriolet*; hackney coachman, cabman.

côcher, *v.a.*, to tread (of birds—*des oiseaux*).

cochère, *adj.f.*, carriage. *Porte* —; carriage-entrance, gate.

cochet, *n.m.*, young cock.

cochevis (kosh-vi), *n.m.*, crested lark.

cochléaria (-klé-), *n.m.*, (bot.) cochlearia, scurvy-grass.

cochon, *n.m.*, hog, pig, boar, poker; (metal.) sow, pig. dross. — *de lait*; sucking-pig. — *d'Inde*; Guinea-pig. *C'est un* —; he is a dirty fellow. *Avoir gardé les* —*s ensemble*; to be hail fellows well met.

cochonnée, *n.f.*, litter (of pigs).

cochonner, *v.n.*, to farrow, to pig. *v.a.*, to do a thing in a slovenly manner, to botch.

cochonnerie (ko-sho-n-rî), *n.f.* nastiness, filth; beastliness, beastly action *en* language, obscenity; trash, rubbish.

cochonnet, *n.m.*, die with twelve sides; jack (at bowls—*jeu de boule*).

coco, *n.m.*, cocoa, cocoa-nut; liquorice-water.

cocon, *n.m.*, cocoon.

cocorli, *n.m.*, (orni.) dunlin; purr; sea-lark.

cocotier (-tié), *n.m.*, cocoa-tree.

cocréancier, *n.m.*, joint-creditor.

cocréte, *n.f.*, (bot.) yellow-rattle. — *des prés*; lousewort.

coction, *n.f.*, coction, boiling.

cocu, *n.m.*, (l.ex.) cuckold.

cocuage, *n.m.*, (l.ex.) cuckoldom.

cocufier, *v.a.*, (l.ex.) to cuckold.

code, *n.m.*, code, collection of laws; law; (phar.) ⊙ dispensatory.

codébit-eur, *n.m.*, **-rice**, *n.f.*, joint-debtor.

codécimateur, *n.m.*, fellow tithe-owner.

codemandeur, *n.m.*, co-plaintiff, joint plaintiff.

codétenteur, *n.m.*, joint-holder.

codex (-dèks), *n.m.*, (pharm.) dispensatory.

codicillaire, *adj.*, contained in a codicil.

codicille, *n.m.*, codicil.

codification, *n.f.*, codification.

codifier, *v.a.*, to codify.

*****codille**, *n.m.*, codille (at ombre).

codonataire, *n.m.f.*, joint donor.

cœcum, *n.m.* V. **cæcum**.

coefficient, *n.m.*, (alg.) coefficient.

coégal, **-e**, *adj.*, coequal.

coégalité, *n.f.*, coequality.

coemption, *n.f.*, coemption.

coéquation, *n.f.*, assessment of taxes.

coercibilité, *n.f.*, (phys.) coercibleness.

coercible, *adj.*, coercible.

coerciti-f, **-ve**, *adj.*, coercive.

coercition, *n.f.*, coercion.

coéternel, **-le**, *adj.*, coeternal.

coéternité, *n.f.*, coeternity.

cœur (keur), *n.m.*, heart, mind, soul; courage, spirit, spiritedness, mettle; stomach; core; depth; hearts (cards—*cartes*); middle, midst. *Mal au* —; qualm. *Serrement de* —; heartburn. *Du fond de son* —; from the bottom of one's heart. *Au* — *dur*; hard-hearted. *De* —; from one's heart, with all one's might. *Avoir le* — *contrit*; to be of a contrite heart. *Le* — *lui saigne*; his heart bleeds. *Avoir à* —, *prendre à*

— : to have at heart, to take anything to heart. *Cela lui tient au —* ; that lies heavy upon his heart. *Avoir quelque chose sur le —* , to have something heavy on one's mind. *Le — me le disait bien* ; my heart misgave me *Si le — vous en dit* ; if you like it. *Il a le — au métier* ; he loves his business. *Il a le — porté à cela* ; he is inclined to it *Avoir le — tendre* ; to be tender-hearted. *Il a le — bien placé* ; his heart is in the right place. *Il n'a point de —* ; he has no spirit. *Sans —* ; heartless. *Avoir le — bas* ; to be mean-spirited. *Avoir le — sur les lèvres* ; to be open-hearted. *Soulèvement de —* ; rising of the stomach. *J'ai mal au —* ; I am sick. *Avoir le — mort* ; to be sick at heart. *Ouvrir, décharger, son — à quelqu'un* ; to unbosom one's self to one. *Il en a le — net* ; he has eased his mind of it. *Au — de l'hiver* ; in the depth of winter. *À contre- —* ; against one's will. *De bon —* ; heartily. *De tout mon —* ; with all my heart. *De gaîté de —* ; in gaiety of heart; wantonly. *Apprendre quelque chose par —* ; to learn a thing by heart. *Dîner par —* ; to dine with Duke Humphrey. *Tant que le — me battra* ; to the last drop of my blood. *Tenir au —* ; to stick in one's stomach. *Avoir le — brisé* ; to be broken-hearted. *Avoir le — fendu* ; to be cut to the heart.

coexistant, -e., *adj.* co-existent.
coexistence. *n.f.,* co-existence.
coexister. *v.n.,* to co-exist.
coffre. *n.m.,* chest, trunk, coffer: (hunt.) carcase; drum (of a mill—*de moulin*); (print.) coffin. — *de sûreté* : strong box. — *de bord* ; sea-chest. *Elle est belle au —* ; she has golden charms. *Un — -fort (—s —s)* ; a strong box. *Avoir le — bon* ; to have a good chest.
coffrer, *v.a.,* (fam.) to imprison.
coffret, *n.m.,* little chest or trunk.
coffretier (-tié), *n.m.,* trunk-maker.
cofidéjusseur, *n.m.,* joint security.
*****cognasse.** *n.f.,* wild quince.
*****cognassier.** *n.m.,* wild quince-tree.
cognat. *n.m.,* cognate.
cognation. *n.f.,* cognation.
*****cognée.** *n.f.,* axe, hatchet. *Mettre la — à l'arbre* ; to lay the axe to the tree; to begin an enterprise. *Aller au bois sans —* ; to go to sea without biscuit.
*****cogne-fétu,** *n.m.* (—, *or* — —s), (pop.) person busy for nothing.
*****cogner,** *v.a.,* to knock in, drive in.
*****se cogner.** *v.r.,* to knock, to hit, to strike.
cogniti-f, -ve, *adj.,* (philos.) capable of knowing.
*****cognoir,** *n.m.,* (print.) shooting-stick.
cohabitation, *n.f.,* cohabitation.
cohabiter, *v.n.,* to cohabit.
cohérence, *n.f.,* coherency.
coherent, -e, *adj.,* coherent.
cohériter, *v.n.,* to inherit conjointly with one or more persons.
cohériti-er, *n.m.,* **-ère,** *n.f.,* co-heir, co-heiress.
cohésion. *n.f.,* cohesion.
cohobation, *n.f.,* (chem.) cohobation.
cohober, *v.a.,* (chem.) to cohobate.
cohorte. *n.f.,* cohort, band, crew, troop.
cohue. *n.f.,* rout, mob, tumultuous crowd, clamorous multitude.
coi, -te, *adj.,* quiet, still, snug.
coiffe, *n.f.,* head dress; caul (of children—*pour enfants*); skull-cap; net; (hot.) galla. — *de chapeau* : lining of a hat.
coiffer, *v.a.,* to put (anything) on one's head; to dress the hair; to infatuate; to throw at any one's head: to make tipsy: (hunt.) to take by the ears; (nav.) to back: to cap (bottles—*bouteilles*); (arch.) to cap. *Être bien*

coiffé : to have one's hair well dressed ; to have a hat that becomes one, and fits well, *Enfant né coiffé* ; child born with a caul upon its head. *Il est né coiffé*: he is born to a good fortune. *sainte Catherine* ; to remain an old maid. *Du vin coiffé* ; mixed wine. — *une bouteille* ; to cap a bottle. *Chien bien coiffé* : dog with a handsome head and long ears. *Cette femme coiffe son mari* ; that woman cuckolds her husband. *Il est coiffé de cette femme* ; he is bewitched with that woman. — *une voile* ; to back a sail.
se coiffer, *v.r.,* to wear (on one's head—*sur la tête*); to dress one's hair; to get intoxicated; to be infatuated with; (nav.) to be taken aback. — *de faux cheveux* : to wear false hair. — *en cheveux* (of a woman—*des femmes*); to wear no cap.
coiffer. *v.n.,* to dress hair; to become; (nav.) to be taken aback.
coiffeu-r, *n.m.,* **-se,** *n.f.,* hairdresser.
coiffure, *n.f.,* head-dress.
coin. *n.m.,* corner, angle, nook, coin; (coin.) stamp; (railways) pin ; (print.) quoin ; clock (of stockings—*des bas*); (tech) gad ; (mec) wedge. *Il n'a pas bougé du — du feu* ; he has never been from home, he has seen nothing of the world.
coïncidence, *n.f.,* coincidence.
coïncident, *adj.,* coincident.
coïncider, *v.n.,* to coincide, to be coincident.
coïndication, *n.f.,* (med.) coindication.
coing (coin), *n.m.,* quince.
coïntéressé, *n.m.,* associate, party having a common interest with another.
coïon. *n.m,* (l.ex.) dastard, dastardly wretch, coward.
coïonner. *v.a.,* (l.ex.) to use one scurvily, to make a fool of one; to call one a coward.
coïonner, *v.n.,* (l ex.) to joke.
coïonnerie (ko-io-n-rî), *n.f.,* (l.ex.) dastardliness, sneakingness; a mean, low action ; bad joke.
coït. *n.m* , coition.
coïte. *n.f.* V. **couette.**
cojouissance, *n.f.,* joint use.
coke, *n.m.,* coke.
col. *n.m.,* neck (of the body—*du corps*); cravat; neck (of bottles; of mountains—*de bouteilles, de montagnes*); pad, stiffener; collar. *Faux —* : collar. — *droit* ; stand-up collar. — *de cravate* : stiffener. — *de la vessie, de la matrice*: neck of the bladder, of the womb.
colarin, *n.m.,* (arch.) gorgerin.
colas, *n.m.,* vulgar name for the raven; a stupid man.
colature, *n.f.,* (pharm.) colature.
colback, *n.m.,* colback (military cap—*coiffure militaire*).
colchique, *n.m.,* meadow-saffron, colchicum.
colcotar, *n.m.,* (chem.) colcothar.
colégataire, *n.m.,* co-legatee.
coléoptère, *adj.,* coleopterous; *n.m.,* coleopter.
coléoptères, *n.m. pl.,* coleoptera.
colère, *n.f.,* passion, anger, wrath, rage, fury. *Accès de —* : fit of passion. *Être en —* : to be angry. *Se mettre en —* ; to get into a passion.
colère, *adj.,* passionate, hasty, choleric.
colérique, *adj.,* choleric, irascible, passionate.
coliart, *n.m.,* (ich.) skate.
colibri. *n.m.,* humming-bird.
colicitant, *n.m.,* (jur.) colitigant.
colifichet, *n.m.,* knick-knack, gew-gaw, trifle, trumpery, toy.

colimaçon, *n.m.*, snail.

colin, *n.m.*, (ich.) coal-fish.

*colin-maillard, *n.m* (*n.p.*), blindman's-buff; blindman (at blindman's-buff); bird-cake

colin-tampon, *n.m.* (*n.p.*), a Swiss beating of drum. (pop) *Je m'en moque comme de —* ; I do not care a fig about it.

colique. *n.f..* colic, griping ; stomach-ache; *pl* , after-pains. — *saturnine* ; painter's colic.

colis, *n.m.*, package.

colisée. *n.m.*, Coliseum, Colosseum.

collaborat-eur. *n.m.*, **-rice**. *n.f.*, (kol-la-), fellow-labourer, assistant. contributor

collaboration (kol-la-), *n.f.*, assistance, contribution.

collaborer, *v.n.*, (of authors, writers— *d'écrivains*) to work together.

collage, *n.m.*, pasting, gluing, sizing (of paper—*de papier*), paper-hanging.

collant, -e. *adj* , tight, close-fitting.

collapsus (-sus), *n.m.*, (med.) collapse.

collataire (kol-la-tè-r), *n.m.*, one who has been collated to a benefice.

collatéral, -e (kol-la-), *adj* , collateral.

collatéral, *n.m.*, (jur.) collateral

⊙**collatérale**, *n.f.*, aisle (of churches— *d'églises*).

collatéralement, *adv* , (jur.) collaterally.

collateur (kol-la-). *n.m..* collator.

collati-f. -ve (kol-la-), *adj.*, collative.

collation (kol-la-cion), *n.f.*, collation.

collation (ko-la-cion), *n.f.*, collation (a light repast—*repas léger*).

collationner (kol-la-cio-né), *v.a.*, to collate, to compare.

collationner (ko-la-cio-né), *v.n.* , to make a light repast ; to take a collation.

colle, *n.f.*, paste, glue ; sham. fib, bouncer, cracker. — *forte* ; glue. — *à bouche* ; mouth-glue. — *de poisson*, isinglass. *Donner une — à quelqu'un* ; to tell any one a fib.

collecte (kol-lèkt), *n.f.*, gathering; collection (of money—*d'argent*) ; collect (prayer— *prière*).

collecteur(ko-lèk-teur),*n.m.*, collector, tax-gatherer.

collecti-f. -ve (kol-lèk-), *adj.*, collective.

collectif (kol-lèk-), *n.m* , collective noun.

collection(kol-lèk-cion), *n.f.*,collection; set.

collectionner (kol-lèk-cio-né), *v.a* , to collect, to make collections of things.

collectionneu-r (kol-lèk-cio-), *n m* , **-se**, *n.f.*, collector.

collectivement (kol-lèk-tiv-man), *adv* , collectively.

collège, *n.m.*, college, school. — *électoral*, assembly of electors; constituency.

collégial, -e *adj.*, collegial ; collegiate. *Église —e* ; a collegiate church.

collégiale, *n.f.*, collegiate church.

collégialement, *adv.*, scholastically.

collégien (-ji-in), *n.m.*, collegian.

collègue (kol-lèg), *n.m.*, colleague.

collement, *n.m.*, (med.) cohesion. — *des paupières*; cohesion of the eyelids.

coller, *v.a.*, to paste; to glue; to size; to stick together ; to clear (with isinglass—*avec de la colle de poisson*); to stump (embarrass any one —*embarrasser*); to hang (paper-hangings— *papier de tenture*).

se coller, *v.r.*, to stick to; to cake; to apply closely to.

coller, *v.n.*, to stick, to adhere; to fit tight (of clothes—*des vêtements*). *Ce pantalon colle bien*; those trousers fit nicely.

collerette (kol-rèt), *n.f.*, collar (for ladies— *de dame*) ; (bot.) involucrum; (tech.) flange.

collet, *n m.*, collar (of a gown, coat—*d'une robe, d'un habit*); cape; bands (for the neck— *pour le cou*); neck (of teeth—*des dents*); (hunt.)

snare ; crown (of anchors—*d'ancres*): (tech.) collet; clergyman. — *montant* ; stand-up collar. — *rabattu* ; laid-down collar. *Petit —* ; one of the cloth, young clergyman. — *monté* : buckram collar. *L'n — monté* ; a person of great affected gravity. — *de mouton* ; neck of mutton. *Prendre, saisir, quelqu'un au —* ; to collar one. *Prêter le — à quelqu'un* ; to cope with one.

colleté.*part.*, (her.) having acollar of another enamel than the body (of animals—*des animaux*).

colleter (kol-té), *v.a.*, to collar one, to seize one by the neck.

se colleter, *v.r* , to collar each other ; to lay hold of each other by the collar.

colleter, *v.n.*, to set snares (for game—*à gibier*).

colleteur, *n.m.*, one who lays snares (for game—*pour le gibier*); (pop) wrangler, fighter.

colleur, *n.m.*, paper-hanger; gluer; paster; bill-sticker; sizer.

collier, *n.m.*, collar ; ring (mark round the neck of certain animals—*marque autour du cou de certains animaux*); bow (of spurs—*des éperons*); (arch , tech.) collar ; necklace. *Cheval de —*; draught-horse. — *de misère*; drudgery. *Donner un coup de —* ; to make a fresh attempt.

⊙**colliger**, *v.a* , to collect passages (of books— *de livres*).

colline, *n.f.*, hill, hillock. *La double —*; Parnassus. *Gagner la —* ; to take to one's heels.

colliquati-f. -ve (kol-li-koua-),*adj.*, (med.) colliquative.

colliquation (kol-li-koua-), *n.f.*, (med.) col-liquation, melting.

collision (kol-li-). *n.f.*, collision.

collocation (kol-lo-), *n.f.*, collocation; setting in order, rank. — *de l'argent*; investing of money.

collodion, *n.m.*, collodion.

colloque (kol-lok), *n.m.*, colloquy, confer-ence, dialogue.

colloquer (kol-lo-ké), *v.a.*, to rank, to place in order; to place.

colluder (kol-lu-dé), *v.n.*, to collude.'

collusion (kol-lu-zion), *n.f.*, collusion, pre-varication. *User de —* ; to prevaricate.

collusoire (kol-lu-zoar), *adj* , collusory, collusive.

collusoirement (kol-lu-zoar-mān), *adv* , collusively.

collyre, *n.m.*, (med.) collyrium, eye-salve.

colmatage. *n.m.*, (agri.) the rising of the level of low-lying lands by means of the mud left by water.

colombage, *n.m.*, (carp) wooden front.

colombe, *n.f.*, dove; (carp.) joist (of a par-tition—*d'une cloison*).

colombier, *n.m.*, dove-cot, pigeon-house; (print.) pigeon-hole, gap. *Faire venir les pigeons au —* ; to bring fish to one's net. —*;* a sort of paper.

colombin, -e *adj.*, columbine, dove-colour.

colombin, *n.m.*, (min.) lead ore; (orni.) stock-dove.

colombine, *n.f.*, pigeon-dung, fowls'-dung; (bot.) columbine.

colombo, *n.m.*, (bot.) calumba, colombo.

colon, *n.m.*, colonist, planter; cultivator ; West Indian settler.

côlon, *n.m.*, (anat.) colon.

colonel, *n.m.*, colonel. *Grade de —;* coloneley.

⊙**colonelle**, *n.f.* and *adj.*, the colonel's company ; of the colonel's company.

colonial, -e *adj.*, colonial.

colonie, *n.f.*, colony, settlement.

colonisation, *n.f.*, colonizing, colonization.

coloniser, *v.a.*, to establish a colony, to colonize.

colonnade, *n.f.*, (arch.) colonnade.

colonne. *n.f.*, column ; pillar ; bed-post ; row (of units, tens—*d'unités, de dizaines, &c.*) ; (milit., nav., phys., print., arch.) column. — *cannelée* ; fluted column. — *plaquée* ; pilaster. — *torse* ; wreathed column.

colonnette, *n.f.*, little column.

colophane, *n.f.*, black rosin, colophony.

coloquinte, *n.f.*, colocynth ; bitter apple.

colorant, **-e**, *adj.*, colouring.

coloration. *n.f.*, colouration.

coloré. **-e**, *part.*, coloured. *Vin* — ; deep-coloured wine. *Teint* — ; fresh-coloured complexion.

colorer. *v.a.*, to colour, to dye ; to varnish ; to colour (to give a false appearance to—*donner une fausse apparence*).

se colorer, *v.r.*, to colour (of a thing—*des choses*).

coloriage, *n.m.*, (paint.) colouring.

colorier, *v.a.*, to colour (engravings, &c.—*estampes, &c.*).

coloris. *n.m.*, colour ; (paint.) colouring.

coloriste, *n m.*, colourer ; colourist.

colossal, **-e**, *adj.*, colossal, giant-like. *Des statues —es* ; colossal statues. [Has no plural masculine.]

colosse. *n.m.*, colossus, giant.

colostrum, *n.m.* (*n.p.*), (med.) colostrum.

colportage, *n.m.*, hawking ; peddling ; pedlery.

colporter, *v.a.*, to hawk about ; to retail, to spread. — *une nouvelle* ; to retail a piece of news.

colporteur, *n.m.*, hawker, pedler.

colure, *n.m.*, (astron., geog.) colure.

colza. *n.m.*, colza, field-cabbage.

columelle, *n.f.*, (bot.) columella.

coma. *n.m.*, (med.) coma.

comateu-x. **-se**. *adj.*, comatose.

combat (kon-ba). *n.m.*, combat, fight, battle ; fighting ; contest, action, engagement, struggle ; strife, warring. — *singulier* ; single combat. — *à outrance* ; mortal combat. — *égal* ; drawn battle. — *simulé* ; sham fight. *Au fort du* — ; in the thick of the fight. *Être hors de* — ; to be disabled. *Faire branle-bas de* — ; (nav.) to clear for action.

combattable. *adj.*, combatable

combattant, *n.m.*, combatant, fighting man, champion ; (orni.) ruff.

combattre, *v.a.*, to fight, to combat ; to wage war against, to battle with, to dispute, to contest. — *contre une maladie* ; to struggle with a disease. — *une opinion* ; to combat an opinion.

se combattre, *v.r.*, to combat ; to contend with each other.

combattre, *v.n.*, to fight, to combat, to war, to contend, to vie with one another, to struggle. — *de politesse* ; to vie with one another in politeness.

⊙combe. *n.f.*, valley.

combien (kon-bi-in), *adv.*, how much, how many ; how ; how far ; how long ; what. *En* — *de temps ?* how long will it take ? — *y a-t-il depuis cela ?* how long is it since that ? — *raut cela ?* what is that worth ? *A* — *évaluez-vous cela ?* at how much do you value that ?

combinaison, *n.f.*, combination ; contrivance.

combinat-eur, *n.m.*, **-rice**, *n.f.*, combiner.

combiné. **-e**, *part.*, united ; (chem.) combined.

combiner, *v.a.*, to combine, to contrive.

se combiner, *v.r.*, to combine, to be contrived.

comble. *n.m.*, heaping (of measure—*de mesures*) ; consummation ; zenith, acme ; summit, height, top, complement. *Ferme des —s* (carp.) ; framing of a roof. *De fond en* — ; from

top to bottom. *Ruiné de fond en* —, utterly ruined. *La mesure est au* — ; the measure is full. *Pour* — *de gloire* ; to complete his glory.

comble, *adj.*, heaped up full to the top.

comblement, *n.m.*, act of filling up.

combler, *v.a.*, to heap, to heap up, to make up, to fill up, to crown ; to cover (deficit) ; to complete ; to overwhelm. — *de faveurs* ; to load with favours.

comblète. *n.f.*, (hunt.) cleft.

combrière, *n.f.*, tunny net.

combuger, *v.a.*, to rinse out (casks—*tonneaux*).

comburant, **-e**, *adj.*, (chem.) burning.

combustible, *adj.*, combustible.

combustible, *n.m.*, fuel, firing ; (chem.) combustible.

combustibilité, *n.f.*, combustibleness, combustibility ; (chem.) deflagrability.

combustion (kon-bus-tion), *n.f.*, combustion, conflagration.

comédie, *n.f.*, comedy, play ; play-house, theatre ; shamming, farce ; players ; play-book. *Donner la* — ; to be the laughing-stock. *Jouer une* — ; to act a play. *Le sujet, l'intrigue, le dénouement, d'une* — ; the subject, plot, catastrophe of a comedy.

comédien, *n.m.*, **-ne**, *n.f.*, (-dl-in, diè-n), comedian, actor, actress, player ; hypocrite, dissembler. *Troupe de —s*, company of actors. *—s ambulants* : strolling players.

comestible, *adj.*, eatable ; edible.

comestible, *n.m.*, eatable ; *pl.*, eatables, provisions, victuals.

cométaire, *adj.*, cometary.

comète, *n.f.*, comet ; kind of game at cards ; kind of riband ; peculiar kind of firework. *chevelue* ; haired comet. — *barbue* ; bearded comet. — *à queue* ; tailed comet. *Vin de la* — ; wine of the year 1811.

cométographie, *n.f.*, cometography

comices. *n.f*, *pl.* (antiq.) comitia.

comicial. **-e**, *adj.*, comitial.

⊙coninge, *n.f.*, (artil.) a very large bomb.

comique, *adj.*, comical, ludicrous, laughable, funny. *Le genre* — ; subjects of a comic nature, comedy. *Acteur* — ; comic actor.

comique, *n.m.*, the comic art, comedy ; comical part ; comic actor or author. *Avoir du* — *dans la figure* ; to have a comic face.

comiquement (-màn), *adv.*, in a comic manner, comically, humorously.

⊙comite, *n.m.*, overseer of a crew of galley-slaves

comité, *n.m.*, meeting of a few persons ; small party ; committee. — *permanent* ; standing committee. *La chambre formée en* — ; a committee of the whole house. *Petit* — ; a small party ; select few. *Diner en petit* — ; to have a small dinner party of intimate friends. — *de lecture* ; a committee for deciding whether or not a new play be fit for representation.

comma, *n.m.*, (print.) colon ; (mus.) comma.

command, *n.m.*, (jur.) he who has charged another to purchase for him ; principal.

commandant, *adj.*, (milit., nav.) commanding.

commandant, *n.m.*, (milit., nav.) commandant, commander. — *de place* ; governor of a fortified town. — *de la marine* ; flag-officer of the navy. — *d'une escadre* ; commodore.

commande. *n.f.*, order. *Ouvrage de* — ; work made to order. *Marchandise de* — ; goods bespoken. *Maladie de* — ; feigned sickness. *Louanges de* — ; forced praise.

commandement, *n.m.*, command, order ; word of command ; manner of commanding ; writ, order ; commandment, precept, law, rule, injunction. *Il a tout à son* — ; he has all things at command. *Il a la langue française a son —;* he is very conversant in the French tongue.

commander, *v.a.,* to command, to order. to govern ; to have the command of ; to bespeak ; to overlook. *Cette tour commande la ville ;* that tower overlooks the town.

commander, *v.n.,* to command, to rule ; to direct ; to order, to bid ; (milit., nav.) to give the word of command. *— à ses passions;* to master one's passions. *— à la route* (nav.) ; to order or direct the course of a ship.

se **commander,** *v.r.,* to control one's self.

commanderie (ko-män-drï), *n.f.,* commandery.

commandeur, *n.m.,* commander (in orders of knighthood—*dans les ordres de chevalerie*).

commanditaire, *n.m.,* sleeping partner.

commandite, *n.f.,* limited joint-stock company.

commanditer, *v.a.,* to supply the funds for a commercial undertaking, to become a sleeping partner.

comme, *adv.,* as, like ; so ; almost, nearly ; as it were, as if ; how, in what way ; so much. *— aussi ;* (jur.) and likewise. *Faites — lui ;* do like him. *— cela;* so so. *Il est — mort;* he is almost dead. *La lumière est — l'une des couleurs ;* light is, as it were, one of the colours. *— vous me traitez ,* how you treat me. *Vous voyez — il travaille;* you see how he works.

comme, *conj.,* as, seeing that, since, because.

commémoraison, *n.f.,* (c.rel.) commemoration, remembrance, mention, of a saint.

commémorati-f, -ve, *adj.,* commemorative.

commémoration (kom-mé-), *n.f.,* (c.rel.) commemoration. *La — des morts;* commemoration of the dead; All-Souls'-Day. *Faire — de quelqu'un ;* (fam.) to make mention of any one.

commémorer, *v.a.,* (neologism) to remember, to recollect.

commençant, *n.m.,* **-e,** *n.f.,* beginner, novice, tyro.

commencement (ko-mäns-män), *n.m.,* beginning, commencement ; setting in. *Au —;* in the beginning, at first. *Les —s sont toujours difficiles;* beginnings are always difficult.

commencer, *v.a.,* to begin, to commence ; to initiate, to impart the first principles to. *— quelqu'un;* to initiate, to begin with one. *— un cheval;* to begin training a horse.

commencer, *v.n.,* to commence, begin. *Lorsqu'il commença de parler;* when he began speaking. *Cet enfant commence à parler;* this child begins to speak. [*Commencer de* indicates an action which will endure; *commencer à* indicates an action which will go progressing.]

commendataire, *adj.,* (canon law—*loi canon*) commendatory.

commende, *n.f.,* (canon law—*loi canon*) commendam.

commensal, *n.m.,* **-e,** *n.f.,* habitual guest; boarder ; officer admitted to the royal table. *Être — d'une maison;* to be habitually a guest in a house. *Être commensaux;* to take one's meals together.

commensalité, *n.f.,* right of admission to the royal table.

commensurabilité, *n.f.,* (math.) commensurableness, commensurability.

commensurable, *adj.,* (math.) commensurable.

commensuration, *n.f.,* (math.) commensuration.

comment, *adv.,* how, in what manner; why, wherefore; what! indeed! *— cela?* how is that? *—! vous voulez . . . ;* what! you wish. . .

comment, *n.m.,* the reason, the why and

the wherefore. *Savoir le pourquoi et le —; ,* know the why and the wherefore.

commentaire, *n.m.,* commentary, comment, exposition; remark. *Point de —!* (fam.) no impertinent remarks!

commentateur, *n.m.,* commentator, annotator.

commenter, *v.a.,* to comment, to write comments upon, to explain, expound, annotate.

commenter, *v.n.,* to criticize; to comment on.

commérage, *n.m.,* gossiping; gossip, tittle-tattle.

commerçable, *adj.,* negotiable.

commerçant, *n.m.,* trader, merchant.

commerçant, -e, *adj.,* commercial, mercantile; trading.

commerce, *n.m.,* commerce. trade, trading, traffic; intercourse, communication, correspondence, acquaintance, communion, conversation : a game at cards. *— des colonies, — avec les colonies;* colonial trade. *Affaires de —;* mercantile affairs. *Femme de —;* tradeswoman. *Fond de —;* business. *Être dans le —;* to be in business, in trade. *Il fait un gros —;* he drives a great trade. *Chambre de —;* chamber of commerce. *— de galanterie;* intrigue. *Lier — avec quelqu'un;* to establish a correspondence with one. *Liez — avec lui;* contract an acquaintance with him. *Être d'un — sûr;* to be a person to be depended upon.

commercer, *v.n.,* to trade, to drive a trade, to traffic with.

commercial. -e, *adj.,* commercial.

commercialement, *adv.,* commercially.

commère, *n.f.,* godmother; gossip. *Cet homme est une vraie —;* that man is a regular gossip. *—, bonne —;* (fam.) a bold, cunning woman, not easily discouraged. *Accommodez-moi, ma —;* a game at cards resembling commerce.

commérer, *v.n.,* to gossip, to tittle-tattle.

commettage, *n.m.,* (nav.) laying of ropes and cables.

commettant, *n.m.,* constituent; employer ; principal; (jur.) warrantor. *Corps de —s;* constituents, constituency.

commettre, *v.a.,* to commit, to perpetrate; to appoint, to delegate, to constitute, to commission, to empower; to commit to one's charge, to entrust, to trust with, to confide; to expose ; to embroil; to set by the ears, to make mischief between ; (nav.) to lay.

se **commettre,** *v.r.,* to commit one's self; to expose one's self.

commination, *n.f.,* (rhet.) commination.

comminatoire, *adj.,* (jur.) comminatory.

comminuti-f, -ve, *adj.,* comminutive.

comminution, *n.f.,* comminution.

commis, -e, *part.,* committed, appointed, exposed ; (nav.) laid.

commis, *n.m.,* clerk; book-keeper; shopman. *Premier —;* head clerk. *— marchand;* merchant's clerk. *— voyageur;* commercial traveller. *— des vivres;* (nav.) steward.

commise, *n.f.,* (feudal jur.—*loi féodale*) forfeit, escheat.

commisération (kom-mi-), *n.f.,* commiseration.

commissaire, *n.m.,* commissary; commissioner ; manager. *— des guerres;* commissary. *— des vivres :* commissary of provisions. *— adjoint ;* deputy commissioner. *— des pauvres ;* member of a charitable board. *— aux saisies réelles;* sequestrator. *— de police;* commissary of police. *— -priseur (—s —s);* auctioneer, appraiser.

commissariat, *n.m.,* commissaryship, trusteeship; (milit.) commissariat.

commission, *n.f.*, commission, trust, charge; commission, commission-trade; errand; mandate, warrant; the holding a trust for a time only; a committee, commission. *Il est allé en —;* he is gone on an errand. *Obtenir — d'un juge;* to obtain a judge's warrant. *— rogatoire;* writ of inquiry. *— en guerre;* warrant or permission from the king to cruise against the enemy. *— d'enquête;* committee of inquiry. *Maison de —;* agency-office. *Membre d'une —;* committee-man. *En —;* (nav.) in commission. *En —;* (com.) on sale or return. *Faire les —s;* to run on errands.

commissionnaire, *n.m.*, factor; porter, errand-boy; messenger. *— de vente;* salesman. *— de roulage;* carrier, wagon office-keeper. *— chargeur;* freight commissioner.

commissionner, *v.a.*, to empower, to commission.

commissoire, *adj.*, (jur.) binding.

commissure, *n.f.*, (anat.) commissure.

commissural, *-e*, *adj.*, commissural.

committimus, *n.m.* (*n.p.*). (jur.) *Lettres de —;* chancery order appointing the court which is to take cognizance of an action.

committitur, *n.m.* (*n.p.*), (jur.) order of the president of a court of justice appointing a judge to hold an inquest.

commodat, *n.m.*, (jur.) gratuitous loan (to be repaid in kind—*d'une chose qu'il faut rendre en nature*); bailment.

commode, *adj.*, commodious, convenient; comfortable; agreeable, easy; good-natured, accommodating. *Une maison —;* a comfortable house.

commode, *n.f.*, chest of drawers, drawers.

commmodément, *adv.*, commodiously, conveniently, comfortably.

commodité, *n.f.*, convenience, accommodation; conveyance. *—s;* water-closet.

commodore, *n.m.*, (nav.) commodore.

commotion, *n.f.*, commotion; shock; (med.) concussion (of the brain—*du cerveau*).

commuable, *adj.*, commutable.

commuer, *v.a.*, (jur.) to commute.

commun, *-e*, *adj.*, common; usual, ordinary, every day; mean, vulgar. *Le sens —;* common sense. *Je n'ai rien de — avec lui;* I have nothing in common with him. *A frais —s;* jointly. *Faire bourse —e;* to have one common stock. *Lieux —s;* common places. *Le droit —;* common law. *D'une —e voix;* unanimously. *Une voix —e;* a vulgar voice. *Le bruit —;* current report. *Cette terre vaut tant de revenu an ée —e,* that land yields so much a year on an average.

commun, *n.m.*, the generality; under-servants; commonalty; common people, the vulgar, the mob. *Vivre sur le —;* to sponge. *L'âne du — est toujours le plus mal bâté;* matters of public concern are commonly neglected. *Le — des hommes;* the generality of men.

communal, *-e*, *adj.*, of the parish; parish; communal.

communauté, *n.f.*, community, society. *— de biens;* community of property (between husband and wife—*entre le mari et la femme*); (jur.) communion.

communaux, *n.m.pl.*, (jur.) pasture grounds, common.

commune, *n.f.*, commune (inhabitants); parish, township (in France); town-hall. *La chambre des —s;* the House of Commons. *Le maire d'une —;* the mayor of a commune. *Assemblée de la —;* vestry.

communément, *adv.*, commonly, usually, generally.

communiant, *n.m.*, *-e*, *n.f.*, communicant.

communicabilité, *n.f.*, communicability.

communicable, *adj.*, communicable.

communicati-f, *-ve*, *adj.*, communicative.

communication, *n.f.*, intercourse, communication. *— de pièces;* (jur.) showing cause. *La — se fait entre avoués;* the showing cause is conducted by lawyers. *En — avec;* open to (mec.).

communicativement, *adv.*, communicatively.

communier, *v.n.*, to communicate, to receive the sacrament.

communier, *v.a.*, to give the communion.

communion, *n.f.*, communion, fellowship; sacrament. *Être retranché de la — des fidèles;* to be turned out of the church, to be excommunicated. *Faire sa première —;* to receive the sacrament for the first time.

communiquer, *v.a.*, to communicate, to impart; to show, to tell, to acquaint. *se communiquer*, *v.r.*, to be communicative, to communicate with (of places—*de lieux*). *Vous vous communiquez trop;* you are too communicative.

communiquer, *v.n.*, to hold or keep up a correspondence with; (nav.) to have a free intercourse after having performed quarantine.

communisme, *n.m.*, communism.

communiste, *n.m.*, communist.

commutati-f, *-ve*, *adj.*, (jur.) commutative.

commutation, *n.f.*, (jur.) commutation.

comocladie, *n.f.*, (bot.) maiden-plum, comocladia.

compacité, *n.f.*, (phys.) compactness.

compact, *-e*, *adj.*, compact; (phys.) dense, solid.

*****compagne**, *n.f.*, female companion; consort, partner; helpmate; playmate; (of animals—*des animaux*) mate. *Fidèle —;* faithful attendant.

*****compagnie**, *n.f.*, society, company; (com.) company; (hunt.) covey; full. *— ordonnancée;* chartered company. *— de commerce;* trading company. *Il n'y a pas si bonne — qui ne se sépare;* the best of friends must part. *Sa maison est le rendez-vous de la bonne —;* his house is the resort of fashionable people. *Dame de —;* lady's companion. *Être de bonne —;* to be well-bred. *Aller en —;* to go together. *Tenir — à quelqu'un;* to keep one company. *Fausser — à quelqu'un;* to desert a company, to fail in one's appointment. *Une — de perdrix;* a covey of partridges. *Être bête de —;* to be fond of company and easily led on by others. *Former une —;* to establish a company. *Règle de —;* fellowship. *Une — d'infanterie;* a company of foot. *Une — de cavalerie;* a troop of horse. *— franche;* independent company.

*****compagnon**, *n.m.*, companion, fellow, associate, co-mate, consort, mate, partner; journeyman; play-fellow, playmate; droll fellow. *— d'école, d'étude;* school-fellow. *— de table;* messmate. *— de jeu;* play-fellow. *— de taverne;* pot-companion. *— d'armes;* companion in arms. *Joyeux —;* jolly fellow, jolly dog. *Traiter de pair à —;* to go cheek by jowl.

*****compagnonnage**, *n.m.*, the time after apprenticeship, trades-union.

comparabilité, *n.f.*, comparability.

comparable, *adj.*, comparable, to be compared.

comparaison, *n.f.*, comparison; simile, similitude. *Toute — cloche;* every comparison is lame. *Il n'y a point de — de vous à lui;* there is no comparison between you and him. *Ce n'est qu'un ignorant en — d'un tel;* he is a mere ignoramus in comparison with such a one. *Par — à* or *avec ce que j'ai fait;* comparatively with what I have done.

comparaître, *v.n.*, to appear. — *devant le tribunal de Dieu;* to appear before the tribunal of God.

comparant, **-e**, *n.* and *adj.*, he or she who makes his or her appearance in court. or before a notary, &c.; appearing.

comparati-f, **-ve**, *adj.*, comparative.

comparatif, *n.m.*, (gram.) comparative, comparative degree.

comparativement (-mān), *adv.*, comparatively.

comparer, *v.a.*, to compare.

ⓢ**comparoir**, *v.n.*, (jur.) to make one's appearance in a court of justice.

comparse, *n.m.*, (thea.) supernumerary.

compartiment, *n.m.*, compartment, division.

comparution, *n.f.*, appearance, forthcoming.

compas, *n.m.*, pair of compasses, compass. — *à trois branches;* triangular compasses. — *à pointes changeantes;* draught compasses. — *de réduction;* proportional compasses. *Faire toutes choses par règle et par —;* to do everything by rule and compass. *Il a le — dans l'œil;* he has a sure eye.

compassement (-pâs-mān), *n.m.*, compassing.

compasser, *v.a.*, to measure with compasses; to proportion; to regulate; to reflect on. *Un homme bien compassé;* a formal, starched, man.

compassion, *n.f.*, compassion, pity, mercy. *Avoir — de quelqu'un, avoir de la — pour quelqu'un;* to take compassion on one, to have compassion for any one.

compatibilité, *n.f.*, compatibility.

compatible, *adj.*, compatible, consistent. *Son humeur n'est pas — avec la mienne;* his temper does not agree with mine,

compatir, *v.n.*, to sympathize with, to compassionate, to agree, to be compatible with.

compatissant, **-e**, *adj.*, compassionate feeling.

compatriote, *n.m.f.*, compatriot, fellowcountryman. fellow-countrywoman.

compendieusement, *adv.*, in brief, compendiously.

compendium (kon-pin-di-om), *n.m.*, compendium, abridgment, summary.

compensable, *adj.*, that may be compensated, compensable.

compensateur, *n.m.*, (horl.) compensating balance. — *magnétique;* compensating apparatus to indicate the deviations of the mariner's compass.

compensat-eur, **-rice**, *adj.*, (horl.) compensative, compensating. *Pendule —;* compensating pendulum.

compensation, *n.f.*, compensation, amends, reparation, satisfaction; set-off. *Faire —;* to compensate, to make amends for.

compensatoire, *adj.*, compensatory.

compenser, *v.a.*, to counter-balance, to set against; to compensate, to make up for. *Rien ne compense la perte de l'honneur;* nothing can make up for the loss of honour.

se **compenser**, *v.r.*, to compensate.

compérage, *n.m.*, comparternity; cheating, trickery.

compère, *n.m.*, godfather; gossip; crony; pal; confederate of a quack. of a thimble-rigger, &c. *Un bon —;* a good companion.

compère-loriot, *n.m.* (--*s* --*s*), (orni.) goldhammer, goldfinch; loriot; stye (on the eye- *à l'œil*).

compétemment (kon-pé-ta-mān), *adv.*, (l.u.) competently.

compétence, *n.f.*, competency, cognizance;

competition; department. *Cela n'est pas de votre —;* that is beyond your sphere.

compétent, **-e**, *adj.*, sufficient, suitable, requisite; (jur.) cognizant; competent. *Il est juge —;* he is a competent judge. *Vous n'êtes pas — pour cela;* you are not fit for that.

compéter, *v.n.*, (jur.) to belong ; to be due; to be cognizable.

compétit-eur, *n.m.*, **-rice**, *n.f.*, competitor.

compétition, *n.f.*, rivalry, contention, strife.

compilateur, *n.m.*, compiler.

compilation, *n.f.*, compilation.

compiler, *v.a.*, to compile.

compitales, *n.f. pl.*, (antiq.) compitalia.

ⓞ***complaignant***, **-e**, *n.* and *adj.*, complainant; complaining.

complainte, *n.f.*, complaint (jur.); lament, complaint, lamentation, moan, plaint, wailing; plaintive ballad.

complaire, *v.n.*, to humour, to please.

se **complaire**, *v.r.*, to delight in.

complaisamment (-zam-an), *adv.*, complaisantly, obligingly.

complaisance, *n.f.*, kindness; complaisance, complacency; (com.) accommodation. —*s;* love, affection. *Abuser de la — de quelqu'un;* to abuse any one's complaisance. *Faire une chose par —;* to do a thing out of complaisance.

complaisant, **-e**, *adj.*, complaisant, affable, civil, obliging; kind.

complaisant, *n.m.*, **-e**, *n.f.*, over-civil person, fawner; go-between.

complant, *n.m.*, (agri.) plantation.

complément, *n.m.*, complement; objective case.

complémentaire, *adj.*, complemental.

compl-et, **-ète**, *adj.*, complete, full, total, perfect. *Un habillement —;* a complete suit of clothes. *Œuvres —ètes;* complete works.

complet, *n.m.*, complement, full number. *Être au —;* to be full.

complètement (kon-plèt-mān), *adv.*, completely, thoroughly.

complétement, *n.m.*, finishing, completion.

compléter, *v.a.*, to complete, to perfect.

compléti-f, **-ve**, *adj.*, (gram.) completive.

complexe, *adj.*, complex; complicated.

complexion, *n.f.*, constitution; disposition, complexion, humour.

complexité, *n.f.*, complexity.

complication, *n.f.*, intricacy, complication.

complice, *n.m.f.* and *adj.*, accomplice, accessory, privy.

complicité, *n.f.*, the being an accomplice.

complies, *n.f. pl.*, (c. rel.) compline.

compliment, *n.m.*, compliment; *pl.*, congratulations. *Faire — à quelqu'un;* to compliment one. *Faites-lui mes —s;* give him, her, my compliments. *Mes —s chez vous;* remember me to all at home. *Je vous en fais mon —;* I wish you joy. *Rengainer son —;* to put up one's compliment.

complimenter, *v.a.*, to compliment, to congratulate.

complimenteu-r, *n.m.*, **-se**, *n.f.*, complimenter.

complimenteu-r, **-se**, *adj.*, complimentary.

compliqué, **-e**, *adj.*, complicate; complicated, intricate.

compliquer, *v.a.*, to render intricate, to complicate, to entangle.

se **compliquer**, *v.r.*, to become complicated.

complot, *n.m.*, plot, conspiracy.

comploter, *v.a.*, to plot.

comploteur, *n.m.*, plotter, schemer.

componction, *n.f.*, compunction, contrition, remorse.

componé, -e, *adj ,* (her.) componed.

comportement, n.m., demeanour, comportment.

comporter, v.a., to permit, to allow. *Le temps le comporte ;* times require it.

se comporter, v.r., to behave, to behave one's self ; to go on. *Se — mal ;* to misbehave. *Il se comportera mieux à l'avenir ;* he will behave better for the future.

composant, n.m., (chem.) component,

composante, n.f., (math.) component.

composé, -e, *adj.,* composed, compound ; complicate ; affected, stiff. *Un mot — ;* a compound word. *Il a l'air extrêmement sérieux et — ;* he looks very grave and formal. *Air — ;* stiff, starched air.

composé, n.m., compound.

composées, n.f. pl., (bot.) compositæ.

composer, v.a., to compose, form, create, compound. *Dieu a composé l'homme d'un corps et d'une âme ;* God composed man of a body and soul. *— sa mine ;* to adjust one's looks. *Il faut savoir se — selon le temps, selon les lieux ;* one must prepare one's self according to time, according to place. *— des almanachs ;* to indulge in chimerical reveries.

composer, v.n., to compound, to compromise, to make up, to adjust; to capitulate. *Il a composé avec ses créanciers ;* he has compounded with his creditors.

composeur, n.m., scribbler, paltry writer.

composite, adj., (arch.) composite.

composite, n.m., the composite order.

compositeur, n.m., composer (of music — de musique); (jur.) compounder ; (print.) compositor. *Amiable — ;* (jur.) compounder, arbitrator.

composition, n.f., composition, construction, composing ; theme, agreement, settlement; capitulation. *Venir à — ;* to come to an agreement. *Un homme de — ;* an easy, tractable person. *Une fille de bonne — ;* a complying girl. *Faire bonne — ;* to grant advantageous terms. *Il est de difficile — ;* he is hard to deal with. *Se rendre par — ;* to surrender upon terms. *Entrer en — ;* to enter into terms of composition.

compost, n.m., (agri.) compost.

composter, v.a., (agri.) to compost.

composteur, n.m., (print.) composing-stick.

⊙**compotateur, n.m.,** bottle-companion.

○**compotation, n.f.,** compotation; drinking bout, a merry-making.

compote, n.f., stewed fruit. *— de pigeons;* stewed pigeons. *Avoir l'œil en — ;* to have a black eye. *Avoir les yeux en — ;* to have a pair of black eyes.

compotier (-tié), n.m., shallow dish in which stewed fruits are served up.

compréhensibilité, n.f., comprehensibleness.

compréhensible, adj., comprehensible.

compréhensi-f, -ve, adj., comprehensive.

compréhension, n.f., comprehension, apprehension, understanding, intelligence.

compréhensivité, n.f., comprehensiveness

comprendre, v.a., to comprehend, to include, to comprise, to contain, to understand, to conceive. *Je comprends fort bien ce que vous me dites ;* I understand very well what you say to me. *— mal ;* to misunderstand. *A ce que je comprends ;* by what I find. *Je ne le comprends pas ;* I do not know what to make of him.

compresse, n.f., (surg.) compress, bolster, pledget. *— fenêtrée ;* perforated compress.

compressibilité n.f., compressibility.

compressible, adj., compressible.

compressi-f, -ve, *adj.,* (surg.) compressive.

compression. n.f., compression, condensation ; (surg.) astriction.

comprimable, adj., compressible.

comprimé, -e, *part.,* (bot.) compressed, flat, condensed ; put down, kept under.

comprimer, v.a., to compress, to condense ; to quell ; to put down, to keep down, to restrain, to curb.

compromettant, adj., injurious, dangerous, compromitting.

compromettre, v.n., to compromise, to implicate; to put to arbitration, to consent to a reference, to refer to the arbitrament of one or more arbitrators.

compromettre, v.a., to expose, to commit, to compromise. *— son autorité, sa dignité ;* to expose one's authority or character.

se compromettre, v.r., to implicate, to compromise, one's self.

compromis, n.m., mutual agreement, compromise. *Mettre en — ;* to submit to arbitration.

compromissaire, n.m., arbitrator, referee.

comptabilité (kon-ta-), n.f., accounts, book-keeping. *Il entend bien la — ;* he has a thorough knowledge of accounts.

comptable (kon-tabl), adj., accountable, responsible. *Agent — ;* accountant ; responsible agent. *Nous sommes —s de nos talents à la patrie ;* we are accountable to our country for our talents.

comptable, n.m., accountant ; responsible agent.

comptant (kon-tân), n.m., ready money, cash. *Au — ;* (com.) for cash. *Payer — ;* to pay ready money. *Avoir du — ;* to be well in cash. *Voilà tout mon — ;* here is all my cash.

comptant, adj., (of money — d'argent) ready ; (of payment) in cash; (com.) prompt.

compte (kont), n.m., account, reckoning, calculation, score; question ; report; profit; esteem, value, regard. *Avez-vous votre — !* have you got your due? *Je n'ai pas mon — ;* I have not my number. *De — fait,* altogether, on computation. *— rond;* even money. *— borgne ;* old money. *Livre de — ;* book of accounts. *Roue de — ;* (horl.) notch-wheel. *Chambre des —s ;* chamber of accounts. *Auditeur des —s;* auditor of the exchequer. *Arrêter, solder, un —, des —s;* to settle accounts. *Arrêté de — ;* account agreed upon. *Pour solde de — ;* in full of all demands. *Faire rendre — ;* to call to account. *Rendre — ;* to give an account. *Avoir un — en banque;* to have money at a banker's. *Mettre en ligne de — ;* to pass to account. *Tenir — ;* to keep an account. *Ne tenir ni — ni mesure;* to leave all at sixes and sevens. *A bon — ;* at a cheap rate. *Être de bon — ;* to be true in one's dealings. *Faire — ;* to depend upon, to expect, to intend. *Il n'y a pas trouvé son — ;* he did not find what he expected. *Ils sont bien loin de — ;* they are much at odds. *Vous m'en rendrez — ;* you shall answer for it. *Il faut lui rendre — de tout ;* we must account to him for everything. *Je prends cela sur mon — ;* I will be accountable for that. *On ne sait à quoi s'en tenir sur son — ;* we do not know what to think of him. *A ce — -là ;* it being so. *Les bons —s font les bons amis ;* short reckonings make long friends. *Faire — d'une personne;* to value a person. *Il n'en fait aucun — ;* he slights him. *Au bout du — ;* when all is done. *En fin de — ;* in the end.

compte-pas, n.m., (—), odometer, pedometer; surveying-wheel. *V.* **odomètre.**

compter (kon-té), v.a., to count, to reckon, to number, to calculate ; to include; to charge; to settle accounts. *— ses pas ;* to walk slowly. *Marcher à pas comptés ;* to walk with measured steps.

compter, *v.n.*, to reckon, to calculate; to intend, to purpose; to think, to expect. *Quand comptez vous partir ?* when do you propose setting out ? *Je compte le voir demain ;* I expect to see him to-morrow. — *sur ;* to depend upon, to rely upon, to count upon ; to anticipate, to expect.

compte rendu, *n.m.*, return, report, statement.

compteur (kon-teur), *n.m.*, counter, accountant, computer; (mach.) tell-tale; (tech.) meter.

comptoir (kon-toàr), *n.m.*, counter; counting-house ; factory, settlement; bar (of a public-house—*de cabaret*, &c.). *Dame de* —; shopwoman; barmaid. *Garçon de* —; barman, barkeeper.

compulser, *v.a.*, to look through a register; to examine, in virtue of a judge's order.

compulsoire, *n.m.*, (jur.) examination of papers in virtue of a judge's order.

comput (kon-put), *n.m.*, computation (of time—*du temps*).

computation, *n.f.*, computation (of time —*du temps*).

computiste, *n.m.*, a computer. computist.

comtal, **-e**, *adj.*, belonging to an earl or a countess.

comtat, *n.m.*, county (of Avignon, *or* — Venaissin).

comte, *n.m.*, count ; earl.

comté, *n.m.*, county ; earldom.

comtesse, *n.f.*, countess.

concasser, *v.a.*, to pound, to bruise, to crush.

concaténation, *n.f.*, concatenation.

concave, *adj.*, concave.

⊙**concave**, *n.m.*, concaveness, concavity, concave.

concavité, *n.f.*, concaveness, concave, concavity.

concavo-concave, *adj.*, concavo-concave.

concavo-convexe, *adj.*, concavo-convex.

concédant, *n.m.*, grantor.

concéder, *v.a.*, to grant, to yield.

concentration, *n.f.*, concentration.

concentré, **-e**, *part.*, concentrated ; concentred ; close, close-tongued. *Un homme toujours* — ; a thoughtful man ; a man who is not communicative. *Haine* —*e ;* suppressed hatred.

concentrer, *v.a.*, to concentrate. — *sa fureur ;* to dissemble one's rage.

se concentrer, *v.r.*, to concentre, to meet in one centre ; to centre.

concentrique, *adj.*, concentric.

concentriquement, *adv.*, concentrically.

concept (kon-sèpt), *n.m.*, conception.

conceptible, *adj.*, conceptible.

conception, *n.f.*, conception ; apprehension ; thought, notion, understanding ; wit. conceit. *Il a la* — *vive, facile, dure ;* he is quick, easy, dull, of apprehension.

concernant, *prep.*, concerning, relating to, touching, about, in reference to.

concerner, *v.a.*, to relate or belong to, to concern, to regard.

concert, *n.m.*, concert ; harmony ; unanimity, concord. — *spirituel ;* oratorio. — *de louanges ;* concurrence of praises. *De* — ; by common consent. *Agir de* — ; to act in concert. *Faire une chose de* — ; to go hand in hand in a business.

concertant, **-e**, *adj.*, in concert (mus.). *Symphonie* —*e ;* symphony performed in concert by two or three or more instruments.

concertant, *n.m.*, **-e**, *n.f.*, performer in a concert.

concerté, **-e**, *adj.*, affected ; studied ; starched ; contrived.

concerter, *v.a.*, to contrive, to concert; to practise for a concert.

⊙**concerter**, *v.n.*, to play in a concert.

se concerter, *v.r.*, to plan together, to concert ; to lay ones' heads together.

concerto, *n.m.* (—*s*), concerto.

concession, *n.f.*, act of concession, grant.

concessionnaire, *n.m.*, grantee. — *d'un privilège ;* patentee.

concetti, *n.m.pl.* (n.s.), witty conceits ; affected thoughts.

concevable, *adj.*, conceivable.

concevoir, *v.a.*, to apprehend, to imagine, to understand, to perceive, to take, to comprehend ; to word, to express; to conceive; to become pregnant. *Elle est hors d'âge de* — ; she is past child-bearing.

conche, *n.f.*, (tech.) brine-pond.

conchoïdal, **-e** (-ko-), *adj.*, (geom.) conchoidal.

conchoïde (-ko-), *n.f.*, (geom.) conchoïd.

conchyliologie (-ki-), *n.f.*, conchology.

conchyliologique (-ki-), *adj.*, conchological.

conchyliologiste (-ki-), *n.m.*, conchologist.

conchyte (-kit), *n.f.*, conchite.

concierge, *n.m.f.*, porter, porteress ; door-keeper.

conciergerie, *n.f.*, guarding of a palace, a mansion, &c. ; porter's lodge ; a prison in Paris.

concile, *n.m.*, an assembly of prelates and doctors, council ; decrees and decisions of a council.

conciliable, *adj.*, reconcilable.

conciliabule, *n.m.*, conventicle. — *en plein air ;* field conventicle.

conciliaire, *adj.*, of or belonging to a council.

conciliairement, *adj.*, in council.

conciliant, **-e**, *adj.*, conciliating, reconciling.

conciliat-eur, *n.m.*, **-rice**, *n.f.*, conciliator; reconciler.

conciliat-eur, **-rice**, *adj.*, conciliatory. conciliating.

conciliation, *n.f.*, conciliation ; reconciliation.

conciliatoire, *adj.*, conciliatory.

concilier, *v.a.*, to reconcile, to conciliate, to accord ; to gain, to procure.

se concilier, *v.r.*, to conciliate. — *les esprits ;* to gain people's good will.

concis, **-e**, *adj.*, concise, brief, short.

concision, *n.f.*, brevity, conciseness.

concitoyen, *n.m.*, **-ne**, *n.f.* (-in, -è-n), fellow-citizen; fellow-townsman or townswoman.

conclave, *n.m.*, assembly of cardinals; conclave.

conclaviste, *n.m.*, conclavist.

concluant, **-e**, *adj.*, conclusive, decisive.

conclure, *v.a.*, to conclude, to finish; to infer; to move. *Qu'en voulez-vous* — *!* what do you infer from that ?

conclure, *v.n.*, to conclude, to infer; to think, to judge. *Cette raison ne conclut pas ;* this reason proves nothing. — *criminellement contre quelqu'un ;* to bring one in guilty.

conclusi-f, **-ve** *adj.*, conclusive.

conclusion, *n.f.*, final decision, conclusion ; end ; inference.

concoct-eur, **-rice**, *adj.*, concoctive.

concoction, *n.f.*, concoction.

concombre, *n.m.*, (bot.) cucumber, — *sauvage ;* horse cucumber.

concomitance, *n.f.*, concomitance, concomitancy.

concomitant, **-e**, *adj.*, concomitant.

concordance, *n.f.*, concordance, agreement ; concord.

concordant. *n.m.*, (mus.) barytone.

concordant, *adj.*, (mus.) concordant.

concordat, *n.m.*, concordat ; compact, agreement ; composition ; bankrupt's certificate. *Bénéfice de —;* (jur.) benefit of the insolvent act. *Sans —;* (jur.) uncertificated (of bankrupts—*des faillis*).

concordataire, *n.m.*, a bankrupt who has obtained a certificate.

concorde, *n.f.*, concord, good understanding, agreement, harmony. *Mettre la — entre des ennemis;* to reconcile enemies.

concorder, *v.n.*, to live in concord, to agree, to concur.

concourant, **-e**, *adj.*, concurrent.

concourir, *v.n.*, to concur, to conspire, to contribute ; to compete ; to unite ; to meet. *Tout concourt à ma ruine;* all things conspire to my ruin. *Être admis à —;* to be allowed to compete. *Ces deux hommes ont concouru pour le prix;* these two men competed for the prize.

concours, *n.m.*, concurrence, co-operation ; concourse ; meeting ; competition. *Son — m'a été fort utile;* his co-operation has been very useful to me. *Se présenter au —;* to compete, to contest for.

concr-et, -ète, *adj.*, (arith., log.) concrete ; (math.) applicate.

concret, *n.m.*, (log.) concrete.

concrétion, *n.f.*, concretion.

concubinage, *n.m.*, concubinage.

concubinaire, *n.m.*, one who keeps a concubine.

concubine, *n.f.*, concubine.

concupiscence, *n.f.*, concupiscence, lust.

concupiscent, -e, *adj.*, concupiscent, libidinous.

concupiscible, *adj.*, concupiscible.

concurremment (-kur-ra-mân), *adv.*, in concurrence.

concurrence (kon-kur-rans), *n.f.*, competition, opposition. *Jusqu'à — de;* to the amount of, to the extent of.

concurrent, *n.m.*, **-e**, *n.f.*, competitor.

concussion. *n.f.*, extortion, peculation. *User de —;* to be guilty of extortion.

concussionnaire, *n.m.*, extortioner, peculator.

concussionnaire, *adj.*, guilty of peculation, of bribery, extortion.

condamnable (-da-na-), *adj.*, condemnable, blamable.

condamnation (-da-na-), *n.f.*, condemnation, judgment, sentence. *Subir sa —;* to undergo one's sentence. *Subir —;* to give up the right of appeal against a sentence. *— par défaut;* judgment by default. *Passer —;* to confess one's self in the wrong.

condamné, *n.m.*, **-e**, *n.f.*, (kon-da-né), convict.

condamner (kondâné), *v.a.*, to condemn, to sentence ; to blame, to censure ; to block up (doors, windows—*portes, fenêtres*) ; to give over (patients—*malades*). *— à une amende;* to fine. *— d'avance;* to prejudge.

condensabilité, *n.f.*, condensability.

condensable, *adj.*, condensable.

condensateur, *n.m.*, (phys.) condenser.

condensation, *n.f.*, condensation.

condenser, *v.a.*, (phys.) to condense *— de nouveau;* to recondense. *Machine à —;* condensing-engine.

se **condenser**. *v.r.*, (phys.) to condense.

condenseur. *n.m.*, (mec.) condenser.

condescendance, *n.f.*, condescension, compliance. *Acte de —:* act of condescension.

condescendant, -e, *adj.*, condescending, complying.

condescendre, *v.n.*, to condescend, to comply, to yield.

condiction, *n.f.*, (Roman law—*droit romain*) action at law for the execution of a stipulation, or recovering a debt.

condiment, *n.m.*, condiment.

condisciple, *n.m.*, condisciple, schoolfellow.

condit, *n.m.*, (pharm.) confect.

condition, *n.f.*, condition, circumstances, nature ; quality, figure, rank. fortune ; station ; situation, place ; offer, terms. *Améliorer sa —;* to better one's circumstances. *Les gens de —;* people of fashion. *Être de —;* to be well born. *Être de basse —;* to be low born. *Chacun doit vivre selon sa —;* every one ought to live according to his station. *Toutes les —s ont leurs désagréments;* every condition has its own troubles. *Il est dans une bonne —;* he has a good place. *— provisionnelle;* proviso. *Sans —;* without a proviso. *Ils se sont rendus à des —s honorables;* they surrendered upon honourable terms. *A —, sous —;* on condition. *Vendre sous —;* to sell upon condition of taking the article back again if not approved. *A — que:* on condition, provided that. *En —;* at service (of servants—*des domestiques*).

conditionné, -e. *adj.*, in a good or bad condition (with *bien* or *mal*).

conditionnel, -le, *adj.*, conditional ; (jur.) provisory.

conditionnel, *n.m.*, (gram.) conditional.

conditionnellement, *adv.*, conditionally, upon condition.

conditionner, *v.a.*, (com.) to put into good condition.

condoléance, *n.f.*, condolence. *Faire un compliment de — à quelqu'un;* to condole with one.

condoma, *n.m.*, a species of antelope.

condor, *n.m.*, condor.

condormant, *n.m.*, **-e**, *n.f.*, (ecc. hist.) a sort of heretic.

⊙*se* **condouloir**, *v.r.*, to condole.

conduct-eur, *n.m.*, **-rice**, *n.f.*, conductor, conductress, leader, guide ; conductor (of omnibuses, &c.).

conduct-eur, -rice, *adj.*, leading ; (phys.) conducting.

conductibilité, *n.f.*, the property of conducting (heat and electricity—*la chaleur et l'électricité*)

conductible, *adj.*, transmitting heat and electricity.

conduction, *n.f.*, (phys.) conduction ; (Roman law—*droit romain*) renting a house.

conduire (conduisant, conduit), *v.a.*, to conduct, to lead, to guide, to convey, to carry, to bring, to take ; to go along with, to accompany, to attend ; to have the command of ; to govern, to rule, to direct. *Conduisez monsieur à sa chambre;* show the gentleman to his room. *— un troupeau;* to drive a flock. *— une affaire;* to carry on a business. *— un jeune homme;* to tutor, train or bring up a youth. *— la conscience de quelqu'un;* to. direct one's conscience. *— un bâtiment, un travail;* to be surveyor of a building, to have the direction of a work.

se **conduire**, *v.r.*, to conduct, to behave, to behave one's self ; to guide one's self. *Il se conduit bien;* he behaves himself well.

conduire, *v.n.*, to conduct, to lead ; to drive. *Ce chemin conduit à la ville;* this road leads to the town. *— à grandes guides;* to drive four-in-hand. *L'art de —;* the art of driving.

conduit, *n.m.*, conduit. duct, passage, pipe ; passage. *— auditif;* auditory passage. *— de la vapeur;* steam-port. *— de vent;* (mach.) blast-pipe.

conduite, *n.f.*, conduct, leading ; management. charge, administration ; behaviour, de

meanour, deportment; guidance. prudence, discretion; water-pipes; (nay.) conduct-money;
(mus.) port (of the voice—*de la voix*). *Se charger
de la — d'une affaire;* to take the management
of a business. *La — d'une pièce de théâtre;* the
disposition of a drama. — *régulière;* orderly
conduct. *Avoir de la —;* to be well-behaved.
Manquer de —; to misconduct one's self, to be
ill-behaved.

condupliqué, *adj.*, (bot.) (of leaves—*des
feuilles*) conduplicated.

condyle, *n.m.*, (anat.) condyle.

condyloïde, *adj.*, condyloid.

cône, *n.m.*, cone; (opt.) pencil; (bot.) strobile.

⊙**confabulateur**, *n.m.*, story-teller, col-
loquist.

⊙**confabulation**, *n.f.*, confabulation.

⊙**confabuler**, *v.n.*, to confabulate, to chat.

confecteur, *n.m.*, confector (Roman antiq.).

confection, *n.f.*, confection, electuary;
general term for the execution of anything.
La — du chyle; the formation of the chyle. *La
— d'un inventaire;* the completing an inventory.

confectionner, *v.a.*, to manufacture, to
make, to finish.

confectionneu-r, *n.m.*, **-se**, *n.f.*, maker,
finisher (of wearing apparel—*d'habillements*).

confédérati-f, **-ve**, *adj.*, confederative.

confédération, *n.f.*, confederation, confederacy.

confédéré, **-e**, *n.* and *adj.*, confederate, associate, federate, confederated.

se **confédérer**, *v.r.*, to confederate.

conférence, *n.f.*, conference; lecture; comparison, collation.

conférer, *v.a.*, to compare, to collate, to
confer, to bestow, to grant. — *un auteur avec
un autre;* to collate two authors.

conférer, *v.n.*, to consult together, to confer.

conferve, *n.f.*, (bot.) conferva.

confesse, *n.*, (c. rel.) confession (to a priest
—*à un prêtre*). [This noun has no gender, is
always accompanied by *à* or *de*, and *never* by
any article.]

confesser, *v.a.*, to confess; to acknowledge,
to avow.

se **confesser**, *v.r.*, to confess one's sins, to confess (to a priest—*à un prêtre*). *Se — au renard;*
to betray one's self.

confesseur, *n.m.*, confessor; father-confes-
sor.

confession, *n.f.*, confession, acknowledgment, avowal. *Donner à quelqu'un le bon Dieu
sans —;* to trust any one with untold gold.

confessionnal, *n.m.*, confessional.

confiance, *n.f.*, confidence, reliance, trust,
dependence, assurance; self-conceit. *Avoir de
la — en quelqu'un;* to repose confidence in any
one. *Donner sa — à quelqu'un;* to confide in
one. *Homme de —;* confidential man of business. *Une personne de —;* a trusty person.
Cela donne de la —; that inspires confidence.

confiant, **-e**, *adj.*, confident, sanguine; self-
conceited.

confidemment (-da-män), *adv.*, in confidence.

confidence, *n.f.*, confidence, secrecy, secret,
disclosure; trust (of benefices). *Être dans la —
de quelqu'un;* to be in one's confidence. *Il était
dans la —;* he was in the secret. *Un échange
de —s;* an exchange of secrets. *Faire une — à
quelqu'un;* to make a disclosure to one. *Faire
une —fausse;* to make a pretended disclosure.
Tenir un bénéfice en —; to hold a living in trust
or for another.

confident, *n.m.*, **-e**, *n.f.*, confident, confidant, confidante.

confidentiaire (-ci-), *n.m.*, one who holds a
living in trust.

confidentiel, **-le** (-ci-), *adj.*, confidential.

confidentiellement (-ci-), *adv.*, confidentially.

confier, *v.a.*, to confide, to intrust, to commit to; to tell in confidence.

se **confier**, *v.r.*, to trust in; to place reliance
on; to unbosom one's self to. *Se — en ses forces;*
to trust to one's strength. *Je me confie à vous;*
I trust to you.

configuration, *n.f.*, configuration.

configurer, *v.a.*, (l.u.) to configurate, to
form.

confinement, *n.m.*, confinement, imprisonment.

confiner, *v.n.*, to border upon; to confine,
to limit.

confiner, *v.a.*, to confine, to imprison.

se **confiner**, *v.r.*, to confine one's self.

confins, *n.m. pl.*, confines, borders, limits.
Aux — de la terre; at the ends of the earth.

confire (confisant, confit), *v.a.*, to preserve; to pickle. *Confit en dévotion;* extremely
devout. — *une peau;* to soak a skin. *C'est un
homme confit;* he is done for.

confirmati-f, **-ve**, *adj.*, confirmatory.

confirmation, *n.f.*, confirmation. *Cela a
besoin de —;* that requires confirmation.

confirmer, *v.a.*, to confirm, to ratify, to
sanction. — *quelqu'un;* (l. ex.) to give any one
a slap in the face.

se **confirmer**, *v.r.*, to be confirmed.

confiscable, *adj.*, confiscable, liable to forfeiture.

confiscant, *adj.*, (jur.) confiscating.

confiscation, *n.f.*, confiscation, forfeiture.

confiserie, *n.f.*, confectionery, confectioner's
shop.

confiseur, *n.m.*, **-se**, *n.f.*, confectioner.

confisquer, *v.a.*, to confiscate, to forfeit.

confit, *n.m.*, preparation for dressing
chamois skins.

confiteor, *n.m.* (—), confiteor. *Dire son —;*
to acknowledge one's fault.

confiture, *n.f.*, preserve; sweetmeat.

confituri-er, *n.m.*, **-ère**, *n.f.*, dealer in preserves, confectioner.

conflagration, *n.f.*, conflagration.

conflit, *n.m.*, contention, strife, contest,
conflict, collision; jarring. — *de juridiction;*
dispute between two or more courts of justice.

confluent, *n.m.*, (geog.) confluence, conflux.

confluent, **-e**, *adj.*, (med.) confluent. *Petite
vérole —;* confluent small-pox.

confluer, *v.n.*, to be confluent.

confondre, *v.a.*, to confound, confuse; to
blend, to mix, to mingle.

conformation, *n.f.*, conformation.

conforme, *adj.*, conformable, congenial,
consonant. *Pour copie —;* a true copy, conformable to the original.

conformé, **-e**, *adj.*, formed, shaped.

conformément, *adv.*, suitably, conformably.

conformer, *v.a.*, to conform.

se **conformer**, *v.r.*, to conform one's self, to
follow, to comply with. *Se — aux circonstances;*
to conform to circumstances.

conformiste, *n.m.f.*, conformist.

conformité, *n.f.*, likeness, agreement, conformity. *En —;* conformably, accordingly.

confort, *n.m.*, help, succour; comfort, ease.

confortable, *adj.*, consolatory, comfortable.

confortant, **-e**, *or* **confortati-f**, **-ve**, *adj.*,
strengthening, comforting.

confortatif, *n.m.*, (med.) corroborant.

confortation, *n.f.*, (l.u.) strengthening.

conforter, *v.a.*, to comfort; (med.) to strengthen; to console.

confraternité, *n.f.*, fraternity.

confrère, *n.m.*, confrier; fellow-member; contemporary.

confrérie, *n.f.*, brotherhood, confraternity.

confrication, *n.f.*, (pharm.) confrication.

confrontation, *n.f.*, confrontation; comparing (of writings).

confronter, *v.a.*, to confront, to stand face to face; to compare, to collate. — *la copie à l'original*; to compare the copy with the original.

confus, -e, *adj*, mixed, blended; ashamed, confused. *Bruit* —; confused rumour.

confusément, *a lv.*, confusedly.

confusion, *n.f.*, confusion; confusedness. *Mettre tout en* —; to disturb every thing. *En* —; confusedly.

confutation, *n.f.*, confutation; refutation.

confuter, *v.a.*, to disapprove, to confute.

congé, *n.m.*, (milit.) leave; liberty, permission; discharge, dismissal; warning, notice (to quit); holiday; congé; permit; (nav.) pass, clearance; (arch) apophysis; escape; (milit.) furlough. *Prendre* —; to take one's leave.

congéable, *adj.*, occupied by a tenant at will.

congédier, *v.a.*, to discharge, to dismiss, to pay off.

congélable, *adj.*, congealable.

congélation, *n.f.*, congelation, congealing; (mas.) rock-work; icicle (on sculptures).

congeler, *v.a.*, to congeal; to coagulate.

se **congeler**, *v.r.*, to congeal, to coagulate.

congénère, *adj.*, congener, congenerous.

congénital, -e, *a lj.*, congenital.

congestion -(jès-tion), *n.f.*, congestion.

conglaire, *n.m.*, (antiq.) congiary.

conglobation, *n.f.*, (rhet.) conglobation.

⊙**conglobé, -e**, *adj.*, conglobate; (anat.) lymphatic; globate, globited.

conglomérat, *n.m.*, (geol.) conglomerate.

conglomération, *n.f.*, conglomeration.

conglomérer, *v.a.*, to conglomerate.

conglutinant -e, *adj.*, conglutinating.

conglutinati-f, -ve, *adj.*, conglutinative.

conglutination, *n.f.*, conglutination.

conglutiner, *v.a.*, to glue together; to thicken, to conglutinate.

congratulation, *n.f.*, congratulation.

congratulatoire, *adj.*, expressing joy, congratulatory.

congratuler, *v.a.*, (jest.) to congratulate, to felicitate.

congre, *n.m.*, conger; conger-eel.

congréer, *v.a.*, (nav.) to worm.

congréganiste, *n.m.f.*, a person belonging to a congregation.

congrégation, *n.f.*, fraternity, congregation; brotherhood. — *des fidèles*, whole body of any church.

congrès, *n.m.*, congress; ⊙an ancient method of proving one's virility or impotency.

congru, -e, *adj.*, suitable, consistent, agreeable to, congruous. *Portion* —*e*; suitable allowance.

congruité, *n.f.*, congruity, consistency, propriety.

congrûment, *adv.*, congruously, properly.

conicine, *n.f.*, (chem.) conia.

conifère, *adj.*, coniferous.

coniforme, *a lj.*, coniform.

***conille**, *n.f.*, (nav.) little corner.

conique, *adj.*, conical.

conite, *n.m.*, (min.) conite.

conjectural, -e. *adj.*, conjectural.

conjecturalement (-ral-màn), *adv.*, conjecturally.

conjecture, *n.f.*, guess, conjecture.

conjecturer, *v.a.*, to conjecture, to guess.

conjoindre, *v.a.*, to conjoin, to join, to unite.

conjoint. -e, *part.*, conjoined, conjunct. *Les futurs* —*s*; the bride and bridegroom that are to be. *Feuilles* —*es*; (bot.) conjugate leaves

conjointement (kon-joint-màn), *adv.*, conjointly, unitedly.

conjoncti-f. -ve. *adj.*, conjunctive.

conjonction, *n.f.*, conjunction; union, connection; coition.

conjonctive, *n.f.*, (anat.) conjunctiva.

conjonctivement, *adv.*, conjunctively.

conjoncture, *n.f.*, conjuncture, juncture.

⊙*se* **conjouir**, *v.r.*, to rejoice with one, to congratulate.

⊙**conjouissance**, *n.f.*, congratulation.

conjugaison, *n.f.*, (gram., anat.) conjugation.

conjugal, -e, *adj.*, conjugal.

conjugalement (-gal-màn), *adv.*, conjugally.

conjugati-f, -ve. *adj.*, (gram.) conjugative, relating to conjugation.

conjuguer (-ghé), *v.a.*, (gram.) to conjugate.

se **conjuguer**, *v.r.*, to be conjugated.

conjungo, *n.m.*, (jest.) wedding, marriage.

conjurateur, *n.m.*, plotter, conspirator; conjurer.

conjuration, *n.f.*, conspiracy, plot; conjuration, exorcism; *pl.*, entreaties.

conjuré, *n.m.*, conspirator, plotter.

conjuré, -e, *part.*, confederate, sworn.

conjurer, *v.a.*, to implore; to conspire, to plot; to swear; to raise evil spirits, to exorcise, to conjure. *Il trouva moyen de* — *la tempête*, he found out a means for appeasing the storm.

connaissable, *adj.*, (l.u.) recognisable, easily known.

connaissance, *n.f.*, knowledge; acquaintance; intercourse; learning, understanding; (hunt.) the print of a stag's foot on the ground; *pl.*, knowledge, attainments, acquirements. *La* — *du bien et du mal*; the knowledge of good and evil. *Prendre* — *d'une chose*; to take notice of a thing. *Prendre* — *d'une cause*; to take cognizance of a case. *Parler en* — *de cause*, *agir avec* — *de cause*. to talk of a thing with a thorough knowledge of the matter, to proceed upon a thorough knowledge of the matter. *Faire* — *avec quelqu'un*; to form an acquaintance with one. *Être en pays de* —; to be among acquaintances. *Ses* —*s sont très-bornées*; his knowledge is very limited.

connaissants, *adj. m. pl.*, (jur.) skilled; acquainted with.

connaissement (-nès-màn), *n.m.*, (com.) bill of lading.

connaisseu-r, *n.m.*, **-se**, *n.f.*, *adj.*, connoisseur, one skilled in a thing.

connaisseu-r, -se, *adj.*, of a connoisseur.

connaître (connaissant, connu), *v.a.*, to know, to be aware of, to perceive; to understand, to be versed in anything; to be acquainted with; to experience. *Je le connais de vue*; I know him by sight. *Faire* —; to make it appear, to prove, to reveal. *Se faire* —, to make one's self known. *Je le ferai* —; I will disclose his conduct. *Dès qu'il est question d'intérêt, il ne connaît plus personne*; in matters of interest, everybody is a stranger to him. *Je ne connais que cela*; that's all I can say. — *à fond*; to know thoroughly. *Connaissez-vous cet homme-là?* are you acquainted with that man?

se **connaître**, *v.r.*, to know one's self; to know each other. *Connais-toi, toi-même; know* thyself. *Il ne se connaît pas ;* he is out of his senses. *Se — en quelque chose ;* to understand a thing, to be a judge of a thing.

connaître, *v.n.*, to know ; to have cognizance, to take cognizance.

conné, -e (ko-n-né), *adj.*, (bot.) connate.

connecter, *v.a.*, to connect ; *se —, v.r.*, to be connected.

connecti-f, -ve *adj.*, (bot.) connective.

connétable, *n.m.*, high constable.

connétable, *n.f.*, high constable's wife.

connétablie, *n.f.*, the court and jurisdiction of the high constable ; residence of the high constable.

connexe (ko-n-nèks), *adj.*, (jur.) connected.

connexion (ko-n-nèk-sion), *n.f.*, connexion, affinity.

connexité (ko-n-nèk-sité), *n.f.*, connexion, connexity.

connivence (ko-n-ni-), *n.f.*, connivance.

connivent, -e (ko-n-ni-), *adj.*, (anat., bot.) connivent.

conniver (ko-n-ni-), *v.n.*, to connive.

connu, *n.m.*, known ; that which is known.

connu, -e, *part.*, known, understood. *Il est — comme le loup blanc ;* he is the common talk of the town.

conoïdal, *adj.*, (bot.) conoidal.

conoïde, *n.m.*, (anat., geom.) conoid.

conoïde, *adj.*, (anat., geom.), conoidical.

conque, *n.f.*, conch, sea-shell ; (anat.) concha, pavilion of the ear.

conquérant, *n.m.*, conqueror.

conquérant, -e, *adj.*, conquering.

conquérir (conquérant, conquis), *v.a.*, to conquer, to subdue ; to gain, to obtain.

conquêt, *n.m.*, (jur.) acquisition.

conquête, *n.f.*, conquest.

consacrant, *adj.*, consecrating.

consacrant, *n.m.*, consecrator.

consacrer, *v.a.*, to consecrate ; to devote ; to hallow, to sanctify ; to sanction, to perpetuate.

se **consacrer**, *v.r.*, to devote one's self.

consanguin, -e (-ghin, -ghi-n), *n.* and *adj.*, (jur.) by the father's side. *Frère —, sœur —e ;* half-brother, half-sister, by the father's side. *Les —s ;* half-brothers and sisters by the father's side.

consanguinité (-gu-i-), *n.f.*, consanguinity.

conscience, *n.f.*, conscience, perception, consciousness ; (print.) work paid by the day ; the compositors paid by the day. *Cri de — ;* qualm of conscience. *— bourrelée ;* gangrened conscience. *— nette ;* clear conscience. *Remords de — ;* remorse, sting of conscience. *Se faire un cas de — d'une chose ;* to make a matter of conscience of a thing. *Il a la — large ;* he is not over scrupulous. *Mettre la main sur la — ;* to lay one's hand upon one's heart. *Il a dit tout ce qu'il avait sur la — ;* he has told his mind without reserve. *Transiger avec sa — ;* to compound with one's conscience. *En — ;* conscientiously.

consciencieusement, *adv.*, conscientiously.

consciencieu-x, -se, *adj.*, conscientious.

conscient, -e, *adj.*, conscious.

conscription. *n.f.*, (milit.) conscription.

conscriptionnel, -le, *adj.*, relating to the conscription.

conscrit, *adj.*, conscript. *Père — ;* Roman senator.

conscrit, *n.m.*, conscript, recruit ; freshman (of schools—*aux écoles*).

consécrateur, *n.m.*, consecrator.

consécration, *n.f.*, consecration.

consécuti-f, -ve, *adj.*, consecutive.

consécutivement (-tiv-mān), *adv.*, consecutively.

*conseil, *n.m.*, counsel, advice ; council ; council-board ; board ; resolution, course, determination ; counsellor. *— de commerce ;* board of trade. *Il ne prend — que de sa tête ;* he does everything by himself, without consulting any one. *La nuit porte — ;* advise with your pillow. *— de guerre ;* court-martial. *— de famille ;* family council ; commission of lunacy.

*conseiller**, *v.a.*, to advise, to counsel, to give advice.

*conseill-er, *n.m.*, -ère, *n.f.*, counsellor, adviser ; councillor ; puisne justice ; judge.

*conseillère, *n.f.*, wife of a counsellor.

*conseilleur, *n.m.*, adviser, (b.s.) one who gives advice unasked, and inopportunely.

consentant, -e, *adj.*, consenting, willing.

consentement (kon-sant-mān), *n.m.*, consent, assent.

consentir, *v.n.*, to consent, to agree, to acquiesce ; to assent to ; (nav.) to spring, to break. *Qui ne dit mot consent ;* silence gives consent.

*consentir, *v.a.*, (jur.) to consent to.

*conséquemment (-ka-mān), *adv.*, consistently ; consequently. *— à ce que nous avions réglé ;* according to our arrangements.

conséquence, *n.f.*, consequence, sequel ; consequent ; inference ; moment, importance ; deduction. *Tirer une — ;* to draw an inference. *Prévoir les —s d'une démarche ;* to foresee the consequences of a measure. *Cela tire à — ;* that will be a precedent. *De peu de — ;* of no consequence, insignificant. *C'est un homme sans — ;* he is a person of no consequence. *Faire l'homme de — ;* to set up for a man of consequence. *Une affaire de nulle — ;* an affair of no moment. *En — ;* accordingly. *En — de vos ordres ;* according to your orders.

conséquent, -e, *adj.*, just, consistent, coherent.

conséquent, *n.m.*, (log., math.) consequent. *Par — ;* consequently, in consequence.

conservat-eur, *n.m.*, -rice, *n.f.*, *adj.*, preserver, guardian, keeper ; conservative. *— des chasses ;* ranger. *— des eaux et forêts ;* commissioner of the woods and forests.

conservation, *n.f.*, preservation, registration (of mortgages—*d'hypothèques*).

conservatoire, *n.m.*, conservatory, school where music and declamation are taught ; Magdalen asylum ; conservatory (of objects of art).

conservatoire, *adj.*, conservative, conservatory.

conserve, *n.f.*, preserve ; (nav.) consort ; (phar.) conserve ; *pl.*, preservers (spectacles—*lunettes*). *Deux vaisseaux vont de — ;* two ships keep company together. *—s au vinaigre ;* pickles.

conservé, -e, *part.*, preserved. *Ce tableau est bien — ;* this painting is well preserved. *Être bien — ;* to bear one's age well.

conserver, *v.a.*, to preserve, to keep ; to maintain. *Une vie réglée conserve et fortifie la santé ;* a regular life preserves and fortifies the health.

se **conserver**, *v.r.*, to be preserved ; to preserve one's self ; to keep (of meat, &c.—*viande, &c.*) ; to bear one's age well. *Son teint s'est bien conservé ;* her complexion is well preserved. *Conservez-vous ;* take care of yourself.

considérable, *adj.*, considerable, notable, eminent, illustrious, important. *Peu — ;* of little importance.

considérablement, *adv.*, considerably.

⊙**considérant, -e**, *adj.*, considering, regardful.

considérant, *n.m.*, (jur.) preamble ; recital.

considération. *n.f.*, consideration; account, regard, sake; note, respect, esteem. *Cela mérite —;* that requires consideration. *C'est à votre — qu'il l'a fait;* it is out of regard for you that he did it. *Faire entrer en —;* to take into consideration. *N'avoir aucune — pour les gens;* to have no regard for people. *Il n'a nulle — dans le monde;* the public hold him in no esteem whatever. *Un homme de —;* a man of note.

considérément, *adv.*, considerately, prudently, thoughtfully.

considérer, *v.a.*, to consider, to take into consideration, to look at, to view, to gaze upon, to regard, to behold, to contemplate; to regard to; to have a consideration for, to value, to esteem, to respect, to look up to; to mind, to look to; to look upon. *Tout bien considéré;* all things rightly considered. *— une chose en elle-même;* to look at a thing in itself. *Il faut bien — les choses avant de s'engager;* you must look before you leap.

se considérer, *v.r.*, to esteem one's self; to hold one's self.

*consignataire, *n.m.*, trustee, depositary; (com.) consignee.

*consignat-eur, *n.m.*, *-rice*, *n.f.*, (com.) consignor.

*consignation. *n.f.*, consignment, deposit; lodgment (banking—*terme de banque*); (jur.) consignation. *Caisse des dépôts et —s;* suitor's fund. *Ces marchandises sont à la — d'un tel;* these goods are consigned to such a one.

*consigne, *n.f.*, (milit.) orders; instructions. *Manquer à la —;* to disregard orders. *Forcer la —;* to force a sentry. *Lever la —;* to revoke orders.

*consigner, *v.a.*, to deposit; to record; to refuse admittance; to keep in (schoolboys, troops—*écoliers, troupes*); (com.) to consign. *Je l'ai consigné à ma porte;* I have left orders not to admit him.

consistance, *n.f.*, consistency, consistence; firmness; stability; credit, consideration; (jur.) matter. *Le temps n'a point de —;* the weather is unsettled. *C'est un esprit qui n'a point de —;* he is a person of no consistency. *Cette nouvelle prend de la —;* this news takes a more likely appearance of truth.

consistant, *-e*, *adj.*, consisting of.

consister, *v.n.*, to be composed, to consist. *Le tout consiste à savoir;* the main point is to know. *Son revenu consiste en rentes;* his revenue consists of property in the funds.

consistoire. *n.m.*, consistory.

consistorial, *-e*, *adj.*, consistorial.

consistorialement, *adv.*, in a consistory.

consolable, *adj.*, consolable.

consolant, *-e*, *adj.*, consoling, comforting, consolatory.

consolat-eur, *n.m.* *-rice*, *n.f.*, comforter, consoler.

consolat-eur, *-rice*, *adj.*, consoling; consolatory.

consolation, *n.f.*, consolation, comfort, solace.

consolatoire, *adj.*, consolatory.

console, *n.f.*, (arch.) console, bracket; pier-table; corbel.

consoler, *v.a.*, to console, to solace, to comfort.

se consoler, *v.r.*, to be consoled; to solace, to console one's self.

consolidant, *n.m.* and *adj.*, (med., surg.) consolidant.

consolidation, *n.f.*, consolidation.

consolidement, *n.m.*, act of consolidating, consolidation.

consolider, *v.a.*, to consolidate.

se consolider, *v.r.*, to consolidate.

consolidés, *n.m. pl.*, consolidated funds, consols.

consommateur, *n.m.*, consumer; (theol.) perfecter. *L'auteur et le — de notre foi;* the author and perfecter of our faith.

consommation, *n.f.*, consummation; consumption.

consommé, *n.m.*, jelly broth, gravy soup.

consommé, *-e*, *part.*, consumed, used; consummated;. consummate; profound; accomplished.

consommer, *v.a.*, to consummate, to complete, to perfect, to finish, to accomplish; to consume, to use.

⊙**consompti-f**, *-ve*, *adj.*, (med.) caustic.

⊙**consomptif**, *n.m.*, (med., surg.) caustic.

consomption, *n.f.*, consumption; destruction; (med.) atrophy, decline. *Être malade de —;* to be in a consumption.

consonance, *n.f.*, consonance, consonancy; concord.

consonant, *-e*, *adj.*, consonant.

consonne, *n.f.*, consonant.

consorts, *n.m. pl.*, (jur.) associates, people connected together, having the same interest; (b. s.) confederates.

consoude, *n.f.*, (bot.) comfrey, consound.

conspirance, *n.f.*, (l. u.) tendency.

conspirant, *-e*, *adj.*, (mec.) conspiring.

conspirateur, *n.m.*, conspirator.

conspiration, *n.f.*, conspiracy, conspiration, plot. *La — des poudres;* the gunpowder-plot.

conspirer, *v.a.* and *n.*, to conspire, to agree together, to concur, to combine; to plot. *Tout conspire à me ruiner;* every thing conspires to my ruin. *— la ruine de l'État;* to plot the ruin of the State.

conspuer, *v.a.*, to spit upon; to despise.

constable, *n.m.*, constable.

constamment (-ta-män), *adv.*, with constancy, steadily, perseveringly; constantly.

constance, *n.f.*, constancy; perseverance; steadiness, steadfastness; firmness, persistence.

constant, *-e*, *adj.*, constant, unshaken; steadfast, persevering, unvarying, invariable; steady, lasting; certain, unquestionable.

constante, *n.f.*, (alg.) constant quantity.

constatation, *n.f.*, authentication; ascertaining, verifying.

constater, *v.a.*, to prove, to verify, to establish undeniably; to ascertain, to state, to declare.

constellation (-tèl-la-), *n.f.*, constellation.

constellé, *-e*. (-tèl-lé), *adj.*, (astrol.) made under a certain constellation; constellated (of stones—*des pierres*).

⊙**conster**, *v.n.*, and *imp.*, (jur.) to be evident; to appear.

consternation, *n.f.*, consternation.

consterner, *v.a.*, to strike with consternation; to astound, to amaze, to dismay, to dishearten. *Cette perte les a tous consternés;* this loss has dismayed them all.

constipation, *n.f.*, constipation, costiveness.

constipé, *-e*, *adj.*, costive, confined in the bowels.

constiper, *v.a.*, to constipate, to bind.

constituant, *-e*, *adj.*, constituent; giving a power of attorney.

constituant, *n.m.*, member of the Constituent Assembly (French hist.).

constituante, *n.f.*, Constituent Assembly (French hist.).

constituer, *v.a.*, to constitute, to make; to place, to put; to raise to an office or dignity; to settle, to assign; to give into custody. *Qui vous a constitué juge?* who made you a judge?

— *quelqu'un prisonnier ;* to commit one to prison. — *une rente ;* to settle an annuity.

se constituer. *v.r.,* to constitute one's self, to form one's self into, to give one's self into custody.

constituti-f. -ve, *adj.,* constitutive.

constitution. *n.f.,* constitution; temper, temperament, complexion of the body; settlement of an annuity; declaration of appointment.

constitutionnalité. *n.f.,* constitutionality.

constitutionnellement (-nèl-màn), *adv.,* constitutionally.

constitutionnel, *n.m.,* constitutionalist.

constitutionnel, -le, *adj.,* constitutional.

constricteur, *n.m.,* (anat.) constrictor.

constriction. *n.f.,* constriction, contraction, compression ; (med.) astriction.

constricti-f. -ve, *adj.,* (med.) constringent.

constringent, -e, *adj.,* constringent.

constructeur, *n.m.,* constructor, builder; ship-builder, shipwright.

construction. *n.f.,* act of building; arrangement and connection of words in a sentence, construction ; building, erection ; structure; ship-building. *Faire de nouvelles —s ;* to erect new buildings. *La — d'une carte géographique;* the construction of a map. *Faire la — d'une phrase ;* to construct a phrase. *Vaisseau de — française ;* French built ship.

constructivité, *n.f.,* (phrenology) constructiveness.

construire (construisant, construit), *v.a.,* to construct, to build, to erect, to rear up, to frame; to arrange; (gram.) to construct. — *une phrase ;* to construct a sentence. — *un poème ;* to frame a poem.

⊙**constupration,** *n.f.,* constupration.

⊙**constuprer,** *v.a.,* to constuprate, to violate, to ravish.

consubstantialité (-sia-), *n.f.,* consubstantiality.

consubstantiation (-sia-), *n.f.,* consubstantiation.

consubstantiel, -le, (-slèl), *adj.,* consubstantial.

consubstantiellement (-slèl-màn), *adv.,* consubstantially.

consul. *n.m.,* consul.

consulaire, *adj.,* consular. *Personnage —;* an ex-consul.

consulairement (lèr-màn), *adv.,* according to the consular court.

consulat, *n.m.,* consulate ; consulship.

consultant, *adj.m.,* consulting. *Avocat —;* chamber-counsellor. *Médecin —;* consulting physician.

consultant, *n.m.,* consulter; person consulted.

consultati-f. -ve, *adj.,* consultative. deliberative. *Avoir voix —ve ;* to have the right of discussion without that of voting.

consultation, *n.f.,* consultation ; conference ; opinion.

consulter, *v.a.,* to consult, to advise with, to take advice of, to deliberate, to confer. — *un avocat ;* to go to a counsel. — *une affaire ;* to examine, to search into, an affair. — *son chevet ;* to advise with one's pillow. *Ils consultèrent ensemble ;* they laid their heads together. *Il en veut — avec ses amis ;* he wishes to confer with his friends about it.

se consulter, *v.r.,* to consider, to reflect, to deliberate ; to be consulted. *La voix de la raison ne se consulte jamais ;* the voice of reason is never consulted.

consulteur, *n.m.,* counsellor of the Pope.

consumant, -e, *adj.,* consuming, devouring.

consumer, *v.a.,* to consume ; to destroy ;

to wear out or away, to drudge out; to squander, to waste, to spend. *Le temps consume toutes choses ;* time wears out every thing. *Cette maladie le consume ;* that disease wastes him to nothing.

se consumer, *v.r.,* to decay, to waste away, to wear out ; to ruin one's self ; to undermine one's health ; to waste one's strength. *Il se consume d'ennui ;* he wastes away with melancholy. *Se — de douleur ;* to pine away with grief.

contabescence, *n.f.,* (med.) consumption.

contabescent, -e, *adj.,* (med.) consumptive.

contact (-takt), *n.m.,* contact, touching, touch ; (mining—*mines*) nip (of the roof or wall —*du ciel ou de la muraille*).

⊙**contadin,** *n.m.,* countryman, peasant, clown, boor.

contagieu-x, -se, *adj.,* contagious, catching ; infectious.

contagion, *n.f.,* contagion, infection. — *de mœurs ;* corruption of manners. *La — du vice ;* the infection of vice.

*****contaille,** *adj.f.,* floss. *Soie —;* floretta, refuse, floss-silk.

contamination, *n.f.,* contamination.

contaminer, *v.a.,* to contaminate.

conte, *n.m.,* story, tale, falsehood, fib. —*s de fées ;* fairy tales. *Réciter un —;* to tell a story. — *en l'air ;* improbable story, fiction. — *fait à plaisir ;* feigned story. — *gras ;* smutty, lascivious story. — *de bonne femme,* — *à dormir debout,* — *bleu,* — *borgne ;* idle, silly story ; old woman's tale ; tale of a cock and bull. *Il brode un peu le —;* he ornaments the story a little. *Ce sont des —s ;* it is only a joke. *C'est un grand faiseur de —s ;* he is a great fibber, a great story-teller.

contemplat-eur, *n.m.,* **-rice,** *n.f.,* contemplator.

contemplati-f. -ve, *adj.,* contemplative.

contemplation. *n.f.,* contemplation, meditation, reflection. *En — de ;* in consideration of, on account of.

contempler, *v.a.,* to contemplate, to behold, to survey, to view, to gaze on.

contempler, *v.n.,* to contemplate, to meditate, to reflect.

contemporain, -e, *adj.,* contemporary, contemporaneous.

contemporain, *n.m.,* **-e,** *n.f.,* contemporary.

contemporanéité, *n.f.,* contemporaneity, contemporariness.

contempt-eur, **·rice,** *adj.,* contemptuous, scornful, insolent, disdainful.

contempt-eur, *n.m.,* **··rice,** *n.f.,* contemner, despiser, scorner.

⊙**contemptible,** *adj.,* contemptible.

contenance (cont-nans), *n.f.,* capacity, capaciousness ; contents ; countenance, posture, look, air, deportment ; (nav.) burden. — *fière ;* haughty air. — *assurée ;* bold look. — *ridicule ;* ridiculous carriage. — *étudiée ;* studied deportment. *Il n'a point de —;* he is quite abashed. *Perdre —;* to be abashed. *Faire perdre —;* to put out of countenance. *Servir de —;* to keep in countenance. *Porter quelque chose par —;* to carry a thing to keep oneself in countenance. *Un éventail sert de —;* a fan keeps in countenance. *Faire bonne —;* to keep one's countenance.

contenant, *n.m.,* holder, container.

contenant, -e, *adj.,* holding, containing.

contendant, -e, *adj.,* contending. *Les parties —es ;* the contending parties, the candidates.

contendant. *n.m.,* contender.

contenir (con-tnir), *v.a.,* to contain ; to

comprise; to hold; to include, to comprehend; to confine; to keep in, to keep within, to restrain; to repress; to hold or keep in check or awe, to rule, to bridle; to dam. *Les gardes avaient peine à — la foule;* the guards could with difficulty keep the crowd in check. *— quelqu'un dans le devoir;* to keep one to his duty. *On ne saurait le —;* there is no keeping him within bounds.

se contenir, *v.r.*, to keep within bounds, to be moderate; to abstain from, to refrain from, to forego; to refrain, to forbear; to contain one's self; to curb one's passions; to keep one's temper.

content, **-e**, *adj.*, content, contented; satisfied, pleased, gratified. *Il est — de sa condition;* he is contented with his condition. *Avoir le visage —;* to look pleased. *Être —;* to be willing, to be satisfied. *Être — de quelqu'un;* to be pleased with one. *Il est bien — de lui-même;* he has a great idea of himself.

contentement (kon-tant-mān), *n.m.*, content, contentment, satisfaction; comfort, pleasure; blessing. *— passe richesse;* contentment is better than riches.

contenter, *v.a.*, to content, to give satisfaction, to satisfy; to please, to gratify, to indulge, to humour. *On ne saurait — tout le monde;* one cannot please every body.

se contenter, *v.r.*, to indulge or gratify oneself; to be satisfied with; to content one's self with, to be content with, to take up with; to rest satisfied with. *Je me contente d'une honnête médiocrité;* I am satisfied with a moderate fortune. *Contentez-vous de cela;* content yourself with that.

contentieusement (-si-euz-mān), *adv.*, contentiously, litigiously.

contentieu-x, -se, *adj.*, litigated, in litigation, in dispute, contested. contended for; controvertible, disputable; litigious, contentious, quarrelsome. *Esprit —;* quarrelsome fellow.

contentieux, *n.m.*, debatable matters, affairs in litigation; *pl.*, disputed claims. *Bureau du —;* office for the settlement of disputed points. *Agent du —;* solicitor.

contentif, *adj.m.*, (surg.) (bandages) retentive.

contention. *n.f.*, contention, contest, debate, strife; eagerness; vehemence, heat; (surg.) keeping reduced (fractures). *— d'esprit;* intense application of mind.

contenu, *n.m.*, contents.

conter, *v.a.*, to tell, to relate. *— des fagots;* to tell idle stories. *En —;* to romance, to tell fibs. *En — de belles, — des sornettes;* to tell what is untrue, trifling or frivolous. *En — à une femme, lui — des douceurs, lui — fleurettes,* to talk soft nonsense to a woman. *S'en faire —;* to listen to soft nonsense.

conter, *v.n.*, to relate, to tell a story. *Il conte bien;* he tells a story well.

conterie, *n.f.*, coarse glass-ware.

⊙**conteste**, *n.m.*, contestation, contest, dispute.

contestable, *adj.*, contestable, controvertible.

contestablement. *adv.*, contestably.

contestant, -e, *adj.*, contending.

contestant, *n.m.*, **-e**, *n.f.*, contesting party, litigant.

contestation. *n.f.*, contestation, contest, dispute, debate; strife, variance, wrangling, bickering; litigation. *En —;* at issue; at variance, at odds. *Hors de toute —;* beyond all contestation, dispute.

contester, *v.a.*, to contest, to dispute; to deny, to contend, to debate. *Il me conteste ma qualité;* he calls my rank in question. *On lui*

conteste cette terre; his right to that estate is disputed.

conteu-r, *n.m.*, **-se**, *n.f.*, story-teller, tale-teller, one who tells or relates stories or tales, narrator, teller; romancer, fibber.

conteu-r, -se, *adj.*, fond of telling tales.

contexte, *n.m.*, context; text (of a deed—*d'un titre*).

contexture, *n.f.*, contexture (of the muscles, &c.—*des muscles, &c.*); texture (of a stuff—*d'une étoffe*).

contigu, -ë, *adj.*, contiguous, adjoining. *Ces deux provinces sont —ës;* these two provinces border on each other. *Mon champ est — à la forêt;* my field is bounded by the forest.

contiguïté, *n.f.*, contiguity.

continence, *n.f.*, continency, chastity.

continent, *n.m.*, continent, mainland.

continent, -e, *adj.*, sober, temperate, chaste, continent; (med.) continent, continuous, unremitting. *Fièvre —e;* unremitting fever.

continental, -e, *adj.*, continental.

contingence, *n.f.*, contingency, casualty.

contingent, *n.m.*, contingent, quota.

contingent, -e, *adj.*, casual, contingent, accidental.

continu, *n.m.*, (philos.) that which is divisible, matter, body, space.

continu, -e, *adj.*, continuous, unintrrupted; continual, continued; unintermitting, incessant. *Basse —e;* (mus.) thorough-bass.

continuateur, *n.m.*, continuator, continuer.

continuation, *n.f.*, continuation; (jur.) continuance.

⊙*à la* **continue**, *adv.*, in process of time.

continuel, -le, *adj.*, continual, uninterrupted, unintermitting, unremitting.

continuellement (-èl-mān), *adv.*, continually, uninterruptedly, unintermittingly, unremittingly.

continuer, *v.a.*, to continue; to proceed with; to go on with; to lengthen, to prolong; to extend.

continuer, *v.n.*, to continue, keep on, go on, run on, extend. *Continuez, je vous prie;* pray, go on. *Continuez à bien faire, et vous vous en trouverez bien;* continue to do well, and you will find the advantage of it. [*Continuer* requires either of the prepositions *à* or *de* to be put before the verb depending upon it. *Pensez-vous que Calchas continue à se taire?* (Racine). *Sésostris continuait de me regarder* . . . . . (Fénelon).]

se continuer, *v.r.*, to be continued.

continuité, *n.f.*, continuity; continuance. *Solution de —;* solution of continuity.

continûment, *adv.*, continuedly; (jur.) continually.

contondant, -e, *adj.*, (surg.) bruising, thumping; (instruments) blunt.

contorniate, *adj.*, (of medals—*médailles*) contourniated.

contorsion, *n.f.*, contortion.

contour, *n.m.*, circuit, circumference; contour, outline; (carp.) curtail; (mas.) quirk.

contourné, -e, *adj.*, (her.) contourne.

contournement, *n.m.*, convolution.

contourner, *v.a.*, to give the proper contour to; to distort, to twist, to deform; to twine round, to twist round; to turn around.

se contourner, *v.r.*, to grow crooked, to become bent, twisted, deformed.

contractant, -e, *adj.*, contracting. *Partie —e;* contracting party; (jur.) covenanter.

contractant, *n.m.*, **-e**, *n.f.*, contractor, stipulator; (jur.) covenanter.

contracté, -e, *part.*, (gram.) contracted, shortened.

contracter, *v.a.*, to make a mutual agreement, to contract; to covenant, to stipulate, to bargain, to make a contract; to shrink, to straiten; to acquire, to get; to catch. — *de bonnes habitudes;* to acquire good habits.

se **contracter**, *v.r.*, to contract, to shrink up, to straiten; to shorten.

contracter, *v.n.*, to contract, make a contract.

contracti-f, -ve, *adj.*, (med.) contractive.

contractile, *adj.*, contractile.

contractilité, *n.f.*, contractility.

contraction, *n.f.*, contraction.

contractuel, -le, *adj.*, (jur.) stipulated, agreed upon.

contracture, *n.f.*, (arch.) diminution; (med.) contraction; (physiology) contraction (of the joints—*des jointures*).

contradicteur, *n.m.*, contradictor; (jur.) adversary, opposer.

contradiction, *n.f.*, contradiction; opposition; inconsistency; discrepancy; (jur.) claim of adverse title. *Esprit de* —; spirit of contradiction.

contradictoire, *adj.*, contradictory; inconsistent. *Jugement* —; judgment after the hearing of all parties.

contradictoirement (-toar-män), *adv.*, contradictorily; inconsistently; (jur.) after the hearing of all parties.

***contraignable**, *adj.*, (jur.) compellable.

***contraignant, -e**, *adj.*, compelling, compulsive; troublesome.

contraindre (contraignant, contraint), *v.a.*, to constrain, to compel, to force, to make, to drive, to necessitate, to impel, to oblige by force; to put a constraint upon; to restrain; to squeeze, to pinch, to cramp, to straiten.

se **contraindre**, *v.r.*, to constrain one's self, to refrain, to forbear.

contraint, -e, *adj.*, forced, stiff, unnatural, affected; cramped, constrained.

contrainte, *n.f.*, constraint, compulsion, coercion; restraint, constraint. *Parler sans* —; to speak freely. *Avec* —; restrainedly. — *par corps;* arrest for debt. *Jugement de* — *par corps;* capias.

contraire, *adj.*, contrary, opposite, adverse, repugnant, inconsistent; opposed, against, adverse; hurtful, bad, prejudicial, not good for. *Le vin vous est* —; wine is bad for you.

contraire, *n.m.*, contrary, opposite. *Le chaud est le* — *du froid;* heat is the opposite of cold. *Au contraire;* on the contrary. *Tout au* —, *bien au* —; quite the contrary, the reverse. *Aller au* — *d'une chose, d'une personne;* to go or speak against a thing, a person.

contrairement (kon-trèr-män), *adv.*, contrarily.

contralte, *n.m. V.* **contralto**.

contralto, *n.m.* (—), (mus.) contralto, counter-tenor.

contrapontiste, *n.m.*, (mus.) contrapuntist.

contrariant, -e, *adj.*, provoking, annoying, vexatious; disappointing.

contrarier, *v.a.*, to contradict, to gainsay; to disappoint; to thwart, to counteract, to baffle, to oppose. *Être contrarié par les vents;* to be wind-bound.

contrariété, *n.f.*, contrariety, contradiction; cross, vexation, impediment, difficulty, obstacle; disappointment. *Quelle* —! how annoying!

contrastant, *adj.*, contrasting.

contraste, *n.m.*, contrast.

contraster, *v.a.*, to contrast.

contraster, *v.a.*, (paint.) to contrast, to put in contrast.

contrat, *n.m.*, contract, deed, instrument,

articles, indenture; agreement, bargain. *Minute d'un* —; draught of a deed. *Un* — *en bonne forme;* a contract in due form. *Dresser un* —; to draw up a deed. *Passer un* —; to sign and seal a deed. — *à la grosse;* (nav.) bottomry; bottomry-bond.

contravention, *n.f.*, contravention, infraction.

contre, *prep.*, against; contrary to; by, near, close, close by. — *le bon sens;* contrary to good sense. *À* — *-cœur;* repugnantly. *Aller* — *vent et marée;* to sail against wind and tide. *Se fâcher* — *quelqu'un;* to be angry with one. *Se battre* — *quelqu'un;* to fight one. *Par* —; as a set-off. *Pour et* —; for and against, pro and con.

contre, *adv.*, near, close. *Tout* —; close by. *Ci-* —; opposite.

contre, *n.m.*, con (the opposite of *pro*); against; the opposite side of the question. *Savoir le pour et le* —; to know the short and long of a matter.

contre-allée, *n.f.* (— *s*), counter-alley.

contre-amiral, *n.m.* (— *-amiraux*), rear-admiral; rear-admiral's flag-ship.

contre-appel, *n.m.* (— *-s*), (fenc.) caveating; second roll call.

contre-approches, *n.f. pl.* (*n.s.*), (fort.) counter-approaches.

contre-attaques, *n.f. pl.* (*n.s.*), (milit.) counterworks.

contre-balancer, *v.a.*, to counterbalance, to counterpoise; to countervail.

se **contre-balancer**, *v.r.*, to counterbalance one another, to be counterbalanced, to be equipoised.

contrebande, *n.f.*, contraband goods, smuggled goods; smuggling. *Un homme de* —; an obnoxious fellow, a black sheep. *Faire la* —; to smuggle, to deal in smuggled goods.

contre-bandé, -e, *adj.*, (her.) counterbarred.

contrebandier, *n.m.*, smuggler, contrabandist.

contre-barré, -e, *adj.* (— *s*), (her.) counterbended.

en **contre-bas**, *adv.*, (arch.) downwards.

contrebasse, *n.f.*, (mus.) double-bass.

contrebassiste, *n.m.*, (mus.) double-bass player.

contre-basson, *n.m.* (— *-s*), (mus.) double bassoon; double bassoon-player.

contre-batterie, *n.f.* (— *-s*), cross-battery, counter-battery; counter-plot.

à **contre-biais**, *adv.*, contrariwise.

à **contre-bord**, *adv.*, (nav.) *Les deux vaisseaux courent à* —; the two vessels are running aboard of each other.

contre-boutant, *n.m.* (— *-s*), counterfort; butment; buttress.

contre-bouter, *v.a.*, to buttress; to support with a raking shore or but.

contre-brasser, *v.a.*, (nav.) to brace about the yards.

contre-calquer, *v.a.*, to take a counterproof of a counterdrawing.

contre-capion, *n.m.* (— *s*), — *de poupe;* the upper part of the false post of a row-galley. — *de proue;* the upper part of the stemson of a galley.

contrecarrer, *v.a.*, to thwart, to oppose.

contre-charme, *n.m.* (— *-s*), countercharm.

contre-châssis, *n.m.* (—), outer-sash; double sash.

contre-chef, *n.m.* (— *-s*), foreman.

contre-civadière, *n.f.* (— *-s*), (nav.) bowsprit topsail.

contre-clef, *n.f.* (— *-s*), (arch.) second stone in the crown of an arch.

contre-cœur, *n.m.* (— —s), chimney-back. *A* —; reluctantly.

contre-coup, *n.m.* (— —s), rebound, repercussion ; counter-blow.

contre-courant, *n.m.* (— —s) counter-current.

contredanse, *n.f.*, quadrille.

contre-déclaration, *n.f.* (— —s), counter-declaration.

contre-dégagement, *n.m.* (— —s), (fenc.) double.

contre-dégager, *v.n.*, (fenc.) to double.

contre-digue, *n.f.* (— —s), embankment, dike, for the strengthening of another.

contredire, *v.a.*, to contradict, to gainsay ; to be inconsistent with ; (jur.) to confute, to disprove, to answer ; (hunt.) to reclaim.

se **contredire**, *v.r.*, to contradict one's self, to contradict one another; to be inconsistent with, to be contradictory to.

contredisant, **-e**, *adj.*, contradicting.

contredisant, *n.m.*, respondent, contradictor.

contredit, *n.m.*, answer, reply, contradiction; (jur.) objection, rejoinder. *Cela est sans* — ; that is beyond all dispute. *Sans* —; incontestably, beyond a doubt.

contrée, *n.f.*, country, region.

***contre-écaille**, *n.f.* (— —s), the reverse side of a shell.

contre-écart, *n.m.* (— —s), (her.) counter-quarter.

contre-écarteler, *v.a.*, (her.) to counter-quarter.

contre-échange, *n.m.* (— —s), exchange.

contre-enquête, *n.f.* (— —s), counter-inquiry.

contre-épaulette, *n.f.* (— —s), epaulet without fringe.

contre-épreuve, *n.f.* (— —s), counter-proof ; spiritless copy, feeble imitation ; counter-deliberation (of deliberative assemblies—*d'assemblées délibérantes*).

contre-épreuver, *v.a.*, (engr.) to take a counter-proof.

contre-espalier, *n.m.* (— —s), an espalier facing another, with a walk between them.

contre-expertise, *n.f.* (— —s), counter-valuation.

contre-étrave, *n.f.* (— —s), (nav.) apron.

contrefaçon, *n.f.*, counterfeiting, counterfeit, pirating, forgery.

contrefacteur, *n.m.*, counterfeiter (of coin, &c.—*de monnaie*, &c.); forger (of bills, &c.—*de lettres de change*, &c.).

contrefaction, *n.f.*, act of forging, counterfeiting, forgery.

contrefaire, *v.a.*, to counterfeit, to imitate, to copy ; to mimic, to ape ; to pirate ; to disguise, to disfigure.

se **contrefaire**, *v.r.*, to dissemble one's character, to play the counterfeit.

contrefaiseur, *n.m.*, mimic, imitator (of animals, persons—*d'animaux, de personnes*).

contrefait, **-e**, *part.*, counterfeit, deformed. *Un homme tout* — ; a deformed man.

contre-fanon, *n.m.* (— —s), (nav.) vertical lines.

contre-fenêtre, *n.f.* (— —s), inside-sash.

contre-fente, *n.f.* (— —s), (surg.) contra-fissure, counter-cleft.

contre-fiche, *n.f.* (— —s), (carp.) brace, strut.

contre-fil, *n.m.* (*n.p.*), the opposite direction. *Le* — *de l'eau*; upward the river. *A* — : backwards.

contre-finesse, *n.f.* (— —s), counter-trick; counter-cunning ; trick for trick.

contre-foc, *n.m.* (— —s), fore-top stay-sail.

contrefort, *n.m.*, counterfort, buttress, pillar, pier ; (geol.) lesser chain ; (of boots and shoes—*de bottes*, &c.) stiffener.

contre-fossé, *n.m.* (— —s), counter-drain.

contre-fracture, *n.f.* (— —s), (surg.) contra-fissure.

contre-fruit, *n.m.* (— —s), (arch.) overspan.

contre-fugue, *n.f.* (mus.), counterfugue.

contre-gage, *n.m.* (— —s), double security, pledge.

contre-gager, *v.a.*, to take security, to take a pledge.

contre-garde, *n.f.* (— —s), counterguard.

⊙**contre-garde**, *n.m.* (— —s), deputy warden of the mint.

contre-hacher, *v.a.*, (engr.) to counterhatch.

contre-hachure, *n.f.* (— —s), counterhatching.

⊙**contre-hâtier** (-tié), *n.m.* (— —s), kitchen fire-dog.

en **contre-haut**, *adv.*, (arch.) upwards.

contre-indication, *n.f.* (— —s), (med.) contra-indication.

contre-indiquer, *v.a.*, (med.) to contra-indicate.

contre-issant, **-e**, *adj.* (— —s), (her.) counter-salient.

contre-jauger, *v.a.*, (carp.) to fit a mortice to a tenon, to countergauge.

contre-jour, *n.m.* (— —s), counter-light, false-light. *A* — : in a false light.

contre-jumelles, *n.f. pl.* (*n.s.*), kennel stones.

contre-lames, *n f.pl.* (*n.s.*), (gauze-making —*manufacture de gaze*) counter-lams.

contre-latte, *n.f.* (— —s), counterlath.

contre-latter, *v.a.*, to counterlath.

contre-lattoir, *n.m.* (— —s), lath-holder, clincher.

contre-lettre, *n.f.* (— —s), (jur.) defeasance, counter-deed.

***contre-maille**, *n.f.* (— —s), a kind of net.

***contre-mailler**, *v.a.*, to doublemesh.

contremaître, *n.m.*, boatswain's mate ; overseer ; foreman.

contremandement, *n.m.*, counter-order, countermand.

contremander, *v.a.*, to countermand.

contremarche, *n.f.*, counter-march ; (carp.) raiser.

contremarcher, *v.n.*, to counter-march.

contre-marée, *n.f.* (— —s), eddy-tide.

contremarque, *n.f.*, countermark ; check (thea.).

contremarquer, *v.a.*, to countermark.

contre-mine, *n.f.* (— —s), countermine.

contre-miner, *v.a.*, to countermine.

contre-mineur, *n.m.* (— —s), counter-miner.

⊙**contre-mont**, *adv.*, upwards ; up-hill against the stream.

contre-mot, *n.m.* (— —s), (milit.) counter-sign.

contre-mouvement, *n.m.* (— —s), counter-movement.

contre-mur, *n.m.* (— —s), (fort.) countermure.

contre-murer, *v.a.* (fort.) to countermure.

contre-opposition, *n.f.* (— —s), counter-opposition.

contre-ordre, *n m.* (— —s), counter-order.

contre-ouverture, *n.f.* (— —s), counter-opening.

contre-partie, *n.f.* (— —s), counterpart; opposite ; contrary ; (mus.) counterpart.

contre-peser, *v.a.*, to counterbalance.

contre-pied *n.m.* (*n.p.*) (hunt.) back-scent ;

the reverse. *Les chiens avaient pris le —;* the dogs went on the back-scent. *Il prend toujours le — de ce qu'on dit;* he always misconstrues what is said.

contre-planche, *n.f.* (— —s), counter-plate.

contre-platine, *n.f.* (— —s), screw-piece.

contre-poids, *n.m.* (—), counterpoise, counterbalance; rope-dancer's balance.

contre-poil, *n.m.* (*a.p.*), wrong way of the hair; of the nap. *A —;* against the grain. *Prendre une affaire à —;* to take a thing in a wrong sense. *Prendre quelqu'un à —;* to shock, to offend, one.

contre-poinçon, *n.m.* (— —s), clincher (instrument).

contrepoint, *n.m.,* (mus.) counterpoint; (nav.) double rope attached to the clue of a sail.

contre-pointer, *v.a.,* to quilt on both sides; to contradict, to run counter; (artil.) to point cannon against other cannon. *— du canon;* to raise a battery against another battery.

contrepoison, *n.m.,* antidote, counterpoison.

contre-porte, *n.f.* (— —s), double-door, baize-door.

contre-poser, *v.a.,* (com.) to set down wrong.

contre-position, *n.f.* (— —s), contra-position.

contre-projet. *n.m.* (— —s), counter-plan.

contre-promesse, *n.f.* (— —s), (jur.) counterbond.

contre-proposition, *n.f.* (— —s), reply, retort.

contre-queue d'aronde, *n.f.* (— —s), (fort.) counter-swallowtail.

****contre-quille,** *n.f.* (— —s), (nav.) kelson.

contre-rail. *n.m.* (— —s), guard-rail.

contre-retable, *n.m.* (— —s), back of the altar-piece.

contre-révolution, *n.f.* (— —s), counter-revolution.

contre-révolutionnaire, *adj.* (— —s), counter-revolutionary.

contre-révolutionnaire, *n.m.* (— —s), counter-revolutionist.

contre-révolutionner, *v.a.,* to effect a counter-revolution.

contre-ronde, *n.f.* (— —s), (milit.) counter round.

contre-ruse, *n.f.* (— —s), counter-trick.

contre-sabord, *n.m.* (— —s), (nav.) port-lid.

à **contre-saison,** *adv.,* out of season.

contre-salut, *n.m.* (— —s), (nav.) answer to a salute.

contre-sanglon. *n.m.* (— —s), girth-leather.

contrescarpe, *n.f.,* (fort.) counterscarp.

contrescarper, *v.a.,* to make a counterscarp.

contre-scel. *n.m.* (— —s), counterseal.

contre-sceller, *v.a.,* to counter-seal.

contreseing. *n.m.,* counter-signature.

contresens, *n.m.,* contrary sense, contrary meaning; wrong construction; wrong translation; wrong meaning; false reading; wrong side (of stuffs, of an affair—*d'étoffes, d'affaires*). *Faire un —;* to mistranslate, to misinterpret, to misconceive. *A —;* in a wrong way, on the wrong side. *Employer une étoffe à —;* to make up a stuff on the wrong side.

****contre-signal,** *n.m.* (— -signaux), counter-signal.

****contresignataire,** *n.m.,* countersigner.

****contresigner.** *v.a.,* to countersign.

****contre-taille,** *n.f.* (— —s), (com.) counter-tally: *pl..* (engr.) cross-lines.

contretemps, *n.m.,* accident, disappointment; mischance; (man.) counter-time; (mus.) syncopation. *A —;* unseasonably, at a wrong time; (mus.) out of time; with syncopation.

contre-terrasse, *n.f.* (— —s), (her.) lower terrace.

contre-tirer, *v.a.,* to counterdraw, to trace; to counterprove.

contre-tranchée, *n.f.* (— —s), (fort.) countertrench.

contrevairé. -e. *adj..* (her.) countervairy.

contrevallation, *n.f.,* (fort.) contravallation.

contrevenant, *n.m.,* -e, *n.f.,* infringer, offender.

contrevenir, *v.n.,* to infringe, to act contrary to, to violate; to transgress.

contrevent, *n.m.,* window-shutter.

contre-vérité, *n.f.* (— —s), irony; mock praise.

contre-visite, *n.f.* (— —s), second search.

contribuable, *n.m.,* tax-payer; contributor.

contribuer, *v.n.,* to contribute, to conduce, to help on, to tend. *— au succès d'une affaire;* to contribute to the success of a business. *Il y a contribué;* he has contributed to it. *On a fait — tout le pays;* the whole country was put under contribution.

contributi-f. -ve, *adj.;* relating to taxation; subjected to a tax.

contribution, *n.f.,* contribution; tax; (com.) average. *—s directes;* direct taxes. *— indirectes;* indirect taxes. *Mettre un pays à —;* to put a country under contribution.

contributoire, *adj.,* what is to be paid. *Portion —;* amount to be paid, assessment.

contributoirement, *adv.,* of taxes.

contrister, *v.a.,* to grieve, to vex, to make sad.

contrit, -e. *adj.,* contrite, penitent.

contrition, *n.f.,* contrition.

contrôle, *n.m.,* control, controller's office; (thea.) check-taker's office; roll, list; stamp (on gold and silver—*sur l'or et l'argent*); stamp office (for gold and silver—*pour l'or et l'argent*); (milit.) muster-roll; control, censure; register, registry-duty. *Porter quelqu'un sur les —s;* to put any one on the rolls. *Rayer quelqu'un des —s;* to strike anyone off the rolls.

contrôler, *v.a.,* to register, to put upon the rolls; to check, to verify, to examine; to control; to censure, to criticize upon; to stamp (gold and silver—*l'or et l'argent*). *— de la vaisselle;* to stamp plate.

contrôleu-r, *n.m.,* -se, *n.f.,* controller, superintendent; censurer, critic, fault-finder; (thea.) check-taker.

controuver, *v.a.,* to forge, to contrive falsely; to invent, to counterfeit, to feign.

controversable, *adj.,* that may be disputed; controvertible.

controverse, *n.f.,* controversy, discussion, disputation, dispute. *Ouvrage de —,* polemics.

controversé, -e, *adj.,* controverted; debated, argued pro and con, agitated.

controverser, *v.a.,* to controvert, to dispute.

controversiste, *n.m.,* controvertist, disputant.

contumace, *n.f.,* contumacy, non-appearance, default. *Condamner par —;* to judge by default. *Purger la —;* to plead against a judgment given in default; contumaciousness, obstinacy, perverseness.

contumace, *n.m.* and *f.,* (jur.) defaulter, one in contumacy.

contumace, *adj.,* contumacious.

contumacer, *v.a..* (l.u.) (criminal law—*jur. crimin.*) to judge by default. *Se laisser —;* to suffer judgment to go by default.

contumax, *adj.*, (l.u.) contumacious.

contumax, *n.m.*, one guilty of contumacy; (canon law—*loi canon*) he who refuses obedience to the laws of the church, notwithstanding censure and admonition.

contus. **-e**, *adj.*, bruised, contused.

contusion. *n.f.*, contusion, bruise.

contusionné. **-e**, *adj.*, (surg.) bruised.

contusionner, *v.a.*, to contuse, to bruise.

convaincant, **-e**, *adj.*, convincing.

convaincre, *v.a.*, to convince; to persuade, to satisfy; to convict.

se convaincre, *v.r.*, to convince one's self, to be convinced.

convaincu, **-e**. *part.*, convinced, convicted.

convalescence, *n.f.*, convalescence. *En pleine* — ; quite convalescent.

convalescent, **-e**, *adj.*, convalescent.

convalescent. *n.m.*, **-e**, *n.f.*, person in a state of convalescence.

convallaire. *n.f.*, convallaria, lily of the valley. *V.* **muguet**.

convenable (conv-nabl), *adj.*, suitable, fit, proper, convenient, apposite, consonant; seasonable; adequate, conformable, accordant, agreeable; meet, seemly, becoming, beseeming; befitting, expedient; fitting, pat. *Peu* — ; indecorous, unfit. *Juger* — ; to deem proper.

convenablement, *adv.*, suitably, fitly, becomingly, seemly, worthily.

convenance, *n.f.*, fitness, congruity; seasonableness (of time—*de temps*), decency, propiety, expediency; seemliness, convenience; *pl.*, propriety, good manners. *Mariage de* — ; prudent marriage. *Blesser les —s;* to offend against propriety. *Braver les —s;* to set all decorum at defiance. *Manquer de — envers quelqu'un,* to be guilty of a breach of good manners towards any one.

⊙**convenant**. **-e**, *adj.*, becoming, agreeable, suitable, seemly.

convenant, *n.m. V.* **covenant**.

convenir, *v.n.*, to agree; to admit, to own, to acknowledge; to suit, to fit, to match, to serve one's turn; to be proper for; to become; to be suitable; to be fit, expedient, convenient, meet, proper. *Je suis convenu d'y aller,* I have agreed to go there. *Cette maison m'a convenu,* the house suited me. *Il convient que vous y alliez;* it is proper you should go there.

se convenir. *v.r.*, to suit each other, to agree.

conventicule, *n.m.*, conventicle.

convention, *n.f.*, convention, agreement, covenant, treaty; *pl.*, conditions, articles, agreement. *Je m'en tiens à la* — ; I stand to the agreement. *Membre de la — nationale,* member of the National Convention (French hist.).

conventionnel. **-le**, *adj.*, conventional.

conventionnel. *n.m.*, member of the National Convention (French hist.).

conventionnellement, *adv.*, by agreement.

conventualité. *n.f.*, monastic life.

conventuel. **-le**, *adj.*, conventual.

conventuel. *n m.*, conventual.

conventuellement, *adv.*, conventually.

convergence. *n.f.*, convergence.

convergent. **-e**, *adj.*, convergent, converging.

converger, *v.n.*, to tend to one point, to converge.

convers, **-e**, *adj.*, employed in a menial capacity, in a convent. *Frère —, sœur —e;* convert.

convers. *n.m.*, (ich.) young shad.

conversation, *n.f.*, conversation, converse, talk, discourse. *Par où entamer la* — ! how shall we begin the conversation? *S'emparer de la* — ; to engross the conversation, *Être à la* — , to be attending to the conversation. *Laisser tomber la* — ; to drop the conversation.

converse, *n.* and *adj. f.*, (log.) converse; (math.) inverted. *Proposition* — (log.); converse proposition. *Proposition* — (math.); inverted proposition.

converser, *v.n.*, to converse, to talk; to discourse, to commune.

conversible, *adj.*, convertible.

conversion. *n.f.*, conversion; transformation; change; converting, changing; (milit.) wheeling. *Quart de* — ; (milit.) wheel of the quarter circle.

converti. *n.m.*, **-e**. *n.f.*, convert. — *au lit de la mort;* clinical convert.

convertible, *adj.*, (theol., fin.) convertible.

convertir. *v.a.*, to convert; to change, to turn; to make a convert; to bring over, to turn, to transform.

se convertir. *v.r.*, to be converted, to turn, to be made a convert.

convertissable. *adj.*, (fin., theol.) convertible.

convertissement (-män), *n.m.*, conversion.

convertisseur, *n m.*, converter.

convexe. *adj.*, convex.

convexité. *n.f.*, convexity.

convexo-concave. *adj.*, convexo-concave.

convexo-convexe, *adj.*, convexo-convex.

conviction. *n.f.*, conviction. *Agir par* — ; to act from conviction. *Avoir la — intime*, to be thoroughly convinced

convictionnel. **-le** *adj.*, convictive.

convictionnellement, *adv.*, (l.u.) convictively.

convié. *n.m.*, **-e**, *n.f.*, guest, one invited to a feast.

il **convient**, *v.imp.*, it is fit, expedient, convenient, becoming, meet. *V.* **convenir**.

convier, *v.a.*, to invite, to request the company of any one; to incite, to urge. — *à un festin,* to invite to an entertainment.

convive, *n.m.f.*, guest. *C'est un bon* — , he is a good companion at table.

convivialité, *n.f.*, conviviality.

convocable. *adj.*, (very l.u.) convocable.

convocation, *n.f.*, convocation, summons.

convoi, *n m.*, funeral procession; funeral; (milit., nav.) convoy; (railways) train. — *de grande vitesse;* fast train. — *de petite vitesse,* — *de marchandises;* goods train. — *direct;* express train. — *omnibus,* slow train. — *de voyageurs,* passenger train. — *parcourant toute la ligne;* through train. — *funèbre;* funeral procession. *Être du* — ; to be at the funeral. *En* — , (nav.) with convoy

⊙**convoitable**. *adj.*, covetable, desirable.

convoiter. *v.a.*, to covet, to hanker after, to conceive a violent passion for.

convoiteur, *n.m.*, **-se**, *n.f.*, (neologism) coveter.

⊙**convoiteux**. **-se**, *adj.*, covetous, lusting after.

convoitise, *n.f.*, covetousness, eager desire; lust.

convol, *n.m.*, (jur.) second marriage.

convoler. *v.n.*, to marry again. — *en secondes,* *en troisiemes, noces*, to marry a second, a third, time.

convoluté. **-e**, *adj.*, (bot.) convoluted.

convoluti-f, **-ve**, *adj.*, (of leaves — *des feuilles*) curling.

convolvulus (-lûs), *n.m.*, (bot.) convolvulus.

convoquer. *v.a.*, to convoke, to convene, to summon, to assemble.

convoyer, *v.a.*, (milit., nav.) to convoy.

convoyeur, *n.* and *adj. m.*, (nav.) convoy (ship—*vaisseau*).

convulsé, -e, *adj.*, (med.) convulsed.

convulsibilité, *n.f.*, (med.) liability to convulsion.

convulsi-f, -ve, *adj.*, convulsive.

convulsion, *n.f.*, convulsion. *Donner des* —*s*; to throw into convulsions. *Tomber en* —*s*; to be seized with convulsions.

convulsionnaire, *adj.*, subject to convulsions.

convulsionnaire, *n.m.f.*, convulsionary (fanatic).

convulsionner, *v.a.*, (med.) to convulse, to produce convulsions.

convulsivement, *adv.*, convulsively.

conyze, *n.f.*, (bot.) conyza, flea-bane.

coobligation, *n.f.*, joint obligation.

coobligé, *n.m.*, joint bondsman.

coopérant, -e, *adj.*, co-operating, concurring

coopérat-eur, *n.m.*, **-rice**, *n.f.*, co-operator, fellow-labourer, fellow-workman.

coopérat-eur, -rice, *adj.*, (l.u.) co-operating.

coopérati-f, -ve, *adj.*, co-operative.

coopération, *n.f.*, concurrent effort of labour, co-operation.

coopérer, *v.n.*, to co-operate.

cooptation, *n.f.*, co-optation.

coopter, *v.a.*, to co-optate.

coordination, *n.f.*, proper arrangement; co-ordination.

coordonnée, *n.f.*, (geom.) co-ordinate.

coordonner, *v.a.*, to establish order among things; to arrange properly.

copahu, *n.m.*, copaiba, copaiva.

copaïer or **copayer**, *n.m.*, copaiba tree.

copal, *n.m.*, copal.

copartageant. -e (-jän,-te), *n.* and *adj.*, joint-sharer; having a joint share.

copeau, *n.m.*, chip, shaving (of wood). *Des* —*s*; shavings.

copeck, *n.m.* (—*s*). *V.* **kopeck**.

copermutant, *n.m.*, one who exchanges with another, permuter.

copermutation, *n.f.*, the act of exchanging, permutation.

copermuter, *v.a.*, to permute, to exchange.

copernicien, -ne (-in, -è-n), *adj.*, Copernician.

cophte or **copte**, *n.m.* and *adj.*, Copt; Coptic. *Un moine* —; a Coptic monk. *La langue* —; the Coptic language.

copie, *n.f.*, copy, transcript; exercise; imitation; task; (print.) copy. — *figurée*; fac-simile. — *au net*; fair copy.

copier, *v.a.*, to copy; to imitate; to mimic, to take off, to ape.

se **copier**, *v.r.*, to be always the same.

copieusement (ko-pieůz-män), *adv.*, copiously, abundantly, heartily (of eating).

copieu-x, -se, *adj.*, copious, plentiful. *Un homme — en paroles*; a man of many words.

copiste, *n.m.*, copier, transcriber, copyist, imitator; music copier.

copreneur, *n.m.*, co-lessee.

copropriétaire. *n.m.f.*, joint-proprietor.

copropriété, *n.f.*, joint property.

copte, *n.m.* *V.* **cophte**.

copter, *v.a.*, to make the clapper of a bell strike on one side only.

coptique, *adj.*, Coptic.

copulati-f, -ve, *adj.*, copulative.

copulation, *n.f.*, copulation.

copule, *n.f.*, (log.) copula.

coq, *n.m.*, cock; weathercock; (horl.) cock. — *d'Inde*; turkey-cock. — *de bruyère*; heath-cock, grouse. — *à queue fourchue*; black heath-

cock. — *de combat*; game-cock. — *des bois*; wood-cock. — *de montre*; cock of a watch. — *des jardins*; costmary. — *du village*, — *de la paroisse*; cock of the walk. *Joute de* —*s*; cock-fight. *Faire jouter des* —*s*; to make cocks fight. *Au chant du* —; at cock-crow. *Être comme un — en pâte*; to live in clover. *Être rouge comme un* —; to have a face like a turkey apple.

coq, *n.m.*, (nav.) cook.

coq-à-l'âne, *n.m.* (—), idle discourse, nonsense, cock-and-bull story. *Il fait toujours des* —; he is always talking nonsense.

coqualin, *n.m.*, striped squirrel.

coquard, *n.m.*, mongrel pheasant.

coquâtre, *n.m.*, (orni.) half-gelded cock.

coque, *n.f.*, shell (of eggs, walnuts, snails—*d'œufs, de noix, de colimaçons*); pearl-shell; (nav.) hull; (conch.) cockle. *Manger des œufs à la* —; to eat boiled eggs — *du Levant*; Indian berry *Je ne donnerai pas une — de noi c de toutes ses promesses*; I would not give a straw for all his promises.

coquecigrue, *n.f.*, idle story, stuff; fiddle-faddle. *À la venue des* —*s*; never.

coquelicot, *n.m.*, wild-poppy, corn-poppy.

⊙**coqueliner**, *v.n.*, (pop.) to crow, to chuck; to run after the girls.

coquelourde, *n.f.*, Pasque-flower, Flora's-bell.

coqueluche (ko-klush), *n.f.*, ⊙hood; favourite, reigning fancy; hooping-cough. *Il est la — des femmes*; he is the favourite of the fair. ⊙**coquelucher**, *v.n.*, to have the hooping-cough.

coqueluchon, *n.m.*, (jest.) hood of a monk's cloak, cowl.

coquemar (kok-mär), *n.m.*, boiler, kettle.

coquereau, *n.m.*, (nav.) hoy, lighter.

coqueret, *n.m.*, winter-cherry.

coquerico, *n.m.*, cock-a-doodle-do.

coquerie, *n.f.*, (nav.) large cooking-room on a wharf.

coqueriquer, *v.n.*, (l.u.) (pers.) to crow.

coqueron, *n.m.*, (nav.) cook-room.

coquet, -te, *adj.*, coquettish.

coquet, *n.m.*, jilt, flirt; cock-boat.

coqueter (kok-té), *v.n.*, (l.u.) to coquet, to flirt; to be a general coquette or lover; to paddle a boat.

coquetier (kok-tié), *n.m.*, poulterer; egg-merchant; egg-cup.

coquette, *n.f.*, coquette, flirt, jilt. *Faire la* —; to coquet.

coquetterie (ko-kè-trì), *n.f.*, coquetry; affectation (in dress—*dans la parure*); flirtation; finicalness. *Une — d'expressions*; far-fetched expressions.

***coquillage**, *n.m.*, shell-fish; shells; shell-work.

***coquillart**, *n.m.*, bed of shells and stones.

***coquille**. *n.f.*, shell (of fruit, of animals—*des fruits, des animaux*) shell; (print.) wrong letter; thumb (of a latch—*d'un loquet*); foot-board (of coach-box—*de siège de cocher*); post demy, small post (paper—*papier*); under-part of a stair-case; (anat.) concha; *pl.*, wares of little value. *Rentrer dans sa* —; to draw in one's horns. *À qui vendez-vous vos* —*s*; it is of no use trying to do me.

***coquilleu-x, -se**, *adj.*, filled with shells, shelly.

***coquillier**, *n.m.*, collection of shells; cabinet of shells.

***coquilli-er. -ère**, *adj.*, conchiferous.

coquin, -e, *adj.*, idle, debauched; free and easy.

5

coquin, n.m., knave, rascal, rogue. *Tour de* —; knavish trick.

⊙*coquinaille**, n.f., pack of rogues, set of rascals.

coquine, n.f., slut, hussy.

coquinerie (ko-ki-n-rî), n.f., knavery, rascally trick, roguery.

cor, n.m., corn; horn, hunting-horn. *Avoir des* —s *aux pieds;* to have corns on one's feet. *À* — *et à cri;* with horn and voice; with hue and cry; with might and main.

coracoïde, adj., (anat.) coracoid.

*corail**, n.m., coral. *Des lèvres de* —; rosy lips.

*coraillère**, n.f., (nav.) boat to fish corals.

*corailleur**, n.m., coral-diver, coral-fisher.

*corailleur**, adj., of coral fishing. *Bateau* —; coral-fisher's boat.

⊙corallin**, -e, adj., red like coral, coralline.

coralline, n.f., (nav.) boat used in fishing for coral; (zool.) coralline.

coralloïde, adj., coralloid.

coralloïde, n.m, coralloid.

coran, n.m., Koran.

corbeau, n.m., crow; raven; (arch.) corbel, mutule; (astron.) corvus; (nav.) grappling-iron

*corbeille**, n.f., flat, wide basket; (arch.) corbel; (fort.) corbeil; clump (of trees— *d'arbres*); wedding presents. *Une* — *de fleurs;* a basket of flowers. — *de mariage;* wedding presents.

*corbeillée**, n.f., basketful.

corbigeau, n.m. ⊙V. **courlis.**

*corbillard**, n.m., ⊙state-coach; hearse; ⊙young raven.

*corbillat**, n.m., young raven.

*corbillon**, n.m., small basket; crambo (a game—*jeu*).

⊙corbin**, n.m., (orni.) crow. V. **bec-de-corbin.**

corbine, n.f., (orni.) carrion-crow.

corbusée, n.f., (orni.) black-neb.

corcelet, n.m. V. **corselet.**

cordage, n.m., cordage, cord, rope; the measuring of wood by the cord. — *en trois;* rope made with three strands. — *de rechange;* spare ropes.

corde, n.f., cord, rope; line; twist, twine, string; (mus.) chord; tone, note; concord; span (of an arch—*d'une arche*); laniard (of buoys—*de bouées*); thread (of cloth—*du drap*); hanging (death by); gallows. — *à danser;* dancing-rope. *Danseur de* —; rope-dancer. — *à boyau;* cat-gut. *Échelle de* —; rope-ladder. *Une* — *de bois;* a cord of wood. *Ne touchez point cette* — *là;* do not harp upon that string. *Toucher la grosse* —; to hit the main point of the question. *Instrument à* —s; stringed instrument. — *de violon;* fiddle-string. *Flatter la* —; to play with delicacy. *Avoir deux* —s *à son arc;* to have two strings to one's bow. *Son habit montre la* —; his coat is threadbare. *Friser la* —; narrowly to escape hanging. *Il y va de la* —; it is a hanging matter. *Filer sa* —; to go the way to the gallows. *Avoir de la* — *de pendu;* to have the devil's own luck.

cordé, -e, part., twisted.

cordé, -e, adj., (bot.) cordated, heart-shaped.

cordeau, n.m., line, cord.

corder, v a., to twist, twine; to wreathe.

cordelette, n f., small cord; string.

cordelier, n.m., cordelier; Franciscan friar; gray-friar.

cordelière, n.f., Franciscan nun; cordelier's girdle; (arch.) twisted fillet.

cordelle, n.f., (nav.) tow-line; ⊙gang, party.

corder, v.a., to cord; to bind with a cord. — *du bois;* to measure wood by the cord.

se corder, v.r., to be corded; to grow stringy.

corderie, n.f., rope-walk, rope-yard; rope-making; (nav.) boatswain's store-room.

cordial, -e, adj., cordial, hearty, sincere.

cordial, n.m., cordial.

cordialement (kor-dial-măn), adv., cordially, heartily, sincerely.

cordialité, n.f., cordiality; heartiness; hearty affection.

cordier, n.m., rope-maker.

cordiforme, adj., cordiform, heart-shaped.

cordon, n.m., twist, string; check-string (of carriages—*de voitures*); cord; fillet, thread, ribbon; order; girdle; plinth, edging of stone; (milit., fort., arch.) cordon; (anat.) funis; edge (of coins—*de pièces de monnaie*); door-rope. — *ombilical;* umbilical cord. — *de chapeau;* hatband. — *de sonnette;* bell pull. *Un* — *bleu;* a knight of the Holy Ghost. — *bleu;* a first-rate cook. *Un* — *rouge;* a knight of the order of St. Louis.

cordonner, v.a., to twist, to twine; to braid.

cordonnerie, n.f., shoemaking, the trade of a shoemaker; shoe-place.

cordonnet, n.m., twist; edging, milling (of coins—*de pièces de monnaie*).

cordonnier, n.m., cordwainer; shoemaker. — *pour femmes;* ladies' shoemaker.

corée, n.m., (poet.) choreus, trochee. V **chorée.**

corégence, n.f., co-regency.

corégent, n.m., -e, n.f., co-regent.

coreligionnaire, n.m.f., co-religionist.

coriace, adj., tough, ropy; niggardly; stringy; cartilaginous. *Un homme* —; a close-fisted fellow.

coriace, -e, adj., coriaceous.

coriaire, adj., fit for tanning; —, n.f. (bot.) V. **corroyère.**

coriambe, n.m., (poet.) choriambus.

coriandre, n.f., (bot.) coriander.

corindon, n.m., (min.) corindon, corundum, adamantine spar.

corinthien, -ne (-in, -è-n), adj., Corinthian.

corinthien, n.m., -ne, n.f., Corinthian.

coris, n.m. V. **cauris.**

corlieu, n.m., curlew.

corme, n.f., (bot.) service-apple.

cormier, n.m., (bot.) service-tree.

cormoran, n.m., sea-raven, cormorant.

cornac, n.m., elephant driver, cornac; showman.

cornage, n.m., (vet.) wheezing.

*cornailler**, v.n., (carp.) to go stiffly; to be clumsily made.

cornaline, n.f., cornelian stone.

cornard, adj., (pop., l.ex.) cuckold.

cornard, n.m., (pop., l.ex.) cornuto, cuckold.

cornardise, n.f., (pop., l.ex.) cuckoldom.

corne, n.f., horn; corner; shoe-horn; dog's ear (on books, leaves—*aux feuilles des livres*); (nav.) gaff, throat; outside rind (of animals' feet—*des pieds de certains animaux*); cap of the Doge of Venice. *Bête à* —s; horned beast. *Essence de* — *de cerf;* spirits of hartshorn. *Faire les* —s *à quelqu'un;* to cry fie for shame to anyone. *Montrer les* —s; to show one's teeth. *Lever les cornes;* to hold up one's head again. *Les* —s *d'un bonnet carré;* the corners of a square cap. *Chapeau à trois* —s; three-cornered hat. *Les* —s *de la lune;* the horns of the moon. *Les* —s *de l'autel;* the horns of the altar. — *d'abondance;* cornucopia, horn of plenty. *Faire une* — *à un livre;* to turn down the corner of a book. *Faire des* —s *à un livre;* to dog's-ear a book.

corné, -e, adj., corneous, horny.

corneau, *n.m.*, (hunt.) offspring of a bulldog and a hound.

cornée, *n.f.*, (anat.) cornea.

cornéenne, *n.f.*, horn-stone.

*****corneille**, *n.f.*, carrion-crow, rook. — *emmantelée ;* hooded-rook. *Bayer aux —s ;* to stand gaping in the air. *Il y va comme une — qui abat des noix ;* he goes at it tooth and nail.

cornement, *n.m.*, tingling of the ears.

cornemuse, *n.f.*, bagpipe: *Joueur de — ;* bagpiper

corner, *v.n.*, to blow, to wind or sound a horn ; (man.) to wheeze ; to tingle (of the ears —*des oreilles*) ; to be tainted (of meat—*de la viande*). *Les oreilles me cornent ;* my ears tingle.

corner, *v.a.*, to blare out, to blurt out, to trumpet. *Il a corné cela par toute la ville ;* he has trumpeted it through the whole town. — *quelque chose aux oreilles de quelqu'un ;* to din a thing into any one's ears.

cornet, *n.m.*, horn, ear-trumpet ; ink-horn; dice-box ; (conch.) cornet. — *de postillon ; post-boy's horn.* — *à bouquin ;* cowherd's horn. — *à piston ;* cornet-a-piston.

cornette, *n.f.*, head-dress, cornet, mob-cap; cornetcy; (nav.) broad pendant.

⊙**cornette**, *n m.*, (milit.) cornet.

corneur, *n.m.*, horn-blower.

corneur, *adj.*, (vet.) that wheezes.

corniche, *n.f.*, (arch.) cornice, surbase.

cornichon, *n.m.*, little horn ; gherkin ; green-horn, ninny.

cornicule, *n.f.*, small horn, cornicle.

corniculé, -e, *adj.*, corniculate, horned.

corni-er, -ère, *adj.*, corner ; relating to the corner. *Pilastre — ;* column at the corner.

cornière, *n.f.*, corner gutter; (print.) corner iron.

cornifle, *n.m.*, (bot.) horn-wort.

*****cornillas**, *n.m*, young rook.

corniste, *n.m.*, cornist, player upon the horn.

*****cornouille**, *n.f.*, dog-berry.

*****cornouiller**, *n.m.*, dog-berry-tree.

cornu, -e, *adj.*, horned; angular, cornered ; extravagant.

cornue, *n.f.*, (chem.) retort.

corollaire, *n.m.*, corollary.

corolle, *n.f.*, (bot.) corol, corolla.

corollifère, *adj.*, corollated, bearing a corolla.

coronaire, *adj.*, (anat.) coronary.

coronal, -e, *adj.*, (anat.) coronal.

coronal, *n.m.*, (anat.) coronal.

coroner (-nèr), *n.m.* (—s), coroner.

*****coronille**, *n.f.*, (bot.) coronilla.

coronoïde, *adj.*, (anat.) coronoid.

coronope, *n.m.*, (bot.) wart-cress. — *de t uelle ;* crow's-foot.

corossol, *n.m.*, (bot.) custard-apple. — *des marais ;* cork-wood.

corossolier, *n.m*, (bot.) anona.

corporal, *n.m.*, (c. rel.) corporale, communion cloth.

corporalité, *n.f.*, corporality.

corporation, *n.f.*, corporation, corporate body.

corporéité, *n.f.*, corporeity.

corporel, -le, *adj.*, corporal, bodily.

corporellement (-män), *adv.*, corporally, bodily.

corporifier, *v.a.*, to corporify, to form into a body.

corps (kor), *n.m.*, body ; person ; substance, thickness, consistence ; company, society, commonalty, college; main point; barrel (of pumps —*de pompes*) ; caudex (of roots—*de racines*); (anat., fort., milit., paint., print., opt.), body ; (of wine, of writing, of sovereigns, of musical instruments, of wearing apparel—*des vias, de l'écriture, de souverains, d'instruments de musique, de vêtements*), body ; corps ; set of men ; (print.) depth, body, of a letter ; shell (of a house, a pulley—*d'une maison, d'une poulie*). — *mort;* dead body. — *morts;* (nav.) moorings. — *glorieux;* glorious body ; costive person. *Un drôle de — ;* a queer fellow. *Se tuer le — et l'âme;* to work one's life and soul out. *Répondre — pour — ;* to be answerable for a person. *Faire — neuf;* to take a new lease of one's life. *Il fait bon marché de son — ;* he makes himself very cheap ; he exposes himself unnecessarily to danger. *Il faut voir ce que cet homme a dans le — ;* we must see what stuff this man is made of. *Enlever un homme comme un — saint;* (prov.) to kidnap a man. *Gagner son pain à la sueur de son — ;* to earn one's bread by the sweat of one's brow. *Tomber rudement sur le — à quelqu'un;* to speak in offensive terms of any one (either in his presence or his absence—*en sa présence ou en son absence*). *C'est un pauvre — ;* he is a poor weak fellow. *Avoir le — dérangé ;* to have one's body out of order. *Passer son épée au travers du — à quelqu'un;* to run any one through the body with one's sword. *Il a le diable au — ;* he is a devil of a fellow. — *de bâtiment;* principal part of a building. — *de logis;* detached building. *Le — du délit;* that which proves a crime, an offence. *Un vin qui a du — ;* a strong-bodied wine. *Prendre du — ;* to grow stout, fat. *Le — du clergé;* the body of the clergy. *Les — de métiers;* the trades' companies. *Ils font—à part;* they are a separate body. *Esprit de — ;* spirit of party. *Un — d'infanterie;* a body of foot. *Un garde du — ;* a life-guard. *Un — de garde;* a guard-house; watch-house; round-house. — *à — ;* hand to hand. *À — perdu;* headlong; desperately. *À bras-le-corps;* by the waist. *Saisir quelqu'un à bras-le— ;* to seize any one round the waist. *N'avoir rien dans le — ;* to have taken no food; to be a person of no pluck. *À son — défendant;* reluctantly, in one's own defence.

corpulence. *n.f.*, corpulence ; stoutness. *Un homme de petite — ;* a stoutish man.

corpulent, -e, *adj.*, corpulent, stout.

corpusculaire, *adj.*, corpuscular.

corpuscule. *n.m.*, corpuscule.

corpusculiste. *n.m.*, corpuscularian.

⊙**corradoux**, or **courradoux**, *n.m.*, (nav.) between decks. *V.* **entrepont**.

correct (-rèct), **-e**, *adj.*, accurate, correct.

correctement, *adv.*, correctly, accurately.

correcteur, *n.m.*, corrector, emendator; (print.) reader ; Superior of a Minimi's convent.

correcti-f, -ve, *adj.*, corrective.

correctif, *n.m.*, corrective.

correction. *n.f.*, correction ; correctness, accuracy; alteration ; reprimand ; reproof; (print.) reading, correcting. *Maison de —*, house of correction.

correctionnel, -le, *adj.*, correctional (of misdemeanours—*de délits*) ; punishable.

correctionnellement, *adv.*, by way of correction (of misdemeanours—*de délits*).

correctivement (-tiv-män), *adv.*, correctively, as a corrective.

correctoire, *n.m.*, book of penance, formulary.

correctrice, *n.f.*, Lady Superior of a convent of Minimi nuns.

corrégidor, *n.m.*, corregidor.

corrélati-f, -ve, *adj.*, correlative.

corrélati-f, *n.m.*, **-ve**, *n.f.*, correlative.

corrélation. *n.f.*, correlation.

correspondance. *n.f.*, correspondence, intercourse ; connexion, relation. *Être en — avec*, *quelqu'un* ; to correspond with any one. *Entretenir une* — *avec quelqu'un ;* to keep up a correspondence with any one. *Voiture de* —; branch-coach. *Service de* —; cross-post.

correspondant, -e, *adj.,* correspondent, corresponding.

correspondant, *n.m.,* correspondent.

correspondre, *v.n.,* to correspond, to communicate, to be in correspondence ; to agree.

corridor, *n.m.,* lobby, corridor, gallery. *Cette porte donne sur le* —; this door opens into the gallery.

corrigé, *n.m.,* corrected copy ; key (book —*livre*).

corrigeant, -e (-jän, -t), *adj.,* correcting.

corriger, *v.a.,* to correct; to rectify; to repair ; to amend ; to reclaim ; to reprove, to reprehend, to chide, to chastise. — *des épreuves ;* (print.) to correct proofs.

se **corriger,** *v.r.,* to correct one's self, to amend, to reform, to be reformed. *Elle s'est bien corrigée de cela ;* she has quite broken herself of that.

corrigible, *adj.,* corrigible.

corroborant, -e (kor-ro-), *adj.,* (med.) corroborant.

corroborant. *n.m.,* (med.) corroborant.

corroborati-f, -ve (kor-ro-), *adj.,* (med.) corroborative.

corroboratif (kor-ro-), *n.m.,* (med.) corroborant.

corroboration (kor-ro-), *n.f.,* (med.) corroboration, strengthening.

corroborer (kor-ro-), *v.a.,* to strengthen, to corroborate.

corrodant, -e, *adj.,* corroding.

corroder (kor-ro-dé), *v.a.,* to corrode.

corroi, *n.m.,* currying of leather; (mas.) claying.

corroirie, *n.f.,* (tech.) currier's shop, currying.

corrompre, *v.a.,* to corrupt; to adulterate, to spoil; to infect, to taint; to pervert; to bribe. *Les mauvaises compagnies corrompent les bonnes mœurs ;* evil communications corrupt good manners. — *des témoins,* to bribe witnesses. *Se laisser* — ; to take a bribe.

se **corrompre,** *v.r.,* to grow corrupt; to become tainted, to fester.

corrompu. -e, *part.,* corrupted; bribed; spoiled; unsound. *Homme* —; *mœurs* —*es ;* debauchee; dissolute manners.

corrosi-f, -ve (kor-rô-), *adj.,* corrosive.

corrosif, *n.m.,* corrosive.

corrosion (kor-rô-zion), *n.f.,* corrosion.

☉**corroyer.** *n.m.* V. **corroyère.**

corroyer, *v.a.,* to curry (leather—*des cuirs*); to prepare clay for puddling; to pug; to beat up. — *du bois;* to plane wood. — *du fer;* to hammer iron. — *du sable;* (pounding—*écraser*) to roll sand.

corroyère, *n.f.,* (bot.) sumac.

corroyeur. *n.m.,* currier.

corrugateur, *n.m.,* (anat.) corrugator.

corrugation, *n.f.,* corrugation, wrinkling.

corrupt-eur, *n.m..* **-rice,** *n.f.,* (kor-rup-), corrupter, spoiler; briber.

corrupt-eur. -rice, *adj.,* corrupting, corrupt, infectious.

corruptibilité (kor-rup-), *n.f.,* corruptibility.

corruptible (kor-rup-), *adj.,* corruptible.

corruption (kor-rup-), *n.f.,* corruption ; tainting, putridity, rottenness; depravity, perversity, defilement; bribery.

cors, *n.m. pl.,* (hunt.) horns ; branches, starts. *Un cerf dix* — ; a full-grown stag.

corsage, *n.m.,* trunk (of the body—*du corps*); body (of a dress—*de robe*).

corsaire, *n.m.,* privateer ; commander of a privateer ; corsair, rover ; shark (person—*personne*).

corsé, *adj.,* (fam.) strong, thick.

corse. *n.m.f.* and *adj.,* Corsican.

corselet. *n.m.,* corselet.

corset, *n.m.,* corset, stays ; bodice ; (surg.) bandage.

corseti-er, *n.m.,* **-ère,** *n.f.,* (-tié, -ti-èr), corset-maker, stay-maker.

cortège, *n.m.,* train, retinue, cortege ; procession ; attendants.

cortès (-tès), *n.f.pl.,* cortes (Spanish parliament—*le parlement espagnol*).

cortical, -e, *adj.,* (bot., anat.) cortical.

cortiqueu-x, -se, *adj.,* (bot.) corticose.

coruscation, *n.f.,* coruscation.

corvéable, *adj.,* (feudalism—*féodalité*) liable to forced labour ; liable to contribution in forced labour.

corvéable, *n.m.,* one liable to forced labour ; one liable to contribution in forced labour.

corvée, *n.f.,* (feudalism—*féodalité*) statute-labour ; fatigue duty done by soldiers ; toil ; drudgery ; bore.

corvette. *n.f.,* corvette, sloop of war.

☉**corvoyeur,** *n.m.,* man employed on forced labour.

corybante, *n.m.,* priest of Cybele.

corybantique, *adj.,* corybantic. —*s, n.f. pl.,* feasts in honour of Cybele.

☉**corybantisme.** *n.m.,* (med.) insanity attended with sleeplessness.

corymbe, *n.m.,* (bot.) cluster, corymb.

corymbé, -e. (bot.) corymbous.

corymbeu-x, -se, *adj.,* (bot.) corymbiated.

corymbifère. *adj.,* (bot.) corymbiferous. —*s, n.f. pl.,* corymbiferous plants.

coryphée, *n.m.,* corypheus ; leader, chief ; principal man ; (theat.) chorus-master.

coryza, *n.m.,* (med.) coryza, cold in the head.

cosaque. *n.m.,* Cossack.

cosaque, *n.f.,* Cossack dance. *Je veux te faire danser une* — ; (pop.) I'll let you know, sir ; I'll give you a taste of the stick.

cosécante, *n.f.,* (geom.) co-secant.

*****coseigneur,** *n.m.,* joint lord of a manor.

cosinus (-si-nûs), *n.m.,* (geom.) co-sine.

cosmétique. *n.m.* and *adj.,* cosmetic.

cosmétique, *n.f.,* art of using cosmetics.

cosmique, *adj.,* (astron.) cosmical.

cosmiquement, *adv.,* (astron.) cosmically.

cosmogonie, *n.f.,* cosmogony.

cosmogonique, *adj.,* cosmogonical.

cosmographe, *n.m.,* cosmographer.

cosmographie, *n.f.,* cosmography.

cosmographique, *adj.,* cosmographical.

cosmolabe, *n.m.,* (astron.) cosmolabe.

cosmologie, *n.f.,* cosmology.

cosmologique, *adj.,* cosmological.

cosmologiste, *or* **cosmologue,** *n.m.,* cosmologist.

cosmopolite, *n.m.,* cosmopolite.

cosmopolite. *adj.,* cosmopolitan.

cosmopolitisme, *n.m.,* cosmopolitism,

cosmorama, *n.m.,* cosmorama.

cosse, *n.f.,* cod, husk, pod ; (nav.) thimble.

cosser, *v.n.,* (of rams—*des béliers*) to butt.

cosson, *n.m.,* (ent.) weevil ; (agri.) new shoot of a vine.

cossu, -e, *adj.,* husked, podded ; substantial, warm, rich. *En conter de* —*es ;* to tell romantic tales.

costal. -e, *adj.,* costal.

costume, *n.m.,* customs, manners, usages ; costume, dress. *Grand* —; full dress. *Petit* — ; undress.

costumer. *v.a.,* to dress in a costume.

se **costumer,** *v.r.,* to dress one's self as, in a costume.

costumier, *n.m.*, costumier, dealer in costumes.

cotangente, *n.f.*, (geom.) co-tangent.

cote, *n.f.*, letter, number, figure (to indicate the order—*pour indiquer le rang, l'ordre*); (com.) quotation; quota, share. *Faire une — mal taillée* ; to compromise claims by mutual agreement.

côte, *n.f.*, rib (of the body, of cloth, of fruit —*du corps, des étoffes, des fruits*) ; (arch., bot., manu.), rib ; (agri.) edge ; hill, declivity; shore, sea-coast. *Fausses —s* ; short ribs. *Se casser une —* ; to break a rib. *Rompre les —s à quelqu'un* ; to break any one's bones. *Mesurer les —s à quelqu'un* ; to thrash any one. *Se mettre à la —* ; (nav.) to run aground. *Ranger la —* ; to coast. *Raser la —* ; to sail along, to hug, the shore. *— à —* ; side by side. *Le long de la —* ; along the hill.

côté, *n.m.*, side; broadside ; way, manner ; flank ; part; slice. *Il a un point de —* ; he has got a stitch in his side. *Le — faible* ; the weak side. *Mettre une bouteille, un tonneau, sur le —* ; to empty a bottle, a cask. *De tous —s* ; on all sides. *— de première* ; (print.) outer form. *— de seconde* ; inner form. *De mon —* ; for my own part. *Ils sont parents du — maternel* ; they are related on the mother's side. *Il est du — gauche* ; he is a natural child. *Se ranger du — de quelqu'un* ; to side with any one. *De quel — êtes-vous ?* whom do you side with ? *Il se met du — du plus fort* ; he takes the strongest side. *A — de* ; by, near. *Être à — de la question* ; to be far from the question. *Donner à —* ; to miss. *De —* ; sideways, aslant, obliquely, aside. *Une vue de —* ; a side-view. *Regarder de —* ; to look askance. *Mettre une chose de —* ; to lay by. *De — et d'autre* ; up and down, here and there, on all sides. *C'est son — faible* ; it is his weak side. *S'asseoir à — de quelqu'un* ; to sit by the side of any one. *Se tenir les —s de rire* ; to shake one's sides with laughing. *De l'autre —* ; in the next room.

coteau, *n.m.*, declivity, slope ; little hill, rising ground.

côtelette (kot-let), *n.f.*, chop, cutlet. *Une — de mouton* ; a mutton chop. *Des —s de veau* ; veal cutlets. *— de porc frais* ; pork chop.

coter, *v.a.*, to number ; to quote. *— le cours des effets publics* ; to quote the price of stocks.

coterie (ko-trî), *n.f.*, coterie, set, club ; gang.

cothurne, *n.m.*, buskin. *Chausser le —* ; to assume the buskin.

cothurné, -e, *adj.*, (antiq.) cothurnated.

côtier (-tié), *adj., n.m.*, coasting ; coasting-pilot.

côtière (-tî-èr), *n.f.*, (gard.) border, sloping bed ; (nav.) (l.u.) coasts, coast-line.

**cotignac (-gna), n.m., quiddany, marmalade of quinces.

*cotillon, n.m., under-petticoat ; cotillon (dance). Il aime le — ; he loves the women. *Régime du —* ; petticoat government.

cotir, *v.a.*, (fruit) to bruise, to damage.

cotisation, *n.f.*, clubbing ; assessment, quota, share.

cotiser, *v.a.*, to assess, to rate.

se **cotiser**, *v.r.*, to rate, to assess ; to unite, to club together.

cotissure, *n.f.*, (fruit) damage, bruising.

coton, *n.m.*, cotton ; down (of fruit and hair on the face—*des fruits, du poil follet*). *— épluché* ; picked cotton. *— brut* ; raw cotton. *— plat* ; darning cotton. *— à tricoter* ; knitting cotton. *— de couleur* ; coloured cotton. *Bobine de —* ; reel of cotton. *Écheveau de —* ; skein

of cotton. *Balle de —* ; bale of cotton. *Toile de —* ; cotton cloth. *Il jette un vilain —* ; he is losing his reputation. *Il jette, il file, un mauvais —* ; he is declining very fast.

cotonnade, *n.f.*, cotton cloth, cotton-check.

cotonné, -e, *part.*, woolly (of hair—*des cheveux*) ; covered with, full of, cotton.

cotonner, *v.a.*, to fill, to cover with, cotton.

se **cotonner**, *v.r.*, to be covered with down, to become downy; to cotton, to nap, to rise with a nap, to become mealy (of vegetables—*des fruits, des légumes*). *Les artichauts et les radis se cotonnent*; artichokes and radishes grow pithy or spongy.

cotonner, *v.n.*, to cotton, to nap, to rise with a nap.

cotonneu-x, -se, *adj.*, pithy, spongy, mealy ; (bot.) downy, cottony.

cotonnier, *n.m.*, cotton-tree.

cotonni-er, -ère, *adj.*, cotton, of cotton.

cotonnière, *n.f.*, (bot.) cotton-weed; cudweed.

cotonnine, *n.f.*, cotton sail-cloth.

côtoyer, *v.a.*, to go by the side ; (nav.) to coast, to coast along ; to keep close to the shore.

cotre, *n.m.*, cutter. *V.* **cutter.**

cotret, *n.m.*, fagot. *Il est sec comme un —* ; he is as thin as a lath. *De l'huile de —* ; stirrup oil, cudgelling.

cottage. *n.m.*, cottage-villa, cottage.

cotte, *n.f.*, ☉petticoat. *— d'armes* ; coat of arms. *— de mailles* ; coat of mail. *— morte* ; the property which a monk leaves behind him after his death.

cotte, *v.m.*, (ich.) bull-head. *— chabot* ; sea-scorpion.

☉**cotteron**, *n.m.*, short, narrow skirt ; [diminut. of **cotte**].

cotut-eur, *n.m.*, **-rice**, *n.f.*, joint-guardian.

cotyle, *n.f.*, (antiq.) a Greek measure nearly equal to half a pint English ; (anat.) cotyla.

cotylédon, *n.m.*, (anat., bot.) cotyledon.

cotylédoné, -e, *adj.*, (bot.) cotyledonous.

cotylier, *n.m.*, (bot.) cotyledon, navel-wort.

cotyloïde, *adj.*, (anat.) cotyloid.

cou, *n.m.*, neck. *— de travers* ; wry-neck. *Sauter, se jeter, au — de quelqu'un*; to fall on a person's neck. *Se casser le —* ; to break one's neck. *Rompre le — à* ; to break the neck of. *Prendre ses jambes à son —* ; to take to one's heels.

couard, *n.m.*, (fam.) coward, dastard.

couard, -e, *adj.*, (fam.) coward, cowardly.

couardement, *adv.*, (fam.) cowardly.

couarder, *v.n.*, (fam.) to act in a cowardly manner.

couardise, *n.f.*, (fam.) cowardice, dastardliness.

couchage, *n.m.*, bedding (for the army—*pour l'armée*); act of lying ; price of a bed (lodging—*logement*).

couchant, *adj.*, setting. *Un chien —* ; a setting dog. *Faire le chien —* ; to crawl and cringe. *Soleil —* ; setting sun.

couchant, *n.m.*, west ; wane, decline.

couche, *n.f.*, bed ; bedstead ; confinement, childbed, lying-in ; delivery, birth ; childbed-linen, swaddling-clothes ; layer, stratum, row; (gard.) hot-bed, bed ; (mining—*mines*) seam ; coat (of varnish, colour—*de vernis, de couleur*); stake (at play—*au jeu*). *La — nuptiale* ; the nuptial bed. *Pendant ses —s* ; during her confinement. *Elle est morte en —s* ; she died in childbed. *Être en, faire ses, —s* ; to be confined, to lie-in. *Heureuse —* ; good delivery. *Fausse —* ; miscarriage. *Partager la — de quelqu'un*, to be the partner of any one's bed.

couché, -e, *part.*, put to bed, in bed, lying down, recumbent, jaçent ; (her.) couchant.

couchée, *n.f.*, place where one stops to sleep when travelling ; bed ; night's lodging.

coucher, *v.a.*, to put to bed ; to lay down ; to lay low ; to lodge ; to knock down ; to incline ; to lay on ; ⊙to stake. — *quelqu'un en joue;* to take aim at any one. — *en joue;* to aim at. ⊙ — *gros;* to play deep. — *par écrit;* to write down.

se coucher. *v.r.*, to go to bed ; to lay one's self down, to lie down, to lie flat ; to set ; to go down. *Allez vous* — ; go to bed. *Il n'est pas encore temps d'aller* —; it is not bed-time yet. *Comme on fait son lit, on se couche;* as you make your bed, so you must lie. *Allez vous* — (fam.) ; go along with you, be off with you. *Le soleil se couche;* the sun is setting.

coucher, *v.n.*, to lie, to sleep ; to lie down, to rest. — *au cabaret;* to sleep at a public-house. — *à la belle étoile;* to sleep in the open air. — *sur la dure;* to sleep upon the bare boards. — *tout habillé;* to sleep with one's clothes on.

coucher, *n.m.*, going to bed, retiring to rest; sleeping ; settlrg. *C'est l'heure de son* —; it is his bed-time. *Le petit* — ; the time from the king's taking leave of the company to his going to bed.

couchette, *n.f.*, bedstead.

coucheu-r, *n.m.*, **-se**, *n.f.*, bed-fellow. *Mauvais* —; troublesome bed-fellow ; disagreeable person.

couchis, *n.m.*, layer.

couci-couci, *adv.*, (fam.) so so, indifferently.

coucou, *n.m.*, cuckoo ; barren strawberry-plant ; wooden clock ; one-horse chaise.

coude, *n.m.*, elbow ; bend, angle ; winding; knee (of machinery—*de machines*). *Donner des coups de* — ; to elbow. *Hausser le* — ; to drink hard, to fuddle.

coudé, -e, *part.*, bent, elbowed ; having an elbow.

coudée, *n.f.*, arm's length ; cubit. *Avoir les* — *franches;* to have elbow room.

cou-de-pied, *n.m.* (—s —), instep.

couder, *v.a.*, to bend, to make an elbow.

se couder. *v.r.*, to elbow, to form an elbow.

coudoyer, *v.a.*, to elbow, to jostle.

se coudoyer, *v.r.*, to elbow, to jostle, one another.

coudraie, *n.f.*, hazel-copse; filbert-orchard.

coudran. *n.m.*, (nav.) tar.

coudranner, *v.a* , (nav.) to soak cords in tar.

coudre, *n.m* , nut-tree, hazel-tree.

coudre (*cousant, cousu*), *v.a.*, to sew, to stitch ; to tack. — *à;* to stitch or sew to. — *du linge;* to sew linen. — *à grands points;* to take long stitches.

⊙**coudrette**, *n.f.*, hazel-copse.

coudrier, *n.m.*, hazel-tree.

couenne (kooa-n), *n.f.*, pig-skin ; (med.) buff.

couenneu-x, -se (kooah-), *adj.*, (med.) containing buff. *Angine—se;* diphtheria.

couette. *n.f.*, ⊙ feather-bed ; (mec.) socket.

coufique. *adj.*, (philol) cufic.

cougourde, *n.f.*, (bot.) bottle-gourd.

couguar (-gar), *n m.*, (mam.) cougar.

coulage, *n.m.*, leakage.

coulamment (koo-la-mån), *adv.*, fluently, freely, readily. *Il parle* — ; he talks fluently.

coulant, -e, *adj.*, flowing ; streamy; smooth ; easy, accommodating; slip (of knots —*de nœuds*). *Style* —; easy, fluent style. *Nœud* —; noose.

coulant, *n.m.*, slide (jewel worn by ladies round the neck—*pierre précieuse que les dames portent au cou*) ; slide (of an umbrella, &c.—*de parapluie, &c.*).

coulé, *n.m.*, (mus.) slur; slide (dance); cast (founding—*fondu*) ; (paint.) first wash.

coulée, *n.f.*, (of writing—*écriture*) running-hand; tapping (metal.) ; (geol.) coulée. *Trou de* — (metal.); tap-hole.

coulement (kool-mån), *n.m.*, running, flow (of liquids).

couler, *v.n.*, to flow, to run ; to glide, to glide along ; to pour, to stream; to trickle, to drop; to leak, to run out ; to ooze ; to glide away, to fly away; to slip; to slide away, to go down ; (founding—*fonte*) to run through the mould ; to touch lightly upon; to be uhed, to be spilt. *Se laisser* — *jusqu'à terre;* to slide down to the ground. *Faire* — ; to shed. *L'échelle va* — ; the ladder will slip. *L'encre ne coule pas;* the ink does not run freely. *Le nez lui coule;* his nose runs. *La chandelle coule;* the candle gutters. *Les larmes lui coulent des yeux;* tears trickle from his eyes. — *sur un fait;* to glide over a fact. — *bas;* to founder, to sink.

couler, *v.a.*, to cast ; to strain ; to slip in ; to pass (time—*le temps*) ; (mus.) to slur; to run down ; to do for; to scald (linen); to fall off, to drop; to sink ; to run smooth, to flow. — *une statue;* to cast a statue. — *une glace;* to cast a plate of glass. — *un vaisseau à fond;* to sink a ship. — *un pas;* to pass smoothly over a step (in dancing—*en dansant*).

se couler, *v.r.*, to slip, to creep, to steal, to slide.

couleur, *n.f.*, colour, paint; favour (ribbon —*ruban*) ; colouring; appearance; suit (at cards—*aux cartes*). —*s aigres;* st.ff colours. —*s amies;* friendly colours. — *éclatante;* deep colour. — *tranchante;* glaring colour. — *solide;* fast colour. — *de feu;* flame colour. — *de rose;* rose colour. *Pâles* — *s* (med.); chlorosis, green sickness. — *locale;* local colouring. — *voyante;* showy colour. — *à l'huile;* oil colour. —*s passantes;* fading colours. *Diversifier, mêler, assortir, les* —*s;* to vary, to blend, to match, colours. *Juger d'une chose comme un aveugle des* —*s;* to talk of a subject without knowing anything about it. *Voir tout* — *de rose;* to see all things in their brightest colours. *Les hommes de* — ; men of colour, mulattoes. *Lampes de* — ; variegated lamps. *Reprendre* — ; to be in favour again; to appear in society again. *Changer de* — ; to change colour. *La* — *lui monta au visage;* the colour came into his face. *Ce rôti a bien pris* —; that roast meat is nicely browned. *L'affaire prend* —; the thing is looking better. *De quelle* — *tourne-t-il?* what are trumps (at cards—*aux cartes*)? *Donner de la* — ; to follow suit. *Prendre* — ; (lansquenet) to stake and cut the cards. *Appliquer les* —*s;* to lay on the colours. *Adoucir, amortir, les* —*s;* to soften, to deaden, colours. *Rehausser les* —*s;* to heighten the colours. *Peindre à pleines* —*s;* to paint with a full brush. *Mettre en* — ; (paint.) to stain. *Style sans* — ; colourless style. *Prendre* — ; to assume a character. *Il l'a trompé sous* — *d'amitié;* he deceived him under a show of friendship. *Sous* — *de;* under the pretext of.

couleuvre, *n.f.*, adder ; (fig.) mortification. *Faire avaler des* —*s à quelqu'un;* to put all sorts of indignities on a person who dares not complain.

couleuvreau, *n.m.*, young adder.

couleuvrée, *n.f.*, (bot.) bryony.

couleuvrine, *n.f.*, culverin ; aspic. *Être sous la* — *d'un autre;* to be dependent on another. *Être sous la* — *d'une place;* to be within reach of a fort.

coulis, *adj.m.* *Vent* — ; wind that comes through cracks and chinks, draught of air.

coulis, *n.m.*, (cook.) cullis, gravy, jelly; (mas.) grout.

coulisse, *n.f.*, groove; sliding board; running string; rib (presses); (print.) galley; (theat.) side-scene; behind the scenes; shutter, door; (exchange language—*terme de bourse*) coulisse, unauthorised part of the exchange; Capel Court; frequenters of the coulisse. — *d'arbalète*; chase of a cross-bow. *Propos de* —*s*; green-room talk. *Faire les yeux en* —; to look out of the corner of one's eyes.

coulisseau, *n.m.*, wooden grooves for beds with castors; guide (engineering—*terme d'ingénieur*).

coulissier, *n.m.*, stock-jobber who transacts business on the exchange without being licensed as a stock-broker.

couloir, *n.m.*, skimming-dish, strainer; (arch.) passage, lobby. ⊙—*de la bile*; biliary duct.

couloire, *n.f.*, colander, sieve, strainer.

coulpe, *n.f.*, (rel.) sin, fault. *J'en dis ma* —; I repent, I ask pardon.

coulure, *n.f.*, running (metal); falling off (fruit).

coumarine, *n.f.*, (chem.) coumarine.

coup (koo), *n.m.*, blow, thump, knock, stroke, hit, stab, thrust, lash; crack (of a whip —*de fouet*); beat (of a drum—*du tambour*); draught (liquids); clap (of thunder—*de tonnerre*); (artil.) charge; move (at chess, draughts —*aux échecs, aux dames*); (fenc.) thrust; gust (of wind—*de vent*); throw (at dice—*aux dés*); shot, report (of fire-arms—*d'armes à feu*); butt (of rams—*de béliers*); time; trick; event; aim; attempt; act; action; deed; kick (with the foot—*avec le pied*); push. —*s*; knocking. — *amorti*; spent shot. *Grand* —; hard blow; last cast. *Porter un* —; to deal a blow. *Petit* —; pat; sip (of liquid—*de liquides*). *Heureux* —; lucky hit. — *monté*; got-up affair. — *mortel*, — *de mort*; death-blow. — *de maître*; master-stroke. — *de jarnac*; unexpected blow. — *de tête*; act of desperation. — *de partie*; decisive blow. — *de poing*; blow with the fist. — *de coude*; push with the elbow. *Un* — *de revers*; back-stroke. *Donner des* —*s de pied*; to kick. — *de massue*; blow with a club; thunder-stroke. — *de bâton*; blow with a stick. *Donner des* —*s de bâton à quelqu'un*; to cudgel any one. *Donner un* — *d'épée*; to deal a sword thrust — *de fleuret*; pass. *Donner des* —*s de fouet*; to lash. — *de dent*; bite. *Au* — *de trois heures*; when the clock strikes three. *Un* — *de sifflet*; a whistle (with the mouth—*avec la bouche*). *Donnez-moi un* — *de peigne*; give me a combing. — *de foudre*; thunder-bolt. — *de sang*; apoplectic fit; congestion of the brain. — *de soleil*; sun-stroke. — *d'air*; cold in the head *or* chest. *Le* — *de grâce*; the coup-de-grace, the finishing stroke. *C'est comme un* — *d'épée dans l'eau*; it is like beating the air. *Un* — *de bec*; a piece of slander. *Assommer quelqu'un de* —*s, rouer quelqu'un de* —*s*; to beat in a cruel manner. *Détourner le* —; to ward off the blow. *Faire son* —, *manquer son* —; to succeed, to fail, in one's project. — *perdu*; random shot. *Donner un* — *de chapeau*; to touch one's hat. *Faire d'une pierre deux* —*s*; to kill two birds with one stone. *Flanquer des* —*s à quelqu'un*; to give any one a thrashing. *Sans* — *férir*; without striking a blow, without firing a shot. *Porter* —; to hit home. *Encore un* —; once more, again; one more blow. *Encore un* — *je vous dis*; once more do I tell you. *D'un seul* —; at one blow; at one swoop. *A* — *perdu*; in vain. *Sous le* — *de*; under the threat of. — *sur* —; one after another, without stopping. *Pour le* —; at,

upon this, thereupon, for once. *Après* —; too late. *A tous* —*s*; at every turn, every moment. *Du premier* —; at the first. *Tout à* —; all of a sudden, suddenly. *Tout d'un* —; at once, all at once. *A* — *sûr*; certainly, to a certainty, unquestionably. *Il a reçu un* — *de fusil*; he has received a gun-shot wound. — *de canon à l'eau*; shot between wind and water. — *de partance*; (nav.) farewell gun; signal for departure. *Un* — *de vent*; a gale. — *de main*; (milit.) coup-de-main, surprise, sudden, unexpected, desperate, attack. *Donner un* — *de main à quelqu'un*; to give one a hand. *Donner un* — *d'épaule à quelqu'un*; to give any one a helping hand, a lift. *Donner un* — *de collier*; to put one's shoulder to the wheel. *Frapper les grands* —*s*; to employ decisive measures. *Asséner un* —; to deal a blow. *Coup d'œil*; glance, look. *Jeter un* — *d'œil sur*; to take a peep at. *Avoir le* — *d'œil juste*; to have a sure eye. *Au premier* — *d'œil*; at first sight. *Cette démarche a porté* —; this step has taken effect. *Un* — *de bonheur*; a lucky hit. *Un* — *de malheur*; an unlucky hit. — *d'étourdi*; rash action. — *de désespoir*; desperate attempt. — *d'essai*; first attempt. — *d'éclat*; striking act. — *de tête*; great piece of wisdom, rash action. — *d'état*; piece of great policy; violent measures. — *d'autorité*; unusual act of authority. *Par un* — *de hasard*; by a mere chance. — *de bonheur*; lucky chance. — *imprévu*; unexpected accident. — *du ciel*; providential hit. —*s et blessures*; (jur.) cutting and maiming. — *de théâtre*; unexpected event; clap-trap. *Il a fait le* —; he has done the deed. *Un* —; once. *Il a encore trois* —*s à jouer*; he has still to play three times. *Tirer un* —; to fire a shot. *Porter un* — *fourré à quelqu'un*; to do any one an ill turn. *Le* — *vaut l'argent*; it is worth trying. *Buvez encore un* —; drink once more. *Boire un grand* —; to drink a large draught. *Buvons un* — *ensemble*; let us take a glass together. *Tuer quelqu'un à* —*s de bâton*; to beat any one to death.

coupable, *adj.*, culpable, guilty, in fault, sinful. *Déclarer quelqu'un* —; to bring any one in guilty. *Se déclarer* —, *non* —; to plead guilty, not guilty.

coupable, *n.m.f.*, guilty person; culprit.

coupage, *n.m.*, cutting; diluting (of wine—*du vin*).

coupant, *n.m.*, edge (of a sword, &c.—*d'une épée, &c.*). *de l'ongle du sanglier*; the edge of a wild boar's foot (hunt.).

coupant, -e, *adj.*, cutting, sharp (instruments).

coupe, *n.f.*, cutting; chopping; felling (of wood—*de bois*); wood felled; cut (style); cut (place); the cut end; felling, a fall of timber; cup; chalice; quaffing-bowl; (arch.) section, plan, slope; division; (astron.) Crater; calice; cup; (theol.) wine; cutting (at cards—*aux cartes*). *La* — *des cheveux*; hair-cutting. *La* — *des pierres*; stone-cutting. *Mettre en* —; to mark for cutting. *La* — *d'un bois taillis se fait tous les neuf ans*; coppice wood is felled every ninth year. *Il a la* — *malheureuse*; he has a very unlucky hand at cutting. *Être sous la* — *de quelqu'un*; to play first (at cards — *aux cartes*); to be in any one's power. *Boire la* — *jusqu'à la lie*; to drink the cup of bitterness to the dregs. — *d'un ouvrage*; division of a work into parts. *La* — *et liaison des scènes*; the division and connexion of the scenes. *La* — *des vers*; the division of verses. *Boire dans une* —; to drink out of a cup.

coupé, *n.m.*, coupee (step in dancing—*pas de danse*); chariot; brougham; front part of a French diligence.

coupé. -e, *part.*, cut, short. laconic. *Un pays* — ; a country intersected with rivers, canals, &c. *Un style* — ; a laconic style. *Du lait* — ; milk and water.

coupe-asperges, *n.m.* (—), (hort.) asparagus-knife.

⊙**coupeau**, *n.m.*, top of a hill.

coupe-bourgeon, *n.m.* (— *s*), vine-grub.

coupe-cercle, *n.m.* (— *s*), round-punch (for cutting out pasteboard—*pour découper du carton*).

coupe-cors, *n.m.* (—), corn-cutter (instrument).

coupe-gorge, *n.m.* (—), cut-throat place ; nest of swindlers ; the dealer turning up his own card first (lansquenet).

coupe-jarret, *n.m.* (— *s*), cut-throat, assassin, ruffian.

coupe-légume, *n.m.* (— *s*), vegetable-cutter.

coupellation (-pèl-la), *n.f.*, (chem.) cupellation ; testing (metal.).

coupelle, *n.f.*, cupell. *Argent de* — ; purest silver. *Essai à la* — ; cupellation. *Mettre à la* — ; to submit to cupellation ; to put to the test.

coupeller, *v.a.*, to test (metals—*les métaux*).

***coupe-paille**, *n.m.* (—), chaff-cutter.

coupe-pâte, *n.m.* (—), dough-knife.

couper, *v.a.*, to cut ; to cut off, to lop, to strike off, to cut down ; to cut out ; to clip, to pare, to cut away, to geld ; to cross, to get before ; to dilute (milk, wine, with water—*du lait, du vin, avec de l'eau*), (milit.) to intercept ; to divide, to intersect, to interrupt ; to intercept, to hinder ; to impede, to get before ; to strike ; to geld ; to cut up, to carve ; to amputate ; to chop. — *menu ;* to mince. — *un habit ;* to cut out a coat. — *par tranches ;* to slice, to cut into slices. — *la queue ;* to dock. *Les sanglots lui coupent la voix ;* her sobs stifle her utterance. — *la bourse à quelqu'un ;* to pick one's pocket. — *le cours d'une rivière ;* to interrupt the course of a river. — *les vivres à une armée ;* to intercept the provisions of an army. — *la parole à quelqu'un ;* to interrupt any one. *Pour — court ;* to be brief, in short. — *le chemin à quelqu'un ;* to stop one's way. — *la ligne ;* (milit.) to break through the line. — *le sifflet à quelqu'un* (pop.); to cut any one's throat.

se **couper**, *v.r.*, to cut one's self ; to be chafed ; to cut ; to wear out ; to burst ; to crack ; to intersect, to intersect one another ; to cross, to intersect ; to contradict one's self, to falter, to equivocate. — *la gorge ;* to cut one's throat ; to fight a duel with any one. — *la main ;* to cut one's hand. *Ce cuir s'est coupé ;* this leather has burst.

couper, *v.n.*, to cut, to cut in (at cards—*aux cartes*) ; to chop. *À qui à* — *?* whose cut is it ? — *dans le vif ;* to cut to the quick. — *court à quelqu'un ;* to cut any one short. — *par le plus court ;* to take the shortest way.

coupe-racine, *n.m.* (— *s*), (agri.) root-breaker.

couperet (koo-prè), *n.m.*, chopper, enameller's file.

couperose (koo-prôz), *n.f.*, copperas ; (med.) stone-pock. — *verte ;* green vitriol. — *blanche ;* white vitriol. — *bleue ;* blue vitriol.

couperosé, -e, (koo-prô-zé), *adj.*, blotched, pimpled.

coupe-tête, *n.m.* (*n.p.*), leap-frog.

coupeu-r, *n.m.*, **-se**, *n.f.*, cutter ; player (lansquenet). — *de bourse ;* pickpocket, cutpurse.

coupeur d'eau, *n.m.*, (orni.) cut-water.

couplage, *n.m.*, one of the sixteen parts composing a float of wood.

couple, *n.f.*, couple (two things of the same kind—*deux choses de même espèce*) ; (of game

—*du gibier*) brace. *Une* — *de bœufs ;* a yoke of oxen. *Une* — *de lièvres ;* a brace of hares.

couple, *n.m.*, couple (two animated beings acting in concert—*deux êtres vivants agissant de concert*) ; pair (of animals, male and female—*d'animaux, mâle et femelle*) ; (nav.) frame. *C'est un* — *bien assorti ;* they are a well-matched couple. *Un* — *de chevaux ;* a pair of horses. *Maître* — ; midship-frame. —*s de remplissage ;* (nav.) filling timber. — *de balancement ;* balance timbers. *Par* —*s ;* in pairs.

coupler, *v.a.*, to couple, to link.

couplet, *n.m.*, couplet, verse ; song ; tirade ; hinge.

coupleter. *v.a.*, to write a song.

⊙**coupletier**, *n.m.*, writer of songs.

coupoir, *n.m.*, cutter (sharp instrument—*outil coupant*) ; blade ; knife ; (print.) cutting-knife ; (foundry—*fonderie*) dressing-bench.

coupole, *n.f.*, spherical vault ; cupola.

coupon, *n.m.*, remnant ; coupon, dividend warrant ; (com.) part (of shares—*d'actions*) ; (theat.) ticket.

coupure, *n.f.*, cut, slit, incision ; suppression, erasion ; (milit.) intrenchment, ditch behind a breach ; (banking term—*terme de banque*) small note. *J'ai une* — *au doigt ;* I have a cut on my finger.

cour, *n.f.*, court (of a sovereign prince—*d'un prince souverain*) ; court of justice ; love-suit, courtship ; yard, court, courtyard. *Basse*- — (—*s* —*s*), back-yard, poultry-yard. — *d'entrée ;* entrance-court, front-court. — *de derrière ;* back-court. *Les gens de la* — ; courtiers. *Eau bénite de* — ; empty promises. *C'est la* — *du roi Pétaud ;* it is Bedlam broken loose. *Faire la* — *à une dame ;* to court a lady. *Mettre hors de* — ; to nonsuit.

courable, *adj.*, (hunt.) that may be hunted.

courage, *n.m.*, courage, daring ; spirit, mettle, fearlessness ; fortitude, greatness of soul ; heart, zeal ; passion, temper. *Prendre* — ; to be of good heart, to pluck up courage. *Manquer de* — ; to be wanting in courage. *Perdre* — ; to be discouraged. *Tenir son* — *à deux mains ;* to summon all one's courage. *Je n'ai pas le* — *de lui refuser ;* I have not the heart to refuse it him. — *!* come ! take courage.

courageusement (-jeûz-mân), *adv.*, courageously, bravely, valiantly, gallantly, fearlessly.

courageu-x, -se, *adj.*, courageous, daring, gallant, valiant, brave, fearless.

⊙**coural**, *n.m.* *V.* **courée.**

couramment (koo-ra-mân), *adv.*, fluently, readily. *Il lit* — : he reads fluently.

courant, -e, *adj.*, current, running, present ; ordinary ; fair, middling (of goods—*de marchandises*) ; lineal (of measures—*de mesures*). *Le mois* — : the present month. *Monnaie* —*e ;* current coin. *Le prix* — ; the current price. *Compte* — ; account current. *Écriture* —*e ;* running-hand.

courant, *n.m.* current, stream, tide ; course, routine ; present price ; present month, instant. *Le* — *du marché ;* the market price. *Le* — *des affaires ;* the course of affairs. *Être au* — *des nouvelles ;* to know the news of the day. *Tenir quelqu'un au* — *de ;* (com.) to keep any one constantly advised of. *Se mettre au* — *de ;* to acquaint one's self with. *Fin* — ; (com.) at the end of the present month. *En* — ; cursorily, in haste.

courante, *n.f.*, courant (a kind of dance—*sorte de danse*) ; running-hand (of writing—*écriture*) ; (l.ex.) looseness, relaxation.

⊙**couranu**, *n.m.* *V.* **courée.**

courbage, *n.m.*, bending, curving.

***courbaril**, *n.m.*, locust-tree.

courbatu, -e, *adj.,* (vet.) foundered, bad in the joints; (med.) affected with the lumbago. *Je me sens tout —;* I have got the lumbago all over me.

courbature, *n.f.,* (vet.) foundering, lameness; (med.) lumbago.

courbaturer, *v.a.,* to bring on the lumbago.

courbe, *adj.,* curved, bent.

courbe, *n.f.,* curve; (nav., carp.) knee; (vet.) curb; turn (in a road—*de route*).

courbement, *n.m.,* bending.

⊙**courbément,** *adv.,* curvedly, crookedly.

courber, *v.a.,* to bend, to warp, to make crooked, to curve, to incurvate; (tech.) to sag, to bow down, to weigh down. *Courbé de vieillesse;* bent with age.

se **courber,** *v.r.,* to bend, to bow; to stoop; to bow down.

courber, *v.n.,* to bow, to bend.

courbet, *n.m.,* bow of a pack-saddle.

courbette, *n.f.,* (man.) curvet; bowing and scraping (of a person—*des personnes*). *Il fait des —s,* he bows and cringes.

courbetter, *v.n.,* (man.) to curvet.

courbure, *n.f.,* curve, curvature, bending, curvation, bend; (tech.) sagging.

*****courcailler,** *v.n.,* to cry like a quail.

*****courcaillet,** *n.m.,* cry of the quail; quailpipe.

courcive, *n.f.* *V.* **coursive.**

courçon, *n.m.,* (artil.) iron hoop, band.

coureau, *n.m.,* small yawl (to load ships—*pour charger les vaisseaux*).

courée, *n.f.,* (nav.) stuff to pay a ship's bottom.

coureur, *n.m.,* runner, racer; courser, hunter; light-porter; running footman; groom; gadder; rambler, rover, stroller; inconstant lover; (milit.) skirmisher; scout. *— de sermons;* sermon-hunter. *— de nuit;* man who keeps late hours.

coureuse, *n.f.,* gadder, street-walker.

coure-vite, *or* **court-vite,** *n.m.* (—), (orni.) courser.

courge, *n.f.,* gourd, pumpion, pumpkin. *— à la moelle;* vegetable marrow.

courir (courant, couru), *v.n.,* to run; to hasten; to hunt, to run after; to ramble, to gad abroad. to run about, to rove, to run up and down; to flow, to stream; to run on; to run along, to extend, to stretch; to prevail, to be prevalent, to be about, abroad; to go round; to be current, to circulate, to be reported; (nav.) to sail. *— à toutes jambes;* to run as fast as possible. *— à bride abattue;* to ride full gallop. *— après;* to run after. *Devancer en courant;* to outrun. *— çà et là;* to run about, up and down; to gad about. *L'année qui court;* the present year. *Au temps, par le temps, qui court;* as times go. *La monnaie qui court;* the current money. *La mode qui court;* the prevailing fashion. *Le bruit court qu'il est mort;* there is a report that he is dead. *Il court bien des maladies;* there is much illness about. *— à l'autre bord;* (nav.) to stand upon the other tack. *— au large;* to stand off. *— à sa perte;* to hasten to one's ruin. *— à l'hôpital;* to be ruining one's self. *— aux armes;* to fly to arms. *— sur le marché de quelqu'un;* to outbid any one. *— à sa fin;* to draw to an end. *Faire — des bruits;* to spread reports. *Faire — une santé;* to make a toast go round.

courir, *v.a.,* to run after, to pursue; to travel over; to hunt; to frequent; to infest; to expose one's self, to run, to take. *— les rues;* to run about the streets. *— la prétantaine;* to gad about. *— les bals, les théâtres;* to frequent balls, theatres. *— le pays;* to rove, to stroll about. *— le monde;* to travel. *Être fou à — les*

rues; to have lost one's wits. *— la poste;* to do a thing precipitately. *— sa vingtième année;* to be in one's twentieth year. *— le plat pays, la mer;* to be a pirate. *— le même lièvre;* to be engaged in the same pursuit.

courlieu, *or* **courlis,** *n.m.,* (orni.) curlew.

couronne, *n.f.,* crown, coronet; wreath; (anat., arch., astron., conch., hort., hunt.) crown; crown (of the teeth—*des dents*); crown (a coin—*pièce d'argent*); (vet.) coronet; (fort.) crown-work. *— civique;* civic crown. *— d'épines;* crown of thorns. *La — du martyre;* the crown of martyrdom. *Décerner une —;* to award a wreath. *— impériale;* (bot.) crown-imperial. *— de pieu;* head of a stake. *— des blés;* rose-campion. *Domaine de la —;* crown-lands. *C'est le plus beau fleuron de sa —;* it is the brightest jewel in his crown. *Traiter de — à —;* to treat from sovereign to sovereign. *— matrimoniale;* (hist. of Scotland—*histoire d'Écosse*) matrimonial crown.

couronné, -e, *part.,* crowned; encompassed; (vet.) broken-kneed; (arch.) capped. *Arbre —;* tree of which the top is withering. *Cheval —;* broken-kneed horse.

couronnement (koo-ro-n-mǎn), *n.m.,* crowning, coronation; (arch.) crowning, coping (of walls—*de murailles*); cap (of blocks—*de poulies*); (nav.) taffarel of a ship.

couronner, *v.a.,* to crown; to decree a crown; to award a prize; to wreath; (arch.) to cap. *— de fleurs;* to crown with flowers. *La fin couronne l'œuvre;* all's well that ends well.

se **couronner,** *v.r.,* to be crowned, to wear a crown; to begin to wither at the top (of trees—*des arbres*); to be broken-kneed (of a horse—*du cheval*).

couronnure, *n.f.,* crown (on a stag's head —*de la tête du cerf*).

⊙**courradoux,** *n.m.* *V.* **entrepont.**

courre, *n.m.,* (hunt.) starting-place; hunting country.

courre, *v.a.,* (hunt.) to run; to hunt.

courrier, *n.m.,* courier, post, post-boy; messenger. *— de la malle;* mail-guard. *Jour de —;* post-day. *Par le — de ce jour;* by to-day's post. *Par le retour du —;* by return of post. *L'heure du —;* post-time. *Faire son —;* to get one's letters ready for the post. *Lire son —;* to read one's letters.

courrière, *n.f.,* (l.u.) wanderer (woman).

courroi, *n.m.,* roller (used by dyers—*de teinturier*).

courroie, *n.f.,* strap, thong. *Allonger la —;* to make the most of one's money. *Serrer la — à quelqu'un;* to diminish any one's supplies.

courroucer, *v.a.,* to provoke to anger, to anger. *Flots courroucés;* angry waves.

se **courroucer,** *v.r.,* to become angry.

courroux, *n.m.,* wrath, anger, rage. *Être en —;* to be angry.

courroyer, *v.a.,* to stretch stuffs just dyed.

courroyeur, *n.m.,* one who stretches stuffs just dyed.

cours, *n.m.,* course, stream, current, running, vent, scope; public drive (place—*place publique*); vogue; currency (of coin—*des monnaies*); progress; continuation; term, space; lectures, course of lectures; (com.) market price; (nav.) voyage. *Donner un libre à sa fureur;* to give full vent to one's rage. *Le — du soleil est d'orient en occident;* the course of the sun is from east to west. *Le — de la vie;* the space of life. *Ce bruit a eu —;* there has been such a report. *Donner — à;* to give currency to. *Salle de —;* lecture-room. *Faire un —;* to give a course of lectures. *Suivre un —;* to attend a course of lectures. *Ce jeune homme a fini ses —;* this young man has finished his studies. *— de ventre;* looseness of the bowels.

Le — des humeurs; the flow of humours. — *légal;* legal tender. *Dernier —;* closing price. *Premier —;* opening price. *Obtenir le —;* (com.) to command a price. *Voyage de long —;* distant voyage.

course, *n.f.*, race, running; run; career; tilt; coursing, hunting, chase; cruise, cruising incursion, privateering; journey, walk; excursion, jaunt; tour; fare; course; (nav.) cruise; length of the stroke (of a piece of machinery— *d'une pièce de machine). Il est léger à la —;* he is swift in the race. *Surpasser à la —;* to outrun. *— de bague;* running at the ring. *— de chevaux;* horse-race. *— au clocher;* steeplechase. *Une — à pied;* a foot-race. *— de chars;* chariot-race. *— par enjeux;* sweepstakes. *— de haies;* hurdle-race. *Aller en —;* to go upon a cruise. *Vaisseau armé en —;* ship armed for cruising, privateer. *Être en —;* to be out. *Faire des —s;* to go on errands. *Faire une — à cheval;* to take a ride. *Faire une — à pied;* to walk out on foot. *Prendre un fiacre à la —;* to take a hackney coach by the distance. *Lutte à la —;* foot-match.

coursier, *n.m.*, charger, steed; (nav.) bow, bow-chase; float-board.

coursive, *n.f.*, (nav.) waist.

courson, *n.m.*, shoot cut down to three or four eyes; vine-shoot.

court, **-e**, *adj.*, short; scanty; brief, concise, succinct; limited. *Être — d'argent;* to be short of money. *Avoir la vue —e ;* to be near-sighted. *Il est revenu avec sa —e honte ;* he came back unsuccessful. *Il veut la faire —e et bonne;* he wishes to have a short but merry life.

court, *n.m.*, the shortest way. *Savoir le — et le long d'une affaire ;* to know the long and the short of an affair.

court, *adv.*, short. *S'arrêter tout —;* to stop short. *Tourner —;* to turn short. *Pour le faire —;* to be short. *Couper — à quelqu'un;* to cut any one short. *Demeurer tout —;* to stop short. *Tenir quelqu'un de —;* to keep one under. *Tout —;* only.

courtage, *n.m.*, (com.) business of a broker; brokerage, commission. *— de change;* billbrokerage. *Faire le —;* to carry on the business of a broker.

courtaud, **-e**, *adj.*, thick-set, dumpy; docked (of dogs, horses—*des chiens et des chevaux). Étriller quelqu'un en chien —,* to give any one a good licking.

courtaud, *n.m.*, **-e**, *n.f.*, short, thick-set person. *Courtaud, courtaud de boutique ;* shop drudge. [In the latter sense, *courtaud* is not used in the feminine.]

courtauder, *v.a.*, to dock (horses—*les chevaux).*

***court-bouillon**, *n.m.* (*—s —s*), a wine-sauce to boil fish in.

court-bouton, *n.m.* (*—s —s*), peg (of a plough—*de charrue).*

courte-botte, *n.m.* (*—s —s*), shrimp of a fellow.

courte boule, *n.f.*, short bowls.

courte haleine, *n.f.*, shortness of breath, asthma.

courtement, *adv.*, (l.u.) with brevity, in few words.

***courte paille**, *n.f.*, cut (piece of straw). *Tirer à la —;* to draw cuts.

courtepointe, *n.f.*, counterpane.

courtepointier (-tié), *n.m.*, counterpanemaker.

courter, *v.a.*, to buy and sell as a broker, as a commission agent.

courtier (-tié), *n.m.*, broker. *— de change;* bill-broker, money-broker. *— non breveté. — marron ;* unlicensed broker. *— maritime;* ship-

broker. *— pour les denrées coloniales;* colonial-broker. *— d'assurances, d'actions;* insurance, share, broker. *— pour les sucres;* sugar-broker. *— de mariage ;* matrimonial agent.

courtière, *n.f.*, matrimonial agent.

courtilière, *n.f.*, mole-cricket.

***courtille**, *n.f.*, the northern outskirts of Paris.

courtine, *n.f.*, (fort.) curtain.

courtisan, *n.m.*, courtier.

courtisane, *n.f.*, courtesan.

courtisanerie, *n.f.*, courtiery; mean fawning.

courtisanesque, *adj.*, courtier-like.

courtiser, *v.a.*, to court, to make court to, to flatter. *— une femme;* to make love to a woman.

court-jointé, **-e**, *adj.* (*— —s*), short-jointed (of horses—*des chevaux).*

courtois, **-e**, *adj.*, courteous, polite, well-bred. *Armes —es ;* courteous arms.

courtoisement (-toaz-màn), *adv.*, in a courteous manner, courteously.

courtoisie, *n.f.*, courteousness, courtesy, kindness, good turn.

à courts jours, *adv.*, having a few days to run (of bills). *Lettre de change à —;* bill which has but a few days to run.

court-vêtu, **-e**, *adj.* (*— —s*), dressed in short clothes.

court-vite, *n.m.* (*—*) *V.* **coure-vite**.

couscous, *n.m.* (*n.p.*), the name of an Arabian dish consisting of very small balls of minced meat and flour fried in oil

couseuse, *n.f.*, stitcher (of books—*de livres).*

cousin, *n.m.*, **-e**, *n.f.*, cousin; friend, crony. *— germain ;* first cousin, cousin german. *— au troisième degré;* third cousin.

cousin, *n.m.*, (ent.) gnat.

cousinage, *n.m.*, relationship of cousin, relation, kindred.

cousiner, *v.a.*, to call cousin.

se **cousiner**, *v.r.*, to call one another cousin.

cousiner, *v.n.*, to sponge, to live on others, to be friends, cronies.

cousinerie (koo-zi-n-rî), *n.f.*, host of cousins.

cousinière, *n.f.*, gnat-veil.

cousoir, *n.m.*, (book-bind.) sewing-press.

coussin, *n.m.*, cushion; pad; (min., surg.) bolster. *— de mire;* bed of a cannon.

coussinet, *n.m.*, small cushion; pad; iron wedge; (surg.) bolster; (arch.) cushion; (railways) chair; pillion (of saddles—*de selles);* (bot.) whortleberry; cranberry.

cousu, **-e**, *part.*, sewed, stitched. *Ses finesses sont cousues de fil blanc;* his tricks are very shallow. *Bouche cousue;* mum's the word. *Être — d'argent;* to be rolling in money.

coût, *n.m.*, (jur.) cost, charge; price, expense.

coûtant, *adj.*, of the cost. *Prix —;* prime cost.

couteau, *n.m.*, knife; ⊙ short sword, dagger. *— à découper;* carving-knife. *À —x tirés;* at daggers drawn. *— pliant;* clasp-knife. *— à ressort;* spring-knife. *— à deux tranchants,* two-edged knife. *Planche à —x ;* knife-board. *Donner un coup de — à quelqu'un;* to stab one with a knife. *Aiguiser ses —x;* to prepare for the engagement. *— poignard;* dagger-knife. *Ils en sont à —x tirés;* they are at daggers drawn.

coutelas (koo-tlâ), *n.m.*, cutlass.

coutelier, *n.m.*, cutler.

coutelière, *n.f.*, knife-case; cutler's wife.

coutellerie (koo-tèl-rî), *n.f.*, trade of a cutler; cutler's shop; cutlery, cutler's ware.

coûter, *v.n.*, to cost; to stand in; to be expensive; to be painful, troublesome, mortifying. *Il lui en coûte beaucoup de dire cela ;* it is very painful to him to say that. *L'argent ne lui coûte rien ;*

he knows not the value of money. *Que coûte-t-il de souhaiter!* there is nothing so easy as wishing. *Tout lui coûte;* every thing is an effort to him. *Coûte que coûte;* come what may; at any price.

coûter, *v.a.,* to cost. *Cela lui coûta la vie;* that cost her her life.

coûteusement, *adv.,* expensively.

coûteu-x, -se, *adj.,* expensive, costly.

coutier (-tié), *n.m.,* tick-maker.

coutil (koo-ti), *n.m.,* ticking. *Fil de —;* drill.

coutre, *n.m.,* plough-share, coulter.

coutume, *n.f.,* custom; habit; practice, usage; ⊙tax; collection of customs. *Selon ma —;* according to my custom. *Comme de —;* as usual. *Avoir — de;* to be used to. *Une fois n'est pas —;* once does not make a habit.

coutumi-er, -ère, *adj.,* common, ordinary, customary; accustomed, used; wonted, habitual. *Pays —;* country governed by common law. ⊙**coutumier,** *n.m.,* customary (book of common law—*livre de coutumes*).

couture, *n.f.,* seam; sewing, stitching; scar. *Rabattre les —s;* to flatten the seams. *Ils ont été battus à plate —;* they were totally routed. *— ouverte;* (nav.) open seam.

couturer, *v.a.,* to seam. *Il a le visage couturé;* his face is seamed.

couturier, *n.* and *adj. m.,* (anat.) sartorious, the tailor's muscle; ⊙seamster.

couturière, *n.f.,* dress-maker, sempstress, mantle-maker.

couvain, *n.m.,* eggs of bees, bugs, &c.

couvaison, *n.f.,* brooding-time, sitting.

couvée, *n.f.,* nest of eggs; brood, covey; (b.s.) generation, race of persons. *D'une —;* at one brood.

couvent, *n.m.,* convent, monastery, nunnery.

couver, *v.a.,* to sit on, to hatch; to brood on, to incubate, to brood, to brew. *— quelqu'un des yeux;* to look tenderly at any one. *— de mauvais desseins;* to brew ill designs. *— une maladie;* to breed a distemper.

se **couver,** *v.r.,* to brood, to sit, to lie hid, to hatch.

couver, *v.n.,* to brood, to sit, to lie hid; to lurk; to smoulder; to prepare secretly.

couvercle, *n.m.,* cover, lid; (tech.) cap, shutter.

couverseau, *n.m.,* cover of the drum (of a mill—*d'un moulin*).

couvert, *n.m.,* table-cloth and covers; cover (plate, spoon, knife, and fork); case containing a spoon, knife, and fork; shelter; covert, shady place, thicket; cover, wrapper. *Mettre le —;* to lay the cloth. *Ôter le —;* to remove the cloth, to clear the table. *Donner le — à quelqu'un;* to shelter any one.

couvert, -e, *part.,* covered; (fort.) covered, hid, hidden, secret; close, concealed; cloudy, overcast (of the weather—*du temps*); obscure, ambiguous (of words—*des mots*); clad, deep-coloured (of wine—*du vin*). *— de plaies;* covered with sores. *— de gloire;* loaded with honour. *Il est toujours bien —;* he is always well clothed. *Mots —s;* ambiguous words. *Pays —;* woody country. *Chemin —;* (fort.) covert-way. *Lieu —;* shady place. *Temps —;* cloudy weather. *À —;* under cover; sheltered, secure. *Se mettre à —;* to shelter one's self. *Être à —;* to have good security, to be safe.

couverte, *n.f.,* glaze, glazing.

⊙**couvertement,** *adv.,* covertly, secretly.

couverture, *n.f.,* cover (of a book—*de livre*); wrapper; coverlet, counterpane, bed-clothes; blanketing; cloak, blind; (com.) guaranty. *— de laine;* blanket. *— de cheval;* horse-cloth. *— piquée;* quilt. *— de selle;* saddle-cloth. *Faire la —;* to turn down the bed.

couverturier, *n.m.,* maker of blankets.

couvet, *n.m.,* earthenware foot-stove.

couveuse, *n.f.,* brooding-hen.

couvi, *adj.,* addle. *Œuf —;* rotten egg.

couvre-chef, *n.m.* (— —s), covering for the head, kerchief.

couvre-feu, *n.m.* (—), curfew, curfew-bell.

couvre-lumière, *n.m.* (— —s), (artil.) apron.

couvre-pied, *n.m.* (— *or* — —s), foot-cover, let.

couvre-plat, *n.m.* (— —s), dish-cover.

couvreur, *n.m.,* tiler, slater. *— en ardoise;* slater. *— en chaume;* thatcher.

couvrir, (couvrant, couvert), *v.a.,* to cover; to envelop; to wrap up; to muffle up; (com., milit.) to cover; (of horse—*du cheval*) to serve, to leap; to excuse, to palliate; to defray (expenses—*des dépenses*); to overflow, to over-spread; to overrun; to protect; to copulate; to leap; to cloak, to keep secret, to disguise. *— un toit;* to roof. *— de honte;* to load with shame. *— sa faute;* to palliate one's fault. *Un bon général doit savoir — sa marche;* a good general ought to know how to conceal his march.

se **couvrir,** *v.r.,* to cover one's self, to put on one's hat, to be covered; to cover *or* defend one's self; to conceal one's self; to get under cover; to be overcast (of the weather—*du temps*); to reimburse one's self. *Couvrez-vous;* put your hat on. *Le temps se couvre;* the weather is overcast.

covenant (kov-nän), *n.m.,* covenant.

covenantaire, *n.m.,* covenanter.

covendeu-r, *n.m.,* **-se,** *n.f.,* joint-vender.

cowpox, *n.m.,* cow-pox.

coxal, *adj.,* (anat.) of the hip, pertaining to the hip.

crabe, *n.m.,* crab-fish.

crabier, *n.m.,* crab-eater.

crac, *int.,* creaking noise, crack. *—! le voilà parti;* he was off in the twinkling of an eye!

crachat, *n.m.,* spittle; slight materials (of buildings—*de bâtiments*); star, grand cross.

crachement (krash-män), *n.m.,* spitting. *— de sang;* spitting of blood.

cracher, *v.a.,* to spit, to spit out, to utter, to come out with; to come down with (money —*de l'argent*). *Tout craché;* very like.

cracher, *v.n.,* to spit, to sputter (of speaking, of pens—*du parler, des plumes*). *— au bassin;* to contribute. *— au nez, au visage, de quelqu'un,* to spit in any one's face.

cracheu-r, *n.m.,* **-se,** *n.f.,* spitter.

crachoir, *n.m.,* spittoon.

crachotement, *n.m.,* spitting often.

crachoter, *v.n.,* to spit often.

craie, *n.f.,* chalk. *Marquer avec de la —;* to chalk. *Marquer à la — les logis que les soldats doivent occuper;* to billet, to quarter soldiers.

craindre, (craignant, craint), *v.a.,* to fear, to apprehend; to be afraid of, to dread, to stand in awe or fear of; to be afraid; to dislike; to be unable to bear. *Il craint d'être découvert;* he fears being discovered. *Il craint que sa femme ne meure;* he fears his wife will die. *Je ne crains pas de le dire;* I do not hesitate to say so. *Ces arbres craignent le froid;* cold will hurt these trees. *Se faire — de quelqu'un;* to keep any one in awe.

crainte, *n.f.,* fear, dread, awe, apprehension. *La — de Dieu;* fear of God. *La — de la mort;* the fear of death. *Retenir quelqu'un par la —;* to keep one in awe. *Sans —;* fearlessly. *Avec —;* fearfully. *— de, de —;* for fear of. *De — que,* for fear of; for fear that, lest. *De — d'être surpris;* for fear of being surprised. *De — qu'il ne le fasse;* lest he should do it.

crainti-f. -ve. *adj.*, fearful, apprehensive, timid, timorous, cowardly.

craintivement. *adv.*, fearfully, timorously.

***cramailler**. *n m.*, (horl.) notch-wheel.

cramoisi, *n.m.*, crimson.

cramoisi, -e. *adj.*, crimson; red, scarlet (of persons—*des personnes*). *Devenir tout* — ; to turn quite red.

crampe. *n.f.*, cramp; torpedo, cramp-fish, numb-fish; (nav.) cramp-iron; hook of a block. *Avoir des* —*s* ; to have the cramp.

crampon, *n.m.*, (bot.) fulcrum. prop; (farriery—*maréchalerie*) calkin ; (hort.) climbing-spur; (mach) click ; cramp-iron, cramp-hook; brace. — *de fer à cheval* ; frost-nails of a horse-shoe.

cramponné. -e. *part.*, (her) having half a potence at both ends, cramponee; (farriery—*maréchalerie*) with calkins.

cramponner, *v.a.*, to cramp, to fasten with a cramp-iron. — *un cheval* ; to shoe a horse with frost-nails, calkins.

se cramponner, *v.r.*, to cling, to fasten to any thing.

cramponnet, *n.m.*, little cramp-iron, tack, loop. — *de targette* ; lock staple.

cran, *n.m.*, notch; (bot.) scurvy-grass, cochlearia, horse-radish; (print.)nick; (vet.) notch, ridge. *D'un* — ; by a notch. *Sa fortune a baissé d'un* — ; his fortune is a notch, a peg, lower.

crâne, *n.m.*, skull, brain-pan, cranium; (pop.) madcap, swaggerer, blusterer.

crânerie (crâ-n-ri), *n.f.*, (pop.) swaggering, blustering.

crangon, *n.m.*, shrimp.

craniologie, *or* **cranologie**, *n.f.*, craniology.

craniologique, *adj.*, craniological.

craniologiste, *n.m.*, craniologist.

craniomètre, *n.m.*, craniometer.

craniométrie, *n.f.*, craniometry.

craniométrique, *adj.*, craniometrical.

cranioscopie, *n.f.*, cranioscopy.

cranologie, *n.f.* V. **craniologie**.

cranson, *n.m.*, scurvy-grass. — *rustique*, horse-radish.

crapaud. *n.m.*,toad ;(artil.) mortar-carriage ; (vet.) crepane, maltworm. *La bave d'un* — ; toad-spittle. *C'est un vilain* — ; he is an ugly toad. *Il est chargé d'argent comme un* — *de plumes*, all the money he has he may put in his eye. — *de gouvernail* ; (nav.) goose-neck. — *de mer* ; toad-fish. — *volant* ; churn-owl. — *de timon* ; pole-end (of a carriage—*d'une voiture*).

***crapaudaille**. *n.f.*, a gang of contemptible people. V. **crépodaille**.

crapaudière, *n.f.*, toad-hole; (fig.) lov, swampy place.

crapaudine, *n.f.*, (min.) bufonite, toad-stone, wolf's-tooth ; leaden grating; valve of an escape pipe ; (vet.) crepane, crack; (bot.) sideritis, iron-wort ; (mec.) socket. *Mettre des pigeons à la* — ; to broil pigeons on a grid-iron with their legs flattened and stretched out.

crapelet, *n.m.*, young toad.

crapone. *n.f.*, (horl.) square flat file.

crapoussin. *n.m.*, -e, *n.f.*, little ill-shaped man or woman, dwarf, shrimp. *Ces gros petits* —*s crèvent comme des mousquets et nous, maigrelets, nous vivons*, these big, short, deformed wretches go off like so many muskets, while we, poor thin beings, live on.

crapule. *n.f.*, low vulgar debauchery; crapulence, intemperance ; gluttony, drunkenness ; low debauched people.

crapuler. *v.n.*, to live in crapulence, to fuddle or drink hard, to give one's self up to all sorts of low debauchery.

crapuleusement, *adv* , intemperately.

crapuleu-x.-se, *adj.*, crapulous, drunken, intemperate. vulgar, debauched.

craque. *n.f.*, fib, humbug.

craquelé, -e. *adj.*, crackled, fissured (of china—*de la porcelaine*).

craquelin (kra-klin), *n.m.*, cracknel.

craquelot (kra-klo), *n.m.*, red-herring.

craquelotière (kra-klo-tièr), *n.f.*, woman who cures herrings.

craquelure. *n.f.*, fissure, crack (in china, pictures. &c.—*de la porcelaine, des tableaux, &c.*).

craquement (krak-mán), *n.m.*, crack, cracking noise; crepitation, creaking. *Un* — *de dents* ; a chattering of the teeth.

craquer, *v.n.*, to creak, to crack, to crackle ; to tell a lie, to boast, to draw the long bow. *Faire* — *ses doigts* ; to make one's fingers snap.

craquerie, *n.f.*, cracking boasting, drawing the long bow, fiction, story, fib, fudge.

craquètement. *n.m.*, crackling ; gabbling (of the stork and other birds—*de la cigogne et d'autres oiseaux*).

craqueter (kra-kté). *v.n.*, to crackle, to crepitate; to gabble (of some birds—*de quelques oiseaux*). *Le laurier craquete au feu* ; laurel crackles in the fire.

craquette. *n.f.*, notch (of a tailor—*de tailleur*); scum (on melted butter—*de beurre fondu*).

craqueu-r, *n.m.*, **-se**, *n.f.*, noisy, boasting fellow; bouncer, braggart.

crase, *n.f.*, (gram.) crasis, contraction of two syllables into one ; (med.) crasis, constitution.

crasiologie, *n.f.*, crasiology.

crassane, *n.f.*, crasane, a sort of pear.

crasse, *n.f.*, dirt, filth, scurf; squalor; niggardliness, stinginess ; coat of filth that collects on a painting; rusticity, bad manners. — *de la tête* ; dandriff. *La* — *des métaux* ; the dross, scum, scale, of metals. *La* — *du collège* ; the rudeness of school

crasse, *adj* , gross, thick, coarse. *Une ignorance* — ; gross ignorance.

crasser. *v.a.*, to foul, to dirty (of fire-arms —*d'armes à feu*).

se crasser, *v r.*, to become foul (of fire-arms —*d'armes à feu*).

crasseu-x.-se. *adj* , dirty, filthy, nasty, squalid, rusty. *Cheveux* — ; greasy hair.

crasseu-x. *n.m.*, **-se**. *n.f.*, sloven, slut; niggard, miser, skin-flint. *Un* — ; a filthy man.

crassule, *n.f.*, a plant having succulent or thick leaves.

cratère, *n.m.*, (geol.) crater ; (antiq) bowl, cup ; (astron.) Crater. Cup.

craticulation, *n.f.*, (paint.) squaring.

craticuler, *v.a.*, (paint.) to square. V. **graticuler**.

cratirites, *n.f.pl.*, wild Grecian figs.

craupécherot, *or* **corbeau pêcheur**, *n.m.*, (orni.) bald-buzzard, osprey, fishing-eagle.

cravache, *n.f* , horsewhip.

cravan. *n.m.*, (orni.) brent-barnacle, brand-goose, brent.

cravate. *n.f.*, cravat, neckcloth, necker-chief — *d'un drapeau* ; knot of a flag-staff.

cravate, *n.m.*, Croat; Croatian horse. *Régiment de* —*s* ; formerly regiment of light cavalry; regiment of Croats. —, *adj.*, Croatian. *Cheval* — ; Croatian horse.

se cravater. *v.r.*, to put on one's cravat.

crayeu-x.-se, *adj.*, chalky

crayon. *n.m.*, chalk; pencil; pencil drawing, portrait in crayons; description of a persoü; sketch. — *noir*; blacklead-pencil. — *d'ardoise*; slate-pencil. — *de pastel*; pastel, crayon. *Affûter un —, donner une pointe à un —*; to point a pencil.

crayonner, *v.a.*, to draw with a pencil; to sketch rudely or imperfectly; to sketch, to trace the outline, to chalk, to delineate; to paint badly.

crayonneur, *n.m.*, (b.s.) dauber.

crayonneu-x, **-se**, *adj.*, chalky.

créadier, *n.m.*, sort of drag-net.

créance, *n.f.*, credence, credit, trust, belief; debt, money owing; influence; (hunt.) command. *Lettres de —*; letters of credence, credentials. *Lettre de —*; letter of credit. *Donner — à une chose*; to give credit to a thing. *Chien de bonne —*; dog under good command. *Oiseau de peu de —* (hawking—*fauconnerie*); bird that will not come back to its master.

créanci-er, *n.m.*, **-ère**, *n.f.*, creditor; (jur.) covenantee, obligee; debtee. — *importun*; dun. — *hypothécaire*; mortgagee.

créat, *n.m.*, (man.) creat.

créateur, *n.m.*, creator, maker.

créat-eur, **-rice**, *adj.*, creative, creating. *Il a le génie —*; he has an inventive genius.

créatine, *n.f.*, (chem.) creatine.

création, *n.f.*, creation; production. *Les merveilles de la —*; the wonders of the creation.

créature, *n.f.*, creature; dependant, tool.

ⓢ**crébèbe**, *n.m.*, V. **cubèbe**.

crécelle, *n.f.*, rattle.

crécerelle, *n.f.*, (orni.) kestrel.

crèche, *n.f.*, manger, crib; infant-asylum; (arch.) starling with a row of stakes.

crédence, *n.f.*, credence, credence-table; buttery, pantry.

crédencier, *n.m.*, pantler, clerk of the buttery, buttery-keeper.

crédibilité, *n.f.*, credibility.

crédit, *n.m.*, credit; trust; authority, interest, influence, sway, power; repute, esteem, name, vogue, favour, request. *Lettre de —*; letter of credit. *Faire —, vendre, donner, à —*; to credit, to give trust, to give credit. *Ouvrir un — à quelqu'un*; to open an account with any one. *Il a bon —*; his credit is good. *Donner — en banque*; to have the transfer booked. *Avoir — en banque*; to be a creditor on the bank-books. *Faire — de la main à la bourse*; to trust no farther than one can see. — *est mort*; old Trust is dead. *Cela l'a mis en —*; that brought him into repute. *A —*; on credit, on trust; to no purpose; gratuitously, without proof, without ground, at random.

créditer, *v.a.*, to trust; to enter upon the credit side of an account, to credit. *Être crédité sur une ville*; to have letters of credit on a town.

créditeur, *n.m.*, creditor. —, *adj.*, *compte —*; creditor's account.

credo, *n.m.* (—), creed, belief.

crédule, *adj.*, credulous, easy of belief.

crédulement, *adv.*, with credulity, credulously.

crédulité, *n.f.*, credulity.

créer, *v.a.*, to create; to invent; to imagine; to produce; to beget; to appoint; to establish. — *un chevalier*; to dub a knight. — *une rente*; to settle a rent or annuity. — *des moyens*; to find means.

*****crémaillère**, *n.f.*, pot-hanger, pot-hook; (horl.) rack; (tech.) rack, toothed rack. *La — d'un cric*; the rack of a jack. *Chaise à —*; spring-back chair. *Pendre la —*; to give a house-warming. *Aller pendre la —*; to go to a house-warming.

*****crémaillon**, *n.m.*, small pot-hook.

crémaster, *n.* and *adj. m.*, (anat.) cremaster.

crémation, *n.f.*, cremation.

crème, *n.f.*, cream; the best part of a thing. *the cream. — fouettée*; whipt cream. *Fromage à la —*; cream-cheese. — *de tartre*; cream of tartar.

crément, *n.m.*, (gram.) increase (of a word —*d'un mot*).

crémer, *v.n.*, to cream, to gather cream.

crémerie, *n.f.*, milk-shop, dairyman's shop.

crémeu-x, **-se**, *adj.*, creamy.

crémi-er, *n.m.*, **-ère**, *n.f.*, milkman, milk-woman.

*****crémillée**, *n.f.*, ward (of a lock—*de serrure*).

crémone, *n.m.*, a Cremona violin.

crénage, *n.m.*, (letter-founding—*fonte de caractères*) kerning.

créné, **-e**, *adj.*, (bot.) crenated, indented.

créneau, *n.m.*, battlement; embrasure; space between the platoons when drawn up in battle array.

crénelage, *n.m.*, (coin.) milling.

crénelé, **-e**, *part.*, *adj.*, (her.) embattled; (bot.) denticulated, crenated.

créneler (kré-n-lé), *v.a.*, to make or form into battlements; to indent, to notch. — *une roue*; to tooth, to cog, a wheel. — *une pièce de monnaie*; to mill a piece of money.

crénelure (kré-n-lur), *n.f.*, the being crenated, notched, or denticulated; (anat.) indentation; (bot.) crenature; crenel.

créner, *v.a.*, (letter-founding—*fonte de caractères*) to kern.

crénerie, *n.f.*, (letter-founding—*fonte de caractères*) kerning.

crénilabre, *n.m.*, (ich.) gold-finny.

crénirostre, *n.m.*, a bird whose beak is indented.

crénon, *n.m.*, first splitting of a block of slate.

crénulé, **-e**, *adj.*, having small notches or indentations.

crénure, *n.f.*, (print.) hole in the bar of a frame.

créole, *n.m.f.*, Creole; West Indian.

créosote, *n.f.*, (chem.) creosote.

crêpage, *n.f.*, glossing of crape.

crêpe, *n.m.*, crape; (fig.) veil. *Il porte un — à son chapeau*; he wears a crape hat-band. — *crépé*; crisped crape. — *lisse*; smooth crape.

crêpe, *n.f.*, pancake.

crêper, *v.a.*, to crisp, to crape, to frizzle. *Cheveux crépés*; frizzed hair.

crépi, *n.m.*, rough-cast, parget.

saint-**crépin**, *n.m.*, Saint Crispin; kit (of a journeyman shoemaker—*d'un ouvrier cordonnier*). *Perdre son saint-crépin*; to lose one's all.

crépine, *n.f.*, fringe (woven on the top—*tissée par le haut*); caul covering the bowels of sheep. *A —*; fringy.

crépir, *v.a.*, to parget, to rough-cast. — *le cuir*; to work leather in grain, to pummel a hide on the flesh side. — *le crin*; to crisp hair.

crépissage, *n.m.*, (mas.) plastering, pargetting, rough-casting.

crépissement, *n.m.*, pargetting, rough-casting; parget.

crépissure, *n.f.*, pargetting, rough-casting.

crépitant, **-e**, *adj.*, crepitating, crackling.

crépitation, *n.f.*, crepitation, crackling.

crépodaille, or **crapaudaille**, *n.f.*, thin crape, gauze-crape.

crépon, *n.m.*, crepon.

crépu, **-e**, *adj.*, crisped, frizzled, crisp, crispy, woolly. *Les nègres ont les cheveux —s*; the hair of negroes is woolly.

crépusculaire, *adj.*, crepuscular. *Lumière* — ; twilight.

crépuscule, *n.m.*, c epuscule, twilight; dawn. — *du soir* ; owl-light. *Le* — *de la raison ;* the dawn of reason.

créquier, *n.m.*, wild plum-tree ; (her.) sort of seven-branched candlestick.

cresane. *n.f.* V. **crassane**.

crescendo, *adv.*, (mus.) crescendo.

créseau, *n.m.*, species of woollen stuff, kersey.

cresserelle, *n.f.* V. **crécerelle**.

cresson. *n.m.*, cress, cresses, water-cress. — *aléncis, de jardin ;* dittander, garden-cress. — *doré ;* golden saxifrage. — *des prés ;* lady's smock. — *sauvage ;* water-plantain. — *de rivière ;* water-rocket.

cressonnière, *n.f.*, cress-bed.

crésus, *n.m.* (—), very rich man. *C'est un* — ; he is a very rich man.

crétacé, -e, *adj.*, cretaceous.

crête. *n.f.*, crest, tuft, comb of a cock or hen ; top-knot ; (anat.) ridge ; (arch.) ridge. — *de morue ;* part of a cod near the head. *Lever la* — ; to be conceited. *Baisser la* — ; to come down a peg. *Rabaisser la* — *à quelqu'un ;* to bring one down a peg. — *d'un fossé ;* bank on the side of a ditch. — *d'une montagne ;* ridge of a mountain. — *d'une grosse vague ;* crest of a billow. — *marine ;* samphire. — *de coq ;* cock's-comb ; hog's-ear shell. *Crête-de-coq* (—*s* —); louse-wort.

crêté, -e, *adj.*, crested, tufted.

crételer, *v.n.*, (of hens—*des poules*) to cackle.

crétin, *n.m.*, (med.) cretin ; idiot. *C'est un* — ; he is an idiot.

crétiniser, *v.a.*, to cause one to become an idiot, a cretin.

crétinisme, *n.m.*, cretinism.

crétique, *adj.*, cretic.

crétois, -e, *n.* and *adj.*, Cretan.

cretonne, *n.f.*, fine linen.

cretons, *n.m.pl.*, residuum of melted tallow and kitchen-stuff, graves — *delard ;* scrapings.

creusage, *n.m.*, deepening, lowering ; ploughing ; digging.

creusement (kreûz-măn), *n.m.*, (l.u.) digging.

creuser, *v.a.*, to dig, to delve ; to hollow, to make hollow, to excavate, to scoop out ; to sink, to deepen. — *la terre ;* to dig the ground. — *un fossé ;* to dig a ditch. — *une question ;* to examine a question thoroughly.

se **creuser**, *v.r.*, to become hollow. — *le cerveau ;* to rack one's brain.

creuser, *v n.*, to dig. — *sous terre ;* to dig underground. — *bien avant ;* to dig deep.

creuset, *n.m.*, crucible, melting-pot ; (chem.) hearth ; test, trial. *Passer par le* — ; to assay, to refine. *Le* — *du bon sens ;* the test of good sense.

creux, *n.m.*, hollow, cavity ; pit, hole, chasm ; gutter, delve ; mould ; mortar, trough ; pit of the stomach. — *planté d'arbres ;* dell planted with trees. — *profond dans une mine ;* groove in a mine. *Le* — *de la main ;* the hollow of the hand. *Il a un bon* — ; he has a fine bass voice. — *d'un vaisseau* (nav.); depth of a ship's hold. — *d'une voile ;* cavity of a sail (which retains the wind—*qui retient le vent*).

creu-x, -se, *adj.*, hollow, cavernous ; deep ; empty, unsubstantial, airy, fantastical, chimerical, extravagant. *Des yeux* — ; eyes sunk in the head. *Avoir les joues* —*ses ;* to have hollow cheeks. *Il a le ventre* — ; his belly is empty. *Un fossé* — *de trois pieds ;* a ditch three feet deep. *Esprit* —. *cerveau* — ; cracked-brain, unfurnished head. *Pensées* —*ses ;* airy notions.

Viande —*se ;* frothy, unsubstantial food. *Songer* — ; to be in a brown study.

crevaille, *n.f.*, guttling, gormandizing, stuffing ; tuck out, blow out.

crevasse. *n.f.*, crevice, chink, rift, crack ; gap, cranny ; (vet.) malt-worm, cratches. *Des* —*s aux mains ;* chaps in the hands.

crevasser, *v.a.*, to split, to crack ; to chap ; to make cracks.

se **crevasser**, *v.r.*, to crack, to split, to gape.

crevé, *n.m.*, **-e**, *n.f.*, (l. ex.) very large person.

crevé, *n.m.*, opening, slash (in sleeves—*des manches, &c.*).

crève-cœur, *n.m.* (—), heart-break, heart-breaking, grief of heart.

crever, *v.a.*, to burst, to break, to split, to crack, to rift, to tear, to rend ; to stave in ; to cram one with victuals. — *une botte ;* to burst a boot. — *les yeux à quelqu'un ;* to put out one's eyes. — *un cheval ;* to kill a horse. *Cela vous crève les yeux ;* that lies under your nose.

crever, *v.n.*, to burst ; to die, to perish. *C'est une médecine à faire* — *un cheval ;* this medicine is enough to kill a horse. — *de graisse ;* to be extremely fat. — *de chaud ;* to be dying with heat. — *de rire ;* to split one's sides with laughing. — *de faim ;* to be dying with hunger. — *d'orgueil ;* to be bursting with pride. — *de biens ;* to wallow in wealth.

se **crever**, *v.r.*, to burst ; to kill one's self. *Se* — *de boire et de manger ;* to cram or stuff till one is ready to burst. *Se* — *de travail ;* to over-work one's self.

crevet, *n.m.*, stay-lace with tags at both ends.

crevette, *n.f.*, prawn, shrimp.

cri, *n.m.*, cry ; scream, screaming ; roar, roaring ; bawling, howling, yell, yelling, outcry, clamour ; whine, whining ; squeak, squeaking. — *de joie, — d'allégresse ;* shout, shouting, hallooing, huzza, acclamation. — *aigre, aigu, perçant ;* scream, shriek, squeak, shrill cry. *Les* —*s des femmes ;* the squalling of women. — *de guerre ;* watchword. — *d'armes ;* (her.) motto. *Jeter un* —, *faire des* —*s, pousser un* — ; to cry out, to scream, to squall, to yell, to roar. *Demander à grands* —*s ;* to demand with a loud voice. *Je poussai un grand* — ; I shrieked. *Jeter les hauts* —*s ;* to cry out. *Le* — *de la nature ;* the voice of nature. *Donner du* — *à la soie ;* to sulphur silk. *A cor et à* — *s :* with hue and cry.

criage, *n.m.*, public crying.

criaillement, *n.m.*, act of wrangling ; brawling ; (of geese—*des oies*) gabbling.

criailler, *v.n.*, to bawl, to brawl, to cry, to clamour ; to scold, to chide ; (of geese—*des oies*) to gabble.

criaillerie, *n.f.*, brawling, clamouring, scolding, wrangling.

criailleu-r, *n.m.*, **-se**, *n.f.*, brawler, bawler, wrangler ; shrew, scold.

criant, -e, *adj.*, crying. *Injustice* — ; crying injustice.

criard, -e, *adj.*, crying, bawling, squalling, noisy ; brawling, clamorous, scolding ; (paint.) discordant ; shrill. *Dettes* —*es ;* dribbling debts, *Voix* — ; shrill voice.

criard, *n.m.*, **-e**, *n.f.*, brawler, clamourer ; scold, shrew.

criarde. *n.f.*, thick gummed cloth which makes a noise ; varnished cloth.

criblage, *n.m.*, sifting.

crible, *n.m.*, sieve ; riddle. *Percé comme un* — ; as full of holes as a sieve ; riddled.

cribler, *v.a.*, to sift, to riddle ; to scan, to examine ; to pepper (a person—*quelqu'un*). — *de coups ;* to shoot, run, or stab through and through all over. *Voile criblée ;* sail much damaged by shots.

cribleu-r, *n.m.*, **-se**, *n.f.*, sifter.

cribleu-x, **-se**, *adj.*, (anat.) pierced like a sieve. sieve-like.

criblier, *n.m.*, sieve-maker.

criblure, *n.f.*, siftings.

cribration, *n.f.*, (chem.) cribration.

cribriforme, *adj.*, cribriform.

cric (krî), *n.m.*, lifting-jack. handscrew; little ratchet-wheel on which the braces of carriages are fixed.

cric-crac (krik-krak), (*onomatopœia*) imitation of the creaking noise produced by breaking or tearing.

cricoïde, *n.m. and adj.*, (anat.) cricoid.

cri-cri, *n.m.* (— —s), (pop.) (ent.) cricket.

crid (krid), *n.m.* V. **criss.**

criée, *n.f.*, proclamation of sale; auction. *Sa maison est en — ;* his house is to be sold by auction. *Audience des —s;* public hall where land and houses are sold by auction.

crier, *v.n.*, to cry, to cry out, to halloo, to shout, to bawl; to scream, to shriek, to screech; to squall, to clamour; to call out; to whine, to pule; to complain loudly, to brawl, to exclaim; to scold; to huzza, to talk loudly; to gabble (of geese—*des oies*); to screech (of owls—*des hiboux*); to troat (of deer—*du cerf, &c.*); to chirp (of grasshoppers and other insects —*de la sauterelle et autres insectes*); to groan (of roe-bucks—*du chevreuil*). — (of doors, &c.—*des portes, &c.*); to creak. — *aux armes;* to cry to arms. — *au secours;* to call out for help. — *au meurtre;* to cry out murder. — *au voleur;* to cry out thieves. — *au feu;* to cry fire. — *à l'injustice;* to exclaim against an injustice. — *au scandale;* to inveigh against a scandal. — *gare;* to cry out beware! take care. — *misère;* to complain of poverty. — *miséricorde;* to cry for mercy. — *famine;* to cry out famine. — *à tue-tête, comme un perdu;* to roar as loud as one can. — *bien fort;* to cry out very loudly. *Les boyaux lui crient;* his bowels rumble. *Il crie avant qu'on l'écorche;* he cries before he is hurt. *Tout le monde crie contre cela;* every body cries out against it.

crier, *v.a.*, to proclaim; to cry; to hawk; to put up; to publish, to blazon. *Cet enfant est perdu, il faut le faire — ;* the child is lost, it must be cried. *Faites — ce paquet de livres;* put up this lot of books.

crierie (krî-rî), *n.f.*, bawling, clamour; wrangling; scolding, brawling.

crieu-r, *n.m.*, **-se**, *n.f.*, bawling man or woman, squaller, bawler; crier; auctioneer; hawker. — *public;* town-crier.

crime, *n.m.*, crime; sin, transgression; guilt, guiltiness, wickedness, sinfulness. — *d'État;* treason. — *de lèse-majesté;* high treason. — *capital;* capital offence, crime; (jur.) felony. — *dénaturé;* unnatural crime. — *noir;* base, foul crime. — *qualifié;* indictable offence. *Il fait un — à son épouse d'être attachée à son serin;* he takes offence at his wife's fondness for a canary-bird. *Jésus-Christ a porté la peine de nos —s;* Christ has suffered for our sins. *Être porté au — ;* to be prone to guilt. *Endurci dans le — ;* hardened in crime.

criminaliser, *v.a.*, to remove a cause to the crown-side, to send over to the crown-side.

criminaliste, *n.m.*, one who is well versed in criminal law; writer on criminal law.

criminalité, *n.f.*, criminalness.

criminel, **-le**, *adj.*, criminal, felonious, guilty. *Juge — ;* a judge that tries on life and death. *Chambre —le, cour —le;* crown-side.

criminel, *n.m.*, **-le**, *n.f.*, criminal, culprit, offender, felon; criminal affair, proceedings before a criminal court. — *d'état;* state criminal.

criminellement (-nèl-mân), *adv.*, criminally, culpably, guiltily.

crin, *n.m.*, hair (of the mane and tail of the horse and other animals—*de la crinière et de la queue du cheval et d'autres animaux*); horse-hair; abrupt termination of a metallic vein. *Un sommier de — ;* hair-mattress. *Se prendre aux —s;* to seize one another by the hair. *À tous —s;* with flowing mane and tail.

crinal, *n.m.*, (surg.) Anel's probe.

crincrin, *n.m.* (*onomatopœia*), sorry fiddle; wretched fiddler.

crinier, *n.m.*, horse-hair worker or seller.

crinière, *n.f.*, lion's mane, horse's mane. *Vilaine — ;* ugly head of hair.

crinoline, *n.f.*, crinoline.

crinon, *n.m.*, crinodes.

criocère, *or* **porte-croix** (—), *n.m.*, (ent.) crioceris.

crique, *n.f.*, creek, cove.

criquet, *n.m.*, bad horse, tit; little man; (ent.) gryllus, locust.

crise, *n.f.*, crisis. *L'affaire est dans sa — ;* the matter is come to a crisis.

crispation, *n.f.*, crispation, shrivelling; thrilling sensation. *Donner des —s à quelqu'un;* to give any one the fidgets.

crisper, *v.a.*, to shrivel, to contract, to make shrink; to thrill, to make thrill, to thrill through; to irritate (the nerves—*les nerfs*); to give any one the fidgets, to fidget.

se **crisper**, *v.r.*, to shrivel, to shrivel up.

crispin, *n.m.*, valet (in Molière's comedies). *C'est un — ;* he looks like a valet. *Jouer les —s* (thea.); to perform the parts of valets.

criss, *n.m.*, creese, Malay dagger.

crissement, *n.m.*, grating of the teeth.

crisser, *v.n.*, to grate (of the teeth—*des dents*).

cristal, *n.m.*, crystal; *pl.*, crystal ware. — *de roche;* rock crystal. — *de mine;* quartz. — *fondu;* factitious crystal. *Le — des eaux;* the clearness of water. *Le Palais de — ;* the Crystal Palace.

cristallerie (-tal-rî), *n.f.*, art of making crystal, of manufacturing crystal; crystal manufactory; glass-house, glass-works.

cristallier, *n.m.*, glass-cutter.

cristallière, *n.f.*, crystal mine.

cristallin, **-e**, *adj.*, crystalline; pellucid.

cristallin, *n.m.*, (anat.) crystalline lens; (astron.) crystalline heaven.

⊙**cristallin**, *n.m.*, coloured transparent crystals.

cristallisable, *adj.*, crystallizable.

cristallisant, **-e**, *adj.*, (chem.) crystallizing.

cristallisation, *n.f.*, crystallizing, crystallization.

cristalliser, *v.a. and n.*, to crystallize; to be converted into crystal. — *la soie;* to let the alum settle upon the silk.

se **cristalliser**, *v.r.*, to crystallize; to candy.

cristallisoir, *n.m.*, crystallizing-pan, crystallizer.

cristallographie, *n.f.*, crystallography.

cristalloïde, *n.f.*, membranous capsule containing the crystalline lens of the eye.

cristallotechnie (-tèk-nî), *n.f.*, art of crystallizing salts.

cristallotomie, *n.f.*, the art of cutting crystals.

criste-marine, *n.f.* V. **passe-pierre.**

criterium (-om), *n.m.*, criterion; touchstone. *L'évidence est le — de la vérité;* evidence is the criterion of truth.

critiquable, *adj.*, that may be criticized; exceptionable.

critique, *n.m.*, critic; censurer, censorious person, carper. *— fâcheux;* fault-finder.

critique, *n.f.*, criticism, censure; science of criticism. critique; critical taste. *La —;* the critics. *Faire de la —;* to write criticisms. *Faire la — d'un ouvrage;* to criticize, to review, a work.

critique, *adj.*, critical; censorious, carping, censuring; alarming; ticklish, momentous. *Humeur —;* censorious temper. *Signes —s;* critical symptoms. *Pouls —;* alarming pulse.

critiquer, *v.a.*, to criticize, to examine; to censure, to blame.

croassement (kro-as-măn), *n.m.*, croak, croaking, cawing (of crows—*des corbeaux, &c.*).

croasser, *v.n.*, to croak, to caw (of crows—*des corbeaux, &c.*).

croate, *n.m.f.* and *adj.*, Croatian.

croc (krô), *n.m.*, hook; crook, grapnel, drag; fang, tusk; canine tooth; dog-tooth; tooth; (l.u.) curling moustache; (nav.) boat-hook. *— de batelier;* waterman's pole. *— de candelette;* hook of the fore-castle. *— à trois branches;* grapnel with three hooks. *— de capon;* cat-hook. *— de palan;* tackle-hook. *Mettre, pendre, au —;* to put, to lay, on the shelf, to lay by. *Mettre les armes au —;* to renounce the army. *Moustaches en —;* curling moustache.

croc (krock), *n.m.*, crackling, crackling noise. *Faire — sous la dent;* to crackle under the teeth.

croc-en-jambe (kro-kăn-), *n.m.* (*—s —*), trip; Cornish hug; dirty trick. *Donner un — à quelqu'un;* to trip up any one's heels; to supplant any one.

croche, *adj.*, crooked, bent.

croche, *n.f.*, (mus.) quaver. *Double —;* semi-quaver. *Triple —;* demi-semi-quaver. *Quadruple —;* double-semi-quaver. *Chanter par —;* to semi-quaver.

crocher, *v.a.*, to hook; to crook (card-teeth —*les dents d'une carde*). *— l'organeau d'une ancre;* to fish the anchor by the ring.

crocher, *v.n.*, (agri.) to produce, to bear. *Les arbres crochent bien;* the trees are full of bearers.

croches, *n.f. pl.*, smith's tongs.

crochet, *n.m.*, hook; steelyard; two-pronged hoe; turn (on a road—*de route*); (surg.) key, crotchet; (erpetology) fang; (arch.) crocket; (anat.) dog-tooth, canine tooth; (dental surg.) wire; ⊙heart-breaker (of curls—*des cheveux*). *— d'une porte;* hasp, clasp. *Clou à —;* tenter-hook. *Des ouvrages au —;* crotchet-work. *Un — de diamants;* a crotchet of diamonds. *— de chiffonnier;* stick with a hook at the end, used by rag-gatherers. *Un — de serrurier;* a picklock. *— d'arbre;* bearer. *—s; pl.*, fangs, tusks; crotchets; braces; ⊙locks of hair. *— de porte-faix;* French porter's stretcher to carry burdens on. *Être sur les —s de quelqu'un;* to live at another person's charge. *Je suis ici sur mes —s;* I live here upon my own charge. *— d'armes;* (nav.) hooks to support the small arms in a cabin. *— de retraite;* eye-bolts in the train of a gun-carriage. *— de bittes;* hooks to fasten the cross-piece to the bits. *— d'épontilles;* hasps of the stanchions between decks.

crochetage (krosh-taj), *n.m.*, porterage.

crocheter (krosh-té), *v.a.*, to pick a lock; to penetrate into a house burglariously.

se crocheter, *v.r.*, (pop.) to fight.

crocheteur, *n.m.*, porter, street-porter. *Injures de —;* billingsgate abuse. *— de serrure;* picklock, housebreaker.

crochetier (-tié), *n.m.*, hook-maker, clasp-maker; maker of porters' stretchers.

crocheton, *n.m.*, small hooks; crotchets.

crocheu, *n.m.*, tool used by rope-makers; a tool to bend card-teeth.

crochu, *-e*, *adj.*, crooked, hooked. *Il a les mains —es;* he is light-fingered.

crocodile, *n.m.*, crocodile. *— d'Amérique;* American crocodile, alligator. *Larmes de —;* treacherous tears.

crocodiléen, *n.m.*, crocodilian.

crocus (-kus), *n.m.*, crocus, saffron.

croie, *n.f.*, a disease of hawks.

croiler, or **croler**, *v.n.*, (hawking—*fauconnerie*) to scour.

croire (croyant, cru), *v.a.*, to believe; to credit, to give credit to; to have faith in, to trust to, to place reliance on; to be advised, persuaded; to think; to deem; to presume, to be of opinion. *Je le crois bien;* I really believe it. *Je n'en crois rien;* I don't believe a word of it. *Il le croit bonnement;* he fairly believes it. *Il ne croit point;* he has no belief. *— une chose trop légèrement;* to believe something too easily. *— conseil;* to be advised. *À l'en croire, tout est perdu;* if he is to be believed, all is lost. *J'en crois à peine mes yeux;* I can hardly believe my eyes. *S'il faut en — les apparences;* if appearances are to be trusted. *Je crois pouvoir le faire;* I think I can do it. *Croyez-vous qu'il le fasse?* do you think he will do it? *Je crois qu'il le fera;* I think he will do it. *Croyez-vous qu'il le fera?* do you think he will do it? *Je ne le crois pas;* I do not think he will. *Il est à — qu'il le veut ainsi;* it is to be presumed that he will have it so.

croire, *v.n.*, to believe, to have faith in, to be a believer; to trust; to credit; to be of opinion; to think; to consider. *— en Dieu;* to believe in God. *— aux revenants;* to believe in ghosts. *— aux miracles;* to believe in miracles. *Je crois bien;* I believe you. *Je crois que non;* I believe not.

se croire, *v.r.*, to think or believe one's self, to consider one's self; to be believed, to be credible. *Cet homme se croit habile;* that man thinks himself skilful. *Cela peut se —;* it is credible.

croisade, *n.f.*, crusade; (astron.) Southern Cross, Crosier.

croisé, *-e*, *part.*, crossed; cross (of the breeds of animals—*des animaux*); twilled, double-milled (of cloth—*des étoffes*); (mill.) promiscuous. *Serge —;* kersey. *Demeurer, se tenir, les bras —s;* to sit with folded arms. *Avoir les jambes —es;* to sit cross-legged. *Feux —s;* cross fire.

croisé, *n.m.*, Crusader; twill; crossing (a step in dancing—*pas de danse*).

croisée, *n.f.*, window; casement, sash; (arch.) cross-aisle, transept; (print.) cross. *— cintrée;* arched window. *—s d'ogives;* pointed arches. *— de l'ancre;* cross of the anchor.

croisement (croaz-măn), *n.m.*, act of crossing; crossing; cross-breeding (of animals—*animaux*).

croiser, *v.a.*, to cross, to lay across, or cross-wise, to set across; to cross out, to strike out, to efface; to thwart; to cross (breeds of animals—*races d'animaux*). *— quelqu'un;* to cross one in his designs. *Des races croisées;* mixed breeds.

croiser, *v.n.*, to lap over; to cruise. *— sur une côte;* to cruise along a coast.

se croiser, *v.r.*, to cross each other, to be crossed, to lie athwart each other; to intersect each other; to thwart one another; to assume the cross, to engage in the holy war. *Ces deux courriers se sont croisés;* these two messengers passed each other on the way.

croisette, *n.f.*, cross-wort; (her.) cresslet; (nav.) pin or bolt used as a fid to a flag-staff.

— *noire. grosse* — (bot.); cheese-rennet, ladies' bed-straw.

croiseur, *n.m.*, cruiser.

croisière, *n.f.*, (nav.) cruise; cruising latitude; sort of tool to mark sea-biscuits; (railways) intersection of two lines.

*****croisille**, *n.f.*, (rope-making—*corderie*) cross-piece.

*****croisillon**, *n.m.*, cross-bar; sash-bar.

croissance, *n.f.*, growth. — *entière*; full growth. *Arrêter dans sa* —; to stunt the growth of.

croissant, *n.m.*, crescent, the moon in her increase; short bout (of a violin—*du violon*); pruning-hook; hedge-bill, hedging-bill; (ich.) moon-fish; curtain-pin (in the form of a crescent—*en forme de croissant*). *En* —; lunated. *Les cornes du* —; the horns of the crescent. *L'empire du* —; the Crescent. — *de cheminée*; chimney-hook. — *de pic ou de gui*; (nav.) throat or jaw of the gaff.

croissant, -e, *adj.*, growing, increasing.

croisure, *n.f.*, the length of the yards (of a ship—*d'un vaisseau*); coat-staves; crossing, mill (in stuffs—*des étoffes*); (poet.) intermixture, mingling.

croît, *n.m.*, increase (of a flock—*d'un troupeau*) by young ones; growth.

croître, (croissant, crû). *v.n.*, to grow, to wax, to grow up, to grow tall, to spring up; to augment, to increase; to lengthen; to swell or swell out, to be swollen; to multiply, to be multiplied or increased; to be grown; to sprout, to shoot. — *trop rapidement*; to outgrow, to overgrow. *Les jours commencent à* —; the days begin to lengthen, to draw out. *Elle ne fait que* — *et embellir*; she grows handsomer every day.

croix, *n.f.*, cross; rood; affliction, trouble, tribulation; star; (coin.) cross; (print.) dagger; (her.) cross. *Sainte* —; holy rood. *Les bras d'une* —; the bars of a cross. *Mettre quelque chose en* —; to put a thing cross-wise. *Avoir les jambes en* —; to sit cross-legged. *Faire le signe de la* —; to cross one's self. *On est allé au-devant de lui avec la* — *et la bannière*; they went to meet him with cross and banner, with great ceremony. *Il faut faire une* — *à la cheminée*; we must make a cross on the chimney, we must score that up. *Jouer à* — *et à pile*; to play at head and tail, to toss. — *de par Dieu, de Jésus*; cross-row, criss-cross-row, primer, horn-book, alphabet. — *de Saint André ou de Bourgogne*; St. Andrew's-cross, Saltier (her.). — *de Saint Antoine*; St. Anthony's-cross. — *de Lorraine*; cross with two bars. *Grand*—; knight grand-cross. *Croix de chevalier* (bot.); caltrops, tribulus. — *de Jérusalem* (bot.); lychnis Chalcedonica. — *sur les câbles*; (nav.) cross in the hawse. *Mettre les vergues en* —; to square the yards. — *du Sud*, — *australe* (astron.); Southern Cross, Crosier.

cromlech, *n.m.*, (—*s*), cromlech.

cromorne, *n.f.*, (mus.) cromorna, cremona.

crône, *n.m.*, (nav.) wheel-crane (on a wharf —*sur un quai*).

croquade, *n.f.*, (paint.) sketch, hasty drawing.

croquant, *n.m.*, poor wretch, fellow; countryman; gristle. —*s*; name given to French peasants who rebelled under Henri IV and Louis XIII.

croquant, -e, *adj.*, crisp, crackling. *Biscuit* —; hard biscuit. *Caractère* —; crispness.

croquante, *n.f.*, crisp-tart; almond-cake.

à la **croque-au-sel**, *adv.*, with salt only. *Manger quelque chose à la* —; to eat a thing with salt only.

croque-lardon. *n.m.* (— —*s*), lick-spittle (l. ex.), lick-dish, sponger.

croque-mitaine, *n.m.* (— —*s*), old bogy, black bogy.

croque-mort, *n.m.* (— —*s*), undertaker's man.

croque-note. *n.m.* (— —*s*), sorry musician, crotchet-monger.

croquer, *v.n.*, to crackle between the teeth, to craunch.

croquer, *v.a.*, to craunch; to devour. to eat hastily; to make the first sketch or rough draught of a drawing or picture, to sketch; to filch, to pilfer; (nav.) to hook or grapple anything. *Il n'a fait que* — *ce poème*; he has only written a sketch of the poem. — *le marmot*; to dance attendance.

croque-sol, *n.m.* (— —*s*). *V.* **croque-note**.

croquet, *n.m.*, crackling gingerbread.

croquette, *n.f.*, (cook.) ball of fried rice or of potatoes.

croqueur, *n.m.*, devourer. gormandizer, glutton; (l.ex.) greedy-gut, greedy-guts.

*****croquignole**. *n.f.*, fillip; sort of hard and dry pastry; cracknel.

*****croquignoler**, *v.a.*, to fillip.

croquis, *n.m.*, (paint.) rough draft, outline, sketch. *Cahier de* —; sketch-book. *Faire le* — *d'une figure*; to sketch a figure.

crosse, *n.f.*, (of bishops—*d'évêque*) crosier; (of muskets—*de fusils*) but-end; bat (to play with—*pour jouer*); cricket (game—*jeu*). *Jouer à la* —; to play at cricket.

crossé, -e, *adj.*, crosiered. *Un abbé* — *et mitré*; a crosiered and mitred abbot.

crosser, *v.a.*, to beat; to scold, to treat any one with contempt; to strike a ball with a bat.

crosser, *v.n.*, to play at cricket; to bat.

crossette, *n.f.*, (agri.) layer; (arch.) return, ear, elbow, ancone.

crosseur, *n.m.*, cricket-player, cricketer.

*****crossillon**, *n.m.*, the curled end of the crosier.

crotale, *n.m.*, (antiq.) crotalum; (zool.) rattlesnake.

crotaphite, *adj.*, *n.m.*, (anat.) crotaphite.

crotte, *n.f.*, dirt, mud, mire; dung. *Il fait bien de la* —; it is very dirty. *Être dans la* —; to be in a state of squalid misery. —*s de brebis*; treadles of sheep. —*s de lapins*; crotels of a rabbit. — *de renard*; scumber.

crotté, -e, *part.*, dirty, squalid; wretched, sorry. — *comme un barbet*; as dirty as a pig. *Un poète* —; a paltry poet. *Il fait bien* — *dans les rues*; the streets are very dirty. — *jusqu'à l'échine*; muddied up to the eyes; draggle-tailed.

crotter, *v.a.*, to dirt, to dirty, to bemire; to daggle, to draggle, to bedraggle; to splash, to spatter, to bespatter. *Se* —; to dirt one's self; to get dirty; to draggle.

crottin, *n.m.*, dung (of horses, sheep, &c. —*des chevaux, des moutons, &c.*).

crou, *n.m.*, (geol.) soil composed of sand and clay.

crouchaut, *n.m.*, crotch, floor-timbers of a boat or ship.

croulant, -e, *adj.*, sinking, crumbling, ready to fall.

croulement (krool-mān), *n.m.*, sinking, falling in or down (of a building, &c.—*d'un édifice, &c.*).

crouler, *v.n.*, to sink, to give way, to fall, to fall in, to crumble, to ruin; to go to ruin.

crouler, *v.a.*, (nav.) to launch; (hunt.) to wag (said of stags when they are frightened—*du* *cerf, &c., quand il s'effraye). Le cerf croule la queue;* the stag wags his tail.

Ⓢ**se crouler,** *v.r.,* to fail in an enterprise; (fig.) to sink in others' estimation.

crouli-er, -ère, *adj.,* quaggy, boggy, swampy, moving.

croup (kroop), *n.m.,* (med.) croup.

croupade, *n.f.,* (man.) croupade.

croupal, -e, *adj.,* pertaining to the croup.

croupe, *n.f.,* croup, crupper, the buttocks (of a horse—*du cheval*), rump; top or brow of a hill; (arch.) hip-roof. *Cheval à — de mulet;* narrow-rumped horse. *Être, aller, monter, en —;* to ride behind another on the same horse. *— d'église;* half-cylinder roof.

croupé, -e, *adj.,* with a rump, crupper. *Cheval bien—;* horse with a fine croup.

Ⓢ**à croupetons,** *adv.,* squatting.

croupi, -e, *adj.,* stagnant. *De l'eau —e;* stagnant water.

croupiader, *v.n.,* to cast an anchor by the stern.

croupier, *n.m.,* croupier (at a gaming-table —*à une table de jeu*); partner (of a gambler—*d'un joueur*).

croupière, *n.f.,* saddle-tie, crupper; (nav.) stern-cable, stern-fast. *Tailler des —s à quelqu'un;* to cut out work for one; (milit.) to put to flight. *Mouiller en —;* to cast anchor by the stern.

croupion, *n.m.,* rump. *Parlement —;* the Rump Parliament.

croupir, *v.n.,* to stagnate; to lie, to wallow. *Cet enfant croupit dans ses langes;* that child is lying in its filth. *— dans le vice dans l'oisiveté;* to wallow in sin, in idleness.

croupissant, -e, *adj.,* standing, stagnating.

croupon, *n.m.,* square hide.

croustade, *n.f.,* dish prepared with crusts.

*croustille, n.f., little crust, crust.

*croustiller, v.n., to bite, eat, or gnaw a crust.

*croustilleusement, adv., (fam., l.u.) comically, with mirth, pleasantly; smuttily.

*croustilleu-x, -se, adj., (fam., l.u.) droll, funny; smutty. *Des contes —x;* smutty tales.

croûte, *n.f.,* crust; cake; coarse painting, daub; (med.) scab, scurf. *La — de dessous;* the under-crust. *Casser une — avec quelqu'un;* to take a crust with any one, to pick a bit with any one. *Ne manger que des —s;* to fare hard.

croûté, -e, *adj.,* crusted, caked, crusty.

croûtelette (kroo-tlèt), *n.f.,* little crust.

se **croûter,** *v.r.,* to cake, to crust.

croûtier (-tié), *n.m.,* picture-broker, dealer in daubs *or* coarse paintings; dauber.

croûton, *n.m.,* small crust; wretched dauber; (cook.) sippet.

croyable, *adj.,* credible, believable, to be believed *or* credited; like, likely. *Cela n'est pas —;* that is not likely.

croyance, *n.f.,* belief, creed, faith, persuasion; opinion; trust, credit. *Fausse —;* misbelief. *La — des chrétiens;* the belief of the Christians. *La — des juifs;* the Jewish creed. *Cela passe toute —;* that exceeds all belief.

croyant, *n.m.,* **-e,** *n.f.,* believer. *Les vrais —s;* true believers.

cru, *n.m.,* growth; invention; making, fabrication. *Boire du vin de son —;* to drink wine of one's own growth. *Des fruits d'un bon —;* fruit of a good soil. *Cela n'est pas de son —;* that thing is not of his own invention.

) **cru, -e,** *adj.,* raw, crude, uncooked; indigestible; unwrought, hard, blunt, harsh, coarse, rough; indecent, smutty, obscene, bawdy; undigested, unconcocted; stiff. *Tout —;* quite raw. *Cuir —;* undressed leather. *Soie —e;*

raw silk. *Métal —;* raw metal, ore. *Eau —e;* hard water. *Couleur —e;* stiff colour. *Une lumière —e;* a stiff light.

à cru, *adv.,* on the bare skin. *Botté à —;* booted without stockings. *Monter à cheval à —;* to ride a horse without a saddle.

cruauté, *n.f.,* cruelty. *User de —;* to employ cruelty.

cruche, *n.f.,* pitcher, jar, jug; stupid person, blockhead, booby, lout, dolt. *Tant va la — à l'eau qu'à la fin elle se casse;* the pitcher goes so often to the well that it comes home broken at last.

cruchée, *n.f.,* pitcherful, jugful, jarful.

crucherie, *n.f.,* (fam.) stupidity, silliness. *Vous ne dites que des —s;* you only utter absurdities.

cruchette, *n.f.* *V.* **cruchon.**

cruchon, *n.m.,* little pitcher.

cruciade, *n.f.,* a tax imposed by the pope for carrying on the holy war.

crucial, -e, *adj.,* crucial, cross-like.

crucifère, *n.f.* and *adj.,* (bot.) cruciferous plant; cruciferous. *—s., n.f. pl.,* cruciferæ.

crucifiement, *or* **crucifiment** (-mân), *n.m.,* crucifixion.

crucifier, *v.a.,* to crucify.

crucifix (-fi), *n.m.,* crucifix, cross. *Manger de —;* great devotee. *Galerie du —;* rood-loft. *Faire le demi —;* (pop.) to beg.

crucifixion, *n.f.,* crucifixion.

cruciforme, *adj.,* cross-shaped, cross-like, cruciform.

erudité, *n.f.,* crudity, crudeness, inconcoction; indecent expression; offensive, harsh words; (paint.) stiffness, crudeness.

crue, *n.f.,* rise, swelling; growth, growing; increase. *La — des eaux;* the swelling of the waters. *— de mer;* surge of the sea. *Cet arbre a pris toute sa —;* that tree is come to its full growth.

cruel, -le, *adj.,* cruel, merciless, pitiless, ruthless, hardhearted; relentlesss, remorseless; sanguinary, murderous, bloodthirsty; hard, inflexible, flinty; grievous, tormenting. *Il fait le —;* he acts a cruel part. *Elle n'est pas — le;* she is kind enough.

cruellement (-èl-mân), *adv.,* cruelly, barbarously; unmercifully, mercilessly, pitilessly, ruthlessly, grievously, severely.

Ⓔ**cruentation,** *n.f.,* (med.) cruentation.

crûment, *adv.,* bluntly, coarsely, roughly, inconsiderately, crudely.

cruor, *n.m.,* (physiology) cruor.

crural, -e, *adj.,* (anat.) crural.

crustacé, -e, *adj.,* crustaceous.

crustacé, *n.m.,* crustacean.

cruzade, *n.f.,* crusade (Portuguese coin—*monnaie portugaise*).

crypte, *n.f.,* crypt; (bot., anat.) crypta. [In the language of botany and anatomy, this word is also used in the masculine.]

cryptogame, *n.f.,* (bot.) aphrodite, cryptogam.

cryptogame, *adj.,* (bot.) cryptogamic.

cryptogamie, *n.f.,* (bot.) cryptogamia.

cryptographie, *n.f.,* cryptography. *V.* **stéganographie.**

cryptographique, *adj.,* cryptographical.

crypto-portique, *n.m.,* (— -s), (arch.) crypto-porticus.

crystal. *V.* **cristal.**

c-sol-ut, *n.m.,* (mus.) c. *Cet air est en —;* this tune is in c.

ct (ab. of **courant**); inst. (instant).

cte, (ab. of **comte**), earl.

ctesse, (ab. of **comtesse**), countess.

cu, *n.m.,* (very l.ex.) *V.* **cul.**

cubage, *n.m.,* *or* **cubature,** *n.f.,* cubature.

cubation, *n.f.*, cubature.

cube, *n.m.*,· (geom., arith.) cube. *Le — de deux est huit;* the cube of 2 is 8.

cube, *adj.*, (arith.. geom.) cubic.

cubèbe, *n.m.*, cubeba.

cuber, *v.a.*, (geom., arith.) to cube.

cubilot. *n.m.*, (metal.) cupola.

cubique, *adj.*, (arith., geom.) cubic.

cubital, -e, *adj.*, (anat.) cubital.

cubitus (-tus), *n.m.*, (anat.) cubitus.

cuboïde. *n.m.*, (anat.) cuboid.

cucubale, *n.m.*, (bot.) cucubalus, berry-bearing campion.

cucurbitacé. -e, *adj.*, cucurbitaceous.

cucurbitacée, *n.f.*, (bot.) cucurbitaceous plant. *—s, n.f. pl.*, cucurbitaceæ.

cucurbite, *n.f.*, (chem.) cucurbit.

*****cueillage** (keu-), *n.m.*, act of gathering.

*****cueille** (keu-), *n.f.*, (agri.) gathering of fruit ; (nav.) width of sail-cloth.

*****cueillette** (keu-ièt), *n.f.*, gathering ; crop (fruit) ; (nav.) mixed cargo ; collection of money for the poor.

*****cueilleu-r** (keu-ieur), *n.m.*, **-se**, *n.f.*, gatherer.

*****cueillir** (keu-), (cueillant, cueilli), *v.a.*, to cull, to pick, to pluck; to gather ; to take up ; (nav.) to coil. *— des fleurs ;* to pluck flowers. *— des lauriers ;* to gather laurels.

*****cueilloir** (keu-). *n.m.*, fruit-basket.

cuider, *n.m.*, fruit-basket.

cuiller or **cuillère** (ku-liér), *n.f.*, spoon — *à soupe;* soup-ladle. *— à café;* tea-spoon. *— à bouche ;* table-spoon. *— à dessert;* dessert-spoon.

*****cuillerée** (ku-), *n.f.*, spoonful, ladleful.

*****cuilleriste**, *n.m.*, spoon-maker.

*****cuilleron**, *n.m.*, bowl of a spoon.

cuir, *n.m.*, hide, skin, leather; strop ; fault of pronouncing *s* for *t*, and vice versa, at the end of words, or of using these letters unnecessarily ; as : *Il est sorti zhier, j'étais à la campagne,* for *Il est sorti hier, j'étais à la campagne.* *—s bruts;* raw hides. *—s apprêtés;* dressed hides. *— à rasoir ;* razor-strop. *Faire du — d'autrui large courroie ;* to make free with other people's money. *Tanner le — à quelqu'un ;* to give any one a hiding. *Faire des —s en parlant ;* to pronounce finals instead of final *t,* and vice versa; or to sound *s* or *t* when there is none at the end of words. *— de Russie ;* Russian leather.

cuirasse, *n.f.*, cuirass, breast-plate. *— à l'épreuve du mousquet ;* ball-proof cuirass. *Le défaut de la — ;* the extremity of the armour, vulnerable part. *On lui a trouvé le défaut de la —;* his weak side has been found. *Endosser la —;* to turn soldier.

cuirassé. -e, *adj.*, armed with a cuirass; ready armed ; hardened ; secret. *Il est —;* he is prepared for anything, he is incapable of feeling remorse. *Vaisseau —;* iron-clad ship. iron-clad.

cuirasser, *v.a.*, to arm with a cuirass; to iron-case (nav.).

se **cuirasser**, *v.r.*, to put on a cuirass.

cuirassier, *n.m.*, cuirassier.

cuire. (cuisant, cuit), *v.a.*, to cook, to do; to boil ; to bake ; to roast ; to broil, to grill ; to dress, to prepare ; to stew ; to burn (of the sun —*du soleil*) ; to ripen ; (physiology) to concoct, to digest. *— la viande;* to do the meat. *— trop;* to overdo. *— des briques;* to burn bricks. *— à l'eau;* to boil. *Faire — des œufs;* to boil eggs.

cuire. *v.n.*, to be cooked, to be done; to be burned; to bake ; to broil ; to boil ; to smart, to burn. *La main me cuit;* my hand smarts. *Vous viendrez — à mon four ;* you will want me

some day, and then I shall be even with you. *Il vous en cuira;* you shall smart for it.

cuisant, -e, *adj.*, sharp, smarting ; piercing, exquisite ; severe ; poignant. *Douleur —e;* violent pain.

cuiseur, *n.m.*, brick-burner.

cuisine, *n.f.*, kitchen ; cookery; the cooks; spice-box ; fare, living ; (nav.) cuddy, caboose, galley. *— bourgeoise;* plain living. *Graisses de — ;* kitchen stuff. *Être chargé de — ;* to be monstrously fat. *Faire la — ;* to cook, to dress victuals. *Chef de — ;* master-cook. *Aide de —;* under-cook. *Fille de —;* maid-cook.

cuisiner, *v.n.*, to cook, to dress victuals.

cuisinier, *n.m.*, cook, man-cook.

cuisinière. *n.f.*, woman-cook ; maid-cook ; Dutch oven, meat-screen.

cuissard, *n.m.*, cuish (armour—*armure*).

cuisse, *n.f.*, thigh, leg (of poultry—*volaille*). *Une — de volaille;* a leg of a fowl.

cuisse-madame, *n.f.* (— —*s*), sort of pear.

cuisson. *n.f.*, dressing (of victuals—*de comestibles*) ; cooking (baking, boiling, roasting. &c. —*cuire au four, bouillir, rôtir, &c.*); smart (pain —*douleur*). *Ressentir une — ;* to smart.

cuissot, *n.m.*, haunch (of venison—*venaison*).

cuistre, *n.m.*, college-fag ; vulgar, pedantic fellow.

cuit, -e. *part.*, cooked, done, boiled, roasted, baked. *Cela est trop —;* that is done too much, overdone (of meat—*viande*). *— au four;* baked.

cuite, *n.f.*, baking ; burning (of bricks, &c. —*de briques*); (manu.) boiling.

cuivre, *n.m.*, copper. *— jaune;* brass. *— vierge;* native copper. *— battu;* wrought copper. *—fondu;* cast-copper. *— en barres;* bar-copper. *—en planches;* sheet-copper. *Fonte de —;* pig-copper.

cuivré, -e, *adj.*, copper-coloured,

cuivrer, *v.a.*, to cover with sheet-copper, to copper.

cuivreux. -se, *adj.*, coppery.

cul (ku), *n.m.* (very l. ex.) breech ; backside; posteriors ; rump ; bottom ; tail (of carts—*de charrettes*) ; top. *— par-dessus tête;* head over heels. *Donner du pied au — à quelqu'un;* to kick any one. *Être à —;* not to know what to do. *Faire le — de poule;* to pout. *— de basse-fosse ;* dungeon. *— de-jatte* (—*s —*); cripple who goes on his posteriors with a bowl under them. *— -de-lampe* (—*s —*); (arch.) bracket; (print.) tail-piece. *— de porc* (nav.); wall-knot. *— -de-sac* (—*s—*); blind alley. *— -de-four* (—*s —*); (arch.) demi-cupola. *— -blanc* (—*s —s*); (orni.) wheat-ear, white-tail, fallow-chat, fallow-finch; snipe.

culasse, *n.f.*, breech (of a cannon, musket, &c.—*de canons, de fusils, &c.*) ; pavilion (of diamonds—*de diamants*).

culbutant, *n.m.*, (orni.) tumbler.

culbute, *n.f.*, somerset; fall, tumble. *Faire la — :* to turn a somerset.

culbuter, *v.a.*, to throw down, to throw down headlong.; to overthrow, to ruin, to upset; to make any one, anything, tumble down ; to do for. *Cette entreprise l'a culbuté ;* this enterprise has ruined him.

culbuter, *v.n.*, to fall head over heels.

culbutis, *n.m.*, things thrown down.

culée, *n.f.*, abutment (of bridges—*de ponts*) ; tail (of a hide—*de peaux*) ; (nav.) stern-way.

culer, *v.n.*, to fall astern, to make stern-way ; to veer (of the wind—*du vent*). *Scier à — ;* to back water.

culier. *adj.*, (l.ex.) of the rectum, pertaining to the rectum.

culière, *n.f.*, gutter-stone, kennel-stone, breech of harness.

culinaire, *adj.*, culinary

culmifère, *adj.*, (bot.) culmiferous.

culminant. *adj.*, culminating; prominent. *Point* —; culminating point.

culmination. *n.f.*, culmination.

culminer, *v.n.*, (astron.) to culminate.

culot, *n.m.*, youngest bird of a brood; youngest of a litter of animals; youngest of a family of children; youngest member of a society; bottom (of lamps, crucibles, &c.—*de lampes, de creusets, &c.*). *Le — d'une pipe;* the black at the bottom of a pipe.

culotte, *n.f.*, small clothes, breeches; rump (of an ox, a pigeon—*de bœuf, de pigeon*). — *de bœuf;* rump of beef.

culotter, *v.a.*, to breech, to put in breeches; to colour (pipe).

se **culotter,** *v.r.*, to put on one's breeches; to get coloured (pipe).

culottier, *n.m.*, breeches-maker.

⊙**culottin,** *n.m.*, newly-breeched boy; tight breeches.

culpabilité, *n.f.*, guiltiness; culpability.

culte, *n.m.*, creed; worshipping; religion; worship. *Rendre un — à;* to worship.

cultivable, *adj.*, cultivable, arable.

cultivat-eur, *n.m.*, **-rice.** *n.f.*, husbandman, cultivator, grower, agriculturist.

cultiva-eur -rice. *adj.*, agricultural.

cultivation, *n.f.*, cultivation.

cultiver, *v.a.*, to cultivate; to till; to improve; to inform. — *la vigne;* to cultivate the vine. — *l'esprit;* to cultivate the mind.

culture, *n.f.*, culture; cultivation. *Être sans —;* to be fallow.

cumin, *n.m.*, (bot.) cumin. — *des prés;* caraway seed.

cumul, *n.m.*, accumulation, junction; plurality of offices, places.

cumulard, *n.m.*, (fam. b. s.) pluralist, placeman.

cumulati-f. -ve, *adj.*, accumulative.

cumulativement (-tiv-mān), *adv.*, in an accumulative manner.

cumuler, *v.a.*, to accumulate.

cumuler, *v.n.*, to be a pluralist of offices, places.

cunéaire, *adj.*, cuneate.

cunéiforme, *adj.*, cuneiform.

cunette, *n.f.*, (fort.) cuvette.

cupide, *adj.*, covetous, greedy.

cupidité, *n.f.*, cupidity; covetousness; concupiscence, lust.

cupidon, *n.m.*, (myth.) Cupid, Love.

cupule, *n.f.*, (bot.) cupule; cup (of acorns—*des glands du chêne*).

curabilité, *n.f.*, curableness.

curable, *adj.*, that may be healed, curable.

curaçao, (ku-ra-so), *n.m.*, Curaçoa.

curage, *n.m.*, cleansing cleaning (of harbours, sewers, &c.—*de ports, d'égouts, &c.*); (bot.) waterpepper.

curare, *n.m.*, curare, poison extracted from the ourari-tree (*lasiostoma curare*).

curatelle. *n.f.*, guardianship; trusteeship.

curat-eur, *n.m.*, **-rice.** *n.f.*, curator, curatrix, trustee; committee (for lunatics—*pour les fous*).

curati-f. -ve, *adj.*, curative.

curatif, *n.m.*, curative agent.

curation, *n.f.*, (med.) treatment.

curcuma, *n.m.*, (bot.) curcuma, turmeric.

cure, *n.f.*, cure, healing; living, benefice, cure; parsonage, rectory; ⊙ care.

curé. *n.m.*, rector, vicar. *C'est Gros Jean qui en remontre à son —;* the clerk wants to teach the parson.

cure-dent, *n.m.* (— —*s*), tooth-pick.

curée. *n.f.*, (hunt.) quarry.

cure-langue, *n.m.* (— —*s*), tongue-scraper.

curement. *n.m.*, cleansing (of harbours, sewers. &c.—*de ports, d'égouts, &c.*).

cure-môle, *n.m.* (— —*s*), dredging-machine.

*****cure-oreille,** *n.m.* (— —*s*), ear-pick.

cure-pied, *n.m.* (— —*s*), horse-picker.

curer, *v.a.*, to cleanse (harbours. sewers, &c. —*ports, égouts, &c.*); to pick (the teeth, the ears —*les dents, les oreilles*). *Se — les dents;* to pick one's teeth.

curette, *n.f.*, scraper.

cureur, *n.m.*, cleanser (of harbours, sewers, &c.—*de ports, d'égouts, &c.*).

curial. -e, *adj.*, vicarial, rectorial. *Maison —e;* parsonage-house.

curiale, *n.m.*, (antiq.) citizen of the 2nd class of the Roman people during the Empire.

curie. *n.f.*, ward; (antiq.) curia.

curieusement (-euz-mān), *adv.*, curious'y, inquisitively; carefully.

curieu-x. -se. *adj.*, curious; inquisitive; fond of; careful. *Il est — de tableaux;* he is fond of pictures.

curieu-x. *n.m.*, **-se,** *n.f.*, inquisitive person, spectator, looker-on; virtuoso; curious fact.

curion, *n.m.*, (antiq.) curio.

curiosité, *n.f.*, curiosity; inquisitiveness; rarity. *Par —;* out of curiosity.

curseur, *n.m.*, (math.) cursor.

cursi-f. -ve, *adj.*, cursive.

cursivement, *adv.*, cursorily.

curucucu, *n.m.*, a serpent of Peru.

curule, *adj.*, curule. *Chaise —;* curule chair.

curure, *n.f.*, dirt (from harbours, sewers, &c.—*de ports, d'égouts, &c.*).

curvati-f. -ve, *adj.*, (bot.) slightly curved.

*****curviligne,** *adj.*, curvilineal.

curvirostre, *adj.*, (orni.) curvirostral.

cuscute, *n.f.*, (bot.) dodder.

cuspide, *n.f.*, cuspis.

cuspidé. -e, *adj.*, (bot.) cuspidated.

cussoné. -e, *adj.*, (tech.) worm-eaten (of wood—*du bois*).

custode. *n.f.*, cloth to cover the pyx in which the host is kept; curtain of the high altar; ⊙ curtain. *Sous la —;* in private.

custode, *n.m.*, warden.

custodie, *n.f.*, part of a province belonging to monks.

custodi-nos, (-nos), *n.m.* (—), one who holds a living in trust.

cutané. -e, *adj.*, cutaneous.

cuticule. *n.f.*, (anat. bot.) cutic'e.

cutter (-tèr), *n.m.* (—*s*), (nav.) cutter.

cuvage, *n.m.*, (tech.) fermenting (of wine —*du vin*); place where wine is fermented.

cuve, *n.f.*, tub, vat, copper. — *de brasseur;* brewing-vat. — *matière;* mash-tub. *Fossé à fond de cuve* (fort.); flat-bottomed ditch. — *de bain;* bathing-tub.

cuveau, *n.m.*, small vat, small tub.

cuvée, *n.f.*, tubful; (fam.) sort. *En voici d'une autre —;* here's one of another sort for you.

cuvelage (kuv-laj), *n.m.*, tubbing (mines).

cuveler (kuv-lé), *v.a.*, to tub (mines).

cuver, *v.n.*, to work, to ferment.

cuver, *v.a.*, to appease; to sleep off the effects of wine. — *son vin*, to sleep one's self sober.

cuvette. *n.f.*, wash-hand basin; basin, cistern (of barometers. steam-engines—*de baromètres, de machines à vapeur*); (fort.) cuvette. *Montre à —;* capped watch.

cuvier, *n.m.*, wash-tub.

cyame, *n.m.*, (ent.) whale-louse.

cyanate, *n.m.*, (chem.) cyanate.

cyanhydrique, *adj.*, (chem.) hydrecyanic, prussic.

cyanogène *n.m.*, (chem.) cyanogen.

cyanomètre, *n.m.*, (phys.) cyanometer.
cyanure, *n.m.*, (chem.) cyanide.
cyathe, *n.m.*, (antiq.) cyathus.
cyclamen (-mè-n), *n.m.*, (bot.) cyclamen, sow-bread.
cycle, *n.m.*, cycle. *Le — solaire;* the solar cycle.
cyclique, *adj.*, cyclical.
cycloïdal, -e, *adj.*, cycloidal.
cycloïde, *n.f.*, (geom.) cycloid.
cyclométrie, *n.f.*, cyclometry.
cyclone, *n.f.*, tornado. [Also masculine.]
cyclope, *n.m.*, Cyclops.
cyclopéen, -ne (-in, -è-n), *adj.*, cyclopean.
*cygne, *n.m.*, swan. *Jeune — ;* cygnet.
cylindracé, -e, *adj.*, (bot.) cylindraceous.
cylindrage, *n.m.*, mangling (of linen).
cylindre, *n.m.*, cylinder; roller; garden-roller; mangle, calender; barrel; rundle. *Passer au — ;* to pass through the mangle.
cylindrer, *v.a.*, to calender; to roll. *— les allées d'un jardin;* to roll the paths of a garden.
cylindrique, *adj.*, cylindric.
cylindroïde, *n.m.*, cylindroid.
cymaise, *n.f.* *V.* **cimaise**.
cymbalaire, *n.f.*, ivy-leaved toad-flax.
cymbale, *n.f.*, cymbal.
cymbalier, *n.m.*, cymbal-player.
cymbiforme, *adj.*, (bot.) cymbiform.
cyme, *n.m.*, (bot.) cyme. *V.* **cime**.
cymrique, *n.m.* and *adj.*, Kymric.
cynanche *or* **cynancie**, *n.f.*, (med.) cynanche.
cynanque, *n.m.*, (bot.) dog's-bane.
cynégétique, *n.f.*, cynegetics. *—, adj.*, relating to hunting, and dogs.
cynips, *n.m.*, (ent.) cynips.
cynique, *adj.*, cynical, snarling, snappish; barefaced, indecent.
cynique, *n.m.*, cynic.
cynisme, *n.m.*, cynicism.
cynocéphale, *n.m.*, (zool.) cynocephalus.
cynoglosse, *n.f.*, (bot.) cynoglossum, hound's-tongue.
cynorrhodon, *n.m.*, (bot.) hip.
cynosure, *n.f.*, (astron.) Cynosure, Little Bear.
cyprès, *n.m.*, cypress, cypress-tree; cypress-wood.
cyprière, *n.f.*, cypress-grove.
cyrénaïque, *adj.*, cyrenaic. *—, n.m.*, cyrenaic philosopher.
cyrillien, *or* **cyrillique**, *adj.* *Alphabet — ;* the Slavonic alphabet invented in the 9th century by St. Cyrillus.
cystique, *adj.*, (anat.) cystic.
cystite, *n.f.*, (med.) cystitis.
cystocèle, *n.f.*, (med.) cystocele.
cystotome, *n.m.*, (surg.) an instrument to cut into the bladder.
cystotomie, *n.f.*, cystotomy.
cytarexylon, *n.m.*, (bot.) fiddle-wood.
cytise, *n.m.*, (bot.) cytisus, bean-trefoil.
cyzicéne, *n.m.*, (Grec. antiq.) guest-chamber.
czar (gzar), *n.m.*, czar.
czarien, -ne (-in-è-n), *adj.*, of the czar.
czarine, *n.f.*, czarina.
czarowitz, *n.m.*, czarowitz.

D

d, *n.m.*, the fourth letter of the alphabet, d.
d', ab. of **de**.
da, *particle*, truly, indeed. *Oui-da;* yes, for-sooth. *Nenni-da, non-da;* no, indeed; no, for-sooth.

da-capo, *adv.*, (mus.) da capo.
dactyle, *n.m.*, (poet.) dactyl.
dactyliomancie, *n.f.*, dactyliomancy.
dactyliographie, *n.f.*, dactyliography.
dactylique, *adj.*, dactylic.
dactylologie, *n.f.*, dactylology.
dactyloptère, *adj.*, (ich.) finger-finned.
dactyloptère, *n.m.*, dactylopterus, flying-fish.
dada, *n.m.*, horse, cock-horse; hobby, hobby-horse. *Aller à — ;* to ride a cock-horse. *Être sur son — ;* to be on one's hobby.
dadais, *n.m.*, booby, clown.
⊙**dagorne**, *n.f.*, one-horned cow; beldam, hag.
dague (dag.), *n.f.*, dirk; *pl.*, tusks (of a wild boar—*du sanglier*); first horns (of a two-year-old deer—*d'un cerf de deux ans*).
daguer (da-ghé), *v.a.*, to stab; (hunt.) to rut.
daguerréotype (-ghér), *n.m.*, daguerreo-type.
daguet (da-ghè), *n.m.*, (hunt.) brocket.
dahlia, *n.m.*, dahlia.
*daigner, *v.n.*, to deign, to be pleased, to condescend, to vouchsafe.
*d'ailleurs. *V.* **ailleurs**.
daim (din), *n.m.*, deer, fallow-deer; buck.
daine (dèn or di-n), *n.f.*, doe.
daintiers (-tié), *n.m.pl.*, (hunt.) dowcets.
dais, *n.m.*, canopy; dais.
⊙**daler** (da-lèr), *n.m.* *V.* **thaler**.
dallage, *n.m.*, paving with flag-stones, flag-ging.
dalle, *n.f.*, slab; flag, flag-stone; slice (of fish—*de poisson*).
daller, *v.a.*, to pave with flag-stones.
dalmatique, *n.f.*, dalmatic (a priest's gar-ment—*vêtement ecclésiastique*).
dalot, *n.m.*, (nav.) scupper-hole, scupper.
⊙**dam** (dan), *n.m.*, hurt; injury; (theol.) pri-vation of the sight of God.
damas, *n.m.*, damask; (bot.) damson; Da-mascus blade.
damasquiner, *v.a.*, to damaskene, to em-boss; to frost (cutlery—*coutellerie*).
damasquinerie (-ki-n-ri), *n.f.*, damasken-ing.
damasquineur, *n.m.*, damaskener, one who damaskens.
damasquinure, *n.f.*, damaskened work; embossing (cutlery—*coutellerie*).
damassé, *n.m.*, damask.
damasser, *v.a.*, to damask.
damasserie (da-mas-ri), *n.f.*, damask linen manufactory.
damasseur, *n.m.*, damask worker.
damassin, *n.m.*, figured linen cloth, diaper.
damassure, *n.f.*, damasking (of linen—*du linge*).
dame, *n.f.*, lady; married lady; nun; dame; man, draught (backgammon—*trictrac*); (draughts—*dames*) draught, man, king, queen; queen (cards, chess—*cartes, échecs*); dam, ram-mer. *—s de charité;* ladies of charity. *—s de France;* princesses of the royal family of France. *— d'honneur;* maid of honour. *Elle fait la — ;* she sets up for a lady. *Notre— ;* Our Lady. *Ma chère — ;* my dear madam. *Jouer aux —s;* to play at draughts. *Aller à — ;* (at draughts—*aux dames*) to go to king. *Aller à — ;* (at chess—*aux échecs*) to go to queen.
dame, *int.*, well! forsooth! *— ! c'est juste;* to be sure! it is right.
dame-jeanne, *n.f.* (*—s —s*), demi-john (large bottle).
damer, *v.a.*, to crown (a man at draughts—*aux dames*); (arch.) to allow half a foot for sloping; to ram. *— le pion à quelqu'un;* to outdo any one.

dameret. *adj. m.*, (l. u.) foppish.
dameret, *n.m.*, lady's man, spark, beau.
damier. *n.m.*, draught-board.
damnable (dâ-nabl) *adj.*, damnable.
damnablement (dä-na-), *adv.*, damnably.
damnation (dâ-na-), *n.f.*, damnation.
damné, -e (dâ-né), *part.*, damned.
damné, -e (dâ-né),*n.m.*, soul damned. *Les*
—*s :* the damned. *Souffrir comme un* —*; to*
suffer horribly. *C'est l'âme —e du ministre;* he
is the tool of the minister.
damner (dâ-né), *v.a.*, to damn.
se **damner** (dâ-né), *v.r.*, to damn one's self.
⊙**damoiseau,** *n.m.*, beau, fop, spark; young
page.
⊙**damoisel.** *n.m.* *V.* **damoiseau.**
⊙**damoiselle,** *n.f.*, damsel.
danché, -e, *adj.*, (her.) indented.
dandin, *n.m.*, ninny.
dandinement (-di-n-män), *n.m.*, jogging,
waddling.
dandiner, *v.n.*, to waddle; to twist (one's
body—*le corps*) about; to occupy one's self
about trifles.
se **dandiner,** *v.r.*, to waddle; to twist (one's
body—*le corps*) about.
dandy, *n.m.*, dandy.
dandysme, *n.m* , dandyism.
danger, *n.m.*, danger, peril, risk. *Braver*
les —*s;* to brave dangers. *Affronter les* —*s;*
to face dangers. *Être en — de;* to be in danger
of.
dangereusement (danj-reuz-mān), *adv.*,
dangerously.
dangereu-x, -se, *adj.*, dangerous.
danois, -e, *adj.*, Danish.
danois, *n m., -e, n.f.,* Dane.
danois, *n.m.*, Danish (language—*langue*)
dane (dog—*chien*).
dans, *prep.*, in, within, into; with, according
to. *Il fait cela* — *le dessein de s'établir;* he
does so with a design to establish himself,
— *un moment;* in a minute. *J'ai beaucoup*
travaillé — *le temps;* I used to study a good
deal formerly.
dansant, -e, *adj.*, dancing. *Soirée* —*e;*
dancing evening-party.
danse,n.f., dance, dancing; beating, hiding.
Aimer la —*;* to like dancing. — *de corde;*
rope-dancing. *Il a une* — *contrainte;* he has a
stiff way of dancing. *Donner une* — *à quelqu'un;*
to make one dance for it. *Entrer en* —*;* to join
the dance.
danser,v.n., to dance. *Elle danse avec grâce;*
she dances gracefully. — *en mesure;* to keep
time in dancing. *Faire* — *quelqu'un;* to lead
one a dance. *Il ne sait sur quel pied* —*;* he
does not know which way to turn.
danser, *v.a.*, to dance. — *un menuet;* to
dance a minuet.
danseu-r, *n.m.*, **-se,** *n.f.*, dancer. — *de*
corde; rope-dancer.
danubien, -ne (-in, -è-n), *adj.*, Danubian.
daphné, *n.m.* (bot.) daphne.
darce, *n.f.* *V.* **darse.**
dard, *n.m.*, dart; sting (insects, serpents);
(bot.) stimulus. *Le* — *d'une abeille;* the sting of
a bee.
darder, *v.a.*, to dart; to shoot forth, to
beam, to hurl. *Le soleil darde ses rayons;* the
sun darts his rays.
⊙**dardeur,** *n.m.*, shooter, dart-flinger.
dariole, *n.f.*, cream-cake.
darne, *n.f.*, slice of certain fish (as salmon,
&c.—*de saumon, &c.*).
darse, *n.f.*, (nav.) wet-dock.
dartre, *n.f.*, skin disease; eruption (of the
skin—*cutanée*); blotch, tetter; herpes. —
farineuse ; pityriasis, dandriff.
dartreu-x, -se, *adj.*, herpetic.

dartreu-x. *n.m.*, **-se,** *n.f.*, person affected
with an eruption.
dataire. *n.m.*, datary (officer in the chancery
of Rome—*officier de la chancellerie du pape*).
date, *n.f.*, date. *A courte* —: short-dated.
A longue —; long-dated. *Prendre* —; to fix a
day. *Je suis le premier en* —; I have the prior
date.
dater, *v.a.*, to date.
dater, *v.n.*, to date; to date from afar; to
form a period; to reckon.
daterie (da-trî), *n.f.*, datary's office.
datif, *n.m.*, (gram.) dative, dative case.
dati-f, -ve, *adj.*, (jur.) dative. *Tutelle* —*ve ;*
dative guardianship.
dation. *n.f.*, (jur.) giving. — *en payement;*
giving in payment.
datisme, *n.m.*, tautology.
datte, *n.f.*, (bot.) date.
dattier, *n.m.*, date-tree.
datura. *n.m.*, (bot.) datura stramonium,
thorn-apple.
daube, *n.f.*, (cook.) a seasoning for meat.
dauber, *v.a.*, (pop.) to cuff, to drub; (fig.)
to banter; to jeer.
daubeur, *n.m.*, jeerer, banterer, sneerer.
daubière, *n.f.*, long stew-pan.
dauphin, *n.m.*, (ich.) dolphin; dauphin
(eldest son of the kings of France—*fils aîné du*
roi de France).
dauphine, *n.f.*, dauphiness (the dauphin's
consort—*la femme du dauphin*).
dauphinelle, *n.f.*, (bot.) lark-spur.
daurade, *n.f.*, (ich.) gilt-head.
d'autant. *V.* **autant.**
davantage, *adv.*, more; longer. *Pas* —*;*
no more. *Je n'en dirai pas* —; I shall say no
more. *Je n'en sais pas* —; I know nothing more
about it. *Ne restez pas* —; do not stay any
longer.
davier, *n.m.*, dentist's forceps; (nav.) davit.
de, *prep.*, of, from, by, with, in, upon, out of,
some, any, for, at, to. *Un piat d'argent;* a silver
dish. *De Paris à Londres;* from Paris to London.
De près, de loin; near, afar. *Faire de son mieux ;*
to do one's best. *Vivre de fruits et de légumes;* to
live on fruit and vegetables. *Sauter de joie;* to
leap for joy. *Se moquer de quelqu'un;* to laugh at
any one. *Il y eut cent hommes de tués;* there were
a hundred men killed. *Il n'y a personne de blessé;*
there is no one wounded. *Plus d'effets et moins*
de paroles; more deeds and fewer words. *Quelque*
chose de bon; something good. *Indigne de vivre;*
unworthy to live. *Le désir d'apprendre;* the
desire of learning. *Avoir besoin d'argent;* to be
in want of money. *Qu'est-ce que de nous !* what
poor creatures we are! *L'un d'entre eux;* one of
them. *D'après l'original;* from the original. *De*
chez vous; from your house. *De par le roi;* in
the king's name. *De ce que;* because. *Les*
hommes d'à-présent; men of the day. *Un coup de*
bâton; a blow with a stick. *Trait de plume;* dash
of the pen. *Un coup de fusil;* a shot. *Signe de*
téte; nod. *Le fils de mon ami;* my friend's son.
Leçons de danse; lessons in dancing. *Un enfant*
d'un bon naturel; a good-natured child. *Une*
lame d'épée; a sword-blade. *Une prise de tabac;*
a pinch of snuff. *Un collier de perles;* a pearl
necklace. *Être d'un repas;* to make one at a
banquet. *N'avez-vous point d'enfants!* have you
no children? [*De* is changed into *d'* before a
vowel or silent *h.*]
dé, *n.m.*, die (for playing—*à jouer*); thimble;
(arch.) coin, block, dado; (nav.) cock (of blocks
—*de poulies*); (coin.) die. — *fermé;* woman's
thimble. — *ouvert ;* tailor's thimble. *Jouer aux*
—*s;* to play at dice. —*s pipés ;* cogged dice.
Avoir le —*;* to be the first to play. *Flatter le*
—*;* to slide the dice; to soften a thing down

À vous le —; now it is your turn. *Le — en est jeté;* the die is cast.

déalbation, *n.f.,* (chem.) dealbation.

débâchage, *n.m.,* untilting (of carts, waggons—*de charrettes, haquets, &c.*).

débâcher, *v.a.,* to uncover a carriage.

débâclage, *n.m.,* clearing (of a port—*d'un port*).

débâcle, *n.f.,* breaking up of the ice (in a river that was frozen—*d'une rivière gelée*); clearing (of a harbour—*d'un port*); overthrow, shock, downfall.

débâclement, *n.m.,* breaking up of the ice.

débâcler, *v.n.,* to break up (of the ice—*de la glace*).

débâcler, *v.a.,* to clear (a harbour—*un port*); to unbar (doors—*portes*). — *les bateaux;* to clear the harbour of boats. — *une porte, une fenêtre;* to unbar a door, a window.

débâcleur, *n.m.,* officer that superintends the clearing of a port.

débagouler, *v.n.,* (l.ex.) to spew, to puke.

débagouler, *v.a.,* (l.ex.) (fig.) to launch into abuse; to insult, to abuse any one foully.

débagouleur, *n.m.,* (i.ex.) scurrilous, foulmouthed railer.

déballage, *n.m.,* unpacking.

déballer, *v.a.,* to unpack.

à la **débandade,** *adv.,* in confusion, helterskelter. *Mettre tout à la —;* to put everything in confusion.

débandement (dé-band-măn), *n.m.,* disbanding; (milit.) leaving the ranks.

débander, *v.a.,* to unbind; to unbend, to loosen. — *un pistolet;* to uncock a pistol. — *quelqu'un;* to take off the handkerchief tied over one's eyes.

se **débander,** *v.r.,* to slacken *or* grow loose, to disband; to get uncocked (of fire-arms—*d'armes à feu*); to grow milder (of the weather—*du temps*). — *l'esprit;* to relax one's mind.

débanquer, *v.a.,* to break the bank (at play —*au jeu*).

débaptiser (dé-ba-tĭ-zé), *v.a.,* to change the name of. *Il jugea à propos de se —;* he thought proper to change his name.

*débarbouiller, *v.a.,* to clean, to make clean, to wash the face.

se **débarbouiller,** *v.r.,* to wash one's face; to extricate one's self.

débarcadère, *n.m.,* landing, landing-place, terminus (of railways).

débardage, *n.m.,* unlading (of wood—*de bois*).

débarder, *v.a.,* to unlade wood; to clear a wood of the trees which have been felled in it.

débardeur, *n.m.,* one who unlades wood; workman who breaks up boats; wharf-porter.

débarqué, *n.m.,-e, n.f.,* person landing. *Un nouveau —;* one just come to town; a raw countryman.

débarquement, *n.m.,* landing, disembarkment.

débarquer, *v.a.,* to disembark, to land, to unship.

débarquer, *v.n.,* to land. *Nous débarquâmes en tel endroit;* we went ashore at such a place.

débarras, *n.m.,* riddance, disencumbrance. *Bon — !* a good riddance!

débarrassé, -e, *part.,* disembarrassed; rid. *Son esprit est —de cet important souvenir;* his mind is released from that troublesome recollection.

débarrassement, *n.m.,* (l.u.) disembarrassment.

débarrasser, *v.a.,* to clear, to clear away, to disencumber, to rid, to disentangle, to disembarrass.

se **débarrasser,** *v.r.,* to disentangle, to extri-

cate one's self from, to rid one's self of, to get clear, to get clear of; to clear, to be cleared (of the road, the way—*d'un chemin, d'une route*).

débarrer, *v.a.,* to unbar. — *une porte;* to unbar a door.

débat, *n.m.,* debate, dispute, discussion. *Vider un —;* to settle a dispute. *À eux le —;* let them settle it between them.

débâter, *v.a.,* to unsaddle; to take off a pack-saddle.

débattre, *v.a.,* to debate, to discuss, to argue. *se* **débattre,** *v.r.,* to struggle, to strive, to flounder, to writhe.

débauche, *n.f.,* debauch; debauchery; lewdness, dissoluteness. *Aimer la —;* to be fond of revelling.

débauché, *n.m.,* debauchee, rake.

débaucher, *v.a.,* to debauch; to entice away; to take one from one's occupations. *se* **débaucher,** *v.r.,* to become debauched; to be led away from one's occupations.

débaucheu-r, *n.m.,* -**se,** *n.f.,* debaucher, seducer.

débet, *n.m.,* debit, balance of an account.

débiffé, -e, *part.,* disordered, out of order. *Visage —;* haggard countenance.

débiffer, *v.a.,* to debilitate, to disorder, to enfeeble. *Être tout débiffé;* to be quite out of sorts.

débile, *adj.,* weakly, weak, feeble. *Avoir le cerveau —;* to have weak brains. *Mémoire —;* weak memory.

débilement (dé-bil-măn), *adv.,* feebly, weakly.

débilitant, *n.m.,* (med.) debilitant.

débilitant, -e, *adj.,* (med.) debilitating.

débilitation, *n.f.,* debilitation, enfeebling.

débilité, *n.f.,* debility, weakness.

débiliter, *v.a.,* to debilitate, to enfeeble.

*débillardement, *n.m.,* (carp.) cutting diagonally.

*débillarder, *v.a.,* (carp.) to cut diagonally.

*débiller, *v.a.,* to take off the horses that draw a boat.

débine, *n.f.,* difficulties, poverty, embarrassment, mess. *Il est tombé dans la —;* he has fallen into poverty.

débit, *n.m.,* sale, traffic; market; retail shop: license to sell; delivery, utterance; debit side (book-keeping—*comptabilité*); (mus.) recitative. *Marchandise de bon —;* commodity that sells well. — *de tabac;* tobacconist's shop. *Porter au — de quelqu'un;* to carry to any one's debit. *Il a un beau —;* he has a fine delivery.

débitage, *n.m.,* cutting up (of stones, timber, &c.—*de pierres, de charpente, &c.*).

débitant, *n.m.,* -**e,** *n.f.,* retailer, dealer. — *en détail, en gros;* retail, wholesale, dealer.

débiter, *v.a.,* to sell; to retail; to give out, to spread, to report, to utter; to debit; to cut up (wood, stone—*le bois, la pierre*). — *en gros, en détail;* to sell, wholesale, by retail. — *son rôle;* to recite one's part. — *des nouvelles;* to spread news.

débit-eur, *n.m.,* -**rice,** *n.f.,* debtor; (jur.) obligor. *Être — de;* to be in debt to.

débiteur, *adj.m.,* debtor. *Compte —;* debtor's account.

débiteu-r, *n.m.,* -**se,** *n.f.,* prattler, newsmonger. *C'est une grande -se de mensonges;* she is a regular fib-teller.

déblai, *n.m.,* cutting; excavating, excavation; rubbish; riddance. *Être en —;* to have been excavated.

déblatérer, *v.n.,* to speak against; to rail at.

déblayer, *v.a.,* to clear away; to clear.

déblocage, *n.m.,* (print.) turning letters.

débloquer, *v.a.,* to raise a blockade; (print.) to turn letters.

déboire, *n.m.*, after-taste; vexation; mortification.

déboisement, *n.m.*, the clearing land of trees. forests.

déboiser, *v.a.*, to clear land of trees, forests.

déboîtement (dé-boat-mān), *n.m.*, disjointing, dislocation.

déboîter, *v.a.*, to put out of joint, to dislocate, to disjoint.

se **déboîter**, *v.r.*, to be dislocated, to become disjointed.

débonder, *v.a.*, to take the bung out of; to loosen, to unbind. — *un étang;* to open the sluice of a pond.

se **débonder**, *v.r.*, to gush, to sluice out, to break out or open, to burst forth, to escape out of the bung-hole; to be relaxed (of a person—*des personnes*).

débonder, *v.n.*, to escape through the bung-hole; to escape through the sluice of a pond; to gush out.

débondonnement, *n.m.*, unbunging.

débondonner, *v.a.*, to take out the bung.

débonnaire, *adj.*, too good-natured; compliant, gentle, easy-tempered.

débonnairement, *adv.*, compliantly, easily.

⊙**débonnaireté**, *n.f.*, compliance.

débord, *n.m.*, edge (of a coin—*d'une pièce de monnaie*); ⊙overflowing; ⊙(med.) defluxion.

débordé, **-e**, *adj.*, overflowed; lewd, dissolute, debauched.

débordement, *n.m.*, overflowing, breaking out, inundation, irruption; dissoluteness, debauchery, lewdness; torrent, flood; (med.) overflow.

déborder, *v.n.*, to overflow, to run over; to project, to bag, to jut out; (nav.) to get clear, to sheer off. *La doublure déborde;* the lining bags. *Cette maison déborde;* that house juts out.

déborder, *v.a.*, to take off the border; to outrun; to go beyond; (milit.) to outflank; to edge (plumber's business—*plomberie*).

se **déborder**, *v.r.*, to overflow; to break, to burst, forth.

débordoir, *n.m.*, edging-tool (of a plumber —*de plombier*).

débosseler (dé-bos-lé), *v.a.*, to take the bruises, the dents, out of.

débotté, *n.m.*, taking the boots off.

débotter, *v.a.*, to pull off boots.

se **débotter**, *v.r.*, to pull off one's boots.

débouché, *n.m.*, opening, expedient; outlet, issue; (com.) market; water-way (of bridges—*de ponts*).

débouchement (dé-boosh-mān), *n.m.*, outlet. market. disemboguement.

déboucher, *v.a.*, to open; to clear; to uncork. — *une bouteille;* to uncork a bottle.

déboucher, *v.n.*, to pass out; to fall into (rivers, &c.—*des rivières*); (milit.) to debouch; to relieve the bowels; to expand the mind. *Au* — *du défilé;* when we had passed the defile.

débouchoir, *n.m.*, lapidary's tool.

déboucler, *v.a.*, to unbuckle, to uncurl. — *une jument;* to unring a mare.

*⊙**débouilli**, *n.m.*, (dy.) boiling.

*⊙**débouillir**, *v.a.*, (dy.) to boil.

déboulonner, *v.a.*, (tech.) to unbolt, to unpin.

débouquement (dé-book-mān), *n.m.*, (nav.) narrow channel; disemboguement.

débouquer, *v.n.*, (nav.) to disembogue.

débourbage, *n.m.*, (metal.) trunking.

débourber, *v.a.*, to cleanse; to take the mud away; (metal.) to trunk. — *une voiture;* to draw a carriage out of the mire.

débourrement (dé-boor-mān), *n.m.*, taking off the fleece.

débourrer, *v.a.*, (man.) to break in; to worm (fire-arms—*les armes à feu*); to polish (a person—*quelqu'un*). — *un jeune homme;* to form or polish a young man. — *un cheval;* to break in a horse.

⊙**débours**. *n.m.*, disbursement, sum laid out.

déboursé, *n.m.*, money laid out, disbursement.

déboursement, *n.m.*, disbursement; outlay, expenditure.

débourser, *v.a.*, to disburse, to expend, to lay out.

debout, *adv.*, upright, on end; up; standing; in existence (of things—*des choses*); ahead (of the wind—*du vent*). *Il se tient* —; he is standing up. *Être* —; to be up, to be stirring. *Allons, —, il est déjà grand jour;* come, get up, it is broad daylight. *Un conte à dormir* —; rigmarole. *Avoir le vent* —; to have the wind ahead.

débouté, *n.m.*, (jur.) dismission.

débouter, *v.a.*, (jur.) to overrule, to reject, to non-suit. *Il a été débouté de sa demande;* his demand was rejected; he was non-suited.

déboutonné, **-e**, *part.*, unbuttoned.

déboutonner, *v.a.*, to unbutton.

se **déboutonner**, *v.r.*, to unbutton one's self; to unbosom one's self.

****débraillé**, **-e**, *part.*, open-breasted. *Tout* —; with one's breast uncovered.

*se **débrailler**, *v.r.*, to uncover one's breast.

****débredouiller**, *v.a.*, (trick-track) to save the lurch.

se ****débredouiller**, *v.r.*, to save the lurch (trick-track).

débridement (dé-brid-mān), *n.m.*, unbridling; dispatching, hurrying over; (surg.) relieving constriction by incision.

débrider, *v.a.*, to unbridle; to dispatch, to hurry; (surg.) to remove constriction by incision.

débrider, *v.n.*, to unbridle one's horse; to halt; to stop. *Sans* —; without stopping; at a stretch.

débris, *n.m.*, remains, wreck, ruins; waste; rubbish.

****débrouillement**, *n.m.*, disentangling, unravelling.

****débrouiller**, *v.a.*, to disentangle, to unravel, to clear up, to explain.

se **débrouiller**, *v.n.*, to unravel; to be disentangled, to be cleared up.

débrutir, *v.a.*, to clear off the rough; to polish (gems—*les pierres précieuses*).

débrutissement (-tis-mān), *n.m.*,, rough-polishing (of gems—*de pierres précieuses*).

débucher, *v.n.*, (hunt.) to start.

débucher, *v.a.*, (hunt.) to dislodge, to start.

débucher, *n.m.*, (hunt.) start. *Il se trouva au* —; he was present at the start.

débusquement, *n.m.*, driving out; dislodging; ousting.

débusquer, *v.a.*, to turn out, to oust; (hunt.) to start, to dislodge.

début, *n.m.*, lead, first cast, or throw; outset; debut; first appearance; beginning. *Voilà un beau* —; that is a fine beginning.

débutant, *n.m.*, **-e**, *n.f.*, actor, actress, appearing for the first time; beginner.

débuter, *v.a.*, to lead, to play first; to begin; to open; to set out; to make one's first appearance. *Il a mal débuté dans le mon[de]* made a bad beginning in life.

débuter, *v.a.*, to drive from the jack (at bowls—*aux boules*); to drive from the mark (at cards—*aux cartes*).

deçà, *prep.*, this side of. —, *de* —, *par* —, *la rivière;* this side of the river. *En* — *de la rivière;* on this side of the river.

deçà, *adv.*, here, on this side. — *et delà ;* here and there, this and that side, up and down. *Jambe —, jambe delà ;* one leg this side, the other that side. *De —, par —, en — ;* this side.

déca (particle used in French weights and measures) deca (ten times the unit).

décacheter (dé-kash-té). *v.a.*, to unseal, to open ; to break open, to break the seal of.

décadaire. *adj .* having ten days.

décade. *n.f.*, decade.

décadence, *n.f.*, decay, decline, wane, downfall.

décadi, *n.m.*, decadi, the tenth day of a decade in the calendar of the first French Republic.

décaèdre, *adj.*, decahedral.

décaèdre, *n.m.*, (geom.) decahedron.

décagone, *n.m.*,(fort., geom.) decagon.

décagone, *adj.*, decangular.

décagramme, *n.m.*, decagram (5·61 drams avoirdupois).

décaisser, *v.a.*, to take out of its box.

décalage, *n.m.*, unwedging.

décaler. *v.a.*, to unwedge.

décalitre, *n.m.*, decalitre (2·2009 gallons).

décalogue, *n.m.*, Decalogue (the ten commandments—*les dix commandements de Dieu*).

décalquer, *v.a.*, to counter-draw.

décaméron, *n.m.*, decameron.

décamètre, *n.m.*, decametre (32·88992 feet).

décampement (dé-kanp-mān), *n.m.*, (milit.) decampment.

décamper, *v.n.*, (milit.) to decamp ; to move off. to walk off ; to pack off.

décanat, *n.m.*, deanery, deanship.

décandrie, *n.f.*, (bot.) decandria.

décantation, *n.f.*, (chem.) decantation.

décanter, *v.a.*, (chem.) to decant, to pour off gently.

décanteur, *n.m.*,(chem., pharm.) decanter.

décapage, *n.m.*, cleaning, scraping (metal).

décaper, *v.n.*, (nav.) to sail beyond a cape.

décaper, *v.a.*, to clean (metal).

décapétalé, **-e**, *adj.*, (bot.) having ten petals.

décaphylle, *adj.*, (bot.) having ten leaves.

décapitation, *n.f.*, decapitation, beheading.

décapiter, *v.a.*, to behead, to decapitate.

décapode, *adj.*, ten-footed, decapodal.

décapole, *n.f.*, Decapolis.

décarreler (dé-kar-lé), *v.a.*, to take up a floor, to unpave.

décastère, *n.m.*, decastere(13·1 cubic yards).

décastyle, *n.m.*, (arch.) decastyle.

décasyllabe, *adj.*, decasyllabic.

décatir, *v.a.*, to spunge woollen cloth.

décatissage, *n.m.*, spunging of woollen cloth.

décatisseur, *n.m.*, spunger of woollen cloth.

décaver, *v.a.*, to win the whole of one of the players' stakes.

décédé, **-e**, *part.*, deceased, dead.

décédé, *n.m.*, **-e**, *n.f.*, deceased; person deceased.

décéder, *v.n.*, to die, to expire, to decease.

déceindre, *v.a.*, to ungird, to loose a girdle.

décélement (-sèl-mān), *n.m.*, disclosure.

déceler, *v.a.*, to disclose, to reveal, to betray.

se **déceler**, *v.r.*, to betray one's self.

décembre, *n.m.*, December.

décemment (dé-sa-mān), *adv.*, in a decent manner, decently.

décemvir (-sèm-), *n.m.*, decemvir.

décemviral, **-e**, *adj.*, decemviral.

décemvirat, *n.m.*, decemvirate.

décence, *n.f.*, decency, propriety.

décennal, **-e** (-sèn-nal), *adj.*, decennial.

décent, **-e**. *adj.*, decent, becoming.

décentralisation, *n.f.*, decentralization.

décentraliser, *v.a.*, decentralize.

décepti-f, **-ve**. *adj.*, deceptive.

déception, *n.f.*, deception.

décerner, *v.a.*, to decree ; to award, to bestow, to issue (a summons—*une assignation*.) — *un mandat d'amener ;* to issue a writ of arrest.

décès. *n.m.*, decease, demise, death.

décevable, *adj.*, deceivable.

décevant, **-e**, *adj.*, deceptive.

décevoir, *v.a.*, to deceive.

déchaînement (-shèn-mān), *n.m.*, unbridling ; wildness (passions); exasperation.

déchaîner, *v.a.*, to unchain; to let loose, to exasperate.

se **déchaîner**, *v.r.*, to free one's self from one's chains; to run riot; to inveigh.

déchanter, *v.n.*, to change one's tone, to lower one's pretensions. to sing another tune. *Je le ferai — ;* I'll make him change his tone.

déchaperonné, **-e**. *adj.*, (of a wall—*d'un mur*) dismantled of its coping.

déchaperonner, *v.a.*, to unhood.

décharge. *n.f.*, unloading, unlading ; lumber-room ; discharge ; release ; exoneration ; (jur.) defence. *Pièce de — ;* lumber-room. *Témoin à — ;* witness for the prisoner. *Entendre les témoins à charge et à — ;* to hear the witnesses for and against.

déchargement, *n.m.*, unloading, unlading.

décharger, *v.a.*, to unload, to unlade, to empty, to vent, to disburden, to lighten; to discharge; to release, to set free; to exonerate; (hort.) to prime; to dismiss. — *sa conscience ;* to clear one's conscience. — *son cœur à quelqu'un ;* to open one's heart to one. — *son fusil sur quelqu'un ;* to discharge one's musket at any one. — *sa bile, sa colère, sur quelqu'un ;* to vent one's bile, to wreak one's anger, upon any one. — *un accusé ;* to exculpate an accused person. *Il a été déchargé de toute accusation;* he was discharged of all blame.

se **décharger**, *v.r.*, to discharge itself (liquids); to disembogue (rivers); to free one's self; to go off of itself (of a gun—*d'un fusil*) ; to change, to fade (of colours—*des couleurs*): to lay the blame. — *d'une faute sur quelqu'un ;* to lay the blame of a fault on any one.

décharger, *v.n.*, to unload; to unlade; to come off (of ink—*de l'encre*).

déchargeur, *n.m.*, unloader, wharf-porter.

décharné, **-e**. *part.*, fleshless ; lean ; emaciated; impoverished. *Visage — ;* gaunt face. *Style — ;* naked style.

décharner, *v.a.*, to strip off the flesh ; to excarnate ; to impoverish, to make lean, to emaciate ; to render meagre, naked.

⊙**décharpir**, *v.a.*, to part persons fighting ; to separate.

déchasser, *v.a.*,(turnery—*terme de tourneur*) to drive out pegs; (dancing—*danse*) déchasser.

déchaumage, *n.m.*, (agri.) digging up the stubble; ploughing up the stubble.

déchaumer, *v.a.*,to plough up the stubble ; to break up fallow-land.

déchaussé, **-e**, *adj.*, bare-footed.

déchaussement (-shôs-mān), *n.m.*, baring the root of a tree; lancing of the gum round a tooth ; baring (of teeth—*des dents*); shrinking of the gums.

déchausser, *v.a.*, to pull off shoes and stockings; to lay bare (trees, teeth, buildings —*arbres, dents, bâtiments*). — *les dents ;* to lay bare the teeth ; to lance the gums.

se **déchausser**, *v.r.*, to take off one's shoes and stockings ; to become bare (of the teeth—*des dents*).

déchaussoir, *n.m.*, gum-lancet.

déchaux, *adj.m.*, bare-footed (of friars—*de moines*).

déchéance, *n.f.*,(jur.)forfeiture; fall, decay.

déchet, *n.m.*, (com.) loss, waste.

déchevelé, -e, *part.*, dishevelled.

décheveler (-shĕ-vlé), *v.a.*, to dishevel.

se décheveler (-shĕ-vlé), *v.r.*, to dishevel one another's hair.

déchevêtrer, *v.a.*, to take the halter off, to unhalter; to disentangle.

se déchevêtrer, *v.r.*, to get one's halter off.

*décheviller, *v.a.*, to unpeg, to unpin.

déchiffrable, *adj.*, that can be deciphered, legible.

déchiffrement, *n.m.*, deciphering.

déchiffrer, *v.a.*, to decipher; to unravel; to make clear.

se déchiffrer, *v.r.*, to be deciphered, to be unravelled.

déchiffreur, *n.m.*, decipherer.

déchiqueté, -e, *part.*, (bot.) laciniate; jagged. *Feuille —e ;* jagged leaf.

déchiqueter (dé-shik-té), *v.a.*, to cut, to slash, to mangle, to cut in long pieces ; to pink.

déchiqueteur (-shik-teur), *n.m.*, he who cuts, slashes, *or* pinks.

⊙**déchiqueture** (-shik-tur), *n.f.*, slashing, cutting, pinking.

déchirage, *n.m.*, ripping up, breaking up, of a ship's planks. *Bois de —;* old ship-timber.

déchirant, -e, *adj.*, heart-rending, harrowing. *Des remords —s*, frightful, wild remorse.

déchiré, -e, *part.*, torn, rent, ragged, tattered. *Être tout —;* to be all in rags. *Chien hargneux a toujours l'oreille —e*, snarling dogs have always sore ears.

déchirement (-shir-mān), *n.m.*, rending, tearing; (surg.) laceration. *— d'entrailles ;* excruciating pain in the bowels. *—s de cœur;* anguish of heart. *—s ;* intestine broils.

déchirer, *v.a.*, to tear, to rend, to lacerate ; to bespatter, to revile, to defame. *— une plaie;* to tear open a wound. *— à coups de fouet,* to lash to pieces. *— quelqu'un à belles dents ;* to pull one to pieces. *— l'oreille ;* to grate on the ear. *— de vieux vaisseaux;* to rip up old vessels. *— la cartouche;* to bite the cartridge. *Être, déchiré de remords ;* to be tortured with remorse. *— son prochain ;* to slander one's neighbour.

se déchirer, *v.r.*, to tear, to be torn, to be rent ; to vilify, to abuse, to defame, each other. *Ce papier se déchire très facilement;* this paper tears very easily. *Je sentis mon cœur —,* I felt my heart breaking.

déchireu-r, *n.m.*, **-se**, *n.f.*, tearer, render; breaker up, ripper up (of boats, ships—*de bateaux, de vaisseaux*).

déchirure, *n.f.*, rent, tear.

déchoir (déchu), *v.n.*, to decay, to fall off, to decline; to forfeit, to lose ; (nav.) not to keep the right course. *— de son rang ;* to fall from one's rank. *Il est fort déchu de sa réputation :* he is greatly fallen in reputation. *— de ses espérances ;* to be less sanguine in one's hopes. *Être déchu d'un droit;* to have forfeited a claim. *Commencer à —;* to begin to fall away.

déchouement, *n.m.*, the setting afloat of a stranded ship.

déchouer, *v.a.*, to get off, to set afloat a ship that is aground.

déchristianiser, *v.a.*, to unchristian.

se déchristianiser, *v.r.*, to lose the character of Christian, to fall from Christianity.

déchu, -e, *part.*, decayed, sunk, fallen. *Ange —;* fallen angel.

déci, particle used in French weights and measures, deci (one-tenth of the unit).

décidé, -e, *adj.*, decided, determined, resolved.

décidément, *adv.*, decidedly, positively.

⊙**décidence**, *n.f.*, the falling of the womb.

décider, *v.a.*, to decide, to determine, to settle ; to induce, to persuade.

décider, *v.n.*, to decide, to determine. *Que le sort décide entre nous ;* let fortune determine between us. *Cet événement décida de mon sort;* that event decided my fate.

se décider, *v.r.*, to decide, to determine, to resolve, to make up one's mind ; to be decided, to be settled. *La victoire s'est décidée en faveur de nos armes :* victory decided for our arms. *Tout se décidait par intérêt;* everything was decided by interest.

décideur, *n.m.*, (l.u.) he who decides or settles peremptorily.

décidu, -e, *adj.*, (bot.) deciduous.

décigramme, *n.m.*, decigram (1·5432 grain).

décilitre, *n.m.*, decilitre (0·176 pint).

déciller. *V.* **dessiller**.

décimable, *adj.*, tithable.

décimal, -e. *adj.*, decimal.

décimateur, *n.m.*, tithe-owner.

décimation, *n.f.*, decimation.

décime, *n.m.*, decime, tenth part of a franc; a war-tax.

⊙**décime**, *n.f.*, tithe, the tenth part.

décimer, *v.a.*, to decimate (to punish every tenth soldier—*punir, mettre à mort un soldat sur dix*); to destroy, to sweep off, to carry off.

décimètre, *n.m.*, decimetre (3·937 inches).

décimo, *adv.*, tenthly.

décintrement, *n.m.*, (arch.) taking away the centres.

décintrer, *v.a.*, (arch.) to take away the centres from an arch.

décintroir, *n.m.*, (tech.) cutting-hammer.

décirer, *v.a.*, to take the wax off.

décisi-f, -ve, *adj.*, decisive, conclusive; positive, peremptory. *C'est un homme —;* he is a positive man. *Prendre un ton —;* to assume a peremptory tone.

décision, *n.f.*, decision; determination. *Une — de droit;* a decision in law.

décisivement (-ziv-mān), *adv*, decisively, peremptorily, positively.

décisoire, *adj.*, (jur.) decisory.

décistère, *n.m.*, decistere (3·53 cubic feet).

déciviliser, *v a.*, to uncivilize.

déclamateur, *n.m.*, declaimer, stump-orator. *Ce n'est qu'un —;* he is a mere declaimer.

déclamatour, *adj.*, declamatory, stilted, bombastic. *Ton —;* high-flown style.

déclamation, *n.f.*, declamation, elocution; manner, art of reciting, declaiming ; abuse, invective. *— oratoire, théâtrale ;* oratorical, theatrical elocution. *Professeur de —;* teacher of elocution. *Il s'est livré à des —s contre sa partie adverse;* he indulged in a strain of invective against his adversary.

déclamatoire, *adj.*, declamatory.

déclamer, *v.a.*, to declaim; to recite; to spout, to mouth out.

déclamer, *v.n.*, to declaim; to recite; to spout, to inveigh.

déclarat-eur, *n.m.*, **-rice**, *n.f.*, declarer.

déclarati-f, -ve, *adj.*, declaratory.

déclaration, *n.f.*, declaration ; disclosure; notification ; (jur.) schedule ; statute (of bankruptcy—*de faillite*); (jur.) affidavit; verdict (of juries—*du jury*). *— d'amour;* declaration of love. *— d'entrée, de sortie ;* declaration of goods (at the custom-house—*à la douane*) on entering, on leaving the town.

déclaratoire, *adj.*, declaratory.

déclaré, -e, *adj.*, declared ; open. *Ennemi —;* declared enemy.

déclarer, v.a., to declare, to make known; to proclaim; to certify; to denounce; to find (guilty, not guilty—*coupable, ou non coupable*). — *sa volonté*; to make known one's will.

se **déclarer**, v.r., to declare, to speak one's mind; to declare one's self, itself; to break out; to set in (of the weather—*du temps*). *La petite vérole s'est déclarée*; the small-pox has broken out. *La victoire s'est déclarée pour nous*; victory declared for us.

déclasser, v.a., to alter the classing.

déclencher, v.a., to unlatch a door, to lift up the latch.

déclic, n.m., (mec.) click; monkey (of a pile-driver—*de sonnette*).

déclimater, v.a., to accustom to a foreign climate.

déclin, n.m., decline, decay; wane (of the moon—*de la lune*); ebb; close; main-spring (of fire-arms—*d'armes à feu*). *L'hiver est sur son* —; winter is drawing to a close.

déclinable, adj., (gram.) declinable.

déclinaison, n.f., (gram.) declension; (astron., phys.) declination. — *de la boussole*; variation of the compass. — *d'un cadran*; declination of a dial.

déclinant, -e, adj., declining. *Cadran* —; declining dial.

déclinatoire, adj., declinatory. *Exception* —; exception.

déclinatoire, n.m., (jur.) declinatory plea, exception.

décliner, v.n., to decline; to be on the wane, to fall off. *Ses forces déclinent beaucoup*; his strength is fast declining. *Ce malade décline tous les jours*; the patient is falling away every day.

décliner, v.a., (gram.) to decline; to state. — *son nom*; to state one's name. — *une juridiction*; to decline, to except to, the jurisdiction of a court of law.

déclive, adj., declivous, sloping; (surg.) dependent.

déclivité, v.f., declivity.

décloîtrer, v.a., to withdraw from a convent.

déclore, v.a., to unclose, to throw open.

déclos, -e, part., unclosed; open.

déclouer, v a., to unnail.

décochement (-kosh-män), n.m., discharge (of arrows, shafts—*de flèches, de traits*); shooting.

décocher, v.a., to discharge, to let fly (arrows—*flèches*); to let fly; to bring out. — *les traits de sa colère contre quelqu'un*; to discharge the shafts of one's anger against any one.

décoction, n.f., (pharm.) decoction.

*décognoir, n.m., (print.) shooting-stick.

décoiffer, v.a., to take off a head-dress, to undress the hair; to take the sealing-wax off the cork of a bottle.

se **décoiffer**, v.r., to undo one's head-dress, to take off one's cap. *Cet enfant se décoiffe toujours*; that child is constantly pulling off its cap.

décollation. n.f., decollation, beheading.

décollement (-kol-män), n.m., ungluing, unpasting, coming off.

décoller, v.a., to behead; to unglue, to deglutinate; to disengage (at billiards—*au billard*).

se **décoller**, v.r., to unglue, to get unglued, to come off.

décolleté, -e, part., in a low dress. *Une femme trop décolletée*; a woman whose bosom is too much uncovered.

décolleter (-kol-té), v.a., to uncover the breast.

se **décolleter**, v.r., to bare one's shoulders; to wear a low-bodied dress.

décolleter, v.n., to leave the neck bare.

décoloration, n.f., decoloration.

décoloré, -e, part., discoloured. *Un teint* —; a discoloured complexion.

décolorer, v.a., to discolour, to take away the colour, to change from the natural hue.

se **décolorer**, v.r., to lose one's colour; to become discoloured. *Ces roses se décolorent*; these roses lose their colour.

décombrer, v.a., to clear away rubbish, to clear rubbish from.

décombres, n.m.pl., rubbish.

décommander, v.a., to countermand.

décompléter, v.a., to render incomplete.

décomposable, adj., decomposable; decompoundable.

décomposé, -e, part., decomposed; decomposite. *Un visage* —; a distorted countenance.

décomposer, v.a., to decompose, to discompose; to decompound. *La terreur décompose le visage*; terror distorts the face.

se **décomposer**, v.r., to decompose, to become decomposed; to be distorted (of the features —*des traits du visage*).

décomposition, n.f., decomposition; discomposition.

décompte (dé-kont), n.m., deduction; deficiency; disappointment. *Trouver du* —; to be disappointed.

décompter (dé-kon-té), v.a., to deduct; to reckon off.

décompter, v.n., to reckon off; to be disappointed; to lose one's illusions.

déconcerté, -e, adj., disconcerted.

déconcerter, v.a., to disconcert, to foil, to baffle.

se **déconcerter**, v.r., to be disconcerted.

déconfire, v.a., to discomfit; nonplus.

déconfiture, n.f., discomfiture; havoc; overthrow; (jur.) insolvency.

déconfort. n.m., discomfort, sorrow.

déconforter, v.a., to discomfort, to grieve.

*déconseiller, v.a., to dissuade.

déconsidération, n.f., disrepute; disesteem, discredit.

déconsidéré, -e, adj., sunk into disrepute.

déconsidérer, v.a., to bring into disrepute.

se **déconsidérer**, v.r., to fall, to sink, into disrepute.

déconstruire, v.a., to take to pieces; to unbuild, to demolish, to pull down; to decompose; (gram.) to construct badly. — *des vers*; to turn verse into prose.

décontenancé, -e, part., out of countenance, abashed.

décontenancer, v.a., to abash, to put out of countenance.

se **décontenancer**, v.r., to be put out of countenance.

déconvenue, n.f., discomfiture, disaster, mishap.

décor, n.m., decoration, ornamental painting; (paint.) graining; pl., (theat.) scenery. — *en bois*; graining in imitation of wood. *Peintre en* —*s*; grainer.

décorateur, n.m., ornamental painter, decorator; scene-painter; grainer.

décorati-f, -ve, adj., decorative, ornamental.

décoration, n.f., decoration, embellishment; star; star of the order of the Legion of Honour; pl., scenery. *Porter une* —; to wear the star of an order.

décorder, v.a., to untwist, to untwine (a rope—*une corde*).

décoré, -e, part., decorated; wearing the insignia of some order of knighthood.

décoré, n.m., knight; knight of the Legion of Honour.

décorer, v.a., to decorate, to ornament; to

dignify; to trim up; to set off; to confer (titles, honours—*des titres, des honneurs*); to confer the knighthood of the Legion of Honour; to paint. — *d'un ordre:* to honour with the order of. *Se* — *d'un titre;* to dignify one's name with a title.

décortication, *n.f.*, stripping off bark, decortication.

décortiquer, *v.a.*, to decorticate;

décorum (-rom), *n.m.*, decorum, decency. *Observer le* — ; to keep decorum. *C'est pour garder le* — ; it is for decency's sake. *Blesser le* — ; to offend against decorum.

découcher, *v.n.*, to sleep out; to stay out all night.

découcher, *v.a.*, to put out of one's bed.

découdre, *v.a.*, to unsew, to unstitch, to rip up.

se **découdre**, *v.r.*, to come unsewed, unstitched.

découdre, *v.n.*, to contend. *Ils veulent en* — ; they are bent on having a brush together.

découlant, -e, *adj.*, flowing.

découlement (-kool-mân), *n.m.*, flowing, dropping, trickling.

découler, *v.n.*, to trickle, to flow, to run; to spring, to proceed. *La sueur découlait de son visage;* the perspiration was running down his face. *C'est de Dieu que les grâces découlent;* our blessings flow from God.

découpage, *n.m.*, (tech.) cutting out, carving out. — *à l'emporte-pièce*, punching.

découpé, -e, *part.*, (paint.) cut out; (bot.) cut.

découpé, *n.m.*, (hort.) mingled bed; parterre.

découper, *v.a.*, to cut into pieces. into shreds; to cut up, to carve; to pink, to slash; to cut out. — *un poulet* ; to carve a fowl. — *une jupe;* to slash a petticoat. — *des figures* ; to cut out figures.

découpeu-r, *n.m.*, **-se**, *n.f.*, person that cuts out.

découple *or* **découpler**, *n.m.*, (hunt.) uncoupling, unleashing of dogs.

découplé, -e, *part.*, uncoupled; strapping. *C'est un gaillard bien* — ; he is a strapping fellow. *Une fille bien* —*e* ; a bouncing girl.

découpler, *v.a.*, to uncouple, to unleash, to let loose.

découpoir, *n.m.*, (tech.) punch, stamping-machine, stamping press.

découpure, *n.f.*, cutting out, pinking, work cut out; cut paper-work.

décourageant, -e (-jân, -t), *adj.*, discouraging, disheartening.

découragement (-raj-mân), *n.m.*, discouragement; despondency. *Tomber dans le* — ; to become discouraged.

décourager, *v.a.*, to discourage, to dishearten, to daunt, to deter.

se **décourager**, *v.r.*, to be discouraged. *Il y a de quoi se* — ; there is enough to discourage one.

décourant, -e, *adj. V.* **décurrent**.

décourber, *v.a.*, to unyoke barge horses

découronner, *v.a.*, to discrown. — *une hauteur*, to sweep the top of a hill of the troops that occupied it.

décours, *n.m.*, decrease; wane (of the moon —*de la lune*).

décousu, -e, *part.*, *adj.*, unsewed, unstitched, ripped; desultory, unconnected. *Style* — ; desultory style. *Des idées* —*es* ; unconnected ideas.

décousure, *n.f.*, unsewing, seam-rent; (hunt.) gash (by a wild boar—*d'un sanglier*).

découvert, -e, *part.*, uncovered, detected, plain; discovered. *Une allée* —*e* ; an open walk. *Un pays* — ; an open country. *À* — ; in the open air; plainly; exposed to the fire of the

enemy. *Être à* — ; (com.) to have no pledge, no security.

découvert, *n.m.*, (com.) uncovered balance; deficit.

découverte, *n.f.*, discovery; (nav.) lookout; (milit.) reconnoitring. *La* — *d'un secret;* the finding out of a secret. *Aller à la* — ; to scout. *Envoyer à la* — *de;* to send to reconnoitre.

découvreur, *n.m.*, discoverer.

découvrir, *v.a.*, to uncover, to expose, to unmuffle, to unroof ; to see, to spy out, to discover, to disclose; to unveil; to find out. — *les racines d'un arbre;* to lay bare the roots of a tree. — *son jeu;* to show one's cards; to betray one's self. *Je lui ai découvert mon cœur ;* I laid my heart open to him. — *une mine d'or;* to discover a mine of gold. — *le pot aux roses;* to find out the intrigue, the plot.

se **découvrir**, *v.r.*, to uncover one's self, to unbosom one's self; to expose one's self; to be detected; to make one's self known; to clear up (of the sky—*du ciel*).

décrasser, *v.a.*, to take off the dirt, to clean. — *la tête* ; to clean the head. *Il faut* — *ce jeune homme;* the young man requires brushing up.

se **décrasser**, *v.r.*, to get the dirt off one's self; to polish one's self, to become polite, elegant.

décréditement (-dit-mân), *n.m.*, discrediting.

décréditer, *v.a.*, to discredit, to disgrace, to bring into discredit.

se **décréditer**, *v.r.*, to sink into discredit, to lose one's credit *or* reputation.

décrépir, *v.a.*, (mas.) to take off plastering, rough-casting, *or* pargeting from walls, &c.

décrépissage, *n.m.*, (mas.) the taking off of plastering, rough-casting *or* pargeting from walls. &c.

décrépit, -e, *adj.*, decrepit.

décrépitation, *n.f.*, decrepitation.

décrépiter, *v.n.*, to decrepitate, to crackle.

décrépitude, *n.f.*, decrepitude.

décret, *n.m.*, decree, fiat ; ☉(jur.) writ.

décrétale, *n.f.*, decretal.

décréter, *v.a.*, to decree; ☉(jur.) to issue a writ against.

décreusage, *n.m.*, ungumming (of silk, thread—*de la soie, du fil*).

décreuser, *v.a.*, to ungum.

décri, *n.m.*, crying down, prohibition ; disrepute, discredit.

décrier, *v.a.*, to decry, to cry down, to discredit, to bring into disrepute.

se **décrier**, *v.r.*, to bring one's self into disrepute ; to cry one another down.

décrire, *v.a.*, to describe. *Cette merveille ne saurait se* — ; that wonder beggars description.

décrocher, *v.a.*, to unhook, to take down.

décroire, *v.a.*, to disbelieve, to discredit.

décroissance, *n.f. V.* **décroissement**.

décroissant, -e, *adj.*, decreasing, diminishing ; decrescent ; (math.) descending.

décroissement(-kroas-mân), *n.m.*, decrease, diminution.

décroître, *v.n.*, to decrease, to diminish.

décrottage, *n.m.*, cleaning of boots, trowsers, &c., soiled with mud.

décrotter, *v.a.*, to rub off the dirt, to clean, to brush off.

se **décrotter**, *v.r.*, to brush the dirt off one's self.

décrotteur, *n.m.*, shoe-boy, shoe-black;

décrottoir, *n.m.*, a scraper (for shoes—*pour la chaussure*).

décrottoire, *n.f.*, shoe-brush, hard brush.

décrue, *n.f.*, decrease; fall (of water—*del'eau*). *La crue et la* — *de l'eau;* the increase and decrease, the rise and fall, of water.

décruer, *v.a.*, (dy.) to scour.

décrûment, *n.m.*, (dy.) scouring.

décrusement, *n.m.*, (dy.) ungumming.

décruser, *v.a.*, to ungum.

déçu, -e, *part.*, deceived; frustrated.

décuire, *v.a.*, to thin (syrup, &c.—*du sirop*). *Ce sirop est trop épais, il faut le —;* this syrup is too thick, it must be thinned.

déculasser, *v.a.*, to unbreech (a gun, &c.—*un fusil, &c.*).

décuple, *adj.*, tenfold, decuple.

décuple, *n.m.*, decuple, tenfold. *Il a gagné le — de ce qu'il avait avancé;* he has gained ten times as much as he laid out.

décupler, *v.a.*, to increase ten times as much, to make tenfold.

décurie, *n.f.*, (antiq.) decury.

décurion, *n.m.*, (antiq.) decurion.

décurrent, -e, *adj.*, (bot.) decurrent.

décursi-f. -ve, *adj.*, decursive.

décussation, *n.f.*, decussation.

décuver, *v.a.*, to put from one cask into another (of wine—*du vin*).

*****dédaigner**, *v.a.*, to disdain, to scorn, to slight, to turn one's nose up at.

*****dédaigneusement** (-eûz-mān), *adv.*, disdainfully, scornfully.

*****dédaigneu-x, -se**, *adj.*, disdainful, scornful. *Faire le —;* to turn up one's nose. *Beauté fière et —se;* proud and haughty beauty.

dédain, *n.m.*, disdain, scorn.

dédale, *n.m.*, labyrinth, maze.

dédamer, *v.n.*, to put a draught out of its place (at draughts—*aux dames*).

dedans, *adv.*, within, in; inside. *Il est là-dedans;* he is within. *En —;* on the inside, within. *Sa porte était fermée en —;* his door was fastened inside. *Donner —;* to be taken in. *Être —;* to be in for it. *Mettre quelqu'un —;* to take any one in. *Se mettre —;* to get taken in, to get into a scrape. *De —;* from within. *Par —;* within, inside.

dedans, *n.m.*, inside; interior. *Du — au dehors;* from within outwards. *Au — et au dehors;* at home and abroad.

dédicace, *n.f.*, dedication (consecration); dedication (of a book—*d'un livre*); inscription.

dédicatoire, *adj.*, (of an epistle—*d'une épître*) dedicatory.

dédier, *v.a.*, to dedicate (to consecrate); to dedicate (books—*des livres*); to inscribe.

dédire, *v.a.*, to gainsay, to unsay, to contradict.

se dédire, *v.r.*, to recant, to retract, to unsay what one has said; to go from one's word, to recede. *Se — de sa promesse;* to go from one's promise. *Il ne peut s'en —;* he cannot go back.

dédit, *n.m.*, unsaying; forfeit, forfeiture; retraction; deed stipulating forfeiture. *Au — de;* on the forfeiture of. *Avoir son dit et son —;* to retract what one says.

dédommagement (maj-mān), *n.m.*, indemnification; compensation, amends, indemnity.

dédommager, *v.a.*, to indemnify, to make amends (for a loss—*pour une perte*); to compensate, to make up.

se dédommager, *v.r.*, to indemnify one's self, to compensate one's self.

dédorer, *v.a.*, to ungild.

se dédorer, *v.r.*, to lose its gilt.

dédoublement, *n.m.*, dividing into two, making one into two.

dédoubler, *v.a.*, to take out the lining; to divide into two; (nav.) to unsheath (a vessel—*un vaisseau*). *— une pierre;* to cut a stone into two parts lengthwise.

déduction, *n.f.*, deduction; inference; taking from defalcation; enumeration, recital.

déduire, (déduisant, déduit), *v.a.*, to take

from, to deduct, to subtract; to draw from, to deduce.

⊙**déduit**, *n.m.*, amusement, pleasant occupation.

déesse, *n.f.*, goddess, female deity.

défâcher, *v.a.*, to pacify.

se défâcher, *v.r.*, to be pacified or pleased again, to cool. *S'il est fâché, qu'il se défâche;* if he is hot, let him cool again.

*****défaillance**, *n.f.*, fainting fit, swoon; exhaustion; extinction (of a family—*d'une famille*); ⊙(chem.) deliquescence. *Tomber en —;* to fall into a swoon.

*****défaillant**, *n.m.*, **-e**, *n.f.*, (jur.) defaulter.

*****défaillant, -e**, *adj.*, falling off; decaying; weak, feeble; faltering, unsteady. *Sa main —e;* his feeble hand. *Ligne —e;* branch of a family without heirs.

*****défaillir**, *v.n.*, to grow faint and weak, to fail; to decay; to swoon, to faint away. *Ses forces défaillent tous les jours;* his strength fails him every day. *Il se sent —;* he feels himself decaying. *Je me sentis —;* I felt I was going to faint.

défaire, *v.a.*, to undo; to take asunder; to unpin; to unrip; to unknit; to make away with; to defeat; to eclipse, to obscure; to emaciate, to make lean, to waste; to discompose, to alter; to free, to deliver, to rid. *— une malle;* to unpack a trunk. *— un nœud;* to untie a knot. *Sa maladie l'a bien défait;* his illness has made him very thin. *Défaites-moi de cet importun;* rid me of that troublesome fellow. *— un marché, — un mariage;* to annul, break off, a bargain, a marriage.

se défaire, *v.r.*, to rid one's self, to get rid of, to get quit of, to ease one's self of, to make away, to forsake, to leave off; to come undone, to become loose; to lose strength and quality (of wine—*du vin*). *Je me suis défait de cette charge;* I got rid of that office. *Se — de son ennemi;* to dispatch one's enemy. *Se — d'un vice;* to leave off a vice. *Se — d'une mauvaise habitude,* to break one's self of a bad habit. *Défaites-vous de vos préjugés;* shake off your prejudices. *Se — de sa marchandise;* to sell off one's wares. *Se — d'un bénéfice;* to give up a benefice. *Se — d'un cheval;* to part with a horse. *Se — d'un domestique;* to discharge a servant. *Ce vin se défait;* this wine is losing its flavour.

défait, -e, *part.*, undone, defeated; meagre, lean, wasted.

défaite, *n.f.*, defeat, overthrow; (com.) sale; evasion, shift, put-off, sham. *Ces marchandises-là sont de bonne —;* those goods command a quick sale. *La — est ingénieuse,* that is an ingenious evasion. *C'est une —;* that is a mere put-off.

défalcation, *n.f.*, defalcation, abatement, deduction.

défalquer, *v.a.*, to take off, to defalcate, to deduct.

se défausser, *v.r.*, (at cards—*aux cartes*) to renounce.

défaut, *n.m.*, defect; fault; flaw, blemish; want; default. *Chacun a ses —s;* every one has his defects. *Il n'y a personne sans—;* there is no man but has his faults. *Cette pièce de porcelaine a un—;* there is a flaw in that piece of china. *Le — du blé, de subsistances;* want of corn, of victuals. *C'est là le — de la cuirasse;* that's his blind side. *Condamner par —;* to cast i.r non-appearance. *Jugement par—;* judgment by default. *Les chiens sont en —;* the hounds are at fault. *Trouver quelqu'un en—;* to find one at fault. *Mettre quelqu'un en—;* to baffle, to foil, one. *Au —, à — de;* in default of, for want of.

défaveur, *n.f.*, disfavour, disgrace.

défavorable, *adj.*, unfavourable.

défavorablement, *adv.*, unfavourably.

défécation, *n.f.*, (pharm.) defecation. *Matière à —;* temper (of sugar—*du sucre*).

défecti-f, -ve, *adj.*, (gram.) defective.

défection, *n.f.*, defection, falling off, disloyalty.

défectivité, *n.f.*, (gram.) defectiveness.

défectueusement (-eûz-măn), *adv.*, defectively.

défectueu-x, -se, *adj.*, defective, imperfect.

défectuosité, *n.f.*, defect, imperfection, flaw.

défendable, *adj.*, that may be defended, defensible, tenable.

défendant, *part.*, defending. *Il l'a tué à son corps —;* he killed him in self-defence. *Faire une chose à son corps —;* to do a thing reluctantly, in self-defence.

défende-ur, *n.m.*, **-resse**, *n.f.*, (jur.) defendant; respondent.

défendre, *v.a.*, to defend, to protect; to shelter, to shield, to support, to uphold, to vindicate; to forbid, to prohibit. *— son ami;* to defend one's friend. *On a défendu le port des armes;* the carrying of arms is prohibited. *La raison nous défend de faire une injustice;* reason forbids us to do an injustice. *— sa maison à quelqu'un;* to forbid any one one's house.

défendre, *v.n.*, (jur.) to defend. *Il a été condamné faute de —;* he was cast for want of being defended.

se défendre, *v.r.*, to defend one's self; to excuse one's self from doing a thing; to clear one's self; to deny a thing; to keep, to shield, one's self from; to help, to forbear. *Cet accusé a voulu se — lui-même;* that prisoner wanted to conduct his own defence. *Il ne peut se — de tant de reproches;* he cannot clear himself from so many imputations.

défens, *n.m.*, (forestry—*eaux et forêts*) defence of forests, order prohibiting the cutting down of trees and the letting in of cattle.

défense, *n.f.*, defence, protection; prohibition, interdiction; apology, vindication, justification; warning, notice; task; (nav.) fender; skid; boom. **—s**, (fort.) outwork, defence; tusk, fang (of boars—*de sangliers*); tusk (elephants). *Se mettre en —;* to stand upon one's defence. *Être hors de —;* not to be in a condition to defend one's self. *Bois en —;* a wood so far grown that cattle may be let into it without danger to the trees. *Cordes de —;* fenders of junk *or* old cable. *Faire —;* to forbid, to prohibit. *Preuves alléguées pour la — d'une cause;* plea. *Donner ses —s;* to answer. *Arrêt de —;* decree to suspend the execution of a former decree. *Armé, muni, de —s;* tusked, fanged (of boars, elephants—*de sangliers, &c.*).

défenseur, *n.m.*, defender, supporter, vindicator, advocate; defender, counsel. *Un nommé d'office;* a defender appointed by the court.

défensi-f, -ve. *adj.*, defensive.

défensive, *n.f.*, safeguard, defensive. *Se tenir sur la —;* to stand upon the defensive.

déféquer, *v.a.*, to defecate.

déférant, -e, *adj.*, complying, condescending, yielding.

déférence, *n.f.*, deference, regard, respect.

déférent, *adj. m.*, deferent. *Cercle —* (anc. astron.); deferent. *Canal —* (anat.); deferent.

déférer, *v.a.*, to confer, to bestow; to tender. *— le serment à quelqu'un;* to tender an oath to, to accuse before one, to put one on his oath. *— quelqu'un en justice;* to impeach one in court. *— quelqu'un à l'inquisition;* to report one to the inquisition.

déférer, *v.n.*, to defer, to yield, to condescend. *— aux sentiments des autres;* to defer to the sentiments of others. *— à quelqu'un;* to pay deference to one.

déferler, *v.a.*, (nav.) to unfurl.

déferler, *v.n.*, to break into foam (of the sea—*de la mer*). *La lame déferle;* the wave bursts into foam.

déferrer, *v.a.*, to unshoe (a horse—*un cheval*); to nonplus, to confound.

se déferrer, *v.r.*, to come off, to fall off, to lose a shoe; to be non-plussed *or* confounded. *Mon lacet se déferre;* the tag is coming off my lace.

défet, *n.m.*, waste sheets (in bookselling *or* printing—*terme de librairie et d'imprimerie*).

*****défeuillaison**, *n.f.*, defoliation.

*****défeuiller**, *v.a.*, to take off the leaves. *Le vent a défeuillé les arbres;* the wind has taken off, blown off, the leaves.

se défeuiller, *v.r.*, to lose the leaves (of trees —*des arbres*). *Les arbres se défeuillent;* the trees are losing their leaves.

défi, *n.m.*, defiance, challenge. *Un cartel de —;* a written challenge. *Envoyer un — à quelqu'un;* to send one a challenge. *Je lui ai fait un — aux échecs;* I challenged him to a game at chess. *Mettre au —;* to set at defiance.

défiance, *n.f.*, distrust, mistrust; diffidence. *Concevoir de la —;* to entertain distrust. *Être dans la —;* to have one's misgivings. *Une sotte — le retient;* he is held back by a foolish diffidence.

défiant, -e, *adj.*, distrustful, mistrustful, suspicious.

déficient, -e, *adj.*, (arith.) deficient.

déficit (-sit), *n.m.*, deficit, deficiency. *Il faut tant pour combler le —,* so much is necessary to make up the deficit.

défier, *v.a.*, to defy, to challenge; to brave, to dare; to set at defiance. *— quelqu'un au trictrac;* to challenge one to play at backgammon. *— les dangers;* to face dangers. *Il ne faut jamais — un fou;* never bid defiance to a madman. *Je vous défie de m'en donner la preuve;* I defy you to give me the proof of it.

défier, *v.n.*, (nav.) to bear off from a thing.

se défier, *v.r.*, to defy, to challenge, each other; to distrust, to mistrust, to suspect. *Je me défie de ses caresses;* I suspect the sincerity of his caresses. *Se — de ses forces,* to distrust one's own strength. *Se — de soi-même;* to distrust one's self.

défigurer, *v.a.*, to disfigure, to mar, to distort, to spoil. *La petite vérole l'a tout défiguré;* the small-pox has quite disfigured him. *— la vérité;* to distort the truth.

se défigurer, *v.r.*, to disfigure one's self, to become disfigured, to become deformed.

défilé, *n.m.*, defile, long narrow pass; strait, difficulty; (milit.) defiling, filing off. *Je ne vois aucun moyen de sortir de ce —;* I see no way of getting out of this difficulty.

défilement, *n.m.*, filing off; (fort.) defilading.

défiler, *v.a.*, to unstring, to unthread; to untwist. *— des perles;* to unstring pearls *— son chapelet;* to say all one has got to say on a subject. *Elle a défilé son chapelet;* she has given up devotion. *Le chapelet se défile;* the association is falling to pieces. *— un ouvrage;* (fort.) to protect a work from being swept on enfilade.

défiler, *v.n.*, to defile, to file off. *Les soldats ne pouvaient — que deux à deux;* the soldiers could only defile two by two.

défiler, *n.m.*, (milit., l.u.) filing off.

défini, *n.m.*, the definite.

défini, -e, *part.*, determined, definite, defined. *Nombre —;* definite number. *Article —;* definite article.

définir, *v.a.*, to define, to determine; to decide; to explain. — *une personne;* to give an idea of a person.

définissable. *adj.*, definable.

définisseur, *n.*.. *h.*, one who defines.

définiteur. *n.m.*, definitor, counsellor *or* assistant (assigned to the general in some religious orders—*imposé a z général dans quelques ordres religieux*).

définiti-f. **-ve**, *adj.*, definitive, peremptory, positive. *En —ve;* definitively. *En —ve, que voulez-vous?* in a word, what do you want?

définition. *n.f.*, definition; decision, determination. *Faire une —;* to give a definition.

définitivement (-tiv-mān), *adv.*, definitively, positively, decidedly.

définitoire, *n.m.*, chapter held by certain monks for the regulation of their order.

déflagration, *n.f.* (chem.) deflagration.

défléchi, **-e**, *adj.*, turned aside, deflected.

défléchir, *v.n.*, to turn from *or* aside.

déflegmation, *n.f.* (chem.) dephlegmation.

déflegmer, *v.a.*, (chem.) to dephlegmate.

défleuraison, *n.f.*, fall of the blossom.

défleurir, *v n*, to shed blossoms.

défleurir, *v.a.*, to nip or strip off blossoms; to take off the bloom of fruit (by handling it—*en le maniant*).

déflexion, *n.f.*, (phys.) deviation, deflection.

défloration, *n.f.*, defloration.

déflorer *v.a.*, to deflour — *un sujet;* to take away the cream of a subject.

⊙**défluer**, *v.n.*, (astrol.) to flow, to recede.

défonçage, *n.m.*, (agri.) deep ploughing.

défoncé, **-e**, *part. Chemin —;* broken road.

défoncement (-fons-mān), *n.m.*, (tech.) staving in, beating in of the head of casks; (agri.) digging up; deep ploughing.

défoncer, *v.a.*, to stave (a cask—*un tonneau*); to knock in the head (of a cask—*d'un tonneau*). — *un terrain;* to dig ground to the depth of two or three feet, clear it of stones, and mix it with compost. — *une peau;* to dip a hide.

se défoncer, *v.r.*, to give way at the bottom; to break up (of roads—*des routes*).

déformation, *n.f.*, deformation.

déformé, **-e**, *adj.*, deformed, out of form.

déformer, *v.a.*, to put out of form, to throw out of shape. *Se —;* to lose the proper form or shape. *Sa taille se déforme;* her figure begins to get deformed.

défouetter, *v.a.*, (book-bind.) to untie.

défourner, *v.a* . to draw out of an oven. — *le pain*, to draw the batch.

défournis, *n.m. pl.*, (nav.) fault, scantiness (of wood—*dans le bois*).

défourrer, *v.a.*, (nav) to unwrap, to take off the envelope.

défrai, *n.m.*, settling the expense of a house, defraying.

défraîchir, *v.a.*, to destroy, to take off. the brilliancy, gloss. *or* freshness of a thing. *Se —, v r..* to lose brilliancy, freshness.

défranciser, *v.a.*, to unfrenchify.

défrayer, *v.a.*. to defray, to bear. the charges of; to amuse; to be the laughing-stock of. — *la compagnie :* to be the laughing-stock of the company.

défrayeur, *n.m.*, one who pays expenses, defrayer.

défrichage. *or* **défrichement** (-frish-mān), *n.m.*, clearing, grubbing up; land so cleared. *Faire le — un terrain :* to clear a piece of ground. *Ce — est en plein rapport cette année :* this piece of cleared land is in full bearing this year.

défricher, *v.a.*, to clear, to grub up: to unravel (l.u.). — *un champ :* to clear a field.

défricheur, *n.m.*, one who clears an untilled piece of ground.

défrisement (-friz-mān), *n.m.*, act of uncurling.

défriser, *v.a.*, to uncurl, to put out of curl; (pop.) to disappoint, to ruffle.

se défriser, *v.r.*, to uncurl, come out of curl.

défroncement, *n.m.*, unplaiting, unfolding.

défroncer, *v.a.*, to undo gathers, folds, or plaits; to unknit (the brows—*les sourcils*). — *le sourcil;* to smooth one's brow.

défroque, *n.f.*, the money and movables which a monk leaves at his decease; cast-off clothes.

défroquer, *v.a.*, to unfrock. *Se —;* to forsake, to renounce one's order (of monks—*de moines*).

défuner, *v.a.*, (nav.) to strip (a mast—*un mât*).

défunt, **-e**, *adj.*, defunct, deceased. *Les enfants du —;* the deceased's children.

dégagé, **-e**, *part.*, disengaged; flippant; bold; easy. *Chambre —e;* room that has a back-door. *Escalier —;* back stairs. *Taille —e;* free, easy figure (pers.). *Air —;* free, easy way.

dégagement (-gaj-mān), *n.m.*, disengagement. clearance; (fenc.) disengaging. *Le — des effets déposés au mont-de-piété;* the redeeming of articles at the pawnbroker's. *Le — de sa parole;* the calling in of one's word. *Le — de la voie publique;* the clearing of the street. *Le — de la poitrine;* the easing of the chest. *Escalier de —;* private staircase.

dégager, *v.a.*, to redeem; to take out of pawn; to free, to disengage, to separate; to evolve. — *sa parole;* to redeem one's word; to withdraw one's word. — *quelqu'un de sa parole;* to release one from his word. — *son cœur;* to disengage one's heart. — *une porte;* to clear a doorway. — *la tête, la poitrine;* to ease, relieve, or lighten the head, the chest. *Il l'a dégagé de ses ennemis;* he disengaged him from his enemies. *Je le dégageai de ses liens;* I freed him from his bonds. — *le fer;* (fenc.) to disengage. *Cet habit dégage la taille;* that coat shows off the shape to advantage. — *les cheveux;* to lighten the hair.

se dégager, *v.r.*, to be cleared from; to extricate, to disengage, to free, to disentangle, to loose one's self; to get away, to get clear; (chem.) to be evolved.

dégaine, *n.f.*, (fam.) awkwardness; ridiculous manners, deportment, &c. *Quelle —!* what a waddle!

dégainer, *v.a.*, unsheathing, drawing (of a sword—*d'une épée, &c.*). *Être brave jusqu'au —;* to be brave till it comes to the push.

dégainer, *v a.*, to draw, to unsheath one's sword; to lug out.

dégaineur. *n.m.*, hector, bully, quarrelsome fellow, professed duellist.

déganter, *v.a.*, to pull off gloves.

se déganter, *v.r.*, to take off one's gloves.

dégarnir, *v.a.*. to disgarnish, to unfurnish, to strip. — *une chambre, une maison;* to unfurnish a room. a house. — *le cabestan;* (nav.) to unring the capstern. — *un vaisseau de ses agrès :* to strip a vessel of its rigging. — *un arbre :* to thin a tree. — *une robe;* to untrim a gown.

se dégarnir, *v.r.*, to strip one's self; to empty, become empty; to grow thin; to wear lighter clothes. *Sa tête se dégarnit;* his hair is growing thin. *La salle se dégarnit;* the house is getting empty. *Il ne faut pas trop se hâter de se —;* people should not be in too great a hurry to put on light clothing.

dégasconner, *v.a.*, to teach a Gascon to

speak good French, to acquire French manners, &c.

dégât, *n.m.*, havoc, damage, depredation, waste. *La grêle a fait un grand —; the hail has made great havoc. *Faire le —; to ravage.

dégauchi, -e, *adj.*, planed, smoothed, straightened.

dégauchir, *v.a.*, to smooth, to plane, to level, to straighten; to form, to polish. — *un jeune homme;* to polish a young man.

dégauchissage, or **dégauchissement** (-shis-mān), *n.m.*, planing, straightening, levelling, smoothing.

dégel, *n.m.*, thaw. *Avoir du —;* to have a thaw. *Être au —;* to thaw (of the weather—*du temps*).

dégeler (dé-jlé), *v.a.n.*, to thaw.

se **dégeler**, *v.r.*, to thaw.

⊙**dégénérat-eur**, -**rice**, *adj.*, degenerating.

dégénération, *n.f.*, degeneration; degeneracy, deterioration.

dégénérer, *v.n.*, to decline, to degenerate. — *de ses ancêtres;* to degenerate from one's ancestors. *L'apoplexie dégénère quelquefois en paralysie;* apoplexy sometimes degenerates into paralysis.

dégénérescence, *n.f.* (med.) *V.* **dégénération**.

dégénérescent, -e, *adj.*, degenerating.

dégingandé, -e, *adj.*, tottering, swinging in one's gait; ill-formed; unconnected.

dégluer, *v.a.*, to take off the bird-lime; to remove the gum from the eyes.

se **dégluer**, *v.r.*, to extricate one's self from bird-lime; to be cleared from gum (of the eyes—*des yeux*).

⊙**déglutir**, *v.a.*, to swallow

déglutition, *n.f.*, deglutition.

***dégobiller**, *v.a.*, (l.ex.) to bring up; to puke, to spew, to vomit, to throw up.

***dégobillis**, *n.m.*, (l.ex.) vomit, spew.

dégoiser, *v.a.n.*, ⊙ to chirp, to twitter; to rattle; to bolt out; to chatter. *En dégoise-t-elle!* how she does rattle on! *Il a dégoisé tout ce qu'il sait;* he blabbed out all he knew.

dégommage, *n.m.*, washing out the gum.

dégommer, *v.a.*, (dy.) to wash out the gum; (pop.) to turn out of office; to oust; to carry off (kill—*tuer*).

dégonder, *v.a.*, to unhinge, to take from its hinge.

se **dégonder**, *v.r.*, to come unhinged, to come off its hinges.

dégonflement, *n.m.*, subsiding, falling, collapsing; reduction.

dégonfler, *v.a.*, to cause a thing to collapse, to cause a swelling to subside; to discharge the gas from a balloon.

se **dégonfler**, *v.r.*, to go down, to be reduced, to subside, to unbosom one's self.

dégor, *n.m*, a discharging tube in a distilling vessel.

dégorgement, *n.m.*, breaking out, overflowing; unstopping. — *d'un tuyau;* cleansing of a pipe.

dégorgeoir (-joar), *n.m.*, priming-iron (of guns—*de canon*); place where waters are discharged; spout.

dégorger, *v.a.*, to clear, to open; to cleanse, to scour.

dégorger, *v.n.*, to discharge one's self, to overflow. *Faire —;* to purge (fish—*du poisson*).

se **dégorger**, *v.r.*, to discharge, to empty itself.

dégoter, *v.a.*, (pop.) to knock down; to oust, to displace, to push off.

dégourdi, -e, *adj.*, quick, sharp, acute, shrewd (pers.); tepid (water, &c.—*eau, &c.*). *C'est un homme bien —;* he is a shrewd fellow.

dégourdi, *n.m.*, -e, *n.f.*, quick, sharp, acute, shrewd man or boy; pert, forward woman or girl.

dégourdir, *v.a.*, to quicken, to revive; to sharpen, to render shrewd; to polish. — *ses jambes;* to stretch one's limbs. *Faire — de l'eau;* to take the chill off water. — *un jeune homme;* to polish a young man.

se **dégourdir**, *v.r.*, to remove the numbness from; to lose the numbness; to become sharp, polished, shrewd; to brighten up.

dégourdissement (-dis-mān), *n.m.*, a quickening, reviving.

dégoût, *n.m.*, disgust, disrelish, loathing; dislike, distaste; mortification. *Il lui a pris du — pour la viande;* he has taken a dislike for meat. *Avoir du — pour la vie;* to be disgusted with life. *On lui a donné bien des—s;* they made him swallow many a bitter pill.

dégoûtant, -e, *adj.*, disgusting, loathsome, distasteful, nauseous; unpleasant, disheartening. *Plaie —e;* disgusting sore.

dégoûté, -e, *n.* and *adj.*, fastidious person; fastidious. *Faire le —;* to be squeamish, fastidious. *C'est un bon —;* he likes good things.

dégoûter, *v.a.*, to disgust; to put out of conceit. *Cela est bien fait pour — quelqu'un du métier;* that is well calculated to disgust any one with the trade. *Il est dégoûté de la vie;* he is disgusted with life.

se **dégoûter**, *v.r.*, to take a disgust, a dislike, a distaste to; to nauseate, to dislike.

dégouttant, -e, *adj.*, dropping, dripping.

dégouttement, *n.m.*, dripping, falling in drops.

dégoutter, *v.n.*, to drop, to trickle, to drip, to dribble. *La sueur lui dégouttait du front;* the perspiration rolled off from his brow. *Faire — du beurre sur de la viande;* to drip butter upon meat.

dégradant, -e, *adj.*, degrading, debasing.

dégradation, *n.f.*, degradation; damage, dilapidation; (paint.) diminution of light and shade. — *de noblesse;* degradation from the order of nobility.

dégrader, *v.a.*, to deprive of dignity, to degrade; to strip; (paint.) to diminish the light and shade; to damage, to dilapidate. — *un bois, une maison;* to damage a wood, a house. *Le temps a dégradé ce monument;* time has dilapidated that monument.

se **dégrader**, *v.r.*, to degrade, to debase, to disgrace one's self; to become damaged, defaced, dilapidated; (jur.) to waste.

dégrafer, *v.a.*, to unclasp, to unhook.

se **dégrafer**, *v.r.*, to become unhooked, unfastened (of garments—*des vêtements*); to unbutton, unhook, unfasten one's clothes.

dégraissage, or **dégraissement**, *n.m.*, cleaning, scouring.

dégraisser, *v.a.*, to scour, to remove greasy stains; to fleece one; to impoverish land, to carry off the soil; (carp.) to beard, to thin; (cook.) to remove fat. — *un bouillon;* to skim the fat off broth. — *un habit;* to scour a coat. *La poudre dégraisse les cheveux;* powder cleans the hair. *Terre à —;* fuller's-earth. *Les ravines dégraissent les terres;* torrents impoverish land (by carrying off the soil).

dégraisseur, *n.m.*, scourer.

dégraissis, *n.m.*, scourings.

dégravoiement, or **dégravoiment**, *n.m.*, (arch.) baring, laying bare (by water—*par l'eau*).

dégravoyer, *v.a.*, (arch.) to bare, to lay bare (of water—*de l'eau*).

degré, *n.m.*, step, stair, staircase; stage, grade, gradation; degree, point, extent; (astron., geol., gram., math., phys.) degree; (of universities—*des universités*) degree. *A un très haut —*, in an eminent degree. *Par —s* ; gradually. *Au suprème —* ; to *n.* superlative degree.

dégréement, *n.m.*, (nav.) unrigging.

dégréer, *v.a.*, (nav.) to unrig. — *un mât* ; to strip a mast.

dégrèvement, (-grèv-mān), *n.m.*, reducing a tax, freeing (from encumbrance—*d'hypothèques*, *&c.*).

dégrever, *v.a.*, to diminish, to reduce (a tax—*un impôt*) ; to free (from encumbrance—*d'hypothèques, &c.*).

dégringolade, *n.f.*, fall, tumble.

dégringoler, *v.n.*, to run down, to tumole down.

dégrisement (-griz-mān), *n.m.*, (fam.) sobering, getting sober.

dégriser, *v.a.*, to sober ; to cool, to bring to one's senses.

dégrossage, *n.m.*, drawing fine ; (wire-drawing—*terme de tréfileur*) reducing.

dégrosser, *v.a.*, (wire-drawing—*terme de tréfleur*) to reduce ; to draw smaller.

dégrossi, *n.m.*, (arts) roughing, rough-hewing, roughing down.

dégrossir, *v.a.*, to chip, to chip off the grosser parts ; to rough-hew, to hew down ; to clear up, to unravel ; to make a rough sketch of. — *un bloc de marbre* ; to chip a block of marble.

dégrossissage, *n.m.*, (arts) roughing, rough-hewing ; roughening down ; (carp.) dressing, trimming.

*****déguenillé**, **-e** (dég-ni-ié), *n.* and *adj.*, tatterdemalion,ragged person ; tattered,ragged, in rags. *Ce monsieur, si bien mis, je l'ai vu tout —* ; that gentleman, now so well dressed, I have seen in rags and tatters. *Un grand —* ; a big tatterdemalion. *Quelle est cette petite —e ?* who is that little girl in rags and tatters ? *Elle était toute —e* ; she was in rags and tatters. *Un habit —* ; a ragged coat.

déguerpir, *v.a.*, (jur.) to quit, to give up.

déguerpir (-ghèr-), *v.n.*, to pack off. *Je le ferai bien —* ; I'll make him pack off. — *au plus vite* ; to pack off as fast as possible.

déguerpissement (-ghèr-pis-mān), *n.m.*, (jur.) quitting ; yielding, giving over.

dégueuler (-gheu-), *v.n.*, (l.ex.) to spew, to vomit.

*****déguignonner** (-ghi-), *v.a.*, to change ill-luck.

déguisement (-ghiz-mān), *n.m.*, disguisement, disguise. *Parlez sans —* ; speak openly.

déguiser (-ghi-), *v.a.*, to disguise, to conceal, to hide. *On le déguisa en femme* ; they disguised him as a woman.

se **déguiser**, *v r.*, to disguise one's self.

dégustateur, *n.m.*, taster (of wines—*de vin*).

dégustation, *n.f.*, tasting (of wines—*de vin*).

déguster, *v.a.*, to taste (wines—*les vins*).

déhâler, *v.a.*, to take off sun-burns.

se **déhâler**, *v.r.*, to clear one's complexion.

déhanché, **-e**, *adj.*, hipped, hipshot.

se **déhancher**, *v.r.*, to waddle, to walk with a waddling motion.

déharnachement (-nash-mān), *n.m.*, un-harnessing.

déharnacher, *v.a.*, to unharness.

déhiscence, *n.f.*, (bot.) dehiscence.

déhiscent, **-e**, *adj*, (bot.) dehiscent.

déhonté, **-e**, *adj.*, shameless, unabashed *C'est un homme —* ; he is a man destitute of shame.

dhors (dé-or), *adv*, out, without, out of doors, abroad, externally ; (nav.) out, at sea. *En —* ; without, outside. *Au —* ; outwardly. *De —* ; from without. *Au dedans et au —* ; at home and abroad. *Mettre quelqu'un —* ; to turn one out of doors.

dehors, *n.m.*, outside, exterior ; *pl.* appearances ; (fort.) out-works ; dependences (of a house—*d'une maison*). *Sauver les —* ; to save appearances.

déicide, *n.m.*, deicide.

déification, *n.f.*, deification.

déifier, *v.a.*, to deify.

déisme, *n.m.*, deism.

déiste, *n.m.*, deist.

déiste, *adj.*, deistical.

déité, *n.f.*, deity, god, goddess.

déjà, *adv.*, already, before, yet.

déjection, *n.f.*, (med.) dejection ; ejection.

se **déjeter**, *v.r.*, to warp (of wood—*du bois*) ; (med.) to deviate.

déjettement (dé-jèt-mān), *n.m.*, warping; deviation.

déjeuner or **déjeuné**, *n.m.*, breakfast, breakfast-service. — *à la fourchette* ; meat breakfast. *Second —* ; luncheon. *Un — de porcelaine* ; a porcelain breakfast-service.

déjeuner, *v.n.*, to breakfast.

déjoindre, *v.a.*, to disjoin (stone, wood—*la pierre, le bois*).

se **déjoindre**, *v.r.*, to become disjoined.

déjouer, *v.a.*, to baffle. — *un projet* ; to baffle a project. — *quelqu'un* ; to baffle one, to foil one.

déjouer, *v.n.*, (fam) to play badly ; (nav.) to wave (of the flag—*du pavillon*).

déjucher, *v.n.*, to unroost, to come down from roost. *Je vous ferai bien — de là* ; I will make you come down from there.

se **déjuger**, *v.r.*, to change, to reverse one's opinion.

delà, *prep.*, beyond ; farther than, on the other side of. *Au —, de —, par —, en —* ; beyond, further on, upwards. *Deçà et —* ; right and left ; all about. *Jambe deçà, jambe —* ; one leg this side, the other that side.

délabré, **-e**, *part.*, tattered, in rags. *Une santé —e* ; shattered health. *Un navire —* ; a shattered vessel. *Terre —e* ; land gone to ruin. *Un estomac —* ; a disordered stomach. *Être —* ; to be all in tatters.

délabrement, *n.m.*, ruin, decay, dilapidation

délabrer, *v.a.*, to shatter, to ruin, to pull to pieces, to destroy, to tear to tatters.

se **délabrer**, *v.r.*, to fall to tatters ; to decay. *Tous mes meubles se délabrent* ; all my furniture is going to wreck.

délacer, *v.a.*, to unlace. — *un corset* ; to unlace stays.

se **délacer**, *v.r.*, to unlace one's self ; to come undone (of stays, strings, &c.—*d'un corset, de cordons, &c.*).

délai, *n.m.*, delay. *User de —* ; to put off, to procrastinate.

délaissé, **-e**, *part.*, abandoned, forlorn. *Des orphelins —s* ; helpless orphans.

délaissement (-lès-mān), *n.m.*, destitution, forlornness, helplessness ; (jur.) abandonment to a mortgagee.

délaisser, *v.a.*, to forsake, to abandon ; to cast off ; to desert, to leave ; to relinquish.

délardement, *n.m.*, (arch.) splay, slope.

délarder, *v.a.*, (arch.) to splay.

délassement (-làs-mān), *n.m.*, remission of attention or application, relaxation ; repose, recreation.

délasser, *v.a.*, to refresh, to relax, to divert. *Le sommeil vous délasse* ; sleep refreshes one. *Un changement d'occupation délasse l'esprit* ; a change of occupation relaxes the mind.

se **délasser**, *v.r.*, to refresh one's self.

délat-eur, *n.m*, **-rice**, *n.f.*, informer, accuser.

délation, *n.f.*, information, informing.

R

délatter, *v.a.*, to unlath.

délavage, *n.m.*, diluting of colour (in drawing and water-colour painting—*dessin et aquarelle*).

délavé, -e, *adj.*, weak, pale (of gems—*de pierres précieuses*) ; diluted (of colours—*des couleurs*).

délaver, *v.a.*, to dilute colour (in drawing and water-colour painting—*dessin et aquarelle*) ; to soak, imbibe with water ; *se —*, *v.r.*, to become soaked, imbibed with water ; to lose colour.

délayant, *n.m.*, (med.) diluent.

délayant, -e, *adj.*, (med.) diluent.

délayement (-lè-i-mân), *n.m.*, diluting.

délayer, *v.a.*, to dilute ; to temper (lime—*de la chaux*) ; to spin out.

deleatur, *n.m.* (—), (print.) dele.

délectable, *adj.*, delicious, delectable, delightful.

délectation, *n.f.*, delectation, delight.

délecter, *v.a.*, (l.u.) to delight.

se **délecter**, *v.r.*, to take delight. *Se — à l'étude ;* to delight in study.

délégant *or* **délégateur**, *n.m.*, **-e, -trice**, *n.f.*, delegator.

délégataire, *n.m. and f.*, delegate.

délégation, *n.f.*, delegation, assignment ; proxy.

délégatoire, *adj.*, containing a delegation.

délégué (-ghé), *n.m.*, delegate, deputy ; proxy.

déléguer (-ghé-), *v.a.*, to delegate ; to assign. *— son autorité ;* to delegate one's authority.

délestage, *n.m.*, (nav.) unballasting.

délester, *v.a.*, to unballast.

délesteur, *n.m.*, (nav.) ballast-heaver.

délétère, *adj.*, deleterious.

délibérant, -e, *adj.*, deliberative.

délibérati-f, -ve, *adj.*, deliberative.

délibération, *n.f.*, deliberation ; resolution. *Mettre une affaire en — ;* to bring a thing under deliberation.

délibéré, -e, *adj.*, deliberate, resolute. *Marcher d'un pas — ;* to walk resolutely.

délibéré, *n.m.*, (jur.) deliberation.

délibérément, *adv.*, deliberately, boldly, resolutely.

délibérer, *v.n.*, to deliberate ; to determine, to resolve. *Il n'y a pas lieu à — ;* there is no room for deliberating. *Il en sera délibéré ;* it shall be taken into consideration.

délicat, -e, *adj.*, delicate, dainty, nice, fastidious, ticklish. *Vous êtes bien — ;* you are very fastidious. *Faire le — ;* to be fastidious. *Affaires —e ;* ticklish affair. *Un homme — ;* a man of delicate health. *Il est — sur le point d'honneur ;* he is very tender in points of honour. *Il est — et blond ;* he is hard to please.

délicatement (-kat-mân), *adv.*, delicately, daintily. *Peu — ;* indelicately.

⊙**délicater**, *v.a.*, to cocker, to fondle, to pamper. *Se —*, *v.r.*, to nurse one's self, to indulge one's self.

délicatesse, *n.f.*, delicacy ; tenderness ; daintiness ; nicety (of language—*de langage*) *Les —s d'une langue ;* the niceties of a language. *La — de sa complexion, de sa santé ;* the delicacy of his constitution, of his health. *— de teint ;* delicacy of complexion. *Avoir une grande — de conscience ;* to have a very scrupulous conscience.

délice, *n.m. sing ;* **délices**, *n.f. pl.*, delight ; deliciousness. *Goûter les —s de la vie ;* to taste the delights of life. *Faire ses —s d'une chose ;* to delight in a thing. *Je faisais les —s de ma mère ;* I was my mother's darling.

délicieusement (-eûz-mân), *adv.*, deliciously, delightfully.

délicieu-x, -se, *adj.*, delicious, delightful.

se **délicoter**, *v.r.*, (man.) to slip the halter.

délictueux, -se, *adj.*, (jur.) unlawful, felonious.

délié, -e, *adj.*, untied, loose ; small, thin, slender, slim ; cunning. *Avoir l'esprit — ;* to be quick, acute. *Avoir la langue —e ;* to have a voluble tongue.

délié, *n.m.*, (penmanship—*écriture*) thin stroke, upstroke.

délier, *v.a.*, to unbind ; to untie ; to liberate, to release, to absolve. *— quelqu'un d'un serment ;* to free one from an oath. *On l'a délié de ses vœux ;* he was liberated from his vows. *se* **délier**, *v.r.*, to come untied, to get unfastened ; to get loose.

délimitation, *n.f.*, settling the limits, boundaries.

délimiter, *v.a.*, to settle the boundaries, the limits.

délinéation, *n.f.*, delineation.

délinquant, *n.m.*, **-e**, *n.f.*, delinquent, offender.

⊙**délinquer**, *v.n.*, (jur.) to offend, to trespass.

déliquescence (-kès-sânss), *n.f.*, (chem.) deliquescence, deliquation.

déliquescent, -e, *adj.*, (chem.) deliquescent.

deliquium, (-kui-om), *n.m.*, (chem.) deliquium.

délirant, -e, *n. and adj.*, (med.) one who is delirious ; delirious, frenzied.

délire, *n.m.*, delirium, frenzy, deliriousness. *Avoir le — ;* to rave. *Tomber en — ;* to become delirious.

délirer, *v.n.*, to be delirious, to rave.

delirium tremens (dé-li-riom-tré-ninss), *n.m.* (*n.p.*), (med.) delirium tremens.

délit, *n.m.*, misdemeanour, delinquency, offence ; (mas.) wrong bed (of stone—*de pierre*) *Prendre quelqu'un en flagrant — ;* to catch one in the very act.

déliter, *v.a.*, (mas.) to lay stones in their wrong bed.

délitescence (-tès-sâns), *n.f.*, (med.) delitescence.

délivrance, *n.f.*, deliverance, delivery ; childbirth.

délivre, *n.m.*, (anat.) after-birth ; heam (of animals—*des animaux*).

délivrer, *v.a.*, to deliver, to release, to set free ; to rid of. *— de prison ;* to deliver from prison. *— de la marchandise ;* to deliver goods. *se* **délivrer**, *v.r.*, to deliver one's self, to free one's self.

délivreur, *n.m.*, deliverer ; distributor of provisions in the Royal Household ; (man.) hostler ; (techn.) one of the two drums of a cotton-machine.

délogement (-loj-mân), *n.m.*, removal ; change of quarters.

déloger, *v.n.*, to remove, to quit, to go from one's house ; to go away, to march off. *— sans trompette ;* to march off in silence, to steal away.

déloger, *v.a.*, to turn out (of house—*d'une maison*) ; to oust ; (milit.) to dislodge.

déloyal, -e, *adj.*, disloyal, false, treacherous, unfair.

déloyalement (déloa-yal-mân), *adv.*, disloyally, treacherously.

déloyauté, *n.f.*, dishonesty, perfidiousness, treachery.

delta, *n.m.*, (geog.) delta.

deltoïde, *adj.*, (anat., bot.) deltoid.

déluge, *n.m.*, deluge, flood. *Un — de larmes ;* a flood of tears. *Un — de paroles ;* a torrent of words.

déluré, *adj.*, wide-awake, ready prepared, sharp.

délustrer, *v.a.*, to take off the lustre, the gloss of.

déluter, *v.a.*, to unlute.

démagogie, *n.f.*, demagogism; demagogues.

démagogique, *adj.*, demagogic, demagogical.

démagogue (-gog), *n.m.*, demagogue.

démaigrir, *v.n.*, (jest.) to recover one's flesh.

démaigrir, *v.a.*, (arch.) to thin.

#démailloter, *v.a.*, to unswathe.

demain, *adv.*, to-morrow. — *matin;* to-morrow morning. — *soir;* to-morrow night. *Après —;* the day after to-morrow *À — les affaires!* we will talk of business another day!

demain, *n.m.*, to-morrow.

démanché, *n.m.*, (mus.) shift.

démanchement (-mansh-măn), *n.m.*, taking off (a handle—*un manche*); being without a handle; (mus.) shift.

démancher, *v.a.*, to take off the handle.

se démancher, *v.r.*, to lose its handle; to go wrong; (mus.) to shift.

démancher, *v.n.*, (nav.) to get out of the channel; (mus.) to shift.

demande, *n.f.*, question, request, petition; demand, suit, inquiry; (com.) order. *Faire sa — par écrit;* to present one's request in writing. *Appuyer une —;* to second a request. *À sotte — point de réponse;* a silly question needs no answer. — (mus.); subject of a fugue.

demander, *v.a.*, to ask, to beg, to request, to sue for, to demand; (jur.) to pray; to desire; to wish, to want; to ask for, to call for; to inquire after; to require; (com.) to order. — *pardon;* to beg pardon. — *l'aumône;* to ask alms. — *son pain;* to beg one's bread. *Que demandez-vous?* what do you want? *N'est-il venu personne me —?* has nobody called for me? *On vous demande;* you are wanted. *Cela demande une explication;* that requires an explanation.

demander, *v.n.*, to ask, to beg; to wish, to request; to require, to demand.

demandeu-r, *n.m.*, **-se**, *n.f.*, asker; applicant.

demande-ur, *n.m.*, **-resse**, *n.f.*, (jur.) demandant, plaintiff.

démangeaison (-jè-zon), *n.f.*, itching; longing. *Avoir une grande — de parler;* to have a great itching to talk.

démanger, *v.n.*, to itch; to long. *La tête me démange;* my head itches. *Les pieds lui démangent;* he longs to go out.

démantèlement (-tèl-măn), *n.m.*, (fort., milit.) dismantling.

démanteler (-man-tlé), *v.a.*, (milit.) to dismantle.

démantibuler, *v.a.*, to break the jaw-bone; to put out of order.

démarcation, *n.f.*, demarcation. *Ligne de —;* line of demarcation.

démarche, *n.f.*, gait, walk; proceeding, measure; application. — *noble;* noble bearing. *Faire une —;* to take a step; to make an application. *On observe toutes ses —s;* all his steps are watched.

démarier, *v.a.*, to annul a marriage.

se démarier, *v.r.*, to get unmarried.

démarquer, *v.a.*, to unmark.

démarquer, *v.n.*, to lose the mark of its age (of a horse—*du cheval*). *Ce cheval démarque;* that horse has lost the mark of its age.

démarrage, *n.m.*, unmooring.

démarrer, *v.a.*, to unmoor. — *un cordage;* to unbend a rope.

démarrer, *v.n.*, to leave her moorings (of a ship—*d'un vaisseau*); to move.

démasquer, *v.a.*, to unmask; to show up — *une batterie;* to unmask a battery.

se démasquer, *v.r.*, to unmask, to take off one's mask. *Il s'est démasqué;* he has pulled off his mask.

démâtage, *n.m.*, (nav.) dismasting.

démâter, *v.a.*, to dismast.

démâter, *v.n.*, to lose her masts (of a ship —*d'un vaisseau*).

démêlage, *n.m.*, combing (of wool—*be laine*).

démêlé, *n.m.*, strife, contest, contention. *Leur — est fini;* their difference is at an end.

démêler, *v.a.*, to disentangle, to separate; to contest; to distinguish; to clear from perplexity, to unravel, to extricate, to untwist, to unfold; to comb somebody's hair with a large comb. *Avoir à — avec;* to have to do with. *Je ne veux rien avoir à — avec lui;* I will have nothing to do with him. — *le vrai d'avec le faux;* to distinguish truth from falsehood.

se démêler, *v.r.*, to unravel; to extricate one's self; to comb one's hair with a large comb.

démêloir, *n.m.*, large hair-comb.

démembrement, *n.m.*, dismemberment; dismembered part.

démembrer, *v.a.*, to tear limb from limb; to dismember, to disjoint.

déménagement (-naj-măn), *n.m.*, removal, removing, change of residence.

déménager, *v.a.*, to remove one's furniture.

déménager, *v.n.*, to remove (to change one's residence—*changer de résidence*). *Sa raison déménage;* he is getting childish.

démence, *n.f.*, insanity, madness, lunacy, mental alienation. *Tomber en —;* to become insane.

se démener, *v.r.*, to stir, to struggle, to make a great bustle, to strive, to toil. *Se — avec vigueur;* to struggle vigorously.

démenti, *n.m.*, lie; contradiction, disappointment. *Donner un — à quelqu'un;* to give any one the lie. *Vous en aurez le —;* you will get the worst of it.

démentir, *v.a.*, to give the lie to, to contradict; to deny; to belie. *Démentirez-vous votre signature?* will you deny your signature? — *sa gloire;* to belie one's fame. *Ses actions démentent ses discours;* his actions belie his language.

se démentir, *v.r.*, to contradict one's self; to belie one's self; to fall off; to flag, to give way. *Cet ouvrage se dément un peu vers la fin;* this work falls off, flags, a little towards the end.

démérite, *n.m.*, demerit.

démériter, *v.n.*, to demerit. *Je n'ai point démérité de vous, auprès de vous;* I have done nothing to forfeit your esteem.

démesuré, -e, *adj.*, huge, immoderate; unbounded, excessive. *Il a une envie —e de vous voir;* he longs excessively to see you.

démesurément, *adv.*, immoderately, inordinately, excessively.

démettre, *v.a.*, to put out of joint, to dislocate; to dismiss, to turn out; (jur.) to over-rule.

se démettre, *v.r.*, to be put out of joint; to resign, to throw up. *Il s'est démis le poignet;* he has dislocated his wrist. — *de son emploi;* to resign one's employment.

démeublement, *n.m.*, unfurnishing; absence of furniture.

démeubler, *v.a.*, to unfurnish.

demeurant, *n.m.*, remainder, residue. *au demeurant*, *adv.*, in other respects; after all.

demeurant, -e, *adj.*, (jur.) dwelling, living, abiding.

demeure, *n.f.*, abode, home, dwelling, lodgings; stay; (jur.) delay. *Changer sa — de —;* to change one's lodgings. *Être en — avec ses créanciers;* to be behindhand with one's creditors. *Mettre en —;* (jur.) to put in suit; to compel, to lay under the necessity. *Être à —;* to be a fixture. *Cela n'est pas à —;* that is only temporary.

demeurer, *v.n.*, to live, to lodge, to reside; to continue, to remain, to rest; to stay; to stand, to stop. *— à la campagne;* to live in the country; *— en arrière;* to stay behind. *— sur son appétit;* not to fully satisfy one's appetite. *Où en êtes-vous demeuré?* where did you leave off? *Demeurons-en là;* let us leave off there, let it go no farther. *La victoire nous est demeurée;* victory remained with us. *— d'accord;* to agree.

demi, *n.m.*, (arith.) half.

demi, -e, *adj.*, half. *Un demi-pied;* half a foot. *Demi-soupir* (mus.); quaver rest. *Un pied et —;* a foot and a half. *Une demi-heure;* half an hour. *Une heure et —e;* an hour and a half. *Entendre à demi-mot (— —s),* to take one's meaning at once. *Demi-cercle (— —s);* semicircle. *En demi-cercle;* semi-circular. *Demi-dieu (— —x);* demi-god. *À fourbe, fourbe et —;* set a thief to catch a thief.

demi. *adv.,* half. *Il est à — fou;* he is half mad. *Faire les choses à —;* to do things by halves.

demie, *n.f.*, the half-hour.

demi-fleuron, *n.m.* (— —s), *V.* **fleuron**.

demi-fortune, *n.f.* (— —s), four-wheeled one-horse carriage.

demi-lune, *n.f.* (— —s), (fort.) half-moon.

⊙**demi-métal**, *n.m.* (— *métaux*). semi-metal.

demi-setier, *n.m.* (— —s), half a pint English.

demi-solde, *n.f.* (*n.p.*), half-pay. *Officier en —;* half-pay officer.

démission, *n.f.*, resignation. *Donner sa —;* to give in one's resignation. *Offrir sa —;* to tender one's resignation.

démissionnaire, *n.m.f.,* resigner.

démissionnaire, *adj.,* that has resigned, thrown up, his commission, vacated his seat.

démitrer, *v.a.,* (l.u.) to unmitre, to take away the mitre of.

démocrate, *n.m.,* democrat.

démocratie, *n.f.,* democracy.

démocratique, *adj.,* democratic.

démocratiquement, *adv.,* democratically.

demoiselle, *n.f.,* young lady; unmarried lady; young girl; gentlewoman; hot waterbottle; dragon-fly; (orni.) Numidian crane; paving beetle. *Une jolie —;* a pretty young lady. *C'est une — bien née;* she is a young lady of good birth.

démolir, *v.a.,* to demolish, to pull down, to subvert, to overthrow, to cut up to nothing.

démolisseur, *n.m.,* demolisher, subverter.

démolition, *n.f.,* demolition; *—s, n.f pl.,* materials (of a demolished building—*matériaux de démolition*).

démon, *n.m.,* devil, fiend; demon; genius. *Petit —;* little demon (child—*enfant*). *Faire le —;* to play the devil. *Quel — vous agite!* what evil spirit torments you?

démonarchiser, *v.a.,* to overthrow monarchical government.

démonétisation, *n.f.,* withdrawal from circulation (of money—*de monnaies*); calling in.

démonétiser, *v.a.,* to withdraw from circulation; to call in (money—*monnaies*).

démoniacal, *adj.,* demoniacal, demoniac.

démoniaque, *n.m.f.,* demoniac, demon, devil.

démonographe, *n.m.,* demonographer.

démonographie, *n.f.,* demonology.

démonologie, *n.f.,* demonology.

démonomanie, *n.f.,* demonomania.

démonstrateur, *n.m.,* demonstrator.

démonstrati-f, -ve, *adj.,* demonstrative.

démonstration, *n.f.,* demonstration.

démonstrativement (-tiv-mán), *adv.,* demonstratively.

démontage, *n.m.,* taking to pieces.

démonter, *v.a.,* to dismount, to unhorse; to nonplus, to baffle; to alter (one's countenance —*son visage*); to take to pieces, to undo; (nav. to supersede, to unship. *— le gouvernail;* to unship the rudder. *— un capitaine;* to supersede a captain.

se démonter, *v.r.,* that may be taken to pieces (of machinery, &c.—*des machines, &c.*); to lose one's countenance, to be nonplussed, disconcerted; to be getting out of order (of machinery, &c.—*de machines, &c.*); to become impaired (of the health—*de la santé*).

démontrable, *adj.,* demonstrable.

démontrer. *v.a.,* to demonstrate, to prove

démoralisat-eur, -rice, *adj.,* corrupting, demoralizing.

démoralisation, *n.f.,* demoralization.

démoraliser. *v.a.,* to demoralize.

⊙**démoraliseur** *n.m.,* corrupter.

démordre, *v.n.,* to let go one's hold; to depart, to desist. *Faire — quelqu'un;* to make one change one's resolution. *Il n'en démordra pas;* he will not abate an inch.

démotique. *adj.,* demotic.

démoucheter, *v.a.,* to take off the button of a foil.

démunir, *v.a.,* to strip a place of ammunition.

se démunir. *v.r.,* to deprive one's self.

démurer, *v.a.,* to unwall, to open.

démuseler (-muz-lé), *v.a.,* to unmuzzle.

dénaire. *adj.,* denary.

dénantir. *v.a.,* to deprive of security.

se dénantir. *v.r.,* to give up securities

dénationaliser *v.a.,* to denationalize.

dénatter, *v.a.,* to unmat (hair—*des cheveux*).

dénaturalisation. *n.f.,* loss of naturalization.

dénaturaliser, *v.a.,* to denaturalize.

dénaturation, *n.f.,* (chem.) debasement, sophistication

dénaturé, -e, *adj.,* unnatural, barbarous.

dénaturer, *v.a.,* to alter the nature of; to deface, disfigure, to change, to misrepresent, to pervert, to distort; (chem.) to debase.

dendrite (din-), *n.f.,* (min.) dendrite.

dendroïde (din-), *adj.,* (bot.) dendroid.

dénégation, *n.f.,* denial

déni. *n.m.,* (jur.) denial, refusal. *— de justice;* refusal of justice (of a judge who refuses to pronounce sentence—*refus d'un juge de prononcer jugement*).

déniaisé, -e, *adj.,* cunning. *Un homme —;* a cunning, crafty man.

déniaiser. *v.a.,* to sharpen the wits; to cheat, to take in a fool.

se déniaiser, *v.r.,* to learn wit, to become sharp, to grow cunning.

déniché, -e. *part.,* gone, flown. *Les oiseaux sont —s;* the birds are flown.

dénicher, *v.a.,* to take out of the nest; to turn out; to hunt out; to find out. *— une statue;* to turn a statue out of its niche.

dénicher, *v.n.,* to forsake its nest (of a bird—*d'un oiseau*); to hasten away; to make off, to run away. *Allons il faut —;* come, be off with you.

dénicheur, *n.m.,* person who goes birds-nesting. *Un — de merles;* sharper.

denier, *n.m.*, (antiq.) denarius; denier; money; cash. funds; rate of interest; (pharm.) scruple; old French copper coin worth 1-13th of a farthing; (coin.) weight of a little above 1¼ grammes. — *à Dieu*; earnest money. *A beaux —s comptants*: in cash, in ready money. *Les —s publics*; the public money. ⊙*Au — vingt-cinq*; four per cent. *Le — de Saint Pierre*; Saint Peter's penny. *Le — de la veuve*; the widow's mite.

dénier, *v.a.*, to deny, to refuse.

dénigrant, *adj.*, disparaging, denigrating.

dénigrement, *n m.*, vilifying, disparagement.

dénigrer, *v.a.*, to disparage, to traduce.

dénombrement, *n.m.*, enumeration, census, list.

dénombrer, *v.a.*, to number.

dénominateur, *n.m.*, (arith.) denominator.

dénominati-f, -ve, *adj.*, denominative.

dénomination, *n.f.*, denomination.

dénominer, *v.a.*, (jur.) to denominate, to mention by name.

dénoncer, *v.a.*, to denounce, to inform, to announce, to lodge information against; to give notice.

dénonciat-eur, *n.m.*, **-rice**, *n.f.*, denunciator, informer.

dénonciation, *n.f.*, denunciation, denouncement, declaration, intimation.

⊙**dénotation**, *n.f.*, denotation.

dénoter, *v.a.*, to describe; to denote, to betoken.

dénouement or **dénoûment**, *n.m.*, event (of intrigues, novels—*d'intrigues, de romans*); denouement, catastrophe (of a play—*d'une comédie, &c.*). *Le — de cette pièce est heureux*; the catastrophe of that play is happy.

dénouer, *v.a.*, to untie, to loose; to give elasticity; to solve (difficulties—*difficultés*); to unravel (plots—*intrigues, &c.*).

se **dénouer**, *v.r.*, to untie, to unravel, to unfold. *Sa langue s'est dénouée à la fin*; he has spoken out at last.

denrée, *n.f.*, commodity. *Il vend bien sa —*; he makes the most of his talents.

dense, *adj.*, dense.

densité, *n.f.*, density.

dent, *n.f.*, tooth; notch, cog. *—s de lait*; first teeth. *—s de sagesse*; wisdom teeth. *—s d'en haut*; upper teeth. *—s d'en bas*, lower teeth. *—s barrées*; dove-tailed teeth. *Faire ses —s*; to cut one's teeth. *Les —s percent à cet enfant*; that child is cutting his teeth. *Les —s lui claquent*; his teeth chatter. *Serrer les —s*; to set the teeth. *Grincer des —s*; to gnash the teeth. *Une — qui branle*; a loose tooth. *Le mal de —s*; the tooth-ache. *Avoir mal aux —s*; to have the tooth-ache. *Les —s lui tombent*; he loses his teeth. *L'alvéole d'une —*; the socket of a tooth *Se curer les —s*; to pick one's teeth. *Le fruit vert agace les —s*; green fruit sets the teeth on edge. *Une vieille sans —*; a toothless hag. *Armé jusqu'aux —s*, armed to the teeth. *N'avoir pas de quoi mettre sous la —*; not to have a morsel to put in one's mouth *Avoir une — contre quelqu'un*; to have an old grudge against one. *Déchirer à belles—s*, to tear to pieces. *Chacun lui donne un coup de —*; every one has a fling at him. *Être sur les —s*; to be tired out. *Montrer les —s à quelqu'un*, to show one's teeth to anyone. *Ne pas desserrer les —s*; not to open one's lips. *Parler entre ses —s*; to speak betwixt one's teeth. *Parler des grosses —s*; to talk big. *Prendre le mors aux —s*; to run away; to be earnest in business. *Rire du bout des —s*; to sham a laugh, to pretend to laugh. *Murmurer entre ses —s*; to speak to one's self. *C'est vouloir prendre la lune avec les —s*; it is aiming at impossibilities. *Les —s d'une roue*; the cogs of a wheel. *Ce couteau a des —s*; that knife is notched.

dentaire, *adj.*, dental.

dentaire, *n.f.*, (bot.) dentaria, toothwort.

dental, -e, *adj.*, (gram.) dental.

dentale, *n.m.*, (conch.) dentalium, dental, tooth-shell.

dentale, *n.f.*, (gram.) dental.

dent-de-lion, *n.m.* (—*s* —), dandelion.

denté, -e, *adj.*, toothed; (bot.) dentated. *Roue —e*; cogged wheel. *Feuille —e en scie*; serrated leaf.

dentée, *n.f.*, bite from a hound; stroke, rip (of a tusk—*d'une défense de sanglier, &c.*).

dentelaire, *n.f.*, (bot.) lead-wort.

dentelé, -e (dant-lé), *adj.*, notched, jagged, denticulated, toothed, indented; (anat.) —, *n m.*, denticulated muscle.

denteler, *v.a.*, to indent, to notch, to jag.

dentelle, *n.f.*, lace, lace-work. *Manchettes à —*, lace ruffles.

dentellière, *n.f.*, lace-woman, lace-maker.

denteluře (dan-tlur), *n.f.*, jagging, notching, denticulation, indenting.

denticulé, -e, *adj.*, (bot.) denticulated, indented.

denticules. *n.m. pl.*, (arch.) denticles.

dentier (-tié), *n.m.*, set of teeth (natural or artificial—*naturelles ou fausses*); (surg.) metal plate on which artificial teeth are set.

dentifrice, *n.m.*, dentifrice. —, *adj.*, good for the teeth; *poudre —*; tooth-powder.

dentiste, *n.m.*, dentist.

dentition, *n.f.*, dentition, cutting of teeth.

denture, *n.f.*, set of teeth; (horl.) teeth range.

dénudation, *n.f.*, denudation.

dénuder, *v.a.*, to denude; to lay bare.

dénué, -e, *adj.*, destitute; void. — *de support*; bereft of support. — *d'esprit*; devoid of wit.

dénuement or **dénûment**, *n.m.*, destitution, deprivation.

dénuer, *v.a.*, to bereave, to strip, to leave destitute.

se **dénuer**, *v.r.*, to strip one's self; to leave one's self bare.

dépaqueter (dé-pak-té), *v.a.*, to unpack.

*****dépareiller**, *v.a.*, to unmatch, to spoil the pair of, to render incomplete. — *des gants*; to unmatch gloves. *Livres dépareillés*; odd books.

déparer, *v.a.*, to undress (altars—*autels*); to strip; to disfigure, to take away the beauty; to disparage.

déparier, *v.a.*, to take away one (of a pair —*d'une paire*); to separate (the male and female of certain animals—*le mâle de la femelle*).

déparler, *v.n.*, to cease talking.

déparquer, *v.a.*, to let the sheep out of a fold; to unpen.

départ, *n.m.*, departure, setting out; (chem.) parting; (metal.) departure. *Être sur son —*; to be on the eve of setting out.

départager, *v.a.*, to destroy by a casting-vote the equality of the division. — *les voix, les suffrages*, to give a casting-vote.

département, *n.m.*, distribution; department (province or business assigned to a particular person—*spécialité, affaire assignée à quelqu'un*). *Les —s de la France*; the departments of France. — *des affaires étrangères*; foreign-office. — *de l'intérieur*; home-office. *Cela n'est pas de son —*; that does not lie in his province.

départemental, -e, *adj.*, departmental.

⊙**départie**, *n.f.*, departure.

départir, *v.a.*, to distribute, to divide, to endow, to bestow.

se départir, *v.r.*, to depart, to desist, to swerve, to deviate. *Il s'est départi de sa demande;* he has desisted from his demand. *Se — de son devoir;* to swerve from one's duty.

dépasser, *v.a.*, to go beyond; to exceed, to surpass; to outsail; to draw out (ribbons, &c.—*rubans, &c.).* — *ses pouvoirs;* to exceed one's power.

dépâtisser, *v.a.*, (print.) to sort and distribute types.

dépavage, *n.m.*, unpaving.

dépave., *v.a.*, to unpave, to take up the pavement.

dépaysé. **-e**, *part.*, away from home. *Se trouver — dans une société;* to feel one's self a stranger in a company.

dépayser (-pè-i-zé), *v.a.*, to take, to send from home; to remove; to put (one—*quelqu'un*) out; to put on a wrong scent. **se dépayser**, *v.r.*, to leave one's home, to go abroad.

dépècement (-pès-mān), *n.m.*, cutting up, cutting in pieces; dismemberment.

dépecer (dép-sé), *v.a.*, to cut up, to carve, to cut in pieces; to dismember. — *une volaille;* to cut up a fowl. — *de la viande;* to carve meat.

dépêche, *n.f.*, despatch (letter on affairs of state—*concernant les affaires de l'état*); (com) correspondence, mail. *Les — s;* the post-bags. *Faire les — s;* to make up the despatches, the mails.

se dépêcher, *v.r.*, to make haste, to look sharp. *Dépêchez-vous;* make haste.

dépêcher, *v.a.*, to send off despatches, a courier, a messenger; to despatch; to be quick, to do things quickly, to hasten; to make away with anyone, to kill. *Travailler à dépêche compagnon;* to hurry over one's work. *Se battre à dépêche compagnon;* to give no quarter in fighting.

dépêcher, *v.n.*, to send off a courier, an express messenger, in haste. *On a dépêché à Vienne;* a courier has been sent to Vienna.

dépeçoir, *n.m.*, chopping-knife.

dépeindre, *v.a.*, to depict; to describe; to paint, to represent.

*****dépenaillé. -e**, *adj.*, (fam.) tattered, ragged, in rags; ill-clad; faded (of the face—*du visage*).

*****dépenaillement**, *n.m.*, raggedness; faded appearance (of the face—*du visage*).

dépendamment (-da-mān), *adv.*, (l.u.) dependently.

dépendance, *n.f.*, dependence; appendage; out-house. *Être dans la — de quelqu'un;* to be dependent on any one. *Tenir quelqu'un dans la —;* to keep any one in a state of dependancy.

dépendant, -e, *adj.*, dependent.

dépendre, *v.a.*, to take down; to unhang.

dépendre, *v.n.*, to depend; to be dependent; to rest. *Cela dépend de moi;* that depends on, rests with, me.

dépens, *n.m. pl.*, expense, cost. *Vivre aux — d'autrui;* to live upon other people's expense. *Faire la guerre à ses —;* to play a losing game. *Il a gagné son procès avec —;* (jur.) he gained his lawsuit with costs.

dépense, *n.f.*, expense; expenditure; outlay; steward's office; pantry; *pl.*, supplies (of parliament—*parlement*). *Comité des —s;* (parliament—*parlement*) committee of supplies. *De folles —s;* extravagant expense. *—s de bouche;* expense for living. *La — du ménage;* household expense. *Sa — excède ses revenus;* his expenditure exceeds his income. *Ne pas plaindre la —;* not to spare expense. *Faire de la —;* to spend money. *Aimer la —;* to like spending money.

dépenser, *v.a.*, to spend, to expend; to consume; (b.s) to waste. *Il aime à —;* he is fond of spending.

dépensi-er. -ère, *n.* and *adj.*, extravagant person, spendthrift; extravagant.

dépensier, *n.m.*, bursar (of a religious community—*d'une communauté religieuse*); (nav.) purser's steward.

déperdition, *n.f.*, deperdition, loss, waste; (med.) discharge.

dépérir, *v.n.*, to perish, to decline, to pine away, to waste, to wither, to dwindle, to waste away, to decay, to go to ruin.

dépérissement (-ris-mān), *n.m.*, wasting away, decay, withering, falling away; withered state (of plants—*des plantes*).

dépersuader, *v.a.*, to dissuade.

dépêtrer, *v.a.*, to disentangle, to extricate, to disengage. **se dépêtrer**, *v.r.*, to get out of; to rid one's self of, to get clear of.

dépeuplement, *n.m.*, depopulation.

dépeupler, *v.a.*, to unpeople, to dispeople, to depopulate, to unstock. — *un colombier;* to unstock a pigeon-house. — *une forêt;* to thin a forest. **se dépeupler**, *v.r.*, to be depopulated, to be unstocked.

⊙**déphlogistiquer**, *v.a.*, to dephlogisticate.

dépiécer, *v.a.* *V.* **dépecer.**

dépilage, *n.m.*, taking off the fleece (of hides —*des peaux*)

dépilati-f. -ve, *adj.*, depilatory.

dépilation, *n.f.*, depilation.

dépilatoire, *n.m.*, depilatory.

dépiler, *v.a.*, to lose the hair (of animals —*des animaux*).

dépiquage, *n.m.*, (agri.) trampling down by horses or mules, of wheat, barley, &c., to replace thrashing.

dépiquer, *v.a.*, to unquilt; to cheer up. — *quelqu'un;* to restore the good humour of any one; (gard.) to transplant. **se dépiquer**, *v.r.*, to recover one's good humour.

dépister, *v.a.*, (hunt.) to track; to ferret out. to hunt out.

dépit, *n.m.*, spite, vexation. *Avoir du —;* to be vexed. *Il pleurait de —;* he wept for vexation. *Faire quelque chose par —,* to do a thing out of spite. *En — de;* in spite of. *Écrire en — du bon sens;* to write in defiance of good sense.

dépiter, *v.a.*, to vex. **se dépiter**, *v.r*, to be vexed, to be in a pet.

dépiteu-x. -se, *adj.*, (hawking—*fauconnerie.*) *Oiseau —;* a hawk that will not come back when it has lost its quarry.

déplacé, -e, *part.*, displaced, misplaced, ill-timed, unbecoming. *Discours —;* speech out of season.

déplacement (dé-plas-mān), *n.m.*, displacement, change of place.

déplacer, *v.a.*, to displace, to misplace, to remove. **se déplacer**, *v.r.*, to change one's place, to leave one's place, one's residence.

déplaire, *v.n.*, to displease, to offend; to incur the displeasure of any one; to be unpleasant, disagreeable. *Ne vous en déplaise;* with your leave. *Sa conduite déplait à tout le monde;* his conduct is disliked by everybody. **se déplaire**, *v.r.*, to dislike, to be displeased with, to displease each other; to pine (of animals, plants—*des animaux et des plantes*). *Je ne me déplairais pas ici;* I should not dislike living here. *Les troupeaux se déplaisent dans ce lieu-là;* the flocks do not thrive in that place.

déplaisance, *n.f.*, dislike, aversion.

déplaisant, -e, *adj.,* unpleasant, disagreeable, annoying, obnoxious.

déplaisir, *n.m.,* displeasure, grief, sorrow, trouble, affliction.

déplantage, *n.m.,* or **déplantation,** *n.f.,* displanting.

déplanter, *v.a..* to displant.

déplantoir, *n.m.,* (gard.) trowel.

déplâtrer, *v.a.,* (mas.) to take off plaster.

déplier, *v.a.,* to unfold ; to lay out (goods—*marchandises*).

déplisser, *v.a.,* to undo the plaits, to unplait.

se **déplisser,** *v.r.,* to come out of plait.

déploiement, or **déploîment** (-dé-ploa-măn), *n.m.,* display, unfolding ; (milit.) deployment.

déplorable. *adj.,* deplorable, lamentable.

déplorablement, *adv.,* deplorably, lamentably.

déplorer, *v.a.,* to deplore, to bewail, to lament. — *la misère humaine;* to deplore the misery of mankind.

déployé, -e, *adj.,* unfolded, displayed, open. *Voguer à voiles —es;* (nav.) to be under full sail.

déployer, *v.a.,* to unfold, to unroll, to unfurl, to set out, to display, to open, to show, to stretch, to spread ; (milit.) to deploy. — *les voiles;* to spread the sails. — *toute son éloquence;* to set forth all one's eloquence.

se **déployer,** *v.r.,* to unroll, to display one's self ; (milit.) to deploy.

déplumé, -e, *adj.,* displumed, unfeathered.

déplumer, *v.a.,* to displume, to deprive of feathers.

se **déplumer,** *v.a.,* to moult, to shed feathers.

dépolir, *v.a.,* to take off the polish. — *du verre,* to rough glass. *Le feu dépolit le marbre;* fire takes the polish off marble.

dépolissage, *n.m.,* (of glass—*du verre*) roughing.

déponent. *adj., n.m.,* (gram.) deponent.

dépopulariser, *v.a.,* to render unpopular.

se **dépopulariser,** *v.r.,* to become unpopular.

dépopulation. *n.m.,* depopulation.

déport. *n.m.,* delay ; (jur.) challenging one's self (of judges, &c.—*de juges, &c.*).

déportation. *n.f.,* deportation (transportation for life—*à vie*).

déporté, *n.m.,* person sentenced to deportation ; transport, convict.

déportement, *n.m.,* misconduct.

déporter, *v.a.,* to deport, to transport for life.

se **déporter.** *v.r.,* to desist from. *Se — de ses prétentions;* to withdraw one's claims.

déposant, -e, *adj.,* depositing ; giving evidence.

déposant, *n.m., -e,** *n.f.,* deponent ; depositor ; bailer.

déposer, *v.a.,* to lay down ; to lay aside ; to strip, to divest, to depose ; to deposit ; to give evidence ; to lodge (a complaint—*une plainte*). *On le déposa de sa charge;* they divested him of his charge. — *son bilan ;* to file one's schedule.

déposer, *v.n.,* to settle, to leave a sediment ; to give evidence.

dépositaire, *n.m.,* depositary, trustee.

déposition, *n.f.,* deposition ; deposing ; evidence. *La — porte que;* the evidence says that.

déposséder, *v.a.,* to dispossess.

dépossesseur, *n.m.,* one who deprives of possession.

dépossession, *n.f.,* dispossession.

déposter, *v.a.,* to drive from a post, to dislodge.

dépôt, *n.m.,* depositing, deposit, trust ; lodgment (of money—*d'argent*); depository, warehouse ; depot, agency ; sediment, settling. — *de mendicité;* poor-house. *Faire un — :* to make a deposit. *En — :* as a deposit in trust ; (com.) on sale.

dépoter. *v.a..* to take out of a pot ; to decant (liquids).

dépotoir. *n.m.,* general deposit of night-soil.

dépoudrer. *v.a.,* to unpowder.

se **dépoudrer,** *v.r.,* to unpowder one's hair.

****dépouille.** *n.f..* spoil ; slough, skin, hide ; wardrobe (of persons deceased—*d'un décédé*); remains ; spoils, booty ; crop ; exuviæ. — *mortelle:* mortal remains. *La — d'un serpent ;* the slough of a serpent. *L'âme quitta sa — mortelle :* the soul forsook its earthly tenement. *Il a laissé sa — à un tel ;* he left his wardrobe to such a one. —*s opimes;* spolia opima. *Il s'enrichit des —s d'autrui;* he enriches himself with the spoils of others.

****dépouillé, -e,** *part.,* stripped ; naked. *Jouer au roi —;* to ruin any one.

****dépouillement** (dè-poo-i-măn), *n.m..* spoliation ; despoiling ; privation ; inspection (of a ballot-box—*du scrutin*); abstract (of an account—*d'un compte*). *Au — du scrutin;* on inspecting the ballot-box.

****dépouiller,** *v.a.,* to unclothe ; to strip ; to skin, to lay bare ; to despoil, to deprive ; to throw off ; to cast off (of insects, &c.—*des insectes*); to lay aside ; to gather (crops—*récoltes*) ; to inspect (a ballot-box—*le scrutin*) ; to present an abstract (of accounts—*de comptes*). — *ses vêtements;* to throw off one's clothes. — *une anguille;* to skin an eel.

se ****dépouiller,** *v.r.,* to shed its skin (of insects and animals—*des insectes et des animaux*) ; to moult ; to divest one's self of ; to dispense with.

dépourvoir, *v.a.,* to leave unprovided or destitute.

se **dépourvoir,** *v.r.,* to leave one's self unprovided. *Se — d'argent;* to leave one's self without cash.

dépourvu, -e, *adj.,* destitute, unprovided, void. *Au —;* unawares.

dépravation, *n.f.,* depravity, depravement ; depravation. *La — de l'estomac;* the disordered state of the stomach. *La — du siècle;* the depravity of the age.

dépravé, -e, *adj.,* vitiated, depraved. *Goût —;* depraved taste. *Jeunesse —e;* depraved youth.

dépraver, *v.a.,* to vitiate, to deprave.

se **dépraver,** *v.r.,* to become vitiated, depraved. *Son goût se déprave;* his taste is vitiated.

déprécati-f, -ve, *adj.,* (theol.) deprecatory.

déprécation, *n.f.,* deprecation.

dépréciat-eur, *n.m.,* **-rice,** *n.f.,* one who depreciates.

dépréciation, *n.f.* depreciation.

déprécier, *v.a.,* to depreciate, to undervalue, to slight.

se **déprécier,** *v.r.,* to depreciate one's self, each other.

déprédat-eur, *n.m.,* **-rice,** *n.f.,* depredator.

déprédat-eur, -rice, *adj.,* depredatory.

déprédation, *n.f.,* plundering, depredation, malversation.

dépréder, *v.a.,* (l.u.) to depredate.

déprendre, *v.a.,* to loosen, to part.

dépression, *n.f.,* hollow, depression, falling in ; (astron., anat., surg.) depression.

déprier, *v.a.,* to disinvite.

déprimer, *v.a.,* to press down, to depress ; to underrate.

se **déprimer,** *v.a.,* to be flattened, depressed.

déprisant, -e, *adj.,* depreciating.

dépriser. *v.a.,* to undervalue, to underrate.

de profundis (-fon-dis), *n.m.,* (c. rel.) de profundis.

depuis, adv., since, since that time. *Je ne l'ai point vu —;* I have not seen him since.

depuis, prep., since. from, after. *— la création du monde;* since the creation of the world. *— peu;* lately. *— quand?* how long since ? *— deux ans:* these two years. *— longtemps;* this great while. *— ce temps-là;* ever after.

depuis que, conj., since. *— que vous êtes parti;* since you went away.

dépurati-f, -ve. adj., depuratory.

dépuration, n.f., depuration.

dépuratoire, adj., depuratory.

dépuré. -e, adj.. depurate.

dépurer. v.a., to depurate.

députation, n.f., deputation; deputyship.

député, n.m., deputy.

députer, v.a., to depute.

députer. v.n., to send a deputation.

déracinement (-si-n-mān), n.m., rooting up, eradication.

déraciner, v.a.; to root up, to pluck up, to pull up by the root, to eradicate. *— un cor;* to cut out a corn. *— un mal;* to eradicate an evil.

se déraciner, v.r., to unroot, to be torn up by the roots.

dérader, v.n., (nav.) to be driven from the anchors and forced out to sea.

déraidir, v a., to unstiffen, to make pliant, to soften.

se déraidir, v.r., to grow pliant, soft, supple.

***déraillement,** n.m., running off the rails.

***dérailler,** v.n., to run off the rails.

déraison. n.f., unreasonableness, want of reason, irrationality, preposterousness.

déraisonnable, adj., senseless, unreasonable, void of reason, preposterous.

déraisonnablement, adv., unreasonably, irrationally, preposterously.

déraisonner, v.n., to reason falsely, to talk nonsense.

dérangé. -e, adj., out of order, deranged, crazy; unwell, out of sorts. *Estomac —;* disordered stomach.

dérangement (dé-rānj-mān), n.m., derangement, discomposure, trouble, embarrassment; disorder, disturbance. *— de l'esprit;* disorder of the mind. *— de la santé,* bad state of health.

déranger, v.a., to derange, to put out of its place, out of order, to displace; to discompose; to disconcert, to incommode, to put out of sorts, to unsettle. *Cela m'a tout dérangé;* that has quite disconcerted me. *La moindre chose le dérange;* the least thing in the world unsettles him.

se déranger, v.r., to be deranged; to get out of order; to be unwell; to trouble one's self; to misconduct one's self; to lead a disorderly life.

déraper, v.n., (nav.) to get atrip. *L'ancre a dérapé;* the anchor is atrip. *Faire — une ancre;* to trip the anchor.

dératé. -e, adj., deprived of spleen, lively; cunning, sharp.

dérater, v.a., to take out, to extract, the spleen.

derby. n.m., derby.

derechef, adv.. over again, afresh, again.

déréglé. -e. adj., irregular. intemperate; exorbitant; unruly; dissolute, profligate. *Vie —e:* irregular life. *Appétit —.* immoderate appetite. *Imagination —e;* disordered imagination. *Désirs —s:* inordinate desires. *Une conduite —e:* disorderly conduct.

déréglement, n.m., intemperateness, exorbitancy; irregularity; unruliness; dissoluteness, licentiousness. *Vivre dans le —;* to lead a disorderly life.

déréglément. adv.. disorderly, inordinately, intemperately, dissolutely.

dérégler, v.a., to put out of order, to disorder.

se dérégler, v.r., to be out of order, to be deranged ; to lead a disorderly life.

dérider, v.a., to unwrinkle, to take away the wrinkles, to smooth. *La joie déride le front;* joy smoothes the brow.

se dérider, v.r., to unbend one's brow; to cheer up.

dérision. n.f., derision. *Par —:* out of derision. *Tourner tout en —;* to turn everything into ridicule.

dérisoire. adj., derisive.

dérivati-f,-ve, adj., derivative.

dérivatif. n.m., derivative.

dérivation, n.f., derivation.

dérive, n.f., drift, lee-way. *En —;* adrift.(*Avoir belle —;* to have good sea-room.

dérivé, -e. adj., derivative.

dérivé, n.m., (gram) derivative.

dériver, v.n.. to be derived; to get clear of the shore; (nav.) to drift; to derive, to proceed from. *D'où faites-vous — ce mot?* what is the derivation of that word?

dériver, v.a., to derive; to divert (of rivers, &c.—*de rivières, &c.*).

derme, n.m., (anat.) derma.

derni-er, -ère, adj., last; highest. greatest, vilest, meanest ; youngest (of a family of children—*d'une famille*); (mus.) closing. *En — lieu;* in the last place. *En — ressort;* ultimately. *Rendre le — soupir;* to breathe one's last. *C'est la —e lettre qu'il ait écrite;* it is the last letter he wrote. *Mettre la —e main à quelque chose;* to put the finishing stroke to a thing. *Une affaire de la —e importance;* an affair of the greatest importance. *Arriver au — degré;* to arrive at the highest degree. *Cela est du — ridicule,* that is excessively ridiculous.

derni-er, n.m., **-ère,** n.f., last; end of the gallery (tennis). *Le — des hommes,* the last of men. *Jusqu'au —;* to the last. *Dernier-né (—s —s):* last born male child.

dernièrement, adv., lately, of late.

dérobé, -e, part.,stolen; spare (of time—*du temps*); (arch.) private. *Escalier —;* private staircase. *Fèves —es;* beans slipped out of their skins. *À la —e;* by stealth, privately. *S'en aller à la —e;* to steal away.

dérober, v.a., to rob, to steal, to pilfer, to plunder, to purloin; to conceal, to hide, to protect, to screen, to shelter; to shell (beans—*des fèves). — quelqu'un à la justice;* to screen any one from justice.

se dérober, v.r., to steal away, to escape, to disappear, to avoid, to shun. *Il s'est dérobé;* he has stolen away. *Se — à la justice,* to fly from justice. *Le vaisseau se déroba bientôt à la vue*; we soon lost sight of the ship.

dérogation, n.f., derogation.

dérogatoire, adj., derogatory.

dérogeance, n.f., forfeiture (of nobility— *de noblesse*).

dérogeant, -e (-jänt, -t), adj., derogating, derogatory.

déroger, v.n., to derogate; to take away. to detract; to condescend; to stoop. *— à l'usage établi,* to derogate from established custom. *— à noblesse;* to forfeit one's nobility.

⊙ **dérouiller.** V. **déraidir.**

dérougir, v.a., to take off the redness.

se dérougir, v.r., to lose its redness.

dérougir, v.n., to lose its redness.

***dérouillement,** n.m., clearing from rust.

***dérouiller.** v.a., to remove. the rust, to polish, to brighten up.

se dérouiller, v.r., to lose its rust; to rub off the rust; to polish up; to read up a subject. *L'esprit se dérouille dans le grand monde;* good company rubs the rust off one's mind.

déroulement (dé-rool-mān), *n.m.*, unrolling; production of the evolute (of curves—*des courbes*).

dérouler, *v.a.*, to unroll; to spread out, to display; (geom.) to produce the evolute. — *les merveilles de la création;* to unfold the wonders of creation.

se **dérouler**, *v.r.*, to unroll; to display itself; to open to the view.

déroute, *n.f.*, rout, defeat, overthrow, ruin. *Mettre une armée en —;* to rout an army. *Mettre quelqu'un en —;* to confuse, to silence any one.

dérouter, *v.a.*, to put out of one's way; to embarrass, to bewilder; to disconcert, to perplex; to baffle. *Je suis tout dérouté;* I am quite out of my latitude.

derrière, *prep.*, behind, behind one's back. *Laisser loin — soi*, to leave far behind one. *Regardez — vous;* look behind you.

derrière, *adv.*, behind. *Par —;* from behind. *Porte de —;* back-door; evasion.

derrière, *n.m.*, hind, hinder part; posteriors; tail-board (of a cart—*d'une charrette*); breech. *Être logé sur le —;* to lodge at the back of the house. *Montrer le —;* to turn tail.

derviche *or* **dervis**, *n.m.*, dervis.

des, *art.pl.*, of the; from the. *V.* **de**.

dès, *prep.*, from, since. — *le point du jour;* from break of day. — *le berceau;* from the cradle. — *à présent;* from this moment, forthwith, henceforth. — *lors;* from that time.

dès que, *conj.*, when, as soon as; since. — *qu'il parut;* as soon as he appeared. — *que vous le souhaitez;* since you wish it.

se **désabonner**, *v.r.*, to withdraw one's subscription (from a newspaper or periodical—*à un journal, &c.*).

désabuser, *v.a.*, to disabuse, to undeceive.

se **désabuser**, *v.r.*, to undeceive one's self. *Désabusez-vous;* undeceive yourself.

désaccord, *n.m.*, disagreement; (mus.) discord. *Être en —;* to be at variance.

désaccorder, *v.a.*, to untune, to put out of tune.

se **désaccorder**, *v.r.*, to get out of tune.

désaccoupler, *v.a.*, to uncouple.

se **désaccoupler**, *v.r.*, to uncouple.

désaccoutumance, *n.f.*, want of custom.

désaccoutumer, *v.a.*, to unaccustom.

se **désaccoutumer**, *v.r.*, to accustom one's self. *Se — de faire une chose;* to leave off doing a thing.

désachalander, *v.a.*, to take away the customers.

désaffection, *n.f.*, disaffection.

désaffectionner, *v.a.*, to lose affection, to cause any one to lose affection (for a person—*pour une personne*).

se **désaffectionner**, *v.r.*, to lose affection (for a person—*pour quelqu'un*).

désaffourcher, *v.a.*, (nav.) to unmoor or heave up an anchor.

désaffubler, *v.a.*, to unmuffle.

désagréable, *adj.*, disagreeable, unpleasant; unacceptable; uncomfortable; obnoxious; unsightly; distasteful. *Nature —;* disagreeableness. *Cela est — à voir;* that is displeasing to the sight.

désagréablement, *adv.*, disagreeably, unpleasantly; unacceptably; uncomfortably; obnoxiously.

désagréer, *v.n.*, to displease. *Cela ne me désagrée pas:* I do not dislike it.

⊙**désagréer**. *v.a.*, to unrig. *V.* **dégréer**.

désagrégation, *n.f.*, disaggregation.

désagréger, *v.a.*, to disaggregate.

désagrément, *n m.*, disagreeableness; unpleasantness; blemish. *Cet état a ses —s;* that condition has its unpleasantness.

désajuster, *v.a.*, to derange, to disturb, to put out of order.

se **désajuster**. *v.r.*, to become deranged, disturbed, to get out of order. *Sa coiffure s'est désajustée;* her head-dress is out of order.

désalignement, *n.m.*, (milit.) unevenness (of ranks of soldiers—*des rangs*).

désaligner, *v.a.*, (milit.) to make uneven (ranks of soldiers—*des rangs*).

se **désaligner**, *v.r.*, (milit.) to fall out of the ranks.

désallier, *v.a.*, to disunite (allies).

se **désallier**. *v.r.*, to break off an alliance.

désaltérant, -e, *adj.*, that quenches thirst.

désaltérer, *v.a.*, to quench the thirst.

se **désaltérer**, *v.r.*, to quench one's thirst.

⊙**désancrer**, *v.n.*, to weigh anchor.

*****désappareiller**. *V.* **dépareiller**.

désapparier, *v.a.*, to separate (birds that have been paired—*des oiseaux qui ont été accouplés*).

désappointement (-point-mān), *n.m.*, disappointment.

désappointer, *v.a.*, to disappoint; ⊙ to strike soldiers off the rolls. — *une pièce d'étoffe* (com.); to cut the threads which keep in position the folds of fabrics.

désapprendre, *v.a.*, to unlearn.

désapprobat-eur, *n.m.*, **-rice**, *n.f.*, one who disapproves.

désapprobat-eur. **-rice**, *adj.*, disapproving. *Un geste —;* a gesture of disapprobation.

désapprobation, *n.f.*, disapprobation, disapproval.

désappropriation, *n.f.*, renunciation (of property—*de propriété*).

se **désapproprier**, *v.r.*, to renounce (property —*la propriété*).

désapprouver, *v.a.*, to disapprove of.

désarçonner, *v.a.*, to dismount, to unsaddle, to unhorse; to baffle, to nonplus.

désargenter, *v.a.*, to unsilver, to drain of money. *Ces emplettes m'ont désargenté;* these purchases have emptied my purse.

se **désargenter**, *v.r.*, to become unsilvered, to lose its plating.

désarmé, -e, *part.*, disarmed, unarmed.

désarmement, *n.m.*, disarming; (nav.) laying up.

désarmer, *v.a.*, to disarm, to unarm; to foil; to uncock (a gun—*un fusil, &c.*); (nav.) to unship (oars—*les rames*); to lay up, to dismantle. *Ses pleurs me désarmèrent;* her tears disarmed me. — *la colère de quelqu'un;* to appease any one's anger. — *un vaisseau;* to dismantle a ship, to lay her up; to pay off the officers and crew.

désarmer, *v.n.*, to disarm; (nav.) to be dismantled.

désarrimer, *v.a.*, (nav.) to alter or shift the stowage in the hold.

désarroi, *n.m.*, disorder, disarray.

désarticulation, *n.f.*, (surg.) amputation in a joint.

désarticuler, *v.a.*, to disjoint.

désassembler, *v.a.*, to take to pieces.

désassocier, *v.a.*, to dissociate.

désassorti, -e, *adj.*, displaced, disarranged; incomplete (of a book—*d'un livre*).

désassortir, *v.a.*, to spoil the match of; to mismatch.

désastre, *n.m.*, disaster.

désastreusement (-treūz-mān), *adv.*, disastrously.

désastreu-x. -se, *adj.*, disastrous.

désavantage, *n.m.*, disadvantage; disadvantageousness. *L'affaire a tourné à leur —;* the business turned out to their disadvantage.

Parler au — de quelqu'un ; to speak disadvantageously of any one.

désavantager.v.a., to deprive of an advantage, to disadvantage.

désavantageusement (-jeuz-mãn), adv., disadvantageously.

désavantageu-x, -se, adj., disadvantageous.

désaveu, n.m., disavowal, denial ; disowning. *Il fait le — de cette action ;* he disowns that action.

désaveugler. v.a.. to undeceive.

désavouer. v.a., to disown, to disclaim, to disavow, to deny. *— sa signature ;* to disown one's signature. *Cette mère a désavoué son enfant ;* that mother has disowned her child.

descellement, n.m., (mas.) unbedding.

desceller, v.a., to unseal ; (mas.) to unbed.

descendance, n.f., descent, lineage.

descendant, -e, adj., descending, going down ; (milit.) coming off duty.

descendant, n.m., -e, n.f., descendant, offspring.

descendant, n.m., (l.u.) ebb-tide.

descendre, v.n., to descend ; to go down ; to go down stairs ; to come, to step, to get down ; to alight ; to stay, to put up ; to fall ; to reach ; to come from ; (nav.) to land ; to ebb, to subside. *Descendez vite ;* make haste and come down. *— de cheval ;* to dismount. *— de voiture ;* to get out of a carriage. *— d'un bateau ;* to get out of a boat. *— dans un puits ;* to go down into a well. *La marée descend ;* it is ebb-tide. *— dans sa conscience ;* to examine one's conscience. *Il descendit à l'hôtel ;* he put up at the hotel. *Nous descendîmes dans une île ;* we landed on an island. *Il vaut mieux monter que —;* it is better to rise than to fall.

descendre, v.a., to descend, to take down, to bring, to let down ; to go, to come, to get down ; to set down ; to land. *Descendez ce tableau ;* take that picture down. *Où vous descendrai-je ?* where shall I set you down ? *— la garde ;* to come off guard.

descente, n.f., descent ; going down ; taking down ; subsiding (of waters—*des eaux*); dismounting ; disembarkment ; (fin.) run ; declivity ; irruption ; rupture, hernia ; (milit.) coming off guard. *La justice a fait une — chez lui ;* the police have searched his house. *La — de la croix ;* the descent from the cross.

descripti-f, -ve, adj., descriptive.

description, n.f., description, inventory.

déséchouer, v.a., (nav.) to get afloat.

désemballage, n.m., unpacking.

désemballer, v.a., to unpack. *On a désemballé les marchandises ;* they have unpacked the goods.

désembarquement,n.m., disembarkment, landing.

désembarquer. v.a., to disembark, to land ; to unship, to unlade.

désemboîter, v.a., to disjoint ; to put out of socket ; to dislocate.

désembourber, v.a., to draw out of the mire.

se **désembourber,** v.r., to get out of the mire.

désemparer, v.n., to quit, to go away.

désemparer, v.a., to quit ; (nav.) to disable. *— un vaisseau ;* to disable a ship.

désempenné (dé-zan-pèn-né), adj., stripped of its feathers.

désempeser, v.a., to unstarch, to take out the starch.

se **désempeser,** v.r., to become unstarched.

désemplir, v.a., to make less full. *— un tonneau ;* to draw from a cask a part of its contents.

se **désemplir.** v.r., to become less full. *Ma bourse se désemplit ;* my purse is getting low.

désemplir, v.n., to grow empty, to become less full. *Sa maison ne désemplit point ;* his house is always full.

désenchantement (-shãnt-mãn), n.m., disenchantment.

désenchanter. v.a., to disenchant.

désenclaver. v.a., to disinclose (land from other lands—*terrain d'autres terrains*).

désenclouer, v.a., to take out a nail. *— un canon ;* to unspike a cannon. *— un cheval ;* to take a nail out of a horse's foot.

désencombrer, v.a., to disencumber ; to remove rubbish.

désenfiler, v.a., to unthread. to unstring. *— une aiguille ;* to unthread a needle.

se **désenfiler,** v.r.. to come unstrung.

désenfler, v.a., to reduce the swelling.

se **désenfler,** v.r., to become less swollen.

désenfler, v.n., to become less swollen ; to cease to be swollen.

désenflure, n.f., diminution, ceasing, of a swelling.

désengrener, v.a., to throw out of gear.

désenivrer, v.a., to sober, to make sober again.

se **désenivrer,** v.r., to get sober again, to recover, to be cured of. *Se — en dormant ;* to sleep one's self sober.

désenlaidir, v.a., to render less ugly.

se **désenlaidir,** v.r., to become less ugly.

désennuyer, v.a., to drive away tedium ; to cheer, to divert.

se **désennuyer,** v.r., to drive away one's tedium ; to divert one's self.

désenrayer, v.a., to unlock or unskid (a wheel—*une roue*).

désenrayer, v.n., to unskid.

désenrhumer, v.a., to cure of a cold.

se **désenrhumer,** v.r., to cure one's cold.

désenrouer, v.a., to cure of hoarseness.

se **désenrouer,** v.r., to cure one's hoarseness.

désensabler, v.a., to get a stranded boat out of the mud or sand.

désensevelir (-sèv-lir), v.a., to unwrap, to exhume (a corpse—*un cadavre*).

désensorceler, v.a., to unbewitch.

désensorcellement, n.m., unbewitching.

désentêter, v.a., to cure of obstinacy.

se **désentêter,** v.r., to be cured of obstinacy. *Il ne peut se — de cette opinion ;* he cannot get that opinion out of his head.

désenverguer (-ghé), v.a., to unbend (sails —*les voiles d'un vaisseau*).

désert, -e, adj., desert, solitary, wild, unfrequented ; abandoned ; deserted.

désert, n.m., desert, solitary place, waste, wilderness. *Il a prêché au —;* he preached in the wilderness.

déserter, v.a., to desert, to abandon, to forsake, to quit, to leave. *— son poste ;* to desert one's post. *— la maison paternelle ;* to forsake the paternal roof. *— les drapeaux ;* to desert one's colours.

déserter, v.n., to desert, to leave. *— à l'ennemi ;* to go over to the enemy.

déserteur, n.m., deserter.

désertion. n.f., desertion.

⊙ à la **désespérade,** adv., desperately, like a madman.

désespérance, n.f., despair, the loss of all hope.

désespérant, -e, adj., desperate, hopeless, discouraging.

désespéré, -e, part., hopeless, desperate ; in despair, despondent, disheartened.

désespéré, n.m., -e, n.f., madman, madwoman ; person deprived of hope ; person in

despair. *Se battre en* —; to fight desperately. *Agir en* —; to behave like a madman.

désespérément, *adv.*, desperately, past recovery.

désespérer, *v.n.*, to despair, to despond, to give up all hope. — *de quelqu'un, de quelque chose;* to despair of any one, of anything; to give up any one, anything, for lost. *Les médecins désespèrent de sa vie;* the physicians despair of his life.

désespérer, *v.a.*, to drive to despair; to vex exceedingly, to torment.

se **désespérer,** *v.r.*, to be in despair, to give one's self up to despair.

désespoir, *n.m.*, despair; hopelessness, desperation, despondency. *Être au* —; to be in despair; to be vexed, grieved. *Mettre au* —; to drive to despair; to vex extremely. *Tomber dans le* —; to sink into despair. *De* —; through despair, through rage.

*****déshabillé** (dé-za-), *n.m.*, dishabille, undress. — *du matin;* morning dress.

*****déshabiller** (dé-za-), *v.a.*, to undress, to take one's clothes off, to strip, to disrobe.

se *****déshabiller** (dé-za-), *v.r.*, to undress one's self.

⊙*****déshabiller** (dé-za-), *v.n.*, to undress.

déshabité, -e, (dé-za-), *adj.*, uninhabited, deserted.

déshabituer (dé-za-), *v.a*, to unaccustom, to break of.

se **déshabituer** (dé-za-), *v.r.*,to unaccustom one's self; to break one's self of. *Se* — *d'une chose,* to leave off doing a thing.

déshérence (dé-zé-), *n.f.*, (jur.) escheat.

déshériter (dé-zé), *v.a.*, to disinherit.

désheurer (dé-zeu-), *v.a.*, (fam., l.u.) to change the hours of one's usual occupations.

se **désheurer** (dé-zeu-), *v.r.*, (fam., l.u.) to change the hours of the usual occupations of one's self.

déshonnête (dé-zo-), *adj.*, immodest, indecent, shameful.

déshonnêtement (dé-zo-nêt-män), *adv.*, indecently, immodestly, shamefully.

déshonnêteté (dé-zo-nêt-té), *n.f.*, (l.u.) indecency, immodesty.

déshonneur (dé-zo-), *n.m.*, dishonour; disgrace, shame, discredit. *Il a mis le comble à son* —; he has put the finishing stroke to his dishonour. *Faire* — *à quelqu'un;* to disgrace one. ⊙*C'est me prier de mon* —; that is asking me to dishonour myself.

déshonorable (dé-zo-), *adj.*, dishonourable, disgraceful.

déshonorablement (dé-zo-), *adv.*, dishonourably.

déshonorant, -e (dé-zo-), *adj.*, dishonourable, disgraceful, shameful.

déshonorer (dé-zo-), *v.a.*, to dishonour, to bring to shame, to bring shame upon, to disgrace. *Il a déshonoré sa famille;* he has dishonoured his family.

se **déshonorer** (dé-zo-), *v.r.*, to dishonour one's self, to disgrace one's self.

desideratum, *n.m.*, *(desiderata),* desideratum.

*****désignati-f, -ve.** *adj.*, indicative.

*****désignation,** *n.f.*, designation, nomination, choice.

*****désigné, -e,** *part.*, appointed, indicated. *A l'heure* —*e;* at the appointed hour.

*****désigner,** *v.a.*, to designate, to describe; to denote, to betoken; to appoint, to fix; to assign, to elect, to nominate, to choose, to point out.

désillusionner, *v.a.*, to undeceive, to free from illusion.

désincorporer, *v.a.*, to disincorporate, to separate, to disunite.

désinence, *n.f.*, (gram.) termination, ending.

désinfatuer, *v.a.*, to disabuse, to undeceive, to dispel the infatuation of.

se **désinfatuer,** *v.r.*, to cease being infatuated.

désinfectant, *adj.*, disinfecting. —, *n.m.*, disinfectant.

désinfecter, *v.a.*, to disinfect, to purify.

désinfection, *n.f.*, disinfection, fumigation.

désintéressé, -e, *adj.*, uninterested; disinterested; unselfish, impartial, unbiassed.

désintéressement (-rès-män), *n.m.*, impartiality; indifference; disinterestedness.

désintéressément, *adv.*, (l.u.) disinterestedly.

désintéresser, *v.a.*, to indemnify; to buy out the interest of.

*****désinterligner,** *v.a*, (print.) to unlead; to make solid.

désinvestir, *v.a.*, to devest.

désinviter, *v.a.*, to recall an invitation.

désinvolture, *n.f.*, easy, graceful, bearing and gait.

désir, *n.m.*, desire, wish; longing. — *déréglé;* inordinate desire. *Au gré de ses* —*s;* agreeably to one's wishes. *Avoir le* — *de;* to have a desire to. *Brûler du* — *de;* to be inflamed with the desire of.

désirable, *adj.*, desirable.

désirer, *v.a.*, to desire, to wish for, to long for. *Que désirez-vous de moi?* what do you wish of me? *Je désire vous parler;* I wish to speak to you. *Cet ouvrage ne laisse rien à* —; this work is most satisfactory in all respects.

désireu-x, -se, *adj.*, desirous, anxious.

désistement, *n.m.*, desistance, desisting; relinquishment.

se **désister,** *v.r.*, to desist from, to give over, to abandon. *Il s'est désisté de ses poursuites;* he gave over his pursuits.

dès lors, *adv.* *V.* **dès.**

désobéir, *v.n.*, to refuse to obey, to disobey. — *au roi;* to disobey the king.

désobéissance, *n.f.*, disobedience; undutifulness; (jur.) contumacy.

désobéissant, -e, *adj.*, disobedient, undutiful.

désobligeamment (-ja-män), *adv.*, disobligingly, unkindly.

désobligeance, *n.f.*, unkindness, lack of complaisance.

désobligeant, -e (-jän, -t), *adj.*, disobliging, unkind, uncivil.

désobligeante (-jant), *n.f.*, carriage for two persons only.

désobliger, *v.a.*, to disoblige, to displease.

désobstruant, -e, *adj.*, (med.) deobstruent.

désobstruant, *n.m.*, (med.) deobstruent.

désobstructi-f, -ve, *adj.*, (med.) deobstruent.

désobstructi-f, *n.m.*, (med.) deobstruent.

désobstruer, *v.a.*, to clear from obstruction, to free, to deobstruct.

désoccupation, *n.f.*, inactivity, want of employment.

désoccupé, -e, *adj.*, unemployed, unoccupied.

désœuvré, -e, *adj.*, unoccupied, idle, unemployed. *Être* —; to be unemployed. *Le temps pèse aux gens* —*s;* time hangs heavily on those who are unemployed.

désœuvrement, *n.m.*, want of occupation, idleness.

désolant, -e, *adj.*; disheartening, grievous, afflicting, distressing, dispiriting; mortifying, provoking, unbearable, tiresome.

désolateur, *n.m.*, spoiler, ravager, destroyer.

désolation, *n.f.*, desolation, disconsolateness, affliction, grief, vexation.

désolé, -e, *part.*, afflicted, disconsolate, broken-hearted, in great distress ; very sorry ; grieved.

désoler, *v.a.*, to desolate, to lay waste, to waste, to devastate ; to afflict, to grieve, to make disconsolate, to drive mad ; to vex ; to pester, to harass, to annoy, to torment. *La mort de son ami le désole ;* the death of his friend grieves him very much. *Ce retard me désole ;* this delay vexes me.

se **désoler**, *v.r.*, to grieve, to give one's self up to affliction, to pine with grief. to be disconsolate.

désopilant. -e, *adj.*, (med.) deobstruent.

désopilant. *n.m.*, (med.) deobstruent.

désopilati-f, -ve, *adj.*, (med.) deobstruent, opening.

désopilation. *n.f.*, (med.) removal of obstruction.

désopiler, *v a.*, (med.) to deobstruct, to clear. *Cela désopile la rate ;* that dispels the spleen.

désordonné. -e. *adj.*, disorderly ; dissolute, unruly, inordinate ; immoderate, extravagant. *Appétit — ;* immoderate appetite. *Il est — dans ses dépenses ;* he is extravagant in his expense.

désordonnément, *adv.*, disorderly, irregularly, inordinately ; immoderately, excessively.

désordonner, *v.a.*, to disorder, to disturb.

désordre. *n.m*, disorder, confusion ; licentiousness ; disorderly life ; riot, debauchery ; discomposure, perturbation ; variance, dissension, discord ; disturbance ; devastation. *Sa coiffure est en — ;* her head-dress is in disorder. *Vivre dans le — ;* to lead a riotous life. *Retirer quelqu'un du — ;* to reclaim one from a licentious life. *Il a l'esprit en — ;* his mind is in a state of perturbation. *Les passions mettent le — dans l'âme ;* the passions discompose the soul. *Faire cesser le — ;* to put an end to the disturbance. *En — ;* in disorder.

désorganisat-eur. -rice, *n.* and *adj.*, disorganizer ; disorganizing.

désorganisation. *n.f.*, disorganization.

désorganiser. *v.a.*, to disorganize.

se **désorganiser**, *v.r.*, to become disorganized.

désorienter, *v.a.*, to put any one out of his reckoning ; to make a person lose his way ; to put out, to disconcert. to put out of countenance. *Être désorienté ;* to lose one's way ; to be out of one's element. *Notre guide était tout à fait désorienté ;* our guide had lost all knowledge of the way.

désormais, *adv.*, henceforth, hereafter, from this time.

désossement (dé-zos-män), *n.m.*, boning. taking out the bones. *Faire le — d'un lièvre ;* to take out the bones of a hare.

désosser, *v.a.*, to bone, to take out the bones. *Une dinde désossée ;* a boned turkey

désourdir (dé-zoor-), *v.a.*, (l.u.) to unweave ; to unravel.

désoxydation. *n.f.*, (chem.) disoxidation. deoxidation.

désoxyder, *v.a.*, (chem.) to disoxidate, to deoxidate.

se **désoxyder**, *v.r.*, to disoxidate, to deoxidize ; to become deoxidized.

désoxygénation. *n.f.*, (chem.) disoxygenation

désoxygéner, *v.a.*, (chem.) to disoxygenate.

se **désoxygéner**, *v.r.*, to become disoxygenated.

despote, *n.m.*, despot.

despotique, *adj.*, despotic. despotical.

despotiquement (-tik-män), *adv.*, despotically.

despotisme, *n.m.*, despotism.

despumation, *n.f.*, (chem.) despumation.

despumer, *v.a.*, (chem.) to despumate, to skim.

desquamation (-koua-), *n.f.*, desquamation.

dessaisir, *v.a.*, to deprive of possession.

se **dessaisir**, *v.r.*, to deprive one's self of, to give up.

dessaisissement (-zis-män), *n.m.*, divesting one's self.

dessaisonner. *v.a.*, (agri.) to plough, manure, or sow land unseasonably and contrary to custom.

dessalé, -e, *part.*, unsalted, soaked ; sharp, cunning.

dessalé, *n.m.*, **-e**. *n.f.*, sharp fellow, sharp woman. knowing person.

dessaler, *v.a.*, to remove salt from meat, &c. by soaking.

se **dessaler**, *v r.*, to become less salt.

dessangler, *v.a.*, to ungirth, to loosen the girth.

desséchant. -e, *adj.*, drying.

desséché, -e, *part.*, dried up ; desiccated. *Des ossements —s ;* dried bones. *Des marais —s ;* drained marshes.

desséchement (-sésh-män), *n m.*, drying up. drainage, dryness ; emaciation.

dessécher, *v.a.*, to dry, to dry up ; to parch ; to drain ; to wither ; to waste, to emaciate. *— le cœur ;* to harden the heart.

se **dessécher**, *v.r.*, to dry up, to become dry ; to be drained ; to wither ; to waste away.

dessein. *n.m*, design, intention, intent ; resolution ; plan, scheme, purpose, view. *Le — en est formé ;* the resolution is taken. *Concevoir un — ;* to conceive a design. *Cacher son — ;* to hide one's purpose. *Former le — de faire une chose ;* to intend to do a thing. *Changer de — ;* to alter one's mind *Avoir — de ;* to intend. *Avoir de grands —s ;* to have great views. *De — prémédité ;* premeditately. *À — ;* designedly, on purpose, intentionally. *Je l'ai fait à — ; I* did it designedly. *À bon — ;* with a good intention. *À — de ;* in order to, with a design to. *À — que ;* that, to the end that. *Sans — ;* undesignedly, unintentionally.

desseller, *v.a.*, to unsaddle, to take off the saddle.

desserre, *n.f.*, (l.u.) loosening. *Être dur à la — ;* to be a close-fisted man.

desserrer, *v.a.*, to loosen, to slacken ; (print.) to unlock.

se **desserrer**, *v.r.*, to get loose.

dessert. *n.m.*, dessert.

desserte. *n.f.*, leavings ; ecclesiastical functions, officiating.

dessertir, *v.a.*, to take precious stones, &c., from their mountings.

desservant, *n.m.*, curate, officiating minister.

desservir, *v.a.*, to take away, to clear the table. to remove the cloth ; to disserve, to do an ill office ; to officiate (of clergymen—*d'ecclésiastiques*). *Il vous a desservi auprès du ministre ;* he has done you an ill turn with the minister.

dessiccati-f, -ve, *adj.*, desiccative, desiccant.

dessiccatif, *n.m.*, desiccative, desiccant.

dessiccation, *n.f.*, desiccation.

dessiller, *v.a.*, to open (eyes—*les yeux*). — *les yeux à quelqu'un ;* to undeceive one.

se **dessiller**, *v.r.*, to open (of one's eyes—*des yeux*).

dessin, *n.m.*, drawing ; design, sketch ; pattern ; draught, plan ; (mus.) arrangement. — *lavé ;* washed drawing. -- *colorié*, coloured drawing. — *haché;* hatched drawing. — *lithographie;* lithographic drawing. — *à la craie;* chalk drawing. *Cette étoffe est d'un joli —;* this stuff is of a pretty pattern.

dessinateur, *n.m.,* draughtsman; designer, pattern-drawer.

dessiné, -e, *part.,* drawn. *Une figure bien —e:* a well-drawn face. *Un jardin bien —;* a garden well laid out.

dessiner, *v.a.,* to draw; to sketch, to delineate; to set off. — *au crayon;* to draw with a pencil. — *de fantaisie, d'après nature, d'après la bosse;* to draw from fancy. from nature, from the bust. *Un vêtement qui dessine bien les formes;* a dress that sets off the figure to advantage.

se **dessiner,** *v.r.,* to be delineated, to be visible, to appear; to assume a form, to be formed; to display one's figure to advantage. *Une terre se dessine dans la brume;* land is visible through the mist.

dessoler, *v.a.,* (agri.) to unsole (animals— *les animaux*); to take off the sole; to change the usual order of the cultivation of land.

dessouder, *v.a.,* to unsolder.

se **dessouder,** *v.r.,* to get unsoldered.

dessoûler, *v.a.,* (pop.) to sober, to make sober; —, *v.n.,* to get sober again.

se **dessoûler,** *v.r.,* (pop.) to get sober again.

dessous, *adv.,* under, underneath, below. *Ci—;* underneath, below. *En—;* underneath; downward; (fig.) sly, artful person.

dessous, *prep.,* under, underneath, beneath. *Je l'ai cherché dessus et — la table;* I have looked for it upon and under the table.

dessous, *n.m.,* lower part; under side; wrong side; worst; lee (of the wind—*du vent*). *Le — du vent;* (nav.) leeward. *Avoir le —;* to be worsted, to have the worst of it. *Au—;* below; under; beneath. *Je suis logé au— de lui;* I lodge below him. *Cet emploi est au— de lui;* that employment is beneath him. *Par—;* under, beneath. *Là—;* there, under there.

dessus, *adv.,* on, upon, over; uppermost. *Il n'est ni — ni dessous;* it is neither on nor under. *Sens — dessous;* upside down, topsy-turvy. *Au —;* above; upwards, *Ci—;* above. *Voyez ci—;* see above. *En—,* on the upper or right side; in the upper part, above; at the top; uppermost. *Cela est noir en — et blanc en dessous;* it is black on the upper side, and white underneath. *Là— ;* on it, on that, on there; to, on, about, this subject; upon this head; on which, thereupon, saying this, with these words. *Passons là—;* let us say nothing about it. *Vous pouvez compter là—;* you may rely upon that. *Par—;* above; over; more, over and above. *Il sauta par—;* he jumped over.

dessus, *prep.,* on, upon. *Ôtez cela de — la t'ble;* take that off the table. *Cela est au— de ses forces;* that is beyond his strength. *Cet homme est au— de la calomnie;* this man is out of the reach of slander. *Il sauta par— — la barrière;* he leaped over the gate. *Par— tout;* above all. *Il a des affaires par— les yeux;* he is over head and ears in business. *Par— le marché;* into the bargain.

dessus, *n.m.,* top, the upper part; upper side, right side; upperhand, advantage; (mus.) treble. *Le — de la tête;* the crown of the head. *Le — de la main;* the back of the hand. *Le — d'un livre;* the cover of a book. *Le — du vent;* (nav.) the weather-gauge *Être au— du vent;* to be to windward. *Bas— (—);* second treble.

destin, *n.m.,* destiny, doom, fate; career. *On ne peut fuir son —;* no one can escape his destiny. *Un — funeste;* a fatal destiny.

destinataire, *n.m.,* person to whom a parcel, a letter, is addressed.

destination, *n.f.,* destination.

destiné, -e *part.,* destined, born. *Il est au barreau;* he is destined for the law. *Un homme — aux grandes choses;* a man born to great things. *Il était — à périr de cette manière;* he was doomed to perish in this way.

destinée, *n.f.,* fate, destiny; doom; career. *Remplir ses —s;* to fulfil one's destiny. *Finir sa —;* to terminate one's career.

destiner, *v.a.,* to destine, to intend, to design, to purpose; to doom. *À qui destine-t-on un si riche présent?* for whom is so rich a present intended?

se **destiner,** *v.r.,* to be destined, intended. *Il se destine au barreau;* he intends to follow the bar.

destituable, *adj.,* removable from office.

destitué, -e, *adj.,* destitute, devoid. — *de bon sens;* devoid of sense.

destituer, *v.a.,* to dismiss, to turn out, to discharge, to remove (from office—*d'une place*).

destitution, *n.f.,* dismissal, removal (from office—*d'une place*).

© **destrier,** *n.m.,* steed, charger, war-horse.

destruct-eur, *n.m.,* **-rice,** *n.f.,* destroyer; ravager, spoiler. *Les soldats sont de grands —s,* soldiers are great spoilers.

destruct-eur, -rice, *adj.,* destructive. destroying, deadly, ruinous. *Fléau —;* deadly scourge.

destructibilité, *n.f.,* destructibility.

destructi-f, -ve, *adj.,* destructive, destroying.

destruction, *n.f.,* destruction.

désuétude (-su-), *n.f.,* disuse, desuetude.

désunion, *n.f.,* disunion, disjunction.

désunir, *v.a.,* to disunite, to disjoin.

se **désunir,** *v.r.,* to disunite, to come asunder.

détachement (dé-tash-mán), *n.m.,* indifference; (milit.) detachment, draught. — *de tout intérêt;* disinterestedness.

détacher, *v.a.,* to detach, to disengage, to loosen, to untie, to unbind, to unfasten; to undo; to separate, to cut off; to give (a blow— *un coup*); (milit.) to draught, to tell off; to take out stains, to clean. — *une épingle;* to take out a pin. — *un ruban;* to loosen a riband. — *une agrafe;* to undo a clasp. — *un soufflet à quelqu'un;* to give any one a box on the ear.

se **détacher,** *v.r.,* to become loosened, unfastened; to come undone; to be detached; to disengage one's self; to break away or off; to come off or away. *Se — d'une femme,* to break off acquaintance with a woman. *Se — du jeu;* to leave off gaming. *Se — du monde;* to break off with the world.

détacheu-r, *n.m.,* **-se,** *n.f.,* scourer.

*détail, *n.m.,* detail; retail; particular, circumstance. *Vendre en —;* to sell by retail. *Je n'ai omis aucun des —s;* I omitted none of the circumstances. *Les —s en sont fort curieux;* the details are very curious.

*détaillant, *n.m.,* **-e,** *n.f.,* retailer.

*détailler, *v.a.,* to cut in pieces; to retail, to sell by retail; to detail, to relate minutely.

détailleu-r, *n.m.,* **-se,** *n.f.,* retailer.

détalage, *n.m.,* taking in goods, putting up goods (that have been exposed in a shop window — *qui ont été mises en montre*).

détaler, *v.a.,* to take in goods (that have been exposed in a shop window—*qui ont été mises en montre*).

détaler, *v.n.,* to take in goods (that have been exposed in a shop window—*qui ont été mises en montre*); to shut up shop; to scamper away.

détalinguer (-ghé), *v.n.,* (nav.) to unbend the cable.

détaper, *v.a.*, to take out the tompion (of a cannon—*d'un canon*).

déteindre, *v.a.*, to take out the dye or colour.

déteindre, *v.n.*, to lose colour, to fade; to come off (of colours—*des couleurs*). *Cette étoffe déteint beaucoup*; this stuff fades very much.

se déteindre, *v.r.*, to lose colour; to fade; to come off (of colours—*des couleurs*).

dételer (dé-tlé), *v.a.*, to unharness, to take out, to unyoke (horses, oxen—*chevaux, bœufs, &c.*).

détendoir, *n.m.*, tool used by weavers to stretch *or* unstretch the chain.

détendre, *v.a.*, to unbend, to slacken, to relax, to loosen, to take down, to unhang. — *un arc*; to unbend a bow. — *son esprit*; to relax one's mind. — *une tapisserie*; to take down a set of hangings. — *une tente*; to strike a tent.

se détendre, *v.r.*, to unbend; to take relaxation, repose.

détendre, *v.a.*, to take down, to unhang (tapestry—*tapisserie*); to strike (tents—*tentes*).

détenir (dé-tnir), *v.a.*, to detain, to withhold, to keep back. — *quelqu'un en prison*; to keep one prisoner.

détente, *n.f.*, trigger (of a gun—*d'un fusil, &c.*); (horl.) detent, stop. *Machine à* —; expansion-engine. *À la* —; in pulling the trigger. *Lâcher la* —; to pull the trigger. *Être dur à la* —; (fig. and fam.) to be close-fisted.

détent-eur, *n.m.*, **-rice**, *n.f.*, holder, detainer.

*****détentillon**, *n.m.*, (horl.) detent, *or* stop, of the minute-hand.

détention, *n.f.*, detention.

détenu, -e *part.*, detained, withheld. — *en prison*; kept in prison. — *prisonnier*; kept a prisoner. *Être* — *pour dettes*; to be in prison for debt.

détenu, *n.m.*, **-e**, *n.f.*, prisoner. *Un* — *politique*; a political prisoner.

détergent, -e *adj.*, (med.) detergent.

déterger, *v.a.*, (med.) to deterge; to absterge, to cleanse. — *une plaie*; to cleanse a wound.

détérioration, *n.f.*, deterioration.

détériorer, *v.a.*, to deteriorate, to impair, to make worse.

se détériorer, *v.r.*, to deteriorate; to become defaced, to become debased; to become the worse for wear.

déterminable, *adj.*, determinable.

déterminant, -e *adj*, determinative, decisive, conclusive.

déterminati-f, -ve *adj.*, (gram.) determinative.

déterminatif, *n.m.*, (gram.) determinative word.

détermination, *n.f.*, determination, resolution, decision, settled purpose.

déterminé, -e *part.*, determined, decided; fixed; resolved on; caused; determinate; ascertained. *Un sens* —; a determinate significication. *Il est* — *à tout*; he is ready for anything.

déterminé, -e *adj.*, determined, bold, steady, resolute. *Un soldat* —; a soldier of undaunted courage.

déterminé, *n.m.*, desperate fellow, resolute man. *Un petit* —; a froward, ungovernable child.

déterminément, *adv.*, absolutely, positively, determinately, expressly, precisely; boldly, resolutely.

déterminer, *v.a.*, to determine, to decide, to settle, to fix; to ascertain; to resolve; to make one resolve *or* take a resolution; to fix the meaning; to lead to, to cause. *C'est moi qui*

l'ai déterminé à cela; it was I made him take that resolution. *Il a déterminé de rebâtir sa maison*; he has resolved to rebuild his house.

se déterminer, *v.r.*, to resolve; to determine; to be determined. *Je ne puis me* — *à rien*; I cannot resolve upon anything.

déterminisme, *n.m.*, (philos.) determinism.

déterré, *n.m.*, person dug up. *Avoir l'air d'un* —; to look like one risen from the dead.

déterrer, *v.a.*, to dig up; to disinter, to take up; to find, to discover, to bring to light, to ferret out, to rout out; to unkennel (foxes—*renards*); to unearth (hunt.). — *une statue antique*; to dig up an antique statue. — *un trésor*; to find a treasure.

déterreur, *n.m.*, one who disinters. — *de saints*; discoverer of the names of saints.

détersi-f, -ve *adj.*, (med.) detersive, abstergent, cleansing.

détersif, *n.m.*, (med.) detergent, detersive.

détestable, *adj.*, detestable, hateful.

détestablement, *adv.*, detestably, abominably.

détestation, *n.f.*, detestation.

détester, *v.a.*, to detest. — *ses péchés*; to abominate one's sins.

détester, *v.n.*, (l.u.) to blaspheme. *Ne faire que jurer et* —; to do nothing but curse and swear.

détiarer, *v.a.*, to deprive of one's tiara; to discrown.

détirer, *v.a.*, to draw out, to stretch. — *une étoffe*; to pull out a stuff. — *des cuirs*; to stretch hides.

détiser, *v.a.*, to rake out (the fire—*le feu*); to still, to quell.

détisser, *v.a.*, to unweave.

détonant, *adj.*, detonating.

détonation, *n.f.*, detonation.

détoner, *v.n.*, to detonate.

détonner, *v.n.*, to be out of tune, to get out of tune; to talk nonsense.

détordre, *v.a.*, to untwist, to unwring.

se détordre, *v.r.*, to come untwisted; ○ to sprain.

détors, -e *adj.*, untwisted. *Du fil* —; untwisted thread.

○ **détorse**, *n.f. V.* **entorse**.

*****détortiller**, *v.a.*, to untwist; to unravel.

se détortiller, *v.r.*, to become untwisted; to unravel.

détorquer, *v.a.*, to distort, to misrepresent. — *un passage*; to distort the meaning of a passage.

détouper, *v.a.*, to unstop, to take out the bung or stopple; to take the tow out of.

*****détoupillonner**, *v.a.*, to prune (orange-trees—*orangers*).

détour, *n.m.*, winding, turning; by-way, circuitous road; shift, evasion, trick, subterfuge. *Le* — *d'une rue*; the turning of a street. *Les* —*s d'un bois*; the windings and turnings of a wood. *Quel* — *vous avez fait!* what a way you went round! *Je connais ses tours et ses* —*s*; I know all his evasions and subterfuges. *Être sans* —; to be sincere. *User de* —*s*; to use evasions.

détourné, -e *part.*, turned away; retired; indirect, oblique. *Des chemins* —*s*; by-ways. *Voie* —*e*; indirect means.

détournement, *n.m.*, turning away, turning aside; embezzlement (of property—*d'argent, &c.*).

détourner, *v.a.*, to turn away, to turn aside, to turn off, to lead off, out of; to divert, to avert, to drive or keep back, to estrange; to secrete; to convey away, to embezzle, to appropriate; to deter, to dissuade. — *la rue*; to turn the eyes away. — *un coup*; to avert a blow.

On l'accuse d'avoir détourné ces fonds; he is accused of having converted these funds to his own use. *Détourner quelqu'un de son devoir;* to make one swerve from his duty. *Cela me détourne de mes occupations;* that draws me away from my business.

se détourner. *v.r.,* to turn away; to turn aside; to go out of the way, to swerve. *Se — de son chemin;* to go out of one's way. *Se — de son devoir;* to swerve from one's duty. *Se — de son travail:* to leave one's work.

détourner, *v.n..* to turn, to turn off.

détracter, *v.a.,* (l.u.) to detract, to traduce, to slander, to speak ill of, to backbite.

détract-eur, *n.m.,* **-rice,** *n.f.,* detracter, slanderer, traducer.

détracteur, *adj.m.,* detractive, detracting.

détraction, *n.f.,* detraction.

détranger. *v.a.,* (hort.) to drive away (insects that injure the plants—*ies insectes nuisibles*).

détraquer, *v.a.,* to spoil a horse's paces, to throw a horse out of his paces; to disorder, to put out of order; to throw into confusion; to lead astray.

se détraquer, *v.r.,* to spoil his paces (of a horse—*du cheval*); to be out of order, to be disordered; to go astray. *Cette montre se détraque;* this watch is out of order. *Sa tête se détraque;* his head is disordered. *Un cheval qui se détraque;* a horse that loses his paces.

détrempe, *n.f.,* distemper, painting in distemper. *Une —;* a sketch in distemper. *Un mariage en —;* a pretended marriage.

détremper, *v.a.,* to dilute, to weaken; to enervate. *— des couleurs;* to dilute colours. *— de la farine avec des œufs;* to beat up flour with eggs. *— de l'acier;* to soften steel.

détresse, *n.f.,* distress, sorrow, grief, trouble. *J'eus pitié de sa —;* I took compassion on his sorrow.

détresser, *v.a.,* to unweave, to unplait.

détriment, *n.m.,* detriment; injury, prejudice; (geol.) remains. *Être au — de;* to be a detriment to.

détrition, *n.f.,* detrition.

détritus (-tûs). *n.m.,* detritus.

détroit, *n.m.,* (geog.) strait; sound, narrow.

détromper, *v.a.,* to undeceive.

se détromper, *v.r.,* to be undeceived; to undeceive one's self.

détrônement (dé-trô-n-män), *n.m.,* dethronement.

détrôner. *v a.,* to dethrone.

détrôneur. *n.m.,* dethroner.

détrousser, *v.a.,* to untuck, to let down; to rifle, to rob. *— les voyageurs;* to plunder travellers.

détrousseur, *n.m.,* highwayman.

détruire (détruisant, détruit), *v.a,* to destroy, to ruin, to exterminate, to subvert, to do away with, to break up. *— une ville de fond en comble;* to raze a town to the ground. *— une armée;* to overthrow an army. *— les animaux nuisibles;* to exterminate noxious animals. *— la santé,* to ruin the health. *— radicalement;* to eradicate.

se détruire, *v.r.,* to fall to ruin, to decay; to destroy each other, to neutralize one another; to destroy one's self.

dette. *n.f.,* debt; score; obligation. *— hypothécaire;* debt upon mortgage. *—s actives;* money owing to us. assets. *—s passives;* debts, liabilities. *—s criardes;* petty debts. Contracter, faire, des *—s;* to contract debts, to run into debt.

Être accablé, perdu, de —s; to be deeply in debt.

*****deuil,** *n.m.,* mourning, grief, sorrow; black clothes, black; mourners; time of mourning. *Habit de —;* mourning clothes. *Grand ~:*

deep mourning. *Petit —;* half mourning. *Demi —;* half mourning. *Personne qui mène le —;* chief mourner. *Voiture de —;* mourning-coach. *Suivre le —;* to be one of the mourners. *Porter le —, être en —;* to be in mourning. *Prendre le —;* to go into mourning. *Faire son — d'une chose;* to make up one's mind to the loss of a thing.

deutéro-canonique, *adj.,* deuterocanonical.

deutéronome, *n.m.,* Deuteronomy.

deux, *adj.,* two, second. *— à —;* two by two. *— fois;* twice. *Personne qui mène le —;* much, twice as many. *De — jours en — jours;* every two days. *De — jours l'un;* every other day. *Regarder quelqu'un entre — yeux;* to stare at one. *Piquer des —;* to clap spurs to one's horse. *Tous —;* both, both together. *Tous les —;* both. *Henri —;* Henry the second. *N'en faire ni un ni —;* to decide at once.

deux, *n.m.,* two; second; (cards, dice—*cartes, dés*) deuce. *Le — du mois;* the second of the month. *On peut faire cela à —;* two can play at that game.

deuxième (deu-zièm), *adj.,* second.

deuxièmement (-zièm-män), *adv.,* secondly.

deux-points, *n.m.* (—), (gram.) colon.

déva, *n.m.,* name of the gods in Indian religion; of evil spirits in Parsee religion.

⊙dévaler, *v.a.,* to let down; to descend, to go or come down. *— les degrés;* to go down the stairs. *— du vin à la cave;* to let wine down into the cellar.

⊙dévaler, *v.n.,* to descend, to go down, to come down.

dévaliser, *v.a.,* to rifle, to strip, to rob, to plunder.

devancer, *v.a.,* to precede, to go before; to get before, to outrun, to outwalk, to outstrip; to take the place of; to have the precedence; to be beforehand, to forestall; to anticipate; to go beyond, to surpass. *Il a devancé le courrier;* he has left the courier behind. *— à cheval;* to outride. *Son génie a devancé son siècle;* his genius was beyond his century. *J'allais vous voir, mais vous m'avez devancé;* I was going to see you, but you are beforehand with me.

devanci-er, *n.m.,* **-ère,** *n.f.,* predecessor; *pl.,* ancestors, forefathers.

devant, *prep.,* before; in front of, over against, opposite to; (nav.) ahead of. *Mettez cela — le feu;* put that before the fire. *Regarder — soi;* to look before one's self. *Ôtez-vous de mon jour;* get out of my light. *Ôtez-vous de moi;* stand out of my sight. *Ils passent par — chez nous;* they pass before our door. *Il marchait — moi;* he walked before me. *Quand il fut — ses juges;* when he was in the presence of his judges. *Par — notaire;* in the presence of a notary.

devant, *adv.,* before; (nav.) ahead. *Passez —;* go before. *Le train de — d'une voiture;* the forewheels of a coach. *Les jambes de —;* the forelegs. *Sens — derrière;* hind part foremost.

devant, *n.m.,* front, the fore-part. *Il est logé sur le —;* he lodges in the front. *Un — de cheminée;* a chimney-board. *Prendre le —;* to set out before; to get before. *Prendre les —s;* to forestall. *Aller, venir, envoyer, au — de quelqu'un;* to go, to come, to send, to meet any one. *Aller au — d'une chose;* to prevent a thing. *Aller au — des désirs de quelqu'un;* to anticipate any one's desires. *Ci —;* before, formerly, heretofore, late.

devantier (-tié), *n.m.,* (fam., l.u.) apron.

devantière (-ti-èr), *n.f.,* riding petticoat.

devanture. *n.f.,* front (of buildings—*d bâtiments*). *La — d'une boutique:* a shop-front.

dévastat-eur, *n.m.*, **-rice**, *n.f.*, destroyer, despoiler, desolater, ravager.

dévastat-eur, **-rice**, *adj.*, devastating, desolating. destructive.

dévastation, *n.f.*, devastation; ravage, havoc.

dévaster, *v.a.*, to devastate, to lay waste, to desolate, to make desolate, to spoil, to ravage.

développable, *adj.*, susceptible of development.

développante (dév-lo-pant), *n.f.*, (geom.) evolvent; involute.

développée, *n.f.*, (geom.) evolute.

développement (dév-lop-màn), *n.m.*, unfolding, opening; development; display; clearing up; (geom.) evolution.

développer (dév-lo-pé), *v.a.*, to open. to unwrap, to unfold; to develop, to expand; to display, to expound, to elucidate, to lay open, to explain; to clear up, to unravel; (arch.) to trace upon a plan. *— le plan d'un ouvrage;* to display the plan of a work. *— un système;* to expound a system.

se **développer**, *v.r.*, to expand; to unfold itself, to display itself, to be unfolded or displayed; to be cleared up, to be unravelled; to extend itself, to spread out, to stretch out or forth, to be stretched out. *Les bourgeons commencent à se —;* the buds are beginning to expand. *Cet enfant se développe;* that child is growing. *La raison se développe;* reason displays itself.

devenir (dé-vnir), *v.n.*, to become, to grow, to get, to turn; to become of, to come to. *— un enfant sage;* to grow a good child. *— honnête homme;* to become an honest man. *— homme de bien;* to grow a good man. *Ces fruits deviennent rouges en mûrissant;* those fruits grow red when ripening. *Cela commence à — fatigant;* that begins to grow tiresome. *— à rien;* to come to nothing. *Que deviendrai-je?* what will become of me? *Qu'est devenu votre frère?* what has become of your brother? *Je ne sais ce qu'il est devenu;* I don't know what has become of him. *Que voulez-vous —?* what profession do you intend to follow, what do you intend to be? *Je ne sais plus que —;* I don't know which way to turn myself. *Faire — fou;* to drive one mad.

déventer, *v.a.*, (nav.) to take the wind out (of the sails of a vessel—*des voiles d'un navire*).

dévergondage, *n.m.*, unbounded licentiousness, shameless way of life; barefaced impudence; dissoluteness.

dévergondé, -e, *n.* and *adj.*, rake; harlot; brazen-faced, lewd, shameless, impudent.

dévergondement, *n.m.*, *V.* **dévergondage**.

dévergonder, *v.a.*, to render shamelessly licentious, to render dissolute.

se **dévergonder**, *v.r.*, to become shamelessly dissolute and licentious; to lose all feeling of shame.

déverguer (-ghé), *v.a.*, to unbend the sails from the yards.

***déverrouiller**, *v.a.*, to unbolt.

devers, *prep.*, ⊙towards, about, near. *Par —;* in one's possession; (jur.) before. *Il vient de — ces pays-là;* he comes from somewhere about those places. *Il a les papiers par — lui;* he is possessed of the papers.

dévers, -e, *adj.*, (arts) bending, jutting out, leaning. *Ce mur est —;* that wall juts out.

dévers, *n.m.*, (tech.) inclination. *Marquer un bois suivant son —;* to mould timber according to its inclination.

déverser, *v.n.*, to bend, to lean, to jut out. *Ce mur déverse;* that wall leans.

déverser, *v.a.*, to bend, to incline; to throw, to cast; to divert (of water—*des eaux*). *— une pièce de bois;* to bend a piece of wood. *— le*

mépris; to throw contempt (upon one—*sur quelqu'un*). *Se —*, *v.r.*, to fall into (of rivers, canals, &c.—*des rivières, des canaux, &c.*).

déversoir, *n.m.*, wear (dam of a river—*barrage de rivière*).

dévêtir, *v.a.*, to undress, to take off the clothes of; (jur.) to divest.

se **dévêtir**, *v.r.*, to take off one's clothes, to undress, to strip, to leave off part of one's clothes; to give up, to divest one's self. *Se — d'un héritage;* to give up an inheritance.

dévêtissement (-tis-màn), *n.m.*, (jur.) giving up, devesting.

déviation, *n.f.*, deviation.

dévidage, *n.m.*, winding (into a skein—*en écheveaux*).

dévider, *v.a.*, to wind (into skeins—*en écheveaux*).

dévideu-r, *n.m.*, **-se**, *n.f.*, winder.

dévidoir, *n.m.*, reel, skein-winder.

dévier, *v.n.*, to swerve; to deviate.

se **dévier**, *v.r.*, to deviate, to swerve. *— de son chemin;* to deviate from one's road. *— de la bonne route;* to deviate from the right way.

devin, *n.m.*, **-eresse**, *n.f.*, diviner, augur, soothsayer.

deviner, *v.a.*, to divine, to foretell, to predict; to guess, to guess at. *Devinez ce que j'ai fait;* guess what I have done. *Cela se devine aisément;* it is easy to divine that. *— une énigme;* to guess an enigma. *En devinant;* at a guess.

devineu-r, *n.m.*, **-se**, *n.f.*, guesser.

⊙**devis**, *n.m.*, talk, chat.

devis, *n.m.*, (com.) estimate. *Donner un —;* to give in an estimate.

. dévisager, *v.a.*, to disfigure, to scratch the face of; (pop.) to stare at any one rudely or threateningly.

se **dévisager**, *v.r.*, to disfigure one another; to scratch each other's faces; (pop.) to stare at each other rudely or threateningly.

devise, *n.f.*, devise, emblem; motto, posy. *La — d'une bague;* the posy of a ring.

deviser, *v.n.*, (fam.) to chat, to talk.

dévisser, *v.a.*, to unscrew.

dévoiement (dé-voa-màn), *n.m.*, looseness, relaxation; (arch.) inclination, slope (of chimney-flues, pipes—*de tuyaux de cheminées, &c.*).

dévoilement (-voal-màn), *n.m.*, unveiling.

dévoiler, *v.a.*, to unveil; to discover, to uncover; to unravel.

se **dévoiler**, *v.r.*, to unveil one's self, to be unveiled, to be disclosed, to be revealed.

dévoîment, *n.m.*, *V.* **dévoiement**.

devoir, *n.m.*, duty; task, exercise. *S'acquitter de son —;* to perform one's duty. *Être à son —;* to be at one's post. *Rentrer dans son —;* to return to one's duty. *— pascal;* the receiving the communion at Easter. *—s seigneuriaux;* manorial fees. *Tenir quelqu'un dans le —;* to keep one to his good behaviour. *Se mettre en — de faire une chose;* to set about doing a thing. *J'irai vous rendre mes —s;* I shall go and pay my respects to you. *Les derniers —s;* funeral rites.

devoir, *v.a.*, to owe, to be in debt; to be bound to. *— une somme d'argent à quelqu'un;* to owe a sum of money to any one. *Il doit partir dans peu de jours;* he is to set out in a few days. *Je dois parler sur ce sujet;* I am to speak about that subject. *Je lui dois tous mes maux;* I owe all my misfortunes to him. *Il ne devrait pas abandonner ses parents;* he ought not to abandon his parents. *Vous devriez vous conduire autrement;* you should behave yourself otherwise. *Nous devons obéir aux lois;* we must obey the laws. *La campagne doit être belle main-*

tenant; the country must be beautiful now. *Il devait partir ce matin;* he was to set out this morning. *Tous les hommes doivent mourir;* all men must die.

se devoir, *v.r.,* to owe one's self : to owe it to one's self. — *à sa patrie, à sa famille;* to owe one's self to one's country, to one's family. *On se doit d'être honorable;* a man owes it to himself to be honourable.

dévole, *n.f.,* having no trick (at cards—*aux cartes*).

dévoler, *v.n.* (cards—*aux cartes*), to lose all the tricks.

dévolu, -e, *adj.,* devolved, escheated. *Terre —e à la couronne;* an escheat. *Procès — à la cour;* cause devolved to the court.

dévolu, *n.m.,* (ecc.) devolution, lapse of right; claim, choice. *Un bénéfice tombé en — ;* a benefice fallen into lapse of right. *Une dame de la cour jeta un — sur lui;* a lady of the court laid a claim to him.

dévolutaire. *n.m.,* (ecc.) one who has obtained a benefice fallen into lapse of right.

dévolutif, -ve, *adj.,* (jur.) which causes a thing to pass from one to another person.

dévolution, *n.f.,* (jur.) devolution; escheat.

dévonien, -ne, *adj.,* (geol.) devonian.

dévorant, -e, *adj.,* devouring; ravenous; consuming; wasting. *Estomac, appétit,—;* ravenous hunger, ravenous appetite. *Un mal —; a* wasting disease. *Soif —e;* burning thirst. *Climat —;* wasting climate.

dévorateur, *n.m.,* devourer, destroyer.

dévorer, *v.a.,* to devour; to eat up; to prey upon, to destroy, to suppress, to squander, to consume; to gaze at eagerly ; to pore over ; to swallow, to conquer, to master; to pocket. *La faim le dévore;* he is almost dying with hunger. *Il a dévoré tout son bien;* he has squandered away all his fortune. *Il est dévoré d'ambition;* he is consumed with ambition. — *sa douleur;* to suppress one's sorrow. — *un affront;* to brook or pocket an affront. — *les livres;* to read over books hastily and greedily. — *quelqu'un des yeux;* to gaze upon, to stare at, any one.

dévoreu-r, *n.m.,* **-se,** *n.f.,* devourer, glutton. — *de livres;* book-worm.

dévot, -e, *adj.,* devout, godly, pious, holy; saintly. *Avoir l'air —;* to have a sanctified look.

dévot, *n m.* **-e,** *n.f.,* devout person; (b.s.) devotee, saint. *Ne vous y fiez pas, c'est un faux —;* put no trust in him, he is a devotee.

dévotement (dé-vot-mãn), *adv.,* devoutly, piously.

⊙**dévotieusement** (-ci-eu-), *adv.,* devotionally.

dévotieux, -se, (-ci-), *adj.,* devout.

dévotion, *n.f.,* devotion; godliness; disposal; devoutness; devotedness. *Être en —;* to be at one's devotion. *Être dans la —;* to be à devotee. *Faire ses —s;* to perform one's devotions ; to receive the communion. *Tout ce qu'il a est à ma —;* all he has is at my disposal.

dévouement (dé-voo-mãn), *n m.,* devotion, devotedness.

dévouer, *v.a.,* to devote; to dedicate; to consign. *Il lui est entierement dévoué;* he is entirely devoted to him. — *quelqu'un au mépris;* to consign any one to contempt.

se dévouer, *v.r.,* to devote one's self, to dedicate one's self. *Se — à la patrie;* to devote one's self to one's country.

dévoyé, *n.m.,* stray sheep (out of the way of salvation—*hors de la voie du salut*).

dévoyer, *v.a.,* to mislead; (arch.) to place obliquely; to cause a looseness (in the bowels—*dévoiement*).

se dévoyer, *v.r.,* ○ to lose one's way; (arch.) to be placed obliquely; (rel.) to go astray. *Il s'est devoyé du chemin de la vérité;* he has gone out of the way of salvation.

dextérité, *n.f.,* dexterity, adroitness, cleverness, skill.

dextre. *adj.,* right-handed; (her.) dexterous.

○**dextre.** *n.f.,* the right hand.

○**dextrement,** *adv.,* dexterously.

dextrine, *n.f.,* (chem.) dextrine.

dey. *n.m.,* dey.

dia ! *int.,* hoi (to make horses turn to the left —*pour faire tourner les chevaux à gauche*). *Il n'entend ni à — ni à hurhau;* there is no making him hear reason. *L'un tire à — et l'autre à hurhau;* they pull different ways.

diabète, *n.m.,* (med.) diabetes.

diabétique, *adj.,* diabetic. —, *n.m.f.,* one suffering with diabetes.

diable (diàbl). *n.m.,* devil; hell; wild child; deuce; truck, drag. *Un ragoût à la —; a* wretchedly bad dish. *Les —s sont déchainés;* hell has broken loose. *Va au —;* go to the devil. *Un bon —;* a good-natured fellow. *Un méchant —;* a mischievous dog. *Un pauvre —;* a poor wretch. *Le — s'en mêle;* the devil is in it. *Le — l'emporte;* the devil take you. *Quel — d'homme est-ce là?* what devil of a fellow is this? *C'est le —;* there's the devil of it. *C'est une — d'affaire;* it is a devilishly bad affair. *Cela ne vaut pas le —;* that is not worth a fig. *Il a le — au corps;* the devil is in him. *Brûler une chandelle au —;* to hold a candle to the devil. *Faire le — contre quelqu'un;* to play the devil with any one. *Faire le — à quatre;* to play the devil. *Tirer le — par la queue;* to be hard up. *Il n'est pas si — qu'il est noir:* he is not so bad as he appears to be. *Au —!* the devil take it. *Allé au —;* gone to the devil. — *de mer;* seacormorant; sea-devil.

diable! *int.,* the devil, the deuce. *Comment —!* how the devil! *Que — avez-vous?* what the devil is the matter with you? *À quoi — s'amuse-t-il?* what the deuce is he about? *De quoi — se mêle-t-il?* why the deuce does he meddle with it?

diablement, *adv.,* devilishly. — *chaud;* devilishly hot.

diablerie, *n.f.,* witchcraft; jugglery; wildness (of children—*des enfants*); piece of devilry. *Il y a quelque — là-dessous;* there is some jugglery in all that.

diablesse, *n.f.,* shrew; she-devil. *Une bonne —;* a good-natured creature. *Une pauvre —;* a poor wretch.

○**diablezot!** *int.,* the devil ! *Vous conseillez de faire cela —!* devil take it, I am not such a fool as to do that.

diablotin, *n.m.,* imp. little devil; troublesome imp; chocolate-lozenge.

diabolique, *adj.,* diabolical, devilish.

diaboliquement (-lik-mãn), *adv.,* diabolically, devilishly.

diachylon, or **diachylum,** *n.m.,* diachylon, diachylum.

diaco, *n.m.,* deacon or chaplain in the order of Malta.

diacode. *n.m.,* diacodium.

diacommatique, *n.f.,* (mus.) the raising of a note to lead to a transition.

diaconal, -e. *adj.,* diaconal.

diaconat, *n.m.,* diaconate, deaconry, deaconship.

diaconesse. *n.f.,* deaconess.

diaconie, *n.f.,* diaconia, deaconry, deaconship.

diacoustique, *n.f.,* diacoustics.

diacre. *n.m.,* deacon.

diadelphie, *n.f.,* (bot.) diadelphia.

diadelphique, *adj.*, (bot.) diadelphian, diadelphic.

diadème. *n.m.*, diadem.

diagnostic, *n.m.*, (med.) diagnostic.

diagnostique. *adj.*, (med.) diagnostic.

diagnostiquer, *v.a.*, to ascertain the diagnostics of a disease.

diagonal. -**e**, *adj.*, diagonal.

diagonale. *n.f.*, (geom.) diagonal.

diagonalement (-nal-mân), *adv.*, diagonally.

diagramme, *n.m.*, (geom.) diagram.

diagraphe. *n.m.*, diagraph.

dialecte. *n.m.*, dialect.

dialecticien (-in), *n m*, dialectician.

dialectique. *n.f.*, dialectics, logic.

dialectique. *adj.*, dialectic, dialectical.

dialectiquement (-tik-mân), *adv.*, dialectically.

dialogique, *adj.*, dialogistic, dialogistical.

dialogisme, *n.m.*, dialogism.

dialogiste, *n.m.*, writer of dialogues, dialogist.

dialogue (-log), *n.m.*, dialogue.

dialoguer (-ghé), *v.a.*, to make several persons speak in character ; (mus.) to make two or more voices, or two or more instruments, reply to each other ; to put in the form of a dialogue.

dialoguer (-ghé), *v.n.*, to compose dialogues ; to speak, to talk ; to converse familiarly with, to chat with.

diamant, *n.m.*, diamond ; (nav.) crown, throat (of anchors—*d'ancre*) ; (horl.) jewel. — *taillé*; cut diamond. — *brut*; rough diamond. — *de nature*; diamond unfit for the wheel. —*s de la couronne*; crown jewels. — *de première eau*; diamond of the first water *Monter un —*; to set a diamond. — *de vitrier*; glazier's diamond.

diamantaire, *n.m.*, diamond-cutter.

diamétral, -**e**, *adj.*, diametrical.

diamétralement (-tral-mân), *adv.*, diametrically. *Sentiments — opposés*; sentiments diametrically opposite to each other.

diamètre, *n.m.*, diameter. *Demi-diamètre*; semi-diameter.

diandrie, *n.f.*, (bot.) diandria.

diandrique, *adj.*, (bot.) having two stamens.

diane, *n.f.*, (nav.) morning-gun ; (milit.) reveille, the beat of drum at daybreak.

diantre, *n m.*, the deuce. *Au — soit l'imbécile!* the deuce take the fool !

diantre, *int.*, the deuce ! the dickens !

diapalme, *n.m.*, (pharm.) a kind of ointment.

diapason, *n.m.*, (mus.) pitch, diapason ; tuning-fork.

diapédèse, *n.m.*, (med) deapedesis.

diaphane, *adj.*, diaphanic, diaphanous, transparent.

diaphanéité, *n.f.*, diaphaneity, transparency.

diaphorèse, *n.f.*, (med.) diaphoresis.

diaphorétique. *adj.*, (med.) diaphoretic.

diaphragmatique, *adj.*, (anat.) diaphragmatic.

diaphragme, *n.m.*, diaphragm, midriff ; partition with an opening through it.

diaphragmite, *n.f.*, (med.) diaphragmatitis.

diaphtore, *n.f.*, (med.) corruption of the aliments in the stomach ; corruption of the fœtus in the womb.

diapré, -**e**, *adj.*, diapered, variegated, diversified. *Un nez —*; a nose covered with red pimples.

diaprer. *v.a.*, to variegate, to diaper.

se diaprer, *v.r.*, to become diapered, to become variegated.

diaprun, *n.m.*, (pharm.) lenitive electuary, confection of senna.

diaprure, *n.f.*, variégation.

diarrhée, *n.f.*, (med.) diarrhœa.

diarthrose, *n.f.*, (anat.) diarthrosis.

diascordium (-om), *n.m.*, (pharm.) diascordium.

diastase, *n.f.*, (surg.) diastasis.

diastole. *n.f.*, (physiology) diastole.

diastrophie. *n.f.*, (surg.) the displacing of the muscles, with or without luxation.

diastyle, *n.m.*, (arch.) diastyle.

diatessaron, *n.m.*, (mus.) diatessaron.

diathèse, *n.f.*, (med.) diathesis.

diatonique, *adj.*, (mus.) diatonic.

diatoniquement, *adv.*, in a diatonic scale, diatonically.

diatragacanthe, *n.m.*, (pharm.) tragacanth powder.

diatribe, *n.f.*, sharp criticism, dissertation, castigation, diatribe.

dicacité, *n.f.*, waggery, causticity.

dichorée (-ko-), *n.m.*, (Latin, Grec. poet.) dichoreus, dichoree.

dichotome (-ko-), *adj.*, (bot.) dichotomous.

dichotomie (-ko-), *n.f.*, (astron.) dichotomy.

dicotylédone, *n.f.*, (bot.) dicotyledon.

dicotylédone, *adj.*, (bot.) dicotyledonous.

dictame, *n.m.*, (bot.) dittany. — *blanc*; fraxinella, bastard dittany. — *faux*; bastard dittany. *Origan —, — de Crète*; dittany of Crete ; Cretan marum.

dictamen (-mèn), *n.m.*, dictate, suggestion, consciousness.

dictateur, *n.m.*, dictator.

dictatorial, -**e**, *adj.*, dictatorial.

dictature, *n.f.*, dictatorship.

dictée, *n.f.*, act of dictating, dictation. *Écrire sous la —*; to write from dictation.

dicter, *v.a.*, to dictate, to indite ; to prompt ; to suggest ; to prescribe. *La raison nous dicte cela*; reason prescribes that.

diction, *n.f.*, diction, elocution, phraseology, style ; delivery.

dictionnaire, *n.m.*, dictionary. — *vivant*, walking dictionary. *À coups de —*; by constant reference to the dictionary. — *de prononciation*; pronouncing dictionary. — *de mots obscurs*; glossary. — *de géographie*; geographical dictionary, gazetteer. — *de marine*; dictionary of naval terms.

dicton, *n.m.*, saying, common saying, byword, saw, proverb ; (l.u.) sarcasm.

dictum (-tom), *n.m.*, (jur.) purview of an act or decree.

didactique, *adj.*, didactic.

didactique, *n.m.*, didactic order ; didactic language.

didactique, *n.f.*, didactic art.

didactiquement, *adv.*, didactically.

didactyle, *adj.*, didactylous.

didascalie, *n.f.*, (antiq.) among the Greeks, directions given by the author of a play to the actors ; the argument of a play.

dideau, *n.m.*, crossing-net.

didelphe, *n.m.* and *adj.*, (zool.) didelphys ; didelphyc.

didyme, *adj.*, (bot.) didymous.

didynamie, *n.f.*, (bot.) didynamia.

dièdre, *adj.*, (geom.) dihedral.

diel, *n.m.*, a kind of French fuller's earth.

diérèse, *n.f.*, (gram.) diæresis.

dièse, *n.m.*, (mus.) diesis, sharp.

diésé, -**e**, *adj.*, (mus.) marked with a diesis, sharp.

diéser, *v.a.*, (mus.) to mark a note to be played sharp; to play a note sharp.

diète, *n.f.*, diet, regimen; diet (an assembly of the states of Germany—*assemblée des états d'Allemagne*). *Faire* —; to diet one's self, to live moderately.

diététique, *adj.*, (med.) dietetical.

diététique, *n.f.*, (med.) dietetics.

diététiste, *n.m.*, (med.) dieter.

diétine, *n.f.*, local diet; cantonal convention. dietine.

dieu, *n.m.*, God. — *tout-puissant*; Almighty God. *Le* — *des armées*, the Lord of Hosts. *Le bon* — : God Almighty; the host. *Croire en* —; to believe in God. *Porter le bon* — *à un malade*; to carry the host to a sick person. *La Fête-Dieu*: Corpus Christi-day. *Un homme de* — : a godly man. *Un Hôtel-Dieu* (—*s* —); an hospital for sick persons. — *vous bénisse*: God bless you. *S'il plaît à* —, *avec l'aide de* —, — *aidant*; God willing, God helping. — *le veuille, plût à* —; God grant it. would to God — *m'en garde*, — *m'en préserve, à* — *ne plaise*; God forbid. — *merci, grâces à* — ; thank God. *Bon* — ! *mon* —! good God! good heavens! *Jurer ses grands dieux*: to swear by all that is sacred. *Au nom de* — ; in God's name. *Pour l'amour de* — ; for God's sake. *Les dieux du paganisme*; the heathen gods. — ! *grand* — ! good God !

dieudonné, *n.m.*, heaven-sent.

diffamant. -e, *adj.*, defamatory.

diffamat-eur, *n.m.*, -**rice**, *n.f.*, defamer, detractor, slanderer, libeller, calumniator.

diffamation, *n.f.*, defamation, aspersion, calumny, slandering, libelling, traducing. — *verbale*, (jur.) slander.

diffamatoire, *adj.*, defamatory, libellous, slanderous.

diffamer, *v.a.*, to defame, to slander, to traduce.

différemment (di-fé-ra-män), *adv.*, differently.

différence, *n.f.*, odds; difference; diversity, disproportion, contrast, disparity. — *marquée*; material difference. — *notable*; wide difference. — *du tirant d'eau*, (nav.) difference in the draught of water.

différencier. *v.a.*, to make a difference, to distinguish; (math.) to differentiate.

différend, *n.m.*, difference, quarrel, dispute; difference (of value—*de valeur*). *Avoir un* — *avec quelqu'un*; to be at variance with any one. *Partager le* — ; to split the difference.

différent. -e, *adj*, different, dissimilar, various, divers, opposite, contrary. — *l'un de l'autre*, unlike. *À des degrés* —*s*; to different degrees. *Il est souvent* — *de lui-même*; he often differs from himself.

différentiel. -**le**, *adj.*, (math.) differential. *Calcul* —, differential calculus.

différentielle, *n.f.*, (math.) differential; fluxion.

différentier, *v.a.*, (math.) to differentiate.

différer, *v.a.*, to defer, to delay, to put off, to postpone, to adjourn. *Ce qui est différé n'est pas perdu*; what is put off is not lost.

différer, *v.n.*, to defer, to put off, to delay.

différer. *v.n*, to differ, to be unlike, to be different; to disagree.

difficile. *adj.*, difficult, hard; nice; particular; wilful (of horses—*des chevaux*). *Un homme* — ; a man hard to please. *Temps* —*s*; hard times. *De* — *accès*, hard to come at. *Il est* — *sur les aliments*. he is nice in his eating. *Faire le* — ; to be difficult to please.

difficilement (-sil-män), *adv.*, with difficulty, with much ado, with great pains, not easily.

difficulté. *n.f.*, difficulty; objection; obstacle,

hindrance, impediment; cross. rub; misunderstanding, quarrel. *Cela ne souffre point de* — ; that admits of no difficulty. — *de respirer*; shortness of breath. *Faire des* —*s sur quelque chose*; to raise objections against any thing. *Faire* — *de quelque chose*; to scruple about any thing. *Trancher la* — : to decide peremptorily. *Avoir des* —*s*, to have crosses. *Il y a entre eux quelque* — ; there is some difference between them. *Sans* — : undoubtedly, without doubt.

difficultueu-x, **-se**, *adj.*, that raises or starts difficulties.

diffluence, *n.f.*, diffluence.

diffluent. -e, *adj.*, diffluent.

diffluer, *v.n.*, to spread diffusely.

difforme, *adj.*, deformed, ill-favoured, misshapen, ugly.

difformer, *v.a.*, to deform, to spoil; to deface (coins, money—*des monnaies*).

difformité, *n.f.*, deformity. *La* — *du vice*, the ugliness of vice.

diffraction, *n.f.*, (opt.) diffraction.

diffus, -e, *adj.*, diffuse, prolix, wordy, verbose, long-winded.

diffusément, *adv.*, diffusely, verbosely, wordily.

diffusion, *n.f.*, diffusion; diffusiveness; prolixity, vagueness, wordiness, verbosity. — *de lumière*; spreading of light. — *de style*; prolixity of style.

digamma, *n.m.* (—), (Grec. gram.) digamma.

digastrique, *adj.*, (anat.) digastric.

digérer, *v.a.*, to digest; to examine, to discuss, to scan, to set in order ; to bear, to brook, to put up with, to suffer. — *de la viande*: to digest meat. *Non digéré*; undigested. *Bien* — *une chose dans son esprit*; to ruminate well upon a thing. *Il ne peut* — *cet affront*; he cannot brook that affront.

digérer, *v.n.*, (chem.) to digest.

digeste, *n.m.*, digest.

digesteur, *n.m.*, (chem.) digester.

digesti-f. **-ve**, *adj.*, digestive.

digestif. *n.m.*, (med.) digestive.

digestion (-tion), *n.f.*, digestion. *Cela aide à la* — : that aids digestion. *Cette entreprise est de dure* — ; this is a laborious enterprise.

digital. -e, *adj.*, digital.

digitale. *n.f.*, (bot.) fox-glove, digitalis.

digitaline, *n.f.*, (chem.) digitaline.

digité. -e, *adj.*, (bot.) digitated, finger-like, fingered.

digitigrade, *n.m.*, (mam.) digitigrade.

diglyphe. *n.m.*, (arch.) diglyph.

****digne**, *adj.*, deserving, worthy. *Un* — *homme*, a worthy man. *Un* — *magistrat*; an upright magistrate. — *de foi*; deserving of credit. *Cela est* — *de lui*; that's just like him. *Il était* — *d'un meilleur sort*; he deserved a better fate.

****dignement**. *adv.*, worthily, deservedly, justly, according to one's deserts; handsomely. *Il s'acquitte* — *de sa charge*, he performs the duties of his office in a worthy manner.

****dignitaire**, *n.m.*, dignitary.

****dignité**, *n.f.*, dignity; stateliness. — *d'un prince*, princeliness. *Il soutient la* — *de son rang*; he maintains the dignity of his station. *Être constitué en* — ; to be raised to power. *Parvenir aux* —*s*; to attain dignity.

digresser, *v.n.*, to depart from the main subject, to digress.

digressi-f, **-ve**, *adj.*, digressive.

digression, *n.f.*, digression. *Faire des* —*s*; to ramble.

digressivement, *adv.*, digressively.

digue (dig), *n.f.*, dike, dam, mound, embankment, bank; bound, obstacle; embankment.

diguement (dig-män), *n.m.*, causeway (ports'

diguer (-ghé), *v.a.*, to dam, to dike; to spur (a horse—*un cheval*).

digyne, *adj.*, (bot.) digynous, having two pistils.

digynie. *n.f.*, (bot.) digynia.

dilacération, *n.f.*, tearing *or* rending, dilaceration, laceration.

dilacérer, *v.a.*, to dilacerate, to lacerate, to tear off *or* to pieces.

⊙**dilaniat-eur**, **-rice**, *adj.*, dilaniating, dilacerating, rending.

dilapidat-eur. *n.m.*, **-rice**, *n.f.*, dilapidator; one who wastes property.

dilapidat-eur, **-rice**, *adj.*, wasteful, extravagant.

dilapidation, *n.f.*, dilapidation, waste.

dilapider, *v.a.*, to dilapidate, to spend inconsiderately, to waste.

dilatabilité. *n.f.*, (phys.) dilatability.

dilatable, *adj.*, (phys.) dilatable.

dilatant, *n.m.*, (surg.) dilating body, agent, instrument.

dilatateur, *n.m.*, (surg.) dilator.

dilatation, *n.f.*, dilatation, expansion, distension; (surg.) enlargement. *La — d'une membrane*; the stretching of a membrane. *La — d'une plaie*; the dilatation of a sore.

dilatatoire, *n.m.* *V.* **dilatateur**.

dilater, *v.a.*, to dilate, to enlarge, to widen; to distend, to expand. *La joie dilate le cœur*; joy gladdens the heart.

se **dilater**, *v.a.*, to dilate, to be dilated; to be distended.

dilatoire. *adj.*, dilatory.

⊙**dilayer**, *v.a.* and *n.*, to postpone, to delay.

dilection, *n.f.*, love, charity.

dilemme (di-lem), *n.m.*, dilemma.

dilettante (di-let-tan-t), *n.m.* and *f.*, (*dilettanti*) dilettante.

dilettantisme (-lèt-tan-), *n.m.*, dilettanteism.

diligemment (-ja-mân), *adv.*, diligently, speedily, promptly.

diligence, *n.f.*, diligence, speed, despatch; diligence, stage-coach; (jur.) suit, proceedings; vigilance, care. *Bureau des —s*; coach-office. *Aller en —*; to go with speed; to go by coach. *User de —*; to use despatch. *À la — d'un tel*; (jur.) at the suit of such a one.

diligent, **-e**, *adj.*, diligent, quick; sedulous, assiduous, mindful.

diligenter, *v.a.*, to hasten, to forward, to push on, to be quick.

se **diligenter**, *v.r.*, to make haste, to use diligence.

diligenter, *v.n.*, to hasten, to be quick.

diluer, *v.a.*, to dilute.

dilution, *n.f.*, dilution.

diluvien, **-ne** (-in,-ène), *adj.*, diluvian.

diluvium (-viome), *n.m.*, (geol.) diluvium.

dimanche, *n.m.*, Sunday, Sabbath, the Lord's-day. *Le — de Pâques*; Easter Sunday. *Le — des Rameaux*; Palm Sunday. *Le — gras*; Shrove Sunday

dime. *n.f.*, tithe.

dimension, *n.f.*, dimension.

dîmer, *v.a.*, to tithe, to levy tithes. *— dans un champ*; to tithe a field. *— au pressoir*; to tithe wine in the press.

dîmer, *v.n.*, to have a right to tithe.

dîmeur, *n.m.*, tithe-gatherer.

diminuer, *v.a.*, to diminish, to lessen, to shorten, to reduce, to retrench, to impair.

diminuer, *v.n.*, to diminish, to lessen, to decrease, to abate.

diminuti-f, **-ve**, *adj.*, diminutive.

diminutif, *n.m.*, diminutive.

diminution, *n.f.*, diminution; abridgment,

curtailing, reduction, abatement; diminishing, lessening. *— de dépense*; retrenchment in expenses. *— des figures*; (her.) rebatement of figures.

dimissoire. *n.m.*, (ecc.) letter dimissory.

dimissorial, **-e**, *adj.*, (ecc.) dimissory.

dinanderie (di-nan-dri), *n.f.*, brass wares.

dinandier, *n.m.*, brasier.

dinatoire, *adj.*, relating to dinner.

dinde, *n.f.*, turkey-hen.

dindon, *n.m.*, turkey-cock; (person—*personne*) goose. *C'est un —*; he is a goose.

dindonneau, *n.m.*, young turkey.

dindonni-er, *n.m.*, **- ère**, *n.f.*, minder of turkeys.

dîné, *or* **dîner**, *n.m.*, dinner. *L'heure du —*; dinner-time.

dînée, *n.f.*, place where travellers stop to dine; dinner of travellers; price of the dinner of travellers.

dîner, *v.n.*, to dine. *Prier quelqu'un de —*; to ask any one to stay to dinner. *Prier à —*; to invite to dine.

dînette. *n.f.*, doll's dinner. *Faire la —*; to play at dinner.

dîneur, *n.m.*, diner; eater.

dinosaurien, *n.m.*, (foss.) deinosaurian.

dinotherium (-té-ri-ome), *n.m.* (*—s*), (foss.) dinotherium, deinotherium.

diocésain, **-e**, *adj.*, diocesan.

diocésain, *n.m.*, **-e**, *n.f.*, inhabitant of a diocese.

diocèse, *n.m.*, diocese

diœcie (di-é-si), *n.f.*, (bot.) diœcia.

dioïque. *adj.*, (bot.) diœcian.

dionée, *n.f.*, (bot.) dionæa, catch-fly plant.

dionysiaque, *adj.*, (antiq.) concerning Bacchus, of Bacchus.

dionysiaques, *or* **dionysies**, *n.f.pl.*, (antiq.) Dionysia.

dioptrique, *n.f.*, (opt.) dioptrics.

dioptrique, *adj.*, dioptrical.

diorama, *n.m.*, diorama.

diorite, *n.m.*, (geol.) green-stone.

diphtongue (-tong), *n.f.*, diphthong.

diploé, *n.m.*, (anat.) diploe.

diplomate, *n.m.*, diplomatist.

diplomatie, *n.f.*, diplomacy.

diplomatique, *n.f.*, diplomatics.

diplomatique. *adj.*, diplomatical.

diplomatiquement (-tik-mân), *adv.*, diplomatically.

diplomatiste, *n.m.*, diplomatist.

diplôme, *n.m.*, diploma.

diplopie, *n.f.*, double vision, diplopia.

dipode, *adj.*, having two feet or two fins.

diptère, *adj.*, (arch., ent.) dipteral.

diptère, *n.m.*, dipteral insect. *—s*; diptera.

diptyques, *n.m.pl.*, (antiq.) diptych, diptychum.

dire (disant, dit), *v.a.*, to tell, to say, to speak, to state, to write, to relate; to think; to believe; to express; to name. *— d'avance*; to say beforehand. *— entre les dents*; to mutter between one's teeth. *Dites votre avis*; give your opinion. *Dis-je*; said I. *On dit*; it is said. *— du bien ou du mal de quelqu'un*; to speak well or ill of any one. *— des injures à quelqu'un*; to call any one names. *— des duretés*; to say harsh things. *— quelque chose à l'oreille*; to whisper any thing in the ear. *Si le cœur vous en dit*; if you have a mind for it. *Le cœur vous en dit-il?* do you like it? *Cela va sans —*; that is understood, that goes without saying, of course, that is a matter of course. *C'est-à-dire*; that is to say. *Pour ainsi —*; if I may say so, *Ce n'est pas à*

— *que;* it does not follow that. *Est-ce à —que?* does it follow that? *Que veut — cela? qu'est-ce que cela veut — ?* what is the meaning of that? *— la messe;* to say mass. *Je ne sais que — de tout cela;* I do not know what to think of all that. *Faire — à quelqu'un;* to make any one say; to send word to any one. *Tout est dit;* all is over. *Cela ne dit rien;* that is nothing to the purpose. *Cela soit dit en passant;* but that by the way. *C'est tout — ;* it is saying all. *Cela vous plait à — ;* you are pleased to say so.

se **dire**, *v.r.*, to call one's self, to style one's self, to give one's self out as; to be called ; to be said.

dire, *n.m.*, what one says, saying, words ; (jur.) allegation. *Le — du défendeur;* the words of the defendant. *Au — de tout le monde;* according to what every body says. *Le bien-dire;* elegance of speech. *Se fier pour quelque chose au — des autres, d'autrui;* to take anything upon trust.

direct (di-rèkt), **-e**, *adj.*, direct, straight ; assessed (of taxes, in England—*des impôts, en Angleterre*). *En ligne —e;* in a straight line.

directe, *n.f.*, (feudal jur.*-loi féodale*) tenure in capite, lordship.

directement, *adv.*, directly, straightforwardly ; point-blank, home, in a direct or straightforward manner. *Aller — à son but;* to go directly to one's object. *— contraire;* quite contrary. *— en face;* just opposite.

direct-eur, *n.m.*, **-rice**, *n.f.*, director, manager, superintendent, overseer, conductor ; directress, conductress, directrix. *— de conscience;* spiritual director. *— de la monnaie;* master of the mint.

direction, *n.f.*, direction, management, directorship ; director's house or office; (math.) bearing ; (mining—*mines*) stretch ; bearing. *Avoir la —;* to preside. *— de créanciers;* meeting of creditors. *Biens en —;* goods placed under the direction of assignees.

directoire, *n.m.*, directory, rubric; guide; the supreme executive council of France in 1795.

directorat, *n.m.*, directorship.

directorial, **-e**, *adj.*, directorial.

dirigeant, **-e** (-jän,-t), *adj.*, directing, acting.

diriger, *v.a.*, to direct ; to guide, to conduct, to manage. *— une maison religieuse;* to govern a convent.

se **diriger**, *v.r.*, to direct one's steps, to go towards ; to make for ; to take pattern from ; to direct, to govern, one's self ; (nav.) to stand in.

dirimant, **-e**, *adj.*, (canon law—*loi canon*) invalidating. *Empêchement — ;* an impediment that invalidates a marriage.

discale, *n.f.*, (com.) tret, tare.

discaler, *v.n.*, (com.) to tare, to diminish.

⊙ **disceptation**, *n.f.*, disceptation, disputation, debate.

discernement, *n.m.*, distinction ; discernment, judgment, discerning. *Âge de — ;* years of discretion.

discerner, *v.a.*, to discern, to distinguish, to know, to discriminate. *— le vrai du faux;* to discern truth from untruth.

disciple, *n.m.*, disciple, pupil, scholar.

disciplinable, *adj.*, disciplinable, governable, tractable.

discipline, *n.f.*, discipline, education, instruction : scourge. *Donner la — ;* to chastise.

discipliner, *v.a.*, to discipline ; to chastise, to scourge.

se **discipliner**, *v.r.*, to be formed to discipline ; to scourge one's self.

discobole, *n.m.*, (antiq.) discobolus.

discoïde, *adj.*, (conch.) having the form of a quoit.

discontinu, **-e**, *adj.*, discontinuous.

discontinuation, *n.f.*, discontinuance, discontinuation.

discontinuer, *v.a.*, to discontinue, to interrupt, to leave off, to suspend, to give over.

discontinuer, *v.n.*, to discontinue, to cease, to leave off.

discontinuité, *n.f.*, discontinuity, discontinuance, discontinuation.

disconvenable, *adj.*, unsuitable, improper.

disconvenablement, *adv.*, improperly, unsuitably.

disconvenance, *n.f.*, incongruity, discrepancy, disagreement, unsuitableness ; dissimilarity, dissimilitude ; disproportion, difference, inequality.

disconvenir, *v.n.*, to deny, to disown. *Il ne disconvient pas du fait;* he does not deny the fact.

discord, *n.m.*, discord.

discord, **-e**, *adj.*, (mus.) out of tune, jarring.

discordance, *n.f.*, discordancy, disagreement, discrepancy; (mus.) inconsonancy; undulation.

discordant, **-e**, *adj.*, discordant, jarring, dissonant, harsh, out of tune ; untunable, tuneless, unmusical; disagreeing, inharmonious, incongruous.

discorde, *n.f.*, discord, disagreement, variance, disunion, dissension, strife. *Pomme de — ;* bone of contention.

discorder, *v.n.*, (mus.) to be out of tune, to be discordant, inconsonant ; to jar.

discoureu-r, *n.m.*, **-se**, *n.f.*, talker; babbler, chatterer, talkative man or woman. *Quel ennuyeux — !* what a chattering bore.

discourir, *v.n.*, to discourse, to descant on, to reason on.

discours, *n.m.*, discourse; speech. *Les parties du —;* the parts of speech. *— oratoire;* set speech. *— en l'air;* idle talking. *C'est un bon —;* it is a good speech. *Faire un —;* to make a speech, to deliver an address, an oration; (parliament—*parlement*) to be upon one's legs.

discourtois, **-e**, *adj.*, discourteous, unmannerly; uncivil.

discourtoisement, *adv.*, uncourteously.

discourtoisie, *n.f.*, discourtesy, unmannerliness, incivility.

discrédit, *n.m.*, discredit, disrepute, disesteem.

discréditer, *v.a.*, to discredit ; to bring into discredit, into disrepute ; to bring discredit on.

discr-et, **-ète**, *adj.*, discreet, considerate, cautious, prudent; wary, circumspect; reserved, secret, close; shy. *Tu veux faire le —;* you affect to be a close fellow. *Quantité —ète;* distinct, discrete, quantity.

discrètement, *adv.*, discreetly, cautiously, circumspectly, warily, prudently, reservedly.

discrétion, *n.f.*, circumspection, prudence ; discretion, reserve, wariness; reservedness, discreetness. *L'âge de — ;* years of discretion. *Agir, parler, avec — ;* to act, to speak warily. *Vivre à — ;* (milit.) to have free-quarters. *Se rendre à — ;* to surrender at discretion. *Se remettre à la — de quelqu'un;* to submit to the will of a person. *Avoir du pain à — ;* to have bread ad libitum.

discrétionnaire, *adj.*, discretionary, discretional.

discrétoire, *n.m.*, council-room (of certain religious communities—*de certaines communautés religieuses*) ; council.

discrimen (-mè-n), *n.m.*, (surg.) bandage for bleeding in the forehead.

disculpation, *n.f.*, disculpation.

disculper, v.a., to disculpate, to exculpate, to vindicate, to clear, to exonerate.

discursi-f. **-ve**, adj., discursive.

⊙**discussi-f**. **-ve**, adj., (med.) discutient.

discussion. n.f., discussion, debate; altercation, strife, wrangling, dispute; (jur.) seizure and sale (of the property of a debtor—des biens d'un débiteur) Faire une — de biens: to distrain, appraise, and expose for sale the goods of a debtor. Sans division ni —; jointly and severally.

discutable, adj., debatable, disputable.

discuter, v.a., to discuss, to debate, to argue; to examine, to argue, to canvass, to inquire into; to scan, to sift, to search into. — un point de droit; to discuss an article of law. — les biens d'un débiteur; to distrain, appraise, and expose for sale the goods of a debtor.

disert, **-e**, adj., copious, fluent.

disertement, adv., copiously, profusely, fluently, fully.

disette, n.f., scarcity, dearth, want; poverty, penury.

⊙**disetteu-x**, **-se**, adj., needy, necessitous.

diseu-r, n.m., **-se**, n.f., teller, speaker, talker. — de bonne aventure; fortune-teller. —de bons mots; jester. — de nouvelles; newsmonger. — de riens; idle talker. Un beau —; a fine talker.

disgrâce, n.f., disgrace, disfavour; misfortune, affliction, downfall.

disgracié, **-e**, part., out of favour. — de la nature; deformed, disfigured, ill-favoured.

disgracier, v.a., to disgrace, to put out of favour.

disgracieusement, adv., awkwardly, ungracefully, unhandsomely.

disgracieu-x, **-se**, adj., ungraceful, uncomely, uncouth, disgracious; disagreeable; unpleasant, awkward.

disgrégation, n.f., (opt.) disgregation; separation.

⊙**disgréger**, v.a., (opt.) to scatter, to separate, to disperse.

disjoindre, v.a., to disjoin, to disunite.

se **disjoindre**, v.r., to come apart or asunder.

disjoncti-f. **-ve**, adj., (gram.) disjunctive.

disjonction, n.f., disjunction, separation; (jur.) severance.

disjonctive, n.f., (gram.) disjunctive.

dislocation, n.f., dislocation, luxation. Il y a —; the bone is out of joint. La — d'une armée; the breaking up of an army.

disloquer, v.a., to dislocate, to disjoint, to put out of joint; to take to pieces (machine); (milit.) to break up (an army—une armée).

disparaître, v.n., to vanish; to vanish out of sight; to get out of the way; to disappear.

disparate, n.f., incongruity, dissimilarity.

disparate, adj., incongruous, dissimilar, disparate.

disparité, n.f., disparity, dissimilarity.

disparition, n.f., disappearance.

dispendieu-x, **-se**, adj., expensive; costly.

dispensaire, n.m., (med.) dispensatory, pharmacopœia; dispensary.

dispensat-eur, n.m., **-rice**, n.f., dispenser.

dispensation, n.f., dispensation, distribution.

dispense, n.f., dispensation, exemption, license, permission.

dispenser, v.a., to exempt; to dispense with; to dispense, to bestow. Dispensez-moi de faire cela; excuse me from doing that. Le soleil dispense à tous sa lumière; the sun dispenses his light to all.

se **dispenser**, v.r., to dispense with; to exempt one's self; to be distributed.

disperser, v.a., to disperse; to scatter, to dispel, to rout.

se **disperser**, v.r., to disperse; to be dispersed, to spread about, to be scattered, to dispel.

dispersion, n.f., dispersion, dispersing, scattering.

dispondée, n.m., (poet.) dispondee.

disponibilité, n.f., (jur.) power of disposal (of property—de biens); (milit.) state of being unattached. Être en —; (milit.) to be unattached.

disponible, adj., free, disposable, unoccupied, disengaged, vacant. Il n'y a pas une place —; there is not one place vacant.

dispos, adj. m., active, nimble, cheerful, well.

disposé, **-e**.part., disposed, inclined; ready; prepared. Un homme bien — pour quelqu'un; a man well disposed towards any one. Mal —; ill-disposed.

disposer, v.a., to dispose, to order, to lay out; to prepare, to make ready, to fit; to incline, to prevail upon.

se **disposer**, v.r., to dispose one's self, to be disposed; to get ready, to prepare; to array one's self.

disposer, v.n., to dispose of; to prescribe, to ordain, to order, to make over; (com.) to draw a bill. Vous pouvez — de moi; you may dispose of me. L'homme propose et Dieu dispose; man proposes and God disposes.

⊙**dispositi-f**, **-ve**, adj., preparatory.

dispositif, n.m., (jur.) purview (of an act, decree, &c.—d'une loi, d'un jugement, &c.). Le — d'un arrêt; the purview of a decree.

disposition, n.f., disposition, arrangement; order; provision; disposal; service; tendency; inclination, aptness; humour; mind, resolution; habit. Les — s d'une loi; the provisions of a law. — testamentaire; (jur.) devise. Il a des gens à sa —; he has people at his disposal. Il a de très bonnes —s pour vous; he is very well disposed towards you. Être en bonne —; to enjoy a good habit of body. Cela est à votre —; that is at your service

disproportion, n.f., disproportion.

disproportionné, **-e**, adj., disproportionate.

disproportionnel, **-le**, adj., disproportional.

disproportionnellement (-nèl-màn), adv., disproportionally.

disputable, adj., disputable, controvertible, contestable.

*****disputailler**, v n., to dispute frequently and about trifles

*****disputaillerie**, n.f., wrangling, idle dispute.

*****disputailleur**, n.m., idle disputer, wrangler.

disputant, n.m., disputant.

dispute, n.f., discussion, disputation, dispute, contest, wrangle, wrangling.

disputer, v.n., to discuss; to argue, to dispute; to contend, to contest, to wrangle. — contre quelqu'un; to dispute with-any one. Ils disputent ensemble; they quarrel. — sur un point de droit; to discuss a point in law. De quoi dispute-t-on? what is the matter in discussion? — de; to vie with each other in.

disputer, v.a., to contend for, to dispute. Il lui dispute le pas; he contends with him for precedence — le passage à quelqu'un; to oppose one's passage.

se **disputer**, v.r., to dispute; to contend for; to wrangle.

disputeu-r, **-se**, n. and adj., wrangler, disputant; disputatious, disputative.

disque, n.m., disc, quoit; (bot.) discus.

disquisition, n.f., disquisition.

disruption, *n.f.*, disruption.

dissecteur, *n.m.*, dissector.

dissection, *n.f.*, dissection. — *des nerfs* ; nevrotomy.

dissemblable, *adj.*, dissimilar, unlike, different.

dissemblablement, *adv.*, dissimilarly.

dissemblance, *n.f.*, dissimilitude, dissimilarity.

dissembler, *v.n.*, to differ, to be unlike.

dissémination, *n.f.*, dissemination ; (bot) semination ; scattering (of seeds—*des graines*).

disséminer, *v.a.*, to disseminate, to scatter.

dissension, *n.f.*, dissension, discord, disunion ; strife.

dissentiment, *n.m.*, dissent, disagreement.

disséquer, *v.a.*, (surg.) to dissect ; to analyse.

disséqueur, *n.m.*, (iron.) dissector. *V.* **dissecteur**.

dissertat-eur, *n.m.*, **-rice**, *n.f.*, dissertator.

dissertati-f, -ve, *adj.*, in the form of a dissertation.

dissertation, *n.f.*, dissertation, treatise ; a formal discourse.

disserter, *v.n.*, to dissert. — *sur un point d'histoire :* to expatiate on a point of history.

dissidence, *n.f.*, scission, dissidence, difference of opinion.

dissident, -e, *n.* and *adj.*, dissident, dissenter ; dissentient, dissident, dissenting.

dissimilaire, *adj.*, dissimilar, different, unlike.

dissimilitude, *n.f.*, dissimilitude, difference, unlikeness.

dissimulat-eur, *n.m.*, **-rice**, *n.f.*, dissembler, hypocrite.

dissimulation, *n.f.*, dissimulation, dissembling ; double-dealing. *Avec —* ; dissemblingly. *User de —* : to dissemble. — *de naissance :* concealment of birth.

dissimulé, -e, *n.* and *adj.*, dissembler ; dissembling, double-faced, artful. *Homme profondément —* : man extremely close. *Caractère —* : artful disposition.

dissimuler, *v.a.*, to dissemble, to conceal, to hide ; to play the hypocrite ; to feign to take no notice of ; to pretend not to do sor' e-thing. — *sa haine :* to dissemble one's hatred. — *une injure*, to take no notice of an insult.

se dissimuler, *v.r.*, to conceal ; to be concealed.

dissimuler, *v.n.*, to dissemble. *Il dissimula qu'il s'en fût aperçu ;* he pretended not to have perceived it.

dissipat-eur, -rice, *n.* and *adj.*, squanderer, spendthrift, prodigal, waster ; lavish, wasteful, extravagant.

dissipation, *n.f.*, dissipation, wasting ; waste ; recreation, relaxation, diversion. *Il s'est ruiné par ses —s :* he ruined himself by his dissipation. *Vivre dans la —* ; to lead a dissipated life.

dissiper, *v.a.*, to dissipate, to scatter, to dispel, to disperse ; to consume, to waste, to squander away, to spend ; to recreate, to divert, to relax. *L'exercice dissipe les humeurs ;* exercise dispels the humours. — *les factions ;* to quell factions — *son bien ;* to squander away one's wealth.

se dissiper, *v.r.*, to divert, recreate, or relax one's self ; to be dispersed, dispelled, or dissipated.

dissitivalve, *adj.*, (mol.) having disjointed valves.

dissolu, -e, *adj.*, dissolute, profligate, lewd, loose, licentious. *Elle est fort —e dans ses mœurs ;* she is very loose in her manners. *Vie —e :* debauched life.

dissoluble, *adj.*, dissoluble, dissolvable.

dissolument, *adv.*, dissolutely, loosely, lewdly, licentiously, riotously.

⊙**dissoluti-f, -ve**, *adj. V.* **dissolvant**.

dissolution, *n.f.*, dissolution ; solution ; dissoluteness, looseness of manners, licentiousness, lewdness ; riot. — *des simples ;* dissolution of herbs. *La — d'un mariage ;* the annulling of a marriage. — *de société ;* dissolution of partnership.

dissolvant, *n.m.*, dissolvent, resolvent, solvent. *L'eau est un grand —* ; water is a powerful dissolvent.

dissolvant, -e, *adj.*, dissolvent, resolvent, solvent.

dissonance, *n.f.*, (mus.) dissonance, discord.

dissonant, -e, *adj.*, dissonant, discordant, jarring.

dissoner, *v.n.*, (mus.) to make a discord, to jar, to be discordant.

dissoudre (dissolvant, dissous), *v.a.*, to dissolve, to break, to break up. *L'eau dissout le sucre ;* water dissolves sugar. — *un mariage ;* to annul a marriage.

se dissoudre, *v.r.*, to dissolve, to be dissolved, to melt ; to break up.

dissou-s, -te, *part.*, dissolved, broken up.

dissuader, *v.a.*, to dissuade, to advise to the contrary.

dissuasi-f, -ve, *adj.*, dissuasive.

dissuasion, *n.f.*, dissuasion.

dissyllabe, *adj.*, (gram.) dissyllabic.

dissyllabe, *n.m.*, (gram.) dissyllable

dissyllabique, *adj.*, dissyllabic.

distance, *n.f.*, distance. *Du Créateur à la créature, la — est infinie ;* the distance from the Creator to the creature is infinite. *Tenir à —* ; to keep at a distance. *Garder sa —* ; to keep one's distance.

distancé, -e, *part.*, distanced.

distancer, *v.a.*, to distance.

distant, -e, *adj.*, distant, remote, far off.

distendre, *v.a.*, (med.) to stretch, to expand, to distend.

se distendre, *v.r.*, (med.) to be distended.

distension, *n.f.*, (med.) distension, tension.

distillable, *adj.*, distillable.

distillateur, *n.m.*, distiller.

distillation, *n.f.*, distillation. *L'art de la —* : distillery.

distillatoire, *adj.*, distillatory.

distiller, *v.a.*, to distil ; to discharge, to vent. — *deux fois ;* to rectify. —*son esprit sur quelque chose ;* to puzzle one's brains about a thing. — *son venin sur quelqu'un ;* to spit out one's venom against any one.

distiller, *v.n.*, to drop, to distil, to drizzle, to trickle, to run by little and little ; to be discharged, vented.

distillerie (-til-ri), *n.f.*, distillery, still-house.

distinct (-tinct), **-e**, *adj.*, distinct, different ; separate ; plain ; clear.

distinctement, *adv.*, distinctly, clearly, plainly.

distincti-f, -ve, *adj.*, distinctive, distinguishing, characteristic. *Caractère —, marque —re :* characteristic.

distinction, *n.f.*, distinction, division ; difference ; eminence, superiority. *Sans —* ; promiscuously, indiscriminately. *Faire — de l'ami et de l'ennemi ;* to distinguish between a friend and a foe. *Un homme de —* ; a man of rank. *Défaut de —* ; want of distinction. *Pur —* ; for distinction, for distinction's sake.

distingué, -e, *adj.*, distinguished, eminent, conspicuous ; gentlemanly ; ladylike ; genteel. *Naissance —e ;* high birth.

distinguer (-ghé), *v.a.*, to discern, to distinguish ; to make a distinction, to discrimi-

nate; to make eminent; to take notice of, to treat with marks of distinction. — *le bien du mal*; to distinguish good from evil. — *une chose d'avec une autre;* to distinguish one thing from another.

se distinguer, *v.r.*, to distinguish *or* signalize one's self, to make one's self eminent; to be distinguished. *Il se distingue par ses talents;* he is distinguished for his talents.

distique, *n.m.*, distich.

distique, *adj.*, (bot.) having flowers *or* leaves in double and opposite rows.

distordre, *v.a.*, (med) to distort. *Se —, v.r..* to become distorted.

distors, -e, *adj.*, distorted, wrested.

distorsion, *n.f..* distortion.

distraction, *n.f.*, separation, subtraction; abstraction, absence of mind, wandering, heedlessness, inattention; recreation, diversion, relief. — *de dépens*; (jur.) awarding expenses. *Il est sujet à des —s;* he is subject to absence of mind.

distraire, *v.a.*, to separate, to subtract; to call off, to take off, to divert from, to distract, to disturb; to divert, to entertain; to turn from. — *quelqu'un de ses juges naturels ;* to deprive any one of his natural judges. *La moindre chose le distrait ;* the least thing takes off his attention. — *des études ;* to disturb from study.

se distraire, *v.r.*, to divert one's attention ; to be disturbed; to divert one's self, to amuse one's self.

distrait, -e, *adj.*, absent (in mind— *d'esprit*); heedless, wandering ; distracted, vacant. *Un homme — ;* an absent man. *Air —, regards —s;* absent air, vacant looks.

distrait, *n.m.*, absent man (in mind— *d'esprit*).

distrayant, -e, *adj.*, diverting, pleasing, entertaining.

distribuer, *v.a.*, to distribute, to deal out, to portion out, to serve out; to dispose, lay out, arrange; (print.) to distribute; (theat,) to cast. — *des aumônes;* to distribute alms. — *un appartement ;* to lay out a suit of rooms.

distribut-eur. *n.m.*, **-rice,** *n.f.*, distributer, bestower, dispenser. — *des vivres;* (nav.) purser's steward, purser's mate.

distributi-f, -ve, *adj.*, distributive.

distribution, *n.f.*, distribution ; division; laying out, disposition; delivery (of letters by post—*des lettres par la poste);* (print.) distribution; (theat.) cast. *La* — *des prix ;* the distribution of prizes. *Ordre de* — ; roll of the creditors who are to receive dividends. *La* — *de cet appartement est commode ;* this suit of rooms is conveniently laid out.

distributivement (-tiv-män), *adv* , distributively.

district (-trik), *n.m.*, district; jurisdiction.

dit, *n.m..* maxim ; saying; ⊕ fable, tale. *Les —s et faits des anciens ;* the acts and sayings of the ancients. *Avoir son — et son dédit ;* to say and unsay.

dit, *-e, part.*, said, spoken ; surnamed, called. *Ce qui fut — fut fait ;* he made his words good. *Aussitôt —, aussitôt fait ;* no sooner said than done. *Susdit ;* above-mentioned.

dithyrambe, *n.m.*, dithyramb ; dithyrambic, dithyrambus.

dithyrambique. *adj.*. dithyrambic.

dito, *adv.*, (com.) Do (ditto).

diton. *n.m.*, (mus.) ditone.

ditriglyphe, *n.m.*, (arch.) ditriglyph.

diurétique, *n.m* and *adj.*, (med.) diuretic.

diurnal, *n.m.*, (c. rel.) diurnal, daily prayerbook.

diurne, *adj.*, (astron., med., ent.) diurnal.

diurne, *n.m.*, (ent.) diurnal insect. —**s,** diurna.

divagat-eur, -rice. *n.* and *adj.*, desultory, rambling speaker ; desultory, rambling.

divagation, *n.f.*, divagation ; wandering, straying ; (jur.) straying (of animals—*des animaux). Se perdre dans les —s;* to lose sight of the question.

divaguer (-ghé), *v.n.*, to be incoherent (either in writing or speaking—*en écrivant ou en parlant),* to ramble, to stray, wander, *or* go from one's subject ; to go astray ; to stray (of cattle—*des bestiaux).*

divan, *n.m.*, divan (council of the Turkish empire—*grand conseil de l'empire turc);* sofa, divan.

divarication, *n.f.*, (med.) divarication.

divariqué. -e, *adj.*, (bot.) straggling.

⊙**dive**, *adj.*, divine.

divergence, *n.f.*, divergence, divergency; difference of opinion.

divergent, -e, *adj.*, divergent ; different ; (bot.) spreading.

diverger, *v.n.*, to diverge.

divers. -e, *adj.*, diverse, various, different, multifarious ; divers, sundry, several.

divers. *n.m.*, (com.) sundries.

diversement, *adv.*, diversely, variously, differently.

diversifier, *v.a.*, to diversify, to vary. — *l'entretien ;* to give variety to the conversation. **se diversifier**, *v.r.,* to be varied, diversified.

diversion, *n.f.*, diversion. *Faire* — *de l'humeur ;* to divert the humour.

diversité, *n.f.*, diversity, variety, difference.

divertir, *v.a.*, to divert ; to embezzle, to convert to one's own use, to make away with, to convey away ; to amuse, to recreate, to delight, to exhilarate. — *des fonds ;* to misapply funds. *Deniers divertis ;* embezzled money.

se divertir, *v.r.*, to take one's pleasure or diversion, to make merry, to divert or recreate one's self; to be diverted or amused, to be merry; to make sport with. *Divertissez-vous bien ;* enjoy yourselves.

divertissant, -e, *adj.*, diverting, entertaining, amusing.

divertissement (-tis-män), *n.m.*, diversion, divertisement, pastime, relaxation ; amusement; entertainment; purloining, embezzlement. *Une comédie avec des —s ;* a comedy with divertisements. — *de deniers ;* embezzling of money.

dividende, *n.m.*, dividend. — *arriéré;* unclaimed dividend. *Faire un* — ; (com.) to declare a dividend.

divin, -e. *adj.*, divine ; godlike ; heavenly. *L'office* — ; divine service. *Ouvrage* — ; most excellent work. *Beauté —e;* heavenly beauty. *Le* — *Platon,* the divine Plato.

divinateur, *n.m.*, **-rice,** *n.f.*, diviner; divineress.

divination, *n.f.*, divination. — *par le feu;* pyromancy.

divinatoire, *adj.*, divinatory ; divining.

divinement (di-vi-n-män), *adv.*, divinely, heavenly.

diviniser, *v.a.*, to deify ; to acknowledge as divine.

divinité, *n.f.*, Divinity, Godhead, deity. *Adorer la —;* to worship the Divinity. *Les —s des eaux, des forêts ;* the water divinities, the deities of the forest. *C'est une —;* she is an angel.

divis, *n.m.*, (l.u) division. *Posséder par — ;* to possess a portion of.

divise, *n.f.*, (her.) narrow band.

diviser, *v.a.*, to divide ; to parcel out; to part, to portion out ; to disunite, to set at variance. — *une quantité ;* to divide a quantity

— *le tout en ses parties ;* to divide the whole into its parts.

se diviser, *v.r.*, to divide ; to be divided ; to be disunited ; to be at variance.

diviseur, *n.m.*, (arith.) divisor.

diviseur, *adj.m.*, divisive, dividing.

divisibilité, *n.f.*, divisibility.

divisible, *adj.*, divisible.

division, *n.f.*, division ; partition ; dividing ; (math., print., rhet., milit., parliament) division ; (nav.) squadron. *Étre en —;* to be at variance.

divisionnaire, *adj.*, divisional ; divisionary, of a division.

divorce, *n.m.*, divorce ; variance. *Faire — avec sa femme ;* to divorce one's wife. *Faire — ;* to renounce. *Ils sont dans un continuel — ;* they are always at variance.

divorcer, *v.n.*, to be divorced. *Elle a divorcé d'avec lui ;* she has been divorced from him.

divulgation, *n.f.*, divulgation.

divulguer (-ghé), *v.a.*, to divulge, to blaze abroad. *— un secret ;* to divulge a secret, to blab out a secret.

dix (dis, in reckoning, and before words it does not qualify ; diz, before a vowel ; di, when followed by a word it qualifies, if it begins with a consonant), *adj.*, ten. *Innocent — ;* Innocent the tenth.

dix, *n.m.*, ten ; tenth.

dix-huit, *adj.*, eighteen, eighteenth.

dix-huit, *n.m.*, eighteen, eighteenth.

dix-huitième, *adj.*, eighteenth.

dixième (-zièm), *adj.*, tenth. *Le — jour ;* the tenth day. *La — fois ;* the tenth time.

dixième, *n.m.*, tenth.

dixième, *n.f.*, (mus.) tenth.

dixièmement (di-zièm-mān), *adv.*, tenthly.

dixme, *n.f.* *V.* **dîme**.

dix-neuf. *adj.*, nineteen, nineteenth.

dix-neuf, *n.m.*, nineteen, nineteenth.

dix-neuvième. *adj.*, nineteenth.

dix-neuvième, *n.m.*, nineteenth.

dix-sept, *adj.*, seventeen, seventeenth.

dix-sept, *n.m*, seventeen, seventeenth.

dix-septième, *adj.*, seventeenth.

dix-septième, *n.m.*, seventeenth.

dizain, *n.m.*, decastich ; (c.rel.) a rosary consisting of ten beads.

dizaine, *n.f.*, ten. *Il y avait une — de personnes ;* there were some ten people.

dizeau, *n m.*, shock of wheat (consisting of ten sheaves—*dix gerbes*).

⊙**dizenier**, *n.m.*, tithing-man.

djinn, *n.m.* (—*s*), (Arabian myth) imp, evil spirit, demon.

d-la-ré, *n.m.*, (mus.) D.

d.m. (ab. for Docteur Médecin) ; M.D. (Medicinæ Doctor).

do, *n.m.*, (mus.) C ; do, ut.

docile, *adj.*, docile, tractable, submissive, manageable. *Enfant — ;* docile child.

docilement (do-sil-mān), *adv.*, with docility.

docilité, *n.f.*, docility, tractableness, manageableness.

docimasie, or **docimastique**, *n.f.*, (metal.) docimacy.

docimastique, *adj.*, docimastic.

dock, *n.m.*, dock.

docte, *adj.*, erudite, learned.

doctement, *adv.*, learnedly, in a learned manner.

docteur, *n.m.*, doctor. *— en théologie, en droit, en médecine ;* doctor of divinity, of law, of medicine.

doctoral, **-e**, *adj.*, doctoral.

doctoralement, *adv.*, doctorally.

doctorat, *n.m.*, doctorship, doctor's degree.

doctorerie (-tor-ri), *n.f.*, disputation for the degree of doctor (of divinity—*en théologie*).

doctoresse, *n.f.*, (jest.) doctoress.

doctrinaire, *n.m.*, lay brother ; doctrinaire. *—, adj.*, lay.

doctrinal, **-e**, *adj.*, doctrinal.

doctrine, *n.f.*, doctrine.

document, *n.m.*, document, title, title-deed.

dodécaèdre, *n.m.*, (geom.) dodecahedron.

dodécagone, *n.m.*, (geom.) dodecagon.

dodécagone. *adj.*, twelve-angled.

dodécagynie, *n.f.*, (bot.) dodecagynia.

dodécandrie, *n.f.*, (bot.) dodecandria.

dodécatémorie, *n.f.*, (astron.) dodecatemorion.

dodiner, *v.a.*, to rock ; to swing.

dodiner, *v.n.*, (horl., l.u.) to oscillate, to vibrate.

se dodiner, *v.r.*, to nurse one's self, to make much of one's self.

dodo, *n.m.*, (fam.) by-by, lullaby ; sleep, bed. *Aller à — ;* to go to lullaby.

dodo, *n.m.*, (pop.) (orni.) dodo. *V.* **dronte**.

dodu. **-e**, *adj.*, plump.

dogaresse, *n.f.*, the wife of a doge.

dogat, *n.m.*, dogate.

doge, *n.m.*, doge.

dogesse, *n.f.*, (l.u.) doge's wife.

dogmatique, *adj.*, dogmatic.

dogmatique, *n.m.*, dogmatics.

dogmatiquement (-tik-mān), *adv.*, dogmatically.

dogmatiser, *v.n.*, to dogmatize ; to teach false dogmas.

dogmatiseur, *n.m.*, dogmatizer.

dogmatiste, *n.m.*, dogmatist.

dogme, *n.m.*, dogma, tenet.

dogre, *n.m.*, Dutch dogger, dogger-boat.

dogue (dog), *n.m.*, mastiff, house-dog ; bull-dog.

doguin, *n.m.*, **-ne**, *n.f.*, (-ghin, -ghi-n), young of the house-dog, mastiff, bull-dog.

doigt (doa), *n.m.*, finger ; toe ; hand ; digit. *Les cinq —s de la main ;* the five fingers of the hand. *Un — du pied ;* a toe. *Avoir sur les —s ;* to get a rap on the knuckles. *Étre à deux —s de sa ruine ;* to be upon the brink of ruin. *Savoir quelque chose sur le bout du — ;* to have a thing at one's fingers' ends. *Mon petit — me l'a dit ;* a little bird told me. *Se mordre les —s de quelque chose ;* to repent of a thing. *Il est à deux —s de la mort ;* he has one foot in the grave. *J'en mettrais le — au feu ;* I would lay my life upon it. *Étre servi au — et à l'œil ;* to be served at a nod. *On le montre au — ;* he is pointed at. *Vous avez mis le — dessus ;* you have hit the nail on the head. *Un — de vin ;* a little drop of wine. *S'en lécher les —s ;* to lick one's lips.

doigter (doa-té), *v.n.*, (mus.) to finger.

doigter, *n.m.*, (mus.) fingering.

doigtier (doa-tié), *n.m.*, finger-stall, thumb-stall.

doit, *n.m.*, (com.) Dr. (debtor).

doitée, *n.f.*, a piece of thread shorter than a needleful.

dol, *n.m.*, (jur.) deceit, fraud.

dolabre, *n.f.*, dowl-axe.

dolage, *n.m.*, smoothing with the adze.

dolce (dol-cé), *adv.*, (mus.) dolce.

doléance, *n.f.*, mournful complaint, lament. *Faire, conter, ses —s ;* to make one's complaints.

dolemment (do-la-mān), *adv.*, mournfully, wofully.

dolent, **-e**, *adj.*, doleful, woful, piteous, mournful.

doler, *v.a.*, to smooth with the adze.

doliman, *n.m.*, doliman.

dollar, *n.m.*, dollar.

dolman, *n.m.*, a hussar's pelisse.

dolmen, *n.m.* (—s), dolmen.

doloire, *n.f.*, adze.

dolomie, *or* **dolomite**, *n.f.*, (min.) dolomite.

dom, *n.m.*, dom; don. *V.* **don**.

domaine, *n.m.*, domain; estate, demesne, possession, property; department, province. *Le — de la couronne;* the crown-lands. *Cela n'est point de mon —;* that is not in my province.

domanial, **-e**, *adj.*, demesnial, of or belonging to a demesne.

domanialiser, *v.a.*, to consolidate several states into one, or unite them to the crown.

dôme, *n.m.*, (arch.) dome, cupola; dome, principal church. — *de verdure;* verdant arch.

domerie, *n.f.*, an abbey (for the reception of the sick—*pour la réception des malades*).

domestication, *n.f.*, domestication (of animals—*des animaux*).

domesticité, *n.f.*, domesticity, the being a servant; the menials *or* servants (of a household—*d'une maison*); domesticated state.

domestique, *adj.*, domestic, homely, home-bred; menial; tame, domesticated.

domestique, *n.m.*, servant, domestic; servants, domestics (of a house—*d'une maison*); household; home. *Il a changé tout son —;* he has changed all his servants. *Il aime son —;* he is fond of his home.

domestique, *n.f.*, woman-servant, maid-servant, servant. — *pour tout faire;* maid, servant, of all-work.

domestiquement (-tik-măn), *adv.*, servant-like, menially.

domestiquer, *v.a.*, to domesticate, to tame.

domicile, *n.m.*, domicile, abode, residence. — *politique;* political residence. — *civil;* ordinary residence, dwelling. *A —;* at one's own house, at home. — *légal;* settlement, legal settlement.

domiciliaire, *adj.*, domiciliary. *Faire une visite — chez quelqu'un;* to search any one's house.

domicilié, **-e**, *adj.*, resident, domiciled, domiciliated. *Il est —;* he is settled, he has taken a house.

se domicilier, *v.r.*, to settle, to dwell in a place.

dominance, *n.f.*, quality of preponderance and prevalence, dominance, rule.

dominant, **-e**, *adj.*, dominant, predominant, reigning, prevalent. *Passion —e;* ruling passion. *Goût —;* reigning taste. *La religion —e;* the established religion.

dominante, *n.f.*, (mus) dominant. *Dans le mode d'ut, sol est la —, et fa la sous-dominante;* in the mode C, G is the dominant, F the sub-dominant.

dominat-eur, **-rice**. *n.* and *adj.*, dominator, ruler; ruling, governing, dominant, domineering, arrogant.

domination, *n.f.*, domination; dominion, rule, sway.

dominer, *v.n.*, to rule, to bear rule or sway, to have the mastery; to dominate, to preponderate, to prevail; to domineer, to lord it; to rise above; to command a view of, to look over; to command; to predominate. *Il faut que la raison domine sur les passions;* reason must prevail over the passions. *Sa tête domine au-dessus de la foule;* his head rises above the crowd. *Cette tour domine sur tous les environs;* that tower overlooks all the surrounding country.

dominer, *v.a.*, to rule, to govern, to sway, to prevail over, to domineer over; to rise above,

to command a view of; to command, to keep in subjection. *La citadelle domine la ville;* the citadel commands the town.

dominicain, *n.m.*, Dominican, Dominican friar.

dominicain, **-e**, *adj.*, Dominican.

dominicaine, *n.f.*, Dominican nun.

dominical, **-e**, *adj.*, dominical. *Lettre —e;* dominical letter. *L'oraison —e;* the Lord's prayer.

dominicale, *n.f.*, Sunday sermon.

domino, *n.m.*, domino. *En —;* in a domino. *Jouer aux —s;* to play at dominoes.

dominoterie, *n.f.*, stained paper.

dominotier (-tié), *n.m.*, dealer in stained paper.

dommage, *n.m.*, damage, injury, hurt, detriment, loss; harm. *Cela me porte —;* that is a loss for me. *Faire du —;* to do harm. *C'est —;* it is a pity. — *s et intérêts, dommages-intérêts;* (jur.) damages.

dommageable (-jabl), *adj.*, hurtful, prejudicial, injurious.

domptable (don-tabl), *adj.*, tameable

dompter (don-té), *v.a.*, to subdue, to subjugate, to quell, to tame. — *ses passions;* to overcome one's passions. — *des animaux;* to tame animals. — *un cheval;* to break in a horse.

se dompter, *v.r.*, to quell, to overcome one's passions.

dompteur (don-teur), *n.m.*, subduer; tamer; vanquisher.

dompte-venin, *n.m.* (—), (bot.) swallow-wort.

don, *n.m.*, gift, donation, present, endowment; knack. *Les —s du ciel;* the gifts of heaven. —*s de la nature;* natural endowments. — *gratuit;* free gift. *Le — de la parole;* the gift of speech. *Il a le — de plaire;* he has the knack of pleasing.

don, *n.m.*, don (Spanish and Portuguese title—*titre espagnol et portugais*)

dona, *n.f.* (—s), lady, (fem. of don).

donataire, *n.m.* donee.

donat-eur, *n.m.*, **-rice**, *n.f.*, donor.

donation, *n.f.*, donation, free gift; deed of gift. —*s de la couronne;* grants of the crown. *Faire — de ses biens;* to make over one's property by deed of gift.

donatisme, *n.m.*, donatism.

donatiste, *n.m.*, Donatist.

donc, *conj.*, therefore; accordingly; then, consequently. *Répondez —;* answer, then. *Qu'ai-je — fait?* what have I done then?

dondon, *n.f.*, (fam., b. s.) plump, jolly, fresh-coloured woman, girl.

donjon, *n.m.*, donjon, turret, castle-keep; dungeon; pavilion.

donjonné, **-e**, *adj.*, turreted.

donnant, **-e**, *adj.*, generous. *Il n'est pas —;* he is not generous.

donne, *n.f.*, deal (at cards—*aux cartes*).

donné, **-e**, *part.*, given.

donnée, *n.f. sing.*, **données**, *n.f. pl.*, datum, data, principles, facts admitted *or* known; notion, idea, information; (math.) known quantity, datum; theme of a play, a poem, &c.

donner, *v.a.*, to give, to bestow, to present with, to make a present of; to give away; to cause; to grant, to confer upon; to ascribe; to deal (at cards—*aux cartes*); to wish (good day, &c.—*bonjour, &c.*); to devote; (com.) to sell, to let have. — *en échange;* to give in exchange. — *tort à quelqu'un;* to blame any one. — *une bague à quelqu'un;* to present a person with a ring. — *sa fille en mariage;* to give one's daughter in marriage. *Qui donne tôt, donne deux fois;* he who gives in time gives twice. — *la vie;* to grant life. — *le bonjour* *à quelqu'un ;* to wish any one a good day. — *un soufflet à quelqu'un ;* to box any one's ears. — *rendez-vous ;* to appoint a place to meet. — *quittance ;* to give a receipt. — *le branle à une affaire ;* to set an affair going. — *le ton ;* to set the fashion. — *la chasse ;* to pursue. — *sa parole ;* to give one's word. — *du chagrin ;* to vex. — *de la peine ;* to trouble. — *les mains à une chose ;* to give one's consent to a thing. — *de l'altesse à quelqu'un ;* to give one the title of highness. — *une baie ;* to humbug. — *sa voix, son suffrage ;* to give one's vote, one's suffrage. — *gain de cause ;* to give up. *Donnez des sièges ;* bring chairs. *Il en donne à tout le monde ;* he makes a fool of everybody. *Je donne beaucoup au hasard ;* I attribute a good deal to chance. *Donnez à boire à ces hommes ;* give those men something to drink. *Donnez-nous à manger ;* give us something to eat. *C'est à vous à — ;* it is your turn to deal. *En — à quelqu'un ;* to beat, to maul, any one ; to cheat any one, to take any one in.

se donner, *v.r.,* to give one's self ; to procure ; to take place (of battles—*batailles*) ; to get ; to abandon, to attach, one's self ; to give one's self out as. *Se — à quelqu'un ;* to abandon, to devote, one's self to any one. *Se — la peine de ;* to take the trouble to. *Se — des airs ;* to give one's self airs. *Se — de la tête contre les murs ;* to run one's head against the wall. *S'en — à cœur joie ;* to indulge one's self to one's heart's content ; to take one's fill of it.

donner, *v.n.,* to give, to give away ; to addict one'sself ; to give one's self up ; to get into the head (of liquors—*des spiritueux*) ; to hit, to strike ; (milit.) to charge ; to deal (at cards —*aux cartes*) ; to yield, to bear, to produce ; to look out ; to look into, to overlook. — *contre un banc de sable ;* to strike on a sand-bank. *Mes fenêtres donnent sur la rue ;* my windows look into the street. — *à penser à quelqu'un ;* to make any one think. — *à parler ;* to furnish occasion for talk. — *dedans ;* to fall into a snare. — *dans une embuscade ;* to fall into an ambuscade. — *dans le piège, dans le panneau ;* to fall into the snare. *Le soleil donne dans ma chambre ;* the sun shines into my room *Ce vin donne dans la tête ;* that wine gets up into the head.

donneu-r, *n.m.,* **-se,** *n.f.,* giver, donor. *Il n'est pas — ;* he is not fond of giving. — *d'eau bénite de cour ;* man of promises only.

don quichotte, *n.m.* (— —s), a man like Don Quixote.

don quichottisme, *n.m.* (*n.p.*), quixotism.

dont. *pron.,* whose, whereof, of which, of whom, for whom, &c. *Dieu — nous admirons les œuvres ;* God whose works we admire. *Ce — il s'agit ;* the business in hand. *L'affaire — je vous ai parlé ;* the business of which I spoke to you.

donzelle, *n.f.,* damsel, wench.

dorade, *n.f.,* (astron., ich.) dorado.

doradille, *n.f.* V. **cétérac.**

doré, -e. *part.,* gilt, gilt over. *Langue —e ;* winning, deceitful tongue. — *sur tranche ,* gilt-edged (of books—*de livres*).

dorée, *n.f.,* (ich.) doree, John-Dory.

dorénavant, *adv..* henceforth, hereafter, for the future, from this time forward.

dorer, *v.a.,* to gild, to gild over — *un pâté ;* to glaze a pie with the yoke of eggs. — *la pilule ;* to gild the pill.

se dorer, *v.r.,* to gild ; to become of a gold colour.

doreu-r, *n.m.,* **-se,** *n.f.,* gilder.

dorien (-in), *n,* and *adj. m.,* Dorian ; Doric.

dorine, *n.f.,* (bot.) golden saxifrage.

dorique, *n.m.* and *adj.,* Doric.

dorloter, *v.a.,* to cocker, to fondle, to pamper ; to coddle.

se dorloter, *v.r.,* to nurse one's self up.

dormant, -e. *adj.,* sleeping, dormant, stagnant ; (com.) dull ; unemployed (of money— *d'argent*). *Eau —e ;* stagnant water. *Manœuvre —e ;* (nav.) standing part of a tackle. *Châssis — ;* fixed sash.

dormant, *n.m.,* (tech., carp.) dormant, dormer, sleeper, post.

dormeu-r, *n.m.,* **-se,** *n.f.,* (pers.) sleeper ; sluggard.

dormeuse, *n.f.,* kind of travelling carriage.

*dormille, *n.f.,* (ich.) loche.

dormir (dormant, dormi), *v.n.,* to sleep, to be asleep ; to be supine ; to be still ; to be dormant (of money—*d'argent*) ; to be stagnant (of water—*d'eau*) ; to do nothing. — *d'un bon sommeil, d'un bon somme ;* to sleep soundly. — *trop longtemps ;* to oversleep one's self. — *la grasse matinée ;* to sleep till late in the day. — *tout debout ;* not to be able to keep one's eyes open. *Qui dort, dîne ;* sleeping is as good as eating. *Il dort comme une marmotte ;* he sleeps like a top. *Il n'y a point de pire eau que l'eau qui dort ;* still water runs deep. *J'ai dormi d'un bon somme ;* I have taken a long nap.

dormir, *n.m.,* sleep.

dormiti-f, -ve, *adj.,* soporific, somnific, somniferous. *Une potion —ve ;* a sleeping draught.

dormitif, *n.m.,* dormitive. *L'opium est un dangereux — ;* opium is a dangerous dormitive.

doronic, *n.m.,* (bot.) doronicum, leopard's-bane.

dorsal, -e, *adj.,* dorsal.

dorsténie, *n.f.,* (bot.) contrayerva.

dortoir, *n.m.,* dormitory.

dorure, *n.f.,* gilding ; glazing (of pastry— *pâtisserie*).

dos, *n.m.,* back. *Sur le — ;* upon the back, on one's back. — *courbé, voûté ;* bent back. *L'épine du — ;* the spine, back-bone. — *d'une montagne ;* ridge of a mountain. *Avoir quelqu'un sur le — ;* to be saddled with somebody. *Tourner le — ;* to take to flight. *Tourner le — à quelqu'un ;* to turn one's back on any one, to forsake any one. *Avoir bon — ;* to have a strong back. *Faire le gros — ;* to set up its back (of a cat—*du chat*) ; to assume the air of a man of importance. — *d'âne ;* shelving ridge. *En — d'âne ;* with a shelving ridge.

dosage, *n.m.,* (chem., pharm.) dosing, proportioning.

dose, *n.f.,* dose ; quantity ; portion. — *légère ;* slight dose.

doser, *v.a.,* to dose.

dossier, *n.m..* back (of a seat—*d'un siège*) ; brief (of a barrister—*d'un avocat*) ; bundle of papers. — *d'un lit ;* head-board of a bed.

dossière, *n.f.,* back (of a cuirass—*de cuirasse*).

dot (dot), *n.f.,* marriage portion ; dowry. *Donner une — à ;* to give a dowry to. *La — d'une religieuse ;* what a nun pays for being admitted into a nunnery. *Coureur de —s ;* fortune-hunter.

dotal, -e, *adj.,* dotal.

dotation, *n.f.,* endowment, dotation.

doter, *v.a.,* to endow, to give a portion, to give a dowry. — *une église ;* to endow a church.

douaire, *n.m.,* jointure, dower, marriage-settlement. *Il lui a assigné dix mille livres de — ;* he has settled ten thousand francs upon her.

douairi-er, -ère, *adj.,* dowager.

douairière, *n.f.,* dowager ; jointress.

douane, *n.f.,* custom-house, custom-duty, duty. *Préposé à la — ;* custom-house officer.

Conseil des —s; board of customs. *Droit de —;* custom-house duty.

douaner, *v.a.,* to clear goods at the custom-house ; to pass through the custom-house.

douanier, *n.m.,* custom-house officer; tide-waiter.

douani-er, -ère, *adj.,* relating to the custom-house, to the customs.

doublage, *n.m.,* (nav.) sheathing. *— de cuivre;* copper-sheathing.

double, *adj.,* double, duplicate; strong (of quality—*qualité*); double, deceitful, arrant; duple. *Partie —;* (com.) double entry.

double, *n.m.,* double; duplicate; counterpart (of a deed—*d'un titre*); (theat.) substitute; an old French coin worth two deniers. *Plus du —;* more than the double. *Mettre une chose en —;* to double a thing. *Jouer quitte ou —;* to play double or quits. *— (mus.);* a turn.

double, *adv.,* double. *Voir —;* to see double.

doublé, *n.m.,* (billiards) doublet.

doubleau, *n.m.,* (carp.) binding joist. *V.* **arc-doubleau.**

double emploi, *n.m.,* anything done twice.

doublement, *n.m.,* doubling.

doublement, *adv.,* doubly, in a double manner.

doubler, *v.a.,* to double; to line (clothes —*vêtements*); (arch.) to fur; (milit., nav., print., theat.) to double; to sheath (a ship—*un vaisseau*). *— le pas;* to go faster. *— un habit de velours;* to line a coat with velvet.

doublet, *n.m.,* (billiards, jewellery, trick-track—*billard, bijouterie, trictrac*) doublet; (linguistics) words having the same derivation, but a slightly different spelling and different meanings, doublets.

doublette, *n.f.,* coupler (of organs — *d'orgues*).

doubleu-r. *n.m.,* **-se,** *n.f.,* doubler.

doublon, *n.m.,* doubloon, Spanish pistole ; (print.) double.

doublure, *n.f.,* lining; (theat.) substitute.

douce-amère, *n.f.* *(—s —s),* woody nightshade, bitter-sweet.

douceâtre, *adj.,* sweetish.

doucement, *(doos-mān), adv.,* slowly, leisurely; gently, softly, tenderly, quietly; blandly; peaceably, calmly, smoothly, placidly; mildly; melodiously; meekly; patiently; comfortably; indifferently, not very well, so so. *Aller tout —;* to be so so.

doucerette, *n.f.,* female of feigned kindness, of pretended good conduct.

doucereu-x, -se, *adj.,* sweetish, mawkish; affectedly mild; mealy-mouthed.

doucet. -te, *adj.,* demure, mild, affected *Faire le —;* to look demure.

doucette, *n.f.,* (bot.) corn salad, lamb's lettuce, valerianella.

doucettement *(-sèt-mān), adv.,* (pop.) gently, softly. *Il va tout —;* he's so so.

douceur, *n.f.,* sweetness; fragrance; softness; mildness; kindness, good-nature; melodiousness, harmony; mellowness; calmness; smoothness; peacefulness; meekness, gentleness; sweet thing; delight, pleasure, comfort; douceur. *Employer la —;* to use gentleness. *Prendre quelqu'un par la —;* to treat any one with kindness. *Goûter les —s de la vie;* to taste the comforts of life. *Les —s de la société;* the delights of society.

douche, *n.f.,* douche, shower-bath. *Donner une — à quelqu'un;* to give any one a douche, a shower-bath.

doucher, *v.a.,* to give a douche, a shower-bath.

doucine, *n.f.,* (arch.) doucine; (carp.) moulding-plane.

doucir, *v.a.,* to polish looking-glasses.

douelle, *n.f.,* (arch.) archivolt, intrados ; facing of a voussoir.

douer, *v.a.,* to endow, to bestow upon. *Dieu l'a douée de grandes vertus;* God has endowed her with great virtues.

*douille, *n.f.,* socket.

*douillet, -te, *n.* and *adj.,* effeminate, delicate person; soft, downy; nice; tender; effeminate; delicate. *C'est un —;* he loves to indulge himself.

*douillette, *n.f.,* wadded dress, wadded great coat.

*douillettement *(doo-ièt-mān), adv.,* softly, tenderly, delicately, effeminately.

douleur, *n.f.,* pain; ache; soreness; anguish, grief, sorrow, affliction; dolor, woe. *Les —s de l'enfantement;* the pangs of childbirth. *— aiguë;* acute pain.

⊙*se* **douloir,** *v.r.,* to grieve, to wail, to lament.

douloureusement *(-reûz-mān), adv.,* grievously.

douloureu-x, -se, *adj.,* painful, tender, smarting, sore; grievous, dolorous, sorrowful; sad. *Cri —;* mournful cry.

doupion, *n.m.,* twin thread (of the cocoon— *du cocon du ver à soie*); double thread, coarse, raw silk.

doute, *n.m.,* doubt; doubtfulness, dubiousness; apprehension, misgiving, distrust. *Mettre en —;* to call in question. *Faire naître des —s;* to give rise to misgivings. *Jeter des —s dans l'esprit;* to fill the mind with distrust. *Sans —;* without doubt, no doubt, doubtless, indubitably. *Sans — que;* no doubt that.

douter, *v.a.,* to doubt, to question, to hesitate, to suspect, to scruple. *Il doute de tout;* he doubts every thing. *Je doute que cela soit;* I doubt whether it be so. *Je doute qu'il veuille le faire;* I doubt whether he will do it. *Je ne doute pas qu'il ne le fasse,* I do not doubt but that he will do it.

se **douter,** *v.r.,* to suspect, to surmise, to conjecture; to distrust, to mistrust, to fear. *Je m'en doutais bien;* I thought so. *Je me doutais qu'il viendrait;* I suspected he would come. *Pouvais-je me — qu'il dût venir sitôt?* could I imagine that he was to come so soon ?

douteur *(doo-), n.m.,* doubter.

douteusement *(doo-teûz-mān), adv.,* doubtfully.

douteu-x. -se, *adj.,* doubtful, dubious, ambiguous, questionable. *D'une manière —se;* doubtfully. *Il est — qu'il le fasse;* it is doubtful whether he do it.

douvain, *n.m.,* wood (for making staves for casks—*merrain*).

douve, *n.f.,* stave; (bot.) spearwort.

dou-x, -ce, *adj.,* sweet; soft, smooth; easy; gentle, mild; fragrant, agreeable, comfortable, charming, pleasant; harmonious; peaceful, calm; unfermented; fresh (of water—*de l'eau*); mellow. *Eau —ce;* fresh water, soft water. *Poisson d'eau —ce;* fresh-water fish. *Senteur —ce;* sweet smell. *Une taille douce;* a copper-plate. *Un billet —;* a love-letter. *Faire les yeux —;* to cast amorous looks. *Il fait bien —;* the weather is very mild. *—ce rêverie;* sweet musing. *Mener une vie —ce;* to lead an easy, agreeable life. *Un — sourire;* a gracious smile. *Il est — comme un agneau;* he is as gentle as a lamb.

doux, *adv.,* gently; submissively. *Filer —;* to be submissive. *Tout —;* softly, gently.

douzaine, *n.f.,* dozen. *Une demi- —;* half a dozen. *À la —, par —;* by the dozen.

douze, *adj.,* twelve, twelfth. *Les — signes du zodiaque;* the twelve signs of the zodiac. *Charles —;* Charles the twelfth.

douze. *n.m.*, twelve, twelfth. *Le — du mois;* the twelfth instant. *Un in— —;* a duodecimo.

douzième, *n.m.,* and *adj.,* twelfth.

douzièmement, *adv.,* twelfthly, in the twelfth place.

*****douzil,** *n.m.,* spigot, peg.

doxologie. *n.f.,* doxology.

doyen. *n.m.,* dean; senior. oldest member.

doyenné (doa-ié-né), *n.m.,* deanship, deanery; dean's-pear.

drachme (drakm), *n.f.,* drachma; dram.

dracocéphale. *n.m.,* (bot.) dragon's-head.

draconien. -ne (-in, -è-n), *adj.,* draconian.

draconte, *n.m.,* (bot.) dragon's-wort.

dragage, *n.m.,* dragging (of a river—*d'une rivière).*

dragée, *n.f.,* comfit, sugar-plum; small shot. *—s lissées;* plain sugar-plums. *Grosse —;* luck-shot. *Avaler la —;* to swallow the pill.

drageoir (dra-jo-ar), *n.m.,* comfit-dish.

drageon (-jon), *n.m.,* (bot.) shoot, sucker.

drageonner (-jo-né), *r.n.,* to put forth shoots or suckers.

dragme. *V.* **drachme.**

dragoman. *V.* **drogman.**

dragon, *n.m.,* dragon; vixen; (astron., erpetology) draco. *— ailé;* flying dragon. *Sa femme est un vrai —;* his wife is a regular termagant.

dragon, *n.m.,* dragoon.

dragonnade. *n.f.,* dragonnade.

dragonne, *n.f.,* sword-knot; violent woman. *À la —;* cavalierly, unceremoniously.

dragonner, *r.a.,* (l.u.) to dragoon; to worry. *se dragonner,* *v.r.,* (l.u.) to torment one's self

dragonnier, *n.m.,* dragon-tree.

draguage (-gaj), *n.m.* *V.* **dragage.**

drague (drag), *n.f.,* dredge; dredging-machine. grains (of a brewery—*d'une brasserie).*

draguer (ghé), *v.a.,* to drag; to dredge. *— une ancre;* to sweep the bottom for a lost anchor.

draguette (-ghèt), *n.f.,* small dredge or drag.

dragueur (-gheur), *n.m.,* dredging-machine.

drain. *n.m.,* drain, draining-pipe.

drainage, *n.m.,* drainage.

draine, *n.f.,* (orni.) missel, missel-bird.

drainer, *v.a.,* to drain.

dramatique, *adj.,* dramatic.

dramatique, *n.m.,* drama, dramatic style.

dramatiser, *v.a.,* to dramatize.

dramatiste, *n.m.f.,* (l.u.) dramatist.

dramaturge, *n.m.,* dramatist. [Often used ironically.]

drame, *n.m.,* drama.

drap (dra), *n.m.,* cloth, sheet, pall. *— fin;* superfine cloth, broadcloth. *Gros —;* coarse cloth. *Être dans de beaux —s;* to be in a fine mess. *Le voilà dans de beaux —s!* he is in a fine pickle. *— mortuaire;* pall. *Tailler en plein —;* to have abundance of means at command.

drapé. -e. *part.,* covered, clothed; hung with black; (bot.) thick, close; woollen. *— à l'antique,* clothed after the antique.

drapeau, *n.m.,* flag, standard, ensign, streamer, colours; rag. *Se ranger sous les —x de;* to serve under, to espouse the cause of.

draper, *v.a.,* to cover with cloth; to hang a carriage with black or other dark-coloured cloth as a sign of mourning; to arrange, to ornament with drapery; (paint., sculpt.) to give drapery to; to censure, to reflect on. *se draper,* *v.r.,* to cover one's self; to envelop one's self; to parade; to assume an air of importance.

draper, *v.n.,* to have a carriage hung with dark-coloured cloth as a sign of mourning.

draperie (drap-ri), *n.f.,* drapery; cloth-trade, cloth-making.

drapi-er, *n.m.,* **-ère,** *n.f.,* draper, woollen-draper.

drapière. *n.f.,* packing-pin.

drastique, *n.m.* and *adj.,* (med.) drastic.

drave. *n.f.,* (bot.) whitlow-grass.

drawback, *n.m.* (—s), drawback.

drayage, *n.m.,* fleshing (of hides—*de peaux).*

drayer, *v.a.,* to flesh (hides—*peaux).*

drayoire, *n.f.,* fleshing-knife.

drayure, *n.f.,* fleshings (of hides—*de peaux).*

drêche, *n.f.,* malt. *Four à —;* malt-kiln. *Faiseur de —;* maltster.

drelin, onomatopœia, tinkling (of a bell—*d'une sonnette).*

dresse, *n.f.,* piece of leather to underlay a shoe.

dresser. *v.a.,* to erect, to straighten, to make straight; to raise, to set up; to hold upright; to spread; to lay (a snare—*un piège);* to pitch (camp); to trim (a boat—*un bateau);* to lay out, to arrange; to make out (accounts—*des comptes);* to draw up (a report—*un rapport);* to prick up (the ears—*les oreilles);* to train (animals—*les animaux).* *— la tête;* to hold the head erect. *Cheval qui dresse les oreilles;* a horse that pricks up his ears. *— des statues;* to erect statues. *— un lit;* to put up a bed. *— une tente;* to pitch, to set up, a tent. *— un buffet;* to lay out a side-board. *— un piège;* to lay a trap. *— un plan;* to draw up a plan. *— des arbres;* to dress trees. *— un cheval;* to train a horse. *— quelqu'un;* to form one. *Dresse la chaloupe!* trim the boat! *— la barre du gouvernail;* to right the helm.

se **dresser,** *v.r.,* to stand on end (of the hair —*des cheveux);* to stand erect; to form one's self.

dresser, *v.n.,* to stand on end. *Les cheveux lui dressèrent sur la tête;* his hair stood on end.

dressoir, *n.m.,* dresser; sideboard.

*****drille,** *n.m.,* ⊙ soldier; fellow. *Un bon —;* a good jovial fellow. *Un pauvre —;* a poor wretch.

*****drilles,** *n.f. pl.,* rags (for making paper—*a faire du papier).*

drisse, *n.f.,* (nav.) haliard; gear.

drogman. *n.m.,* dragoman.

drogue (drog), *n.f.,* drug; rubbish; stuff; drogue, a card-game played by soldiers and sailors. *N'être que de la —;* to be nothing but trash, rubbish.

droguer (-ghé), *v.a.,* to drug, to physic. *se droguer,* *v.r.,* to physic one's self.

droguer, *v.n.,* to play at drogue; (pop.) to dance attendance.

droguerie (dro-gri), *n.f.,* drugs, drug-trade.

droguet (-ghè), *n.m.,* drugget.

droguetier (-ghè-tié), *n.m.,* drugget-weaver.

droguier (-ghié), *n.m.,* medicine-chest.

droguiste (-ghist), *n.m.,* druggist.

droit, -e, *adj.,* straight, right, plumb; direct; upright, erect; just, righteous; stand-up (collars—*cols.*) *Ligne —e;* straight line. *En —e ligne;* in a straight line. *Remettre quelqu'un dans le — chemin;* to put any one in the right way again. *Tenir la tête —e;* to hold one's head upright. *Il est — comme un cierge;* he is as straight as an arrow. *Le côté —;* the right-hand side. *Un col —;* a stand-up collar.

droit, *n.m.,* right; equity; law; authority; claim, title; fee; due (tax—*impôt);* duty, custom-duty. *Les —s de l'hospitalité;* the rights of hospitality. *Jouir de ses —s;* to enjoy one's rights. *Faire — à chacun;* to do every one justice. *Le — des gens;* the law of nations. *Renoncer à ses —s;* to give up one's right. *—*

d'aînesse; birthright, primogenitureship. — *de péage,* toll. *A bon —;* with good reason.

droit, *adv.,* straight, straight on, directly; honestly, uprightly. *A tort ou à —;* right or wrong. *A qui de —;* whom it may concern. *Aller tout —;* go straight on. *Aller — au but;* to go straight to the mark. *— comme ça;* (nav.) right on.

droite, *n.f.,* right hand, right; right side; right-hand side. *A —;* on the right. *Prendre la —;* to turn to the right. *Tourner à —;* to turn to the right.

droitement (droat-mān), *adv.,* uprightly, sincerely; rightly, with judgment, judiciously.

droiti-er, -ère (-tié, -tiè-r), *adj.,* right-handed.

droiture, *n.f.,* uprightness, integrity, honesty, rectitude. *En —;* directly, in a direct manner.

drolatique, *adj.,* amusing, laughable, pleasant.

drôle, *adj.,* droll, jocose, ludicrous; comical, strange, funny. *Il est fort —;* he is very ludicrous. *Un — de corps;* a queer fellow.

drôle, *-n.m.,* rogue; rascal, blackguard; scoundrel; sharp fellow.

drôlement (drôl-mān),*adv.,* comically, facetiously, jocosely.

drôlerie (drôl-ri), *n.f.,* drollery, droll thing.

drôlesse, *n.f.,* vile, worthless woman; hussy.

dromadaire, *n.m.,* dromedary.

drome, *n.f.,* float, raft.

dronte, *n.m.,* (orni.) dodo.

drosère, *n.f.,* (bot.) sun-dew.

drosse, *n.f.,* (nav.) truss.

drouine, *n.f.,* tinker's sack.

drouineur, *or* **drouinier,** *n.m.,* tinker.

droussage, *n.m.,* the carding and oiling of wool before spinning it.

drousser, *v.a.,* to card and oil wool.

droussette, *n.f.,* large card for wool.

drousseur, *n.m.,* carder, workman who cards and oils wool.

dru, -e, *adj.,* fledged (of birds—*des oiseaux*); brisk, lively, smart; close-planted, thick-set.

dru, *adv.,* thick, thickly. *Les balles tombaient — comme grêle;* the bullets fell as thick as hail.

druide, *n.m.,* druid.

druidesse, *n.f.,* druidess.

druidique, *adj.,* druidical.

druidisme, *n.m.,* druidism.

drupacé, -e, *adj.,* (bot.) drupaceous.

drupe, *n.m.,* (bot.) drupe.

dryade, *n.f.,* Dryad; (bot.) dryas.

du, *art. m.,* (contraction of *de le*) of the, from the, by the; some, any.

dû, *n.m.,* due, what is owed, what is owing; duty.

dû, due, *part.* (of *devoir*). due, owed. *J'aurais — faire cela;* I ought to have done that.

dualisme, *n.m.,* dualism.

dualiste, *n.m.,* dualist, manichean.

dualité, *n.f.,* duality.

dubitati-f, -ve. *adj.,* dubitative.

dubitation, *n.f.,* dubitation.

duc, *n.m.,* duke; (orni.) horn-owl. *Grand- —* (*-s —s*); grand-duke; great horn-owl.

ducal,-e,aadj.,*ducal. *Grand- —* (*— -ducaux*), grand-ducal.

ducat, *n.m.,* ducat.

ducaton, *n.m.,* ducatoon.

duché, *n.m.,* dukedom, duchy.

duchesse, *n.f.,* duchess; a kind of sofa; a kind of pear. *Lit à la —;* four-post bedstead.

ducroire, *n.m.,* (com.) del credere.

ductile, *adj.,* ductile.

ductilité, *n.f.,* ductility, ductileness.

*****duègne,** *n.f.,* duenna.

duel, *n.m.,* duel; (gram.) dual number. *Appeler en —;* to challenge.

duelliste, *n.m.,* duellist.

☉**duire,** *v.n.,* to suit.

duite, *n.f.,* woof of cloth, weft.

dulcification, *n.f.,* dulcification

dulcifier, *v.a.,* to dulcify

dulcinée, *n.f.,* dulcinea.

dulie, *n.f.,* dulia (worship of saints among Catholics—*culte des saints parmi les catholiques*)

dûment, *adv.,* duly.

dune, *n.f.,* down (of sand—*de sable*).

dunette, *n.f.,* (nav.) poop.

duo, *n.m.* (*—s*), (mus.) duo, duet, duetto.

duodécimal, -e. *adj.,* duodecimal.

duodénal, -e, *adj.,* of the duodenum.

duodénum (-nom), *n.m.,* (anat.)duodenum.

duodi, *n.m.,* duodi, second day of the decade in the calendar of the first French Republic.

dupe, *n.f.,* dupe; gull.

duper, *v.a.,* to dupe, to deceive, to gull, to take in.

duperie (du-pri), *n.f.,* dupery, trickery.

dupeu-r, *n.m.,* **-se,** *n.f.,* cheat, trickster.

duplicata, *n.m.* (*—*), duplicate.

duplication, *n.f.,* duplication.

duplicature, *n.f.,* (anat.) duplicature.

duplicité, *n.f.,* duplicity; double-dealing, deceit.

☉**duplique,** *n.f.,* (jur.) rejoinder.

☉**dupliquer,** *v.n.,* (jur.) to rejoin, to put in a rejoinder.

dupondius, *n.m.* (*—*), (antiq.) dupondius.

duquel, *pron.,* of which, from which. *V.* **lequel** and **dont.**

dur, -e, *adj.,* hard; tough; obdurate, harsh, merciless, unkind, unfeeling, hard-hearted. *Il a les traits —s;* his features are harsh. *L' regard —;* a harsh look. *Des vers —s;* harsh verses. *Un esprit —;* a dull understanding. *Marchandise —e à la vente;* goods of slow sale. *Avoir l'oreille —e;* to be dull of hearing. *Le temps est —;* the weather is severe. *Tableau —;* stiff painting; harsh painting.

dur, *adv.,* hardly; firmly. *Il entend —;* he is hard of hearing.

durabilité, *n.f.,* durableness.

durable, *adj.,* durable, lasting, solid.

durablement, *adv.,* durably, lastingly.

duracine, *n.f.,* sort of peach.

durant, *prep.,* during. *— sa vie, sa vie —;* during his lifetime.

dur-bec, *n.m.* (*—s —s*), (orni.) hawfinch.

durcir, *v.a.,* to harden, to make hard, to make tough; to indurate.

se **durcir,** *v.r.,* to harden, to indurate, to grow hard.

durcir, *v.n.,* to harden, to become hard; to stiffen; to indurate.

durcissement (-sis-mān), *n.m.,* hardening, stiffening; induration.

dure, *n.f.,* bare ground; bare floor. *Coucher sur la —;* to sleep on the ground, on the bare floor.

durée, *n.f.,* duration, continuance. *Être de longue —e;* to be durable.

durement (-dur-mān), *adv.,* hard; hardly, harshly, sharply, roughly, rigorously.

dure-mère, *n.f.* (*n.p.*), (anat.) dura mater.

durer, *v.n.,* to last, to continue; to remain; to endure. *Une étoffe qui dure;* a stuff that wears well. *Le temps lui dure;* time hangs heavy upon him. *Ne pouvoir — en place;* to be unable to remain any where. *Faire vie qui dure;* to take care of one's money, to think of to-morrow. *Ne pouvoir — dans sa peau;* to be ready to jump out of one's skin.

duret. -te, *adj.*, (l.u.) somewhat hard, rather tough.

dureté (dur-té), *n.f.*, hardness, toughness; harshness, austerity, unkindness; hard-favouredness; stiffness. *La — du fer;* the hardness of iron. *Avoir une — d'oreille;* to be hard of hearing. *La — de son regard;* the sternness of his look. *— de cœur;* hard-heartedness.

duretés, *n.f. pl.*, harsh, offensive words.

*durillon, *n.m.*, callosity, hard skin; corn (on the foot—*aux pieds*).

⊙**durillonner**, *v.n.*, to become hard.

se **durillonner**, *v.r.*, to become covered with warts, callosities.

duriuscule, *adj.*, (jest.) somewhat hard, tough, hardish.

duumvir (du-om-), *n.m.*, duumvir.

duumvirat, *n.m.*, luumvirate.

duvet, *n.m.*, down; wool, nap.

duveté. -e, (duv-té) *adj.*, (of birds—*des oiseaux*) downy.

duveteu-x, -se, *adj.*, (fruit) downy.

dynamètre, *n.m.*, dynameter.

dynamique, *n.f.*, dynamics.

dynamique, *adj.*, dynamical.

dynamisme, *n.m.*, name given to the doctrine of Newton.

dynamite, *n.f.*, dynamite.

dynamomètre, *n.m.*, dynamometer.

dynaste, *n.m.*, (antiq.) kinglet, petty sovereign.

dynastie, *n.f.*, dynasty.

dynastique, *adj.*, dynastic.

dyscole, *adj.*, (l.u.) who departs from an established opinion; difficult to live with.

dyscrasie, *n.f.*, (med.) dyscrasy.

dysenterie (dis-sant-ri), *n.f.*, dysentery.

dysentérique, *adj.*, dysenteric.

dysopie, *n.f.*, dysopsy.

dysorexie, *n.f.*, dysorexy.

dyspepsie, *n.f.*, dyspepsia.

dysphagie, *n.f.*, dysphagia.

dysphonie, *n.f.*, dysphony.

dysphorie, *n.f.*, dysphoria.

dyspnée, *n.f.*, dyspnœa.

dysurie, *n.f.*, dysury.

E

e, *n.m.*, the fifth letter of the alphabet, e.

e, abbreviation of *Éminence, Excellence*.

eau, *n.f.*, water; rain, perspiration; tea (of herbs—*tisane*); liquid; wash; *pl.*, (nav.) track, wake; lustre, gloss; *pl.*, watering-place. — *bénite;* holy water. — *douce*, fresh water, soft water. — *dure;* hard water. — *de mer;* sea-water. — *saumâtre;* brackish water. — *mère;* mother-water (chem.). — *de source;* spring-water. — *courante;* running water. — *morte;* still water. — *panée;* toast and water. *Morte —*(n.p.): neap-tide. — *forte* (n.p.); aqua fortis. *Grandes —x;* high flood (of rivers—*des rivières*). *Hautes —x;* high water. — *bénite de cour;* empty promises, blarney. — *dormante;* stagnant water. *Aller aux —x;* to go to a watering-place. *Porter de l'— à la mer;* to carry coals to Newcastle. *Ils se ressemblent comme deux gouttes d'—;* they are as like as two peas. *Il n'est pire — que celle qui dort;* smooth waters run deep. *Cela s'en est allé en — de boudin;* that came to nothing at all. *Aller à l'—;* to take the water (of a dog—*du chien*). *Un jet d'—;* a water-spout. *Une pièce d'—, une nappe d'—;* a sheet of water. —*x jaillissantes;* spouting waters. *Passer l'—;* to cross the water. *Au bord de l'—;* on the water-side. *Nager entre deux —x;* to swim under water;

to waver between two parties. *À fleur d'—;* even with the water. *Faire venir l'— au moulin;* to bring grist to the mill. *Mettre de l'— dans son vin;* to lower one's pretensions. *Pêcher en — trouble;* to fish in troubled water. *Cela fait venir l'— à la bouche;* that makes one's mouth water. *Lancer un navire à l'—;* to launch a ship. *Faire de l'—;* (nav.) to water, to take in fresh water. *Faire une voie d'—;* to spring a leak. — -*de-vie* (—*x* —); brandy. — *de rose;* rose-water. — *d'arquebusade;* arquebusade water. *Il tombe de l'—;* it rains. *Il est tout en —;* he is in a great perspiration. *Suer sang et —;* to toil and moil. *Donner — à un drap;* to give a gloss to a piece of cloth. *Maître des —x et forêts;* ranger of the woods and forests. *Eaux-fortes;* etchings, collection of etchings.

ébahi, -e, *adj.*, wondering, aghast.

*s'***ébahir**, *v.r.*, to wonder at, to be amazed, to be surprised.

ébahissement (-is-mān), *n.m.*, wonderment, amazement, astonishment.

ébarbage, *n.m.*, (arts) paring, paring away; (engr.) edging off; scraping.

ébarber, *v.a.*, to pare, to strip (quills—*plumes d'oie*); (engr.) to edge off, to scrape. — *un plat;* to edge a dish off.

ébarboir, *n.m.*, (arts) parer.

ébat, *n.m.*, (fam.) diversion, pastime, sport, gambol. *Prendre ses —s;* to sport. [Generally used in the plural.]

ébattement (é-bat-mān), *n.m.*, balancing (of a vehicle—*d'une voiture*); (jest.) diversion, pastime, sport, gambol.

*s'***ébattre**, *v.r.*, to sport, to take one's pleasure.

ébaubi, -e, *adj.*, (fam., jest.) amazed, astonished.

ébauche, *n.f.*, sketch, rough draught, drawing, outline.

ébaucher, *v.a.*, to make the first draught, to draw an outline of, to sketch, to rough-hew; to delineate; (mas.) to boast.

ébaucheur, *adj.*, (tech.) roughing.

ébauchoir, *n.m.*, (sculp.) boasting-tool.

⊙*s'***ébaudir**, *v.r.*, (jest.) to frolic.

⊙**ébaudissement**, *n.m.*, frolicking.

ebbe, *or* **èbe**, *n.m.*, (nav.) ebb, reflux, low water.

ébène, *n.f.*, ebony, ebon. *Des cheveux d'—;* raven locks.

ébéner, *v.a.*, to ebonize.

ébénier, *n.m.*, ebony-tree, ebon-tree.

ébéniste, *n.m.*, cabinet-maker.

ébénisterie, *n.f.*, cabinet-work.

⊙**éberner**, *v.a.* *V.* **ébrener**.

éblouir, *v.a.*, to dazzle; to fascinate. *Le soleil nous éblouit;* the sun dazzles us. *C'est une beauté qui éblouit;* she is a dazzling beauty.

éblouissant, -e, *adj.*, dazzling, transplendent. *Une beauté —e;* a transplendent beauty.

éblouissement (-is-mān), *n.m.*, dazzling.

*éborgner, *v.a.*, to make blind of one eye, to put out one eye.

*s'***éborgner**, *v.r.*, to make one's self blind of one eye; to put out each other's eyes.

⊙**éborgner**, *n.m.*, road-scraper.

*ébouillir, *v.n.*, to boil down, to boil away. *Cette sauce est trop ébouillie;* that sauce is boiled away too much. *Ne laissez point tant — le pot;* do not let the pot boil away so much.

éboulement (é-bool-mān), *n.m.*, falling in, falling down. — *de terre;* landslip.

ébouler, *v.n.*, to fall in, to fall down.

*s'***ébouler**, *v.r.*, to fall in, to fall down, to tumble. *Ce rempart s'éboule;* the rampart is falling in.

éboulis, *n.m.*, rubbish, fallen ground.

ébourgeonnement (-jo-n-mān), *n.m.*, (hort.) nipping of the buds.

ébourgeonner (-jo-né), *v.a.*, (hort.) to nip off the buds.

ébouriffé, -e. *adj.*, disordered, in disorder ; in a flutter. *Elle arriva tout —e ;* she came in with her head-dress all disordered. *Qu'avez-vous donc ? vous voilà tout — ;* what is the matter with you ? you are all of a flutter.

ébousiner, *v.a.*, (mas.) to clean off.

ébranché, -e, *adj.*, branchless.

ébranchement (é-bransh-mān), *n.m.*, (hort.) pruning, lopping.

ébrancher, *v.a.*, (hort.) to prune, to lop.

ébranlement (é-branl-mān), *n.m.*, shock, concussion, shaking ; perturbation, trouble.

ébranler, *v.a.*, to shake, to move ; to disturb. *Les vents ont ébranlé cette maison ;* the winds have shaken that house. *— la résolution de quelqu'un ;* to shake any one's resolution. *Sa fidélité ne fut jamais ébranlée ;* his fidelity was never shaken.

s'ébranler, *v.r.*, to shake, to be shaken, to be disturbed ; (milit.) to move. *Quand les deux armées s'ébranlèrent ;* when the two armies moved.

ébrasement (é-brâz-mān), *n.m.*, (arch.) splaying.

ébraser, *v.a.*, (arch.) to splay.

ébrécher, *v.a.*, to notch, to make a notch in (a knife, razor, &c.—*à un couteau, à un rasoir, &c.*); to impair. *Ses folles dépenses ont ébréché sa fortune ;* his extravagant living has made a gap in his fortune.

s'ébrécher, *v.r.*, to be notched, to break off a piece of one's tooth—*une dent*).

ébrener, *v.a.*, (l. ex.) to clean an infant.

ébriété, *n.f.*, ebriety.

⊙*ébrillade,** *n.f.*, (man.) ebrillade.

ébrouement, *n.m.*, sneezing ; snorting (of a horse—*du cheval*).

ébrouer, *v.a.*, (dy.) to wash.

s'ébrouer, *v.r.*, (man.) to snort ; to sneeze (of cattle—*des bestiaux*).

ébruiter, *v.a.*, to make known ; to spread about (a report—*une rumeur*).

s'ébruiter, *v.r.*, to be made known, to be noised about.

ébuard, *n.m*, wooden wedge.

ébullition, *n.f.*, boiling, ebullition.

écachement, *n.m.*, bruising, crushing.

écacher, *v.a.*, to crush, to squash, to squeeze flat. *Nez écaché ;* flat nose.

*écaille,** *n.f.*, scale ; shell ; chipping (porcelain). *Des —s d'huître ;* oyster-shells. *Peigne d'— ;* tortoise-shell comb.

*écaillé, -e,** *adj.*, scaly.

*écaill-er,** *n.m.*, **-ère,** *n.f.*, oyster-man, oyster-woman.

*écailler,** *v.a.*, to scale.

s'écailler, *v.r.*, to peel off, to scale, to scale off ; to chip off.

*écailleu-x, -se.** *adj.*, scaly, squamous.

écale, *n.f.*, shell (of peas, &c.—*de pois, &c.*), hull (of nuts, &c.—*de noix, &c.*). *— de noix ;* walnut-shell.

écaler, *v.a.*, to shell (beans, peas—*des fèves, des pois*); to hull (almonds, nuts—*des amandes, des noix, &c.*).

s'écaler, *v.r.*, to shell, to be shelled.

*écarbouiller,** *v.a.*, (pop.) to crush.

écarlate, *n.f.* and *adj.*, scarlet.

écarlatine. *V. scarlatine.*

*écarquillement** (-mān), *n.m.*, (fam) opening (of one's eyes, legs—*des yeux, des jambes*).

*écarquiller,** *v.a.*, (fam.) to open. *— les jambes ;* to spread one's legs. *— les yeux ;* to open, to strain one's eyes.

écart, *n.m.*, step aside, digression, swerving, error ; (man.) strain ; (écarté) cards rejected. *Il fit un — pour éviter le coup ;* he stepped aside to avoid the blow. *Faire un — ;* to step aside.

Faire un — dans un discours ; to make a digression in a speech. *Les —s de l'imagination ;* the flights of the imagination. *Ce cheval s'est donné un — ;* that horse has strained himself. *Les —s de la jeunesse ;* the errors of youth. *Faire son — ;* to lay out one's cards. *À l'— ;* aside, apart, by one's self, in retirement. *Mettre à l'— ;* to put by, to lay aside. *Il le prit à l'— ;* he took him aside. *Se mettre, se tenir, à l'— ;* to keep aloof, to stand aside. *Laisser à l'— ;* to leave aside, to shun ; to omit.

écarté, *n.m.*, ecarté (cards—*jeu de cartes*).

écarté, *part.*, remote, lonely.

écartelé, -e. *adj.*, quartered, torn to pieces ; (her.) quartered.

écartèlement, *n.m.*, tearing to pieces, quartering.

écarteler, *v.a.*, to quarter, to tear to pieces ; (her.) to quarter.

écartelure, *n.f.*, (her.) quartering.

écartement, *n.m.*, putting aside ; removal ; separation ; (surg.) diastasis.

écarter, *v.a.*, to set aside, to remove ; to waive ; to pass over ; to dispel ; to widen ; to keep from ; to disperse, to scatter, to avert ; to discard one's cards (at cards—*aux cartes*). *— une mauvaise pensée ;* to dismiss an evil thought. *— un coup ;* to ward off a blow.

s'écarter, *v.r.*, to turn aside ; to deviate ; to err ; to ramble ; to swerve ; to remove. *S'— de son sujet ;* to go from one's subject. *S'— de son chemin ;* to go out of one's way. *S'— de son devoir ;* to swerve from one's duty. *La foule s'écarta ;* the crowd made way.

*écartillement,** *n.m. V.* **écarquillement.**

*écartiller,** *v a. V.* **écarquiller**

⊙**écaveçade,** or **écavessade,** *n.f.*, (man.) motion given to the head of a horse.

ecce homo (èk-sé-), *n.m.* (—), ecce homo ; (fig.) thin, pale person.

ecchymose (é-ki-), *n.f.*, (med.) ecchymosis.

ecchymosé (éki-), *adj.*, being in a state of ecchymosis, bruised.

ecclésiaste, *n.m.*, Ecclesiastes (a book of the Old Testament—*livre de l'Ancien Testament*).

ecclésiastique, *adj.*, ecclesiastic, clerical.

ecclésiastique, *n.m.*, clergyman, ecclesiastic ; Ecclesiasticus (a book of the Apocrypha—*un des livres sapientiaux*).

ecclésiastiquement (-tik-mān), *adv.*, ecclesiastically.

écervelé, -e, *adj.*, hare-brained, mad-brained, rash, giddy. *Une tête —e,* a mad-cap.

écervelé, *n.m.*, **-e,** *n.f.*, mad-cap ; hare-brained person.

échafaud, *n.m.*, scaffold ; (arch.) stage. *Mourir sur un — ;* to die on a scaffold.

échafaudage, *n.m.*, scaffolding, pompous preparations ; display.

échafauder, *v.n.*, to scaffold, to erect scaffolding.

échafauder, *v.a.*, to make preparations for a work ; ⊙ to pillory.

s'échafauder, *v.r.*, to make preparations ; to make scaffolding ; (fig.) to raise one's self, to support one's self, to find supporters.

échalas, *n.m.*, prop for a vine. *C'est un — ;* he is as thin as a lath.

échalassement, *n.m.*, (hort.) propping.

échalasser, *v.a.*, to prop vines, &c.

échalier, *n.m.*, fence made with the branches of trees.

échalote, *n.f.*, shallot, eschalot.

échampir, *v.a.*, (house paint.—*terme de peintre en bâtiments*) to set off. *V.* **réchampir.**

échancré, -e, *part.*, hollowed out ; (bot.) emarginated ; sloped.

échancrer, *v.a.*, to slope, to hollow out.
échancrure, *n.f.*, hollowing, sloping, slope.
échange, *n.m.*, exchange, barter. *Un — de compliments*; an exchange of compliments.
échangeable (-jabl), *adj.*, exchangeable.
échanger, *v.a.*, to exchange, to interchange. *— une propriété contre une autre*; to exchange one property for another. *Ils échangèrent quelques coups de poing*; they exchanged a few blows.
échanson, *n.m.*, cup-bearer.
échansonnerie (-so-n-ri), *n.f.*, cup-bearers of a prince ; a king's wine-cellars.
*__échantillon__, *n.m.*, sample, pattern, specimen ; (nav.) scantling.
*__échantillonnage__, *n.m.*, sampling ; gauging.
*__échantillonner__, *v.a.*, to sample, to gauge.
échanvrer, *v.a.*, to hatchel.
échappade, *n.f.*, (engr.) slip.
échappatoire, *n.f.*, shift, subterfuge, creep-hole, put-off, evasion.
échappé, *n.m.*, -e, *n.f.*, a person who has made his *or* her escape ; a horse of mongrel breed. *Un — de galères*; an escaped convict. *Un — des petites-maisons*; a madman, a crack-brained fellow.
échappée, *n.f.*, prank ; sally, snatch ; (arch.) rounding off ; space for carriages to turn in. *Faire quelque chose par —s*; to do a thing by snatches, by fits and starts. *— de vue*; vista. *— de lumière*; (paint.) accidental light.
échappement, *n.m.*, (horl.) escape, scapement. *— à recul*; recoil-escapement. *— à repos*; dead beat. *— de la vapeur*; (mec.) puff.
échapper, *v.n.*, to escape, to make one's escape, to get away, to get out of, to avoid, to shun, to fly, to break, out. *Laisser —*; to overlook, to pass over, to let pass. *Faire — un prisonnier*; to favour a prisoner's escape. *— à la fureur des ennemis*; to escape the rage of the enemy. *— du naufrage*; to escape from shipwreck. *Rien n'échappe à sa prévoyance*; nothing escapes his foresight. *Cela m'est échappé de la mémoire*; that has slipped my memory. *Laisser — l'occasion*; to let slip an opportunity. *Laisser — un mot*; to drop a word. [When *échapper* means *to avoid, to be preserved*, it requires the preposition *à*: *On échappe à l'orage*. When it means *to steal away, to leave a place*, it requires the preposition *de*: *On échappe de prison*.]
échapper, *v.a.*, to escape, to avoid ; (man.) to put to the greatest speed. *L'— belle*; to have a narrow escape. *— le danger*; to avoid danger ; *— la côte*; to escape stranding.
s'échapper, *v.r.*, to get loose, to get away, to escape, to steal away, to slip out; to vanish, to disappear ; to forget one's self. *Il s'est échappé jusqu'à dire*; he forgot himself so far as to say.
écharbot, *n m.*, (bot.) water-chesnut, water-caltrops.
écharde, *n.f.*, prick, prickle (of a thistle—*du chardon*) ; splinter.
échardonner, *v.a.*, to clear of thistles.
échardonnoir, *n.m.*, weed-hook.
écharner, *v.a.*, to excarnate ; (curriery—*corroierie*) to flesh.
écharnoir, *n.f.*, (curriery—*corroierie*) fleshing-knife.
écharnure, *n.f.*, (curriery—*corroierie*) scrapings or parings of hides.
écharpe, *n.f.*, scarf ; sling ; (nav.) shell of a pulley or block ; (engineering—*terme d'ingénieur*) surface-table ; water-table ; (her.) scarp. *Changer d'—*; to be a turncoat, to change sides, to rat. *Avoir le bras en —*; to have one's arm in a sling. *Le canon tire en —*; the cannon fires slanting. *Coup d'épée en —*; slanting cut.

Avoir l'esprit en —; to be heedless, absent, inattentive.
écharper, *v.a.*, to slash, to cut; to cut to pieces. *Il lui a écharpé le visage*; he gave him a slash across the face. *— un régiment*; to cut a regiment to pieces.
échars, **-e**, *adj.*, ⊙ of a coin below the legal standard. *Vents —*; (nav.) shifting winds, light and variable winds.
⊙**échars**, *n.m.*, what is wanting in the legal standard of a coin.
écharser, *v.n.*, (nav.) to veer, to shift about, to change often ; ⊙—, *v.a.*, to lower the standard of coins.
échasse, *n.f.*, (orni.) stilt-bird. *— à manteau noir*; long-legged plover.
échasse, *n.f.*, stilt; tressel, trussel (of stages —*tréteaux*) ; upher. *d'échafaud*; upher, scaffolding-pole. *Il est toujours monté sur des —s*; he is always on stilts, in buckram.
échassier, *n.m.*, (orni.) grallic.
échauboulé, **-e**, *adj.*, (med.) full of pimples.
échauboulure, *n.f.*, (med.) pimple, blotch, rash, pustule.
échaudage, *n.m.*, lime-wash ; white-washing (of walls—*pour les murs*).
échaudé, *n.m.*, simnel (kind of pastry—*pâtisserie*). *— au beurre*; simnel with butter.
échaudé, **-e**, *adj.*, part., scalded. *Chat — craint l'eau froide*; a burnt child fears the fire.
échauder, *v.a.*, to scald.
s'échauder, *v.r.*, to burn one's self ; to burn one's fingers. *Il s'y est échaudé*; he burned his fingers in that business.
échaudis, *n.m.*, (nav.) triangular shape.
échaudoir, *n.m.*, scalding-house ; scalding-tub.
échauffaison, *n.f.*, (med.) an overheating of one's self ; breaking out of the skin.
échauffant, **-e**, *adj.*, heating.
échauffe, *n.f.*, heap. *Mettre les peaux en —*; to heap the hides.
échauffé, *n.m.*, odour (caused by excessive heat—*causée par une chaleur excessive*). *Sentir l'—*; to have or exhale a hot smell.
échauffée, *n.f.*, first operation of salt-makers in warming their oven.
échauffement (é-shôf-mān), *n.m.*, heating; over-excitement.
échauffer, *v.a.*, to warm, to heat, to over-heat; to excite, to inflame, to irritate, to anger ; to vex. *Échauffez la chambre*; warm the room. *Les épices échauffent le sang*; spices heat the blood. *Cela lui échauffe la bile*; that provokes him.
s'échauffer, *v.r.*, to grow warm, to over-heat one's self; to grow angry, to fly into a passion, to chafe, to fume, to grow high (of quarrels—*querelles*). *La chambre s'échauffe*; the room is growing warm. *Il s'est échauffé à marcher*; walking has made him warm. *La querelle s'échauffe*; the quarrel is getting hot. *Le jeu s'échauffe*; they are playing deep. *S'— sur la voie*; (hunt.) to follow the chase eagerly.
échauffourée, *n.f.*, a rash, headlong, or blundering enterprise ; skirmish, affray.
échauffure, *n.f.*, red pimple.
échauguette (-ghèt), *n.f.*, (milit.) watch-box, watch-tower.
échauler, *v.a.* V. **chauler**.
échaux, *n.m.pl.*, channels, furrows (to receive water for watering or draining fields—*vour l'irrigation ou le drainage des champs*).
échéance, *n.f.*, falling due, expiration. *— commune*; average maturity. *— prochaine*; near approach of maturity. *À courte —*; at a short date, short-dated. *À longue —*; at a long date;

long-dated. *Jusqu'à l'—;* until maturity, till due. *Payer une lettre de change à l'—;* to pay a bill of exchange on its coming due; to discharge at maturity.

échec, *n.m.*, check; blow; loss. *Donner —;* to check. — *et mat;* checkmate. *Être — et mat;* to be checkmated. *Il a souffert un grand —;* he has suffered a dreadful blow. *Tenir un homme en —;* to have a man under one's thumb. *Tenir une armée en —;* to keep an army at bay.

échecs (é-shè), *n.m.pl.*, chess; board and set of chess-men; chess-men. *Jouer aux —;* to play at chess.

échelette, *n.f.*, rack (for pack-saddles, carts &c.—*de bâts, charrettes, &c.*); (orni.) wall-creeper.

échelier, *n.m.*, peg-ladder.

échelle, *n.f.*, ladder; ladder-staircase; scale; (nav.) quarter-deck ladder. — *brisée;* folding-ladder. — *de siège;* scaling-ladder. — *de corde;* rope-ladder. — *de meunier;* trap-ladder. — *à incendie;* fire-ladder, fire-escape. — *de jardin ou de tapissier;* pair of steps. — *de dunette;* poop-ladder. — *de commandement;* accommodation-ladder. — *campanaire;* bell-founder's diapason. —*s du Levant;* sea-ports in the Levant. *Faire la courte —;* to mount upon one another's shoulders. *Faire à quelqu'un la courte —;* to assist any one in his endeavours. *Sentir l'—;* to deserve hanging. *Après lui il faut tirer l'—;* he has left nothing to be done, nothing can be better.

échelon (ésh-lon), *n.m.*, round (of a ladder —*d'une échelle*), step, stepping-stone; (milit.) echelon. *Descendre d'un —;* to come down a step. *Marcher en —s;* to march in echelons.

échelonner, *v.a.*, to draw up in echelons; to arrange according to gradation. — *un corps d'infanterie;* to draw up a body of infantry in echelons.

s'échelonner, *v.r.*, to be arranged or drawn up in echelons.

échenal, *or* **écheneau**, *n.m.*, wooden gutter of a roof; (metal.) earth-gutter into which the molten metal falls to be conducted to the mould.

*échenillage**, *n.m.*, clearing, ridding of caterpillars.

*écheniller** (ésh-ni-), *v.a.*, to rid plants of caterpillars.

*échenilleur**, *n.m.*, one who rids plants of caterpillars; a bird living on caterpillars.

*échenilloir**, *n.m.*, instrument used for ridding plants of caterpillars.

écheno. *V.* **échenal.**

échoir. *V.* **échoir.**

écheveau (ésh-vo), *n.m.*, hank, skein. *Dévider un —;* to reel, to wind off, a skein.

échevelé, -e (é-shèv-lé), *adj.*, dishevelled, whose hair hangs loose; disordered.

échevette, *n.f.*, small skein.

échevin (ésh-vin), *n.m.*, eschevin, sheriff, alderman.

échevinage, *n.m.*, eschevinage, shrievalty, sheriffdom, sheriffship.

échidné (é-kid-), *n.m.*, (zool.) echidna.

échi-f, -ve, *adj.*, (hunt.) voracious, greedy.

échiffe, *or* **échiffre**, *n.m.*, (arch.) partition-wall of a stair.

*échignole**, *n.f.*, (tech.) button-maker's spindle.

*échillon**, *n.m.*, water-spout, column of clouds and water.

échimose, *n.f. V.* **ecchymose.**

échine, *n.f.*, spine, back-bone, chine; (arch.) echinus, ovolo. *Une maigre —;* a thin lank person. *Crotté jusqu'à l'—;* spattered, or splashed, up to the neck.

échinée, *n.f.*, (cook.) chine, chine-piece.

échiner, *v.a.*, to break the back, to kill, to murder; to beat unmercifully.

s'échiner, *v.r.*, to knock one's self up with work; to work one's self to death.

échinite (éki-), *n.m.*, (foss.) petrified sea-hedgehog, echinite.

échinope (éki-), *n.m.*, (bot.) echinops, globe-thistle.

échinophore (éki-), *n.f. and adj.*, (bot.) prickly parsnip; echinophora; (conch.) unival-vular shell.

échioïde (-é-ki-), *n.m.*,(bot.) *V.* **vipérine.**

échiqueté, -e (é-shik-té), *adj.*, cheekered; (her.) checkee.

échiquier, *n.m.*,chess-board; court of exchequer; square net. *Ouvrage fait en —;* checker-work.

écho (é-ko), *n.m.*, echo. *Le jeu des —s;* echo-stop (in organs—*d'orgues*). —*s de lumière;* (paint.) reverberations of light.

échoir (échéant, échu), *v.n.*, to expire, to be out, to lapse, to devolve; to chance, to happen, to fall, to fall out; to fall to. *Le premier payement doit — à Noël;* the first payment falls due at Christmas. *Cette lettre de change est échue;* that bill of exchange is due. *Cela lui est échu en partage;* that fell to him by lot. *Si le cas y échoit, s'il y échet, le cas échéant;* the case occurring.

échomètre (é-ko-), *n.m.*, echometer.

échométrie (é-ko-), *n.f.*, echometry.

échoppe, *n.f.*, booth, stall; round *or* flat graver; scalper, scorper, burin.

échopper, *v.a.*, to work with a flat or round graver; to scorp.

échouage, *n.m.*, (nav.) stranding. *Lieu d'—;* place proper for running a vessel aground.

échouement, *n.m.*, running aground, stranding.

échouer, *v.n.*, to run aground *or* on shore, to cast away, to run against, to hit, to strand, to be stranded; to miscarry; to be disappointed. *La frégate échoua contre un rocher;* the frigate struck upon a rock. *Il échoue dans tous ses desseins;* all his designs miscarry.

échouer, *v.a.*, (nav.) to strand, to run aground.

écimer, *v.a.*, to top, to pollard (a tree—*des arbres*).

éclaboussement, *n.m.*, splashing, bespattering.

éclabousser, *v.a.*, to splash, to bespatter.

éclaboussure, *n.f.*,splash, the dirt *or* water one is splashed with; (nav.) spoon-drift.

éclair, *n.m.*, lightning, flash of lightning; (chem.) shine. —*s de chaleur;* heat-lightning. *Il a passé comme un —;* he shot by like lightning. *Faire des —s;* to lighten.

éclairage, *n.m.*, lighting, illumination.

éclaircie, *n.f.*, (nav.) clear spot in a cloudy sky; glade.

éclaircir, *v.a.*, to clear, to brighten to clarify; to thin, to make thin; to clear up to elucidate, to illustrate, to explain, to throw a light on. *Cet auteur éclaircit bien des vérités;* that author clears up many truths. — *une difficulté;* to clear up a difficulty. *Le temps éclaircit la vérité;* time brings truth to light. — *quelqu'un;* to enlighten any one, to instruct. to inform, any one. *Il faut l'en —;* he must be informed of it. — *une peau;* to gloss a skin.

s'éclaircir, *v.r.*, to clear, to brighten, to become clear or bright, to grow light; to be solved; to be explained, to be elucidated. *Le temps s'éclaircit;* the weather is clearing up. *Son teint commence à s'—;* her complexion begins to grow clear. *s' — d'une chose;* to inquire about or into a business, to inform one's self about a thing, to clear up a matter. *Il faut* s'— *sur cette affaire ;* that affair must be cleared up.

éclaircissement (-sis-män), *n.m.*, clearing up, explanation, illustration; elucidation; hint, light, discovery, insight. *Avoir un —, en venir à un — avec quelqu'un ;* to have an explanation, to come to an explanation, with any one.

éclaire, *n.f.*, (bot.) celandine. *La grande —;* swallow-wort, tetter-wort. *La petite —;* crowfoot, pilewort.

éclairer, *v.a.*, to light, to give light to; to illuminate; to carry a light before one, to show a light to one; to enlighten, to instruct; to observe, to watch; (milit.) to reconnoitre; (paint.) to throw light in, to put light in. *Le soleil éclaire la terre;* the sun lights, gives light to, the earth. *Éclairez monsieur;* light the gentleman. *Les bonnes lectures éclairent l'esprit;* the reading of good books enlightens the mind. *Il faut l'— de près ;* he must be watched closely. *— une question ;* to throw a light upon a question. **s'éclairer,** *v.r.,* to become enlightened; to instruct one another.

éclairer, *v.n.,* to sparkle, to shine, to brighten; *v. imp.,* to lighten. *Il éclaire ;* it lightens.

éclaireur, *n.m.,* (milit.) scout. *Aller en —;* (milit.) to scout.

éclanche, *n.f.,* shoulder of mutton.

éclat, *n.m.,* shiver; splinter (of wood, stone, brick, &c.—*de bois, de pierre, de brique, &c.);* brightness, refulgence, radiancy, resplendency, glitter, effulgence; clap, crash, noise; lustre, pomp, richness, magnificence, glory, gaudiness (of colours—*des couleurs);* rumour, uproar. *Un — de pierre;* a piece of stone flown off. *Un — de bombe;* a splinter of a bomb. *On ne saurait soutenir l'— du soleil;* there is no bearing the glare of the sun. *L'— des yeux;* the brilliancy of the eyes. *L'— et la pompe de son style;* the splendour and pomp of his style. *Un — de rire;* a burst of laughter. *Un grand — de voix;* a loud shout. *L'— des habits;* the magnificence of dress. *Action d'—;* bold stroke. *Des personnes d'—;* eminent persons. *Cette action a fait —;* that action has made a great deal of noise. *Voler en —s;* to be shivered, to fly into a thousand pieces.

éclatant, -e, *adj.,* bright, sparkling, glittering, brilliant, radiant, dazzling, striking, effulgent, shining, signal, glorious; piercing, loud, shrill. *Tout — de lumière;* all radiant with light. *Son —;* shrill sound. *Bruit —;* crash. *Actions —es ;* splendid exploits. *Vengeance —e;* signal vengeance.

éclater, *v.n.,* to split, to shiver, to break in pieces, to burst; to crack, to clap; to cry out, to exclaim against, to fly into, to break out; to blaze out; to shine, to sparkle, to glitter, to flash, to irradiate. *Une bombe éclate en tombant;* a bomb bursts on falling. *Le tonnerre vient d'—;* there has just been a clap of thunder. *— de rire;* to burst out laughing. *— en injures;* to burst forth into abuse. *L'incendie éclata pendant la nuit;* the fire broke out during the night. *Sa colère a éclaté;* his passion burst forth. *Sa joie éclata;* his joy broke forth. *Faire —;* to shiver, to shatter; to splinter; to snap, to burst, to cause to explode; to vent, to give vent to; to brighten, to blaze forth; to show, to discover, to make appear.

s'**éclater,** *v.r.,* to split, to shiver, to fly into fragments, to burst.

éclectique, *n.m.* and *adj.,* eclectic.

éclectisme, *n.m.,* eclecticism.

éclipse, *n.f.,* eclipse. *— de soleil, de lune ;* an eclipse of the sun, of the moon. *Faire une —;* to vanish. *Son intelligence est sujette à des —s;* his understanding is apt to be cloudy.

éclipser, *v.a.,* to eclipse; to throw into the shade. *La lune éclipse le soleil;* the moon eclipses the sun.

s'**éclipser,** *v. r.,* to be eclipsed *or* darkened, to disappear, to vanish. *Il s'éclipsa tout d'un coup ;* he suddenly disappeared.

écliptique, *n.f.* and *adj.,* (astron.) ecliptic.

éclisse, *n.f.,* (surg.) splint; splinter; cheesewattle; wood split thin to make the sides of lutes and violins, of pails, tubs, casks, &c.

éclisser, *v.a.,* (surg.) to splint.

éclogue, *n.f.* V. **églogue.**

éclopé, -e, *n.* and *adj.,* cripple; foot-sore, lame. *Il est tout —;* he is quite lame.

écloper, *v.a.,* to lame; to make lame, footsore; s'—; *v.r.,* to become lame, foot-sore.

éclore, *v.n.,* to hatch; to blow, to open; to break, to dawn. *Les poulets commencent à —;* the chickens begin to peep out of the shell. *Ils éclosent à merveille;* they come out charmingly. *Faire — des oiseaux;* to hatch birds. *Le soleil fait — les fleurs;* the sun makes the flowers blow, open.

éclosion, *n.f.,* hatching; blowing.

écluse, *n.f.,* lock, guard-lock, sluice, dam, mill-dam, wear, weir, flood-gate. *— de moulin;* mill-gate. *— à sas;* lift-lock. *— à vannes;* sliding flood-gate. *Déversoir à —;* weir. *— à marée montante;* tide-gate.

éclusée, *n.f.,* sluice-full of water.

écluser, *v.a.,* (engineering—*terre d'ingénieur)* to build locks in a canal *or* river; to take a boat through a lock.

éclusier, *n.m.,* sluice-keeper, lock-keeper.

écobuage, *n.m.,* (agri.) weeding and burning the weeds.

écobuer, *v.a.,* to weed a field and burn the weeds.

écœurer, *v.a.,* to disgust; (fig.) to shock; to dishearten.

écofrai, *or* **écofroi,** *n.m.,* (tech.) cutting-board.

écoinçon, *or* **écoinson,** *n.m.,* (mas., carp.) diagonal, angle-tie; angle stuff-bead ; (carp.) jamb (of doors—*de portes);* (carp.) reveal (of windows—*de fenêtres).*

écolâtre, *n.m.,* (theol.) doctor, teacher.

école, *n.f.,* school; scholastic philosophy. *Petite —;* day-school. *Maître d'—;* schoolmaster. *Camarade d'—;* school-fellow. *— de droit;* law-school. *— de marine;* naval school. *— d'équitation;* riding-school. *— de natation;* swimming-school. *— communale;* parish-school. *— d'enseignement mutuel;* Lancasterian school. *Cela sent l'—;* that savours of pedantry. *Faire —;* to be at the head of a school. *Dire les nouvelles de l'—;* to tell tales out of school. *Faire l'— buissonnière;* to play truant. *Faire une —;* (backgammon—*trictrac)* to forget to mark one's points, to be pegged. *Envoyer à l'—;* to peg. *Faire une —;* to commit a stupid blunder.

écoli-er, *n.m.,* **-ère,** *n.f.,* school-boy, school-girl, pupil, scholar, learner. *En —;* scholar-like. *Prendre le chemin des —s;* to go round about. *Ce n'est qu'un —;* he is but a novice.

éconduire, *v.a.,* to show out; to put off, to refuse, to deny. *Il nous éconduit poliment;* he gives us a polite refusal.

économat, *n.m.,* stewardship; bursary-steward's office.

économe, *adj.,* economical, saving. *C'est une femme —;* she is a thrifty woman. *Être — de louanges;* to be sparing of praise.

économe, *n.m.,* steward, housekeeper, manager, economist, purser (of colleges, hospitals, &c.—*de collèges, hôpitaux, &c.).*

économie, *n.f.,* economy; thrift. *Vivre avec —;* to live economically. *Faire des —s; to* put by money, to save money. *L'— de l'univers;* the disposition of the universe. *L'— du corps humain;* the harmony of the human body. *L'— d'un discours;* the management or disposition of a speech.

économique, *adj.*, economic, economical. *Ménage —;* economical housekeeping. [*Économique* is applied to things only.]

économie, *n.f.*, economics.

économiquement (-mik-mān),*adv.*, economically.

économiser, *v.a.*, to economize, to save, to husband. *— ses forces;* to husband one's strength.

économiste, *n.m.*, economist.

écope, *n.f.*, (nav) scoop.

écorce, *n.f.*, bark, rind ; outside, surface. *Ôter l'—;* to peel. *Cet homme n'a que l'— ;* he is but a superficial, a shallow man. *Juger du bois par l'—;* to judge of the inside by the outside.

écorcement, *n.m.*, barking (of trees—*d'arbres*).

écorcer, *v.a.*, to bark, to strip.

écorché, *n.m.*, (paint.) figure without skin for the study of the muscles.

à écorche-cul, *adv.*, (l.ex.) sliding on the ground ; against the grain, unwillingly.

écorchée, *n.f.*, (conch.) conus.

écorchement, *n.m.*, excoriation ; flaying, skinning.

écorcher, *v.a.*, to flay, to skin ; to gall, to peel off, to rub off the bark; to take off the skin ; to fleece. *— l'anguille par la queue;* to begin at the wrong end. *Cela écorche les oreilles;* that grates on one's ears. *Ce procureur écorchait ses clients;* that attorney fleeced his clients. *— le français;* to speak broken French, to murder the French language.

s'écorcher, *v.r.*, to tear off one's skin, to get skinned, to gall.

écorcherie, *n.f.*, knacker's yard ; inn in which travellers are fleeced; fleecing.

écorcheur, *n.m.*, knacker; flayer; fleecer.

écorchure, *n.f.*, scratch, excoriation ; slight wound.

écorner, *v.a.*, to break the horns, the corners, of; to curtail, to impair, to lessen, to diminish. *Ce taureau est écorné;* that bull has one of his horns broken.

écornifler, *v.a.*, to sponge, to hang on.

écorniflerie, *n.f.*, sponging, hanging on.

écornifleu-r, *n.m.*, **-se**, *n.f.*, sponger, hanger-on.

écornure, *n.f.*, corner broken off, breaking at the edges.

écossais, **-e**, *n.* and *adj.*, Scotchman; Scotchwoman ; Scotch.

écossaise, *n.f.*, plaid, plaid-stuff.

écosser, *v.a.*, to shell (peas or beans—*des pois, des fèves*).

écosseu-r, *n.m.*, **-se**, *n.f.*, one that shells.

écot, *n.m.*, share (of a reckoning—*d'une dépense*); reckoning ; score; company ; stump (of a tree—*d'un arbre*). *Payez votre —;* pay your share. *Parlez à votre —;* speak to your own company ; mind your own business.

***écouailles**, *n.f. pl.*, coarse wool.

écoulement (é-kool-mān), *n.m.*, flowing, running, draining; (com.) sale. *L'— de l'eau;* the flowing of water. *L'— de nos produits;* the sale of our commodities.

écouler, *v.a.*, to pour away; to sell.

s'écouler, *v.r.*, to run or flow away; to pass away, to glide away ; to slip away; (com.) to go off. *L'eau s'écoule;* the water flows away. *L'argent s'écoule;* money slips away. *Le temps s'écoule;* time glides away. *Ces marchandises s'écoulent vite;* these goods sell fast.

écourgeon. *V.* **escourgeon**.

écourter, *v.a.*, to shorten, to dock, to crop; to curtail. *— un chien;* to crop a dog. *Cheval écourté;* cropped horse.

écoutant, -e. *n.* and *adj.*, listener, hearer; listening, attending. *Avocat —;* briefless barrister.

écoute, *n.f.*, hiding-place for listening; (nav.) sheet (cordage). *Être aux —s;* to be on the watch, on the look out.

écouter, *v.a.*, to listen; to hearken; to give hearing; to hear; to pay attention to. *— à la porte;* to listen at the door. *— les avis de quelqu'un;* to listen to any one's advice. *— la raison;* to listen to reason. *Écoutez;* hark ye, look here. *Il n'écoute personne;* he minds nobody. *Ne l'écoutez pas!* never mind him! *Se faire —;* to obtain a hearing.

s'écouter, *v.r.*, to like to hear one's self; to be over careful of one's self. *Il s'écoute trop;* he nurses himself too much.

écouteu-r, *n.m.*, **-se**, *n.f.*, listener. *C'est un — aux portes;* he is an eaves-dropper.

écouteux, *adj.*, skittish (of horses—*des chevaux*).

***écoutille**, *n.f.*, (nav.) hatchway. *Fermer les —s;* to shut down the hatches.

écoutoir, *n.m.*, ear-trumpet.

***écouvillon**, *n.m.*, scovel (of ovens—*de four*); sponge (of a cannon—*de canon*).

***écouvillonner**, *v.a.*, to sweep with a scovel; to sponge (a cannon—*un canon*).

écran, *n.m.*, screen ; hand-screen; fire-screen.

écrasant, -e, *adj.*, crushing; humiliating ; exorbitant, excessive.

écrasé, -e. *part.*, crushed, ruined. *Nez —;* flat nose. *Taille —e;* squat figure (pers.).

écrasement (é-krāz-mān), *n.m.*, crushing; crush; bruising; squashing; overwhelming ; destruction, ruin.

écraser, *v.a.*, to crush; to bruise; to weigh down, to overwhelm; to bear down; to run over; to ruin; to squash. *— des groseilles;* to squash gooseberries. *J'ai manqué d'être écrasé par un carrosse;* I was near being run over by a coach. *Être écrasé de travail;* to be overwhelmed with work. *— d'impôts;* to crush with taxes. *— ses rivaux;* to crush one's rivals.

écrémer, *v.a.*, to take off the cream, to skim ; to take the best of.

écrêter, *v.a.*, to sweep off the top of a work, to dismantle with shot ; to cut off the comb of a cock.

écrevisse, *n.f.*, crawfish, crayfish; (astron.) Cancer. *Une — de mer;* a lobster. *Rouge comme une —;* as red as a lobster.

s'écrier, *v.r.*, to cry out, to exclaim. *S'— d'admiration, de douleur;* to exclaim with admiration, to cry out from pain.

***écrille**, *n.f.*, grate, to prevent fish in ponds from getting out.

écrin, *n.m.*, casket, jewel-box.

écrire (écrivant, écrit), *v.a.*, to write; to spell ; to pen, to set down. *— quelque chose sur un registre;* to enter a thing in a register. *Papier à —;* writing-paper. *— à un ami;* to write to a friend.

s'écrire, *v.r.*, to sign one's self, to write one's name ; to be written, to be spelled ; to write to each other.

écrit, *n.m.*, writing, written agreement; pamphlet. *Mettre, coucher, par —;* to set a thing down in writing.

écrit, -e. *part.*, writ, written. *Cela était — au ciel;* that was written above. *Il est — que je ne gagnerai jamais;* I am fated never to win.

écriteau. *n.m.*, bill (poster); board.

écritoire, *n.f.*, ink-horn; inkstand. *— portative;* pocket ink-horn.

écriture, *n.f.*, writing, hand, handwriting; scripture. — *coulée*; secretary-hand, running-hand. *Mauvaise* —; scrawl. *L'Écriture sainte*; the Holy Scripture, the Bible. *Commis aux* —*s*; copying clerk.

***écrivailler**. *v.a.*, to write much, fast, and badly.

***écrivaillerie**, *n.f.*, scribbling.

***écrivailleur**. *n.m.* *V.* **écrivassier**.

***écrivain**. *n.m.*, writer, author; writing-master; clerk of a ship of war. — *public*; public scrivener, petition writer.

écrivant, -e, *adj.*, writing.

écrivassier, *n.m.*, scribbler.

écrou. *n.m.*, nut of a screw; female screw; entry in the gaol-book. *Livre, registre, d'*—; gaol-book.

écrouelles. *n.f.pl.*, king's evil, scrofula.

écrouelleu-x. -**se**, *adj.* and *n.*, scrofulous; person affected with the king's evil.

écrouer, *v.a.*, to enter in the gaol-book.

écroues, *n.f. pl.*, bills of expense of the royal kitchen.

écrouir. *v.a.*, to hard-hammer (metal).

écrouissement, *n.m.*, hardening with a hammer.

écroulé, -**e**, *part.*, fallen down, overthrown. *Un mur* —; a fallen wall. *Un empire* —; an overthrown empire.

écroulement, (é-krool-màn), *n.m.*, falling in, falling down.

s'écrouler, *v.r.*, to fall in, to fall down. to fall to pieces. *Cet édifice vient à* —; that building fell down. *La terre s'érroula*; the ground gave way.

écroûter, *v.a.*, to cut off the crust. *Il ne faut pas ainsi* — *le pain*; you must not cut the crust off the loaf in that manner.

écru, -**e**, *adj.*, unbleached. *Fil* —, *soie* —*e*; raw thread, raw silk. *Toile* —*é*; brown holland.

écrues, *n.f.pl.*, wood of new and spontaneous growth.

ectropion, *n.m.*, (med.) eversion of the eyelids.

ⓒ**ectype**, *n.f.*, ectype.

écu, *n.m.*, shield; ⓒcrown, an obsolete French coin;. ⓒhalf a crown; money, cash; copy-paper. *Amasser des* —*s*; to hoard up money. *C'est le père aux* —*s*; he is a monied man.

écuage. *n.m.*, scutage, land-tax.

écubier, *n.m.*, (nav.) hawse-hole.

***écueil** (ékeu-i), *n.m.*, reef, rock; peril, danger; *Donner sur un* —; to strike against a rock. *Le monde est plein d'*—*s*; the world is full of rocks.

écuelle. *n.f.*, porringer. *Laver les* —*s*; to wash the dishes. *Des lavures d'*—*s*; dish-water, hog-wash.

écuellée, *n.f.*, porringer-full.

écuisser, *v.a.*, to splinter (trees—*des arbres*).

éculer. *v.a.*, to tread down at heel (shoes —*des souliers, &c.*). *J'écule tous mes souliers*; I tread all my shoes down at heel.

s'éculer, *v.r.*, to wear down at the heel (of shoes—*chaussures*).

écumage, *n.m.*, skimming.

écumant. -**e**, *adj.*, foaming; frothy. *La mer* —*e*; the foaming sea.

écume, *n.f.*, froth, foam; scum. dross; dregs. *L'*— *de la mer*; the foam of the sea. *L'*— *de certains métaux*; the dross of some metals. *L'*— *d'un cheval*; the foam of a horse. *Jeter de l'*—; to foam. *Quand il est en colère, l'*— *lui sort de la bouche*; when he is in a passion, the foam comes out of his mouth. — *de mer*; white talc.

œcuménicité, *n.f.* *V.* **œcuménicité**.

œcuménique. *a.lj.* *V.* **œcuménique**.

œcuméniquement, *adv.* *V.* **œcuméniquement**.

écumer. *v.n.*, to foam, to froth. *La mer écume*; the sea foams. *Il écumait de rage*; he foamed with rage.

écumer. *v.a.*, to skim; to pick up; to range. — *le pot*; to skim the pot. — *les marmites*; to be a sponger. — *les mers*; to scour the seas.

écumeur. *n.m.*, skimmer, collector; parasite. — *de marmites*; sponger, hanger-on. — *de mer*; sea-robber, sea-rover.

écumeu-x, -**se**, *adj.*, frothy.

écumoire. *n.f.*, skimmer, scummer.

écurer. *v.a.*, to scour, to cleanse. — *de la vaisselle*; to scour dishes.

***écureuil**. *n.m.*, squirrel.

écureur. *n.m.*, -**se**, *n.f.*, scourer of kitchen utensils. — *de puits*; well-cleanser.

écurie, *n.f.*, stable; stabling; equipage. *Valet d'*—; stable-boy.

écusson, *n.m.*, escutcheon; shield, coat of arms: (arch.) knob; (hort., nav.) escutcheon.

écussonner, *v.a.*, (hort.) to bud, to inoculate.

écussonnoir, *n.m.*, (hort.) budding-knife.

écuyer, *n.m.*, esquire, squire; equerry; riding-master; rider; wall hand-rail (of a stair-case—*d'un escalier*). *Il est bon* —; he is a good horseman. — *tranchant*; carver. — *de cuisine*; head cook (of princes, &c.).

écuyère, *n.f.*, horsewoman, female equestrian performer.

eczéma, *n.m.* (n.p.), (med.) eczema.

edda. *n.f.* (—*s*), edda.

éden (é-dè-n), *n.m.*, Eden.

édenté, -**e**, *adj.*, toothless. *Vieille* —*e*; toothless hag. *Un peigne* —; a comb with broken teeth.

édenter. *v.a.*, to wear out, to break the teeth of objects such as combs, saws, &c.; to pull off the teeth of any one as a punishment, a torture; to cause any one to lose his teeth. *La vieillesse nous édente*; old age causes us to lose our teeth.

s'édenter, *v.r.*, to lose its teeth (combs, saws, &c.—*peignes, scies, &c.*).

édentés, *n.m.pl.*, (zool.) edentata.

édicter. *v.a.*, to enact *Peines édict'es par la loi*; penalties enacted by law.

édifiant, -**e**, *adj.*, edifying.

édificateur, *n.m.*, (l.u.) builder.

édification, *n.f.*, building (temples); edification.

édifice. *n.m.*, edifice, building, pile; structure, fabric. *L* — *social*; the structure of society.

édifier. *v.a.*, to build (temples); to edify, to improve.

édile, *n.m.*, edile.

édilité, *n.f.*, edileship.

édit, *n.m.*, edict.

éditer. *v.a.*, to publish (a book—*un livre*).

éditeur. *n.m.*, publisher.

édition, *n.f.*, edition. —*princeps*; original edition.

édredon, *n.m.*, eider-down; eider-down coverlet.

éducat-eur, -**rice**, *n.* and *adj.*, educator; that which imparts education.

éducation, *n.f.*, education: breeding, rearing (of animals—*des animaux*); training; manners. *Faire l'*— *d'un jeune homme*; to educate a young man. *Tenir une maison d'*— *de demoiselles*; to keep a boarding school for young ladies. *Il n'a point d'*—; he has no breeding.

édulcoration. *n.f.*, edulcoration.

édulcorer, *v.a.*, (pharm.) to edulcorate, to sweeten.

éduquer, *v.a.*, (pop.) to bring up, to educate, children.

éfaufiler, *v.a.*, to pull out the threads of (textile fabrics—*de tissus*).

effaçable. *adj.*, that may be effaced.

effacement, *n.m.*, effacing, effacement. (fig.) *L'— des caractères ;* lack of moral vigour, of firmness and will.

effacer, *v.a.*, to efface, to expunge; to wear out ; to rub out ; to strike out; to blot out; to scrape out, to scratch out; to wash away, to obliterate : to eclipse, to throw into the shade. — *une chose de la mémoire;* to efface a thing from the memory. — *ses péchés par ses larmes,* to wash out one's sins by one's tears. *Il a effacé la gloire de ses ancêtres ;* he has effaced the glory of his ancestors.

s'effacer, *v.r.*, to get obliterated ; to wash out ; to wear away ; to keep in the back-ground. *Il s'effaça pour éviter le coup;* he drew in to avoid the blow. -

effaçure, *n.f.*, blot, blotting out, obliteration, erasure.

effaner, *v.a.*, (agri.) to take away the leaves.

effaré, **-e**, *part.*, wild. *Un visage —;* a haggard, wild-looking face.

effarement, *n.m.*, bewilderment, distraction.

effarer, *v.a.*, to terrify, to scare.

s'effarer, *v.r.*, to be scared, to look wild.

effarouchant, **-e**, *adj.*, terrifying, startling.

effaroucher, *v.a.*, to scare away ; to startle, to give umbrage.

s'effaroucher, *v.r.*, to be scared, to be startled, to take umbrage. *Mon cheval s'est effarouché;* my horse took fright.

effecti-f, **-ve**, *adj.*, effective. *C'est un homme —;* he is a man of his word.

effectif, *n.m.*, (milit.) effective force.

effection, *n.f.*, (geom.) effection.

effectivement (-tiv-mān), *adv.*, in effect, really, actually, indeed, in effect.

effectuer, *v.a.*, to effect, to execute, to accomplish ; to bring about; to work out.

s'effectuer, *v.r.*, to be effected, executed, accomplished.

effémination, *n.f.*, effeminacy.

efféminé, **-e**, *adj.*, effeminate, womanish. *Air —;* effeminate look.

efféminer, *v.a.*, to effeminate, to enervate. *Les voluptés efféminent l'âme et le corps ;* voluptuousness enervates the body and the soul.

effendi, or **efendi** (è-fân-di), *n.m.*, effendi (a title among the Turks—*titre de fonctionnaires turcs*).

effervescence, *n.f.*, effervescence. *Calmer l'— des passions;* to cool the ferment of the passions.

effervescent, **-e**, *adj.*, effervescent.

effet, *n.m.*, effect, performance, intent, execution ; purpose; funds; stocks; power (mec.); bill of exchange, bill ; *pl.*, goods ; luggage (of a traveller—*d'un voyageur*); moveables, chattels. *Produire de l'—;* to make an impression. *Ces choses-là font un vilain —;* those things look very ill. *Souscrire un —;* to sign a bill. — *à échoir ;* running bill. *Faire les fonds d'un —;* to provide for a bill. *Faire honneur à un —;* to honour a bill. *À double —;* double acting (mec.). *En —;* in reality, indeed. *Pour cet —;* to that end, to that purpose. *À l'— de ;* to the end that, with a view to. *À quel —? to* what purpose ?

*effeuillaison, *n.f.*, fall of the leaves.

*effeuillement, *n.m.*, stripping off the leaves

*effeuiller, *v.a.*, to strip off leaves.

*s'effeuiller, *v.r.*, to lose its leaves (of a tree, a flower—*d'un arbre, d'une fleur*). *Les roses s'effeuillent;* the roses are shedding their leaves.

efficace, *adj.*, efficacious. *Ce remède est — contre les poisons ;* this remedy is efficacious in cases of poisoning.

efficace, *n.f.*, efficacy, efficiency, virtue.

efficacement (-kas-mān), *adv.*, efficaciously, efficiently.

efficacité, *n.f.*, efficacy, efficiency.

efficient, **-e**, *adj.*, efficient.

effigie, *n.f.*, effigy. *Pendre en —; to* hang in effigy.

effigier, *v.a.*, to make an effigy.

effilé, *n.m.*, fringe worn in deep mourning.

effilé, **-e**, *adj.*, slender, slim. *Avoir la taille —e ;* to have a thin, slender figure.

effiler, *v.a.*, to unweave, to ravel out, to unravel; to thin (the hair—*les cheveux*); (hunt.) to tire out the dogs.

s'effiler, *v.r.*, to ravel, to ravel out ; to taper.

effilocher, or **effiloquer**, *v.a.*, to ravel out, to undo (silk—*de la soie*).

effiloques. *n.f.pl.*, untwisted silk (for making wadding—*pour faire de la ouate*).

effilure, *n.f.*, thread ravelled.

efflanquer, *v.a.*, to make lean. *Style efflanqué;* meagre style.

effleurer, *v.a.*, to take off the surface; to pick (flowers—*des fleurs*); to skim over, to glance at ; to graze, to touch upon.

effleurir, *v.a.*, (chem.) to effloresce.

s'effleurir, *v.r.*, to effloresce.

efflorescence, *n.f.*, efflorescence.

efflorescent, **-e**, *adj.*, efflorescent.

effluence, *n.f.*, (phys.) effluence.

effluent, **-e**, *adj.*, (phys.) effluent.

effluve, *n.m.*, effluvium.

effondrement, *n.m.*, (agri.) digging deep.

effondrer, *v.a.*, (agri.) to dig deep, to break in. — *une volaille;* to draw a fowl.

s'effondrer, *v.r.*, to fall in ; to give way.

*effondrilles, *n.f.pl.*, grounds, sediment, dregs.

s'efforcer, *v.r.*, to strain, to strive, to make an effort, to exert one's self ; to struggle, to endeavour, to attempt.

effort, *n.m.*, effort, exertion, endeavour ; force, strength; (nav., vet.) strain. *Faire de vains — s;* to make useless efforts. *L'— de l'eau a rompu cette digue;* the force of the water has broken down that dyke. *Ce cheval a un —;* that horse is strained. *Faire un — sur soi-même ;* to do one's self violence.

effraction, *n.f.*, breaking, breaking open. *Vol avec —;* burglary.

effraie, *n.f.*, white barn-owl.

effrayant, **-e**, *adj.*, frightful, fearful, dreadful.

effrayé, **-e**, *part.*, afraid, daunted.

effrayer, *v.a.*, to fright, to frighten, to terrify, to dismay.

s'effrayer, *v.r.*, to be frightened, to be startled, to take fright. *Il s'effraie de peu de chose;* he is soon frightened.

effréné, **-e**, *adj.*, unbridled, unruly. *Passions —es;* ungovernable passions.

effriter, *v.a.*, (agri.) to exhaust land.

s'effriter, *v.r.*, (agri.) to become exhausted (of land—*d'un terrain*).

effroi, *n.m.*, fright, terror, consternation. *Trembler d'—;* to tremble with fright. *Porter partout l'—;* to carry consternation everywhere.

effronté, **-e**, *n.* and *adj.*, shameless, brazen-faced person; shameless, bold, brazen-faced. *Une femme —e ;* a bold creature.

effrontément, *adv.,* impudently, boldly, shamelessly.

effronterie (é-front-rî), *n.f.,* effrontery, boldness, impudence, brazenness. *Il est plein d'—;* he is full of impudence. *Il a eu l'— de me menacer;* he had effrontery enough to threaten me. *Payer d'—;* to brazen it out.

effroyable, *adj.,* frightful, dreadful, horrid, horrible; shocking; prodigious. *Elle est d'une laideur —;* she is frightfully ugly.

effroyablement, *adv.,* frightfully, horribly, dreadfully. *Elle est — laide;* she is frightfully ugly.

effusion, *n.f.,* effusion, pouring out, shedding. *— de tendresse;* flow of tenderness.

éfourceau, *n.m.,* two-wheeled timber-carriage.

égagropile, *n.m.,* (vet) wool-ball.

égal, -e, *adj.,* equal, uniform, like, alike; even, level, same. *Tout lui est égal;* it is all one to him. *Une humeur —e;* an even temper.

égal, *n.m.,* **-e,** *n.f.,* equal. *A l'— de;* in comparison of, as much as, equal to. *Traiter d'—;* to treat as one's equal. *Sans —;* matchless.

également (é-gal-män), *adv.,* equally, alike, uniformly.

égaler, *v.a.,* to equal, to make even, level; to come up to, to match; to compare, to parallel. *Il égale les anciens;* he is equal to the ancients.

s'égaler, *v.r.,* to render one's self equal.

égalisation, *n.f.,* equalization.

égaliser, *v.a.,* to equalize, to make level; to square accounts. *L'amour égalise toutes les conditions;* love brings all ranks to the same level. *— un terrain;* to level a piece of ground.

égalitaire, *adj.,* referring to political equality.

égalité, *n.f.,* equality, levelness; evenness, uniformity; (geom.) congruity. *A — de mérite;* where there is equality of merit. *— d'âme;* equanimity.

égard, *n.m.,* regard, consideration, respect. *Avoir —;* to pay regard. *Avoir — à quelque chose;* to be regardful of any thing. *Avoir des —s pour;* to have consideration for, to pay regard to. *Eu — à;* considering. *Eu — à la qualité;* considering the quality. *Avoir de grands —s pour quelqu'un;* to show any one great deference. *Par — pour;* out of regard for. *Par — pour vous;* for your sake. *A l'— de;* respecting; with regard to. *A cet —;* in this respect. *—;* Court which sat at Malta to try litigations between the Knights of Malta.

égaré,-e, *part.,* strayed; misguided, misled, roving. *Des yeux —s;* wild looks. *Esprit —;* wandering mind. *Il a l'esprit —;* his mind is disordered. *Brebis —es;* lost sheep.

égarement (é-gar-män), *n.m.,* straying, losing one's way; mistake, error; wildness (of the look—*du visage*); disorder, ill conduct. *Les —s des philosophes;* the errors of philosophers. *Le cœur a ses — comme l'esprit;* the heart has its errors as well as the head. *— d'esprit;* mental alienation.

égarer, *v.a.,* to mislead, to misguide; to bewilder; to impair (intellect); to lead astray, to lead into error; to mislay. *— quelque chose;* to mislay anything.

s'égarer, *v.r.,* to lose one's way, to stray; to err; to mistake; to be led into error; to go astray; to ramble; to lose one's self. *Il s'est égaré de son chemin;* he has lost his way. *Il s'égara dans la forêt;* he lost himself in the forest.

égarotté, -e, *adj.,* (man.) wither-wrung.

égayer, *v.a.,* to enliven, to divert, to make cheerful, to lighten, to elevate (the spirits—*le moral*), to cheer, to cheer up; to thin (trees—*des arbres*). *— un appartement;* to make an apartment lighter.

s'égayer, *v.r.,* to make merry, to make one's self merry, to divert one's self, to sport, to cheer up. *Il faut vous égayer;* you must cheer up. *Nous nous égayâmes à ses dépens;* we made merry at his expense.

égide, *n.f.,* Ægis (shield of Jupiter, or Pallas—*bouclier de Jupiter et de Pallas*); shield, buckler, breast-plate. *Il me sert d'—;* he is my shield.

égilops (-lops), *n.m.,* (med.) egilops.

églantier (-tié), *n.m.,* (bot.) eglantine, brier, dog-brier. *— odorant;* sweet-brier.

églantine, *n.f.,* (bot.) eglantine, hip.

églefin, *n.m.,* (ich.) haddock.

église, *n.f.,* church. *L'— anglicane;* the church of England. *Un homme d'—;* a churchman, a clergyman. *Gueux comme un rat d'—;* as poor as a church-mouse. *Les états de l'—;* the states of the church.

églogue (-log), *n.f.,* eclogue, æglogue.

⊖**égoïser,** *v.n.,* to egotize.

égoïsme, *n.m.,* egotism, selfishness; (philos.) egoism.

égoïste, *adj.,* egotistic; selfish. *Elle est très —;* she is very selfish.

égoïste, *n.m.f.,* egotist; (philos.) egoist. *C'est un —;* he is an egotist.

égopode, *n.m.,* (bot.) goat-weed, goutwort.

égorger,*v.a.,* to cut the throat, to slaughter, to butcher, to kill.

égorgeur, *n.m.,* slaughterer, murderer.

*s'égosiller, *v.r.,* to make one's throat sore with speaking, to make one's self hoarse.

égotisme, *n.m.,* egotism.

égotiste, *n.m.f.,* (l.u.) egotist.

égout, *n.m.,* running or falling of water; sink, drain, sewer; projecting roof.

égouttage, *n.m.,* drainage; draining.

égoutter, *v.a.,* to drain, to drip.

égoutter, *v.a.,* to drain, to let drop.

s'égoutter, *v.r.,* to drop, to drain.

égouttoir, *n.m.,* drain.

égoutture, *n.f.,* drainings, drippings.

égrainer. *V.* **égrener.**

s'égrainer. *V.* **s'égrener.**

égrapper, *v.a.,* to take off grapes from the bunch.

*égratigner, *v.a.,* to scratch, to claw. *Le chat l'a égratigné;* the cat has scratched him. *S'il ne mord, il égratigne;* if he does not bite he scratches.

*égratigneu-r, *n.m.,* **-se,** *n.f.,* one who scratches, scratcher.

*égratignure, *n.f.,* scratch (on the skin—*à la peau*); slight wound. *Il ne saurait souffrir la moindre —;* he does not know how to bear the least thing.

*égravillonner, *v.a.,* to remove a tree from the earth, and clear its roots from the soil adhering to them before replanting it.

égrefin, *n.m.* *V.* **églefin.**

égrenage. *n.m.,* shelling (grains); picking (grapes—*le raisin*) from the bunch; (arts) ginning.

égrener, *v a.,* to shell (grain); to pick from the bunch (grapes—*raisin*); (arts) to gin.

s'égrener, *v.r.,* to shell (grain); to fall (of grapes—*raisin*).

*égrillard, -e, *adj.,* sprightly, brisk.

*égrilloir, *n.m.,* grate to keep the fish in a pond.

égrisée, *n.f.,* diamond-dust.

égriser, *v.a.,* to clean (diamonds—*diamants*).

égrisoir. *n.m..* diamond-dust box.

égrugeoir (-joàr), *n.m.*, kind of wooden mortar to reduce salt, sugar, &c., to powder.

égruger, *v.a.*, to pound, to bruise. — *du sel;* to pound salt.

égueulé, *n.m.*, **-e**, *n.f.* (égheulé), (pop.) vulgar, rude person.

égueulement (é-gheul-mān), *n.m.,* (artil.) breaking at the mouth of a cannon.

égueuler (égheulé), *v.a.*, to break off the mouth or neck of glass and other vessels.

s'égueuler, *v.r.*, to bawl till one's throat is sore; (artil.) to break at the mouth (of a gun— *d'un canon*).

égyptien, **-ne** (-si-in, -si-èn), *adj.*, Egyptian.

égyptien, *n.m.*, **-ne**, *n.f.*, Egyptian; gipsy.

eh, *int.*, ah! well! — *bien!* well! — *bien, soit;* well, be it so.

éhanché, **-e**, *adj.* V. **déhanché**.

éherber, *v.a.* V. **sarcler**.

éhonté, **-e**, *adj.*, shameless, brazen-faced.

éhouper, *v.a.*, to lop off the top (of a tree— *d'un arbre*).

eider, *n.m.* (—*s*), (orni.) eider, eider-duck.

éjaculateur, *adj.*, (anat.) ejaculatory.

éjaculation, *n.f.*, throwing out with force, discharge; ejaculation (fervent prayer—*prière fervente*).

éjaculatoire, *adj.* V. **éjaculateur**.

éjaculer, *v.a.*, (anat.) to throw out, to ejaculate, to discharge.

élaboration, *n.f.*, elaboration.

élaboré, **-e**, *adj.*, elaborate, wrought, laboured.

élaborer, *v.a.*, to elaborate, to work out.

élagage, *n.m.*, (hort.) lopping; branches lopped off.

élaguer (-ghé), *v.a.*, to lop, to prune; to curtail, to cut down. *Élaguez ces détails inutiles;* cut out those useless particulars.

élagueur, *n.m.*, (hort.) pruner.

élan, *n.m.*, start, spring, flight, glow, soaring; burst, outburst, transport (of the soul—*de l'âme*); (mam.) elk, moose-deer. *Par —s;* by starts. *Prendre un —;* to take a spring, a flight.

élancé, **-e**, *adj.*, slender, slim, thin, lank.

élancement, (é-lāns-mān), *n.m.*, shooting, twitch (of pain—*d'une douleur*); *pl.*, transports (of the soul—*de l'âme*).

élancer, *v.a.*, (l.u.) to dart, to shoot.

s'élancer, *v.r.*, to bound, to shoot, to shoot forth, to rush, to dash, to spring; to take one's flight. *Il s'élança sur son cheval;* he leaped on horseback. *Il s'élança parmi les ennemis;* rushed upon the enemy. — *sur quelqu'un;* to spring upon any one. *Mon âme s'élança vers Dieu;* my soul lifted itself up to God.

élancer, *v.n.*, to shoot, to twitch (of pain—*d'une douleur*).

élapion, *n.m.*, (orni.) kite. — *martinet;* swallow-tailed kite.

élargir, *v.a.*, to stretch, to widen, to make wider, to let out; to enlarge, to release, to set at liberty. — *un habit;* to let out a coat. — *ses quartiers;* to extend one's quarters. — *un compas;* to open a pair of compasses.

s'élargir, *v.r.*, to widen, to become wider; to enlarge; to stretch; to enlarge one's estate.

élargissement (-jis-mān). *n.m.*, widening, enlarging; release, discharge (from prison).

élargissure, *n.f.*, piece let in to widen anything.

élasticité, *n.f.*, elasticity.

élastique, *adj.*, elastic

élatine. *n.f.*, (bot.) water-wort.

élavé, *adj.*, (hunt.) soft and palish, (of the coat of dogs, &c.—*du poil des chiens, &c.*).

elbeuf, *n.m.*, Elbeuf-cloth.

eldorado, *n.m.* (—*s*), El Dorado.

éléatique, *adj.*, eleatic.

électeur, *n.m.*, elector.

électi-f, **-ve**, *adj.*, elective.

élection, *n.f.*, election, return. *Temps, lieu d'—* (surg.); most favourable time, place, for performing an operation. *Solliciter des suffrages aux —s;* to solicit votes at the elections.

électoral, **-e**, *adj.*, electoral. *Priver du droit —;* to disfranchise.

électorat, *n.m.*, electorate.

électrice, *n.f.*, Elector's consort, Electress.

électricité, *n.f.*, electricity.

électrique, *adj.*, electric. *Secousse —;* electric shock. *Conducteur —;* electric conductor.

électrisable, *adj.*, electrifiable.

électrisant, **-e**, *adj.*, electrifying.

électrisation, *n.f.*, electrification.

électriser, *v.a.*, to electrify.

s'électriser, *v.r.*, to be electrified, to electrify.

électro-aimant, *n.m.* (— —*s*), electro-magnet.

électro-chimie, *n.f.* (*n.p.*), electro-chemistry.

électro-dynamique, *n.f.* (*n.p.*), electro-dynamics.

électro-magnétisme, *n.m.* (*n.p.*), electro-magnetism.

électromètre, *n.m.*, (phys.) electrometer.

électro-négati-f, **-ve**, *adj.*, electro-negative.

électrophore, *n.m.*, (phys.) electrophorus.

électro-positi-f, **-ve**, *adj.*, electro-positive.

électroscope, *n.m.*, (phys.) electroscope.

électuaire, *n.m.*, electuary.

élégamment (-ga-mān), *adv.*, elegantly.

élégance, *n.f.*, elegance, elegancy. *L'— du style;* elegancy of style.

élégant, **-e**, *n.* and *adj.*, gentleman, lady, of fashion; elegant, fashionable.

élégiaque, *adj.*, elegiac.

élégiaque, *n.m.*, elegist.

élégie, *n.f.*, elegy.

élément, *n.m.*, element. *La chasse est son —;* hunting is his element.

élémentaire, *adj.*, elementary, elemental.

élémi, *n.m.*, (pharm.) elemi.

éléphant, *n.m.*, elephant.

éléphantiasis (-tia-zis), *n.f.*, (med.) elephantiasis.

éléphantin, **-e**, *adj.*, elephantine.

élevage, *n.m.*, (agri.) breeding (of cattle, horses, &c.—*des bestiaux, chevaux, &c.*).

élévateur, *adj.*, *n.m.*, (anat.) elevator, levator.

élévation, *n.f.*, elevation, lifting up, raising; rising ground, height, eminence; (persp.) view; exaltation; greatness (of soul—*d'âme*); nobleness; (c. rel.) elevation of the host; rise (of prices—*de prix*); raised plan. *Il lui doit son —;* he is indebted to him for his elevation. *Il a beaucoup d'—;* he possesses great elevation of mind. — *dans le style;* loftiness of style. — *de côté;* side view of a building—*d'un bâtiment*).

élévatoire, *n.m.*, (surg.) elevator.

élève, *n.m.f.*, pupil, scholar; student; (nav.) midshipman. *Ce précepteur ne quitte jamais son —;* that tutor never leaves his pupil.

élève, *n.f.*, (agri.) breeding (of cattle, horses &c.—*des bestiaux, chevaux, &c.*).

élevé, (él-vé), **-e**, *part.*, raised, grand; heroic, eminent, stately; high (of prices—*de prix*); exalted. *C'est un jeune homme bien —;* he is a very well-bred youth.

élever, (él-vé), *v.a.*, to raise, to raise up, to exalt, to lift up; to cast up, to ennoble; to erect, to rear up, to set up; to augment, to increase; to run up (of accounts—*comptes*); to bring up, to breed, to rear; to educate, to train up, to nurse, to foster. — *quelqu'un aux nues;* to extol any one to the skies. — *la voix;* to raise one's voice. *Il a élevé le prince;* he brought up the prince. *J'ai pris de la peine à — ces plantes;* I took some trouble to raise those plants. — *la jeunesse dans la crainte de Dieu;* to bring up children in the fear of God.

s'**élever**, *v.r.*, to arise; to ascend, to mount, to go up, to run up; to amount; to be elevated; to increase, to augment; to run up (of accounts —*comptes*); to be started. *Une tempête s'éleva;* a storm arose. *Les vapeurs s'élèvent de la terre;* vapours rise from the earth. *Celui qui s'élève sera abaissé;* he who exalts himself shall be humbled. *Les vagues s'élevèrent haut;* the waves rolled high.

éleveur (él-veur), *n.m.*, elevator, levator; cattle-breeder.

élevure (él-vur), *n.f.*, pimple, blotch.

elfe, *n.m.*, elf (fairy—*génie de l'air*).

élider, *v.a.*, (gram.) to make an elision, to elide.

s'**élider**, *v.r.*, to be elided, to be cut off. *Cette lettre s'élide;* that letter is elided.

éligibilité, *n.f.*, eligibility.

éligible, *adj.*, eligible.

s'**élimer**, *v.r.*, to wear out, to rub out.

élimination, *n.f.*, elimination, dismissal, expulsion.

éliminer, *v.a.*, to eliminate, to strike out, to expel.

élingue (é-ling), *n.f.*, (nav.) sling, strop.

élinguer (-ghé), *v.a.*, (nav.) to sling.

élire, *v.a.*, to elect, to choose, to return.

élision, *n.f.*, elision.

élite, *n.f.*, choice, pick. *L'— de l'armée;* the choice men, the pick, of the army. *J'ai eu l'— de ses livres;* I have had the pick of his books.

élixir, *n.m.*, elixir.

elle, *pron.*, she, her, it; **elles**, *pl.*, they, them. *Je parle d'—;* I speak of her. *Je reviens à —;* I return to her. *Je lui parle;* I am speaking to her. *Je les lui donne à elle-même;* I give them to herself. *Je les vois, —s et leur frère;* I see them and their brother.

ellébore, *n.m.*, (bot.) hellebore. — *noir;* Christmas-thorn, black hellebore. *Avoir besoin d'—;* not to be in one's right senses.

elléborine, *n.f.*, (bot.) helleborine, bastard hellebore.

ellipse (è-lips), *n.f.*, (gram., geom.) ellipsis.

ellipsoïde, *n.m.*, (geom.) ellipsoid.

ellipticité, *n.f.*, ellipticity.

elliptique, *adj.*, elliptical.

elliptiquement, *adv.*, elliptically.

elme (Feu Saint), *n.m.*, corposant, Castor and Pollux.

élocution, *n.f.*, elocution.

éloge, *n.m.*, eulogium, eulogy, panegyric, encomium, praise, commendation. *Digne d'—;* praiseworthy. *Faire soi-même son —,* to sound one's own praises. *Faire l'— d'un auteur;* to speak in praise of an author.

élogieu-x, **-se**, *adj.*, full of praise, eulogistic.

élogiste, *n.m.*, eulogist, writer of panegyrics.

*ï**éloigné**, **-e**, *part.*, removed, distant, wide, remote, far. *Temps —s;* distant times. *Cause —e;* remote cause. *Il est fort — de le croire;* he is far from believing it. *Se tenir —;* to keep away, to stand aloof. *D'une manière —e;* distantly.

*ï**éloignement** (é-loagn-màn), *n.m.*, removal, removing; distance, remoteness; aversion, estrangement, unwillingness. *On voit Paris dans l'—;* Paris is seen in the distance. *Avoir de l'— pour le travail;* to have an aversion for work.

*ï**éloigner**, *v.a.*, to remove, to put away, to send away; to dismiss; to discard; to repudiate; to remove further; to waive; to avert; to banish; to drive away; to put off, to delay, to retard; to alienate, to estrange; to indispose. — *un sujet;* to waive a subject. — *les soupçons;*

to discard suspicion. — *quelqu'un de;* to indispose any one towards. — *quelqu'un de son pays;* to send any one away from his country. *Éloignez de vous ces mauvaises pensées;* dismiss such evil thoughts.

s'*ï**éloigner**, *v.r.*, to go away, to remove; to forsake; to withdraw; to ramble; to swerve; to be different, to differ, to dislike; (paint.) to appear in the distance; to be alienated. *Ne vous éloignez pas;* don't go out of the way. — *de son devoir;* to deviate from one's duty. — *de son sujet;* to ramble from one's subject. *Cette opinion s'éloigne de la mienne;* that opinion differs from mine.

élongation, *n.f.*, elongation; digression.

élonger, *v.a.*, (nav.) to sheer off.

éloquemment (-ka-màn), *adv.*, eloquently.

éloquence, *n.f.*, eloquence. — *mâle;* manly eloquence. — *de la tribune;* parliamentary eloquence.

éloquent, **-e**, *adj.*, eloquent.

élu, *n.m.*, **-e**, *n.f.*, person elect, elect.

élu, **-e**, *part.*, elected, chosen, elect, appointed.

élucidation, *n.f.*, elucidation.

élucider, *v.a.*, to elucidate.

élucubration, *n.f.*, lucubration.

éluder, *v.a.*, to elude, to evade. — *une question;* to evade a question. — *une promesse;* to evade the performance of a promise.

élyme, *n.m.*, (bot.) elymus.

élysée, *n.m.*, (myth.) Elysium.

élysée, *adj.*, Elysian. *Les champs —s;* the Elysian Fields.

élyséen, **-ne** (-in, -è-n), *adj.*, Elysian.

élysiens (-in), *adj.m.pl.*, (myth.) Elysian.

élytre, *n.m.*, (ent.) elytron, wing-shell.

elzévir, *n.m.*, Elzevir edition.

elzévirien, **-ne**, *adj.*, of an Elzevir edition.

émaciation, *n.f.*, emaciation.

émacié, **-e**, *adj.*, emaciated.

*ï**émail**, *n.m.*, enamel. — *de Hollande;* Dutch blue. *Peindre en —;* to enamel. *Peinture en —;* enamelling, enamelled picture. *Peintre en —;* enameller.

*ï**émailler**, *v.a.*, to enamel.

*ï**émailleur**, *n.m.*, enameller.

*ï**émaillure**, *n.f.*, enamelling.

émanation, *n.f.*, emanation.

émancipation, *n.f.*, emancipation.

émanciper, *v.a.*, to emancipate.

s'**émanciper**, *v.r.*, to take up too much liberty, to get too free. *Vous vous émancipez trop;* you are rather too free.

émaner, *v.n.*, to emanate.

émargement, *n.m.*, writing on the margin; marginal note; signature on the margin.

émarger, *v.a.*, to write, to sign, on the margin; (fig.) to receive one's salary; (tech.) to diminish the breadth of the margin of engravings, &c.

émarginé, **-e**, *adj.*, (bot.) emarginated.

émasculation, *n.f.*, emasculation.

émasculer, *v.a.*, to emasculate.

embabouiner, *v.a.*, (fam., l.u.) to wheedle; to gammon.

emballage, *n.m.*, packing up; package. *Toile d'—;* packing-canvas, pack-cloth.

emballer, *v.a.*, to pack up; to pack off; (fam. jest.) to send away, to pack off any one.

emballeur, *n.m.*, packer; (pop.) bragger.

embander, *v.a.*, to tie up; to swaddle (a child—*un petit enfant*).

embarcadère, *n.m.*, terminus; wharf.

embarcation, *n.f.*, small boat, craft.

embardée, *n.f.*, (nav.) yaw, lurch.

embarder, *v.a. and n.*, (nav.) to yaw, to lurch.

embargo, *n.m.*, embargo. *Lever l'—;* to

7 *

take off an embargo. *Mettre un — sur ;* to lay an embargo on.

*embarillé, -e, *adj.,* barrelled up.

*embariller, *v.a.,* to barrel, to barrel up.

embarquement, *n.m.,* embarkation, embarking, shipping.

embarquer, *v.a.,* to embark, to ship, to put on ship-board ; to take on board ; to see off. *On l'a embarqué dans une méchante affaire ;* he has been drawn into a bad affair.

s'embarquer, *v.r.,* to embark, to take shipping ; to engage.

embarras, *n.m.,* incumbrance, hinderance, impediment ; embarrassment, intricacy, fuss ; perplexity, puzzle ; (med.) derangement. *Cet homme fait bien de l'—;* that man makes a great fuss. *Être dans l'—;* to be in difficulties. *Mettre quelqu'un dans l'—;* to perplex any one. *Se mettre dans l'—;* to get into embarrassment, into a scrape. *Je suis dans l'— ;* I am at a loss.

embarrassant, -e, *adj.,* embarrassing, puzzling ; perplexing, encumbering, cumbersome, troublesome.

embarrassé, -e, *part.,* embarrassed, entangled, perplexed, obstructed. *Être—;* to be at a loss.

embarrasser, *v.a.,* to embarrass, to encumber, to obstruct ; to clog, to trouble, to confound, to puzzle ; to come amiss to ; to insnare. *Être embarrassé de sa personne ;* not to know what to do with one's self. *Que cela ne vous embarrasse point ;* do not trouble yourself about it. *Cette question l'a embarrassé ;* that question perplexed him. *Il est embarrassé de répondre ;* he is at a loss for an answer. *— une rue ;* to obstruct a street.

s'embarrasser, *v.r.,* to entangle one's self, to be embarrassed, entangled ; to be solicitous about ; (med.) to be affected. *Il ne s'embarrasse de rien;* he troubles himself about nothing. *Sa langue s'embarrasse;* his tongue begins to falter ; his speech is impeded.

embasement, *n.m.,* (arch.) continuous pedestal (under the mass of a building—*sous la masse d'un bâtiment*).

embatage, *n.f.,* casing of wheels.

⊙*embatailler, *v.a.,* to furnish with battlements, to embattle.

embâter, *v.a.,* to put on a pack-saddle ; to saddle, to encumber. *On l'a embâté d'une affaire bien désagréable ;* they have saddled him with a very disagreeable job.

embâtonner, *v.a.,* (l.u.) to arm with a cudgel.

embatre, *v.a.,* to case (a wheel—*une roue*).

embauchage, *n.m.,* hiring (workmen—*des ouvriers*); tampering, gaining over, enticing away.

embaucher, *v.a.,* to hire (workmen— *des ouvriers*); to entice away, to tamper with.

embaucheur, *n.m.,* one who entices away ; recruiting-officer ; recruiter.

embauchoir, *n.m.,* boot-tree.

embaumement, (an-bôm-măn), *n m.,* embalming.

embaumer, *v.a.,* to embalm ; to perfume, to scent.

embaumeur, *n.m.,* embalmer.

embéguiner (-ghi-), *v.a.,* to muffle up ; to infatuate, to bewitch.

s'embéguiner, *v.r.,* to be infatuated, to be bewitched.

embellie, *n.f.,* (nav.) fine weather (after foul weather—*après une tempête*)

embellir, *v.a.,* to embellish, to beautify ; to adorn. *— un conte ;* to embellish a tale.

s'embellir, *v.r.,* to beautify, to improve in beauty.

embellir, *v.n.,* to beautify, to grow handsomer. *Elle ne fait que croître et —;* she grows taller and handsomer every day.

embellissement (-lis-măn), *n.m.,* embellishment, improvement, adornment.

s'emberlucoquer, *v.r.,* (fam.) to be prepossessed with, to be wedded to.

*embesogné, -e, *adj.,* (fam., jest.) busy, busily engaged.

embêter, *v.a.,* (triv.) to stupify, to stultify, to besot ; to annoy, to plague ; to tease, to torment ; to worry ; to aggravate.

s'embêter, *v.r.,* (triv.) to feel dull, bored.

emblavage, *n.m.,* (agri.) sowing with corn.

emblaver, *v.a.,* to sow with corn.

emblavure, *n.f.,* piece of land sown with corn.

d'emblée, *adv.,* at the first, in a trice ; at the first onset.

emblématique, *adj.,* emblematical.

emblème, *n.m.,* emblem. *Être l'— de ;* to be emblematical of. *Une couronne est l'— de la royauté ;* a crown is the emblem of royalty.

emboire, *v.a.,* to imbibe ; (sculp.) to coat (with oil or wax—*à l'huile ou à la cire*).

s'emboire, *v.r.,* (paint.) to get dull ; to become confused.

⊙emboiser, *v.a.,* to coax, to wheedle.

⊙emboiseu-r, *n.m.,* -se, *n.f.,* coaxer, wheedler.

emboîtement (ăn-boat-măn), *n.m.,* fitting, jointing, clamping.

emboîter, *v.a.,* to joint ; to set (bones—*les os*) ; to clamp, to fit, to fit in. *— le pas ;* (milit.) to lock up.

s'emboîter, *v.r.,* to fit, to fit in.

emboîture, *n.f.,* socket, clamp ; (pottery—*poterie*) collar. *L'— des os ;* the juncture of the bones.

embolie, *n.f.,* (med.) embolism.

embolisme, *n.m.,* embolism.

embolismique, *adj.,* embolismic, embolismal.

embonpoint, *n.m.,* plumpness, corpulence, stoutness, obesity. *Prendre de l'— ;* to pick up flesh. *Perdre son — ;* to fall away, to lose flesh.

embordurer, *v.a.,* (l.u.) to put in a frame, to frame.

embossage, *n.m.,* (nav.) bringing the broadside to bear.

embosser, *v.a.,* (nav.) to bring the broadside to bear.

s'embosser, *v.r.,* (nav.) to be brought to bear.

embouché, -e, *part.,* entered (of boats—*des bateaux*). *Être mal — ;* to be foul-mouthed, impertinent.

emboucher, *v.a.,* to put to one's mouth (wind instruments—*instruments à vent*) ; to prompt ; to bit (a horse—*un cheval*). *Il l'a bien embouché ;* he has given him a good prompting.

s'emboucher, *v.r.,* (of rivers—*des rivières*) to fall into ; to empty, to discharge itself.

embouchoir, *n.m.,* boot-tree.

embouchure, *n.f.,* mouth-piece (of wind-instruments—*d'instruments à vent*); mouth (of a river, of a harbour—*d'une rivière, d'un port*) ; out-fall (engineering—*terme d'ingénieur*).

embouer, *v.a.,* (pop.) to cover with mud.

embouquement, *n.m.,* (nav.) entering a strait.

embouquer, *v.n.,* (nav.) to enter a strait.

embourbé, -e, *part.,* bemired. *Il jure comme un charretier — ;* he swears like a trooper.

embourber, *v.a.,* to put in the mire ; to bemire. *— quelqu'un dans une mauvaise affaire;* to get any one into a troublesome affair.

s'**embourber**, *v.r.*, to sink in the mud, to stick in the mire; to be involved in any disagreeable affair.

embourrer. *V.* **rembourrer**.

embourser, *v.a.*, to put in one's purse.

emboutir, *v.a.*, (gold.) to scoop out; (coppersmith's work—*terme de chaudronnier*) to beat out; (arch.) to ornament with sheet-iron mouldings; to cover wood-ornaments with sheets of lead to exclude water.

embranchement, *n.m.*, branch. branching off; branch-road; branch-line (railways).

embrancher, *v.a.*, (carp.) to put together.

s'**embrancher**, *v.r.*, to branch off; to branch of roads—*de routes*).

embrasé, -e, *part.*, burning, in flames.

embrasement (an-brâz-măn), *n.m.*, conflagration, burning.

embraser, *v.a.*, to fire, to set on fire, to kindle, to inflame. *La guerre a embrasé toute l'Europe*; war has thrown all Europe into a conflagration.

s'**embraser**, *v.r.*, to kindle, to take fire, to glow, to be inflamed. *Cette matière s'embrase facilement*; that stuff easily catches fire.

embrassade, *n.f.*, embrace, hug.

embrasse, *n.f.*, curtain-arm, curtain-band.

embrassé, -e, *part.*, embraced. *Ils se tenaient—s*; they remained locked in each other's arms.

embrassement (an-bras-măn), *n.m.*, embrace.

embrasser, *v.a.*, to embrace, to clasp; to kiss; to encompass, to encircle, to comprehend, to comprise, to take in, to include; to seize, to avail one's self of, to undertake. *Qui trop embrasse, mal étreint*; grasp all, lose all. — *une opinion*; to embrace an opinion. — *la querelle de quelqu'un*; to espouse any one's quarrel. — *la profession des armes*; to embrace the profession of arms. — *une occasion*; to seize, to avail one's self of, an opportunity.

s'**embrasser**, *v.r.*, to embrace, to kiss, one another.

embrasseu-r, *n.m.*, -**se**, *n.f.*, (fam., l.u.) embracer, kisser.

embrassure, *n.f.*, band of iron put round a beam *or* chimney to prevent its splitting.

embrasure, *n.f.*, embrasure; recess (of doors and windows—*de portes et de fenêtres*).

embrayer, *v.a.*, to engage (mec.).

embrener, *v.a.*, (l.ex.) to dirty with fecal matter. *S'—dans quelque affaire;* to entangle one's self into an ugly piece of business.

embrèvement, *n.f.*, (carp.) mortise.

embrever, *v.a.*, (carp.) to mortise.

embrigadement, *n.m.*, the forming into brigades of the agents of the civil authority; (milit.) brigading.

embrigader, *v.a.*, (milit.) to brigade; to form into brigades the agents of the civil authority.

embrocation, *n.f.*, embrocation.

embrocher, *v.a.*, to spit, to put upon the spit. — *quelqu'un;* to run any one through the body.

****embrouillé**, -e, *part.*, perplexed, intricate.

****embrouillement** (an-brou-i-măn), *n.m.*, embroiling, confusion, intricacy, perplexity.

****embrouiller**, *v.a.*, to embroil, to confuse, to confound, to perplex, to obscure. *Il m'a embrouillé l'esprit;* he has quite confounded my thoughts.

s'**embrouiller**, *v.r.*, to embroil, to perplex, one's self; to become intricate; to get confused.

embrouilleu-r, *n.m.*, -**se**, *n.f.*, one who throws things into confusion.

embruiné, -e, *adj.*, (agri.) spoiled by drizzling rain.

embrumé, -e, *adj.*, foggy, misty.

embrun, *n.m.*, (nav.) spray.

embryogénie. *n.f.*, embryogeny.

embryographie. *n.f.*, embryography.

embryologie. *n.f.*, embryology.

embryon. *n.f.*, embryo; (bot.) germ; little bit of a man.

embryonnaire. *adj.*, embryonic.

embu. *n.m.*, (paint.) dark, dull appearance (of pictures—*des tableaux*).

embûche, *n.f.*, snare, ambush. *Dresser des —s;* to lay snares.

embuscade. *n.f.*, ambuscade; ambush; lurking-place, snare. *Être en —;* to be lying in wait.

embusquer, *v.a.*, to ambuscade.

s'**embusquer**, *v.r.*, to lay in ambuscade.

émender, *v.a.*, to amend.

émeraude (é-mrôd), *n.f.*, emerald.

émergence, *n.f.*, (phys.) emersion, emergence.

émergent, *adj.*, (phys.) emergent.

émerger, *v.n.*, to emerge.

émeri (é-mri), *n.m.*, (min.) emery.

****émerillon**, *n.m.*, whirl (for weaving—*pour tisser*); (nav.) swivel-hook.

****émerillon**, *n.m.*, (orni.) stone-falcon, merlin.

****émerillonné**, -e, *adj.*, brisk, sprightly.

émérite, *adj.*, emerited.

émersion, *n.f.*, emersion.

émérus, *n.m.*, (bot.) bastard-senna, colutea

****émerveillement**, *n.m.*, wonder, astonishment.

****émerveiller**, *v.a.*, to astonish, to amaze.

s'**émerveiller**, *v.r.*, to marvel, to wonder, to be astonished. *Il s'émerveille de tout ce qu'il voit;* he is amazed at all he sees.

émétique, *n.m.* and *adj.*, emetic, puke, vomit; emetical.

émétiser, *v.a.*, (pharm.) to add emetic to a mixture.

émettre, *v.a.*, to put in circulation, to emit, to issue, to give out, to put forth, to express.

émeute, *n.f.*, riot, disturbance. *Chef d'—;* ringleader.

émeutier (-tié), *n.m.*, rioter.

émier, *v.a.*, to crumble.

émietter, *v.a.*, to crumble.

s'**émietter**, *v.r.*, to crumble.

émigrant, -e, *n.* and *adj.*, emigrant; emigrating.

émigration, *n.f.*, emigration, migration.

émigré, *n.m.*, -e, *n.f.*, emigrant.

émigrer, *v.n.*, to emigrate.

éminoé, *n.m.*, (cook.) mince-meat.

émincer, *v.a.*, to mince (meat—*de la viande*).

éminemment (-na-măn), *adv.*, eminently, in a high degree.

éminence, *n.f.*, eminence; eminency, rising ground, height.

éminent, -e, *adj.*, eminent, high, lofty, conspicuous.

éminentissime, *adj.*, most eminent.

émir, *n.m.*, Ameer, Emeer, Emir.

émissaire, *n.m.*, emissary; (tech.) overflow pipe, over-flow channel. *Bouc —;* scapegoat.

émission, *n.f.*, emission, isue, putting into circulation.

emmagasinage, *n.m.*, warehousing.

emmagasiner, *v.a.*, to warehouse. — *des marchandises;* to lay goods in a magazine.

emmaigrir, *v.a.* *V.* **amaigrir**.

****emmaillotement**, *n.m.*, swaddling.

****emmailloter**, *v.a.*, to swaddle, *to* swathe, to bind up in swaddling clothes.

emmanchement (an-mansh-măn), *n.m.*, (paint., sculpt.) joining; putting a handle,

emmancher, r.a., to put a handle to; to begin, to set about. *Affaire mal emmanchée;* ill-managed affair.

s'emmancher, v.r., to be begun; to be done. *Cela ne s'emmanche pas ainsi;* that is not the way to set to work.

emmancher, c.n., (nav.) to enter the channel.

emmancheur, n.m., handle-maker.

emmanchure, n.f., arm-hole.

emmannequiner, v.a., to put in hampers; to basket (plants—*des plantes*).

emmantelé, -e, adj., covered with a cloak; (fort.) ⊕fortified. *Corneille —e;* hooded-crow.

⊙**emmanteler**, r.a., (fort.) to fortify.

emmariné, -e, adj., accustomed to the sea.

emmariner, v.a., to furnish (a ship—*un vaisseau*) with seamen; to accustom to the sea.

s'emmariner, v.r., to be manned (of a ship —*d'un vaisseau*); to accustom one's self to the sea.

emmêlé, -e, adj., entangled.

emmêler, v.a., to entangle; s'—, v.r., to get entangled.

emménagement (an-mé-naj-mān), n.m., removal into another house; removal; pl., (nav.) internal arrangements, accommodations.

emménager, v.n., to move in.

s'emménager, v.r., to move in.

emménagogue, n.m. and adj., (med.) emmenagogue.

emmener (an-mné), v.a., to carry away, to take away, to lead away, to fetch away, to convey away. *Il l'a emmené dans son carrosse;* he took him away in his coach. *Emmenez-le!* off with him!

emmenotter, v.a., to handcuff, to manacle.

emmeuler, v.a., to stack hay.

emmiellé, -e, adj., honeyed, sweet, soft. *Paroles —es;* honeyed words.

emmieller, v.a., to honey; to sweeten with honey; to cajole.

emmiellure, n.f., (vet.) a resolvent plaster.

emmitoufler, v.a., to muffle up.

emmortaiser, v.a., to mortise, to set in a mortise.

s'emmortaiser, v.r., to mortise.

emmotté, -e, adj., (of trees—*d'arbres*) with earth round the root.

emmuseler, v.a., to muzzle.

émoi, n.m., emotion, anxiety, flutter. *Mettre en —;* to put in a flutter. *Étre en —;* to be agitated.

émollient, -e, adj., emollient, softening medicine.

émollient, n.m., emollient. *Faire usage des —s;* to make use of emollients.

émolument, n.m., emolument, fee, perquisite.

émolumentaire, adj., proceeding from emoluments.

émolumenter, v.n., to profit; to get fees, perquisites.

émonctoire, n.m., (med.) emunctory.

émondage, n.m.; pruning, lopping (trees—*arbres*).

émonde, n.f., dung of birds of prey.

émonder, v.a., to prune, to lop.

émondes, n.f. p'., branches lopped off; trash.

émondeu-r, n.m., -se, n.f., pruner.

émotion, n.f., emotion; stir, commotion. *Éprouver beaucoup d'—;* to be much moved.

émotter, v.a., (agri.) to break clods of earth.

émottoir, n.m., (agri.) roller, clod-breaker.

émoucher, v.a., to drive flies away.

s'émoucher, v.r., to beat away the flies.

émouchet, n.m., sparrow-hawk. *Donner*

l'— à une peau; to soak a hide, divested of its horns, ears, and tail.

émouchette, n.f., fly-net (for horses—*pour les chevaux*).

émoucheu-r, n.m., -se, n.f., (pers.) fly-fanner.

émouchoir, n.m., fly-flap.

émoudre, v.a., to whet, to grind, to sharpen. — *des couteaux;* to grind knives. *Faire — des ciseaux;* to have scissors ground.

émouleur, n.m., grinder (of sharp instruments—*d'instruments tranchants*).

émoulu, -e, part., ground. *Frais — de;* fresh from, just come from. *Il est frais — du collège;* he is just from college. *Combattre à fer —;* to fight with sharp weapons; to fight in earnest and desperately.

émoussage, n.m., (agri.) emuscation.

émoussé, -e, part., blunt; dull. *Un esprit —;* a dull mind. *Des sens —s;* deadened senses. *État —;* bluntness.

émousser, v.a., to make blunt; to take off the edge; to dull; to take the moss off trees; to deaden. — *un rasoir;* to take the edge off a razor.

s'émousser, v.r., to get blunt; to become dull; to be, to become, deadened. *La pointe de ce couteau s'est émoussée;* the point of this knife is blunted.

émoussoir, n.m., moss-scraper.

***émoustillé**, -e, adj., brisk, sprightly.

***émoustiller**, v.a., to exhilarate, to put into spirits.

émouvant, adj., touching, moving, affecting, stirring.

émouvoir, v.a., to move, to stir up; to agitate, to provoke; to rouse; to raise; to affect, to touch. *Il sait l'art d'— les passions;* he has the art of stirring up the passions. *Il est ému de crainte;* he is moved with fear. — *une sédition;* to raise a sedition.

s'émouvoir, v.r., to rise; to be roused; to be stirred up. *Il s'émut une grande tempête,* there arose a great storm. *Il s'émut à la vue du péril;* he was troubled at the sight of the danger. *Il s'émeut de rien;* the least thing concerns him.

***empaillage**, n.m., stuffing (animal).

***empaillement**, n.m., bottoming (with straw —*en paille*); stuffing (animal).

***empaillé**, -e, part., stuffed.

***empailler**, v.a., to pack in straw; to stuff (birds—*oiseaux*); to put straw bottoms in chairs. — *des ballots;* to pack up bales in straw. — *une plante;* to wrap straw round a plant. *Ce naturaliste empaille fort bien les oiseaux;* that naturalist stuffs birds very cleverly.

***empailleu-r**, n.m., -se, n.f., chair-mender; bird-stuffer.

empalement (an-pal-mān), n.m., empalement; (tech.) paddle-door.

empaler, v.a., to empale.

empan, n.m., span.

empanacher, v.a., to plume, to adorn with a plume. — *un casque;* to adorn a helmet with a plume.

empanner, v.a., (nav.) to bring to.

empaqueter (an-pak-té), v.a., to pack up, to make up into a bundle, to do up.

s'empaqueter, v.r., to wrap up. *Il s'empaqueta dans son manteau;* he wrapped himself up in his cloak.

s'emparer, v.r., to possess one's self of; to make one's self master of; to take possession of, to seize, to secure; to engross (conversation); to master. — *d'un héritage;* to seize upon an inheritance. — *de l'esprit de quelqu'un;* to circumvent any one.

empâtement, n.m., stickiness, clamminess; cramming (of fowls—*de la volaille*); (surg.) puffiness; (arch.) water-table.

empâter, *v.a.*, to make clammy, sticky; to cram (fowls—*volaille*); (paint.) to impaste. *Cela m'a empâté les mains;* that has made my fingers sticky.

empattement, *n.m.*, footing, foundation (of walls —*de murs*); (tech.) platform (of a crane— *de grue*).

empaumer,*v.a.*, to grasp; to take possession of; to gain over; (at tennis—*à la paume*) to strike with the palm of the hand or with a bat. — *la voie;* (hunt.) to catch the scent.

empaumure, *n.f.*, upper part of the head of a stag or roebuck; palm-piece of a glove.

empêché, -e,*part.*, hindered, at a loss. *Être — de sa personne;* to be greatly embarrassed.

empêchement (an-pêsh-män), *n.m.*, hinderance, obstacle, impediment, opposition, obstruction. *Lever tous les —s;* to remove all obstacles. *Apporter de l'— à quelque chose;* to throw impediments in the way of any thing. *Je n'y mets point d'—;* I do not oppose it.

empêcher, *v.a.*, to oppose, to prevent; to hinder, to obstruct, to impede, to put a stop to. — *un mariage;* to oppose a marriage. *Cette muraille empêche la vue;* this wall obstructs the prospect. *Cela n'empêcha pas qu'il ne le fît;* that did not prevent him from doing it. *Il m'empêche de travailler;* he hinders me from working. *L'un n'empêche pas l'autre;* the one does not preclude the other.

s'empêcher, *v.r.*, to forbear, to refrain from, to keep from. *Il ne saurait — de médire;* he cannot forbear slandering. *Je ne saurais m'empêcher de le faire;* I cannot help doing it.

***empeigne**, *n.f.*, upper leather (of a shoe—*d'une chaussure*); vamp.

empennelage, *n.m.*, backing an anchor.

empenneler, *v.a.*, to back an anchor.

empenner, *v.a.*, to feather arrows.

empereur, *n.m.*, emperor.

empesage, *n.m.*, starching.

empesé, -e, *part*, starched.

empeser, *v.a.*, to starch. — *un jabot;* to starch a frill.

empeseu-r, *n.m.*, **-se**, *n.f.*, starcher.

empester, *v.a.*, to infect, to taint.

empêtré, -e, *part.*, entangled.

empêtrer,*v.a.*, to entangle, to embarrass to hamper. — *quelqu'un dans une mauvaise affaire;* to engage any one in a disagreeable affair.

s'empêtrer, *v.r.*, to become entangled hampered, embarrassed. *Le cheval s'est empêtré les pieds;* the horse has got his feet entangled.

emphase, *n.f.*, magniloquence, pomposity; tumid style; emphasis.

emphatique, *adj.*, bombastic, tumid.

emphatiquement (-tik-män), *adv.*, bombastically, pompously.

emphractique, *n.m.adj.*, (pharm.) emphractic.

emphysème, *n.m.*, (med.) emphysema.

emphytéose, *n.f.*, long lease.

emphytéote, *n.m.*, tenant on a long lease.

emphytéotique, *adj.*, emphyteutic. *Bail —;* very long lease. *Redevance —;* ground-rent.

empierrement, *n.m.*, ballasting; broken stones; metalled road.

empierrer, *v.a.*, to metal (roads—*les routes*).

empiétement,*n.m.*, encroaching, encroachment.

empiéter,*v.a.*,to encroach,to make encroachments, to intrench upon, to invade.

empiéter,*v.n.*, to encroach. *La mer empiète sur la côte;* the sea encroaches upon the coast. *Il empiète sur mes droits;* he encroaches upon my rights.

empiffrer, *v.a.*, to cram, to stuff (with food —*de la nourriture*).

s'empiffrer, *v.r.*, to cram, to stuff.

empilement, *n.m.*, piling; stacking (of wood—*du bois*).

empiler, *v.a.*, to pile; to stack. — *du bois;* to pile up wood.

empire, *n.m.*, empire, sovereignty; authority; reign; sway, dominion, command, ascendency; dominions. *Bas- —;* Lower Empire. *L'humide —;* (poet.) the sea. — *d'Occident, d'Orient;* the Western, the Eastern, Empire. *Vous avez un — absolu sur moi:* you have an absolute command over me. *Avoir de l'— sur quelqu'un;* to sway any one. *Traiter quelqu'un avec —;* to treat one imperiously,with haughtiness. *Avoir de l'— sur soi;* to have the command of one's passions. *Se disputer l'—;* to contend for rule.

empirée, *n.m.* V. **empyrée**.

empirer, *v.a.*, to make worse.

empirer, *v.n.*, to grow worse. *Sa maladie empire chaque jour;* his illness gets worse every day.

empirique, *adj.*, empiric, empirical.

empirique, *n.m.*, empiric.

empiriquement, *adv.*, empirically.

empirisme, *n.m.*, empiricism.

emplacement (an-plas-män), *n.m.*, site, ground, piece of ground, place.

emplanture, *n.f.*, (nav.) step (of a mast— *d'un mât*).

emplâtre, *n.m.*, plaster, salve, ointment; sickly person; helpless creature. *Mettre un — à;* (med.) to put a plaster on. *Mettre un — à une affaire;* to patch up a business. *C'est un véritable —;* he is fit for nothing.

emplette, *n.f.*, purchase. *Faire — de quelque chose;* to purchase anything.

emplir, *v.a.*, to fill, to fill up.

s'emplir, *v.r.*, to fill.

emploi, *n.m.*, employ, employment; situation, place, post; entry (cf accounts—*des comptes*); (theat.) line of business; (fin.) appropriation. — *abusif;* misemployment. *Faux —;* false item (of accounts—*comptes*). *Faire un bon — de son temps;* to make a good use of one's time. *Double —;* useless repetition. *Donner de l'—;* to give employment.

employé, *n.m.*, clerk, person employed, employé.

employer, *v.a.*, to employ, to use, to make use of; to bestow; to spend. *Bien — son temps;* to employ one's time well. — *son temps à l'étude;* to spend one's time in study. — *une phrase;* to use a phrase. — *mal;* to misemploy. — *le vert et le sec;* to leave no stone unturned. *Je l'ai employé à cela;* I set him to work on that. — *une somme en recette;* (com.) to enter a sum as received.

s'employer, *v.r.*, to employ, to exert, one's self; to use one's interest. — *pour quelqu'un;* to use one's interest for any one.

emplumer, *v.a.*, (mus) to quill. — *un clavecin;* to quill a harpsichord.

s'emplumer, *v.r.*, to feather one's nest; (pop) to pick up one's flesh. *Il s'est bien emplumé dans cette maison;* he feathered his nest well in that house.

empocher, *v.a.*, (fam.) to pocket. *Il empoche tout ce qu'il gagne;* he pockets all his winnings.

***empoigner**, *v.a.*, to grasp, to seize, to lay hold of; to take up, to take into custody. *Cela est trop gros, on ne saurait l'—;* that is too thick, it is impossible to grasp it. *Je vous ferai —;* I will have you taken up.

s'empoigner, *v.r.*, to lay hold of each other. *Ils se sont empoignés;* they laid hold of each other, they had a set to.

empointer, *v.a.*, to point (pins, needles —*épingles, aiguilles*).

s'empiffrer, *v.r.*, to cram, to stuff.

empointeur, *n.m.*, pointer (of pins, needles —*d'épingles, d'aiguilles*).

empois. *n.m.*, starch.

empoisonné, *-e, part.*, poisoned; poisonous.

empoisonnement (-poâ-zo-n-mǎn), *n.m.*, poisoning.

empoisonner, *v.a.*, to poison; to infect; to mar, to corrupt; to imbitter, to envenom. *Ces maximes sont capables d'— la jeunesse*; these maxims are calculated to corrupt the young. *S'—, v.r.*, to poison one's self.

empoisonneu-r, *n.m.*, *-se, n.f.*, poisoner, corrupter; wretched cook.

empoisser, *v.a.* V. **poisser**.

empoissonnement (-poâ-so-n-mǎn), *n.m.*, stocking with fish.

empoissonner, *v.a.*, to stock (a pond—*un étang*) with fish.

emporté, *-e, adj.*, fiery, passionate, hot, hot-headed. *Un caractère violent et —*; a hot and passionate temper.

emportement, *n.m.*, transport; passion, fit of passion; hastiness.

emporte-pièce, *n.m.*, punch (instrument); puncher; cutting-out machine; fly-press; sarcastic person; severe satirist.

emporter, *v.a.*, to carry away, to take away, to sweep away, to convey away; to remove (stains—*les taches*); to carry off (kill—*tuer*); to entail, to involve. *Le vent a emporté mon chapeau*; the wind has blown my hat off. *Cette maladie l'a emporté*; that illness carried him off. *— de haute lutte*; to carry with a high hand. *La jeunesse se laisse — aux plaisirs*; youth suffers itself to be hurried away by pleasures. *L'— sur*; to prevail, to have the advantage, to get the better of, to preponderate, to overcome, to outbalance, to surpass. *L'amour l'emporte souvent sur la raison*; love often gets the better of reason. *Il l'a emporté sur tous ses concurrents*; he has carried it over all his competitors. *Cette considération l'emporte sur toutes les autres*; that consideration outweighs every other.

s'emporter, *v.r.*, to fly into a passion; to declaim, to inveigh; to rail at; to run away (of horses—*des chevaux*). *— contre le vice*; to declaim against vice. *— comme une soupe au lait*; to take fire like gunpowder.

empoter, *v.a.*, (hort.) to inclose in pots, to pot.

empourpré, *-e, adj.*, purple, purpled, empurpled.

empourprer, *v.a.*, *s'—, v.r.*, to purple.

empreindre, *v.a.*, to imprint, to stamp; to impress; to tincture.

empreinte, *n.f.*, mark, stamp, print, impression; (paint.) first coat. *L'— d'un cachet*; the stamp of a seal. *Son ouvrage porte l'— de son esprit*; his work bears the stamp of his wit.

empressé, *-e, adj.*, active; assiduous; officious; eager. *Il paraît fort — auprès d'elle*; he appears very assiduous in his attentions to her. *Des soins empressés*; assiduous attentions.

empressement (an-prèss-mǎn), *n.m.*, eagerness, earnestness; assiduous attention; alacrity, promptness. *Avec —*; eagerly, earnestly, cheerfully, industriously. *Il a beaucoup d'— à vous servir*; he is very anxious to serve you. *Trop d'—*; overforwardness.

s'empresser, *v.r.*, to be eager, earnest, forward, to be ardent. *— de parler*; to hasten to speak.

emprisonnement (-zo-n-mǎn), *n.m.*, imprisonment, confinement, custody. *— cellulaire*; solitary confinement.

emprisonner, *v.a.*, to imprison, to confine.

emprunt, *n.m.*, borrowing, loan. *Il est toujours aux —s*; he is always borrowing. *Argent d'—*; borrowed money. *Une beauté d'—*; an artificial beauty.

emprunter, *v.a.*, to borrow. *— de l'argent à quelqu'un*; to borrow money of any one. *Nom emprunté*; assumed name.

emprunteu-r, *-se, n.* and *adj.*, borrower; borrowing, prone to borrow; not original.

empuantir, *v.a.*, to cause an ill smell, to infect.

s'empuantir, *v.r.*, to stink, to have a bad odour.

empuantissement (-tis-mǎn),*n.m.*, stench.

empyème, *n.m.*, (med.) empyema.

empyrée, *n.m.* and *adj.*, empyrean; empyreal.

empyreumatique, *adj.*, empyreumatical.

empyreume, *n.m.*, empyreuma.

ému, *-e, part.*, moved, affected. *Fort —*, much affected.

émulat-eur, *n.m.*, *-rice, n.f.*, (l.u.) emulator, rival, imitator.

⊖**émulati-f**, *-ve, adj.*, emulative.

émulation, *n.f.*, emulation.

émule, *n.m.*, rival, competitor, emulator.

émulgent, *-e, adj.*,(anat.) emulgent.

émulsi-f, *-ve, adj.*, emulsive.

émulsion, *n.f.*, emulsion.

émulsionner, *v.a.*, to mix an emulsion with.

en, *prep.*, in, into, within, on, to, at, like, in the form of, as a, out of, by, for. *De l'ai mise — pension*; I have put her to a boarding-school. *— haut*; above, up stairs. *— bas*; below, downstairs. *— avant*; forward. *— arrière*; backward, behind. *— dedans*; within. *— dehors*; without. *Aller — France*; to go to France. *En tout temps*; at all times. *— hiver*; in winter. *Être — bonne santé*; to be in good health. *— nourrice*; at nurse. *— prière*; at prayers. *Vivre — roi*; to live like a king. *Agir — furieux*; to act as a madman. *Être — robe de chambre*; to be in one's dressing-gown. *— dépit de lui*; in spite of him. *De plus — plus*; more and more. *Voir — songe*; to see in a dream. *Il l'aborda — riant*; he came up to her with a smile. *— passant*; by the way. *— colère*; in a passion. *— guerre*; at war. *— paix*; at peace. *Tomber — décadence*; to fall into decay. *— trois jours*; in three days. *Être — ville*; to be out.

en, *pron.*, *m.f. sing.* and *pl.*, of him, of her, of it, its, of them, their; from him, from her, from it, from them; by him, by her, by it, by them; about him, about her, about it, about them; thence, from thence; some, any. *Avez-vous de l'argent*? have you any money? *J'— ai*; I have some. *Vous — parlez toujours*; you are always speaking of him. *Il — est mort un*; one of them is dead. *J'— suis bien aise*; I am very glad of it. *J'— suis fâché*; I am sorry for it. *J'— suis surpris*; I wonder at it. *Qu'— dites-vous?* what do you say to it? *Je n'— ai point*; I have none. *— voulez-vous?* will you have any? *Donnez-m'—*; give me some. *C'est un bœuf, j'— vois les cornes*; it is an ox, I see its horns. *Si vous voulez voir de beaux tableaux, il — a*; if you desire to see fine pictures, he has got some. *Il — est des femmes comme des enfants*; it is with women as with children. *Il — est de cela comme de la plupart des choses*: it is the same with that as with most other things. *Après cela ils — vinrent aux mains*; after that they came to blows. *— vouloir à quelqu'un*; to have a grudge against any one. *S'— aller*; to go away. *S'— retourner*; to return. *C'— est fait*; it is over. *Il s'— faut de beaucoup*; there wants a great deal. *Il ne sait où il — est*; he knows not where he is. *Il — tient*; he is caught. *Voulez-vous — être?* will you make one? *Parlez-lui —*; speak to him of it. *Il veut — découdre*; he wants to fight it out.

énallage, *n.f.*, (gram.) enallage.
énamourer, *v.r.*, to fall in love.
enarrhement, *n.m.* *V.* **arrhement**.
enarrher. *v.a.* *V.* **arrher**.
énarthrose, *n.f.*, (anat.) enarthrosis.
encablure, *n.f.*, (nav.) cable length.
encadré, **-e**, *part.*, framed.
encadrement, *n.m.*, framing, frame.
encadrer, *v.a.*, to frame, to encircle; to introduce, to insert. *Faire — un tableau;* to have a picture framed. *S'—*, *v.r.*, to be introduced, inserted, enclosed.
encadreur, *n.m.*, picture-frame maker.
encager, *v.a.*, to cage, to put in a cage.
encaisse, *n.f.*, (fin., com.) cash in hand, metallic reserve.
encaissé, **-e**, *part.*, encased; embanked. *Cette rivière est —e;* that river is deeply embanked.
encaissement (ân-kès-mân), *n.m.*, packing in cases; packing; putting in boxes; embankment (of rivers—*des rivières*); (fin.) collection.
encaisser, *v.a.*, to encase, to pack; to put in a box; to embank (rivers—*rivières*); (fin.) to collect; to lay down a base (to roads—*routes*).
encan, *n.m.*, auction, public sale. *Vente à l'—;* sale by public auction. *Mettre à l'—;* to put up for sale. *Vendre à l'—;* to sell by auction.
***encanailler**, *v.a.*, to degrade by introducing low company.
***s'encanailler**, *v.r.*, to keep low company. *Gardez-vous de vous encanailler;* beware of keeping low company.
encapuchonné, **-e**, *part.*, cowled.
encapuchonner, *v.a.*, to put on a cowl.
s'encapuchonner, *v.r.*, to wear a cowl; to put on a cowl; (man.) to arch the neck (of horses —*des chevaux*).
encaquement, *n.m.*, packing; putting into a keg of herrings—*des harengs*).
encaquer, *v.a.*, to barrel; to cram up. — *des harengs;* to barrel herrings.
encaqu-eur, *n.m.*, **-euse**, *n.f.*, one that barrels; packer (of beef, pork, fish—*de bœuf, de porc, de poisson*).
encarter, *v.a.*, (print.) to insert as a cancel.
s'encarter, *v.r.*, to be inserted as a cancel.
en-cas, *n.m.* (—), sun-shade large enough to be used as an umbrella; anything kept ready in case of need.
encastelé, **-e**, *adj.*, hoof-bound (of a horse— *du cheval*).
s'encasteler, *v.r.*, (of a horse—*du cheval*) to be hoof-bound.
encastelure, *n.f.*, being hoof-bound (of a horse—*du cheval*).
encastrement, *n.m.*, fitting; fitting in.
encastrer, *v.a.*, to fit, to fit in.
s'encastrer, *v.r.*, to fit, to fit in.
encaustique, *n.f.* and *adj.*, (paint.) encaustic.
encavement (ân-kav-mân), *n.m.*, putting into a cellar.
encaver, *v.a.*, to put in a cellar.
encav-eur, *n.m.*, cellar-man.
enceindre, *v.a.*, to enclose, to encircle, to encompass, to surround. — *de murailles —* to enclose with walls.
enceinte, *adj.f.*, pregnant, in the family-way; enceinte.
enceinte, *n.f.*, circuit, circumference; enclosure, precincts; place; (fort.) enceinte. *Mur d'— continue;* wall of circumvallation. *Dans cette —;* within these walls.
encens, *n.m.*, incense, frankincense; fragrance; praise. *Brûler de l'— sur les autels;* to burn incense on the altars. *Donner de l'— à quelqu'un;* to praise any one.

encensement (an-sâns-mân), *n.m.*, incensing.
encenser, *v.a.*, to incense, to perfume with frankincense; to flatter.
encenseur, *n.m.*, flatterer.
encensoir, *n.m.*, censer, perfuming-pan; (astron.) Ara; (fig.) ecclesiastical power. *Mettre la main à l'—;* to meddle with ecclesiastical affairs. *Donner de l'— par le nez, casser le nez à coups d'—;* to flatter fulsomely.
encéphale, *n.m.*, encephalon, brain.
encéphalique, *adj.*, (anat.) encephalic.
encéphalite, *n.f.*, inflammation of the brain.
encéphalocèle, *n.f.*, encephalocele, hernia of the brain.
enchaînement (ân-shèn-mân), *n.m.*, chaining; concatenation, chain, series.
enchaîner, *v.a.*, to chain up, to chain, to bind in chains, to chain down, to captivate; to link, to connect. *Sa beauté enchaîna tous les cœurs;* her beauty captivated every heart.
s'enchaîner, *v.r.*, to link, to be connected.
enchaînure, *n.f.*, (tech.) chain; connection, chain-work.
enchanteler (ân-shân-tlé), *v.a.*, to arrange timber in a yard; to set (casks—*des tonneaux*) on gawntrees.
enchantement (ân-shân-tmân), *n.m.*, enchantment, delight. *Par —;* by enchantment. *Il est dans l'—;* he is delighted.
enchanter, *v.a.*, to enchant, to bewitch, to fascinate, to charm, to gratify. *Elle est enchantée de son mari;* she is enchanted with her husband. *Je suis enchanté de pouvoir vous être utile;* I am overjoyed to be of any service to you.
enchante-ur, **-resse**, *n.* and *adj.*, enchanter, enchantress, bewitcher; enchanting. *Voix —resse;* enchanting voice.
enchaperonner, *v.a.*, to hood (a hawk—*un faucon*); to hood.
encharner, *v.a.*, (trunk-making—*layeterie*) to put hinges to.
enchâsser, *v.a.*, to enchase, to enshrine; to insert; to introduce; to set. — *dans de l'or;* to set in gold. — *un diamant;* to set a diamond. — *une anecdote dans un discours;* to introduce an anecdote into a speech.
enchâssure, *n.f.*, setting; insertion; introduction.
enchausser, *v.a.*, (gard.) to cover with straw or dung.
enchère, *n.f.*, bidding (at an auction—*à une vente publique*); auction. *Vente à l'—, aux —s;* sale by auction. *Couvrir une —;* to make a higher bid. *Vendre à l'—, aux —s;* to sell by auction. *Folle —;* bidding what one cannot pay. *Mettre aux —s;* to bring to the hammer; to put up to auction. *Payer la folle —;* to pay dear for one's rashness. *Il est à l'—;* he is to be bought by the highest bidder.
enchérir, *v.a.*, to bid for, to outbid, to over-bid; to raise (prices—*des prix*).
enchérir, *v.n.*, to bid, to outbid; (fig.) to surpass, to outdo, to go further; to rise (in price—*de prix*). *La volaille a enchéri;* poultry has risen in price.
enchérissement (-ris-mân), *n.m.*, rise, increase, advance in price.
enchérisseur, *n.m.*, bidder (at an auction —*à une enchère*).
enchevêtré, **-e**, *part.*, entangled; confused.
s'enchevêtrer, *v.a.*, to put on a halter, to halter; to entangle.
s'enchevêtrer, *v.r.*, to get a foot entangled in the halter; to get entangled; to get confused, embarrassed.

enchevêtrure, *n.f.*, (carp.) binding; injury in the foot of a horse.

enchifrené, -e, *part.*, stuffed up (of the nose—*du nez*). *Je suis tout* —; my nose is stuffed up.

enchifrènement (-èn-mán), *n.m.*, stuffing up (of the nose—*du nez*); rheum, cold in the head.

enchifrener, *v.a.*, to stop up the nose (by a cold—*rhume de cerveau*).

enchiridion (-ki-), *n.m.*, (antiq.) manual, enchiridion.

enchymose (-ki-), *n.f.*, (med.) cutaneous hyperæmia.

enclave, *n.f.*, piece of enclosed land; boundary, limit; recess (of a lock on a river—*d'une porte d'écluse*).

enclavé, -e, *part.*, enclosed.

enclavement (an-kiav-mán), *n.m.*, enclosing (of land—*d'un terrain, d'un pays*).

enclaver, *v.a.*, to enclose (land within other land—*un terrain, un pays*).

s'enclaver, *v.r.*, (of land—*d'un terrain, d'un pays*) to be enclosed (in other land—*par un autre terrain ou pays*).

enclin, -e, *adj.*, inclined, prone, addicted *Il est* — *au bien;* he is inclined to good.

enclitique, *n.f.*, (gram.) enclitic.

encloîtrer, *v.a.*, to cloister.

enclore, *v.a.*, to enclose, to fence in, to take in.

enclos, *n.m.*, enclosure, close.

enclouer, *v.a.*, to prick animals (in shoeing them—*en les ferrant*); to spike (a gun—*un canon*).

enclouure, *n.f.*, prick (in the foot of an animal—*au pied d'un cheval, &c.*); difficulty, obstacle, hinderance.

enclume, *n.f.*, anvil; (anat.) incus. *Billot d'* —; anvil-block. *Être entre le marteau et l'* —; to be between the anvil and the hammer. *Remettre sur l'* —; to remodel.

enclumeau, *or* **enclumot**, *n.m.*, hand-anvil.

encoche, *n.f.*, notch (on a tally, on the bolt of a lock—*sur une taille, au pène d'une serrure*).

encocher, *v.a.*, to notch. — *une flèche;* to fit an arrow in the bow.

encoffrer, *v.a.*, to put in a coffer; to lay up; to cage.

*encoignure, *or* **encognure** (an-ko-gnur), *n.f.*, corner; buffet (that stands in a corner—*propre pour un coin*).

encollage, *n.m.*, sizing.

encoller, *v.a.*, to size.

encolure, *n.f.*, neck and shoulders of a horse; (b.s.) appearance (of a person—*d'une personne*). *Il a l'* — *d'un sot;* he looks like a fool.

encombrant, *adj.*, bulky, cumbering, encumbering.

encombre, *n.m.*, clog, impediment, hinderance, obstacle.

encombrement, *n.m.*, obstruction.

encombrer, *v.a.*, to obstruct, to incumber, to embarrass.

*à l'*encontre, *prep.*, counter, against. *Aller à l'* — *de quelque chose;* to run counter to a thing.

encorbellement (-bèl-mán), *n.m.*, (arch.) corbelling, projecting.

encore, *adv.*, yet, still, more, again; once more; further; moreover; besides, however. *Il n'est pas* — *venu;* he is not come yet. *À sept heures j'attendais'* —; at seven o'clock I was still waiting. — *!* what, again? *Outre l'argent, on lui donna* — *un cheval;* besides the money, he had, moreover, a horse given to him. — *s'il voulait m'envoyer dire;* if, however, he would send me word. *Vous servez-vous* — *de ce livre?* are you still using that book? *Il est* — *plus*

riche que son frère; he is still richer than his brother. *Quoi* —*!* what else? — *moins;* still less. *Prenez* — *un verre de vin;* take another glass of wine. — *une fois je vous dis;* I tell you once more.

encore, *conj.*, even, yet. — *que;* though, although.

encorné, -e, *adj.*, horned.

encourageant, -e, *adj.*, encouraging.

encouragement (-raj-mán), *n.m.*, encouragement, incitement, incentive.

encourager, *v.a.*, to encourage, to stimulate, to be a promoter of. *S'* —, *v.r.*, to encourage each other.

encourir, *v.a.*, to incur, to draw down upon one's self, to fail under. — *le mépris de tout le monde;* to draw general contempt upon one's self.

encrage, *n.m.*, (print.) inking.

encrassement, *n.m.*, fouling (of fire-arms —*des armes à feu*).

encrasser, *v.a.*, to make dirty, to dirty; to make greasy; to foul (fire-arms—*armes à feu*).

s'encrasser, *v.r.*, to grow greasy, to become dirty; to debase one's self; to become fouled (of fire-arms—*d'armes à feu*).

encre, *n.f.*, ink. — *à écrire;* writing ink. — *d'imprimerie;* printing ink. — *de Chine;* Indian ink. *C'est la bouteille à l'* —; there's no seeing through that. *Tacher d'* —; to ink. *Écrire de bonne* — *à quelqu'un;* to write in strong terms to any one. *Être dans la bouteille à l'* —; to be in the secret.

encrer, *v.a.*, (print.) to ink.

encrier, *n.m.*, inkstand, ink-horn; (print.) ink-trough. *Table d'* —; (print.) ink-table.

encroué, *adj.*, entangled (of the branches of a tree—*des branches d'arbres*).

encroûté, -e, *part.*, full of prejudices. *Être* — *de préjugés;* to be full of prejudices. &c.

encroûter, *v.a.*, to crust; to plaster a wall, &c.

s'encroûter, *v.r.*, to crust, to get hard, to become heavy; to become stupid.

encuirasser, *v.a.*, to cover with a cuirass.

s'encuirasser, *v.r.*, to put on one's cuirass; to get covered with dirt; to become hardened.

encuvement (án-kuv-mán), *n.m.*, putting into a vat.

encuver, *v.a.*, to put into a vat.

encyclique, *n.f.* and *adj.*, encyclical letter; encyclical.

encyclopédie, *n.f.*, encyclopædia.

encyclopédique, *adj.*, encyclopedic.

encyclopédiste, *n.m.*, encyclopedist.

endécagone, *n.m.* and *adj.*, (geom.) hendecagon.

endémique, *adj.*, endemical.

endenté, -e, *adj.*, indented; furnished with teeth.

endenter, *v.a.*, (carp.) to indent; to cog, to tooth.

endetter, *v.a.*, to cause to run into debt; to run into debt.

s'endetter, *v.r.*, to run into debt, to contract debts.

endévé, -e, *n.* and *adj.*, (fam., l.u.) irritable, passionate person; impatient, irritable, passionate.

endêver, *v.r.*, to be mad, to be vexed. *Faire* — *quelqu'un;* to vex any one; to make any one mad.

endiablé, -e, *adj.*, possessed (by a devil—*du diable*); wicked, horrible.

endiablé, *n.m.*, -e, *n.f.*, person possessed. *C'est un* —: he is like one possessed.

endiabler, *v.n.*, to wish one's self at the devil, to be in a passion.

endiguement, *n.m.*, damming in ; damming up.

endiguer (-ghé), *v.a.*, to dam in ; to dam up.

s'endimancher, *v.r.*, to put on one's Sunday clothes.

endive, *n.f.*, endive.

endoctriner, *v.a.*, to indoctrinate, to teach ; to give his cue (to any one—*quelqu'un*).

endoctrineur, *n.m.*, one who indoctrinates.

endolori, -e, *adj.*, painful, aching.

endolorir, *v.a.*, to make sore, tender.

endommagement (-maj-mân), *n.m.*, endamagement, loss, injury.

endommager, *v.a.*, to damage, to injure.

s'endommager, *v.r.*, to be damaged; to become deteriorated.

endormeur, *n.m*, cajoler, wheedler, flatterer, coaxer.

endormi, -e, *part.*, asleep, sleeping ; sleepy, drowsy, sluggish; benumbed. *J'ai la jambe—e ;* my leg is benumbed.

endormi, *n.m.*, **-e**, *n.f.*, sleepy person ; sleepy head ; person asleep. *Faire l'—;* to sham sleep.

endormir, *v.a.*, to lull asleep, to send to sleep ; to rock to sleep ; to wheedle, to amuse, to deceive; to benumb, to lull. *Endormez cet enfant :* rock that child to sleep. *Sa conversation vous endort;* his conversation sends you to sleep. *Cela m'a endormi la jambe;* that has benumbed my leg.

s'endormir, *v.r.*, to fall asleep, to go to sleep, to slumber ; to be lulled into security. *— du sommeil de la tombe;* to sleep the sleep of death. *— dans le vice ;* to be steeped in vice. *Il s'est endormi sur cette affaire;* he was wanting in vigilance in that business. *— sur le rôti;* to neglect what requires most attention.

endos. *n.m.*, (com.) endorsement.

endosmose. *n.f.* (phys.) endosmose.

endosse, *n.f.*, (fam.) trouble; burden.

endossement (ân-dôsmân), *n m.*, (com.) endorsement. *V.* **endos**, which is more frequently used.

endosser, *v.a.*, to put on the back; to buckle on; to put on; to saddle ; (com.) to endorse. *— une lettre de change ;* to endorse a bill of exchange. *— le harnais;* to put on the harness.

endosseur, *n.m.*, (com.) endorser.

endroit, *n.m.*, place, part, passage ; point; right side (of a stuff—*d'une étoffe*). *Voilà l'où il est blessé;* this is the place he is wounded in. *Son plus bel —;* any one's, any thing's, best side. *— faible;* weak point. *- sensible;* sensitive point.

enduire (enduisant, enduit), *v.a.*, to do over, to lay over, to coat. *— une muraille de plâtre;* to do a wall over with plaster.

enduit, *n.m.*, coat, coating, layer; glaze, glazing.

endurant, -e *adj.*, patient under injury. *Peu —;* impatient of injury.

endurci, -e, *part.*, hardened, obdurate, inured, callous. *Un cheval — aux coups;* a horse inured to blows. *Pécheur —;* hardened sinner.

endurci, *n.m.*, **-e**, *n.f.*, hardened sinner.

endurcir, *v.a.*, to harden, to make hard, to inure ; to render obdurate, to steel ; to indurate ; to render callous. *Le travail endurcit le corps;* labour hardens the body. *L'avarice avait endurci son cœur;* avarice had steeled his heart.

s'endurcir, *v.r.*, to harden, to grow hard ; to be steeled ; to become callous ; to indurate.

endurcissement (-sis-mân). *n.m.*, hardness; hardness of heart, obduracy; callousness.

endurer. *v.a.*, to endure, to bear ; to suffer,

to allow, to put up with, to permit. — *to froid ;* to bear cold.

onéorème, *n.m.*, (med.) eneorema.

énergie, *n.f.*, force, energy. *Avec —;* with energy. *Sans —;* of no energy. *L'— des passions ;* the force of the passions. *Doué d'—;* endowed with energy.

énergique, *adj.*, energetic, energetical, forcible. *Remède —;* powerful remedy.

énergiquement (-jik-mân), *adv.*, energetically.

énergumène, *n.m.*, demoniac.

énervation. *n.f.*, enervation.

énervement, *n.m.*, state of an enervated person.

énerver, *v.a.*, to enervate, to unnerve.

s'énerver, *v.r.*, to become enervated.

enfaîteau. *n.m.* (mas.) ridge tile.

enfaîtement (ân-fêt-mân), *n.m.*, (arch.) ridge (on the tops of houses—*sur les toits*).

enfaîter, *v.a.*, to roof a house.

enfance, *n.f.*, infancy, childhood; childishness, puerility. dotage; childish action. *Première —;* earliest infancy. *Dès mon —;* from my infancy. *Sortir de l'—;* to emerge from childhood. *Être en —;* to be in one's dotage. *Tomber en —;* to become childish.

enfant, *n.m.f.*, child ; infant; native ; (jur.) issue. *Avoir des —s;* to have children. *— adoptif ;* adopted child. *L'— prodigue ;* the prodigal son. *L'— à naître ;* the unborn child. *— trouvé;* foundling. *— naturel ;* natural child. *Un — de famille;* a young gentleman. *— de la balle;* child that follows his father's profession. *Un — à la mamelle;* an infant at the breast. *Un — mort-né ;* a still-born child. *Discours d'—;* childish language. *— de chœur;* singing-boy. *Les —s perdus ;* (milit.) the forlorn hope. *Faire l'—;* to play like a child. *C'est bien l'— de sa mère;* he is a chip of the old block. *En travail d'—;* in labour. *C'est un bon —;* he is a good child, he is a good fellow. *Voilà une belle —;* that is a fine girl. *Les —s de France;* the children of the King of France, the children of the eldest son of the King of France.

enfantement (ân-fân-tmân), *n.m.*, childbirth.

enfanter. *v.a.*, to bear, to bring forth ; to bring to light; to give birth to. *Les guerres civiles enfantent mille maux;* civil wars give birth to a thousand evils.

***enfantillage**, *n.m.*, child's play.

enfantin, -e *adj.*, infantine, childish.

enfariner, *v.a.*, to flour, to sprinkle with flour. *Être enfariné de quelque science;* to have a smattering of some science. *Être — d'une mauvaise doctrine;* to be prepossessed in favour of a bad doctrine. *Il est venu nous dire cela la gueule enfarinée* (triv.); he came, full of stupid confidence, to tell us that.

enfer (an-fèr), *n.m.*, hell, infernal regions. *Au fond de l'—;* in the bottom of hell. *Les peines de l'—;* the torments of hell. *L'— s'est déchaîné contre moi;* hell is let loose against me. *Tison d'—;* hell-hound. *Un feu d'—;* a devil of a fire.

enfermé, *n.m.*, confined air. *Sentir l'—;* to smell close.

enfermer, *v.a.*, to shut, to shut in; to shut up; to lock up; to enclose ; to coop up, to conceal ; to comprehend, to comprise. *— un homme dans une prison;* to lock a man up in prison. *C'est un homme à — ;* that man ought to be confined in a mad-house. *— à clef;* to keep under lock and key. *— un parc de murailles;* to wall in a park.

s'enfermer. *v.r.*, to lock one's self up, to seclude one's self; to lock, to lock up ((f a thing —*des objets*).

enferrer, *v.a.*, to run any one through with a sword, &c., to transfix.

s'enferrer, *v.r.*, to run one's self through with a sword, &c. ; (fig.) to injure one's self.

enficeler, *v.a.*, to tie with a string.

enfilade, *n.f.*, suite (of chambers—*de chambres*) ; string (of phrases) ; (milit.) enfilade.

enfiler, *v.a.*, to thread, to string ; to pierce, to run any one through with a sword, &c. ; to engage in ; (milit.) to enfilade. — *une aiguille ;* to thread a needle. — *des perles ;* to string pearls; to lose one's time. — *un discours ;* to begin a long-winded speech. — *un homme ;* to run a man through the body.

s'enfiler, *v.r.*, to be run through, to be pierced; to get engaged in.

enfileur, *n.m.*, header (in pin-making—*manufacture des épingles*) ; prattler; (pop.) cheat, wheedler.

enfin, *adv.*, in fine, finally, at length, in short, after all, at last. — *elle est venue ;* at last she is come.

enflammé, **-e**, *part.*, on fire, in flames, ignited.

enflammer, *v.a.*, to set on fire, to fire, to kindle; to inflame, to heat; to incense, to provoke.

s'enflammer, *v.r.*, to take fire, to be kindled, to be inflamed, to blaze ; to be incensed ; to ignite. *On vit tout le vaisseau —;* they saw the whole ship in a blaze.

enflé, **-e**, *part.*, swelled, inflated, puffed up, bloated; (lit.) bombastic.

enfler, *v.a.*, to swell, to swell out, to blow out, to bloat; to puff up, to distend, to elate, to excite ; to inflate. *Les pluies ont enflé la rivière;* the rains have swelled the river. *Le vent enflait nos voiles;* the wind swelled our sails. — *son style ;* to swell one's style.

s'enfler, *v.r.*, to swell, to grow turgid. *La voile s'enfle;* the sail swells. — *d'orgueil ;* to be puffed up with pride.

enflure, *n.f.*, bloatedness, swelling; bombast, turgidness. — *du style ;* turgidness of style.

enfoncé, **-e**, *part.*, broken open, sunken. *Des yeux enfoncés:* sunken eyes. — *!* (pop.) dished ! done for !

enfoncement (ân-fons-mân), *n.m.*, sinking, sinking down; breaking in; recess; (paint.) back-ground.

enfoncer, *v.a.*, to sink, to sink to the bottom ; to drive in; to break in; to outwit, to surpass; to ruin, to blow up. — *un clou dans la muraille ;* to drive a nail into the wall. — *son chapeau ;* to pull one's hat over one's eyes. — *un bataillon ;* to break a battalion.

s'enfoncer, *v.r.*, to sink, to sink down ; to break down ; to bury one's self; to plunge; to fail, to make a mess of. — *dans un bois ;* to dive into a wood. *Cet homme s'enfonce dans l'étude;* that man buries himself in study. — *dans la débauche ;* to plunge into debauchery.

enfoncer, *v.n.*, to sink.

enfonceur, *n.m.*, one who breaks in or through anything. — *de portes ouvertes ;* braggart.

enfonçure, *n.f.*, cavity; boards (of a bedstead—*d'un bois de lit*) ; bottom pieces (of casks —*de tonneaux*).

enforcir, *v.a.*, to strengthen.

s'enforcir, *v.r.*, to gather strength ; to grow stronger.

enforcir, *v.n.*, to gather strength, to get strength.

enfouir, *v.a.*, to hide *or* bury in the ground, to cover with earth.

enfouissement (ân-foo-is-mân), *n.m.*, hiding in the ground.

enfouisseu-r, *n.m.*, **-se**, *n.f.*, burier, hider in the ground.

enfourcher, *v.a.*, to bestride, to straddle.

enfourchure, *n.f.*, (hunt.) forked head (of a stag— *du cerf*).

'enfourner, *v.a.*, to put in the oven. — *le pain;* to put the bread in the oven. *Bien —, mal —;* to make a good, a bad, beginning.

s'enfourner, *v.r.*, to get into a difficult road, into a blind alley, into a scrape.

enfreindre (enfreignant, enfreint), *v.a.*, to infringe, to violate. — *un traité ;* to infringe a treaty. — *les lois;* to transgress the laws.

enfroquer, *v.a.*, (b.s.) to make one turn monk or friar.

s'enfroquer, *v.r.*, (b.s) to turn monk.

s'enfuir, *v.r.*, to run away, to take flight, to escape ; to run off ; to elope; to run out, to leak. *Ils s'étaient enfuis de la prison;* they had made their escape from prison. *La bouteille s'enfuit;* the bottle leaks.

enfumé, **-e**, *part.*, smoked, smoky.

enfumer, *v.a.*, to smoke, to fill with smoke, to smoke out. — *un renard ;* to smoke out a fox.

engagé, *n.m.*, soldier enlisted.

engagé, **-e**, *part.*, engaged ; (nav.) in action, water-logged. *La clef est —e dans la serrure ;* the key sticks in the lock. *Vaisseau —;* water-logged ship.

engageant, **-e** (-jăn,-t), *adj.*, engaging, winning, pleasing. *Il a des manières —es;* he has winning manners.

engageantes, *n.f.pl.*, short under-sleeves with lace cuffs.

engagement (ân-gaj-mân), *n.m.*, pledging, pawning; engagement (promise—*promesse*) ; enlisting ; (milit.) bounty ; (milit.) action ; *pl.*, (com.) liabilities. *Entrer dans un —;* to enter into an engagement. *Manquer à un —;* to fail in an engagement.

engager, *v.a.*, to pawn, to pledge; to engage, to induce, to invite ; (milit.) to enlist ; to hire ; to bind ; (b.s.) to involve ; to unite ; to compel. — *ses meubles;* to pledge one's furniture. — *son cœur;* to engage one's heart. *Cela ne vous engage à rien;* that binds you to nothing. — *quelqu'un dans une mauvaise affaire ;* to entangle any one into a disagreeable affair. — *le combat;* to begin the action. — *un soldat;* to enlist a soldier. — *une clef dans une serrure;* to entangle a key in a lock.

s'engager, *v.r.*, to engage one's self, to be a security, to promise, to take upon one's self, to undertake, to bind one's self ; to hire one's self ; to enlist ; to entangle one's self, to get involved. — *pour un ami;* to stand bound for a friend. — *dans une mauvaise affaire ;* to get involved in a bad business. *Le combat ne tarda pas à —;* the battle soon began.

engagiste, *n.m.*, tenant (of crown lands— *de terres royales*).

engainer, *v.a.*, to sheathe

engeance (an-jăns), *n.f.*, breed, brood (animal) ; (b.s.) race (pers.). *Des poules d'une grande —;* hens of a large breed. *Maudite —;* cursed race.

engelure (an-jlur), *n.f.*, chilblain.

engendrer, *v.a.*, to beget, to engender, to generate, to procreate ; to breed, to spawn. — *des enfants ;* to beget children. *Chaque animal engendre son semblable;* every animal procreates its species. *Ne pas — la mélancolie ;* to be of a very gay disposition. *Le mauvais air engendre des maladies ;* bad air breeds diseases. *L'oisiveté engendre le vice;* idleness begets vice. *La familiarité engendre le mépris ;* familiarity begets contempt.

s'engendrer, *v.r.*, to be bred, engendered; to breed.

engeoler, *v.a.*, *V.* **enjôler**.

engeoleur, *n.m.* *V.* **enjôleur.**

⊙**enger**, *v.a.*, to hamper, to cumber, to burden.

engerber, *v.a.*, to sheaf, to heap up.

engin, *n.m.*, machine, engine.

englober, *v.a.*, to unite ; to put, to throw, together.

engloutir, *v.a.*, to swallow up, to devour ; to ingulf ; to absorb; to dissipate, to squander away. *La mer a englouti bien des richesses ;* the sea has swallowed up many riches.

*s'***engloutir**, *v.r.*, to be swallowed up, to be ingulfed.

engloutissement,*n.m.*, ingulfing, swallowing up.

engluer, *v.a.*, to lime, to daub with birdlime.

*s'***engluer**, *v.r.*, to be caught, to stick in birdlime (of birds—*des oiseaux*) ; to lime one's self ; to be caught, to be taken in (pers.).

engoncer, *v.a.*, to cramp. *Cet habit vous engonce fort ;* that coat cramps you very much.

engorgement, *n.m.*, obstruction, stopping up.

engorger, *v.a.*, to obstruct, to block up, to choke up, to stop up ; (med.) to congest.

*s'***engorger**, *v.r.*, to be obstructed, choked up ; (med.) to be congested.

engouement, *or* **engoûment** (ân-goo-mân), *n.m.*, infatuation ; (med. vet.) obstruction. *On ne saurait le faire revenir de son —; it* is impossible to cure him of his infatuation.

engouer, *v.a.*, to obstruct the throat ; to infatuate.

*s'***engouer**, *v.r.*, to obstruct one's throat ; to be obstructed ; to be infatuated. — *d'une femme,* to be infatuated with a woman.

engouffrer, *v.a.*, to ingulf, to swallow up.

*s'***engouffrer**, *v.r.*, to be ingulfed ; to blow hard (of the wind in a narrow passage—*du vent dans un passage étroit*) ; to run into. *Le vent s'est engouffré dans la cheminée ;* a gust of wind has rushed into the chimney. *Que de fortunes se sont engouffrées dans cette entreprise !* how many fortunes have been swallowed up in that enterprise!

engoulé, -e, *adj.*, swallowed up ; (Her.) engoulee.

engouler, *v.a.*, to swallow up.

engoulevent (ân-gool-vân), *n.m.*, (orni.) fern-owl ; goat-sucker.

engourdi, -e, *adj.*, torpid, heavy, dull.

engourdir, *v.a.*, to benumb, to make torpid ; to dull, to make languid, to enervate. *Le froid engourdit les mains ;* cold benumbs one's hands. *L'oisiveté engourdit l'esprit ;* idleness benumbs the mind.

*s'***engourdir**, *v r.*, to get benumbed ; to become torpid, enervated, enfeebled.

engourdissement (ân-goor-dis-mân),*n.m.*, numbness, torpor, enervation. *Avoir un — au bras;* to have a numbness in the arm. *Tirer quelqu'un de son —;* to rouse any one from his torpor.

engrais, *n.m.*, rich pasture ; fatting ; manure, soil. *Mettre des bœufs à l'—;* to put oxen to fatten.

engraissement (ân-grès-mân), *n.m.*, fattening ; corpulence.

engraisser, *v.a.*, to fatten, to cram (fowls—*volaille*); to manure. — *des bestiaux;* to fatten cattle.

*s'***engraisser**, *v.r.*, to fatten, to grow fat, stout ; to grow rich ; to grow thick or ropy. — *des misères publiques ;* to fatten on the public misery.

engraisser, *v.n.*, to become corpulent ; to fatten ; to thrive.

engranger, *v.a.*, (agri.) to get in, to house.

engravement (ân-grav-man), *n.m.*, (nav.) running aground in the sand.

engraver, *v.a.*, to run aground in the sand (of boats and ships—*bateaux, vaisseaux*) ; (nav.) to place, to hide, things in the ballast.

engraver, *v.n.*, *s'—, v.r.*, (nav.) to get embedded in the sand.

engrêlé, -e, *adj.*, (her.) engrailed.

engrêler, *v.a.*, (her.) to engrail ; to purl (lace—*dentelle*).

engrêlure, *n.f.*, purl (of lace—*dentelle*); (her.) engrailing.

engrenage, *n.m.*, gear (mec.). *A—;* serrated. *Roue d'— ;* brake-wheel.

engrener, *v.a.*, to put corn (in the millhopper—*dans la trémie*) ; to feed with corn ; to throw into gear, to engage (mec.).

*s'***engrener**, *v.r.*, to work into each other (of toothed wheels—*roues dentées*) ; to be put in gear (mec.). *Ces roues s'engrènent bien ;* these wheels work into each other well.

engrener, *v.n.*, to put corn (into the millhopper—*dans la trémie*) ; to work into each other (of toothed wheels—*roues dentées*) ; to begin. *Il a bien engrené ;* he has begun well.

engrenure, *n.f.*, working into each other (of wheels—*roues dentées*).

engri, *n.m.*, (mam.) a genus of leopard found in Congo.

engrosser, *v.a.*, (l.ex.) to make pregnant.

*s'***engrumeler**, *v.r.*, to clod, to coagulate.

*****enguenillé, -e** (ân-g-), *part.*, tattered.

*****enguenillér**, *v.a.*, to clothe in tatters.

s'*enguenillér**, *v.r.*, to be clothed in tatters.

enhardir, *v.a.*, to embolden. *Ce succès l'avait enhardi ;* that success had emboldened him.

*s'***enhardir**, *v.r.*, to make bold, to grow bold. *Il s'est enhardi à parler en public ;* he made bold to speak in public.

enharmonique, *adj.*, (mus.) enharmonic.

enharnachement, *n.m.*, harnessing, trappings.

enharnacher, *v.a.*, to harness ; to rig out, to deck out. *Vous voilà plaisamment enharnaché ;* you are oddly accoutred.

enherber, *v.a.*, to turn into pasture land.

énigmatique, *adj.*, enigmatical.

énigmatiquement (-tik-mân), *adv.*, enigmatically.

énigme, *n.f.*, enigma, riddle. *Deviner une —;* to guess a riddle. *Vous parlez par —s;* you speak in riddles. *Proposer une —;* to put a riddle. *Mot d'une — ;* answer to a riddle.

enivrant, -e, *adj.*, intoxicating.

enivré, -e, *part.*, intoxicated.

enivrement, *n.m.*, intoxication. *L'— de l'amour ;* the intoxication of love.

enivrer, *v.a.*, to inebriate, to intoxicate ; to elate. *La bière enivre comme le vin ;* beer inebriates as well as wine. *La prospérité nous enivre ;* prosperity intoxicates us.

*s'***enivrer**, *v.r.*, to get intoxicated ; to be elated. *Il s'est enivré à ce repas ;* he got intoxicated at that dinner. — *d'espérance ;* to be elated with hope. — *de son vin ;* to drink alone and to excess ; to have too good an opinion of one's self.

enjambée, *n.f.*, stride. *Faire de grandes —s;* to take long strides.

enjambement (ân-jân-bmân), *n.m.*, (poet.) beginning a clause in one verse and completing it in the next.

enjamber, *v.n.*, to stride ; to project, to encroach upon ; (poet.) to begin a clause in one verse, and to finish it in the next.

enjamber, *v.a.*, to stride over, to bestride — *le ruisseau ;* to stride over the gutter.

enjaveler (ān-ja-vlé), *v a.*, (agri.) to sheaf.

enjeu, *n.m.*, stake (at play—*au jeu*). *Retirer son* —; to withdraw one's stake; to declare off.

enjoindre, *v.a.*, to enjoin, to charge. *Cela m'a été enjoint;* this has been enjoined to me. *Dieu nous enjoint d'observer ses lois;* God commands us to observe his laws. *Il lui est enjoint de;* he is enjoined to.

enjôler, *v.a.*, to coax, to wheedle. —*une femme;* to coax a woman.

enjôleu-r, *n.m.*, **-se;** *n.f.*, wheedler, coaxer.

enjolivement (-liv-mān), *n.m.*, embellishment, ornament.

enjoliver, *v.a.*, to embellish, to set off.

enjoliveur, *n.m.*, (b.s.) embellisher.

enjolivure, *n.f.*, set-off, ornament, embellishment.

enjoué, -e, *adj.*, playful, sprightly; lively, sportive. *Il a l'humeur —e;* he is of a playful humour. *Il écrit d'un style —;* he writes in a sportive style.

enjouement, *or* **enjoûment** (ān-joo-mān), *n.m.*, playfulness, sportiveness, sprightliness. *Avec —;* playfully, lively.

enkysté, -e, *adj.*, (med.) encysted.

enlacement (ān-las-mān), *n.m.*, lacing, entwining; interweaving.

enlacer, *v.a.*, to lace; to entwine; to twist; to interlace; to clasp; to interweave. — *quelqu'un dans ses bras;* to entwine any one in one's arms.

s'enlacer, *v.r.*, to entwine; to twist.

enlaidir, *v.a.*, to make ugly, to disfigure.

enlaidir, *v.n*, to grow ugly, to be disfigured.

enlaidissement (-dis-mān), *n.m.*, growing ugly; disfigurement.

enlèvement (ān-lèv-mān), *n.m.*, carrying off; removal; carrying off forcibly, kidnapping; abduction; translation (to heaven—*aux cieux*); buying up, monopoly. *L'— des Sabines;* the rape of the Sabines.

enlever, *v.a.*, to lift, to raise; to carry, to carry off; to carry away; to rescue; to pick out; to carry away forcibly, to kidnap; to take off, to clear away, to remove; to sweep off; to charm, to delight. *On lui a enlevé sa femme;* his wife has been carried off. *On lui a enlevé ses meubles;* his furniture has been carried off. *Enlevez cela de dessus la table;* take that off the table. — *une place* (milit.); to carry a town. — *la peau;* to flay the skin. *La mort l'a enlevé à la fleur de son âge;* death swept him off in his prime. — *des taches;* to take out stains. — *tous les prix;* to carry off all the prizes. *Ses discours enlèvent tout le monde;* his speeches charm everybody.

s'enlever, *v.r.*, to rise; to come off, to peel off; to come out; to go off (of goods for sale —*de marchandises*); to get into a passion.

☉enlevure, *n.f. V.* **élevure**.

enlier, *v.a.*, (mas.) to bond, to give a bond (stones, bricks—*pierres, briques*).

enluminer, *v.a.*, to colour, to illuminate, to flush (the complexion—*le teint*); (lit.) to overload with ornaments.

s'enluminer, *v.r.*, to rouge, to paint. — *la trogne* (triv.); to get a red nose (from drinking —*par la boisson*). *Visage enluminé;* inflamed face.

enlumineu-r, *n.m.*, **-se**, *n.f.*, map *or* print colourer; illuminator.

enluminure, *n.f.*, colouring; illuminating; redness (of the face—*du visage*); overcolouring (style).

ennéagone (è-n-né-), *n.m.*, (geom.) enneagon.

ennéagone, *adj.*, nonagon, enneagon.

ennéandrie (è-n-né-), *n.f.*, (bot.) enneandria.

ennemi, *n.m.*, **-e**, *n f.*, (è-n-mi), enemy, foe; thing prejudicial. — *déclaré;* open enemy. *C'est autant de pris sur l'—;* it is so much gained from the enemy.

-ennemi, -e; *adj.*, hostile, inimical, hurtful, prejudicial; (paint.) unfriendly. *La fortune —e;* adverse fortune. *L'armée —e;* the enemy's army.

ennoblir, *v.a.*, to ennoble. *Les sciences et les arts ennoblissent une langue;* sciences and arts ennoble a language.

s'ennoblir, *v.r.*, to be ennobled, exalted.

ennui, *n.m.*, tediousness, weariness; tedium, spleen, vexation; tiresome thing.

ennuyant.-e, *adj.*, annoying, tedious, irksome. *Cela est fort —;* that is very irksome. *Temps —;* tiresome weather.

ennuyer, *v.a.*, to tire, to weary, to be tiresome, to be tedious, to tease, to annoy, to bother. *Cela m'ennuie;* that annoys me. *Cela m'ennuie à la mort;* that bores me to death.

s'ennuyer,*v.r.*,to be wearied,to have a tedious time of it, to tire one's self, to feel dull. *Il s'ennuie de tout;* every thing is tedious to him.

ennuyeusement (ān-nui-leûz-mān), *adv.*, tediously, irksomely.

ennuyeu-x, -se, *n.* and *adj.*, tiresome person, bore; tedious, wearisome, tiresome, annoying. *Temps —;* tiresome weather. *Livre —;* tedious book.

énoncé, *n.m.*, statement; (geom.) enunciation.

énoncer, *v.a.*, to state, to express, to declare, to utter, to word, to enunciate.

s'énoncer, *v.r.*, to express one's self; to be expressed. *Il s'énonce bien;* he expresses himself well. *Il n'a pas le don de —;* he has not the gift of expressing himself clearly.

énonciati-f, -ve, *adj.*, enunciative, enunciatory.

énonciation, *n.f.*, enunciation, utterance; statement.

***enorgueillir** (ān-nor-ghè-yir), *v.a.*, to make proud, to elevate. *Les succès l'enorgueillissent;* success makes him proud.

***s'enorgueillir** (ān-nor-ghè-yir), *v.r.*, to be, to grow proud of, to be puffed up, to become elated.

énorme, *adj.*, enormous, huge. *Crime —;* heinous crime.

énormément, *adv.*, enormously.

énormité, *n.f.*, enormousness, hugeness, vastness; enormity.

énouer, *v.a.*, to pick cloth; to burl.

☉enquérant, -e, *adj.*, inquisitive.

s'enquérir (s'enquérant, enquis), *v.r.*, to inquire, to make an inquiry. *Il faut — de la vérité du fait;* we must inquire into the truth of the fact.

enquerre, *v.a.*, ☉ to inquire. *Armes à —;* (her.) false arms.

enquête, *n.f.*, inquiry, inquest, inquisition. — *en matière criminelle;* criminal information. *Ordonner une —;* to direct an inquiry to be made.

s'enquêter, *v.r.*, to inquire, to care for.

enraciner, *v.a.*, to root. *Des préjugés enracinés;* inveterate prejudices.

s'enraciner, *v.r.*, to take root. *Il ne faut pas laisser — les maux;* evils must not be suffered to grow inveterate.

enragé, -e. *part.*, mad, rabid, desperate, raging, enraged. *Un chien —;* a mad dog.

enragé, *n.m.*, madman.

enrageant, -e (-jān, -t), *adj.*, vexing, maddening.

enrager, *v.n.*, to be mad, to run mad, to go mad to be enraged. *Faire —;* to madden. —

de faim; to be ravenously hungry. — *contre quelqu'un;* to be enraged against any one. *Il n'enrage pas pour mentir;* he makes nothing of telling lies.

enraiement, *or* **enrayement,** *n.m.,* putting on the skid, the drag.

enrayer, *v.a.,* to set the spokes in a wheel; to skid (a wheel—*une roue*), to put on the drag; (agri.) to plough the first furrow ; (fig.) to stop ; to keep down, to moderate, to stem.

enrayer, *v.n.,* to put on the drag, to skid (a wheel—*une roue*); (fig.) to keep down, to moderate, to check.

enrayure, *n.f.,* drag, skid (of a wheel—*d'une roue*).

enrégimenter, *v.a.,* to embody, to form into regiments.

enregistrement, *n.m.,* registering, registry, entry, enrolment. *Faire l'—;* to register.

enregistrer, *v.a.,* to register, to enter in a register, to enrol.

enrhumer, *v.a.,* to give a cold to. *Je suis enrhumé;* I have a cold. *Être enrhumé du cerveau;* to have a cold in the head.

s'enrhumer, *v.r.,* to catch cold.

enrichi, *n.m.,* **-e,** *n.f.,* person that has enriched himself; upstart, stuck-up person.

enrichir, *v.a.,* to enrich, to make rich; to adorn, to embellish. *Le commerce enrichit un pays;* trade enriches a country. — *son esprit;* to enrich one's mind.

s'enrichir, *v.r.,* to grow rich, to thrive; to be stored. — *des dépouilles d'autrui;* to grow rich with the spoils of others.

enrichissement (-shis-mān), *n.m.,* enriching, embellishment, adornment.

enrôlement (ān-rôl-mān), *n.m.,* enlisting, enrolment.

enrôler, *v.a.,* to enlist, to enrol.

s'enrôler, *v.r.,* to enrol one's self, to enlist.

enroué, -e, *adj.,* hoarse.

enrouement, *or* **enroûment** (ān-roo-mān), *n.m.,* hoarseness.

enrouer, *v.a.,* to make hoarse.

s'enrouer, *v.r.,* to become, to get, hoarse.

*enrouiller, *v.a.,* to rust, to make rusty. *L'humidité enrouille le fer;* damp rusts iron.

*s'enrouiller, *v.r.,* to grow rusty.

enroulement (ān-rool-mān), *n.m.,* rolling up; (arch.) scroll.

enrouler, *v.a.,* to roll, to roll up.

s'enrouler, *v.r.,* to roll one's self up; to roll up.

enrubanner, *v.a.,* to ornament with ribbons. *S'—,* *v.r.,* to deck one's self with ribbons; to adorn one's self too much.

ensablement, *n.m.,* sand-bank; ballasting.

ensabler, *v.a.,* to run aground upon a sand-bank.

s'ensabler, *v.r.,* to run aground on a sand-bank.

ensacher, *v.a.,* to bag.

ensaisinement, *n.m.,* (feudal law—*féodalité*) acknowledging a purchaser of land as a tenant.

ensaisiner, *v.a.,* (feudal law—*féodalité*) to acknowledge a purchaser of land as a tenant.

ensanglanter, *v.a.,* to make bloody, to stain with blood. *La terre était ensanglantée;* the earth was soaked with blood.

*enseignant, -e, *adj.,* teaching.

*enseigne, *n.f.,* mark, sign, sign-board; ensign; ensigncy; streamer (flag—*drapeau*). *À bonnes —s;* deservedly; on sure grounds. *Être logé à même —;* to be in the same predicament.

*enseigne, *n.m.,* ensign; midshipman. — *de vaisseau;* midshipman.

*enseignement (ān-sègn-mān), *n.m.,* pre-

cept, instruction, teaching; tuition; lesson, ⊙(jur.) *pl.,* proof.

*enseigner, *v.a.,* to teach, to instruct; to show, to inform. — *des enfants;* to teach children. — *la jeunesse;* to teach youth. — *les mathématiques;* to teach mathematics. *Enseignez-nous le chemin;* show us the way.

ensellé, -e, *adj.,* saddle-backed.

ensemble, *adv.,* together, conjointly, at the same time. *Mêler —;* to mix together. *Ils ne sont pas bien —;* they are at variance. *Le tout —;* the whole.

ensemble, *n.m.,* whole, ensemble; uniformity; harmony. *Tout cela forme un assez bel —;* all that forms a very handsome whole. *Morceau d'—;* a piece of music harmonized for several voices.

ensemencement (āns-mäns-mān), *n.m.,* (agri.) sowing.

ensemencer, *v.a.,* to sow (ground—*un terrain*). — *un champ;* to sow a field.

enserrer, *v.a.,* ⊙to contain, to enclose; (gard.) to put into a greenhouse.

ensevelir (ān-sě-vlir), *v.a.,* to shroud, to put in a shroud; to bury; to swallow up; to engross; to absorb. — *les morts;* to bury the dead. *Être enseveli dans le chagrin;* to be absorbed in grief.

s'ensevelir, *v.r.,* to be buried; to bury one's self.

ensevelissement (ān-sě-vlis-mān), *n.m.,* putting in a shroud; burying, burial.

ensevelisseu-r, *n.m.,* **-se,** *n.f.,* one who puts a dead body into a shroud or winding-sheet.

ensorceler, *v.a.,* to bewitch. *Cette femme l'a ensorcelé;* that woman has bewitched him.

ensorceleu-r, *n.m.,* **-se,** *n.f.,* bewitcher.

ensorcellement (-sèl-mān), *n.m.,* bewitchment.

ensoufrer, *v.a.,* to dip in brimstone.

ensuite, *adv.,* after, afterwards, then. *Vous irez là —;* you will go there afterwards. — *il me dit;* then he told me. *Et —?* what then? — *de quoi;* after which.

ensuite, *prep.,* after. — *de cela;* after that. — *de quoi;* after which.

⊙**ensuivant,** *adj.,* following. *V.* **suivant.**

s'ensuivre, *v.r.,* to follow, to result, to ensue, to spring. *Il s'ensuit que vous avez tort;* it follows that you are in the wrong. *Il ne s'ensuit pas que j'aie tort;* it does not follow that I am wrong. *De grands malheurs s'ensuivirent;* great misfortunes resulted from it. [This verb is only used in the third person, singular and plural.]

entablement, *n.m.,* (arch.) entablature; entablement; tablet.

s'entabler, *v.r.,* (man.) to entable.

entacher, *v.a.,* to taint, to infect; to sully, to tarnish.

*entaille, *n.f.,* notch, gash; (carp.) mortise; groove.

*entailler, *v.a.,* to notch; to cut away.

*entaillure, *n.f.,* notch.

entame, *n.f.,* first cut (of a loaf—*d'un pain*).

entamer, *v.a.,* to make an incision, to cut, to make the first cut; to broach, to begin; (milit.) to break through; (b.s.) to encroach upon; (b.s.) to impair; to prevail upon. — *la peau;* to cut the skin. — *le pain;* to make the first cut in a loaf. — *une matière;* to begin, to enter upon, a subject. *Se laisser —;* to suffer an encroachment. — *la réputation de quelqu'un;* to injure any one's reputation.

entamure, *n.f.,* cut; first cut; incision.

entassement (ān-tas-mān), *n.m.,* heap, accumulation, pile.

entasser, *v.a.,* to heap, to heap up; to pile up; to hoard, to hoard up; to accumulate; to cram; to huddle, to pack together. — *des écus;*

to hoard up money. *Personne entassée;* thick-set person.

entasseur, *n.m.,* hoarder, money-saving person.

ente, *n.f.,* graft, tree bearing a graft; (paint.) handle (of a brush—*d'un pinceau*).

entendement (än-tand-män), *n.m.,* understanding; judgment, head, sense.

entendeur, *n.m.,* hearer, understander. *À bon — demi-mot suffit;* a word to the wise is sufficient.

entendre, *v.a.,* to hear; to understand; to know; to expect, to require, to intend; to mean. *À vous —;* according to you. *J'ai entendu dire;* I heard some people say. *Il n'y a point de pire sourd que celui qui ne veut pas —,* no one is so deaf as he who will not hear. *— les témoins;* to hear the witnesses. *Il entend un peu l'anglais;* he understands English a little. *— mal;* to misunderstand. *Entendons-nous;* let us come to a right understanding. *— à demi-mot;* to take the hint. *Donner à —;* to give to understand. *Ne pas — malice;* to do or say anything without meaning any harm. *Il a fait allusion à votre disgrâce, mais sans y — malice;* he alluded to your mishap, but he did not mean any harm. *— raison;* to listen to reason. *— raillerie;* to take a joke. *Il n'entend pas raillerie;* he cannot take a joke. *Il n'entend pas la raillerie;* he is no hand at jokes. *— la messe, les vêpres;* to attend mass, vespers. *Il entend bien son métier;* he knows his trade very well. *Cet homme n'entend rien aux affaires;* that man knows nothing about business. *Qu'entendez-vous par là?* what do you mean by that? *Chacun fait comme il l'entend;* everybody does as he thinks proper.

s'entendre, *v.r.,* to hear one another; to understand one another; to be heard; to be understood; to lay their heads together; to act in concert with, to have a secret understanding with; to come to an arrangement with; to agree with, to be on good terms with; to be skilful in; to be a judge of. *Le bruit est si grand qu'on ne s'entend pas;* there is so much noise that we cannot hear one another speak. *Le canon de Waterloo s'entendait à dix lieues du champ de bataille;* the cannon of Waterloo was heard at a distance of ten leagues from the field of battle. *On l'accuse de — avec l'ennemi;* he is accused of acting in concert with the enemy. *— à une chose;* to be skilful in a thing. *Il ne s'entend pas mal à cela;* he has a pretty good knack at that. *— en une chose;* to understand how to do a thing. *Il s'entend en musique;* he understands music. *Je m'entends bien;* I know very well what I mean. *Ils s'entendent pour me nuire;* they have laid their heads together to injure me. *Ils s'entendent comme larrons en foire;* they are as thick as thieves together. *Cela s'entend, cela s'entend bien;* let it be understood; of course, as a matter of course, to be sure.

entendre, *v.n.,* to hear, to hear of; to approve of, to consent to; to listen to. *— dur;* to be hard of hearing. *— clair;* to be quick of hearing. *Ne savoir auquel —;* not to know whom to listen to. *Il n'entend pas de cette oreille-là;* he is deaf on that side. *J'entends que vous restiez avec moi;* I expect you to remain with me.

entendu, -e, *adj.,* intelligent, skilful. *Un homme bien — aux affaires;* a very intelligent man in business.

enténébrer, *v.a.;* to involve in darkness; to wrap in darkness, in night.

entente, *n.f.,* meaning; skill, judgment, understanding. *Mots à double —;* ambiguous words. *L'— est au diseur;* every body under-

stands his own meaning best. *L'— au coloris;* skill in colouring.

enter, *v.a.,* to graft, to ingraft. *— de nouveau;* to regraft. *— en écusson;* to bud, to in-eye.

entérinement (-ri-n-män), *n.m.,* judicial ratification, confirmation.

entériner, *v.a.,* to ratify, to confirm.

entérique, *adj.,* (med.) enteric.

entérite, *n.f.,* (med.) enteritis.

enterrement (än-tèr-män), *n.m.,* burial, funeral, interment. *Billet d'—;* invitation to a funeral. *Être prié d'un —;* to be invited to a funeral.

enterrer, *v.a.,* to bury, to inter, to inhume; to survive, to eclipse, to surpass; to end, to terminate; to sink (of money—*de l'argent*). *— son secret;* to bury one's secret. *Molière a enterré tous ses devanciers;* Molière threw all his predecessors into the shade. *— la synagogue avec honneur;* to terminate an affair with honour.

s'enterrer *v.r.,* to bury one's self; to see no company; to go with his head to the ground (of a horse—*du cheval*).

en-tête, *n.m.* (*— -s*), heading; head. *— de facture;* bill-head.

entêté -e, *n.* and *adj.,* stubborn person; obstinate, wayward, self-willed, stubborn; infatuated. *— comme un âne;* as stubborn as a mule. *Il est — d'une folle;* he is infatuated with a foolish woman.

entêtement (än-tê-tmän), *n.m.,* stubbornness, waywardness; obstinacy; infatuation. *Son — le perdra;* his stubbornness will be his ruin.

entêter, *v.a.,* to affect the head, to disturb the head, to intoxicate; to prepossess, to infatuate, to render vain; to head (pins—*ler épingles*). *Vin qui entête;* heady wine. *Les louanges nous entêtent;* praises are apt to make us conceited.

s'entêter, *v.r.,* to become stubborn, wayward, obstinate; to be infatuated with, to take a strong fancy to.

entêteu-r, *n.m.,* **-se,** *n.f.,* header (of pins—*d'épingles*).

enthousiasme, *n.m.,* enthusiasm, rapture, ecstasy.

enthousiasmer, *v.a.,* to enrapture, to render enthusiastic. *Il est enthousiasmé de cette musique;* he is in rapture with that music.

s'enthousiasmer, *v.r.,* to become enthusiastic.

enthousiaste, *n.m.f.,* enthusiast.

enthousiaste, *adj.,* enthusiastic.

enthymème, *n.m.,* (log.) enthymeme.

entiché, -e, *part.,* (l.n.) beginning to spoil (fruit); tainted, marred; infatuated. *Fruit —;* spoiled fruit.

enticher, *v.a.,* to taint, to infect; to infatuate. *Vous l'avez entiché de ce système;* you have tainted him with that system.

enti-er, ère (-tié, -tiè-r), *adj.,* entire, whole, complete, total; obstinate, positive, self-willed; (arith.) integral. *Une —e soumission;* complete submission. *Cheval —;* stone-horse, stallion, entire horse. *Pain —;* whole loaf. *Nombre —;* (arith.) integral.

entier (-tié), *n.m.,* entireness; (arith.) integral. *En son —;* at full length.

entièrement (än-tiè-män), *adv.,* entirely, wholly. *— ruiné;* utterly ruined.

entité, *n.f.,* (philos.) entity.

entoilage, *n.m.,* linen or other material to which lace is sewed; sewing on linen cloth; sewing on of lace; pasting on canvass.

entoiler, *v.a.*, to sew upon cloth, to sew upon lace; to mount upon canvass.

entoir, *n.m.*, (hort.) grafting-knife.

entomologie, *n.f.*, entomology.

entomologique, *adj.*, entomological.

entomologiste, *n.m.*, entomologist.

entonnement (än-to-n-män), *n.m.*, putting into a cask, barrelling.

s'entonner, *v.r.*, (of the wind) to rush into, to blow down. *Le vent s'entonne dans la cheminée;* the wind blows down the chimney.

entonner, *v.a.*, to tun, to barrel, to put into casks; (mus.) to begin (singing a tune—*à chanter*); to intonate, to strike up; to celebrate. *Il entonne bien* (pop.); he drinks hard. *— une chanson à boire;* to strike up a drinking song.

entonnerie (än-to-n-rï), *n.f.*, place where beer is barrelled.

entonnoir, *n.m.*, funnel; (anat.) funnel. *Fleurs en —;* funnel-shaped flowers.

entorse, *n.f.*, sprain; strain, twist, shock. *Il s'est donné une — au pied;* he has sprained his foot.

*entorti̓lage, *n.m.*, entanglement; subterfuge, equivocal discourse.

*entortillé, -e, *part.*, twined, winded about. *Style —;* perplexed style.

*entortillement, *n.m.*, winding about, twining, twisting, entanglement. *L'— d'un serpent;* the twisting of a serpent.

*entortiller, *v.a.*, to wrap, to roll about, to wind, to coil; to twist, to distort; to get round, to get the better of. *Laissez-moi, vous m'entortillez* (pop.); leave me alone, you perplex me.

s'entortiller, *v.r.*, to twist round, to wind round; to twine.

entour, *n.m.*, [always employed in the plural, save in the adverbial expression, *À l'—;* around]. *—s;* environs, adjacent parts; persons around any one (friends, relations, servants, &c.—*amis, parents, serviteurs, &c.*). *Prendre les —s;* to gain over to one's interest the persons around any one.

entourage, *n.m.*, frame; whatever surrounds an object; mounting (of jewellery—*bijouterie*); confidents, advisers, friends, servants, relations, &c.

entourer, *v.a.*, to enclose, to surround. *— une ville de murailles;* to encompass a town with walls. *Entouré de terre;* land-locked. *— quelqu'un de soins;* to treat any one with all manner of attentions.

entournure, *n.f.*, turning up; sloping (of sleeves—*de manches*).

en-tout-cas, *n.m.* (—), a large sun-shade that may be used as an umbrella.

s'entr'accorder, *v.r.*, to agree together.

s'entr'accuser, *v.r.*, to accuse one another.

entr'acte, *n.m.* (— —*s*), (thea.) interval between the acts; interlude, intermede. *Dans l'—;* between the acts. *Faire de longs —s;* to be long between the acts, to keep the curtain down a long time.

s'entr'admirer, *v.r.*, to admire one another.

s'entr'aider, *v.r.*, to help, to aid, one another.

*entrailles, *n.f.pl.*, entrails, bowels, intestines, inward parts; numbles; bowels (affection). *Elle a pour moi des — de mère;* she has a motherly affection for me. *Cet acteur a des —s;* this actor has feeling. *Les —s de la miséricorde de Dieu;* the tender mercies of God.

s'entr'aimer, *v.r.*, to love one another.

entrain, *n.m.*, warmth; heartiness; spirit, spirits; animation.

entraînant, *-e, *adj.*, that carries away, that hurries on, that hurries away; capti-

vating, seductive. *Un style —;* an overpowering style. *Éloquence —e;* winning eloquence.

entraînement (än-trè-n-män), *n.m.*, impulse, sway, prevalence; rapture, enthusiasm; temptation, allurement. *L'— des passions;* the sway of the passions.

entraîner, *v.a.*, to carry away, to sweep off; to hurry away, to hurry along; to draw, to bring, to win, to gain, over; to drag away, along; to entail, to involve; to train (racehorses—*chevaux de course*). *— les cœurs;* to gain over all hearts. *— quelqu'un dans l'erreur;* to hurry any one into error. *— quelqu'un dans le crime;* to hurry any one on to crime. *La guerre entraîne après elle bien des maux;* war entails many evils.

entrait, *n.m.*, (carp.) tie-beam.

entrant, *-e, *adj.*, winning, engaging, insinuating; entering office. *Les conseillers —s;* the newly appointed councillors. *—, n.*, person coming in. *Les —s et les sortants;* persons coming in and going out.

s'entr'appeler, *v.r.*, to call one another.

entrave, *n.f.*, clog, hinderance, obstacle, impediment, shackle; *pl.*, horse-lock; trammels, fetters. *Le génie ne peut point souffrir d'—;* genius will not be fettered.

entraver, *v.a.*, to shackle, to clog; to fetter, to trammel; to hinder, to impede. *— un cheval;* to shackle a horse.

s'entr'avertir, *v.r.*, to give one another notice, to warn one another.

entre, *prep.*, between, betwixt; among, amongst; in. *— le ciel et la terre;* between heaven and earth. *Regarder quelqu'un — les deux yeux;* to stare at any one. *Être — deux vins;* to be half seas over. *— chien et loup;* between lights, in the twilight. *Ils résolurent — eux;* they resolved among them. *— autres;* among others. *Je le mettrai — vos mains; I* will deliver it into your hands. *Cela soit dit — nous;* that is between ourselves.

*entre-bâillé, -e, *adj.*, ajar, half open. *Laissez la porte —e;* leave the door ajar.

*entre-bâiller, *v.a.*, to half open.

s'entre-baiser, *v.r.*, to kiss one another.

s'entre-battre, *v.r.*, to beat one another, to fight together.

s'entre-blesser, *v.r.*, to wound one another.

entrechat, *n.m.*, (dancing—*danse*) cut, cutting, caper, entrechat.

s'entre-chercher, *v.r.*, to seek one another, to look for one another.

s'entre-choquer, *v.r.*, to knock, to clash, to beat, to dash, against one another; to interfere.

entre-colonne, *n.f.* (— —*s*), or **entre-colonnement**, *n.m.* (— —*s*), (arch.) intercolumniation.

s'entre-connaître, *v.r.*, to know each other.

entrecôte, *n.f.*, (cook.) meat between the ribs.

entre-coupe, *n.f.* (— —*s*), (arch.) empty space between two vaults constructed one over the other.

entrecoupé, *-e, *part.*, broken (of words—*mots*). *Mots —s;* broken words.

entrecouper, *v.a.*, to traverse, to cross, to intersect; to stop, to interrupt, to break off. *Les soupirs entrecoupent la voix;* sobs stop the speech.

s'entrecouper, *v.r.*, to cut or cross one another; to interrupt one another; (vet.) to hit or chafe one leg against the other when walking (horses—*chevaux*).

s'entre-croiser, *v.r.*, to cross one another.

s'entre-déchirer, *v.r.*, to tear one another to pieces,

s'entre-défaire, *v.r.*, to defeat one another.

s'entre-détruire, *v.r.*, to destroy one another.

entre-deux, *n.m.* (—), intermediate space; partition; (cook.) middle (of a cod—*d'une morue*), the part between the head and the tail; insertion (lace—*dentelle*); (nav.) trough of the sea.

entre-deux, *adv.*, (l.u.) betwixt and between.

s'entre-dévorer, *v.r.*, to devour one another; to ruin one another.

s'entre-dire, *v.r.*, to tell one another. — *des injures;* to call one another names.

s'entre-donner, *v.r.*, to give one another.

entrée, *n.f.*, entry, entrance; mouth; entering, coming in; reception; beginning; introduction, inlet; (cook.) entry; admission-money, entrance-money; custom-duty; entree (dancing—*danse*). *L'— d'un port;* the mouth of a harbour. — *et sortie d'un acteur;* entrance and exit of an actor. *Avoir ses —s;* to have free admission, to be on the free-list of a theatre. *Droit d'—;* custom-duty. *Payer l'—;* to pay a town-due; (custom-house —*douane*) to pay duty. *Tuyau d'—;* (tech.) inlet-pipe. ⊙ *D'—;* at first, at the first.

s'entre-fâcher, *v.r.*, to tease one another.

entrefaites, *n.f.pl.*, interval, meantime. *Dans ces —, sur ces —;* in the meanwhile.

entrofilet, *n.m.*, a short newspaper article.

s'entre-fouetter, *v.r.*, to whip or lash one another.

s'entre-frapper, *v.r.*, to strike one another.

entrogent, *n.m.*, (fam.) shrewdness, tact. *Cet homme fera son chemin, il a de l'—;* that man will get on, he possesses tact.

s'entr'égorger, *v.r.*, to cut each other's throat; to kill one another.

s'entre-haïr, *v.r.*, to hate each other.

s'entre-heurter, *v.r.*, to knock or beat one against the other.

entrelacement (-las-mān), *n.m.*, interweaving, wreathing, blending, intertwining.

entrelacer, *v.a.*, to interlace, to intertwine, to interweave, to weave, to braid; to plash; to wattle. — *des chiffres;* to blend ciphers. *Des branches entrelacées;* interwoven branches.

s'entrelacer, *v.r.*, to entwine, to twist, to wreath.

entrelacs (-lâ), *n.m.pl.*, (arch., paint.) twine

entrelardé, **-e**, *part.*, interlarded.

entrelarder, *v.a.*, to interlard; to insert between. — *un discours de passages grecs et latins;* to interlard a discourse with Greek and Latin passages.

***entre-ligne**, *n.m.* (——*s*), space between lines, interlineation; (print.) space-line, lead.

s'entre-louer, *v.r.*, to praise one another, to laud one another.

entre-luire, *v.n.*, to glimmer.

s'entremanger, *v.r.*, to eat one another.

entremêler, *v.a.*, to intermingle, to inter-mix.

s'entremêler, *v.r.*, to intermingle, to inter-mix; to meddle. *Des nuances qui s'entremêlent;* shades which are blended together.

s'entre-mesurer, *v.r.*, to measure each other.

entremets (-mè), *n.m.*, (cook.) side-dish, entremets.

entremetteu-r, *n.m.*, **-se**, *n.f.*, go-between, manager, mediator; procurer; procuress.

s'entremettre, *v.r.*, to interpose, to interfere, to intermeddle; to meddle.

entremise, *n.f.*, interposition, mediation, intervention, interference; medium, agency; (nav.) carling. *Par l'— de la presse;* through the medium of the press.

s'entre-mordre, *v.r.*, to bite one another.

s'entr'empêcher, *v.r.*, to hinder, to thwart, each other.

entre-nœud, *n.m.* (——*s*), (bot.) internode.

s'entre-nuire, *v.r.*, to hurt one another, to injure each other.

s'entre-pardonner, *v.r.*, to pardon one another.

s'entre-parler, *v.r.*, to speak to one another, to talk together.

entrepas, *n.m.*, (man.) ambling pace.

s'entre-percer, *v.r.*, to run each other through, to pierce each other.

***s'entre-piller**, *v.r.*, to plunder one another.

***entre-pointillé**, **-e**, *adj.*, (engr.) composed of line and dotted engraving.

entrepont, *n.m.*, (nav.) between decks. *Dans les —;* between decks.

entreposage, *n.m.*, (custom-house—*douane*) bonding.

entreposer, *v.a.*, (custom-house—*douane*) to bond, to put in bond; to store, to warehouse.

entreposeur, *n.m.*, (custom-house—*douane*) bonded-warehouse-keeper; warehouse-keeper.

entrepositaire, *n.m.*, (custom-house—*douane*) bonder.

entrepôt, *n.m.*, staple, mart, emporium; (custom-house—*douane*) bond; bonded warehouse; store. — *fictif;* town warehouse. — *réel;* king's warehouse, queen's warehouse, bonded warehouse. *Mutation d'—;* removal to another warehouse; removal of bonded goods. *Port à l'—;* bonded port; warehousing port. *En —;* in bond. *Faire une mutation d'—;* to remove goods to another warehouse. *Mettre en —;* to bond. *Réintégrer dans l'—;* to rewarehouse.

s'entre-pousser, *v.r.*, to push each other.

entreprenant, **-e**, *adj.*, enterprising, adventurous, venturous; daring, bold.

entreprendre, *v.a.*, to undertake, to attempt, to take in hand, to take upon one's self; to contract for, to contract to; to adventure, to offer, to venture; to trouble. — *quelqu'un;* to set upon any one, to fall foul of any one, to banter or jeer any one.

entreprendre, *v.n.*, to encroach on, to infringe upon; to undertake.

entrepreneur, *n.m.*, master-builder; contractor. — *de diligences;* coach proprietor. — *de maçonnerie;* master-mason. — *de pompes funèbres;* undertaker.

entrepreneuse, *n.f.*, maker.

entrepris, **-e**, *adj.*, that has lost the use of his limbs; disconcerted. *Il est — d'un bras;* he has lost the use of an arm.

entreprise, *n.f.*, enterprise, undertaking, attempt; usurpation, violence; contract; (com.) concern, establishment. *À —;* by contract. *Par —;* by contract. *Ouvrage à l'—;* work by contract. — *par masse de travaux;* contract by the lump. *Il échoue dans ses —s;* he miscarries in his undertakings. — *générale des messageries;* general coach and conveyance office.

s'entre-produire, *v.r.*, to produce each other.

s'entre-quereller, *v.r.*, to quarrel with each other.

entrer, *v.n.*, to enter, to come in, to go in, to get in, to walk in, to march in, to drop in, to step in; to pierce, to run into; (astron.) to house; (nav.) to let in. — *bien avant,* to penetrate far. — *une seconde fois;* to re-enter. *Faire —;* to send in. *Faire — un vaisseau dans un bassin;* to dock a ship. — *dans le monde;* to enter the world. — *en possession;* to take possession. — *au service de quelqu'un;* to enter any one's service. — *dans sa vingtième année* to enter one's twentieth year. — *en jeu;* to come into play. *Vous n'entrez pas dans ma pensée;* you mistake my meaning. — *dans les intérêts de quelqu'un;* to side with any one. — *dans les goûts;* to be of one's taste. — *en danse;* to begin to dance. *Faire — quelque chose dans un discours;* to introduce something into a speech. *Il y entre pour un cinquième;* he is engaged for one-fifth. *Cet article n'entre pour rien dans mes demandes;* this article has nothing to do with my demands. *On ne saurait lui rien faire — dans la tête;* there is no driving anything into his head. *On n'entre pas ici;* no admittance here.

s'entre-regarder, *v.r.*, to look at, to stare at one another.

s'entre-regretter, *v.r.*, to regret each other.

s'entre-répondre, *v.r.*, to answer one another.

s'entre-saluer, *v.r.*, to salute one another.

s'entre-secourir, *v.a.*, to help, to succour, one another.

entresol, *n.m.*, mezzanino, entresol (suite of apartments between the ground floor and the first floor).

entre-sourcils, *n.m.* (—), space between the eyebrows.

s'entre-soutenir, *v.r.*, to support one another.

s'entre-souvenir, *v.r.*, to half remember.

s'entre-suivre, *v.r.*, to follow each other, to succeed each other.

*entretaille, *n.f.*, (engr.) interline; (dancing—*danse*) change of foot.

*s'entre-tailler. V. **s'entrecouper** (vet.).

*entretaillure, *n.f.*, (vet.) cutting, crepance, crepane.

s'entre-talonner, *v.r.*, to tread on each other's heels; to follow each other closely.

entre-temps, *n.m.* (—), interval.

ⓒ**entretènement** (-tè-n-mān), *n.m.*, maintenance, support, keeping, preservation.

entretenir (ān-tré-tnir), *v.a.*, to hold, to hold together, to keep up; to keep in repair, to keep in good order; to keep, to preserve, to maintain; to cherish; to converse, to talk with; to entertain; — *les chemins;* to keep the roads in repair. — *la paix;* to maintain peace. *Il entretient fort agréablement la compagnie;* he entertains the company very agreeably.

s'entretenir, *v.r.*, to hold, to keep; to be sustained, to be maintained, to be supported, to be kept up; to maintain, to keep, to support one's self; to subsist; to converse with, to discourse with, to commune with, to talk to. — *avec quelqu'un;* to discourse with any one. — *par lettres;* to converse by letters. — *de quelqu'un;* to speak of one. *Il s'entretient du jeu;* he lives by gambling. — *avec soi-même;* to meditate, to reflect. — *avec Dieu;* to reflect on the Holy Word of God.

entretien (-tiin), *n.m.*, maintenance, keeping, living, livelihood; keeping in repair; conversation, discourse, talk; communication, conference. *Faire l'— du public;* to be the talk of the parish. *Un homme d'un agréable —;* a man of agreeable conversation.

entretoile, *n.f.*, inserted cut-work.

entretoise, *n.f.*, (carp.) tie-beam, intertie, cross-bar; cross-piece.

s'entre-toucher, *v.r.*, to touch one another.

s'entre-tuer, *v.r.*, to kill each other.

s'entre-vendre, *v.r.*, to sell to each other; to sell each other, to betray each other.

entre-voie, *n.f.* (— —*s*), (railways) the six-foot way.

entrevoir, *v.a.*, to have a glimpse of, to peep in, to discover a little of; to have misgivings, to foresee. — *quelqu'un;* to have a glimpse

of any one. *J'entrevois de grands obstacles;* I anticipate great difficulties.

s'entrevoir, *v.r.*, to have a meeting, interview, conference; to see, to visit, each other.

entrevous, *n.m.*, (carp.) interjoist.

entrevoûter, *v.a.*, to plaster a space between two joists.

entrevue. *n.f.*, interview, meeting.

*entripaillé, **-e**, *adj.*, (l.ex.) big-bellied.

s'entr'obliger, *v.r.*, to oblige each other.

entr'ouïr, *v.a.*, (l.u.) to hear imperfectly.

entr'ouvert, **-e**, *part.*, partly open, ajar; (man.) sprained in the shoulder-joint.

entr'ouverture, *n.f.*, (vet.) result of a sprain of the shoulder-joint.

entr'ouvrir, *v.a.*, to open a little, to half-open. — *une porte;* to set a door ajar.

s'entr'ouvrir, *v.r.*, to open, to gape; to be ajar.

enture, *n.f.*, (gard.) incision, cut (for grafting—*de greffe*).

énumérateur, *n.m.*, enumerator.

énumérati-f, **-ve**, *adj.*, enumerative.

énumération, *n.f.*, enumeration.

énumérer, *v.a.*, to enumerate, to count, to reckon.

envahir, *v.a.*, to invade, to overrun, to encroach upon.

envahissant, **-e**, *adj.*, invading.

envahissement (-is-mān), *n.m.*, overrunning, invasion, encroachment.

envahisseur, *n.m.*, invader.

envaser, *v.a.*, to fill up, to choke with mud (ports, rivers, &c.—*ports, rivières, &c.*); to sink and stick in the mud.

s'envaser, *v.r.*, (nav.) to stick fast in the mud; to become filled up and choked with mud (of ports, canals, &c.—*ports, canaux, &c.*).

enveloppe (ān-vlop), *n.f.*, wrapper, cover, covering; envelope; exterior; (anat.) coat; casing (of cylinders—*de cylindres*); tunic (of the eye—*de l'œil*); (fort.) envelope; (mec.) case, casing; (tech.) cage; (metal.) mould. *Écrire sous l'— de quelqu'un;* to write under another person's cover.

enveloppé, **-e**, *part.*, enveloped, ambiguous, equivocal. *Il a l'esprit —;* his head is confused. *Être — dans un désastre;* to be involved in a misfortune.

enveloppement (ānv-lop-mān), *n.m.*, enveloping, wrapping up, envelopment.

envelopper, *v.a.*, to envelop, to wrap up, to cover, to fold up, to do up, to put up; to muffle; to beset, to inclose, to environ, to hem in, to surround; to involve, to implicate; to cover, to disguise. — *quelque chose de papier;* to wrap anything up in paper. — *l'ennemi;* to hem in the enemy.

s'envelopper, *v.r.*, to cover or wrap one's self up, to envelop one's self, to muffle one's self up; to involve one's self.

envenimer, *v.a.*, to infect with venom, to poison, to envenom, to irritate, to inflame, to exasperate. — *une plaie;* to irritate a wound. *Il l'a envenimé contre moi;* he has exasperated him against me.

s'envenimer, *v.r.*, to be envenomed; to fester, to rankle.

enverger, *v.a.*, to garnish with little willow branches.

enverguer (-ghé), *v.a.*, (nav.) to fasten the sails to the yards.

envergure, *n.f.*, (nav.) extent of sail upon the yards; spread of a bird's wings when extended.

envers (ānvèr), *prep.*, towards, to. *Je vous défendrai — et contre tous;* I will defend you against everyone.

envers, *n.m.*, wrong side. *À l'—;* on the

wrong side ; inside out. *Il a l'esprit à l'—* ; he is wrong-headed.

à l'envi, *adv.,* in emulation of one another, emulously. *À l'— l'un de l'autre ;* in emulation of one another. *Ils travaillent à l'— l'un de l'autre ;* they strive who shall work most.

enviable. *adj.,* enviable.

envie. *n.f.,* envy, enviousness ; wish, desire, longing, hankering, inclination ; mark (which some children have when they are born— *marque de naissance*) ; hangnail. *L'— le dévore ;* he is eaten up with envy. *Sécher d'— ;* to pine away with envy. *Faire — ;* to raise envy. *Porter — à quelqu'un ;* to envy any one. *Avoir — de ;* to have a mind to. *J'ai grande — d'aller la voir ;* I have a great mind to pay her a visit. *Avoir — de dormir ;* to feel an inclination to sleep. *On lui en a donné — ;* they have set him agog upon it. *L'— lui en est passée ;* his longing is over. *Il m'en a ôté l'— ;* he has put me out of conceit with it. *Passer son — de quelque chose ;* to satisfy one's longing for any thing. *— de femme grosse ;* longing of a woman with child. *Il a une — au visage ;* he has a mark on his face.

envié, -e, *part.,* envied. *Il est — de tout le monde ;* he is envied by every body.

⊙**envieilli, -e,** *adj.,* inveterate, long-established, old, of long standing ; hardened. *V.* **endurci, invétéré.**

⊙**envieillir,** *v.a.,* to make one look old. *V.* **vieillir.**

envier, *v.a.,* to envy, to be envious of, to grudge ; to desire, to long for, to wish for. *Je ne lui envie point sa bonne fortune ;* I do not envy his good fortune.

envieu-x, -se, *adj.,* envious, jealous.

enviné, -e, *adj.,* smelling of wine. *Ce baril est — ;* that cask smells of wine.

environ, *adv.,* about, thereabouts. *Son armée est d'— dix mille hommes ;* his army consists of about ten thousand men.

environnant, -e, *adj.,* surrounding.

environner, *v.a.,* to surround ; to encompass, to beset ; to environ. *— d'une balustrade ;* to enclose with a rail. *Les gardes qui environnaient le prince ;* the guards who stood round the prince. *L'éclat qui l'environne ;* the splendour which surrounds him.

environs, *n.m.pl.,* environs ; vicinity, neighbourhood.

envisager, *v.a.,* to look, to stare, in the face, to eye, to face ; to consider, to look upon, to look at. *— de sang froid le péril ;* to look coolly on danger.

envoi, *n.m.,* sending ; thing sent, packet, parcel, package, goods forwarded ; goods to be forwarded ; (lit.) envoy ; (nav.) order to put the helm alee. *Compléter un — ;* to make up a parcel ; *Faire un — ;* to send off a parcel or package. *Lettre d'— ;* letter of advice.

s'envoiler, *v.r.,* (metal.) to warp, to bend.

envoisiné, -e, *adj.,* that has got neighbours.

envoisiner, *v.a.,* to surround with neighbours.

s'envoler, *v.r.,* to fly away, to take wing ; to be carried off (by the wind—*par le vent*) ; to disappear. *L'oiseau s'est envolé ;* the bird is flown.

envoûtement, *n.m.,* magical charm.

envoûter, *v.a.,* to cast a spell on any one, by transfixing a waxen image representing such person.

envoyé, *n.m.,* envoy ; deputy ; messenger. *L'— de Dieu ;* the messenger of God. *-e, n.f.,* an envoy's wife.

envoyer, *v.a.,* to send, to forward ; to transmit. *— un paquet à quelqu'un ;* to send a parcel to any one. *Je vous envoie mon domestique ;* I send you my servant. *— chercher ;* to send for.

— au diable, — à tous les diables : to send to the devil. *— paître, — promener ;* to send off, to send about one's business ; to send any one off with a flea in his ear. *— en prison ;* to commit, to commit to prison. *Envoie !* (nav.) a-lee !

envoyeur, *n.m.,* sender. *-, adj.m.,* (post office—*postes*) despatching. *Bureau — ;* despatching office.

éolien, -ne, (-liin, -liè-n), *adj ,* Eolian, Eolic. *Harpe —ne ;* Eolian harp.

éolien, *n.m.,* Eolic (dialect).

éolipyle, *n.m.,* (phys.) æolipile.

éolique, *adj.,* Eolic, Eolian.

épacte, *n.f.,* (astron.) epact.

*épagneul, -e, n.f., spaniel.

épais, -se, *adj.,* thick ; heavy, dull, gross. *Mur — de deux pieds ;* wall two feet thick. *Brouillard — ;* thick fog. *Ignorance —se ;* gross ignorance. *Un homme — ;* a blockhead. *Avoir la langue —se ;* to speak thick. *Des cheveux — ;* thick hair.

épais, *n.m.,* thickness.

épais, *adv.,* thick, thickly. *Semer — ;* to sow thick.

épaisseur, *n.f.,* thickness ; depth ; density.

épaissir, *v.a.,* to thicken, to make thick, to incrassate.

s'épaissir, *v.r.,* to become thick, to get thick, to grow thick ; to become big, to grow large ; to become heavy or dull. *Sa langue s'épaissit ;* he begins to speak thick.

épaissir, *v.n.,* to thicken, to become thick ; to get stout, to grow stout, to become stout.

épaississement (-sis-mân), *n.m.,* thickening, thickness.

épamprage, *or* **épamprement,** *n.m.,* lopping off the leafy branches of a vine.

épamprer, *v.a.,* to lop off the leafy branches of, to prune, a vine.

épanchement (é-pânsh-mân), *n.m.,* pouring out, shedding ; overflowing, effusion. *— de cœur ;* opening of one's heart. *— d'amitié ;* effusion of friendship.

épancher, *v.a.,* to pour out ; to open. *— son cœur ;* to open one's heart.

s'épancher, *v.r.,* to be discharged, poured out, to escape ; to open one's heart, to unbosom one's self.

épandre, *v.a.,* to pour out, to scatter, to strew, to throw here and there.

s'épandre, *v.r.,* to spread out, to be scattered.

épanorthose, *n.f.,* (rhet.) epanorthosis.

épanouir, *v.a.,* to expand, to smooth, to brighten up. *— la rate ;* to make merry, to drive away the spleen.

s'épanouir, *v.r.,* (of flowers—*des fleurs*) to blow, to expand, to open ; to brighten up. *Son visage s'épanouit ;* his face brightened up.

épanouissement (-noo-is-mân), *n.m.,* blowing (of flowers—*des fleurs*) ; (fig.) expansion.

éparcet, *n.m.* *V.* **esparcet, esparcette.**

s'éparer, *v.r.,* (man.) to jerk, to fling out ; to kick.

*épargnant, -e, adj., sparing, saving, economical ; parsimonious.

*épargne, n.f., economy, saving, savingness, sparingness ; ⊙treasury. *— mesquine ;* shabby saving. *Avec — ;* sparingly. *Aller à l'— ; user d'— ;* to save, to be saving. *Il vit de ses —s ;* he lives on his savings. *Aller à l'— des mots ;* to be sparing of words. *Caisse d'—, caisse d'— et de prévoyance ;* savings-bank. *Tailler, graver, en — ;* (engr.) to reserve.

*épargner, v.a., to save, to lay up, to lay by, to spare, to husband, to economize ; to spare (not to inflict pain on, to pardon—*ménager, pardonner*). *— son bien ;* to save one's wealth. *On ne lui épargne pas l'argent ;* they are not sparing

of money with him. *Ne m'épargnez pas;* do not spare me.

s****épargner**, *v.r.*, to spare one's self ; to spare one another.

***épargner**, *v.n.*, to economize, to be saving, to be sparing. — *sur sa toilette;* to save in dress.

***éparpillement**, *n.m.*, scattering, dispersing, dispersion.

***éparpiller**, *v.a.*, to scatter, to strew about, to spread, to throw here and there. — *ses troupes;* to scatter one's troops.

épars, -e, *adj.*, scattered, dispersed; (of hair —*des cheveux*) dishevelled; thin (of plants— *des plantes*). *D'une manière —e;* stragglingly.

éparvin, or **éparvin**, *n.m.*, (vet.) spavin. — *osseux, sec;* blood-spavin; string-halt.

épaté, -e, *adj.*, with the foot broken off (of glasses—*des verres*); flat (of noses—*du nez*).

épater, *v.a.*, to break the foot off (a glass— *d'un verre*); to flatten.

s'épater, *v.r.*, to sprawl.

épaulard, *n.m.*, (ich.) ork.

épaule, *n.f.*, shoulder; start (of wheels—*de roues*). *Des —s larges;* broad shoulders. *Hausser les —s;* to shrug up one's shoulders. *Faire hausser les —s à quelqu'un;* to make any one shrug his shoulders. *Plier les —s;* to put up with. *Prêter l'— à quelqu'un;* to back any one. *Faire une chose par-dessus l'—;* to leave a thing undone; to do a thing over the left. *L'— d'un bastion;* the flank of a bastion. —*s d'un vaisseau;* bows of a ship.

épaulée, *n.f.*, push (with the shoulders— *des épaules*); (cook.) fore-quarter of mutton without the shoulder. —*s;* shouldering. *Faire une chose par —s;* to do a thing by fits and starts.

épaulement (é-pôl-mān), *n.m.*, a shouldering-piece, covert; shoulder; (fort.) epaulment, demi-bastion, breast-work.

épauler, *v.a.*, to break the shoulder, to splay; to help, to back, to countenance, to shoulder up, to prop; to press to the shoulder (of rifles—*fusils*). — *des troupes;* to cover troops. *Bête épaulée;* animal with a sprained shoulder; (fig., fam.) a perfect fool; a dishonoured woman.

épaulette, *n.f.*, shoulder-strap; shoulder-piece; epaulet. — *à gros grains, — à graine d'épinards;* (milit.) epaulet with large bullion worn by field and general officers.

épave, *adj.*, (jur.) stray.

épave, *n.f.*, (jur.) waif; stray; estray. —*s maritimes, —s de mer;* wreck.

épeautre, *n.m.*, spelt, great barley; bearded wheat.

épée, *n.f.*, sword; (fig.) brand, steel; swordsman. *Charger l'— à la main;* to charge sword in hand. *Un homme d'—;* a swordsman, a soldier. *Mettre l'— à la main;* to draw one's sword. *Se battre à l'—;* to fight with swords. *Passer l'— au travers du corps;* to run a man through the body. *Presser quelqu'un l'— dans les reins;* to bear hard upon any one. *Son — est vierge;* his sword has never been fleshed. *N'avoir que la cape et l'—;* to have nothing but one's nobility; to have no other fortune but one's sword. *Il est brave comme l'— qu'il porte;* he is true to the backbone. *L'— use le fourreau;* the sword wears out the scabbard. *C'est un coup d'— dans l'eau;* it is beating the air. *Passer au fil de l'—;* to put to the edge of the sword, to put to the sword. *Être, en être, aux —s et aux couteaux;* to be at daggers drawn. *Jouer de l'— à deux talons;* to take to one's heels. *Son — est trop courte;* his arm is not long enough. *C'est son — de chevet;* he is his bosom friend, his constant companion.

épeiche, *n.f.*, (orni.) golden oriole, witwall.

épeler (é-plé), *v.a.*, to spell. *Épelez ce mot,* spell that word. — *mal;* to misspell.

épellation, *n.f.*, naming the letters of a word spelling.

épenthèse, *n.f.*, (gram.) epenthesis.

épenthétique, *adj.*, (gram.) epenthetical.

éperdu, -e, *adj.*, distracted, aghast. *Tout — d'amour;* quite distracted with love.

éperdument, *adv.*, distractedly, passionately, desperately.

éperlan, *n.m.*, (ich.) smelt, sparling, sprat.

éperon (épron), *n.m.*, spur; wrinkle (in the corner of the eye—*rides au coin de l'œil*); (arch.) buttress, counterfort; (nav.) head of a ship; (fort.) spur. *Donner de l'— à un cheval;* to clap spurs to a horse. *Chausser les —s;* to put on spurs. *Cheval qui n'a ni bouche ni —;* horse that obeys neither rein nor spur. *Il a besoin d'—s;* he wants spurring. *Chausser les —s à quelqu'un;* to put spurs on any one.

éperonné, -e, (é-pro-né), *adj.*, spurred; wrinkled (of the eyes—*des yeux*). *Elle a les yeux —s;* she has wrinkles in the corners of her eyes.

éperonner, *v.a.*, to spur.

éperonnier, *n.m.*, spur-maker; Indian peacock.

épervier, *n.m.*, (orni.) hawk, sparrow-hawk; cast-net.

épervière, *n.f.*, (bot.) hawkweed.

épervin, *n.m.* V. **éparvin**.

éphèbe, *n.m.*, (Grec. antiq.) a youth of 18 years of age.

éphélide, *n.f.*, (med.) ephelis; freckle.

éphémère, *adj.*, ephemeral.

éphémère, *n.f.*, ephemera, day-fly.

éphémérides, *n.f. pl.*, ephemerides.

éphod (é-fod), *n.m.*, (Jewish antiq.—*antiq. juive*) ephod.

éphore (é-for), *n.m.*, (Grec. antiq.) ephor.

épi, *n.m.*, ear of corn; awn. — *bien garni;* well-filled ear. — *de cheveux;* tuft of hair. — *de diamants;* cluster of diamonds. — *d'eau;* pond-weed. — *de faîte;* (arch.) top of the crown-post. *Assembler en —;* to scarf.

épiaire, *adj.*, (antiq.) continuous (of a fever— *fièvre*).

épice, *n.f.*, spice; *pl.,* ⊙judges' fees. *Pain d'—;* gingerbread. *Fine —;* sharp fellow, knowing blade. *Dans les petits sacs sont les bonnes —s;* little and good (pers.). *Herbe aux —s;* all-spice.

épicène, *adj.*, (gram.) epicene.

épicer, *v.a.*, to spice; ⊙(of judges—*de juges*) to charge too high fees.

épicerie (é-pi-sri), *n.f.*, spices, grocery; grocery-business. *Petite —;* chandlery.

épichérème (-ké-), *n.m.*, (log.) epichirema.

épici-er, *n.m.,* **-ère**, *n.f.*, grocer. *Il faut envoyer ce livre à l'—;* this book must go to the butter-shop.

épicrâne, *n.m.*, (anat.) epicranium.

épicurien, -ne (-iin, -iè-n), *n.* and *adj.*, epicure; epicurean.

épicurisme, *n.m.*, epicureanism, epicurism.

épicycle, *n.m.*, (astron.) epicycle.

épicycloïde, *n.f.*, (geom.) epicycloid.

épidémie, *n.f.*, epidemic.

épidémique, *adj.*, epidemic, epidemical.

épidendre, *n.m.*, (bot.) epidendrum.

épiderme, *n.m.*, epidermis, cuticle, scarf skin.

épidermique, *adj.*, (anat.) epidermic, epidermical.

épididyme, *n.m.*, (anat.) epididymis.

épié, -e, *part.*, eared, awny, awned; (fig.) awn-like.

épier, *v.n.*, to ear, to shoot into ears.

épier, *v.a.*, to watch. to be a spy upon. *Il épie ce que vous faites;* he is a spy upon your actions. *On épie vos démarches;* your steps are dogged.

épierrement, *n.m.*, clearing land of stones.

épierrer, *v.a.*, to take away, to clear away stones.

épieu, *n.m.*, boar-spear.

épigastre, *n.m.*, (anat.) epigastrium.

épigastrique. *adj.*, (anat.) epigastric.

épiglotte, *n.f.*, (anat.) epiglottis.

épigrammatique, *adj.*, epigrammatic, epigrammatical.

épigrammatiquement, *adv.*, epigrammatically.

épigrammatiser, *v.n.*, to write epigrams.

épigrammatiste, *n.m.*, epigrammatist.

épigramme, *n.f.*, epigram.

épigraphe, *n.f.*, epigraph.

épigraphie, *n.f.*, epigraphics, epigraphy.

épigraphique, *adj.*, pertaining to epigraphy.

épigyne. *adj.*, (bot.) epigynous.

épilatoire, *adj.*, depilatory.

épilepsie, *n.f.*, (med.) epilepsy. *Attaque d'—;* epileptic fit. fit of epilepsy.

épilep-dque, *n.m.f.*, and *adj.*, epileptic; epileptical.

épiler, *v.a.*, to depilate.

s'épiler, *v.r.*, to pluck out one's grey hairs.

épileu-r, *n.m.*, **-se**. *n.f.*, depilator (pers.).

*épillet, *n.m.*, (bot.) spikelet.

épilobe, *n.m.*, (bot.) willow-herb.

épilogue (-log), *n.m.*, epilogue.

épiloguer (-ghé). *v.n.*, to carp at, to censure, to criticize, to find fault with. *Il épilogue sur tout;* he finds fault with everything.

épiloguer, *v.a.*, to criticize, to find fault with, to carp at.

épilogueur (-gheur), *n.m.*, critic, fault-finder.

épinard (-när), *n.m.*, (bot.) spinage. *—s;* (cook.) spinage. *— -fraise;* strawberry-blite, strawberry-spinach. *— sauvage;* all-good, *Épaulettes à graine d'—s;* epaulets with large bullion.

épine. *n.f.*, thorn; prickle; rub, obstacle, difficulty; bristling point (metal.). *— blanche;* hawthorn; berberry. *— dorsale, du dos;* spine; back-bone. *Noble —;* hawthorn. *— noire;* German acacia; blackthorn, sloe. *Avoir une — au pied;* to have a thorn in one's side. *Tirer à quelqu'un une — du pied;* to relieve one from great embarrassment. *Être sur les —s, sur des —s;* to be upon pins and needles. *Il n'y a pas de roses sans —s;* no rose without a thorn, no joy without alloy. *Les —s de la chicane;* the thorny points of the law.

épines, *n.f.pl.*, (metal.) bristling points.

épinette, *n.f.*, (mus.) spinet; (bot.) North-American fir-tree.

épineu-x, **-se**, *adj.*, thorny. prickly; knotty, ticklish. *Arbres —;* thorny trees. *Pomme —se;* (bot.) stramony, thorn-apple *Question —se;* ticklish question.

épine-vinette, *n.f.*, berberry. barberry.

ⓒ**épingare**, *n.m.*, (artil.) one-pounder.

épingle, *n.f.*, pin. *—s;* pin-money; gratuity, douceur. *Attacher avec une —;* to pin. *Il est toujours tiré à quatre —s;* he is always as neat as hands can make him; he always looks as if he had just stepped out of a bandbox. *Tirer son — du jeu;* to get out of a scrape. *À coups d'—s;* inch by inch. *— à cheveux;* hairpin. *Ôter les —s;* to unpin.

épinglé. *adj.*, corded. *Velours —;* light corded velvet.

épingler, *v.a.*, to pin.

épinglette, *n.f.*, (artil.) priming-iron; priming-wire; (mining—*mines*) piercer;(tech.) pricker.

épingli-er, *n.m.*, **-ère**, *n.f.*, pin-maker; dealer in pins.

épinière, *adj.f.*, (anat.) spinal. *Moelle —;* spinal marrow.

épiniers, *n.m.pl.*, (hunt.) brake, thicket.

épinoche, *n.f.*, (com.) best coffee; (ich.) stickleback.

épiphanie, *n.f.*, Epiphany.

épiphonème. *n.m.*, (rhet.) epiphonema.

épiphora, *n.m.*, (med.) epiphora.

épiphyse, *n.f.*, (anat.) epiphysis.

épiploon. *n.m.*, (anat.) epiploon.

épique. *adj.*, epic.

épiscopal, **-e**, *adj.*, episcopal.

épiscopal, *n.m.*, episcopalian.

épiscopalement. *adv.*, episcopally.

épiscopat. *n.m.*, episcopate, episcopacy.

épiscopaux, *n.m.pl.*, Episcopalians.

ⓒ**épiscopiser**, *v.a.*, to aspire to a bishopric to assume the airs and manners of a bishop.

épisode, *n.m.*, episode.

épisodique.*adj.*, episodical.

épispastique, *n.m.* and *adj.*, (med.) epispastic.

épisperme. *n.m.*, (bot.) seed-coat, episperm, aril, arillus.

épisser, *v.a.*, (nav.) to splice.

épissoir, *n.m.*, (nav.) fid, splicing-fid; marline-spike.

épissure. *n.f.*, (nav.) splice.

épistolaire, *adj.*, epistolary.

épistolaire. *n.m.*, letter-writer.

épistoli-er. *n.m.*, **-ère**, *n.f.*, letter-writer; (c.rel.) lectionary.

épistolographe, *n.m.*, Greek or Latin letter writer.

épistyle (*n.m.*, (arch.) epistyle.

épitaphe. *n.f.*, epitaph.

épitase. *n.f.*, (dramatic lit.) epitasis.

épithalame, *n.m.*, epithalamium, wedding-song.

épithème, *n.m.*, (pharm.) epithem.

épithète, *n.f.*, epithet.

épitoge, *n.f.*, a hood worn by the first presidents of courts of justice.

épitomé, *n.m.*, epitome.

épître, *n.f.*, epistle.' letter. missive. *Les —s des Apôtres;* the epistles of the Apostles. *— dédicatoire;* dedicatory epistle. *Le côté de l'—;* the right-hand side of the altar.

épitrope. *n.f.*, (rhet.) epitrope.

épizootie (-ii), *n.f.*, epizooty.

épizootique, *adj.*, epizootic. *Maladie —;* epizootic distemper.

*éplaigner, *v.a.*, (manu.) to raise the nap of the cloth, to tease, to teasel.

éploré, **-e**. *adj.*, in tears, weeping. *Une mère —e;* a mother in tears.

éployé, **-e**, *adj.*, (her.) spread (of the eagle *—de l'aigle*).

épluchage, *n.m.*, (manu.) picking.

épluchement (é-plush-män), *n.m.*, cleaning. picking.

éplucher, *v.a.*, to pick. to clean, to sift; to examine minutely. *— la vie de quelqu'un;* to examine minutely into any one's life. *— un ouvrage;* to examine a work minutely.

s'éplucher, *v.r.*, to pick itself (of certain animals).

éplucheu-r, *n.m.*, **-se**, *n.f.*, picker; fault-finder.

éplucheuse, *n.f.*, picker (instrument).

épluchoir, *n.m.*, paring-knife.

épluchure. *n.f.*, paring; *pl.*, orts, refuse.

épode, *n.f.*, epode.

épointé. **-e**, *adj.*, (of a dog—*d'un chien*) that has broken its thigh; (of a horse—*d'un cheval*) that has sprained its haunches. *Ce chien est* —; that dog has broken his thigh.

épointer, *v.a.*, to break off the points.

s'épointer, *v.r.*, to have its point broken off.

*épointillage, *n.m.*, (tech.) removing of orts from newly manufactured woollen cloth.

*épointiller, *v.a.*, (tech.) to remove orts from newly manufactured woollen cloth.

épointure, *n.f.*, (of horses, dogs—*du cheval, du chien*) hip-shot.

épois, *n.m.pl.*, trochings (of a deer—*du cerf*).

éponge, *n.f.*, sponge. *Passer l'— sur quelque action;* to obliterate the recollection of an action. *Presser l'—;* to squeeze the sponge; to exact too much. *Il boit comme une —;* he drinks like a fish.

éponger, *v.a.*, to sponge; to sponge up.

épongier, *n m.*, (l.u.) sponge-man.

*épontille, *n.f.*, (nav.) stanchion, prop.

*épontiller, *v.a.*, to prop, to shore.

éponyme, *n.m.* and *adj.*, (antiq.) eponyme.

épopée, *n.f.*, epopee.

époque, *n.f.*, epoch; period, time, era. *Faire —;* to form an era. *Dès cette —;* from that time. *À l'— de;* at the time of.

époud^er, *v.a.*, (l.u.) to dust. *V.* **épousseter**.

épouffé, **-e**, *adj.*, (fam.) out of breath.

s'épouffer, *v.r.*, to steal away, to scamper off; to get out of breath from laughing.

*épouiller, *v.a.*, (l.ex.) to louse.

*s'épouiller, *v.r.*, (l.ex.) to louse one's self.

époule, **espole**, *or* **espoule**, *n.f.*, (manu.) thread put on the bobbin before placing it in the shuttle.

épouleur, **espoleur**, *or* **espouleur**, *n.m.*, workman who puts the thread upon the shuttle.

époulin, **espolin**, *or* **espoulin**, *n.m.*, (manu.) small shuttle.

époumoner, *v.a.*, to tire the lungs of.

s'époumoner, *v.r.*, to tire one's lungs.

*épousailles, *n.f.pl.*, espousals, nuptials, wedding.

épouse, *n.f.*, spouse, bride, wife.

épousé, **-e**, *part.*, married, wedded.

épousée, *n.f.*, bride, wife. *Mener l'— à l'église;* to lead the bride to church.

épouser, *v.a.*, to marry, to take in marriage, to wed, to espouse, to embrace. — *une héritière;* to marry an heiress. — *les intérêts d'autrui;* to espouse the interests of others.

s'épouser, *v.r.*, to marry each other.

épouseur, *n.m.*, man who intends to marry.

épousseter (é-pous-té) *v.a.*, to dust, to wipe off the dust; to beat the dust out of; to bather, to dust (beat—*rosser*). — *quelqu'un;* to dust any one's jacket for him.

s'épousseter, *v.r.*, to wipe the dust off one's self.

époussette, *n.f.*, dusting-rag, duster, épouti, *n.m.*, orts (in cloth—*dans le drap*).

époutieuse (-tieuz), *n.f.*, picker (of cloth—*de drap*).

époutir, *v.a.*, to pick, to clean (cloth—*le drap*).

épouvantable, *adj.*, frightful, dreadful, tremendous. *Laideur —;* frightful ugliness. *À un degré —;* to a frightful degree.

épouvantablement, *adv.*, frightfully, dreadfully, tremendously.

*épouvantail, *n.m.*, scare-crow; bugbear; (orni.) sea-swallow. *C'est un — de chenevière;* she is a perfect scarecrow.

épouvante, *n.f.*, terror, dismay, affright. *Porter l'— dans le pays ennemi;* to carry terror into the enemy's country. *L'— les a*

pris; they were seized with dismay. *Frapper d'—;* to dismay, to affright.

épouvantement, *n.m.*, terror, the acme of terror.

épouvanter, *v.a.*, to terrify, to frighten, to appal, to scare. *Il l'épouvantait par ses menaces;* he terrified him with his threats.

s'épouvanter, *v.r.*, to be frightened, terrified; to take fright.

époux, *n.m.*, spouse, husband, bridegroom; *pl.*, husband and wife. *Futur —;* intended husband.

épreindre (épreignant, épreint), *v.a.*, to squeeze out, to press.

épreinte, *n.f.*, tenesmus.

s'éprendre, *v.r.*, to become enamoured.

épreuve, *n.f.*, trial, proof, test, ordeal; (print.) proof, revise. *J'en ai fait l'—;* I have tried it, made a trial of it. *Passer par de rudes —s;* to go through hard trials. *Mettre à l'—;* to make a trial of, to put to the test. *À l'— du feu;* proof against fire. *À l'— des balles;* ball-proof. *À l'— de l'eau;* water-proof. *À toute —;* proof against every thing. *Courage à toute —;* courage proof against every thing. — *judiciaire;* ordeal. *Temps d'—;* probation — *chargée;* (print.) foul proof. — *peu chargée;* (print.) clean proof. *Corriger une —;* (print.) to correct a proof. *Première — d'auteur;* (print.) reader's proof. *Seconde — d'auteur;* (print.) revise. *Troisième — d'auteur;* (print.) second revise. — *avant la lettre;* (engr.) proof before letters. *Tirer une —;* (print.) to pull a proof.

épris, **-e**, *adj.*, taken, smitten. *Il en est —;* he is smitten with her.

éprouver, *v.a.*, to try, to prove; to put to the proof; to feel, to experience, to meet with. — *la fidélité de quelqu'un;* to try any one's fidelity. — *une douleur;* to feel a pain. — *des malheurs;* to meet with misfortunes. — *un canon;* to test a cannon.

éprouvette, *n.f.*, gauge; eprouvette (for testing gunpowder—*pour éprouver la poudre*). *sel d'epsom,* *n.m.*, Epsom salts.

eptacorde, *n m.* *V.* **heptacrode**.

eptagone, *n.m.* *V.* **heptagone**.

épucer, *v.a.*, to catch the fleas of; to clear of fleas.

s'épucer, *v.r.*, to catch one's fleas.

épuisable, *adj.*, exhaustible.

épuisé, **-e**, *part.*, drained; spent; worn-out; thread-bare; out of print; done up; exhausted. *Terre —e;* exhausted ground.

épuisement (é-puiz-mān), *n.m.*, draining; draining off; exhaustion. *L'— des finances;* the low state of the finances. *Tuyau d'—;* exhausting-pipe.

épuiser, *v.a.*, to exhaust, to spend, to drain, to use up. *Ses débauches ont épuisé ses forces;* his debaucheries have exhausted his strength. — *une matière;* to exhaust a subject. *Leurs ressources étaient épuisées;* their resources were exhausted.

s'épuiser, *v.r.*, to be exhausted, to waste, to wear out, to exhaust one's self. — *à force de travail;* to exhaust one's self by dint of work.

épulide, *or* **épulie**, *n.f.*, (surg.) epulis.

épulons, *n.m.pl.*, (antiq.) epulones.

épulotique, *n.m.* and *adj.*, (pharm.) epulotic.

⊙épurati-f, **-ve**, *adj.*, depurating.

épuration, *n.f.*, purification, purifying, refining, refinement. — *du sang;* purifying of the blood.

épuratoire, *adj.*, purifying.

épure, *n.f.*, (arch.) diagram.

épurement, *n.m.*, purifying.

épurer, *v.a.*, to purify, to clear, to clarify,

to refine ; to purge. — *de l'eau bourbeuse ; to* clear muddy water. — *de l'or ;* to refine gold.

s'épurer, *v.r.,* to be purified, to grow finer.

épurge. *n.f.,* (bot.) caper-spurge.

équarrir, *v.a.,* (tech.) to square.

équarrissage. *n.m.,* (carp.) squareness ; scantling ; flaying and cutting up (horses—*les chevaux*). *Dix pouces d'* — ; ten inches square.

équarrissement. *n.m.,* (tech.) squaring.

équarrisseur, *n.m.,* knacker.

équateur (é-koua-), *n.m.,* equator, equinoctial line.

équation (é-koua-), *n.f.,* (alg.) equation. — *du premier degré ;* (alg.) simple equation. *Poser une* — ; to state an equation.

équatorial, -e (é-koua-), *adj.,* equatorial ; —, *n.m.,* equatorial (instrument).

équerre, *n.f.,* set square. *Dresser à l'—;* to square. *À fausse* — ; out of square. *Courbe à* — ; (nav.) square knee.

équestre (ékuèstr), *adj.,* equestrian.

équiangle (é-kui-), *adj.,* (geom.) equiangular.

équidifférent, -e (é-kui-), *adj.,* equidifferent.

équidistant, -e (é-kui-), *adj.,* (geom.) equidistant.

équilatéral, -e (é-kui-), *adj.,* (geom.) equilateral.

équilatère (é-kui-), *adj.,* (geom.) equilateral.

équilibre, *n.m.,* equilibrium, equipoise, poise, balance. *Mettre en* — ; to poise. *Faire l'—;* to make things equal. *Perdre l'—;* to lose one's equilibrium, one's balance.

équilibrer, *v.a.,* to poise; to place in equilibrium.

équinoxe, *n.m.,* equinox. — *d'automne ;* autumnal equinox. — *de printemps ;* vernal equinox.

équinoxial. -e, *adj.,* equinoctial. *Ligne —e ;* equinoctial line.

équipage, *n.m.,* equipage, carriage ; equipment ; dress ; plight ; crew (of a ship—*d'un vaisseau*). *Avoir son* — ; to keep one's carriage. *Être dans un triste* — ; to be badly equipped. *Être en triste* — ; to be in a sad plight. — *de Jean de Paris ;* brilliant equipage. — *de Bohême ;* sorry equipage. *Maître d'—;* (nav.) boatswain.

équipe, *n.f.,* (nav.) train of boats ; set, gang (of workmen—*d'ouvriers*).

équipée, *n.f.,* foolish enterprise ; freak, frolic.

équipement (é-kip-màn), *n.m.,* outfit, fitting out, equipment.

équiper. *v.a.,* to equip, to fit out, to stock, to furnish ; to ill-treat, to pay out. — *une flotte ;* to fit out a fleet.

s'équiper. *v.r.,* to fit one's self out ; to dress up.

équipet, *n.m.,* (nav.) locker.

équipollence, *n.f.,* (l.u.) equipollence.

ⓒ**équipollent,** *n.m.,* equipollent, equivalent. *À l'—;* in proportion.

ⓒ**équipollent, -e,** *adj.,* equipollent, equivalent.

ⓞ**équipoller,** *v.a.,* to be equivalent, to be of the like value.

équipondérance (é-kui-), *n.f.,* equipondérance.

équitable, *adj.,* equitable, upright, just.

équitablement, *adv.,* equitably, justly.

équitant, -e (é-kui-), *adj.,* (bot.) (of leaves —*des feuilles*) equitant.

ⓞ**équitati-f, -ve,** *adj.,* (bot.) equitant.

équitation (é-kui-), *n.f.,* equitation, riding, horsemanship.

équité, *n.f.,* equity. justice.

équivalemment (-la-màn), *adv.,* in an equivalent manner.

équivalence, *n.f.,* equivalence.

équivalent, -e *adj.,* equivalent.

équivalent, *n.m.,* equivalent.

équivaloir, *v.n.,* to be equivalent.

équivalve, *adj.,* (conch.) equivalve.

équivoque, *adj.,* equivocal, ambiguous, doubtful, uncertain. *Un homme* — ; a man of doubtful character.

équivoque, *n.f.,* equivocation ; ambiguity ; (paint.) defect, fault. *User d'—s ;* to equivocate.

équivoquer, *v.n.,* to equivocate, to speak ambiguously.

s'équivoquer, *v.r.,* to use one word for another, to make a mistake, to be mistaken.

érable, *n.m.,* maple, maple-tree. — *blanc:* sycamore. — *à sucre;* sugar-maple.

éradication, *n.f.,* eradication.

érafler, *v.a.,* to scratch slightly, to graze.

éraflure, *n.f.,* slight scratch.

*****éraillé,-e,** *part.,* frayed ; blood-shot (of the eyes—*des yeux*); (nav.) (of cables and ropes—*des câbles, cordes, &c.*) chafed, galled.

*****éraillement,** *n.m.,* (med.) eversion of the eyelids ; fraying, fretting, unweaving.

*****érailler,** *v.a.,* to fray, to fret, to unweave.

***s'érailler,** *v.r.,* to fray ; (nav.) to chafe ; to become blood-shot (of the eyes—*des yeux*). *La gaze est sujette à* —; gauze is apt to fray.

*****éraillure,** *n.f.,* fret.

*****ératé, -e,** *part.,* spleened; sprightly, lively, gay, arch, shrewd. *Un petit garçon* —; a sprightly little boy.

érater, *v.a.,* to pull out the spleen ; to spleen.

s'érater, *v.r.,* to run one's self out of breath, to lose one's breath through running.

ère, *n.f.,* era, æra, epoch.

érèbe, *n.m.,* (myth.) Erebus.

érecteur, *n.m.* and *adj.,* (anat.) erector (muscle).

érectile, *adj.,* (anat.) erectile.

érection, *n.f.,* erection, erecting; establishment, raising.

éreinter, *v.a.,* to break any one's back; to tire out, to knock up.

s'éreinter, *v.r.,* to break one's back, to tire one's self out, to be knocked up ; to drudge, to toil and moil.

érémitique, *adj.,* hermetical, eremitical.

érésipélateu-x, -se, *adj.,* (med.) erysipelatous.

érésipèle, *n.m.,* (med.) erysipelas, St. Anthony's fire; (vet.) wild-fire.

éréthisme, *n.m.,* (med.) erethismus.

ergastule, *n.f.,* (Rom. antiq.) slaves' prison.

ergo, *conj.,* (log.) ergo; then, therefore. — *-glu,* — *-gluc* (fam., jest.); ergo, nothing at all.

ergot, *n.m.,* spur (of certain birds—*de certains oiseaux*); (agri.) ergot, spur; (pharm.) ergota; (nav.) taggle; dew-claw (of a dog—*du chien*); (vet.) ergot. *Être sur ses —s ;* to get on one's high horse. — *de coq ;* cock's-spur, panic-grass.

ergotage, *n.m.* V. **ergoterie.**

ergoté, -e, *adj.,* spurred, having a dew-claw (of a dog—*du chien*). *Un coq bien* — ; a well-spurred cock. *Seigle* — ; spurred rye.

ergoter, *v.n.,* to cavil, to wrangle. *Il ergote sur tout;* he finds fault with everything.

ergoterie (èr-gotri), *n.f.,* cavilling; quibbling, quibble.

ergoteu-r, *n.m.,* **-se,** *n.f.,* caviller, quibbler.

ergotisme, *n.m.,* cavilling, quibbling, quibble; (med.) ergotism.

éridan, *n.m.,* (astron.) Eridanus.

ériger, *v.a.,* to erect, to raise, to rear, to institute.

s'ériger, v.r., to erect one's self into ; to set

up for, to pretend to be. — *en censeur public ;* to set up for a public censor.

*érigne, *or* **érine,** *n.f.,* (surg.) hook.

érigone, *n.f.,* (astron.) Virgo.

ermin, *n.m.,* duty paid at the customhouses in the Levant.

erminette, *or* **herminette,** *n.f.,* (carp.) adze.

ermitage, *n.m.,* hermitage.

ermite, *n.m.,* hermit.

érodé, -e, *adj.,* (tech.) eroded, gnawed.

érosion, *n.f.,* erosion.

érotique, *adj.,* erotic.

érotomanie, *n.f.,* erotomania, nymphomania.

erpétologie, *n.f.,* erpetology.

errant, -e (èr-rän, -t), *adj.,* wandering, roving, errant. *Chevalier — ;* knight-errant. *Le juif — ;* the wandering Jew.

errant, *n.m.,* (religious expression) lost sheep.

errata (èr-ra-ta), *n.m.* (—), errata.

erratique, *adj.,* (med., astron.) erratic.

erratum, *n.m.* (—), erratum. *V.* **errata.**

erre, *n.f.,* course, way; (nav.) way (of a ship—*d'un vaisseau*); *pl.,* track (of a stag—*d'un cerf*). *Aller grand' — ;* to go very fast. *Marcher sur les — s de quelqu'un;* to tread in any one's footsteps.

errements (èr-män), *n.m. pl.,* traces, track, manner, way. *Reprendre les anciens — d'une affaire;* to fall into the old track again.

errer (èr-ré), *v.n.,* to wander, to ramble, to stray, to range, to rove, to roll ; to err, to mistake, to be mistaken. — *partout ;* to ramble about. — *çà et là;* to ramble about, to stroll up and down. *Aller errant ;* to wander up and down.

erreur (èr-reur), *n.f.,* error, illusion, mistake. *Sauf — ;* errors excepted. *Commettre une — ;* to commit an error. *Tirer quelqu'un de son — ;* to convince any one of his error.

errhin, *n.m.,* (med.) errhine.

errhin, e, *adj.,* (med.) errhine.

erroné, -e (èr-ro-né), *adj.,* erroneous, mistaken, false, unsound.

erronément, *adv.,* erroneously.

ers (èr), *n.m.,* tare, fitch, lentil.

erse, *n.f.,* (nav.) iron cringle. — *s de poulies ;* block-strops.

erse, *adj.,* Erse (Gaelic, Irish, Highland Scotch—*gaélique, irlandais, écossais*).

érubescent, -e, *adj.,* erubescent, reddening.

érucage, érucago, *or* **érucaguo** (-kag), *n.f.,* (bot.) rocket.

éructation, *n.f.,* eructation, belching.

éructer, *v.a.,* (l.u.) to eructate, to belch.

érudit, -e, *adj.,* erudite, learned.

érudit, *n.m.,* scholar, learned man.

érudition, *n.f.,* learning, erudition.

érugineu-x, -se, *adj.,* eruginous.

érupti-f, -ve, *adj.,* (med.) eruptive.

éruption, *n.f.,* act of breaking forth, eruption; cutting (of teeth—*des dents*).

érysipélateu-x, -se, *adj. V.* **érésipélateux.**

érysipèle, *n.m. V.* **érésipèle.**

ès, *art.,* (contraction of *en les*), in, of. *Maître — arts;* master of arts.

escabeau, *n.m.,* stool.

escabelle, *n.f.,* stool.

escache, *n.f.,* scatch, bit for horses.

escadre, *n.f.,* (nav.) squadron, fleet. *Chef d'— ;* vice-admiral.

*escadrille, *n.f.,* (nav.) small squadron ; squadron of brigs, cutters, and gun-boats.

escadron, *n.m.,* (milit.) squadron (of horse —*de cavalerie*).

escadronner, *v.n.,* to manœuvre (of cavalry —*de cavalerie*).

escalade, *n.f.,* scaling a wall; (milit.) escalade.

escalader, *v.a.,* to scale, to climb over; (milit.) to escalade. — *un mur ;* to scale a wall.

escale, *n.f.,* (nav.) putting in. *Faire — dans un port;* to put into a port.

escalier, *n.m.,* staircase, stairs. — *en limaçon;* winding staircase. — *dérobé;* private staircase. — *de commandement* (nav.); companion-ladder.

escalin, *n.m.,* a coin of the Netherlands worth about 6d. (Of. 64c.)

escalope, *n.f.,* (cook.) a kind of stew.

escamotage, *n.m.,* juggling.

escamote, *n.f.,* juggler's-ball.

escamoter, *v.a.,* to juggle, to juggle away ; to pilfer, to shuffle out of, to ease of. *On lui a escamoté sa bourse ;* they eased him of his purse.

escamoteur, *n.m.,* juggler.

escamper, *v.n.,* to scamper away.

escampette, *n.f.,* scampering. *Il a pris de la poudre d'— ;* he has scampered away.

escapade, *n.f.,* prank, freak, spree, frolic, lark. *Faire une — ;* to have a lark.

escape, *n.f.,* (arch.) shaft, lower part of the shaft, of a column.

*escarbille, *n.f.,* coal cinders.

escarbot, *n.m.,* (ent.) horn-beetle.

escarboucle, *n.f.,* (min.) carbuncle.

escarcelle, *n.f.,* (jest.) purse. *Il a rempli son — ;* he has filled his purse.

escargot, *n.m.,* snail, edible snail.

escarmouche, *n.f.,* skirmish. — *de route;* (milit.) running fight. *Aller à l'— ;* to go out to skirmish.

escarmoucher, *v.n.,* to skirmish.

escarmoucheur, *n.m.,* skirmisher.

escarole, *n.f.,* (bot.) endive.

escarotique, *n.m.* and *adj.,* (med.) escharotic, caustic.

escarpe, *n.f.,* (fort.) scarp, escarp.

escarpé, -e, *adj.,* steep, steepy, cragged.

escarpement, *n.m.,* (fort.) escarpment.

escarper, *v.a.,* to cut steep; (milit.) to escarp.

escarpin, *n.m.,* pump (shoe). *Jouer de l'— ;* to run away, to take to one's heels.

escarpolette, *n.f.,* swing, see-saw. *Il a la tête à l'— :* he is a hare-brained fellow.

escarre, *n.f.,* (med.) eschar; slough; ⊙(fig.) gap.

escaveçade, *n.f.,* (man.) jerk (with the cavesson).

escient, *n.m.,* (l.u.) knowledge. *À son — ;* to his knowledge, wittingly. *À bon — ;* in earnest; wittingly.

esclaire, *n.m.,* (hawking—*fauconnerie*) bird of prey which has a long body and flies well.

esclandre, *n.m.,* fracas; disaster ; circumstance that causes scandal.

esclavage, *n.m.,* slavery; bondage ; thraldom ; inthralment. *Réduire à l'— ;* to enslave, to reduce to slavery.

esclave, *n.m.f.,* slave; bondman. *Commandeur d'—s ;* slave-driver. *Propriétaire d'—s;* slave-owner. *Produit par le travail des —s;* slave-grown. *On est — dans cette maison ;* one is a slave in that house.

esclave, *adj.,* slavish. *Avoir une âme — ;* to have a slavish, base disposition.

escobard, *n.m.,* equivocator, shuffler.

escobarder, *v.n.,* to equivocate, to prevaricate.

escobarderie, *n.f.,* prevarication, shuffling, subterfuge.

⊙**escoffion,** *n.m.,* cap worn formerly by women.

escogriffe, *n.m.,* sharper, shark, sponger; tall, ill-made man.

escompte (ès-cont), *n.m.*, discount. *A* — ; **at a discount**. *Faire l'* — ; to discount.

escompter (ès-conté), *v.a.*, to discount, to cash. — *un billet ;* to cash a bill.

escompteur (ès-kon-teur), *n.m.*, (com.) discounter.

escope, *n.f.*, V. **écope**.

escopette, *n.f.*, carbine.

escopetterie, *n.f.*, volley of carbines, &c.

escorte, *n.f.*, escort ; (nav.) convoy. *Servir d'* — *à ;* to serve for an escort to, to guard. *Bâtiment d'* — ; convoy-ship

escorter, *v.n.*, to escort. — *la caisse militaire ;* to escort the military chest.

escouade, *n.f.*, (milit.) squad.

escourgée,*n.f.*,scourge (of leather—*de cuir*).

escourgeon (-jon), *n.m.*, winter-barley.

escousse, *n.f.*, (l.u.) spring, run, start (before leaping— *avant de sauter*). *Prendre son* — ; to take a spring.

escrime, *n.f.*, fencing. *Salle d'* — ; fencing-school. *Être hors d'* — ; to be put off one's guard; to be at one's wit's end.

escrimer, *v.n.*, to fence ; to have a trial of skill.

s'escrimer, *v.r.*, to apply one's self diligently, to strive ; to try ; to be skilful in ; to have some knowledge of.

escrimeur, *n.m.*, fencer.

escroc (ès-krô), *n.m.*, sharper, swindler, black-leg.

escroquer, *v.a.*, to swindle, to cheat.

escroquerie (ès-kro-krî), *n.f.*, swindling, swindle, cheating.

escroqueu-r, *n.m.*, -**se**, *n.f.*, cheat, swindler.

escubac. V. **scubac**.

esculape, *n.m.* (—*s*), Esculapius ; (fam.) a clever physician.

esculent, **-e**, *adj.*, (l.u.) edible, eatable, esculent.

escurial, *n.m.*, Escurial.

e-si-mi, *n.m.*,(mus.) E.; in vocal music. mi.

ésope, *n.m.* (—*s*). Æsop; (fam.) hunchback. *C'est un* — ; he is a hunchback.

ésotérique, *adj.*, esoteric.

espace, *n.m.*, space, room, place, volume. —*s imaginaires ;* imaginary space. *Court — de temps ;* short space of time.

espace, *n.f.*, (print.) space.

espacement (ès-pas-mân), *n.m.*, (arch.) interval, interspace ; (print.) spacing.

espacer, *v.a.*, to leave a space between ; (print.) to space.

espade, *n.f.*, tewing-beetle (for hemp—*d chanvre*).

espader, *v.a.*, to tew hemp.

espadeur, *n.m.*, hemp-beater.

espadon, *n.m.*, espadon (sword— *grande épée à deux mains ; sabre*) ; (ich.) sword-fish.

espadonner, *v.n.*, to fight with the espadon.

*****espagnol**, **-e**, *n.* and *adj.*, Spaniard; Spanish. *La langue* —*e ;* the Spanish tongue.

*****espagnol**, *n.m.*, Spanish (language—*langue*).

*****espagnolette**, *n.f.*, baize ; French window fastening.

espalier, *n.m.*, (hort.) espalier ; fruit-wall. *Venir en* — ; to grow on an espalier.

espalmer, *v.a.*, (nav.) to grave.

esparcet, *n.m.*, **esparcette**, *n.f.*, French honey-suckle ; esparcet ; sainfoin.

espargoute, *n.f.* V. **spergule**.

espars, *n.m.*, (nav.) spar.

espèce, *n.f.*, species, kind, sort; (jur.) case; *pl.*, specie, ready money, hard cash; (theol.) element. *L'* — *humaine ;* mankind. *Payer en* — ; to pay in cash.

espérance, *n.f.*, hope, confidence, expectation. *Dans l'* — ; in expectation. *Se nourrir*

d' — ; to feed on hope. *Vivre d'* — ; to live on hope. *Mettre son — en Dieu ;* to put one's hope in God. *Répondre à ses* —*s ;* to answer one's expectations.

espérer,*v.a.*, to hope, to hope for, to expect; to trust. *Il espère une meilleure fortune ;* he hopes for a better fortune. *Je n'espère plus rien ;* I have no further hopes.

espérer, *v.n.*, to hope, to be hopeful of ; to put one's trust in. *J'espère en Dieu ;* I put my trust in God.

espiègle. *n.m.f.* and *adj.*, frolicsome child ; frolicsome, waggish.

espièglerie, *n.f.*, frolic, roguish trick.

espingole, *n.f.*, blunderbuss.

espion, *n.m.*, **-ne**, *n.f.*, spy.

espionnage, *n.m.*, espionage ; occupation of a spy, spying.

espionner, *v.a.*, to spy.

esplanade, *n.f.*, esplanade.

espoir, *n.m.*, hope, expectance. *Avoir l'* — *de;* to be in hopes of. *Mettre son — dans ;* to set one's hopes on. *Sans — ;* hopeless.

espole, *n.f.* V. **époulle**.

espoleur, *n.m.* V. **époulleur**.

espolin, *n.m.* V. **époullin**.

esponton, *n.m.*, spontoon.

espoule, *n.f.* V. **époulle**.

espouleur, *n.m.* V. **époulleur**.

espoulin, *n.m.* V. **époullin**.

espringale, *n.f.*, a kind of sling formerly in use in the armies.

esprit, *n.m.*, spirit, soul, ghost, shade ; mind, sense, understanding, wit, intellect ; humour, disposition, temper, character ; meaning ; spirit, spirituous liquor; (gram.) breathing. — *malin ;* evil spirit, fiend. — *follet ;* goblin. *Dieu est un* — ; God is a spirit. *Le Saint-* —, *l'* — *Saint ;* the Holy Ghost. — *doux* (Grec. gram.); soft breathing. — *rude* (Grec. gram.); hard breathing. — *borné, étroit ;* narrow intellect. — *dérangé ;* disordered mind. — *immonde* (biblical expression); unclean spirit. *Cultiver l'* — ; to cultivate the mind. *Un homme d'* — ; a man of parts, a sensible man. *Un ouvrage d'* — ; a work of talent. *Un bel* — ; a wit. *Un — fort ;* a free-thinker. — *présent ;* ready wit. *S'alambiquer l'* — ; to puzzle one's brains. *Un homme à l'* — *étroit ;* a narrow-minded man. *Aliéner l'* — *à quelqu'un ;* to drive any one mad. *Avoir l'* — *sain ;* to be of sound mind. *Avoir de l'* — ; to be intelligent, to be witty, to be sensible. *Avoir l'* — *aux talons ;* to be unconscious of what is doing, to go a wool-gathering. *Dépourvu d'* — ; destitute of intellect. *Faire de l'* — ; to play the wit. *C'est un — de contradiction ;* he is of a contradictory spirit. *Faire revenir l'* — *à quelqu'un ;* to bring any one to his senses. *Où avait-il l'* — *quand ?* where were his wits when? what was he thinking of when ? *Vous n'avez pas saisi l'* — *de cet auteur ;* you have not understood the meaning of that author. *Reprendre ses* —*s ;* to recover one's senses; to come to one's self again. *Ne pas avoir l'* — *tranquille ;* to be uneasy in one's mind. *Rendre l'* — ; to give up the ghost. *Venir dans l'* — ; to come into one's mind. *Passer pour un homme d'* — ; to pass for a wit. —*s animaux ;* animal spirits. —, *de ;* animus.

esquicher, *v.n.*, *s'* —; *v.r.*, (reversis) to play a low card in order not to win a trick. *S'* — (fig.); to answer evasively.

*****esquif**, *n.m.*, skiff.

*****esquille**, *n.f.*, splinter (of a bone—*d'un os*).

esquinancie, *n.f.*, quinsy.

esquine, *n.f.*, (man.) horse's loins; (bot.) China-root. *Un cheval fort d'* — ; a horse strong in his loins. (bot.) V. **squine**.

esquipot, *n.m.*, (fam.) money-box.

esquisse, *n.f.*, sketch, outline, rough drawing. *Cahier d'—s;* sketch-book. *Faire l'— de;* to make a sketch of. *L'— d'un poème;* the sketch of a poem.

esquisser, *v.a.*, (paint.) to sketch, to outline. — *une figure;* to sketch a figure.

esquiver, *v.a.*, to evade, to avoid, to elude. — *un importun;* to avoid a troublesome man.

s'esquiver, *v.r.*, to escape, to slip away, to steal away, to give the slip, to make off.

esquiver, *v.n*, to slip away, to make off; to avoid.

essai, *n.m*, trial. essay, attempt; sample; testing, assaying (metal.). *Donner, prendre, à l'—;* to give, to take, on trial. *Faire son coup d'—;* to make one's first attempt. *Faire l'— de;* to make a trial of. — *sur la peinture;* essay on painting. *Faire l'— de l'or;* to assay gold. *Pour —;* by way of trial.

essaim (è-sin), *n.m.*, swarm; multitude.

essaimer, *v.n.*, to swarm. *Cette ruche a essaimé;* that hive has swarmed.

essanger, *v.a.*, to soak (foul linen—*du linge sale*).

essarder, *v.a.*, (nav.) to clean with a mop, to swab.

essartement, *n.m.*, grubbing, clearing (of lands—*d'un terrain*).

essarter, *v.a.*, to clear (of wood, thistles—*du bois, des chardons*); to assart

essayer, *v.a.*, to try; to essay, to attempt, to make a trial of; to assay. — *de l'or,* to assay gold. — *une chose;* to try a thing.

s'essayer, *v.r.*, to try one's strength, one's ability, to make attempts, to try one's hand. *Il s'est essayé à peindre;* he has tried his hand at painting.

essayer, *v.n.*, to try, to attempt, to make a trial. *Essayez de le persuader;* try to persuade him. — *de marcher;* to try to walk.

essayerie, *n.f.*, assay-office (of the mint—*de l'hôtel des monnaies*).

essayeur, *n.m.*, assayer. — *des monnaies;* assayer of the mint.

esse, *n.f.*, S; linch-pin (of the axle-tree of a coach—*d'un essieu de voiture*); fore-lock (of gun-carriages—*d'affûts*).

esséminer, *v.a.*, (l.u.) to disperse; to scatter.

essence, *n.f.*, essence; substance; species (of trees—*d'arbres*). — *de romarin;* essence of rosemary. — *de la vie;* heart's blood.

essénien, *n.m.*, Essene.

essentiel, -le (-cièl), *adj.*, essential, material. *C'est à le point —;* that is the main point.

essentiel (-cièl), *n.m.*, essential, essential point, main point.

essentiellement (-sièl-mān), *adv.*, essentially, materially.

essette, *n.f.*, hammer with one end round and the other sharp.

esseulé, -e, *adj.*, (fam., l.u.) solitary, abandoned.

essieu, *n.m.*, axle-tree.

essor, *n.m.*, flight; soaring, soar; strain; swing, play, scope. *Donner l'— à;* to give wings to, to give scope to. *L'— du génie;* the soaring of genius. *Prendre son —;* to take one's flight.

essorant, -e, *adj.*, (her.) soaring. *Un oiseau —;* (her.) a soaring bird.

essorer, *v.a.*, to hang in the air in order to dry.

s'essorer, *v.r.*, to soar away and come back with difficulty (of falcons—*des faucons*).

*essoriller, *v.a.*, to cut the ears (of a dog—*d'un chien*); to crop short (hair—*les cheveux*). — *un chien;* to crop a dog.

essoufflé, -e, *part.*, breathless; out of breath. *Être tout —;* to be quite out of breath.

essoufflement, *n.m.*, panting, breathlessness.

essouffler, *v.a.*, to put out of breath; to wind (horses—*les chevaux*). *S'—, v.r.,* to put one's self out of breath.

essui, *n.m.*, drying-place, drying-house.

essuie-main, *n.m.* (—, or —*s*), towel.

essuie-plume, *n.m.* (—, or —*s*), pen-wiper.

essuyer, *v.a.*, to wipe, to wipe off, to wipe away, to wipe dry; to sustain, to support, to bear, to endure, to go through, to undergo. — *les larmes de quelqu'un;* to dry up any one's tears, to console any one. — *des affronts;* to endure affronts. — *un refus;* to meet with a refusal.

s'essuyer, *v.r.*, to dry one's self. — *les mains, la figure;* to wipe one's hands, one's face.

est (èst), *n.m.*, east. *D'—;* eastern, easterly. *Un vent d'—;* an easterly wind. *À l'—;* to the east, eastward.

estacade, *n.f.*, stockade; boom (of a harbour—*d'un port*).

estafette, *n.f.*, courier, express; (milit.) estafet.

estafier, *n.m.*, (b.s.) tall footman, lanky Jack; hector, bully.

estafilade, *n.f.*, cut (in the face—*au visage*), gash; rent (in clothes—*aux vêtements*).

estafilader, *v.a.*, to slash, to cut (in the face—*au visage*).

estagnon, *n.m.*, a copper bottle.

estame, *n.f.*, worsted, knitted worsted.

estamet, *n.m.*, a common woollen fabric.

estaminet, *n.m.*, coffee-house and smoking-room; smoking divan.

estampage, *n.m.*, stamping (metal.).

estampe, *n.f.*, print, engraving, cut; stamp. *Magasin d'—s;* print-shop; (tech.) stamping-machine, punch.

estamper, *v.a.*, to stamp; to punch (horse-shoes—*les fers à cheval*).

*estampille, *n.f.*, stamp (instrument, mark).

*estampiller, *v.a.*, to stamp.

estanc, *adj.m.*, (nav.) well closed. *Un navire —;* (nav.) a well closed ship.

estance, *n.f.*, (nav.) stanchion.

ester, *v.n.*, (jur.) to appear in court.

estère, *n.f.*, straw mat.

⊙**esterlin,** *n.m.*, a weight formerly used by goldsmiths.

esteuble, *n.f.* V. **éteule.**

esthétique, *n.f.*, æsthetics.

esthétique, *adj.*, æsthetical.

estimable, *adj.*, estimable. *Avoir des qualités —s;* to have estimable qualities.

estimateur, *n.m.*, appraiser, appreciator, valuer.

estimatif, *adj.*, estimative. *État —;* estimate.

estimation, *n.f.*, estimation, appraising, valuation, estimate. *Faire une — de;* to appraise, to estimate.

estime, *n.f.*, esteem, regard, estimation; (nav.) reckoning. *Avoir de l'— pour;* to hold in esteem. *Être perdu d'— et de réputation;* to have lost one's reputation, and the esteem of every one

estimer, *v.a.*, to estimate, to value; to rate; to esteem, to regard, to prize, to consider, to deem, to account. — *des meubles;* to value furniture. — *trop;* to overrate. *J'estime sa vertu;* I esteem his virtue.

s'estimer, *v.r.*, to esteem, to prize, one's self; to set a value on one's self; to consider one's self; to esteem one another.

estival, -e, *adj.*, estival, summer.

estivation, *n.f.*, (bot.) estivation; (zool.)

8

torpor into which crocodiles, some serpents and fishes fall during a few days of the hot season.

estive, n.f., (nav.) cargo of cotton, wool, and other elastic substances.

estiver, v.a., (nav.) to press the cargo down; to turn cattle out to grass during summer.

estoc, n.m., tuck (sword—*épée*); point of a sword; trunk, stock (of trees—*d'arbres*). *Frapper d'— et de taille;* to thrust and cut. *Parler d'— et de taille;* to talk at random. *Dites-vous cela de votre —?* do you say that out of your own head? *Être réduit à blanc —;* to be done up.

estocade, n.f., (fenc.) stoccado, stoccade, thrust; unexpected attack.

estocader, v.n., (fenc.) to thrust, to make passes, to lunge.

estomac (-ma), n.m., stomach; fore-part of the belly (of a fowl—*de volaille*). *Avoir mal à l'—;* to have the stomach-ache. *Ardeur d'—;* heartburn. *Soulever l'—;* to turn the stomach. *Tiraillements d'—;* twitching pains in the stomach. *Le creux de l'—;* the pit of the stomach.

s'estomaquer, v.r., (fam.) to take offence; not to be able to brook; to exhaust one's self by speaking. *Il s'est estomaqué;* he is vexed.

estompe, n.f., stump (for drawing—*pour dessiner*). *Dessin à l'—;* stump-drawing.

estomper, v.a., (drawing—*dessin*) to stump.

estouffade, n.f. V. **étouffée**.

estrade, n.f., estrade, stage. ☉*Battre l'—;* to scout. *Batteurs d'—;* ☉scouts; (fam.) strollers, trampers, vagrants.

estragon, n.m., (bot.) tarragon.

☉**estramaçon**, n.m., two-edged sword. *Coup d'—;* stroke with the edge of a sword.

estramaçonner, v.r., (jest., l.u.) to strike with the edge of a sword.

estrapade, n.f., strappado; gibbet used for the strappado; (man.) estrapade. *Donner l'— à son esprit;* to put one's brains upon the rack.

estrapader, v.a., to give the strappado.

estrapasser, v.a., (man.) to overwork, to override.

estraper, v.a., to mow (stubble—*un chaume*).

estrope, n.f., (nav.) strop.

estroper, v.a., (nav.) to strop.

estropiat, n.m., (fam.) lame mendicant soldier; lame beggar.

estropié, n.m., -e, n.f., cripple.

estropié, -e, part., crippled, disabled. *Être — d'un bras;* to have an arm disabled. *Passage —;* mutilated passage.

estropier, v.a., to cripple, to lame, to maim, to disable; to mangle, to murder, to spoil. *Il fut estropié à tel siège;* he was lamed at such a siege. *— un passage;* to mutilate a passage. *— un rôle;* (theat.) to murder a part.

estuaire, n.m., (geog.) estuary.

esturgeon (-jon), n.m., (ich.) sturgeon.

esule, n.f., (bot.) esula.

et (é), conj., and. *—...—;* both ... and. *—vous — moi;* both you and I. [The final *t* of *et* is never pronounced.]

étblage, n.m., price of, what is paid for, stabling.

étable, n.f., stable (for oxen, sheep, goats—*pour bœufs, moutons, chèvres*); stall; cattle-shed; cattle-house; pig-sty, hog-sty, sty. *S'aborder de franche —;* (nav.) to run right into one another, to run foul of one another.

établer, v.a., to put in a stable, to stable.

étabi, n.m., bench (joiner's, &c.—*de menuisier, &c.*); shop-board (tailor's—*de tailleur*).

établi, -e, part., established.

établir, v.a., to establish, to set, to fix, to

erect, to set up, to set up in business; to institute, to found, to aver, to make good (statements—*assertions*); to assert; to prove, to make out, to show; to induct; to strike (balance); to impose (a tax—*un impôt*). *— sa fille;* to settle one's daughter. *— sa fortune, son crédit;* to establish one's fortune, one's credit. *— un fait;* to state a matter of fact. *— par des exemples;* to prove, to make good, by examples.

s'établir, v.r., to establish one's self, to fix one's residence, to take up one's residence; to settle down, to settle (marry—*se marier*); to set up shop; to set up in business, to set up for one's self, to set up. *Il est venu — en France;* he came to settle in France. *Il s'songs à —;* he thinks of settling.

établissement (-blis-mẚn), n.m., establishment, establishing; setting up, fixing, erecting; proving, making out, showing; imposition (of taxes—*d'impôts*); settling; setting up in business. *L'— d'un fait;* the stating of a matter of fact. *Les hôpitaux sont des —s très-utiles;* hospitals are highly useful institutions. *L'— de ses enfants;* the settling of one's children. *Frais de premier —;* first expenses. *Dans l'—;* on the premises.

étage, n.m., story, floor; flight (of stairs—*escaliers, marches*); (geol., mining—*mines*) layer, stratum. *Il demeure au troisième —;* he lives on the third floor. *Il y a des hommes d'esprit de tout —;* there are wits of every degree. *C'est un sot à triple —;* he is a consummate fool. *Avoir un menton à double —;* to have a double chin.

étager, v.a., to taper (the hair—*les cheveux*).

étagère, n.f., what-not, shelves.

étague (é-tag), n.f., (nav.) hoisting the yards.

étal, n.m., stay, shore; prop, strut. (nav.) *— de misaine;* fore-stay. *— d'artimon;* mizzen-stay. *— du grand mât;* main-stay.

étaie, n.f., (her.) chevron half the ordinary breadth.

☉**étaiement**, n.m., propping, staying, shoring, supporting, bearing up. V. **étayement**.

étaim, (é-tin), n.m., fine carded wool.

étain, n.m., tin; pewter. *— fin;* pure tin. *— commun;* block tin. *— métallique;* white tin. *—oxydé;* tin-stone. *— en feuilles;* tin-foil. *— de glace;* tin-glass.

étal, n.m., butcher's stall; butcher's shop.

étalage, n.m., laying out, exposing of goods for sale; goods exposed for sale; shop-window; window; stallage; finery, fine clothes; showing off, ostentatious display. *Cela n'est bon qu'à servir d'—;* that will only serve for show. *Faire — de son esprit;* to make a show of one's wit. *Faire de l'—;* to make a show, to show off.

étalagiste, n.m., stall-keeper.

étale, adj., (nav.) still; slack (of the water—*de la mer*); settled (of the wind—*du vent*).

étalé, -e, part., patulous, spread, unfolded, displayed.

étaler, v.a., to expose for sale; to put in the shop-window; to spread, to spread out; to show, to set forth, to display, to make a show or parade of, to show off.

s'étaler, v.r., to be exposed for sale; to be hung up in the window; to be displayed, to be spread out; to stretch one's self out, to sprawl; to show one's self off, to show off. *— sur l'herbe;* to stretch one's self at full length on the grass.

étalier, n.m., journeyman-butcher.

étalinguer (-ghé), v.a., (nav.) to clinch.

étalingure, n.f., (nav.) clinch.

étalon, n.m., stallion; standard (of weights and measures—*des poids et mesures*.)

étalonnage, or **étalonnemen**

stamping (of weights and measures—*des poids et mesures*); gauging.

étalonner, *v.a.*, to stamp (weights and measures—*poids et mesures*); to gauge.

étalonneur, *n.m.*, officer who stamps weights and measures.

étamage, *n.m.*, tinning; quicksilvering, foliation; plating.

étambot (*formerly* étambord), *n.m.*, (nav.) stern-post.

étambrai, *n.m.*, (nav.) partner (of a mast or capstern—*d'un mât, d'un cabestan*).

étamer, *v.a.*, to tin; to plate (glass—*du verre*); to foliate, to quicksilver. — *un miroir;* to plate a looking-glass.

étameur, *n.m.*, tinner; silverer.

étamine, *n.f.*, stamin; tammy; bolting-cloth; bolter; bunting; (bot.) stamen, male organ, thrum. *Passer par l'—;* to sift. *Il a passé par l'—:* he has been strictly examined.

étaminé, -e, *adj.*, (bot.) stamened.

étamineuse, *adj.f.*, (bot.) having stamina, but no petals or leaves.

étaminier, *n.m.*, stamin-maker.

étamper, *v.a.*, to punch (horse-shoes—*des fers à cheval*).

étampure, *n.f.*, the holes of a horse-shoe.

étamure, *n.f.*, melted tin, tinning, material for tinning.

étanche, *adj.*, water-tight; air-tight; steam-tight.

étanché, *part.*, of a ship in which a leak has been stopped.

étanchement (é-tänsh-män), *n.m.*, stanching; stopping; quenching, slaking. *L'— du sang;* the stopping of blood.

étancher, *v.a.*, to stanch; to stop; to slake, to quench. — *le sang;* to stop the blood. — *la soif;* to quench the thirst. — *un vaisseau;* (nav.) to free a ship of water.

étançon, *n.m.*, prop, stay, supporter, shore; (nav.) stanchion.

étançonner, *v.a.*, to prop, to underprop, to stay, to support, to shore.

étanfiche, *n.f.*, quarry-stratum.

étang, *n.m.*, pond, fish-pond; pool. *Peupler un — ;* to stock a pond. *Pêcher un — ;* to drag a pond.

étape, *n.f.*, store-house; rations; forage; halting place. *Brûler l'—;* to pass by a halting-place without stopping.

étapier, *n.m.*, (milit.) distributor of rations.

état, *n.m.*, state; commonweal, commonwealth; state, case, condition; position, circumstance, plight, predicament, account; list, register, inventory, estimate; establishment; calling, profession, station; office; *pl.*, dominions; (med.) acme; (milit.) list, muster-roll. *Il est en — de payer;* he is able to pay, he is in a condition to pay. *En quelque — que soit l'affaire;* however the matter may stand. *Se mettre en — de défense;* to put one's self in a state of defence. *Mettre en —;* to prepare. *Tenir une chose en —:* to keep a thing ready; to keep a thing in its place. *Tenir en —;* to keep in suspense. *L'— -major (—s —s);* (milit.) staff, staff-office. *—s généraux;* states-general. *Tenir un grand —:* to keep a large establishment. *Ministre, secrétaire, d';* minister, secretary, of state. *Coup d'—;* stroke of state-policy. *Homme d'—;* statesman. *Affaires d';* state affairs. *Raison d'—:* state-policy. *Les —s-Unis d'Amérique;* the United States of Northern America.

étau, *n.m.*, vice. *Les mâchoires de l'—;* the chops of the vice. — *à main:* hand-vice.

étayement.(-tê-män), *n.m.*, staying, shoring, shoring up, propping, supporting.

étayer, *v.a.*, to stay, to prop, to bear up, to support, to shore.

ctc., *conj.*, (ab. of et cætera), &c.

et cætera. *conj.*, et cætera.

été, *n.m.*, summer; prime (of life—*de la vie*). — *chaud, brûlant;* warm, scorching, summer. *Au milieu de l'—;* in the middle of summer. *Être dans son —:* to be in one's prime.

*éteigneu-r, *n.m.*, **-se**, *n.f.*, (pers.) extinguisher.

*éteignoir, *n.m.*, extinguisher (instrument).

éteindre(*éteignant, éteint), *v.a.*, to put out, to extinguish, to quench, to appease; to exterminate, to destroy, to obliterate; to soften (colours—*couleurs*); to wear out; to liquidate (a debt—*une dette*); to strike out. *Éteignez la chandelle;* put out the candle. — *de la chaux;* to slake lime. — *la soif;* to quench the thirst. *L'âge éteint le feu des passions;* age quenches the fire of the passions. — *une pension;* to buy up, to redeem, an annuity. — *une obligation;* to cancel an obligation. — *le souvenir de;* to obliterate the recollection of. — *une couleur;* to soften down a colour.

s'éteindre, *v.r.*, to be extinguished, to be put out, quenched; to go out; to die away, to die out; to decrease, to diminish, to be diminished; to be slaked (of lime—*de la chaux*). *Le feu s'éteint;* the fire is going out. *Cette maison va —;* that family will soon die out, will soon be extinct.

éteint, e, *part.*, put out, extinguished, out, extinct. *Mon feu est —;* my fire is out. *Elle a la voix —e;* her voice is scarcely audible. *Des yeux —s;* dull eyes.

étendage, *n.m.*, lines to hang things to dry upon; drying-room.

étendard, *n.m.*, standard, colours, banner, flag. *Arborer, déployer, planter, un —;* to hoist, to display, to plant, a standard. *Lever l'— de la révolte;* to raise the standard of a rebellion.

étendeuse, *n.f.*, (spinning—*filature*) stretcher.

étendoir, *n.m.*, drying-room; (print.) peel.

étendre, *v.a.*, to spread, to stretch, to expand, to distend; to lay out; to lengthen, to prolong, to draw out; to lay dead, to kill one on the spot; to enlarge, to extend, to widen; to wire-draw; to lay on (colours—*couleurs*); to overthrow, to throw down. — *du beurre sur du pain;* to spread butter upon bread. — *son armée;* to extend one's army. — *du linge;* to lay out linen. — *le bras;* to stretch out one's arm. — *les ailes;* to spread the wings. — *son commerce;* to extend one's trade.

s'étendre, *v.r.*, to stretch one's self out, to sprawl; to reach, to extend; to expatiate, to dwell; to lengthen, to grow out; to draw out, to launch. *Il s'étendit tout de son long sur l'herbe;* he laid himself at full length upon the grass. *Aussi loin que la vue peut —;* as far as the eye can reach. — *sur un sujet;* to expatiate, to dwell, upon a subject.

étendu, e, *part.*, stretched, spread, extended. *Du linge — sur l'herbe;* linen laid out on the grass. *Un empire fort —;* a wide extended empire. *La vue est ici fort —e;* the prospect is very wide here. *Des connaissances —es;* extensive knowledge. *Il a une voix très —e;* he has great compass of voice. *C'est un esprit fort —;* he is a man of vast intellect.

étendue, *n.f.*, extent, extensiveness, expanse; compass, length. *Dans toute son —;* to the full. *La vaste — des mers;* the wide expanse of the sea. *Grande — de voix;* great compass of voice.

éternel, -le, *adj.*, eternal, everlasting, ever-during, endless, ever-living. *Dieu seul est* — ; God alone is eternal. *Le Père* — ; God Almighty.

éternel. *n.m.*, Eternal, God ; Everlasting.

éternelle. *n.f.* V. **immortelle**.

éternellement (-nèl-mān), *adv.*, eternally, to all eternity, everlastingly ; for ever, perpetually ; incessantly, continually, for evermore.

éterniser, *v.a.*, to eternize. — *son nom ;* to immortalize one's name.

s'éterniser, *v.r.*, to be perpetuated, to be rendered eternal.

éternité, *n.f.*, eternity, everlastingness. *De toute* — ; from all eternity.

éternue, *n.f.*, (bot.) fiorin.

éternuement, or **éternûment**, *n.m.*, sneezing, sneeze.

éternuer, *v.n.*, to sneeze.

éternueu-r. *n.m.*, **-se**, *n.f.*, sneezer.

étésien, *adj.*, etesian.

étêtement (é-têt-mān), *n.m.*, pollarding, topping.

étêter. *v.a.*, (hort.) to top, to pollard ; to take off the heads (of nails, pins—*de clous, d'épingles*).

⊙**éteuf** (é-teu), *n.m.*, ball (at tennis—*au jeu de paume*).

éteule, or **esteuble**, *n.f.*, stubble.

éther (é-tèr), *n.m.*, ether.

éthéré, **-e**, *adj.*, ethereal.

éthérifier, *v.a.*, to etherialize; to etherize.

s'éthérifier, *v.r.*, to become etherized.

éthérisation, *n.f.*, (chem.) etherification; (med.) the producing sleep by means of ether.

éthériser, *v.a.*, (chem.) to etherealize; (med.) to produce insensibility by means of ether.

éthiopien, *n.m.*, **-ne**, *n.f.*, Ethiopian.

⊙**éthiops** (é-tiops), *n.m.*, (chem.) æthiops.

éthique, *n.f.*, ethics, morals.

éthique, *adj.*, ethic.

ethmoïdal. **-e**, *adj.*, (anat.) ethmoidal. *L'os* — ; ethmoidal bone.

ethmoïde, *n.m.*, (anat.) ethmoid.

ethnarchie, *n.f.*, ethnarchy.

ethnarque, *n.m.*, ethnarch.

ethnique, *adj.*, ethnic ; ethnical.

ethnographe. *n.m.*, ethnologist.

ethnographie, *n.f.*, ethnography.

ethnographique, *adj.*, ethnographical.

ethnologie, *n.f.*, ethnology. ethnography.

ethnologue, *n.m.*, ethnologist, ethnographer.

ethnologique, *adj.*, ethnologic, ethnological.

éthologie, *n.f.*, ethology.

éthologique, *adj.*, ethologic.

éthopée, *n.f.*, description of human passions and manners.

étiage (é-tiaj), *n.m.*, low-water mark.

étier (é-tié), *n.m.*, ditch that conveys seawater to a salt-marsh.

étincelant, **-e** (é-tin-slän. -t), *adj.*, sparkling, glittering, flashing, twinkling, glistening. *Étoile* —*e;* twinkling star. *Des yeux* —*s;* sparkling eyes.

étincelé, *adj.*, (her.) a field seme of sparks.

étinceler (é-tin-slé), *v.n.*, to sparkle, to flash, to gleam, to twinkle, to glitter. *Les yeux lui étincellent de colère;* his eyes are sparkling with anger. *Cet ouvrage étincelle d'esprit;* that work sparkles with wit.

étincelette, *n.f.*, little spark.

étincelle. *n.f.*, spark, flash of fire, nill. *Jeter des* —*s;* to throw out sparks. *Il n'a pas une* —*de bon sens;* he has not one spark of good sense.

étincellement (-sèl-mān), *n.m.*, sparkling, twinkling, glistening, scintillation.

étiolement (é-tiol-mān), *n.m.*, etiolation (of plants—*des plantes*) ; (med.) chlorosis.

étioler, *v.a.*, to etiolate (plants—*plantes*).

s'étioler, *v.r.*, to etiolate (of plants—*des plantes*).

étiologie, *n.f.*, (med.) etiology.

étique, *adj.*, hectic ; consumptive ; lean, lank. emaciated.

étiqueter (é-tik-té), *v.a.*, to label, to ticket. — *des marchandises ;* to ticket goods.

étiquette, *n.f.*, ticket, label; etiquette. *Condamner sur l'*— *du sac;* to condemn without examining. *Tenir à l'*—; to be particular in respect to etiquette.

étire, *n.f.*, stretching-iron (of curriers—*des corroyeurs*).

étirer, *v.a.*, to stretch ; (tech.) to lengthen, to wire-draw.

s'étirer, *v.r.*, to stretch one's self out.

étisie, *n.f.*, consumption, decline.

étoffe, *n.f.*, stuff ; cloth ; condition, quality. —*s;* (print.) wear and tear. — *drapée;* woollen cloth. *Il y a de l'*— *chez lui ;* (of a person—*d'une personne*) he has got some stuff in him. *C'est une belle* — *que le velours;* a fine stuff is velvet.

étoffé, **-e**, *adj.*, stuffed (of furniture—*de meubles*); comfortably off. *Discours bien* —*;* well-arranged speech ; speech full of capital things. *Maison bien* —*e;* well-furnished house. *Homme bien* — ; man in good circumstances.

étoffer, *v.a.*, to stuff, to furnish with materials.

étoile, *n.f.*, star ; (man.) blaze ; centre (of walks in parks—*des allées d'un park*) ; star-wheel ; asterisk ; (print., fort.) star. *À la lumière des* —*s;* by starlight. — *polaire;* polar-star. —*s fixes;* fixed stars. —*s errantes;* wandering stars. — *tombante, filante;* shooting star. *Coucher à la belle* — ; to sleep in the open air. *Né sous une mauvaise* —; born under an unlucky star.

étoilé, **-e**, *adj.*, starry ; full of stars, studded with stars. *La voûte* —*e;* the spangled vault. *Bouteille* —*e;* starred bottle (cracked—*fêlée*).

étoiler, *v.a.*, to star, to stud with stars; to crack; to blaze (mark with a star—*marquer d'une étoile*).

s'étoiler, *v.r.*, to star, to crack.

étole, *n.f.*, (c.rel.) stole.

étonnamment (é-to-na-mān), *adv.*, astonishingly, wonderfully.

étonnant. **-e**. *adj.*, astonishing, surprising, wonderful, marvellous.

étonné. **-e**. *part.*, astonished. *Être* — *de;* to be astonished at.

étonnement (é-ton-mān). *n.m.*, astonishment, amazement; admiration, wonder; ⊙shock. *Frapper d'*— ; to strike with amazement. *Remplir d'*— ; to fill with astonishment. *Je ne reviens pas de mon* — ; I cannot recover from my astonishment. *Tout le monde est dans l'*—; every body is amazed. *A l'*— *de tout le monde;* to the astonishment of every body.

• **étonner**, *v.a.*, to astonish, to amaze, to startle; to astound, to stun. *Je suis étonné qu'il ne m'en ait rien dit;* I am astonished that he should have told me nothing about it.

s'étonner, *v.r.*, to be astonished, to be amazed, to wonder. *Il ne s'étonne de rien;* he is astonished at nothing.

étouffade, *n.f.* V. **étouffée**.

étouffant, **-e**, *adj.*, suffocating, sultry, close. *Chaleur* —*e;* suffocating heat.

étouffé, **-e**, *part.*, stifled ; suppressed.

étouffée, *n.f.*, (cook.) estoufade.

étouffement (é-toof-mān), *n.m.*, suffocation, stifling.

⌐touffer, *v.a.*, to suffocate, to choke, to

throttle, to smother, to stifle, to suppress; to hush up; to deaden (sound—*un son*). *Les mauvaises herbes étouffent le blé;* weeds choke up the corn. — *ses plaintes;* to smother one's complaints. — *une affaire;* to hush up an affair. — *une révolte;* to suppress a revolt. — *la voix;* to drown the voice.

étouffer, *v.n.,* to be choking, to be choked; to be suffocated. *J'étouffe ici;* I am suffocated here. — *de rire;* to choke with laughter.

étouffoir, *n.m.,* extinguisher (for charcoal—*à charbon*) ; damper (piano).

étoupe, *n.f.,* tow, oakum. *Mettre le feu aux —s;* to add fuel to the flame. — *goudronnée;* tarred oakum.

étouper, *v.a.,* to stop (with tow or oakum—*avec de l'étoupe ou de la filasse*) ; (nav.) to calk. *S'— les oreilles;* to stop one's ears with cotton.

*étoupille, *n.f.,* (artil.) quick-match.

*étoupiller, *v.a.,* (artil.) to furnish with quick-matches.

*étoupillon, *n.m.,* (artil.) toppin.

étourdeau, *n.m.,* young capon.

étourderie, *n.f.,* giddiness, heedlessness, thoughtlessness, giddy act, blunder. *Il fait toujours des —s;* he is always committing some giddy act or other.

étourdi, -e, *adj.,* stunned; giddy, dizzy, thoughtless, heedless; giddy-headed.

étourdi, *n.m.,* **-e,** *n.f.,* rattle-head, madcap, romp. *C'est une —e;* she is a giddy creature. *À l'—e;* giddily, heedlessly. *Jeter à l'—;* to blurt out.

étourdiment, *adv.,* inconsiderately, heedlessly, thoughtlessly.

étourdir, *v.a.,* to stun, to deafen, to make dizzy, to make giddy; to astound; to din; te assuage (pain); to parboil. — *la grosse faim;* to stay the stomach. — *de la viande;* to parboil meat. — *de l'eau;* to take off the cold of the water.

s'étourdir, *v.r.,* to divert one's thoughts; to be preoccupied; to try to forget. *Il s'étourdit sur son chagrin;* he tries to forget his grief.

étourdissant, -e, *adj.,* stunning, deafening, astounding. *Un bruit —;* a deafening noise.

étourdissement (-dis-măn), *n.m.,* stunning, dizziness, giddiness; amazement; stupor; shock. *Il a des —s;* he is subject to swimmings in the head. *Le premier — passé;* when the first shock was over.

étourneau, *n.m.,* (orni.) starling; giddy person; presumptuous young man; flea-bitten horse.

étourneau, *adj.,* flea-bitten (of horses—*des chevaux*).

étrange. *adj.,* strange, odd, queer, novel; uncouth. *Chose —!* strange! strange to say! *Voilà un homme —;* that is a strange man. *C'est une personne bien —;* she is a very queer sort of a person.

étrangement (é-tranj-măn), *adv.,* strangely, queerly.

étrang-er, -ère, *adj.,* strange; foreign; unknown; irrelevant; outlandish. *Ministre des affaires —ères;* minister for foreign affairs. *Être — à une science;* to be unacquainted with a science. *Un fait — à la cause;* a fact unconnected with the case. *Corps —;* extraneous body. *Une langue —e;* a foreign language.

étrang-er, *n.m.,* **-ère,** *n.f.,* foreigner, stranger, alien; foreign parts. *C'est un —;* he is a foreigner. *À l'—;* abroad. *Passer à l'—;* to go abroad.

⊙étranger, *v.a.,* to estrange, to drive away.

s'étranger, *v.r.,* (hunt.) to leave, to abandon a country, to disappear from a country (of game—*du gibier*).

étrangeté (é-tranj-té), *n.f.,* strangeness; oddness, queerness.

⊙étranglant, -e, *adj.,* overwhelming, amazing.

étranglé, -e, *part.,* scanty, too narrow. *Discours —;* speech too much compressed.

étrangle-loup, *n.m.* (—), (bot.) true-love.

étranglement, *n.m.,* strangling; (med.) strangulation.

étrangler, *v.a.,* to strangle, to throttle, to choke, to stifle; to make too little, too narrow, to make scanty. *Cet habit est étranglé;* that coat is too scanty. — *une affaire;* to slur over a business.

s'étrangler, *v.r.,* to strangle one's self.

étrangler, *v.n.,* to be choked, to be strangled.

*étranguillon (-ghi-ion), *n.m.,* (vet.) strangles. *Poire d'—;* choke-pear.

étrape, *n.f.,* small sickle.

étraper, *v.a.,* to cut down the stubble with a sickle.

étraquer, *v.n.,* (hunt.) to track (on the snow—*sur la neige*).

étrave, *n.f.,* (nav.) stem.

être (étant, été), *v.n.,* to be; to belong; to have; to stand; to take part in; to come, to go; to lie; to belong, to prove to be; to turn out to be. — *en bonne santé;* to be in good health. — *fatigué;* to be tired. — *à quelque chose;* to be doing anything. *Y —;* to be at home; to have hit it. *J'y suis;* I have it. *Je suis des vôtres;* I make one of you. *Je n'en suis plus;* I cry off. *Il n'en est rien;* such is not the case, it is nothing of the sort. — *sage;* (of children—*des enfants*) to be good. — *bien avec quelqu'un;* to be on good terms with any one. — *mal avec quelqu'un;* to be on bad terms with any one. — *de moitié;* to go half. *Hé bien, soit;* well, let it be so. *Ainsi soit-il;* so be it. *Ce tableau est du Poussin;* this picture is by Poussin. *Il est de Paris;* he is a native of Paris. *Cet enfant est à moi;* that child belongs to me. *Cela n'est pas;* it is not so. *Si ce n'est que;* except that. *N'eût été que;* had it not been for. *Il en sera de nous comme des autres;* it will be with us as with others. *Ce sont eux qui;* it is they who. *Je suis à vous dans un moment;* I shall be at your service, with you, in a moment. *Sa maison est entre deux collines;* his house stands between two hills. *Qu'est-ce que c'est?* what is it? *C'est à vous de parler;* it is for you to speak. *Où en êtes-vous?* where are you? where did you leave off? *Je ne sais pas où j'en suis;* I do not know how I am situated, I do not know what I am about. *Il est à présumer;* it is to be presumed. *Il n'est pas en moi de l'éviter;* it does not depend upon me to avoid it. *En êtes-vous encore là?* do you still believe that? *Il en sera ce qu'il plaira à Dieu;* it will be as God pleases. *J'en serai de moitié;* I will go in for half. *J'y suis pour un tiers;* I am in for a third part. *C'en est fait de lui;* it is all over with him. *Voilà où nous en sommes;* such is our present situation. *Il ne sait où il en est;* he does not know where he is; he does not know what he is about. *Que sera-ce de?* what will become of? *Vous y êtes;* you have hit it. *Cela n'en est pas;* that does not belong to it. *Je suis tout à vous;* I am entirely at your service. (fam.) *Si j'étais de vous;* were I in your place. *Je n'y suis pour personne;* I am at home to no one. *Madame n'y est pas;* my mistress is not at home. *Quoi qu'il en soit;* at all events, be that as it may. *En — pour son argent;* to get clear of anything with the loss of one's money. *En — pour vingt francs;* to be in for it to the tune of twenty francs.

être, *n.m.,* being, existence; trunk (of a

tree—*d'un arbre*). *Les* —*s d'une maison; the* parts, ins and outs of a house. *L'* — *Suprême;* the Supreme Being. *Non* —; nonentity. *Bien*— —; welfare, comforts of life. *Il sait tous les* —*s de cette maison;* he knows all the ways about that house. *Couper à blanc* —; (of trees—*des arbres*) to cut down to the root.

étrécir, *v.r.*, to narrow, to make narrower; to take in (clothes—*vêtements*). — *un cheval;* (man.) to cause a horse to narrow.

s'étrécir, *v.r.*, to shrink, to narrow, to become narrower.

étrécissement (-sis-màn), *n.m.*, shrinking, narrowing, straitening.

étrécissure, *n.f.*, straitness, narrowness.

étreindre (étreignant, étreint), *v.a.*, to bind, to tie, to tie up; to press, to clasp.

étreinte, *n.f.*, knot; clasping, pressing; embrace. *De douces* —*s;* sweet embraces.

étrenne (é-trè-n), *n.f.*, handsel; *pl.*, new year's gift. *Donner des* —*s à quelqu'un;* to give any one a new year's gift.

étrenner (é-trè-né), *v.a.*, to give a new year's gift, to give a Christmas-box; to handsel. *Il l'a étrenné d'une montre;* he gave him a watch for his new year's gift.

***étrésillon,** *n.m.*, prop, stay.

***étrésillonner,** *v.a.*, to prop, to stay.

étrier, *n.m.*, stirrup; iron-hook; (surg.) stirrup-bandage; strap. *Il est ferme sur ses* —*s;* he is firm in his stirrups. *Vin de l'*—; stirrup-cup. *Il a toujours le pied à l'*—; he is never out of the saddle. *Courir à franc* —; to ride full speed. *Faire perdre les* —*s à quelqu'un;* to put any one out of countenance.

***étrille,** *n.f.*, curry-comb.

***étriller,** *v.a.*, to curry, to comb (a horse— *un cheval*); to fleece; to give a thrashing to.

étriper, *v.a.*, to gut (animal). *Aller à étripe cheval;* to ride a horse furiously.

étriqué, -e. *adj.*, scanty; curtailed. *Habits* —*s;* scanty clothes, coat.

étrivière, *n.f.*, stirrup-leather. *Donner les* —*s à quelqu'un;* to give any one a thrashing.

étroit, -e, *adj.*, narrow, tight, strait, close; intimate. *Habit* —; tight coat. *Esprit* —; narrow mind. *Être dans une* —*e amitié avec quelqu'un;* to be on the most intimate terms with any one. *À l'*—; narrowly. *Être à l'*—; to be pinched, to be poor. *Vivre à l'*—; to live sparingly.

étroitement (é-troat-màn), *adv.*, closely, tightly, narrowly. — *uni;* closely united.

étroitesse, *n.f.*, narrowness; straitness; tightness, closeness.

étronçonner, *v.a.*, to lop off (the heads of trees—*la tête d'un arbre*).

étrusque, *adj.*, Etruscan.

étude, *n.f.*, study; (in colleges—*dans les collèges*) school-room, time of study; (paint.) academical figure; office, chambers, practice (of attorneys—*de gens de loi*); disguise, art, affectation; *pl.*, education. *Cabinet d'*—; study. *Maître d'*—; usher (in colleges—*dans les collèges*). *Avoir de l'*—; to be a man of attainment. *Il me fais une* — *de;* I make it a study to. *Il a fait ses* —*s;* he has finished his education. *Il a fait de bonnes* —*s;* he has had a good education. *Être sans* —; to have no education.

étudiant, *n.m.*, student. — *en droit;* law student. — *en médecine;* medical student.

étudié, -e. *part.*, studied, affected. *Langage* —; studied language. *Tableau fort* —; elaborate piece of painting.

étudier, *v.n.*, to study; to practise (music).

étudier, *v.a.*, to study; to be studious of; to practise (music). — *la nature;* to study nature. — *son rôle;* to study one's part. — *un discours;* to study a speech.

s'étudier, *v.r.*, to study, to make it one's study.

étui, *n.m.*, case, box; sheath, wing-sheath; needle-case. — *de chapeau;* hat-case.

étuve, *n.f.*, sweating-room; (manu.) stove, drying-stove.

étuvée. *n.f.*, stewed meat.

étuvement (é-tuv-màn), *n.m.*, bathing, fomenting (of a wound—*d'une blessure*).

étuver, *v.a.*, to bathe, to foment (a wound— *une blessure*); (cook.) to stew.

⊙**étuviste,** *n.m.*, bath-keeper.

étymologie, *n.f.*, etymology.

étymologique, *adj.*, etymological.

étymologiquement, *adv.*, etymologically.

étymologiser, *v.n.*, to etymologize.

étymologiste, *n.m.*, etymologist.

eubages, *n.m.pl.*, Gaulish Druids.

eucharistie (eu-ka-ris-ti), *n.f.*, Eucharist.

eucharistique, *adj.*, eucharistical.

eucologe, *n.m.*, euchology.

eucrasie, *n.f.*, (med.) eucrasy.

eudiomètre, *n.m.*, eudiometer.

eudiométrie, *n.f.*, eudiometry.

eudiométrique, *adj.*, eudiometric.

eufraise, *n.f.*, (bot.) euphrasy, eyebright.

euh, *int.*, aha! euh! Euh! so, so.

eulogie, *n.f.*, ⊙ (rel.) consecrated bread; *pl.*, (Grec. rel.) broken remnants of the host.

euménide, *n.f.*, (myth.) Fury.

eunuque, *n.m.*, eunuch.

eupatoire, *n.f.*, (bot.) eupatory.

euphémique, *adj.*, euphemistic.

euphémisme, *n.m.*, euphemism.

euphonie, *n.f.*, euphony.

euphonique, *adj.*, euphonical.

euphorbe, *n.m.*, (bot.) euphorbia, spurge; (pharm.) euphorbium.

euphorbiacées, *n.f.pl.*, (bot.) euphorbiaceæ.

européen, -ne (-in, è-n), *n.* and *adj.*, European.

eurythmie, *n.f.*, eurythmy.

eustache, *n.m.*, cheap clasp-knife.

eustyle, *n.m.*, (arch.) eustyle.

eutychéen, *or* **eutychien,** *n.m.*, eutychian.

eux, *pron. m.pl.*, they; them. — -*mêmes;* themselves. *Entre* —; between them.

évacuant, -e, *adj.*, (med.) evacuant.

évacuant, *n.m.*, (med.) evacuant.

évacuatif, -ve, *adj.*, (med., l.u.) evacuant.

évacuation, *n.f.*, evacuation; ejection. *L'*— *d'une place;* the evacuation of a place.

évacuer, *v.a.*, to evacuate; to throw off, to eject, to clear. — *les humeurs;* to evacuate the humours. *Faites* — *la salle;* clear the room. — *une place;* to evacuate a place.

s'évacuer, *v.r.*, to make one's escape, to escape, to break loose. *Les prisonniers se sont évadés;* the prisoners have made their escape.

évagation, *n.f.*, evagation.

évaluable, *adj.*, ratable, that may be set at a certain value.

évaluation, *n.f.*, valuation, estimate. *L'*— *d'une perte;* the estimate of a loss.

évaluer, *v.a.*, to value, to estimate, to rate.

évangélique, *adj.*, evangelical.

évangéliquement (-lik-màn), *adv.*, evangelically.

évangéliser, *v.a.*, to evangelize, to preach the Gospel to. — *les nations;* to evangelize the world.

évangéliser, *v.n.*, to evangelize, to preach the Gospel.

évangéliste, *n.m.*, Evangelist. *Les quatre* —*s;* the four Evangelists.

évangile. *n.m.*, Gospel. *Côté de l'*—; left-hand side of the altar. *Prêcher l'*—; to preach the Gospel. *Il croit cela comme l'*—: he takes that for Gospel. *Prendre tout pour paroles d'*—;

to take all for Gospel. *L'— du jour;* the current news.

s'évanouir, *v.r.*, to faint, to swoon, to swoon away; to vanish, to disappear. *Cette nouvelle l'a fait —;* that news made her swoon.

évanouissement (-noo-is-mān), *n.m.*, swoon, swooning away, fainting fit, syncope. *Revenir d'un —;* to recover from a swoon.

évaporable, *adj.*, evaporable.

évaporati-f, -ve, *adj.*, causing evaporation.

évaporation, *n.f.*, evaporation; giddiness, thoughtlessness.

évaporatoire, *adj.*, evaporating.

évaporé, -e, *n.* and *adj.*, giddy, thoughtless person; evaporate, evaporated; (pers.) giddy, heedless. *Un jeune homme —;* a giddy-brained youth.

évaporer, *v.a.*, to evaporate, to give vent, to pour out in words. *— son chagrin;* to give vent to one's grief.

s'évaporer, *v.r.*, to evaporate; to get giddy, heedless. *Il commence à —;* he begins to be irregular in his conduct.

évasé, *part.*, widened. *Nez —;* nose with wide nostrils.

évasement (-vâz-mān), *n.m.*, width (at the mouth of a vase, &c.—*à l'ouverture d'un vase, &c.*); (arch.) splay.

évaser, *v.a.*, to widen (an opening—*une ouverture*); to spread, to extend; (arch.) to splay. *— un tuyau;* to widen a pipe. *— un arbre;* to extend a tree.

évasi-f, -ve, *adj.*, evasive.

évasion, *n.f.*, escape, flight, elopement.

évasivement, *adv.*, evasively.

évasure, *n.f.*, the splayed opening of a vase; splay.

évêché, *n.m.*, bishopric; episcopate; bishop's house.

évection, *n.f.*, (astron.) evection.

*évoil, *n.m.*, (l.u.) awakening; (fig.) warning, hint, alert. *En —;* on one's guard; on the watch.

éveillé, -e, *adj.*, awake, brisk, lively, sprightly. *Elle est fort —;* she is very gay.

*éveiller, *v.a.*, to awake, to awaken, to wake, to rouse, to animate. *— les soupçons;* to awake suspicion.

*s'éveiller, *v.r.*, to awake, to wake up; to get animated. *Elle s'est éveillée en sursaut;* she awoke with a start.

événement (é-vé-n-mān), *n.m.*, event, occurrence; emergency. *À tout —;* at all events. *En cas d'—;* upon an emergency.

évent, *n.m.*, vapidness, deadness; open air; vent-hole; air-hole; (artil.) windage. *Sentir l'—;* to smell vapid. *Avoir la tête à l'—;* to be thoughtless.

*éventail, *n.m.*, fan. *Fenêtre en —;* fan-light.

*éventailliste, *n.m.*, fan-maker.

éventaire, *n.m.*, flat basket used by women to hawk about fish, fruit, flowers, &c.

éventé, -e, *part.*, fanned; flat, dead; giddy, thoughtless. *Vin —;* dead wine. *Un homme —;* a giddy man.

éventer, *v.a.*, to fan, to winnow (corn—*le blé*); to air; to deaden (liquors—*liqueurs*); to let get flat; to injure by exposure to the air; to discover (mine); to divulge.

s'éventer, *v.r.*, to fan one's self, to evaporate, to pall, to become flat; to be divulged; to get abroad; to take vent.

éventoir, *n.m.*, fire-fan.

éventrer, *v.a.*, to embowel, to disembowel, to eviscerate, to gut (fish—*poisson*); to rip up, to break open; to open (a pie—*un pâté*).

s'éventrer, *v.r.*, to rip open one's bowels.

éventualité, *n.f.*, uncertainty, contingency.

éventuel, -le, *adj.*, eventual, contingent. uncertain.

éventuel, *n.m.*, grant, capitation-fee accorded to professors of French public schools and universities.

éventuellement (-tuèl-mān), *adv.*, eventually, contingently.

évêque, *n.m.*, bishop. *— in partibus;* bishop in partibus. *Devenir d'— meunier;* to descend from peer to peasant.

éversion, *n.f.*, eversion, overthrow.

s'évertuer, *v.r.*, to struggle, to strive, to exert one's self. *Je m'évertue à le faire;* I do all I can to accomplish it.

évhémérisme, *n.m.*, Evemerus's system of interpreting mythology.

éviction, *n.f.*, (jur.) ejection. ejectment.

évidement, *n.m.*, scooping out, hollowing; groove, hollow.

évidemment (-da-mān), *adv.*, evidently, obviously.

évidence, *n.f.*, evidence, obviousness. *Mettre en —;* to make evident. *Être en —;* to be conspicuous.

évident, -e, *adj.*, evident, plain, clear, obvious, ostensive.

évider, *v.a.*, to hollow, to groove, to scoop out; to unstarch.

évidoir, *n.m.*, tool (for hollowing wind instruments—*pour évider les instruments à vent*).

évidure, *n.f.*, (tech.) hollowing, sloping.

évier, *n.m.*, sink.

évincer, *v.a.*, to evict, to eject; to oust. *Il a été évincé;* he was turned out.

évitable, *adj.*, avoidable; evitable.

évitage, *n.m.*, (nav.) swinging; swinging-room.

évitée, *n.f.*, (nav.) swinging; berth, swinging-room. *Le vaisseau fait son —;* the ship is swinging. *Avoir son —;* to have a wide berth (of a ship—*d'un vaisseau*).

évitement (é-vit-mān), *n.m.*, (railways) siding, shunting. *Gare, voie, d'—;* shunting-line.

éviter, *v.a.*, to shun, to avoid, to evade. *Une chose qui ne peut pas être évitée;* an unavoidable thing. *— les périls;* to avoid dangers. *— les mauvaises compagnies;* to shun bad company. *On ne peut — sa destinée;* there is no avoiding one's destiny.

s'éviter, *v.r.*, to avoid each other; to spare one's self.

éviter, *v.n.*, (nav.) to swing. *— au vent;* to stem the wind. *— à la marée;* to stem the tide.

évocable, *adj.*, (jur.) that can be evoked.

évocation, *n.f.*, evocation, raising up (of spirits—*d'esprits*).

évocatoire, *adj.*, (jur.) that can cause evocation.

évoluer, *v.n.*, (nav., milit.) (l.u.) to perform evolutions.

évolution, *n.f.*, evolution.

évolutionnaire, *adj.*, (milit., nav.) relating to evolutions.

évoquer, *v.a.*, to evoke, to raise up, to conjure up; to call up. *— à un tribunal supérieur;* (jur.) to appeal to a superior court.

évulsion, *n.f.*, (tech.) evulsion.

ex (èks), (prefix) ex.

ex abrupto, *adv.*, suddenly, unexpectedly.

exacerbation, *n.f.*, (med.) exacerbation.

exact, -e (èg-zakt), *adj.*, exact, accurate, correct, precise, punctual; close. *— e analyse;* close analysis. *Les sciences —es;* the exact sciences. *— à;* exact in. *Homme — à tenir sa parole;* man exact in keeping his word.

exactement, *adv.*, exactly, punctually, accurately.

exacteur, *n.m.*, exactor.

exaction, *n.f.*, exaction, extortion.

exactitude, *n.f.*, exactness, punctuality, exactitude; correctness, accuracy, precision, closeness. *Agir avec —;* to be punctual.

exaèdre. *n.m.* and *adj. V.* **hexaèdre**.

exagérat-eur, *n.m.*, **-rice**, *n.f.*, exaggerator.

exagérati-f, -ve, *adj.*, exaggeratory.

exagération. *n.f.*, exaggeration.

exagérer, *v.a.*, to exaggerate, to magnify.

exagone, *n.m.* and *adj. V.* **hexagone**.

exaltation, *n.f.*, exaltation, exalting.

exalté, -e, *n.* and *part.*, enthusiast; person over-excited; exalted, elated; over-excited; heated, feverish.

exalter, *v.a.*, to exalt, to extol, to magnify, to glorify, to cry up; to excite, to elate; to over-excite; (chem.) to exalt, to purify.

s'exalter. *v r.*, to become excited, elated, to rise to a high pitch; to be over-excited; to extol, to magnify, to cry up one another.

examen (-min), *n.m.*, examination, investigation, survey. — *préliminaire* (of universities—*d'universités*); little-go. *Jury d'—:* board of examiners. *Faire l'— d'un livre;* to examine a book. *Après mûr —;* after mature examination. — *de conscience;* self-examination. *Se préparer à un —;* to prepare for an examination.

examinat-eur, *n.m.*, **-rice**, *n.f.*, one who examines, examiner. — *supérieur pour les mathématiques* (universities—*des universités*); moderator.

examiné, -e. *part*, examined.

examiner, *v.a.*, to examine, to inquire into, to inspect, to survey, to look at; to weigh, to discuss, to consider, to explore. — *à fond;* to examine thoroughly. — *rapidement;* to examine rapidly, to run over.

s'examiner, *v.r.*, to examine, to search one's self; to examine one's own conscience; to examine, to observe, one another attentively. — *à fond sur une affaire;* thoroughly to examine one's self upon a subject.

exanthémateu-x, -se, *adj.*, (med.) exanthematous.

exanthématique, *adj.*, (med.) exanthematous.

exanthème. *n.m.*, (med.) exanthema.

exarchat (-ka), *n.m.*, exarchate.

exarque. *n.m.*, exarch.

exaspérant, -e, *adj.*, exasperating.

exaspération, *n.f.*, exasperation.

exaspéré, -e, *part.*, exasperated, enraged, incensed.

exaspérer, *v.a.*, to exasperate, to enrage, to incense.

s'exaspérer, *v.r.*, to become, to get, to grow exasperated, enraged, incensed.

exaucement(ég-zôs-mán), *n.m.*, (of prayers, vows—*de prières, de vœux*) granting, hearing.

exaucer, *v.a.*, to hearken to, to hear favourably; to grant. *Dieu exauce les prières des humbles;* God gives ear to the prayers of the humble.

excavation, *n.f.*, excavation, excavating.

excaver. *v.a.*, to excavate, to hollow.

excédant, -e, *adj.*, exceeding; tiresome, unbearable.

excédent, *n.m.*, overplus; surplus; over-weight; (arith.) excess.

excéder, *v.a.*, to exceed, to go beyond; to wear out, to tire out. *Il a excédé son pouvoir;* he has exceeded his power. — *quelqu'un de coups;* to beat and bruise any one unmercifully.

s'excéder, *v.r.*, to be worn out; to wear out; to weary, to tire, one's self out. — *de débauches;* to wear one's self out with debauchery. — *de travail;* to over-work one's self; to work too hard.

excellemment (èk-sè-la-mán), *adv.*, excellently.

excellence, *n.f.*, excellence, excellency. *Par —;* pre-eminently, above all. *Votre —;* your Excellence. *Donner de l'—;* (fam.) to call any one Excellence.

excellent. -e, *adj.*, excellent.

excellentissime, *adj.*, most excellent.

exceller, *v.n.*, to excel, to be eminent, to transcend, to be transcendant. *Il excelle en poésie;* he excels in poetry.

excentricité, *n.f.*, eccentricity.

excentrique. *adj.*, eccentric. *Cercles —s;* (geom.) eccentric.

excentrique, *n.m.*, (mec.) eccentric-wheel.

excepté, *prep.*, except, excepting, save, but. — *que;* except that.

excepter, *v.a.*, to except.

exception, *n.f.*, exception; (jur.) exception; (jur.) plea; (jur.) bar. — *déclinatoire* (jur.); plea to the jurisdiction. — *péremptoire* (jur.); demurrer. — *d'incompétence* (jur.); foreign plea. — *tirée de l'aveu, des actes de la partie;* estoppel. *À l'— de;* with the exception of, except, excepting.

exceptionnel, -le, *adj.*, containing an exception, exceptional.

excès, *n.m.*, excess, immoderation, waste; intemperance, riot, debauchery; (jur.) ill-usage, outrage, violence; (geom., arith.) excess. *Les — de la jeunesse;* the excesses of youth. *À l'—, avec —, jusqu'à l'—;* to excess, excessively, immoderately. *Faire un —;* to commit an excess, to be guilty of an excess.

excessi-f, -ve, *adj.*, excessive, extravagant, exorbitant.

excessivement (-siv-mán), *adv.*, excessively, to excess.

exciper, *v.n.*, (jur.) to allege an exception.

excipient, *n.m.*, (pharm.) excipient.

excise, *n.f.*, excise; excise-office. *L'— est, en Angleterre, ce que les contributions indirectes sont en France;* the excise in England is the same thing as the *contributions indirectes* in France.

exciser, *v.a.*, (surg.) to amputate, to cut off.

excision, *n.f.*, (surg.) excision.

excitabilité, *n.f.*, excitability.

excitable, *adj.*, excitable.

excitant, -e, *adj.*, (med.) exciting.

excitant, *n.m.*, (med.) excitant.

excitat-eur, *n.m.*, **-rice**, *n.f.*, exciter.

excitati-f, -ve, *adj.*, excitative.

excitation, *n.f.*, exciting, excitation, excitement. — *à la haine et au mépris du gouvernement* (jur.); contempt against the government.

excitement (èk-sit-mán), *n.m.*, (med.) excitement.

exciter, *v.a.*, to excite, to provoke, to stir up, to cause, to inspire, to arouse, to rouse; to urge, to stimulate, to encourage, to inspirit, to animate, to quicken, to instigate, to prompt, to spur; to inflame, to irritate. — *les soldats à combattre;* to excite the troops to fight. — *la pitié;* to excite pity. — *un chien contre quelqu'un;* to set a dog at any one.

s'exciter, *v.r.*, to excite, to animate, to encourage one's self; to animate, to encourage one another.

exclamati-f, -ve, *adj.*, (gram.) of exclamation. *Point —;* note of exclamation.

exclamation, *n.f.*, exclamation. *Point d'—;* note of exclamation.

s'exclamer, *v.r.*, to exclaim, to cry out.

exclure, *v.a.*, to exclude, to debar, to shut out, to keep from, to bar, to leave out.

exclusi-f, -ve, *adj.*, exclusive.

exclusion, *n.f.*, exclusion.

exclusivement (-ziv-mán), *adv.*, exclusively.

excommunication, n.f., excommunication.

excommunié, n.m., **-e**, n.f., excommunicate. *Avoir un visage d'—;* to look pale and wretched.

excommunier, v.a., to excommunicate.

excoriation, n.f., (surg.) excoriation.

excorier, v.a., (surg.) to excoriate.

excrément, n.m., excrement. *— de la terre;* dregs of mankind, scum of the earth.

excrémenteu-x -se, or **excrémentiel, -le**, or **excrémentitiel, -le**, adj., excrementitious, excremental, excrementitial.

excrét-eur, or **excrétoire**, adj. m., (physiology) excretory, excretive.

excrétion, n.f., (physiology) excretion.

excroissance, n.f., excrescence, excrescency.

excursion, n.f., excursion, inroad; digression, rambling; trip. *En —;* on an excursion. *Faire une —;* to make an excursion, to take a trip.

excusable, adj., excusable, pardonable, venial; (jur.) by misadventure (homicide).

⊙**excusation**, n.f., (jur.) excusation, plea.

excuse, n.f., excuse, apology; (jur.) plea, excusation. *Faire des —s;* to make an apology. *Je vous fais —;* I beg your pardon.

excuser, v.a., to excuse, to exculpate, to pardon; to bear with; to apologize for. *Il l'a excusé auprès du roi;* he has apologized for him to the king. *On doit — les fautes de la jeunesse;* one ought to bear with the faults of youth.

s'excuser, v.r., to excuse, to exculpate one's self; to throw the blame on; to decline; to apologize, to make an apology. *Le capitaine s'est excusé sur son lieutenant;* the captain cast the blame upon his lieutenant. *— de faire une chose;* to decline doing a thing.

exeat (èg-zé-at), n.m., pass, leave (to go out of one diocese into another—*pour passer d'un diocèse dans un autre). Donner à quelqu'un son —;* to send off, to discard, to dismiss, any one. *Donner un —;* to give one leave to go out (in colleges—*dans les collèges*).

exécrable, adj., execrable.

exécrablement, adv., execrably.

exécration, n.f., execration. *Il est en — à tout le monde;* he is held in abhorrence by every body.

exécratoire, adj., execratory.

exécrer, v.a., to execrate, to hold in execration.

exécutable, adj., feasible, practicable.

exécutant, n.m., (mus.) performer, player.

exécuter, v.a., to execute, to perform; to accomplish, to achieve, to fulfil; (jur.) to distrain; (jur.) to serve; to put to death. *J'exécuterai ce que j'ai promis;* I shall perform what I promised. *— un arrêt;* to execute a sentence.

s'exécuter, v.r., to be performed, to be done, to take place; to sell off (one's property for the benefit of creditors—*ses biens au profit des créanciers*); to sacrifice one's self; to yield, to comply.

exécut-eur, n.m., **-rice**, n.f., executor, executrix; executioner, hangman. *— testamentaire;* executor, executrix. *Livrer à l'—;* to deliver over to the executioner.

exécuti-f. -ve, adj., executive.

exécution, n.f., execution, accomplishment, performance, achievement, fulfilment. *Mettre des ordres à —;* to put orders into execution. *L'— de ce travail ne répond pas au plan;* the execution of this work does not come up to the plan. *L'— d'un morceau de musique;* the performance of a piece of music. *Homme d'—;* resolute man. *Ordre d'—;* (of a criminal—*d'un criminel*) death-warrant, warrant for execution. *Procéder à l'—;* to do execution on criminals.

exécutoire, n.m. and adj., (jur.) writ of execution; executory.

exèdre, n.m., (arch.) exedra.

exégèse, n.f., exegesis.

exégétique, adj., exegetical.

exemplaire, adj., exemplary.

exemplaire, n.m., model, pattern; copy (of printed books, engravings, &c.—*de livres, de gravures, &c.). J'ai trois —s de ce livre-là;* I have three copies of that book. *J'ai un bel — de cette médaille;* I have a fine copy of that medal.

exemplairement (-plèr-mān), adv., exemplarily.

exemple, n.m., example, pattern; precedent, instance; copy, copy-slip; copy (imitation of the copy—*imitation de l'exemple). Proposer un —;* to offer an example. *Ne vous réglez pas sur son —;* do not take a pattern from him. *Faire un — de quelqu'un;* to make an example of any one. *Prendre — sur quelqu'un;* to take example from any one. *Il n'y en a point d'—;* there is no precedent for it, there is no example of such a thing. *Donnez-m'en un —;* give me an instance. *Citer un —;* to quote an instance. *Un dictionnaire sans —s est un squelette;* a dictionary without examples is a skeleton. *À l'— de;* in imitation of. *Par —;* for instance, for example; indeed! bless me! upon my word! upon my honour! *Par —, voilà qui est fort!* upon my honour, that is rather too good a joke! *Sans —;* extraordinary, unexampled, unparalleled.

exempt, -e (èg-zān, -t), adj., exempt, exempted, free from.

exempt, n.m., ecclesiastic exempted from the jurisdiction of the ordinary; ⊙officer commanding in the absence of the captain and lieutenants. *— de police;* police officer.

exempter (èg-zan-té), v.a., to exempt, to free; to dispense, to excuse.

s'exempter, v.r., to exempt one's self from, to dispense with.

exemption (èg-zānp-sion), n.f., exemption, immunity; dispensation. *Lettre d'— des droits de douane;* (com.) bill of sufferance.

exequatur (-koua-), n.m. (—), exequatur.

exercer, v.a., to exercise, to train up; to perform, to practise, to exert; to follow, to carry on (a trade—*un métier, &c.*); (milit.) to drill. *— des soldats;* to drill soldiers. *— sa mémoire;* to exercise one's memory. *— la patience de quelqu'un;* to try any one's patience. *— l'hospitalité;* to be hospitable. *— la médecine;* to practise medicine.

s'exercer, v.r., to exercise, to practise; to exercise, to train, one's self; to exert one's self.

exercer, v.n., to practise; to visit (manufacturers and others who sell excisable articles —*ceux qui vendent des articles sujets aux droits d'octroi*). *Avocat qui n'exerce plus;* retired barrister.

exercice, n.m., exercise, practice, use; work, labour, trouble, fatigue; inspection (of an officer of the indirect taxes—*des commis des droits réunis*); (administration) receipts and expenditure during a certain time; (milit.) drill; drilling. *Entrer en —;* to commence one's functions. *Sortir d'—;* to finish one's term of service. *L'— d'une profession;* the exercise of a profession. *Faire l'—;* to exercise. *Faire faire l'— à des soldats;* to drill, to train, soldiers. *Prendre de l'—;* to take exercise. *Se tenir en —;* to keep one's self in practice. *— à feu;* rifle, carbine exercise. *— de piété;* practice of piety.

exérèse, n.f., (surg.) extraction, amputation, cutting off.

exergue (èg-zèrg), n.m., exergue.

8*

exfoliati-f, -ve, *adj.*, (surg., pharm.) exfoliative.

exfoliation, *n.f.*, (surg.) exfoliation.

s'exfolier, *v.r.*, to exfoliate.

exhalaison, *n.f.*, exhalation, effluvium.

exhalant, *n.m.* and *adj.*, (anat.) exhaling vessel ; exhaling.

exhalation, *n.f.*, exhalation.

exhaler, *v.a.*, to send forth, to exhale ; to breathe ; to vent ; to emit. *Ces fleurs exhalent une douce odeur;* these flowers emit a sweet smell. *— sa colère;* to vent one's anger.

s'exhaler, *v.r.*, to be emitted, to be exhaled ; to give vent to, to indulge in. *— en plaintes, en menaces;* to give vent to one's complaints, to indulge in threats.

exhaussement (ĕg-zōs-mǎn), *n.m.*, (arch.) height ; raising up, making higher.

exhausser, *v.a.*, (arch.) to raise, to raise up, to run up, to make higher.

exhérédation, *n.f.*, (jur.) disinheriting, exheredation, disinheritance.

exhéréder, *v.a.*, (jur.) to exheredate, to disinherit.

exhiber, *v.a.*, to exhibit, to produce, to show. *— ses papiers, son passeport;* to produce one's papers, one's passport.

exhibition, *n.f.*, (jur.) exhibition, producing, exhibiting. *— publique;* public exhibition.

exhilarant, -e, *adj.*, exhilarating.

exhortati-f, -ve, *adj.*, exhortative.

exhortation, *n.f.*, exhortation.

exhortatoire, *adj.*, exhortatory.

exhorter, *v.a.*, to exhort. *— à la paix;* to exhort to peace.

exhumation, *n.f.*, exhumation, disinterment.

exhumer, *v.a.*, to exhume, to dig out of the ground ; to disinter ; to bring to light.

exigeant, -e, (-jän, -t), *adj.*, unreasonable, particular, exacting too much ; troublesome, hard to please.

exigence, *n.f.*, unreasonableness ; claim, demand ; exigency, exigence (that which circumstances require—*des circonstances). Selon l'— du cas;* as occasion shall require.

exiger, *v.a.*, to exact, to require, to demand. *— des égards;* to require respect. *— le payement d'une dette;* to exact the payment of a debt.

exigibilité, *n.f.*, the quality of being exigible.

exigible, *adj.*, exigible, demandable.

exigu, -ë, *adj.*, scanty, slender, slight, petty, small. *Repas —;* scanty repast.

exiguïté, *n.f.*, scantiness, slenderness, slightness, smallness.

exil, *n.m.*, exile, banishment. *Envoyer en —;* to banish.

exilé, *n.m.*, **-e**, *n.f.*, exile.

exiler, *v.a.*, to exile, to banish.

s'exiler, *v.r.*, to exile one's self ; to withdraw, to seclude, one's self. *Il s'est exilé du monde;* he has withdrawn himself from the world.

⊙exilité, *n.f.*, smallness, slightness.

existant, -e, *adj.*, existing, in being, existent, extant.

existence, *n.f.*, existence, being: *Mettre un terme à son —;* to put an end to one's existence.

exister, *v.n.*, to exist ; to be in existence, to live ; to be extant. *Cette dette n'existe plus;* this debt is extinct. *Les ouvrages qui existent;* the works which are extant.

exocet, *n.m.*, (ich.) exococtus, flying fish.

exode, *n.m.*, Exodus; exode.

exomphale, *n.f.*, (surg.) exomphalus.

exonération, *n.f.*, exoneration.

exonérer, *v.a.*, to exonerate, to unload, to free from.

exophtalmie, *n.f.*, exophthalmia.

exophtalmique, *adj.*, exophthalmic.

exorable, *adj.*, exorable.

exorbitamment (-ta-mǎn), *adv.*, exorbitantly, excessively, extravagantly.

exorbitant, -e, *adj.*, extravagant, exorbitant, excessive. *Dépense —e;* extravagant expense.

exorciser, *v.a.*, to exorcise, to conjure ; to exhort, to urge.

exorcisme, *n.m.*, exorcism.

exorciste, *n.m.*, exorcist, exorciser.

exorde, *n.m.*, exordium.

exosmose, *n.f.*, (phys.) exosmose, exosmosis.

exostose, *n.f.*, (med., bot.) exostosis.

s'exostoser, *v.r.*, (surg.) to form an exostosis.

exotérique, *adj.*, exoteric.

exotique, *adj.*, exotic.

expansibilité, *n.f.*, expansibility.

expansible, *adj.*, expansible, expansive.

expansi-f, -ve, *adj.*, expansive; unreserved, open-hearted. *Une âme —ve;* an overflowing heart.

expansion, *n.f.*, expansion. *Avoir de l'—;* to be open, unreserved, communicative.

expatriation, *n.f.*, expatriation.

expatrier, *v.a.*, to expatriate.

s'expatrier, *v.r.*, to expatriate one's self.

expectant, -e, *adj.*, expectant.

expectant, *n.m.*, expectant.

expectati-f, -ve, *adj.*, expectant.

expectative, *n.f.*, expectation, hopes, prospect ; (jur.) expectancy. *Il est dans l'—;* he is in expectation. *Avoir l'— de quelque chose;* to have the expectation of any thing.

expectorant, -e, *adj.*, expectorant.

expectorant, *n.m.*, expectorant.

expectoration, *n.f.*, expectoration ; sputa.

expectorer, *v.a.*, to expectorate.

expédient, *n.m.*, expedient; shift ; ⊙(jur.) compromise. *Homme d'—;* man for an expedient. *En être aux —s;* to be reduced to expedients. *Son dernier —;* one's last shift.

expédient, *adj.m.*, expedient, fit, meet, proper, advisable.

expédier, *v.a.*, to despatch, to perform, to send off ; to forward; to clear (at the custom-house—*à la douane*) ; to draw up. *— des marchandises;* to forward goods. *— un acte;* to draw up a deed.

expéditeur, *n.m.*, sender ; (nav.) shipper.

expéditi-f, -ve, *adj.*, expeditious, quick

expédition, *n.f.*, expedition, despatch; sending, shipment ; copy (of a deed—*d'un titre*) ; clearance (at the custom-house—*à la douane*) ; *pl.*, despatches. *Faire l'— de;* (com.) to forward. *Le courrier attend ses —s;* the courier is waiting for his despatches. *Homme d'—;* man quick in business. *L'— d'Égypte;* the expedition to Egypt.

expéditionnaire, *adj.*, expeditionary.

expéditionnaire, *n.m.*, sender ; copying-clerk.

expérience, *n.f.*, experience ; trial, experiment. *Faire une —;* to make an experiment. *Des —s de chimie;* experiments in chemistry. *Je sais cela par —;* I know that by experience. *Parler par —;* to speak from experience.

expérimental, -e, *adj.*, experimental.

expérimentateur, *n.m.*, experimentalist.

expérimenté, -e, *adj.*, experienced.

expérimenter, *v.a.*, to experiment, to try by use, to experience.

expert, -e, *adj.*, expert.

expert, *n.m.*, appraiser; surveyor; expert.

expertement, *adv.*, expertly.

expertise, *n.f.*, survey (of specially-appointed surveyors—*d'experts nommés exprès*); report, appraisement. *Faire une* —; to make a survey.

expertiser, *v.a.*, to make a survey.

expiation. *n.f.*, expiation, atonement. *En* — *de;* as an atonement for. *Faire* — *de;* to make an atonement for.

expiatoire, *adj.*, expiatory. *Sacrifice* —; sin-offering.

expier. *v.a.*, to expiate, to atone for; to pay (for a deed—*une mauvaise action*).

expirant, *-e*, *adj.*, expiring.

expirateur, *adj.m.*, (anat.) expiratory.

expiration, *n.f.*, expiration.

expirer, *v.n.*, to expire; to breathe one's last; to die away; to come to an end. *Mon bail a expiré hier;* my lease was out yesterday.

expirer, *v.a.*, to breathe out; to exhale, to expire.

expléti-f, *-ve*, *adj.*, (gram.) expletive.

explétif, *n.m.*, (gram.) expletive.

explicable, *adj.*, explicable, explainable.

explicateur, *n.m.*, explainer, cicerone.

explicati-f, *-ve*, *adj.*, explicative, explaratory.

explication, *n.f.*, explanation, explication, interpretation. *Avoir une* — *avec;* to have an explanation with. *L'* — *des phénomènes de la nature;* the explanation of the phenomena of nature. *Cela demande* —; that requires an explanation.

explicite, *adj.*, explicit.

explicitement (-cit-màn), *adv.*, explicitly.

expliquer, *v.a.*, to explain, to express, to declare, to teach, to expound; to construe, to illustrate. *Expliquez-moi ce que cela signifie;* explain to me what that means. — *une énigme;* to solve a riddle. — *une doctrine;* to expound a doctrine.

s'expliquer, *v.r.*, to explain one's self; to have an explanation; to be explained.

exploit, *n.m.*, exploit, achievement, feat, deed; (jur.) writ. *Signifier un* —; to serve a writ.

exploitable, *adj.*, that may be worked, that may be cultivated, that may be turned to account; improvable; (jur.) distrainable. *Cette mine est encore* —; that mine may still be worked.

exploitant, *adj.m.*, (jur.) acting, serving writs.

exploitation, *n.f.*, working; improving (lands—*les terres*); cultivation (of wood—*des bois*); employing, using. — *d'un champ* (agri.); cultivation of a field. — *par compartiments* (mining—*mines*); panel-work. — *par grande taille* (mining—*mines*); long work. *Champ d'* —; working-place. *Matériel d'* —; working-stock. *En* —; being worked; in activity. *Mettre en* —; to work.

exploiter, *v.a.*, to work; to improve; to cultivate for sale; to win (mining—*mines*); to use; to make the most of. — *une mine;* to work a mine. — *un bois;* to cultivate a wood for sale. — *une place;* to make the most of a situation. — *la curiosité publique;* to speculate upon public curiosity.

⊙**exploiter**, *v.n.*, to serve writs.

exploiteur, *n.m.*, (b.s.) person who takes advantage of others—*d'autrui*), who works, who uses (others—*les autres*); achiever of feats.

explorateur. *n.m.*, explorer.

explorat-eur, *-rice*, *adj.*, exploratory.

exploration, *n.f.*, exploration.

explorer, *v.a.*, to explore.

explosible. *adj.*, explosive.

explosi-f, *-ve*, *adj.*, explosive.

explosion, *n.f.*, explosion; bursting, blowing up.

exponentiel, *-le*, *adj.*, (alg.) exponential.

exportateur, *n.m.*, exporter.

exportation, *n.f.*, exportation.

exporter, *v.a.*, to export.

exposant, *n.m.*, *-e*, *n.f.*. petitioner: exhibitor; (math.) exponent. index.

exposé, *n.m.*. statement; account, outline; (jur.) recital. *Faire un* —; to draw up a statement.

exposer, *v.a.*, to expose, to expose to view, to show, to exhibit; to endanger, to hazard, to venture, to render liable, to make liable, to lay open; to state, to set forth; to expound, to explain. — *en vente;* to expose for sale. — *sa vie;* to venture one's life. — *ses sentiments;* to state one's sentiments. — *un système;* to unfold a system. — *un corps mort sur un lit de parade;* to lay out a dead body in state.

s'exposer, *v.r.*, to expose one's self; to be exposed, to be liable, to lay one's self open, to lie open. *Il s'expose à la risée de tout le monde;* he makes himself the laughing-stock of everybody.

exposeur, *v.a.* and *n.*, to explain; to exhibit. *Je ne connais personne qui expose mieux;* I know no one who can explain a thing better. *Ce peintre n'a pas encore exposé;* that painter has not yet exhibited.

exposition, *n.f.*, exhibition, exposing; exposure; lying-in-state (of dead bodies—*d'un corps mort*); situation, aspect, statement, explanation. *La grande* —; the Great Exhibition. *Maison dans une* — *agréable;* house with an agreeable aspect. *Faire une fidèle* — *de toutes ses raisons;* to give a faithful account of all one's reasons.

exprès, *-se*, *adj.*, express, positive. *La loi est* — *se sur ce point;* the law is positive on that point.

exprès, *n.m.*, express (messenger—*messager*).

exprès, *adv.*, expressly, purposely, on purpose. *Il semble fait* — *pour cela;* he seems to be cut out for it.

express, *n.m.* and *adj.*, (railways) express, express train. *Le train* —; the express train.

expressément, *adv.*, expressly.

expressi-f, *-ve*, *adj.*, expressive.

expression, *n.f.*, expression, expressiveness. *L'* — *de la joie;* the expression of joy. *Son regard est plein d'* —; his look is full of expression. — *imaginaire;* (alg.) imaginary, impossible, binomial. *La plus simple* —; (math.) the lowest terms. *Réduire à la plus simple* —; to reduce to the lowest terms.

exprimable, *adj.*, expressible.

exprimer, *v.a.*, to express, to press out, to squeeze out; to be expressive of; to declare, to utter, to tell; to word. — *le suc d'une plante;* to squeeze the juice out of a plant.

s'exprimer, *v.r.*, to express one's self; to be expressed. — *par la physionomie;* to be expressed by the physiognomy.

ex professo, *adv.*, ex professo.

expropriation, *n.f.*, (jur.) dispossession. — *forcée;* appropriation. *Jury d'*—(jur.); valuation jury.

exproprier, *v.a.*, (jur.) to take possession of the landed property of a debtor, to dispossess; to appropriate.

expulser. *v.a.*, to expel, to thrust out, to turn out, to eject; to put out.

expulsi-f, *-ve*, *adj.*, (med.) expulsive.

expulsion, *n.f.*, expulsion, extrusion; (jur.) ejection; ejectment.

expurgatoire, *adj.*, expurgatory. *Index* —; expurgatory index.

expurger, *v.a.*, to expurgate.

exquis, *-e*, *adj.*, exquisite. *Vin* —; delicious wine. *Avoir un goût* —; to have an exquisite taste.

exquisement (-kìz-mān), *adv.*, exquisitely.

exsangue, *adj.*, bloodless, anæmic; that has lost much blood.

exsiccation, *n.f.*, (chem.) exsiccation.

exsuccion, *n.f.*, exsuction.

exsudation, *n.f.*, exsudation, exudation.

exsuder, *v.n.*, to exude. to perspire.

c **extant**, **-e**, *adj.*, (jur.) existing.

extase, *n.f.*, ecstacy, trance; rapture. *Ravir en —:* to transport to ecstacy. *Être ravi en —;* to go into rapture. *Tomber en —;* to fall into a trance.

s'extasier, *v.r.*, to be enraptured, to be in rapture; to be in ecstacy.

extatique, *adj.*, ecstatic, rapturous.

extenseur, *n.m.* and *adj.*, (anat.) extensor.

extensibilité, *n.f.*, extensibility.

extensible, *adj.*, extensible, tensible; tensile.

extensi-f, **-ve**, *adj.*, extending, expanding.

extension, *n.f.*, extension; tension; extent. *in* **extenso**, *adv.* *V.* **in extenso**.

exténuation, *n.f.*, extenuation, feebleness, debility.

exténuer, *v.a.*, to extenuate, to enfeeble, to weaken, to debilitate. *Sa maladie l'a fort exténué;* his illness has weakened him very much.

extérieur, **-e**, *adj.*, exterior, external, outward; foreign.

extérieur, *n.m.*, exterior, outside; foreign countries, abroad. *Les nouvelles de l'—;* news from abroad. *À l'intérieur et à l'—;* at home and abroad.

extérieurement (-eur-mān), *adv.*, externally, outwardly.

exterminat-eur, **-rice**, *n.* and *adj.*, destroyer, exterminator; exterminating, destroying.

exterminati-f, **-ve**, *adj.*, exterminating.

extermination, *n.f.*, extermination.

exterminer, *v.a.*, to exterminate, to destroy.

externat, *n.m.*, day-school.

externe, *adj.*, external, exterior, outward, outdoor.

externe, *n.m.*, day-scholar; (of hospitals—*des hopitaux*) dresser.

extinction, *n.f.*, extinction, extinguishment; destruction, abolition; redemption (of annuities—*d'annuités, de rentes viagères*); liquidation, settlement (of debts—*de dettes*); quelling, suppression (of disturbances—*d'émeutes*); extermination; quenching; slacking (of lime—*de la chaux*). — *des racines*; (alg., arith.) evolution. — *de voix*; loss of voice. *A l'— des feux, des bougies*; (at auctions—*aux enchères*) by inch of candle. *Jusqu'à —, jusqu'à — de chaleur naturelle*; till one is exhausted.

extirpateur, *n.m.*, extirpator, destroyer; (agri.) weeder; weeding-tool, spud.

extirpation, *n.f.*, excision, extirpation; uprooting, destruction, weeding up.

extirper, *v.a.*, to extirpate, to root out, to pull up, to exterminate, to cut off. — *un cancer*; to cut out a cancer.

extorquer, *v.a.*, to extort, to wrest, to worm out of.

extorsion, *n.f.*, extortion.

extra, *n.m.* (—), extra, something extra. *C'était ma fête et nous avons fait un —, un peu d'—;* it was my birthday, so we had something extra, something a little extra. *Plat d'—;* extra dish.

extractif, *n.m.*, (chem.) extractive, extract.

extracti-f, **-ve**, *adj.*, extractive.

extraction, *n.f.*, extraction; origin, descent, lineage. *L'— d'une dent;* the drawing of a tooth.

extradition, *n.f.*, extradition.

extrados, *n.m.*, (arch.) extrados.

extradossé, **-e**, *adj.*, (arch.) extra-dossed.

extraire (extrayant, extrait), *v.a.*, to extract, to draw, to take out; to make extracts from; to take a prisoner from one prison to another, or before a magistrate. — *un livre*; to make an abridgment of a book.

extrait, *n.m.*, substance extracted, extract; epitome; spirit; abstract. — *de naissance, de baptême, de mariage*; certificate of birth, baptism, marriage. — *mortuaire*; certificate of death. — *authentique*; certified copy of a document.

extrajudiciaire, *adj.*, extrajudicial.

extrajudiciairement, *adv.*, extrajudicially.

extra-muros (-rôs), *adv.*, out of the walls of a city, assembly, &c., off the stones (of London—*de Londres*).

extraordinaire, *adj.*, extraordinary, unusual. *Il n'y a rien d'— à cela;* there is nothing extraordinary in that. *Question —;* rack (torture). *Visage —;* odd face.

extraordinaire, *n.m.*, extraordinariness, extraordinary thing, uncommon thing.

extraordinairement (-nèr-mān), *adv.*, extraordinarily, unusually; oddly. *Procéder contre quelqu'un;* (jur.) to prosecute any one criminally.

extrapassé, **-e**, *part.*, (paint.) beyond natural limits. *V.* **strapassé**.

extrapasser, *v.a.*, (paint.). *V.* **strapasser**.

extravagamment (-ga-mān), *adv.*, extravagantly, unreasonably.

extravagance, *n.f.*, extravagance, folly, wildness; mad action. *J'ai pitié de son —; I pity his folly. Il a dit mille —s;* he said a thousand extravagant things.

extravagant, **-e**, *n.* and *adj.*, extravagant, wild person; extravagant, wild. *C'est un —;* he is a mad fellow.

extravagante, *n.f.*, (c.rel.) extravagant, papal constitution. *Les —s;* decretal epistles of the pope.

extravaguer (-ghé), *v.n.*, to talk idly, to rave, to talk like a madman.

extravasation, *or* **extravasion**, *n.f.*, (med.) extravasation.

extravasé, **-e**, *adj.*, extravasated. *Sang —;* extravasated blood.

s'extravaser, *v.r.*, to be extravasated.

extrême, *adj.*, extreme, utmost, excessive.

extrême, *n.m.*, extreme, utmost, point *Jusqu'à l'—, à l'—;* to an extreme. *Il se jette dans les —s*, he runs into extremes. *Les —s se touchent;* extremes meet.

extrêmement (èks-trêm-mān), *adv.*, extremely.

extrême-onction, *n.f.* (n.p.), (c.rel.) extreme unction.

in **extremis** (i-nèks-tré-mìs), *adv.*, (jur.) at the point of death.

extrémité, *n.f.*, extremity, extreme; excess, last moment. *A l'—;* to extremity, at a push; dying. *Passer d'une — à l'autre;* to pass from one extreme to another. *Pousser à la dernière —;* to drive to extremity.

extrinsèque, *adj.*, extrinsical. *Valeur — des monnaies;* value assigned to coins independently of their actual weight.

exubérance, *n.f.*, exuberance.

exubérant, **-e**, *adj.*, exuberant.

exulcérati-f, **-ve**, *adj.*, (med.) producing ulcers.

exulcération, *n.f.*, (med.) exulceration.

exulcérer, *v.a.*, (med.) to exulcerate.

exutoire, *n.m.*, (med.) issue.

ex-voto, *n.m.* (—). votive offering.

f. *n.m.f.*, the sixth letter of the alphabet, f.

fa, *n.m.*, (mus.) fa ; F.

fabagelle, *n.f.*,**fabago**, *n.m.*,(bot.) fabago.

fable, *n.f.*, fable, story ; untruth ; tale ; mythology. *Être la — de tout le monde ;* to be the table-talk of every body.

fabliau, *n.m.*, ancient tale in verse.

fablier, *n.m.*, fabulist ; book of fables.

fabricant, *n.m.*, manufacturer.

fabricateur, *n.m.*, (b.s.) fabricator, maker. *— de fausse monnaie ;* coiner of base money. *— de nouvelles ;* forger of news.

fabrication, *n.f.*,fabrication, manufacture ; forgery. *La — d'un faux acte ;*the forging of a deed.

fabricien (-si-in), or **fabricier**, *n.m.*, administrator of the property of a parish, vestryman.

fabrique, *n.f.*, building (of churches—*d'églises*) ; vestry-board ; property of a parish church ; making, fabrication ; (manu.) works ; manufactory ; forging. *Marchandises de — ;* goods of inferior quality. *Prix de — ;* cost price.

fabriquer, *v.a.*, to manufacture ; to fabricate ; to coin (money—*monnaie*) ; to forge.

fabuleusement (-leûz-mân), *adv.*, fabulously.

fabuleu-x, -se, *adj.*, fabulous, fictitious.

fabuliste, *n.m.*, fabulist.

façade, *n.f.*, front (of an edifice); frontage ; facade.

face, *n.f.*, front ; fore-part (of a building—*d'un édifice*) ; face ; state ; aspect, appearance ; countenance ; surface. *La — de la mer ;* the surface of the sea. *Une — réjouie ;* a jolly face. *Faire — à ;* to face. *À la — de ;* in the presence of. *En — de ;* in the face of ; opposite. *Couvrir la — à quelqu'un ;* to give any one a dab in the face. *— de réprouvé ;* sinister-looking countenance. *— de carême ;* pale face. *Faire volte- — ;* to face about. *Faire — à ses affaires ;* to meet one's engagements. *Les affaires ont bien changé de — ;* things have taken quite another aspect. *— à — ;* face to face. *Vu de — ;* seen from the front. *De prime — ;* at first.

facé, -e, *adj.*, (l.u.) faced. *Un homme bien — ;* a full-faced man.

facer, *v.a.*, (basset—*bassette*) to turn up as first card the same card as that on which a player has staked.

facétie (-ci), *n.f.*, facetiousness, jest, joke, witty saying. *Recueil de —s ;* jest-book.

facétieusement (-sieûz-mân), *adv.*, facetiously, jestingly.

facétieu-x, -se (-ci-), *adj.*, facetious.

facette, *n.f.*, facet, face. *Diamant taillé à —s ;* diamond cut facet-wise.

facetté, -e, *part.*, faceted.

facetter, *v.a.*, to cut into facets.

fâché, -e, *adj.*, angry, displeased ; sorry, vexed. *Il est — de vous avoir offensé ;* he is sorry he has offended you. *Être — contre quelqu'un ;* to be angry with any one. *Être — d'un malheur ;* to be sorry for a misfortune.

fâcher, *v.a.*, to anger, to make angry, to offend, to vex, to displease. (imp. l.u.). *Il me fâche d'être forcé de vous dire ;* I am sorry to be obliged to tell you. *Soit dit sans vous — ;* with all due deference.

se fâcher, *v.r.*, to be angry, to get into a passion, to be offended. *Ne vous fâchez pas ;* do not be angry.

fâcherie (fâ-shri), *n.f.*, angry feeling ; disagreement ; vexation.

fâcheusement, *adv.*, unpleasantly, inopportunely, disagreeably.

fâcheu-x, -se, *adj.*, grievous, sad, troublesome, vexatious ; difficult ; cross, peevish. *C'est un — personnage ;* he is a troublesome personage. *Il est — que vous n'ayez pas été averti à temps ;* it is a pity that you were not told in time.

fâcheux, *n.m.*, troublesome fellow, pesterer, teaser, bore.

facial, -e, *adj.*, (anat.) facial. *Angle — ;* facial angle.

⊙**faciende**, *n.f.*, (b.s.) cabal, intrigue, clique.

faciès (fa-siès), *n.m.*, (med.) facial expression.

facile, *adj.*, facile, easy ; yielding, complying ; voluble ; weak. *Un homme de — accès ;* a man easy of access. *Style — ;* easy style. *Un homme — ;* a man of an easy temper. *Tout cela est plus — à dire qu'à faire ;* all that is easier to say than to do.

facilement (fa-sil-mân), *adv.*, easily, readily, yieldingly.

facilité, *n.f.*, facility, ease, easiness, readiness ; fluency (of speech—*à parler*) ; quickness (of understanding—*d'intelligence*) ; (com.) accommodation. *Il a une grande — à parler ;* he has great fluency of speech.

faciliter, *v.a.*, to facilitate, to make easy.

façon, *n.f.*, make ; making, workmanship ; shape, fashion ; (agri.) dressing ; way, manner ; look, appearance, mien ; compliment ; affectation ; ceremony ; attention ; *pl.*, ceremony. *À la — de ;* after the manner of. *De cette — ;* in this manner. *La — d'un habit ;* the make, the cut, of a coat. *Prendre à — ;* to make up ladies', gentlemen's, own materials. *Tailleur à — ;* tailor who makes up your own materials. *Donner à — ;* to put out to make. *C'est sa — de penser ;* it is his way of thinking. *De — ou d'autre ;* somehow or other, somehow. *En aucune — ;* by no means, in no wise. *De quelque — que ce soit ;* anyhow. *Un homme de bonne — ;* a well-looking man. *Cela n'a ni mine ni — ;* that has neither grace nor shape. *En donner de la bonne — à quelqu'un ;* to give it to any one well. *S'en donner de la bonne — ;* to go on at a fine rate. *Faire des —s ;* to be ceremonious. *Un homme plein de —s ;* a ceremonious man. *Point de —s ;* no ceremony. *Sans —s ;* without ceremony. *Pourquoi faites-vous tant de —s ?* why do you stand so much on ceremonies ? *De — que ;* in such a way as, so that.

faconde, *n.f.*, (fam.) talkativeness, loquacity ; ⊙eloquence. *Avoir de la — ;* to have the gift of the gab.

façonné, -e, *part.*, figured (of stuffs—*des étoffes*) ; wrought.

façonner, *v.a.*, to make, to make up, to fashion, to figure,to form,to adorn, to embellish, to work, to polish ; to accustom, to use.

se façonner, *v.r.*, to use one's self to. *Les peuples qui ont connu la liberté ne se façonnent point au joug ;* those nations that have enjoyed liberty cannot accustom themselves to the yoke.

façonner, *v.n.*, (fam.) to be ceremonious.

façonnerie (fa-so-n-ri), *n.f.*, figuring (of stuffs—*des étoffes*).

façonni-er, -ère, *adj.*, ceremonious,precise, formal.

fac-similaire, *adj.*, exactly copied, imitated.

fac-similé, *n.m.*, facsimile.

fac-similé, *part.*, copied exactly.

fac-similer, *v.a.*, to facsimile.

factage, *n.m.*, porterage.

facteur, *n.m.*, maker ; (arith., com.) factor ;

postman, letter-carrier. — *de pianos*; piano-forte-maker. — *d'orgues*; organ-builder.

factice, *adj.*, factitious, artificial.

facticement (-tis-män), *adv.*, factitiously, in a factitious manner.

factieu-x, -se, *adj.*, factious, mutinous, seditious.

factieux, *n.m.*, factionist.

faction, *n.f.*, faction; sentry, duty of a sentinel. *Être en* —, *faire* —; to be on duty. *Entrer en* —; to go on duty. *Relever de* —; to relieve sentry.

factionnaire, *n.m.*, sentinel, sentry.

factorage, *n.m.*, (com.) factorage.

factorerie (-tor-rĭ), *n.f.*, (com.) factory.

factotum, *n.m.* (—*s*), factotum.

factrice, *n.f.*, (com.) female agent. factor.

factum (-tom), *n.m.* (—*s*), (jur.) statement of a case.

facture, *n.f.*, composition (of music, verse); (com.) bill of parcels; invoice, bill. *Tête de* —; bill-head. *Livre de* —*s*: invoice-book. *Faire une* —; to make out an invoice.

facturer, *v.a.*, to invoice.

⊙**facturier**, *n.m.*, manufacturer.

facule, *n.f.*, (astron.) facula.

facultati-f, -ve, *adj.*, optional. *Bref* —; pope's license.

faculté, *n.f.*, faculty, ability, propriety, power, virtue, quality; talent; *pl.*, means, property. —*s intellectuelles*; mind, intellectual faculties. *Il a la* — *de parler en public*; he has a talent for public speaking.

fadaise, *n.f.*, trifle, stuff, fiddle-faddle, silliness, silly thing.

fade, *adj.*, insipid, unsavoury, tasteless, heavy, dull.

fadement, *adv.*, heavily, dully, spiritlessly, insipidly.

fadeur, *n.f.*, insipidity, insipidness, unsavouriness, tastelessness; silliness; insipid compliment.

fagot, *n.m.*, fagot, bundle; idle story. *Âme d'un* —; small sticks of a fagot. *Bois de* —; bavin. *Il y a* —*s et* —*s*; all things of the same sort are not alike. *Sentir le* —; to be suspected of heresy. *Conter des* —*s*; to tell idle stories. *Prendre un air de* —; to warm one's self by the blaze of a fagot. *Être habillé comme un* —; to be dressed in a slovenly, slatternly, manner.

fagotage, *n.m.*, fagot-making, fagot-wood.

fagoté, -e, *part.*, dressed in a slovenly manner. *Comme le voilà* —; how slovenly dressed he is.

fagoter, *v.a.*, to fagot, to make into fagots; to jumble together; to dress in a slovenly manner, to dress a fright. *Peut-on* — *ainsi un enfant?* how can people make such a fright of a child? *se fagoter*, *v.r.*, to dress one's self in a slovenly manner, to dress one's self a fright. *Cette femme semble prendre à tâche de* —; that woman seems to do her best to make a fright of herself.

fagoteur, *n.m.*, fagot-maker; bungler; scribbler.

fagotin, *n.m.*, small fagot; monkey dressed in man's clothes; clown (of a quack—*d'un charlatan*).

fagoue, *n.f.*, pancreas; sweetbread of veal.

⊙**faguenas** (-fag-nä). *n.m.*, rank smell (proceeding from dirty people—*émanant d'un corps sale ou échauffé*).

faible, *adj.*, weak, feeble, faint, deficient; helpless; light (coin.); small (of number—*des nombres*); (mus.) thin. *Homme* —; weak man. — *de corps et d'esprit*; weak in body and mind. *Le plus* — *est toujours écrasé*; the weakest goes to the wall. *Le côté* — *d'une chose*; the weak side of a thing.

faible, *n.m.*, weak person; weak side, weak part, weakness, blind side. foible. *Avoir du* — *pour*; to have a partiality for. *Protéger le* — *contre le fort*; to protect the feeble against the strong. *Je le tiens par son* —; I have got him by his blind side.

faiblement, *adv.*, weakly, faintly, feebly; slenderly, poorly; helplessly.

faiblesse, *n.f.*, weakness, feebleness, faintness, fainting fit, swoon; slenderness, deficiency, defect; foible; lightness (coin.); invalidness; invalidity. *Avoir de la* — *pour quelqu'un*; to be partial to any one. *Sentir de la* —; to feel faint. *Tomber en* —; to swoon away, to be seized with a fainting fit. *Il lui a pris une* —; she, he, was taken with a fainting fit. *Avoir de fréquentes* —*s*; to be subject to fainting fits. *Une femme qui a eu une faiblesse*; a woman that has made a slip, a mistake.

faiblir, *v.n.*, to become weak; to abate; to slacken, to give way, to relax.

faïence, *n.f.*, crockery, crockery-ware; faience. — *Anglaise*; blue, yellow, crockery-ware; earthenware.

faïencerie (fa-ian-srĭ), *n.f.*, crockery-ware factory; crockery-ware.

faïenci-er, *n.m.*, **-ère**, *n.f.*, dealer in crockery-ware, crockery-ware man, crockery-ware woman.

*****faille**, *n.f.*, (geol.) out-throw, excavation; (mining—*mines*) fault; Flemish grosgrain silk; female head-dress used in Flanders.

*****failli**, *n.m.*, **-e**, *n.f.*, bankrupt.

*****faillibilité**, *n.f.*, liability to err, fallibility.

*****faillible**, *adj.*, liable to err, fallible.

*****faillir**, *v.n.*, to err, to miss; to fail; to trespass; to transgress; to mistake, to be mistaken; to be extinct; to be on the point of; to be well nigh; to fail, to be a bankrupt. *Il a failli*; he missed his aim. *Les plus doctes sont sujets à* —; the most learned are liable to be mistaken. *Jouer à coup faillant*; to take the place of him who misses. *Le cœur me faut*; I am ready to faint. *J'irai sans* —; I will go without fail. *Il a failli tomber*; he was near falling. *Il s'en faut beaucoup*, *il s'en faut de beaucoup*; very far from it. *Peu s'en faut*; very near. *Tant s'en faut*; far from it.

*****faillite**, *n.f.*, bankruptcy, failure. *Être en* —; to be a bankrupt. *Faire* —; to fail, to become a bankrupt. *Ouverture d'une* —; docket. *Faire déclarer l'ouverture d'une* —; to strike a docket. *Syndicat de* —; commission of bankruptcy. *Déclaration de* —; declaration of insolvency.

faim (fin), *n.f.*, hunger; (fig.) thirst. *Avoir* —; to be hungry. *Mourir de* —; to starve, to be dying with hunger. — *canine*; rabid hunger. *Apaiser la* — *de quelqu'un*; to stay any one's hunger. *Un meurt-de-* —; a starveling. *Faire mourir de* —; to starve out. *Réduire par la* —; to starve out. *Se laisser mourir de* —; to starve one's self to death. *La* — *chasse le loup hors du bois*; hunger will break through stone walls. — *insatiable des richesses*; insatiable thirst for riches.

faim-valle, *n.f.* (*n.p.*), (vet.) hungry-evil.

faine, *n.f.*, (bot.) mast, beech-nut.

fainéant, -e, *n.* and *adj.*, sluggard, loiterer; idle, lazy, slothful, sluggish.

fainéanter, *v.n.*, to be idle, to be indolent.

fainéantise, *n.f.*, idleness, laziness, slothfulness.

faire (faisant, fait), *v.a.*, to make, to do; to create, to bear, to exert; to construct, to frame; to coin; to counterfeit; to work, to effect, to perform; to celebrate (festivals—*des fêtes*); to play (a game—*à un jeu*); to play off (tricks—*des tours*); to prosecute (studies—*des études*); to raise (troops—*des troupes*); to have (children—*des enfants*); (nav.) to make for, to set (sail— *voile*); to receive, to take in (a supply —*une fourniture, une provision*); to build (nests—*des nids*); to offer up (prayers—*des prières*); to carry on (a trade—*un métier*); to compose (books—*des livres*); to take (a ride, a walk, a religious vow—*une promenade à pied, à cheval, ou en voiture; un vœu religieux*); to follow (profession); to inflict (injuries—*du mal*); to pay (attention); to oblige; to practise, to transact, to commit, to perpetrate; to exercise, to discharge; to fashion, to form, to improve; to use, to accustom, to inure, to train up; to act, to personate, to affect, to set up for, to sham, to counterfeit; to wage; to lay (eggs—*des œufs*); to charge for, to sell; to be; to render; to give out, to tell; to cause; to get; to bring; to bid, to order. *À* —; to be done; — *un voyage;* to perform a journey. *Avoir beaucoup à —, avoir fort à —;* to have a great deal to do. *Donner fort à — à quelqu'un;* to give any one a great deal of trouble. *Cela fera tout aussi bien;* that will do just as well. *Se laisser —;* to let others do as they like with one. *N'avoir rien à —;* to have nothing to do. *Faites ce que vous voudrez, je ne m'en soucie pas;* do your worst. I care not. *Qu'y —?* what is to be done? *Dieu a fait le ciel la terre;* God made heaven and earth. — *des enfants;* to have children. — *et dire sont deux;* saying and doing are different things. *Cet écolier a-t-il fait son thème?* has that boy done his exercise? — *sa besogne;* to do one's work. — *tous ses efforts, tout son possible;* to do one's utmost. *À tout —;* fit for everything; of all work. *Bonne à tout;* servant of all work. *Être à tout —;* to be fit for anything. — *du bien, du mal;* to do good, harm. — *une bonne œuvre;* to do a good work. — *la charité;* to bestow charity, to do good. — *l'aumône;* to give alms. — *un mauvais coup;* to do a bad action. — *une sottise;* to do a foolish act. — *des bassesses;* to behave meanly. — *son devoir;* to discharge one's duty. — *son apprentissage;* to serve one's apprenticeship. — *un tour de jardin;* to take a turn in the garden. — *le tour du jardin;* to walk round the garden. — *une promenade;* to take a walk. — *une lieue à pied;* to walk a league. *Il fait bien ses affaires;* he is getting on well. — *une chambre;* to clean a room. — *la couverture;* to turn down the bed. — *les foins;* to make hay. — *la moisson;* to get in the harvest. *Que ferez vous de votre fils?* what will you do with your son? *Il est fait au chaud et au froid;* he is used to heat and cold. *Les affaires font les hommes;* business makes men. *Que faites-vous aujourd'hui?* what are you going to do to-day? *Je n'ai rien à faire;* I have nothing to do. *Je n'ai que — de lui;* I do not want him. *Je n'ai que — de lui ni de ses visites;* I neither want him nor his visits. — *la revue d'une armée;* to review an army. — *des recrues;* to recruit. — *la médecine;* to practise medicine. — *des armes;* to fence. — *un grand négoce;* to carry on a great trade. — *la cuisine;* to dress meat, to cook. — *un métier;* to exercise a trade. *Il ne sait pas — son métier;* he does not know his trade. — *le roi;* to personate the king. — *l'amant;* to act the lover. — *le savant;* to set up for a learned man. *Elle ne fait œuvre de ses dix doigts;* she never does a thing. — *le malade;* to sham illness. — *la sourde oreille;* to pretend to be deaf, to turn a deaf ear. — *mine de, —semblant de;* to feign, to pretend. *Il faisait semblant de n'en rien savoir;* he pretended to know nothing about it. *Que voulez-vous que j'y fasse?* what can I do. how can I help it? *Ce petit garçon fait le mutin;* that little boy is refractory. *Cela fait toutes mes délices;* that is all my delight. *On le faisait mort;* they gave out that he was dead. *Faites-le entrer;* bid him

come in. show him in. *Il le fit mettre à mort;* he ordered him to be put to death. *Je le lui ai fait avoir;* I have procured it for him. — *bâtir;* to have built. — *aller une machine; to set a* machine going. — *venir;* to send for. — *dire une leçon à quelqu'un;* to hear any one say his lesson. *Cela fait beaucoup;* that makes a great difference. *Cela ne fait rien;* that makes no difference. — *entendre à quelqu'un;* to give any one to understand. — *voir;* to show. — *connaître;* to make known. — *savoir;* to inform. *Faites-moi savoir de vos nouvelles;* let me hear from you. — *accueil;* to welcome. — *affront;* to affront. — *attention;* to pay attention, to mind. — *banqueroute;* to become a bankrupt. — *bonne chère;* to live well. — *bonne mine à quelque chose;* to put a good face on anything. — *carême;* to keep lent. — *cas de;* to value, to have a good opinion of. — *peu de cas de;* to make light of. *Ne — cas que de l'argent;* to value nothing but money. — *compassion;* to raise compassion. — *une confidence à quelqu'un;* to trust a secret to any one. — *conscience;* to scruple. — *déshonneur;* to disgrace. — *don;* to make a donation, a present of. — *envie;* to raise envy. — *feu;* to fire. — *front;* to face. — *montre de;* to make a parade of. — *de l'eau* (nav.); to take in fresh water. — *du bois, du biscuit* (nav.); to furnish with wood, with biscuit. — *eau* (nav.); to make water, to leak. — *force de voiles;* to crowd sail. — *voile* (nav.); to make for, to set sail. *Je ne ferai rien de la sorte;* I shall do nothing of the kind.

se **faire**, *v.r.*, to be done, to be made; to happen; to take place; to be; to grow; to become; to use one's self to, to be used to, to accustom one's self; to give one's self out as; to set up for; to pretend. *Quelle idée vous faites-vous de cet homme-là?* what is your idea of that man? *Si cela peut se —;* if that can be done. *Je me suis fait au bruit de la rue;* I have accustomed myself to the noise of the street. — *à la fatigue;* to inure one's self to fatigue. — *à tout;* to accustom one's self to everything. — *médecin;* to become a physician. *Il se fait plus riche qu'il ne l'est;* he gives himself out for being richer than he is. — *des amis;* to make one's self friends. — *aimer;* to make one's self beloved. — *voir;* to show one's self. — *saigner;* to get one's self bled. — *mal;* to hurt one's self. *Comment cela se fait-il?* how is that? — *un devoir de;* to make it a duty to. *Il se fait tard;* it is getting late. *Paris ne s'est pas fait en un jour;* Rome was not built in a day.

faire, *v.n.,* to do, to make; to act; to mean, to signify; to look; to deal (at cards—*aux cartes*); to be; to fit; to arrange, to manage. — *pour quelqu'un;* to supply any one's place, to act for any one. — *bien;* to do right. — *mal;* to do wrong. *Il n'en veut — qu'à sa tête;* he will only do as he pleases. *C'est à — à vous;* you are well able to do it. *C'est bien à — à vous de;* does it become you to? *C'est à — à moi le lui parler;* it is my business to speak to him. *Il ne fait que sortir et rentrer;* he does nothing but go out and in. *Il ne fait que de sortir;* he has just gone out. *Qu'est-ce que cela fait là?* what does that do there? *Qu'est-ce que cela fait?* what does that signify? *Qu'est-ce que cela vous fait?* what is that to you? *Cela ne me fait rien;* that is nothing to me. *Ces deux choses font fort bien ensemble;* these two things look very well together. *L'or fait bien avec le vert;* gold looks very well upon green. *Faites qu'il soit content;* see that he is satisfied. *Rien n'y faisait;* nothing would do. *Il fait chaud;* it is hot. *Il fait froid;* it is cold. *Il fait beau;* it is fine. *Il fait cher vivre à Londres;* living is dear in London. *Il fait bon ici;* it is comfortable here. *À qui à*

—? whose deal is it? *Je viens de —;* I have just dealt.

faire. *n.m.,* doing, execution; (fine arts—*beaux-arts*) manner, style.

faisable, *adj.,* practicable, allowable, feasible.

faisan. *n.m.,* **faisane,** *n.f.,* pheasant. *Une poule —e;* a hen-pheasant. *Coq —;* cock-pheasant. *— noir, de montagne;* black heath-cock.

faisances, *n.f. pl.,* dues over and above the rent.

faisandeau, *n.m.,* young pheasant.

faisandé, -e, *part.,* having a flavour of game, high.

faisander, *v.a.,* to keep game till it gets a high flavour.

se faisander, *v.r.,* to get a flavour of game, to get high.

faisanderie (-dri), *n.f.,* pheasantry.

faisandier, *n.m.,* pheasant-breeder.

faisant, -e, *adj.,* acting, doing.

faisceau, *n.m.,* bundle; sheaf (of arrows—*de flèches*); (anat.) fasciculus; pile (of arms—*de fusils*); (arch.) cluster; (opt.) pencil; (fig.) union; *pl.,* (antiq.) fasces. *—d'armes;* pile of arms. *Mettre les armes en —x:* to pile arms. *En —;* (arch.) clustered. *— de rayons;* (opt.) pencil of rays.

faiseu-r, *n.m.,* **-se,** *n.f.,* maker; (b.s.) swindler; maker, monger, doer. *— de vers;* scribbler of verses. *— de systèmes;* system-monger. *Mangez de ce pâté, c'est du bon —;* try a piece of this pie, it is made by a first-rate hand. *Les grands diseurs ne sont pas les —s;* great talkers are little doers. *— d'affaires;* person of a not very honourable calling, as an usurer, &c

fait, *n.m.,* fact, act, deed; case; matter, business, point, point in question; what suits; share. *C'est un — bien constaté;* it is a well-known fact. *Par le seul —;* by the simple fact, ipso facto. *Prendre quelqu'un sur le —;* to catch any one in the act. *Prendre — et cause pour quelqu'un;* to take any one's part. *Voies de —;* violence, assault. *Pour venir au —;* to come to the point. *Au —;* in fact, in point of fact. *Être au — de;* to be acquainted with; to be aware of. *Il est au — de cette affaire;* he is well acquainted with that affair. *C'est un — à part;* that is another matter. *De —;* indeed, certainly. *Il est de — que;* it is a fact that. *Les hauts —s d'un guerrier;* the exploits of a warrior. *Voilà mon —;* that is just what I want. *Mettre en —;* to lay down as a fact. *Être sûr de son —;* to be sure of any thing, to be sure of what one states. *C'est votre —;* that just suits you. *Dire à quelqu'un son —;* to tell any one your mind. *Au — et au prendre;* at the scratch, when it comes to the scratch. *En venir au — et au prendre;* to come to the scratch. *Se mettre au — de;* to acquaint one's self with. *Trouver le — de quelqu'un;* to find what any one wants. *Donner son — à quelqu'un;* to pay any one out. *Mettre quelqu'un au —;* to acquaint any one with the point in question. *Tout à —;* entirely, completely, quite. *Si —;* yes, yes indeed. *Vous n'y êtes pas allé. Si —;* you did not go there. Yes, I did; yes, indeed I did.

fait, -e, *part.,* made, done, fit, qualified; grown, full grown, grown up *Ce qui est —, est —;* what is done, cannot be undone. *Un homme —;* a grown-up man. *De compte —;* upon computation. *Comme le voilà —!* how ill he looks! *Tenez cela pour —;* consider it done. *Cela vaut —;* that is as good as done. *C'est de lui;* he is undone. *C'en est — de;* it is all over with. *Ce qui est — n'est pas à faire;* what is done is done. *Aussitôt dit, aussitôt —;* no sooner said than done. *Tout —;* ready made, cut and dry. *C'est bien —;* it serves him, her, you,

them, right. *Est-ce —!* have you done? is it done? *C'est un grand pas de —;* it is a great step towards it. *C'est comme un — exprès;* it seems done on purpose. *Cela est — pour moi, cela semble — pour moi; cela n'est — que pour moi;* such things happen to me alone, such is my luck.

faitage, *n.m.,* ridge (of a house—*d'une maison*); roofing.

faîte, *n.m.,* top, summit, pinnacle; zenith; height; ridge, coping (of building—*de bâtiment*). *Le — des honneurs:* the height of honours. *— de cheminée;* chimney-top.

fait exprès, *n.m.,* thing done intentionally.

faîtière (-tièr), *adj.,* of the ridge. *Tuile —;* ridge-tile, pantile. *Lucarnes — s;* sky-lights.

faîtière, *n.f.,* ridge-tile, pantile.

faix (fè), *n.m.,* weight, burden. *Plier sous le —;* to sink under the weight.

fakir, *n.m.,* fakir (Mahommedan monk-moine mahométan).

falaise, *n.f.,* cliff. *Les blanches —s d'Albion;* the white cliffs of England.

falaiser, *v.n.,* (of the waves—*des vagues*) to break against the cliffs.

falbala, *n.m.,* furbelow.

falcade, *n.f.,* (man.) falcade.

falcidie, or **falcidienne,** *adj.f.,* (Rom. law.) falcidian.

falciforme. *adj.,* (bot.) falcate, falcated.

○**fallace.** *n.f.,* deceit, fraud.

fallacieusement (fal-la-sieuz-mān), *adv.,* fallaciously.

fallacieu-x. -se (fal-la-), *adj.,* fallacious.

falloir, *v.imp.,* must, should, ought; to be necessary, requisite; to be obliged; to need, to stand in need of, to want. *Il faut le faire;* it must be done. *Il faut que je fasse cela;* I must do that. *Il faut que j'y aille;* I must go there. *Il fallait venir plus tôt;* you ought to have come sooner. *Il faudra le satisfaire;* you must satisfy him. *Il aurait fallu s'y prendre ainsi;* you should have gone to work thus. *Faut-il le demander?* need you ask? *Je ne sais ce qu'il lui faut;* I do not know what he wants. *Il me faut de l'argent;* I must have some money. *J'en ai plus qu'il ne m'en faut;* I have more than I want. *Combien vous en faut-il?* how much do you want? *Que lui faut-il pour sa peine?* how much must he have for his trouble? *Faites cela comme il faut;* do that properly, well. *Il fait ce qu'il faut;* he does what is requisite. *Des gens comme il faut;* well-bred people. *Un homme comme il faut;* a gentlemanly man. *Il se vante de ne pas me craindre, il faudra voir!* he boasts that he does not fear me, but wait a bit! *Il me menace d'un procès, c'est ce qu'il faudra voir!* he threatens me with an action, but we shall see!

s'en falloir, *v.r.,* to be wanting; to be far; to be near, to be on the point. *Il s'en fallut de peu que je ne fusse écrasé;* I was near being run over. *Peu s'en est fallu que je ne mourusse;* I was near dying. *Il s'en faut de beaucoup que la somme y soit;* the sum is far from being complete. *Il s'en faut de beaucoup que l'un ait autant de mérite que l'autre;* the one is far from possessing as much merit as the other. *Il s'en faut de beaucoup;* very far from it. *Il s'en faut de peu qu'il ne soit aussi grand que son frère;* he is nearly as tall as his brother. *Tant s'en faut que; far from.* Tant s'en faut qu'il consente *qu'au contraire il fera tout pour l'empêcher;* he is so far from consenting that he will, on the contrary, do all he can to prevent it. *Tant s'en faut qu'au contraire;* (fam. jest.) on the contrary, quite the reverse. [When *s'en falloir* is preceded by a negative, or accompanied by a word implying a negative sense, as *peu, guère,* *presque, rien*, or if the phrase implies doubt, or has an interrogative meaning, the dependent clause is accompanied by the negation *ne*; but when *s'en falloir* is neither preceded by a negation, nor accompanied by any of the above words, the dependent clause does not take the negative particle.]

falot, *n.m.*, large lantern, tallow-lamp.

falot, -e, *adj.*, comical, droll, laughable, funny.

falotement, *adv.*, comically, amusingly, ludicrously.

falourde, *n.f.*, bundle of fire-wood.

falquer, *v.n.*, (man.) to make falcades.

falques, *n.f.pl.*, (man.) falcade ; (nav.) wash-board.

falsificateur, *n.m.*, falsifier ; debaser.

falsification, *n.f.*, falsification, adulteration, debasement.

falsifié, -e, *adj.*, adulterated.

falsifier, *v.a.*, to falsify, to adulterate, to debase. — *les métaux ;* to adulterate metals. — *de la monnaie ;* to debase coin.

falun, *n.m.*, broken shells used to manure land, falun, shell-marl.

faluner, *v.a.*, to manure with shell-marl.

falunière, *n.f.*, falun pit, shell-marl pit.

fâme, *n.f.*, (jur.) character, good name, fame.

famé, -e, *adj.*, famed. *Bien —;* of good repute. *Homme mal —;* man of bad character.

famélique, *n.m.f.* and *adj.*, starveling; starving, famishing. *Auteur —;* starving author. *Il a bien l'air d'un —;* he has quite the mien of a poor starving wretch.

fameu-x, -se, *adj.*, famous, famed, celebrated, renowned, notorious; (iron.) precious. — *imbécile;* precious fool. — *voleur;* notorious thief.

familiariser, *v.a.*, to accustom to, to familiarize.

se **familiariser**, *v.r.*, to familiarize one's self; to make one's self familiar, to grow familiar; to accustom, to use, one's self to; to become tame (animal).

familiarité, *n.f.*, familiarity, familiar terms. *Vivre sur le pied de la plus grande —;* to be on the most familiar terms.

famili-er, -ère, *adj.*, familiar, free, intimate, unconstrained.

famili-er, *n.m.*, **ère**, *n.f.*, familiar. *C'est un des —s du prince ;* he is one of the familiar companions of the prince.

familièrement (-mân), *adv.*, familiarly.

*****famille**, *n.f.*, family, kindred, race, tribe. *Être chargé de —;* to have a large family. *Il a un air de —;* he has a family likeness about him. *Affaires de —;* domestic concerns. *Chef de —;* head of a family.

famine, *n.f.*, famine. *Crier — sur un tas de blé;* to complain of poverty in the midst of plenty.

fanage, *n.m.*, (agri.) turning of grass ; hay-maker's pay ; leaves of a plant.

fanaison, *n.f.* V. **fenaison**.

fanal, *n.m.*, lantern of a ship ; signal-light, watch-light, beacon.

fanariote, *n.m.f.* V. **phanariote**.

fanatique, *n.m.f.*, and *adj.*, fanatic ; fanatical, bigoted.

fanatiser, *v.a.*, to fanaticize.

fanatisme, *n.m.*, fanaticism, bigotry.

fandango, *n.m.*, fandango (Spanish dance— *danse espagnole*).

fane, *n.f.*, fallen leaves ; dead leaves ; envelope (of a flower— *de la fleur*).

fané, -e, *adj.*, faded.

faner, *v.a.*, to spread grass ; to spread hay ; to fade, to tarnish.

se **faner**, *v.r.*, to fade, to fade away, to

droop, to tarnish. *Cette femme commence à —;* that woman begins to fall off.

faneu-r, *n.m.*, **-se**, *n.f.*, haymaker.

fanfan, *n.m.*, darling, duck (child— *enfant*).

fanfare, *n.f.*, flourish, flourish of trumpets. *Sonner une —;* to strike up a flourish.

fanfaron, *adj.m.*, blustering, swaggering, bragging, boasting.

fanfaron, *n.m.*, blusterer; swaggerer; boaster, braggart. *Faire le —;* to play the braggart.

fanfaronnade, *n.f.*, blustering, bragging, boasting.

fanfaronnerie (-ro-n-rî), *n.f.*, blustering, swaggering, bragging, boasting.

fanfreluche, *n.f.*, bawble, gewgaw.

fange, *n.f.*, mire, mud, dirt ; vileness ; degradation.

fangeu-x, -se, *adj.*, miry, muddy, dirty.

fanion, *n.m.*, (milit.). V. **fanon**.

fanon, *n.m.*, dewlap (of oxen— *des bœufs*); fetlock (of horses— *du cheval*); fin (of whales— *de la baleine*); (c.rel.) fanon; (milit.) pennon.

fanons, *n.m. pl.*, (surg.) the name of bandages for a broken arm or thigh.

fantaisie, *n.f.*, imagination ; fancy ; whim, crotchet, odd fancy ; fantasticalness. *Il a eu la — d'aller voyager ;* he has taken it into his head to set out to travel. *Vivre à sa —;* to live according to one's own fancy. *Cela est-il à votre —?* is that to your liking? *Il lui prit — d'aller le voir ;* she took a fancy to pay him a visit. *Par —;* out of pure whim. *Objets de —;* fancy articles. *Avoir une —;* to fancy. *Avoir des —s;* to be fanciful.

fantasmagorie, *n.f.*, phantasmagoria, dissolving view.

fantasmagorique, *adj.*, phantasmagorical.

fantasmagoriquement, *adv.*, phantasmagorically.

fantasque, *adj.*, fantastic, fantastical, fanciful, whimsical, capricious, odd.

fantasquement, *adv.*, (l.u.) fantastically, fancifully, whimsically.

fantassin, *n.m.*, foot-soldier.

fantastique, *adj.*, fantastic, fantastical, fanciful, chimerical.

fantastiquement (-tik-mân), *adv.*, fantastically.

fantoccini (fân-tot-shee-nee), *n.m. pl.*, fantoccini (puppets— *marionnettes*).

fantôme, *n.m.*, phantom, spectre, shadow.

fanum (fa-nom), *n.m.*, (—), (antiq.) fane, temple.

faon (fân), *n.m.*, doe, fawn.

faonner (fa-né), *v.n.*, to fawn.

faquin, *n.m.*, scoundrel, mean rascal, puppy.

faquinerie (fa-ki-n-rî), *n.f.*, rascally action, rascally meanness.

faquir, *n.m.* V. **fakir**.

farandole, *n.f.*, farandole (Provencial dance— *danse provençale*).

faraud, *n.m.*, a vulgar fellow proud of smart clothes, a snob, a swell.

farce, *n.f.*, (cook.) stuffing, forced meat ; farce (thea.) ; drollery ; tomfoolery ; practical joke ; waggish trick. *Tirez le rideau, la — est jouée ;* let down the curtain, the farce is ended. *Faire une — à quelqu'un ;* to play any one a trick. *Faire ses —s;* to sow one's wild oats.

farceur, *n.m.*, player in a farce ; droll person ; dog (pers.), rogue. *Faire le —;* to be droll.

farcin, *n.m.*, (vet.) farcin. farcy.

farcineu-x, -se, *adj.*, affected with farcy.

farcir, *v.a.*, to stuff, to cram.

se **farcir**, *v.r.*, to stuff, to cram.

fard, *n.m.*, paint, varnish; disguise, dissimulation. *Parlez-moi sans —;* speak to me without disguise. *Se mettre du — à la figure ;* to paint one's face.

fardage, *n.m.,* (nav.) dunnage.

fardé, -e, *part.,* painted.

fardeau, *n.m.,* burden, load, weight ; mash (for brewing—*terme de brasseur*) ; mass (mining mines). *Imposer un — à quelqu'un ;* to put a burden on any one. *S'imposer un — ;* to take a burden on one's self.

farder, *v.a.,* to paint (the face—*le visage*) ; (fig.) to varnish, to gloss over.

se **farder,** *v.r.,* to paint one's face, to paint. *Elle se farde ;* she paints.

farder, *v.n.,* to sink, to give way ; (nav.) to swell out (of sails—*des voiles*). *Ce mur commence à — ;* this wall is beginning to sink.

fardier, *n.m.,* dray for carrying stone.

farfadet, *n.m.,* goblin, familiar spirit ; frivolous man.

*farfouiller,** *v.a.* and *n.,* to rummage.

faribole, *n.f.,* idle story, trifle.

farinacé, -e, *adj.,* farinaceous.

farine, *n.f.,* flour, meal ; farina. *Fleur de —;* flour. *Folle —;* mill-dust. *Marchand de —;* flour-dealer. *Gens de même —;* birds of a feather. *Donner dans la —* (paint.) ; to paint in a wishy-washy manner. *D'un sac à charbon il ne saurait sortir de blanche* (prov.) ; what can you expect from a pig but a grunt ?

fariner, *v.a.,* to flour.

farinet, *n.m.,* one-faced die.

farineu-x, -se, *adj.,* white with flour; mealy, farinaceous.

farinier, *n.m.,* flour-dealer.

farinière, *n.f.,* meal-tub.

farlouse, *n.f.,* (orni.) titlark, titling.

farniente, *n.m.* (n.p.), leisure, repose.

farouch, or **farouche,** *n.m.,* (agri.) clover, clover-grass.

farouche, *adj.,* wild ; fierce ; sullen ; unsociable ; shy. *Regard —;* fierce look. *Cette femme est bien — ;* that woman is very shy.

farrago, *n.m.,* farrago.

fasce, *n.f.,* (her.) fesse.

fascé, -e, *adj.,* (her.) fessy.

fascia, *n.m.,* (anat.) fascia.

fasciculaire, *adj.,* (bot.) fascicular.

fascicule, *n.m.* (bot.) fascicle, small bundle (of plants, herbs—*de plantes*) ; fasciculus (number of a work—*livraison d'un ouvrage*).

fasciculé, -e, *adj.,* (bot.) fasciculate, fasciculated.

fascié, -e, *adj.,* fasciated.

fascinage, *n.m.,* (fort.) work made with fascines ; the making of fascines.

fascinat-eur, -rice, *adj.,* fascinating.

fascination, *n.f.,* fascination.

fascine, *n.f.,* (fort.) fascine ; fagot, hurdle, bavin.

fasciner, *v.a.,* to fascinate.

faséole, *n.f.,* phasel, kidney-bean, French bean, haricot, phaseolus.

fashion, *n.f.,* fashion ; fashionable world.

fashionable, *n.m.f.* and *adj.,* fashionable.

fasier, *v.n.,* (nav.) (of sails—*des voiles*) to shiver. *Mettre à — ;* (nav.) to spill.

faste, *n.m.* (n.p.), pomp, ostentation, display, vain show, pageantry. *Étaler un grand — ;* to make a great display.

fastes, *n.m. pl.,* fasti, annals ; records. *Les — de l'histoire ;* the annals of history.

fastidieusement (-euz-mǎn), *adv.,* tediously, irksomely.

fastidieu-x, -se, *adj.,* irksome, tedious, wearisome.

fastigié, -e, *adj.,* fastigiate, fastigiated.

fastueusement (euz-mǎn), *adv.,* magnificently, ostentatiously, pompously, splendidly, gorgeously.

fastueu-x, -se, *adj.,* ostentatious, pompous, gorgeous, showy, magnificent.

fat (fat), *n.* and *adj. m.,* fop, coxcomb ; foppish, coxcomical. *Affectation de — ;* foppery. *En — ;* foppishly. *C'est un — :* he is a coxcomb.

fatal, -e, *adj.,* fatal. *Terme — ;* (jur.) expiration of a delay. *Ces remèdes ont été —s au malade ;* those remedies proved fatal to the patient.

fatalement (fa-tal-mǎn), *adv.,* fatally.

fatalisme, *n.m.,* fatalism.

fataliste, *n.m.,* fatalist.

fatalité, *n.f.,* fatality.

fatidique, *adj.,* fatidical.

fatigant, -e, *adj.,* fatiguing, toilsome, irksome, wearisome, tiresome.

fatigue, *n.f.,* fatigue, toil, hardship, weariness. *Excéder de — ;* to wear out with fatigue, to tire out. *Un homme de — ;* a man capable of resisting fatigue. *Supporter la — ;* to stand fatigue. *Rompre à la — ;* to accustom to fatigue.

fatigué, -e, *part.,* fatigued, jaded ; (paint.) overworked. *Des chevaux —s ;* jaded horses. *La manière de ce peintre est —e ;* the manner of that painter is overworked.

fatiguer (-ghé), *v.a.,* to fatigue, to tire, to weary, to harass, to tease ; (paint.) to overwork. *La lecture fatigue la vue ;* reading fatigues the sight. *— un champ ;* to impoverish a field. *— une salade ;* to mix a salad.

se **fatiguer,** *v.r.,* to fatigue one's self ; to tire one's self ; to be jaded.

fatiguer, *v.n.,* to fatigue one's self ; to be fatiguing ; (nav.) to work. *— à l'ancre ;* (nav.) to ride hard. *Ne pas — à l'ancre ;* (nav.) to ride easy. *Ne pas — à cheval* (man.) ; to ride easy.

fatras, *n.m.,* rubbish, trash, stuff, medley, litter, confusion ; balderdash.

fatrassier, *n.m.,* untidy man, indulging in untidiness.

fatuité, *n.f.,* fatuity, self-conceit, foppishness.

faubert, *n.m.,* (nav.) swab, mop.

fauberter, *v.a.,* (nav.) to swab, to mop.

fauberteur, *n.m.,* (nav.) swabber.

faubourg (fô-boor), *n.m.,* outskirt, faubourg, part of a town without the gates ; suburb.

faubourien, -ne (-iǐn, è-n), *adj.,* pertaining to the faubourgs.

faubourien, *n.m.,* inhabitant of a faubourg.

fauchage, *n.m.,* mowing.

fauchaison, *n.f.,* mowing-time.

fauché, *n.f.,* mowing ; mowing-time.

fauchée, *n.f.,* day's mowing.

faucher, *v.a.,* to reap, to mow, to cut down. *— les prés ;* to mow the meadows.

faucher, *v.n.,* (man.) to throw the fore-legs sideways in walking (of a horse—*du cheval*).

fauchet, *n.m.,* hay-rake.

fauchette, *n.f.,* (gard.) small hedge-knife.

faucheur, *n.m.,* mower, reaper ; field-spider.

faucheur, or **faucheux,** *n.m.,* field-spider.

*faucille,** *n.f.,* sickle, reaping-hook.

*faucillon,** *n.m.,* bill-hook.

faucon, *n.m.,* (orni.) falcon ; hawk.

fauconneau, *n.m.,* ☉ (artil.) falconet ; (orni.) young hawk.

fauconnerie (fô-co-n-rî), *n.f.,* falconry, hawking.

fauconnier, *n.m.,* falconer. *Monter à cheval en — ;* to mount a horse the off-side.

fauconnière, *n.f.,* hawking-pouch, saddle-bag.

faufiler, *v.a.,* to tack, to baste (needle-work —*ouvrage à l'aiguille*).

se **faufiler,** *v.r.,* to insinuate one's self, to ingratiate one's self ; to intrude ; to curry favour. *Il se faufile partout ;* he intrudes himself in everywhere.

faulx, *n.f.* *V.* **faux.**

faune, *n.m.*, (myth.) faun.

faune, *n.f.*, (zool.) fauna.

faussaire, *n.m.f.*, forger (of writing—*d'écrit*); person guilty of forgery. *Poursuivre comme —;* to prosecute for forgery.

faussement (fôs-mān), *adv.*, falsely, erroneously, untruly.

fausser, *v.a.*, to bend; to warp; to strain; to falsify; to pervert; to violate; (mus.) to put out of tune; to strain (a lock, a key—*une serrure, une clef*). *— une cuirasse;* to indent a cuirass. *—sa parole;* to violate one's word. *— compagnie à quelqu'un;* to give any one the slip.

se **fausser**, *v.r.*, to bend; to be warped, perverted.

fausset, *n.m.*, spigot, peg; (mus.) falsetto. *Chanter en —;* to sing in falsetto. *Trou de —;* vent-hole.

fausseté (fôs-té), *n.f.*, falsity, falseness, falsehood, duplicity, insincerity, deceitfulness, treachery.

faute, *n.f.*, fault, mistake, error; want, scarcity, dearth. *A — de;* (jur.) in default of. *Faire une —;* to make a fault. *Ne pas se faire —, de;* not to be sparing of. *Relever une —;* to point out a fault. *Surprendre quelqu'un en —;* to find any one at fault. *A qui la — ?* whose fault is it? *— de;* for want of. *— d'orthographe;* wrong spelling. *Ne vous en faites pas —;* do not spare it. *Il est mort — de secours;* he died for want of help. *Sans —;* without fail.

***fauteuil**, *n.m.*, arm-chair; chair (speaker's, president's seat—*siège de président*); academic chair. (of the French Academy—*place à l'académie française*). *— à la Voltaire;* reclining arm-chair. *Occuper le —;* to fill the chair.

faut-eur, *n.m.*, **-rice**, *n.f.*, abettor, favourer, fomenter. *Être — de;* to abet. *Les —s d'un crime;* the abettors of a crime.

fauti-f, **-ve**, *adj.*, faulty; at fault.

fauve, *adj.*, fawn-coloured, tawny. *Bêtes —s;* fallow-deer, stag, &c.

fauve, *n.m.*, *sing.*, (hunt.) deer, fallow-deer.

fauvette, *n.f.*, (orni.) warbler. *Petite —;* garden-warbler, redwing. *— babillarde;* white-throat. *— à tête noire;* blackcap.

faux (fô), *n.f.*, scythe; (anat.) falx.

fau-x, **-sse**, *adj.*, false, untrue, erroneous, wrong; spurious; unsound; base, counterfeit; artificial, imitation; fictitious, mock, sham, pretended; insincere, double, treacherous, deceitful; (mus.) out of tune; forged. *Acte —;* (jur.) forgery. *— témoin;* false witness. *Chose —sse;* untruth. *—sse doctrine;* erroneous doctrine. *—sse monnaie;* counterfeit money. *— brave;* braggadocio, swaggerer. *—sse démarche;* wrong step. *Voix —sse;* voice out of tune. *— brillant;* tinsel. *—sse équerre;* bevel. *—sse fenêtre;* blank, sham, window. *Faire — bond;* not to keep an engagement.

faux, *n.m.*, falsehood, forgery; false. *Discerner le vrai d'avec le —;* to discern truth from falsehood. *Crime de —;* crime of forgery. *Un —;* a forgery. *Commettre un —;* to commit a forgery. *Poursuivre pour —;* to prosecute for forgery. *Arguer de —;* to accuse, to tax, as false. *S'inscrire en — contre une chose;* to undertake to prove that a thing is false.

faux, *adv.*, erroneously, falsely, wrongfully; (mus.) out of tune. *Il chante —;* he sings out of tune. *A —;* falsely, unjustly. *Être accusé à —;* to be accused unjustly. *Porter à —;* (arch.) to be out of perpendicular, not to be upright. *Cette poutre porte à —;* that post is not upright.

faux-fuyant, *n.m.* (— —s), by-place; subterfuge, evasion, creep-hole.

faveur, *n.f.*, favour, boon; interest; vogue.

A la — de; by favour of, under cover of. *En — de;* in behalf of, in favour of. *Demander une —;* to ask a favour. *Être en —;* to be in favour, in vogue. *Prendre —;* to get into favour, into vogue. *Mettre en —;* to bring into favour, into vogue.

favorable, *adj.*, favourable, propitious. *Le ciel vous soit — !* heaven befriend you ! *Cela lui est —;* that is favourable for him.

favorablement, *adj.*, favourably.

favori, **-te**, *n.* and *adj.*, favourite.

favori, *n.m.*, whisker. *Il a de beaux —s;* he has fine whiskers.

favoriser, *v.a.*, to favour, to befriend, to countenance; to aid, to assist.

favoritisme, *n.m.*, favouritism.

fayard (fa-iar), *n.m.*, (bot.) beech.

fayence, &c. *V.* **faïence**, &c.

☉**féage**, *n.m.*, feoffment.

☉**féal**, **-e**, *adj.*, trusty, faithful.

☉**féal**, *n.m.*, trusty, faithful friend. *A nos amis et féaux;* to our trusty and well-beloved friends.

☉**féauté**, *n.f.*, fealty.

fébricitant, **-e**, *n.* and *adj.*, (med.) feverpatient; labouring under fever.

fébrifuge, *n.m.* and *adj.*, febrifuge.

fébrile, *adj.*, febrile.

fécale, *adj.*, fecal. *Matière —;* feces, excrement.

fèces, *n.f.pl.*, (pharm.) sediment; (med.) feces.

fécial, *n.m.* and *adj.*, (Rom. antiq.) fecial.

fécond, **-e**, *adj.*, fecund, fruitful, prolific, fertile, rich, teeming, voluminous. *Mine —e;* rich mine. *Avoir l'esprit —;* to have a fertile imagination. *Être — en;* to teem.

fécondant, **-e**, *adj.*, fertilizing, genial.

fécondation, *n.f.*, fecundation, impregnation; fructification.

féconder, *v.a.*, to fecundate, to impregnate; to make fruitful, to fertilize. *— un champ;* to fertilize a field.

fécondité, *n.f.*, fecundity, fruitfulness, fertility.

fécule, *n.f.*, fecula.

féculence, *n.f.*, feculency.

féculent, **-e**, *adj.*, feculent.

féculerie, *n.f.*, manufactory of fecula.

fédéral, **-e**, *adj.*, federal.

fédéraliser, *v.a.*, (neologism) to make federate. *Se —,* *v.r.*, to be formed into a federation.

fédéralisme, *n.m.*, federalism.

fédéraliste, *n.m.*, federalist.

fédérati-f, **-ve**, *adj.*, federate, federative. *Alliance —ve;* federative alliance.

fédération, *n.f.*, federation.

fédéré, **-e**, *n.* and *adj.*, federate.

fée, *n.f.*, fairy; fay. *Comme une —;* fairy-like.

féerie, *n.f.*, fairy art, enchantment; fairyland.

féerique, *adj.*, fairy.

feindre (feignant, feint), *v.a.*, to feign, to dissemble, to pretend, to sham. *— de la joie;* to counterfeit joy. *— une maladie;* to sham an illness.

feindre, *v.n.*, to feign, to sham. *Il possède l'art de —;* he knows the art of dissembling.

feint, **-e**, *part.*, feigned, counterfeit, pretended, sham. *Amitié —e;* pretended friendship.

feinte, *n.f.*, feint; pretence, dissimulation; (mus.) accidental; (print.) friar. *User de —;* to dissemble. *Il fit une —;* (fenc.) he made a feint.

☉**feintise**, *n.f.*, feint, pretence, sham.

feld-maréchal, *n.m.* (— *maréchaux*), Field-Marshal.

feldspath, *n.m.*, (min.) feldspar, feldspath.

feldspathique. *adj.*, (min.) feldspathic.

fêlé. -e, *part.*, cracked (of glass—*du verre*); cracked (pers.); delicate (of the chest—*de la poitrine*). *Il a la tête —e ; he is cracked.

fêler, *v.a.*, to crack (glass—*verre*).

se fêler, *v.r.*, to crack (of glass—*du verre*).

félicitation. *n.f.*, felicitation, congratulation. *Lettre de — ;* congratulatory letter.

félicité. *n.f.*, felicity, bliss, happiness.

féliciter, *v.a.*, to congratulate, to felicitate, to give joy.

se féliciter, *v.r.*, to congratulate one's self.

félin. -e, *adj.*, feline.

fellah, *n.m*, (— *s*), fellah, Egyptian peasant.

félon. -ne, *u.* and *adj.*, (l.u.) traitor; felon; felonious.

félonie, *n.f.*, (feudalism—*féodalité*) treason towards one's lord.

felouque, *n.f.*, (nav.) felucca.

fêlure. *n.f.*, crack, chink, fissure.

femelle, *n.f.* and *adj.*, female; hen. [Applied *only* to animals.]

féminin. -e, *adj.*, feminine, female, womanish, woman-like, effeminate. *Genre — ;* feminine gender. *Sexe — ;* female sex.

féminin. *n.m.*,.(gram.) feminine.

féminiser, *v.a.*, (gram.) to make feminine, to make of the feminine gender.

femme (famme), *n.f.*, woman; wife, married woman. *Une — auteur ;* an authoress. *Mari et — ;* man and wife. *Une — sage ;* a well-conducted woman. *Une sage— ;* a midwife. — *de chambre ;* waiting-woman, lady's maid. — *de charge ;* housekeeper. — *de journée,* — *de ménage ;* char-woman. — *en puissance de mari ;* (jur.) feme-covert. *Avoir — ;* to have a wife. *Avoir — et enfants ;* to have a wife and children. *Prendre — ;* to take a wife. *Bonne — ;* good, obliging woman; old woman; simple, superstitious woman.

femmelette (fa-mlèt), *n.f.*, silly, weak woman ; effeminate man.

fémoral.-e, *adj.*, (anat.) femoral.

fémur, *n.m.*, (anat.) femur, thigh-bone; (vet.) hurl-bone. *Tête du — ;* head, apophysis of the femur.

fenaison, *n.f.*, hay-time, hay-harvest; hay-making.

fendant. *n.m.*, hector, bully. *Faire le — ;* to play the bully.

fenderie (fan-drî), *n.f.*, slitting (of iron into rods—*du fer en tringles, barres, &c.*); slitting-mill.

fendeur, *n.m.*, cleaver, slitter, splitter. — *de roues ;* wheel-cutter.

se fendiller, *v.r.*, to slit ; to chink; to crack.

fendoir, *n.m.*, cleaver (instrument).

fendre, *v.a.*, to cleave, to split, to rive, to crack, to cut open, to rend, to rip ; to break ; to burst. — *du bois ;* to cleave wood. *Un navire qui fend l'eau ;* a ship that ploughs the sea. — *les airs ;* to cut the air. — *la presse ;* to squeeze through the crowd. — *les bataillons de l'ennemi ;* to break through the battalions of the enemy.

se fendre, *v.r.*, to cleave, to burst asunder, to split, to slit; to chap, to chink, to rive, to gape ; (fenc.) to lunge.

fendre, *v.n.*, to be ready to split ; to break, to burst. *La tête me fend ;* my head is ready to split.

fendu. -e, *part.*, cleft, split, cloven. *Des yeux bien —s ;* large, well-formed eyes.

fêne, *n.f.*, *V.* **faîne**.

fenestré. -e, *adj.*, (bot.) cancellate; (ent.) fenestrate.

fenêtrage, *n.m.*, windows.

fenêtre, *n.f.*, window, casement; (anat.) aperture. — *à châssis ;* sash-window. — *en baie, en saillie ;* bay, bow, window ; (Gothic arch.) oriel-window, oriel. — *à coulisse, en guillotine ;* sash-window. — *en éventail ;* fanlight. — *en ogive* (arch.); Gothic window. *Con damner une — ;* to block up a window. *Regarder par la — ;* to look out at the window. *Jeter par la — ;* to throw out of the window, to be a spendthrift, to play at ducks and drakes with one's property.

fenil, *n.m.*, hayloft.

fenouil.*n.m.*, fennel; fennel-seed. — *puant ;* anet. — *de mer ;* sea-samphire. — *de porc ;* sulphur-wort, hog's-fennel.

fenouillet, *n.m.*, (bot.) fennel-apple.

fenouillette, *n.f.*, (bot.) fennel-apple ; fennel-water.

fente, *n.f.*, slit, chink, cleft, chap, flaw; gap, cranny, crevice ; (min.) rent ; cleavage ; (nav.) spring.

fenton, *n.m.*, iron-cramp, iron-tie.

fenugrec, *n.m.*, (bot.) fenu-greek.

féodal. -e, *adj.*, feudal.

féodalement, *adv.*, according to the feudal law.

féodalité, *n.f.*, feudality, feudalism.

fer (fèr), *n.m.*, iron; head, point ; sword, brand, steel ; tag ; (nav.) spindle (of vanes—*de girouettes*). — *s ;* iron-work ; irons, chains, fetters. — *battu ;* wrought-iron. — *fondu ;* cast-iron. — *impur ;* iron-ore. — *doux ;* soft iron. — *aigre ;* brittle iron. — *laminé ;* rolled iron. — *oligiste, spéculaire ;* (min.) iron-glance. — *rouvecin ;* red-scar iron. — *de carillon ;* bar iron. *Le — d'une pique ;* the head of a pike. — *de lacet,* — *d'aiguillette ;* tag of a lace. *Le — et le feu ;* fire and sword. — *en barres ;* bar-iron. — *à cheval ;* horse-shoe ; (fort.) horse-shoe ; (man.) horse-shoe bat, — *à marquer ;* marking-iron. — *dur ;* hard iron — *à cheval cramponné,* — *à cheval relevé ;* horse-shoe with calkins. — *de fenderie ;* slit iron. — *de fonte ;* cast-iron. — *à glace ;* frost-shoe. — *de lance ;* (arch.) stanchion. — *à repasser ;* iron, box-iron, flat-iron. — *à souder ;* soldering-iron. *Bande, piece, de — ;* (tech.) strap. *Bois de — ;* iron-wood. *Fil de — ;* iron wire. *Fonte de — ;* cast-iron. *Limaille de — ;* iron-dust, iron-filings. *Marchand de — ;* dealer in iron, ironmonger. *Mine de — ;* (min.) iron-ore. *Minerai de — ;* iron-ore ; iron-stone. *Ouvrage en — ;* iron-work. *Scorie de — ;* iron-dross. *Usine de — ;* iron-works. *A tête de — ;* strong-headed, resolute, determined. — *d'arc-boutant ;* (nav.) goose-neck of a boom. — *de gaffe ;* (nav.) boat-hook. — *à calfat,* — *de calfat ;* calker's iron, calking-iron. *Petits, —s ;* punches (book-bind.) *Avoir toujours quelque — qui cloche ;* to have always some screw loose. *Battre le — ;* to fence, to tilt. *Battre le — pendant qu'il est chaud ;* to strike the iron while it is hot, to make hay while the sun shines. *Être aux —s, être dans les —s ;* to be fettered, bound, to be in chains ; to be in prison, in captivity. *Être condamné à cinq ans de —s* (milit.); to be condemned to five years' imprisonment. *Employer le — et le feu ;* to use the knife and cautery; to employ violent means. *Être un corps de — ;* to be made of iron. *Mettre les —s au feu ;* to put the irons in the fire, to fall to work. *Porter le — et la flamme dans ;* to ravage with fire and sword. *Tomber les quatre —s en l'air ;* to fall upon one's back. *Ne tenir ni à — ni à clou ;* to be badly fastened, badly arranged. *Cela ne vaut pas les quatre —s d'un chien ;* that is not worth a fig, a straw. *Cet enfant userait du — ;* that child wears out his things in a frightful manner. *Être sur le —;* (nav.) to be at anchor. *Notre navire était depuis trois jours sur le —;* our ship had been lying at anchor for three days.

fer (cheptel de), *n.m. V.* **cheptel.**

fer-blanc, *n.m.,* (*—s —s*) tin, tin-plate; latten.

ferblanterie, *n.f.,* tin-ware.

ferblantier (-tié), *n.m.,* tinman.

fer-chaud, *n.m.* (*n.p.*), (med.) cardialgia, heartburn, pyrosis.

féret. *n.m.,* (min.) hematite.

férial, -e, *adj.,* (ecc.) ferial (of the days—*des jours*).

férie, *n.f.,* (antiq.) feriæ; (ecc.) feria.

férié, -e, *adj.,* of holidays. *Jour —;* holiday.

○**férir,** *v.a.,* to strike. *Sans coup —;* without striking a blow.

ferlage, *n.m.,* (nav.) furling.

ferler, *v.a.,* (nav.) to furl.

fermage, *n.m,* rent (of a farm—*d'une ferme*); rent; (jur.) rent-charge. *Refus de payer le —;* denial of rent.

fermant, -e. *adj.,* closing. *Meuble —;* piece of furniture provided with a lock.

ferme, *n.f.,* farm, farm-house; farming (letting out on lease—*affermer*); (carp.) trussed girder; main couple; truss; (carp.) rib (of centerings, roofs—*d'un comble*); (thea.) set-piece. *— triangulaire;* (carp.) truss. *Emplacement de —;* farmstead. *Régisseur de —;* farmbailiff. *Maîtresses —s* (carp.); principal rafters bearing on the girders. *—s de remplage* (carp.); middle rafters. *Donner, bailler, à —;* to let, to farm, to farm let. *Monter une —;* to stock a farm.

ferme, *adj.,* firm, steady, fast; fixed, steadfast; strong, stout; stiff; unshaken, constant, resolute. *Être — à cheval;* to sit firm in the saddle. *Elle lui dit d'un ton —;* she told him firmly. *Avoir le poignet —;* to have a strong wrist.

ferme, *adv.,* firmly, fast, hard. *Frapper —;* to strike hard. *Tenir —;* to hold fast.

ferme *int.,* cheer up !

fermement, *adv.,* firmly, steadily, fixedly, steadfastly, strongly, stoutly.

ferment, *n.m.,* ferment; leaven; yeast.

fermentable, *adj.,* fermentable.

fermentati-f, -ve, *adj.,* fermentative.

fermentation, *n.f.,* fermentation, working.

fermenter, *v.a.,* to ferment, to rise, to work. *La pâte fermente;* the dough rises.

fermentescible, *adj.,* fermentable.

fermer, *v.a.,* to shut, to shut up, to fasten, to close, to close up; to encompass; to enclose. *— la porte;* to shut the door. *— la porte au nez de quelqu'un,* to shut the door in any one's face. *— la porte à clef;* to lock the door. *— la porte à double tour;* to double-lock the door. *— la porte au verrou;* to bolt the door. *— un robinet;* to stop a cock. *— les yeux sur quelque chose;* to wink at anything. *— les yeux à la lumière;* to shut one's eyes against conviction. *— l'oreille aux médisances;* to close one's ears against slander. *— la bouche à quelqu'un;* to stop any one's mouth. *— boutique;* to shut up shop. *— les yeux à, de, quelqu'un qui vient de mourir;* to close the eyes of one who has just died. *— l'écurie quand les chevaux sont partis* (prov.); to shut the stable when the horse is out.

se **fermer,** *v.r.,* to shut, to shut up, to close, to be closed, to be enclosed, to be encompassed. *Cette plaie se fermera bientôt;* that wound will soon close up. *Un cœur qui se ferme à la pitié;* a heart that is shut against pity.

fermer, *v.n.,* to shut, to be shut.

fermeté, *n.f.,* firmness; constancy, steadiness, steadfastness, stability.

fermeture, *n.f.,* closing, shutting; (carp.) lock-smith—*serrurerie*); fastening; (nav.) plank (of a ship's side in the intervals between the wales—*bordages de vaisseau entre les préceintes*).

fermeur, *n.m.,* (anat.) closer.

fermier, *n.m.,* husbandman, farmer; tenant. *— général;* farmer-general.

fermière, *n.f.,* farmer's wife.

fermoir, *n.m.,* clasp.

fermure, *n.f. V.* **fermeture** (nav.).

féroce, *adj.,* ferocious, fierce. *Homme brutal et —;* brutal and savage man. *Bête —;* wild beast.

férocité, *n.f.,* ferocity, fierceness.

***ferraille.** *n.f.,* old iron.

***ferrailler,** *v.n.,* to fence; (b.s.) to fight (with swords—*à l'épée*); to wrangle.

***ferrailleur,** *n.m.,* dealer in old iron; fighter (with a sword—*à l'épée*); wrangler, disputer.

ferrandinier, *n.m.,* silk-weaver.

ferrant, *adj.,* that shoes horses. *Maréchal —;* farrier.

ferré, -e, *part.,* shod; metalled; stoned; chalybeate (of water—*de l'eau*); skilled, versed in. *Chemin —;* metalled road. *Eau —-e;* chalybeate water. *— à glace;* rough-shod; skilled in.

ferrement (fèr-màn), *n.m.,* iron tool; putting fetters on convicts, *pl.,* iron-work, ironing.

ferrer, *v.a.,* to bind, to hoop, with iron. *— une canne;* to put a ferrule on, to tip, a cane. *— un lacet;* to tag a lace. *— un cheval;* to shoe a horse. *— à glace;* to rough-shoe.

ferret, *n.m.,* tag (of a lace—*d'un lacet*). *Je ne voudrais pas en donner un — d'aiguillette;* I would not give a straw, a fig, a rush, for it.

ferreur, *n.m.,* tagger (of aiglets—*d'aiguillettes*).

ferrière, *n.f.,* tool-bag (of farrier's, &c. —*de maréchaux, &c.*).

ferrifère, *adj.,* ferriferous.

ferronnerie (fé-ro-n-ri), *n.f.,* iron-store; iron-foundry.

ferronni-er, *n.m.,* **-ère,** *n.f.,* ironmonger.

ferronnière. *n.f.,* any jewel worn by women, and fixed on the forehead by a gold chain.

ferrugineux, *n.m.,* (pharm.) medicament containing iron.

ferrugineu-x, -se, *adj.,* ferruginous. *Eau —se;* chalybeate wate.

ferrure, *n.f.,* iron-work; shoeing (animal).

fertile, *adj.,* fertile, fruitful, teeming. *— en blé;* abounding with corn.

fertilement (-til-màn), *adv.,* fertilely, abundantly, fruitfully, plenteously.

fertilisable, *adj.,* that can be fertilized.

fertilisant, -e, *adj.,* fertilizing.

fertilisation, *n.f.,* fertilization.

fertiliser, *v.a.,* to fertilize, to manure.

fertilité, *n.f.,* fertility, fecundity, fruitfulness.

féru, -e, *part.,* smitten; stung to the quick.

férule, *n.f.,* ferule, rod; stroke, cut (with a ferule); (bot.) ferula, giant-fennel.

fervemment (-va-màn), *adv.,* fervently.

fervent, -e, *adj.,* fervent. *— dans la piété;* fervent in piety.

ferveur, *n.f.,* fervour, fervency.

fescennin, -e, *adj.,* (antiq.) fescennine.

fesse, *n.f.,* buttock, breech. *—s;* (nav.) tuck.

fesse-cahier, *n.m.* (*—,* or *— —s*), quill driver; literary hack.

fessée, *n.f.,* whipping, flogging.

fesse-mathieu, *n.m.* (*— —r*), miser, hunks, skinflint, close-fist, pinch-fist.

fesser, *v.a.,* to whip the breech; to flog, to whip. *— le cahier;* to drive the quill, to be a literary hack.

fesseu-r, *n.m.*, **-se**, *n.f.*, flogger.
fessier, *n.m.*, breech; (anat.) gluteus.
fessi-er, **-ère**, *adj.*, (anat.) gluteal.
fessu, **-e**, *adj.*, (pop.) large-breeched.
festin, *n.m.*, feast. banquet, regale. *Faire* —, *faire un* —; to feast, to banquet.
festiner, *v.a.*, (jest.) to feast, to entertain.
festiner, *v.n.*, (jest.) to banquet, to feast, to make merry.
festival, *n.m.*, festival (musical entertainment).
feston, *n.m.*, festoon; scallop.
festonner, *v.a.*, to festoon; to scallop.
festoyer, *v.a.*, to entertain; to feast.
fête, *n.f.*, holiday, festival; saint's day; festivity; feast, merry-making. — *carillonnée*; high festival; great holiday. — *patronale*; patron saint's day. *Jour de sa* —; one's saint's day; one's birthday. *Un jour de* —; a holiday. —*s mobiles*; moveable feasts. — *légale*; bank holiday. *Troubler la* —; to mar the pleasure (of the company—*de la société*). *Faire* — *à quelqu'un*; to make any one kindly welcome. *Se faire de* —; to intermeddle. *Se faire une* — *de*, *se faire*—*de*; to look forward with pleasure to. *Payer sa* —; to entertain one's friends on one's birthday *or* saint's day, to keep one's birthday *or* saint's day. *Ce n'est pas tous les jours* —; Christmas comes but once a year.
fête-dieu, *n.f.* (*n.p.*), Corpus Christi.
fêter, *v.a.*, to keep holiday, to keep, to celebrate, to observe, as a holiday; to entertain, to feast. — *quelqu'un*; to receive any one with open arms; to make any one very welcome. *C'est un saint qu'on ne fête pas*; he is a person without credit *or* authority.
fetfa, *n.m.*, decision of a mufti on a point of law or religion.
fétiche, *n.m.*, fetich.
fétichisme, *n.m.*, feticism, fetichism.
fétide, *adj.*, fetid, rank.
fétidité, *n.f.*, fetidness, offensiveness.
fêtoyer, *v.a.* *V.* **festoyer.**
fétu, *n.m.*, straw; fig (thing of little value —*chose de peu de valeur*). *Tirer au court* —; to draw lots, to draw cuts. *Cela ne vaut pas un* —; that is not worth a fig. *Un cogne-* —; a fussy person.
fétu-en-cul, *n.m.* (—) *V.* **paille-en-queue.**
fétus, *n.m.* *V.* **fœtus.**
feu, *n.m.*, fire, burning, conflagration, combustion; fire-place; chimney; set of fire-irons; family, household, house; light, signal-light, torch-light; brunt (of fire-arms—*des armes à feu*); brilliancy, lustre; heat, ardour, flame, passion; vivacity, spirit; animation, mettle; liveliness, sprightliness; (feudalism—*féodalité*) hearth; (milit.) firing; (vet.) fire; (theat.) extra pay. — *follet*; ignis fatuus, Jack-with-a-lantern, will-with-the-wisp. — *grisou*; fire-damp. —*de joie*; bonfire. *Mettre le* — *à une chose*; to set a thing on fire. *Prendre l'air du* —; to warm one's self. *Se tenir au coin du* —; to keep in the chimney-corner. *Mettre le pot au* —; to put the pot on the fire. *Couleur de* —; flame-colour. — *grégeois*; Greek fire. — *Saint-Elme*; corpsant, Castor and Pollux. — *Saint-Antoine*; St. Anthony's fire. *Il n'a jamais vu le* —; he has never smelt gun-powder. *Mettre tout à* — *et à sang*; to put every thing to fire and sword. *Brûler un homme à petit* —; to kill a man by inches. *C'est le* — *et l'eau*; they are as opposite as fire and water. *J'en mettrais ma main au* —; I would lay my life upon it. *Il n'y a point de* — *sans fumée*; there is no smoke without fire. *Se jeter dans le* — *pour éviter la fumée*; to jump out of the frying-pan into the fire. *Il y a tant de* —*x dans ce village*; there are so many chimneys, so many

families, in this village. *Garniture de* —; set of fire-irons. *N'avoir ni* — *ni lieu*; to have neither house nor home. *Le* — *dont il brûle*; the flame that consumes him. *Ce vin a trop de* —; that wine is too fiery. *Il prend* — *aisément*; he takes fire easily. *Il jette* — *et flamme*; he frets and fumes. *Il a jeté tout son* —; he has spent all his fire. — *bien nourri*, — *bien servi*; (milit.) galling, smart, well-sustained fire. — *rasant*; (milit.) flank fire. — *coulant*; (milit.) running-fire. *Triste* —, — *triste*; dull fire. —*vif*; (milit.) brisk fire. — *d'artifice*; fireworks. —*x de Bengale*; blue-lights. — *de cheminée*; chimney on fire. — *d'enfer*; very brisk fire. scorching fire. *Boîte à* —; coal-box (locomotive). *Bouche à* —; piece of ordnance. *Coffre à* —; (nav.) fire-chest. *Coup de* —; shot; shot-wound. *Fer à donner le* —, *fer à mettre le* —; cauterizing iron. *Lance à* —; match. *À l'épreuve du* —; fire-proof. *Sous le* — *de*; upon the spur of. *Activer le* —; to rouse the fire. *Attiser le* —; to poke, to stir, the fire. *Cesser le* —; (milit.) to leave off firing. *Condamner au* —; to condemn to the stake. *Crier au* —; to cry fire! *Donner le* — *à*; (vet.) to sear. *Faire* —; (milit.) to fire, to give fire. *Courir comme au* —; to run after eagerly. *Faire* — *qui dure*, to -husband one's property; to take care of one's health. *Faux* —; flash in the pan; *faire faux* —; to miss fire, to flash in the pan. *Faire long* —; to hang fire; to fire at a long distance. *Faire* — *des quatre pieds*; to exert one's self to the uttermost. *Jeter ses premiers* —*x*; to sow one's wild oats. *Jeter de l'huile sur le* —; to add fuel to the flame. *Se jeter dans le* — *pour quelqu'un*, *se mettre au* — *pour quelqu'un*; to go through fire and water for any one. *Mettre le* — *au four*; to heat the oven. *Mettre le* — *sous le ventre à quelqu'un*; to urge any one to do a thing. *Donner le* — *chaud*, *trop ardent*, *à la viande*; to roast meat before too fierce a fire. *Montrer une chose au* —; to dry a thing by the fire; to warm a thing through by the fire. *Soutenir le* —; (milit.) to stand fire. *Soutenir un* —; (milit.) to keep up a fire. *Ne voir que du* — *à quelque chose*; to be dazzled by anything, not to understand something. *Le* — *a pris à la maison*; the house has caught fire. *Le* — *lui sort par les yeux*; his eyes flash fire. *Feu!* (milit.) fire!
feu, **-e**, *adj.*, late, deceased, defunct. *Le* — *roi*; the late king. *La* —*e reine*, — *la reine*; the late queen. — *les princes*, *les* —*s princes*; the late princes.
feudataire, *n.m.*, feudatory.
feudiste, *n.m.* and *adj.*, feodist.
*****feuillage**, *n.m.*, foliage, leaves, leafage; (bot.) frond; frondescence.
*****feuillaison**, *n.f.*, (bot.) foliation.
*****feuillant**, *n.m.*, feuillant, monk of the order of St. Bernard.
*****feuillantine**, *n.f.*, feuillantine, nun of the order of St. Bernard; (cook.) a kind of puff-paste.
*****feuillard**, *n.m.*, hoop-wood.
*****feuille**, *n.f.*, leaf; sheet (of paper, metal — *de papier*, *métal*, &c.); paper, newspaper, journal; foil (of mirrors—*de miroirs*); way-bill (of public coaches, &c.—*de voitures publiques*, &c.); list; veneer (cabinet-making—*ébénisterie*). —*s*; (arch.) foils; foliation; feathering. *L'aisselle d'une* —; the axil of a leaf. *Trembler comme la* —; to shake like an aspen-leaf. *Vin de deux* —*s*; wine two years old. — *de papier*; sheet of paper. — *volante*; loose sheet; flying sheet. — *de décharge*, — *de rebut*; (print.) waste-sheet. — *hebdomadaire*; weekly paper. — *quotidienne*; daily newspaper. — *de route*; (of public coaches—*de voitures publiques*) way-bill; (milit.) route of the road.

*feuillé, -e, adj., (her.) leafy; (bot.) foliate.
*feuillé, n.m., (paint.) foliage, leafage.
*feuillée, n.f., bower, green arbour.
*feuille-morte, n.m., feuillemort, foliomort.
*feuille-morte, adj. invariable, feuillemort, foliomort.
*feuiller, v.n., to come into leaf; (paint.) to paint the foliage of a picture.
*feuilleret, n.m., fillister, fillister-plane.
*feuillet, n.m., leaf (two pages of a book—deux pages de livre); (com.) folio; (mam.) fech; (min.) thin plate; (bot.) gill, gills. — à poing; hand-saw. Tournez le —; turn over the leaf. — refait; (print.)cancel. Faire une corne à un —; to turn down a leaf.
*feuilletage (feu-il-taj), n.m., puff-paste.
*feuilleté, -a, part.,(min.) foliated. Gâteau —; puff; buttered-roll.
*feuilleter (feu-il-té), v.a., to turn over, to peruse, to run over.
*se feuilleter, v.r., (min.) to split into thin plates.
*feuilletis, n.m., the part in slate which is easily divided into thin lyers; the cutting edge of diamonds.
*feuilleton (feu-il-ton), n.m., feuilleton (that part of journals devoted to literary articles, critiques, &c.); fly-sheet.
*feuilletoniste, n.m., writer of feuilletons.
*feuillette, n.f., wine-cask containing 35·5 gallons.
*feuillu, -e, adj., leafy; (bot.) folious.
*feuillure, n.f., (carp.) rebate.
feurre, n.m., straw (for chair bottoms—pour fond de chaise).
feutrabilité, n.f., felting quality.
feutrage, n.m., felting.
feutre, n.m., felt; hat; (saddlery—sellerie) packing.
feutrer, v.a., to felt; (saddlery—sellerie) to pack.
feutrier, n.m., felt-maker.
feutrière, n.f., felt-cloth.
fève, n.f., bean; broad bean; berry; chrysalis (of silk-worms—du ver à soie); (vet.) lampas. —s de haricot; kidney-beans. —s de marais; broad beans. — de Tonka; Tonquin bean. Roi de la —; twelfth-night king.
féverole (fèv-rol), n.f., horse-bean; dried kidney-bean; bean.
février, n.m., (bot.) three-horned acacia, honey-locust, &c., genus gleditchia.
février, n.m., February.
fez, n.m. (—), fez, a red woollen cap worn by the Turks.
fi! int., fie! fie. — donc; fie! for shame. Faire — d'une chose; to turn up one's nose at a thing.
fiacre, n.m., hackney-coach; hack-carriage. Place de —s; hackney-coach stand. Cocher de —; hackney-coachman.
*fiançailles, n.f.pl., betrothing, affiancing.
fiancé, n.m., -e, n.f., person affianced, betrothed.
fiancer, v.a., to betroth, to affiance.
fibre, n.f., fibre, filament; (fig.) affections.
fibreu-x, -se, adj., fibrous, fibrose; stringy.
*fibrille, n.f., (anat.) fibril.
*fibrilleu-x, -se, adj., fibrillous.
fibrine, n.f., (chem.) fibrine.
fic, n.m., (med.) ficus; (vet.) fig.
ficelé, -e. part., (pop.) dressed; dressed out.
ficeler (fi-slé), v.a., to bind, to tie, with string. — de fil de fer; to wire.
ficelier, n.m., reel, roller (for string—à ficelle)
ficelle, n.f., pack-thread, twine, string. Montrer la —; to betray the secret motive.
fichant, -e, adj., (fort.) darting. Feu —; darting fire.

fiche, n.f., pin (for a hinge—de charnière); fish (at cards—aux cartes).
fiché, -e, part., driven in; (her.) fitchee.
ficher, v.a. (past part., fiché, fichu), to drive in, to thrust in, to fasten in; (mas.) to pin up; (pop.) to give in a rude manner; to throw aside. — un clou; to drive in a nail.
se ficher, v.r., (pop.) to throw one's self down, on, &c.; to laugh at, to make game of.
fichet, n.m., ivory peg (to mark at trick-track—pour marquer au trictrac).
fichtre! int., (pop.) the deuce! the devil; plague!
fichu, n.m., neckerchief. Corps de —; habit-shirt.
fichu, -e, part. (of ficher), (pop.) pitiful; deuced; done for; thrown aside; rudely given.
ficoïdes, n.f.pl., (bot.) ficoïdeæ.
⊙fictice, adj., supposed, imaginary, fictitious.
ficti-f, -ve, adj., fictitious, imaginary.
fiction, n.f., fiction, figment.
fictionnaire, adj., fictitious, founded on fiction.
fictivement (-tiv-mān), adv., fictitiously.
fidéicommis, n.m., (jur.) trust, fideicommissum. Violation du —; breach of trust.
fidéicommissaire, n.m., (jur.) feoffee, trustee.
fidéicommissariat, n.m., (jur.) trusteeship.
fidéjusseur, n.m., (jur.) fidejussor.
fidéjussion, n.f. V. cautionnement.
fidèle, adj., loyal, true, trusty, faithful. Traducteur —; correct translator. Copie —; exact copy. Mémoire —; retentive, good, memory.
fidèle, n.m.f., faithful friend. —s; (rel.) believers.
fidèlement (fi-dèl-mān), adv., faithfully, truly, loyally, trustily; accurately, exactly.
fidélité, n.f., fidelity, faithfulness, loyalty, fealty; secrecy; exactness, accuracy; retentiveness (of the memory—de la mémoire); (jur.) allegiance. — éprouvée; tried fidelity. Prêter serment de —; to take an oath of fidelity.
fiduciaire, n.m., (jur.) fiduciary.
fiduciaire, adj., (jur.) in trust.
fief (fièf), n.m., (feudalism—féodalité) fee, fief.
fieffé, -e, adj., (fam.,pop.) arrant, downright, regular. Fripon —; arrant knave.
fieffer, v.a., to enfeoff.
fiel, n.m., gall; hatred, bitterness, rancour, spleen. Vésicule du —; gall-bladder. Amer comme —; as bitter as gall. Un homme plein de —; a man full of malice. Il a vomi tout son —; he has vented all his spleen.
fiente, n.f., dung (of some animals—de quelques animaux). Appliquer un banc de —; (manu.) to dung.
fienter, v.a., to dung.
fier, v.a. to trust, entrust.
se fier, v.r., to trust to; to rely, to depend, upon; to put one's trust in. Je me fie à vous —; I trust to you. Fiez-vous-y (iron.); do not trust to that. Bien fou qui s'y fie; more fool he who trusts to it.
fi-er (fi-èr), -ère, adj., proud, high-spirited, haughty, stout, bold; (her.) fierce. Femme —ère et impérieuse; proud, imperious woman. Il est — de son mérite; he is proud of his merit.
fier-à-bras, n.m. (—), bully, hector.
fièrement, (fièr-mān). adv., proudly, arrogantly, haughtily, soundly, stoutly, boldly; (pop.) preciously, finely, famously.
⊙fierte, n.f., shrine; St. Roman's shrine.
fierté, n.f., pride, haughtiness, arrogance; boldness; intrepidity. Rabaisser, rabattre, la — de quelqu'un; to bring down, to humble, any one's pride.

fièvre, n.f., fever, feverishness, restlessness, inquietude; pl., (med.) ague. — ardente; burning fever. — chaude; violent fever. — éphémère; quotidian fever. — hectique; hectic fever. — intermittente; intermittent fever, ague. — lente; hectic. — puerpérale; puerperal fever. — de lait; milk fever. — tierce; tertian fever. — tremblante; ague. — de cheval; violent fever. — des prisons; typhus, gaol fever. Accès de —; fit of fever; fit of the ague. Trembler la —; to shake with fever. Sortir de —; to recover from a fever. Donner la —; to put in a fever. Tomber de — en chaud mal; to fall from the frying-pan into the fire. Que la — le serre! plague take him! plague on him! Avoir la —; to be feverish.

fiévreu-x,-se, adj., feverish; liable to fever; occasioning fever; (med.) febrific; full of fever (of a place—d'un lieu); restless.

fiévreux, n.m., fever-patient. Salle des —; fever-ward.

fiévrotte, n.f., slight fever.

fifre, n.m., fife; fifer.

figement (fij-măn), n.m., congealing, congealment, coagulation, curdling.

figer, v.a., to congeal, to coagulate, to curdle, to curd.

se figer, v.r., to congeal, to coagulate, to curdle, to curd.

figue (fig), n.f., (bot.) fig. Moitié—, moitié raisin; partly willingly, partly unwillingly; half well, half ill. Faire la — à; to despise, to treat with contumely; to brave, to defy.

figuerie (fi-grî), n.f., fig-ground.

figuier (fi-ghié), n.m., fig-tree; (orni.) fig-eater. — d'Adam; — des banians (bot.); banian, banyan-tree. — d'Inde; opuntia, Indian fig-tree.

⊕figuline, n.f., pot, vase, of earthenware.

figurabilité, n.f., figurability.

figurant, n.m., -e, n.f., (theat.) figurant (dancer—danseur), supernumerary, super.

figurati-f, -ve, adj., figurative, typical; (Grec. gram.) characteristic.

figurative, n.f., (Grec. gram.) characteristic.

figurativement (-tiv-măn), adv., figuratively.

figure, n.f., figure, form, shape; countenance, face; court-card (at cards—aux cartes); diagram; representation; symbol, type; (mus.) figured passage. Faire —; to make, to cut, a figure. À la —; to one's face, in one's teeth.

figuré, n.m., (gram.) figurative sense.

figuré, -e. part., figured; figurative; (mus.) figured; (math.) figural. Sens —; figurative sense.

figurément, adv., figuratively.

figurer, v.a., to figure, to represent, to typify.

se figurer, v.r., to imagine, to fancy, to figure to one's self.

figurer, v.n., to look well, to match, to suit; to make, to cut a figure; to flourish; to dance in figures; (theat.) to be a supernumerary, to super.

figurine, n.f., (paint.) little figure, minor figure.

figurisme, n.m., opinion of those who consider the events of the Old Testament as a figure of those of the New Testament.

figuriste, n.m., figurist.

fil, n.m., thread; edge; grain; chain, string, series; crack, flaw (in marble and other stones—du marbre et des pierres); stream, current (of water—d'eau). — de caret; rope-yarn. — à voile; sail-twine. — d'emballage; pack-thread. — à plomb; plumb-line, plumb-rule. — de la bonne Vierge; air-threads, gossamer.

— d'archal, — de fer; iron wire. — de laiton; brass wire. — d'Écosse; cotton. Le — d'une épée; the edge of a sword. — d'Ariane; Ariadne's thread; clue. Grillage en — métallique; wire-work. À — fin; fine-grained (of wood —du bois). À gros —; coarse-grained (of wood —du bois). Aller de — en aiguille; to go from one thing to another. Aller contre le —; to go against the stream; to go against the grain. Aller de droit —; to go straightforward. Avoir du — à retordre; to have work cut out for one. Donner du — à retordre à quelqu'un; to cut out work for any one. Donner le — à; to whet, to sharpen, to put an edge on. Faire un —; to spin a yarn. Mettre, passer, au fil de l'épée; to put to the edge of the sword. Ôter le — de; to take the edge off. Suivre le — de; to go with the stream.

filage, n.m., spinning; (bot.) cotton-rose; cud-weed.

filagramme. V. **filigrane**.

filaire, n.f., (ent.) filaria.

filament, n.m., filament, thread.

filamenteu-x, -se, adj., thready, stringy; (bot.) filamentous.

filandière, n.f., spinster, spinner. Les sœurs —s; the fates.

filandres, n.f.pl., gossamer, air-threads; strings (of leguminous plants—des légumineuses).

filandreu-x, -se, adj., stringy, thready.

filant, -e, adj., (liquids) flowing gently; (of stars—étoiles) shooting.

filasse, n.f., harl, tow (of flax, hemp—du lin, du chanvre); bast; (bot.) harl.

filassi-er, n.m., -ère, n.f., flax-dresser, dealer in flax.

filateur, n.m., manager, proprietor, of a spinning-factory; spinner.

filatrice, n.f., (tech.) silk-winder (pers.).

filature, n.f., spinning; spinning-mill; spinning-ground; rope-walk; spinning. Champ de —; spinning-ground.

file, n.f., row, rank, file. Ranger par —; to draw up in file. Chef de —; front-rank man. Par — à droite! right wheel!

filé, n.m., thread (of gold or silver—d'or ou d'argent). — d'or; gold wire. — d'argent; silver wire.

filer, v.a., to spin; to conduct, to carry on; to spin out; (nav.) to veer. Machine à —; spinning-machine. — sa corde; to go the way to the gallows.

filer, v.n., to rope; (milit.) to file; (of cats—des chats) to purr; to shoot (of ships, of stars—des vaisseaux, des étoiles); to flare (of lights—des lumières); to cut one's stick, to take one's self off. Il faut —; we must be off. Allons, filez; come, cut your stick. Ce sirop file; this sirup is ropy. — doux; to be all submission, to put up with an insult, an affront.

filerie (fi-lrî), n.f., wire-drawing; wire-mill.

filet, n.m., string, filament, small thread; fibre; (bot.) fillet; chine; (arch.) bead (of liquor —des liqueurs); bed moulding; runner (of strawberries—des fraises); (anat.) fœnum; (print.) rule; string (of the tongue—de la langue); (man.) bridon; net; snare. — d'or; fillet of gold. Un — de vinaigre; a dash of vinegar. Il n'a pas le —; he has a well-oiled tongue. — d'une vis; thread of a screw. Prendre au —; to catch in a net. Faiseur de —s; net-maker. Faire tomber dans un —; to insnare.

fileur, n.m., spinner; wire-drawer; (fam.) truant.

fileuse, n.f., spinner, spinster.

filial, -e, adj., filial.

filialement (-al-măn), adv., filially.

filiation, n.f., filiation; (fig.) connection — des idées; connection of ideas.

filiculo, *n.f.,* (bot.) filicula.

filière, *n.f.,* draw-plate; screw-plate; (carp.) purlin.

filiforme, *adj.,* (bot.) filiform.

filigrane, *n.m.,* filigrane, fillagree, filigree; water-mark in paper.

filin, *n.m.,* (nav.) cordage.

filipendule, *n.f.,* (bot.) dropwort.

***fille,** *n.f.,* girl, female, lass, maiden; daughter; servant-maid; spinster. *Petite— :* grand-daughter. *Arrière-petite— ;* great grand-daughter. *Belle— ;* daughter-in-law; step-daughter. *—s d'honneur ;* maids of honour. *— de chambre :* lady's-maid. *— de service ;* house-maid, chambermaid. *— de boutique ;* shop-woman.

***fillette,** *n.f.,* lass, young girl.

***filleul.** *n.m.,* godson.

filleule, *n.f.,* goddaughter.

filoche, *n.f.,* net-work.

filon, *n.m.,* metallic vein, lode.

filoselle, *n.f.,* floss-silk.

filou, *n.m.,* pickpocket, sharper, cheat.

filouter, *v.a.,* to pickpocket; to cheat, to swindle.

filouterie (fi-lout-ri), *n.f.,* picking pockets, swindling; cheating, filching.

fils (fiss), *n.m.,* son; offspring. *Un — dénaturé ;* an unnatural son. *Petit— ;* grand-son. *Arrière-petit— ;* great grand-son. *Beau— ;* son-in-law; step-son. *— de famille ;* young man living under the authority of his parents, or belonging to a good family. *Être bien — de son père ;* to be one's father's own child, to be a chip of the old block.

filtrage, *n.m.,* filtering, straining.

filtrant, -e, *adj.,* filtering, straining.

filtration, *n.f.,* filtration, filtering, straining, percolation.

filtre, *n.m.,* filter; filtering-machine; philter, love potion. *V.* **philtre.**

filtrer, *v.a.,* to filter, to strain; to percolate. *Pierre à — ;* filtering-stone.

se **filtrer,** *v.r.,* to filter, to be filtered.

filure, *n.f.,* spinning (quality of what is spun *— de ce qui est filé*).

fin, *n.f.,* end, conclusion, termination, issue, expiration, aim, design, view, object, intention. *Mettre — à ;* to put an end to. *Tirer à sa — ;* to draw towards an end. *Étre à sa — ;* to be at one's last shift. *La — couronne l'œuvre ;* all is well that ends well. *Aller, tendre, à ses — s ;* to pursue one's point. (jur.) *— de non-recevoir ;* exception. *À ces — s ;* for this, for that. end. *Mener à bonne — ;* to bring to an end to succeed. *Cheval à toute — ;* horse fitted to ride and drive. *À telle — que de raison ;* to serve for all available purposes; at any rate, for such purpose as may be required. *À la — ;* at last, at length. In the end, in the long run.

fin, -e, *adj.,* fine, thin, refined; acute, ingenious; delicate, polite; shrewd, cunning, sly; small (of handwriting — *d'écriture*). *— es herbes;* sweet herbs. *Diamant — ;* real diamond. *Des traits — s ;* delicate features. *Il a l'oreille — e ;* he has a delicate ear. *Un — voilier ;* a swift sailer. *Avoir le nez — ;* to have a good nose. *C'est un — matois ;* he is a knowing one. *Le — mot ;* the main point. *Je n'entends pas le — mot de tout ceia ;* I cannot understand the secret of all that ; I don't see the force of that.

fin, *n.m.,* sharp fellow, keen fellow; gist, main point (metal.) pure metal. *Savoir le fort et le — de quelque chose ;* to be thoroughly acquainted with anything, to know the long and the short of anything. *— contre — n'est pas bon à faire doublure ;* diamond cut diamond. *Jouer au plus — ;* to play the politician with. *Écrire en — ;* to write small hand.

⊙**finage,** *n.m.,* (jur.) territory of a parish.

final, -e, *adj.,* final, last, finishing.

finale, *n.m.,* (mus.) finale.

finale, *n.f.,* (gram.) last syllable.

finalement (fi-nal-màn), *adv.,* finally, lastly.

finance, *n.f.,* cash, ready money ; finance. financiers ; *pl.,* finances. *Projet de loi de — :* bill of supply.

⊙**financer,** *v.a.,* to pay a fine for a privilege.

financer, *v.n.,* to lay out money; to come down with one's money.

financier, *n.m.,* financier.

financi-er. -ère. *adj.,* financial.

finasser, *v.n.,* to act cunningly, to finesse.

finasserie (fi-na-sri), *n.f.,* finesse.

finasseu-r, *n.m.,* **-se.** *n.f.,* artful person.

finassi-er, *n.m.,* **-ère,** *n.f. V.* **finasseur.**

finaud; -e. *n.* and *adj.,* sly, artful, cunning person, sly-boots; sly, artful.

finement (fi-n-màn), *adv.,* artfully, cunningly, slily, ingeniously, shrewdly.

finesse, *n.f.,* fineness; delicacy; ingenuity; finesse, artifice, craftiness, slyness, craft, shrewdness. *User de — ;* to play cunning. *Faire — d'une chose ;* to make a secret of a thing. *Entendre — à une chose ;* to give a malicious turn to a thing. *Des — s cousues de fil blanc;* artifices easily seen through.

finet, -te, *adj.,* (l.u.) sly, subtle, cunning.

finette, *n.f.,* thin stuff, tissue.

fini, -e, *part.,* finished, ended, complete. *C'est une affaire — e ;* that affair is settled.

fini, *n.m.,* finish, high finish; finite, limited extent. *Donner le — à ;* to finish off.

finir, *v.a.,* to finish, to complete, to end; to terminate; to finish off; to put an end to.

finir, *v.n.,* to finish ; to terminate, to conclude; to be at an end, to be over; to expire. *En — avec ;* to put an end to. *— bien,* to come to a good end. *Il n'en finira jamais ;* he will never come to an end.

finisseu-r, *n.m.,* **-se,** *n.f.,* finisher.

finnois, -e, *n.* and *adj.,* Finn ; Finnish.

fiole, *n.f.,* phial.

fion, *n.m.,* (pop.) finishing touch, last touch; knack.

fioritures, *n.f. pl.,* (mus.) graces.

firmament, *n.m.,* firmament.

firman, *n.m.,* firman.

fisc, *n.m.,* public treasury, fisc.

⊙**fiscal,** *n.m.,* (feudalism — *féodalité*) the lord's solicitor.

fiscal, -e, *adj.,* fiscal. *Avocat, procureur — (feudalism — féodalité);* the lord's solicitor.

fiscalité, *n.f.,* (b.s.) zeal for the interests of the public treasury.

fissipare, *adj.,* (zool. bot.) fissiparous.

fissipède, *n.m.* and *adj.,* fissiped.

fissirostre, *adj.,* (orni.) fissirostral.

fissirostres, *n.m. pl.,* (orni.) fissirostres.

fissure, *n.f.,* fissure, cleft ; crack, rent.

fistulaire, *adj.,* fistular, fistuliform.

fistule, *n.f.,* fistula.

fistuleu-x, -se, *adj.,* fistulous ; fistular.

fixation, *n.f.,* fixation ; appointing, fixing, rating, assessment.

fixe, *n.m.,* appointed, regular salary ; settled weather ; *pl., les — s ;* (astron.) fixed stars ; (chem.) fixed bodies.

fixé, *n.m.,* oil-painting stuck upon glass.

fixe, *adj.,* fixed, settled, steady, certain, stationary, regular. *Prix — ;* set price. (milit.) *— ! eyes — front !*

fixement, *adv.,* fixedly.

fixer, *v.a.,* to fix, to fasten ; to settle ; to determine. *— un jour ;* to appoint a day. *— ses regards sur quelqu'un ;* to fix one's eyes upon any one. *— les regards de quelqu'un ;* to attract any one's eyes.

se **fixer**, *v.r.*, to fix, to be fixed, to settle, to be settled. — *à quelque chose ;* to fix upon anything.

fixité, *n.f.*, fixity, fixedness.

flabelliforme, *adj.*, (bot.) fan-shaped.

flaccidité, *n.f.*, flabbiness, flaccidity.

flache, *n.f.*, hole in the pavement ; (carp.) flaw.

flacon, *n.m.*, flagon ; small bottle.

flagellant, *n.m.*, flagellant.

flagellation, *n.f.*, flagellation, scourging, lashing.

flageller (fla-jèl-lé), *v.a.*, to flagellate, to scourge, to lash.

flagelliforme, *adj.*, flagelliform, whip-shaped.

flageoler, *v.n.*, to tremble, to shake (of horses' legs—*des jambes du cheval*).

flageolet, (fla-jo-lè), *n.m.*, flageolet ; young haricot-bean.

flagorner, *v.a.*, to flatter servilely ; to fawn upon, to palaver.

flagornerie, *n.f.*, sycophantry, palaver.

flagorneu-r, *n.m.*, **-se** *n.f.*, sycophant, toad-eater.

flagrant, **-e**, *adj.*, flagrant. *En — délit ;* in the very fact.

flair, *n.m.*, (hunt.) scent.

flairer, *v.a.*, to smell, to scent. *Flairez ce bouquet ,* smell that nosegay. — *quelque chose ;* to smell a rat.

flaireur, *n.m.*, (l.u.) smeller. — *de cuisine ;* parasite.

flamand, -e, *n.* and *adj.*, Fleming ; Flemish.

flamant, *n.m.*, (orni.) flamingo.

flambant, **-e**, *adj.*, blazing, flaming ; (her.) flaming.

flambe, *n.f.*, (bot.) vulgar name of several kinds of irises.

flambé, **-e**, *adj.*, singed ; ruined, done for. *Il est —;* he is done for. *Mon argent est —;* my money is gone.

flambeau, *n.m.*, flambeau, link, taper, torch ; candlestick ; light, luminary. *Porte- — (—x) ;* link-boy. *Le — du jour ;* the luminary of day. *Les — x de la nuit ;* the stars.

flamber, *v.a.*, to singe, to purify by fire ; to inflame ; to fire. — *une volaille ;* to singe a fowl.

flamber, *v.n.*, to blaze, to flame.

flamberge, *n.f.*, (jest.) sword. *Mettre — au vent ;* to draw one's sword.

flamboyant, **-e**, *adj.*, flaming, blazing. *Étoile —e ;* blazing star.

flamboyer, *v.n.*, to flame, to blaze.

flamine, *n.m.*, (antiq.) flamen.

flamme, *n.f.*, flame, blaze, fire ; ardour ; (nav.) pendant ; (vet.) fleam. *Ce feu ne fait point de —;* that fire does not blaze. *Jeter de la —;* to flame. *Être en —;* to flame, to be in a flame. *Tout en —;* all in a flame. *Jeter feu et —;* to fret and fume.

flammèche, *n.f.*, flake of fire.

flammette, *n.f.*, (vet.) fleam.

flan, *n.m.*, custard ; a coin before it is stamped.

flanc (flan), *n.m.*, flank, side ; entrails ; womb, bosom (of persons—*des personnes*) ; (nav.) breast. *Se battre les —s ;* to exert one's self to no purpose. *Par le — droit ;* (milit.) to the right about. *Prêter le — à ;* to lay one's self open to.

flanchet, *n.m.*, flank of beef , part of a cod below the fins.

flanconade, *n.f.*, (fenc.) flanconade.

flandrin, *n.m.*, tall ungainly fellow.

flanelle, *n.f.*, flannel.

flâner, *v.a.*, to lounge, to saunter, to stroll.

flânerie (flâ-n-rî), *n.f.*, lounging ; lounge ; stroll ; sauntering.

flâneu-r, *n.m.*, **-se**, *n.f.*, lounger, stroller, saunterer

flanquant. **-e**, *adj.*, (fort.) flanking. *Bastion —;* flanking bastion.

flanquement (flank-mān), *n.m.*, (fort.) flanking.

flanquer, *v.a.*. (arch., fort.) to flank ; to defend, to secure, to guard ; to deal (a blow—*un coup*) ; to strike ; to throw ; to toss. — *un soufflet à quelqu'un ;* to give any one a box on the ear.

se **flanquer**, *v.r.*, to throw one's self ; to fall ; to poke, to intrude.

flaque, *n.f.*, small pool, puddle.

flaquée, *n.f.*, dash of water.

flaquer, *v.a.*, (l.u.) to dash (water or any other liquid—*un liquide*).

flasque, *adj.*, lank, feeble, weak, flabby.

flasque, *n.m.*, cheek (of gun-carriages—*d'affûts de canons*).

flasque, *n.f.*, flask, powder-flask, powder-horn.

flatir, *v.a.*, (coin.) to flatten.

flatoir, *n.m.*, (coin.) flattening-hammer.

flâtrer, *v.a.*, to burn with a red hot key-shaped iron the head of a dog bitten by a mad animal.

flatter, *v.a.*, to flatter, to tickle ; to gloss over ; to cajole ; to caress, to endear, to make much of, to stroke, to coax, to fawn ; to smooth ; to touch gently (musical instruments). *Elle aime à s'entendre —;* she likes to be flattered. *Un portrait flatté ;* a flattering likeness. *La musique flatte l'oreille ;* music soothes the ear. *Le chien flatte son maître ;* the dog fawns upon his master.

se **flatter**, *v.r.*, to flatter one's self. *Il se flatte qu'on aura besoin de lui ;* he flatters himself that he will be wanted.

flatterie (fla-trî), *n.f.*, flattery, adulation, fawning.

flatteu-r, **-se**, *adj.*, flattering, complimentary ; fawning.

flatteu-r, *n.m.*, **-se**, *n.f.*, flatterer.

flatteusement (-teuz-mān), *adv.*, flatteringly.

flatueu-x, **-se**, *adj.*, causing flatulency ; windy.

flatulence, *n.f.*, flatulence, windiness.

flatulent, **-e**, *adj.*, flatulent, windy.

flatuosité, *n.f.*, flatulency.

fléau, *n.m.*, (agri.) flail ; scourge, plague ; beam (of a balance) ; iron bar (to fasten folding gates—*pour fermer les portes à deux battants*). *La guerre est un terrible —;* war is a dreadful scourge.

flèche, *n.f.*, arrow ; (astron.) sagitta ; spire (of a steeple—*d'un clocher*) ; (trick-track) point ; (nav.) pole ; perch (of carriages—*de voitures*) ; (fort.) bonnet ; (arch.) rise. *Tirer une — ;* to let fly an arrow. *Les —s de l'amour ;* the darts of love. *Faire — de tout bois ;* to leave no stone unturned. *Il ne sait plus de quel bois faire — ;* he is put to his last shift, he is at his wit's end. — *de lard ;* flitch of bacon.

fléchier, *n.m.*, arrow-maker.

fléchière, *n.f.*, (bot.) arrow-head.

fléchir, *v.a.*, to bend, to bow ; to move, to melt ; to persuade, to touch. — *le genou ;* to bend the knee.

fléchir, *v.n.*, to bend, to bow, to yield, to give way, to stagger, to waver. *Ce bois rompra plutôt que de —,* that wood will break before it bends.

fléchissement (-shis-màn), *n.m.*, bending, giving way.

fléchisseur, *n.* and *adj. m.*, (anat.) flexor.

flegmasie, *n.f. V.* **phlegmasie**.

flegmatique, or **phlegmatique**, *adj.*, (med.) phlegmatic, pituitous ; cold, dull, sluggish, phlegmatic (of the mind—*du caractère*). —, *n.*, cold, dull, phlegmatic person.

flegme, or **phlegme**, n.m.,phlegm,coldness.
flegmon, n.m. V. **phlegmon**.
flegmoneu-x, **-se**, adj. V. **phlegmo-neux**.
flétan, **flételet**, or **fleton**, n.m.,(ich.) flounder.
flétrir, v.a., to wither, to dry up, to cause to fade, to blight, to blast; to tarnish, to blemish, to brand, to disgrace, to stain, to dishonour, to stigmatize. L'âge flétrit la beauté; age causes beauty to fade.
se flétrir, v.r., to fade, to wither, to tarnish; to dishonour one's self; to be branded, to be stigmatized. Sa beauté commence à —; her beauty begins to fade.
flétrissant, **-e**, adj., dishonouring.
flétrissure, n.f., fading, decaying, withering; blemish, blot, brand, discredit, disgrace; stigma.
fleur, n.f., flower, bloom, blossom; choice, best, pick; flourish; (pharm.) flour. —s d'arbre; blossoms of a tree. Être dans la — de son âge; to be in the prime of one's age. Être dans toute sa —; to be in its prime (of a thing—des choses). Avoir la — d'une chose; to have the best of a thing. Semer de —s; to strew with flowers. —s blanches; whites, fluor-albus. À — de; even with, level with. À — de terre; even with the ground.
fleuraison, or **floraison**,n.f., efflorescence, blowing-time of flowers.
fleur de lis, n.f., fleur-de-lis.
fleurdelisé, **-e**, part., marked with a fleur-de-lis.
fleurdeliser, v.a., to mark with a fleur-de-lis.
fleuré, adj., (her.) flowery, flowered.
fleurer, v.n., to smell, to exhale. Cela fleure bon; that smells nice.
fleuret, n.m., silk ferret; (fenc.) foil.
fleureté, (her.) V. **fleuré**.
fleurette, n.f., little flower, floweret; amorous discourse, gallant speech. Conteur de —s; sayer of gallant things.
fleuri, **-e**, part., flowery, florid, agreeable. Teint —; florid complexion. Écrire d'une manière —e; to write in a florid style.
fleurir, v.n., to flower, to blow; to bloom, to blossom; to thrive, to be in repute, to flourish, to prosper. Cet arbre fleurissait tous les ans deux fois; this tree blossomed twice every year. Cet auteur florissait sous le règne de —; that author flourished under the reign of. Les arts et les sciences florissaient alors; arts and sciences flourished then. [When used figuratively, in the sense of to be prosperous, the verb fleurir is irregular in the present part., which is florissant, and in the 3rd persons, singular and plural, of the imperfect of the indicative which are florissait, florissaient.]
fleurir, v.a., to ornament with flowers.
se fleurir, v.r., to ornament one's self with flowers.
fleurissant, **-e**, adj., blossoming, blooming, blowing. Les prés —s; the flowery meadows.
fleuriste, n.m.f., florist, floriculturist; artificial-flower-maker; (in compound words—dans les mots composés) flower. Jardinier —; flower-gardener, nursery-man. Jardin —; flower-garden.
fleuron, n.m., flower-work (paint., &c.); jewel, ornament; (print.) tail-piece. C'est le plus beau — de sa couronne; it is the brightest jewel in his crown.
fleuronné, **-e**, adj., (bot.) having florets; (paleography) ornamented. (her.) V. **fleuré**.
fleuve, n.m., river (which falls into the sea), stream; (myth., paint., sculpt.) river-god. Le bord d'un —; the bank of a river. L'embouchure

d'un —; the mouth of a river. Le — de la vie, the stream of life.
flexibilité, n.f., flexibility, flexibleness, pliancy.
flexible, adj., flexible, pliable, pliant.
flexion, n.f., flexion, bending.
flexueu-x, **-se**, adj., (bot.) flexuous.
flexuosité, n.f., (bot.) flexuosity.
flibot, n.m., (nav.) fly-boat.
flibustier (-tié), n.m., buccaneer, freebooter.
flic-flac, n.m., (onomatopœia) crack of the whip; (in dancing—danse) flick-flack.
flint-glass, n.m., flint-glass.
flocon, n.m., flake; flock, tuft. Un — de laine; a flock of wool. Il tombait de la neige à gros —s; it snowed in great flakes.
floconneux, **-se**, adj., flaky.
fionflon, n.m., tol-de-rol (chorus).
floraison, n.f. V. **fleuraison**.
floral, **-e**, adj., (bot.) floral. Jeux floraux; floral games.
flore, n.f., (bot.) anthology, flora; (myth.) Flora.
floréal, n.m., Floreal, the eighth month of the calendar of the first French republic, from April 20th to May 19th.
florence, n.m., sarcenet.
florencé, **-e**, adj., (her.) flowery.
florentin, **-e**, n. and adj., Florentine.
florentine, n.f., florentine.
florès (-rès), adv., figure, dash. Faire —; to make a show, to cut a dash.
florifère, adj., (bot.) floriferous.
florin, n.m., florin.
florissant, **-e**, adj., prosperous, flourishing.
floriste, n.m., florist.
flosculeu-x, **-se**, adj., (bot.) floscular, flosculous.
floss, n.m., (metal.) floss.
flot, n.m., wave, billow, flood, surge; tide, flood-tide; crowd (of persons—de personnes); stream, torrent. Les —s de la mer; the waves of the sea. Le bruit des —s; the roaring of the waves. Mettre un vaisseau à —; to set a ship afloat. Être à —; to be afloat. À —s; in streams, in torrents; in crowds.
flottable, adj., navigable (for rafts and loose wood—pour les radeaux et le bois).
flottage, n.m., floating of wood.
flottaison, n.f., (nav.) load water-line.
flottant, n.m.,(of hydraulic wheels—de roues hydrauliques) float.
flottant, **-e**, adj., floating, flowing; irresolute, wavering, fluctuating.
flotte, n.f., fleet; cable-buoy; (fishing—pêche) float.
flotté, **-e**, part., floated. Bois —; float-wood.
flottement (flot-mān), n.m., wavering, irresolution; (milit.) undulation.
flotter, v.n., to float, to waft; to be irresolute, to fluctuate, to waver. Faire — du bois; to float wood. — entre la crainte et l'espérance; to fluctuate between hope and fear. —, v.a., (nav.) to ease off, to slacken (cable).
flotteur, n.m., raftsman; (nav.) cable-buoy; water-gauge.
*****flottille**, n.f., flotilla.
flou, n.m., (paint.) softness of touch. — d'un pinceau; softness of a brush.
flou, adj., (paint.) light and soft.
flou, adv., (paint.) lightly.
flouer, v.a., to steal; to diddle out of.
flouerie (floū-ri), n.f., cheating.
floueur, n.m., sharper, cheat, gull-catcher.
flou-flou, n.m. (—), rustling of silk.
fluant, **-e**, adj., transient; badly sized (of paper — du papier).
fluate, n.m., (chem.) fluate.

fluaté, -e, *adj.*, fluate of. *Chaux —e;* fluate of lime.

fluctuant, *adj.*, fluctuating.

fluctuation. *n.f.*, fluctuation.

fluctueu-x, -se, *adj.*, fluctuating.

fluente, *n.f.*, (math.) fluent.

fluer, *v.n.*, to flow, to run.

fluet, -te, *adj.*, thin, spare, lean.

flueurs. *n.f.pl.*, (med.) fluor-albus, whites.

fluide, *adj.*, liquid.

fluide, *n.m.*, fluid.

fluidité, *n.f.*, fluidity, fluidness.

fluor, *n.m.*, (chem.) fluorine; (min.) fluor ; fluor-spar. *Spath —;* fluor, fluor-spar.

fluorine, *n.f.*, (chem.) fluorine ; (min.) fluorid.

flûte, *n.f.*, (nav.) flute; (mus.) flute; French roll. *Jouer de la —;* to play the flute. *— allemande, traversière;* German flute. *Ce qui vient de la — s'en retourne au tambour;* lightly come, lightly go. *Ajuster ses —s;* to tune one's pipes; to prepare one's measures. *Accordez vos —s;* settle it between you.

flûté, -e, *adj.*, soft, fluted, fluty.

flûteau, *n.m.*, child's whistle; (bot.) water-plantain.

flûter, *v.n.*, to play on the flute; to drink hard; to tipple.

flûteu-r, *n.m.*, **-se,** *n.f.*, (b.s.) player on the flute.

flûtiste, *n.m.*, flutist, flute-player.

fluvial, -e, *adj.*, fluvial.

fluviatile, *adj.*, fluviatile.

flux (flu), *n.m.*, flux, flow. influx, flood; stream, rising ; (at cards—*aux cartes*) flush.

fluxion, *n.f.*, inflammation; *pl.*, (math.) fluxions. *Une — de poitrine;* an inflammation of the lungs.

fluxionnaire, *adj.*, (l.u.) subject to inflammation.

foarre, foerre, fouarre, *n.m.*, straw.

foc, *n.m.*, (nav.) jib. *Grand —;* standing-jib.

focal. *adj.*, focal.

fœtus (fé-tus), *n.m.*, fœtus.

foi, *n.f.*, faith, belief; fidelity ; trust; credit, evidence; proof, testimony; (milit.) parole; fealty. *N'avoir ni — ni loi;* to regard neither law nor Gospel. *Ma —!* really ! faith ! *Fausser sa —;* to break one's faith. *— de gentilhomme;* as I am a gentleman, on the word of a gentleman. *Garder sa —;* to keep one's faith. *Manquer à sa —;* to break one's faith. *Bonne —;* honesty. plain-dealing. *Mauvaise —;* dishonesty. *Un homme de bonne —,* an honest man. *Ajouter — à quelque chose;* to give credit to anything. *Avez-vous — à ces contes-là ?* do you give credit to such stories? *En — de quoi;* in testimony whereof. *De bonne —;* sincerely, honestly, uprightly, in earnest. *Agir de bonne —;* to act fairly.

foible. *V.* **faible.**

foie, *n.m.*, liver. *Maladie de —;* liver-complaint.

foin, *n.m.*, hay, grass. *Meule de —;* haystack. *Grenier à —;* hayloft. *Faire les —s;* to make hay. *Mettre du — dans ses bottes;* to feather one's nest.

foin ! *int.*, plague ! deuce ! *— de lui!* deuce take him !

foire, *n.f.*, (l. ex.) diarrhœa; fair (market); fairing. *La — n'est pas sur le pont ;* there is no occasion to be in such a hurry. *Ils s'entendent comme larrons en —;* they are as thick as thieves together.

foirer, *v.n.*, (l.ex.) to have diarrhœa.

foireu-x, -se, *adj.*, (l.ex.) lax, relaxed. — *n.*, one who is relaxed. *Avoir la mine —se;* to look pale, sick.

fois, *n.f.*, time (repetition). *Une — par an ;*

once a year. *Deux — par semaine;* twice a week. *Plusieurs —;* several times. *De — à autre;* from time to time. *Une autre —;* another time. *Une — pour toutes;* once for all. *Une — autant;* as much again. *À la —, tout à la —;* all together, all at once. *Autant de — que, toutes les — que;* as often as. *Une — n'est pas coutume;* once does not make a habit. *À plusieurs —;* repeatedly. *Mille — pour une;* once for a thousand. *Y regarder à deux —;* to look at it twice. *N'en pas faire à deux —;* not to hesitate a moment. *Trois — trois;* three times three.

foison. *n.f.*, plenty, abundance. *À —;* plentifully, abundantly.

foisonner, *v.n.*, to abound ; to increase (of animals—*des animaux*).

fol. -le, *adj.* *V.* **fou.**

folâtre. *adj.*, gamesome, sportive, frolicsome, playful.

folâtrer. *v.n.*, to play, to sport, to toy, to romp, to frolic. *En folâtrant;* sportively, wantonly.

folâtrerie, *n.f.*, frolic, prank, toying, wanton trick.

foliacé. -e. *adj.*, foliaceous.

foliaire, *adj.*, relating to leaves, of leaf, of leaves.

foliation, *n.f.*, (arch.) feathering; (bot.) foliation.

folichon. -ne, *n.* and *adj.*, wag, frolicsome person; gamesome, wanton, sportive, frolicsome. *Un petit —;* a little wag.

folie, *n.f.*, madness, folly. lunacy, frenzy ; piece of folly, foolery, foolishness, foolish thing; country residence. *Un accès de —;* a fit of madness. *Faire une —;* to do a foolish act. *Qui fait la — la boit ;* as you brew so you must drink. *Aimer à la —;* to love to distraction. *À la —;* madly.

folié, -e, *adj.*, foliated.

folio, *n.m.*, folio. *Un in- — (—);* a folio book. *— recto;* first page. *— verso;* second page.

foliole, *n.f.*, (bot.) foliole.

follement (fol-mǎn), *adv.*, madly, foolishly, dotingly, extravagantly.

follet. -te. *adj.*, wanton, playful, frolicsome; downy (of hair—*poil*). *Poil —;* down. *Feu —;* ignis fatuus, will-o'-the-wisp, will-with-the-wisp. jack-with-a-lantern. *Esprit —;* goblin.

follet, *n.m.*, goblin; ignis fatuus, will-o'-the-wisp, will-with-the-wisp, jack-with-a-lantern.

folliculaire, *n.m.*, (b.s.) pamphleteer.

follicule, *n.m.*, follicle.

follicule, *n.f.*, (pharm.) pod (of senna—*du séné*).

fomentation, *n.f.*, fomentation.

fomenter. v.a., to foment. *— des troubles;* to excite troubles. *— une querelle;* to stir up a quarrel.

foncé. -e. *adj.*, dark (of colour—*couleur*).

foncement (fons-mǎn), *n.m.*, sinking (of wells—*de puits*).

foncer, v.a., to put a bottom to (a cask—*à un tonneau*); to sink (wells—*puits*).

fonceur, *n.m.*, sinker (of wells—*de puits*).

fonci-er, -ère, *adj.*, landed ; ⊙ skilled, learned. *Contribution — ère;* land-tax.

foncièrement (-sièr-mǎn), *adv.*, thoroughly, completely; at bottom.

fonction, *n.f.*, functions, office; *pl.*, functions, duty, office. *Entrer en —;* to enter on one's functions. *Faire ses —s;* to perform one's duties. *Sortir de —;* to retire from office.

fonctionnaire. *n.m.*, one who holds an office, functionary; officer.

fonctionnel, -le, *adj.*, functional.

fonctionnement, *n.m.*, acting, operating, working.

fonctionner, *v.n.*, to work, to act.

fond, *n.m.*, bottom, ground; groundwork; foundation; depth; centre, heart, further end, most remote part; main point; basis; (paint.) background; *pl.*, (print.) inner margin; (thea.) back-scene; (mining—*mines*) underground; recess; (nav.) flooring. *Sans* —; bottomless. *Tomber au* —; to fall to the bottom. *Le* — *d'un carrosse;* the back of a coach. — *de lit;* wooden bottom of a bed. *Faire* — *sur;* to depend upon. *Le* — *d'un bois;* the heart of a forest. *Il faut venir au* —; we must get to the bottom. *Voir le* — *du sac;* to search a thing to the bottom. *Velours à* — *d'or;* velvet with a gold ground. *Des arbres occupent le* — *du tableau;* trees occupy the back-ground of the picture. *Le* — *d'un miroir;* the back of a looking-glass. *Bas*— (— *s*); deep water. *Haut*—(—*s*); shallow water. *Perdre* —; to get, to swim, beyond one's depth. *Couler à* —; (nav.) to sink, to run down. *À* —; thoroughly, fully, to the bottom, perfectly. *Il possède cette science à* —; he is thoroughly master of that science. *Au* —; in the main, at the bottom. *De* — *en comble;* wholly, from top to bottom. *Il est ruiné de* — *en comble;* he is utterly ruined.

fondamental, **-e**. *adj.*, of the foundation; fundamental, essential.

fondamentalement (-tal-män) *adv.*, fundamentally.

fondant, **-e**. *adj.*, melting.

fondant, *n.m.*, flux.

fondat-eur, *n.m.*, **-rice**, *n.f.*, founder.

fondation, *n.f.*, foundation; groundwork; bottoming (of roads—*des routes*); endowment; establishment. *La* — *d'une colonie;* the establishment of a colony.

fondé, *n.m.*, person authorized to act for another. — *de pouvoir, de procuration;* private attorney; agent acting under power of attorney.

fondé, **-e**. *adj.*, that has a foundation, founded; (fin.) consolidated. *Il est* — *à;* he has a right to.

fondement (fond-män), *n.m.*, foundation; groundwork; basis; fundament. *Jeter les* —*s de la paix;* to lay the foundations of peace. *Ce bruit est sans* —; that report is without foundation.

fonder, *v.a.*, to lay the foundation, to build, to erect, to found; to ground, to establish, to endow. — *un empire;* to lay the foundation of an empire.

se fonder, *v.r.*, to rely, to be grounded, to be founded. — *sur l'analogie;* to be founded upon analogy.

fonderie (fon-dri), *n.f.*, foundry, foundery, founding; melting-house, smelting-house. — *de caractères d'imprimerie;* letter-foundry.

fondeur, *n.m.*, founder, melter; smelter (of ore—*de minerai*). — *en caractères d'imprimerie;* letter-founder.

fondoir, *n.m.*, melting-house (for melting fat, tallow—*pour les suifs*).

fondre, *v.a.*, to melt, to dissolve, to cast; (paint.) to soften; to blend. — *une cloche;* to cast a bell.

se fondre, *v.r.*, to melt; to dissolve; to blend, to coalesce; to be cast; to diminish, to disappear suddenly.

fondre, *v.n.*, to melt down; to melt away; to dissolve; to burst (into tears—*en larmes*); to dart, to pounce; to make a stoop (of birds—*des oiseaux*); to fall away. *Il fondit sur lui;* he pounced upon him. — *en larmes;* to burst into tears.

fondrière, *n.f.*, bog, quagmire, slough.

***fondrilles**, *n.f.pl.*, grounds, sediment, dregs.

fonds (fôn), *n.m.*, land, soil, ground; landed property; funds, stock, capital, principal, cash, ready money; stock in trade, business; *pl.*, funds, stocks. *Biens*— —; land. *Acheter des* —; to put money in the funds. *Mettre de l'argent à* — *perdu;* to sink money. *Spéculer sur les* — *publics;* to speculate in the public funds. *Céder son* —; to give up one's business. *Être en* —; to be in cash. *Faire rentrer des* —; to get in money. *Ce marchand a vendu son* —; that tradesman has sold his business. *Un* — *inépuisable de science;* an inexhaustible stock of science.

fondue, *n.f.*, (cook.) cheese and eggs.

fonger, *v.n.*, to blot (of paper—*du papier*).

fongible, *adj.*, (jur.) that may be replaced in kind.

fongosité, *n.f.*, (med.) fungus.

fongueu-x -se, (-gheû, -z), *adj.*, (med.) fungous, proud.

fongus (-gus), *n.m.*, (med.) fungus.

fontaine, *n.f.*, fountain; spring. *De l'eau de* —; spring water. *Il a été à la* — *de Jouvence;* he has been to the mill, he has renewed his youth.

fontainier. *V.* **fontenier.**

fontanelle, *n.f.*, (anat.) fontanel.

fontange, *n.f.*, topknot (ribbon—*ruban*).

fonte, *n.f.*, melting, casting, cast; cast-iron; brass; smelting; (print.) font, fount; holster (of saddles—*de selles*). *Fer de* —; cast-iron. *Jeter en* —; to cast.

fontenier, *n.m.*, fountain-maker.

fonticule, *n.m.*, (surg.) issue.

fonts (fôn), *n.m.pl.*, font. *Tenir quelqu'un sur les* —; to stand godfather, godmother, to any one.

for, *n.m.*, (l.u.) tribunal, conscience. — *extérieur;* temporal jurisdiction of the church. — *intérieur;* spiritual jurisdiction; conscience.

forage, *n.m.*, boring; drilling; (feudalism—*féodalité*) due upon wine.

forain, **-e**. *adj.*, foreign, alien, outlandish. *Marchand* —: hawker. *Rade* —*e* (nav.); open roadstead. *Spectacle* —; show (at fairs—*aux foires*).

foraminé, *adj.*, foraminous.

forban, *n.m.*, pirate, sea-robber, corsair.

forçage, *n.m.*, (coin.) overweight.

forçat, *n.m.*, galley-slave, convict.

force, *n.f.*, strength, might, force; forcibleness, power; violence, constraint, necessity; command, vigour, energy, efficacity; fortitude, resolution; *pl.*, troops, forces; (nav.) press (of sail—*de voiles*). *Les* —*s lui manquent;* his strength fails him. *Frapper de toute sa* —; to strike as hard as one can. *Mettre des* —*s sur pied;* to raise forces. *Assembler ses* —*s;* to muster one's forces. *Les* —*s de terre;* land-forces. *La* — *de la vérité;* the power of truth. *Céder à la* — *majeure;* to yield to superior force. *User de* —, *employer la* —; to use forcible means. *Faire* — *de voiles;* to crowd all sail. *Maison de* —; house of correction, bridewell. *Il n'a ni* — *ni vertu;* he has neither valour nor virtue. *À* — *de;* by dint of, by strength of. *À* — *de bras;* by strength of arm. *À*—*d'argent;* with large sums of money. *De* —, *par* —; forcibly, by force, by forcible means. *À toute* —; by all means. *Travailler à* —; to work hard. *Il m'est* — *de;* it is absolutely necessary for me to.

force, *adv.*, much, a great quantity of, a great deal of; many, a great many, a great number of. *Je leur fis* — *compliments;* I paid them an abundance of compliments.

forcé, **-e**. *part.*, forced, unnatural; (man.) overreached. *Vent* — (nav.); violent, boisterous wind.

forcément, *adv.*, forcibly, by force, compulsively; necessarily.

forcement, *n.m.*, forcing, compelling. — *de recette;* exercise of the right of compelling public officials to refund the public Treasury for the taxes they have neglected to recover.

forcené, -e, *n.* and *adj.*, madman, madwoman; furious, mad, infuriate; enraged.

forceps (-séps), *n.m.*, (surg.) forceps.

forcer, *v.a.*, to force, to compel, to constrain; to impel ; to break open, to wrench, to wrest, to bend, to break through; (hunt.) to emboss; to run down, to hunt; — *une porte;* to break open a door. — *une clef ;* to force a key. — *un cheval ;* to override a horse. — *la nature;* to force nature. — *sa voix ;* to strain one's voice. — *de voiles;* to crowd all sail.

se **forcer**, *v.r.*: to strain, to strain one's self ; to do violence to one's feelings.

forces, *n.f.pl.*, shears.

forclore, *v.a.*, (jur.) to foreclose.

forclusion, *n.f.*, (jur.) foreclosure, foreclosing.

foré, -e, *part.*, bored, perforated; piped (of keys— *des clefs*).

forer, *v.a.*, to bore, to drill, to perforate, to pierce.

forestier, *n.m.*, ranger, forester.

foresti-er, -ère, *adj.*, forest, pertaining to forests. *Enlever au régime des lois —ères;* to disafforest.

forêt, *n.f.* forest, forest-land, wood-land. *Conversion en —;* afforestation. *Convertir en —;* to afforest. *Déclarer ne plus être —;* to disafforest.

foret. *n.m.*, gimlet, borer, drill.

forfaire, *v.n.*, to fail in one's duty ; to trespass; to prevaricate. *Il a forfait à l'honneur;* he has forfeited his honour.

forfaire, *v.a.*, to forfeit (fief).

forfait, *n.m.*, crime, offence, transgression; contract. *Entreprendre à —;* to contract by the job.

forfaiture, *n.f.*, forfeiture ; prevarication.

⊙**forfante**, *n.m.*, romancer, quack, charlatan.

forfanterie (-fan-trī), *n.f.*, romancing, bragging, puffing, boasting.

forficule, *n.f.*, (ent.) earwig.

forge, *n.f.*, forge, smithy; melting-house. —*s;* iron-works. *Grosse— :* large forge. — *de campagne;* (milit.) travelling forge.

forgeable (-jabl), *adj.*, that may be worked by fire and the hammer.

forger, *v.a.*, to forge, to hammer ; to invent, to contrive, to forge, to coin. — *des nouvelles;* to fabricate news. — *des mots ;* to coin words.

se **forger**, *v.r.*, to create, to imagine, to conjure up.

forgeron, *n.m.*, smith, blacksmith. *En forgeant on devient —;* practice makes perfect.

forgeur, *n.m.*, forger, contriver, inventor, fabricator. — *de contes, de nouvelles ;* forger of tales, of news.

forhuer, or **forhuir**, *v.n.*, (hunt.) to blow, to wind (a horn — *un cor*).

forjet, *n.m.*, jutting out (of a wall—*d'un mur*).

forjeter, *v.n.*, (arch.) to jut out.

forlancer, *v.a.*, (hunt.) to dislodge, to start (game—*le gibier*).

⊙**forligner**, *v.n.*, to degenerate, to fall off ; to forfeit one's honour. *Elle a forligné;* she has made a false step.

forlonger, *v.a.*, to spin out, to lengthen, to protract.

se **forlonger**, *v.r.*, to be spun out, to be drawn out; (hunt.) to run a length. *Le cerf s'était forlongé ;* the stag had got ahead.

forlonger, *v.n.*, (hunt.) to forsake the country, to run a length (of a stag—*du cerf*).

se **formaliser**, *v.r.*, to take exception, offence, to feel offended, to feel affronted.

formalisme, *n.m.*, formalism.

formaliste, *adj.*, formal, precise, ceremonious. *Il est trop — :* he is too precise.

formaliste, *n.m.*, formalist.

formalité, *n.f.*, formality, form, ceremony. *Défaut de —, manque de —;* (jur.) informality.

formariage. *n.m.*, (feudal-law—*féodalité*), marriage between serfs belonging each to a different lord.

format, *n.m.*, form, size (of a book—*de livres*).

format-eur, -rice, *adj.*, formative, creative.

formation, *n.f.*, formation.

forme, *n.f.*, form, shape, figure, make; mode, mould, frame; body (of a hat — *d'un chapeau*) ; mould (in paper-making — *manufacture du papier*) ; (print.) form; seat; stall (of a choir — *dans un chœur*); bed of gravel; (vet.) ring-bone ; (nav.) dock. — *de soulier ;* last of a shoe. *Mettre des souliers en —;* to put shoes on the last. — *de chapeau ;* hat block. *Sans autre — de procès;* without any further formality. *En —;* formally. — *de procédure;* law proceeding. *En la — qui suit;* as follows. *Argument en —;* formal argument. *Pour la —;* for form's sake.

formel, -le, *adj.*, formal, express, precise, plain, explicit.

formellement (-mèl-mäṅ), *adv.*, formally, expressly, precisely, strictly.

former, *v.a.*, to form, to frame, to fashion, to make, to bring up, to cut out, to mould, to season ; (jur.) to array (a panel — *une liste de jurés*). — *une difficulté ;* to start a difficulty. — *une plainte;* to lodge a complaint. — *un jeune homme ;* to train up a youth.

se **former**, *v.r.*, to be made, formed ; to be bred, to form, to take, to assume a form, to come to some shape, to improve; to resolve one's self into (a committee, &c.—*en comité, &c.*). — *une idée de quelque chose ;* to form an idea of anything. *Il se formera avec le temps ;* he will become polished in time.

formica-leo, *n.m.* (—), myrmeleon, antlion.

formicant, *adj.*, (med.) (of the pulse — *du pouls*) weak and frequent.

formication, *n.f.*, (med.) formication.

formidable, *adj.*, formidable, dreadful, frightful ; tremendous.

formier, *n.m.*, last-maker.

formique, *adj.*, (chem.) formic.

formuer, *v.a.*, (hawking—*fauconnerie*) to mew.

formulaire, *n.m.*, formulary.

formule, *n.f.*, formula, form ; prescription. — *d'algèbre ;* algebraic formula.

formuler, *v.a.*, (med.) to write a prescription in due form ; to detail, to state; (jur.) to draw up in due form ; (alg.) to reduce to a formula.

fornicat-eur, *n.m.*, **-rice**, *n.f.*, fornicator.

fornication, *n.f.*, fornication.

forniquer, *v.n.*, to fornicate.

forpaître, or **forpaiser**, *v.n.*, (hunt.) to feed at a distance from the covert.

⊙**fors**, *prep.*, save, except, but.

forsenant, *adj.*, (hunt.) eager after the game (of dogs—*des chiens*).

fort, -e, *adj.*, strong, stout, powerful, violent, plentiful, copious ; severe (of illness—*d'une maladie*) ; sturdy, robust, lusty, hardy, able-bodied, vigorous, able ; hard, painful, difficult ; skilful, clever; high (of wind—*du vent*); heavy (of ground, of rain—*d'un terrain, de la pluie*). *Avoir la tête —e, l'esprit —;* to have a strong mind. *Un esprit — :* a free-thinker. *Un coffre-*

—, a strong box, a safe. *Colle —e*; glue-hold. *Terre —e*; heavy ground. *Place —e*; strong hold. *Expression —e*; significant expression. — *de poids*; overweight, too heavy. *À plus —e raison*; so much the more. *Le plus — en est fait*; the hardest part is over. *Être — aux échecs*; to play at chess very well. *Se faire —*; to undertake, to take upon one's self. *Se porter — pour quelqu'un*; to answer for any one. *Trouver plus — que soi*; to meet with more than one's match. *C'est plus — que moi*; I cannot help it. *C'est trop —, c'est par trop —*; it is too bad.

fort, *n.m.*, strongest part of a thing; thickest part (of a wood—*d'un bois*); stronghold, fort; strength; skill; depth, heat, height; centre. *Le — d'une affaire*; the main point of a business. *La critique est son —*; criticism is his .forte. *Dans le — de l'hiver*; in the depth of winter. *Dans le — de sa colère*; in the height of his passion. *Dans le — du combat*; in the heat of the fight. *Au — de la tempête*; in the height of the storm. — *de la halle*; porter (of the corn-exchange at Paris—*à la halle au blé de Paris*).

fort,*adv.*, very,very much,highly,extremely, vastly, exceedingly; hard, forcibly. — *bien*; very well. *Il pleut —*; it rains fast. *Frapper —*; to strike hard.

forte, *adv.*, (mus.) forte.

fortement, *adv.*, strongly, vigorously, with force, stoutly, forcibly, much; exceedingly.

forte-piano, *n.m.* (— —s), piano.

forteresse (for-très), *n.f.*, fortress, stronghold.

fortifiant, **-e**, *adj.*, strengthening, fortifying, invigorating.

fortifiant, *n.m.*, (med.) tonic.

fortification, *n.f.*, fortification; redoubt.

fortifier, *v.a.*, to fortify, to strengthen, to invigorate; to corroborate, to confirm. — *un camp*; to fortify a camp. *Le bon vin fortifie l'estomac*; good wine strengthens the stomach. *se fortifier*, *v.r.*, to fortify one's self, to gather strength, to grow strong; to make one's self a proficient; to gain proficiency; to make one's self better acquainted; to become skilled.

fortin, *n.m.*, (milit.) fortlet, little fort.

à fortiori (-cio-), *adv.*, à fortiori, much more.

fortitrer, *v.n.*, (hunt.) to avoid relays.

fortrait, **-e**, *adj.*, (of horses—*des chevaux*) overfatigued.

fortraiture,*n.f.*, overfatigue (of a horse—*du cheval*).

fortuit, **-e**, *adj.*, fortuitous, casual. *Cas —*; mere chance.

fortuitement(-tu-it-mān),*adv.*,fortuitously, casually, accidentally, by chance.

fortune, *n.f.*, fortune, chance, risk, hazard, wealth; (myth.)Fortune. *La — lui rit*; fortune smiles upon him. *Avoir de la —*; to possess property. *Artisan de sa —*; architect of one's own fortune. *La — du pot*; pot-luck. *Bonne —*; good luck, good fortune. *Mauvaise —*; ill-fortune, ill-luck. *Courir après la —*; to hunt after fortune. *Brusquer la —*; to tempt fortune. *Faire —*; to make a fortune. *Être en —*; to be lucky, to be in luck's way. *Manger sa —*; to squander one's fortune. *Il faut faire contre mauvaise — bon cœur*; we must bear up against bad fortune. — *de mer*; sea risks.

fortuné, **-e**, *adj.*, fortunate, lucky; happy.

⊙**fort-vêtu** (for-vê-tu), *n.m.*, person dressed above his condition.

forum (fo-rom), *n.m.*, (antiq.) forum.

forure, *n.f.*, bore, hole drilled.

fosse, *n.f.*, hole, pit, den, grave; (hort.) trench. *Basse- —*; dungeon. *Avoir un pied dans la —*; to have one foot in the grave. — *de*

céleri; celery-trench. — *aux lions*; lion's den; (nav.) boatswain's store-room. *Mettre dans la —*; to lay in the grave.

fossé, *n.m.*, ditch, drain; (fort.) moat, fosse. *Mourir au bord d'un —*; to die in a ditch. *Sauter le —*; to pass the Rubicon.

fossette,*n.f.*,dimple;(play)chuck-farthing. — *de l'estomac*; pit of the stomach.

fossile, *n.m.* and *adj.*, fossil.

fossoyage, *n.m.*, ditching; grave-digging.

fossoyer, *v.a.*, to ditch, to dig a trench round.

fossoyeur, *n.m.*, ditcher, grave-digger; sexton.

fou, **fol**, **-le**, *adj.*, mad, foolish, wild, insane, senseless, frolicsome; playful; excessively fond; distracting (of pain—*d'une douleur*); excessive. *Un fol espoir*; a foolish hope. *Devenir —*; to go mad. *Être — de*; to be mad for; to be passionately fond of. *Que vous êtes—*! how foolish you are!

fou, *n.m.*, **folle**, *n.f.*, madman, madwoman; madcap; mad-brain; jester, fool; bishop (at chess—*aux échecs*); (orni.)booby. *Maison de —s*; lunatic asylum. *Faire le —*; to play the fool. *Plus on est de —s, plus on rit*; one fool makes many; the more, the merrier.

fouace, *n.f.*, buttered roll.

fouage, *n.m.*, (feudalism—*féodalité*) fuage, hearth-money, hearth-penny.

*fouaille, *n.f.*, (hunt.) quarry.

*fouailler, *v.a.*, to lash, to whip.

foudre, *n.f.*,thunder,thunderbolt,lightning. *Coup de —*; clap of thunder. *La — est tombée sur*; a thunderbolt fell on. *Lancer la —*; to hurl the thunderbolt. *Être tué par la —*; to be killed by lightning.

foudre, *n.m.*, thunderbolt; great orator; great warrior, captain, hero; a large cask, a tun. *Un — de guerre*; a thunderbolt of war.

foudroiement, or **foudroîment** (foo-droa-mān), *n.m.*, striking with a thunderbolt.

foudroyant, **-e**, *adj.*, terrible, crushing, dreadful; fulminating; withering.

foudroyer, *v.a.*, to strike with thunder; to batter with cannon and mortars; to fulminate, to blast; to crush, to ruin, to confound.

fouée, *n.f.*, bat-fowling.

fouenne, *n.f.* V. **faîne**.

fouet, *n.m.*, whip, horsewhip, lash; whipcord; whipping; cat, cat-o'-nine-tails. *Faire claquer un —*; to crack a whip. *Faire claquer son —*; to sound one's own trumpet. *Donner le — à quelqu'un*; to whip any one. *Donner des coups de — à*; to whip. *Poulie à —* (nav.); tailblock.

fouetté, **-e**, *part.*, whipt, whipped; streaked (of flowers and fruit—*des fleurs et des fruits*). *De la crème —e*; whipt cream. *Tulipe —e*; streaked tulip.

fouetter,*v.a.*, to whip,to horsewhip, to lash, to scourge, to flog; (nav.) to lash; (nav.) to flap back against the masts (of sails—*des voiles*). *Il n'y a pas là de quoi — un chat*; it is a mere trifle. *Il a bien d'autres chiens à —*; he has other fish to fry.

fouetter, *v.a.* and *n.*, to cut (of the wind—*du vent*); to beat (of the hail, rain, snow—*de la grêle, de la pluie, de la neige*); to sweep (of cannon—*du canon*).

fouetteur, *n.m.*, flogger, whipper.

fougade,or **fougasse**,*n.f.*,(milit.)fougade, fougass.

fouger, *v.n.*, (hunt.) to grub (of wild boars—*du sanglier*).

fougeraie (fou-jrè), *n.f.*, fern-plot; ferny ground.

fougère, *n.f.*, (bot.) fern; brake; (fig.) drinking glass. — *aquatique, fleurie, royale*;

flowering fern, king's fern. — *impériale, femelle*; brake. — *musquée*; sweet fern.

fougon, *n.m.*, (nav.) cook's galley, caboose.

fougue (foug), *n.f.*, fury, passion, transport, heat, ardour, fire, spirit, spiritedness, mettle. *Dans la — de la colère*; in the heat of passion. *La — de la jeunesse*; the impetuosity of youth. *Un cheval qui a trop de —*; a horse that has too much mettle.

fougueu-x, -se (-gheû, -z), *adj.*, fiery, hot, hasty, impetuous, ardent, spirited, animated, passionate, mettlesome, high-mettled. *Cheval —*; spirited horse. *Passions —ses*; unruly passions.

*fouille, *n.f.*, excavating; excavation; digging; (arch.) getting.

*fouille-au-pot, (l.ex.) *n.m.* (—), scullion, turnspit.

*fouiller, *v.a.*, to excavate, to dig; to search, to pry into, to rummage; (paint., sculpt.) to sink. — *une mine*; to work a mine. — *quelqu'un*; to search any one. *Fouillez dans votre poche*; examine your pocket.

*se fouiller, *v.r.*, to search one's pockets, to feel in one's pockets; to search one another.

*fouiller, *v.n.*, to dig, to search, to rummage, to ransack. — *dans sa mémoire*; to ransack one's brain.

*fouillis, *n.m.*, confusion, medley.

fouine, *n.f.*, (mam.) martin, beech-martin; martlet; (agri.) pitchfork, fork; (fishing—*pêche*) gig, fishgig, fizgig, gaff.

fouiner, *v.n.*, to sneak away, to steal away, to slink off, to steal off.

fouir, *v.a.*, to dig, to delve.

fouissement (foo-is-mân), *n.m.*, digging.

foulage, *n.m.*, (manu.) fulling.

foulant, -e, *adj.*, pressing down. *Pompe —e*; forcing-pump.

foulard, *n.m.*, silk handkerchief.

foule, *n.f.*, crowd, throng, multitude, concourse, mob, press, shoal, fry, herd, common herd; (manu.) fulling. *Venir en —*; to flock, to throng together. *Entrer en —*; to crowd in. *La — des draps*; (manu.) the fulling of cloth. *Sortir de la —; se tirer de la —*; to rise above the common herd.

foulé, -e, *part.*, trodden down, trampled upon, oppressed; (manu.) milled.

foulée, *n.f.*, pile (of skins—*des peaux*); tread (of steps—*des pas*); *pl.*, (hunt.) foiling, fusee, slot; (man.) appui.

fouler, *v.a.*, to tread, to trample on, to trample down, to grind down, to oppress; to gall (animal); to sprain; (agri.) to jam; (manu.) to full; (manu.) to mill; (hunt.) to beat (a wood—*un bois*). — *la vendange*; to press the grapes. — *aux pieds*, to trample under foot. — *du drap*; to full cloth. — *un chapeau*; to work a hat. — *un cheval*; to override a horse.

se fouler, *v.r.*, to sprain one's self. — *le pied*; to sprain one's foot.

fouler, *v.n.*, (print.) to give impression.

foulerie (foo-lrî), *n.f.*, fullery.

fouleur, *n.m.*, wine-presser; fuller.

fouloir, *n.m.*, (manu.) beater; (artil.) rammer.

fouloire, *n.f.*, (manu.) fulling-board.

foulon, *n.m.*, fuller. *Chardon à —*; (bot.) teasel, fuller's thistle. *Moulin à —*; fulling-mill. *Terre à —*; fuller's-earth.

foulonnier, *n.m.*, fuller.

foulque, *n.f.*, (orni.) coot.

foulure, *n.f.*, sprain, strain; (manu.) fulling; (manu.) milling; *pl.*, (hunt.) foiling, fusee, slot (of a stag—*du cerf*); (vet.) warbles.

four, *n.m.*, oven; bakehouse; kidnapping-house; dark room; furnace; kiln; (metal.) hearth. *Mettre le pain au —*; to put the batch into the oven. — *de campagne*; portable oven. — *à briques*; brick-kiln. — *à chaux*; lime-kiln. *Gueule de —*; kiln-hole. *Des petits —s*; (cook.) small cakes. *Pièces de —*; (cook.) pastry. *Charger le —*; to heat the oven. *Ce n'est pas pour vous que le — chauffe*; that is not for you. *Vous viendrez cuire à mon —, je vous y attends*; you will have need of me some day, and then I will be revenged, even, with you. *Faire —*; to be unsuccessful, to fail, to break down (fam., thea.).

fourbe, *n.f.*, cheat, imposture, low villany, knavery.

fourbe, *n.m.f.*, cheat; knave, cozener.

fourbe, *adj.*, cheating, knavish, cozening. *Il a l'esprit — et rusé*; he has a crafty, cunning disposition.

fourber, *v.a.*, to cheat, to take in, to gull, to bubble, to trick.

fourberie, *n.f.*, cheat, knavery, cozenage, deceit.

fourbir, *v.a.*, to furbish, to brighten, to polish, to polish up.

fourbisseur, *n.m.*, furbisher; sword-cutler.

fourbissime, *adj.*, most knavish.

fourbissure, *n.f.*, furbishing; rubbing up.

fourbu, -e, *adj.*, (vet.) foundered; diseased in the feet. *Rendre —*; to founder.

fourbure, *n.f.*, foundering; founder in the feet.

fourche, *n.f.*, fork, pitchfork. —*s patibulaires*; forked gibbet. —*s Caudines*; Caudine forks. *Faire la —*; to fork, to branch off. *Faire une chose à la —*; to do a thing carelessly.

fourché, -e, *part.*, forked, split; cloven; (her.) fourchee. *Croix —e*; (her.) cross four-chee.

fourcher, *v.n.*, to fork; to branch off; to trip (of the tongue—*de la langue*). *Chemin qui fourche*; road that branches off. *La langue lui a fourché*; his tongue tripped.

se fourcher, *v.r.*, to fork, to branch off.

fourcher, *v.a.*, (agri.) to fork.

fourchet, *n.m.*, (vet.) foot-rot.

fourchetée, *n.f.*, forkful.

fourchette, *n.f.*, fork; rest (of a musket—*d'un fusil*); forset (of gloves—*des gants*); sleeve-bit (of a shirt—*d'une chemise*); prop (of carts—*des charrettes*). *Les dents d'une —*; the prongs of a fork. *Déjeuner à la —*; to take a meat breakfast. — *du pied d'un cheval*; the frog of a horse's foot.

fourchon, *n.m.*, prong.

fourchu, -e, *adj.*, forked; cloven; furcate. *Barbe —e*; forked beard. *Pied —*; cloven foot. *Chemin —*; road branching off. *Menton —*; chin indented in the middle.

fourchure, *n.f.*, furcation.

fourgon, *n.m.*, van, carriage; (milit.) waggon; poker (of ovens—*de fours*); (railways) van. *La pelle se moque du —*; it's the kettle calling the pot.

fourgonner, *v.n.*, to poke the fire (of an oven—*d'un four*); to stir, to poke the fire; to poke, to fumble, to rummage.

fourmi, *n.f.*, ant, pismire, emmet. *Avoir des —s dans l'oreille*; to feel a tingle in one's ear.

fourmilier, *n.m.*, ant-eater.

fourmilière, *n.f.*, ant-hill, ant-nest; swarm.

fourmi-lion, *n.m.*, (—*s* —*s*). *V.* **formica-leo**.

*fourmillement, *n.m.*, tingling.

*fourmiller, *v.n.*, to swarm, to abound with, to be full of, to crawl with; to feel a tingling, to tingle. *Les vers fourmillent dans ce fromage*; that cheese is crawling with maggots.

fournage, *n.m.*, price of baking.

fournaise, *n.f.*, furnace.

fourneau, *n.m.*, stove, furnace; (milit.) chamber (mine); *pl.*, (nav.) cook's galley. —

de cuisine; kitchen stove. — *portatif;* portable furnace. *Le — d'une pipe;* the bowl of a pipe. *Haut —;* blast furnace.

fournée, *n.f.,* a batch, baking.

fourni-er, *n.m.,* **-ère,** *n.f.,* oven-keeper; parish-baker.

fournil (-ni), *n.m.,* bakehouse.

fourniment, *n.m.,* ⊙powder-flask, powder-horn; (milit.) belt, shoulder-belt.

fournir, *v.a.,* to furnish, to provide, to supply, to stock, to store; to make up, to complete; to draw a bill. — *l'armée de vivres;* to supply the army with provisions. — *des défenses;* to furnish means of defence.

se **fournir,** *v.r.,* to furnish, to supply, one's self.

fournir, *v.n.,* to contribute, to supply, to be sufficient, to suffice. — *à la dépense;* to bear the expense.

fournissement (-nis-mān), *n.m.,* (com.) share of capital; capital.

fournisseur, *n.m.,* contractor, tradesman, purveyor, supplier.

fourniture, *n.f.,* furnishing, providing, supplying; supply, provision. *Il fait les —s de la maison;* he provides for the family. — *de salade;* dressing of a salad. *Faire — de;* to supply.

fourrage, *n.m.,* fodder, provendor; forage; (artil.) wad, wadding; foraging-party. — *vert;* green fodder, grass. — *sec;* dry fodder, hay. *Envoyer au —;* to send out a foraging.

fourrager, *v.n.,* to forage; to pilfer, to plunder. — *dans un champ;* to forage in a field — *au vert;* to forage for grass. — *au sec;* to forage for hay.

fourrager, *v.a.,* to forage, to ravage; to rummage; to rake.

fourragère. *adj.f.,* fit for fodder. *Plantes —s;* plants fit for fodder.

fourrageur, *n.m.,* forager.

fourré, *n.m.,* thicket, brake.

fourré, -e, *part.,* interchanged; secret; underhand (of blows—*d'un coup*); woody (of countries—*d'un pays*); mixed (of hay, straw—*du foin, de la paille*); furred (of clothing—*des vêtements*); plated (of medals—*des médailles*). *Bois —;* wood full of thickets and briars. *Pays —;* country full of woods, hedges, &c. *Coup —;* underhand trick, thrust. *Paix —e;* peace suddenly patched up. *Médaille —e;* plated medal. *Des langues —es;* stuffed pig, sheep, or neat's tongues.

fourreau, *n.m.,* case, scabbard, sheath, cover; child's frock. *L'épée use le —;* the sword wears out the scabbard. *Coucher dans son —;* to sleep in one's clothes.

⊙**fourrelier** (foor-lié), *n.m.,* scabbard-maker

fourrer, *v.a.,* to put, to thrust; to cram, to stuff; to beat, to knock; to line with fur; (nav.) to serve (cables and ropes—*câbles et cordages*). *Fourrez cela dans l'armoire;* put that away into the cupboard. *Il fourre du latin dans ses discours;* he stuffs his speeches with Latin. — *quelque chose dans la tête de quelqu'un;* to beat a thing into any one's brains. *Il fourre son nez partout;* he pokes his nose everywhere.

se **fourrer,** *v.r.,* to get, to creep, in; to intrude one's self, to poke one's self in; to wear warm clothing. *Il se fourre partout;* he thrusts himself in everywhere. *Ne savoir où —;* not to know where to hide one's self.

fourreur, *n.m.,* furrier.

fourrier, *n.m.,* harbinger; (milit.) quartermaster.

fourrière, *n.f.,* pound. *Mettre un cheval en —;* to pound a horse.

fourrure, *n.f.,* fur; (her.) vair; (nav.) service.

fourvoiement (-voa-mān), *n.m.,* (l.u.) going astray, wandering.

fourvoyer, *v.a.,* to mislead, to lead astray, to lead into error.

se **fourvoyer,** *v.r.,* to go astray, to stray; to err grossly.

fouteau, *n.m.,* beech, beech-tree.

foutelaie, *n.f.,* plantation of beech-trees.

foyer, *n.m.,* fire-grate, hearth, hearthstone; (thea.) lobby, green-room; focus; *pl.,* home. — *des acteurs* (thea.); green-room. — *du public* (thea.); lobby. *Combattre pour ses —s;* to fight for one's home. *Aimer à garder son —;* to like quiet, and to lead a secluded life.

frac, *n.m.,* evening dress coat.

fracas, *n.m.,* crash, noise; din, bustle, fuss. *Avec —;* with a crash. *Faire du — dans le monde;* to make a noise in the world.

fracasser, *v.a.,* to break to pieces, to shatter.

se **fracasser,** *v.r.,* to break to pieces, to shatter.

fraction, *n.f.,* breaking; fraction; portion; (arith.) fraction.

fractionnaire, *adj.,* fractional.

fractionnement, *n.m.,* dividing into fractions.

fractionner, *v.a.,* to divide into fractions.

fracture, *n.f.,* breaking (with violence—*avec violence*); rupture; (surg.) fracture.

fracturé, -e, *adj.,* (surg.) fractured.

fracturer, *v.a.,* (surg.) to fracture.

se **fracturer,** *v.r.,* (surg.) to fracture.

fragile, *adj.,* fragile; brittle; frail. — *comme du verre;* as brittle as glass. *Fortune —;* frail fortune.

fragilité, *n.f.,* fragility; brittleness; frailty.

fragment, *n.m.,* fragment, piece, scrap.

fragmentaire, *adj.,* fragmentary, fragmental.

fragon, *n.m.,* (bot.) butcher's broom.

frai, *n.m.,* spawn, spawning (of fish—*des poissons*); fry (young fish—*petits poissons*); roe, hard roe (of fish—*de poisson*).

fraîchement (frèsh-mān), *adv.,* coolly, freshly; coldly; newly, recently.

fraîcheur, *n.f.,* coolness, freshness, bloom; floridness, ruddiness; lustre, brilliancy; (nav.) flow of wind. *La — de ces fleurs;* the freshness of these flowers. *La — du teint;* the floridness of the complexion.

fraîchir, *v.n.,* to freshen, to blow fresh.

frairie, *n.f.,* (fam.) entertainment, merry-making, merriment. *Faire —, être en —;* to make merry, to be merry-making.

fra-is, -îche, *adj.,* cool, fresh, coldish; recent, new, youthful; florid, ruddy. *Temps —;* cool weather. *Eau —îche;* cold water. *Des nouvelles —îches;* fresh news. *Des œufs —;* new-laid eggs. *Du pain —;* new bread. *Plaie toute —îche;* raw wound. *Du saumon —;* fresh salmon. *Des troupes —îches;* fresh troops. *Un teint —;* a florid complexion.

frais, *n.m.,* cool, coolness, freshness; cool spot; (nav.) gale. *Mettre du vin au —;* to cool wine. *Il fait —;* it is cool. *Prendre le —;* to take the air, to go out for an airing. *Bon —, joli —;* (nav.) fresh gale. *Grand —;* hard, strong gale.

frais, *n.m.pl.,* expense, expenses; charge, charges. *Faux —;* incidental expenses. *Menus —;* petty expenses. *Les —d'un procès;* the costs of a lawsuit. *Tous — faits;* clear of all charges. *À grands —;* very expensively. *À peu de —;* with little expense, cheap. *Constituer quelqu'un en —;* to put any one to expense. *Se mettre en —;* to put one's self to expense. *Recommencer sur nouveaux —;* to begin anew, to begin over again.

fraise, *n.f.,* (bot.) strawberry; ruff; (fort.)

fraise; (hunt.) start; crow. —s des bois; wood-strawberries. — de veau; calf's crow.

fraisement (frèz-mān), n.m., (arch.) starling; (fort.) fraising.

fraiser, v.a., to plait, to ruffle; (fort.) to fraise; to knead dough thoroughly well.

fraisette, n.f., small ruff.

fraisier, n.m., strawberry-plant.

fraisil (-zi), n.m., coal-dross.

framboise, n.f., (bot.) raspberry. —sauvage, blackberry.

framboisé, -e, part., flavoured with raspberries; having a flavour of raspberries.

framboiser, v.a., to give a taste of raspberry.

framboisier, n.m., raspberry-bush, raspberry-plant.

framée, n.f., Frankish lance.

franc (fran), n.m., franc (French coin worth 9·69 pence). Au marc le —; at the rate of so much in the pound.

franc, -he (fran, frānsh), adj., free, unconstrained, exempt from; frank, downright, open, sincere; entire, full; complete; true, real; mere; arrant; staunch, right; very; whole, clear; (paint.) bold. — de port; post-paid. Compagnie —he; free-company. Cœur —; open heart. Être — du collier; to draw freely (of horses—des chevaux); (fig.) to be always ready to come forward. Un — charlatan; a downright quack. Une —he coquette; an arrant jilt. — Taupins. V. **taupins**.

franc, adv., frankly, freely, plainly, openly, sincerely; clean, quite, completely, entirely.

franc, n.m., (hort.) seedling.

fran-c, -que, n. and adj., Frank; Frankish.

français, -e, adj., French. La langue —e; the French tongue. À la —e; after the French fashion.

français, n.m., -e, n.f., Frenchman, French-woman.

français, n.m., French. Entendre le —; to understand French. Parler —; to speak French; to speak plainly, to call a spade a spade.

franc-alleu, n.m. (—s —s). V. **alleu**.

francatu, n.m., a kind of apple.

de **franc-étable**, adv., (nav.) of two ships running into each other, and striking each other's prow.

franc-fief, n.m. (—s —s), a fief possessed by a commoner.

franc-funin, n.m. (—s —s), (nav.) white hawser.

franchement (frānsh-mān), adv., frankly, freely, openly, plainly, sincerely, unreservedly, ingenuously, boldly. J'avoue — que; I frankly acknowledge that.

franchir, v.a., to leap, to get over; to clear; to pass, to pass over, to overstep; to break through; to cross; to surmount. Il a franchi le fossé; he has jumped over the ditch — une barrière; to clear a bar. — les montagnes; to cross the mountains. — les bornes du devoir; to overstep the bounds of duty. — le pas; to take a resolution. — le mot; to let out the word. — une difficulté; to overcome a difficulty.

franchise, n.f., franchise, exemption, immunity, freedom (of a city—d'une ville); frankness, sincerity, openness, candour, plainness; (paint.) boldness, freedom. Parler avec —; to speak with frankness. — du coloris; (paint.) freedom of colouring.

francisation, n.f., gallicizing; registering as a French ship.

franciscain, n.m., franciscan friar, grey friar.

franciser, v.a., to Frenchify.

se **franciser**, v.r., to Frenchify one's self, to become Frenchified.

francisque, n.f., Frankish battle-axe.

franc-maçon, n.m. (—s —s), freemason.

franc-maçonnerie, n.f. (n.p.), freemasonry.

franco, adv., free of expense. Écrire —; address, post-paid.

francolin, n.m., (orni.) francolin.

franc-parler, n.m. (n.p.), liberty of speech.

franc-quartier, n.m. (—s —s), (her.) quarter, franc-quarter.

franc-réal, n.m. (—s —s), sort of pear.

Ⓞ**franc-salé**, n.m. (—s —s), right to take salt from the excise salt-store without paying the tax.

Ⓞ**franc-tenancier**, n.m. (—s —s), free-holder.

franc-tireur, n.m. (—s —s), (milit.) irregular sharp shooter.

frange, n.f., fringe, valance.

frangé, -e, adj., (bot.) fimbriate.

franger, v.a., to fringe.

franger, or **frangier**, n.m., fringe-maker.

frangipane, n.f., kind of pastry.

frangipanier, n.m., (bot.) red jasmine.

franque, adj.f., Frankish.

franquette, n.f., (l.u.) frankness. À la bonne —; frankly, freely, sincerely.

frappant, -e, adj., striking, impressive.

frappe, n.f., (coin.) stamp; (type-founding —fonderie de caractères) set of matrices.

frappé, -e, part., stuck; iced (of liquids—des boissons); strong and close (of cloth—du drap); powerful, forcible. — d'étonnement; struck with wonder. Vers bien —s; spirited verses.

frappé, n.m., (mus.) fall (of the foot—du pied).

frappe-main, n.m. (n.p.), hot-cockles (game—jeu).

frappement (frap-mān), n.m., striking (of the rock by Moses—du rocher par Moïse).

frapper, v.a., to strike, to smite, to slap, to tap, to hit; to make an impression; to ice (liquids—boissons); (nav.) to seize. — vivement; to rap. — avec le pied; to stamp. — légèrement; to pat. — la terre du pied; to stamp one's foot upon the ground. — de la monnaie; to stamp money. — un coup; to strike a blow.

se **frapper**, v.r., to strike one's self; to strike one another; to have one's mind filled with sinister thoughts.

frapper, v.n., to knock, to strike, to rap. — à la porte; to knock at the door. — juste; to hit home. Entendre — ; to hear a knock.

frappeu-r, n.m., -se, n.f., beater; striker.

frasque, n.f., freak, whim, sudden, unexpected prank.

frater (-tèr), n.m., surgeon's boy; sawbones; village barber; (milit., nav.) barber.

fraternel, -le, adj., fraternal, brotherly.

fraternellement (-nèl-mān), adv., fraternally.

fraterniser, v.n., to fraternize.

fraternité, n.f., fraternity, brotherhood.

fratricide, n.m., fratricide.

fraude (frōd), n.f., fraud, deceit, imposition, fraudulency. En —; fraudulently. Faire une —; to commit a fraud. Passer en —; to smuggle.

frauder, v.a., to defraud.

fraudeu-r, n.m., -se, n.f., defrauder, smuggler.

frauduleusement (-leûz-mān), adv., fraudulently.

frauduleu-x, -se, adj., fraudulent.

fraxinelle, n.f., (bot.) fraxinella, white dittany, bastard dittany.

Ⓞ**frayant, -e**, adj., expensive.

frayer, v.a., to trace out, to open, to mark

out · to rub against, to graze, to brush. *Qui n'est pas frayé;* unbeaten, untrodden. *Chemin frayé;* beaten path. *Le coup n'a fait que — sa botte;* the blow only grazed his boot.

se frayer, *v.r.,* to open, to prepare (a way— *une voie*); to carve out.

frayer, *v.n.,* to wear away; to keep company, to frequent, to be on good terms; (of fishes—*des poissons*) to milt. *Ces deux hommes ne frayent pas ensemble;* these two men do not agree together.

frayère, *n.f.,* spot where fishes come to spawn.

frayeur, *n.f.,* fright, terror, dread, fear. *Être saisi de —;* to be seized with terror.

frayoir, *n.m.,* (hunt.) rub.

frayure, *n.f.,* (hunt) rubbing.

fredaine, *n.f.,* frolic, prank.

⊙**fredon,** *n.m.,* (mus) trill.

fredonnement (-do-n-măn), *n.m.,* humming, singing without words.

fredonner, *v.a.* and *n.,* to hum. *— un air;* to hum an air.

frégate, *n.f.,* frigate; (orni.) frigate-bird.

frégaton, *n.m.,* frigatoon.

frein, *n.m.,* bit, bridle; curb, check; brake; drag (of carriages—*de voitures*); (anat.) frænum, ligament. *Ronger son —;* to champ the bit; to fret one's self. *Mettre un — à sa langue;* to bridle one's tongue. *Il faut mettre un — à sa cruauté;* his cruelty must be curbed.

frelampier, *n.m.,* scamp, rascally fellow.

frelatage, *n.m.,* adulteration, sophistication.

frelater, *v.a.,* to adulterate, to sophisticate. *Ce vin est frelaté;* this wine is adulterated. *Ouvrages frelatés;* spurious works.

frelaterie (-la-trï), *n.f.,* sophistication, adulteration. *V.* **frelatage.**

frelateur, *n.m.,* sophisticator, adulterator.

frêle, *adj.,* frail; faint, weak.

⊙**frêler,** *v.n.,* to crackle (as hair, wool, feathers —*cheveux, laine, plumes*).

freloche, *n.f.,* gauze-net.

frelon, *n.m.,* (ent.) hornet; (bot.) knee-holly.

freluche, *n.f.,* tuft (of silk, &c.—*de soie, &c.*).

freluquet, *n.m.,* puppy, coxcomb.

frémir, *v.n.,* to shudder, to tremble, to quiver, to shake; to vibrate, to murmur, to moan; to simmer. *— de colère ·* to tremble with anger. *J'entendais — le feuillage;* I heard the leaves rustling. *La mer frémit;* the sea boils.

frémissant, -e, *adj.,* quivering, trembling.

frémissement (-mis-măn) *n.m.,* shudder, shuddering, quivering, trembling; roaring; vibration; murmuring (of water—*de l'eau*); simmering. *— cataire* (med.) thrill purring tremor of the heart.

frêne, *n.m.,* ash, ash-tree.

frénésie, *n.f.,* frenzy. *Tomber en —;* to be seized with frenzy.

frénétique, *adj.,* distracted, frantic, raving.

frénétique, *n.m.f.,* raving person.

fréquemment (-ka-măn), *adv.,* frequently, often.

fréquence, *n.f.,* frequency; quickness (of the pulse—*du pouls*).

fréquent, -e, *adj.,* frequent. *Pouls—;* quick pulse.

fréquentati-f, -ve, *adj.,* (gram.) frequentative.

fréquentatif, *n.m.,* (gram.) frequentative.

fréquentation, *n.f.,* frequenting, frequentation; company (persons—*personnes*).

fréquenter, *v.a.,* to frequent, to keep company with, to resort to; to receive the sacrament frequently.

fréquenter, *v.n.,* to frequent, to visit often, to associate with; to converse with.

frère, *n.m.,* brother: fellow-Christian; friar,

monk. *— aîné;* elder brother. *— cadet;* younger brother. *—s jumeaux;* twins. *Demi—;* half-brother. *— consanguin;* brother by the father's side. *— utérin;* brother by the mother's side. *— de lait;* foster-brother. *Beau- — (−x −s);* brother-in-law. *— lai, — convers;* lay-brother. *— chapeau;* assistant brother. (poet.) *— chapeau;* useless verse only introduced for the rhyme. *Faux —;* false brother, false friend. *— d'armes;* brother in arms.

fresaie, *n.f.,* (orni.) white-owl. *V.* **effraie.**

fresque, *n.f.,* fresco. *Peindre à —;* to paint in fresco.

fressure, *n.f.,* pluck. *— de veau;* calf's pluck. *— de cochon;* harslet, haslet.

fret (frè), *n.m.,* freight. *Prendre du —;* to take in freight.

fréter, *v.a.,* to let a ship to freight, to charter; to freight.

fréteur, *n.m.,* freighter; charterer.

fréttillant, -e, adj., frisky.

*frétillement, n.m , frisking, wriggling.

frétiller, v.n., to frisk, to wriggle. *Les pieds lui frétillent;* he is impatient to be off. *La langue lui frétille;* his tongue itches to speak.

fretin, *n.m.,* fry, young fish; trash, rubbish.

frette, *n.f.,* (tech.) iron hoop.

fretté, -e, *adj.,* (her.) fretty.

fretter, *v.a.,* to hoop.

freux, *n.m.,* rook. *Lieu habité par des —;* rookery.

friabilité, *n.f.,* friability.

friable, *adj.,* friable.

friand, -e, *adj.,* dainty, nice, fond. *Avoir le goût —;* to have a nice taste. *Un morceau —;* a delicate morsel. *Être — de;* to be fond of.

friand, *n.m.,* **-e,** *n.f.,* epicure, dainty person.

friandise, *n.f.,* daintiness, dainty, nicety. *Aimer les —s;* to be fond of dainties.

fricandeau, *n.m.,* (cook.) fricandeau.

fricassée, *n.f.,* (cook.) fricassee.

fricasser, *v.a.,* to fricassee; (pop.) to squander away, to waste, to dissipate.

fricasseur, *n.m.,* bad cook.

friche, *n.m.,* waste (uncultivated ground— *terrain inculte*). *Laisser une terre en —;* to let a piece of ground lie fallow.

fricot, *n.m.,* (pop.) ragout, stew.

fricoter, *v.n.,* (pop.) to feast; (fig., pop.) *— v.a.,* to squander.

fricoteur, *n.m.,* (pop.) feaster; fast liver; (milit.) a bad soldier.

friction, *n.f.,* friction.

frictionner, *v.a.,* (med.) to rub.

se **frictionner,** *v.r.,* (med.) to rub one's self.

frigidité, *n.f.,* frigidity.

frigorifique, *adj.,* frigorific.

frileu-x, -se, *adj.,* chilly.

frimaire, *n.m.,* Frimaire, the third month of the calendar of the first French republic, from November 21st to December 20th.

frimas, *n.m.,* rime, hoar-frost.

frime, *n.f.,* (triv.) show, pretence. *Il n'en a fait que la —;* he only made a show of it, it was all pretence.

fringale, *n.f.,* (fam.) sudden and unusual feeling of hunger. *Avoir la —;* to feel hungry all of a sudden.

fringant, -e, *adj.,* brisk, nimble, frisky. *Cheval —;* frisky horse.

fringuer (-ghé), *v.n.,* to frisk (of horses— *des chevaux*), to skip.

⊙**friolerie** (frio-lrï), *n.f.,* dainty.

friolet, *n.m.,* sort of pear.

⊙**fripe,** *n.f.,* rag; scrap; eatable.

friper, *v.a.,* to rumple; to spoil, to wear out; (pop.) to gobble down. to eat greedily, to devour; (pop.) to waste, to dissipate, to squander.

se friper, *v.r.*, to get rumpled.

friperie (fri-pri), *n.f.*, frippery, old clothes; old clothes' trade; rag-fair. *Se jeter, tomber, sur la — de quelqu'un;* to fall foul of any one.

fripe-sauce, *n.m.* (—), (l.ex.) greedy-gut, glutton; bad cook.

fripi-er, *n.m.*, **-ère**, *n.f.*, dealer in old clothes, dealer in old furniture.

fripon, -ne, *adj.*, knavish, roguish, rascally.

fripon, *n.m.*, **-ne**, *n.f.*, knave, rogue, cheat, swindler, rascal. *Un tour de —;* a knavish trick.

friponneau, *n.m.*, little rogue, rascal, cheat.

friponner, *v.a.* and *n.*, to cheat, to pick a pocket; to trick out of a thing, to pilfer, to steal.

friponnerie (-po-n-rî), *n.f.*, knavish trick, roguishness, knavery.

friquet, *n.m.*, tree-sparrow.

frire, *v.a.* and *n.*, to fry. *Il n'y a rien à —* (pop.); there is nothing to eat, there is nothing to be gained *Il n'a plus de quoi —;* he is quite ruined.

frise, *n.f.*, (arch.. paint., sculpt.) frieze; dread-nought. *Cheval de —* (fort.); cheval-de-frise.

friser, *v.a.*, to curl (hair—*les cheveux*), to frizzle, to crisp; to graze, to glance upon, to touch lightly, to brush.

se friser, *v.r.*, to curl, to curl one's hair; to fall into curl.

friser, *v.n.*, to curl; (print.) to slur.

frisotter, *v.a.*, (b.s.) to curl, to frizzle.

se frisotter, *v.r.*, (b.s.) to curl, to frizzle one's self.

frisquette, *n.f.*, (print.) frisket.

frisson, *n.m.*, shivering, cold fit; chilliness; slight emotion. *Avoir le —;* to have the shivers. *Cela donne le —;* that makes one shudder.

frissonnant, *adj.*, shuddering, shivering.

frissonnement (-so-n-mǎn), *n.m.*, shivering, chilliness.

frissonner, *v.n.*, to shiver, to shudder.

frisure, *n.f.*, curling, curliness; curls.

frit, -e, *part.*, (pop.) ruined, undone. *Il est —;* he is undone. *Tout est —;* all is over.

fritillaire, *n.f.*, (bot.) fritillary.

fritte, *n.f.*, (glass-making—*manufacture du verre*) frit.

friture, *n.f.*, frying; thing fried; fried fish; butter for frying.

frivole, *adj.*, frivolous, trifling. *Amusements —s;* trifling amusements. *Homme —;* frivolous man.

frivolité, *n.f.*, frivolity, frivolousness.

froc, *n.m.*, frock, garment (monk's—*de moine*). *Prendre le —;* to turn monk. *Jeter le — aux orties;* to throw off one's frock; to abandon one's profession.

frocard, *n.m.*, (b.s.) monk, priestling.

froid, *n.m.*, cold, coldness, chilliness, frigidity; unconcern; lukewarmness, dulness, reservedness. *Transir de —;* to benumb with cold. *Il est tout raide de —;* he is quite stiff with cold. *Avoir —;* to be cold. *Mourir de —;* to be starved with cold. *Grelotter de —;* to shiver with cold. *Prendre —;* to catch cold. *Il y a du — entre eux;* there is a coolness between them.

froid, -e, *adj.*, cold, frigid, lifeless; lukewarm, cool, indifferent, dispassionate, dull. *Temps —;* cold weather. *— comme glace;* as cold as ice. *Tempérament —;* cold constitution. *Un homme —;* a cold sort of a man. *Un homme de sang —;* a cool-headed man. *Battre — à quelqu'un;* to be cold to any one.

froidement (froa-dmǎn), *adv.*, coldly, frigidly, lukewarmly, dispassionately, lifelessly.

froideur, *n.f.*, coldness, chilliness; lukewarmness, indifference, coolness.

⊙**froidir**, *v.n.*, to grow cold.

froidure, *n.f.*, coldness (of the weather—*du temps*); cold, (fig.) winter.

⊙**froidureu-x**, **-se**, *adj.*, chilly.

froissement (froas-mǎn), *n.m.*, bruising, rumpling; (fig.) clashing; hurt, slight, affront.

froisser, *v.a.*, to bruise, to strike, to dash, to clash with; to rumple; to gall, to offend, to hurt. *Sa chute lui a froissé la cuisse;* he bruised his thigh by his fall. *— une étoffe;* to rumple a stuff.

se froisser, *v.r.*, to get offended.

froissure, *n.f.*, bruise, rumple.

frôlement (frôl-mǎn), *n.m.*, grazing, rustling.

frôler, *v.a.*, to graze, to touch lightly in passing.

se frôler, *v.r.*, to graze, to touch each other lightly in passing.

fromage, *n.m.*, cheese. *— mou;* soft cheese. *— à la crème;* cream-cheese. *— bien gras;* rich cheese.

fromag-er, *n.m.*, **-ère**, *n.f.*, cheesemonger.

fromager, *n.m.*, cheese-mould; (bot.) silk-cotton-tree.

fromagerie (-ma-jrî), *n.f.*, cheese-dairy, cheese-trade.

fromageu-x, **-se**, *adj.*, cheesy.

froment, *n.m.*, wheat.

fromentacée, *adj.f.*, (bot.) frumentaceous.

fromental, *n.m.*, rye-grass; oat-grass.

froncement (frons-mǎn), *n.m.*, contraction, knitting (of the brows—*des sourcils*); frowning; frown.

froncer, *v.a.*, to contract (the brow—*les sourcils*); to knit, to wrinkle; to purse (the lips—*les lèvres*); to gather (needle-work—*couture*).

se froncer, *v.r.*, to contract, to wrinkle.

froncis, *n.m.*, (needle-work—*couture*) gather, fold.

frondaison, *n.f.*, (bot.) foliation.

fronde, *n.f.*, sling; (surg.) bandage for the chin; Fronde (French hist.).

fronder, *v.a.*, to sling, to fling; to blame, to censure; to reflect upon.

fronderie (fron-drî), *n.f.*, (French hist.) riot of the Fronde; riot, disturbance.

frondeur, *n.m.*, slinger; censurer, fault-finder, critic.

front, *n.m.*, forehead, brow, face, front; boldness, impudence, brass. *La jeunesse au — riant;* youth with its smiling face. *— d'airain;* brazen-face. *Le — d'un bâtiment;* the front of a building. *De —;* in front, abreast.

frontal, *n.m.*, frontal; frontal (instrument of torture); (surg.) head-bandage.

frontal, -e, *adj.*, (anat.) frontal.

fronteau, *n.m.*, frontlet; frontal; (nav.) breast-work.

frontière (-ti-èr), *n.f.*, frontier, border, confine, limit.

frontispice, *n.m.*, frontispiece.

fronton, *n.m.*, (arch.) pediment, frenton; (nav.) breast-work.

frottage, *n.m.*, rubbing; dry-rubbing.

frottée, *n.f.*, (pop.) a sound beating.

frottement (frot-mǎn), *n.m.*, rubbing, friction.

frotter, *v.a.*, to rub; to rub down; to dry-rub; to bang, to pommel. *Se faire —;* to get a drubbing.

se frotter, *v.r.*, to rub one's self; to provoke (any one—*à quelqu'un*); to meddle (with anything—*à quelque chose*). *— les yeux;* to rub one's eyes. *Ils se sont bien frottés l'un l'autre;* they have banged one another finely. *Ne vous y* *frottez pas ;* do not meddle with it. *Ne vous frottez pas à lui ;* do not provoke him.

frotter, *v.n.,* to rub.

frotteur, *n.m.,* rubber. dry-rubber (of floors —*de planchers*).

frottis. *n m.,* (paint.) coat. over a picture. of a light transparent colour to imitate certain conditions of nature.

frottoir, *n.m.,* rubbing-cloth, razor-cloth.

frouer. *v.n.,* to pipe, to call (birds—*oiseaux*).

frou-frou, *n.m.,* (— —*s*), rustling of silk. &c.

fructidor, *n.m.,* Fructidor, the twelfth month of the calendar of the first French republic, from August 18th. to September 16th.

fructification. *n.f.,* fructification.

fructifier, *v.n.,* to be fruitful, to fructify

fructueusement (-eûz-măn), *adj.,* fruitfully, profitably.

fructueu-x, -se, *adj.,* fruitful ; fertile, profitable.

frugal, -e. *adj.,* frugal.

frugalement (-gal-măn), *adv.,* frugally.

frugalité, *n.f.,* frugality.

frugivore. *adj.,* frugivorous.

fruit, *n.m.,* fruit ; dessert ; offspring ; advantage. benefit, profit ; (mas.) batter. *Les —s de la terre ;* the fruits of the earth. *— hâtif ;* early fruit. *— indigène ;* native fruit. *— tardif ;* late fruit. *— à noyau ;* stone fruit. *— à pépin ;* kernel fruit. *Avec — :* profitably. *Être — sec* (school—*écoles*) ; to be plucked. *Faire — sec* (school—*écoles*) ; to pluck, to reject at an examination. *Tirer du — de ;* to derive benefit from.

fruité, -e, *adj.,* (her.) fructed.

fruiterie (frui-trï), *n.f.,* fruit-loft, fruit-trade.

fruiti-er, -ère. *adj.,* fruit, fruit-bearing. *Arbre — ;* fruit-tree.

fruiti-er, *n.m.,* **-ère,** *n.f.,* fruiterer, greengrocer.

frusquin, *n.m.,* (triv.) one's all. *Son saint — ;* one's all.

fruste, *adj.,* defaced, corroded (of coins, medals—*de monnaies. médailles, &c.*).

frustratoire. *adj.,* frustratory.

frustrer, *v.a.,* to defraud, to frustrate. to disappoint ; to baffle. *Il a frustré ses créanciers ;* he has defrauded his creditors.

fuchsia, *n.m.,* fuchsia.

fuchsine, *n.f.,* (chem.) fuchsine, an aniline red dye.

fucus (-kus), *n.m.,* (bot.) fucus, wrack, sea-wrack.

fugace, *adj.,* fugitive ; flying ; fleeting ; transient.

fugiti-f, -ve. *adj.,* fugitive, gliding, flitting ; transient. fleeting, short-lived. *Des plaisirs —s ;* transient pleasures. *Poésies —s ;* fugitive poetry.

fugiti-f. *n.m.,* **-ve.** *n.f.,* fugitive, runaway.

fugue (fug), *n.f.,* (mus.) fugue ; wild prank, lark. *Faire une — ;* to betake one's self to one's heels ; to have a lark.

fuie *n.f.,* small pigeon-house.

fuir, (fuyant, fui), *v.n.,* to flee, to fly ; to run away ; to elude. to shun. to avoid ; to shift about ; to leak ; (paint.) to appear at a distance. *Le temps fuit ;* time flies. *Ce tonneau fuit ;* this cask leaks.

fuir, *v.a.,* to fly, to avoid, to shrink from, to shun. *— l'ennemi ;* to fly from the enemy. *se fuir,* *v.r.,* to fly from one's self ; to shun, to avoid each other.

fuite, *n.f.,* flight, running away, avoiding, shunning ; evasion, shift, subterfuge ; running out, leakage. *Prendre la — ;* to run away. *Mettre en — ;* to put to flight.

fulgurant, *adj.,* (meteorology) attended

with lightning ; (med.) sharp and quickly recurring (of pains—*de douleurs*).

fulguration, *n.f.,* (chem.) fulguration ; lightning. '

fulgurite, *n.m.,* (phys.) fulgurite.

fuligineu-x, -se. *adj.,* fuliginous.

fuliginosité, *n.f.,* fuliginosity.

fulmicoton, *n.m.,* (chem.) gun-cotton.

fulminant, -e, *adj.,* fulminant, fulminating.

fulminate. *n.m.,* (chem.) fulminate.

fulmination. *n.f.,* fulmination.

fulminer. *v.n.,* to storm, to thunder ; (chem.) to fulminate. to explode.

fulminer, *v.a.,* (ecc.) to fulminate, to issue forth.

fulminique, *adj.,* (chem.) fulminic.

fumage. *n.m.,* colouring (of silver wire—*de fil d'argent*).

fumant, -e, *adj.,* smoking, reeking, fuming. *— de colère ;* fuming with rage.

fumé, *n.m.,* (engr.) smoke-proof.

fumée, *n.f.,* smoke ; fume, reek ; vanity, phantom, bubble ; (hunt.) *pl.,* fumet, dung of deer. *Des tourbillons de — :* volumes of smoke. *La — d'un volcan ;* the smoke of a volcano. *S'exhaler en — ;* to evaporate in smoke. *Il n'y a point de — sans feu ;* there is no smoke without fire.

fumer, *v.n.,* to smoke ; to reek ; to fret and fume.

fumer, *v.a.,* to smoke, to smoke-dry ; (agri.) to dung, to manure. *— des jambons ;* to smoke hams. *— un champ ;* to dung a field. *— une pipe ;* to smoke a pipe.

fumerolle, *n.f.,* fumarole.

fumeron (fu-mron), *n.m.,* half-burnt charcoal.

fumet, *n.m.,* flavour (of meat; of wines—*de viande, de vins*) ; raciness. *Ce vin a un bon — ;* that wine has a fine flavour.

fumeterre (fum-tèr), *n.f.,* (bot.) fumitory, fumiter.

fumeur, *n.m.,* smoker (of tobacco—*de tabac*).

fumeu-x, -se, *adj.,* fumous, fumy.

fumier, *n.m.,* manure, dung, muck ; dung-hill ; trash, rubbish. *Mourir sur un — ;* to die in a ditch.

fumifuge, *adj.,* expelling smoke.

fumigation, *n.f.,* fumigation.

fumigatoire, *adj.,* (med.) fumigating.

fumiger, *v.a.,* to fumigate.

fumiste, *n.m.,* chimney-doctor, funist.

fumivore, *n.m.* and *adj.,* smoke-consumer ; smoke-consuming.

fumoir, *n.m.,* (tech.) smoking-shed, smoking-house ; (in a private house—*dans une maison particulière*) smoking-room.

fumure, *n.f.,* (agri.) dressing ; dunging, manuring.

funambule, *adj.,* funambulatory.

funambule, *n.m.,* funambulist, rope-dancer.

funèbre, *adj.,* funeral, mournful, melancholy, ominous.

***funérailles,** *n.f. pl.,* funeral.

funéraire, *adj.,* funeral.

funeste, *adj.,* fatal ; melancholy ; baneful.

funestement, *adv.,* fatally.

fungus (fon-gus), *n.m.* *V.* **fongus.**

funicule, *n.m.,* (bot.) funiculus, funicle.

funin, *n.m.,* (nav.) white hawser.

fur, *n.m.* *À — et à mesure, au — et à mesure ;* in proportion. *On le paye au — et à mesure de l'ouvrage ;* he is paid in proportion to the quantity of work done.

furet, *n.m.,* ferret. *Chasser au — ;* to hunt with a ferret. *C'est un — ;* he is a ferreter.

fureter (fur-té), *v.n.,* to ferret, to ferret out, to search out, to rummage.

fureter, *v.a.*, to ferret out, to hunt after news.

fureteur (fur-teur), *n.m.*, ferreter. — *de nouvelles ;* news-hunter.

fureur, *n.f.*, fury, madness, rage, wildness ; mania, passion. *Quand il entre en — ;* when he gets into a fury. *Lorsque la — le prend ;* when he is seized with a fit of fury. *Cette actrice fait — ;* that actress is quite the rage. *Être transporté de — :* to be transported with fury. *Mettre un taureau en — :* to rouse a bull to madness. *La — des vents ;* the fury of the winds. *Il a la — du jeu ;* he has a passion for gaming. *Avec — :* furiously.

furfuracé, *adj.*, furfuraceous.

furibond, -e, *n.* and *adj.*, subject to fits of fury ; furious-looking.

furie, *n.f.*, fury, rage ; (myth.) Fury. *Entrer en — , se mettre en — ;* to fall into, to get into, a fury. *La — de la tempête ;* the fury of the tempest. *Dans la — du combat ;* in the heat of the battle. *C'est une — ;* she is a fury.

furieusement (-eû-măn), *adv.*, furiously ; prodigiously, with a vengeance.

furieu-x, -se, *adj.*, furious, mad, enraged, raging, fierce : monstrous, confounded, tremendous. *Il est — dans le combat ;* he is furious in the *fight. Tempête —se ;* raging storm. *C'est un — mangeur ;* he is a tremendous eater.

furolles, *n.f.pl.*, fiery exhalations.

furoncle, *n.m.*,(med.)furuncle,boil ; gathering ; (vet.) ambury.

furti-f, -ve, *adj.*, furtive, stealthy, secret. *Entrer d'un pas — ;* to steal in. *Regard — ;* furtive look.

furtivement (-tiv-măn), *adv.*, furtively, by stealth, secretly.

fusain, *n.m.*, (bot.) prickwood, spindle-tree.

fusant, *adj.*, fusing.

fusarolle, *n.f.*, (arch.) fusarole.

fuseau, *n.m.*, spindle ; distaff.

fusée, *n.f.*, spindleful ; (vet.) splint, splinter ; (surg.) fistula ; (artil., her., horl..) fusee ; rocket ; barrel (of a _kitchen-jack—de tourne-broche). Avoir une — à démêler avec quelqu'un ;* to have a bone to pick with any one. *Une — volante ;* a rocket.

fuséen, *n.m.*, (artil.) soldier trained to fire rockets.

fuselé, -e, *adj.*, slender, spindle-shaped.

fuser, *v.n.*, to expand, to spread ; to dissolve.

fusibilité, *n.f.*, fusibility.

fusible, *adj.*, fusible.

fusiforme, *adj.*, (bot.) spindle-shaped, fusiform.

fusil (-zi), *n.m.*, steel (to strike a light ; to sharpen knives—*briquet ; pour aiguiser les couteaux*) ; tinder-box ; musket, gun. *Pierre à — ;* flint. *Il fut tué d'un coup de — ;* he was killed by a musket shot. *Un coup de — ;* the report of a musket. *— à deux coups ;* double-barrelled gun. *— de chasse ;* fowling-piece. *— de munition ;* musket. *— à piston ;* percussion-musket. *— à vent ;* air-gun. *— Gras ;* the name of the rifle in use in the French army since 1872.

fusilier, *n.m.*, fusileer.

***fusillade,** *n.f.*, discharge of musketry.

***fusiller,** *v.a.*, to shoot.

***se fusiller,** *v.r.*, to fire at each other.

fusion, *n.f.*, fusion, coalition ; melting ; blending.

fusionner, *v.a.* and *n.*, to operate a union between political parties, *or* commercial companies, to amalgamate.

⊙**fuste,** *n.f.*, (nav.) rowing and sailing ship.

fustet, *n.m.*, Venetian shumac, fustic.

fustigation, *n.f.*, fustigation, whipping, flogging.

fustiger, *v.a.*, to flog, to scourge, to whip.

fût, *n.m.*, stock (of a gun or pistol—*d'un fusil, d'un pistolet*) ; shaft (of a column—*d'une colonne*) ; cask ; barrel (of a drum—*d'un tambour*).

futaie, *n.f.*, forest of high, lofty trees. *Demi- — ;* forest of half-grown trees. *Haute — .* forest of full-grown trees.

***futaille,** *n.f.*, small cask. *— en botte ;* barrel-staves.

futaine, *n.f.*, fustian.

futé, -e, *adj.*, sharp, cunning, sly.

futée, *n.f.*, joiner's putty.

f-ut-fa, *n.m..* (mus.) F; (vocal mus.) fa.

futile, *adj.*, futile, frivolous.

futilité, *n.f.*, futility, triflingness.

futur, -e, *adj.*, future.

futur, *n.m.,* **-e,** *n.f.*, intended (husband, wife —*mari, femme*). *Sa —e ;* his intended wife.

futur, *n.m.*, futurity ; (gram.) future.

futurition, *n.f.*, futurition.

fuyant, -e, *adj.*, flying, fleeing ; fading (of colours—*des couleurs*) ; (paint.) tapering. *Échelle —e ;* tapering scale.

fuyard, *adj.*, apt to run away ; fugitive.

fuyard, *n.m.*, **-e,** *n.f.*, fugitive, runaway.

G

g, *n.m.*, the seventh letter of the alphabet, g.

gaban, *n.m.* V. **caban.**

gabare, *n.f.*, lighter, flat-bottomed barge, store-ship, transport-ship.

gabari, *or* **gabarit,** *n.m..* mould (of a ship —*d'un vaisseau*) ; (railways) carriage-gauge.

gabarier, *n.m.*, lighterman ; master of a store-ship.

⊙**gabatine,** *n.f..* deceit. *Donner de la — à quelqu'un ;* to humbug any one.

gabegie, *n.f.*, (pop.) fraud, deceit.

gabelage (ga-blaj), *n.m.*, time for drying salt ; mark to distinguish the magazine salt from the smuggled.

gabeler (ga-blé), *v.a.*, to dry (salt—*sel*) in the magazine of the excise-office.

gabeleur (ga-bleur), *n.m.*, gabel-man.

gabelle, *n.f.*, gabel (tax upon salt—*impôt sur le sel*). *Frauder la — ;* to defraud the excise.

gabet, *n.m.*, vane (of mathematical instruments—*d'instruments de mathématiques*).

gabier, *n.m.*, (nav.) top-man.

gabion, *n.m.*, (fort.) gabion.

gabionnade, *n.f.*, (milit.) field fortification, gabionnade.

gabionner, *v.a.*, (fort.) to cover with gabions.

gâche, *n.m.*, staple (of a lock or for a wall—*de serrure, ou pour un mur*).

gâcher, *v.a.*, to mix mortar ; to bungle, to make a mess of ; to sell under price.

gâchette, *n.f.*, tumbler (of a musket—*d'un fusil, &c.*) ; follower (of a lock—*d'une serrure*).

gâcheur, *n.m.*, mason's labourer ; bungler ; one who sells under price.

gâcheu-x, -se, *adj.*, splashy, sloppy. *Chemin — ;* sloppy road.

gâchis, *n.m.*, slop, mess, pickle. *Faire du —, to make a slop, to make a mess. Être dans le —. avoir du — ;* to be in a mess, in a pickle.

gade, *n.m.*, (ich.) codfish.

gadoïde, *n.m.*, (ich.) codfish.

gadouard, *n.m.*, nightman.

gadoue, *n.f.*, filth, night-soil.

gaélique, *n.m.* and *adj.* Gaelic.

gaffe, *n.f.*, (nav.) gaff, boat-hook.

gaffer, *v.a.*, (nav.) to hook (with the boat-hook—*avec une gaffe*).

gage, *n.m.*, pawn, pledge; security; token, testimony; forfeit (play—*a certains jeux*); (jur.) bailment. —*s*; wages, hire, pay. *Prêter sur* —*s*; to lend money on pawned articles. *Préter sur* —*s*; pawnbroker. *Mettre en* —; to pawn. *Donner en* —; to pawn. *Jouer aux* —*s*; to play at forfeits. *Casser aux* —*s*; to dismiss, to discharge.

⊙**gage-mort**, *n.m.* (—*s* —*s*). *V.* **mort-gage**.

gager, *v.a.*, to hire; to lay, to lay a wager, to hold a wager, to bet; to pay wages to, to pay. — *avec quelqu'un, contre quelqu'un*; to lay a wager with, against any one. *Je gage que je le ferai*; I will bet that I do it. — *le double contre le simple*; to bet two to one. — *sa vie*; to lay one's life. *Gage que si, gage que non*; (elliptical and fam.) phrases—*expressions elliptiques et familières*) I bet it is, I bet it is not.

gagerie (gaj-rî), *n.f. V.* **saisie**.

gageu-r, *n.m.*, -**se**, *n.f.*, better, wagerer.

gageure (ga-jur), *n.f.*, bet, wager. *Faire une* —; to lay a wager. *Soutenir la* —; to persist in an enterprise or in an opinion; to stick to a thing.

gagiste *adj.*, (jur.) by pledge. *Créancier* —; pledgee, bailee.

gagiste. *n.m.*, hireling; (thea.) supernumerary, one who receives hire; (jur.) pledgee, bailee.

*****gagnage**, *n.m.*, pasturage, pasture-land, grazing-land; (hunt.) ground where deer feed.

*****gagnant**, *n.m.*, -**e**, *n.f.*, winner (at play, in a lottery—*au jeu, à une loterie*).

*****gagnant**, -**e**, *adj.*, winning (at play, in a lottery),

*****gagne-denier**. *n.m.* (— —*s*), labourer, labouring man, day-labourer.

*****gagne-pain**, *n.m.* (—), means of subsistence, livelihood, daily bread.

*****gagne-petit**, *n.m.* (—), knife-grinder.

*****gagner**, *v.a.*, to gain, to make; to earn, to get; to win; to prevail upon; to gain over, to bribe; to allure, to attract, to entice; to carry, to make one's self master of; to prepossess; to deserve; to seize, to come over; to reach, to get to, to come to, to arrive at; to catch. -- *son pain à la sueur de son front*; to earn one's bread by the sweat of one's brow. — *sa vie avec peine*; to work hard for one's living. *Vous n'y gagnez rien*; you will gain nothing by it. — *une bataille*; to gain a battle. — *un pari*; to win a bet. — *la partie*; to win the game. — *son procès*; to gain one's cause. *Je n'ai pu — cela sur lui*; I could not prevail upon him to do that. — *quelqu'un*; to win any one's money (at play—*au jeu*). — *quelqu'un*; to draw, to gain, any one over. — *la contrescarpe*; to carry the counterscarp. *J'y gagnai une pleurésie*; I got a pleurisy there. — *un rhume*; to catch a cold. *La faim me gagne*; I am beginning to feel hungry. — *le logis*; to reach home. — *du chemin*, — *du pays*; to gain ground; to get forward, to get on. — *du temps*; to gain time. — *du pied*, — *les champs*; to run away, to scour away. — *le devant*; to get the start. — *quelqu'un de vitesse*; to get the start of any one; to be beforehand with him. — *le dessus*; to get the better of. — *un raisseau*; to gain ground on a ship. — *la volonté d'un cheval*; to break, to subdue, a horse.

*****se gagner**. *v.r.*, to gain, to earn, to make, to acquire; to be catching, to be contagious.

*****gagner**, *v.n.*, to gain, to make, to earn, to get, to reach; to win (at cards, in a lottery—*aux cartes, à une loterie*). — *à être connu*; to improve upon acquaintance.

*****gagneu-r**, *n.m.*, -**se**, *n.f.*, winner, gainer.

gai, -**e**, *adj.*, gay, merry, lively, mirthful, cheerful; blithe, buxom, gladsome, pleasant; (mus.) allegro. *Vert* —; light green. *Temps —;*

cheerful weather. *Il a le vin* —; he is very merry in his liquor. — *comme un pinson*; as gay as a lark, as merry as a grig. *Être fort* —; to be in excellent spirits.

gai, *adv.*, (l.u.) gaily, merrily.

gaïac, *n.m.*, gayac, (bot.) guaiac, guaiacum, holy-wood, wood of life; Indian wood. *Bois de* —; lignum-vitæ; (bot.) lignum-vitæ tree. *Gomme, résine, de* —; guaiacum.

gaiement, or **gaîment** (ghè-mãn), *adv.*, gaily, merrily, cheerfully, cheerily, briskly, blithely, jovially, laughingly; willingly, heartily.

gaieté, or **gaîté**, *n.f.*, gaiety, merriment, mirth, glee; cheerfulness, blitheness, merriness, mirthfulness, jovialness, sportiveness, good humour; sportful words; frolic, youthful frolic. *Cheval qui a de la* —; (man.) mettlesome horse. *De* — *de cœur*; wantonly, out of mere wantonness.

*****gaillard**, -**e**, *adj.*, joyful, joyous, jovial, jolly, merry, lively; blithe, buxom, light-hearted; libertine, wanton; broad; tipsy; elevated (half-tipsy—*gris*); cool, fresh (of the wind—*du vent*). *Nous étions tous un peu* —*s*; we were all rather elevated (tipsy). *Vent* —; cool wind.

gaillard, *n.m.*, lively, merry, jovial fellow; fellow, blade, jolly dog. *Gros* —; great big fellow. *Petit* —; sly dog. *Grand* — *résolu*; determined dog.

gaillard, *n.m.*, (nav.) castle. — *d'arrière*; quarter-deck. — *d'avant*; forecastle. *Sur le* — *d'avant*; before the mast.

*****gaillarde**, *n.f.*, gaillard (dance—*danse*); wanton; (print.) bourgeois.

*****gaillardement**. *adv.*, joyously, merrily, blithely; boldly, briskly.

*****gaillardise**. *n.f.*, sprightliness, liveliness, frolicsomeness, mirth, jollity; broad, free, wanton language. *Dire des* —*s*; to make use of free, wanton language.

*****gaillet**. *n.m.*, (bot.) joint-grass; cheese-rennet; cleavers. — *grateron*; goose-grass.

gain, *n m.*, gain, profit, emolument, lucre; winning, gaining. — *de la bataille*; winning of the battle. — *net*; clear gain, net profit. —*s nuptiaux*, —*s de survie*; (jur.) whatever is left to the survivor (husband or wife—*mari ou femme*). *Amour du* —; love of lucre. — *de jeu*; winnings. *Tirer du* — *de*; to profit by. *Vivre de son* —; to live by one's winnings. *Avoir* — *de cause*; to carry a cause. *Donner* — *de cause*; to yield. *Se retirer sur son* —; to leave off playing after having won.

gaine. *n.f.*, scabbard, sheath; (bot.) case; ochrea; (archi.) terminal; (nav.) canvass-edging. — *de pavillon*; canvass-edging of an ensign.

gainier, *n.m.*, sheath-maker, scabbard-maker; (bot.) judas-tree.

gaîté. *V.* **gaieté**.

gala. *n.m.*, gala.

galactomètre, *n.m.*, lactometer.

galamment (ga-la-mãn), *adv.*, gracefully, with a good grace; with gallantry, courteously, in a courtly manner; handsomely, genteelly, gallantly, bravely, nobly.

galane, *n f.*, (bot.) tortoise-flower.

galanga, *n.m.*, (bot.) galangale, galanga.

galant, -**e**, *adj.*, honest, upright; civil; liberal, generous; gallant, courteous; fine, genteel. *C'est un* — *homme*; he is a man of honour. *Un homme* —; a man of gallantry (towards the ladies—*pour les dames*). *Un billet* —; a love-letter. *Humeur* —*e*; gay humour. *En* — *homme*; like an honest man, gallantly. *Manières* —*es*; gallant manners. *Femme* —*e*; courtezan.

galant, *n m.*, gallant, wooer, sweetheart, suitor, lover; brisk fellow. *Faire le* —; to court the ladies. *Un vert galant*; a brisk spark, a devoted admirer of the fair sex. — *d'hiver*; *bot.*) snow-drop.

galanterie (ga-lan-tri), *n.f.*, politeness, gallantry (towards the ladies—*pour les dames*), flattering, courteous compliment; present; intrigue, affair of gallantry; syphilis. *Dire des —s*; to say soft things. *Ce n'est qu'une —*; it is but a compliment.

galantin, *n.m.*, dangler, beau.

galantine, *n.f.*, dish of white meat served cold; (bot.) snow-drop. — *perce-neige*; snow-drop.

⊙**galantiser**, *v.a.*, to dangle after. *Se —*, *v.r.*, to admire one's self.

galaxie, *n.f.*, (astron.) Galaxy, Milky-Way.

galbanum (-nom), *n.m.*, (bot.) galbanum. *Donner du — à quelqu'un*; to put a sham upon any one.

galbe, *n.m.*, (arch.) graceful sweep; entasis; swelling; outline (of the face—*du visage*).

gale, *n.f.*, itch; scab; mange; scurf (of vegetables, fruit—*des légumes et des fruits*). *Être méchant comme la —*; to be very spiteful. *N'avoir pas la — aux dents*; to be a glutton.

galé, *n.m.*, gale, sweet-willow, Dutch myrtle.

galéace, or **galéasse**, *n.f.*, (nav.) galeas.

galée, *n.f.*, (print.) galley. *Coulisse de —*; galley-slice.

galéga, *n.m.*, (bot.) galego, goat's rue. *V.* lavanèse.

galène, *n.f.*, (min.) galena. — *de fer*; wolfram. *Fausse —*; mock-lead.

galénique, *adj.*, (med.) galenic, galenical.

galénisme, *n.m.*, (med.) galenism.

galéniste, *n.m.*, (med.) galenist.

galéobdolan, *n.m.*, (bot.) yellow archangel.

galéopsis, *n.m.*, (bot) galeopsis; stinking dead-nettle, blind-nettle.

se galer, *v.r.*, (pop.) to scratch, to rub, one's self. —, *v.a.*, to scratch, to claw.

galère, *n.f.*, galley, row-galley; organ-builder's plane; Spanish waggon. *Être condamné aux —s*; to be condemned to the galleys. *Tenir —*; to maintain a galley. *Vogue la —*; come what may. *Qu'allait-il faire dans cette —!* what business had he there? *C'est une vraie —*; it is terrible hard work, terrible drudgery.

galerie (ga-lri), *n.f.*, gallery, lobby, corridor; (nav.) stern-gallery, balcony; passage; (mec.) foot-board; (mining—*mines*), level, draft; (thea.) gallery; customary walk. *Petite —*; (arch.) heading; (mining—*mines*) creep-hole. — *principale*; (arch.) body-range (of vaults—*d'une arche*); (mining—*mines*) board. — *d'allongement*; (mining—*mines*) main level. — *d'écoulement*; (engineering—*terme d'ingénieur*) drainage, drain-gallery, (mining—*mines*) adit; offtake; drift; thirl. — *du faux pont* (nav.); gangway. — *en saillie* (arch.); bartizan.

galérien (-riin), *n.m.*, galley-slave.

galerne, *n.f.*, (nav.) north-westerly wind.

galet, *n.m.*, shuffle-board; pebble, shingle; gravel; (locksmith's work—*serrurerie*) roller.

galetas (gal-tâ), *n.m.*, garret; hole, miserable lodging.

galette, *n.f.*, broad thin cake; sea-biscuit.

galeu-x, -se, *adj.*, itchy; scabby; mangy; scurfy (of plants, trees—*des végétaux*). *Chien —*; mangy dog. *Brebis —se*; scabby sheep. *Arbre —*; scurfy tree.

galeu-x, *n.m.*, **-se**, *n.f.*, one infected with the itch.

galhauban, *n.m.*, (nav.) back-stay. *Rides de —s*; laniards of the back-stays. —*s volants*; preventer back-stays.

galimafrée, *n.f.*, (cook.) hodge-podge, hash.

galimatias (-tiâ), *n.m.*, fustian, nonsense; balderdash.

galion, *n.m.*, (nav.) galleon.

galiote, *n.f.*, galliot; half-galley, bark, boat; (bot.) bennet. — *à bombes*; bomb-ketch. — *de Hollande*; track-scout.

galipot, *n.m.*, white resin.

galle, *n.f.*, oak-apple, gall. *Noix de —*; gall-nut. —*s de chêne*; oak-leaf galls.

gallican, -e (gal-li-), *adj.*, Gallican.

gallicanisme, *n.m.*, Gallicanism (doctrine of the French Church—*doctrine de l'église française*).

gallicisme (gal-li-). *n.m.*, gallicism.

gallinacé, -e, *adj.*, (orni.) gallinaceous.

gallinacés (gal-li-), *n m.pl.*, (orni.) gallinæ, the gallinaceous tribe.

galline, *n.f.*, (ich.) sapphirine garnet; swallow-fish; tub-fish.

gallique (gal-lik), *adj.m.*, (chem.) gallic. *Acide —*; gallic acid.

gallique, *adj.*, Gallic.

gallois, -e, *adj.*, Welsh.

gallois, *n.m.*, **-e**, *n.f.*, Welshman; Welshwoman.

gallois, *n.m.*, Welsh language.

gallon, *n.m.*, (measure of capacity) gallon.

galoche, *n.f.*, galosh, clog; (nav.) clamp *Un menton de —*; a long-pointed chin. — *de fer*; (nav.) hanging clamp.

galon, *n.m.*, galoon, lace; grocer's round box; petty officers' stripes.

galonner, *v.a.*, to lace, to adorn with gold or silver-lace. *Habit galonné*; laced coat.

galonnier, *n.m.*, gold-lace maker; silver-lace maker.

galop (ga-lô), *n.m.*, gallop; (dance—*danse*) gallopade; (pop.) scolding, reprimand. *Petit —*; hand gallop. — *raccourci, demi —*; canter. — *étendu*; overreaching gallop.

galopade, *n.f.*, galloping; gallop. *Faire une —*; to have a gallop.

galopant, -e, *adj.*, that progresses fast (of pulmonary consumption—*de la phtisie*).

galoper, *v.n.*, to gallop; to run on; to run about; to dance the gallopade. *Faire — un cheval*; to make a horse gallop. *Le temps galope*; time flies swiftly.

galoper, *v.a.*, to gallop; to pursue; to run after; to seize. *La fièvre le galope*; he has a fit of ague.

galopin, *n.m.*, errand boy; young rogue; blackguard.

⊙**galoubet**, *n.m.*, (mus.) galoubet (flute).

galuchat, *n.m.*, dog-fish skin; shark-skin.

galvanique, *adj.*, galvanic. *Pile —*; galvanic battery, galvanic trough.

galvaniser, *v.a.*, to galvanize.

galvanisme, *n.m.*, galvanism.

galvanomètre, *n. m.*, galvanometer.

galvanoplastie, *n.f.*, electrotype.

galvauder, *v.a.*, to abuse; to scold; to mess, to spoil.

gambade, *n.f.*, skip, gambol. *Payer en —s*; to shuffle with one, to pay in excuses.

gambader, *v.n.*, to gambol, to skip, to romp, to frisk.

gambette, *n.f.*, (orni.) red-shank.

gambier, *n.m.*, iron bar (used in glass manufactories—*manufacture du verre*).

*gambiller, *v.n.*, to wag one's legs, to kick about one's legs.

gambit, *n.m.*, (at chess—*aux échecs*) gambit.

gamelle, *n.f.*, (milit., nav.) porringer, platter, mess. *Camarade de —*; messmate. *Manger à la même —*; to eat out of the same dish, to mess together.

gamin, *n.m.*, boy, lad, urchin, chit; blackguard, idle boy, little dirty idle lad.

gamme, *n.f.*, (mus.) gamut, scale. — *chromatique*; chromatic scale. *Etre hors de —*; to be off the hinges. *Changer de —*; to alter one's conduct. *Chanter la* — *à quelqu'un* ; to chide any one soundly. *Mettre quelqu'un hors de* — ; to put any one out, to disconcert any one. *Je lui ai répondu sur la même* — ; I answered him in the same tone.

ganache. *n.f.*, lower jaw (of a horse—*du cheval*) ; thick-skulled fellow, lout, dolt, booby, blockhead.

ganer. *v.n.*, (ombre) to renounce dealing.

ganga. *n.m.*, (orni.) grouse.

ganglion. *n.m.*, (surg.) ganglion ; spavin (in horses—*chez le cheval*).

ganglionnaire. *adj.*, (anat.) ganglionary.

gangrène. *n.f.*, gangrene, mortification. *Il a la* —*à la jambe ;* his leg has mortified.

gangrené, -e, *adj.*, gangrened, mortified.

gangrener. *v.a.*, to gangrene, to mortify. *Se* —; *v.r.*, to become gangrened, to be mortified ; to grangrene ; (fig.) to canker.

gangreneu-x,-se, *adj.*, (med.) gangrenous.

gangue (gang), *n.f.*, (mining — *mines*) gangue, vein-stone.

ganivet, *n.m.*, small penknife ; (surg) small knife.

gano, (ombre) let me have the deal, I have the king.

ganse, *n.f.*, bobbin ; edging ; cord ; loop (of diamonds—*de diamants*). — *de soie* ; silk-cord.

gant, *n.m.*, glove ; gauntlet. — *pour faire des armes* ; fencing-glove. — *de Notre-Dame* (bot.); throatwort. *Baguette à* —*s;* glove-stick. *Souple comme un* — ; as soft as a glove. *L'amitié passe le* —, excuse my glove. *Jeter le* —, to throw down the gauntlet, to challenge. *Ramasser, relever, le* — ; to take up the gauntlet, to accept the challenge. *Aller à quelqu'un comme un* — ; to fit any one like a glove; to suit any one to a T. *Se donner les* —*s ;* to attribute to one s self the success, merit (of a thing—*de quelque chose*).

gantelée, *n.f.*, (bot.) foxglove, throatwort. *Campanule* — ; throatwort.

gantelet (gan-tlè), *n.m.*, gauntlet ; handleather (for bookbinders, hatters, shoemakers, saddlers—*de relieurs, chapeliers, cordonniers, selliers*) ; (surg.) glove-bandage.

ganter, *v.a.*, to glove, to fit with gloves ; to fit (of gloves—*des gants*). *Cela me gante ;* that just suits me.

se ganter, *v.r.*, to put on one's gloves.

ganterie (gan-trî), *n.f.*, glove-making ; glove trade.

gant-ier, *n.m.*, **-ière,** *n.f.* (-tier, -ti-àr), glover.

***gantiller,** *n.m.*, (bot.) throatwort.

garage, *n.m.*, (railways) shunting ; (on rivers, canals, &c.—*sur les rivieres, les canaux, &c.)* putting into a wet dock.

garançage, *n.m.*, (dy.) madder dyeing, maddering.

garance, *n.f.*, (bot.) madder, madder-root. *Petite* — ; squinancy. — *robée ;* barked madder.

garancer, *v.a.*, (dy.) to madder.

garanceur, *n.m.*, (dy.) madder-dyer.

garancière, *n.f.*, madder-ground.

garant, *n.m.*, **-e,** *n.f.*, guarantee ; surety, security ; voucher ; warrantor ; (nav.) tackle-fall. *Se rendre* — ; to warrant. *J'en suis* —; I answer for it.

garanti, *n.m.*, **-e,** *n.f.*, warrantee.

garantie (-ti), *n.f.*, warranty ; guaranty ; warranting, guaranteeing ; making good ; security, voucher. — *accessoire ;* (jur.) collateral security. *Sous-* — (— —*s*) ; counterbound. — *de droit ;* (jur.) implied warranty. *Être* — *à quelqu'un de quelque chose ;* to pledge one's self to any one for anything.

garantir, *v.a.*, to guarantee ; to warrant ; to

vouch for : to ensure : to make good, to indemnify; to keep from ; to protect. to defend. *Je lui ai garanti le fait ;* I vouched for the fact to him. *Je ne vous le garantis pas ;* I will not warrant it to you. — *quelqu'un de toutes poursuites ;* to secure any one against all demands. — *du froid ;* to keep from cold. **se garantir,** *v.r.*, to secure one's self. to preserve one's self, to shelter one's self ; to keep clear of. to steer clear of.

garat. *n.m.*, sort of calico.

garbure. *n.f.*, (cook.) sort of thick porridge.

garcette, *n.f.*, (nav.) gasket. knittle, sennit, sinnet; cat-o'-nine-tails, cat.

garçon, *n.m.*, boy, lad ; bachelor ; journeyman, man ; shop-boy, shopman; waiter; groom; (nav.) younker. *C'est un rieux* — ; he is an old bachelor. *Faire le mauvais* — ; to hector. to bluster. *Se faire beau* — ; to riot, to lead a dissipated life. *Brave* — ; brave fellow ; good fellow. *Premier* — ; foreman. — *tailleur ;* journeyman tailor.

garçonner, *v.n.*, to hoiden, to romp.

garçonnière, *n.f.*, romp, tom-boy, hoiden.

garde, *n.f.*, keeping; defence; watching; guard; watch; nurse; custody, charge, ward (of a lock—*d'une serrure*); fly-leaf (of books —*d'un livre*); low card (at cards—*aux cartes*); (fenc.) ward, guard; (nav.) anchor-watch; care, heed. *Avoir la* — *d'un poste ;* to have the defence of a post. — *avancée;* advance-guard. *Faire la* —, *être de* — ; to be upon guard. *Monter la* — ; to mount guard. *Monter une* — *à quelqu'un ;* to reprimand any one severely. *Descendre la* — ; to come off guard. *Relever la* — ; to relieve guard. *La*— *montante;* soldiers who are going on guard. *La* — *descendante;* those who are coming off guard. *Officier de* — ; officer on guard. — *du corps;* life-guards. *Un corps de* — ; a guard-house. — *à vous;* attention. *Faire bonne* — ; to keep good watch. — *d'enfants;* dry nurse. *Avoir en* — ; to have in one's keeping. *Donner en* — *à quelqu'un ;* to commit to one's keeping. *Dieu vous ait en sa sainte* — ; may God have you in his holy keeping. *Se tenir en* — ; to be upon one's guard. *Il a toujours* — *à carreau;* he is always guarded against, ready for every thing. *Fruit de* — ; fruit that will keep. *Prenez* — *à cela ;* take care of that. *Prenez* — *de tomber;* take care not to fall. *Prendre* — ; to mind. *Il prend* — *à un sou;* he looks at a penny. *Ne prenez pas* — *à moi;* do not mind me. *Il m'offense sans y prendre* — ; he offends me without meaning it. *Se donner de* — *de quelqu'un, de quelque chose;* to be on one's guard against any one, any thing. *S'en donner jusqu'à la* — ; to take pleasure to the full. *Être hors de* — ; to be completely ignorant of an affair. *N'avoir* — *de faire une chose;* not to have the inclination to do a thing, to be far from doing a thing; not to be fool enough to do a thing ; to be unable to do a thing. *Il n'a* — *de tromper, il est trop honnête homme;* he is too honest to think of cheating. *Je n'ai* — *d'y aller ;* I am not such a fool as to go there. *Nous n'avons* — *d'en douter ;* far be it from us to doubt it. *Être sur ses* —*s; se tenir sur ses* —*s;* to be upon one's guard. *A la* —! guard, guard! watch. watch !

garde. *n.m.*, keeper, warden, warder ; guard. — *des sceaux;* keeper of the seals. — *des rôles;* — *des archives;* master of the rolls. — —*national ;* national guard. — *du commerce;* sheriff's officer, bailiff. — *de nuit ;* watchman. — *du corps;* life-guardsman. *Les* —*s du corps;* the life-guards.

garde-barrière, *n.m.* (—, or — *s* — *s*), gate-keeper.

garde-bois, *n.m.* (—. *or* —*s* —), forest-keeper.

garde-bourgeoise. *n.f.* (—*s* —*s*), (jur.) right of the surviving parent to enjoy the property of his *or* her children until they attained a certain age.

garde-boutique. *n.m.* (—. *or* — —*s*), commodity that will not go off, old shopkeeper.

garde-cendre, *n.m.* (—. *or* — —*s*). fender.

garde-champêtre, *n.m.* (—*s* —*s*), field-keeper. keeper.

garde-chasse, *n.m.* (—, *or* —*s* —*s*), game-keeper.

garde-chevron. *n.m.* (— —*s*), barge-board; verge-board.

garde-chiourme, *n.m.* (—, *or* —*s* —), convict-keeper.

garde-corps, *n.m.* (—), rail, hand-rail; (nav.) life-line; swifter (of capstans—*de cabestans*).

garde-côte. *n.m.* (—*s* —*s*), cruiser, guard-ship. —*s des côtes*; military guards for the defence of the coast in time of war.

garde-crotte, *n.m.* (—), splash-board.

garde-étalon, *n.m.* (—, *or* —*s* —*s*), stallion-keeper.

garde-feu, *n.m.* (—, *or* — —*x*), fire-guard; fender; match-tub.

garde-forestier, *n.m.* (—*s* —*s*), forester; (jur.) walker.

garde-fou. *n.m.*(— —*s*), parapet(of bridges, quays—*de ponts, de quais*); rail, hand-rail; (nav.) life-line; swifter (of capsterns—*de cabestans*).

garde-frein, *n.m.* (—*s* —*s*). brakesman.

garde-magasin. *n.m.* (—, *or* —*s* —*s*), keeper of a store-house; warehouse-keeper, warehouse-man; commodity that will not go off, old shop-keeper.

garde-malade, *n.m.f.* (—, *or* —*s* —*s*), nurse for the sick, watcher.

garde-manche, *n.m.* (— —*s*). half-sleeve.

garde-manger, *n.m.* (—), outtery, larder. pantry; safe.

garde-marteau, *n.m.* (—, *or* —*s* —*x*), hammer-keeper (official charged with the task of marking with a hammer the trees to be cut down in a forest—*fonctionnaire chargé de marquer les arbres à couper dans une forêt*).

garde-ménagerie, *n.m.* (—, *or* — —*s*), (nav.) ship's butcher.

garde-meuble, *n.m.* (—, *or* — —*s*), store-room, lumber-room.

garde-nappe, *n.m.* (—. *or* — —*s*), mat (to keep a dish from the table—*pour protéger la nappe ou la table*).

garde-national, *n.m.* (—*s-nationaux*), national guard.

garde-nationale, *n.f.* (—*s* —*s*), national guard.

garde-noble, *n.f.* (—*s* —*s*), (jur.) guardian-ship of a nobleman's children giving to the surviving parent the right to enjoy the property of his *or* her children until they were of age.

garde-note, *n.m.* (—*s* —*s*), notary.

garde-pêche, *n.m.* (—, *or* —*s* —*s*), river-keeper, water-bailiff.

garder, *v.a.,* to keep, to preserve; to lay up, to lay by, to save; to tend, to take care of, to look after, to look to, to nurse; to guard, to protect, to defend; to observe; to keep down, to keep on (one's stomach—*sur l'estomac*). *Je garde cela pour moi;* I keep that for myself. *Gardez votre place;* keep your place. — *la chambre;* to keep one's room. — *la maison;* to take care of the house. — *un secret;* to keep a secret. *Je garde cet argent pour mon voyage;* I lay up this money for my journey, *En donner*

à —; to impose upon. *Je la lui garde bonne;* I have got a rod in pickle for him. — *un enfant;* to take care of a child. — *les bestiaux;* to tend cattle. — *les enjeux;* to keep the stakes. — *le mulet;* to dance attendance. *Dieu m'en garde;* God forbid, heaven preserve me from it. — *le silence;* to keep silence. — *la bienséance;* to observe decency. — *son ban;* to complete one's period of exile. — *un malade;* to tend a sick person. — *à vue;* not to lose sight of. — *sa dignité, son rang;* to maintain, to uphold one's dignity, one's rank. — *les commandements;* to observe. to keep the commandments. — *sous clef;* to keep locked up. — *une médecine;* to keep a dose of medicine on one's stomach.

se **garder,** *v.r.,* to keep; to keep down, to keep in; to beware; to take care not; to abstain. to refrain; to guard. *Gardez-vous bien de faire cela;* take care not to do that. *Gardez-vous d'ennemis;* beware of enemies. *Ce fruit ne peut — longtemps;* this fruit cannot keep, cannot be kept, long.

garde-robe, *n.m.* (— —*s*), apron(to preserve a lady's dress—*pour garantir la robe*).

garde-robe, *n.f.* (— —*s*), wardrobe; water-closet, privy; (bot.) southern-wood.

garde-temps, *n.m.* (—), time-piece, chronometer.

gardeur-r, *n.m.,* **-se,** *n.f.,* keeper; herd. — *de cochons;* swineherd.

garde-vaisselle, *n.m.* (—, *or* —*s* —), gentle-man of the ewry, yeoman of the scullery.

garde-vente, *n.m.* (—, *or* — —*s*), wood-merchant's agent.

garde-vue, *n.m.* (—), screen for the eyes.

gardien, *n.m.,* **-ne,** *n.f.,* (-in, -è-n), guar-dian; keeper; door-keeper; trustee; warden (prison); (jur.) bailiff's man, broker's man; superior (of a Franciscan convent—*d'un couvent de Franciscains*). *Dieu est notre meilleur —;* God is our best guardian. — *de la sainte barbe;* (nav.) gunner's mate. — *de la fosse aux lions;* boatswain's mate.

gardien, -ne, *adj.,* tutelary, guardian. *L'ange —;* the guardian angel.

gardon, *n.m.,* (ich.) roach.

gare! *int.,* clear the way; make way; take care; look out! — *de là!* clear the way there! — *de devant!* make way before! — *l'eau! — l'eau là-bas!* take care below! — *le fouet! — le bâton!* beware of the rod! beware of the stick!

gare, *n.f.,* wet-dock; (railways) platform; terminus. — *d'arrivée,* — *de départ;* terminus. — *d'évitement* (railways); siding, shunting line, loop line. *Chef de —* (railways); station-master.

garenne (ga-rè-n), *n.f.,* (of rabbits, hares) vivary, warren. — *forcée, privée;* enclosed warren.

garennier, *n.m.,* warrener, warren-keeper.

garer, *v.a.,* to secure, to fasten. — *un bateau;* to fasten a boat in a wet-dock; to dock a boat.

se **garer,** *v.r.,* to keep in shore (of boats—*des bateaux*); to keep out of the way; to get out of the way. *Il faut — d'un fou;* we must get out of the way of a madman.

gargantua, *n.m.* (—*s*), a glutton.

gargariser, *v.a.,* to gargle, to gargarize.

se **gargariser,** *v.r.,* to gargle one's throat.

gargarisme, *n.m.,* gargarism, gargle; gargling.

gargotage. *n.m.,* ill-dressed victuals.

gargote, *n.f.,* cheap eating-house; cook-shop.

gargoter, *v.n.,* to frequent low eating-houses; to tipple; to eat and drink in a slovenly manner.

gargoti-er, *n.m.,* **-ère,** *n.f.,* (-tié, -ti-èr), low eating-house keeper; bad cook.

*gargouillade,** *n.f.,* step in dancing.

*gargouille, n.f., gargoyle, water-shoot.
*gargouillement. n.m., rumbling, rattling (of water in the stomach—*de l'estomac*).
*gargouiller, v.n., to dabble, to paddle (in water—*dans l'eau*).
*gargouillis, n.m., splashing (of water—*de l'eau*) from a water-spout.
gargousse, n.f., cannon-cartridge. *Papier à* — ; cartridge-paper.
gargoussier, n.m., (nav.) cartridge-box.
garigue, n.f., (l.u.) waste-land, waste.
garnement, n.m., good-for-nothing fellow, scapegrace.
garni, n.m., furnished lodgings. *Loueur, loueuse en* — ; lodging-house keeper. *Être en* —, *loger en* — ; to live in furnished lodgings.
garni, -e, part., garnished; furnished, trimmed. *Maçonnerie* —*e;* masonry filled up in the middle. *Chambres* —*es;* furnished rooms.
garnir, v.a., to furnish, to provide, to stock; to ornament, to trim, to garnish, to adorn; to line; to fill, to occupy; (nav.) to rig; to quilt; to serve. — *une maison;* to furnish a house. — *une boutique;* to stock a shop. — *une chemise;* to trim a shirt. — *une robe;* to trim a gown; to line a gown.
se garnir, v.r., to furnish one's self; to provide one's self; to stock one's self; to fill, to be filled; to protect one's self.
garnisaire, n.m., tax-gatherer's bailiff.
garnison, n.f., garrison; (jur.) bailiff's men.
garnissage, n.m., trimming (of clothes—*des vêtements*), facing. *Bois de* — ; facing-board.
garnisseur-, n.m., -se, n.f., trimmer.
garniture, n.f., furniture, trimming; garniture; garnish, garnishing; lining; set; (nav.) rigging. *La* — *d'une chemise;* the trimming of a shirt. *La* — *d'une épée:* sword ornaments. *Une* — *de diamants;* a set of diamonds.
garou, n.m., (bot.) spurge-flax.
garrot, n.m., (vet.) withers; bending lever; (surg.) tourniquet; packing-stick. *Cheval blessé sur le* — (vet.); horse wither-wrung. (fig.) *Être blessé sur le* — ; to have been injured in one's reputation.
garrotte, n.f., garote, strangulation.
garrotter, v.a., to bind (with cords—*avec des cordes*), to tie down; to pinion.
garrulité, n.f., (l.u.) garrulity, loquacity.
gars, n.m., lad, young fellow.
garus, n.m., Garus (elixir).
gascon, -ne, adj., Gascon.
gascon, n.m., -ne, n.f., Gascon; boaster, braggart.
gascon, n.m., Gascon language.
gasconisme, n.m., Gasconism.
gasconnade, n.f., gasconade, boast. *Dire des* —*s;* to gasconade.
gasconner, v.n., to speak Gascon, to speak with a Gascon accent; to gasconade, to brag.
*gaspillage, n.m., disorder; waste, wasting, squandering.
*gaspiller, v.a., to confuse, to throw into disorder; to waste, to lavish, to squander, to consume, to fritter away. — *son temps;* to waste one's time. — *son argent;* to squander, to fritter, one's money away.
*gaspilleu-r, n.m., -se, n.f., waster, spendthrift.
gaster (-tèr), n.m., (med.) stomach.
gastéropodes, n.m.pl., (zool.) gasteropods.
gastralgie, n.f., (med.) gastralgia.
gastriloque, n.m., (l.u.) gastriloquist, ventriloquist.
gastrique, adj., gastric.
gastrite, n.f., gastritis.
gastro, a prefix from Gr. γαστήρ, γαστρός.
gastrologie, n.f., gastrology.
gastronome, n.m., gastronomist.
gastronomie, n.f., gastronomy.

gastronomique, adj., gastronomic.
gastroraphie, n.f., (surg.) gastroraphy.
gastrotomie, n.f., (surg.) gastrotomy.
gâté. -e, adj., part., spoiled, damaged, tainted. *Viande* —*e;* tainted meat. *Enfant* — ; spoiled child.
gâteau, n.m., cake; honey-comb; (surg.) pledget. — *des rois;* Twelfth-night cake. — *de miel;* honey-comb. *Avoir part au* — ; to share in the booty, to have a finger in the pie. *Partager le* — ; to go halves.
gâte-enfant, n.m.f. (—, *or* — —s), person who spoils children.
gâte-métier, n.m. (—, *or* — —s), person who spoils a trade.
gâte-papier, n.m. (—), scribbler, paltry writer.
gâte-pâte, n.m. (—), bad pastry-cook, bad baker; bungler.
gâter, v.a., to spoil, to damage, to hurt, to injure, to impair; to taint, to corrupt, to deprave. *La grêle a gâté les vignes;* the hail has damaged the vines. *Le soleil gâte la viande;* the sun taints meat. — *du papier;* to waste, to blot, paper, to scribble. — *un enfant;* to spoil a child.
se gâter, v.r., to taint, to spoil; to be spoiled, to become corrupt. *Ce vin commence à* — ; that wine begins to spoil. *Le temps se gâte;* the fine weather is breaking up.
gâterie (gâ-trî), n.f., attention that spoils (any one—*quelqu'un*).
gâte-sauce, n.m. (—, *or* — —s), scullion; (b.s.) bad cook.
gâte-tout, n.m. (—), mar-all.
gâteu-r, n.m., -se, n.f., spoiler. — *d'enfants;* children's spoiler.
gâteu-x, n.m., -se, n.f., paralytic, insane paralytic, who have lost control over their excretory organs.
gatte, n.f., (nav.) manger.
gattilier, n.m., (bot.) chaste-tree, vitex, agnus-castus.
gauche, (gôsh), adj., left; crooked; clumsy, awkward. *Le côté* — ; the left side. *La main* — ; the left hand. *Un air* — ; an awkward air. *Des manières* —*s;* uncouth manners.
gauche, n.f., left-hand; left-hand side; left side; (milit.) left wing, left flank. *A* — ; on the left, to the left. *Tournez à* — ; turn to the left. *Donner à* — ; to be in the wrong box.
gauchement (gôsh-män), adv., awkwardly, uncouthly, clumsily.
gauch-er, -ère, n. and adj., left-handed person; left-handed.
gaucherie (gô-shrî), n.f., awkwardness, clumsiness; clumsy action.
gauchir, v.n., to turn aside, to step aside, to flinch; to become warped; to dodge, to prevaricate.
gauchir, v.a., to warp; to pervert.
se gauchir, v.r., to warp.
gauchissement, n.m., (carp.) warping.
gaude, n.f., (bot.) dyer's-weed; pl., hasty-pudding.
se gaudir, v.r., to rejoice; to make game.
gaudriole, n.f., broad joke, smutty talk.
gaudron, n.m. V. godron.
gaudronné, -e, adj., (bot.) repand.
gaufrage, n.m., goffering.
gaufre, n.f., honey-comb; waffle (thin cake —*pâtisserie légère et mince*); victim; dupe.
gaufrer, v.a., to goffer.
gaufreu-r, n.m., -se, n.f., gofferer.
gaufrier, n.m., waffle-iron, goffer-iron
gaufrure, n.f., goffering.
gaule, n.f., pole; switch.

gauler, v.a., to beat trees with a long pole, to knock down (fruit).

gaulis, n.m., small wood, small branches.

gaulois, **-e**, adj., Gaulish,Gallic; (fig.) old-fashioned.

gaulois, n.m., **-e**. n.f., Gaul; frank person.

gaulois, n.m., Gallic language. (fig.) C'est du — ; it is an old-fashioned expression.

gaupe, n.f., slut, trollop.

gaure, n.m., Gueber, Guebre.

se **gausser**, v.r., (pop.) to banter, to jeer, to make game of. Il se gausse de tout le monde; he banters every body.

gausserie (gô-srî), n.f., bantering, making game.

gausseu-r, n.m., **-se**, n.f., banterer.

gausseu-r, **-se**, adj., bantering, mocking.

gavauche, n.m., (nav.) disorder, confusion.

gave, n.m., torrent, mountain river (in the Pyrenees—des Pyrénées).

gaver, v.a., (pop.) to cram (with food—de nourriture). Se —, v.r., to cram one's self with food.

gavion, n.m., (pop.) throat, wizen.

gavotte, n.f., gavot (kind of dance—danse).

gayac, n.m. V. gaïac.

gaz (gäz), n.m., gas; (med.) flatus. — étouffant; choke-damp. Éclairage au — ; lighting with gas. Un conduit de — ; a gas-pipe. Bec de — ; gas-burner. Jet de — ; jet of gas. Usine à — ; gas-works. Fermer le bec de — ; to turn off the gas. Ouvrir le bec de — ; to turn on the gas. Réservoir de — ; gas-holder.

gaze, n.f., gauze.

gazéifier, v.a., (chem.) to gassify.

se **gazéifier**, v.r., to gassify.

gazéiforme, adj., (chem.) having the form of gas.

gazelle, n.f., gazelle.

gazer, v.a., to cover with gauze; to gloss over.

Ⓒ **gazetier** (gâz-tié), n.m., (b.s.) gazetteer.

gazetin (gâz-tin), n.m., (l.u.) little gazette.

gazette, n.f., gazette ; newsmonger.

gazeu-x, **-se**, adj., (chem.) gaseous.

gazier, n.m., gauze-maker; gas-fitter.

gazomètre, n.m., gasometer.

gazométrie, n.f., gasometry.

gazon, n.m., grass; turf; (fort.) gazon. Parterre de — ; grass-plot. Abonder en — ; to abound in grass. Produire du — ; to sward.

gazonnant, adj., (gard.) producing grass.

gazonnement (ga-zo-n-măn), n.m., turfing, covering with turf.

gazonner, v.a., to cover with turf, to turf.

*****gazouillement**, n.m., chirping, warbling (of birds—des oiseaux); purling, bubbling (of a brook—d'un ruisseau); prattle.

*****gazouiller**, v.n., to chirp, to warble; to prattle ; to twitter; to lisp; to murmur. Cet enfant commence à — ; that child begins to prattle.

Ⓒ **gazouillis**, n.m., warbling, twitter.

geai (jè), n.m., (orni.) jay.

géant, n.m., **-e**, n.f., giant, giantess. Aller à pas de — ; to stride like a giant.

géant, **-e**, adj., gigantic.

gecko, n.m., (zool.) gecko.

géhenne (-è-n), n.f., gehenna, hell.

geindre (geignant, geint), v.n., to whine, to moan.

gélatine, n.f., gelatin.

gélatineu-x, **-se**, adj., gelatinous.

gélatinifier, v.a., to gelatinate.

se **gélatinifier**, v.r., to gelatinate.

gelé, **-e**, part., frozen, frost-bitten. Il a le bec — ; he is tongue-tied.

gelée, n.f., frost; (cook.) jelly. — blanche; white frost, hoar-frost. — de groseille ; currant jelly.

geler, v.a., to freeze. Je suis tout gelé de froid; I am quite frozen with cold.

se **geler**, v.r., to freeze.

geler, v.n., to freeze. La rivière a gelé ; the river is frozen. Les doigts lui ont gelé; his fingers were frozen. Il gèle ; it freezes. Il gèle à pierre fendre; it freezes as hard as it can.

géli-f, **-ve**, adj., (of trees, of stones—d'arbres, de pierres) ; cracked by the frost.

Ⓒ **geline**, n.f., hen, fat hen.

gelinotte, n.f., young fat pullet. — des bois ; hazel-hen.

gélivure, n.f., crack caused by frost.

gémara, n.m.,Gemara, the second part of the Talmud.

gémeaux, n.m.pl., (astron.) Gemini, the Twins; (agri.) meadows mowed twice a year.

gémin-é, **-e**, adj., (bot.) geminate, double ; (jur.) reiterated.

gémir, v.n., to groan, to moan, to sigh ; to lament, to bewail. — de douleur ; to groan with pain. — sous le joug ; to groan under the yoke. Je gémis de votre erreur; I bewail your error. — sur les pécheurs; to bewail over sinners.

gémissant, **-e**, adj., moaning, lamenting.

gémissement gé-nis-măn). n.m., groan, moan, wail; complai t, lamentation; groaning, moaning, bewailing. Les —s des blessés; the groans of the wounded. Pousser un — ; to utter a groan.

Ⓒ **gemma**, n.m., (bot.) gem.

gemmation (jèm-ma-), n.f., gemmation, budding.

gemme, adj., of gems. Des pierres —s ; gems. Sel — ; rock salt.

gemme, n.f., (bot.) gem ; leafy bud; (min.) gem.

gemmer, v.n., to bud, to germinate.

gemmer, v.a., to incise, to tap pines to obtain resin.

gemmiforme, adj., (bot.) bud-shaped.

gemmipare (jèm-mi-), adj.; gemmiparous.

gémonies, n.f.pl., (antiq.) gemoniæ.

génal, adj., (anat.) of the cheek.

gênant, **-e**, adj., troublesome, embarrassing, uneasy, difficult; incommodious, that causes restraint.

gencive, n.f., gum (of the teeth).

gendarme, n.m., man-at-arms; gendarme; dragoon (woman—femme); (b.s.) thief-taker; flaw (in a diamond—dans un diamant); pl., sparks (of fire—de feu). C'est un vrai — ; she is a regular dragoon.

gendarmer, v.a., to dragoon.

se **gendarmer**, v.r., to resist, to struggle; to fly into a passion ; to get into a rage.

gendarmerie, n.f., gendarmery (French horse and foot police).

gendre, n.m., son-in-law.

gêne, n.f., Ⓒrack, torture; constraint, difficulty, uneasiness; inconvenience, annoyance, trouble; torment; narrow circumstances; embarrassment, pecuniary difficulty. Être à la — ; to be uneasy, uncomfortable. Sans — ; unconstrained, unrestrained, without ceremony. Mettre à la — ; to put to trouble. Se mettre l'esprit à la — ; to rack one's brains. Être sans — ; to be free and easy. Se donner de la — pour quelque chose ; to make one's self uneasy about any thing.

gên-é, **-e**, part., constrained, uneasy; short of cash. Air — ; constrained air.

généalogie, n.f., genealogy.

généalogique, adj., genealogical.

généalogiste, n.m., genealogist.

génépi, or **génipi**, n.m., (bot.) a variety of artemisia, growing in the Alps. — noir; artemisia spicata. — blanc; artemisia mutellina.

gêner, *r.a.*, to impede, to obstruct; to trouble, to inconvenience, to incommode, to be in the way of any one; to put restraint upon; to disturb, to embarrass, to annoy; to cramp. *Ce soulier me gêne;* this shoe pinches me. *La présence de cet homme me gênait;* the presence of that man annoyed me. *Il me gêne dans mes projets;* he impedes me in my plans.

se gêner, *r.r.*, to constrain one's self, to put one's self out of one's way, to put one's self to inconvenience. *On ne doit pas — entre amis;* there is no need of ceremony among friends. *Il ne se gêne pas;* he does not stand on ceremony, he makes himself quite at home.

général, *n m.*, (log., milit.) general. *En —;* in general, generally.

général, -e, *adj.*, general.

généralat, *n.m.*, generalship.

générale, *n.f.*, (milit.) fire-drum, general.

généralement (-ral-män), *adv.*, generally, in general.

généralisat-eur, -rice, *adj.*, generalizing.

généralisation, *n.f.*, generalization.

généraliser, *r.a.*, to generalize.

généralissime, *n.m.*, generalissimo.

généralité, *n.f.*, generality.

générat-eur, -rice, *adj.*, generating, generative, genial.

générat-eur, *n.m.*, **-rice**, *n.f.*, generator, generant.

générati-f, -ve, *adj.*, generative.

génération, *n.f.*, generation, descent, production; genesis. *De — en —;* from generation to generation.

généreusement (-reûz-män), *adv.*, generously, bountifully, munificently; stoutly, bravely.

généreu-x, -se, *adj.*, generous, noble; liberal, benevolent, bountiful; courageous, noble.

générique, *adj.*, generic.

générosité, *n.f.*, generosity, liberality, benevolence, bountifulness.

genèse, *n.f.*, Genesis.

genestrolle, *n.f.*, (bot.) dyer's-broom, green-weed.

genêt, *n.m.*, (bot.) broom; jennet, genet (Spanish horse—*cheval d'Espagne*).

généthliaque, *n.m.*, genethliac.

généthliaque, *adj.*, genethliacal.

genette, *n.f.*, (mam.) genet, civet; (bot.) genista.

à la genette, *adv.*, with short stirrups (of riding—*équitation*).

génevois, -e, *n.* and *adj.*, Genevese.

genévrier, *n.m.*, juniper-tree.

géniculé, -e, *adj.*, (bot.) geniculated.

génie, *n.m.*, genius; spirit; (milit.) engineers. *Suivre son —;* to follow the bent of one's genius. *Le — d'une langue;* the genius of a language. *Le corps du —* (milit.); the corps of engineers.

genièvre, *n.m.*, juniper-berry; juniper-tree; gin.

génisse, *n.f.*, heifer.

génital, -e, *adj.*, genital. *Les parties —es;* the genitals.

géniteur, *n.m.*, (b.s.) generator.

génitif, *n.m.*, (gram.) genitive. *Au —;* in the genitive case.

⊙génitoires, *n.m.pl.*, genitals.

⊙géniture, *n.f.*, (jest.) offspring.

génois, -e, *n.* and *adj.*, Genoese.

genope, *n.f.*, (nav.) seizing, lashing.

genoper, *r.a.*, (nav.) to seize, to lash.

genou, *n.m.*, knee; (nav.) lower futtock; (mec.) ball and socket; *pl.*, lap. *Être à —x;* to be on one's knees. *Se mettre à —x;* to kneel. *Tenir un enfant sur ses —c;* to hold a child on one's lap. *Fléchir le —;* to bend the knee,

Tomber aux —x de quelqu'un; to fall at any one's feet. *— de la rame;* arm of an oar.

***genouillère**, *n.f.*, knee-piece (of armour—*d'une armure*); top (of a boot—*des bottes*); knee-cap; pulley-piece.

génovéfain, *n.m.*, canon of the Church of Ste Geneviève.

genre, *n.m.*, genus; species; kind, sort; fashion, taste; style, manner; gender; (paint.) genre. *Le — humain;* mankind. *Un — de vie;* a course of life. *Il a un — qui lui est propre;* he has a style peculiar to himself. *Le — tragique;* the tragic style. *De bon —;* gentlemanly, lady-like. *De mauvais —;* ungentlemanly, unlady-like.

gens (jän), *n.m.* (*pl.* of Gent), people, persons, men, hands; domestics, servants, attendants. *Ce sont des — fort dangereux, de fort dangereuses —;* they are very dangerous people. *Des — fins, de fines —;* cunning folks. *Tous les — de bien;* all honest people. *Tous les habiles —;* all people of skill. *Toutes les vieilles —*, all old people. *Les petites —;* humble people. *— de lettres;* men of letters. *— de guerre;* soldiers. *— d'église;* churchmen. *— d'affaires;* men of business. *Le droit des —;* the law of nations. *Il y a — et —;* there are people of all sorts. *Les vieilles — sont prudents;* old people are prudent. [*Gens* requires all adjectives that follow it to be in the masculine, and all those that precede it to be in the feminine. The masculine, however, is used before Gens, when the word *tous* alone precedes it, or when *tous* is accompanied by an adjective having the same termination for both genders. When Gens more particularly refers to men, as in the expressions, *Gens de lettres, Gens de loi*, &c., the adjectives that precede Gens are also put in the masculine.]

gent, *n.f.* (*sing.* of Gens), (jest.) nation people, race, tribe. *La — marécageuse;* the marshy tribe.

⊙gent, -e, *adj.*, fair, comely.

gentiane, *n.f.*, (bot.) gentian.

gentianelle, *n.f.*, (bot.) gentianella.

gentil (-ti), *n.* and *adj.m.*, Gentile.

gentil, -le, *adj.*, pretty; (iron.) ridiculous, pretty, fine. *Un — métier!* a fine occupation, indeed! *Un — enfant;* a pretty child.

gentil, *n.m.*, **-le**, *n.f.*, pretty person. *Faire le —;* to affect graceful manners.

***gentilhomme** (-ti-lom), *n.m.* (*gentilshommes*) (ti-zom), nobleman, gentleman. *— d lièvre;* poor country squire.

***gentilhommerie** (-ti-io-mrî), *n.f.*, nobility, gentility.

***gentilhommière** (-ti-io-mièr), *n.f.*, small country-seat.

gentilité, *n.f.*, Gentile nations; heathenism.

***gentillâtre**, *n.m.*, lordling.

***gentillesse**, *n.f.*, prettiness, gracefulness; pretty thing, pretty thought; (b.s.) pretty trick; fine trick. *Voilà de vos —s;* these are your fine tricks.

gentiment, *adv.*, prettily, gracefully; (iron.) nicely.

génuflexion, *n.f.*, genuflexion, kneeling

géocentrique, *adj.*, (astron.) geocentric.

géodésie, *n.f.*, geodesy.

géodésique, *adj.*, geodesical.

géognosie, *n.f.*, geognosy.

géognostique, *adj.*, geognostic.

géogonie, *n.f.*, geogony.

géogonique, *adj.*, geogonic.

géographe, *n.m.*, geographer. *Ingénieur-— (-s -s);* geographical engineer.

géographie, *n.f.*, geography. *Cartes de —;* geographical maps.

géographique, *adj.*, geographical.

géographiquement, *adv.,* geographically.

geôlage (jô-), *n.m.,* gaol fee.

geôle (jôl), *n.f.,* gaol, jail, prison.

geôlier (jô-lié), *n.m.,* gaoler, jailer.

goôlière, *n.f.,* gaoler's wife.

géologie, *n.f.,* geology.

géologique, *adj.,* geological.

géologue (-log), *n.m.,* geologist.

géomance, or **géomancie,** *n.f.,* geomancy.

géomancien (-ci-in), *n.m.,* geomancer.

géométral, -e, *adj.,* geometrical. *Plan* —; ground-plot.

géométralement (-tral-mǎn), *adv.,* geometrically.

géomètre, *n.m.,* geometrician, geometer.

géométrie, *n.f.,* geometry.

géométrique, *adj.,* geometrical.

géométriquement. (-trik-mǎn), *adv.,* geometrically.

géoponique, *adj.,* geoponic.

géorama, *n.m.,* georama.

géorgien, -ne, *n.* and *adj.,* Georgian.

géorgique, *adj.,* Georgic.

géorgiques, *n.f.pl.,* Virgil's Georgics.

géoscopie, *n.f.,* geoscopy.

géranium (-om), *n.m.,* (bot.) geranium.

gérance, *n.f.,* management; managership.

gérant, *n.m.,* manager, conductor; (com.) principal; responsible editor (of a paper—*d'un journal*).

gérant, -e, *adj.,* managing.

gerbe, *n.f.,* sheaf.

gerbée, *n.f.,* bundle of straw in which some grains of corn remain.

gerber, *v.a.,* to make up into sheaves. — *des tonneaux,* to pile casks upon each other.

gerbière, *n.f.,* cart to carry the sheaves into the barn.

gerboise, *n.f.,* (mam.) jerboa.

gerce, *n.f.,* (ent.) (pop.) tinea, clothes-moth.

gercer, *v.a.,* to chap; to crack. *Le froid gerce les lèvres;* cold weather chaps the lips.

segercer, *v.r.,* to chap, to crack.

gercer, *v.n.,* to chap, to crack.

gerçure, *n.f.,* chap; crack; chink, cleft.

gérer, *v.a.,* to manage.

gerfaut, *n.m.,* (orni.) gerfalcon.

germain, -e, *adj.,* german, first. *Cousin* —, *cousine* —*e;* cousin-german, first-cousin. *Issu de* —; second-cousin. *Il a le* — *sur moi;* he is cousin-german to my father, to my mother.

germain, *n.m.,* **-e,** *n.f.,* (jur.) brother, sister of the whole blood.

germain, -e, *n.* and *adj.,* German, native of ancient Germany.

germandrée, *n.f.,* (bot.) germander.

germanique, *adj.,* Germanic.

germanisme, *n.m.,* germanism.

germe, *n.m.,* germ; bud; seed; sprout, shoot; (bot.) ovarium. *Pousser des* —*s;* to sprout.

germer, *v.n.,* to shoot, to spring up, to sprout, to bud. *Le blé commence à* —; the corn is beginning to spring up.

germinal, -e, *adj.,* germinal.

germinal, *n.m.,* Germinal, the seventh month of the calendar of the first French republic, from March 21st to April 19th.

germinatif, -ve, *adj.,* germinal.

germination, *n.f.,* (bot.) germination.

germoir, *n.m.,* malt-house.

gérondif, *n.m.,* (gram.) gerund.

géronte, *n.m.* (—*s*), weak-minded old man.

gerzeau, *n.m.,* (bot.) (pop.) fennel-flower.

gésier, *n.m.,* gizzard; pannel (of a hawk— *du faucon*).

Ⓞ**gésine,** *n.f.,* confinement, lying-in.

Ⓞ**gésir,** *v.n.,* to lie. *Ci-gît;* here lies.

gesse, *n.f.,* (bot.) vetch.

gestation, *n.f.,* gestation.

geste, *n.m.,* gesture; action; movement, sign. *Faire des* —*s;* to gesticulate.

geste, *n.f.,* (old French literature) gest, achievement. *Chanson de* —; heroic poem.

Ⓞ**gestes,** *n.m.pl.,* great deeds, heroic achievements.

gesticulat-eur, *n.m.,* **-rice,** *n.f.,* gesticulator.

gesticulation, *n.f.,* gesticulation.

gesticuler, *v.n.,* to gesticulate too much in speaking.

gestion, *n.f.,* management, administration.

geyser, *n.m.* (—*s*), geyser.

giaour, *n.m.* (—*s*), giaour.

gibbeu-x, -se, *adj.,* gibbous.

gibbon, *n.m.,* (mam.) gibbon.

gibbosité, *n.f.,* gibbosity, gibbousness.

gibecière (ji-bsièr), *n.f.,* game-bag; pouch, bag, poke; juggler's pocket. *Faire des tours de* —; to play tricks of leger-de-main.

gibelet, *n.m.,* gimlet. *Il a un coup de* —; he is cracked.

gibelin, *n.m.,* (Italian hist.) Ghibeline.

gibelotte, *n.f.,* (cook) gibelot, ragout of rabbits.

giberne, *n.f.,* cartridge-box.

gibet, *n.m.,* gibbet, gallows.

gibier, *n.m.,* game. — *à plume;* feathered game. *Gros* —; forest game. *Menu* —; small game. — *dérobé;* poached game. — *de galère,* — *de potence;* — *de grève;* Newgate-bird, gaol-bird, gallows-bird, gallows-swinger. *Pièce de* —; head of game. *Ce n'est pas là votre* —; that is no affair of yours. *Ce n'est pas de son* —; that is not his fancy; that is beyond his capacity.

giboulée, *n.f.,* shower, hail-shower. — *de mars;* April shower.

giboyer, *v.n.,* to go hunting, shooting; to hunt, to shoot.

giboyeur, *n.m.,* huntsman, hunter; dealer in game.

giboyeu-x, -se, *adj.,* full of game.

gifle, *n.f.,* slap in the face; box on the ear.

gifler, *v.a.,* to slap in the face; to box the ears of.

gigantesque, *adj.,* gigantic, colossal.

gigantomachie, *n.f.,* (antiq) gigantomachia.

gigogne, *n.f. Mère* —; a woman having many children.

gigot, *n.m.,* leg of mutton; *pl.,* (man.) hind legs of a horse; legs, shanks (of persons—*des personnes*). *Étendre ses* —*s;* to stretch one's legs. *Des manches à* —; leg of mutton sleeves.

gigoté, -e, *adj.,* (horses, dogs—*chevaux, chiens*) strong-limbed.

gigoter, *v.n.,* to spurn, to kick (of animals); to be continually shaking the legs.

gigue (jig), *n.f.,* shank; jig. *Avec ses grandes* —*s, il tient tout le devant de la cheminée;* with his long shanks, he takes up all the front of the fire-place.

gilet, *n.m.,* waistcoat, vest. — *de flanelle;* flannel waistcoat. — *d'armes;* fencing-jacket.

gileti-er, *n.m.,* **-ère,** *n.f.,* waistcoat maker.

gille, *n.m.,* clown, ninny, simpleton; large fishing-net. *Faire* —; to go away, to cut one's stick; (pop.) to become a bankrupt.

gimblette, *n.f.,* biscuit having the form of a ring.

gindre, *n.m.,* baker's workman.

gingas, *n.m.,* ticking, tick.

gingembre, *n.m.,* (bot.) ginger.

gingeolier, *n.m.,* (bot.) lote, jujube-tree.

ginguet, -te (-ghè, -ghèt), *adj.,* weak, sorry, worthless, short, scanty. *Habit* —; scanty coat. *Esprit, style* —; frivolous mind, frivolous style.

ginguet, *n.m.*, weak wine, bad wine.
ginseng, *n.m.*, (pharm.) ginseng.
gipsy, *n.m.f.*, (*gipsies*) gipsy.
girafe, *n.f.*, (mam.) giraffe, cameleopard.
girande, *n.f.*, girande (collection of several jets of water—*faisceau de jets d'eau*); girande, bouquet (fireworks—*feu d'artifice*).
girandole, *n.f.*, girandole, branched-candle-stick; set of diamonds, sprig of precious stones; (fireworks—*feu d'artifice*) girandole; (bot.) epara.
girasol, *n.m.*, (min.) girasol.
giratoire, *adj.*, gyral.
giraumon, *or* **giraumont**, *n.m.*, (bot.) pompion; pumpkin.
girofle, *n.m.*, (bot.) clove. *Un clou de —*; a clove. *Griffe de —*; clove-stalk.
giroflée, *n.f.*, gilliflower, stock-gilliflower. *—jaune*; wallflower. *Donner à quelqu'un une —à cinq feuilles*; to give any one a box on the ear.
giroflée, *adj.*, of clove. *Cannelle —*; (com.) clove-bark.
giroflier, *n.m.*, (bot.) clove-tree.
girolle, *n.f.*, edible agaric, a variety of mushroom.
giron, *n.m.*, lap; (arch.) tread (of a step—*d'une marche d'escalier*); (her.) gyron. *Le — de l'église*; the bosom, the lap, the pale, of the Church.
gironde, *n.f.*, (French hist.) Girondist party.
girondin, *n.m.*, (French hist.) Girondist, Girondin.
gironné, *adj.*, (her.) gyronny.
girouette, *n.f.*, weathercock, vane. *— à fumée*; smoke-disperser. *Fer de —*; spindle of a vane. *C'est une —*; he is a mere weather-cock.
gisant, **-e**, *adj.*, lying (ill, dead—*malade, blessé, mort*). *Meule —e*; bed, bedder, bedetter, nether millstone.
gisement (jiz-mân), *n.m.*, (nav.) bearing; (min.) layer, bed. *—s houillers*; coal-measures.
gît, third person sing. of the present indicative of the verb *Gésir*; lies (sick, dead—*malade, blessé, mort*). *Son cadavre — sur la terre*; his body lies on the ground. *Ci —*; here lies (expression used in epitaphs).
gitan-o, *n.m.*, **-a**, *n.f.* (*—s*), Spanish word for gipsy.
gîte, *n.m.*, home, lodging-place; lodging, resting-place, quarters; nether millstone; form, seat (of hares—*du lièvre*); (mining—*mines*) layer; stratum, bed, deposit. *Un lièvre va toujours mourir au —*; a person likes to end his days in his native place. *Dernier —*; long home.
gîter, *v.a.*, to lodge, to sleep.
se **gîter**, *v.r.*, to lodge, to sleep.
givre, *n.m.*, hoar-frost, rime.
givre, *n.f.*, (her.) serpent.
givré, **-e**, *adj.*, (her.) enveloped with a serpent.
glabre, *adj.*, (bot.) glabrous, smooth, without down.
glaçant, **-e**, *adj.*, freezing; icy, chilling.
glace, *n.f.*, ice; coach-window; glass, plate-glass; looking-glass; flaw (in a diamond—*dans un diamant*). *Banc de —*; field of ice. *Clarté de la —*; ice-blink. *Montagne de —*; iceberg. *Froid comme —*; as cold as ice. *Mettre du vin à la —*; to put wine to ice, to ice wine. *Champagne frappé de —*; iced champagne. *Boire à la —*; to drink iced water. *Rompre la —*; to break the ice. *Prendre une — à l'orange*; to take an orange-ice.
glacé, **-e**, *part.*, frozen, frosted, iced; freezing, nipping, biting, icy; chilling, cold, icy-cold, clay-cold.

glacée, *n.f.*, (bot.) ice-plant. *V.* **glaciale**.
glacer, *v.a.*, to freeze, to ice; to freeze up, to congeal, to chill; to strike; to glaze; to frost; to hide the seams (of a garment—*d'un vêtement*). *Un air froid glace le visage*; cold air freezes the face. *Ce récit nous glaça d'horreur*; this recital struck us with horror. *— des confitures*; to ice sweetmeats. *— de la viande*; to glaze meat. *— une doublure*; to stitch down a lining. *— la soie*; (dy.) to alum the silk.
se **glacer**, *v.r.*, to freeze, to chill; to become weak, to grow feeble.
glacer, *v.n.*, to freeze.
glaceu-x, **-se**, *adj.*, having flaws, flawed (of precious stones—*des pierres précieuses*).
glaciaire, *adj.*, (geol.) glacial. *Période —*; ice period.
glacial, **-e**, *adj.*, frozen, glacial, icy, frigid. *Air —*; nipping air. *Vent —*; freezing wind. *Mine —*; cold looks. *Mer —, océan —*; (geog.) Frozen Ocean.
glaciale, *n.f.*, (bot.) ice-plant.
glacier, *n.m.*, glacier; field, mass of ice; coffee-house keeper; dealer in ice.
glacière, *n.f.*, ice-house.
glacis, *n.m.*, (paint.) glazing; (fort.) glacis; (arch.) talus, weathering.
glaçon, *n.m.*, piece of ice. *Petit —*; icicle.
gladiateur, *n.m.*, gladiator.
glaïeul, *n.m.*, (bot.) gladiole, sword-grass, corn-flag, iris. *— puant*; spurgewort, stinking gladwin. *— des marais*; gladwin iris, yellow water-flag.
glaire, *n.f.*, glair.
glairer, *v.a.*, to glair.
glaireu-x, **-se**, *adj.*, glairy.
glaise, *n.f.*, clay; potter's earth.
glaise, *adj.*, loamy, clayey. *Terre —*; loam, clay.
glaiser, *v.a.*, to loam, to marl. *— des terres*; to marl land.
glaiseu-x, **-se**, *adj.*, clayey, marly, loamy.
glaisière, *n.f.*, marl-pit, clay-pit.
glaive, *n.m.*, sword; blade, steel. *Le — de la justice*; the sword of justice. *Le — vengeur*; the avenging sword. *Le — de la parole*; the power of eloquence. *Puissance du —*; power of the sword, of life and death.
glama, *or* **lama**, *n.m.*, (mam.) glama, lama.
glanage, *n.m.*, gleaning.
gland, *n.m.*, acorn; tassel; (anat.) glans. *— de mer*; (conch.) acorn, acorn-fish, acorn-shell. *— de terre*; (bot.) earth-nut.
glande, *n.f.*, (anat.) gland; kernel. *Endurcissement des —s*; scirrhosity. *— lymphatique*, lymphatic gland.
glandé, **-e**, *adj.*, (vet.) glandered; (her.) acorned.
glandée, *n.f.*, pannage, crop of acorns.
glandulaire, *adj.* *V.* **glanduleux**.
glandule, *n.f.*, (anat.) glandule.
glanduleu-x, **-se**, *adj.*, glandulous, glandular.
glandulifère, *adj.*, (anat.) glanduliferous.
glane, *n.f.*, handful of corn gleaned; *pl.*, gleanings. *Faire —*; to glean. *— d'oignons*; rope of onions. *— de poires*; bunch of pears.
glaner, *v.a. and n.*, to glean.
glaneu-r, *n.m.*, **-se**, *n.f.*, gleaner.
glanure, *n.f.*, gleanings.
glapir, *v.n.*, to yelp (of puppies and foxes —*des jeunes chiens et des renards*); to screech, to scream, to squeak (of persons—*des personnes*). *Il glapit au lieu de chanter*; he screeches instead of singing.
glapissant, **-e**, *adj.*, (of puppies and foxes —*des jeunes chiens et des renards*) yelping; shrill; screeching, screaming, squeaking (of persons —*des personnes*).

glapissement (-pis-măn), *n.m.*, (of puppies and foxes—*des jeunes chiens, des renards*) yelping; screeching, scream, squeaking (of persons —*des personnes*).

glas, *n.m.*, knell; passing-bell. — *funèbre;* funeral-knell, death-bell. *Sonner le* —; to ring the knell, to toll the knell.

glaucome, *n.m.*, (med.) glaucoma.

glauque, *adj.*, glaucous.

glèbe, *n.f.*, glebe, ground, land. *Esclaves de la* —, *serfs de la* —; serfs. *Être attaché à la* —; to be bound to the soil.

gléchome (-kom), *n.m.*, ground-ivy.

glène, *n.f.*, (anat.) glene, socket; (nav.) coil.

gléner, *v.a.*, (nav.) to coil.

glénoïdal, -e, *adj.*, (anat.) glenoid. *Cavité —e de l'omoplate;* glenoid cavity of the scapula.

glénoïde, *adj.*, (anat.) glenoid.

glénoïdien, -ne (-in, -è-n), *adj.*, (anat.) glenoid.

glette, *n.f.*, (métal.) litharge; dross.

glissade, *n.f.*, sliding, slide; slipping; slip; (dancing—*danse*) glissade. *Faire une* —; to have a slide; to make a slip, to make a false step.

glissant, -e, *adj.*, slippery. *Il fait* —; it is slippery walking. *Pas* —; delicate affair, ticklish affair. *Terrain* —; slippery, tender ground.

glissé, *n.m.*, (dancing—*danse*) glisse.

glissement (glis-măn), *n.m.*, slipping; sliding.

glisser, *v.n.*, to slip, to slip over; to slide; to glance over, to slur over; to make little, no impression; to slide; **to** glance. *L'échelle glissa;* the ladder slipped. — *sur la glace;* to slide. *Cela m'a glissé des mains;* that slipped through my fingers. *Glissons là-dessus;* let us pass over that.

glisser, *v.a.*, to slip, to slip in; to slide, to slide in; to insinuate, to introduce. *Il glissa sa main dans ma poche;* he slipped his hand in my pocket.

se glisser, *v.r.*, to slip, to slide, to creep, to steal in; to insinuate one's self.

glisseur, *n.m.*, slider.

glissoire, *n.f.*, slide.

globe, *n.m.*, globe, sphere, orb. *Le — de la terre;* the globe of the earth. *Le — céleste;* the celestial globe. — *de feu;* fire-ball.

in **globo**. *V.* **in globo**.

globulaire, *n.f.*, globularia, French daisy.

globulaire, *adj.*, globular.

globule, *n.m.*, globule.

globuleu-x, -se, *adj.*, globulous, globular, globous.

gloire, *n.f.*, glory; glorification; halo; aureola. *Vaine* —; vain glory. *Être la — de;* to be the glory of. *Se faire une — de quelque chose;* to glory in anything. *Mettre sa — à;* to glory in. *Il aspire à toutes les* —*s;* he aims at all kinds of glory.

⊙**gloméré, -e**, *adj. V.* **aggloméré**.

⊙**glomérer**, *v.a. V.* **agglomérer**.

gloria, *n.m.* (—), coffee with brandy in it.

gloriette, *n.f.*, recess (in a garden—*dans un jardin*).

glorieusement (-euz-măn),*adv.*,gloriously.

glorieu-x, -se, *adj.*, glorious; (rel.) glorified, blessed; vainglorious, conceited, self-conceited; proud.

glorieu-x, -se, *n.f.*, -se, *n.f.*, braggart, boaster; vainglorious person. *Faire le* —; to be a braggart.

glorification, *n.f.*, glorification.

glorifier, *v.a.*, to glorify, to give glory to.

se glorifier, *v.r.*, to glory in, to boast.

gloriole, *n.f.*, vainglory.

glose (glōz), *n.f.*, gloss; glozing; carping; parody.

gloser, *v.a.*, to gloss; to gloze, to criticize, to carp at, to find fault with.

gloser, *v.n.*, to carp at, to find fault with.

gloseu-r, *n.m.*, -se, *n.f.*, carper; find-fault.

glossaire, *n.m.*, glossary.

glossateur, *n.m.*, glossologist.

glossite, *n.f.*, (med.) inflammation of the tongue.

glossographe, *n.m.*, glossographer.

glossographie, *n.f.*, glossography.

glossologie, *n.f.*, glossology.

glossopètre, *n.m.*, (geol.) petrified fish teeth.

glotte, *n.f.*, (anat.) glottis.

glougloter, or **glouglouter**, *v.n.*, to gabble (of a turkey—*du dindon*).

glouglou, *n.m.*, gurgling.

gloume, *n.m. V.* **glume**.

gloussement (glous-măn), *n.m.*, clucking (of hens—*de la poule*).

glousser, *v.n.*, to cluck (of hens—*de la poule*).

glouteron (glou-tron), *n.m.*, (bot.) burdock.

glouton, -ne, *adj.*, gluttonous, greedy.

glouton, *n.m.*, -ne, *n.f.*, glutton; (mam.) glutton.

gloutonnement (-to-n-măn), *adv.*, gluttonously, greedily.

gloutonnerie (-to-n-rī), *n.f.*, gluttony.

glu, *n.f.*, bird-lime, lime.

gluant, -e, *adj.*, glutinous, sticky, limy.

gluau, *n.m.*, lime-twig. *Tendre des* —*x;* to set lime-twigs.

glucose, *n.f.*, (chem.) glucose.

gluer, *v.a.*, to lime; to make sticky.

glui, *n.m.*, barley straw.

glume, *n.f.*, (bot.) glume, husk.

gluten (-tèn), *n.m.*, gluten.

glutinati-f, -ve, *adj.*, agglutinative.

glutination, *n.f. V.* **agglutination**.

glutineu-x, -se, *adj.*, glutinous, viscous.

glutinosité, *n.f.*, glutinosity, viscidity, viscosity, viscousness; stickiness.

glycérine, *n.f.*, glycerin.

glycine, *n.f.*, (bot.) glycin, a Chinese plant.

glyconien, or **glyconique**, *adj.*, glyconian.

glycose, *n.f. V.* **glucose**.

glyphe, *n.m.*, (arch.) glyph.

glyptique, *n.f.*, glyptics.

glyptographie, *n.f.*, glyptography.

gnaphale, *n.m.*, (bot.) cudweed, everlasting.

gneiss, *n.m.*, (min.) gneiss.

gnome, *n.m.*, gnome.

gnomide, *n.f.*, gnome.

gnomique, *adj.*, gnomical, sententious.

gnomon, *n.m.*, gnomon, pin of a dial.

gnomonique, *n.f.*, gnomonics, dialling.

gnose, *n.f.*, (theol.) gnosis; (philos.) gnosticism,

gnosticisme, *n.m.*, gnosticism.

gnostiques, *n.m.pl.*, gnostics.

tout de **go**, *adv.*, freely, unceremoniously.

gobbe, *n.f.*, poisoned ball (for a dog—*pour les chiens*).

gobelet (go-blè), *n.m.*, goblet, mug, drinking-cup; juggler's box; buttery (of palaces—*d'un palais*); officers of the buttery. *Joueur de* —*s;* juggler. *Tour de* —; juggler's trick.

gobelin (go-blin), *n.m.*, goblin, evil spirit.

gobelins, *n.m. pl.*, Gobelins, manufacture of tapestry at Paris.

gobelotter (go-blo-té), *v.n.*, to tipple.

gobe-mouches, *n.m.* (—), (orni.) fly-catcher; (bot.) fly-trap; simpleton; gull; trifler; ninny.

gober, *v.a.*, to gulp down, to swallow; to swallow down, to believe easily; to nab. *Il gobe* des mouches; he trifles away his time. Je ne vais pas — cela; I am not going to swallow that. — le morceau; to swallow the bait, to be caught, taken in.

goberge, n.f., cross bar (of a bedstead—d'un bois de lit); handle (of a joiner's press—d'une presse de menuisier).

se **goberger**, v.r., to enjoy one's self; to take one's ease, to lounge.

gobet, n.m., gobbet. Prendre quelqu'un au —; to seize any one when he least expects it.

gobeter (gob-té), v.a., (mas.) to point.

gobeur, n.m., swallower; gull (person—personne).

gobin, n.m., (fam., l.u.) a little hunchback.

*__godaille__, n.f., tippling, drinking.

*__godailler__, v.n., to tipple.

*__godailleur__, n.m., tippler.

godelureau, n.m., popinjay, coxcomb, fop.

godenot, n.m., puppet, juggler's puppet; (b.s.) ill-shaped man, punch.

goder, v.n., to crease (of clothes—des vêtements); to pucker (of needle-work—d'ouvrage à l'aiguille).

godet, n.m., drinking-cup (with no handle—sans anse); calyx (of a flower—de fleur); cup (of a lamp—de lampe).

godiche, n. and adj., simpleton, ninny.

godichon, -ne, n. and adj., silly, simple.

*__godille__, n.f., (nav.) scull.

*__godiller__, v.n., (nav.) to scull.

*__godilleur__, n.m., (nav.) sculler.

godiveau, n.m., (cook.) force-meat pie.

godron, n.m., ⊙plait; (arch.) godroon.

godronner, v.a., ⊙to plait round; to make godroons on.

goéland, n.m., (orni.) gull.

goélette, n.f., (nav.) schooner.

goémon, n.m., sea-wrack.

⊙**goet**, n.m. V. **gouet**.

goétie (-ci), n.f., goety.

⊙**goffe**, adj., ill-shaped, awkward.

*__gogaille__, n.f., (pop.) merry-making.

à **gogo**, adv., in clover. Être à —; to live in clover.

goguenard, -e (gog-nâr), adj., bantering, jeering.

goguenard, n.m., -e, n.f., banterer, jeerer.

goguenarder (gog-nar-dé), v.n., to jeer, to banter.

goguenarderie, n.f., jeering, jeer, bantering.

goguettes, n.f.pl., merry story, merry saying. Être en —; to be in a merry mood. Chanter — à quelqu'un; to abuse any one.

goinfre, n.m., gormandizer.

goinfrer, v.n., to gormandize.

goinfrerie, n.f., gormandizing.

goitre, n.m., goitre, wen; (bot.) struma.

goitreu-x, -se, adj., goitrous.

goitreu-x, n.m., **-se**, n.f., person affected with a goitre; (orni.) pelican.

golfe, n.m., gulf.

gommage, n.m., gumming.

gomme, n.f., gum; (med.) gummatum. — arabique; gum arabic. — -gutte (—s —s); gamboge. — élastique; India rubber.

gommer, v.a., to gum.

gomme-résine, n.f. (—s —s), gum-resin.

gommeu-x, -se, adj., gummous, gummy.

gommier, n.m., gum-tree.

gomphose, n.f., (anat.) gomphosis.

gond, n.m., hinge (for doors, gates—de portes); pintle (of a rudder—de gouvernail). Hors des —s; unhinged; (fig.) enraged, beside one's self.

gondole, n.f., gondola.

gondoler, v.n., (tech.) to warp (of wood—du bois).

gondolier, n.m., gondolier.

gonfalon, or **gonfanon**, n.m., gonfalon, gonfanon.

gonfalonier, n.m., gonfalonnier.

gonflement, n.m., swelling; tumidness.

gonfler, v.a., to swell, to puff up, to inflate, to fill with wind. Des yeux gonflés; swollen eyes.

se **gonfler**, v.r., to swell, to swell up, to be swollen.

gonfler, v.n., to swell, to swell up.

gong, n.m., (—s), gong.

gonin, n.m., knave, rogue, rascal.

goniomètre, n.m., goniometer.

goniométrie, n.f., goniometry.

gonne, n.f., sea-cask, barrel.

gonorrhée, n.f., gonorrhœa.

gord, n.m., fishing-net with poles fixed in a river.

gordien (-di-in), adj.m., Gordian. Nœud —; Gordian knot.

gordius (-us), n.m., hair-worm, gordius.

⊙**gore**, n.f., sow.

goret, n.m., (jest.) young pig; (nav.) hog.

goreter, v.a., (nav.) to hog.

gorge, n.f., throat, gullet; neck and shoulders (of a woman—d'une femme); breast, neck; mouth, orifice; defile, strait, narrow pass; (fort.) gorge; groove (of a pulley—d'une poulie); roller (of maps, &c.—de cartes géographiques, &c.). Un mal de —; a sore throat. À pleine —; at the top of one's voice. Couper la — à quelqu'un; to cut any one's throat; to ruin any one. Prendre quelqu'un à la —; to seize any one by the throat. Rire à — déployée; to laugh immoderately. Rendre —; to disgorge, to refund. Elle a la — belle; she has a beautiful breast. Faire des —s chaudes de quelque chose; to ridicule, to laugh, at any thing.

gorge-de-pigeon, adj. invariable, iridescent, shot (of colours—couleur).

gorge-de-pigeon, n.m. (n.p.), shot-colour.

gorgée, n.f., draught; quantity taken at a time; mouthful.

gorger, v.a., to gorge.

se **gorger**, v.r., to gorge one's self.

gorgeret, n.m., (surg.) gorget, gorgeret.

⊙**gorgerette**, n.f., gorget.

gorgerin, n.m., gorget (armour—armure); (arch.) gorgerin.

gorgone, n.f., (myth.) Gorgon; (zool.) gorgonia.

*__gorille__, n.m., (mam.) gorilla.

gosier, n.m., throat, gullet; (anat.) fauces. Coup de —; (mus.) breath. Avoir le — sec; to be always thirsty. S'humecter le —; to wet one's whistle.

gossampin, n.m., silk-cotton-tree.

gothique, adj., pertaining to the Goths, Gothic. Écriture —; black letter.

gothique, n.m., Gothic.

gothique, n.f., (print.) old English.

gouache, n.f., painting in water-body colour.

gouailler, v.a., (pop.) to chafe, to tease.

gouailleu-r, n.m., **-se**, n.f., chafer, joker, teaser.

⊙*__goudille__, n.f. V. **godille**.

⊙*__goudiller__, v.n. V. **godiller**.

⊙*__goudilleur__, n.m. V. **godilleur**.

goudron, n.m., tar.

goudronnage, n.m., tarring.

goudronner, v.a., to tar; to pay with tar.

goudronnerie (-dro-n-ri), n.f., tar-works.

gouet, n.m., (bot.) arum, cuckoo-pintle.

gouffre, n.m., gulf; whirlpool.

gouge, n.f., gouge.

gouger, v.a., to gouge.

gouine, n.f., (pop.) street-walker.

goujat, *n.m.*, soldier's servant; mason's labourer; blackguard.

goujon, *n.m.*, gudgeon. *Faire avaler le — à quelqu'un;* to gull any one.

goule, *n.f.*, ghoul.

goulée, *n.f.*, (pop.) mouthful.

goulet, *n.m.*, narrow entrance of a harbour.

goulette, *n.f.* V. **goulotte**.

gouliafre, *n.m.*, (pop.) glutton.

goulot, *n.m.*, neck (of a bottle, &c.—*de bouteille, &c.*).

goulotte, *n.f.*, water-channel.

goulu, -e *adj.*, gluttonous, greedy.

goulu, *n.m.*, **-e**, *n.f.*, glutton, greedy person.

goulûment, *adv.*, gluttonously, greedily.

goum, *n.m.* (—s), (milit.) native contingent furnished to the French army in Algeria by every tribe.

*****goupille**, *n.f.*, (tech.) pin; peg; bolt.

*****goupiller**, *v.a.*, (tech.) to pin.

*****goupillon**, *n.m.*, aspersorium; aspergill; holy-water sprinkler; bottle-brush.

*****goupillonner**, *v.a.*, to cleanse with a bottle-brush.

gourbi, *n.m.* (—s), hut, cabin.

gourd, -e, *adj.*, benumbed.

gourde, *n.f.*, (bot.) gourd; calabash; piaster (a coin—*monnaie*); flask.

gourdin, *n.m.*, cudgel, club; (nav.) rope's end.

gourdiner, *v.a.*, (pop) to cudgel.

goure, *n.f.*, adulterated drug.

gourer, *v.a.*, (pop.) to adulterate drugs; to cheat.

goureur, *n.m.*, adulterator of drugs; cheat, trickster.

gourgandine, *n.f.*, (pop.) street-walker.

gourgane, *n.f.*, broad bean, bean.

gourgouran, *n.m.*, an Indian silk fabric.

gourmade, *n.f.*, punch, cuff.

gourmand, -e, *adj.*, gluttonous, greedy.

gourmand, *n.m.*, **-e**, *n.f.*, glutton.

gourmander, *v.a.*, to chide, to reprimand, to reprove harshly; to check, to curb; (cook.) to lard.

gourmandise, *n.f.*, gluttony, greediness.

gourme, *n.f.*, (med.) ringworm of the scalp; (vet.) glanders. *Jeter sa—;* to have a running at the nose (of a horse—*du cheval*); to have a rash (of children—*des enfants*); to sow one's wild oats (of a young man—*d'un jeune homme*).

gourmé, -e, *part.*, curbed; affectedly grave.

gourmer, *v.a.*, to curb (a horse—*un cheval*); to box, to thump.

se **gourmer**, *v.r.*, to thump, to pommel, each other.

gourmet, *n.m.*, connoisseur in wine; winetaster; judge of good living.

gourmette, *n.f.*, (man.) curb, curb-chain. *Lâcher la — à quelqu'un;* to loosen any one's reins a little, to give any one more scope.

gournable, *n.f.*, (nav.) tree-nail.

gournabler, *v.a.*, (nav.) to drive in the tree-nails.

goussant, or goussaut, *n.m.*, thick-set horse.

gousse, *n.f.*, pod, husk. — *d'ail;* clove of garlic.

gousset, *n.m.*, fob; arm-pit; odour of the arm-pits; gusset (of a shirt—*de chemise*); (carp.) brace. *Vider un —;* to pick a pocket.

goût, *n.m.*, taste, savour, relish; smell; inclination, liking; style, manner, fashion. *Avoir du — pour;* to like, to have a liking for, to be fond of. *Avoir le — de;* to taste of. *Avoir le — difficile;* to be difficult to please, to be nice, particular. *Relever le —;* to give a relish. *Avoir le — dépravé;* to have one's mouth out of taste. *Cela plaît au —;* that is pleasing to the taste. *Avoir bon —;* to taste nice. *Viande de haut —;*

highly-seasoned meat. *Ce pain a un — de noisette;* that bread tastes of nuts. *Être de son —;* to be palatable; to hit one's fancy. *C'est un critique plein de —;* he is a critic of great taste. *Chacun a son —;* every one to his liking. *Prendre — à une chose;* to take a liking to a thing. *Trouver une chose à son —;* to find a thing to one's liking. *Il ne faut point disputer des —s;* there's no accounting for tastes. *De bon —;* in good taste. *De mauvais —;* in bad taste, vulgar. *Ces vers sont dans le — de Racine;* these verses are in the style of Racine. *Faire une chose par —;* to do a thing from taste. *Cela est-il de votre —?* is that to your taste? *Satisfaire ses —s;* to satisfy one's tastes.

goûter, *v.a.*, to taste, to relish; to like, to approve of; to enjoy; to smell. *Voulez-vous — notre vin?* will you taste our wine? *Goûtez ce tabac;* smell this snuff. *Ce prédicateur est bien goûté;* that preacher is very much liked. — *les plaisirs de la table;* to enjoy the pleasures of the table. — *le repos;* to enjoy repose.

se **goûter**, *v.r.*, to be tasted. *Une sauce doit toujours —;* a sauce ought always to be tasted.

goûter, *v.n.*, to taste, to smell; to lunch; to try, to make a trial of; to approve of. *Goûtez de ce vin;* try this wine.

goûter, *n.m.*, repast taken between dinner and supper; lunch.

goutte, *n.f.*, drop, small quantity; dram; (arch., pharm.) drop; (med.) gout. — *à —;* drop by drop. *Mère —;* unpressed wine. *Boire la —;* to take a drop (of liquor—*d'eau-de-vie*). *Boire une —;* to drink a drop. *Ils se ressemblent comme deux —s d'eau;* they are as like as two peas. — *sciatique;* sciatica, hip-gout. — *vague;* wandering gout. *Accès de —;* attack of the gout. *Être travaillé de la —;* to suffer from the gout.

goutte, *adv.*, (l.u.) in the least, at all. *Il ne voit —;* he does not see at all. *N'entendre —;* not to hear at all; not to understand in the least.

gouttelette (gou-tlèt), *n.f.*, small drop.

goutteu-x, -se, *adj.*, gouty.

goutteu-x, *n.m.*, **-se**, *n.f.*, gouty person.

gouttière, *n.f.*, gutter of a roof; spout (for rain-water—*pour eau de pluie*); cornice (of a carriage—*d'une voiture*); fore-edge (of a book—*d'un livre*); (anat.) groove; (nav.) *pl.*, water-way. — *de plomb;* leaden spout.

gouvernable, *adj.*, governable.

*****gouvernail**, *n.m.*, rudder, helm. *Tenir le —;* to be at the helm.

©**gouvernance**, *n.f.;* a town ward in the Netherlands.

gouvernant, -e, *adj.*, governing, ruling.

gouvernant, *n.m.*, governor, ruler. *Les —s;* those who govern.

gouvernante, *n.f.*, governor's wife; governante, governess; housekeeper (of a single man —*d'un célibataire*).

gouverne, *n.f.*, guidance, government. *Je vous dis cela pour votre —;* I tell you that for your guidance.

gouvernement, *n.m.*, government; management; governorship; government-house; (nav.) steering. *En son —;* under his management.

gouvernemental, -e, *adj.*, of the government.

gouverner, *v.a.*, to govern, to rule, to command, to manage, to direct, to regulate, to look to, to take care of; to husband; to bring up (children—*enfants*); to breed (animal); (nav.) to steer; to rein up (a horse—*un cheval*). — *un ménage;* to direct a household. — *quelqu'un;* to rule any one. — *un vaisseau;* to steer a ship. *C'est lui qui gouverne la barque;* it is he who is

entrusted with the conduct of the enterprise.
Il gouverne bien sa barque; he conducts his affairs well.

se gouverner, *v.r.*, to govern one's self; to behave one's self; to be governed.

gouverner, *v.n.*, to govern, to rule; to manage; (nav.) to steer, to answer the helm.

gouverneur, *n.m.*, governor, ruler, tutor.

goyave, *n.f.*, (bot.) guava (fruit).

goyavier, *n.m.*, (bot.) guava (tree—*arbre*).

grabat, *n.m.*, pallet. stump-bed. *Être sur le —;* to be on a sick-bed.

grabataire, *n.* and *adj.*, bedrid person, bedrid. bedridden.

grabuge, *n.m.*, (triv.) wrangling. quarrel, squabble, brawl.

grâce, *n.f.*, grace; favour, pardon; king's. queen's, pardon; mercy. indulgence; gracefulness, elegance; *pl.*, thanks; *pl.*, (myth.) Graces. *Accorder une —;* to grant a favour. *De —;* for mercy's sake! pray! I pray you! *Bonnes —s;* good graces; head curtains (of a bed—*d'un lit*). *Actions de —;* thanksgiving. *À la — de;* at the mercy of. *Demander — à;* to ask pardon of, to crave quarter of. *Faire une — à quelqu'un;* to do any one a favour. *Faire — à quelqu'un;* to forgive any one; to pardon any one. *Se mettre dans les bonnes —s de quelqu'un;* to get into any one's good graces. *Rentrer en —;* to get into favour again. *Il est dans les bonnes —s du roi;* he is in the king's good graces. *Perdre les bonnes —s de quelqu'un;* to lose any one's good graces. *Trouver — devant quelqu'un;* to find favour in any one's sight. *L'an de —;* the year of grace, in the year of our Lord. *Rendre —s au ciel;* to return thanks to heaven *Dire ses —s;* to say grace. *— à Dieu;* thank God. *Je vous rends —;* I thank you. *Sans —;* graceless *Avec —;* graceful. *Faire une chose de bonne —;* to do a thing with a good grace. *Sacrifier aux —s;* to sacrifice to the Graces.

graciable, *adj.*, (jur.) pardonable.

gracier, *v.a.*, (jur.) to pardon.

gracieusement (-eûz-măn),*adv.*,graciously, kindly, gracefully.

⊖gracieuser, *v.a.*, to show kindness to.

gracieuseté, *n.f.*, graciousness; acknowledgment, gratuity.

gracieu-x, **-se**, *adj.*, graceful, pleasant, courteous, gracious, kind, obliging.

gracilité, *n.f.*, gracility; shrillness.

gradation, *n.f.*, gradation; climax.

grade, *n.m.*, grade, rank; degree.

gradé, *adj.m.*, that has a rank (applied only to petty officers—*des sous-officiers et caporaux*).

gradin, *n.m.*, step; shelf; bench; tier; *pl.*, benches rising one above the other, tiers.

graduation, *n.f.*, graduation; drying-house (in salt-works—*dans les salines*).

gradué, *n.m.*, graduate (of a university—*d'une université*).

gradué. **-e**, *adj.*, *part.*, graduated, progressive. *Cours de themes —;* progressive course of exercises.

graduel. **-le**, *adj.*, gradual.

graduel. *n.m.*, (c.rel.) gradual.

graduellement (-ĕl-măn), *adv.*, gradually

graduer, *v.a.*, to graduate. *Se faire —;* to graduate. to take a degree.

graffite, *n.m.*, drawing on the walls of the antique towns of Italy.

*graillement, *n.m.*, hoarseness

*grailler, *v.n.*, (hunt.) to call the dogs (by sounding the horn—*avec le cor de chasse*)

*graillon. *n.m.*, broken meat; burned meat scrap; smell of burnt meat or fat. *Marie —;* slattern, slut.

*graillonner, *v.n.*, to hawk up phlegm; to have a smell of burnt meat or fat.

*graillonneu-r. *n.m.*, -se, *n.f.*, (l.ex.) person who often spits, or hawks.

grain, *n.m.*, grain, berry. bead; squall. *Gros —s;* wheat and rye. *Menus —s;* spring corn. *Un — de raisin;* a grape. *— de chapelet;* bead of a chaplet. *Un rosaire à gros —s;* a rosary of great beads. *Un — de sel;* a grain of salt. *Il n'a pas un — de bon sens;* he has not a grain of sense. *Il a un — de folie dans la tête;* he is cracked. *Être dans le —;* to be in a good thing. *Poules de —;* corn-fed pullets. *Catholique à gros —s;* lax Catholic.

graine, *n.f.*, seed; berry; set (persons—*personnes*); eggs (of silkworms—*de vers à soie*). *Monter en —;* to run to seed. *C'est une mauvaise — que les écoliers;* school-boys are a sad set. *— d'Avignon;* French berry. *— de lin*, linseed. *— de vers à soie;* silkworm's eggs. *— de niais;* thing only calculated to delude the most simple. *C'est de la — de niais;* why, a fool would not be taken in by it. *Cette fille monte en —;* that woman is likely to die an old maid.

grainer, *v.n.* *V.* **grener**

grainetier (grè-n-tiè), *V.* **grènetier**.

grainetis (grè-n-ti), *n.m.*, (coin.) punch. puncheon.

graini-er, *n.m.*, **-ère**, *n.f.*, seedsman, seeds woman.

graissage, *n.m.*, greasing, grease.

graisse, *n.f.*, fat, fatness, grease; (pharm.) tallow. *— de rôti;* dripping. *— de cuisine*, kitchen-stuff.

graisser, *v.a.*, to grease, to make greasy; to make dirty. *— la patte à quelqu'un;* to give any one a sop, to fee any one. *— ses bottes*, (pop.) to prepare to set out, to prepare for kingdom come.

graisser, *v.n.*, to be oily (of wine—*du vin*).

graisseu-x. **-se**, *adj.*, greasy; fatty.

graissier, *n.m.*, grease-merchant.

gralle, *n.m.*, (orni.) grallie, wading bird.

grallipède, *adj.*, grallatory, long-legged (of birds—*des oiseaux*).

gramen (-mèn), *n.m.*, gramineous plant.

graminée, *adj.f.*, gramineous; grammeal.

graminée, *n.f.*, gramineous plant; *—s*, gramineæ, gramineaceæ.

graminiforme, *adj.*, graminifolious.

grammaire, *n.f.*, grammar. *— raisonnée*, analytical grammar.

grammairien, *n.m.*, **-ne**, *n.f.* (-in.-è-h), grammarian.

grammatical. **-e**, *adj.*, grammatical. *Correction —e;* grammatical correctness, good grammar.

grammaticalement (-kal-măn), *adv.*, grammatically.

grammatiste, *n.m.*, grammatist.

gramme, *n.m.*, gramme (15 438 grains troy).

grand. **-e**, *adj.*, great, large; high, lofty, tall; wide; big; capacious, huge; grand; broad (of daylight—*du jour*); grown up. *Homme —;* tall man. *— homme;* great man. *Une —e personne;* a grown-up person. *Les blés sont déjà —s;* the corn is already high. *— bal;* grand ball. *Il fut — dans l'adversité;* he was great in adversity. *Un — personnage;* a great personage. *Il n'a pas — argent;* he has not much money. *Le — prêtre;* the high-priest. *Le — monde;* the fashionable world. *J'ai eu grand'peur;* I was greatly frightened. *La grand'messe (— —s);* high mass. *Grand'garde (— —s)* (milit.) outpost. *—es eaux;* floods. *Voleur de — chemin;* highwayman. *Le — ressort;* the main-spring. *Il est — jour; it is broad daylight. *— livre;* ledger. *— livre de la dette publique,* *—livre;* list of the creditors of the State.

grand, *n.m.*, grandee; nobleness, grandeur, grandness; *pl.*, the great, great people. *Tran-*

cher du —; to carry it with a high hand. Du petit au —; comparing little things with great ones. Promesse de — n'est pas héritage; one must not trust the promises of the great. En —; on a large scale; in grand style; (paint.) at full length (portraits).

grand-duc, n.m. (—s —s), grand-duke.

grand-ducal, adj.m. (— -ducaux); **grand-ducale**, adj.f. (— —s), of a grand-duke.

grandelet, -te (gran-dlè, -t), adj., biggish, pretty tall.

grandement (gran-dmän), adv., grandly, nobly; greatly, vastly, highly, extremely, largely, very much.

grandesse, n.f., grandeeship (title of a Spanish grandee—titre d'un grand d'Espagne).

grandeur, n.f., size; height; length; breadth; bulk, bulkiness; greatness, largeness, magnitude, hugeness, bigness; tallness; might; grandeur, nobleness. Ils sont de même —; they are of the same size. Mépriser les —s de ce monde; to despise the grandeurs of this world. De — naturelle; as large as life. Il a un air de — qui impose; he has an air of grandeur that commands respect. — d'âme; magnanimity. Regarder quelqu'un du haut de sa —; to look down upon any one.

grandiose, adj., grand, imposing.

grandiose, n.m., grandeur.

grandir, v.n., to grow; to grow up, to spring up; to grow tall, to grow big; to increase. Cet enfant grandit à vue d'œil; that child grows so fast that one may even see it. — trop pour ses habits; to grow out of one's clothes.

se grandir, v.r., to make one's self taller by standing on one's toes; to become taller, to grow taller; to grow; to become greater, to raise one's self, to rise. La médiocrité croit — en rabaissant le mérite; mediocrity believes it raises itself by running down merit.

grandissime, adj., very great, very large.

grand'mère, n.f. (— —s), grandmother.

grand-oncle, n.m. (—s —s), great-uncle.

grand-père, n.m. (—s —s), grandfather, grandsire.

grand'tante, n.f. (— —s), great-aunt.

grange, n.f., barn. Batteur en —; thrasher.

granit (-nit), n.m., (min.) granite.

granitelle, adj., (min.) granitel.

granitique, adj., (min.) granitic.

granivore, adj., granivorous.

granulation, n.f., granulation.

granule, n.m., (bot.) granule.

granulé, -e, part., granulated, granular.

granuler, v.a., to granulate.

se granuler, v.r., to granulate.

granuleu-x, -se, adj., granulous, granular, granulated.

graphique, adj., graphic, graphical. Représentation —; (math.) scheme.

graphiquement, adv., graphically.

graphite, n.m., (min.) graphite; plumbago.

graphomètre, n.m., (math.) graphometer.

grapin, n.m. V. grappin.

grappe, n.f., bunch (of grapes, currants—de raisin, de groseilles); cluster (of fruit—de fruits); (artil.) grape, grapeshot; (vet.) grape, wart. Mordre à la —; to bite at the hook, to swallow the bait. Croître en —; to cluster.

*****grappillage**, n.m., gleaning (in a vineyard—dans une vigne).

*****grappiller**, v.a. and n., to glean grapes; to glean; to gain a trifle, to make a little profit.

*****grappilleu-r**,n.m., **-se**, n.f.,grape-gleaner; gleaner; petty extortioner.

*****grappillon**, n.m., little bunch of grapes.

grappin, n.m., (nav.) grapple, grappling, grapnel-iron. — à main; hand grappling. —

de brûlot; fire grappling. Jeter le — sur quelqu'un; to get any one into one's clutches.

gras, -se, adj., fat, fleshy, plump, full of fat, corpulent, obese; greasy, oily, unctuous; rich; broad, indecent; (paint.) thick; (print.) thick-faced (of letters—de caractères). — comme un moine: as fat as a mullet, as a pig, as butter. Dormir la —se matinée; to sleep all the morning; to rise late. Il en fait ses choux —; he feathers his nest with it. Ce cheval a la vue —se; this horse is dim-sighted. Cette sauce est trop —se; this gravy is too rich. Soupe —se; meat soup. Dîner —; meat dinner. Du vin —; thick wine. De l'encre —se; thick ink. Terre —se; heavy clayey soil. Terres — ses; fat ground. Du son —; fine bran. Jour —; meat-day. Les jours —; shrove days, shrove-tide. Avoir la langue —se; to speak thick. Temps —; hazy weather. Cette comédie est trop —se; this comedy is too broad. Le pavé est —; the pavement is slippery. Cet homme n'en est pas plus —; this man is none the better for it.

gras, n.m., fat, fleshy part; meat; meat diet; calf (of the leg—de la jambe). Faire —, manger —; to eat meat.

gras-cuit, adv., (of bread—du pain) heavy.

gras-double, n.m. (— —s), tripe.

gras-fondu, n.m. (n.p.), or **gras-fondure**, n.f. (n.p.), (vet.) molten-grease.

gras-mollet, n.m. (— —s), (ich.) lump-fish.

grassement (grâs-män), adv., plentifully, largely; liberally; comfortably. Payer —; to pay generously. Vivre —; to live comfortably.

grasset, -te, adj., fattish, pretty fat, pretty plump.

grasset, n.m., (vet.) stifle; stifle-joint.

grassette, n.f., (bot.) butterwort, sanicle.

grasseyement, n.m., thick pronunciation.

grasseyer, v.n., to speak thick (by pronouncing the letter r in a peculiar manner, like many Parisians).

*****grassouillet, -te**, adj., plump.

grat (gra), n.m., place scratched by fowls.

grateron, n.m., (bot.) scratch-weed; goose-grass; cleavers.

graticuler, v.n., (paint.) to square.

gratification, n.f., gratuity, bounty, encouragement.

gratifier, v.a., to confer on, to bestow on; to attribute, to ascribe. — quelqu'un de ses bévues; to father one's blunders upon somebody else. — quelqu'un d'un coup de poing; to bestow a blow with one's fist on any one.

gratin, n.m., scraping of a dish or saucepan. — d'un plat, d'une casserole); burned part.

gratiole (-ci-), n.f., (bot.) gratiola, hyssop. — officinale; hedge-hyssop.

gratis (gra-tis), adv., gratis, for nothing, gratuitously.

gratis, n.m., exemption from cost; free gift.

gratitude, n.f., gratitude, gratefulness, thankfulness.

gratte, n.f., (nav.) scraper. — double; double-headed scraper.

gratté, -e, part., scratched.

gratte-boësse, n.f. (—), scratching-brush for gilding.

gratte-boësser, v.a., to scratch with the brush in gilding.

gratte-cul, n.m. (— —s), (bot.) canker, dog-rose. Il n'est point de si belle rose qui ne devienne —; all beauties are subject to decay.

gratte-langue, n.m. (— —s), tongue-scraper.

gratteleu-x, -se (gra-tleû, -z), adj., itchy.

grattelle, n.f., (med.) a rash with some itching.

gratte-navire, n.m. (— —s), ship-scraper.

gratte-papier, n.m. (—, or — —s), scribbling drudge, quill-driver.

gratter, *v.a.*, to scratch, to scrape. *Trop cuit, trop parler nuit ;* too much scratching inflames a wound, and too much talking does great harm. — *quelqu'un où il lui démange ;* to talk of a thing that pleases any one.

se **gratter**, *v.r.*, to scratch one's self ; to scrape one's self. *Qui se sent galeux se gratte ;* let him whom the cap fits wear it.

grattoir, *n.m.*, scratching-knife, scraper, eraser.

gratton, *n.m.*, (adj., (bot.) *V.* **grateron**.

gratuit, -e, *adj.*, gratuitous, free. *Supposition —e ;* gratuitous supposition.

gratuité, *n.f.*, gratuity, free gift.

gratuitement (-tui-tmän), *adv.*, gratuitously ; free, for nothing ; groundlessly.

grauwacke, *n.f.*, (geol., min.) graywacke, greywacke ; grit-rock.

gravatier (-tié), *n.m.*, rubbish-carter.

gravati-f, -ve, *adj.*, (med.) dull, heavy.

gravats (-vä), *n.m.pl. V.* **gravois**.

grave, *adj.*, heavy ; grave, serious, solemn, sedate, demure, sober ; weighty, of importance ; grievous ; low, deep, hollow, flat. *Contenance, mine, —;* solemn look. *Blessure —;* grievous wound. *Note —;* low note. *Ton —;* deep tone. *Accent —;* grave accent.

grave, *n.m.*, gravity ; heavy body. *Passer du — au gai ;* to pass from grave to gay. *Chute des —s* (phys.) ; descent of bodies.

grave, *n.f.*, beach, strard in Newfoundland.

gravé, -e, *part.*, engraved. *Être — de petite vérole ;* to be marked, seamed, with the smallpox ; to be pock-marked.

gravelée (gra-vlée), *adj.f.*, crude. *Cendre —;* pearl ashes.

graveleu-x, -se (gra-vleü, -z), *adj.*, troubled with gravel ; gravelly, sandy, gritty ; obscene, smutty. *Terroir —;* gravelly soil. *Fruit —;* stony fruit. *Crayon —;* gritty pencil.

graveleux, *n.m.*, (med.) person troubled with gravel.

gravelle, *n.f.*, (med.) gravel.

gravelure (gra-vlur), *n.f.*, obscenity, broadness, immodest discourse, smut, smuttiness.

gravement (gra-vmän), *adv.*, gravely, seriously, solemnly, soberly ; grievously ; (mus.) deeply.

graver, *v.a.*, to engrave ; to grave ; to impress, to imprint. — *à l'eau-forte ;* to etch. — *en creux* (engr.) ; to sink.

se **graver**, *v.r.*, to be engraved ; to be graven, to be impressed, imprinted. — *quelque chose dans l'esprit ;* to impress any thing on one's mind.

graveur, *n.m.*, engraver. — *à l'eau-forte ;* etcher.

gravier, *n m.*, gravel, grit ; *pl.*, (med.) gravel. *Couvrir de —;* to gravel.

gravière, *n f.*, (agri.) vetch and lentils ; (orni.) plover.

gravir, *v.a.* and *n.*, to crawl up, to clamber, to clamber up, to climb, to climb up.

gravitation, *n.f.*, (phys.) gravitation.

gravité, *n.f.*, gravity ; seriousness, solemnity, demureness, sedateness, graveness ; weight, importance, grievousness ; (mus.) flatness, lowness. *Centre de —;* centre of gravity. — *du son ;* deepness of sound.

graviter, *v.n.*, (phys.) to gravitate.

gravois, *n.m.*, coarse plaster ; rubbish (of plaster—*de plâtre*). *Enlever les —;* to carry away the rubbish.

gravure, *n.f.*, engraving, graving ; cut, print. — *sur pierre ;* stone-engraving. — *au burin ;* stroke-engraving. — *en creux ;* die-sinking ; intaglio. — *en taille-douce ;* copperplate-engraving. — *au trait ;* line-engraving. — *sur acier ;* steel-engraving. — *sur bois ;* wood-en-

graving. — *en caractères d'imprimerie ;* letter-engraving. — *en pierres fines ;* seal-engraving ; engraving on precious stones.

gré, *n.m.*, will, wish ; liking, pleasure ; mind. *De bon —;* willingly. *Contre son —;* unwillingly. *Il y est allé de son —;* he went of his own accord. *Cela est-il à votre —?* is that to your liking ? *Elle est assez à mon —;* I like her well enough. *Bon — mal —, de — ou de force ;* whether one will or no, willing or unwilling, willy nilly, nolens volens. *Se laisser aller au — des flots ;* to commit one's self to the mercy of the waves. *Ses crins flottaient au — du vent ;* his mane waved in the wind. *Prendre, avoir, recevoir en —;* to take in good part, to ap prove of. *Prendre en —;* to receive with resignation ; to take a liking to. *Savoir —, bon —, beaucoup de —, à quelqu'un de quelque chose ;* to be pleased, to be content, with any one for anything. *Savoir mauvais — à quelqu'un de quelque chose ;* to be discontented, to be displeased, with any one for anything. *Je lui en sais bon —;* I take it kindly of him.

grèbe, *n.m.*, (orni.) grebe. — *huppé ;* great-crested grebe.

grec, -que, *adj.*, Greek, Grecian. *La langue —que ;* the Greek tongue.

grec, *n.m.*, **-que**, *n.f.*, Greek, Grecian ; miser ; sharper, black-leg, cheat. *Être — en quelque chose ;* to be very skilful in anything ; to be a dab at anything.

grec, *n.m.*, Greek language. *C'est du — pour moi ;* that is Greek, Hebrew, to me.

gréciser, *v.a.*, to grecize, to hellenize.

grécisme, *n.m.*, grecism.

gréciste, *n.m.*, Grecian ; Hellenist, Greek scholar.

grecque, *n.f.*, Greek woman, Grecian woman ; (arch.) fret, fret-work ; bookbinder's saw ; saw. *Orner de —s* (arch.) ; to fret. *Orné d'une —* (arch.) ; fretty.

grecquer, *v.a.*, (bookbind.) to saw-bind.

gredin, *n.m.*, **-e**, *n.f.*, scrub, scoundrel, low blackguard ; kind of little dog with long hair ; lapdog.

gredinerie (-di-n-ri), *n.f.*, blackguardism.

gréement, *n.m.*, (nav.) rigging.

gréer, *v.a.*, (nav.) to rig.

gréeur, *n.m.*, (nav.) rigger.

greffe, *n.m.*, (jur.) registry, record-office ; registrar's office.

greffe, *n.f.*, graft, grafting, engraftment. — *à l'anglaise ;* whip-grafting. — *par approche ;* graft by approach. — *en couronne ;* crown-graft. — *en écusson ;* shield-graft ; graft by gems ; budding. — *en fente ;* chink-graft, cleft-graft. — *shoulder-graft. — en flûte ;* flute-graft. *Lever une —;* to take a graft.

greffer, *v.a.*, to graft.

greffeur, *n.m.*, grafter.

greffier, *n.m.*, registrar, recorder, clerk of the court ; master of the rolls ; prothonotary.

greffoir, *n.m.*, grafting-knife.

grégaire, *adj.*, gregarious.

grège, *adj.*, raw (of silk—*de la soie*).

grégeois (-joâ), *adj.*, only used in *Feu —;* Greek fire ; wild fire.

grégorien, -ne (-in, -è-n), *adj.*, Gregorian.

grègue (grèg), *n.f.*, breeches. *Tirer ses —s ;* to run away, to cut one's stick. *Laisser ses —s ;* to lay one's bones (to die—*mourir*).

grêle, *n.m.*, (of trumpets, horns—*de trompettes, de cors de chasse*) highest tone.

grêle, *n.f.*, hail, hail-storm ; (of the eyelid—*de la paupière*) grando, hailstone, chalazion. *Grain de —;* hailstone. — *de coups ;* shower of blows.

grêle, *adj.*, slender, slim, lank ; shrill. *Des jambes —s ;* slim legs. *Voix —;* shrill voice. *Intestins —s* (anat.) ; small intestines.

grêlé, -e, *part.*, ravaged by hail; pock-marked, seamed with the small-pox. *Cet homme a été —*; that man has suffered great losses. *Un homme —*; a man pitted with small-pox. *Il est un peu —*; he is rather low in the world.

grêler, *v. imp.*, to hail. *Il grêle*; it hails.

grêler, *v.a.*, to ravage by hail, to ruin.

grelin, *n.m.*, (nav.) warp; stream-cable; (Ich.) coal-fish. *— en queue de rat*; pointed stream-cable.

grêlon, *n.m.*, large hail-stone.

grelot, *n.m.*, little bell; hawk's bell. *Attacher le —*; to bell the cat, to take the first step in a difficult enterprise. *Trembler le —*; to tremble, to shake, so that one's teeth chatter.

grelotter, *v.n.*, to quake, to shiver (with cold —*de froid*).

grément, *or* gréement, *n.m.*, (nav.) rigging.

grémial, *n.m.*, (c. rel.) gremial (eccl. ornament).

grémil, *n.m.*, (bot.) gromwell, gromil.

*grémillet, *n.m.*, (bot) scorpion-grass, scorpion's-tail.

grenade, *n.f.*, pomegranate; (milit.) grenade.

grenadier, *n.m.*, pomegranate-tree; pomegranate; (milit.) grenadier. *— sauvage* (bot.); wild pomegranate. *Jurer comme un —*; to swear like a trooper. *C'est un —, c'est un vrai —*; she is a regular dragoon.

grenadière, *n.f.*, ⊙grenade-pouch; upper band (of a rifle—*de fusil*). *Mettre son fusil à la —*; (milit.) to sling one's musket.

*grenadille, *n.f.*, (bot.) grenadilla, passion-flower.

grenadin, *n.m.*, (cook.) small fricandeau.

grenadine, *n.f.*, grenadine (silk—*soierie*).

*grenaille, *n.f.*, granulated metal; refuse corn.

*grenailler, *v.a.*, to granulate.

*se grenailler, *v.r.*, to granulate.

grenat, *n.m.*, (min.) garnet; great humming-bird.

grené, *n.m.*, (engr.) stippling.

greneler, *v.a.*, to grain (leather—*cuir*).

grener, *v.n.*, to seed, to run to seed; to produce seed.

grener, *v.a.*, to granulate, to corn; to grain (leather—*cuir*); (engr.) to stipple. *— de la poudre à canon*; to corn gunpowder.

greneterie (grè-n-tri), *n.f.*, seed trade.

grenetier (grè-n-tié), *n.m.*, -ère, *n.f.* (grè-n-tié), seedsman; seedswoman.

grenetis (grè-n-ti), *n.m.*, milling, engrailed ring round a piece of coin; milling punch.

grenettes, *n.f. pl.*, Avignon-berry, French-berry.

grenier, *n.m.*, granary, corn-loft, loft, cock-loft; garret; (nav.) floor-ceiling (of a ship —*d'un navire*). *— au foin*; hayloft. *En —*; in the granary, in store; (nav.) in bulk. *Aller du — à la cave, de la cave au —*; to talk in an unconnected manner, to tell a long rigmarole. *Charger en —*; (nav.) to load in bulk.

*grenouille, *n.f.*, frog; (print.) frog.

⊙*grenouiller, *v.n.*, to guzzle, to tipple, to sot.

*grenouillère, *n.f.*, place full of frogs; marshy place; fen; (b.s.) damp, unhealthy house.

*grenouillet, *n.m.*, (bot.) Solomon's-seal, knee-grass.

*grenouillette, *n.f.*, (med.) ranula; (bot.) buttercup; frogbit. *V.* ranule.

grenu, -e, *adj.*, seedy, full of corn; granulous. *Épi bien —*; ear very full of corn. *Cuir*

bien —; leather that has a good grain. *Huile —e*; clotted oil. *Marbre —*; grained marble.

grès, *n.m.*, sandstone; stoneware; (min.) grit, grit-stone, grit-rock. *— à bâtir*; free-stone. *— des rémouleurs*; grindstone.

⊙gréseu-x, -se, *adj.*, sandy, gritty.

*grésil, *n.m.*, sleet.

*grésillement, *n.m.*, shrivelling, shrivelling up; wrinkling (as parchment does in the fire —*comme le parchemin dans le feu*); shrivelled state.

*grésiller, *v.imp.*, to sleet.

*grésiller, *v.a.*, to shrivel, to shrivel up, to wrinkle.

*grésillonner, *v.n.*, to chirp (of the cricket —*du grillon*).

g.-ré-sol, *n.m.*, (mus.) G; (vocal mus.) sol

gresserie (grè-srî), *n.f.*, sandstone, grit, freestone; stoneware; sandstone quarry.

grève, *n.f.*, strand; Grève (a square at Paris, where capital punishments formerly took place—*place de Paris où se faisaient autrefois les exécutions*); strike of workmen. *Faire —*; to strike (of workmen—*ouvriers*).

grevé, *n.m.*, (jur.) heir of entail.

grever, *v.a.*, to wrong, to injure; to burden; to encumber (with debt, &c.—*de dettes, §c.*). *Un pays grevé d'impôts*; a country burdened with taxes. *Terre grevée d'hypothèques*; estate encumbered with mortgages. *Terre non grevée*; unencumbered estate.

grianneau, *n.m.*, young heath-cock; young grouse.

griblette, *n.f.*, (cook.) hash of broiled meat.

*gribouillage, *n.m.*, scrawl; daub (paint.).

*gribouille, *n.m.*, simpleton, blockhead.

*gribouiller, *v.a.*, to scrawl (writing—*écriture*); to daub (paint.).

*gribouillette, *n.f.*, scramble, scrambling. *Attraper quelque chose à la —*; to scramble for any thing. *Jeter quelque chose à la —*; to make a scramble of anything. *À la —*; negligently.

grièche, *adj.*, (l.u.) prickly. *Ortie — (—s —s)*; sting-nettle. *Pie — (—s —s)*; shrike; shrew, scold.

grief (gri-èf), *n.m.*, grievance, wrong, injury; complaint. *Faire un — à quelqu'un*; to do any one an injury. *Redresser un —*; to redress an injury. *—s, —s et contredits* (jur.); plea.

gri-ef, -ève, *adj.*, grave, grievous.

grièvement (-èv-màn), *adv.*, grievously, sorely, gravely, greatly.

grièveté (-èv-té), *n.f.*, enormity, gravity, heinousness.

griffade, *n.f.*, clawing, scratch.

griffe, *n.f.*, claw; fang; pounce, talon; grasp; (gard.) bulb; stamped facsimile of a signature; (tech.) catch; music-pen. *Je suis sous ses —s*; I am in his clutches. *Donner un coup de — à quelqu'un*; to do any one an ill office; to speak ill of any one. *Apposer sa — à*; to put one's signature to.

griffer, *v.a.*, (falconry—*fauconnerie*) to take with the claws, to claw; to scratch (of cats—*des chats*).

griffon, *n.m.*, griffin, griffon, gypaetos.

griffonnage, *n.m.*, scrawl, scrawling, scribbling, scribble.

griffonner, *v.a.*, to scrawl; to scribble.

griffonneu-r, *n.m.*, -se, *n.f.*, scrawler, scribbler.

*grignon, *n.m.*, hard piece of the crusty side of a loaf; residuum of olives.

*grignoter, *v.a.*, to nibble; to get something (some profit—*faire un petit profit*).

*grignotis (-ti), *n.m.*, (engr.) crispness.

grigou, *n.m.*, beggarly fellow, miserable wretch; sordid miser.

gril (gri), *n.m.*, gridiron. *Être sur le — ;* to be upon thorns, to be be in a stew.

*****grillade**, *n.f.*, broiled ham; toast (of bread, of cheese—*de pain, de fromage*).

*****grillage**, *n.m.*, light iron-railing; wire-work; (metal.) roasting. *— de bois :* (arch.) frame of timber.

*****grille**, *n.f.*, grate; grating; railing. *— de fer ;* iron-railing.

*****griller**, *v.a.*, to enclose with iron rails ; to rail in ; to grate ; (cook.) to broil ; (metal.) to roast; to scorch (of the sun—*du soleil*).

*se**griller**, *v.r.*, to be scorched ; to be parched ; to be roasted.

*****griller**, *v.n.*, (cook.) to broil ; to be on thorns, in hot water.

*****grillet**, *n.m.*, or *****grillette**, *n.f.*, (her.) hawk's bell.

*****grilleté**, *-e*, *adj.*, (her., falconry—*fauconnerie*) belled.

*****grilletier** (-tié), *n.m.*, maker of grates.

*****grillon**, *n.m.*, (ent.) cricket. *— domestique ;* house-cricket. *— -taupe* (*—s —s*), taupe— (*—s —s*); fen-cricket, mole-cricket.

*****grillotter**, *v.n.*, to chirp like the cricket.

grimaçant, *-e*, *adj.*, grimacing, grinning.

grimace, *n.f.*, grimace, wry face ; humbug, cant ; box with a pin-cushion top. *Faire la — ;* to make faces. *Faire des —s à quelqu'un ; —;* to make faces at any one, to grin at any one. *Cet habit fait la — ;* that coat puckers.

grimacer, *vn.*, to make faces, wry faces ; to grin ; to pucker (of clothes—*des vêtements*).

grimacerie (-ma-sri), *n.f.*, (l.u.) making faces ; dissimulation.

grimaci-er, *-ère*, *adj.* and *n.*, grimacing ; simpering ; dissembling ; canting ; maker of grimaces ; simperer ; dissembler, canting person.

grimaud, *-e*, *adj.*, (l.u.) (of children—*des enfants*) cross, ill-tempered.

grimaud, *n.m.*, urchin, brat ; scribbler, sorry writer.

grime, *n.m.*, ⊙brat ; (thea.) old man. *Il joue les —s ;* (thea.) he plays the old men.

grimelin, *n.m.*, (b.s.) brat, urchin.

*se**grimer**, *v.r.*, (thea.) to paint wrinkles on one's face to play old men, old women, duennas, &c.

grimoire, *n.m.*, conjuring book; obscure language ; illegible scrawl. *Il sait le — ;* he knows what he is about. *C'est du — pour lui ;* it is Greek to him.

grimpant, *-e*, *adj.*, (bot.) climbing.

grimpart, *n.m.*, (orni.) nut-hatch.

grimper, *v.n.*, to climb, to climb up, to clamber up, to creep up (of plants—*des plantes*).

grimpereau, *n.m.* **V. grimpart.**

grimpeurs, *n.m. pl.*, (orni.) climbers.

grincement (grins-man), *n.m.*, gnashing, grinding (of the teeth—*des dents*).

grincer, *v.a.*, to gnash (the teeth—*les dents*) ; to grate. *Faire — les dents ;* to make the teeth grate, to set the teeth on edge.

grincer, *v.n.*, to grind ; to gnash ; to grate. *— des dents :* to grind one's teeth. *La porte grinça sur ses gonds rouillés ;* the door grated in turning on its rusty hinges.

grincheu-x, *-se*, *adj.*, ill-tempered, peevish, crabbed.

gringalet, *n.m.*, weak, slender man ; man of no consistency.

gringolé, *-e*, *adj.*, (her.) snake-headed.

gringotter, *v.n.*, to twitter (of birds—*des oiseaux*) ; to hum.

gringotter, *v.a.*, to hum a tune badly.

gringuenaude, *n.f.*, (l.ex.) dirt.

griotte, *n.f.*, marble with red and brown spots ; a variety of large black cherries.

griottier, *n.m.*, (bot.) agriot-tree.

grippe, *n.f.*, (l.u.) fancy, whim ; hobby ; (med.) influenza. *Prendre quelqu'un en —, se prendre de — contre quelqu'un ;* to take a dislike to any one.

grippé, *part.*, (med.) shrunk, contracted (of the face—*du visage*) ; (of persons—*des personnes*) suffering with influenza.

grippeminaud (grip-minó), *n.m.*, grimalkin, a cat.

gripper, *v.a.*, to gripe, to clutch, to seize, to snatch up; to nab ; to crib.

*se**gripper**, *v.r.*, to shrivel ; to take a dislike to.

grippe-sou. *n.m.* (*—, or — —s*), pinchpenny ; curmudgeon.

gris, *-e*, *adj.*, gray ; gray-headed ; tipsy, fuddled. *Cheveux — ;* gray hair. *Lettres —es ;* (print.) flourished letters. *Temps — ;* raw weather. *Faire mine —e à quelqu'un ;* to look black at any one. *La nuit tous les chats sont — ;* in the dark, all cats are gray. *Papier — ;* brown paper.

gris, *n.m.*, gray. *— cendré ;* ash-gray. *— pommelé ;* dappled gray.

*****grisaille**, *n.f.*, cameo with a gray ground ; hair partly gray.

*****grisailler**, *v.a.*, to paint gray.

grisâtre, *adj.*, grayish.

griser, *v.a.*, to make tipsy, to fuddle.

*se**griser**, *v.r.*, to be intoxicated, to get tipsy, to be fuddled.

griser, *v.n.*, (dy.) to turn gray.

griset, *n.m.*, (orni.) young goldfinch.

grisette, *n.f.*, gray gown, russet gown ; (orni.) white-throat ; grisette, work girl.

grisoller, *v.n.*, to warble (of the lark—*de l'alouette*).

grison, *-ne*, *adj.*, gray, gray-haired, gray-headed.

grison, *n.m.*, gray-beard (old man—*vieillard*) ; donkey, ass (person) ; a footman dressed in gray clothes for the performance of a secret errand.

grisonnant, *adj.*, getting gray (of the hair—*des cheveux*).

grisonner, *v.n.*, to grow gray (of hair—*des cheveux*).

grisou, *n.m.*, (mining—*mines*) fire-damp.

grive, *n.f.*, (orni.) thrush. *Il est soûl comme une — ;* he is as drunk as a fiddler.

grivelé, *-e* (gri-vlé), *adj.*, speckled.

⊙**grivelée**, *n.f.*, illicit, secret petty profit.

griveler, *v.a.n.*, to make illicit petty profit.

grivelerie, *n.f.*, getting illicit petty profit.

⊙**griveleur**, *n.m.*, one who makes illicit petty profit.

grivois, *-e*, *adj.*, jolly ; smutty.

grivois, *n.m.*, jolly companion.

grivoise, *n.f.*, a jolly canteen-woman, sutler's wife.

grog, *n.m.*, grog.

*****grognard**, *-e*, *adj.*, grumbling, growling.

*****grognard**, *n.m.*, *-e*, *n.f.*, grumbler, growler ; old soldier of the first French Empire.

*****grognement**, *n.m.*, grunt, grunting, growling, grumbling.

*****grogner**, *v.n.*, to grunt, to growl, to grumble.

*****grogneu-r**, *-se*, *adj.* and *n.*, grumbling, growling ; grumbler, growler.

*****grognon**, *adj. m.f.*, grumbling, growling.

*****grognon**, *n.m.f.*, grumbler, growler.

groin, *n.m.*, snout (of a hog—*du sanglier*).

grolle, *n.f.*, (orni.) rook.

grommeler (grom-lé), *v.n.*, to grumble, to mutter ; to grunt.

⊙**grommeleu-x**, *-se*, *adj.* and *n.*, grumbling ; muttering.

grondant, *-e*, *adj.*, scolding ; roaring, rumbling.

grondement, *n.m.*, rumbling, roaring.

gronder. *v.n.,* to growl, to grumble, to mutter; to snarl; to rumble, to roar.

gronder. *v.a.,* to chide, to scold, to reprimand.

gronderie (-dri), *n.f.,* scolding, chiding.

grondeu-r, -se, *adj.,* grumbling, scolding.

grondeu-r, n.m., -se, *n.f.,* scold; grumbler.

grondin, *n.m.,* (ich.) red gurnet.

groneau, *n.m.,* gray gurnet.

grom, *n.m.* (—*s*), groom.

gros, -se, *adj.,* large, big, great, bulky; pregnant, with child, loud (of laughter—*du rire*); dark (of colour—*couleur*); rough (of the voice—*voix*); heavy (of cavalry—*cavalerie*); coarse, thick; rich, substantial; foul, bad (of the weather—*du temps*); high. — *bon sens;* plain good sense. — *mots;* oaths. *Les — poissons mangent les petits;* the large fish prey upon the small. —*se somme d'argent;* great sum of money. — *drap;* coarse cloth. — *souliers;* thick shoes. —*se viande;* butcher's meat. — *lourdaud;* blockhead. *Un — marchand;* a substantial tradesman. — *temps;* foul weather. *La mer est —se;* the sea is high. *Une —se femme;* a stout woman. *Une femme —se;* a pregnant woman.

gros. *n.m.,* large part; bulk, mass; main body (of an army—*d'une armée*); large hand (writing—*écriture*); (com.) wholesale. *Vendre en —;* to sell wholesale.

gros, *adv.,* much. *Gagner —;* to earn, to win much.

gros-bec, *n.m.* (——*s*), (orni.) grossbeak.

gros canon, *n.m.,* (print.) French canon.

*****groseille,** *n.f.,* red-currant, white-currant; gooseberry. — *à maquereau,* — *verte;* gooseberry.

*****groseillier,** *n.m.,* red-currant-tree, white-currant tree; gooseberry-bush. — *noir* (l.u.); black-currant-tree. *V.* **cassis.**

*****groseillon,** *n.m.,* small currant.

gros-jean, *n.m.* (——*s*), a vulgar fellow, a countryman. *Être — comme devant;* to be no better off than before after endeavouring to better one's self. — *en remontre à son curé;* to teach one's grandmother how to suck eggs.

grosse. *n.f.,* gross (twelve dozen—*douze douzaines*); large hand (writing—*écriture*); bottomry; (jur.) copy.

grosserie (grô-srī). *n.f.,* ironmongery, wholesale. *Il ne fait que la —;* he is a wholesale dealer only.

grossesse, *n.f.,* pregnancy, gestation.

grosseur, *n.f.,* bigness, largeness, size, bulk; swelling.

grossi-er, -ère, *adj.,* coarse, thick; homely, plain, common; clumsy, rough, rude; unpolished, uncivilized; unmannerly, scurrilous; churlish, unpolite, uncouth, boorish. *Des meubles —s;* clumsy furniture. *Mœurs —ères;* unpolished manners. *Vous êtes bien —;* you are very unmannerly. *Il m'aborda d'un air —;* he accosted me rudely. *Erreur —ère;* gross mistake.

grossièrement (-sièr-măn), *adv.,* coarsely, rudely, roughly, uncouthly, boorishly, unmannerly, scurrilously; churlishly; grossly, indecently.

grossièreté (-sièr-té), *n.f.,* coarseness, grossness; rudeness, clownishness, roughness, unpoliteness, bluntness, unmannerliness; coarse language, scurrility; clumsiness, awkwardness; churlishness. *Il lui a dit des —s;* he said rude things to him.

grossir, *v.a.,* to make bigger, greater; to enlarge, to augment, to increase; to swell, to swell out; to magnify.

se grossir, *v.r.,* to grow bigger, larger; to

increase in size; to increase, to augment, to be increased; to swell; to magnify.

grossir. *v.n.,* to get big, large; to grow stout; to magnify; to enlarge; to swell out.

grossissant, *adj.,, magnifying. Verre —;* magnifier.

grossissement (-sis-măn). *n.m.,* magnifying.

grosso-modo. *adv.,* summarily.

grossoyer, *v.a.,* to engross, to copy in a large hand.

grotesque, *n.m.* and *adj.,* grotesque; grotesque figure; grotesque dancer.

grotesquement. *adv.,* grotesquely.

grotte. *n.f.,* grotto, grot; crypt.

*****grouillant, -e,** *adj.,* (pop.) stirring, moving about; swarming, crawling. *Tout — de vermine;* crawling with vermin.

*****grouillement** (groo-), *n.m.,* (pop.) rumbling (of the intestines—*des intestins*).

*****grouiller,** *v.n.,* (pop.) to stir, to move; to rumble (of the intestines—*des intestins*); to shake (the head with old age—*la tête de vieillesse*); to swarm. *Le ventre me grouille;* my belly rumbles. *La tête lui grouille;* his head shakes. *Cela grouille de vermine;* that crawls with vermin.

group (groop), *n.m.,* (com.) bag of money.

groupe, *n.m.,* group, cluster. — *de sculpture;* group of sculpture.

grouper, *v.a.,* to group.

se grouper, *v.r.,* to form into groups, to be grouped.

grouper, *v.n.,* (paint.) to group.

gruau, *n.m.,* oat-meal; gruel, groats; (tech.) small crane. *Farine de —;* groats.

grue, *n.f.,* (orni., tech.) crane; (astron.) Grus; simpleton, goose. *Faire le pied de —;* to dance attendance.

⊙**gruerie,** *n.f.,* court of the justices in eyre; rights of the king in connection with the woods possessed by private individuals.

gruger, *v.a.,* to craunch, to eat, to eat up, to devour. — *du sucre;* to craunch sugar.

grugerie, *n.f.,* squandering.

grume. *n.f.,* bark left on felled trees.

grumeau, *n.m.,* clod, clot, lump, *Des —x de sang;* clots of blood.

se grumeler, *v.r.,* to clot.

grumeleu-x,-se(gru-mleû,-z),*adj.,* clotted, grumous; rugged, rough. *Sang —;* clotted blood. *Poires —ses;* rough pears.

gruyer, *n.m.,* a justice in eyre.

gruy-er, -ère, *adj.,* of the crane. *Faucon —,* hawk trained to fly the crane. *Faisan —;* crane-pheasant. ⊙*Seigneur —;* lord having certain rights on the woods of his vassals.

gruyère, *n.m.,* Gruyere cheese.

guano (gooa-no), *n.m.,* guano.

gué (ghé), *n.m.,* ford. *Passer une rivière à —;* to ford a river. *Sonder le —;* to sound a person.

guéable (ghé-), *adj.,* fordable.

guèbre, *n.m. V.* **gaure.**

guédasse. *n.f.,* weed-ashes.

guède (ghèd), *n.f.,* (dy.) woad, dyer's-woad, pastel.

guéder (ghé-dé), *v.a.,* to dye with woad; ⊙to gram, to stuff (with food—*de nourriture*). ⊙*se guéder,* *v.r.,* to cram one's self with food.

guéer (ghé-é), *v.a.,* to ford. — *un cheval;* to water a horse (in a river—*dans une rivière*). — *du linge;* to wash linen (in a river—*dans une rivière*).

guelfe. *n.m.,* (Italian hist.) Guelph.

*****guenille** (ghé-), *n.f.,* rag, tatter; rubbish, trifle.

*****guenilleu-x,-se,** *adj.,* tattered, ragged, in rags.

*****guenillon** (ghé-), *n.m.,* little rag.

guenipe (ghě-), *n.f.*, slut, dirty slut, trollop; street-walker.

guenon (ghě-), *n.f.*, (mam.) monkey; she-monkey; fright, ugly woman; strumpet.

guenuche (ghě-), *n.f.*, young she-monkey.

guépard, *n.m.*, (mam.) cheetah, hunting-leopard of India.

guêpe (ghêp), *n.f.*, (ent.) wasp. — *-frelon* (—*s* —*s*); hornet. *Mouche*— (—*s* —*s*); wasp-fly.

guêpier, *n.m.*, wasps' nest; (orni.) bee-eater; scrape, difficulty. *Donner, tomber, dans un* —; to get into a scrape.

ⓞ**guerdon** (ghěr-), *n.m.*, guerdon, recom-pense, reward, meed.

ⓞ**guerdonner**, *v.a.*, to requite, to reward, to recompense.

guère, or **guères** (ghèr), *adv.*, but little, not much, not very; not long; hardly, scarcely, very few. *N'avoir* — *d'argent;* to have but little money. *Il n'est* — *sage;* he is not very wise. *Il ne tardera* — *à venir;* it will not be long before he comes. *Il ne s'en faut* —; it wants but little. *N'avoir* — *plus;* to have little more. *N'avoir* — *moins;* to have little less. *Il n'y a* — *que les rois qui puissent;* scarcely any but kings are able to.

guéret (ghé-rè), *n.m.*, (agri.) land ploughed, but not sown.

guéridon (ghé-), *n.m.*, gueridon, round table, loo-table.

guérilla (ghé-), *n.f.*, guerilla (small army of irregulars).

guérilla, *n.m.*, guerilla-soldier.

guérir (ghé-), *v.a.*, to heal, to cure. *Pou-voir de* —; sanativeness. — *la fièvre;* to cure a fever. — *quelqu'un d'une erreur;* to free any one from an error. *Cela ne me guérira de rien;* that will be of no use to me.

se guérir, *v.r.*, to recover, to be cured, to heal, to be healed, to recover one's health, to mend; to get rid, to be rid. — *de ses préventions;* to get rid of one's prejudices. *Médecin, guéris-toi toi-même;* physician, heal thyself.

guérir, *v.n.*, to heal, to heal up; to recover, to be cured; to get rid, to be rid. *On ne guérit point de la peur;* fear admits of no cure.

guérison (ghé-), *n.f.*, recovery, healing, cure. *Il doit sa* — *à tel remède;* he owes his cure to such and such a remedy.

guérissable, *adj.*, curable.

guérisseu-r, *n.m.*, **-se**, *n.f.*, (b.s.) healer, curer.

guérite (ghé-), *n.f.*, sentry-box; turret, watch-tower. *Gagner la* —; to scamper away, to take to one's heels.

guerre (ghèr), *n.f.*, war; warfare; strife, dissension. — *à mort;* war to the knife. — *de plume;* ink-and-paper war. *Vaisseau de* —; man-of-war. *Petite* —; sham fight; minor opera-tions of war, as scouting, surprising convoys, cutting off communications, &c. *Cri de* —; war-cry. *Foudre de* —; great warrior. *Gens de* —; military men. *Place de* —; fortified town. *Nom de* —; nickname. *Aller à la petite* —; to go a pillaging. *Faire la* — *avec;* to serve with, to be a fellow-soldier. *Faire la* — *à ses passions;* to struggle with one's passions. *Faire la* — *à;* to be at war with. *Il lui en fit la* —; he railed him for it. *Faire la* — *à l'œil;* to keep watch in order to profit by circumstances. *Faire bonne* — *à quelqu'un;* to deal fairly with any one. *De bonne* —; by fair play. *À la* — *comme à la* —; one must suit one's self to the times. *Qui terre a,* — *a;* money always brings care. *Moitié* —, *moitié marchandise;* armed (of ships—*des vais-seaux*); (fig.) half-willingly, half-compulsorily. *Faire une chose de* — *lasse;* to do a thing against one's will, after long resistance.

guerri-er, **ère**, *n.* and *adj.*, warrior; female warrior; warlike; martial.

guerroyant, **-e**, *adj.*, martial, fond of war.

guerroyer, *v.n.*, to make war, to wage war, to war.

guerroyeur, *n.m.*, man fond of war.

guet (ghè), *n.m.*, watch; watching; sentinel. — *de nuit;* patrol, night-watch. *Mot du* —; watchword. *Maison du* —; round-house. *Crier au* —; to call the watch. *Étre au* —, *avoir l'œil au* —, *l'oreille au* —; to be on the watch, to be on the look-out. *Ce chien est de très bon* —; this is a very good watch-dog. *Se donner le mot du* —; to act in concert. *Faire le* —; to watch, to keep watch; to look out, to be on the look out.

guet-apens (ghè-ta-pän), *n.m.* (—*s* —), am-bush, ambuscade; wilful injury; lying in wait. *De* —; by lying in wait. *Dresser un* — *à;* to waylay.

guêtre (ghè-tr), *n.f.*, gaiter. *Grande* —; legging. *Tirer ses* —*s;* to run away, to cut one's stick. *Laisser ses* —*s quelque part;* to leave one's bones somewhere.

guêtré, **-e**, *adj.*, gaitered.

guêtrer, *v.a.*, to put on gaiters, to gaiter.

se guêtrer, *v.r.*, to put on one's gaiters.

guêtrier, *n.m.*, gaiter-maker.

guetter (ghè-té), *v.a.*, to lie in wait for, to watch for, to be upon the watch for; to dog, to watch; to wait for, to await. *Le chat guette la souris;* the cat watches for the mouse.

guetteur, *n.m.*, (nav.) signal-man, look-out-man.

gueulard (gheu-lar), *n.m.*, furnace-mouth.

gueulard, *n.m.*, **-e**, *n.f.*, (pop.) brawler, bawler; glutton.

gueule (gheul), *n.f.*, mouth, jaws, chops. — *renversée* (arch.); ogive. *À* — *dépourvue de dents* (ich.); leather-mouthed. *En* — (bot.); labiated. *La* — *d'un chien;* the mouth of a dog. *Mettre quelqu'un à la* — *du loup;* to put any one in the clutches of his enemy. — *fraîche* (triv.); person always ready to eat. *Homme fort en* — (triv.); abusive man. *Femme trop forte en* — (triv.); woman that has an ill tongue. *Il n'a que de la* — (triv.); he is all talk. *Donner sur la* — *à quelqu'un* (triv.); to give any one a slap on the chops. *Il est venu la* — *en-farinée* (triv.); he came blundering and confidently. *Il a la* — *pavée* (triv.); his throat is paved. *Il a la* — *morte* (triv.); he is down in the mouth. *La* — *d'un sac;* the mouth of a sack.

gueule-de-loup, *n.f.* (—*s* —), (bot.). *V.* **muflier**.

gueulée, *n.f.*, (l.ex.) large mouthful; in-decent expression.

gueuler (gheu-lé), *v.n.*, (pop.) to bawl, to squall, to clamour, to mouth.

gueuler, *v.a.*, (hunt.) to take up, to seize.

gueules, *n.m.*, (her.) gules. *Porter de* —; to bear gules.

*gueusaille (gheu-), *n.f.*, parcel of beggars, low set, rabble.

gueusailler, *v.n.*, to beg, to mump.

gueusant, **-e** (gheu-), *adj.*, begging, mump-ing.

gueusard, *n.m.*, beggar, scoundrel, black-guard, ragamuffin.

gueuse (gheuz), *n.f.*, pig-iron; beggar; bad woman.

gueuser, *v.a.* and *n.*, (fam.) to beg.

gueuserie (gheû-zrî), *n.f.*, beggary, beg-garliness; trash.

gueuset, *n.m.*, pig-iron.

gueu-x, **-se**, *adj.*, poor, beggarly, wretched.

— *comme un rat d'église;* as poor as a church-mouse.

gueux, *n.m.,* beggar; knave, rascal. raga-muffin, scoundrel. *Tas de — ;* pack of scoun-drels. — *revêtu;* upstart.

gui (ghi), *n.m.,* mistletoe; (nav.) main-boom (of a sloop, of a brig—*d'un sloupe, d'un brick*).

guibre (ghi-br), *n.m.,* (nav.) cut-water.

guichet (ghi-shè), *n.m.,* wicket; grating; door; shutter.

guichetier (ghish-tié), *n.m.,* turnkey.

guide (ghid), *n.m.,* guide; guide-book; text-book; (milit.) flugelman, fugleman.

guide, *n.f.,* rein (of a bridle—*de bride*). *Conduire à grandes —s;* to drive four-in-hand.

guide-âne, *n.m.* (—, *or* — —s), guide-book.

guide-chaîne, *n.m.* (—, *or* — —s), (horl.) guard, ratchet.

guide-main, *n.m.* (—, *or* — —s), (of the piano-forte) chiroplast, hand-guide.

guider (ghi-dé), *v.a.,* to guide, to lead to conduct; to direct. — *un vaisseau;* to steer a ship.

guidon (ghi-), *n.m.,* (milit.) field-colours, guidon; (nav.) broad pendant; (mus.) direction.

guifette (ghi-), *n.f.,* (orni.) sea-swallow.

*guignard (ghi-), *n.m.,* (orni.) dotterel.

*guigne (ghi-), *n.f.,* white-heart cherry.

*guigner (ghi-), *v.a.,* (fam.) to peep. — *une charge;* to have an eye on an office.

*guigner, *v.n.,* to leer.

*guignette (ghi-), *n.f.,* (orni.), common sand-piper.

*guignier (ghi-), *n.m.,* white-heart cherry-tree.

*guignon (ghi-), *n.m.,* (fam.) bad luck, ill-luck. *Avoir du — ;* to be unlucky. *Être en — ;* to have a run of ill-luck.

guigue (gig), *n.f.,* (nav.) gig.

*guildive (ghi-), *n.f.,* (l.u.) rum.

☉guilée (ghi-), *n.f.,* shower of rain.

*guillage (ghi-), *n.m.,* working (of beer—*de la bière*).

*guillaume (ghi-), *n.m.,* rebate-plane.

*guilledin (ghi-), *n.m.,* English gelding (horse—*cheval*).

*guilledou (ghi-), *n.m.,* (pop.) places of ill-fame. *Courir le — ;* to frequent places of ill-fame.

*guillemet (ghi-), *n.m.* (print) inverted commas.

*guillemeter, *v.a.,* to put between inverted commas.

*guillemot (ghi-), *n.m.,* (orni.) guillemot.

*guilleret, -te (ghi-), *adj.,* sprightly, gay, lively. *Il a l'air — ;* he has a sprightly air.

*guilleri (ghi-), *n.m.,* chirping (of sparrows —*des moineaux*).

*guillocher (ghi-), *v.a.,* (arch.) to enrich with guilloche; to engine-turn.

*guillochis (ghi-), *n.m.,* (arch.) guilloche; engine-turning.

*guillotine (ghi-), *n.f.,* guillotine.

*guillotiné, *n.m.,* -e, *n.f.,* a guillotined con-vict.

*guillotinement, *n.m.,* guillotining.

*guillotiner, *v.a.,* to guillotine, to behead.

guimauve (ghi-), *n.f.,* marsh-mallow.

guimaux (ghi-), *n.m.* pl., fields mowed twice a year.

guimbarde (ghin-), *n.f.,* guimbard, jew's-harp; long cart.

guimpe (ghinp), *n.f.,* inside chemisette; veil (for nuns—*de religieuse*).

guinard, *n.m.,* (ich.) red gurnet.

guindage (ghin-), *n.m.,* (nav.) hoisting.

guindant (ghin-), *n.m.,* (nav.) hoist (of flags — *de pavillons*).

guinde, *n.f.* **guinda, guindeau,** *n.m.,* (nav.) windlass.

guindé, -e, *part.,* stiff, strained, forced. unnatural. *Cet homme est toujours — ;* that man is always as stiff as a poker.

guinder (ghin-dé), *v.a.,* to hoist, to strain, to force; (nav.) to sway up.

*se guinder, *v.r.,* to be strained; to be forced.

guinderesse (ghin-drès), *n.f.,* (nav.) top-rope.

guinderie (ghin-dri), *n.f.,* constraint, stiff-ness.

guinée (ghi-), *n.f.,* guinea: long cloth.

guingan (ghin-), *n.m.,* gingham.

guingois (ghin-ghoa), *n.m.,* crookedness. *De— ;* awry, cross-grained *Marcher tout de— ;* to walk crookedly. *Avoir l'esprit de — ;* to be cross-grained.

guinguette (ghin-ghèt), *n.f.,* public-house (out of town—*hors de ville*); tea-garden; (fam.) small country-house.

guiorant, -e, *adj.,* (of rats and mice—*rats et souris*) squeaking.

guiorer (ghi-), *v.n.,* (of rats and mice—*rats et souris*) to squeak.

guipon (ghi-), *n.m.,* (nav.) mop.

guipure (ghi-), *n.f.,* guipure.

guirlande (ghir-), *n.f.,* garland, wreath; girdle (of jewels—*de pierreries*); (arch.) belt (of a column—*de colonne*). *Orné de —s;* adorned with garlands.

guise (ghiz), *n.f.,* manner, way; fancy, humour. *En — de;* by way of. *Chacun vit à sa — ;* every body lives as he likes.

guitardin (ghi-), *n.m.,* (bot.) fiddle-wood.

guitare (ghi-), *n.f.,* guitar. *Jouer, pincer, de la — ;* to play the guitar.

guitariste, *n.m.,* guitarist, guitar-player.

guiterne (ghi-), *n.f.,* prop (to support the shears which are employed to mast or dis-mast a ship—*arc-boutant pour le support des machines à mâter*).

guit-guit (ghi-gbi), *n.m.* (—s —s), a va-riety of humming-birds.

guiton (ghi-), *n.m.,* (nav.) six hours' watch.

guivre, *n.f.* *V.* **givre.**

gulf-stream, *n.m.* (n.p.), (geog.) Gulf-stream.

gumène, *n.f.,* (her.) cable (of an anchor—*d'ancre*).

gustatif, *adj.m.,* (anat.) (of nerves) gusta-tory, hypoglossal.

gustation *n.f.,* tasting, gustation.

gutta-percha (-ka), *n.f.* (n.p.), gutta percha.

gutte, *V.* **gomme.**

guttier, *n.m.,* (bot.) a variety of hebraden-dron yielding a resin resembling gamboge.

guttifères, *n m.pl.,* (bot.) guttiferæ.

guttural, -e (gut-tu-), *adj.,* guttural.

gutturale, *n.f.,* guttural.

gymnase (jim-nâz), *n.m.,* gymnasium.

gymnasiarque, *n.m.,* gymnasiarch.

gymnaste, *n.m.,* gymnast.

gymnastique, *n.f.,* gymnastics.

gymnastique, *adj.,* gymnastic.

gymnique, *adj.,* gymnic.

gymnique, *n.f.,* gymnic.

gymnosophiste, *n.m.,* gymnosophist.

gymnosperme, *adj.,* (bot.) gymnospermous.

gymnospermie, *n.f.,* (bot.) gymnospermia.

gymnote, *n.m.,* gymnotus. — *électrique;* electric eel.

gynandre, *adj.,* (bot.) gynandra.

gynandrie, *n.f.,* (bot.) gynandria.

gynécée, *n.m.,* the women's part of the house, gyneceum, gynæceum.

gynécocratie (-ci), *n.f.,* gynæcocracy.

gynécocratique, *adj.,* of a gynæcocracy.

gypaète, *n.m.,* (orni.) griffin, bearded grif-fin, gypætos.

gypse, *n.m.*, gypsum, parget; plaster-stone.
gypseu-x, -se, *adj.*, gypseous.
gyratoire. *adj. V.* **giratoire**.
gyromancie, *n.f.*, gyromancy.
gyrovague, *n.m.*, wandering monk.

H

[All words in which the *h* is aspirated, are marked thus †.]

h, *n.m.f.*, the eighth letter of the alphabet, h.
†**ha!** *int.*, ah ! ha !
habeas corpus. *n.m.* (*n.p.*), habeas-corpus.
habile. *adj.*, able, clever, skilful; expert, sharp, quick; qualified; capable; (nav.) able-bodied. *Un homme* —; an able man. — *dans les affaires;* skilful in business.
habilement (a-bil-män), *adv.*, cleverly, skilfully, ably; dexterously.
habileté (a-bil-té), *n.f.*, ability, skill, cleverness, skilfulness.
habilitation. *n.f.*, (jur.) habilitation, qualification.
habilité, *n.f.*, (jur.) competency.
*habiliter, *v.a.*, (jur.) to qualify.
*habillage, *n.m.*, (cook.) trussing poultry for the spit.
*habillement. *n.m.*, clothes, clothing, dress, wearing apparel, attire. — *complet*. entire suit of clothes.
*habiller, *v.a.*, to dress, to clothe; to make clothes for; to wrap up; to become; (cook.) to prepare. *Ce tailleur m'habille;* that tailor makes my clothes, works for me. *Il habille bien,* he works well. *Cette étoffe vous habille bien;* that stuff becomes you very well. — *une pensée en vers;* to clothe a thought in verse. — *de la volaille;* to draw and truss fowls. — *du poisson;* to gut and scale fish. — *du cuir;* to dress leather.
s'habiller, *v.r.*, to dress one's self ; to find one's own clothes; to abuse each other. *Cet homme s'habille bien;* that man dresses well.
† **habilleu-r**, *n.m.*, **-se**, *n.f.*, (thea.) dresser; skin-dresser.
habit, *n.m.*, garment, dress, apparel, garb; coat, dress coat; *pl.*, clothes, wearing apparel. — *bourgeois;* private clothes. — *complet;* suit of clothes. — *habillé;* dress coat. — *de cheval;* riding-coat. —*s de deuil;* mourning. *Porter un — râpé;* to wear a shabby coat L'— *ne fait pas le moine;* it is not the cowl that makes the friar; it is not the coat that makes the man.
habitable, *adj.*, inhabitable.
habitacle, *n.m.*, ⊙ habitation; (nav.) binnacle.
habitant, *n.m.*, **-e**, *n.f.*, inhabitant, resident, inmate; denizen. *Les —s des bois;* the denizens of the woods.
habitation, *n.f.*, habitation, residence, abode, dwelling-place; place of abode; settlement (in a colony—*dans une colonie*); (zool., bot.) habitat, haunt. *Maison d'—;* (jur.) dwelling-house.
habiter, *v.a.*, to inhabit, to dwell in, to live in, to reside in, to frequent. — *un lieu;* to live in a place.
habiter, *v.n.*, to inhabit; to dwell in; to reside in; (jur.) to cohabit.
habitude. *n.f.*, habit, custom, use; (b.s.) trick. *Il ne fait pas une habitude de cela;* he does not make a custom of it. L'— *est une autre nature;* use is a second nature. *Faire quelque chose par — ;* to do a thing from habit. *Faire perdre une vilaine — à quelqu'un ;* to break any one of a bad habit, of a nasty trick.

habitué, -e, *part.*, used, accustomed.
habitué, -e, *n.f.*, frequenter, customer. *Les —s d'un café;* the regular customers of a coffee-house.
habituel, -le, *adj.*, habitual, customary, usual.
habituellement(-èl-män), *adv.*, habitually, customarily, usually.
habituer, *v.a*, to use, to accustom, to habituate, to inure. — *les jeunes gens à la fatigue;* to inure young men to fatigue.
s'habituer, *v.r.*, to accustom, to inure, one's self. *Je m'y habituerai;* I shall get used to it. — *au climat;* to inure one's self to the climate.
†**hâbler**, *v.n.*, to brag, to boast, to draw the long-bow.
†**hâblerie**. *n.f.*, bragging, boasting, drawing the long-bow.
†**hâbleu-r**. *n.m.*, **-se**, *n.f.*, bragger, boaster.
†**hache**, *n.f.*, axe, hatchet. — *d'armes;* battle-axe. *Fait à coups de —;* clumsily made. *Avoir un coup de — ;* to be crack-brained.
†**haché, -e**, *adj.*, (style) abrupt.
*†**hache-paille**, *n.m.* (—), chaff-cutter.
†**hacher**, *v.a.*, to chop, to hew, to cut to pieces; (engr.) to hatch; (cook.) to hash, to mince. — *menu;* to chop small; (cook.) to mince. — *en morceaux;* to cut to pieces.
†**hachereau** (ha-shrô), *n.m.*, little axe, hatchet.
†**hachette**. *n.f.*, hacking-knife, hatchet.
†**hachis**, *n.m.*, (cook.) minced meat, hash.
†**hachisch**, *n.m.* (*n.p.*), haschisch.
†**hachoir**, *n.m.*, chopping-board; chopping-knife; chaff-cutter.
†**hachure**, *n.f.*, (engr.) hatching.
†**hagard, -e**, *adj.*, haggard, wild.
hagiographe, *n.m.*, hagiographer.
hagiographe, *adj.*, hagiographic.
hagiographie, *n.f.*, hagiography.
hagiologique, *adj.*, hagiological.
†**haha**, *n.m.*, ha-ha, haw-haw.
†**hahé!** *int.*, (hunt.) tally-ho !
†**hai!** *int.*, hey ! well ! indeed ! bless me !
†**haie**, *n.f.*, hedge, hedgerow; beam of a plough; row, line. — *vive;* quickset hedge. *Se ranger en — ;* to form a line. *Fermer d'une — ;* to hedge in.
†**haïe!** *int.*, (carter's cry—*cri de charretier*) gee ho !
*†**haillon**, *n.m.*, rag, rags, tatters.
†**haine**, *n.f.*, hate, hatred; spite. *Avoir de la — pour, avoir en —;* to hate. *Porter de la — à;* to feel hatred towards.
†**haineusement**, *adv.*, hatefully, spitefully.
†**haineu-x, -se**, *adj.*, hateful, malignant, spiteful.
†**haïr**, *v.a.*, to hate, to detest, to loathe. — *cordialement ;* to hate heartily. — *comme la peste;* — *à la mort;* to feel a deadly hatred towards.
†**haire**, *n.f.*, hair-shirt.
†**haïssable**, *adj.*, hateful, odious.
†**halage**, *n.m.*, towage, towing. *Chemin de —;* towing-path.
†**halbran**, *n.m.*, young wild-duck.
†**halbrené, -e**, *adj.*, ragged feathered (of a bird—*d'un oiseau*) ; ragged, in a sad pickle.
†**halbrener**, *v.n.*, to shoot wild ducks.
†**hâle**. *n.m.*, heat of the sun; burning sun; burning heat. *Le — fane tout;* the heat of the sun dries up everything.
†**hâlé, -e**. *part.*, sun-burnt; swarthy; tanned.
haleine, *n.f.*, breath, wind. *Perdre l'—;* to get out of breath. *Reprendre —;* to recover one's breath. *Courir à perte d'—;* to run one's self out of breath. *Tout d'une —;* with the

same breath. *Un ouvrage de longue —*; a long-winded work.

halenée, *n.f.*, smell, whiff. *— d'ail*; whiff of garlic.

halener. *v.a.*, to smell the breath of; (hunt.) to get scent of.

haler, *v.a.*, (nav.) to haul. to heave; to set. to excite. *— un bateau à la cordelle*; to tow a boat. *— un bâtiment*; to track a vessel. *— le vent*; to haul the wind. *— un chien sur quelqu'un*; to set a dog at any one.

hâler, *v.a.*, to tan, to burn (of the sun—*du soleil*).

se **hâler**, *v.r.*, to become sun-burnt.

haletant, **-e**, *adj.*, out of breath, panting, puffing.

haleter (hal-té), *v.n.*, to blow, to puff, to pant for breath.

haleur, *n.m.*, tracker.

halieutique, *adj.*, relating to fishing.

halieutiques, *n.m.pl.*, halieutics.

halitueu-x, **-se**, *adj.*, (med.) halituous.

hallage, *n.m.*, market-duty, hallage

hallali, *n.m.*, (stag-hunting—*chasse au cerf*) flourish of the horn at the death; (call. shouts at the same moment—*appel, cris au même moment*) halloo.

halle, *n.f.*, market; market-place, market-house. *Langage des —s*; Billingsgate language. *Aller à la —*; to go to market.

hallebarde (hal-bard), *n.f.*, halberd.

hallebardier, *n.m.*, halberdier.

hallier, *n.m.*, thicket; market-keeper; any one who sells on a market.

hallucination (hal-lu-), *n.f.*, hallucination.

halluciné. **-e**, *adj.* and *n.*, (med.) one having hallucinations.

halo, *n.m.*, halo.

hâloir, *n.m.*, drying-room (for hemp—*pour le chanvre*).

halot, *n.m.*, rabbit burrow.

halotechnie, *n.f.*, (chem.) part of chemistry relating to the preparation of salts.

halte, *n.f.*, halt; stand, stop; halting-place; resting-place. *Faire —*; to halt. *— là!* hold! stop there!

haltère, *n.m.*, (antiq.) weights of stone or lead carried in the hands during athletic exercises; (modern gymnastics—*gymnastique moderne*) dumb-bells.

halurgie, *n.f.*, making or extracting salts.

hamac, *n.m.*, hammock. *Haut les —s* (nav.); up all hammocks.

hamadryade, *n.f.*, (myth.) Hamadryad, wood-nymph.

hameau, *n.m.*, hamlet.

hameçon (am-son), *n.m.*, hook, fish-hook; bait. *Mordre à l'—*; to take the bait.

hameçonné, **-e**, *adj.*, hooked.

hameçonner, *v.a.*, to hook; to take in (by specious words—*par des paroles captieuses*).

hampe, *n.f.*, staff (of a lance, &c.—*de lance, &c.*); handle (of a brush—*de brosse*); flower-stalk.

han, *n.m.*, heave (of a workman striking a heavy blow—*d'un ouvrier frappant un coup avec effort*).

hanap, *n.m.*, goblet.

hanche, *n.f.*, hip, haunch; (nav.) quarter. *Les poings sur les —s*; with one's arms akimbo.

hauchoan, *n.m.*, Brazilian buzzard.

hanebane, *n.f.* *V.* **jusquiame**.

hangar, *n.m.*, shed, cart-shed, cart-house.

hanneton (ha-n-ton), *n.m.*, may-bug, cock-chafer; thoughtless person. *C'est un —*; he is a giddy fellow.

hanovrien, **-ne** (-in, -è-n), *adj.*, Hanoverian

hanovrien, *n.m.*, **-ne**, *n.f.*, Hanoverian.

hanscrit, *n.m.* *V.* **sanscrit**.

hanse, *n.f.*, Hanse-Towns. *La — Teutonique*; the Hanse-Towns.

hanséatique, or **anséatique**, *adj.*, Hanseatic.

hansière, *n.f.*, (nav.) hawser. *V.* **haussière**.

hanter, *v.a.*, to haunt, to frequent, to frequent the society of. *Dis-moi qui tu hantes et je te dirai qui tu es*; tell me the company you keep, and I will tell you what you are.

hanter, *v.n.*, to frequent. *— chez quelqu'un*; to frequent any one's house.

⊙**hantise**, *n.f.*, (b.s.), keeping company with, intercourse.

happe, *n.f.*, axle-tree bed (of carriages—*de voitures*); cramp-iron.

happe-chair, *n.m.* (—), grasp-all.

happelourde (ha-ploord), *n.f.*, paste, imitation of a precious stone; a horse of fine appearance but no strength; well-dressed fool.

happer, *v.a.*, to snap, to snap up; to catch, to lay hold of, to nab.

haquenée (ha-knée), *n.f.*, ambling nag; ill-made, ungainly, woman. *Aller sur la — des cordeliers*; to trudge along on foot.

haquet (ha-kè), *n.m.*, dray.

haquetier (hak-tié), *n.m.*, drayman.

harangue, *n.f.*, harangue, speech, address, oration. *La tribune aux —s*; the rostrum.

haranguer (-ghé), *v.a.*, to harangue.

haranguer, *v.n.*, to harangue, to hold forth, to speechify.

harangueu-r (-gheur), *n.m.*, **-se**, *n.f.*, haranguer, orator; speech-maker, speechifier.

haras, *n.m.*, stud (of breeding horses and mares). *— (orni)*. *V.* **ara**.

harasse, *n.f.*, crate.

harasser, *v.a.*, to harass, to tire out, to weary, to overtire, to jade.

harceler, *v.a.*, to harass, to torment; to gall. *— l'ennemi*; to harass the enemy.

harcèlement, *n.m.*, harassing, torment.

harde, *n.f.*, herd (of deer—*de cerfs, &c.*); leash (for dogs—*de chiens*).

harder, *v.a.*, (hunt.) to leash dogs four and four, or six and six together.

hardes, *n.f. pl.*, wearing apparel, attire, clothes.

hardi, **-e**, *adj.*, hardy, bold, daring, intrepid, impudent. *Air —*; impudent look. *Manières —es*; audacious manners. *Ce musicien a le jeu —*; this musician has a bold manner of playing.

hardiesse, *n.f.*, boldness, hardihood, hardiness, fearlessness; assurance; impudence, audacity. *Avoir la — de dire*; to have the boldness to say. *Il y a beaucoup de — dans ce dessin*; there is great boldness in this drawing. *— de style, d'expression*; boldness of style, of expression.

hardiment, *adv.*, boldly, fearlessly, daringly, impudently. *Marcher — à l'ennemi*; to march boldly against the enemy.

hare! *int.*, (hunt.) halloo!

harem (ha-rèm), *n.m.*, harem.

hareng (ha-ran), *n.m.*, herring. *— frais*; fresh herring. *— saur*; red herring. *La caque sent toujours le —*; what is bred in the bone will never come out of the flesh.

harengaison (-ghè-zon), *n.f.*, herring-season.

harengère, *n.f.*, herring-woman; fish-woman; fish-fag.

harengerie (ha-ran-jri), *n.f.*, herring-market.

harenguet (-ghè), *n.m.*, (ich.) herring-cob.

⊙*hargnerie, *n.f.*, squabble, wrangling.

*hargneu-x, **-se**, *adj.*, cross; cross-grained; snappish; peevish, surly, crusty; snarling; vicious (of horses—*des chevaux*). *Chien —*; snarling dog; quarrelsome fellow.

†**haricot**, *n.m.*, kidney-bean ; (cook.) stew of mutton and turnips. —*s verts;* French beans. —*s d'Espagne ;* scarlet runners.

†**haridelle**, *n.f.*, jade, hack, sorry horse.

†**harle**, *n.m.*, (orni.) merganser.

harmonica, *n.m.*, harmonica ; musical glasses.

harmonie, *n.f.*, harmony ; unison, concord ; union ; keeping ; (mus) harmonics. *Avec* — ; harmoniously. *En* — ; in time, in keeping. *Sans* — ; inharmonious, unmusical. *Donner de l'* — *à ;* to give harmony to.

harmonier, *v.a.* *V.* **harmoniser.**

s'**harmonier**, *v.r.* *V.* **s'harmoniser.**

harmonieusement (-euz-mān), *adv.*, harmoniously, musically.

harmonieu-x, -se, *adj.*, harmonious. musical ; friendly (of colours—*des couleurs*). *Sons* — ; harmonious sounds. *Couleurs —ses ;* friendly colours.

harmonique, *n.m. and adj.*, harmonics ; harmonic, harmonical.

harmoniquement (-nik-mān), *adv.*, harmoniously.

harmoniser, *v.a., s'* —, *v.r.*, to harmonize.

harmoniste, *n.m.;* harmonist.

harmonium, *n.m.*, (mus.) harmonium.

harmoste, *n.m.*, (Gr. antiq.) Spartan governor of a conquered town.

†**harnachement** (har-nash-mān), *n.m.*, harness ; harnessing.

†**harnacher**, *v.a.*, to harness.

harnacheur, *n.m.*, harness-maker, dealer ; person that harnesses.

harnais, *or* **harnois**, *n.m.*, harness ; horse-trappings, trappings. *Endosser le* — *;* to turn soldier. *Cheval de* — ; draught-horse.

†**haro**, *n.m.*, hue and cry. *Crier* — *sur quelqu'un;* to set up a hue and cry after any one.

†**harpagon**. *n.m.*, miser.

se †**harpailler**, *v.r.*, to wrangle. to squabble.

†**harpaye**, *n.f.*, (orni.) harpy-falcon, marsh-harrier.

†**harpe**, *n.f.*, harp; (conch.) harp-shell. *Pincer de la* — *;* tó play the harp. — *éolienne;* Eolian harp.

†**harpé, -e**, *adj.*, well-made (of greyhounds—*lévriers).* *Un lévrier bien* — *;* a well-shaped greyhound.

†**harpeau**, *n.m.*, (nav.) grappling-iron.

†**harpège**, *n.m.* *V.* **arpège.**

†**harpéger**, *v.n.* *V.* **arpéger.**

†**harper**, *v.a.*, to gripe, to grapple —, *v.n.*, (man.) to raise the legs without bending them (of horses—*chevaux.*)

se † **harper**, *v.r.*, to grapple one another.

†**harpie**, *n.f.*, harpy

†**harpin**, *n.m.*, boat-hook; a kind of carbuncle (in cattle—*des bestiaux).*

harpiste, *n.m.f.*, harpist, player on the harp.

†**harpon**, *n m.*, harpoon, spear ; fish-spear.

†**harponner**, *v a.*, to harpoon, to spear.

†**harponneur**, *n.m.*, harpooner.

†**hart**, *n.f.*, withe (for binding fagots—*pour lier les fagots*) ; rope, halter. *C'est un homme qui mérite la* —*;* he is a man who deserves hanging

haruspice, *n m. V.* **aruspice.**

†**hasard**, *n.m.*, chance, accident, casualty, hazard, risk. *Jeu de* — ; game of chance *Coup de* — ; lucky chance. *Une chose de* —, a second-hand thing. *Au* —, at random, at a venture. *À tout* — ; at all events. *Par* — ; by chance, accidentally. *S'abandonner au* — ; to give one's self up to chance. *Jeter quelque chose au* —; to leave anything to chance. *Courir le* —; to run the risk.

†**hasardé, -e**, *part.*, hazarded ; (cook.) tainted.

†**hasarder**, *v.a.*, to hazard, to risk. to venture, to run the risk. *Il hasarde son argent au jeu ;* he ventures his money at gaming.

se †**hasarder**, *v.r.*, to hazard, to venture. to risk. — *à faire une chose ;* to venture to do a thing.

†**hasardeusement** (-deûz-mān), *adv.*. hazardously, venturesomely.

†**hasardeu-x, -se,** *adj.*, hazardous, venturous, venturesome, unsafe.

†**haschisch**, *n.m.*, (n.p.). *V.* **hachisch.**

†**hase**, *n.f.*, doe-rabbit. doe-hare.

hast, *n.m.*, staff. *Armes d'* — : weapons fixed on a long staff, such as lances. &c.

hastaire, *n.m.*, (antiq.) spearman, hastarius.

†**haste**, *n.f.*, (antiq.) spear.

†**hasté -e,** *adj.*, (bot.) hastated.

†**hastiforme,** *adj.*, (bot.) halberd-shaped, hastated.

†**hâte**, *n.f.*, hurry; haste. *En* — ; in haste. *À la* — ; in a hurry, in haste. *Avoir* —; to be in haste. *Faire une chose à la* —; to do a thing in a hurry. *S'éloigner à la* —; to hasten away. *Revenir en toute* —; to hasten back.

†**hâtelet** (hâ-tlè), *n.m.*, small skewer, small silver skewer.

†**hâter**, *v.a.*, to hasten, to forward, to expedite ; to hurry, to hurry on; to hurry over; to push on, to force (fruit).

se †**hâter**, *v.r.*, to make haste, to hurry, to hurry one's self. *Hâtez-vous de partir ;* make haste and set off.

†**hâteur**, *n.m.*, cook charged with the roasting of meat in the royal kitchen.

†**hâtier**, *n.m.*, spit-rest.

†**hâti-f, -ve,** *adj.*, forward; precocious, premature; (hort.) early. *Fruit* —; early fruit.

†**hâtiveau**, *n.m.*, (hort.) hasty pear ; early pea.

†**hâtivement** (hâ-ti-vmān), *adv.*, (hort.) early.

†**hâtiveté** (hâ-tiv-té), *n.f.*, earliness, forwardness.

†**haubans**, *n.m.pl.*, (nav.) shrouds. *Grands* — ; main-shrouds. — *de misaine ;* fore-shrouds.

†**haubergeon**, *n.m.*, small hauberk.

†**haubert**, *n.m.*, hauberk.

†**hausse**, *n.f.*, (com.) rise, advance ; (print.) overlay ; block (for raising anything—*pour élever les objets*) ; (of a rifle—*d'un fusil*) backsight. *À la* — ; (com.) on the advance. *Jouer à la* —; (com.) to speculate on a rise. *Joueur à la* —; speculator on a rise. — *d'archet ;* nut of a fiddle-bow.

†**hausse-col**, *n.m.* (— —s), gorget.

†**haussement** (hôs-mān), *n.m.*, raising. — *d'épaules ;* shrug of the shoulders.

†**hausser**, *v.a.*, to raise, to raise up, to lift up ; to augment; (com.) to advance. — *les épaules ;* to shrug up one's shoulders. — *la voix ;* to raise one's voice. — *les gages ;* to raise the wages. — *le coude ;* to drink hard.

se †**hausser**, *v.r.*, to be raised ; to rise, to raise one's self ; to clear up (of the weather—*du temps*); to increase ; (com.) to rise. — *sur la pointe des pieds;* to stand upon tip-toe.

†**hausser**, *v.n.*, to rise ; to get higher ; to increase. *La rivière a bien haussé ;* the river has risen very high. *Le change hausse ;* the rate of exchange is rising. *Les actions haussent;* the price of shares is rising. *La rente hausse;* the funds are rising.

†**haussier**, *n.m.*, bull, speculator on a rise in the public funds.

haussière. *V.* **aussière** and **hansière.**

†**haut, -e,** *adj.*, high ; tall ; lofty, chief, principal; upper; elevated; loud (of sound—*son*);

haughty. *Au plus — degré;* in the highest degree. *Les —es régions de l'air;* the upper regions of the air. *Il a juré, la main —e;* he swore with uplifted hand. *Marcher la tête —e;* to walk with the head erect. *Il peut aller partout la tête —e;* he can hold up his head wherever he goes. *La marée, la mer, est —e;* it is high water. *Avoir la voix —e;* to have a loud voice. *Lire à —e voix;* to read aloud. *Crier à —e voix;* to cry out loudly. *Pousser les —s cris;* to complain loudly. *Prendre le — ton;* to talk in a high strain. *Une personne de — rang;* a person of high rank. *—s faits;* great deeds. *Voici bien du — style;* this is a lofty style indeed. *Crime de —e trahison;* crime of high-treason. *Le — commerce;* the higher branches of commerce. *Messe —e;* high mass. *La chambre —e;* the upper house. *Le — -Canada;* Upper Canada. *Le — bout de la table;* the upper end of the table. *Un homme —;* a haughty man. *Viande de — goût;* high-seasoned meat. *Jeune cadet de — appétit;* extravagant young fellow. *Les —es cartes;* the court-cards. *Tenir la bride —e à quelqu'un;* to keep a tight hand over any one.

†**haut,** *n.m.,* height; top; summit; upper part; (mus.) high notes. *Le — d'une rue;* the top of a street. *Il est en —;* he is up stairs. *Je demeure dans une chambre d'en —;* I live in an upper room. *De — en bas;* downward. *Tomber de son —;* to fall flat down; to be thunderstruck. *Il y a du — et du bas dans la vie;* there are ups and downs in life. *Le — d'un clocher;* the top of a steeple. *Regarder quelqu'un de — en bas;* to eye any one from head to foot; to look down upon any one. *Traiter quelqu'un de — en bas;* to treat any one contemptuously. *Cette maison a quarante pieds de —;* this house is forty feet high.

†**haut,** *adv.,* high; loud; aloud, loudly. *Montez plus —;* go up higher. *Ainsi qu'il a été dit plus —;* as has already been said. *Reprendre les choses de plus —;* to begin farther back. *Parlez plus —;* speak louder. *Tout —;* aloud. *Parler —;* to speak aloud, to speak out. *— le pied;* off with you; let us be off at once. *Faire — le pied;* to vanish, to disappear; to run away. *Renvoyer des chevaux — le pied;* to send horses away without saddles or harness. *— la main;* with a high hand; off hand; in a high-handed manner. *Mener un cheval — la main;* to hold a tight rein on a horse.

☉†**haut-à-bas,** *n.m.* (—), hawker, pedlar.
' †**haut-à-haut,** *n.m.* (—), (hunt.) halloo.
†**hautain, -e,** *adj.,* haughty, supercilious.
†**hautainement** (hô-tè-n-mân), *adv.,* haughtily, superciliously.
†**hautbois** (hô-boâ), *n.m.,* hautboy; hautboy-player.
☉†**haut-de-chausses,** *or* **haut-de-chausse,** *n.m.* (—s —, *or* —s —s), small-clothes; trunk-hose.
†**haute-contre,** *n.f.* (—s —), (mus.) countertenor.
†**haute lisse,** *n.f.,* tapestry hangings.
†**hautement** (hô-tman), *adv.,* aloud, boldly, resolutely.
†**haute paye,** *n.f.,* extra pay; one who receives extra pay.
†**hautesse,** *n.f.,* highness (the Sultan's title —titre du Sultan).
☉†**haute-taille,** *n.f.* (—s —s), (mus.) uppertenor.
†**hauteur,** *n.f.,* height, altitude; rising ground, eminence; depth; elevation; firmness, haughtiness; superciliousness. *La — d'une montagne;* the height of a hill. *Mur à — d'appui;* wall breast-high. *La — d'un bataillon;* the depth of a battalion. *La — d'un*

astre; the altitude of a star. *Prendre la — du soleil;* to take the sun's altitude. *Être à la — d'une île* (nav.); to be off an island. *La — de ses conceptions;* the loftiness of his ideas. *Être à la — de quelqu'un;* to comprehend any one. *Être à la — du siècle;* to keep pace with the age. *Parler avec —;* to speak haughtily. *Avec —;* imperiously.

†**haut-fond,** *n.m.* (—s —s), (nav.) shoal.
†**haut-le-corps,** *n.m.* (—), skip, start.
†**haut-le-pied,** *n.m.* (—), person with no fixed residence; scoundrel.
†**hautur-ier, -ière,** *adj.,* of the high seas.
†**hauturier,** *n.m.,* sea-pilot.
†**hâve,** *adj.,* pale, wan; emaciated.
†**haveron** (ha-vron), *n.m.,* wild oats.
†**havir,** *v.a.,* to scorch (meat—viande).
se †**havir,** *v.r.,* to scorch, to be scorched (of meat—de la viande).
†**havir,** *v.n.,* to scorch (of meat—de la viande).
†**havre,** *n.m.,* haven, harbour, port.
†**havresac,** *n.m.,* knapsack, wallet.
†**hé !** *int.,* ho ! ah ! hey ! I say !
☉†**heaume** (hòm), *n.m.,* helm, helmet; (nav.) tiller, bar.
hebdomadaire, *adj.,* weekly.
hebdomadier, *n.m.,* one on duty for a week in convents and chapters.
héberge, *n.f.,* (jur.) the point at which a wall ceases to be common to two buildings of unequal height.
héberger, *v.a.,* to lodge, to entertain, to harbour.
hébété, -e, *n.f.,* dolt, blockhead.
hébéter, *v.a.,* to stupify, to besot; to dull.
hébraïque, *adj.,* Hebrew, Hebraic.
hébraïquement, *adv.,* Hebraically.
hébraïsant, *n.m.,* Hebraist.
hébraïsme, *n.m.,* Hebraism.
hébreu, *n.* and *adj.m.,* Hebrew; Hebraic.
hécatombe, *n.f.,* hecatomb.
hectare, *n.m.,* hectare (2 acres, 1 rood, 35 perches).
hectique, *adj.,* (med.) hectic.
hectisie, *n.f.,* (med.) consumption.
hectogramme, *n.m.,* hectogramme (3·527 oz. avoirdupois).
hectolitre, *n.m.,* hectolitre (22·009668 imperial gallons).
hectomètre, *n.m.,* hectometre (328·09167 British statute feet).
hégémonie, *n.f.,* supremacy; (antiq.) supremacy which belonged to one town in the Greek federations.
hégire, *n.f.,* hegira (Mahometan era—ère des Mahométans).
heiduque, *n.m.,* Hungarian foot-soldier.
hein ! *int.,* hey !
hélas, *int.,* alas ! ah !
hélépole, *n.f.,* (antiq.) an engine of war used by the Greeks in the siege of towns.
†**héler,** *v.a.,* (nav.) to hail, to speak (a ship —un vaisseau). —, *v.n.,* to hail, to call.
hélianthe, *n.m.,* (bot.) helianthus, sunflower.
hélianthème, *n.m.,* (bot.) helianthemum, rock-rose.
héliaque, *adj.,* (astron.) heliacal.
héliastes, *n.m.pl.,* (antiq.) heliasts.
hélice, *n.f.,* helix, screw.
hélicon, *n.m.,* Helicon.
héliocentrique, *adj.,* heliocentric.
héliographie, *n.f.,* heliography.
héliographique, *adj.,* heliographic.
héliomètre, *n.m.,* heliometer.
hélioscope, *n.m.,* helioscope.
héliotrope, *n.m.,* (bot.) heliotrope; sunflower; (min.) heliotrope, blood-stone.

hélix. *n.m.*, (anat.) helix.

hellanodices. *or* **hellanodiques.** *n.m.pl.*, the judges of the Olympic games.

hellébore, *n.m.* *V.* **ellébore.**

helléborine, *n.f.* *V.* **elléborine.**

hellènes (èl-lè-n), *n.m.pl.*, Hellenes.

hellénique, *adj.*, Hellenic.

hellénisme, *n.m.*, Hellenism.

helléniste, *n.m.*, Hellenist.

helminthe, *n.m.*, (zool., med.) generic name of intestinal worms.

helminthologie, *n.f.*, helminthology.

⊙**hélose,** *n.f.*, (med.) helosis.

helvétique, *adj.*, Helvetic.

†**hem!** *int.*, hem !

hématite, *n.f.*, (min.) hematite.

hématocèle, *n.f.*, (surg.) hematocele.

hématologie, *n.f.*, hematology.

hématose, *n.f.*, hæmatosis, sanguification.

hématurie, *n.f.*, (med.) hæmaturia.

hémérocalle, *n.f.*, (bot.) hemerdeallis.

hémi, a prefix from Greek ἡμί, half, semi.

⊙**hémicoptère,** *n.m.* *V.* **phénicoptère.**

hémicycle, *n.m.*, hemicycle.

hémine, *n.f.*, (antiq.) hemina, cotyla, about half a pint.

hémiplégie, *or* **hémiplexie,** *n.f.*, (med.) hemiplegy, hemiplegia.

hémiptère, *n.m.*, (ent.) hemipter.

hémiptère, *adj.*, hemipteral.

hémisphère, *n.m.*, hemisphere.

hémisphérique, *adj.*, hemispheric.

hémistiche, *n.m.*, hemistich.

hémoptoïque, *adj.*, (med.) who spits blood.

hémoptysie, *n.f.*, hæmoptysis.

hémorragie, *n.f.*, hemorrhage.

hémorroïdal, -e, *adj.*, hemorrhoidal.

hémorroïdale, *n.f.*, (anat.) hemorrhoidal artery.

hémorroïdes, *n.f.pl.*, hemorrhoids, piles.

hémorroïsse, *n.f.*, (Biblical hist.) woman troubled with the bloody flux.

hémostatique, *adj.*, (med.) styptic.

hendécagone. *n.m.*, (geom.) hendecagon.

hendécasyllabe, *n.m.*, hendecasyllable.

†**hennir** (ha-), *v.n.*, to neigh.

†**hennissement** (ha-). *n.m.*, neighing.

⊙**hépar,** *n.m.*, (chem.) hepar.

hépatique, *adj.*, hepatic.

hépatique, *n.f.*, (bot.) liverwort.

hépatite, *n.f.*, hepatitis, inflammation of the liver ; (min.) hepatite, liver-stone.

heptacorde, *n.m.*, heptachord.

heptagonal, -e, *adj.*, heptagonal.

heptagone, *n.m.* and *adj.*, heptagon ; heptagonal.

heptaméron, *n.m.*, heptameron.

heptandre, *adj.*, heptandrian.

heptandrie, *n.f.*, heptandria.

heptangulaire, *adj.*, heptangular.

heptaphylle, *adj.*, (bot.) heptaphyllous.

heptarchie, *n.f.*, heptarchy.

heptarchique, *adj.*, heptarchic.

héraldique, *adj.*, heraldic.

†**héraut,** *n.m.*, herald.

herbacé, -e *adj.*, (bot.) herbaceous.

herbage, *n.m.*, herbage, grass, pasture, pasture-ground.

herbager, *n.m.*, grazier.

herbe, *n.f.*, herb, grass. *Brin d'—* ; blade of grass. *—s potagères* ; pot-herbs. *— marine* ; sea-weed. *— militaire* ; milfoil. *— de la Saint-Jean* ; ground-ivy. *— de Saint-Jean* ; mugwort. *Bouillon aux —s* ; herb soup. *Mettre un cheval à l'—* ; to put a horse out to grass. *Blé en —* ; corn in the blade. *Mauvaises —s* ; weeds. *Mauvaise — croît toujours* ; ill weeds grow apace. *Manger son blé en —* ; to spend one's money

before one gets it. *Couper l'— sous le pied à quelqu'un* ; to supplant any one, to oust any one. *C'est un docteur en —* ; he is a doctor in embryo. *Il a marché sur quelque mauvaise —* ; he has got out of bed the wrong way. *— à l'ambassadeur, à la reine (tabac)* ; snuff, tobacco. *— aux charpentiers, à la coupure (millefeuille)* ; milfoil. *— aux chats (marum)* ; cat-thyme. *— aux chantres (vélar)* ; hedge-mustard, hedge-garlic. *— aux cuillers (cochlearia)* ; scurvy-grass, cochlearia. *— aux écus (nummulaire)* ; money-wort. *— aux gueux (clématite)* ; clematis, climber. *— aux Patagons (hydrocotyle)* ; hydrocotyle. *— au pauvre homme (gratiole)* ; hyssop. *— aux perles (grémil)* ; gromwell, gromil. *— du siège (scrofulaire)* ; figwort. *— aux verrues (héliotrope)* ; heliotrope.

*herbeiller, *v.n.*, (hunt.) to graze.

herber, *v.a.*, to lay on the grass. *— de la toile* ; to lay linen cloth on the grass (to bleach it—*pour la blanchir*).

herberie, *n.f.*, bleaching-ground for wax.

herbette, *n.f.*, (poet.) short grass.

herbeu-x, -se, *adj.*, grassy, herbous.

herbier, *n.m.*, herbal, herbarium.

herbière, *n.f.*, herb-woman.

herbivore, *adj.*, herbivorous.

herbivore, *n.m.*, herbivorous animal.

herborisation, *n.f.*, herborization, herborizing, herborizing excursion.

herboriser, *v.n.*, to herborize.

herboriseur, *n.m.*, collector of plants.

herboriste, *n.m.*, herbalist, herborist ; dealer in medicinal herbs.

herboristerie, *n.f.*, herb trade, herbalist's shop.

herbu, -e, *adj.*, grassy, covered with grass.

hercotectonique, *n.f.*, art of fortifying.

hercule, *n.m.*, (astron.) Hercules.

herculéen, -ne (-in, -èn), *adj.*, Herculean.

†**here,** *n.m.*, sorry fellow, poor wretch ; poor devil ; game at cards.

héréditaire, *adj.*, hereditary, heritable, inheritable.

héréditairement, *adv.*, hereditarily.

hérédité, *n.f.*, heirship, right of inheritance, succession ; hereditary right ; inheritance.

hérésiarque, *n.m.*, heresiarch.

hérésie, *n.f.*, heresy. *Il ne fera point d'—* ; he will not set the Thames on fire.

héréticité, *n.f.*, heretical nature.

hérétique, *n.m.f.* and *adj.*, heretic, heretical.

†**hérissé, -e,** *adj.*, rough, shaggy, brushy, bristling ; (bot.) hairy, prickly. *Cheveux —s, poil —* ; shaggy hair. *Un pédant — de grec et de latin* ; a pedant bristling with Greek and Latin.

†**hérisser,** *v.a.*, to bristle, to bristle up, to erect ; to arm ; to lard. *Le lion hérisse sa crinière* ; the lion bristles up his mane. *Les piquants qui hérissent la tige du rosier* ; the prickles that arm the stalk of a rose-bush. *— son style de néologismes* ; to lard one's style with neologisms.

se†**hérisser,** *v.r.*, to stand on end, to stand erect ; to bristle, to bristle up ; to be bristling with, to be armed ; to be covered.

†**hérisser,** *v.n.*, to bristle, to bristle up. *Les cheveux lui hérissent à la tête* ; the hair on his head stands on end.

†**hérisson,** *n.m.*, (mam.) hedgehog, urchin ; (fort.) herisson ; canting-wheel ; sprocket-wheel ; sprocket ; rag-wheel ; spur-wheel *Jeune —* (mam.) ; hedgepig. *— de mer* (ich.) ; sea-hedgehog.

†**hérissonné, -e,** *adj.*, (her.) crouching.

†**héritage,** *n.m.*, heritage, inheritance, heirdom. *—s libres* ; (jur.) fee-simple. *—s substitués* ; (jur.) fee-tail.

hériter, *v n.*, to inherit, to be heir; to obtain by inheritance; to succeed.

hériter, *v.a.*, to inherit. *Il n'a rien hérité de son père;* he inherited nothing from his father.

hériti-er, *n.m.,* **-ère,** *n.f.* (-tié, -ti-èr), heir, heiress, inheritor, inheritrix. — *institué, testamentaire;* (jur.) heir under a will; devisee. — *naturel;* (jur.) heir of one's body. — *par substitution;* heir of entail. — *légitime;* lawful heir. — *universel;* sole heir. — *présomptif;* heir-apparent. *Il est — de son oncle;* he is heir to his uncle.

hermaphrodisme, *n.m.*, hermaphrodism.

hermaphrodite, *n.m.* and *adj.*, hernaphrodite; hermaphroditic, hermaphroditical, androgynal, androgynous.

hermeline, *n.f.*, (her.) sable.

herméneutique, *n.f.* and *adj.*, hermeneutics; hermeneutic, hermeneutical.

hermès (èr-mès), *n.m.*, (sculpt.) Mercury's head.

hermétique, *adj.*, hermetic, hermetical. *Science —;* hermetical science. *Colonne —;* (sculpt.) column with a man's head (for capital —*pour chapiteau*).

hermétiquement (-tik-mān), *adv.*, hermetically, closely.

hermine, *n.f.*, (mam.) ermine; hermine; winter-weasel; (her.) ermine; ermine (fur—*fourrure*). — *d'été;* (mam.) stoat.

herminé. -e, *adj.*, (her.) ermined.

herminette, *or* **erminette,** *n.f.*, (carp.) adze. — *courbée;* hollow adze.

hermitage, *or* **ermitage,** *n.m.*, hermitage. *Vin de l'—;* hermitage.

hermite, *or* **ermite,** *n.m.*, hermit.

†**herniaire,** *adj.*, hernial. *Bandage —;* truss.

†**herniaire,** *n.f.*, (bot.) rupture-wort.

†**hernie,** *n.f.*, hernia, rupture. — *ombilicale;* umbilical hernia.

herniole, *n.f.*, (bot.) rupture-wort.

†**hernutes,** *n.m.pl.*, Moravians, the United Brethren.

hérodiens (-in), *n.m.*, (Bibl. hist.) Herodians.

héroï-comique, *adj.*, heroi-comic; mock-heroic.

héroïde, *n.f.*, heroic epistle.

héroïne, *n.f.*, heroine.

héroïque, *adj.*, heroic. *Poème —;* heroic poem. *Temps —s;* heroic ages.

héroïquement (-ik-mān), *adv.*, heroically.

héroïsme, *n.m.*, heroism.

†**héron,** *n.m.*, heron. — *crabier;* crab-eater. *Masse de —;* heron plume.

†**héronneau,** *n.m.*, young heron.

†**héronner,** *v.n.*, (hawking—*fauconnerie*) to fly at the heron.

†**héronni-er. -ère,** *adj.*, heron-like; thin, lank, meagre; (hawking—*fauconnerie*) trained to fly the heron. *Oiseau —;* a hawk as fast-flying and thin as a heron. ⊙ *Femme —ère;* skinny, high-hipped woman. ⊙ *Cuisse —ère;* long lank thigh.

†**héronnière,** *n.f.*, heronry.

†**héros** (-rô), *n.m.*, hero.

herpes marines, *n.f.pl.*, certain things cast on shore by the sea, such as amber and ambergris.

herpès, *n.m.*, (med.) herpes, tetters.

herpétique, *adj.*, (med.) herpetic.

†**hersage,** *n.m.*, (agri.) harrowing of a field.

†**herschel,** *n.m.*, (astron.) Georgium Sidus, Herschel, Uranus.

†**herse,** *n.f.*, harrow; (fort.) portcullis, herse; candlestick (used in Catholic churches—*employé*

dans les églises catholiques*); (nav.) iron oringle; (bot.) caltrop.

†**thersé,- e,** *part.* and *adj.*, (agri.) harrowed; (her.) with a herse.

†**therser,** *v.a.*, (agri.) to harrow.

†**therseur,** *n.m.*, harrower.

hésitation, *n.f.*, hesitation; stammering, faltering.

hésiter, *v.n.*, to hesitate, to falter, to hum and haw, to be at a stand, to stick, to stop, to waver; to be doubtful, to demur. *Faire —;* to stagger. *Sans —;* unhesitatingly.

hétairie, *or* **hétérie,** *n.f.*, (antiq.) political association public or secret; (modern.) political association to free Greece from the Turkish yoke.

hétéroclite, *adj.*, (gram.) heteroclite, heteroclitic, heteroclitical, anomalous; eccentric, odd, whimsical. *Manières —s;* eccentric manners. *Visage —;* odd face. *Bâtiment —;* irregular building.

hétérodoxe, *adj.*, heterodox.

hétérodoxie, *n.f.*, heterodoxy.

hétérogame, *adj.*, (bot.) heterogamous.

hétérogène, *adj.*, heterogeneal, heterogeneous, dissimilar, incongruous.

hétérogénéité, *n.f.*, heterogeneity, heterogeneousness.

hétérosciens (-si-in), *n.m.pl.*, (geog.) Heteroscians, Heteroscii.

hetman, *n.m.*, hetman.

†**hêtre,** *n.m.*, beech, beech-tree.

heu, *n.m.*, (nav.) hoy.

heu! *int.*, alas! lackaday! hey! ah! aye!

⊙**heur,** *n.m.*, luck, good fortune. *Il n'y a qu'heur et malheur en ce monde;* chance is everything.

heure, *n.f.*, hour; o'clock; time, time of day; *pl.*, primer (prayer-book—*livre de prières*). *Belle —;* (b.s.) nice hour, pretty hour. *Une bonne, grande, grosse —;* a good, a full, hour. — *dernière, dernière —;* last moments. — *marquée, désignée, dite;* appointed hour. — *suprême;* dying hour, hour of death, last moments. —*s en sus;* afterhours, over-hours (of workmen—*d'ouvriers*). *Ami, homme, de toutes les —s;* friend who is always welcome, friend always ready to oblige. *Livre d'—s;* (c. rel.) primer. *Une paire d'—s;* a primer. *Un mauvais quart d'—;* a bad, a disagreeable, time. *Quart d'— de Rabelais;* paying time, settling time, trying time. *J'y serai dans une —;* I will be there within an hour. *Quelle — est-il?* what o'clock is it? *Il est une — et demie;* it is half past one. *Sur les une —;* about one o'clock. *L'horloge a sonné deux —s;* the clock has struck two. *Chercher midi à quatorze —s;* to look for a thing where it is not to be found, to run a wild-goose chase. *Mettre une montre à l'—;* to set a watch. *Il est l'— de dîner;* it is dinner-time. *À l'— qu'il faut;* in due time. *Vous venez à l'— qu'il fallait;* you come in the very nick of time. *Je le ferai à mes —s perdues;* I will do it in my leisure hours. *Donner —;* to fix an hour. *L'— du berger;* the propitious hour for wooers. *De bonne —;* betimes, early, soon. *Venez de meilleure —;* come sooner. *À cette —, à l'— qu'il est;* now, at present, at this present time. *Pour l'—;* at present. *Tôt à l'—;* by-and-by, presently; not long ago, just now. *D'une — à l'autre;* from one moment, from one minute, to the other. *D'— à autre;* now and then. *À la bonne —;* in good time; well and good. *Les Heures;* (myth.) the Hours (*Horæ*).

heureusement (eu-reûz-mān), *adv.*, happily, luckily; successfully, fortunately, prosperously; by good luck; well. *Il imagine — les choses;* he has a happy fancy.

heureu-x -se, *adj.*, happy; blessed, blissful; lucky, fortunate; successful; prosperous, favour-

able, auspicious; pleasing, prepossessing; good;
excellent, rare. *Tous les hommes veulent être —;*
all men wish to be happy. *Une —se vieillesse;*
a happy old age. *Il est né — ;* he was born lucky.
Des couches —ses; a happy delivery (of a woman).
Un génie —; a felicitous genius. *Être —;* to be
lucky. *— au jeu;* lucky at gaming. *Il est —
d'avoir eu votre protection;* he is happy in having
had your protection.

†**heurt,** *n.m.*, collision; blow; shock, knock;
mark left by a blow.

†**heurtement,** *n.m.*, hiatus.

†**heurter,** *v.a.*, to run against, to knock
against, to strike against, to hit against; to hit,
to strike; to run foul of; to jostle; to shock, to
hurt, to offend, to disoblige; (paint.) to colour
hard. *— quelqu'un;* to run against any one.
Ce vaisseau a heurté l'autre; this ship ran foul
of the other. *— les préjugés de;* to shock the
prejudices of. *Dessin heurté;* drawing roughly
coloured.

se†**heurter,** *v.r.*, to strike, to hit, one's self; to
strike against one another, to run foul of each
other; to come into collision; to jostle one
another; to clash. *-- à la tête;* to hit one's self
on the head. *Les boucs se heurtent de leurs têtes;*
goats butt at one another with their heads.

†**heurter,** *v.n.,* to strike, to knock, to hit; to
dash, to knock (at a door—*à une porte*).

⊙†**heurtoir,** *n.m.*, knocker (of a door—*de
porte*), (arch.) sill.

hexacorde, *n.m.*, (mus.) hexachord.

hexaèdre, *n.m.* and *adj.*, (geom.) hexahedron; hexahedral.

hexagonal, -e, *adj.,* hexagonal

hexagone, *n.m.* and *adj.,* (geom.) hexagon;
hexagonal.

hexamètre, *n.m.* and *adj.,* hexameter;
hexametrical.

hexandre, *adj.,* (bot.) hexándrous.

hexandrie, *n.f.,* (bot.) hexandria.

hexaples, *n.m.pl.,* (theol.) Hexapla.

hiatus (ia-tus), *n.m.*, hiatus.

†**hibou,** *n.m.*, owl; melancholic, unsociable
person. *— commun;* (orni.) long-eared owl. *—
scops;* (orni.) scops-eared owl. *Faire le —;* to
mope like an owl.

†**hic,** *n.m.*, knot, difficulty (of a business—*dans
une affaire*), rub.

†**hidalgo,** *n.m.*, hidalgo.

†**hideusement** (-deûz-màn), *adv.*, hideously,
frightfully, horribly, dreadfully, shockingly.

†**hideu-x, -se,** *adj.,* hideous, frightful, horrible, dreadful, shocking.

†**hie,** *n.f.,* beetle, paving-beetle, rammer (of
pavier*—de paveurs*) *Battre à la —;* to ram.

†**hièble,** *n.f.,* (bot.) danewort, dwarf-elder.

hiémal, -e, *adj.,* wintery, hyemal. *Plantes
—es,* winter-plants.

†**hiement** (hi-màn), *n.m.*, grating, creeking
(of machines); ramming.

hier (i-ièr), *adv.*, yesterday. *— matin;* yesterday morning. *— au soir;* last night. *Avant-
—;* the day before yesterday. *La nuit d'—;*
yesterday night, yesternight. *Homme d'—;*
upstart.

†**hier** (hi-é), *v.a.* and *n.*, to ram; (of machines) to creak.

hiérarchie, *n.f.,* hierarchy.

hiérarchique, *adj.,* hierarchical.

hiérarchiquement (-shik-màn), *adv.,*
hierarchically.

†**hiérarque,** *n.m.,* hierarch.

hiératique, *adj.,* hieratic.

hiéroglyphe, *n.m.*, (antiq.) hieroglyph,
hieroglyphic.

hiéroglyphique, *adj.,* hieroglyphical,
hieroglyphic.

hiéroglyphiquement (-fik-màn), *adv.,*
hieroglyphically.

hiéronique, *n.m.*, conqueror in the sacred
games.

hiéronymite, *n.m.*, hieronymite, monk of
the Spanish order of the Hieronymites.

hiérophante, *n.m.*, (Grec. antiq.) hierophant.

hilarant, -e, *adj.,* exhilarating. *Gaz —;*
(chem.) laughing gas.

hilarité, *n.f.,* hilarity; cheerfulness; mirth.

†**hile.** *n.m.*, (bot.) hilum.

hindoustani.*n.m.,*(*n.p.*)(philology) hindu-
stanee, hindostany (language)

hippiatrique, *n.f.,* veterinary art.

hippique, *adj.,* hippic.

hippocampe, *n.m.,* (myth., zool.) hippo-
campus, hippocamp, sea-horse.

hippocentaure, *n.m.,* (antiq.) hippocentaur.

hippocras (-krâs), *V.* **hypocras.**

hippocratique, *adj.,* hippocratic.

hippocrène, *n.f.,* (myth.) Hippocrene.

hippodrome, *n.m.,* hippodrome; race-
course.

hippodromie, *n.f.,* horse-racing.

hippogriffe, *n.m.,* hippogriff, winged horse.

hippolithe, *n.f.,* (vet.) hippolith.

hippomane, *n.m.,* hippomane.

hippopotame, *n.m.,* hippopotamus, river-
horse, sea-horse.

hirondelle, *n.f.,* (orni.) swallow. *— domestique, — de cheminée;* house-swallow. *— rustique, — de fenêtre;* martin. *— de rivière, — de
rivage;* sand-martin. *— de mer;* sea-gull;
(ich.) swallow-fish; tub-fish; tub. *Pierre d'—;*
swallow-stone. *Une — ne fait pas le printemps;*
one swallow does not make a spring.

hispide, *adj.,* (bot.) hispid, strigous.

hispidité, *n.f.,* (bot.) hispidity, strigosity.

†**hisser,** *v.a.,* to hoist, to hoist up, to heave,
to heave up, to raise, to haul up; to haul out
(sails—*les voiles*); to sway up (yards—*les vergues*).
— promptement; (nav.) to trice.

se†**hisser,** *v.r.,* to raise one's self up.

histologie, *n.f. V.* **histologie.**

histoire, *n.f.,* history, tale, story, narration;
long rigmarole; idle story, untruth, falsehood.
— faite à plaisir; feigned story. *Faiseur d'—s;*
story-teller. *Peintre d'—;* historical painter.
Tableau d'—; historical picture, history piece.
C'est une autre —; that is quite another story.
Voilà bien des —s; what a fuss you make about it.

histologie, *n.f.,* histology.

⊙**historial, -e,** *adj.,* historical.

historien (-ri-in), *n.m.,* historian.

historienne, *n.f.,* (l.u.) historian.

historier, *v.a.,* to embellish, to ornament,
to grace with ornaments.

historiette, *n.f.,* little story story.

historiographe, *n.m.,* historiographer.

historique, *adj.,* historical. *Cela est —;*
that is historical, a matter of fact.

historique, *n.m.,* history (recital of facts—
exposé de faits).

historiquement (-rik màn), *adv.,* historically.

histrion, *n.m.,* histrion, actor, stage-player;
player; (b.s.) mountebank.

histrionique, *adj.,* histrionic.

histrionner, *v.n.,* (jest.) to act, to perform
plays; to play.

hiver (i-vèr), *n.m.,* winter. *— doux;* mild
winter. *— rude;* severe winter. *Cœur de l'—;*
mid-winter. *Queue de l'—;* latter end of winter.
Au cœur, au milieu, au plus fort, de l'—; in the
depth of winter.

⊙**hivernade,** *n.f.,* wintering, hyemation;
(bot.) growing in winter.

hivernage, *n.m.,* winter, winter time;
wintering place; (agri.) winter-fallowing;
winter-fodder.

16

hivernal, -e, *adj.*, (l.u.) wintery.

hiverner, *v.n.*, to winter.

hiverner, *v.a.*, (agri.) to winter-fallow.

†**hiverner**, *v.r.*, to inure one's self to cold.

†**ho**! *int.*, ho! hoa! oh! hoy! (nav.) ahoy!

†**hobereau** (ho-brô), *n.m.*, (orni.) hobby; country squire; troublesome neighbour.

†**hoc**, *n.m.*, hock (game at cards—*jeu de cartes*). *Cela lui est* —; he is sure of that.

†**hoca**, *n.m.*, hoca (game of chance—*jeu de hasard*).

†**hoche**, *n.f.*, (of tallies—*de tailles*) notch, nick.

†**hochement** (hosh-mān), *n.m.*, shaking, tossing, wagging (of the head—*de la téte*).

†**hochepied**, *n.m.*, heron-hawk.

†**hochepot**, *n.m.*, (cook.) hodge-podge, hotch-potch.

†**hochequeue**, *n.m.*, (orni.) nut-hatch, wagtail.

†**hocher**, *v.a.*, to jog, to shake, to wag, to toss. — *la téte*; to shake one's head.

†**hocher**, *v.n.*, (man.) to shake the bit.

†**hochet**, *n.m.*, coral, rattle (for children—*pour les enfants*); toy. *Il y a des* —*s pour tout âge*; every age has its hobby.

†**hogner**, *v.n.*, (l.u., pop.) to grumble, to growl.

†**hoir**, *n.m.*, (jur.) heir.

hoirie, *n.f.*, (jur.) inheritance.

†**holà**! *int.*, holla! hoa! (nav.) holloa! ho, there!

†**holà**, *n.m.*, stop; end. *Mettre le* —; to put a stop to a fray.

†**hôlement**, *n.m.*, hooting (of owls—*du hibou*).

†**hôler**, *v.n.*, to hoot (like an owl—*en hibou*).

†**hollandais, -e**, *n.* and *adj.*, Dutchman; Dutchwoman; Dutch.

†**hollandais**, *n.m.*, Dutch language.

†**hollandé, -e**, *adj.*, dressed (of quills—*plumes d'oie*). *Batiste* —*e*; strong thick cambric.

†**hollander**, *v.a.*, to dress (quills—*plumes d'oie*).

holocauste, *n.m.*, holocaust, burnt-offering; sacrifice.

holographe, *adj. V.* **olographe**.

holothurie, *n.f.*, holothuria, trepang.

†**hom**! *int.*, hum! humph!

†**homard**, *n.m.*, (ich.) lobster. — *femelle*; hen lobster. — *mâle*; cock lobster.

hombre, *n.m.*, (game at cards—*jeu de cartes*) ombre.

homélie, *n.f.*, homily; sermon.

homéopathe, *n.m.* and *adj.*, (med.) homeopathist.

homéopathie, *n.f.*, (med.) homeopathy.

homéopathique, *adj.*, homeopathic.

homérique, *adj.*, Homeric.

homicide, *n.m.*, homicide, man-slayer; manslaughter. — *involontaire*; manslaughter. — *volontaire*; voluntary homicide; wilful murder. — *commandé par la nécessité actuelle de la légitime défense*; (jur.) chance-medley. — *non qualifié crim n'i délit*; (jur.) justifiable homicide. — *par imprudence*; homicide by misadventure.

homicide, *adj.*, murderous, homicidal. *Des yeux* —*s*; killing eyes.

⊙**homicider**, *v.a.*, to murder, to slay, to kill.

hommage, *n.m.*, homage; service; acknowledgment, token, gift, testimony; *pl.*, respects, homage. *Faire* — *à quelqu'un*; to do homage to any one. *Rendre* — *à la vérité*; to do homage to truth. *Rendre ses* —*s à quelqu'un*; to pay one's respects to any one. — *de reconnaissance*; token of gratitude.

hommagé, -e, *adj.*, held by homage.

hommager, *n.m.*, homager.

hommasse, *adj.*, masculine, manlike (of women—*des femmes*).

homme, *n.m.*, man; (triv., pop.) husband, old man. *Dieu créa l'*— *à son image*; God cre-

ated man after his own image. — *d'église*, *d'épée*, *de lettres*; churchman, military man, literary man. — *du monde*; man of the world. *C'est un* — *à tout*; he is a man of all work. *C'est un* — *à pendre*; he is a man who ought to be hanged. *C'est un* — *pauvre* —; he is a poor weak fellow. *C'est un* — *pauvre*; he is a poor man. *C'est un très bon* —; he is a very good man. *Bon* —; good, virtuous man; good-natured, simple, easy man; old fellow; old codger. — *bon*; kind-hearted, good, virtuous, man. *Brave* —; good man; good fellow, good chap. — *brave*; brave, daring man. — *de paille*; man-of-straw. — *de bois* (man.); fagot; dumb-jockey. — *à tout faire*; jack of all trades. — *des bois* (mam.) mantiger, mantichor, wild man, baboon. *Enlèvement d'*—; (jur.) man-stealing. *Herbe à pauvre* —; (bot.) hedge-hyssop. *La perle des* —*s*; (fam.) a trump of a man, a trump. *Il n'y a téte d'*— *qui ose*; no man alive, no man living, would dare. *C'est un* — *que cet* —*là*; he is a man every inch of him. *C'est le dernier des* —*s*; he is the worst of men, the greatest villain alive. *Voilà mon* —; that is the man for my money.

⊙**hommeau**, *n.m.*, little man.

homme-dieu, *n.m.*, (n.p.) Man-God, Jesus-Christ.

homocentrique, *adj.*, (astron.) homocentric.

homogène, *adj.*, homogeneal, homogeneous.

homogénéité, *n.f.*, homogeneity, homogeneousness, homogenealness.

homologati-f, -ve, *adj*, homologative, affirmative.

homologation, *n.f.*, (jur.) confirmation, approval, homologation.

homologue, (-log) *adj.*, (geom.) homologous, similar, like.

homologuer (-ghé), *v.a.*, (jur.) to confirm, to homologate.

homoncule, or **homuncule**, *n.m.*, (fam.) little man.

homonyme, *adj*, homonymous.

homonyme, *n.m.*, homonym; namesake.

homonymie, *n.f.*, homonymy.

homophonie, *n.f.*, homophony.

honchets, *n.m.pl. V.* **jonchets**.

†**hongre**, *n.m.* and *adj.*, (vet.) gelding; gelded; emasculated. —, *cheval* —; gelding.

†**hongré**, *part.*, gelded, gelt.

†**hongrer**, *v.a.*, to geld (a horse—*un cheval*).

†**hongrois, -e**, *n.* and *adj.*, Hungarian.

†**hongrois**, *n.m.*, Hungarian language.

†**hongroyeur**, *n.m.*, tanner of Hungary-leather.

honnête, *adj.*, honest, upright, virtuous, becoming, seemly, decent, modest, decorous; handsome; genteel; suitable, proper, befitting; civil, kind, courteous, polite, moderate, reasonable. *Un* — *homme*; an honest man. *Une* — *femme*; a virtuous woman. — *garçon*; honest fellow. *Récompense* —; handsome reward. *Prétexte* —; fair pretence. *Prix* —; reasonable price. *Aisance, fortune,* —; decent competency. *Un homme* —; a civil man. *Cet habit est encore* —; this coat is still respectable (fit to be worn — *bon à porter*).

honnête, *n.m.*, honesty, probity.

honnêtement, *adv.*, honestly, uprightly, honourably, virtuously; becomingly, decently, modestly, decorously, handsomely, genteelly; suitably, properly, befittingly; civilly, kindly, courteously, politely, handsomely (liberally —*libéralement*); moderately, reasonably.

honnêteté (o-nêt-té), *n.f.*, honesty, probity, uprightness, integrity; modesty, decency; chasteness, chastity, virtue; propriety, fitness, sultableness, decorum; laudableness, praiseworthiness; respectability, decorum; politeness, courtesy, kindness. *Blesser les règles de l'—;* to offend against the rules of propriety. *Faire une — à quelqu'un;* to make any one an acknowledgment, a present; to be civil, courteous, polite, to any one.

honneur, *n.m.,* honour; credit; court-card, bonour (at cards—*aux cartes*). —*s;* regalia (crown jewels—*joyaux et attributs royaux*). *Affaire d'—;* affair of honour. *Chevalier d'—;* gentleman in waiting. *Croix d'—;* cross of the Legion of Honour. *Dame d'—;* lady of honour. lady in waiting. *Fille d'—;* maid of honour. *Demoiselle d'—;* bride's-maid. *Garçon d'—;* bride's-man, best man. *Membre de la Légion d'—;* member of the Legion of Honour. *Parole d'—;* word of honour. *Parole d'—; ma parole d'—;* upon my honour. *Partie d'—;* rubber (at cards —*aux cartes*); conquering game. *D'—;* honourable; honorary. *Non en homme d'—;* dishonourably; ungentlemanlike, ungentlemanly. *En —;* in honour, in request. *Sauf votre —;* saving your presence. *Être en —;* to be honoured; to be in favour, in request. *Faire — à;* to do credit to, to be an honour to; (com.) to honour, to meet (bills). *Faire — à ses affaires;* to meet one's engagements. *Faire à quelqu'un l'— de quelque chose;* to ascribe the honour of any thing to any one. *Faire les —s;* to do the honours. *Se faire — de quelque chose;* to consider, to esteem, anything an honour; to take a pride in anything; to be proud of anything; to take credit for anything. *Faire réparation d'—;* to make an apology. *Ne jouer que l'—, ne jouer que pour l'—;* to play for love. *Se piquer d'—;* to feel one's honour piqued. *Prendre tout au point d'—;* to be too nice, too delicate, on the point of honour. *En sortir à son —, en sortir avec —;* to come off with honour. *Tenir à — de;* to esteem it an honour to. *S'en tirer avec —;* to come off with honour. *D'—, sur mon —;* upon my honour. *Foi d'homme d'—;* as I am a man of honour. *À tout seigneur tout —;* give honour where it is due. *Vous me faites —;* you do me an honour. *Briguer les —s;* to seek for honours.

†**honni,** *part.,* dishonoured, disgraced. — *soit qui mal y pense;* evil be to him who evil thinks.

†**honnir.** *v.a.* to dishonour, to disgrace.

honorabilité. *n.f.,* honourableness.

honorable. *adj.,* honourable; respectable, creditable, reputable; proper, suitable.

honorablement. *adv.,* honourably; respectably, creditably; properly, suitably; nobly, sumptuously, splendidly.

honoraire. *adj.,* honorary, titular, titulary.

honoraire. *n.m.,* fee; salary. *Les —s d'un avocat;* a barrister's fee.

honorer. *v.a.,* to honour, to pay honour to; to do credit to, to be an honour to. *Honore ton père et ta mère;* honour thy father and mother. *Il honora l'assemblée de sa présence;* he honoured the assembly with his presence.

s'honorer. *v.r.,* to acquire honour; to do one's self honour; to think, to consider, to deem, to esteem it an honour; to pique one's self on, to take a pride in.

ad **honores** (-rès), *adv.,* (l.u.) honorary, ad honorem.

honorifique. *adj.,* honorific, honorary.

†**honte,** *n.f.,* shame; disgrace, reproach, scandal, infamy. *Mauvaise —;* bashfulness. *Sans —;* shameless, unblushing; shamelessly, unblushingly. *Avoir — de faire une mauvaise action;* to be ashamed of doing a bad action. *Rougir de —;* to blush for shame. *Faire — à quelqu'un;* to make one ashamed. *Il est la —*

de sa famille; he is the disgrace of his family. *Revenir avec sa courte —;* to return without success; to return affronted. *Avoir toute — bue;* to be lost to all shame, to all sense of shame, to all feeling of shame. *Perdre toute —;* to lose all shame, all sense of shame, all feeling of shame. *Regarder comme une —;* to look on, to hold, as a disgrace. *Que — ne vous fasse dommage* (prov.); don't be ashamed to do what is right.

†**honteusement** (-teûz-mān), *adv.,* shamefully, disgracefully, ignominiously, infamously, scandalously.

†**honteux, -se,** *adj.,* ashamed; bashful, shy; shameful, disgraceful, scandalous, disreputable, discreditable. *Il a l'air —;* he has a bashful look. *Pauvres —;* modest poor *Une conduite —se;* disgraceful conduct. *Les parties —ses;* the secret parts, pudenda. *Morceau —;* last piece in the dish (at table). *Il n'y que les — qui perdent;* a close mouth catches no flies. *Jamais — n'eut belle amie;* faint heart never won fair lady.

hôpital. *n.m.,* hospital; alms-house, poorhouse. — *ambulant;* field-hospital. *Vaisseau- — (-x-hôpitaux);* hospital-ship. *Aller à l'—;* to go to the workhouse; to go to the dogs. *Prendre le chemin de l'—;* to be on the highway to ruin; to go the way to the workhouse.

hoplite, *n.m.,* (antiq.) hoplite.

†**hoquet,** *n.m.,* hiccough, hiccup, hickup. — *de la mort;* death-rattle. *Avoir le —;* to have the hiccoughs, the hiccups. *Faire passer le —;* to stop the hiccoughs, the hiccups.

†**hoqueton** (hok-ton), *n.m.,* hoqueton (short coat or cassock—*casaque courte*); ☉ police-officer, policeman.

horaire. *adj.,* horary, horal.

†**horde,** *n.f.,* horde.

☉†**horion,** *n.m.,* (jest.) bang, thump, violent blow.

horizon, *n.m.,* horizon. *À l'—;* on the horizon. *Monter sur l'—* (astron.); to ascend.

horizontal. -e, *adj.,* horizontal.

horizontalement (-tal-mān), *adv.,* horizontally.

horloge. *n.f.,* clock; time-keeper; (nav.) glass. — *d'eau;* clepsydra. *Monter une —;* to wind up a clock. — *de sable;* hour-glass. — *qui marche huit jours;* eight-day clock.

horloger. *n.m.,* clockmaker, watchmaker.

horlogère, *n.f.,* clockmaker's wife, watchmaker's wife.

horlogerie (-lo-jrî), *n.f.,* watchmaking, clockmaking; clock-work; horology.

hormis, *prep.,* except, excepting, but, save, saving.

horographie, *n.f.,* horography.

horoscope, *n.m.,* horoscope. *Tirer l'— de quelqu'un;* to calculate any one's nativity.

horreur (or-reur), *n.f.,* horror, dread, detestation, abomination; awe; enormity; fright (very ugly person—*individu très laid*). *Être saisi d'—;* to be seized with horror. *J'ai — d'y penser;* I dread to think of it. *Une belle —;* an awful spectacle, sight. *Inspirer l'— du vice;* to inspire a horror for vice. *Il est en — à toute la terre;* he is abhorred by all the earth. *On m'a dit des —s de cet homme-là;* I have been told shocking things of that man.

horrible (or-ribl), *adj.,* horrible, horrid, hideous, frightful, shocking, dreadful, fearful. *Il fait un temps —;* it is shocking weather.

horriblement (or-ri-), *adv.,* horribly, horridly, shockingly, hideously, frightfully.

horripilation (or-ri-), *n.f.,* (med.) horripilation.

†**hors,** *prep.,* out; beyond; but, except, save. — *de saison;* out of season. — *de doute;* with

out question, · without doubt. — *de prix ;* extremely dear. — *de combat ;* disabled. *Je suis tout — de moi-même ;* I am quite beside myself. — *d'ici ;* away with you, out of my sight. — *cela, nous sommes d'accord ;* except that, we agree. — *d'œuvre ;* outside the subject ; digression.

thors-d'œuvre, *n.m.* (—), out-work · digression ; (cook.) side-dish.

hortensia, *n.m.,*(bot.)hortensia, hydrangea.

horticole, *adj.,* horticultural.

horticulteur, *n.m.,* horticulturist ; horticultor.

horticultural, -e, *adj.,* horticultural.

horticulture, *n.f.,* horticulture. *Exposition d' — ;* flower-show.

hosanna (o-za-n-na), *n.m.* (—s), Hosanna.

hospice, *n.m.,* hospital ; alms-house. — *des enfants trouvés ;* foundling hospital. — *des aliénés ;* lunatic asylum.

hospitali-er, -ère, *adj.,* hospitable.

hospitali-er, *n.m.,* **-ère,** *n.f.,* hospitaller.

hospitalièrement, *adv.,* hospitably.

hospitalité, *n.f.,* hospitality.

hospodar, *n.m,* hospodar.

hostie, *n.f.,* (Jewish antiq.) offering ; victim, sacrifice ; (c.rel.) host, consecrated wafer.

hostile, *adj.,* hostile, inimical, adverse.

hostilement (os-til-mān), *adv.,* hostilely, adversely.

hostilité, *n.f.,* hostility ; enmity.

hôte, *n.m.,* host ; landlord, innkeeper, publican ; guest ; lodger ; inhabitant. *Table d'—;* table d'hote, ordinary. *Qui compte sans son — compte deux fois ;* he who reckons without his host must reckon again.

hôtel, *n.m.,* mansion, large house ; hotel, inn. — *de ville ;* town-hall. — *des monnaies ;* mint. *L'— -Dieu ;* the principal hospital of a town. *Maître d'— ;* steward. *Descendre à l'— ;* to put up at an inn, at an hotel. *Être à l'— ;* to stay, to lodge, at an hotel, at an inn.

hôteli-er, *n.m.,* **-ère,** *n.f.,* innkeeper, host, hostess, landlord, landlady, of an inn.

hôtellerie(-tè-lrī),*n f.,* inn, hotel, hostelry.

hôtesse, *n.f.,* hostess ; landlady of an inn, guest, visitor ; lodger.

thotte, *n.f.,* dosser, basket (to carry things in upon one's back—*pour porter sur le dos*). — *de cheminée ;* basket funnel.

thottée, *n.f.,* basketful.

thottentot, *n.m.,* **-e,** *n.f.,* Hottentot.

thottereau, *or* † **hotteret,** *n.m.,* garden-basket.

hotteu-r, *n.m.,* **-se,** *n f.,* basket-carrier.

thouache, *or* **houaiche,** *n.f.,* *or* **ouaiche,** *n.m.,* (nav.) wake of a ship. *V.* **sillage**

theublon, *n.m.,* hop. — *sauvage ;* wild hop, hedge-hop. *Four à — ;* hop-kiln. *Perche à — ;* hop-pole.

theublonner, *v.a.,* to hop.

theublonnière, *n.f.,* hop-ground, hop-garden, hop-field, hop-yard.

theucre, *n.m.* *V.* **hourque.**

thoue, *n.f.,* (agri.) hoe.

thouer, *v.a.* and *n.,* to hoe, to dig.

***thouille,** *n f.,* pit-coal, coal, sea-coal. — *flambante ;* inflammable coal, open-burning coal. — *grasse ;* smith-coal. — *maigre ;* uninflammable coal, close-burning coal. — *schisteuse ;* slate-coal. — *sèche ;* glance-coal ; (min.) culm. — *de moyenne grosseur ;* cob-coal. *Bateau pour le transport de la — ;* coal-barge *Chargeur de — ;* coal-whipper. *Dépôt de — ;* coal-depot, coal-wharf. coal-store. *Mine de — ;* coal-mine, coal-pit. *Exploiter une mine de — ;* to work a coal-mine.

***thouill-er, -ère,** *adj.,* coal, coaly. *Terrains*

—s ; coal-fields. *Exploiter un terrain — ; to* work a coal-field. *Gisements —s ;* coal-measures.

***thouillère,** *n.f.,* coal-mine, coal-work, colliery. *Exploitant de — ;* coal-master. *Propriétaire de — ;* coal-owner, coal-proprietor.

***thouilleur,** *n.m.,* collier, coal-miner.

***thouilleu-x, -se,** *adj.,* containing coal, coaly.

thoulan,n.m., (—s). *V.* **uhlan.**

†**houle,** *n.f.,* (nav.) rolling wave, surge, swell (of the sea—*de la mer*) ; skillet, iron pot.

†**thoulette,** *n.f.,* crook, sheep-hook ; crosier ; trowel ; spatula.

†**thouleu-x, -se,** *adj.,* (nav.) swelling. *Mer —se ;* rolling sea.

†**thoulque,** *n.f. V.* **Houque.**

†**thoupi** (hoop), *int.,* (hunt.) holla!

†**thouper,** *v.a.,* (hunt.) to hoop ; to shout (to one's companion—*à un compagnon*).

*se***houper,** *v r.,* to shout to each other.

†**thouppe,** *n.f.,* tuft ; top-knot ; tassel. — *d poudrer ;* powder-puff.

†**thouppé, -e,** *adj.,* (bot.) tufted, crested.

†**thouppée,** *n.f.,* (nav.) swell (of a wave—*d'une vague*), surge.

†**thouppelande** (hoo-pland), *n f ,* big coat (great coat—*pardessus*).

†**thoupper,** *v.a.,* to tuft. — *de la laine ;* to tuft, to comb, wool.

†**thouque,** *n.f.,* (bot.) feather-grass.

†**thoura,** *int. V.* **hourra.**

†***thourailler,** *v.n.,* (hunt.) to hunt with bad hounds.

†***thouraillis,** *n.m.,* (hunt.) pack of good-for-nothing hounds.

†**thourdage,** *n.m.,* rough-walling, pugging.

†**thourder,***v.a.,* to rough-work, to rough-wall, to pug.

†**thourdi,** *n.m.,* (nav.) wing-transom.

†**thourdis,** *n.m. V.* **hourdage.**

†**thouret,** *n.m.,* (hunt.) bad hound.

†**thouri,** *n.f.,* houri.

†**thourque,** *n.f.,* (nav.) hooker.

†**thourra,** *n.m.* (—s), cry of the Cossacks marching to the enemy ; sudden and unexpected charge of irregulars, or light cavalry accompanied with shouts ; hurra, hurra.

†**thourvari,** *n.m.,* (hunt.) cry used by huntsmen to call back the dogs ; uproar.

†**thousard,** *n.m. V.* **hussard.**

†**housé,** *adj.,* booted ; dirty-booted.

†**houseaux,** *n.m, pl.,* leggings.

***thouspiller,** *v.a.,* to pull, to touse, to worry, to mob, to tug ; to abuse, to cut up.

***se* **thouspiller,** *v.r.,* to tug, to touse, to worry each other ; to wrangle.

⊙***houspillon,** *n.m.,* small quantity of wine or liquor poured into the glass as a final sip.

†**thoussage,** *n.m.,* dusting, sweeping (with a feather-broom—*avec un plumeau*).

†**thoussaie,** *n.f.,* holly-grove.

†**thoussard,** *n.m. V.* **hussard.**

†**thousse,** *n.f.,* housing. horse-cloth ; saddle-cloth, hammer-cloth ; cover (for a bed, chair, &c.—*de lit, de chaise, &c*).

†**thoussé, -e,** *adj.,* (her.) clothed (of a horse—*d'un cheval*).

†**thousser,** *v.a.,* to dust, to sweep (with a hair or feather-broom—*avec un plumeau*).

†**thoussine,** *n.f.,* switch.

†**thoussiner,** *v.a,* to switch ; to beat, to thrash.

†**thoussoir,** *n.m.,* whisk ; birch-broom ; feather-broom.

†**thousson,** *n.m.,* (bot.) knee-holly, butcher's-broom.

†**thoux,** *n.m.,* holly, holly-tree. — *frelon (—s), petit — ;* butcher's-broom.

†**thoyau,** *n.m.,* mattock ; pickaxe

⊙†**huaille,** *n.f.,* mob, populace.

†**huard**, *n.m.*, ospray, ospiey, sea-eagle.

†**hublot**, or **hulot**, *n.m.*, (nav.) small port-hole.

†**huche**, *n.f.*, kneading-trough; trough; bin-hopper (of a mill—*d'un moulin*).

†**hucher**, *v.a.*, (hunt.) to whistle.

†**hue!** *int.*, gee! gee ho! (carter's exclamation to go to the right-hand side—*cri de charretier pour faire aller les chevaux à droite*).

†**huée**, *n.f.*, shouting, shout; hooting.

†**huer**, *v.a.* and *n.*, to shout after, to hoot at; to hoot.

†**huette**, *n.f.* *V.* **hulotte**.

†**huguenot**, **-e** (hug-no, -t), *n.* and *adj.*, Huguenot.

†**huguenote**, *n.f.*, stove with a saucepan on it; pipkin. *Des œufs à la —;* eggs dressed with mutton gravy.

†**huguenotisme**, *n.m.*, (l.u.) Huguenotism.

†**huhau!** *int.*, gee! gee up! (carter's exclamation—*cri de charretier*). *V.* **hue**.

hui, *adv.*, (jur.) this day, to-day.

huilage, *n.m.*, oiling.

huile, *n.f.*, oil. — *douce;* sweet oil. — *rance;* rancid oil. — *de ricin;* castor-oil. — *de navette;* rape-oil. — *de lin;* linseed-oil. — *de baleine;* train-oil, whale-oil. — *comestible;* salad-oil. — *à brûler;* lamp-oil. — *de cotret;* stirrup oil (thrashing—*volée de coups de bâton*). — *de bras;* elbow grease (labour, pains —*travail*). *Cet ouvrage sent l'—;* that work smells of the lamp. *Jeter de l'—, sur, dans, le feu;* to add fuel to the flame. *Donner une bonne ration d'— de cotret à quelqu'un;* to give any one a good dose of stirrup oil. *Tache d'—;* stain of oil; (fig.) irremediable evil, lasting shame.

huiler, *v.a.*, to oil; to anoint with oil.

huilerie, *n.f.*, oil-manufactory, oil-shop.

huileu-x, **-se**, *adj.*, oily, greasy.

huilier, *n.m.*, cruet-stand.

huilière, *n.f.*, (nav.) oil-pitcher.

⊙**huis**, *n.m.*, door. *A — clos;* with closed doors, in private.

huisserie (ui-srî), *n.f.*, door-frame.

huissier, *n.m.*, usher; door-keeper; tip-staff, sheriff's officer, bailiff; gentleman-usher. — *audiencier;* crier of the court.

†**huit** (*huit*, before a vowel, a silent *h*, and at the end of the phrase; *hui* before a word beginning with a consonant, when *huit* qualifies it), *adj.*, eight; eighth. *Dans — jours, d'aujourd'hui en —;* this day week.

†**huit**, *n.m.*, eight; eighth. *Le — du mois;* the eighth day of the month.

†**huitain**, *n.m.*, stanza of eight verses.

†**huitaine**, *n.f.*, eight days. *Dans la —;* in the course of the week.

†**huitième** (hui-ti-èm), *adj.*, eighth.

†**huitième**, *n.m.*, eighth.

†**huitième**, *n.f.*, eighth class, eighth form (of public schools—*collèges*).

†**huitièmement**, *adv.*, eighthly.

huître, *n.f.*, oyster. — *marinée;* pickled oyster. — *à l'écaille;* oyster in the shell. *Cloyère d'—s;* basket of twenty-six dozen of oysters. *Frai d'—s;* oyster-brood. *Ouvrir une — ;* to open an oyster. *C'est une — à l'écaille;* he is a blockhead.

huitrier, *n.m.*, (orni.) oyster-catcher.

†**hulan**, *n.m.* (—s). *V.* **uhlan**.

†**hulotte**, *n.f.*, owlet.

humain, **-e**, *adj.*, human; humane. *Le genre — ;* mankind.

humain, *n.m.*, human being, man.

humainement, *adv.*, humanly; humanely.

humaniser, *v.a.*, to humanize, to civilize; to soften, to mollify.

s'**humaniser**, *v.r.*, to become humanized; to

comply with, to come down to the intellectual level of others.

humaniste, *n.m.*, humanist.

humanitaire, *adj.* and *n.m.*, friend of mankind.

humanité, *n.f.*, humanity; human nature; mankind; *pl.*, humanities.

humble, *adj.*, humble; lowly, meek. *Votre très humble serviteur;* your very humble servant.

humblement, *adv.*, humbly; meekly. *Demander — pardon;* to humbly beg pardon.

humectant, **-e**, *adj.*, refreshing, moistening, emollient.

humectant, *n.m.*, food, drink that moistens, refreshes; (med.) emollient.

humectation, *n.f.*, moistening, wetting.

humecter, *v.a.*, to wet, to moisten, to damp.

s'**humecter**, *v.r.*, to be moistened; to refresh one's self. — *le gosier;* to wet one's whistle (to drink—*boire*).

†**humer**, *v.a.*, to inhale, to suck in. — *l'air;* to inhale the air.

huméral, **-e**, *adj.*, (anat.) humeral.

humérus (-rús), *n.m.*, (anat.) humerus.

humeur, *n.f.*, humour; temper, disposition, turn of mind, mood, caprice, fancy, whim; ill-humour. —*s froides;* king's evil, scrofula. *Elle a l'— gaie;* she is of a cheerful disposition. *Être d'— à faire quelque chose;* to be disposed to do anything. *Être de bonne —;* to be in a good humour. *Être de mauvaise —;* to be out of temper. *Avoir de l'—;* to be out of temper. *Avec —;* peevishly, crossly.

humide, *n.* and *adj.*, moisture, humidity; humid, watery; damp, wet, moist, liquid.

humidement (u-mid-màn), *adv.*, (l.u.) in a damp house.

humidité, *n.f.*, humidity, humidness, dampness, moisture, wateriness, wetness.

humiliant, **-e**, *adj.*, humiliating.

humiliation, *n.f.*, humiliation, abasement.

humilier, *v.a.*, to humble, to humiliate, to take down, to bring down. *Dieu humilie les superbes;* God humbleth the proud.

s'**humilier**, *v.r.*, to humble, to abase, one's self.

humilité, *n.f.*, humility, humbleness, meekness, lowliness.

humoral, **-e**, *adj.*, (med.) humoral.

humorisme, *n.m.*, (med.) humoralism.

humoriste, *adj.*, peevish, ill-tempered; humoristic.

humoriste, *n.m.*, ill-tempered, peevish, person; humorist; (med.) humoralist.

humoristique, *adj.*, humoristic.

humus (u-mús), *n.m.*, soil.

†**hun**, *n.m.*, Hun.

†**hune**, *n.f.*, (nav.) top. *La grande —;* the main-top. *La — de misaine;* the fore-top. *La — d'artimon;* the mizzen-top.

†**hunier**, *n.m.*, top-sail. *Le grand —;* the main-top sail. *Le petit —;* the fore-top-sail.

†**huppe**, *n.f.*, (orni.) pewet; tuft, top-knot (of a bird—*d'oiseau*).

†**huppé**, **-e**, *adj.*, tufted, crested (of birds—*des oiseaux*); (fam.) high in station, well off. *Les plus —s y sont pris* (prov.); the most skilful may be deceived.

•**thure**, *n.f.*, head (of a wild boar, of certain fish—*du sanglier, de quelques poissons*). — *de saumon;* jowl of a salmon. *Vilaine —;* ragged head of hair.

†**hurhau!** *int.*, gee! gee ho! (carter's exclamation—*cri de charretier*). *V.* **hue**.

†**hurlement**, *n.m.*, howl, howling, roar; yell, yelling, shriek.

†**hurler**, *v.n.*, to howl, to yell; to roar, to bellow. *Il faut hurler avec les loups,* you must do as those with whom you are.

†**hurleur**, *n.m.*, howler.

Ⓞ**thurluberlu**, *adv.*, (jest.) inconsiderately.

†**thurluberlu**, *n.m.*, (jest.) giddy goose, hare-brained person.

†**hussard**, *n.m.*, hussar.

à la †**hussarde**, *adv.*, like hussars; by rapine, by pillage.

†**hutte**, *n.f.*, hut, cottage.

se†**hutter**, *v.r.*, to make a hut, to lodge in a hut.

   hyacinthe, *n.f.*, (bot., min.) hyacinth. *V.* **jacinthe**.

   hyades, *n.f.*, (astron.) Hyades.

   hyalin, -e, *adj.*, hyaline.

   hyalode, *adj.*, of the colour of glass.

   hybride, *n.* and *adj.*, hybrid, mongrel.

   hydatisme, *n.m.*, (med.) the noise produced by the fluctuation of the liquid in an abscess.

   hydr, hydro, prefix from Greek ὕδωρ.

   hydragogue (-gog), *n.m.*, (med.) hydragogue.

   hydrate, *n.m.*, (chem.) hydrate.

   hydraté, *adj.*, (chem.) hydrated.

   hydraulique, *n.f.* and *adj.*, hydraulics; hydraulic. *Bélier* — (phys.); water-ram. *Ouvrages* —*s;* water-works. *Puissance* —; water-power.

   hydre, *n.f.*, hydra.

   hydrocèle, *n.f.*, hydrocele.

   hydrocéphale, *n.f.*, hydrocephalus.

   hydrochlorate, *n.m.*, (chem.) hydrochlorate.

   hydrochlorique, *adj.*, (chem.) hydrochloric.

   hydrocotyle, *n.f.*, (bot.) hydrocotyle.

   hydrodynamique, *n.f.* and *adj.*, hydrodynamics; hydrodynamic.

   hydrogène, *n.m.*, (chem.) hydrogen.

   hydrogéné, -e, *adj.*, (chem.) hydrogenated, combined with hydrogen.

   hydrogéner, *v.a.*, to hydrogenize.

   hydrographe, *n.m.*, hydrographer.

   hydrographie, *n.f.*, hydrography.

   hydrographique, *adj.*, hydrographical.

   hydrolithe, *n.f.*, hydrolite.

   hydrologie, *n.f.*, hydrology.

   hydromancie, *n.f.*, hydromancy.

   hydromel, *n.m.*, hydromel. — *vineux;* metheglin.

   hydromètre, *n.m.*, hydrometer.

   hydrométrie, *n.f.*, hydrometry.

   hydrométrique, *adj.*, hydrometrical.

   hydrophane, *n.f.*, (min.) hydrophane.

   hydrophobe, *n.m.f.* and *adj.*, person affected with hydrophobia; hydrophobic.

   hydrophobie, *n.f.*, hydrophobia.

   hydropique, *n.m.f.* and *adj.*, person affected with dropsy; dropsical.

   hydropisie, *n.f.*, dropsy

   hydropneumatique, *adj.*, hydropneumatic.

   hydroscope, *n.m.*, one whose trade is to look for sources and springs.

   hydroscopie, *n.f.*, the art of looking for springs, sources.

   hydrostatique, *n.f.* and *adj.*, hydrostatics; hydrostatical.

   hydrosulfate, *or* **hydrosulfure**, *n.m.*, (chem.) hydrosulphate, hydrosulphuret.

   hydrosulfurique, *adj.*, hydrosulphuric. *Acide* —; hydrosulphuric acid.

   hydrothérapie, *n.f.*, (med.) hydropathy.

   hydrothérapique, *adj.*, hydropathic.

   hydrothorax (-raks), *n.m.*, hydrothorax.

   hydrotique, *adj.*, hydrotic.

   hydrure, *n.m.*, (chem.) hydruret.

   hyémal, -e, *adj.* *V.* **hiémal**.

   hyémation, *n.f.*, hyemation.

   hyène, *n.f.*, hyena.

   hygiène, *n.f.*, hygiene.

   hygiénique, *adj.*, hygienic.

   hygrologie, *n.f.*, (med.) hygrology.

---

   hygromètre, *n.m.*, hygrometer.

   hygrométrie, *n.f.*, hygrometry.

   hygrométrique, *adj.*, hygrometrical.

   hymen (i-mèn), *or* **hyménée**, *n.m.*, Hymen; marriage, wedlock. *Le flambeau de l'* —; the torch of Hymen.

   hymen, *n.m.*, (anat.) hymen.

   hyménoptère, *n.m.* and *adj.*, hymenopter; hymenopteral.

   hymne, *n.m.*, hymn (in honour of God, of a hero—*en l'honneur de Dieu, d'un héros*).

   hymne, *n.f.*, hymn (sung in churches—*d'église*). *Recueil d'* —*s;* hymn-book.

   hyoïde, *n.m.* and *adj.*, (anat.) hyoid bone, tongue-bone; hyoid.

   hypallage, *n.f.*, (gram.) hypallage.

   hyperbate, *n.f.*, (gram.) hyperbaton.

   hyperbole, *n.f.*, (rhet.) hyperbole; (math.) hyperbola.

   hyberbolique, *adj.*, hyperbolic; hyperbolical.

   hyperboliquement (-lik-mān), *adv.*, hyperbolically.

   hyperborée, *or* **hyperboréen, -ne** (-in, èn), *adj.*, hyperborean.

   hyperboréens, *n.m. pl.*, (Grec. antiq.) Hyperboreans.

   hypercatalectique, *adj.*, hypercatalectic.

   hypercritique, *n.m.*, hypercritic.

   hyperdulie, *n.f.*, hyperdulia (worship of the Virgin Mary—*culte de la sainte Vierge*).

   hypertrophie, *n.f.*, (med.) hypertrophy. — *du cœur;* hypertrophy of the heart.

   hypertrophié, *adj.*, in a state of hypertrophy, enlarged.

   hypèthre, *n.f.*, (arch.) hypethral.

   hypnotique, *adj.*, (med.) hypnotic.

   hypocondre, *n.m.*, (anat.) hypochondria.

   hypocondriaque, *or* **hypocondre**, *n.m.f.* and *adj.*, (med.) hypochondriac, hypochondriacal.

   hypocondrie, *n.f.*, hypochondriasis.

   hypocras, *n.m.*, hippocras.

   hypocrisie, *n.f.*, hypocrisy. *Avec* —; hypocritically.

   hypocrite, *n.m.f.* and *adj.*, hypocrite; hypocritical.

   hypocritement, *adv.*, hypocritically.

   hypogastre, *n.m.*, (anat.) hypogastrium.

   hypogastrique, *adj.*, hypogastric.

   hypogée, *n.m.*, (arch.) hypogeum.

   hypoglosse, *n.m.* and *adj.*, (anat.) hypoglossal nerves; hypoglossal, under the tongue.

   hypoglottide, *n.f.*, (pharm.) a lozenge.

   hypophylle, *adj.*, (bot.) hypophyllous.

   hypopyon, *n.m.*, hypopium.

   hypostase, *n.f.*, (theol.) hypostasis.

   hypostatique, *adj.*, (theol.) hypostatical.

   hypostatiquement (-tik-mān), *adv.*, hypostatically.

   hypostyle, *adj.*, (antiq.) of a building, the ceiling of which is supported by columns.

   hypoténuse, *n.f.* (geom.) hypotenuse.

   hypothécaire, *adj.*, on mortgage. *Créancier* —; mortgagee.

   hypothécairement (-kèr-mān), *adv.*, by mortgage.

   hypothèque, *n.f.*, mortgage. *Créancier sur* —; mortgagee. *Débiteur sur* —; mortgager. *Donner en* —; to give as a mortgage. *Éteindre, purger, une* —; to pay off a mortgage. *Il est bien hypothéqué;* he is very inform.

   hypothéquer, *v.a.*, to mortgage. *Il est bien hypothéqué;* he is very inform.

   hypothèse, *n.f.*, hypothesis, supposition. *Par* —; by supposition.

   hypothétique, *adj.*, hypothetical.

   hypothétiquement (-tik-mān), *adv.*, hypothetically.

   hypotypose, *n.f.*, (rhet.) hypotyposis.

hypsomètre, *n.m.*, an instrument indicating the altitude of a place by the temperature at which water begins to boil in such a place.

hypsométrie, *n.f.*, altimetry, hypsometry.

hysope, *n.f.*, (bot.) hyssop.

hystérie, *n.f.*, hysteria, hysterics.

hystérique, *adj.*, hysteric, hysterical.

hystérite, *n.f.*, (med.) hysteritis.

hystérocèle, *n.f.*, (med.) hysterocele.

hystérologie, *n.f.*, (rhet.) hysterology, hysteron-proteron.

hystérotome, *n.m.*, (surg.) an instrument to perform hysterotomy.

hystérotomie, *n.f.*, (surg.) hysterotomy.

I

i, *n.m.*, the ninth letter of the alphabet, i. *Il met les points sur les —* ; he is scrupulously exact ; he is very finicking.

iambe, *n.m.*, (poet.) iambus.

iambique, *adj.*, iambic.

ibid, ab. of ibidem.

ibidem (-dèm), *adv.*, ibidem, the same.

ibis (i-bis), *n.m.*, (orni.) ibis.

⊙**icel-ui**, *m.*, -le, *f.*, *pron.*, (jur.) this ; that.

ichneumon, *n.m.*, (mam., ent.) ichneumon ; ichneumon-fly.

ichnographie (ik-no-), *n.f.*, ichnography ; ground-plan.

ichnographique, *adj.*, ichnographic.

ichor (i-kor), *n.m.*, (med.) ichor.

ichoreu-x. **-se**, *adj.*, (med.) ichorous.

ichtyocolle (ik-ti-), *n.f.*, isinglass, fish-glue.

ichtyographie, *n.f.*, ichthyography.

ichtyographique, *adj.*, ichthyographic.

ichtyolithe, *n.m.*, ichthyolite.

ichtyologie, *n.f.*, ichthyology.

ichtyologique, *adj.*, ichthyological.

ichtyologiste, *n.m.*, ichthyologist.

ichtyophage, *n.m.f.* and *adj.*, ichthyophagist ; ichthyophagous.

ichtyosaure, *n.m.*, (geol.) ichthyosaurus.

ici, *adv.*, here, hither, in this place ; now. *Il a passé par —* ; he passed this way. *Venez —* ; come here. *D'—* ; hence. *D'— là* ; from here to there ; between this and then. *— près* ; hard by. *Par —* ; through here, this way. *— bas* ; here below. *Jusqu'—* ; till now, up to this time, hitherto ; down to here.

icoglan, *n.m.*, page of the Sultan.

iconoclaste, *n.m.*, iconoclast.

iconographe, *n m.*, iconographer.

iconographie, *n.f.*, iconography.

iconographique, *adj.*, iconographical.

iconolâtre, *n.m.*, iconolater.

iconolâtrie, *n.f.*, iconolatry, image-worship.

iconologie. *n.f.*, iconology.

iconomaque, *n.m.*, one opposed to the worship of images.

iconostase. *n.f.*, large screen with three doors, separating the altar from the nave in Greek churches.

icosaèdre. *n.m.*, (geom.) icosahedron.

icosandre, *adj.*, icosandrous.

icosandrie, *n.f.*, (bot.) icosandria.

ictère. *n.m.*, (med.) icterus, jaundice.

ictérique, *adj.*, icteric, icterical.

id, ab. of idem.

ide, *n.m.*, (piquet) name of each of the two tricks played to decide a bet.

idéal. **-e**. *adj.*, ideal.

idéal. *n.m.*, ideal. *Le beau —* ; the beau-ideal.

idéaliser, *v.a.*, to idealize, to form ideas.

idéalisme. *n.m.*, idealism.

idéaliste, *n.m.*, idealist.

idée, *n.f.*, idea, notion, perception ; conceit, fancy ; sketch, outline ; mind, head ; thought ; taste ; just a taste. *Selon nos —s* ; according to our notions. *En —* ; in imagination, ideally. *Il me vient à l'—* ; it occurs to me. *Avoir une —* : to have an idea. *N'avoir pas d'— de* ; to have no notion of. *Se faire une —* ; to form an idea. *Il me revient en —, à l'—, que . . ;* it recurs to me that. *Changer d'—* ; to alter one's mind. *Se mettre dans l'—* ; to take it into one's head. *Ôter une chose de l'— de quelqu'un ;* to get a thing out of any one's head. *Donner une — d'ail à quelque chose ;* to give any thing just a taste of garlic. *On ne peut lui ôter cela de l'—* ; one cannot get that out of his head. *Il me vient une —* ; an idea strikes me. *Perdre l'— de* ; to lose all recollection of. *— creuse ;* empty notion. *— fixe ;* fixed idea. *— plaisante ;* odd conceit.

idem (i-dèm), *adv.*, idem, ditto.

identification, *n.f.*, identification.

identifier, *v.a.*, to identify.

s'identifier. *v.r.*, to identify one's self. to become identified ; to identify.

identique, *adj.*, identical, the same.

identiquement (-tik-màn), *adv.*, identically.

identité, *n.f.*, identity, sameness.

idéographie, *n.f.*, ideography.

idéographique, *adj.*, ideographic.

idéologie, *n.f.*, ideology.

idéologique, *adj.*, ideological.

idéologue, *n.m.*, ideologist.

ides (id), *n.f.pl.*, (antiq.) ides.

⊙**idiocrase**, *n.f.* V. **idiosyncrasie**.

idio-électrique, *adj.*, idio-electric.

idiogyne, *adj.*, (bot.) having the stamina separated from the pistil.

idiomatique, *adj.*, idiomatic.

idiome, *n.m.*, idiom, dialect, language.

idiopathie, *n.f.*, (med.) idiopathy ; (philos.) inclination.

idiopathique, *adj.*, idiopathic.

idiosyncrasie, *n.f.*, idiosyncrasy, idiocrasy, peculiarity of constitution.

idiot, **-e**, *n.* and *adj.*, idiot, natural fool ; fool ; idiotic, foolish.

idiotie (-ci), *n.f.*, (med.) idiocy, idiotcy, imbecility.

idiotisme, *n.m.*, (gram.) idiom, idiotism ; (med.) idiocy, idiotcy.

⊙**idoine**, *adj.*, fit, proper.

idolâtre, *n.m.f.* and *adj.*, idolater ; idolatrous. *Elle est — de ses enfants ;* she dotes on her children.

idolâtrer, *v.n.*, to worship idols.

idolâtrer. *v.a.*, to idolize, to be extremely fond of, to dote upon. *Il idolâtre cette femme ;* he idolizes that woman.

idolâtrie, *n.f.*, idolatry. *Il l'aime à l'—* ; he loves her to idolatry ; he idolizes her.

idolâtrique, *adj.*, idolatrous.

idole, *n.f.*, idol. *C'est une vraie —* ; she is nothing but a wax-doll ; she is a perfect block-head. *Il se tient là comme une —* ; he stands there like a statue. *Faire son — de* ; to idolize.

idylle, *n.f.*, idyl.

if, *n.m.*, yew, yew-tree ; triangular stand for illumination lamps.

*****igname**, *n.f.*, Indian potato ; yam.

*****ignare**, *n.m.* and *adj.*, dunce, ignoramus ; illiterate, ignorant.

igné, **-e** (ig-né), *adj.*, igneous.

ignicole (ig-ni-), *n.m.* and *adj.*, ignicolist, fire-worshipping.

ignition (ig-ni-), *n.f.*, ignition.

ignivore (ig-ni), *adj.*, ignivorous.
*ignobilité, *n.f.*, ignobleness, baseness, vileness.
*ignoble, *adj.*, ignoble, vile.
*ignoblement, *adv.*, ignobly, vilely.
*ignominie, *n.f.*, ignominy.
*ignominieusement(-eûz-mān),*adv.*,ignominiously.
*ignominieu-x, -se, *adj.*, ignominious.
*ignoramment (-ra-mān), *adv.*, ignorantly, unknowingly.
*ignorance, *n.f.*, ignorance; error, mistake, blunder. — *crasse*; sordid ignorance. *Par* —; from ignorance. *Être dans l'* — *de*; to be ignorant of. *Prétendre cause d'* —; to plead ignorance.
*ignorant, -e, *n.* and *adj.*, ignoramus, ignorant person; ignorant, illiterate, unlearned; unacquainted with.
*ignorantin, *n.m.* and *adj.*, ignorant. —*s;* *frères* —*s;* lay-brothers devoted to the elementary instruction of the poor.
*ignorantissime, *adj.*, most ignorant, profoundly ignorant.
*ignoré, -e, *part.*, unknown.
*ignorer, *v.a.*, to be ignorant of, not to know, to be unacquainted with. *J'ignore l'art de* *flatter;* I am a stranger to the art of flattery. *S'ignorais qu'il fût arrivé;* I was ignorant of his having arrived.
*s'ignorer, *v.r.*, not to know one's self; to be ignorant of one's own capabilities.
iguane, *n.m.*, (zool.) iguana.
il, *pron.m.*, he; it, there; *pl.*, ils, they. — *me parle;* he speaks to me. — *fait froid;* it is cold. — *y a des gens;* there are persons. — *s'éleva un murmure;* there arose a murmur.
île, *n.f.*, island, isle. —*s sous le vent;* Leeward Islands. —*s du vent;* Windward Islands.
iléon, *n m.*, (anat.) ileum.
iles, *n.m. pl.*, (anat.) the lower sides of the abdomen, the flanks. *Os des* —; os ilium, hip, haunch-bone.
iléum, *n.m.* *V.* iléon.
iléus (-ûs), *n.m.*, (med.) ileus; iliac passion.
iliade. *n.f.*, Iliad.
iliaque, *adj.*, (anat.) iliac.
ilion, or ilium, *n.m.*; (anat.) coxa, haunchbone.
illégal, -e (il-lé), *adj.*, illegal, unlawful.
illégalement(il-lé-gal-mān),*adv.*, illegally, unlawfully.
illégalité (il-lé-), *n.f.*, illegality, unlawfulness.
illégitime (il-lé-), *adj.*, illegitimate; unlawful, unjust; spurious.
illégitimement(il-lé-),*adv.*, illegitimately, uniawfully.
illégitimité (il-lé-), *n.f.*, illegitimacy, unlawfulness, spuriousness.
illettré, -e (il-lè-),*adj.*, illiterate,unlettered.
illibéral, -e (il-li-), *adj.*, illiberal; mean; mechanical, of artisans, mechanics.
illibéralement (il-li-), *adv.*, illiberally; meanly.
illibéralité, *n.f.*, illiberality, meanness.
illicite (il-li-), *adj.*, illicit, unlawful.
illicitement (il-li-cit-mān), *adv.*, illicitly, unlawfully.
illimitable (il-li-), *adj.*, illimitable.
illimité, -e (il-li-), *adj.*, unlimited, unbounded, boundless.
illisible (il-li-), *adj.*, illegible.
illisiblement (il-li-), *adv.*, illegibly.
illogicité (il-lo-), *n.f.*, illogicalness.
illogique (il-lo-), *adj.*, illogical.
illogiquement (il-lo-jik-mān), *adv.*, illogically.
illuminateur (il-lu-), *n m.*, illuminator.

illuminati-f, -ve(il-lu-),*adj.*, illuminative.
illumination (il-lu-), *n.f.*, illumination.
illuminé, -e (il-lu-), *adj.*, illuminated, enlightened.
illuminé, *n.m.*, -e, *n.f.*, illuminee.
illuminer (il-lu-), *v.a.*, to illuminate; to illumine; to illume; to enlighten the mind.
illuminisme (il-lu-), *n.m.*, illuminism.
illusion (il-lu-), *n.f.*, illusion, self-deception, self-delusion, delusion. *Faire* — *à quelqu'un;* to appear to somebody different from what one actually is. *Se faire* — *à soi-même;* to deceive one's self.
illusoire (il-lu-), *adj.*, illusive, illusory, delusive.
illusoirement (il-lu-zoar-mān), *adv.*, illusively, fallaciously.
illustration (il-lus-), *n.f.*, illustration, illustriousness; illumination; explanation.
illustre (il-lu-), *adj.*, illustrious, eminent.
illustre, *n.m.*, illustrious man, worthy.
illustrer (il-lu-), *v.a.*, to illustrate; to render illustrious; to illuminate.
s'illustrer,*v.r.*, to render one's self illustrious
illustrissime (il-lu-), *adj.*, most illustrious.
îlot, *n.m.*, islet.
ilote, *n.m.*, helot.
ilotisme, *n.m.*, helotism.
image, *n.f.*, image, likeness, resemblance; picture. *Cet enfant est l'* — *de son père;* this child is the very image of his father.
imag-er, *n.m.*, -ère, *n.f.*, image-vendor.
imagerie (i-ma-jri). *n.f.*, image-trade; picture-trade.
imaginable, *adj.*, imaginable
imaginaire. *adj.*, imaginary, visionary; (math.) imaginary, impossible. *Espaces* —*s;* imaginary realms.
imaginati-f, -ve, *adj.*, imaginative.
imagination.*n f.*, imagination, conception, fancy, conceit; thought.
imaginative, *n.f.*, imagination, fancy, imaginative faculty.
imaginer,*v.a.*, to imagine, to conceive, to contrive.
s'imaginer, *v.r.*, to imagine one's self, to imagine, to think, to fancy, to believe. *Imaginez-vous;* fancy.
iman, *n m.*, iman (Mohammedan priest).
imaret, *n.m.*, a sort of inn and hospital for the poor in Turkey.
imbécile,*adj.*,imbecile, foolish, silly, simple.
imbécile. *n.m.f.*, idiot, fool, simpleton.
imbécilement (-sil-mān), *adv.*, foolishly, stupidly.
imbécillité, *n.f.*, imbecility, idiotcy, stupidity, foolishness.
imberbe, *adj.*, beardless.
imbiber, *v.a.*, to imbibe, imbue; to soak; to steep.
s'imbiber, *v.r.*, to imbibe, to soak.
imbibition, *n.f.*, imbibition.
imbrication, *n.f.*, imbrication.
⊙imbricée, *adj.* *V.* imbriqué.
imbrim (in-bri-m), *n.m.*, (orni.) loon
imbriqué, -e, *adj.*, (bot.) imbricated.
*imbroglio (-bro-lio), *n.m.* (—*s*), imbroglio, confusion, intricacy, perplexity.
imbu, -e,*adj.*, imbued, impressed, tinctured.
imbuvable, *adj.*, undrinkable.
imitable, *adj.*, imitable.
imitat-eur, -rice, *adj.*, imitative.
imitat-eur. *n.m.*, -rice, *n.f.*, imitator.
imitati-f, -ve, *adj.*, imitative *Les arts* – *s;* the imitative arts.
imitation, *n.f.*, imitation. *À l'* — *de;* in imitation of.
imiter. *v.a.*, to imitate, to copy, to mimic, to take off.

immaculé. -e (im-ma-), *adj.*, immaculate, spotless.

immanent. -e (im-ma-), *adj.*, immanent.

immangeable (im-man-jabl), *adj.*, uneatable.

immanquable (im-man-), *adj.*, infallible, certain.

immanquablement (im-man-), *adv.*, infallibly, certainly, without fail.

immarcescible (im-mar-), *adj.*, immarcescible, unfading.

immatérialisme (im-ma-), *n.m.*, immaterialism.

immatérialiste (im-ma-), *n.m.*, immaterialist.

immatérialité (im-ma-), *n.f.*, immateriality, immaterialness. *L'— de l'âme ;* the immateriality of the soul.

immatériel, -le (im-ma-), *adj.*, immaterial, incorporeal.

immatériellement (im-ma-té-ri-èl-män), *adv.*, immaterially, incorporeally.

immatriculation (im-ma-), *n.f.*, matriculation.

immatricule (im-ma-), *n.f.*, (jur.) matriculation; registering.

immatriculer (im-ma-), *v.a.*, to matriculate. *Se faire —;* to get one's name entered.

immédiat, -e (im-mé-), *adj.*, immediate.

immédiatement (im-mé-diat-män), *adv.*, immediately; directly.

⊙**immémorant, -e** (im-mé-), *adj.*, unmindful, forgetful.

immémorial, -e (im-mé-), *adj.*, immemorial.

immémorialement (im-mé-), *adv.*, immemorially.

immense (im-mäns), *adj.*, immense, infinite, boundless.

immensément (im-män-), *adv.*, immensely.

immensité (im-män-), *n.f.*, immensity, infiniteness.

immensurable (im-män-), *adj.*, immensurable.

immerger (im-mèr-), *v.a.*, to immerge, to immerse.

immérité, -e (im-mé-), *adj.*, undeserved, unmerited.

immersi-f, -ve (im-mèr-), *adj.*, by immersion.

immersion (im-mèr-), *n.f.*, immersion.

immeuble (im-meu-bl), *adj.*, (jur.) real (of estate—*des biens*).

immeuble, *n.m.*, estate, real estate; fixture.

immigrant (im-mi-), *n.m.*, **-e**, *n.f.*, immigrant.

immigration (im-mi-), *n.f.*, immigration.

immigrer (im-mi-), *v.n.*, to immigrate.

imminence (im-mi-), *n.f.*, imminence, impendency.

imminent, -e (im-mi-), *adj.*, imminent, impending. *Péril —;* imminent danger.

s'immiscer (si-mi-sé), *v.r.*, to interfere, to take upon one's self; to meddle with; to enter upon. *— dans les affaires des autres;* to meddle with other people's business.

immiscibilité (im-mis-), *n.f.*, immiscibility.

immiscible (im-mis-), *adj.*, immiscible.

immission (im-mi-), *n.f.*, immission.

immixtion (im-miks-tion), *n.f.*, blending; (jur.) entering on possession; unasked, unwarrantable interference.

immobile (im-mo-), *adj.*, immovable, motionless.

immobilement, *adv.*, immovably.

immobili-er, -ère (im-mo-), *adj.*, real (of estate—*des biens*).

⊙**immobilier**, *n.m.*, landed property.

immobilisation (im-mo-), *n.f.*, (jur.) the conversion of personal property into real estate.

immobiliser (im-mo-), *v.a.*, to convert personal property into real estate.

immobilité (im-mo-), *n.f.*, immobility, immovability.

immodération, *n.f.*, immoderation.

immodéré, -e (im-mo-), *adj.*, immoderate, intemperate.

immodérément (im-mo-), *adv.*, immoderately, intemperately.

immodeste (im-mo-), *adj.*, immodest, indecent.

immodestement (im-mo-), *adv.*, immodestly, indecently.

immodestie (im-mo-dès-ti), *n.f.*, immodesty, indecency.

immolateur (im-mo-), *n.m.*, immolator, sacrificer.

immolation (im-mo-), *n.f.*, immolation, sacrificing.

immoler (im-mo-lé), *v.a.*, to immolate, to sacrifice, to slay ; to laugh at, to ridicule.

s'immoler, *v.r.*, to immolate, to sacrifice, one's self ; to sacrifice one's feelings; to stand ridicule. *— pour sa patrie;* to sacrifice one's self for one's own country. *Il s'est immolé de bonne grâce;* he stood the joke very well.

immonde (im-mond), *adj.*, unclean, impure.

immondice (im-mon-), *n.f.*, filth, dirt; (Bibl.) uncleanliness, impurity.

immondicité (im-mon-), *n.f.*, (Bibl.) uncleanness.

immoral. -e (im-mo-), *adj.*, immoral.

immoralité (im-mo-), *n.f.*, immorality.

immortaliser (im-mor-), *v.a.*, to immortalize.

s'immortaliser, *v.r.*, to immortalize one's self.

immortalité (im-mor-), *n.f.*, immortality.

immortel, -le (im-mor-), *adj.*, immortal, everlasting.

immortel, *n.m.*, **-le**, *n.f.*, immortal

immortelle, *n.f.*, (bot.) everlasting, American cudweed.

immortellement, *adv.*, immortally.

immortification (im-mor-), *n.f.*, (theol.) immortification.

immortifié, -e (im-mor-), *adj.*, unmortified.

immuable (im-mu-), *adj.*, immutable, unalterable, unchangeable. *Dieu seul est —;* God alone is immutable.

immuablement (im-mu-), *adv.*, immutably, unalterably, unchangeably.

immunité (im-mu-), *n.f.*, immunity, unchangeableness.

immutabilité (im-mu-), *n.f.*, immutability, unchangeableness.

⊙**immutable** (im-mu-). *V.* **immuable**.

impair, -e, *adj.*, odd, uneven.

impairement (in-pèr-män), *adv.*, (math.) unevenly.

impalpabilité, *n.f.*, impalpability.

impalpable, *adj.*, impalpable.

impanation *n.f.*, (theol.) impanation.

impardonnable, *adj.*, unpardonable.

imparfait, -e, *adj.*, imperfect, unfinished, incomplete.

imparfait, *n.m.*, (gram.) imperfect, imperfect tense.

imparfaitement (-fèt-män), *adv.*, imperfectly.

imparisyllabique, *adj.*, (gram.) imparasyllabic.

imparité *n.f.*, inequality, imparity.

impartageable (-jabl), *adj.*, indivisible.

impartial, -e. *adj.*, impartial. *Historien —;* impartial historian.

impartialement (-sial-män). *adv.*, impartially.

impartialité, *n.f.*, impartiality.

impartibilité, *n.f.*, (feudal law—*loi féodale*) impartibility.

impartible, *adj.*, impartible.

impasse, *n.f.*, land without egress; blind alley; inextricable difficulty, dead-lock.

impassibilité, *n.f.*, impassibility, impassibleness, undisturbedness.

impassible, *adj.*, impassible, impassive, undisturbed, unmoved.

impassiblement, *adv.*, impassively, undisturbedly.

impastation, *n.f.*, (mas.) impastation.

impatiemment (-sia-mān), *adv.*, impatiently, eagerly.

impatience, *n.f.*, impatience; restlessness, eagerness. *L'— dans les douleurs;* impatience under sufferings. *Donner des —s;* to put out of all patience. *Être dans l'— de faire une chose;* to be impatient to do a thing.

impatient, -e, *adj.*, impatient; anxious, restless, eager. *— de briser ses fers;* impatient to shake off one's fetters.

impatientant, -e, *adj.*, provoking, vexing.

impatienter, *v.a.*, to make impatient, to tire one's patience, to put out of patience; to provoke.

s'impatienter, *v.r.*, to lose one's patience, to become impatient.

s'impatroniser, *v.r.*, (b.s.) to become master (of a house, of a family—*d'une maison, d'une famille*).

impayable, *adj.*, invaluable, admirable, worth any money; inimitable, funny, extraordinary.

impayé, -e, *adj.*, unpaid.

impeccabilité (in-pèk-ka-), *n.f.*, impeccability.

impeccable, *adj.*, impeccable.

impénétrabilité, *n.f.*, impenetrability, imperviousness.

impénétrable, *adj.*, impenetrable, impervious; unfathomable, inscrutable. *Un homme —;* a very close man.

impénétrablement, *adv.*, impenetrably.

impénitence, *n.f.*, impenitence. *Mourir dans l'—;* to die impenitent.

impénitent, -e, *n.* and *adj.*, impenitent.

impenses, *n.f.pl.*, (jur.) expenses (for repairs, improvements—*pour réparations et améliorations*).

impérati-f, -ve, *adj.*, imperative. *Prendre un ton —;* to assume an imperative tone.

impératif, *n.m.*, (gram.) imperative.

impérativement (-tiv-mān), *adv.*, imperatively.

impératoire, *n.f.*, (bot.) masterwort.

impératrice, *n.f.*, empress.

imperceptible, *adj.*, imperceptible.

imperceptiblement, *adv.*, imperceptibly.

imperdable, *adj.*, (of law-suits, of games —*de procès, de jeux*) that cannot be lost.

imperfectibilité, *n.f.*, imperfectibility.

imperfectible, *adj.*, imperfectible.

imperfection, *n.f.*, imperfection.

imperforation, *n.f.*, (med.) imperforation.

imperforé, -e, *adj.*, (med.) imperforated.

impérial, -e, *adj.*, imperial.

impériale, *n.f.*, roof, outside (of a coach—*d'une diligence*); all-fours (cards—*aux cartes*); imperial serge; (bot.) imperial; melon pompion; imperial (under the lip—*à la lèvre inférieure*).

impérialement (-al-mān), *adv.*, imperially.

impérialiste, *n.m.*, imperialist.

impériaux, *n.m.pl.*, imperialists (German troops, ministers—*ministres, troupes de l'empereur d'Allemagne*).

impérieusement (-eûz-mān), *adv.*, imperiously.

impérieu-x, -se, *adj.*, imperious, haughty, supercilious, domineering; lordly.

impérissabilité, *n.f.*, imperishableness.

impérissable, *adj.*, imperishable.

impérissablement, *adv.*, imperishably.

impéritie (-ci), *n.f.*, incapacity; unskilfulness, ignorance.

imperméabilité, *n.f.*, impermeability.

imperméable, *adj.*, impermeable, impervious. *— à l'air;* air-tight. *— à l'eau;* water-proof.

impermutabilité, *n.f.*, (phys.) impermutability.

impermutable, *adj.*, that is not permutable.

impersonnalité, *n.f.*, (philos.) impersonality.

impersonnel, -le, *adj.*, impersonal.

impersonnel, *n.m.*, (gram.) impersonal verb.

impersonnellement (-nèl-mān), *adv.*, (gram.) impersonally.

impersuasible, *adj.*, impersuasible.

impertinemment (-na-mān), *adv.*, impertinently, insolently, sillily, foolishly, nonsensically.

impertinence, *n.f.*, impertinence, insolence, sauciness; impertinent thing; nonsense, silliness, offensive thing.

impertinent, -e, *n.* and *adj.*, impertinent person, saucy person, sauce-box; impertinent, saucy, insolent, pert.

imperturbabilité, *n.f.*, imperturbability.

imperturbable, *adj.*, imperturbable.

imperturbablement, *adv.*, imperturbably.

impétigo, *n.m.*, (med.) impetigo, moist tetter, ringworm.

impétrable, *adj.*, (jur.) impetrable.

impétrant, -e, *n.m.*, *-e*, *n.f.*, (jur.) grantee; candidate (for a degree—*diplômé*).

impétration, *n.f.*, (jur.) impetration.

impétrer, *v.a.*, (jur.) to impetrate.

impétueusement (-eûz-mān), *adv.*, impetuously, vehemently, violently, forcibly.

impétueu-x, -se, *adj.*, impetuous, vehement, violent, boisterous; headlong.

impétuosité, *n.f.*, impetuosity, impetuousness; force, vehemence, boisterousness. *L'— des vents;* the fury of the wind.

impie, *adj.*, impious, ungodly, reprobate.

impie, *n.m.f.*, impious man, impious woman, ungodly person, reprobate.

impiété, *n.f.*, impiety, ungodliness.

impitoyable, *adj.*, pitiless, unpitying; merciless, unmerciful; ruthless, unrelenting, unsparing.

impitoyablement, *adv.*, pitilessly, unpityingly; mercilessly, unmercifully; ruthlessly, unrelentingly, unsparingly.

implacabilité, *n.f.*, implacability, implacableness.

implacable, *adj.*, implacable.

implacablement, *adv.*, implacably.

implantation, *n.f.*, implantation.

implanter, *v.a.*, to implant; to plant.

s'implanter, *v.r.*, to be planted, to be fixed, to be lodged.

implexe, *adj.*, implex.

implication, *n.f.*, implication, involving, entangling; contradiction.

implicite, *adj.*, implicit; tacit, implied.

implicitement (-sit-mān), *adv.*, implicitly, tacitly.

impliquer, *v.a.*, to implicate, to involve, to entangle; to imply, to infer. *Cela implique contradiction;* that implies a contradiction.

impliquer, *v.n.*, to involve contradiction.

imploration, *n.f.*, supplication, imploration.

implorer, *v.a.*, to implore, to call upon, to

crave, to supplicate, to beg, to entreat, to beseech.

impoli, -e, *adj.*, impolite, unpolite, uncourteous, uncivil, rude.

impolice, *n.f.*, (l.u.) impolicy.

impoliment, *adv.*, unpolitely, uncourteously, uncivilly, rudely.

impolitesse, *n.f.*, impoliteness, unpoliteness, incivility, rudeness; impolite thing, rude thing. *Il m'a fait une —;* he has been guilty of a piece of rudeness towards me.

impolitique, *adj.*, impolitic.

impolitiquement, (-tik-mãn), *adv.*, in an impolitic manner.

impondérabilité, *n.f.*, (phys.) imponderability.

impondérable, *adj.*, (phys.) imponderable, imponderous.

impopulaire, *adj.*, unpopular.

impopulairement (-lèr-mãn), *adv.*, unpopularly.

impopularité, *n.f.*, unpopularity.

imporeu-x, -se, *adj.*, imporous.

imporosité, *n.f.*, imporosity.

importable, *adj.*, (com.) importable.

importance, *n.f.*, importance, consequence, moment; consideration, weight, consequentialness. *D'—;* of consequence, of moment; consequentially; soundly, thoroughly. *Corriger quelqu'un d'—;* to punish any one soundly. *De la dernière —;* of the greatest importance, of the highest importance. *Avoir de l'—;* to be of importance, of moment, of consequence. *Homme d'—;* man of consequence. *Se donner des airs d'—;* to give one's self consequential airs. *Faire l'homme d'—;* to set up for a man of importance, to play the man of consequence.

important, -e, *adj.*, important, of consequence, of moment; momentous, weighty. *Question — e;* weighty question. *Un homme —;* a man of note. *Peu —;* immaterial.

important, *n.m.*, essential, chief, point; consequential man. *Faire l'—;* to set up for a man of importance; to give one's self an air of importance.

importateur, *n.m.*, (com.) importer.

importation, *n.f.*, importation; (com.) imports.

importer, *v.imp.*, to import, to be of moment, to be of consequence, to concern; to matter, to signify. *Il n'importe pas;* it is no matter, it is of no consequence, it does not matter, it does not signify. *N'importe;* no matter, never mind. *Que m'importe?* what matters it to me? *Que vous importe?* of what consequence is it to you? *Qu'importe?* what does it matter?

importer, *v.a.*, (com.) to import; to import, to introduce. *— des expressions étrangères;* to introduce foreign expressions.

importun, -e, *n.* and *adj.*, tiresome person, troublesome, intruder; importunate, troublesome, tiresome; obtrusive; irksome. *Il est — par ses questions;* he is troublesome with his questions. *Visite — e;* obtrusive visit. *Être —;* to intrude; to be troublesome.

importunément, *adv.*, (l.u.) importunely, importunately, troublesomely, obtrusively.

importuner, *v.a.*, to importune, to pester, to trouble, to annoy, to plague, to incommode; to tease. *— ses débiteurs;* to dun one's debtors.

importunité, *n.f.*, importunity.

imposable, *adj.*, taxable.

imposant, -e, *adj.*, imposing, commanding; striking; stately. *Attitude — e;* commanding attitude.

imposer, *v.a.*, to impose hands on any one in confirmation *or* ordination; to lay on; to impose, to enjoin, to prescribe; to lay; to tax; to charge, to impute; to thrust upon, to force upon; (print.) to impose. *C'est au vainqueur d'— la*

loi aux vaincus; it is for the conqueror to prescribe laws for the conquered. *— des peines;* to inflict punishment. *— silence;* to impose silence. *— des droits;* to lay duties. *— un pays;* to tax a country. *— un nom;* to give a name. *Je ne prétends pas vous — mon opinion;* I don't pretend to force my opinion upon you.

s'imposer, *v.r.*, to obtrude, to be obtrusive, to obtrude one's self; to impose a tax upon one's self.

imposer, *v.n.*, to awe, to overawe, to keep in awe. *C'est un homme dont la présence impose;* he is a man whose presence overawes. *Sa mine impose;* his looks impose on people. *En —;* to lie, to tell an untruth. *En — à quelqu'un;* to impose upon any one.

imposition, *n.f.*, imposition; tax; impost; assessment; (print.) imposition *— des mains;* laying on of hands. *— d'un tribut;* imposition of a tribute. *— d'une peine;* infliction of a punishment. *Lever les —s;* to levy taxes.

impossibilité, *n.f.*, impossibility. *— physique;* physical impossibility. *Être de toute —;* to be utterly impossible. *Se trouver dans l'— de faire quelque chose;* to find it impossible to do a certain thing; to be utterly unable to do a certain thing.

impossible, *n.m.*, impossibility: a great deal. *Je ne puis pas faire l'—;* I cannot do impossibilities. *À l'— nul n'est tenu;* there is no doing impossibilities; there is no flying without wings. *Gagner l'—;* to gain enormously. *Chercher l'—, vouloir trouver l'—;* to look for a mare's nest.

imposte, *n.f.*, (arch.) impost, moulding.

imposteur, *adj.*, deceitful. *Des oracles —s,* juggling oracles.

imposteur, *n.m.*, impostor.

imposture, *n.f.*, imposture, cheat.

impôt, *n.m.*, tax, duty; impost. *— sur chaque feu;* hearth-money. *— sur chaque tête;* poll-tax. *Lever des —s;* to levy taxes. *Percevoir les —s;* to collect the taxes.

impotence, *n.f.*, (med.) impotency; weakness.

impotent, -e, *adj.*, (med.) impotent, infirm.

⊙**impourvu, -e**, *adj.*, unprovided. *À l'—;* unawares, on a sudden. *V.* **dépourvu** and **improviste**.

impraticabilité, *n.f.*, impracticability, impracticableness.

impraticable, *adj.*, impracticable; untractable, unmanageable; uninhabitable. *L'humidité rend cette chambre — pendant l'hiver;* the damp renders this room uninhabitable during the winter.

imprécation, *n.f.*, imprecation. *Faire des —s;* to use, to utter, imprecations; to imprecate, to curse. *Charger d'—s;* to load with imprecations.

imprécatoire, *adj.*, imprecatory.

***imprégnation**, *n.f.*, impregnation.

***imprégner**, *v.a.*, to impregnate.

*s'**imprégner**, *v.r.*, to be impregnated.

imprenable, *adj.*, impregnable.

⊙**impréparation**, *n.f.*, impreparation.

imprescriptibilité, *n.f.*, imprescriptibility.

imprescriptible, *adj.*, imprescriptible.

impresses, *adj.pl.* *V.* **intentionnelles**.

impression, *n.f.*, impression; impress, print; printing; edition; (paint.) priming. *Faute d'—;* press error, misprint. *L'— d'un sceau;* the impression of a seal. *Frais d'—;* printing expenses. *Être susceptible d'—;* to be impressible. *Produire une —;* to produce an impression.

impressionnable, *adj.*, impressionable, sensitive; impressive,

impressionner, *v.a.*, to impress, to make an impression on; to move.

imprévoyance, *n.f.*, want of foresight, improvidence.

imprévoyant, -e, *adj.*, wanting foresight, improvident.

imprévu. -e, *adj.*, unforeseen, unexpected, unthought of. unlooked for.

imprimable. *adj.*, fit to be printed.

imprimé, *n.m.*, printed book, printed paper.

imprimer, *v.a.*, to imprint, to impress, to stamp, to print, to implant, to instil; to give (motion); (paint.) to prime. — *un livre;* to print a book. — *un sceau sur de la cire;* to imprint a seal upon wax. *Se faire —;* to appear in print.

imprimerie (in-pri-mri), *n.f.*, printing; printing-office, printing establishment

imprimeur, *n.m.*, printer; pressman. — *en taille-douce;* copperplate printer. — *lithographe;* lithographic printer.

imprimure, *n.f.*, (paint.) priming.

improbabilité, *n.f.*, improbability, unlikelihood

improbable, *adj.*, improbable, unlikely.

improbablement, *adv.*, improbably.

improbat-eur -rice, *n.* and *adj.*, censurer; disapprobatory.

improbation, *n.f.*, disapprobation.

improbe. *adj.*, dishonest.

improbité, *n.f.*, improbity, dishonesty.

improductibilité, *n.f.*, quality of that which cannot be produced.

improductible, *adj.*, which cannot be produced.

improducti-f. -ve, *adj.*, unproductive.

improductivement (-tiv-măn), *adv.*, unproductively.

impromptu, *n.m.*, (—, *or* —s), impromptu.

impromptu, -e, *adj.*, impromptu, extemporary.

impropice, *adj.*, unpropitious.

impropre, *adj.*, improper. *Terme —*, improper expression.

improprement, *adv.*, improperly.

impropriété, *n.f.*, impropriety (of language —*de langage*).

improuver, *v.a.*, to disapprove, to disapprove of.

improvisat-eur, *n.m.*, **-rice**, *n.f.*, improvisatore, extemporary speaker, extemporizer.

improvisation, *n.f.*, improvisation, extemporaneous speaking; (mus.) voluntary.

improviser, *v.a.*, to improvise, to produce extempore, to make extempore.

improviser, *v.n.*, to extemporize, to speak extempore.

à l'improviste, *adv* , on a sudden, unawares, unexpectedly. *Prendre à l'—;* to catch any one unawares, napping.

imprudemment (-da-măn), *adv.*, imprudently, unadvisedly, indiscreetly, incautiously.

imprudence, *n.f.*, imprudence, unadvisedness; indiscretion, imprudent act, imprudent thing. *Faire une —;* to do an imprudent thing.

imprudent, -e, *n.* and *adj.*, imprudent, fool-hardy person; imprudent, unadvised, unwise, incautious.

impubère, *adj.*, in a state of impuberty.

impudemment (-da-măn), *adv.*, impudently, audaciously, shamelessly.

impudence, *n.f.*, impudence, audaciousness, shamelessness; impudent thing, impudent conduct, piece of impudence.

impudent, -e, *n.* and *adj.*, impudent person, shameless person, brazen-face; impudent, saucy, shameless, brazen-faced.

impudeur, *n.f.*, immodesty, wantonness.

impudicité, *n.f.*, impudicity, immodesty, unchasteness, lewdness, lasciviousness, lewd act.

impudique, *adj.*, unchaste, lewd, immodest, impure.

impudiquement (-dik-măn), *adv.*, immodestly, unchastely, lewdly, lustfully, impurely.

⊙***impugner**, *v.a.*, to impugn.

impuissance, *n.f.*, impotence, impotency; inability, incapacity, powerlessness.

impuissant, -e, *adj.*, impotent; powerless.

impulsi-f. -ve, *adj.*, impulsive.

impulsion, *n.f.*, impulsion, impulse; impetus; suggestion. *Par —;* by impulse. *Donner l'— à;* to give an impulsion, an impetus to.

impunément, *adv.*, with impunity.

impuni, -e, *adj.*, unpunished. *Laisser un affront —;* to put up with an affront.

impunité, *n.f.*, impunity.

impur, -e, *adj.*, impure, unchaste, immodest.

impurement (in-pur-măn), *adv.*, impurely, immodestly.

impureté (in-pur-té), *n.f.*, impurity, immodesty.

imputabilité, *n.f.*, imputableness.

imputable, *adj.*, imputable, attributable: to be deducted.

imputati-f, -ve *adj.*, imputative.

imputation, *n.f.*, imputation; charge; deduction.

imputer, *v.a.*, to impute, to attribute, to ascribe to, to charge with; to deduct. — *une faute à quelqu'un;* to attribute a fault to any one. — *à crime;* to impute as a crime. *On vous imputera cela à négligence;* it will be imputed to your negligence. — *une somme payée sur le principal;* to deduct a payment from the principal.

s'imputer, *v.r.*, to be attributed, imputed; to attribute to one's self. *La faute ne peut — qu'à votre imprudence;* the fault can only be attributed to your imprudence.

imputrescible, *adj.*, imputrescible.

in (prefix used in composition as a particle of negation, as in *infini;* it is also used as an augmentative prefix, as in *incorporer*), in, un. [Before *b, m, p, in* is changed into *im;* and before *l* and *r*, into *il* and *ir*. When *in* comes before a consonant, as in *insu*, it has the nasal sound; but when placed before a vowel, as in *inégal*, it is sounded like *een* in English; and when coming before *n*, it has also the sound of the English *een*, as in *innocent*.]

inabondance, *n.f.*, want of abundance, scarcity.

inabordable, *adj.*, inaccessible, unapproachable.

inabordé, -e, *adj.*, unvisited, unapproached.

inabrité, -e, *adj.*, unsheltered.

inabstinence, *n.f.*, intemperance.

inacceptable, *adj.*, unacceptable.

inaccessibilité, *n.f.*, inaccessibility, inaccessibleness.

inaccessible, *adj.*, inaccessible, unapproachable. *Le port est — aux vaisseaux de guerre;* the port is inaccessible to men of war.

inaccommodable, *adj.*, irreconcilable, that cannot be made up.

inaccomplissement, *n.m.*, unaccomplishment.

inaccord, *n.m.*, (gram.) want of concord.

inaccordable, *adj.*, that cannot be granted; that cannot be made to agree; untunable.

inaccostable, *adj.*, (l.u.) inaccessible. *C'est un homme —;* nobody can come near the man.

inaccoutumé, -e, *adj.*, unaccustomed, uncustomary, unwonted, unusual.

inacheté, -e, *adj.*, (l.u.) unbought.

inachevé, -e (i-nash-vé), *adj.*, unfinished, uncompleted, incomplete.

inacti-f, -ve, *adj.*, inactive, inert.

inaction, *n.f.*, inaction.

inactivement (-tiv-măn), *adv.*, inactively.

inactivité, *n.f.*, inactivity.

inadéquat,-e (-koua, -t), *adj.*, inadequate, incomplete.
inadhérent, -e, *adj.*, not adherent.
inadmissibilité, *n.f.*, inadmissibility.
inadmissible, *adj.*, inadmissible.
inadmission, *n.f.*, non-admission.
inadouci, -e, *adj.*, unsoftened, unmitigated.
inadvertance, *n.f.*, inadvertence, inadvertency, oversight. *Par —* ; from inadvertence, inadvertently, by an oversight.
inaimable, *adj.*, (l.u.) unamiable.
inaliénabilité, *n.f.*, quality of being inalienable.
inaliénable, *adj.*, inalienable.
inaliéné. -e, *adj.*, unalienated.
inalliable, *adj.*, that cannot be alloyed, that cannot be combined.
inaltérabilité, *n.f.*, inalterability, unchangeableness.
inaltérable, *adj.*, inalterable, unalterable, unchangeable, invariable.
inamical, -e, *adj.*, unfriendly.
inamicalement (-kal-mān), *adv.*, in an unfriendly manner.
inamissibilité, *n.f.*, (theol.) quality of that which cannot be lost.
inamissible, *adj.*, (theol.) which cannot be lost.
inamovibilité, *n.f.*, irremovability.
inamovible, *adj.*, irremovable.
inamusable, *adj.*, (l.u.) that cannot be amused.
inanimation, *n.f.*, want of animation.
inanimé, -e, *adj.*, inanimate, lifeless.
inanité, *n.f.*, inanity, emptiness. [Only used figuratively.]
inanition, *n.f.*, inanition. *Mourir d'—* ; to die from inanition, from starvation.
inapaisé, -e, *adj.*, unappeased.
inapercevable, *adj.*, imperceptible, unperceivable.
inaperçu, -e, *adj.*, unperceived, unobserved.
inappétence, *n.f.*, (med.) inappetence, inappetency, want of appetite.
inapplicabilité, *n.f.*, inapplicability.
inapplicable, *adj.*, inapplicable.
inapplication, *n.f.*, inapplication.
inappliqué, -e, *adj.*, inattentive, heedless, unmindful.
inappréciable, *adj.*, inappreciable ; inestimable, invaluable.
inappréciablement, *adv.*, inappreciably.
inapprivoisable, *adj.*, untamable.
inapte, *adj.*, (l.u.) unapt, unfit.
inaptitude, *n.f.*, inaptitude, unaptness, unfitness.
inarticulé, -e, *adj.*, inarticulate. *Des sons —s* ; inarticulate sounds.
⊙**inartificiel. -le**. *adj.*, artless, real, true.
⊙**inartificiellement**, *adj.*, artlessly, really, truly.
inassermenté, *adj.*, unsworn.
inassimilable, *adj.*, that is not assimilable.
inassorti, -e, *adj.*, ill-assorted.
inassoupi, -e, *adj.*, sleepless.
inassouvi, -e, *adj.*, unsatiated.
inattaquable, *adj.*, unassailable ; unimpeachable.
inattendu, -e, *adj.*, unexpected, unforeseen, unhoped for.
inattenti-f, -ve, *adj.*, inattentive, unmindful.
inattention, *n.f.*, inattention.
inaugural. -e, *adj.*, inaugural.
inauguration, *n.f.*, inauguration.
inaugurer, *v.a.*, to inaugurate.
inavouable, *adj.*, that is not avowable.
inca, *n.m.*, Inca.
incalculable, *adj.*, incalculable. innumerable.

incalculablement, *adv.*, incalculably.
incalomniable, *adj.*, that cannot be calumniated.
incamération, *n.f.*, incameration.
incamérer, *v.a.*, to unite lands to the pope's domains.
incandescence, *n.f.*, incandescence.
incandescent, -e. *adj.*, incandescent.
incantation, *n.f.*, incantation.
incapable, *adj.*, incapable ; unable, unfit, incompetent. *Il est — de lâcheté* ; he is incapable of cowardice. *C'est un homme —* ; he is a man of no capacity. *Rendre —* ; to incapacitate.
incapacité, *n.f.*, incapacity, incapability, inability, unfitness, disability, disqualification. *Frapper d'—* ; to incapacitate. *Être frappé d'—* ; to be under a disqualification.
incarcération, *n.f.*, incarceration.
incarcérer, *v.a.*, to incarcerate.
incarnadin, -e, *adj.*, carnation-coloured; flesh-coloured.
incarnadin, *n.m.*, carnation-colour.
incarnat, -e, *adj.*, carnation-coloured, flesh-coloured.
incarnat, *n.m.*, carnation ; carnation-colour.
incarnation, *n.f.*, incarnation.
incarné, -e, *adj.*, incarnate.
s'incarner, *v.r.*, to become incarnate.
incartade, *n.f.*, thoughtless insult ; prank folly.
incendiaire, *n.m.f.* and *adj.*, firer, incendiary.
incendie, *n.m.*, fire, conflagration. *— par malveillance* ; incendiary fire, arson. *Appareil de sauvetage pour les —s* ; fire escape. *Arrêter un —* ; to get a fire under.
incendié, *n.m.*, -e, *n.f.*, sufferer by fire.
incendier, *v.a.*, to burn, to burn down ; to set fire to.
incertain, -e, *adj.*, uncertain, questionable ; unsettled, unsteady, inconstant. *Le temps est bien —* ; it is very unsettled weather.
incertain, *n.m.*, what is uncertain, uncertainty.
incertainement, *adv.*, (l.u.) doubtfully.
incertitude, *n.f.*, uncertainty ; unsteadiness, fickleness, unsettledness ; incertitude. *L'— du temps* ; the unsettled state of the weather.
incessamment (-sa-mān), *adv.*, immediately, directly ; incessantly.
incessant, -e, *adj.*, incessant.
incessible, *adj.*, inalienable.
inceste, *n.m.*, incest, incestuous person.
inceste, *adj.*, incestuous.
incestueusement (-eûz-mān), *adv.*, incestuously.
incestueu-x, -se, *n.* and *adj.*, incestuous person ; incestuous.
incharitable, *adj.*, (l.u.) uncharitable.
inchoati-f, -ve (-ko-), *adj.*, and *n.m.*, (gram.) inchoative, inceptive ; inchoative verb.
incidemment (-da-mān), *adv.*, incidentally.
incidence, *n.f.*, incidence, incidency.
incident, *n.m.*, incident, occurrence ; (b.s., jur.) difficulty.
incident, -e, *adj.*, incidental.
incidentaire, *n.m.*, (l.u.) cavilier, a disputatious man.
incidenter, *v.n.*, (jur.) to raise incidents ; (b.s.) to start difficulties.
incinération, *n.f.*, incineration.
incinérer, *v.a.*, to incinerate.
inconcis, -e, *adj.*, uncircumcised.
incirconcis, *n.m.*, uncircumcised man. (Bibl.) *Les —* uncircumcision, the Gentiles.

incirconcision, *n.f.*, uncircumcision. [Only used figuratively.]

incise. *n.f.*, (gram.) incidental, parenthetic clause.

incisé, -e, *adj.*, incised, cut, gashed, notched.

inciser. *v a.*, to incise, to make an incision; (hort.) to tap.

incisi-f. -ve, *adj.*, incisive. *Dents —ves;* incisors.

incision. *n.f.*, incision.

incisive. *n.f.*, incisive tooth; incisor.

incitant, -e. *adj.*, (med.) inciting.

incitant. *n. m.*, (med.) incitant.

incitat-eur. *n.m.*, **-rice.** *n.f.*, inciter.

incitatif. -ve, *adj.*, inciting.

incitation. *n.f.*, incitement, incentive, instigation; (med.) stimulus.

inciter, *v.a.*, to incite; to excite; to instigate.

incivil. -e, *adj.*, uncivil, unmannerly.

incivilement (-vil-mǎn), *adv.*, uncivilly, unmannerly.

incivilité. *n f.*, incivility.

incivique. *adj.*, unpatriotic.

incivisme, *n.m.*, incivism, want of patriotism.

inclémence. *n.f.*, inclemency.

inclément, -e, *adj.*, inclement.

inclinaison. *n f.*, inclination.

inclinant, -e. *adj.*, inclined.

inclination. *n.f.*, inclination, bow; stooping; bias; proneness, attachment, passion. *Par —;* from inclination. *Mariage d'—;* love-match.

incliner. *v.a.*, to incline, to slope; to stoop; to bow; to bend.

s'incliner, *v.r.*, to incline; to bow, to bend, to bow down; (geol.) to dip.

incliner, *v.n.*, to incline, to lean, to be disposed, to be inclined.

inclus, -e, *adj.*, enclosed. *Ci- —;* herein inclosed.

incluse, *n.f.*, an inclosed letter; inclosed.

inclusi-f. -ve *adj.*, inclusive; inclosing.

inclusivement (-ziv-mǎn), *adv.*, inclusively.

incoercible. *adj.*, incoercible.

***incognito,** *adv.*, incognito.

***incognito,** *n.m.*, incognito. *Garder l' —;* to live incognito.

incohérence. *n.f.*, incoherence.

incohérent. -e, *adj.*, incoherent.

incolore, *adj.*, colourless.

incomber. *v.n.*, to be incumbent on any one; to be a duty.

incombustibilité. *n.f.*, incombustibility.

incombustible, *adj.*, incombustible.

incommensurabilité, *n.f.*, incommensurability.

incommensurable, *adj.*, incommensurable.

incommode. *adj.*, inconvenient, incommodious, importunate, troublesome.

incommodé, -e, *part.*, indisposed, unwell; distressed (of ships—*des vaisseaux*). *Être —;* to be indisposed. *Un vaisseau —;* a ship in distress.

incommodément, *adv.*, incommodiously, inconveniently.

incommoder, *v.a.*, to incommode, to inconvenience, to trouble; to disturb, to annoy, to disagree with. *Si cela ne vous incommode pas;* if it be no trouble to you. *J'ai peur de vous —;* I am afraid of being troublesome to you.

s'incommoder, *v.r.*, to inconvenience one's self; to make one's self ill.

incommodité *n..f*, inconvenience, incom-

---

modiousness, indisposition; distress (of a ship—*d'un vaisseau*). *Signal d'—* (nav.); signal of distress.

incommuable. *adj.*, incommutable.

incommunicable, *adj.*, incommunicable.

incommutabilité. *n.f.*, incommutability.

incommutable, *adj.*, (jur.) that cannot be dispossessed; of which one cannot be dispossessed.

incommutablement, *adv.*, (jur.) incommutably.

incomparable, *adj.*, incomparable, matchless, unequalled.

incomparablement. *adv.*, incomparably.

incompatibilité, *n.f.*, incompatibility, inconsistency.

incompatible, *adj.*, incompatible, inconsistent.

incompatiblement, *adv.*, incompatibly, inconsistently.

incompétemment (-ta-mǎn), *adv.*, incompetently.

incompétence, *n.f.*, incompetence, incompetency.

incompétent, -e, *adj.*, incompetent.

incomplaisance, *n.f.*, want of complaisance; unkindness.

incompl-et -ète, *adj.*, incomplete, imperfect.

incomplètement (-plet-mǎn), *adv.*, incompletely, imperfectly.

incomplexe. *adj.*, incomplex.

incompréhensibilité, *n f.*, incomprehensibility, incomprehensibleness; unintelligibility; unscrutableness.

incompréhensible. *adj.*, incomprehensible, unintelligible, inscrutable.

incompréhensiblement. *adv.*, incomprehensibly.

incompressibilité. *n.f.*, incompressibility.

incompressible, *adj.*, incompressible.

incompris. -e, *adj.*, not understood.

inconcevable, *adj.*, inconceivable; strange, wonderful.

inconcevablement, *adv.*, inconceivably.

inconciliable, *adj.*, irreconcilable.

inconciliablement. *adv.*, irreconcilably.

inconduite. *n.f.*, misconduct.

incongelable, *adj.*, uncongealable.

incongru, -e. *adj.*, incongruous; unfit, unseemly, indecorous.

incongruité, *n.f.*, incongruity; impropriety, unseemliness; gross indecency.

incongrûment, *adv.*, incongruously, improperly, in an unseemly manner, indecorously.

inconnu, -e, *adj.*, unknown.

inconnu, *n.m., -e, n.f.*, unknown person; unknown; stranger.

inconnu. *n.m.* (n.p.), the unknown, that which is unknown.

inconnue, *n.f.*, (math.) unknown quantity.

inconscience, *n f.*, unconsciousness.

inconscient, *adj.*, unconscious.

inconséquemment, *adv.*, inconsistently.

inconséquence, *n.f.*, inconsistency.

inconséquent, -e. *adj.* and *n.*, inconsistent; inconsistent person.

inconsidération, *n.f.*, inconsiderateness.

inconsidéré, -e. *adj.*, inconsiderate, thoughtless, incautious.

inconsidérément, *adv.*, inconsiderately, thoughtlessly, incautiously.

inconsistance, *n.f.*, inconsistency.

inconsistant, *adj.*, inconsistent.

inconsolable, *adj.*, inconsolable, not to be comforted, disconsolate.

inconsolablement, *adv.*, inconsolably; disconsolately.

inconsolé, *adj.*, unconsoled.

inconstamment, *adv.*, inconstantly, unsteadily.

inconstance, n.f., inconstancy, fickleness, waveringness, unsteadiness ; changeableness, variableness. L'— d'un amant ; the fickleness of a lover. L'— du temps ; the changeableness of the weather.

inconstant, -e, adj., inconstant, fickle, wavering, changeable ; variable, unsettled, unsteady.

inconstitutionnalité, n.f., absence of constitutionality.

inconstitutionnel, -le, adj., unconstitutional.

inconstitutionnellement(-nèl-màn), adv., unconstitutionally.

incontestable, adj., incontestable, indisputable, unquestionable.

incontestablement, adj., incontestably, indisputably, unquestionably.

incontesté, -e, adj., uncontested, uncontradicted ; uncontended for.

incontinence, n.f., incontinency.

incontinent. -e, adj., incontinent, unchaste.

incontinent, adv., (l.u.) at once, directly, immediately.

incontradiction, n.f., absence of contradiction, agreement.

incontroversable, adj., incontrovertible.

inconvenable, adj., unbecoming, unsuitable.

inconvenablement, adv., unbecomingly.

inconvenance, n.f., impropriety, indecorousness, indecorum ; unseemliness.

inconvenant. -e, adj., improper, unbecoming, unseemly.

inconvénient, n.m., inconvenience, inconveniency. Je ne vois pas d'— à cela : I see no inconvenience in, I have no objection to, that.

inconvertible, adj., unconvertible.

incoordination, n.f., absence of co-ordination.

incorporalité, n.f., incorporality.

incorporation, n.f., incorporation.

incorporéité, n.f., incorporeity.

incorporel, -le, adj., incorporeal.

incorporer, v.a., to incorporate ; to embody. — un régiment dans un autre ; to incorporate one regiment with another.

s'incorporer, v.r., to incorporate, to embody.

incorrect. -e, adj., incorrect.

incorrectement, adv., incorrectly.

incorrection, n.f., incorrectness, inaccuracy.

incorrigibilité, n.f., incorrigibility, incorrigibleness.

incorrigible, adj., incorrigible, irreclaimable.

incorrigiblement, adv., incorrigibly.

incorrompu. -e, adj., (l.u.) incorrupt, pure.

incorruptibilité, n.f., incorruptibility, incorruptibleness.

incorruptible, adj., incorruptible.

incorruption, n.f., incorruption, incorruptness.

incrassant. -e, adj., (med.) incrassating, nutritive.

incrassant. n.m., (med.) nutritive.

incrédibilité, n.f., incredibility, incredibleness.

incrédule, adj., incredulous, unbelieving.

incrédule, n.m.f., unbeliever ; infidel.

incrédulité, n.f., incredulity ; unbelief.

incréé, -e, adj., increate, increated.

incriminable, adj., that may be incriminated, prosecuted.

incrimination, n.f., (jur.) crimination.

incriminer, v.a., to incriminate.

incroyable, adj., incredible.

incroyable, n.m., French dandy (1795-1799).

incroyablement, adv., incredibly.

incroyant, n.m., unbeliever.

incrustation, n.f., incrustation.

incruster, v.a., to incrust, to inlay.

s'incruster, v.r., to become incrusted.

incubation, n.f., incubation.

incube, n.m., incubus.

incuit, n.m., underdone part of roast meat.

incuit, -e, adj., underdone (of roast meat— d'un rôti).

inculpable, adj., (jur.) liable to crimination.

inculpation, n.f., crimination, accusing.

inculpé, n.m., -e, n.f., (jur.) prisoner.

inculper, v.a., to accuse, to criminate.

inculquer, v.a., to inculcate.

s'inculquer, v.r., to be inculcated.

inculte, adj., uncultivated ; untilled, unploughed, waste ; unpolished, rude. Terres —s, waste lands.

inculture, n.f., (l.u.) inculture.

incunable, n.m. and adj., incunabula ; relating to incunabula.

incurabilité, n.f., incurability.

incurable, n.m.f. and adj., incurable.

incurablement, adv., incurably.

incurie, n.f., carelessness, thoughtlessness.

incurieusement, adv., incuriously.

incurieu-x. -se, adj, incurious.

incuriosité, n.f., incuriosity.

incursion, n.f., incursion, inroad. Faire des —s : to make incursions.

incuse, adj. and n.f., with one or both sides sunk (of medals—des médailles).

inde, n.m., (dy.) indigo, indigo-blue.

*indébrouillable, adj., that cannot be unravelled.

indécemment, adv., indecently.

indécence, n.f., indecency.

indécent. -e, adj., indecent.

indéchiffrable, adj., undecipherable, illegible, inexplicable.

indécis, -e, adj., undecided, doubtful ; indeterminate, undefined. Il était — ; he was wavering.

indécision, n.f., indecision, waveringness.

indéclinabilité, n.f., the condition of being indeclinable.

indéclinable, adj., (gram) indeclinable.

indécomposable, adj., indecomposable.

indécrottable, adj., (pop.) unpolished, rude, incapable of cultivation.

indéfectibilité, n.f., indefectibility.

indéfectible, adj., indefectible.

indéfendable, adj., indefensible.

indéfini. -e, adj., indefinite, unlimited.

indéfiniment, adv., indefinitely.

indéfinissable. adj., indefinable, undefinable, unaccountable.

indélébile, adj., indelible.

indélébilité, n.f., indelibility.

indéliberé, -e, adj., indeliberate.

indélicat, -e, adj., indelicate ; unhandsome.

indélicatement (-ka-tmàn), adv., indelicately, unhandsomely.

indélicatesse, n.f., indelicacy ; unhandsomeness.

indemne (in-dèm-n), adj., (jur.) indemnified. Rendre — ; to indemnify.

indemnisation, n.f., indemnification.

indemniser (in-dèm ni-zé), v.a., to indemnify, to make good.

s'indemniser, v.r., to indemnify one's self.

indemnité, n.f., indemnity.

indéniable, adj., undeniable.

indépendamment (-da màn), adv., independently.

indépendance, n.f., independence.

indépendant, -e, adj., independent.

indépendant, n.m., Independent.

indéracinable, adj., that cannot be eradicated.

indescriptible, adj., indescribable.

indésirable, adj., undesirable.

indestructibilité, n.f., indestructibility.

indestructible, *adj.*, indestructible.

indéterminable, *adj.*, indeterminable.

indétermination, *n.f.*, indetermination, irresolution.

indéterminé, -e, *adj.*, indeterminate, unlimited.

indéterminément, *adv.*, indeterminately.

indevinable, *adj.*, that cannot be guessed.

indévot. -e, *adj.*, indevout, irreligious.

indévotement, *adv.*, indevoutly; in an irreligious manner.

indévotion, *n.f.*, indevotion, irreligion.

index (in-dèks), *n.m*, index, table of contents; forefinger. — *expurgatoire;* expurgatory Index. *Mettre à l'—;* to prohibit.

indicateur, *adj.*, indicating.

indicateur, *n.m.*, indicator; (anat.) index.

indicatif, *n.m.*, (gram.) indicative mood.

indicati-f, -ve, *adj.*, indicative.

indication, *n.f.*, indication, information; sign.

indice, *n.m.*, indication, indicator, sign, mark, token.

indicible, *adj.*, inexpressible, unspeakable, ineffable.

indiciblememt, *adv.*, unspeakably, ineffably.

indiction, *n.f.*, indiction; convocation.

indicule, *n.m.*, (l.u.) slight indication.

indien, -ne (-in, -è-n), *n.* and *adj.*, Indian.

indienne, *n.f.*, printed calico, printed cotton.

indienneur, *n.m.*, calico-printer.

indifféremment (-ra-mān), *adv.*, indifferently, with indifference.

indifférence, *n.f.*, indifference, unconcern; inclination.

indifférent, -e, *adj.*, indifferent; unconcerned; immaterial. *Il lui est — de sortir ou de rester;* it is indifferent to him whether he goes out or not.

indifférent, *n.m.*, **-e**, *n.f.*, one who is indifferent to persons or things. *Faire l'—;* to feign indifference.

indigence, *n.f.*, indigency, poverty.

indigénat, *n.m.*, the right of the indigenes of a country; naturalization (in Poland— *en Pologne*); the quality of being indigene.

indigène, *n.m.f.* and *adj.*, indigene; native.

indigent, -e, *adj.* and *n.*, indigent, needy, necessitous; poor person.

indigéré, -e, *adj.*, undigested, indigested; crude.

indigeste, *adj.*, indigestible, undigested; crude.

indigestible, *adj.*, (l.u.) indigestible.

indigestion, *n.f.*, indigestion.

indigète, *adj.*, (antiq.) of the country.

*__indignation__, *n.f.*, indignation. *Avec —;* indignantly. *Faire éclater son —;* to give vent to one's indignation.

*__indigne__, *adj.*, unworthy, undeserving; infamous, worthless, scandalous *Il est — de vivre;* he is unworthy to live. — *de succéder;* (jur.) disqualified to inherit.

*__indigne__. *n.m.*, worthless, infamous wretch; (jur.) one debarred by law from inheriting, in consequence of injury done to the deceased.

*__indigné. -e__, *part.*, indignant. *Être —;* to be indignant.

*__indignement__, *adv.*, unworthily, infamously, scandalously.

*__indigner__. *v.a.*, to render indignant; to raise the indignation of.

*s'__indigner__. *v.r.*, to be indignant.

*__indignité__, *n.f.*, indignity; unworthiness, worthlessness; infamy. scandalous thing.

indigo, *n.m.*, indigo.

indigoterie, *n.f.*, indigo manufactory.

indigotier (-tié), *n.m.*, indigo-plant.

indiquer, *v.a.*, to indicate, to show, to point out; to direct to, to inform of. to acquaint with, to appoint. *Indiquez-moi la demeure de;* show me the dwelling of. *Voulez-vous m'— le chemin de l'église?* will you show me the way to the church? *Au lieu indiqué;* at the appointed place.

indirect, -e, *adj.*, indirect.

indirectement, *adj.*, indirectly.

indisciplinable, *adj.*, indisciplinable; indocile, unruly, ungovernable.

indiscipline, *n.f.*, indiscipline.

indiscipliné, -e, *adj.*, undisciplined.

indiscr-et, -ète, *adj.*, indiscreet, inconsiderate, unwary; inquisitive; injudicious; telltale, unable to keep a secret.

indiscrètement (-krèt-mān), *adv.*, indiscreetly, inconsiderately; unadvisedly, injudiciously, unguardedly.

indiscrétion, *n.f.*, indiscretion, inconsiderateness, imprudence, unwariness; piece of indiscretion, indiscreet thing.

indiscutable, *adj.*, incontestable, unquestionable, indisputable.

indispensabilité, *n.f.*, indispensableness.

indispensable, *adj.*, indispensable.

indispensablement, *adv.*, indispensably.

indisponible, *adj.*, that cannot be disposed of.

indisposé, -e, *adj.*, indisposed, unwell.

indisposer, *v.a.*, to indispose; to render, to make unwell; to disaffect, to disincline, to estrange, to set against.

*s'__indisposer__, *v.r.*, to be indisposed; to be unwell.

indisposition, *n.f.*, indisposition; disinclination.

indisputable, *adj.*, indisputable.

indissolubilité, *n.f.*, indissolubility.

indissoluble, *adj.*, indissoluble.

indissolublement, *adv.*, indissolubly.

indistinct. -e, *adj.*, indistinct, confused.

indistinctement, *adv.*, indistinctly.

indistinction, *n.f.*, indistinction.

individu, *n.m.*, individual. *Avoir soin de son —;* to take care of one's self, of number one.

individualisation, *n.f.*, individualization.

individualiser, *v.a.*, to individualize.

individualisme, *n.m.*, individualism.

individualité, *n.f.*, individuality.

individuel. -le, *adj.*, individual.

individuellement (duèl-mān), *adv.*, individually.

indivis, -e, *adj.*, (jur.) undivided.

indivis, *n.m.*, (jur.) joint-tenancy. *Par —;* in joint-tenancy.

indivisé, -e, *adj.*, undivided.

indivisément, *adv.*, indivisibly.

indivisibilité, *n.f.*, indivisibility.

indivisible, *adj.*, indivisible.

indivisiblement, *adv.*, indivisibly.

indivision, *n.f.*, joint-possession, copartnery; joint-tenancy.

in-dix-huit. *n.m.* and *adj.* (—), (print.) decimo-octavo, in eighteen, eighteenmo.

indocile. *adj.*, indocile, unmanageable.

indocilité, *n.f*, indocility, untractableness.

indocte. *adj.*, illiterate. ignorant.

indo-germanique, *adj*, Indo-German (languages—*langues*).

indolemment (-la-mān), *adv.*, indolently.

indolence, *n.f.*, indolence, sluggishness, sloth.

indolent. -e. *n.* and *adj.*, indolent person; indolent, sluggish, slothful.

indomptable, *adj.*, indomitable; untamable. ungovernable.

indomptablement. *adv.*, indomitably, untamably.

indompté, -e, *adj.*, untamed, wild; uncontrollable.

indou, *n.m.*, Hindoo.

in-douze, *n.m.* and *adj.* (—), (print.) duodecimo, in twelve, twelvemo.

indu, -e, *adj.*, undue, unseasonable. *Heure —e*, unseasonable hour.

indubitable, *adj.*, indubitable.

indubitablement, *adv.*, indubitably, undoubtedly, unquestionably.

induction, *n.f.*, (philos.) induction, inference; (phys.) induction; (l u.) instigation, suggestion, incitement.

induire (induisant, induit), *v.a.*, to induce, to lead, to infer. *— en erreur;* to lead into error.

indulgence, *n.f.*, lenity, leniency, indulgence. *User d'— envers;* to use indulgence to. *Avoir de l'— pour;* to be indulgent to; to make allowance for.

indulgent, -e, *adj*, lenient, indulgent, considerate.

indult (in-dult), *n.m.*, indult, indulto.

indultaire, *n.m.*, (canon law—*droit canon*) one who had a right to a living in virtue of an indult of the Pope.

indûment, *adv.*, unduly.

induration, *n.f.*, (med.) induration.

induré, *adj.*, (med.) indurated.

industrie, *n.f.*, -skill, ingenuity; business, trade; manufactures, arts and manufactures; industry. *Vivre d'—;* to live by one's wits. *Chevalier d'—;* swindler, sharper.

industriel, *n.m.*, manufacturer, trader.

industriel, -le, *adj.*, industrial, manufacturing. *Les produits —s;* the productions of arts and manufactures. *Richesses —ies;* commercial wealth.

industrieusement (-eûz-măn), *adv.*, ingeniously, skilfully.

industrieu-x, -se, *adj.*, ingenious, skilful.

induts, *n.m.pl.*, assistant priests.

inébranlable, *adj.*, immovable; resolute; unmoved, unshaken, steady, firm.

inébranlablement, *adv.*, immovably, steadily, resolutely.

inédit, -e, *adj.*, inedited, unpublished.

ineffabilité, *n.f.*, ineffability, unspeakableness.

ineffable, *adj.*, ineffable, inexpressible, unutterable.

ineffablement, *adv.*, ineffably.

ineffaçable, *adj.*, indelible.

ineffaçablement, *adv.*, indelibly.

inefficace, *adj.*, inefficacious, ineffective, ineffectual, unavailing.

inefficacement, *adv.*, inefficaciously.

inefficacité, *n.f.*, inefficacy, ineffectualness, inefficaciousness.

inégal, -e, *adj.*, unequal; uneven.

inégalement, *adv.*, unequally, unevenly

inégalité, *n.f.*, inequality; unevenness.

inélégamment, *adv.*, inelegantly.

inélégance, *n.f.*, inelegance.

inélégant, -e, *adj.*, inelegant.

inéligibilité, *n.f.*, ineligibility.

inéligible, *adj.*, ineligible.

inéluctable, *adj.*, inevitable, unavoidable.

inénarrable, *adj.*, unspeakable.

inepte, *adj.*, inept, unfit, foolish, silly.

ineptement, *adv.*, ineptly.

ineptie (-ci), *n.f.*, ineptness, ineptitude, foolishness, absurdity.

inépuisable, *adj.*, inexhaustible.

inépuisablement, *adv.*, inexhaustibly.

inerme, *adj.*, (bot.) inermous.

inerte, *adj.*, inert, sluggish.

inertie (-ci). *n.f.*, inertia; inertness; indolence, inactivity. *Force d'— ;* inertia, vis inertiæ.

inespérable, *adj.*, that cannot be hoped.

inespéré, -e, *adj.*, unhoped, unlooked for, unexpected.

inespérément, *adv.*, (l.u.) unexpectedly.

inestimable, *adj.*, inestimable.

inestimé, -e, *adj.*, unesteemed.

inévitable, *adj.*, inevitable, unavoidable.

inévitablement, *adv.*, inevitably, unavoidably.

inexact, -e, *adj.*, inexact, inaccurate.

inexactement, *adv.*, inaccurately, incorrectly.

inexactitude, *n.f.*, inexactness, inaccuracy, incorrectness.

inexcusable, *adj.*, inexcusable, unjustifiable, unwarrantable.

inexcusablement, *adv.*, inexcusably, unjustifiably.

inexécutable, *adj.*, impracticable.

inexécuté, -e, *adj.*, unexecuted.

inexécution, *n.f.*, inexecution.

inexercé -e, *adj.*, unexercised, unpractised.

inexigible, *adj.*, that cannot be demanded.

inexorable, *adj.*, inexorable, inflexible, unrelenting.

inexorablement, *adv.*, inexorably.

inexpérience, *n.f.*, inexperience.

inexpérimenté, -e, *adj.*, inexperienced, inexpert.

inexpiable, *adj.*, inexpiable.

inexpié, *adj.*, unatoned.

inexplicable, *adj.*, inexplicable, uncountable.

inexplicablement, *adv.*, inexplicably.

inexpliqué, *adj.*, unexplained.

inexploité, *adj.*, (of land—*d'un terrain*) untilled, uncultivated; (mines, &c.) unworked.

inexploré, *adj.*, unexplored.

inexplosible, *adj.*, unexplosive.

inexprimable, *adj.*, inexpressible, unutterable, unspeakable.

inexpugnable, *adj.*, inexpugnable, impregnable.

inextensible, *adj.*, that is not extensible.

in extenso (i-nèks-tin-sô), *adv.*, in extenso, fully, at full length.

inextinguible (gu-i-), *adj.*, inextinguishable, unquenchable. *Soif — ;* quenchless thirst.

in extremis, *adv.* V. extremis (in).

inextricable, *adj.*, inextricable.

inextricablement, *adv.*, inextricably.

*****infaillibilité**, *n.f.*, infallibility, infallibleness.

*****infaillible**, *adj.*, infallible. *Dieu seul est — ;* God alone is infallible.

*****infailliblement**, *adv.*, infallibly; without fail.

infaisable, *adj.*, impracticable.

infamant, *adj.*, infamous, ignominious.

⊙**infamation**, *n.f.*, (jur.) mark of infamy.

infâme, *adj.*, infamous, base; squalid, filthy, nasty. *D'une manière — ;* infamously.

infâme, *n.m.f.*, infamous person; person branded with infamy.

infamie, *n.f.*, infamy, ignominy; baseness, infamous action

infant, *n.m.*, -**e**, *n.f.*, Infante; Infanta (of Spain, of Portugal—*d'Espagne, de Portugal*).

infanterie (in-fan-tri), *n.f.*, infantry. — *légère;* light infantry.

infanticide, *n.m.f.*, infanticide, murderer, murderess, of a child.

infanticide, *n.m.*, infanticide; child-murder.

infatigabilité, *n.f.*, indefatigability, indefatigableness.

infatigable, *adj.*, indefatigable, unwearied, unweary.

infatigablement, *adv.*, indefatigably, unweariedly.

infatuation, n.f., infatuation.
infatuer, v.a., to infatuate.
s'infatuer, v.r., to be infatuated.
infécond, -e, adj., infecund, infertile, unfruitful, barren, sterile.
infécondité, n.f., infecundity, infertility, unfruitfulness, barrenness, sterility.
infect (in-fèkt), **-e,** adj., infectious.
infectant, adj., infecting; tainting; offensive (of smell—d'odeur).
infecter, v.a., to infect, to taint.
infection, n.f., stench; infection; infectious disease.
infélicité, n.f., infelicity, unhappiness.
inféodation, n.f., infeodation, infeoffment.
inféoder, v.a., to infeoff; to entail.
s'inféoder, v.r., to be infeoffed.
infère, adj., (bot.) inferior, lower.
inférer, v.a., to infer, to conclude, to deduce.
inférieur, -e, adj., inferior, subordinate, lower, nether; under, petty, below.
inférieur, n.m., inferior.
inférieurement (-eur-măn), adv., in an inferior manner.
infériorité, n.f., inferiority.
infernal, -e, adj., infernal, hellish. Pierre —e; lunar caustic.
infernalement, adv., infernally.
infertile, adj., infertile, unfruitful; sterile, barren.
infertilisable, adj., that cannot be made fertile.
infertilité, n.f., infertility, unfruitfulness, barrenness.
infester, v.a., to infest, to harass, to annoy; to overrun.
infidèle, adj., unfaithful, faithless; untrue, unbelieving.
infidèle, n.m.f., unfaithful person; infidel, unbeliever.
infidèlement, adv., unfaithfully, faithlessly.
infidélité, n.f., infidelity, faithlessness, unfaithfulness; inaccuracy, unbelief.
infiltration, n.f., infiltration.
s'infiltrer, v.r., to infiltrate; (fig.) to spread.
infime, adj., (of ranks—du rang) lowest.
infini, -e, adj., infinite, boundless, endless; numberless.
infini, n.m. (n.p.), infinite. À l'—; to infinity, ad infinitum, infinitely.
infiniment, adv., infinitely, without end; exceedingly, extremely. Il a — d'esprit; he has a great deal of wit.
infinité, n.f., infinity, infiniteness, infinitude.
infinitésimal, -e, adj., infinitesimal, infinitely small. Quantité —e; infinitesimal quantity.
infinitif, n.m. and adj., (gram.) infinitive, infinitive mood.
infirmati-f, -ve, adj., annulling, invalidating.
infirmation, n.f., invalidation.
infirme, n.m.f. and adj., an invalid; infirm, weak, feeble, frail.
infirmer, v.a., to invalidate, to nullify.
infirmerie, n.f., infirmary.
infirmi-er, n.m., **-ère,** n.f., person who waits upon the sick in an infirmary; nurse of an infirmary.
infirmité, n.f., infirmity, weakness.
inflammabilité, n.f., inflammability.
inflammable, adj., inflammable.
inflammation, n.f., inflammation.
inflammatoire, adj., inflammatory.
inflation, n.f., (med.) inflation.
infléchi, -e, adj., (opt.) inflected.
infléchir, v.a., (opt.) to inflect.

s'infléchir, v.r., (opt.) to be inflected.
inflexibilité, n.f., inflexibility, inexorableness.
inflexible, adj., inflexible; unrelenting, unbending, inexorable.
inflexiblement, adv., inflexibly, inexorably.
inflexion, n.f., inflection; inflexion; variation.
inflicti-f, -ve, adj., inflictive.
infliction, n.f., infliction.
infliger, v.a., to inflict.
s'infliger, v.r., to inflict one's self; to impose on one's self. — des privations; to impose privations on one's self.
inflorescence, n.f., (bot.) inflorescence.
influence, n.f., influence; sway. Avoir de l'— sur; to have influence over. Avoir beaucoup d'— sur; to have great influence over.
influencer, v.a., to influence.
influent, -e, adj., influential.
influer, v.n., to influence, to sway.
influx, n.m., (tech.) influx.
in-folio, n.m. and adj. (—), (print.) folio.
information, n.f., inquiry; inquest. Aller aux —s; to make inquiries; to go for a servant's character. Prendre des —; to make inquiries.
informe, adj., unformed; shapeless. Étoiles —s; unformed stars.
informé, n.m., (jur.) investigation, inquiry, inquest.
informer, v.a., to inform; to acquaint, to give information, to apprise.
s'informer, v.r., to inquire, to make inquiries; to ask. Il s'est informé de votre santé; he inquired after your health.
informer, v.n., (jur.) to inquire into, to investigate.
infortiat, n.m. (n.p.), the middle part of Justinian's Digest, place between the older and the newer Digest.
infortune, n.f., misfortune, adversity.
infortuné, -e, n. and adj., unfortunate, unhappy, ill-fated, wretched person; unfortunate, unhappy, ill-fated, wretched.
infracteur, n.m., infractor, infringer, violator.
infraction, n.f., infraction, infringement, breach, violation.
infranchissable, adj., insurmountable, insuperable.
infrangible, adj., infrangible.
infréquenté, -e, adj., unfrequented.
infructueusement, adv., fruitlessly, to no purpose, in vain.
infructueu-x, -se, adj., unfruitful, fruitless, unavailing.
infus, -e, adj., intuitive.
infuser, v.a., to infuse, to steep. — à froid; to make a cold infusion.
s'infuser, v.r., to be infused.
infusibilité, n.f., infusibility.
infusible, adj., unfusible.
infusion, n.f., infusion; intuition.
infusoir, n.m., (surg.) instrument to introduce liquids into the veins.
infusoires, n.m.pl. and adj., (zool.) infusoria; infusorial, infusory.
***ingagnable,** adj., that cannot be won, that cannot be gained.
ingambe, adj., nimble, brisk.
s'ingénier, v.r., to strive, to tax one's ingenuity. Je m'ingénie à le faire; I strive all I can to accomplish it.
ingénieur, n.m., engineer. — civil; civil engineer. — constructeur de vaisseaux; mastershipwright. Art de l'—; engineering — des mines; mining engineer. — des ponts et chaussées; civil engineer of the government for

bridges and roads in France. — -*géographe* (–s –s); geographer. — -*opticien* (–s –s); optician.

ingénieusement, *adv.*, ingeniously.

ingénieu-x, -se, *adj.*, ingenious.

ingéniosité, *n.f.*, ingenuity.

ingénu, -e, *adj.*, ingenuous, frank, open, candid.

ingénu, -e, *n.m.*, *n.f.*, ingenuous person, artless person; (Rom. antiq.) born free-man.

ingénuité, *n.f.*, ingenuousness, frankness, openness, candidness, simplicity.

ingénument, *adv.*, ingenuously, frankly, openly, candidly.

ingérence, *n.f.*, interference, meddling, dabbling.

ingérer, *v.a.*, (physiology) to introduce into the stomach through the mouth.

s'ingérer, *v.r.*, to meddle with. — *dans les affaires d'autrui*; to meddle with other people's business.

ingestion (-jès-ti-on), *n.f.*, (physiology) introducing into the stomach through the mouth.

in globo, *adv.*, in a lump.

inglorieu-x. -se, *adj.*, inglorious.

ingouvernable, *adj.*, ungovernable.

ingrat, -e, *n.* and *adj.*, unthankful, ungrateful, ingrate person; ungrateful, ingrate, unthankful, thankless; unprofitable, unfruitful; sterile; unpleasant.

ingratitude, *n.f.*, ingratitude, unthankfulness, thanklessness, piece of ingratitude.

ingrédient (-di-àn), *n.m.*, ingredient.

inguérissable, *adj.*, incurable.

inguinal, -e.(-gu-i-), *adj.*, inguinal.

ingurgitation, *n.f.*, (med.) introduction of a liquid into the throat.

inhabile, *adj.*, unqualified; incapable, unskilful, unfit.

inhabilement, *adv.*, unskilfully.

inhabileté, *n.f.*, inability, unskilfulness, incompetency, incapacity.

inhabilité, *n.f.*, (jur.) incompetency; disability.

inhabitable, *adj.*, uninhabitable.

inhabité, -e, *adj.*, uninhabited.

inhabitude, *n.f.*, want of habit.

inhalation, *n.f.*, inhalation.

inharmonie, *n.f.*, want of harmony.

inharmonieu-x, -se, *adj.*, inharmonious, unmusical.

inhérence, *n.f.*, inherence.

inhérent, -e, *adj.*, inherent.

⊙**inhiber**, *v.a.*, to inhibit, to prohibit, to forbid.

inhibition, *n.f.*,(jur.)inhibition,prohibition.

inhonoré, -e, *adj.*, (l.u.) unhonoured.

inhospitali-er, -ère, *adj.*, inhospitable; unfriendly.

inhospitalièrement, *adv.*, inhospitably.

inhospitalité, *n.f.*, inhospitality.

inhostile, *adj.*, unhostile.

inhumain, -e, *adj.*, inhuman.

inhumainement (i-nu-mè-n-màn), *adv.*, inhumanly.

inhumanité, *n.f.*, inhumanity.

inhumation, *n.f.*, inhumation, interment.

inhumectation, *n.f.*, (l.u.) want of humidity, dryness.

inhumer, *v.a.*, to inhume, to bury, to inter.

inimaginable, *adj.*; unimaginable, incomprehensible, inconceivable.

inimitable, *adj.*, inimitable.

inimitablement, *adj.*, inimitably.

inimitié, *n.f.*, enmity, hatred, antipathy. *Avoir de l'— pour*; to bear enmity to.

inintelligence, *n.f.*, lack of intelligence.

inintelligent, *adj.*, unintelligent.

inintelligible, *adj.*, unintelligible.

inintelligiblement, *adv.*, unintelligibly.

ininterrompu, *adj.*, uninterrupted.

inique, *adj.*, iniquitous; unrighteous.

iniquement(i-nik-màn),*adv.*, iniquitously.

iniquité, *n.f.*, iniquity; unrighteousness.

initial, -e,*adj.*, initial.

initiale, *n.f.*, initial.

initiat-eur, *n.m.*, **-rice**, *n.f.*, one who initiates.

initiati-f, -ve,*adj.*, initiatory.

initiation, *n.f.*, initiation.

initiative, *n.f.*, initiative. *Prendre l'—*; to take the initiative.

initié, -e, *adj.*, initiated.

initié, *n.m.*, person initiated.

initier, *v.a.*, to initiate, to admit.

injecter, *v.a.*, to inject.

injection, *n.f.*, injection.

injonction, *n.f.*, injunction. *Faire — à*; to enjoin.

injouable, *adj.*, that cannot be played, acted.

injudicieu-x, -se, *adj.*, injudicious.

injure, *n.f.*, insult, injury, wrong; *pl.*, abuse, abusive language. *Dire des —s à quelqu'un*; to call any one names, to abuse any one. *Faire — à quelqu'un*; to wrong any one. *Avoir toujours l'— à la bouche*; to be abusive, to be foulmouthed.

injurier, *v.a.*, to abuse, to call names, to rail at, to insult.

injurieusement (-eûz-màn), *adv.*, injuriously, wrongfully, abusively, reproachfully, revilingly.

injurieu-x, -se, *adj.*, injurious, wrongful; reproachful, abusive, offensive, reviling.

injuste, *adj.*, unjust, unfair, wrong, wrongful.

injuste, *n.m.*, unjust, wrong; unjust person.

injustement, *adv.*, unjustly, wrongly, wrongfully, unfairly.

injustice, *n.f.*, injustice; wrong, act of injustice.

injustifiable, *adj.*, unjustifiable.

⊙**inlisible**, *adj.* V. *illisible*.

in manus, *nm.* (–), (c. rel.) prayer said at the point of death.

in naturalibus. V. *naturalibus* (in).

innavigable, *adj.*, unnavigable, not navigable.

inné, -e, *adj.*, innate, inborn, inbred.

innervation, *n.f.*, (physiol.) innervation .

innocemment (ino-sa-màn), *adv.*, innocently, harmlessly; simply, sillily, foolishly.

innocence, *n.f.*, innocence, guiltlessness; harmlessness, inoffensiveness; simplicity, silliness.

innocent, -e,*adj.*, innocent,guiltless; harmless, inoffensive; simple, silly. *Il a été reconnu —*; he was found not guilty. *Se déclarer —*; to plead not guilty. *Tenir pour —*; to hold guiltless.

innocent, *n.m.*, **-e**, *n.f.*, innocent person ; simpleton, idiot. *Le massacre des —s*; the Massacre of the Innocents. *Tourte d'—s*; pigeon-pie made with young pigeons.

innocenter, *v.a.*, to find not guilty, to declare innocent.

innocuité, *n.f.*, innocuousness, harmlessness.

innombrable, *adj.*, innumerable, numberless.

innombrablement, *adv.*, innumerably.

innomé, -e, *adj.*, (jur.) unnamed, nameless.

innominé, *adj.*, (anat.) nameless, unnamed.

innovat-eur, *n.m.*, **-rice**, *n.f.*, innovator.

innovation, *n.f.*, innovation.

innover, *v.n.*, to innovate, to make innovations.

inobservable, *adj.*, that is not observable.

inobservance, *n.f.*, non-observance.
inobservation, *n.f.*, non-observance.
inoccupé, -e.*adj.*, unoccupied, unemployed.
in-octavo, *n.m.* and *adj.* (—), (print.) octavo, in octavo.
inoculateur, *n.m.*, inoculator.
inoculation, *n.f.*, inoculation.
inoculer, *v.a.*, (med.) to inoculate.
s'inoculer, *v.r.*, (med.) to inoculate one's self; to be inoculated.
⊙**inoculiste**, *n.m.*, partisan of inoculation.
inodore. *adj.*, inodorous, inodorate, scentless, void of smell.
inoffensi-f, -ve. *adj.*, inoffensive.
inoffensivement, *adv.*, inoffensively.
inofficieu-x. **-se**, *adj.*, (jur.) inofficious; securing-advantages to one heir to the detriment of the others; disinheriting the lawful heir without a cause.
inofficiosité, *n.f.*, (jur.) act of securing advantages to one to the detriment of the others; act of disinheriting the lawful heir without a cause.
inondation, *n.f.*, inundation, overflow, flood, deluge.
inonder, *v.a.*, to inundate, to overflow, to deluge; to overrun, to overspread, to pour into, to overwhelm.
inopiné, -e, *adj.*, unforeseen, unexpected, unlooked for.
inopinément, *adv.*, unawares, unexpectedly.
inopportun, -e, *adj.*, inopportune, unseasonable.
inopportunément, *adv.*, inopportunely.
inopportunité, *n.f.*, inopportuneness, unseasonableness.
inorganique, *adj.*, inorganical.
inosculation, *n.f.*, (anat.) inosculation, anastomosis.
inouï, -e. *adj.*, unheard of.
inoxydable, *adj.*, which cannot be oxygenized.
in pace, *n.m.* (—), prison in a convent.
in-partibus. *V.* **partibus** (in).
in petto (-pèt-to),*adv.*, in petto, in secret.
in-plano, *n.m.* and *adj.* (—), (print.) broadside.
in-promptu, *n.m.* *V.* **impromptu**.
inqualifiable, *adj.*, that cannot be qualified.
inquart, *n.m.*, (chem.) quartation.
in-quarto (-kooar-), *n.m.* and *adj.* (—), (print.) quarto, in quarto.
inqui-et, -ète. *adj.*, unquiet, anxious, uneasy; restless. *Il a l'humeur—ète;* he is of a restless temper.
inquiétant, -e, *adj.*, alarming, causing uneasiness.
inquiéter, *v.a.*, to make uneasy, to disquiet; to disturb, to trouble.
s'inquiéter, *v.r.*, to be anxious, to be uneasy, to make one's self uneasy, to alarm one's self.
inquiétude, *n.f.*, anxiety, uneasiness, disquietude; solicitude, restlessness. *Avoir des —s sur la santé de quelqu'un;* to be uneasy about any one's health. *Donner de l'— à;* to make uneasy. *Il est sans — sur l'avenir;* he is without anxiety for the future. *Soyez sans — là-dessus;* make yourself easy on that score. *Avoir des —;* to be uneasy.
inquisiteur, *n.m.*, inquisitor.
inquisition, *n.f.*, inquisition.
inquisitorial, -e, *adj.*, inquisitorial.
insaisissable, *adj.*, unseizable; imperceptible.
insalubre, *adj.*, insalubrious, unhealthy, unwholesome.
insalubrité, *n.f.*, insalubrity, unhealthfulness, unwholesomeness.

insanité, *n.f.*, insanity.
insatiabilité, *n.f.*, insatiableness.
insatiable, *adj.*, insatiable, insatiate.
insatiablement, *adv.*, insatiably.
insciemment, *adv.*, unwittingly, unknown to one's self.
inscription, *n.f.*, inscription; registry, entry; term (of schools—*terme d'école*); (fin.) stock-receipt; inscribing. — *hypothécaire;* registry of mortgage. — *de faux;* allegation of forgery. *Avoir toutes ses —s;* (of students—*des étudiants*) to have kept all the terms. *Prendre ses —s;* to enter one's name for the terms.
inscrire, *v.a.*, to inscribe, to enter; to register; to empannel (jury).
s'inscrire, *v.r.*, to inscribe one's self; to enter one's name.
inscrutabilité, *n.f.*, inscrutability, inscrutableness; unsearchableness.
inscrutable, *adj.*, inscrutable, unfathomable.
inscrutablement, *adv.*, inscrutably.
⊙**insçu**. *V.* **insu**.
insécable, *adj.*, insecable, indivisible.
insecte, *n.m.*, insect.
insecticide, *adj.*, having the power of killing insects.
insectivore, *adj.*, insectivorous.
insécurité, *n.f.*, insecurity.
in-seize, *n.m.* and *adj.* (—), (print.) sixteen, in sixteen.
insensé, -e, *n.* and *adj.*, insane, madman, mad woman; maniac; unwise person; fool; insane, mad; foolish, senseless.
insensibilité, *n.f.*, insensibility, unconsciousness, unfeelingness.
insensible, *adj.*, insensible, unconscious, unfeeling; hard-hearted, imperceptible. *Être — au froid;* to be insensible to cold.
insensiblement, *adv.*, insensibly, imperceptibly.
inséparabilité, *n.f.*, inseparableness.
inséparable, *adj.*, inseparable.
inséparablement, *adv.*, inseparably.
inséparables, *n.m.f.pl.*, persons that cannot be separated; (orni.) love-birds.
insérer, *v.a.*, to insert, to put in.
insermenté, *adj.*, unsworn.
insertion, *n.f.*, insertion.
insidieusement (-eûz-mǎn), *adv.*, insidiously.
insidieu-x, **-se**, *adj.*, insidious.
*****insigne**, *adj.*, signal, notorious.
*****insigne**, *n.m.*, badge; *pl.*, insignia.
*****insignifiance**, *n.f.*, insignificance.
*****insignifiant, -e**, *adj.*, insignificant.
insincère, *adj.*, insincere.
insinuant, -e, *adj.*, insinuating.
insinuatif, -ve, *adj.*, (l.u.) insinuating.
insinuation, *n.f.*, insinuation; hint, suggestion, intimation; ⊙ (jur.) registration.
insinuer, *v.a.*, to insinuate; to hint, to suggest; to instil.
s'insinuer, *v.r.*, to insinuate, to penetrate, to creep, to worm one's self.
insipide, *adj.*, insipid, tasteless, unsavoury, dull, flat.
insipidement (-pid-mǎn), *adv.*, insipidly; dully.
insipidité, *n.f.*, insipidity, insipidness, unsavouriness, tastelessness; dulness.
insistance, *n.f.*, insistence.
insister, *v.n.*, to insist; to persist, to urge, to press, to lay stress. *.Il insiste à demander;* he persists in demanding.
insociabilité, *n.f.*, unsociableness.
insociable, *adj.*, unsociable.
insociablement. *adv.*, unsociably.

insocial, -e, *adj.,* unsocial.

insolation, *n.f.,* insolation : sun-stroke.

insolemment (-la-män), *adv.,* insolently.
impudently, saucily.

insolence, *n.f.,* insolence, impertinence,
sauciness.

insolent, -e, *adj.* and *n.,* insolent, pert,
saucy, impudent; insolent person.

insolidité, *n.f.,* want of solidity.

insolite, *adj.,* unusual.

insolitement, *adv.,* unusually.

insolubilité, *n.f.,* insolubility.

insoluble, *adj.,* insoluble.

insolvabilité, *n.f.,* insolvency.

insolvable, *adj.,* insolvent.

insomnie (in-som-nî), *n.f.,* restlessness,
wakefulness; *pl.,* sleepless nights.

insondable, *adj.,* unfathomable

insouciance, *n.f.,* carelessness, thoughtlessness, heedlessness, listlessness.

insouciant, -e, *adj.,* careless, thoughtless,
heedless, listless.

insoucieu-x, -se, *adj.,* careless.

insoumis, *n.m.,* (milit. jur.) conscript,
recruit who does not join his regiment after
receiving an order to do so.

insoumis, -e, *adj.,* unsubdued.

insoutenable, *adj.,* indefensible, insupportable, unbearable.

inspecter, *v.a.,* to inspect, to survey.

inspect-eur, *n.m.,* **-rice,** *n.f.,* inspector,
superintendent, surveyor.

inspection, *n.f.,* inspection, survey; superintendence; view, sight. *Passer à l'—;* (milit.)
to undergo inspection. *A la première —:* at
first sight. *Faire l'— de;* to examine, to survey, to inspect.

inspirat-eur, -rice, *adj.* and *n.,* inspiring;
inspiratory; inspirer.

inspirateur, *n.m.,* (anat.) inspiratory
muscle.

inspiration, *n.f.,* inspiration, suggestion;
inhaling.

inspiré, *n.m.,* **-e,** *n.f.,* person inspired (by
Heaven—*du ciel*).

inspirer, *v.a.,* to inspire; to breathe; to
suggest, to prompt; to instil; to inhale.

instabilité, *n.f.,* instability. *L'— de la
fortune;* the instability of fortune.

instable, *adj.,* unstable, mutable.

installation, *n.f.,* installation; instalment; induction.

installer, *v a.,* to instal, to induct.

s'installer, *v.r.,* to instal one's self; to place
one's self.

instamment (ins-ta-män), *adv.,* earnestly,
urgently.

instance, *n.f.,* entreaty, solicitation; (jur.)
instance; *pl.,* urgency. *Faire de grandes, de
vives, —s:* to entreat earnestly.

instant, *n.m.,* instant, moment, trice. *A
l'—;* instantly, immediately. *Dans un —:* in
an instant. *Je reviens à l'—;* I shall return
immediately.

instant, -e, *adj.,* earnest, pressing, urgent.

instantané, -e, *adj.,* instantaneous.

instantanéité, *n.f.,* instantaneousness.

instantanément, *adv.,* instantaneously.

instar, *adv.,* like. *A l'— de;* like; in
imitation of.

instauration, *n.f.,* establishment, establishing, institution, instituting, founding.

instigat-eur, *n.m.,* **-rice,** *n.f.,* instigator,
inciter.

instigation, *n.f.,* instigation.

instiguer (-ghé), *v.a.,* (l.u.) to instigate.

instillation (-til-la-), *n.f.,* instillation.

instiller (ins-til-lé), *v.a.,* to instil.

instinct (-tin), *n.m.,* instinct.

instincti-f, -ve, *adj.,* instinctive.

instinctivement, *adv.,* instinctively.

⊙**instituant,** *n.m.,* (jur.) plaintiff.

institué, *n.m.,* (jur.) tenant in tail.

instituer, *v.a.,* to institute, to establish, to
appoint.

institut, *n.m.,* institution, order, institute.

institutes, *n.f. pl.,* (jur.) institutes.

institut-eur, *n.m.,* **-rice,** *n.f.,* institutor,
tutor; governess; schoolmaster; schoolmis-
tress.

institution, *n.f.,* institution, establishment; school, seminary; (jur.) settlement. —
de demoiselles; seminary for young ladies.
Chef d'—: head of an academy.

instructeur, *n.m.* and *adj.,* (milit.) instructor; (l.u.) instructor. *Sergent —;* drill-
sergeant.

instructi-f, -ve, *adj.,* instructive.

instruction, *n.f.,* instruction ; education;
information, attainments ; lesson ; direction;
(jur.) inquiry, examination. *L'— de la jeunesse;*
the instruction of youth. *Avoir de l'—;* to be
well educated. *—s détaillées;* particular instructions. *Sans —;* untaught, uneducated.
Donner des —s; to give directions. *Juge d'—;*
examining judge, inquiry-judge.

instruire (instruisant, instruit), *v.a.,* to
instruct, to teach, to inform, to apprise, to
acquaint; to train; (jur.) to investigate, to
examine, to proceed. — *la jeunesse;* to instruct
youth.

s'instruire, *v.r.,* to instruct, to inform, to
improve, one's self; to form the subject of an
inquiry, to be under examination.

instruisable, *adj.,* (l.u.) teachable.

instruit, -e, *part.,* instructed ; informed;
learned, well informed.

instrument, *n.m.,* instrument; implement,
tool; underling. — *tranchant;* edge-tool. —*s
aratoires,* agricultural implements. *Servir
d'—;* to be instrumental.

instrumentaire, *adj.,* (jur.) required by
law. *Témoin —;* witness (required by law) to
a deed.

instrumental, -e, *adj.,* instrumental.

instrumentation, *n.f.,* (mus.) composition of the instrumental part.

instrumenter, *v.n.,* (jur.) to act; to draw
up deeds, indentures, &c.; to compose instrumental music.

instrumentiste, *n.m.,* instrumental performer.

à l'insu, *prep.,* unknown to. *A mon —; à
votre —;* unknown to me, unknown to you. *A
l'— de son père;* unknown to his father.

insubmersible, *adj.,* that cannot be submerged.

insubordination, *n.f.,* insubordination.

insubordonné, -e, *adj.,* insubordinate.

insuccès, *n.m.,* failure, want of success.

insuffisamment, *adv.,* insufficiently.

insuffisance, *n.f.,* insufficiency.

insuffisant, -e, *adj.,* insufficient, inadequate.

insufflation, *n.f.,* insufflation.

insuffler, *v.a.,* (med.) to breathe in.

insulaire, *n.m.f.* and *adj.,* islander; insular.

insultant, -e, *adj.,* insulting.

insulte, *n.f.,* insult, affront. *Avec —;* insultingly. *Faire une — à quelqu'un;* to offer an
insult to any one. *Supporter une —;* to brook an
insult.

insulter, *v.a.,* to insult, to affront.

insulter, *v.n.,* to insult.

insupportable, *adj.,* insupportable, insufferable, intolerable.

insupportablement, *adv.,* insupportably,
insufferably, intolerably.

insurgé, -e, *part.,* insurgent ; in insurrection.

insurgé, *n.m.*, insurgent.

insurgence, *n.f.*, insurrection.

insurgents, *n.m.pl.*, name of a Hungarian militia.

s'insurger, *v.r.*, to revolt, to rise in insurrection.

insurmontable, *adj.*, insurmountable, insuperable, invincible.

insurmontablement, *adv.*, insurmountably, insuperably.

insurrection, *n.f.*, insurrection.

insurrectionnel,-le, *adj.*, insurrectionary.

intact (in-takt), **-e** *adj.*, intact, entire, whole, untouched; unblemished, untainted, irreproachable.

intactile, *adj.*, intangible.

***intaille,** *n.f.*, (engr.) intaglio.

intangibilité, *n.f.*, intangibility.

intangible, *adj.*, intangible.

intarissable, *adj.*, inexhaustible, that never dries up.

intégral, -e, *adj.*, integral, whole, entire.

intégrale, *n.f.*, (math.) integral, fluent.

intégralement(-gral-măn), *adv.*, integrally, entirely.

intégralité, *n.f.*, integrality, entireness.

intégrant, -e, *adj.*, integral, integrant.

intégration, *n.f.*, (math.) integration.

intègre, *adj.*, honest, upright, just.

intégrer, *v.a.*, (math.) to integrate.

intégrité, *n.f.*, integrity, uprightness, probity; soundness; entireness.

intellect (in-tèl-lèkt), *n.m.*, intellect, understanding.

intellecti-f, -ve, *adj.*, intellective.

intellection, *n.f.*, intellection.

intellectuel, -le, *adj.*, intellectual.

intelligence(-tèl-li-), *n.f.*, intellect; intelligence; understanding; knowledge; good understanding, harmony; correspondence; spirit, spiritual being; skill, ability. *En bonne — avec;* on good terms with. *Être d'—;* to be leagued together. *— étroite;* narrow intellect.

intelligent, -e (-tèl-li-), *adj.*, intelligent, sharp.

intelligibilité (-tèl-li-), *n.f.*, intelligibility, intelligibleness.

intelligible (-tèl-li-), *adj.*, intelligible; audible; intellectual.

intelligiblement(-tèl-li-),*adv.*, intelligibly, audibly.

intempéramment (-ra-măn), *adv.*, intemperately, immoderately.

intempérance, *n.f.*, intemperance, insobriety, excess.

intempérant, -e, *adj.*, intemperate.

intempéré, -e, *adj.*, intemperate.

intempérie, *n.f.*, inclemency, intemperateness.

intempesti-f, -ve, *adj.*, unseasonable, untimely, intempestive.

intempestivement, *adv.*, at an unseasonable time, at an untimely moment.

intendance, *n.f.*, administration, direction, management, superintendence; the office, the house, of an intendant; (milit.) commissariat.

intendant,*n.m.*,intendant, steward; (milit.) commissary. *— de la liste civile;* intendant of the civil list.

intendante, *n.f.*, intendant's lady

intense, *adj.*, intense, violent, severe.

intensité, *n.f.*, state of being strained or stretched, intensity, intenseness.

intensivement, *adv.*, intensely.

intenter, *v.a.*, to enter; to bring; to commence *— une action contre quelqu'un;* to bring an action against any one.

intention, *n.f.*, intention; intent, purpose, design: view. *— présumée criminelle;* implied

malice. *A l'— de;* on account of. *Dans l'— de;* with a view to. *Avoir l'— de;* to intend to.

intentionné, -e, *adj.*, intentioned. *Une personne bien —e;* a well-intentioned person.

intentionnel, -le, *adj.*, intentional.

intentionnelles, *adj.f.pl.*, (antiq.) supposed, intended. *Espèces impresses, espèces —;* images which, the ancients supposed, came out of bodies to make an impression on the senses.

intercadence,*n.f.*, (med.)irregular beating of the pulse.

intercadent, *adj.*, irregular (of the pulse—*du pouls*).

intercalaire, *adj.*, intercalary. *Jour —;* intercalary day. *Vers —s;* burden of a song.

intercalation, *n.f.*, intercalation.

intercaler, *v.a.*, to intercalate.

intercéder, *v.n.*, to intercede.

intercepter, *v.a.*, to intercept.

interception, *n.f.*, (phys.) interception.

intercesseur, *n.m.*, intercessor, interceder.

intercession, *n.f.*, intercession.

intercostal, -e, *adj.*, (anat.) intercostal.

intercurrent, -e, *adj.*, (med.) intercurrent.

interdiction, *n.f.*, interdiction, prohibition; suspension; laying under an interdict; privation of the exercise (or civil rights—*des droits civils*).

interdire, *v.a.*, to interdict, to prohibit, to forbid; to suspend; to amaze, to confound, to stupify; (jur.) to declare a man incapable of managing his own affairs. *— l'entrée à quelqu'un;* to shut any one out.

interdit, -e, *part.*, abashed, confused.

interdit, *n.m.*, interdict, person interdicted.

intéressant, -e, *adj.*, interesting.

intéressé, -e, *part.*, interested; selfish.

intéressé, *n.m.*, party interested.

intéresser, *v.a.*, to interest; to concern; to give a share to; (surg.) to injure. *Cela ne vous intéresse en rien;* that does not concern you at all.

s'intéresser, *v.r.*, to take an interest in, to be interested, to be concerned for; to have an interest, to be concerned.

intérêt, *n.m.*, interest, concern, share; *pl.*, interest. *Avoir un — à;* to have an interest, a share, in. *Il est de mon — de le faire;* it is my interest to do it. *Il y va de mon —;* it concerns my interest. *Favoriser les —s de quelqu'un;* to promote any one's interest. *C'est l'— qui nous guide;* it is interest that guides us. *Cet argent porte —;* this money bears interest.

interférence, *n.f.*, (opt.) interference.

interférer, *v.n.*, to interfere.

interfolier, *v.a.*, to interleave.

intérieur, -e, *adj.*, interior, internal, inner, inward.

intérieur, *n.m.*, interior, inside, home, private life. *Ministre de l'—;* Secretary of State for the home department.

intérieurement, *adv.*, inwardly, internally.

intérim (-rim), *n.m.*, interim. *Dans l'—;* in the interim.

intérimaire, *adj.*, provisional, temporary.

interjection, *n.f.*, (gram.) interjection ;(jur.) lodging (of an appeal—*d'un appel*).

interjeter,*v.a.*,(jur.)to lodge (an appeal—*un appel*).

***interligne,** *n.f.*, (print.) lead.

interligne,n.m.*,(mus.) space; space between two written or printed lines.

***interligner,** *v.a.*, (print.) to lead.

interlinéaire, *adj.*, interlineary.

interlinéation, *n.f.*, interlineation.

interlinéer, *v.a.*, to interline

interlocut-eur, *n.m.*, **-rice,** *n.f.*, interlocutor, interrogator.

interlocution, *n.f.*, interlocution.

interlocutoire, *n.m.* and *adj.*, (jur.) inter-

locutory decree; interlocutory. *Arrêt —; in-*
terlocutory judgment.

interlope. *adj.,* interloping.

interlope, *n.m.,* interloper (vessel—*navire*).

interloquer. *v.a.,* ⊙ to give an interlocutory
judgment; to nonplus, to put to a nonplus.

intermaxillaire, *adj.,* (anat.) intermax-
illary.

intermède, *n.m.,* interlude; (chem.) intermediate.

intermédiaire, *adj.,* intermediate, intervening.

intermédiaire, *n.m.,* medium, intermediate agent. *Par l'— de;* through the medium
of.

intermédiat, -e, *adj.,* intermediate.

interminable, *adj.,* interminable.

intermission, *n.f.,* intermission.

intermittence, *n.f.,* intermission; cessation.

intermittent, -e, *adj.,* intermittent.

intermonde, *n.m.,* intermundane space.

intermusculaire, *adj.,* (anat.) intermuscular.

internat, *n.m.,* boarding-school; house-sur-
geoncy (of hospitals—*d'un hôpital*).

international, -e, *adj.,* international.

interne, *n.m.f.,* (of schools—*dans les écoles*)
boarder; (of hospitals—*des hôpitaux*) house-
surgeon; clinical clerk.

interne, *adj.,* internal, interior; indoor.
Élève —; boarder (in school—*à l'école*).

interner. *v.a.,* to send into, to confine in,
the interior of a country.

internissable, *adj.,* that cannot be sullied.

internonce, *n.m.,* internuncio.

interosseu-x, -se, *adj.,* (anat.) interosseous.

interpellat-eur, *n.m.,* **-rice,** (-pèl-la-), *n.f.,*
one who calls upon, who questions.

interpellation (-pèl-la-), *n.f.,* interpellation, summons; question (in parliament—*au
parlement*).

interpeller (-pèl-lé), *v.a.,* to summon, to
call upon, to require, to challenge, to question.

interpolateur, *n.m.,* interpolator.

interpolation, *n.f.,* interpolation.

interpoler, *v.a.,* to interpolate.

interposé, -e, *part.,* interposed.

interposer, *v.a.,* to interpose.

s'interposer, *v.r.,* to interpose, to come
between.

interposition, *n.f.,* interposition; intervention.

interprétati-f, -ve, *adj.,* interpretative.

interprétation, *n.f.,* interpretation, construction. *— erronée;* misconstruction. *Donner une mauvaise — à;* to misconstrue.

interprète, *n.m.,* interpreter, expounder.

interpréter, *v.a.,* to interpret, to expound.

*interrègne (-tèr-rè-), *n.m.,* interregnum.

interrogant, *adj.,* (l.u.) (gram.) interrogative, of interrogation. *Point —;* note of interrogation.

interrogat-eur, *n.m.,* **-rice,** *n.f.,* interrogator, examiner.

interrogati-f, -ve, *adj.,* interrogative.

interrogation, *n.f.,* interrogation, question.
Point d'—; note of interrogation.

interrogatoire, *n.m.,* examination. *Subir
un —;* to undergo an examination. *— contradictoire;* cross-examination.

interroger, *v.a.,* to interrogate, to question;
to consult. *— l'histoire;* to consult history.
— contradictoirement; to cross examine.

s'interroger, *v.r.,* to examine one's self, to
interrogate each other.

interroi (-tèr-roa), *n.m.,* (antiq.) regent;
one who at Rome held the regal office between
the death of one king and the election of
another.

interrompre, *v.a.,* to interrupt, to cut off,
to break off.

s'interrompre, *v.r.,* to interrupt one's self,
to leave off.

interrupt-eur, -rice. *n.* and *adj.,* interrupter; causing interruption.

interruption, *n.f.,* interruption.

intersection, *n.f.,* intersection.

interstellaire (-stèl-lèr), *adj.,* (astron.) interstellar.

interstice, *n.m.,* interstice.

intertropical, *adj.,* intertropical.

intervalle, *n.m.,* interval, interstice. *Par
—s;* at intervals.

intervenant, -e, *n.* and *adj.,* (jur.) intervening party; intervening.

intervenir. *v.n.,* to intervene, to interfere;
to interpose; to happen, to occur. *Faire —;*
to bring, to call, in.

intervention, *n.f.,* intervention, interference.

interversion, *n.f.,* interversion.

intervertir. *v.a.,* to intervert, to change.

intestable. *adj.,* (jur.) intestable.

intestat, *n.m.,* and *adj. invariable,* (jur.)
intestate. *Héritier ab —;* heir of one that dies
intestate.

intestin, *n.m.,* intestine.

intestin, -e, *adj.,* intestine.

intestinal, -e, *adj.,* (anat.) intestinal.

intimation, *n.f.,* intimation; legal notice.

intime, *n.m.f.* and *adj.,* intimate; inmost.
C'est mon ami —; he is my intimate friend.

intimé, -e, *n.f.,* (jur.) appellee.

intimement (-tin-màn), *adv.,* intimately.

intimer, *v.a.,* to notify, to give legal notice
of. *On lui intima l'ordre de partir;* they notified
to him the order to depart.

intimidation, *n.f.,* intimidation.

intimider, *v.a.,* to intimidate.

s'intimider, *v.r.,* to be intimidated.

intimité, *n.f.,* intimacy, close connection.

intitulé, -e, *part.,* entitled.

intitulé, *n.m.,* title (of deeds, books—*de
titres, de livres*).

intituler, *v.a.,* to entitle, to call.

s'intituler, *v.r.,* to entitle one's self, to call
one's self.

intolérable, *adj.,* intolerable, insufferable,
insupportable.

intolérablement, *adv.,* intolerably, insufferably.

intolérance, *n.f.,* intolerance.

intolérant, -e, *adj.,* intolerant.

intolérantisme, *n.m.,* intolerance.

intonation, *n.f.,* intonation.

intorsion, *n.f.,* intorsion.

intoxication, *n.f.,* (med.) poisoning produced by living in a poisonous atmosphere.

intrados, *n.m.,* or **douelle,** *n.f.,* (arch.)
intrados.

intraduisible, *adj.,* untranslatable.

intraitable, *adj.,* untractable, ungovernable,
unmanageable, unruly, difficult; refractory.

intra-muros, *adv.,* inside a town.

intransiti-f, -ve (-zi-), *adj.,* (gram.) intransitive.

intrant, *n.m.,* in the University of Paris, the
name formerly given to him who appointed the
Rector.

in-trente-deux, *n.m.,* and *adj.* (—), (print.)
in thirty-two.

intrépide, *adj.,* intrepid, dauntless, undaunted, fearless, resolute; bold.

intrépidement (-pi-dman), *adv.,* intrepidly,
fearlessly.

intrépidité, *n.f.,* intrepidity, dauntlessness,
boldness, undauntedness, fearlessness.

intrigant, -e, *adj.* and *n.,* intriguing; intriguer; trimmer.

intrigue (in-trig), *n.f.*, intrigue; scrape, difficulty; plot. — *accessoire;* under-plot. *Démêler, dénouer, une* — ; to unravel an intrigue.

intrigué. -e, *part.*, puzzled, perplexed.

intriguer (-ghé), *v.a.*, to puzzle, to perplex. **s'intriguer**, *v.r.*, to intrigue; to take pains, to put one's self to much trouble to bring a piece of business to a successful issue.

intriguer, *v.n.*, to intrigue, to plot.

intrigueu-r, *n.m.*, **-se**, *n.f.*, intriguer.

intrinsèque, *adj.*, intrinsic, intrinsical.

intrinsèquement (-sèk-mān), *adv.*, intrinsically.

introduct-eur, *n.m.*, **-rice**, *n.f.*, introducer

introducti-f. -ve, *adj.*, (jur.) of the first process, introductory.

introduction, *n.f.*, introduction; preamble; (jur.) previous proceedings.

introductoire, *adj.*, introductory, preliminary.

introduire (introduisant, introduit), *v.a.*, to introduce, to show in, to bring, to bring in; to conduct; to put. — *adroitement;* to shuffle in. — *imperceptiblement;* to slide in. — *de force;* to thrust in.

s'introduire, *v.r.*, to introduce one's self; to get in, to gain admittance; to enter; to be introduced, to be brought in; to intrude, to intrude one's self. — *partout;* to intrude everywhere.

introït (-it), *n.m.*, (c. rel.) introit.

intromission, *n.f.*, (phys.) intromission.

intronisation, *n.f.*, enthroning (of bishops —*d'évêque*).

introniser, *v.a.*, to install (a bishop— *un évêque*) ; to enthrone.

introuvable, *adj.*, undiscoverable, not to be found.

introuvé, -e, *part.*, unfound.

intrus, -e, *part.* and *n.*, intruded, obtruded; intruder.

intrusion, *n.f.*, intrusion.

intuiti-f, -ve, *adj.*, intuitive.

intuition, *n.f.*, intuition.

intuitivement (-ti-vmān), *adv.*, intuitively.

intumescence (-mès-sans,) *n.f.*, intumescence.

intumescent, -e, *adj.*, intumescent.

intussusception, *n.f.*, (med., physiology) intussusception, introsusception.

inule, *n.f.*, (bot.) inula.

inuline, *n.f.*, (chem.) inulin.

inusable, *adj.*, that cannot be worn out.

inusité, -e, *adj.*, unused, not in use, obsolete.

inutile, *adj.*, useless, fruitless, profitless; unnecessary; unavailing, needless, unserviceable, vain, of no use.

inutilement (-til-mān), *adv.*, uselessly, fruitlessly, unprofitably, to no purpose, vainly, needlessly.

inutilité, *n.f.*, inutility, uselessness, unprofitableness; useless thing.

invagination, *n.f.*, (med.) intussusception.

invaincu, -e, *adj.*, unvanquished, unconquered.

invalidation, *n.f.*, invalidation.

invalide, *adj.*, invalid; infirm; (milit., nav.) disabled.

invalide, *n.m.* and *f.*, invalid; (milit.) invalid, pensioner. — *externe;* out-pensioner.

invalidement (-lid-mān), *adv.*, invalidly, without force, without effect.

invalider, *v.a.*, to invalidate, to make of no force, to make void.

invalidité, *n.f.*, invalidity.

invariabilité, *n.f.*, invariableness, invariability.

invariable, *adj.*, invariable, unchangeable, unalterable. *Mot* —; indeclinable word.

invariablement, *adv.*, invariably, unchangeably, unalterably.

invasion, *n.f.*, invasion; inroad.

invective, *n.f.*, invective — *sanglante;* bitter invective.

invectiver, *v.n.*, to inveigh.

invendable, *adj.*, unsaleable.

invendu, -e, *adj.*, (com.) unsold.

inventaire, *n.m.*, inventory. *Bénéfice d'*—; (jur.) non-liability to debts beyond assets descended.

inventer, *v.a.*, to invent, to find out, to contrive, to devise; to imagine, to forge, to fabricate. *Il n'a pas inventé la poudre;* he will never set the Thames on fire.

invent-eur, -rice, *n.* and *adj.*, inventor, contriver, deviser; inventive.

inventi-f. -ve, *adj.*, inventive.

invention, *n.f.*, invention, contrivance; inventing, contriving; device, trick; (c. rel.) discovery of relics; festival in honour of such discovery. *Brevet d'*—; patent. *Vivre d'*—; to live upon one's wits.

inventorier, *v.a.*, to inventory.

inversable, *adj.*, that cannot be upset.

inverse, *adj.*, inverse, inverted. *En raison* —; in inverse ratio. *En sens* —; in the contrary direction. *Être en raison* — *de;* to be in inverse ratio to.

inverse, *n.m.*, reverse, contrary. *Faire juste l'*—; to do just the contrary, to do the exact contrary.

inversement, *adv.*, inversely.

inversion, *n.f.*, (gram.) inversion.

invertébré, -e, *adj.* and *n.*, invertebral; invertebrate.

inverti, -e, *adj.*, inversed, reversed.

investigat-eur, -rice, *n.* and *adj.*, investigator, explorer; investigating, investigative, scrutinizing, inquiring; inquisitive.

investigation, *n.f.*, investigation.

investir, *v.a.*, to invest, to vest; to surround, to block up; to put in possession.

investissement (-tis-mān), *n.m.*, (milit.) investment.

investiture, *n.f.*, investiture.

invétéré, -e, *part.*, inveterate. *Haine —e;* inveterate hatred.

s'invétérer, *v.r.*, to grow inveterate, to become inveterate. *Cette maladie s'est invétérée;* this disorder has grown inveterate.

invincibilité, *n.f.*, invincibleness.

invincible, *adj.*, invincible, insuperable, unconquerable, insurmountable.

invinciblement, *adv.*, invincibly, insuperably, unconquerably, insurmountably.

in-vingt-quatre, *n.m.* and *adj.* (—).(print.) twenty-four, in twenty-four.

inviolabilité, *n.f.*, inviolability; inviolableness.

inviolable, *adj.*, inviolable, inviolate.

inviolablement, *adv.*, inviolably.

inviolé, -e, *adj.*, inviolate.

invisibilité, *n.f.*, invisibility, invisibleness

invisible, *adj.*, invisible.

invisiblement, *adv.*, invisibly.

invitation, *n.f.*, invitation.

invitatoire, *n.f.*, (c.rel.) invitatory.

invité, -e *n.m.*, *n.f.*, guest.

inviter, *v.a.*, to invite, to bid, to beg; to allure, to incite, to attract, to tempt. — *à dîner;* to invite to dinner.

invocation, *n.f.*, invocation.

involontaire, *adj.*, involuntary.

involontairement (-tèr-mān), *adv.*, involuntarily.

involucral, -e, *adj.*, (bot.) involucral, pertaining to an involucrum.

involucre, *n.m.*, (bot.) involucrum, involucre : cover.

involuti-f, -ve, adj., (bot.) involute, involuted.

involution, n.f., (jur.) involvement, complication.

invoquer, v.a., to invoke, to call upon, to cry unto, to invocate ; to appeal to.

iuvraisemblable, adj., unlikely, improbable.

·invraisemblablement, adv., improbably, unlikely.

invraisemblance, n.f., unlikeliness, unlikelihood, improbability ; unlikely thing, improbable thing.

invulnérabilité, n.f., invulnerability, invulnerableness.

invulnérable, adj., invulnerable.

iavulnérablement, adv., invulnerably.

iode, n.m.; (chem.) iodine.

iodé, -e, adj, (chem.) iodized.

iodeux, adj, (chem.) iodous.

iodique, adj., (chem.)-iodic.

iodure, n.m., (chem.) ioduret, iodide.

ioduré, -e, adj.,(chem.)ioduretted, containing an iodide.

ionien, -ne (-in, -e-n), adj, Ionian, Ionic.

ionien, n.m., Ionic.

ionique, adj., Ionic. L'ordre —; the Ionic order.

iota, n.m.. iota ; jot, tittle.

iotacisme, n.m.,(gram.)frequent repetition of the letter i.

ipécacuana, n.m., ipecacuanha.

ipso facto, adv., by the fact.

iranien, -ne, adj., (philology) iranic.

irascibilité, n.f., irascibleness, irascibility.

irascible, adj., irascible, irritable.

⊙**ire,** n.f., wrath, anger, ire.

iridium, n.m. (n.p.), (chem.) iridium.

iris (i-ris), n.m., iris, rainbow; (anat.) iris; (bot.) iris, iris-root, orris, orris-root. Pois d'—; (pharm.) issue-peas.

irisation, n.f., (phys.) iridescence.

irisé, -e, adj., rainbow-coloured, irised, irisated, irisate, variegated ; iridescent.

ir¹andais, -e, n. and adj., Irishman, Irishwoman ; Irish.

irlandais. n m., Irish language.

ironie, n.f., irony.

ironique. adj., ironic, ironical.

ironiquement, adv., ironically.

iroquois. n.m.. Iroquois ; lout.

irrachetable(ir-rash-tabl),adj., unredeemable.

irradiation (ir-ra-), n.f., irradiation.

irradier (ir-ra-), v.n., to irradiate.

irraisonnable(ir-rè-),adj., irrational ; void, destitute of reason.

irraisonnablement (ir-rè-), adv., irrationally.

irrationnel, -le, adj., irrational.

irrationnellement. adv., i rationally.

irréalisable, adj., that cannot be done.

irrecherchable, adj., not to be looked for ; not to be sued.

irréconciliable (ir-ré-),adj., irreconcilable.

irréconciliablement (ir-ré-), adv., irreconcilably.

irréconcilié, -e (ir-ré-), adj., unreconciled.

irrécouvrable, adj., irrecoverable.

irrécusable (ir-ré-), adj., unexceptionable, unobjectionable.

irrécusablement, adv., unexceptionably ; unobjectionably.

irréductibilité (ir-ré-), n.f., irreducibleness.

irréductible (ir-ré-), adj., irreducible, unreducible.

irréfléchi, -e (ir-ré-), adj., thoughtless, heedless, inconsiderate, unguarded.

irréflexion (ir-ré-), n.f., thoughtlessness, heedlessness, inconsiderateness.

irréformable (ir-ré-), adj., unchangeable, irrevocable.

irréfragable (ir-ré-), adj., irrefragable, irrefutable.

irréfragablement (ir-ré-), adv., irrefragably, undeniably, irrefutably.

irréfutable (ir-ré-), adj., irrefutable.

irréfuté, adj., not refuted, not disproved.

irrégularité (ir-ré-), n.f., irregularity.

irréguli-er, -ère (ir-ré-), adj., irregular ; (math.) scalene.

irrégulièrement (ir-ré-),adv., irregularly.

irréligieusement (ir-ré-), adv., irreligiously, profanely.

irréligieu-x, -se (ir-ré-). adj., irreligious.

irréligion (ir-ré-), n.f., irreligion.

irrémédiable (ir-ré-), adj., irremediable, not to be remedied, helpless, irretrievable.

irrémédiablement (ir-ré-), adv., irremediably ; irrecoverably.

irrémissible (ir-ré-), adj., irremissible, unpardonable.

irrémissiblement (ir-ré-), adv., irremissibly, unpardonably.

irréparable (ir-ré-), adj., irreparable, irretrievable, irrecoverable.

irréparablement(ir-ré-),adv., irreparably, irretrievably, irrecoverably.

irrépréhensible (ir-ré-), adj., irreprehensible, irreproachable, irreprovable.

irréprhensiblement (ir-ré-), adv., irreprehensibly, irreproachably, irreprovably.

irrépressible. adj., irrepressible.

irrprochable (ir-ré-),adj., irreproachable, irreprovable, unexceptionable.

irréprochablement (ir-ré-), adv., irreproachably, irreprovably, unexceptionably.

irrésistibilité (ir-ré-), n.f., irresistibility ; irresistibleness.'

irrésistible (ir-ré-), adj., irresistible.

irrésistiblement (ir-ré-),adv., irresistibly.

irrésolu, -e (ir-ré-), adj., irresolute, wavering, undetermined.

irrésoluble (ir ré-), adj., irresolvable.

irrésolument (ir-ré-), adv., irresolutely.

irrésolution (ir-ré-). n.f., irresolution.

irrespectueusement, adv., disrespectfully.

irrespectueu-x, -se, adj., disrespectful.

irrespirable. adj., irrespirable.

irresponsabilité. n.f., irresponsibility.

irresponsable, adj., irresponsible.

irrévéremment (ir-ré-vé-ra-mán), adv., irreverently.

irrévérence, n.f., irreverence, disrespect.

irrévérencieu-x, -se adj., irreverent ; disrespectful.

irrévérent, -e. adj., irreverent.

irrévocabilité (ir-ré-),n.f.,irrevocableness

irrévocable. adj., irrevocable.

irrévocablement, adv., irrevocably.

irrigable. adj., that can be irrigated.

irrigateur, n.m., watering-engine.

irrigation (ir-ré-), n.f., irrigation.

irriguer, v.a., to irrigate.

irritabilité (ir-ri-), n.m., irritability.

irritable, adj., irritable.

irritant, -e, adj., irritating, provoking ; (med.) irritant ; (jur.) vital.

irritant. n.m., (med.) irritant.

irritation. n.f., irritation ; exasperation.

irrité, -e. part., irritated, exasperated, excited ; angry. Une mer —e ; an angry sea.

irriter (ir-ri-té), v.a., to irritate ; to incense, to anger, to exasperate ; to provoke, to excite, to enrage. Vous irritez sa colère ; you provoke his anger. Il est irrité contre vous ; he is exasperated with you.

s'irriter. *v.r.*, to be irritated; to be angry, provoked, exasperated.

irroration (ir-ro-), *n.f.*, irroration.

irruption (ir-rup-), *n.f.*, irruption.

isabelle, *adj.*, dun-coloured (of horses—*des chevaux*); dove-coloured (of birds—*des oiseaux*).

isabelle, *n.m.*, Isabel; dun (horse—*cheval*); dove-colour (of birds—*oiseaux*).

isard. *n.m.*, (mam.) name given in the Pyrenees to the antelope chamois.

ischion (-ki-), *n.m.*, (anat.) ischium.

ischurétique (-ku-). *adj.*,(med.) ischuretic.

ischurie (-ku-), *n.f.*, (med.) ischury, ischuria.

isiaque, *adj.*, pertaining, relating, to Isis.

isinglass,*n.m.* V. **ichtyocolle** and **colle de poisson.**

islam, *n.m.*, islam, religion of Mahomet.

islamisme, *n.m.*, islamism.

isocéle, *adj.*, (geom.) isosceles.

isochromatique (-kro-),*adj.*, isochromatic.

isochrone (izo-krô-n), *adj.*, isochronal, isochronous.

isochronisme, *n.m.*, isochronism.

isolant, -e, *adj.*, (phys.) insulating. *Corps* —; insulating body.

isolation, *n.f.*, isolation, insulation.

isolé, -e, *adj.*, *part.*, isolated, lonely: detached, insulated, solitary. *Lieu* —; lonely place.

isolement (i-zol-mān), *n.m.*, loneliness, isolation.

isolément, *adv.*, separately.

isoler, *v.a.*, to isolate, to insulate, to detach, to separate.

s'isoler, *v.r.*, to isolate one's self, to shun society.

isoloir, *n.m.*,(phys.) insulator.

isomère. *adj.*, (min. chem.) isomeric.

isotherme, *adj.*, isothermal.

israélite (iz-), *n.m.,f.* and *adj.*, Israelite; Israelitic, Israelitish, Jewish. *Un bon* —; a plain, simple man.

issu, -e, *adj.*, born, descended, sprung.

issue, *n.f.*, issue, egress, outlet; end, event; refuse grain; offal (of animals—*d'animaux*).

isthme, *n.m.*, isthmus.

isthmiques, *adj.m.pl.*, (antiq.) Isthmian. *Jeux* —; Isthmian games.

itague (i-tag), *n.f.*, (nav.) runner-tie. — *de la drisse des huniers*; tie of the top-sails.

italianiser, *v.a.*, to Italianize.

italianisme, *n.m.*, Italianism.

italien, -ne (-in, -è-n), *n.* and *adj.*, Italian.

italien. *n.m.*, Italian language.

italique, *n.m.* and *adj.*, italics; italic.

item (i-tem), *adv.*, also, moreover.

item, *n.m.* (—), item.

itérati-f, -ve, *adj.*, iterative, repeated.

itérativement (-tiv-mān),*adv.*, repeatedly.

ithos, *n.m.*, that part of rhetoric which relates to manners and customs.

itinéraire, *n.m.* and *adj.*, itinerary.

iule, *n.m.*, (ent.) julus. V. **jule.**

ive, *or* **ivette,** *n.f.*, (bot.) iva.

ivoire, *n.m.*, ivory. *D'*—; ivory. — *des dents;* ivory of the teeth.

ivoirier, *n.m.*, ivory-turner.

ivraie, *n.f.*, darnel, tare; rye-grass. *Séparer l'*— *d'avec le bon grain;* to separate the tares from the wheat.

ivre. *adj.*, drunk, inebriated, intoxicated. *A moitié* —; half-tipsy, half-seas-over. — *mort;* dead drunk. — *de joie;* intoxicated with joy.

ivresse, *n.f.*, drunkenness, ebriety, inebriation, intoxication.

ivrogne, *n.m.* and *adj.*, drunkard; drunken, tipsy, given to drink.

ivrogner, *v.n.*,(pop.) to fuddle, to fuddle one's self, to sot, to guzzle, to get drunk.

ivrognerie, *n.f.*, inebriation, drunkenness, intoxication.

ivrognesse, *n.f.*, (pop.) drunkard, drunken woman.

ixia, *n.f.*,(bot.) ixia.

J

j, *n.m.*, the tenth letter of the alphabet, j.

⊙**jà,** *adv.*, already.

jable, *n.m.*, cross-groove (cooper's work—*tonnellerie*).

jabler, *v.a.*, to cross (cooper's work—*tonnellerie*).

jabot, *n.m.*, frill (of a shirt—*d'une chemise*); crop (of a bird—*des oiseaux*). *Faire* —; to give one's self airs. *Se remplir le* —; to have a blow-out.

jaboter, *v.n.*, to prattle, to chatter.

jacasse, *n.f.*,(pop.) chatterer, prater, talkative female.

jacasser, *v.n.*, to chatter (of the magpie—*de la pie*); (fig.) to prate, to jabber.

jacée, *n.f.*, (bot.) knapweed.

jacent, -e, *adj.*, (jur.) in abeyance.

jachère, *n.f.*, fallow, fallow-ground. *Terre en* — : fallow-land.

jachéré, -e, *part.*, fallowed.

jachérer, *v.a.*, to fallow.

jacinthe, *or* **hyacinthe,** *n.f.*, (bot., min.) hyacinth.

jacobée, *n.f.*, (bot.) ragwort.

jacobin, -e, *adj.*, Jacobinical.

jacobin, *n.m.*, jacobin friar, monk; Jacobin, ultra radical of the French revolution.

jacobinisme, *n.m.*, Jacobinism.

jacobite, *n.m.* and *adj.*, Jacobite.

jaconas, *n.m.*, jaconet.

jacot, *n.m.* V. **jacquot.**

jacquerie, *n.f.*, rising of the French peasants against the nobility in 1358; rising of peasants.

jacques, *or* **jacques bonhomme,** *n.m.*, nickname designating the French peasants as a class.

jacquot, *or* **jacot,** *n.m.*, poll; poll-parrot; pug (monkey—*singe*).

jactance, *n.f.*, boasting, bragging, boast.

⊙**se jacter,** *v.r.*, to swagger, to brag.

jaculatoire, *adj.*, ejaculatory.

jade. *n.m.*, (min.) jade.

jadelle, *n.f.*, (orni.) coot.

jadis (jâ-dis), *adv.*, of old, in times of yore formerly.

jaguar, *n.m.* (zool.) jaguar.

jaïet, *n.m.* V. **jais.**

jaillir, *v.n.*, to spout, to spout out, to gush, to gush out, to spurt out; to spring, to burst out.

jaillissant, -e, *adj.*, spouting, gushing; springing.

jaillissement, *n.m.*, spouting out, gushing out.

jais, *n.m.*, jet.

jalage, *n.m.*, (feudalism—*féodalité*) duty on wine.

jalap (ja-lap), *n.m.*, jalap.

jale, *n.f.*, large bowl.

⊙**jalet,** *n.m.*, pebble-stone, pebble.

jalon (ja-lon), *n.m.*, levelling-staff; surveying-staff offset-staff; landmark

jalonnement, *n.m.*, (land surveying—*lever des plans*) placing of offset staves in ground to be surveyed; (milit.) placing javelin-men to mark out a direction.

jalonner, *v.n.*, to fix staves in the ground; to place landmarks.

Jalonneur, *n.m.*, (milit.) javelin-man (to mark out a direction—*pour indiquer la direction*).

Jalousement, *adv.*, jealously.

Jalouser, *v.a.*, to be jealous of.

se Jalouser, *v.r.*, to be jealous of each other.

Jalousie, *n.f.*, jealousy; fear, uneasiness, umbrage; blind, Venetian blind; (bot.) three-coloured amaranth. *Par* —; out of jealousy. *Donner de la* — *à quelqu'un;* to make any one jealous.

Jalou-x, -se, *n.* and *adj.*, jealous person; jealous; desirous, anxious; inclining on one side (of a carriage, of a ship—*d'une voiture, d'un vaisseau*). *Il est* — *de votre gloire;* he is jealous of your glory. — *d'acquérir de la gloire;* desirous of acquiring glory. — *de plaire;* anxious to please.

Jamais, *adv.*, never, ever. *Je ne la vois* —; I never see her. *Si* — *je deviens riche;* if ever I grow rich.

Jamais, *n.m.*, time without end. *Au grand* —; for ever and ever, to all eternity.

Jambage, *n.m.*, jamb (of a door—*de porte*); hanger (in writing—*écriture*).

Jambe, *n.f.*, leg. *Courir à toutes* —*s;* to run at full speed. *Prendre ses* —*s à son cou;* to betake one's self to one's heels. *Être haut en* —; to be long-legged. *Cela ne lui rend pas la* — *mieux faite;* he is none the better for it.

Jambé, -e, *adj.*, legged. *Bien* —; well made about the legs. *Mal* —; badly made about the legs.

Jambette, *n.f.*, small pocket-knife; (carp.) jamb.

Jambi-er, -ère. *adj.*, (anat.) of the leg.

Jambon, *n.m.*, ham, gammon of bacon.

Jambonneau, *n.m.*, small ham.

Jan, *n.m.*, (trick-track) jan.

Janissaire, *n.m.*, janizary, janissary.

Jansénisme, *n.m.*, Jansenism.

Janséniste, *n.m.* and *adj.*, Jansenist.

Jante, *n.f.*, felly (of a wheel—*de roue*).

Janvier, *n.m.*, January.

Japon, *n.m.*, Japan-ware.

Japonais, -e, *n.* and *adj.*, Japanese.

Japonais, *n.m.*, Japanese language.

Jappement (ja-pmän), *n.m.*, yelping (of dogs—*du chien*).

Japper, *v.n.*, to yelp.

○**Jaque**, *n.f.*, coat. — *de mailles;* coat of mail.

Jaquemart, *n.m.*, jack of a clock; clock-house.

Jaquette, *n.f.*, jacket; tunic.

Jaquier, *n.m.*, species of fig-tree.

Jarde, *n.f.* *V.* **jardon**.

Jardin, *n.m.*, garden. — *d'agrément;* pleasure-garden. — *potager;* kitchen-garden. — *fruitier;* fruit-garden. — *des plantes;* botanical garden. — *suspendu;* pendent garden.

Jardinage, *n.m.*, gardening; garden-ground; garden-stuff.

Jardiner, *v.n.*, to garden.

Jardinet, *n.m.*, small garden.

Jardineuse, *adj.f.*, (of emeralds—*émeraudes*) spotty, dark.

Jardinier, *n.m.*, gardener. — *fleuriste* (—*s* —*s*); florist — *maraîcher;* kitchen-gardener.

Jardini-er, -ère, *adj.*, of the garden, pertaining to the garden. *Plantes* — *ères*, garden-plants.

Jardinière, *n.f.*, gardener's wife; garden-woman; low ruffle; flower-stand; kind of vegetable soup.

Jardon, *n.m.*, or **jarde**, *n.f.*, (vet.) jardes; curbs.

Jargon, *n.m.*, jargon, gibberish, lingo; cant; (min.) jargoon, jargon, gray or brown zircon.

Jargonner, *v.a.n.*, to talk jargon, to say in jargon.

○**Jarni !** *int.*, by Heaven! by the Lord!

Jarousse, *or* **Jarrosse**, *n.f.*, (bot.) vetch.

Jarre, *n.f.*, jar.

Jarret, *n.m.*, ham, hamstring; (arch.) projection. — *de veau;* knuckle of veal. *Couper les* —*s à un cheval;* to hamstring a horse. *Coupe-* (— —*s*); ruffian, bully. *Être ferme sur ses* —*s;* to keep one's countenance. *Avoir du* — *; to be a good walker, a good dancer (who is not easily fatigued—*qui ne se fatigue pas aisément*).

Jarreté, -e (jar-té), *adj.*, close-hammed; (arch.) protuberant.

Jarretière (jar-tièr), *n.f.*, garter. *L'ordre de la* —; the Order of the Garter. *Ne pas aller à la* — *à quelqu'un;* to be nothing compared to any one.

Jars (jâr), *n.m.*, (orni.) gander. *Il entend le* —; he is no fool.

Jas, *n.m.*, (nav.) stock, anchor-stock.

Jaser, *v.n.*, to prate, to chatter, to gabble, to chat, to babble; to blab, to tattle. — *comme une pie, comme une pie borgne;* to chatter like a magpie.

Jaserie (jâ-zrî), *n.f.*, prating, chattering; prate, chatter; twaddle.

Jaseu-r, *n.m.*, **-se**, *n.f.*, prater, chatterer; chatter-box; (orni.)chatterer. *Grand* — (orni.); Bohemian chatterer, wax-wing.

Jasmin, *n.m.*, (bot.) jasmine, jessamine.

Jaspe, *n.m.*, (min.) jasper.

Jaspé, -e, *part.*, jasperated; marbled.

Jasper, *v.a.*, to marble.

Jaspure, *n.f.*, marbling.

Jatte, *n.f.*, bowl, platter; (nav.) manger. *Cul-de-jatte* (—*s* —); cripple deprived of the use of his legs or thighs.

Jattée, *n.f.*, bowlful, platterful.

Jauge(jôj), *n.f.*, gauge; gauging-rod; (nav.) tonnage, burden. — *d'eau;* water-gauge.

Jaugeage (jô-jaj), *n.m.*, gauging.

Jauger, *v.a.*, to gauge, to measure; to take the gauge of.

Jaugeur, *n.m.*, gauger.

Jaunâtre, *adj.*, yellowish.

Jaune, *adj.*, yellow.

Jaune, *n.m.*, yellow. — *d'œuf*, yolk of an egg.

Jaunet, *n.m.*, buttercup; bachelor's-buttons; (pop.) yellow-boy, gold coin.

Jaunir, *v.a.*, to make yellow, to dye yellow; (arts) to yellow.

Jaunir, *v.n.*, to grow yellow, to turn yellow.

Jaunissage, *n.m.*, (arts) yellowing.

Jaunissant, -e, *adj.*, turning yellow, yellowing; ripening.

Jaunisse, *n.f.*, jaundice; (vet.) yellows.

Javart, *n.m.*, (vet.) quittor.

Javeau, *n.m.*, sand-bank.

Javeler (ja-vlé), *v.a.*, to bind (corn—*du blé*) in sheaves.

Javeleur (ja-vleur), *n.m.*, reaper that lays the corn upon the furrow, that gathers the corn into bundles; binder.

Javeline (ja-vli-n), *n.f.*, javelin.

Javelle, *n.f.*, small sheaf; small bundle (of corn left to dry—*de blé laissé à sécher*).

Javelot (ja-vlo), *n.m.*, javelin.

○**Jayet** (ja-iè), *n.m.* *V.* **jais**.

je, *pron.*, I. — *dis;* I say. *Parlé* —*!* do I speak?

Je (ab. of **Jeune**), Jr. (junior).

Jean (jan), *n.m.*, John. *La Saint* —; midsummer.

Jeannette (ja-nèt), *n.f.*, spinning-jenny.

Jectisses, *adj.f.pl.*, of earth, soil, rubbish, &c., used to raise, or level a piece of ground, fill up an excavation, &c.; (mas.) any stone small enough to be placed by hand.

Jéhovah, *n.m.*, Jehovah.

Jéjunum, *n.m.*, (anat.) jejunum.

⊙jennet, *n.m.*, *V.* **genet.**

jenny, *n.f.*, jenny (cotton-frame—*métier à filer le coton*).

jérémiade, *n.f.*, jeremiad.

jérose, *n.f.*, (bot.) rose of Jericho.

jésuite, *n.m.*, jesuit. — *en robe courte, de robe courte;* lay jesuit.

jésuitique, *adj.*, jesuitic, jesuitical.

jésuitisme, *n.m.*, jesuitism.

jésus, *n.m.*, long royal, super royal (paper—*papier*).

jet (jè), *n.m.*, casting, throwing, throw; shoot, sprout; casting (metal.); (agri.) tiller; jet (of water—*d'eau*); new swarm (of bees—*d'abeilles*). *Le — d'un filet;* the casting of a net. *Un — de pierre;* a stone's throw. — *de lumière;* ray of light. *Le — d'une draperie;* (paint.) the position of a drapery. — *d'eau;* water-spout, jet d'eau. — *d'abeilles;* swarm of young bees. *D'un seul —;* at one stroke. *Faire le —;* (com., nav.) to throw (goods—*marchandises*) overboard. — *de marchandises* (nav., com., jur.); jetsam, jetson, jettison.

jeté, *n.m.*, jeté (dancing—*danse*).

jeté, -e, *part.*, cast, thrown. *Le dé, le sort, en est —;* the die is cast, the thing is resolved on.

jetée, *n.f.*, jetty, pier. — *de port;* jetty-head, pier-head.

jeter, *v.a.*, to throw, to cast, to fling, to hurl; to throw down, to cast down, to fling down; to hurl down; to mould; to shoot, to shoot out, to shoot forth, to send forth; to disembogue, to empty. — *l'ancre;* to cast anchor. — *un soupir;* to heave a sigh. — *les fondements d'une maison;* to lay the foundation of a house. — *de profondes racines;* to take deep root. — *les yeux sur quelqu'un;* to cast one's eyes on any one. — *à la mer* (nav.); to throw overboard — *bas* (dy.); to take out of the copper. — *une draperie;* to dispose the drapery (paint). — *ses cartes;* to play one's cards. *Ce cheval jette sa gourme;* that horse has the glanders. — *de l'huile sur le feu;* to add fuel to the flame. *se jeter*, *v.r.*, to throw one's self, to cast one's self, to fling one's self; to fall on, to fall upon (attack—*attaquer*); to shoot; to strike out, to launch out; to be thrown down, to be thrown away; to disembogue, to fall, to empty one's self (of rivers—*des rivières*). — *sur l'ennemi;* to rush upon the enemy. — *au cou de quelqu'un;* to fall on any one's neck. — *à tort et à travers;* to dash through thick and thin.

jeton, *n.m.*, counter, token.

jeu, *n.m.*, play; sport; fun; game; gaming, gambling; acting (of actors—*d'acteurs*); stake; (of organs—*d'orgues*) stop; (nav.) set; (nav.) suit; (mec.) length of stroke; (teeh.) play. — *d'enfant;* child's play. *Les —x de l'enfance,* the sports of infancy. — *de cartes;* card-game; pack of cards. *Bonheur au —;* good luck at play. — *de hasard;* game of chance. *De bon —;* by fair play. *Couper —;* to discontinue playing, to go off with one's winnings. *Tenir le — de quelqu'un;* to play for any one. — *de bourse;* stock jobbing, *J'ai beau —;* I have a good game. *Il a le — serré;* he plays a sure game. *Avoir beau —;* to have a good chance. *Cacher son —;* to cover one's designs *Jouer bien son —;* to play one's cards well. *Faire bonne mine à mauvais —;* to put a good face on a bad business. *Bon —;* bon argent; in good earnest. *Le — ne vaut pas la chandelle;* it is not worth the trouble, it is not worth powder and shot. *Se piquer au —;* to persist in playing. *Mettre au —;* to stake. *Jouer gros —;* to play high. *Jouer petit —;* to play low. *Ils sont à deux de —;* they are upon even terms. *Un — de quilles;* a set of nine-pins. — *d'échecs;* set of chess-men. *Je sais son jeu;* I know his

way. — *de voiles,* complete suit of sails. *Avoir du —* (tech.); to have too much play; not to be steady. — *de mots;* pun, playing upon words. — *d'esprit;* piece of wit. — *x floraux;* floral games.

jeudi, *n.m.*, Thursday. *Le — gras;* Shrove Thursday. *La semaine des trois —s;* when two Sundays come together; *i.e.,* never.

à jeûn, *adv.*, fasting. *Je suis encore à —;* I have not breakfasted yet.

jeune, *adj.*, young; younger, junior; youthful. — *homme;* young man, lad, youngster. — *s gens;* young men. — *personne;* young girl, young lady. *Homme encore —;* man who is still young. — *premier.* — *première* (thea.); the actor, actress, who performs the parts of lovers.

jeune, *n.m.,* (l.u.) young person. — *de langue;* young man studying the Oriental languages.

jeûne, *n.m.*, fasting; fast.

jeunement (jeu-n-màn), *adv.*, (hunt.) just. *Cerf de dix cors —;* stag just turned ten years.

jeûner, *v.n.*, to fast.

jeunesse, *n.f.*, youth, youthful days; youthfulness; young people; (pop.) lad; (pop.) young girl. *La — passe vite;* youth passes quickly. *Avoir un air de —;* to have a youthful look. *J'ai rencontré une — fort jolie* (pop.); I met a very pretty young girl.

jeunet, -te, *adj.*, very young.

jeûneu-r, *n.m.*, **-se**, *n.f.*, faster.

***joaillerie**, *n.f.*, jeweller's trade or business; jewellery, jewels.

***joailli-er**, *n.m.*, **-ère**, *n.f.*, jeweller.

jobard, *n.m.*, ninny, simpleton.

jobarderie, *n.f.*, silliness, fool's trick, stupid action.

jobet, *n.m.*, (metal.) iron wire of a mould.

joc, *n.m.*, state of repose (used in speaking of mills—*des moulins*). *Mettre le moulin à —,* to stop the mill.

jockey, *n.m.* (-s), jockey.

jocko, *n.m.*, (mam.) pongo.

jocrisse, *n.m.*, cotquean; simple awkward servant.

joie, *n.f.*, joy, joyfulness; gladness; glee, mirth; jovialness. *Être ravi, comblé, de —,* to be overjoyed, to be transported with joy. *Ne pas se sentir de —;* to be ready to leap out of one's skin for joy, to be unable to contain one's self for joy. *Faire la — de quelqu'un,* *être la — de quelqu'un,* to be any one's joy. *Pleurer de —;* to weep for joy. *Feu de —;* bonfire.

***joignant**, *prep.*, next to, contiguous to, adjoining.

***joignant, -e**, *adj.*, adjoining, next to, adjacent, contiguous.

joindre (joignant, joint), *v.a.*, to join, to adjoin, to put together, to unite, to fix together, to connect; to add; to annex, to join with; to overtake; to come up to; (arch.) to fay. — *les mains;* to clasp the hands. — *l'utile à l'agréable;* to unite the useful and the agreeable. *se joindre*, *v.r.*, to join, to unite, to be joined, to be united; to be adjoining, to be adjacent, to be contiguous; to be added, to consort, to meet (find one another—*se trouver*).

joindre, *v.n.*, to join. *Ces planches ne joignent pas;* these planks do not join.

joint, *n.m.*, joint; seam, junction. — *articulé;* knuckle joint. *Trouver le —;* to find out the best manner of arranging an affair.

joint, -e, *part.*, joined, united, added; jointed. *Prier quelqu'un à mains —es;* to beg hard. *Vous trouverez ci — copie de sa lettre;* you will find herewith a copy of his letter.

jointé, -e, *adj.*, (of a horse—*du cheval*) jointed.

jointée, *n.f.*, double handful.

jointi-f. -ve, *adj.*, (arch.) joined, closed.

jointoiement (-toa-män), *n.m.*, grouting, pointing (of walls—*des murs*).

jointoyer, *v.a.*, to grout, to point (walls—*murs*).

jointure, *n.f.*, joint, articulation.

joli, -e, *adj.*, pretty, pleasing, neat, genteel; fine, good; nice. *Un — enfant;* a pretty child. *Il est dans un — état;* he is in a nice state, in a pretty mess.

joli, *n m.*, pretty, what is pretty.

joliet, -te, *adj.*, rather pretty.

joliment, *adv.*, prettily, pleasingly; (b. s.) finely; (fam.) much, many.

jolite, *n.f.*, violet-stone.

jonc (jon), *n.m.*, rush; Malacca-cane; keeper (ring—*bague*). — *marin;* sea-rush. — *odorant;* camel's-hay.

jonchaie, *n.f.*, rush-bed, plantation of rushes.

jonché, -e, *part.*, strewed.

jonchée, *n.f.*, strewing (of flowers, &c.—*de fleurs, &c.*). — *de crème;* cream-cheese.

joncher, *v.a.*, to strew.

jonchets, *n.m. pl.*, spilikins (game—*jeu*).

jonciforme, *adj.*, rush-shaped, rush-like.

jonction, *n.f.*, junction, joining.

jongler, *v.n.*, to juggle.

jonglerie, *n.f.*, juggling, hocus-pocus.

jongleur, *n.m.*, juggler.

jonque, *n.f.*, junk (Chinese vessel—*vaisseau chinois*).

*jonquille, *n.f.*, (bot.) jonquil.

joseph (papier), *n.m.*, silver-paper, tissue-paper.

jouable, *adj.*, that may be performed (of music and plays—*de pièces de musique et de théâtre*).

jouail, *n.m.* V. **jas**.

*jouailler, *v.n.*, to play for diversion.

joubarbe, *n.f.*, (bot.) sengreen; house-leek.

joue, *n.f.*, cheek. *Coucher, mettre, en —;* to aim at, to take aim at. *En — !* (milit.) present!

joué, -e, *part.*, played; mocked, made game of. *On m'a —;* I have been made game of, a fool of. *Pièce touchée, pièce —e;* (at draughts, trick-track, chess—*aux dames, au trictrac, aux échecs*) if you touch your piece, you must move it.

jouée, *n.f.*, (arch.) reveal.

jouer, *v.a.*, to play; to stake; to move; to perform, to act; to feign, to imitate; to make game of, to deceive. — *une partie;* to play a game. *Ne — que l'honneur;* to play for love. — *quelque chose;* to play for something. — *quelqu'un;* to make a fool of any one. — *un tour à quelqu'un;* to play any one a trick. — *une comédie;* to act a comedy. — *un rôle;* to play a part. — *la comédie;* to act a sham part. — *un air sur le violon;* to play a tune on the violin. *Ce papier joue le velours;* this paper looks like velvet.

se jouer, *v.r.*, to sport, to play, to make game of, to baffle; to do with the greatest facility. — *de quelqu'un;* to make a fool of any one. *La fortune se joue des hommes;* fortune makes sport of mankind. — *à quelqu'un;* to meddle with any one who is more than one's match.

jouer, *v.n.*, to play, to sport; to trifle; to run the risk; to explode (mine); to speculate (on the funds—*sur les fonds publics*); to work, to work loose (mec). — *aux cartes;* to play at cards. *A qui à — ?* whose turn is it to play? *C'est à moi à —;* it is my turn to play. — *au volant;* to play at shuttlecock. — *à jeu sûr;*

to play without risk. — *au plus fin;* to vie in cunning with. — *à quitte ou double;* to play double or quits. — *de son reste;* to stake one's all. — *de malheur;* to be unfortunate. *Il joue à se faire tuer;* he ventures his life. — *du violon;* to play upon the violin. *Faire —;* to set going. *Ils jouent bien au billard;* they play well at billiards. — *des talons;* to betake one's self to one's heels. — *des gobelets;* to juggle. *Ne — que pour l'honneur;* to play for love.

jouet, *n.m.*, plaything, toy; laughing-stock; jest; sport. *Être le — de la fortune;* to be the sport of fortune.

joueu-r, *n.m.*, **-se**, *n.f.*, player; gamester, gambler. *Mauvais — de violon;* cat-gut scraper. *Beau —;* agreeable person at play. — *à la baisse* (exchange language—*terme de bourse*); bear. — *à la hausse* (exchange language—*terme de bourse*); bull.

joufflu, -e, *n. and adj.*, chub-cheeked person; chub-cheeked.

joug (joog), *n.m.*, yoke. *Mettre les bœufs au —;* to yoke the oxen. *S'affranchir du —;* to throw off the yoke.

jouir, *v.n.*, to enjoy, to possess, to be in possession of. — *de l'embarras de quelqu'un;* to enjoy any one's embarrassment. *Les animaux jouissent de la faculté de;* animals possess the faculty of. *Il est si occupé qu'on n'en peut — un instant;* he is so much occupied that one cannot have a minute's conversation with him.

jouissance, *n.f.*, enjoyment, possession; (fin.) interest payable; use (of a garden, house, &c.—*d'un jardin, d'une maison, &c.*).

jouissant, -e, *adj.*, enjoying, in full possession.

joujou, *n.m.*, plaything, toy.

jour, *n.m.*, day, daytime, daylight, light; gap, opening; facility, means. *A court —;* short-dated (of bills—*lettres de change*). *A long —;* long-dated (of bills—*lettres de change*). *A chaque — suffit sa peine;* sufficient unto the day is the evil thereof. *A la pointe du —;* at the break of day. — *s caniculaires;* dog-days. *Le — et la nuit;* day and night. *Il commence à faire —;* it begins to be light. *Petit —;* morning twilight. *Il fait —;* it is daylight. *Grand —;* broad daylight. *Le — baisse;* the day declines. *A la chute du —;* at nightfall. *Demi-—,* twilight, feeble light. *Il est — chez lui;* he is up. *En plein —;* in open daylight. *Brûler le —;* to shut out daylight. *Donner le —;* to give birth. *Mettre au —;* to bring to light. *Se faire —;* to make one's way. *Tous les —s;* every day. *De nos —s;* in our days, at present. *Un — ou l'autre;* some day or other. *Du — que;* since the day when. *Quinze —s;* a fortnight. *Un — de fête;* a holiday. — *de l'an;* new-year's day. — *ouvrier, ouvrable;* working-day. — *gras;* flesh-day. — *maigre;* fish-day. *Les —s gras;* shrove-tide. *Donner, souhaiter, le bon — à quelqu'un;* to wish any one good morning. *Être de —;* to be upon duty. *Il donne tant par —;* he gives so much a day. *Il me remet de — en —;* he puts me off from day to day. *Je l'attends de — en —;* I expect him every day. *Faire son bon —;* (triv.) to receive the sacrament. *Mourir plein de —s;* to die full of days. *Vivre au — la journée, vivre au — le —;* to live from hand to mouth. *Bon —, bonne œuvre;* the better the day, the better the deed. *Faire du — la nuit;* to turn day into night. *Le goût du —;* the reigning fashion. *Être dans son bon —;* (paint.) to be in a good light; to be on one's good behaviour. *Se mettre à tous les —s;* to make one's self cheap. *L'auteur de vos jours;* the author of your being. *Si je*

rois — *à cela* ; if I can see through it. *À* — ;
open, open-worked. *Broderie à* — ; open-
worked embroidery. *Mettre à* — ; to bring up
to date.

journal, *n m.*, journal, diary; newspaper;
(com.) day-book. — *nautique* (nav.); log-book.
Tenir un — ; to keep a diary.

journali-er, -ère, *adj.*, daily; diurnal; uncertain. inconstant. changeable.

journalier, *n.m.*, journeyman, day-labourer.

journalisme, *n.m.*, journalism.

journaliste, *n.m.*, journalist.

journée, *n.f.*, day ; day's work; day's wages;
day's journey. *Toute la* — ; all day long. *Travailler à la* — ; to work by the day. *Homme de*
— ; day-labourer. *Femme de* — ; charwoman.

journellement (-nèl-mǎn), *adc.*, daily,
every day.

joute, *n.f.*, joust, just, tilt. — *de coqs* ; cock-
fight.

jouter, *v.n.*, to joust, to tilt ; to argue.

jouteur, *n.m.*, tilter ; antagonist, adversary.

jouvence, *n.f.*, (l.u.) youth. *Fontaine de
Jouvence* ; fountain of youth.

jouvenceau, *n.m.*, (jest.) lad, stripling,
young fellow.

jouvencelle, *n.f.*, (jest.) lass, young girl.

Ojouxte, *prep.*, near.

jovial, -e, *adj.*, jovial, jocund, joyous.

jovialement (jo-vial-mǎu), *adv.*, jovially,
joyously.

jovialité, *n.f.*, mirth, noisy mirth.

joyau, *n.m.*, jewel. — *x de la couronne* ;
crown-jewels.

joyeusement (joa-yeûz-mǎn), *adv.*, cheerfully, joyfully, merrily.

joyeuseté (joa-yeûz-té), *n.f.*, joke, jest.

joyeu-x, -se, *adj.*, joyful, merry, cheerful,
mirthful; gladsome. *Bande* — *se* ; joyous band.

jubé, *n.m.*, rood-loft. *Venir à* — ; to come to.

jubilaire, *adj.*, of jubilee.

jubilation, *n.f.*, jubilation, festivity, rejoicing.

jubilé, *n.m.*, jubilee. *Faire son* — ; to perform all the acts of devotion stipulated in the
jubilee bull.

jubilé, *adj.*, of fifty years' standing.

jubiler, *v.n.*, to make merry, to exult.

juc, *n.m.*, roost, perch.

juché, -e, *part.*, perched, roosted. *Cheval*
— . (man.) boulet (horse whose pastern joint of
the hind legs is too forward—*cheval dont le
boulet est trop en avant.* V. **boulet** and
bouleté

jucher, *v.n.*, to roost, to perch.

se jucher, *v.r.*, to roost, to perch.

juchoir, *n.m.*, roosting-place.

judaïque, *adj.*, Judaical, Jewish.

judaïquement (-ik-mǎn), *adv.*, Judaically.

judaïsant, *adj.*, judaizing.

judaïser, *v.n.*, to judaize.

judaïsme, *n.m.*, Judaism.

judas, *n.m.*, Judas (treacherous person—
traître); peep-hole. *Baiser de* — ; treacherous
kiss. *Poil de* — ; carroty hair.

judelle, *n.f.*, (orni.) coot.

judicatum solvi, *adj. invariable*, (jur.)
caution — ; bail which a foreigner must give before beginning an action against a French subject before a French court.

judicature, *n.f.*, judicature, magistracy.

judiciaire, *adj.*, judiciary, judicial, legal.

judiciaire, *n.f.*, judgment; sagacity.

judiciairement (-èr-mǎn), *adv.*, judicially,
legally, by authority of justice.

judicieusement (-eûz-mǎn), *adv.*, judiciously, considerately. discreetly.

judicieu-x, -se, *adj.*, judicious, wise, discreet.

juge, *n.m.*, judge ; justice. — *de paix* ,
justice of the peace. — *de camp*, stickler. —
d'instruction ; examining magistrate. *Se constituer en* — *de* ; to erect one's self into a judge of
jugé, -e, *part.*, judged. *Bien* — ; well
judged.

jugeable (ju-jabl), *adj.*, amenable to a
tribunal.

jugement (juj-mǎn), *n.m.*, judgment,
opinion, view; trial, sentence. — *par défaut* ;
judgment by default. *Mettre quelqu'un en* — ;
to put any one on his trial, to bring any one up
for trial. *Rendre un* — ; to deliver judgment.
Rendre un — *contre* ; to sentence. *Prononcer un*
— ; to give judgment, to pass sentence. *Subir
un* — ; to be under sentence. *Passer en* — ; to
be brought up for trial. *Mettre quelqu'un
en* — ; to indict any one. *Je me rends à votre*
— ; I bow to your judgment.

juger, *v.a.*, to judge; to conjecture, to think,
to believe, to imagine ;. to try ; to bring to trial ;
to sentence. — *à propos* ; to think proper.
se juger, *v.r.*, to judge one's self; to deem, to
think, one's self ; (jur.) to be tried, to be heard.
Vous en jugez-vous capable? do you think yourself equal to it ? *Cette affaire se jugera demain* ;
(jur.) this affair will be heard, will come on, to-
morrow.

juger, *v.n.*, to judge ; to pass sentence ; to
give judgment; to deem, to think. — *sur
l'étiquette du sac* ; to judge by the label. —
d'autrui par soi-même ; to judge of others by
one's self. *Jugez de la profondeur de son humilité* ; judge of the extent of his humility.

jugulaire, *adj.*, (anat.) jugular.

jugulaire, *n.f.*, (anat.) jugular vein ; strap
(of a soldier's hat—*de shako*).

juguler, *v.a.*, to choke; to torment; to cheat
out of ; to ruin.

jui-f, -ve, *n.* and *adj.*, Jew; Jewess; Jewish.
Le — *errant*; the wandering Jew.

*juillet, *n.m.*, July.

juin, *n.m.*, June.

juiverie (jui-vrî), *n.f.*, jewry (Jews' ward in
a town—*quartier des Juifs dans une ville*); Jew's
bargain.

jujube, *n.m.*, jujube. *Pâte de* — ; jujube
lozenges.

jujubier, *n.m.*, jujube-tree.

jule, *n.m.*, (ent.) iulus ; (bot.) catkin ; an
Italian coin worth about three pence.

julep (ju-lèp). *n.m.*, julep.

julien, -ne (-li-in,-è-n), *adj.*, Julian.

julienne, *n.f.*, (bot.) rocket; (cook.) vegetable soup.

jumart, *n.m.*, jumart.

jume-au, -lle, *n.* and *adj.*, twin ; (anat.)
twin muscles ; twin-born ; twin; double (fruit).
Des cerises —*lles*; double-cherries. *Frères* —*aux*,
twin brothers.

jumelé, -e, *adj.*, (her.) bar-gemel.

jumeler, *v.a.*, to strengthen with cheeks;
to match (things—*objets*). — *un mât* (nav.); to
fish a mast.

jumelle, *n.f.*, twin ; *pl.*, double opera-glass ;
(carp.) cheeks, side-beams ; (her.) gemel;(nav)
fish (of masts and yards—*de mâts et de
vergues*). —*s de rechange* ; (nav.) spare fishes.

jument, *n.f.*, mare.

jungle, *n.f.*, jungle.

junon, *n.f.*, (astron.) Juno.

junte, *n.f.*, junta (Spanish council—*conseil
espagnol*).

jupe, *n.f.*, petticoat ; skirt (of a gown—*de
robe*).

jupiter (-tèr), *n.m.*, (astron.) Jupiter.

jupon, *n.m.*, short petticoat.

jurande, *n.f.*, wardenship (of a company of

tradesmen—*d'un métier*); wardens (of a company of tradesmen—*d'un métier*).

jurassique, *adj.*, (geol.) Oolitic and Liassic, Jurassic.

⊙**jurat**, *n.m.*, alderman (of Bordeaux).

juratoire, *adj.*, by oath. *Caution* —; oath taken by any one to appear in court when required.

juré, -e, *adj.*, sworn.

juré, *n.m.*, juror, juryman; member of a board of examination. *Récuser un* —; to challenge a juror.

jurement (jur-màn), *n.m.*, oath. *Proférer un* —; to utter an oath.

jurer, *v.a.*, to swear; to vow; to take an oath of; to blaspheme. — *la ruine de quelqu'un;* to swear any one's destruction.

se jurer, *v.r.*, to swear to one another. *Nous nous jurâmes une éternelle amitié;* we swore eternal friendship to each other.

jurer, *v.n.*, to swear; to blaspheme; to contrast (of colours—*des couleurs*); to squeak (of musical instruments—*d'instruments de musique*); to jar, to clash (of sound—*des sons*). *Il ne faut — de rien;* we must swear to nothing. *Il jure comme un charretier;* he swears like a trooper.

jureur, *n.m.*, swearer.

⊙**juri**. *V.* jury.

juridiction, *n.f.*, jurisdiction; department, province. *Ce n'est pas de sa* —; it is not in his province.

juridictionnel, -le, *adj.*, jurisdictional.

juridique, *adj.*, legal, juridical, judicial.

juridiquement (-dik-màn), *adv.*, juridically, judicially.

jurisconsulte, *n.m.*, jurisconsult, lawyer.

jurisprudence, *n.f.*, jurisprudence.

juriste, *n.m.*, jurist.

juron, *n.m.*, oath. *Gros* —; tremendous oath. *Lâcher un* —; to rap out an oath.

jury, *n.m.*, jury; board of examination. — *mi-parti étranger;* party-jury. *Banc du* —; jury-box. *Chef du* —; foreman of the jury. *Former un tableau, une liste, du* —; to impannel a jury. *Juger par le* —; to try by jury. *Récuser un* —; to challenge a jury. — *de jugement;* petty-jury.

jus, *n.m.*, juice; gravy (of meat—*de viande*). *Plein de* —; juicy.

jusant, *n.m.*, (nav.) ebb, ebb-tide.

jusque, jusques (in poet. and st. e.), *prep.*, to, even, as far as, till, until; down to; up to. *Depuis Paris jusqu'à Londres;* from Paris to London. *Jusqu'au ciel;* up to the skies. *Depuis le premier jusqu'au dernier;* from the first to the last. *Jusqu'à demain;* till to-morrow. *Jusqu'à quand?* how long? till when? *Jusqu'à présent;* till now. *Jusqu'où?* how far? *Jusqu'ici;* till now; down to here. — *-là;* up to that time. *Jusqu'à ce que;* until. *Jusqu'à ce que cela soit fait;* till it be done. *Il a vendu jusqu'à sa chemise;* he has sold the very shirt off his back.

jusquiame, *n.f.*, hyosciamus, henbane.

jussion, *n.f.*, command, royal command, order.

⊙**justaucorps** (-kor), *n.m.*, close coat.

⊙**juste**, *n.m.*, jacket (worn by country-women —*de paysanne*).

juste, *adj.*, just, equitable, lawful, appropriate; apposite; right; upright, righteous; fit, proper, exact; tight. *Dieu est* —: God is just. — *Dieu! — ciel!* good God! just heaven! *Un homme* —; a righteous man. *Vos souliers sont trop —s;* your shoes are too tight. *Ma montre est* —; my watch is right.

juste, *n.m.*, upright man, virtuous man; what is just. *La science du* —; the knowledge of what is just.

juste, *adv.*, just, exactly, accurately, precisely; (mus.) true. *Chanter* —; to sing true, in time, in tune. *Il raisonne* —; he reasons closely. *Au* —; exactly, precisely, just.

justement, *adv.*, justly, honestly, precisely.

justesse, *n.f.*, justness, accuracy, exactness; appropriateness, precision. *Avec* —; with precision, appropriately.

justice, *n.f.*, justice; righteousness; jurisdiction; fairness; courts of justice; execution. *Faire — à;* to do justice to. *Rendre — à;* to do justice to. *Rendre la* —; to administer justice. *Se faire* —; to do one's self justice. *Cour de* —; court of law, of judicature. *Appeler quelqu'un en* —; to sue any one. *Déni de* —; refusal of justice. *Que — soit faite;* let execution be done.

justiciable, *n.m.f.* and *adj.*, person amenable to a tribunal; amenable.

justicier, *v.a.*, to punish corporally; to execute.

justicier, *n.m.*, justiciary; lover of justice.

justifiable, *adj.*, justifiable.

justifiant, -e, *adj.*, justifying.

justificati-f, -ve, *adj.*, justifying, justificative, justificatory.

justification, *n.f.*, justification, vindication, proof; (print.) justification.

justifier, *v.a.*, to justify, to vindicate, to prove, to make good; (print.) to justify.

se justifier, *v.r.*, to justify, to clear, to vindicate, one's self.

justifier, *v.n.*, (print.) to justify.

jute, *n.m.*, jute.

juteu-x, -se, *adj.*, juicy.

juvénile, *adj.*, juvenile, youthful.

juvénilement (-nil-màn), *adv.*, boyishly, childishly, in a juvenile manner.

juvénilité, *n.f.*, youth, youthfulness.

se juxtaposer, *v.r.*, to be in juxtaposition.

juxtaposition (juks-ta-), *n.f.*, juxtaposition.

K

k, *n.m.*, the eleventh letter of the alphabet, k.

kabak, *n.m.*, public-house (in Russia—*en Russie*).

kabin, *n.m.*, indemnification paid by a Turk to the wife he repudiates.

kahouanne, *n.f.*, loggerhead turtle.

kaïmac, *n.m.* (—*s*), sherbet in use in the East.

kakatoès, *n.m.*, (orni.) cockatoo. *V.* cacatois.

kaléidoscope, *n.m.*, kaleidoscope.

⊙**kalendes**, *n.f.pl. V.* calendes.

kali, *n.m.*, (bot.) kali.

kamichi (-shi), *n.m.*, (orni.) horned-screamer (palamedea).

kan, *n.m.*, khan.

kandjar, or kangiar, *n.m.* (—*s*), Asiatic and African dagger.

kanguroo, or kangourou (-goo-roo.), *n.m.*, (mam.) kangaroo.

kantisme, *n.m.*, Kantism.

kantiste, *n.m.*, Kantist.

kaolin, *n.m.*, kaolin, porcelain clay.

karabé, *n.m. V.* carabé.

karat, *n.m. V.* carat.

karata, *n.m.*, (bot.) a variety of aloe.

karl, *n.m.*, a kind of spice.

katakoua, *n.m. V.* kakatoès.

keepsake, *n.m.*, keepsake.

képi, *n.m.*, military cap.

kératophyte, *n.m.*, name given by ancient naturalists to polypary formations, transparent like horn.

kermès (-mès), *n.m.*, (ent.) kermes; (chem.) kermes-mineral.

kermesse, *n.f.,* a fair (in the Netherlands—*dans les Pays-bas*).

khédive, *n.m.* (—*s*), Khedive, viceroy of Egypt.

kilo, *n.m.,* (ab. of **kilogramme**) kilo.

kilogramme, *n.m.,* kilogram (2·2055 lbs. avoirdupois).

kilolitre, *n.m.,* kilolitre (220·09663 gallons).

kilomètre, *n.m.,* kilometre(1093·6389 yards).

kilométrique, *adj.,* pertaining to the kilometre.

⊙**kina-kina,** *n.m.* V. **quinquina.**

⊙**kinancie,** *n.f.* V. **esquinancie.**

king, *n.m.,* king (sacred book of the Chinese—*livre sacré des Chinois*).

kinine, *n.f.* V. **quinine.**

kino, *n.m.,* (pharm.) kino.

kiosque, *n.m.,* kiosk (eastern pavilion—*pavillon dans le goût oriental*).

kirsch-wasser, *n.m.,* kirschwasser.

klephte, *n.m.* V. **clephte.**

knout (knoot), *n.m.,* knout.

kopeck, *n.m.* (—*s*), kopeck (Russian coin worth about half a penny—*monnaie de cuivre russe = cinq centimes*).

koran, *n.m.,* Koran. V. **coran.**

kouan, *n.m.,* (bot.) cochineal, cochineal-fig.

kremlin (krèm-lin), *n.m.,* Kremlin (the palace of the czars at Moscow—*palais des czars à Moscou*).

kreutzer (-zèr) *n.m.,* kreutzer (German coin—*monnaie allemande*).

kurtchis, *n.m.,pl.,* a Persian cavalry corps composed of nobles.

kymrique, *adj.* V. **cymrique.**

kynancie, *n.f.,* (med.). V. **cynancie.**

kyrielle, *n.f.,* litany ; (fig.) string (long list—*longue liste*); long tedious story.

kyste, *n.m.,* (med.) cyst, cystis.

kystique, *adj.,* (med.) cystic.

kystotome, *n.m.,* (surg.). V. **cystotome.**

kystotomie, *n.f.,* (surg.). V. **cystotomie.**

L

l, *n.m.f.,* the twelfth letter of the alphabet, l.

l', *art.,* (contraction of le and la) the. V. **le.**

l', *pron.,* (contraction of le and la) him, her, it.

la, *art.f.,* the. V. **le.**

la, *pron.,* her it. V. **le.**

là, *adv.,* there, thither, then (of time—*de temps*). —*bas ;* down there. —*haut,* above, up there. *Çà et* —; here and there, up and down, all about. —*dessus ;* on there; upon that; thereupon. *Mettez le livre* —*dessus :* put the book on there. —*dessus, il me dit :* upon that, he said to me. —*dessous :* under there. —*dedans ;* within. *De* —; thence, from thence ; from that time, from that cause. *Il n'est pas* —; he is not there, he is absent. *Par* —; that way. *Jusque* —; till then, till that time. *Ce n'est pas* —*que je vise ;* that is not the thing I aim at. *Celui-là, celle-là ;* that. *Ceux-là, celles-là ;* those.

là là, *int.,* now then ! there ! there now !

là là, *adv.,* so so, indifferently.

la, *n.m.,* (mus.)la ; A. *l'rendre le* —; to tune one's instrument.

labarum (-rom), *n.m.,* labarum (Constantine's imperial standard—*étendard impérial de Constantin*).

labeur, *n.m.,* labour, work, toil ; (print.) book-work. *Terres en* —; tilled lands.

labial, -e, *adj.,* labial. *Offres* —*es ;* (jur.) offer to pay without exhibiting the money.

labiale, *n.f.,* (gram.) labial.

labié, -e, *adj.,* (bot.) labiate, labiated.

labiée, *n.f.,* labiated plant.

labile, *adj.,* labile, bad (of the memory—*de la mémoire*); (bot.) deciduous. *Mémoire* —; bad memory.

laboratoire, *n.m.,* laboratory.

laborieusement (-eûz-mān), *adv.,* laboriously, painfully.

laborieu-x, -se, *adj.,* laborious, industrious, hard-working, assiduous, toilsome, painful.

labour, *n.m.,* ploughing, tillage. *Terres de* —; ploughed lands. *Donner un* —; *à une terre ;* to till, to dress, a piece of ground. *Donner un* —*à une vigne :* to dress a vine.

labourable, *adj.,* arable. *Terres* —*s ;* arable lands.

labourage, *n.m.,* tillage, husbandry ; ploughing, tilling.

labourer, *v.a.,* to plough, to till ; to dig, to turn up ; to rip up, to rip open ; to toil through. —*sa vie ;* to toil through life.

labourer, *v.n.,* to plough, to till ; to drudge; to toil and moil ; (nav.) to come home, to drag (of anchors—*des ancres*); (of ships—*des vaisseaux*) to graze the bottom (with the keel—*de la quille*); (of horses—*des chevaux*) to stumble.

laboureur, *n.m.,* husbandman, ploughman, tiller.

labyrinthe, *n.m.,* labyrinth, maze.

lac, *n.m.,* lake.

lacer, *v.a.,* to lace ; to line (of dogs—*du chien*).

se **lacer,** *v.r.,* to lace one's self.

lacérable, *adj.,* lacerable.

lacération, *n.f.,* laceration.

lacéré, -e, *part.,* (bot.) lacerate, lacerated.

lacérer, *v.a.,* to lacerate ; (jur.) to tear up, to destroy.

lacerne, *n.f.,*(antiq.) lacerna, a kind of cloak worn by the Romans.

laceron, *n.m.,* (bot.) sow-thistle. V. **laiteron.**

lacet, *n.m.,* lace ; springe ; braid ; bow-string (to strangle—*pour étrangler*); zigzags, turnings of mountain-roads; *pl.,* toils. *Ferrer un* —; to tag a lace. *Mouvement de* —; side rolling motion of carriages on railways.

lâche, *adj.,* loose, slack, lax ; slothful, sluggish ; faint-hearted ; mean-spirited, dastardly ; cowardly, base, mean, shameful. *Ce nœud est trop* —; this knot is too loose.

lâche, *n.m.,* coward, craven, dastard.

lâché, -e, *part.,* slackened, loose.

lâchement (lâsh-mān), *adv.,* sluggishly, slothfully, loosely, dastardly, cowardly.

lâcher, *v.a.,* to slacken, to relax, to loose, to make loose, to loosen ; to let go, to let slip, to cast off, to throw off ; to let out, to unbind ; to let loose, to release. — *la bride à un cheval ;* to loosen the reins of a horse. — *pied,\ — le pied ;* to retreat, to turn tail ; to waver, to be irresolute. — *sa proie ;* to let go one's prey. — *un prisonnier ;* to release a prisoner. — *prise ;* to let go one's hold. — *une arme à feu ;* to fire a gun. — *un soufflet à quelqu'un ;* to give any one a box on the ear. — *une parole,* — *un mot ;* to let out a word. — *le mot, la parole ;* to speak the word. — *une bordée* (nav.); to fire a broadside.

se **lâcher,** *v.r.,* to slacken, to grow loose, to become loose, to slip ; to go off ; to give a loose to one's tongue, to let out.

lâcher, *v.n.,* to slacken, to grow slack, to become slack, to grow loose, to become loose; to slip, to go off. *Si le fusil vient à* —; if the gun happens to go off.

lâcheté (lâsh-té), *n.f.,* cowardice, cowardliness, dastardy, dastardliness, baseness ; base action ; meanness, act of cowardice

lacinié, -e, *adj.*, (bot.) laciniate, laciniated, jagged.

laciniure, *n.f.*, (bot.) jag.

lacis, *n.m.*, net-work; (anat.) plexus.

lack, *n.m.* (—s), lac, lack. *Un — de roupies;* a lac of rupees.

laconique, *adj.*, laconic, laconical.

laconiquement (-nik-män), *adv.*, laconically.

☉**laconiser**, *v.n.*, to live sparingly; to be laconic, to speak laconically.

laconisme, *n.m.*, laconism, laconicism.

lacrymal, -e, *adj.*, lachrymal. *Sac —;* (anat.) lachrymal bag.

lacrymatoire, *n.m.*, (Roman antiq.) lachrymatory.

lacrymatoire, *adj.*, (Roman antiq.) lachrymary.

lacs (lä), *n.m.*, string; gin, springe. — *d'amour;* love-knot.

lactate, *n.m.*, (chem.) lactate.

lactation, *n.f.*, lactation.

lacté, -e, *adj.*, lacteal, milky, lacteous; chyliferous. *La voie —e* (astron.); the Milky-Way.

lactescence, *n.f.*, lactescence.

lactescent, -e, *adj.*, (bot.) lactescent.

lactifère, *adj.*, lactiferous.

lactique, *adj.*, (chem.) lactic.

lactomètre, *n.m.*, lactometer. *V.* **galactomètre**.

lactucarium, *n.m.*, (pharm.) lactucarium.

lacune, *n.f.*, gap, hiatus; interruption, blank; (bot.) air-cell, lacuna.

lacustre, *adj.*, lacustral, lacustrine.

ladanum, *n.m.*, (n.p.) ladanum, a gum-resin.

ladre, *adj.*, leprous; measly (of pigs—*du cochon*); insensible, unfeeling; mean, sordid, stingy, scurvy, scaly; niggardly; churlish.

ladre, *n.m.*, **-sse**, *n.f.*, leper; sordid person, scurvy person, shabby person. *Maison de —s;* lazar-house. *Un vrai —;* a regular curmudgeon. — *vert;* sordid fellow, stingy churl.

ladrerie, *n.f.*, leprosy; measles; sordid avarice, stinginess, sordidness, scurviness, scaliness, lazar-house.

lady (lè-di), *n.f.*, (*ladies*), lady.

lagon, *n.m.*, lagoon.

lagophtalmie, *n.f.*, (med.) lagophthalmia.

☉**lague** (lag), *n.f.*, (nav.) track, wake (of a ship—*d'un vaisseau*). *V.* **sillage**.

lagune, *n.f.*, lagune, lagoon.

lai, -e, *adj.*, lay.

lai, *n.m.*, layman; lay (small poem—*petit poème*); complaint, lament.

laïc. *V.* **laïque**.

laîche, *n.f.*, (bot.) sedge.

laid, -e, *adj.*, ugly, ill-favoured, ill-looking; plain; unseemly, unhandsome, unbecoming. — *comme le péché;* as ugly as sin. *Ce que vous dites là est bien —;* what you say is very unbecoming.

laid, *n.m.*, ugly part, ugliness; bad side; naughty boy.

laide, *n.f.*, plain girl; naughty girl.

laidement, *adv.*, uglily.

laideron (lè-dron), *n.f.*, ugly girl, ugly woman; ugly creature.

laideur, *n.f.*, ugliness, uncomeliness; ill-favouredness; deformity; unseemliness; unbecomingness. *La — du vice;* the ugliness of vice.

laie, *n.f.*, wild sow; riding-lane (through a forest—*dans une forêt*).

lainage, *n.m.*, woollen stuff; fleece; teaseling.

laine, *n.f.*, wool; worsted. — *de Berlin;* Berlin-wool. — *d'agneau;* lamb's-wool. *Flocon de —;* flock of wool. *Bêtes à —;* lanigerous

animals (rams, sheep, lambs—*moutons, &c.*). *Se laisser manger la — sur le dos;* to suffer one's self to be fleeced; to put up with everything. *De —;* woollen.

lainer, *v.a.*, to tease (wool—*la laine*).

lainerie (lè-n-ri), *n.f.*, woollen goods; woollens; place for shearing sheep; art of manufacturing woollens; wool-market; teaseling-shop.

laineu-r, *n.m.*, **-se**, *n.f.*, teaseler.

laineuse. *n.f.*, teaseler (woman—*ouvrière*); gig (machine for carding wool—*machine à carder la laine*).

laineu-x, -se, *adj.*, woolly, fleecy; (bot.) downy, woolly; lanate, lanated.

laini-er, -ère. *adj.*, of wool.

lainier, *n.m.*, wool-stapler; wool-comber, wool sorter.

laïque, *n.m.* and *adj.*, layman; lay, laic, laical. *Les —s;* the laity.

lais, *n.m.*, standard-tree; alluvion.

laisse, *n.f.*, string; leash; slip; (hawking—*fauconnerie*) lune. — *de lévriers;* leash of greyhounds. *Mener quelqu'un en —;* to hold any one in leading-strings, to lead any one by the nose. *En —;* in a leash.

laissées, *n.f.pl.*, dung (of bears, wild boars —*d'ours, de sangliers*).

laisser, *v.a.*, to leave, to quit, to desert, to abandon; to leave, to bequeath; to suffer, to permit, to let. to allow; to let alone; to omit; to leave off; to leave out; to give up. — *tout à l'abandon;* to leave everything in disorder. — *tout aller;* to neglect everything. — *tout traîner;* to let everything lie about in disorder, to keep nothing in its proper place. — *la vie à quelqu'un;* to spare any one's life. — *quelqu'un en paix, en repos;* to let any one alone, to let any one be. — *quelqu'un;* to leave any one behind. — *quelqu'un maître d'une chose;* to leave any one free to act as he pleases in anything. — *là quelqu'un;* to leave any one, to give up any one. — *là quelque chose;* to leave off, to discontinue, to give up, any thing. — *quelqu'un pour ce qu'il est;* to take no notice of, not to mind, a person. *Il y a à prendre et à — dans ces choses;* you must pick and choose from these things; there are good and bad ones among these things. *A prendre ou à laisser;* to be taken or left alone; take it or leave it. — *une chose à un certain prix;* to dispose of a thing for a certain price. *On n'a qu'à le — faire;* one needs only let him alone. *Laissez donc!* stuff, nonsense! *Laissez-moi faire;* leave it to me. — *aller;* to let go. — *sortir;* to let out. *Cela ne laisse pas que d'être vrai;* it is true nevertheless.

se laisser, *v.r.*, to allow one's self, to suffer one's self. — *conduire;* to suffer one's self to be led. — *aller à ses passions;* to give one's self up to one's passions. — *tomber;* to fall. — *mourir;* to die. — *aller à la tentation;* to give one's self up to temptation. — *aller à la douleur;* to abandon one's self to grief. — *lire;* to be readable, pleasant to read. — *manger,* — *boire;* to be palatable.

laisser-aller, *n.m.*, (n.p.) ease, freedom, unrestraint; easiness, yieldingness.

laisser-courre, *n.m.*, (n.p.) (hunt.) place where the dogs are loosened.

laissez-passer, *n.m.* (—), permit, leave, permission.

lait, *n.m.*, milk; white, glair (of eggs—*d'œufs*). *Fièvre de —;* milk-fever. *Frère de —;* foster-brother. *Sœur de —;* foster-sister. *Cochon de —;* sucking-pig. *Petit —,* (n.p.) — *clair;* whey. — *coupé;* milk and water. — *de beurre;* buttermilk. — *de poule;* mulled egg. — *écrémé;* skim-milk. *Être au —;* to be made with milk; to be confined to milk diet. *Vache* à — ; dairy-cow, milch cow. *Bouillir du* — *à quelqu'un* ; to please any one. — *de chaux*; whitewash. *Riz au* — : rice milk.

laitage, *n.m.,* milk food. *Régime de* — ; milk diet.

laitance, or **laite,** *n.f.,* (ich.) milt, melt, soft roe.

laité, -e, *adj.,* soft-roed.

laitée, *n.f.,* litter (of a bitch—*d'une chienne*). *V.* **portée.**

laiterie (lè-tri), *n.f.,* dairy; dairy-room; dairy-farm, milk-farm.

laiteron (lè-tron), *n.m.,* (bot.) sow-thistle; hare's-lettuce.

laiteu-x, -se, *adj.,* lacteous, milky.

laitier (-tié), *n.m.,* (metal.) dross; slag. — *des volcans* ; fragments of lava.

laitier (-tié), *n.m.,* milkman.

laitière, *n.f.,* milkwoman, milkmaid, dairy-maid ; milch cow ; woman with a great deal of milk. *Cette vache est une bonne* — ; this cow gives a great deal of milk.

laitière, *adj.,* milch, yielding milk (of cows —*des vaches*). *Vache* — ; milch cow.

laiton, *n.m.,* latten, brass. *Fil de* — ; brass wire.

laitue, *n.f.,* (bot.) lettuce. — *pommée*,; cabbage-lettuce. — *romaine* ; cos-lettuce.

laize, *n.f.,* width (of a stuff—*d'une étoffe*).

là là, *adv. V.* **là.**

là là! *int. V.* **là.**

lama, *n.m.,* Lama (of the Tartars—*des Tartares*).

lama, or **llama,** *n.m.,* (mam.) lama, glama.

lamanage, *n.m.,* coasting-pilotage, harbour-piloting.

lamaneur, *n.m.,* harbour-pilot, coasting-pilot.

lamantin, *n.m.,* (zool.) *V.* **lamentin.**

lambdoïde, *adj.,* (anat.) lambdoidal.

lambeau, *n.m.,* rag, tatter; shred, strip, fragment, scrap; ribbon (of flesh—*de chair*); bit.

lambel, *n.m.,* (her.) label.

lambin, -e, *n.* and *adj.,* loiterer, dawdler; slow, drawling.

lambiner, *v.n.,* to drawl, to loiter, to dawdle.

lambourde, *n.f.,* (carp.) joist, summer-tree ; (mas.) soft stone.

lambrequins, *n.m. pl.,* (her.) mantle; (arch.) scallop.

lambris, *n.m.,* panelling; wainscot; ceiling ; (poet. st. e.) mansion, palace; magnificent decoration of a mansion. *Les célestes* —(poet.); Heaven. — *feint* ; imitation panelling.

lambrissage, *n.m.,* wainscoting, panelling.

lambrisser, *v.a.,* to panel; to wainscot.

lambruche, or **lambrusque,** *n.f.,* (bot.) wild vine.

lame, *n.f.,* plate, sheet (metal.); (anat.) lamina; blade; sword, swordsman; (nav.) billow, surge, wave; hussy; (bot.) gill; wire (of gold, of silver—*d'or, d'argent*). *Fine* — ; sly hussy (of a woman—*d'une femme*). *Entre deux* —*s* ; in the trough of the sea. *Emporté par une* — ; washed away. *La* — *use le fourreau* ; the steel wears away the scabbard ; the mind wears out the body. *Bonne* — ; good swordsman.

lamé, -e, *adj.,* laminated.

lamelle, *n.f.,* lamella.

lamellé, -e, *adj. V.* **lamelleux.**

lamelleu-x, -se (la-mèl-leû),*adj.,* lamellate, lamellated, lamellar ; laminate, laminated ; scaly, exfoliate.

lamentable, *adj.,* lamentable, woful; mournful, rueful.

lamentablement, *adv.,* lamentably, mournfully, wofully, ruefully.

lamentation, *n.f.,* lamentation, bewailing, wailing; lamenting, lament.

lamenter. *v.a.,* to lament, to bewail, to bemoan, to mourn, to mourn over.

se **lamenter,** *v.r.,* to lament, to mourn, to moan, to bewail.

lamenter, *v.n.,* (l.u.) to lament.

lamentin, *n.m.,* lamentin. lamantin, sea-cow, sea-maid, mermaid, manatee.

lamie, *n.f.,* (antiq., ent.) lamia; (ich.) white shark.

lamier, *n.m.,* (bot.) lamium; archangel.

laminage, *n.m.,* (metal.) flatting (of gold —*de l'or*) ; rolling.

laminer, *v.a.,* (metal.) to flat (of gold—*de l'or*); to roll.

laminerie, *n.f.,* (metal.) rolling-mills.

lamineur, *n.m.,* (metal.) workman employed in rolling-mills.

lamineu-x, -se, *adj. V.* **cellulaire.**

laminoir, *n.m.,* (metal.) flatting-machine, rolling-mill.

lampadaire, *n.m.,* lamp-post.

lampadiste, *n.m.,* (antiq.) lampadist.

lampadophore, *n.m.,* (antiq.) torch-bearer.

lampas (-pâss), *n.m.,* (vet.) lampass; a silk fabric. *Humecter le* — ; to drink wine (pop.).

lampassé, -e, *adj.,* (her.) langued.

lampe, *n.f.,* lamp. — *d'Argand* ; Argand lamp. — *d'argent* ; silver lamp. — *de sûreté,* — *de Davy* ; safety-lamp. *Dessous de* — ; lamp-stand. *Arranger une* — ; to trim a lamp. *Sentir la* — ; to smell of the lamp.

lampée, *n.f.,* (pop.) tumblerful (of drink— *de boisson*).

lamper. *v.a.* and *n.,* (pop.) to toss off (drink—*boisson*) ; to guzzle.

lamperon (lanp-ron), *n.m.,* wick-holder (of a lamp—*d'une lampe*).

lampion, *n.m.,* grease-pot, illumination-lamp ; church-lamp.

lampiste, *n.m.,* lamp-maker ; lamp-lighter.

⊙**lampon.** *n.m.,* lampoon.

*****lamprillon,** *n.m. V.* **lamproyon.**

lamproie, *n.f.,* lamprey.

lamproyon, *n.m.,* young lamprey.

lampyre, *n.m.,* lampyris, glow-worm.

lance, *n.f.,* lance, spear ; staff, flag-staff. *Rompre une* — *pour quelqu'un* ; to take up the cudgels for any one. *Baisser la* — ; to strike one's flag, to give in.

lancéolaire, *adj.,* (bot.) lanceolate, lanceolated (of leaves—*des feuilles*).

lancéolé, -e, *adj.,* (bot.) lanceolate, lanceolated.

lancer, *v.a.,* to dart, to fling, to hurl, to throw, to cast, to launch; to shoot, to issue forth ; to issue (a warrant—*un mandat*). — *un javelot* ; to dart a javelin. — *une pierre* ; to fling a stone. — *un regard de colère* ; to dart an angry look. — *des regards* ; to cast looks. — *une flèche* ; to shoot an arrow. — *un cheval* ; to push on a horse. — *un vaisseau* ; to launch a ship.

se **lancer,** *v.r.,* to dart, to spring; to rush, to make a rush ; to launch; to start; to fly.

lancer, *v.n.,* (of a ship—*d'un vaisseau*) to yaw.

lancette, *n.f.,* (surg.) lancet. *Donner un coup de* — ; to lance.

lancier, *n.m.,* (milit.) lancer.

lancière, *n.f.,* waste-gate (of a mill-dam— *d'un biez de moulin*).

lancinant, -e, *adj.,* shooting (of pain— *d'une douleur*).

lançoir, *n.m.,* mill-gate (of water-mills—*de moulin à eau*).

landamman, *n.m.,* landamman (magis-

trate in some of the Swiss cantons—*magistrat suisse).*

landau, *n.m.* (*landaus*), landau.

lande, *n.f.,* waste land, moor.

landgrave, *n.m.,* landgrave.

landgraviat, *n.m.,* landgraviate.

landgravine, *n.f.,* wife of a landgrave.

landier, *n.m.,* kitchen fire-dog.

landwehr, *n.f.* (*—s*), landwehr.

laneret (la-n-rè), *n.m.,* (orni.) lanneret, shrike.

langage, *n.m.,* language, tongue, speech. *Le — des oiseaux ;* the language of birds. *Le — des yeux ;* the language of the eyes. *Le — des fleurs ;* the language of flowers. *Changer de —;* to change one's tone. *Ils tiennent tous le même —;* they all hold the same language.

lange, *n.m.,* swaddling-cloth.

langoureusement (-reûz-mān), *adv.* languishingly.

langoureu-x, -se, *adj.,* whining, languishing, consumptive. *Faire le — auprès d'une femme ;* to act the whining lover to a woman.

langouste, *n.f.,* spiny lobster, sea-crayfish.

langue (lāng), *n.f.,* tongue; language; neck (of land—*de terre*). *Une mauvaise —;* a slanderous tongue. *C'est une mauvaise —;* he, she, is a slanderous person. *Tirer la —;* to put out one's tongue. *Avoir la — liée ;* to be tongue-tied. *Avoir la — bien pendue ;* to have an oily tongue; to have the gift of the gab. *Avoir la — grasse ;* to speak thick. *Avoir un mot sur le bout de la —;* to have a word at the tip of one's tongue. *La — lui a fourché ;* his, her, tongue tripped. *Prendre —;* to obtain intelligence of what is going on, of the state of anything. *Coup de —;* backbiting. *Donner des coups de à ;* to slander, to cast reflections on. *Jeter sa — aux chiens ;* to give up endeavouring to guess. *Votre énigme est trop difficile, je jette ma — aux chiens ;* your riddle is too difficult, I give it up. *Beau parler n'écorche point la —;* good words cost nothing. *— vivante ;* living language. *— morte ;* dead language. *— vulgaire ;* vulgar tongue. *Maître de —s ;* teacher of languages. *Quelle —!* what a tongue he, she, has! *Sa — va toujours ;* his tongue never stops.

langue-de-serpent, *n.f.* (*—s —*), (bot.) serpent's-tongue, adder's-tongue; (geol.) serpent's-tongue, petrified fish teeth.

languette (-ghèt), *n.f.,* tongue (thing shaped like a tongue—*objet ayant la forme d'une langue*); key (of musical instruments—*d'instruments de musique*); index (of a balance—*de balance*).

langueur (-gheur), *n.f.,* languidness, languor; *pl.,* debility. *Maladie de —;* lingering illness; decline. *Il ne sent point les — de l'âge ;* he does not suffer the debility of old age.

langueyer (-ghè-ié), *v.a.,* to examine the tongue of a hog to see whether he is diseased or not.

langueyeur (-ghè-ieur), *n.m.,* examiner of hogs' tongues.

languier (-ghié), *n.m.,* smoked hog's tongue and throat.

languir (-ghir), *v.n.,* to languish, to linger, to pine, to pine away, to droop, to be sickly, to fade; to flag. *— de misère ;* to languish in misery. *— d'amour ;* to pine away for love. *La conversation languit ;* the conversation flags.

languissamment (-ghi-sa-mān), *adv.,* languishingly, droopingly, lingeringly.

languissant, -e, *adj.,* languid, languishing, lingering, pining, drooping, sickly, fading; (com.) dull.

lanice, *adj.,* of wool. *Bourre —;* flock of wool.

lanier, *n.m.,* (orni.) lanner, lanneret, shrike.

lanière, *n.f.,* thong.

lanifère, *adj.,* lanigerous, laniferous.

lanigère, *adj.* *V.* **lanifère.**

laniste, *n.m.,* (antiq.) buyer, trainer, or seller of gladiators.

lansquenet (lans-kĕ-nè), *n.m.,* lansquenet (card game—*jeu de cartes*); lansquenet (German foot soldier—*fantassin allemand*).

lantanier, *n.m.,* (bot.) lantana.

lanterne, *n.f.,* lantern; (arch.) lantern, lantern-tower, lantern-light; spy-place; (mec.) lantern-wheel; trundle; assay-balance glass-case; *pl.,* fooleries; idle stories, nonsense. *— sourde ;* dark-lantern. *— magique ;* magic-lantern. *Il veut faire croire que des vessies sont des —s ;* he would have one believe that the moon is made of green cheese. *Mettre à la —;* to hang up at the lamp-post (French revolution). *À la —!* to the lamp-post with him, her, them!

lanterner, *v.n.,* to dally, to trifle, to trifle away one's time ; to be irresolute.

lanterner, *v.a.,* to trifle with, to make a fool of ; to tire with idle stories.

lanternerie, *n.f.,* irresolution; trifling difficulty ; trifling, dallying; nonsense, nonsensical stuff.

lanterni-er, *n.m.,* **-ère,** *n.f.,* trifler, babbler; (l.u.) lantern-maker, lamplighter.

lantiponnage, *n.m.,* nonsense.

lantiponner, *v.a.n.,* to talk nonsense, to plague with nonsensical stuff.

lanturlu, *n.m.* or **lanturlu,** *adv.,* stuff. *Il lui a répondu —;* stuff! he replied to him.

lanugineu-x, -se, *adj.,* lanuginous, downy.

laper, *v.a.n.,* to lap, to lick up.

lapereau (la-prô), *n.m.,* young rabbit.

lapidaire, *n.m.,* lapidary.

lapidaire, *adj.,* lapidary. *Style —;* lapidary style.

lapidation, *n.f.,* lapidation, stoning to death.

lapider, *v.a.,* to lapidate, to stone to death; (fig.) to attack, to tear to pieces.

lapidification, *n.f.,* lapidification.

lapidifier, *v.a.,* to lapidify.

se**lapidifier,** *v.r.,* to lapidify, to become lapidified.

lapidifique, *adj.,* lapidific.

lapin, *n.m.,* **-e,** *n.f.,* rabbit, buck-rabbit, doe-rabbit.

lapis, or **lapis lazuli** (-pis), *n.m.* (*—*), lapis lazuli.

lapon, *n.m.,* **-ne,** *n.f.,* Laplander.

laps (laps), *n.m.,* lapse (of time—*de temps*).

laps, -e, *adj.,* fallen back to heresy.

laquais (la-kè), *n.m.,* lackey, footman.

laque, *n.f.,* lac, lake. *Gomme —;* gum-lake. *— en bâtons ;* stick-lake. *— en grain ;* seed-lac.

laque, *n.m.,* lacker.

laquelle, *pron.f.,* which, who, that.

laquer, *v.a.,* to lacker, to varnish.

laqueu-x, -se, *adj.,* of the nature of lac; lake-coloured.

laraire, *n.m.,* (ant.) the lares' domestic altar.

larcin, *n.m.,* larceny; theft, pilfering; robbery; thing stolen; spoil. *Faire un —;* to commit a theft. *Faire un doux —;* to steal a kiss.

lard (lâr), *n.m.,* bacon, pig's fat. *Flèche de —;* flitch of bacon. *Tranche de —;* rasher of bacon. *Il fait du —;* he grows fat by sleeping.

larder, *v.a.,* to lard, to stick; to interlard; to run through, to pierce. *— un discours de citations ;* to interlard a speech with quotations. *— de coups d'épée ;* to run through with a sword. *— de la viande ;* to lard meat.

lardoire, *n.f.,* larding-needle.

lardon, *n.m.,* piece of pig's fat; thin slice of bacon; joke, cut, jest.

lare (lâr), *n.m.*, (myth.) Lare, household god.

large, *adj.*, broad, wide, large; great, grand; lax. *Ce champ est plus long que* — ; this field is longer than it is wide. *Une rue — de soixante pieds;* a street sixty feet wide.

large, *n.m.*, breadth, width; (nav.) offing. *Porter au* — ; (nav.) to bear off from the land. *Au* — ! keep off! *Gagner le* — ; to stand out to sea. *Cette rue a soixante pieds de* — ; this street is sixty feet wide. *Au* — ; spaciously, abroad. *Être au* — ; to be abroad, to be at one's ease. *Être logé au* — ; to have a great deal of room. *Au long et au* — ; in length and width, far and wide.

large, *adv.*, wide; grandly. *Ce cheval va trop* —, that horse goes too wide.

largement, *adv.*, largely, abundantly, amply, fully, plentifully, grandly.

largesse, *n.f.*, largess, liberality, bounty, munificence. *Faire des* —*s au peuple;* to be liberal to the people.

largeur, *n.f.*, breadth, width; wideness, broadness.

larghetto (-ghèt-tô), *adv.*, (mus.) larghetto.

largo, *adv.*, (mus.) largo.

largue (larg), *n.m.*, (l.u.) (nav.) offing.

largue, *adj.*, (nav.) large; flowing. *Écoutes* —*s;* (nav.) flowing sheets. *Vent* — ; oblique wind.

larguer (-ghé), *v.a.*, (nav.) to cast off; to let run (ropes—*cordages*); to let out (reefs—*ris*).

larigot, *n.m.*, ⊙flute. *Boire à tire*- — ; to drink hard.

larix (la-riks), *n.m.* V. **mélèze**.

larmaire, *adj.*, (bot.) tear-shaped.

larme, *n.f.*, tear; drop. *Pleurer à chaudes* —*s;* to shed bitter tears. *Verser des* —*s;* to shed tears. *Fondre en* —*s;* to melt into tears.

larmier, *n.m.*, (arch.) larmier, corona, drip-stone; coping; eye-vein (of the horse—*du cheval*).

larmières, *n.f.pl.*, or **larmiers**, *n.m.pl.*, openings under the eyes of the stag.

larmiers, *n.m.pl.*, (vet.) the sides of the forehead, the temples, of the horse.

larmoiement (-moa-män), *n.m.*, wateriness of the eyes.

larmoyant, -e, *adj.*, weeping, in tears.

larmoyer, *v.n.*, to cry, to shed tears.

larmoyeu-r, *n.m.*, **-se**, *n.f.*, weeper, one who weeps easily, frequently, about trifles.

larron, *n.m.*, thief; (print.) bite; (bookbind.) leaf folded in and not cut.

larronneau, *n.m.*, little thief; pilferer.

larronnesse, *n.f.*, a female thief.

larve, *n.f.*, (ent.) larva.

larves, *n.f.pl.*, (antiq.) ghosts, spectres, evil genii.

laryngé, -e, *adj.*, laryngeal.

laryngien, -ne (-in, -è-n), *adj.*, laryngean.

laryngite, *n.f.*, (med.) laryngitis.

laryngotomie, *n.f.*, (surg.) laryngotomy.

larynx (la-rinks), *n.m.*, (anat.) larynx.

las! (lâ) *int.*, alas!

las, -se, *adj.*, tired, weary, fatigued. — *de travailler;* tired with working. *Un — d'aller;* a lazy fellow. *Faire quelque chose de guerre —se;* to do a thing for the sake of peace and quietness.

lascar, *n.m.*, lascar (East Indian sailor, gunner—*matelot indien*).

lasci-f, -ve, *adj.*, lascivious, lewd, lustful, wanton, libidinous.

lascivement (las-siv-män), *adv.*, lasciviously, lewdly.

lasciveté (las-siv-té), *n.f.*, lasciviousness, lewdness, lust, lustfulness.

laser (-zèr), *n.m.*, (bot.) laserwort.

lassant, -e, *adj.*, tiresome, wearisome, fatiguing.

lasser, *v.a.*, to tire, to weary. to fatigue.

se **lasser**, *v.r.*, to tire, to grow tired, to be fatigued, to be wearied.

lassitude, *n.f.*, lassitude, weariness.

last, *or* **laste**, *n.m.*, (com., nav.) last (two tons weight—*deux tonneaux*, 4,000 kil.).

lasting (-tingh), *n.m.*, lasting (stuff—*étoffe*).

latanier, *n.m.*, a palm-tree, latania, growing in Mauritius.

latent, -e, *adj.*, latent, hid, concealed.

latéral, -e, *adj.*, lateral, side.

latéralement (-ral-män), *adv.*, laterally; sideways.

à **latere**. V. **légat**.

lathyrus, *n.m.*, (bot.) lathyrus.

laticlave, *n.m.*, (antiq.) laticlave.

latin, -e, *adj.*, Latin; (nav.) lateen. *La langue* —*e;* the Latin language.

latin, *n.m.*, Latin. *Il est au bout de son* —: he is at his wit's end. *Du — de cuisine;* dog Latin.

latiniser, *v.a.*, to latinize.

latinisme, *n.m.*, latinism.

latiniste, *n.m.*, latinist.

latinité, *n.f.*, latinity. *La basse* — ; low Latin.

latitude, *n.f.*, latitude; extent; climate. *Prendre une* — ; to take a latitude.

latitudinaire, *adj.*, latitudinarian.

latomie, *n.f.*, (antiq.) latomia.

latrie, *n.f.*, latria.

latrines, *n.f.pl.*, privy.

latte, *n.f.*, lath.

latter, *v.a.*, to lath.

lattis, *n.m.*, lathing, lath-work.

laudanum, *n.m.*, laudanum.

laudati-f, -ve, *adj.*, laudatory.

laudes (lôd), *n.f.pl.*, (c. rel.) lauds.

lauréat, *adj.*, laureate.

lauréole, *n.f.*, (bot.) spurge-laurel.

laurier, *n.m.*, laurel, bay-tree. — *-rose;* oleander, rose-bay. *Couronne de* — ; wreath of laurel. *Couronné de* —*s;* crowned with laurels, laurelled.

laurose, *n.m.*, (bot.) oleander, rose-bay.

lavabo (-bô), *n.m.*, wash-stand; (c. rel.) prayer at washing the hands; (c. rel.) napkin.

lavage, *n.m.*, washing; slops; wash.

lavanche, *or* **lavange**, *n.f.* V. **avalanche**.

lavande, *n.f.*, (bot.) lavender. — *commune*, — *officinale;* common lavender.

lavandier, *n.m.*, yeoman of the laundry.

lavandière, *n.f.*, (l.u.) laundress, washerwoman; (orni.) wagtail.

lavanèse, *n.f.*, (bot.) goat's-rue.

lavaret, *n.m.*, (icht.) gwiniad, fresh-water herring.

lavasse, *n.f.*, shower of rain (l.u.); slopy sauce; wash.

lave, *n.f.*, lava.

lavé, -e, *part.*, washed. *Couleur* —*e* (paint.); light colour. *Cheval de poil bai* — ; light-bay horse.

lavement (la-vmän), *n.m.*, (c. rel.) washing; (med.) injection, clyster.

laver, *v.a.*, to wash, to wash off, to cleanse; to wash up; to lave, to bathe; to absolve, to declare innocent. — *la tête à quelqu'un;* to blow any one up; to rate any one soundly.

se **laver**, *v.r.*, to wash, to wash one's self. — *les mains;* to wash one's hands. — *d'un crime;* to clear one's self of a crime. *Je m'en lave les mains;* I will have nothing to do with it, I wash my hands of it.

⊙**laver**, *v.n.*, to wash, to wash one's hands.

lavette, *n.f.*, dish-cloth, dish-clout.

laveu-r, *n.m.*, **-se**, *n.f.*, washer, scourer. —*se de vaisselle;* scullion, scullery-maid. — *de mines;* buddler.

lavis, *n.m.*, wash, colouring. *Dessin fait au* —; washed drawing.

lavoir, *n.m.*, washing-place, wash-house; scullery; (metal.) buddle; rubbing-board.

lavure, *n.f.*, dish-water, hogwash; (gold.) washing; *pl.*, goldsmith's sweepings. — *de vaisselle*; dish-water; (fig.) weak, tasteless broth.

laxati-f, -ve, *adj.*, laxative, opening.

laxatif, *n.m.*, (pharm.) laxative.

laxité, *n.m.*, (med.) laxity, looseness.

layer, *v.a.*, to cut a path through a forest.

layetier(-tié), *n.m.*, box-maker, packing-case maker.

layette, *n.f.*, drawer, box; baby-linen.

layetterie (lè-iè-trî), *n.f.*, baby-linen making; baby-linen trade.

layeur. *n.m.*, person that lays out paths in forests.

lazaret, *n.m.*, lazaretto, lazar-house.

lazariste, *n.m.*, Lazarite, Lazarist (monk—*moine*).

lazarone, *n.m.* (*lazaroni*), lazarone.

lazuli. *V.* **lapis**.

lazulite, *n.m.*, (min.) lazulite, azure-stone.

lazzi, *n.m.* (—, *or* —s), piece of buffoonery, jest, joke.

le, *art.m.*, **la**, *f.*, **les**, *pl.m.f.*, the.

le, *pron.m.*, **la**. *f.*, **les**, *pl.m.f.*, him, her, it, them; so. *Je les vois*; I see them. *Je le vois*; I see him, it. *Il l'aime*; he loves him, it. *Je l'aime*; I love her. *Donnez-le-moi*; give it me. *La voici*; here she is. *Je suis enrhumée, mes femmes le sont aussi*; I have got a cold, so have my women.

lé, *n.m.*, breadth (of linen, &c.—*de la toile, &c.*).

lèche, *n.f.*, thin slice.

léché, -e, *part.*, licked. *Tableau* —; (paint.) laboured picture.

à lèche-doigts, *adv.*, (l.u.) in small quantities, niggardly, meanly, sparingly, just enough to taste.

lèchefrite (lèsh-frit), *n.f.*, dripping-pan.

lécher, *v.a.*, to lick, to lick up; (paint.) to labour.

se lécher. *v.r.*, to lick one's self. *S'en* — *les doigts*; to lick one's fingers at it.

leçon, *n.f.*, lesson; lecture; reading, lection. *Vraie* —; true reading (of a text—*d'un texte*). —*s publiques*; public lectures. *Il a pris des* —*s d'un tel*; he took lessons of such an one. *Faire la* — *à quelqu'un*; to give any one a lecture, to lecture any one.

lect-eur, *n.m.*, **-rice**. *n.f.*, reader, lecturer, professor. — *bénévole*; gentle reader.

lectisterne, *n.m.*, (antiq.) a feast offered to the gods.

lecture. *n.f.*, reading; perusal. *Il a beaucoup de* —; he is well-read. *Savant par la* —; well-read. *Cabinet de* —; reading-room, circulating-library.

légal, **-e**, *adj.*, legal, lawful, legitimate.

légalement (-gal-mān), *adv.*, legally, lawfully. legitimately.

légalisation. *n.f.*, (jur.) authentication.

légaliser, *v.a.*, (jur.) to authenticate.

légalité, *n.f.*, legality. lawfulness.

légat, *n.m.*, legate (of the pope—*du pape*). — *à latere*; legate à latere.

légataire, *n.m.f.*, (jur.) legatee. — *universel*; residuary legatee.

légation. *n.f.*, legateship, legation.

légatoire. *adj.*, (antiq.) of a province ruled by a governor appointed by the Emperor of Rome.

lège, *adj.*, (nav.) light.

légendaire. *n.m.*, legendary.

légende, *n.f.*, legend; legendary story; legend (of a medal or coin—*d'une médaille, d'une pièce de monnaie*).

lég-er, -ère, *adj.*, light (not heavy); easy; nimble, active; fickle, unsteady, light-headed; feeble, frivolous, trifling, slight, inconsiderate, thoughtless. *Faire à la* —*e*; to slight over. — *comme une plume*; as light as a feather. *Cheval* — *à la main*; light-borne horse. *Vin* —; light wine. *Être* — *à la course*; to be nimble-footed. *Cavalerie* —*e*; light-horse. *Avoir la tête* —*e*; to be hare-brained. *Une faute* —*e*; a small fault. *Être vêtu à la* —*e*; to be lightly dressed.

légèrement (lé-jèr-mān), *adv.*, lightly, slightly; nimbly, swiftly, cursorily, thoughtlessly.

légèreté (lé-jèr-té), *n.f.*, lightness, nimbleness, swiftness; fickleness, unsteadiness; levity, frivolity, volatibility; inconsiderateness, thoughtlessness; slight fault. *La* — *d'un cerf*; the fleetness of a stag.

légion, *n.f.*, legion. — *d'honneur*; Legion of Honour. — *de parents*; host of relations.

légionnaire, *n.m.* and *adj.*, legionary; knight of the Legion of Honour.

législat-eur. -rice, *adj.* and *n.* legislating, law-giving; legislator; legislatress, legislatrix; law-giver, law-maker. *Moïse fut le* — *des Hébreux*; Moses was the legislator of the Jews.

législati-f, -ve, *adj.*, legislative.

législation, *n.f.*, legislation.

législature, *n.f.*, legislature.

légiste, *n.m.*, legist, civilian.

légitimaire, *adj.*, (jur.) secured by law to the heir; of the heir entitled to the portion secured by law.

légitimation, *n.f.*, legitimation; recognition. — *des pouvoirs d'un ambassadeur*; recognition of an ambassador in his official capacity.

légitime, *adj.*, just, lawful, legitimate, rightful, justifiable. *Enfant* —; legitimate child, child born in wedlock.

légitime, *n.f.*, (jur.) portion that a child has by law in his parent's estate.

légitimement (-tim-mān), *adv.*, legitimately, lawfully, justly, rightfully, fairly, justifiably.

légitimer, *v.a.*, to legitimate; to justify, to apologize; to legalize; to recognize. *L'ivresse ne légitime aucune mauvaise action*; drunkenness does not justify any bad action.

légitimiste, *n.m.f.*, legitimist.

légitimité, *n.f.*, legitimacy, lawfulness, rightfulness, fairness; justifiableness.

legs (lè), *n.m.*, legacy, bequest, gift by will.

léguer (lé-ghé), *v.a.*, to leave, to leave by will, to demise, to bequeath.

légume, *n.m.*, vegetable, herb; pulse; legume, legumen.

légumineuses, *n.f. pl.*, (bot.) leguminosæ.

légumineux. *n.m.pl.*, vegetables.

légumineu-x, -se, *adj.*, leguminous.

lemme (lèm), *n.m.*, (geom.) lemma.

lémures. *n.m.pl.*, (Roman antiq.) lemures.

lémuriens (-in), *n.m.pl.*, (mam.) lemuridæ.

lémuries, *n.f.pl.*, (Roman antiq.) lemuria.

lendemain (lān-dmin), *n.m.*, morrow, next day, day after, following day. *Le* — *de ses noces*; the day after one's marriage. *Penser au* —; to think of the morrow, of to-morrow.

lendore, *n.m.f.*, dawdle, dawdling person.

lénifier, *v.a.*, (med.) to lenify.

léniti-f, -ve, *adj.*, (med.) lenitive.

lénitif, *n.m.*, (med.) lenitive, emollient.

lent, -e, *adj.*, slow, tardy; remiss; lingering. — *à parler*; slow of speech. — *à payer*; tardy in one's payments. *Fièvre* —*e*; slow fever, low fever, continued fever.

lente, *n.f.*, (ent.) nit.

lentement (lān-tmān), *adv.*, slowly, tardily, remissly.

lenteur, *n.f.*, slowness, tardiness, remissness.

lenticulaire, *or* **lenticulé**, **-e**, *adj.*, lenticular, lentiform.

lenticule, *n.f.*, (bot.) duck-meat, duck's-meat, duck-weed.

lentiforme, *adj.*, lentiform, lenticular.

lentigineu-x, **-se**, *adj.*, (med.)lentiginous; freckled.

lentigo, *n.m.*, (med.) lentigo; freckles.

*****lentille**, *n.f.*, (bot.) lentil; freckle; lens; pendulum-bob. *Avoir le visage couvert de —s;* to have one's face covered with freckles.

*****lentilleu-x**, **-se**, *adj.*, (l.u.) freckled.

lentisque, *n.m.*, (bot.) lentisk, mastic-tree.

léonin, **-e**, *adj.*, leonine. *Vers — s;* leonine verses.

léonure, *or* **léonurus**, *n.m.*, (bot.) mother-wort.

léopard, *n.m.*, leopard.

lépas, *n.m.*, (conch.) limpet, patella.

lépidoptère, *n.m.* and *adj.*, (ent.) lepidopter, lepidoptera; lepidopterous.

lépisme, *n.m.*, (ent.) bookworm.

lèpre, *n.f.*, leprosy.

lépreu-x, **-se**, *n.* and *adj.*, leper; leprous.

léproserie (lé-prô-zrî), *n.f.*, lazar-house; hospital for lepers.

lepte, *n.m.*, (ent.) leptus. *— automnal;* wheal-worm.

lepte, *n.f.*, (bot.) a triphyllous plant of the order Celastraceæ.

lequel. *pron. m.*, **laquelle**, *f.*, **lesquels**, *pl.m.*, **lesquelles**, *pl.f.*, who, whom, that, which; (interrogatively) which one, which. *Lequel, laquelle, vous plaît davantage?* which pleases you best? *Lequel, laquelle, préférez-vous?* which one do you prefer?

lérot, *or* **liron**, *n.m.*, (mam.) garden-dormouse.

les, *definite art.* and *pr. pl.*, the; them. *V.* **le**.

lèse, *adj.*, high-treason. [Only employed in connection with some other word.]

lèse-faculté, *n.f.* (*n.p.*), (jest.) high-treason against the faculty, disregarding a physician's advice.

lèse-humanité, *n.f.* (*n.p.*), high-treason against humanity.

lèse-majesté, *n.f.* (*n.p.*), high-treason; (jur.) leze-majesty.

lèse-nation, *n.f.* (*n.p.*), high-treason against the nation.

léser. *v.a.*, to wrong, to injure.

lésine, *n.f.*, niggardliness; stinginess.

lésiner, *v.n.*, to be niggardly, parsimonious, stingy, mean.

lésinerie (lé-zi-n-rî), *n.f.*, stinginess, meanness, niggardliness; stingy act.

lésineu-r, **-se**, *adj.*, niggardly, stingy, mean, parsimonious.

lésion, *n.f.*, wrong, injury; (surg.) lesion, hurt; loss (at play—*au jeu*). *Se faire une — ;* (med.) to meet with an injury.

lesse, *n.f.* *V.* **laisse**.

lessive, *n.f.*, lye-washing, wash; washing; linen washed; (chem.) lixivium. *Donner sa — à laver;* to give one's dirty linen to be washed. *Faire la — du gascon* (prov.); to turn one's shirt *or* neckerchief when it is dirty. *Faire une —, une forte, une furieuse, — ;* to sustain a loss, a heavy loss (at play—*au jeu*).

lessiver, *v.a.*, to wash in lye.

lessiveu-r, *n.m.*, **-se**, *n.f.*, lye-washer.

lest (lèst), *n.m.*, (nav.) ballast.

lestage, *n.m.*, (nav.) ballasting.

leste, *adj.*, brisk, nimble, active; clever; unceremonious, unscrupulous; indecorous.

lestement, *adv.*, briskly, cleverly; freely; indecorously.

lester, *v.a.*, (nav.) to ballast.

se lester, *v.r.*, to take in ballast; to line one's stomach, to lay in a stock of provisions. *Je me suis bien lesté avant de me mettre en route;* I lined my stomach well before setting out on my journey.

lesteur, *n.m.*, boat to carry ballast, lighter, ballast-lighter.

léthargie, *n.f.*, lethargy.

léthargique, *adj.*, lethargic, lethargical.

léthé, *n.m.*, (myth.) Lethe.

léthifère, *adj.*, lethiferous.

lettre, *n.f.*, letter; (print.) letter, type. *—s;* literature, letters. *Prendre une chose à la —, au pied de la —;* to take a thing literally, in a literal sense, to the letter. *Rendre à la —;* to render word for word, literally. *— de change;* bill of exchange. *— de crédit;* letter of credit; credentials. *—s patentes;* letters patent. *— de cachet* (French hist.); lettre-de-cachet, arbitrary warrant. *—s de marque;* letters of mark. *— de mer* (nav.); pass. *— affranchie;* paid letter. *— recommandée;* registered letter. *— refusée, — morte, — au rebut, — tombée en rebut;* dead letter. *Boîte aux —s;* letter-box. *Expédition des —s;* despatch of letters. *Jeter, mettre, une — à la poste;* to post a letter. *Ce sont —s closes;* that is a secret. *Un homme de —s;* a man of letters. *Les belles- —s;* polite literature.

lettré, **-e**, *adj.*, lettered, literate, literary.

lettrine, *n.f.*, (print.) heading, reference.

leu, *n.m.*, old French for *loup*, wolf; still in use in the expression: *à la queue leu leu;* one after the other, in a file. *À la queue — — ;* a child's game.

leucorrhée, *n.f.*, (med.) leucorrhœa, whites.

leur, *personal pron.*, to them, them. *Je le — donne;* I give it to them. *Je — ai dit cela;* I told them that. *Donnez-le- —;* give it to them.

leur, *possessive adj.*, their. *Le —, la —, les —s*, possess. pron., theirs. *J'aime mieux ma maison que la — ;* I like my house better than theirs. *Je ne veux rien du — ;* I want nothing of theirs.

leurre, *n.m.*, lure; decoy; bait. *Se laisser prendre à un — ;* to be caught in a snare, to swallow a bait.

leurrer, *v.a.*, to lure; to entice, to decoy, to trapan.

se leurrer, *v.r.*, to be ensnared, entrapped; to delude one's self. *Ces oiseaux ne se leurrent pas facilement;* these birds are not to be easily entrapped.

levain, *n.m.*, leaven, barm, yeast; remains; germ. *Pain sans —;* unleavened bread.

levant, *n.m.* and *adj.*, East, Levant. *Du — au couchant;* from east to west; rising, orient.

levantin, **-e**, *n.* and *adj.*, Levantine.

levantine, *n.f.*, levantine (silk cloth—*soierie*).

lève, *n.f.*, large, wooden spoon to raise the bowl in playing at mall.

levé, *n.m.*, (mus.) rise (of the foot, of the hand—*du pied, de la main*).

levé, **-e**, *part.*, lifted up, raised; up, risen (out of bed—*hors du lit*). *Votre maître est-il — ?* is your master up?

levée, *n.f.*, gathering (fruits, &c) ; levying; raising ; (post-office—*de la poste*) collection ; embankment; breaking up, rising, recess; swell (of the sea—*de la mer*); trick (at cards—*aux cartes*). *Faires des —s de soldats;* to raise soldiers.

lever, *v.a.*, to lift, to lift up, to heave, to raise up, to pull up; (hunt.) to start, to flush; to take up, to hold; to remove, to take away; to take out; to gather, to collect; to raise, to levy; to survey, to make a survey. *Levez la tête;* hold up your head. *— les oreilles;* to prick up one's ears. — *la main sur quelqu'un*; to lift up one's hand against any one. — *le camp;* to break up the camp. — *quelqu'un;* to help any one up. — *le masque;* to throw off the mask. — *un plan;* to draw, to take a plan; to survey, to make a survey.

se **lever**, *v.r.*, to rise, to get up ; to stand up ; to break up; to start up ; to make a stand ; (of the sea—*de la mer*) to heave. *Il se lève de bon matin;* he rises early. — *précipitamment;* to start up.

lover, *v.n.*, to come up, to be up (of plants —*des plantes*); to ferment, to rise. *Faire — un lièvre;* to start a hare.

lever, *n.m.*, rising; levee; surveying. *Au — du soleil;* at sun-rise. — *des plans;* land-surveying.

lever-dieu, *n.m.* (—), (c. rel.) raising of the host.

léviathan, *n.m.*, leviathan.

levier, *n.m.*, lever ; hand-spike; (horl.) arm; crowbar. *La force du —;* the power of the lever. *Le point d'appui d'un —;* the fulcrum of a lever.

levis, *adj.*, for drawing up. *Pont- —;* draw-bridge.

lévite, *n.m.*, Levite.

lévite, *n.f.*, (l.u.) frock-coat ; surtout ; woman's dress.

lévitique; *n.m.*, Leviticus.

levrauder, *v.a.*, (l.u.) to harass, to pester.

levraut, *n.m.*, leveret, young hare.

lèvre, *n.f.*, lip. *Je l'ai sur le bord des —s;* I have it at my tongue's end. *Il a le cœur sur les —s;* his heart is on his lips.

levretté, -e, *adj.*, like a greyhound.

levrette, *n.f.*, greyhound ; harrier-bitch.

lévrier, *n.m.*, greyhound, harrier.

levron, *n.m.*, young greyhound, young harrier.

levure, *n.f.*, yeast. barm.

lexicographe, *n.m.*, lexicographer.

lexicographie, *n.f.*, lexicography.

lexicographique, *adj.*, lexicographical.

lexicologie, *n.f.*, lexicology.

lexique, *n.m.*, lexicon, dictionary.

lez, *prep.*, near.

lézard, *n.m.*, lizard.

lézarde, *n.f.*, crevice in a wall.

lézardé, -e, *adj.*, cracked (of walls—*des murs*).

lézarder, *v.a.*, to crack (of walls—*murs*).

se **lézarder**, *v.r.*, to crack, to become cracked.

liais, *n.m.*, finely-grained, hard, building limestone.

liaison, *n.f.*, joining, conjunction ; connexion ; intimacy ; up-stroke (of writing—*écriture*) ; (mus.) slur, binding-note.

liaisonner, *v.a.*, (mas.) to bind (stones—*pierres*).

liane, *n.f.*, (bot.) bind-weed.

liant, -e, *adj.*, supple, flexible. pliant ; forming connections easily; affable, mild. *Un esprit —:* a gentle temper.

liard, *n.m.*, liard (0·125 penny) ; half a farthing.

liarder, *v.n.*, to contribute in small sums; to pay by farthings.

lias, *n.m.*, (geol.) Lias.

liasique *or* **liassique**, *adj.*, (geol.) Liassic.

liasse, *n.f.*, bundle, file of papers.

libage, *n.m.*, (mas.) ashlar.

libation, *n.f.*, libation. *Faire des —s;* to offer up libations.

libelle, *n.m.*, libel, lampoon.

libeller (li-bèl-lé), *v.a.*, (jur.) to draw up judicial documents.

libelliste, *n.m.*, libeller.

libellule, *n.f.*, (ent.) libellula, dragon-fly.

liber (li-bèr), *n.m.*, (bot.) liber.

libera, *n.m.* (—s), (c.rel.) prayer for the dead.

libéral, -e, *adj.*, liberal, generous, bounteous. free-hearted, open-handed.

libéral, *n.m.*, liberal.

libéralement (-ral-mān), *adv.*, liberally. bountifully, largely, generously, bounteously.

libéralisme, *n.m.*, liberalism.

libéralité, *n.f.*, liberality; donation. bounty.

libérat-eur, *n.m.*, **-rice**, *n.f.*, deliverer, liberator. rescuer.

libérati-f, **-ve**, *adj.*, freedom-giving, liberating.

libération, *n.f.*, deliverance, discharge, riddance.

libéré, -e, *part.*, liberated, discharged. *Forçat —;* returned convict.

libérer, *v.a.*, to discharge, to liberate, to free. se **libérer**, *v.r.*, to be liberated, to be discharged ; to pay off one's debts.

liberté, *n.f.*, liberty, freedom, franchise. *On a rendu la — aux prisonniers;* the prisoners were restored to liberty. *Mettre en —;* to set at liberty.

liberticide, *adj.*, liberticide.

libertin, -e, *adj.*, libertine. licentious; idle (of children—*des enfants*).

libertin, *n.m.*, **-e**, *n.f.*, libertine, rake; idle (of children—*des enfants*) ; ⊙ unbeliever.

libertinage, *n.m.*, libertinism, debauchery; wildness ; ⊙ irreligion. *Vivre dans le —;* to lead a life of libertinism.

libertiner, *v.n.*, to be a libertine, to be rakish; to be idle (of children—*des enfants*).

se **libertiner**, *v.r.*, to be a libertine; to play the idler (of children—*des enfants*).

libidineu-x, -se, *adj.*, libidinous.

ad libitum. *V.* **ad libitum**.

libraire, *n.m.*, bookseller.

librairie, *n.f.*, book-trade, bookselling; bookseller's shop.

libration, *n.f.*, (astron.) libration.

libre, *adj.*, free; at liberty ; unguarded, unconfined ; bold, broad ; rid, exempt; unstamped (of paper—*papier*). *Il a tout son temps —;* all his time is his own. — *à vous de sortir ou de rester;* stay or go, which you please. *Cette place est —;* that seat is unoccupied. *Avoir le champ —;* to have free scope for action.

libre-échange, *n.m.*, (n.p.) free-trade.

libre-échangiste, *n.m.* (— -s), free-trader.

librement, *adv.*, freely, without restraint ; boldly. *En user —;* to make free with it.

librettiste, *n.m.*, the author of the words of an opera.

libretto, *n.m.* (—s, or *libretti*), words of an opera, libretto.

lice, *n.f.*, lists ; field, arena ; (tapestry—*tapisserie*) warp; (mam.) bitch-hound. *Entrer dans la —, en —;* to enter the lists. *Haute —,* high warp. *Basse —;* low warp.

licence, *n.f.*, license, leave ; permission ; liberty, licentiousness; licentiate's degree.

licencié, *n.m.*, licentiate.

licenciement (-sī-mān), *n.m.*, (milit.) disbanding.

licencier, *v.a.*, to disband (troops—*troupes*).

se **licencier**, *v.r.*, to grow licentious, to take liberties.

licencieusement (-eûz-mān), *adv.*, licentiously, lewdly, dissolutely.

licencieu-x, -se, *adj.*, licentious, dissolute.

licet (-sèt), *n.m.* (—), (l.u.) permission. leave.

lichen (li-kè-n), *n.m.*, (bot.) lichen.

licitation, *n.f.*, sale by auction of the property of co-proprietors.

licite, *adj.*, licit. lawful. allowable.

licitement (-sit-mān), *adv.*, lawfully, lictly.

liciter, *v.a.*, to sell by auction the property of co-proprietors.

licol, *n.m. V.* **licou.**

licorne, *n.f.*, unicorn. — *de mer ;* narwhal.

licou, *n.m.*, halter.

lictour, *n.m.*, lictor.

lie, *n.f.*, lees, dregs, grounds. *Boire jusqu'à la —* ; to drink to the dregs. *La — du peuple ;* the scum of the people.

☉**lie**, *adj.*, merry.

lié, **-e**, *part.*, tied, bound, connected. *Une sauce bien —e ;* a thick sauce.

liège, *n.m.*, cork ; cork-tree.

liéger, *v.a.*, to cork (a net—*un filet*).

liégeu-x, **-se**, *adj.*, like cork, corky.

lien (li-in), *n.m.*, band, rope, strap ; *pl.*, bonds, chains, irons. *Briser, rompre, ses —s ;* to break one's bonds. — *conjugal ;* matrimonial bond.

lienterie, *n.f.*, (med.) lientery.

lientérique, *adj.*, lienteric.

lier, *v.a.*, to bind, to bind down ; to fasten, to tie, to tie down, to tie up ; to join ; to thicken ; to link, to connect. *C'est un fou à — ;* he ought to be put in a strait-jacket. — *une sauce ;* to thicken a sauce. — *des notes ;* (mus.) to slur notes. — *commerce avec quelqu'un ;* to establish a connection with any one.

se**lier**, *v.r.*, to bind ; to tie ; to thicken ; to become acquainted with ; to become intimate with ; to form a connection.

lierre, *n.m.*, (bot.) ivy. — *terrestre ;* ground-ivy. — *grimpant ;* tree-ivy.

☉**liesse**, *n.f.*, mirth, gaiety, merriment.

lieu, *n.m.*, place, spot, ground ; family ; cause, reason, occasion ; *pl.*, premises ; water-closet. *En tout — ;* everywhere. *En aucun — ;* nowhere. *Se porter sur les —x ;* to go to the spot. *En premier — ;* in the first place. *Les saints —x ;* the holy shrines. *S'allier en bon — ;* to marry into a good family. *—x communs ;* common-place topics. *Il n'y a pas — de craindre ;* there is no cause to fear. *Vous avez donné — à cela ;* you are the occasion of it. *Il m'a tenu — de père ;* he has been a father to me. *Avoir — ;* to take place, to happen. *—x d'aisances ;* water-closet. *Être au — et place de quelqu'un ;* to represent any one. *Au — de ;* in the place of, instead of, in lieu of. *Au — que ;* whereas, when on the contrary, while.

lieue, *n.f.*, league (two ard a half miles English).

lieur. *n.m.*, binder (of sheaves, hay, &c.—*de gerbes, de foin, &c.*).

lieutenance (lieu-tnäns), *n.f.*, lieutenant-ship, lieutenancy.

lieutenant, *n.m.*, lieutenant. — *en premier, en second ;* first lieutenant, second lieutenant. *Sous- — (— —s) ;* ensign.

☉**lieutenante**, *n.f.*, the wife of a judge whose title was lieutenant.

lièvre, *n.m.*, hare. *Bec-de- — (—s —) ;* hare-lip. *Il ne faut pas chasser deux —s à la fois ;* one must not have too many irons in the fire.

ligament, *n.m.*, (anat.) ligament.

ligamenteu-x, **-se**. *adj.*, ligamentous.

ligature, *n.f.*, ligature.

lige, *adj.*, liege. *Fief — ;* vassalage.

***lignage**, *n.m.*, lineage.

***lignager**, *n.m.*, person of the same descent.

***ligne**, *n.f.*, line ; path ; swath (of grass—*de l'herbe*) *Être en première — ;* to hold the first rank. *Être hors de — ;* to be out of the line, beyond comparison. *Il ne fait pas ses —s droites ;* he does not keep his lines straight. *À la — ;* a new line, a break. — *à pêcher ;* fishing-line. *Pêcher à la — ;* to angle. *Troupe de — ;* troops of the line.

***lignée**, *n.f.*, lineage, progeny, offspring. issue.

***ligner**, *v.a.*, (carp.) to draw lines on.

***lignerolle**, *n.f.*, (nav.) twine.

***lignette**, *n.f.*, twine (for nets—*à filet*).

***ligneul**, *n.m.*, shoemaker's thread.

***ligneu-x**, **-se**, *adj.*, (bot.) ligneous, woody.

lignite (lig-nit), *n.m.*, lignite, brown-coal.

ligue (lig), *n.f.*, league ; plot.

liguer (lighé), *v.a.*, to unite in a league.

se**liguer**, *v.r.*, to league.

ligueu-r, *n.m.*, **-se**, *n.f.*, leaguer.

ligulé, **-e**, *adj.*, (bot.) ligulate ; strap-shaped.

lilas, *n.m.*, lilac.

lilas, *adj.*, lilac-coloured.

liliacée, *n.* and *adj. f.*, liliaceous plant ; liliaceous.

lilliputien, **-ne**, *adj.*, of somebody, or something exceedingly small, lilliputian.

limace, *n.f.*, slug ; (mec.) Archimedes screw.

limaçon, *n.m.* snail (anat.) cochlea. *Escalier en — ;* winding-staircase.

***limaille**, *n.f.*, filings.

limande, *n.f.*, (ich.) dab.

limas, *n.m. V.* **limace.**

limbe, *n.m.*, limb, border.

limbes, *n.m.pl.*, (theol.) limbo, limbus.

lime, *n.f.*, file ; (bot.) sweet lemon. *Les dents d'une — ;* the teeth of a file. — *douce ;* smooth file. — *sourde ;* dead file.

limer, *v.a.*, to file.

limeur, *n.m.*, filer.

limier, *n.m.*, blood-hound, lime-hound ; police-spy.

liminaire, *adj.*, said of a prologue or epistle serving as a preface to a book.

limitati-f, **-ve**, *adj.*, limiting.

limitation, *n.f.*, limitation.

limitativement, *adv.*, limitedly, with limitation.

limite, *n.f.*, limit, landmark, boundary, bound, confine.

limité, **-e**, *part.*, limited.

limiter, *v.a.*, to limit, to bound ; to circumscribe, to confine.

limitrophe, *adj.*, neighbouring. bordering.

limon, *n.m.*, slime, ooze ; clay ; (bot.) lemon ; shaft (of a carriage—*de voiture*) ; string-board (of a staircase—*d'escalier*).

limonade, *n.f.*, lemonade.

limonadi-er, *n.m.*, **-ère**, *n.f.*, maker, seller, of lemonade ; coffee-house keeper.

limoneu-x, **-se**, *adj.*, muddy, turbid ; containing mud.

limonier, *n.m.*, shaft-horse ; (bot.) lemon-tree.

limonière, *n.f.*, four-wheeled carriage having two shafts.

limousin, *n.m.*, rough-waller, mason.

limousinage, *n.m.*, rough-walling ; ashlar-work.

limousine, *n.f.*, cloak of thick coarse wool worn by carmen and peasants.

limousiner, *v.a.*, to rough-wall.

limpide. *adj.*, limpid, clear.

limpidité, *n.f.*, limpidness, clearness.

limure, *n.f.*, filing ; filings.

lin, *n.m.*, flax. *Graine de — ;* linseed. *Toile de — ;* linen-cloth.

linacées, *n.f.pl. V.* **linées.**

linaire, *n.f.*, (bot.) toad-flax.

linceul, *n.m.*, winding-sheet, shroud.

linéaire. *adj.*, linear.

linéal. **-e**, *adj.*, lineal, in a direct line.

linéament. *n.m.*, trace, lineament, feature.

linées, *n.f.pl.*, (bot.) plants of the flax kind.

linette, *n.f.*, flax-seed.

linge. *n.m.*, linen ; cloth. — *propre ;* clean linen. *Changer de — ;* to change one's linen.

ling-er, *n.m.*, **-ère**. *n.f.*, linendraper.

lingère, *n.f.*, keeper of a fancy linen-shop ;

seamstress (to take care of the linen **in** colleges, boarding schools. &c.—*de collèges, pensions, &c.*).

lingerie (ün-jrî), *n.f.*, linen trade, linen-drapery; hosiery; place where the linen is kept in colleges, hospitals, &c.

lingot, *n.m.*, ingot, bullion; (hunt.) slug. — *d'or*; ingot of gold. *Or en* — ; gold in bullion.

lingotière (-ti-èr), *n.f.*, ingot-mould; (metal.) foss.

lingual, -e (-gooal), *n.f.* and *adj.*, (anat., gram.) lingual.

lingue (lîngh), *n.f.*, (ich.) ling.

linguet (-ghè), *n.m.*, (nav.) poll of the capstern.

linguiforme (-gooi-), *adj.*, linguiform, like a tongue.

linguiste (-gooist), *n.m.*, linguist.

linguistique (-gooistik), *n.f.*, linguistics.

lini-er, -ère, *adj.*, of flax. *Industrie —ère*; linen-trade, manufacturing of linen-cloth; flax-spinning.

linière, *n.f.*, flax field.

liniment, *n.m.*, (pharm.) liniment.

linon, *n.m.*, lawn.

linot, *n.m.*, (orni.) cock-linnet.

linotte, *n.f.*, hen-linnet. *C'est une tête de* — ; he is a foolish fellow, he has not too much brains. *Siffler la* — ; (pop.) to drink hard; to be in limbo.

linteau, *n.m.*, (carp.) head-piece, lintel.

lion, *n.m.*, (mam.) lion; dandy; (astron.) Leo. *Jeune* — ; lion's cub, whelp, young lion. — *marin*; sea-wolf. *Dent-de—* (*—s* —); (bot.) dandelion. *Un* — *rugissant*; a roaring lion. *Coudre la peau du renard à celle du* — ; to join cunning to strength. *C'est l'âne couvert de la peau du* — ; he is the ass with the lion's skin. *C'est un* — ; (of a young man—*d'un jeune homme*) he is a dandy.

lionceau, *n.m.*, (mam.) young lion, lion's whelp, cub.

lionne. *n.f.*, (mam.) lioness; fashionable woman of easy virtue.

lionné, -e, *adj.*, (her.) rampant.

lioube, *n.m.*, (nav.) scarf by which a jury-mast is attached to the stump of a mast.

lipogrammatique, *adj.*, lipogrammatic.

lipogrammatiste, *n.m.*, lipogrammatist, letter-dropper.

lipogramme, *n.m.*, lipogram.

lipome, *n.m.*, (med.) lipoma, adipose wen.

lipothymie, *n.f.*, (med.) lipothymy.

lippe, *n.f.*, blobber-lip, thick lip. *Faire sa* — , *la* — , *faire une grosse, une vilaine*, — (fam.); to pout.

◊**lippée**, *n.f.*, (fam.) mouthful; meal. [In the latter sense this word is only used with the adj. *franche*.] *Franche* — ; a good meal that costs nothing. *Chercheur de franches —s*; spunger.

lippitude, *n.f.*, (med.) lippitude, blearedness.

lippu, -e, *adj.*, blobber-lipped, thick-lipped.

liquation (-cooa-), *n.f.*, liquation, eliquation.

liquéfaction, *n.f.*, liquefaction.

liquéfiable, *adj.*, liquefiable.

liquéfier, *v.a.*, to liquefy.

se **liquéfier**, *v.r.*, to liquefy.

liquet, *n.m.*, (hort.) small baking pear.

liqueur, *n.f.*, liquid; liquor, spirits; liqueur cordial. *Vin de* — ; sweet wine. *—s fraîches*; refreshing liquors. *Marchand de —s spiritueuses*; dealer in spirits.

liquidambar, *n.m.*, (bot.) liquid-amber.

liquidateur, *n.m.*, liquidator.

liquidation, *n.f.*, liquidation, settling; settlement; winding up.

liquide, *adj*, liquid, watery; clear; net (of money—*d'argent*), *La plaine* — ; the watery plain

liquide, *n.m.*, liquid, fluid; spirit, spirituous liquor.

liquide, *n.f.*, (gram.) liquid.

liquider, *v.a.*, to liquidate, to settle, to discharge; to wind up.

se **liquider**, *v.r.*, to liquidate, to settle, to discharge one's debts.

liquidité, *n.f.*, liquidness, liquidity, fluidity.

liquoreu-x, *-se*, *adj.*, cordial, sweet.

liquoriste, *n.m.*, dealer in liqueurs.

lire (lisant, lu), *v.a.*, to read. *Continuer de* — ; to read on. — *tout bas*; to read low. — *à haute voix*; to read with a loud voice. — *dans la pensée de quelqu'un*; to read any one's thoughts.

liron, *n.m.* *V.* **loir** and **lérot**.

lis (lis), *n.m.*, (bot.) lily. — *asphodèle*; lily-daffodil. *Fleur de* — (her.); flower-de-lis, flower-de-luce.

liséré, *n.m.*, strip (of riband—*de ruban*); border, edging.

li, lisérer, *v.a.*, to border with piping.

liseron (li-zron), *n.m.*, (bot.) bind-weed.

liset, *n.m.*, (bot.) *V.* **liseron**.

liseu-r, *n.m.*, *-se*, *n.f.*, reader.

lisible, *adj.*, legible, readable.

lisiblement, *adv.*, legibly.

lisière, *n.f.*, list (of cloth—*du drap*); strings, leading-strings; border, skirt. — *de toile*; selvage of linen-cloth. — *d'un bois*; outskirts, verge, of a wood.

lissage, *n.m.*, (tech.) smoothing, glossing; (nav.) fixing of the ribands or rails of a ship.

lisse, *adj.*, smooth, sleek, glossy.

lisse, *n.f.*, hand-rail, hand-railing; (nav.) sheer-rails, drift-rails, riband — *s de porte-haubans*; sheer-rails. —*s de la rabattue*; drift-rails. —*s de couronnement*; upper rails of the stern. —*s de grande rabattue*; quarter-rails. —*s de l'éperon*; rails of the head. —*s de bastingage*; rails of the nettings. —*s des couples*; ribands. — *du fort*; extreme breadth line. — *des façons*; floor-riband. —*s des œuvres mortes*; ribands of the upper-works. —*s de plat-bord*; drift-rails. — *de vibord*; waist-rail. —*s de la herpe*; rails of the head. — *de hourdi*; wing-transom. — (tapestry—*tapisserie*); *V.* **lice**.

lisser, *v.a.*, to smooth, to gloss, to polish.

lisseu-r, *n.m.*, *-se*, *n.f.*, polisher.

lissoir, *n.m.*, polisher (tool—*outil*).

lissure, *n.f.*, polishing, sleeking.

liste, *n.f.*, list, roll, catalogue. — *civile*; civil list. — *des jurés*; (jur.) panel of jurors.

listeau, *n.m.*, (nav.) rim used to fill the openings of ribands *or* rails; (arch.) listel, list, fillet.

listel, *n.m.* (*listeaux*), (arch.) listel, list, fillet.

liston, *n.m.*, (her.) scroll.

lit, *n.m.*, bed; bedstead; layer; stratum; channel. — *de plume*; feather-bed. — *de parade*; bed of state. — *de repos*; couch. — *de sangle*; folding-bed. — *volant* (nav.); cot. — *à quenouilles*, — *à colonnes*; four-post bedstead, four-poster. *Quenouille de* — ; *colonne de* — ; bedpost. *Descente de* — ; carpet for the bedside. *Bois de* — ; bedstead. *Se mettre au* — ; to go to bed. *Garder le* — ; to keep one's bed. *Ils font — à part*; they sleep in separate beds. *Il a des enfants de deux —s*; he has children by two wives. *Ruelle de* — ; bed-side. — *de dessous*; understratum (of a quarry—*carrière*). — *de la mer*; bed of the sea. — *du vent*; (nav.) the wind's eye. *Tenir le* — *du vent*; to go close to the wind. — *de marée*; tide way. — *de Procuste*; the bed of Procustes; (fig.) tyrannical custom, rule, law, &c.

litanies, *n.f.pl.*, litany, prayers; long-winded story.

liteau, *n.m.,* haunt (of a wolf—*de loup*); coloured stripes (on napkins—*sur les serviettes*).
litée, *n.f.,* (hunt.) haunt, lair.
literie, *n.f.,* bedding.
litharge. *n.f.,* (min.) litharge.
lithargé, -e, or **lithargiré, -e,** *adj.,* adulterated with litharge.
lithiase, or **lithiasie,** *n.f.,* (med.) lithiasis.
lithoclaste, *n.m.,* (surg.) lithoclast (instrument).
lithocolle, *n.f.,* lithocolla.
lithogénésie, *n.f.,* lithogenesy.
lithographe, *n.m.,* lithographer. *Imprimeur* —; lithographic printer.
lithographie. *n.f.,* lithography; lithograph; lithographic printing-office.
lithographier, *v.a.,* to lithograph.
lithographique, *adj.,* lithographic.
lithoïde, *adj.,* lithoidal.
lithologie, *n.f.,* lithology.
lithologue, *n.m.,* lithologist.
lithontriptique, *n.m.* and *adj.,* (med.) lithontriptic.
lithophage, *adj.,* lithophagous.
lithophylle, *n.f.,* lithophyl.
lithophyte, *n.m.,* lithophyte.
lithosperme, *n.m.,* (bot.) lithospermum; gromil, gromwell.
lithotome, *n.m.,* (surg.) lithotome.
lithotomie, *n.f.,* (surg.) lithotomy.
lithotomique, *adj.,* (surg.) lithotomic.
lithotomiste, *n.m.,* (surg.) lithotomist.
lithotriteur, *n.m.,* (surg.) lithotritor.
lithotritie, (-tri-ci), *n.f.,* (surg.) lithotrity.
litière (-tièr), *n.f.,* litter; stable-litter. *Il est sur la* —; he is in the straw (of a horse—*du cheval*); he is sick abed (pers.). *Faire* — *de quelque chose;* to throw a thing about like dirt.
litigant, -e, *adj.,* engaged in litigation.
litige. *n.m.,* litigation, suit at law. *En* —; litigated.
litigieu-x, -se, *adj.,* litigious (of things—*des choses*). *Esprit* —; litigious spirit.
litispendance, *n.f.,* (jur.) pendency.
litorne, *n.f.,* (orni.) litorn, field-fare.
litote, *n.f.,* (rhet.) litotes.
litre, *n.f.,* black band, with the coat of arms of a deceased person, hung down a church.
litre. *n.m.,* litre (1·760 pint).
litron, *n.m.,* ancient measure of capacity, about the sixteenth part of a bushel.
littéraire, *adj.,* literary.
littérairement, *adv.,* literarily.
littéral, -e, *adj.,* literal.
littéralement (-ral-män), *adv.,* literally, word for word, verbatim.
littéralité, *n.f.,* literality, literalness.
littérateur, *n.m.,* literary man, scholar, man of letters.
littérature, *n.f.,* literature, scholarship, learning.
littoral, -e, *adj.,* littoral, belonging to the sea-coast.
littoral, *n.m.,* coast, sea-shore.
lituite, *n.m.,* (foss.) lituite.
liturgie, *n.f.,* liturgy.
liturgique, *adj.,* liturgic, liturgical.
liturgiste, *n.m.,* writer on the liturgy.
lituus, *n.m.* (—), (antiq.) lituus, augur's wand; a clarion, a curved trumpet.
liure, *n.f.,* cord, cart-rope; (nav.) seizing, lashing, gammoning (of the bowsprit—*du beaupré*).
livarde, *n.f.,* cord; (nav) sprit (of a shoulder of mutton sail—*devoile rectangulaire*). *Voile à* —; sprit-sail.
livarder, *v.a.,* (nav.) to sprit.
livide, *adj.,* livid.

lividité, *n.f.,* lividness.
livrable, *adj.,* (com.) deliverable.
livraison, *n.f.,* delivery (of goods—*de marchandises*); part, number (of a book—*d'un livre*).
livre, *n.m.,* book. — *manuscrit, imprimé;* manuscript, printed book. — *en feuilles;* book in sheets. — *cartonné;* book in boards. — *broché;* stitched book. — *épuisé;* book out of print. *Collationner un* —; to collate a book. *Mettre un* — *au jour;* to publish a book. *Un dévoreur de* —*s;* a bookworm (pers.). *Parler comme un* —; to speak like a book. *Traduire à* — *ouvert;* to translate at sight. *Chanter à* — *ouvert;* to sing at sight. — *de compte;* book of accounts. *Grand* —; ledger. — *journal;* daybook. — *de caisse;* cash-book. *Teneur de* —*s;* book-keeper. *Tenir les* —*s;* to keep the books, to keep the accounts. *Grand-* —, *grand* — *de la dette publique;* list of the creditors of the State.
livre, *n.f.,* pound (1lb., 1oz., 10 1-4 dr. avoirdupois); livre (coin.); franc. — *sterling;* pound sterling (twenty shillings—*vingt schellings, environ 25 frcs.*). — *parisis;* Paris livre (one shilling—*un schelling*). — *tournois;* Tours livre (tenpence—*dix pence*).
livrée, *n.f.,* livery; livery-servants. — *de noce;* wedding-favours.
livrer, *v.a.,* to deliver; to deliver up, over; to betray; to give up. — *de la marchandise à;* to deliver goods to. — *bataille;* to engage battle. — *un assaut;* to make an assault. — *une place à l'ennemi;* to deliver up a place to the enemy. — *une ville au pillage;* to give up a town to pillage. — *son âme à la douleur;* to yield one's soul up to grief.
se livrer, *v.r.,* to deliver one's self up, over; to give one's self up, over; to surrender one's self; to devote, to dedicate, to apply, one's self; to confide, to trust, one's self; to riot in; to expose one's self.
livret, *n.m.,* little book; workman's certificate; multiplication-table; book (at cards—*aux cartes*). — *de batteur d'or;* gold-beater's mould.
lixiviation, *n.f.,* (chem.) lixiviation.
lixiviel, -le, *adj.,* (chem., pharm.) lixivial.
lixivium (-om), *n.m.,* (chem.) lixivium.
llama, *n.m.* V. **lama.**
lobe, *n.m.,* lobe; lobe of the ear; (arch.) cusp; (arch.) foil.
lobé, -e, *adj.,* (bot.) lobed, lobate.
lobélie, *n.f.,* (bot.) lobelia, cardinal-flower. — *enflée;* Indian tobacco, emetic weed.
lobiole, *n.f.,* small lobe (in lichens—*des lichens*).
lobulaire, *adj.,* lobulary.
lobule, *n.m.,* (anat.) lobule.
local, -e, *adj.,* local.
local, *n.m.,* habitation, ground occupied by a building; premises.
localisation, *n.f.,* localization.
localiser, *v.a.,* to localize.
se localiser, *v.r.,* to become, to be, located.
localité, *n.f.,* locality, place.
locataire, *n.m.f.,* tenant, renter, lodger; (jur.) lessee. — *à bail;* lessee. *Recevoir des* —*s;* to take in tenants. — *en vertu d'un bail;* leaseholder.
locati-f. -ve, *adj.,* of or belonging to the tenant. *Valeur* —*ve;* value in rent.
location, *n.f.,* letting, letting out; hiring; renting; (jur.) location.
locatis (-tis), *n.m.,* (fam. l.u.) hired horse, jade.
loch, *n.m.,* (nav.) log. *Table de* —; log-book. *Jeter le* —; to heave the log.
loche, *n.f.,* (ich.) loach, groundling.
locher, *v.n.,* (of a horse's shoe—*d'un fer à cheval*) to be loose. *Il y a là quelque fer qui loche;* there is a screw loose there.

lochet, *n.m.*, narrow spade.

lochial, **-e**, *adj.*, (med.) lochial.

lochies, *n.f.pl.*, (med.) lochia.

locman. *n.m.*, coasting pilot.

locomobile, *n.f.*, (agri., manu.) movable steam-engine.

locomot-eur. -rice, *adj.*, (anat.) promoting, producing locomotion.

locomoti-f. -ve, *adj.*, locomotive.

locomotion. *n.f.*, locomotion.

locomotive, *n.f.*, locomotive, locomotive-engine.

locrenan, *n.m.*, (coarse cloth—*toile grossière*) lockram.

locuste. *n.f.*, (ent.) locust; (zool.) shrimp.

locution. *n.f.*, expression, mode, form of speech. locution.

lods, *n.m.pl.*, (feudal law—*féodalité*) only used in the expression: — *et ventes*, lord's due on sales of inheritances.

lof, *n.m.*, (nav.) loof, luff. *Aller au* —; to sail near the wind. *Être au* —; to be to the windward. *Tenir le* — ; to keep the weather-gauge. — *pour* —! to the weather-side! *Couple de* —; loof-frame. *Largue le* —! up tacks and sheets! *Bouter le* —; to trim all sharp. — *tout!* luff round! — *à la risée!* ease the ship! *Virer* —*pour* —; to tack, to veer the ship.

lofer, *v.n.*, (nav.) to luff.

logarithme, *n.m.*, (math.) logarithm.

logarithmique, *adj.*, logarithmic, logarithmical, logarithmetical, logarithmetic.

logarithmique, *n.f.*, logarithmic curve.

loge, *n.f.*, lodge, hut, box; booth; cell; den; actor's dressing-room. — *d'un chien;* kennel of a dog. *Ouvreuses de* —*s;* box-openers. — *grillée;* latticed box. — *découverte;* open box. *Premières* —*s* (thea.) ; first tier of boxes. *Tenir une* — (freemasonry—*franc-maçonnerie*) ; to hold a lodge. — *du tigre,* tiger's den.

logeable (lo-jabl), *adj.*, inhabitable, tenantable.

logement (lo-jmăn), *n.m.*, lodgings; house-room; (milit.) lodgment; (nav.) room. — *garni;* furnished lodgings.

loger, *v.n.*, to lodge, to live, to put up. — *chez soi;* to live at home. — *dans une auberge;* to put up at an inn. — *à la belle étoile;* to lodge in the open air.

loger, *v.a.*, to lodge, to harbour, to give a lodging, to house; to stable. — *des soldats;* to quarter soldiers.

se loger, *v.r.*, to lodge, to take up one's lodgings.

logette. *n.f.*, little cabin.

logeu-r, *n.m.*, **-se**, *n.f.*, lodging-house keeper.

logicien (-in), *n.m.*, logician.

logique, *n.f.* and *adj.*, logic ; logical.

logiquement, *adv.*, logically.

logis, *n.m.*, house, dwelling, lodging, lodging-house, home. *Corps de* —; main building. *On m'attend au* —; they wait for me at home. *Bon* — *à pied et à cheval;* good accommodation for man and horse.

logographe, *n.m.*, early Greek historian and prose writer.

logogriphe, *n.m.*, logogriph, riddle.

logomachie. *n.f.*, logomachy, war of words.

logos, *n.m.* (n.p.), (theol.) God the Word; (in Plato's Philos.—*philosophie platonicienne*) the Creator of all things.

loi, *n.f.*, law ; power, dominion ; authority ; rule. *Homme de* —; lawyer. *Projet de* — (parliament) bill. *Présenter un projet de* — ; to bring in a bill. *Rejeter un projet de* —; to throw out a bill. — *annonaire ; V.* **annonaire.**

loin, *adv.*, far, far off, a great way off, at a distance, remote, distant. *De* — *en* —; at great intervals, at a distance from each other. *Revenir de* —; to have a narrow escape. *Aller chasser au* —; to go a hunting a great way off. — *du monde;* far from the world. — *d'ici;* a great way off. — *d'ici!* be gone! — *des yeux,* — *du cœur;* out of sight, out of mind. *Bien* — *de;* instead of ; far from. *Bien* — *que;* far from, so far from. *Bien* — *que cela soit;* it is so far from being so.

lointain, **-e**, *adj.*, remote, far distant. *Pays* —; remote country.

lointain, *n.m.*, distance. *Le* — *d'un tableau;* the back-ground of a picture.

loir, *n.m.*, (mam.) dormouse.

loisible, *adj.*, lawful, allowable.

loisir, *n.m.*, leisure, spare time. *J'ai du* —; I am at leisure. *Êtes-vous de* —? are you at leisure? *À* —; leisurely, at leisure.

lok, *n.m. V.* **looch.**

lollard, *n.m.* (—*s*), Lollard.

lombaire, *adj.*, (anat.) lumbar.

lombard, *n.m.*, pawnbrokery. *V.* **mont-de-piété.**

lombard, *n.m.*, **-e**, *n.f.*, Lombard.

lombes, *n.m.pl.*, lumbal region, loins.

lombric, *n.m.*, (ent.) dew-worm, earth-worm, lob-worm.

lombrical. **-e**, *adj.*, lumbrical.

lomentacé, **-e**, *adj.*, (bot.) lomentaceous.

lompe, *n.m.*, (ich.) lump-fish, sea-owl.

londrin, *n.m.*, light woollen cloth, an imitation of London cloth.

long, **-ue** (lŏn, lŏng), *adj.*, long, slow, tedious. *Le temps est* — *à qui attend;* time appears very long to one in expectation. — *à manger,* — *à tout;* slow at meat, slow at everything. *De* —*ue main;* of long standing.

long, *n.m.*, length. *Cela a dix aunes de* —; that is ten ells in length. *Être couché, étendu, tout de son* —; to lie at full length. *Prendre le plus* —; to go the longest way about. *Tout le* —; all along. *Tout au* —; along, at large, at full.

long, *adv.*, much, a great deal.

longanimité, *n.f.*, longanimity, forbearance, long-suffering.

longe, *n.f.*, loin; tether. *Une* — *de veau;* a loin of veal.

longer, *v.a.*, to go, to walk, along.

longévité, *n.f.*, longevity.

longimétrie, *n.f.*, longimetry.

longitude, *n.f.*, (geog.) longitude. *Prendre les* —*s;* to take the longitude.

longitudinal, **-e**, *adj.*, longitudinal.

longitudinalement, *adv.*, longitudinally.

long-jointé, **-e**, *adj.*, (man.) long-jointed.

longrine, *or* **longuerine**, *n.f.*, (carp.) girder.

longtemps (lŏn-tăn), *adv.*, long, a long while, a great while. *Il y a* — *que je ne l'ai vu;* I have not seen him for a great while.

longue (long), *n.f.*, long syllable. *À la* —; with time, in the long run.

longuement (long-măn), *adv.*, long, a long time, a great while.

longuet, **-te**, *adj.*, longish, somewhat long, pretty long, at great length.

longueur (-gheur), *n.f.*, length, longness; slowness, tediousness; prolixity. *Trois pieds de* —; three feet in length. *En* —; lengthwise. *Tirer les choses en* —; to delay, to cause delays, to cause any affair to linger on.

longue-vue, *n.f.* (—*s* —*s*), small telescope, spy-glass.

looch (lok), *n.m.*, (pharm.) loch.

lopin, *n.m.*, (pop.) lump ; bit, morsel (of eatables—*de comestibles*).

loquace (-kooas), *adj.*, loquacious, talkative.

loquacité (-kooa-), *n.f.*, loquacity, talkativeness.

loque, *n.f.*, rag, tatter.
loquèle (-kuèl), *n.f.*, small talk.
loquet, *n.m.*, latch.
loqueteau (lok-to), *n.m.*, little latch.
loquette, *n.f.*, (pop.) little piece, small bit.
lord, *n.m.* (—s), lord.
lorette, *n.f.*, lorette, lady of easy virtue.
lorgnade, *n.f.*, ogle, side-look, glance.
lorgner, *v.a.*, to leer, to ogle; to look through an opera-glass; to quiz; to have an eye on. — *une charge;* to have an eye on an office.
lorgnerie, *n.f.*, ogling, side-glance.
lorgnette, *n.f.*, opera-glass.
lorgneu-r, *n.m.*, *-se*, *n.f.*, ogler.
lorgnon, *n.m.*, eye-glass, quizzing-glass.
loriot, *n.m.*, (orni.) oriole.
lors, *adv.*, then. *Dès* —; from that time. — *de;* at the time of.
lorsque, *conj.*, when. — *j'arrivai;* when I arrived.
⊙**los**, *n.m.*, praise.
losange, *n.m.*, (math.) lozenge; lozenge-moulding.
losangé, *-e*, *adj.*, (math.) in lozenges; (her.) lozengee, lozengy.
lot (lô), *n.m.*, lot; portion, share; prize. *Le* — *qui lui est échu;* the portion which has fallen to his share. *Le gros* —; the first prize in a lottery.
loterie (lo-tri), *n.f.*, lottery; raffle. *Mettre à la* —; to put in the lottery. *Gagner à la* — to win in the lottery. *Faire une* —; to raffle.
loti, *-e*, *part.*, divided into lots. *Le voilà bien* —; he has made a good choice.
lotier (-tié), *n.m.*, (bot.) lotus, lotos.
lotion, *n.f.*, lotion, washing; ablution.
lotir, *v.a.*, to divide into lots, to share.
lotissage, *n.m.*, (chem.) assaying, averaging.
lotissement (-tis-mǎn), *n.m.*, dividing into lots, lotting.
loto, *n.m.*, loto (game of chance—*jeu de hasard*).
lotophages, *n.m.pl.*, Lotophagi (people of ancient Africa who fed on lote berries—*peuple de l'Afrique ancienne qui se nourrissait de lotus*).
lotte, *n.f.*, (ich.) lote.
lotus, *or* **lotos** (-tús, -tôs), *n.m.*, (bot.) lote.
louable, *adj.*, laudable, praiseworthy, commendable.
louablement, *adv.*, laudably, commendably, in a manner deserving praise.
louage, *n.m.*, letting out, hire, hiring, renting. *Donner à* —; to let out, to hire. *Prendre à* —; to rent. *Un cheval de* —; a hired horse.
louange, *n.f.*, praise, commendation. *Donner des* —*s;* to bestow praise.
louanger, *v.a.*, to bepraise, to flatter, to praise.
louangeu-r, *-se*, *n.* and *adj.*, praiser, flatterer, commender, panegyrist; encomiastic.
louche, *adj.*, squint-eyed; dubious, ambiguous, equivocal; not clear.
louche, *n.m.*, ambiguity, equivocalness. *Il y a du* — *dans sa conduite;* there is something suspicious in his conduct.
louche, *n.f.*, soup-ladle.
loucher, *v.n.*, to squint.
louchet, *n.m.*, grafting implement.
louer, *v.a.*, to let, to let out, to rent, to hire, to hire out, to lease; to take, to rent. — *une maison à quelqu'un;* to rent any one a house.
se louer, *v.r.*, to hire one's self out; to be let.
louer, *v.a.*, to praise, to commend, to laud.
se louer, *v.r.*, to laud, to praise, one's self. — *de quelqu'un;* to be well pleased with any one; to be satisfied with any one.
loueu-r, *n.m.*, *-se*, *n.f.*, hirer, one who lets out; ⊙praiser, flatterer.
lougre, *n.m.*, lugger.

louis, *n.m.*, louis (an old French coin equal to nineteen shillings). — *d'or;* louis d'or.
loup (loo), *n.m.*, wolf; (med.) lupus; black velvet mask; packing stick. *Manger comme un* —; to eat like a wolf. *Un saut de* —; a ha-ha. *Entre chien et* — : in the dusk of the evening. *Enfermer le* — *dans la bergerie;* to shut the wolf up in the sheepfold; to cure a disease hastily; to drive in a disease. *Marcher à pas de* —; to walk cautiously like a thief. *Mettre quelqu'un à la gueule du* —; to throw any one into the lion's mouth. *Il est connu comme le* — *blanc;* he is known by everybody. *Quand on parle du* — *on en voit la queue;* talk of the devil and he is sure to appear. *La faim chasse le* — *hors du bois;* hunger will break through stone walls. *Il faut hurler avec les* —*s;* when you are at Rome, you must do as they do at Rome. *Qui se fait brebis, le* — *le mange;* daub yourself with honey and you will never want flies.
loup-cerve, *n.f.* (—*s* —*s*), (mam.) she-lynx.
loup-cervier, *n.m.* (—*s* —*s*), lynx.
loupe, *n.f.*, magnifying-glass, lens, eye-glass; (med.) wen.
loupeu-x, *-se*, *adj.*, wenny.
loup-garou, *n.m.* (—*s* —*s*), man-wolf; bug-bear; owl, surly dog; churlish fellow.
lourd, *-e*, *adj.*, heavy; lumpish, unwieldy; dull, clumsy, thick-headed; awkward.
lourdaud, *n.m.*, *-e*, *n.f.*, awkward person; blockhead, loggerhead.
lourdement, *adv.*, heavily; clumsily; grossly.
lourderie, *n.f.*, gross blunder.
lourdeur, *n.f.*, heaviness; sluggishness; dulness.
⊙**lourdise**, *n.f.*, gross blunder.
⊙**loure**, *n.f.*, loure (dance—*danse*).
lourer, *v.a.*, (mus.) to join the notes.
loustic, *n.m.*, comical companion.
loutre, *n.f.*, otter. — *marine;* sea-otter.
⊙**louvat**, *n.m.*, young wolf. *V.* **louveteau**.
louve, *n.f.*, she-wolf; wanton woman; (tech.) sling.
louver, *v.a.*, (tech.) to sling.
louvet, *-te*, *adj.*, fox-coloured (of horses—*chevaux*).
louveteau (loov-to), *n.m.*, young wolf.
louveter (loov-té), *v.n.*, to whelp (of wolves—*des loups*).
louveterie (loov-tri), *n.f.*, wolf-hunting train.
louvetier, *n.m.*, head of the Royal wolf-hunting train; landowner who has pledged himself to keep a wolf-hunting train.
louviers, *n.m.*, Louviers cloth.
louvoyage, *n.m.*, (nav.) tacking about.
louvoyer, *v.n.*, (nav.) to tack about; to ply by boards; to manœuvre.
louvre, *n.m.*, Louvre (public edifice in Paris); palace, magnificent house.
lover, *v.a.*, (nav.) to coil.
loxodromie, *n.f.*, (nav.) loxodromics.
loxodromique, *adj.*, loxodromic.
loyal, *-e*, *adj.*, honest, loyal, honourable, true, fair, fair-dealing, straightforward, upright; (com.) of good quality, unadulterated. *Un* — *chevalier;* a true knight.
loyalement (loa-yal-mǎn), *adv.*, fairly, loyally, honestly, faithfully, uprightly.
loyauté, *n.f.*, loyalty, honesty, honourableness, fairness, fair-dealing, integrity.
loyer, *n.m.*, hire, rent. *Donner à* —; to let. *Prendre une maison à* —; to hire a house. *Les* —*s sont élevés dans ce quartier;* rents are high in this neighbourhood.
lozange, *n.f.* *V.* **losange**.
lubie, *n.f.*, crotchet, maggot, whim. *Il lui prend souvent des* —*s;* he often takes whims into his head.

lubricité, *n.f.*, lubricity, lechery, lewdness.

lubrifier; *v.a.*, to lubricate.

lubrique, *adj.*, lecherous, lewd, lascivious.

lubriquement (-brik-mǎn), *adv.*, lasciviously, lecherously, lewdly.

lucarne, *n.f.*, sky-light, dormer-window, garret-window.

lucet, *n.m.*, (bot.) whortle-berry.

lucide, *adj.*, lucid.

lucidité, *n.f.*, lucidness.

lucifer (-fèr), *n.m.*, Lucifer, Phosphor, Phosphorus.

luciole, *n.f.*, glow-worm; firefly.

lucrati-f, -ve, *adj.*, lucrative.

lucre, *n.m.*, lucre.

lucubrateur, *n.m.*, lucubrator.

lucubration, *n.f.* *V.* **élucubration**.

lucullus, *n.m.* (—), a rich man fond of luxurious living; one who receives company sumptuously.

luette, *n.f.*, (anat.) uvula.

lueur, *n.f.*, glimmer, glimmering, light, glimpse, gleam. — *blafarde;* pale glimmer. *Faible —;* faint glimmer. *Une — d'espérance;* a glimpse of hope. *Jeter une faible —;* to glimmer.

lugubre, *adj.*, lugubrious, doleful, dismal, mournful.

lugubrement, *adv.*, dolefully, dismally, mournfully.

lui, personal pron., he; him, to him; her, to her; it, to it. *C'est —;* it is he. *Parlez-lui;* speak to him, to her. *Donnez-lui-en;* give him some.

luire (luisant, lui), *v.n.*, to shine, to glitter; to gleam. *Quand le soleil luit:* when the sun shines. *La clarté qui nous luit;* the light which shines upon us. *Le soleil luit pour tout le monde;* the sun shines for everybody.

luisant, -e, *adj.*, glistening, glittering, shining; shiny, glossy. *Un ver —;* a glow-worm.

luisant, *n.m.*, gloss.

luisante, *n.f.*, (astron.) brilliant star.

luites, *n.f.pl.*, (hunt.) *V.* **suites**.

lumachelle, *n.f.*, (min.) lumachella, shell-marble.

lumbago (lon-), *n.m.*, lumbago.

lumière, *n.f.*, light; touch-hole (of a fire-arm—*d'arme à feu*); information; intelligence, knowledge; insight, luminary; (paint) light. *A la — de;* by the light of. *Éteindre une —;* to put out a light. *Mettre en —;* to demonstrate. *Être privé de la —;* to have lost one's sight. *La — du soleil, du jour;* the light of the sun, of day. *La — de la raison;* the light of reason.

***lumignon**, *n.m.*, snuff (of a candle—*de chandelle*); wick (of a lamp—*de lampe*); candle end.

luminaire, *n.m.*, luminary, light; lights (of a church—*d'église*). *Le — d'un enterrement;* funeral torches.

lumineusement (-neûz-mǎn), *adv.*, luminously.

lumineu-x, -se, *adj.*, luminous.

lunaire, *adj.*, lunar.

lunaire, *n.f.*, (bot.) lunary, moonwort.

lunaison, *n.f.*, lunation.

lunatique, *adj.* and *n.m.f.*, moon-struck; fantastical, whimsical; moon-struck, fantastical, whimsical person.

lundi, *n.m.*, Monday.

lune, *n.f.*, moon. (ich.) — *de mer;* sun-fish. *La — est dans son plein;* the moon is full. *Pleine —, nouvelle —;* full moon, new moon. *Clair de —;* moon-light. — *rousse;* April moon. *Vouloir prendre la — avec les dents;* to attempt impossibilities. *Avoir des —s;* to have whims. *Faire un trou à la —;* to decamp, to moonshine it. *La — de miel;* the honeymoon.

lunetier, *n.m.*, spectacle-maker; spectacle-seller.

lunette, *n.f.*, spy-glass, eye-glass; telescope; merry-thought (of a fowl—*de volaille*); seat (of a close-stool, a water-closet—*de chaise percée ou de privé*); (arch.. fort.. man.) lunette; rim (of a watch case—*de montre*); *pl.*, spectacles. — *d'approche;* spy-glass, telescope. — *de poche;* pocket spy-glass. *Porter des —s;* to wear spectacles.

luniforme, *adj.*, luniform, moon-shaped.

lunisolaire, *adj.*, lunisolar.

lunule, *n.f.*, (geom.) lune.

lunulé, -e, *adj.*, (bot.) lunulate.

lupercales, *n.f.pl.*, (antiq.) lupercalia.

lupin, *n.m.*, (bot.) lupine.

luron, *n.m.*, **-ne**, *n.f.*, jolly fellow, determined fellow; buxom, bouncing girl.

lusiade, *n.f.*, Lusiad (Camoens' epic poem).

lustrage, *n.m.*, (manu.) lustring.

lustral, -e, *adj.*, lustral.

lustration, *n.f.*, lustration.

lustre, *n.m.*, lustre, brilliancy, brightness; renown, distinction, gloss; splendour; candle-stick, chandelier ornamented with drops of cut glass; lustre, space of five years.

lustré, -e, *part.*, that has a gloss upon it, glossy.

lustrer, *v.a.*, to give a lustre, a gloss, to.

lustrine, *n.f.*, lustring (silk stuff—*soierie*).

lustucru, *n.m.*, simpleton; what-do-you-call-him.

lut (lut), *n.m.*, (chem.) luting.

luter, *v.a.*, (chem.) to lute.

luth (lut), *n.m.*, (mus.) lute.

luthéranisme, *n.m.*, Lutheranism.

luthérien, -ne (-in, -è-n), *n.* and *adj.*, Lutheran.

luthier, *n.m.*, lute-maker.

lutin, *n.m.*, hobgoblin, imp; most lively person; wild child. *Faire le —;* to play the deuce.

lutin, -e, *adj.*, roguish, waggish.

lutiner, *v.a.*, to plague, to tease, to pester.

lutiner, *v.n.*, to tear about, to play the deuce.

lutrin, *n.m.*, reading-desk, choristers.

lutte, *n.f.*, wrestling; struggle, contest, strife. *S'exercer à la —;* to practice wrestling. *De haute —;* by main force. *De bonne —*, by fair play.

lutter, *v.n.*, to wrestle; to struggle, to contend, to strive. — *contre la tempête;* to struggle with the storm. — *contre la tentation;* to struggle against temptation.

lutteur, *n.m.*, wrestler.

luxation, *n.f.*, (surg.) luxation, dislocation.

luxe, *n.m.*, luxury. *Objets de —;* fancy goods.

luxé, *part.*, luxated, dislocated.

luxer, *v.a.*, (surg.) to lux, to luxate, to dislocate.

se **luxer**, *v.r.*, to become luxated.

luxueu-x, -se, *adj.*, magnificent, rich, sumptuous.

luxure, *n.f.*, lust, lewdness.

luxuriance, *n.f.*, luxuriance.

luxuriant, -e, *adj.*, luxuriant.

luxurieusement, *adv.*, lustfully, lewdly.

luxurieu-x, -se, *adj.*, lustful, lewd, libidinous, wanton.

luzerne, *n.f.*, lucern, lucern-grass.

luzernière, *n.f.*, lucern field.

lycanthrope, *n.m.*, person affected with lycanthropy.

lycanthropie, *n.f.*, lycanthropy.

lycée, *n.m.*, lyceum, college.

lycéen (-in), *n.m.*, collegian.

lychnide, *n.f.*, (bot.) lychnis.

lyciet, *n.m.*, (bot.) lycium.

lycopode, *n.m.*, (bot.) lycopodium, wolf's-claw, club-moss.

lydien, -ne, *n.* and *adj.*; Lydian.

lymphatique, *adj.*, (med.) lymphatic.

lymphe, *n.f.*, (med.) lymph; (bot.) sap.

lynx (links), *n.m.*, lynx. *Avoir des yeux de* —; to be lynx-eyed.

lyre, *n.f.*, lyre; (fig.) talent of the poet, poetry; (astron., anat.) lyra. *Jouer de la* —; to play the lyre.

lyrique. *n.* and *adj.*, lyric; lyrical. *Vers* —*s*; lyrical verses. *Poète* —; lyrical poet.

lyrisme, *n.m.*, dignified and poetic style; poetic enthusiasm.

lysimachie, *n.f.*, lysimachia, loose-strife, willow herb. — *bleue*; purple loose-strife. — *jaune*; willow-herb.

lysimaque, *n.f.*, (bot.) loose-strife.

lythrode, *n.f.*, (min.) lythrode.

M

m (me), *n.m.*, (-ème), *n.f.*, the thirteenth letter of the alphabet, m.

m. (ab. of Majesté), M., Majesty; (ab. of Monsieur) Mr., Mister.

m', (contraction of Me), me. *V.* **me.**

ma, *possessive adj.f.*, my. [*Mon* is used for the feminine before a vowel or *h* mute.] — *chère*; my dear. *Mon âme*; my soul. *V.* **mon.**

m.a., (ab. of *Maison Assurée*) house insured.

mab, *n.f.*, Mab (queen of the fairies).

macabre, *adj.*, used only in the expression: *danse* —; the dance of death, as shown in engravings of the 14th and 15th centuries.

macadam, *n.m.*, road metal.

macadamiser, *v.a.*, to macadamize.

macaque, *n.m.*, dog-faced monkey.

macaron, *n.m.*, macaroon.

macaronée, *n.f.*, (poet.) macaronic.

macaroni, *n.m.*, macaroni.

macaronique, *adj.*, (poet.) macaronic.

macédoine, *n.f.*, dish consisting of a medley of fruit *or* vegetables; medley.

macer, *v.a. V.* **masser.**

macération, *n.f.*, maceration.

macérer, *v.a.*, to macerate.

machabées (-ka-), *n.m. pl.*, Maccabees (the two last books of the old Testament—*les deux derniers livres de l'ancien Testament*).

mâche, *n.f.*, (bot.) corn-salad, lamb's-lettuce.

mâchecoulis, *or* **mâchicoulis**, *n.m.*, (fort.) machicolation.

mâche-dru, *n.m.* (—), (pop.) glutton.

mâchefer (mâsh-fèr), *n.m.*, dross of iron, scoria, hammerslag; offal, puddler's offal.

mâchelière. *n.f.* and *adj.*, jaw-tooth, grinder, of the jaw. *Dents* —*s*; jaw-teeth.

machemoure, *n.f.*, remains of ship biscuit.

mâcher, *v.a.*, to chew, to masticate, to champ; to eat ravenously. — *à vide*; to chew the air; (fig., fam.) to delude one's self with false expectations. — *de haut*; (fam.) to eat without appetite. *Il faut lui* — *tous ses morceaux*; every thing must be ready made to his hand. *Ne pas* — *ce qu'on pense*; not to hesitate saying what one feels, not to mince matters, to speak one's mind.

se mâcher, *v.r.*, to be chewed.

mâcheu-r, *n.m.*, **-se**, *n.f.*, high feeder, great eater, muncher. — *de tabac*; chewer of tobacco.

machiavélique, *adj.*, Machiavelian.

machiavélisme, *n.m.*, Machiavelism.

machiavéliste, *n.m.*, Machiavelian.

mâchicatoire, *n.m.*, masticatory.

mâchicoulis, *n.m. V.* **mâchecoulis.**

machinal, -e, *adj.*, mechanical.

machinalement, *adv.*, mechanically.

machinateur, *n.m.*, machinator, plotter, contriver.

machination, *n.f.*, machination; plot; contrivance.

machine. *n.f.*, machine, engine; machinery, piece of mechanism; intrigue. — *pneumatique*; air-pump. — *soufflante*; blowing-machine. — *à colonne d'eau*; water-pressing machine. — *à détente de vapeur*; expansion steam-machine. — *à simple effet*; single-acting machine. — *à double effet*; double-acting machine. — *à basse pression*; low-pressure engine. — *à haute pression*; high-pressure engine. — *à moyenne pression*; mean-pressure engine. — *à vapeur*; steam-engine. — *de vingt chevaux*; engine of twenty horse power. — *à mâter* (nav.); sheers (for masting ships). *La* — *va bien, fonctionne bien*; the machine, the engine, works well. —*s de théâtre*; machinery of a theatre. *La* — *ronde*; (poet., fam.) the earth, the Universe. *C'est une pure* —, *ce n'est qu'une* —; (of persons without energy—*des gens sans caractère*) he, she, is a mere machine.

machiner, *v.a.*, to machinate, to contrive, to plot, to plan. *Il machine votre perte*; he is plotting your ruin.

machiniste, *n.m.*, machinist, engineer, engine-man.

mâchoire, *n.f.*, jaw, jawbone. *Jouer*, *s'escrimer, de la* —; to set one's chops going, to eat with avidity. *C'est une* —; he is a blockhead. *Avoir la* — *pesante, lourde*; to express one's self awkwardly, without elegance or sprightliness. — *d'étau*; vice chops. —*s de chien de fusil*; chops of the cock of a flint gun.

mâchonner, *v.a.*, to chew with difficulty; to mumble, to munch. *Que mâchonnez-vous entre vos dents?* what are you mumbling between your teeth?

mâchure, *n.f.*, defect in the nap (of cloth —*du drap*).

mâchurer, *v.a.*, to daub, to smear; to blacken; (print.) to maculate.

macis, *n.m.*, mace.

m.a.c.i., (initial letters of the words *Maison Assurée contre l'Incendie*), house insured against fire (equivalent to the plates of the various fire-offices seen on houses in England).

maclage, *n.m.*, act of mixing glass (when in the furnace—*dans le four*).

macle, *n.f.*, (bot.) water-caltrops; (min.) macle; sort of net; (her.) mascle. *V.* **macre.**

macler, *v.a.*, to mix hard and soft glass together in the furnace.

maçon, *n.m.*, mason, bricklayer; mason, freemason. *C'est un vrai* —; he is a bungler.

maçonnage, *n.m.*, mason's work, masonry.

maçonner, *v.a.*, to do mason's work, masonry; to plaster; to bungle, to do badly. *Voyez comme il a maçonné cela*; see in what a slovenly manner he has done that.

maçonnerie (-so-n-rî), *n.f.*, masonry, mason's work; stone-work; masonry, freemasonry. — *en liaison*; bound masonry. — *brute*; ashlar. — *de blocaille*; rubble-work. — *maillée*; net-work.

maçonnique, *adj.*, masonic.

macque, *n.f.*, brake (mallet to beat hemp —*maillet à battre la chanvre*).

macquer, *v.a.*, to beat, to break hemp.

macre, *or* **macle**, *n.f.*, (bot.) water-caltrops.

macreuse, *n.f.,* (orni.) black-diver, king-duck. *Avoir un sang de* —; to have a cold, frigid disposition.

macrocosme, *n.m.,* (philos.) macrocosm.

macroure, *adj.,* (zool.) macrourous; (bot.) spiked.

maculature, *n.f.,* (print.) macule, waste sheet of printed paper; coarse brown paper.

macule, *n.f.,* stain, spot; (astron.) macula. *Agneau sans.*— ; lamb without spot.

maculer, *v.a.,* to blot, to spot, to maculate.

maculer, *v.n.,* (print.) to become maculated, blotted

madame, *n.f.,* madam, mistress, my lady, ma'am. *Monsieur vaut bien* — ; the husband is as good as the wife. *Faire la* —; to give one's self airs of consequence, to play the grand lady. *C'est une grosse* — (pop.); she is a rich lady.

madapolam, *n.m.,* strong calico from Madapolam.

madéfaction, *n.f.,* (pharm.) madefaction.

madéfier, *v.a.,* (pharm.) to madefy.

madeleine, *n.f.* (—s), only used in : *pleurer comme une* — ; to weep like a Magdalen.

madelonnette (ma-dlo-nèt), *n.f.,* repentant woman. —*s;* Magdalen asylum (for repentant women—*pour les pécheresses repentantes*); a prison for women in Paris.

mademoiselle (mad-moa-zèl), *n.f.,* miss.

madère, *n.m.,* Madeira; Madeira wine.

madone, *n.f.,* madona, madonna.

madrague (-drag), *n.f.,* (fishing—*terme de pêche*) tunny-net.

madras (-dràs), *n.m.,* Madras neckerchief.

madré,-e, *adj.,* speckled, spotted; cunning, sly. *C'est un* — *compère;* he is a sly fellow, a knowing card.

madré *n.m.,* **-e,** *n.f.,* cunning, sharp, sly person. *Un fin* — ; a cunning blade.

madrépore, *n.m.,* (polypes) madrepore.

madrier, *n.m.,* (fort.) madrier; piece of timber; joist.

madrigal, *n.m.,* madrigal.

madrure, *n.f.,* speckling, spotting; mottling.

maëstral, *n.m.* *V.* **mistral.**

mafflé,-e, or **mafflu,-e,** *n.* and *adj.,* (fam., l.u.) chub-cheeked person; chub-cheeked.

magasin, *n.m.,* magazine, warehouse, store-house; shop, store; stock; magazine (serial—*ouvrage périodique*); basket (of a coach—*d'une voiture*). — *de nouveautés;* linendraper's shop. *Marchandise en* — ; stock. *Le* — *des jeunes Demoiselles;* the Young Ladies' Magazine.

magasinage, *n.m.,* warehousing; warehouse-rent. *Droit de* —; store dues.

⊙**magasiner,** *v.a.* *V.* **emmagasiner.**

magasinier, *n.m.,* warehouse-keeper.

magdaléon, *n.m.,* (pharm.) magdaleon.

mage, *n.m.,* magian. —*s; magi,* wise men of the East. *L'adoration des* —*s;* the adoration of the wise men.

⊙**mage,** or **maje,** *adj.,* first, chief. [Only used in the expression : *juge* — : chief-justice.]

magicien, *n.m.,* **-ne,** *n.f.* (-in, -ě-n), magician.

magie, *n.f.,* magic. — *blanche;* natural magic. — *noire;* black art, witchcraft. *La* — *du style, de la poésie;* the magic of style, of poetry.

magique, *adj.,* magic, magical. *Baguette* — ; magic wand. *Lanterne* — ; magic-lantern.

magisme. *n.m.,* magianism.

magister (-tèr), *n.m.,* country schoolmaster; pedant.

magistère, *n.m.,* grand mastership of the order of Malta ; ⊙ (chem., pharm.) magistery.

magistral, **-e** *adj.,* magistral, authoritative, dictatorial. *Parler d'un ton* —; to speak in an authoritative toπe. *Ligne* —*e ;* principal

outline. *Compositions* —*es ;* medicaments composed according to a physician's prescription.

magistralement (-tral-màn), *adv.,* magisterially.

magistrat, *n.m.,* magistrate ; corporation municipal council (in some French towns—*dans quelques villes de France*).

magistrature, *n.f.,* magistracy. — *assise :* the judges. — *debout;* body of public prosecutors. *V.* **parquet.**

*****magnanerie,** *n.f.,* magnanerie, place where silk-worms are reared, silk-worm nursery.

*****magnanier,** *n.m.,* silk-worm cultivator ; foreman in a magnanerie.

*****magnanime,** *adj.,* magnanimous, high-minded.

*****magnanimement,** *adv.,* magnanimously.

*****magnanimité,** *n.f.,* magnanimity, high-mindedness.

magnat (mag-na), *n.m.,* nobleman, magnate (in Hungary and Poland—*en Hongrie et en Pologne*).

⊙*****magne,** *adj.,* great.

*****magnésie,** *n.f.,* magnesia.

magnésium, *n.m.* (n.p.), (chem.) magnesium.

*****magnétique,** *adj.,* magnetic.

*****magnétiser,** *v.a.,* to magnetize.

*****magnétiseur,** *n.m.,* magnetizer.

*****magnétisme,** *n.m.,* magnetism.

magnificat (mag-ni-fi-kat), *r.m.,* magnificat (hymn to the Virgin Mary—*cantique de la Vierge*).

*****magnificence,** *n.f.,* magnificence.

*****magnifico,** *n.m.,* magnifico (grandee of Venice—*grand de Venise*).

*****magnifier,** *v.a.,* to magnify, to extol, to exalt.

*****magnifique,** *adj.* and *n.,* magnificent, gorgeous, splendid, grand; ostentatious, vain man; what is magnificent.

*****magnifiquement** (-fik-màn), *adv.,* magnificently, gorgeously, splendidly, grandly.

magnolia, or **magnolier** (mag-no-), *n.m.,* (bot.) magnolia.

magot, *n.m.,* (mam.) magot ; baboon ; booby; ill-favoured man ; grotesque figure (of china, &c.—*de porcelaine, &c.*); hoard of money, hidden treasure.

mahaleb, *n.m.,* (bot.) mahaleb.

⊙**maheutre,** *n.f.,* sleeve.

⊙**maheutre,** *n.m.,* Protestant soldier of the 16th century (French hist.).

mahogon, or **mahogoni,** *n.m.,* (bot.) mahogany.

mahométan, -e, *n.* and *adj.,* Mahometan, Mohammedan.

mahométisme, *n.m.,* Mahometanism, Mohammedanism.

mai, *n.m.,* May ; may-pole. *Bois de* —; (bot.) hawthorn. *Planter le* — ; to set up the may-pole.

maidan, *n.m.* (—*s*), market-place (in the East).

maie, *n.f.,* (nav.) sort of trough bored full of holes, wherein to drain newly tarred cordage; kneading-trough.

maïeur, *n.m.,* (local ex.) mayor.

maigre, *adj.,* meagre, lean, thin, spare, slender; poor, sorry; (of coal—*de la houille*) close-burning. — *échine;* bare-bones (pers.) — *comme un hareng;* as lean as a shotten herring, as thin as a lath. *Jours* —*s;* fish-days. *Repas* —; lenten entertainment. *Soupe* —; herb soup. — *chère;* poor living. — *repas ;* sorry meal. *Sujet* —; barren subject. *Écriture* ; scraggy handwriting.

maigre, *n.m.,* lean; (ich.) umbrina ; any food save meat. *Faire* —; to abstain from flesh. *Traiter en* —; to treat with fish. *En* —; (carp.) sharply, scantily.

maigrelet, -te, *adj.*, thin, thinnish, lean, spare.

maigrement, *adv.*, meagrely, poorly, sorrily, sparingly.

maigret, -te. *adj.*, lean, poor, thin, spare.

maigreur, *n.f.*, leanness, meagreness; slenderness, thinness, sorriness, poorness, spareness.

maigrir, *v.n.*, to grow lean, to become lean; to grow thin, to become thin; to fall away. *Il maigrit à vue d'œil;* he grows perceptibly thinner.

*****mail**, *n.m.*, mallet; mall (game—*jeu*); mall (place—*endroit*).

*****maille**, *n.f.*, mesh; stitch; mail; speck (on the wings of partridges—*sur les ailes de la perdrix*); web (in the eye—*à l'œil*); haw (in the eyes of animals—*dans les yeux des animaux*); ancient small coin. *Cotte de* —*s*; coat of mail. *Ils ont toujours — à partir ensemble;* they have always a crow to pluck with each other, a bone to pick with one another. *N'avoir ni sou ni* —; not to have a farthing.

*****maillechort**, *n.m.*, German silver.

*****mailler**, *v.n.*, to grow speckled (of partridges—*de la perdrix*).

*****maillet**, *n.m.*, mallet, beetle.

*****mailloche**, *n.f.*, mallet, beetle.

*****maillot**, *n.m.*, swaddling-band; swaddling-clothes.

*****maillure**, *n.f.*, (hawking—*fauconnerie*) spots and speckles on the plumage of hawks.

main, *n.f.*, hand; hand-writing; lead (at cards—*aux cartes*); hook (at the end of a well-rope—*de corde à puits*); handle; hand-shovel; body-loop (of carriages—*de voitures*); paw (of some animals—*de quelques animaux*). *— de papier;* quire of paper. *En lever la* —, to take one's oath of it. *Mettre l'épée à la* —; to draw one's sword. *Mettre le pain à la* — *à quelqu'un;* to put one in the way of making a livelihood. *Donner la* — *à quelqu'un;* to give one's hand to any one, to assist any one, to give any one a hand. *Baiser les* —*s à quelqu'un;* to kiss any one's hands. *Tendre la* —; to hold out one's hand, to lend a helping hand. *Donner les* —*s à une chose;* to consent to a thing. *Cheval de* —; led horse. *Cela est sous votre* —; that is under your nose. *Il est sous za* — ; he depends upon him. *Mettre la* — *sur quelqu'un;* to lay hands upon any one. *Il n'y va pas de* — *morte;* he strikes hard. *Tenir la* — *à quelque chose;* to take anything in hand. *Un coup de* —; (milit.) bold, unexpected attack, surprise; a bold stroke. *Tour de* —; sleight of hand. *En venir aux* —*s;* to come to blows. *Faire* — *basse sur;* to lay violent hands on, to plunder. *Tenir la* — *haute à quelqu'un;* to keep a tight hand over any one. *Mettre la dernière* — *à un ouvrage;* to put the finishing stroke to a work. *Battre des* —*s* ; to clap one's hands. *Faire crédit de la* — *à la bourse;* to trust no further than one can see. *Mettre la* — *à une chose;* to set one's hand to a thing. *Il a la* — *bonne;* he is very handy. *Mettre la* — *à l'œuvre;* to set about a work. *Être en* —; to be in hand, to have in hand. *Avoir la* — *légère;* to be free with one's hand. *J'ai toujours l'argent à la* —; I am always laying out money. *Il en a les* —*s nettes;* his hands are clean of it. *Je m'en lave les* —*s;* I wash my hands of it. *J'en mettrais ma* — *au feu;* I would stake my life on it. *Ils se tiennent tous par la* —: they go hand in hand together. *Froides* —*s, chaudes amours;* a cold hand, a warm heart. *Avoir la* —; to have the deal, to lead, to play first. *Avoir la* — *crochue;* to be light-fingered. *À la* —; in hand, by hand; ready. *À deux* —*s;* with both hands. *À pleines* —*s;* largely, liberally, plentifully. *À toutes* —*s;* fit for

anything; (man.) fitted to ride and drive. *De longue* —; long since, of old standing. *De* — *en* —; from one to another, from hand to hand. *En un tour de* —; in a trice. *— courante* (com.); waste-book.

main chaude, *n.f.*, hot cockles (game—*jeu*).

main-d'œuvre, *n.f.* (—*s* —), workmanship, handicraft, manual labour.

mainette. *n.f.*, (bot.) coral club-top.

main-forte, *n.f.* (*n.p.*), assistance, help rendered to officers of justice.

mainlevée, *n.f.*, (jur.) replevin; withdrawal.

mainmise. *n.f.*, (jur.) seizure.

mainmortable. *adj.*, (jur.) subject to mortmain.

mainmorte, *n.f.*, (jur.) mortmain.

maint, -e, *adj.*, many. — *homme;* many a man. —*e fois;* many a time.

maintenant (min-tnän), *adv.*, now, at this time, at present, nowadays, by this time.

maintenir (min-tnir), *v.a.*, to sustain, to keep together; to maintain; to keep up; to secure.

se **maintenir**, *v.r.*, to hold out, to keep up, to be kept up, to be maintained. — *dans les bonnes grâces de;* to keep one's self in the good graces of.

maintenue, *n.f.*, possession adjudged upon a full trial.

maintien (-ti-in), *n.m.*, maintenance, preservation; keeping up; carriage, deportment, bearing.

maiolique, *or* **majolique**, *n.f.*, old Spanish or Italian earthenware, faience.

mairain, *n.m.* *V.* **merrain**.

maire, *n.m.*, mayor.

mairie, *n.f.*, mayoralty; town-hall.

maïs (mah-is), *n.m.*, maize, Indian wheat.

mais (mè), *conj.*, but; why. — *encore;* but yet. —, *qu'ai-je fait?* why, what have I done? — *oui;* —, *non;* why, yes; why, no. *Je n'en puis* —; I cannot help it.

maison, *n.f.*, house, household, home, habitation; family, race; firm. *Le devant, le derrière, d'une* —; the front, the back, of a house. — *de campagne;* country-house, country-seat. — *de seigneuriale;* mansion. — *de ville*, — *commune;* town-hall. *Tenir* —; to be a house-keeper. *Faire* — *nette;* to dismiss all the servants in one's household at the same time. *Faire* — *neuve;* to get new servants. *Garder la* —; to keep at home. *Petites* —*s;* mad-house. — *garnie;* furnished house. — *d'éducation:* school, boarding-school. — *de jeu;* gaming-house. *La* — *du roi;* the king's household.

maisonnée, *n.f.*, whole house or family.

maisonnette, *n.f.*, small house, cottage.

maître, *n.m.*, master, owner, proprietor; instructor, teacher, governor, director; chief, head; (nav.) boatswain. — *d'école;* school-master. — *de pension;* boarding-school master. — *d'étude;* usher. — *à danser*, — *de danse;* dancing-master. — *d'armes;* fencing-master. — *ès-arts;* master of arts. — *d'hôtel;* steward, major-domo. *Un petit-* (—*s* —*s*); a beau, a dandy. *Se rendre* — *de la conversation;* to engross the whole conversation. *Vous êtes le* — *d'y aller;* it is at your option to go there. *Il a trouvé son* —; he has met with his match. *Tel* —, *tel valet;* like master, like man. *Compter de clerc à* —; to render a minute account. *Heurter en* —; to rap hard. — *clerc;* chief clerk (of a lawyer—*d'un homme de loi*). *Le* —*autel* (—*s* —*s*); the high-altar. — *câble;* sheet cable. — *d'équipage;* boatswain (of a ship of war—*d'un vaisseau de guerre*). — *canonnier;* master-gunner. — *de port;* harbour-master. — *de vaisseau;* commander of a merchant-ship. *Ce tableau est d'un* grand —; that picture is by a great master. *Coup de* —; masterly stroke. *Main de* —; masterly hand. *Un* — *gonin*; an arch cheat.

maîtresse,*n.f.*,mistress; teacher,governess; landlady. *Petite* —; lady of studied elegance.

maîtrise, *n.f.*, freedom (of a company— *d'une compagnie*).

maîtriser, *v.a.*, to master, to domineer, to lord,.to get master, to get under; to overcome, to subdue. — *ses passions*; to overcome one's passions.

majesté, *n.f.*, majesty. *Crime de lèse*—; high-treason.

majestueusement(-eûz-măn),*adv*.,majestically.

majestueu-x, **-se**, *adj.*, majestic.

majeur, *n.m.*, a male of full age, major; (mus.) major mode.

majeur, **-e**, *adj.*, major, greater; important; of full age; (mus.) major. *Force* —*e*; superior force.

majeure, *n.f.*, (log.) major; a female of full age; ⊙public disputation in divinity (in universities—*terme d'université*).

major, *n.m.*, major. *État*— (milit.): staff.

majorat, *n.m.*, landed property attached to a title so as to descend with it; entailed estate.

majordome. *n.m.*, major-domo.

majorité, *n.f.*, majority, full age. *Arriver à sa* —; to come of age.

majuscule, *n.f.* and *adj.*, capital; large, capital letter.

maki. *n.m.*, (mam.) lemur.

makis, or **maquis**, *n.m.*, thicket (in Corsica—*en Corse*).

mal, *n.m.*,evil,ill;harm,pain, ache,sickness, distemper,complaint;hardship; mischief; misfortune. — *du pays*; homesickness, nostalgia. *Les maux de la vie*; the evils of life. *Rendre le bien pour le* —; to return good for evil. *De deux maux il faut choisir le moindre*; of two evils,choose the least. *Il a eu plus de peur que de* —; he was more frightened than hurt. *Il faut éviter le* — *et faire le bien*; do good and shun evil. *Quel* — *y a-t-il à cela?* what harm is there in that? *Induire quelqu'un à* —; to lead any one into evil. *Penser à* —; to mean harm. *Il a* — *au côté*; he has a pain in his side. *Un* — *de tête*; a headache. *La tête me fait* —; my head aches. — *de dents*; toothache. — *d'yeux*; sore eyes. *Vous me faites* —; you hurt me. — *d'aventure*; whitlow. — *de mer*; sea-sickness. — *de cœur*; qualmishness. *Tomber de fièvre en chaud* —; to fall out of the frying-pan into the fire. *Di-e du* — *de son prochain*; to speak ill of one's neighbour. *Prendre en* —; to take offence at. *Tourner en* —; to misinterpret; to put a wrong construction on. *J'ai* — *à la tête*; I have the headache.

mal, *adv.*, ill, wrong, amiss, badly; uncomfortably; on bad terms. *Il écrit* —; he writes badly. *Cela va* —; that goes on badly. *Vous vous y prenez* —; you go the wrong way to work. *Cet habit vous sied* —; that coat does not become you. *De* — *en pis*; worse and worse. *Se trouver* —; to faint. *Mettre* — *avec*; to set at variance with. *Être* — *dans ses affaires*; to be low in the world. *Être* — *avec quelqu'un*; to be on bad terms with any one. — *à propos*: improperly, unseasonably. *Pas* —; not a little, not a few. *Être fort* —: to be very ill. *Trouver* —; to find amiss. *C'est* — *à lui de*; it is wrong of him to.

malachite (-kit), *n.f.*, (min.) malachite.

malacie, *n.f.*, (med.) malacia, vitiated appetite.

malacologie, *n.f.*, malacology.

malactique, *n.m.* and*adj.*,(med.) emollient.

malade, *adj.*, sick, ill, diseased; unwell, poorly, bad. — *à la mort*; sick unto death. *Avoir l'air* —; to look ill. *Bras* —; sore arm. *Ces plantes sont* —*s*; those plants are diseased. *Rendre* —; to make ill.

malade. *n.m.f.*, sick person, invalid ; patient.

maladie, *n.f.*, illness, sickness, malady, disease, complaint, disorder, distemper; passion, fondness. ⊙ — *du pays*; homesickness, nostalgia.

maladi-f, **-ve**, *adj.*, sickly, unhealthy.

⊙**maladiveté** (-div-té), *n.f.*, sickliness, unhealthiness.

maladministration, *n.f.*, maladministration.

⊙**maladrerie**, *n.f.*, hospital for lepers.

maladresse,*n.f.*,awkwardness,clumsiness, unskilfulness, awkward thing.

maladroit, **-e**, *n.* and*adj.*, awkward person; awkward, clumsy, unskilful. *Vous êtes un* — *!* what an awkward fellow you are! *C'est une* —*e*; she is an awkward woman.

maladroitement (-droat-măn). *adv.*, clumsily, awkwardly.

malaga, *n.m.*, Malaga (wine).

malaguette, or **maniguette**, *n.f.*, malaguetta-pepper.

malai, or **malais**, **-e**, *n.* and *adj.*, Malay.

malai, *n.m.*, Malay language.

malaise, *n.m.*, uncomfortableness, uneasiness. *Sentir du* —; to. feel uncomfortable. *Être dans le* —; to be straitened in one's circumstances.

malaisé, **-e**, *adj.*, hard, difficult; inconvenient; straitened in circumstances.

malaisément, *adv.*, with difficulty, with trouble.

malandre, *n.f.*, (vet.) malanders; rottenness of the knots (in timber—*des bois de charpente*).

malandreu-x, **-se**, *adj.*, having rotten knots (of wood—*des charpentes*).

malandrin, *n.m.*, brigand, highwayman. —*s*: name given to the bands of brigands which infested France in the 14th century.

⊙**mal-animé**, **-e**, *adj.*, evil-minded.

malappris, **-e**, *adj.* and *n.*, unmannerly; ill-bred person.

malart, *n.m.*, wild drake.

malavisé, **-e**,*adj.*, ill-advised, imprudent.

malaxer, *v.a.*, (pharm.) to work up.

malbâti, **-e**, *n.*,'and *adj.*, ill-favoured person; ill-shaped.

⊙**malcontent**, *n.m.*, disaffected man, malcontent, malecontent. *Les* —*s* (French hist.); the Malecontents, name of a party at the court of Charles IX.

⊙**malcontent**, **-e**, *adj.*, displeased, dissatisfied, discontented, malcontent, malecontent.

maldisant, **-e**, *n.* and *adj.*, slanderer; slanderous.

mâle, *n.m.*, male; cock.

mâle, *adj.*, male, manly, manful ; masculine, he. *Perdrix* —; male partridge. *Des contours* —*s*; masculine outlines. *Des figures* —*s*; masculine figures. *Air* —; manliness.

malebête (mal-bêt), *n.f.*, (l.u.) dangerous person.

⊙**malebosse**. *n.f.*, great hump.

malédiction,*n.f.*, malediction, curse. *Donner sa* — *à*: to bestow a malediction on.

malefaim (mal-fin), *n.f.*, gnawing hunger.

maléfice, *n.m.*, witchcraft.

maléficié, **-e**, *adj.*, bewitched.

maléfique, *adj.*, (astrol.) malevolent.

malemort, *n.f.*, tragic death; bad end.

malencontre, *n.f.*, mishap, mischance.

malencontreusement (-treûz-măn),*adv.*, unluckily, untowardly.

malencontreu-x, -se, *adj.*, unlucky, untoward. *Évènement —;* untoward event.

mal-en-point, *adv.*, badly off; in a sorry plight.

malentendu, *n.m.*, misunderstanding, misapprehension.

malepeste! (mal-pèst), *int.*, the devil! plague on it!

mal-être, *n.m.* (*n.p.*), uncomfortableness, uneasiness, painful sensation.

malevole, *adj.*, (fam. l.u.) malevolent, evildisposed.

malfaçon, *n.f.*, bad work; cheat, trickery.

malfaire, *v.n.*, to do evil.

malfaisance, *n.f.*, (l.u.) evil-doing.

malfaisant, -e, *adj.*, malevolent, mischievous, unhealthy; injurious, prejudicial. *Nourriture —e;* unwholesome food.

malfait, -e, *adj.*, ill-made, ill-shaped, deformed; badly done; ill-advised.

malfaiteur, *n.m.*, malefactor, evil-doer.

malfamé, -e, *adj.*, ill-famed.

malgracieusement, *adv.*, ungraciously, rudely.

malgracieu-x, -se, *adj.*, rude, ungracious.

malgré, *prep.*, in spite of; notwithstanding, against the will of. *Il l'a fait — moi;* he did it in spite of me. *— cela;* nevertheless.

malhabile, *adj.*, unskilful, awkward.

malhabilement, *adv.*, unskilfully, awkwardly.

malhabileté (-bil-té), *n.f.*, unskilfulness, awkwardness.

malherbe, *n.f.*, deadly carrot.

malheur, *n.m.*, misfortune; mischance, mishap; unhappiness, unluckiness; unfortunate thing. *Par —;* unhappily, unluckily. *Avoir du —;* to have ill luck. *Jouer de —;* to be unlucky. *Être en —;* to have a run of ill luck. *Porter —;* to bring ill luck. *Il n'y a qu'heur et — en ce monde;* hap and mishap govern the world. *C'est un petit —;* that is but a slight misfortune. *Un — ne vient jamais seul;* misfortune never comes alone. *À quelque chose — est bon;* it is an ill wind that blows nobody good. *Quel —!* what an unfortunate thing! *— à vous!* woe be to you! *— aux vaincus!* woe to the vanquished!

malheureusement (-reûz-mãn), *adv.*, unfortunately, unluckily, unhappily. *— il est ruiné;* unhappily he is ruined.

malheureu-x, -se, *adj.*, unfortunate, unlucky; unhappy; miserable, wretched, poor, needy. *Il est né —;* he was born unfortunate. *Il mène une vie fort —se;* he leads a most unhappy life. *Faire une fin —se;* to come to an unhappy end.

malheureu-x, *n.m.*, **-se**, *n.f.*, unhappy person, wretched being; poor wretch, wretch. *Ce — fera une mauvaise fin;* that wretch will come to an ill end.

malhonnête, *adj.*, dishonest; impolite. *Des manières —s;* rude manners.

malhonnêtement (-nêt-man), *adv.*, dishonestly; unpolitely, rudely, uncivilly.

malhonnêteté (-nêt-té), *n.f.*, impoliteness, rudeness; rude action. *Il est d'une — révoltante;* he is shockingly rude.

malice, *n.f.*, malice, maliciousness, spite; roguishness, archness; prank, waggish thing, roguish thing, trick.

malicieusement (-eûz-mãn), *adv.*, maliciously, malignantly; archly, roguishly, slily.

malicieu-x, -se, *adj.*, malicious, malignant, mischievous; roguish, waggish, arch. *Un enfant —;* a roguish child. *Un cheval —;* a vicious horse.

***malignement**, *adv.*, malignantly.

***malignité**, *n.f.*, malignity, malice.

malin, *n.m.*, the devil.

mali-n, *-gne, *adj.*, malicious, mischievous, malignant; waggish, arch, roguish; shrewd; sly. *Pensées —gnes;* malignant thoughts. *L'esprit —, le — esprit;* the evil one, Satan. *Un regard —;* an arch look. *Il est trop — pour se laisser attraper;* he is too shrewd to be caught. *Fièvre —gne;* malignant fever.

mali-n, *n.m.*, *-gne*, *n.f.*, malignant, malicious person; sly, shrewd, acute person; knavish person. *C'est un —;* he is a sly one.

maline, *n.f.*, (nav.) spring-tide.

malines, *n.f.*, Mechlin, Mechlin lace.

malingre, *adj.*, poorly, sickly, weakly.

malintentionné, -e, *n.* and *adj.*, evilminded person, evil-minded, ill-disposed. *Il est — à votre égard;* he is ill-disposed towards you.

malique, *adj.*, (chem.) malic.

malitorne, *n.* and *adj.*, awkward, ungainly, person; awkward, ungainly.

mal-jugé, *n.m.* (*n.p.*), (jur.) erroneous judgment.

mallard, *n.m.*, small grindstone.

malle, *n.f.*, trunk; pedlar's box; mail, mailcoach. *Faire, défaire, sa —;* to pack, to unpack, one's trunk.

malléabilité (mal-lé-), *n.f.*, malleableness.

malléable (mal-lé-), *adj.*, malleable.

malléole, *n.f.*, (anat.) malleolus, ankle-bone.

malle-poste, *n.f.* (— *s* —*s*), mail-coach.

malletier (mal-tié), *n.m.*, (l.u.) trunk-maker.

mallette, *n.f.*, little trunk.

mallier, *n.m.*, shaft-horse of a mail-coach.

malmener, *v.a.*, to use ill, to maltreat; to bully, to abuse.

malotru, *n.m.*, **-e**, *n.f.*, ill-bred person; uncouth person.

***malpeigné**, *n.m.*, dirty fellow, dirty pig.

malplaisant, -e, *adj.*, unpleasant, disagreeable.

malpropre, *adj.*, dirty, slovenly, squalid.

malproprement, *adv.*, dirtily, slovenly, squalidly.

malpropreté, *n.f.*, dirtiness, uncleanliness, slovenliness.

malsain, -e, *adj.*, unhealthy, sickly; unwholesome. *Cet air est —;* that air is unwholesome.

malséant, -e, *adj.*, unbecoming, unseemly.

malsonnant, -e, *adj.*, ill-sounding, offensive.

malt (malt), *n.m.*, malt.

maltage, *n.m.*, maltage.

malté, -e, *adj.*, malted.

malteur, *n.m.*, maltman, maltster.

⊙**maltôte**, *n.f.*, exaction upon the people, extortion.

⊙**maltôtier** (-tié), *n.m.*, tax-gatherer, exciseman.

maltraiter, *v.a.*, to maltreat; to treat harshly, to use ill.

malvacée, *n.* and *adj.f.*, malvaceous plant; malvaceous.

***malveillance**, *n.f.*, malevolence, ill-will.

***malveillant, -e**, *adj.*, malevolent, malignant.

***malveillant**, *n.m.*, evil-minded person.

malversation, *n.f.*, malversation.

malverser, *v.n.*, to be guilty of malversation.

malvoisie, *n.f.*, Malmsey.

malvoulu, -e, *adj.*, (l.u.) disliked.

maman, *n.f.*, mamma. *Bonne —, grand'—;* grandmother. *Une grosse —;* a fat woman.

mamelle, *n.f.*, breast; teat; udder. *Un enfant à la —;* a child at the breast.

mamelon (ma-mlon), *n.m.*, nipple, pap, teat; dug (of animals—*des animaux*); pap (of a mountain—*d'une montagne*).

mamelonné, -e, *adj.*, mammilated,

mamelu, -e (ma-mlu), *adj.*, full-breasted.
mameluk (ma-mlook), *n.m.*, Mameluke.
mamillaire (-mil-lèr), *adj.*, (anat.) mammiliary.
mammaire (mam-mèr), *adj.*, (anat.) mammary.
mammalogie (mam-ma-), *n.f.*, mammalogy.
mammalogiste (mam-ma-), *n.m.*, mammalogist.
mammifère (mam-mi-), *n.m.* and *adj.*, mammifer ; mammiferous.
mammiforme (mam-mi-) *adj.*, mammiform.
mammon, *n.m.*, Mammon.
mammouth, *n.m.*, mammoth.
m'amour, obsolete abbreviation of *ma amour*, my love. —*s*, marks of love, caresses.
manant, *n.m.*, ☉peasant; clown, clodhopper.
*mancenille, *n.f.*, (bot.) manchineel.
*mancenillier, *n.m.*, manchineel-tree.
manche, *n.m.*, handle; neck (of musical instruments—*d'instruments de musique*) ; fingerboard (of a violin—*du violon*) ; tail (of a plough —*de charrue*). *Il branle dans le* — ; he hesitates ; he totters. *Jeter le* — *après la cognée* ; to throw the handle after the hatchet.
manche, *n.f.*, sleeve ; (geog.) channel ; (at play—*au jeu*) rubber ; (nav.) flexible pipe, hose. *Bouts de* — ; half-sleeves. *Grandes* —*s* ; puddingsleeves. —*s pendantes* ; hanging-sleeves. *Avoir une personne dans sa* — ; to have a person at one's disposal. *C'est une autre paire de* —*s* ; that is quite another thing. —*à vent* ; (nav.) wind-sail.
manchette, *n.f.*, cuff, ruffle ; (print.) side-note.
manchon, *n.m.*, muff.
manchot, -te, *n.* and *adj.*, one-handed, one-armed person ; one-handed, one-armed. *Il n'est pas* — ; he is no fool.
manchot, *n.m.*, (orni.) pinguin.
mancienne (-si-èn), *n.f.*, mealy-tree, wayfaring-tree.
mandant, *n.m.*, (jur.) employer ; (com.) principal.
mandarin, *n.m.*, mandarin.
mandarine, *n.f.*, a variety of orange.
mandarinier, *n.m.*, (bot.) a variety of orange-tree native of Manilla.
mandat, *n.m.*, (jur.) warrant, mandate ; (com.) draft ; check ; order. — *de comparution* ; summons to appear. — *d'arrêt* ; warrant.
mandataire, *n.m.*, mandatory ; proxy.
mandater, *v.a.*, to deliver an order for the payment of ; to deliver an order for.
mandement (mān-dmān), *n.m.*, mandate, order, mandamus ; charge (of a bishop to his clergy—*d'un évéque à son clergé*).
mander, *v.a.*, to write, to write word, to send word, to send for. *Je lui ai mandé de venir* ; I have sent him word to come. *On a mandé le médecin* ; the physician was sent for.
mandibule, *n.f.*, (anat.) mandible, jaw.
☉***mandille**, *n.f.*, a footman's overcoat.
mandoline, *n.f.*, mandolin.
mandore, *n.f.*, mandore (sort of lute—*espèce de luth*).
mandragore, *n.f.*, (bot.) mandrake.
*mandrill, *n.m.*, (mam.) mandrill.
mandrin, *n.m.*, mandrel.
manducation, *n.f.*, manducation.
manéage, *n.m.*, (nav.) hand-work.
manége, *n.m.*, manege, horsemanship ; riding-school ; manœuvres, by-play.
mânes, *n.m.pl.*, manes, shade, ghost.
manganèse, *n.m.*, manganese.
mangeable (-jabl), *adj.*, eatable.
*mangeaille (-jā-i), *n.f.*, food (for birds, cats, &c.—*pour les oiseaux, les chats, &c.*) ; (b.s.) victuals.

mangeant, -e (-jän, -t), *adj.*, eating. *Être bien* — ; to eat heartily.
mangeoire (-joâr), *n.f.*, manger, crib.
manger, *v.a.*, to eat; to eat up; to consume; to squander away, to run through. *Salle de* —; dining-room. — *son bien* ; to squander one's property. *Je le mangerais* ; I could eat him. — *ses mots* ; to clip one's words. *Les gros poissons mangent les petits* ; might overcomes right.
se manger, *v.r.*, to eat each other ; to eat each other up ; to hurt each other ; (gram.) to be cut off, elided.
manger, *v.n.*, to eat ; to take one's meals ; to feed. *Il mange dans la main* ; he eats out of your hand (of an animal). *Donnez-moi à* — ; give me something to eat.
manger, *n.m.*, eating, victuals, food.
mangerie (man-jrī), *n.f.*, (pop.) eating; exaction, extortion, imposition.
mange-tout, *n.m.* (—), prodigal, spendthrift, squanderer.
mangeu-r, *n.m.*, **-se**, *n.f.*, eater ; great eater ; spendthrift. *Un* — *de viandes apprétées* ; a lazy fellow. — *de petits enfants* ; braggart.
mangeure (-jur), *n.f.*, place nibbled (by mice, &c.—*par les souris, &c.*).
mangle, *n.f.*, (bot.) the fruit of the mangrove.
manglier, *n.m.*, (bot.) mangrove, mangle.
mangonneau, *n.m.*, mangonel (an engine formerly used for throwing stones—*machine de guerre employée autrefois pour lancer des pierres, &c.*).
mangoustan, *n.m.*, (bot.) mangostan.
mangouste, *n.f.*, (mam.) ichneumon ; mangostan (fruit).
mangue (mang), *n.f.*, (bot.) mango.
manguier (-ghié), *n.m.*, (bot.) mango-tree.
maniable, *adj.*, easy to be handled, workable ; tractable, manageable.
maniaque, *n.m.f.* and *adj.*, person having a mania.
manichéen (-in), **-ne**, *n.* and *adj.*, Manichean.
manichéisme, *n.m.*, Manicheism.
manichordion (-kor-), *n.m.*, manichord, manicordon.
manicle, *n.f.* V. **manique**.
manie, *n.f.*, mania ; passion.
maniement, or **maniment**, *n.m.*, handling ; management. — *des armes* ; manual exercise. *Le* — *des deniers* ; the management of money.
manier, *v.a.*, to feel, to handle ; to touch ; to use, to manage, to govern. *Il sait bien* — *le ciseau* ; he knows well how to handle the chisel. — *une affaire* ; to manage a business.
manier, *v.n.*, (man.) to act (of a horse—*du cheval*).
manière, *n.f.*, manner, way ; sort, kind ; style, mannerism. *La* — *dont je lui ai parlé* ; the way in which I spoke to him. *De* — *ou d'autre* ; somehow or other. *Chacun a sa* — ; every one has his own way. — *de parler* ; mode of speech. *De la bonne* — ; handsomely. *Par* — *d'acquit* ; for form's sake. *La* — *de ce peintre est grande* ; that painter's style is grand. *De la même* — ; in the same manner. *Il a des* —*s agréables* ; he has pleasing manners. *De* — *que* ; so that.
maniéré, -e, *adj.*, affected. *Air* — ; affected air.
maniériste, *n.m.*, mannerist.
manieur, *n.m.*, handler, person who handles.
manifestation, *n.f.*, manifestation.
manifeste, *adj.*, manifest, evident.
manifeste, *n.m.*, manifesto.

manifestement. *adv.*, manifestly.

manifester. *v.a.*, to manifest, to make known. — *sa pensée ;* to make known one's thought.

se manifester. *v.r.*, to manifest one's self. to be made manifest.

manigance. *n.f.*, manœuvre, underhand dealing.

manigancer. *v.a.*, to contrive, to plot.

maniguette, *n.f. V.* **malaguette**.

manille, *n.f.*, (at cards—*aux cartes*) manille.

manioc. **manihot**. *or* **manioque**, *n.m.*, (bot.) manioc, manihot.

manipulaire, *n.m.* and *adj.*, (antiq.) commander of the maniple ; manipular.

manipulateur, *n.m.*, manipulator.

manipulation, *n.f.*, manipulation.

manipule, *n.m.*, handful ; (c.rel., antiq., pharm.) maniple.

manipuler, *v.a.* and *n.*, to manipulate.

manique, *or* **manicle**, *n.f.*, hand-leather.

maniveau, *n.m.*, osier-stand.

manivelle, *n.f.*, handle, winch, crank. *La — d'un gouvernail ;* the whip-staff of a helm.

manne (mâ-n), *n.f.*, manna. — *en larmes :* manna in flakes. — *céleste ;* manna from Heaven.

manne (ma-n), *n.f.*, hamper.

mannequin (ma-n-kin), *n.m.*, hamper; small hamper; (paint.) lay-figure; insignificant person. *Figure qui sent le — ;* unnatural figure.

mannequiné, **-e**. *adj.*, unnatural. *Ces figures sont —es ;* (paint.) those figures are unnatural, smack of the lay-figure.

manœuvre, *n.f.*, manœuvre; (nav.) rope; working (a ship—*un vaisseau*); (milit.) drill. **—s**, *pl. ;* (nav.) rigging. —*s courantes ;* running-rigging. —*s dormantes ;* standing-rigging. *Officier qui entend la — ;* officer expert in working a ship. *Amarrer une — ;* to make a rope fast.

manœuvre, *n.m.*, workman, journeyman, mason; bungler; crafty person. *Ce n'est qu'un — ;* he is a mere mechanic. *Travail de — ;* manual labour.

manœuvrer, *v.a.* and *n.*, to manœuvre ; to work (a ship—*un vaisseau*). — *les voiles ;* to work the sails. *Faire — des soldats ;* to drill soldiers.

manœuvrier, *n.m.*, sailor well skilled in working a ship ; general, officer well skilled in handling troops.

manoir, *n.m.*, manor, mansion, manorhouse.

manomètre, *n.m.*, (phys.) manometer.

manométrique, *adj.*, (phys.) manometrical.

manouvrier, *n.m.*, day-labourer.

manquant, **-e**, *n.* and *adj.*, absentee; missing, absent, wanting, short.

manque, *n.m.*, want. *Il a trouvé dix francs de — ;* he has found ten francs wanting. — *de ;* for want of.

manqué, **-e**. *part.*, defective; abortive. *Une affaire —e ;* a failure. *Un poète — ;* a would-be poet.

manquement (man-kmân), *n.m.*, omission, failure, want.

manquer, *v.n.*, to miss, to fail ; to be wanting ; to be wanting in respect ; to be deficient ; to miss fire ; to stand in need of ; to forfeit, to break ; to be insolvent ; to be near, to have like ; to be out, in want, of ; to decay ; to miscarry ; to give way. *Arme à feu qui manque :* a fire-arm that misses fire. *Marchand qui a manqué :* bankrupt merchant. *Le cœur lui manque :* she faints. *Les forces lui manquent ;* his strength fails him. *Le pied lui a manqué :* his foot slipped. *L'argent lui manque ;* he is short

of money. *Rien ne vous manquera :* you shall want for nothing. *La poudre leur manque ;* they are in want of powder. *L'affaire a manqué :* the business has miscarried. — *à son devoir :* to fail in one's duty. — *à sa parole :* to break one's word. — *à un rendez-vous :* to break an appointment. *Je n'y manquerai pas :* I will not fail. *Il ne manque de rien :* he wants for nothing. *Il ne manque pas de vanité ;* he does not want for vanity. — *de parole ;* to fail in one's promise. — *d'argent ;* to be in want of money. *Ne manquez pas de vous y trouver :* do not fail to be there. *Il a manqué de tomber ;* he was very near falling. — *à quelqu'un.* — *de respect à quelqu'un ;* to be disrespectful to somebody. *Il manque de tout ;* he is destitute of all the necessaries of life.

manquer. *v.a.*, to miss, to lose. *Il a manqué son coup ;* he has missed his aim. — *une occasion :* to lose an opportunity.

mansarde, *n.f.*, garret.

mansardé, **-e**, *adj.*, attic, garret provided with a window.

manse, *n.f.*, (feudality—*féodalité*) quantity of land sufficient to maintain a family ; (of abbeys—*d'abbayes*). *V.* **mense**.

mansuétude, *n.f.*, mildness, meekness, gentleness.

mante, *n.f.*, mantle (woman's—*de femme*); (ent.) — *religieuse ;* praying mantis.

manteau, *n.m.*, cloak ; mantle ; mask, pretence ; (her.) mantling. *S'envelopper de son — ;* to wrap one's self up in one's cloak. *Le — royal ;* the royal mantle. *Cela se vend sous le — ;* that is sold clandestinely. *Garder les —x ;* to stand sentinel; to take no share in it. — *de cheminée ;* mantel-piece.

mantelet (man-tlè), *n.m.*, short cloak ; mantlet ; (fort.) mantlet. —*s de sabords ;* (nav.) port-lids ; (of a coach—*d'une calèche*) apron.

mantelure (man-tlur), *n.f.*, hair on a dog's back different from that on the body.

*mantille, *n.f.*, mantilla.

manuel, **-le**, *adj.*, performed by the hand, manual.

manuel, *n.m.*, manual, hand-book.

manuellement (-èl-mān), *adv.*, from hand to hand, manually.

manufacture, *n.f.*, manufacture; manufactory ; mill, factory.

manufacturer, *v.a.*, to manufacture.

manufacturi-er, **-ère**, *adj.*, manufacturing.

manufacturier, *n.m.*, manufacturer.

manumission, *n.f.*, manumission.

in **manus**, *n.m. V.* **in manus**.

manuscrit, **-e**, *adj.*, manuscript, written with the hand.

manuscrit, *n.m.*, manuscript.

manutention, *n.f.*, management ; (l.u.) act of upholding, maintenance ; (milit.) bakehouse.

mappemonde (map-mond), *n.f.*, map of the world.

maque, *n.f. V.* **macque**.

maquer, *v.a. V.* **macquer**.

maquereau (ma-krô), *n.m.*, (ich.) mackerel, (l.ex.) pimp, pander; reddish spot on one's legs, produced by approaching a fire too much to warm one's self.

maquerellage, *n.m.*, (l.ex.) panderism.

maquerelle, *n.f.*, (l.ex.) procuress.

maquette, *n.f.*, (sculpt.) rough model (in clay, wax, &c., on a small scale—*d'argile, de cire, &c., en petit*).

*maquignon, *n.m.*, (b.s.) horse-dealer ; horse-jockey ; jockey ; jobber. — *de charges ;* (b.s.) agent for the sale of offices. — *de mariages ;* (b.s.) matrimonial agent.

*maquignonnage, *n.m.*, (b.s.) horse-dealing; jockeyship; underhand work; jobbing.

*maquignonné, -e, *part.*, trimmed up for sale, bishoped (of horses—*des chevaux*).

*maquignonner, *v.a.*, (b.s.) to jockey, to trim, to bishop (a horse for sale—*un cheval à vendre*); to job: to carry on any illicit trade.

*maquilleur, *n.m.*, (nav.) mackerel-boat.

maquis, *n.m. V.* **makis.**

marabout, *n.m.*, marabout: ill-favoured man, copper kettle; (orni.) argil, hurgil; argil feathers; a kind of ribbon.

maraicher, *n.m.*, kitchen-gardener.

marais, *n.m.*, marsh, fen, bog, swamp, morass; low lying kitchen-garden ground (Paris). *Dessécher un —*, to drain a marsh. *— salants;* salt-pits.

marasca, *n.m.*, (hort.) sour cherry with which maraschino is made.

marasme, *n.m.*, (med.) marasmus, consumption.

marasquin, *n.m.*, maraschino.

marâtre, *n.f.*, step-mother; unkind, harsh mother.

maraud, *n.m.*, **-e**, *n.f.*, scoundrel, rascal; slut, jade.

maraudage, *n.m.*, marauding. freebooting.

*maraudaille, *n.f.*, rabble, base vulgar.

maraude, *n.f.*, marauding.

marauder, *v.n.*, to maraud.

maraudeur, *n.m.*, marauder.

maravédis, *n.m.*, maravedi (small Spanish copper.coin worth little less than a farthing—*petite monnaie de cuivre espagnole = un centime et demi*).

marbre, *n.m.*, marble; marble, slab, stone for grinding colours, &c.; (print.) imposing-stone, slab; *pl.*, works, statues, &c., made of marble; samples of various kinds of marble. *Il est de —;* he is made of stone. *— jaspé;* variegated marble. *Plaque de —;* slab of marble. *—s d'Arundel;* Arundel marbles. *— filandreux;* fibrous marble. *— terrasseux;* terrene marble. *— du gouvernail;* (nav.) barrel of the steering-wheel.

marbré. -e, *part., adj.*, marbled. *Du papier —;* marbled paper.

marbrer, *v.a.*, to marble.

marbrerie, *n.f.*, marble-cutting, marble-work, marble-yard; marble-works.

marbreur, *n.m.*, marbler.

marbrier, *n.m.*, marble-cutter, marble-polisher.

marbrière, *n.f.*, quarry of marble.

marbrure, *n.f.*, marbling.

marc (mar). *n.m.*, mark. *Poids de —;* eight-ounce weight. *Au — la livre;* so many shillings in the pound. *— d'or;* a duty paid to the king by the titularies of certain offices.

marc (mar), *n.m.*, residuum (of any thing squeezed, boiled, or strained—*de toute chose pressée, bouillie ou filtrée*). *— de raisin;* skins of grapes after the last pressing. *— de café;* grounds, grouts of coffee.

marcassin, *n.m.*, young wild boar, grice.

marcassite, *n.f.*, (min.) marcasite.

marceline, *n.f.*, coloured silk fabric; (min.) red silicate of manganese.

· marchand, *n.m.*, **-e**, *n.f.*, merchant, dealer, tradesman, shopkeeper, store-keeper; buyer, customer; bidder (at auctions—*aux enchères*); (orni.) surf-scoter. *— en gros;* wholesale dealer. *— en détail;* retailer. *— fripier;* slopseller. *Petit —;* chandler. *— ambulant, forain;* itinerant dealer. *N'est pas — qui toujours gagne:* we must expect to meet with losses sometimes. *Y a-t-il — !* is there a bidder, does any one bid ? (at auctions—*aux en-*

chères). *Trouver —;* to find a customer, a purchaser.

marchand, -e. *adj.*, merchantable, marketable, vendible; mercantile, trading; navigable (of rivers—*rivières*). *Prix —;* trade price, wholesale price. *Place -e;* trading place. *Vaisseau —;* merchantman, merchant-ship. *Capitaine —;* merchant-captain. *Marine -e;* merchant-service.

marchandage, *n.m.*, task-work, piece-work.

*marchandailler, *v.n.*, to haggle.

marchande, *n.f.*, tradeswoman, trading-woman. *— lingère;* woman who keeps a linen-shop. *— d'herbes;* herb-woman. *— d'huitres;* oyster-woman. *— de modes;* milliner.

marchander, *v.a.*, to cheapen, to bargain for, to haggle for, to chaffer for ; to spare; to hesitate to expose. *Ne pas — quelqu'un;* not to spare any one, not to mince matters with any one. *Il ne marchande pas sa vie;* he does not hesitate to expose his life.

marchander, *v.n.*, to haggle, to chaffer, to stand haggling, to bargain ; to be at a stand, to be irresolute, to hesitate.

marchandeur, *n.m.*, task-master.

marchandise, *n.f.*, merchandise, goods, ware, commodity. *Faire valoir sa —;* to cry up one's goods, to set one's self off. *— qui plaît est à demi-vendue;* please the eye and pick the purse.

marche, *n.f.*, walk; walking; gait, march ; progress, advance; procession; step, stair ; move (at chess, drafts—*aux échecs, aux dames*); conduct; way of proceeding; military frontier, border; marches, borders, between England and Wales, also between England and Scotland. *Ce vaisseau a une — avantageuse:* that vessel is a fast sailer. *Vaisseau construit pour la —;* ship built to sail very fast; clipper. *— des astres;* course of the stars. *Faire une fausse —;* to play a false move. *— d'un poème;* progress of a poem. *— d'escalier;* step of a staircase. *— d'un tour;* treadle of a lathe. *— de deux heures;* walk of two hours, two hours' walk. *La — de cet homme a été louche dans l'affaire;* the conduct of that man in the affair has been suspicious. *— militaire, — triomphale;* military, triumphal, march. *L'armée est en —;* the army is on the march.

marché, *n.m.*, market, market-place; market-time; bargain, purchase. *— au blé, aux herbes, au poisson;* corn, grass, fish-market. *Bon —;* cheapness. *Conclure un —;* to strike a bargain. *Acheter, vendre, à bon —;* to buy, to sell cheap. *Avoir bon — de;* to obtain cheaply an advantage over. *Faire bon — d'une chose;* to hold any thing cheap, not to spare a thing. *Mettre le — à la main à quelqu'un;* to offer any one to break off a bargain. *Vous n'en serez pas quitte à si bon —;* you shall not get off so easily. *On n'a jamais bon — de mauvaise marchandise;* the best is cheapest. *Il le paiera plus cher qu'au —;* he shall smart for it, he shall repent it. *— d'or;* excellent bargain, great bargain. *Meilleur —;* cheaper. *C'est un — donné;* it is for nothing, it is absolutely given away. *Par-dessus le —;* into the bargain. *Le — tient tous les jours;* the market is held every day.

marchepied (marsh-pié), *n.m.*, stepping-stone; towing-path; foot-board; step (of a coach, altar, &c.—*d'une voiture, d'un autel, &c.*), *pl.*, (nav.) foot-ropes of the yards. *Servir de —;* to serve as a stepping-stone.

marcher, *v.n.*, to walk, to step; to tread; to go, to travel, to march; to sail, to run, to ply; to move on. *— en avant, en arrière, à* *reculons ;* to walk forward, to walk backward, — *à grands pas, sur la pointe du pied ;* to stride along, to walk on tiptoe. — *à quatre pattes ;* to go on all-fours. — *à pas de loup ;* to walk with stealthy steps. — *sur les traces de quelqu'un ;* to follow in any one's footsteps. — *sur les talons de quelqu'un ;* to tread on any one's heels. — *sur des épines ;* to tread on thorns. — *de front ;* to march abreast. *Faire — la cavalerie ;* to march the cavalry. *Ce régiment marche ;* that regiment marches. — *droit ;* to walk straight. *Je le ferai — droit ;* I will take care that he behaves well. *Cette montre marche bien ;* this watch goes well. *Ce navire marche bien ;* this vessel sails well. — *sur quelque chose ;* to tread upon anything. — *égal à ;* to be equal to. — *à l'ennemi ;* to march upon the enemy. — *à tâtons ;* to grope one's way.

marcher, *n.m.,* walking, walk ; gait ; ground (on which one walks—*sur lequel on marche*).

marcher, *v.a.,* (hat-making—*chapellerie*) to press.

marcheu-r, *n.m.,* **-se,** *n.f.,* pedestrian, walker. *Bon — ;* (nav.) fast-sailing, swift-sailing, vessel ; fast sailer.

marcottage, *n.m.,* (hort.) layering.

marcotte, *n.f.,* (hort.) layer.

marcotter, *v.a.,* (hort.) to layer.

mardelle. *V.* **margelle.**

mardi, *n.m.,* Tuesday. — *gras ;* Shrove-Tuesday. — *saint ;* Tuesday before Easter; Tuesday in Passion-week.

mare, *n.f.,* pool, pond ; trough (used by cider brewers—*employé dans la fabrication du cidre*).

marécage, *n.m.,* marsh, bog, fen, swamp.

marécageu-x, -se, *adj.,* marshy, fenny, swampy, boggy. *Pays —, terrain — ;* marshy land.

maréchal, *n.m.,* farrier, shoeing-smith ; marshal, field-marshal. — *des logis ;* sergeant (in the cavalry). — *ferrant ;* farrier. — *vétérinaire ;* farrier and veterinary surgeon. — *de camp ;* brigadier, brigadier-general. — *de France ;* Marshal of France. *Grand — ;* grand marshal ; earl marshal.

maréchalat, *n.m.,* dignity of a Marshal of France.

maréchale, *n.f.,* field-marshal's lady.

maréchalerie, *n.f.,* farriery.

⊙**maréchaussée,** *n.f.,* court and jurisdiction of the Marshals of France ; mounted police.

marée, *n.f.,* tide ; sea-fish. *Haute —, pleine — ;* high water. *Basse — ;* low water. *La — monte ;* the tide is coming in. *La — descend ;* the tide is going down, running down. *Prendre la — ;* to take the opportunity of the tide. — *montante ;* flood. — *descendante ;* ebb. — *qui porte au vent ;* wind-tide. *Aller contre vent et — ;* to pursue one's course in spite of all difficulties. *Avoir vent et — ;* to sail with wind and tide. *Vendeur de — ;* fishmonger. *Cela arrive comme — en carême ;* that comes like fish in Lent. *Ce qui vient de flot s'en retourne de — ;* lightly come, lightly go. *La — n'attend personne ;* time and tide wait for no man.

marelle, *n.f.,* scotch-hopper, hopscotch.

maremme, *n.f.,* marshy land, marshes on the sea-shore (in Italy—*en Italie*).

marengo (-ring-go), *n.m.,* Oxford grey (colour—*couleur*).

marengo, *n.f.,* (cook.) marengo, fowl fricassed with mushroom.

margarine, *n.f.,* (chem.) margarin.

margarique, *adj.,* (chem.) margaric.

margay, *n.m.,* (mam.) margay, Cayenne cat.

marge, *n.f.,* margin (of paper, books—*du papier, de livres*) ; freedom, latitude ; time. *Écrire une note en — ;* to make a marginal note. *Laisser assez de — à quelqu'un ;* to give any one sufficient scope. *Nous avons de la — ;* we have time enough.

margelle, *n.f.,* curb (of a well—*d'un puits*).

marger, *v.a.,* (print.)to gauge the furniture of.

margeur, *n.m.,* (print.) compositor who places the sheets under the strings of the machine.

marginal, -e, *adj.,* marginal.

marginé, -e, *part.,* margined, marginated.

marginer, *v.a.,* to margin.

margot, *n.f.,* magpie, mag ; talkative woman.

margotin, *n.m.,* small bundle of fagots.

***margouillet,** *n.m.,* (nav.) truck.

***margouillis** (-goo-yee), *n.m.,* (fam.) puddle, dirty plash, sludge ; (fig.) difficulty ; embarrassment. *Laisser quelqu'un dans le — ;* to leave any one in the lurch.

margrave, *n.m.f.,* (title of nobility in Germany) margrave ; margravine.

margraviat, *n.m.,* margraviate.

marguerite, *n.f.,* daisy ; pearl ; (nav.) messenger. *Reine— (—s —s) ;* China-aster, China-star. *Faire — ;* to clap a messenger on the cable. *Jeter des —s devant les pourceaux ;* to cast pearls before swine.

***marguillerie,** *n.f.,* churchwardenship.

***marguillier,** *n.m.,* churchwarden.

mari, *n.m.,* husband, spouse. *Affranchissement de la puissance de — ;* (jur.) discoverture. *État de la femme en puissance de — ;* (jur.) coverture. *En puissance de — ;* (jur.) covert, under coverture.

mariable, *adj.,* marriageable.

mariage, *n.m.,* marriage, matrimony, wedlock ; match ; wedding ; fortune, portion. — *d'inclination ;* love match. — *de raison,* — *de convenance ;* prudent match. — *en détrempe ;* pretended marriage. — *sous la cheminée ;* marriage under the rose. *Contrat de — ;* marriage contract, marriage treaty, marriage articles. *Promettre en — ;* to promise in marriage. *Rechercher une jeune fille en — ;* to solicit the hand of a young girl. *Prendre en — ;* to take to wife. — *de conscience ;* private marriage.

marié, *n.m.,* married man ; bridegroom. —*s,* married people. *Nouveaux —s ;* new-married couple.

mariée, *n.f.,* married woman ; bride. *Se plaindre que la — est trop belle ;* to find fault with a good bargain.

marier, *v.a.,* to marry, to match ; to blend ; to unite. *Il a fort bien marié sa fille ;* he has married his daughter very advantageously. — *la vigne avec l'ormeau ;* to marry the vine with the elm. — *des couleurs ;* to blend colours.

se marier, *v.r.,* to marry, to espouse, to wed, to be married to ; to match, to ally, to unite. *Il s'est marié très richement ;* he has made a very rich match. *Elle est en âge de — ;* she is of age to marry.

marie-salope, *n.f.* (—s —s), mud-barge.

marieu-r, *n.m.,* **-se,** *n.f.,* match-maker.

marin, -e, *adj.,* marine ; seafaring ; sea. *Avoir le pied — ;* to get one's sea-legs ; not to be put out of countenance.

marin, *n.m.,* mariner, seaman, seafaring man, sailor. — *d'eau douce ;* fresh-water sailor.

marinade, *n.f.,* marinade (pickled meat fried—*viande marinée frite*) ; souse ; pickles.

marine, *n.f.,* sea-affairs ; sea-service ; navigation ; marine ; navy ; naval forces ; taste, smell, of the sea ; (paint.) sea-piece *Officier de — ;* naval officer. — *marchande ;* mercantile, navy. — *militaire*; royal navy. *Soldats, troupes, de la* — ; marines. *Terme de* — ; sea-term. *Sentir la* —, *avoir un goût de* — ; to taste of the sea.

mariné. -e. *part.*, marinated, pickled; (her.) marine. *Des marchandises* —*es*; merchandise damaged by being too long at sea.

mariner. *v.a.*, to marinate, to pickle, to souse ; (nav.) to jerk.

maringouin, *n.m.*, (ent.) musquito.

marinier, *n.m.*, waterman, bargeman, lighterman.

marionnette, *n.f.*, puppet, marionnette; short woman; frivolous, weak-minded woman; *pd* . puppet-show.

marital, -e, *adj.*, marital, pertaining to a husband.

maritalement (-tal-mān), *adv.*, maritally, as man and wife, matrimonially.

maritime, *adj.*, maritime, naval.

maritorne, *n.f.*, ill-made, dirty woman.

marivaudage, *n.m.*, excessively refined style ; mannerism.

marjolaine, *n.f.*, (bot.) sweet marjoram.

⊙**marjolet,** *n.m.*, fop, little coxcomb.

marli, *n.m.*, catgut, thread gauze.

***marmaille,** *n.f.*, (fam.) brats, lot of little brats.

marmelade, *n.f.*, marmalade. *Cette viande est en* — ; that meat is done to a jelly. *Mettre en* — ; to beat to a jelly. *Avoir la mâchoire en* —: to have one's jaw smashed.

marmenteau, *adj.*, reserved (of trees—*des arbres*).

marmite, *n.f.*, pot, saucepan, boiler, copper. *Elles servent à faire bouillir la* — ; they help to make the pot boil. *Écumeur de* —*s* ; spunger. *Nez en pied de* — ; broad pug nose.

⊙**marmiteu-x, -se,** *n.* and *adj.*, (fam.) pitiful, poor wretch ; sad, wretched, whimpering, whining, pitiful.

marmiton, *n.m.*, scullion, kitchen drudge.

marmonner, *v.a.* and *n.*, (pop.) to mutter, to grumble, to growl.

marmoréen, -ne, *adj.*, marmorean.

marmose, *n.f.*, (mam.) marmose.

marmot, *n.m.*, ⊙ monkey ; (mam.) marmoset ; puppet, grotesque figure ; brat. *Croquer le* — ; to dance attendance, to kick one's heels, to wait.

marmotte, *n.f.*, brat (little girl); (mam.) marmot ; woman's head-dress formed of a handkerchief tied round the head ; (nav.) match-tube.

marmotter, *v.a.* and *n.*, to mutter, to mumble.

marmouset, *n.m.*, grotesque figure ; young monkey (little boy—*petit garçon*); fire-dog, and-iron (ornamented with a figure at the end—*orné d'une figure*).

marnage, *n.m.*, (agri.) marling, chalking, claying.

marne, *n.f.*, (agri.) marl, chalk, clay.

marner, *v.a.*, (agri.) to marl, to chalk, to clay.

marneron, *n.m.*, (agri.) marler, marl-digger.

marneu-x, -se, *adj.*, marly.

marnière, *n.f.*, marl-pit, clay-pit.

maronite, *n.m.f.* and *adj.*, Maronite.

maronner, *v.n.*, (pop.) to grumble, to growl.

maroquin, *n.m.*, morocco-leather, morocco. — *du Levant* ; Turkey-leather.

maroquiner, *v.a.*, to morocco.

maroquinerie (-ki-n-rī), *n.f.*, morocco-leather manufacture.

maroquinier, *n.m.*, morocco-tanner.

marotique, *adj.*, marotic (imitation of Marot's style).

marotisme, *n.m.*, marotism (imitation of Marot's style).

marotte, *n.f.*, fool's bauble : fancy, folly,

whim, hobby. *Chacun a sa* — ; every body has his hobby.

maroufle, *n.m.*, ragamuffin ; booby, clod-hopper.

maroufle, *n.f.*, (paint.) lining-paste.

maroufler, *v.a.*, (paint.) to line.

marquant, -e. *adj.*, conspicuous, striking. *Personne* —*e* ; person of note, of distinction.

marque, *n.f.*, mark, cipher. stamp; (com.) private mark ; brand (with a hot iron—*avec un fer chaud*) ; badge ; trace ; sign ; token ; proof, instance ; counter (at play—*de jeu*) ; pit (of the small-pox—*de la petite vérole*). — *de fabricant* ; manufacturer's mark. — *de la douane* ; custom-house stamp. — *d'honneur* ; badge of honour. *Homme de* — ; man of note. *Donner à quelqu'un une* — *d'estime* ; to give any one a proof of esteem. *Lettres de* — ; letters of mark for seizing vessels. *Ville de* — ; coinage-town. — *de beau temps*; signs of fine weather. —, *une* — *que j'ai fait cela* ; as a proof that I did that. *Faire porter ses* —*s à quelqu'un* ; (fam.) to leave one's mark on any one.

marqué, -e, *part.*, marked, evident. — *de la petite vérole* ; pitted with the small-pox. *Homme* — *au bon coin* ; a man of the right stamp. *Ouvrage* — *au bon coin* ; excellent work. *Attentions* —*es* ; marked attentions. *Il est né* — ; he was born with a mark. *Avoir les traits* —*s* ; to have strongly-marked features.

marquer, *v.a.*, to mark, to stamp ; to brand ; to stigmatize ; to leave marks ; to score up ; to mark out, to trace out ; to mark down, to note ; to betoken, to bespeak, to denote ; to tell, to mention, to write ; to show, to give marks of, to testify. — *son jeu* ; to mark one's points at play. *Je lui ai marqué que* ; I wrote to him that. — *à quelqu'un sa reconnaissance* ; to show one's gratitude to any one. — *à quelqu'un ce qu'il doit faire* ; to specify to any one what he has to do.

marquer, *v.n.*, to make its appearance (of a thing—*des choses*) ; to be remarked, to be evident ; to be remarkable, distinguished ; to be of note ; to be shone upon (of sun-dials—*de cadrans solaires*) ; to mark, to show age by the teeth (of horses—*du cheval*) ; (fenc.) to make a full pass. *Cela marquerait trop* (fam.); that would attract too much attention. *Cet homme ne marque point* ; that man is in no way remarkable.

marqueter, *v.a.*, to speckle, to spot, to inlay.

marqueterie (-kè-trī), *n.f.*, marquetry, chequered-work, chequer-work, inlaid-work, inlaying, mosaic, patch-work.

marqueteur, *n.m.*, inlayer.

marquette, *n.f.*, cake (of virgin wax—*de cire vierge*).

marqueur (-keur), *n.m.*, marker, scorer.

marquis, *n.m.*, marquis, marquess. — *de Carabas* ; (jest.) great landed proprietor. *Faire le* — ; to give one's self airs of consequence.

marquisat, *n.m.*, marquisate.

marquise, *n.f.*, marchioness ; marquee.

marquiser, *v.a.*, to style any one a marquis, *se* **marquiser,** *v.r.*, to assume the title of marquis.

marraine, *n.f.*, godmother.

marre, *n.f.*, mattock.

⊙**marri, -e,** *adj.*, sorry, grieved, concerned, troubled.

marron, *n.m.*, (bot.) large French chestnut ; chestnut ; ⊙large curl tied with a riband; cracker (fire-works—*pièce d'artifice*) ; (milit.) mark ; (print.) work printed clandestinely ; chestnut-colour. — *d'Inde* ; horse-chestnut. — *d'eau* ; water-caltrops fruit.

marron, *adj. invariable*, maroon, chestnut-colour.

marron, -ne, *adj.*, fugitive, runaway (of

slaves—*d'esclaves*) ; wild (of animals that have been tame—*l'animaux domestiques redevenus sauvages*) ; (com.) unlicensed, interloping. *Courtier* — ; (com.) unlicensed broker. *Cochon* —; wild hog.

marron, *n.m.*, **-ne**, *n.f.*, runaway slave ; maroon ; free black slave (of the West Indies—*aux Indes Occidentales*).

marronnage, *n.m.*, state of a runaway slave ; running away (of slaves—*d'esclaves*).

Ⓞ**marronner**, *v.a.*, to curl the hair with curling tongs.

marronnier, *n.m.*, (bot.) French chestnuttree, chestnut-tree. — *d'Inde ;* horse-chestnuttree.

marrube, *n.m.*, (bot.) madwort ; marrubium, horehound ; bugle-weed.

mars (mars), *n.m.*, March ; (chem.) Mars (Iron—*le fer*) ; (astron.) Mars ; (fig., poet.) war. *Giboulées de* — ; April showers. *Les* — ; *pl.*, seed sown in spring. *Champ de* — ; (milit.) large drilling ground ; (hist.) assembly of the nation held in March.

marseillaise, *n.f.*, Marseillaise hymn ; Marseillaise.

marsouin, *n.m.*, (mam.) porpoise, sea-hog ; ugly wretch. *Vilain* — ; ugly disagreeable man.

marsupial, **-e**, *adj.*, (natural hist.) marsupial.

marsupiaux, *n.m.pl.*, (natural hist.) marsupialia.

martagon, *n.m.*, (bot.) martagon, mountainlily, Turk's-cap.

marte, *n.f.* V. **martre**.

marteau, *n.m.*, hammer, clapper ; knocker ; (ich.) hammer-fish ; hammer-oyster. *Être entre le* — *et l'enclume ;* to be in an embarrassing position. — *à deux mains :* sledge-hammer. — *d'une arbalète :* cross. *Graisser le* — ; to fee the porter. *Avoir un coup de* — ; to be cracked in the upper story.

martel, *n.m.*, hammer. [Only used in : *Avoir* — *en tête ;* to be very uneasy.]

martelage, *n.m.*, (tech.) hammering.

martelé, **-e**, *part.*, hammered ; (mus.) brilliant and distinct. *Vaisselle* —*e ;* hammered plate. *Vers* —*s ;* laboured verses.

marteler, *v.a.*, to hammer ; to torment, to tease, to vex. *Il martèle ses vers ;* he labours his verses.

martelet, *n.m.*, little hammer.

marteleur, *n.m.*, hammerman.

martial, **-e**, *adj.*, martial, warlike, soldierly. *Code* —, *législation* —*e ;* articles of war.

martin, *n.m.*, (orni.) pastor. *La Saint-* — ; Martinmas.

martinet, *n.m.*, (orni.) martinet, martlet, swift, sea-martin ; flat candlestick, hand-candlestick ; tilt-hammer ; cat-o'-nine-tails. — *de pie ;* (nav.) peak-haliards of the mizzen.

martingale, *n.f.*, (nav., man.) martingale. *Jouer à la* — ; to play double or quits.

martinisme, *n.m.*, martinism.

martiniste, *n.m.*, martinist.

martin-pêcheur, *n.m.* (—*s* —*s*), (orni.) king-fisher.

martin-sec, *n.m.* (—*s*—*s*), a kind of pear.

martre, *n.f.*, (mam.) martin, sable. — *zibeline ;* sable. *Prendre* — *pour renard ;* to take a cow for a bull.

martyr, *n.m.*, **-e**, *n.f.*, martyr. *Il est le* —*de cette femme ;* he is a martyr to that woman. *Le commun des* —*s ;* the common herd.

martyre, *n.m.*, martyrdom. *Souffrir le* — ; to suffer martyrdom. *Faire souffrir le* — *à quelqu'un ;* to make any one suffer martyrdom.

. **martyriser**, *v.a.*, to make any one suffer martyrdom ; to torment.

martyrologe, *n.m.*, martyrology.

martyrologiste, *n.m.*, martyrologist.

marum (-rom), *n.m.*, (bot.) cat-thyme.

mascarade, *n.f.*, masquerade, mask.

mascaret, *n.m.*, eddy of water, violent eddy of the tide ; bar (of harbours—*de ports*).

mascaron, *n.m.*, (arch.) mask.

masculin, **-e**, *adj.*, masculine, male. *Fief* —: fee in tail male.

masculin, *n.m.*, (gram.) masculine.

masculiniser, *v.a.*, to give the masculine gender to a person or object.

masculinité, *n.f.*, masculineness, masculinity.

masque, *n.m.*, mask ; blind, cloak, pretence ; masker, masquerader, mummer ; (paint.) head ; (arch.) mask. *Il a un bon* — : (of actors—*des acteurs*) his features are expressive. *Lever le* —; to pull off the mask.

Ⓞ**masque**, *n.f.*, ugly woman ; naughty little girl.

masqué, **-e**, *part.*, masked. *Être toujours* —; to be always close. *Bal* —; masked ball, masquerade.

masquer, *v.a.*, to mask, to conceal, to cloak ; (milit.) to mask.

*se***masquer**, *v.r.*, to be masked, to mask ; to disguise one's self.

massacrant, **-e**, *adj.*, cross, peevish. *Humeur* —*e ;* awful temper.

massacre, *n.m.*, massacre, butchery ; slaughter, havoc ; bungler, botcher ; (hunt.) head (of a deer newly killed—*tête de faure tué récemment*).

massacrer, *v.a.*, to massacre, to butcher, to slay, to slaughter ; to bungle, to botch. *Cet acteur a massacré son rôle ;* that actor murdered his part. — *des hardes, des meubles ;* to spoil clothes, furniture.

massacreur, *n.m.*, slaughterer, slayer ; bungler.

massage, *n.m.*, shampooing.

masse, *n.f.*, mass, heap, lump ; hoard ; stock ; mace ; (jur.) creditors, estate (of bankrupts—*de faillis*) ; (com.) capital stock, capital ; (tech.) sledge-hammer. — *des biens :* (jur.) estate. — *des biens immeubles ;* (jur.) real estate. — *des biens meubles :* (jur.) personal estate. — *de plume ;* fifty pounds of feathers. — *de héron ;* heron's crest, tuft. — *d'eau ;* typha, reed-mace. *En* — ; in a body, in the mass, by the bulk. *Les* —*s :* the people as a whole, the million.

Ⓞ**masse**, *n.f.*, stake, pool (at play—*au jeu*).

massement, *n.m.*, (milit.) massing of troops.

massepain (mas-pin), *n.m.*, marchpane.

masser, *v.a.*, (milit.) to mass troops ; Ⓞto stake, to put into the pool (at play—*au jeu*) ; (paint.) to mass ; to shampoo.

massette, *n.f.*, (bot.) mace-reed, reed-mace ; cat-tail, cat's-tail. — *à larges feuilles ;* great cat-tail.

massicot, *n.m.*, (chem.) massicot, masticot.

massier, *n.m.*, mace-bearer.

massi-f, **-ve**, *adj.*, massive, bulky ; lumpish ; massy. *Figure d'argent* — ; figure of solid silver, of massive silver. *Avoir l'esprit* — ; to be dull-minded.

massif, *n.m.*, (gard.) group (of trees, flowers—*d'arbres, de fleurs*) ; solid mass, group, block ; wall (of an oven—*de four*) ; (mas.) solid mass.

massivement (-siv-măn), *adv.*, massively, heavily, solidly.

massorah, or **massore**, *n.f.*, masora, massora, masorah.

massorète, *n.m.*, masorite.

massorétique, *adj.*, massoretic, masoretic, masoretical.

massue, *n.f.*, club. *Coup de* — ; dreadful blow, heavy blow, calamity.

mastic, *n.m.*, mastic ; cement ; putty.

mastication, *n.f.,* mastication.

masticatoire, *n.m.,* (med.) masticatory.

mastigadour. *n.m.,* (vet.) mastigador, slabbering-bit (of a bridle—*de bride*).

mastiquer, *v.a.,* to putty ; to cement.

mastodonte, *n.m.,* (fos.) mastodon.

mastoïde, *adj.,* (anat.) mastoid. *Apophyse* —: mastoid process.

mastoïdien, -ne (-in, -è-n), *adj.,* (anat.) pertaining to the mastoid process.

masturbation, *n.f.,* masturbation, self-pollution.

masturber, *v.a.,* to pollute.

se **masturber.** *v.r.,* to commit self-pollution.

masulipatan, *n.m.,* calico coming from Masulipatan.

masure, *n.f.,* ruins (of a house—*d'une maison*) ; ruins ; hovel.

mat (mat), **-e,** *adj.,* unpolished, dead, dull ; heavy ; (chess) mated, check-mated. *Or* — ; unpolished gold. *Coloris* — ; dim colouring. *Broderie* —*e* ; heavy embroidery.

mat (mat), *n.m.,* (chess) mate ; (tech.) deadening. *Donner, faire, échec et* — ; to checkmate.

mât (mâ), *n.m.,* mast ; pole. *Le grand* — ; the main-mast. — *de perroquet* ; top-mast. — *de beaupré* ; bowsprit. — *de misaine* ; fore-mast. — *d'artimon* ; mizzen-mast. *Bas—de misaine* ; lower fore-mast. *Petit* — *de hune* ; top-mast. — *de perroquet de fougue* ; mizzen top-mast. — *de perruche* ; mizzen top-gallant-mast. — *à pible* ; pole mast. — *vertical* ; mast on end. —*s inclinés vers l'arrière* ; masts hanging abaft. — *d'un brin* ; mast of one piece of wood only. — *d'assemblage* ; made mast. — *forcé* ; mast which is sprung. — *jumelé, reclampé, renforcé* ; mast fished (in a weak place or opposite any spring—*à un endroit faible, ou sur une fissure*). — *de pavillon* ; ensign staff. —*s de hune de rechange* ; spare top-masts. —*s majeurs* ; standing masts. *Aller à* —*s et à cordes* ; to scud under bare poles. —*s venus à bas* ; disabled masts. *Lieu d'un* — ; station of a mast. *Mettre les* —*s de hune* ; to heave the top-masts on end.

matador, *n.m.,* matador ; matadore (at play—*au jeu*) ; influential person, big wig.

mâtage, *n.m.,* masting (of a ship—*d'un vaisseau*).

⊙ **matagraboliser,** *v.a.,* (jest.) to give one's self more trouble with a thing than it is worth.

matamore, *n.m.,* hector, bully.

⊙ **matassins,** *n.m.pl.,* matachin (grotesque dance—*danse bouffonne*) ; the men who danced it.

maté, *n.m.,* (bot.) mate (*ilex paraguensis*).

mâté, -e, *adj.,* (nav.) masted. — *en caravelle* ; fitted with pole top-masts. — *en chandelier* ; masted upright. — *en frégate* ; having bent, inclined, masts. — *en semaque* ; masted for a sprit which crosses the sail diagonally. — *en vaisseau* ; masted as a ship of the line. — *en fourche* ; masted with a gaff. — *à pible* ; pole masted. — *en polacre* ; masted with three pole masts and square sails. — *en heu* ; masted for a sprit. — *en galère* ; masted as a galley. *Haut* —, *trop* — ; over-masted.

matelas (ma-tlâ), *n.m.,* mattress. — *d'un carrosse* ; squab, cushion, of a coach. — *de bourre* ; flock-bed. — *à air* ; air mattress.

matelasser (ma-tla-sé), *v.a.,* to cover with a mattress, to stuff.

matelassi-er, *n.m.,* **-ère,** *n.f.,* mattress-maker.

matelot (ma-tlô), *n.m.,* seaman, sailor ; (nav.) ship. *Bon* — ; able seaman. — *de première classe* ; able-bodied seaman. — *à deniers* ; seaman entered for a certain time. — *à mariage* ; seaman entered for the whole voyage. *Vaisseau* — ; good company-keeper.

matelotage (ma-tlo-taj), *n.m.,* seamanship ; seaman's wages, pay.

matelote (ma-tlot), *n.f.,* (cook.) matelote. *À la* — ; seamanlike, sailor's fashion.

mâter, *v.a.,* to mast ; to toss up (the oars —*les rames*). *Machine à* — ; sheers. *Machine à* — *flottante* ; sheer-hulk.

mater, *v.a.,* to mortify, to harass (with corporal hardships—*corporellement*) ; to bring down, to break down, to curb ; to check-mate. *On a maté son orgueil* ; his pride has been sadly brought down.

mâtereau, *n.m.,* (nav.) small mast ; juffer, pole, staff.

matérialiser, *v.a.,* to materialize.

matérialisme, *n.m.,* materialism.

matérialiste, *n.m.f.* and *adj.,* materialist ; materialistic.

matérialité, *n.f.,* materiality, materialness.

matériaux, *n.m.pl.,* materials.

matériel, -le, *adj.,* material ; coarse, gross, rough ; massy, heavy, dull. *Il est* — ; he is a matter-of-fact man. *Faux* — ; (jur.) forgery.

matériel, *n.m.,* materials, stock, working-stock ; stores. —*d'une armée* ; baggage, ammunition, artillery, &c., of an army. — *de siège* ; materials, apparatus for a siege. — *d'une imprimerie* ; stock of materials of a printing-office.

matériellement (-rièl-mān), *adv.,* materially ; coarsely, grossly, roughly.

maternel, -le, *adj.,* maternal, motherly. *Parents* —*s* ; relations by the mother's side. *Langue* —*le* ; mother-tongue.

maternellement (-nèl-mān), *adv.,* maternally.

maternité, *n.f.,* maternity.

mâteur, *n.m.,* (nav.) mast-maker.

mathématicien (-siin), *n.m.,* mathematician.

mathématique, *n.f.,* mathematics. —*s pures* ; pure, speculative, mathematics. —*s mixtes* ; mixed mathematics. *Étudier les* — ; to study mathematics. [Rarely used in the singular.]

mathématique, *adj.,* mathematical.

mathématiquement (-tik-mān), *adv.,* mathematically.

matière (ma-ti-èr), *n.f.,* matter ; subject, cause, reason, motive. — *brute,* — *première* ; raw material. —*s d'or et d'argent* ; bullion. *S'élever au-dessus de la* — ; to soar above matter. *Être enfoncé dans la matière* ; to be smothered in matter ; to be heavy. — *purulente* ; purulent matter. *Donner* — *à parler* ; to give occasion for speaking. *En* — *de* ; in point of, in affairs of.

matin, *n.m.,* morning, noon, forenoon ; prime. *Demain* — ; to-morrow morning. *Se lever de grand* — ; to rise very early. *Un beau* — ; some fine day.

matin, *adv.,* early, early in the morning.

mâtin, *n.m.,* mastiff ; rascal, cur.

matinal, -e, *adj.,* morning ; early (of a person accidentally rising early).

matinalement, *adv.,* early.

mâtineau, *n.m.,* little mastiff.

matinée, *n.f.,* morning. *Dormir la grasse* — ; to lie in bed late in the morning.

mâtiner, *v.a.,* to serve (of a mastiff—*du mâtin*) ; to abuse.

matines, *n.f.pl.,* matins.

matineu-x, -se, *adj.,* generally rising early (of persons—*des personnes*).

matini-er, -ère, *adj.,* morning. [Only used in: *l'étoile* —*ère* ; the Morning-Star.]

matir, *v.a.,* to deaden (metals—*métaux*).

matois, -e, *adj.* and *n.,* cunning, artful, sly ; cunning person, sly person. *C'est un fin* — ; he's a cunning blade.

matoiserie (ma-toa-zrî), *n.f.*, cunning, slyness.

matou, *n.m.*, tom-cat ; ugly person.

matras (-trâ), *n.m.*, (chem.) matrass.

matricaire, *n.f.*, (bot.) matricaria, feverfew.

matrice, *n.f.*, matrix, womb ; (com.) matrice ; (min.) matrix ; standard weight, measure.

matrice, *adj.*, mother. *Église —;* mother-church. *Langue —;* mother-tongue. *Couleurs —s ;* primitive colours.

matricide, *n.m.*, matricide.

matriculaire, *n.m.* and *adj.*, matriculate ; matriculated.

matricule, *n.f.* and *adj.*, register, matricula ; matriculation, certificate of matriculation ; matriculation. *Registre —;* matriculation book.

matrimonial, **-e**, *adj.*, matrimonial.

matrone, *n.f.*, matron.

matte, *n.f.*, (metal.) matt.

maturati-f, **-ve**, *adj.*, (med.) maturative.

maturatif, *n.m.*, (med.) maturant.

maturation, *n.f.*, maturation, ripening.

mâture, *n.f.*, masting, masts, mast-store ; wood for masts.

maturité, *n.f.*, maturity, ripeness. *Avec —;* maturely, with maturity.

matutinal, **-e**, *adj.*, (l.u.) matutinal.

maubêche, *n.f.*, (orni.) knot.

mandire (maudissant, maudit), *v.a.*, to curse, to imprecate.

○**maudisson**, *n.m.*, (fam.) curse.

maudit, **-e**, *part.*, cursed. *— soit le maladroit !* dence take the clumsy rascal !

maugréer, *v.n.*, to fume, to curse and swear.

maupiteu-x, **-se**, *adj.* and *n.*, ○ cruel, pitiless. *Faire le —;* to complain, to lament, without so much reason as one wishes to make believe.

maure, *n.m.* *V.* **more**.

maures-ue, *adj.* *V.* **moresque**.

mauricaud, *adj.* *V.* **moricaud**.

mausolée, *n.m.*, mausoleum.

maussade, *adj.*, sulky, sullen ; unpleasant, dull, tedious ; awkward ; slovenly, clumsy.

maussadement (mô-sad-mân), *adv.*, disagreeably, sullenly, peevishly.

maussaderie (mô-sa-drî), *n.f.*, unpleasantness, sullenness.

mauvais, **-e**, *adj.*, bad, ill, evil; mischievous, ill-natured ; injurious ; (print.) battered (of letters—*des caractères*) ; unhandsome. *— nouvelle ;* bad news. *— livre ;* mischievous book. *Avoir —e mine ;* to look ill. *Prendre quelque chose en —e part ;* to take a thing in an ill sense. *—e tête ;* hot-headed person. *— sujet ;* worthless fellow, rascal, scoundrel.

mauvais, *n.m.*, bad. *Il faut prendre le bon et le —;* one must take the good with the bad.

mauvais, *adv.*, bad, wrong. *Sentir —;* to have a bad smell. *Il fait —;* it is bad weather. *Trouver — que ;* to take it ill that.

mauve, *n.f.*, mallow ; (orni.) sea-gull.

mauviette, *n.f.*, lark ; lath (thin person—*personne fort maigre*).

mauvis, *n.m.*, (orni.) mavis, song-thrush, throstle.

maxillaire, *adj.*, pertaining to the jaw, maxillary.

maxime, *n.f.*, maxim. *Tenir pour —;* to hold it as a maxim.

maximum, *n.m.* (**-s**), (math.) (*maxima*), maximum ; acme.

mayonnaise, *n.f.*, (cook.) mayonnaise.

mazarinade, *n.f.*, song, pamphlet, against Cardinal Mazarin.

mazette, *n.f.*, tit (sorry horse—*mauvais petit cheval*) ; person of no strength, of no ardour ; awkward person (at play—*au jeu*).

md., (ab. of Marchand) shopkeeper.

mde., (ab. of Marchande) shopkeeper.

me, *pron.*, me ; to me. *Il — blâme ;* he blames me. *Vous — parlez ;* you speak to me. *— voici ;* here I am.

meâ-culpâ. *n.m.* (—), expression taken from the *Confiteor. Dire, faire, son —;* to repent ; to confess one's faults to one's self or to others.

méandre, *n.m.*, meander.

méat, *n.m.*, (anat.) meatus.

mécanicien (-in), *n.m.*, mechanician ; machinist, mechanic ; engine-maker ; engine-man.

mécanique, *n.f.*, mechanics ; mechanism ; machine, machinery, piece of machinery. *Une belle —;* a fine machine.

mécanique, *adj.*, mechanic, mechanical.

mécaniquement (-ni-kmân), *adv.*, mechanically.

mécaniser, *v.a.*, to use as a machine ; (pop.) to tease, to plague. *— les hommes ;* to use men as mere machines.

mécanisme, *n.m.*, mechanism.

mécène, *n.m.*, a protector of science, art, and literature.

méchamment (mé-sha-mân), *adv.*, wickedly, spitefully, maliciously, ill-naturedly.

méchanceté (mé-shans-té), *n.f.*, wickedness, spitefulness, mischievousness ; crossness, naughtiness, ill-nature ; ill-natured thing, piece of ill-nature.

méchant, **-e**, *adj.*, bad, wretched, worthless ; wicked, dishonest ; sorry, paltry ; wicked, ill-natured, mischievous, malicious ; wayward, naughty, unkind. *— homme ;* a wicked man. *Il a la mine —e ;* he has an ill-natured look. *Un — poète ;* a paltry poet.

méchant, *n.m.*, **-e**, *n.f.*, wicked person ; evil doer ; naughty child. *Dieu punira les —s ;* God will punish the wicked. *Faire le —;* to be fractious (of a child—*des enfants*).

mèche, *n.f.*, wick (of a lamp or candle—*de lampe, de chandelle, &c.*); tinder ; match ; screw (of cork-screws, wimbles, &c.—*de tire-bouchons, vilbrequins, &c.*) ; centre-bit ; whip-lash. *Découvrir, éventer, la —* (milit.) ; to discover the enemy's match by means of a countermine ; to find out the secret of a plot. *— de cheveux;* lock of hair.

○**méchef**, *n.m.*, mischief, mischance ; harm.

mécher, *v.a.*, to fumigate with brimstone.

mécompte (mé-kont), *n.m.*, miscalculation, disappointment. *Il a trouvé bien du —;* he has met with great disappointments.

mécompter, *v.n.*, to strike wrong (of clocks —*des horloges, des pendules*).

se **mécompter** (mé-kon-té), *v.r.*, to miscalculate ; to be disappointed ; to be out in one's reckoning. *Il s'est mécompté dans son raisonnement ;* he is out in his reasoning.

méconium (-om), *n.m.*, (med.) meconium.

méconnaissable, *adj.*, not easy to be known again.

méconnaissance. *n.f.*, unthankfulness, ungratefulness, ingratitude.

méconnaissant, **-e** *adj.*, unthankful, ungrateful, unmindful.

méconnaître. *v.a.*, not to know again, not to recognize ; to disown, not to know ; to ignore, to slight, not to appreciate. *Il méconnaît ses parents ;* he disowns his relations.

se **méconnaître**, *v.r.*, to forget one's self.

méconnu, **-e**, *part.*, unacknowledged ; unrecognized ; ignored, disowned.

mécontent, **-e**, *adj.*, dissatisfied, ill-satisfied,

discontented. *Il est — de vous;* he is displeased with you. *Vous êtes — de tout;* you are discontented with everything.

mécontent, *n.m.*, **-e**. *n.f.*, dissatisfied person; malecontent. *C'est un —;* he is a discontented man.

mécontentement (-tan-tmän), *n.m.*, discontent, discontentedness, dissatisfaction, displeasure. *Donner du — à:* to displease.

mécontenter. *v.a.*, to discontent, to dissatisfy, to displease.

mécréance, *n.f.*, infidelity, unbelief, irreligion.

mécréant, *n.m.*, unbeliever, infidel.

mécroire, *v.n.*, to disbelieve.

*médaille, *n.f.*, medal ; (arch.) medallion. *Chaque — a son revers;* everything has its good and its bad side. *Tourner la —;* to turn the tables.

*médaillé, *n.m.* and *adj.*, of him who has received a medal as a reward.

*médaillier, *n.m.*, cabinet of medals.

*médailliste, *n.m.*, medallist.

*médaillon, *n.m.*, medallion ; locket.

médecin (mé-dsin), *n.m.*, physician, doctor. *Faire venir le —;* to send for the physician. *Il est abandonné des —s;* the doctors have given him up. *Docteur médecin;* doctor of physic. *Un — d'eau douce;* a water-gruel doctor. *Le temps est un grand —;* time cures all.

médecine (mé-dsi-n), *n.f.*, medicine, physic. *Étudiant en —;* medical student. *— légale;* forensic medicine.

médeciner (mé-dsi-né), *v.a.*, to physic.

se **médeciner**, *v.r.*, to physic one's self.

médial, -e, *adj.*, (gram.) median.

médian, -e, *adj.*, (anat.) mesial.

médianoche, *n.m.*, meat-supper after midnight.

médiante, *n.f.*, (mus.) mediant.

médiastin, *n.m.*, (anat.) mediastine.

médiat, -e. *adj.*, mediate.

médiatement (mé-dia-tmän), *adv.*, mediately.

médiat-eur, *n.m.*, **-rice**, *n.f.*, mediator, mediatrix.

médiation. *n.f.*, mediation.

médiatisation. *n.f.*, mediatization.

médiatiser, *v.a.*, to mediatize.

médical, -e, *adj.*, medical. *Matière —e;* materia medica.

médicament, *n.m.*, medicament.

médicamentaire, *adj.*, concerning medicines.

médicamenter, *v.a.*, to physic.

se **médicamenter**, *v.r.*, to physic one's self.

médicamenteu-x, -se, *adj.*, medicamental.

médication, *n.f.*, medication.

médicinal, -e, *adj.*, medicinal.

médimne, *n.m.*, (antiq.) medimnus.

médiocre, *adj.*, mediocre, middling, ordinary.

médiocre, *n.m.*, mediocrity.

médiocrement, *adv.*, middlingly, indifferently, tolerably.

médiocrité, *n.f.*, mediocrity ; competence (fortune).

médique, *adj.*, Median.

médire, *v.n.*, to slander, to speak ill, to backbite, to traduce. *— de son prochain;* to speak ill of one's neighbour.

médisance, *n.f.*, slander, scandal, backbiting; piece of slander.

médisant, -e. *adj.* and *n.*, slanderous, scandalou ; slanderer. *Il ne faut pas croire les —s;* slanderers are not to be credited.

méditati-f, -ve, *adj.* and *n.*, meditative; meditative person.

méditation. *n.f.*, meditation.

méditer, *v.a.*, to meditate, to think over ; to contemplate, to plan. *— la ruine de quelqu'un ;* to meditate any one's ruin.

méditer, *v.n.*, to contemplate. *Passer sa vie à —:* to spend one's life in meditation.

méditerrané, -e, *adj.*, mediterranean, mediterraneous. *La mer —e;* the Mediterranean Sea.

méditerranée, *n.f.*, the Mediterranean Sea.

méditerranéen. -ne, *adj.*, pertaining to the Mediterranean Sea.

medium (-om), *n.m.* (—*s*). medium.

médius, *n.m.*, middle-finger.

médullaire (mé-dul-ler), *adj.*, medullary.

méduse, *n.f.*, (zool.) medusa, sea-nettle, jelly-fish.

meeting, *n.m.* (—*s*), meeting.

méfaire, *v.n.*, to do evil.

méfait, *n.m.*, misdeed.

méfiance, *n.f.*, mistrust, distrust.

méfiant, -e, *adj.*, mistrustful, distrustful.

se **méfier**. *v.r.*, to mistrust, to distrust.

mégalosaure, *or* **mégalosaurus**, *n.m.*, (foss.) megalosaurus.

mégarde, *n.f.*, inadvertence. *Par —;* inadvertently.

mégathérium, *n.m.* (—*s*), (foss.) megatherium.

mégère, *n.f.*, (myth.) Megæra; shrew, vixen.

mégie, *n.f.*, tawing, leather-dressing.

mégisser, *v.a.*, to taw.

mégisserie (mé-gi-sri), *n.f.*, tawing, leather-dressing.

mégissier, *n.m.*, tawer, leather-dresser.

*meilleur, -e *adj.*, better, best. *Le —;* the best. *Ceci est bon, mais cela est —;* this is good, but that is better.

*meilleur, *n.m.*, best; best wine. *Le — du conte;* the best of the story.

meistre, *or* **mestre**, *n.m.*, (nav.) mast, main mast. *Mât de —;* main mast (of ships with lateen sails—*des bâtiments à voiles latines*).

mékhitariste, *n.m.*, a monk of the Armenian convent in the St. Lazar Island near Venice.

mélampyre, *n.m.*, (bot.) cow-wheat.

mélancolie, *n.f.*, melancholy; melancholiness. *Chasser la —;* to drive away melancholy. *Il n'engendre point la —;* he is a merry mortal.

mélancolique, *adj.*, melancholy, dismal, gloomy. *Séjour —;* dismal abode.

mélancoliquement (-lik-män), *adv.*, melancholy, in a melancholy manner, sadly.

mélange, *n.m.*, mixture, mingling; medley; mash, (for brewing—*à brasser*); *pl.*, miscellaneous works, miscellanea. *Un bonheur sans —;* unalloyed happiness.

mélanger, *v.a.*, to mix, to mingle, to blend, to mash, to intermix, to mash.

se **mélanger**, *v.r.*, to mix, to mingle ; to be mashed.

mélasse, *n.f.*, molasses, treacle.

melchite (-kit), *n.m.*, name formerly given by heretics to the Syrian Orthodox Christians; applied in modern time to Eastern Christians who have partly adopted the doctrine and rites of the Greek Church.

mêlé, -e, *part.*, mixed.

mêlée, *n.f.*, conflict; fray, fight; altercation, dispute.

mêler, *v.a.*, to mingle, to mix, to mix up; to blend, to jumble ; to bring in, to implicate; to shuffle (cards—*cartes*); to entangle. *— du fil;* to entangle thread. *— les cartes;* to shuffle the cards. *— une serrure;* to force a lock. *Il* *est* **mêlé** *dans une mauvaise affaire;* he is mixed up in a bad piece of business.

se mêler, *v.r.*, to mingle, to be mingled, to be mixed; to tamper; to blend; to trouble one's self; to intermeddle. *— dans la foule;* to mingle with the crowd. *— de;* to meddle. to intermeddle. *Mêlez-vous de vos affaires;* mind your own business. *De quoi vous mêlez-vous? what business is that of yours? — ensemble;* to commingle.

mélèze, *n.m.*, (bot.) larch-tree.

mélianthe, *n.m.*, (bot.) honey-flower.

mélilot, *n.m.*, (bot.) melilot, sweet-trefoil.

méli-mélo, *n.m.* (—), (fam.) medley.

mélinet, *n.m.*, (bot.) honeywort.

mélisse, *n.f.*, (bot.) balm-mint, garden-balm.

mellifère, *adj.*, melliferous.

mellifères, *n.m.pl.*, melliferous insects.

mellification, *n.f.*, mellification.

mellifue, *adj.*, mellifluous.

mellifluité, *n.f.*, mellifluence.

mellithe, *n.f.*, honey-stone, mellite.

mélodie, *n.f.*, melody, melodiousness.

mélodieusement (-eûz-măn), *adv.*, melodiously, musically.

mélodieu-x, -se, *adj.*, melodious, musical, tuneful.

mélodique, *adj.*, (mus.) melodious; agreeable to the rules of melody.

mélodramatique, *adj.*, melodramatic.

mélodramaturge, *n.m.*, author of melodramas.

mélodrame, *n.m.*, melodrama.

mélomane, *n.m.*, melomaniac, person music-mad.

mélomanie, *n.f.*, melomania.

melon, *n.m.*, melon. *— musqué;* musk-melon. *— d'eau;* water-melon.

melongène, *or* **mélongène,** *n.f.*, mad-apple, egg-plant.

melonnière, *n.f.*, melon-ground.

mélopée, *n.f.*, (mus.) melopœia.

méloplaste, *n.m.*, (mus.) a board with a stave drawn on for the tuition of vocal music.

mémarchure, *n.f.*, sprain (in a horse's leg *— du cheval*).

membrane, *n.f.*, (anat.) membrane, film; (ornl.) web.

membraneu-x, -se, *adj.*, membranous, filmy.

membre, *n.m.*, member; limb; (nav.) rib. *Les —s d'une famille;* the members of a family. *Les —s du corps humain;* the limbs of the human body.

membré, -e, *adj.*, limbed. *Bien —;* having well made and well proportionate limbs.

membru, -e, *adj.*, large-limbed, stout-limbed.

membrure, *n.f.*, the limbs of the human body; cord (to measure fire-wood—*pour mesurer le bois à brûler*); ribs, timbers (of a ship); (carp.) split-board.

même, *adj.*, same; self; very. *Une seule et —origine;* one and the same origin. *C'est la — chose;* it is all one. *Moi-même;* myself. *Eux—s;* themselves. *C'est la bonté —;* she is goodness itself. *La chose —;* the very thing.

même, *adv.*, even, also, likewise. *Il lui a tout donné, — ses habits;* he has given him everything, even to his clothes. *Les plus sages — le font;* even the wisest do it. *Quand — il me l'aurait dit;* even though he had said it me. *À — de;* able to. *Mettre à —;* to enable. *Vous êtes à — de rendre service à cet honnête homme;* you are able to do that honest man a service. *Il vous a mis à — de le faire;* he has enabled you to do it. *De —;* the same; so; like. *Faites de —;* do the same. *Tout de —;* all the same,

in the same manner. *De — que;* in the same manner as, so as, as.

même, *n.m.*, same, same thing. *Cela revient au —;* it comes to the same thing.

mêmement, *adv.*, also, even, likewise.

mémento (-min-), *n.m.* (—*s*), memento.

mémoire, *n.f.*, memory, recollection, remembrance. *Avoir une — de lièvre;* to have a very short memory. *Je n'en ai pas la moindre —;* I have not the slightest remembrance of it. *De — d'homme on n'a vu telle chose;* such a thing has not been seen within the memory of man. *Des choses dignes de —;* things worthy of commemoration. *Remettre dans la —,* conserver la *— de;* to remind, to remember. *Rappeler quelque chose à la — de quelqu'un;* to bring any thing to any one's recollection, to remind any one of anything. *En — de;* in memory of. *Réhabiliter la — d'un défunt;* to reinstate the fame of a dead person. *À la — de;* in memory of. *Si j'ai bonne —;* if I remember rightly.

mémoire, *n.m.*, memorial; memorandum; bill, account. *Dresser un —;* to draw up a memorial. *— acquitté;* bill receipted. *— d'apothicaire;* exorbitant bill.

mémorable, *adj.*, memorable.

mémorandum (-dom), *n.m.*, memorandum; memorandum-book; memorial.

mémorati-f, -ve, *adj.*, (fam.) recollecting. *Être — de quelque chose;* to remember any thing.

mémorial, *n.m.*, memorial; (com.) waste-book.

mémorialiste, *n.m.*, memorialist.

menaçant, -e, *adj.*, menacing, threatening. *D'une manière —e;* threateningly.

menace, *n.f.*, menace, threat. *— en l'air;* empty threat. *Paroles de —;* threatening words, menacing words.

menacer, *v.a.*, to threat, to threaten, to menace; to forebode, to portend. *--de la main;* to threaten with the hand. *L'air nous menace d'un orage;* the air threatens us with a storm. *— ruine, — de tomber;* to totter.

ménade, *n.f.*, (antiq.) priestess of Bacchus, bacchanal.

ménage, *n.m.*, housekeeping, household; housewifery, house; household goods; family; husbandry, economy, saving. *Tenir — en —;* to keep house, to be a housekeeper. *Entrer en —;* to begin housekeeping. *Rompre son —;* to leave off housekeeping. *Dépense de —;* household expenses. *— de garçon;* bachelor's household. *Faire bon —;* to live well together. *Pain de —;* household bread. *Toile de —;* homespun cloth. *Femme de —;* charwoman. *Elle entend bien le —;* she is a good housewife. *Vivre de —;* to live sparingly.

ménagement (-na-jmăn), *n.m.*, regard, respect, circumspection, caution, discretion; management, conduct.

ménager, *v.a.*, to husband, to manage with economy, to spare, to be sparing, to save, to be saving; to take care of, to be careful of, to conduct carefully; to treat with caution, to treat gently, to treat kindly, to treat with respect; to reserve; to procure, to prepare; to manage, to manage. *— son bien;* to husband one's fortune. *— quelqu'un;* to treat any one with respect, consideration. *Je n'ai rien à —;* I have no measures to keep. *Pour — notre faiblesse;* in condescension to our weakness. *— les termes;* to weigh what one says. *— l'occasion;* to improve an opportunity. *— ses forces;* to spare one's strength. *— ses amis;* to forbear being troublesome to one's friends. *— son crédit;* to make a prudent use of one's credit. *Je lui ai ménagé une place;* I helped him to a situation,

— une agréable surprise; to prepare, to procure, an agreeable surprise. — *une étoffe;* to make the most of a stuff. — *un escalier dans un bâtiment;* to contrive a staircase in a house. — *la chèvre et le chou;* to hold with the hare and run with the hounds.

se **ménager**. *v.r.*, to take care of one's self; to spare one's self; to behave with care, with caution, to conduct one's self cautiously. — *avec quelqu'un;* to keep in, to keep on good terms, with any one. — *entre deux partis contraires;* to steer successfully between two adverse parties, and remain friendly with both.

ménager, *v.n.*, to save, to save up. *Il ménage pour ses enfants;* he is saving up for his children.

ménag-er, -ère, *adj.*, thrifty, saving, sparing, provident, frugal.

ménager, *n.m.*, economist; thrifty, saving, frugal, sparing man. *Être bon — du temps;* to husband one's time well.

ménagère, *n.f.*, economist; economical housewife; thrifty, saving, frugal, sparing woman; housewife; housekeeper.

ménagerie (-na-jiı),*n.f*, menagery; ⊙poultry-yard.

ménageu-r, *n.m.*,**-se**, *n.f.*,(l.u.) person treating others with care, caution, circumspection.

mendiant, -e, *n.* and *a fj.*, beggar, mendicant; beggarman; beggarwoman; (c.rel) mendicant-friar, mendicant; begging, mendicant. *Les quatre —s;* the four orders of mendicant friars; raisins, figs, almonds, and nuts

mendicité, *n.f.*, beggary, mendicity; beggars; vagrancy.

mendier. *v.a.* and *n.*, to beg; to beg for; (b.s.) to solicit meanly, to implore. *Il mendie son pain;* he begs his bread.

meneau, *n.m.*, (arch.) mullion.

menée, *n.f.*, underhand dealing, secret practice, plot, conspiracy; track. *Suivre la —;* (hunt.) to follow the track.

mener, *v.a.*, to carry, to conduct, to lead, to bring; to direct, to head, to command, to guide; to introduce, to take; to take along with; to amuse; to lead about. — *les bêtes aux champs;* to drive the cattle to the fields. — *paître les vaches;* to take, to drive, the cows to grass. — *quelqu'un en prison;* to convey any one to gaol. — *un enfant par la lisière;* to conduct a child in leading-strings. — *quelqu'un à la baguette;* to rule any one with a tight hand. — *tambour battant;* to carry it with a high hand over. — *un grand train;* to make a clatter. — *le branle;* to take the lead. *Menez-moi chez le ministre;* introduce me to the minister.

mener, *v.n.*, to drive; to lead, to conduct, to go. *Ce chemin mène à la ville;* this road leads to the town. *Cela ne mène à rien;* that leads to nothing, that is of no use.

ménestrel, *n.m.*, minstrel.

ménétrier, *n.m.*, fiddler.

meneur, *n.m.*, driver; agent for wet-nurses; leading man, ringleader.

meneuse, *n.f.*, female agent for wet-nurses.

menhir, *n.m.* (-s), (archæology) menhir.

méniane, *n.f.*, (arch.) a kind of balcony in Italian houses.

ménianthe, *n.m.*, (bot.) bog-bean, marsh-trefoil.

menin, *n.m.*, young nobleman attached to the person of the Dauphin (French hist.).

méninge, *n.f.*, (anat.) meninges. ·

méningite, *n.f.*, (med.) meningitis.

ménippée, *adj.* and *n.f.*, of satires in the style of those of the philosopher Menippus. *Satire —, la —;* a satire which appeared in 1593 against the party of the Ligue (French hist.).

ménisperme, *n.m.*, (bot.) menispermum, moon-seed.

ménisque, *n.m.*, (opt.) meniscus.

ménologe, *n.m.*, menology.

menotte, *n.f.*, (fam.) little hand (of a child —*d'un enfant*); *pl.*, handcuffs, manacles.

mense, *n.f.*, (of abbeys—*d'abbayes*) income, revenue, stock; ⊙table, board (food—*nourriture*).

mensonge, *n.m.*, lie, falsehood, untruth, story; error, illusion, vanity. *Débiter des —s;* to utter lies. *Tout petit —, — de rien, — d: marchand;* white lie.

mensong-er, -ère, *adj.*, lying, untrue, deceitful, false, counterfeit.

mensongèrement, *adv.*, falsely, deceitfully.

menstrue, *n.m.*, (chem.) menstrum.

menstruel, -le. *adj.*, (med.) menstrual. *Flux —;* menses, catamenia.

menstrues,*n.f.*, (physiology) menses, catamenia.

mensuel, -le. *adj.*, monthly.

mensuellement, *adv.*, monthly.

mensurabilité, *n.f.*, mensurability.

mensurable. *adj.*, mensurable.

mental, -e, *adj.*, mental.

mentalement (-tal-mān), *adv.*, mentally.

menterie (man-trī), *n.f.*, story, fib, falsehood, untruth.

menteu-r, -se, *adj.*, lying, false, deceitful.

menteu-r, *n.m.*, **-se**. *n.f.*, liar, story-teller. *Un — de profession,* a confirmed liar.

menthe, *n.f.*, (bot.) mint. — *aquatique;* water-mint. — *verte*, spearmint.

mention, *n.f.*, mention, mentioning, naming.

mentionner. *v.a.*, to mention, to make mention of.

mentir (mentant, menti), *v.n.*, to lie, to tell a lie, a story, a falsehood, an untruth; to fib. *Gardez-vous bien de —;* beware of lying. *Il en a menti;* he is a liar. *Il n'enrage pas pour —;* he does not stick at a lie. *Se — à soi-même;* to belie one's self. *A beau — qui vient de loin;* (prov.) travellers see strange things. *Sans —, à ne point —;* to tell the truth, in fact, indeed.

menton, *n.m.*, chin. — *en galoche* turned up chin. — *à double étage;* double chin — *qui avance;* prominent chin. *Avoir deux —s;* to be double-chinned.

mentonnet, *n.m.*, (mec.) ear, tipper.

mentonni-er, -ère, *adj.*, (anat.) relating to the chin.

mentonnière, *n.f.*, chin-piece; bandage for the chin.

mentor (min-), *n.m.*, mentor, guide, tutor.

menu, -e, *adj.*, small, slender, spare, thin, inconsiderable. *Le — peuple;* the common people. —*s plaisirs;* pocket-money.

menu, *n.m.*, minute detail, particulars. *Le — d'un repas;* the bill of fare of an entertainment. *Un paquet de —;* a bundle of small linen.

menu, *adv.*, small. *Il pleuvait dru et —;* the rain fell fine and fast. *Marcher, trotter, dru et —;* to walk fast, but with short steps.

***menuaille**, *n.f.*, small money; fry, small fish; trash.

menuet,*n.m.*. minuet

menuiser, *v.a.* and *n*, to do carpenter's work.

menuiserie (-nui-zrī), *n f.*, joinery, joiner's work; carpentry.

menuisier, *n.m.*, joiner, carpenter and joiner. — *en bâtiments;* house-carpenter.

menuisière, *n.f.*, carpenter's wife.

menuisière, *adj.f.*, (ent.) carpenter. *Abeille —,* carpenter-bee.

méphitique, *adj.*, mephitic.

méphitisme, *n.m.*, mephitis, mephitism.

méplat, *n.m.*, (paint.) flat, flat part.

méplat, **-e**. *adj.*, (carp., paint.) flat.

seméprendre, *v.r.*, to mistake; to make a mistake; to be mistaken; (fig.) to forget one's self, to be wanting in respect. *Vous vous méprenez ;* you mistake; you forget yourself.

mépris, *n.m.*, contempt, scorn, contumely; *pl.*, contumelious language, contemptuous treatment. *Avoir du — pour quelqu'un ;* to feel contempt for any one. *Au — des lois :* in defiance of the laws. *Témoigner du — pour ;* to evince contempt for. *Tomber dans le — ;* to fall into contempt. *La familiarité engendre le — ;* familiarity breeds contempt.

méprisable. *adj.*, contemptible, despicable.

méprisablement, *adv.*, despicably.

méprisant. **-e**, *adj.*, contemptuous, scornful, contumelious.

méprise, *n.f.*, mistake, oversight, misunderstanding; misapprehension. *Lourde — ;* gross mistake. *Faire une grande — ;* to make a great mistake.

mépriser, *v.a.*, to contemn, to despise, to scorn ; to slight.

mer (mèr), *n.f.*, sea, deep; jar (frequently replenished—*qu'on remplit à mesure qu'elle se vide*). *La haute — ;* main sea; high sea. — *basse — ;* shallow sea. *Port de — ;* sea-port. *Un coup de —* (nav.); a sea. *Homme de — ;* seafaring man. *Loup de — ;* expert seaman. *D'outre- — ;* beyond the seas. *En pleine — ;* on the open sea, on the high seas. *Chercher quelqu'un par — et par terre;* to look for any one high and low. *C'est la — à boire;* it is an endless task. *Porter de l'eau à la — ;* to carry coals to Newcastle. *La — est belle;* the sea is smooth. *Tenir la — ;* to keep at sea. *Jeter, tomber, à la — ;* to throw, to fall, overboard. *Recevoir un coup de — ;* to ship a sea. *Gros coup de —,* heavy sea. *Mettre à la — ;* to put to sea. *Pouvoir tenir la — ;* (nav.) to be seaworthy (of a ship—*d'un vaisseau*).

mercantile, *adj.*, mercantile.

***mercantille**, *n.f.*, (l.u.) petty trading; hucksterage.

mercenaire, *adj.*, mercenary, venal.

mercenaire, *n.m.*, mercenary, hireling.

mercenairement (-nèr-màn), *adv.*, mercenarily.

mercerie, *n.f.*, mercery, haberdashery.

merci, *n.f.* (n.p.), mercy. *Crier — ;* to cry for mercy. *Don d'amoureuse — ;* lady's favour. *Être, se mettre, à la — de quelqu'un ;* to be, to place one's self, at any one's mercy.

merci, *n.m.*, thanks; thank you. *Dieu — ;* thank God !

merci, *adv.*, thank you, I have had quite enough, I'd rather not.

merci-er. *n.m.*, **-ère**. *n.f.*, mercer, haberdasher. *Petit — ;* haberdasher.

mercredi. *n.m.*, Wednesday. — *des Cendres ;* Ash-Wednesday.

mercure, *n.m.*, (astron.) Mercury; quicksilver.

mercuriale, *n.f.*, harangue, lecture, reprimand, censure, rebuke; rating; averages, average prices of grain; (bot.) mercurialis.

mercuriel, **-le**, *adj.*, mercurial. *Onguent — ;* mercurial ointment.

mère, *n.f.*, mother. *Belle- — (—s —s) ;* mother-in-law. *Grand'— (— —s),* (pop.) — *grand (—s —) ;* grandmother. *Dure- — (n.p.) ;* dura mater. *Pie-— (n.p.) ;* pia mater. *Eau— ;* mother water. *L'oisiveté est la — de tous les vices ;* idleness is the mother of all vices. — *nourrice ;* foster-mother. *La — patrie ;* the mother-country.

mère, *adj.*, mother; primitive. — *goutte ;* unpressed wine. — *laine ;* the finest wool.

mérelle. *n.f.* *V.* **marelle**.

méridien (-in), *n.m.*, meridian.

méridien. **-ne**. *adj.*, meridian.

méridienne (-di-è-n), *n.f.*, afternoon nap; meridian line. *Faire la — ;* to take an afternoon nap.

méridional, **-e**, *adj.*, meridional, southern.

meringue (-ringh), *n.f.*, meringue (cake—*pâtisserie*).

mérinos (-nôs), *n.m.*, merino sheep · merino (stuff—*étoffe*).

merise, *n.f.*, wild cherry.

merisier. *n.m.*, wild cherry-tree.

méritant. **-e**, *adj.*, meritorious, worthy.

mérite, *n.m.*, merit, worth; desert, attainments. *Il sera traité selon ses — s ;* he shall be dealt with according to his deserts. *Se donner le — de quelque chose ;* to assume the merit of anything. *Se faire un — de ;* to make a merit of.

mériter, *v.a.* and *n.*, to deserve, to merit. *Il mérite d'être récompensé ;* he deserves to be rewarded. *Cette nouvelle mérite confirmation ;* that news requires confirmation. *Cela ne mérite pas qu'on en parle ;* that is not worth mentioning.

mérithalle, *n.m.*, (bot.) internode.

méritoire, *adj.*, meritorious.

méritoirement (-toâr-màn), *adv.*, meritoriously.

merlan, *n.m.*, (ich.) whiting; (b.s.) journeyman hair-dresser.

merle, *n.m.*, (orni.) blackbird. — *aquatique ;* water-ouzel. *C'est un fin — ;* he is a cunning blade. *Dénicheur de —s ;* person not to be trusted.

merlette, *n.f.*, (her.) martlet.

merlin, *n.m.*, (nav.) marline; cleaver, chopper (tool—*outil*).

merlon, *n.m.*, (fort.) merlon.

merluche, *n.f.*, (ich.) dried haddock; salt-cod.

merlus, *n.m.*, haddock.

merrain, *n.m.*, (hunt.) horn (of deer—*de fauve*); (cooperage—*tonnellerie*) clap-board.

***merveille**, *n.f.*, wonder, marvel. *À — ;* admirably done, wonderfully well. *Faire des —s ;* to perform wonders. *Promettre monts et —s ;* to promise wonders. *Mes affaires vont à — ;* my affairs go on admirably.

***merveilleuse**, *n.f.*, affected lady.

***merveilleusement** (-eûz-màn), *adv.*, wonderfully, admirably; wonderfully well.

***merveilleu-x**, **-se**, *adj.*, wonderful, wondrous, marvellous.

***merveilleux**, *n.m.*, marvellous, exquisite; coxcomb.

mes (mè), *adj. m.f.pl.*, my.

mésadvenir, *or* **mésavenir**, *v.imp.*, (l.u.) to come to any harm.

mésair, *or* **mézair**, *n.m.*, (man.) passage.

mésaise, *n.m.*, uncomfortableness, uneasiness.

mésalliance, *n.f.*, misalliance, disparagement.

mésallier, *v.a.*, to disparage; to marry to any one of an inferior rank.

se mésallier, *v.r.*, to disparage one's self; to contract a misalliance.

mésange, *n.f.*, titmouse, tomtit.

mésarriver, *v.imp.*, to come to any harm, to happen unluckily.

mésaventure. *n.f.*, mischance, mishap.

mésembryanthème, *n.m.*, (bot.) fig-marigold.

mésentère. *n.m.*, (anat.) mesentery.

mésentérique, *adj.*, (anat.) mesenteric.

mésestime, *n.f.*, bad opinion (about any one —*de quelqu'un*).

mésestimer, *v.a.*, to disesteem, to undervalue, to depreciate.

mésintelligence, *n.f.*, misunderstanding.

mésinterpréter, *v.a.*, to misinterpret, to misconstrue.

mesmérisme, *n.m.*, mesmerism.

mésoffrir, *v.n.*, to underbid.

mesquin, -e, *adj.*, mean, shabby ; paltry, poor.

mesquinement (-ki-n-màn), *adv.*, shabbily, meanly.

mesquinerie (-ki-n-rî), *n.f.*, meanness, shabbiness ; mean thing.

mess, *n.f.* (—), (milit.) mess, officers' table.

message, *n.m.*, message ; errand.

messag-er, *n.m.*, **-ère**, *n.f.*, messenger, forerunner ; carrier. *Les hirondelles sont les —ères du printemps ;* swallows are the forerunners of spring.

messagerie (mé-sa-jri), *n.f.*, stage-coach office ; stage-coach, coach, stage.

messaline, *n.f.*, a dissolute woman.

messe, *n.f.*, (c.rel.) mass. — *haute, grand'—* (— —s) ; high mass, grand mass. *Petite —, — basse ;* low mass. — *des morts, — de requiem ;* mass for the dead.

messéance, *n.f.*, unseemliness, unbecomingness.

messéant, -e, *adj.*, unseemly, unbecoming.

messeigneurs, *n.m.pl.*, my lords.

messeoir (mé-soâr), *v.n.*, to be unbecoming ; not to befit.

Ⓞ**messer** (-sèr), *n.m.*, mister, master.

messidor, *n.m.*, Messidor, the tenth month of the calendar of the first French republic, from June 19th to July 18th.

messie, *n.m.*, Messiah.

messier, *n.m.*, keeper of crops, of vineyards.

messieurs (mè-sieû), *n.m.pl.*, gentlemen, Messrs.

messire, *n.m.*, sir, squire.

messire jean, *n.m.* (—s —s), a variety of pear.

mestre, *n.m.* (nav.). *V.* **meistre**.

Ⓞ**mestre de camp**, *n.m.*, colonel of a horse or infantry regiment. — *général ;* brigadier-general.

Ⓞ**mestre de camp**, *n.f.*, the first company of a regiment.

mesurable, *adj.*, measurable.

mesurage, *n.m.*, measurement, measuring.

mesure, *n.f.*, measure ; dimension ; (mus.) measure, bar ; (fenc.) proper distance ; (poet.) metre, measure ; bound ; extent, limit ; decorum ; propriety. *Il a comblé la —;* he has heaped up the measure. *Au fur et à — que :* in proportion as ; according to. *Observer la — ;* to keep time. *Chanter en — ;* to keep time in singing. *Ne point garder de — avec une personne ;* to have no regard, no consideration, for a person. *Cette idée passe la — de son esprit ;* that idea is beyond the compass of his capacity. *Outre — ;* excessively, beyond measure. *À — que ;* in proportion as. *À — ;* in proportion, accordingly. *À — que l'un avançait, l'autre reculait ;* as one advanced, the other retired. *Vous n'avez qu'à travailler, et on vous paiera à — ;* you need only work, and you'll be paid accordingly. *Sans — ;* beyond all measure, immeasurable, unguardedly.

mesuré, -e, *part.*, measured, cautious ; circumspect. *Il est très — dans ses discours ;* he is very circumspect in what he says.

mesurer, *v.a.*, to measure ; to proportion, to compare, to consider. — *les autres à son aune ;* to measure other people's corn by one's own bushel. *À brebis tondue Dieu mesure le vent ;* God tempers the wind to the shorn lamb. — *ses discours ;* to be cautious in what one says.

se **mesurer**, *v.r.*, to measure one's self ; to be measured ; to vie, to contend ; to try one's strength ; to measure swords.

mesureur, *n.m.*, measurer, meter.

mésuser, *v.n.*, to misuse, to abuse, to make an ill use of.

métabole, *n.f.*, (rhet.) metabola.

métacarpe, *n.m.*, (anat.) metacarpus.

métacarpien, -ne, *adj.*, metacarpal.

métacentre, *n.m.*, (geom. nav.) metacentre.

métachronisme (-kro-), *n.m.*, metachronism.

métacisme, *n.m.*, metacism.

Ⓞ***métail**, *n.m.*, metallic composition ; metal.

métairie, *n.f.*, land held on condition that the landlord shall receive a settled portion of the produce ; small farm.

métal, *n.m.*, metal. — *vierge ;* native ore. *blanc anglais ;* Britannia metal. — *appliqué sur un autre ;* charge. — *précieux ;* precious metal.

métalepse, *n.f.*, (rhet.) metalepsis.

métallifère (-tal-li-), *adj.*, metalliferous.

métallique (-tal-lik), *adj.*, metallic.

Ⓞ**métallique**, *n.f. V.* **métallurgie**.

métallisation (-tal-li-), *n.f.*, (chem., metallization.

métalliser (-tal-li-), *v.a.*, (chem.) to metallize.

métallographie (-tal-lo-), *n.f.*, metallography.

métalloïde, *n.m.*, (chem.) metalloid.

métallurgie (-tal-lur-), *n.f.*, metallurgy.

métallurgique (-tal-lur-), *adj.*, metallurgic.

métallurgiste (-tal-lur-), *n.m.*, metallurgist.

métamorphique, *adj.*, metamorphic.

métamorphisme, *n.m.*, metamorphism.

métamorphose, *n.f.*, metamorphosis, transformation.

métamorphoser, *v.a.*, to metamorphose, to transform.

se **métamorphoser**, *v.r.*, to metamorphose one's self, to be metamorphosed.

métaphore, *n.f.*, (rhet.) metaphor.

métaphorique, *adj.*, metaphorical.

métaphoriquement (-rik-màn), *adv.*, metaphorically.

métaphrase, *n.f.*, metaphrase.

métaphraste, *n.m.*, metaphrast.

métaphysicien (-in), *n.m.*, metaphysician.

métaphysique, *n.f.*, metaphysics.

métaphysique, *adj.*, metaphysical.

métaphysiquement (-zik-màn), *adv.*, metaphysically.

métaphysiquer, *v.n.*, (fam.) to subtilize.

métaplasme, *n.m.*, (gram.) metaplasm.

métastase, *n.f.*, (med.) metastasis.

métatarse, *n.m.*, (anat.) metatarsus.

métathèse, *n.f.*, (gram.) metathesis.

métayage, *n.m.*, leasing farms on condition that the farmer shall give to the owner a settled portion of the produce.

métay-er, *n.m.*, **-ère**, *n.f.*, metayer, farmer holding land on condition of yielding to the owner a settled portion of the produce ; small farmer.

*méteil, *n.m.*, meslin (mixture of wheat and rye—*mélange de froment et de seigle*). *Pass :— ;* mixture consisting of two thirds of wheat and one of rye.

*méteil, *adj.*, of wheat mixed with rye.

métempsycose, *n.f.*, metempsychosis, transmigration of souls.

métempsycosiste, *n.m.f.*, one who believes in metempsycosis.

métemptose, *n.f.*, (astron.) metemptosis.

météore, *n.m.*, meteor.

météorique, *adj.*, meteoric.

météorisation, *n.f.*, (vet.) wind.

météorisé, -e, *adj.*, (med.) flatulent.

météorolithe, *n.m.*, meteorolite, aerolite.

météorologie, *n.f.*, meteorology.

météorologique, *adj.*, meteorological.

méteque, *n.m.*, (antiq.) an alien who was suffered to settle at Athens on paying a tax, but without enjoying civil rights.

méthode, *n.f.*, method ; custom, way. *Cet homme a une étrange* — ; that man has a strange way with him.

méthodique, *adj.*, methodical, systematical.

méthodiquement (-dik-măn), *adv.*, methodically, systematically.

méthodisme, *n.m.*, methodism.

méthodiste, *n.m.f.*, methodist.

méticuleusement, *adv.*, fastidiously, minutely.

méticuleu-x, -se, *adj.*, over-scrupulous, fastidious.

métier (-tié), *n.m.*, trade, handicraft, business, calling, craft, profession ; loom, frame ; framework. *Avoir le cœur au* — ; to have one's heart in a thing. *Il n'a pas le cœur au* — ; his heart does not go with his profession. *Le* — *des armes*; the profession of arms. *Il est du* — ; he is in the same trade, he belongs to the same fraternity. *C'est un tour de son* — ; that's a trick of his. *Chacun son* —, *et les vaches sont bien gardées;* every one to his trade. *Les hypocrites font* — *et marchandise de la dévotion* ; hypocrites make a trade of devotion.

méti-f, -ve, *adj.* V. **métis**.

métis (-tis), **-se**, *n.* and *adj.*, mongrel; of mongrel breed, half-bred.

métonomasie, *n.f.*, metonomasy.

métonymie, *n.f.*, (rhet.) metonymy.

métope, *n.f.*, (arch.) metope.

métoposcopie, *n.f.*, metoposcopy.

métoposcopique, *adj.*, metoposcopical.

mètre, *n.m.*, metre (1·093633 yards) ; (poet.) metre.

métrer, *v.a.*, to measure by the metre.

métrète, *n.f.*, (antiq.) measure of capacity, amphora ; quadrantal.

métreur, *n.m.*, (arch.) measurer (using the metre for his measurements); appraiser, valuer.

métrique, *n.f.*, scansion, versification.

métrique, *adj.*, metrical.

métrologie, *n.f.*, metrology.

métromane, *n.m.f.*, metromaniac.

métromanie, *n.f.*, metromania.

métropole, *n.f.*, metropolis, capital.

métropolitain, -e, *adj.*, metropolitan. *Église* —*e*; mother-church.

métropolitain, *n.m.*, metropolitan, bishop, archbishop.

métrorrhagie, *n.f.*, (med.), metrorrhagia, uterine hemorrhage.

mets (mê), *n.m.*, dish (food—*nourriture*).

mettable, *adj.*, that may be worn, wearable.

metteur, *n.m.*, putter. — *en œuvre* ; setter, mounter of jewels, &c —*de pierreries, &c.*). — *en pages;* (print.) maker-up, clicker.

mettre (mettant, mis), *v.a.*, to put ; to put out, to put in, to invest (money—*de l'argent*) ; to put on, to wear ; to place, to lay, to set ; to bring ; to reduce, to carry; to employ. — *au jour;* to bring to light ; to give birth to. — *à jour;* to bring up to date. — *en ordre ;* to set in order. — *la charrue devant les bœufs;* to put the cart before the horse. — *des paroles en musique;* to set words to music. — *de la prose en vers;* to turn prose into verse. — *du fard, du rouge;* to paint one's face. — *par écrit ;* to put in writing. — *une chose au net;* to write a thing out fair. — *un habit;* to put on a coat. — *le couvert;* to lay the cloth. — *un officier aux arrêts;* to put an officer under arrest. — *quelqu'un en état de;* to enable any one to. — *une chose en état à quelqu'un;* to persuade any one to do a thing. — *un livre au jour;* to publish a book. — *un vaisseau à l'eau;* to launch a ship.

— *quelqu'un à la besace ;* to reduce any one to beggary. — *un arrêt à exécution;* to execute a decree. — *bas;* to bring forth, to litter. — *quelqu'un dehors;* to turn any one out of doors. — *quelqu'un au fait;* to inform any one of a thing, of what is going on, of the state of affairs. — *quelqu'un à l'amende;* to fine any one. — *quelqu'un à la raison;* to bring any one to reason. — *deux personnes mal ensemble;* to set two persons by the ears. — *une affaire en compromis;* to submit a thing to arbitration. — *quelqu'un en peine;* to make any one uneasy. — *quelqu'un en colère;* to put any one into a passion. — *quelqu'un au désespoir;* to drive any one to despair. — *ordre à ses affaires;* to put one's affairs in order. *Il met son nez partout;* he thrusts his nose everywhere. — *en pages* (print) ; to make up, to click. *se* **mettre**, *v.r.*, to put one's self ; to sit down ; to dress; to begin; to stand. — *à table ;* to sit down at table. — *à la fenêtre;* to place one's self at the window. — *en danger;* to get into danger. — *en colère;* to put one's self into a passion. — *sur son quant-à-soi ;* to give one's self airs. — *dans le commerce;* to turn tradesman; to take to trade. — *à son aise;* to take one's ease. — *sur les rangs pour une charge ;* to enter one's self as a candidate for a place. — *en voyage;* to set out upon a journey. — *bien;* to dress well. — *mal avec quelqu'un;* to fall out with any one. *La peste se mit dans l'armée;* the plague broke out in the army. *Il se met à tout;* he turns his hand to everything. — *à parler;* to begin to speak.

mettre, *v.n.*, to set, to put. — *en mer;* to put to sea.

meublant, -e, *adj.*, serving to furnish; fit for furniture.

meuble, *n.m.*, household goods, furniture; piece of furniture; utensil. — *de famille;* heirloom. *Se mettre dans ses* —*s;* to furnish apartments of one's own.

meuble, *adj.*, movable; personal. *Biens—s et immeubles;* personal property. *Terre* —; mellow land.

meublé, -e, *part.*, furnished. *Être bien* —; to have one's house, one's rooms, nicely furnished.

meubler, *v.a.*, to furnish, to stock, to store. — *sa mémoire;* to store one's memory. — *une maison;* to furnish a house. — *une ferme;* to stock a farm.

se **meubler**, *v.r.*, to get furniture of one's own.

meubler, *v.n.*, to look well, to be ornamental.

meuglement, *n.m.* V. **beuglement**.

meugler, *v.n.* V. **beugler**.

meulard, *n.m.*, large millstone; grindstone.

meule, *n.f.*, millstone ; grindstone ; burr (of a deer's head—*de tête de fauve*) ; (agri.) cock, stack, rick ; (ich.) sun-fish. — *inférieure,* *gisante;* nether millstone, bedder. — *supérieure;* upper millstone, runner. — *de fromage;* large cheese shaped like a millstone.

meulerie, *n.f.*, millstone-works.

meulier, *n.m.*, millstone-maker.

meulière, *n.f.* and *adj.*, millstone, millstone-quarry ; for millstone. *Pierre* — ; stone fit for making millstones ; millstone.

meunerie (meû-n-ri), *n.f.*, trade of a miller.

meunier, *n.m.*, miller ; (ich.) pollard.

meunière, *n.f.*, miller's wife ; (orni.) long-tailed titmouse.

meurt de faim, *n.m.* (-). V. **mourir**.

meurtre, *n.m.*, murder, manslaughter. *Crier au* — ; to cry murder ; to complain bitterly.

meurtri, -e, *part.*, bruised, black and blue, contused. *Il est tout* —*de coups;* he is quite covered with bruises.

meurtri-er, **-ère**, *n.* and *adj.*, assassin, murderer; murderess; murdering, murderous.

meurtrière, n.f., (fort.) loophole; (arch.) balistraria.

meurtrir. v.a., to bruise, to contuse, to make black and blue.

meurtrissure. n.f., bruise, contusion.

meute. n.f., pack (of hounds—de chiens). Chef de —; whipper-in. leader of the band.

⊙**mévendre**, v.a., to undersell.

mévente. n.f., ⊙underselling; (com.) not selling, lack of sale.

mézair, n.m. V. **mésair**.

mézéréon. n.m., (bot.) mezereon.

mezzanine, n.f., (arch.) mezzanine.

mezzo-termine, n.m. (—), medium, middle course.

mezzo-tinto, n.m. (—), mezzotinto.

mgr. (ab. of Monseigneur,) my lord.

mi, invariable particle. mid, middle, half. Joined to the names of the months, or to the word carême, it forms with them feminine compound nouns which require the article: la mi-carême; Mid-Lent. La mi-août; the middle of August. It may also be joined to the nouns corps, jambe, chemin, mur, côte, terme, sucre, when the compound words thus formed require the preposition à and do not admit of the article: à mi-côte; half way up the hill. À mi-corps; up to the waist. V. **mi-parti**.

mi, n.m., (mus.) E, mi.

miasmatique, adj., miasmatic.

miasme. n.m., miasma, miasm.

miaulement (miôl-män), n.m., mewing (of cats—du chat).

miauler, v.n., to mew (of cats—du chat).

mica, n.m., (min.) mica, glimmer, glist, Muscovy glass.

micacé, **-e**, adj., micaceous.

micaschiste, n.m., (min.) mica-schist.

miche, n.f., round loaf; small loaf.

michel (la Saint-), n.f., Michaelmas.

micmac, n.m., secret practice, underhand dealing, intrigue.

micocoulier, n.m., (bot.) nettle-tree.

microcosme, n.m., microcosm.

micrographie, n.f., micrography.

micromètre, n.m., (astron.) micrometer.

microscope. n.m., microscope; magnifying-glass. Voir tout avec un —; to exaggerate everything.

microscopique, adj., microscopic, microscopical.

microzoaire. n.m., (zool.) microscopic animalcule. infusory.

miction, n.f., (med.) micturition.

midi. n.m, noon, noonday, noontide, mid-day, twelve o'clock (in the day); south; southern aspect. À —; at noon, at twelve o'clock. Le — de la vie; the meridian of life. À l'heure de —; at the hour of twelve. — est sonné; it has struck twelve. Chercher — à quatorze heures; to look for knots in a bulrush. — vrai; true meridian. — moyen; mean meridian. Les régions du —; the regions of the south.

mie. n.f., crum, crumb (soft part of bread—partie molle du pain); ⊙crum, crumb (very little bit—miette).

mie, adv., (l u.) not.

mie, n.f., (ab. of amie) dear, sweet, love; nurse. Ma —; my darling, my sweet, my love. Il appelle sa —; he calls his nurse.

miel, n.m., honey. Mouche à —; honey-bee. Rayon de —; honey-comb. Ruche à —; bee-hive. ⊙— aérien; manna. On prend plus de mouches avec du — qu'avec du vinaigre; fair means go farther than foul.

miellat, n.m., (bot.) honey-dew.

miellé, **-e**, adj., honey-coloured; honeyed, sweet, covered with honey.

mielleusement (-eûz-män), adv., sweetly, honey-like.

mielleu-x, **-se**, adj., honeyed, fair-spoken. Paroles —ses; honeyed words.

mien. **-ne** (mi-in, mi-è-n), adj., (l.u.) mine. Un — frère; a brother of mine. Le —, la —ne, les —s, les —nes, pron., mine. my own. Je ne demande que le —; I only ask for my own. Les —s; my friends, my relations. Faire des miennes; to play my tricks. [Used as adjective in the singular only, and always with the indefinite article un, une.]

miette, n.f., crumb, little bit.

mieux. adv., better; rather, best, more. J'aimerais —; I had rather. En —; for the better. De — en —; better and better. Je me porte le — du monde; I am as well as can be. Le — que je pourrai; as well as I can. Il a fait du — qu'il a pu; he has done his best. À qui — —; in emulation of one another. C'est on ne peut —; it cannot be better.

mieux, n.m., better; best. Le — est l'ennemi du bien; let well alone, beware in bettering a thing you do not make it worse. Il y a du — dans son état; he is better. Faire de son —, faire da — qu'on peut; to do one's best, to do the best one can. Au —; at best; for the best. Pour le —; for the best.

mieux, adj., better. Il n'y a rien de —; there is nothing better.

mièvre, adj., (fam.) arch, roguish; affected style of writing. Cet enfant est bien —; that child is very arch.

mièvrerie, or **mièvreté**, n.f., (fam.) roguishness, archness; piece of roguery, prank; affectedness in writing.

*****mignard**, **-e**, adj., delicate, pretty; mincing. Manières —es; mincing manners.

*****mignardement**, adv., delicately, daintily, mincingly.

*****mignarder**. v.a., to cocker, to fondle, to cuddle, to indulge. — un enfant; to cocker a child. — son style; to affect prettiness in one's style.

*****mignardise**, n.f., delicacy, delicateness; mincing; fondling, cockering, cuddling; (bot.) feathered pink. Il a de la — dans son langage; he is somewhat mincing in his language.

*****mignon**, **-ne**, adj., delicate, pretty, neat, tiny. Bouche —ne; pretty, small mouth. Pied —; neat foot. Argent —; spare money.

*****mignon**, n.m., darling, fondling, favourite; minion.

*****mignonne**, n.f., darling, fondling, favourite; a kind of pear; (print.) emerald, minion.

*****mignonnement**, adv., delicately, finely, nicely.

*****mignonnette**, n.f., minionette (sort of lace—espèce de dentelle); ground pepper; (bot.) feathered pink.

⊙*****mignoter**, v.a., (fam.) to fondle, to cocker; to cuddle.

⊙se **mignoter**, v.r., (fam.) to cocker one's self, to nurse one's self.

⊙*****mignotise**, n.f., (fam.) blandishment, endearment; caress.

migraine, n.f., megrim, headache.

migration, n.f., migration.

migratoire, adj., migratory.

mijaurée, n.f., (fam.) affected woman.

mijoter, v.a., (cook.) to cause to simmer; (fam.) to fondle, to cocker; (fig.) to contrive, to plot, to brew.

se **mijoter**, v.r., (fam.) to cocker one's self, to nurse one's self.

mikado. n m. (—s), Mikado.

mil, adj., one thousand. [Used for the first thousand in dates of the Christian era only.] L'an — huit cent cinquante; the year one thousand eight hundred and fifty.

mil. *n.m.*, (bot.) millet.

milady (-lè-), *n.f.* (*miladies*), my lady.

milan, *n.m.*, (orni.) kite.

milandre. *n.m.*, (ich.) tope.

milésiaque, *adj.*, of Miletus; applied to the fables and tales of Aristides of Miletus.

miliaire. *n.f.* and *adj.*, (med., anat.) miliaria; miliary. *Fièvre —;* miliaria, miliary fever.

milice, *n.f.*, militia; soldiery. soldiers; ⊙ war, warfare. *Soldat de la —;* militiaman. *Tirer pour la —;* to draw for the militia.

milicien (-si-in), *n.m.*, militiaman.

milieu, *n.m.*, middle, midst, heart, centre; expedient, medium, mean. *Au — de la foule;* in the midst of the crowd. *Au beau —;* in the very middle. *Au — des hommes;* among men. *L'air est le — dans lequel nous vivons;* the air is the medium in which we live. *Il faut savoir garder le juste —;* we must know how to observe the golden mean.

milieu. *adj.*, middle. [Only used in the expression: *le point —;* the middle point.]

militaire, *n.m.* and *adj.*, military man, soldier, military, soldiery; soldierly, soldierlike, warlike, military. *L'art, la discipline, —;* military art, discipline.

militairement (-tèr-mān), *adv.*, militarily.

militant, -e, *adj.*, (theol.) militant. *L'église —e;* the church militant.

militer. *v.n.*, to militate. *Cette raison milite pour moi;* that reason militates in my favour.

mille, *n.m.* and *adj.*, thousand, a thousand, one thousand. *Les — et une nuits;* the thousand and one nights. *On a dit cela — et — fois;* that has been said thousands of times. *Le premier —;* the first thousand.

mille, *n.m.*, mile (measure of length—*mesure de longueur*=1,609 mètres).

***mille-feuille,** *n.f.* (—),(bot.) milfoil.

mille-fleurs. *n.f.* (—), all-flower. *Eau de —;* cow's stale; oil of cow-dung. *Huile de —;* oil of cow-dung. *Rossolis de —;* cordial of all-flower.

millénaire (mil-lé-). *adj.*, millenary.

millénaire. *n.m.*, millennium; millenarian.

millénarisme, *n.m.*, millenarianism.

⊙**millepède.** *n.m. V.* **mille-pieds.**

mille-pertuis, *n.m.* (—), (bot.) St.-John's-wort.

mille-pieds, *n.m.* (—), (ent.) myriapod.

millépore, *n.m.*, millepore.

millésime (mil-lé-zi-m), *n.m.*, date, year, of a medal. coin, monument.

***millet,** *n.m.*, (bot.) millet grass, millet.

milliaire. *n.m.* and *adj.*, milestone; miliary. *Borne —, pierre —;* milestone. *— doré; (milliarum aureum)* the milestone set up by Augustus in the forum.

milliard, *n.m.*, one thousand millions.

milliasse. *n.f.*, (fam.) thousands (vast number —*grand nombre*).

millième, *n.m.* and *adj.*, thousandth.

millier, *n.m.*, thousand, thousand-weight. *— de fer;* thousand-weight of iron. *Un — d'arbres;* a thousand trees, thousands of trees. *On en trouve par —s;* they are to be found in thousands.

milligramme, *n.m.*, milligram (French weight; ·0154 grain).

millilitre, *n.m.*, millilitre (French measure; ·06103 cubic inch).

millimètre, *n.m.*, millimetre (French measure; ·03937 inch).

million. *n.m.*, million.

millionième, *n.m.* and *adj.*, millionth.

millionnaire. *n.m.f.* and *adj.*, millionaire; person extremely rich; worth millions. *C'est un —, il est —;* he is a millionaire, he is worth millions.

millouin, *or* **milouin,** *n.m.*, (orni.) poach-ard.

milord (-lor), *n.m.* (*milords*), lord; (pop.) rich man. *C'est un —;* he is a nabob.

milréis (-is), *n.m.*, millree (Portuguese coin —*monnaie portugaise*).

mime, *n.m.* and *adj.*, (antiq.) mime; mimer; mimic; mimical.

mimer, *v.a.*, to mimic.

mimique, *n.f.* and *adj.*, art of imitating, mimicry; mimic, mimical.

mimosa, *n.f.*, (bot.) mimosa, the sensitive-plant. [In botanical language mimosa and all other names of plants ending in *a* are masculine.]

mimule, *n.m.*, (bot.) monkey-flower.

minable, *adj.*, (fam.) pitiful, very shabby.

minage, *n.m.*, (feudalism—*féodalité*) toll levied on corn sold at market, corn duty.

minaret, *n.m.*, minaret.

minauder, *v.n.*, to be affected in one's manners, to be lackadaisical.

minauderie (mi-nô-drī), *n.f.*, affected, lackadaisical manners, lackadaisicalness.

minaudi-er, -ère, *adj.* and *n.*, affected, lackadaisical; affected, lackadaisical person.

mince. *adj.*, thin, slender, puny, shallow, poor, slight. *Esprit —;* shallow wit. *C'est un homme mince;* he is but a shallow man. *Taille —;* slim, slender, waist.

mine, *n.f.*, look, aspect, mien, appearance; show. *Il a la — trompeuse;* he has a deceitful look. *— fière;* proud look. *Il ne faut pas juger des gens à la —;* people should not be judged by their looks. *Homme de bonne —;* good-looking man. *Avoir bonne —;* to look well. *Avoir mauvaise —;* to look ill. *Il a la — d'être riche;* he looks like a rich man. *J'ai bien la — de payer vos folies;* it seems very likely that I shall have to pay for your follies. *Faire — d'être fâché;* to pretend to be angry. *Faire bonne — à quelqu'un;* to look pleasant at any one. *Faire bonne — à mauvais jeu;* to put a good face on the matter. *Faire la — à quelqu'un;* to pout at any one. *Faire la —;* to look displeased. *Payer de —;* to be all outside show.

mine, *n.f.*, mine; ore; source, store; mine (French measure, 78 litres); (Grec. antiq.) mina. *— d'or;* gold-mine. *— de charbon de terre;* coal-pit. *Le puits de la —;* the shaft of the mine. *— de plomb;* lead-mine; plumbago, black-lead pencil. *— d'argent cornée;* soft silver-ore. *— d'argent rouge;* silver-ore mixed with arsenic and sulphur. *— à bocarder;* ore rough from the mine. *— élevée;* upright mine. *— profonde;* mine with downward lodes. *— sèche;* hard ore. *—s vives;* rich mines. *Faire jouer une —* (milit.); to spring a mine. *Éventer la —* (milit.); to discover and destroy the enemy's mine; (fig.) to see through an intrigue and prevent it.

miner, *v.a.*, to mine, to undermine. to sap; to hollow, to waste, to wear away; to consume, to waste by slow degrees, to prey upon. *— un bastion* (milit.); to mine a bastion. *L'eau mine la pierre;* water wears away stone. *Cette maladie le mine;* that disease is wearing him away.

mineral, *n.m.*, ore. *— lavé;* buddled ore. *Extraire le —;* to dig ore. *— brut;* raw ore.

minéral —, *n.m.*, mineral.

minéral, -e, *adj.*, mineral.

minéralisateur, *n.m.*, (chem., min.) mineralizer.

minéralisateur, -rice, *adj.*, (chem., min.) mineralizing.

minéralisation, *n.f.* (chem., min.) mineralization.

minéraliser, *v.a.*, (chem., min.) to mineralize.

minéralogie, *n.f.*, mineralogy.

minéralogique, *adj.*, mineralogical, mineralogic.

minéralogiste, n.m., mineralogist.
⊙**minéralogue** (-log), n.m. V. **minéralogiste.**

minerve, n.f., (myth.) Minerva; (fam.) head, brain. *Tirer quelque chose de sa* —; to draw, to get, any thing from one's head. from one's brains.

minet, n.m., **-te,** n.f., puss, kitten.

mineur, n.m., miner, underminer, pitman.

mineur, -e, adj., minor, under age; minor, less, lesser; (mus.) minor. *Frère* —; Minorite, Franciscan.

mineur, n.m., **-e,** n.f., minor, (jur.) infant.

mineur, n.m., (mus.) minor-mode; (in convents — *dans les couvents*) minor.

mineure. n.f., (log.) minor; ⊙public disputation in divinity (at universities—*terme d'université*).

miniature, n.f., miniature. *Portrait en* —; miniature-portrait. *Peintre en* —; miniature-painter.

miniaturiste, n.m., miniature-painter.

mini-er, -ère, adj., pertaining, relating to mines.

minière, n f., earth, sand, or stone in which metal or mineral is found.

à **minimâ,** adv., (jur.) *Appel* —; appeal by the public prosecutor when he considers a sentence as too lenient.

minime, adj., very small, very slender, very trifling, trifling, inconsiderable.

⊙**minime,** n.f., (mus.) minim.

minime, n.m., Minim (monk—*moine*).

minimum (-nom), n.m. (—s), (math.) (*minima*), minimum.

ministère, n.m., ministry, agency; administration, department; minister's office; ministration. *Cela n'est pas de mon* — ; that does not belong to my office. *Le — des affaires étrangères, de l'intérieur, de la guerre;* the foreign, the home, the war, office.

ministériel, -le, adj., ministerial.

ministériellement (-rièl-mân), adv., ministerially.

ministre, n.m., minister; clergyman; servant. *Le premier* —; the prime minister, the premier. — *d'état;* minister of state. *Les —s de l'autel;* the priests.

minium (-om), n.m. (n.p.), (min.) minium, red lead.

minois, n.m., pretty face.

minon, n.m., puss; kitten.

minoratif, n.m., (med.) laxative, gentle aperient.

minorati-f, -ve, adj., laxative.

minorité, n.f., minority, nonage, (jur.) infancy.

minot, n.m., ⊙minot (French measure, 39 litres); (nav.) bumkin.

minotaure, n.m., (myth.) minotaur.

minoterie, n.f., flour export trade; flour mill.

minotier, n.m., miller, flour dealer; the owner of a *minoterie* (which see above).

minuit, n.m., midnight, twelve o'clock at night. *En plein* —; at the dead of night, in the middle of the night.

minuscule, adj., (of letters—*des lettres*) small.

minuscule, n.f., (print.) small capital.

minute, n.f., minute (of time—*de temps*); moment, instant; small hand (writing—*écriture*); first draught, rough draught, minute, copy; draught; (astron., arch., geom.) minute. *Homme à la* —; punctual man. *Faire la — de;* to make a rough draught of; to take minutes of. *Sablier de* —; minute-glass.

minuter, v.a., to draw up, to make a rough draught; to minute down; (l.u.) to design; to intend, to purpose.

minuterie (mi-nu-trî), n.f., (horl.) minute wheel-work; minute-wheels; minutes marked on a dial.

minutie (-ci), n.f., trifle, minutiæ.

minutieusement (-ci-eûz-mân), adv., minutely.

minutieu-x, -se, adj., minute; circumstantial.

mioche, n.m.f., (fam.) brat (little child—*petit enfant*).

mi-parti, -e, adj., bipartite, divided into two equal but different parts. *Les avis ont été —s;* the votes were equally divided.

miquelet (mi-klè), n.m., (in former times) Spanish bandit; (in modern use) a soldier for the guard of the Spanish provincial governors.

⊙**miquelot** (mi-klô), n.m., pilgrim that begs his way to any shrine dedicated to Saint Michael. *Faire le* —; to put on a sanctified, a sanctimonious, air.

mirabelle, n.f., (bot.) mirabelle (plum—*prune*).

miracle, n.m., miracle, wonder. *A* —; miraculously, extremely well, wonderfully well. *Faiseur de —s;* miracle-monger. *Crier* —; to cry wonder. *Crier au* —; to declare a thing a miracle. *Opérer des —s;* to work miracles.

miraculeusement (-leûz-mân), adv., miraculously, wonderfully.

miraculeu-x, -se, adj., miraculous, wonderful, marvellous.

mirage, n.m., mirage; looming.

miramolin, n.m., name given to the Calif of the Arabs by the writers of the middle age.

mirauder, or **miroder,** v.a., to dress; to gaze at. — *un œuf;* to try an egg (by holding it up to the light—*en le tenant à la lumière*).

mire, n.f., (artil.) aim; (of firearms—*d'armes à feu*) foresight. *Prendre sa* —; to take aim. *Point de* —; point aimed at; object, end, in view.

miré, adj., (hunt.) whose tusks are curved inwards (of boars—*du sanglier*).

mirer, v.a., to aim, to take aim, to aim at, to have in view; to look at. — *une place;* to aim at a situation. — *des œufs;* to try eggs (by holding them up to the light—*en les tenant à la lumière*).

se **mirer,** v.r., to look at one's self in a glass; to admire one's self. — *dans ses plumes;* to take pride in one's beauty and dress.

mirer, v.n., (nav.) to loom, to appear indistinctly; (of precious stones—*des pierres précieuses*) to have but few angles, few facets; to take aim.

miretto, n.f., (bot.) Venus's-looking-glass. V. **miroir.**

mirifique, adj., wonderful, marvellous; admirable.

mirliflore, n.m., exquisite, fop, dandy, coxcomb.

mirlirot, n.m., corruption of **mélilot,** which see.

mirliton, n.m., reed-pipe.

mirmidon, or **myrmidon,** n.m., (hist.) Myrmidon; shrimp, pigmy (pers.).

miroder, v.a. V. **mirauder.**

miroir, n.m., mirror, looking-glass, glass; (opt.) mirror; speculum. *Étamer un* —; to foliate a looking-glass. — *ardent;* burning-mirror. *Des œufs au* —; fried eggs. — *de Vénus;* (bot.) Venus's-looking-glass.

miroitant, -e, adj., reflecting like a mirror.

miroité, -e, adj., (of horses—*du cheval*) dapple-bay.

miroitement, n.m., reflexion of the light by polished surfaces; flashing, brilliancy.

miroiter, v.n., to reflect light, to flash, to shine.

miroiterie (mi-roa-trî), n.f., looking-glass trade or business.

miroitier (-tié), *n.m.*, looking-glass maker.

miroton, *n.m.*, (cook.) miroton (dish composed of meats already cooked—*mets composé de viandes déjà cuites*).

mis, (abbreviation of Marquis).

misaine, *n.f.*, (nav.) fore. *Mât de —*; foremast. *Voile de —*; foresail.

misanthrope, *n.m.*, misanthrope, misanthropist, man-hater.

misanthropie, *n.f.*, misanthropy.

misanthropique, *adj.*, misanthropic; misanthropical.

miscellanées, *n.m.pl.*, miscellanea, miscellany.

mischna, *n.m.* (*n.p.*), mischna, mishna.

miscibilité, *n.f.*, miscibility.

miscible, *adj.*, miscible.

mise, *n.f.*, laying, placing; dress, manner of dressing; stake; bidding (at auctions—*aux enchères*); (l.u.) circulation (of coin—*de monnaie*). *— à l'eau*; launch (of a ship—*d'un vaisseau*). *— hors*; (com.) outlay. *Cet homme est de —*; that man is presentable. *Cette raison n'est pas de —*; that reason will not pass. *Cette étoffe n'est pas de —*; that stuff is not worn, not in fashion, not fashionable. *Avoir une — simple*; to wear a plain dress. *Sa — était de cinq francs*: he had staked five francs. *— en possession*; taking possession. *— en accusation*; bringing up for trial. *— en liberté*; enlargement. *— en scène*; (thea.) getting up of a dramatic piece. *— en vente*; putting up for sale. *— en œuvre*; working of any thing. *— en pages*; (print.) clicking, making-up. *— en train*; (print.) making ready.

mise, (abbreviation of Marquise).

miser, *v.n.*, (local ex.) to bid (at auctions —*aux enchères*).

misérable, *adj.*, miserable. wretched; wicked; sorry, worthless.

misérable, *n.m.f.*, wretch, miserable wretch, miscreant. *C'est un —*; he is a villain. *C'est une —*; she is a wretch.

misérablement, *adv.*, miserably, wretchedly; worthlessly, wickedly.

misère, *n.f.*, misery, wretchedness, distress, want; trouble, plague, grievous thing; trifle, trifling thing. *Il est mort de faim et de —*; he died of starvation and want. *Le monde n'est que — et vanité*: the world is but misery and vanity. *Prendre le collier de —*; to make one's self a drudge.

miséréré, *n.m.*, (med.) iliac passion; (e.rel.) miserere (51st psalm).

miséricorde, *n.f.*, mercy, tenderness, mercifulness; pardon, quarter, grace, forgiveness, pitifulness; small seat. *Crier —*; to cry for mercy. *Il ne mérite point de —*; he deserves no mercy. *Faire —*; to show mercy. *À tout péché —*; one ought to forgive all offences. *—! il va se tuer*; mercy upon me! he will kill himself.

miséricordieusement (-eûz-măn), *adv.*, mercifully, compassionately.

miséricordieu-x, -se, *adj.*, merciful, compassionate, forgiving, pitiful.

miss, *n.f.* (—), miss, young lady.

missel, *n.m.*, missal; mass-book.

mission, *n.f.*, mission. *Envoyer en —*; to send on a mission. *Remplir une —*; to perform a mission.

missionnaire, *n.m.*, missionary.

missive, *n.f.* and *adj.*, missive.

mistigri, *n.m.*, pam (card game —*jeu de cartes*).

mistral, or **maëstral**, *n.m.*, (local ex.) north-west wind.

mistriss, *n.f.* (*n.p.*), Mrs.

mitaine, *n.f.*, mitten.

mite, *n.f.*, (ent.) mite; maggot.

mithra, *n.m.*, (antiq.) Mithra, the Sun (Persia).

mithridate, *n.m.*, (pharm.) mithridate. *Vendeur de —*; quack; braggadocio.

mitigation, *n.f.*, mitigation.

mitigé, -e, *part.*, mitigated. *Peine —e*; mitigated penalty.

mitiger, *v.a.*, to mitigate, to soften, to make less severe.

miton, *r.m.*, woman's mitten.

mitonner, *v.n.*, to lie soaking or stewing; to soak, to stew.

mitonner, *v.a.*, to cocker, to fondle, to cuddle. *— quelqu'un*; to humour any one. *— une affaire*; to prepare an affair gradually. *Il aime qu'on le mitonne*: he likes to be cockered. *se mitonner*, *v.r.*, to nurse one's self, to cocker one's self; (cook.) to simmer.

mitoyen, -ne (mi-toa-yin, -iè-n), *adj.*, middle; intermediate. *Mur —*; party-wall. *Cloison —ne*; partition wall between two rooms. *Mitoyenne de —*; partition wall between two rooms.

mitoyenneté (-toa-ie-n-té), *n.f.*, joint property claims of two neighbours to a wall, hedge, or ditch.

*****mitraillade**, *n.f.*, discharge, fire of grape-shot.

*****mitraille**. *n.f.*, ☉ old iron; grapeshot; case-shot, canister-shot, canister; small charge, coppers; (nav.) langrage, langrel-shot. *Charge à —*; case-shot.

mitrailler, *v.a.* and *n.*, to fire grapeshot, canister-shot.

mitrailleuse, *n.f.*, (artil.) mitrailleuse, mitrailleur.

mitre, *n.f.*, mitre; chimney-pot (shaped like a mitre—*en forme de mitre*).

mitré, -e, *adj.*, mitred.

mitron, *n.m.*, journeyman baker.

mixte, *adj.*, mixed; mixt; (bot.) common (of buds—*des boutons*).

mixte, *n.m.*, mixed body.

*****mixtiligne**, *adj.*, (geom.) mixtilineal, mixtilinear.

mixtion (miks-ti-on), *n.f.*, (pharm.) mixture, mixtion, mixing.

mixtionner (miks-tio-né), *v.a.*, to mix, to mingle.

mixture, *n.f.*, (pharm.) mixture.

mlle, (ab. of Mademoiselle).

mm., (ab. of Messieurs).

mme, (ab. of Madame).

mnémonique, *adj.*, mnemonic, mnemonical.

mnémonique or **mnémotechnie**, *n.f.*, mnemonics, mnemotechny.

mobile, *adj.*, movable; changeable, unsteady, variable; quick, lively.

mobile, *n.m.*, mover, spring, motive power; a soldier of the *garde mobile*. *Premier —*; prime mover; *primum mobile*; ringleader. *L'intérêt est le plus grand — des hommes*: interest is the prime mover of human actions.

mobile, *n.f.*, *garde mobile* (corps).

mobiliaire, *adj.*, movable, personal.

mobili-er, -ère, *adj.*, movable; personal, of personal property. *Succession —ère*; inheritance of personal property.

mobilier, *n.m.*, movables, furniture.

mobilisable, *adj.*, (milit.) that can be mobilized.

mobilisation, *n.f.*, act of making movable; giving by agreement the quality of personal property to real property; (milit.) mobilization.

mobiliser, *v.a.*, to convert into movables; to give by agreement the quality of personal property to real property; (milit.) to draft for active service, to mobilize.

mobilité, *n.f.*, mobility. variableness, inconstancy, unsteadiness, unfixedness. *—*—*de caractère*; versatility of disposition.

mocassín, *n.m.*, moccassin (shoe—*chaussure*).

modale. *n.f.* and *adj.*, (log.) modal.

modalité, *n.f.*, (log.) modality.

mode, *n.f.*, mode, fashion, vogue ; way ; *pl.*, millinery. *C'est la dernière* — : it is the newest fashion. *Un habit à la* — ; a fashionable coat. *Se mettre à la* — ; to dress in the fashion. *Être à la* — ; to be in fashion. *Du bœuf à la* — ; beef a-la-mode.

mode. *n.m.*, (gram , log., mus.) mode. mood.

modelage (mo-dlaj), *n.m.*, modelling.

modelé (mo-dlé), *n.m.*, (sculp.) model (imitation).

modèle. *n.m.*, model, copy, pattern. — *d'écriture* ; copy-slip. *Conformez-vous au* — ; keep to the pattern. *Faire le métier de* — ; to serve as a model. — *parfait* ; perfect model, paragon.

modeler (mo-dlé), *v.a* , to model, to form, to shape.

se modeler, *v.r.*, to take for one's pattern. to take pattern. *Il se modèle sur son frère* ; he takes pattern by his brother.

modeler. *v.a.*, to model.

modeleur (mo-dleur), *n.m.*, modeller.

modénature, *n.f.*, (arch.) proportion, profile and sweep of a cornice moulding.

modérat-eur, *n.m.*, **-rice**, *n.f.*, moderator. moderatrix.

modération, *n.f.*, moderation ; abatement, diminution ; mitigation.

modéré, -e, *adj.*, moderate, reasonable.

modérément, *adv.*, moderately, in moderation.

modérer, *v.a.*, to moderate, to abate; to restrain, to restrict ; to lessen, to reduce. — *ses passions* ; to curb one's passions. — *le zèle de quelqu'un* ; to cool any one's zeal.

se modérer, *v.r.*, to moderate, to moderate one's self, to keep one's temper ; to restrain one's self. *Le temps s'est modéré* ; the weather has become more temperate.

moderne, *adj.*, modern. *À la* — ; in the modern style.

moderne. *n.m.*, modern.

moderner, *v.a.*, (arch., l.u.) to modernize.

moderniser, *v.a.*, to modernize.

moderniste, *n.m.*, modernist.

modeste. *adj.*, modest, unassuming.

modestement, *adv.*, modestly.

modestie, *n.f.*, modesty, coyness.

modicité. *n.f.*, smallness, moderateness.

modificati-f. -ve, *adj.*, modifying.

modificatif. *n.m.*, (gram.) modifying word.

modification, *n.f.*, modification.

modifier. *v.a.*, to modify.

*modillon, *n.m.*, (arch.) modillion.

modique. *adj.*, moderate, small.

modiquement (-dik-mân), *adv.*, moderately.

modiste, *n.m.f.*, man-milliner ; milliner.

modulation, *n.f.*, modulation.

module. *n.m.*, (arch.) module ; (alg.) modulus: diameter of medals—*de médailles*.

moduler. *v.a.* and *n.*, to modulate.

moelle, *n.f.*, marrow, pith, medulla. *Os à* —. marrow-bone. — *d'arbre* ; pith of a tree.

moelleusement, *adv.*, softly, with softness : (paint.) with mellowness.

moelleux, *n.m* , (paint.) mellowness ; softness.

moelleu-x. -se. *adj.*, full of marrow. marrowy : pithy ; soft ; mellow. *Voix —se* ; mellow voice. *Vin —* ; mellow vine. *Discours* —; pithy discourse.

moellon, *n.m.*, ashlar. *Maçonnerie de* — ; ashlar-work.

O mœuf, *n.m.* (gram.) mood.

mœurs (meurs), *n.f. pl.*, manners, morals, habits, inclinations, ways ; customs. *Avoir des* —; to be a man of morals. *N'avoir pas de* — ; to be immoral. *Un homme sans* — ; an unprincipled man. *Les — des animaux* ; the habits of animals.

mofette. *or* **moufette**, *n.f.*, (l.u.) firedamp (mines) ; ☉(chem.) any poisonous gas; (mam.) mephitic weasel. — *atmosphérique*, azote. azotic gas.

mogol. *n.m.*, Mogul.

☉**mohatra**. *adj.*, (law) usurious. *Contrat* — ; usurious agreement for selling at a high price on credit. and repurchasing at once at a low price but for cash.

moi. *personal pron.*, I, me, to me. — *! trahir le meilleur de mes amis !* what ! I betray my best friend ! *C'est* — ; it is I. *Venez à* —; come to me *Quant à* — : as for me. —*-même* ; myself. *À* — *!* help! help ! *Parlez-* —; speak to me. *Donnez-le-* — ; give it me.

moi, *n.m.*, self.

moïdore. *n.m.*, moidore (Portuguese coin —*monnaie portugaise*).

*moignon. *n.m.*, stump (of amputated limbs. of branches of a tree cut off—*d'un membre amputé, d'une branche d'arbre coupée*).

*moinaille, *n.f.*, (b.s.) monks.

moindre. *adj.*, less, least. *La — chose* ; the least thing. *Je n'en ai pas le — souvenir* ; I have not the least remembrance of it.

moine. *n.m.*, monk, friar ; wooden warming-pan ; (print.) friar. — *lai* ; lay-monk. *Gras comme un* — ; as fat as a pig. *L'habit ne fait pas le* — ; it is not the cowl that makes the friar.

moineau, *n.m.*, sparrow. *Tirer sa poudre aux —x* ; to waste one's powder and shot.

moinerie (moa-n-rî), *n.f.*, monkhood.

moinesse, *n.f.*, (jest.) nun.

*moinillon. *n.m.*, petty monk.

moins. *adv.*, less. under, wanting, to ; minus. *Parlez* — ; speak less. *C'est — que rien* ; it is next to nothing. *Ni plus ni* — ; neither more nor less. *Il ne s'agit de rien — que de sa vie* ; nothing less than his life is at stake. *Il n'est rien — que sage* ; he is anything but prudent. *Il n'y a rien de — vrai que cette nouvelle* ; no news can be further from the truth than this. *Il est une heure — un quart* ; it wants a quarter to one. *A* — ; for less. *Vous ne l'aurez pas à* — ; you shall not have it for less. *À — de* ; for less than ; unless. *À — que* ; unless. —*value* (—*s*) ; inferior value.

moins. *n.m.*, least, less ; (alg.) minus. *C'est le — que vous puissiez faire* ; it is the least you can do. *Pas le — du monde* ; not in the least. *Au —* ; at least.

moirage, *n.m.*, (manu.) watering (stuffs, &c.—*d'étoffes, &c.*).

moire. *n.f.*, (manu.) watering ; moire.

moiré, -e, *adj.*, (manu.) watered.

moirer, *v.a.*, (manu.) to water (stuffs—*les étoffes*).

mois. *n.m.*, month ; monthly allowance ; month's pay.

moise. *n.f.*, (carp.) couple.

moiser, *v.a.*, (carp.) to bridge over.

moisi. *n.m.*, mouldiness, mustiness.

moisi, -e. *part.*, mouldy, musty.

moisir, *v.a.*, to mould. to make mouldy, to make musty.

se moisir, *v.r.*, to grow mouldy, to grow musty.

moisir. *v.n.*, to grow mouldy, musty.

moisissure *n.f.*, mouldiness, mustiness.

moissine. *n.f.*, a bundle of vine-branches with the grapes hanging to them.

moisson, *n.f.*, harvest ; harvest-time.

moissonner, *v.a.*, to reap, to cut down, to crop, to mow. — *un champ;* to reap a field.

moissonneu-r, *n.m.*, **-se**, *n.f.*, reaper, harvestman, harvest-woman.

moissonneuse, *n.f.*, (agri.) reaping machine.

moite, *adj.*, moist, damp.

moiteur, *n.f.*, moisture, dampness.

moitié (-tié), *n.f.*, moiety, half; (fam.) better half, wife. *C'est trop cher de — ;* it is too dear by half. *Je l'ai laissé à — chemin ;* I have left him half way. *Être de — avec quelqu'un;* to go halves with any one.

moitié, de moitié, à moitié, *adv.*, half, by half.

moka, *n.m.*, moka. *Du café —;* moka coffee.

mol, *adj.m.* V. **mou**.

molaire, *n.f.* and *adj.*, molar-tooth, mill-tooth, jaw-tooth; molar.

môle, *n.m.*, mole, jetty-head; pier.

môle, *n.f.*, (med.) mole.

moléculaire, *adj.*, molecular.

molécule, *n.f.*, molecule, particle.

molène, *n.f.*, (bot.) mullen, mullein.

molestation, *n.f.*, molestation.

molester, *v.a.*, to molest, to trouble.

molette, *n.f.*, rowel (of a spur—*d'éperon*) ; (vet.) windgall ; muller (for colours—*pour broyer les couleurs*).

molinisme, *n.m.*, molinism.

moliniste, *n.m.*, molinist.

molinosisme, *n.m.*, quietism, Molino's system.

mollah, *n.m.* (—s), Mollah.

mollasse, *adj.*, flabby, flimsy.

molle, *n.f.*, (ich.) sun-fish.

molle, *n.f.* V. **mou**.

mollement (mol-män), *adv.*, softly, slackly; feebly; effeminately. *Vivre —;* to live an effeminate life.

mollesse, *n.f.*, softness, laxness; slackness, tameness, weakness, indolence; effeminacy. *Vivre dans la — ;* to live in effeminacy.

mollet, -te, *adj.*, soft; light (of bread—*du pain*). *Des œufs —s:* soft-boiled eggs. *Lit — ;* soft bed. *Pain — ;* light bread.

mollet, *n.m.*, calf (of the leg—*de la jambe*).

molleton (mol-ton), *n.m.*, swan-skin.

mollification, *n.f.*, mollification, softening.

mollifier, *v.a.*, to mollify, to soften.

mollir, *v.n.*, to soften, to grow soft; to slacken, to flag, to abate, to faint, to yield. *Le vent mollit;* the wind slackens.

mollusque, *n.m.*, mollusk.

molosse, *n.m.*, (Latin, Gr. poet.) a foot of three long syllables ; house-dog, large mastiff ; a genus of American bats.

moly, *n.m.*, a plant mentioned by Homer; wild garlic.

molybdène, *n.m.*, (min.) molybden, molybdena.

moment, *n.m.*, moment ; (mec.) momentum. *Attendez un —;* stop a moment. *Il a des —s de bonté ;* he has fits of kindness. *Voici le — de se décider ;* now is the time for decision. *Un —,* j'ai à vous parler; one moment, I want to speak to you. *Au — de;* on the point of, just as. *Au — où, au — que ;* the instant that. *Du — que;* as soon as. *Du — que vous le voulez ;* since you will have it. *Je l'attends d'un — à l'autre;* I expect him every moment. *Dans le — ;* in a moment, in a minute. *En ce — ;* at this moment. *À tout —, à tous —s ;* every instant, at every turn.

momentané, -e, *adj.*, momentary.

momentanément, *adv.*, momentarily, for the moment.

momerie (mô-mri), *n.f.*, mummery.

momie (mô-), *n.f.*, mummy; dark thin person.

mon, *possessive adj.m.*, **ma**, *f.*, **mes**, *pl.m.f.*, my. *Mon père, ma mère et mes enfants;* my father, mother and children. *Mon âme;* my soul. *Mon unique ressource:* my only resource. *Mon bon et digne ami;* my good and worthy friend. [*Mon* is used instead of *ma* before a vowel or silent *h*.]

monacal, -e, *adj.*, monachal.

monacalement (-kal-män), *adv.*, like a monk.

monachisme (-shism), *n.m.*, monachism.

monade, *n.f.*, monad.

monadelphié, *n.f.*, (bot.) monadelphia.

monandrie, *n.f.*, (bot.) monandria.

monarchie (-shi), *n.f.*, monarchy.

monarchique (-shik), *adj.*, monarchical, monarchic.

monarchiquement (-shik-män), *adv.*, monarchically.

monarchiser (-shi-zé), *v.a.*, to monarchize.

monarchiste (-shist), *n.m.*, monarchist.

monarque, *n.m.*, monarch.

monastère, *n.m.*, monastery, convent.

monastique, *adj.*, monastic, monastical.

monaut, *adj.m.*, one-eared (animal).

monceau, *n.m.*, heap.

mondain, -e, *n.* and *adj.*, worldling; worldly, worldly-minded; mundane ; earthly.

mondainement (-dè-n-män), *adv.*, mundanely, worldly.

mondanité, *n.f.*, worldliness, worldly vanities.

monde, *n.m.*, world, universe; mankind, men ; people ; company. *Faire le tour du — ,* to sail round the world. *L'autre — ;* the next world. *Dans l'autre — ;* hereafter. *Il n'est plus du — ;* he is dead. *L'an du — ;* in the year of the world. *Il voit beaucoup de — ;* he sees a great deal of company. *Peu de —, pas grand — ;* few people, not many people. *Avoir du — ;* to have company ; to be accustomed to society. *Connaître son — ;* to know whom one has to deal with. *Le mieux du — ;* the best in the world. *Le beau — ;* people of fashion. *Le petit — ;* little people. *Ainsi va le — ;* such is the world. *Tout votre — est-il arrivé?* is all your company come? *Venir au — ;* to come into the world.

monde, *adj.*, (rel.) clean.

mondé, -e, *part.*, cleansed. *De l'orge — ;* hulled barley.

monder, *v.a.*, to cleanse ; to hull (barley, &c.—*orge, &c.*)

mondificati-f, -ve, *adj.*, (med.) cleansing.

mondifier, *v.a.*, (med.) to cleanse, to wash.

monétaire, *adj.*, monetary.

monétisation, *n.f.*, making and stamping money; minting.

monétiser, *v.a.*, to give currency to paper-money.

moniteur, *n.m.*, monitor, adviser.

monition, *n.f.*, (ecc.) monition.

monitoire, *n.m.*, *adj.*, (ecc.) monitory.

monitorial, -e, *adj.*, (ecc.) monitory.

monnaie, *n.f.*, coin, money; change ; mint; coinage; currency. *Hôtel de la — ;* the mint. *Fausse — ;* counterfeit coin. *Battre — ;* to coin money; to raise money. *Papier — ;* paper-money. *— de compte;* nominal, imaginary, money. *— courante;* current money. *— faible;* light money. *— légale ;* legal tender. *Petite — ;* small change. *Donnez-moi la — d'un franc;* give me change for a franc. *Payer en — de singe ;* to laugh at one's creditors, instead of paying them. *Rappeler la — ;* to call in money.

○**monnaierie**, *n.f.*, smithery (at the mint —*à l'hôtel des monnaies*).

monnayage, *n.m.*, coining.

monnayer, *v.a.*, to coin.

monnayeur, *n.m.*, coiner, minter. *Faux —*; coiner of base money.

mono, a prefix from Gr. μόνος.

monocéros, *n.m.*, monoceros, unicorn, narwhal.

monochrome, *n.m.* and *adj.*, monochrome; monochromatic.

monocle, *n.m.*, single eye-glass.

monocorde, *n.m.*, monochord.

monocotylédone, *n.f.* and *adj.*, (bot.) monocotyledon, endogen; monocotyle, mon-ocotyledonous, endogenous.

monodie, *n.f.*, monody.

monœcie (-nè-sî), *n.f.*, (bot.) monœcia.

monogame, *n.m.f.* and *adj.*, monogamist; monogamous.

monogamie, *n.f.*, monogamy.

monogrammatique, *adj.*, monogrammatic, monogrammic.

monogramme, *n.m.*, monogram.

monographie, *n.f.*, monography.

monoïque, *adj.*, (bot.) monœcious, mon-œcian.

monolithe, *n.m.* and *adj.*, monolith; monolithic, monolithal.

monologue (-log), *n.m.*, monologue; solilo-quy.

monomane, *n.m.f.* and *adj.*, monomaniac; monomaniacal.

monomanie, *n.f.*, monomania.

monôme, *n.m.*, (alg.) monome.

monopétale, *adj.*, (bot.) monopetalous.

monophylle, *adj.*, (bot.) monophyllous.

monopole, *n.m.*, monopoly.

monopoleur, *n.m.*, monopolist.

monopoliser, *v.a.*, to monopolize.

monoptère, *adj.*, (arch.) monopteral.

monorime, (poet.) with but one rhyme, being a monorhyme.

monosépale, *adj.*, (bot.) monosepalous.

monosperme, *adj.*, (bot.) monospermous.

monostique, *n.m.*, monostich.

monosyllabe, *n.m.* and *adj.*, (gram.) monosyllable; monosyllabic.

monosyllabique, *adj.*, monosyllabic.

monothéisme, *n.m.*, monotheism.

monothéiste, *n.m.* and *adj.*, monotheist; monotheistic.

monothélisme, *n.m.*, monothelitism.

monothélite, *n.m.*, monothelite.

monotone, *adj.*, monotonous.

monotonie, *n.f.*, monotony.

monotriglyphe, *n.m.*, (arch.) mono-triglyph.

mons, *n.m.*, ab. of Monsieur, sir; used in contempt, but not in writing.

*monseigneur, *n.m.* (*messeigneurs, nossei-gneurs*), my lord.

*monseigneur, *n.m.* (—*s*), crowbar (used by burglars— *employé par les voleurs*).

*monseigneuriser, *v.a.*, (jest.) to style my lord one who has no right to it.

monsieur (meu-sieu), *n.m.*, sir, gentleman; this gentleman, the gentleman. — *A.* ; Mr. *A. Non,* —; no sir. — *dit* ; the gentleman says; this gentleman says; Mr. (so-and-so) says. *Faire le* —; to play the fine gentleman. *C'est un vilain* —; he is a disagreeable fellow. *Mon-sieur;* the king of France's brother.

monstre, *n.m.*, monster.

monstrueusement (-eûz-măn), *adv.*, monstrously, prodigiously.

monstrueu-x, -se, *adj.*, monstrous, pro-digious.

monstruosité, *n.f.*, monstrosity, anomaly.

mout, *n.m.*, mount, mountain. *Le* — *Etna.* mount Etna. *Aller par* —*s et par vaux;* to go

over hill and dale. — *-de-piété* (—*s* —); mont-de-piété, lombard, lombard-house. *Commission-naire au* —*-de-piété;* pawnbroker.

montage, *n.m.*, carrying up; taking up; (arts) mounting, setting, putting together.

*montagnard, -e, *adj.*, inhabiting the mountains.

*montagnard, *n.m., -e*, *n.f.*, mountaineer, highlander; democrat of the Convention and of the National Assembly of France, 1793.

*montagne, *n.f.*, mountain; party of the democrats in the Convention and in the National Assembly of France, 1793. *Chaîne de* —*s;* range, ridge, of mountains. *La* — *a enfanté une souris;* the mountain has brought forth a mouse.

*montagneu-x, -se, *adj.*, mountainous, hilly.

montanisme, *n.m.*, montanism.

montaniste, *n.m.*, montanist.

montant, *n.m.*, upright; amount, sum total; ⊙next for promotion; (carp.) upright, door-post; high flavour.

montant, -e, *adj.*, ascending, rising; flowing, coming in; high-necked (of dresses— *des robes*); (milit.) relieving. *Un chemin* — *;* an up-hill road. *La marée* —*e;* the flowing tide. *Une robe* —*e;* a high-necked dress. *La garde* —*e* (milit.) ; the relieving guard.

monte, *n.f.*, (of animals—*des animaux*) season for covering.

montée, *n.f.*, stair, staircase, pair of stairs; acclivity, ascent; (arch.) height.

monter, *v.n.*, to go up, to come up, to get up, to ascend, to mount, to ride; to rise; to come in; to grow up, to shoot, to increase; to amount. — *et descendre;* to go up and down. — *sur un arbre;* to climb up a tree. — *à sa chambre;* to go up to one's room. — *à cheval;* to ride on horseback. — *en chaire;* to mount the pulpit. *Montez!* come up! up with you! — *sur le Parnasse;* to turn poet. *La marée monte;* the tide is coming in.

monter, *v.a.*, to mount, to carry up, to lift up; to make up; to raise, to prepare; to wind up; to mount, to ride; to put together; to furnish, to supply. — *une montre;* to wind up a watch. — *un diamant;* to set a diamond. — *sa lyre;* to tune one's lyre. — *le gouvernail;* to hang the rudder. — *un vaisseau;* to have the command of a vessel. — *la garde;* to mount guard. — *un cheval;* to mount a horse; to train a horse.

se monter, *v.r.*, to amount; to rise; to be irritated; to supply one's self, to take in a stock, a supply.

monteur, *n.m.*, setter, mounter (of jewel-lery — *de joyaux*).

montgolfière, *n.f.*, fire-balloon.

monticule, *n.m.*, hillock.

montie (-ti), *n.f.*, (bot.). *V.* mouron.

mont-joie, *n.f.* (—*s* —), title of the first king at arms in France; ancient war-cry of the French.

⊙**mont-joie**, *n.f.* (—*s* —), heap of stones (to commemorate any event—*en mémoire d'un événement*).

montoir, *n.m.*, horse-block. *Cheval doux au* —; an easy horse to get upon.

montrable, *adj.*, that can be shown.

montre, *n.f.*, watch; sample; show, parade; show-case, show-window. — *à réveil;* alarum-watch. — *à répétition;* repeating-watch. — *à double boîte;* double-cased watch. — *à savon-nette;* hunting-watch. — *détraquée;* watch out of order. *Il est une heure à ma* —; it is one o'clock by my watch. *Faire* — *de son esprit;* to show off one's wit.

montrer, *v.a.*, to show, to exhibit, to point out; to teach; to set forth. — *une chose au doigt;* to point out a thing. — *la porte à* quelqu'un; to show any one the door. — quelqu'un du doigt; to point one's finger at any one. Se faire — du doigt; to get pointed at. Cela montre la corde; that is threadbare.

se **montrer**, v.r., to show one's self; to appear; to prove one's self; to look.

montreur, n.m., shower.

montueu-x, **-se**, adj., hilly, mountainous.

monture, n.f., animal for riding; nag; mounting, setting (of gems—des pierreries); head-stall (of a bridle—de bride). — d'un fusil; stock of a gun. — d'éperon; spur leather.

monument, n.m., monument; tomb.

monumental, **-e**, adj., monumental.

moquable, adj., deserving of mockery.

moque, n.f., (nav.) dead-eye, dead-block. — à un trou; heart. — de civadière de tréiingage; sprit-sail sheet-block.

se **moquer**, v.r., to mock, to make game of, to make fun of, to make a fool of, to ridicule, to laugh at; to jest; to scoff at. On s'est moqué de lui; they laughed at him. Se faire—de soi; to get laughed at. Je m'en moque; what do I care for it. Vous vous moquez, je pense; you are in jest, I suppose.

moquerie (mo-kri), n.f., mockery, scoff, jeer, derision.

moquette, n.f., Wilton carpet ; decoy-bird.

moqueu-r, **-se**, adj., mocking, jeering, deriding.

moqueu-r, n.m., **-se**, n.f., derider, mocker, quiz. — d'Amérique; mocking-bird.

*morailles, n.f.pl., horse-twitchers.

*moraillon, n.m., hasp.

moraine, n.f., (geol.) moraine.

moral, **-e**, adj., moral.

moral, n m., mental faculties, mind; spirit, spirits (of troops— des troupes).

morale, n.f., ethics; morals, moral philosophy, morality; rebuke, lecture. Il faut lui faire une bonne —; you must give him a good lecture.

moralement (-ral-mån), adv., morally.

moralisation, n.f., moralization.

moraliser, v.n, to moralize.

moraliseur, n.m., (b.s.) moralizer.

moraliste, n.m., moralist, moralizer.

moralité, n.f., morality, morals; moral reflection.

moraves, adj., Frères moraves. V. hernutes.

morbide, adj., (paint., sculpt.) having morbidezza; (med.) morbid.

morbidesse, n.f., (paint.) morbidezza; suppleness, ease, elegance of attitude, manners, gait.

morbifique, adj., morbific.

morbleu! int., zounds!

morce, n.f., curb-stone, binding-stone.

morceau, n.m., bit, piece, morsel; fragment. — délicat; tit-bit. Aimer les bons —x; to love good things. Il a ses —x taillés; he has just enough to live on; he must not go beyond his orders. Manger un —; to eat a morsel. — d'ensemble; (mus.) concerted piece. Mettre en —x; to tear to pieces.

morceler, v.a., to parcel, to parcel out.

morcellement (-sèl-man), n.m., dividing into parcels, parcelling out.

mordacité, n.f., mordacity, corrosiveness; virulency, bitterness, sarcasm.

mordant, **-e** adj., biting; cutting, sarcastic. C'est un homme — ; he is a sarcastic man. Style —; sarcastic style.

mordant, n.m., (dy., gilding) mordant; sarcasm, keenness.

mordicant, **-e**, adj., mordant, corrosive; smart, biting, satirical.

mordicus (-kus), adv., tenaciously, stoutly.

⊙**mordienne** (-di-èn), s.f., only used in the

phrase: à la grosse —; unceremoniously, bluntly.

*mordiller, v.a., to nibble.

mordoré, **-e**, adj., reddish brown.

mordorure, n.f., reddish brown.

mordre, v.a., to bite, to nibble; to corrode, to gnaw; to carp at, to find fault with. — la poussière; to bite the dust. Chien qui aboie ne mord pas; barking dogs do not bite.

se **mordre**, v.r., to bite one's self. — la langue; to bite one's lip. S'en mordre les doigts; to repent of it.

mordre, v.n., to bite, to nibble; to eat away; to hold fast, to take to, to like; to criticize; to censure; (print.) to cover. Je n'ai jamais pu — au Latin; I was never able to take to Latin. Il ne saurait y —; it is beyond his reach; he will never attain it.

mordu, **-e**, adj., (bot.) premorse.

more, n.m., Moor; blackamoor.

⊙**moreau**, adj., extremely black. Cheval —; jet-black horse.

morelle, n.f., (bot.) nightshade.

morène, n.f., (bot.) frogbit.

moresque, adj., Moorish, moresque.

moresque, n.f., morris-dance; (paint.) moresque.

moret, or **mouret**, n.m., (bot.) whortleberry.

morfil, n.m., wire edge (of knives, of razors —de couteaux, de rasoirs, &c.); elephant's tusks after they are removed from the animal, ivory.

morfondre, v.a., to chill.

se **morfondre**, v.r., to catch cold, to be chilled; to wait in vain, to dance attendance; (vet.) to morfounder. La pâte se morfond; the dough is losing its heat.

morfondure, n.f., (vet.) morfoundering.

morganatique, adj., morganatic; left-handed (of marriages—mariages).

morgeline, n.f., (bot.) chickweed.

morgue (morg), n.f., stately look; proud, haughty lock, haughtiness; ⊙room at the entrance of a prison; morgue,dead house.

⊙**morguer** (ghé), v.a., to dare, to defy.

moribond, **-e**, adj. and n., dying, in a dying state; person in a dying state.

moricaud, **-e**, n and adj., blackamoor; black.

morigéner, v.a., to school, to reprimand.

*morille, n.f., (bot.) moril.

*morillon, n.m., black grape; (orni.) tufted duck.

morillons, n.m.pl., (jewel. — joaillerie) rough emeralds.

morion, n.m., morion.

morne, n.m., small mountain (West Indies — Indes Occidentales).

morne, adj., dull, gloomy, mournful, dejected.

morné, **-e** adj., (her.) said of a lion without teeth, claws, or tail; ⊙blunted (of arms— des armes).

mornifle, n.f., slap in the face.

morose, adj., morose, sullen, sour.

morosité, n.f., moroseness, sullenness, surliness.

morphée, n.m , Morpheus. (fig.) Être dans les bras de —; to be asleep. Les pavots de —; sleep.

morphine, n.f., morphia.

morpion, n.m., (l.ex.) crab-louse.

mors, n.m., bit (of a bridle—de bride). Les chevaux prirent le — aux dents; the horses ran away. Prendre le — aux dents; to take fright; to run headlong into pleasure; to fly into a passion.

morse, n.m., morse, sea-horse, walrus.

morsure, n.f., bite, biting.

mort, n.f., death, decease; (hunt.) mort. Avoir la — sur les lèvres; to look like death. Avoir la — dans l'âme; to be sick at heart.

Être à l'article de la —; to be at the point of death. *Mourir de sa belle* —; to die a natural death. *Mettre la* — *dans l'âme à quelqu'un;* to be the death of any one. *Il a la* — *entre les dents;* he has one foot in the grave. *À* —; mortally. to death. *Les affres de la* —; the terrors of death.

mort, -e, part., dead, defunct; lifeless, insensible; dormant; stagnant; still, inanimate. *Un enfant* —*-né* (— —*s*); a still-born child. *Une fille* —*-née* (— —*s*); a still-born girl. *Le feu est* —; the fire is out. *Argent* —; money lying dead. *Couleur* —*e;* faint colour. —*e-saison* (—*s* —*s*); slack season. — *marée;* neap tide. *Tête* —*e;* (chem.) caput mortuum. *Il n'y va pas de main* —*e;* he strikes like a blacksmith. —*e la bête,* — *le venin;* dead men do not bite. *Mort-bois;* V. **bois.** *Morte-eau; eau morte;* V. **eau.** *Morte-paye;* V. **paye.**

mort, n.m., **-e,** n.f., dead person, deceased; dead body, corpse. *Enterrer les* —*s;* to bury the dead. *Le jour des* —*s;* All Souls'-day.

mortadelle, n.f., Italian sausage.

***mortaillable,** adj., (feudalism—*féodalité*) in bondage.

mortaise, n.f., mortise.

mortalité, n.f., mortality.

mortel, -le, adj., mortal, deadly.

mortel, n.m., **-le,** n.f., mortal.

mortellement (-tèl-măn), adv., mortally. deadly.

mort-gage, n.m. (—*s* —*s*), (jur.) mortgage, security of which the usufruit, although received by the creditor, is not applied to the reduction of the debt.

mortier (-tié), n.m., (artil.. mas.) mortar; mortier (cap of the president of a court of justice—*bonnet de président de cour de justice*); mortar (vessel—*à piler*).

mortifère, adj., mortiferous.

mortifiant, -e, adj., mortifying, humiliating.

mortification, n.f., mortification.

mortifier, v.a., to mortify. — *de la viande;* to make meat tender.

se **mortifier,** v.r., to mortify.

mort-ivre, adj. V. **ivre mort.**

mortuaire, adj., mortuary. *Drap* —; pall. *Registre* —; register book of deaths. *Extrait* —; certificate of death.

morue, n.f., cod, codfish.

morve, n.f., snot; (vet.) glanders.

morveau, n.m., (1. ex) dry mucus.

morveu-x, -se, adj., snotty; (vet.) glandered. *Cheval* —; horse that has the glanders. *Qui se sent* —*se mouche* (prov.); let him whom the cap fits wear it.

morveu-x, n.m., **-se,** n.f., (in contempt—*par mépris*) child, brat, young man.

morvolant, n.m., silk mixed with floss.

mosaïque, adj., Mosaic, of, from Moses.

mosaïque, n.f., mosaic, mosaic-work, tesselated pavement.

mosaïste, n.m., workman who does mosaic-work.

mosarabe, n.m. V. **mozarabe.**

moscouade, n.f., muscovado (unrefined sugar—*sucre brut*).

mosquée, n.f., Mosque, Mosk.

mot, n.m., word; expression; saying, sentence; motto; answer (to a riddle—*à une énigme*). *À bon entendeur, demi* — *suffit;* a word to the wise is sufficient. — *usité, inusité;* word in use, word not in use. — *à double entente;* double entendre, ambiguous word. *Jeu de* —*s;* play upon words. — *forgé;* coined word. *Gros* —*s;* abusive words. *Trancher le* —; to speak out. *Ne dire* —; not to utter a word.

Qui ne dit — *consent;* silence gives consent. *Donner le* — *à quelqu'un;* to give any one the word, the cue. *Bon* —; witticism. — *pour rire;* jest, joke. *Avoir le* — *pour rire;* to be jocose, to crack one's joke. *Il lui a dit un* — *à l'oreille;* he whispered a word in his ear. *Prendre quelqu'un au* —; to take any one at his word. *Ils se sont donné le* —; they understand one another. — *à* —, — *pour* —; word for word. *En un* —; in a word, in short. *À ces* —*s;* at those words, so saying.

***motelle,** n.f., (ich.) burbot.

motet, n.m., (mus.) motet.

moteur, n.m., mover, author; motive power, impellent, impeller; (anat.) motor.

mot-eur, -rice, adj., motive.

motif, n.m., motive, incentive, incitement; ground, cause; (mus.) subject. *Pour quel* —? on what ground? on what score? *Faire valoir les* —*s* (jur); to show cause.

motion, n.f., motion. *Faire, appuyer, faire adopter, une* —; to make, to support, to carry, a motion.

motiver, v.a., to allege, to assign, as a motive; to be the cause of.

motte, n.f., clod; ball of earth; turf, (fuel—*à brûler*).

se **motter,** v.r., (hunt.) to lurk behind a clod.

motteux, n.m. (orni.) fallow-finch.

motu proprio, adv., from one's own impulse.

motus! (-tûs). int., mum! silence!

mou, mol, adj.m., **molle,** f., soft, mellow; weak; slack, feeble, nerveless; inactive; sluggish; tame. effeminate. *Cire molle;* soft wax. *Poires molles;* mellow pears. *Un homme mou et efféminé;* a soft effeminate man. *Une molle oisiveté;* effeminate idleness. *Style mou;* nerveless style. *Mer molle* (nav.); slack water. [*Mol* is used before a vowel or *h* mute.]

mou, n.m., soft; slack (of a rope—*d'un cordage*); lights (of some animals—*de quelques animaux*).

mouchard, n.m., or **mouche,** (1 u.) n.f., police-spy, informer.

moucharder, v.a., to inform, to spy.

mouche, n.f., fly; patch (on the face—*pour le visage*); beauty-spot; button (of a foil—*de fleuret*); (astron.) musca. *Prendre la* —; to take offence easily. *Gober les* —*s;* to stand gaping with one's mouth open. *Faire d'une* — *un éléphant;* to make a mountain of a molehill. *Quelle mouche vous a piqué!* why, what's the matter with you? *Des pieds de* —*s;* scrawl (writing—*écriture*). —*s volantes* (med.); muscæ volitantes, motes in the eyes. *Faire des pieds de* —*s;* to write an illegible scrawl. *C'est une fine* —; he, she is a sly one. *Chiures de* —; fly-blows. —*-guêpe* (—*s* —*s*) (ent.); wasp-fly.

moucher, v.a., to wipe the nose of ; to snuff; ☉ (fam.) to spy, to dog. *Mouchez cet enfant;* wipe that child's nose. — *une chandelle;* to snuff a candle.

se **moucher,** v.r., to blow one's nose. *Mouchez-vous;* blow your nose. *Ne pas* — *du pied;* to be up to snuff; to be no fool.

moucher, v.n., to blow one's nose.

moucherolle, n.m., (orni.) fly-catcher..

moucheron, n.m., gnat, very small winged insect; snuff (of a candle—*de chandelle, &c.*).

mouchet, n.m., (orni.) bog-rush.

moucheté, -e, adj., spotted. *Cheval* —, dappled, spotted horse. *Fleuret* —; foil with a button on the point.

moucheter, v.a., to spot, to speckle.

mouchettes, n.f.pl., snuffers.

moucheture, n.f., spot, speck, speckle; (surg.) scarification; pl., spottedness, speckledness.

moucheur, n.m., candle-snuffer.

12 *

mouchoir, *n.m.*, handkerchief. — *de cou ;* neckerchief. *Jeter le* —; to throw the handkerchief.

mouchure, *n.f.*, snuff (of a candle—*de chandelle, &c.*).

mouçon, *n.f.* V. **mousson**.

moudre (moulant, moulu), *v.a.*, to grind, to mill. — *du blé ;* to grind corn. — *de coups ;* to beat soundly. *J'ai le corps tout moulu ;* I am bruised all over.

moue, *n.f.*, pouting ; wry face. *Faire la* — *à quelqu'un ;* to make a wry face at any one. *Faire la* — ; to pout.

mouée, *n.f.*, (hunt.) reward.

mouette, *n.f.*, (orni.) gull.

moufette, *n.f.* V. **mofette**.

mouflard, *n.m.*, -e, *n.f.*, (pop.) one having a big, fat, face

moufle, *n.f.*, (mec.) tackle ; tackle-block ; fingerless glove.

mouflé, -e, *adj.*, used only in *poulie* —*e ;* single pulley connected with others in a tackle-block.

moufle, *n.m.*, (chem.) muffle.

mouflon, *n.m.*, (zool.) moufflon.

***mouillage**, *n.m.*, anchorage, anchoring, place. *Être au* —; to be at anchor. *Aller au* —; to stand for the anchoring-place.

***mouillé**, -e, *part.*, wet, watery ; (of the letter *l*—*de la lettre l*) liquid. *Poule* —*e ;* milksop (pers.).

***mouille-bouche**, *n.f.* (— *or*, — —s), a kind of pear.

***mouiller**, *v.a.*, to wet ; to moisten, to steep. — *l'ancre* (nav.) ; to let go the anchor.

***mouiller**, *v.n.*, (nav.) to anchor.

***mouillette**, *n.f.*, sippet (to eat boiled eggs with—*de pain*).

***mouilloir**, *n.m.*, water-can (in which women dip their fingers when they spin—*pour mouiller les doigts en filant*).

***mouillure**, *n.f.*, wetting, watering.

moujik, *n.m.*, (—s), moujik, Russian peasant.

moulage, *n.m.*, moulding ; grinding, milling ; mill-work, machinery of a mill ; ☉ measuring (of wood—*du bois à brûler*).

moule, *n.m.*, matrix, mould, cast ; netting-pin. *Faire un* — ; to take a cast. *Jeter en* —; to cast in a mould. *Cela ne se jette pas en* — (prov.) ; that cannot be done easily.

moule, *n.f.*, (conch.) muscle.

moulé, -e, *part.*, *adj.*, moulded ; cast ; printed. *Lettre*—*e ;* printed letter. *Chandelle* —*e ;* moulded candle.

moulé, *n.m.*, (pop.) printed characters; writing having the shape of printing type.

mouler, *v.a.*, to cast, to mould.

se mouler, *v.r.*, to mould one's self. — *sur un autre ;* to frame one's conduct by another's.

mouleur, *n.m.*, moulder.

moulin, *n.m.*, mill. — *à blé ;* corn-mill. — *à vent ;* wind-mill. — *à bras ;* hand-mill. — *à café ;* coffee-mill. *C'est un* — *à paroles ;* she is a chatterbox. *Faire venir l'eau au* — ; to bring grist to the mill.

moulinage, *n.m.*, (manu.) silk-throwing.

mouliner, *v.a.*, to eat wood (of worms—*des vers*) ; to throw (silk—*la soie*).

moulinet, *n.m.*, small windlass ; small mill. *Faire le* — *avec une épée ;* to twirl a sword about.

moulineur, or **moulinier**, *n.m.*, silk-thrower.

☉**moult** (moo), *adv.*, much, very much.

moulu, -e, *part.*, ground ; bruised.

moulure, *n.f.*, (arch.) moulding.

mourant, -e, *n.* and *adj.*, dying person ; dying, expiring ; fading.

mouret, *n.m.* V. **moret**.

mourine, *n.f.*, (ich.) eagle-ray.

mourir (mourant, mort), *v.n.*, to die, to depart this life ; to perish, to drop off, to go off, to expire, to stop ; to go out (of fire—*du feu*). *Être mort au monde ;* to be dead to the world. — *de faim ;* to die of starvation ; to starve. — *de soif ;* to be dying with thirst. — *de froid ;* to starve with cold. — *d'envie ;* to long for. — *de chagrin ;* to die of a broken heart. *Il la fera* — *de chagrin ;* he will break her heart. — *de rire ;* to die with laughing. *C'est un meurt de faim ;* he is a pauper, a starveling.

se mourir, *v.r.*, to be dying ; to be going out (of fire—*du feu*). *Cet homme se meurt ;* this man is dying.

mouron, *n.m.*, (bot.) pimpernel ; chickweed ; (ent.) eft.

mourre, *n.f.*, game in which two persons quickly show to each other, their fingers raised and shut, for the number of the former to be guessed.

mousquet, *n.m.*, musket.

☉**mousquetade**, *n.f.*, musket-shot.

☉**mousquetaire**, *n.m.*, musketeer.

mousqueterie (-kè-trî), *n.f.*, musketry, volley of musketry.

mousqueton, *n.m.*, musketoon.

mousse, *n.f.*, moss ; froth, foam ; lather. *Pierre qui roule n'amasse pas de* — ; a rolling stone gathers no moss.

mousse, *n.m.*, cabin-boy, ship-boy.

☉**mousse**, *adj.*, blunt, dull (of edged instruments—*d'instruments tranchants*).

mousseline (moos-ii-n), *n.f.*, muslin.

mousser, *v.n.*, to froth, to foam, to effervesce, to lather. *Faire* — ; to froth ; to puff.

mousseron (moos-ron), *n.m.*, mushroom.

mousseu-x, -se, *adj.*, foaming, frothy. *Rose* —*se ;* moss-rose.

moussoir, *n.m.*, chocolate-stick.

mousson, *n.f.*, monsoon.

moussu, -e, *adj.*, mossy, full of moss.

moustache, *n.f.*, moustache, mustachio, mustache ; whisker (of animals—*des animaux*). *Relever sa* — ; to twirl up one's mustache. *Brûler la* — *à quelqu'un ;* to fire a pistol in any one's face. *Donner sur la* — *à quelqu'un ;* to hit any one in the face.

moustiquaire, *n.f.*, musquito-net.

moustique, *n.m.*, musquito.

moût, *n.m.*, must (wine not fermented—*vin non fermenté*) ; wort.

moutard, *n.m.*, (pop.) brat.

moutarde, *n.f.*, mustard. *Graine de* —; mustard-seed. *S'amuser à la* —; to stand trifling one's time away.

moutardier, *n.m.*, mustard-pot ; mustard-maker ; (orni.) black-martin, swift.

☉**moutier**, *n.m.*, convent, monastery.

mouton, *n.m.*, sheep ; mutton ; sheep-leather ; prison-spy ; rammer ; beetle, monkey (rammer) ; foaming wave. *Un troupeau de* —*s ;* a flock of sheep. *Revenons à nos* —*s ,* let us return to our subject.

☉***moutonnaille**, *n.f.*, flock of sheep.

moutonné, -e, *adj.*, fleecy.

moutonner, *v.a.* and *n.*, to make woolly, fleecy ; to curl, to frizzle ; (nav.) to foam.

moutonneu-x, -se, *adj.*, woolly ; foamy (of waves—*de la mer*).

moutonni-er, -ère, *adj.*, sheep-like.

mouture, *n.f.*, grinding ; price for grinding ; meslin of wheat, rye, and barley. *Tirer d'un sac deux* —*s ;* to take double profit on anything.

mouvance, *n.f.*, (feudalism—*féodalité*) tenure.

mouvant, -e, *adj.*, moving, animated, busy. *Sable* —; quick-sand.

mouvement (moov-mān), *n.m.*, movement, motion ; move, manœuvre ; fluctuation ; (mus.)

time; (paint.) animation, life; spirit; impulse, emotion, disturbance, commotion; stir, bustle; (horl.) works. *Se donner du* —; to bestir one's self. *Le* — *du style*; animation of style. *Les* —*s oratoires*; bursts of eloquence. — *naturel*; natural impulse. *Faire une chose de son propre* —; to do a thing of one's own accord.

mouver, *v.a.*, (gard.) to loosen, to stir.

mouvoir (mouvant, mu), *v.a.*, to move, to stir; to prompt, to stir up, to actuate; to excite. *se* **mouvoir**. *v.r.*, to move.

moxa. *n.m.*, (surg.) moxa.

moye (moa), *n.f.*, soft part (of stone—*de la pierre*).

moyen (moa-yin), *n.m.*, means, way, manner; medium; power; (jur.) plea; (log.) mean; (math.) middle term; *pl.*, means; pecuniary circumstances; parts. *Il n'y a pas* — *de faire cela*; there is no means of doing that. *Je n'en ai pas le* —; I have not the ability to do it; I can't afford it. *Le* — *de lui parler?* how can one speak to him? *Contribuer chacun selon ses* —*s*; to contribute each according to his means. *Il a beaucoup de* —*s*; he is very clever. *Voies et* —*s*; ways and means. *Au* — *de*; by means of, with the help of.

moyen, -ne (moa-yin, -yè-n), *adj.*, mean, middle, middle-sized. *Le* — *âge*; the middle ages. *Terme* —; average, mean, on an average.

moyennant (moa-iè-nän), *prep.*, by means of, with the help of.

moyennant que, *conj.*, provided that.

moyenne, *n.f.*, average; (math.) mean, medium. — *approximative*; rough average. *Sur une* — *de*; at an average of. *En* —; on an average.

⊙**moyennement** (moa-iè-n-män), *adv.*, moderately, indifferently.

⊙**moyenner**, *v.a.*, to mediate.

moyeu, *n.m.*, nave (of a wheel—*de roue*); preserved plum; ⊙yolk of an egg.

mozarabe, *n.m.*, Muzarab.

mozarabe, *or* **mozarabique**, *adj.*, muzarabic.

mr, (ab. of Monsieur), Mr., Mister.

ms., Msc. (ab. of Manuscrit), Ms., Manuscript.

mss, (ab. of Manuscrits), Mss., Manuscripts.

muable. *adj.*, mutable.

muance, *n.f.*, (mus.) changing a note.

mucate, *n.m.*, mucic acid combined with a base.

à **muche-pot**. *adv.* *V.* **musse-pot** (à).

mucilage, *n.m.*, mucilage.

mucilagineu-x, -**se**, *adj.*, mucilaginous.

mucosité, *n.f.*, mucus.

mucus (-kus), *n.m.*, mucus.

mue, *n.f.*, moulting; moulting season; cast-skin, slough; mew, coop (cage). *Être en* —; to be moulting.

mue, *adj.*, only used in *rage* —; dumb madness (of dogs—*des chiens*).

muer, *v.n.*, to moult, to cast its skin; to mew. *Ce chien mue*; that dog is moulting. *Sa voix mue*; his voice is breaking.

muet, -te, *adj.*, dumb, mute, speechless; silent (of letters—*des lettres de l'alphabet*). *Il est sourd-* —, — *et muet*; he is deaf and dumb. *La frayeur le rendit* —; terror struck him dumb. *Scène* —*te*; dumb show.

muet, *n.m.*, -**te**, *n.f.*, dumb man, dumb woman.

muette. *n.f.*, mew; hunting-lodge.

muezin. *n.m.* (—s), muezzin.

mufle. *n.m.*, muffle, muzzle (of animals—*des animaux*); snout (of persons—*des personnes*). — *de veau* (bot.); snap-dragon, calf's snout.

mufleau, *n.m.*, (bot.) snap-dragon, calf's snout.

muflier, *n.m.*, (bot.) snap-dragon, calf's snout.

mufti, *or* **muphti**, *n.m.* (—*s*), mufti.

muge. *n.m.*, (ich.) mullet.

mugir, *v.n.*, to bellow, to low; to roar. *Il mugissait de colère*; he was roaring with passion.

mugissant, -**e**, *adj.*, bellowing, roaring.

mugissement (-jis-män), *n.m.*, bellowing, lowing; roaring.

⊙**mugot**, *n.m.* *V.* **magot**.

muguet (-ghè), *n.m.*, (bot.) lily of the valley, May-lily; ⊙ (fam.) beau, fop.

mugueter (mug-té), *v.a.*, (fam., l.u.) to play the fop.

⊙**muid**, *n.m.*, hogshead (measure).

mulâtre, *adj.*, mulatto.

mulâtr-e, *n.m.*, -**esse**, *n.f.*, mulatto.

⊙**mulcter**, *v.a.*, (jur.) to fine, to punish; to vex, to ill-treat.

mule, *n.f.*, slipper; she-mule; *pl.*, chilblains in the heels, kibes; (vet.) chaps. *La* — *du pape*; the pope's slipper. *Baiser la* — *du pape*; to kiss the pope's toe. *Ferrer la* —; to get the market-penny.

mulet, *n.m.*, he-mule; (bot., orni.) mule; (ich.) mullet. *Garder le* —; to be kept waiting, to dance attendance.

muletier (mul-tié), *n.m.*, muleteer.

mulle, *n.m.*, (ich.) surmullet.

⊙**mulle**, *n.f.* *V.* **caillette**.

mulle. *adj.*, (com.) of inferior quality (of madder—*de la garance*).

mulot, *n.m.*, field-mouse.

multangulaire, *adj.*, (bot.) multangular.

multangulé, -e, *adj.*, multangular.

multi, a prefix from Latin *multus*.

multicapsulaire, *adj.*, (bot.) multicapsular.

multicolore, *adj.*, of many colours.

multifide, *adj.*, (bot.) multifid.

multiflore, *adj.*, (bot.) multiflorous.

multiforme, *adj.*, multiform.

multilatère. *adj.*, multilateral.

multiloculaire, *adj.*, (bot.) multilocular.

multinôme, *n.m.*, (l.u.) (alg.) multinominal. *V.* **polynôme**.

multipare, *adj.*, multiparous.

multipartite, *adj.*, (bot.) multipartite.

multipède, *adj.*, multiped.

multiple. *n.m.* and *adj.*, (arith.) multiple.

multipliable, *adj.*, multipliable.

multipliant, *adj.*, multiplying.

multiplicande, *n.m.*, (arith.) multiplicand.

multiplicateur, *n.m.*, (arith.) multiplier.

multiplication, *n.f.*, multiplication. *Table de* —; multiplication table.

multiplicité, *n.f.*, multiplicity.

multiplier, *v.a.*, to multiply.

se **multiplier**, *v.r.*, to multiply; to be repeated.

multiplier, *v.n.*, to multiply.

multitude, *n.f.*, multitude.

multivalve. *n.f.* and *adj.*, multivalve; multivalvular.

municipe. *n.m.*, a town, especially in Italy, subject to Rome but governed by its own laws.

municipal, -e, *adj.*, municipal.

municipal, *n.m.*, municipal officer; municipal guard.

municipalité, *n.f.*, municipality.

munificence, *n.f.*, munificence, bounty.

munir, *v.a.*, to provide with, to supply.

se **munir**, *v.r.*, to provide one's self, to be provided, to be supplied.

munition, *n.f.*, ammunition; *pl.*, military stores. —*s de bouche*; provisions; —*s de guerre*; ammunition.

munitionnaire, *n.m.*, (milit.) contractor, commissary.

muphti, *n.m.* *V.* **mufti**.

muqueu-x, -se, *adj.*, mucous.

mur,n.m., wall. — *mitoyen* ; partition-wall. — *de clôture* ; inclosure-wall. — *d'appui* ; breast-high wall. *Mettre quelqu'un au pied du* — ; to nonplus any one.

mûr, -e, *adj.*, ripe, mature ; worn out, shabby (of clothes—*des vêtements*). *L'âge* — ; mature age. *Du vin* —; wine fit to be drunk.

*muraille, n.f., thick, high wall ; rampart.

*muraillement, n.m., (mas.) walling.

mural, -e *adj.*, mural.

mûre, n.f., (bot.) mulberry. — *sauvage* ; blackberry.

mûrement (mûr-mân), *adv.*, maturely. *J'y ai* — *réfléchi* ; I have maturely reflected on it.

murène, n.f., (ich.) muræna.

murer, v.a., to wall ; to wall up.

murex (-rèks), n.m., (conch.) murex.

muriate, n.m., (chem.) muriate.

muriatique, *adj.*, (chem.) muriatic. *Acide* — ; muriatic acid.

mûrier, n.m., mulberry-tree.

mûrir, v.n., to ripen, to grow ripe, to mature.

mûrir, v.a., to ripen, to mature.

murmurant, -e, *adj.,* murmuring, babbling ; muttering, grumbling.

murmurat-eur, n. and *adj.*m., murmurer, grumbler ; murmuring, discontented.

murmure, n.m., murmur ; murmuring, grumbling, muttering ; whispering ; prattling ; babbling. — *d'approbation*; murmur of approbation.

murmurer, v.n., to murmur, to grumble, to mutter; to whisper ; to gurgle, to prattle, to babble.

murmurer, v.a., to mutter, to whisper. *Que murmurez-vous là?* what are you muttering there ?

se **murmurer,** v.r., to be whispered, to be whispered about.

murrhin, -e, *adj.,* murrhine.

musagète, *adj.,* (myth.) chief of the Muses; (of Apollo—*d'Apollon*).

*musaraigne, n.f., (mam.) shrew-mouse.

musard, -e, n. and *adj.,* loiterer, dawdler ; loitering, dawdling.

musarder, v.n., to loiter, to dawdle.

musarderie, n.f., loitering, trifling ; dawdling.

musc, *or* **porte-musc,** n.m. (—), (mam.) musk, musk-deer.

musc, n.m., musk (scent—*matière odorante*).

muscade, n.f., nutmeg ; juggler's ball. *Noix* — ; nutmeg.

muscadet, n.m., muscadet (wine—*rin*).

muscadier, n.m., nutmeg-tree.

muscadin, n.m., musk-lozenge ; beau, dandy.

muscat,n.m. and *adj.*, muscatel muscadine, muscadel (a kind of grapes, of wine, of pears—*espèce de raisin, de vin, de poires*).

muscatelline,n.f.,(bot.) adoxa, moschatel.

muscle, n.m., muscle.

musclé, -e, *adj.,* having the muscles strongly marked.

musculaire, *adj.,* muscular.

musculature, n.f., (sculpt., paint.) muscularity.

muscule, n.m., (Rom. antiq.) mantelet, shed (engine of war—*engin de guerre*).

musculeu-x, -se, *adj.,* muscular, brawny, musculous.

muse, n.f., Muse.

muse, n.f., (hunt.) beginning of rutting-time.

museau, n.m., muzzle, snout, nose.

musée, n.m., museum.

museler (mu-zlé), v.a., to muzzle, to gag.

muselière, n.f., muzzle (for an animal's snout—*pour empêcher un animal de mordre ou de manger*).

muser, v.n., to loiter, to trifle ; (hunt.) to begin to rut.

muserolle (muz-rol), n.f., nose-band, musrole.

musette, n.f., bagpipe; tune for the bagpipe ; nose-bag (for horses—*pour les chevaux*).

muséum (-om). n.m. (—s), museum.

musical, -e, *adj.*, musical.

musicalement (-kal-man), *adv.*, musically.

musicien, n.m., -ne, n.f. (-in, -è-n), musician.

musico, n.m. (—s), in the Netherlands a low music hall.

musicomane, n.m., (l.u.) person extremely fond of music. *V.* **mélomane.**

musicomanie, n.f., (l.u.) passion for music. *V.* **mélomanie.**

musi-f, *or* **mussi-f, -ve,** *adj.*, (chem.) mosaic. *Or*— ; mosaic-gold, ormolu.

musique, n.f., music ; band, musicians. *Mettre des vers en* — ; to set verses to music. *Être réglé comme un papier de* — ; to be as regular as clock-work. *Nous ferons de la* — ; we will have music.

musqué, -e, *adj.,* musked, perfumed ; studied, unnatural ; odd, strange.

musquer, v.a., to perfume with musk, to musk.

se **musquer,** v.r., to scent one's self with musk.

à **musse-pot,** *adv.,* in concealment.

*O*se **musser,** v.r., to hide one's self; to lurk in a corner.

mustelle, n.f., (ich.) whistle-fish.

musulman, -e, n. and *adj.*, Mussulman ; Mahometan. Mohammedan.

*O***musurgie,** n.f., (mus.) musurgy.

mutabilité, n.f., mutability.

mutation, n.f., mutation, change.

muter, v.a., to put sulphur in wine.

mutilat-eur, -rice, n. and *adj.*, mutilator; mutilating.

mutilation, n.f., mutilation; maiming.

mutiler, v.a., to mutilate ; to maim.

mutin, -e, *adj.,* obstinate, stubborn, unruly, fractious ; riotous.

mutin, n.m., -e, n.f., obstinate person; refractory child; mutineer, rioter.

mutiné, -e, *part.,* mutinous, riotous. *Peuple* — ; riotous people. *Les flots* —s ; the raging waves.

se **mutiner,** v.r., to mutiny, to be refractory, unruly. *Cet enfant se mutine* ; that child gets unruly.

mutinerie (-ti-n-ri), n.f., mutiny, riot ; unruliness.

mutisme, n.m., dumbness.

mutualité, n.f., mutuality.

mutuel, -le, *adj.,* mutual, reciprocal. *Société de secours* —s ; benefit society.

mutuellement (-èl-mân), *adv.,* mutually, reciprocally.

mutule, n.f., (arch.) mutule.

myélite, n.f., (med.) inflammation of the spinal marrow.

myographie, n.f., myography.

myologie, n.f., myology.

myope, n.m.f. and *adj.*, myope, short-sighted person ; short-sighted.

myope, n.m., (ent.) conops.

myopie, n.f., myopia, myopy, short-sightedness.

myose, n.f., (med.) mycsis.

myosotis, n.m., (bot.) myositis, scorpion-grass.

myotomie, n.f., myotomy.

myriade, *n.f.,* myriad.

myriagramme, *n.m.,* myriagramme (22·0485 lbs. avoirdupois).

myriamètre, *n.m.,* myriametre (6·2138 miles).

myriapode, *n.m.,* (ent.) myriapod.

myrmidon. *n.m. V.* **mirmidon.**

myrobolan, *n.m.,* (bot.) myrobalan.

myrobolan, -te. *adj.,* (pop.) prodigious, wonderful; splendid, grand, magnificent.

myrobolanier, *n.m.,* myrobalan-tree.

myrrhe, *n.f.,* myrrh.

myrrhis (mir-ris), *n.m.,* (bot.) myrrhis.

myrte, *n.m.,* myrtle.

myrtiforme. *adj.,* myrtiform.

myrtille, *n.f.,* (bot.) bilberry.

mystagogue (-gog), *n.m.,* (antiq.) mysta-\ gogue.

mystère, *n.m.,* mystery. *Étudier les —s de la nature ;* to study the mysteries of nature. *Sans autre — ;* without further ado. *Approfondir un — ;* to look into a mystery. *Mettre du — à ;* to make a mystery of.

mystérieusement (-eûz-măn), *adv.,* mysteriously.

mystérieu-x, -se, *adj.,* mysterious.

mysticisme, *n.m.,* mysticism.

mysticité, *n.f.,* mysticism.

mystificateur, *n.m.,* hoaxer.

mystification, *n.f.,* hoaxing, hoax, mystification.

mystifier, *v.a.,* to hoax, to mystify.

mystique, *adj.,* mystical, mystic.

mystique, *n.m.f.,* (pers.) mystic.

mystique, *n.f.,* (philos.) the study of spirituality.

mystiquement (-tik-măn), *adv.,* mystically.

mystre, *n.m.,* (antiq.) Greek measure for liquors.

mythe, *n.m.,* myth, fable.

mythique, *adj.,* mythic, mythical.

mythologie, *n.f.,* mythology.

mythologique, *adj.,* mythological, fabulous.

mythologiste, *or* **mythologue,** *n.m.,* mythologist.

myure, *adj.,* (med.) sinking (of the pulse— *du pouls*). *Pouls — ;* sinking pulse.

N

n (èn), *n.f.* (ne), *n.m.,* the fourteenth letter of the alphabet, n.

n' (contraction of Ne), not.

nabab, *n.m.,* nabob.

nababie, *n.f.,* nabobship.

nabatéen (-té-in), **-ne** (-té-è-n), *adj.,* applied by the Arabs to the language and literature of the Assyrians.

nabot, *n.m.,* **-e,** *n.f.,* (jest.) shrimp (pers.), dwarf.

nacarat, *n.m.,* nacarat.

nacarat, *adj. invariable,* of the colour of nacarat.

nacelle, *n.f.,* wherry; (arch.) scotia, casement.

nacre. *n.f.,* mother of pearl.

nacré, -e, *adj.,* nacreous.

nadir, *n.m.,* (astron.) nadir.

naffe, *n.m.,* orange-flower. [Only used in : *eau de —,* a scent in which orange-flower is the chief ingredient.]

nage, *n.f.,* swimming; (fig.) profuse perspiration. *À la — ;* swimming, by swimming. *Passer la rivière à la — ;* to swim over the river. *Se jeter à la — ;* to leap into the water. *Être tout en — ;* to be all in a perspiration.

nagée, *n.f.,* (l.u.) stroke in swimming.

nagement (na-jmän), *n.m.,* swimming (of fish—*des poissons*).

nageoire, *n.f.,* fin (of a fish—*de poisson*); cork, bladders, &c., to hold up a person learning to swim ; piece of wood floating in a pail, &c., to keep the water steady.

nager, *v.n.,* to swim; to float; to abound, to roll ; to welter; (nav.) to row. *Il nage comme un poisson ;* he swims like a fish. *— dans l'opulence ;* to roll in riches. *— entre deux eaux ;* to waver ,between two parties. *— dans son sang ;* to be weltering in one's blood. *— à culer* (nav.); to back, to back water.

nageu-r, *n.m.,* **-se,** *n.f.,* swimmer; (nav.) rower.

naguère, *or* **naguères** (na-ghèr), *adv.,* lately, but lately, but now.

naïade, *n.f.,* (myth.) naiad.

naï-f, -ve. *adj.,* naive, native, artless, ingenuous; plain, unaffected, natural; candid; simple. *Grâce —ve;* native grace. *Réponse —ve;* simple answer.

naïf, *n.m.,* (lit., paint.) nature without art.

nain (nin), **-e** (nè-n), *n.* and *adj.,* dwarf; dwarfish. *— jaune ;* Pope Joan (card game— *jeu de cartes*). *Arbres —s ;* dwarf trees.

naïre, *n.m.,* Indian chief (Malabar).

naissance, *n.f.,* birth; nativity; descent, extraction; beginning, dawn, rise. *Le lieu de sa — ;* one's birth-place. *Jour de —, anniversaire de la — ;* birth-day. *Être de haute — ;* to be high-born. *Prendre — de;* to originate in. *Donner — à ;* to give rise to.

naissant, -e, *adj.,* newly-born ; dawning; budding, rising; infant; beginning, nascent. *Une fortune —e ;* a rising fortune.

naître (naissant, né), *v.n.,* to be born, to come into the world; to originate, to arise ; to rise, to dawn, to spring up. *Il est né poète; he was born a poet. Les fleurs naissent sous ses pas;* flowers spring up under her steps. *Cela peut faire — des soupçons;* that may give rise to suspicion.

naïvement (-iv-măn), *adv.,* ingenuously, plainly, candidly, naively, artlessly.

naïveté (-iv-té), *n.f.,* native simplicity, ingenuousness, artlessness; simple thing; naivete.

nanan, *n.m.,* sweetmeats, goody (childish— *enfantin*).

nankin, *n.m.,* nankeen.

nanti, -e, *part.,* stocked, furnished with. *Être — ;* to hold as a pledge.

nantir, *v.a.,* to give as a pledge.

se nantir, *v.r.,* to hold as a pledge; to provide one's self ; to take possession.

nantissement (-tis-măn), *n.m.,* security, pledge.

napée, *n.f.,* (myth.) forest-nymph, mountain-nymph.

napel, *n.m.,* (bot.) monk's-hood.

naphte, *n.m.,* naphtha.

napiforme, *adj.,* (bot.) napiform.

napoléon, *n.m.,* napoleon (French gold coin, worth 15s. 10½d.—*pièce d'or de 20 francs*).

napolitain, -e, *n.* and *adj.,* Neapolitan.

nappe, *n.f.,* cloth, table-cloth; (hunt.) dead animal's skin; net for catching birds. *— d'eau;* sheet of water.

napperon (na-pron), *n.m.,* napkin (small table-cloth—*petite nappe*).

narcisse, *n.m.,* (bot.) daffodil, narcissus. *C'est un — ;* he is enamoured of himself.

narcotine, *n.f.,* narcotine.

narcotique, *n.m.* and *adj.,* narcotic.

narcotisme, *n.m.,* (med.) narcotism.

nard, *n.m.*, (bot., pharm.) nard; (bot.) spike-nard.

nargue (narg), *n.f.*, pshaw, pish. *Dire —de;* to snap one's finger at. *— de l'amour;* a fig for, a plague on, love.

narguer (-ghé), *v.a.*, to defy, to set at defiance.

narguilé, *n.m.*, narghileh, Turkish, Persian pipe.

narine. *n.f.*, nostril.

narquois, -e; *n.* and *adj.*, sharper, swindler; banterer; cunning, sly. *Parler —;* to talk slang.

narrat-eur, *n.m.*, **-rice**, *n.f.* (nar-ra-), narrator.

narrati-f, -ve (nar-ra-), *adj.*, narrative, narratory.

narration (nar-ra), *n.f.*, narration, narrative.

narré (nar-ré), *n.m*, narrative, narration, recital.

narrer (nar-ré), *v.a.*, to narrate, to relate, to tell.

narthex, *n.m.*, (archæology) vestibule in front of the nave in ancient basilicas, reserved for new converts, energumens, and penitents.

narval, *n.m.*, (mam.) narwhal, sea-unicorn.

nasal. -e, *adj.*, nasal. *Son —;* nasal sound.

nasale, *n.f.*, (gram.) nasal.

nasalement, *adv.*, (gram.) with a nasal sound.

nasaliser, *v.a.*, to render nasal, to nasalize.

nasalité, *n.f.*, (gram.) nasal sound.

nasard, *n.m.*, organ-stop, to imitate the human voice.

nasarde, *n.f.*, fillip, rap on the nose.

nasarder, *v.a.*, to fillip, to rap on the nose; to jeer, to banter; to defy, to persecute.

naseau, *n.m.*, nostril (of animals–*des animaux*). *Un fendeur de —x;* a swaggerer, a braggart.

nasi, *n.m.*, President of the Sanhedrim.

*****nasillant, -e**, *adj.*, speaking through the nose.

*****nasillard. -e**, *n.* and *adj.*, snuffler, person who speaks through his nose; snuffling.

*****nasillement**, *n.m.*, speaking through the nose.

*****nasiller**, *v.n.*, to speak through the nose, to snuffle.

*****nasilleu-r**, *n.m.*, **-se**, *n.f.*, one that speaks through his nose, snuffler.

*****nasillonner**, *v.n.*, to speak a little through the nose.

nasse, *n.f.*, bow-net (for catching fish–*filet de pêche*). *Il est dans la —;* he is in a scrape.

nasselle, *n.f.*, net made with rushes.

natal, -e, *adj.*, natal, native. *Lieu —;* birth-place. *Pays—;* native country. *Jour —;* birth-day.

natation, *n.f.*, swimming.

natatoire, *adj.*, swimming.

nati-f, -ve, *adj.*, native, natural. *Il est —de;* he is a native of. *Or —;* native gold.

natif, *n.m.*, native.

nation, *n.f.*, nation.

national, -e *adj.*, national. *Assemblée –e;* national assembly. *Garde –e;* national guard (corps). *Garde —;* national guard (man–*homme*).

nationalement (-nal-mān), *adv.*, nationally.

nationaliser, *v.a.*, to nationalize.

se nationaliser, *v.r.*, to become nationalized.

nationalité, *n.f.*, nationality.

nationaux, *n.m.pl.*, natives.

nativité, *n.f.*, nativity, birth.

natron, or **natrum**, *n.m.*, (min.) natron.

natte, *n.f.*, mat, matting; straw-mat; plait (of hair, silk, &c.–*de cheveux, de soie, &c.*).

natter. *v.a.*, to mat; to plait.

nattier, *n.m.*, mat-maker; straw-plaiter.

in naturalibus, *adv.*, (fam.) in a state of nakedness.

naturalisation. *n.f.*, naturalization.

naturaliser, *v.a.*, to naturalize.

naturalisme, *n.m.*, naturalism, naturalness.

naturaliste. *n.m.*, naturalist.

naturalité, *n.f.*, the being a native.

nature, *n.f.*, nature; kind. *Don de la —;* gift of nature. *L'habitude est une seconde —;* use is a second nature. *La — humaine;* human nature; mankind. *Payer en —;* to pay in kind. *L'art perfectionne la —;* nature is improved by art. *Prendre la — pour modèle;* to take nature as a model. *Dessiner d'après —;* to draw from nature.

naturel, -le. *adj.*, natural, native, inborn, innate, inherent, genial; plain, home-bred.

naturel, *n.m.*, native; nature, naturalness; temper, constitution; feeling; life. *Les —s du pays;* the natives of the country. *— fort et robuste;* strong constitution. *Un homme d'un mauvais —, d'un bon —;* an ill-natured, a good-natured, man. *Au —;* naturally, to the life; (cook.) cooked plain.

naturellement (-rèl-mān), *adv.*, naturally, by nature; genuinely.

naufrage, *n.m.*, shipwreck, wreck. *Faire —;* to be wrecked.

naufragé, -e, *n.* and *adj.*, person ship-wrecked; wrecked, shipwrecked.

naulage, *n.m.*, freight (on the Mediterranean–*usité dans la Méditerranée*).

naumachie, *n.f.*, naumachy (spectacle representing a sea-fight–*représentation d'un combat naval*).

nauséabond, -e *adj.*, nauseous.

nausée, *n.f.*, nausea; disgust.

nautile, *n.m.*, (mol.) nautilus.

nautique, *adj.*, nautical, nautic.

nautiquement, *adv.*, nautically.

nautoni-er, *n.m.*, **-ère**, *n.f.*, (poet.) pilot, mariner.

naval, -e, *adj.*, naval. *Combat —;* sea-fight.

○**navée**, *n.f.*, boat-load.

navet, *n.m.*, turnip; (hort.) root.

navetier (nav-tié), *n.m.*, maker of shuttles.

navette, *n.f.*, (ecc.) incense-box; (bot.) rape, rape-seed; netting-needle, shuttle. *Faire la —;* to go and come back again, once or several times.

naviculaire. *adj.*, (anat., bot.) navicular.

navigabilité, *n.f.*, navigableness, seaworthiness.

navigable. *adj.*, navigable.

navigateur, *n.* and *adj.m.*, navigator; seafaring.

navigation, *n.f.*, navigation, voyage.

naviguer (-ghé), *v.n.*, to navigate, to sail. *— en pleine mer;* to sail in the open sea.

○**naville**, *n.f.*, small irrigation canal.

navire, *n.m.*, vessel, ship. [Not applied to men of war–*ne s'applique pas aux vaisseaux de guerre.*] *Couler à fond un —;* to sink a ship. *Un — marchand;* a merchantman.

navrant, -e, *adj.*, heart-rending.

navré, -e, *part.*, broken-hearted. *Avoir le cœur —;* to be broken-hearted.

navrer, *v.a.*, to wound, to distress; to rend the heart. *Cela me navre le cœur;* that rends my heart.

○**navrure**, *n.f.*, wound, contusion.

nazaréen (-ré-in), *n.m.*, **-ne** (-ré-è-n), *n.f.*, Nazarite, Nazarene.

n.b., (ab. of Nota Bene) N.B., Nota Bene.

n.d., (ab. of Notre Dame) our Lady.

ne, *adv.*, no, not. *Je — veux pas;* I will not. *Cela — vaut rien;* that is good for nothing. *Il — cesse de gronder;* he does not cease scolding. *Je n'ose lui parler;* I dare not speak to him. *Je —*

peux me taire; I cannot remain silent. *Je — saurais vous dire*: I cannot tell you. *Je crains que cela — soit*; I fear that it is so. *Je — doute pas que cela ne soit*: I do not doubt it. *A moins que cela — soit*; unless that is so. *Il — fait que dormir*; he does nothing but sleep. *- . . . . que*; only, but. *Il n'a fait que cela*; he only did that. *Il — le fera plus*; he will not do it again. [*Ne* is contracted into *n'* before a vowel or a silent *h*.]

né, -e. *part.*, born. — *de la mer*: sea-born. *Bien —*: of good birth. *Nouveau- —*, *m.* (— —*s*, *nouveau- —e. f.* (— —*s*); newly-born. *Mort- —*, *m.* (— —*s*), *mort- —e, f.* (— —*s*); still-born.

néanmoins. *adv.*, nevertheless, however, for all that.

néant, *n.m.*, nothing, naught, nothingness. *C'est un homme de —*; he is a man of nothing. *Mettre au —*; to annul, to set at naught.

nébride, *n.f.*, fawn-skin worn at the feast of Bacchus.

nébuleuse, *n.f.*, (astron.) nebula.

nébuleu-x, -se, *adj.*, nebulous, cloudy.

nébulosité, *n.f.*, nebulosity.

nécessaire, *adj.*, necessary, requisite, needful. *La respiration est — à la vie*; respiration is necessary to life.

nécessaire, *n.m.*, necessaries; dressing-case; work-box. *Se refuser le —*; to refuse one's self the necessaries of life.

nécessairement (-sèr-màn), *adv.*, necessarily.

nécessitante, *adj.f.*, absolute; (theol.) compulsory.

nécessité, *n.f.*, necessity, necessariness; exigence; need, want. — *n'a point de loi*; necessity knows no law. *Faire de — vertu*; to make a virtue of necessity. *La — est la mère de l'invention*; necessity is the mother of invention. *Les —s de la nature*; the wants of nature. *De —*; of necessity, necessarily.

nécessiter, *v.a.*, to compel, to force; to necessitate.

nécessiteu-x, -se, *adj.*, necessitous, needy.

nécessiteux, *n.m.*, pauper.

nec plus ultra, *n.m.* (*n.p.*), ne plus ultra.

nécrologe, *n.m.*, obituary.

nécrologie, *n.f.*, necrology, obituary.

nécrologique, *adj.*, necrologic, necrological.

nécromance, or **nécromancie,** *n.f.*, necromancy.

nécromancien (-ci-in), *n.m.*, **-ne** (-ci-è-n), *n.f.*, necromancer.

nécromant, *n.m.*, necromancer.

nécropole, *n.f.*, necropolis.

nécrose, *n.f.*, (med.) necrosis.

nectaire, *n.m.*, (bot.) nectarium, nectary, honey-cup.

nectar, *n.m.*, nectar.

nef, *n.f.*, nave (of a church—*d'église*); (poet.) ship. *Moulin à —*; mill built upon a boat.

néfaste, *adj.*, (antiq.) of solemn festivals, of rest; inauspicious, of evil omen, unlucky. *Jour —*: day of mourning.

néfle, *n.f.*, (bot.) medlar.

néflier, *n.m.*, (bot.)medlar-tree.

négatif, *n.m.*, (photograph.) negative.

négati-f, -ve, *adj.*, negative.

négation, *n.f.*, negation, negative.

négative, *n.f.*, negative, refusal.

négativement (-tiv-màn),*adv.*, negatively.

négligé, -e, *part.*, neglected, unheeded. *Style —*; careless style. *Extérieur —*; slovenly exterior.

négligé, *n.m.*, undress, negligee.

négligeable, *adj.*, (math.) that can be neglected. *Quantité —*; small quantity which can be left aside.

négligement (-gli-jmàn), *n.m.*, (arts) neglecting.

négligemment (-ja-màn), *adv.*, negligently, carelessly.

négligence, *n.f.*, negligence, neglect.

négligent, -e, *adj.* and *n.*, negligent. *neglectful, remiss, careless; negligent person.*

négliger, *v.a.*, to neglect, to omit, to slight, to pass over, to disregard, to pass by. *se négliger,* *v.r.*, to neglect one's self. *Il commence à —*; he begins to be careless in his person.

négoce, *n.m.*, trade, traffic, business. *Faire un gros —*; to carry on a large trade.

négociabilité, *n.f.*, negotiability.

négociable, *adj.*, negotiable, transferable.

négociant, *n.m.*, merchant.

négociat-eur, *n.m.*, **-rice,** *n.f.*, negotiator, transactor.

négociation, *n.f.*, negotiation, transaction.

négocier, *v.n.*, to negotiate, to trade.

négocier, *v.a.*, to negotiate; to be in treaty for. — *un mariage*; to negotiate a marriage. *se négocier,* *v.r.*, to be negotiating (of a thing —*des choses*).

*****négraille,** *n.f.*, negro-race.

nègre, *n.m.*, negro.

négrerie, *n.f.*, negro-yard.

négresse, *n.f.*, negress.

négrier, *n.* and *adj.m.*, slave-ship, slaver; slave-dealer. *Capitaine —*; captain of a slave-ship. *Bâtiment —*: slave-ship.

*****négrillon,** *n.m.*, **-ne,** *n.f.*, little negro.

négromancien, négromant, *n.m.* V. **nécromancien, nécromant.**

neige, *n.f.*, snow. *De gros flocons de —*; large flakes of snow. *Amas de —*; snow-drift. *Boule de —*; snow-ball. *Il est tombé de la —*; there has been a fall of snow.

neiger, *v. imp.*, to snow. *Il neige*; it snows.

neigeu-x, -se, *adj.*, snowy. *Temps —*; snowy weather.

nélumbo, *n.m.*, (bot.) nelumbium.

néméen (-in), *adj.m.*, Nemean.

néméennes, *n.f.pl.*, Pindarus' odes on the victories won at the Nemean Games.

nénies, *n.f.pl.*, (antiq.) funeral dirge.

nenni (na-ni), *adv.*, (fam.) no, not at all. — *da*; no, indeed; certainly not.

nénufar, *n.m.*, nenuphar, water-lily, water-rose.

néo, a prefix from Gr. *véos*.

néocore, *n.m.*, (antiq.) official who swept and guarded a temple.

néographe, *n.m.* and *adj.*, one who wishes to introduce a new way of spelling.

néographisme, *n.m.*, new way of spelling.

néo-latin, *adj.*, applied to the seven modern languages derived from Latin.

néologie, *n.f.*, neology.

néologique, *adj.*, neological.

néologisme, *n.m.*, neologism.

néologiste, *n.m.*, neologist.

néologue, *n.m.*, (b.s.) neologist.

néoménie,*n.f.*,(antiq.)neomenia; ⊙(astron.) new moon.

néophyte, *n.m.f.*, neophyte.

néo-platonicien (-ci-in), **-ne** (-ci-è-n), *n.* and *adj.* (— —*s*), Neoplatonist. *École — ne*; the Neoplatonists' school.

néo-platonisme, *n.m.* (*n.p.*), Neoplatonism.

néotérique, *adj.*, neoteric.

népenthès, *n.m.*, (antiq.) nepenthe; (bot.) nepenthes.

néphralgie, *n.f.*, nephralgia, nephralgy.

néphrétique, *n.m.* and *adj.*, (med.) nephritic; person affected with renal colic.

néphrétique, *n.f.*, renal colic.

néphrite, *n.f.*, nephritis.

népotisme, *n.m.*, nepotism.

neptune, *n.m.*, (astron., myth.) Neptune; (fig.) the sea.

neptunien, -ne, adj., (geol.) neptunian.

néréide, n.f., (myth) Nereid.

nerf (nèrf), n.m., nerve, sinew; fortitude; (book-bind.) cord, slip of tape. Attaque de —s; fit, nervous attack. [The f is mute in nerf, when used in the pl., and in nerf de bœuf.]

nerf-férure, n.f. (—s —s), (vet.) overreach.

nérite, n.f., (conch.) nerite.

néroli, n.m., neroli.

nerprun, n.m., (bot.) buckthorn, purging buckthorn.

⊙**nervaison**, n.f., (med.) nervous system.

⊙**nerval, -e**, adj., acting upon the nerves, nervine.

nervé, -e, part., nerved.

nerver, v.a., to cover with sinews. — un livre; (book-bind.) to cord a book.

nerveu-x, -se, adj., nervous; sinewy, wiry, vigorous. Être —; to be nervous. Bras —; sinewy arm.

nervin, n. and adj. m., nervine.

nervure, n.f., (arch.) nerve; (bot.) nerve (of a leaf—de feuille); (book-bind.) slips of tape, cording; (ent.) nervure; (carp.) rib.

nestor, n.m. (—s), the oldest and most respectable man of a body, association, assembly, &c.

nestorianisme, n.m., Nestorianism.

nestorien, -ne (-in, -è-n), adj. and n., Nestorian.

net, -te, adj., clean, neat, pure; clear, fair, empty; plain, distinct; easy, perspicuous; (com.) net. Une chambre — te; a clean room. Un cheval sain et — : a horse warranted sound and free from any defect. Ce vin est —; that wine is clear. Une écriture — te; a fair hand. Avoir la voix — te; to have a clear voice. Je veux en avoir le cœur —; I will be satisfied about it. Faire maison — te; to dismiss all the servants in one's household at the same time. Une réponse — te; a plain answer. Son bien est —; his estate is clear. Une pensée — te; a clear thought. Il a l'esprit —; he has a clear understanding.

net, n.m., fair copy. Mettre au — ; to copy fair.

net, adv., clean, entirely; plainly, freely, flatly. Il me l'a refusé tout —, he flatly refused me.

nettement (nèt-màn), adv., neatly; cleanly; clearly; distinctly; frankly, plainly, flatly. Parlez-lui — ; speak to him plainly, freely.

netteté (nèt-té), n.f., cleanness, cleanliness; neatness, clearness, distinctness, plainness, blamelessness. Voir avec — ; to see with distinctness. — dans la voix; clearness of voice.

nettoiement (né-toa-màn), n.m., cleaning, cleansing, clearing.

nettoyage, n.m. V. **nettoiement**.

nettoyer, v.a., to clean, to cleanse, to make clean, to scour, to wipe. — un habit; to clean a coat. — les biens d'une maison; to pay off the debts of a firm. — le tapis; to sweep the stakes. — la tranchée (milit.); to drive the besiegers from their trench. — une maison (fig. fam.); to carry off the furniture.

se nettoyer, v.r., to clean one's self. — les dents; to clean one's teeth.

neuf, n. and adj., nine, ninth. Un — de cœur; a nine of hearts. [Neuf is pronounced neu when it precedes an adj. or a n. beginning with a consonant : and neuv, if the adj. or n. begins with a vowel or a silent h.]

neuf, n.m., new; something new. À —; anew, again; like new De —; new. Habiller de —; to dress in new clothes. Donnez-nous du —; give us something new.

neu-f, -ve, adj., new; raw, green, young. Maison — ve; new house. Faire corps —; to take a new lease of one's life. Il est tout — dans

ce métier; he is quite new to that business. Une pensée — ve; a new thought.

neume, n.m., (plain-chant) the singing of notes without words on one vowel. —s; signs used in the middle age for the notation of plain chant.

neutralement (-tral-màn), adv., (gram.) neutrally.

neutralisant, n.m. and adj., (chem.) neutralizing body; neutralizing.

neutralisation, n.f., neutralization.

neutraliser, v.a., to neutralize.

se neutraliser, v.r., to counteract each other.

neutralité, n.f., neutrality.

neutre, n.m. and adj., neuter; neutral. Pavillon —; neutral flag. Nom —; neuter noun. Verbe —; neuter verb. Sel —; neutral salt.

neuvaine, n.f., (c.rel.) neuvaines.

neuvième, n.m. and adj., ninth. Il est le —, elle est la—, de sa classe; he, she, is the ninth in his, in her, class.

neuvième, n.f., (mus.) ninth.

neuvièmement (-vièm-màn), adv., ninthly.

neveu, n.m., nephew. Petit- — (—s —x); grandnephew. — à la mode de Bretagne; cousin once removed. Nos —x, nos derniers —x, nos arrière- —x; our posterity, our children's children.

névralgie, n.f., neuralgia.

névralgique, adj., (med.) neuralgic.

névritique, n. and adj.m., (med.) neurotic.

névrographie, n.f., neurology.

névrologie, n.f., neurology.

névroptère, adj., neuropteral, neuropterous.

névroptère, n.m., neuropteran.

névrose, n.f., (med.) nervous affection, nervous disorder, neurose.

névrotomie, n.f., neurotomy.

newtonianisme (neu-), n.m., Newtonianism.

newtonien, -ne (neu-to-ni-in, -è-n), adj., Newtonian.

newtonien, n.m., newtonian.

nez (né), n.m., nose; face; scent (of dogs—des chiens). — aquilin; aquiline nose. — retroussé; turned up nose. — écrasé, épaté; flat nose, pug nose. Il s'est cassé le —; he has broken his nose. Donner sur le — à quelqu'un; to strike any one on the nose. Regarder quelqu'un sous le —; to stare any one in the face. Ne voir pas plus loin que son —; to see no farther than one's nose. Avoir bon —; to have a good nose. Il saigne du —; his nose bleeds. Au — de quelqu'un; under one's nose. Rire au — de quelqu'un; to laugh in any one's face. Fermer la porte au — à quelqu'un; to shut the door in any one's face. — à —; face to face. Parler du —; to speak through the nose. Fourrer son — dans une affaire; to thrust one's nose into a business. Mener quelqu'un par le —; to lead any one by the nose. Donner du — en terre; to miscarry. Tirer les vers du — à quelqu'un; to pump any one. Jeter quelque chose au — de quelqu'un; to throw a thing in any one's teeth. Il a bon —; he is a sagacious man. Il a un pied de —; he looks foolish at it; he is sadly disappointed. Faire un pied de — à; to laugh at.

ni, conj., neither; nor; or. Il n'est — bon — mauvais; it is neither good nor bad. — moi non plus; nor I either.

niable, adj., that may be denied, deniable.

niais, -e, n. and adj., ninny, simpleton; silly, simple. Il a l'air —; he has a silly look.

niaisement (niè-màn), adv., sillily, foolishly.

niaiser, v.n., to stand trifling, to play the fool, to faddle.

niaiserie (-èz-rî), n.f., silliness, foolishness, simplicity; silly thing, trifle, foolery, nonsense.

⊙**nice**, adj., foolish, silly.

niche, *n.f.*, niche; trick, prank. *Faire une —
à*; to play a trick upon.

nichée, *n.f.*, nest (of young birds—*de petits
oiseaux*); brood; crew, set. *Une — de souris;
e.* brood of mice.

nicher, *v.a.*, to nestle. *Qui vous a niché là?*
who put you there?

se nicher, *v.r.*, to nestle. to nestle one's self;
to poke one's self; to put one's self. *Où la vertu
va-t-elle — !* where will virtue take up its abode
at last?

nicher, *v.n.*, to nestle, to make a nest.

nichet, *n.m.*, nest-egg.

nichoir, *n.m.*, breeding-cage.

nickel, *n.m.*, (metal.) nickel.

nicodème, *n.m.*, noodle. *C'est un grand —;*
he is a great noodle.

nicotiane (-ci-), *n.f.*, (bot.) nicotiana.

nicotine, *n.f.*, nicotine.

nictation, *n.f.*, nictation, nictitation.

nicter, *v.n.*, (vet.) to nictate.

nictitation, *n.f.* *V.* **nictation**.

nid, *n.m.*, nest; berth, post. *Petit à petit
l'oiseau fait son —;* little strokes fell great oaks.
Trouver la pie au —; to find what one is looking
for. *Un — à rats;* a hovel, a mere hole. —
d'oiseau; bird's nest.

nidification, *n.f.*, nidification.

nidoreu-x. -se, *adj.*, nidorous.

nièce, *n.f.*, niece. *Petite- — (—s —s)*, grand-
niece. — *à la mode de Bretagne;* cousin, once
removed.

nielle, *n.f.*, smut, blight; (bot.) rose-campion.

nielle, *n.m.*, niello, inlaid enamel-work.

nieller, *v.a.*, (agri.) to smut, to blast, to
blight; to inlay with enamel-work.

nielleur, *n.m.*, (gold.) enameller of niello.

niellure, *n.f.*, (gold.) art of the enameller of
niello.

nier, *v.a.*, to deny, to gainsay. *Il nie que
cela soit;* he denies it is so.

nigaud, -e. *n.* and *adj.*, booby, simpleton,
silly fellow; silly, foolish. *Un grand —;* a
great booby.

nigaud. *n.m.*, (orni.) booby, gannet.

nigauder, *v.n.*, to play the fool, to trifle.

nigauderie (-gô-drî), *n.f.*, silliness, tom-
foolery; foolish trick.

nigelle, *n.f.*, (bot.) fennel-flower.

nihilisme, *n.m.*, nihilism.

nihiliste, *n.m.f.* and *adj.*, nihilist, nihilistic.

nilgaut, *n.m.*, (zool.) nylghau, nylgau,
neelghau.

*nille**, *n.f.*, tendril (of a vine—*de la vigne*).

nilomètre, *n.m.*, nilometer.

nimbe, *n.m.*, (paint.) nimbus.

nippe, *n.f.*, clothes, apparel; things; furniture. [Mostly used in the plural.]

nipper, *v.a.*, to fit out, to rig out.

se nipper. *v.r.*, to rig one's self out. *Il s'est
bien nippé;* he rigged himself out very well.

nique, *n.f.*, (fam., l.u.) sign of mockery or
contempt. *Faire la — à quelqu'un;* to mock any
one. *Faire la — à la fortune;* to despise riches.

nitée, *n.f.* *V.* **nichée**.

nitouche, *n.f.*, demure hypocrite. *Sainte—;*
demure-looking person. *Faire la sainte —;* to
look as if butter would not melt in one's mouth.

nitrate, *n.m.*, nitrate.

nitre, *n.m.*, nitre.

nitreu-x. -se, *adj.*, nitrous.

nitrière, *n.f.*, nitre-bed.

nitrification, *n.f.*, nitrification.

se nitrifier, *v.r.*, to nitrify.

nitrique, *adj.*, nitric.

nitrite, *n.m.*, nitrite.

nitrogène, *n.m.*, and *adj.*, nitrogen, nitrogenous.

nitroglycérine, *n.f.*, (chem.) nitroglycerine.

nitro-muriatique, *adj.*, nitro-muriatic.

niveau, *n.m.*, level. — *d'eau;* water-level.
— *à bulle d'air;* spirit-level. *Au — de;* on a
level with, even with.

niveler (ni-vlé), *v.a.*, to make even, to take
the level of, to level.

niveleur (ni-vleur), *n.m.*, leveller.

nivellement (-vèl-màn), *n.m.*, levelling.

nivéole, *n.f.*, (bot.) snow-flake.

nivereau, *n.m.*, or **niverolle**, *n.f.*, snow-
bird.

☉**nivet**, *n.m.*, (pop.) dishonest profit of agents.

nivôse, *n.m.*, Nivôse, fourth month of the
calendar of the first French republic, from
December 21st or 22nd, to January 19th or
20th.

nobiliaire, *n.m.*, nobiliary.

nobiliaire, *adj.*, of the nobility, aristocratic.

nobilissime, *n.m.*, (antiq.) nobilissimus.

nobilissime, *adj.*, most noble.

noble, *adj.*, noble, great, elevated. *Être de
— sang;* to be of noble blood. *Il a l'air —;* he
has a noble look.

noble, *n.m.*, noble, nobleman.

noblement, *adv.*, nobly. *Vivre —;* to live
like a noble.

noblesse, *n.f.*, nobility; nobleness, loftiness.
La haute —; the higher nobility. *La petite —;*
the inferior nobility. — *de cœur;* nobleness of
heart. — *de style;* loftiness of style.

noce, *n.f.*, wedding, wedding-party; *pl.*,
marriage, nuptials, wedding. *Habit de —s;*
wedding suit. *Tant qu'à des —s* (prov. pop.);
plentifully. *N'être pas à la —;* to be in no
pleasant situation. *Gâteau de —;* bride-cake.

nocher, *n.m.*, (poet.) pilot. *Caron, le pâle
—;* Charon, the grim ferryman.

noctambule, *n.m.f.*, noctambulist.

noctambulisme, *n.m.*, noctambulism.

nocturne, *adj.*, nocturnal, nightly.

nocturne, *n.m.*, (rel.) nocturn; (mus.)
notturno.

nocturnement, *adv.*, (l.u.) by night.

☉**nocuité**, *n.f.*, nocuousness, culpability.

nodosité, *n.f.*, nodosity; (surg.) node.

nodule, *n.m.*, nodule.

nodus, *n.m.*, (surg.) node.

noël, *n.m.*, Christmas; Christmas-carol. *Les
fêtes de —;* the Christmas holidays. *À la fête
de —, à la —;* at Christmas.

nœud (neu), *n.m.*, knot; stress, difficulty,
intricacy, knotty point; tie, bond, band; knuckle;
knob; node (med., bot., astron., lit). — *serré*,
hard knot. — *coulant;* noose. *Un — de diamants;*
a knot of diamonds. — *d'amour;* love-knot.
Bois plein de —s; wood full of knots. *Voilà le
— de l'affaire;* there lies the difficulty of the
business. *Resserrer les —s de l'amitié;* to
tighten the bonds of friendship. *Le — de
la gorge;* Adam's apple. — *d'une pièce
dc théâtre;* the knot of a play. —*s d'une
planète;* nodes of a planet. — *de bouline;* (nav.)
bowline-knot. — *de bois* (nav.); limber-hitch.
Nous filons douze —s par heure; we make twelve
knots an hour. *Le — gordien;* the Gordian
knot.

noir. -e, *adj.*, black; swarthy; foul, dirty;
dark, gloomy; black and blue; dismal; base,
wicked, heinous; brown (of bread — *du pain*).
— *comme jais;* black as jet. *Des yeux —s;* black
eyes. *Blé —;* buckwheat. *Bêtes —es;* black
game. *Une chambre —e,* a dark room. *Un
temps —;* gloomy weather. *Il a une humeur
—e,* he has a gloomy temper. *Des idées —es;*
gloomy ideas. *Un — attentat;* a black
crime. *Avoir l'âme —e;* to have a bad heart.
Rendre —; to blacken.

noir. *n.m.*, black ; negro; (agri.) brown-rust.
— *de fumée;* lamp-black. — *d'ivoire;* ivory-
black. *Teindre en —;* to dye black. *Porter le*

—; to be in mourning. *Broyer du* — ; to have the dismals.

noirâtre. *adj.*. blackish.

noiraud, -e, *adj.*. dark, of a dark complexion.

noirceur, *n.f.*, blackness; black spot; heinousness, baseness. treacherous action, foul thing. *La — de son crime ;* the blackness of his crime. *La — æe son âme ;* the baseness of his soul.

noircir. *v.a.*, to black. to blacken, to make black, to stain, to smut; to sully, to traduce. *Le soleil noircit le teint ;* the sun tans the complexion. — *la réputation de quelqu'un ;* to sully any one's character.

se **noircir**, *v.r.*, to blacken. to grow black. — *la barbe ;* to blacken one's beard. *Cela s'est noirci à la fumée ;* that has become blackened in the smoke. *Le temps se noircit ;* the weather begins to grow cloudy.

noircir, *v.n.*, to blacken, to grow black.

noircissure, *n.f.*, black spot.

noire, *n.f.*, (mus.) crotchet.

noise. *n.f.*, quarrel. *Chercher — à quelqu'un ;* to pick a quarrel with any one.

noisetier (noaz-tié), *n.m.*, nut tree, hazeltree.

noisette. *n.f.*, nut, hazel-nut.

noix (noa), *n.f.*, walnut.nut; kernel; (of meat —*de la viande*) pope's eye; tumbler (of firearms—*d'armes à feu*); plug (of cocks—*de robinets*); grinding-wheel (of coffee-mills—*de moulins à café*). — *de galle ;* gall-nut. *Coquille de —;* walnut-shell. *La — du genou ;* the kneecap. — *d'acajou ;* cashew-nut. — *muscade ;* nutmeg. — *vomique ;* nux vomica. *Brou de —;* walnut husk. — *de terre, terre- — (—);* earth-nut. pig-nut.

noli me tangere (-mé-tan-jé-ré-), *n.m.* (—), (bot.) noli me tangere, touch me not.

nolis.'or nolisement. *n.m.*, freight (in the Mediterranean—*dans la Méditerranée*).

noliser, *v.a.*, to freight (in the Mediterranean—*dans la Méditerranée*).

nom (non), *n.m.*, name; fame, celebrity; (gram.) noun. *Un — propre, un — de baptême ;* a proper, a christian, name. *Je ne le connais que de —;* I only know him by name. — *de guerre ;* nickname. *Il nomme les choses par leur —;* he calls every thing by its name. *Au — de;* in the name of. *De —;* in name. — *social ;* name of the firm. *Décliner son — ;* to give in one's name. *Changer de —;* to change one's name. — *collectif ;* collective noun. — *substantif,* — *adjectif ;* substantive noun, adjective noun.

nomade. *n.m.* and *adj.*, nomade, nomad; nomadic, wandering. *Peuples —s ;* nomadic tribes.

nomancie. '*n.f.*, nomancy.

nomarque. *n.m.*. (antiq.) chief of an Egyptian nome or province.

nombrable, *adj.*, (l.u.) countable.

nombrant. *adj.*, (math.) abstract.

nombre. *n.m.*. number; numerousness; quantity; quorum; harmony. *Mettre au — de ;* to number among. — *compétent :* quorum (of members of any body—*des membres d'un corps*). *Surpasser en — ;* to outnumber. — *pair ;* even number. — *impair ;* odd number. — *premier ;* primary number. *Être du —, au — des savants ;* to be one of the learned. *Vous n'êtes pas du — ;* you are not one. *Dans le — ;* among the number. *Il y a du — dans ces vers :* there is harmony in these verses. — *abstrait.* — *nombrant ;* abstract number. — *concret.* — *nombré ;* concrete number. — *d'or* (astron.) golden number. *N'être pas en — (of assemblies—d'assemblées) ;* not to form a quorum.

nombré, -o, *part.*, (math.) concrete; numbered.

nombrer, *v.a.*. to number, to compute, to sum up.

nombreu-x. **-se.** *adj.*, numerous; harmonious. *Style —;* harmonious style.

nombril (non-bri), *n.m.*.(anat.) navel, umbilic, umbilicus; (bot.) hilum, umbilicus.

nome, *n.m.*. (antiq.) nome.

nomenclateur, *n.m.*, nomenclator.

nomenclature, *n.m.*, nomenclature.

nominal, -e, *adj.*, nominal. *Appel — ;* call of the names.

nominalement, *adv.*, nominally.

nominalisme, *n.m.*, (philos.) nominalism.

nominaliste, *n.m.* (*nominaux*), (philos. Nominalist.

nominataire, *n.m.*, (ecc.) nominee.

nominateur, *n.m.*, (ecc.) nominator.

nominatif, *n.m.*, (gram.) nominative.

nominati-f, -ve, *adj.*, of names.

nomination, *n.f.*, nomination, appointment.

nominativement (-tiv-mān), *adv.*, by name.

nommé, -e, *part.*, named, said. *Le — Jacques ;* one James by name. *À jour — ; at the appointed day. *À point — ;* in the nick of time.

nommément, *adv.*, namely; particularly.

nommer, *v.a.*, to name, to call, to give a name; to nominate, to elect. — *quelqu'un son héritier ;* to institute any one one's heir.

se **nommer,** *v.r.*, to state one's name; to be called. *Comment se nomme-t-il ?* what is his name?

nomothète, *n.m.*, (antiq.) nomothete.

non, *adv.*, no, not. — *pas, s'il vous plaît ;* not so, if you please. *Vous ne l'aimez pas, ni moi — plus ;* you do not like it, nor I either. *Je crois que —;* I think not. *Je dis que —;* I say no. —*-da;* no indeed, certainly not.

non-activité, *n.f.* (n.p.), (milit.) being unattached (of officers—*d'officiers*).

nonagénaire, *adj.*, of ninety, ninety years of age. —, *n.m. f.*, nonagenarian.

nonagésime, *adj.*, nonagesimal.

nonagone, *n.m.*, nonagon.

nonandre, *adj.*, (bot.) having nine stamens.

⊙**nonante,** *adj.*, ninety.

⊙**nonantième,** *adj.*. ninetieth.

nonce, *n.m.*, nuncio.

nonchalamment (-la-mān), *adv.*, carelessly, indolently, heedlessly.

nonchalance, *n.f.*, carelessness, heedlessness, remissness, nonchalance.

nonchalant, -e, *n.* and *adj.*, careless, listless person; careless, heedless, listless, remiss.

nonchaloir, *n.m.*, nonchalance.

nonciature, *n.f.*, nunciature.

non-conformiste, *n.m.* (— —s), nonconformist.

non-conformité. *n.f.*(n.p.), nonconformity.

none, *n.f.*, (c.rel.) none ; (antiq.) ninth hour (3 o'clock p.m.—*3 heures après midi*).

nones. *n.f.pl.*, (antiq.) nones.

non-être, *n.m.* (n.p.), (philos.) non-entity, non-existence.

nonidi. *n.m.*, nonidi, ninth day of the decade of the calendar of the first French republic.

non-intervention, *n.f.* (n.p.), (pol.) non-intervention.

nonius (-ûs), *n.m.*, (math.) nonius, sliding rule.

non-jouissance. *n.f.* (n.p.), non-enjoyment.

non-lieu, *n.m.* (n.p.), (jur.) not sufficient cause to give rise to an action at law, or to a prosecution.

non-moi, *n.m.* (*n.p.*), (philos.) all that which is not self.

ñonnain, *n.f.*, (jest.) nun.

nonne. *n.f.*, nun.

nonnerie, (no-n-ri), *n.f.*, (jest) nunnery.

nonnette. *n.f.*, (jest.) nun; sort of gingerbread; (orni.) ospray.

nonobstant, *prep.*, notwithstanding, in spite of.

nonobstant que. *conj.*, notwithstanding, although.

non-ouvré, **-e**, *adj.*, (of raw materials—*matières premières*) unwrought.

non-pair. *adj.*, not even, odd (of numbers).

*nonpareil, -le, *adj.*, nonpareil, matchless, unparalleled.

*nonpareille,*n.f.*,nonpareil; narrow ribbon; nonpareil (apple, small sugar-plum—*pomme, petite dragée*); (print.) nonpareil.

non-payement,*n.m.* (——*s*), non-payment.

non plus ultra, *n.m.* *V.* **nec plus ultra**.

non-prix. *n.m.* (—). (com.) undervalue.

non-résidence, *n.f.* (*n.p.*), non-residence.

non-sens, *n.m.* (—), nonsense.

nonuple, *adj.*, ninefold.

nonupler, *v.a.*, to increase nine times.

non-usage, *n.m.* (*n.p.*), disuse.

non-valeur, *n.f.*(——*s*), unproductiveness; bad debt.

⊙**non-vue**, *n.f.* (*n.p.*), (nav.) misty weather, fog.

nopal, *n.m.* (—*s*),(bot.) nopal.

nord, *n.m.*, North; north-wind. ——*est*. north-east; north-east wind. — -*ouest*; north-west; north-west wind.

nord, *adj.*, North (pole).

noria, *n.f.* (—*s*), (mec.) noria, Persian-wheel.

normal, **-e**, *adj.*, normal. *École —e*; normal school. *État —*; healthy state.

normale, *n.f.*, (geom.) normal, perpendicular.

normand, **-e**, *adj.*, Norman; equivocal (of answers—*réponses*); feigned (reconciliation). *Réponse —e*; ambiguous answer.

normand. *n.m.*, **-e**, *n.f.*, Norman. *Répondre en —*; to give an evasive answer. *C'est un fin —*; he is a crafty fellow.

norne, *n.f.*, (Scandinav. mythol.) Norn. *Les trois —s*; the three Norns; or fates, the present, the past, and the future.

nos, *adj. m.f. pl.*, our.

nosographie. *n.f.*, nosography.

nosologie. *n.f.*, nosology.

nosologiste, *n.m.*, nosologist.

nosseigneurs, *n.m.pl.*, my lords.

nostalgie, *n.f.*, nostalgia, home-sickness.

nostoc, *n.m.*, (bot.) nostoch.

nota, *n.m.* (—), observation. note, marginal note.

notabilité, *n.f.*, (com.) respectability; principal person.

notable, *adj.*, notable. remarkable, considerable, of influence. *Faits —s*; remarkable doings; remarkable facts.

notable. *n.m.*, principal; (hist. of France) notable; leading man.

notablement. *adv.*, notably, considerably.

notaire. *n.m.*, notary. — *public*; public notary. *C'est comme si le — y avait passé*; it is as good as a bond.

notamment (no-ta-män). *adv.*, specially, especially, particularly, namely.

notariat. *n.m.*, profession of a notary.

notarié. **-e**. *adj.*, notarial.

notation. *n.f.*, notation.

note. *n.f.*, note, mark, remark; bill; account; minute, memorandum. — *infamante*; brand of infamy. *Chanter sur une autre —*; to change one's tune. *Chanter la —*; to sol-fa. *Bien atta-*

quer la —; to make a note tell. (mus.)— *sensible*; leading note.

noter, *v.a.*. to note, to note down; to mark; to observe. to notice, to take notice. *Notez bien cela*; observe that well. *Cela est à —*; that is worth noting down.

⊙**noteur**, *n.m.*, music copier.

notice. *n.f.*, notice; account: sketch; review (in newspapers—*dans les journaux*).

notification, *n.f.*, notification.

notifier, *v.a.*, to notify.

notion, *n.f.*, notion. idea, knowledge. *Selon la — que j'en ai*; according to my notion of it.

notoire. *adj.*, notorious.

notoirement (no-toar-män), *adv.*, notoriously.

notoriété, *n.f.*, notoriety, evidence.

notre, *adj. m.f.* (*nos*), our. — *maison*; our house. '— *père*; our father. *Nos frères et nos sœurs*; our brothers and sisters. *Nos père et mère*; our father and mother.

nôtre, *possessive pron. m.f.* (*nôtres*). ours. *C'est votre ami et le —*; it is your friend and ours. *Le —*; our own, ours. *Les —s*; pl., our people, our relations, our friends. *Celui-là est-il des —s?* is that man one of our people? *Ne serez-vous pas des —s?* won't you make one of us? *Voilà leur maison, celle-ci est la —*; there is their house, this one is ours.

notre-dame, *n.f.*, our Lady; festival in honour of our Lady; Notre-Dame (name of churches—*nom d'église*).

notule, *n.f.*, short note (added to ancient texts—*ajoutée à des textes anciens*).

noue, *n.f.*, gutter-lead; pantile; pasture ground.

noué, **-e**, *part.*, tied, rickety. *Enfant —*; rickety child. *Une pièce de théâtre bien —e*; a well-plotted dramatic piece.

nouement (noo-män), *n.m.*, knotting.

nouer, *v.a.*, to tie, to knot; to get up, to concoct.

se nouer. *v.r.*, to attach, to fasten one's self; to grow rickety.

nouer, *v.n.*, (hort.) to knot.

nouet, *n.m.*, little bag (that contains a substance to be infused or boiled—*contenant quelque chose à infuser ou à bouillir*).

noueu-x, **-se**, *adj.*, knotty, knotted, full of knots, nodose.

nougat, *n.m.*, almond-cake.

nouilles or **noules**, *n.f.pl.*, German cake.

noulet, *n.m.*, gutter (of a roof—*de toit*).

noumène *n.m.*..(in Kant's philos.) noumenon, *i.e.*, the facts which occur in the soul.

nourrain, *n.m.*, fry (fish—*poisson*). *V.* **alevin**.

nourri, **-e**, *part.*, nourished, fed; rich. *Feu bien —*; very close fire. *Une couleur —e*; (paint.) thick-laid. colour. *Blé, grain. bien —*; well-filled corn. *Style —*; copious style.

nourrice, *n.f.*, nurse; wet-nurse, fostermother. *Mettre un enfant en —*, to put a child out to nurse.

nourricier. *n.m.*, foster-father, fosterer.

nourrici-er. **-ère**,*adj.*, nutritive, nutritious. *Pere —*; foster-father.

nourrir,*v.a.*. to nourish, to nurture; to feed, to keep, to maintain, to sustain; to suckle. to nurse, to foster; to supply; to bring up, to rear up, to keep alive; to cherish. *Le bois nourrit le feu*; wood feeds the fire. *La Sicile nourrissait Rome*; Sicily supplied Rome with provisions. *L'étude nourrit l'esprit*; study strengthens the understanding. *L'espérance nourrit l'amour*, hope keeps love alive.

se nourrir. *v.r.*, to feed, to live, to support one's self; to live, to feed upon. *Se bien nourrir*; to live well.

nourrissage, *n.m.*, feeding (of cattle—*des bestiaux*).

nourrissant, **-e**, *adj.*, nutritive, nourishing.

nourrisseur, *n.m.*, cow-keeper.

nourrisseur, *adj.*, (tech.) feeding.

nourrisson, *n.m.*, foster-child, nurse-child, nursling, suckling.

nourriture, *n.f.*, nourishment, food, diet, board, living, livelihood; nurture. *Son travail lui procure la* — ; he finds a livelihood by his labour. *Faire des* —*s ;* to breed cattle, fowls, etc.

nous, *personal pron.*, we, us; to us; each other. — *disons ;* we say. *Il* —*aime ;* he loves us. *Vous* — *parlez ;* you speak to us. — - *mêmes ;* ourselves. — *autres ;* we. — — *aimons ;* we love each other.

nouure, *n.f.*, rickets; (hort.) knotting.

nouveau, **nouvel**, *adj.*, *m.*, **nouvelle**, *f.*, new, recent. *Le nouvel an ;* the new year. *De* —*le date ;* recently. *De* —*le mode ;* new fashioned. *Recommencer sur nouveaux frais ;* to begin anew. *Un homme* — ; an upstart. *Un habit* — ; a coat of a new fashion. *Un nouvel habit ;* a fresh coat. — *venu*, newly-come. *Un* — *venu ;* a new-comer; *des nouveaux venus ;* new-comers. *Une nouvelle venue ;* new-comer (female); *des nouvelles venues*, new-comers (females). — *débarqué ;* person just come up from the country. [Nouvel is used for the masculine before a vowel or an *h* mute.]

nouveau, *n.m.*, new, something new. *À* —*;* on new account. *De* — ; anew; again. *Qu'y a-t-il de* —*!* what is the news?

nouveau-né, *n.m.*, (— —*s*); **nouveau-née**, *n.f.*, (— —*s*), new-born babe.

nouveauté, *n.f.*, newness, novelty; change, innovation ; *pl.*, fancy articles. *Magasin de* —*s;* repository of fancy articles ; linendraper's shop. *C'est une* — *que de vous voir ;* it is a rarity to see you.

nouvelle, *n.f.*, news, tidings, intelligence, account ; novelet. *Quelles sont les* —*s !* what is the news? *Débiter des* —*s ;* to spread news. —*s de basse cour ;* idle rumours. *Envoyer savoir des* —*s de quelqu'un ;* to send to know how any one is. *Mandez-moi de vos* — ; let me hear from you. *Ne faites rien que vous n'ayez de mes* — *;* do nothing till you hear from me. *Vous aurez de mes* —*s ;* you shall hear from me. *Point de* —*s, bonnes* —*s ;* no news is good news. *Recevoir des* —*s de ;* to hear from.

nouvellement (noo-vèl-măn), *adv.*, newly, lately, recently.

nouvelleté (-vèl-té), *n.f.*, (jur.) dispossession, trespass.

nouvelliste, *n.m.*, newsmonger ; novelist.

novale, *n.f.*, land newly broken up ; *pl.*, tithes on new land.

novat-eur, **-rice**, *n.* and *adj.*, innovator ; innovating.

novation, *n.f.*, (jur.) substitution.

novelles, *n.f.pl.*, (Roman law—*droit romain*) novels, Justinian's constitutions. [It is used in the *sing.* in speaking of one of them : *La novelle X ;* Novel X.]

novembre, *n.m.*, November.

novice, *adj.*, novice, inexperienced. *Une main* — ; an inexperienced hand.

novice, *n.m.f.*, novice ; (nav.) apprentice. *Il est encore* — *dans son métier ;* he is yet but a novice in his trade.

noviciat, *n.m.*, novitiate, probationership ; part of the convent where novices live; apprenticeship.

○**novissimé**, *adv.*, very lately.

noyade (noa-yad), *n.f.*, drowning.

noyale, or **noyalle** (noa-yal), *n.f.*, sailcloth.

noyau (noa-yô), *n.m.*, stone (of fruit—*de fruit*); nucleus; core (of statues, of casts—*de statues, de moules*) ; (metal.) core; noyau (cordial). — *de pêche ;* stone of a peach. *Fruits à* — ; stone-fruit.

noyé, **-e** (noa-yé), *part.* and *n.*, drowned, drowning ; a drowned person.

noyer (noa-yé), *n.m.*, walnut-tree.

noyer (noa-yé), *v.a.*, to drown ; to put under water, to swamp, to deluge ; (paint.) to confuse (colours—*des couleurs*). — *son chagrin dans le vin ;* to drown one's cares in wine.

se **noyer** (noa-yé), *v.r.*, to be drowned, to drown one's self. — *dans le sang ;* to wallow in blood. *C'est un homme qui se noie ;* his affairs begin to take a bad turn.

noyon (no-yon; noa-yon; né-yon), *n.m.*, scratch, mark (at bowls—*aux boules*).

noyure (no-yur; noa-yur), *n.f.*, countersink (for nails, screws, &c.—*de clous, de vis, &c.*).

nu, **-e**, *adj.*, naked, bare, uncovered ; plain, open, without disguise, destitute. *Il était tout* — ; he was quite naked. *Il avait la tête* —*e, il était nu-tête ;* he was bare-headed. *Aller nu-pieds ;* to go barefoot. *Un va-nu-pieds* (—) ; a poor destitute wretch. *Observer quelque chose à l'œil* — ; to observe anything with the naked eye. *C'est la vérité toute* —*e ;* it is the naked truth. — *e propriété* (jur.); property without the usufruct of it. — *propriétaire* (jur.); owner who is not possessed of the usufruct of his property.

nu, *n.m.*, (paint.) nude, nudity ; naked (of a wall—*d'un mur*); *pl.*, (Bibl.) naked. *À* — ; naked, bare. *Monter un cheval à* — ; to ride a horse bare-backed.

nuage, *n.m.*, cloud ; mist ; (fig.) darkness; gloom, sadness, dejection. *Le ciel est couvert de* —*s ;* the sky is covered with clouds. *Un* — *de poussière ;* a cloud of dust.

nuageu-x, **-se**, *adj.*, cloudy. *Un ciel* — ; a cloudy sky.

nuaison, *n.f.*, (nav.) time of a steady set breeze.

nuance, *n.f.*, shade, hue, tint. *Les* —*s des caractères ;* the shades of characters.

nuancer, *v.a.*, to shade, to tint. — *des couleurs ;* to shade colours.

nubécule, *n.f.*, (med.) nubecula.

nubile, *adj.*, marriageable, nubile.

nubilité, *n.f.*, state of being marriageable.

nudité, *n.f.*, nudity, nakedness.

nue, *n.f.*, cloud ; *pl.*, skies. *Élever jusqu'aux* —*s ;* to extol to the skies. *Se perdre dans les* —*s ;* to lose one's self in the clouds. *Tomber des* —*s ;* to fall from the clouds, to be amazed.

nuée, *n.f.*, cloud ; storm ; swarm, host, flock, shower. *Une* — *de barbares ;* a swarm of barbarians. *Une* — *de traits ;* a shower of darts.

nuement. *V.* **nûment**.

nuer, *v.a.*, to shadow (colours of silks, &c. —*les couleurs de soies, &c.*); to blend different colours in one another.

nuire (nuisant, nui), *v.n.*, to hurt, to prejudice, to do hurt, to harm, to annoy, to wrong. *Il cherche à me* — ; he seeks to do me harm. *Le froid nuit à la santé ;* cold is hurtful to health. *se* **nuire**, *v.r.*, to hurt, to injure one's self ; to hurt, to injure, each other.

nuisible, *adj.*, hurtful, detrimental, prejudicial, injurious, noxious.

nuit, *n.f.*, night, night-time ; darkness. *Bonnet de* — ; night-cap. *À la* — *tombante ;* when it is quite dark. *Passer la* — ; to sit up all night. *L'astre des* —*s ;* the orb of night. *Il fait* — ; it is night. *Il se fait* — ; night is coming on. *La* — *de l'ignorance ;* the darkness of ignorance. *De* — ; by night, in the nighttime, nightly. *Effet de* — ; (paint.) night-piece. *Je vous souhaite une bonne* — ; I wish you good

night. *La — porte conseil ;* advise with your pillow.

nuitamment (-ta-mān), *adv.*, by night, in the night, nightly.

nuitée, *n.f.*, lodging ; night's work.

nul, -le. *pron.*, no one, nobody, not one. — *n'ose en approcher ;* nobody dares come near him.

nul, -le. *adj.*, no, not any ; void, of no force, null, invalid. *—le part ;* nowhere. *Sans — égard ;* without any regard. *Rendre — ;* to nullify. *C'est un homme — ;* he is a cipher.

nulle. *n.f.*, (cryptography—*stéganographie*) graphic sign that is meaningless, superfluous.

nullement (nul-mān), *adv.*, not at all, by no means.

nullifier (nul-li-fié), *v.a.*, to nullify.

nullité (nul-li-té), *n.f.*, nullity ; (jur.) flaw. *La — d'un acte ;* the nullity of a deed. *Cet homme est d'une parfaite — ;* that man is a downright cipher.

nûment. *adv.*, nakedly, openly.

numéraire. *n.m.* and *adj.*, metallic currency, specie, cash ; legal (of *coin—des espèces*). *Valeur — ;* legal value, legal tender.

numéral, -e, *adj.*, numeral.

numérateur. *n.m.*, (arith.) numerator.

numération, *n.f.*, (arith.) numeration.

numérique. *adj.*, numerical.

numériquement (-rik-mān), *adv.*, numerically.

numéro, *n.m.*, number ; (com.) size. *Donnez-moi le — de sa maison ;* give me the number of his house. *Voyez le — cinq ;* see number five. *Il entend le —* (pop.) ; he understands his business.

numérotage, *n.m.*, numbering.

numéroter, *v.a.*, to number, to mark with a number.

numismate. *n.m.*, numismatologist.

numismatique, *adj.*, numismatic.

numismatique, *n.f.*, numismatics.

numismatographie, *n.f.*, numismatography.

nummulaire, *n.f.*, (bot.) moneywort.

nummulite, *n.f.*, nummulite.

nuncupatif. *adj.* m., nuncupatory, nuncupative. *Testament — ;* nuncupative will.

nundinales, *adj. f. pl.*, (antiq.) nundinal, nundinary.

nuptial, -e, *adj.*, nuptial.

nuque. *n.f.*, nape (of the neck—*du cou*).

nutation. *n.f.*, (astron., bot.) nutation.

nutriti-f, -ve, *adj.*, nutritive, nutritious, nourishing.

nutrition. *n.f.*, nutrition.

nyctage du Pérou, *n.f.*, (bot.) marvel of Peru, mirabilis.

nyctalope. *n.m.f.*, nyctalops.

nyctalopie, *n.f.*, nyctalopia, nyctalopy.

nymphe, *n.f.*, nymph ; (ent.) nymph, grub ; (anat.) *pl.*, nymphæ.

nymphéa, *n.m.*, (bot.) nenuphar, white water-lily.

nymphéacées, *n.f. pl.* (bot.) nymphæaceæ.

nymphée, *n.f.* or *m.*, (antiq.) nymphæum.

nymphomanie, *n.f.*, nymphomania.

O

o, n.m., the fifteenth letter of the alphabet, o.

o. (ab. of Ouest), W., West.

o ! *int.*, O !

oasis (o-a-zis), *n.f.*, oasis.

obclavé, -e, *adj.*, (bot.) obovate.

obconique. *adj.*, (bot.) obconic, obconical.

obcordé, -e, *adj.*, (bot.) obcordate.

obédience, *n.f.*, permission to leave one convent for another; functions (in a convent—*dans un couvent*); jurisdiction (of the pope—*du pape*); (Bibl.) obedience.

obédiencier. *n.m.*, priest doing duty in another's benefice.

obédientiel, -le (-ci-èl), *adj.*, (ecc.) pertaining, relating to obedience ; (Bibl.) obediential.

obéir, *v.n.*, to obey, to comply with, to be obedient ; to bend, to yield. *Pour — à,* in obedience to. *Il faut lui — ;* he must be obeyed. *Se faire — ;* to make one's self obeyed.

obéissance, *n.f.*, obedience ; dominion (of princes). *Prêter — à un prince ;* to yield dominion to a prince. *Être sous l' — de père et mère ;* to be under the legal authority of one's father and mother. *Être d'une grande — ;* to be very obedient.

obéissant, -e, *adj.*, obedient, pliant.

obélisque, *n.m.*, obelisk.

obérer, *v.a.*, to run in debt. *C'est un homme fort obéré ;* he is greatly in debt.

s'obérer, *v.r.*, to involve one's self in debt.

obèse, *adj.*, obese.

obésité, *n.f.*, obesity.

obier, *n.m.*, guelder-rose. [This word is sometimes, but incorrectly, spelt *aubier*.]

obit (o-bit), *n.m.*, (c.rel.) obit.

obituaire, *n.m.* and *adj.*, (c. rel.) obituary ; ⊙ (ecc.) one appointed by the pope to a benefice vacant by the death of the titulary.

objecter, *v.a.*, to object, to reproach with.

objecti-f, -ve, *adj.*, objective.

objectif, *n.m.*, (opt.) object-glass ; (philos., milit.) object ; aim, end.

objection, *n.f.*, objection. *Repousser une — ;* to overthrow an objection. *Aller au-devant d'une — ;* to meet an objection.

objectivement. *adv.*, objectively.

objectivité, *n.f.*, objectivity.

objet, *n.m.*, object, subject, matter, business ; aim, end, view, drift, purport ; article ; *pl.*, goods. *Un — de risée ;* a laughing-stock. *Être l'— de la raillerie ;* to be the object of raillery. *Il n'a pour — que son intérêt ;* his only view is self-interest. *Il vend toute sorte d'—s ;* he deals in all sorts of articles. *—s de première nécessité ;* articles of indispensable use.

objurgation, *n.f.*, objurgation.

oblat, *n.m.*, ⊙ lay monk ; a monk of the order of the Immaculate Conception.

oblation. *n.f.*, oblation, offering.

obligataire, *n.m.*, (com., fin.) bond-holder.

obligation, *n.f.*, obligation, (com., fin., jur.) bond. *Remplir ses —s ;* to fulfil one's obligations. *Vous êtes dans l'— de lui répondre ;* you are bound to answer him. *Être dans l'— de ;* to be under an obligation to. *Porteur d'— ;* (com.) bond-holder.

obligatoire. *adj.*, obligatory, incumbent.

obligatoirement (-tôar-mān), *adv.*, obligatorily, compulsorily.

obligé, *n.m.*, indentures (of apprenticeship —*d'apprentissage*).

obligé, *n.m.*, -e. *n.f.*, (jur.) obligor.

obligé, -e, *part.*, obliged ; necessary. *Je suis — de sortir ;* I am obliged to go out.

obligeamment (-ja-mān), *adv.*, obligingly.

obligeance (-jans), *n.f.*, kindness.

obligeant, -e, *adj.*, obliging, kind.

obliger, *v.a.*, to oblige, to bind ; to compel ; to gratify. *Votre devoir vous y oblige ;* you are bound in duty to do it. *— un apprenti ;* to bind apprentice.

s'obliger, *v.r.*, to bind one's self.

obliger. *v.n.*, to impose obligations ; to oblige, to favour.

oblique. *adj.*, oblique, slanting ; indirect. *Pont — ;* oblique-bridge, skew-bridge.

obliquement (o-blik-măn), *adv.*, obliquely, crookedly, indirectly, aslant.

obliquer, *v.n.*, to walk in an oblique direction.

obliquité, *n.f.*, obliquity; obliqueness; slant.

oblitération, *n.f.*, obliteration.

oblitérer, *v.a.*, to obliterate.

s'oblitérer, *v.r.*, to be obliterated; (l.u.) to fall into disuse, to disappear.

oblong, **-ue**, *adj.*, oblong.

obole, *n.f.*, obole. *N'avoir pas une —;* not to be worth a groat.

obombrer, *v.a.*, (Bibl.) to overshadow.

obreptice, *adj.*, obreptitious.

obrepticement (-tis-măn), *adv.*, by concealing the truth.

obreption, *n.f.*, concealment of the truth, reticence, obreption.

obscène, *adj.*, obscene.

obscénité, *n.f.*, obscenity, obsceneness.

obscur, **-e**, *adj.*, obscure, dark. *Il fait —;* it is dark. *Naissance —e;* mean birth. *Couleur —e;* dark colour. *Clair- (—s —s);* (paint.) light and shade.

obscurcir, *v.a.*, to obscure, to darken, to dim. *— la vue;* to dim the sight.

s'obscurcir, *v.r.*, to become obscure, dark; to grow dim. *Le soleil s'obscurcit;* the sun is obscured. *Le ciel s'obscurcit;* the sky is overcast. *Son esprit s'obscurcit;* his understanding is becoming clouded.

obscurcissement (-sis-măn), *n.m.*, obscuration, darkness, dimness.

obscurément, *adv.*, obscurely, confusedly, dimly.

obscurité, *n.f.*, obscurity, gloom, darkness. *A travers l'— de la nuit;* through the obscurity of the night.

obsécration, *n.f.*, (rhet.) obsecration.

obséder, *v.a.*, to beset; to possess (of evil spirits—*du malin esprit*).

obsèques (ob-sèk-), *n.f.pl.*, obsequies.

obséquieusement, *adv.*, obsequiously.

obséquieu-x, **-se**, *adj.*, obsequious.

obséquiosité, *n.f.*, obsequiousness.

observable, *adj.*, observable.

observance, *n.f.*, observance.

observantin, *n.m.*, observant (monk of the order of St. Francis—*religieux de l'observance de Saint-François*).

observat-eur, **-rice**, *n.* and *adj.*, observer; observant, observing. *Un esprit —;* an observing mind.

observation, *n.f.*, observance; observation, remark. *Être en —;* to be on the look-out.

observatoire, *n.m.*, observatory.

observer, *v.a.*, to observe, to mind, to notice; to watch, to keep a watch over; to fulfil, to perform. *— les lois;* to observe the laws. *Lui avez-vous fait — que?* did you observe to him that?

s'observer, *v.r.*, to be circumspect, to look about one's self; to eye each other.

obsession, *n.f.*, besetting, obsession; being possessed (by evil spirits—*du malin esprit*).

obsidiane, *or* **obsidienne**, *n.f.*, (min.) obsidian.

obsidional, **-e**, *adj.*, obsidional. *Couronne —e;* obsidional crown.

obstacle, *n.m.*, obstacle, bar, impediment, obstruction. *Lever un —;* to remove an impediment. *Rencontrer un —;* to meet with an obstacle. *Faire naître un —;* to give rise to an obstacle.

obstétrical, **-e**, *adj.*, obstetric, obstetrical.

obstétrique, *n.f.*, obstetrics.

obstination, *n.f.*, obstinacy, pertinacity, stubbornness.

obstiné, **-e**, *adj.*, obstinate; self-willed; stubborn.

obstinément, *adv.*, obstinately, stubbornly.

obstiner, *v.a.*, to make obstinate.

s'obstiner, *v.r.*, to be obstinate, to be obstinately resolved, to insist on. *— à une chose;* to be obstinate in a thing. *Il s'obstine dans son opinion;* he is obstinate in his opinion.

obstructi-f, **-ve**, *adj.*, obstructive, obstruent.

obstruction, *n.f.*, obstruction, stoppage.

obstrué, **-e**, *adj.*, obstructed, stopped.

obstruer, *v.a.*, to obstruct, to stop up.

obtempérer, *v.n.*, (jur.) to obey; to submit, to comply. *— à un ordre;* to obey an order.

obtenir, *v.a.*, to obtain, to procure, to get. *— satisfaction d'un outrage;* to obtain satisfaction for an insult.

s'obtenir, *v.r.*, to be obtained.

obtention, *n.f.*, (jur.) obtainment, purchase.

obturateur, *n.m.*, (anat.) obturatorius; lid, cover.

obturat-eur, **-rice**, *adj.*, (anat.) relating to the obturatorius; covering, stopping.

obturation, *n.f.*, (surg.) covering, stopping.

obtus, **-e**, *adj.*, obtuse, dull, blunt. *Angle —;* obtuse angle. *Esprit —;* dull mind.

obtusangle, *adj.*, obtuse-angular.

obtusangulé, **-e**, *adj.*, (bot.) obtuse-angled.

obus (o-buz), *n.m.*, (artil.) shell.

obusier, *n.m.*, (artil.) howitzer.

obvention, *n.f.*, (eco.) obventions.

obvers, *or* **obverse**, *n.m.*, obverse.

obvier, *v.n.*, to obviate. *— à un inconvénient;* to obviate an inconvenience.

oc, *adv.*, (in Old Provencial) yes. *Langue d'—;* langue d'oc.

oca, *n.m.*, (bot.) oca.

occase, *adj.*, (astron.) occasive.

occasion, *n.f.*, opportunity, occasion; cause, reason. *Il faut attendre l'—;* an occasion must be waited for. *Profiter d'une —;* to take advantage of, to improve, an opportunity. *En toute —;* on all occasions. *A votre —;* for your sake. *D'—;* accidentally; second-hand. *Marchandise d'—;* second-hand goods.

occasionnel, **-le**, *adj.*, occasional.

occasionnellement (-nèl-măn), *adv.*, occasionally.

occasionner, *v.a.*, to occasion, to cause.

occident, *n.m.*, West. *D'—;* western.

occidental, **-e**, *adj.*, occidental, western, westerly. *Les Indes —es;* the West Indies.

occidentaux, *n.m.pl.*, natives, inhabitants, of the Western countries.

occipital, **-e**, *adj.*, occipital.

occiput (-put), *n.m.*, occiput.

☉**occire**, *v.a.*, to slay, to kill.

☉**occis**, *part.*, killed, slain.

☉**occiseur**, *n.m.*, murderer, killer, slayer.

occision, *n.f.*, ☉killing; slaughter.

occlusion, *n.f.*, (med.) closing, shutting up.

occultation, *n.f.*, (astron.) occultation.

occulte, *adj.*, occult.

occupant, **-e**, *n.* and *adj.*, occupant, possessor; occupier; occupying; (jur.) concerned as the attorney.

occupation, *n.f.*, occupation, business, employment, work. *Donner de l'— à quelqu'un;* to cut out work for any one.

occupé, **-e**, *adj.*, busy, employed, engaged.

occuper, *v.a.*, to occupy, to employ, to busy. *— une maison;* to occupy a house. *— la place de quelqu'un;* to be in any one's place. *Il faut — les jeunes gens;* youth ought to be employed.

s'occuper, *v.r.*, to occupy one's self; to be busy, to apply one's self, to attend to. *— à lire;* to be occupied in reading. *Je m'occupe de votre affaire;* I am occupied about your affair.

occuper, *v.n.*, (jur.) to be concerned as the attorney, to appear.

occurrence (o-kur-rans), n.f., occurrence, emergency.

occurrent, -e, adj., (l.u.) occurring.

océan, n.m., ocean.

⊙**océane,** adj.f., of the ocean. Mer —; ocean.

océanide, n.f., (myth.) Oceanide, nymph of the Sea, daughter of the Ocean.

océanique, adj., oceanic.

ocellé, -e, adj., ocellated.

ochlocratie (o-klo-cra-ci), n.f., ochlocracy.

⊙**ochre,** n.f. V. **ocre.**

ocre, n.f., ochre.

ocreu-x, -se, adj., ochry, ochreous.

octaèdre, n.m., (geom.) octahedron.

octaédrique, adj., (geom.) octahedral.

octandre, adj., (bot.) octandrian, octandrous.

octandrie, n.f., (bot.) octandria.

octant, n.m., octant; quadrant.

⊙**octante,** adj., eighty, fourscore.

⊙**octantième** (-tièm), adj., eightieth.

octarchie (-shi), n.f., octarchy.

octave, n.f., octave; eight.

octavin, n.m., octave-flute.

octavo, adv., eighthly. V. **in-octavo.**

octavon, n.m., **-ne,** n.f., mustee, person one-eighth black.

octidi, n.m., octidi, eighth day of the decade in the calendar of the first French republic.

octil, adj.m., (astron.) octile.

octobre, n.m., October.

octogénaire, n.m.f. and adj., octogenary, octogenarian.

octogone, n.m. and adj., octagon; octagonal.

octostyle, adj., octostylar.

octroi, n.m., grant; town-due.

octroyer, v.a., to grant.

octuple, adj., eightfold, octuple.

octupler, v.a., (l.u.) to increase eightfold.

oculaire, adj., ocular. Témoin —; eye-witness. Verre —; eye-glass.

oculaire, n.m., (opt.) eye-glass.

oculairement (-lèr-màn), adv., ocularly.

oculiste, n.m., oculist.

odalisque, n.f., odalisk, odalisque.

ode, n.f., ode.

odelette, n.f., (poet.) odelet.

odéon, or **odéum,** n.m., Odeon.

odeur, n.f., odour, smell, scent, fragrancy. N'être pas en — de sainteté auprès de quelqu'un; not to be in the good graces of any one.

odieusement (-eûz-màn), adv., odiously, hatefully.

odieu-x,-se, adj., odious, hateful, loathsome. Se rendre —; to make one's self odious.

odomètre, n.m., odometer, pedometer. V. **pédomètre.**

odontalgie, n.f., odontalgia, toothache, odontalgy.

odontalgique, n.m. and adj., odontalgic.

odontoïde, adj., (anat.) odontoid.

odontologie, n.f., (anat.) odontology.

odorant, -e, adj., odoriferous, fragrant, sweet-smelling.

odorat, n.m., smell; smelling. Cela blesse l'—; that is offensive to the smell.

odoriférant, -e, adj., odoriferous, fragrant, sweet-scented.

odyssée, n.f., Odyssey.

œcuménicité, n.f., œcumenicity.

œcuménique, adj., œcumenical.

œcuméniquement, adv., œcumenically.

œdémateu-x, -se, adj., edematous.

œdème, n.m., (med.) œdema.

œdipe, n.m., a man who easily guesses riddles, &c.

œgagre (égagr), n.m., wild goat.

*****œil** (eu-ye), n.m. (yeux), eye; hole (in bread, cheese); (print.) face; bubble (of soup —de la soupe); lustre (of precious stones—des pierres précieuses); eye (of a needle, &c.—d'une aiguille, &c.) Clin d'—; twink. En un clin d'—; in the twinkling of an eye. Un beau coup d'—; a fine prospect. Le premier coup d'—; the first sight. D'un coup d'—; at a glance. Avoir mal aux yeux; to have sore eyes. Regarder quelqu'un du coin de l'—; to glance at any one. Regarder quelqu'un entre les deux yeux; to look any one in the face. Ouvrir de grands yeux; to stare, to stare with one's eyes wide open. Avoir l'— à quelque chose; to have an eye upon any thing. Avoir l'— sur quelqu'un; to watch any one. Suivre de l'—; to follow with the eye, to watch, to look at. Le soleil me donne dans les yeux; the sun dazzles my eyes. Cela lui blesse les yeux; that is an eyesore to him. À vue d'—; visibly. Donner dans l'— à quelqu'un; to take any one's fancy. Faire les yeux doux; to look lovingly. Dévorer quelqu'un des yeux; to look any one through and through. Couver des yeux; to look lovingly on. Dévorer une chose des yeux; to look upon a thing with greedy eyes. Cela saute aux yeux; that stares one in the face. Avoir un bandeau sur les yeux; to be blindfolded. Pour vos beaux yeux; for your pretty face. Je lui ai poché l'—; I gave him a black eye. Il a de bons yeux; he is sharp-sighted. Il n'a des yeux que pour elle; he sees nothing but her. Fermer les yeux sur quelque chose; to wink at anything.

œil-de-bœuf, n.m. (—s —), bull's eye, round or oval window; a waiting-room in the royal palace at Versailles.

œil-de-chat, n.m. (—s —), (min.) cat's-eye.

œil-de-perdrix, n.m. (yeux —), soft corn (on the foot— aux pieds).

œil-de-serpent, n.m. (—s —), (min.) serpentine-stone.

œil-d'or, n.m. (—s —), (ich.) gold-finny.

*****œillade,** n.f., glance, ogle, sheep's eye. Jeter des —s; to cast glances.

œillère, adj.f., of the eye. Dent —; canine tooth.

*****œillère,** n.f., eye-flap, blinker (of a horse—d'un cheval); canine tooth.

*****œillet,** n.m., (bot.) carnation, pink; (nav.) eye; eyelet; eyelet-hole. — de poète; sweet-william.

*****œilleton,** n.m., (hort.) offset; layer.

*****œillette,** n.f., field-poppy.

œnanthe, n.f., (bot.) watery drop-wort.

œnologie, n.f., wine-making.

œnomancie, n.f., (antiq.) œnomancy (divination by wine—divination au moyen du vin).

œnomètre, n.m., œnometer (instrument for ascertaining the strength of wine— instrument pour mesurer le degré de force du vin).

œnophore, n.m., (antiq.) wine vessel.

œsophage, n.m., œsophagus, gullet.

œsophagien, -ne (-in, -è-n), adj., pertaining to the œsophagus.

œstre, n.m., (ent.) œstrus, gad-fly.

œuf (euf), n.m. (œufs) (eû), egg; pl., roe (of a fish—du poisson). —s pochés; poached eggs. —s à la coque; eggs in the shell. —s brouillés; buttered eggs. — couvi; addle egg. — frais; new-laid egg. —s sur le plat, —s au miroir; fried eggs. Plein comme un —; as full as an egg. Il tondrait sur un —; he would skin a flint. Mettre tous ses —s dans un panier; to risk all in one enterprise.

œuvé, -e, adj., hard-roed (of fish—poisson).

œuvre, n.f., work, piece of work; deed, act; bezel (of a stone—d'une pierre précieuse); church-wardens' pew; fabric (fund appropriated for the repairs of a church—fabrique, revenu d'une paroisse). — de piété, — de charité, act of piety, of charity. —s pies; pious works. l'œu — de *génie* ; a work of genius. *La fin couronne l' —* ; all is well that ends 'well. *A l'— on connait l'ouvrier* ; the workman is known by his work. *Bon jour, bonne —* ; the better day, the better deed. *Maître des hautes —s* ; hangman. *Maître des basses —s* ; nightman. *Mettre en —* ; to make use of, to work up; to set (jewellery *—joaillerie*). *Mettre tout en —* ; to leave no stone unturned. *—s inédites* ; unpublished works. *—s posthumes* ; posthumous works. *—s mélées* ; miscellaneous works, miscellanea.

cœuvre, *n.m.*, work ; (arch.) clear ; works of musicians and engravers; performance ; (metal.) argentiferous lead. *Travailler au grand —* ; to seek the philosopher's stone. *Dans —* ; (arch.) clear, in the clear. *Hors d' —* ; (arch.) from out to out. *Sous —* ; (mas.) underpinning.

offensant, -e, *adj.*, offensive, obnoxious.

offense, *n.f.*, offence, transgression, trespass. *Demander réparation d'une —* ; to demand satisfaction for an offence. *Pardonner les —s* ; to forgive offences. *Expier une —* ; to atone for an offence.

offensé, *n.m.*, offended party.

offenser, *v.a.*, to offend, to give offence; to hurt ; to be offensive to, to offend against. *Le coup lui a offensé le cerveau* ; the blow hurt his brain. *— la délicatesse* ; to shock delicacy. **s'offenser**, *v.r.*, to be offended, to take exception, to take offence at.

offenseur, *n.m.*, offender.

offensi-f, -ve, *adj.*, offensive (attack—*attaque*).

offensive, *n.f.*, offensive.

offensivement (-siv-mān), *adv.*, offensively (of an attack—*d'une attaque*).

offerte, *n.f.*, or **offertoire**, *n.m.*, (c.rel.) offertory.

office, *n.m.*, office ; duty ; employment, functions; service, turn ; worship. *Avocat nommé d'—* ; advocate appointed by the judge. *Faire quelque chose d'—* ; to do a thing of one's own accord. *C'est un — d'ami que vous lui avez rendu* ; it is a friendly turn you have done him. *Rendre un mauvais — à quelqu'un* ; to do any one an ill turn. *L'— divin* ; divine service, churchtime. *Exercer un —* ; to hold an office. *Le saint-—* ; the holy-office, the Inquisition.

office, *n.f.*, servants' hall, pantry ; *pl.*, dependencies of the kitchen.

official, *n.m.*, (ecc.) official.

officialité, *n.f.*, officiality.

officiant, *n.* and *adj. m.*, officiating priest, officiating clergyman : officiating.

officiante, *n.f.*, officiating nun.

officiel, -le, *adj.*, official.

officiellement (-èl-mān), *adv.*, officially.

officier, *v.n.*, to officiate; to do one's duty at table, to eat heartily.

officier, *n.m.*, officer ; butler, steward. *— de marine* ; naval officer. *— d'état-major* ; staff-officer. *—supérieur* ; field-officer. *Sous-officier* ; non-commissioned officer. *—s de la bouche* ; king's cooks. *—s du gobelet* ; king's butlers.

officieusement (-eûz-mān), *adv.*, officiously, obligingly.

officieu-x, -se, *n.* and *adj.*, busy-body ; officious, obliging.

officinal, -e, *adj.*, (pharm.) officinal.

officine, *n.f.*, an apothecary's laboratory.

offrande, *n.f.*, offering, present.

offrant, *adj.m.*, bidding. *Au plus — et dernier enchérisseur* ; to the highest and last bidder.

offre, *n.f.*, offer, tender. *Faire une —* ; to make an offer.

offrir (offrant, offert), *v.a.*, to offer, to propose, to tender : to present; to afford. to give, to yield ; to bid. *— un present*; to offer a present.

s'offrir, *v.r.*, to offer, to propose one's self; to offer.

offuscation, *n.f.*, (astron.) transient diminution of the brightness of the sun.

offusquer, *v.a.*, to obscure, to darken. to dazzle; to offend. *Le soleil m'offusque les yeux*, the sun dazzles my eyes. *Cet artiste a un rival qui l'offusque* ; that artist has a rival who stands in his light.

ogival, -e, *adj.*, (arch.) pointed.

ogive, *n.f.*, ogive. pointed arch.

*****ognon**, *n.m.* V. **oignon**.

*****ognonet**, *n.m.* V. **oignonet**.

*****ognonière**, *n.f.* V. **oignonière**.

ogre, *n.m.*, ogre. *Il mange comme un —* ; he eats like a wolf.

ogresse, *n.f.*, ogress.

oh! *int.*, O ! ho !

oidium, *n.m.* (*n.p.*), (agri.) oidium. vine-mildew.

oie, *n.f.*, (orni.) goose ; simpleton, ninny. *Plume d' —* ; goose-quill. *— de mer* ; merganser. *Contes de ma mère l' —* ; tales of mother goose. *Jeu de l' —* ; game of goose.

*****oignon**, *n.m.*, onion; bulb, bulbous root ; bunion. *Regretter les —s d'Égypte* ; to sigh for the flesh-pots of Egypt. *Chapelet d'—s* ; rope of onions. *Un — de tulipe* ; a tulip root. *Être en rang d'—* ; to be all in a row. *Se mettre en rang d' —* ; to take one's place in a row.

*****oignonet**, *n.m.*, ognonet (summer pear —*poire d'été*).

*****oignonière**, *n.f.*, onion-bed.

oil, *adv.*, (old French) yes. *Langue d'—* ; langue d'oïl.

☉**oïlle** (o-ye), *n.f.*, (cook.) olio.

oindre (oignant, oint), *v.a.*, to anoint. *Vieux —* ; cart-grease.

oing (oin), *n.m.*, hog's-grease, cart-grease.

oint, *n.m.*, anointed. *L'— du Seigneur* ; the Lord's anointed.

oiseau, *n.m.*, bird ; creature (pers.) ; (mas.) hod. *— de proie* ; bird of prey. *Tirer aux —x* ; to go fowling. *Tirer l'—* ; to shoot at a bird. *— moqueur* ; mocking-bird. *Chasse aux —x* ; fowling. *Plan à vue d'—* ; bird's-eye view. *Il est comme l'— sur la branche* ; he is unsettled. *La belle cage ne nourrit pas l'—* ; a fine cage does not fill a bird's belly. *Petit à petit l'— fait son nid* ; little strokes fell great oaks. *À vol d'—* ; as the crow flies, in a straight line. *— mouche (—x —s)* ; humming-bird. *— trompette*; (orni.) trumpeter. *—x de passage* ; birds of passage. *—x de basse-cour* ; fowls. *—x royageurs*; migratory birds.

oiseler (oa-zlé), *v.a.*, (hawking —*fauconnerie*) to train a bird.

oiseler, *v.n.*, to catch birds.

oiselet (oa-zlè), *n.m.*, little bird.

oiseleur (oa-zleur), *n.m.*, bird-catcher.

oiselier, *n.m.*, bird-seller.

oisellerie (oa-zèl-ri), *n.f.*, bird-catching ; bird-trade.

oiseu-x, -se. *adj.*, indolent, idle. *Mener une vie —se* ; to live in idleness. *Paroles —ses* ; idle words.

oisi-f, -ve, *adj.*, doing nothing, idle, unoccupied ; uninvested (of money—*argent*).

oisif, *n.m.*, idler.

*****oisillon**, *n.m.*, young bird.

oisivement (oa-ziv-mān), *adv.*, idly.

oisiveté (oa-ziv-té), *n.f.*, idleness. *Croupir dans l'—* ; to wallow in sloth.

oison, *n.m.*, gosling ; ninny, simpleton.

☉**oisonnerie**, *n.f.*, excessive simplicity.

oléacées. *n.f.pl.*, (bot.) oleaceæ.

oléagineu-x, -se, *adj.*, oleaginous, oily.

oléandre, *n.m.*, (bot.) oleander, rose-bay.

oléifère, *adj.*, oil-bearing.

oléine. *n.f.*, (chem.) oleïn.
oléique, *adj.*, (chem.) oleic.
oléracé. -e. *adj.*, oleraceous.
olfacti-f. -ve. *adj.*, olfactory.
oliban, *n.m.*, (pharm.) olibanum.
olibrius (-ûs). *n.m.*, conceited fool person of great pretensions.
oliette. *n.f.* V. œillette.
oligarchie. *n.f.*, oligarchy.
oligarchique, *adj.*, oligarchical.
oligarque. *n.m.*, partisan of an oligarchy.
oligiste, *adj.*. (min.) oligist.
olim. *n.m.* (—), registers of the Parliament of Paris.
olinde. *n.f.*, Olinda sword-blade.
olivaire, *adj.*, olivary.
olivaison, *n.f.*, olive season. crop of olives.
olivâtre. *adj.*, olivaceous. olive-green.
olive. *n.f.*, (bot.) olive; (arch.) olive-moulding. *Branche, rameau, d'—*; olive branch.
olivète. *n.f.*, (bot.). V. œillette.
olivettes. *n.f.pl.*, sort of dance after the olives are gathered.
olivier, *n m.*, olive-tree, olive.
ollaire, *adj.f.*, soft (of certain stones which are easy to cut—*sorte de pierre facile à tailler*). *Pierre —*; potstone.
olla podrida, *n.f.* (—). olio; olla podrida.
olographe, *adj.*, holographic, holographical. *Testament —*; will written with the testator's own hand.
olographe. *n.m.*, holograph.
olonier; *n.m.*, (bot.) strawberry-tree; cane-apple.
olympe, *n.m.*, Olympus.
olympiade. *n.f.*, Olympiad.
olympien (-pi-in), **-ne** (-pi-è-n), *adj.*, Olympian.
olympique. *adj.*, Olympic.
ombelle, *n.f.*, (bot.) umbel.
ombellé, -e (on-bèl-lé), *adj.*, (bot.)umbellar, umbellated.
ombellifère (-bèl-li-), *n.f.* and *adj.*, (bot.) umbelliferous plant; umbelliferous.
ombellule (on-bèl-lul), *n.f.*, (bot)umbellet, umbellule.
ombilic, *n.m.*, (anat.) umbilic, umbilicus. navel; (bot.) hilum, umbilicus.
ombilical, -e. *adj.*, umbilic, umbilical. *Cordon —*; umbilical cord, navel.
ombiliqué, -e, *adj.*, (bot.) umbilicate, umbilicated.
embrager, *v.a.*, to shade.
ombrageu-x, -se, *adj.*, skittish (of horses —*des chevaux*); easily taking umbrage. *Cheval —*; skittish horse.
ombre. *n.f.*, shade; shadow; spirit; background. *S'endormir à l'— d'un arbre*; to sleep in the shade of a tree. *Se mettre à l'—*; to get into the shade. *L'— suit le corps*; the shadow follows the body. *Couvrir d'—*; to shade. *Les —s de la nuit*; the shades of night. *Avoir peur de son —*; to be afraid of one's own shadow. *Faire — à quelqu'un*; to eclipse any one. to throw any one into the shade. to give umbrage to any one. *—s chinoises*; shadow works. *Couvert d'—*; shady.
ombre, *n.m.*. (ich.) umbra; ombre (card game—*jeu de cartes*). *— de rivière*; red charr, grayling.
ombre (terre d'), *n.f.*, black-ochre.
ombré, -e. *part.*, tinted, shaded.
ombrelle. *n.f.*, parasol.
ombrer, *v.a.*, (drawing, paint.) to tint, to shade.

ombreu-x. -se. *adj.*. umbrageous; shady.
ombromètre, *n.m.*, ombrometer, rain-gauge.
oméga, *n.m.*, omega.
omelette (o-mlèt), *n.f.*, omelet.
omettre, *v.a.*. to omit. to leave out.
omission, *n.f.*. omission. *Sauf erreur ou —*; errors excepted.
omnibus, *n.m.*, omnibus.
omnipotence. *n.f.*, omnipotence.
omnipotent. *adj.*. omnipotent.
omniprésence. *n.f.*, omnipresence, ubiquity.
omniprésent. -e. *adj.*, ubiquitary, omnipresent.
omniscience. *n.f.*, omniscience.
omnium (-om), *n.m.*, (fin.) omnium.
omnivore, *adj.*, omnivorous.
omoplate, *n.f.*, omoplate, scapula. shoulder-blade.
omphalode, *n.m.*, (bot.) omphalode.
on. *pron.*, one, they, we, you, people. men, somebody. *— croirait*; one would think. *— dit*; they say; it is said. *— s'imagine*; people think. *— croit*; it is thought. *— me l'a dit*; I was told so. *Que dira-t-on?* what will people say? *Se moquer du qu'en dira-t-on*; not to care what people say. *Croire sur un — dit, sur des — dit*; to believe upon hearsay. *Si l'on me croit*; if I am believed.
onagre, *n.m.*, (mam., antiq.) onager; (bot.) œnothera.
onanisme, *n.m.*, onanism.
⊙**onc. onques,** *adv.*, never.
once, *n.f.*, (weight—*poids*) ounce; (mam.) ounce.
oncial, *n.m.*, (l.u.) V. onciale.
onciale, *n.* and *adj. f.*, uncial.
oncle, *n.m.*, uncle.
onction, *n.f.*, unction; anointing; grace, impressiveness. *L'extrême —*; (o. rel.) extreme unction.
onctueusement (-eûz-mân), *adv.*, impressively.
onctueu-x, -se, *adj.*, unctuous, oily. impressive. *Une terre —se*; fat earth. *Un sermon —*; an impressive sermon.
onctuosité, *n.f.*, unctuousness, oiliness.
onde, *n.f.*, wave; watering. *L'— amère*; the briny sea. *Passer l'— noire*; to cross the Stygian lake. *Les —s d'un bois veiné*; the waves of a piece of veined wood.
ondé, -e, *adj.*, undulated, watered.
ondée, *n.f.*, shower.
ondin, *n.m.*, **-e,** *n.f.*, genius of the water, Undine.
ondoiement (-doa-mân), *n.m.*, private baptism.
ondoyant, -e. *adj.*, undulating, waving, flowing. *Fumée —e*; waving smoke. *Vagues —es*; waving billows.
ondoyer, *v.n.*, to undulate, to rise in billows, to wave.
ondoyer. *v.a.*, to baptize privately.
ondulant. *adj.*, undulating.
ondulation. *n.f.*, undulation; waving.
ondulatoire, *adj.*, undulatory.
ondulé, *adj.*, undulate, undulated.
onduler, *v.n.*, to undulate, to wave.
onduleu-x, -se, *adj.*, undulating, flowing waving.
onéraire. *adj.*, (jur.) acting, accountable.
onéreu-x. -se, *adj.*, burdensome, onerous.
ongle. *n.m.*, nail (of fingers, claws—*des doigts, des pattes, &c.*); claw; hoof. *Couper, rogner, ses —s*; to cut, to gnaw, one's nails. *Coup d'—s.* scratch. *Jusqu'au bout des —s*: to one's fingers ends. *Rogner les —s à quelqu'un*; to clip any one's wings.

onglée, *n.f.*, numbness of the fingers.
onglet, *n.m.*, (bot.) aiglet; (engr.) graver; (print.) one leaf cancel. *Assemblage à —; mitre* (joinery—*menuiserie*).
onglette, *n.f.*, (engr.) flat graver.
onguent (on-gan), *n.m.*, ointment.
onguentaire (on-gan-tèr), *a j.*, unguentary.
onguiculé, -e (-gu-i-), *adj.*, unguiculate, unguiculated.
onguiforme (-gu-i-), *adj.*, ungulate.
ongulé, -e, *adj.*, hoofed.
onirocritie (-cri-ci), *or* **onirocritique**, *n.f.*, interpretation of dreams, oneiroscopy.
oniromance, *or* **oniromancie**, *n.f.*, oneiromancy.
onocrotale, *n.m.*, (orni.) pelican.
onomatopée, *n.f.*, (gram.) onomatopœia.
ontologie, *n.f.*, ontology.
ontologique, *adj.*, ontological.
ontologiste, *n.m.*, ontologist.
onyx (o-niks), *n.m.* and *adj.* invariable, onyx.
onze, *n.m.* and *adj.*, eleven, eleventh. [*Onze, onzième*, do not admit of being preceded by *l'*, say, therefore, *le onze, du onze, au onzième*. The final *s* or *z* of any word preceding *onze, onzième*, are not carried forward to the latter.] *Le — du mois*; the eleventh of the month.
onzième, *n.m.* and *adj.*, eleventh.
onzième, *n.f.*, (mus.) eleventh.
onzièmement (on-zièm-mān), *adv.*, eleventhly, in the eleventh place.
oolithe, *n.m.*, oolite.
oolithique, *adj.*, oolitic.
opacité, *n.f.*, opaqueness.
opale, *n.f.*, opal.
opaque, *adj.*, opaque.
opéra, *n.m.*, opera, opera-house. *C'est un —; it is a perfect imbroglio.
opérant, -e, *adj.*, operating.
opérat-eur, *n.m.*, **-rice**, *n.f.*, operator; mountebank, quack.
opération, *n.f.*, operation, working, performance; (fin.) transaction. *Subir une —; to undergo an operation. Terminer une —; to close a transaction.
opérer, *v.n.*, to work, to operate. *Cette médecine commence à —; that medicine begins to operate.
opérette, *n.f.*, a little opera.
opes, *n.m. pl.*, (arch.) opes; (mas.) scaffold-holes.
ophicléide, *n.m.*, ophicleide.
ophidien, -ne (-di-in,-è-n), *adj.*, ophidian.
ophidiens (-di-in), *n.m.pl.*, ophidians, ophidia.
ophioglosse, *n.m.*, (bot.) ophioglossum. *V.* **langue-de-serpent**.
ophiologie, *n.f.*, ophiology.
ophiologiste, *n.m.*, ophiologist.
ophite, *n.m.*, (min.) ophite.
ophtalmie, *n.f.*, ophthalmia, ophthalmy.
ophtalmique, *adj.*, ophthalmic.
ophtalmographie, *n.f.*, ophthalmography.
ophtalmologie, *n.f.*, ophthalmology.
ophtalmoscope, *n.m.*, ophthalmoscope.
opiacé, -e, *adj.*, (med.) containing opium.
opiat, *n.m.*, opiate.
opilati-f, -ve, *adj.*, (med.) oppilative.
opilation, *n.f.*, (med.) oppilation.
opiler, *v.a.*, (med.) to oppilate.

opimes, *adj. f. pl.*, opima. *Dépouilles —; opima spolia.
opinant, *n.m.*, speaker, person that gives his opinion.
opiner, *v.n.*, to speak, to give one's opinion. *Les juges opinèrent à la mort; the judges' opinion was for death. — du bonnet; to vote blindly; to adopt the opinions of others.
opiniâtre, *adj.*, stubborn, obstinate, headstrong, self-willed. *Le combat fut —; the fight was obstinate. Un mal —; an obstinate disease.
opiniâtre, *n.m.f.*, stubborn person. *Je hais les —s; I hate stubborn people.
opiniâtrément, *adv.*, obstinately, stubbornly.
opiniâtrer, *v.a.*, to contradict, to tease; to maintain a thing obstinately.
s'opiniâtrer, *v.r.*, to be obstinate. *Ils s'y sont opiniâtrés; they obstinately persisted in it.
opiniâtreté, *n.f.*, obstinacy, stubbornness. *Il suit son entreprise avec —; he pursues his scheme with pertinacity.
opinion, *n.f.*, opinion, vote. *Chacun motiva son —; every one gave his reasons for his opinion. Les —s sont partagées; opinions are divided. Résumer les —s; to sum up the opinions. Recueillir les —s; to collect the votes. C'est une affaire d'—; it is a mere matter of opinion. Il a bonne — de lui-même; he has a great opinion of himself.
opisthodome, *n.m.*, (antiq.) opisthodome.
opisthographe, *adj.*, (paleography—*paléographie*) written on both sides.
opium (o-piom), *n.m.*, opium.
oplomachie *n.f.*, (antiq.) a fighting with heavy arms; the art of fencing.
opobalsamum (-sa-mom), *n.m.*, (pharm.) opobalsam, balm of Gilead.
opodeldoch, *or* **opodeltoch**, *n.m.*, opodeldoc.
opossum (-som), *n.m.*, (mam.) opossum.
opportun, -e, *adj.*, opportune, convenient, seasonable, timely, well-timed.
opportunément, *adv.*, opportunely, seasonably.
opportunité, *n.f.*, opportuneness, seasonableness, expediency.
opposable, *adj.*, opposable.
opposant, -e, *n.* and *adj.*, opponent, adversary; opposing, opposite, adverse.
opposé, -e, *adj.*, opposite, contrary; facing; disinclined. *Deux armées —es l'une à l'autre; two armies opposed one to the other.
opposé, *n.m.*, opposite, reverse, contrary. *Il est tout l'— de son père; he is quite the opposite of his father.
opposer, *v.a.*, to oppose; to put in opposition; to place against; to plead, to urge. — *la force à la force; to oppose force to force.
s'opposer, *v.r.*, to be opposed, to set one's self against, to resist, to stem, to object, to combat. — *à quelque chose; to be opposed to anything.
opposite, *n.m.*, (l.u.) opposite, contrary. *C'est tout l'— de l'autre; it is quite the opposite of the other. À l'—; over, against, opposite. À l'— du camp; opposite the camp.
opposition, *n.f.*, opposition, resistance; (jur.) attachment. *Former — à la publication des bans; to forbid the bans. Le parti de l'—; the opposition party.
oppresser, *v.a.*, to oppress, to depress, to deject. *L'excès de nourriture oppresse l'estomac; excess of food oppresses the stomach. La chagrin l'oppresse; grief oppresses him.
oppresseur, *n.m.*, oppressor.
oppressi-f, -ve, *adj.*, oppressive.

oppression, *n.f.,* oppression. — *de poitrine;* oppression in the chest.

oppressivement (-siv-män), *adv.,* oppressively.

opprimant, -e, *adj.,* oppressing.

opprimé. -e, *part.,* oppressed.

opprimer, *v.a.,* to oppress. *Malheur à ceux qui oppriment!* woe to the oppressors!

opprobre, *n.m.,* opprobrium, shame. *Être l'— de sa famille;* to be the disgrace of one's family.

optati-f, -ve, *adj.,* optative.

optatif, *n.m.,* (gram.) optative.

opter, *v.n.,* to choose. *Il faut qu'il opte entre ces deux emplois;* he must choose the one or the other of those two employments.

opticien (-si-in), *n.m.,* optician.

optime (-mé), *adv.,* bravo, capital, very well, perfectly well.

optimisme, *n.m.,* optimism.

optimiste, *n.m.f.* and *adj.,* optimist; of optimists.

option, *n.f.,* option, choice. *Avoir l'—;* to have the choice. *Je vous en laisse l'—;* I leave you the choice.

optique, *adj.,* optic, optical. *Le nerf —;* the optic nerve. *Illusion —;* optical illusion.

optique, *n.f.,* optics; perspective. *Les illusions de l'—;* the deceptions of optics. *L'— du théâtre;* stage illusion.

opulemment (-la-män), *adv.,* opulently.

opulence, *n.f.,* opulence, wealth.

opulent, -e, *adj.,* opulent, wealthy.

opuntia (o-pon-sia), *n.f.,* (bot.) opuntia, prickly-pear.

opuscule, *n.m.,* opuscule, tract.

or, *n.m.,* gold; (her.) or. — *affiné;* refined gold. *Paillettes d'—;* gold spangles. *Vaisselle d'—;* gold plate. — *monnayé;* gold specie. — *vierge;* native gold. *Acheter quelque chose au poids de l'—;* to pay very dear for anything. *Être tout cousu d'—;* to roll in riches. *C'est de l'— en barre;* it is as good as ready money. *Il dit d'—:* he talks most sensibly. *Promettre des monts d'—;* to promise whole mountains of gold. *Tout ce qui reluit n'est pas —;* all is not gold that glitters. *Le nombre d'—* (astron.); the golden number. *L'âge d'—;* the golden age. *Des jours filés d'— et de soie;* happy days, halcyon days.

or, *conj.,* but, now. — *sus, commençons;* now, let us begin. — *çà;* now, well now.

oracle, *n.m.,* oracle. *En —;* like an oracle.

orage, *n.m.,* storm, tempest. *Nous aurons de l'—;* we shall have a storm. *Un — mêlé d'éclairs et de tonnerre;* a storm with thunder and lightning. *L'— gronde;* the storm rages. *Chercher un abri contre l'—;* to seek shelter from the storm. *Le temps est à l'—;* the weather is stormy. *Laisser passer l'—;* to let the storm blow over. *Les —s des passions;* the tempests of the passions.

orageusement, *adv.,* tempestuously, turbulently, boisterously.

orageu-x, -se, *adj.,* stormy, tempestuous; agitated, restless. *Une mer —se;* a tempestuous sea. *Saison —se;* stormy season. *Mener une vie —se;* to lead an agitated life.

oraison, *n.f.,* speech; oration; orison, prayer. *Une — funèbre;* a funeral oration. *Faire une —;* to say a prayer. *L'— dominicale;* the Lord's prayer.

oral, *n.m.,* veil (used by the pope, and formerly by women; also by the Jewesses out of doors—*porté par le pape; porté autrefois par les femmes, et par les Juives quand elles étaient en public).*

oral, -e, *adj.,* oral.

oralement (-al-män), *adv.,* orally.

orange, *n.f.,* orange. — *douce;* sweet orange. *Écorce d'—;* orange-peel. *Rouelle d'—;* slice of orange. *Fleur d'—;* orange flower.

orangé, -e. *adj.,* orange-coloured.

orangé, *n.m.,* orange-colour.

orangeade (-jad), *n.f.,* orangeade.

orangeat (-ja), *n.m.,* candied orange-peel.

oranger, *n.m.,* orange-tree; orange-man.

orangère. *n.f.,* orange-woman.

orangerie (o-ranj-ri), *n.f.,* orange-house; orange-grove, orangery.

orangiste, *n.m.,* orange-grower; orange-man.

orang-outang, *n.m.,* orang-outang.

orateur. *n.m.,* orator, speaker. — *éloquent, véhément;* eloquent, vehement, orator.

oratoire, *adj.,* oratorial, oratorical. *Débit —;* oratorical delivery. *Art —;* oratory.

oratoire. *n.m.,* oratory (room in a private house devoted to prayer—*chambre consacrée à la prière*); Oratory (religious order—*ordre religieux).*

oratoirement (-toâr-män), *adv.,* oratorically, oratorically.

oratorien (-in), *n.m.,* Oratorian.

oratorio, *n.m.,* (mus.) oratorio.

orbe, *n.m.,* (astron.) orbit; orb; (ich.) orbis, orb-fish.

orbe, *adj.,* (surg.) causing contusion (of blows —*de coups).*

orbiculaire, *adj.,* orbicular.

orbiculairement (-lèr-män), *adv.,* orbicularly.

orbiculé. -e, *adj.,* (bot.) orbicular, orbiculate, orbiculated.

orbitaire, *adj.,* (anat.) orbital.

orbite, *n.f.,* (astron.) orbit; (anat.) orbit, socket. *L'— de l'œil;* the socket of the eye.

orcanète, *n.f.,* (bot.) orchanet, alkanet, dyer's-bugloss, dyer's-gromwell.

orchestique (-kès-), *n.f.* and *adj.,* (antiq.) the art of dancing; relating to dancing.

orchestration (-kès-), *n.f.,* (mus.) scoring.

orchestre (-kès-) *n.m.,* orchestra; band.

orchestrer (-kès-), *v.a.,* (mus.) to score.

orchidées (-ki-), *n.f.pl.,* (bot.) orchidaceæ.

orchis (or-kis), *n.m.,* (bot.) orchis, foolstone, bee-flower, gnat-flower.

ord, *adj.,* ugly, dirty.

ordalie. *n.f.,* ordeal.

ordinaire, *adj.,* ordinary, common, usual, customary. *Le cours — de la nature;* the usual course of nature. *Le train — de la vie;* the ordinary course of life.

ordinaire, *n.m.,* ordinary; ordinary practice; daily fare; (milit.) mess; ordinary allowance; *pl.,* menses. *C'est un homme au-dessus de l'—;* he is above the common run. *À l'—;* as usual. *D'—, pour l'—;* usually, ordinarily.

ordinairement (nèr-män), *adv.,* ordinarily, usually, commonly.

ordinal, *adj.m.,* ordinal.

ordinand, *n.m.,* candidate for ordination.

ordinant, *n.m.,* ordaining bishop.

ordination, *n.f.,* ordination.

ordo, *n.m.* (—), ordo, book regulating the order of the daily service in the church.

ordon, *n.m.,* timber-frame for the support of a tilt-hammer.

ordonnance, *n.f.,* order, ordering, ordonnance, ordinance; (milit.) orderly; (med.) prescription. *Habits d'—;* regimentals. *Officier d'—;* orderly officer.

ordonnancement, *n.m.,* written order of payment.

ordonnancer, *v.a.,* (fin.) to order the payment of (in writing—*par écrit).*

ordonnateur, *n.m.,* ordainer; orderer.

ordonnat-eur, -rice, adj., ordaining; ordering.

ordonné, -e, part., ordered, prescribed; ordained. Charité bien —e commence par soi-même; charity begins at home. Une tête mal —e; a confused head.

ordonnée, n.f.. (geom) ordinate.

ordonner, v.a., to ordain, to order, to regulate; to direct, to command, to enjoin, to prescribe, to decree; to confer holy orders. Il est plus aisé d'— que d'exécuter; it is easier to order than to execute. Mon devoir me l'ordonne; my duty commands me to do it. Le médecin a ordonné la saignée; the physician has prescribed bleeding.

ordre, n.m., order, mandate; class; tribe; pl., holy orders. Maintenir l'—; to maintain order. Traiter les choses par —; to treat things in their order. Marcher en — de bataille; to march in battle array. Il est le premier créancier en —; he stands first on the list of creditors. Cet homme n'a pas d'—; that man has no order with him. Cela n'est pas dans l'—; that is not in order, not right. L'ancien — de choses; the old order of things. J'y mettrai —; I shall look to it. Un esprit du premier —; an intellect of the highest order. Un talent du premier —; a first-rate talent. Donner ses —s; to give one's orders. Un'— par écrit; a written order. De quel — faites-vous cela! by whose order do you do that? Prendre les —s; to go into orders. Conférer les —s; to ordain. — de chevalerie; order of knighthood. — d'architecture; order of architecture. En bon —; in good order.

ordure, n.f., filth. dirt. dust; excrement; dirty thing; pl., sweepings. Panier aux —s; dirt basket.

orduri-er, -ère, n. and adj., dirty person; ribald; filthy.

oréade, n.f., (myth.) oread:

⊙**orée,** n.f., border, skirt of a wood or forest.

*****oreillard, -e,** adj., (of horses—des chevaux) lop-eared.

*****oreille,** n.f., ear, hearing; tie (of shoes—de souliers); fluke (of anchors—d'ancres); earthboard (of ploughs—de charrues); pl., ears (c. a bale—de ballots); end-teeth (of combs—de peignes). Le tympan de l'—; the drum of the ear. Se boucher les —r; to stop one's ears. Avoir mal aux —s; to have the earache. Avoir un tintement d'—s; to have a tingling in one's ears. Boucle d'—; ear-ring. Parler à l'—à quelqu'un. dire un mot à l'— à quelqu'un; to whisper in any one's ear, to say a word in any one's ear. Prêter l'— à; to lend an ear to. Faire la sourde —; to turn a deaf ear. Échauffer les —s à quelqu'un; to provoke any one. Donner sur les —s à quelqu'un; to box any one's ears Avoir la puce à l'—; to have a flea in one's ear, to be uneasy. Se faire tirer l'—; to be very reluctant. Il ne se fait guère tirer l'—; he does not need much entreaty. Être endetté par-dessus les —s; to be over head and ears in debt. Avoir les —s rebattues de quelque chose; to have one's ears dunned with a thing. Ventre affamé n'a point d'—s; a hungry belly has no ears. Avoir les —s délicaes; to have delicate ears. Avoir les —s chastes; to have chaste ears. Il a bonne —; he has a quick ear. Il a l'— dure; he is dull of hearing. Il a de l'—; he has a delicate ear. Cela lui entre par une — et sort par l'autre; that goes in at one ear and out at the other. Tirer l'— à quelqu'un; to pull any one's ears.

*****oreiller,** n.m., pillow. Une taie d'—; a pillow-case.

*****oreillère,** n.f., (ent.) earwig.

*****oreillette,** n.f.. (anat.) auricle; (bot., conch.,

zool.) ear. —s du cœur (anat.); auricles of the heart.

*****oreillon,** n.m., part of a helmet covering the ear; (zool.) eminence of the ears of bats; (med.) mumps [in this sense. generally used in the plural]; pl., cuttings of hides employed to make glue.

orémus (-mus), n.m. (—), oremus (prayer—prière).

oréographie, n.f. V. orographie.

ores. or **ors.** adv., only used in d'— et déjà; from this moment.

orfèvre, n.m., goldsmith, silversmith. — bijoutier; goldsmith and jeweller.

orfèvrerie, n.f., goldsmith's trade, silversmith's trade; jewellery.

orfévri, -e, adj., wrought by the goldsmith, by the silversmith.

orfraie, n.f., sea-eagle, ospray.

orfroi, n.m., orfrays (fringe of gold—tissu d'or).

organdi, n.m., book-muslin.

organe, n.m., organ; voice, medium. L'— de la vue; the organ of sight. Cet acteur manque d'—; that actor has no voice.

organeau, n.m., (nav.) ring.

organique, n.f., (antiq.) instrumental music; mechanics, machines.

organique, adj., organic. Loi —; organic law.

organisat-eur, -rice, n. and adj., one who organizes; organizing.

organisation, n.f., organization.

organisé, -e, part., organized. Une tête bien —e; a well-organized mind.

organiser, v.a., to organize. — une armée; to organize an army.

s'organiser, v.r., to become organized.

organisme, n.m., organism.

organiste, n.m., organist.

organsin, n.m., organzine.

organsinage, n.m., organzining.

organsiner, v.a., to organzine.

orgasme, n.m., (med.) orgasm.

orge, n.f., barley. — mondé; hulled barley. — perlé; pearl barley. Faire ses —s; to feather one's nest. [Orge is masculine with the adjectives mondé and perlé.]

orgeat (or-ja), n.m., orgeat (liquor).

orgelet, or **orgeolet,** n.m., (med.) stye.

orgiaque, adj., (antiq.) of the orgies or feasts in honour of Bacchus; of revelry.

orgie (or-jî), n.f., orgy; (antiq.) pl., orgies.

orgue (org), n.m., **orgues,** n.f.pl., (mus.) organ; (fort.) orgues. Buffet d'—; organ-case. — de Barbarie; barrel-organ, street-organ. Point d'—; organ point. — de mer; organ-pipe coral.

*****orgueil** (or-gheu-), n.m., pride, arrogance. Être enflé, bouffi, d'—; to be puffed up with pride. Noble —; hones t pride.

orgueilleusement (or-gheu-leûz-mân), adv., proudly, haughtily.

orgueilleu-x, -se, n. and adj., proud, haughty person; proud, haughty.

orichalque, n.m., (antiq.) orichalcum, orichalch.

orient, n.m., East, Orient; water (of pearls —des perles). Les peuples d'—; the Eastern nations. L'empire d'Orient; the Eastern Empire. Commerce d'Orient; the East India trade.

oriental. -e, adj., oriental, eastern. Indes —es; India. East India.

orientaliste, n.m., orientalist.

orientaux, n.m.pl., Orientals.

orienté, -e, part., (nav.) set (of sails—des voiles). Bien —; in a good aspect. Mal —; in a bad aspect. Carte bien —e; map exactly drawn.

orientement (oriant-mân), n.m., (nav.) trim (of sails—des voiles).

orienter, v.a., to set towards the East; (nav.) to trim (sails—*les voiles*). — *un cadran*, to set a quadrant.

s'orienter, v.r., to find out the East; to discover where one is; to see what one is about. *Laissez-moi m'—*; let me see where I am.

orifice, n.m., orifice, aperture, hole.

oriflamme, n.f., oriflamme.

origan, n.m., (bot.) origanum, marjoram.

originaire, adj., originally. come from; native. *Il est — d'Italie.* he is of Italian origin.

originairement (-nèr-màn), adv., originally, primitively.

original, -e, adj., original, primitive; eccentric, queer, odd. *Consulter l'édition —e*; to consult the original edition. *Le texte —*; the original text. *C'est un génie —*; he is an original genius. *Avoir un caractère —*, to have a.i eccentric character.

original, n.m., original (not the copy—*œuvre première*); strange character; queer fellow; (mam.) elk. *C'est un — sans copie*; he is uncommonly odd. *Copié sur l'—*; copied from the original.

originalement (-nal-màn), adv., originally, in an original manner.

originalité, n.f., originality; eccentricity.

origine, n.f., origin, fountain, source. *L'— d'un mot*; the origin of a word. *Il était de bass*—; he was of mean origin. *Dans l'—*; originally. *Dès l'—*; from the very beginning, from the very first.

originel, -le, adj., original, primitive. *Péché —*; original sin.

originellement (-nèl-màn), adv., originally.

***orignal**, or **original**, n.m., elk. [Used in Canada instead of *élan*—*employé au Canada au lieu de élan*.]

***orillard**, -e. V. **oreillard**.

***orillon**, n.m., (fort.) orillon ; (of a plough—de *charrue*) mould-board ; (of a porringer—d'*écuelle*) handle; pl., (med.) mumps, (for which *oreillons* is also used).

orin, n.m., (nav.) buoy-rope (of an anchor—d'*ancre*).

orion, n.m., (astron.) Orion.

oripeau, n.m.. Dutch gold ; tinsel ; foil.

orle. n.m.,(arch.) orle, orlet, orlo ; (her.) orle.

orléans, n.m., light.woollen cloth employed for summer wear.

ormaie, or **ormoie**. n.f., elm-grove.

orme, n.m., elm. *Attendre sous l' —* : to wait till doomsday.

ormeau, n.m., young elm.

***ormille**, n.f., hedge of young elms.

ormin, n.m., (bot.) annual clary.

ormoie, n.f. V. **ormaie**.

orne, n.m. (bot.) ornus, flowering-ash.

orné, -e, part., adorned, ornamented.

ornemaniste, n.m., (arch.) ornament-maker.

ornement, n.m., ornament. *Elle est l'— de son sexe*; she is the ornament of her sex.

ornemental, adj., ornamental.

ornementation, n.f., ornamentation.

orner, v.a., to adorn, to ornament, to decorate, to grace, to embellish. *Les vertus ornent l'âme*; virtues adorn the soul. — *son esprit*; to adorn one's mind.

ornière, n.f., rut (of a road—*de route*); old track, beaten path. *Il est retombé dans l'—*, he is fallen back into the old track again.

ornithogale, n.m., (bot.) ornithogalum, star-of-Bethlehem.

ornitholithe, n.m., ornitholite.

ornithologie, n.f., ornithology.

ornithologiste, or **ornithologue**, n.m., ornithologist.

ornithomance, or **ornithomancie**, n.f., ornithomancy.

ornithorynque, n.m., (zool.) ornithorhynchus.

orobanche, n.f., (bot.) orobanche, broom-rape, strangleweed.

orobe, n.f., (bot.) orobus, bitter-vetch.

orographie, n.f., orography.

orologie, n.f., orology.

oronge, n.f., (bot.) orange-agaric. *Fausse —* ; amanita muscaria.

***orpailleur**, n.m.. gold-finder.

orphelin, -e, n. and adj., orphan.

orphelinat, n m., orphan-asylum, orphanage.

orphéon, n.m., choral society.

orphéoniste, n.m., member, pupil, of a choral society.

orphie, n.f., garfish.

orphique, adj., Orphic.

orphique, n.m., votary of Orpheus; pl., poems attributed to Orpheus.

orphiques, n.f.pl., (antiq.) orgies, feasts in honour of Bacchus.

orpiment, n.m., orpiment.

orpimenter, v.a., to colour with orpiment.

orpin, n.m., (bot.) orpine ; (min.) orpiment.

orque, n.m., (ich.) ork. V. **épaulard**.

ors, adv. V. **ores**.

***orseille**, n.f., (bot.) orchal, archil.

ort, adj. invariable, (com.) gross weight. *Peser —*: to weigh gross weight.

***orteil**, n.m.. toe ; great toe. *Se dresser sur ses —s*; to stand on tip-toe.

orthodoxe, adj., orthodox.

orthodoxie, n.f., orthodoxy.

orthodromie, n.f., orthodromy.

orthoépie, n.f., orthoepy.

orthogonal, -e, adj., orthogonal.

orthogonalement, adv., in a right angle.

orthogone, adj., (geom.) orthogonal.

orthographe, n.f., orthography, spelling. *Faute d'—*; mistake in spelling.

orthographie, n.f., (arch., bot., geom., persp.) orthography.

orthographier, v.a. and n., to spell.

orthographique, adj.. orthographical, orthographic. *Dessin —*; orthographical drawing.

orthographiste, n.m., orthographer.

orthopédie, n.f., orthopædy.

orthopédique, adj., orthopædic.

orthopédiste, n.m.. orthopædist.

orthopnée, n.f., orthopnœa.

orthoptère, n.m. and adj., orthopterous insect; orthopterous.

orthoptères, n.m.pl., orthoptera, orthopterans.

ortie (or-tï), n.f., nettle; (vet.) rowel.

ortive, adj., (astron.) ortive.

ortolan, n.m., (orni.) ortolan.

orvale, n.f., (bot.) clary, orval.

orvet, n.m., (erpetology) slow-worm.

orviétan, n.m., orvietan. *Marchand d'—*; quack-doctor.

oryctographie, n.f., oryctography.

oryctologie, n.f., oryctology.

oryctologiste, or **oryctologue**, n.m., oryctologist.

os (ô), n.m., bone. *L'— de la jambe*: the shin-bone. — *de l'épaule* : shoulder-blade. *Jusqu'à la moelle des —* : to the backbone. *Elle n'a que la peau et les —* : she is nothing but skin and bone. *Rompre les — a quelqu'un*; to beat any one unmercifully.

oscillant, -e, adj., oscillating.

oscillation (-sil-la-), n.f., oscillation, vibration.

oscillatoire (-sil-la-), adj., oscillatory.

osciller (os-sil-lé), v.n., to oscillate, to vibrate, to fluctuate.

oscitant, -e adj.. (med.) oscitant.

oscitation, n.f., oscitancy.

osculat-eur, -rice, adj., (geom.) osculatory.

osculation, n.f., (geom.) osculation.

osé, -e, adj., bold.

***oseille**, n.f., sorrel.

oser, v.a., to dare, to be so bold as, to venture. Vous n'osez rien; you won't venture any thing.

oser, v.n., to dare. Je n'oserais, je n'ose; I dare not. Si j'ose le dire; if I may venture so to speak. Oserai-je le dire? can I venture to say it? Oseriez-vous le blâmer? would you dare to blame him?

oseraie (ô-zrè), n.f., osier-bed.

osier, n.m., osier, withy. Un panier d'—; a wicker-basket.

osmazôme, n.f., (chem.) osmazome.

osmium, n.m. (n.p.), (chem.) osmium.

osmonde, n.f., (bot.) osmund.

ossature, n.f., (anat.) osseous frame, skeleton.

osselet (o-slè), n.m., ossicle; knuckle-bone; (vet.) osselet.

ossements (os-män), n.m.pl., bones (of dead bodies, of dead animals—de corps morts et d'animaux).

osseu-x, -se, adj., bony.

ossianique, adj., of Ossian.

ossification, n.f., ossification.

ossifier, v.a., to ossify.

s'ossifier, v.r., to ossify.

ossu, -e, adj., that has large bones, bony.

ossuaire, n.m., ossuary.

ostéine, n.f., (chem.) substance extracted from bones.

ostensible, adj., ostensible.

ostensiblement, adv., ostensibly.

ostensoir, or **ostensoire**, n.m., (c.rel.) monstrance, remonstrance.

ostentat-eur, -rice, n. and adj., ostentatious person; ostentatious.

ostentation, n.f., ostentation, show. Faire — de ses richesses; to make a show of one's wealth.

ostéocolle, n.f., osteocolla, bone-glue.

ostéocope, adj., of the bones. Douleur —; osteocope.

ostéogénie, n.f., osteogeny.

ostéographie, n.f., osteography.

ostéolithe, n.m., petrified bone.

ostéologie, n.f., osteology.

ostéotomie, n.f., osteotomy.

ostracé, -e, adj., of the nature of the oyster.

ostracisme, n.m., ostracism.

ostracite, n.f., (foss.) ostracite.

ostrogot, n.m., Ostrogoth; barbarian. Vous me prenez pour un —; you take me for a barbarian.

otage, n.m., hostage, pledge. En —; as an hostage.

otalgie, n.f., otalgia.

ôté, prep., except save. — cela, je ferai tout; I'll do everything but that.

ôter, v.a., to take away; to remove; to deprive; to take off; to take out; to pull off. Ôtez cette table de là; take that table away. Ôtez la nappe; take away the cloth. Je ne puis m'— cela de la tête; I can't get that out of my head. — sa cravate, son manteau, son chapeau, ses souliers; to take off one's neckcloth, one's cloak, one's hat, one's shoes. — son gilet; to pull off one's waistcoat. — son chapeau à quelqu'un; to take off one's hat to one. On lui a ôté sa place; they have taken his situation from him. Cette eau ôte les taches; that water takes out stains.

s'ôter, v.r., to remove; to get away; to be removed, to be taken away, to take one's self away. Ôtez-vous de devant mes yeux; get out of my sight. Ôtez-vous du chemin; stand out of the way.

ottoman, -e, n. and adj., Ottoman.

ottomane, n.f., ottoman (sofa).

ou, conj., or, either, or else. Mort — vif; either dead or alive.

où, adv., where, whither; at which; in which; to which; when, that. — suis-je? where am I? — allez-vous? where are you going? D'—? whence? D'— est-il? what countryman is he? D'— savez-vous cela? how do you know that? D'— vient que? how is it that? Par—? which way? L'état — il est; the condition in which he is. Le but — il tend; the object he aims at. — en êtes vous avec lui? upon what terms are you with him? Partout —; wherever. Le moment — je vous ai quitté; the moment when I left you.

⊙**ouaiche**, n.m., (nav.). V. **houache** and **sillage**.

⊙***ouaille**, n.f., sheep; pl., flock (of a pastor —d'un curé, d'un pasteur).

ouais! int., heyday! dear me! bless my soul!

ouate, n.f., wadding, padding; cotton-wool.

ouater, v.a., to wad, to pad.

oubli, n.m., forgetfulness, neglect, oblivion. Mettre en —; to forget. Ensevelir dans l'—; to bury in oblivion. Tomber dans l'—; to sink into oblivion, to fall into neglect.

oubliable, adj., liable to be forgotten; that deserves to be forgotten.

⊙**oubliance**, n.f. V. **oubli**.

oublie, n.f., a kind of very thin pastry.

oublier, v.a., to forget, to be unmindful of. — son devoir; to forget one's duty. N'oubliez pas les pauvres; remember the poor. — une injure; to forget an injury.

s'oublier, v.r., to forget one's self; to neglect one's affairs. Les parvenus s'oublient facilement; upstarts easily forget themselves.

oubliettes, n.f.pl., oubliettes, dungeon.

oublieur, n.m., vendor of thin pastry.

oublieu-x, -se, adj., forgetful, oblivious.

ouest (ou-èst), n.m., West, westerly, western. Un vent d'—; a westerly wind.

ouf! int., Oh!

oui, adv., yes. — -da; yes, indeed, willingly. Il ne m'a répondu ni — ni non; he gave me no positive answer. Il a dit que — ; he said yes. **oui**, n.m., yes. Dire le grand —; to marry. Le — et le non; yes and no.

ouï, -e, part., heard. J'ai — dire; I have heard say.

ouï-dire, n.m. (—), hearsay.

ouïe, n.f., hearing. Avoir l'— bonne; to be quick of hearing.

ouïe, n.f., hole (of a violin, &c.—des violons, &c.); pl., gills (of fish—de poisson).

***ouillage**, n.m., ullage; filling up of a cask of wine.

ouiller, v.a., to replace in a cask of wine the quantity which has disappeared by leakage, absorption, &c.

ouïr, v.a., to hear.

ouistiti, n.m., striated monkey.

ouragan, n.m., hurricane.

ourdir, v.a., to warp; to plot, to brew. — une toile; to warp a cloth. — une trahison; to plot a treacherous design. — un complot; to hatch a plot.

ourdissage, n.m., warping.

ourdisseu-r, n.m., **-se**, n.f., warper.

ourdissoir, n.m., warp-beam.

ourdissure, n.f., warping.

ourler, v.a., to hem (needle-work—ouvrage à l'aiguille).

ourlet, n.m., hem.

ours (oors), n.m., bear. Un — mal léché; an unlicked cub. Il ne faut pas vendre la peau de l'— avant qu'on l'ait pris; one must not sell the bear's skin before he is caught. C'est un —; he is a bear. Chasse à l'—; bear-hunt.

ourse, *n.f.*, she-bear: (astron.) Ursa. *La grande —* ; Ursa Major, the Greater Bear. *La petite —* ; Ursa Minor, the Lesser Bear.

oursin, *n.m.*, sea-urchin.

ourson, *n.m.*, bear's cub.

ourvari, *n.m. V.* **hourvari**.

outarde, *n.f.*, (orni.) bustard.

outardeau, *n.m.*, (orni.) young bustard.

outil (oo-ti), *n.m.*, tool, implement.

¹**outillage**, *n.m.*, stock of tools.

¹**outillé, -e**, *adj.*, furnished with tools.

¹**outiller**, *v.a.*, to furnish with tools.

outrage, *n.m.*, outrage, gross insult; injury. *Souffrir un —* ; to brook an outrage. *Faire un — à* ; to commit an outrage on.

outrageant, -e (-jän, -t), *adj.*, outrageous; contumelious, reproachful.

outrager, *v.a.*, to outrage. *— la pudeur* ; to commit an outrage on decency.

outrageusement (-jeûz-män), *adv.*, outrageously, contumeliously.

outrageu-x, -se, *adj.*, outrageous.

outrance, *n.f.*, extreme; excess. *Combat à —* ; combat to the death.

outre, *n.f.*, leather-bottle.

outre, *adv.*, further, beyond. *Passer —* ; to go on, to take no notice of a thing; (jur.) to proceed. *D' en —* ; through and through.

outre, *prep.*, beyond; besides, in addition to, above. *D'— -mer* ; from beyond the seas. *— cela* ; besides that.

outre que, *conj.*, besides.

outré, -e, *adj.*, exaggerated, incensed; strained. *Pensée —e* ; extravagant thought. *Des louanges —es* ; extravagant praise. *Il est — en tout* ; he is extravagant in every thing.

outrecuidance, *n.f.*, presumption.

outrecuidant, -e, *adj.*, overweening, presumptuous.

☉**outrecuidé, -e**, *adj.*, presumptuous, overweening.

outrément, *adv.*, (l.u.) excessively, beyond measure.

outremer, *n.m.*, ultra-marine (colour—*couleur*).

outrepasse, *n.f.*, extra-cuttings (of wood—*de bois*).

outrepasser, *v.a.*, to go beyond, to exceed.

outrer, *v.a.* and *n.*, to exaggerate; ☉to overwhelm ; to incense; to strain. *— un cheval* ; to strain a horse. *C'est un homme qui outre tout* ; he is a man who overdoes every thing.

ouvert, -e, *part.*, open, unfortified (of towns —*des villes*). *A livre —* ; at sight, on opening the book. *Parler à cœur —* ; to speak with open heart. *Chanter à livre —* ; to sing at sight. *Compte —* ; running account.

ouvertement, *adv.*, openly.

ouverture, *n.f.*, opening; aperture, chink; overture, beginning ; orifice; width (of a door —*d'une porte*). *Faire des —s de paix* ; to make overtures of peace. *L'— était bien belle* ; the overture was very fine.

ouvrable, *adj.*, working. *Jour —* ; working-day.

ouvrage, *n.m.*, work, piece of work; performance, workmanship; job. *— de brique* ; brickwork. *Se mettre à l'—* ; to set to work. *— à l'aiguille* ; needle-work.

ouvragé, -e, *adj.*, wrought.

ouvrant, -e, *adj.*, opening. *A jour —* ; at the break of day, at daybreak.

ouvré, -e, *adj.*, (of textile fabrics—*du linge*) diapered; wrought.

ouvreau, *n.m.*, side-hole (of furnaces—*de fourneaux*).

ouvrer, *v.a.*, to work; to diaper; to coin. *— la monnaie* ; to coin money.

☉**ouvrer**, *v.n.*, to work.

ouvreu-r, *n.m.*, **-se**, *n.f.*, opener ; (thea.) box-keeper.

ouvrier, *n.m.*, workman, artisan; mechanic, operative, journeyman. *A l'œuvre on connaît l'—* ; the workman is known by his work.

ouvri-er, **-ère**, *adj.*, operative, working. *Jour —* ; working-day. *La classe —ère* ; the working-classes. *Cheville —ère* ; pole-bolt (of a coach—*d'une voiture*) ; (fig.) prime mover.

ouvrière, *n.f.*, workwoman.

ouvrir (ouvrant, ouvert), *v.a.*, to open, to set upon ; to sharpen (the appetite—*l'appétit*); to broach (opinion). *— la terre* ; to dig open the earth. *Cela ouvre l'appétit* ; that sharpens the appetite. *— son cœur à quelqu'un* ; to unbosom one's self to any one.

s'ouvrir, *v.r.*, to open, to disclose one's self. *— un passage* ; to make one's self a way. *— à quelqu'un* ; to open one's mind to any one.

ouvrir, *v.n.*, to open.

ouvroir, *n.m.*, workshop; gratuitous industrial school for poor girls.

ovaire, *n.m.*, (anat.) ovary; (bot.) ovary, ovarium.

ovalaire, *adj.*, (anat.) oval.

ovale, *n.m.* and *adj.*, oval.

ovariotomie, *n.f.*, (surg.) amputation of a diseased ovary.

ovation, *n.f.*, ovation.

ove, *n.m.*, (arch.) ovolo.

oviducte, *n.m.*, (anat.) oviduct.

ovine, *adj.*, ovine.

ovipare, *n.m.* and *adj.*, oviparous animal; oviparous.

ovoïde, *adj.*, ovoid.

ovule, *n.m.*, (physiology—*physiologie*) ovule, ovulum.

oxalate, *n.m.*, (chem.) oxalate.

oxalide, *n.f.*, (bot.) oxalis.

oxalique, *adj.*, oxalic.

oxycrat, *n.m.*, oxycrate (beverage—*breuvage*).

oxydabilité, *n.f.*, oxidability.

oxydable, *adj.*, oxidable.

oxydation, *n.f.*, oxidation.

oxyde, *n.m.*, (chem.) oxide.

oxyder, *v.a.*, (chem.) to oxidate.

s'oxyder, *v.r.*, to be, to become oxidized.

oxygénable, *adj.*, (chem.) oxygenizable.

oxygénation, *n.f.*, (chem.) oxygenation.

oxygène, *n.m.*, (chem.) oxygen.

oxygéner, *v.a.*, (chem.) to oxygenate.

oxygone, *adj.*, (geom.) oxygonal, oxygonial.

oxymel, *n.m.*, oxymel.

oxyrrhodin, *n.m.*, (pharm.) oxyrrhodine.

oyant, *n.m.*, **-e**, *n.f.*, (jur.) auditor.

ozène, *n.f.*, ozena.

ozone, *n.m.*, (chem.) ozone.

P

p, *n.m.*, the sixteenth letter of the alphabet, p.

p. (initial letter of Père), father (priest—*prêtre*).

p. (initial letter of Pour), (com.) per.

pacage, *n.m.*, pasture-land.

pacager, *v.n.*, (jur.) to pasture.

in pace, *n.m. V.* **in pace**.

pacha, *n.m.*, (-s), pacha. bashaw.

pachalik (pa-ka-lik), *n.m.*, (-s), pachalic.

pachyderme, *n.m.* and *adj.*, pachyderm; pachydermatous.

pacificat-eur, -rice, *n.* and *adj.*, pacificator, pacifier; pacifying.

pacification, *n.f.*, pacification, peace-making.

pacifier, *v.a.*, to pacify, to appease.

pacifique, *adj.*, pacific, peaceable, peaceful.

pacifiquement (-fīk-măn), *adv.*, peacefully, peaceably.

pacotille, *n.f.*, (com.) venture ; quantity, stock. *Marchandises de* — ; slops, slop-made, ready-made, cheap, goods ; salework.

pacta conventa, *n.m.pl.*, pacta conventa, covenant between the King of Poland and the nation.

pacte, *n.m.*, compact, pact, agreement.

pactiser, *v.n.*, to covenant,.to make a compact with.

pactole, *n.m.*, Pactolus ; (fig.) a source of great wealth.

padischâ, *n.m.* (—*s*), a title of the Sultan of Turkey.

padou, *n.m.*, ferret (ribbon—*ruban*).

padouane, *n.f.*, Paduan coin (imitation of an ancient medal—*imitation de médailles antiques*).

pæan (pé-ăn), *n.m.*, pæan.

pagaie, *n.f.*, paddle. *Aller à la* — ; (nav.) to paddle.

paganisme, *n.m.*, paganism, heathenism.

pagayer, *v.a.* and *n.*, (nav.) to paddle.

page, *n.m.*, page (person—*domestique*). *Être hors de* — ; to be one's own master.

page, *n.f.*, page (of a book—*de livre*); *Le haut, le bas, d'une* — ; the top, the bottom, of a page. *Mettre en* —*s* ; (print.) to make up, to click. *Metteur en* —*s* ; clicker, maker-up.

pagination, *n.f.*, paging.

paginer, *v.a.*, to page, to folio.

***pagne**, *n.m.*, cotton drawers (worn by negroes—*de sauvages*).

***pagnon**, *n.m.*, black superfine Sedan cloth.

☉***pagnote**, *n.m.*, dastard, poltroon.

☉***pagnoterie**, *n.f.*, cowardly action ; stupid thing.

pagode, *n.f.*, pagod, pagoda.

paie, *n.f.* V. **paye**.

paiement, *or* **paîment** *n.m.* V. **payement**.

païen, -ne, *n.* and *adj.*, pagan, heathen. *Les dieux des* —*s* ; the gods of the pagans.

***paillard, -e**, *n.* and *adj.*, (l.ex.) wanton, lewd person ; libidinous, lewd.

***paillarder**, *v.n.*, (l.ex.) to practise lewdness.

***paillardise**, *n.f.*, (l.ex.) lechery, lewdness.

***paillasse**, *n.f.*, straw mattress, palliasse.

***paillasse**, *n.m.*, clown, merry-andrew.

***paillasson**, *n.m.*, straw-matting ; straw-mat ; mat.

***paille**, *n.f.*, straw ; chaff ; flaw (of gems, of metals—*des pierres précieuses, des métaux*); (manu.) chip ; mote. *Menue* — , chaff. *Brin de* — ; bit of straw. *Chapeau de* — ; straw-hat. *Homme de* — ; man-of-straw. *Un feu de* — ; straw fire, sudden, short blaze. *Tirer à la courte* — ; to draw lots, to draw cuts. *Rompre la* — *avec quelqu'un* ; to fall out with any one. *Ce diamant a une* — ; that diamond has a flaw in it.

***paille**, *adj. invariable*, straw-coloured.

***paillé, -e**, *adj.*, (her.) diapered ; covered with straw ; flawy (of metals—*des métaux*); straw-coloured.

***paille-en-queue**, *n.m.* (—), tropic-bird, phaeton.

***pailler**, *n.m.*, farm-yard, heap of straw. *Chapon de* — ; barn-door capon. *Être sur son* — ; to be in one's stronghold.

***pailI-er, -ère**, *adj.*, of farm-yards.

***paillet**, *adj.*, pale (of red wine—*du vin rouge*).

***pailleté**, *adj.*, spangled.

***paillette**, *n.f.*, spangle.

***pailleu-r**, *n.m.*, **-se**, *n.f.*, dealer in straw.

***pailleu-x, -se**, *adj.*, flawy (of metals—*des métaux*). *Du fer* — ; flawy iron.

***paillon**, *n.m.*, large spangle ; piece of solder.

pain, *n.m.*, bread, loaf ; cake (of colour, &c. —*de couleur*, &c.). *Un* — ; a loaf. *Du* — ; some bread. *Un petit* — ; a roll. — *mollet* ; soft bread. *Du* — *bis* ; brown bread. *Du* — *frais, du* — *tendre* ; new bread. *Du* — *rassis* ; stale bread. — *de munition* ; ammunition bread. — *sans levain* ; unleavened bread. — *de ménage* ; home-made bread. *Manger son* — *blanc le premier* ; to have the best first. — *chapelé* ; rasped bread. *Il sait son* — *manger* ; he knows how to shift for himself. — *quotidien* ; daily bread. *Mettre à quelqu'un le* — *à la main* ; to give any one his bread. *Avoir son* — *cuit* ; to have a competency, to have enough to live on. — *de sucre* ; sugar-loaf. — *de savon* ; cake of soap. — *bénit* ; consecrated bread. *Un* — *à cacheter* ; a wafer. — *d'épice* ; gingerbread.

pair *adj.*, even (of numbers—*des nombres*); like, similar. *Non* —; odd. — *ou non*; even or odd.

pair, *n.m.*, peer ; equal ; par ; equality ; fellow ; (of birds—*des oiseaux*) mate. *Le change est au* —; the exchange is at par. *Au* — ; at par ; not behindhand (with one's task—*dans son travail*). *Être jugé par ses* —*s* ; to be tried by one's peers. *Sans* —; matchless. *Nous voilà* — *à* — ; now we are even. *De* —; on a par, on an equality. *Aller de* — *avec quelqu'un* ; to go cheek by jowl with any one. *Marcher de* —*avec* ; to be on an equal footing with. *Traiter quelqu'un de* — *à compagnon* ; to be hail-fellow well met with any one. *Hors de* — ; above one's equals.

paire, *n.f.*, pair, brace, couple. *Une* — *de bœufs* ; a pair of oxen. *Une* — *de ciseaux* ; a pair of scissors. *Les deux font la* —; the two make a pair.

pairement (pèr-măn), *adv.*, (arith.) evenly.

pairesse, *n.f.*, peeress.

pairie, *n.f.*, peerage.

paisible, *adj.*, peaceable, peaceful, quiet. *Sommeil* — ; peaceful sleep. *Mener une vie* — ; to lead a peaceful life.

paisiblement, *adv.*, peaceably, peacefully.

paisson, *n.f.*, pasture (in forests—*dans les forêts*).

paitre (paissant, pu) *v.a.* and *n.*, to graze, to feed. *Mener* — *des moutons* ; to drive the sheep to pasture. *Envoyer* —*quelqu'un* ; to send any one about his business. *Allez* —; go about your business.

se **paître**, *v.r.*, to feed.

paix, *n.f.*, peace ; quiet ; (c.rel.) osculatory, pax. *Troubler la* — *de* ; to disturb the peace of. *Garder la* —; to keep the peace. — *fourrée, plâtrée* ; hypocritical peace, patched-up peace. *Laissez-moi en* —; let me alone. *Il a fait sa* — ; he has made his peace. *Ne donner ni* — *ni trève à quelqu'un* ; to leave any one no rest. *La* — *du cœur* ; peace of heart.

paix ! *int.*, peace ! be quiet !

pal, *n.m.* (—*s*, *or* **paux**), pale (punishment—*supplice*); (her.) pale.

paladin, *n.m.*, paladin. *C'est un vrai* —; he is a perfect knight-errant.

palais, *n.m.*, palace ; court of justice ; hall ; palate (of the mouth—*de la bouche*) ; taste. *Terme de* — ; law term. *Style du* —, *style de* — ; law style.

palan, *n.m.*, (nav.) tackle.

palançons, *n.m.pl.*, (mas.) props to support mud-walls till they are dry.

palanque, *n.f.*, (fort.) blindage, blind.

palanquin, *n.m.*, palanquin.

palastre, *n.m.*, case (of a lock—*de serrure*).

palatale, *n.* and *adj.f.*, (gram.) palatal.

palatin, -e, *adj.*, Palatine.

palatin, *n.m.*, Palatine.

palatin, -e, *adj.*, (anat.) of the palate.

palatinat, *n.m.*, Palatinate.

palatine, *n.f.*, wife of a Palatine; Palatine princess; fur-tippet; tippet.

pale, *n.f.*, sluice, flood-gate; blade (of an oar —*de rame*); paddle-board; (c.rel.) pall (square paste-board covered with muslin or stuff, and laid upon the chalice—*carton carré couvert de toile blanche pour couvrir le calice*).

pâle, *adj.*, pale, wan, pallid; ghastly. — *comme la mort;* as pale as death. — *de colère;* pale with rage. *Un peu* —; palish. *Bleu* —; pale blue. —*s couleurs;* (med.) chlorosis, green-sickness. *Cet ouvrage est d'un style* —; the style of that work is tame.

palée, *n.f.*, row of stakes, of pales.

palefrenier (pal-frĕ-nié), *n.m.*, groom.

palefroi (pal-froa), *n.m.*, palfrey.

paléographe, *n.m.*, paleographer.

paléographie, *n.f.*, paleography (study of ancient writings—*science des écritures anciennes*).

paléontologie, *n.f.*, paleontology.

paléontologique, *adj.*, paleontological.

paléontologiste, *n.m.*, paleontologist.

paléothérium, *n.m.* (—*s*), (foss.) paleothere, paleotherium.

paleron (pa-lron), *n.m.*, shoulder-blade, shoulder-bone (of certain animals—*de quelques animaux*).

palestine, *n.f.*, (print.) two-line pica.

palestre, *n.f.*, (antiq.) palestra.

palestrique, *adj.*, (antiq.) palestrian, pal-estic.

palestrique, *n.f.*, (antiq.) palestra (exercises).

palet, *n.m.*, quoit. *Jouer aux* —*s;* to play at quoits.

paletot (pal-to), *n.m.*, paletot; great coat.

palette, *n.f.*, battledore; (paint.) pallet, palette; (surg.) pallet; (gilding—*dorure*) pallet; (horl.) pallet; (tech.) float-board. *Sentir la* —; to smack of the pallet.

palétuvier, *n.m.*, (bot.) mangrove, mangle; button-tree.

pâleur, *n.f.*, paleness, wanness, pallidness, ghastliness. — *mortelle;* death-like paleness.

pali, *n.m.*, (philol.) Pahli, Pali. *Étudier le* —; to study Pahli, the Pali language.

pali, **-e**, *adj.*, (philol.) Pali, of Pali. *La langue* —*e;* the Pahli language.

palier, *n.m.*, landing-place (of a stair-case—*d'escalier*); stair-head. *Demeurer sur le même* —: to live on the same floor. *Un homme est fort sur son* —; every man is a king in his own house.

palière, *n.f.*, top-stair.

palification, *n.f.*, (engineering—*terme d'in-génieur*) palification.

palimpseste, *n.m.*, palimpsest.

palingénésie, *n.f.*, palingenesia, palingen-esy.

palinod, *n.m.*, palinod (verses made in honour of the Immaculate Conception of the Blessed Virgin—*poème en l'honneur de l'Immaculée Conception de la Vierge*).

palinodie, *n.f.*, palinody, recantation. *Chanter la* —; (fam., fig.) to retract, to recant.

pâlir, *v.n.*, to grow, to turn, to become pale, to wan, to pale. *Son étoile pâlit;* his star is on the wane.

pâlir, *v.a.*, to turn, to make pale; to bleach. *Le vinaigre pâlit les lèvres;* vinegar bleaches the lips.

palis, *n.m.*, pale, fence of pales; space enclosed by pales.

palissade, *n.f.*, palisade, palisado; paling; wooden fence; (fort.) stockade.

palissader, *v.a.*, to fence with palisades, to palisade; (fort.) to stockade.

palissage, *n.m.*, (hort.) paling up.

palissandre, *or* **palixandre**, *n.m.*, violet ebony.

pâlissant, *adj.*, turning pale, waning.

palisser, *v.a.*, (hort.) to pale up.

palisson, *n.m.*, (furriers—*terme de mégisserie*) softening-iron; softening-board.

paliure, *n.m.*, (bot.) dry hawthorn (to make hedges—*pour faire des haies*).

palixandre, *n.m.* V. **palissandre**.

palladium (pal-la-diom), *n.m.*, Palladium; (fig.) palladium; (chem.) palladium.

pallas (pal-lâs), *n.f.*, (astron.) Pallas.

palle, *n.f.*, (c.rel.) V. **pale**.

palliati-f, -ve (pal-li-), *adj.*, (med.) palliative.

palliatif, *n.m.*, palliative.

palliation (pal-li-), *n.f.*, palliation.

pallier (pal-lié), *v.a.*, to excuse; to palliate.

pallium (pa-li-om), *n.m.*, pallium, pall (of bishops, archbishops—*d'évêque, d'archevêque*).

palma-christi, *n.m.* (—), (bot.) castor-oil plant, palma Christi; oil-nut; oil-tree. *Huile de* —; (pharm.) castor-oil.

palmaire, *adj.*, (anat.) relating to the palm of the hand; (orni.) webbed.

palme, *n.f.*, palm, palm-tree; palm-branch; victory, triumph. *Remporter la* —; to bear away the palm. *La* — *du martyre;* the crown of martyrdom. *Huile de* —; palm-oil.

palme, *n.m.*, palm, hand's breadth.

palmé, -e, *adj.*, palmated; webbed; fin-toed; (bot.) handed.

palmette, *n.f.*, palm-leaf (ornament—*orne-ment*).

palmier, *n.m.*, palm-tree, palm. — *en éven-tail;* macaw-tree. — *huileux;* palm-oil-tree. — *du Japon,* — *à sagou;* sago-tree. — *marin;* sea-palm-tree. — *nain;* dwarf-palm.

palmifère, *adj.*, (bot.) palmiferous.

palmipède, *adj.*, (orni.) palmiped, fin-footed, web-footed.

palmipède, *m.n.*, (orni.) palmiped.

palmiste, *n.m.*, (bot.) palmetto, cabbage-tree.

palmite, *n.m.*, sap of palm-trees.

palombe, *n.f.*, (orni.) wood-pigeon.

palonnier, *n.m.*, whipple-tree (of a coach—*d'une voiture*).

palot, *n.m.*, (pop.) clown, clod-hopper.

pâlot, -te, *adj.*, palish, wannish.

palpable, *adj.*, palpable.

palpablement, *adv.*, palpably.

palpe, *n.f.*, (ent.) palp, feeler.

palpébral, -e, *adj.*, (anat.) palpebral.

palper, *v.a.*, to feel, to palp; to feel about. — *de l'argent;* to get money into one's fingers, to finger money.

palpitant, -e, *adj.*, palpitating, panting. *Cœur* —; throbbing, beating, heart. *Des membres* —*s;* quivering limbs.

palpitation, *n.f.*, palpitation; throbbing, throb.

palpiter, *v.n.*, to palpitate, to throb; to pant. *Le cœur lui palpite;* his heart flutters. *Il palpite d'amour;* he is panting with love.

palplanche, *n.f.*, sheeting-pile (mas.).

palsambleu! par la sambleu! *int.*, zounds! forsooth!

paltoquet, *n.m.*, clown, clownish fellow.

paludéen, -ne (dé-in, -dé-è-n), *adj.*, palu-dal, marsh. *Fièvre* —*ne;* marsh-fever.

palus (-lûs), *n.m.*, (geog.) marsh, moor, fen.

palustre, *adj.*, paludal.

pâmer, *v.n.*, to swoon away. *Faire* — *de rire;* to make any one split his sides with laughter, to make any one die with laughter.

se pâmer, *v.r.*, to swoon away, to swoon; to faint, to faint away. — *de joie;* to be transported with joy.

13

pâmoison, *n.f.*, swoon, fainting fit. *Tomber en —;* to fall into a swoon, to swoon, to faint away.

pampa, *n.f.* (—s) (-pass), pampas.

pampe, *n.f.*, corn-blade.

pamphlet, *n.m.*, pamphlet.

pamphlétaire, *n.m.*, pamphleteer.

pamphlétier, *n.m.*, pamphleteer.

pampiniforme, *adj.*, (anat.) pampiniform.

pamplemousse, *n.f.*, (bot.) shaddock.

pampre, *n.m.*, vine-branch full of leaves; vine-leaf; (arch.) pampre, vine-branch.

pan, *n.m.*, flap, lappet; skirt; large piece (of a wall); side. *— d'un habit;* flap of a coat. *— de muraille;* large piece of a wall. *— coupé;* (carp.) cant. *A —s coupés;* (carp.) cantwise. *Tour à six —s;* six-sided, six-fronted, tower.

pan! *int.*, slap! flap!

panacée, *n.f.*, panacea, nostrum.

panache, *n.m.*, plume, plume of feathers; (bot.) streaks of colour (in a flower—*dans une fleur*); cap, top (of a church lamp—*d'une lampe d'église*); (arch.) triangular part of an arch.

panaché, -e, *part.*, striped, streaked, variegated. *Tulipe —e, rose —e;* striped tulip, striped rose. *Glace —e;* (cook.) fruit ice-creams of various kinds and colours mixed together.

panacher, *v.n.*, **se panacher,** *v.r.*, to become streaked, to become striped, to become variegated; to be streaked, to be striped.

panachure, *n.f.*, (of flowers, fruit—*de fleurs, de fruits*) variety of colours, variegation; streak, stripe.

panade, *n.f.*, (cook.) bread-soup, panada, panado.

se panader, *v.r.*, to strut, to go strutting along.

panage, *n.m.*, pannage.

panais, *n.m.*, (bot.) parsnip.

panard, *adj.*, (of a horse—*cheval*) crooklegged.

panarine, *n.f.*, (bot.) whitlowwort.

panaris, *n.m.*, (med.) panaris, whitlow.

panathénaïque, *adj.*, (antiq.) of the Panathenæa.

panathénées, *n.f.pl.*, (Grecian antiq.) Panathenæa.

pancaliers, *n.m.*, (bot.) Pancaliers cabbage.

pancarte, *n.f.*, toll-table; tariff; paper, writing; placard; visitor's book. *De vieilles —s;* old writings.

pancrace, *n.m.*, (antiq.) pancratium.

pancratiaste (-ci-ast), *n.m.*, (antiq.) pancratist.

pancratiaste, *adj.*, (antiq.) pancratic, pancratical.

pancréas (-às), *n.m.*, (anat.) pancreas, sweet-bread.

pancréatique, *adj.*, (anat.) pancreatic.

pandanées, *n.f.pl.*, (bot.) pandanaceæ.

pandectes, *n.f.pl.*, (Roman jur.) pandects.

pandémonium (-ni-om), *n.m.* (—s), pandemonium.

pandiculation, *n.f.*, (med.) pandiculation.

pandit, *n.m.* (—s), Pandit, Pundit.

pandore, *n.f.*, Pandora. (fig.) *La boîte de —;* source of evils.

pandour, *n.m.*, pandour (Hungarian soldier); coarse, brutal man.

pané, -e, *part.*, (cook.) covered with bread crumbs. *De l'eau —e;* toast and water.

panégyrique, *n.m.*, panegyric.

panégyriste, *n.m.*, panegyrist.

paner, *v.a.*, (cook.) to crumb, to cover with bread crumbs.

panerée (pa-n-rée), *n.f.*, basketful (mostly said of fruit—*principalement appliqué aux fruits*).

paneterie (pa-n-tri), *n.f.*, pantry (of public establishments—*d'établissements publics*).

panetier (pa-n-tié), *n.m.*, pantler, master of the pantry.

panetière (pa-n-tièr), *n.f.*, bag or satchel wherein shepherds put their bread; pouch.

pangolin, *n.m.*, (mam.) pangolin, shorttailed manis.

panic, *n.m.*, (bot.) panic, panic-grass.

panicule, *n.f.*, (bot.) panicle.

paniculé, -e, *adj.*, paniculate, paniculated, panicled.

panier, *n.m.*, basket, hamper, pannier; scuttle; beehive made of straw or osiers; hooppetticoat. *— d'osier;* wicker-basket. *— à claire-voie;* open-worked basket. *— à ouvrage;* workbasket. *— percé;* spendthrift. *Adieu —s, vendanges sont faites;* it is all over with me, us, &c. *Voûte à anse de —;* (arch.) elliptical vault.

panification, *n.f.*, panification.

panifier, *v.a.*, to make bread.

panique, *n.f.* and *adj.*, panic, sudden fright; panical, panic. *Panique, terreur —;* panic, panical fright.

panis (pa-nis), *n.m.*, (bot.) panic, panicgrass.

panne, *n.f.*, shag, plush; fat; (carp.) purlin; face (of a hammer—*de marteau*). *Culotte de —;* plush-breeches. *Être en —;* (nav.) to lie to. *Mettre en —;* (nav.) to bring to, to heave to. *Se tenir en —;* (nav.) to lie to. *Ce cochon n'a presque point de —;* this pig has scarcely any fat. *Être dans la —* (pop.); to be hard up, to be in difficulties.

panné, *adj.*, (pop.) shabby, poor, penniless.

panneau, *n.m.*, square, panel; snare, trap; panel (of a saddle—*de selle*). *— de lambris;* wainscot panel. *— de porte;* tympan of a door. *Donner dans le —;* to fall into the snare.

panneauter, *v.n.*, (hunt.) to set snares, to set traps.

pannelle, *n.f.*, (her.) poplar leaf.

panneton (pa-n-ton), *n.m.*, (locksmith's work—*serrurerie*) key-bit; catch of an espagnolette; long basket in which bakers put the dough.

pannicule, *n.m.*, (anat.) adipose membrane; cellular tissue.

panonceau, *n.m.*, scutcheon.

panoplie, *n.f.*, panoply.

panorama, *n.m.*, panorama.

panoramique, *adj.*, panoramic.

pan pan, *onomatopœia*, rat-tat-tat; bang, slap, flap.

pansage, *n.m.*, dressing, rubbing, grooming of a horse.

panse, *n.f.*, paunch, belly; rumen, cud (of ruminating animals—*des ruminants*). *Grosse —;* pot-belly, paunch. *Avoir les yeux plus grands que la —;* to have eyes bigger than one's belly. *— d'a;* oval of an *a*. *Il n'a pas fait une — d'a;* he has done nothing at all, he has not done a stroke.

pansé, -e, *part.*, dressed. *Il est bien —;* he has eaten a pretty quantity.

pansement (pans-mân), *n.m.*, dressing (of wounds—*de blessures*); rubbing, grooming (of a horse—*d'un cheval*). *V.* **pansage.**

panser, *v.a.*, to dress (wounds—*des blessures*); to groom (a horse—*un cheval*).

pansu, -e, *adj.*, pot-bellied, tun-bellied, bigbellied.

pantalon, *n.m.*, pantaloons, pair of pantaloons; trousers, pair of trousers; pantaloon (pantomime). *— collant;* tight trousers.

pantalonnade, *n.f.*, pantaloon's dance, buffoonery; false demonstration, absurd subterfuge.

pantelant, -e (pan-tlân, -t), *adj.*, panting, heaving; palpitating. *Chair —e;* quivering flesh.

panteler (pan-tlé), *v.n.*, to gasp for breath, to pant.

pantenne (-tè-n), *n.f.*, (nav.) situation of a ship riding with her yards apeak. *Vergues en —* ; yards placed obliquely, and sails badly trimmed. *Vaisseau en —* ; ship which rides apeak.

panthée, *adj.f.*, pantheistic (statues, figures).

panthéisme, *n.m.*, Pantheism.

panthéiste, *n.m.*, pantheist.

panthéistique, *adj.*, pantheistic, pantheistical.

panthéon, *n.m.*, pantheon.

panthère, *n.f.*, (mam.) panther.

pantière (-tièr), *n.f.*, (hunt.) draw-net.

pantin, *n.m.*, dancing Jack, puppet ; (b.s.) great gesticulator.

pantographe, *n.m.*, pantograph.

pantographie, *n.f.*, pantography.

pantographique, *adj.*, pantographic, pantographical.

pantoiement, *n.m.*, (hawking—*fauconnerie*) pantess.

pantois, *adj.*, ⊙panting, out of breath ; astonished, stupefied, aghast.

pantomètre, *n.m.*, (geom.) pantometer.

pantomime, *n.m.*, pantomime, pantomimist.

pantomime, *n.f.*, dumb-show ; pantomime.

pantomime, *adj.*, pantomimic, pantomimical.

pantoufle, *n.f.*, slipper. *Être en —* ; to be in one's slippers. *Soulier en —* ; slip-shod shoe, shoe down at heel. *Raisonner comme une —* ; to reason like a jackass. *Fer à —* ; pantonshoe, panton.

pantoufler, *v.n.*, to reason like a jackass.

pantouflerie, *n.f.*, stupid conversation ; piece of nonsense, piece of absurdity.

pantouflier, *n.m.*, slipper-maker.

paon (pan), *n.m.*, (orni.) peacock ; (astron.) Pavo. — *sauvage des Pyrénées* ; ruff, reeve. — *bleu* ; peacock-fish. *Queue-de- —* (min.) ; iridescent sulphate of copper.

paonne (pa-n), *n.f.*, (orni.) pea-hen.

paonneau (pa-nô), *n.m.*, (orni.) pea-chick.

papa, *n.m.*, papa, dad, daddy.

papable, *adj.*, that may be made pope.

papal, -e, *adj.*, papal.

papas (pa-pâ), *n.m.*, pope (priest of the Levant—*prêtre chrétien en Orient*).

papauté, *n.f.*, papacy, popedom, pontificate.

papavéracées, *n.f.pl.*, (bot.) papaveraceæ

papaye, *n.f.*, (bot.) papaw (fruit).

papayer, *n.m.*, papaw-tree ; papaw.

pape, *n.m.*, Pope, head of the Catholic Church; (orni.) papa.

papegai (pap-ghè), *n.m.*, (orni.) popinjay ; a wooden bird to shoot at.

papelard (pa-plar), *n.m.*, (fam.) hypocrite.

papelard, -e, *adj.*, (fam.) hypocritical. *Air, ton, —* ; sanctified air, tone.

papelardise (pa-plar-diz), *n.f.*, (fam.) hypocrisy, sanctimony, sanctimoniousness.

papeline, *n.f.*, poplin.

papelonné, *adj.*, (her.) covered with scales.

paperasse (pa-ras), *n.f.*, old paper ; waste paper ; (b.s.) paper.

paperasser, *v.n.*, to rummage papers; to scribble paper.

paperassier, *n.m.*, scribbler; man who likes to amass old papers.

paperassi-er, -ère, *adj.*, red-tape ; formal.

papesse, *n.f.*, papess.

papeterie (pap-tri), *n.f.*, paper-mill ; paper-making ; paper-trade ; paper-manufacture ; paper-manufactory ; stationery. *Magasin de —* ;

papetier (pap-tié), *n.m.*, paper-maker ; stationer.

papier, *n.m.*, paper. — *à écrire* ; writing-paper. — *brouillard* ; blotting-paper. — *gris* ; brown paper. *Main de —* ; quire of paper. *Cahier de —* ; paper-book ; quarter of a quire of paper. — *cassé* ; outside sheets. — *chantonné* ; wrinkled paper. — *serpente, — de soie* ; silver-paper. — *blanc* ; white paper, blank paper. — *collé* ; sized paper. — *non collé* ; unsized paper. — *mécanique* ; machine-made paper, machine-paper. — *peint, — teint* ; stained-paper. — *de verre* ; glass-paper. — *soufflé, — velouté* ; flock-paper. —*s de bord* ; (nav.) ship's papers. —*coquille* ; demy paper, post-demy paper. — *Jésus* ; super-royal paper, long-royal paper. — *pelure* ; foreign paper, foreign post-paper. *Couteau à —* ; paper-knife, paper-cutter. *Fabricant de — peint* ; paper-stainer. — *rayé* ; striped paper. — *du Nil* ; papyrus. — *naturel* ; fossil paper. ⊙—*s-nouvelles* ; newspapers. *Être bien dans les —s de quelqu'un, être bien sur les —s de quelqu'un* ; to be in any one's good books, good graces. *Être mal dans les —s de quelqu'un, être mal sur les —s de quelqu'un* ; to be out of any one's good books. *Ôtez cela de vos —s* ; cross that out of your book. *Brouiller, gâter, du —* ; to waste, to spoil paper. ⊙—*journal* (com.) ; day-book. — *volant* ; flying-sheet. — *timbré* ; stamped paper. — *-monnaie* ; paper-money.

papilionacé, -e, *or* *papilionacé, -e*, *adj.*, (bot.) papilionaceous.

papillaire, *adj.*, (anat.) papillary.

papille, *n.f.*, (anat.) papilla.

papillon, *n.m.*, (ent.) butterfly ; butterfly (pers.) — *de nuit* ; moth.

papillonner, *v.n.*, to flutter about from one thing to another.

papillotage, *n.m.*, twinkling (of the eyes—*des yeux*) ; putting in paper. in curl-papers (of the hair—*des cheveux*) ; (print.) mackling, slurring.

papillote, *n.f.*, curl-paper (for the hair—*pour les cheveux*) ; sweetmeat in paper ; chocolate in paper ; spangle (of gold or silver—*d'or ou d'argent*) ; (cook.) paper. *Côtelette en —* ; cutlet fried in paper.

papilloter, *v.a.*, to put hair in paper.

papilloter, *v.n.*, to twinkle ; to dazzle, to be gaudy; (print.) to slur.

papisme, *n.m.*, papism, popery.

papiste, *n.m.f.*, papist.

papiste, *adj.*, papistic, papistical ; popish.

pappeu-x, -se, *adj.*, (bot.) downy, pappous.

papule, *n.f.*, (med.) papula, pimple.

papyracé, -e, *adj.*, thin and dry like paper ; papyraceous.

papyrus, *n.m.*, (bot.) paper-rush ; papyrus.

pâque, *n.f.*, Passover.

pâque, *or* **pâques**, *n.m.*, Easter. *Quinzaine de —s* ; Passion-week and Easter week. *Semaine de —s* ; Easter week. (In the following expressions *Pâques* is feminine plural: —*s fleuries* ; Palm-Sunday. —*s closes* ; Low-Sunday. *Faire ses —s* ; to receive the Sacrament at Easter). [*Pâque* is very rarely used in the sense of *Easter*.]

paquebot (pak-bô), *n.m.*, packet-boat, packet. — *à vapeur* ; steam-packet. — *de poste* ; mail-packet.

pâquerette, *n.f.*, (bot.) Easter-daisy.

paquet, *n.m.*, bundle, parcel ; packet; mail ; trick ; lump (pers.) ; (print.) slip. *Faire un —* ; to make up a parcel. *Faire son —* ; to pack up one's traps, to pack up. *Hasarder le —* ; to engage in a doubtful enterprise. *Faire ses —s pour l'autre monde* ; to set out for the long journey, to kick the bucket. *Faire un — sur quelqu'un* ; to backbite anyone. *Donner un — à*

quelqu'un; to play off a trick on any one.
Donner à quelqu'un son —; to give any one a good answer, to silence any one. *Recevoir son —, recevoir ses —s;* to be discharged. to be sent to the right-about, to get the sack. *Cette femme est un vrai —;* that woman is a regular lump. *Le — d'Angleterre, d'Espagne;* the English, the Spanish, mail.

paqueter, *v.a.*, to bundle. to bind up in parcels, to roll up.

paquetier (pak-tié), *n.m.*, (print.) piecehand.

paquette, *n.f.*, (bot.) ox-eye daisy.

paqueur, *n.m.*, salt-fish packer.

pâquis, *n.m.*, feeding ground (frequented by game—*fréquenté par le gibier*); pasture.

par, *prep.*, by, through, out of, about, into, in, from, for, for the sake of, at, with; during. *De — le roi;* in the king's name. *Je l'ai fait — cette raison;* I did it for that reason. *Il a fait cela — crainte;* he did that out of fear, from fear, through fear. *Il entra — la porte;* he entered by the door. *Je compris — là;* I understood from that. *— passe-temps;* by way of diversion. *Cela se fait — tout pays;* that is done in all countries. *— où!* which way? *— ici;* this way. *— là;* that way. *— deçà;* this side. *— delà;* that side. *— dedans;* within. *— dehors;* without. *— -devers;* by, with. *— -dessus;* over, above. over and above. *— -dessus les maisons;* above the houses. *— -dessous;* under, underneath. *— devant;* before, forwards. *— derrière;* behind, backwards. *— le haut.* *— en haut;* towards the top, upwards. *— le bas, — en bas;* downwards. *Prenez-le — le bras;* take his arm. *— le passé;* formerly. *— -ci — là;* here and there; off and on. *— aventure;* by chance. *— devant* (jur.); in the presence of. *Il a passé — Paris;* he passed through Paris. *Se promener — les rues;* to walk about the streets. *Jeter — la fenêtre;* to throw out of the window. *Il faut en passer — là;* people must put up with it. *Elle conclut — le supplier de;* she concluded by beseeching him to. *Distribuer — chapitres;* to divide into chapters. *Aller — bandes;* to go in companies. *Couper — morceaux;* to cut in pieces, into pieces. *Donner tant — tête;* to give so much per head, for each person. *Une guinée — soldat;* a guinea each soldier.

para, *n.m.* (—*s*), para, Turkish coin worth about half a penny.

parabase, *n.f.*, (antiq.) parabasis, a sort of prologue in ancient Greek comedy.

parabolain, *n.m.*,(Roman antiq., ecc.) parabolanus, parabolan.

parabole, *n.f.*, (geom.) parabola; parable. *Les —s de Salomon;* the proverbs of Solomon.

parabolique, *adj.*, parabolic, parabolical.

paraboliquement (-lik-mān), *adv.*, parabolically.

paracentèse, *n.f.*, (surg.) paracentesis, tapping.

⊙**parachèvement**, *n m.*, ending, finishing; completion.

⊙**parachever**, *v.a.*, to finish, to end, to complete.

parachronisme(-kro-),*n.m.*,parachronism.

parachute, *n.m.*, parachute.

paraclet, *n.m.*, (Bibl.) Paraclete.

parade, *n.f.*, parade; show, state, pageant, pageantry; (fenc.) parade, parrying; (milit.) parade; burlesque scenes outside shows at fairs. *Chambre de —;* state-room. *Lit de —;* bed of state. *Faire — d'une chose;* to make a parade, a display, of a thing. *Faire —;* (nav.) to dress a ship with flags. *Ne pas être heureux à la —;* not to be quick at repartee, to be a bad hand at repartee.

parader, *v.n.*, to show one's self; to cruise.

Faire — un cheval; to show off the paces of a horse.

paradigme, *n.m.*, (gram.) paradigm.

paradis, *n.m.*, paradise; (thea.) upper gallery. *Le — terrestre;* earthly paradise. *Celuici est un —;* this place is a heaven on earth. *Oiseau de —;* bird of paradise. *Pomme de —;* apple of paradise. *Sur ma part du —;* as I hope to be saved.

paradisier, *n.m.*, (orni.) bird of paradise.

paradoxal, -e, *adj.*, paradoxical.

paradoxalement, *adv.*, paradoxically.

paradoxe, *n.m.*, paradox.

⊙**paradoxe**, *adj.*, paradoxical.

paradoxisme, *n.m.*, (rhet.) paradoxy.

parafe, or **paraphe**, *n.m.*, flourish (added to one's signature—*ajouté après la signature*); initials and flourish; paraph.

parafer, or **parapher**, *v.a.*, to put one's flourish, dash, or initials to.

paraffine, *n.f.*, (chem.) paraffine.

parage, *n.m.*, (nav.) latitude, quarter; place; (l.u.) extraction, descent, lineage. *De haut —;* of high degree.

paragoge, *n.f.*, (gram.) paragoge.

paragogique, *adj.*, (gram.) paragogic, paragogical.

paragraphe, *n.m.*, paragraph.

⊙**paraguante** (-gooant), *n.f.*, present (for a service rendered—*en reconnaissance d'un service*); douceur.

paraître (paraissant, paru), *v.n.*, to appear, to make one's appearance, to be seen, to be visible; to make a show, to make some figure; to seem, to look; to come out, to be published; (nav.) to heave in sight. *— en mer;* to loom. *Commencer à —;* to appear, to come in sight. *Ces raisons paraissent bonnes;* these reasons seem to be good. *Quand votre ouvrage paraîtra-t-il!* when will your work be published? *Chercher à —;* to endeavour to make an appearance, to cut a figure. *Il n'y a rien qui n'y paraisse;* that is very evident, very clear. *Faire —;* to show, to discover, to exhibit. *Il paraît;* it appears. *Il y paraît;* there are appearances of it, it is evident. *Il n'y paraît pas;* there is no appearance of, there are no signs of it.

paralipomènes, *n.m.pl.*, (Bibl.) Paralipomena.

paralipse, *n.f.*, (rhet.) paralipsis.

parallactique, *adj.*, (astron.) parallactic.

parallaxe, *n.f.*, (astron.) parallax.

parallèle, *adj.*, (geom.) parallel.

parallèle, *n.f.*, (geom) parallel; (fort.) parallel.

parallèle, *n.m.*, parallel, comparison; (geog.) parallel, circle of latitude. *Mettre en —;* to draw a parallel between, to compare.

parallèlement, *adv.*, parallel, in parallel lines.

parallélépipède, or **parallélipipède**, *n.m.*, (geom.) parallelopiped.

parallélisme, *n.m.*, parallelism.

parallélogrammatique, *adj.*, (geom.) parallelogrammic.

parallélogramme, *n.m.*,(geom.) parallelogram. *— articulé* (mec.); parallel-joint. *— de Watt;* (mec.) parallel motion.

parallélographe, *n.m.*, parallel-ruler.

paralogisme, *n.m.*, paralogism.

paralyser, *v.a.*, (med.) to paralyze; to render powerless, to paralyze.

paralysie, *n.f.*, (med.) paralysis, palsy. *Tomber en —;* to be struck with palsy, to have a paralytic stroke.

paralytique, *n.m.f.* and *adj.*, paralytic; paralytical, palsied.

paramètre, *n.m.*, (geom.) parameter.

parangon, n.m., ⊙paragon, model, comparison, parallel; (jewellery—*joaillerie*) paragon. *Gros* — (print.); double pica. *Petit* — (print.); paragon. *Cela est sans* —; that is without a parallel, unparalleled. *Faire le* — *d'une chose avec une autre;* to compare one thing with another.

parangon, adj. *invariable*, (jewellery—*joaillerie*) without defect, perfect. *Diamant* —; diamond without a blemish.

parangonnage, n.m., (print.) justifying, justification.

parangonner, v.a., ⊙to compare, to make comparison of; (print.) to justify.

parant, -e, adj., ornamental, decking, adorning.

paranymphe, n.m., ⊙supporter, paranymph; (antiq.) paranymph.

parapet, n.m., parapet, parapet-wall, breastwork.

paraphe, **parapher**. V. **parafe**, **parafer**.

paraphernal, -e, adj., (jur.) paraphernal. *Biens paraphernaux;* paraphernal property, paraphernalia.

paraphernaux, n.m.pl., (jur.) paraphernalia, wife's property.

paraphimosis (-zis), n.m., (surg.) paraphimosis.

paraphrase, n.f., paraphrase.

paraphraser, v.a. and n., to paraphrase.

paraphraseu-r, n.m., **-se**, n.f., (b.s.) amplifier.

paraphraste, n.m., paraphrast.

paraplégie, n.f., (med.) paraplegia.

parapluie, n.m., umbrella.

parasange, n.f., (antiq.) parasang (Persian measure of distance—*mesure itinéraire des Perses*).

parasélène, n.f., (astron.) paraselene.

parasite, n.m., parasite.

parasite, adj., parasitic, parasitical; sycophantic; superfluous, recurring too frequently. *Plantes —s;* parasitical plants. *Insectes —s;* parasitic insects. *Mots —s;* superfluous, redundant words.

parasitisme, n.m., (med.) parasitism.

parasol (-sol), n.m., parasol. *Plante en* —; umbelliferous plant.

paratitlaire, n.m., (jur.) author of paratitla.

paratitles, n.m.pl., (jur.) paratitla, paratitles.

paratonnerre, n.m., conductor, lightning-rod, lightning-conductor; (nav.) marine conductor, conductor.

paravent, n.m., screen, folding-screen.

parbleu! int., zounds! forsooth!

parc, n.m., park; pen (for cattle—*pour les bestiaux*); sheepfold; bed (of oysters—*d'huîtres*); (artil.) park; warren (for game—*à gibier*); (agri.) sheepwalk; (nav.) locker. — *de construction;* yard (for ships—*de vaisseaux*). *Les murailles d'un* —; the walls of a park.

parcage, n.m., folding (of sheep—*de moutons*); penning (of cattle—*de bestiaux*).

parcellaire, adj., by small portions. *Cadastre* —; register of lands divided into small portions.

parcellaire, n.m., register of the survey of lands made by small portions.

parcelle, n.f., particle, portion; instalment. — *du sol;* portion of the soil. *Payer par —s;* to pay by instalments.

parceller, v.a., to portion out.

parce que, conj., because, inasmuch as, forasmuch as; why, wherefore.

parchemin, n.m., parchment; pl., titles of nobility; descent, pedigree. *Allonger le* —; to lengthen deeds uselessly. *Il est fier de ses —s;* he is proud of his pedigree.

parcheminerie (-mi-n-rî), n.f., parchment-making; parchment-factory; parchment-trade.

parcheminier, n.m., parchment-maker.

parcimonie, n.f., parsimony, sparingness.

parcimonieusement, adv., parsimoniously.

parcimonieu-x, -se, adj., parsimonious, sparing.

parcourir, v.a., to travel over, to go over, to run over, to perambulate, to take a survey; to look over; to peruse; to turn over the leaves (of a book—*d'un livre*). *Il a parcouru toute l'Asie;* he has travelled all over Asia. — *la ville;* to survey the town. — *un livre;* to look through a book. *Je l'ai parcouru;* I have read it cursorily.

parcours, n.m., line travelled over by a public conveyance; commonage.

pardessus, n.m., overcoat.

pardon, n.m., pardon, forgiveness; pl. (c. rel.) indulgences. *Je vous demande* —; I beg your pardon. —; excuse me.

pardonnable, adj., pardonable, excusable, that may be forgiven.

pardonné, -e, part., pardoned, forgiven.

pardonner, v.a., to pardon, to forgive; to spare, to excuse. — *les offenses;* to forgive offences. — *une erreur à quelqu'un;* to excuse an error in any one. *Pardonnez à ma franchise de vous dire cela;* excuse my frankness in telling you that. *Pardonnez-moi;* pardon me; excuse me.

paréage, or **pariage**, n.m., (feudal law—*féodalité*); joint possession of the same estate by two lords.

⊙**paréatis**, n.m. (—), in former times a permission to distrain pursuant to an order of a court of another jurisdiction than that in which the distraint was to take place.

parégorique, n.m. and adj., (med.) paregoric.

*****pareil, -le**, adj., like, alike, equal; similar, such. *Je n'ai rien vu de* —; I never saw the like. *Sans* —; peerless, matchless. *C'est un homme sans* —; he has not his match.

pareil, n.m., equal, fellow, match. *Il a trouvé son* —; he has found his match. *Fréquentez vos —s;* keep company with your equals.

pareille, n.f., similar treatment. *Rendre la — à quelqu'un;* to serve any one the same, to pay any one out, to be even with any one.

*****pareillement**, adv., similarly; in the same way, likewise, too.

parélie. V. **parhélie**.

parelle, n.f., (bot.) parella, patience.

parement (par-mān), n.m., ornament; facing (of dress—*d'habit*); cuff (of sleeves—*de manches*); large stick (of a fagot—*d'un fagot*); (arch.) facing; altar-cloth; curb-stone.

parementer, v.a., (arch.) to face.

parenchymateu-x, -se, adj., parenchymatous.

parenchyme, n.m., (anat., bot.) parenchyma; diploe (of leaves—*des feuilles*).

parénèse, n.f., parenesis.

parénétique, adj., parenetic.

parent, n.m., **-e**, n.f., relation, relative; kinsman, kinswoman, kin; pl., parents, father and mother; relatives, relations, connexions, kindred. — *paternel;* relation by the father's side. — *maternel;* relation by the mother's side. *Un bon ami vaut mieux qu'un* —; a good friend is better than a kinsman. *Grands—s;* grandfather and grand-mother. *Proche* —; near relative; (jur.) next of kin.

⊙**parentage**, n.m. V. **parenté**.

parenté, n.f., relationship, consanguinity,

kindred; relations, relatives, kinsfolk, connexions, family.

parentèle, *n.f.*, (fam.). *V.* **parenté**.

parenthèse, *n.f.*, parenthesis. *Par —;* by way of parenthesis, by-the-by, by-the-way. *Entre —s;* in parenthesis.

parer, *v.a.*, to adorn, to set off, to set out, to deck, to embellish; to shelter; to guard; to parry, to ward off; (nav.) to clear; to pare (horse's hoofs—*le sabot d'un cheval*). *— un coup;* to ward off a blow. *— du cuir;* to dress leather. *— du cidre;* to make cider ferment. *— un agneau;* to dress a lamb. *— un cap;* (nav.) to clear a cape. *— un câble;* to clear a cable. *— une ancre;* to clear an anchor. *— un enfant;* to dress out a child. *Il est assez paré de sa bonne mine;* his good appearance sets him off sufficiently.

se parer, *v.r.*, to adorn one's self; to dress; to dress one's self out; to screen, to guard one's self; to make a show, to boast. *Elle se pare d'une manière ridicule;* she decks herself out in a ridiculous manner.

parer, *v.n.*, (fenc.) to parry; to screen, to defend; to guard. *— et porter en même temps;* to parry and thrust at the same time. *On ne peut pas — à tout;* one can't guard against everything.

parère, *n.m.*, (com.) opinion of merchants on matters of commerce.

parésie, *n.f.*, (med.) slight palsy.

paresse, *n.f.*, idleness, sloth, laziness, indolence. *— d'esprit;* sluggishness of intellect, indolence of mind.

paresser, *v.n.*, to give one's self up to idleness, to idle.

paresseusement (-eûz-mân), *adv.*, lazily, idly, slothfully.

paresseu-x, -se, *n.* and *adj.*, sluggard, idle, lazy person; lazy, idle, slothful, sluggish, indolent.

paresseux, *n.m.*, (mam.) sloth.

pareur, *n.m.*, (tech.) finisher.

parfaire, *v.a.*, to perfect, to complete, to make up.

parfait, -e, *adj.*, perfect, finished; accomplished, complete. *Dieu seul est —;* God alone is perfect. *Accord —;* (mus.) perfect chord. *Cela est fait et —;* that is completely finished.

parfait, *n.m.*, perfection; (gram.) perfect. *Plus-que- —;* preterpluperfect. *Au —;* (gram.) in the perfect.

parfaitement (-fèt-mân), *adv.*, perfectly, completely, exactly.

parfilage, *n.m.*, undoing the threads (of textile fabrics—*de tissus*); picking out the threads.

parfiler, *v a.* and *n.*, to undo the threads (of textile fabrics—*de tissus*); to pick out the threads of.

parfois, *adv.*, sometimes, occasionally, now and then.

parfondre, *v.a.*, to fuse (enamel—*émail*).

parfournir, *v.a.*, to render complete, to make up.

parfum (-fun), *n.m.*, perfume, odour, scent, fragrance. *Le — des fleurs;* the fragrance of flowers. *Répandre un —;* to spread a perfume.

parfumer, *v.a.*, to perfume, to sweeten, to scent. *Les fleurs parfument l'air;* the flowers perfume the air.

se parfumer, *v.r.*, to use perfumes, to perfume one's self.

parfumerie (-fu-mrî), *n.f.*, perfumery.

parfumeu-r, *n.m.*, **-se**, *n.f.*, perfumer.

parfumoir, *n.m.*, perfuming-dish.

parhélie, or **parélie**, *n.m.*, parhelion, mock-sun.

pari, *n.m.*, bet, wager, stake. *Faire un —;* to lay a bet. *Tenir le —;* to take the bet.

paria, *n.m.*, paria.

pariade, *n.f.*, (hunt.) pairing-time (of partridges—*des perdrix*).

parier, *v.a.*, to bet, to lay a wager.

pariétaire, *n.f.*, (bot.) parietary.

pariétal, *adj.m.*, (anat.) parietal.

pariétal, *n.m.*, (anat.) parietal-bone.

parieur, *n.m.*, bettor.

parisette, *n.f.*, (bot.) paris.

parisien, -ne, *n.* and *adj.*, Parisian.

parisienne, *n.f.*, (print.) pearl; Parisienne (patriotic song—*chant patriotique*).

Ⓞ**parisis** (-zîs), *adj.*, of Paris (of coins—*monnaie*).

parisyllabique (-sil-la-bik), *adj.*, (gram.) parisyllabic.

parité, *n.f.*, parity, comparison, parallel case.

parjure, *n.m.f.* and *adj.*, perjurer; perjured, forsworn.

parjure, *n.m.*, perjury, false oath.

se parjurer, *v.r.*, to perjure, to forswear, one's self, to be forsworn.

parlage, *n.m.*, empty talk, prattle.

parlant, -e, *adj.*, speaking; (her.) allusive, canting. *Ce portrait est —;* that is a speaking portrait. *Cet homme est peu —;* that man is not talkative.

parlement, *n.m.*, parliament. *Contraire aux usages du —;* unparliamentary.

parlementaire, *n.m.* and *adj.*, bearer of a flag of truce; parliamentarian; parlementary. *Un vaisseau —;* a cartel-ship.

parlementer, *v.n.*, to parley, to come to a parley.

parler, *v.n.*, to speak, to talk, to commune, to discourse, to converse. *Façon de —;* mode of speaking. *— distinctement;* to speak distinctly. *— à l'oreille;* to whisper. *— en public;* to speak in public. *— trop;* to speak too much. *Il parle mal de vous;* he speaks ill of you. *Faire — de soi;* to make one's self a matter of talk. *— à un sourd;* to speak to a post. *Cela ne vaut pas la peine d'en —;* it is not worth mentioning. *Cela parle tout seul;* the thing speaks for itself. *Il en parle bien à son aise;* it is easy for him to say so. *Je lui apprendrai à —;* I will teach him to govern his tongue. *Il trouvera à qui —;* he shall meet with his match. *— en l'air;* to talk at random. *— à cheval à quelqu'un;* to speak to any one imperiously. *— de la pluie et du beau temps;* to talk of indifferent matters. *— d'abondance;* to speak on the spur of the moment. *Il a bien fait — de lui;* he has got much talked of. *— en maître;* to speak peremptorily.

parler, *v.a.*, to speak (a language—*une langue*). *— français;* to speak French. *Il parle bien sa langue;* he speaks his language well.

se parler, *v.r.*, to speak to each other; to be spoken (of languages—*langages*). *Elles se parlent des yeux;* they speak to each other with their eyes.

parler, *n.m.*, utterance, way of speaking. *Avoir son franc —;* to be free-spoken. *Jamais beau — n'écorche la langue;* fair words are always the best.

parlerie, *n.f.*, prating, talkativeness.

parleu-r, *n.m.*, **-se**, *n.f.*, speech-maker, talker. *Un beau —;* a good speaker.

parli-er, -ère, *adj.*, (l.u.) talkative.

parloir, *n.m.*, parlour.

parmentière (-tièr), *n.f.*, (bot.) potato.

parmesan, *n.m.*, Parmesan cheese.

parmi, *prep.*, among, amongst, amid, amidst.

parnasse, *n.m.*, Parnassus. *Les nourrissons du —;* the nurslings of Parnassus. *Le — français;* French poetry, French poets.

parnassien, -ne (-in, -èn), *adj.*, pertaining to Parnassus, Parnassian.

parnassien, *n.m.*, (jest.) son of Parnassus, poet.

parodie, *n.f.*, parody.

parodier, *v.a.*, to parody.

parodiste, *n.m.*, author of a parody.

paroi, *n.f.*, wall, partition; (anat.) coat, wall. *Les —s d'un vase;* the interior sides of a vase. *Les —s de l'estomac;* the coats, the walls of the stomach.

paroisse, *n.f.*, parish, parish-church; parishioners. *Être de deux —s;* not to be fellows (of things—*des choses*).

paroissial, -e, *adj.*, parochial, parish.

paroissien (-in), *n.m.*, **-ne** (-è-n), *n.f.*, parishioner.

paroissien, *n.m.*, catholic prayer-book.

parole, *n.f.*, word; speech, language; saying, sentiment; utterance, voice; eloquence; promise; (milit.) parole. *Il traîne ses —s;* he drawls his words. *Il a perdu la —;* he has lost the use of his tongue. *Porter la —;* to speak, to be the spokesman. *Adresser la — à quelqu'un;* to address any one. *Prendre la —;* to begin to speak, to address the house (in Parliament—*au parlement*). *Avoir la —;* to be allowed to speak; to be upon one's legs (in Parliament—*au parlement*). *Demander la —;* to request permission to speak. *Céder la —;* to decline speaking, to give up one's turn for speaking. *Couper la — à quelqu'un;* to interrupt any one speaking. *Ses mémorables;* notable sayings. *Il a la — lente;* his utterance is slow. *Il a la — tremblante;* his voice falters. *La puissance de la —;* the might of eloquence. *Engager sa —;* to promise, to pledge one's word. *Tenir —, sa —;* to keep one's word, to be as good as one's word. *Donner sa —;* to give one's word. *Dégager sa —;* to recall one's word. *Se dédire de sa —, manquer de —;* to go from one's word. *Il est prisonnier sur —;* he is prisoner upon parole. *Il est homme de —;* he is a man of his word. *— d'honneur;* word of honour. *Ils ont eu des —s;* words passed between them. *Se prendre de —s;* to have words.

paroli, *n.m.*, double stake (at faro, &c.—*au pharaon*, &c.). *Faire —;* to double. *Rendre le — à quelqu'un*, to outdo any one.

paronomase, *n.f.*, paronomasy.

paronomasie, *n.f.*, resemblance between words of different languages.

paronychie, *n.f.*, (med.) paronychia, whitlow.

paronyme, *n.m.* and *adj.*, (gram.) paronyme; paronymous.

paronyque, *n.f.*, (bot.) whitlowwort.

parotide, *n.f.* and *adj.*, (anat.) parotis, parotid gland; (med.) parolitis, mumps; parotid.

parotidien, -ne (-in, -è-n), *adj.*, (anat.) parotid.

parotidite, *n.f.*, (med.) parolitis, mumps; (vet.) vives.

paroxysme, *n.m.*, (med.) paroxysm, fit.

parpaing (-pin), *n.m.*,(mas.) perpend-stone.

parque, *n.f.*, (myth.) Fate, fatal sister; *pl.*, Fates.

parquer, *v.a.*, to fold, to pen, to pen up, to enclose; (artil.) to park. *— des bœufs;* to pen cattle. *— des moutons;* to fold sheep.

se parquer, *v.r.*, to be placed in an enclosure; (artil.) to be parked.

parquer, *v.n.*, to be penned, to be penned up (of cattle—*des bestiaux*); (artil.) to be parked.

parquet, *n.m.*, bar (of a court of justice—*d'un tribunal*); office of the public prosecutor; the public prosecutor and his officers; wood flooring (of room—*d'un chambre*); back (of a looking-glass—*d'un miroir*); (nav.) locker. *— à boulets;* (nav.) shot-locker.

parquetage, *n.m.*, flooring.

parqueter, *v.a.*, to floor.

parqueterie (-kè-tri), *n.f.*, making wood flooring.

parqueteur, *n.m.*, maker of wood floors.

parrain, *n.m.*, godfather, sponsor; ⊙second (in a duel—*dans un duel*); soldier selected by the culprit in a military execution to blindfold him.

parricide, *n.m.* and *adj.*, parricide; matricide; parricidal, murderous.

parse, or parsi, *n.m.* and *adj.*, Parsee; pertaining to Parsee, of Parsee. [*Parse* is more frequently used as an adjective than *Parsi*.]

parsemer, *v.a.*, to strew, to spread, to besprinkle. *— un chemin de fleurs;* to strew a path with flowers. *Le ciel est parsemé d'étoiles;* the skies are spangled with stars.

part, *n.f.*, share, part, portion; concern, interest; part, side. *Voilà votre —, voici la mienne;* there is your share, here is mine. *Être de — avec quelqu'un;* to go shares with any one. *Faire la — à quelqu'un;* to give any one his share. *Entrer en — avec quelqu'un;* to go shares with any one. *Avoir — à quelque affaire;* to have a share in any business. *Avoir — au gâteau;* to share in the profits of anything, to have a finger in the pie. *Prendre — à;* to participate in, to be a party to. *La — que je prends à votre douleur;* my concern for your affliction. *Faire part de quelque chose à quelqu'un;* to give any one a share of anything; to apprise any one of anything. *Billets de faire —;* circular letters to announce a birth, a death, &c. *Faire la — des accidents;* to make allowance for accidents. *Prendre en bonne —;* to take in a good sense. *Prendre en mauvaise —;* to take amiss. *Je le sais de bonne —;* I have it from good hands. *Dites-lui de ma —;* tell him from me. *Saluez-le de ma —;* remember me to him. *Je prends cela de la — d'où il vient;* I take it from whence it comes. *Je vais quelque —;* I am going somewhere. *On ne le trouve nulle —;* he is not to be found anywhere. *Autre —;* somewhere else. *Nulle —;* nowhere. *En quelque — que;* wherever. *D'une — il considérait que;* on one side he considered that. *De — et d'autre, de toutes —s;* on either side, on all sides. *De — en —;* through and through. *À —;* apart, aside. *Mettre à —;* to set apart. *Il le tira à —;* he took him aside. *C'est un fait à —;* that is a particular case. *Raillerie à —;* in good earnest, without joking.

part (part), *n.m.*, (jur.) child, infant, birth.

partage, *n.m.*, share, lot, portion; partition; sharing, distribution, division. *— égal;* equal division. *Faire le — du butin;* to divide the booty. *La prudence est le — des vieillards;* prudence is proper to old age. *Faire le — de;* to divide.

partageable (-jabl), *adj.*, divisible into shares.

partageant (-jàn), *n.m.*, (jur.) sharer.

partager, *v.a.*, to share; to give a share; to divide, to parcel, to portion, to distribute; to partake of, to participate in, to take part in. *Partagez cela entre vous;* divide that between you. *— le butin;* to share the booty. *Les avis se trouvent partagés;* the votes are divided. *Il faut — le différend;* we must split the difference. *Je partage votre joie;* I participate in your joy.

se partager, *v.r.*, to divide, to be divided.

partager, *v.n.*, to share, to receive a share.

partance, *n.f.*, (nav.) setting sail, departure. *Coup de —;* signal for sailing; sailing-gun. *En —;* on the point of sailing.

partant, *adv.*, therefore, and therefore, thus.

partenaire, *n.m.f.*, partner (at play or in dancing—*au jeu, à la danse*).

parterre, *n.m.*, flower-garden, parterre;

(thea.) pit; audience, public. *Réjouir le —;* to please the audience.

parthénogénèse, *n.f.*, (ent.) parthenogenesis.

parthénon, *n.m.*, Parthenon.

parti, *n.m.*, party, side, part, cause; resolution, choice, ways, means, expedient, course, method; offer, condition; use, advantage; calling, profession; (milit.) detachment; match (marriage—*mariage*). *Chef de —;* leader of a party. *Entrer dans un —;* to join a party. *Être du bon —;* to be on the right side. *Être du de;* to be on the side of. *Prendre le — de quelqu'un;* to take any one's part. *Homme de —;* party man. *Esprit de —;* party spirit. *Il a pris son —;* he has formed his resolution. *J'ai pris le — de me taire;* I chose to be silent. *C'est un — pris;* his mind is made up. *À — pris point de conseil;* when a man's mind is made up, advice is useless. *Voilà le — qu'il nous faut prendre;* this is what we must do. *C'est le — le plus court;* that is the shortest way. *C'est un bon —;* it is a very good offer. *Faire un mauvais — à quelqu'un;* to do any one harm. *Il cherche à tirer — de tout;* he endeavours to turn everything to account. *Il a épousé un bon —;* he has made a good match. *Tirer le meilleur — de quelque chose;* to make the best of anything.

partiaire (-ci-èr), *adj.*, (jur.) that gives a portion of the produce of the land for rent.

partial, -e (-ci-al), *adj.*, partial, biassed.

partialement (-cial-mãn), *adv.*, partially, with partiality.

se **partialiser** (-cia-li-), *v.r.*, to be partial *or* biassed.

partialité (-cia-li-), *n.f.*, partiality.

in **partibus**, *adv.*, in partibus. *Un évêque — ;* a bishop in partibus.

participant, -e. *adj.*, participating.

participant, *n.m.*, -e, *n.f.*, participant.

participation, *n.f.*, participation, privity. *La — aux droits;* the participation of rights. *Cela s'est fait sans ma —;* that was done unknown to me.

participe, *n.m.*, (gram.) participle.

participer, *v.n.*, to partake, to participate, to have a share in, to be a party to. *Je participe à votre douleur;* I share in your sorrow. *Le mulet participe du cheval et de l'âne;* the mule partakes of both the horse and the ass.

particulariser, *v.a.*, to particularize. — *un fait;* to give the particulars of a fact.

particularisme, *n.m.*, (rel. pol.) particularism.

particulariste, *n.m.*, (pol.) particularist.

particularité, *n.f.*, particular, particularity.

particule, *n.f.*, particle.

particuli-er, ère, *adj.*, particular, peculiar, private; circumstantial, singular. *L'intérêt — doit céder à l'intérêt général;* private interest must give way to the public interest. *On lui a donné une chambre —ère;* they gave him a private room. *Le cas est fort —;* the case is altogether singular. *Il a un talent —;* he has a peculiar talent. *Un esprit —;* an odd kind of man.

particulier. *n.m.*, particular individual, private individual; (pop.) fellow. *Ce n'est qu'un simple —;* he is only a private man. *Que nous veut ce — ?* what does that fellow want with us? *En —;* in particular, in private. *Être en son —;* to be in one's own room. *Il faut le voir en —;* you must see him privately. *En mon —;* as for me.

particulièrement (-lièr-mãn), *adv.*, particularly, peculiarly, especially.

partie (-tî), *n.f.*, part, match; project; line of business; (com.) parcel; ⊙ (bookkeeping—*tenue des livres*) entry; (play—*au jeu*) game;

party; contracting party; *pl.*, pudenda. *Air d quatre —s;* tune in four parts. *Tenir bien sa — ;* to act one's part well. *Vous en êtes en — cause;* you are partly the cause of it. *Faire une — de piquet;* to play a game at piquet. — *nulle;* drawn game. *Un coup de —;* masterly stroke, decisive blow. *La — n'est pas égale;* it is not an equal match. *Quitter la —;* to give up, to throw up the game. *Voulez-vous être de la — !* will you be one of us? *Lier une —;* to form a project (for amusement). — *carrée;* pleasure party consisting of two gentlemen and two ladies. — *fine;* secret pleasure party. — *adverse;* adverse party. — *intéressée;* party concerned. *Avoir affaire à forte —;* to have to deal with more than one's match. *Qui n'entend qu'une — n'entend rien;* he who hears one side only, hears nothing. (book-keeping—*tenue des livres*) — *double;* double entry. — *simple;* single entry. *En —;* partly. — *bien, — mal;* partly well, partly ill.

partiel, -le (-ci-èl), *adj.*, partial.

partiellement (-cièl-mãn), *adv.*, partially, by instalments.

partir (partant, parti), *v.n.*, to set out, to start, to go, to go away, to depart; to be off, to spring (of birds—*des oiseaux*); to come, to proceed; to flow from; to go off (of firearms—*des armes à feu*). — *du port;* to sail from the harbour. *Faire —;* to send off. *Il part comme l'éclair;* he is off like lightning. *Faire partir un lièvre;* to start a hare. — *d'un éclat de rire;* to burst out into a fit of laughter. — *comme un trait;* to dart off like an arrow. *La bombe part du mortier;* the bomb is shot from the mortar. *Cela part d'un bon cœur;* that flows from a good heart. *Cet ordre part de sa colère;* that order is the result of his passion. *À — du règne de;* from the reign of. *À — d'aujourd'hui;* from this day forward.

partir, *v.a.*, to part, to divide. [Only used in: *Ils ont toujours maille à —;* they are always squabbling.]

partir, *n.m.*, (man.) start.

partisan, *n.m.*, partisan.

partiti-f, -ve. *adj.*, (gram) partitive.

partition, *n.f.*, (mus.) score.

partner, *n.m.f.*(—*s*). *V.* **partenaire**.

partout, *adv.*, everywhere. — *où;* wherever.

parturition, *n.f.*, (med.) parturition.

parure, *n.f.*, attire, dress, finery, ornament. — *de diamants;* set of diamonds. *Meubles de même;* furniture that matches.

parvenir, *v.n.*, to attain, to arrive, to come, to reach, to succeed. — *à ses fins;* to attain one's aim.

parvenu, -e, *part.*, arrived.

parvenu, *n.m.*, parvenu, upstart.

parvis, *n.m.*, parvis (place in front of a church—*place devant la grande porte d'une église*); space round the tabernacle of the temple of Jerusalem; (poet.) enclosure, hall, vestibule.

pas, *n.m.*, step, pace; footstep, stride, walk, gait; progress, precedence; passage (of arms—*d'armes*). *Marcher d'un — léger;* to walk with a light step. *Il le suit — à —;* he follows him step by step. *À petits —;* slowly. *Il n'y a qu'un —;* it is but a step hence. *Il marche à grands —;* he takes long strides. *Marcher à — comptés;* to walk very slowly. *Faire un — en arrière;* to draw back a little. *Aller, marcher, à — de loup;* to go softly. *Retourner sur ses —;* to go back, to retrace one's steps. *Aller à — mesurés;* to proceed with circumspection. *Faire un faux —;* to make a false step. — *de clerc;* blunder. *Avoir le —;* to have precedence. *De ce —;* directly, at once. *Mettre un cheval au —;* to walk a horse. — *accéléré* (milit.); **quick time.** — *redoublé* (milit.); **double quick time.** *Marcher sur les* — *de quelqu'un ;* to tread in any one's footsteps. *Se tirer d'un mauvais* — *;* to get out of a scrape. *Sauter le* — *;* to take a resolution. — *d'une vis ;* furrow of a screw. — *de fusée :* (horl.) turn of a fusee. *Aller au* — *;* to walk (of a horse—*d'un cheval*).

pas, *adv.,* no; not, not any. — *un ;* not one. *Je ne veux* — *;* I will not. — *du tout ;* not at all. *Presque* — *;* scarcely any. *Je n'ai* — *de livre ;* I have no book.

pascal, -e. *adj.,* paschal.

pas-d'âne, *n.m.* (—), sharp bridle-bit; basket-hilt (of a sword—*d'une épée*); (bot.) colt's-foot.

pasigraphie, *n.f.,* pasigraphy.

pasquin, *n.m.,* pasquin.

pasquinade, *n.f.,* pasquinade.

⊙**pasquiniser,** *v.a.,* to lampoon, to satirize.

passable, *adj.,* passable, tolerable, middling.

passablement, *adv.,* passably, tolerably, indifferently, middlingly.

passacaille, *n.f.,* a kind of dancing lapsed into disuse.

passade, *n.f.,* passing through a place without stopping; (man.) passade.

passage, *n.m.,* passage; arcade; thoroughfare; transition; passage-money; toll. *Oiseaux de* — *;* birds of passage. — *à niveau* (railways) ; crossing. *Ôtez-vous du* — *;* stand out of the way. *Se faire* — *;* to make, to cut one's way through.

passager, *v.a.* and *n.,* (man.) to passage. — *un cheval ;* to passage a horse.

passag-er, -ère, *adj.,* passing, transient, transitory, fugitive.

passag-er, *n.m.,* **-ère,** *n.f.,* passenger; person passing through a place ; traveller.

passagèrement (-jèr-mān), *adv.,* transiently, for a short time.

passant, *n.m.,* passenger, passer-by.

passant, -e, *adj.,* much frequented. *Un chemin* — *;* a much frequented thoroughfare. *Une rue* —*e ;* a much frequented street.

passation, *n.f.,* (jur.) drawing up a title-deed, a contract.

passavant, *n.m.,* pass, permit (of the custom-house—*de la douane*); (nav.) gangway.

passe, *n.f.,* pass, situation, state ; (print.) overplus; (fenc.) pass, passado ; port (at billiards—*au billard*); channel (for harbours, of rivers—*de ports, de rivières*); odd money ; stake (at play—*au jeu*); (geog.) track. *Être en* — *d'avoir quelque emploi ;* to be in a fair way to procure employment. *Il est en fort belle* — *;* he has a very fine prospect before him.

passe, *adv.,* let it be so. — *encore pour cela ;* well, let that be too.

passé, -e, *part..* past, gone, over. *Il a trente ans* —*s ;* he is past thirty. *La pluie est* —*e ;* the rain is over.

passé, *n.m.,* past, time past, things past ; (gram.) past tense.

passé, *prep.,* except ; after.

passe-campane, *n.f.* (—), (vet.) capellet.

passe-carreau, *n.m.* (— —*x*), sleeve-board.

passe-cheval, *n.m.* (— -*chevaux*), ferry-boat for horses.

passe-debout, *n.m.* (—), permit for transit (of the custom-house—*douanes*).

passe-dix, *n.m.* (—), passage (play—*jeu de dés*).

passe-droit, *n.m.* (— —*s*), favour; injustice, wrong.

passée, *n.f.* (hunt.) time when a flight of woodcocks pass by. *Tuer des bécasses à la* —*;* to shoot woodcocks as they fly by.

passe-fleur, *n.f.* (— —*s*), (bot.) a species of anemone.

passéger. *v.n.* *V.* **passager.**

passe-lacet, *n.m.* (— —*s*), bodkin.

passement (pâs-mān), *n.m.,* lace (of gold, silk, &c., for clothes or furniture—*d'or, de soie,* &c., *pour les vêtements et les meubles*).

passementer (pâs-man-té), *v.a.,* to lace (clothes, furniture—*les vêtements et les meubles*).

passementerie (pâs-man-trî), *n.f.,* lace-making, lace-trade.

passementi-er (-tié), *n.m.,* **-ère** (-tièr), *n.f.,* lace-maker, lace-man, lace-woman.

***passe-méteil,** *n.m.,* meslin (mixture of two-thirds of wheat and one-third of rye—*mélange de deux tiers de blé et d'un de seigle*).

passe-parole, *n.m.* (—),(milit.) pass-parole.

passe-partout, *n.m.* (—), master-key, pass-key, latch-key; (engr.) passe-partout ; (print.) factotum ; compass-saw. *L'argent est un bon* — *;* money gains admittance everywhere.

passe-passe, *n.m.* (—), sleight of hand. *Tour de* — *;* legerdemain ; hocus-pocus.

passe-pied, *n.m.* (— —*s*), passe-pied (dance —*danse*).

passe-pierre, *n.f.* (—, *or* — —*s*), samphire, sea-samphire.

passepoil, *n.m.,* piping (for clothes—*de vêtements*).

passeport, *n.m.,* passport; pass; (fig.) recommendation.

passer, *v.n.,* to pass, to pass on, to pass along, to pass away; to die, to expire; to pass for, to be considered; to pass muster; to fade (of flowers—*des fleurs*). *Cette fleur est passée ;* that flower is faded. — *en sautant ;* to skip over. — *par ;* to pass through. *Laisser* — *;* to overlook. *Il a passé par la ville ;* he passed through the town. *Passez par ici ;* come this way. — *outre ;* to go beyond. *Il a passé par de rudes épreuves ;* he has gone through several trials. *Mes beaux jours sont passés ;* my best days are over. *La fantaisie m'en est passée ;* my fancy is over. *Faire* — *un mal ;* to cure an illness. *Il passera un jour par mes mains ;* one day or other he will fall into my hands. *Cela est passé en proverbe ;* that has become a proverb. *Il faut en* — *par là ;* we must submit. *Il ne lui passe rien ;* he forgives him nothing. — *chez ;* to call on. *Je passerai chez vous demain ;* I will call on you to-morrow. *Cela m'a passé de l'esprit ;* that has slipped my memory. *Il a été passé par les armes ;* he was shot.

passer, *v.a.,* to pass, to cross, to go over; to slip, to exceed, to surpass; to utter (base coin—*de la fausse monnaie*); to strain (liquids —*des liquides*); to run (tape, &c.—*un ruban, un cordon,* &c.); to put on (wearing apparel—*les vêtements*); to dress (skins, stuffs—*les peaux, les étoffes*); to omit, to leave out; to allow, to grant, to pardon. — *la rivière ;* to pass over the river. — *la rivière à la nage ;* to swim over the river. *Passez votre chemin ;* go your way. — *son habit ;* to put on one's coat. *Je n'y entends rien, cela me passe ;* I do not understand anything about it, it is beyond my comprehension. — *son temps à se divertir ;* to spend one's time in amusement. — *son envie d'une chose ;* to gratify one's desire for a thing. — *sous silence ;* to take no notice of. *Passez cet endroit ;* pass over that place. *Passez-moi cet article ;* pass me that article. — *condamnation sur soi-même ;* to pass sentence on one's self. — *une obligation ;* to enter into a bond. — *un soldat par les baguettes ;* to make a soldier run the gauntlet. — *tout le monde au fil de l'épée ;* to put everybody to the sword. *Voulez-vous me* — *cela !* will you hand, pass, me that?

se **passer,** *v.r.,* to pass, to pass away; to fade; to decay, to fall off : to happen; to be satisfied;

13*

to forbear, to do without, to make shift. *L'oc-casion se passe;* the opportunity slips away. *Les fleurs se passent en un jour;* flowers decay in one day. *Je dois l'avertir de tout ce qui se passe;* I ought to inform him of everything that happens. - *Il se passe de peu;* he is satisfied with little. *Il ne saurait se — de vin;* he can-not do without wine.

passerage, *n.f.*, (bot.) pepperwort.
passereau (pâ-srô), *n.m.*, (orni.) sparrow.
passerelle (pâ-srèl), *n.f.*, foot-bridge.
passerine (pâ-sri-n) *n.f.*, (bot.) sparrow-wort.
passerinette (pâ-sri-nèt), *n.f.*, (orni.) red-wing.
passe-rose, *n.f.* (— —s), (bot.) hollyhock.
passe-temps, *n.m.* (—), pastime.
passeur, *n.m.*, ferry-man.
passe-velours, *n.m.* (—), (bot.) coxcomb, flower-gentle.
passe-vin (pâs-vin), *n.m.* (—), wine-strainer.
⊙**passe-volant,** *n.m.* (— —s), interloper, intruder; (milit.) fagot.
passibilité, *n.f.*, passibility.
passible, *adj.*, passible; liable.
passi-f, -ve, *adj.*, passive. *Dette —ve;* debt.
passif, *n.m.*, (gram.) passive; (com.) liabili-ties, debts.
passiflore, *n.f.*, (bot.) granadilla, passion-flower.
passion, *n.f.*, passion; love; fondness. *Commander à ses —s;* to rule one's passions. *Déclarer sa —;* to declare one's love. *Il a la — des médailles;* he has a passion for medals. *De—, avec —;* passionately.
passionné, -e, *adj.*, passionate, impas-sioned, passionately fond. *Amant —;* passionate lover. *Il est — pour la gloire;* his passion is glory.
passionnément, *adv.*, passionately, fondly.
passionner, *v.a.*, to impassion.
se passionner, *v.r.*, to be impassioned, en-amoured. *Vous vous passionnez trop;* you are too ardent.
passivement (-siv-mǎn), *adj.*, passively.
passiveté, *or* **passivité,** *n.f.*, passiveness.
passoire, *n.f.*, colander, strainer.
pastel, *n.m.*, pastel; crayon; (bot.) woad, dyer's woad.
pastenade, *n.f.*, (bot.) parsnip.
pastèque, *n.f.*, water-melon.
pasteur, *n.m.*, pastor, minister; clergy-man; shepherd.
pastiche, *n.m.*, (paint.) pasticcio; imitation (of an author—*d'un auteur*); (mus.) medley.
*pastille,** *n.f.*, lozenge.
pastisson, *n.m.* V. **pâtisson.**
pastoral, -e, *adj.*, pastoral.
pastorale, *n.f.*, pastoral.
pastoralement (-ral-mǎn), *adv.*, pastorally.
pastoureau, *n.m.*, little shepherd boy.
pastourelle, *n.f.*, shepherd girl; (dance—*danse*) pastourelle.
pat (pat), *n.m.*, stalemate (at chess—*aux échecs*).
patache, *n.f.*, (nav.) patache; coach, pub-lic conveyance (not suspended—*non suspendue*).
patagon, *n.m.*, patacoon (Spanish coin—*monnaie espagnole*).
pataquès (-kès), *n.m.*, (fam.) fault which consists in sounding a *t* for an *s*, and an *s* for a *t.*
patarafe, *n.f.*, scrawl.
patard, *n.m.*, an obsolete French coin worth a farthing.
patarin, *n.m.* V. **albigeois** and **vaudois.**
patate, *n.f.*, (bot.) batatas, sweet potato.
patatras! *int.*, crack! thump! slap! bang!

pataud, *n.m.*, pup with large paws. *Être à nage— —;* to swim (of dogs after being thrown into the river—*d'un chien jeté à l'eau*); (pers.) to struggle to get out of the water; to be in clover.
pataud, -e, *adj.*, (pers.) ill made.
patauger, *v.n.*, to splash, to walk in the mire; to become entangled, embarrassed.
patchouli, *n.m.*, patchouli.
pate, *n.f.* V. **patte.**
pâte, *n.f.*, paste, dough; constitution, temper; kind, sort; (print.) pie. — *brisée;* short paste. — *feuilletée;* puff paste. — *cro-quante;* crisp paste. *Mettre la main à la —;* to do a thing one's self. *C'est une bonne — d'homme;* he is a good-natured fellow. *Une bonne — de femme;* a good-natured woman.
pâté, *n.m.*, pie, pasty; blot (of ink —*d'encre*); block (of buildings—*de bâtiments*), (print.) pie. *Un — de venaison;* a venison pasty. *Faire le —;* to pack the cards (at play—*au jeu*). *Un gros —;* a plump chub-faced child. *Faire un —;* to make a blot.
pâtée, *n.f.*, paste (to fatten poultry—*pour la volaille*); mess (for dogs or cats—*pour les chiens et les chats*).
patelin (pa-tlin), *n.m.*, (fam.) wheedler.
patelin, -e, *adj.*, (fam.) wheedling. *Air —;* wheedling look.
patelinage (pa-tli-), *n.m.*, (fam.) wheedling.
pateliner (pa-tli-), *v.n.*, (fam.) to wheedle.
pateliner, *v.a.*, (fam.) to manage adroitly.
patelineu-r, *n.m.*, **-se,** *n.f.*, (fam.) wheedler.
patelle, *n.f.*, (conch.) limpet.
patemment (-ta-), *adv.*, evidently, obvious-ly, publicly.
patène, *n.f.*, (c.rel.) paten, patin.
patenôtre (pa-tnôtr), *n.f.*, paternoster; Lord's prayer; *pl.*, (pop.) beads of a rosary.
⊙**patenôtrier,** *n.m.*, bead-maker.
patent, -e, *adj.*, patent; obvious, manifest. *Lettres —es;* letters patent.
patentable, *adj.*, that can be taxed as carrying on a trade.
patente, *n.f.*, license (for the exercise of a trade—*pour exercer un commerce*); (nav.) bill of health.
patenté, -e, *n.* and *adj.*, licensed dealer; licensed.
patenter, *v.a.*, to license.
pater (pa-tèr), *n.m.* (—), Lord's prayer, paternoster; great bead (of a chaplet—*d'un chapelet*).
patère, *n.f.*, window-screw; (arch., antiq.) patera.
⊙**paterne,** *adj.*, (jest.) fatherly.
paternel, -le, *adj.*, paternal, fatherly. *Parents —s;* relations on the father's side. *Bénédiction —le;* father's blessing. *Amour —;* fatherly love.
paternellement (-nèl-mǎn), *adv.*, pater-nally, fatherly.
paternité, *n.f.*, paternity, fathership.
pâteu-x, -se, *adj.*, doughy, clammy; milky (of gems—*des pierreries*); muddy (of roads—*des routes*). *Chemin —;* muddy road.
pathétique, *adj.*, pathetic, affecting, mov-ing, touching.
pathétique, *n.m.*, pathos; patheticalness.
pathétiquement (-tik-mǎn), *adv.*, patheti-cally.
pathognomonique, *adj.*, pathognomonic.
pathologie, *n.f.*, pathology.
pathologique, *adj.*, pathologic.
pathologiste, *n.m.*, pathologist.
pathos (pa-tôs), *n.m.*, (b.s.) pathos, fustian, rant.
patibulaire, *adj.*, patibulary.

/patiemment (pa-sia-màn), *adv.*, patiently, with patience.

| patience, *n.f.*, patience, endurance, forbearance; puzzle (game—*jouet*). *Un jeu de —;* a puzzle. *Avoir de la —;* to have patience. *Être à bout de —;* to be out of patience, to lose patience. *Prendre son mal en —;* to bear one's misfortune patiently. *Perdre —;* to lose patience. *Perdre toute —;* to lose all patience. *Prendre —;* to take patience.

patience, *n.f.*, (bot.) patience, dock.

patient, -e, *adj.*, patient, enduring, forbearing.

patient, *n.m.*, sufferer; patient; culprit (about to be executed—*qui va être exécuté*).

patienter, *v.n.*, to take patience.

patin, *n.m.*, skate; sill (of a stair-case—*d'escalier*).

patine, *n.f.*, patina (fine rust on medals—*vert-de-gris des médailles antiques, &c.*).

patiner, *v.n.*, to skate.

patiner, *v.a.*, to handle, to fumble, to paw; (l.ex.) to touch indiscreetly.

patineur, *n.m.*, **-se**, *n.f.*, skater.

patineur, *n.m.*, (l.ex.) one who is fond of touching.

pâtir, *v.n.*, to suffer; to drudge. *Vous en pâtirez;* you'll suffer for it.

pâtis, *n.m.*, pasture-ground.

pâtisser, *v.n.*, to make pastry.

pâtisserie, *n.f.*, pastry; pastry-business.

pâtissi-er, *n.m.*, **-ère**, *n.f.*, pastry-cook.

pâtissoire, *n.f.*, pastry-board, pastry-table.

pâtisson, *n.m.*, (bot.) squash-melon.

patois, *n.m.*, patois, dialect peculiar to certain French provinces.

pâton, *n.m.*, bolus (for fattening poultry—*pour engraisser la volaille*).

patraque, *n.f.*, rubbish, trumpery thing; bad watch; person of a broken-down constitution; gimcrack.

pâtre, *n.m.*, herdsman, shepherd.

ad patres (pa-très), *adv.*, (triv.) to kingdom come. *Envoyer quelqu'un —;* to knock any one on the head, to kill.

patriarcal, -e, *adj.*, patriarchal.

patriarcat, *n.m.*, patriarehate, patriarchship.

patriarche, *n.m.*, patriarch.

patrice, *n.m.*, patrician.

patriciat, *n.m.*, dignity of a patrician; order of patricians; patriciate.

patricien, -ne (-in, -è-n), *n.* and *adj.*, patrician.

patrie, *n.f.*, native country, native land, home.

patrimoine, *n.m.*, patrimony, inheritance.

patrimonial, -e, *adj.*, patrimonial.

patriote, *n.m.f.* and *adj.*, patriot; patriotic.

patriotique, *adj.*, patriotic.

patriotiquement (-tik-màn), *adv.*, like a patriot, patriotically.

patriotisme, *n.m.*, patriotism.

Ⓒ**patrociner**, *v.n.*, (jest.) to argue.

patron, *n.m.*, patron; patron saint; master (of a house—*maître d'une maison*); (fam.) governor; principal; (nav.) cockswain; master (of slaves—*d'esclaves*); (canon law—*loi canon*) advowee; pattern, model; (tech.) templet. *— d'un vaisseau marchand;* master of a merchantman. *— de chaloupe;* cockswain of a long-boat. *Je veux parler au —;* I want to speak to your master, to the governor. *Faire un —;* to take a pattern.

patronage, *n.m.*, patronage; advowson.

patronal, -e, *adj.*, patronal.

patronat, *n.m.*, (Rom. hist.) protection, patronizing.

Ⓒ**patroniser**, *v.a.*, to patronize.

Ⓒ**dès le patron-jaquet, dès le patron-minet**, *adv.*, very early, at daybreak.

patronne, *n.f.*, patroness; female guardian saint.

patronner, *v.n.*, to take the pattern of; to stencil.

patronner, *v.a.*, to patronize.

patronnesse, *adj.f.*, patronizing, supporting. *Dame —;* lady who gives her patronage.

patronymique, *adj.*, patronymic.

***patrouillage**, *n.m.*, (l.u.) mess made by paddling; puddle.

***patrouille**, *n.f.*, patrol. *Faire la —;* to patrol.

***patrouiller**, *v.n.*, (pop.) to paddle, to puddle, paw about; (milit.) to patrol.

***patrouiller**, *v.a.*, (pop.) to handle things in a dirty manner; to spoil things by handling them in a clumsy, dirty manner.

***patrouillis**, *n.m.*, mess made by paddling, puddle.

patte, *n.f.*, paw (of animals—*d'animal*); flap (of pockets—*de poche*); foot (of birds, of glasses—*d'oiseau, de verre*); leg (of an insect—*d'insecte*). *— de chien;* dog's paw. *— d'oie;* foot of a goose. *Des —s d'araignée;* spider's legs. *—s d'écrevisse;* claws of a crawfish. *Marcher à quatre —s;* to go on all fours. *Passer sous la — de quelqu'un;* to fall into any one's clutches. *Mettre la — sur quelqu'un;* to lay one's claws upon any one. *Donner un coup de — à quelqu'un;* to pass a severe remark on any one, in his presence *or* in his absence. *Graisser la — à quelqu'un;* to give any one a sop, to fee any one. *—s de mouches;* scrawl.

patte-d'oie, *n.f.* (*—s —*), (bot.) goose-foot; intersection of several roads; crow's foot (wrinkle round the eye).

Ⓒ**patte-pelu**, *n.m.* (*——s*), **patte-pelue**, *n.f.* (*——s*), wolf in sheep's clothing; crafty hypocrite.

pattu, -e, *adj.*, rough-footed.

pâturage, *n.m.*, pasture, pasture-ground grazing.

pâture, *n.f.*, food, pasturage.

pâturer, *v.n.*, to pasture.

pâtureur, *n.m.*, (milit.) pastor.

paturin, *n.m.*, (bot.) meadow-grass. *— comprimé;* wire-grass.

patvron, *n.m.*, pastern.

paucité, *n.f.*, (l.u.) paucity.

paulette, *n.f.*, tax formerly paid for permission to dispose of one's office.

paulo-post-futur, *n.m.*, (gram.) paulo-post-future.

paulownia, *n.m.*, (bot.) paulownia.

paume, *n.f.*, palm (of one's hand—*de la main*); tennis (game—*jeu*).

paumelle, *n.f.*, sort of barley; hand-leather.

paumer, *v.a.*, (pop.) to give a punch. *— la gueule à quelqu'un* (triv.); to give any one a punch in the face.

paumier, *n.m.*, keeper of a tennis-court.

paumoyer, *v.a.*, (nav.) to underrun (cables).

paumure, *n.f.*, upper part of the head (of a stag—*du cerf*).

paupérisme, *n.m.*, pauperism.

paupière, *n.f.*, eyelid; eyelash; (fig.) eye, eyes. *Fermer la —;* to shut one's eyes; to sleep; to die.

pause, *n.f.*, pause, stop, rest.

pauser, *v.a.*, (mus.) to pause, to make a pause.

pauvre, *adj.*, poor, needy, wretched; paltry, sorry. *Une langue —;* a poor language. *Un* *sujet* —; a barren subject. *Le* — *homme!* poor silly fellow! *Un homme* — : a poor man. *C'est un* — *poète;* he is a wretched poet. *Un* — *hère, un* — *diable;* a poor devil.

pauvre, *n.m.*, poor person, pauper. —*s houteux;* poor people who are ashamed to beg.

pauvrement, *adv.*, poorly, beggarly.

pauvresse, *n.f.*, poor woman, beggar-woman, beggar-girl.

pauvret, *n.m.*, **-te**, *n.f.*, poor creature, poor thing.

pauvreté, *n.f.*, poverty, indigence, need; sorry thing. — *n'est pas vice;* poverty is no crime.

pavage, *n.m.*, pavement, paving.

pavane, *n.f.*, pavan (dance—*danse*).

se **pavaner**, *v.r.*, to strut, to strut along.

pavé, *n.m.*, paving-stone; pavement; paved road. *Être sur le* — ; to be without employment, without a home. *Battre le* — ; to idle about town. *Tâter le* — ; not to walk firmly. *Le haut du* — ; the wall side. *Tenir le haut du* —; to hold the first rank. *Brûler le* — ; to drive like the wind. *Être sur le* — *du roi;* to be on the king's highway.

pavement (pav-mān), *n.m.*, paving; pavement.

paver, *v.a.*, to pave.

pavesade, *n.f.*, (nav.) pavisade.

paveur, *n.m.*, pavier, paver, pavior.

pavie, *n.m.*, cling-stone.

*****pavillon**, *n.m.*, pavilion, summer-house; flag, standard; (c.rel.) veil of the tabernacle; bell (of a trumpet—*de trompette*). *Amener son* —; to strike her flag (of a ship—*d'un vaisseau*). — *blanc;* flag of truce. — *de poupe;* ensign. *Hisser le* —; to hoist the flag. *Baisser* —; to yield.

pavois, *n.m.*, shield; (nav.) armour.

pavoisement, *n.m.*, (nav.) dressing with colours, flags.

pavoiser, *v.a.*, (nav.) to adorn with flags.

pavot, *n.m.*, (bot.) poppy.

payable, *adj.*, payable.

payant, **-e**, *adj.*, paying. *Carte* —*e;* bill (at an eating-house—*au restaurant*).

payant, *n.m.*, **-e**, *n.f.*, payer, person that pays.

paye (pè-ye), *n.f.*, pay, salary; wages; (fam.) paymaster. *Une bonne* —; a good paymaster. *Morte-* — (—*s* —*s*); old servant kept and p. id without doing any work; tax-payer who cannot pay his taxes; ⊙soldier kept in a garrison in time of peace and of war. *Haute* — (milit.); extra pay for good conduct stripes.

payement (pè-mān), *n.m.*, payment. *Jour de* —; pay-day. *Non-* — (—*s*); non-payment.

payen, -ne, *adj.* *V.* **païen**.

payer, *v.a* , to pay, to pay for, to pay off, to pay away, to recompense, to reward. — *trop;* to overpay. — *argent comptant;* to pay down. *Se faire* —; to get paid, to get one's money. *Qui répond paye;* the bail must pay. — *quelqu'un d'ingratitude;* to be ungrateful to any one. — *de belles paroles;* to pay with fine speeches. — *le tribut à la nature;* to pay the debt of nature. — *en même monnaie;* to pay in like coin. — *les violons;* to pay the piper. — *d'effronterie;* to brazen it out. — *d'audace;* to face it out. *Il me la payera;* he shall pay for it; I'll be revenged on him for it. *Vous en payerez la folle enchère;* you shall pay dear for your rashness.

se **payer**, *v.r.*, to be satisfied; to be bought. — *de raisons;* to be satisfied with reasons. *Cela ne peut pas* —; that cannot be bought, that cannot be had for money.

payeu-r, *n.m.*, **-se**, *n.f.*, paymaster; payer.

pays (pè-yee), *n.m.*..country, fatherland, birthplace, native place, home ; (pop.) fellow-countryman. *Gagner* —: to get up. *Courir le* — : to be upon the ramble. *Battre du* — : to wander about. *Être en* — *de connaissance:* to be among acquaintances. *Savoir la carte du* —; to know one's ground, one's people. — *perdu:* out of the way place. — *natal;* native country. *De quel* — *êtes-vous?* what countryman are you? *Avoir le mal du* — ; to be homesick. *Nul n'est prophète en son* —; no man is a prophet in his own country. *Il est bien de son* —; he is very simple, very credulous. *A vue de* —; at first sight.

paysage (pè-i-zaj), *n.m.*, landscape; landscape-painting.

paysagiste (pè-i-za-jist), *n.m.*, landscape-painter.

paysan (pè-i-zan), *n.m.*, **-ne** (-za-n), *n.f.*, countryman; countrywoman; peasant.

paysannerie (pè-i-za-n-ri), *n.f.*, manners of the peasantry.

payse, *n.f.*, (pop.) fellow countrywoman.

péage. *n.m.*, toll; toll-house.

péager; *n.m.*, toll-gatherer.

peau, *n.f.*, skin, hide, peel; (fig , fam.) person. — *d'oignons;* onion-peel. — *de fruit*. skin of fruit. *Ôter la* —: to peel. *Contes de* — *d'âne;* nursery tales. *Être dans la* — *de quelqu'un;* to be in any one's shoes.

peausserie (pô-sri), *n.f.*, peltry; skinner's trade.

peaussier (pô-sié), *n.m.*, skinner.

peaussier, *adj.*, (anat.) cutaneous (muscle).

⊙**peautre**, *n.m.*, place of ill repute. [Only used in the popular expression : *Envoyer au* —; to send to the devil.]

pébrine, *n.f.*, a kind of epidemic among silk-worms.

pec, *adj.*, recently salted (of herrings—*harengs*).

pécari, *n.m.*, peccary, South American wild boar.

peccable (pèk-kabl), *adj.*, peccable.

*****peccadille**, *n.f*, peccadillo.

⊙**peccant, -e** (pèk-kān, -t), *adj.*, (med.) morbid, not healthy, peccant.

peccata, *n.m.*, (—), (pop.) an ass; fool, dolt, blockhead.

peccavi (pèk-ka-vi), *n.m.* (—), peccavi.

pêche, *n.f.*, (bot.) peach. — *hâtive;* early peach. — *tardive;* late peach.

pêche, *n.f.*, fishing, angling. *La* — *à la ligne;* angling. *Aller à la* —; to go a fishing.

péché, *n.m.*, sin, trespass. — *originel;* original sin. — *mignon;* besetting sin. — *grave;* heinous sin. — *irrémissible;* unpardonable sin. *Racheter ses* —*s;* to redeem one's sins. *A tout* — *miséricorde;* we should not require the death of a sinner. *Rechercher les vieux* —*s de quelqu'un;* to examine into the past life of any one.

pécher, *v.n.*, to sin, to transgress, to trespass ; to offend. — *contre la bienséance;* to offend against decency. *Ce n'est pas par là qu'il pèche;* that is not his failing.

pêcher, *v.a.* and *n.*, to fish; to angle; to fish for. — *à la ligne;* to angle for, to fish for, with a rod and line. — *un étang;* to draw a pond. — *en eau trouble;* to fish in troubled waters. — *au plat;* to take what one likes out of the dish. *Où avez-vous pêché cela ?* where did you pick that up?

pêcher, *n.m.*, peach-tree.

pécheresse (pé-shrès), *n.f.* *V.* **pécheur**.

pêcherie (pê-shri), *n.f.*, fishing-place; fishery.

pêche-ur. *n.m.*, **-rasse**. *n.f.*, sinner.

pêcheu-r, *n.m.*, **-se**, *n.f.*, fisher, angler, fisherman, fisherwoman. — *à la ligne;* angler. *Ligne de* —; fishing-line.

pêcheur, *adj.*, fishing.

pécore, *n.f.*, stupid creature, blockhead.

pecque, *n.f.*, conceited woman (abusive expression—*terme injurieux*).

pectiné, **-e**, *adj.*, pectinal, like the teeth of a comb.

pectoral, **-e**, *adj.*, pectoral.

pectoral, *n.m.*, breast-plate (of the high-priest of the Jews—*du grand prêtre des Juifs*); (med.) pectoral.

péculat, *n.m.*, peculation. *Être coupable de* —: to peculate.

péculateur, *n.m.*, (l.u.) peculator.

pécule, *n.m.*, stock of money saved up by one in the power of another, by a slave, for instance.

pécune, *n.f.*, ready money, cash.

pécuniaire, *adj.*, pecuniary.

pécunieu-x, **-se**, *adj.*, monied, that has money.

pédagogie, *n.f.*, pedagogy.

pédagogique, *adj.*, pedagogical.

pédagogue, *n.m.*, pedagogue.

pédale, *n.f.*, pedal; treadle; foot-board.

pédané, *adj.*, formerly said of judges who tried cases standing up.

pédant, **-e**, *n.* and *adj.*, pedant; pedantic.

pédantiser, *v.n.* V. **pédantiser**.

pédanterie (pé-dan-tri), *n.f.*, pedantry.

pédantesque, *adj.*, pedantic.

pédantesquement, *adv.*, pedantically.

pédantiser, *v.n.*, to play the pedant, to assume a pedantic air, way, or bearing.

pédantisme, *n.m.*, pedantry.

pédéraste, *n.m.*, pederast.

pédérastie, *n.f.*, pederasty.

pédestre, *adj.*, pedestrian.

pédestrement, *adv.*, on foot. *Aller* —; to go on foot.

pédicelle, *n.m.*, (bot.) pedicle, pedicel.

pédiculaire, *adj.*, pedicular.

pédiculaire, *n.f.*, (bot.) pedicularis, louse-wort.

pédicule, *n.m.*, (bot.) peduncle; (med.) neck.

pédiculé, **-e**, *adj.*, pedicellate.

pédicure, *n.m.* and *adj.*, corn-cutter; corn-cutting.

pédiluve, *n.m.*, (med.) pediluvium, foot-bath.

pédimane, *n.m.* and *adj.*, (mam.) pedimane; pedimanous.

pédomètre, *n.m.*, pedometer.

pédon, *n.m.*, courier on foot, runner.

pédonculaire, *adj.*, (bot.) peduncular.

pédoncule, *n.m.*, (bot.) peduncle, flower-stalk.

pédonculé, **-e**, *adj.*, (bot.) pedunculate.

pégase, *n.m.*, Pegasus.

pehlvi, *n.m.* and *adj.*, Huzvâresh or Pehlevi.

*peignage, *n.m.*, combing, wool-combing.

*peigne, *n.m.*, comb; (paint.) graining-tool. — *fin;* small-toothed comb. — *à démêler;* wide-toothed comb.

*peigné, **-e**, *part.*, combed. *Un jardin bien* —; a well-kept garden. *Un mal* — or *un malpeigné:* a dirty, ill-dressed, fellow.

*peigner, *v.a.*, to comb; (pop.) to beat, to drub.

se **peigner**, *v.r.*, to comb one's self; (pop.) to beat each other.

*peigneur, *n.m.*, **-se**, *n.f.*, (manu.) comber.

*peignier, *n.m.*, comb-maker.

*peignoir, *n.m.*, dressing-gown; bathing-gown.

*peignures, *n.f.pl.*, hair combed out.

peindre (peignant, peint), *v.a.*, to paint, to portray; to describe, to depict. — *d'après nature;* to paint from nature. — *à l'huile;* to

paint in oil. — *l'histoire;* to paint historical subjects. — *le portrait;* to take likenesses. *Se faire* —; to sit for one's portrait. *Fait à* —; very handsome. *Il nous a peint sa détresse;* he drew us a picture of his distress.

se **peindre**, *v.r..* to paint one's self; to be represented. *La douleur se peignait sur son visage;* his face was the picture of grief.

peine, *n.f.*, punishment, penalty, pain; affliction, misery; uneasiness, trouble, anxiety, labour; pains; reluctance. *Proportionner la* — *au délit;* to proportion the penalty to the offence. *Sous les* —*s de droit;* on pain of being punished according to law. *Partager les* —*s de quelqu'un;* to share any one's troubles. *Il n'y a que des* —*s dans la vie;* the world is full of affliction. *Cela fait* — *à voir;* it hurts one to see that. *À chaque jour suffit sa* —; sufficient for the day is the evil thereof. *Je suis en* — *de savoir ce qu'il deviendra;* I am at a loss to know what will become of him. *Faire de la* — *à quelqu'un;* to pain any one. *Être dans la* —; to be in trouble. *Se mettre en* — *de;* to trouble one's self about. *Je voudrais vous épargner cette* —; I would willingly spare you that trouble. *Cela n'en vaut pas la* —: it is not worth while. *Il a de la* — *à parler;* he is scarcely able to speak. *Il a de la* — *à marcher;* he can hardly walk. *Il a eu beaucoup de* — *à en venir à bout;* he had much ado to bring it about. *J'ai* — *à le croire;* I can hardly believe it. *Un homme de* —; a labourer. *Ce n'est pas la* — ; it is not worth while. *À* —; hardly, scarce, scarcely. *À* — *sait-il lire;* he can hardly read. *À grand'* —; with great trouble, with much difficulty.

peiné, **-e**, *part.*, pained, grieved; laboured, elaborate. *Un ouvrage* —; a laboured piece of work.

peiner, *v.a.*, to pain, to make uneasy, to put to trouble; to fatigue.

se **peiner**, *v.r.*, to take pains.

peiner, *v.n.*, to labour, to toil; to be reluctant.

peint, **-e**, *part.*, painted, drawn. *Toiles* —*es;* printed calicoes.

peintre, *n.m..* painter. — *de paysage;* landscape-painter. *Un* — *en bâtiments;* a house-painter.

peinturage, *n.m.*, painting (on wood, on a wall, &c.—*sur bois, sur un mur, &c.*); daub.

peinture, *n.f.*, painting; paint; picture, portraiture; painters' work; colours. — *à l'huile;* oil-painting. — *en détrempe;* distemper-painting. — *en mosaïque;* mosaic-painting. *En* —; in painting, in appearance.

peinturer, *v.a.*, (l.u.) to paint (with one colour only—*d'une seule couleur*).

peintureur, *n.m.*, bad painter, dauber. V. **barbouilleur**.

pékin, *n.m.*, pekin (textile fabric—*tissu de soie*).

pelade, *n.f.*, alopecy, alopecia, scurf.

pelage, *n.m.*, colour of the hair (of animals—*des animaux*).

pélagianisme, *n.m.*, pelagianism, Pelagius' tenets.

pélagien, **-ne** (-in, -è-n), *adj.*, pelagian.

pélagique, *adj.*, pelagic, pelagian, pertaining to the sea.

pélamide, *n.f.*, (ich.) pelamis.

pélard (pe-lar), *adj.*, barked (of wood—*bois*).

pélasgique, *adj.*, pertaining to the Pelasgians.

pelé, **-e**, *adj.*, bald-pated man; ragamuffin. *Il n'y avait que quatre* —*s et un tondu;* there was nothing but rag, tag, and bobtail.

pêle, *n.m.* V. **pêne**.

pêle-mêle, *adv.*, pell-mell, confusedly, helter skelter.

pêle-mêle, *n.m.*, pell-mell.

peler, *v.a.*, to strip of the hair, to make bald; to pare, to peel, to scald (pigs—*cochons*). — *un cochon de lait*; to scald a sucking pig. — *un arbre*; to peel a tree. — *des amandes*; to peel almonds.

se peler, *v.r.*, to come off (of the hair—*du poil*); to peel off.

peler, *v.n.*, to peel off (of the skin—*de la peau*).

pèlerin (pèl-rin), *n.m.*, **-e** (-ri-n), *n.f.*, pilgrim, traveller; hypocrite, dissembler.

pèlerin, *n.m.*, (orni.) peregrine falcon.

pèlerinage (pel-ri-), *n.m.*, pilgrimage. *Aller en* —; to go on a pilgrimage.

pèlerine (pèl-ri-n), *n.f.*, tippet.

pélican, *n.m.*, pelican.

pelin, *n.m.*, lime-pit (for hides—*pour les peaux*).

pelisse, *n.f.*, pelisse.

pellagre, *n.f.*, (med.) pellagra.

pelle, *n.f.*, shovel. *La — se moque du fourgon*; the pot calls the kettle black. *Ôter avec la* —; to shovel out.

pellée, pellerée, pelletée (pèl-rée, pèl-tée), *n.f.*, shovelful.

pelleron (pèl-ron), *n.m.*, baker's shovel.

pelleterie (pèl-tri), *n.f.*, furriery; peltry.

pelleti-er, *n.m.*, **-ère**, *n.f.*, furrier.

pellicule (pèl-li-kul), *n.f.*, pellicle.

pellucide (pel-lu-), *adj.*, (phys.) pellucid.

pelotage, *n.m.*, making skeins into balls; goat-skins from the East done up in balls; (at billiards and tennis—*au billard et à la paume*) playing without observing the rules of the game.

pelote (plot), *n.f.*, pin-cushion; clew of thread; pellet; blaze (on a horse's forehead—*sur le front d'un cheval*). — *de neige*; snow-ball. *Faire sa* —; to save up a sum of money.

peloter (plo-té), *v.a.*, to make up into a ball; to bang, to cuff, to beat.

se peloter, *v.r.*, to roll round; to bang each other; to dispute.

peloter, *v.n.*, (at tennis—*à la paume*) to knock the ball about without playing regularly.

peloton (plo-ton), *n.m.*, ball (made of things wound round—*de fil, de soie, de laine, &c.*); lump (of fat—*de graisse*); (milit.) company; tennis-ball; group, knot (of people—*de gens*). *Ils entraient par* —s; they entered by groups. *Se mettre en* — ; to roll one's self up like a ball. *Feu de* — ; fire by company.

pelotonner (plo-to-né), *v.a.*, to wind into balls.

se pelotonner, *v.r.*, to gather into knots, into groups; to gather into a round mass; to roll one's self up.

pelouse (plooz), *n.f.*, lawn, green sward; grassplot.

peltaste, *n.m.*, (antiq.) targeteer.

pelte, *n.f.*, (antiq.) target, small buckler.

pelté, -e, *adj.*, (bot.) peltated.

pelu, -e, *adj.*, hairy. [Only used in **patte-pelu**, which see.]

peluche (plush), *n.f.*, shag, plush, cotton and woollen drugget.

peluché, -e, *adj.*, shaggy.

pelucher (plu-shé), *v.n.*, to become shaggy.

pelure (plur), *n.f.*, paring, peel.

pelvien, -ne (-in, -è-n), *adj.*, (anat.) pelvic.

pemphigus, *n.m.*, (med.) pemphigus.

*****penaille**, *n.f.*, rags; (b.s.) monks.

*****penaillerie**, *n.f.*, rags; set of ragamuffins; (b.s.) monks.

*****penaillon**, *n.m.*, rag.

pénal, -e, *adj.*, penal.

pénalité, *n.f.*, penal system.

penard, *n.m.*, old fox (pers.), old libertine.

pénates, *n.m.pl.*, (antiq.) penates, household gods.

penaud, -e, *n.* and *adj.*, person abashed, sheepish person; abashed, sheepish.

penchant, *n.m.*, slope, declivity; inclination, propensity, bent, penchant. *Le — d'une montagne*; the slope of a mountain. *Suivre son* —; to follow one's bent. *Se laisser aller à son* — ; to indulge one's propensity.

penchant, -e, *adj.*, shelving, sloping, declining.

penchement (pansh-mān), *n.m.*, stoop, stooping.

pencher, *v.a.*, to incline, to lean, to bend, to stoop. — *la tête*; to stoop the head. — *un vase*; to incline a vase.

se pencher, *v.r.*, to bend, to bend over, to stoop. — *sur le bord d'un précipice*; to bend over the brink of a precipice.

pencher, *v.n.*, to lean; to slope, to incline, to be disposed. *Il penche vers le nord*; it leans to the north. — *vers la clémence*; to lean to mercy. — *vers, du côté de*; to incline towards, to lean on the side of.

pendable, *adj.*, hanging, that deserves hanging, abominable. *Cas* —; hanging matter. *Un tour* —; an abominable trick.

pendaison, *n.f.*, hanging on the gallows.

pendant, *prep.*, during.

pendant que, *conj.*, whilst, while.

pendant, *n.m.*, thing pendent, thing hanging; counterpart, pendant, fellow; frog (of a sword-belt—*de baudrier, de ceinturon*). — *d'oreille*; ear-ring. *Il faut un — à ce tableau*; this picture requires its fellow. *C'est son* —; he is his counterpart.

pendant, -e, *adj.*, pendent, hanging, pending, depending; standing (of crops—*blés, fruits, &c.*). *Oreilles —es*; hanging ears. *Marcher les bras —s*; to walk with one's arms dangling. *Le procès est* —; the cause is pending.

pendard, *n.m.*, **-e**, *n.f.*, rascal, rogue, scoundrel; jade.

pendeloque (pan-dlok), *n.f.*, ear-drop; pendant, drop.

pendentif, *n.m.*, (arch.) pendentive.

penderie (pen-dri), *n.f.*, ☉hanging (putting to death—*supplice*); (tech.) drying-house.

pendeur, *n.m.*, hangman, executioner; (nav.) pennant (rope—*cordage*), span.

*****pendiller**, *v.n.*, to hang, to dangle.

pendre, *v.a.*, to hang, to hang up, to suspend. — *de la viande au croc*; to hang up meat on a hook. — *des voleurs*; to hang robbers. *Il ne vaut pas la corde pour le* — ; he is not worth hanging. *Il dit pis que — de vous*, he says everything that is bad of you.

se pendre, *v.r.*, to hang one's self.

pendre, *v.n.*, to hang, to hang up, to hang down, to be suspended. *Les joues lui pendent*; his cheeks are flabby. *Autant lui en pend à l'oreille*; the same may happen to himself, he had better look to himself.

pendu, *n.m.*, one that has been hanged. *Il est sec comme un* — ; he is as thin as a lath. *Avoir de la corde de — dans sa poche*; to have the devil's own luck.

pendu, -e, *part.*, hanged, hung. *Aussitôt pris, aussitôt* — ; no sooner said than done. *Il est toujours — à ses côtés*; he is always dangling after him. *Avoir la langue bien —e*; to have a well-oiled tongue.

pendule, *n.f.*, (horl.) time-piece, chimney clock, ornamental clock. — *détraquée*; clock out of order. *Remonter une* — ; to wind up a clock.

pendule, *n.m.*, pendulum.

penduliste, *n.m.*, case-maker for time-pieces.

pêne, *n.m.*, bolt (of a lock—*de serrure*).
pénétrabilité, *n.f.*, penetrability.
pénétrable, *adj.*, penetrable.
pénétrant, -e, *adj.*, penetrating, piercing, keen, impressive. *Il fait un froid —;* it is piercing cold. *Avoir l'œil —;* to have a penetrating eye.
pénétrati-f. -ve, *adj.*, (l.u.) penetrating.
pénétration, *n.f.*, penetration, acuteness. *Avoir une grande — d'esprit;* to have great acuteness of mind.
pénétré, -e, *part.*, penetrated. *— de douleur;* grieved to the heart. *Avoir l'air —;* to seem deeply concerned.
pénétrer, *v.a.*, to penetrate, to enter, to pierce; to pervade ; to fathom; to impress ; to imbue. *La pluie a pénétré mon habit;* the rain has penetrated my coat. *— quelqu'un;* to see through any one. *Son état m'a pénétré;* his situation deeply moved me.
se pénétrer, *v.r.*, to penetrate each other; to impress one's self ; to impress one's mind.
pénétrer, *v.n.*, to penetrate; to pervade; to pierce, to get in. *Il pénétra bien avant dans le pays;* he went a great way into the country.
pénible, *adj.*, painful, laborious; troublesome.
péniblement, *adv.*, painfully, laboriously.
péniche, *n.f.*, (nav.) pinnace.
pénicillé, -e, *adj.*, (anat.) pencil-shaped.
pénil, *n.m.*, (anat.) mons veneris.
péninsulaire, *adj.*, peninsular.
péninsule, *n.f.*, peninsula.
pénitence, *n.f.*, penitence, penance, punishment. *La — est une vertu chrétienne;* penitence is a Christian virtue. *Faire — de ses péchés;* to do penance for one's sins. *Faire —;* to fare poorly. *Mettre un enfant en —;* to punish a child.
pénitencerie (-tän-srî), *n.f.*, penitentiary's court ; penitentiary (office at the court of Rome —*office à la cour de Rome*).
pénitencier, *n.m.*, reformatory; penitentiary, priest vested with the power of absolving in cases reserved to the bishop.
pénitent, -e, *n.* and *adj.*, penitent, repentant. *Pécheur —;* contrite sinner.
pénitentiaire (-ci-èr), *adj.*, penitentiary. *Maison —;* penitentiary.
pénitenti-aux(-ci-ô),**-elles**(-ci-èl),*adj.pl.*, penitential.
pénitentiel (-ci-èl), *n.m.*, penitential.
pennage, *n.m.*, (hawking—*fauconnerie*) plumage.
penne (pè-n), *n.f.*, beam-feather (of a hawk —*du faucon*) ; feather; (orni.) feather of the tail or wing; (nav.) peak of a mizzen or lateen sail.
penné. *adj.*, (bot.) pennate, pennated.
penniforme, *adj.*, penniform.
pennon (pè-n-non), *n.m.*, pennon.
pénombre, *n.f.*, penumbra.
penon, *n.m.*, (nav.) dog-vane.
pensant, -e, *adj.*, thinking. *Bien —;* right-thinking, well-disposed, right-minded. *Mal —;* evil-thinking, evil-disposed.
pensée, *n.f.*, thought, idea, conception ; mind, belief, opinion; design; meaning; sketch, first draught ; (bot.) pansy, heart's-ease. *La dame de ses —s;* one's lady-love. *— ultérieure;* after-thought. *S'accoutumer à la — de la mort;* to habituate one's self to the idea of death. *Parler contre sa —;* to speak against one's conviction, opinion. *Concevoir de vastes —s;* to conceive vast projects. *Entrer dans la — de quelqu'un;* to conceive and approve of any one's meaning. *Lire dans la — de quelqu'un;* to read any one's thoughts. *Cela m'est venu dans la —;* that came into my mind. *S'entretenir avec ses —s;* to hold converse with one's thoughts.
penser, *v.n.*, to think, to reflect, to meditate, to deem, to be of opinion ; to hope ; to be on the point, to be near, to have like ; to take heed, to take care. *L'homme pense;* man thinks. *— à quelque chose;* to think of any thing. *Il est venu sans qu'on y pensât;* he came unexpectedly. *C'est un homme qui pense bien;* he is a man who has sound notions. *Il l'a fait sans y —;* he did it unwittingly. *À quoi pensez-vous, de faire cela?* what do you mean by doing that? *— à mal;* to have some ill design, to mean harm. *Il pensait à me surprendre;* he thought to surprise me. *Il a pensé mourir;* he nearly lost his life. *J'ai pensé tomber;* I was near falling. *À ce que je pense;* to my mind, in my mind, in my opinion. *Façon de —;* way of thinking. *— à soi;* to look to one's self, to take care of one's self.
penser, *v.a.*, to think, to think of. *Il ne dit jamais ce qu'il pense;* he never says what he thinks. *— du bien de;* to think well of. *— quelque chose pour faire réussir une affaire;* to think of something to bring a matter to a successful termination. *Que pensez-vous de cela?* what think you of that?
penser, *n.m.*, inward reasoning, thought.
penseur, *n.m.* and *adj.*, thinker; thinking, reflecting.
pensi-f, -ve, *adj.*, pensive, thoughtful.
pension, *n.f.*, pension, annuity, payment; board ; board and lodging ; boarding-house; boarding-school ; livery (of horses—*des chevaux*); (milit.) mess. *Prendre quelqu'un en —;* to receive any one as a boarder. *Se mettre en —;* to go to a boarding-house. *— bourgeoise;* family boarding-house. *Mettre ses chevaux en —;* to put one's horses out at livery. *Mettre son fils en —;* to place one's son at a boarding-school. *— de demoiselles;* young ladies' boarding-school, seminary for young ladies. *— de jeunes gens;* young gentlemen's boarding-school, boarding-school for young gentlemen, seminary for young gentlemen. *— de retraite;* retiring pension. *Obtenir une —;* to obtain a pension. *— viagère;* life-annuity. *Demi- —;* board.
pensionnaire, *n.m.f.*, boarder ; pensioner; pensionary (in Holland—*de Hollande*). *Demi- —;* day-boarder. *Prendre des —s;* to take in boarders.
pensionnat, *n.m.*, boarding-school.
pensionner, *v.a.*, to pension.
pensum (pin-som), *n.m.* (—s), imposition, task (at school—*d'écolier*). *Donner pour —;* to give as a task.
pent, penta, prefix from Gr. πέντε.
pentacorde, *n.m.*, (mus.) pentachord.
pentagone, *n.m.* and *adj.*, (geom., fort.) pentagon; pentagonal.
pentamètre, *n.m.* and *adj.*, pentameter.
pentandrie, *n.f.*, (bot.) pentandria.
pentaphylle, *adj.*, (bot.) pentaphyllous.
pentapole, *n.f.*, (ancient geog.) pentapolis (country having five cities—*territoire comprenant cinq villes principales*).
pentarchie, *n.f.*, pentarchy (government by five rulers—*gouvernement de cinq chefs*).
pentateuque, *n.m.*,(Bible) Pentateuch, first five books of Moses.
pentathle, *n.m.*, (Grec. antiq.) the five exercises.
pente, *n.f.*, declivity, inclination. slope, descent; acclivity, ascent ; valance (of a bed—*de lit*); (nav.) sides (of an awning—*d'une tente*); propensity, bent. *Le terrain va en —;* the ground shelves down. *Avoir de la — au plaisir;* to have a natural propensity for pleasure.
pentecôte (pant-kôt), *n.f.*, Whitsuntide, Pentecost. *Le temps de la —;* Whitsuntide. *Dimanche de la —;* Whitsunday.
pentière (-tièr), *n.f.* *V.* **pantière.**

penture, *n.f.*, iron-work, iron-brace; (tech.) hinge. — *de sabords* (nav.); googings of the port-lids. — *s en fer à cheval;* scuttle-hinges.

pénultième (-ti-èm), *adj.*, last but one; (gram.) penultimate.

pénultième, *n.f.*, (gram.) penult, penultima.

pénurie, *n.f.*, penury, want, scarcity.

péone, *n.f.* V. **pivoine** (bot.).

péotte, *n.f.*, large gondola used in the Adriatic.

péperin, *n.m.*, peperine (volcanic stone—*pierre volcanique*).

pépie, *n.f.*, pip (disease of birds—*maladie de la volaille*). *Elle n'a point la* —; she is not tongue-tied. *Il a la* —; he is for ever drinking.

pépier, *v.n.*, to chirp, to pip.

pépin, *n.m.*, (bot.) kernel, pip. — *de raisin;* grapestone.

pépinière, *n.f.*, (hort.) nursery.

pépiniériste, *n.m.*, nursery-man.

pépite, *n.f.*, (min.) nugget.

péplon, *or* **péplum**, *n.m.*, (antiq.) lady's cloak.

pepsine, *n.f.*, (chem. pharm.) pepsin.

percale, *n.f.*, cotton cambric.

percaline, *n.f.*, glazed cotton (for lining—*pour doublure*); (book-bind.) cloth.

perçant, -e, *adj.*, piercing, sharp, keen, shrill. *Froid* —; piercing cold. *Vent* —; sharp wind. *Des yeux* —*s;* sharp, piercing eyes. *Des cris* —*s;* piercing cries. *Voix* —*e;* shrill voice. **en perce**, *adv.*, broached, tapped. *Mettre en* —; to prick, to pierce. *Mettre du vin en* —; to broach a cask of wine.

percé, -e, *part.*, pierced, bored. *Habit* —; coat in holes. *Avoir le cœur* —; to be struck to the heart. *Maison bien* —*e;* well-lighted house. *Paysage bien* —*e;* well-opened landscape. *Chaise* —*e;* close-stool. *Il est bas* —; he is low in purse. *Fruits* —*s de vers;* worm-eaten fruits. *C'est un panier* —; money burns in his pocket, he is a spendthrift.

perce-bois, *n.m.* (—). (ent.) borer.

percée, *n.f.*, *or* **percé**, *n.m.*, opening (in a wood—*dans un bois*), vista, glade. *Faire une* — *dans les bataillons ennemis;* to hew a passage through the enemy's battalions.

***perce-feuille**, *n.f.* (— —*s*), (bot.) thorough-wax.

perce-forêt, *n.m.* (— —*s*) (fam., l.u.), determined sportsman.

perce-lettre, *n.m.* (— —*s*), bodkin (wherewith holes used to be made in paper or parchment for inserting the strings to which seals were attached—*instrument pour faire dans les lettres et papiers des trous qui recevaient les cordons auxquels on attachait les cachets de cire*).

percement, *n.m.*, piercing, opening.

perce-mousse, *n.f.*, *or* **perce-neige**, *n.f.* (—), (bot.) snow-drop.

***perce-oreille**, *n.m.* (— —*s*), (ent.) earwig.

perce-pierre, *n.f.* (— —*s*). V. **passe-pierre**.

percepteur, *n.m.*, collector (of taxes—*des impôts*); gatherer. — *des impôts;* tax-gatherer.

perceptibilité, *n.f.*, liability to being collected, as taxes, &c.; the quality of being perceptible, perceptibility.

perceptible, *adj.*, collectible; perceptible, perceivable.

perception, *n.f.*, the faculty of perceiving, perception; gathering, collecting.

percer, *v.a.*, to bore, to drill, to pierce, to tap, to broach, to open; to penetrate, to see through; to thrill; (engineering—*terme d'ingénieur*) to tunnel; to wet through (of rain—*de la pluie*). — *avec un foret;* to drill, to pierce. — *d'outre en outre;* to run through and through. — *un ais;* to bore a plank. — *un*

tonneau; to tap a cask. — *un escadron;* to cut a passage through a squadron. — *avec le bec;* to peck through. — *d'un coup d'épée;* to run through with a sword. — *l'avenir;* to dive into futurity. *Les os lui percent la peau;* his bones are coming through his skin. — *un abcès;* to lance, to open an abscess. — *une forêt;* to open, to make a road through a forest. — *une porte dans un mur;* to open a door in a wall.

se percer, *v.r.*, to bore, to be bored.

percer, *v.n.*, to pierce, to pierce through, to break, to break through, to come out, to come through, to open; to appear, to peep out, to peep forth, to transpire; to show one's self, to discover one's self, to manifest one's self; to rise, to make one's way, to get on; to make one's way through a crowd. *Les dents vont bientôt* — *à cet enfant;* that child's teeth will soon come through, that child will soon cut his teeth. *Cette tumeur percera d'elle-même;* that tumour will break, burst, of itself. — *par son mérite;* to rise, to make one's way, by one's merit. *Si compacte que soit la foule, perçons toujours;* however dense the crowd may be, let us break through it all the same.

perces, *n.f.pl.*, holes of wind instruments.

perceur, *n.m.*, borer.

percevoir, *v.a.*, to receive, to gather, to collect (taxes—*les impôts*); (philos.) to perceive.

perche, *n.f.*, perch, pole; perch (measure—*mesure*); (hunt.) horns; (ich.) perch. — *commune;* barse. *Petite* —; cole-perch. *Grande* — (pers.); walking rushlight.

perché, *n.m.*, the being perched (of birds—*des oiseaux*). *Au* —; when perched.

percher, *v.n.*, to perch.

se percher, *v.r.*, to perch one's self, to perch.

percheron, *n.m.*, horse, native of the French province Perche.

perchlorure, *n.m.*, (chem.) bichloride, perchloride.

perchoir, *n.m.*, roost.

perclus, -e, *adj.*, (med.) impotent. *Avoir le cerveau* —; to be wanting in sense, in judgment.

perçoir, *n.m.*, piercer (to tap casks—*pour percer les tonneaux*).

perçu, -e, *part.*, collected.

percussion, *n.f.*, percussion, verberation.

percutante, *adj.*, (artil.) percussion. *Fusée* —; percussion-fuse.

perdable, *adj.*, losable.

perdant, -e, *n.* and *adj.*, loser; losing.

perdition, *n.f.*, waste, wreck, ruin; perdition, destruction. *S'en aller en* —; to go to ruin, to go to wreck and ruin.

perdre, *v.a.*, to lose, to be deprived of, to be out of pocket; to waste, to ruin, to be the ruin of, to undo, to corrupt, to debauch; to spoil; (nav.) to carry away; (nav.) to cast away; (tech.) to discharge (water—*de l'eau*). — *la santé;* to lose one's health. — *la raison;* to lose one's reason. — *haleine;* to lose one's breath. — *la tête;* to lose one's wits. — *une gageure;* to lose a wager. — *quelqu'un de réputation;* to defame any one. — *l'occasion;* to lose the opportunity. — *courage;* to despond. — *une chose de vue;* to lose sight of a thing. *Ses débauches le perdront;* his debauchery will ruin him. *L'inondation a perdu les blés;* the inundation has spoilt the crops.

se perdre, *v.r.*, to be lost, to lose one's self, to lose one's way, to stray; to be cast away; to have a rambling way of arguing; to be nonplussed; to disappear, to fall into disuse; to ruin one's self; to go to ruin, to go to wreck and ruin; to spoil, to be spoilt; (nav.) to be carried away; (nav.) to be cast away; to hole one's own ball (at billiards—*au billard*).

perdre, *v.n.*, to lose, to be a loser, to be out of pocket; (nav.) to ebb. *La marée perd;* the tide is ebbing.

perdreau, *n.m.*, (orni) young partridge.

perdrigon, *n.m.*, Perdrigon-plum.

perdrix, *n.f.*, (orni.) partridge. — *grise;* common partridge. — *rouge;* red-legged partridge. *Couple de* —; brace of partridges.

perdu, -e. *part.*, lost, ruined, wasted; bewildered; undermined; spoilt; stray, forlorn. — *de dettes;* over head and ears in debt. — *de réputation;* ruined in reputation. *Courir, crier, comme un* —; to run, to cry, like mad, like a madman. *Tirer à coup* —; to shoot at random. *Pays* —; out of the way, deserted land. *À corps* —; head-long, desperately. *Heures* —es; spare time, leisure hours. *Un bienfait n'est jamais* —; a good action never remains unrewarded. *Enfants* —s (milit.); forlorn hope.

Ⓞ**perdurable**, *adj*, perdurable, lasting, permanent.

Ⓞ**perdurablement**, *adv.*, for ever, perdurably.

père, *n.m.*, father, parent; sire. — *de famille;* father of a family. *Nos* —s; our forefathers. —s *du désert;* old anchorites. *Le saint* —, *le très saint* —. *notre saint* —, *notre très saint* —, *le* — *des fidèles le* — *des Chrétiens* (c. rel.); the pope. — *spirituel;* ghostly father, father confessor. *Beau-* — (—*x* —s); father-in-law; step-father. — *nourricier;* foster-father. — *la joie;* frank, gay, and hearty fellow. — *aux écus;* man with a great deal of money. *De* — *en fils;* from father to son, from sire to son. — *noble* (thea.); first old man. *Dormir, s'endormir, avec ses* —s, to sleep with one's fathers.

pérégrination, *n.f.*, peregrination.

pérégrinité, *n.f.*, (jur.) being a foreigner, alienism.

péremption, *n.f.*, (jur.) limitation.

péremptoire, *adj.*, peremptory.

péremptoirement (-tôar-män), *adv*, peremptorily.

Ⓞ**pérennial**, **-e** (-rè-n-nial). *adj.*, perennial.

pérennité. *n.f.*, perpetuity.

péréquation, *n.f.*, assessment, assessing of taxes.

perfectibilité. *n.f.*, perfectibility.

perfectible, *adj.*, perfectible.

perfection. *n.f.*, perfection. *Le plus haut degré de* —; the acme of perfection. *La* — *en personne;* perfection in person, the pink of perfection. *En* —; to perfection.

perfectionnement (-sio-n-män), *n.m.*, improvement. *Leçons de* —; finishing lessons.

perfectionner, *v.a.*, to perfect; to improve; to improve on. — *ce que les autres ont inventé;* to improve on the inventions of others.

se **perfectionner**. *v.r.*, to perfect one's self; to improve one's self; to improve.

perfide, *n.m.f.* and *adj.*, perfidious, treacherous, false, false-hearted person; perfidious, treacherous, false. *Le* — *m'a trahi;* the perfidious man betrayed me.

perfidement (-fid-män), *adv.*, perfidiously, falsely, treacherously, basely.

perfidie, *n.f.*, perfidy, perfidiousness; treachery; false-heartedness, treacherousness; treacherous action, treacherous thing. *Faire une* —; to commit an act of perfidy.

perfolié, -e, *adj.*, (bot.) perfoliate, perfoliated.

perforant, -e. *adj.*, perforating; perforative.

perforateur. *n.m.*, (tech.) perforator.

perforati-f, -ve, *adj.*, (surg.) perforative.

perforation, *n.f.*, perforation.

perforer, *v.a.*, to perforate.

péri. *n.m.*, peri (Persian fairy—*fée, génie des contes persans*).

périanthe, *n.m.*, (bot.) perianth, perianthium.

périapte. *n.m.*, periapt.

péribole, *n.m.*, (arch.) peribolus.

péricarde, *n.m.*, (anat.) pericardium.

péricardite, *n.f.*, (med.) pericarditis.

péricarpe. *n.m.*, (bot.) seed-vessel, pericarp.

périchondre, *n.m.*, (anat.) perichondrium.

péricliter, *v.n.*, to be in danger, in jeopardy.

péricrâne, *n.m.*, (anat.) pericranium.

péridot. *n.m.*, chrysolite, peridot.

péridrome, *n.m.*, (arch.) peridrome.

périgée. *n.m.* and *adj.*, (astron.) perigee, perigeum; in its perigee.

périgueux (-gheü), *n.m.*, (min.) Perigord stone.

périhélie, *n.m.* and *adj.*, (astron.) perihelion, perihelium; in its perihelion.

* **péril**, *n.m.*, peril, danger, jeopardy, hazard, risk. *Au* — *de ma vie;* at the hazard of my life. *Être en* — *de la vie;* to have one's life in danger. *Prendre une affaire à ses risques et* —s; to take the event of an affair upon one's self.

* **périlleusement**, *adv.*, perilously, dangerously, hazardously.

* **périlleu-x, -se**, *adj.*, perilous, dangerous, hazardous.

périmer, *v.n.*, (jur.) to be barred by limitation.

périmètre, *n.m.*, (geom.) perimeter.

périnéal, -e, *adj.*, relating to the perinæum.

périnée, *n.m.*, (anat.) perinæum.

période. *n.f.*, period (revolution); (med.) period; (astron.) period; (chron.) period; (gram.) period, sentence; (mus.) phrase. — *lunaire:* lunar period. — *bien arrondie;* well-rounded period. — *embarrassée;* involved period. — *carrée;* flowing period, full period.

période, *n.m.*, pitch, summit, acme, period. *Démosthène et Cicéron ont porté l'éloquence à son plus haut* —; Demosthenes and Cicero carried eloquence to its highest pitch. *Long* — *de temps;* long period of time

périodicité, *n.f.*, periodicity.

périodique, *adj.*, periodic, periodical; (arith.) recurring, circulating. *Fraction* — (arith.); circulating, recurring decimal, repetend. *Fraction* — *composée* (arith.); mixed circulating decimal. *Style* —; full style.

périodiquement (-dik-män), *adv.*, periodically.

périœciens (pé-ri-è-si in), *n.m.pl.*, (geog.) periœciens, periœci, perlecians.

perioste, *n.m.*, (anat.) periosteum.

périostose, *n.f.*, (med.) periostitis.

péripatéticien, -ne (-ci-in, -è-n), *n.* and *adj.*, Peripatetic.

péripatétisme, *n.m.*, Peripateticism.

péripétie (-pé-ci), *n.f.*, sudden turn of fortune; (thea.) catastrophe, event.

périphérie, *n.f.*, (geom.) periphery.

périphrase, *n.f.*, periphrasis, periphrase, circumlocution.

périphraser, *v.n.*, to periphrase, to talk in a roundabout way, to express by circumlocution.

périple, *n.m.*, (ancient geog.) periplus.

péripneumonie, *n.f.*, (med.) peripneumonia, peripneumony.

périptère, *n.m.* and *adj.*, (arch.) periptery; peripteral

périr. *v.n.*, to perish, to die, to be lost, to be destroyed, to sink, to fall off; (jur.) to be barred by limitation. — *de froid;* to perish with cold. *Tôt ou tard les méchants périssent malheureusement.* sooner or later the wicked come to an untimely end. *Faire* — *une armée,* to destroy an army. *L'instance est périe* (jur.); the suit is barred by limitation.

périsciens (-si-in), *n.m.pl.*, (geog.) Peris-
clans, Periscii.
périssable, *adj.*, perishable.
péristaltique, *adj.*, (med.) peristaltic.
péristole, *n.f.*, (physiolog.) the peristaltic
motion of the intestines.
péristyle, *n.m.* and *adj.*, (arch.) peristyle;
ornamented with a peristyle.
périsystole, *n.f.*, (physiolog.) perisystole.
péritoine, *n.m.*, (anat.) peritoneum.
péritonite, *n.f.*, (med.) peritonitis.
perkale, perkaline. *V.* **percale, percaline.**
perlasse, *n.f.*, pearlash.
perle, *n.f.*. pearl; bead (of bracelets, necklaces, &c.—*de bracelets, de colliers, &c.*); (print.)
pearl; (arch.) bead; (pharm.) pearl. *Nacre de
—;* mother of pearl. — *baroque;* irregular
pearl. *Jeter des —s devant les pourceaux;* to cast
pearls before swine. —*s fines;* native pearls.
Semence de —s; the smallest pearls. *Herbe aux
—s;* gromwell, gromil. *C'est la — des hommes;*
he is the best of men. *Nous ne sommes pas ici
pour enfiler des —s;* we are not here to pick straws.
Faire la —; to froth, to froth up (of brandy—*de
l'eau-de-vie*).
perlé, -e, *adj.*. pearled, set with pearls;
pearly; beady; boiled twice (of sugar—*du sucre*);
(her.) pearled; (mus.) brilliant and delicate.
Bouillon —; pearly broth. *Orge —;* pearl-
barley.
perler, *v.n.*, to bead, to form globules.
perli-er, -ère, *adj.*, of pearl. *Huître —ère;*
pearl-oyster.
perlière, *n.f.*, (bot.) cudweed.
perlimpinpin, *n.m.*, used only in: *poudre de
—;* quack's powder (pop.).
perlon, *n.m.*, (ich.) swallow-fish, sapphirine-
gurnet, tub-fish.
perlure, *n.f.*, (hunt.) curling (of horns—*du
bois des fauves*).
permanence, *n.f.*, permanence, permanency. *Armée en —;* standing army. *L'assemblée s'est déclarée en —;* the assembly declared
its sittings permanent.
permanent, -e, *adj.*, permanent; (mec.)
constant.
perméabilité, *n.f.*, permeability, perviousness.
perméable, *adj.*, permeable, pervious.
permesse, *n.m.*, (poet.) Permessus.
permettre, *v.a.*, to permit, to allow, to suffer,
to give leave, to let. *Permettez-moi de vous
dire;* allow me to tell you, let me tell you. *Les
médecins lui ont permis le café;* the physicians
have allowed him coffee. *Dieu permet souvent
que les méchants prospèrent;* God often permits
the wicked to prosper.
se **permettre**, *v.r.*, to permit, to allow, to suffer
one's self; to indulge; to indulge one's self; to
take the liberty.
permis, -e, *part.*, lawful. *S'il m'est — de le
dire;* if I may say so. *À vous — de;* you may.
Est-il — d'entrer! may I come in?
permis, *n.m.*, permit, licence. — *de chasse;*
shooting-license.
permission, *n.f.*, permission, allowance,
leave, permit. *Avec votre —;* by your leave.
Abuser de la —; to go beyond bounds. *Prendre
la — sous son bonnet;* to take French leave.
permixtion (-miks-ti-on), *n.f.*, permixtion.
permutable, *adj.*, (gram.) commutable.
permutant, *n.m.*, permuter.
permutation, *n.f.*, permutation, exchange,
change. — *de consonnes;* transposition of consonants.
permuter, *v.a.*, to exchange. — *une cure
contre un bénéfice simple;* to exchange a rectory
against a sinecure benefice.
se **permuter**, *v.r.*, (gram.) to permute.

pernicieusement (-euz-mān), *adv.*, perniciously, mischievously, hurtfully, injuriously,
prejudicially.
pernicieu-x, -se, *adj.*, pernicious, mischievous, hurtful, injurious, prejudicial. — *à la
santé;* pernicious to the health.
Ⓞ**pernocter**, *v.n.*, to spend the night.
péroné, *n.m.*, (anat.) fibula.
péronnelle, *n.f.*, silly, talkative woman.
péroraison, *n.f.*, peroration;
pérorer, *v.n.*, to harangue; to hold forth;
to speechify.
péroreur, *n.m.*, haranguer, speechifier.
pérot, *n.m.*, tree of the age of two cuttings.
Pérou, *n.m.*, Peru. *Ce n'est pas le —;* it is
no great thing.
péroxyde, *n.m.*, (chem.) peroxide
perpendiculaire, *n.f.* and *adj.*, perpendicular. *Abaisser une —;* to let fall a perpendicular. *Élever une —;* to raise a perpendicular.
perpendiculairement (-lèr-mān), *adv.*,
perpendicularly.
perpendicularité, *n.f.*, perpendicularity.
perpendicule, *n.m.*, (l.u.) perpendicle.
perpétration, *n.f.*, (jur.) perpetration.
perpétrer, *v a.*, (jur.) to perpetrate.
perpétuation, *n.f.*, perpetuation.
perpétuel, -le, *adj.*, perpetual, never-
ceasing, endless.
perpétuellement (-èl-mān), *adv.*, perpetually, everlastingly.
perpétuer, *v.a.*, to perpetuate.
se **perpétuer**, *v.r.*, to be perpetuated.
perpétuité, *n.f.*, perpetuity. *À —;* for
ever; for life. *Condamner aux travaux forcés à
—;* to sentence to penal servitude for life.
perplexe, *adj.*, perplexed, embarrassed,
irresolute; perplexing.
perplexité, *n.f.*, perplexity.
perquisition, *n.f.*, perquisition, search.
Mandat de —; search-warrant. *Lancer un
mandat de —;* to issue a search-warrant.
perré, *n.m.*, (arch.) water-wings.
perrin-dandin, *n.m.*, an ignorant, greedy
judge.
perron, *n.m.*, steps before a house; (arch.)
perron.
perroquet, *n.m.*, (orni.) parrot; parrot
(pers.); (nav.) gallant-sail, gallant. *Parler
comme un —;* to talk like a parrot.
perruche, *n.f.*, she-parrot; perroquet.
perruque, *n.f.*, wig, periwig, peruke. — *à
nœuds;* bobwig, bobtail-wig. *Tête à —;* barber's
block; prejudiced old man.
perruquier, *n.m.*, wig-maker, peruke-
maker; hair-dresser.
perruquière, *n.f.*, barber's wife.
Ⓞ**pers, -e**, *adj.*, bluish.
persan, -e, *n.* and *adj.*, Persian.
persan, *n.m.*, Persian language.
persane, *n.f.*, Persian woman.
perse, *n.f.*, (geog.) Persia; Persian woman;
chintz.
perse, *n.m.*, (ancient hist.) Persian man.
persécutant, -e, *adj.*, troublesome, teasing.
persécuter, *v.a.*, to persecute, to trouble, to
importune, to tease.
persécut-eur, -rice, *n.* and *adj.*, persecutor, troublesome man or woman; persecuting.
persécution, *n.f.*, persecution.
persée, *n.m.*, (astron.) Perseus.
persévéramment (-ra-mān), *adv.*, perseveringly.
persévérance, *n.f.*, perseverance, steadiness, industry.
persévérant, -e, *adj.*, persevering, steady,
industrious.
persévérer, *v.n.*, to persevere, to be steadfast, to persist in one's opinion. — *dans un
dessein;* to persevere in a design.

persicaire, *n.f.*, (bot.) water-pepper.
persicot, *n.m.*, persecot, persicot.
persienne, *n.f.*, Venetian shutter.
persiflage,*n.m.*,quizzing,bantering,banter.
persifler, *v.a.*, to quiz, to smoke, to banter.
persifleur, *n.m.*, banterer, quiz.
persil, *n.m.*, (bot.) parsley. — *d'âne*;
beaked parsley. — *des 'marais*; sium angusti-
folium.
*****persillade**, *n.f.*, (cook.) slices of boiled beef
with vinegar and parsley.
*****persillé, -e**, *adj.*, spotted (of cheese—*du
fromage*).
persique, *adj.*, (arch.) Persian, Persic.
persistance, *n.f.*, persistence, persistency.
persistant, -e, *adj.*, (bot.) persistent, persisting.
persister, *v.n.*, to persist, to stand to. *Il
persiste à nier*; he persists in denying. *Il persiste dans son sentiment*; he persists in his
opinion.
personnage, *n.m.*, personage, person;
(theat.) character, part. *C'est un sot* — ; he is a
silly fellow. *Il joue bien son* — ; he plays his
part well.
personnalité, *n.f.*, personal feeling; self-
love, selfishness; personality; personal remark.
personnat, *n.m.*, sort of benefice in a cathedral which gave its holder precedence over the
simple canons.
personne, *n.f.*, person, man, woman, child,
female; (gram., theol.) person. *Jeune*
— ; young lady, young girl. *Parlant à sa* — ;
(jur.) speaking to him in person. *Les* —*s de
condition*; people of fashion. *Sans acception de
—s*; without respect of persons. *Il est bien fait
de sa* — ; he has a handsome person. *J'y étais
en* — ; I was there in person. *Avoir soin de
sa* — ; to take care of one's self. *Il aime sa* — ;
he loves his dear self. *Payer de sa* — ; to expose one's self to danger. *A la première,
seconde, troisième* — ; (gram.) in the first,
second, third, person.
personne, *pron. m.*, nobody, no man, none,
no one; any body, any one. *Il n'y a* — *à la
maison*; there is nobody at home. *Je doute
que* — *y réussisse*; I doubt whether any one will
succeed in it.
personnée, *n.* and *adj.f.*, (bot.) personate,
masked flower; personate, masked.
personnel, -le, *adj.*, personal; selfish.
personnel, *n.m.*, ☉personal character;
staff, all the persons composing any establishment; (milit., nav.) personnel.
personnellement (-nèl-mān), *adv.*, personally.
personnification, *n.f.*, personification.
personnifier, *v.a.*, to personify; to impersonate.
perspecti-f, -ve, *adj.*, perspective.
perspective, *n.f.*, perspective, view; prospect. — *aérienne*; aerial perspective. *Cela
borne la* — ; that bounds the prospect. —
riante; delightful prospect. *Il a la* — *d'une
grande fortune*; he has the prospect of a large
fortune. *En* — ; in the distance; in prospect,
in expectation.
perspicace, *adj.*, perspicacious.
perspicacité, *n.f.*, perspicacity.
perspicuité, *n.f.*, perspicuity.
perspiration, *n.f.*, (med.) perspiration.
persuader, *v.a.*, to persuade, to make to
believe, to convince, to satisfy. *J'en suis per-
suadé*; I am convinced of it.
se **persuader**, *v.r.*, to persuade, to convince
one's self: to be persuaded.
persuader, *v.n.*, to persuade. to convince.
persuasi-f, -ve, *adj.*, persuasive.
persuasion,*n.f.*, persuasion; belief,opinion.
L'éloquence a pour but la — ; the object of elo-

quence is persuasion. *Agir à la* — *d'un autre*,
to act by the persuasion of another.
perte, *n.f.*, loss, losings; ruin, waste, wastefulness; (med.) flooding. *Faire une* — ; to meet
with a loss. *Être en* — ; to be a loser. *Courir
à sa* — ; to go to ruin. — *de temps*; waste of
time. *La* — *du Rhône*; (geog.) place where the
Rhone disappears beneath the rocks. *Vendre
à* — ; to sell at a loss. *En pure* — ; to no purpose. *A* — *de vue*; farther than one can see.
pertinacité, *n.f.*, pertinacity.
pertinemment (-na-mān), *adv.*, pertinently.
pertinence, *n.f.*, pertinency.
pertinent, -e, *adj.*, pertinent.
pertuis, *n.m.*, (geog.) straits; sluice, narrow opening in a flood-gate.
pertuisane, *n.f.*, partisan. halberd.
perturbat-eur, -rice, *n.* and *adj.*, disturber; disturbing.
perturbation, *n.f.*, perturbation; disturbance, commotion.
pervenche, *n.f.*, (bot.) periwinkle.
pervers. -e, *adj.*, perverse, froward, untoward, wicked.
pervers, *n.m.*, perverse, froward person;
wrong-doer.
perversion, *n.f.*, perversion.
perversité, *n.f.*, perversity, perverseness,
frowardness, untowardness.
pervertir, *v.a.*, to pervert, to be pervertive
of, to be a perverter of.
pervertissable, *adj.*, pervertible.
pervertissement (-tis-mān), *n.m.*, perversion, corruption.
pervertisseur, *n.m.*, perverter, corrupter.
pesade, *n.f.*, (man.) pesade.
pesage, *n.m.*, the action of weighing.
pesamment (pĕ-za-mān), *adv.*, heavily,
ponderously, weightily, lumpishly.
pesant, -e,*adj.*, heavy, ponderous, weighty;
unwieldy, lumpish; cumbersome; sluggish,
slow; full weight. *Fardeau* — ; heavy burthen.
Cheval — *à la main*; hard-mouthed horse. *Il
a la main* — *e*; he has a heavy hand. *Il a
l'esprit* — ; his mind is dull. *Joug* — ;heavy yoke.
Un louis d'or — ; a louis d'or of the full weight.
pesant, *n.m.*, weight. *Il vaut son* — *d'or*;
he is worth his weight in gold.
pesant, *adv.*, weight, in weight.
pesanteur,*n.f.*, weight, heaviness, weightiness; sluggishness, dulness, slowness, unwieldiness; ponderosity, ponderousness; (phys.)
force of gravity, gravity. — *de téte*; heaviness
in the head. — *d'esprit*; dulness of mind.
pesée, *n.f.*, weighing; all that is weighed
at once. *Faire une* — ; to weigh.
pèse-liqueur, *n.m.* (—, *or* — *s*), hydrometer.
peser, *v.a.*, to weigh; to ponder, to consider.
— *les raisons de quelqu'un*; to weigh any one's
arguments. — *ses paroles*; to weigh one's
words.
peser, *v.n.*, to weigh, to be of weight, to be
heavy; to bear upon; to lean; to dwell upon.
Viande qui pèse sur l'estomac; meat that lies
heavy upon the stomach. *Cela me pèse sur
le cœur*; that lies heavy upon my heart. — *sur
un levier*; to bear upon a lever.
peseur, *n.m.*, weigher.
peson, *n.m.*, steelyard.
pessaire, *n.m.*, (med.) pessary.
pessimisme, *n.m.*, way of thinking, opinion
of the pessimist.
pessimiste. *n.m.*, pessimist.
peste, *n.f.*, plague, pestilence, pest, torment.
La flatterie est la — *des cours*; flattery is the
pest of courts. *.*— *soit du fou!* plague on the
fool !

peste. *adj.*, sly, arch.

peste! *int.*, plague! deuce!

pester, *v.n.*, to inveigh against, to bluster. *Il peste contre ses juges ;* he rails at his judges.

pestifère, *adj.*, (l.u.) pestiferous, pestilential.

pestiféré, -e, *n.* and *adj.*, person infected with the plague; infected with the plague.

pestilence. *n.f.*, pestilence.

pestilent, -e, *adj.*, pestilential.

pestilentiel, -le (-ci-èl), *adj.*, pestilential, infectious, contagious.

pet, *n.m.*, (l. ex.) *Un — de nonne ;* apple-fritter.

pétale, *n.m.*, (bot.) petal, flower-leaf.

pétalé, -e, *adj.*, (bot.) petalous.

pétalisme, *n.m.*, (antiq.) petalism.

pétalite, *n.f.*, petalite.

pétaloïde, *adj.*, petaloid.

pétarade. *n.f.*, (of animals—*des animaux*) farting ; noise with one's mouth.

pétard, *n.m.*, (milit.) petard ; (fireworks —*pièce d'artifice*) cracker.

pétarder, *v.a.*, to blow up with a petard.

pétardier, *n.m.*, one who makes petards.

pétase. *n.m.*, (antiq.) petasus ; broad-brimmed hat.

pétaud, *n.m. C'est la cour du roi — ;* it is Bedlam broke loose.

pétaudière, *n.f.*, bear-garden, confused company.

pétéchial, -e, *adj.*, (med.) petechial. *Fièvre —e ;* petechial fever.

pétéchies, *n.f.pl.*, (med.) petechiæ.

pet-en-l'air, *n.m.* (—), man's short morning gown.

péter, *v.n.*, (l. ex.) to burst ; to break ; to snap ; to crackle, to bounce ; (of fire-arms—*des armes à feu*) to explode, to burst.

péteu-r, *n.m.*, *-se*, *n.f.*, (l. ex.) sorry fellow.

****pétillant, -e**, *adj*, crackling, sparkling.

****pétillement**, *n.m.*, crackling, sparkling.

****pétiller**, *v.n.*, to crackle ; to sparkle ; to long to do a thing. *Son ouvrage pétille d'esprit ;* his work sparkles with wit. *Ses yeux pétillent ;* his eyes sparkle. — *d'impatience ;* to boil with impatience.

pétiolaire (-ci-), *adj.*, (bot.) petiolary.

pétiole (-ci-), *n.m.*, (bot.) petiole.

pétiolé, -e (-ci-), *adj.*, (bot.) petiolate.

petit, -e, *adj.*, little, small, diminutive, short, unimportant, petty ; grand (of one's children's children, of one's nephew's children, of one's niece's children—*des descendants*). — *fils (— s—)* ; grand-son. *Un — homme ;* a little man. *Un homme — ;* a mean man. *Un — roi ;* a petty king. *Le — peuple ;* the common people. *Le — monde ;* the common people. —*e guerre. V.* **guerre**. — *collet ;* young clergyman. —*e vérole ;* small-pox. *De la —e bière ;* small-beer. — *à — ;* by degrees. — *-maître (—s —s)* ; coxcomb. —*e maîtresse (—s —s)* ; lady of studied elegance. — *à — l'oiseau fait son nid ;* small strokes fell great oaks. *En —, au — pied ;* in miniature, on a small scale.

petit, *n.m.* -**e**, *n.f.*, little child ; dear, darling ; young one ; whelp, pup, kitten, cub. *Les —s d'une chienne ;* the whelps of a bitch. *Les —s d'une truie ;* the litter of a sow. *Faire des —s ;* to bring forth young ones. *Pauvre — ;* poor little fellow.

petitement (pëtit-män), *adv*, little ; slenderly, meanly, poorly. *Il est logé — ;* he has a small lodging.

petite-oie, *n.f.* (*n.p.*). (cook.) giblets ; ☉stockings, gloves, hat and other minor parts of clothing ; ☉minor tokens of love.

petitesse, *n.f.*, smallness, littleness, short-ness, meanness. — *d'âme ;* meanness of soul. — *d'esprit ;* narrowness of mind. *C'est une — à lui ;* it is a mark of littleness on his part.

petit-gris, *n.m.* (—*s* —), minever, Siberian squirrel.

pétition, *n.f.*, petition. *Faire une — ;* to draw up, to address, a petition. *Faire présenter une — ;* to petition. — *de principe* (log.) ; petitio principii, begging the question.

pétitionnaire, *n.m.f.*, petitioner.

pétitionnement, *n.m.*, petitioning (in writing—*par écrit*).

pétitionner, *v.n.*, to make a request, to petition.

pétitoire, *adj.*, (jur.) claiming the right of property in real estate.

pétitoire, *n.m.*, (jur.) claim of the right of property in real estate.

peton, *n.m.*, foot (of children—*d'enfant*) ; little foot.

pétoncle, *n.m.*, (conch.) scallop.

pétreau, *n.m.*, (gard.) sucker (of a tree—*d'arbre*).

pétrée, *adj f.*, (geog.) stony. [Only used in *Arabie — :* Arabia Petræa.]

pétrel. *n.m.*, (orni.) petrel.

pétreu-x, *-se*, *adj.*, (anat.) stone-like.

pétri, -e, *part.*, kneaded. *C'est un homme tout — de salpêtre ;* he is a passionate man. — *d'ignorance :* full of ignorance.

pétrifiant. -e, *adj.*, petrifactive.

pétrification, *n.f.*, petrifaction, petrification.

pétrifier, *v.a.*, to petrify.

se pétrifier, *v.r.*, to petrify, to become stone.

pétrifique, *adj.*, petrific.

pétrin, *n.m.*, kneading-trough ; scrape, hobble. *Se mettre dans le — ;* to get into a scrape.

pétrir, *v.a.*, to knead ; to mould.

pétrissable, *adj.*, that can be kneaded ; (fig.) yielding, submissive, obedient, easily led.

pétrissage. *n.m.*, kneading.

pétrisseur. *n.m.*, *-se*, *n.f.*, kneader, journeyman-baker.

pétrole, *n.m.*, petrol, rock-oil.

pétroleu-r, *n.m.*, *-se*, *n.f.*, malefactor who commits arson by means of petroleum.

pétrosilex (-lèks), *n.m.*, (min.) petrosilex.

in **petto** (i-n pèt-to), *adv.*, in petto, secretly.

pétulamment (-la-män), *adv.*, petulantly.

pétulance, *n.f.*, petulancy.

pétulant, -e, *adj.*, petulant.

☉**petun**, *n.m.*, tobacco, snuff.

☉**petuner**, *v.n.*, to take snuff ; to smoke tobacco.

pétunia, *n.m.*, (bot.) petunia.

pétunse, or pétunzé, *n.m.*, petunse (stone used for making porcelain—*feldspath à porcelaine*).

peu, *adv.*, little, few. — *ou point ;* little or nothing. *Ni — ni point ;* none at all. — *d'argent ;* little money. — *d'hommes ;* few men. — *aimable ;* not very amiable. *Fort — ;* very little. *Quelque — ;* a little. *Si — que ;* however little. *Si — que rien ;* very little. *Tant soit — ;* ever so little. — *à — ;* by degrees. *Dans —, dans — de temps ;* in a little time. *Dans — de jours ;* in a few days. *À — près, à — de chose près ;* nearly, about. *Attendez un — ;* wait a little.

peu. *n.m.*, little, few. *Le — que je vaux :* the little that I am worth. *Encore un — ;* a little longer ; a little more. *Se contenter de — ;* to be contented with little.

peulvan, or peulven, *n.m.*, (archæology —*archéologie*) menhir.

peuplade, *n.f.*, people emigrating to populate a country ; colony ; tribe.

peuple, *adj.*, (l.u.) vulgar, common.

peuplé, -e, *adj.*, peopled ; stocked.

peuple, *n.m.*, people, nation ; multitude,

vulgar; fry (fish—*petit poisson*); sucker (of a plant—*d'une plante*); ☉ (bot.) poplar; (techn.) deal-wood. *C'est un homme du* —; he is one of the common people. *Le menu* —, *le bas* —, *le petit* —; the common people. *La lie du* —; the scum of the people. *Mettre du* — *dans un étang;* to stock a pond with fry.

peuplement, *n.m.*, peopling; stocking a poultry-yard, a pond; planting new trees in woods.

peupler, *v.a.*, to people, to populate; to stock with inhabitants; to stock with animals; to plant trees, vines, &c.

se **peupler**, *v.r.*, to become peopled.

peupler, *v.n.*, to multiply, to breed.

peuplier, *n.m.*, poplar.

peur, *n.f.*, fear, fright. *Avoir* —; to be afraid. *Avoir grand'peur;* to be in great fear. *Mourir de* —; to be frightened to death. *Faire* — *à quelqu'un;* to frighten any one. *Sans* —; fearless. *En être quitte pour la* —; to get off for the fright. *Avoir* — *de son ombre;* to be afraid of one's shadow. *De* — *de;* for fear of. *De* — *que;* lest, for fear that. *De* — *qu'il ne le sache;* lest he should know it.

peureu-x, -se, *adj.*, fearful, timorous.

peut-être, *adj.*, perhaps, may be, perchance. — *viendra-t-il,* — *qu'il viendra;* perhaps he will come. — *que oui;* perhaps so.

peut-être, *n.m.*, perhaps. *Il n'y a pas de* —; there is no perhaps in the case.

phaéton, *n.m.*, phaeton.

phagédénique, *adj.*, (med.) phagedenic.

phagédénisme, *n.m.*, (med.) phagedena.

phalange, *n.f.*, phalanx; (anat.) phalanx.

phalanger, *n.m.*, (mam.) phalanger.

phalangite, *n.m.*, soldier of a phalanx.

phalanstère, *n.m.*, phalansterium.

phalanstérien, -ne (-in,-è-n), *n.* and *adj.*, phalansterian.

phalaris (-ris), *n.m.*,(bot.) phalaris, canary-grass.

phalarope, *n.m.*, (orni.) phalarope.

phalène, *n.f.*, (ent.) moth.

phalence, *or* **phaleuque**, *n.m.* and *adj.*, (Gr. and Lat. poet.) hendecasyllable; hendecasyllabic.

phallique, *adj.*, relating to the Bacchic orgies, and to the emblem that was solemnly borne therein, phallic.

phallus, *n.m.*, (antiq.) phallus, the emblem that was solemnly borne in procession in the Bacchic orgies; (bot.) morell, latticed mushroom.

phanariote, *n.m.f.*, Greek of the upper class, living in the Phanar quarter of Constantinople.

phanérogame, *n.f.* and *adj.*, (bot.) phanerogamic plant; phanerogamian, phanerogamic, phanerogamous.

phantaisie, *n.f.* V. **fantaisie**.

phantasmagorie, *n.f.* V. **fantasmagorie**.

phantasmagorique, *adj.* V. **fantasmagorique**.

pharaon, *n.m.*, Pharaoh, common name given to all the Egyptian Kings before the Persians conquered Egypt.

pharaon, *n.m.*, faro, pharaon (card game—*jeu de cartes*).

pharaonique, *adj.*, Pharaonic.

phare, *n.m.*, light-house, beacon, beacon-light.

*****pharillon**, *n.m.*, a grate in which fishermen keep a fire to attract and catch fish at night.

pharisaïque, *adj.*, Pharisaic, Pharisaical.

pharisaïsme, *n.m.*, Pharisaism.

pharisien (-zi-in), *n.m.*, **-ne** (-zi-è-n), *n.f.*, Pharisee.

---

pharmaceutique, *n.f.* and *adj.*, pharmaceutics; pharmaceutical.

pharmacie, *n.f.*, pharmacy; chemist's shop; apothecary's shop, apothecary's business; medicine chest; dispensary (in hospitals—*dans les hôpitaux*).

pharmacien (-in), *n.m.*, apothecary; chemist and druggist.

pharmacologie, *n.f.*, pharmacology.

pharmacologique, *adj.*, relating to pharmacology.

pharmacopée, *n.f.*, pharmacopœia.

pharmacopole, *n.m.*, (jest.) pharmacopolist; vendor of drugs.

pharyngite, *n.f.*, (med.) pharyngitis.

pharynx, *n.m.*, pharynx.

phase, *n.f.*, phase, phasis; aspect; stage, period.

phaséole, *n.f.* V. **faséole**.

phébé, *n.f.*, (poet.) the moon.

phébus (-bús), *n.m.*, (myth.) Phœbus; bombast, fustian. *Parler* —; to speak bombast. *Donner dans le* —; to write fustian.

phénicien, -ne (-ci-in, -ci-è-n), *n.* and *adj.*, Phœnician.

phénicoptère, *n.m.*, (orni.) phenicopter, flamingo.

phénique, *adj.*, (chem.) carbolic, phenic.

phénix (fé-niks), *n.m.*, phenix, fabulous bird; (astron.) Phenix. *C'est le* — *des beaux esprits;* he is the phenix of wits.

phénol, *n.m.*, phenol.

phénoménal, -e, *adj.*, phenomenal.

phénomène, *n.m.*, phenomenon. *C'est un* — *que de vous voir ici;* it is quite a miracle to see you here.

phil, *or* **philo,** a prefix from Gr. φίλος.

philanthrope, *n.m.*, philanthropist.

philanthropie, *n.f.*, philanthropy.

philanthropique, *adj.*, philanthropic.

philharmonique, *adj.*, philharmonic.

philhellène, *n.m.f.*, philhellenist.

philippique, *n.f.*, philippic.

phillyrée, *n.f.*, (bot.) phillyrea.

philologie, *n.f.*, philology.

philologique, *adj.*, philological.

philologue, *n.m.*, philologist.

philomathique, *adj.*, philomathic.

philomèle, *n.f.*, (poet.) philomela.

philosophale, *adj.f.*, philosopher's. *Pierre* —; philosopher's stone.

philosophe, *n.m.*, philosopher.

philosopher, *v.n.*, to philosophize.

philosophie, *n.f.*, philosophy; (print.) small pica.

philosophique, *adj.*, philosophical.

philosophiquement (-fik-mãn), *adv.*, philosophically.

philosophisme, *n.m.*, philosophism.

philosophiste, *n.m.*, philosophist.

philotechnique (-tèk-nik), *adj.*, philotechnic.

philtre, *n.m.*, philter.

phimosis (-zis), *n.m.*, (med.) phimosis.

phlébite, *n.f.*, (med.) inflammation of the internal membrane of the veins.

phlébotome, *n.m.*, (surg.) an instrument for bleeding.

phlébotomie, *n.f.*, phlebotomy.

phlébotomiser, *v.a.*, to phlebotomize.

phlébotomiste, *n.m.*, phlebotomist.

phlegmagogue, *adj.*, expectorant.

phlegmasie, *n.f.*, phlegmasy.

phlegmatique, *adj.* V **flegmatique**.

phlegme, *n.m.* V. **flegme**.

phlegmon, *n.m.*, (med.) phlegmon.

phlegmoneu-x, -se, *adj.*, (med.) phlegmonous.

☉ **phlogistique**, *n.m.*, (chem.) phlogiston.

phlogose, *n.f.*, (med.) inflammation.

phlox, *n.m.*, (bot.) phlox.
phlyctène, *n.f.*, (ined.) bulla, blister.
phœnicure, *n.m.*, (orni.) red-start, red-tail.
pholade, *n.f.*, (conch.) pholas.
phonétique, *adj.*, phonetic.
phonique, *n.f.* and *adj.*, phonics; phonic.
phonolithe, *n.m.*, (min.) phonolite.
phonomètre, *n.m.*, (phys.) an instrument to measure the intensity of sound.
phoque, *n.m.*, (mam.) phoca, seal, sea-dog.
phormion, *or* **phormione**, *n.m.*, (bot.) phormium.
phosphate, *n.m.*, (chem.) phosphate.
phosphite, *n.m.*, (chem.) phosphite.
phosphore, *n.m.*, phosphorus.
phosphorescence, *n.f.*, phosphorescence.
phosphorescent, **-e**, *adj.*, phosphorescent.
phosphoreux, *adj.*, phosphorous.
phosphorique, *adj.*, phosphoric.
phosphure, *n.m.*, phosphuret.
phosphuré, **-e**, *adj.*, phosphuretted.
photographe, *n.m.*, photographist, photographer.
   photographie, *n.f.*, photography.
   photographier, *v.a.*, to photograph.
   photographique, *adj.*, photographic.
   photolithographie, *n.f.*, photolithography.
   photomètre, *n.m.*, (phys.) photometer.
   photométrie, *n.f.*, photometry.
   photométrique, *adj.*, photometric.
   photophobie, *n.f.*, (med.) photophobia.
   photosphère, *n.f.*, (astron.) photosphere.
phrase, *n.f.*, phrase, sentence. — *faite;* Idiomatic phrase. *Faire des —s;* to talk in set phrases. — *toute faite;* common-place, common topic.
   phraséologie, *n.f.*, phraseology.
   phraser, *v.a.* and *n.*, (mus.) to mark the phrases; to form phrases, to phrase.
   phraseur, *or* **phrasier**, *n.m.*, (fam.) phraseologist; prolix, verbose, tedious writer *or* talker.
phratrie, *n.f.*, (antiq.) at Athens the third part of a tribe.
phrénésie, **phrénétique**. *V.* **frénésie**, **frénétique**.
phrénique, *adj.*, (anat.) phrenic.
phrénologie, *n.f.*, phrenology.
phrénologique, *adj.*, phrenologic.
phrénologiste, *or* **phrénologue**, *n.m.*, phrenologist.
phrygien, **-ne**, *adj.*, phrygian. *Bonnet —;* the red cap worn during the French Revolution. *Mode —* (mus.); lively, warlike kind of music in use among the ancient Greeks.
phtiriasis, *n.f.*, (med.) pedicular disease.
phtisie, *n.f.*, (med.) phthisis, consumption. *Avoir la —;* to be in a consumption.
phtisique, *n.m.f.* and *adj.*, consumptive person, person in consumption; phthisical, consumptive.
phylactère, *n.m.*, phylactery.
phylarque, *n.m.*, (antiq.) phylarch.
phyllithe, *n.m.*, phyllite.
phylloxera, *n.m.* (—), (ent., agri.) phylloxera.
physicien (-in), *n.m.*, natural philosopher.
physico-mathématique, *adj.*, physico-mathematical.
physiocrate, *n.m.*, economist who believes that wealth is founded upon agriculture.
physiognomonie *n.f.*, physiognomy (art).
physiognomonique, *adj.*, physiognomic.
physiographie, *n.f.*, physiography.
physiographique, *adj.*, physiographical.
physiologie, *n.f.*, physiology.
physiologique, *adj.*, physiological.
physiologiste, *n.m.*, physiologist.

physionomie, *n.f.*, physiognomy, countenance, aspect, look; physiognomy (art).
physionomiste, *n.m.*, physiognomist.
physique, *n.f.*, physics, natural philosophy.
physique, *adj.*, physical.
physique, *n.m.*, natural constitution of a man; exterior.
physiquement (fi-zik-mān), *adv.*, physically.
phytographie, *n.f.*, phytography.
phytolithe, *n.m.*, phytolite, petrified plant.
phytologie, *n.f.*, phytology.
piaculaire, *adj.*, expiatory.
⊙**piaffe**, *n.f.*, ostentation; ostentatious display; excessive luxury, in clothes, coaches, &c.
piaffer, *v.n.*, (man.) to paw the ground; ⊙to make a show.
   piaffeur, *adj.m.*, pawing the ground (of horses—*des chevaux*).
*piailler, *v.n.*, to bawl, to squall. *Des enfants qui piaillent toujours;* children constantly screaming.
   *piaillerie, *n.f.*, bawling, squalling.
   *piailleu-r, *n.m.*, **-se**, *n.f.*, scold; squaller, bawling man or woman.
pian, *n.m.*, (med.) yaws.
pianino, *n.m.* (—s), upright piano.
pianiste, *n.m.f.*, pianist.
piano, *adv.*, (mus.) piano, softly.
piano (—s), *or* **piano-forte** (—s —), *or* **forte-piano** (— —s), *n.m.*, piano-forte. — *à queue;* grand piano. — *carré;* square piano. *Grand — droit;* cabinet piano. *Jouer du —;* to play on the piano.
piast, *or* **piaste**, *n.m.*, descendant of the ancient Polish families.
piastre, *n.f.*, piaster (coin).
piaulard, *n.m.*, puler, whiner.
piauler, *v.n.*, to pule, to whine; (of chickens—*des poussins*) to pip.
pible, *n.m.*, (nav.) pole. *Mât à —;* pole-mast.
pic, *n.m.*, pick, pickaxe; (nav.) gaff; (orni.) woodpecker; peak (of a mountain—*de montagne*); pique (at the game of piquet—*au piquet*). *À —;* perpendicularly; (nav.) apeak; (pop.) just in time.
pica, *n.m.*, (med.) pica.
picader, *n.m.* (—s), picador.
picard, **-e**, *n.* and *adj.*, Picardian.
picholine, *n.* and *adj.f.*, pickled olive; pickled.
⊙**picorée**, *n.f.*, pilfering, plundering. *Aller à la —;* to go a plundering, marauding.
picorer, *v.n.*, ⊙to go marauding, plundering; to plagiarize.
   picoreur, *n.m.*, ⊙marauder; plagiarist.
picot, *n.m.*, splinter (of wood—*de bois*); purl (of lace—*de dentelle, &c.*).
picoté, **-e**, *part.*, pricked, marked. *Il est — de petite vérole;* he is pitted with the small-pox.
picotelle, *n.f.*, (orni.) nut-hatch.
picotement (pi-kot-mān), *n.m.*, prickling, tingling, itching.
picoter, *v.a.*, to prick, to tingle; to provoke, to tease; to peck (of birds—*des oiseaux*); (man.) to touch gently with the spur.
   se **picoter**, *v.r.*, to tease, to irritate, to torment, each other.
picoterie (pi-ko-tri), *n.f.*, (fam.) teasing.
picotin, *n.m.*, peck (of oats—*d'avoine*).
picrate, *n.m.*, (chem.) carbazotate, picrate.
picrique, *adj.*, (chem.) carbazotic, picric.
pic-vert, *n.m.* (—s —s). *V.* **pivert**.
pie, *n.f.*, (orni.) magpie, pie. — *-grièche* (—s —s); shrike; shrew, a very scold. *Elle jase comme une —;* she chatters like a magpie. *Il croit avoir trouvé la — au nid;* he thinks he has made a great discovery.

pie, *adj.*, (l.u.) pious, charitable; (of horses —*des chevaux*) piebald.

pièce, *n.f.*, piece, trick; head (of cattle, of poultry, game—*des bestiaux, de la volaille, du gibier*); apartment; puncheon (of oil, wine, &c. —*d'huile, de vin, &c.*); piece of ordnance, cannon; document; joint (of cooked meat—*de viande*). *Mettre en* —*s;* to pull, to tear, to pieces. *Être armé de toutes* —*s;* to be armed cap-a-pie. *Il emporte la* —; he stings to the quick. *Rassemblage de* —*s;* patchwork. — *de vin;* puncheon of wine. — *d'eau;* sheet of water. *Une* — *d'artillerie;* a piece of ordnance. —*s de campagne;* field-pieces. —*s de batterie;* heavy ordnance. — *de théâtre;* play. *Être bien près de ses* —*s;* to have very little money. *Jouer une* — *à quelqu'un;* to play any one a trick. *Une bonne* — ; a cunning blade.

piécette, *n.f.*, a small Spanish silver coin.

pied (pié), *n.m.*, foot; footing; track; leg (of furniture—*de meubles*), stalk (of plants—*de plantes*). *Les doigts du* —; the toes. — *bot;* club-foot, club-footed. *Avoir des cors aux* —*s;* to have corns on one's feet. *Le cou-de-* — (—*s* —); the instep. *Marcher sur la pointe du* —; to walk on tip-toe. *Un coup de* — ; a kick. *Donner des coups de* —; to kick. *Aller à* —; to go on foot. *Taper du* —; to stamp. *Marcher* —*s nus;* to walk barefoot. *Mettre sous ses* —*s;* to trample on. *Les* —*s de devant;* the fore-feet. *Petits-* —*s* (—); small fowl, small game. — *plat, plat* —; flat foot; (fig.) knave, mean rascal. — *poudreux;* vagabond, rascal, scoundrel. *Une coutume qui prend* — ; a custom that gets footing. *Perdre* —; to get out of one's depth. *Avoir* —; not to be beyond one's depth. —*s et poings liés;* tied hand and foot. *Lâcher* —; to give way. *Prendre* — *sur quelque chose;* to take any thing as a precedent. *Ne savoir sur quel* — *danser;* to be put to one's last shift. *Sauter à* —*s joints;* to jump with feet joined. *Tenir le* — *sur la gorge de quelqu'un;* to attempt to force any one to do any thing. *Tenir* — *à boule;* to stick to one's work. *Couper l'herbe sous le* — *à quelqu'un;* to supplant any one. *Il a été sur* — *toute la nuit;* he has been up all night. *De* — *en cap;* cap-a-pie. *Haut le* —; be off with you; let us be off at once. *Faire haut le* —; to vanish, to disappear; to run away. *Haut-le-* —, *n.m.* (—), (fam.) a man with no fixed residence; a scoundrel. *Renvoyer des chevaux haut le* —; to send horses away without saddles or harness. *Au* — *de la lettre;* strictly speaking, literally. *Si vous lui donnez un* —, *il en prendra quatre;* give him an inch and he'll take an ell. *Il a trouvé chaussure à son* —; he has found just what he wanted; he has met with his match. *Il s'est tiré une épine du* —; he pulled a thorn out of his foot. *Être en* —; to be in the exercise of one's functions. *De* — *ferme;* without stirring, firmly. *Être assis au* — *d'un arbre;* to be seated at the foot of a tree. *Un* — *de céleri;* a stick of celery. *Le* — *du lit;* the foot of the bed. *Le* — *d'une table;* the leg of a table. — *de mât;* heel of a mast. *Cela a tant de* —*s de long;* that is so many feet long. — *à* — ; step by step; by degrees. *Sur le* — *de;* at the rate of. *D'arrache-* —; without intermission. *Au petit* —; on a small scale.

pied-à-terre, *n.m.* (—), temporary lodging; country-box (house—*maison*).

pied-d'alouette, *n.m.*, (—*s* —), (bot.) larkspur.

pied-de-coq, *n.m.* (—*s* —), (bot.) cock's-foot-grass.

pied-de-lion, *n.m.* (—*s* —), (bot.) lion's-foot.
pied-de-poule, *n.m.* (—*s* —), (bot.) crow-foot.

pied-de-veau, *n.m.* (—*s* —), (bot.) cuckoo-pint.

pied-d'oiseau, *n m.* (—*s* —), (bot.) bird's-foot.

pied-droit, *n.m.* (—*s* —*s*), (arch.) pier; pie droit.

piédestal, *n.m.*, (arch.) pedestal.

pied-fort, *n.m.* (—*s* —*s*), (coin.) a gold, silver or copper coin thicker than others, and coined as standard.

piédouche, *n.m.*, (arch.) piedouche, small pedestal for a bust, a vase, &c.

piège, *n.m.*, snare, trap, decoy. *Tendre, dresser, un* —; to set a snare. *Prendre au* —; to catch in a trap. *Il a donné, il est tombé, dans le* —; he fell into the snare.

pie-grièche, *n.f.*, (—*s* —*s*), (orni.) shrike; (pers.) shrew.

pie-mère, *n.f.* (n.p.), (anat.) pia mater.

*****pierraille**, *n.f.*, broken stone.

pierre, *n.f.*, stone, flint; (fig.) steel, rock; gem; (med.) calculus. — *de taille;* freestone. — *à aiguiser;* whetstone, grindstone. — *précieuse;* gem, precious stone. — *fausse;* artificial gem; paste. — *à fusil;* flint. — *à cautère;* potential cautery. — *d'achoppement;* stumbling-block. — *de touche;* touchstone. *La* — *philosophale;* the philosopher's stone. *Il gèle à* — *fendre;* it freezes extremely hard. *Jeter la* — *à quelqu'un;* to attack any one (in words— *en paroles*). *Jeter des* —*s dans le jardin de quelqu'un;* to throw out insinuations about any one. — *d'attente;* (mas.) toothing; (fig.) stepping-stone. — *angulaire;* corner-stone. — *d'évier;* gutter-stone, kitchen-sink. — *milliaire;* milestone.

pierrée, *n.f.*, (engineering—*terme d'ingénieur*) rumbling drain.

pierreries (pièr-ri), *n.f.pl.*, jewels, precious stones.

pierrette, *n.f.*, little stone, pebble.

pierreu-x, **-se**, *n.* and *adj.*, person afflicted with the stone; stony, flinty; calculous.

pierrier, *n.m.*, swivel-gun.

pierrot, *n.m.*, house-sparrow; clown, merry-andrew.

pierrures, *n.f.pl.*, (hunt.) pearls.

piété, *n.f.*, piety. *Des gens sans* — ; ungodly persons.

piéter, *v.n.*, to put one's foot on the mark (at games—*à quelques jeux*).

piéter, *v.a.*, ⊙to set against. — *l'étrave, l'étambord, le gouvernail* (nav.); to mark the numbers of feet on the stem, on the stern-post, on the rudder.

⊙*se* **piéter**, *v.r.*, to resist.

piétinement (-ti-n-mān), *n.m.*, moving the feet; stamping.

piétiner, *v.n.*, to stamp, to move one's feet about. — *de colère;* to stamp with anger.

piétiner, *v.a.*, to tread, to trample, under foot, to trample on.

piétisme, *n.m.*, pietism.

piétiste, *n.m.*, pietist.

piéton, *n.m.*, **-ne**, *n.f.*, pedestrian, foot-passenger; postman in rural districts.

piètre, *adj.*, (fam.) shabby, wretched; pitiful.

piètrement, *adv.*, (fam.) pitifully, wretchedly, shabbily.

piètrerie, *n.f.*, (l.u.) pitiful thing, wretched stuff.

piette, *n.f.*, (orni.) weasel-coot.

pieu, *n.m.*, stake, pile.

pieusement (pi-eûz-mān), *adv.*, piously, devoutly.

pieuvre, *n.f.*, (mol.), octopus, poulp.

pieu-x, **-se**, *adj.*, pious, godly, religious, holy.

piffre, *n.m.*, **-sse**, *n.f.*, (l.ex.) stout person ; glutton.

se **piffrer**, *v.r.*, (l.ex.) to eat greedily, to excess.

pigeon (-jon), *n.m.*, pigeon, dove ; dupe, gull. — *culbutant;* tumbler. — *à grosse gorge;* cropper. — *ramier;* wood-pigeon. — *voyageur;* carrier-pigeon. *Des—s à la crapaudine;* broiled pigeons.

pigeonneau (-jo-no), *n.m.*, young pigeon.

pigeonnier (-jo-nié), *n.m.*, pigeon-house, dove-cot.

pigment, *n.m.*, (anat.) pigment.

****pigne**, *n.f.*, (metal.) pena gold, pena silver ; (bot.) kernel of the fir-apple.

****pignocher**, *v.n.*, to eat without appetite.

****pignon**, *n.m.*, gable end (of a house—*de maison*); kernel (of a fir-apple—*de pomme de pin*); (mec.) pinion. *Avoir — sur rue;* to have a house of one's own.

pignorati-f, -ve, *adj.*, (jur.) having the power of buying again.

pilaire, *adj.*, pertaining to the hair.

pilastre, *n.m.*, (arch.) pilaster.

pilau, *n.m.*, pillaff (stewed rice—*ragoût de riz*).

pile, *n.f.*, pile, heap ; pier (of a bridge—*de pont*); mole (mas.); (arch.) tambour ; (of coins —*de pièces de monnaie*) reverse, pile. *Mettre en —;* to pile up. — *de cuivre;* pile of weights. — *voltaïque,* — *de Volta,* — *galvanique;* voltaic, galvanic battery. — *ou face, croix ou —;* head or tail, man or woman. *Jouer à — ou face, à croix ou —;* to play at head or tail, to toss.

pile-culée, *n.f.* (—*s* —*s*), abutment-pier.

piler, *v.a.*, to pound.

pileur, *n.m.*, pounder, beater.

pileu-x, -se, *adj.* V. **pilaire**.

pilier, *n.m.*, pillar, column, post ; (pers.) support, supporter. — *de cabaret;* tavern-haunter, perpetual tippler. — *butant;* butting pillar. — *de carrière;* pillar, support of a quarry.

****pillage**, *n.m.*, pillage, plunder. *Livrer au —;* to give up to plunder. *Tout y est au —;* every one there plunders just as he likes.

****pillard, -e**, *n.* and *adj.*, pillager, plunderer ; pillaging, plundering.

****piller**, *v.a.*, to pillage, to plunder. to ransack ; to purloin, to pilfer ; to attack (of dogs—*des chiens*). — *une ville;* to plunder a town. *Ce chien pille tous les autres chiens ;* that dog attacks, flies at, all the other dogs.

****pillerie**, *n.f.*, pillage, plunder, pilfer, extortion.

****pilleur**, *n.m.*, pillager, plunderer, pilferer.

pilon, *n.m.*, pestle ; stamper. *Mettre au —;* to tear up (books—*livres*).

pilonnage, *n.m.*, (tech.) pugging ; pounding.

pilonner, *v.a.*, (tech.) to pug ; to pound.

pilori, *n.m.*, pillory. *Mettre quelqu'un au —* (fig.); to defame somebody.

pilorier, *v.a.*, to pillory, to put in the pillory.

piloris, *n.m.*, (mam.) musk-rat.

piloselle, *n.f.*, (bot.) mouse-ear.

pilot (pi-lô), *n.m.*, (tech.) heap of salt ; pile, stake of timber.

pilotage, *n.m.*, pile-driving, piling ; (nav.) piloting.

pilote, *n.m.*, pilot. — *côtier;* coasting pilot. — *lamaneur;* coasting, harbour, river pilot. — *hauturier;* sea pilot.

piloter, *v.a.* and *n.*, (tech.) to pile, to drive piles in.

piloter, *v.a.*, (nav.) to pilot ; (fig., fam.) to guide, to serve as a guide.

pilotin, *n.m.*, (nav.) pilot-boy.

pilotis, *n.m.*, piling, pile-work ; stilt (of bridges—*de ponts*).

pilule, *n.f.*, (pharm.) pill. *Dorer la —;* to gild the pill.

pilum, *n.m.* (—), (antiq.) heavy javelin of the Roman infantry.

pimbêche, *n.f.*, impertinent woman. *Quelle —! what a minx !*

piment, *n.m.*, pimento, capsicum, all-spice.

pimpant, -e, *adj.*, fine, spruce, smart.

☉**pimpesquée**, *n.f.*, affected woman.

pimprenelle, *n.f.*, (bot.) pimpernel, burnet. — *d'Afrique;* honey-flower.

pin, *n.m.*, (bot.) pine-tree, pine, Scotch fir. *Pomme de —;* fir-cone ; fir-nut ; fir-apple.

pinace, *n.f.* V. **pinasse**.

pinacle, *n.m.*, pinnacle. *Mettre quelqu'un sur le —;* to praise any one to the skies. *Il est sur le —;* he is as high as he can go.

pinaie, *n.f.*, pine-plantation.

pinasse, *or* **pinace**, *n.f.*, (nav.) pinnace.

pinastre, *n.m.*, (bot.) pinaster.

pinçard, *adj.*, wearing the shoe at the toe (of a horse—*du cheval*).

pince, *n.f.*, pliers, nippers ; tongs ; hold ; gripe ; crow, crowbar (lever—*levier*); sharp-pointed fold (in garments, &c.—*dans les vêtements, &c.*); toe (of a horse's foot—*du pied du cheval*); claw (of a lobster—*du homard*); edge (of a deer's hoof—*du pied du cerf*); (surg.) forceps. *Petites —s;* tweezers. —*s à sucre;* sugar-tongs. —*s d'un cheval;* horse's fore-teeth. — *d'un fer à cheval;* front of a horse-shoe. *Prendre une bûche avec la —;* to take up a log with the tongs. *Être menacé de la —, craindre la —;* to be in danger of being arrested. to fear being arrested. *Gare la —;* mind you are not sent to prison. *Avoir la — forte, la — rude;* to have a good gripe.

pincé, -e, *adj.*, affected, stiff.

pinceau, *n.m.*, pencil, brush. *Trait, coup, de —;* dash, stroke, of the pencil. *Avoir un beau —* (paint.); to have a fine touch.

pincée, *n.f.*, pinch (quantity taken between the thumb and fingers—*quantité prise entre le pouce et un doigt*).

pincelier, *n.m.*, (paint.) dip-cup.

****pince-maille**, *n.m.* (—, *or* —*s*), pinch-penny, skinflint.

pincement, *n.m.*, (agri.) nipping off of the heads of buds.

pince-nez, *n.m.* (—), double eye-glass.

pincer, *v.a.*, to pinch, to press, to hold fast, to gripe ; to bite ; to nip, to nip off ; to rally, to reproach ; to surprise, to catch ; to play (the guitar, harp, &c.—*de la guitare, de la harpe, &c.*); (nav.) to hug. — *les petits bourgeons d'un arbre;* to nip off the small buds of a tree. — *de la harpe;* to play upon the harp. — *quelqu'un;* to give any one a nip. *Il pince en riant;* he can nip and laugh. — *le vent* (nav.); to hug the wind.

se **pincer**, *v.r.*, to pinch one's self.

pincer, *v.n.*, to pinch, to rally, to reproach ; to play (the guitar, harp, &c.—*de la guitare, de la harpe, etc.*); (man.) to place the spur very near the horse without touching it.

pince-sans-rire, *n.m.* (—), sly, malicious person.

pincette, *n.f.*, *or* **pincettes**, *n.f.pl.*, tongs, tweezers, nippers. *On ne le toucherait pas avec des —s;* a person would not touch him with a pair of tongs.

pinchina, *n.m.*, thick, coarse woollen cloth.

pinçon, *n.m.*, mark left on the skin by a severe pinch.

pinçure, *n.f.*, pinching, pinch ; crease (in cloth—*dans le drap*).

pindarique, *adj.*, pindaric.

pindariser, *v.n.*, to speak affectedly ; to talk fustian, bombast ; to write fustian, bombast.

pindariseur, *n.m.*, ranter, talker of fustian, bombast; writer of fustian, bombast.

pinde, *n.m.*. Pindus; (fig.) poets, poetry. *Les déesses du* —; the Muses.

pinéal, -e. *adj.*, (anat.) pineal.

pineau. *n.m.*. black Burgundy grape.

pingouin, or **pinguin**, *n.m.*, (orni.) penguin; auk.

pingre, *n.m.* and *adj.*, (pop.) miser; avaricious, mean.

pinne, or **pinne marine**, *n.f.*, (mol.) pinna.

pinné. -e, *adj.*, (bot.) pinnate, pinnated.

pinnule, *n.f.*, pinule (of mathematical instruments—*d'instruments de mathématiques*).

pinque, *n.f.*, (nav.) pink.

pinson, *n.m.*, (orni.) finch; chaffinch. *Gai comme un* —; as gay as a lark.

pintade, *n.f.*, (orni.) Guinea-fowl, pintado.

pinte, *n.f.*, pint (obsolete measure—*ancienne mesure*).

pinter, *v.n.*, to tipple, to guzzle.

pioche. *n.f.*, pickaxe, mattock.

piocher, *v.a.*, to dig.

piocher, *v.n.*, to dig ; to fag, to work hard, to study hard. *Il a tant pioché qu'il a terminé l'ouvrage en un mois:* he has worked away so hard that he has finished the work in a month.

piocheur, *n.m.*, digger; hard-working student.

pioler. *V.* **piauler**.

pion, *n.m.*, pawn (at chess—*aux échecs*); man (at draughts—*aux dames*); man without property or resources; usher (in a school—*de collège, d'école*). *Damer le* — *à quelqu'un*; to outdo any one.

pione. *n.f. V.* **pivoine** (bot.).

pionner, *v.n.*, to take pawns (at chess—*aux échecs*).

pionnier, *n.m.*, pioneer.

piot (piô), *n.m.*, (pop.) wine

piote. *n.f.*, a species of gondola.

pioupiou (pioo-), *n.m.*, (—s), (pop.) foot-soldier, worm-crusher.

pipe, *n.f.*, pipe, tobacco-pipe; pipe (cask—*tonneau*).

pipeau, *n.m.*, pipe, oaten pipe, shepherd's pipe; bird-call; limed twig; snare.

pipée, *n.f.*, catching birds with a bird-call.

piper, *v.a.*, to catch birds with a bird-call; to deceive, to trick; to dupe, to cheat ; to prepare (cards—*cartes*) ; to load, to cog (dice—*dés*).

piperesse. (st.e.)fem. of **pipeur**, which see.

⊙**piperie** (pi-prî), *n.f.*, cheating (at play—*au jeu*); deceit, trickery.

pipeu-r, -se, *n.* and *adj.*, cheat, trickster (at play—*au jeu*); cheat, deceiver ; cheating, deceitful.

pipi, *n.m.*, (triv.) urine, water. *Faire* —; to piddle.

pipi, or **pitpit**, *n.m.*, (orni.) titling, titlark, pipit.

piquant, -e. *adj.*, prickly, stinging; sharp, pungent; biting, nipping; cutting, keen; lively, piquant, pointed, smart. *De la moutarde* — *e* ; hot mustard. *Froid* — ; biting cold. *Des mots* —*s*; pointed words, cutting words. *Il a une conversation* —*e*; his conversation is lively. *Elle a l'air* —; she has a lively air.

piquant, *n.m.*, prickle, quill (of porcupines —*du porc-épic*); pungency, point; piquancy. *Le* — *de la chose;* the point of the matter.

pique, *n.f.*, pike (weapon—*arme*); ⊙ pike-man; pique, quarrel. *Bois de* — ; pikestaff. *Demi*— ; short pike. *Être à cent* — *s de* ; to be far off in guessing. *Être à cent* —*s au-dessus, au-dessous, de quelqu'un, de quelque chose* ; to be far above, below, anyone, anything. *Petite* — ; slight pique, quarrel, tiff. *Par* —; out of pique.

pique, *n.m.*, spade (at cards—*aux cartes*).

piqué, -e, *part.*, quilted ; larded. *Jupon* — ; quilted petticoat. *Poulet* —; larded chicken.

piqué, *n.m.*, quilting.

pique-assiette, *n.m.* (—, *or* —*s*), spunger.

pique-bœuf. *n.m.* (—, *or* —*s*), cattle-drover; (orni.) buphaga, beefeater.

pique-nique, *n.m.* (—*s*), picnic. *Faire un* —; to have a picnic.

piquer, *v.a.*, to prick; to goad ; to sting; to bite ; to quilt ; to stitch ; to lard ; to stick ; to prick off, to mark off; to be piquant ; to excite, to stimulate, to urge on, to goad on ; to pique, to gall, to nettle ; to spur ; (surg.) to puncture. — *les absents* ; to prick off the absent. — *d'honneur*, to pique. — *quelqu'un jusqu'au sang;* to prick any one to the blood. — *des bœufs*; to goad oxen. *Quelle mouche le pique?* what has put him into a passion ? — *une jupe*; to quilt a petticoat. — *de la viande*; to lard meat. — *un cheval* ; to spur a horse. — *la curiosité de quelqu'un* ; to excite any one's curiosity. *Il en fut piqué*; he was nettled at it.

se **piquer**, *v.r.*, to prick one's self, to sting one's self ; to be offended, to be nettled, to feel affronted, to be piqued ; to pride one's self, to plume one's self, to pique one's self, to take a pride in ; to turn sour; to become spotted. — *d'honneur*; to make it a point of honour. — *au jeu*; to grow warm in play. *Ce papier se pique*; this paper is becoming spotted, covered with spots. *Ce vin se pique*; this wine is turning sour.

piquer, *v.n.*, to sting ; to be piquant ; (man.) to spur. — *des deux*; to spur a horse on both sides; (fig. fam.) to go very fast ; to strive.

piquet, *n.m.*, picket, peg, stake ; (milit.) picket; piquet (card game—*jeu de cartes*). *Être au* — ; to be in the corner, to stand still in one place (as a punishment in schools—*punition d'écolier*). *Être de* — (milit.); to be on picket duty. *Planter le* — ; to pitch the tents, to take up one's quarters. *Lever le* — ; to strike the tents ; to decamp. *Aller planter le* — *chez quelqu'un*; to take up one's quarters with any one.

piquette. *n.f.*, paltry wine; sour wine.

piqueur, *n.m.*, outrider; marker who notes down the names of persons absent; (cook.) one who lards (meat, &c.—*la viande, &c.*); (man.) stud-groom; (hunt.) whipper-in, huntsman. — *d'assiettes* ; spunger. — *d'écurie*; head-groom. — *de vin* ; wine-taster.

piqueu-r. *n.m.*, **-se**, *n.f.*, stitcher.

piquier, *n.m.*, pikeman.

piqûre, *n.f.*, pricking, prick, sting, puncture ; worm-hole ; (needlework—*ouvrage à l'aiguille*) quilting, stitching; (vet.) warbles.

pirate. *n.m.*, pirate, corsair, buccaneer ; extortioner.

pirater, *v.n.*, to pirate, to exercise piracy, to commit piracy.

piraterie (pi-ra-trî), *n.f.*, piracy ; act of piracy ; extortion.

pire, *adj.* and *n.m.*, worse, worst. *Le remède est* — *que le mal* ; the remedy is worse than the disease. *Le* — ; the worst. *Il n'y a* — *sourd que celui qui ne veut pas entendre:* none are so deaf as those who will not hear. *Il n'y a* — *eau que l'eau qui dort* ; still waters run deep.

piriforme. *adj.*, (anat.) pear-shaped.

pirogue (pi-rog). *n.f.*, pirogue.

pirole, *n.f.*, (bot.) winter-green.

pirouette. *n.f.*, pirouette; whirligig; subterfuge.

pirouetter. *v.n.*, to pirouette; to turn about.

pirrhonien. -ne. *adj. V.* **pyrrhonien**.

pirrhonisme. *n.m. V.* **pyrrhonisme**.

pis, *n.m.*, udder, dug (of cows, &c.—*des vaches, &c.*).

pis, *adv.* and *n.m.*, worse, worst. *Le* — *qui*

puisse arriver ; the worst that can happen.
Mettre quelqu'un au —; to bid any one do his
worst. *De mal en —, de — en —;* worse and
worse. *Qui — est;* what is worse. *Mettre les
choses au —:* to suppose the worst.

pis aller, *n.m.,* worst ; last shift. *Au —;*
at the worst ; let the worst come to the worst ;
when the worst comes to the worst. *C'est
votre —;* it is your last shift.

pisciculture, *n.f.,* pisciculture, fish culture.

piscine. *n.f.,* piscina.

piscivore, *adj.,* piscivorous.

pisé, *n.m.,* pise (mas.).

pissasphalte, *n.m.,* pissasphalt.

pissat, *n.m.,* piss, urine.

pissement (pis-mān), *n.m.,* (med.) evacuation by the urethra.

pissenlit, *n.m.,* (bot.) dandelion; pissabed.

pisser, *v.a.* and *n.,* to piss ; to make water,
to urine.

pisseu-r, *n.m.,* **-se,** *n.f.,* pisser.

pissoir, *n.m.,* public urinal.

pissoter, *v.n.,* to piss often.

pissotière, *n.f.,* public urinal; paltry fountain.

pistache, *n.f.,* pistachio, pistachio-nut.

pistachier, *n.m.,* pistachio-tree.

piste, *n.f.,* track, footprints, trace. *Suivre
quelqu'un à la —;* to trace any one. *Suivre un
lièvre à la —;* to follow the scent of a hare.

pistil, *n.m.,* (bot.) pistil.

pistole, *n.f.,* pistole (gold coin of Spain—
monnaie d'or espagnole). *Il est cousu de —s ;* he
is rolling in riches.

pistolet, *n.m.,* pistol. *Un coup de —;* a
pistol-shot. *Tirer un coup de —;* to shoot off a
pistol. *— d'arçon ;* holster-pistol.

piston, *n.m.,* sucker (of a pump—*de pompe*);
piston. *Fusil à —;* percussion-gun.

pitance, *n.f.,* pittance, allowance of food (in
monasteries, prisons—*des couvents, des prisons*).
Maigre —; short allowance. *Aller à la —;* to
go to market.

pitaud, *n.m.,* **-e,** *n.f.,* clown, lubberly person.

pite, *n.f.,* (bot.) agave.

piteusement (pi-teŭz-mān), *adj.,* piteously,
wofully, sadly.

piteu-x, -se, *adj.,* piteous, pitiable, woful.
Faire —se mine ; to look rueful. *Faire —se
chère ;* to fare badly.

pitié, *n.f.,* pity, compassion. *Émouvoir la —
de quelqu'un ;* to move any one's pity. *Cela est
digne de —;* that is deserving of pity. *Regarder
quelqu'un d'un œil de —;* to look upon one with
an eye of pity. *Il vaut mieux faire envie que —;*
better be envied than pitied. *C'est grande —,
c'est grand' —;* it is a great pity. *Vos menaces
me font —;* your threats move my pity. *Il
raisonne à faire —;* he reasons pitifully. *Regarder quelqu'un en —;* to despise any one.

piton, *n.m.,* screw-ring; (geog.) peak.

pitoyable, *adj.,* pitiful, pitiable, piteous;
compassionate: contemptible.

pitoyablement, *adv.,* pitifully, piteously;
wretchedly.

pitpit, *n.m.* V. **pipi** (orni.).

pittoresque (pit-to-rèsk), *adj.,* picturesque,
graphic.

pittoresquement (pit-to-rèsk-mān), *adv.,*
picturesquely, in a picturesque manner.

pituitaire, *adj.,* pituitary.

pituite, *n.f.,* pituite, phlegm.

pituiteu-x, -se, *adj.,* pituitous, phlegmatic.

pivert, *n.m.,* (orni.) green woodpecker.

pivoine, *n.m.,* (orni.) bullfinch,gnat-snapper.

pivoine, *or* **péone,** *or* **pione,** *n.f.,* (bot.)
piony, peony.

pivot, *n.m.,* pin, pivot ; (hort.) tap-root.

C'est le — sur lequel l'affaire tourne ; he is the
main hinge on which the business turns. *— de
meule de moulin ;* spindle of a mill.

pivotant, -e, *adj.,* (bot.) tap-rooted. *Racine
—e* (bot.); tap-root.

pivoter, *v.n.,* to turn on a pivot.

pizzicato, *n.m.* and *adv.* (—), (mus.) pizzicato.

placabilité, *n.f.,* placableness.

placable, *adj.,* placable.

placage, *n.m.,* plating (metal.); veneering
(of wood—*des bois*) ; patchwork.

placard, *n.m.,* placard; (print.) slip; cupboard (in a wall—*dans un mur*); (carp.) door-
leap. *Porte en —;* panel-door.

placarder, *v.a.,* to placard, to post up. *—
un avis au public ;* to post up a public notice.

place, *n.f.,* place, room, seat; post, employment, office, town, stronghold; fortress; square.
Retenir des —s à la diligence ; to secure seats in
a stage-coach. *Mettre chaque chose à sa —;* to
put everything in its place. *Faire — à quelqu'un ;* to make room for any one. *Il a été tué
sur la —;* he was killed upon the spot. *Il ne
saurait demeurer en —;* he can never stand
still. *Mettez-vous à ma —;* put yourself in my
place. *Si j'étais à votre —;* if I were in your
place. *— de confiance;* place of trust. *Un
homme en —;* a man in office. *— d'armes ;*
place of arms, stronghold. *La — n'est pas
tenable;* one cannot stay in that place. *— de
fiacres;* hackney-coach stand. *Une voiture de
—;* a hackney-coach. *La tête, la fin, de la —;*
the top, the bottom of the stand. *Avoir crédit
sur la —;* (com.) to have credit in the market.
— marchande; place good for trade, trading
town.

placé, -e, *part.,* placed. *Il est bien —;* he
has a good place, situation. *Il a le cœur bien —;*
his heart is in the right place. *Cela n'est pas
bien —;* that is ill-timed.

placement (plas-mān), *n.m.,* placing ;
(com.) sale; putting out, investing, investment
(money—*argent*). *Bureau de —;* intelligence-
office ; registry-office (for servants, &c.—*pour
domestiques, &c.*).

placenta (-sin-ta), *n.m.,* (anat., bot.) placenta.

placer, *n.m.* (—*s*), (gold digging) placer.

placer, *v.a.,* to place, to put, to seat, to dispose, to set, to invest. *— de l'argent à la banque ;*
to lodge money in the bank. *— de l'argent sur
l'État;* to invest money in the funds. *Il place
bien ce qu'il dit ;* what he says is to the purpose.
— quelqu'un ; to get any one a place. *— son affection en bon lieu ;* to love a deserving person.
se placer, v.r., to place one's self ; to obtain a
situation.

placet, *n.m.,* petition ; ⊙stool.

placeu-r, *n.m.,* **-se,** *n.f.,* person that places
(servants, &c.—*les domestiques, &c.*).

placide, *adj.,* placid, calm.

placidement, *adv.,* placidly.

placidité, *n.f.,* placidity, quietness.

placi-er, *n.m.,* **-ère,** *n.f.,* owner of a market-
place, underletter of standings; (com.) town
traveller.

plafond, *n.m.,* ceiling. *— en voussure ;* cove
— en corniche ; soffit.

plafonnage, *n.m.,* ceiling.

plafonner, *v.a.,* to make a ceiling.

plafonneur, *n.m.,* ceiling-maker, plasterer.

plagal, *adj.,m.,* (mus.) plagal.

plage, *n.f.,* shore, sea-shore. *— de sable ;*
sandy beach. *Vaisseau jeté sur la —;* ship
stranded on the beach.

plagiaire, *n.m.,* plagiarist, plagiary.

plagiat, *n.m.,* plagiarism.

⊙**plaid,** *n.m.,* plea. *Être sage au retour des —s ;*

to lose liking for litigations after losing a lawsuit.

plaid (plè), *n.m.*, plaid (Scotch garment—*manteau écossais*).

plaidable, *adj.*, pleadable.

plaidant, *adj.*, pleading. *Avocat —;* barrister, pleader.

plaider, *v.a.*, to plead, to argue; to be at law, to litigate. *— quelqu'un;* to sue any one at law. *— le faux pour savoir le vrai;* to plead the wrong side in order to get at the right.

plaider, *v.n.*, to plead; to be at law.

plaideu-r, *n.m.*, **-se**, *n.f.*, litigant.

plaidoirie, *n.f.*, barrister's, counsel's speech; pleading.

☞**plaidoyable**, *adj.*, (jur.) of the sitting-day, of the hearing-day, of a Court.

plaidoyer, *n.m.*, defence, speech at the bar.

plaie, *n.f.*, sore, wound; plague, evil. *Panser une —;* to dress a sore. *— envenimée;* rankling sore. *Frapper d'une —;* to smite with a plague. *Mettre le doigt sur la —;* to point out the evil.

plaignant, **-e**, *n.* and *adj.*, (jur.) complainant, prosecutor; complaining.

plain, **-e**, *adj.*, plain, even, flat. *En —e campagne;* in open country. *Chambres de — pied,* **—pied** (—); rooms on one floor. *—chant* (*n.p.*); plain chant.

plaindre (plaignant, plaint), *v.a.*, to pity, to compassionate, to commiserate; to grudge. *Je vous plains;* I pity you. *Il est à —;* he is to be pitied. *— sa peine;* to grudge one's pains. *— le pain qu'ils mangent;* to grudge the very bread they eat. *Il ne plaint rien à ses enfants,* he grudges his children nothing.

se plaindre, *v.r.*, to complain, to groan, to moan; to grudge. *J'ai bien lieu de me plaindre de vous;* I have good reason to complain of you. *— en justice;* to lodge a complaint in court.

plaine, *n.f.*, a plain.

plainte, *n.f.*, complaint, plaint; groaning. *Porter —;* to lodge a complaint.

plainti-f, **-ve**, *adj.*, plaintive, querulous, complaining, doleful.

plaintivement (-tiv-măn), *adv.*, plaintively, mournfully, dolefully.

plaire (plaisant, plu), *v.n.*, to please, to be agreeable; to delight. *— à quelqu'un;* to please any one. *Cela vous plait à dire;* you are pleased to say so. *Plait-il!* what do you say? *Je ferai ce qu'il vous plaira;* I will do what you please. *Il ne me plaît pas que vous y alliez;* I do not like that you should go there. *Si cela ne vous plait pas;* if you are averse to it. *Plût à Dieu;* would to God. *À Dieu ne plaise;* God forbid.

se plaire, *v.r.*, to delight in, to take pleasure in; to like, to love; to be pleased with. *Il se plaît à faire du mal;* he delights in doing mischief.

plaisamment (plè-za-măn), *adv.*, humorously, pleasantly; ludicrously, laughably.

plaisance, *n.f.*, pleasure. *Maison de —;* villa. *Bateau de —;* pleasure boat.

plaisant, **-e**, *adj.*, pleasant; humorous, ludicrous, comical, pretty. *C'est le plus — homme du monde;* he is the most jocose fellow alive. *Ce sont de —es gens* (iron.); they are pretty people. *Il vous a fait un — régal;* he gave you a pleasant entertainment. *C'est un — personnage;* he is a pretty fellow.

plaisant, *n.m.*, jester; humour; ludicrousness. *Il fait le —;* he plays the jester. *Un mauvais —;* a sorry jester. *Le — de l'aventure;* the laughable part of the adventure.

plaisanter, *v.a.*, to joke, to banter, to jeer.

plaisanter, *v.n.*, to jest, to joke, to make merry. *Il plaisante sur tout;* he jests about everything. *C'est un homme qui ne plaisante pas;*

he is no jester. *Il ne plaisante pas là-dessus;* he is no jester on that score.

plaisanterie, *n.f.*, pleasantry, jesting, joking, jest, joke; mockery. *— de bon ton, de mauvais ton;* genteel, vulgar, pleasantry. *— légère, piquante;* light, pointed, pleasantry. *Cela est dit par —;* that is said in jest. *— à part;* without jesting. *Il sait manier, il manie bien, la —;* he knows how to turn, to manage, a jest well.

plaisir, *n.m.*, pleasure, delight, joy; recreation, diversion, sport, entertainment; will, consent, approbation; favour, courtesy, kindness, good turn. *Faire —;* to give pleasure. *Se faire un — de;* to take pleasure in. *Se faire un — de son devoir;* to make a pleasure of one's duty. *Prendre — à quelque chose;* to delight in any thing. *Cela fait — à voir;* that is a pleasant sight. *Nul — sans peine;* no joy without alloy. *La peine passe le —;* the pain exceeds the pleasure. *Partie de —;* pleasure party. *Jouer pour le —, pour son —;* to play for love, for diversion. *Menus —s;* pocket-money. *Faites-moi un —;* do me a favour. *À —;* carefully; at one's ease. *Un conte fait à —;* a made up story, a tale, a lie. *Par —;* for pastime, for sport; (fam., l.u.) by way of trial.

plamée, *n.f.*, lime used in building after serving to remove hair from hides.

plan, *n.m.*, plane; plan, draught, design, model; scheme, project; ground, perspective. *— incliné;* inclined plane. *Arrière— (—-—s);* (paint.) back-ground. *— d'arrimage* (nav.); tier. *— de niveau;* datum line. *Lever des —s,* surveying. *Faire le — de;* to survey. *— à vue d'oiseau;* bird's-eye view. *— en relief;* plan in relief. *Lever un —;* to take a plan. *Faire l'élévation d'un —;* to give a raised plan.

plan, **-e**, *adj.*, even, plain, level, flat.

planche, *n.f.*, board, plank; (engr.) plate; (gard.) bed, border. *—s d'un bateau;* planks, ribs, of a boat. *Faire la —;* to float on one's back. *Monter sur les —s;* to tread the boards. *S'appuyer sur une — pourrie;* to lean upon a rotten staff. *Faire la — aux autres;* to show others the way. *— à débarquer;* gangboard of a boat. *— de salut;* sheet anchor.

planchéiage, *n.m.*, boarding, planking, flooring.

planchéier, *v.a.*, to plank, to floor with planks.

plancher, *n.m.*, floor; ceiling; (nav.) stage. *— parqueté;* inlaid, wooden floor. *— carrelé;* brick, stone floor. *Frotter un —;* to scrub a floor. *Le — des vaches;* dry land. *Sauter au —;* to jump to the ceiling.

planchette, *n.f.*, little board; (math.) plane table.

plançon, or **plantard**, *n.m.*, sapling; slip of willow, &c.

plane, *n.m.* *V.* **platane**.

plane, *n.f.*, drawing-knife; turning chisel; spoke-shave.

planer, *v.n.*, to hover, to tower; to soar; to look down (from on high—*de haut*). *Un milan qui plane;* a kite hovering. *— sur les difficultés;* to soar above difficulties.

planer, *v.a.*, to make smooth, to plane, to planish. *— un morceau de bois;* to plane a piece of wood. *— le cuivre;* to beat copper smooth. *— une peau;* to strip the wool off a skin.

planétaire, *adj.*, planetary.

planétaire, *n.m.*, planetarium, orrery.

planète, *n.f.*, planet.

planeur, *n.m.*, (manu.) planisher.

planimétrie, *n.f.*, (geom.) planimetry.

planisphère, *n.m.*, planisphere.

in **plano**, *adv.* *V.* **in plano**.

plant, *n.m.*, set, twig, plant, young plant,

slip, plantation. — *de vigne ;* slip of vine. *Jeune* — ; vineyard newly set ; plantation of young trees.

plantage, *n.m.,* planting ; plantation (of sugar-canes, tobacco, &c.—*de cannes à sucre, de tabac, &c.*).

plantain. *n.m.,* (bot.) plantain.

plantard, *n.m. V.* **plançon.**

plantation, *n.f.,* planting ; plantation.

plante, *n.f.,* sole of the foot ; (bot.) plant. — *ligneuse ;* ligneous plant. — *fibreuse ;* fibrous plant. — *herbacée ;* herbaceous plant. *Le jardin des* —*s ;* the botanical garden. —*s marines ;* marine plants. —*s parasites ;* parasitical plants. —*s à tuyau ;* culmiferous plants.

planter, *v.a.* and *n.,* to plant, to set, to fix. — *des oignons, des pois;* to plant onions, peas. — *des bornes;* to set bounds. — *le piquet en quelque lieu;* to take up one's quarters in any place. — *là quelqu'un;* to leave any one in the lurch, to give any one the slip. *Maison bien plantée ;* house well seated. *Cheveux bien plantés;* hair well placed.

se **planter**, *v.r.,* to be planted ; to place one's self.

planteur, *n.m.,* planter.

plantigrade, *n.m.* and *adj.,* plantigrade animal ; plantigrade ; *pl.,* plantigrada, plantigrades.

plantoir, *n.m.,* dibble.

planton, *n.m.,* (milit.) orderly. *Être de* —; to be on orderly's duty.

plantule. *n.f.,* (bot.) plantule.

plantureusement (-reûz-măn), *adv.,* (fam.) plentifully, copiously.

plantureu-x, -se, *adj.,* plentiful, copious ; abundant.

planure, *n.f.,* shavings (of wood—*de bois*).

plaque, *n.f.,* plate ; slab ; badge. — *de fonte ;* plate of cast iron. — *de porte-faix ;* badge of a porter. — *tournante* (railways); turning plate.

plaqué, *n.m.,* plated metal.

plaqué, -e. *part.,* plated.

plaqueminier, *n.m.,* (bot.) ebony-tree.

plaquer, *v.a.,* to plate ; to lay on. — *du bois ;* to veneer wood. — *des bijoux ;* to plate jewels.

plaquette, *n.f.,* small thin book ; a small copper coin.

plaqueur, *n m.,* veneerer ; plater.

plasticité, *n.f.,* plasticity.

plastique, *n.f.* and *adj.,* plastic art ; plastic.

plastron, *n.m.,* breast-plate ; (fenc.) plastron ; laughing-stock, butt ; drill-plate.

plastronner, *v.a.,* to put a plastron on (any one—*à quelqu'un*).

se **plastronner,** *v.r.,* to put on a plastron, to plastron one's self.

plat, *n.m.,* dish ; (nav.) mess ; sheet (of glass—*de verre*) ; flat side (of anything—*d'un objet*). — *d'argent ;* silver dish. — *apprêté ;* made dish. — *réchauffé ;* warmed-up dish. *Camarade de* — ; messmate. — *de l'équipage* (nav.) ; mess for seven men. *Servir un* — *de son métier ;* to give a specimen of one's work. *C'est un* — *de son métier ;* this is one of his tricks. —*s de balance;* scales of a balance. *Des coups de* — *d'épée ;* strokes with the flat side of a sword.

plat, -e. *adj.,* flat ; dull, insipid, spiritless. *Un pays* — : a flat country. *Cheveux* —*s ;* straight hair. *Elle a la physionomie* —*e ;* she has an unmeaning countenance. *Vin* — ; flat wine. *Cheval* —, lank horse. *Avoir le ventre* — ; to have an empty belly. *Sa bourse est bien* —*e ;* his purse is very low. *Son armée a été battue à* —*e couture ;* his army has been utterly defeated. *Un pied* —. *un* — *pied :* a worthless

fellow. *Un style* — ; a flat style. *C'est un* — *personnage;* he is a dull fellow.

platane, *n.m.,* plane-tree, platane.

plataniste. *n.m.,* (antiq.) grove of platanes.

plat-bord, *n.m.* (—*s* —*s*), (nav.) gunwale, gunnel, port-last. *Lisses de* — ; drift-rails.

plateau, *n.m.,* wooden scale ; waiter, tray, tea-tray ; upland, table-land.

plate-bande, *n.f.* (—*s* —*s*), (arch., hort.) plat-band ; border. — *de baie ;* lintel of a door or window.

platée, *n.f.,* (arch.) massive foundation under the whole area of the building ; dishful.

plate-forme, *n.f.* (—*s* —*s*), platform. — *de batterie ;* platform of a battery. — *de fondation* (carp.) ; sleepers.

plate-longe, *n.f.* (—*s* —*s*), kicking-strap (for horses—*de chevaux*) ; (man.) leading-rein.

platement (plat-măn), *adv.,* flatly, dully, rigidly, without spirit.

plateur, *n.f..* (jest., l u.) flatness.

plateure, *n.f.,* (metal.) vein which, after sinking vertically or obliquely, assumes a horizontal direction.

platine, *n.f.,* (print.) platine ; lock (of fire-arms—*d'armes à feu*) ; (tech.) plate. —*s de montre :* plates of a watch. — *de serrure ;* plate of a lock.

platine, *n.m.,* (metal.) platinum.

platise, *n.f.,* (l.u.) dull, senseless writing or words.

platitude, *n.f.,* platitude, dullness ; flatness.

platonicien, -ne (si-in, si-èn), *n.* and *adj.,* Platonist ; Platonic.

platonique, *adj.,* Platonic.

platonisme, *n.m.,* Platonism.

plâtrage, *n.m.,* plaster-work, plastering ; unsolid work.

plâtras, *n.m.,* old plaster-work ; rubbish

plâtre, *n.m.,* plaster ; (b.s.) paint (on the face—*sur la figure*). *Enduire de* — ; to coat with plaster. — *cuit ;* calcined plaster. *Battre quelqu'un comme* —; to beat any one to a mummy.

plâtré, -e, *part.,* plastered. *Visage* — ; painted face. *Paix* —*e ;* patched-up peace.

plâtrer, *v.a.,* to plaster ; to patch up, to piece up ; (agri.) to manure with plaster.

se **plâtrer,** *v.r.,* (b.s.) to paint one's self. *Elle se plâtre* (b.s.) ; she paints her face.

plâtreu-x, -se, *adj.,* chalky.

plâtrier, *n.m.,* plasterer.

plâtrière, *n.f.,* chalk-pit, plaster-quarry.

plausibilité, *n.f.,* plausibleness.

plausible. *adj.,* plausible.

plausiblement, *adv.,* plausibly.

plèbe, *n.f.,* common people.

plébéien, -ne (-in, -è-n), *n.* and *adj.,* plebeian.

plébiscite, *n.m.,* plebiscitum.

pléiade. *n.f.,* **pléiades,** *n.f. pl.,* Pleiades ; the seven stars.

⊙**pleige,** *n.m ,* (jur.) pledge.

⊙**pleiger,** *v.a.,* (jur.) to pledge.

plein, -e. *adj.,* full, filled, replete ; copious. *Rivière* —*e de poissons ;* river well stocked with fish. *Livre* — *d'érudition :* book stored with learning. *Homme* — *d'esprit ;* man full of wit. — *comme un œuf ;* as full as an egg. — *e lune :* full moon. *Une chienne* —*e ;* a bitch with young. —*e récolte :* plentiful crop. *Voguer à* —*es voiles :* to go with full sails. *Arbre en* — *vent ;* tree in the open air. *Être en* —*e mer ;* to be out at sea. *En* —*e rue ,* in the middle of the street *En* — *jour :* in broad daylight. *En* — *midi .* at high noon. *En* — *e nuit ;* in the dead of night. *En* —*e paix ;* in the midst of peace. *Avoir le cœur* — ; to have one's heart full. *Donner à* —*e*

main, à —es mains ; to give, to bestow, largely.
Porter — (nav.) ; to keep the sails full.
plein, n.m., full part ; plenum. Dans le — ; in the middle. À pur et à — ; fully, to the full, entirely.
plein, adv., full. — les deux mains ; both hands full. En — ; fully, entirely. À pur et à — ; altogether, completely. Tout —, a great many, numbers, very many.
pleinement, adv., fully, to the full.
plénière, adj.f., plenary. Indulgence — ; plenary indulgence. Cour —, plenary court.
plénipotentiaire, n.m. and adj., plenipotentiary.
plénitude, n.f., plenitude, fulness.
pléonasme, n.m., pleonasm.
pléonastique, adj., pleonastic.
plésiosaure, n.m., (foss.) plesiosaur, plesiosaurus.
pléthore, n.f., plethora.
pléthorique, adj., plethoric.
pleu-pleu, or **plui-plui,** n.m. (—), green woodpecker.
pleurant, -e, adj., weeping, crying.
pleurard, n.m., puling, squalling child.
pleure, n.f., (anat.). V. **plèvre.**
pleure-misère, n.m. (—), miser always complaining of poverty ; curmudgeon.
pleurer, v.n., to cry, to weep, to shed tears, to bewail, to mourn. — comme un enfant ; to cry like a child. — amèrement ; to weep bitterly. — à chaudes larmes ; to shed bitter tears. — de joie ; to weep for joy. — à volonté ; to cry at will. — sur quelqu'un ; to weep over any one. — sur ses péchés ; to weep for one's sins.
pleurer, v.a., to weep, to bewail ; to lament ; to mourn ; to grudge. — son père ; to mourn one's father.
pleurésie, n.f., pleurisy.
pleurétique, adj., pleuritic.
pleureu-r, n.m., **-se,** n.f., weeper ; mourner.
pleureur, n.m., (mam.) weeper, sapajou (monkey—singe).
pleureu-r.-se, adj., weeping, crying, mournful, tearful. Saule — ; weeping willow.
pleureuses, n.f.pl., bands of cambric formerly worn on the sleeves at the beginning of mourning.
pleureu-x, -se, adj., weeping, crying.
pleurnichement (-nish-män), n.m., whine, whining.
pleurnicher, v.n., to snivel, to whimper, to whine.
pleurnicherie (-nl-shrl), n.f., whining.
pleurnicheu-r, n.m., **-se,** n.f., whimperer, sniveller.
pleuronecte, n.m., (ich.) pleuronectes.
pleuropneumonie, n.f., (med.) pleuropneumonia.
pleurs, n.m.pl., tears ; crying, weeping ; bleeding (of a vine—de la vigne). Des —touchants, moving tears. Verser, répandre, des — ; to shed tears. Essuyer ses — ; to dry one's tears.
pleutre, n.m., coward ; contemptible fellow.
pleuvoir (pleuvant, plu), v.imp., to rain. Il pleut à verse ; it pours with rain. — à petites gouttes ; to drizzle. — des hallebardes ; to rain pitchforks, to rain cats and dogs. L'argent y pleut ; it rains riches there. — à seaux ; to rain in torrents. Comme s'il pleuvait ; in quantities, a great quantity.
plèvre, n.f., (anat.) pleura.
plexus (plèk-sus), n.m., (anat.) plexus.
pleyon, n.m., osier-tie.
pli, n.m., plait, fold, bend, wrinkle, crease. Cet habit ne fait pas un — ; that coat has not a wrinkle in it. Sous le même — ; under the same cover. Fouiller dans tous les —s et replis, sonder tous les —s et replis, du cœur ; to search into the

inmost recesses of the heart. Un faux — ; a crease (in stuffs—dans les étoffes). Il a pris son — ; he has taken his bent. Avoir des —s au front ; to have wrinkles in one's forehead. Le — du bras : the bend of the arm.
pliable, adj., pliable, pliant, bending, flexible, supple.
pliage, n.m., folding.
pliant, -e, adj., pliant, pliable, bending, flexible, supple. Siège — ; a folding-stool.
pliant, n.m., folding-stool, fold-stool.
plica, n.m., (med.). V. **plique.**
plicatile, adj., (bot.) plicate, twining.
pliciforme, adj., in the form of a fold.
plie, n.f., (ich.) plaice.
plié, -e, part., folded.
plié, n.m., bend of the knee in dancing.
pliement (pli-män), n.m., act of folding.
plier, v.a., to fold, to fold up ; to bend ; to bring under. — une lettre ; to fold a letter. — du linge ; to fold up linen. — les voiles ; to furl the sails. — bagage ; to decamp, to pack off. — les genoux ; to bend one's knees. — son esprit aux volontés d'autrui ; to bend one's mind to the will of others.
se plier, v.r., to be folded, bent ; to bow, to bend. Se ne saurais me — à cela ; I cannot stoop to that.
plier, v.n., to bend ; to yield ; to give way. Faire — un arc ; to bend a bow. Il vaut mieux — que rompre ; better bend than break. — sous l'autorité de quelqu'un ; to yield to any one's authority. L'infanterie plia ; the infantry gave way.
plieu-r, n.m., **-se,** n.f., folder.
plinthe, n.f., (arch.) plinth.
plioir, n.m., folding-knife.
plique, n.f., (med.) plica.
plissement (plis-män), n.m., folding ; plaiting.
plisser, v.a., to plait.
plisser, v.n., to form plaits.
plissure, n.f., plaiting.
ploc, n.m., (nav.) sheathing hair.
plomb (plon), n.m., lead, shot ; plumb-line, plummet ; custom-house seal ; sink. Menu — ; small shot. — en saumon ; pig-lead. Jeter son — sur quelque chose ; to have an eye upon anything. Mine de — ; black-lead pencil, lead. — de vitres ; came. À — ; perpendicularly, directly ; perpendicular. Tomber à — ; to plumb.
plombage, n.m., leading, lead work.
plombagine, n.f., plumbago, black-lead.
plombé, -e, part., leaded, leady. Dent —e, tooth that has been stopped. Il a le teint — ; he has a livid complexion.
plomber, v.a., to lead ; to mark or stamp with lead ; to stop (a tooth—une dent) ; to plumb. — le faîte d'un toit ; to lead the ridge of a roof. — un mur ; to plumb a wall.
plomberie (plon-brî), n.f., plumbery ; lead-making ; lead-manufactury ; lead-works.
plombeur, n.m., custom-house officer who affixes the lead-stamp on merchandise.
plombier, n.m., plumber.
plombifère, adj., plumbiferous.
plongé, -e, part., immersed ; dipped (of candles—chandelles) ; sunk (in despair—dans le désespoir). Chandelle —e, dipped candle.
plongeant, -e (-jän, -t), adj., plunging. Vue —e ; view from a height. Feu — ; fire (of musketry, &c.—de mousqueterie, &c.) coming from above.
plongée, n.f., (fort.) talus of the parapet.
plongement, n.m., plunging, dipping ; dip ; (of ships and carriages—de vaisseaux et de voitures) pitching.

plongeon (-jon), *n.m.*, (orni.) diver. *Faire le —;* to dive; to duck; to flinch.

plonger, *v.a.*, to plunge, to dip, to immerse. *— quelqu'un dans la douleur;* to plunge any one into grief.

se **plonger**, *v.r.*, to plunge. *— dans la douleur;* to abandon one's self to grief.

plonger, *v.n.*, to dive, to dip; to duck; to take a downward direction; to pitch (of ships, of carriages—*de vaisseaux et de voitures*).

plongeur, *n.m.*, plunger, diver. *Cloche de —;* diving-bell.

plongeur, *adj.*, (hydr.) plunging.

ploquer, *v.a.*, to apply sheathing hair (to a ship's bottom—*à la carène d'un vaisseau*).

ployable, *adj.*, pliable, easy to bend.

ployer, *v.a.*, to bend, to bow; to fold up.

se **ployer**, *v.r.*, to be bent, to be folded; to bend, to give way.

ployer, *v.n.*, to bend; to yield, to submit.

pluche. *V.* **peluche.**

pluie, *n.f.*, rain; shower (abundance—*abondance*). *Un jour de —;* a rainy day. *Il tombe de la —;* it rains. *Petite — abat grand vent;* a little rain lays a great dust. *Après la —, le beau temps;* after clouds, fair weather. *— battante;* pelting rain. *Le temps est à la —;* it looks likely to rain. *Faire la — et le beau temps;* to make both rain and sunshine, to do what one pleases. *Parler de la — et du beau temps;* to talk of indifferent things.

plui-plui, *n.m.* *V.* **pleu-pleu.**

plumage, *n.m.*, plumage, feathers.

** **plumail**, *n.m.*, feather-broom.

plumasseau, *n.m.*, quill (for harpsichords —*pour clavecins*); feather (of arrows—*de flèches*); (surg.) pledget; feather-broom, duster.

plumasserie (-ma-sri), *n.f.*, feather-trade.

plumassier, *n.m.*, feather-merchant.

plume, *n.f.*, feather, quill, pen. *— d'acier;* steel pen. *Tailler une —;* to mend, to cut a pen. *Mettre la main à la —;* to take pen in hand. *Se laisser aller au courant de la —;* to write off-hand, to be guided by one's pen. *— de corbeau;* crow-quill. *La belle — fait le bel oiseau;* fine feathers make fine birds. *Il est au poil et à la —;* he is fit for anything. *Il y a laissé de ses —s;* he has been stripped of his feathers. *Passer la — par le bec à quelqu'un;* to baffle any one. *La fente d'une —;* the slit of a pen. *Le bec d'une —;* the nib of a pen. *Une bonne —;* a good penman. *Jeter la — au vent;* to allow chance to decide.

plumeau, *n.m.*, feather-broom, duster; penstand.

plumée, *n.f.*, penful (of ink—*d'encre*); plucking goose-feathers; quantity of feathers plucked from a bird.

plumer, *v.a.*, to pluck, to plume; to fleece. *— une volaille;* to pluck a fowl. *— quelqu'un;* to fleece any one. *— la poule sans la faire crier;* to fleece the sheep without making it bleat.

plumet, *n.m.*, plume, ostrich feather; plume of feathers.

plumetis (plum-ti), *n.m.*, tambouring (embroidering—*broderie*).

plumeu-x, -se, *adj.*, (bot.) plumous, feathery.

plumipède, *n.m.*, plumiped.

plumitif, *n.m.*, (jur.) minute-book.

plum-pudding, *n.m.* (— —s). *V.* **pouding.**

plumule, *n.f.*, (bot.) plumule.

plupart, *n.f.*, most, most part, the greatest part; generality, most people. *La — du monde prétend;* most people say. *La — de ses amis l'abandonnèrent;* most of his friends forsook him. *La — écrivent;* most people write. *Pour la —;* mostly. *Les hommes sont pour la — intéressés;*

the generality of men are selfish. *La — du temps;* generally.

pluralité, *n.f.*, plurality.

pluriel, -le, *adj.*, (gram.) plural.

pluriel, *n.m.*, (gram.) plural.

plus, *adv.*, more, over, most; also, moreover; further; besides; plus. *— aimable que sage;* more lovely than wise. *— savant que lui;* more learned than he. *Il a — d'argent que;* he has more money than. *Il m'en coûte — qu'à vous;* it costs me dearer than you. *Il a — de vingt ans;* he is above twenty. *Nous sommes — qu'à moitié persuadés;* we are more than half convinced. *Je n'y retournerai —;* I will go there no more. *— je la vois, — je la hais;* the more I see her, the more I hate her. *— loin, further. — près, de — près;* nearer. *— de larmes;* no more tears. *N'avoir — rien;* to have nothing left. *Il y a — ; what is more. Il y en a tant et —; there is abundance of it. Au —, tout au —; at most. Il a tout au — trente ans;* he is thirty at most. *De —; besides, moreover, again, furthermore, nay. De —, il faut remarquer;* you must observe besides. *D'autant —; the more so. De — en —; more and more. Il s'enrichit de — en —;* he grows richer and richer every day. *Ni — ni moins;* neither more nor less. *Vous avez beau dire, il n'en sera ni — ni moins;* you may talk as much as you please, it will be so. *— ou moins;* more or less, thereabout. *Qui —, qui moins;* some more, some less. *Sans — différer;* without further delay. *Sans — de façon;* without any more ado. *— tard, — loin, — près;* later, farther, nearer.

plus, *n.m.*, more; most. *Le — que je puisse faire;* the most I can do.

plusieurs, *pron.* and *adj.*, *m.f.pl.*, several, many.

plus-pétition, *n.f.* (n.p.), (jur.) demand exceeding the rights of the plaintiff.

plus-que-parfait (plus-kĕ-par fè), *n.m.* (n.p.), (gram.) pluperfect tense.

plus-value, *n.f.* (— —s), (fin.) superior value.

plutonique, *adj.*, (geol.) plutonic.

plutôt, *adv.*, rather, sooner. *— mourir que faire une lâcheté;* rather die than do a dishonourable thing.

pluvial, *n.m.*, (c. rel.) pluvial.

pluvial, *adj.*, of rain.

pluvier, *n.m.*, plover.

pluvieu-x, -se, *adj.*, rainy, showery. *Un jour —;* a rainy day.

pluviomètre, *n.m.*, pluviameter, rain-gauge, udometer.

pluviôse, *n.m.*, Pluviose, fifth month of the calendar of the first French republic, from January 20th to February 18th or 19th.

pneumatique, *n.f.* and *adj.*, pneumatics; pneumatic. *Machine —;* air-pump.

pneumatocèle, *n.f.*, (med.) pneumatocele.

pneumatologie, *n.f.*, pneumatology.

pneumatose, *n.f.*, (med.) pneumatosis.

pneumonie, *n.f.*, pneumonia.

pneumonique, *n.m.f.* and *adj.*, (med.) person suffering with pneumonia; pneumonic.

pnyx, *n.m.*, (antiq.) the Pnyx (at Athens—*d'Athènes*).

pochade, *n.f.*, (paint.) rough sketch.

poche, *n.f.*, pocket; pouch; sack; bag; small fiddle; crop (of a bird—*d'oiseau*); sack (of an abscess—*d'un abcès, &c.*); (needlework—*ouvrage à l'aiguille*) pucker; wrinkle (in clothes—*dans les vêtements*). *Fouiller dans ses —s;* to search one's pockets. *Un mouchoir de —;* a pocket handkerchief. *Mettre en —;* to pocket. *Jouer de la —;* to pull out one's purse, to come down with the money. *Acheter chat en —;* to buy a pig in a poke.

poché, -e, *part.*, blotted (of writing—*écriture*); poached (of eggs—*des œufs*); black (of the eyes—*des yeux*). *Des œufs* —*s*; poached eggs. *Avoir les yeux* —*s au beurre noir*; to have eyes black and blue.

pocher, *v.a.*, to poach; to bruise. — *les yeux à quelqu'un*; to give any one a pair of black eyes.

pocheter (posh-té), *v.a.*, to keep in one's pocket.

pocheter, *v.n.*, to be kept in one's pocket.

pochette, *n.f.*,⊙pocket; net (for rabbits—*à lapins*); small fiddle. kit.

podagraire, *n.f.*, (bot.) goatweed, goutwort.

podagre, *n.f.*, podagra, gout in the feet.

podagre, *n.m.f.* and *adj.*, gouty person; afflicted with the gout, gouty, podagrical.

podestat, *n.m.*, podesta (magistrate in Italy —*magistrat italien*).

podium, *n.m.* (—), (antiq., arch.) podium.

podosperme, *n.m.*, (bot.) funiculus.

pœcile, *n.m.*, (Grec. antiq.) pœcile.

poêle, *n.f.*, frying-pan. *Tomber de la* — *dans le feu*; to jump out of the frying-pan into the fire.

poêle, *or* **poile**, *n.m.*, stove; the room in which the stove is placed.

poêle, *n.m.*, pall; (c. rel.) canopy.

poêlette, *n.f.*, small pan.

poêlier, *n.m.*, stove-maker.

poêlon, *n.m.*, saucepan.

poêlonnée, *n.f.*, saucepanful.

poème, *n.m.*, poem.

poésie, *n.f.*, poetry; poesy.

poète, *n.m.*, poet; poetess. *Méchant* —; wretched poet. — *lauréat*; poet laureate. *Elle est* — ; she is a poetess.

poétereau (po-é-trô), *n.m.*, poetaster.

poétesse, *n.f.*, (l.u.) poetess.

poétique, *n.f.* and *adj.*, poetics; poetical.

poétiquement (-tik-mân), *adv.*, poetically.

poétiser, *v.n.*, ⊙ to versify, to poetize; to make poetical.

poids (poâ), *n.m.*, weight; burden; moment. importance. *Le* — *d'un fardeau*; the weight of a burden. *Cela est le* — ; that is weight. *Un* — *de dix livres*; a ten pound weight. *Avoir du* —; to weigh. *Faire bon* —; to give good weight. *Vendre une chose au* — *de l'or*; to sell a thing extremely dear. *Le* — *des affaires*; the weight of business.

*****poignant, -e**, *adj.*, poignant; acute, keen. *Remords* — ; poignant remorse.

*****poignard**, *n.m.*, poniard, dagger. *Coup de* —; stab. *Ce fut un coup de* — *pour elle*; she was wounded to the heart by it.

*****poignarder**, *v.a.*, to poniard, to stab with a poniard.

se **poignarder**, *v.r.*, to poniard, to stab one's self with a poniard.

poigne, *n.f.*, (pop.) grasp of the hand; (fig.) strength.

*****poignée**, *n.f.*, handful; handle; hilt (of swords, &c.—*d'épée*, *&c.*). *A* — ; by the handful. *Jeter de l'argent à* — ; to throw money about by handfuls.

*****poignet**, *n.m.*, wrist; wrist-band (of linen —*du linge*); cuff (of a gown—*d'un vêtement*).

poil, *n.m.*, hair (of animals—*des animaux*); hair (of persons; other than that of the head—*des personnes*; excepté de la tête); wool (of some animals—*de quelques animaux*); beard; nap (of cloth, of hats—*du drap, des chapeaux*); colour (of horses—*des chevaux*); (bot.) bristle, wool. —*follet*; down; soft hair. — *de drap*; nap of cloth. *Monter un cheval à* — ; to ride a horse bare back. *Il y a laissé de son* — ; he was pretty well fleeced there. *Un chien qui est au* — *et à la*

plume; a dog for feather and leather. *Être au* — *et à la plume*; to be fit for anything. *Faire le* — *à un cheval*; to trim a horse. *De quel* — *est ce cheval?* of what colour is that horse? — *bai*; bay.

poile, *n.m.* *V.* **poêle**.

poilu, -e, *adj.*, shaggy; hairy; (bot.) bristly, pilose.

*****poincillade**, *n.f.*, (bot.) Barbadoes flower-fence.

poinçon, *n.m.*, punch, puncheon; bodkin; puncheon (cask—*tonneau*); (carp.) king-post; stamp (of coins—*des monnaies*).

poinçonnage, *n.m.*, marking with a stamp, stamping.

poinçonner, *v.a.*, to mark with a stamp, to stamp.

poindre, *v.n.*, to peep, to dawn, to break. *Le jour commençait à* —; day was beginning to break. *Le poil commence à lui* — *au menton*; his beard begins to appear.

poindre, *v.a.*, (l.u.) to sting. *Oignez vilain, il vous poindra*; *poignez vilain, il vous oindra*; save a thief from the gallows and he will cut your throat. *Quel taon vous point?* why, what's the matter with you?

poing, *n.m.*, fist, hand closed. *Coup de* —; punch. cuff. *Se battre à coups de* —; to fight with fisticuffs. *Fermer le* —; to clinch one's fist. *A* —*fermé*; with clinched fist. *Faire le coup de* — *avec quelqu'un*; to have a set-to with any one. *Il sait faire le coup de* — ; he knows how to box. *Pieds et* —*s liés*; bound hand and foot.

point, *adv.*, no, not; not at all; none. *Je ne l'ai* — *vu*; I have not seen him. *Il n'a* — *d'argent*; he has no money. — *du tout*; not at all. — *d'amitié sans vertu*; there can be no friendship without virtue.

point, *n.m.*, point; dot; full stop; period; speck; hole (of a strap, &c.—*de courroies, §c.*); break (of day—*du jour*); (needlework—*ouvrage à l'aiguille*) stitch; moment, difficulty; (nav.) tack (of the sheets—*des voiles*); — *de côté*; pain in the side, stitch. *Un* — ; full stop. — *et virgule*; semicolon. *Deux-* —*s*; colon. — *d'interrogation*; note of interrogation. — *d'admiration*, — *d'exclamation*; note of exclamation. *Lettre de deux* —*s* (print.); two-line letter. *Il ne met jamais de* — *sur les i*; he never dots his i's. *Mettre les* —*s sur les i*; to dot one's i's; to be very punctilious. — *d'orgue*; (mus.) pause. — *d'appui*; fulcrum. — *d'Angleterre*; Brussels point (lace). *Faire venir quelqu'un à son* —; to bring any one over to one's own views. *Il fut sur le* — *d'être tué*; he was very near being killed. *A* — ; in the nick of time. *A* — *nommé*; at the appointed time. *Tout vient à* — *à qui sait attendre*; patience and time bring everything to bear. *Un* — *fait à temps en sauve mille*; a stitch in time saves nine. *L'affaire est réduite à ce* — ; the business is come to that point. *Au plus haut* —; to the utmost pitch. *Au dernier* —; to the highest degree. *C'est un* — *arrêté*; it is a thing agreed on. *Avoir un* — *de côté*; to have a stitch in one's side. *Faire un* — *à* (needlework—*ouvrage à l'aiguille*); to put a stitch in. — *de vue*; point of view, prospect. — *du vent* (nav.); tack. — *d'honneur*; point of honour. *De tout* —; in all points, in every respect. *De* — *en* —; exactly, in every point. —*s cardinaux*; cardinal points. — *du compas*; point of the sea-compass.

pointage, *n.m.*, (artil., nav.) pointing, levelling.

pointal, *n.m.*, (carp.) prop.

pointe, *n.f.*, point (sharp end—*bout aigu*):

(print.) bodkin; pungency, tartness, sharpness; witticism; tack, tin-tack (nail—*clou*); etching-needle; head (of an arrow, of a lance—*d'une flèche, d'une lance*); (fenc.) small sword; (agri., geog.) point. *La* — *d'une épée*; the point of a sword. — *d'une plume*; nib of a pen. *La* — *du jour*; the break, the dawn, of day. *Marcher sur la* — *du pied*; to walk on tiptoe. *Tourner la* — *du pied en dehors*; to turn one's toes out. *Tailler en* —; to cut point-wise. *Se terminer en* —; to end in a point. *Faire une* — (milit.); to deviate from the line; (fig.) to turn aside. *Pousser sa* —; to pursue one's point. — *d'une épigramme*; point of an epigram. *Faire la* — (man.); to rear. — *de terre*; foreland.

pointé, -e, *adj.*, pointed.

pointement (point-mǎn), *n.m.*, (artil.) pointing, levelling.

pointer, *v.a.*, to pierce, to stick; to stab; to prick, to mark; to point; to dot; to sharpen; (print.) to register. — *la carte* (nav.); to point the chart. — *un canon*; to point a cannon.

pointer, *v.n.*, to point, to dot; to spring up, to soar, to fly high; (man.) to rear.

pointeur, *n.m.*, pointer, marker; (artil.) artillery-man who points the gun.

***pointillage**, *n.m.*, (engr.) dotting, stippling.

***pointillé**, *n.m.*, (engr.) dotting, stippling.

***pointille**, *n.f.*, trifle, trifling point; bickering, cavil, about a trifling subject.

***pointiller**, *v.n.*, to dot, to stipple; to cavil.

***pointiller**, *v.a.*, to nettle, to tease.

***pointillerie**, *n.f.*, bickering, cavilling.

***pointilleu-x, -se**, *adj.*, cavilling, particular, punctilious. *Un critique* —; a carping critic. — *sur le cérémonial*; punctilious with respect to ceremony.

pointu, -e, *adj.*, pointed, sharp, sharp-pointed, peaked. *Chapeau* —; sugar-loaf hat.

pointure, *n.f.*, (print.) point; (of shoes—*des chaussures*) size.

poire, *n.f.*, (bot.) pear; weight (of a steel-yard—*d'une balance romaine*). — *d'angoisse*; choke-pear. *Entre la* — *et le fromage*; at dessert. — *à poudre*; powder-horn, powder-flask. *Garder une* — *pour la soif*; to lay up something for a rainy day. —*s secrètes*; pear-bit (of a bridle—*mors*). — *de Messire Jean*; a kind of very sweet pears.

poiré, *n.m.*, perry.

poireau, or **porreau**, *n.m.*, (bot.) leek; (vet.) wart.

poirée, *n.f.*, (bot.) white beet.

poirier, *n.m.*, pear-tree.

pois, *n.m.*, (bot.) pea. *Cosse de* —; pea-cod. — *ramés*; branch peas. — *carrés*; marrow-fats. — *chiches*; chick-peas. — *cassés*; split peas. *Il donne un* — *pour avoir une fève*; he gives a sprat to catch a herring.

poison, *n.m.*, poison.

poissard, -e, *adj.*, vulgar, low. *Style* —; Billingsgate style.

poissarde, *n.f.*, fishwoman.

poisser, *v.a.*, to pitch, to do over with pitch; to make sticky.

poisseu-x, -se, *adj.*, pitchy.

poisson, *n.m.*, fish; small measure of capacity, about half a gill; *pl.*, (astron.) Pisces. — *de mer, de rivière*; sea-fish, river-fish. *Colle de* —; isinglass. — *d'avril*; April fool's errand. — *rouge*; gold-fish. — *juif*; hammer-fish. *Donner un* — *d'avril à quelqu'un*; to make an April fool of any one. *Être comme le* — *hors de l'eau*; to be like a fish out of water.

***poissonnaille**, *n.f.*, small fish.

poissonnerie (-so-n-rî), *n.f.*, fish-market.

poissonneu-x, -se, *adj.*, abounding in fish.

poissonnier, *n.m.*, fishmonger.

poissonnière, *n.f.*, fishmonger (woman); fish-kettle.

poitrail, *n.m.*, breast (of a horse—*du cheval*); breast-piece (of harness—*de harnais*); (arch.) breast-summer.

poitrinaire, *n.m.f.* and *adj.*, person in a decline; consumptive.

poitrine, *n.f.*, chest, breast; brisket. *Avoir la* — *découverte*; to have one's breast open. *Une fluxion de* —; an inflammation of the lungs. *Il a bonne* —; he has got good lungs.

poivrade, *n.f.*, pepper sauce.

poivre, *n.m.*, pepper. — *en grains*; whole pepper. — *de la Jamaïque*; all-spice, Jamaica-pepper.

poivrer, *v.a.*, to pepper, to put pepper in.

poivrier, *n.m.*, pepper-plant; pepper-box.

poivrière, *n.f.*, spice-box; pepper-box; (fort.) sentry-box built of stone in the angle of a bastion.

poix, *n.f.*, pitch; shoemakers' wax. *Cela tient comme* —; that sticks like pitch.

polacre, or **polaque**, *n.f.*, (nav.) polacca, polacre.

⊙**polacre**, or **polaque**, *n.m.*, Polack (Polish horseman—*cavalier polonais*).

polaire, *adj.*, polar. *Étoile* —; polar star. *Cercle* —; polar circle.

polarisation, *n.f.*, polarization.

polariser, *v.a.*, to polarize.

polarité, *n.f.*, (phys.) polarity.

polder (pol-dèr), *n.m.*, polder, tract of low land reclaimed from the sea by means of high embankments in Holland and Belgium.

pôle, *n.m.*, (astron., geog.) pole. — *arctique*; arctic pole. — *antarctique*; antarctic pole. —*s de l'aimant*; magnetic poles.

polémarque, *n.m.*, (antiq.) polemarch.

polémique, *n.f.* and *adj.*, polemics; polemic, polemical.

polémoscope, *n.m.*, polemoscope.

polenta, *n.f.*, (n.p.), a sort of pap, made of maize flour, used in Italy.

poli, -e, *adj.*, polished; polite, civil; refined; bright. *C'est un homme* —; he is a polite man.

poli, *n.m.*, polish.

police, *n.f.*, police; (print.) fount; policy (of insurance—*d'assurance*). — *d'assurance*; policy of insurance. *Commissaire de* —; commissary of police. *Espion de* —; police-spy. *Être mandé à la police*; to be sent for to the police-office. *Faire la* — *d'une salle*; to keep order in a hall. *Salle de* — (milit.); guard-room. *Bonnet de* —; foraging-cap.

policer, *v.a.*, to establish policy; to civilize.

polichinelle, *n.m.*, punch, merry-andrew.

⊙**poliment**, *n.m.*, polishing. *V.* **polissage**.

poliment, *adv.*, politely.

polir, *v.a.*, to polish, to polish up, to brighten, to burnish; to make polite, to civilize. — *un discours*; to polish a discourse. — *une langue*; to polish a language.

se **polir**, *v.r.*, to polish (of a thing—*des choses*).

polissage, *n.m.*, polishing.

polisseu-r, -se, *n.f.*, polisher.

polissoir, *n.m.*, polisher (tool—*outil*).

polissoire, *n.f.*, shining-brush.

polisson, *n.m.*, blackguard; low fellow, raga-muffin; mischievous child.

polisson, -ne, *adj.*, mischievous, idle, black-guard.

polissonne, *n.f.*, girl who runs about the streets.

polissonner, *v.n.*, to play the blackguard.

polissonnerie (-so-n-rî),*n.f.*,blackguardism, blackguard trick.

polissure, *n.f.*, polishing.

politesse, *n.f.*, politeness, good breeding,

polite thing. *Faire une —;* to do a polite thing.

politique, *adj.*, political.

politique. *n.m.*, politician, statesman. *C'est un rusé —;* he is a crafty politician.

politique, *n.f.*, policy; politics. *Étudier la —;* to study politics. *Sonder la profondeur de la —;* to sound the depths of politics. *Parler —;* to talk on politics. *— extérieure;* foreign politics; foreign policy.

politiquement (-tik-mān), *adv.*, politically, politicly.

politiquer, *v.n.*, (fam.) to talk politics.

polka, *n.f.*, polka.

polker. *v.n.*, to dance the polka.

poli. *n.m.* (*n.p.*), (pol.) poll.

pollen (pol-lè-n), *n.m.*, (bot.) pollen.

pollicitation (pol-li-), *n.f.*, (jur.) pollicitation.

pollué, -e (pol-lué), *adj.*, polluted.

polluer (pol-lué), *v.a.*, to pollute, to defile, to profane.

se **polluer**. *v.r.*, to pollute one's self.

pollution (pol-lu-), *n.f.*, pollution, profanation.

polonais. -e. *adj.*, Polish.

polonais, *n.m.*, Pole; Polonese (language).

polonaise, *n.f.*, Pole (woman); (mus.) polonaise.

poltron. -ne. *n.* and *adj.*, coward, poltroon; cowardly, dastardly, chicken-hearted.

poltronnerie (-tro-n-ri), *n.f.*, cowardice, poltroonery.

poly, a prefix from Gr. πολύς.

polyacoustique, *adj.*, polyacoustic.

polyadelphie, *n.f.*, polyadelphia.

polyandrie. *n.f.*, (bot.) polyandria.

polyarchie. *n.f.*, polyarchy.

polychreste, *adj.*; (pharm.) polycrest.

polychrome, *adj.*, (tech.) of many colours.

polyèdre. *n.m.*, (geom.) polyhedron.

polygala, *or* **polygale**, *n.m.*, (bot.) polygala, milkwort.

polygame. *n.m.f.* and *adj.*, polygamist; polygamous.

polygamie, *n.f.*, polygamy; (bot.) polygamia.

polygarchie. *n.f. V.* **polyarchie**.

polyglotte, *n.m. f.* and *adj.*, polyglot.

polygone, *n.m.* and *adj.*, (fort., geom.) polygon; polygonal, polygonous.

polygraphe, *n.m.*, polygraph (instrument for multiplying copies of a writing—*machine pour faire mouvoir plusieurs plumes en même temps*); author who writes on many different subjects.

polygraphie, *n.f.*, polygraphy; that part of a library which contains the works of authors who have written on various subjects.

polygynie. *n.f.*, polygynia.

polymathie. *n.f.*, polymathy, knowledge of many arts and sciences.

polymathique, *adj.*, polymathic.

polymorphe, *adj.*, polymorphous.

polymorphisme, *n.m.*, polymorphy.

polynôme, *n.m.*, (alg.) polynome, polynomial.

polype. *n.m.*, polyp, polype, polypes, polypus. *— du nez;* polypus in the nose.

polypétale, *adj.*, (bot.) polypetalous.

polypeu-x, -se, *adj.*, (med.) polypous.

polyphone, *adj.*, polyphonic.

polyphylle, *adj.*, polyphyllous.

polypier, *n.m.*, polypier, coral.

polypode, *n.m.*, (bot.) polypody.

polyptique. *n.m.*, (feudality—*féodalité*) register of rents, taxes, &c., due to a lord.

polyscope. *n.m.*, polyscope.

polyspaste, *n.m.*, polyspast.

polysperme, *adj.*, polyspermous.

polystyle, *adj.*, (arch.) polystyle.

polysyllabe. *n.m.* and *adj.*, polysyllable; polysyllabic, polysyllabical.

polysyllabique, *adj.*, polysyllabic, polysyllabical.

polysynodie. *n.f.*, administrative system in which the minister of every department is replaced by a board.

polytechnicien, *n.m.*, a pupil of the Paris Polytechnic School.

polytechnique (-tèk-nik), *adj.*, polytechnic. *École —;* Polytechnic School.

polythéisme, *n.m.*, polytheism.

polythéiste. *n.m.* and *adj.*, polytheist; polytheistic, polytheistical.

polytric, *n.m.*, (bot.) golden maiden-hair, hair-moss.

pomerium, *or* **pomœrium**, *n.m.* (—), (antiq.) the space left free from buildings within and without a town.

pomifère, *adj.*, pomiferous.

pommade. *n.f.*, pomatum (for the hair—*pour les cheveux*); (man.) vault, vaulting. — *pour les lèvres;* lip-salve.

pommader, *v.a.*, to pomatum.

pomme, *n.f.*, apple; ball, knob; head (of a cabbage, of a lettuce, of a walking-stick—*de chou, de laitue, de canne*). — *sauvage; crab*, crab-apple. — *d'Adam;* Adam's apple. — *de discorde;* apple of discord, bone of contention. — *d'amour;* tomato. — *de terre;* potato. — *de chêne;* oak-apple. — *de coloquinte;* bitter-apple. — *de pin;* fir-apple. — *de chou, de laitue;* head of a cabbage, of a lettuce. — *de canne;* head of a cane. — *de lit;* ball at the top of a bed-post. — *s de pavillon* (nav.); trucks of the ensign-staff. —*s de girouette* (nav.); acorns of the vanes.

☉**pommé**, *n.m.*, cider.

pommé, -e. *part.*, grown to a round head, cabbaged; (fig.. fam.) complete, downright. *Laitue —e;* cabbage-lettuce. *Un fou —;* a downright fool. *Une sottise —e;* an egregious blunder.

pommeau, *n.m.*, pommel (of saddles, swords —*de selle, d'épée*).

pommelé, -e. *adj.*, dappled; cloudy (with dappled clouds—*de nuages pommelés*). *Cheval gris- —;* dapple-grey horse.

se **pommeler** (po-m-lé), *v.r.*, to become dappled. *Le ciel s'est pommelé;* the sky is grown dappled.

pommelle, *n.f.*, roller-bolt (of carriages—*de voitures*); grating (of pipes—*de tuyaux*).

pommer, *v.n.*, (hort.) to cabbage, to grow to a round head.

pommeraie (po-mrè), *n.f.*, orchard of apple-trees.

pommette, *n.f.*, pommel, knob, ball; cheek-bone.

pommier, *n.m.*, apple-tree; apple-roaster.

pomoyer, *v.n.*, (nav.) to underrun (cables).

pompe, *n.f.*, pomp; splendour. *Marcher en grande —;* to march in great state. — *funèbre;* funeral pomp. — *du style;* loftiness of style. *Entrepreneur de —s funèbres;* undertaker.

pompe, *n.f.*, pump. *Piston d'une —;* plug, sucker, of a pump. — *à feu;* steam-pump. — *à incendie;* fire-engine. — *est éventée;* the pump blows. *La — est haute;* the pump sucks. *La — se décharge;* the pump has lost water. *À la —!* (nav.) pump ship, ho!

pomper, *v.n.*, to pump.

pomper, *v.a.*, to pump, to suck up. — *l'humidité;* to suck up the moisture.

pompeusement (-peûz-mān), *adv.*, pompously, with great pomp.

14

pompeu-x, -se. *adj.*, pompous, stately. *Style, discours,* — *:* lofty style, speech.

pompier, *n.m.,* fireman; pump-maker.

pompon, *n.m.,* ornament of a head-dress or gown; (milit.) tuft.

pomponné, -e, *part.,* decked out, tricked out.

pomponner, *v.a.,* (fam.) to ornament, to deck out, to dress. — *son style;* to trick out one's style.

se **pomponner,** *v.r.,* (fam.) to dress one's self up. *Cette femme aime à — ;* that woman is fond of dressing herself up.

⊙**ponant,** *n.m.,* west; ocean (in contradistinction from the Mediterranean—*par opposition à la Méditerranée*).

ponçage, *n.m.,* act of rubbing with pumicestone.

ponce, *n.f.,* pumice; (drawing—*dessin*) pounce. *Pierre* — *;* pumice-stone.

ponceau, *n.m.,* (bot.) corn-poppy; onearched bridge; red colour, poppy-colour.

ponceau, *adj.,* poppy-coloured.

poncer, *v.a.,* to pumice; (drawing—*dessin*) to pounce. — *de la vaisselle;* to rub plate with pumice-stone.

ponceu-x, -se, *adj.,* pumiceous.

poncif, *n.m.* *V.* **poncis.**

poncire, *n.m.,* large odorous lemon.

poncis, *n.m.,* (drawing, engr.) drawing pounced.

ponction, *n.f.,* (surg.) puncture, tapping.

ponctualite, *n.f.,* punctuality.

ponctuation, *n.f.,* punctuation; vowelpoints (in Oriental languages—*des langues orientales*).

ponctué, -e, *part.,* punctuated, dotted. *Plante* —*e;* dotted plant. *Ligne* —*e;* dotted line.

ponctuel, -le, *adj.,* punctual, exact.

ponctuellement (-èl-mān), *adv.,* punctually, exactly.

ponctuer, *v.a.,* to punctuate, to point.

pondage, *n.m.,* poundage (duty per pound —*droit levé sur les marchandises en Angleterre*).

pondérabilité, *n.f.,* ponderability.

pondérable, *adj.,* ponderable.

pondération, *n.f.,* (phys.) ponderation; poising, balancing.

pondérer, *v.a.,* to poise, to balance.

pondeuse, *n.f.,* layer (of hens—*des poules*).

pondre, *v.a.,* to lay eggs.

poney, *n.m.,* pony.

pongo, *n.m.,* (main.) pongo.

pont, *n.m.,* bridge; deck (of a ship—*d'un vaisseau*); flap (of trousers—*de pantalons*). — *levis* (—*s* —); drawbridge. — *tournant;* swingbridge. — *dormant:* fixed bridge. — *suspendu;* suspension-bridge. *Faire un* — *d'or à quelqu'un;* to make any one great pecuniary concessions. — *aux ânes:* asses' bridge. *La foire n'est pas sur le* — (prov.); there is no need to be in such a hurry. *Les* —*s et chaussées:* bridges and roads, department of the government including everything connected with the making and repairing of roads, bridges, canals, &c. — *volant* (nav.); hanging stage. *Premier* — *;* lower deck. *Second* — *;* upper deck of a two-decker. *Troisième* — *;* upper deck of a three-decker. *Faux* — *;* spar-deck. — *arqué;* cambered deck. — *coupé;* half-deck.

pont-aqueduc. *n.m.* (—*s* —*s*). aqueductbridge.

ponte, *n.f.,* laying of eggs.

ponte, *n.m.,* punter (cards—*aux cartes*); (ombre) ponto, the ace of hearts or diamonds.

ponté, -e, *adj.,* decked (of a ship—*d'un vaisseau*).

ponter, *v.n.,* (play—*au jeu*) to punt.

pontet, *n.m.,* trigger-guard (of fire-arms—*d'armes à feu*); saddle-tree.

pontife, *n.m.,* pontiff. *Le souverain* — *:* the sovereign pontiff, the pope.

pontifical, *n.m.,* pontifical.

pontifical, -e, *adj.,* pontifical.

pontificalement (-kal-mān), *adv.,* pontifically.

pontificat, *n.m.,* pontificate.

pontin, *adj.,* Pontine. *Les marais* —*s;* the Pontine marshes, between Rome and Naples.

pont-levis, *n.m.* (—*s* —), drawbridge; flap (of trousers—*de pantalons*); (man.) pontlevis.

pont-neuf, *n.m.* (—*s* —*s*), street-ballad, popular song.

ponton, *n.m.,* pontoon, bridge of boats; hulk.

pontonage, *n.m.,* bridge-toll; hire of a ferryboat; pontage.

pontonnier, *n.m.,* toll-gatherer; (milit.) pontonier, pontonnier.

pontuseau, *n.m.,* water-line (in papermaking—*manufacture du papier*).

pope, *n.m.,* pope, (priest of the Greek church —*prêtre de l'église grecque*).

popeline, *n.f.,* poplin.

poplité, -e, *adj.,* (anat.) popliteal.

populace, *n.f.,* populace, mob.

populaci-er, -ère, *adj.,* pertaining to the populace.

populaire, *adj.,* popular, vulgar.

populairement (-lèr-mān), *adv.,* popularly.

populariser, *v.a.,* to popularize, to make popular.

se **populariser,** *v.r.,* to make one's self popular.

⊙**popularisme,** *n.m.,* seeking popularity.

popularité, *n.f.,* popularity.

population, *n.f.,* population.

populéum (-om), *n.m.,* (pharm.) unguentum populi.

populeu-x, -se, *adj.,* populous.

populo, *n.m.* (—*s*), (jest.) plump little boy.

poracé, -e, *adj.,* (med.) porraceous.

porc (pork), *n.m.,* hog, pig, pork; porker. — *frais;* pork. *Côtelette de* —*;* pork-chop. [The final *c* of *porc* is silent before words beginning with a consonant.]

porcelaine, *n.f.,* porcelain, china, chinaware.

porcelainier, *n.m.,* workman in a porcelain manufactory.

porc-épic (por-ké-pik), *n.m.* (—*s* —*s*), porcupine.

porchaison, *n.f.,* wild-boar season.

porche, *n.m.,* porch.

porcher, *n.m.,* -**ère,** *n.f.,* swineherd.

porcherie, *n.f.,* pig-sty.

porcine, *adj.f.,* porcine.

pore, *n.m.,* pore.

poreu-x, -se, *adj.,* having pores, porous.

porisme, *n.m.,* (geom.) porism; (antiq.) corollary.

porosité, *n.f.,* porosity.

porphyre, *n.m.,* (min.) porphyry; (pharm.) porphyry grinding-table.

porphyrisation. *n.f.,* grinding (with a muller—*au moyen d'une molette*), pulverization.

porphyriser, *v.a.,* to grind: to porphyrize.

porque, *n.f.,* sow; (nav.) rider. — *de fond;* floor-riders. *Allonges de* — *:* futtock-riders. *Aiguillettes de* — *;* upper futtock-riders.

porracé, -e, *adj.* *V.* **poracé.**

porreau, *n.m.* *V.* **poireau.**

porrection, *n.f.,* (c.rel.) presentation of the instruments used in the ministry in conferring minor orders.

porrigo, *n.m.,* (med.) porrigo.

port, *n.m.,* port, haven, harbour; wharf: postage, carriage (of parcels—*de paquets*); aspect; presence, portliness; (nav.) burden; (mus.) a grace-note, portamento. — *de mer;* sea-

port. *Prendre* —, *surgir au* — ; to come into harbour, to land ; to attain one's end. *Arriver à bon* — ; to come safe into harbour ; to arrive safely. *Franc de* — ; post-paid (of letters—*des lettres, &c.*). *Faire naufrage au* — ; to be wrecked in port. —*de lettres;* postage. —*payé;* post-paid. *Permis de* — *d'armes;* licence to carry arms. — *de voix;* (voc. mus.) portamento-voice. *Elle a un* — *de reine;* her walk is that of a queen. *Le* — *d'une plante* (bot.); the aspect of a plant. — *permis* (nav.); weight of goods and luggage allowed free on board ship to officers, sailors and passengers.

portable, *adj.,* that can be worn, wearable.

portage, *n.m.,* portage (at water-falls in America—*aux chutes d'eau en Amérique*); conveyance, porterage ; (nav.) *V. port permis* under **port.**

*portail, *n.m.,* front gate (of a church—*d'église*); door-way, portal.

portant, -e, *adj.,* bearing. *L'un — l'autre;* one with another. *Il est bien* — ; he is in good health. *Tirer sur quelqu'un à bout* — ; to shoot at any one quite close.

portati-f, -ve, *adj.,* portable.

porte, *adj.,* (anat.) portal. *Veine* —; portal vein.

porte, *n.f.,* gate, gateway, door-way, door; eye (for hooks—*d'agrafes*); defile (of mountains —*de montagnes*); the Sublime Porte. *Les* —*s d'une ville;* the gates of a town. —*s d'enfilade;* suite of doors. — *cochère;* court-gate, yard-gate. — *à deux battants;* folding-doors. — *battante;* baize-door. — *vitrée;* glass-door. — *croisée* (—*s* —*s*); terrace or garden glass-door. *Mettre quelqu'un à la* — ; to turn any one out of doors. *Fermer la* — *au nez de quelqu'un;* to shut the door in any one's face. — *de derrière;* back-door ; shift. *Prendre la* — ; to take to the door. *Refuser la* — ; to deny admittance. *A* —*s ouvrantes;* at the opening of the gates. *A* — *close;* with closed doors. —*s d'un bassin;* gates of a dock. *La* — *ottomane;* the Ottoman, the Sublime Porte.

porté, -e, *part.,* carried, inclined, prone. *Il est* — *par la loi que;* it is provided by the law that. *Il est* — *à médire;* he is prone to back-biting.

* porte-aiguille, *n.m.* —, (surg.) instrument used to carry a needle into a deep cavity.

*porte-aiguille, *n.m.* (—, *or* — —*s*), needle-case.

porte-allumettes, *n.m.* (—), match-box.

Ⓒ **porte-arquebuse,** *n.m.* (—), king's gun-bearer.

porte-assiette, *n.m.* (—, *or* — —*s*), plate-stand.

Ⓒ **porte-auge,** *n.m.* (—), hodman, mason's labourer.

porte-baguette, *n.m.* (—), pipe (of muskets, pistols—*de fusils, de pistolets*).

porte-baïonnette, *n.m.* (—, *or* — —*s*), bayonet-belt.

porteballe, *n.m.,* pedlar, packman.

porte-barres, *n.m.* (—), pole-ring.

porte-bossoir, *n.m.* (— —*s*), (nav.) supporter of the cat-head.

porte-bougie, *n.m.* (—), (surg.) guide for a bougie.

porte-carabine, *n.m.* (—), carbine-swivel.

porte-cartes, *n.m.* (—), card-rack.

portechape, *n.m.,* cope-bearer.

portechoux, *n.m.,* horse for carrying vegetables to market.

porte-cigare, *n.m.* (—), cigar-holder.

porte-cigares, *n.m.* (—), cigar-case.

porte-clefs, *n.m.* (—), turnkey; (mus.) key-board.

portecollet, *n.m.,* pad, stiffener (for collars —*de collets*).

porte-collier, *n.m.* (— —*s*), (nav.) belaying-cleat which supports the collar of the stay.

portecrayon, *n.m.,* pencil-case.

porte-croix, *n.m.* (—), cross-bearer.

porte-crosse, *n.m.* (—), crosier-bearer ; (milit.) carbine-bucket.

porte-cure-dent, *n.m.* (— —*s*), tooth-pick case.

porte-dieu, *n.m.* (—), priest that carries the host to sick persons.

porte-drapeau, *n.m.* (—), (milit.) ensign-bearer, ensign.

portée, *n.f.,* brood, litter; reach (of the hand, arm—*de la main, du bras*); reach (of the mind—*de l'esprit*), capacity, compass ; import (extent of signification); shot (of a missile weapon—*d'une arme de jet*); (artil.) range ; (arch.) pitch ; bearing; resting-point ; (mus.) staff, stave. *Hors de la* — *du canon;* beyond the range of cannon. *A la* — *du fusil;* within gun-shot. *Cela n'est pas à ma* — ; that is not within my reach. *Être à la* — *de la voix de quelqu'un;* to be within hearing. *Cet ouvrage n'est pas à ma* — ; that work is not within my compass. *Cela passe ma* — ; that is beyond my compass. *Se mettre à la* — *de quelqu'un;* to come down to the level of any one. *Esprit d'une haute* — ; an intellect of great range. *La* — *d'un raisonnement;* the scope of an argument.

Ⓒ**porte-enseigne,** *n.m.* (—), standard-bearer.

porte-épée, *n.m.* (—), sword-bearer ; sword-belt, sword-hanger.

porte-éperon, *n.m.* (—, *or* — —*s*), spur-strap.

porte-étendard, *n.m.* (—), standard-bearer ; cornet.

porte-étriers, *n.m.* (—), stirrup-strap.

porte-étrivières, *n.m.* (—), stirrup-bar.

*porte-éventail, *n.m.* (—), fan-carrier.

portefaix, *n.m.,* porter, street-porter.

porte-fer, *n.m.* (—), horse-shoe case.

*portefeuille, *n.m.,* portfolio ; pocket-book ; bill-case. *Tout son bien est en* — ; all his property is invested in bills. *Cet auteur a plusieurs ouvrages en* — ; that author has several works by him in manuscript.

porte-flambeau, *n.m.* (—, *or* — —*x*), light-bearer ; torch-bearer; linkman.

porte-fourchette, *n.m.* (—, *or* — —*s*), knife rest.

porte-fromage, *n.m.* (—), cheese-tray.

porte-gargousse, *n.m.* (—), (nav.) cartridge-box.

porte-hache, *n.m.* (—), (milit.) axe-case.

porte-haubans, *n.m.* (—), (nav.) chain-wale, channel.

porte-huilier, *n.m.* (—), cruet-stand.

porte-lettres, *n.m.* (—), letter-case.

porte-liqueurs, *n.m.* (—), liquor-frame.

porte-lof, *n.m.* (—, *or* — —*s*), (nav.) bumkin.

porte-malheur, *n.m.* (—), ill omen, person who brings ill-luck.

porte-malle, *n.m.* (—). *V.* **porteballe.**

portemanteau, *n.m.,* portmanteau ; row of pegs (for cloaks, hats—*pour chapeaux, pardessus, &c.*).

porte-mèche, *n.m.* (—), wick-holder (of lamps—*de lampe*); (surg.) tent-probe.

portement, *n.m.,* (paint.) carrying. — *de croix;* carrying the cross.

porte-mitre, *n.m.* (—), mitre-bearer.

porte-monnaie, *n.m.* (—), flat purse.

porte-montre, *n.m.* (—), watch-stand.

porte-montres, *n.m.* (—), show-case for watches.

porte-mors, *n.m.* (—), heading-rein.

porte-mouchettes, *n.m.* (—), snuffers-tray.

porte-mousqueton, *n.m.* (—), carbine-swivel.

porte-muso, n.m. (—). V. muse (mam.).
porte-objet, n.m. (—, or — —s), part of microscopes for holding the object viewed.
porte-page, n.m. (—), (print.) page-paper.
porte-parapluies, n.m. (—), umbrella-stand.
porte-pièce, n.m. (—, or — —s), shoemaker's punch.
porte-pierre, n.m. (—), (surg.) caustic-case.
porte-pipe, n.m. (—), pipe-case.
porté-plume, n.m. (—, or — —s), pen-holder.
porte-plumes, n.m. (—), pen-case.
porte-queue, n.m. (—, or — —s), train-bearer.
porter (-tèr), n.m., porter (beer—bière).
porter, v.a., to carry, to bear; to bring; to support; to wear; to convey; to measure; to bring forth, to yield, to produce; to declare, to manifest, to induce, to prompt, to prevail, to excite, to persuade, to contain, to import. — un fardeau; to carry a burthen. L'un portant l'autre; one with another, upon an average. Vous en porterez le péché; the sin will lie at your door. Il ne porte jamais d'argent sur lui; he never carries money about him. — un habit; to wear a coat. — le deuil; to be in mourning. — perruque; to wear a wig. — ses cheveux; to wear one's own hair. — une bague au doigt; to wear a ring en one's finger. Il a porté la livrée; he has worn a livery. Elle porte la culotte; she wears the breeches. — l'épée; to wear a sword. — les armes; to carry arms, to shoulder arms. — la tête haute; to carry one's head high. — le bras en écharpe; to carry one's arm in a sling. — son pied, en dedans; to tread inwardly. — bien ses bras en dansant; to have a good air with one's arms in dancing. Le — haut; to carry it high. — la main à l'épée; to lay one's hand upon one's sword. — une botte (fenc.); to make a thrust. Cela porte coup; that hits home. — ses vues bien haut; to have great designs. Somme qui porte intérêt; sum that yields interest. L'enfant qu'elle porte; the child that she bears. Il en portera la peine; he will suffer for it. Vin qui porte bien l'eau; wine that bears water very well. Ils l'ont porté à la vengeance; they have excited him to revenge. Être porté à la vertu; to be inclined to virtue. L'ordre du roi ne porte pas cela; the king's order does not declare that. L'arrêt porte condamnation; the sentence carries condemnation along with it. La déclaration porte que; the declaration expresses that. — amitié à quelqu'un; to bear any one friendship. — respect; to respect. — envie; to envy. — bonheur; to bring good luck. — préjudice; to be prejudicial. — témoignage; to bear witness. — son jugement sur quelque chose; to pass one's judgment upon any thing. — une santé; to drink a toast.
se porter, v.r., to be, to do (of health—de la santé); to tend, to incline; to be inclined, to be disposed; to be worn; to proceed; to repair; to move; to stand forth; to be prone. Comment vous portez-vous? how do you do? — bien; to be well. Ne pas — bien, to be unwell. — sur les lieux; to repair to the place. Cette pièce réussit, la foule s'y porte; that piece takes, the people go in crowds to see it. Il se porte au bien; he is well inclined. Il s'est porté à cela lui-même; he took to that of himself. — fort pour quelqu'un; to answer for any one, to become security for any one.
porter, v.n., to bear, to rest, to lie; (artil., man.) to carry; (nav.) to stand, to bear off; (her.) to bear; to aim at; to hit, to take effect; to reach; to bear young, to go with young (of animals—des animaux). Le carrosse porte sur

la flèche; the coach bears upon the pole. Un raisonnement qui porte à faux; an inconclusive argument. Tous les coups que l'on tire ne portent pas; all the shots fired do not carry home. Ce vin porte à la tête; that wine gets into the head. Sa vue porte loin; his eye reaches far. — au nord-ouest; to stand to the north-west. Les voiles portent; the sails are full. — de gueules (her.); to bear gules.
porte-respect, n.m. (—), weapon carried for self-defence; mark of dignity; person of an imposing exterior.
porte-rideau, n.m. (— —x), curtain-pole.
porte-rôtie, n.m. (— —s), toast-stand, toast-rack.
porte-scie, n.m. (—, or — —s), (ent.) saw-fly. Insectes —; insects provided with a hand-saw-like ovipositor.
porte-tapisserie, n.m. (—), frame for tapestry.
porte-trait, n.m. (—, or — —s), trace-strap, trace-robin.
porteu-r, n.m., -se, n.f., porter; bearer; (com.) holder. Le — d'une lettre; the bearer of a letter. Payable au —; payable to the bearer.
porte-vent, n.m. (—), (mus.) wind-canal (of organs—des orgues).
porte-verge, n.m. (—, or — —s), verger.
porte-vergue, n.f. (—), (nav.) iron-horse.
porte-vis, n.m. (—), screw-piece.
porte-voix, n.m. (—), speaking-trumpet.
portier (-tié), n.m., porter, door-keeper.
portière (-ti-èr), n.f., curtain before a door; coach-door; portress.
portière, adj.f., of an age to bear (of cows, &c.—des vaches, &c.).
portion, n.f., portion, part, share; allowance. — de nourriture; allowance of food. Diminuer la — de quelqu'un; to shorten any one's allowance.
portioncule, n.f., (l.u.) a small portion.
portique, n.m., portico.
portor, n.m., portor, black marble with deep yellow veins.
○**portraire**, v.a., to pourtray.
portrait, n.m., portrait, likeness, picture. Peintre de —s; portrait painter. — en grand; portrait on a large scale. — à l'huile; portrait in oil. — en pied; full length portrait. — flatté; flattering portrait. — chargé; caricature.
portraiture, n.f., ○ portrait. Livre de — (paint.); drawing-book.
portugais, n.m. Portuguese (language).
portugais, -e, n. and adj., Portuguese.
portugaise, n.f., (nav.) lashing and crossing of the head of sheers.
portulan, n.m., (nav.) a book containing the situation of ports, their description, hours of the tides, &c.
posage, n.m., laying; laying down.
pose, n.f., laying, laying down; posture, attitude; hanging (of bells—de sonnettes); stationing (of sentries—de sentinelles).
posé, -e, part., laid, set, poised. Cela —, il s'ensuit que; this being granted, it follows that. Un homme bien — dans le monde; a man well situated, in a good position.
posé, -e, adj., sedate, staid, sober.
posément, adv., sedately, staidly.
poser, v.a., to place, to set, to lay down; to suppose, to admit, to grant; to post up; to hang (bells—sonnettes); (mus.) to set; (arith.) to put down. — le pied; to set one's foot down. Posez votre paquet; lay down your bundle. — l'arme à terre; to ground arms. — les armes; to lay down one's arms. — une figure; to put a figure in the proper position. — la première pierre d'un édifice; to lay the first stone

of an edifice. — *à sec;* to lay down dry. — *à cru;* to erect timber frame-work, &c., without a foundation. — *à plat;* to lay down flat. — *une sonnette;* to hang a bell. — *des gardes;* to post guards. — *en fait;* to lay down as a fact. — *une question;* to state a question. *Posons que cela soit;* let us suppose it to be so. *Il pose bien sa voix;* he gives his voice the proper pitch.

se **poser,** *v.r.,* to assume an attitude; to pitch (of birds—*des oiseaux*).

poser, *v.n.,* to bear, to rest, to lean; to take a posture, to stand, to sit for one's portrait.

poseur, *n.m.,* one who lays down stones, &c.; layer. — *de sonnettes;* bell-hanger.

poseu-r, *n. m.,* **-se,** *n.f.,* one who is affected in his manners, attitude, &c., a prig, a snob.

positi-f, -ve, *adj.,* positive, certain, practical. *Ce fait est — ;* it is a positive fact. *Un esprit — ;* a practical understanding. *C'est un homme — ;* he is a matter-of-fact man. *Elle ne m'avait rien promis de — ;* she had given me no positive promise.

positif, *n.m.,* positive reality ; (gram.) positive.

position, *n.f.,* position, situation; posture; stand, place; station of life; circumstances. — *embarrassante;* involved circumstances. *Fausse — * (arith.); false position. *Dans une bonne — ;* well off. *Dans une — peu élevée;* of little respectability. *Être en — de;* to be able to. *Quelle est sa — ?* how is he circumstanced?

positivement (-tiv-mǎn), *adv.,* positively, exactly.

positivisme, *n.m.,* (philos.) positivism.

positiviste, *n.m.,* (philos.) positivist, partisan of positivism.

pospolite. *n.f.,* pospolite, the Polish nobility when assembled in arms.

possédé, *n.m.,* **-e,** *n.f.,* person possessed. *Un homme — du démon;* a man possessed with the devil. *Il se démène comme un — ;* he lays about him like a madman.

posséder. *v.a.,* to possess, to be possessed of, to be master of, to enjoy, to own, to hold, to have, to be worth (of a person—*des personnes*); to be acquainted with. — *un emploi;* to hold an employ. *Les vertus qu'il possède;* the virtues he is possessed of. — *le cœur d'une personne;* to possess any one's heart. *L'ambition le possède;* he is possessed with ambition. *Le diable le possède;* the devil torments him. *Bien — une langue;* to be thoroughly master of a language. *Bien — son sujet;* to have a thorough command of one's subject.

se **posséder,** *v.r.,* to command one's temper, to command one's self, to master one's passions. *Ne — point;* to be beside one's self. *Il ne se possède pas de joie;* he is ready to leap out of his skin for joy.

possesseur, *n m.,* possessor, owner, master; occupant, occupier. — *légitime;* lawful possessor.

possessif, *n.m. and adj.,* (gram.) possessive case; possessive.

possession. *n.f.,* possession, occupation. *Mettre en — ;* to give possession, to invest. — *antérieure;* preoccupancy. *Prise de — ;* taking possession. — *injuste.* wrongful possession.

possessoire, *adj.,* (jur.) possessory. *Action — .* possessory action.

possessoire, *n.m.,* (jur.) possession (of real property—*de biens immeubles*).

posset, *n.m.,* posset.

possibilité, *n.f.,* possibility.

possible. *adj.,* possible. *Il est — de le faire;* it is possible to do it. *Il est — qu'il le fasse;* he may possibly do it. *Venez le plus tôt — ;* come as early as you can.

possible, *n.m.,* possibility, utmost *Faire*

tout son — ; to do one's utmost. *Je ferai tout mon — ;* I'll do whatever lies in my power.

postal, -e, *adj.,* relating to the post-office, postal.

postcommunion, *n.f.,* (c.rel.) post-communion.

postdate. *n.f.,* (l.u.) postdate.

postdater, *v.a.,* to postdate.

poste, *n.m.,* post; guard-house; place, employment; (nav.) berth; station (of a ship—*d'un vaisseau*). — *de chirurgiens;* surgeons' berth. — *des malades;* cockpit. — *de combat;* quarters. — *d'un vaisseau;* station of a ship in a fleet. *Être à — fixe dans un lieu;* to be stationed in a place. *Être à son — ;* to be at one's post.

poste, *n.f.,* post, post-house; post-stage; post-office; mail; buck-shot. *Aller en — ;* to travel post. *Courir la — ;* to ride post. *Chevaux de — ;* post-horses. *Maître de — ;* post-master. — *restante;* till called for.

posté. -e, *part.,* placed, stationed.

postel, *n.m.,* kind of thistle used in cloth manufactories.

poster, *v.a.,* to station, to place, to post.

postérieur, -e. *adj.,* posterior.

postérieur. *n.m.,* posteriors.

postérieurement (-eur-mǎn), *adv.,* subsequently.

à **posteriori.** *adv.,* (log.) a posteriori.

postériorité, *n.f.,* posteriority.

postérité, *n.f.,* posterity, issue. *En appeler à la — ;* to appeal to posterity. *Transmettre son nom à la — la plus reculée;* to transmit one's name to the remotest posterity. *Passer à la — ;* to be handed down to posterity.

postes. *n.f.pl.,* (arch.) Vitruvian scroll.

postface, *n.f.,* address placed at the end of a work, after-address.

⊙**postfixe,** *n.m.,* (gram.) postfix, termination.

posthume, *n.m.* and *adj.,* posthumous child; posthumous. *Œuvres —s;* posthumous works. *Un fils — ;* a posthumous son. *C'est un — ;* he is a posthumous child.

postiche. *adj.,* superadded; false, misplaced; (milit.) doing another's duty provisionally. *Dents —s;* false teeth. *Cheveux —s;* false hair. *Caporal — ;* soldier doing corporal's duty.

*** postillon,** *n.m.,* postillion; post-boy; (trick-track) mark above the half.

postposer, *v.a.,* ⊙to put after; (book-bind.) to transpose.

postpositi-f, -ve, *adj.,* (gram.) postpositive.

postposition, *n.f.,* postposition.

postscénium, *n.m.* (—), postscenium.

post-scriptum (-tom), *n.m.* (—), postscript.

postulant, *n.m.,* **-e,** *n.f.,* postulant, candidate.

postulat. *n.m.,* postulate.

postulation, *n.f.,* being concerned as the attorney; (canon law—*loi canon*) application for a dispensation.

postulatum. *n.m.* (*postulata*), (philos.) postulate. *V.* **postulat.**

postuler. *v.a.,* to solicit; to apply for; (ecc.) to apply for a dispensation. — *une place;* to put up for a place.

postuler, *v.n.,* to be concerned as the attorney.

posture, *n.f.,* posture, attitude, situation, condition.

pot, *n.m.,* pot, jug; tankard; (stationery—*papeterie*) foolscap; ⊙ pot, morion, helmet. *Mettre en — ;* to pot. — *de chambre;* chamber-pot. *Bête comme un — ;* as stupid as a post. *Mettre le — sur le feu.* to put the pot on the fire. *Courir la fortune du — ;* to take pot-luck. — *pourri;* hotch-potch; jar filled with all sorts of flowers; medley. — *à feu* (artil.); fireball.

— -au-féu (—); meat to be boiled to make soup,
broth. Tourner .autour du —; to beat about
the bush. Gare le — au noir; beware of the
danger. Découvrir le — aux roses; to find out
the secret. Il en payera les —s cassés; he will
pay for the damage. C'est le — de terre contre
le — de fer; it is the earthen pot against the
iron pot.

potable, adj., drinkable.

potage, n.m., porridge, soup. —aux herbes;
vegetable soup. Il ne trouva que cela pour tout
—; that's all he found.

potager, n.m., kitchen-stove; kitchen-
garden; soup-pan.

potag-er, -ère, adj., oleraceous. Herbes,
plantes —ères; pot-herbs.

potamot, n.m., (bot.) pond-weed.

potasse, n.f., potash. —d'Amérique; pearlash.

potassium (-siom), n.m., potassium.

pot-de-vin, n.m. (—s —), gratuity; premium; good-will; bonus; bribe.

pote, adj., (fam.) big, swollen, sore (of the
hand—de la main).

poteau, n.m., post, stake. —cornier; corner-
post.

potée, n.f., potful; houseful (of children—
d'enfants); putty (of tin—d'étain); (metal.)
moulding, luting loam. —d'étain; pewter.

potelé, -e, (po-tlé), adj., plump, fat.

potelet (po-tlè), n.m., (carp.) strut.

potence, n.f., gallows, gibbet; prop; crutch
in the form of a T; sliding rule for measuring
the height of men and horses; (nav.) gallows-
bit; (horl.) potence. Gibier de —; Newgate
bird.

potentat, n.m., potentate.

potentiel. -le, (-ci-èl), adj., (med., gram.)
potential.

potentiellement (-ci-èl-), adv., potentially.

potentille, n.f., (bot.) cinque-foil.

poterie (-tri), n.f., pottery, earthenware.

poterne, n.f., (fort.) postern.

potiche, n.f., China or Japan vase.

potier (-tié), n.m., potter. Terre à —;
potter's clay. —d'étain; pewterer.

potin, n.m., pinchbeck.

potion, n.f., (med.) potion, draught.

potiron, n.m., pumpkin, pompion, pumpion.

⊙**potron-jaquet**, or **potron-minet**, n.m.
V. **patron-jaquet.**

pou, n.m., louse. Des —x; lice.

pouacre, n.m. and adj., (pop.) niggard;
nasty fellow; niggardly; nasty.

pouah! int., faugh!

pouce, n.m., thumb; inch. Il s'en mordra
les —s; he will repent of it. Serrer les —s à
quelqu'un; to wrest a secret from any one.
Mettre les —s; to give in.

poucet, n.m., small thumb. Le petit —;
Tom Thumb.

poucettes, n.f.pl., manacles (for the thumbs
—pour les pouces).

poucier, n.m., thumb-stall.

pou-de-soie, n.m. (—x —), or **pout-de-
soie**, n.m. (—s —), (silk—soierie) paduasoy.

pouding, n.m., pudding.

poudingue (-dingh), n.m., pudding-stone.

poudre, n.f., dust; powder; gunpowder.
—d'or; gold dust. Sucre en —; powdered
sugar. Réduire en —; to pulverize. Jeter de la
— aux yeux de quelqu'un; to throw dust into the
eyes of any one, to impose on any one. Du tabac
en —; snuff. Du café en —; ground coffee. —
à canon; gunpowder. La soute aux —s (nav.);
the powder magazine. Il n'a pas inventé la —;
he is no conjuror; he will never set the Thames
on fire. Mettre le feu aux —s; to fan the flame.

poudrer, v.a., to powder the hair.

se poudrer, v.r., to powder one's hair.

poudrette, n.f., dried night soil.

poudreu-x, -se, adj., dusty, powdery. C'est
un pied —; he is a vagabond.

poudrier, n.m., sand-box, pounce-box;
gunpowder-maker.

poudrière, n.f., powder-mill; powder-
magazine; sand-box.

poudroyer, v.n., to rise (of the dust—de la
poussière); to be dusty (of roads—des routes).

pouf, n.m., bombastic advertisement, puff.
Faiseur de —s; puffer. Faire des —s; to disappear without paying one's debts.

pouf, adv., plump, bang.

pouf, adj., invariable, crumbling (of stones—
des pierres).

pouffer, v.n., to burst out (into laughter).
[Only used in: — de rire; to burst out into
laughter.]

*****pouillé**, n.m., register of benefices.

*****pouiller**, v.a., (pop.) to rail at, to abuse.

*****se pouiller**, v.r., (pop.) to abuse each other.

*****pouilles**, n.f.pl., abuse, abusive language.
Il m'a chanté —; he abused me.

*****pouilleux, -se**, n. and adj., lousy person;
beggarly fellow; lousy.

*****pouillot**, n.m., (orni.) pewet.

*****poulailler**, n.m., poulterer; hen-house;
poultry-house; poultry-cart.

poulain, n.m., foal, colt; (med.) bubo.

poulaine, n.f., (nav.) figure-head.

poulan, n.m., (at cards—aux cartes) pool.

poularde, n.f., fat pullet.

poule, n.f., female of the cock, hen; pool
(play—au jeu). Jeune —; pullet. —d'Inde;
turkey-hen. —d'eau; moor-hen. Faire venir
la chair de —; to make one's flesh creep, to make
one shudder. Plumer la — sans la faire crier;
to pluck the hen without making it scream. —
mouillée; milk-sop (pers.).

poulet, n.m., chicken; love-letter; (stationery—papeterie) note-paper.

poulette, n.f., young hen, pullet; lass.

⊙**poulevrin**, n.m., priming powder, priming
powder-horn. V. **pulvérin.**

pouliche, n.f., filly, colt, foal.

poulie, n.f., pulley; (nav.) block.

poulier, v.a., to hoist, to draw, with a
pulley.

poulierie, n.f., block-shed; block-manufac-
ture.

poulieur, n.m., block-maker.

⊙**poulin, -e**. V. **poulain, pouliche.**

pouliner, v.n., to foal (of mares—des juments).

poulinière, n.f. and adj., breeding mare;
breeding (of mares—des juments).

pouliot, n.m., (bot.) penny-royal.

poulpe, n.f. V. **pulpe.**

poulpe, n.m., (mol.) octopus, poulp.

pouls (poo), n.m., pulse. — déréglé; irregular pulse. — faible; low pulse. — élevé; high
pulse. — formicant; small, weak and frequent
pulse. Se tâter le —; to consult one's own
strength. Tâter le — à quelqu'un; to feel any
one's pulse. Le — lui bat; his pulse beats.

poult-de-soie, n.m. (—s —). V. **pou-de-
soie.**

poumon, n.m., lung, lungs.

poupard, n.m., (triv.) babe, baby.

poupart, n.m., a species of large crab.

poupe, n.f., poop, stern. Bâtiment à — carrée; square-sterned vessel. Bâtiment à —étroite;
lute-sterned vessel. Vent en —; stern-wind.
Mettre vent en —; to bear away before the wind.
Mouiller en —; to moor by the stern. Avoir le
vent en —; to sail before the wind; to be in
luck's way.

poupée, n.f., doll; puppet; (arch.) poppy-
head; (hort.) crown-graft; bunch of hemp or

flax tied to the distaff. *Enter en —* (hort.);
to graft in the bark.

poupin, -e, *n.* and *adj.,* (fam.) person affectedly smart in dress; dashing.

poupon, *n.m.,* **-ne,** *n.f.,* plump, chub-cheeked baby, boy, girl. *Ma —ne;* my darling.

pour, *prep.,* for; on account of; in order; towards; to; though, notwithstanding. *— tou-jours, — jamais;* for ever. *— le moins;* at least. *— cet effet;* therefore, and therefore. *— ainsi dire;* as it were, so to say. *Il fera cela — vous;* he will do that for your sake. *On l'a laissé — mort;* he was left for dead. *— qui me prenez-vous?* whom do you take me for? *Je le tiens — mon ami;* I take him to be my friend. *— moi;* for my part, as for me. *— ce qui est de moi, j'y con-sens;* for my part I consent to it.

pour, *n.m.,* for, pro. *Les — et les contre;* the pros and cons.

pourana, *n.m.* (n.p.), Purana, sacred poem containing the theology of the Hindoos.

pourboire, *n.m.,* drink-money. *Demander un —;* to ask for something to get drink with.

pourceau, *n.m.,* hog, pig, swine. *Étable à —x;* hog-sty. *— de mer;* sea-hog, porpoise. *C'est un vrai —;* he is a perfect hog.

pourchasser, *v.a.,* to pursue, to seek eagerly.

pourfendeur, *n.m.,* (l.u.) killer. *— de géants;* giants' killer, braggadocio.

pourfendre, *v.a.,* (fam.) to cleave asunder, to cleave; to kill outright.

pourir, *v.n V.* **pourrir.**

pourissage, or **pourrissage,** *n.m.,* (tech.) retting.

pourissoir, or **pourrissoir,** *n.m.,* (tech.) retting vat.

pouriture, *n.f. V.* **pourriture.**

pourlécher, *v.a.,* (l.u.) to lick.

se pourlécher, *v.r.,* (fam.) to lick one's lips; (fig.) to hug one's self; to anticipate a pleasure.

pour lors, *adv.,* then, after that; at that time.

pourparler, *n.m.,* parley.

pour peu que, *conj.,* ever so little, however so little.

pourpier, *n.m.,* (bot.) purslain.

pourpoint, *n.m.,* doublet. *A brûle-—;* quite close; to one's face.

pourpre, *n.m.,* purple (colour—*couleur*); (med.) purples; (her.) purpure.

pourpre, *adj.,* purple.

pourpre, *n.f.,* purple (stuff—*étoffe*); purple-dye; purple-fish; (fig.) sovereign dignity; cardinalate. *Porter la —;* to wear the purple. *Être né dans la —;* to be born in a palace.

pourpré, -e, *adj.,* purpled, purple. *Fièvre —e;* purpura, petechial fever.

pourprier, *n.m.,* (mol.) purpura.

pourpris, *n.m.,* enclosure.

pour que, *conj.,* in order that, so that, to.

pourquoi, *adv.,* why, wherefore. *— cela?* why so? *— pas?* why not?

pourquoi, *conj.,* why, for what, upon what account. *Demandez-moi —;* I don't know why. *C'est —;* therefore.

pourquoi, *n.m.,* the reason why; the why and the wherefore. *Je voudrais bien savoir le —;* I would fain know the why and the wherefore.

pourri, *n.m.,* rottenness, rotten part.

pourri, -e, *part.,* rotten. *Pomme —e;* rotten apple. *Pierre —e;* rotten stone.

pourrir, *v.n*, to rot, to grow rotten.

pourrir, *v.a.,* to rot, to make rotten; to mature (a cold—*un rhume*); to ripen.

se pourrir, *v.r.,* to get rotten.

pourrissage, *n.m. V.* **pourissage.**

pourrissant, -e, *adj.,* rotting.

pourrissoir, *n.m. V.* **pourissoir.**

pourriture, *n.f.,* rot, rottenness, putrefaction; (agri.) brown rust; (vet.) rot.

poursuite, *n.f.,* pursuit, chase; prosecution; persecution; (jur.) suit, proceedings. *In-tenter des —s* (jur.); to institute proceedings, to take proceedings. *La — du plaisir a plus de charmes que le plaisir même;* the pursuit of pleasure has more charms than pleasure itself.

poursuivant, *n.m.,* candidate; suitor, wooer; (jur.) prosecutor, plaintiff. *— d'armes;* pursuivant at arms.

poursuivant, *adj.,* pursuing; (jur.) suing.

poursuivre, *v.a.,* to pursue, to hunt, to chase; to endeavour to obtain, to seek for; to persecute, to annoy, to beset; (jur.) to sue; (jur.) to prosecute. *— quelqu'un en justice;* to prosecute any one at law. *— l'ennemi;* to pursue the enemy. *— un procès;* to carry on a law-suit. *— une charge;* to endeavour to obtain an office. *— une pension;* to solicit a pension. *— son discours;* to proceed with one's discourse. *— son chemin;* to proceed on one's way, to pursue one's road.

se poursuivre, *v.r.,* to be pursued, to be continued; (jur.) to be sued; to be prosecuted.

poursuivre, *v.n.,* to pursue, to continue. *Poursuivez; il est beau de m'insulter ainsi;* goon; it is a noble thing of you to insult me thus.

pourtant, *adv.,* however, howsoever, yet, still, for all that, notwithstanding, though, nevertheless.

pourtour, *n.m.,* periphery, circumference.

pourvoi, *n.m.,* (jur.) appeal (for reversal of judgment—*pour la cassation d'un jugement, d'un arrêt*). *— en grâce;* petition for mercy.

pourvoir, *v.n.,* to see to, to look to; to provide, to supply; to nominate, to appoint. *Pour-voyez à cette affaire;* look to that business *— à sa subsistance;* to provide for one's support. *— à un bénéfice;* to prefer to a living, to appoint to a living, to nominate to a living.

pourvoir, *v.a.,* to invest with, to put in possession of; to provide, to supply, to furnish, to stock; to endow. *— une place de vivres;* to provide a garrison with victuals. *Ce père a bien pourvu tous ses enfants;* that father has made a handsome provision for all his children.

se pourvoir, *v.r.,* to provide one's self to apply, to sue, to make application for. *— en jus-tice;* to sue at law. *— par appel;* to enter an appeal. *— en cassation;* to make application for a reversal of judgment. *— en grâce;* to petition for mercy.

☉pourvoirie, *n.f.,* provision-store.

pourvoyeur, *n.m.,* purveyor, provider.

pourvu que, *conj.,* provided that. *— vous le fassiez;* provided you do it.

pousse, *n.f.,* shoot, sprout; (vet.) heaves, shortness of breath, broken wind, asthma; ☉bailiffs (sheriff's officers); a disease of wines.

poussé. -e, *part.,* pushed. *Ce cheval est — de nourriture;* this horse has been fed too much. *Du vin —;* turbid, diseased wine.

☉pousse-cul, *n.m.* (—, or — —s), bum-bailiff.

poussée, *n.f.,* pushing, thrusting; push, thrust. *Donner la — à quelqu'un;* to pursue any one vigorously; to follow up any one closely. *Faire une belle —* (fam., iron.); to do a mighty fine thing.

pousse-pieds, *n.m.* (—). *V.* **anatife.**

pousser, *v.a.,* to push, to give a push to, to thrust, to give a thrust to; to shove, to shove on, to drive, to drive on, to impel; to strike, to throw, to hit; to carry on, to extend, to forward; to send forth, to shoot forth, to put out, to put forth (of plants—*des plantes*); to urge, to stir up, to provoke, to impel, to incite, to instigate; to bring forward, to assist forward, to help on; to utter (a groan—*un gémissement, un* *cri*); to heave, to fetch (a sigh—*un soupir*). — *en avant ;* to push on. — *dehors ;* to thrust out. — *un cheval ;* to push on a horse. — *le temps avec l'épaule* (prov.); to endeavour to gain time. — *la porte au nez de quelqu'un ;* to slam the door in any one's face. — *le dé ;* to throw the die. — *une botte* (fenc.); to make a thrust. — *un mur plus loin ;* to carry a wall further. — *un raisonnement trop loin ;* to carry an argument too far. — *à bout ;* to shock greatly ; to cause to lose all patience. — *une affaire à bout ;* to carry a thing to a successful termination. — *une tranchée ;* to forward a trench. — *des cris ;* to utter cries. — *des soupirs ;* to heave sighs. *Vous me poussez trop ;* you urge me too far. *C'est un tel qui l'a poussé ;* it was so and so that pushed him forward. — *sa pointe ;* to pursue one's point. *On l'a poussé à se battre ;* they set him on to fight. — *quelqu'un de questions ;* to question any one closely. *Les arbres commencent à — des boutons ;* the trees begin to put forth buds.

se **pousser**, *v.r.*, to push forward, to push one's self forward, to be pushed forward, to be pushed, to be carried ; to push forward one another. *La plaisanterie ne doit pas — jusqu'à l'offense ;* joking ought not to be carried so far as to give offence. — *de nourriture ;* to eat too much.

‹ **pousser**, *v.n.*, to sprout, to sprout forth, to shoot, to shoot forth (of plants—*des plantes*); to be broken-winded (of horses—*des chevaux*); to grow (of the hair, nails—*des cheveux, des ongles*); to push forward, to push on, to go on; to bulge, to jut out. *Les blés poussent déjà ;* the corn is already coming up. *Ce mur pousse en dehors ;* this wall bulges outwards. *Poussons jusqu'à la forêt ;* let us push forward as far as the forest.

poussette, *n.f.*, pushpin (game—*jeu*).

pousseu-r, *n.m.*, **-se**, *n.f.*, pusher, shover; utterer (of sighs—*de soupirs*).

poussier, *n.m.*, coal-dust ; gunpowder-dust; turf-dust.

poussière, *n.f.*, dust, powder; (bot.) pollen, male-seed. *Nuage de — ;* cloud of dust. — *de la mer ;* spray. *Réduire en — ;* to reduce to dust. *Jeter de la — aux yeux de quelqu'un ;* to throw dust into any one's eyes. *Tirer quelqu'un de la — ;* to raise any one from the dunghill. *Il fait de la — ;* it is dusty, the roads are dusty.

poussiéreu-x, -se, *adj.*, dusty.

poussif, *n.m.*, (pop.) pursy man.

poussi-f, -ve, *adj.*, (pop.) pursy ; (vet.) short-breathed, short-winded, broken-winded.

poussin, *n.m.*, chick, young chicken. — *qui ne fait que d'éclore ;* chick just out of its shell.

poussinière, *n.f.*, (pop.) (astron.) Pleiades.

poussoir, *n. m.*, (horl.) pusher ; driver (dentist's instrument—*instrument de dentiste*).

poussolane. *V.* **pozzolane**.

pout-de-soie, *n.m.* (—*s —*). *V.* **pou-de-soie**.

poutre, *n.f.*, beam ; mote.

poutrelle, *n.f.*, small beam ; (carp.) stop-plank.

pouvoir, *v.n.*, to be able, can, may. — *marcher ;* to be able to walk. *Je ne puis vous répondre ;* I cannot answer you. *N'en — plus ;* to be worn out, to be completely exhausted, to be tired out, to be done up. *N'en — mais, ne — mais d'une chose* (fam.); not to have had any share, anything to do, in a thing. *Pouvait-il mais de cela?* was that at all his fault, could he possibly help that? *Puisse-t-il réussir ;* may he succeed. *Il peut arriver que ;* it may happen that. *Il pourrait survenir une circonstance qui changeât la face des choses ;* some circumstance might arise which would change the whole face of matters. *Je n'y puis rien ;* I

cannot help it. *Je puis ne pas le faire ;* I may not do it. *Je ne puis pas le faire ;* I cannot do it.

pouvoir, *v.a.*, can do, to be able to do; to have power. *Je ne puis rien à cela ;* I can do nothing in that business. *Vous pouvez tout sur lui ;* you have great power over him. *Je ne crois pas le — ;* I do not think I can do it.

se **pouvoir**, *v.r.imp.*, to be possible. may be, can be. *Cela se peut ;* that may be, that is possible. *Cela ne se peut pas ;* that is impossible.

pouvoir, *n.m.*, power ; sway, authority. *Il est en son — de ;* he has it in his power to. *Le feu a le — de ;* fire has the power of. *Avoir une chose en son — ;* to have a thing in one's possession. *Étre fondé de — ;* to have power of attorney. *Il a plein — de ;* he has full powers to. *Abuser de son — ;* to abuse one's power. *Avoir un —* (jur.); to have a power of attorney, a letter of attorney.

pouzzolane, or **pozzolane**, *n.f.*, (—*s*), pozzolana, puzzolana, pozzuolana.

pp., ab. of the word *Pères*, fathers, applied to ecclesiastics.

pragmatique, *n.f.* and *adj.*, pragmatic sanction ; pragmatic.

prairial, *n.m.*, Prairial, ninth month of the calendar of the first French republic, from May 20th to June 18th.

prairie, *n.f.*, meadow, prairie, savannah. —*s artificielles ;* grounds sown with grass, clover.

praline, *n.f.*, burnt almond.

praliner, *v.a.*, to burn with sugar (like burnt almonds—*comme les pralines*).

prame, *n.f.*, (nav.) pram, prame.

praticabilité, *n.f.*, practicableness, practicability.

praticable, *adj.*, practicable, feasible, possible; passable (of roads—*des routes*). *Si la chose est — ;* if the thing be practicable. *Les chemins ne sont pas —s ;* the roads are not passable, the roads are not practicable. *Porte —, fenêtre —* (thea.); real door, real window.

praticables, *n.m. pl.*, (thea.) real, not painted, objects.

praticien (-si-in), *n.m.* and *adj.*, practitioner ; (sculpt.) rough-hewer ; practising. *Médecin — ;* practising physician.

pratiquant, -e, *adj.*, of one who regularly observes his religious duties.

pratique, *n.f.*, practice, practical part, observance, usage; dealing, doing, customer, custom ; practice (of attorneys, notaries, physicians—*d'avoués, de notaires, de médecins*); Punch's whistle, squeaker; (nav.) pratique. *Mettre en — ;* to put into practice, to practise. *Faire de sourdes —s ;* to carry on clandestine dealings. *C'est une bonne — ;* he is a good customer. *Donner — à un vaisseau* (nav.); to admit a vessel to pratique. *Cet avoué entend bien la — ;* that attorney is well versed in the practice of the law. *Terme de — ;* law-term. *Obtenir, recevoir, —* (nav.); to take pratique.

pratique, *adj.*, pertaining to practice, practical, experienced. *Étre — d'un lieu* (nav.); to be a good pilot for a place.

pratiquement (-tik-măn), *adv.*, practically.

pratiquer, *v.a.*, to practise, to exercise ; to frequent, to converse with, to keep company with ; to tamper with, to obtain ; (arch.) to contrive. — *la vertu ;* to practise virtue. — *la médecine ;* to practise physic. *Se garder de — les méchants ;* to avoid associating with the wicked. — *un chemin ;* to open a road. — *un trou ;* to make a hole. — *des intelligences ;* to get intelligence. — *des témoins ;* to suborn witnesses.

se **pratiquer**, *v.r.*, to be in use, to be practised, to be customary. *Cela ne se pratique point ;* that is not usual.

pratiquer, *v.n.*, to practise; (nav.) to have free intercourse.

pré, *n.m.*, meadow, small mead ; paddock ; ground, place where a duel is fought. *Se trouver sur le* —; to be upon the ground.

préadamites, *n.m.pl.*, Christian sectarians who believed that men had been in existence before Adam.

préalable, *adj.*, previously·necessary; previous.

préalable, *n.m.*, necessary preliminary; preliminary. *Au* —; previously, first of all.

préalablement, *adv.*, previously, first of all.

préambule, *n m.*, preamble. *Point de* —; none of your prefacing.

préau, *n.m.*, yard, courtyard (of a convent or prison—*d'un couvent, d'une prison*).

prébende, *n.f.*, prebend, prebendaryship.

prébendé, -e, *adj.*, that enjoys a prebend.

prébendier, *n.m.*, prebendary.

précaire, *adj.*, precarious; uncertain.

précairement (-kèr-män), *adv.*, precariously.

précaution, *n.f.*, precaution; caution. *Prendre des* —*s auprès de quelqu'un;* to proceed warily with any one. *User de* —*;* to use caution.

précautionner, *v.a.*, to warn, to caution.

se précautionner, *v.r.*, to be cautious, to guard against, to take precautions. — *contre le chaud;* to guard against heat.

précédemment (-da-män), *adv.*, before, previously.

précédent, -e, *adj.*, precedent, preceding, foregoing.

précédent, *n.m.*, something done or said previously : precedent.

précéder, *v.a.*, to precede, to go before, to go first ; to have the precedency. *Il était précédé par, il était précédé de;* he was preceded by.

préceinte, *n.f.*, (nav.) wale, bend. ribband. — *basse, première* —, *seconde* —; main wale. *Troisième et quatrième* —; channel-wale.

précepte, *n.m.*, precept, rule ; prescript, command.

précepteur, *n.m.*, tutor, private tutor, preceptor.

préceptoral, -e, *adj.*, preceptorial

préceptorat, *n.m.*, tutorage, tutorship.

précession, *n.f.*, (astron.) precession. — *des équinoxes;* precession of the equinoxes.

prêche, *n.m.*, sermon (protestant); protestant church, meeting-house. *Quitter le* —; to cease to be a protestant; to turn catholic.

prêcher, *v.a.*, to preach, to hold forth, to preach up, to extol, to praise. — *la parole de Dieu;* to preach the word of God. *Ne* — *que malheur et misère;* to announce nothing but bad news; to be always complaining of the hardness of the times. — *les fidèles;* to exhort the faithful. — *toujours la même chose;* to be always repeating the same thing. — *un converti;* to wish to persuade a person of that of which he is already convinced. — *ses exploits;* to extol, to boast, of one's exploits.

prêcher, *v.n.*, to preach. — *d'exemple;* to set the example, to practise what one preaches. — *sur la vendange;* to preach over one's cups. *On a beau — à qui n'a cœur de bien faire;* to reprove a fool is but lost labour.

prêcheu-r, *n.m.*, **-se**, *n.f.*, (fam.) preacher, sermonizer. *Frère* —; Dominican friar.

précieuse, *n.f.*, conceited, finical or precise woman : prude.

précieusement (-eûz-män), *adv.*, preciously, carefully; (paint.) very elaborately.

précieu-x, -se, *adj.*, precious, costly, valuable ; affected, finical, precise, over-uice, *Pierres*

—*ses;* precious stones. *Il n'y a rien de si — que le temps;* there is nothing so precious as time. *Tableau d'un fini* —; picture elaborately finished.

précieux, *n.m.*, affectation, affectedness ; affected man.

préciosité, *n.f.*, (l.u.) affectation, affectedness : preciseness.

précipice, *n.m.*, precipice. *Il marche sur le bord du* —; he walks on the brink of a precipice. *On l'a tiré du* —; he has been rescued from destruction.

⊙**précipitable**. *adj.*, precipitable.

précipitamment (-ta-män), *adv.*, precipitately, hurriedly, rashly, precipitously, precipitantly, headlong.

précipitant, *n.m.*, (chem.) precipitant.

précipitation, *n.f.*, precipitation, precipitance, precipitancy ; (chem.) precipitation.

précipité, -e, *part.*, precipitated, precipitate ; rash, hasty, sudden. — *de haut en bas;* hurried headlong from top to bottom. *Course — e;* hasty flight. *Marcher à pas* —*s;* to walk with hurried steps. *Départ* —; sudden departure.

précipité, *n.m.*, (chem.) precipitate. *Un — de mercure;* a precipitate of mercury.

précipiter, *v.a.*, to precipitate, to throw, to hurl ; to hurry; (chem.) to precipitate. — *sa retraite;* to hurry one's retreat. — *ses pas;* to quicken one's steps.

se précipiter, *v.r.*, to precipitate one's self ; to rush, to dash ; to spring forth, to dart, to run. — *sur quelqu'un;* to rush upon any one.

préciput, *n.m.*, portion of an estate or inheritance, which falls to one of the coheirs over and above his equal share with the rest ; benefit stipulated in the marriage contract in favour of the surviving wife or husband.

précis, *n.m.*, summary, abstract, compendium, epitome.

précis, -e, *adj.*, precise, distinct, exact, strict, formal, just. *Venir à l'heure* —; to come exactly at the time appointed. *Prendre des mesures* —*es;* to take just measures.

précisément, *adv.*, precisely, exactly, just; just so.

préciser, *v.a.*, to state precisely.

précision, *n.f.*, precision, preciseness.

précité, *adj.*, (jur.) aforenamed, aforesaid.

précoce, *adj.*, precocious. *Fruit* —; early fruit. *Un esprit* —; a precocious mind.

précocité, *n.f.*, precociousness, precocity.

précompter (-kon-té), *v.a.*, to deduct beforehand.

préconçu, -e, *adj.*, preconceived.

préconisation, *n.f.*, preconisation, declaration of the pope that a bishop appointed by his sovereign has the requisite qualities.

préconiser, *v.a.*, to extol, to cry up, to praise; to preconise, to declare that a bishop appointed by his sovereign has the requisite qualities.

préconnaissance, *n.f.*, foreknowledge.

préconnaître, *v.a.*, to foreknow.

précordial, -e, *adj.*, (anat.) precordial.

précurseur, *n.m.*, forerunner, precursor, harbinger.

prédécéder, *v.n.*, to die first, to predecease.

prédécès, *n.m.*, predecease.

prédécesseur, *n.m.*, predecessor.

prédestinatien (-si-in), *n.m.*, predestinarian.

prédestination, *n.f.*, predestination. — *à la grâce;* predestination to be saved.

prédestiné, -e, *n.* and *adj.*, one of the elect ; elect. *Avoir un visage de* —; to have a happy-looking face.

11 *

prédestiner, v.a., to predestinate.
prédéterminant, adj., (theol.) predetermining.
prédétermination, n.f., predetermination.
prédéterminer, v.a., to predetermine.
prédial, -e, adj., predial. Des rentes —es; ground-rents.
prédicable, adj., (log.) predicable.
prédicament, n.m., (log.) predicament.
prédicant, n.m., (b.s.) protestant preacher.
prédicat, n.m., (log., gram.) predicate.
prédicateur, n.m., preacher.
prédication, n.f., preaching. La — de l'évangile; the preaching of the gospel.
prédiction, n.f., prediction.
prédilection, n.f., predilection, partiality.
prédire, v.a., to predict, to foretell, to forebode. — l'avenir; to foretell the future.
prédisposant, -e, adj., (med.) predisposing.
prédisposer, v.a., (med.) to predispose.
prédisposition, n.f., (med.) predisposition.
prédominance, n.f., predominance.
prédominant, -e, adj., predominant, prevalent.
prédominer, v.n., to predominate, to prevail.
prééminence, n.f., pre-eminence.
prééminent, -e, adj., pre-eminent.
préemption, n.f., pre-emption.
préétablir, v.a., to pre-establish.
préexistant, -e, adj., pre-existent.
préexistence, n.f., pre-existence.
préexister, v.n., to pre-exist.
préface, n.f., preface, preamble, exordium, introduction.
préfectoral, adj., pertaining, relating to a French prefect.
préfecture, n.f., prefectship, prefecture; prefect's house, prefect's offices.
préférable, adj., preferable.
préférablement, adv., preferably.
préférence, n.f., preference. De —; in preference.
préférer, v.a., to prefer, to choose.
préfet, n.m., (Rom. antiq.) prefect; chief magistrate of each department in France; chief inspector of school studies in France; chief magistrate for the police of Paris.
préfinir, v.a., (jur.) to fix a term, a delay, within which certain acts are to be performed.
préfix (-fiks), -e, adj., (jur.) prefixed, appointed.
préfixe, n.m. and adj., (gram.) prefix; prefixed.
préfixion, n.f., (jur.) settled time, prefixion.
préfloraison, n.f., (bot.) prefloration.
préfoliation, n.f., (bot.) foliation, vernation.
prégnation, n.f., gestation (of animals—des animaux).
préhensile, adj., prehensile.
préhistorique, adj., pre-historic, pre-historical.
préjudice, n.m., prejudice, hurt, detriment, injury. Il a obtenu cela à mon — ; he obtained that to my prejudice. Cela vous portera —; that will be detrimental to you. Au — de sa parole; to the detriment of his word. Sans — de mes droits; without prejudice to my claims.
préjudiciable, adj., prejudicial, detrimental, injurious.
préjudiciaux, adj.m.pl., payable (of costs —des dépens) before subsequent proceedings can be taken.
préjudiciel, -le, adj., (jur.) interlocutory. Question —le; interlocutory question, to be decided previous to the principal action.
préjudicier, v.n., to prejudice, to do prejudice, to be prejudicial, to be detrimental, to

hurt, to injure. S t négligence a préjudicié à ses affaires; his negligence has been very prejudicial to his affairs.
préjugé, n.m., presage, presumption, prejudice; (jur.) precedent. Exempt de —s; free from prejudices. Homme sans —; unprejudiced man. Se défaire de ses —s d'enfance; to divest one's self of one's early prejudices. Dissiper les —s; to remove prejudices.
préjuger, v.a., to prejudge; (jur.) to give an interlocutory judgment.
prélart, or **prélat**, n.m., (nav.) tarpauling.
se prélasser, v.r., to assume an air of affected gravity, dignity, haughtiness.
prélat, n.m., prelate; (nav.) V. **prélart**.
prélation, n.f., right that children had to succeed to their father's offices.
prélature, n.f., prelacy.
prèle, or **presle**, n.f., (bot.) horsetail, shave-grass.
prélegs (-lè), n.m., legacy giving the preference to one of the legatees.
préléguer (-ghé), v.a., to give a legacy with preference.
préler, v.a., to rub with horsetail.
prélèvement (-lèv-màn), n.m., previous deduction.
prélever (prél-vé), v.a., to deduct, to take off first.
préliminaire, n.m. and adj., preliminary.
préliminairement, adv., preliminarily.
prélire, v.a., (print.) to read a first time.
prélude, n.m., prelude.
préluder, v.n., to prelude, to flourish, to play a prelude. — à une chose par une autre; to make one thing a prelude to another.
prématuré, -e, adj., premature, untimely.
prématurément, adv., prematurely.
prématurité, n.f., prematureness.
préméditation, n.f., premeditation.
prémédité, -e, part., premeditated. Un dessein —; a premeditated design.
préméditer, v.a., to premeditate.
prémices, n.f.pl., first-fruits.
premi-er, -ère, adj., first; foremost; premier; chief, principal; former, ancient, old, primitive, primeval. Nos —s parents; our first parents. Les —s temps du monde; the early ages of the world. Au — abord; at first view. — en date; senior. En — lieu; in the first place. ☉ —pris; wretched-looking man; il a l'air d'un — pris; he looks wretched. — venu; first comer. — né (—s —s); first-born.
premier, n.m., first; first floor; leader. Jeune —, m., jeune —ère, f. V. **jeune**. Il demeure au — ; he lives on the first floor.
premièrement (-mièr-màn), adv., first, firstly, in the first place.
prémisses, n.f.pl., (log.) premises.
prémonitoire, adj., (med.) premonitory.
prémontrés, n.m.pl., Premonstrants, a regular order of canons of Prémontré in Picardy (France).
prémotion, n.f., (theol.) premotion.
prémunir, v.a., to forewarn, to caution, to provide before hand.
se prémunir, v.r., to provide, to be provided. — contre le froid; to be provided against the cold.
prenable, adj., that may be taken, pregnable.
prenant, -e, adj., (of a person—des personnes) having to receive money; prehensile. Queue —e; prehensile tail.
prendre (prenant, pris), v.a., to take; to take up; to lay hold of; to seize; to apprehend; to fetch; to assume; to contract; to pick out; to snatch; to catch (a cold—un rhume); to imbibe; to call for (any one—quelqu'un); to attack (of diseases—des maladies); to collect (votes); **to**

contract (diseases, engagements—*maladies, engagements*); to help one's self to. — *garde*; to take heed. — *parti pour quelqu'un*; to take any one's part. — *feu*; to take fire. — *soin d'une chose*; to take care of a thing. — *les armes*; to take up arms. — *une ville d'assaut*; to take a town by storm. — *médecine*; to take physic. — *du tabac*; to take snuff. — *congé de quelqu'un*; to take leave of any one. — *la rue à droite*; to take the street on the right. — *le plus court*; to take the shortest way. — *les devants*; to go before. — *bien son temps*; to hit the time well. — *naissance*; to take its rise (of things—*des choses*). — *fait et cause pour quelqu'un*; to take any one's part, to undertake any one's defence. — *quelqu'un sur le fait*; to take one in the fact. — *exemple sur quelqu'un*; to take an example from any one. — *avis de quelqu'un*; to take any one's advice. — *les avis*; to collect the votes. — *intérêt, — part à*; to take part in, to be a party to, to be concerned in, to be a partaker of, to be interested in. — *l'air*; to take an airing — *bien le sens d'un auteur*; to catch an author's meaning. *Vous prenez mal mes paroles*; you misconstrue my words. — *une chose en bonne part*; to take a thing well, in good part. — *les choses de travers*; to take things amiss, the wrong way. — *bien ou mal une affaire*; to go the right or the wrong way to work in a business. — *les choses comme elles viennent*; to take things as they come. *l'occasion aux cheveux*; to take time by the forelock. *À tout —*: upon the whole, in the main. *Ne savoir pas — quelqu'un*; not to know how to deal with any one. *Il en a pris sa bonne part*; he has had his share of it. *Il m'a pris en amitié*; he has conceived a friendship for me. *Je vous y prends*; now I have caught you. *Si la curiosité me prend d'y aller*; if my curiosity prompts me to go there. *L'envie lui prit d'y aller*; the fancy took him to go there. *Il prend beaucoup sur lui*; he assumes much, he takes much on himself. *Cela prend forme*; that begins to come into shape. *Ce qui est bon à — est bon à rendre*; take all that is offered, you may give it back when you please. — *terre* (nav.); to land. — *le vent* (nav.); to sail near the wind. — *le large* (nav.); to stand out to sea.

se prendre, *v.r.*, to be taken, to be caught; to catch, to cling; to freeze, to congeal (of liquids —*des liquides*); to begin, to go to work. *Le sirop se prendra bientôt*; the syrup will soon be congealed. — *à pleurer*; to begin to cry. *Se bien prendre à une chose*; to go the right way to work at a thing. *De la manière dont il s'y prend*; as he goes to work. — *d'amitié pour quelqu'un*; to take a liking for any one. — *de paroles avec quelqu'un*; to have high words with any one. *S'en prendre à*; to blame, to lay the blame on. *S'en prendre à quelqu'un*; to lay the fault upon any one.

prendre, *v.n.*, to take, to turn; to take root; to congeal, to freeze; to succeed; to burn up, to begin to burn; to curdle (of milk—*du lait*). *Bien lui a pris d'avoir été averti*; it was well for him he was told of it. *Il lui en prendra mal*; evil will betide him. *Il lui prit une fièvre*; he was attacked by fever.

prendre, *n.m.*, act of taking. *Au fait et au —*; at the scratch, when it comes to the scratch.

preneu-r, *n.m.*, **-se**, *n.f.*, taker; lessee; (of animals—*d'animaux*) catcher; (com.) purchaser, buyer.

preneur, *adj.m.*, (nav.) that takes a prize.

prénom (-non), *n.m.*, Christian name; prenomen.

prénotion, *n.f.*, prenotion, surmise, conjecture.

préoccupation, *n.f.*, preoccupation, prepossession of the mind.

préoccupé, **-e**, *part.*, preoccupied, absorbed in mind; prejudiced, biassed. *Avoir l'esprit — de quelque chose*; to have one's mind absorbed in any thing.

préoccuper, *v.a.*, to engross; to preoccupy the mind, to prepossess, to prejudice, to bias.

préopinant, *n.m.*, **-e**, *n.f.*, previous speaker; last speaker.

préopiner, *v.n.*, to vote before another.

préordination, *n.f.*, preordination.

préordonner, *v.a.*, to preordain, to predetermine.

préparant, *adj.*, (anat.) spermatic. *Vaisseaux —s*; spermatic duct.

préparateur, *n.m.*, preparer.

préparatif, *n.m.*, preparation, preparative.

préparation, *n.f.*, preparation.

préparatoire, *n.m.* and *adj.*, preparative, preliminary.

préparer, *v.a.*, to prepare, to fit; to provide; to make ready; (agri.) to till. — *les voies à quelqu'un*; to pave the way for any one. **se préparer**, *v.r.*, to prepare, to prepare one's self, to get ready. — *pour un voyage*; to get ready for a journey. — *au combat*; to prepare for battle. *Préparez-vous à le recevoir*; prepare to meet him. *Voilà un orage qui se prépare*; there is a storm brewing.

prépondérance, *n.f.*, preponderance, preponderancy.

prépondérant, **-e**, *adj.*, preponderant. *Voix —e*; casting-vote.

préposé, *n.m.*, custom or excise officer.

préposer, *v.a.*, to set over, to charge with.

prépositi-f, **-ve**, *adj.*, (gram.) prepositive. *Locution —ve*; prepositive expression.

préposition, *n.f.*, (gram.) preposition.

prépuce, *n.m.*, prepuce, foreskin.

prérogative, *n.f.*, prerogative.

près, *prep.*, by, near, nigh, close to, hard by, nearly. *S'asseoir — de quelqu'un*; to sit by any one. *Il demeure ici —*; he lives close by. *Voir l'ennemi de —*; to see the enemy near at hand. *Combattre de —*; to fight hand to hand. *Suivre de —*; to follow close. *À cela —*; save that, that excepted, with that exception; nevertheless, for all that. *À beaucoup —*; by a great deal, nothing near. *Tout —*; very near. *À peu —*; pretty near, nearly. *De — et de loin*; far and nigh.

présage, *n.m.*, presage, omen, foreboding. *Un oiseau de sinistre —*; a bird of evil omen. *Mes —s sont accomplis*; my forebodings are fulfilled.

présager, *v.a.*, to presage, to forebode, to portend, to conjecture.

se présager, *v.r.*, to be foreboded, to be presaged.

pré-salé, *n.m.* (—*s —s*), mutton from sheep that have fed in meadows watered by the sea.

presbyopie, *n.f.*, (opt.) presbyopy, farsightedness, presbyopia.

presbyte, *n.m.f.* and *adj.*, presbyte; farsighted person; presbyopic; far-sighted.

presbytéral, **-e** *adj.*, priestly. *Maison —e*; parsonage, vicarage.

presbytéranisme, *n.m.* V. **presbytérianisme**.

presbytère, *n.m.*, parsonage, parsonagehouse, vicarage; ⊙ presbytery.

presbytérianisme, *n.m.*, presbyterianism.

presbytérien, **-ne** (-ri-in, -ri èn), *n.* and *adj.*, presbyterian.

presbytie (-ci), *n.f.*, (opt.) presbyopy, farsightedness, presbyopia.

presoience, *n.f.*, prescience, foreknowledge, foresight.

prescriptible, *adj.*, prescriptible.

prescription, *n.f.*, (jur.) limitation ; prescription, precept. *Interruption de la* — ; (jur.) bar to a limitation. *Établi par* — ; prescriptive. *Se perdre par* — (jur.); to be lost by limitation. —*s médicales ;* medical prescriptions.

prescrire, *v.a.*, to prescribe, to direct, to order, to enjoin. — *des lois ;* to prescribe laws. — *un régime ;* to prescribe a diet.

se **prescrire**, *v.r.*, (jur.) to be lost by limitation.

prescrire, *v.n.*, to be lost by limitation.

préséance (pré-séans), *n.f.*, precedence, precedency. *Avoir la* — *sur ;* to take precedency over.

présence, *n.f.*, presence ; sight, view. *Faire acte de* — ; to make one's appearance. *Mettre en* — ; to bring face to face. *En* — *de ;* in presence of. *En ma* — ; before me. *Deux armées qui sont en* — ; two armies that are in sight of each other. — *d'esprit ;* presence of mind.

présent, *n.m.*, present, present time ; present, gift ; (gram.) present, present tense. *Donner en* — ; to give as a present. *Faire* — *quelque chose à quelqu'un ;* to make a present of any thing to any one. *Dès à* — ; from this time. *À* — ; at present. *Pour le* — ; for the present. *Jusqu'à* — ; till now.

présent -e, *adj.*, present. *Être* — ; to be present, to stand by.

presentable, *adj.*, that may be presented, presentable.

presentat-eur, *n.m.*, **-rice**, *n.f.*, presenter (to benefices—*à un bénéfice*).

présentation, *n.f.*, presentation, presentment. *À* — (com.) ; on presentation, upon demand. *En retard de* — (com.) ; overdue.

présentement (-zant-mān), *adv.*, now, at present.

présenter, *v.a.*, to present, to offer, to hold out, to introduce. — *ses lettres de créance ;* to exhibit one's credentials. — *les armes ;* to present arms. —*une personne à une autre ;* to introduce one person to another. — *à quelqu'un ses respects ;* to pay one's respects to any one.

se **présenter**, *v.r.*, to present one's self, to appear, to come forward, to offer one's self ; to occur. *Il s'est présenté à moi ;* he presented himself before me. *Cet homme se présente bien ;* that man has a good address. *Une affaire qui se présente bien ;* a thing that looks well. *Il se présenta une difficulté ;* a difficulty occurred.

présenter, *v.n.*, (nav.) to stem. — *au vent ;* to stem the wind.

présenteur, *n.m.*, (l.u.) presenter.

préservat-eur, **-rice**, *adj.*, preservative.

préservatif-f, -ve, *adj.*, preservative.

préservatif, *n.m.*, preservative.

préservation, *n.f.*, preservation.

préserver, *v.a.*, to preserve, to defend, to keep. *Le ciel m'en préserve !* heaven preserve me from it !

se **préserver**, *v.r.*, to preserve one's self. to guard against, to keep off. — *d'une maladie ;* to keep off a disease.

présidence, *n.f.*, presidency, presidentship.

président, *n.m.*, president, chairman, speaker (in the House of Commons—*de la chambre des communes*). — *d'âge ;* president by seniority.

présidente, *n.f.*, lady president ; president's lady.

présider, *v.a.*, to preside, to be president of, to be chairman of. — *une compagnie ;* to preside over a company.

présider, *v.n.*, to preside, to be president

or chairman ; to be in the chair ; to direct. — *à une assemblée ;* to preside over an assembly. — *à la direction d'un ouvrage ;* to have the management of a work.

présides, *n.m. pl.*, Spanish penal colonies, presides.

⊙**présidial**, *n.m.*, presidial, inferior court of judicature.

⊙**présidial, -e**, *adj.*, presidial.

⊙**présidialement** (-al-mān), *adv.*, without appeal.

présompti-f, -ve, *adj.*, presumptive, apparent, presumed (of heirs—*des héritiers*).

présomption, *n.f.*, presumption, presumptuousness, self-conceit.

présomptueusement (-eûz-mān), *adv.*, presumptuously.

présomptueu-x, -se, *adj.*, presumptuous, presuming, self-conceited.

presque, *adv.*, almost, nearly, all but. *Un ouvrage* — *achevé ;* a work nearly finished. *Je ne l'ai* — *pas vu ;* I scarcely saw him. — *jamais ;* hardly ever.

presqu'île, *n.f.* (— —*s*), peninsula.

⊙**presqu'ombre**, *n.f. V.* **pénombre.**

pressage, *n.m.*, pressing.

pressamment (-sa-mān), *adv.*, pressingly, earnestly.

pressant, -e, *adj.*, pressing, urgent, earnest, importunate ; acute (of pain—*de douleurs*).

presse, *n.f.*, press (newspapers, machine— *journaux, machine*) ; printing-press ; crowd, throng ; impress (forcing men into the service— *enrôlement forcé*) ; press-gang ; urgency ; (bot.) a variety of peach. — *à copier ;* copying-machine. — *d'imprimerie ;* printing-press. — *à satiner ;* hot-press, cold-press. *La* — *y est ;* people flock there ; it has a great run. *Cet ouvrage est sous* — ; this work is in the press. *Mettre sous* — ; to send to press, to go to press.

pressé, -e, *adj.*, in haste, in a hurry ; urgent. *Vous êtes bien* — ; you are in a great hurry. *Cela n'est pas* — ; there's no hurry for that.

pressée, *n.f.*, pressful ; pressing.

pressément, *adv.*, (l.u.) hurriedly, hastily.

pressentiment, *n.m.*, presentiment, misgiving, foreboding. *Avoir un* — *de fièvre ;* to feel a threatening of fever.

pressentir, *v.a.*, to have a presentiment of ; to ascertain the intentions of ; to sound. — *quelqu'un ;* to sound any one. *Il faut le* — ; we must sound him.

presse-papiers, *n.m.* (—), paper-weight.

presser, *v.a.*, to press, to squeeze ; to crowd, to throng ; to hasten, to hurry ; to urge, to be pressing with, to importune ; to be hard upon ; to exaggerate ; to impress (sailors —*des matelots*). — *une éponge ;* to squeeze a sponge. *On pressa si fort les ennemis ;* they pressed so hard upon the enemy. — *vivement un siège ;* to carry on a siege vigorously. — *une entreprise ;* to push an enterprise with vigour. *Il pressa son départ ;* he hastened his departure.

se **presser**, *v.r.*, to press, to squeeze ; to crowd; to be in a hurry, to make haste, to hurry. — *de faire une chose ;* to make haste to do a thing. *Pressons-nous ;* let us make haste.

presser, *v.n.*, to be urgent ; to be acute (of pain—*des douleurs*).

presseur, *n.m.*, presser.

pressier, *n.m.*, (print.) pressman.

pression, *n.f.*, pressure. *Machine à vapeur à haute* —, *à moyenne* —, *à basse* — ; steam-engine of high pressure, of mean pressure, of low presure.

pressis, *n.m.*, (l.u.) gravy, juice.

pressoir, *n.m.*, press ; press-room ; wine-press.

pressurage. *n.m.*, pressure (of fruit—*des fruits*); pressing.

pressurer, *v.a.*. to press (grapes or apples —*du raisin, des pommes*); to squeeze; to grind down, to oppress. — *une orange ;* to squeeze an orange. — *la bourse de quelqu'un ;* to drain any one's purse. *Il ne songe qu'à vous — :* his only thought is how he can squeeze money out of you.

pressureur, *n.m.*, presser (of fruit—*de fruits*).

prestance, *n.f.*, imposing deportment, bearing, carriage.

prestant, *n.m.*, diapason (of an organ—*d'orgue*).

prestation. *n.f.*, taking (of an oath—*de serment*); prestation (payment in kind—*payement en nature*).

preste, *adj.*, agile, nimble, quick, smart. *C'est un homme — et habile ;* he is a clever fellow.

preste, *adv.*, presto, quick.

prestement, *adv.*, nimbly, quickly.

prestesse, *n.f.*, agility, quickness, nimbleness.

prestidigitateur, *n.m.*, juggler.

prestidigitation, *n.f.*, jugglery, legerdemain.

prestige. *n.m.*, enchantment, fascination; deception, illusion ; magic spell ; prestige.

prestigieu-x, -se, *adj.*, enchanting, bewitching, illusive.

prestimonie, *n.f.*, (canon law—*loi canon*) prestimony.

presto, *adv.*, (mus.) presto.

prestolet, *n.m.*, priestling.

présumable, *adj.*, presumable.

présumer, *v.a.*, to presume, to conjecture. — *trop de quelqu'un ;* to presume too much upon any one. — *trop de soi ;* to be too assuming. *Il est d — ;* it is to be supposed.

présupposer (-su-pô-zé), *v.a.*, to presuppose.

présupposition, *n.f.*, presupposition.

présure, *n.f.*, rennet, runnet.

prêt, *n.m.*, loan ; (milit.) advance-money.

prêt, -e, *adj.*, ready, in readiness, prepared, willing. *Tenir — ;* to keep ready. *Tenez-vous — à partir :* be ready for starting.

pretantaine, *n.f. Courir la — ;* to ramble about, to gad up and down.

prêté, -e, *part.*, lent.

prêté, *n.m.*, (l.u.) thing lent. *C'est un — rendu ;* it is but tit for tat.

prétendant, *n.m.*, **-e**, *n.f.*, claimant, candidate; suitor, wooer; pretender (to the throne —*au trône*).

prétendre, *v.a.*, to claim, to lay claim to, to pretend to. *Que prétendent ces misérables ?* what do these wretches pretend to ?

prétendre, *v.n.*, to lay claim to; to pretend, to mean ; to maintain. *Je prétends que mon droit est incontestable ;* I maintain that my claim is incontestable.

prétendu, -e, *adj.*, pretended, feigned, sham. *C'est un — bel esprit ;* he is a would-be wit.

prétendu, *n.m.*, **-e**, *n.f.*, intended, future husband, future wife. *Voilà mon — ;* there is my intended.

prête-nom. *n.m.* (— —*s*), one that lends his name to another.

pretantaine, *n.f. V.* **pretantaine**.

prétentie-x, -se, *adj.*, ...assuming.

prétention, *n.f.*, pretention, claim. *Venir à bout de ses — s :* to make good one's claims. *Sa — est mal fondée ;* his demand is groundless. *Il a des — s à l'esprit ;* he has pretensions to wit.

C'est un homme sans — s ; he is a man of no pretensions. *Cette femme a encore des — s ;* that woman still makes pretensions to beauty. *Se désister d'une — ;* to relinquish a claim.

prêter, *v.a.*. to lend. to give, to attribute, to father ; to take (oath—*serment*). — *de l'argent à intérêt ;* to lend money on interest. — *secours ;* to lend a helping hand. — *main-forte à quelqu'un ;* to assist any one, to come to any one's assistance. — *l'oreille :* to give ear. — *serment ;* to take oath. — *foi et hommage ;* to take an oath of allegiance. — *le collet à quelqu'un ;* to try one's strength with any one. — *le flanc ;* to expose one's self.

se **prêter**, *v.r.*, to give way to ; to indulge ; to humour ; to countenance, to favour.

prêter, *v.n.*, to lend ; to give, to stretch (of a thing—*des choses*). *Ce cuir-là prête comme un gant ;* that leather stretches like a glove.

prêter, *n.m.*, loan. *C'est un — à ne jamais rendre ;* it is a loan never to be repaid.

prétérit (-rit), *n.m.*, (gram.) preterit.

prétérition, *n.f.*, (rhet.) preterition ; pretermission.

prétermission, *n.f. V.* **prétérition**.

prêteu-r, *n.m.*, **-se**, *n.f.*, lender. — *sur gages ;* pawnbroker.

préteur. *n.m.*, (antiq.) pretor.

prétexte, *n.m.*, pretext, pretence. — *spécieux ;* plausible pretence. *Faux — ;* false pretence. *Sous—de le secourir ;* under pretence of assisting him.

prétexte, *n.* and *adj.f.*, (Rom. antiq.) prætexta, tunic.

prétexter, *v.a.*, to pretend, to feign, to affect, to sham.

pretintaille, *n.f.*, furbelow; (fig.) accessory, appendage, incidental profit.

pretintailler, *v.a.*, to furbelow, to trim (a dress—*une robe*).

prétoire, *n.m.*, (antiq.) pretorium.

prétorien, -ne (-in, -è-n), *adj.*, (antiq.) pretorian.

prétorien, *n.m.*, (antiq.) pretorian (soldier).

***prêtraille**, *n.f.*, (b.s.) priesthood.

prêtre. *n.m.*, priest, clergyman. *Il s'est fait —;* he has taken orders. — *habitué ;* parish priest. *Grand — ;* high priest.

prêtresse, *n.f.*, priestess.

prêtrise, *n.f.*, priesthood.

préture, *n.f.*, pretorship.

preuve. *n.f.*, proof, evidence, testimony, token ; (com.) proof-sample ; proof (of spirits—*des spiritueux*). *En venir à la — ;* to come to the proof. *Faire — de noblesse ;* to prove one's nobility. *Il a fait ses — s ;* he has given proofs of his capacity. *Faire — de courage ;* to prove one's self a man of courage. *Servir de — ;* to serve as a proof. — *s induites des circonstances ;* (jur.) circumstantial evidence.

preux, *n.* and *adj.m.*, valiant knight, gallant knight : worthy ; gallant, valiant, stout, worthy.

prévaloir, *v.n.*, to prevail. *La faveur prévaut souvent sur le mérite ;* favour frequently prevails over merit.

se **prévaloir**, *v.r.*, to take advantage, to avail one's self. — *de sa naissance ;* to take advantage of one's birth.

prévaricateur, *n.m.*, prevaricator; betrayer of one's trust.

prévaricat-eur, -rice, *adj.*, prevaricating.

prévarication, *n.f.*, prevarication; betrayal of one's trust.

prévariquer. *v.n.*, to prevaricate, to betray one's trust.

prévenance (pré-vnans), *v.f.*, kindness, kind attention.

prévenant. -e. *adj.*, prepossessing; ready to oblige, to anticipate any one's wishes, kind. *La grâce — e de Dieu;* God's predisposing grace. *Il a un air — ;* he has a prepossessing look.

prévenir (pré-vnir), *v.a.*, to go before, to precede, to come before, to be beforehand with, to get the start of, to anticipate; to prevent, to hinder; to prepossess; to prejudice: to predispose, to bias, to inform, to warn. — *le mal:* to prevent evil. — *les objections;* to anticipate objections. — *les besoins de quelqu'un;* to anticipate any one's wants. *Il m'a fait — de son arrivée:* he sent me information of his arrival. *On vous en avait prévenu;* you had information of it.

se **prévenir,** *v.r.,* to be prepossessed, to be prejudiced. — *en faveur de quelqu'un;* to take a liking to any one.

préventi-f. -ve *adj.*, preventive.

prévention, *n.f.,* prepossession, prejudice, bias; prevention, preventing; accusation: (jur.) prosecution; (jur.) state of being impeached, state of being arraigned. *Donner des —s contre soi;* to raise prejudices against one's self. *Vaincre les —s de quelqu'un;* to overcome any one's prejudices.

préventivement, *adv.,* in a preventive manner; (jur.) while awaiting trial, on suspicion.

prévenu, *n.m.,* **-e,** *n.f.,* (jur.) prisoner (before trial—*avant le jugement*), the accused.

prévision, *n.f.,* prevision.

prévoir, *v.a.,* to foresee. *Il faut tout — ;* we must provide against every thing.

prévôt, *n.m.,* provost; (nav.) marshal. *Grand —, grand — de l'armée* (milit.); provost-marshal. — *de salle d'armes;* fencing-master's assistant.

prévôtal, -e, *adj.,* relating, pertaining to a provost.

prévôtalement (-tal-mān), *adv.,* by a provost-court.

prévôté, *n.f.,* provostship.

prévoyance, *n.f.,* foresight, forethought. *Rien n'échappe à sa —;* nothing escapes his foresight.

prévoyant, -e, *adj.,* provident.

priapée, *n.f.,* obscene picture; obscene poem.

priapisme, *n.m.,* (med.) priapism.

prié, *n.m.,* **-e,** *n.f.,* person invited, guest.

prie-dieu, *n.m.* (—), praying-desk.

prier, *v.a.* and *n.,* to pray; to entreat, to beseech, to call upon, to beg, to implore, to supplicate, to request; to invite, to bid. — *quelqu'un d'une grâce;* to request a favour of any one. *Il m'a prié de l'accompagner;* he begged me to accompany him. *On m'a prié de le faire;* I have been requested to do it. *Je vous en prie;* I beg of you. — *à dîner;* to invite to dinner. — *de dîner;* to beg to stay at dinner.

prière, *n.f.,* prayer, suit, request, entreaty. *Instante — ;* earnest prayer. *Faire une — à quelqu'un;* to make a request to any one. *Être en — ;* to be at prayers. *Faire une chose à la — de quelqu'un;* to do a thing at any one's request, at any one's entreaty. *Dire ses —s. faire sa —,* *faire ses —s:* to say one's prayers.

prieur, *n.m.,* prior (superior of a convent—*supérieur de couvent*).

prieure, *n.f.,* prioress.

prieuré, *n.m.,* priory.

prima donna, *n.f.* (*prime donne*), the first female singer in an opera.

primage, *n.m.,* (com.) primage (allowance paid to the captain of a ship—*bonification accordée au capitaine d'un vaisseau*).

primaire, *adj.,* primary. *École — ;* elementary school.

primat, *n.m.,* primate, metropolitan.

primatial, -e (-ci-al), *adj.,* primatial, primatical.

primatie (-ma-ci), *n.f.,* primacy, primateship.

primauté, *n.f.,* primacy, supremacy, preeminence; playing first (at cards. *dice—aux cartes, aux dés*). *Gagner quelqu'un de — ;* to anticipate any one, to be beforehand with any one.

prime, *adj.,* (alg.) accented. *b', b — ;* b', b accented.

prime, *n.f.,* premium, bounty; (c.rel.) prime (first canonical hour succeeding lauds—*première heure canonique après laudes*); (fenc.) prime; primero (card game—*jeu de cartes*); (com.) prime wool; (jewellery—*joaillerie*) pebble; (exchange language—*terme de bourse*) agio; (customs—*douanes*) drawback. *À — ;* at a premium.

de **prime abord,** *adv.,* at first.

de **prime face,** *adv.,* at first, *prima facie.*

primer, *v.n.,* to play first, to lead (at play—*au jeu*); to take the lead, to excel, to surpass. *Il prime en tout;* he excels in everything.

primer, *v.a.,* to surpass, to excel; to give a prize (at an agricultural show—*à un concours agricole*). *Il prime tous les autres;* he excels all the others.

de **prime-saut,** *adv.,* all at once, at the first effort.

prime-sauti-er, -ère, *adj.,* quick (of thought—*de la pensée*), ready-witted; thoughtless, inconsiderate, heedless. *Les Français ont, en général, l'esprit — ;* the French are, in general, ready-witted.

primeur, *n.f.,* first of the season (of vegetables, fruit, flowers, wine, &c.—*des légumes, des fruits, des fleurs, du vin, &c.*); early fruit; early vegetables; early flower; early sentiment, first love. *Les fruits sont chers dans la — ;* fruit is dear in the early part of the season, fruit is dear when it first comes in. *Certains vins ne sont pas bons dans la — ;* certain wines are not good when they are new. *Servir à table un plat de —s;* to serve up a dish of early vegetables.

Ⓞ**primevère,** *n.m.,* spring season.

primevère, *n.f.,* primrose, cowslip, oxlip.

primicériat, *n.m.,* dignity, office of primicerius, dean, in some churches.

primicier, *n.m.,* primicerius, dean (of some churches—*dans quelques églises*).

primidi, *n.m.,* Primidi, first day of the decade in the calendar of the first French republic.

primipilaire, *or* **primipile,** *n.m.,* (Roman antiq.) primipilus.

primiti-f, -ve, *adj.,* primitive, primeval, primogenial, original; (gram.) primitive, original.

primitif, *n.m.,* (gram.) primitive.

primitivement (-tiv-mān), *adv.,* primitively, originally.

primo, *adv.,* firstly, first, in the first place.

primogéniture, *n.f.,* primogeniture.

primordial, -e, *adj.,* primordial.

primordialement (-al-mān), *adv.,* primordially.

primulacées, *n.f. pl.,* (bot.) primulaceæ.

prince, *n.m.,* prince. *Vivre en — :* to live like a prince. *Dîner de — :* princely dinner.

princeps (-sèps), *adj. invariable,* (print.) earliest, first (edition).

princerie (prin-sri), *n.f.,* deanery, deanship (in certain churches—*dans certaines églises*).

princesse, *n.f.*, princess. *Oui, ma —;* (fam.) yes, my charmer.

princi-er, ère, *adj.*, princely, like a prince.

princier, *n.m.*, primicerius, first dignitary (of certain churches—*dans certaines églises*). *V.* **primicier**.

principal, -e, *adj.*, principal, chief, main; (astron.) primary.

principal, *n.m.*, principal thing, principal point, chief point, material point; principal, capital (money—*argent*); principal, head-master (of a communal college—*d'un collège communal*); (jur.) principal cause of action. *Pour vous, le — est que vous ayez soin de votre santé;* the principal thing for you to do is to take care of your health. *Payer le — et l'intérêt;* to pay both principal and interest.

principalat, *n.m.*, head-mastership of a communal college.

principalement (-pal-män), *adv.*, principally, chiefly.

⊙**principalité**, *n.f. V.* **principalat**.

principat, *n.m.*, the Imperial dignity among the Romans.

principauté, *n.f.*, principality, princedom.

principe, *n.m.*, beginning, source, outset, origin, principle; *pl.*, principles, rudiments. *Dès le —;* from the very origin. *Établir, poser, un —;* to establish, to lay down, a principle. *Partir d'un —;* to set out from a principle. *Homme sans —s;* unprincipled man. *L'amour-propre est le -- de presque toutes nos actions;* self-love is the cause of almost all our actions.

principion, principule, *n.m.*, petty prince.

printani-er, ère, *adj.*, spring. *Fleurs —ères;* spring-flowers. *Étoffes —ères;* stuffs for spring, spring stuffs.

printemps (-tän), *n.m.*, spring, springtime; prime, bloom. *Le — de sa vie;* the morning of life. *Dans le — de sa vie;* in the prime of one's days. *Au — de ses jours;* in the bloom of one's youth.

à priori, *adv.*, à priori.

priorité, *n.f.*, priority.

pris, -e, *part.*, taken, caught. *Homme bien — dans sa taille;* well-shaped man. *Cet homme est — de vin;* that man is in liquor, that man is the worse for liquor. *Premier- —; V.* **premier**.

prisable, *adj.*, estimable, valuable.

prise, *n.f.*, taking, capturing, capture; prize; hold, handle, purchase; quarrel; dose; pinch; *pl.*, fighting. *La — d'une ville;* the taking of a town. *-- de possession;* taking possession. *— de possession d'un bénéfice;* induction to a living. *— d'habit* (c. rel.); taking the habit. *Décret de — de corps;* writ of arrest. *Part de —;* prize-money. *Amariner une —;* to man a prize. *Être de bonne —;* to be a lawful prize. *Lâcher —;* to let go one's hold. *Donner — à la critique;* to lay one's self open to criticism, to expose one's self to criticism; to give a hold to criticism. *Donner — sur soi à son ennemi;* to give one's enemy an advantage over one's self. *— de tabac;* pinch of snuff. *En venir aux —s;* to grapple with one another, to come to blows. *Les deux chiens sont aux —s;* the two dogs are fighting. *Être aux —s avec la mauvaise fortune;* to be struggling with adversity. *Être aux —s avec la mort;* to be on the point of death, to be in great danger.

prisée, *n.f.*, estimate, appraisement. *Faire la — de;* to make an estimate of.

priser, *v.a.*, to prize, to rate, to value, to set a price on, to appraise, to estimate; to esteem, to have an esteem for.

se priser, *v.r.*, to be valued, to be esteemed; to think a great deal of one's self, to set a high value on one's self.

priser, *v.a.* and *n.*, to take snuff.

priseu-r, *n.m.*, **-se**, *n.f.*, snuff-taker.

priseur, *adj.*, who appraises. *Commissaire —;* appraiser, auctioneer. *Expert — assermenté;* sworn appraiser.

prismatique, *adj.*, prismatic.

prisme, *n.m.*, prism.

prismoïde, *n.m.* and *adj.*, prismold; prismoidal.

prison, *n.f.*, prison, gaol, jail; imprisonment, confinement. *S'échapper de —;* to break out of prison. *— d'état;* state prison. *Être dans la — de saint Crépin;* to wear shoes which pinch. *Être condamné à la — perpétuelle;* to be condemned to imprisonment for life. *Envoyer en —;* to send to prison.

prisonni-er, *n.m.*, **-ère**, *n.f.*, prisoner. *— d'état;* state-prisoner.

privati-f, -ve, *adj.*, (gram.) privative; (jur.) in severalty.

privation, *n.f.*, privation, deprivation, bereavement. *Vivre de —s;* to lead a life of privation. *Être dans la —;* to be in a state of privation. *La — de la vue;* the loss of sight.

privativement (-tiv-män), *adv.*, exclusively.

privauté, *n.f.*, extreme familiarity. *Prendre des —s.* to take liberties.

privé, -e, *part.*, deprived. *Corps — de vie;* lifeless body. *Homme — de sa raison;* man deprived of his reason.

privé, -e, *adj.*, private; tame (animal). *Vie —e;* private life. *De son autorité —e;* of one's own authority.

⊙**privément**, *adv.*, familiarly.

priver, *v.a.*, to deprive; to bereave; to tame (animal). *— quelqu'un de ses biens;* to deprive any one of his property. *Je ne veux pas vous — de cela;* I won't rob you of that.

se priver, *v.r.*, to deprive one's self.

privilège, *n.m.*, privilege; (jur.) preference, (thea.) licence. *Accorder un — à;* to grant a privilege to; to license (printers—*imprimeurs*). *Priver de ses —s;* to deprive any one of his privileges; to disfranchise. *Atteinte portée aux —s;* breach of privilege. *Les —s de la noblesse;* the privileges of the nobility.

privilégié, -e, *adj.*, privileged, exempt; (thea.) licensed; (jur.) entitled to preference (of creditors—*de créanciers*). *Lieu —; privileged place. *C'est un être —;* he is a privileged being.

privilégié, *n.m.*, privileged person.

privilégier, *v.a.*, to grant a privilege, to privilege.

prix, *n.m.*, price, cost, value, worth; estimation; reward; prize. *— fait;* settled price. *Mettre un — à;* to set a price upon. *— excessif;* extravagant price. *Juste —;* moderate price. *Une chose de —;* a thing of great value. *Hors de —;* extravagantly dear. *Une chose qui n'a point de —;* a thing that is invaluable. *Vendre à tout —;* to sell at any price. *Mettre la tête d'un homme à —;* to set a price upon a man's head. *— fixe* (com.); set price, no abatement. *À quelque — que ce soit;* cost what it will. *La vertu trouve son — en elle-même;* virtue is its own reward. *Remporter le —;* to carry off the prize. *Au — de;* at the expense of, in comparison with. *À vil —;* under price, dirt-cheap. *— courant* (com.); current price, market price. *— coûtant;* cost price.

probabilisme, *n.m.*, probabilism.

probabilité, *n.f.*, probability, likelihood.

probable, *adj.*, probable, likely. *Cela est bien peu —;* that is any thing but probable.

probablement, *adv.*, probably, likely.

probante, *adj.f.*, probatory (of documents
—*de titres*); convincing (arguments). *En forme*
—; in an authentic form. *Raison* —; convincing reason.

probation, *n.f.*, probation.

probatique, *adj.*, only used in : *piscine* —;
the reservoir near the Temple in which Hebrew
Priests washed the animals that were to be
sacrificed.

Ⓒ**probatoire**, *adj.*, probatory.

probe, *adj.*, honest, upright ; of probity.
Homme —; man of probity.

probité, *n.f.*, probity, honesty, integrity,
uprightness. — *éprouvée ;* tried probity.

problématique, *adj.*, problematical.

problématiquement (-tik-mān), *adv.*,
problematically.

problème, *n.m.*, problem. *Poser un* —; to
state a problem. *Résoudre un* —; to solve a
problem.

proboscide, *n.f.*, (natural hist., her.) proboscis.

proboscidiens, *n.m.pl.*, (zool.) probosci-
dians, proboscideæ.

procédé, *n.m.*, behaviour, proceeding, way
of acting ; process, operation ; *pl.*, delicate,
gentlemanly manners. *Avoir des* —*s ;* to be
delicate in one's manners, to behave handsomely. *Manquer aux* —*s :* to behave in an
unhandsome manner. *C'est un homme à* —*s ;*
he is a gentlemanly man. — *chimique ;*
chemical process.

procéder, *v.n.*, to proceed, to come from ;
to arise ; to behave, to conduct one's self ; (jur.)
to proceed. — *criminellement contre quelqu'un ;*
to proceed criminally against any one. *Cela
procède bien ;* that goes on very well.

procédure, *n.f.*, (jur.) proceedings ;
practice.

procès, *n.m.*, lawsuit, suit, action, trial,
process. *Être en* —; to be at law. *Intenter
un* —, *faire un* —, *à quelqu'un ;* to bring an
action against any one, to institute proceedings
against any one. *Gagner son* —: to gain
one's suit. *Perdre son* —; to be cast. *Juger
un* — *en faveur de quelqu'un ;* to give judgment
in one's behalf. *Faire le* — *à quelqu'un ;* to try
any one, to bring any one to trial ; to call any
one to account. *Sans autre forme de* —; without any more ado.

processi-f, -ve. *adj.*, litigious.

procession, *n.f.*, procession.

processionnal, *n.m.*, (c. rel.) processional.

processionnel, -le, *adj.*, processional.

processionnellement (-nèl-mān),*adv.*, in
procession.

procès-verbal, *n.m.* (— *verbaux*), proces
verbal, authentic written minute, *or* report, of
an official act *or* proceeding; proceedings,
report.

prochain, -e, *adj.*, near, nearest, next,
approaching, near at hand, nigh, approximate,
proximate. *Village* —; neighbouring village.
Le mois —; next month. *La semaine* —*e ;* next
week. *Son départ est* —; his departure is nigh
at hand.

prochain, *n.m.*, neighbour, fellow-creature.

prochainement (-shè-n-mān), *adv.*, in a
short time, shortly, soon.

proche, *adj.*, near, next, near at hand,
neighbouring, nigh. *La ville la plus* —; the
nearest town. — *parent ;* near relation.

proche, *prep.*, near, nigh.

proche, *adv.*, near, nigh. *De* — *en* —; from
place to place ; gradually, one after another.
Le choléra s'étendit rapidement de — *en* —; the
cholera spread rapidly from place to place.

proches, *n.m.pl.*, near relations, near relatives ; relations, relatives, kinsmen, kin, kindred.

prochronisme, *n.m.*, prochronism.

proclamateur, *n.m.*, proclaimer.

proclamation, *n.f.*, proclamation. *Faire
une* —; to make a proclamation. *Publier une*
—; to publish a proclamation.

proclamer, *v.a.*, to proclaim, to cry out, to
give out, to announce, to trumpet.

proclitique, *n.m.* and *adj.*, (gram.) unaccented word ; unaccented.

procombant, -e, *adj.*, (bot.) procumbent.

proconsul, *n.m.*, (Roman hist.) proconsul.

proconsulaire, *adj.*, (Roman hist.) proconsular.

proconsulat, *n.m.*, (Roman hist.) proconsulship.

procréation, *n.f.*, procreation.

procréer, *v.a.*, to procreate.

procurateur, *n.m.*, procurator (of Genoa
and Venice—*de Gênes et de Venise*).

procuratie (-ci), *n.f.*, (at Genoa and Venice
—*à Gênes et à Venise*) procuratorship, dignity
of a Procurator ; a Procurator's palace.

procuration, *n.f.*, procuration, power of
attorney, letter of attorney, warrant of attorney;
power, warrant, proxy (deed —*titre*).

procuratrice, *n.f.* V. **procureur**.

procurer, *v.a.*, to procure, to obtain, to
help to, to get. — *une charge à quelqu'un ;* to
procure, to obtain, to get, an office for any one.
se procurer, *v.r.*, to procure, to obtain, to get
for one's self ; to be procured, to be obtained,
to be procurable. — *de l'argent ;* to obtain
money. *Ce poisson se procure très-difficilement ;*
this fish is procured with great difficulty.

procur-eur, *n.m.*, **-atrice**, *n.f.*, proxy.
Agir par —; to act by proxy.

procureur, *n.m.*, ⓞsolicitor, attorney, procurator; ⓞ — *fiscal* (feudalism—*féodalité*); lord's
attorney; purveyor (of monastic orders—*dans
les ordres religieux*). — *général ;* Attorney
General. — *du roi*, — *impérial*, — *de la république ;* public prosecutor.

ⓞ**procureuse**, *n.f.*, (jest.) attorney's wife,
solicitor's wife.

prodigalement (-gal-mān), *adv.*, prodigally, extravagantly, lavishly.

prodigalité, *n.f.*, prodigality, profusion,
extravagance, lavishness; act of prodigality,
act of extravagance.

prodige, *n.m.*, prodigy, wonder, marvel.

prodigieusement (-eûz-mān), *adv.*, prodigiously, wonderfully, wondrously, marvellously ; stupendously.

prodigieu-x, -se, *adj.*, prodigious, wondrous, wonderful, marvellous ; vast, stupendous.

prodigue, *adj.*, prodigal, profuse, lavish,
wasteful. *L'enfant* —; the prodigal son.

prodigue, *n.m.*, prodigal, spendthrift.

prodiguer (-ghé), *v.a.*, to lavish, to waste,
to squander away, to be prodigal of, to be lavish
of, to throw away. — *sa vie ;* to throw away
one's life.

se prodiguer, *v.r.*, to be lavished, to be
thrown away ; to offer one's self. *Les courtisans
se prodiguent à tous ;* courtiers are continually
offering their services to every one.

ⓞ**proditoirement**,*adv.*,(jur.)treacherously.

prodrome, *n.m.*, introduction, preface ;
(med.) premonitory symptoms.

product-eur, -rice, *adj.*, productive, producing.

producteur, *n.m.*, (polit. econ.) producer.

productibilité, *n.f.*, producibleness.

productible, *adj.*, producible.

producti-f, -ve, *adj.*, productive.

production, *n.f.*, act of producing, production ; (jur.) exhibition (of deeds—*de titres*);
(jur.) deeds exhibited ; (anat.) process, growth.

produire (produisant, produit), *v.a.*, to
produce, to bring forth ; to bear, to yield, to be

worth ; to be productive of, to be the cause of ; to show, to exhibit ; to make known. *Ce pays produit de l'or ;* this country produces gold. — *des titres ;* to show title-deeds. — *des témoins ;* to produce witnesses. *Cette charge produit dix mille francs par an ;* this office is worth ten thousand francs a year. *La guerre produit de grands maux ;* war is productive of great evils. — *un jeune homme dans le monde ;* to introduce a young man into society, to bring out a young man.

se **produire**, *v.r.*, to introduce one's self, to make one's way ; to be produced, brought forth.

produire, *v.n.*, (jur.) to deliver particulars, to show title-deeds.

produit, *n.m.*, produce, product, yield ; production ; (arith., geom.) proceeds. *Il vit du* — *de sa terre ;* he lives on the produce of his land. —*s agricoles ;* agricultural produce. — *chimique ;* chemical product. — *net* (com.) ; net proceeds.

proéminence, *n.f.*, prominence, prominency, protuberance.

proéminent, -e, *adj.*, prominent, protuberant.

profanateur, *n.m.*, profaner.

profanation, *n.f.*, profanation.

profane, *adj.*, profane.

profaner, *v.a.*, to profane, to defile, to pollute. *C'est* — *le talent que de faire cela ;* it is a profanation of talent to do that.

profecti-f, -ve, *adj.*, (jur.) of the property coming to one by inheriting from one's father, mother or any other ascendant.

proférer, *v.a.*, to utter, to speak. — *des menaces ;* to utter threats.

prof-ès, -esse, *n.* and *adj.*, professed friar ; professed nun ; professed.

professer, *v.a.*, to profess, to make a profession of ; to exercise, to practise, to teach, to be a professor of, to lecture on. — *le plus grand respect pour quelqu'un ;* to profess the greatest respect for any one. — *une science ;* to teach a science. — *un métier ;* to practise a trade, to exercise a calling.

professer, *v.a.* and *n.*, to be a professor, to be a lecturer ; to lecture, to teach.

professeur, *n.m.*, professor ; teacher ; lecturer ; practiser (of an art or calling—*d'un art, d'une profession*). *Chaire de* —; professorship. — *en droit ;* professor of law.

profession, *n.f.*, profession, declaration ; profession (occupation), calling ; trade, business. *Il fait* — *de bel esprit ;* he sets up for a wit. *De quelle* — *est-il ?* what is his profession ? *Dévot de* —; professed devotee.

professionnel, -le, *adj.*, professional.

ex **professo**, *adv.*, ex professo ; thoroughly ; in a professional manner.

professoral, -e, *adj.*, professorial.

professorat, *n.m.*, professorship ; teaching.

profil, *n.m.*, profile, side face ; (drawing—*dessin linéaire*) section. *Un visage de* —; a face in profile.

profiler, *v.a.*, to profile.

profit, *n.m.*, profit, gain, emolument, benefit, utility ; improvement, progress ; use. *Au* —; *or the benefit of, for the use of.* — *net ;* clear profit. *Il ne m'en revient aucun* —; I get no advantage by it. *Mettre tout à* —; to improve every thing to the best advantage. *Faire son* — *de ;* to make a profit by. *Tirer du* — *de ;* to profit by. —*s éventuels,* perquisites.

profitable, *adj.*, profitable.

profiter, *v.n.*, to profit, to gain ; to benefit, to avail one's self ; to improve. — *sur des marchandises ;* to profit by goods. *Faire* — *son argent ;* to derive profit from one's money. — *des bons avis,* to profit by good advice. — *de*

l'occasion ; to avail one's self of, to improve, the opportunity. *Les biens mal acquis ne profitent point ;* ill gotten goods never prosper. — *en sagesse ;* to improve in wisdom. *C'est un terrain où rien ne profite ;* it is a soil where nothing thrives.

profond, -e, *adj.*, deep, profound, consummate ; heavy (of sighs—*soupirs*) ; dark (of the night—*nuit*). *Un* — *sommeil,* a sound sleep. —*e révérence ;* low bow, low courtesy. *Science* —*e ;* profound learning. *Puits* —; deep well. *Un savant* —; a profound scholar. *Un* — *penseur ;* a profound thinker. *Un* — *scélérat ;* a consummate villain. *Nuit* —*e ;* dark night.

profond, *n.m.*, depth, abyss.

profondément, *adv.*, deep, profoundly, soundly. *Saluer* —; to bow low. *Dormir* —; to sleep soundly.

profondeur, *n.f.*, depth ; profoundness, profundity ; penetration.

profusément, *adv.*, profusely.

profusion, *n.f.*, profusion, profuseness. *Donner avec* —; to give profusely, lavishly. *Faire des* —*s ;* to spend with profusion.

Ⓞ**progéniture**, *n.f.*, (jest.) progeny, offspring.

prognathe, *adj.*, (ethnology) prognathous.

prognathisme, *n.m.*, (ethnology) the being prognathous.

prognostic, *n.m.* V. **pronostic**.

prognostique, *adj.*, (med.) prognostic.

programme, *n.m.*, programme, bill. — *de spectacle ;* play-bill.

progrès, *n.m.*, progress ; advancement, improvement, proficiency. — *d'une maladie ;* progress of a disease. *Faire des* — *dans les études ;* to make progress in study. *Faire des* — *dans la vertu ;* to improve in virtue. *Il a fait de grands* —*s ;* he is greatly improved.

progresser, *v.n.*, to progress, to improve.

progressi-f, -ve, *adj.*, progressive.

progression, *n.f.*, progression.

progressivement (-siv-mān), *adv.*, progressively.

prohiber, *v.a.*, to forbid, to interdict, to prohibit.

prohibiti-f, -ve, *adj.*, prohibitive, prohibitory.

prohibition, *n.f.*, prohibition, interdiction.

prohibitionniste, *n.m.*, (com.) prohibitionist.

proie, *n.f.*, prey. *Oiseaux de* —; birds of prey. *Être en* — *à la douleur ;* to be a prey to grief. *Être ardent à la* —; to be eager after booty. *Partager la* —; to divide the spoil. *Être en* — *à ses valets ;* to be pilfered by one's own servants.

projectile, *n.m.* and *adj.*, projectile.

projection, *n.f.*, projection.

projecture, *n.f.*, (arch.) projecture.

projet, *n.m.*, project, scheme, design, plan, first sketch ; rough draft. *Former, concevoir, un* —; to lay, to contrive, a scheme. *Homme à* —*s ;* schemer, projector.

projeter (proj-té), *v.a.*, to project, to plan, to contrive, to scheme ; to contemplate, to intend ; to project, to throw forward, to cast forward ; to project, to delineate. — *un grand ouvrage ;* to project a great work. — *d'aller à la campagne ;* to contemplate going into the country. *La terre projette son ombre ;* the earth throws forward its shadow.

se **projeter**, *v.r.*, to project, to jut out, to shoot out, to be prominent.

projeter, *v.n.*, to form projects.

projeteu-r, *n.m.*, **-se**, *n.f.*, projector, person full of projects ; schemer.

prolapsus, *n.m.*, (med.) prolapsus, prolapse. — *de la luette ;* prolapse of the uvula.

prolégomènes, *n.m.pl.*, prolegomena.
prolepse. *n.f.*, (rhet.) prolepsis.
proleptique, *adj.*, (med.) proleptic, proleptical.
prolétaire, *n.m.* and *adj.*, proletary; proletarian.
prolétariat, *n.m.*, proletariat.
prolifère, *adj.*, (bot.) proliferous.
prolifique, *adj.*, prolific.
prolixe, *adj.*, prolix, tedious, diffuse, verbose.
prolixement, *adv.*, prolixly.
prolixité, *n.f.*, prolixity, prolixness.
prologue (-log), *n.m.*, prologue.
prolongation, *n.f.*, prolongation, delay.
prolonge, *n.f.*, (artil.) binding rope, lashing; (artil.) small ammunition-waggon.
prolongement (-lonj-mân), *n.m.*, prolongation.
prolonger. *v.a.*, to prolong. to lengthen, to protract, to lengthen out, to draw out; (geom.) to produce; (nav.) to bring alongside; to sail along. — *une trève*; to prolong a truce. — *un quai*; to prolong a quay. — *le temps*; to spin out the time. — *le terme d'un payement*; to give a longer time for payment.
se prolonger, *v.r.*, to be prolonged; to extend, to be prolonged. *Les débats se sont prolongés fort avant dans la nuit*; the debates were prolonged until a late hour of the night.
promenade (pro-mnad), *n.f.*, walking, walk; walk, promenade (place); ambulatory, deambulatory. — *à pied*; walk. — *à cheval*; ride, ride on horseback. — *en voiture*; drive, airing; drive, ride in a carriage. — *en bateau*; row, sail. *Faire une* — ; to take a walk; to go for a walk. *Faire une* — *en voiture*; to take a drive, to go for a drive. *La* — *est belle aujourd'hui*; it is beautiful weather for a walk, it is beautiful weather for walking, to-day.
se promener (pro-mné), *v.r.*, to walk, to take a walk, to go for a walk, to promenade; to wander, to extend. — *à cheval*; to ride, to take a ride, to go out riding. — *en voiture*; to take a drive, to take an airing, to drive out. — *sur l'eau*; to go on the water; to go for a row; to go for a sail. *Du haut de Montmartre la vue se promène sur toute la ville de Paris*; from the top of Montmartre the eye wanders over all the city of Paris. *Envoyer quelqu'un* — ; to send any one packing. *Qu'il aille* — ; let him go and be hanged. *Allez vous promener*; go about your business.
promener, *v.a.*, to take out for a walk, to take out walking; to take, to take out, for an airing, for a drive; to take, to take out, for a ride; to take out (animal); to turn (one's eyes, looks—*ses yeux, ses regards*); to lead about, to take about. — *sa vue sur une assemblée*; to glance one's eye over an assembly. — *ses rêveries*; to carry one's reveries abroad. — *quelqu'un*; to bandy any one about.
promeneu-r, *n.m.*, **-se**, *n.f.*, person that takes another out to walk; walker, pedestrian; rider, person taking a ride; person taking a drive.
promenoir, *n.m.*, walk, place for walking.
promesse, *n.f.*, promise, word; promissory note, note of hand. *Tenir sa* — ; to keep one's promise. *Satisfaire à sa* — ; to be as good as one's word. *Vendre avec* — *de garantir*; to warrant one's commodities good.
promettant, *n.m.*, (jur.) promiser, promisor.
prometteu-r, *n.m.*, **-se**, *n.f.*, promiser.
promettre, *v.a.*, to promise. *Il m'a promis d'ivenir*; he promised me that he would come. ε — *et tenir sont deux*; it is one thing to promise, another to perform. *Voilà un temps qui promet lu chaud*; this weather forebodes heat.

se promettre, *v.r.*, to promise one's self; to purpose, to resolve.
promettre, *v.n.*, to promise, to be promising, to bid fair. *Ce jeune homme promet beaucoup*; that is a very promising young man.
prominence, *n.f.*, prominence.
prominent, **-e**, *adj.*, prominent.
prominer, *v.n.*, to rise above; to be prominent.
promis, **-e**, *part.*, promised. *La terre* — *e*; the promised land. *Chose* — *e, chose due*; one is bound in honour to perform what he promises.
promiscuité. *n.f.*, promiscuousness; promiscuous intercourse.
promission, *n.f.*, (Bibl.) promise. *La terre de* — ; the land of promise.
promontoire, *n.m.*, (geog.) promontory, headland.
promoteur, *n.m.*, promoter.
promotion, *n.f.*, promotion.
promouvoir, *v.a.*, to promote, to prefer, to raise, to advance.
prompt, **-e** (prôn, pront), *adj.*, prompt, quick, ready; sudden, speedy, swift; hasty, passionate. *-e réponse*; quick answer. *Il a la repartie* — *e*; he is quick at repartee. *Il est* — *à servir ses amis*; he is prompt in serving his friends. *Avoir l'esprit* — ; to have a quick understanding.
promptement (prôn-tmân), *adv.*, promptly, quickly, readily, suddenly, speedily, swiftly; hastily, passionately.
promptitude (prôn-ti-tud), *n.f.*, promptitude, speed, speediness; quickness, readiness, suddenness, swiftness; hastiness, passion.
promulgation, *n.f.*, promulgation.
promulguer (-ghé), *v.a.*, to promulgate.
pronaos, *n.m.* (—), (arch., antiq.) pronaos.
pronateur, *n.* and *adj. m.*, (anat.) pronator.
pronation, *n.f.*, (anat.) pronation.
prône, *n.m.*, (c.rel.) sermon (after or before mass—*avant ou après la messe*); lecture, rebuke, sermon. *Recommander quelqu'un au* — ; to recommend any one to the prayers of the congregation; to complain of any one so as to cause him to be severely treated or reprimanded.
prôner, *v.a.*, to cry up, to extol, to preach up, to commend, to praise, to set forth; to preach to, to lecture; (l.u.) to preach.
prôner, *v.n.*, to lecture, to remonstrate.
prôneur, *n.m.*, (l.u.) preacher.
prôneu-r, *n.m.*, **-se**, *n.f.*, puffer, trumpeter; chider, rebukeful prattler, rebuker.
pronom (-non), *n.m.*, (gram.) pronoun.
pronominal, **-e**, *adj.*, pronominal.
pronominalement (-nal-mân), *adv.*, (gram.) pronominally.
prononçable, *adj.*, pronounceable.
prononcé, *n.m.*, (jur.) judgment delivered.
prononcé,-e, *adj.*, decided, decisive; (paint., sculpt.) prominent. *Les muscles en sont bien* — *s*; the muscles are very prominent. *Caractère* — ; decided character. *Goût* — ; decided taste.
prononcer, *v.a.*, to pronounce, to articulate, to utter, to give utterance to; to give; to deliver; to make; to declare; (jur.) to find, to give in; (paint.) to delineate strongly, to bring out, to give prominence to. — *un discours*; to deliver a discourse, to make a speech. — *une sentence*; (jur.) to pass sentence.
se prononcer, *v.r.*, to pronounce one's self, to declare one's self, to speak out, to express one's sentiments; to show one's self, to manifest one's self.
prononcer, *v.n.*, to pronounce; to declare one's sentiment, to decide.
prononciation, *n.f.*, pronunciation; utterance. — *d'une sentence*; passing sentence.

— **nette**, *distincte;* clear, distinct, pronunciation. — *vicieuse, locale;* vicious, local pronunciation. *Il a la — belle;* he has a fine utterance.

pronostic, *n.m.*, prognostic, prognostication; (med.) prognostic, prognosis.

pronostiquer, *v.a.*, to prognosticate.

pronostiqueur, *n.m.*, prognosticator.

propagande, *n.f.*, propaganda.

propagandiste, *n.m.*, propagandist.

propagateur, *n.m.*, propagator, spreader.

propagation, *n.f.*, propagation, spread, spreading, diffusion. *La — d'une maladie;* the spread of a disease. *La — des vérités;* the spread of truth. *La — des connaissances;* the diffusion of knowledge.

propager, *v.a.*, to propagate, to spread, to spread abroad, to diffuse.

se **propager**, *v.r.*, to be propagated, to be diffused, to be spread abroad; to propagate, to spread.

propension, *n.f.*, propensity, tendency, inclination, bent, disposition.

prophète, *n.m.*, prophet, seer. *Personne n'est — dans son pays;* no man is a prophet in his own country.

prophétesse, *n.f.*, prophetess.

prophétie (-ci), *n.f.*, prophecy, prophesying.

prophétique, *adj.*, prophetic, prophetical.

prophétiquement (-tik-mān), *adv.*, prophetically.

prophétiser, *v.a.*, to prophesy.

prophylactique, *adj.*, (med.) prophylactical, prophylactic.

prophylactique, *or* **prophylaxie**, *n.f.*, (med.) the science of prophylactic medicine.

propice, *adj.*, propitious, favourable. *Le ciel soit — à ses vœux;* heaven favour his wishes. *Rendre —;* to render propitious, to propitiate.

propitiation, *n.f.*, propitiation.

propitiatoire, *n.m. and adj.*, propitiatory, mercy-seat; propitiatory.

propolis (-lis), *n.f.*, propolis.

proportion, *n.f.*, proportion, relation, ratio. --*gardée;* in proportion. *À —;* proportionable, proportional; proportionably, proportionately, proportionally. *À — de;* in proportion to.

proportionnalité, *n.f.*, proportionality, proportionateness.

proportionné, -e, *adj.*, proportioned; suited.

proportionnel, -le, *adj.*, proportional.

proportionnelle, *n.f.*, (math.) proportional.

proportionnellement (-nèl-mān), *adv.*, proportionably, proportionately.

proportionnément, *adv.*, proportionally, proportionately, in proportion to.

proportionner, *v.a.*, to proportion, to adjust, to fit, to accommodate, to suit. — *sa dépense à son revenu;* to proportion one's expenditure to one's revenue.

se **proportionner**, *v.r.*, to be proportioned; to proportion one's self, to suit one's self.

propos, *n.m.*, discourse; talk, words; purpose, resolution, design; *pl.*, idle remarks, tattle, talk. *Changeons de —;* let us talk of something else. — *de table;* table-talk. — *interrompu;* desultory talk. *Je me moque des —;* what do I care for people's tattle! *À — (—)* (substantive); seasonableness, pertinentness, pertinency, propriety. *À — (adj.);* seasonable, proper, fit, to the purpose. *À — (adv.);* seasonably, opportunely, pertinently, apropos. *Venir fort à —,* to come in the nick of time. *Elle fait chaque chose à —;* she does everything at a proper time. *Mal à —;* ill-timed, unseasonable, unseasonably. *Hors de —;* unseasonably; not

to the purpose, impertinent, impertinently. *À tort et mal à —;* wrongfully and without a cause. *À —, j'ai oublié de vous dire l'autre jour;* now I think of it, I forgot to tell you the other day. *Il s'est fâché à — de rien;* he got angry for nothing at all. *Il est venu me quereller à — de bottes;* he came to quarrel with me without any earthly reason. *À quel — ?* what about ? *À — de quoi?* for what reason ? why ? *À tout —;* at every turn, ever and anon. *À — de;* with respect to.

proposable, *adj.*, that can be proposed.

proposant, *n.m.*, French protestant student in divinity.

proposant, *adj.m.*, (c. rel.) proposing.

proposer, *v.a.*, to propose, to propound, to move, to make a motion; to offer; to designate. — *un sujet à traiter;* to propose a subject for writing on. — *une question;* to propound a question. — *quelqu'un pour exemple;* to propose any body as a pattern.

se **proposer**, *v.r.*, to propose one's self, to offer one's self; to be proposed, to be offered ; to propose, to purpose, to intend.

proposer, *v.n.*, to propose. *L'homme propose et Dieu dispose;* man proposes and God disposes.

proposition, *n.f.*, proposition; motion; proposal. *Pains de —;* show-bread. *Faire des —s à quelqu'un;* to make any one proposals. —*s de paix;* proposals for peace.

propre, *adj.*, own; very, same, self-same, very same; adapted, appropriate, calculated, fit, fitted; qualified, proper, suitable ; clean, proper; neat, tidy; nice; accurate, right, correct. *C'est son — fils;* it is his own son. *Les qualités —s à quelque chose;* the qualities peculiar to anything. *En main —;* in one's own hands. *Amour— (—s —s);* self-love, conceit. *Nom —;* proper name. *Ce sont ses —s paroles;* those are his very words. *Il est — à tout;* he is fit for anything. *Le mot —;* the proper word. *Il est toujours fort —;* he is always very neat. *Avoir une écriture —;* to write a neat hand.

propre, *n.m.*, characteristic, peculiar quality, property, part; (gram.) proper sense, literal sense; (jur.) real estate, real property ; (c.rel.) particular prayers. *Le — des oiseaux est de voler;* it is the property of birds to fly. *Avoir en —;* to own. *N'avoir rien en —;* to have no property. *Posséder en —;* to possess in one's own right. *Le — et le figuré;* the literal and figurative sense. *Prendre un mot au —;* to use a word in its literal sense.

proprement, *adv.*, properly, correctly, rightly; literally; cleanly; neatly, tidily. — *dit;* properly called, properly so called. *À — parler;* properly speaking. *S'habiller —;* to dress neatly.

propret, -te, *adj.*, spruce, neat.

propreté, *n.f.*, cleanness, cleanliness; spruceness, neatness, niceness.

propréteur, *n.m.*, (Roman hist.) propretor.

propriétaire, *n.m.f.*, owner; proprietor; proprietress; landlord; landlady; freeholder. *Nu — (jur.);* owner who is not possessed of the usufruct of his property.

propriété, *n.f.*, property; ownership; estate; peculiar quality, essential faculty; propriety, correctness (of words, terms—*de mots, de termes*). — *littéraire;* copyright. *Nue — (jur.);* property without the usufruct of it. *Doter quelqu'un d'une —;* to settle an estate upon any one. *Violer la —;* to trespass. —*s;* lands, estates.

propulseur, *n.m.*, (tech.) propeller. — *d hélice;* screw-propeller.

propulsion, *n.f.*, propulsion.

propylées, *n.m pl.*, (arch.) propylæum.

prorata, *n.m.*, proportion. *Au — de ; pro rata.*

prorogati-f. -ve, *adj.*, that prolongs time.

prorogation, *n.f.*, prolongation; prorogation (of parliament—*du parlement*).

proroger, *v.a.*, to prolong time, to protract; to prorogue (parliament—*le parlement*).

prosaïque, *adj.*, prosaic; dull.

prosaïquement, *adv.*, prosaically, in a dull manner.

prosaïser, *v.n.*, to write prose.

prosaïsme, *n.m.*, the defect of being prosaic in verse; (fig.) prosiness, dulness. *Le — de la vie :* the prosiness of life.

prosateur, *n.m.*, prose-writer, prosaist.

proscenium (-sé-ni-om), *n.m.*, (antiq.) proscenium.

proscripteur, *n.m.*, proscriber.

proscription, *n.f.*, proscription.

proscrire, *v.a.*, (proscrivant, proscrit), to proscribe, to outlaw ; to expel, to banish.

proscrit, *n.m.*, **-e**, *n.f.*, proscribed person, exile, outlaw. *Figure de — ;* disagreeable face, displeasing face.

prose, *n.f.*, prose; (c.rel.) prose. *Mettre en — ;* to turn into prose.

prosecteur, *n.m.*, (anat.) prosector.

prosélyte, *n.m.f.*, proselyte.

prosélytisme, *n.m.*, proselytism.

prosodie, *n.f.*, (gram.) prosody.

prosodique, *adj.*, prosodial, prosodical.

prosopopée, *n.f.*, (rhet.) prosopopœia.

prospectus (-tus), *n.m.*, prospectus.

prospère, *adj.*, prosperous, thriving; propitious, favourable.

prospérer, *v.n.*, to prosper, to be prosperous, to be successful, to thrive, to speed.

prospérité, *n.f.*, prosperity, well-being. *Avoir un visage de — ;* to have a face that betokens prosperity.

prostate, *n.f.*, (anat.) prostate, prostate gland.

prostatique, *adj.*, (anat.) prostate, prostatic.

prosternation, *n.f.*, prosternation.

prosternement, *n.m.*, prosternation.

prosterner, *v.a.*, to prostrate.

se **prosterner**, *v.r.*, to prostrate one's self, to fall down.

prosthèse, *n.f.*, (gram.) prosthesis; (surg. l.u.) prosthesis. *V.* **prothèse**.

prostituée, *n.f.*, prostitute.

prostituer, *v.a.*, to prostitute.

se **prostituer**, *v.r.*, to prostitute one's self.

prostitution, *n.f.*, prostitution.

prostration, *n.f.*, prostration, prosternation; (med.) prostration.

prostyle, *n.m.* and *adj.*, (arch.) prostyle ; provided with a prostyle.

protagoniste, *n.m.*, principal character in a theatrical piece, protagonist.

protase, *n.f.*, protasis.

protatique, *adj.*, protatic.

prote, *n.m.*, (print.) overseer.

protect-eur, -rice, *n.* and *adj.*, protector, protectress, patron, patroness, patronizer, fosterer, protective, patronizing, fostering.

protection, *n.f.*, protection, defence; support, patronage, countenance; (nav.) cover.

protectionniste, *n.m.* and *adj.*, (com.) protectionist.

protectorat, *n.m.*, protectorate, protectorship.

protée, *n.m.*, Proteus.

protégé, *n.m.*, **-e**, *n.f.*, protégé; protégée.

protéger, *v.a.*, to protect, to defend; to patronize, to countenance. *— contre le mal ; to* shield from harm.

protestant. -e, *n.* and *adj.*, Protestant.

protestantisme, *n.m.*, Protestantism.

protestation, *n.f.*, protestation, protest. — *d'amitié ;* profession of friendship. *Faire insérer une — dans le procès-verbal ;* to enter a protest.

protester, *v.a.*, to protest; to vow. *Je vous le proteste sur mon honneur,* I swear to you on my honour. *— une lettre de change ;* to protest a bill of exchange.

protester, *v.n.*, to protest. *— de nullité ; to* protest against the validity of a deed.

protêt, *n.m.*, (com.) protest. *— faute de payement ;* protest for non-payment. *Faire signifier un — ;* to give warning of a protest.

prothèse, *n.f.*, (surg.) prosthesis.

proto, a prefix from Gr. πρῶτος.

protocanonique, *adj.*, of the books of Scripture which were generally admitted as inspired writings even before there was any canon law ; not belonging to the Apocrypha.

protocarbure, *n.m.*, (chem.) carburet.

protochlorure, *n.m.*, (chem.) protochloride

protocole, *n.m.*, protocol ; formulary.

protomartyr, *n.m.*, protomartyr.

protonotaire, *n.m.*, protonotary.

protosyncelle, *n.m.*, in the Greek church, the vicar or substitute of a Patriarch *or* of a Bishop.

prototype, *n.m.*, prototype.

protoxyde. *n.m.*, (chem.) protoxide.

protubérance, *n.f.*, (anat.) protuberance.

protubérant, *adj.*, protuberant.

protuteur, *n.m.* (jur.) person who manages the affairs of a minor in the stead of the guardian.

⊙**prou**, *adv.*, enough, much. *Ni peu ni — ;* neither little nor much. *Peu ou — ;* little or much.

proue, *n.f.*, (nav.) prow, stem.

prouesse, *n.f.*, prowess, valour ; (iron.) feat of valour.

prouvable, *adj.*, provable.

prouver, *v.a.*, to prove, to show ; to make good, to substantiate ; to be a proof of, to give proof of.

provéditeur, *n.m.*, proveditor.

provenance (pro-vnâns), *n.f.*, (com.) production.

provenant, -e (pro-vnan, -t), *adj.*, proceeding, accruing, arising.

provençal -e, *n.* and *adj.*, Provencial.

provende, *n.f.*, (l.u.) provision ; (agri.) provender.

provenir (pro-vnir), *v.n.*, to spring, to accrue, to issue, to proceed, to come from.

proverbe, *n.m.*, proverb, saying. *Devenir —, passer en — ;* to become a proverb, to become proverbial.

proverbial. -e. *adj.*, proverbial.

proverbialement (-al-mân), *adv.*, proverbially.

providence, *n.f.*, Providence (of God—*de Dieu*.)

providentiel. -le, *adj.*, providential.

*provignement. *n.m.*, layering of vines.

*provigner, *v.a.*, to layer vines.

*provigner. *v.n.*, (agri.) to increase; ⊙ to augment, to increase.

provin, *n.m.*, layer of a vine.

province. *n.f.*, province, country. *Les gens de — ;* country people. *Il a encore l'air de — ;* he has still something of the country in his manners.

provincial. *n.m.*, provincial, superior of a monastic fraternity.

provincial -e *n.* and *adj.*, provincial, country. country-like. *Manières —es ;* country manners.

provincialat, *n.m.*, provincialship (of convents—*de couvents*).

provincialisme, *n.m.*, (gram.) provincialism.

proviseur. *n.m.*, master, provisor, headmaster, principal of a government college.

provision. *n.f.*, provision, stock, store, supply ; (fam.) hoard ; (com.) stock on hand ; provisional maintenance. *Par —;* provisionally. in the mean time. *Faire ses —s ;* to provide one's self with necessaries. *Faire sa — de bois ;* to take in. to lay in. one's stock of wood.

provisionnel. -le, *adj.*, provisional.

provisionnellement (-nèl-män), *adv.*, provisionally.

provisoire. *n.m.*, provisional state.

provisoire, *adj.*, provisional.

provisoirement (-zoar-män), *adv.*, provisionally.

provisorat, *n.m.*.provisorship,head-mastership of a government college.

⊙**provisorerie**, *n.f.* V. **provisorat**.

provocant. *adj.*, provoking.

provocat-eur. -rice. *n.* and *adj.*, provoker ; instigator,abettor ; provoking,instigating,abetting. *Agent —;* hired plotter, agent of the police.

provocation. *n.f.*, provocation, instigation. — *en duel ;* challenge to fight.

provoquer. *v.a.*, to provoke, to incense, to call forth, to promote ; to instigate ; to challenge. — *des applaudissements ;* to call forth applause. — *en duel ;* to challenge.

proxène. *n.m..* (antiq.) proxene.

proxénète, *n.m.*, (com.) ⊙ broker; a pimp, a pander.

proximité, *n.f.*, proximity, nearness, near relationship. *Le théâtre est à sa —;* the theatre is in his neighbourhood. *Il y a — de sang entre vous et moi ;* you and I are nearly related by the ties of blood.

proyer. *n.m.*, (orni.) common bunting.

prude, *n.f.* and *adj.*, prude ; prudish.

prudemment (-da-män), *adv.*, prudently, discreetly, wisely, cautiously.

prudence. *n.f.*, prudence ; discretion.

prudent. -e,*adj.*,prudent, cautious, discreet.

pruderie (pru-drî), *n.f.*, prudery.

⊙**prud'homie**. *n.f.*, uprightness, integrity, probity.

prud'homme, *n.m.*, skilful *or* able person (in an art or trade—*dans un métier ou une profession*) ; ⊙ upright, honest man. *Conseil des—s :* council of experts, of the most experienced masters and workmen of a calling or trade, whose task it is to decide all disputes.

prune, *n.f.*. plum. — *de Brignoles ;* prunello. — *sauvage ;* skeg. — *de mirabelle ;* mirabelle plum. — *de reine-Claude ;* greengage. — *de Damas ;* damson. *Ce n'est pas pour des —s ;* it is not for nothing.

pruneau, *n.m.*, prune.

prunelaie (pru-n-lè), *n.f.*, place planted with plum-trees.

prunelle. *n.f.*,(bot.) sloe, bullace ; (woollen stuff—*étoffe de laine*) prunella, prunello ; (anat.) pupil, apple of the eye. *Jouer de la —;* to cast sheep's eyes, to ogle. *Jus de —;* very sour, very bad wine.

prunellier, *n.m.*, (bot.) sloe-tree, bullace-tree.

prunier. *n.m..* (bot.) plum-tree.

prurigineu-x, -se, *adj.*, (med.) pruriginous.

prurit. *n.m.*, (med.) prurience. pruriency, pruritus.

prussiate. *n.m..* (chem.) prussiate.

prussien,-ne (-in.-è-n),*n.* and *adj.*, Prussian.

prussique, *adj.*, (chem.) prussic. *Acide —;* prussic acid.

prytane, *n.m.*, (Grec. antiq.) prytanis.

prytanée, *n.m.*, (Grec. antiq.) prytaneum.

p.s., initial letters of postscriptum, P.S., postscript.

⊙**psallette**. *n.f.*, school for singing boys.

psalmiste. *n.m.*, psalmist.

psalmodie. *n.f.*, psalmody ; sing-song.

psalmodier. *v.n.* and *a.*, to recite, to chant, psalms; to read, to recite in a sing-song manner.

psaltérion, *n.m.*, (mus.) psaltery.

psammite, *n.m.*, (min.) psammite, gray-wacke *or* greywacke.

psaume, *n.m.*, psalm.

psautier (-tié), *n.m.*, psalter, psalm-book; (c. rel.) chaplet of 150 beads ; nun's veil.

pseudo, a prefix from Gr. ψεῦδος.

pseudonyme, *adj.*, pseudonymous.

psora, *or* **psore**. *n.f.*, (med.) psora, itch.

psorique, *adj.*, (med) psoric, itchy.

psyché. *n.f.*, (myth.) Psyche ; Psyche-glass, cheval-glass.

psychique. *adj.*, psychical.

psychologie (-ko-). *n.f.*, psychology.

psychologique (-ko-), *adj.*, psychologic, psychological.

psychologiste, *or* **psychologue** (-ko-), *n.m.*, psychologist.

psylle. *n.m.*, snake-charmer.

ptérodactyle, *n.m.*, (foss.) pterodactyl.

ptyalisme, *n.m.*, (med.) ptyalism.

puamment (pu-a-män), *adv.*, stinkingly; (fig., fam.) impudently, in a barefaced manner.

puant. **-e**, *adj.*, stinking ; impudent, barefaced. *Devenir —;* to begin to stink. *Mensonge —;* impudent lie. — *menteur ;* impudent liar.

puant. *n.m.*, (pop.) stinkard.

puanteur, *n.f.*, stink, stench, offensive smell.

pubère, *adj.*, pubescent, that has attained the age of puberty.

puberté, *n.f.*, puberty.

pubescence, *n.f.*, (bot.) pubescence.

pubescent. -e, *adj.*, (bot.) pubescent.

pubien, -ne (-in, -è-n), *adj.*, (anat.) pubic.

pubis, *n.m.* and *adj.*, (anat.) os pubis ; pubic. *Os —;* os pubis, pubic bone, share-bone ; pubes.

publi-c, -que, *adj.*, public; notorious. *Rendre —;* to make public, to publish.

public, *n.m.*, public. *En —;* publicly.

publicain, *n.m.*, (Rom. antiq.) publican ; farmer of the public revenue; extortioner.

publicateur, *n.m.*, (jur.) publisher.

publication, *n.f.*, publication ; action of publishing.

publiciste, *n.m.*, publicist.

publicité, *n.f.*, publicity, notoriety.

publier, *v.a.*, to publish, to make public, to proclaim, to celebrate, to trumpet forth. — *quelque chose sur les toits :* to proclaim anything from the house-tops, to trumpet forth anything. — *une ordonnance :* to issue an ordonnance.

publiquement (-blik-män), *adv.*, publicly, in public.

puce, *n.f.*, (ent.) flea. *Herbe aux —s ;* fleabane, fleawort. — *d'eau ;* water-beetle. — *de mer ;* psyllus marinus. — *de terre ;* earth-puceron. *Avoir la — à l'oreille :* to have a flea in one's ear, to be uneasy. *Mettre à quelqu'un la — à l'oreille ;* to give any one cause for uneasiness.

puce, *adj.*, puce, puce-coloured.

puceau, *n.m.*, (l.ex.) youth.

pucelage(pu-slaj),*n.m.*,(l.ex.)maidenhead; (mol.) cowry.

pucelle, *n.f.*, (fam.) maid. maiden ; (ich.) shad. *La — d'Orléans ;* the Maid of Orleans, Joan of Arc.

puceron (pu-sron), *n.m.*, (ent.) puceron, plant-louse.

puddlage, *n.m.*, (metal.) puddling.

puddler (-dlé), *v.a.*, (metal.) to puddle.

puddleur, *n.m.*, (metal.).puddler.

pudeur, *n.f.*, bashfulness. shame ; modesty, decency. — *virginale ;* virgin bashfulness.

pudibond, -e, *adj.*, bashful. modest.

pudicité, *n.f.*, modesty, pudicity, chastity.

pudique, *adj.*, chaste. modest, bashful.

pudiquement (-dik-mån), *adv.*, chastely, purely.

puer, *v.n.* and *a.*, to stink, to have an offensive smell ; to smell of ; to stink of. *Il pue le vin ;* he stinks of wine.

puéril, -e, *adj.*, juvenile, boyish ; puerile, childish.

puérilement (-ril-mån), *adv.*, puerilely, childishly.

puérilité. *n.f.*, puerility, childishness.

puerpéral, -e, *adj.*, puerperal.

puff(puf, peuf), *n.m.*, exaggerated statement, puff. *Faire le — ;* to puff.

puffin, *n.m.*, (orni.) puffin.

pugilat, *n.m.*, pugilistic art, pugilism.

pugile. *n.m.*, (antiq.) pugilist, boxer.

pugiliste, *n.m.*, pugilist, boxer.

puine, *n.m.*, (forestry—*gruerie*) wood of little value, such as brambles, broom, furze, &c. *V. mort-bois* under **bois.**

puiné, -e, *n.* and *adj.*, younger brother, younger sister ; younger.

puis, *adv.*, then, afterwards, after that, next. *Et — ;* and besides, and then. *Et — ?* what then ? what next ? well ?

puisage, *n.m.*, drawing water.

puisard, *n.m.*, cesspool ; (mining) sump, water-sump.

puisatier, *n.m.*, well-sinker.

puiser, *v.a.*, to draw, to fetch up, to take, to borrow ; to imbibe. — *de l'eau à la rivière ;* to draw water out of the river. — *à la source ;* to draw from the source, to go to the fountain-head. — *des opinions ;* to imbibe opinions.

puiser, *v.n.*, to draw, to borrow, to take ; (nav.) to make water. *C'est un auteur qui puise partout ;* he is an author who borrows from all quarters.

puisque, *conj.*, since, seeing, seeing that, inasmuch as.

puissamment (-sa-mån), *adj.*, powerfully, forcibly, potently ; extremely, very. *Il est — riche ;* he is exceedingly rich.

puissance. *n.f.*, power ; dominion, sway, empire ; ability,force ; virtue,quality, property ; (mining—*mines*) thickness (of layers or lodes—*des couches, des veines*) ; (mec.) power, horse-power. *Toute — (n.p.);* omnipotence, almighty power. *Haute — ;* high-mightiness (title—*titre*). *Cette femme est en — de mari;* that woman is under the control of her husband. *Soumettre à sa — ;* to bring under one's dominion. *Traiter de — à — ;* to treat on equal terms. — *motrice ;* moving power.

puissant, -e,*adj.*, powerful, potent, mighty ; lusty, stout, corpulent ; wealthy, rich. — *prince ;* mighty prince. *Famille —e ;* influential family. *Le Tout— (n.p.);* the Almighty. *Il est tout— auprès du prince ;* he can do any thing with the prince.

puits (pui), *n.m.*, well, hole for water ; pit, shaft ; well-hole (of staircases—*d'escalier*) ; (nav.) well-room. — *commun ;* public well. — *à pompe ;* pump-well. — *à roue ; à poulie ;* draw-well. — *artésien ;* artesian well. — *perdu ;* drain-well, blind-well. — *de mine ;* shaft of a mine. — *d'aérage ;* air-shaft. *C'est un — de science ;* he is extremely learned. *La vérité est au fond d'un — ;* truth lies at the bottom of a well.

pullulation, *n.f.*, rapid increase. swarming.

pulluler (pul-lu-), *v.n.*, to increase, to multiply. to pullulate, to swarm.

pulmonaire, *adj.*, (anat., med.)pulmonary. *Phtisie — ;* pulmonary disease, consumption.

pulmonaire, *n.f.*, (bot.) pulmonaria, pulmonary. *Grande — ;* lungwort ; sage of Jerusalem, Jerusalem cowslip. — *des Français ;* golden lung-wort. — *de chêne ;* liverwort.

pulmonie, *n.f.* V. **pneumonie**.

pulmonique, *n.m.f.* and *adj.*, a person affected with consumption ; consumptive.

pulpation, *n.f.*, (pharm.) reducing to pulp.

pulpe, *n.f.*, pulp ; pap. — *cérébrale* (anat.) ; cerebral substance.

pulper, *v.a.*, (pharm.) to reduce to pulp.

pulpeu-x, -se, *adj.*, (bot.) pulpous, pulpy.

pulsati-f, -ve, *adj.*, (med.) pulsative, pulsatory.

***pulsatille**, *n.f.*, (bot.) pasque-flower, pulsatilla.

pulsation, *n.f.*, beating of the pulse, pulsation ; (phys.) pulse.

pulvérat-eur, -rice. *n.* and *adj.*, (zool.) pulverulent bird ; pulverulent.

pulvérescence, *n.f.*, pulverulence.

pulvérescent, -e, *adj.*, pulverulent.

pulvérin, *n.m.*, priming powder ; priming powder-horn ; mist (from water-falls—*des chutes d'eau*).

pulvérisation, *n.f.*, pulverization.

pulvériser, *v.a.*, to reduce to powder, to pulverize ; to annihilate ; to reduce to atoms.

pulvérulent, -e, *adj.*, (bot.) pulverulent ; easy to reduce into powder.

pumicin, *n.m.*, palm-oil.

punais, -e, *adj.*, affected with ozæna.

punaise, *n.f.*, bug ; (ent.) bug. *Cousain de —s ;* nest of bugs.

punaisie, *n.f.*, ozæna.

punch (ponsh), *n.m.*, punch (beverage—*breuvage*).

punique, *adj.*, punic.

punir, *v.a.*, to punish, to chastise. *Puni de mort ;* punished with death.

punissable, *adj.*, punishable.

punisseur, *n.m.* and *adj.*, avenger, punisher ; avenging, punishing.

punition, *n.f.*, punishment. *Par — ;* as a punishment.

pupillaire (-pil-lèr), *adj.*, pupillary.

pupillarité (-pil-la-), *n.f.*, (jur. l.u.) nonage, minority.

pupille, *n.m.f.*, ward, pupil (under the care of a guardian—*sous l'autorité d'un tuteur*).

pupille, *n.f.*, pupil, apple of the eye.

pupitre, *n.m.*, desk. scrutoir.

pur, -e, *adj.*, pure, genuine. unadulterated ; unspotted ; clean, clear, unmingled, unalloyed ; mere, downright. *Une lumière —e ;* a clear light. *Un ciel — ;* a clear, cloudless sky. *Être en état de —e nature ;* to be stark naked. *Du vin — ;* wine without water, pure wine. *Obligation —e et simple ;* unconditional obligation. *C'est la —e vérité ;* it is the unvarnished truth. *Par —e bonté ;* out of mere kindness. —*e sottise ;* downright nonsense. *Ce fruit est du poison tout — ;* that fruit is downright poison. *Félicité —e ;* unalloyed happiness. *Une réputation —e :* an untarnished reputation. *Une gloire —e ;* unsullied glory. *Un trait —, un dessin —* (drawing) ; a clean stroke, a clean drawing. *À —et à plein ;* unreservedly, entirely. *En —e perte ;* in vain, to no purpose.

pureau, *n.m.*, part uncovered (of slates, tiles—*d'ardoises, de tuiles*).

purée, *n.f.*, soup made with peas, beans. &c.; pea-soup.

purement (-pur-mān), *adv.*, purely, genuinely, merely, only ; innocently. — *et simplement :* unconditionally.

pureté (pur-té), *n.f.*, pureness, purity, gentleness, innocence; chastity. *La — de la foi ;* the purity of faith. *La — des mœurs ;* the purity of morals. — *de style ; purity of style.* — *du goût :* purity of taste.

purgati-f, -ve, *adj.,* purgative.

purgatif, *n.m.,* purgative.

purgation, *n.f.,* purgation, purgative, purge.

purgatoire, *n.m.,* purgatory.

purge, *n.f.,* ⊙purge. — *d'hypothèques* (jur.); paying off of a mortgage.

purger, *v.a..* to purge, to purge away; to cleanse, to purify, to clear. — *un malade;* to purge a sick person. — *son bien de dettes;* to clear one's estate.

se **purger,** *v.r.,* to purge one's self, to purify one's self.

purifiant, -e, *adj.,* purifying, cleansing.

purificateur, *n.m.,* purificator.

purification. *n.f,* purification.

purificatoire, *n.m.,* (c.rel.) purificatory.

purifier, *v.a.,* to purify, to cleanse; to refine; to try (metal). — *le langage ;* to refine the language.

se **purifier,** *v.r.,* to purify one's self, to purify, to refine.

puriforme, *adj.,*(med.) puriform.

purin, *n.m.,* (agri.) liquid manure.

purisme, *n.m.,* purism.

puriste, *n.m.,* purist.

puritain, -e, *n.* and *adj.,* Puritan.

puritanisme, *n.m.,* Puritanism.

purpurin, -e, *adj.,* purplish.

purpurine, *n.f.,* purple, bronze.

purulence, *n.f.,* purulence, purulency.

purulent, -e. *adj.,* purulent.

pus. *n.m..* (med.) pus, matter.

pusillanime (-zil-la-), *adj.,* pusillanimous, faint-hearted.

pusillanimité (-zil-la-), *n.f.,* pusillanimity, faint-heartedness.

pustule, *n.f.,* pustule, pimple, blotch; (bot.) blister.

pustulé, -e, *adj.,* (bot.) blistered.

pustuleu-x, -se, *adj.,* pustulous.

putain, *n.f.,* (l.ex.) street-walker, prostitute, strumpet.

putassier, *n.m.,* (l.ex.) one who frequents prostitutes.

putati-f, -ve, *adj.,* putative, reputed, supposed.

putois. *n.m..* polecat.

putréfaction, *n.m.,* putrefaction.

putréfait. -e, *adj.,* (l.u.) putrefied.

putréfié. -e, *part.,* putrefied.

putréfier. *v.a.,* to putrefy.

se **putréfier.** *v.r..* to putrefy.

putrescible. *adj.,* that can become putrescent.

putride, *adj.,* (med.) putrid.

putridité, *n.f.,* putridness, putridity.

pygargue, *n.m.,* pygarg, pygargus; sea-eagle.

pygmée, *n.m.,* pigmy, dwarf.

pylône, *m.n..* (antiq., arch.) porch of Egyptian temples.

pylore, *n.m.,* (anat.) pylorus.

pyloride, *n.f.,* bivalve shell.

pylorique, *adj.,* (anat.) pyloric.

pyracanthe, *n.f.,* (bot.) pyracanth.

pyrale, *n.f.,* (ent.) pyralis.

pyramidal, -e, *adj.,* pyramidal, pyramidic, pyramidical.

pyramidalement (-dal-mān), *adv.,* pyramidally, pyramidically.

pyramide. *n.f.,* pyramid.

pyramider, *v.n.,* to rise like a pyramid ; to tower ; to stand in a pyramidal form.

pyrèthre, *n.m.,* (bot.) Spanish camomile, feverfew.

pyrétologie, *n.f.,* pyretology.

pyriforme, *adj.* *V.* **piriforme.**

pyrique, *adj.,* pyrotechnic, pyrotechnical.

pyrite, *n.f.,* (min.) pyrites.

pyriteu-x, -se, *adj.,* (min.) pyritic, pyritical.

pyrolâtrie, *n.f.,* the worship of fire, pyrolatry.

*pyroligneux, *adj.,* pyrolignous.

pyrologie, *n.f.,* pyrology.

pyromancie. *n.f.,* pyromancy.

pyromètre, *n.m.,* pyrometer.

pyrophore, *n.m.,* pyrophorus.

pyroscaphe, *n.m.,* (nav.) steamer, steam boat.

pyrosis, *n.f.,* (med.) pyrosis.

pyrotechnie (-tèk-), *n.f.,* pyrotechnics, pyrotechny.

pyrotechnique (-tèk-), *adj.,* pyrotechnic, pyrotechnical.

pyroxène, *n.m.,* (min.) pyroxene.

pyrrhique, *adj.,* Pyrrhic.

pyrrhique, *n.m.,* (poet.) Pyrrhic.

pyrrhique, *n.f.,* (antiq.) Pyrrhic (military dance—*danse militaire*).

pyrrhonien, -ne (-in, -è-n), *n.* and *adj..* Pyrrhonist, Pyrrhonean ; Pyrrhonic.

pyrrhonisme, *n.m.,* Pyrrhonism.

pythagoricien, -ne (-in, -é-n), *n.* and *adj.,* Pythagorean ; Pythagoric, Pythagorical.

pythagorique, *adj..* Pythagoric, Pythagorical.

pythagorisme. *n.m..* Pythagorism.

pythie, *n.f..* (antiq.) the Pythia, priestess of the Pythian Apollo.

pythien (-tiin), *adj.,* Pythian.

pythique. *adj..* Pythian.

pythiques, *n.f.pl.,* Pindarus' odes.

python, *n.m.,* (zool.) python.

pythonisse, *n.f.,* (antiq.) pythoness; witch.

Q

q, *n.m.,* the seventeenth letter of the alphabet, q.

qu', contraction of *Que.*

quacre. *n.m.* *V.* **quaker.**

quadernes (kooa-dèrn), *n.m.pl.,* two fours (tricktrack).

quadragénaire (kooa-). *n.* and *adj.,* person forty years old ; of forty years of age; of forty.

quadragésimal, -e (kooa-), *adj.,* quadragesimal.

quadragésime (kooa-), *n.f.,* Quadragesima.

quadrangle (kooa-), *n.m.,* quadrangle.

quadrangulaire (kooa-), *adj.,* quadrangular, four-cornered.

quadrangulé. -e (kooa-), *adj.,* quadrangular.

⊙**quadrat,** *adj.,* (astrolog.) quadrate. — *aspect ;* quartile. *V.* **quadrature.**

quadrat, *n.m.,* (print.) quadrat. *V.* **cadrat.**

quadratin, *n.m.,* (print.) m. quadrat. *Demi-* — ; (print.) n. quadrat. *V.* **cadratin.**

quadratique (kooa-) *adj.,* quadratic.

quadratrice (kooa-) *n.f.,* (geom.) quadratrix.

quadrature (kooa-), *n.f.,* (astron., geom.) quadrature ; (astrolog.) quartile.

quadrature, *n.f.,* (horl.) movement, dialwork. *V.* **cadrature.**

quadraturier, *n.m.*. (horl.) movement-maker.

☉**quadre, quadrer**. *V*. **cadre, cadrer**.

quadricapsulaire (kooa-), *adj.*, (bot.) quadricapsular.

quadricorne (kooa-), *adj.*, quadricornous.

quadridenté, -e (kooa-), *adj.*, (bot.) quadridentate.

quadriennal. *V*. **quatriennal**.

quadrifide (kooa-), *adj.*, (bot.) quadrifid, four-cleft.

quadrige (kooa-). *n.m.*, (antiq.) quadriga.

quadrijumeaux (kooa-), *adj.m.pl.*, (anat.) quadrigemina. *Tubercules* — ; *corpora quadrigemina.*

quadrilatéral, *adj.*, quadrilateral.

quadrilatère (kooa-), *n.m.*, (geom.) quadrilateral.

__quadrillage__, *n.m.*, pavement of square stones, flags.

__quadrille__. *n.f.*. troop of horse (in a tournament—*dans un carrousel*).

__quadrille__. *n.m.*, (caid game, mus., dancing —*jeu de cartes*, mus., *danse*) quadrille.

quadrillé. *adj.*, (of cloths—*des étoffes*) checkered, plaid ; (of paper—*du papier*) ruled both ways, in squares.

quadrillion (kooa-), *n.m.*, one thousand billions.

quadrilobé, -e (kooa-), *adj.*, (bot.) quadrilobate.

quadriloculaire (kooa-), *adj.*, (bot.) quadrilocular.

quadrinôme (kooa-), *n.m.*, (alg.) quadrinomial.

quadriparti, -e (kooa-), *adj.*, (bot.) quadripartite.

quadripartition (kooa-), *n.f.*, (l.u.) quadripartition.

quadriphylle (kooa-), *adj.*, (bot.) quadriphyllous.

quadrirème. (kooa-). *n.m.*. quadrireme.

quadrisyllabe (kooa-dri-sil-lab),*n.m.*,quadrisyllable.

quadrivalve (kooa-), *adj.*, (bot.) quadrivalve, quadrivalvular.

☉**quadrivium**. *n.m.* (n.p.), quadrivium.

quadrumane (kooa-),*n.m.* and *adj.*, (mam.) quadruman ; quadrumanous.

quadrupède (kooa-). *n.m.* and *adj.*, quadruped : four-footed ; quadruped.

quadruple (kooa-), *n.m.* and *adj.*, quadruple, fourfold ; (Spanish coin—*monnaie espagnole*) a doubloon.

quadruple, *n.f.*, Spanish gold coin worth 85 francs, about £3 8s.

quadrupler (kooa-), *v.a.*, to quadruple, to quadruplicate : to increase fourfold.

quadrupler. *v.n.*. to be quadrupled ; to increase fourfold.

quai. *n.m.*,quay, wharf. *Droit de* — ; wharfage.

quaiage. *n.m.* *V*. **quayage**.

quaiche. *n.f.*, (nav.) ketch.

quaker. or **quacre** (kooa-kr). *n.m.*, quaker.

quakeresse (kooa-kres), *n.f.*. quakeress.

quakérisme (kooa-), *n.m.*. quakerism.

qualifiable, *adj.*. that can be called. named. styled, described. entitled.

qualificateur, *n.m.*. (c. rel.) qualificator.

qualificati-f, -ve, *adj.*, (gram.) qualifying.

qualificatif. *n.m.*, (gram.) qualificative.

qualification. *n.f.*. title, name.

qualifié, -e, *part.*, qualified. called, named.

qualifier. *v.a.*. to qualify, to call ; to entitle to style. to name. — *quelqu'un de fourbe;* to call any one a knave.

se qualifier. *v.r.*. to call one's self, to style one's self.

qualité, *n.f.*. quality ; qualification. accom-plishment ; title. *Il n'a pas les —s requises pour cela* ; he is not qualified for that. *En* — *de* ; in the capacity of, in the character of.

quand, *adv.*. when. *Depuis* —? since when ? *Depuis* — *est-il arrivé?* how long has he been arrived ? *Jusqu'à* —? how long ? till when ?

quand, *conj.*. though, although. — *même*; though, although, even if. — *même elle voudrait*: even if she were willing.

☉**quanquam**. (koo-an-koo-am), *n.m.* (—). Latin oration delivered by a student on examination day.

quanquan, *n.m.* *V*. **cancan**.

quant à, *adv.*. as to, as for. concerning, respecting. — *à cela*; as for that. *Se mettre sur son* — *à-soi*. *sur son* —*à-moi*; to give one's self airs. *Tenir, se tenir sur, son* — *à-soi*, *son* —*à-moi*; to assume a proud and reserved air ; to answer with circumspection.

quantes, *adj.f.pl.*, only employed in the two phrases. *Toutes fois et* —, *toutes et* —*fois que*; whenever, as often as.

quantième, *n.m.*, day (of the month—*du mois*). *Quel est le* — *du mois?* what day of the month is it ?

quantitati-f, -ve, *adj.*, quantitative.

quantité, *n.f.*, quantity ; deal, number, multitude. *Quelle* —! what a lot !

quantum (koo-an-tom)*n.m.*.(—s), quantum.

quarantaine, *n.f.*, about forty ; age of forty ; quarantine. *Faire la* — ; to perform quarantine. *Lever la* —; to admit to pratique. *Purger sa* — ; to clear one's quarantine.

quarante. *n.m.* and *adj.*, forty. *Les* —; the members of the French Academy, who are forty in number.

quarantie (-ti), *n.f.*, tribunal of the forty at Venice.

quarantième (-tièm), *n.m.f.*, and *adj.*, fortieth.

quarderonner, *v.a.*, (arch.) to round off.

quarre, quarré, quarreau, quarrement, quarrer, quarrure. *V*. **carre, carré**, &c.

quart (kar), *n.m.*, quarter, fourth ; point (of the compass—*de la boussole*); quart (measure—*mesure*); (nav.) watch. *Un* — *d'heure*; a quarter of an hour. *Médire du tiers et du* —; to speak ill of every body. — *de cercle* ; quadrant. *Officier de*— (nav.); officer of the watch. *Faire son* — ; to be upon the watch. — *de nuit* ; night-watch. *Faire bon* — ; to keep a good look-out. *Le premier* — ; the starboard-watch. *Bon* —! (nav.) all's well !

quart, -e, *adj.*, fourth : (med.) quartan. *Fièvre* —*e* : quartan ague, quartan.

quartaine, *adj.f.*, (pop.) quartan. *Fièvre* — : quartan ague.

quartan, *n.m.*, (hunt.) fourth year (of wild boars—*du sanglier*).

quartanier, *n.m.*, wild boar, four years old.

quartation. *n.f.*, (metal.) quartation.

quartaut. *n.m.*. cask containing the fourth part of a hogshead.

quarte, *n.f.*, (mus.) fourth ; (fenc.) quarte ; (piquet) quart ; ☉half a gallon.

quartenier, *n.m.*, local police officer.

quarteron. *n.m.*. **-ne**, *n.f.*, quadroon, quateron.

quarteron, *n.m.*, the fourth part of a pound : or of a hundred. *Demi*— ; the eighth part of a pound ; or of a hundred.

quartidi (koo-ar-), *n.m.*, Quartidi, fourth day of the decade in the calendar of the first French republic.

quartier (-tié) *n.m.*, quarter, fourth part ; piece. part : quarter (of a town, of the moon—*d'une ville, de la lune*) ; ward ; district ; neighbourhood ; flap (of a saddle—*de selle*); gammon (of bacon—*de lard*); block (of stone—*de pierre*); (arch., her., milit., vet.) quarter; descent; *pl.* quarters. *Un — de lard :* half a flitch of bacon. *— de soulier ;* quarter of a shoe. *— général* (milit.); head-quarters. *Être en —* (milit.); to quarter. *Demander —;* to beg for quarter, for mercy. *Il ne donne point de — à ses débiteurs ;* he is eternally dunning his debtors. *On n'y fait — à personne :* they spare nobody there.

quartier-maître, *n.m.* (*—s —s*), (milit., nav.) quarter-master.

⊙**quartier-mestre**, *n.m.* (*—s —s*), (milit.) quarter-master.

quartile (kooa-), *adj.*, (astron) quartile. *— aspect :* quartile aspect, quartile.

⊙**quartinier**, *n.m.* *V.* **quartenier**.

quarto. *V.* **in-quarto**.

quarto (kooar-to), *adv.*, fourthly.

quartz (kooar-tz), *n.m.*, (min.) quartz.

quartzeu-x, -se (kooa-), *adj.*, (min.) quartzose, quartzy.

quasi, *n.m.*, (cook.) thick end of a loin of veal.

quasi, *adv.*, (fam.) almost, nearly ; quasi.

quasi-contrat, *n.m.* (*— —s*), (jur.) quasi contract, implied contract.

quasi-délit, *n.m.* (*— —s*), (jur.) injury caused involuntarily.

quasiment, *adv.*, almost, nearly.

quasimodo, *n.f.*, (c.rel.) Quasimodo. *Dimanche de la —;* Low-Sunday.

quassia (kooa-), *n.f.*, (pharm.) quassia.

quassier (kooa-sié), *n.m.*, (bot.) staves-wood, quassin.

quaternaire (kooa-), *adj.*, quaternary.

quaterne, *n.m.*, quaternary.

quaterné. -e, *adj.*, (bot.) quaternate.

⊙**quatorzaine**, *n.f.*, (jur.) fortnight.

quatorze, *n.m.*, and *adj.*, fourteen, fourteenth.

quatorzième, *n.m. f.* and *adj.*, fourteenth, fourteenth day.

quatorzièmement, *adv.*, fourteenthly.

quatrain, *n.m.*, quatrain.

quatre, *adj.*, four, fourth. *Un de ces — matins ;* one of these fine days. *Marcher à — pattes ;* to go upon all fours. *Être tiré à — épingles ;* to look as if one had just come out of a bandbox.

quatre, *n.m.*, four; fourth. *Se mettre en — pour quelqu'un ;* to do any thing to serve any one. *Crier comme — ;* to cry out lustily.

quatre-temps, *n.m.pl.*, Ember-days.

quatre-vingtième, *n.m.f.* and *adj.*, eightieth.

quatre-vingts, *adj.*, eighty. *— millions ;* eighty millions. *L'homme vit — ans, et le chien n'en vit que dix ;* man lives eighty years, and the dog but ten. *Ils étaient — ;* there were eighty of them. *Quatre-vingt-un ;* eighty-one. *Quatre-vingt-dix ;* ninety. *Quatre-vingt-dix-neuf ;* ninety-nine. [*Quatre-vingts* takes no *s* when it precedes another number. It likewise takes no *s* when employed in dates of the Christian era : *L'an mil sept cent quatre-vingt ;* the year 1780.]

quatrième, *n.m.* and *adj.*, fourth ; fourth floor ; pupil of the fourth class.

quatrième, *n.f.* and *adj.*, fourth : fourth class (in schools—*dans les collèges*); (piquet) quart.

quatrièmement, *adv.*, fourthly.

quatriennal, -e (-è-n-nal), *adj.*, quadrennial.

quatrillion (kooa-), *n.m.* *V.* **quadrillion**.

quatuor (kooa-), *n.m.* (*—*), (mus.) quartet, quartette.

quayage. *n.m.*, v harfage, keyage.

que, *relative pron.*, whom, that, which, what.

Qu'est-ce — c'est ! what is it *! — dites-vous !* what do you say ? *— dit-on de nouveau !* what news have you to tell us? *Il ne sait — faire ;* he does not know what to do. *L'homme — vous voyez ;* the man whom you see. *Le livre qu'il a reçu ;* the book which he received.

que, *conj.*, that; how; how much, how many; if; as, when; unless, without; till, until; yet ; lest, for fear that; in order that, for; before ; since; so; than; let; because; why; only, nothing but. *J'avoue — cela est surprenant ;* I acknowledge that that is surprising. *Afin —;* that, in order that. *De sorte — ;* so that. *S'il le souhaite, et — vous le vouliez ;* if he desires it, and you also wish it. *Je ne serai point content — je ne le sache ;* I shall never be contented, until I know it. *Attendez qu'il vienne ;* wait till he comes. *Il me verrait périr, qu'il n'en serait pas touché ;* even if he were to see me die, he would not be concerned at it. *Approchez, — je vous embrasse ;* draw near, in order that I may kiss you. *N'approchez pas de ce chien, de peur qu'il ne vous morde ;* do not go near that dog, lest he should bite you. *Il n'y a qu'une heure qu'il est parti ;* it is but an hour since he left. *On le régala — rien n'y manquait ;* they treated him in such a way that nothing was wanting. *À peine eut-il achevé de parler qu'il expira ;* he had hardly done speaking, when he expired. *Le mari est plus raisonnable — la femme ;* the husband is more reasonable than the wife. *Plutôt — de le faire ;* rather than do it. *Tout savant qu'il est, il a bien peu de jugement ;* learned as he is, he has very little judgment. *C'est à la cour qu'on apprend les manières polies ;* it is at court that one learns politeness. *Qu'il parle ;* let him speak. *Je vous assure — cela est ainsi ;* I assure you that it is so. *Je doute — cela soit ainsi ;* I doubt whether it is so. *C'est une passion dangereuse — le jeu ;* gaming is a dangerous passion. *C'est être sage — de vivre ainsi ;* it is like a wise man to live so. *C'est en vain — je me fatigue ;* it is in vain that I toil and moil. *C'est — je ne savais pas — vous y étiez ;* it was because I did not know that you were there. *Il y a dix ans — je l'aime ;* I have loved her for these ten years. *Je ne suis pas si fou — de le croire ;* I am not such a fool as to believe it. *Il est tout autre — vous ne disiez ;* he is quite different to what you said. *— Dieu vous bénisse !* God bless you. *— j'agisse contre ma conscience !* how can I do a thing against my conscience ! *— vous aimez à parler !* how much you like to talk ! *Qu'elle est grande !* how tall she is ! *Qu'il y a de sots dans le monde !* how many fools there are in the world ! *Le malheureux qu'il est !* what a wretched man he is ! *— ne parlez-vous !* why do you not speak ? *— ne fait-il pas pour s'enrichir !* what does he not do to grow rich ? *— ne puis-je vous rendre service !* would to God that I could serve you ! *, — n'ai-je le temps !* oh, that I had time ! *Je ne sors point — je ne m'enrhume ;* I never go out without catching cold. *Je n'ai — faire de ;* I have no business with, I have nothing to do with ; I have no need of. *Je n'ai — faire de vous dire ;* I need not tell you. *Il ne fait — boire et manger ;* he does nothing but eat and drink. *Nous ne faisons — de commencer*, we are but just beginning. *Je dis — oui ;* I say yes. *Il croit — non ;* he believes not. *Je gage — si ;* I lay it is. *Tant bien — mal ;* partly well, partly ill. *Allez, sot — vous êtes ;* go, blockhead that you are. *Le moyen — je souffre cela ?* how can I bear that ? *Ce n'est pas trop — cela ;* that's not too much.

quel, -le, *adj.*, what. *— homme est-ce !* what sort of a man is he? *—le heure est-il !* what o'clock is it ? *—le pitié !* what a pity ! *—le taille !* what a shape ! *—le que soit votre inten-*

tion; whatever your intention is. — *qu'il soit;* whatever he be, whoever he be. *Tel* —; indifferent, so so.

quelconque, *adj.*, whatever, any, any whatsoever. *D'une manière* —; in any way whatever, any how. *Nonobstant opposition* —; notwithstanding any opposition whatsoever.

quellement (kèl-măn), *adv.*, (l.u.) in any way whatever. *Tellement* — indifferently, so so.

quelque, *adj.*, some, any, a few; whatever, whatsoever. *Adressez-vous à* — *autre;* apply to somebody else. — *jour;* some day or other. *Il y a* —*s années;* some years ago. *J'ai* —*s amis dans cette ville;* I have a few friends in this town. — *part;* somewhere. — *peu d'argent;* some little money. —*s efforts que vous fassiez;* whatever efforts you make. *En* — *lieu qu'il soit;* wherever he is. *En* — *temps que ce soit;* at any time.

quelque, *adv.*, however, howsoever; some, about. — *riches qu'ils soient;* however rich they may be.

quelquefois, *adv.*, sometimes.

quelques-uns, *n.m.pl.*, **-unes**, *n.f.pl.*, some, some people; any; a few.

quelqu'un, *n.m.*, **-e**, *n.f.*, somebody, some one; any body, any one.

quémander, *v.n.*, to beg importunately and clandestinely.

quémandeu-r, *n.m.*, **-se**, *n.f.*, one who begs importunately and secretly.

qu'en-dira-t-on, *n.m.* (*n.p.*), public talk. *Se moquer du* —; to laugh at public talk.

quenelle, *n.f.*, (cook.) ball of forcemeat put into a pie.

quenotte, *n.f.*, (fam.) tooth (of young children—*des petits enfants*).

*****quenouille**, *n.f.*, distaff; distaffful; tree cut in the form of a distaff. — *de lit;* bedpost. *En* —; like a distaff. *Tomber en* —; to fall to the female line. *Coiffer une* —; to cover a distaff.

*****quenouillée**, *n.f.*, distaffful.

*****quenouillette**, *n.f.*, a small distaff; (bot.) distaff-thistle. —*s de la poupe* (nav.); sterntimbers.

quérable, *adj.*, (jur.) of a debt to be applied for by the creditor.

quercitron, *n.m.*, (bot.) quercitron.

querelle, *n.f.*, quarrel, quarrelling, brawl, broil, wrangling. — *légère;* slight quarrel. — *d'Allemand;* groundless quarrel. *Faire une* — *à;* to quarrel with. *Chercher* — *à;* to pick a quarrel with. *Vider une* —; to settle a quarrel. *Susciter une* — *à;* to raise a quarrel.

quereller, *v.a.*, to quarrel with, to pick a quarrel with.

se quereller, *v.r.*, to quarrel, to wrangle, to have words.

quereller, *v.n.*, to quarrel, to wrangle.

querelleu-r, **-se**, *adj.* and *n.*, quarrelsome; quarreller, wrangler.

quérimonie (kué-), *n.f.*, request to an ecclesiastical judge to obtain permission to publish a monitory.

⊙**quérir**, *v.a.*, to fetch. [Only employed in the infinitive with *Aller, Envoyer, Venir.*] *Aller* —; to go and fetch. *Envoyer* —; to send for.

questeur (kuès-), *n.m.*, questor.

question (kès-tion), *n.f.*, question, interrogation; query; (jur.) issue; question (torture). *Faire une* —; to ask a question. *De quoi est-il* —? what's the matter? *Résoudre une* —; to solve a question. *Sortir de la* —; to wander from the question. *Si c'est une* — *à faire;* if it is a fair question. *Il est* — *de;* it is in contemplation to. *Après cela il fut* — *de moi;* then my affair came on the carpet. *Mettre en* —; to question: to

call in question. *Mettre à la* —; to put to the rack, to torture.

questionnaire (kes-tio-nèr), *n.m.*, examination questions; book of questions; torturer.

questionner (kès-tio-né), *v.a.*, to question, to interrogate; to ask questions.

questionneu-r, *n.m.*, **-se**, *n.f.*, questioner, querist.

questure (kuès-), *n.f.*, questorship; questors' office.

quête, *n.f.*, quest, search; collection, gathering; (hunt.) beating about; (nav.) rake. *Se mettre en* — *de;* to go in quest of.

quêter, *v.a.*, to be in quest or search of; to make a gathering or collection; (hunt.) to search.

quêteu-r, *n.m.*, **-se**, *n.f.*, collector, gatherer.

queue (keû), *n.f.*, tail; stalk, stem; (l.u.) hone; hogshead; end, extremity; rear; (of documents—*de titres, &c.*) label; billiard-cue; handle (of a frying-pan, of mills—*de poêles à frire, de moulins*); train (of robes, gowns—*de robes*); file, string (of persons—*de personnes*). —*d'aronde* (—*s*—); (carp.) dove-tail. — *écourtée;* bob-tail. — *de-cheval* (—*s* —) (bot.); horsetail. — *de-lion* (—*s* —) (bot.); lion's-tail; motherwort. — *de-pourceau* (—*s* —) (bot.); hog's-fennel. *Demi*— (— —*s*); half a hogshead. *La* — *d'un paon;* a peacock's train. *La* — *d'une robe;* the train of a gown. — *de moulin;* millhandle. — *de poêle;* handle of a frying-pan. *La* — *de l'armée;* the rear of the army. *Avoir les ennemis en* —; to have the enemy at one's heels. *Il est à la* —; he is behind. *Faire* —; to stand in a line. *À* —*d'aronde* (carp.); dovetailed. *À la* — *leu leu.* *V.* **leu.**

queussi-queumi, *adv.*, neither more nor less, neither better nor worse, just the same.

queuter, *v.n.*, to strike two balls at once (at billiards—*au billard*).

queux, or **queue** (keû), *n.f.*, hone, whetstone.

⊙**queux**, *n.m.*, cook.

qui, *relative pron.*, who, whoever, whom, whomsoever, which, that; what; some. *L'homme* — *pense;* the man who thinks. *Les chevaux* — *tirent;* the horses that draw. *De* — *parle-t-il?* whose book is he speaking of? *À* — *est ce livre?* whose book is this? *Dites-moi* —; tell me who. *Je ne sais pas* —; I don't know who. *C'est à* — *l'aura;* it is who shall have her. — *pis est;* what is worse. — *plus est;* what is still more than that. *Je sais* — *vous voulez dire;* I know whom you mean. — *est là?* who's there? — *d'entre vous oserait?* which of you would dare? *Ils étaient dispersés* — *çà, qui là;* they were dispersed some one way, some another. — *que ce soit,* — *que ce puisse être;* whoever, whosoever it be. *Je n'ai vu* — *que ce soit;* I have seen nobody. *Il ne se défiait de* — *que ce fût;* he mistrusted nobody. — *que ce soit, il s'en repentira;* let him be who he will, he shall repent it.

quia (kui-a), *adv.*, (l.u.) naught. *Être à* —; to be at a loss, to be at a stand, to be nonplussed. *Mettre à* —; to nonplus, to put to a stand.

quibus (kui-bus), *n.m.*, (pop.) property, wealth. *Avoir du* —; to be warm; to have plenty of money.

quiconque (ki-kŏnk), *pron.*, whoever, whosoever; whomsoever, whichever.

quida-m (ki-dăn), *n.m.*, **-ne** (ki-da-n), *n.f.*, (jur.) quidam; person of name unknown; a certain person, one.

quiddité (kuid-di-té), *n.f.*, quiddity.

quiescent, **-e** (kui-). *adj.*, quiescent.

⊙**qui-et**, **-ète**, *adj.*, quiet, at rest.

quiétisme, *n.m.*, quietism.

quiétiste, *n.m.f.* and *adj.*, quietist.

quiétude, *n.f.*, quietude.

*****quignon**, *n.m.*, (fam.) hunch (great piece—*gros morceau*).

☉*****quillage**, *n.m.*, keelage, duty levied on merchant ships entering French ports for the first time. *V.* **ancrage**.

*****quille**, *n.f.*, skittle; (nav.) keel. *Jeu de —s;* game of skittles, set of skittles; skittle-ground. *Donner à quelqu'un son sac et ses —s;* to send any one packing.

*****quiller**, *v.n.*, to throw for partners or for first play at skittles.

*****quillette**, *n.f.*, osier plant.

*****quillier**, *n.m.*, skittle-ground.

*****quilloir**, *n.m.*, (nav.) reel-stick.

*****quillon**, *n.m.*, cross-bar of the hilt of a sword.

quina, *n.m.* *V.* **quinquina.**

quinaire, *n.m.*, (antiq.) quinarius.

quinaire (kui-), *adj.*, (math.) quinary.

☉**quinaud, -e**, *adj.*, abashed, ashamed.

*****quincaille**, *n.f.*, ironmongery, hardware.

*****quincaillerie**, *n.f.*, ironmongery, hardware.

*****quincaillier**, *n.m.*, ironmonger, hardware-man.

quinconce, *n.m.*, quincunx.

quindécagone (kuin-), *n.m.*, (geom.) quindecagon.

quindécemvir (kuin-dé-sèm-vir), *n.m.*, quindecemvir.

quindécemvi-at, *n.m.*, quindecemvirate.

quine, *n.m.*, two fives (tricktrack); five winning numbers (in a lottery—*à la loterie*).

quinine, *n.f.*, extract of quinquina, quinine.

quinola, *n.m.*, knave of hearts (reversi).

quinquagénaire (kuin-koua-), *n.m.f.* and *adj.*, person fifty years old; fifty years old.

quinquagésime (kuin-koua-), *n.f.*, Quinquagesima.

☉**quinque** (kuin-kué), *n.m.*, (mus.) quintet.

quinquédenté, -e (kuin-kué-), *adj.*, (bot.) quinquedentate.

quinquennal, -e (kuin-kuèn-nal), *adj.*, quinquennial.

☉**quinquennium**, *n.m.* (n.p.), a five years' course of philosophy and theology.

quinquenove, *n.m.*, a game at dice.

quinquerce (kuin-kuèrs), *n.m.*, (antiq.) quinquertium.

quinquérème (kuin-kué-), *n.f.*, quinquereme.

quinquet, *n.m.*, Argand lamp; lamp.

quinquina, *n.m.*, quinquina; Peruvian bark; (bot.) cinchona.

quint, *n.m.* and *adj.*, (l.u.) fifth. *Charles —;* Charles the Fifth. *Sixte —;* Sextus the Fifth.

quintaine, *n.f.*, (man.) quintain.

quintal, *n.m.*, quintal, hundred-weight.

quintan, *n.m.*, (man.) quintain.

quintane, *adj.*, quintan, of five days (of fevers—*fièvre*).

quinte, *n.f.*, (mus.) fifth; quint (piquet); fit (of coughing—*de toux*); freak, whim; (fenc.) quinte; tenor violin; (man.) dead stop.

quinte, *adj.f.*, of five days (of fevers—*fièvre*). *Fièvre —;* a five-day fever. *V.* **quintaine**.

*****quintefeuille**, *n.f.*, (bot.) cinque-foil.

quintessence, *n.f.*, quintessence: marrow.

quintessencier, *v.a.*, to draw the quintessence out of: to refine, to be critical.

quintette (kuin-tèt), *n.m.*, (mus.) quintet, quintetto.

quinteu-x -se, *adj.*, fanciful, whimsical; making dead stops (of a horse—*du cheval*).

quintidi (kuin-), *n.m.*, Quintidi, fifth day of the decade in the calendar of the first French republic.

quintil -e, (kuin-), *adj.*, (astron.) quintile. *— aspect;* quintile.

quintillion, *n.m.*, one trillion.

quintuple (kuin-), *n.m.* and *adj.*, quintuple, fivefold.

quintupler (kuin-), *v.a.*, to quintuple, to increase fivefold.

quinzain, *n.m.*, fifteen each (at tennis—*à la paume*).

quinzaine, *n.f.*, about fifteen; fortnight.

quinze, *n.m.* and *adj.*, fifteen; fifteenth. *— jours;* fortnight. *D'aujourd'hui en —;* this day fortnight. *Les —-vingts;* Quinze-Vingts, hospital in Paris for three hundred blind men. *Un —-vingts;* an inmate or Quinze-Vingts.

quinzième, *n.m.* and *adj.*, fifteenth; fifteenth day; (mus.) fifteenth.

quinzièmement, *adv.*, fifteenthly, in the fifteenth place.

quipos, *n.m.* (n.s.), quippa, quippo.

quiproquo, *n.m.* (—s), mistake.

quittance, *n.f.*, receipt. *— pour solde de compte*, receipt in full.

quittancer, *v.a.*, to write a receipt on; to receipt.

quitte, *adj.*, discharged (from debt—*d'une dette*); quit, quits, clear; free, rid. *Jouer à — ou double;* to play double or quits. *Tenir —;* to release, to disengage. *Je suis — d'un grand embarras;* I am rid of a great deal of trouble. *Je vous tiens — de votre parole;* I release you from your word. *Vous n'en serez pas — à si bon marché;* you shall not come off so cheaply. *Il en fut — pour la peur;* he got off for his fear.

quittement, *adv.*, (jur.) entirely, without debt or incumbrance.

quitter, *v.a.*, to quit, to leave, to part with; to leave off; to *take off (to lay aside, to desist from); to give up, to give over; to depart (life —la vie). Je vous quitte pour un instant;* I leave you for a moment. *— père et mère;* to quit father and mother. *— ses habits;* to take off one's clothes. *— une charge;* to give up an office. *J'aime mieux — que disputer;* I rather choose to give up than to dispute. *Il a quitté le service;* he has quitted the service. *— le commerce;* to leave off trade. *— la chasse;* to give over hunting. *— la partie;* to give up the game. *Qui quitte la partie la perd;* who leaves off the game, loses.

quitus (kui-tus), *n.m.* (—), (fin.) discharge.

qui va là? or **qui-va-là**, *n.m.*, who goes there? *Avoir réponse à tout, hormis à —;* to be unable to answer an objection which ought to have been foreseen. *Avoir réponse à —;* to be stopped by no difficulty; to have always an answer ready.

qui vive? or **qui-vive**, *n.m.*, (milit.) challenge-word; who goes there? *Être sur le —;* to keep a good look-out, to be upon the qui vive.

*****quoailler**, *v.n.*, (of a horse—*du cheval*) to shake its tail.

quoi, *pron.*, which, what. *— que vous disiez;* whatever you may say. *Dites-moi en — je puis vous servir;* tell me in what I can serve you. *C'est en — vous vous trompez;* you are mistaken in that. *À — passez-vous le temps?* how do you spend your time? *À — bon tant de façons?* why so much ceremony? *À propos de —!* on what occasion? with respect to what? *Avoir de — —* (pop.); to be rich. *Il n'y a pas de —;* it is not worth mentioning; there is no reason for it. *— qu'il en soit;* be that as it may. *Nous avons de — le faire;* we have the means to do it.

quoi! *int.*, what! how! *—. vous avez fait cela?* what! have you done that? *— donc, vous osez me résister en face!* how then I dare you resist me openly?.

quoique, *conj.,* although, though. *Quoiqu'il soit pauvre ;* although he is poor.

quolibet, *n.m.,* quibble, pun, sorry joke.

quote-part, *n.f.* (*—s —s*), quota, portion, share.

quotidien, -ne (-in, -è-n), *adj.,* daily, quotidian, diurnal. *Notre pain — ;* our daily bread.

quotient, *n.m.,* (arith.) quotient.

quotité, *n.f.,* quota, portion, share.

R

r (èr), *n.f.,* (re) *n.m.,* the eighteenth letter of the alphabet, r.

rabâchage, *n.m.,* tautology ; tiresome repetition ; tiresome repetitions in discourse.

rabâcher, *v.n.* and *a.,* (fam.) to make tiresome repetitions, to repeat the same thing over and over again ; to repeat over and over.

rabâcherie (-bâ-shri), *n.f.,* eternal repetition.

rabâcheu-r, *n.m.,* **-se,** *n.f.,* person who makes tiresome repetitions, who eternally repeats the same thing.

rabais, *n.m.,* abatement, reduction, diminution. *Vendre, donner, au — ,* to sell at reduced prices. *Être au — ;* to be fallen in price. *Il les a pris au — ;* he has taken them by contract.

rabaissement (-bès-mān), *n.m.,* diminution of value.

rabaisser, *v.a.,* to lower ; to abate, to diminish, to lessen ; to depreciate, to humble. *— sa voix ;* to lower one's voice. *— les monnaies ;* to depreciate the coin. *— les taxes ;* to lower the taxes. *— l'orgueil de quelqu'un ;* to humble any one's pride.

raban, *n.m.,* (nav.) rope-band, gasket, knittle.

rabanner, *v.a.,* (nav.) to fit a sail with rope-bands and earings.

rabat, *n.m.,* band (for the neck—*de cou*) ; end of the roof (of a tennis-court—*d'un jeu de paume*) ; beating about for game.

rabat-joie, *n.m.* (—), sad balk, anything that checks our joy, damper, wet blanket. *C'est un — ;* he is an enemy to all joy, a regular wet blanket.

rabattre, *v.a.,* to bring down, to lower, to beat down, to lay ; to abate, to diminish, to deduct ; to humble ; to revoke. *Le vent rabat la fumée ;* the wind beats down the smoke. *— un coup ,* to ward off a blow. *Il n'en veut rien — ;* he won't bate an inch on it. *— l'orgueil de quelqu'un ,* to bring down any one's pride. *— le gibier ;* to beat up the game.

se rabattre, *v.r.,* to beat down ; to turn off, to change one's road ; to fall back upon, to come down, to lower one's pretensions ; to limit one's self.

rabattre, *v.n.,* to turn under ; to turn off, to change one's direction.

rabattue, *n.f.,* (nav.) hances *or* falls of the fife-rails.

rabbaniste, *n.m.* V. **rabbiniste.**

rabbi, *or* **rabbin,** *n.m.,* rabbi, rabbin. [*Rabbi* is used only before the names of Jewish doctors and does not admit of the article, as : *Je suis de l'opinion de rabbi Aben :* I am of the same opinion as Rabbi Aben. It is also used in addressing Jewish doctors : *Que dites-vous, rabbi, de cette interprétation ?* what do you think, Rabbi, of this interpretation ? *Rabbin* is used in any other'case]

rabbinage, *n.m.,* rabbinism.

rabbinique, *adj.,* rabbinical.

rabbinisme, *n.m.,* rabbinism.

rabbiniste, *or* **rabbaniste,** *n.m.,* rabbinist.

rabdologie, *n.f.,* rhabdology.

rabdomancie, *or* ☉ **rabdomance,** *n.f.,* rhabdomancy.

rabêtir, *v.a.* and *n.,* to stupify, to make dull or stupid ; to grow dull or stupid.

rabiole, *n.f.* V. **rave.**

rabique, *adj.,* (med.) hydrophobie ; of rabies, of canine madness.

râble, *n.m.,* back of a hare or rabbit ; (chem) rake ; (b.s.) back (of a person—*de personne*).

râblu, -e, *adj.,* thick-backed (of a hare or rabbit—*du lièvre, du lapin*) ; (pers.) broad-backed, that has a good back.

râblure, *n.f.,* (nav) rabbet, channel. *— de la quille ;* rabbet of the keel.

rabonnir, *v.a.,* to improve.

rabot, *n.m.,* plane ; beater (to move lime—*pour remuer de la chaux*) ; road-scraper.

rabotage, *n.m.,* (carp) planing.

raboter, *v.a.* and *n.,* to plane, to smooth with a plane ; to polish.

raboteur, *n.m.,* planer, moulding-worker.

raboteu-x, -se, *adj.,* knotty, rough ; rugged, cragged, craggy ; uneven, harsh.

rabougri, -e, *part.,* stunted. *Un petit homme — ;* a stunted little fellow.

rabougrir, *v.n.,* to be stunted.

se rabougrir, *v.r.,* to become stunted.

*rabouilère, *n.f.,* rabbit's nest.

raboutir, *v.a.,* to piece, to join end to end.

rabrouer, *v.a.,* to snub, to give sharp answers to.

rabroueu-r, *n.m.,* **-se,** *n.f.,* snappish person.

racage, *n.m.,* (nav.) parrel. *Pommes de — ;* trucks of a parrel. *Bigots de — ;* ribs of a parrel. *Bâtard de — ;* parrel-rope. *Drosse de — ;* parrel-truss.

racahout, *n.m.* (*n.p.*), racahout, a nutritious fecula.

*racaille, *n.f.,* rabble, riffraff ; rubbish, trash.

racambeau, *n.m.,* (nav.) traveller.

raccommodage, *n.m.,* mending, repairing, darning.

raccommodement (-mod-mān), *n.m.,* reconciliation, reconcilement.

raccommoder, *v.a.,* to mend, to repair ; to piece, to patch, to botch ; to adjust, to set right ; to improve, to correct ; to reconcile, to make friends again ; to darn. *Faire — quelque chose ;* to have anything mended. *On les a raccommodés :* they have been reconciled.

se raccommoder, *v.r.,* to be reconciled ; to make it up again. *Le mari et la femme se sont raccommodés ;* the husband and wife are friends again.

raccommodeu-r, *n.m.,* **-se,** *n.f.,* mender, patcher.

raccord, *n.m.,* joining, junction.

raccordement, *n.m.,* (arch.) levelling ; union, junction.

raccorder, *v.a.,* to join, to unite.

raccourci, *n.e.part.,* shortened, abbreviate too short. *À bras —s :* with might and main

raccourci, *n.m.,* epitome, abridgment ; (paint.) foreshortening. *En — ;* abridged, briefly ; (persp.) foreshortened.

raccourcir, *v.a.,* to shorten, to make shorter ; to contract ; to curtail ; (persp.) to foreshorten.

se raccourcir, *v.r.,* to shorten, to grow or become shorter ; to contract one's self ; to shrink.

raccourcir, *v.n.,* to shorten, to become shorter ; to shrink.

raccourcissement (-sis-mān), *n.m.,* shortening, contraction.

raccoutrement, *n.m.*, mending of clothes.

raccoutrer, *v.a.*, to mend clothes.

se **raccoutumer**, *v.r.*, to accustom, to use, one's self again.

raccroc (ra-kro), *n.m.*, lucky hit.

raccrocher, *v.a.*, to hook again; to hang up again ; to recover, to get again. *Raccrochez ce tableau ;* hang up this picture again, — *son argent ;* to recover one's money.

se **raccrocher**, *v.r.*, to cling; to adhere; to)etrieve one's self. — *à une chose;* to cling to a thing.

raccrocheuse, *n.f.*, (pop.) street-walker.

race, *n.f.*, race ; stock, breed ; (agri.) variety. *Un cheval de* —; a thoroughbred horse. *Ce chien est de bonne* —; this dog is of a good breed. *Croiser les* —s; to cross the breeds. — *de vipères;* generation of vipers. *La* — *future :* future ages. *Les bons chiens chassent de* —. it runs in bl., her, their, blood. *Cette fille chasse de* —; that girl is a flirt like her mother.

rachat, *n.m.*, repurchase, redemption, recovery, ransom. *Vendre à faculté de* —; to sell with power of redemption.

rachetable (rash-tabl), *adj.*, redeemable.

racheter (rash-té), *v.a*, to buy back again, to purchase ; to ransom, to buy off, to redeem ; to compensate, to make up for ; to atone, to atone for. — *une rente ;* to redeem an annuity. — *les prisonniers;* to ransom the prisoners. — *ses vices par ses vertus;* to redeem one's vices by one's virtues.

se **racheter**, *v.r.*, to redeem one's self ; to be compensated, to be made up for.

racheu-x, **-se**, *adj.*, knotty (of wood—*du bois*).

rachever (rash-vé), *v.a.*, (pop.) to finish (anything begun—*une chose commencée*).

rachidien, **-ne** (-in, -èn), *adj.*, (anat.) spinal, vertebral.

rachis (ra-shis), *n.m.*, (anat.) spinal, vertebral column, spine ; (bot.) stalk.

rachitique, *adj.*, (med.) rickety ; (bot.) blighted. stunted.

rachitique. *n.m.f.*, rickety person, person suffering with rickets.

rachitis (-tis), *n.m.*, rachitis ; rickets.

rachitisme, *n.m.*. rachitis ; rickets ; (agri.) white blight.

racinage, *n.m.*, alimentary roots ; (dy.) decoction of walnut husks, of walnut peel.

racinal, *n.m.*, (carp.) sole ; sill.

racine, *n.f.*, root ; radix. *Fruits pendants par les* —s; standing crops. — *carrée* (arith.); square root. — *cubique;* cube root. *Prendre* —; to take root.

raciner, *v.n.*. to strike root.

raciner, *v.a.*, to dye with roots.

rack. *n.m.*, arrack. rack (liquor). *V.* **arack**.

racle. *n.f.*, (nav.) scraper (used to clean a ship's side, deck, &c.—*pour le nettoyage des vaisseaux*).

racle-boyau. *n.m.* (—), catgut-scraper, fiddler.

raclée. *n.f.*. (pop.) beating, drubbing.

racler. *v.a.*. to clear away by rubbing. to scrape, to scrape off; to strike (a measure—*une mesure*); to rake. — *le boyau ;* to scrape the fiddle.

racleur. *n.m.*. catgut-scraper.

racloir. *n.m.*, scraper, road-scraper.

racloire. *n.f.*, strike (of measures—*de mesures*).

raclure, *n.f.*, scrapings.

racolage. *n.m.*, enticing men to enlist, kidnapping.

racoler, *v.a.*, to entice men to enlist, to kidnap.

racoleur. *n.m.*, one who entices men to enlist, crimp.

raconter, *v.a.*, to relate, to tell, to narrate, to recount.

raconteu-r, *n.m.*, **-se**, *n.f.*, relater. teller.

racornir, *v.a.*, to make as hard as horn ; to make hard, to harden ; to dry up, to shrivel, to shrivel up.

se **racornir**, *v.r*, to grow hard, to harden; to shrivel, to shrivel up, to dry up.

racornissement (-nis-màn), *n.m.*, hardening. shrivelling, drying up.

racquit, *n.m.*, winning back.

racquitter, *v.a.*, to win back again; to indemnify.

se **racquitter**, *v.r.*, to win back again; to retrieve one's losses (at play—*au jeu*).

rade, *n.f.*, (nav.) road, roadstead. — *foraine;* open road. *Vaisseau en* —; roader *Aller en* —; to go into the road.

radeau, *n.m.*, raft.

rader, *v.a.*, (nav.) to anchor in a roadstead; to strike (a measure—*une mesure*). — *un vaisseau ;* to anchor a ship in a road.

radeur, *n.m.*, salt-measurer.

radiaire, *n.m.* and *adj.*, (zool.) radiary; radiated. —s, radiata.

radial, **-e**, *adj.*, (anat.. geom.) radial.

radiant, **-e**, *adj.*, radiant.

radiation, *n.f.*, eradiation, irradiation ; obliteration, erasure, crossing out, striking out.

radical, **-e**, *adj.*, radical.

radical, *n.m.*, radical.

radicalement (-kal-màn), *adv.*, radically.

radicalisme, *n.m.*, radicalism.

radicant, **-e**, *adj.*, (bot.) radicant.

radication, *n.f.*, radication.

radicelle, *n.f.*, (bot.) radicle.

radicule, *n.f.*, (bot.) radicle.

radié, **-e**. *adj.*, (bot.) radiant, radiated, stellated ; (her.) radiant.

radier, *n.m.*, (arch.) inverted arch ; floor (of a lock on a canal—*d'une écluse*); apron (of docks, of basins— *de docks, de bassins*) ; radish-plate.

radier, *v.a.*, to strike out.

radieu-x, **-se**, *adj.*, radiant, beamy, shining

radiomètre, *n.m.*, (astron.) radiometer.

radis, *n.m.*, radish.

radius (-us), *n.m.*, (anat.) radius.

radoire, *n.f.*, strike (of measures—*pour mesures*).

radotage, *n.m.*, nonsense, idle talk, drivelling stuff ; dotage.

radoter, *v.n.*, to rave, to dote, to talk idly, to wander.

radoterie (ra-do-trî), *n.f.*, nonsense, unmeaning absurdity, idle words.

radoteu-r, *n.m.*, **-se**, *n.f.*, dotard, driveller. *Vieille* —*se :* trifling old woman.

radoub (-doob), *n.m.*, (nav.) repair, refitting of a ship. *Cale de* —; graving slip. *Forme de* —; gravingdock. *Vaisseau en* —; ship undergoing repairs.

radouber, *v.a.*, (nav.) to refit, to repair.

se **radouber**, *v.r.*, (nav.) to be repaired.

radoubeur, *n.m.*, (nav.) calker.

radoucir, *v.a.*, to soften, to make milder, to render milder, to appease, to pacify.

se **radoucir**, *v.r.*, to soften, to grow milder, to become milder, to get milder; to grow soft, to become soft, to get soft ; to subside, to be appeased, to be pacified; to relent, to relax, to soften down.

radoucissement (-sis-màn), *n.m.*, becoming milder, getting milder (of the weather—*du temps*) : mitigation, allaying.

rafale, *n.f.*, (nav.) squall.

raffe. *n.f.* *V.* **rafle**.

raffermir, *v.a.*, to harden, to make firm ; to fasten ; to establish, to confirm, to settle, to secure, to fortify, to strengthen. *Cet événement raffermit son autorité ;* that event strengthened

his authority. — *le courage de quelqu'un*; to put any one in heart again.

seraffermir. *v.r.*, to grow stronger, to gather strength; to be established, to become established, to be confirmed, to become confirmed. *Sa santé se raffermit*; his health improves.

raffermissement (-mis-măn), *n.m.*, strengthening; confirmation, establishment, fastening, securing.

raffinage, *n.m.*, refining.

raffiné. *n.m.*, name given in France to the lewd dandies and duellists of the end of the 16th century.

raffiné, **-e**, *adj.*, refined; keen, sharp, subtle.

raffinement (ra-fi-n-măn), *n.m.*, refinement, affected nicety.

raffiner, *v.a.*, to refine.

seraffiner, *v.r.*, to refine, to be refined, to become refined.

raffiner, *v.n.*, to refine. — *sur le point d'honneur*; to be very nice upon the point of honour.

raffinerie (ra-fi-n-ri), *n.f.*, refinery; sugar-refinery, refining.

raffineur. *n.m.*, refiner. — *de sucre*; sugar-refiner, sugar-baker.

raffoler. *v.n.*, to dote, to be passionately fond, to be distractedly in love. *Il raffole de cette femme*; he is distractedly in love with that woman.

raffolir, *v.n.*, (l.u.) to become mad, to go mad.

rafistoler, *v.a.*, (fam.) to mend clothes.

rafle, **raffle**, *or* **râpe**, *n.f.*, grape-stalk stripped of all its fruit; (dice—*aux dés*) pair-royal. *Faire* — (fam.); to sweep off the stakes; to sweep off every thing.

rafler, *v.a.*, (fam.) to sweep away, to sweep off, to carry off.

seraflouer, *v.a.*, (nav.). *V.* **renflouer**.

rafraîchir. *v.a.*, to cool; to refresh, to restore, to invigorate, to repair, to recruit, to renew, to freshen, to freshen up, to renovate, to rub up, to crop, to cut, to trim (cut the ends of—*couper l'extrémité*); (milit.) to relieve; to rest. — *du vin*; to cool wine. — *le sang*; to refresh the blood. — *un tableau*; to clean up a picture. — *une tapisserie*; to restore a piece of tapestry. — *les cheveux*; to clip the hair. — *la mémoire*; to refresh one's memory. — *une muraille*; to repair a wall. — *une place*; to supply a garrison with fresh men and provisions. *Ces troupes sont fatiguées, il faut les mettre dans de bons quartiers pour les* —; these troops are worn out, they must be sent into good quarters to rest.

serafraîchir, *v.r.*, to cool, to grow cool, to become cool; to take refreshment, to refresh one's self; to be refreshed; to recruit one's self; to recruit one's strength, to rest one's self. *Venez vous rafraîchir*; come and take some refreshment. *Le vent se rafraîchit*; the wind freshens.

rafraîchir, *v.n.*, to cool, to become cool; to be refreshing.

rafraîchissant, **-e**, *adj.*, cooling, refrigerative.

rafraîchissant, *n.m.*, (med.) refrigerant.

rafraîchissement (-shis-măn), *n.m.*, cooling; cooling effect; *pl.*, refreshments; provisions, supplies. *Faire les* —*s* (nav.); to take in fresh provisions.

rafraîchissoir, *n.m.*, cooler.

*ragaillardir, *v.a.*, to make merry, to render merry, to render cheerful, to enliven, to cheer, to cheer up.

rage, *n.f.*, (med.) rage, fury, incensement; mania; rabies, hydrophobia, rabies canina, ca-

---

nine madness. *Écumer de* —; to foam with rage. *Avoir la* —; to be mad (of animals—*des animaux*). *Il a la* — *d'écrire*; he has a mania for writing. *Il l'aime à la* —; he loves her to distraction. *Il a la* — *du jeu*; he has a passion for gambling. *Faire* —; to be quite the rage; to cause great disorder. *Dire* — *de quelqu'un*; to say all imaginable harm of any one. *Quand on veut noyer son chien, on dit qu'il a la* —(prov.); give a dog a bad name and hang him.

rager, *v.n.*, (fam.) to be in a passion; to sulk, to be angry.

rageu-r, *n.m.*, **-se**, *n.f.*, a peevish person.

ragot, *n.m.*, (hunt.) solitary wild boar, not quite three years old.

ragot, **-e**, *adj.*, dumpy, thick and short; thick set; squat (animal).

ragoût, *n.m.*, (cook.) ragout; stew; hash; pleasure.

ragoûtant, **-e**. *adj.*, relishing, savoury; pleasing, tempting. *Morceau* —; tit-bit. *Ce mets-là n'est guère* —; that dish is not very savoury.

ragoûter, *v.a.*, to revive one's stomach, to restore the appetite; to quicken, to stir up.

seragoûter, *v.r.*, to restore one's appetite.

ragrafer, *v.a.*, to clasp again, to re-clasp, to hook again.

ragrandir, *v.a.*, to enlarge again; to enlarge.

seragrandir, *v.r.*, to be enlarged again; to become larger.

ragréer, *v.a.*, (arch.) to finish, to finish off, to give the finishing touch to; to restore, to renovate, to do up; to pare, to prune; (nav.) to rig anew. — *un ouvrage de menuiserie*; to finish a piece of joiner's work. — *une branche d'arbre*; to prune a branch of a tree.

seragréer, *v.r.*, (nav.) to repair; to procure, to obtain fresh rigging.

ragrément, *n.m.*, finishing, finishing off; restoration, renovation, doing up; pruning, paring (of trees—*des arbres*).

ragué (ra-ghé), *adj.*, (nav.) chafed, rubbed, galled.

raïa, *n.m.*, rajah, raja.

raide, *adj.*, stiff, rigid; tight; tough; steep; swift, rapid; (nav.) taught. — *de froid*; stiff with cold. *Peau* —; tough skin. *Montagne* —; steep mountain. — *comme une barre de fer*; as stiff as a poker. *Se tenir* —; to stand stiff. *Vol* —; rapid flight. *Le cours de la rivière est* —; the current of the river is rapid.

raide, *adv.*, quickly, swiftly; vigorously; tightly; toughly.

raideur, *n.f.*, stiffness, rigidity; inflexibility; tightness; toughness; steepness; swiftness, velocity.

*raidillon, *n.m.*, ascent (in a road—*d'une route*).

raidir, *v.a.*, to stiffen, to render inflexible, to render rigid; to tighten; to toughen; (nav.) to haul taught.

seraidir, *v.r.*, to stiffen; to become, to grow, to get stiff; to become inflexible, to get inflexible; to bear up, to resist; to withstand; to bristle up; to toughen.

raidir, *v.n.*, to stiffen; to become, to grow, to get, stiff; to tighten; to toughen.

raie, *n.f.*, line, stroke; streak, stripe; (of hair—*des cheveux*) parting; (agri.) furrow; (ich.) ray, skate. *À* —*s*; striped. *Faire sa* —; to part one's hair. *Étoffe à* —*s*; striped stuff. (ich.) — *bouclée*; thornback. — *mobular*; angel-fish.

raifort, *n.m.*, (bot.) radish, horse-radish.

rail, *n.m.*, (railways) rail. — *ondulé*; fish-bellied rail. — *à ornière*; tram-rail. *Distance des* —*s dans œuvre*; gauge of way.

*railler, v.a., to bante·, to jeer, to rally, to joke, to jest.
se railler, v.r., to jest, to joke, to mock, to make game of.
*railler, v.n., to jeer, to scoff; to joke, to jest, to laugh at. — de tout; to jeer at every thing. Ne raillez pas davantage; no more of your jeering. Je ne raille pas: I am not joking.
*raillerie, n.f., raillery, bantering, jesting, jest, joke, banter, jeer, mockery. Tourner une chose en —; to make a jest of a thing. Entendre la — ; to joke well, to be a good hand at joking. Entendre — ; to take a joke, to take a jest. C'est une — de croire que; it is ridiculous to think that. — à part, sans — ; seriously, in good earnest. La — en est-elle? (fam.) is it allowable to joke on the matter?
*railleu-r,-se, n. and adj., banterer, jeerer, joker, scoffer, jester; bantering, jeering, joking, jesting, fond of raillery. D'un air —; sneeringly.
railway, n.m., railway.
rainceau. n.m. V. rinceau.
raine, n.f. (local expr.) frog.
rainette, n.f., (erp.) tree-frog ; (bot.) V. reinette.
rainure, n.f., groove ; rabbet ; furrow, slot-hole.
raiponce, n.f., (bot.) rampion, rampion bell-flower.
raire, or réer, v.n., (hunt.) to bell.
rais, n.m., spoke (of a wheel—deroue) ; ☉beam, ray (of light—de lumière); (her.) beam. — de cœur; (arch.) ogee.
raisin, n.m., grapes. Une grappe de — ; a bunch of grapes. Un grain de — ; a grape. Un pépin de — ; a grapestone. — de Corinthe; grocer's currants. Des —s secs ; raisins. — d'Amérique (bot.) ; poke-weed. — d'ours; bear's whortle-berry. — de renard (bot.) ; herb-Paris, true-love. Grand — ; royal (paper—papier).
raisiné, n.m., preserve of pears, quinces and grapes.
raisinier, n.m., (bot.) grape-tree.
raison, n.f., reason, sense, judgment, rationality ; satisfaction ; proof, ground ; motive ; rate; consideration ; (com.) firm ; share; ratio ; (jur) claim. — sociale; firm; name of a firm. Sans —; groundless, groundlessly. Il n'a point de — ; he wants sense, he is deficient in sense. Mariage de — ; prudent marriage. Parler — : to talk sense. to talk sensibly. Avoir — ; to be right. Vous avez — ; you are right Donner — à quelqu'un ; to decide in favour of any one. Plus que de — ; more than is reasonable, more than one ought. Entendre — ; to listen to reason. Mettre quelqu'un à la — ; to bring any one to reason. Comme de —; as it is fit, of course. Être de —; imaginary being. Où force domine — n'a point lieu; where force bears the sway, there's no room for reason. Tirer— d'une injure; to obt..in satisfaction for an injury. Se faire — soi-même; to do one's self justice, to take the law into one's own hands. Rendre — de sa conduite; to give an account of one's conduct. Puissante —; powerful argument. — probable; probable proof. Point tant de —s; none of your arguments. Grande —; great cause. Bonne —; good grounds. À plus forte ; with greater reason. Pour — de quoi; for which cause, wherefore. Pour — à moi connue; for reasons best known to myself. À — de, en — de; in proportion to; according to; at the rate of. En — de; by reason of; in consideration of. À telle fin que de — ; to serve in case of need; at all events; in any case.
raisonnable, adj., rational, reasonable.

thinking, sensible; conscionable, just ; proper, right ; adequate ; moderate ; tolerable. Pension — ; reasonable pension. Prix — ; moderate price.
raisonnablement. adv., reasonably, sensibly, agreeably to reason, justly, rationally ; moderately, pretty well ; tolerably.
raisonné, -e adj., supported by reasoning and by proof ; analytical. Grammaire —e ; methodical grammar.
raisonnement (rè-zo-n-mǎn), n.m., reasoning ; rationality, argument, ratiocination. Faire des —s à perte de vue; to reason vaguely, to wander from the point. Point de —s; no answers ; let me have none of your answers.
raisonner, v.n., to reason, to argue, to discourse ; to answer ; (nav) to lie to (in order to be searched—pour montrer ses passeports). C'est le propre de l'homme de — ; reasoning is proper to man. — faux, to reason falsely. Faire — un vaisseau (nav.) ; to oblige a ship to come near and speak.
raisonner, v.a., to reason, to apply one's reason to ; to examine, to study; (nav.) to bring to and search.
raisonneu-r, -se, n. and adj., reasoner, arguer ; logician ; impertinent answerer ; impertinent, insolent ; answering when reprimanded.
rajah, or raja, n.m., raja, rajah.
rajeunir, v.a., to make young ; to make look younger, to give a young look ; to restore to youth ; to prune, to lop (trees—les arbres).
se rajeunir, v.r., to make one's self look younger.
rajeunir, v.n., to grow young again ; to be restored to youth ; to look young again.
rajeunissant, -e, adj., giving a youthful appearance to.
rajeunissement (-nis-mǎn), n.m., growing young again, making young again.
rajustement, n.m., readjustment ; putting in order.
rajuster, v.a., to readjust, to put to rights, to put in order again ; to reconcile. — un habit ; to arrange a coat. On les a rajustés; they have been reconciled.
se rajuster, v.r., to put one's self or one's dress in order.
râle, n.m., (orni.) rail ; rattling in the throat. — de la mort ; death-rattle.
râlement (râl-mǎn), n.m., rattling in the throat, death-rattle.
ralentir, v.r., to abate, to slacken ; to lessen. to diminish, to moderate, to mitigate. — sa course ; to slacken one's pace.
se ralentir, v.r., to slacken ; to abate, to relax. to diminish ; to grow remiss.
ralentissement (-tis-mǎn), n.m., slackening, relenting, abatement, cooling.
râler, v.n., to have a rattling in the throat.
ralingue (-lin-g), n.f., (nav.) bolt-rope (of a sail—d'une voile). — de fond ; foot-rope. — de chute ; leech-rope. — de têtière ; head-rope. Mettre une voile en — : to let fly the sheets of a sail. Mets en — ! let the sails touch!
ralinguer (-ghé), v.a., (nav.) to sew the bolt-ropes to. — une voile; to sew the bolt-ropes to a sail.
ralinguer, v.n., (nav.) to let fly the sheets of a sail loose to the wind; to fly loose to the wind (of sails—des voiles) ; to shiver.
ralliement (-li-mǎn), n.m., rallying, rally. Mot de — ; rallying-word, countersign. Signe de — ; rallying sign. Point de — ; rallying-place.
rallier, v.a., to rally. — le navire au vent (nav.) ; to haul the wind again ; to bring the ship to the wind

serallier, *v.r.*, to rally.

rallonge. *n.f.*, piece that serves to lengthen. — *d'une table ;* leaf of a table.

rallongement (ra-lonj-män), *n.m.*, lengthening.

rallonger, *v.a.*, to make longer, to lengthen.

rallumer, *v.a.*, to light again ; to rekindle, to kindle again, to light up anew.

serallumer, *v.r.*, to light again ; to burst, to break out again ; to rekindle.

ramadan, or **ramazan**, *n.m.*, (Mahometan religion) Ramadan.

ramadouer, *v.a.*, to soften by caresses or flattery.

ramage. *n.m.*, flowers (on stuffs—*sur les étoffes*) ; flowering ; singing. chirping, warbling (of birds—*des oiseaux*) ; prattle. prattling (of persons—*des personnes*) ; ramage.

ramager, *v.n.*, (l.u.) to warble (of birds—*des oiseaux*).

ramaigrir, *v.a.* and *n.*, to make lean again ; to grow lean again.

***ramaillage**. *nm.*, scraping off the hair (of skins—*des peaux*).

***ramailler**. *v.a.*, to scrape off the hair of skins before they are shamoyed.

ramaire, *adj.*, (bot.) belonging to the branches.

ramas. *n.m.*, collection, heap ; set, troop, lot. *Un — de bandits ;* (fam.) a set of robbers.

ramasse. *n.f.*, sledge (used on mountains —*employé dans les montagnes*).

ramassé. -e, *adj.*, thick-set ; squat ; (bot.) clustered. *Corps — ;* thick-set body. *Taille —e ;* squat figure.

ramasser. *n.m.*, (l.u.) picking up. *Cela ne vaut pas le —* (prov., fam.); that is not worth picking up.

ramasser, *v.a.*, to collect, to gather, to get together, to rake together; to assemble ; to pick up, to take up ; (pop.) to belabour ; to draw in a mountain-sledge. — *toutes ses forces ;* to muster all one's troops.

seramasser, *v.r.*, to assemble, to gather together ; to be assembled ; to roll itself up (animal) ; to pick one's self up, to get up again after a fall.

ramasseur, *n.m.*, collector; mountain sledge-driver.

ramassis, *n.m.*, confused collection, heap.

ramazan, *n.m.* V. **ramadan**.

rambour, *n.m.*, a kind of apple.

rame. *n.f.*, oar ; ream (of paper—*de papier*); (hort.) stick. prop (for peas—*pour les pois*); (manu.) tenter-frame. *Être à la — ;* to tug at the oar ; to work hard. *Mettre un livre à la — ;* to sell a book for waste-paper.

ramé. -e, *adj.*, branch-(of peas); bar, double-head (of shot—*boulets, balles*) ;(hunt.) of a young stag whose antlers are beginning to appear. *Balles —es ;* double shot. *Boulets —s ;* bar-shot.

rameau, *n.m.*, bough. branch (of a tree—*d'arbre*); branch. subdivision ; (anat.) branch. *Le dimanche, le jour, des —x :* Palm-Sunday.

ramée. *n.f.*, arbour made of entwined branches ; branches with their leaves.

ramendable, *adj.*, (tech.) that can be mended.

ramendage, *n.m.*, (tech.) mending with gold leaf.

ramender, *v.a.*, to lower the price of provisions. (pop.); (agri.) to manure again ; to mend gilding ; to dye again.

ramender. *v.n.*, (pop.) to fall in price (of provisions—*des denrées*).

ramener, *v.a.*, to bring again : to bring back; to throw again (dice—*aux dés*); to retrieve; to restore to health; to reclaim ; (man.) to lower its head ; to recall ; to pacify, to bring over. — *une vieille mode :* to bring an old fashion up again. — *quelqu'un à son devoir ;* to bring any one back to his duty. — *à la maison ;* to bring home.

seramener, *v.r.*, (man.) to carry its head. — *bien ;* to carry its head well.

☉**ramentevoir** (ra-mant-voar), *v.a.*, to call back to memory. — *une chose à quelqu'un ;* to remind any one of a thing.

☉**seramentevoir**, *v.r.*, to call to mind.

ramequin (ram-kin), *n.m.*, (cook.) ramekin, cheese-cake.

ramer, *v.n.*, to row, to pull; to tug at the oar ; to work hard.

ramer, *v.a.*, to stick peas ; to prop plants.

ramereau (ra-mrô), *n.m.*, young ringdove.

ramette, *n.f.*, (print.) job-case.

rameur, *n.m.*, rower, oarsman.

rameux. -se, *adj.*, branching, branchy, ramous. *Tige —se ;* branchy stalk.

ramier, *n.m.*, ringdove.

ramification, *n.f.*, ramification.

seramifier, *v.r.*, to ramify, to separate in branches, to branch out.

***ramilles**, *n.f.pl.*, twigs.

ramingue (ra-min-ghi), *adj.*, (man.) restive.

ramoitir, *v.a.*, to moisten, to make damp.

seramoitir, *v.r.*, to become damp.

ramollir, *v.a*, to soften, to make soft; to enervate. — *les cuirs*, to soak the hides. *La volupté ramollit les cœurs ;* voluptuousness enervates the heart.

seramollir, *v.r.*, to soften, to grow soft; to relent

ramollissant, -e, *adj.*, (med.) softening, emollient.

ramollissant, *n.m.*, (med.) emollient.

ramollissement (-lis-mân), *n.m.*, softening.

ramon. *n.m.*, garden-broom (made of branches of trees—*fait de branches*).

ramonage, *n.m.*, sweeping of a chimney.

ramoner, *v.a.*, to sweep a chimney.

ramoneur, *n.m.*, chimney-sweeper.

rampant, -e. *adj.*, creeping, crawling; cringing, crouching, servile; (her.) rampant. *Lierre —*, creeping-ivy. *Âme —e ;* cringing creature. *Style — ;* mean style.

rampant, *n.m.*, (arch.) coping.

rampe *n.f.*, flight of stairs; stairs; hand-rail, baluster; (thea.) foot-lamps, foot-lights; (engineering—*terme d'ingénieur*) inclined plane.

rampement (rânp-mân), *n.m.*, creeping, crawling (reptiles).

ramper, *v.n.*, to creep, to crawl; to crouch, to cringe. *Son style rampe ;* his style is low, flat.

rampin. *adj.m.*. (of a horse—*du cheval*) going on the tip of the hoofs of its hind feet. *V.* **pinçard**.

ramure. *n.f.*, antlers (of a stag—*du cerf*); the whole of the branches of a tree.

rancart. *n.m.*, (fam.) refuse, waste. *Mettre au — ;* to throw aside.

rance, *adj.*, rancid.

rance *n.m.*, rancidness. *Sentir le — ;* to smell rancid.

rancette. *n.f.*, sheet-iron (for stove pipes—*pour tuyaux de poêle*).

ranche. *n.f.*, round of a rack-ladder; rack (of a crane—*de grue*).

rancher. *n.m.*, rack-ladder; roost-ladder.

rancidité, or **rancissure**, *n.f.*, rancidness, rancidity.

rancio, *adj.*, (of Spanish wine—*des vins d'Espagne*) grown yellow.

rancir, *v.n.*, to grow rancid.

rancissure. *n.f. V.* **rancidité**.

rançon, *n.f.*, ransom. *Mettre à — ;* to set a ransom upon.

ranconnement (-so-n-măn), *n.m.*, ransoming, exaction, extortion.

ranconner, *v a.*, to ransom; to set a ransom on; to levy contributions; to impose upon.

rançonneu-r, *n.m.*, **-se**, *n.f.*, (fam , l.u.) extortioner.

rancune, *n.f.*, rancour, spite, grudge, ill-will, malice. *Vieille* —; old grudge. *Il lui garde* —; he owes him a grudge. *Sans* —; without malice.

rancuni-er, **-ère**, *adj.*, rancorous, spiteful.

randonnée, *n.f.*, (hunt.) round, circuit (of game—*au gibier*); ⊙ (fig.) long walk.

rang (ran), *n.m.*, row, range; rank (degree, station—*degré, position*); order; class; rate (of ships—*des vaisseaux*); (print.) frame; (nav.) tier (of cables—*aux cordages*); tier (of boxes in theatres—*de loges au théâtre*). *Dernier* —; lowest rank. *Au même* —; in the same row. *À son* —; in one's turn. *De premier* —; first rate. *Occuper un* — *élevé;* to rank high. *Tenir un* —; to hold a rank, to make a figure. *Se mettre sur les —s;* to enter the lists, to come forward (as a candidate—*comme candidat*); to put up for; to stand for. *Être sur les —s;* to be a candidate. *Il aspire au premier* —; he aspires to the first place. *Mettre au* —; to reckon amongst. *En* — *d'oignon;* in a row. *V.* **oignon.**

rangé, **-e**, *part.*, steady; pitched (of battles —*bataille*). *Bataille* —*e;* pitched battle. *En bataille* —*e;* in a pitched battle. *Un homme* —; a steady man.

rangée, *n.f.*, row, range, file.

rangement, *n.m.*, arranging, putting in order.

ranger, *v.a.*, to range, to put in ranks, to arrange; to put, to set, in order; to set to rights; to subdue, to subject; to rank; to reckon; to keep back; to put out of the way; (nav.) to sail close to; (milit.) to draw up (soldiers—*des soldats*). — *des gens deux à deux;* to place people two and two. — *des livres;* to set books in order. — *une armée en bataille;* to draw up an army in battle array. *Les gardes firent* — *le peuple;* the guards kept the people back. *Rangez cette table;* put that table back, out of the way. — *la terre, la côte;* (nav.) to hug the shore. — *le vent;* (nav.) to haul close to the wind.

se **ranger**, *v.r.*, to make room, to draw back, to step aside, to clear the way, to get out of the way; to reform, to take to regular habits; to draw up (of carriages, of troops—*des voitures, des troupes*); to fall in (of soldiers—*des soldats*). *Il se rangea dans un coin;* he drew aside into a corner. *Ranger-vous donc!* make room, will you! *Les troupes se rangèrent en bataille;* the troops drew up in order of battle. — *à l'avis de quelqu'un;* to embrace the opinion of any one. *Le vent se range à l'arrière* (nav.); the wind veers aft.

ranimer, *v.a.*, to restore, to revive, to animate; to reanimate; to stir up; to enliven. — *les couleurs d'un tableau;* to revive the colours of a picture. *Le printemps ranime toute la nature;* the spring revives all nature.

se **ranimer**, *v.r.*, to revive, to recover, to be restored to health; to brighten up, to be enlivened; to cheer up. *La nature se ranime;* nature revives.

ranule, *or* **grenouillette**, *n.f.*, (med) ranula.

ranz, *n.m.*, ranz. — *des vaches;* ranz des vaches, celebrated Swiss air.

rapace, *adj.*, ravenous, rapacious; (metal.) wasting.

rapace, *n.m.*, rapacious person; rapacious bird. —*s* (orni.); birds of prey.

rapacité, *n.f.*, rapacity, ravenousness; rapaciousness.

râpage, *n.m.*, rasping.

rapaiser, *v.a.*, to pacify, to appease again.

rapatelle, *n.f.*, horse-hair-cloth (for sieves —*pour tamis*).

rapatriage, *n.m.*, reconciliation, reconcilement.

rapatriement (-trî-măn), *n.m.*, the sending back of shipwrecked sailors, or other aliens to their country by consuls; return of troops from distant countries; (l.u.) reconciliation, reconcilement.

rapatrier, *v.a.*, to send back foreigners to their own land; to reconcile, to set to rights, to make friends again. *On les a rapatriés;* they have been reconciled.

se **rapatrier**, *v.r.*, to be reconciled; to be friends again.

râpe, *n.f.*, grater; rasp; stalk, stem of grapes. *V.* **rafle**; *pl.* (vet.) malanders.

râpé, *n.m.*, fresh grapes put into a vessel of spoiled wine to improve it; rappee. — *de copeaux;* chips to refine wine.

râpé, **-e**, *part.*, (of clothes—*des vêtements*) shabby. *Du tabac* —; rappee. *Un habit* —; a threadbare coat.

râper, *v.a.*, to grate, to rasp.

rapetasser (rap-ta-sé), *v.a.*, to patch, to patch up, to piece, to botch.

rapetasseu-r, *n.m.*, **-se**, *n.f.*, botcher, piecer.

rapetisser (rap-ti-sé), *v.a.*, to belittle, to shorten, to make less, shorter, smaller.

se **rapetisser**, *v.r.*, to become little, to lessen, to shrink; to be humble, to lower one's self.

rapetisser, *v.n.*, to become little, to lessen to grow short.

râpette, *n.f.*, (bot.) goose-grass.

rapide, *adj.*, rapid, swift, quick, fleet. *À l'aile* —; swift-winged.

rapide, *n.m.*, rapid.

rapidement (-pid-măn), *adv.*, rapidly, swiftly, fleetly, lightly, fast.

rapidité, *n.f.*, rapidity, swiftness, fleetness.

rapiéçage, *n.m.*, patching (of clothes—*de vêtements*).

rapiècement (-plès-man), *n.m.*, piecing, patching, botching.

rapiécer, *v.a.*, to piece, to botch, to patch.

rapiécetage (-piés-taj), *n.m.*, piecing, patching; anything patched; patchwork.

rapiéceter (-piés-té), *v.a.*, to patch, to piece, to botch; to piece all over. — *des meubles;* to botch up furniture.

rapière, *n.f.*, (jest.) rapier.

rapin, *n.m.*, (fam.) painter's young apprentice; (b.s.) dauber.

rapine, *n.f.*, rapine, plunder, pillage, robbery, plundering, pillaging, spoil.

rapiner, *v.n.* and *a.*, to pillage, to rob, to pilfer.

rapineu-r, *n.m.*, **-se**, *n.f.*, plunderer, pilferer, pillager.

*** rappareiller**, *v.a.*, to get the fellow of, to match.

rapparier, *v.a.*, to find one to complete a pair, to match.

rappel, *n.m.*, recall, recalling, revocation; (milit.) drums beating to arms; unpaid part (of a salary—*d'appointements*). — *à l'ordre;* call to order. — *de lumière* (paint); distribution of light. *Battre le* — (milit.); to beat to arms.

rappeler (ra-plé), *v.a.*, to call again, to call back; to recall, to call home; to recall to mind. *Je m'en allais, et il m'a rappelé;* I was going, and he called me back. — *quelqu'un à la vie;* to restore any one to life. — *un homme à son devoir;* to recall a man to his duty. — *quelqu'un à l'ordre;* to call any one to order. — *ses*

15

esprits; to recover one's self. — *le temps passé;* to recall the past to mind. *Rappelez-moi à son souvenir;* remember me to him. — *sa mémoire;* to endeavour to call to mind, to trace back in one's memory. — *la lumière* (paint.); to distribute the light.

se **rappeler,** *v.r.,* to recollect, to remember, to recall to mind. — *quelque chose;* to remember anything. *Vous rappelez-vous ce fait?* do you remember that fact? *Je me le rappelle parfaitement;* I recollect it very well. *Je me rappelle que vous me l'avez dit;* I recollect you told it me. *Je me rappelle d'avoir fait cela;* I recollect having done that.

rappeler, *v.n.,* (milit.) to beat to arms.

rapport, *n.m.,* bearing; revenue, produce; report, account, information, relation, testimony; tale, story; return; statement; affinity, analogy, resemblance, similitude; harmony, correspondence, uniformity; connection, reference; communication, intercourse, concern; tendency, reference; ratio, proportion; reimbursement, refunding; rising (in the stomach —*de l'estomac*). *Étre en* — ; to be productive, to be in bearing (of land, &c.—*de terres, &c.*). *Étre en plein* — ; to be in full bearing; to be very productive. *Belle montre et peu de* — ; a fine show and a small crop. *Faire un* — ; to draw up a report, to make a return. *Aimer à faire des* —*s;* to love to tell tales. *Il en a fait son* — ; he has given in his report. *Le style n'est pas en* — *avec le sujet;* the style is not in harmony with the subject. *Avoir* — *à;* to relate to, to refer to; to have relation with. *Il n'y a aucun* — *entre ces choses;* there is no connection between these things. *Mettre une personne en* — *avec une autre;* to bring a person in contact with another. *Par* — *à;* with reference to. *Il a fait cela par* — *à vous;* he did that on account of you. *Sous le* — *de;* with respect to. *Terres de* — ; artificial soil. *Pièces de* — ; patch-work, inlaid work.

rapportable, *adj.,* (jur.) that must be refunded.

rapporté, -e, *part.,* brought back. *Ouvrage de pièces* —*es;* inlaid work. *Terres* —*es;* artificial soil.

rapporter, *v.a.,* to bring again, to bring back, to carry back; to bring away, to bring home; to bring home again; to carry home; to account for; to revoke, to recall; to report, to tell, to relate; to give an account of; to cite, to quote; to direct, to refer to; to ascribe, to attribute; to yield, to bear; to bring in; to reimburse; (book-keeping—*comptabilité*) to carry; to trace; to set down. *Il n'en a rapporté que des coups;* he only got blows by it. *Il a fallu* — *une bordure à cette tapisserie;* it has been necessary to put a border to these chamber-hangings. — *un fait comme il s'est passé;* to relate a fact as it happened. *Il rapporte tout;* he tells everything. — *tout à soi;* to aim at nothing but one's private interest. — *l'effet à sa cause;* to refer the effect to its cause. *Une terre qui rapporte beaucoup;* an estate that yields a good revenue. *Des arbres qui rapportent beaucoup;* trees that bear a great deal of fruit. *Son argent lui rapporte six pour cent;* his money brings him in six per cent. *Cette mauvaise action ne lui rapportera rien;* this bad action will avail him nothing. — *du journal au grand livre;* to post from the journal to the ledger.

se **rapporter,** *v.r.,* to agree, to correspond, to tally, to coincide; to relate, to refer, to have a reference to, to allude to, to be allied, related to. *Ces deux couleurs se rapportent bien;* these two colours agree well together. *S'en rapporter à;* to refer one's self to. *Je m'en rapporte à votre témoignage;* I trust to your evidence. *S'il faut s'en rapporter aux anciennes traditions;* if we are

to believe ancient traditions. *Je m'en rapporte à qui que ce soit;* I will refer the thing to any body. *Je m'en rapporte à votre serment;* I put it to your oath.

rapporter, *v.n.,* to fetch and bring (of the dog—*du chien*); to bring in, to produce; to tell tales; to pay well, to be profitable.

rapporteur, *n.m.,* reporter; (geom.) protractor. — *d'un comité;* committee reporter.

rapporteu-r, *n.m.,* **-se,** *n.f.,* tell-tale, tale-bearer.

rapprendre, *v.a.,* to learn again, to learn anew.

rapprivoiser, *v.a.,* to tame again.

rapprochement (-prosh-mān), *n.m.,* drawing, placing near, bringing together; junction; reconcilement, reconciliation; putting together, comparing; comparison.

rapprocher, *v.a.,* to draw near again, to approach again; to bring together; to set in opposition, to compare; to bring nearer. — *deux personnes;* to bring two persons together, to reconcile two persons. *Rapprochez ces deux planches;* put these two planks closer. — *un cerf;* to put hounds on the track of a stag.

se **rapprocher,** *v.r.,* to come near again; to come, to draw, nearer; to approach, to begin to be friends again, to become reconciled.

rapsode, *n.m.,* (Grec. antiq.) rhapsodist.

rapsodie, *n.f.,* rhapsody; rambling composition.

rapsodiste, *n.m.,* rhapsodist.

rapt, *n.m.,* abduction, rape.

râpure, *n.f.,* raspings.

raquetier, *n.m.,* racket-maker; battledore-maker.

raquette, *n.f.,* racket, battledore; snow-shoe; (bot.) Indian fig, opuntia.

rare, *adj.,* rare, uncommon, extraordinary; unusual; scarce; thin, scanty; (med.) slow (of the pulse—*du pouls*). *Devenir* — *comme les beaux jours;* to become quite a stranger. *Se rendre* — ; to make one's self scarce.

raréfacti-f, -ve, *adj.,* rarefying.

raréfaction, *n.f.,* (phys) rarefaction.

raréfiable, *adj.,* (phys.) that can be rarefied.

raréfiant, -e, *adj.,* rarefying.

raréfier, *v.a.,* to rarefy.

rarement (rar-mān), *adv.,* rarely, seldom, unfrequently, not often.

rarescible, *adj.,* that may be rarefied, rarefiable.

rareté (rar-té), *n.f.,* rarity, rareness, scarcity.

rarissime, *adj.,* very rare.

ras, -e, *adj.,* close-shaved, short-haired; shorn, shaved, close, bare; smooth, open, flat; short-naped. *Un chien à poil* — ; a short-haired dog. *Il a la tête* —*e;* his head is shorn. *Il a le menton* — ; he has a bare, smooth, chin. *Il porte la barbe* —*e;* he shaves close. *Du velours* — ; shorn velvet. *Étoffe* —*e;* smooth stuff. *Serge* —*e;* napless serge. —*e campagne;* open country. *Vaisseau* —, or *vaisseau* — *à l'eau;* strait-sheered ship. *Faire table* —*e;* to throw aside old notions.

ras, *n.m.,* short-nap cloth. — *de carène* (nav.); shipwright's floating stage. *Au* — *de, à* — ; nearly level with. — *de marée* (nav.); *V.* **raz.**

rasade, *n.f.,* bumper, brimmer. *Boire* — ; to drink off a bumper.

rasant, -e, *adj.,* (fort.) rasant; (milit.) flank. *Vue* —*e;* view of a flat, open country.

rasement (râz-mān), *n.m.,* (milit.) razing to the ground.

raser, *v.a.,* to shave; to shave off, to demolish, to pull down; to graze, to touch; to skim over; to lay flat. *Se faire* — ; to get one's self shaved. — *une maison;* to pull down a

house. — *un vaisseau;* to cut down a ship.
Une balle lui rasa le visage; a ball grazed his
face. — *la côte* (nav.); to hug the coast.

se **raser,** *v.r.,* to shave, to shave one's self, to
be shaved. *Cette perdrix se rase;* this partridge
keeps close to the ground.

raser, *v.n.,* to shave; to pass very close to;
(vet.) to raze. *Ce cheval rase;* this horse razes.

rasibus (-bus), *prep.,* (pop.) quite close.
Couper —; to cut off quite close.

rasoir, *n.m.,* razor. *Pierre à —;* hone.
Cuir à —; razor-strop. *Repasser un —;* to set a
razor.

rason. *n.m.,* (ich.) razor-fish.

○**raspation,** *n.f.,* (chem.) rasping.

○**raspatoire,** *n.m.,* (surg.) raspatory.

rassade, *n.f.,* glass-bead, bugle.

rassasiant, -e, *adj.,* satiating, filling, cloying.

rassasiement (-zi-mān), *n.m.,* satiety; being
satiated. *Le — des plaisirs;* the surfeit of
pleasures.

rassasier, *v.a.,* to sate, to satiate; to satisfy,
to fill; to cloy, to glut. *Être rassasié d'une chose;*
to be tired of a thing. *Il n'est jamais rassasié
d'argent;* he can never have enough money.

se **rassasier,** *v.r.,* to be satiated; to sate
one's self; to be cloyed. *Il faut craindre de —
des plaisirs;* we must beware of sating ourselves
with pleasure.

rassemblement, *n.m.,* assembling; muster,
mustering, collecting; riotous meeting, mob;
assemblage. *Disperser un —;* to disperse a mob.

rassembler, *v.a.,* to collect, to assemble, to
reassemble, to gather together, to bring
together again; to put together again; to get
together. — *des troupes;* to muster troops. —
des faits pour composer une histoire; to collect
facts, in order to compose a history. — *des
matériaux pour un ouvrage;* to collect materials
for a work.

se **rassembler,** *v.r.,* to assemble, to gather together, to congregate, to meet, to muster. —
en foule; to flock, to crowd.

rasseoir (ra-soâr), *v.a.,* to seat again, to
reseat; to replace, to put in its place again; to
settle, to calm. — *une statue sur sa base;* to
replace a statue on its base. — *une pierre;* to
replace a stone. *Donnez-lui le temps de — ses
esprits;* give him time to recover himself.

se **rasseoir,** *v.r.,* to sit down again, to be
seated again; to settle (of liquids—*des liquides*);
to be composed.

rasseoir. *v.n.,* to settle (of liquids—*des
liquides*). *Laissez — ce café;* let that coffee
settle.

rasséréner, *v.a.,* to make serene, to clear
up; to restore serenity to. *Le soleil parut et
rasséréna le temps;* the sun shone out and
cleared up the weather.

se **rasséréner,** *v.r.,* to clear up, to grow serene.

rassiéger, *v.a.,* to besiege again; to beset
again.

rassis, -e, *part.,* set down again; settled.

rassis, *adj.,* cool, staid, sedate. *Du pain —;*
stale bread. *De sang —;* in cool blood. *De
sens —;* with sound judgment. *Esprit —;*
sedate mind.

rassis, *n.m.,* old horse-shoe put on again
with new nails.

rassortiment, *n.m.,* matching (of colours,
materials, &c.—*des couleurs, des étoffes, &c.*);
sorting; taking in a stock of goods for a
season, &c.

rassortir, *v.a.,* to match again.

○**rassoté, -e,** *part.,* (fam.) bewitched, infatuated.

○**rassoter,** *v.a.,* (fam.) to bewitch. *On l'a
rassoté de cette fille;* they have bewitched him
with that girl.

rassurant, -e, *adj.,* tranquillizing; encouraging, comforting.

rassurer, *v.a.,* to strengthen; to remove
one's fears; to consolidate; to make firm; to
tranquillize, to reassure. — *un homme dans la
foi;* to strengthen a man in the faith.

se **rassurer,** *v.r.,* to tranquillize one's self; to
recover one's self, to be reassured; (of the
weather—*du temps*) to settle, to clear up.
Rassurez-vous; be tranquillized; keep up your
courage.

rat, *n.m.,* rat; whim, maggot. — *d'eau;*
water-rat. — *de Pharaon;* ichneumon. *Mort
aux —s;* rat's-bane. *Un nid à —s;* a sorry
lodging. *Gueux comme un — d'église;* as poor
as a church mouse. *A bon chat bon —;* set a
thief to catch a thief. — *de cave;* small wax
taper; exciseman. *Avoir des —s;* to be whimsical.

ratafia, *n.m.,* ratafia.

ratang, *n.m.,* ratan.

ratanhia, *n.m.,* (bot., med.) rhatany.

ratatiné, -e, *adj.,* shrivelled, shrivelled up;
shrunk. *Un petit vieillard —;* a little withered
old man.

se **ratatiner,** *v.r.,* to shrink, to shrivel, to
shrivel up.

***ratatouille,** *n.f.,* (cook.) bad stew, cag-
mag.

rate, *n.f.,* spleen, milt. *Avoir des vapeurs
de —;* to be troubled with the spleen. *Épanouir
la —;* to drive away the spleen, to make merry,
S'épanouir la —; to drive away one's spleen, to
be merry.

râteau, *n.m.,* (agri.) rake; (horol., nav.)
rack.

râtelage (râ-tlaj), *n.m.,* (agri.) act of
raking.

râtelée (râ-tlée), *n.f.,* raking; rakeful.

râteler (râ-tlé), *v.a.,* to rake.

râteleur (râ-tleur), *n.m.,* raker.

râtelier, *n.m.,* rack (in stables—*d'écurie*);
set of teeth; (milit.) arm-rack; (nav.) rack.
Manger à plus d'un —; to have more than one
string to one's bow. *Mettre les armes au —;* to
quit the service.

ratelle, *n.f.,* disease of pigs.

rater, *v.n.,* to miss fire; to flash in the pan.
Son fusil rata; his gun missed fire.

rater, *v.a.,* to miss; not to obtain; to fail.
— *une charge;* to miss a place.

○**rati-er, -ère** (-tié, -tièr), *adj.,* whimsical.

ratière (-tièr), *n.f.,* rat-trap.

ratification, *n.f.,* ratification.

ratifier, *v.a.,* to ratify.

***ratillon,** *n.m.,* little rat.

ratine, *n.f.,* ratteen.

ratiné, -e, *adj.,* friezed.

ratiner, *v.a.,* (manu.) to frieze.

ratiocination, *n.f.,* ratiocination, reasoning.

ratiociner, *v.a.,* to ratiocinate, to reason.

ration, *n.f.,* ration, allowance. *Mettre à la
—;* to allowance. — *diminuée;* short allowance.

rational. *n.m.,* breastplate (of the High
Priest of the Jews).

rationalisme, *n.m.,* rationalism.

rationaliste, *n.m.,* rationalist.

rationalité, *n.f.,* rationality.

rationnel, -le, *adj.,* rational. *Horizon —;*
rational horizon. *Quantité —le;* rational quantity.

rationnellement (-nèl-mān), *adv.,* rationally.

rationnement, *n.m.,* short allowance of
provisions to soldiers, &c.

rationner, *v.a.*, to allowance, to put on short allowance.

ratissage, *n.m.*, scraping, raking.

ratisser, *v.a.*, to rake; to scrape, to scrape off.

ratissoire, *n.f.*, scraper.

ratissure, *n.f.*, scrapings.

raton, *n.m.*, (mam.) raccoon.

rattacher, *v.a.*, to tie again, to tie up again; to fasten again, to fasten up again; to connect, to attach. — *par une chaîne;* to chain up again. — *une question à une autre;* to connect one question with another.

se **rattacher**, *v.r.*, to be tied; to fasten, to be fastened; to fasten upon: to be attached to, to be connected or allied with. *Cette question se rattache à de grands intérêts;* that question is connected with great interests.

ratteindre, *v.a.*, to retake, to catch again, to take again; to overtake, to come up with.

rattendrir, *v.a.*, to soften again, to make tender again.

rattiser, *v.a.*, to stir up the fire again; to stir up again.

rattraper, *v.a.*, to retake, to catch again, to overtake, to come up with, to recover. *On a ratrapé le prisonnier;* the prisoner has been retaken. *On ne m'y rattrapera pas;* I shall not be caught so again.

rature, *n.f.*, erasure, scratch; word crossed out.

raturer, *v.a.*, to efface; to blot out; to erase; to scrape (skins—*les peaux*).

raucité, *n.f.*, raucity, hoarseness.

rauque, *adj.*, hoarse.

ravage, *n.m.*, ravage, havoc. *Faire des —s;* to make ravages.

ravager, *v.a.*, to ravage, to lay waste, to spoil.

ravageur, *n.m.*, ravager, spoiler.

ravale, *n.f.*, roller (to smooth the ground).

ravalement (-val-mān), *n.m.*, (l.u.) debasement, disparagement; (mas.) rough-casting. *Piano à —;* piano-forte with a double row of keys.

ravaler, *v.a.*, to swallow again; to put down, to lower; to debase, to disparage; (mas.) to rough-cast. — *la gloire de;* to run down the glory of.

se **ravaler**, *v.r.*, to debase one's self; to lower one's self.

ravaudage, *n.m.*, mending (of old clothes —*de vieux habits*); botching, bungling; darning stockings.

ravauder, *v.a.*, to mend (old clothes—*les vieux habits*); to botch, to botch up; to revile; to plague, to teaze, to bustle about (in-doors— *dans une maison*); to darn stockings.

ravauderie (-vô-drî), *n.f.*, silly stuff, nonsense.

ravaudeu-r, *n.m.*, **-se**, *n.f.*, mender (of stockings, old clothes—*de bas, de vieux habits*); botcher, patcher; silly talker.

rave, *n.f.*, long radish, radish.

ravelin (ra-vlin), *n.m.*, (fort.) ravelin.

ravenelle (ra-vnèl), *n.f.*, wall-flower.

ravi, -e, *part.*, carried away, transported; raptured; ravished. *Être — de joie;* to be overjoyed. *J'en suis —;* I am overjoyed at it. — *d'admiration;* carried away by one's admiration. *Je suis — que vous la connaissiez;* I am delighted that you know her.

ravière, *n.f.*, radish-bed.

ravigote, *n.f.*, (cook.) kind of sauce.

ravigoter, *v.a.*, (pop.) to revive.

se **ravigoter**, *v.r.*, to revive, to recover one's strength.

ravilir, *v.a.*, to debase, to disgrace, to degrade, to lower.

ravin, *n.m.*, ravine.

ravine, *n.f.*, mountain torrent; ravine.

ravinement, *n.m.*, hollowing of land by rain water into a narrow channel.

raviner, *v.a.*, to hollow land into narrow channels (of rain water—*occasionnés par la pluie*).

ravir, *v.a.*, to carry off; to take away; to ravish; to charm, to delight, to enrapture. — *une femme;* to ravish a woman. — *le bien d'autrui;* to steal the property of another. — *l'honneur à une fille;* to dishonour a girl. *On lui a ravi son plus doux espoir;* he has been robbed of his dearest hope. *À —;* wonderfully well, to admiration, admirably. *Elle chante à —;* she sings admirably.

ravisement, *n.m.*, thinking better of, altering one's mind.

se **raviser**, *v.r.*, to alter one's mind, to bethink one's self; to think better of it.

ravissant, -e, *adj.*, rapacious, ravenous; admirable, ravishing, delightful, lovely, enchanting. *Une beauté —e;* a ravishing beauty. *Cette femme est —e;* she is a most charming woman.

ravissement (-vis-mān), *n.m.*, rape (of Helen, of Proserpine, &c.—*d'Hélène, de Proserpine,&c.*); transport, rapturous transport, ravishment. *Il était dans le —;* he was in raptures. — *de joie;* transport of joy.

ravisseur, *n.m.*, ravisher.

***ravitaillement**, *n.m.*, revictualling.

***ravitailler**, *v.a.*, to revictual.

raviver, *v.a.*, to make a fire burn up; to revive; to reanimate; to brighten up, to cheer. — *un tableau;* to revive a picture.

se **raviver**, *v.r.*, to revive.

ravoir, *v.a.*, to get again, to have again; to get back.

se **ravoir**, *v.r.*, to recover one's strength, to get about again; to pick up, to pick up one's crumbs.

rayé, -e *part.*, striped, streaked; (artil.) rifled; scratched, scratched out, crossed out. *Vaisselle —e;* scratched plate. *Des mots —s;* words crossed out. *Canon —;* rifled cannon.

rayer, *v.a.*, to scratch, to scratch out; to cross *or* strike out, to erase, to expunge; to streak, to stripe; (artil.) to rifle. — *une étoffe;* to stripe a stuff. *Rayez cela de vos papiers;* strike that out of your books. — *le canon d'un fusil;* to rifle a gun-barrel.

rayère, *n.f.*, loop-hole (in towers—*dans les tours*).

ray-grass, *n.m.* (*n.p.*), (agri.) rye-grass.

rayon, *n.m.*, ray, beam; (geom.) radius; spoke (of a wheel—*de roue*); (ich.) ray; (agri.) furrow; shelf; comb (of honey—*de miel*). — *de lumière;* ray of light. *Faisceau de —s* (opt.); pencil of rays. *Un — d'espérance;* a ray of hope. *À dix lieues de —, dans un — de dix lieues;* within a radius of ten leagues. *Une étoile à cinq —s;* a star with five rays. — *de miel;* honeycomb.

rayonnant, -e, *adj.*, radiant, shining, sparkling, beaming. — *de lumière;* beaming with light.

rayonné, -e, *adj.*, radiated, stellated.

rayonnée, -e, *adj.*, (zool.) radiary. — *s;* radiata.

rayonnement (rè-io-n-mān), *n.m.*, radiance; radiancy; (phys.) radiation. *Le — des astres;* the radiation of the stars.

rayonner, *v.n.*, to radiate, to irradiate; to shine; to beam. *Son visage rayonne de joie;* his face is radiant with joy.

rayure, *n.f.*, stripe (of textile fabrics—*des étoffes*); rifling (fire-arms—*des armes à feu*).

raz, *n.m.*, (nav.) race, bore. — *de marée;* eagre.

razzia, *n.f.* (—s), (milit.) raid.

ré, *n.m.*, (mus.) D ; (vocal mus.) re, ray.

re, **ré**, prefix from Latin *re. red.*

réact-eur, -rice, *n.* and *adj.*, (pol., l.u.) reactionist ; reactionary.

réacti-f, -ve, *adj.*, reactive.

réactif, *n.m.*, (chem.) reagent.

réaction, *n.f.*, reaction.

réactionnaire, *n.m.f.* and *adj.*, reactionist ; reactionary.

réadmettre, *v.a.*, to readmit, to admit again.

réadmission, *n.f.*, readmission, readmittance.

réadopter, *v.a.*, to readopt.

réadoption, *n.f.*, act of adopting again.

réaggrave, *n.f.*, (canon law—*loi canon*) reaggravation.

réaggraver, *v.a.*, (canon law—*loi canon*) to censure by a reaggravation.

réagir, *v.n.*, to react.

réajournement, *n.m.*, readjournment.

réajourner, *v.a.*, to readjourn.

réal, *n.m.* (*réaux*), or **réale**, *n.f.* (*réales*), real (Spanish coin—*monnaie espagnole*).

réal, -e, *adj.*, royal, of the royal galley.

réale, *n.f.*, royal galley.

réalgar, *n.m.*, (min.) realgar.

réalisable, *adj.*, that can be made real ; of money that can be converted into land ; of ventures that can be converted into money.

réalisation, *n.f.*, realization ; (fin.) conversion into money.

réaliser, *v.a.*, to realize ; to convert into money.

se **réaliser**, *v.r.*, to be realized.

réalisme, *n.m.*, realism.

réaliste, *n.m.*, realist.

réalité, *n.f.*, reality ; (theol.) real presence.

réapparition, *n.f.*, reappearance.

réappel, *n.m.*, second call, second calling over.

réappeler, *v.a.*, to call over a second time.

réapposer, *v.a.*, to reaffix, to put on again, to set on again ; to reappend.

réapposition, *n.f.*, reaffixing, reappending ; putting on again.

réarmement, *n.m.*, arming again, re-arming.

réarmer, *v.a.*, to arm again.

réarpentage, *n.m.*, resurvey.

réarpenter, *v.a.*, to resurvey.

réassemblage, *n.m.*, reassemblage.

réassembler, *v.a.*, to reassemble, to gather together again.

réasservir, *v.a.*, to subjugate again.

*réassignation, *n.f.*, new summons.

*réassigné, -e, *part.*, summoned again.

*réassigner, *v.a.*, to reassign, to resummon, to summon again.

réassurance, *n.f.*, reinsurance, reassurance.

réassurer, *v.a.*, to reinsure, to reassure.

réatteler, *v.a.*, (of horses—*des chevaur*) to put to again.

Ⓞ *in* **reatu**, *adv.*, (jur.). *Être* —; to be impeached of a crime.

*rebâiller, *v.n.*, to yawn again.

rebaiser, *v.a.*, to kiss again.

rebaisser, *v.a.*, to lower again, to let down again.

rebander, *v.a.*, to bind again ; to bind up again ; to tie up again ; to put another bandage (over the eyes—*sur les yeux*).

rebaptisant (-ba-ti-), *n.m.*, rebaptizer.

rebaptisation (-ba-ti-), *n.f.*, baptizing again.

rebaptiser (-ba-ti-), *v.a.*, to rebaptize.

rébarbati-f, -ve, *adj.*, stern, crabbed, cross. *Visage* —; crabbed countenance.

rebâter, *v a.*, to put a pack-saddle on again.

rebâtir, *v.a.*, to rebuild, to build again.

rebattre, *v a.*, to beat again ; to repeat, to tell over and over ; to shuffle again (cards—*les cartes*).

rebattu, -e, *part.*, hackneyed, trite. *Un conte* —; an old worn-out story. *J'en ai les oreilles* —*es :* I am sick of hearing it so often.

rebaudir, *v.a.*, (hunt.) to caress (dogs—*les chiens*).

Ⓞ **rebec**, *n.m.*, rebeck.

rebelle, *n.m.f.* and *adj.*, rebel ; rebellious, disobedient ; (med.) obstinate ; (metal.) refractory. —*à la justice:* disobedient to justice. *Un sujet* — *à la poésie;* a refractory subject for verse. *Une fièvre* — *aux remèdes;* an obstinate fever. *C'est une beauté* — *:* she is an unfeeling beauty. *Substances* —*s* (metal.); refractory substances, substances hard to melt.

se **rebeller**, *v.r.*, to rebel, to rise in rebellion, to revolt.

rébellion, *n.f.*, rebellion. *Faire* — *à la justice :* to resist justice.

rebénir, *v.a.*, to bless again ; to consecrate anew.

se **rebéquer**, *v.r.*, to be saucy, to be impertinent.

rebercer, *v.a.*, to rock again.

se **rebercer**, *v.r.*, to rock one's self again.

se **rebiffer**, *v.r.*, to resist, to refuse obedience ; to refuse bluntly.

reblanchir, *v.a.*, to wash again ; to blanch again, to bleach again ; to whitewash again.

rèble, or **rièble**, *n.m.*, (bot.) goose-grass ; cleavers.

reboire, *v.a.*, to drink again.

reboisement, *n.m.*, planting with trees land once occupied by forests.

reboiser, *v.a.*, to plant with trees land once occupied by forests.

rebondi, -e, *adj.*, plump, round, chubby. *Des joues* —*es ;* chubby cheeks.

rebondir, *v.n.*, to rebound.

rebondissement (-dis-mân), *n.m.*, rebounding.

rebord, *n.m.*, border (of clothes—*de vêtements*); ledge; brim.

reborder, *v.a.*, to put a new border to ; to border again. — *une robe ;* to put a new border to a gown. *— des souliers ;* to bind shoes anew.

rebotter, *v.a.*, to make boots again for; to boot somebody again.

se **rebotter**, *v.r.*, to put on one's boots again.

rebouchement, *n.m.*, stopping up again.

reboucher, *v.a.*, to stop up again ; to block up again ; to stuff up ; to cork again. — *un trou ;* to stop up a hole again. — *une bouteille ;* to cork a bottle again.

se **reboucher**, *v.r.*, to get stuffed up again ; to bend. *L'épée se reboucha contre sa cuirasse;* the sword bent against his cuirass.

*rebouillir, *v.n.*, to boil again.

rebouisage, *n.m.*, cleaning and polishing of hats.

rebouiser, *v.a.*, to clean and polish hats.

rebourgeonner, *v.n.*, to bud again.

rebours, *n.m.*, wrong side (of a stuff—*d'une étoffe*); wrong way (of the grain—*contre-poil*); contrary, reverse. *À* —, *au* —; the wrong way; against the grain, backwards. *Marcher à* —; to walk backwards.

rebours, -e, *adj.*, (fam.) cross, cross-grained, crabbed.

rebouteu-r, *n.m.*, -se, *n.f.*, bone-setter.

reboutonner, *v.a.*, to button again.

se **reboutonner**, *v.r.*, to button one's clothes again.

Ⓞ **rebrasser**, *v.a.*, to turn up (one's sleeves, hat, &c.—*ses manches, son chapeau, &c.*).

rebrider, *v.a.*, to bridle again.

rebrocher, *v.a.*, to stitch books again.

rebroder. *v.a.*, to re-embroider.

*rebrouiller, *v.a.*, to embroil again, to mix again, to confound again, to entangle again.

rebroussement (-broos-măn), *n.m.*, turning back; being turned back; (geom.) retrogression.

à rebrousse-poil, *adv.*, against the hair; the wrong way; against the grain.

rebrousser, *v. a.*, to turn up (the hair—*les cheveux*). — *chemin;* to go back.

rebuffade, *n.f.*, rebuff, repulse.

rébus (-bus), *n.m.*, rebus; pun.

rebut, *n.m.*, repulse, rejection, refusal; refuse; trash; waste, rubbish, trumpery; riffraff. *Marchandises de —* : waste goods. *Papier de —;* waste paper. *Mettre au —;* to throw aside. *Être au —;* to be thrown aside. *Mettre une lettre au —;* to send a letter to the dead-letter office.

rebutant. -e. *adj.*, repulsive, forbidding, loathsome. *Travail —;* tedious work. *Air —;* forbidding look. *Homme —;* repulsive man.

rebuter. *v.a.*, to repulse, to rebuff, to thrust away; to reject, to refuse; to disgust, to shock. - *- des excuses;* to refuse an apology. *Il a rebuté ces marchandises;* he rejected those goods.

se rebuter, *v.r.*, to be discouraged or disheartened, to be rebuffed. *Il se rebute aisément;* he is easily disheartened.

recacher, *v.a.*, to hide again.

recacheter (-kash-té), *v.a.*, to seal again.

récalcitrant, -e, *adj.*, stubborn, refractory, perverse, reluctant.

récalcitrer, *v.n.*, to be restive, to kick (of the horse—*du cheval*); (l.u.) to be refractory; to resist.

récapitulati-f, -ve, *adj.*, recapitulatory.

récapitulation, *n.f.*, recapitulation, summing up.

récapituler, *v.a.*, to recapitulate, to sum up.

recarder. *v.a.*, to card again.

recarreler (-kar-lé), *v.a.*, to pave a floor anew.

recasser. *v.a.*, to break again; (agri.) to break up stubble-land, to give a first ploughing to.

recassis, *n.m.*, (agri) stubble-land that has been broken up.

recéder, *v.a.*, to restore again, to let have back again; to give up again.

recel, *n.m.*, (jur.) receiving of stolen goods.

recélé, *n.m.*, (jur.) concealment of goods belonging to a society, a succession, &c.

recélement (-sèl-măn), *n.m.*, concealing, concealment (of malefactors—*de malfaiteurs*); receiving (of stolen goods—*d'objets volés*).

recéler, *v.a.*, to conceal (malefactors—*des malfaiteurs*); to receive (stolen goods—*des objets volés*); to embezzle; to conceal, to contain. — *des effets;* to conceal things. *La terre recèle de grands trésors;* the earth conceals, contains, great treasures.

recéler, *v.n.*, (hunt.) to be concealed.

receleu-r, *n.m.*, **-se,** *n.f.* (ré-cě-), receiver of stolen goods.

récemment (-sa-măn), *adv.*, recently, newly, lately.

recensement (-săns-măn), *n.m* , census; statement; numbering, verification.

recenser, *v.a.*, to take the census; to verify again, to examine.

recension, *n.f.*, (philos.) comparison of an edition of an ancient book with manuscripts; book revised and edited by a critic.

récent, -e. *adj.*, recent, new, late. *Nouvelle —e;* recent news.

recepage, *n.m.*, (agri.) cutting down close to the ground.

recepée, *n.f.*, part cut down of a wood.

receper, *v.a.*, (agri.) to cut down close to the ground ; to cut down.

récépissé, *n.m.*, receipt (for documents, papers—*de titres, de pieces, &c.*); acknowledgment of receipt.

réceptacle, *n.m.*, receptacle; (bot.) torus.

réceptibilité, *n.f.*, (l.u.) receptibility.

réception, *n.f.*, receiving, receipt, reception; levee, drawing-room; entertainment. *Accuser — d'une lettre;* to acknowledge the receipt of a letter. *Bonne —;* welcome, good reception.

réceptivité, *n.f.*, (l.u.) receptivity.

recercler, *v.a.*, to hoop anew, to put new hoops to.

recette, *n.f.*, receipt (what is received—*ce qui est reçu*); recipe (prescription of ingredients for any composition—*de cuisine, de pharmacie, &c.*); receiver's office.

recevabilité, *n.f.*, (jur) admissibility.

recevable, *adj.*, receivable, fit to be received; admissible, allowed.

receveu-r, *n.m.*, **-se,** *n.f.*, receiver, collector (of taxes—*d'impôts*).

recevoir, *v.a.*, to receive, to accept, to take, to take in, to let in; to welcome; to admit; to allow of; to entertain. — *bien:* to receive well; to welcome. — *une opinion:* to admit an opinion. — *la foi;* to receive the faith. *Je reçois vos offres;* I accept your offers. *Son livre a été bien reçu;* his book has taken well. — *une excuse;* to accept an excuse. — *une proposition;* to accept a proposal.

recevoir, *v.n.*, to receive, to receive company; to hold a levee, a drawing-room. *On recevra:* there will be company; a drawing-room, a levee, will be held.

recez (-ré-sè), *n.m.*, recess (minute of the deliberations of the German diet—*acte contenant les délibérations de la diète d'Allemagne*).

réchampir. or **échampir.** *v.a.*, (house-painting, gilding—*peinture en bâtiment, dorure*) to set off.

rechange, *n.m* , change of anything; spare things; (com.) re-exchange; (nav.) spare stores. *Des habits de —;* spare clothes. *J'en ai de —;* I have some in reserve. *Mâts de hune de —;* spare top-masts.

rechanger, *v.a.*, to change again.

rechanter, *v.a.*, to sing again; to tell often.

réchapper, *v.n.*, to escape, to recover. (pop.) *Un réchappé de la potence:* a villain.

rechargement, *n.m.*, reloading, loading again.

recharger. *v.a.*, to load again; to recharge; (milit.) to make a second charge; to charge again, to enjoin over again. — *les ennemis;* to charge the enemy again.

rechasser, *v.a.* and *n.*, to drive away again: to drive back.

rechasser, *v.a.*, to hunt again.

réchaud. *n.m.*, chafing-dish.

réchauffage. *n.m.*, warming up; giving as new what is old; plagiarism; reheating; (metal.) balling.

réchauffé, *n.m.*, food, &c., warmed up; something that is stale, old.

réchauffé, -e. *adj.*, warmed again.

réchauffement, *n.m.*, (hort.) lining.

réchauffer, *v.a.*, to heat again, to make warm again, to make hot again, to warm again, to warm up; to reanimate, to rekindle. *Faire — la soupe;* to warm up the soup. — *une couche* (hort.); to manure a bed anew.

se réchauffer, *v.r.*, to warm one's self, to get one's self warm, to grow warm; to rekindle, to become warmer, to warm.

réchauffoir, *n.m.*, plate-warmer, dish-warmer.

rechausser, *v.a.*, to put on shoes or stockings again ; to set new cogs to a wheel ; (agri., hort.) to mould, to mould up ; (mas.) to line the foot of, to underpin. — *un arbre ;* to mould up a tree. — *un mur ;* to underpin a wall.

rêche, *adj.*, rough (to the taste, touch—*au goût, au toucher*) ; crabbed (of persons—*des personnes*).

recherche, *n.f.*, search, seeking, quest, pursuit ; research, inquiry, investigation ; examination, scrutiny ; studied elegance, neatness, laboured refinement, studied refinement ; addresses, courtship, suit ; (mas.) research, mending (with tiles or slates—*avec des tuiles ou des ardoises*). *Travailler à la — de la vérité ;* to labour in the search after truth. — *exacte ;* strict search. *Faire la — d'une chose ;* to search for a thing. *Style naturel et sans — ;* natural and unaffected style. *Il fait la — d'une veuve ;* he is courting a widow.

recherché, -e, *adj.*, choice, exquisite ; affected, far-fetched, sought after, run after, in great request, in great demand. *Parure —e ;* elegant dress. *Expression —e ;* far-fetched expression. *Ornements —s ;* choice ornaments.

rechercher, *v.a.*, to seek again, to look again for, to seek, to seek for, to seek after, to look for, to search, to search for, to search after ; to investigate, to search into, to inquire into ; to make an inquiry into ; to institute an inquiry into, to enter into an inquiry on ; to call to account ; to endeavour to obtain, to desire, to aspire to ; to run after, to court, to seek ; to solicit in marriage, to ask in marriage, to woo, to court, to solicit the hand of ; to finish, to finish off, to polish ; (man.) to animate. — *les secrets de la nature ;* to seek after the secrets of nature. *On rechercha sa vie ;* they made inquiries into his mode of life. — *un cheval ;* to animate a horse.

rechercheur, *n.m.*, researcher, inquisitor.

***rechigné, -e**, *adj.*, grim, grim-faced, glum, surly, sulky, cross, crabbed.

***rechignement**, *n.m.*, sulking, frowning, sullenness.

***rechigner**, *v.n.*, to look sulky, sullen, grim, sour, crabbed.

○**rechoir**, *v.n.*, to fall again ; to relapse, to have a relapse.

rechute, *n.f.*, fresh fall, new fall, relapse.

récidive, *n.f.*, recidivation, relapse ; second offence, repetition of an offence. *Il y a — ;* it is not the first offence. *Être en — ;* to be an old offender.

récidiver, *v.n.*, to fall again into the same fault ; to repeat the same offence ; to commit the same crime again.

récidiviste, *n.m.*, one who commits again a crime or an offence for which he has been previously convicted ; habitual criminal.

récif, rescif, or **ressif**, *n.m.*, (nav.) reef of rocks.

récipé, *n.m.*, recipe, medical prescription ; receipt.

récipiendaire, *n.m.*, new member.

récipient, *n.m.*, (chem.) recipient, receiver ; cistern, well.

réciprocation, *n.f.*, reciprocation.

réciprocité, *n.f.*, reciprocity, reciprocalness, reciprocation.

réciproque, *n.m.*, like. *Rendre le — ;* to return the like ; to give like for like.

réciproque, *n.f.*, (math., log.) converse.

réciproque, *adj.*, reciprocal, mutual ; (math.) converse, reciprocal.

réciproquement (-prok-mān), *adv.*, reciprocally, mutually ; (math.) conversely.

recirer, *v.a.*, to wax again.

récit, *n.m.*, recital, relation, account, narration, statement ; (mus.) recitative.

récitant, -e, *adj.*, (mus.) solo.

récitateur, *n.m.*, reciter, repeater.

récitatif, *n.m.*, (mus.) recitative.

récitation, *n.f.*, reciting, recitation ; repetition.

réciter, *v.a.*, to recite, to rehearse ; to repeat, to say ; to tell, to relate, to give an account of, to recount ; (mus.) to sing in recitative ; to play in recitative. *Récitez votre leçon ;* say your lesson.

réciter, *v.n.*, (mus.) to perform a recitative ; to recite (at schools—*à l'école*).

réclamant, *n.m.*, **-e**, *n.f.*, (jur.) claimant.

réclamation, *n.f.*, claim, demand ; complaint, protestation ; opposition, objection. *Être en — ;* to have made an objection, a complaint, a demand.

réclame, *n.m.*, (hawking—*fauconnerie*) cry, sign, to bring back a hawk to the lure or to the fist.

réclame, *n.f.*, (print.) catch-word ; primer ; (of newspapers—*journalisme*) editorial announcement ; (c.rel.) part of the short response recited in the versicle) ; (thea.) cue (last words of couplets—*derniers mots des couplets*).

réclamer, *v.a.*, to implore, to entreat, to beseech ; to reclaim, to claim back, to redemand, to demand back again ; to claim, to demand ; (hunt.) to call off ; (hawking—*fauconnerie*) to bring back ; (jur.) to lay claim to, to claim. — *son droit ;* to claim one's right. — *un oiseau ;* to bring back a hawk. — *les chiens ;* to call off the dogs.

se réclamer, *v.r.*, to be reclaimed, to be demanded ; to say one is known to a person ; to make use of the name of any one. *Voyant qu'on allait le maltraiter, il se réclama d'un tel ;* seeing that they were about to ill-treat him, he said he was known to so-and-so.

réclamer, *v.n.*, to oppose, to object, to protest, to complain, to make a complaint, to make objection. *Je réclame contre cela ;* I oppose that. *Personne ne réclame ?* does nobody make any objection ?

reclouer, *v.a.*, to nail again.

○**reclure**, *v.a.*, to shut up, to confine, to cloister up, to sequester.

reclus, -e, *n.* and *part.*, recluse, monk, nun ; cloistered up, shut up, sequestered.

reclusion, or **réclusion**, *n.f.*, reclusion, retirement, seclusion ; (jur.) confinement, imprisonment.

***recogner**, *v.a.*, to hit again, to strike again ; to beat back, to drive back.

récognitif (-cog-), *adj.m.*, (jur.) ratifying a liability. *Acte — ;* ratification of a liability, stating the consideration thereof.

récognition (-cog-), *n.f.*, recognition.

recoiffer, *v.a.*, to dress the head or hair again ; to re-adjust the head-dress ; to cap again, to re-cap (bottles—*des bouteilles*).

recoin, *n.m.*, corner, nook, by-place ; innermost recess.

récolement (-kol-mān), *n.m.*, (jur.) reading the preceding evidence to a witness ; examination ; verification.

.récoler, *v.a.*, (jur.) to read the previous evidence to a witness ; to examine.

○**récollection** (-kol-lèk-), *n.f.*, (devotional style—*spiritualité*) contemplation.

recollement, *n.m.*, pasting or gluing again ; (of a wound—*d'une blessure*) healing.

recoller, *v.a.*, to paste again.

récollet, *n.m.*, **-te**, *n.f.*, recollet (Franciscan friar or nun—*religieux, religieuse de l'Ordre réformé de St. François*).

Ⓞ*se* **récolliger**, *v.r.*, (rel.) to collect one's self.

récolte, *n.f.*, harvest, crop; collection. *Temps de la —* ; harvest time. *Faire la —* ; to get in the harvest.

récolter, *v.a.*, to reap, to get in. *se* **récolter**, *v.r.*, to be got in (of crops—*des moissons*).

recommandable, *adj.*, commendable, recommendable.

Ⓒ**recommandaresses**, *n.f.pl.*, formerly women appointed to keep booking offices for wet nurses.

Ⓞ**recommandataire**, *n.m.*, detaining creditor.

recommandation, *n.f.*, recommendation; esteem ; (jur.) detainer. *Lettre de —* ; letter of introduction.

Ⓞ**recommandatoire**,*adj.*,recommendatory.

recommander, *v.a.*, to recommend, to charge, to enjoin, to request ; (jur.) to detain, to give a notice to stop. *Je vous recommande le secret ;* I recommend you to be secret.

se **recommander**, *v.r.*, to recommend one's self, itself. *Cette chose se recommande d'elle-même ;* the thing is its own recommendation. *Je me recommande à son souvenir ;* I beg him not to forget me.

recommencement, *n.m.*, recommencement, beginning anew.

recommencer, *v.a.*, to recommence, to begin again. *— la guerre ;* to begin war afresh. *— de plus belle,* — *sur nouveaux frais ;* to begin again with fresh vigour, to begin again worse than ever. *C'est toujours à — ;* there is never an end of it.

recommencer, *v.n.*, to recommence, to begin again.

recommenceu-r, *n.m.* **-se**, *n.f.*, one who begins again.

récompense. *n.f.*, reward, recompense ; requital ; compensation, amends ; indemnity. *En — ;* in return ; as a recompense.

récompenser, *v.a.*, to reward, to requite, to recompense, to remunerate ; to make amends, to compensate ; to requite ; to make up for, to repay. *— le temps perdu ;* to make up for lost time.

se **récompenser**, *v.r.*, to make up for, to make amends.

recomposer. *v.a.*, to recompose.

recomposition, *n.f.*, recomposition.

recompter (-kon-té), *v.a.*, to count again.

réconciliable. *adj.*, reconcileable.

réconciliat-eur, *n.m.*, **-rice**, *n.f.*, reconciler.

réconciliation, *n.f.*, reconciliation, reconcilement.

réconcilier, *v.a.*, to reconcile, to conciliate; to make friends again. *On les a réconciliés ;* they have been reconciled. *— une église ;* to consecrate a church anew.

se **réconcilier**, *v.r.*, to be reconciled, to become friends again. *Il s'est réconcilié avec son père :* he has made it up with his father.

réconduction (tacite), *n.f.*, (jur.) holding premises upon the same conditions without actually renewing the lease after its expiration.

reconduire, *v.a.*, to reconduct, to lead back, to show out; to accompany, to see home, to accompany to the door.

reconduite, *n.f.*, accompanying out, or to the door; seeing out, seeing home. *Faire la —;* to accompany out, home.

reconfirmer, *v.a.*, to confirm again.

Ⓞ**réconfort**, *n.m.*, comfort, relief.

Ⓞ**réconfortation**, *n.f.*, cheering up, comforting.

réconforter, *v.a.*, to cheer up, to strengthen, to fortify, to comfort; to cheer.

reconfrontation, *n.f.*, confronting again.

reconfronter, *v.a.*, to confront again.

reconnaissable, *adj.*, recognizable.

reconnaissance, *n.f.*, gratitude, thankfulness; recognition ; examination ; acknowledgment ; reward, return; confession ; recognizance; (milit., nav.) reconnoitring, reconnoitring party. *Avoir de la — ;* to be grateful. *Témoigner sa — ;* to testify one's gratitude. *Faire une — ;* to reconnoitre.

reconnaissant, **-e**, *adj.*, grateful, thankful. *— de ;* thankful for.

reconnaître, *v.a.*, to recognize, to know again ; to know; to find out, to discover ; to acknowledge, to confess, to admit, to allow ; to be grateful; (milit) to reconnoitre. *Je ne le reconnais plus;* he is grown out of my knowledge. *Se faire — ;* to make one's self known. *On a reconnu sa trahison;* his treachery was discovered. *— un enfant ;* to own a child.

se **reconnaître**, *v.r.*, to know one's self ; to see one's self ; to know where one is; to make out ; to come to one's self ; to collect one's self ; to acknowledge one's fault. *Il se reconnaît dans son fils ;* he sees himself in his son. *Je commence à me reconnaître ;* I begin to know where I am.

reconquérir. *v.a.*, to reconquer, to regain. *— l'estime de quelqu'un ;* to recover the esteem of any one.

reconstitution, *n.f.*, (jur.) substitution.

reconstruction, *n.f.*, reconstruction, rebuilding.

reconstruire, *v.a.*, to build again.

reconsulter, *v.a.*, to consult again.

reconter, *v.a.*, to tell again, to relate over again.

recontinuer, *v.a.*, to resume continuing.

recontracter, *v.a.*, to contract again.

reconvention. *n.f.*, (jur.) cross demand.

reconventionnel, **-le**, *adj.*, (jur.) (of demands—*d'actions en justice*) cross.

reconvoquer, *v.a.*, to convene again, to call together again.

recopier, *v.a.*, to copy again.

*****recoquillement**, *n.m.*, curling up, turning up, shrivelling ; being dog's-eared (of leaves of books—*de feuilles de livres*).

*****recoquiller**, *v.a.*, to curl up (in the shape of a shell—*en forme de coquille*); to turn up, to shrivel up ; to dog's-ear (leaves of books—*les feuilles d'un livre*).

*****se* **recoquiller**, *v.r.*, to turn up, to curl up, to be dog's-eared (of leaves—*de feuilles de livres*).

recorder, *v.a.*, to rehearse (a lesson—*une leçon*) ; to learn by heart; to tie again with a cord; to twist again; to measure firewood again.

se **recorder**, *v.r.*, to concert with any one.

recorriger, *v.a.*, to correct again, to revise.

recors. *n.m.*, bailiff's follower.

recoucher, *v.a.*, to put to bed again, to lay flat again.

se **recoucher**, *v.r.*, to go to bed again.

recoudre, *v a.*, to sew again, or stitch again.

recoupe, *n.f.*, rubble, stone-chips; chippings: pollard.

recoupement (-coop-mãn), *n.m.*, (arch.) offset.

recouper, *v.a.*, to cut again.

recoupette, *n.f.*, coarse meal.

recourber, *v.a.*, to bend round, to make crooked.

se **recourber**, *v.r.*, to grow crooked, to bend.

recourir, *v.n.*, to run again; to have recourse to, to apply to. *— aux remèdes ;* to have recourse to remedies.

recours. *n.m.*, recourse; refuge, resort; help, resource. *— en cassation ;* petition of appeal. — *en grâce;* petition for pardon.

Ⓒ**recousse,** *n.f.,* rescue; recapture of a ship. *V.* rescousse.

recousu, -e, *part.,* sewed, stitched again.

recouvrable, *adj.,* (fin.) recoverable.

Ⓒ**recouvrance,** *n.f.,* recovering.

recouvrement, *n.m.,* recovery, regaining; (fin.) payment; (horl.) lid; cap (of a watch—*de montre*); (arch.) overlapping; *pl.,* debts due to one. — *de la santé;* recovery of one's health. *Faire un état de —;* to draw up a statement of debts due. *Faire un —;* to recover an outstanding debt.

recouvrer, *v.a.,* to recover, to regain,.to get again. — *ses forces;* to recover one's strength. — *son bien;* to recover one's fortune.

recouvrir, *v.a.,* to cover again; to cover, to mask, to hide.

se **recouvrir,** *v.r.,* to cover one's self again; to be covered again; to be hidden again, to become cloudy again.

recracher, *v.a.* and *n.,* to spit out again; to spit again.

récréance, *n.f.,* provisional possession of the revenue of a living. *Lettres de —;* (diplomacy) letters of recall.

récréati-f, -ve, *adj.,* recreative.

récréation, *n.f.,* recreation, amusement, diversion; play (of children—*d'enfants*). *Jour de —;* play-day. *Être en —;* to be at play.

recréer, *v.a.,* to recreate, to create again.

récréer, *v.a.,* to recreate, to divert, to amuse.

se **récréer,** *v.r.,* to divert, to amuse one's self, to take recreation.

récrément, *n.m.,* (med.) recrement.

récrémenteu-x, -se, *or* **récrémentitiel, -le,** *adj.,* (med.) recremental, recrementitious.

recrépir, *v.a.,* to parget again, to roughcast; to give a fresh coat of plaster to; to paint (one's face—*son visage*); to patch up. — *un vieux mur;* to replaster an old wall. — *un vieux conte;* to dress up an old story.

recreuser, *v.a.,* to dig up again, to dig deeper.

Ⓒ**recri,** *n.m.,* exclamation; cry.

se **récrier,** *v.r.,* to exclaim; to utter an exclamation; to cry out. *Il n'y a pas de quoi —;* there is nothing to excite our wonder, there is no need of crying out.

récrimination, *n.f.,* recrimination.

récriminatoire, *adj.,* recriminatory.

récriminer, *v.n.,* to recriminate.

récrire, *v.a.,* to write over again; to write again; to rewrite.

recroître, *v.n.,* to grow again; to spring up again.

*se **recroqueviller,** *v.r.,* to shrivel, to shrivel up.

recrotter, *v.a.,* to dirty again.

recru, -e, *adj.,* quite tired, worn out, knocked up.

recrudescence, *n.f.,* recrudescence.

recrudescent, -e, *adj.,* recrudescent.

recrue, *n.f.,* recruiting; recruit; recruits. *Faire des —s;* to raise recruits.

recrutement (re-krut-mȧn), *n.m.,* recruiting, recruitment.

recruter, *v.a.,* to recruit.

se **recruter,** *v.r.,* to recruit.

recruteur, *n.* and *adj. m.,* recruiter; recruiting.

recta, *adv.,* punctually, exactly.

rectangle, *adj.,* (geom.) rectangular, right-angled.

rectangle, *n.m.,* rectangle.

rectangulaire, *adj.,* rectangular, right-angled.

recteur, *n.m.,* rector (of a parish. of an aca-demy—*d'une paroisse, d'une académie*); provost.

rect-eur, -rice, *adj.,* which directs. (chem.) ☉ *Esprit —;* aromatic. (zool.) *Pennes rectrices;* tail-feathers.

rectifiable, *adj.,* rectifiable.

rectificateur, *n.m.,* rectifier.

rectificatif, -ve, *adj.,* rectifying.

rectification, *n.f.,* rectification; (jur.) amendment.

rectifier, *v.a.,* to rectify.

se **rectifier,** *v.r.,* to be rectified.

***rectiligne,** *adj.,* rectilineal, rectilinear.

rectitude, *n.f.,* rectitude, uprightness.

recto, *n.m.* (—*s*), first page of a leaf; odd page.

rectoral, -e, *adj.,* rectorial.

rectorat, *n.m.,* rectorship, rectorate.

rectrice, *n.f.,* (orni.) tail-feather. V.

recteur, *adj.*

rectum (-tom), *n.m.* (—), (anat.) rectum.

reçu, *n.m.,* receipt. *Au — de;* on receipt of. *Donnez-moi un — de ce que je vous remets;* give me a receipt for what I leave with you.

***recueil,** *n.m.,* collection, selection.

***recueillement,** *n.m.,* contemplation, meditation.

***recueilli, -e,** *part.,* gathered, collected; meditative. *C'est un homme très —;* he is a very meditative man.

***recueillir,** *v.a.,* to gather, to get in; to reap; to get together,.to collect; to pick up; to receive. — *une succession;* to inherit an estate. — *ses esprits;* to collect one's self. — *ses forces;* to collect one's strength. — *les voix;* to collect the votes.

se **recueillir,** *v.r.,* to collect one's self, to collect one's thoughts; to wrap one's self up in pious meditation. — *en soi-même;* to retire within one's self.

recuire, *v.a.,* to cook *or* do again; to boil over again; to bake over again; (manu.) to anneal. — *des métaux;* to anneal metals.

recuit, -e, *part.,* boiled, baked, *or* roasted again. *Cela est cuit et —;* that is done to rags.

recuit, *n.m.,* *or* **recuite,** *n.f.,* annealing (of metals, glass—*des métaux, du verre*); reheating (liquids—*des liquides*).

recul, *n.m.,* recoil; kicking (of fire-arms—*des armes à feu*).

reculade, *n.f.,* falling back; retreat; backing (of carriages—*des voitures*). *Honteuse —;* shameful retreat. *Faire une —;* to make a retreat.

reculé, -e, *part.,* put back; distant, remote; backward, behind (in learning—*en savoir*). *La postérité la plus —e;* the remotest posterity.

reculée, *n.f.,* (l.u.) space allowing to move back. *Feu de —;* (l.u.) roasting fire.

reculement (-kul-mȧn), *n.m.,* drawing back; backing (of carriages—*des voitures*); breech (of saddles—*des selles*).

reculer, *v.a.,* to pull back; to put back; to put off, to defer; to extend.

se **reculer,** *v.r.,* to draw back; to go further off; to put back; to be extended, to sit further off.

reculer, *v.n.,* to go back, to fall back, to draw back; to retreat, to recede; to give ground; to recoil; to rein back (a horse—*un cheval*). *Il faut — pour mieux sauter;* one must go back to take a better leap. *Il est trop avancé pour —;* he is too far engaged to retreat. *En reculant;* in going backwards.

à **reculons,** *adv.,* backwards; the wrong way.

Ⓒ**récupérable,** *adj.,* that may be recovered, retrieved, recoverable.

récupérer, *v.a.,* to recover, to retrieve; to get back.

15 *

se **récupérer**, *v.r.*, to recover; to retrieve one's losses.

récurer, *v.a.* V. écurer.

récurrent, -e (-kur-rän, -t), *adj.*, (med.) recurrent, returning.

récursoire, *adj.*, (jur.) which can give rise to recourse, or to an appeal.

récusable, *adj.*, (jur.) liable to exception, that may be challenged.

récusation, *n.f.*, (jur.) challenge, exception.

récuser, *v.a.*, to challenge (witnesses, jurors, &c.—*des témoins, les jurés, &c.*).

se **récuser**, *v.r.*, to excuse one's self (of judges, jurors—*des juges, des jurés*); to decline judging or voting.

rédacteur, *n.m.*, writer (of a deed—*d'un titre*); clerk (in a public office—*d'une administration publique*); editor; writer (of periodicals—*de journaux, &c.*). — *d'un journal;* editor of a newspaper. — *en chef:* principal editor.

rédaction, *n.f.*, drawing up (deeds, &c.— *titres, &c.*); wording; editing (periodicals— *journaux, &c.*); editors.

redan, *n.m.*, (fort.) redan; (arch.) skewback.

redanser, *v.n.*, to dance again.

⊙**rédarguer** (-gu-hé), *v.a.*, to rebuke, to reprove.

reddition (rèd-di-), *n.f.*, (jur.. milit.) surrender, reduction; giving in (of accounts— *de comptes*). — *de compte;* giving in of accounts.

redébattre, *v.a.*, to debate again.

redéclarer, *v.a.*, to declare again.

redédier, *v.a.*, to dedicate anew.

redéfaire, *v.a.*, to undo again.

redéjeuner, *v.n.*, to breakfast again

redélibérer, *v.a.*, to deliberate upon again, to consider again.

⊙**redélivrer**, *v.a.*, to set at liberty a second time.

redemander, *v.a.*, to redemand, to ask again : to ask back again.

redemeurer, *v.n.*, to dwell or live again.

redémolir, *v a.*, to demolish *or* pull down again.

rédempteur, *n.m.*, redeemer, saviour.

rédemption, *n.f.*, redemption; ransom (of Christian captives—*de captifs chrétiens*).

rédemptoriste, *n.m.*, Redemptorist.

redépêcher, *v.a.*, to despatch again.

redescendre, *v.n.*, to go or come down again.

redescendre, *v.a.*, to take down again.

redevable, *n.m.f.* and *adj.*, debtor; indebted; beholding, beholden. *Je suis votre —, or je vous suis —;* I am your debtor.

redevance, *n.f.*, rent; due, service; (feudalism—*féodalité*) fine.

⊙**redevanci-er**, *n.m.*, -**ère**, *n.f.*, tenant owing rent, due, or service.

redevenir (rě-dě-vnir), *v.n.*, to become again.

redévider, *v.a.*, to wind again.

redevoir, *v.a.*, to remain in one's debt, to owe still.

rédhibition, *n.f.*, (jur.) action at law to render a sale null and void.

rédhibitoire, *adj.*, (jur.) rendering a sale null and void.

rédiger, *v.a.*, to draw out; to draw up; to write out; to word.

se **rédimer**, *v.a.*, to redeem one's self.

redingote, *n.f.*, surtout, frock-coat.

redire, *v.a.*, to repeat, to say again, to tell again; to find fault. *Trouver à — à;* to find fault with, to find amiss, to complain of. *Je n'y trouve rien à —;* I see nothing amiss in it.

rediseu-r, *n.m.*, -**se**, *n.f.*, tautologist, repeater; tell-tale.

redistribuer, *v.a.*, to distribute again.

redistribution, *n.f.*, fresh distribution.

redite, *n.f.*, (b.s.) repetition.

redompter (-don-té), *v a.*, to subdue again.

redondance, *or* **rédondance**, *n.f.*, superfluity of words, redundancy.

redondant, *or* **rédondant**, -e, *adj.*, redundant.

redonder, *or* **rédonder**, *v.n.*, to be redundant.

redonner, *v.a.*, to give again, to give back again; to restore; to deal again (at cards—*aux cartes*).

se **redonner**, *v.r.*, to give one's self up again; to give way again; to indulge again in.

redonner, *v.n.*, to give one's self up again; to fall again into; to take to again; (milit.) to charge again.

redorer, *v.a.*, to gild over again, to regild.

redormir, *v.n.*, to sleep again.

⊙**redoublant**, *n.m.*, pupil that remains a second year in the same class.

redoublé, -e, *part.*, redoubled, increased; repeated. *Pas —* (milit.); double quick time. *Rimes —es :* double rhymes.

redoublement, *n.m.*, redoubling, increase ; reduplication; (med.) paroxysm.

redoubler, *v.a.*, to redouble, to increase, to reiterate ; to increase greatly; to put a new lining to. — *ses soins ;* to be doubly careful.

redoubler, *v.n.*, to increase; to redouble; ⊙to continue two years in the same class (at school —*au collège*). — *de soins ;* to be doubly diligent.

redoul, *or* **roudou**, *n.m.*, (bot.) coriaria myrtifolia, tanners' sumac.

redoutable, *adj.*, formidable, redoubtable.

redoute, *n.f.*, (fort.) redoubt; ridotto (public entertainment—*lieu de plaisir*).

redouter, *v.a.*, to dread, to fear. *Il n'est pas à —:* he is not to be dreaded.

redressement (-drès-män), *n.m.*, making straight, straightening; re-erection; redress; relief (from a grievance—*d'un grief*).

redresser, *v.a.*, to make straight, to make straight again, to straighten; to re-erect; to set up again; to put right; to correct, to reform, to put to rights, to set to rights; to redress; to overreach. — *la tête;* to hold up one's head. — *des griefs ;* to redress grievances.

se **redresser**, *v.r.*, to become straight again; to get straight again; to bridle up; to stand erect again; to set upright; to be set right, to be redressed. *Redressez-vous ;* sit up.

redresseur, *n.m.*, redresser, avenger, righter.

réducteur, *n.m.*, (surg.) apparatus for reducing a dislocation.

réductible, *adj.*, reducible.

réducti-f, -**ve**, *adj.*, reductive.

réduction, *n.f.*, reduction; subjugation; (com.) allowance, abatement; (chem., math., surg.) reduction.

réduire (réduisant, réduit), *v.a.*, to reduce, to diminish; to subdue, to subjugate; to compel; to oblige; (chem., math., surg.) to reduce. — *une place;* to reduce a stronghold. — *une histoire;* to curtail a history.

se **réduire**, *v.r.*, to be reduced; to diminish; to reduce one's self; to be subdued; to come to, to amount.

réduit, *n.m.*, retreat, small habitation; lodging; (fort.) reduct.

réduplicati-f, -**ve**, *adj.*, (gram.) reduplicative.

réduplicatif, *n.m.*, (gram.) reduplicative.

réduplication, *n.f.*, reduplication.

réédification, *n.f.*, rebuilding.

réédifier, *v.a.*, to rebuild.

rééditer, *v.a.*, to publish anew (of books— *des livres*)

réel, -le. *adj.*, real, true; actual; substantial.
réélection, *n.f.*, re-election.
rééligibilité, *n.f.*, re-eligibility.
rééligible, *adj.*, re-eligible.
réélire, *v.a.*, to re-elect.
réellement (-èl-măn), *adv.*, really; in reality.
réengendrer, *v.a.*, to regenerate.
réer, *v.n.* V. **raire.**
réescompte, *n.m.*, (com.) rediscount.
réescompter, *v.a.*, (com.) to rediscount.
réexaminer, *v.a.*, to examine anew.
réexpédier, *v.a.*, to forward again, to send off again.
réexpédition, *n.f.*, forwarding again, sending off again.
réexportation. *n.f.*, re-exportation.
réexporter, *v.a.*, to re-export.
refâcher, *v.a.*, to vex again, to anger again.
se **refâcher,** *v.r.*, to grow angry *or* vexed again.
refaçonner, *v.a.*, to form again, to do *or* make again.
réfaction, *n.f.*, (com.) rebate.
refaire, *v.a.*, to do again, to do over again, to remake; to make anew; to begin anew; to recommence ; to deal again (at cards—*aux cartes*) ; to be refreshing; to refresh ; to mend, to repair. — *de la viande,* to warm meat up again.
se **refaire,** *v.r.*, to refresh one's self; to recover one's strength.
refait, *n.m.*, drawn game (at play—*au jeu*); (hunt.) new horns.
refait, -e, *part.*, done again; (of timber—*des bois de charpente*) squared, prepared for use; (nav.) twice laid (of cordage or stuff—*des cordages ou du suif*). *C'est un cheval —;* it is a made horse.
refaucher, *v.a.*, to mow again.
réfection, *n.f.*, repairs; ○repairs to buildings; refection (meal of religious communities —*repas des communautés religieuses*) ; sustenance, food, nourishment; recovery of strength by rest and food.
réfectoire, *n.m.*, refectory, dining-room.
refend, *n.m.*, splitting ; (arch.) channel (in wall—*dans un mur*). *Mur de —;* (arch.) partition-wall. *Bois de —;* cleft timber.
refendre, *v.a.*, to cleave or split again; to quarter (timber—*bois de charpente*); to saw into slabs (stone—*la pierre*); to saw or cut lengthwise.
référé, *n.m.*, (jur.) application to a judge sitting in chambers. *En —;* in chambers.
référence, *n.f.*, reference.
référendaire, *n.m.*, referendary.
référendariat, *n.m.*, referendarship.
référer, *v.a.*, to refer; to ascribe. *En— à;* to refer to.
se **référer,** *v.r.*, to refer, to have a reference; to refer, to leave to, to confide. *S'en référer à l'avis de quelqu'un;* to refer to the opinion of any one.
référer, *v.n.*, to report again, to make a report.
refermer, *v.a.*, to shut again. — *une plaie;* to close a wound.
se **refermer,** *v.r.*, to shut again; to close again.
referrer, *v.a.*, to shoe again (animal).
*****refeuilleter,** *v.a.*, to turn over again, to turn over and over (the leaves of a book—*un livre*); to read again cursorily.
reficher, *v.a.*, to thrust or stick in again, to drive in again.
refiger, *v.n.*, to congeal again.
se **refiger,** *v.r.*, to congeal again.
refixer, *v.a.*, to fix again.
réfléchi, -e. *adj.*, reflected; reflecting; deliberate ; considerate; reflective; (bot.) reflex. *Action —e;* deliberate action. *Crime —;* pre-

meditated crime. *Opinion peu —e;* hasty opinion. *Personne —e;* reflective person. *Homme peu — ;* inconsiderate man.
réfléchir, *v.a.*, to reflect, to reflect back; to throw back; to reverberate.
se **réfléchir,** *v.r.*, to reflect, to be reflected.
réfléchir, *v.n.*, to reflect, to reflect on, to think, to consider, to ponder.
réfléchissant, -e, *adj.*, reflecting.
réfléchissement (-shis-măn), *n.m.*, reflection, reverberation.
réflecteur, *n.* and *adj. m.*, reflector; reflective, reflecting.
reflet, *n.m.*, reflection, reflex (of light or colours—*de la lumière, des couleurs*).
refléter, *v.a.*, to reflect (light or colour—*la lumière, les couleurs*).
se **refléter,** *v.r.*, to reflect, to be reflected.
refleurir, *v.n.*, to blossom again, to blow again, to flower again ; to flourish again.
réflexe, *adj.*, reflex.
réflexibilité, *n.f.*, reflexibility.
réflexible, *adj.*, reflexible.
réflexi-f, -ve, *adj.*, throwing back, reflective.
réflexion, *n.f.*, reflection ; thought. *Par —;* with reflection. *Faire —;* to reflect. *Avez-vous fait vos—s?* have you considered? *Un homme de —;* a thinking man. *Toute — faite;* all things considered.
refluer, *v.n.*, to reflow, to flow back, to ebb.
reflux, *n.m.*, reflux, refluctuation; ebb, ebbing.
○**refonder,** *v.a.*, (jur.) to refund.
refondre, *v.a.*, to refound, to melt again; to recast, to cast again, to mould anew ; to improve; to remodel; (nav.) to repair. — *la monnaie;* to recoin the money. — *un ouvrage;* to remodel a work. — *un vaisseau;* to repair a ship thoroughly.
refonte, *n.f.*, refounding, recasting (metal.); recoinage, recoining; remodelling; (nav.) thorough repair.
reforger, *v.a.*, to forge again.
réformable, *adj.*, reformable, that may be reformed ; (jur.) reversible.
réformat-eur, *n.m.*, **-rice,** *n.f.*, reformer.
réformation. *n.f.*, reformation, amendment. *La — des monnaies;* re-stamping of the coin.
réforme. *n.f.*, reform, reformation, amendment; (milit.) reduction. *Traitement de —* (milit.); half-pay. *Être mis à la —* (milit.); to be put on half-pay. *Être en —* (milit.); to be on half-pay. *Congé de —* (milit.) ; discharge.
réformé, -e, *part.*, reformed. *La religion —e;* the Protestant religion. *Un officier —;* a half-pay officer.
réformé, *n.m.*, reformer, reformist.
réformer, *v.a.*, to reform, to mend, to improve. — *ses mœurs;* to reform one's morals. — *sa vie;* to mend one's life. — *les abus;* to reform abuses. — *son train;* to reduce the number of one's servants. — *les monnaies;* to re-stamp the coin. — *des troupes;* to discharge troops. — *un officier;* to put an officer on half-pay. — *un soldat;* to discharge a soldier.
se **réformer,** *v.r.*, to reform ; to be reformed.
reformer, *v.a.*, to form again, to form anew.
se **reformer,** *v.r.*, to form again, to be formed anew.
réformiste, *n.m.*, reformer, reformist.
refortifier, *v.a.*, to fortify again.
refouetter, *v.a.*, to whip again.
*****refouillement,** *n.m.*, (sculpt.) sinking cavities deeper in order better to set off the prominent parts.

*refouiller, *v.a.*, to dig again; to search again; (sculpt.) to sink deeper.

refoulement (re-fool-mǎn), *n.m.*, driving back; ebbing the tide—*de la marée*. *Le — des eaux;* the flowing back of the waters. *Le — de la marée;* the ebbing of the tide. *Le — d'une armée;* the driving back of an army.

refouler, *v.a.*, to drive back, to repel; to compress; (artil.) to ram.

refouler, *v.n.*, to ebb; to flow back. *La marée refoule;* the tide is ebbing.

refouloir, *n.m.*, cannon-rammer.

refournir, *v.a.*, to furnish again, to stock anew.

réfractaire, *adj.*, refractory, stubborn, obstinate, rebellious.

réfractaire, *n.m.*, (milit.) conscript, recruit who does not join his regiment.

réfracter, *v.a.*, (phys.) to refract.

se réfracter, *v.r.*, to be refracted.

réfracti-f, -ve, *adj.*, refractive.

réfraction, *n.f.*, (phys.) refraction.

refrain, *n.m.*, refrain, burden of a song; constant theme; (nav., l.u.) flowing back of billows after breaking on rocks, surf. *C'est son —;* it is his constant theme; he is always harping upon it.

réfrangibilité, *n.f.*, refrangibility.

réfrangible, *adj.*, refrangible.

refrapper, *v.a.*, to strike again, to knock again. *— la monnaie;* to re-stamp the coin.

réfréner, *v.a.*, to bridle, to restrain; to curb, to repress.

réfrigérant, -e, *adj.*, refrigerant.

réfrigérant, *n.m.*, (chem.) refrigeratory; (med.) refrigerant.

réfrigérati-f, -ve, *adj.*, (med.) refrigerative.

réfrigératif, *n.m.*, (med.) refrigerative.

réfrigération, *n.f.*, (chem.) refrigeration.

⊙**réfrigératoire**, *adj.*, refrigerative.

réfringent, -e, *adj.*, refracting.

refrire, *v.a.*, to fry again.

refriser, *v.a.*, to curl again.

refrogné, -e, *or* **renfrogné, -e**. *part.*, frowning, scowling. *Air —;* scowling look.

*refrognement, *or* **renfrognement**, *n.m.*, frown, knitting of one's brows.

*se refrogner, *or se* **renfrogner**, *v.r.*, to frown, to knit one's brows.

refroidi, -e, *part.*, chilled, cooled.

refroidir, *v.a.*, to cool, to chill.

se refroidir, *v.r.*, to cool, to grow cold *or* cool; to slacken, to relax.

refroidir, *v.n.*, to cool, to become cold.

refroidissement (-dis-mǎn), *n.m.*, cooling, coolness; coldness. *Le — d'une passion;* the cooling of a passion.

refrotter, *v.a.*, to rub again.

refuge, *n.m.*, refuge, shelter. *— assuré;* sure refuge. *Lieu de —;* place of safety.

réfugié, -e, *n.m.*, *-e*, *n.f.*, refugee.

se réfugier, *v.r.*, to take refuge, shelter.

refuir, *v.n.*, (hunt.) to double.

refuite, *n.f.*, (hunt.) shift, doubling; (l.u.) shuffling, evasion.

refus, *n.m.*, refusal, denial; thing refused. *Essuyer un —;* to meet with a refusal. *Un — net;* a flat refusal. *Cela n'est pas de —;* that is not to be refused. *Ce n'est pas à son —;* it is not in his choice. *Enfoncer un pieu jusqu'à — de mouton* (tech.); to ram a pile in until driven home. *Ce pieu est au —;* this pile is set, driven home.

refusable, *adj.*, that can be refused.

refuser, *v.a.*, to refuse; to deny; to decline, not to accept. *— des présents;* to refuse presents. *— la porte à quelqu'un;* to deny any one admittance.

se refuser, *v.r.*, to deny one's self, to deprive one's self of; not to permit; to grudge one's self; to shun, to avoid; to withstand, to resist. *Il se refuse le nécessaire;* he denies himself the necessaries of life.

refuser, *v.n.*, to refuse; to decline; (man.) to refuse to advance; (nav.) to scant (of the wind—*du vent*).

refuseu-r, *n.m.*, *-se*, *n.f.*, refuser.

réfutable, *adj.*, refutable.

réfutateur, *n.m.*, refuter, confuter.

réfutation, *n.f.*, refutation, confutation, disproof.

réfuter, *v.a.*, to refute, to confute.

*regagner, *v.a.*, to regain, to get again, to win back, to recover; to retrieve; to rejoin, to reach, to gain over. *— le dessus;* to get the upper hand again. *— le vent sur l'ennemi* (nav.); to get the weather-gauge of the enemy. *— quelqu'un;* to gain any one over. *— la maison;* to return home, to reach home.

*regaillardir, *v.a.*, to make merry, to enliven, to revive. *V.* **ragaillardir**.

regain, *n.m.*, aftermath, after-grass.

régal, *n.m.*, feast, entertainment; treat; pleasure. *C'est un — pour moi;* it is a treat for me.

régalade, *n.f.*, (fam.) drinking by throwing the head back and pouring the liquid down one's throat; rousing fire; treating; treat.

régalant, -e, *adj.*, amusing, pleasant.

régale, *n.m.*, (mus.) regal.

régale, *n.f.*, right belonging formerly to the kings of France of enjoying the revenues of vacant bishoprics.

régale, *adj.f.*, (l.u.) royal. *Eau —;* aqua regia, nitro-hydrochloric acid.

régalement (-gal-mǎn), *n.m.*, ⊙assessment; levelling (of ground—*de terrain*); ⊙equalization (of shares of an inheritance—*des parts d'un héritage*).

régaler, *v.a.*, to regale, to treat, to feast, to entertain; ⊙to assess taxes; to level (ground—*un terrain*).

se régaler, *v.r.*, to feast, to entertain or treat one another; to regale one's self; to enjoy one's self.

régalien (-in), *adj.m.*, of the rights of the crown.

régaliste, *n.m.*, the holder of a living granted by the king.

regard, *n.m.*, look; gaze; stare; glance; (astrol.) aspect; two pictures looking at one another; *pl.*, eyes; attention, notice; (tech.) draft-hole. *— tendre;* tender look. *Lancer un —;* to dart a look. *Jeter ses —s de côté et d'autre;* to look about. *Jeter un — sur*, to cast a glance at. *Adoucir ses —s;* to soften one's countenance. *Fixer les —s de quelqu'un;* to catch any one's eye; to be looked up to. *Au — sombre;* dull-eyed. *En —;* opposite. *Au — de;* with regard to, concerning, in comparison with.

regardant, *n.m.*, beholder, looker-on, spectator.

regardant, -e, *adj.*, too strict, particular; economical, near, saving.

regarder, *v.a.*, to look at; to look on; to behold; to face, to be opposite, to look into; to consider, to mind, to look up to; to regard, to concern. *— quelqu'un;* to look at any one. *— quelqu'un fixement;* to stare at any one. *— par un trou;* to look at through a hole. *— quelqu'un en pitié;* to look at any one with a pitiful eye. *— quelqu'un de haut en bas;* to look down upon any one with contempt. *— comme;* to look upon as, to consider as, to repute. *Cela vous regarde;* that concerns you.

se regarder, *v.r.*, to look at one's self; to look at each other; to look upon one's self as;

to consider one another as ; to be opposite to each other ; to be in front of each other.

regarder, *v.n.*, to look, to face. to be opposite, to front ; to mind, to pay regard to. *Ma chambre regarde sur le jardin ;* my room overlooks the garden. *Regardez-y bien ;* take heed.

regarnir, *v.a.*, to furnish again ; to retrim.

régate, *n.f.*, regatta, boat-race.

regayer, *v.a.*, to comb hemp.

regayoir, *n.m.*, hemp-comb.

regayure, *n.f.*, refuse of hemp.

regazonnement, *n.m.*, planting land with grass.

regazonner, *v.a.*, to plant land with grass.

regel, *n.m.*, new frost, freezing again.

regeler, *v.n.*, to freeze again.

régence, *n.f.*, regency.

régénérat-eur, -rice, *n.* and *adj.*, regenerator ; regenerating, reproducing.

régénération, *n.f.*, regeneration.

régénérer, *v.a.*, to regenerate.

se **régénérer**, *v.r.*, to be regenerated.

régent, -e, *adj.*, regent.

régent, *n.m.*, regent ; master (of a college—*d'un collège*) ; governor (of the bank of France—*de la banque de France*) ; name of a large diamond of the French crown.

régenter, *v.a.* and *n.*, ⊙ to teach ; (fig.) to domineer, to bluster, to hector.

regermer, *v.n.*, to regerminate.

régicide, *n.m.* and *adj.*, regicide ; regicidal.

régie, *n.f.*, administration ; administration of the taxes ; excise.

regimbement, *n.m.*, kicking (of horses—*des chevaux*) ; resistance.

regimber, *v.n.*, to kick (of horses—*des chevaux*) ; to resist.

régime, *n.m.*, regimen ; diet ; form of government ; rule ; law ; (gram.) object, objective case. *Mettre au —* ; to diet.

régiment, *n.m.*, regiment.

régimentaire, *adj.*, regimental.

région, *n.f.*, region.

régional, *adj.*, pertaining to a region, to a district.

régir, *v.a.*, to govern, to rule ; to administer, to manage.

régisseur, *n.m.*, manager.

régistrateur, *n.m.*, registrar, registrary (in the Pope's chancellor's office—*à la chancellerie papale*).

registre, *n.m.*, register ; register (of an organ—*d'un orgue*) ; (mus.) draw-stop ; (print.) register ; damper (of chimneys—*de cheminées*) ; valve (of a steam-engine—*de machine à vapeur*). *Rapporter sur un —* ; to enter in a register. *Il est sur mes —s ;* I have him in my books.

régistrer, *v.a.*, to register.

régitre, *n.m. V.* **registre**.

régitrer, *v.a. V.* **registrer**.

règle, *n.f.*, rule, ruler ; order ; pattern, model, example ; (arith.) sum ; *pl.*, menses, courses. *Cela est de —* ; that is the rule. *Dans les —s ;* according to rule. *Être en —, se mettre en —* ; to be in due form, to have everything in order. *— à coulisse ;* sliding rule.

réglé, -e, *adj.*, ruled ; regulated, regular, steady. *— comme un papier de musique ;* as regular as clock-work. *Une vie —e ;* a regular life. *À des heures —es ;* at regular hours. *Il a le pouls — ;* his pulse is regular.

règlement, *n.m.*, regulation: laws, by-laws ; standing order ; settlement (of accounts—*de comptes*). *Violer le —* ; to commit a breach of order. *Vous manquez au —* ; you break the rules. *— de compte ;* settlement of an account.

réglément, *adv.*, regularly.

réglementaire, *adj.*, that relates to regulations.

réglementation, *n.f.*, making regulations.

réglementer, *v.a.* and *n.*, to make regulations.

régler, *v.a.*, to rule, to regulate, to square ; to order ; to settle ; to determine, to decide. *— sa dépense ;* to regulate one's expenses. *— ses affaires ;* to settle one's affairs. *— une pendule ;* to set a clock right. *— un différend ;* to settle a difference.

se **régler**, *v.r.*, to regulate one's self by ; to imitate, to follow the example of, to be guided ; to be regulated. *— sur la vertu ;* to be guided by virtue. *Je ne me règle pas sur cela ;* I don't go by that.

réglet, *n.m.*, (print.) rule ; (arch.) girth.

réglette, *n.f.*, (print.) reglet.

régleu-r, *n.m.*, **-se**, *n.f.*, ruler (of paper—*de papier*).

réglisse, *n.f.*, liquorice. *Du jus de —* ; Spanish liquorice. *— en bâton ;* stick liquorice.

réglure, *n.f.*, ruling (of paper—*de papier*).

*****régnant, -e**, *adj.*, reigning, prevailing ; prevalent ; predominating.

*****règne**, *n.m.*, reign ; prevalence ; crown (over the high altar in churches—*au dessus du maître-autel*) ; kingdom ; tiara (of the pope—*du pape*). *— animal ;* animal kingdom. ⊙ *Être en —* ; to be the fashion.

*****régner**, *v.n.*, to reign, to govern, to rule, to bear sway, to prevail ; to be in fashion ; (arch.) to reach. *La maladie qui règne ;* the prevailing disease.

regnicole, *n.m.f.* and *adj.* (rĕg-ni-), (jur.) native.

regonflement, *n.m.*, rising of water, when stopped by some obstacle ; swelling anew.

regonfler, *v.n.*, to swell, to overflow (of water when stopped by an obstacle—*des eaux arrêtées par quelque obstacle*).

regonfler, *v.a.*, to swell again ; to inflate, to fill again.

regorgement, *n.m.*, overflowing (of fluids —*des fluides*).

regorger, *v.n.*, to overflow, to run over, to abound with ; to be glutted. *Cette province regorge de blé ;* that province abounds in corn. *— de santé ;* to have a redundancy of health.

regouler, *v.a.*, (pop.) to snub, to give a sharp answer to ; to surfeit.

regoûter, *v.a.*, to taste again.

regrat, *n.m.*, (l.u.) huckstering ; huckster's shop ; ⊙ retail salt-shop.

regrattage, *n.m.*, (mas.) regrating.

regratter, *v.a.*, to scratch again ; to scrape again ; (mas.) to regrate.

regratter, *v.n.*, to huckster ; (l.u.) to haggle ; to make illegitimate petty profits.

regratterie (-gra-trì), *n.f.*, huckster's trade ; huckstery, huckster's wares.

regratti-er, *n.m.*, **-ère**, *n.f.*, huckster, huckstress, regrater.

regreffer, *v.a.*, to graft again.

regres, *n.m.*, right to retake a living after resigning it ; right to retake an office after selling it.

regret, *n.m.*, regret. *Avoir du —* ; to feel regret. *J'ai — que vous n'ayez pas vu cette pièce ;* I regret that you have not seen that play. *À —* ; with regret, with reluctance, grudgingly.

regrettable, *adj.*, to be lamented, regretted.

regretter, *v.a.*, to regret. *Tout le monde le regrette ;* he is regretted by everybody. *Je regrette qu'il ne soit pas ici ;* I regret that he is not here.

regrossir, *v.a.*, (engr.) to make thicker.

reguinder (-ghin-), *v.a.*, to hoist up again.

se **reguinder**, *v.r.*, to soar again (of a hawk—*du faucon*).

régularisation, *n.f.*, putting in order.

régulariser, *v.a.*, to put in order.

régularité, *n.f.*, regularity, strict observance of rules; strictness; ecclesiastical state.

régulateur, *n.m.*, regulator; standard. *Le — d'une horloge;* the regulator of a clock.

régulat-eur, -rice, *adj.*, regulating.

régule, *n.m.*, (chem.) pure metal.

réguli-er, -ère, *adj.*, regular; punctual, exact.

régulier, *n.m.*, regular (of monks—*des moines*).

régulièrement (-lier-mān), *adv.*, regularly, punctually.

réhabilitation, *n.f.*, rehabilitation.

réhabiliter, *v.a.*, to rehabilitate, to reinstate; to restore to.

se **réhabiliter**, *v.r.*, to rehabilitate one's self, to reinstate, to re-establish one's self.

réhabituer, *v.a.*, to use, to habituate, again.

se **réhabituer**, *v.r.*, to habituate one's self again.

rehacher, *v.a.*, to mince again.

rehanter, *v.a.*, to frequent again.

rehasarder, *v.a.*, to venture again.

rehaussé, -e, *adj.*, heightened, enhanced; set off, enriched.

rehaussement (-hôs-mān), *n.m.*, raising, heightening; increase of value (of coin—*des monnaies*).

rehausser, *v.a.*, to raise, to heighten, to set off, to enrich; to set forth, to extol, to cry up, to enhance, to raise the value of.

rehauts (ré-hô), *n.m.pl.*, (paint.) lightest parts of a picture.

reheurter, *v.a.*, to knock, to hit, again.

réimportation, *n.f.*, (com.) re-importation.

réimporter, *v.a.*, to import again.

réimposer, *v.a.*, to reassess; to lay on again; (print.) to reimpose.

réimposition, *n.f.*, further assessment; (print.) reimposing.

réimpression, *n.f.*, reprinting; reprint.

réimprimer, *v.a.*, to print again.

rein, *n.m.*, kidney; *pl.*, loins, reins, back. *Douleur dans les —s;* pain in the loins. *Poursuitre quelqu'un l'épée dans les —s;* to pursue any one close. *Il a les —s forts:* he is strong-backed. *Chute des —s;* fall of the back. *Les —s d'une voûte;* the haunches of a vault.

reinaire, *adj.*, (bot.) having the shape of a kidney; reniform.

réincorporer, *v.a.*, to reincorporate.

reine, *n.f.*, queen. *— régnante;* reigning queen, queen regnant. *— mère;* queen mother. *— douairière;* queen dowager. *Faire la —;* to act the queen. *- -des-prés (—s —)* (bot.); meadow-sweet.

reine-claude, *n.f.* (*—s —*), (bot.) greengage.

reine-marguerite, *n.f.* (*—s —s*), (bot.) China-aster. *Chinese starwort, starwort. V.* **marguerite**.

reinette, *n.f.*, russet; rennet; pippin. *— d'Angleterre;* golden pippin.

réinfecter, *v.a.*, to reinfect, to taint again.

réinstallation, *n.f.*, reinstalment.

réinstaller, *v.a.*, to reinstal.

reinté, -e, *adj.*, loined, strong-backed.

réintégrande, *n.f.*, (jur.) restoring to the possession of one's property.

réintégration, *n.f.*, reinstatement; (com.) re-warehousing.

réintégrer, *v.a.*, to reinstate; to re-warehouse.

réinventer, *v.a..* to invent anew.

réinviter, *v.a.*, to invite again.

reis, *n.m.* (—), chief. *— -effendi;* Turkish Secretary of state.

réitérati-f, -ve, *adj.*, repeated.

réitération, *n.f.*, reiteration.

réitérer, *v.a.*, to reiterate.

reître, *n.m.*, reiter (German horse soldier of the 14th and 15th centuries—*cavalier allemand du 14e et du 15e siècle*). *C'est un vieux —;* he is an old fox.

*__rejaillir__, *v.n.*, to gush, to gush out, to spurt out, to fly out, to stream, to spring out, to spout, to spout out; to reflect, to be reflected, to flash; to fly back; to rebound, to cast a reflection.

*__rejaillissement__ (-is-mān), *n.m.*, gushing, gushing out, spouting, spouting forth, springing out, spurting, spurting out; reflection, flashing (of light—*de la lumière*); rebounding, flying back (of a solid body—*d'un corps solide*).

rejaunir, *v.n.*, to grow yellow again.

rejet, *n.m.*, rejection; throwing out; young shoot, sprig, sprout; (geol.) out-throw; (fin.) carrying.

rejetable, *adj.*, that may be rejected, rejectable.

rejeter (rěj-té), *v.a.*, to throw again; to drive back, to throw back; to cast *or* throw up, *or* out; to throw, to throw away; to put forth (of plants —*des plantes*); to refuse to accept, to reject; to set aside; to deny; (fin.) to carry. *— le blâme sur;* to throw the blame on. *— un compte sur;* to carry an account to.

se **rejeter**, *v.r.*, to have recourse to.

rejeter, *v.n.*, to shoot (of plants—*des plantes*).

rejeton (rěj-ton), *n.m.*, (bot.) shoot, sprout; (hort.) offset; scion; offspring.

rejoindre, *v.a.*, to rejoin, to join again. to join; to reunite; to meet again; to overtake.

se **rejoindre**, *v.r.*, to join again, to be joined together again; to reunite, to meet again.

rejointoiement (-toa-mān), *n.m.*, (mas.) rejointing.

rejointoyer, *v.a.*, (mas.) to rejoint.

rejouer, *v.a.*, to play again; to act again.

rejouer, *v.n.*, to play again; to recall a move (at draughts and chess—*aux dames et aux échecs*).

réjoui, -e, *n.* and *adj.*, jovial, joyous, merry person; jovial, joyous, merry. *Un gros —;* a jovial man.

réjouir, *v.a.*, to rejoice, to gladden, to delight, to divert, to entertain, to make merry; to cheer, to exhilarate. *Cette couleur réjouit la vue;* that colour pleases the eye. *Le vin réjouit le cœur;* wine makes the heart glad.

se **réjouir**, *v.r.*, to be *or* to make merry, to enjoy one's self; to rejoice; to delight, to delight one's self.

réjouissance, *n.f.*, rejoicing; coarse meat; *pl.*, rejoicings, merry-making. *En signe de —;* as a sign of rejoicing.

réjouissant, -e. *adj.*, jovial, joyous, cheerful; gladsome, rejoicing, cheering.

relâchant, -e, *adj.*, loosening, opening, laxative, relaxing.

relâchant, *n.m.*, opening medicine, laxative.

relâche, *n.m.*, intermission; discontinuance; rest, respite; relaxation; (thea.) no performance. *Il y a — au théâtre ce soir;* there is no performance at the theatre this evening.

relâche, *n.f.*, (nav.) any place fit to put into; putting into port; calling at a port.

relâché. -e, *adj.*, loose, remiss, lax. *Morale —e;* loose doctrine.

relâchement (-lâsh-mān), *n.m.*, slackness, looseness, laxness; slackening, loosening, relaxing; diminution, abatement; relaxation, rest; remissness; laxity (of morals—*des mœurs*). *— des nerfs;* relaxing of the nerves. *— dans les mœurs;* looseness of manners. *— de courage;* faint-heartedness.

relâcher, *v.a.*, to slacken, to loose, to loosen,

to unbend, to relax; to let go, to release, to set at liberty; to yield, to give up, to abate.

se relâcher, *v.r.*, to grow slack *or* loose; to slacken, to abate, to give way, to relax, to fall off; to flag; to get milder (of the weather—*du temps*). — *l'esprit*; to unbend one's mind, to take relaxation.

relâcher, *v.n.*, to abate, to remit, to relax; (nav.) to put into port.

relais. *n.m.*, relay (fresh horses—*chevaux frais*); stage (where fresh horses are taken—*où l'on prend des chevaux frais*); (hunt.) relay; opening (in carpet-making—*manufacture des tapis*); (fort.) *V.* **berme**. *Être de* —; to be unemployed, to have nothing to do.

relaissé,*adj.m.* (hunt.), resting (of hares—*du lièvre*).

relaisser, *v.n.*, (hunt.) to rest (of hares—*du lièvre*).

relancer,*v.a.*,(hunt.) to start again; to turn out again; to urge, to rouse, to answer sharply, to put down, to take up (by an answer—*par une réponse*). — *quelqu'un*; to put any one down; to take any one up (by an answer—*par une réponse*).

relaps, -e (re-laps), *n.* and *adj.*, relapser; relapsed; relapsed into heresy.

rélargir, *v.a.*, to widen, to let out (clothes —*des vêtements*).

rélargissement (-jis-män). *n.m.*, widening; letting out (clothes—*des vêtements*).

relater, *v.a.*, (jur.) to relate, to state.

relateur, *n.m.*, (l.u.) relater.

relati-f, -ve, *adj.*, relative, relating.

relatif, *n.m.*, (gram.) relative.

relation, *n.f.*, relation, reference; respect, account, recital; statement; connection; *pl.*, relations, connection, intercourse. *Être en — avec quelqu'un*; to be connected with any one, to be in correspondence with any one. — *exacte*; exact account.

relationnaire, *n.m.*, narrator, relater.

relativement (-tiv-män). *adv.*, relatively.

relativité, *n.f.*, relativeness.

relatter, *v.a.*, to lath anew.

relaver, *v.a.*, to wash again.

relaxation, *n.f.*, (jur., med.) laxness; enlargement; relaxation. — *d'un prisonnier*; release of a prisoner.

relaxé, *adj.*, relaxed, slackened.

relaxer, *v.a.*, to relax · to enlarge; to release (a prisoner—*un prisonnier*).

relayer,*v.a.*, to take the place of, to relieve, any one.

se relayer, *v.r.*, to relieve one another.

relayer, *v.n.*, to take fresh horses.

relégation, *n.f.*, (jur.) banishment; exile; relegation.

reléguer (-ghé), *v.a.*, to banish; to send off; to shut up; to consign; to relegate.

se reléguer, *v.r.*, to shut one's self up, to seclude one's self.

relent, *n.m.*, mustiness, mouldiness. *Sentir le —*; to smell mouldy.

'relevailles (rel-vä-ye), *n.f.pl.*, churching of a woman.

relevant, -e (rel-vän, -t), *adj.*, held, being holden.

relevé (rel-vé), *n.m.*, abstract, extract, statement; shifting of a horse's shoe. *Faire un — de compte*; to make an abstract of an account.

relevé, -e (rel-), *adj.*, raised; high, exalted, lofty. *Une condition —e*; a high rank. *Pensée —e*; noble thought. *De la viande d'un goût —*: high-seasoned meat.

relevée (rel-), *n.f.*, (jur.) afternoon. *De —*; in the afternoon.

relèvement (re-lèv-män), *n.m.*, raising

again; statement, account; (nav.) rising, bringing afloat.

relever (rel-vé), *v.a.*, to raise again, to lift up again; to restore; to raise; to heighten, to relieve, to set off; to cry up, to extol; to notice, to remark; to take up; to give a relish to; to liberate, to free; to criticize; (nav.) to take the bearings of. — *des fortifications*; to restore fortifications. — *un fossé*: to raise up the banks of a ditch. — *le courage de quelqu'un*; to raise any one's courage. *Relevez votre robe*; tuck up your gown. — *les bords d'un chapeau*; to turn up the rim of a hat. — *un mot*; to criticize a word. — *la tête*; to raise one's head again. *La parure relève la bonne mine*; dress sets off a good countenance. — *une action*; to extol an action. — *quelqu'un*; to raise any one. *Se faire — de ses vœux*; to get one's vows annulled. — *la garde*; to relieve guard. — *une sentinelle*; to relieve a sentry. — *un vaisseau*; to bring a ship afloat again. — *l'ancre*; to shift the position of the anchor. — *une côte*; to take the bearings of a coast. — *le quart* (nav.); to set the watch.

se relever. *v.r.*, to rise again; to get up again, to rise; to rise up, to get up; to recover, to retrieve one's self; to relieve each other.

relever.*v.n.*, to recover; to get better; to turn up; to depend; to be dependent; to be amenable. — *de maladie*; to recover from illness.

releveur, *n.m.* and *adj.*, (anat.) levator; elevator.

reliage, *n.m.*, hooping (of casks—*de tonneaux*).

relief, *n.m.*, relief, relievo, embossment; embossing; set-off. *Bas-*(— —s); bas-relief, bass-relief, basso-relievo, low-relief. *Haut, plein —*, — *entier*; high-relief, alto-relievo. *Demi-*— (— —s); demi-relievo. *Ouvrage de —*; work in relief. *Donner du —*; to set off; to give relief; to make conspicuous.

⊙**reliefs**, *n.m.pl.*, remains, leavings (from the table—*de la table*).

relier, *v.a.*, to hoop (casks—*des tonneaux*); to bind (books—*des livres*).

relieur, *n.m.*, binder, bookbinder.

religieuse, *n.f.*, nun.

religieusement (-eûz-män), *adv.*, religiously.

religieu-x, -se, *adj.*, religious, spiritual; exact, strict, punctual.

religieux, *n.m.*, friar, monk.

religion, *n.f.*, religion; religious worship; piety, godliness, faith. — *La — épure l'âme*; religion purifies the mind. *Se faire une — d'une chose*; to make a thing a matter of conscience. — *réformée*; protestant religion.

religionnaire. *n.m.*, Protestant.

religiosité, *n.f.*, ⊙excessive scrupulousness in religious matters; religiousness.

relimer, *v.a.*, to file again; to polish; to work up.

reliquaire, *n.m.*, reliquary; shrine.

reliquat. *n.m.*, balance, remainder of an account; remains (of a disease—*d'une maladie*); ⊙remains of a feast.

reliquataire, *n.m.*, debtor owing a balance; debtor.

relique, *n.f.*, relic. *Les —s d'un saint*; the shrine of a saint. *Je n'ai pas grand'foi à ses —s*; I have not much confidence in him.

relire, *v.a.*, to read over again.

reliure, *n.f.*, binding (of books—*de livres*).

relocation. *n.f.*, (jur.) letting anew.

reloger, *v.a.* and *n.*, to lodge again, to dwell again.

relouer, *v.a.*, to let again; to underlet; to rent again.

reluire, *v.n.*, to shine, to glitter. *Tout ce*

qui reluit n'est pas or; all is not gold that glitters.

reluisant, -e, *adj.,* bright, shining, glittering.

reluquer, *v.a.,* to cast sheep's eyes on; to ogle; to leer upon.

remâcher, *v.a.,* to chew again, to ruminate; to revolve in one's mind.

remaçonner, *v.a.,* to repair (mas.).

*****remaillage,** *n.m.,* scraping (of hides—*des peaux*).

*****remailler,** *v.a.,* to scrape (hides—*les peaux*).

*****rémailler,** *v.a.,* to enamel again.

remander, *v.a.,* to send word again.

remaniement, or **remaniment,** *n.m.,* handling again; touching again; (print.) overrunning; doing over again, repairing.

remanier, *v.a.,* to handle again; to touch again; to repair; to retouch, to do over again; (print.) to overrun. — *le papier* (print.); to turn the paper.

remarchander, *v.a.,* to haggle again.

remarcher, *v.n.,* to walk or go again; to march again.

remarier, *v.a.,* to marry again, to join again in matrimony.

se **remarier,** *v.r.,* to marry a second time; to be married again.

remarquable, *adj.,* remarkable, observable, conspicuous.

remarquablement, *adv.,* remarkably.

remarque, *n.f.,* remark; notice. *Digne de —;* worthy of notice.

remarquer, *v.a.,* to mark again, to make another mark; to note, to observe, to notice, to take notice; to remark, to distinguish. *Se faire —;* to attract notice, to distinguish one's self.

se **remarquer,** *v.r.,* to be remarked, noticed.

remasquer, *v.a.,* to mask again.

se **remasquer,** *v.r.,* to put on one's mask again.

remballer, *v.a.,* to pack up again.

rembarquement, *n.m.,* re-embarkation.

rembarquer, *v.a.,* to re-embark; to ship again.

se **rembarquer,** *v.r.,* to re-embark; to take shipping again; to go on board again; to engage again.

rembarrer, *v.a.,* to repel, to repulse; to give a sharp answer to, to set down. *Il a été bien rembarré;* he was served as he deserved.

remblai, *n.m.,* filling up; embankment.

remblayer, *v.a.,* to embank, to fill up (with rubbish—*avec des terres, des gravois*).

remboîtement (-boat-mān), *n.m.,* setting (of a bone—*d'un os*); fitting in again, clamping.

remboîter, *v.a.,* to set (a bone—*un os*); to fit in again, to clamp (pieces of joinery—*des pièces de menuiserie, de charpente*).

rembourrage, or **rembourrement** (ran-boor-), *n.m.,* stuffing, stuffing out.

rembourrer, *v.a.,* to stuff (with flock or hair—*de laine ou de crin*); to stuff out.

se **rembourrer,** *v.r.,* (pop.) to stuff (to eat gluttonously—*manger à l'excès*).

remboursable, *adj.,* repayable, to be reimbursed; (fin.) redeemable.

remboursement, *n.m.,* reimbursement, repayment.

rembourser, *v.a.,* to reimburse, to repay, to refund.

se **rembourser.** *v.r.,* to reimburse one's self, to repay one's self.

rembraser, *v.a.,* to kindle again.

rembrasser, *v.a.,* to embrace again.

rembruni, -e, *adj.,* brown, dark, gloomy, dull. *Un air —;* a gloomy look. *Teint —;* dark complexion.

rembrunir, *v.a.,* to make dark or darker, to darken; to cloud; to render sad, sorrowful.

se **rembrunir,** *v.r.,* to get or grow darker; to become cloudy, gloomy; to become sad, melancholy.

rembrunissement (-nis-mān), *n.m.,* darkening, becoming darker.

rembuchement (-bûsh-mān), *n.m.,* (hunt.) return to the wood.

se **rembucher,** *v.r.,* (hunt.) to return to the wood.

remède, *n.m.,* remedy; (med.) clyster. *Sans —;* without remedy, past recovery. *Susceptible de —;* remediable. *Être dans les —s;* to take remedies. *Se mettre dans les —s;* to take remedies, physic. *Un — à tous maux;* a plaster for all sores. *Le grand —;* the grand remedy, mercury.

remédiable, *adj.,* remediable.

remédier, *v.n.,* to remedy. — *à un mal;* to remedy an evil. — *aux inconvénients;* to remedy inconveniences. *On ne saurait y —;* that can't be helped.

remêler, *v.a.,* to mix again; to shuffle, again.

⊙**remembrance,** *n.f.,* remembrance.

⊙**remémorati-f, -ve,** *adj.,* commemorative.

⊙**remémorer,** *v.a.,* to put in mind of, to remind of.

⊙*se* **remémorer,** *v.r.,* to recollect.

remener, *v.a.,* to take back, to lead back; to carry back, to bring back (a person or an animal—*une personne ou un animal*).

remerciement, or **remerciment,** *n.m.,* thanks. *Faire des —s;* to return thanks.

remercier, *v.a.,* to thank, to give or return thanks; to decline; not to accept; to discharge. — *Dieu de ses bienfaits;* to thank God for his favours. *Je vous remercie;* I thank you.

réméré, *n.m.,* (jur.) redemption. *Faculté de —;* power of redemption. *Vente à —;* sale with right of redemption.

remesurer, *v.a.,* to measure again.

remettre, *v.a.,* to put again, to put on again, to wear again; to put back, to put back again, to set again; to lay again; to set (a bone —*un os*); to restore, to reinstate; to recover, to make well; to reassure; to remove; to deliver, to give up; to return, to deliver up; to put off, to delay; to remit, to forgive; to leave one the care of; to entrust. — *à la voile;* to set sail again. — *l'épée dans le fourreau;* to put up one's sword. — *une armée sur pied;* to raise new forces. — *dans l'esprit;* to remind. — *quelqu'un;* to recollect one, to know one again. *Je vous remets;* I recollect your face. — *en bon ordre;* to restore to order. — *en bonne intelligence;* to reconcile, to reunite. *Le voilà tout à fait remis;* he is quite recovered. — *l'esprit;* to soothe the mind. — *une lettre à son adresse;* to deliver a letter to its address. *Faire —;* to have something, to cause something to be, delivered, conveyed. — *de l'argent;* to remit money. — *d'un jour à l'autre;* to put off from day to day. — *une chose à la décision de quelqu'un;* to refer a matter to any one.

se **remettre,** *v.r.,* to apply one's self again; to resume; to set one's self again; to call to mind; to recover, to grow well again; to recover; to compose, one's self; (hunt.) to light (of birds—*des oiseaux*); to resign one's self; to refer, to rely. — *à table;* to sit down again to table. *Remettez-vous;* compose yourself. — *une chose;* to recollect a thing. *S'en remettre à;* to refer to; to trust to. *S'en remettre à quelqu'un;* to refer a thing to any one.

remeubler, *v.a.,* to refurnish.

rémifère, *adj.,* (zool.) of remipeds.

réminiscence, *n.f.,* reminiscence.

rémipède, *n.m.,* (zool.) remiped.

remisage, *n.m.*, putting a carriage into the coach-house.

remise, *n.f.*, giving up; delivery; delay; deferring; remittance; reduction, abatement; commission, allowance ; 'coach-house ; (hunt.) cover (for game—*pour le gibier*); place of lighting-(of partridges—*de perdrix*). *Il use toujours de* —; he always delays. *La* — *d'une audience ;* the putting off of a hearing. *Faire une* —; to make a remittance, to remit. *Il est sous la* —; he is on the shelf.

remise, *n.m.*, coach let on hire; livery-coach.

remiser, *v.a.*, to put a coach in the coach-house.

rémissible, *adj.*, remissible, pardonable, excusable.

rémission, *n.f.*, remission, indulgence, mercy.

rémissionnaire, *n.m.*, criminal who has obtained his pardon.

rémittent, -e, *adj.*, (med.) remitting.

*remmailloter (ran-ma-), *v.a.*, to wrap up in swaddling-clothes again.

remmancher (ran-man-), *v.a.*, to put a new haft or handle to.

remmener (ran-mné), *v.a.*, to take back, to carry back, to lead back (a person or an animal —*une personne ou un animal*).

remodeler (-mo-dlé), *v.a.*, to model anew.

rémolade or **remolade**, *n.f.* *V.* **rémoulade**.

remole. *n.f.* *V.* **remous**.

©rémolliati-f,-ve, rémollient,-e. rémolliti-f. -ve, *adj.*, (med.) emollient, mollifying, softening.

remontage, *n.m.*, new-fronting (of boots—*de bottes*) ; (tech.) remounting, putting together again pieces of machinery, &c.

remonte, *n.f.*, (milit.) remounting ; (of studs —*terme de haras*) new leap.

remonter, *v.n.*, to reascend ; to go up again ; to go back (with reference to time—*du temps*) ; to rise, to rise again, to remount. — *à cheval ;* to get on horseback again. — *sur sa bête ;* to recover one's loss. — *à la source, à l'origine d'une chose ;* to trace a thing back to its origin.

remonter, *v.a.*, to reascend ; to go up again ; to put together again ; to remount (cavalry—*de la cavalerie*); to rise (of public securities—*de la rente, &c.*); to fit up ; to stock ; to go up ; to wind up (a watch, a clock—*une montre, une horloge*). — *une rivière ;* to ascend a river. — *une montre ;* to wind up a watch. — *des bottes ;* to new-front boots. — *un fusil ;* to new-stock a gun ; to put together again the various parts of a musket. — *quelqu'un ;* to revive the spirits of any one. — *un magasin ;* to stock a warehouse anew.

se remonter, *v.r.*, to stock one's self again ; to wind up (watches, &c.—*montres, &c.*); (fig.) to recover one's strength, health.

remontoir, *n.m.*, key (for winding up clocks—*pour remonter les horloges, &c.*); keyless action (in watches—*de montre*).

remontrance, *n.f.*, remonstrance.

remontrant, *n.m.*, remonstrant.

remontrer, *v.a.*, to demonstrate, to represent, to show, to show again ; to remonstrate ; (hunt.) to show where the game has passed. *C'est gros Jean qui remontre à son curé ;* it is teaching one's grandmother how to suck eggs.

se remontrer, *v.r.*, to show one's self again.

rémora, *n.m.* (—*s*),(ich.) remora ; suck-fish ; (fig.) hindrance, impediment, obstacle.

remordre, *v.a.* and *n.*, to bite again anything or anybody ; to attack again ; to try again ; (fig., of conscience) to torment, to rack.

remords (re-mor), *n.m.*, remorse, compunction. *Avoir des* —*s ;* to feel remorse.

rémore, *n.f.* *V.* **rémora**.

remorquage, *n.m.*, (nav.) towing.

remorque, *n.f.*, towing (a ship—*un vaisseau*): *Prendre à lc* —; to take in tow. *Se mettre à la* —; to get into tow. *Câble de* —; tow-line.

remorquer, *v.a.*, (nav.), to tow, to drag.

remorqueur, *n.m.*, tug, towing-vessel.

remorqueuse, *n.f.*, (railways) a particular kind of locomotive.

à rémotis (-tiss), *adv.*, (l.u.)aside. *Mettre à* —; to put by.

remoucher, *v.a.*, to snuff the candle again ; to wipe again the nose of.

se remoucher, *v.r.*, to blow one's nose again.

remoudre, *v.a.*, to grind again (corn, &c.).

rémoudre, *v.a.*, to sharpen, to whet, again.

*remouiller, *v.a.*, to wet again.

rémoulade, *n.f.*, (cook.) sharp mustard-sauce ; (vet.) charge, sprain-ointment.

rémouleur, *n.m.*, grinder, knife-grinder.

remous, *n.m.*, eddy.

*rempaillage, *n.m.*, putting a new straw bottom to a chair.

*rempailler, *v.a.*, to put a new straw bottom to a chair.

*rempailleu-r, *n.m.*, **-se**, *n.f.*, chair-mender.

rempaquement (-pak-man), *n.m.*, barrelling of herrings.

rempaqueter (-pak-té), *v.a.*, to pack up again.

remparer, *v.a.*, to fortify, to make a fortification ; to cover.

se remparer, *v.r.*, to fortify one's self by means of ramparts ; to take possession again.

rempart, *n.m.*, rampart, bulwark.

remplaçant, *n.m.*, substitute.

remplacement (-plas-man), *n.m.*, replacing ; fresh supply ; (fin.) reinvestment. *Bureau de* —; office for providing substitutes for the army. *Le* — *a été aboli en France par la loi de 1872 ;* the replacing of recruits by substitutes was abolished in France by law in 1872. *En* — *de ;* instead of, in place of.

remplacer, *v.a.*, to replace, to take the place of ; to serve as a substitute ; to reinvest. *Vous le remplacerez pendant son absence ;* you will fill his place during his absence. *Se faire* —; to get replaced ; to get a substitute.

se remplacer, *v.r.*, to be replaced ; to get a fresh supply of any thing.

remplage, *n.m.*, the filling up (of wine-vessels—*de pièces de vin*). — *de muraille ;* stones to fill the inside of a wall.

rempli, *n.m.*, tuck, fold.

rempli, -e, *adj.*, full, replete.

remplier, *v.a.*, to make a tuck, to turn in.

remplir, *v.a.*, to fill again ; to fill, to fill up ; to cram, to stuff ; to take up, to occupy ; to supply, to furnish ; to fulfil, to discharge ; to perform ; to answer, to come up to ; to pay back. *Il remplit bien son temps ;* he employs his time well. — *un poste ;* to hold a post. — *ses engagements ;* to fulfil one's engagements. — *une tâche ;* to perform a task. — *l'attente de quelqu'un ;* to answer any one's expectation.

se remplir, *v.r.*, to fill one's self ; to cram or stuff one's self ; to fill, to become full.

remplissage, *n.m.*, filling ; filling up ; filling out ; rubbish, trash.

remplisseuse, *n.f.*, (needle-work—*ouvrage à l'aiguille*) filler-in.

remploi, *n.m.*, (jur.) re-investment.

remployer, *v.a.*, to use again.

remplumer, *v.a.*, to feather again ; (mus.) to quill anew.

se remplumer, *v.r.*, to get new feathers ; to retrieve one's loss ; to get stout again ; to pick up.

rempocher, *v.a.*, to pocket again.
rempoisonner (ràn-poa-zo-né), *v.a.*, to poison again.
rempoissonnement (ràm-poa-so-n-màn), *n.m.*, re-stocking with fish.
rempoissonner (ràn-poa-so-né), *v.a.*, to re-stock with fish.
remporter, *v.a.*, to carry *or* take back; to carry away *or* off, to take away *or* off; to get, to obtain; to bear off. — *un prix*; to carry off a prize. — *la victoire*; to get the victory.
rempotage, *n.m.*, (gard.) potting; potting up again.
rempoter, *v.a.*, (gard.) to pot; to pot again.
remprisonnement, *n.m.*, reimprisonment.
remprisonner, *v.a.*, to reimprison.
remprunter, *v.a.*, to borrow again.
remuage, *n.m.*, moving, stirring.
remuant, **-e**, *adj.*, restless, stirring; unquiet; turbulent.
remue-ménage, *n.m.* (—), stir, rummage; disturbance, bustle, confusion.
remuement, *or* **remûment**, *n.m.*, stirring; moving, commotion, disturbance.
remue-queue, *n.m.* (—). *V.* **hochequeue.**
remuer, *v.a.*, to move; to stir; to rouse; to turn up; to affect; to change the linen of a baby. — *la tête*; to shake one's head. — *des meubles*; to rummage furniture.
se **remuer**, *v.r.*, to stir, to move; to stir one's self; to fidget.
remuer, *v.n.*, to stir, to move; to make a disturbance; to fidget.
remueu-r, *n.m.*, **-se**, *n.f.*, mover, stirrer; workman employed in turning corn about in a granary to prevent it spoiling.
remueuse, *n.f.*, nurse especially employed to wash a baby.
Ⓖ **remugle**, *n.m. V.* **renfermé.**
rémunérateur, *n.m.*, rewarder, remunerator, requiter.
rémunérati-f, **-ve**, *adj.*, remunerative.
Ⓖ **rémunératti-f**, **-ve**, *adj.*, remunerative.
rémunération, *n.f.*, remuneration, reward.
rémunératoire, *adj.*, remuneratory.
rémunérer, *v.a.*, to remunerate, to reward.
renâcler, *v.n.*, (pop.) to snuff, to snort (in anger—*de colère*); to turn up one's nose; to be unwilling, to be reluctant.
renaissance, *n.f.*, second birth, coming to life again; regeneration, revival, renewal; renaissance.
renaissant, **-e**, *adj.*, springing up again, growing again, growing up again, reviving.
renaître, *v.n.*, to be born again; to grow again, to come again; to appear again, to spring up again, to rise again. *Toute la nature renaît;* all nature revives. *Le jour renaît;* day reappears. — *à la vie;* to return to life. — *au bonheur;* to be restored to happiness.
rénal, **-e**, *adj.*, (anat.) renal.
renard, *n.m.*, (mam.) fox; (mam.) dog-fox; fox, cunning dog, sly fellow; (astron.) Fox; (engineering—*terme d'ingénieur*) leak; (pop.) vomit. — *américain;* raccoon. *Queue-de* — (—*s* —) (bot.); prince's-feather. — *marin;* sea-ape. *Fin* —; cunning dog, cunning fox. *Se confesser au* — *;* to tell one's secret to a traitor. *Le* — *prêche aux poules;* the devil rebukes sin.
renarde, *n.f.*, (mam.) she-fox.
renardeau, *n.m.*, fox's cub.
renarder, *v.n.*, to play the fox; (pop.) to vomit.
renardier, *n.m.*, fox-catcher.
renardière, *n.f.*, fox's burrow.
Ⓖ **renasquer**, *v.n. V.* **renâcler.**
roncaissage, *or* **rencaissement**, *n.m.*,

(hort.) putting again trees or shrubs into wooden boxes; (fin.) putting again into the cash box.
rencaisser, *v.a.*, to put again trees or shrubs into wooden boxes; (fin.) to put again into the cash box.
renchéri, **-e**, *adj.*, risen in price, higher-priced; particular, nice (of a person—*des personnes*).
renchéri, *n.m.*, **-e**, *n.f.*, particular person, nice person. *Faire le* —; *faire la* —*e;* to be mighty particular, to be exceedingly delicate.
renchérir, *v.a.* and *n.*, to raise the price of; to grow dear, to get dearer. — *sur;* to improve upon; to go beyond.
renchérissement (-ris-màn), *n.m.*, rising, raising of the price of a commodity.
renclouer, *v.a.*, (milit.) to spike guns again.
*rencogner**, *v.a.*, (fam.) to drive, to get, into a corner.
rencontre, *n.f.*, encounter, rencounter, accidental meeting; accident, chance; collision; meeting; accidental fight; opportunity, occurrence, case; juncture. *Aller, venir, à la* — *de quelqu'un;* to go to meet, to come to meet, any one. *Marchandise de* —; second-hand things. *Roue de* — *d'une horloge;* balance-wheel of a clock. *Vaisseaux de* — (chem.); vessels fitting into each other.
rencontre, *n.m.*, (her.) rencounter.
rencontrer, *v.a.*, to meet, to meet with, to fall in with; to light upon; to find, to encounter; to meet, to encounter (in a hostile manner —*hostilement*).
se **rencontrer**, *v.r.*, to meet, to meet each other, to meet with each other, to be met with; to be seen; to agree, to coincide; to meet, to encounter (in a hostile manner—*hostilement*). *Nos idées se rencontrent;* our ideas coincide, our ideas tally. *Cela ne se rencontre pas tous les jours;* that does not happen, that is not met with every day.
rencontrer, *v.n.*, to have good *or* ill luck, to be fortunate *or* unfortunate; to guess; to speak to the purpose, to make a hit. *Vous avez bien rencontré;* you have hit the right nail on the head. *Le limier rencontre;* the blood-hound is on the scent.
rencorser, *v.a.*, to make a new body (to a gown—*à une robe*).
rendage, *n.m.*, (tech.) produce of raw materials; daily produce of a lime-kiln.
rendant, *n.m.*, **-e**, *n.f.*, (jur.) one who renders an account.
rendement (rand-màn), *n.m.*, produce, yield.
se **rendetter**, *v.r.*, to run into debt again, to get into debt again, to contract fresh debts.
rendeu-r, *n.m.*, **-se**, *n.f.*, one who renders, restorer.
rendez-vous, *n.m.* (—), rendezvous, meeting, appointment; place of meeting, place of resort. *Donner un* — *à quelqu'un;* to make an appointment with any one. *Prendre* —; to make an appointment; to agree on a rendezvous, on an appointment.
rendonnée, *n.f. V.* **randonnée.**
rendormir, *v.a.*, to lull asleep again, to lull to sleep again, to send to sleep again. *Cet enfant s'est réveillé, il faut tâcher de le* —; that child has awakened, we must try to send it off to sleep again.
se **rendormir**, *v.r.*, to fall asleep again, to go to sleep again.
rendoubler, *v.a.*, to turn in, to turn down; to fold up, to double up.
rendre, *v.a.*, to render, to return, to restore, to give back, to give again; to pay back, to repay, to refund, to pay again; to deliver up,

to yield, to yield up, to give up, to render up, to give back; to surrender, to give up; to carry, to convey, to transport, to take; to cast up, to cast out, to eject, to void, to throw up, to throw off one's stomach; to do, to pay, to give; to make; to produce, to bear, to bring in; to translate; to pay, to reward; to express, to convey, to represent; to issue; to exhale, to emit, to send forth, to give out; (jur.) to remit; (jur.) to surrender; (jur.) to return, to find, to bring in; to give in; to give (verdict). — *à chacun ce qui lui appartient;* to render every one his own. *Rendez-moi mon reste;* give me my change. — *de l'ouvrage;* to take home work. — *le salut;* to return a salute. — *hommage;* to render homage. *Je vous rends grâce;* I return you thanks. — *ses respects, ses devoirs à quelqu'un;* to pay one's respects, one's duty, to any one. — *compte;* to give an account. — *visite;* to pay a visit. — *à quelqu'un sa visite;* to return any one his visit. — *justice à quelqu'un;* to do any one justice. — *la justice;* to administer, to dispense justice. — *service à quelqu'un;* to do any one a service. — *la pareille;* to return like for like. — *le bien pour le mal;* to return good for evil. — *avec usure;* to return with interest. *Dieu vous le rende!* may God reward you! — *la santé;* to restore one's health. — *un prisonnier à la liberté;* to restore a prisoner to liberty. *L'expérience l'a rendu sage;* experience has made him wise, has taught him wisdom. — *une place* (milit.); to surrender a town. — *les armes;* to lay down one's arms. — *une médecine;* to throw up a dose of physic. — *gorge;* to refund. — *raison;* to account for, to give a reason. *Rendez-moi raison de votre conduite;* explain your conduct to me. — *raison à quelqu'un;* to give any one satisfaction, to fight a duel. — *un arrêt;* to issue a decree. — *témoignage;* to bear witness. — *à quelqu'un sa parole;* to release any one from his promise. — *l'âme;* to give up the ghost. — *le pain bénit* (c.rel.); to make the bread-offering. ☉ — *le bord* (nav.); to come into port; to lay up. — *un paquet,* — *une lettre;* to take a parcel, a letter, to its destination. — *des marchandises en un lieu;* to take, to carry, to convey goods to a place. *Montez dans ma voiture, en deux heures je vous rendrai là;* get into my carriage, in two hours I will take you there. *Ce fermier rend tant de sa ferme;* that farmer pays so much for his farm.

se **rendre**, v.r., to make one's self, to render one's self; to become, to turn; to go, to repair, to proceed, to resort; to wait upon any one; to flow; to yield, to surrender, to surrender one's self, to give one's self up; to be worn out, to be tired out, to be exhausted. — *partie contre quelqu'un;* to declare against any one. — *à son devoir;* to go where one's duty calls. *Le sang se rend au cœur;* the blood flows to the heart. — *prisonnier;* to surrender one's self prisoner. *Je me rends;* I am tired out; I give up.

rendre, v.n., to lead (of roads—*des routes*); to evacuate, to void; to run (of wounds—*des plaies*).

rendu, -e, part., arrived; rendered; delivered; exhausted, tired out, knocked up. *Je suis —;* I am quite exhausted. *Cheval qui est —;* horse overspent.

rendu, n.m., return, tit for tat.

renduire, v.a., to plaster anew; to daub over again; to give a new coating.

rendurcir, v.a., to make harder.

se **rendurcir,** v.r., to become harder; to become hardened.

rêne, n.f., rein. *Prendre les —s;* to take the reins.

renégat, n.m., **-e.** n.f., renegade.

reneiger, v.n., to snow again.

rêner, v.a., to bridle (a horse—*un cheval*).

rénette, n.f., (vet.) paring knife.

rénetter, v.a., (vet.) to make furrows in a horse's hoof with a paring knife.

renettoyer, v.a., to clean again.

renfaîtage, n.m., repairing the top of a roof.

renfaîter, v.a., to mend the top of a roof.

renfermé, n.m., fustiness; musty; close, confined, air. *Sentir le —;* to smell close.

renfermer, v.a., to shut up, to confine; to comprehend, to include.

se **renfermer,** v.r., to shut one's self up, to confine one's self. — *en soi-même;* to retire within one's self.

renfiler, v.a., to thread again, to new-string.

renflammer, v.a., to rekindle.

se **renflammer,** v.r., to be rekindled.

renflé, -e, adj., swollen, swelling; (bot.) inflated.

renflement, n.m., swelling, enlargement; (bot.) struma.

renfler, v.n., to swell, to swell out.

renflouage, n.m., (nav.) getting a ship afloat again.

renflouer, v.a., (nav.) to get a ship afloat again.

renfoncement (-fons-mān), n.m., cavity; hollow; (print.) indentation; (arch.) break; (paint.) background.

renfoncer, v.a., to pull further on; to pull one's hat over one's eyes; (print.) to indent.

renforcé, -e, adj., strong, thick; substantial; wealthy; stout; thick-set, downright, regular. *Des vers —s de pensées;* verses very rich in thought. *C'est un bourgeois —;* he is a substantial, purse-proud citizen. *Un bidet —;* a strong thick-set nag. *Une étoffe —e;* a thick strong stuff. *Sottise —e;* downright stupidity.

renforcement, n.m., reinforcing, strengthening.

renforcer, v.a., to reinforce; to strengthen; to augment, to increase. — *le son d'un instrument;* to increase the sound of an instrument.

se **renforcer,** v.r., to gather strength; to increase, to grow stronger; (milit.) to be reinforced.

renformir, v.a., (mas.) to mend (a wall, &c.—*un mur, &c.*).

renformis, n.m., (mas.) pargetting, plastering, new coat; repairing (of a wall—*d'un mur*).

renfort, n.m., reinforcement, supply, relief.

*****renfrogné, renfrognement,** se **renfrogner.** *V.* **refrogné, refrognement,** se **refrogner.**

rengagement (-gaj-mān), n.m., re-engagement; (milit.) re-enlistment; pledging, pawning again.

rengager, v.a., to engage again, to re-engage; (milit.) to re-enlist; to pledge, to pawn again. — *un domaine;* to mortgage a domain. — *son cœur;* to engage one's heart again.

se **rengager,** v.r., to engage again, to re-engage; (milit.) to re-enlist.

rengaine, n.f., (pop.) thread-bare, commonplace repetition; harping on; worn-out expedient.

rengainer, v.a., to sheath, to put up. — *une épée;* to put up a sword. *Rengainez votre compliment;* forbear your compliment.

rengainer, v.n., to sheath one's sword, to put up one's sword.

rengorgement, n.m., bridling up, carrying one's head high.

se **rengorger,** v.r., to carry it high, to carry one's head high, to bridle up.

rengraisser, *v.a.*, to fatten again.
se rengraisser, *v.r.*, to grow fat. stout, again; to become fat again, to fatten again.
rengraisser, *v.n.*, to grow fat, to become fat, stout, again.
Ⓔ**rengrégement** (-grèj-màn), *n.m.*, increase, augmentation of a malady.
Ⓔ**rengréger**, *v.a.*, se **rengréger**, *v.r.*, to increase, to augment (of a malady, a pain, &c. —*d'un mal, d'une douleur, &c.*).
rengrénement (-grè-n-màn), *n.m.*, (coin.) re-coinage.
rengréner, *v.a.*, to put corn again in the mill-hopper; (coin.) to coin again, to re-coin, to re-stamp; (mec.) to throw into gear again, to engage again.
reniable, *adj.*, deniable.
reniement, *or* **reniment**, *n.m.*, denying, disowning; denial of St. Peter.
renier, *v.a.*, to deny, to disown; to abjure, to disclaim, to renounce, to forswear. — *sa religion ;* to abjure one's religion.
renier, *v.n.*, to abjure one's religion; to abjure.
Ⓔ**renieur**, *n.m.*, profane swearer, blasphemer.
reniflement, *n.m.*, sniffing.
renifler, *v.n.*, to sniff; to turn up one's nose; to manifest unwillingness.
reniflerie, *n.f.*, sniffing.
renifleu-r, *n.m.*, **-se**, *n.f.*, sniffer.
rénitence, *n.f.*, (med.) renitency.
rénitent, **-e**, *adj.*, (med.) renitent.
renne (rè-n), *n.m.*, reindeer.
renom (-nòn), *n.m.*, renown, fame, reputation, report, note, name.
renommé, **-e**, *adj.*, renowned, famous, noted, celebrated, famed.
renommée, *n.f.*, renown, fame, name, reputation, report; (myth.) Fame. *Bonne — vaut mieux que ceinture dorée;* a good name is better than riches.
renommer, *v.a.*, to name again, to re-elect; to render renowned, to render famous, to make renowned, to make famous. *Se faire —;* to spread one's fame.
se renommer, *v.r.*, to make use of the name of any one.
renonce, *n.f.*, renounce, revoke (at cards— *aux cartes*).
renoncement (-nòns-màn), *n.m.*, renouncing, renouncement. — *à soi-même;* self-denial, abnegation.
renoncer, *v.n.*, to renounce, to give up, to surrender; to forego, to relinquish, to lay down, to disclaim, to waive; to revoke, to renounce (at cards—*aux cartes*). — *à la couronne;* to renounce the crown. — *à une succession:* to give up an inheritance. — *à sa foi;* to renounce one's faith.
renoncer, *v.a.*, to renounce, to disclaim, to disown, to deny.
renonciat-eur, *n.m.*, **-rice**, *n.f.*, (jur.) renouncer.
renonciation, *n.f.*, renunciation, renouncement.
renonculacées, *n.f.pl.*, (bot.) ranunculaceæ.
renoncule, *n.f.*, (bot.) ranunculus, crowfoot, spearwort.
renouée, *n.f.*, (bot.) polygonum, knotberry, knot-grass.
Ⓔ**renouement**, *or* **renoûment**, *n.m.*, renewing, renewal.
renouer, *v.a.*; to knot again, to tie again; to tie; to put together; to resume, to renew. — *amitié;* to be friends again. — *l'amitié de parents;* to reconcile relations. — *une affaire;* to resume a business.
renouer, *v.n.*, to resume one's relations, to resume one's connexion.

renou-eur, *n.m.*, **-euse**, *n.f.* *V.* **rebouteur**.
Ⓔ**renouveau**, *n.m.*, (fam. poet.) springtime.
renouvelable, *adj.*, renewable.
renouveler (-noo-vlé), *v.a.*, to renew, to renovate, to revive, to resuscitate; to refresh. — *une idée;* to revive an idea. — *un usage;* to revive a custom. — *le souvenir d'une chose;* to refresh one's remembrance of a thing.
se renouveler, *v.r.*, to be renewed. to be revived. — *dans le souvenir de quelqu'un;* to remind any one of one's self.
renouveler, *v.n.*, to renew. — *de jambes;* to walk briskly again with renewed strength. — *d'appétit ;* to eat again with a fresh appetite. — *d'attention;* to redouble one's attention. — *d'ardeur;* to be more eager.
renouvellement (-vèl-màn), *n.m.*, renewing, renewal, reviving; reiteration, repetition; increase, redoubling.
rénovat-eur, **-rice**, *adj.*, renovating.
rénovation, *n.f.*, renovation.
* **renseignement**, *n.m.*, information, intelligence; account; indication, direction; *pl.*, reference. *Prendre des—s ;* to make inquiries. *Aller aux —s;* to go and make inquiries. *Bureau de —s;* intelligence-office.
* **renseigner**, *v.a.*, to teach again, to instruct again; to inform, to show, to tell, to direct.
rensemencement, *n.m.*, (agri.) sowing again.
rensemencer, *v.a.*, (agri.) to sow again.
rentamer, *v.a.*, to cut again, to begin again; to resume. — *un discours;* to resume a conversation.
rentassé, **-e**, *adj.*, thick-set.
rentasser, *v.a.*, to heap up again
rente, *n.f.*, yearly income, revenue; rent, annuity; stock. funds; pension. *Vivre de ses —s;* to live upon one's property. — *foncière;* ground-rent. — *viagère;* life-annuity. *Le taux de la —;* the price of stocks. *La — hausse;* the stocks are rising. *Acheter des —s ;* to buy stock. *Faire une — à;* to allow a pension to.
renté, **-e**, *adj.*, who has an income; endowed (of public establishments—*des établissements publics*). *Bien —;* rich, wealthy.
renter, *v.a.*, to allow a yearly income to; to endow (public establishments—*des établissements publics*).
renti-er, *n.m.*, **-ère**, *n.f.*, stockholder, fund-holder, annuitant; independent gentleman; independent lady.
rentoilage, *n.m.*, garnishing anew with cloth. — *d'un tableau;* stretching a picture upon new cloth.
rentoiler, *v.a.*, to furnish, to garnish with new cloth, to put new cloth (to a thing —*à quelque objet*). — *un tableau;* to stretch, to paste, an old painting on new canvas.
rentrage, *n.m.*, bringing in, taking in.
rentraîner, *v.a.*, to carry away again, to lead away again, to draw on, in, again.
rentraire (rentrayant, rentrait), *v.a.*, to fine-draw, to darn, to renter.
rentraiture, *n.f.*, fine-drawing, rentering, darn, darning; joining on.
rentrant, *adj.*, (geom., fort.) re-entering.
rentrant, *n.m.*, person that takes the place of him who has lost (at play—*au jeu*). *On demande un —;* a new player is wanted.
rentrayeu-r, *n.m.*, **-se**, *n.f.*, fine-drawer.
rentré, **-e**, *part.*, (med.) suppressed, driven in. *Humeur —e;* humour driven in. *Sueur —e:* checked perspiration.
rentrée, *n.f.*, re-entrance; re-opening; reappearance; (com.) in-coming, receipt, payment, getting-in; returns; (hunt.) return. *A la — des classes:* at the re-opening of school, at the

conclusion of the vacation, of the holidays. *Cet acteur a fait sa* — (thea.); that actor has made his re-appearance. — *des impôts;* receipt of the taxes. *Ce revenu est d'une — difficile;* this revenue is slow in coming in.

rentrer. *v.n.*, to enter again, to return, to come in again, to go in again, to get in again; to re-enter, to join again; to become again, to get again; to recover; to reopen (of courts of law, schools, colleges, &c.—*des tribunaux, des collèges, des écoles, &c.*); to make one's reappearance, to reappear (of an actor—*des acteurs*); to return to, to resume; (med.) to be suppressed, to be driven in; (engr.) to retouch; to be got in, to come in (of money—*d'argent*); to buy in (at cards—*aux cartes*). — *en possession;* to regain possession. — *en grâce;* to reingratiate one's self. — *en soi-même;* to descend into one's self. — *en son bon sens;* to come to one's senses again. — *en charge;* to return to one's place. — *en condition;* to go to service again. — *en fureur;* to fly into a passion again, to get into a passion again. *Faire —;* to drive in. *Il m'est rentré beau jeu;* I have taken in fine cards. — *dans la ville;* to return to town. *Cet acteur rentre ce soir;* that actor makes his reappearance this evening.

rentrer, *v.a.*, to take in, to bring in, to put in; (med.) to drive in; (nav.) to bowse in; to house guns; (print.) to indent. *Voici le moment de — les foins;* now is the season for getting in the hay. — *une ligne;* (print.) to indent a line.

renvahir, *v.a.*, to invade again.

renvelopper (ran-vlo-pé), *v.a.*, to wrap up again.

renvenimer (rān-vni-), *v.a.*, to make (a wound, a sore—*une plaie*) fester again, rankle again.

renverger, *v.a.*, to edge baskets.

à la **renverse,** *adv.*, backwards, upon one's back. *Tomber à la —;* to fall backwards.

renversé, -e, *part.*, thrown down; (her.) inverted. *Il a l'esprit —;* his brain is turning. *C'est le monde — ;* it is the world turned upside down. *Encolure —e* (man.); pliant neck.

renversement, *n.m.*, reversing, overturning, throwing down, throwing over, overthrowing; turning upside down; deranged, confused, disordered state; subversion, destruction; (surg.) retroversion, prolapse; (mus.) inversion, revert, reversing; (arith.) inversion; (nav.) ⊙ transshipment. *V.* **transbordement.** — *d'un état;* overthrow of a state. — *des lois;* subversion of the laws. — *d'esprit;* turning of the brain. — *de la paupière* (med.); eversion of the eyelid.

renverser, *v.a.*, to reverse, to turn upside-down, to turn topsy-turvy; to throw down, to upset, to tumble down, to overthrow, to overturn; to spill; to turn (the brain—*la cervelle, l'esprit*); to destroy, to ruin; (milit.) to put to flight, to rout, to put to the rout; to invert; (surg.) to retrovert; (nav.) ⊙ to trans-ship. *V.* **transborder.** — *à coups de canon;* to batter down. — *la table;* to upset the table. — *un bataillon;* to break, to overthrow, a battalion. — *un état;* to overthrow a state. *Ceci lui renversera l'esprit;* this will turn his brain. — *l'encre;* to spill the ink, to knock the ink over.

se **renverser,** *v.r.*, to fall down, to turn upside-down, to upset, to be upset, to be thrown down, to overset, to be overset, to capsize; to be capsized, to be spilt; to throw one's self back, to fall back, to lie on one's back; (milit.) to be thrown into disorder, to be thrown back; (surg.) to be retroverted.

renverseur, *n.m.,* overthrower; subverter; inverter,

renvi, *n.m.*, revy, what is laid above the stakes, at cards.

renvier, *v.n.*, to revy, to lay above the stakes, at cards.

renvoi. *n.m.*, sending back, returning, return, sending away, dismission; dismissal, discharge; referring, sending; adjournment; caret, reference (in books, writings, &c.—*dans les livres, les écrits, &c.*); (jur.) reference to another judge; *pl.*, (med.) rising of the stomach. *De —;* returnable. — *du son;* reverberation of sound. *Chevaux de —;* return horses. — *de troupes;* dismissal of troops. — *de la cause à huitaine;* adjournment of the cause till that day week.

renvoyer, *v.a.*, to send again; to send back again, to return; to send away, to dismiss; to discharge; to refer; to put off; to drive back; to throw back; to reflect (light or heat—*la lumière ou la chaleur*); to repeat, to reverberate (sound—*le son*). — *un ministre;* to dismiss a minister. — *un domestique;* to discharge a servant. — *une femme;* to repudiate a wife. *On a renvoyé l'affaire à huitaine;* the cause has been adjourned for eight days. — *la balle à quelqu'un;* to give one as good as he sends. — *un accusé;* to acquit an accused person. — *un plaideur de sa demande;* to refuse a suitor his demand. — *le lecteur à une note;* to refer the reader to a note.

réoccupation, *n.f.*, reoccupying.

réoccuper, *v.a.*, to occupy again, to reoccupy.

réopiner, *v.n.*, to deliver one's opinion again.

réorchestrer, *v.a.*, (mus.) to compose a new score.

réordination, *n.f.*, second ordination, re-ordination.

réordonner, *v.a.*, to ordain again, to re-ordain.

réorganisation, *n.f.*, reorganization.

réorganiser, *v.a.*, to reorganize.

se **réorganiser,** *v.r.*, to be reorganized.

réouverture, *n.f.*, re-opening. *La — d'un théâtre;* the re-opening of a theatre. *La — d'un magasin;* the re-opening of a commercial establishment, shop.

repaire, *n.m.*, haunt, den (of a wild beast—*d'une bête féroce*); (hunt.) dung of hares, wolves, &c.; (tech.) *V.* **repère.** — *de voleurs;* den of thieves, haunt of thieves.

repaître, *v.n.*, (l.u.) to feed, to take refreshment; to bait.

repaître, *v.a.*, (l.u.) to feed, to nourish. *Il faut — ces animaux;* these animals must be fed. — *quelqu'un d'espérances;* to feed any one with hopes.

se **repaître,** *v.r.*, to feed on; to feast on; to delight in. *Il se repaît d'espérances vaines;* he feeds on vain hopes.

répandre, *v.a.* and *n.*, to spill, to shed, to diffuse, to scatter, to distribute, to bestow, to give out, to spread, to pour out, to exhale, to spread abroad, to propagate. — *des larmes,* to shed tears. — *des bienfaits;* to bestow benefits. *Le soleil répand la lumière;* the sun scatters light. — *un bruit;* to spread a report, to propagate a report. — *son sang;* to shed one's blood. — *des aumônes;* to distribute alms. — *l'alarme;* to spread the alarm. — *son cœur;* to open one's heart.

se **répandre,** *v.r.*, to be spilt, to be shed, to be diffused, to be spread, to be scattered, to be distributed, to be bestowed, to be given out, to be poured out, to be exhaled, to be spread abroad, to be propagated; to flow, to spread, to go abroad, to get abroad; to burst out, to break out, to launch out, to fly out;

to frequent society, to go into society. *La lumière se répand beaucoup plus vite que le son;* light flows, travels much more quickly than sound. *La nouvelle de la victoire se répandit en un instant;* the news of the victory was spread abroad in an instant. — *en compliments;* to break out, to launch out, into compliments. — *en invectives;* to burst out, to launch out, into abuse. — *dans le monde;* to go out into society.

répandu, -e, *part.*, spilt, shed. *Être fort — dans le monde;* to go out into society, to mix a great deal in society, to go out a great deal.

réparable, *adj.*, repairable.

reparaître, *v.n.*, to reappear, to appear again, to appear anew, to make one's reappearance.

réparat-eur, -rice, *n.* and *adj.*, restorer, repairer; restorative, reparative. — *de torts;* redresser of grievances.

réparation, *n.f.*, repairing, mending; reparation, amends, satisfaction; *pl.*, repair, repairs. *Faire — à quelqu'un;* to make amends to any one.

réparatoire, *adj.*, reparative.

réparer, *v.a.*, to repair, to mend; to make amends for, to atone for, to redeem; to indemnify; to make up for; to re-establish, to recover, to recruit. — *ses affaires;* to mend one's fortune. — *ses forces;* to recruit one's strength. — *son honneur;* to retrieve one's honour. — *sa faute;* to make amends for one's faults. — *ses pertes;* to retrieve one's loss. — *des torts;* to redress grievances. — *le temps perdu;* to make up for lost time.

répareur, *n.m.,* (tech.) repairer.

réparition, *n.f.,* (astron.) reappearance of a star after an eclipse. *V* **réapparition.**

reparler, *v.n.,* to speak again.

repartie (-tî), *n.f.*, repartee, rejoinder, reply. *Avoir la — prompte, être prompt à la —;* to be quick at repartee. *Faire une —;* to make a repartee.

repartir, *v.n.*, to set out again, to set off again.

repartir, *v.a.* and *n.*, to reply, to answer, to repartee, to retort.

répartir, *v.a.*, to divide, to distribute; to portion out; to assess. — *les contributions;* to assess taxes.

répartiteur, *n.* and *adj.m.*, assessor; assessing (of taxes—*des impôts*).

répartition, *n.f.*, division, distribution; assessment.

repas, *n.m.*, meal, repast. — *de noces;* wedding entertainment. — *en gras;* meat dinner; meat breakfast. — *en maigre;* fish dinner; fish breakfast. *Faire un —;* to make a meal. *Faire ses —, prendre ses —;* to take one's meals.

repassage, *n.m.*, ironing (of linen—*du linge*); dressing (of a hat—*d'un chapeau*); grinding, setting, honing, whetting (of cutlery—*de coutellerie*); (agri.) raking.

repasser, *v.n.,* to pass again; to pass by again; to call again, to look in again. — *chez quelqu'un;* to call again on any one, to look in again on any one.

repasser, *v.a.,* to pass again, to repass; to cross again, to carry over again; to iron, to iron out; to grind, to set, to hone, to whet; to turn over, to think over, to revolve; to go over, to look over; to repeat; (dy.) to dye again; to curry a second time (leather—*les cuirs*); (fig., pop.) to beat; to find fault with, to abuse, to scold. — *une leçon;* to look over a lesson. — *du linge;* to iron linen. — *la lime sur;* to re-polish. — *quelque chose dans son esprit;* to re-volve a thing in one's mind. — *quelqu'un;* to

beat, to abuse, any one. — *sur un cuir;* to strop. — *sur la pierre;* to set, to whet. — *sur la meule;* to grind.

se repasser, *v.r.*, to be ironed; to be ground, sharpened, whetted.

repasseur, *n.m.,* pointer (of pins—*d'épingles*); grinder. — *de couteaux;* knife-grinder.

repasseuse, *n.f.,* ironer.

repassoir, *n.m.,* grinding-stone. — *à crayon;* pencil-pointer.

repaver, *v.a.*, to pave anew, to repave, to pave again.

repayer, *v.a.*, to pay again.

repêcher, *v.a.*, to fish up again; to take out of the water; to take out again, to take up again.

repeindre, *v.a.*, to paint again; to retouch, to touch up.

repeint, *n.m.*, (paint.) re-painted *or* restored parts of a picture.

repenser, *v.n.*, to think of again, to reconsider, to revolve.

repentance, *n.f.*, repentance, contrition.

repentant, -e, *adj.*, repentant, penitent.

repentie (-tî), *adj. n.f.*, penitent. *Les filles —s;* religious institution for penitent women.

se repentir (repentant, repenti), *v.r.*, to repent, to rue. — *de ses fautes;* to repent one's faults. *Il s'en repentira;* he will rue it.

repentir, *n.m.*, repentance, contrition, compunction, penitence; (paint.) pentamento, correction.

repercer, *v.a.*, to pierce again, to bore again; to tap again.

répercussi-f, -ve, *adj.*, (med.) repellent.

répercussif, *n.m.*, (med.) repellent.

répercussion, *n.f.*, repercussion; reverberation.

répercuter, *v.a.*, to repercuss, to drive back; to reverberate, to echo; to reflect; (med.) to repel, to drive in.

reperdre, *v.a.*, to lose again.

repère, *n.m.*, (arts) bench-mark; (mec.) datum.

répertoire, *n.m.*, table, list, catalogue; repertory; (com.) alphabet, alphabetical index. *Pièce qui fait partie du —, pièce restée au —* (thea.); stock-piece. *Être un —* (pers.); to be a living chronicle.

*répétailler, *v.a.*, to repeat over and over again.

répéter, *v.a.*, to repeat; to say again, to tell again; to repeat, to recite; to reflect; (jur.) to claim again, to demand again; to give private lessons to, to be private tutor to; (thea.) to rehearse. *Faire — à quelqu'un sa leçon;* to hear any one say his lesson. *Il répète ces deux élèves* (at school—*terme d'école*); he is private tutor to these two boys. — *une comédie;* to rehearse a comedy. — *une chose contre quelqu'un* (jur.); to claim a thing from any one.

se répéter, *v.r.*, to be repeated; to copy one's self; to be renewed; always to say the same thing.

répétiteur, *n.m.*, tutor, private master; assistant professor (of certain schools—*dans quelques collèges*); (nav.) repeater, repeating-ship.

répétition, *n.f.*, repetition; (jur.) recovering money paid for another; recovering money which one has paid too much; private tuition; (thea.) rehearsal. *Montre à —;* repeating-watch, repeater. *Faire des —s;* to teach in private, to give private tuition, to give private lessons.

repétrir, *v.a.*, to knead again; to form again.

repeuplement, *n.m.*, repeopling, stocking again. — *d'un étang;* re-stocking of a pond.

repeupler, *v.a.*, to repeople; to stock again. — *un étang;* to re-stock a pond.

se **repeupler**, *v.r.*, to be repeopled ; to be re-stocked.

repic, *n.m.*, repeek (piquet). (fig., fam.) *Faire quelqu'un — et capot ;* to nonplus any one.

repiquage, *n.m.*, (agri., gard.) transplantation of a young plant.

repiquer, *v.a.*, to prick again ; (hort.) to prick ; (agri.) to transplant ; (engineering—*terme d'ingénieur*) to pick up.

répit, *n.m.*, respite, reprieve, delay ; rest, breathing-time.

replacement (-plas-mān), *n.m.*, replacing, putting again, setting again ; placing (servants, &c.—*domestiques*, &c.) in a situation again ; reinvestment (of funds—*d'argent*).

replacer, *v.a.*, to replace, to put in place again ; to reinvest (funds—*de l'argent*).

replaider, *v.a.*, (jur.) to replead.

replantation, *n.f.*, replantation.

replanter, *v.a.*, to replant.

replâtrage, *n.m.*, re-plastering ; plastering, plastering up ; botching up, patching up ; insincere reconciliation, imperfect reconciliation.

replâtrer, *v.a.*, to replaster ; to plaster, to plaster up, to botch, to botch up, to patch up.

repl-et, **-ète**, *adj.*, obese, bulky, corpulent, stout, lusty, portly.

réplétion, *n.f.*, repletion, stoutness, fatness, surfeit.

repleuvoir, *v.i.*, to rain anew, again.

repli, *n.m.*, fold ; plait ; crease ; recess ; winding, sinuosity ; turning ; coil. *Les —s du serpent ;* the coils of the serpent. *Les plis et les —s du cœur humain ;* the inmost recesses, the innermost recesses, of the human heart.

repliement, *or* **reploiement**, *n.m.*, (milit.) falling back.

replier, *v.a.*, to fold again, to fold up again ; to wind, to twist, to writhe, to coil ; (milit.) to force back ; to draw back.

se **replier**, *v.r.*, to twist one's self, to wind one's self, to fold one's self, to writhe ; to turn, to turn up ; to bend up ; to wind, to coil ; (milit.) to fall back. — *sur soi-même :* to turn one's thoughts inwardly, to retire within one's self ; (man.) to turn suddenly round.

réplique, *n.f.*, reply, answer ; rejoinder ; (mus.) repeat ; (thea.) cue.

répliquer, *v.a.* and *n.*, to reply, to answer ; to rejoin, to return, to retort ; (jur.) to reply, to rejoin, to put in a rejoinder.

reploiement, *n.m.* V. **repliement**.

replonger, *v.a.*, to plunge again, to dip again, to duck again, to re-immerse, to immerse again.

se **replonger**, *v.r.*, to plunge anew, to plunge one's self anew, to plunge one's self again.

replonger, *v.n.*, to dive again, to dive anew.

reployer, *v.a.*, *se* **reployer**, *v.r.* V. **replier**, *se* **replier**.

repolir, *v.a.*, to repolish, to polish again, to polish anew.

répondant, *n.m.*, bail, surety, security ; (in schools—*terme d'école*) respondent ; clerk (who makes the responses in the church service—*qui répond la messe*).

répondre, *v.a.*, to answer, to reply, to write back ; to make the responses to.

répondre, *v.n.*, to answer, to reply ; to answer, to write back ; to lead, to go (of roads —*de routes*) ; to reach, to be heard (of sound—*du son*) ; to make a suitable return ; to correspond, to respond, to agree, to come up, to satisfy, to answer ; to be answerable, to be accountable, to be responsible, to be security ; (man.) to obey, to answer ; to maintain a thesis. — *à ceux qui appellent :* to answer those who call. — *ad rem ;* to give a direct answer, to answer to the point. — *en Normand ;* to answer

equivocally, to give a shuffling answer. *Pour — à ;* in answer to, in reply to. *Ces allées répondent au canal ;* these walks lead to the canal. — *à l'attente publique ;* to answer public expectation, to come up to public expectation. *Ne pas — à l'attente publique ;* not to answer public expectation, not to come up to public expectation, to fall short of public expectation. *Tout répond à nos vœux ;* everything falls out according to our wishes. *Qui pourrait — de l'événement ?* who could answer for the event ? *Je ne vous réponds que de moi ;* I only answer for myself. *Je vous en réponds ;* I answer for it ; I'll be bound for it !

se **répondre**, *v.r.*, to answer one's self ; to answer each other ; to correspond, to suit, to agree ; to sympathize, to sympathize with each other. *Nos cœurs se répondent ;* our hearts sympathize.

répons, *n.m.*, response (at church—*à l'église*) ; (print.) response.

réponse, *n.f.*, answer, reply ; response ; (jur.) joinder. — *à une réplique* (jur.) ; rejoinder. *À sotte demande point de — ;* a foolish question deserves no answer. — *de Normand ;* equivocal, shuffling, answer. *Faire — ;* to answer, to make answer. *Faire une — ;* to give an answer.

report, *n.m.*, (book-keeping—*comptabilité*) carrying over, carrying forward, bringing forward ; sum carried over, amount brought forward ; continuation, prolongation. *Faire un — ;* to bring forward ; (exchange language—*terme de bourse*) to make a continuation.

reporter (-teur), *n.m.* (—s), reporter (of a newspaper—*journalisme*).

reporter, *v.a.*, to carry back again, to carry back, to take back ; to trace back, to trace ; (book-keeping—*comptabilité*) to carry forward, to carry over.

se **reporter**, *v.r.*, to go back ; to return ; to be carried back.

reporter, *v.n.*, to make a continuation, a prolongation ; (exchange language—*terme de bourse*) to carry on.

repos, *n.m.*, rest ; stillness ; repose, ease, quiet, peace, tranquillity ; pause ; resting-place ; (carp.) quarter-pace. *En — ;* at rest. *Se tenir en — ;* to keep quiet. *Être en — ;* to be at ease. *Mettre en — ;* to make easy. *Laissez-moi en — ;* let me alone. *Lit de — ;* couch. *Mettre un fusil dans son —, au — ;* to half-cock a musket. *Échappement à — * (horl.) ; dead beat.

reposée, *n.f.*, (hunt.) lair.

reposer, *v.a.*, to place again, to lay again, to set again ; to rest (on anything—*sur quelque chose*) ; to lay ; to repose, to settle ; to refresh ; (milit.) to ground arms. *Cela repose la vue ;* that relieves the eye. — *la tête ;* to refresh, to ease the head.

se **reposer**, *v.r.*, to rest one's self, to rest, to repose, to lay one's self down, to lie down ; to rely on, to confide in ; to settle, to settle down ; to pause ; to light (of birds—*des oiseaux*). — *après le travail ;* to rest after labour. *Il faut que l'esprit se repose ;* the mind has need of repose. — *sur ;* to depend on, to rely on. — *sur quelqu'un ;* to rely on, to depend on, any one. — *sur quelqu'un pour une affaire ;* to entrust any one with an affair.

reposer, *v.n.*, to rest, to lie ; to repose ; to lay one's self down, to lie down ; to settle. *Laisser — * (agri.) ; to lay up (ground—*une terre*).

reposoir, *n.m.*, altar set up in the streets for a procession ; resting-place ; pause.

repoussant, **-e**, *adj.*, repulsive, repulsory, forbidding, repelling.

repoussement (-poos-mān). *n.m.*, recoil (of fire-arms—*d'armes à feu*). V. **recul**, which is more frequently used.

repousser, *v.a.*, to repel; to drive back; to beat back, to force back, to push back; to thrust back, to thrust away; to repulse. to repel, to resent; to rebuff; to shoot out again (of plants —*des plantes*); (print.) to prick in. — *l'ennemi;* to repulse the enemy. — *la force par la force;* to repel force by force. — *la tentation;* to repel temptation. — *une demande;* to reject a demand.

repousser, *v.n.*, to be repulsive; to recoil; to kick (of fire-arms—*des armes à feu*); to spring up, to come up again, to shoot up (of plants— *des plantes*); to grow again (of the hair—*des cheveux*).

repoussoir, *n.m.*, driving-bolt; punch (of a dentist—*de dentiste*); (paint.) set-off.

répréhensible, *adj.*, reprehensible.

répréhensi-f, **-ve**, *adj.*, reprehensive.

répréhension, *n.f.*, reprehension.

reprendre, *v.a.*, to take again; to take back; to take up again; to take to again; to catch again; (of diseases—*de maladies*) to return; to recover; to resume, to begin again; to rebuke; to take up, to reprove; to find fault with; (arch.) to underpin. — *connaissance:* to recover one's senses. — *une ville;* to take a town again. — *ses habits d'hiver;* to take to one's winter clothing again. *On ne m'y reprendra plus;* I will not be caught at it again. — *ses forces;* to recover one's strength. — *courage;* to take courage again. — *ses esprits;* to recover one's senses. — *haleine;* to recover one's breath, to breathe again; to take breath. — *le dessus;* to get the upper hand again. — *un mur sous œuvre, en sous-œuvre, par-dessous œuvre;* to underpin a wall. — *aigrement;* to reprove, to take up, sharply.

se reprendre, *v.r.*, to correct one's self, to take one's self up; to be caught again; (of wounds—*de plaies*) to close up again, to heal.

reprendre, *v.n.*, to take root again; (of wounds—*de plaies*) to close up again; to begin to recover; to begin again; to reply, to answer; to return; (man.) to change its pace; to freeze again (of rivers—*des rivières*); to return (of diseases—*de maladies*). *Cet arbre a bien repris;* this tree has taken root very well. *Le froid a repris;* the cold has set in again. *Cette mode a repris:* this fashion has come in again.

preneu-r, *n.m.*, **-se**, *n.f.*, carper, fault-finder.

*****représaille**, *n.f.*, reprisal, retaliation. *User de* —*s;* to make reprisals. *Lettres de* —*s;* letters of marque and reprisal.

représentant, *n.m.*, representative; representant.

représentati-f, **-ve**, *adj.*, representative.

représentation, *n.f.*, representation, exhibition, production, performance; display, show; appearance, mien; air; empty coffin and pall; remonstrance; (philos.) representativeness; (jur.) succession. *Il a une belle —;* he has a stately appearance, a noble deportment.

représenter, *v.a.*, to represent, to present again; to show; to show again; to exhibit; to lay before; to produce; to reflect; to depict; to describe; to look like, to resemble; to perform, to act (a play—*une pièce de théâtre*); to be the representative of; to stand in the place of. *Il se fit — les registres;* he had the registers laid before him. *Cela est représenté au naturel;* that is depicted to the life.

se représenter, *v.r.*, to present one's self again; to appear again; to make one's appearance again; to fancy, to imagine, to picture to one's self; to occur; to present itself again (of a thing—*d'une chose*).

représenter, *v.n.*, to represent, to set forth; to maintain, to keep, one's dignity; to have an imposing appearance.

répressi-f, **-ve**, *adj.*, repressive.

répression, *n.f.*, repression.

reprêter, *v.a.*, to lend again.

reprier, *v.a.*, to pray again.

réprimable, *adj.*, repressible, (that may be repressed.

réprimande, *n.f.*, reprimand, reproof. rebuke. *Faire une — à quelqu'un;* to reprimand any one.

réprimander, *v.a.*, to reprimand, to reprove. to rebuke, to upbraid; to lecture.

réprimant, **-e**, *adj.*, repressive.

réprimer, *v.a.*, to repress, to restrain, to curb, to quell, to keep down, to check. — *le vice;* to put down vice. — *l'orgueil;* to check pride. — *ses désirs;* to check one's desires. — *les abus;* to repress abuses. — *ses passions;* to curb one's passions.

repris, **-e**, *part.*, retaken, resumed, taken up again; reset (of a bone—*d'un os*).

repris de justice. *n.* and *adj.m.*, liberated convict. *Il a été —;* he is a liberated convict.

reprise, *n.f.*, resumption; retaking; taking back; recovery; reconquest; revival; renewal; darn; (mus.) repetition, mark of repetition; (arch.) underpropping, underpinning; (man.) lesson; recapture (of a ship—*d'un vaisseau*). *A plusieurs* —*s;* several times, repeatedly. *La* — *d'un procès;* the renewal of a lawsuit. *Faire des* —*s;* to darn. *Faire des* —*s perdues;* to fine-draw.

repriser, *v.a.*, to darn.

réprobat-eur, **-rice**, *adj.*, reproving, censuring.

réprobation, *n.f.*, reprobation.

reprochable, *adj.*, reproachable.

reproche, *n.m.*, reproach; expostulation; *pl.*, (jur.) exception, objections to the admissibility of a witness. *Un homme sans —;* a man free from reproach. *Faire un — à quelqu'un de quelque chose;* to reproach any one with anything. *Faire des* —*s amers à;* to reproach bitterly. *S'attirer des* —*s;* to incur reproach.

reprocher, *v.a.*, to reproach, to expostulate, to upbraid, to rebuke. — *à une personne quelque chose;* to reproach a person with anything. *Il lui a reproché ses défauts;* he reproached him with his faults. — *les morceaux à quelqu'un;* to grudge any one every bit he eats. — *des témoins* (jur.); to object to the admissibility of witnesses.

se reprocher, *v.r.*, to reproach one's self; to grudge one's self.

reproduct-eur, **-rice**, *adj.*, reproductive.

reproductibilité, *n.f.*, reproducibleness.

reproductible. *adj.*, reproducible.

reproducti-f, **-ve**, *adj.*, reproductive.

reproduction, *n.f.*, reproduction; reprinting, republication.

reproduire, *v.a.*, to produce again, to reproduce; to reprint, to republish.

se reproduire. *v.r.*, to come again; to be reproduced; to show one's self again; to occur again.

repromettre, *v.a.*, to promise again.

réprouvable, *adj.*, censurable, reprehensible, blamable.

réprouvé, *n.m.*, (theol.) reprobate. *Il a un visage de —;* he has a sinister-looking face.

réprouver, *v.a.*, to prove again.

réprouver, *v.a.*, to disapprove of, to disapprove, to reprobate.

reps (rèps), *n.m.*, repp (silk or woollen fabric —*étoffe de soie ou de laine*).

reptile, *n.m.* and *adj.*, reptile; creeping. *C'est un —;* he is a crawling wretch, a reptile.

républicain, **-e**, *n.* and *adj.*, republican.

républicaniser, *v.a.*, to make republican.

républicanisme, *n.m.*, republicanism.

republication, *n.f.*, republication.

republier, *v.a.*, to republish.

république, *n.f.*, republic; commonwealth. *La — des lettres;* the republic of letters.

répudiation, *n.f.*, repudiation, renunciation; rejection.

répudier, *v.a.*, to repudiate, to put away; to renounce, to reject.

*__répugnance__. *n.f.*, repugnance, dislike; reluctance, unwillingness, loathness. *J'ai de la — à le faire;* I am reluctant to do it. *Avec —;* with reluctance, reluctantly, repugnantly.

*__répugnant__, -e, *adj.*, repugnant.

*__répugner__, *v.n.*, to be repugnant, to be contrary, to clash with; to feel repugnance at; to feel reluctant. *Cela répugne au sens commun;* that is contrary to common sense. *Cet homme me répugne;* that man is my aversion. *Cela me répugne;* I have an aversion for that. *Il me répugne de vous entretenir d'un pareil sujet;* it is repugnant to me to talk to you on such a subject.

répulluler, *v.n.*, to repullulate; to abound, to swarm; to increase fast.

répulsi-f, -ve, *adj.*, (phys.) repulsive, repelling.

répulsion, *n.f.*, (phys.) repulsion; (fig.) aversion, disgust.

repurger, *v.a.*, to purge again.

réputation, *n.f.*, reputation, character, repute. *Avoir la — de;* to have the reputation of, to pass for. *Je ne vous connaissais que de —;* I only knew you by report. *En —;* in repute, in request. *Se faire une —;* to get a reputation. *Se mettre en —;* to get into repute. *Avoir de la —;* to have reputation, to have a name. *Être en — de;* to have the reputation of. *Perdre quelqu'un de —;* to ruin any one's reputation, character.

réputer, *v.a.*, to repute, to account, to reckon.

requérable, *adj.*, (jur.) that must be asked for by the creditor himself.

requérant, -e, *n.* and *adj.*, (jur.) plaintiff, applicant; suing.

requérir (requérant, requis), *v.a.*, to request, to beg; to require, to demand; to claim, to summon. *C'est lui qui m'en a requis;* he requested me to do it.

requête, *n.f.*, request, petition, demand, application; (hunt.) cast; a note on the horn to call back the dogs after a check, in order to make a cast. *Faire une —;* to make a request, a demand. *On accorda sa —;* his demand was granted.

requêter, *v.a.*, (hunt.) to search again, to make a cast.

requiem (-kui-èm), *n.m.*, requiem.

requin, *n.m.*, (ich.) shark.

requinqué, -e, *adj.*, (fam., iron.) spruce.

*se**requinquer**, *v.r.*,(fam., iron.) to deck one's self out.

requint, *n.m.*, (feudalism—*féodalité*) twenty-fifth (a *+ax—impôt*).

requis, -e. *part.*, requested, required, requisite. *Il a l'âge —;* he has the proper age.

réquisition, *n.f.*, requisition, application. *À la — ae;* at the application of.

réquisitoire,*n.m.*, (jur.) public prosecutor's address to the court.

resaluer, *v.a.*, to salute, to bow to, again.

resceller, *v.a.*, to seal again.

rescif (rè-cif), *n.m.* V. **récif**.

rescindant, *n.m.*, (jur., ant.) demand to annul an act or judgment.

rescinder, *v.a.*, (jur.) to annul. to rescind.

rescision (rès-si-zi-on), *n.f.*, (jur.) annulment, rescission.

rescisoire(rès-si-zoar),*n.m.*,(jur.)rescissory.

⊙**rescontre**, *n.m.*, (com.) bill-book.

rescousse, *n.f.*, ⊙ retaking of a person *or* of a thing carried off by force; help, rescue. *À la — :* help! help!

rescription, *n.f.*, order for the payment of money; check.

rescrit, *n.m.*, rescript; bull, rescript, edict of the Pope.

réseau, *n.m.*, net. net-work; (anat.) plexus; (arch.) tracery; (geom.) train (of triangles).

résection (ré-cèk-si-on), *n.f.*, (surg.) amputation of part of a diseased *or* broken bone.

réséda, *n.m.*, (bot.) reseda, mignonnette.

réséquer (ré-cé-), *v.a.*, (surg.) to perform *résection*, which see above.

réservation. *n.f.*, reserve, reservation.

réserve, *n.f.*, reserve, reservation, caution. *Se tenir sur la —;* to be reserved. *À la — de;* with the reservation of. *En —;* in reserve, in store. *Mettre en —;* to reserve, to lay by. *Sans —;* without reserve, unreservedly.

réservé, -e, *adj.*, reserved, cautious, wary, circumspect, shy.

réserver, *v.a.*, to reserve, to save, to set apart, to lay by, to lay up.

*se**réserver**, *v.r.*, to reserve, to reserve to one's self; to wait for an opportunity; to be kept. — *la réplique;* to reserve the right of replying. *Je me réserve de faire cela;* I am waiting for an opportunity to do that.

réserviste, *n.m.*, (milit.) reserve-man.

réservoir, *n.m.*, reservoir, tank for water; fish-pond, cistern, well ; (anat.) receptacle.

résidant, -e, *adj.*, resident, residing.

résidence, *n.f.*, residence, place of abode, dwelling, living. *Établir sa — à;* to fix one's abode at.

résident, *n.m.*, resident, minister at a foreign court.

résider, *v.n.*, to reside, to dwell, to live; to lie.

résidu, *n.m.*, settlement (of liquids—*de liquides*); residue; (arith.) remainder ; (chem.) residuum.

*__résignant__. *n.m.*, resigner.

*__résignataire__, *n.m.*, resignee.

*__résignation__, *n.f.*, resignation.

*__résigner__, *v.a.*, to resign, to give up.

*se**résigner**, *v.r.*, to resign one's self, to submit.

résiliation, *n.f.*, cancelling, annulling.

résiliement, *or* **résiliment**, *n.m.* V. **résiliation**.

résilier, *v.a.*, to cancel, to annul.

résille, *n.f.*, hair-net, a Spanish head-dress for females.

résine, *n.f.*, resin, rosin; colophany. *Un pain de —;* a cake of resin.

résineu-x, -se, *adj.*, resinous.

résinifère, *adj.*, yielding resin, resiniferous.

résipiscence (-zi-), *n.f.*, resipiscence, repentance. *Venir à —;* to repent.

résistance, *n.f.*, resistance, opposition ; (med.) obstinacy. *Pièce de —* (cook.); solid joint. *Sans —;* unresistingly. *Faire de la —;* to make resistance, to resist.

résistant, *adj.*, tough, firm, unyielding.

résister, *v.n.*, to resist, to oppose, to withstand ; to endure. — *à l'ennemi;* to resist the enemy. — *à la tentation;* to withstand temptation. *Je n'y saurais plus —;* I can no longer endure it.

résistible, *adj.*, resistible.

résolu, -e, *part.*, resolved on, decided, determined on, settled.

résolu. -e, *adj.*, resolute, bold, determined, stout-hearted.

résoluble, *adj.*, solvable. resolvable.

résolument, *adv.*, resolutely, boldly.

résoluti-f, -ve, *adj.*, (med.) resolutive; resolvent; discutient.

résolutif, *n.m.*, (med.) resolutive, resolvent.

résolution, *n.f.*, resolution, solution, decision, determination; resolve; (jur.) cancelling. *Avec —;* resolutely, stoutly. *Changer de —;* to alter one's mind. *— d'un contrat:* (jur.) cancelling of a contract.

résolutoire, *adj.*, (jur.) having the power of rendering void.

résolvant, -e, *adj.*, *n.m.*, (med.) resolvent.

résonance, *n.f.*, resonance.

résonnant, -e, *adj.*, resonant; sounding, sonorous. *Voix claire et —e;* clear and sonorous voice. *Un violon bien —;* a well-sounding violin.

résonnement (-zo·n·măn), *n.m.*, resound, resounding, clanking.

résonner, *v.n.*, to resound; to clank.

résorber (-zor-), *v.a.*, (med.) to reabsorb.

se résorber (-zor-), *v.r.*, (med.) to be reabsorbed.

résorption (-zor-), *n.f.*, reabsorption.

résoudre (résolvant, résolu), *v.a.*, to resolve; to dissolve, to melt; to solve; to decide, to settle; (jur.) to cancel, to make void; to resolve on, to determine on (a thing—*une chose*); to determine; to decide on; to persuade. *— une tumeur* (med.); to resolve a tumour. *— un problème;* to solve a problem. *— une question;* to settle a question. *— un bail;* to cancel a lease. *A-t-on résolu la paix ou la guerre?* has peace or war been resolved on?

se résoudre, *v.r.*, to resolve, to be resolved, to be solved; to dissolve, to be dissolved; to determine; to be prevailed upon. *L'eau se résout en vapeur;* water is resolved into vapour. *— à;* to resolve on; to bring one's self to. *A quoi vous résolvez-vous?* what resolution have you come to? *Je ne saurais m'y résoudre;* I cannot bring myself to it.

résous, *part.*, resolved, dissolved, melted. [*Résous* has no feminine.]

respect (rès-pè), *n.m.*, respect, regard, reverence, deference, dutifulness; ⊙relation, reference. *Porter — à quelqu'un;* to show respect to any one. *Manquer de — envers quelqu'un;* to be wanting in respect towards any one. *Assurer quelqu'un de ses —s;* to present one's respects to any one. *Présenter ses —s à quelqu'un;* to pay one's respects to any one. *Se faire porter —;* to make one's self respected. *Imprimer le — à;* to impress with respect, to awe. *Tenir en —;* to keep in awe. *Sauf votre —;* saving your presence.

respectable (rès-pèk-), *adj.*, respectable, venerable.

respecter (rès-pèk-), *v.a.*, to respect, to reverence, to revere. *— la vieillesse;* to respect old age.

se respecter (rès-pèk-té), *v.r.*, to respect one's self; to respect each other.

respecti-f, -ve (rès-pèk-), *adj.*, respective.

respectivement (rès-pèk-tiv-măn), *adv.*, respectively.

respectueusement (rès-pèk-tu-euz-măn), *adv.*, respectfully, reverentially, dutifully.

respectueu-x, -se (rès-pèk-), *adj.*, respectful, reverential, dutiful.

respirable (rès-), *adj.*, respirable, vital.

respiration (rès-), *n.f.*, respiration, breathing. *Difficulté de —;* shortness of breath. *Avoir la — coupée;* to be unable to fetch one's breath.

respiratoire (rès-pi-ra-toar), *adj.*, respiratory.

respirer (rès-pi-ré), *v.n.*, to breathe, to respire; to take breath, to rest; to long for. *Il a de la peine à —;* he can scarcely breathe. *— après quelque chose;* to long for any thing, to desire any thing ardently.

respirer (rès-), *v.a.*, to breathe, to inhale;

to thirst after, to long for. *Il ne respire que la vengeance;* he thirsts after vengeance.

resplendir (rès-plăn-), *v.n.*, to shine brightly; to be resplendent.

resplendissant, -e (rès-plăn-), *adj.*, resplendent, bright, glittering.

resplendissement (rès-plăn-dis-măn), *n.m.*, resplendence.

responsabilité (rès-), *n.f.*, responsibility, liability.

responsable (rès-), *adj.*, responsible, answerable, liable.

responsi-f, -ve (rès-), *adj.*, (jur.) responsory.

ressac (rè-sak), *n.m.*, (nav.) surf.

*****ressaigner** (rè-sè-), *v.a.* and *n.*, to bleed again.

ressaisir (-rè-sè-zir), *v.a.*, to seize again, to take again, to recover possession of.

se ressaisir (rè-sè-zir), *v.r.*, to seize again, to recover possession of.

ressasser (rè-sa-sé), *v.a.*, to sift again; to bolt again; to examine minutely; to scrutinize.

ressaut (rè-sô), *n.m.*, (arch.) ressault.

ressauter (rè-sô-té), *v.a.n.*, to leap again; (arch.) to project.

ressécher (rè-sé-), *v.a.*, to dry again.

resseller (rè-sè-lé), *v.a.*, to saddle again.

ressemblance (rè-săn-), *n.f.*, resemblance, likeness. *Se tromper à la —;* to be deceived by the likeness.

ressemblant, -e (rè-săn-), *adj.*, resembling, like.

ressembler (rè-săn-), *v.n.*, to resemble, to be like, to take after. *Le fils ressemble à son père;* the son resembles his father. *Ce portrait vous ressemble peu;* this portrait is not much like you.

se ressembler (rè-săn-), *v.r.*, to resemble one another, to be like each other, to be alike; to be uniform. *Ils se ressemblent comme deux gouttes d'eau;* they are as like as two peas. *Qui se ressemble, s'assemble;* birds of a feather flock together.

ressemelage (rè-sè-mlaj), *n.m.*, soling, new soling (of boots or shoes—*de chaussures*); new footing (of stockings—*de bas*).

ressemeler (rè-sè-mlé), *v.a.*, to sole anew (boots or shoes—*des chaussures*); to foot anew (stockings—*des bas*).

ressemer (rè-sè-mé), *v.a.*, to sow again.

ressenti, -e (rè-săn-), *part.*, felt; (paint.) strongly expressed.

ressentiment (rè-săn-), *n.m.*, slight return, attack, touch (of disease, pain—*d'un mal, d'une douleur*); desire of vengeance, resentment. *Avec —;* resentingly. *Plein de —;* resentful.

ressentir (rè-săn-), *v.a.* to feel, to experience; to manifest, to show; to have a sense of. *— du malaise;* to feel uncomfortable. *Elle ressent vivement cette injure;* she feels that insult deeply.

se ressentir (rè-săn-), *v.r.*, to feel the effects of, to perceive, to resent; to feel (disease, pain —*un mal, une douleur*). *Il se ressent encore de ses pertes;* he still feels the effects of his losses. *— d'une injure;* to resent an injury.

resserrement (rè-sèr-măn), *n.m.*, contraction; (med.) stricture, contraction. *— d'argent;* restriction in the circulation of money.

resserrer (rè-sè-ré), *v.a.*, to tie again; to tie tighter, to bind tighter, to compress, to contract, to straighten; to rivet; to put up again; to keep more closely; to restrain, to confine; (print.) to lock up again; (nav.) to take in sails again; (milit.) to close again. *— une rivière dans son lit;* to confine a river to its bed. *Le froid resserre les pores;* cold contracts the pores.

se resserrer (rè-sè-ré), *v.r.*, to contract, to be contracted; to be narrower, closer; to confine one's self; to be compressed; to become tighter;

ressif (rè-sif), *n.m.* *V.* **récif.**

ressort (rè-sor), *n.m.,* spring; elasticity; energy; activity, force; means. *Faire —;* to fly back. *Il n'agit que par —;* he only acts at the instigation of others. *Faire jouer tous ses —s;* to use every effort.

ressort (rè-sor-), *n.m.,* extent of jurisdiction; department. province; (jur.) resort. *En dernier —;* (jur.) in the last resort: without appeal. *Cela n'est pas de mon —;* that is not my province.

ressortir (rè-sor-), *v.n.,* to go out again; to be set off (of a thing—*d'une chose*). *Faire —;* to bring forward, to show off.

ressortir (rè-sor-), *v.n.,* (jur.) to be under the jurisdiction of; to be appealable to a court.

ressortissant -e, (rè-sor-), *adj.,* (jur.) appealable.

ressouder (rè-soo-), *v.a.,* to solder again.

ressource (rè-soors), *n.f.,* resource, expedient; *pl.,* resources. *Faire —;* to procure resources. *C'est ma dernière —;* that is my last shift. *— désespérée;* despeiate expedient. *Un malheur sans --;* an irreparable misfortune. *Je suis perdu, ruiné, sans —;* I am irretrievably ruined. *Il n'y a point de —;* there's no help for it. *C'est un homme de —;* he is a man fertile in expedients.

Ⓒ**ressouvenance** (rè-soo-vnans), *n.f.,* remembrance.

ressouvenir (rè-soo-vnir), *n.m.,* remembrance, recollection.

se ressouvenir (rè-soo-vnir), *v.r.,* to recollect, to remember. *Faire ressouvenir;* to put in mind. *Vous en ressouvient-il?* do you remember it?

ressuage (rè-), *n.m.,* (tech.) sweating; (metal.) eliquation.

ressuer (rè-), *v.n.,* (metal.) to eliquate; (tech.) to sweat.

ressui (rè-), *n.m.,* lair, where animals dry themselves of dew or rain.

ressusciter (rè-), *v.a.,* to resuscitate, to raise from the dead, to bring to life again, to revive.

ressusciter (rè-), *v.n.,* to rise from the dead, to come to life again, to be resuscitated.

ressuyer (rè-), *v.n.,* to wipe, to dry, again.

se ressuyer (rè-), *v.r.,* to dry; to air (of linen —*du linge*).

restant. -e, (rès-), *adj.,* remaining, left. *Poste —e;* till called for.

restant (rès-), *n.m.,* remainder, rest.

Ⓞ**restaur** (rès-), *n.m.,* (com.). *V.* **ristourne.**

restaurant, -e (rès-), *adj.,* restorative.

restaurant (rès-), *n.m.,* restorative; eatinghouse, dining-rooms.

restaurat-eur, *n.m.,* **-rice,** (rès-), *n.f.,* restorer.

restaurateur (rès-), *n.m.,* eating-house keeper.

restaurati-f, -ve (rès-) *adj.,* (med) restorative.

restauration (rès-), *n.f.,* restoration. reestablishment.

restaurer (rès-), *v.a.,* to restore; to reestablish; to revive. *— ses forces;* to restore one's strength.

se restaurer (rès-), *v.r.,* to take refreshment.

reste, *n.m.,* rest, remainder, remnant, remains, residue, scrap, relic, leavings; *pl.,* mortal remains. *Avoir de —;* to have something left and to spare. to have remaining. *De —;* left, remaining, enough and more than enough. *Les —s mortels;* mortal remains. *Les —s de l'antiquité;* the remains of antiquity. *Et le —;* and so forth, et cætera *Faire son —;*

to stake all the money one has left. *Jouer de son —;* to play one's last stake. *Donner son — à quelqu'un;* to give it to, to abuse, to beat any one. *Il ne demanda pas son —;* he did not wait for any thing more, he sneaked off. *Être en —;* to be behindhand, to be in arrears. *Il n'y a rien de —;* there is nothing left. *J'en ai de —;* I have more than enough. *Du —;* however, nevertheless. *Au —;* besides.

rester, *v.n.,* to remain, to be left; to stay, to stop, to continue, to keep; (mus.) to hold; (nav.) to bear. *C'est tout ce qui me reste;* that is all I have left. *Il reste quelque argent;* there is some money left. *Que me reste-t-il à faire!* what remains for me to do? *Il me reste à vous dire;* I have still to tell you. *Il resta à Rome après notre départ;* he staid at Rome after our departure. *Il est resté stupéfait;* he stood thunder-struck. *Restez tranquille;* keep quiet, keep still. *— chez soi;* to stay at home. *Où en sommes-nous restés?* where did we leave off? *Restons-en là;* let us stop there.

restituable (rès-), *adj.,* repayable, to be restored, to be refunded.

restituer (rès-), *v.a.,* to restore, to return, to give back again, to refund. *— un passage d'un livre;* to restore a passage in a book.

restituteur (rès-), *n.m.,* restorer (of the texts of authors—*des textes d'anciens auteurs*); also said of the Emperors who have had medals made in memory of their predecessors.

restitution (rès-), *n.f.,* restitution, restoration; (jur.) relief.

restreindre (rès-), (restreignant, restreint), *v.a.,* to restrict, to restrain, to limit, to confine, to stint.

se restreindre (rès-), *v.r.,* to restrain one's self, to limit one's self.

restricti-f, -ve (rès), *adj.,* restrictive.

restriction (rès-), *n.f.,* restriction, restraint; reserve. *— mentale;* mental reservation.

restringent, -e (rès-), *adj.,* (med.) (l.u.) astringent.

restringent. *n.m.,* (med) (l.u.) astringent.

résultant, -e, *adj.,* resulting, arising, resultant.

résultante. *n.f.,* (mec.) resultant.

résultat, *n.m.,* result.

résulter, *v.n.,* to result, to follow. to be the consequence. *Que résulte-t-il de là?* what follows from that? *Qu'en peut-il —?* what can be the consequence of it.

résumé, *n.m.,* recapitulation, summary; abridgment; epitome; short account; resumé; (jur.) summing up of a judge. *Au —, en —;* upon the whole, after all, to sum up.

résumer, *v.a.,* to recapitulate, to sum up, to give a summary. *— un discours;* to give a summary of a speech.

se résumer, *v.r.,* to recapitulate, to sum up; to be summed up.

résumption (-zoup-sion), *n.f.,* resumption.

résurrecti-f, -ve, *adj.,* life-giving, life-restoring.

résurrection. *n.f.,* resurrection, rising.

résurrectionniste, *n.m.,* resurrectionist, stealer of dead bodies.

retable, *n.m.,* (arch.) altar screen.

rétablir, *v.a.,* to re-establish, to restore, to repair; to recover; to re-instal; to set up again. *— son honneur;* to retrieve one's honour. *— sa santé;* to recover one's health. *— quelqu'un;* to set any one up again.

se rétablir, *v.r.,* to recover one's health; to be re-established, restored, repaired. *Le crédit commence à —;* credit is beginning to be restored.

rétablissement (-blis-màn), *n.m.,* reestablishment, restoration, repairing, recovery, reinstatement, revival, recovery of health.

Sans espoir de — ; past recovery. — *dans les bonnes grâces de quelqu'un*; restoration to any one's good graces. — *du commerce*; revival of commerce.

retaille, n.f., (manu.) piece cut off.

retailler, v.a., to cut, to mend again (pens, pencils—*les plumes, les crayons*); to prune again.

rétamage, n.m., tinning over again.

rétamer, v.a., to tin over again.

rétameur, n.m., tinker.

retaper, v.a., ⊙to cock (a hat—*un chapeau*); to do up (a hat—*un chapeau*); to dress and powder (a wig—*une perruque*). — *les cheveux*; to turn up the hair.

retard, n.m., delay; (mus.) retardation; slowness (of a clock—*d'une horloge, d'une pendule, d'une montre*). *Apporter du* — ; to cause delay. *Éprouver du* — ; to suffer delay. *Être en* — ; to be late; to be in arrears; to be backward, to be behind time. *Votre montre est en* — *de deux minutes*; your watch is two minutes too slow.

retardataire, n.m. and adj., person in arrears; recruit that has not joined his regiment; in arrears; late, behindhand, tardy.

retardat-eur,-rice, adj., (phys.) retarding.

retardation, n.f., (phys.) retardation.

retardement, n.m., delay, retardment.

retarder, v.a., to retard, to delay, to defer, to put off; to hinder; to put back (clocks and watches—*horloges, pendules, montres*). — *une horloge* : to put a clock back.

retarder, v.n., to lose, to go too slow (of clocks and watches—*horloges, pendules, montres*); to come later. *Ma montre retarde*; my watch loses. *Sa fièvre retarde tous les jours d'environ une heure*; his fit of ague comes on one hour later every day.

retâter, v.a., to touch and feel again; to grope about again; to try, to begin again.

se **retâter, v.r.**, to examine, to see, to ponder on, to revolve in one's mind, to consider.

reteindre, v.a., to dye again.

retendre, v.a., to bend again; to stretch or pull again, to stretch again, to spread again.

retenir, v.a., to get again; to get hold of again; to retain, to keep, to withhold, to keep back; to reserve; to curb; to bespeak, to hire; to secure; to detain, to keep, to confine; to hold back, to hinder; to restrain, to keep from; to remember; (arith.) to carry. — *l'accent de son pays*; to retain the accent of one's country. *Posez sept et retenez deux* (arith.); set down seven and carry two. — *un logement*; to hire a lodging. — *une place à la diligence*; to bespeak a place in the coach. — *un domestique*; to engage a servant. *Il ne saurait* — *sa langue*; he cannot restrain his tongue. — *sa colère*; to bridle one's anger. *Qu'est-ce qui vous retient*? what hinders you? *Je ne sais ce qui me retient*; I know not what hinders me. — *une poutre* (carp.); to secure a beam. — *quelqu'un*; to detain any one.

se **retenir, v.r.**, to keep back, to forbear; to control one's self; to stop; to seize hold; (man.) to hold back.

retenir, v.n., to hold back (of horses—*des chevaux*); to breed (of mares, &c.—*des juments, &c.*).

rétenti-f, -ve, adj., retentive.

rétention, n.f., reservation, retention; (jur.) retaining.

rétentionnaire, n.m., (jur.) detainer, one who detains.

retentir, v.n., to resound, to ring, to re-echo.

retentissant, -e, adj., resounding, ringing, echoing. *Voûte* —*e*; echoing vault.

retentissement (-tis-mān), **n.m.**, resounding, echo, re-echoing.

retentum (ré-tin-tom), **n.m.**, mental reserve; (jur.) ⊙tacit clause.

retenu, -e (ré-tnu), **adj.**, circumspect, reserved, cautious, discreet, wary ; prudent, coy, shy.

retenue, n.f., reservedness, reserve, discretion, circumspection, caution, prudence; (fin.) stoppage. *Il faut avoir de la* — ; one must observe propriety. *Être en* — ; to be kept in (at school—*à l'école*).

reterçage, *or* **retersage, n.m.**, second dressing (of vines—*des vignes*).

retercer, *or* **reterser, v.a.**, to dress vines again.

rétiaire (-ci-èr), **n.m.**, (antiq.) net-fighter (a kind of gladiator—*sorte de gladiateur*).

réticence, n.f., reserve, concealment; (rhet.) reticence.

réticulaire, adj., (anat.) reticular.

réticule, n.f., reticule (of a telescope—*d'un télescope*).

réticulé, -e, adj., (arch., bot.) reticulated.

réti-f, -ve, n. and adj., restive person; restive.

rétiforme, adj., retiform.

rétine, n.f., (anat.) retina.

⊙**retirade, n.f.**, (fort.) retirade.

retiration, n.f., (print.) printing of the 2nd page, of the inner form, reteration, backing.

retiré, -e, adj., retired, lonesome, secluded.

retirement (-tir-mān), **n.m.**, (surg.) contraction of the nerves and muscles.

retirer, v.a., to re-draw, to draw again; to draw back; to withdraw; to draw out; to take away; to redeem, to recover; to receive; to lodge, to shelter; to fire off again; to remove (from school, prison—*de l'école, de prison*); to derive profit. — *sa parole*; to call back one's word. — *quelqu'un de prison*; to remove any one from prison. — *des choses qui étaient en gage*; to take things out of pawn. — *son enjeu*; to withdraw one's stakes. — *de la gloire*; to derive glory.

se **retirer, v.r.**, to retire, to withdraw, to go away; (of water—*des eaux*) to subside, to recede; to retire from; to leave; to quit; to shrink, to contract. *Retirez-vous*; leave the room; be off; (jur.) you can go down (to witnesses—*aux témoins*). *Il s'est retiré du service*; he has quitted the service. — *du commerce*; to retire from business. — *en lieu de sûreté*; to retire to a place of safety. *Il se retire de bonne heure*; he keeps good hours. *Ils se retirèrent chacun chez eux*; they retired to their respective homes.

retirer, v.n., to withdraw, to ebb, to go down (of the tide—*de la marée*).

⊙**retoiser, v.a.**, to measure again.

retombée, n.f., (arch.) springing of an arch.

retomber, v.n., to fall again; to relapse, to fall down again; to fall. — *malade*; to fall ill again. — *dans la même faute*; to relapse into the same fault. *Le blâme retombe sur lui-même*; the blame falls upon himself.

retondre, v.a., to shear again; (arch.) to clean off, to cut away useless ornaments.

retordage, n.m., (manu.) twisting.

retordement, n.m., (manu.) twisting.

retordeur, n.m., twister, throwster.

retordre, v.a., to wring again, to twist again; to twist (silk, thread—*soie, fil*). *Donner du fil à* — *à quelqu'un*; to cut out work for any one, to give any one a great deal of trouble.

rétorquer, v.a., to retort.

retors, -e, adj., twisted; artful, cunning. *Un homme* — ; a cunning man.

rétorsion, n.f., act of retorting.

retorte, n.f., (chem.) retort. *V.* **cornue.**

*retortiller, v.a.**, to twist again.

retouche, *n.f.,* (paint.) retouching.

retoucher, *v.n.,* to touch again, to retouch ; to touch up, to improve.

retoucher, *v.a.,* to retouch again, to touch up, to improve.

retour, *n.m.,* return, coming back ; turning ; winding ; conversion ; (jur.) reversion ; (arch.) return ; thing given in ; acknowledgment ; decline of life ; artifice, trick ; vicissitude ; (nav.) homeward voyage. *Le — du printemps :* the return of the spring. *À mon — ;* on my return. *Sans — ;* for ever, irreparably, irrecoverably, irretrievably. *Être de — ;* to have returned. *Être sur son — ;* to be upon the point of returning. *Être sur le — ;* to be upon the decline of life, to be going downhill. *Avoir de fâcheux —s :* to be odd, whimsical. *Il n'y a point de — avec lui ;* there is no peace to be made with him ; there is no end to his resentment. *Amour qui n'est pas payé de — ;* unrequited love. *À beau jeu beau —,* one good turn deserves another. *La fortune a ses —s.* fortune has her vicissitudes. *— de chasse ;* luncheon after hunting. *Quel — me donnerez-vous !* what will you give me to boot ? *Faire un — sur soi-même ;* to examine one's self. *En — de ;* in return for. *Je serai de — à midi ;* I shall be back at twelve.

retourne, *n.f.,* turn-up card, trump-card, trumps.

retourner, *v.n.,* to return, to go again, to go back, to go back again ; to turn up (at cards *—aux cartes*). *— sur ses pas ;* to retrace one's steps. *— en arrière ;* to turn back. *— à son travail ;* to return to one's work. *N'y retournez pas ;* don't do that again. *Il retourne cœur ;* hearts are trumps. *oyons de quoi il retourne* (pop.) ; let us see what's going on.

retourner, *v.a.,* to turn, to turn up ; to revolve, to turn over ; to turn (clothes*—des vêtements*). *— un habit ;* to turn a coat. *— du foin ;* to turn hay. *— une carte ;* to turn up a card.

se **retourner,** *v.r.,* to turn, to turn round ; to turn one's self. *S'en retourner :* to return home, to go back again, to turn back.

retracer, *v.a.,* to trace again, to retrace, to trace ; to recount, to relate.

se **retracer,** *v.r.,* to retrace, to recall to mind, to remember ; to return, to recur.

rétractation, *n.f.,* retractation, recantation.

rétracter, *v a,* to retract, to recall, to recant.

se **rétracter,** *v.r.,* to retract ; to make a retraction ; to recant. *— de ce qu'on a dit ;* to retract what one has said.

rétractile, *adj.,* retractile.

rétractilité, *n.f.,* retractility.

rétraction, *n.f.,* (med.) retraction.

retraduire, *v.a.,* to translate again.

retraire, *v a,* (jur.) to redeem an estate.

retrait, -e, *adj.,* lean, shrunk (grain) ; shrunk (of wood *—du bois*).

retrait, *n.m.,* (jur.) redemption, regaining possession ; withdrawal (of a bill in parliament, of money from a bank *—d'un projet de loi, d'argent d'une banque*) ; (arch.) off-set ; shrinking, contraction (of clay, metals *—de l'argile, des métaux*). *— conventionnel ;* (jur.) re-emption. *Le — d'un projet de loi ;* the withdrawal of a bill in parliament. *— d'emploi* (milit.) ; being unattached, being on half-pay by punishment (of officers *—officiers*).

retraite, *n.f.,* retreat ; retiring ; retirement ; refuge, hiding-place, haunt, lurking-place ; retiring pension, pension ; shrinking, contraction (of clay, of metals *—de l'argile, des métaux*) ; (arch.) offset ; nail (in the foot of a horse *—dans l'ongle d'un cheval*) ; (milit.) tattoo ; (com.)

redraft. *Battre en — ;* to retreat, to draw off. *Sonner la — ;* (hunt.) to call off the hounds ; (milit.) to sound a retreat. *Donner — à quelqu'un ;* to shelter any one, to harbour any one. *— de roleurs ;* resort, den, of thieves. *Donner à quelqu'un sa — ;* to pension any one off. *Battre la —* (milit.) ; to beat the tattoo. *Officier en — ;* retired officer.

retraité, -e, *n.* and *adj.,* one who is pensioned off, superannuated ; on the retired list. *Officier — ;* officer on the retired list. *Un — ;* one who is pensioned off.

retranchement (-trǎnsh-mǎn), *n.m.,* retrenchment, abridging, curtailment ; (milit.) retrenchment, intrenchment. *Forcer quelqu'un dans ses —s ;* to force any one in his stronghold.

retrancher, *v.a.,* to retrench, to curtail, to cut short ; to cut off ; (arith.) to subtract ; to take away, to abridge ; to deduct ; (milit. to intrench. *— un camp ;* to intrench a camp.

se **retrancher,** *v.r.,* to restrain one's self ; to confine one's self ; to retrench, to curtail one's expenses ; (milit.) to intrench one's self

retranscrire, *v.a.,* to copy out again.

***retravailler,** *v.a.,* to work again, to do over again.

retraverser, *v.a.,* to cross, to traverse again.

retrayant, *n.m.,* **-e,** *n.f.,* (jur.) party recovering possession ; repurchaser ; re-emptor.

rêtre. *n.m.* V. **reitre.**

rétréci, -e, *adj.,* narrow, cramped, contracted, confined.

rétrécir, *v.a.,* to take in, to straiten, to make narrower, to contract ; to narrow, to cramp ; to shrink ; to limit. *— l'âme ;* to narrow the soul. *— un cheval* (man.) ; to make a horse narrow.

se **rétrécir,** *v.r.,* to become narrow, to grow strait ; to shrink, to contract ; to be cramped, contracted, straitened.

rétrécir, *v.n.,* to narrow, to shrink up.

rétrécissement (-sis-mǎn), *n.m.,* narrowing, shrinking, cramping ; contracting ; narrowness, contractedness ; (med.) stricture.

rétreindre, *v.a.,* to hammer out a piece of metal.

retremper, *v.a.,* to temper again (metal.) ; to give renewed force to.

se **retremper,** *v.r.,* to acquire renewed strength.

rétribué, -e, *adj.,* remunerated, rewarded.

rétribuer, *v.a.,* to remunerate, to requite, to reward ; to give a salary, a fee, to.

rétribution, *n.f.,* retribution, reward.

rétroacti-f, -ve. *adj.,* retroactive.

rétroaction, *n.f.,* retroaction.

rétroactivement (-tiv-mǎn), *adv.,* retroactively.

rétroactivité, *n.f.,* retroactive quality.

rétroagir, *v.n.,* to have a retroactive effect.

rétrocéder, *v.a.,* (jur.) to reconvey ; to reassign.

rétrocession, *n.f.,* (jur.) retrocession, redemise, reconveyance.

rétrogradation, *n.f.,* (astron.) retrogradation, retrogression, retrocession.

rétrograde. *adj.,* retrograde.

rétrograder, *v.n.,* to retrograde, to go backward ; to go back.

rétrospecti-f, -ve. *adj.,* retrospective.

retroussé, -e, *part.,* turned up, tucked up, cocked up. *Nez — ;* snub nose, turned-up nose. *Avoir le bras — ;* to have one's sleeves tucked up.

retroussement (-troos-mǎn), *n.m.,* turning up, tucking up, cocking up.

retrousser, *v.a.,* to turn up, to tuck up, to cock ; to tie up ; (nav.) to truss up sails. *—*

sa robe; to tuck up one's gown. — *sa moustache;* to turn up one's moustaches.

se retrousser, *v.r.,* to turn up, to cock up; to turn up, to tie up; to tuck up one's gown.

retroussis, *n.m.,* cock, flap (of a hat—*d'un chapeau*); boot-top, top (of a boot—*de botte*); facing (of a uniform, livery—*d'un uniforme, d'une livrée*).

retrouver, *v.a.,* to find again, to recover; to recognize; to meet again.

se retrouver, *v.r.,* to find one another again; to find one's self again; to be found again; to be met with again.

rets (ré), *n.m.,* net, netting, snare.

réunion, *n.f.,* reunion, union,' junction; meeting, assembly; company. *Salle de —;* assembly-room. *Maison de —;* meeting-house.

réunir, *v.a.,* to reunite, to join again, to bring together again, to reannex; to unite, to join, to bring together, to annex; to collect, to assemble, to muster; to call together, to combine; to reconcile, to unite. — *des faits;* to collect facts.

se réunir, *v.r.,* to reunite, to unite, to join, to join again, to unite again; to be united, to be joined, to be collected; to meet (at an appointed place—*à un endroit indiqué*); to gather, to collect, to come together, to assemble, to muster, to club together, to combine, to blend, to be blended.

réussir, *v.n.,* to succeed, to prosper, to thrive, to be successful, to have success. — *à faire quelque chose;* to succeed in doing any thing. *Il a mal réussi;* he was unsuccessful. *Ce projet n'a pas réussi;* that design did not succeed. *Tout ce qu'il entreprend lui réussit;* everything he undertakes thrives with him. *Les pommiers réussissent dans ce terrain;* apple-trees thrive in this soil.

réussite, *n.f.,* success; issue, end, event, result; successfulness.

revacciner, *v.a.,* to revaccinate.

revalidation, *n.f.,* (jur.) rendering valid again.

revalider, *v.a.,* (jur.) to make valid again.

revaloir, *v.a.,* to return like for like; to be even with. *Il me le revaudra;* he shall pay for it, I will be even with him.

revanche, *n.f.,* revenge, retaliation; return; revenge (at play—*au jeu*). *Avoir sa —;* to have one's revenge; to have one's turn. *Prendre sa —;* to take vengeance; to return like for like. *En —;* by way of retaliation; in return.

revancher, *v.a.,* (fam.) to defend; to revenge; to return like for like.

se revancher, *v.r.,* (fam.) to defend one's self; to be revenged; to revenge; to return like for like; to have one's turn. — *d'un bienfait;* to return a benefit.

revancheur, *n.m.,* (l.u.) defender.

rêvasser, *v.n.,* to have troubled dreams, to have unquiet dreams; to dream; to muse. — *à une affaire;* to muse over a matter, to ponder over a matter.

rêvasserie (-va-srī), *n.f.,* unconnected dreams; musing, dreaming.

rêvasseur, *n.m.,* dreamer, muser.

rêve, *n.m.,* dream; idle fancy, day-dream, vision.

revêche, *adj.,* sharp, harsh, rough; stubborn, unruly, cross, untractable, ill-natured, dogged, cross-grained. *Diamant —;* diamond not polishable in all its parts.

rêve-creux, *n.m.* (—), dreamer, fancymonger.

*****réveil,** *n.m.,* waking, awaking; waking-time; (horl.) alarum, alarm; alarm-watch,

alarm-clock; (milit.) reveille. *À mon —;* on my awaking.

.*réveille-matin, *n.m.* (—), alarm-clock, alarum; chanticleer, cock; disturber of morning repose; (bot.) wartwort, spurge.

*****réveiller,** *v.a.,* to awake, to wake, to rouse, to rouse up, to call up; to stir up, to quicken, to revive. — *des souvenirs fâcheux;* to recall disagreeable recollections.

*****se réveiller,** *v.r.,* to wake, to awake, to wake up, to awaken; to revive; to be roused, to be renewed, to be awakened. *Sa haine se réveilla;* his hatred was roused. — *de son assoupissement;* to awake from one's lethargy. — *en sursaut;* to start up out of one's sleep.

*****réveillon,** *n.m.,* collation in the middle of the night; (paint.) strong touch of light.

révélat-eur, *n.m.,* **-rice,** *n.f.,* informer, revealer, discoverer, detector. — *d'un complot;* revealer of a plot. *Être le — de ses complices;* to be the impeacher of one's accomplices; (jur.) to be king's, queen's, evidence.

révélation, *n.f.,* revelation; discovery, disclosure; (jur.) information.

révéler, *v.a.,* to reveal, to discover, to lay open, to disclose, to detect; to betray; (fam., pop.) to blab.

revenant, -e, *adj.,* pleasing, prepossessing. *Physionomie —e;* pleasing physiognomy.

revenant (rĕ-vnän), *n.m.,* ghost, spirit. *Il y a des —s dans cette maison;* that house is haunted.

revenant-bon, *n.m.* (—*s* —*s*), perquisite; bonus; advantage, gain, emolument.

revendeu-r, *n.m.,* **-se,** *n.f.,* retail-dealer, retailer; dealer in old clothes; regrater. — *se à la toilette;* old clothes-woman.

revendication, *n.f.,* (jur.) claiming, demand. *Action en —* (jur.); action in pursuit of a claim.

revendiquer, *v.a.,* to claim, to demand; to reclaim.

revendre, *v.a.,* to sell again; to regrate. *Il en a à —;* he has enough of it, and to spare. *En — à quelqu'un;* to be deeper than any one.

revenir (rĕ-vnir), *v.n.,* to come again, to come back, to come back again, to return, to recover, to recover one's self; to get over, to come to one's self, to come to; to be restored; to occur, to recur, to present one's self; to resume, to reconsider; to alter one's mind, to change one's opinion, to recant, to retract; to be undeceived; to come over to, to adopt, to embrace; to retrieve; to be reconciled, to be appeased, to be pacified; to cost, to stand in; to amount, to come to; to be tantamount to; to please, to suit, to match; to arise, to accrue, to result, to proceed; to appear, to haunt, to walk; (jur.) to claim on a guarantee. *Faire — quelqu'un;* to call any one back. *Son nom ne me revient pas;* I do not recollect his name. *Revenons à notre propos, à nos moutons;* let us resume, let us return to, our subject, to our business. *J'en reviens toujours là que;* I still persist in thinking that. — *à la charge;* to return to the charge. — *à ses moutons;* to return to one's subject. — *sur une matière;* to return to a subject. — *d'une maladie;* to recover from a fit of illness. *Il revient à vue d'œil;* he recovers visibly. — . *à soi;* to recover one's senses, to come to one's self again, to come to, to revive; to resume one's serenity; to reform, to be reformed, to be reclaimed, to return to the right path. — *d'une frayeur;* to recover from a fright. — *en santé;* to recover one's health. *La jeunesse revient de loin;* those that have youth on their side easily recover from the most dangerous fits of illness. — *sur l'eau;* to get afloat again, to recover one's losses. *Ne pas — de;* to wonder at. *En — d'une belle;* to have had a narrow escape. *Je reviens à l'avis d'un tel ;* I come over to such an one's opinion. *Je n'en reviens pas ;* I cannot recover from my astonishment. *— de ses préjugés ;* to shake off one's prejudices. *— de ses folies ;* to leave off one's old pranks. *Je suis revenu de ces amusements-là ;* I do not care for those amusements any more. *— sur le compte de quelqu'un ;* to have a better opinion of any one. *Quand on m'a fait de ces tours, je ne reviens pas ;* when people play me such tricks as those I never forgive them. *Son humeur ne me revient pas ;* his humour does not please me. *Les deux choses reviennent au même ;* the two things amount to the same, come to the same, are tantamount to the same. *Cet habit revient à tant ;* that coat costs so much. *Il ne m'en revient rien ;* I get nothing by it. *De la viande qui revient ;* meat that rises in one's stomach. *Le vin fait — le cœur ;* wine cheers the heart. *Faire — de la viande* (cook.); to parboil meat ; to broil meat a little.

revente, *n.f.,* resale; selling again, reselling; regrating. *De —;* second-hand. *Lit de —;* second-hand bed.

reventer, *v.a.,* (nav.) to fill a sail again.

revenu (rĕ-vnu), *n.m.,* revenue, income, rent. *État des —s ;* rental. *—s casuels ;* perquisites.

revenue, *n.f.,* young wood (of a coppice—*d'un taillis*).

rêver, *v.n.,* to dream, to be in a dream; to rave, to be light-headed; to talk idly ; to have a wandering mind, to muse; to think, to reflect, to consider. *Il rêve tout éveillé ;* he dreams wide awake. *J'ai rêvé longtemps sur cette affaire ;* I thought a long time about that affair. *Je regagnai mon hôtellerie en rêvant ;* I trudged back to my inn in a thoughtful mood.

rêver, *v.a.,* to dream, to long for, to desire ardently, to dream of. *Il ne rêve que fortune ;* he thinks of nothing but riches.

réverbérant, -e, *adj.,* (of heat, light—*chaleur, lumière*) reverberating; producing reverberation.

réverbération, *n.f.,* reverberation (of light, heat—*de la lumière, de la chaleur*); reverberation, repercussion (of sound—*du son*). *La — des rayons du soleil ;* the reverberation of the solar rays.

réverbère, *n.m.,* reflector, reverberatory plate; street lamp. *Feu de —* (chem.); reverberated fire.

réverbérer, *v.a.* and *n.,* to reverberate (of heat, light—*de la lumière, de la chaleur*).

reverdie, *n.m.,* (nav.) return of the high tide.

reverdir, *v.a.* and *n.,* to paint green again; to become green again; to grow young again; to reblossom; (fig.) to grow influential, powerful again. *Planter là quelqu'un pour —;* to leave any one in the lurch ; to give any one the slip. *Il faut — ces barreaux ;* these iron-bars must be painted green again.

reverdissement (-dis-măn), *n.m.,* growing green again.

révéremment (-ra-măn), *adv.,* reverently.

révérence, *n.f.,* reverence, veneration; bow, courtesy. *Avec —;* reverently. *Faire une profonde —;* to make a low bow, a low courtesy. *Tirer sa — à quelqu'un* (jest.); to make one's bow to any one.

révérencielle, *adj.f.,* reverential. *Crainte —;* reverential awe.

révérencieusement (-euz-man), *adv.,* reverentially.

révérencieu-x, -se, *adj.,* reverential; bowing and scraping.

révérend, -e, *adj.,* reverend. *Très —;*

right reverend. [Sometimes used as a noun in the masculine.]

révérendissime, *adj.,* most reverend.

révérer, *v.a.,* to revere, to reverence, to venerate, to hold in veneration.

rêverie (rĕ-vrî), *n.f.,* revery, musing; dream; raving, delirium. *Tomber en —;* to fall into a revery.

revernir, *v.a.,* to glaze again, to varnish over again.

⊙**reverquier**, *n.m. V.* **revertier**.

revers (-vèr), *n.m.,* back, reverse; facing (of clothes—*de vêtements*); lapel (of a coat—*d'un habit*); back stroke; top (of boots—*de bottes*); reverse, change for the worse. *Coup de —;* back-handed stroke. *Donner un —;* to hit a back stroke. *Le — de la médaille;* the reverse of the medal. *Le — de la tranchée* (fort.); the reverse of the trench.

réversal, -e, *adj.,* (jur.) of a written agreement by which an equivalent is agreed to be given for some contract entered into.

reverseau, *n.m.,* flashing-board (for doors or windows—*de porte et de fenêtre*).

reversement, *n.m.,* (nav.) trans-shipment. *V.* **transbordement**.

reverser, *v.a.,* to pour out again ; to pour off ; (nav.) to trans-ship. (*V.* **transborder**); (com.) to transfer, to carry.

reversi, or **reversis**, *n.m.,* reversis (card game—*jeu de cartes*).

réversibilité, *n.f.,* (jur.) the quality of that which is revertible.

réversible, *adj.,* (jur.) revertible.

réversion, *n.f.,* (jur.) reversion.

revertier (-tiè), *n.m.,* sort of back-gammon.

⊙**revestiaire**, *n.m.,* revestry, revestiary.

revêtement (-vê-tmăn), *n.m.,* (arch., mas.) covering, lining, coating, casing, facing; (fort.) revetement ; (joinery—*ébénisterie*) veneering.

revêtir, *v.a.,* to clothe; to give clothes to, to invest; to dress; to put on, to assume; to endow a person with; to bestow on a person; (mas.) to line, to cover. *— les pauvres ;* to clothe the poor. *— un habit ;* to put on a coat. *— ses pensées d'un style brillant ;* to clothe one's thoughts in a brilliant style. *— la figure de quelqu'un ;* to put on the air of some-one. *Les formes que revêt la pensée ;* the forms that thought assumes, takes, adopts. *— un personnage ;* to assume a character. *Je me suis dépouillé de cet emploi pour l'en —;* I threw up this employment in his favour, to bestow it on him. *— une terrasse de gazon ;* to cover a terrace with turf.

se **revêtir**, *v.r.,* to clothe one's self, to array one's self, to invest one's self, to dress, to put on, to assume, to take; to be invested.

rêveu-r, -se, *n.* and *adj.,* dreamer, muser; thoughtful, pensive, museful, musing.

revient (rĕvi-in), *n.m.,* (com.) only used in: *prix de —;* net cost.

revirade, *n.f.,* (backgammon) back-game.

revirement (re-vir-măn), *n.m.,* sudden change; (nav.) tacking; (com. and fin.) transfer. *— de parties* (com.); transfer.

revirer, *v.n.,* (nav.) to tack about, to tack, to put about ; to turn round; to change sides, to be turn-coat, to rat. *Il a reviré de bord ;* he has ratted.

revisable, *adj.,* that can be revised.

reviser, *v.a.,* to revise, to review, to examine.

reviseur, *n.m.,* reviser, examiner.

revision, *n.f.,* revisal, revision, re-examination, review. *Sujet à —;* questionable. *— de procès ;* rehearing. *Faire la — d'une feuille* (print.); to revise a sheet. *Conseil de —* (milit.); the board that examines the recruits and decides whether or not they are to be admitted into the army.

revivification, *n.f.,* (chem.) revivification, vivification.

revivifier, *v.a.,* to revive, to revivify, to vivify; to regenerate.

revivre, *v.n.,* to come to life again; to live again; to revive. *Faire —;* to bring to life again. *Les pères revivent dans leurs enfants;* fathers live again in their children.

révocabilité, *n.f.,* revocableness.

révocable, *adj.,* revocable, reversible, repealable.

©**révocati-f, -ve.** *adj.,* revocatory.

révocation, *n.f.,* revocation, repeal, revoking, recall.

révocatoire, *adj.,* revocatory.

revoici, *prep.,* (fam., jest) here . . . again. *Me —;* here am I again.

revoilà, *prep.,* (fam., jest) there . . . again. *Les revoilà!* there they are again!

revoir, *v.a.,* to see again; to meet again; to revise, to review, to re-examine.

se **revoir,** *v.r.,* to see, to meet, each other again; to be seen again. *Nous nous reverrons;* we shall see one another again.

revoir, *n.m.,* seeing, meeting, again. *Au —;* good-bye, till we meet again.

revoler, *v.n.,* to fly again, to fly back.

revolin, *n.m.,* (nav.) eddy wind.

révoltant, -e, *adj.,* revolting.

révolte, *n.f.,* revolt, rebellion.

révolté, *n.m.,* rebel.

révolter, *v.a.,* to cause to revolt *or* rebel, to stir up; to rouse, to excite; to shock, to be revolting to.

se **révolter,** *v.r.,* to revolt, to rebel, to be indignant.

révolter, *v.n.,* to revolt, to rebel.

révolu, -e, *adj.,* revolved, accomplished.

révoluti-f, -ve, *adj.,* (bot.) revolute.

révolution, *n.f.,* revolution.

révolutionnaire, *n.m. and adj.,* revolutionist; revolutionary.

révolutionnairement (-sio-nèr-màn)*,adv.,* in a revolutionary manner.

révolutionner, *v.a.,* to revolutionize.

revolver (ré-vol-vèr), *n.m.,* revolver.

revomir, *v.a.,* to vomit, to throw up again; to vomit again; to bring up.

révoquer, *v.a.,* to recall (an ambassador, &c.—*un ambassadeur, &c.*); to dismiss (a clerk, an officer, an official, &c.—*un employé, un officier, un fonctionnaire, &c.*); to revoke, to repeal. — *en doute;* to call in question.

revouloir, *v.a.,* to wish again, to wish again for.

revue, *n.f.,* review; magazine; survey, examination, revision. *Faire la — de;* to examine, to survey. *Faire une — de ses papiers:* to examine one's papers. *Passer en —* (milit.); to review. *Être gens de —;* to meet often.

révulsi-f, -ve, *adj.,* (med.) revulsive.

révulsif, *n.m.,* (med.) revulsive.

révulsion, *n.f.,* revulsion.

rez, *prep.,* (l.u.) level with, even with. — *pied,* — *terre;* even *or* level with the ground.

rez-de-chaussée, *n.m.* (—), ground-floor; level with the ground. *Au —;* on the ground-floor.

rhabdologie, *n.f.* V. **rabdologie.**

rhabdomancie, *n.f.* V. **rabdomancie.**

*****rhabillage,** *n.m.,* repairing, mending, botching, patching.

*****rhabillement,** *n.m.* V. **rhabillage.**

*****rhabiller,** *v.a.,* to dress again, to clothe anew; to mend, to patch up.

*****rhabilleu-r,** *n.m.,* -**se,** *n.f.* V. **rebouteur.**

rhagade, *n.f.,* (med.) rhagade, crack, chap, fissure.

rhapontic, *n.m.,* (bot.) bastard monk's-rhubarb, rheum rhaponticum.

rhapsode, *n.m.,* **rhapsodie,** *n.f.,* **rhapsodiste,** *n.m.* V. **rapsode, rapsodie, rapsodiste.**

rhénan, -e, *adj.,* (geog.) Rhenish.

rhésus (-zus), *n.m.,* pig-tailed baboon.

rhéteur, *n.m.,* rhetorician.

rhétien, -ne, (ti-in, -tiè-n), *adj.,* (geog.) Rhetian.

rhétoricien (-si-in), *n.m.,* rhetorician.

rhétorique, *n.f.,* rhetoric. *Figure de —;* rhetorical figure. *Faire sa —;* to be in the class of rhetoric.

rhin, *n.m.,* (geog.) Rhine. *Vin du —;* Rhenish wine.

rhinante, *n.f.,* (bot.) cock's-comb.

rhingrave, *n.m.,* the ancient title of the governors and judges of the German towns on the Rhine.

rhingrave, *n.f.,* formerly a sort of knee-breeches.

rhinocéros (-ros), *n.m.,* rhinoceros.

rhinoplastie, *n.f.,* (surg.) rhinoplasty.

rhodium (-om), *n.m.,* (min.) rhodium.

rhododendron, *n.m.,* (bot.) rhododendron; rose-bay.

rhombe, *n.m.,* (geom.) rhomb, rhombus; (ich.) rhombus.

rhomboèdre, *n.m.,* (geom.) rhombohedron.

rhomboïdal, -e, *adj.,* rhomboidal.

rhomboïde, *n.m.,* (anat., geom.) rhomboid.

rhubarbe, *n.f.,* rhubarb. — *blanche;* white jalap. — *des moines;* monk's-rhubarb, herb-patience.

rhum (rom), *n.m.,* rum.

rhumatique, *adj.,* rheumatic.

rhumatisant, -e, *n. and adj.,* a person suffering with rheumatism; rheumatic.

rhumatismal, -e, *adj.,* rheumatic.

rhumatisme, *n.m.,* rheumatism.

rhumb, *n.m.* V. **rumb.**

rhume, *n.m.,* cold. — *de cerveau;* cold in the head. *Un gros —;* a violent cold. — *de poitrine;* cold on the chest. *Attraper un —;* to catch a cold.

rhus (rus), *n.m.* V. **sumac.**

rhythme, *n.m.* V. **rythme.**

rhythmique, *adj.* V. **rythmique.**

rhyton, *n.m.,* (Grec. antiq.) horn-shaped drinking vase.

©**raillerie,** *n.f.,* frequent laughing.

riant, -e, *adj.,* laughing, smiling, cheerful; pleasant.

ribambelle, *n.f.,* long list, string; host, lot (of people—*de gens*).

ribaud, -e. *n. and adj.,* (l.ex.) ribald.

ribauderie (-bô-dri), *n.f.,* ribaldry.

ribaudure, *n.f.,* crease, fold (in cloth—*dans le drap*).

riblette, *n.f.,* (cook.) collop; rasher.

©**ribleur,** *n.m.,* (pop.) night-walker. prowler.

ribord, *n.m.,* (nav.) garboard streak.

ribordage, *n.m.,* (nav.) damage done by one ship to another in running foul of her in a port, or in the roads; indemnity for the damage thus done.

ribote, *n.f.,* (pop.) debauch, intoxication. *Être en —;* to be intoxicated, drunk; to be on the spree.

riboter, *v.n.,* (pop.) to get intoxicated, drunk; to be on the spree.

riboteu-r, *n.m.,* -**se,** *n.f.,* (pop.) drunkard; person on the spree.

ricanement (-ka-n-màn), *n.m.,* chuckling, sneering.

ricaner, *v.n.,* to chuckle, to sneer.

ricanerie (-ka-n-ri), *n.f.,* sneer, chuckling.

ricaneu-r, -se, *n. and adj.,* sneerer; sneering.

ric-à-ric, *adv.*, (fam.) rigorously, strictly.

richard, *n.m.*, monied man ; rich fellow.

riche, *n.m.* and *adj.*, rich man ; rich, wealthy, opulent ; copious ; valuable, precious. *Un — parti ;* a good match (marriage). — *moisson ;* copious harvest. *Langue — :* copious language. *— taille :* high stature. *Le mauvais —;* the rich man of the Gospel.

richement (rish-män), *adv.*, richly, opulently, copiously.

richesse, *n.f.*, riches, wealth, wealthiness, opulence ; copiousness ; richness. *La — du sol ;* the richness of the soil. *La — d'une langue ;* the copiousness of a language. *Contentement passe —,:* contentment is better than riches.

richissime, *adj.*, (fam.) excessively rich.

ricin, *n.m.*, (bot.) palma Christi, ricinus communis. *Huile de — ;* castor-oil.

ricocher, *v.n.*, (artil.) to ricochet.

ricochet, *n.m.*, duck and drake (rebound on the water—*sur l'eau*) ; series ; chain, succession ; (artil.) ricochet. *Faire des —s* (artil.) ; to ricochet ; to make ducks and drakes on the water. *Feu à —* (artil.) ; ricochet-firing. *C'est la chanson du — ;* it is the same thing over and over again. *Cette nouvelle est venue par — ;* that news was spread indirectly.

rictus, *n.m.*, grin, grinning.

ride, *n.f.*, wrinkle (on the face—*au visage*) ; (bot.) wrinkle ; ripple (on the water—*sur l'eau*) ; (nav.) laniard. *—s des haubans ;* laniards of the shrouds.

ridé, -e, *adj.*, wrinkled ; (bot.) rugose. *Une pomme —e ;* a shrivelled apple.

rideau, *n.m.*, curtain ; screen (of trees—*d'arbres*) ; (fort.) rideau. *Tirer le — ;* to draw the curtain. *Baisser le —* (thea.) ; to drop the curtain. *Lever de —* (thea.) ; short, amusing play given at the beginning of the evening.

ridelle, *n.f.*, staff-side (of a cart, &c.—*de charrette*).

rider, *v.a.*, to wrinkle (the skin—*la peau*) ; to shrivel ; to crumple ; to ripple (water—*l'eau*) ; to corrugate.

se rider, *v.r.*, to wrinkle, to shrivel, to shrivel up ; to ripple (of water—*de l'eau*).

ridicule, *adj.*, ridiculous. *Se rendre — ;* to make one's self ridiculous.

ridicule, *n.m.*, ridicule, ridiculousness ; ridiculous person, ridiculous thing. *Tomber dans le — ;* to become ridiculous. *Tourner quelqu'un en — ;* to ridicule any one.

ridiculement (-kul-män),*adv.*,ridiculously.

ridiculiser, *v.a.*, to ridicule, to make ridiculous.

ridiculité, *n.f.*, (l.u.) ridiculousness, ridiculous thing.

rièble, *n.m.* *V.* **rèble**.

rien (ri-in), *n.m.*, nothing, nought, not any thing ; anything ; mere nothing, trifle, mere trifle. *Pour — ;* for nothing, for a mere trifle. *— de plus beau ;* nothing finer. *On ne fait — de — ;* nothing can be made out of nothing. *Je n'en ferai — ;* I shall do nothing of the sort. *Cette montre ne vous sert à — ;* that watch is of no use to you. *Cet homme ne m'est — ;* that man is nothing to me. *Cela ne fait — :* that does not matter. *Tout comme si de n'était :* as if nothing at all was the matter. *Ne faites semblant de — :* pretend not to mind it, not to see it. *Je ne pense à — moins qu'à cela ;* nothing is further from my thoughts than that. *Ce n'est — moins que cela :* it is quite another thing, it is any thing but that. *En moins de — :* in the twinkling of an eye. *— au moins ne me fera oublier cela ;* nothing in the world will make me forget that. *Moins que — :* very little. *S'il y a — qui me plaise ;* if anything pleases

me. *Y a-t-il — de nouveau ?* Is there any news ? *N'aboutir a — :* to come to nothing.

rieu-r, *n.m.*, **-se**, *n.f.*, laugher. *Il a les —s de son côté ;* he has the laughers on his side.

riflard, *n.m.*, old umbrella ; (carp.) horseplane ; parting-tool (for stones—*à pierre*).

rigaudon, *n.m.* *V.* **rigodon**.

rigide, *adj.*, rigid, strict, harsh, severe.

rigidement (-jid-män), *adv.*, rigidly, strictly, harshly.

rigidité, *n.f.*, rigidness, rigidity, strictness.

rigodon, *n.m.*, rigadoon.

rigole, *n.f.*, trench, little ditch or furrow, little gutter for water to pass through ; culvert (of roads—*de routes*).

rigorisme, *n.m.*, rigorism, rigorousness, austerity ; hypercriticism.

rigoriste, *n.m.* and *adj.*, rigorist ; hypercritic ; over-rigid, over-severe ; hypercritical.

rigoureusement (-reûz-män), *adv.*, rigorously, severely, strictly, harshly.

rigoureu-x, -se, *adj.*, rigorous, stern, harsh ; strict ; severe, sharp.

rigueur (-gheur), *n.f.*, rigour, severity ; harshness ; sternness, sharpness. *La — du sort ;* the sternness of fate. *Traiter quelqu'un avec — ;* to be severe with any one. *Cette règle est de — ;* this rule is indispensable. *Jouer de — ;* to play the strict rule of the game. *La — de l'hiver ;* the inclemency of the winter. *À la — ;* rigorously, strictly.

***rillettes**, *n.f.pl.*, potted meat of pork.

***rimaille**, *n.f.*, (b.s.) rhyming.

***rimailler**, *v.n.*, to make sorry verses.

***rimailleur**, *n.m.*, sorry rhymer.

rime, *n.f.*, rhyme ; *pl.*, verse. *—s croisées ;* alternate rhymes. *Il n'y a ni — ni raison dans ce qu'il dit ;* there is neither rhyme nor reason in what he says.

rimer, *v.n.* and *a.*, to rhyme.

rimeur, *n.m.*, rhymer ; poetaster.

rinçage, *n.m.*, rinsing.

rinceau, *n.m.*, (arch.) foliage ; (her.) bough.

rincer, *v.a.*, to rinse. *Il a été bien rincé* (pop.) ; he has been well drenched ; he has been well served out.

se rincer, *v.r.*, to rinse. *— la bouche ;* to rinse one's mouth.

rinçure, *n.f.*, slops (weak wine, &c.—*rin faible, &c.*), *pl.*, slops (in which any thing has been rinsed—*eau sale*).

rinforzando, *adv.*, (mus.) rinforzando.

ringard, *n.m.*, (tech.) fire-iron.

ringrave, *n.m.f.* *V.* **rhingrave**.

Ⓞ**riolé, -e**, *adj.*, streaked.

rioter, *v.n.*, to giggle, to titter.

rioteu-r, *n.m.*, **-se**, *n.f.*, giggler, titterer.

riotte, *n.f.*, little quarrel between friends.

***ripaille**, *n.f.*, feasting, junketting. *Faire — :* to feast, to junket.

ripe, *n.f.*, (sculpt.) scraper.

riper, *v.a.*, (sculpt.) to scrape.

ripopée, *n.f.*, slops, mixture of the bottom of several bottles of wine ; drippings of casks ; slop ; medley ; slipslop ; bad wine.

riposte, *n.f.*, smart reply, repartee ; (fenc.) parry and thrust.

riposter, *v.n.*, to repartee, to make a smart reply ; to make a return ; to return it ; (fenc.) to parry and thrust. *Il riposta d'un soufflet ;* he returned it with a slap in the face.

ripuaire, *adj.*, riparian. [Applied to the ancient German tribes that lived on the banks of the Rhine, and to their laws.]

rire (riant, ri), *v.n.*, to laugh ; to be merry ; to look pleasant, to smile ; to be in jest, to joke, to make game of ; to trifle ; to favour ; to scoff at. *Éclater de — ;* to break out into laughter, to burst out laughing. *Étouf-*

16

fer de —; to be suffocating with laughter. *Se tenir les côtes de* —; to split one's sides with laughing. *Pâmer de* —; to die with laughing. *Avoir le mot pour* —; to be facetious, to be ready with one's joke. — *à gorge déployée*; to laugh immoderately. — *du bout des dents*, — *jaune*; to laugh the wrong side of one's mouth. — *dans sa barbe*, — *sous cape*; to laugh in one's sleeve. — *de quelqu'un*; to laugh at any one. *Apprêter à* —; to make one's self a laughing-stock. *Rira bien qui rira le dernier*; they laugh best who laugh last. *Cela fait* —; that makes one laugh. *Il n'y a pas là de quoi* —; there's nothing to laugh at in that. *Et de* —; and they began to laugh. — *aux anges*; to laugh beyond measure; to laugh to one's self. — *aux dépens d'autrui*; to laugh at another's expense. *Nous rirons bien*; we shall be very merry. *La fortune lui rit*; fortune smiles upon him. *Est-ce que vous riez?* are you jesting? *Vous voulez* —; you are jesting. *Je le disais pour* —; I said it in jest. — *de bon cœur*; to laugh heartily. *Pour* —; in play, for fun. *Pincer sans* —; to nip on the sly without laughing, to jest bitingly. **serire**, *v.r.*, to laugh; to make sport, to jest, to trifle, to scoff. *On se rit de lui*; he is laughed at.

rire, *n.m.*, laugh; laughter, laughing; giggle; grin. *De grands éclats de* —; loud laughter. *Un* — *moqueur*; a sneer. *Un* — *niais*; a silly laugh. *Un gros* —; a horse-laugh. — *étouffé*; suppressed laugh; giggle. *Accès de* —; fit of laughter. *Partir d'un éclat de* —; to burst out laughing.

ris, *n.m.*, laugh, smile, laughter; (nav.) reef (of sails—*des voiles*); (cook.) sweet-bread. *Un* — *forcé*; a forced laugh. *Un* — *moqueur*; a sneer. *Prendre un* — (nav.); to take in a reef. — *de veau* (cook.); sweet-bread.

risban, *n.m.*, (fort.) battery for the defence of a port.

risdale, *n.f. V.* **rixdale**.

risée, *n.f.*, laugh, laughter, mockery, derision; butt, laughing-stock; (nav.) gust, squall, flow. *Être la* — *de tout le monde*; to be the laughing-stock of every one.

riser, *v.a.*, (nav.) to strike a sail.

risette, *n.f.*, little child's laugh.

risibilité, *n.f.*, risibility.

risible, *adj.*, risible; comical, laughable.

risiblement, *adv.*, laughably.

risquable, *adj.*, adventurous, hazardous; that may be ventured.

risque, *n.m.*, risk, hazard, peril. *J'en courrai le* —; I will run the risk of it. *À tout* —; at all risks. *À ses* —*s et périls*; at one's risk. *Au* — *de*; at the risk of.

risquer, *v.a.*, to risk, to hazard, to venture, to run the risk of. — *sa vie*; to venture one's life. — *le combat*; to give the battle. *Qui ne risque rien n'a rien*; nothing venture, nothing win. — *le paquet*; to risk all. **serisquer**, *v.r.*, to risk, to venture.

rissole, *n.f.*, (cook.) a kind of meat pie.

rissolé, -**e**, *part.*, (cook.) brown, browned. *Il a le visage* —; his face is sun burnt.

rissoler, *v.a.*, (cook.) to roast brown. **serissoler**, *v.r.*, (cook.) to roast brown.

ristorne, or **ristourne**, *n.f.*, (com.) cancelling an insurance.

ristorner or **ristourner**, *v.a.*, (com.) to cancel an insurance; to carry to another account.

rit, or **rite**, *n.m.*, rite.

ritournelle, *n.f.*, (mus.) ritornello, flourish.

ritualiste, *n.m.*, ritualist.

rituel, *n.m.*, ritual, prayer-book.

rivage, *n.m.*, shore, sea-shore, beach; bank (of rivers—*des rivières*); water-side. *Être jeté*

sur le —; to be thrown ashore. *Quitter le* —; to put off.

rival, -**e**, *n.* and *adj.*, rival. *Ils sont rivaux de gloire*; they are rivals in glory.

rivaliser, *v.n.*, to rival, to vie, to compete, to strive, to strive with, to emulate. *Ils ont rivalisé d'efforts*; they vied with each other in efforts.

rivalité, *n.f.*, rivalry, rivalship, competition, emulation.

rive, *n.f.*, shore, bank (of rivers—*des rivières*); border, skirt (of woods—*des bois*). *On n'y voit ni fond ni* — (prov.); it is beyond any man's comprehension.

river, *v.a.*, to rivet, to clinch. — *à quelqu'un son clou*; to give any one a clincher, to silence any one.

riverain (ri-vrin), *n.m.*, one who lives on the bank of a river; one who possesses property situated along a forest.

riverain, -**e**, *adj.*, bordering (on rivers or woods—*d'une rivière, d'un bois*); possessing property situated along a forest, road, or street.

rivet, *n.m.*, rivet.

rivière, *n.f.*, river. *Bras d'une* —; branch of a river. *Gens de* —; watermen. *La* — *est marchande*; the river is navigable. *Les petits ruisseaux font les grandes* —*s*; many a mickle makes a mickle. *Mettre les peaux en* —; to soak the skins. — *de diamants*; diamond necklace, stream of diamonds.

rivoir, *n.m.*, rivetting-hammer.

rivure, *n.f.*, hinge-pin.

rixdale, *n.f.*, rix-dollar.

rixe, *n.f.*, combat, conflict, fight, scuffle; brawl, dispute, affray; quarrel.

riz (ri), *n.m.*, (bot.) rice. — *au lait*; rice-milk. *Gâteau de* —; rice-pudding, rice-cake.

rize, *n.m.*, rize (Turkish coin—*monnaie de compte turque*).

rizière, *n.f.*, rice-field, rice-plantation.

rob, *n.m.*, (pharm.) rob; rubber (whist).

robe, *n.f.*, gown, robe, dress, frock; coat (of certain animals—*de quelques animaux*); husk, peel (of certain vegetables, fruit—*de quelques légumes et fruits*); cloth (clergymen—*ecclésiastiques*); long robe (lawyers—*gens de loi*). — *de femme*; dress, gown. — *d'enfant*; frock. — *de chambre*; morning-gown, dressing-gown. *Gens de* —; gentlemen of the long robe.

rober, *v.a.*, to bark (madder—*la garance*). — *un chapeau*; to rub a hat. — *la garance*; to bark the madder.

robin, *n.m.*, (b.s.) limb of the law, lawyer.

robin, proper name used in the following familiar and proverbial expressions: *Toujours souvient à* — *de ses flûtes*; people like to remember the tastes and inclinations of their youth. *C'est un plaisant* —; he is a contemptible fellow.

robinet, *n.m.*, cock (instrument for drawing off liquor); tap, plug. — *à deux eaux, à deux faces, à deux fins*; double-valve cock. *Fermer le* —; to turn off the cock. *Ouvrir le* —; to turn on the cock.

robinier, *n.m.*, (bot.) robinia, common acacia, locust-tree.

roborati-f, -**ve**, *adj.*, (med.) (l.u.) roborant.

robre, *n.m.*, rubber (whist). *V.* **rob**.

robuste, *adj.*, robust, hardy, sturdy.

robustement, *adv.*, robustly, hardily, lustily, stoutly.

roc, *n.m.*, rock (isolated mass of stony matter—*masse de pierre isolée*); crook, castle (at chess—*aux échecs*).

***rocaille**, *n.f.*, rock-work, grotto-work.

***rocailleur**, *n.m.*, grotto-maker, rock-work-maker.

***rocailleu-x**, -**se**, *adj.*, pebbly, stony, flinty; rugged, rough.

rocambeau, n.m., (nav.) iron ring holding the sails round the mast.

rocambole, n.f., (hort.) rocambole; a trite poor joke; ☉the piquancy, the point, of an occurrence.

roccelle, n.f., (bot.) archil.

roche. n.f., rock (stony mass, isolated or not —masse de pierre, isolée ou non); rock (insensibility—insensibilité), flint, steel. Cœur de —; heart of flint. Homme de la vieille —; man of the old stamp. Il y a quelque anguille sous —; there is some snake in the grass. — crayeuse, chalk rock.

rocher, n.m., rock (high, and rising in a point—élevé en pointe); (conch.) murex. Plein de —s; rocky. Cœur de —; heart of flint. — escarpé; steep rock.

☉rocheraie (ro-shrê). n.f., (orni.) stock-dove.

rochet, n.m., rocket (surplice—surplis); (horl.) rack, ratch; (of machinery—machines); clink; (locksmith's work—serrurerie) ratchet.

rocheu-x, -se, adj., (geol.) rocky.

rock, or rouc, n.m., rock, fabulous bird of the Eastern tales.

rococo, n.m. and adj., antiquated style; bad taste in the arts; antiquated, old, old-fashioned.

rocou, rocouer, rocouyer. V. roucou, roucouer, roucouyer.

rôder, v.n., to roam, to rove, to ramble; to prowl.

rôdeur, n.m., roamer, rover, rambler; vagrant; prowler.

rodomont, n.m., rodomont, blusterer, ranter, braggadocio, bully.

rodomontade, n.f., rodomontade, boasting, bluster, bravado, swaggering.

rogation, n.f., (Roman jur.) rogation, draft of a law presented to the people.

rogations, n.f.pl., (c.rel.) rogation. Jours des —; rogation-days. Semaine des —; rogation week.

rogatoire, adj., (jur.) of examination. Commission —; commission of inquiry.

rogaton, n.m., scraps, broken meat; waste paper.

roger-bontemps, n.m. (—s —), (fam.) a jolly fellow.

*rogne, n.f., inveterate itch; mange; (vet.) scab.

*rognement, n.m., cutting, paring, clipping.

*rogne-pied, n.m. (—), (vet.) paring-knife.

*rogner, v.a., to clip, to cut (at the extremities—aux extrémités); to pare, to crop, to prune, to lop; to cut off, to cut short, to pare off. — la vigne; to prune the vine. — un livre; to cut a book. — la monnaie; to clip coin. — les ongles à quelqu'un; to clip any one's wings.

*rogneu-r, n.m., -se, n.f., clipper (of coin—de monnaie).

*rogneu-x, -se, adj., itchy, mangy, scabbed, scurvy.

*rognoir, n.m., (book-bind.) plough; cutting-press.

*rognon. n.m., kidney; (pop.) loins; hip; testicle (of some animals—de certains animaux). Blessure aux—s d'un cheval; navel-gall. Mine en —s (metal.); kidney-shaped ore.

*rognonner. v.n., to growl, to grumble.

*rognure. n.f., paring, clipping, cutting; pl., refuse, leavings.

rogomme. n.m., dram, spirits. Voix de —; croaking voice, hoarse voice, drunkard's voice.

rogue (rog). adj., (fam.) proud, haughty.

roi, n.m., king. De par le —; in the king's name. Vive le —; long live the king. Le jour des —s; Twelfth-day. Gâteau des —s; twelfth-cake. Vivre en —; to live like a king. C'est la cour du — Pétaud; it is Bedlam broke loose. — d'armes; king at arms.

roide. adj. V. raide.

roitelet (roa-tlê), n.m., petty king, king-let; (orni.) wren, kinglet. — huppé; golden-crested wren. — triple bandeau; fire-crested wren.

rôle. n.m.. roll, scroll; list, catalogue; (thea.) part, character, À tour de —; in turn, by rotation. Jouer bien son —; to play one's part well. — de combat (nav.); quarter-bill. — de quart; watch-bill. — d'équipage (nav.); muster-roll. Sortir de son —; to be out of character.

rôler, v.n., (b.s.) to lengthen written documents in order to increase costs (of attorneys —des avoués).

rôlet, n.m., (l.u.) character, part. Jouer bien son —; to play one's part well. Être au bout de son —; to be at one's wits' end.

rollier, n.m., (orni.) roller.

romain, -e, adj., Roman; Romish; (print.) Roman. À la —e; Roman-like. L'Église —e; the church of Rome. Calendrier —; Romish calendar. Laitue —e; cos lettuce.

romain, n.m., -e, n.f., Roman.

romain, n.m., (print.) Roman, primer. Gros —; great primer. Petit —; long primer.

romaine, n.f., steelyard; (bot.) cos lettuce.

romaïque, n.m. and adj., Romaic, modern Greek language; Greek, Grecian.

romaïque, n.f., the Greek national dance.

roman, n.m., novel, romance, marvellous tale, romancing tale; Romance (language—langue); Romanish. Cela tient du —; that is like a romance. C'est une aventure de —; is is a romantic adventure.

roman, -e, or romance, adj., Romanic, Romance.

romance, n.f., (mus.) ballad, song.

romancero, n.m. (—s), collection of short epic poems of ancient Spanish poets; collection of ancient poetry in any language.

romancier, n.m., romance-writer; novelist, novel-writer.

romane, adj., (arch.) romanesque.

romanesque, n. and adj., romanticness; fanciful, romantic; romantical.

romanesquement, adv., romantically, in a romantic manner.

romaniser, v.a. and n., to impart an air of fiction to; to make the Roman influence prevail; to turn men into Romans; (philolog.) to write Eastern languages in Roman characters; to follow the dogma of the Romish church.

romanticisme, n.m., romanticism.

romantique, n.m. and adj., romanticness; romanticist; romantic, romantical.

romantiquement (-tik-mân), adv., romantically.

romantisme, n.m., romanticism.

romarin, n.m., (bot.) rosemary.

rompement (ronp-mân), n.m., only used in: — de tête; mental fatigue.

rompre, v.a., to break, to break asunder, to snap; to break off. to dissolve; to train. to break in, to train up, to use: to divert, to turn off; (phys.) to refract; (med.) to rupture; (paint.) to blend. — un criminel; to break a criminal upon the wheel. — la tête à quelqu'un; to break any one's head. — les chemins; to spoil the roads, to break up the roads. — la glace; to break the ice. — le cou à quelqu'un; to break any one's neck. to ruin any one. — les couleurs; to blend the colours. — la mesure (fenc.); to retire in parrying. — le grain germé; to turn the barley. — les bor-

dages (nav.); to rip off planks. — *le sommeil de quelqu'un;* to interrupt the sleep of any one. — *un coup;* to deaden a blow. — *le silence;* to break silence. — *les chiens* (hunt.); to call off the dogs. — *l'eau à un cheval;* to interrupt a horse in drinking. — *un traité;* to break off a treaty. — *son ménage;* to break up housekeeping. — *le carré* (milit.); to break up the square. — *une armée;* to disband an army. — *la paille;* to break off (an agreement, a bargain, &c.—*un accord, un marché, &c.*); to break off, to fall out with, to become the enemy of any one. — *son serment;* to break one's oath. — *le jeûne;* to break one's fast. — *sa prison;* to break out of prison. — *son ban;* to break one's ban. — *un homme aux affaires;* to train a man up to business. — *un cheval;* to break a horse, to break in a horse. *À tout — ;* to the utmost. *Cet acteur a été applaudi à tout — ;* that actor was applauded to the skies.

serompre, *v.r.*, to break, to break off, to snap, to break up, to break asunder; to discontinue; (phys.) to refract; (med.) to rupture.

rompre, *v.n*, to break, to break asunder, to break off, to snap, to break up; to discontinue, to have done. — *court;* to break short, to break short off. — *en visière avec quelqu'un;* to tell any one the truth to his face; to quarrel suddenly with any one.

rompu, -e, *part.*, broke, broken, snapped. *Être — aux affaires;* to be used to business. *Tout — de fatigue;* quite worn out with fatigue. *Travailler à bâtons —s;* to work by fits and starts. *Nombre —* (l.u.); fraction.

ronce, *n.f.*, (bot.) bramble, brier; blackberry-bush; blackberry-tree; (fig.) thorn.

ronceraie, *n.f.*, brake.

rond, -e, *adj.*, round; rotund; frank, easy, plain-dealing; even (of money, accounts—*d'argent, de comptes*). — *comme une boule;* as round as a ball. *Un peu — ;* roundish. *Du fil — ;* coarse thread. *Voix —e;* full voice. *Compte — ;* even account. *C'est un homme tout — ;* he is a plain-dealing man. *Figure de —e bosse* (sculpt.); figure in alto-relievo. *Période —e ;* full and rounded period.

rond, *n.m.*, round, orb, ring, circle. *Danser en — ;* to dance in a ring. — *d'eau;* circular basin of water.

rondache, *n.f.*, round buckler, round shield.

ronde, *n.f.*, round; patrol; taole song, roundelay; (mus.) semibreve; round hand (writing *—écriture*). *Faire la — ;* to go the rounds. *À la — ;* round about. *Boire à la — ;* to drink all round. *Passer à la — ;* to hand round, to pass round.

rondeau, *n.m.*, rondeau (French poet.); (mus.) rondo.

rondelet, -te (rŏn-dlè, -t), *adj.*, roundish, plump, plumpish.

rondelettes, *n.f.pl.*, sail-cloth made in Brittany.

rondelle, *n.f.*, round shield; rundle, ring; washer (of a wheel—*de roue*); sculptor's rounded chisel.

rondement (rŏn-dmăn), *adv.*, roundly; quickly; briskly, vigorously; plainly, frankly. *Il va — en besogne;* he goes briskly to work.

rondeur, *n.f.*, roundness, rotundity; fulness, flow; openness, plain dealing; curve, compass (of a piece of timber used in ship-building—*de charpente de membrure*).

rondin, *n.m.*, billet, round log, cudgel.

rondiner, *v.a.*, to cudgel. — *d'importance;* to cudgel soundly.

rondon, *n.m.*, (hawking—*fauconnerie*) swoop, impetuosity. *En — ;* impetuously.

road-point, *n.m.* (—s —s). (arch.) apsis; place where several roads, or walks, meet.

ronflant, -e, *adj.*, snoring; sonorous, high-sounding; loud.

ronflement, *n.m.*, snoring, snore; roaring, peal, rumbling; humming; snorting (of horses —*des chevaux*). — *des vents;* roaring of the wind. — *d'une toupie;* humming of a top.

ronfler, *v.n.*, to snore; (of horses—*des chevaux*) to snort; (of cannon, thunder, &c.—*du canon, du tonnerre*) to roar; (of organs—*des orgues*) to peal; (of spinning-tops—*des toupies*) to hum.

ronfleu-r, *n.m.*, **-se**, *n.f.*, snorer.

ronge, *n.m.*, (hunt.) ruminating. *Le cerf fait le — ;* the stag is ruminating.

rongeant, -e, *adj.*, gnawing, devouring, corroding; (med.) corrosive.

*rongemaille, n.m. (—), nibble (rat). Maître — ; squire nibble.

ronger, *v.a.*, to gnaw, to nibble, to pick; to waste, to consume, to eat up, to corrode; to fret, to torment, to prey upon (the mind—*l'esprit, la conscience*). — *un os;* to pick a bone. — *son frein;* to champ the bit; to fret inwardly, to chafe. — *ses ongles;* to bite one's nails. *La rouille ronge le fer;* rust corrodes iron. *Donner un os à — à quelqu'un* (fig.); to bestow, to grant any one a favour; to cut out work for any one, to give any one some trouble.

rongeur, *n.* and *adj. m.*, (mam.) rodent; gnawing, biting; corroding; consuming. *Ver — ;* never-dying worm.

roquefort, *n.m.*, Roquefort cheese.

roquelaure, *n.f.*, requelaur (sort of cloak —*sorte de manteau*).

roquentin, *n.m.*, dotard, gray-beard.

roquer, *v.n.*, to castle, to rook (at chess—*aux échecs*).

roquet, *n.m.*, pug-dog; (fam.) dog, cur (person—*personne*).

roquette, *n.f.*, (bot.) rocket. — *sauvage;* wild rocket.

roquille, *n.f.*, gill (of wine—*de vin*).

rosace, *n.f.*, (arch.) rose; rose-work; (Gothic arch.) rose-window.

rosacé, -e, *adj.*, (bot.) rosaceous.

rosacées, *n.f.pl.*, (bot.) rose-tribe, rosaceæ.

rosage, *n.m.*, (bot.) oleander, rose-bay; (dy.) rosing.

rosagine, *n.f.*, (bot.) rose-bay.

rosaire, *n.m.*, rosary.

rosat, *adj.*, (pharm.) of roses. *Miel — ;* honey of roses.

rosbif, *n.m.* (—s), roast-beef.

rose, *n.f.*, rose; (arch.) rose-window; rose-diamond. *Couleur de — ;* rose-coloured. — *d'Inde;* African marigold. *Laurier — (—s —s);* rose-laurel. — *gueldre;* Guelder-rose. — *de diamants;* cluster of diamonds in the form of a rose. *Diamant en — ;* rose-cut diamond. *Découvrir le pot aux —s;* to find out the secret. *Il n'est point de — sans épines;* there is no rose without a thorn.

rose, *adj.*, rose, rosy, pink; rose-coloured.

rose, *n.m.*, rose-colour.

rosé, -e, *adj.*, roseate, rosy.

roseau, *n.m.*, reed, reed-cane; reed-grass. — *de marais;* common marsh-reed. — *cultivé;* evergreen reed. — *odorant;* sweet-flag. *Lieu planté de —x;* reed-bank. *Plein de —x;* reedy. *Couvert de —x;* reeded. *C'est un — peint en fer;* he looks very firm, but in fact he is a weak-minded and irresolute man.

rose-croix, *n.m.* (—s —), Rosicrucian.

rosée, *n.f.*, dew; (vet.) oozing blood. — *du soleil;* (bot.) sun-dew. — *du matin;* morning-dew. *Goutte de — ;* dew-drop.

roselet (rŏ-zlè), *n.m.*, (mam.) stoat.

roselière, *n.f.*, reed-bank.

roselle, *n.f.*, (orni.) redwing.

roséole, *n.f.*, (med.) roseola.

roserale (rŏz-rè), n.f., rosery.

rosette, n.f., rosette; small rose; rose-diamond, rose; red ink; red chalk; (ich.) grey gurnard; (metal.) cake; (orni.) redwing, swine-pipe; (hat-making—*chapellerie*) tip; (paint.) rosette, roset. *Diamant à* —; rose-diamond.

rosier, n.m., rose-tree, rose-bush.

rosière, n.f., young girl who has obtained the rose as a reward for good conduct; (ich.) minnow, pink.

roson, n.m. V. **rosace**.

rosse, n.f., jade, sorry horse; (ich.) roach.

rosser, v.a., to belabour, to lick, to thrash, to curry, to maul soundly, to drub, to give a drubbing to.

*rossignol, n.m., (orni.) nightingale; pipe, flute (made of bark—*d'écorce*); stop (of organ—*d'orgue*); picklock; (carp.) wedge; shopkeeper (old article—*vieille marchandise invendable*). — *d'Arcadie*; jackass. — *de muraille;* (orni.) redstart.

*rossignoler, v.n., (fam.) to imitate the nightingale's song.

rossinante, n.f., Rosinante (sorry horse—*rosse*).

rossinante, n.m., Rosinante, Don Quixote's horse.

rossolis, n.m., rossolis (liquor—*liqueur*); (bot.) sun-dew.

roster, v.a. V. **rouster**.

rostral, -e, adj., rostral.

rostre, n.m., (zool.) rostrum.

rostré, -e, adj., rostrate, rostrated.

rostres, n.m.pl., (antiq.) rostrum; (arch.) rostrum.

rosture, n.f. V. **rousture**.

rot, n.m., (l.ex.) belch, eructation.

rôt, n.m., roast, roast meat; first course. *Gros* —; joint of meat. *Petit* —; roast of game.

rotacé, -e, adj., (bot.) rotate, rotated.

rotang, n.m. V. **rotin**.

rotateur, n. and adj. m., (anat.) rotator; rotatory.

rotateurs, n.m.pl., (zool.) rotatories.

rotation, n.f., rotation.

rotatoire, adj., rotatory.

rotatoires, n.m.pl., (ent.) rotifers, rotatories, wheel-animals, wheel-insects, wheel-animal-cules.

rote, n.f., rota (court of Rome—*juridiction de Rome*).

roter, v.n., (l.ex.) to belch.

rôti, n.m., roast, roast meat.

rôtie (-tî), n.f., toast. *Une* —; a piece of toast.

rotifère, n.m., (ent.) rotifer, wheel-animal.

rotiforme, adj., (zool.) wheel-shaped.

rotin, n.m., (bot.) rotang; rattan, rattancane.

rôtir, v.a., to roast; to broil; to toast (bread—*pain*); to burn, to parch. — *au four;* to bake. *N'être bon ni à* — *ni à bouillir;* to be fit for nothing.

se rôtir, v.r., to parch, to burn, to roast one's self.

rôtir, v.n., to roast, to broil, to toast.

rôtisserie (-ti-srî), n.f., cook-shop.

rôtisseu-r, n.m., **-se**, n.f., keeper of a cookshop. — *en blanc;* keeper of a cock's shop who keeps meat ready to be roasted.

rôtissoire, n.f., roasting screen, roaster, Dutch oven.

rotonde, n.f., rotunda, rotundo; rotunda (inside back part of a diligence—*de diligence*).

rotondité, n.f., rotundity, roundness; plumpness, fatness.

rotule, n.f., (anat.) patella, knee-pan, kneecap.

roture, n.f., commonalty, plebeian state. *Il est né dans la* —; he is of ignoble birth.

roturi-er, -ère, n. and adj., commoner, plebeian, of mean birth; vulgar, mean. ⊙*Air* —; vulgar air.

roturièrement (-rièr-mān), adv., after the manner of plebeians; meanly, commonly, vulgarly.

rouage, n.m., wheelwork, wheels; machinery; (horl.) movement.

rouan, -ne, adj., (of horses—*des chevaux*) roan.

rouan, n.m., roan horse.

rouanne, n.f., brand-iron, used by excise officers for marking wine casks.

rouanner, v.a., to brand, as excise officers do.

rouannette, n.f., (carp.) timber-marker.

rouble, n.m., rouble, ruble (Russian coin—*monnaie russe*).

rouc, n.m. V. **rock**.

rouche, n.f., (nav.) a ship's hull.

roucou, n.m., (bot.) annotto, arnotto, arnotto-tree, roucou; (dy.) annotto, arnotto, roucou.

roucouer, v.a., to paint with annotto, arnotto.

se roucouer, v.r., to paint one's self with arnotto.

roucoulement (-kool-mān), n.m., cooing (pigeons).

roucouler, v.n. and a., to coo (pigeons); to warble, to warble forth. — *aux pieds d'une femme;* to make love to a woman in a maudlin, spooney, silly manner.

roucouyer, n.m., (bot.) roucou, roucou-tree, annotto, arnotto, arnotto-tree.

roudou, n.m. V. **redoul**.

roue, n.f., wheel; (torture) wheel; (artil.) truck. — *d'affût de canon;* truck of a gun-carriage. — *d'une horloge;* clock-wheel. *Pousser à la* —; to push the wheel, to help. *Mettre des bâtons dans les* —*s;* to thwart, to put spokes into the wheels. *Un paon fait la* —; a peacock spreads his tail. *Cet homme fait la* —; that man struts about. *Faire la* —; to tumble over and over, to do the windmill. — *de compte* (horl.); notch-wheel. — *dentée;* toothed-wheel. — *de rencontre* (horl.); balance-wheel. — *de câble* (nav.); coil. — *de gouvernail;* steering-wheel. *Mettre à la* —; to rack, to put to the rack.

roué, n.m., roué; rake, profligate; trickster.

roué, -e, adj., (of deer's horns—*bois du cerf*) close.

rouelle, n.f., round slice, round; (vet.) rowel. — *de citron;* slice of lemon. — *de veau;* fillet of veal.

rouennerie (rooa-n-rî), n.f., printed cotton goods.

rouer, v.a., to break upon the wheel; to crush; to jade. — *quelqu'un de coups;* to beat any one unmercifully. *Être roué de fatigue;* to be jaded with fatigue. — *un câble;* to coil a cable.

rouerie (roo-rî), n.f., rakish, profligate act, action of a roué; trickery.

rouet, n.m., small wheel; spinning-wheel; purr (of a cat—*du chat*); cog-wheel of a mill. — *de tisserand;* weaver's cloth-beam. — *d'arquebuse;* lock of an arquebuse. *Faire le* —; to purr (as a cat does—*du chat*).

rouette, n.f., (tech.) osier-twig.

roue-vis, n.f. (—*s* —), screw-wheel.

rouge, adj., red; blood-red; blood-shot; red-hot. *Fer* —; red-hot iron. *Boulets* —*s;* red-hot balls. *Cuivre* —; copper. — *trogne;* red face.

rouge, n.m., red; red paint, rouge; redness, blush; (orni.) shoveller. — *vif;* vivid red,

bright red. — *brun ;* brownish red. — *d'écarlate ;* scarlet. — *sanguin ;* blood red. — *de garance ;* madder.

rouge, *adv.*, only used in : *Se fâcher tout — ;* to get seriously angry.

rougeâtre (-jâtr), *adj.*, somewhat red, reddish.

rougeaud, -e (-jô, -d), *n.* and *adj.*, red-faced person ; ruddy-faced, red-faced, ruddy.

rouge-bord, *n.m.* (—*s —s*), bumper (of red wine—*de vin rouge*).

rouge-gorge, *n.m.* (—*s —s*), (orni.) redbreast, robin redbreast.

rougeole (-jol), *n.f.*, (med.) measles, rubeola.

rouge-queue, *n.m.* (—*s —s*), red-start, redtail.

rouget, *n.m.*, (ich.) gurnet, red gurnet ; red surmullet ; (ent.) wheal-worm.

rougette, *n.f.*, (mam.) pteropus.

rougeur, *n.f.*, redness, ruddiness ; blush, glow, colour ; *pl.*, (med.) rosy-drop. *La — lui est montée au visage ;* the colour came into her cheeks.

rougir, *v.n.*, to redden, to grow red ; to colour, to colour up, to blush. — *de honte ;* to blush with shame. — *de colère ;* to redden with anger. —*jusqu'au blanc des yeux ;* to blush up to the eyes, to colour up to the eyes. *Faire — quelqu'un ;* to put any one to the blush.

rougir, *v.a.*, to redden ; to mix red wine with water.

roui, *n.m.*, steeping, soaking, maceration ; retting ; fustiness.

*****rouille**, *n.f.*, rust, rustiness (of metals—*des métaux*) ; flaw (of mirrors—*des miroirs*) ; (bot.) mildew, blight, blast. *La — mange le fer ;* rust corrodes iron. *La — du temps ;* the rust of time. *Ces froments sont chargés de — ;* this wheat is mildewed.

*****rouillé, -e**, *adj.*, rusty.

*****rouiller**, *v.a.*, to rust, to make rusty ; to blight ; to impair.

se **rouiller**, *v.r.*, to rust, to grow rusty ; to get rusty, to become rusty; to rust, to be impaired.

*****rouilleu-x**, **-se**, *adj.*, ferruginated.

*****rouillure**, *n.f.*, rustiness, rust.

rouir, *v.a.*, to steep, to soak, to macerate (hemp, flax—*le chanvre, le lin*), to ret.

rouir, *v.n.*, to be retted.

rouissage, *n.m.*, soaking, steeping, retting (of flax or hemp—*du lin, du chanvre*).

roulade, *n.f.*, roll, rolling ; (mus.) roulade ; (cook.) collar. *Faire une — de* (cook.) ; to collar.

roulage, *n.m.*, rolling ; carriage (of goods—*de marchandises*) ; waggon-office ; waggon. — *accéléré ;* fly-waggon.

roulant, -e, *adj.*, rolling ; easy (of roads—*des routes*) ; (surg.) moving (of veins—*des veines*). *Chemin — ;* easy way. *Feu —* (milit.) ; running fire. *Presse —e* (print.) ; press at work.

rouleau, *n.m.*, roll ; roller ; rolling-pin ; roll, twist (of tobacco—*de tabac*) ; coil (of a rope—*d'une corde*) ; (med.) roller ; (print.) roller ; (tech.) sheave. — *de papier ;* roll of paper. *Plier en — ;* to roll up. *Être au bout de son — ;* to be at one's wits' end. — *d'imprimeur ;* printer's roller.

roulée, *n.f.*, (pop.) thrashing, drubbing.

roulement (rool-mān), *n.m.*, rolling, roll ; (mus.) roll ; roll (of a drum—*de tambour*) ; rotation ; volutation. — *d'yeux ;* rolling of the eyes.

rouler, *v.a.*, to roll, to roll up ; to wind, to wind up ; to revolve, to turn over ; to pass, to pass away. — *une chose dans sa tête ;* to turn a thing over in one's mind. — *sa vie ;* to pass one's life. — *carrosse ;* to ride in one's carriage, to keep a carriage.

se **rouler**, *v.r.*, to roll one's self, to roll, to tumble ; to wallow ; to wind.

roulor, *v.n.* to roll, to revolve ; to tumble ; to toss ; to ramble, to wander. to stroll ; to keep going ; to succeed by rotation ; to be plentiful (of a thing—*d'une chose*). *Faire — la presse ;* (print.) to set the press a-going. — *sur l'or et sur l'argent ;* to roll in riches. *Tout roule là-dessus ;* all turns upon that. *Ils roulent ensemble ;* they take their turns. *Faire — ;* to keep going.

roulet, *n.m.*, hatter's roller.

roulette, *n.f.*, roller. truckle, little wheel ; truckle-bed ; ⊙hand-chaise, Bath-chair ; caster ; roulette (game—*jeu*) ; (geom.) cycloid. *Lit à —s ;* bedstead on casters. — *de relieur ;* bookbinder's fillet.

rouleur, *n.m.*, (ent.) vine-fretter, vine-grub.

rouleuse, *n.f.*, name of a kind of caterpillar.

roulier, *n.m.*, waggoner, carter.

roulis, *n.m.*, (nav.) rolling. labouring ; roll.

rouloir, *n.m.*, rolling-board (for wax-candles —*à bougies*).

roupie, *n.f.*, (East Indian coin—*monnaie indienne*) rupee ; (l.ex.) snivel. *Avoir la — ;* to snivel.

roupieu-x, **-se**, *adj.*, (l.u.) snively.

*****roupiller**, *v.n.*, (pop.) to doze, to slumber.

*****roupilleu-r**, *n.m.*, **-se**, *n.f.*, (pop.) dozer, slumberer.

roure, *n.m.*, (bot.) English oak.

roussâtre, *adj.*, reddish, ruddy.

, **rousseau**, *n.* and *adj.m.*, (fam.) red-haired man ; red-haired.

rousselet (roo-slè), *n.m.*, (bot.) russet pear.

rousserolle (roo-srol), *n.f.*, (orni.) great sedge-warbler.

roussette, *n.f.*, (orni.) bog-rush ; (ich.) dogfish, bounce ; (mam.) pteropus.

rousseur, *n.f.*, redness, freckle. *Avoir des —s, avoir des taches de — ;* to be freckled.

roussi, *n.m.*, smell of burning ; ⊙Russian leather.

roussin, *n.m.*, strong thick-set stallion. — *d'Arcadie ;* ass, jackass.

roussir, *v.a.* and *n.*, to make reddish ; to singe, to scorch (by fire—*au feu*) ; to dye of a rusty colour, of a fawn-colour ; to grow red, to turn red ; to singe, to scorch.

roussissage, *n.m.*, dying reddish.

rouster, *or* **rusturer**, *v.a.*, (nav.) to woold, to wind (ropes—*des cordages*).

rousture, *or* **rosture**, *n.f.*, (nav.) woolding, winding (ropes—*de cordages*).

rout (raoot), *n.m.* (—), rout (assembly—*assemblée*).

*****routailler**, *v.a.*, (hunt.) to track with the bloodhound, to track.

route, *n.f.*, road, horse-way, way ; route, direction, path, course ; (nav.) track, course, way, run ; riding (in a forest—*dans une forêt*) ; track, path (of planets, comets—*des astres*). *Grand— (—s)* ; highway. — *ordinaire ;* common road. — *de traverse ;* cross road. *Il est resté en —, he remained behind. Il est en — ;* he is on his way. *Prendre la — de :* to take the way to. *Faire — ;* to travel. *Faire —* (nav.) ; to sail. *À la — !* (nav.) steer the course ! *Porter à — ;* to make a straight course. *Faire fausse — ;* (nav.) to alter the course. — *estimée ;* (nav.) dead reckoning. *Feuille de — (milit.) ; route ; way-bill (of public conveyances —de voitures publiques). On lui a tracé sa — ;* his road is marked out. *La — de la gloire ;* the road to glory. *La — de la vertu ;* the path of virtue.

routier (-tié), *n.m.*, (geog.) tract-chart ; person who knows the roads well. *Vieux — ;* old stager.

routi-er, -ère, *adj.*, of roads. *Carte —ère ;* road-map.

routiers, *n.m.pl.*, name given in France

during the middle ages to bands of plunderers, of highwaymen ; also to light troops.

routine, *n.f.*, routine ; rote (frequent repetition of sounds—*répétition fréquente des mêmes sons*). *Par* — ; by routine, by rote.

routiner, *v.a.*, (l.u.) to habituate, to accustom one to a thing by routine.

routini-er, **-ère**, *n.* and *adj.*, person acting by routine ; of routine.

routoir, *n.m.*, retting-pond ; retting-pit.

rouverin (roo-vrin), *adj.m.*, (metal.) blistered, brittle, hot, short.

rouvieux, or **roux-vieux**, *n.* and *adj.m.* (*n.p.*), (vet.) mange ; mangy.

rouvre, *n.m.*, (bot.) English oak.

rouvrir, *v.a.*, to open again. — *une plaie ;* to reopen a wound.

rou-x, **-sse**, *adj.*, reddish, red-haired, russet. *Homme* — ; red-haired man. *Vents* — ; cold dry winds. *Lune —sse ;* April moon.

roux, *n.m.*, reddish colour ; russet ; (mam.) field-mouse ; (cook.) brown butter sauce. — *ardent ;* fiery red.

roux-vieux, *n.m.* V. **rouvieux**.

royal, **-e** (roa-yal), *adj.*, royal, regal, kingly, kinglike.

royale (roa-yal), *n.f.*, tuft of beard just below the underlip.

royalement (roa-yal-mān), *adv.*, royally, regally, in a kingly manner.

royalisme (roa-ya-), *n.m.*, royalism.

royaliste (roa-ya-), *n.m.f.* and *adj.*, royalist.

royaume (roa-yôm), *n.m.*, kingdom, realm.

royauté (roa-yô-), *n.f.*, royalty. *Abdiquer la* — ; to abdicate the throne. *Les marques de la* — ; the regalia.

r.p., initial letters of *Révérend Père ;* reverend father.

rr., abbreviation of *Royales*, royal.

ru, *n.m.*, channel supplied by a little stream.

ruade, *n.f.*, kick (of horses, &c.—*des chevaux, &c.*); *pl.*, kicking. *Détacher une* —; to give a kick.

rubabelle, or **rubace**, *n.f.*, rubicel, rubicelle.

ruban, *n.m.*, ribbon ; (arch.) beading. *Garniture de —s ;* set of ribbons. — *de fil ;* tape. — - *d'eau* (—*s*—) (bot.); bur-reed, sparganium ramosum. *Canon à —s ;* twisted gun-barrel. —*s de la glotte*, —*s vocaux* (anat.); vocal cords. — *de soie ;* silk ribbon. — *de velours ;* velvet ribbon.

rubané, **-e**, *part.*, (zool.) striped ; flattened, ribbon-like. *Canon* — ; twisted gun-barrel.

rubaner, *v.a.*, to trim with rubans ; to arrange flax and hemp fibres ; to divide wax into bandelets ; to twist a band of iron to turn it into gun-barrels.

rubanerie (-ba-n-rī), *n.f.*, ribbon-weaving ; ribbon-trade.

rubani-er, **ère**, *adj.*, ribbon. *Industrie —ère ;* ribbon-manufacturing, ribbon-trade.

rubanier, *n.m.*, ribbon-weaver ; (bot.) bur-reed.

rubanière, *n.f.*, ribbon-weaver.

rubarbe, *n.f.* V. **rhubarbe**.

rubasse, *n.f.*, (min.) coloured quartz.

rubéfaction, *n.f.*, (med.) rubefaction.

rubéfiant, **-e**, *adj.*, (med.) rubefacient.

rubéfiant, *n.m.*, (med.) rubefacient.

rubéfier, *v.a.*, (med.) to rubify.

⊙**rubeline**. *n.f.* V. **rouge-gorge**.

rubescent, **-e**, *adj.*, rubescent.

rubiacé, **-e**, *adj.*, red coloured.

rubiacées, *n.f.pl.*, plants of the madder family.

rubican, *n.m.* and *adj.*, rubican colour ; rubican.

rubicon, *n.m.*, Rubicon. *Passer le* — ; to take a desperate step.

rubicond, **-e**,*adj.*, rubicund.

rubification, *n.f.*, rubification.

rubigineu-x, **-se**, *adj.*, ferruginated.

⊙**rubine**, *n.f.*, (chem.) ruby. — *d'argent ;* red-silver, ruby-silver. — *d'arsenic ;* realgar.

rubis, *n.m.*, ruby ; red pimple. *Faire — sur l'ongle ;* to drink to the last drop. *Payer — sur l'ongle ;* to pay to the last farthing.

rubricaire, *n.m.*, rubrician, rubricist.

rubricateur, *n.m.*, artist who illuminated manuscripts in the middle ages.

rubrique, *n.f.*, method ; head ; title ; trick ; ruddle, red chalk ; (canon law—*loi canon*) —*s*, *pl.*, rubric. *Sous la — de ;* under the head of.

ruche, *n.f.*, hive ; swarm ; (needle-work—*ouvrage à l'aiguille*) quilling, frilling, ruche. — *d'abeilles ;* bee-hive. *Châtrer une* — ; to. cut away the wax and honey from a hive. — *marine ;* sponge inhabited by aquatic animals.

rucher, *n.m.*, stand for bees ; apiary.

rucher, *v.a.*, (needlework—*ouvrage à l'aiguille*) to quill, to frill.

rudâni-er, **ère**, *adj.*, (l.u.) surly, churlish.

rude, *adj.*, harsh, rough, rugged, uneven ; sharp, rude, hard ; disagreeable ; grating ; violent, fierce ; severe, bitter ; rigid, strict ; formidable ; uncouth, unpolished ; impetuous, boisterous ; troublesome. *Avoir la peau* — ; to have a rough skin. *Une — épreuve ;* a severe trial. *Chemin* — ; rugged road. *Avoir la voix* — ; to have a harsh voice. *Des manières —s ;* rough, coarse, manners. *Un — assaut ;* a fierce assault. *Les temps sont —s ;* times are hard. *Des paroles —s ;* harsh words.

rudement (ru-dmān), *adv.*, roughly, ruggedly, harshly, sharply, severely, strictly ; tumultuously, violently, impetuously, rudely *Traiter* — ; to treat roughly. *Aller — en besogne ;* to work hard.

rudenté, **-e**, *adj.*, (arch.) cabled (of columns —*colonnes*).

rudenture, *n.f.*, (arch.) cabling, rudenture.

rudéral, *adj.*, (bot.) of a plant that grows in rubbish.

rudesse, *n.f.*, harshness ; roughness ; ruggedness ; severity ; tumultuousness ; fierceness, violence ; austerity, strictness ; troublesomeness ; rude thing, coarse thing ; rudeness.

rudiment, *n.m.*, rudiment. *Il en est encore aux —s ;* he is still in his rudiments.

rudimentaire, *adj.*, rudimental, elementary, rudimentary.

rudoyer, *v.a.*, to use roughly, harshly ; to speak harshly to ; to ill-treat (a horse—*un cheval*).

rue, *n.f.*, street ; (bot.) rue. — *passante ;* much frequented street. *Courir les —s ;* to run much the streets ; to be in everybody's mouth (of news —*des nouvelles*) ; to be common (of a thing—*des choses*). — *de traverse ;* cross-street. — *écartée ;* back street. *Il est fou à courir les —s ;* he is stark mad. — *de chèvre ;* goat's-rue.

ruelle, *n.f.*, lane, alley ; bed-side.

rueller, *v.a.*, to mould (vines—*les vignes*).

ruer, *v a.*, (l.u.) to fling, to hurl, to cast ; to throw. — *de grands coups ;* to deal heavy blows.

se ruer, *v.r.*, to throw one's self ; to rush upon.

ruer, *v.n.*, to kick (of horses, &c.—*des chevaux, &c.*).

rueu-r, **-se**, *adj.*, (man.) that kicks. *Cheval* — ; horse which kicks.

rufian (-fi-ān), or **rufien** (-fi-in), *n.m.*, a lewd pimp, a pander.

rugine, *n.f.*, (surg.) rugine, scalp.

ruginer, *v.a.*, (surg.) to scalp.

rugir, *v.n.*, to roar.

rugissant, **-e**, *adj.*, roaring.

rugissement (-jis-mān), *n.m.*, roaring, roar.

rugosité, *n.f.*, rugosity, wrinkle.

rugueu-x, **-se** (-gheû, -z), *adj.*, rugose, wrinkled.

ruilée, n.f., (arch.) verge.

ruine, n.f., ruin, decay ; overthrow. *Tomber en — s ;* to fall to ruins. *Tomber en — ;* to run to ruin. *Courir à sa — ;* to go to ruin ; to go to wreck and ruin. *Battre en — (milit.) ;* to batter down.

ruiné, -e, adj., ruined. *Son crédit est ruiné ;* his credit is gone. *Un tempérament — ;* a worn-out constitution.

ruiner, v.a., to ruin, to lay waste ; to spoil ; to undo, to overthrow. *— un cheval ;* to spoil a horse.

se **ruiner**, v.r., to decay ; to fall to decay ; to ruin one's self ; to be ruined, spoilt.

ruineu-x, -se, adj., falling to ruin ; ruinous.

ruinure, n.f., (carp.) bearing.

ruisseau, n.m., brook, stream, rivulet ; gutter, street-kennel. *Petit — ;* rivulet, brook.

ruisselant, -e (rui-slân, -t), adj., streaming, running.

ruisseler (rui-slé), v.n., to gush, to stream ; to trickle, to trickle down.

⊙**ruisselet** (rui-slè), n.m., rivulet.

rum, n.m. V. **rhum.**

rumb (romb), n.m., (nav.) rhumb.

rumen (-mè-n), n.m., rumen, paunch.

rumeur, n.f., rumour, report, clamour, uproar, noise.

ruminant, -e, adj., ruminant, ruminating.

ruminant, n.m., (mam.) ruminant.

rumination, n.f., rumination, chewing the cud.

ruminer, v.n., to ruminate, to chew the cud ; to muse on, to ponder upon, to think over.

ruminer, v.a., to ruminate ; to think over, to muse over. *Que ruminez-vous là !* what are you musing on there ?

runes, n.f.pl., runes, runic characters.

runique, adj., runic.

⊙**ruption**, n.f., (paint.) ruption.

⊙**ruptoire**, n.m., (surg.) potential cautery.

rupture, n.f., breaking, rupture ; bursting ; (med.) rupture, hernia ; fracture ; (paint.) mixture of colours. *La — d'un os ;* the fracture of a bone. *La — d'un tendon ;* the rupture of a sinew. *La — d'un mariage ;* the breaking off of a match.

rural, -e, adj., rural.

ruse, n.f., artifice, wile, deceit, craft, ruse, cunning, trick ; (hunt.) double. *User de — s ;* to use deceit.

rusé, -e. adj., artful, deceitful, cunning, crafty, sly, subtle, designing. *Un — matois ;* a sharp blade.

ruser, v.n., to use deceit, craft, guile ; (hunt.) to double.

russe, n.m.f. and adj., Russian.

rustaud, -e, adj., (fam.) boorish, rustic, coarse, uncouth.

rustaud, n.m., (fam.) rustic ; clod-hopper.

rustaudement (-tô-dmân), adv., (fam.) V. **rustiquement.**

rustauderie (-tô-drî), n.f. (fam.). V. **rusticité.**

rusticité, n.f., rusticity, clownishness, churlishness, uncouthness.

rustique, adj., rural, rustic, country ; artless, boorish. *Vie — ;* country life. *Ouvrage — ;* rustic work. *Manières — s ;* rustic manners. *Langage — ;* boorish language.

rustique, n.m., (arch.) rustic order.

rustiquement (-tik-mân), adv., rustically, rudely, clownishly, boorishly, uncouthly.

rustiquer, v.a., (arch.) to rusticate, to jag out.

rustre, n.m. and adj., boor, clown ; boorish, clownish, rude.

rusturer, v.a. V. **rouster.**

rut (rut), n.m., rut (of deer—*du cerf*).

rutabaga, n.m., (agri.) Swedish turnip, ruta-baga.

rutilant, -e, adj., rutilant.

rutoir, n.m., (manu.) retting-pit ; retting-pond.

rythme, n.m., rhythm, rhythmus.

rythmique, adj., rhythmical.

S

s (èss), n.f., (se), n.m., the nineteenth letter of the alphabet, s. [S is added for the sake of euphony to the second *pers. sing.* of the imperative of verbs of the first conjugation before *y*, as : *vas-y ;* go there ; and also before *en,* as : *donnes-en ;* give some.]

s', contraction of **se.**

sa, adj.f., his, her, one's, its. V. **son.**

sabbat, n.m., Sabbath, seventh day of the week among the Jews ; Sabbath (sabbatic year *—année sabbatique*) ; nocturnal meeting of witches ; racket, uproar, tumult, scolding. *— de chats ;* caterwauling. *Faire un — ;* to make an uproar. *Faire un beau — à quelqu'un ;* to scold one well.

sabbataire, n.m., Sabbatarian ; Seventh-day Baptist.

sabbatine, n.f., examination, thesis passed by students in the first year of their course.

sabbatique, adj., sabbatical (of years—*des années*).

sabbatisme, n.m., sabbatism.

sabéen (-in), adj., sabian.

sabéisme, *or* **sabaïsme**, n.m., Sabianism.

sabellianisme, n.m., sabellianism.

sabellien (-li-in), n.m., sabellien.

sabine, n.f., (bot.) savin.

sabisme, n.m., Sabianism.

sable, n.m., sand ; gravel ; (h.u.) hour-glass ; (her.) sable. *Banc de — ;* sand-bank. *— mouvant ;* shifting sand.

sablé, -e, adj., laid with sand.

sabler, v.a., to gravel, to sand, to cover with sand or gravel ; to drink off. *— un verre de vin ;* to toss off a glass of wine.

sableu-x, -se, adj., sandy.

sablier, n.m., hour-glass ; (nav.) glass ; sand-box ; (bot.) sand-box.

sablière, n.f., sand-pit, gravel-pit, sablière ; (carp.) sablière, raising-piece ; (arch.) wall-plate ; torsel.

sablon, n.m., sand, small sand.

sablonner, v.a., to scour with sand.

sablonneu-x, -se, adj., sandy, gritty.

sablonnier, n.m., seller of sand.

sablonnière, n.f., sand-pit, gravel-pit.

sabord, n.m., (nav.) port, port-hole.

sabot, n.m., sabot, wooden shoe, horse's hoof ; shoe (of carriages—*de voitures*) ; (conch.) turban, turban-shell ; socket (of furniture—*de meubles*) ; top (play-thing—*jouet*) ; sorry fiddle. *Dormir comme un — ;* to sleep like a top. *Il est venu à Londres en — s* (fig.) ; when he came to London he wore hobnailed shoes.

saboter, v.n., to spin a top ; to make a noise with one's shoes ; v.a., to arm the end of a stake with an iron socket ; (pop.) to do work quickly but slovenly.

sabotier (-tié), n.m., maker of, wearer of, wooden shoes.

sabotière, n.f., dance of people in wooden shoes.

sabouler, v.a., (pop.) to push about, to toss about ; to scold, to rate.

sabre, n.m., sabre ; broadsword.

⊙**sabrenas**, n.m., cobbler ; bungler.

⊙**sabrenasser**, v.a. V. **sabrenauder.**

⊙**sabrenauder**, *v.a.*, to cobble, to botch, to bungle.

sabrer, *v.a.*, to strike *or* cut with a sabre, to sabre; to hurry over. — *une affaire*; to hurry over a business.

sabretache, *n.f.*, (milit.) sabretache.

sabreur, *n.m.*, (fam.) brave soldier, but no strategist.

⊙**sabuleu-x**, **-se**, *adj.*, gritty.

saburral, **-e**, *adj.*, (med.) relating to indigestion.

saburre, *n.f.*, (med.) indigestion.

sac, *n.m.*, sack, bag; knapsack; sackcloth; (surg.) sac; bag, pouch (of certain animals—*de quelques animaux*); plunder, sack, sacking, pillage, ransacking. — *de nuit*; carpet-bag. — *à ouvrage*; work-bag. *Homme de* — *et de corde*; Newgate-bird. — *à vin*; drunkard. *Cul-de- —(—s —)*; blind alley. *Mettre quelqu'un au* —; to nonplus any one. *Tirer d'un — deux moutures*; to take double fees. *Voir le fond du* —; to sift a business to the bottom. — *de blé*; sack of wheat. — *de procès*; lawyer's bag. *Donner communication de son* — (jur.); to communicate papers. *Remplir son* — (fam., pop.); to fill one's belly. *Donner à quelqu'un son* —; to send one about his business, to give any one the sack. *Vider son* —; to exhaust one's budget, to have one's say out. *Mettre une ville à* —; to plunder, to sack a town.

saccade, *n.f.*, (man.) saccade, jerk (with a bridle—*de la bride*); check, rebuke, reproof, reprimand; scolding, rating; (fig.) sudden, brusque movement; fit, start. *Par —s*; by fits and starts.

saccadé, **-e**, *part.*, by jerks. *Style* —; abrupt style.

saccader, *v.a.*, (man.) to jerk, to twitch.

saccage, *n.m.*, havoc, confusion, confused heap.

saccagement (sa-kaj-mān), *n.m.*, sack, sackage, sacking, pillaging, ransacking, plunder.

saccager, *v.a.*, to sack, to ransack, to pillage, to plunder; to throw into confusion.

saccageur, *n.m.*, plunderer; sacker.

saccharate (sak-ka-),*n.m.*,(chem.) saccharated. — *de chaux*, saccharated solution of lime.

sacchareu-x, **-se** (sak-ka-), *adj.*, saccharine.

saccharifère (sak-ka-), *adj.*, sacchariferous.

saccharimètre (sak-ka-), *n.m.*, saccharometer.

saccharin, **-e** (sak-ka-), *adj.*, saccharine.

saccharique (sak-ka-), *adj.*, saccharic.

saccharure (sak-ka-), *n.m.*, (pharm.) sugar of. — *d'aconit*; sugar of aconite.

sacciforme (sak-si-), *adj.*, (bot.) bagged.

sacerdoce, *n.m.*, priesthood.

sacerdocratie (-ci), *n.f.*, government of priests.

sacerdotal, **-e**, *adj.*, sacerdotal.

sachée, *n.f.*, sackful, bagful.

sachem (sa-shèm), *n.m.*, sachem (Indian chief—*chef indien*).

sachet, *n.m.*, satchel, little bag or sack; scent-bag.

sachet, *n.m.*, **-te**, *n.f.*, friar, nun, of the Order of the Sack or of the Penitence of Jesus Christ.

sacoche, *n.m.*, saddle-bag; money-bag.

sacramentaire, *n.m.*, sacramentarian.

sacramental, **-e**, *or* **sacramentel**, **-le**, *adj.*, sacramental. *Mots sacramentaux*; decisive words.

sacramentalement (-tal-mān), *or* **sacramentellement**, *adv.*, sacramentally.

sacre, *n.m.*, anointing, coronation of a king; (orni.) saker; (fig.) ⊙ a villain. — *d'un évêque*; consecration of a bishop.

sacré, **-e**, *adj.*, sacred, holy, consecrated;

(l.ex.) damned, cursed, confounded; (anat.) sacral.

sacrement, *n.m.*, Sacrament; Matrimony. Marriage. *S'approcher des —s*; to go to Confession and receive the Sacrament. *Saint* —; Holy Sacrament; (c.rel.) Host; (c.rel.) monstrance. *Administrer les derniers —s à quelqu'un*; to administer the last Sacrament to any one. *Recevoir le* —; to receive the Sacrament, to take the Sacrament. *Office du saint* —; Communion-service.

sacrer, *v.a.*, to anoint, to crown, a king; to consecrate a bishop.

sacrer, *v.n.*, to curse, to swear.

sacret, *n.m.*, (hawking—*fauconnerie*) sakeret.

sacrificateur, *n.m.*, sacrificer. *Souverain* —; high-priest.

sacrificatoire, *adj.*, sacrificial.

sacrificature, *n.f.*, office of sacrificer.

sacrifice, *n.m.*, sacrifice, offering, peace-offering. — *d'action de grâces*, — *de louange* (Bibl.); thanksgiving.

sacrifier, *v.a.*, to sacrifice, to make offerings; to immolate; to devote time to a thing. — *des victimes*; to sacrifice victims. — *tout à ses intérêts*; to sacrifice every thing to one's interest.

sacrifier, *v.n.*, to sacrifice.

sacrilège, *n.m.*, sacrilege.

sacrilège, *n.m.f.* and *adj.*, sacrilegist, sacrilegious person; sacrilegious.

sacrilègement (-lèj-mān), *adv.*, sacrilegiously.

sacripant, *n.m.*, hector, bully, swaggerer, rodomont.

sacristain, *n.m.*, sexton; sacristan.

sacristie, *n.f.*, sacristy, vestry, vestry-room; audit-house (of cathedrals—*des cathédrales*); church plate, sacred vases, &c.; church fees.

sacristine, *n.f.*, vestry-nun.

sacro, *adj. invariable*, (rel.) holy. — *-saint*; very, doubly holy; (anat.) sacro.

sacrum,*n.m.*,(anat.)sacrum. *Os —*; sacrum, sacral bone.

saducéen (-cé-in), **-ne** (-cé-è-n), *n.* and *adj.*, Sadducee; Sadducean.

saducéisme, *n.m.*, Sadducism.

⊙**saette**, *n.f.* *V.* **sagette**.

safran, *n.m.*, (bot.) saffron; crocus. — *bâtard*; meadow-saffron, mock-saffron, bastard-saffron, safflower. — *de gouvernail* (nav.); after-piece of a rudder.

safrané, **-e**, *adj.*, saffron, saffroned; yellow (of the face—*du visage*).

safraner, *v.a.*, to saffron.

safranière, *n.f.*, saffron-plantation.

safranum (-nom), *n.m.*, (chem.) safflower.

⊙**safre**, *adj.*, (pop.) greedy, gluttonous.

safre, *n.m.*, (chem.) zaffre, zaffer.

saga, *n.f.*, saga, legend of the northern nations of Europe.

sagace, *adj.*, sagacious, acute, shrewd.

sagacité, *n.f.*, sagacity, sagaciousness, quickness, acuteness, shrewdness.

sagamore, *n.m.*, sagamore (Indian chief —*chef indien*).

sage, *adj.*, sage, wise, wary, rational, discreet, judicious, prudent; cool, sober, staid, well-behaved, steady, virtuous, modest; quiet, gentle. *Des lois —s*; wise laws. *Conduite* —; steady, prudent conduct. — *politique*; wise policy. *Être* —; (of children—*des enfants*) to be good, to be a good child.

sage; *n.m.*, wise man, sage.

sage-femme, *n.f.* (—*s* —*s*), midwife.

sagement (saj-mān), *adv.*, sagely, wisely, prudently, discreetly, judiciously, warily, soberly, steadily.

16 *

sagesse, *n.f.*, wisdom, sageness; moderation, discretion, prudence; steadiness, sobriety; goodness (of children—*des enfants*); gentleness (of animals—*des animaux*). *Prix de —; prize for good behaviour.*

○**sagette**, *or* **saette**, *n.f.*, arrow; (bot.) arrow-head; adder's-tongue.

sagine, *n.f.*, (bot.) pearl-grass, pearl-wort.

sagittaire, *n.m.*, (astron.) Sagittarius.

sagittaire, *n.f.*, (bot.) arrow-head, adder's-tongue.

sagittale, *adj.f.*, (anat.) sagittal.

sagitté, **-e**, *adj.*, (bot.) sagittate, arrow-headed.

sagou, *n.m.*, sago.

sagouier, *or* **sagoutier**, *n.m.*, (bot.) sago-tree.

sagouin, *n.m.*, **-e**, *n.f.*, (mam.) sagoin, she-sagoin; slovenly fellow, slovenly woman.

sagum (-gom), *n.m.*, (Roman antiq.) sagum.

s.a.i., initial letters of *Son Altesse Impériale*, His *or* Her Imperial Highness.

saie, *n.f.*, (antiq.) sagum (cloak—*manteau*); brush (used by goldsmiths—*d'orfèvre*); a light kind of serge.

*****saignant**, **-e**, *adj.*, bleeding, bloody; rare, rear, nearly raw, underdone (of roast meat—*de viande rôtie*).

*****saignée**, *n.f.*, (surg.) phlebotomy, bleeding, blood-letting; quantity of blood abstracted; small of the arm; trench (for draining—*de drainage*); (fig.) heavy payment, expense; drain.

*****saignement** (-măn), *n.m.*, bleeding. *— de nez;* bleeding at the nose.

*****saigner**, *v.a.*, to bleed, to let blood; (cook.) to kill; to drain; to get money out of, to bleed any one.

*se*****saigner**, *v.r.*, to bleed one's self, to drain one's self.

*****saigner**, *v.n.*, to bleed. *Je saigne du nez;* my nose bleeds. *— du nez;* to show the white feather, to want courage. *Le cœur me saigne;* it grieves me to the very heart.

*****saigneur**, *n.m.*, (fam., l.u.) bleeder, partisan of bleeding; blood-letter.

*****saigneu-x**, **-se**, *adj.*, bloody. *Bout —;* scrag end, neck of lamb, mutton, veal.

*****saillant**, **-e**, *adj.*, jutting out, projecting; striking, forcible, remarkable; (her.) salient.

*****saillant**, *n.m.*, (fort.) the salient angle of any work.

*****saille!** *archaic 2nd pers. sing. of the imperative of the verb saillir,* (nav.) haul! (word of command—*commandement*).

*****saillie**, *n.f.*, jutting out, projecture; prominence; start, sudden gush, spurt; sudden fit, sally; flash of wit, witticism; (arch.) jettee, bearing out; (arch.) rabbet, ledge; (of a steam-engine—*de machine à vapeur*) spindle.

*****saillir**, *v.n.*, (*irregular*), (arch.) to project, to jut, to jut out, to protrude, to rabbet; (paint.) to stand out. *Faire —;* to bring out. *Qui saille;* prominent. *Cette corniche saille trop;* that cornice projects too much.

*****saillir**, *v.a.*, (*regular*), (of animals—*des animaux*) to leap, to cover, to serve.

*****saillir**, *v.n.*, (*regular*), to gush, to spout out (of liquids—*des liquides*). *V.* **jaillir**, which is much more generally used.

sain, **-e**, *adj.*, sound, hale, healthy, sane, wholesome; (nav.) clear. *— de corps et d'esprit;* sound in body and mind. *Revenir — et sauf;* to return safe and sound. *Jugement —;* sound judgment. *Nourriture —;* wholesome food.

sainbois, *n.m.*, (bot.) spurge-flax.

saindoux, *n.m.*, lard.

sainement (sè-n-măn), *adv.*, soundly, rationally, judiciously, healthily, wholesomely.

sainfoin, *n.m.*, (bot.) sainfoin.

saint, **-e**, *adj.*, holy, sacred, godly, sainted; sanctified; consecrated, saintly. *— homme;* godly man. *L'Écriture —e;* Holy-Writ. *La semaine —e;* holy-week. *Le vendredi —;* Good-Friday. *La —-Jean;* Midsummer. *La —-Martin;* Martinmas-day. *Le —-siège;* the holy see. *—-père;* holy father, the Pope. *Le —-Esprit, l'Esprit —;* the Holy Ghost, the Holy Spirit. *Le —-empire romain, le —-empire;* once the name of the German empire. *— office;* the holy-office, a name for the Inquisition. *Mal —-Jean, mal de —;* falling sickness. *Rendre —;* to sanctify. *Lieu —;* sanctuary. *Terre —e;* consecrated ground; Holy Land. *Feu —-Antoine;* Saint Anthony's fire, erysipelas. [Saint is written with a capital letter and joined to the following name by a hyphen, when such name does not designate a saint: *la Saint-Jean;* Midsummer.]

saint, *n.m.*, **-e**, *n.f.*, saint, patron saint, patron. *— d'une ville;* patron saint of a town. *Mettre au nombre des —s;* to canonize. *Il ne sait à quel — se vouer;* he does not know which way to turn himself. *Le — des —s;* the holy of holies.

saint-augustin, *n.m.* (*n.p.*), Saint Augustine; (print.) Englich.

sainte-barbe, *n.f.* (—), (nav.) powder-magazine, gun-room.

saintement (sint-măn), *adv.*, holily, sacredly.

sainte nitouche, *n.f.* (*n.p.*), a sanctimonious-looking person. *Faire la — —;* to sham Abraham.

sainteté (sint-té), *n.f.*, holiness, sanctity, sacredness; Holiness (the Pope); (b.s.) saintship.

saint-germain, *n.m.* (—), (hort.) Saint Germain, a kind of pear.

saint-simonien, *n.m.*, **-ne**, *n.f.* (—-s), Saint-Simonian.

saint-simonisme, *n.m.* (*n.p.*), system of the Count of Saint-Simon.

saïque, *n.f.*, (nav.) saic.

saisi, *n.m.*, (jur.) person distrained.

saisie, *n.f.*, seizure, distress; caption. *— immobilière;* distress on real property. *— mobilière;* distress on movable goods, distress on personal property.

saisie-arrêt, *n.f.* (—s —), (jur.) attachment; garnishment (in London—*à Londres*).

saisie-brandon, *n.f.* (—s —), (jur.) execution on growing crops.

saisie-exécution, *n.f.* (—s —), (jur.) execution; distress.

saisie-gagerie, *n.f.* (—s —), (jur.) execution by way of security for house-rent.

saisie-revendication, *n.f.* (—s —), (jur.) attachment of goods claimed pending litigation of the claim.

saisine, *n.f.*, (jur.) seizin; (nav.) seizing, lashing.

saisir, *v.a.*, to seize, to seize upon, to catch, to lay hold of, to catch hold of, to get hold of, to take, to take hold of; to strike, to come upon, to impress; to embrace, to avail one's self of; to understand, to perceive, to discern, to comprehend; to attack; (jur.) to distrain; (jur.) to vest; (jur.) to attach. *— quelqu'un au collet;* to collar any one. *— l'occasion;* to seize the opportunity. *La peur les a saisis;* they were struck with fear. *— un tribunal d'une affaire;* to lay an affair before a court.

se **saisir**, *v.r.*, to seize, to catch hold, to lay hold; to arrest, to apprehend.

saisir-arrêter, *v.a.*, (jur.) to attach; (in London—*à Londres*) to garnish.

saisissable, *adj.*, distrainable, seizable; attachable.

saisissant, -e, *adj.,* (of cold—*du froid*) keen, sharp, piercing; striking, thrilling, startling.

saisissant, -e, *n.* and *adj.,* (jur.) distrainer, execution creditor; distraining.

saisissement (-zis-mān), *n.m.,* shock, chill, violent impression, pang.

saison, *n.f.,* season; proper time, moment. *Arrière-* — (— —*s*); latter end of the season, latter end of autumn. *La* — *est avancée;* the season is forward. *Morte-* —(—*s* —*s*) ; (com.) dull, dead season. *Morte* —; winter. *En temps et en* —; in due season. *Être en pleine* — ; to be in their prime (of flowers and fruits—*fleurs et fruits*). *Ces mets ne sont plus de* —; those dishes are out of season.

salade, *n.f.,* salad, salading; mess (for horses—*pour les chevaux*); sallet (kind of helmet—*sorte de casque*). *Retourner, fatiguer, la* — ; to mix the salad.

saladier, *n.m.,* salad-dish, salad-bowl.

salage, *n.m.,* salting.

salaire, *n.m.,* wages, pay, hire; recompense, reward. *Toute peine mérite* — ; the labourer is worthy of his hire.

salaison, *n.f.,* salting provisions; salt-provision.

salamalec, *n.m.,* (jest.) low bow.

salamandre, *n.f.,* salamander.

salangane, *n.f.,* (orni.) esculent swallow.

salant, *adj.,* salt; only used in : *Marais* — ; salt-marsh.

salarié, -e, *n.* and *part.,* person receiving a salary; hireling; placeman; paid.

salarier, *v.a.,* to pay; to give wages or a salary to.

salaud, -e, *n.* and *adj.,* sloven, dirty fellow; dirty woman, slut; slovenly, sluttish.

sale, *adj.* and *n.m.f.,* dirty, nasty, foul ; soiled ; filthy, low, coarse dirty person, sloven. *Vaisseau* — (nav.); foul ship. *Des paroles* —*s;* dirty words.

salé, *n.m.,* salt-pork. *Du petit* —; pork newly-salted; pickled pork.

salé, -e, *adj.,* salted, salt, briny; keen, biting ; coarse, broad. *Un peu* —; saltish. *Sources* —*es;* salt-springs. *Raillerie* —*e;* biting raillery. *Un propos* —; a coarse remark.

salement (sal-mān), *adv.,* dirtily, nastily, filthily, slovenly.

salep (sa-lèp), *n.m.,* salep, salop.

saler, *v.a.,* to salt, to salt down; to corn (beef —*le bœuf*); to overcharge for (goods—*les marchandises*); to overcharge (customers—*les pratiques, les clients*).

se saler, *v.r.,* to be salted (of a thing—*des choses*).

saleron (sal-ron), *n.m.,* bowl of a salt-cellar.

saleté (sal-té), *n.f.,* dirt, soil, dirtiness, nastiness, filthiness; filth, dirty rubbish; dirty thing ; coarseness, ribaldry .

saleur, *n.m.,* salter, curer.

salicaire, *n.f.,* salicaria; purple willow.

salicole, *adj.,* relating to the production of salt.

salicoque, *n.f.,* prawn.

salicor, *n.m.,* or **salicorne,** *n.f.,* (bot.) glasswort, saltwort.

⊙**salicot,** *n.m.* V. **salicoque.**

salicotte, *n.f.,* (bot.) saltwort.

'saliens, *n.m.pl.* and *adj.,* (antiq.) the name of the priests of Mars at Rome: the name of a Frankish tribe.

salière, *n.f.,* salt-cellar; salt-box; hollow over the eyes (of horses—*des chevaux*); hollow behind the collar-bone (of persons—*des personnes*).

salifère, *adj.,* saliferous.

salifiable, *adj.,* (chem.) salifiable.

salification, *n.f.,* (chem.) salification.

salifier, *v.a.,* to salify.

saligaud, *n.m.,* -e, *n.f.,* (pop.) dirty person; dirty thing; sloven; slut.

***salignon,** *n.m.,* salt-cat.

salin, -e, *adj.,* saline, salinous.

salin, *n.m.,* salt-marsh; raw salt.

saline, *n.f.,* salt provisions, salt-fish; salt-mine, salt-works.

salinier, *n.m.,* the owner and worker of salt works.

salique, *adj.,* salic. *Loi* —; salic law.

salir, *v.a.,* to dirt, to dirty, to soil, to stain, to taint.

se salir, *v.r.,* to dirty one's self ; to get dirty; to soil; to sully one's reputation.

salissant, -e, *adj.,* that soils, that gets dirty. *Une couleur* —*e;* a colour that soon soils.

salisson, *n.f.,* (pop.) young slut.

salissure, *n.f.,* spot of dirt.

salivaire, *adj.,* (anat.) salivary.

salivation, *n.f.,* (med.) salivation.

salive, *n.f.,* saliva; spittle.

saliver, *v.n.,* to spit; to be under salivation, to salivate.

salle, *n.f.,* hall, room ; ward (in hospitals— *d'hôpital*); (thea.) house ; arbour (of gardens— *dans un jardin*). — *à manger;* dining-room. *La* — *du commun;* the servants' hall. — *d'audience;* audience-chamber. — *de spectacle ;* play-house. — *de billard ;* billiard-room. — *d'armes;* fencing-school. — *de danse;* dancing-room, dancing-school. — *de verdure;* green arbour. — *d'asile,* infant-school.

salmigondis, *n.m.,* (cook.) hotch-potch, salmagundi; medley.

salmis, *n.m.,* ragout of game previously roasted.

saloir, *n.m.,* salt-box; salting-tub.

salon, *n.m.,* drawing-room; saloon, parlour; exhibition (of paintings, of works of art—*de peinture, de sculpture, &c.*) ; *pl.,* fashionable world.

salope, *n.* and *adj.f.,* slut; disorderly woman; slovenly, sluttish. *C'est une vraie* —; she is a perfect slut. *Marie-* — (—*s* —*s*); mud-boat.

salopement (-lop-mān), *adv.,* (pop.) sluttishly.

saloperie (-lo-prî), *n.f.,* slovenliness, slut-tishness ; coarse language.

salorge, *n.m.,* loaf of salt.

salpêtrage, *n.m.,* nitrification.

salpêtre, *n.m.,* saltpetre. *Ce n'est que du* — ; he takes fire, his blood is up, in a moment.

salpêtrer, *v.a.,* to throw saltpetre (over a space of ground—*sur un terrain*); to nitrify (a wall—*un mur*); to throw out, to produce, saltpetre.

se salpêtrer, *v.r.,* to nitrify, to throw out saltpetre (of walls, &c.—*des murs, &c.*).

salpêtreu-x, -se, *adj.,* saltpetrous.

salpêtrier, *n.m.,* saltpetre-maker.

salpêtrière, *n.f.,* saltpetre-works. *La* —; an asylum for old women and insane females in Paris.

***salsepareille,** *n.f.,* sarsaparilla.

salsifis (-fi), *n.m.,* (bot.) salsify. — *sauvage,* — *des prés;* goat's-beard. — *noir,* — *d'Espagne;* viper's-grass.

saltation, *n.f.,* saltation.

saltimbanque, *n.m.,* mountebank, buffoon.

⊙**saluade,** *n.f.,* bowing; making a low bow.

salubre, *adj.,* salubrious, wholesome, healthful, healthy.

salubrité, *n.f.,* salubrity, healthfulness, wholesomeness.

saluer, *v.a.,* to salute, to bow to; to hail, to greet ; to proclaim. — *la compagnie;* to bow to the company. *Je vous salue, j'ai l'honneur*

rous — (in letters—*fin de lettre*); your servant. your humble servant. — *le soleil;* to hail the sun. *Saluez-le de ma part;* remember me to him. — *de onze coups de canon;* to fire a salute of eleven guns.

se **saluer**, *v.r.*, to bow to, to salute. each other.

salure, *n.f.*, saltness, brine.

salut, *n.m.*, safety; (rel.) salvation; salute, bow; salutation; hail; (c.rel.) benediction; greeting form in official deeds. *Il a cherché son* — *dans la fuite;* he sought for safety in flight. *Un profond* —; a low bow. *Faire un* —; to make a bow; (nav., milit.) to fire a salute.

salutaire, *adj.*, salutary, wholesome, advantageous, beneficial.

salutairement (-tèr-mān), *adv.*, salutarily, beneficially.

salutation, *n.f.*, salutation; salute; bow. *Recevez mes* —*s;* yours truly (in letters—*fin de lettre*).

ⓒ**salvage**, *n.m.* *V.* **sauvetage**.

salvanos (-nôs), *n.m.* (—), (nav.) life-buoy.

ⓢ**salvations**, *n.f.*, (jur.) rejoinder.

salve, *n.f.*, (artil.) salute, volley. *Une* — *d'applaudissements;* a round of applause.

salvé, *n.m.* (—), (c.rel.) Salve Regina.

samaritain (-tin), -**e**, (-tè-n), *n.* and *adj.*, Samaritan.

samedi (sa-m-di), *n.m.*, Saturday.

samscrit, -**e**, *adj.* *V.* **sanscrit**.

san-benito, *n.m.* (—), san benito.

sancir, *v.n.*, (nav.) to founder, to sink.

sanctifiant, -**e**, *adj.*, sanctifying.

sanctificateur, *n.m.*, sanctifier.

sanctification, *n.f.*, sanctification.

sanctifier, *v.a.*, to sanctify, to make holy, to keep holy, to hallow.

sanction, *n.f.*, sanction; assent (of parliament—*du parlement*).

sanctionner, *v.a.*, to sanction.

sanctuaire, *n.m.*, sanctuary; (of the temple at Jerusalem—*du temple de Jérusalem*) holy of holies; (of churches—*des églises*) chancel; (fig.) church.

sandal, or **santal**, *n.m.*, sandal-wood, sandal.

sandale, *n.f.*, sandal; fencing-shoe.

sandalier, *n.m.*, sandal-maker.

sandaraque, *n.f.*, (bot.) sandarack, pounce.

sandjak, sandjiak, or **sandjiakat**, *n.m.* *V.* **sangiac**.

sandwich (-ooitch), *n.m.*, sandwich.

sang, *n.m.*, blood; race, parentage, relationship, kindred. *Un homme de* —; a blood-thirsty man. *Le baptême de* — (theol.); martyrdom without baptism. *Mettre à feu et à* —; to put to fire and sword. *Suer* — *et eau;* to toil and moil. *Se battre au premier* —; to fight till the blood runs. *Cela glace le* —; that curdles one's blood. *Cela est dans le* —; that runs in the blood.

sang-de-dragon, *n.m.* (—), (bot.) dragon's-blood.

sang-froid, *n.m.* (*n.p.*), coolness, composure. *sang-froid. De* —; in cold blood; with composure; sober-minded. *Perdre son* —; to lose one's temper.

sangiac, or **sangiacat**, *n.m.*, sangiac; district, province; governor (in Turkey—*en Turquie*).

sanglade, *n.f.*, lash, cut (with a whip—*de fouet*).

sanglant, -**e**, *adj.*, bloody, covered with blood; outrageous, very offensive. cutting. *Affront* —; outrageous affront. *Satire* —*e;* cutting satire.

sangle, *n.f.*, strap, band; girth (of saddles—*de selles*).

sangler, *v.a.*, to bind with a girth. to girth. to strap. — *un coup de poing;* to deal a blow.

Avoir été sanglé; to have been beaten. ill-used.

se **sangler**, *v.r.*, to lace one's self tightly.

sanglier, *n.m.*, wild boar. — *de mer;* sea-hog.

sanglot, *n.m.*, sob; *pl.*, sobbing. —*s entrecoupés;* broken sobs.

sangloter, *v.n.*, to sob.

sangsue (san-sü), *n.f.*, leech; blood-sucker. extortioner.

sanguification (-gu-i-), *n.f.*, sanguification.

sanguifier (-gu-i-), *v.a.*, to sanguify.

se **sanguifier**, *v.r.*, to sanguify.

sanguin, -**e** (-ghin, -ghi-n), *adj.*, of blood, sanguine; sanguineous. blood-coloured.

sanguinaire (-ghi-), *adj.*, sanguinary, bloody, murderous, bloodthirsty.

sanguinaire, *n.f.*, (bot.) bloodwort.

sanguine (-ghi-n), *n.f.*, red chalk, blood-stone.

sanguinelle (-ghi-), *n.f.*, (bot.) gatter-tree.

sanguinolent, -**e** (-ghi-), *adj.*, (med.) tinged with blood.

sanhédrin, *n.m.*, sanhedrim.

sanicle, *n.f.*, (bot.) sanicle.

sanie, *n.f.*, sanies.

sanieu-x, -**se**, *adj.*, sanious.

sanitaire, *adj.*, sanitary.

sans, *prep.*, without; but for, had it not been for, were it not for. — *amis;* friendless. — *doute;* without doubt. — *cela;* were it not for that. — *quoi;* otherwise. — *y penser;* unawares, unthinkingly.

sans-cœur, *n.m.f.*, (pop.) heartless, unfeeling person.

sanscrit, *n.m.*, Sanscrit (language).

sanscrit, -**e**, *adj.*, Sanscrit.

sans-culotte, *n.m.* (— —*s*), ragged fellow; sans-culotte. ultra, violent republican.

sans-culottides, *n.f.pl.*, the five supernumerary days to complete the year in the calendar of the first French republic; also the festivals held during those days.

sans-dent, *n.f.* (— —*s*), toothless old woman.

sans-fleur, *n.f.* (— —*s*), a sort of apple.

sansonnet, *n.m.*, (orni.) starling.

sans-peau, *n.f.* (—), summer-pear.

sans que, *conj.*, without. *Il a passé* — *que je l'aie aperçu;* he passed without my seeing him.

sans-souci, *n.m.* (—), careless, indifferent man, jolly fellow.

santal, *n.m.* *V.* **sandal**.

santaline, *n.f.*, (chem.) santalin.

santé, *n.f.*, health, healthiness; soundness; toast to the health. *Comment va la* —! how is your health? *Maison de* —; private hospital. *Bureau de* —; board of health. *Billet de* —; certificate of health. *Boire à la* —*de quelqu'un;* to drink any one's health.

santoline, *n.f.*, (bot.) santolina. [Sometimes, but improperly, used for *santonine*, which see.]

santon, *n.m.*, santon; a santon's tomb (in Algeria).

santonine, *n.f.*, (bot.) artemisia santonica; (chem.) santonin.

sanve, *n.f.*, (bot.) charlock, *sinapis arvensis*.

saoul, *adj.* *V.* **soûl**.

saouler, *v.a.* *V.* **soûler**.

sapa, *n.m.*, (pharm.) grape-jelly.

sapajou, *n.m.*, (mam.) sapajou; (fig. pers.) monkey.

sapan, *n.m.*, sapan-wood.

sape, *n.f.*, (milit.) sap. *Aller à la* — (milit.); to sap.

saper, *v.a.*, to sap, to undermine. to cut away.

sapeur, *n.m.*, (milit.) sapper.

saphène, *n.f.*, (anat.) saphena.

saphique, *n.m.* and *adj.*, (Grec. poet.) sapphic.

saphir, *n.m.*, sapphire.

saphirine, *n.f.*, (min.) blue chalcedony.

sapide, *adj.*, sapid, tastable, tasteful.

sapidité, *n.f.*, sapidity, sapidness.

sapience, *n.f.*, ☉sapience, wisdom; (theol.) Wisdom, the book of Solomon.

sapientiaux, *adj.m.pl.*, (Bibl.) sapiential.

sapin, *n.m.*, fir, fir-tree; (pop.) hackney-coach. *Sentir le —;* to have one foot in the grave.

sapine, *n.f.*, fir-plank.

sapinière, *n.f.*, forest of fir-trees.

saponacé,-e, *adj.*, saponaceous.

saponaire, *n.f.*, (bot.) soapwort.

saponification, *n.f.*, saponification.

saponifier, *v.a.*, to saponify.

s'saponifier, *v.r.*, to saponify.

saporifique, *adj.*, saporific.

sapote, *or* *sapotille,* *n.f.*, sapota (fruit).

sapotier, *or* *sapotillier,* *n.m.*, sapota (tree).

sar, *n.m.* V. **sart.**

sarabande, *n.f.*, saraband (dance—*danse*).

sarbacane, *n.f.*, air-cane; pea-shooter.

sarbotière, *n.f.* V. **sorbétière.**

sarcasme, *n.m.*, sarcasm.

sarcastique, *adj.*, sarcastic; sarcastical.

sarcelle, *n.f.*, (orni.) teal.

sarclage, *n.m.*, (gard.) weeding.

sarcler, *v.a.*, (gard.) to weed.

sarcleur, *n.m.*, weeder.

sarcloir, *n.m.*, weeding-hook, hoe.

sarclure, *n.f.*, weedings.

sarcocèle, *n.m.*, (surg.) sarcocele.

sarcocolle, *n.f.*, sarcocolla.

sarcocollier, *n.m.*, (bot.) sarcocol-tree, *pænea mucronata.*

sarcologie, *n.f.*, sarcology.

sarcomateu-x, -se, *adj.*, (surg.) sarcomatous.

sarcome, *n.m.*, (surg.) sarcoma.

sarcophage, *n.m.*, sarcophagus; coffin, representation of a coffin (at a funeral ceremony—*à une cérémonie funèbre*).

sarcophage, *n.m.* and *adj.*,(med.), caustic, corrosive, escharotic.

☉sarcotique, *n.m.* and *adj.*, (med.), sarcotic.

sardanapale, *n.m.*, effeminate man.

sarde, *n.m.f.* and *adj.*, Sardinian.

sarde, *n.f.*, (ich.) whale; scomber; a kind of sardine *or* pilchard caught on the coasts of Brazil.

sardine, *n.f.*, pilchard, sardine.

sardoine, *n.f.*, (min) sardonyx.

sardonien,-ne (-ni-in, -ni-è-n), *adj.*, sardonian.

sardonique, *adj.*, sardonic.

sargasse, *n.f.*, sargassum, gulf-weed.

sarigue, *n.m.*, opossum.

sarisse, *n.f.*, (antiq.) sarissa, the phalanx's long pike.

sarment, *n.m.*, vine-shoot.

sarmenteu-x, -se, *adj.*, (bot.) sarmentose, sarmentous.

saronide, *n.m.*, the name of a class of Gaulish priests.

sarracénique, *adj.*, Saracenic.

sarrasin, *n.m.* and *adj.*, Saracen; (arch.) Saracenic.

sarrasin, *n.m.*, buckwheat.

sarrasine, *n.f.*, (fort.) sarasin, sarrasine, portcullis, herse.

sarrau, *n.m.*, smock-frock.

sarrette, *n.f.*, (bot.) saw-wort.

sarriette, *n.f.*, (bot.) savory; common marum.

sarrot, *n.m.* V **sarrau.**

sart, or sar, *n.m.*, sea-wrack.

sas, *n.m.*, bolting-sieve; sieve; chamber (of locks—*d'écluse*). *Passer au —;* to sift. *Passer au gros —;* to examine superficially.

sassafras, *n.m.*, (bot.) sassafras.

sasse, *n.f.*, (nav.) scoop.

sassement (sâs-mân), *n.m.*, sifting.

sassenage (sas-naj), *n.m.*, Sassenage cheese.

sasser, *v.a.*, to sift, to bolt; to winnow; to scan, to scrutinize.

sasset, *n.m.*, little sieve.

satan, *n.m.*, Satan.

satanas, *n.m.*, (fam.) Satan.

satané, *adj.*, (fam.) roguish, wanton, mischievous.

satanique, *adj.*, satanic, satanical.

satellite (-tèl-lit), *n.m.*, satellite.

satellite, *adj.*, (anat.) companion. [Only used in: *veines —s; venæ comites;* companion veins, those which run in company with an artery.]

satiété, *n.f.*, satiety, surfeit, fulness. *Manger jusqu'à —;* to eat to satiety.

satin, *n.m.*, satin.

satinade, *n.f.*, satinet.

satinage, *n.m.*, satining; glazing (of paper —*du papier*).

satiné, -e, *adj.*, satin-like; glazed (of paper —*du papier*). *Peau —e;* skin as soft as velvet.

satiner, *v.a.*, to satin; to glaze (paper—*du papier*).

satiner, *v.n.*, to become as soft as satin.

satire, *n.f.*, satire; lampoon. — *piquante;* cutting satire. — *personnelle;* lampoon.

satirique, *n.m.* and *adj.*, satirist; satirical.

satiriquement (-rik-mân), *adv.*, satirically.

satiriser, *v.a.*, to satirize.

satiriste, *n.m.f.*, satirist.

satisfaction, *n.f.*, satisfaction, atonement. *Donner de la —;* to give satisfaction.

satisfactoire, *adj.*, (theol.) satisfactory.

satisfaire, *v.a.*, to satisfy, to please; to supply (wants—*des besoins*); to give satisfaction to (to make amends—*faire réparation*). — *sa passion;* to gratify one's passion. — *l'attente de quelqu'un:* to answer any one's expectation.

se satisfaire, *v.r.*, to satisfy one's self, to indulge one's-self.

satisfaire, *v.n.*, to satisfy; to discharge; to perform, to execute; to gratify, to indulge. — *à ses engagements;* to meet one's engagements.

satisfaisant, -e, *adj.*, satisfactory.

satisfait, -e, *adj.*, satisfied, contented, pleased.

satisfecit, *n.m.* (—), written attestation of sa'isfaction.

satrape, *n.m.*, satrap.

satrapie, *n.f.*, satrapy.

saturable, *adj.*, saturable.

saturant, -e, *adj.*, saturant.

saturation, *n.f.*, saturation.

saturer, *v.a.*, to saturate; to surfeit.

saturnales, *n.f.pl.*, Saturnalia.

saturne, *n.m.*, (astron., chem.) Saturn.

saturnien, *adj.*, (Lat. poet) a very ancient Latin verse in which the cæsura is constant.

saturnin, -e, *adj.*, (med.) lead. *Colique —e;* lead colic.

satyre, *n.m.*, satyr.

satyre, *n.f.*, (Grec. antiq.) satyric tragedy.

satyriasis (-zis), *n.m.*, (med.) satyriasis.

satyrion, *n.m.*, (bot.) satyrion, satyrium, standard-grass, stander-grass.

satyrique, *adj.*, pertaining to satyrs, satyric.

sauce, *n.f.*, (cook.) sauce. — *relevée;* rich, highly-seasoned, sauce. — *douce;* sweet sauce. *Il n'est — que d'appétit;* a good appetite is the best sauce. *On ne sait à quelle — le mettre;* one does not know what to do with him. *Faire la — à quelqu'un;* to give any one a smart rebuke. *Être dans la —;* to be in a pickle.

sancé, -e, *part.,* drenched, soused. *Médailles —es ;* plated medals.

saucer, *v.a.,* to dip in sauce; to sop, to souse; to scold; to rail harshly and contemptuously. — *quelqu'un ;* to scold any one.

saucière, *n.f.,* sauce-boat.

saucisse, *n.f.,* small sausage.

saucisson, *n.m.,* large sausage; (artil.) saucisson, saucisse; (fort.) bundle of fagots or fascines.

sauf, -ve, *adj.,* safe, unhurt, unscathed. *Il en est revenu sain et — ;* he is returned safe and sound.

sauf, *prep.,* saving, save, except, but; reserving. — *erreur ;* errors excepted. — *correction ;* under correction. — *votre respect ;* saving your presence.

sauf-conduit, *n.m.* (— —s), safe-conduct.

sauge, *n.f.,* (bot.) sage.

saugrenu, -e, *adj.,* absurd, ridiculous.

saule, *n.m.,* willow. — *pleureur ;* weeping willow.

saumâtre, *adj.,* brackish, briny.

saumon, *n.m.,* (ich.) salmon; (metal.) pig; (nav.) kentledge. — *mariné ;* pickled salmon. — *de fonte ;* pig-iron.

saumoné, -e, *adj.,* salmon. *Truite — e ;* salmon-trout.

saumoneau, *n.m.,* (ich.) young salmon.

saumure, *n.f.,* brine, pickle.

saunage, *n.m.,* salt-trade. *Faux— (n.p.);* contraband salt-trade.

sauner, *v.n.,* to make salt.

saunerie (sô-n-rî), *n.f.,* salt-house; salt-works.

saunier, *n.m.,* salt-maker. *Faux— (— —s);* contraband salt-trader.

saunière, *n.f.,* salt-box.

saupiquet, *n.m.,* (cook.) high-flavoured sauce.

saupoudrer, *v.a.,* to powder; to sprinkle with salt, pepper, &c.; to strew; to sprinkle; (fig.) to intersperse.

saur, *adj.,* red (of herrings—*harengs*). [This word is an abbreviation of *saure,* which see below.]

saure, *adj.,* yellowish brown; sorrel (of horses—*chevaux*); red (of herrings—*des harengs*). *Un hareng — ;* a red herring. *Un cheval — ;* a sorrel horse.

saurer, *v.a.,* to smoke (herrings—*harengs*).

sauret, *adj.,* (l.u.) red (of herrings—*harengs*).

sauriens (-in), *n.m.pl.,* saurians; lizards.

saurin, *n.m.,* milt-herring just smoked.

saussaie, *n.f.,* plantation of willows.

saut, *n.m.,* leap, jump, skip; spring; waterfall; (man.) vault, leap. *Faire un — ;* to take a leap. — *de carpe ;* somerset. — *de Breton ;* tripping up any one's heels. — *de loup ;* ha-ha. *Il s'élança tout d'un — ;* he sprang forward at one bound. *Au — du lit ;* on getting up, on getting out of bed. — *de mouton* (man.); goat-leap.

sautage, *n.m.,* exploding, blasting (mines).

saute, *n.f.,* (nav.) sudden veering of the wind.

sauté, *n.m.,* (cook.) stew.

sauté, -e, *adj.,* (cook.) stewed.

sautelle, *n.f.,* vine-shoot transplanted with its root.

sauter, *v.n.,* to leap, to leap off, to jump, to skip; to spring; (nav.) to veer, to shift (of the wind—*du vent*); to blow up (to explode—*faire explosion*); to kick the bucket (to die—*mourir*); to be discharged (of a person—*des personnes*). — *en avant ;* to leap forward. — *par-dessus une muraille ;* to leap over a wall. — *de joie ;* to jump for joy. *Faire — un bastion ;* to blow up a bastion. *Faire — la banque ;* to break the bank. — *au collet de quelqu'un ;* to collar any

one. *Cela saute aux yeux ;* that stares one in the face. — *aux nues ;* to jump up to the ceiling. *Le vent saute* (nav.); the wind shifts. — *en l'air ;* to bounce up. — *à bas de son lit ;* to jump out of one's bed.

sauter, *v.a.,* to leap, to leap over; to overlook, to pass over; to leave out, to skip. — *un fossé ;* to leap over a ditch. *Il a sauté une phrase ;* he has skipped a sentence.

sautereau (sô-trô), *n.m.,* jack (of harpsichords—*de clavecins*).

sauterelle (sô-trèl), *n.f.,* grasshopper, locust; (carp.) level (instrument).

saute-ruisseau, *n.m.* (— —x), errand-boy.

sauteu-r, *n.m., -se,* *n.f.,* leaper, jumper, tumbler, mountebank; (man.) vaulter.

sauteuse, *n.f.,* a kind of dance.

***sautillant, -e,** *adj.,* hopping, skipping.

***sautillement,** *n.m.,* hopping, skipping.

***sautiller,** *v.n.,* to hop, to skip.

sautoir (sô-toar), *n.m.,* form of a saint Andrew's cross; (her.) saltier; (cook.) stew-pan; (horl.) jumper. *En — ;* cross-wise; (her.) saltier-wise. *Porter son bagage en — ;* to have one's baggage slung over one's shoulder.

sauvage, *n.m.f.* and *adj.,* savage, wild man; wild woman; savage, wild, untamed; shy; unsociable; uncivilized; rude, brutal, barbarous.

sauvagement, *adv.,* wildly; savagely.

sauvageon (-jon), *n.m.,* (agri.) wild stock.

sauvagerie (sô-va-jrî), *n.f.,* unsociableness; shyness.

sauvagesse, *n.f.,* uncivilized female; (fam.) a woman destitute of education and manners, a scold, a shrew.

sauvagin, *n.m.,* taste, smell of water-fowl.

sauvagin, -e, *adj.,* fishy (in taste—*goût*).

sauvagine, *n.f.,* wild water-fowl; odour of water-fowl; (com.) common unprepared peltry.

sauvegarde (sôv-gard), *n.f.,* safe-keeping, safeguard; shield, buckler, protection. — *s de beaupré* (nav.); man-ropes of the bowsprit.

sauvegarder (sôv-gardé), *v.a.,* to protect, to guard.

sauve-qui-peut, *n.m.* (—), head-long flight rout; extreme confusion; panic.

sauver, *v.a.,* to save, to deliver, to rescue; to keep, to be the salvation of; to economize; to conceal; to excuse, to vindicate. *Sauve qui peut ;* save himself who can. — *les apparences ;* to save appearances. — *les défauts d'un ouvrage ;* to conceal the imperfections of a work. — *la vie à quelqu'un ;* to save any one's life.

se **sauver,** *v.r.,* to escape, to make one's escape, to run away; to abscond; to make off; to take refuge; to retrieve one's self; to indemnify one's self; to work out one's salvation.

sauvetage (sôv-taj), *n.m.,* (nav.) salvage. *Canot de — ;* life-boat. *Appareil de — pour les incendies ;* fire-escape.

⊙**sauveté,** *n.f.,* safety.

sauveteur (sôv-teur), *n.m.,* salvor.

sauvette, -e, *n.f.,* duck-stone (game—*jeu*).

sauveur, *n.m.* and *adj.,* saver, deliverer; Saviour, Redeemer; (Bibl.) all-saving.

sauve-vie, *n.f.* (—), (bot.) wall-rue.

savamment (-va-män), *adv.,* learnedly, knowingly.

savane, *n.f.,* savannah.

savant, -e, *adj.,* learned, skilful. *Une main —e ;* a skilful hand.

savant, *n.m.., -e,* *n.f.,* scholar, learned person. *Les —s ;* the literati.

savantasse, *n.m.,* pedantic scholar. [Sometimes spelt *savantas* in poetry.]

savate, *n.f.,* old shoe; (nav.) shoe; bungler. *Traîner la — ;* to be as poor as Job.

savaterie (-va-trî), *n.f.,* place where old shoes are sold.

saveter (sav-té), *v.a.*, to cobble; to bungle, to botch.

savetier (sav-tié), *n.m.*, cobbler; bungler, botcher.

saveur, *n.f.*, savour, relish; sapor.

savoir (sachant, su), *v.a.*, to know, to have a knowledge of, to be aware of; to understand; to be sensible of; to be acquainted with. *Il n'en sait rien ;* he knows nothing about it. *Puisque vous en savez tant ;* since you know so much about it. *Faire — ;* to notify, to acquaint. *Je ne sais ;* I don't know. *Je ne sais que faire ;* I don't know what to do. *Pas que je sache ;* not that I know, not to my knowledge. *Il sait son pain manger ;* he knows what he is about. *Il sait le grec ;* he understands Greek. *Il sait la médecine ;* he has a knowledge of physic. — *vivre ;* to know how to behave. *Il ne sait pas vivre ;* he has no manners. *Il ne sait ni A ni B ;* he does not know A from B. *Je lui en sais le meilleur gré du monde ;* I am highly pleased with him for it. *Je ne sais qu'en croire ;* I know not what to think of it. *Je le sais de bonne part ;* I have it from good hands. *Si on vient à — cela ;* if that comes to be known. *Je ne saurais qu'y faire ;* I cannot help it. *Je ne sais où j'en suis ;* I do not know which way to turn.

savoir, *v.n.*, to know, to be learned, to be a scholar, to be a person of learning. —, *à — ;* viz., namely, that is to say, to wit. *se* **savoir**, *v.r.*, to become known. *Tout se sait avec le temps ;* everything becomes known in process of time.

savoir, *n.m.*, knowledge, learning, scholarship.

savoir-faire. *n.m.* (*n.p.*), management; tact ; wits. *Il vit de son — ;* he lives by his wits.

savoir-vivre, *n.m.* (*n.p.*), good manners, good breeding.

savoisien, -ne, *adj.* and *n.*, Savoyard ; of, from, Savoy.

savon, *n.m.*, soap ; rebuke, scolding ; soaping. *Donner un — à quelqu'un ;* to reprimand any one, to blow any one up. — *marbré ;* mottled soap. — *parfumé ;* scented soap.

savonnage, *n.m.*, soaping; washing with soap. *Eau de — ;* soap-suds.

savonner, *v.a.*, to soap ; to wash with soap, to lather ; (pop.) to reprove, to scold, to blow up. *se* **savonner**, *v.r.*, to bear washing, to wash (of fabrics—*des étoffes*). *Cette étoffe se savonne ;* this material will wash, will bear washing.

savonnerie (-vo-n-ri), *n.f.*, soap-house, soap-trade ; soap-works.

savonnette, *n.f.*, wash-ball ; soap-ball.

savonneu-x, -se, *adj.*, soapy.

savonnier, *n.m.*, soap-boiler, soap-manufacturer ; (bot.) soapberry-tree.

savourement (-voor-mān), *n.m.*, savouring.

savourer, *v.a.*, to savour ; to relish.

savouret, *n.m.*, marrow-bone (of beef or pork—*de bœuf ou de porc*).

savoureusement (-reuz-mān), *adv.*, savourily.

savoureu-x, -se, *adj.*, savoury.

savoyard, *n.m.*, **-e**, *n.f.*, Savoyard. [Very rarely used in this sense for which *Savoisien*, see it above, has been substituted on account of the popular and familiar meaning attributed to *savoyard*, which is : ill-mannered, rude, unmannerly.]

saxatile, *adj.*, saxatile.

saxifrage, *adj.*, saxifragous.

saxifrage, *n.f.*, (bot.) saxifrage.

saxon. -ne, *n.* and *adj.*, Saxon.

saynète, *n.f.*, a little play of the Spanish stage.

sayon, *n.m.*, sayon, kind of great coat formerly worn by soldiers.

sbire, *n.m.*, sbirro.

scabellon, *n.m.*, (arch.) socle, small pedestal.

scabieuse, *n.f.*, (bot.) scabious.

scabieu-x, -se, *adj.*, (med.) scabious, scabby.

scabreu-x, -se, *adj.*, scabrous, rugged, rough ; dangerous, difficult, slippery ; delicate; ticklish.

scalde, *n.m.*, (antiq.) Scandinavian poet.

scalène, *adj.*, (geom.) scalene, scalenous.

scalpel, *n.m.*, scalpel.

scalper, *v.a.*, to scalp.

scalpeur, *n.m.*, scalper.

scammonée, *n.f.*, scammony.

scandale, *n.m.*, scandal ; scandalousness, offence ; exposure. *Faire du — ;* to make an exposure.

scandaleusement (-leuz-mān), *adv.*, scandalously.

scandaleu-x, -se, *adj.*, scandalous.

scandaliser, *v.a.*, to scandalize. *se* **scandaliser**, *v.r.*, to be scandalized. *Il se scandalise de tout ;* he is scandalized at everything.

scander, *v.a.*, to scan.

scape, *n.m.*, (bot.) flower-bearing stem, scape.

scaphandre, *n.m.*, cork-jacket (for swimming—*pour se soutenir sur l'eau*); diving apparatus.

scaphoïde, *adj.*, scaphoid.

scapin, *n.m.*, knave, rogue, low born scoundrel, scamp.

scapolite, *n.m.*, (min.) scapolite.

scapulaire, *n.m.*, scapular, scapulary ; (surg.) shoulder-band.

scapulaire, *adj.f.*, (anat., orni.) scapular.

scarabée, *n.m.*, (ent.) scarabæus, beetle.

scaramouche, *n.m.*, scaramouch.

scare, *n.m.*, (ich.) scarus, parrot-fish.

scarieu-x, -se, *adj.*, (bot.) scarious.

scarificateur, *n.m.*, (surg.) scarificator; scarifier (instrument).

scarification, *n.f.*, scarification.

scarifier, *v.a.*, to scarify.

scariole, *n.f.* *V.* **escarole**.

scarlatine, *n.* and *adj.f.*, (med.) scarlatina; scarlet. *Fièvre — ;* scarlet fever.

scazon, or **scazon**, *n.m.*, (Lat. poet.) iambic verse with a spondee on the sixth foot.

sceau, *n.m.*, seal ; impression of a seal ; act of confirmation ; sanction. —*x de l'Etat ;* Seals of the State. *Garde des —x ;* Keeper of the Seals. — *de Notre Dame* (bot.) ; black briony. *Apposer son — ;* to affix one's seal. *Rompre un — ;* to break a seal.

⊙**scel**, *n.m.* *V.* **sceau**.

scélérat, -e, *adj.*, flagitious, nefarious, villanous.

scélérat, *n.m.*, scoundrel, villain ; unprincipled wretch. *C'est un grand — ;* he is a great villain.

scélératesse, *n.f.*, villainy, atrociousness, flagitiousness.

scélite, *n.f.*, stone having the shape of the human leg.

scellé, *n.m.*, waxen stamp placed officially on locks, closets, &c. ; seals. *Apposer les —s ;* to affix the seals. *Lever les —s ;* to take off the seals. *Bris de — ;* the unlawful breaking of the seals.

scellement (sèl-mān), *n.m.*, sealing ; fastening.

sceller, *v.a.*, to put an official seal to, to seal, to seal up ; to ratify ; to make fast ; (mas.) to bed.

scelleur, *n.m.*, sealer.

scène, *n.f.*, scene ; (thea.) stage, scenery.

La mise en — d'une pièce (thea.); the getting-up of a piece. *Faire une — à quelqu'un ;* to have a row with any one, to blow any one up. *Être en —* (thea.); to be upon the stage.

scénique, *adj.*, scenical, scenic.

scénographie, *n.f.*, scenography.

scénographique, *adj.*, scenographical.

scénopégie, *n.f.*, the feast of tabernacles.

scepticisme, *n.m.*, scepticism.

sceptique, *n.m.* and *adj.*, sceptic, sceptical.

sceptre (sèp-tr), *n.m.*, sceptre; sway, dominion.

schabraque, *or* **chabraque** (sha-), *n.f.*, shabrack.

schah (shâ), *n.m.*, shah (of Persia—*de Perse*).

schako (sha-), *n.m.* *V.* **shako.**

schall (shâl), *n.m.* *V.* **châle.**

scheik (shèk), *n.m.* *V.* **cheik.**

schelling (shê-lin), *n.m.* (—*s*), shilling.

schenante (shê-), *n.m.*, (bot.) lemon-grass.

schène (skê-n), *n.m.*, (antiq.) schene, Egyptian measure of length; about six miles and a half.

schérif (shé-), *n.m.* (—*s*). *V.* **chérif** and **shérif.**

scherzo (skèr-), *n.m.* (*scherzi*), (mus.) sportive piece in a symphony.

schiite (shi-it), *n.m.*, shiite, schismatic Mahometan.

schismatique (shis-), *n.m.* and *adj.*, schismatic; schismatical.

schisme (shism), *n.m.*, schism.

schiste (shist), *n.m.*, (min.) schist, slate.

schisteu-x, **-se** (shis-), *adj.*, schistous.

schlague (shlag), *n.f.*, (milit.) flogging.

schlich (shlik), *n.m.*, (min.) slick.

schnapan (shna-), *n.m.* *V.* **chenapan.**

scholastique (sko-). *V.* **scolastique.**

scholie (sko-). *V.* **scolie.**

schooner (shoo-nèr, skoonèr), *n.m.*, (nav.) schooner.

schorl (shorl), *n.m.*, (min.) schorl.

sciage, *n.m.*, sawing.

sciagraphie, *n.f.* *V.* **sciographie.**

sciatérique, *adj.*, sciatherical.

sciatique, *n.f.* and *adj.*,(anat.,med.)sciatica; hip-gout; sciatical.

scie, *n.f.*, saw; (ich.) saw-fish; (pop.) trouble, bore (tiresome thing—*ennui*). — *à main ;* hand-saw. — *de scieur de long ;* pit-saw.

sciemment (si-a-màn), *adv.*, wittingly, knowingly.

science, *n.f.*, knowledge, science, learning. *Posséder une —à fond;* to be thoroughly master of a science. *S'adonner aux —s;* to devote one's self to the sciences. *La — infuse;* intuition.

scientifique, *adj.*, scientific, scientifical.

scientifiquement (-fik-màn), *adv.*, scientifically.

scier, *v.a.*, to saw; to reap, to cut down. — *du bois;* to saw wood. — *le dos à quelqu'un* (pop.); to bore any one.

se **scier**, *v.r.*, to saw, to be cut with a saw.

scier, *v.n.*, to saw; (nav.) to back water. — *à culer* (nav.); to back, to back water.

scierie(si-rî),*n.f.*, saw-mill.

scieur, *n.m.*, sawyer; reaper. *Fosse de — de long;* saw-pit.

scille, *n.f.*, (bot.) squill.

scillitique, *adj.*, (pharm.) of squill.

scinder, *v.a.*, to divide (motion, question).

scinque, *n.m.*, (erpelotogy) skink.

scintillant, **-e** (-til-làn, -t), *adj.*, scintillant.

scintillation (-til-la-), *n.f.*, scintillation.

scintillement (sin-til-màn), *n.m.*, scintillating, scintillation.

scintiller (-til-lé), *v.n.*, to scintillate.

sciographie, *n.f.*,(arch.) sciagraphy.

sciographique, *adj.*, (arch.) sciagraphical.

scion, *n.m.*, (bot.) scion, shoot.

scioptique, *adj.*, (opt.) scioptic.

scirpe, *n.m.*, (bot.) club-rush.

scissile, *adj.*, scissible.

scission, *n.f.*, secession; division of opinions. *Faire — ;* to secede.

scissionnaire, *n.m.* and *adj.*, seceder; seceding.

scissure, *n.f.*, (anat.) fissure.

sciure, *n.f.*, saw-dust, saw-powder.

sclarée, *n.f.*, (bot.) clary.

sclérophtalmie, *n.f.*, (med.) ophthalmy, inflammation of the conjunctiva.

sclérotique, *n.f.*, (anat.) sclerotic.

scolaire, *adj.*, academic ; of schools.

scolarité, *n.f.*, (ancient jur.) rights of a University student ; time of study required to obtain degrees.

scolastique, *adj.*, scholastical ; academic ; of schools.

scolastique, *n.m.*, scholastic, school-man.

scolastique, *n.f.*, scholasticism.

scolastiquement (-tik-màn), *adv.*, scholastically.

scoliaste, *n.m.*, scholiast.

scolie, *n.f.*, scholium ; (Grec. antiq) table-song.

scolie, *n.m.*, (geom.) scholium

scolopendre, *n.f.*, (bot.) hart's-tongue; (ent.) scolopendra, centiped.

scombre, *n.m.*, (ich.) scomber.

scorbut, *n.m.*, scurvy.

scorbutique, *n.m.* and *adj.*, person affected with the scurvy ; scorbutic.

scordium (-diom), *n.m.*, (bot.) water-germander.

scorie, *n.f.*, (metal.) scoria, dross.

scorification, *n.f.*, (metal.) scorification.

scorificatoire, *n.m.*, a kind of crucible used in cupellation on a large scale.

scorifier, *v.a.*, to scorify.

scorpioïde, *n.f.*, (bot.) scorpion's-tail.

scorpiojelle, *n.f.*, scorpion oil.

scorpion, *n.m.*, (astron.) Scorpion; (ent.) scorpion.

scorpione, *n.f.*, (bot.) scorpion-grass, scorpion's-tail.

scorsonère, *n.f.*, (bot.) viper's-grass.

scotie (-tî), *n.f.*, (arch.) scotia ; casement.

scribe, *n.m.*, scribe, writer.

scripteur, *n.m.*, writer of the pope's bulls.

scrofulaire, *n.f.*, (bot.) figwort.

scrofules, *n.f.pl.*, scrofula, king's evil.

scrofuleu-x, **-se**, *n.* and *adj.*, scrofulous person ; scrofulous.

scrotocèle, *n.f.*, (surg.) scrotocele.

scrotum (-tom), *n.m.* (—), (anat.) scrotum.

scrupule, *n.m.*, scruple ; scrupulosity, qualm ; scrupulousness; scruple(weight—*poids*). *Avoir des —s;* to be scrupulous. *Lever des —s;* to remove scruples. *Je m'en ferais — ;* I should scruple to do it.

scrupuleusement (-leûz-màn), *adv.*, scrupulously, strictly, exactly.

scrupuleu-x, **-se**, *n.* and *adj.*, over nice, overscrupulous person ; scrupulous, nice, rigorous, precise.

scrutat-eur, **-rice**, *n.m.* and *adj.*, investigator, explorer, searcher, scrutinizer ; (of a ballot—*d'un vote*) scrutator ; investigating, searching, scrutinizing.

scruter, *v.a.*, to scrutinize, to search closely, to scrutinize.

scrutin, *n.m.*, ballot, balloting. — *indivduel;* balloting for a single individual. *Dépouiller le —;* to ascertain the result of the ballot.

scubac, *n.m.* *V.* **usquebac.**

sculptable(skul-tabl),*adj.*, to be sculptured ; to be carved.

sculpter (skul-té), *v.a.*, to sculpture, to carve.

sculpteur (skul-teur), *n.m.*, sculptor, carver.

sculptural (skul-tu-), *adj.*, sculptural.

sculpture (skul-tur), *n.f.*, sculpture, carving; carved work.

scutiforme, *adj.*, scutiform, having the shape of a buckler.

scylla, *n.m.*, Scylla. *V.* **charybde**.

scytale, *n.f.*, (antiq.) a staff, used in Sparta, as a cypher to write dispatches.

scytale, *n.m.*, a species of snake.

scythe, *n.m.f.* and *adj.*, Scythian.

se, *pron.*, one's self, himself, herself, itself, themselves; one another, each other. *Il — ruine;* he is ruining himself. *Elle — lasse;* she tires herself. *Ils s'aiment;* they love one another. *Cela — peut;* that may be. *Ils — connaissent;* they know each other. *Ils — parlent;* they speak to each other.

séance, *n.f.*, seat (right of sitting—*droit de siéger*) ; sitting (time of meeting of deliberative assemblies—*temps que dure une assemblée*) ; meeting ; sitting (for one's portrait—*pour faire faire son portrait*). *Avoir —;* to have a seat. *Lever la —;* to close the meeting. *Faire une —;* to sit (at table, at play, &c.—*à table, au jeu, &c.*).

séant, *part.*, (jur.) sitting.

séant, *n.m.*, sitting upright. *Étre sur son —, se mettre sur son —;* to sit up in bed.

séant, -e, *adj.*, fitting, seemly, becoming.

seau, *n.m.*, pail, bucket. *Il pleut à —x;* it rains in torrents.

sébacé, -e, *adj.*, sebaceous.

sébeste, *n.m.*, sebesten-plum.

sébestier (-tié), *n.m.*, (bot.) sebesten-plum-tree.

sébifère, *adj.*, (bot.) yielding tallow.

sébile. *n.f.*, wooden bowl.

sec, sèche, *adj.*, dry; lean, spare; barren; plain; unornamented; cold, unfeeling, sharp; dissatisfied (of looks—*de l'air, de la mine*); (paint.) hard; dried (of fruit, flowers, leaves, fish, &c.—*des fruits, des fleurs, des feuilles, du poisson, &c.*); severe (of reprimands—*d'une réprimande*). *Des mains sèches;* lean hands. *Un homme —;* a spare man. *Coup —;* smart stroke. *Avoir le gosier —;* to be very dry. *Il a le pouls —;* his pulse is sharp. *Étre à —;* to have no money. *Cœur —;* unfeeling heart. *Mine sèche;* dissatisfied look. *Perte sèche;* dead loss.

sec, *n.m.*, dryness; fodder; dry weather. *À —;* dried up; (nav.) under bare poles. *Mettre un étang à —;* to drain a pond. *Vaisseau à —;* ship under bare poles.

sec, *adv.*, dryly, sharply. *Boire —;* to drink hard. *Répondre —;* to answer sharply.

sécable, *adj.*, scissile.

sécant, -e, *adj.*, (geom.) secant.

sécante, *n.f.*, (geom.) secant.

sécateur, *n.m.*, (gard.) pruning-shears.

sécession, *n.f.*, secession.

séchage, *n.m.*, drying.

sèche, *or* **seiche**, *n.f.*, cuttle-fish.

sèchement (sèsh-mãn), *adv.*, dryly; sharply; barrenly, without ornament, plainly.

sécher, *v.a.*, to dry, to dry up.

se **sécher**, *v.r.*, to dry one's self; to dry (of a thing—*d'une chose*).

sécher, *v.n.*, to dry, to wither. *Faire — du linge;* to spread out linen to dry. *— sur pied;* to pine away.

sécheresse (sè-shrès), *n.f.*, dryness; drought; sharpness, barrenness.

sécherie (sé-shri), *n.f.*, (manu.) drying-house.

séchoir, *n.m.*, (manu.) drying-room; (tech.) dryer.

second, -e (sè-gon, -d), *adj.* second. *Eau —e;* (chem.) lye-water.

second (sè-gõn), *n.m.*, second, assistant ; second story, second floor. *Il demeure au —;* he lives on the second floor. *En —;* second, second in command; (nav.) mate.

secondaire (se-gon-dèr), *adj.*, secondary, accessory.

secondairement (se-gon-dèr-mãn), *adv.*, secondarily, accessorily.

seconde (se-gond), *n.f.*, second (of time—*durée de temps*); second class (in schools—*dans les collèges*); (mus.) second.

secondement (se-gon-dmãn), *adv.*, secondly, in the second place.

seconder (se-gon-dé), *v.a.*, to second, to assist; to favour, to back, to support.

secondine (se-gon-di-n), *n.f.*, (bot.) secundine; *pl.*, secundines, after-birth.

secoûment, *n.m. V.* **secoûment**.

secouer, *v.a.*, to shake, to shake off; to jolt, to toss; to discard. *— la tête;* to shake one's head. *— le joug;* to shake off the yoke.

se **secouer**, *v.r.*, to shake one's self, to take exercise; to move about.

secoûment, *or* **secouement**, *n.m.*, shaking.

secourable, *adj.*, helpful, willing to help.

secourir, *v.a.*, to succour, to assist, to relieve, to help, to be a succourer of.

secours, *n.m.*, help, relief, succour, assistance; chapel of ease. *Donner du —;* to render assistance. *Crier au —;* to cry for help.

secousse, *n.f.*, shake, shock; blow, concussion, toss, tossing, jerk; (fig.) difficulties.

secr-et, -ète, *adj.*, secret, private, hidden, undiscovered, reserved, silent. *Tenir —; to keep secret. *Escalier —;* back-stairs.

secret, *n.m.*, secrecy; secret; solitary confinement; secret drawer. *C'est mon —;* that is not a fair question. *Le — de plaire;* the secret of pleasing. *Mettre un prisonnier au —;* to put a prisoner in solitary confinement. *En —;* secretly, privately, in private.

secrétaire, *n.m.*, secretary; escritoire; (orni.) secretary-bird. *— d'ambassade;* secretary to an embassy. *— d'état;* secretary of state.

secrétairerie (-tèr-rî), *n.f.*, secretary's office.

secrétariat, *n.m.*, secretaryship; secretary's office.

secrète, *n.f.*, (c.rel.) secret prayer.

secrètement (-krèt-mãn), *adv.*, secretly, privately, in secret.

sécréter, *v.a.*, (physiology) to secrete.

sécréteur, *adj.*, secretory.

sécrétion, *n.f.*, (physiology) secretion.

sécrétoire, *adj.*, secretory.

sectaire, *n.m.*, sectarian, sectary.

sectateur, *n.m.*, votary.

secte, *n.f.*, sect. *Faire —;* to form a sect.

secteur, *n.m.*, (geom.) sector.

section, *n.f.*, section.

sectionnement, *n.m.*, dividing into parts; division.

sectionner, *v.a.*, to divide into parts; to divide.

séculaire, *adj.*, secular, coming once in a century; a hundred years old; venerable. *Un chêne —;* a venerable oak.

sécularisation, *n.f.*, secularization.

séculariser, *v.a.*, to secularize.

sécularité, *n.f.*, secular jurisdiction.

sécul-ier, -ère, *adj.*, secular, worldly.

séculier, *n.m.*, laic, layman.

séculièrement (-lièr-mãn), *adv.*, secularly.

secundo (se-gõn-), *adv.*, secondly.

sécurité, *n.f.*, security.

sedan, *n.m.*, Sedan-cloth.

sédanoise, *or* **parisienne,** *n.f.,* (print.) pearl.

sédati-f, -ve, *adj.,* (med.) sedative.

sédatif, *n.m.,* sedative.

sédentaire, *adj.,* sedentary.

sédiment, *n.m.,* sediment, settlings, grounds, dregs, lees.

sédimentaire, *adj.,* sedimentary.

séditieusement (-si-euz-mân), *adv.,* seditiously.

séditieu-x, se, *adj.,* seditious.

séditieux, *n.m.,* rebel.

sédition, *n.f.,* sedition. *Faire une —;* to occasion a sedition. *Éteindre une —;* to quash a sedition.

séduct-eur, -rice, *n.* and *adj.,* seducer, enticer; seductive, enticing.

séduction, *n.f.,* seduction, enticement; subornation. *— de témoins;* bribing of witnesses. *La — des richesses;* the allurements of wealth.

séduire (séduisant, séduit), *v.a.,* to seduce, to delude, to beguile; to suborn, to bribe; to bewitch. *— des témoins;* to bribe witnesses.

séduisant, -e, *adj.,* seductive, seducing; delusive, bewitching, tempting. *Offres —es;* tempting offers.

segment, *n.m.,* (geom.) segment.

segmentaire, *adj.,* segmental.

ségrairie, *n.f.,* woods possessed in common.

ségrais, *n.m.,* separate wood.

ségrégation, *n.f.,* segregation.

ségrégativement (-tiv-mân), *adv.,* separately.

seiche, *n.f. V.* **sèche.**

séide, *n.m.,* fanatical partisan of a political or religious chief; (b.s.) murderer.

seigle, *n.m.,* (bot.) rye. *— ergoté;* spurred rye.

*seigneur, *n.m.,* lord; the Lord. *Petit —;* lordling. *— suzerain;* lord paramount. *Notre —;* our Lord. *À tout — tout honneur;* honour to whom honour is due.

*seigneuriage, *n.m.,* seigniorage (duty on coinage—*droit sur la fabrication des monnaies*).

*seigneurial, -e, *adj.,* seigneurial, manorial.

*seigneurie, *n.f.,* seigniory, lordship; manor. *Votre —;* your lordship.

seime, *n.f.,* (vet.) wire-heel.

sein, *n.m.,* breast, bosom; heart (midst—*milieu*); middle; womb (midst—*milieu*). *Au — de l'église;* in the bosom of the church. *Le . de l'éternité;* the womb of eternity. *Donner le — à un enfant;* to give a child the breast.

seine, *n.f.,* fish-net, sein.

seing (sin), *n.m.,* sign manual, signature. *Blanc —;* signature in blank. *— privé;* private seal.

seize, *n.m.* and *adj.,* sixteen, sixteenth.

seizième, *n.m.f.* and *adj.,* sixteenth.

seizièmement, *adv.,* sixteenthly.

séjour, *n.m.,* stay, abode, residence, sojourn; continuance; dwelling, habitation. *Permis de —;* permission to reside. *L'humide —;* the watery regions, the deep.

⊙séjourné, *adj.,* rested, refreshed.

séjourner, *v.n.,* to stay, to sojourn, to make a stay, to tarry; to remain, to continue.

sel, *n.m.,* salt; wit. *— gris;* bay salt. *De bon —;* properly salted. *À la croque au —;* with salt only. *— gemme;* rock-salt. *— marin;* sea-salt. *— Anglais;* Epsom salts. *Couche de —;* bed of salt *— attique;* Attic wit.

sélaciens, *n.m.pl.,* (ich.) cartilaginous fishes.

sélam, *or* **sélan** *n.m.* (—*s*), a bouquet, the arrangement of the flowers of which is used as a kind of writing, in the East.

sélection, *n.f.,* selection.

sélénieux, *adj.,* (chem.) selenious.

sélénite, *n.f.,* (chem.) selenite.

séléniteu-x, -se, *adj.,* selenitic.

sélénium (-om), *n.m.,* (chem.) selenium.

sélénographie, *n.f.,* selenography.

sélénographique, *adj.,* selenographical.

selle, *n.f.,* saddle; stool, relief of the bowels; (med.) motion. *— de femme;* side-saddle, lady's saddle. *Cheval .de —;* saddle-horse. *Aller à la —;* to go to the stool. *Être toujours en —;* never to be out of one's saddle. *À tous chevaux;* common saddle; commonplace discourse. *La première —;* the best horse in the stable. *— de calfat* (nav.); caulking-box.

seller, *v.a.,* to saddle.

se **seller,** *v.r.,* (agri.) to harden.

sellerie (sèl-ri), *n.f.,* saddlery, saddle-room.

sellette, *n.f.,* ⊙ seat of culprits; (fig.) stool of repentance; bed (of a carriage—*de voiture*); shoe-black's box; collar (of a plough—*de charrue*); (nav.) caulking-box.

sellier, *n.m.,* saddler.

selon, *prep.,* according to, agreeably to, conformably to, pursuant to. *On l'a traité — son mérite;* he was treated according to his deserts. *— moi;* in my opinion. *C'est —;* it is according to circumstances, that depends on circumstances.

selon que, *conj.,* as, according as.

*semailles, *n.f.pl.,* sowing; seed; sowing-time.

semaine, *n.f.,* week; week's work; week's wages; week's pocket-money. *À la —;* by the week. *Prêter à la petite —;* to lend small sums of money for a short time at an exorbitant interest. *— sainte;* Holy Week.

semainier, *n.m.,* officer, monk, *or* actor, on duty for the week; case of seven razors; letter-rack.

semainière, *n.f.,* nun *or* actress on duty for the week.

sémaphore, *n.m.,* semaphore.

semaque, *n.f.,* fishing-boat, fishing-smack.

semblable, *adj.,* like, alike, not unlike, similar. *— à un torrent;* like a torrent.

semblable, *n.m.,* like; fellow; fellow-creature.

semblablement, *adv.,* likewise, too, also.

⊙semblance, *n.f.,* resemblance, semblance, look.

semblant, *n.m.,* appearance, semblance, seeming. *Faux —;* hypocritical show, pretence. *Faire —;* to feign, to pretend, to dissemble. *Il fait — de ne pas le voir;* he pretends not to see it. *Ne faire — de rien;* to take no notice of any thing.

sembler, *v.n.,* to seem, to appear. *Cela me semble ainsi;* it appears so to me. *Il semble:* it seems, it appears, it would appear. *Il me semble que je le vois;* I think I see him. *Il lui semble que;* he fancies that. *Que vous en semble?* what do you think of it? *Il lui semble que cela n'est rien;* he thinks it is nothing. *Si bon lui semble;* if he thinks fit.

semé, -e, *part.,* sowed, sown. *— d'étoiles;* bespangled with stars. *— de fleurs;* strewed with flowers.

séméiologie, *n.f.,* semeiology.

séméiotique, *n.f.,* semeiotics.

semelle, *n.f.,* sole (of boots, shoes—*de chaussures*); foot (of stockings—*de bas*); length of a foot; (carp.) sleeper; dormant-tree; shoe (of an anchor—*d'ancre*). *Battre la —;* to pad the hoof, to tramp. *Reculer d'une —;* to give ground a foot. *— de dérive* (nav.); lee-board.

semence, *n.f.,* seed; seeds; fine sprigs (small nails—*petits clous*); (fig.) cause. *— de perles;* seed-pearl. *— d'un procès;* cause of a lawsuit. *— de diamant;* diamond-sparks.

semencine, *n.f.*, (pharm.) one of the three kinds of wormwood.

semen-contra (sé-mè-n-), *n.m.* (*n.p.*), (pharm.) semen-contra, worm-seed.

semer, *v.a.*, to sow, to scatter; to spread; to strew, to sprinkle, to disseminate. — *du blé;* to sow wheat. — *de l'argent;* to scatter money. — *la discorde;* to sow discord. — *des fleurs;* to strew flowers. *Il faut — pour recueillir;* one must sow before he can reap.

semestral, -e (-mès-), *adj.*, half-yearly.
⊙**semestre** (-mès-), *adj.*, half-yearly.

semestre (-mès-), *n.m.*, half-year; six months; half-year's duty; half-year's income; (milit.) six months furlough. *Entrer en —;* to enter one's six months' duty. *Congé de —;* six months' furlough.

semestriel, -le (-mès-), *adj.*, half-yearly.

semestrier (-mès-), *n.m.*, (milit.) soldier absent on a six months' furlough.

semeur, *n.m.*, seedsman, sower; disseminator.

semi, *adj. invariable*, semi, demi, half.

semi-arien, -ne, *adj.* and *n.* (— —s), Semi-Arian.

semi-circulaire, *adj.*, semicircular.

semi-double, *adj.*, semi-double.

semi-flosculeu-x, -se, *adj.*, (bot.) semiflosculous.

***sémillant, -e**, *adj.*, brisk, lively, frisky, sprightly.

semi-lunaire, *adj.*, semi-lunar.

séminaire, *n.m.*, seminary, clerical college.

séminal, -e, *adj.*, seminal.

séminariste, *n.m.*, seminarist.

sémination, *n.f.*, semination.

semi-pélagiens, *n.m.pl.* (*n.s.*), Semi-Pelagians.

semi-périodique, *adj.*, semi-periodic.

semi-preuve, *n.f.* (— —s), imperfect proof, beginning of a proof.

semis, *n.m.*, seed-plot.

sémitique, *adj.*, Semitic.

semi-ton, *n.m.* (— —s), (mus.) semitone.

semoir, *n.m.*, (agri.) seed-lip; drill-machine.

semonce, *n.f.*, rebuke, reprimand, lecture.

semoncer, *v.a.*, to reprimand, to lecture.

⊙**semondre**, *v.a.*, to invite (to a ceremony—*à une cérémonie*).

⊙**semonneur**, *n.m.*, a messenger who carries invitations to a ceremony.

semoule, *n.f.*, semoule, semolina.

semper-virens (sin-pèr-vi-rins), *n.m.* and *adj.* (—), (bot.) a kind of honey-suckle; sempervirent, evergreen.

sempiternel, -le (sin-), *adj.*, sempiternal, everlasting.

sénat, *n.m.*, senate; senate-house.

sénateur, *n.m.*, senator.

sénatorerie, *n.f.*, endowment, residence, of a senator.

sénatorial, -e, *adj.*, senatorial.

sénatorien, -ne (-in, -è-n), *adj.*, senatorial, senatorian.

sénatrice, *n.f.*, senator's lady.

sénatus-consulte (-tus-), *n.m.* (— —s), senatus-consultum.

senau, *n.m.*, (nav.) snow, sort of vessel.

séné, *n.m.*, senna.

sénéchal, *n.m.*, seneschal.

sénéchale, *n.f.*, seneschal's wife.

sénéchaussée, *n.f.*, seneschal's jurisdiction; seneschal's court.

seneçon (sè-n-son). *n.m.*, (bot.) groundsel.

senegrain, senègre, or senegré, *n.m.*, (bot.) fenugreek.

senelle, *n.f.*, *V.* **cenelle**.

sénestre, *adj.*, ⊙left; (her.) sinister.

sénevé (sé-n-vé), *n.m.*, (bot.) charlock, black mustard.

⊙**sénieur**, *n.m.*, senior, oldest in functions.

sénile, *adj.*, senile.

sénilité, *n.f.*, senility, old age.

senne, *n.f.* *V.* **seine**.

sens (sänss), *n.m.*, sense, senses; understanding, judgment; intellect; sensibleness; reason, intelligence; opinion, sentiment; meaning, import; way, direction. *Reprendre ses —;* to come to one's senses. *Bon —:* good sense. — *commun;* common-sense. — *propre;* proper sense. — *figuré;* figurative sense. *Ce mot a deux —;* that word has two meanings. *Il abonde en son —;* he is wedded to his opinion. *J'abonde dans votre —;* I am of your opinion. — *devant derrière;* the hind part foremost. — *dessus dessous;* upside down, topsy-turvy. *Être dans son bon —;* to be in one's right senses. *Mettre quelqu'un hors de son bon —;* to drive any one out of his senses. *En — inverse;* in a contrary direction.

sensation, *n.f.*, sensation. *Éprouver une —;* to experience a sensation. *Faire —;* to cause a sensation.

sensé, -e, *adj.*, sensible, intelligent.

sensément, *adv.*, sensibly.

sensibilité, *n.f.*, sensibility, sensitiveness, feeling; tenderness, soreness; tender-heartedness. *Avoir de la — pour la gloire;* to be sensible to glory.

sensible, *adj.*, sensible (receiving impressions—*capable de sensation*); perceptible, obvious, palpable, evident; feeling, sensitive; visible (horizon); tender, sore (of flesh—*douloureux*). *Il se montra — à ma douleur;* he seemed affected with my sorrow. — *à l'amitié;* sensible of friendship. *C'est son endroit —;* that's his sensitive part. (mus.) *note —;* leading note.

sensible, *n.f.*, (mus.) leading note.

sensiblement, *adv.*, sensibly, obviously, perceptibly, greatly.

sensiblerie, *n.f.*, sentimentality.

sensiti-f, -ve, *adj.*, sensitive.

sensitive. *n.f.*, (bot.) sensitive plant.

sensorial, *adj.*, (physiol.) sensorial.

sensorium (-om), *n.m.*, sensorium.

sensualisme, *n.m.*, sensualism.

sensualiste, *n.m.f.* and *adj.*, sensualist; sensual.

sensualité, *n.f.*, sensuality.

sensuel, -le, *n.* and *adj.*, sensualist; sensual, voluptuous.

sensuellement (-èl-män), *adv.*, sensually.

⊙**sente**, *n.f.* *V.* **sentier**.

sentence, *n.f.*, sentence; maxim; judgment; decree. — *de mort;* sentence of death.

⊙**sentencié**, *n.m.*, -e. *n.f.*, convict.

⊙**sentencier**, *v.a.*, (criminal law—*droit criminel*) to condemn, to pass sentence, to sentence.

sentencieusement (-euz-män), *adv.*, sententiously.

sentencieu-x, -se, *adj.*, sententious.

sentène, *n.f.*, thread of a skein. *V.* **centaine**.

senteur, *n.f.*, scent, fragrance, perfume. *Pois de —;* sweet peas.

sentier (-tié), *n.m.*, path, foot-path, track. — *battu;* beaten track.

sentiment, *n.m.*, feeling, sensation; sentiment; perception; sense, consciousness, sensibility; opinion. *Avoir le — des convenances;* to have a sense of propriety. *Juger par —;* to judge from feeling. — *d'honneur;* sentiment of honour. — *d'amour;* feeling of love. *Selon mon —;* in my opinion.

sentimental. -e *adj.*, sentimental.

sentimentalement. *adv.*, sentimentally.

sentimentalité, *n.f.*, sentimentality, sentimentalism.

sentine, *n.f.*, (nav.) well-room (of a ship—*d'un vaisseau*); (fig.) sink of vice.

sentinelle, n.f., sentinel, sentry. — *perdue*; forlorn sentinel. *Faire* —; to keep sentry, to be on the watch.

sentir (sentant, senti), v.a., to feel, to be sensible of, to have a sense of; to smell, to scent; to taste, to have a taste of, to savour; to look like. *Il ne sent pas les affronts;* he is not sensible of affronts. — *une fleur;* to smell a flower. *Cette carpe sent la bourbe;* this carp tastes of the mud. *Faire — quelque chose.à quelqu'un;* to impress any one with a sense of any thing. *Il sent les choses de loin;* he foresees things afar off.

se **sentir**, v.r., to feel one's self, to know one's self, to be sensible; to be conscious, to feel. *Il se sentait mourir;* he felt himself dying. *Il ne se sent pas de froid,* he is quite benumbed with cold. *Il se sent bien;* he knows himself very well.

sentir, v.n., to feel; to smell, to have an odour; to have a bad smell. — *bon;* to smell nice. — *mauvais;* to smell bad. *Cette viande commence à —;* this meat begins to have a bad smell.

seoir (soâr), v.n., to suit, to become. *Il vous sied mal de;* it ill becomes you to.

seoir (soâr), v.n., (l.u.) to sit.

séparable, adj., separable.

séparation, n.f., separation, disjunction; parting; partition. — *de corps et de biens; divorce a mensâ et thoro.*

séparatiste, n.m., separatist.

séparément, adv., separately; disjunctively.

séparer, v.a., to separate, to sever, to disunite, to divide, to part, to set apart, to drive asunder, to disjoin; to divorce. — *le bon grain d'avec le mauvais;* to separate the good seed from the bad. — *les cheveux sur le front;* to part the hair on the forehead. — *deux hommes qui se battent;* to part two men fighting.

se **séparer**, v.n., to separate, to sever, to part; to break up (of assemblies—*d'assemblées*); to come off. *Il n'y a si bonne compagnie qui ne se sépare;* the best friends must part at last.

sépia, n.f., sepia.

seps (sèps), n.m., (erpetology) seps.

sept (sèt), n.m. and adj., seven, seventh.

ⓒ**septante** (sèp-), adj., seventy.

septante (sèp-), n.m., the seventy Greek translators of the Old Testament. *Version des —;* the Septuagint.

septembre (sèp-), n.m., September.

septembriseur (sèp-), n.m., (French hist.) septembrist, author of the massacres of September, 1792.

septénaire (sèp-), n.m. and adj., septenary.

septennal.-e (sèp-tè-n-nal), adj., septennial.

septennalité (sèp-tè-n-na-), n.f., seven years' duration.

septentrion (sèp-), n.m., North; (astron.) Lesser Bear.

septentrional, -e, (sèp-), adj., North, Northern.

septidi (sèp-), n.m., septidi, the seventh day of the decade of the calendar of the first French republic.

septième (sè-tièm), n.m f. and adj., seventh: seventh day.

septième (sè-tièm), n.f., sequence of seven cards; (mus.) seventh; (piquet) septieme.

septièmement(sè-tièm-mân),adv.,seventhly.

septier (sè-tié), n.m. V. setier.

septillion (sèp-), n.m., (arith.) one quadrillion.

septimo (sèp-), adv., seventhly.

septique (sèp-), adj., (med.) septical, septic.

septuagénaire (sèp-), n.m.f. and adj., septuagenarian; septuagenary.

septuagésime (sèp-), n.f., septuagesima.

septuor (sèp-), n.m. (—), (mus.) a piece for seven voices, or seven instruments.

septuple (sèp-), n.m. and adj., septuple, sevenfold.

septupler (sèp-), v.a., to increase sevenfold.

sépulcral, -e, adj., sepulchral, cadaverous. *Voir —e;* cavernous voice.

sépulcre, n.m., sepulchre, tomb.

sépulture, n.f., burial, sepulture, interment, vault (tomb—*tombe*). *La — ecclésiastique;* Christian burial. *Privé de —;* left unburied.

séquelle, n.f., (fam.) gang, crew (of persons —*de personnes*); set, host (of things—*de choses*).

séquence, n.f., sequence (at cards—*aux cartes*); (c. rel.) sequence.

séquestration, n.f., sequestration.

séquestre, n.m., sequestration; sequestrator; deposit, depository. *Mettre en —;* to sequester.

séquestrer, v.a., to sequester; to put away.

se **séquestrer**, v.r., to sequester one's self.

séquin, n.m., sequin (gold coin—*monnaie d'or*).

*****sérail**, n.m, seraglio.

séran, n.m., hatchel, flax comb.

sérançage, n.m., hatchelling.

sérancer, v.a., to hatchel, to dress (flax or hemp—*lin, chanvre*).

séranceur, n.m., hatcheller, flax or hemp-dresser.

sérançoir, n.m., hatchel, flax-comb.

sérancolin, n.m., Serancolin marble.

sérapéum, n.m. (—s), Serapeum (Egyptian temple of Serapis).

séraphin, n.m., seraph.

séraphique, adj., seraphic.

sérasquier, n.m., seraskier, pacha commanding the troops of a province.

serbocal, n.m., small glass cylinder.

serdeau, n.m., officer of the royal household who received the dishes removed from the royal table; dining-hall of the nobles in waiting; place where the remains of the royal table were sold.

serein, n.m., night-dew, evening-damp.

serein (sè-rin), -e (sè-rè-n), adj., serene, placid.

sérénade, n.f., serenade. *Donner une — à;* to serenade.

sérénissime,adj.,most serene (title—*titre*).

sérénité, n.f., serenity, sereneness; placidness; equanimity. *La — du temps;* the sereneness of the weather. *Avec —;* serenely.

séreu-x, -se, adj., (med.) serous, watery.

ser-f (sèrf), -ve (sèrv), n. and adj., serf; in bondage, of serfs.

serfouette (sèr-), n.f., hoe.

serfouir (sèr-), v.a., to loosen the ground with a hoe; to hoe.

serfouissage (sèr-), n.m., (gard.) hoeing.

serge (sèrj), n.f., serge.

sergent (sèr-), n.m., sergeant; (joiner's tool —*outil de menuisier*) cramp. —*d'armes*, sergeant-at-arms. — *de ville;* policeman.

ⓒ**sergenter** (sèr-), v a., to dun; to plague, to bore.

ⓒ**sergenterie** (sèr-jan-tri), n.f., sergeant-ship.

serger, or **sergier** (sèr-), n.m., serge-maker.

sergerie (sèr-), n.f., serge-manufactory, serge-trade.

séricicole, adj., of silk husbandry.

sériciculture, n.f., silk culture.

série, n.f., series.

sérieusement (-euz-mân), adv., seriously, gravely, in earnest; coolly, gravely.

sérieu-x, -se, *adj.*, serious, grave, staid; earnest, real. *Mine —se;* serious look. *Querelle —se;* serious quarrel.

sérieux, *n.m.*, seriousness, earnestness; (thea.) serious business. *Garder son — ;* to preserve one's gravity, to keep one's countenance. *Prendre son — ;* to grow serious. *Au — ;* in earnest.

serin (sĕ-rīn), *n.m.*, **-e** (sĕ-ı̆-n), *n.f.*, canary, canary-bird.

seriner (sĕ-), *v.a.*, to teach with the bird-organ. *— un oiseau ;* to teach a bird with the bird-organ.

serinette (sĕ-), *n.f.*, bird-organ; singer of no power.

seringa (sĕ-). *n.m.*. (bot.) syringe.

seringue (sĕ-ringh), *n.f.*, syringe, squirt.

seringuer (sĕ-rin-ghé), *v.a.*, to syringe, to squirt. *— un vaisseau* (nav.); to rake a ship.

serment (sèr-), *n.m.*, oath ; *pl.*, swearing. *Faux — ;* false oath. *Préter — ;* to take an oath, to be sworn. *Rompre son —, manquer à son — ;* to break one's oath.

⊙**sermenté, -e** (sèr-), *adj.* V. **assermenté.**

sermon (sèr-), *n.m.*, sermon, admonition.

sermonnaire (sèr-), *n.m.* and *adj.*, collection of sermons; author of sermons; adapted to sermons.

sermonner (sèr-), *v.a.*, (b.s.) to sermonize, to preach, to lecture.

sermonneur (sèr-), *n.m.*, (b.s.) sermonizer, preacher, lecturer.

sérosité, *n.f.*, serosity, wateriness.

serpe (sèı̆p), *n.f.*, bill, bill-hook, hedge-bill, pruning-bill. *C'est fait à la — ;* it is done in a bungling manner.

serpent (sèr-), *n.m.*, serpent, snake, adder; (mus.) serpent, serpent player. *— à sonnettes ;* rattle-snake. *Œil-de- — (—s —);* (jewel-*raillerie*) serpent's eye. *Langue-de- — (—s —);* (bot.) serpent's-tongue.

serpentaire (sèr-), *n.f.*, (bot.) serpentaria, snake-root; dragon's-wort.

serpentaire (sèr-), *n.m.*, (astron.) Serpentarius; (orni.) secretary, serpent-eater.

serpente (sèr-), *n.f.*, silver-paper.

serpenteau (sèr-), *n.m.*, young serpent ; (fire-work—*pièce d'artifice*) serpent.

serpenter (sèr-), *v.n.*, to meander, to wind, to serpentine.

serpentin, -e (sèr-), *adj.*, serpentine (of marble; of a horse's tongue—*du marbre, de la langue du cheval*).

serpentin (sèr-), *n.m.*, worm (of a still—*d'alambic*).

serpentine (sèr-), *n.f.*, serpentine-stone ; serpentine-marble ; (bot.) ophioxylon, snake-wood.

serpette (sèr-), *n.f.*, pruning-knife, garden-knife.

serpigineu-x, -se (sèr-), *adj.*, (med.) serpiginous.

****serpillière** (sèr-), *n.f.*, packing-cloth.

serpolet (sèr-), *n.m.*, (bot.) wild thyme.

serratule (sèr-ra-), *n.f.*, (bot.) serratula, saw-wort.

serre (sèr-), *n.f.*, green-house; conservatory; talon, claw (of birds—*d'oiseau*); pressure (of fruit—*de fruits*). *— chaude ;* hot-house. *Avoir la — bonne ;* to have a strong grasp.

serré, -e (sè-ré), *part.*, close, compact, tight, fast ; crowded ; close-fisted, covetous, (bot.) serrate, serrated; small (of writing—*criture*). *Un nœud — ;* a tight knot. *Drap bien — ;* close-woven cloth. *J'ai le cœur — ;* my heart is oppressed with grief.

serré (sè-ré), *adv.*, very much ; hard (of freezing—*du froid*); impudently (of lying—*de mensonge*). *Jouer — ;* to play prudently.

serre-bosse (sèr-), *n.f.* (—), (nav.) shank-painter.

serre-étoupe (sèr-), *n.m.* (—), stuffing-box.

serre-file (sèr-), *n.m.* (— —s), (milit.) supernumerary; supernumerary rank; (nav.) sternmost ship.

serre-frein (sèr-), *n.m.* (— —s), (railways) guard in charge of the brakes.

serrement (sèr-mǎn), *n.m.*, pressing, clasping; squeeze, squeezing. *— de cœur;* oppression of the heart ; heart-burning.

serrément (sè-ré-), *adv.*, niggardly.

serre-nez (sèr-). *n.m.* (—), (man.) twitch.

serre-nœud (sèr-), *n.m.* (— —s), (surg.) ligature-tightener.

serre-papiers (sèr-), *n.m.* (—), paper-holder, set of pigeon-holes for papers.

serrer (sè-ré), *v.a.*, to press, to press closely; to tighten, to squeeze, to grasp, to wring ; to crowd, to condense, to put close together ; to tie (a knot—*un nœud*) ; (print.) to lock, to lock up ; to oppress (the heart—*le cœur*) ; (milit.) to close (the ranks—*les rangs*); to clinch (one's fist, one's teeth—*le poing, les dents*); to put away ; to clasp, to draw close. *— la main à quelqu'un ;* to shake any one by the hand, to shake hands with any one. *— un nœud ;* to tighten a knot. *— le bouton à quelqu'un ;* to urge any one. *Cela serre le cœur ;* that oppresses the heart. *— les rangs* (milit.) ; to close the ranks. *— son écriture ;* to write close. *— les dents ;* to clinch one's teeth. *— le poing ;* to clinch one's fist. *— la forme* (print.) ; to lock up the form. *— la muraille ;* to pass close to the wall. *— son style ;* to make one's style concise. *— les voiles ;* to take in the sails. *Serrez vos livres ;* put your books away. *— les bl:s ;* to house the corn.

se **serrer** (sè-ré), *v.r.*, to press each other close; to sit close, to lie close ; to stand close ; to crowd.

serre-tête (sèr-), *n.m.* (—), head-band; night-cap.

serrette (sè-rèt), *or* **sarrette**, *n.f.*, (bot.) serratula, saw-wort.

serron (sè-). *n.m.*, seroon.

serrure (sè-rur), *n.f.*, lock. *— de sûreté ;* safety lock. *Crocheter une — ;* to pick a lock.

serrurerie (sè-rur-rī), *n.f.*, locksmith's trade, locksmith's work.

serrurier (sè-), *n.m.*, locksmith.

sertir (sèr-), *v.a.*, to set a stone in the bezel of a ring.

sertissure (sèr-), *n.f.*, setting of a stone in the bezel of a ring.

sérum (-rom), *n.m.*, serum.

servage (sèr-), *n.m.*, servitude, bondage.

serval (sèr-), *n.m.*, (mam.) serval.

servant (sèr-), *adj.*, serving, in waiting.

servant (sèr-), *n.m.*,(artil.) gunner, stationed by the side of a gun to serve it.

servante (sèr-), *n.f.*, servant-maid, maid-servant ; servant ; dumb-waiter ; (print.) frisket-stand.

serviable (sèr-), *adj.*, serviceable, willing to do services, obliging.

service (sèr-), *n.m.*, service ; duty, attendance ; divine service ; set (collection) ; course (of dishes at meals—*aux repas*). *Se mettre en — ;* (of servants—*de domestiques*) to go to service. *Être au — de ;* to be in the service of. *Qu'y a-t-il pour votre — ?* what can I do for you ? *Il a trente ans de — ;* he has served thirty years. *Être de — ;* to be on duty. *Il m'a rendu un bon — ;* he did me a good service.

serviette (sèr-), *n.f.*, napkin, towel.

servile (sèr-), *adj.*, servile, menial; slavish, cringing.

servilement (sèr-vil-mǎn), *adv.*, servilely, slavishly.

servilité (sèr-), n.f., servility, servileness, slavishness.

servir (sèr-), (servant, servi), v.a., to serve, to wait on, to attend, to be serviceable, to be of service ; to be of use ; to help ; (fin.) to pay (interest—des intérêts) ; to supply (with goods—des marchandises) ; (c.rel.) to assist the priest (at mass—à la messe). — son maître à table ; to wait upon one's master at table. Être réduit à — ; to be obliged to go to service. — sa patrie ; to serve one's country.

se servir (sèr-), v.r., to serve one's self, to be served, to be served up (of dishes—des mets). — de; to use, to employ, to make use of ; to avail one's self of. — mal de sa raison ; to make a bad use of one's reason. Servez-vous ; help yourself.

servir (sèr-), v.n., to serve, to be of use, to serve up, to bring in dinner or supper ; to be employed, to be conducive. On a servi ; dinner, supper, is upon the table. — sur mer, sur terre ; to serve in the navy, in the army. Cela ne sert à rien ; that is of no use. Cela sert à plusieurs choses ; that is employed for several things. À quoi sert-il? of what use is it? Il ne sert à rien ; it is of no use. Il ne sert à rien de s'emporter ; it is of no use to fly into a passion. Ce trou me sert de maison ; this hole serves me for a house. Cela sert de pain ; that does instead of bread. Il m'a servi de père ; he has been as a father to me. Cela ne sert de rien ; that is of no avail.

serviteur (sèr-), n.m., servant. — de Dieu; servant of God. — de l'État; servant of the State. Votre—! your servant; I beg to be excused.

servitude (sèr-), n.f., servitude.

ses (sè), adj.pl., his, her, its, one's. V. son.

sésame, n.m., (bot.) sesame, sesamum.

sésamoïde, adj. m., (anat.) sesamoid.

séséli, n.m., (bot.) seseli.

sesquialtère (sès-kui-), adj., (math.) sesquialter. sesquialteral.

sessile (sès-sil), adj., sessile.

session (sè-), n.f., session, sitting; term (of law courts—des tribunaux).

sesterce (sès-), n.m., (Rom. antiq.) sesterce.

sétacé, -e, adj., setaceous.

séthim (-tim), n.m., (bot.) shittim.

*setier (sè-tié), n.m., an obsolete measure, varying according to place.

sétigère, adj., (bot.) setigerous, bristly.

séton, n.m., seton.

*seuil, n.m., threshold (of a door—de porte), groundsill.

seul, -e, n. and adj., one; alone, by one's self ; single ; mere, only, sole. Tout — ; all alone.

seulement (seul-màn), adv., only, but, solely, merely. Un mot — ; but one word.

seulet, -te, adj., (l.u.) alone, by one's self.

sève, n.f., sap; pith; vigour. Cet arbre est en — ; the sap of that tree is rising.

sévère, adj., severe, stern, harsh, rigid, strict. Un juge — ; a stern judge.

sévèrement (-vèr-màn), adv., severely, harshly ; sternly; strictly.

sévérité, n.f., severity, rigidness, strictness, sternness. User de — envers quelqu'un; to use any one with severity.

séveu-x, -se, adj., (bot.) sappy.

sévices, n.m.pl., (jur.) cruelty, assault.

sévir, v.n., to use with rigour; (jur.) to commit cruelty.

sevrage (sè-), n.m., weaning

sevrer (sè-), v.a., to wean.

sèvres, n.m., porcelain, china manufactured at Sèvres.

sevreuse (sè-), n.f., nurse who weans children.

sexagénaire (sèg-za-), n.m.f. and adj., sexagenarian, sexagenary.

sexagésimal (sèg-za-), adj., (math.) sexagesimal.

sexagésime (sèg-za-), n.f., sexagesima.

sexangulaire (sèk-sàn-), adj., sexangular.

sex-digitaire (sèks-), n.m.f. and adj. (— —s), six-fingered person; six-fingered.

sex-digital, -e (sèks-), adj., six-fingered; six-toed.

sexe (sèks), n.m., sex; fair sex. Le beau — ; the fair sex.

sexennal, -e (sèk-sè-n-nal), adj., sexennial.

sextant (sèks-), n.m., sextant.

sexte (sèkst), n.f., (c.rel.) sixth canonical hour; sixth; the sixth book of Pope Boniface VIII.'s Decretals.

sextidi (sèks-), n.m., sextidi, sixth day of the decade of the calendar of the first French republic.

sextil, -e (sèks-), adj., (astrol.) Aspect —; sextile.

sextillion (sèks-), n.m., (arith.) one thousand trillions.

sextule (sèks-), n.m., apothecaries' weight, about 65 grains.

sextuor (sèks-), n.m. (—), (mus.) a piece for six voices or instruments.

sextuple (sèks-), n.m. and adj., sextuple, sixfold.

sextupler (sèks-), v.a., to increase sixfold.

sexualité (sèk-sua-), n.f., sexuality.

sexuel, -le (sèk-su-èl), adj., sexual.

sgraffite, n.m. V. graffite.

shako (sha-), n.m., (milit.) shako.

shall, n.m. V. châle.

sheling, n.m. V. schelling.

shérif (shérif), n.m., sheriff.

si, conj., if; whether; ⊙nevertheless. — vous le faites; if you do it. — je l'avais vu; had I seen it. S'il vient; if he comes. S'ils veulent; if they like. — bien que; so that. — ce n'est que; unless, except.

si, adv., so, so much; however; yes. N'allez pas — vite; do not go so fast. — petit qu'il soit; however little he is, little as he is. Je dis que —; I say yes. Je gage que —; I lay it is so. — fait vraiment; yes indeed. Vous ne l'avez pas vu. —, je l'ai vu; you have not seen it. Yes, I have seen it.

si, n.m., (mus.) B, si.

sialagogue, n.m., (med.) sialogogue.

sialisme, n.m., (med.) ptyalism.

siamois, -e, n. and adj., Siamese.

siamoise, n.f., Siam cotton.

sibarite, n.m. V. sybarite.

sibilant, -e, adj., hissing, sibilant.

sibylle, n.f., sibyl.

sibyllin, adj., sibylline.

sicaire, n.m., hired assassin.

siccati-f, -ve, adj., siccative.

siccatif, n.m., siccative.

siccité (sik-si-), n.f., siccity, dryness.

sicilien, -ne (-in, -èn), n. and adj., Sicilian.

sicilique, n.m., apothecaries' weight, about 97¾ grains.

sicle, n.m., shekel.

sicomore, n.m. V. sycomore.

sidéral, -e, adj., sideral, sidereal.

sidéritis, n.m. V. crapaudine.

sidéroxylon, n.m., iron wood.

siècle, n.m., century, hundred years ; age, time; world; period. Les mœurs de notre —; the manners of our age. Il y a un — qu'on ne vous a vu; we have not seen you for an age. À tous les —, aux —s des —s, dans tous les —s des -s : for ever and ever.

siège, n.m., seat, coach-box; bench (of a court of justice—d'un tribunal); bishopric, see;

dickey (of a carriage—*d'une voiture*); (milit.) siege. *Le — d'un cocher;* a coachman's box. *Le saint- — :* the holy see. *Le cerveau est le — de la raison:* the brain is the seat of reason. *Lever le— :* to raise the siege.

siéger. *v.n.*, to hold one's see (of bishops—*des évêques*); to sit (of assemblies or courts—*d'assemblées, de tribunaux*); to be seated; to lie (of a thing—*des choses*).

sien, -ne (si-in, si-è-n), *pron.*, his, hers, its; one's own. *Mon père et le sien;* my father and his, hers. *Ma sœur et la sienne;* my sister and his, hers.

sien, *n.m.*, **-ne**, *n.f.*, one's own property; his own, her own, one's own. *Chacun le — n'est pas trop;* every one his own is all fair. *Faire des —nes;* to play one's pranks. *Les —s;* one's people, relations and friends. *À chacun le —;* to each his own.

sieste, *n.f.*, siesta, afternoon's nap. *Faire la —;* to take one's afternoon's nap.

sieur. *n.m.*, (jur.) mister.

sifflable, *adj.*, that deserves to be hissed.

sifflant, -e, *adj.*, hissing, whistling, sibilant; wheezing.

sifflement, *n.m.*, whistling, whistle; hissing, hiss; whiz, whizzing (of the wind, an arrow, &c.—*du vent, d'une flèche, &c.*); wheezing.

siffler, *v.n.*, to whistle, to hiss, to whiz; to wheeze.

siffler, *v.a.*, to whistle; to hiss at; to sing (of birds—*des oiseaux*); to prompt. —*quelqu'un;* to prompt any one. *— une pièce;* to hiss a piece. *-- un acteur;* to hiss an actor.

sifflerie, *n.m.*, hissing.

sifflet, *n.m.*, whistle, catcall; windpipe; (nav.) boatswain's call. *Un coup de —* a whistling. *Couper le — à quelqu'un* (triv.); to cut any one's throat; to dumfound any one.

siffleu-r, *n.m.*, **-se**, *n.f.*, whistler, hisser.

siffleur, *n.m.*, (orni.) wood-wren.

siffleu-r, **-se**, *adj.*, whistling, that whistles (of birds—*des oiseaux*); that wheezes (of horses —*des chevaux*).

sigillé, -e (-jil-lé), *adj.*, of bole (fine clay—*argile fine*).

sigisbée, *n.m.*, cicisbeo.

sigle, *n.m.*, initial letter or letters used as abbreviations in ancient writings, monuments and medals, especially Latin.

sigmoïde, *adj.*, (anat.) sigmoid, sigmoidal.

*__signal__, *n.m.*, signal; signal word.

*__signalé, -e__, *adj.*, signal.

*__signalement__, *n.m.*, description of a man.

*__signaler__, *v.a.*, to give the description of; to point out; to mark out; to give a signal; to signalize.

*se __signaler__. *v.r.*, to signalize one's self.

*__signataire__, *n.m.f.*, signer, subscriber.

*__signature__, *n.f.*, signature, sign, sign-manual; signing.

*__signe__. *n.m.*, sign, mark; beck, beckon, nod; indication, token, badge; omen: mark (on the skin—*sur la peau*). *Faire — de la main;* to beckon with the hand. *— de la tête;* nod. *Faire le — de la croix:* to cross one's self.

*__signer__, *v.a.*, to sign, to subscribe.

*se __signer__, *v.r.*, to cross one's self; to make the sign of the cross.

signer. *v.n.*, to sign, to subscribe one's self.

signet (si-nè), *n.m.*, small sign; tassel, mark (for books—*de livre*).

⊙*__signifiance__. *n.f.*, significance, token, testimony.

*__signifiant, -e__, *adj.*, (theol.) significant, significative.

*__significati-f, -ve__. *adj.*, significative, significant.

*__signification__. *n.f.*, signification : meaning, sense; (jur.) legal notice.

*__significativement__, *adv.*, with force, significantly.

*__signifier__, *v.a.*, to signify, to mean, to notify, to intimate; (jur.) to serve a notice, a deed. *Que signifie ce mot?* what is the meaning of this word?

*se __signifier__, *v.r.*, (jur.) to be served.

sil, *n.m.*, yellow ochre (of the ancients—*des anciens*).

silence, *n.m.*, silence, stillness; (mus.) silence. *Faire —;* to keep silence, to be silent. *Rompre le —:* to break silence. *Imposer —;* to command silence. *Passer une chose sous —;* to pass a thing over in silence. *Réduire au —;* to silence.

silencieusement (-euz-mān), *adv.*, silently.

silencieu-x, -se, *adj.*, silent, still.

silène, *n.m.*, (myth.) Silenus; Satyr, attendant of Bacchus; (ent.) a butterfly of southern Europe.

silène, *n.f.*, (bot.) catch-fly.

silex (-lèks), *n.m.*, silex, flint.

silhouette, *or* **silouette**, *n.f.*, silhouette.

silicate, *n.m.*, (chem.) silicate.

silice, *n.f.*, (chem.) silica.

siliceu-x, -se, *adj.*, silicious.

silicique, *adj.*, (chem.) silicic.

silicium, *n.m.*, (chem.) silicon, silicium.

silicule, *n.f.*, (bot.) silicle, silicula.

siliculeu-x, -se, *adj.*, (bot.) siliculous, siliculose.

silique, *n.f.*, (bot.) siliqua, silique.

siliqueu-x, -se, *adj.*, (bot.) siliquous, siliquose.

*__sillage__, *n.m.*, (nav.) track, steerage-way, wake.

sille, *n.m.*, Greek satirical poem.

*__siller__, *v.n.*, (l.u.) (nav.) to run ahead.

*__siller__, *v.a.*, (hawking—*fauconnerie*) to close the eyes (of a hawk—*d'un faucon*).

*__sillet__, *n.m.*, nut (of stringed instruments—*d'instruments à cordes*).

*__sillomètre__, *n.m.*, (nav.) sillometer, log.

*__sillon__, *n.m.*, (agri.) furrow, ridge; track, trail (of light—*de lumière*); wake (of ships—*des vaisseaux*); (anat.) groove; wrinkle; (poet.) *pl.*, fields, plains.

*__sillonner__, *v.a.*, to furrow, to plough; to ridge, to cut; (anat.) to groove.

silo, *n.m.*, pit for preserving grain.

silouette, *n.f.* V. **silhouette**.

silphium (-fiom), *n.m.*, (n.p.) silphium, laser.

silure, *n.m.*, (ich.) silurus.

silurien, -ne (ri-în, -è-n), *adj.*, (geol.) silurian.

silves, *n.f.pl.* V. **sylves**.

simagrée, *n.f.*, grimace, affected way; *pl.*, affectation.

simaise, *n.f.* V. **cimaise**.

simarouba, *n.m.*, (bot.) simaruba.

simarre, *n.f.*, ⊙simare, woman's gown; gown of some judges.

simbleau, *n.m.*, (carp.) radius-line.

similaire, *adj.*, similar.

similarité, *n.f.*, similarity, likeness.

similitude, *n.f.*, similitude, similarity; comparison: (rhet.) simile.

similor, *n.m.*, similor.

simoniaque, *n.m.* and *adj.*, simoniac; simoniacal.

simonie, *n.f.*, simony.

simoun (-moon), *n.m.*, simoon, simoom.

simple, *adj.*, simple, single; only, only one, but one, bare, mere; common, private (of soldiers—*soldats*); plain, unadorned, simple-minded; silly. *Des souliers à — semelle:* single-soled shoes. *Un — soldat:* a common soldier, a private. *— comme un enfant;* as simple as a

child. *Une — lettre;* a single letter, only one letter. *Un homme —;* an unpretending man.

simple,*n.m.,* simple, medicinal plant; (mus.) simple air.

simplement, *adv.,* simply, only, solely, merely, singly; plainly, without any ornament; artlessly; silily.

⊙**simplesse,** *n.f.,* simplicity, simpleness.

simplicité, *n.f.,* simplicity, simpleness, artlessness, plainness; silliness.

simplification, *n.f.,* simplification.

simplifier, *v.a.,* to simplify.

simulacre, *n.m.,* image of an idol; phantom; shadow; appearance, feint, sham. *Un — de combat;* a sham fight.

simulation, *n.f.,* (jur.) feigning.

simulé, -e, *adj.,* fictitious, feigned, false, pretended, counterfeit, sham.

simuler, *v.a.,* to feign, to sham. *— une attaque;* to make a false attack.

simultané, -e, *adj.,* simultaneous.

simultanéité, *n.f.,* simultaneousness, simultaneity.

simultanément, *adv.,* simultaneously.

sinapisé, -e, *adj.,* (med.) infused with mustard.

sinapisme, *n.m.,* sinapism, mustard-plaster.

sincère, *adj.,* sincere, true, open-hearted.

sincèrement (-sèr-mān), *adv.,* sincerely, truly, plainly, ingenuously.

sincérité, *n.f.,* sincerity, sincereness, open-heartedness.

sincipital, -e, *adj.,* pertaining to the sinciput.

sinciput (-put), *n.m.,* sinciput.

sindon, *n.m.,* Christ's shroud; (surg.) pledget.

sinécure, *n.f.,* sinecure.

sinécuriste, *n.m.,* sinecurist.

sine quâ non, *adj.inv.,* sine quâ non, indispensable.

singe, *n.m.,* ape, monkey, baboon; monkey (of pile-drivers—*de mouton*); windlass; pantograph (copying-machine—*machine à copier*). *Payer en monnaie de —;* to laugh at a man instead of paying him.

singe, *adj.,* (l.u.) apish.

singer, *v.a.,* to ape, to mimic.

singerie (sin-jrī), *n.f.,* apish trick, grimace, trick; mimicry.

singe-ur, -resse, *adj.,* that apes, apish.

singeur, *n.m.,* ape (imitator—*imitateur*).

singulariser, *v.a.,* to render singular, odd. *se* **singulariser,** *v.r.,* to render one's self singular, odd.

singularité, *n.f.,* singularity; peculiarity; oddness.

singuli-er, -ère, *adj.,* singular; peculiar; odd; single (combat). *Combat —;* single combat.

singulier, *n.m.,* (gram.) singular.

singulièrement (-lèr-mān), *adv.,* singularly, peculiarly, in a singular manner, oddly.

sinistre, *adj.,* sinister, inauspicious. *Présage —;* sinister foreboding. *Augure —;* unlucky omen.

sinistre, *n.m.,* accident, disaster.

sinistrement, *adv.,* sinistrously.

sinologue (-log), *n.m.,* one versed in the Chinese language.

sinombre, *adj.,* (of a lamp—*des lampes*) shadowless.

sinon, *conj.,* otherwise, else, or else; except, save, if not.

sinon que, *conj.,* save that; except.

sinople, *n.m.,* (her.) sinople, vert; (min.) a variety of quartz.

sinué, -e, *adj.,* (bot.) sinuate.

sinueu-x, -se, *adj.,* sinuous, winding, meandering.

sinuosité, *n.f.,* sinuosity, winding, meandering.

sinus (-nus), *n.m.,* (math.) sine; (anat.) sinus.

siphilis, *n.f.* V. **syphilis.**

siphilitique, *adj.* V. **syphilitique.**

siphon, *n.m.,* siphon; water-spout (at sea—*en mer*).

sire, *n.m.,* sire, title given to kings and emperors in addressing them; ⊙sir (lord). *Un pauvre —;* a poor wretch.

sirène, *n.f.,* siren, mermaid, sea-maid.

sirius (-us), *n.m.,* (astron.) Sirius.

siroco, *or* ⊙**siroc,** *n.m.,* Sirocco.

sirop, *n.m.,* syrup.

siroter, *v.a.,* to sip.

siroter, *v.n.,* to sip.

sirsacas, *n.m.,* Indian cotton-cloth.

sirtes, *n.f.pl.* V. **syrtes.**

sirupeu-x, -se, *adj.,* syrupy.

sirvente, *n.m.,* sirvente.

sis, -e, *adj.,* (jur.) seated, situate, situated.

sison, *n.m.,* honeywort.

sistelle, *n.f.,* (orni.) nut-hatch.

sistre, *n.m.,* (antiq.) sistrum, Egyptian timbrel.

sisymbre, *n.m.,* (bot.) sisymbrium.

sisyphe, *n.m.,* Sisyphus. *Le rocher de —;* long, profitless, and hard work; work which is soon destroyed and must be done over and over again.

site, *n.m.,* site, landscape, scenery.

sitôt, *adv.,* so soon, as soon.

sitôt que, *conj.,* as soon as.

situation, *n.f.,* situation, site; state; (nav.) bearing of coasts.

situé, -e, *adj.,* situate, situated, lying.

situer, *v.a.,* to place.

six, *n.m. and adj.,* six, sixth; sixth day. [For the pronunciation of this word, V. **dix.**]

⊙**sixain,** *n.m.* V. **sizain.**

sixième (si-zièm), *n.m. and adj.,* sixth; sixth day (of a period—*d'une période*); pupil in the sixth class (at school—*au collège*).

sixième (si-zièm), *n.f.,* six cards of the same suit (cards—*jeux de cartes*); sixth class (at school—*au collège*); (piquet) seizième.

sixièmement (si-zièm-mān), *adv.,* sixthly.

sixte (sikst), *n.f.,* (mus.) sixth.

sizain, *n.m.,* stanza of six lines; six packs of cards.

sizette, *n.f.,* sizette (card game—*jeu de cartes*).

slave, *n.m.f. and adj.,* Slav.

sloop, *or* **sloupe** (sloop), *n.m.,* (nav.) sloop.

smalah, *n.f.* (*n.p.*), smalah, among the Arabs the camp of a powerful chief and a sort of movable chief town.

smalt, *n.m.,* smalt, blue glass.

smérinthe, *n.m.,* (ent.) hawk-moth.

*****smille,** *n.f.,* (mas.) scapple-axe.

*****smiller,** *v.a.,* (mas.) to scapple.

sobre, *adj.,* sober, sparing, temperate, abstemious (in eating and drinking—*dans le manger et le boire*).

sobrement, *adv.,* soberly, moderately, temperately, sparingly, abstemiously.

sobriété, *n.f.,* sobriety, soberness, temperance, moderation, abstemiousness. *La — est utile à la santé;* sobriety is good for the health.

sobriquet, *n.m.,* nickname. *Donner un — à;* to nickname.

soc, *n.m.,* ploughshare.

sociabilité, *n.f.,* sociability, sociableness, good fellowship.

sociable, *adj.,* sociable, social.

sociablement, *adv.,* sociably, socially.

social, -e, *adj.,* social; (com.) of a firm.

socialement (-sial-män), *adv.*, socially, in a social manner.

socialisme, *n.m.*, socialism.

socialiste. *n.m.f.*, socialist.

sociétaire, *n.m.f.* and *adj.*, member of a society, of a company.

société, *n.f.*, society; company. partnership. — *de commerce;* trading company. — *anonyme;* joint-stock company. *Homme de mauvaise* — : ungentlemanly man. *Faire une* — *avec quelqu'un;* to enter into partnership with any one. *Règle de* — (arith.); fellowship, rule of fellowship.

socinianisme, *n.m.*. Socinianism.

socinien, -ne (ni-in, -è-n), *n.* and *adj.*, Socinian.

socle, *n.m.*, (arch.) socle, pedestal, socket. — *continu:* basement.

socque, *n.m.*. clog, galoche.

socratique. *adj.*, socratic.

sodium (-om), *n.m.*..(chem.) sodium.

sodomie, *n.f.*, sodomy.

sodomite. *n.m.*, sodomite.

sœur (seur), *n.f.*, sister ; nun. — *s germaines;* sister of the whole blood. — *s consanguines;* sisters by the father's side. — *s utérines;* sisters by the mother's side. — *s jumelles;* twin sisters. — *de lait;* foster-sister. *Demi* — ; sister by the father's, *or* by the mother's side, step-sister. *Belle* — ; sister in law. *Les neuf* — *s;* the Muses. the sacred Nine. — *laie,* — *converse;* lay-sister.

sœurette, *n.f.*, little sister, dear little sister.

sofa. *n.m.*, sofa, ottoman.

soffite, *n.m.*, (arch.) soffit.

sofi, *or* **soufi**, *n.m.* (—*s*), Mahometan philosophers whose tenets are a kind of pantheism.

sofi. *or* **sophi**, *n.m.*, Sofi, Sophi, a title of the King of Persia.

soi, *pron.*, one's self, self, itself. *Penser à* — ; to think of one's self. *Être à* — ; to be one's own master.

soi-disant, *adj.*, self-styled, would-be.

soie. *n.f.*, silk ; hair (of a few species of dogs—*de quelques sortes de chiens*) ; bristle (of hogs—*de cochons, de sangliers*); tongue (of knives, swords—*de couteaux, d'épées, &c.*) ; (vet.) *V.* **seime** — *de bourre;* floss-silk. — *crue,* — *grège;* raw silk. — *plate;* floss-silk. *Des jours filés d'or et de* — ; happy days.

soierie (soa-ri), *n.f.*, silk, silk-trade ; silk-manufactory; *pl.*, silks, silk goods.

soif, *n.f.*, thirst. *Avoir* — ; to be thirsty. *Avoir grand'* — ; to be very thirsty. *Mourir de* — ; to be almost choked with thirst. *Étancher sa* — ; to quench one's thirst. — *des richesses;* thirst for riches. *Garder une poire pour la* — ; to lay up something for a rainy day.

*soigner, *v.a.*, to take care of, to look after, to attend, to attend to, to mind, to nurse. — *un malade:* to take care of a sick person.

*se soigner, *v.r.*, to take care of one's self, to nurse one's self.

*soigneusement (-eûz-män), *adv.*, carefully.

*soigneu-x, -se, *adj.*, careful, regardful ; solicitous ; mindful.

soi-même. *pron.*, one's self; itself.

soi-mouvant. *adj.*, (philos.) self-moving.

soin, *n.m.*. care. attendance on; *pl.*, attentions. *Avoir* — *de quelque chose;* to take care of any thing. *Je vous en laisse le* — ; I leave it to your care. *Rendre des* — *s à quelqu'un;* to pay attentions to any one. *Petits* — *s;* little attentions. *Être aux petits* — *s avec quelqu'un;* to be all attention to any one. *Manque de* — ; carelessness.

soir. *n.m.*, evening, night. *Du matin au* — ;

from morning till night. *Bon* — ; good evening. *Hier* —, *hier au* — ; last evening, last night. *Ce* — ; this evening, to-night.

soirée, *n.f.*, evening (duration of the evening—*durée de la soirée*); evening party. *Aller en* — ; to go out to a party, to an evening party. *Passer la* — ; to spend the evening.

soit, *adv.*. be it so, let it be so, well and good, I grant it. *Hé bien,* —; well, be it so. *Ainsi* — *-il;* so be it.

soit, *conj.*, either, whether, or. — *l'un,* — *l'autre;* either one or the other. — *que;* (with a verb—*avec un verbe*) whether.

soixantaine (soa-sän-tè-n), *n.f.*, about sixty, sixty years of age.

soixante (soa-sänt), *n.m.* and *adj.*, sixty. — *dix;* seventy. — *douze;* seventy-two.

soixanter (soa-sän-té), *v.n.*, to reckon sixty (piquet).

soixantième (soa-sän-tièm), *n.m.* and *adj.*, sixtieth.

sol, *n.m.*. soil ; ground ; ground-plot; (mus.) G, sol; (coin.) ⊙ *V.* **sou**.

⊙**solacier**, *v.a.*, to solace, to comfort, to cheer.

⊙**se solacier**, *v.r.*, to divert one's self.

solaire, *adj.*, solar. *Cadran* — ; sun-dial.

solandre, *n.f.*, (vet.) solander.

solanées, *n.f.pl.*, (bot.) solanaceæ.

solanum (-nom), *n.m.*, (bot.) solanum.

solbatu, -e, *adj.*, (of horses—*des chevaux*) surbated.

solbature, *n.f.*, (vet.) quitter, quitter-bone.

soldanelle, *n.f.*, (bot.) soldanella; convolvulus soldanella.

soldat, *n.m.*, soldier. — *de la milice;* militiaman. *Simple* — ; private soldier.

soldatesque, *n.f.* and *adj.*, soldiery; soldier-like.

solde, *n.f.*, (milit.) pay. *Demi* — ; half-pay.

solde, *n.m.*, (com.) balance. *Pour* — *de tout compte;* in full of all demands.

solder, *v.a.*, to pay; to keep in pay; to liquidate. — *un compte;* to settle an account. — *des troupes;* to pay troops.

sole, *n.f.*, sole (of animals) ; (agri.) break; (ich.) sole ; (arch.) sleeper. — *battue* (vet.); quitter, quitter-bone.

soléaire, *adj.*, (anat.) solear.

solécisme, *n.m.*, solecism.

*soleil, *n.m.*, sun; sunflower; (c. rel.) monstrance; sun-fish; (print.) squabble. — *couchant;* sun-set. *Se chauffer au* — ; to bask in the sun. *Le* — *luit pour tout le monde;* the sun shines upon all alike. *Il fait du* — ; the sun shines. *Coup de* — ; sun stroke, coup-de-soleil. *Le* — *se couche;* the sun is setting, is going down. *Il fait un beau* — ; the sun is shining beautifully.

solen (-lè-n), *n.m.*, (conch., surg.) solen.

solénite, *n.f.*, (fos.) solenite.

solennel, -le (so-la-nèl), *adj.*, solemn.

solennellement (-la-nèl-män), *adv.*, solemnly.

solennisation (-la-ni-) *n.f.*, solemnization.

solenniser (-la-ni-), *v.a.*, to solemnize.

solennité (-la-ni-), *n.f.*, solemnity, solemnness.

solfatare, *n.f.*, (geol.) solfatara.

solfège. *n.m.*. (mus.) solfeggio.

solfier, *v.a.*, (mus.) to solfa.

soli, plural sometimes found, as well as *solos,* of **solo**, which see.

solidaire, *adj.*, conjointly liable ; jointly and separately liable.

solidairement (-dèr-män), *adv.*, conjointly; jointly and separately.

solidarité, *n.f.*, joint liability ; joint and separate liability.

solide, *adj.*, solid, strong, firm; steadfast.

fast; substantial; solvent. *Un jugement —;* a sound judgment.

solide, *n.m.*, solid; solid body; solid figure; reality.

solidement (-lid-mān), *adv.*, solidly, substantially; firmly; soundly.

solidification, *n.f.*, solidification.

solidifier, *v.a.*, to solidify, to concrete.

se solidifier, *v.r.*, to solidify, to become solid; to acquire solidity.

solidité, *n.f.*, solidity, substantialness; steadfastness, stability, firmness, soundness.

soliloque, *n.m.*, soliloquy.

solin, *n.m.*, (arch.) space between two joists or rafters.

solipède, *n.m.* and *adj.*, soliped; solipedous.

soliste, *n.m.*, solo singer, solo player.

solitaire, *adj.*, solitary, lonely, lonesome; desert.

solitaire, *n.m.*, solitaire, recluse, solitary; brilliant (diamond—*diamant*).

solitairement (-tèr-mān), *adv.*, solitarily, lonesomely.

solitude, *n.f.*, solitude, loneliness.

solive, *n.f.*, joist.

soliveau, *n.m.*, small joist.

sollicitable, *adj.*, that may be solicited.

sollicitation (sol-li-), *n.f.*, solicitation, entreaty, instigation.

solliciter (sol-li-), *v.a.*, to solicit ; to incite, to urge; to entreat; to induce; to canvass. — *son payement;* to urge one to pay.

solliciteur, *v.a.*, to solicit.

solliciteu-r, *n.m.*, **-se**, (sol-li-), *n.f*, solicitor, solicitress, canvasser.

sollicitude (sol-li-), *n.f.*, solicitude, anxiety. *Avoir de la — pour;* to be solicitous, anxious, for.

solo, *n.m.* (—), (mus.) solo.

solstice, *n.m.*, solstice. — *d'été;* summer solstice.

solsticial, -e *adj.*, solstitial.

solubilité, *n.f.*, solubility.

soluble, *adj.*, solvable; soluble.

solution, *n.f.*, solution; dissolution; (math.) solution; resolution; (jur.) discharge.

solvabilité, *n.f.*, solvency.

solvable, *adj.*, solvent.

somatologie, *n.f.*, somatology.

sombre, *adj.*, dark, sombre, dull, gloomy, overcast; melancholy, sad. *Temps —;* gloomy weather. *Cette nuit est bien —;* this is a very dark night. *Lumière —;* dull light. *Couleurs —s;* sombre colours. *Le royaume —;* the infernal regions.

sombrer, *v.n.*, (nav.) to founder, to go down.

sommaire, *n.m.* and *adj.*, summary, compendium, abridgment, abstract; summary, compendious.

sommairement (-mèr-mān), *adv.*, summarily, briefly, succinctly.

sommation, *n.f.*, summons; (jur.) process, summons; (math.) summation. *Signifier une — à quelqu'un;* to serve a summons on any one.

somme, *n.f.*, burden; sum (quantity—*quantité*); amount; (math.) sum; (lit.) summary, compendium. *Bête de —;* beast of burden. — *totale;* sum-total. — *toute, en —;* finally, in short.

somme, *n.m.*, nap (sleep—*sommeil*). *Je n'ai fait qu'un — toute la nuit;* I slept without awaking all night.

*sommeil, *n.m.*, sleep. *Avoir —;* to be sleepy. *J'ai bien —;* I am very sleepy. *Profond —;* deep sleep. *Cela porte au —;* that inclines one to sleep. — *agité;* restless sleep. *Dormir d'un profond —;* to sleep soundly. *Être dans un — léthargique;* to be entranced. *Accablé de —;* overpowered with sleep. *Il n'en peut plus de —;* he is quite worn out for want of sleep, he is un-

able to keep awake. *Le — me gagne;* I am getting sleepy.

*sommeiller, *v.n.*, to slumber.

sommeli-er, *n.m.*, **-ère**, *n.f.*, butler.

sommellerie (so-mèl-ri), *n.f.*, butler's place; pantry, buttery.

sommer, *v.a.*, to summon, to call upon, to charge, to challenge; (math.) to sum up, to cast up. — *quelqu'un de sa parole;* to call upon any one to fulfil his promise. — *une place de se rendre* (milit.); to summon a stronghold to surrender.

sommet, *n.m.*, top, apex, summit ;pinnacle ; acme, zenith ; crown, top (of the head—*de la tête*); (bot.) vertex; (arch.) crown; (geom.) apex, vertex.

sommier, *n.m.*, pack-horse ; hair-mattress ; wind-chest (of an organ—*d'un orgue*); wrest-plank (of pianos); (arch.) brest-summer, summer; register-book; (print.) winter. — *élastique;* spring mattress.

sommité (som-mi-), *n.f.*, summit, top, apex; head, principal part.

somnambule (som-nān-), *n.m.f.* and *adj.*, somnambulist.

somnambulisme, *n.m.*, somnambulism.

somnifère (som-ni-). *n.m.* and *adj.*, (med.) narcotic ; somniferous, somnific, narcotic.

somnolence (som-no-), *n.f.*, somnolence, somnolency.

somnolent, -e *adj.*, (med.) somnolent.

somptuaire, *adj.*, sumptuary.

somptueusement (-euz-mān), *adv.*, sumptuously.

somptueu-x, -se, *adj.*, sumptuous.

somptuosité, *n.f.*, sumptuous, sumptuosity.

son, *n.m.*, bran; (phys.) sound. — *aigu;* shrill sound. — *de cloches;* ringing of bells. — *du tambour;* beat of the drum, sound of the drum.

son, sa, ses, *adj.*, his, her, its, one's. *Son frère, sa sœur et ses enfants;* his brother, sister, and children. *Son âme;* his, her, soul. [*Son* is used for the *fem.* instead of *sa* when the word following begins with a vowel or a silent *h*.]

sonate, *n.f.*, (mus.) sonata.

sondage, *n.m.*, sounding ; (mining—*mines*) boring.

sonde, *n.f.*, plummet, fathom-line; (nav.) sounding-line, sounding-lead; (surg.) probe; (manu.) proof-stick; (mining—*mines*) bore; *pl.*, (nav.) soundings. *Jeter la —* (nav.); to heave the lead, to sound.

sonder, *v.a.*, to sound, to try the depth, to fathom; to scrutinize, to explore ; to probe, to search. — *le terrain;* (mining—*mines*) to bore; (fig.) to see how matters stand. — *le gué;* to reconnoitre, to see how matters stand. — *la côte;* to sound the depth along the coast. — *une plaie;* to probe a wound. — *un fromage;* to pierce a cheese. — *quelqu'un;* to sound, to pump, any one.

sonder, *v.n.*, (nav.) to heave the lead, to sound, to take soundings.

sondeur, *n.m.*, (nav.) leadsman.

songe, *n.m.*, dream, dreaming. *Faire un —;* to have a dream. *Voir en —;* to see in a dream, to dream.

songe-creux, *n.m.* (—), dreamer, a visionary; mischief-maker.

⊙**songe-malice**, *n.m.* (—, or — —s), mischief-maker.

songer, *v.n.*, to dream, to muse; to think, to mean; to intend, to devise, to purpose, to propose, to consider. — *profondément;* to think deeply. — *à quelque chose;* to think of anything. *Songez à ce que vous faites;* mind what you are about. *Sans y —;* unawares, unthinkingly. *Il songe à se marier;* he thinks of marrying. — *creux;* to be a visionary. *Songez-y, songez-y bien;* mind what you are about: beware.

songer, *v.a.*, to dream (in one's sleep—*pendant le sommeil*); to dream, to imagine, to think of. — *une comédie;* to think of a comedy, to imagine a comedy. *Ne — que bals, que fêtes;* to think of nothing but balls, fêtes.

songeur, *n.* and *adj.m.*, (l.u.) dreamer; thoughtful, dreamy.

⊙**sonica**, *adv.*, in the nick of time, just in time. *On allait partir sans lui, il est arrivé —;* they were going to set out without him, when he arrived just in the nick of time. *Il a gagné* — (basset—*bassette*); he has gained just in the nick of time.

sonna, or **sunna**, *n.f.*, Sunna (book of the Mahommedans—*livres des traditions de la religion mahométane*).

*****sonnaille**, *n.f.*, bell (attached to the neck of cattle—*pour les bestiaux*).

*****sonnailler**, *v.n.*, (fam.) to ring often and without necessity, to be constantly ringing.

*****sonnailler**, *n.m.*, head of cattle that wears a bell and goes ahead of a flock or herd; bellwether of sheep—*des moutons*).

sonnant, **-e**, *adj.*, sounding, that has a clear sound; sonorous. *Espèces —es;* hard cash, money down, ready money. *À sept heures —es;* just as the clock was striking seven.

sonner, *v.n.*, to sound, to emit a sound; to chink, to ring; to strike (of clocks—*des horloges, des pendules*); to toll; to ring the bell. *Faites — cet écu;* ring that crown-piece. — *de la trompette;* to sound the trumpet. — *du cor;* to blow the French horn. *Voilà midi qui sonne;* the clock is striking twelve, it is striking twelve.

sonner, *v.a.*, to sound, to ring; to toll; to strike (of watches, clocks—*des montres, des horloges, des pendules*); to wind (of wind instruments—*des instruments à vent*); (milit.) to sound. — *les cloches;* to ring the bells. — *le dîner;* to ring for dinner. — *ses gens;* to ring for the servants. — *le boute-selle* (milit.); to sound to horse. *Ne — mot;* not to say a word, not to let the least hint drop. — *la messe;* to ring the bells for mass.

sonnerie (so-n-rî), *n.f.*, ring of bells; bells; (horl.) striking part, clock-work; (milit.) sound of the trumpet.

sonnet, *n.m.*, sonnet.

sonnette, *n.f.*, little bell; (tech.)pile-driver; engraver's mallet. *Cordon de —;* bell-pull. *Agiter la —, tirer la —;* to ring, to ring the bell. to pull the bell.

⊙**sonnettier**, *n.m.*, bell-maker.

sonneur, *n.m.*, bell-ringer.

sonnez (-né), *n.m.*, two sixes (at backgammon—*trictrac*).

sonomètre, *n.m.*, sonometer.

sonore, *adj.*, sonorous. *Voix —;* sonorous voice.

sonorité, *n.f.*, sonorousness.

sopeur, *n.f.*, **sopor**, *n.m.*, (med.) deep, comatous sleep.

sopha, *n.m.* V. **sofa**.

sophi, *n.m.* V. **sofi**.

sophisme, *n.m.*, sophism; *pl.*, sophistry.

sophiste, *n.m.*, sophist.

sophistication, *n.f.*, sophistication; adulteration.

sophistique, *adj.*, sophistic, sophistical.

sophistiquer, *v.a.*, to sophisticate, to adulterate.

sophistiquer, *v.n.*, to play the sophist, to act the sophist.

sophistiquerie (-ti-krî), *n.f.*, sophistry, sophistication, adulteration.

sophistiqueur, *n.m.*, subtilizer, sophisticator, adulterator.

sophore, *n.m.*, (bot.) sophora.

sophronistes, *n.m.pl.*, (antiq.) Athenian magistrates.

soporati-f, **-ve**, *adj.*, soporiferous, soporific.

soporeu-x, **-se**, *adj.*, (med.) soporous.

soporifère, or **soporifique**, *n.m.* and *adj.*, soporific; soporiferous.

soprano, *n.m.*, (mus.) soprano, treble voice.

sor. V. **saure**.

sorbe, *n.f.*, (bot.) sorb.

sorbet, *n.m.*, sherbet.

sorbetière, *n.f.*, ice-pail.

sorbier, *n.m.*, (bot.) sorb. — *domestique;* service, service-tree. — *sauvage, — des oiseaux;* quick-beam, quick-beam tree, roan-tree, mountain ash, wicken, wicken-tree.

sorbonique, *n.f.*, one of three theses that graduates had to go through in the Sorbonne to obtain a higher degree.

sorboniste, *n.m.*, Sorbonist.

sorbonne, *n.f.*, Sorbonne, seat of the university of Paris.

sorcellerie (-sèl-rî), *n.f.*, sorcery, witchcraft, witchery, enchantment.

sorcier, *n.m.*, sorcerer, wizard; conjuror, magician, enchanter. *Il n'est pas grand —;* he is no conjuror.

sorcière, *n.f.*, sorceress, witch, enchantress. *Vieille —;* old hag. *Sabbat des —;* witches' Sabbath.

sordide, *adj.*, sordid, dirty, filthy, mean, covetous, niggardly. — *avarice;* base avarice.

sordidement (-did-mân), *adv.*, sordidly, meanly, niggardly, stingily.

sordidité, *n.f.*, sordidness.

soret. V. **sauret**.

sorgho, *n.m.*, (bot.) sorghum, sorgo.

sorite, *n.m.*, (log.) sorites.

sorne, *n.f.*, scum, slag, dross.

sornette, *n.f.*, idle talk, idle story, stuff. *Conter des —s;* to talk nonsense.

sororal, **-e**, or **sororial**, **-e**, *adj.*, of a sister, sisterly.

sort, *n m.*, fate, destiny, lot; existence; spell, charm. *Le — des armes;* the fate of arms, the chances of war. *Tirer au —;* to cast lots, to draw lots. *Le — en est jeté;* the die is cast. *Jeter un — à quelqu'un;* to throw a spell, over any one. *Jeter un — sur quelque chose;* to throw a spell over anything. *Être son —;* to be one's lot, to fall to one's lot. *Faire un — à quelqu'un;* to procure any one an existence.

sortable, *adj.*, suitable.

sortablement, *adv.*, suitably.

sortant, *n.m.*, person going out; person leaving office, a dignity, a place. *Les entrants et les —s;* those that were going in, and those that were going out.

sortant, **-e**, *adj.*, leaving office; drawn, coming out (of numbers in lotteries—*de numéros à une loterie*).

sorte, *n.f.*, sort, kind, species; manner, way. *Parler de la bonne — à quelqu'un;* to reprimand any one severely. *En aucune —;* in no wise. *De telle —;* to such a degree, in such a way. *De quelque — que ce soit;* in any way. *De la —;* thus, so, in that manner, in that way. *De — que, en — que;* so that. *De toute —, de toutes —s;* of every kind, of all kinds.

sortie (-tî), *n.f.*, going out, coming out, departure, leaving; egress, outlet, issue, way out, tirade; (customs—*douanes*); exportation; (thea.) exit; (milit.) sally, sortie; low cards (at cards—*aux cartes*). *À la — du dîner;* on leaving the dinner-table. *Droit de —;* export duty. *Faire une — à quelqu'un;* to give any one a good blowing up, to blow any one up.

Faire une — (milit.); to make a sally; to make a tirade. *Fausse —* (thea.); wrong exit.

sortilège, *n.m.,* sorcery, witchcraft.

sortir (sortant, sorti), *v.n.* (*irregular*), to go out, to go forth, to come, to come out, to come forth, to emerge, to proceed, to issue; to get out, to come off; to rise; to depart, to swerve, to deviate; to proceed, to come; to result; to ensue; to wander (from a subject—*du sujet*); to start (of the eyes—*des yeux*); to spring up, to come up; to peep out, to shoot out (milit.); to sally forth, to sally out; (thea.) to exit, to make one's exit; to spring, to be born; to run off (locomotives); (paint.) to project, to be in relief. *— de la chambre;* to go out of the room. *Il est sorti;* he is gone out. *Il vient de —;* he is just gone out. *Il est sorti ce matin;* he went out this morning. *La rivière est sortie de son lit;* the river has overflowed its banks. *Faire — un homme de prison;* to get a man out of prison. *— du port;* to leave the harbour. *— de maladie;* to recover from illness. *— de son devoir;* to deviate from one's duty. *— des bornes de la bienséance;* to overstep the rules of decency. *— de cadence* (mus.); to be out of time. *Les yeux lui sortent de la tête;* his eyes start out of his head.

sortir, *v.a.* (*irregular*), to get out, to bring out, to take out, to carry out; to extricate. *Sortez ce cheval;* bring out that horse. *— des fleurs;* to put flowers out in the open air. *— un enfant;* to take a child out.

sortir, *v.a.* (*regular*), (jur.) to obtain, to have.

sortir, *n.m.,* going out, leaving, quitting, coming out, rising. *Au — du lit;* on getting out of bed.

sosie, *n.m.,* person very much resembling another.

⊙**sostère,** *n.f.* *V.* **zostère.**

sot, -te, *n.* and *adj.,* fool, blockhead; stupid, silly, foolish, senseless. (triv.) *— animal;* foolish creature. *Le voilà bien —;* he looks rather foolish now. *Il est resté —;* he looked somewhat foolish. *À —te demande point de réponse;* a silly question needs no answer.

sotie, *n.f.,* kind of satirical drama played in France in the 15th and 16th centuries.

sot-l'y-laisse, *n.m.* (—), parson's nose (of poultry— *de la volaille*).

sottement (sot-mān), *adv.,* sillily, foolishly, senselessly.

sottise, *n.f.,* silliness, folly; silly thing, foolish trick, nonsense, foolishness; indecency; insult; *pl.,* abuse, abusive language. *Dire des —s à quelqu'un;* to abuse any one, to call any one names.

sottisier, *n.m.,* (fam.) collection of indecent tales or songs; person that says indecent things.

sou, *n.m.,* sou, sou-piece; halfpenny. *N'avoir pas le —, n'avoir pas un —;* to be penniless, not to be worth a farthing, not to be worth a groat. *Être sans le —;* not to have a halfpenny, not to have a halfpenny in one's pocket.

soubarbe, *n.f.* *V.* **sous-barbe.**

soubassement (-bâs-mān), *n.m.,* bed-valance; (arch.) basement, sub-basement. *— d'une colonne* (arch.); pattern of a column.

soubresaut, *n.m.,* sudden leap *or* start, (med.) subsultus.

soubrette, *n.f.,* (thea.) waiting-woman, abigail.

soubreveste, *n.f.,* sleeveless upper coat.

soubuse, *n.f.,* (orni.) harrier.

souche, *n.f.,* stump, stock, stub, stem (of trees— *des arbres*); block; blockhead; head, founder (genealogy); chimney-neck, chimney-shaft, chimney-stalk; (bot.) subterranean stock;

counterfoil (of passports, &c.— *de passeports, &c.*); voucher (of cheques, receipts, &c. *—de chèques, de reçus, &c.*); tally. *C'est une —;* he is a blockhead. *Faire —;* to be the first of a branch, to be the founder of a family. *— de cheminée;* stock of chimneys. *— d'enclume;* anvil-block.

souchet, *n.m.,* (bot.) gallingale; (mas.) ragstone; (orni.) shoveller, shoveller-duck.

souchetage (soosh-taj), *n.m.,* act of counting the stocks, the stubs, in a forest.

soucheteur (soosh-teur), *n.m.,* surveyor of stocks, stubs, in a forest.

souci, *n.m.,* care, anxiety; (bot.) marigold; (orni.) golden-crested wren. *Sans —;* free from care. *Avoir —;* to take care. *Avoir des —s;* to have cares. *Être dévoré de —;* to be careworn. *C'est le moindre de mes —s;* that gives me but little concern. *— d'eau, — des marais* (bot.); marsh-marigold. *— des champs* (bot.); wild marigold; cow-marigold. *— figue* (bot.); fig-marigold.

se**soucier,** *v.r.,* to care, to mind, to be concerned, to concern one's self, to be anxious, to be uneasy. *Il ne s'en soucie guère;* he cares little for it. *Il ne se soucie de rien;* he cares for nothing. *Je ne m'en soucie plus;* I do not care any more about it. *— comme de l'an quarante;* not to care a rush.

soucieu-x, -se, *adj.,* anxious, full of care.

soucoupe, *n.f.,* saucer; salver.

soudain, -e, *adj.,* sudden, unexpected, unlooked-for.

soudain, *adv.,* suddenly, on a sudden, all of a sudden.

soudainement (-dè-n-mān), *adv.,* suddenly, on a sudden, all of a sudden.

soudaineté (-dè-n-té), *n.f.,* suddenness, unexpectedness.

soudan, *n.m.* (—s), name given formerly to the Mahometan princes, especially to the King of Egypt.

soudard, *or* **soudart,** *n.m.,* (fam.) weather-beaten soldier.

soude, *n.f.,* (min.) soda; (bot.) glasswort.

souder, *v.a.,* to solder, to weld.

se**souder,** *v.r.,* to unite, to consolidate.

soudiviser, *v.a.* *V.* **subdiviser.**

soudoir, *n.m.,* soldering-iron.

soudoyer, *v.a.,* to pay troops; to keep in pay.

⊙**soudre,** *v.a.,* to solve.

soudrille, *n.m.,* (fam.) lewd, thievish soldier.

soudure, *n.f.,* solder; soldering, welding.

soufflage, *n.m.,* glass-blowing; blowing; (nav.) sheathing.

soufflant, -e, *adj.,* blowing.

souffle, *n.m.,* breath, breathing; (fig.) inspiration, influence.

soufflement, *n.m.,* blowing.

souffler, *v.n.,* to blow; to breathe; to complain; to seek the philosopher's stone. *— aux oreilles de quelqu'un;* to whisper in any one's ear. *— dans ses doigts;* to blow one's fingers. *Il n'oserait —;* he dares not complain.

souffler, *v.a.,* to blow, to blow out; to breathe, to breathe out; to inflate; to whisper; to huff (at draughts— *aur dames*); (nav.) to sheathe; to prompt. *— le feu;* to blow the fire. *— le chaud et le froid;* to blow hot and cold. *— un comédien;* to prompt a player. *— l'orgue;* to blow an organ. *— à quelqu'un un emploi;* to forestall any one and obtain a situation he was trying for. *— un vaisseau;* to sheath a ship. *— les canons* (artil.); to scale the guns. *Ne pas — mot;* not to speak.

soufflerie, *n.f.,* bellows (of an organ— *d'un orgue*); ⊙alchymy.

soufflet, *n.m.,* bellows, pair of bellows; head

(of a carriage—de voiture); box on the ear, slap in the face; affront, mortification; humiliation.

souffletade, n.f., (l.u.) slapping in the face.

souffleter, v.a., to slap in the face, to box the ears of.

⊙**souffleteur,** n.m., person that slaps another's face.

souffleur, n.m., (zool.) a species of dolphin. Les —s; cetaceans.

souffleu-r, -se, n. and adj., blower, organ-blower; panter; prompter; glass-blower; alchymist; panting (of horses—des chevaux). — d'orgue; organ-blower. Cheval —; panting horse.

soufflure, n.f., (metal.) flaw; seedy glass.

souffrable, adj., (l.u.) that may be endured, sufferable.

souffrance, n.f., suffering, sufferance; endurance.

souffrant, -e, adj., suffering, in pain; patient; enduring; unwell, poorly, ailing; diseased. La partie —e; the diseased part.

souffre-douleur, n.m. (—), drudge; fag; butt, laughing-stock.

souffreteu-x, -se, adj., miserable, unwell, poorly.

souffrir (souffrant, souffert), v.a., to suffer, to bear, to endure, to abide; to undergo, to sustain, to stand; to tolerate; to permit, to let, to allow, to put up with; to admit of. — la douleur; to endure pain. — la fatigue; to bear fatigue. — un assaut; to stand an assault. — un affront; to put up with an affront. Je ne saurais — cet homme-là; I cannot endure that man. Il souffre tout à ses enfants; he is too indulgent to his children. Pourquoi souffrez-vous cela? why do you bear that? Cela ne souffre point de retardement; that admits of no delay.

souffrir, v.n., to suffer, to suffer pain, to be in pain; to be pained; to be a sufferer; to be injured. — de la tête; to feel a pain in one's head.

soufi, n.m. V. **sofi.**

soufrage, n.m., sulphuration.

soufre, n.m., sulphur, brimstone. Fleur de —; flour of brimstone.

soufrer, v.a., to do over with brimstone, to dip in brimstone, to sulphur.

soufrière, n.f., sulphur-mine.

soufroir, n.m., sulphuring-stove.

sougarde, n.f. V. **sous-garde.**

sougorge, n.f. V. **sous-gorge.**

souhait, n.m., wish, desire. A —; at one's heart's ease, according to one's desire, as one would have it.

souhaitable, adj., desirable, to be wished for.

souhaiter, v.a., to wish, to wish for, to long for. Je vous souhaite le bonjour; I wish you good day. Il serait à — que, &c.; it is to be wished that, &c. Que souhaitez-vous? what do you wish for? Je vous en souhaite, je t'en souhaite; I wish you may get it.

⊙**souhaiteu-r,** n.m., **-se,** n.f., wisher.

soui, n.m., soy (sauce).

*****souille,** n.f., (hunt.) wallowing place (of wild boars— du sanglier); bed (impression made by the bottom of a ship on the mud—enfoncement produit dans la vase par un navire échoué).

*****souiller,** v.a., to soil, to dirty, to stain, to blemish, to sully, to defile, to contaminate. se **souiller,** v.r., to soil, to get dirty; to sully, to tarnish.

*****souillon,** n.m.f., scullion; sloven, slut.

*****souillure,** n.f., dirt, spot of dirt; spot, stain; blot, impurity; contamination, pollution, defilement.

soûl, -e (soo, -l), adj., glutted; surfeited, drunk, tipsy; cloyed, satiated. — comme une grive; as drunk as a lord. Il est — de musique; he is surfeited with music.

soûl (soo), n.m., one's fill, one's bellyful. Boire et manger son —; to eat and drink one's bellyful

soulageant, -e (-jän, -t), adj., easing; comfortable; relieving.

soulagement (-la-jmän), n.m., relief, ease, alleviation, assuagement; solace, help. Cela me donne du —; that gives me ease (of any one in pain—de quelqu'un qui souffre). C'est un — à ses peines; it is an alleviation of his troubles.

soulager, v.a., to relieve, to ease, to lighten; to alleviate, to allay, to assist, to comfort. — le mal; to alleviate the pain. se **soulager,** v.r., to relieve one's self.

⊙**soûlant, -e,** adj., (l.ex.) filling, satiating.

soûlard, n.m., **-e,** n.f., (pop.) drunkard.

⊙**soulas,** n.m., solace, comfort.

⊙**soûlaud,** n.m., **-e,** n.f., (pop.) drunkard.

soûler, v.a., to fill, to glut, to satiate, to surfeit; to intoxicate, to make drunk. se **soûler,** v.r., to glut one's self, to satiate one's self; to get intoxicated; to riot, to get drunk. — de plaisirs; to riot in pleasures.

souleur, n.f., (fam.) fright.

soulèvement (-lèv-män), n.m., rising (of the stomach—de l'estomac); swelling (of the waves—des vagues); insurrection, revolt; indignation.

soulever (sool-vé), v.a., to raise; to lift, to heave up, to take up; to lift up; to excite, to stir up; to urge to insurrection; to excite to action; to raise the indignation of; to make indignant; to moot (question). se **soulever** (sool-), v.r., to raise one's self, to rise; to swell; to be urged to action; to be urged to indignation, to be indignant; to rise to revolt, to rise in insurrection, in arms. La mer commence à —; the sea begins to swell.

soulever (sool-), v.n., to rise, turn to (of the stomach—de l'estomac). Le cœur me soulève; my stomach rises.

soulier, n.m., shoe. —s ferrés; hobnailed shoes. Être dans ses petits —s; to be in a critical situation.

soulier-botte, n.m. (—s —s). Blucher boot.

*****soulignement,** n.m., underlining.

*****souligner,** v.a., to underline.

⊙**souloir,** v.n., to be wont, to use.

soulte, or **soute,** n.f., (jur.) payment made by a party to a joint owner on division, to equalize the value of the parts divided.

soumettre, v.a., to subdue, to submit, to bring under subjection, to subject; to overcome; to subjugate; to refer. — un pays; to subdue a country. se **soumettre,** v.r., to submit, to yield, to be submissive to give way; to succumb.

soumission, n.f., submission, submissiveness, subjection, obsequiousness, mark of respect; tender for a contract; contract; deed of contract; (jur.) bond; subscription. —s cachetées; sealed tenders.

soumissionnaire, n.m.f., party that makes a tender for a contract.

soumissionner, v.a., to make a tender for.

soupape, n.f., plug, valve. — dormante; fixed valve. — à clapet; clack-valve. — à gorge; throttle valve. — de sûreté; safety-valve.

soupçon, n.m., suspicion; surmise, conjecture, taste, smack (small quantity—petite quantité). Un — d'ail; just a taste of garlic.

soupçonnable, adj., suspicious, liable to be suspected.

soupçonner, v.a., to suspect, to surmise.

soupçonneu-x, -se, adj., suspicious, inclined to suspect others.

soupe, *n.f.*, soup, slice of bread for soup, sippet. — *à perroquet*; bread steeped in wine. *Ivre comme une* —; as drunk as a lord. *Trempé comme une* —; drenched, wet to the skin. — *grasse*; meat soup. — *maigre*; vegetable soup. — *au lait*; milk porridge.

soupente, *n.f.*, loft; brace (of a coach—*de voiture*); strap (of a horse—*d'un cheval*).

souper, *v.n.*, to sup, to take supper.

souper, *or* **soupé**, *n.m.*, supper.

soupeser, *v.a.*, to weigh in the palm of the hand.

soupeu-r, *n.m.*, **-se**, *n.f.*, person who takes supper.

soupied, *n.m. V.* **sous-pied**.

soupière, *n.f.*, tureen, soup-tureen.

soupir, *n.m.*, sigh, breath; breathing; gasp; (mus.) crotchet-rest; *pl.*, sighing. *Jeter, pousser, des* —*s*; to heave sighs. *Rendre le dernier* —; to give up the ghost.

*soupirail**, *n.m.*, air-hole, vent-hole.

soupirant, *n.m.*, wooer.

soupirer, *v.n.*, to sigh; to gasp; to long. — *de douleur*; to sigh for grief. — *après une chose*; to long for a thing.

soupirer, *v.a.*, to breathe, to breathe forth, to sigh.

soupireur, *n.m.*, (fam.) sigher.

souple, *adj.*, supple, pliant, flexible, yielding. *Un esprit* —; a compliant temper.

souplement, *adv.*, pliantly, flexibly, compliantly.

souplesse, *n.f.*, suppleness, pliantness, flexibility, facility, compliance. *La* — *de l'osier*; the pliantness of the osier. *Tours de* —; cunning tricks. *Sa voix a de la* —; there is a degree of flexibility in his voice.

*souquenille**, *n.f.*, long coarse linen gabardine.

source, *n.f.*, source, spring, fountain, fountain-head; well-spring. — *d'eau*; spring. — *qui ne tarit jamais*; spring that never dries. *La* — *de tous les biens*; the source of all blessings. *Prendre sa* —; to take its rise (of rivers—*des rivières*).

sourcier, *n.m.*, one who claims to be possessed of the means to find out sources, and springs of water.

sourcil, (-ci), *n.m.*, eye-brow, brow. *Froncer le* —; to knit one's brow.

sourcili-er, -ère, *adj.*, (anat.) superciliary.

*sourciller**, *v.n.*, to knit one's brows; to frown; (of water—*de l'eau*) to spring. *Sans* —; without moving a muscle.

*sourcilleu-x, -se**, *adj.*, haughty, proud; cloud-topped; uneasy, melancholy. *Montagnes* —*ses*; lofty mountains.

sourd, -e, *adj.*, deaf; dull, hollow (of sound —*du son*); insensible, dead; (math.) ⊙surd; secret, underhand; rumbling. *Voix* —*e*; hollow voice. *Il court un bruit* —; it is whispered about. *Lanterne* —*e*; dark lantern. *Lime* —*e*; dead file. *Douleur* —*e*; dull pain. *Menées* —*es*; underhand dealing.

sourd, *n.m.*, -**e**, *n.f.*, deaf person; (ent.) salamander (local ex.). *Frapper comme un* —; to strike hard. *Faire le* —; to lend a deaf ear. *Il n'est pire* — *que celui qui ne veut pas entendre*; none is so deaf as he who will not hear. — *et muet*; deaf and dumb.

sourdaud, *n.m.*, person who is dull of hearing.

sourdeline, *n.f.*, Italian bag-pipe.

sourdement, *adv.*, with a hollow voice; dully (of sound—*du son*); secretly; in an underhand manner.

sourdine, *n.f.*, sordet, sordine (of a trumpet—*de trompette*); damper (piano). *À la* —; secretly, on the sly.

sourd-muet, *n.m.* (—*s* —*s*), **sourde-**

muette, *n.f.* (—*s* —*s*), deaf and dumb person.

sourdon, *n.m.*, (conch.) cockle.

sourdre, *v.n.*, to spring, to issue, to arise; (nav.) (of a cloud—*d'un nuage*) to rise.

souriant, *adj.*, smiling.

souriceau, *n.m.*, little mouse.

souricière, *n.f.*, mouse-trap.

souriquois, -e, *adj.*, (jest.) of mice. *La gent* —*e*; the mouse tribe.

sourire, *v.n.*, to smile; to countenance; to be agreeable, to please (of a thing—*des choses*). — *à quelqu'un*; to smile upon any one.

sourire, *or* **souris**, *n.m.*, smile. — *moqueur*; sneer.

souris, *n.f.*, mouse; mouse-colour; venison-bit (of a leg of mutton—*de gigot*); (milit.) saucisse, saucisson (to fire a mine—*pour mettre le feu à une mine*); (vet.) nasal cartilage (of the horse—*du cheval*). *Pas de* — (fort.); flight of steps leading to the moat. *Chauve-* — (—*s* —); bat.

souris, *adj. invariable*, mouse-coloured. *Cheval* —; mouse-coloured horse.

sournois, -e, *n.* and *adj.*, dissembler, artful person; dissembled, artful, cunning, sly.

sournoisement, *adv.*, slyly, cunningly, on the sly.

sournoiserie, *n.f.*, slyness, artfulness, cunning.

sous, *prep.*, under, beneath; upon; with; in; sub; deputy. — *le lit*; under the bed. — *terre*; underground. *Affirmer* — *serment*; to swear upon oath. — *silence*; in silence. — *peu de jours*; in a few days. — *peu de temps*; in a little while. — *-gouverneur* (—*s*); deputy-governor.

sous-affermer, *v.a.*, to underlet; to take an under-lease.

sous-agent, *n.m.f.* (—*s*), under-agent.

sous-aide, *n.m.f.* (—*s*), under-assistant.

sous-amendement, *n.m.* (—*s*), additional amendment; amendment to an amendment.

sous-amender, *v.a.*, to make an additional amendment.

sous-arbrisseau, *n.m.* (—*x*), (bot.) suffrutex; undershrub.

sous-axillaire, *adj.*, (bot.) sub-axillary.

*sous-bail**, *n.m.* (—*baux*), under-lease.

sous-barbe, *n.f.* (—*s*), under part of the lower jaw (of horses—*des chevaux*); (nav.) short prop. — *de beaupré*; bob-stay.

sous-bibliothécaire, *n.m.* (—*s*), under-librarian, sub-librarian.

sous-chantre, *n.m.* (—*s*), sub-chanter.

sous-chef, *n.m.* (—*s*), second head-clerk.

sous-chevron, *n.m.* (—*s*), (carp.) under-rafter.

sous-clavi-er, -ère, *adj.*, (anat.) sub-clavian.

sous-clavier, *n.m.* (—*s*), (anat.) sub-clavius.

sous-clerc, *n.m.* (—*s*), under-clerk.

sous-comité, *n.m.* (—*s*), sub-committee.

sous-commissaire, *n.m.* (—*s*), (nav.) issuing-commissary.

sous-contrefort, *n.m.* (—*s*), stiffener (of boots, shoes—*de chaussures*).

sous-costal, -e, *adj.*, (anat.) sub-costal.

souscripteur, *n.m.*, subscriber; (com.) underwriter.

souscription, *n.f.*, subscription; signature; contribution.

souscrire, *v.a.*, to subscribe, to sign. — *un contrat*; to subscribe a contract.

souscrire, *v.a.*, to subscribe; to assent; to underwrite.

souscrivant, *n.m.*, under-writer.

sous-cutané, -e, *adj.*, subcutaneous.

sous-délégué, *n.m.* (—*s*), sub-delegate.

sous-déléguer, *v.a.*, to subdelegate.

sous-diaconat, *n.m.* (— —*s*), subdeaconship, subdeaconry.

sous-diacre, *n.m.* (— —*s*), subdeacon.

sous-diviser, *v.a.* V. **subdiviser.**

sous-division, *n.f.* (— —*s*), subdivision.

sous-dominante, *n.f.* (— —*s*), (mus.) subdominant.

sous-double, *adj.*, (math.) subduple.

sous-doublé, -e, *adj.*, (math.) sub-duplicate.

sous-doyen, *n.m.* (— —*s*), sub-dean.

sous-doyenné, *n.m.* (— —*s*), sub-deanery, sub-deanship.

sous-entendre, *v.a.*, to understand (to mean without expressing—*avoir dans la pensée, mais ne pas exprimer*).

se **sous-entendre,** *v.r.*, to be understood. *Cela se sous-entend ;* that is understood. *Cette condition se sous-entend toujours ;* this condition is always understood, is a matter of course.

sous-entendu, *n.m.* (— —*s*), thing understood.

sous-entente, *n.f.* (— —*s*), mental reservation.

sous-entrepreneur, *n.m.* (— —*s*), sub-contractor (of public works—*de travaux publics*).

sous-espèce, *n.f.* (— —*s*), sub-species.

sous-faîte, *n.m.* (— —*s*), (carp.) under-ridge-board.

sous-ferme, *n.f.* (— —*s*), (jur.) under-lease.

sous-fermer, *v.a.*, to underlet ; to take an under-lease.

sous-fermi-er, *n.m.*, **-ère,** *n.f.* (— —*s*), (jur.) under-lessee.

sous-fondation, *n.f.* (— —*s*), subpavement (of roads).

sous-fréter, *v.a.*, to underlet (ships—*vaisseaux*).

sous-garantie, *n.f* (— —*s*), (jur.) counterbond.

sous-garde, *n.f.* (—), trigger-guard and its accessories (of fire-arms—*d'armes à feu*).

sous-genre, *n.m.* (— —*s*), subgenus.

sous-gorge, *n.f.* (—), throat-band (of a bridle—*de bride*).

sous-gouverneur, *n.m.* (— —*s*), deputy-governor.

sous-greffier, *n.m.* (— —*s*), deputy-registrar.

sous-inféodation, *n.f.* (— —*s*), (feudal law—*droit féodal*) subinfeudation.

sous-intendance, *n.f.* (— —*s*), (milit.) residence, offices, charge, and circuit of a deputy-commissary.

sous-intendant, *n.m.* (— —*s*), (milit.) deputy-commissary, sub-commissary.

sous-lecteur, *n.m.* (— —*s*), sub-reader.

sous-lieutenance, *n.f.* (— —*s*), (artill.) sub-lieutenancy ; (milit.) ensigncy ; (nav.) second-lieutenancy.

sous-lieutenant, *n.m.* (— —*s*), (artil.) sub-lieutenant ; (milit.) ensign ; (nav.) second-lieutenant.

sous-locataire, *n.m.f.* (— —*s*), under-tenant.

sous-location, *n.f.* (— —*s*), under-letting, under-tenancy.

sous-louer, *v.a.*, to underlet ; to under-hire.

sous-maître, *n.m.* (— —*s*), usher, under-master, assistant (at a school—*d'école*).

sous-maîtresse, *n.f.* (— —*s*), teacher (in a school—*d'école*).

sous-marin, -e. *adj.*, submarine ; submersed ; underset (of currents—*courants*).

sous-maxillaire, *adj.*, (anat.) sub-maxillary.

sous-multiple, *n.m.* (— —*s*), (arith.) sub-multiple.

sous-normale, *n.f.* (— —*s*), (geom.) sub-normal ; sub-perpendicular.

sous-occipital, -e, *adj.*, sub-occipital.

en **sous-œuvre,** *adv.*, (arch.) under. *Reprendre un mur en —;* to underpin a wall.

sous-officier, *n.m.* (— —*s*), non-commissioned officer.

sous-orbiculaire, *adj.*, suborbicular, sub-orbiculate.

sous-ordre, *n.m.* (— —*s*), subordinate ; division among himself and his opposing creditors of a sum of money adjudged to a creditor.

sous-perpendiculaire, *n.f.* V. **sous-normale.**

sous-pied, *n.m.* (— —*s*), strap (of trousers —*de pantalon*).

sous-précepteur, *n.m.* (— —*s*), under-tutor.

sous-préfecture, *n.f.* (— —*s*), sub-prefecture.

sous-préfet, *n.m.* (— —*s*), sub-prefect.

sous-prieur, *n.m.* (— —*s*), sub-prior.

sous-prieure, *n.f.* (— —*s*), sub-prioress.

sous-sacristain, *n.m.* (— —*s*), under-sexton, under-sacristan.

sous-secrétaire, *n.m.* (— —*s*), under-secretary.

sous-secrétariat, *n.m.* (— —*s*), under-secretaryship.

sous-seing, *n.m.* (— —*s*), private deed.

sous-sel, *n.m.* (— —*s*), (chem.) sub-salt.

***soussigné, -e,** *part.*, undersigned, under-written. *Nous* —*s certifions ;* we, the under-signed, certify.

***soussigner,** *v.a.*, only used in the past participle, which see above.

sous-sol, *n.m.* (— —*s*), (agri.) sub-soil, sub-stratum.

sous-tangente, *n.f.* (— —*s*), (geom.) sub-tangent.

sous-tendante, *n.f.* (— —*s*), (geom.) sub-tense chord-line.

sous-tendre, *v.a.*, (geom.) to subtend.

sous-titre, *n.m.* (— —*s*), (print.) sub-head.

soustraction, *n.f.*, (arith., jur.) subtraction ; taking away.

soustraire (soustrayant, soustrait), *v.a.*, to take away, to remove ; to shelter, to screen ; (arith.) to subtract.

se **soustraire,** *v.r.*, to escape, to avoid ; to flee ; to exempt one's self. — *au châtiment ;* to avoid punishment. — *à la tyrannie ;* to flee from tyranny. — *à la justice ;* to fly from justice, to abscond.

sous-traitant, *n.m.* (— —*s*), sub-contractor (of public works—*de travaux publics*).

sous-traité, *n.m.* (— —*s*), sub-contract (for public works—*de travaux publics*).

sous-traiter, *v.a.*, to make a sub-contract, to sub-contract.

sous-triple, *adj.*, (math.) sub-triple.

sous-triplé, -e, *adj.*, (math.) sub-triplicate. *En raison —e ;* in a sub-triplicate ratio.

soustylaire, *n.f.*, substyle, substylar line (of a dial—*d'un cadran solaire*).

sous-variété, *n.f.* (— —*s*), sub-variety.

sous-ventrière, *n.f.* (— —*s*), belly-band.

soutache, *n.f.*, braid of a hussar's shako ; narrow braid.

soutacher, *v.a.*, to braid (needle-work—*ouvrage à l'aiguille*).

soutane, *n.f.*, cassock.

soutanelle, *n.f.*, short cassock.

soute, *n.f.*, (nav.) store-room. — *aux poudres ;* (nav.) powder-magazine, powder-room. V. **soulte.**

soutenable (soo-tnabl), *adj.*, maintainable ; supportable, tenable.

soutenance, *n.f.*, the sustaining a thesis.

soutenant (soo-tnăn), *n.m.*, mooter (student —*étudiant*).

soutènement (tè-n-măn), *n.m.*, (arch.) support; (jur.) written explanation.

souteneur (soo-tneur), *n.m.*, bully; supporter (of bad things—*de mauvais lieux*).

soutenir (soo-tnir), *v.a.*, to support, to sustain, to bear, to bear up; to hold, to hold up; to keep up, to uphold; to assert, to maintain; to uphold, to back, to stand by; to countenance, to favour; to prop, to prop up; to strengthen; to afford (an expense—*dépense*); to endure, to bear up against. — *une famille*; to support a family. — *la conversation*; to keep up the conversation. — *son rang*; to support one's rank. — *le combat*; to maintain the fight. — *la lumière*; to bear the light. *Il ne peut — la raillerie*; he cannot bear joking. *Le vin vous soutient*; wine strengthens you. — *une thèse*; to sustain a thesis. — *un siège*; to sustain a siege. *se* **soutenir**, *v.r.*, to support one's self; to sustain one's self; to stand up, to keep one's self up; to bear up; to hold out; to succeed; to continue one's success. *Elle se soutient bien*; she holds out very well. *Son style ne se soutient pas*; his style is not sustained.

soutenu, -e, *adj.*, supported, sustained; continued; elevated. *Discours bien —*; well-sustained discourse. *Style soutenu*; elevated style.

souterrain, -e, *adj.*, subterraneous, subterranean. *Voies —es*; underhand practices.

souterrain, *n.m.*, cave, subterrane; subterraneous place, vault; tunnel; underground.

souterrainement, *adv.*, underground; (fig.) in an underhanded manner, secretly.

soutien (-ti-in), *n.m.*, stay, prop, support; maintenance; sustenance; stiffening; supporter, upholder, vindicator.

soutirage, *n.m.*, racking, drawing off (of liquors—*de liqueurs*).

soutirer, *v.a.*, to rack, to draw off (liquors —*liqueurs*); to get out of (to obtain—*obtenir*).

soutrait, *n.m.*, shelf of a paper-maker's press.

⊙**souvenance** (soo-vnans), *n.f.*, remembrance, recollection.

souvenez-vous-de-moi, *n.m.* (—), (bot.) marsh scorpion-grass.

souvenir (soo-vnir), *n.m.*, remembrance, recollection, memory; keepsake; memorandum-book; letter-rack. *Rappeler une chose au — de quelqu'un*; to remind any one of a thing. *se* **souvenir**, *v.r.*, to remember; to call to mind, to recollect; to bear in mind. — *du temps passé*; to remember past times. *Je m'en souviendrai*; I shall remember it. *S'il m'en souvient bien*; if I recollect rightly.

souvent, *adv.*, often, oftentimes, frequently, many times. *Peu —*; rarely.

⊙**souventefois** (-vant-foa), *adv.*, oftentimes.

souverain, -e (soo-vrin, -vrè-n), *n.* and *adj.*, sovereign; supreme, superlative, sovereign. *Au — degré*; to a sovereign degree.

souverain, *n.m.*, sovereign (coin—*pièce de monnaie*).

souverainement (soo-vrè-n-măn), *adv.*, sovereignly, supremely, superlatively.

souveraineté (souv-rè-n-té), *n.f.*, sovereignty, dominion; dominions.

soy, *n.m. V.* **souï**.

soyeu-x. -se, *adj.*, silky, silken.

spaciousment (-euz-măn), *adv.*, spaciously.

spacieu-x, -se, *adj.*, spacious, roomy.

spadassin, *n.m.*, (b.s.) fighter.

*****spadille**, *n.m.*, spadilla (at ombre—*jeu d'ombre*).

spahi, *n.m.*, spahi, Turkish horse soldier; native horse soldier serving in the French army in Algeria.

spalme, *n.m.*, (nav.) paying-stuff.

spalmer, *v.a.*, to grave, to pitch, to pay (a ship—*un vaisseau*). *V.* **espalmer**

spalt, *n.m.*, (min.) spalt.

sparadrap (-dra-p), *n.m.*, (pharm.) cerecloth.

spare, *n.m.*, (ich.) gilt-head.

spargoule, *or* **spargoute**, *n.f. V.* **spargule**.

spartan, *or* **sparton**. *n.m.*, (nav.) rope made of esparto.

sparte, *n.f.*, (bot.) esparto; mat-weed.

sparterie, manufacture of esparto; esparto articles.

spartiate, *n.m.f.* and *adj.*, Spartan.

sparton, *n.m. V.* **spartan**.

spasme, *n.m.*, spasm.

spasmodique, *adj.*, spasmodic.

spasmologie, *n.f.*, spasmology.

spath (spat), *n.m.*, (min.) spar. — *perlé*; pearl spar. — *fluor*; fluor-spar.

spathacé, -e, *adj.*, (bot.) spathaceous.

spathe, *n.f.*, (bot.) spatha, spathe.

spathique, *adj.*, (min.) sparry, spathic.

spatule, *n.f.*, spatula; (orni.) spoon-bill.

spécial, -e, *adj.*, special, especial, peculiar, particular; professional (of a person—*des personnes*). *Les hommes spéciaux*; professional men.

spécialement (-al-măn), *adv.*, especially, peculiarly, particularly.

spécialiste, *n.m.*, (med.) specialist. *Médecin —*; specialist.

spécialité, *n.f.*, peculiarity, speciality; line of business.

spécieusement (-euz-măn), *adv.*, speciously.

spécieu-x, -se, *adj.*, specious.

spécificati-f. -ve. *adj.*, specifying.

spécification, *n.f.*, specification.

spécifier, *v.a.*, to specify.

spécifique, *n.m.* and *adj.*, specific.

spécifiquement (-fik-măn), *adv.*, specifically.

spécimen (-mè-n), *n.m.* (—s), specimen.

spectacle, *n.m.*, play, spectacle; play-house, performance; sight. *Salle de —*; play-house. *Être en —*; to be exposed to public view. *Se donner en —*; to expose one's self to public view. *Programme de —*; play-bill. *Aller au —*; to go to the play.

spectat-eur. -rice, *n.m.* and *adj.*, spectator, looker on, by-stander; *pl.*, (thea.) audience; looking on.

spectral, *adj.*, (opt.) spectral; pertaining to the spectrum.

spectre, *n.m.*, spectre, phantom; (phys.) spectrum.

spéculaire, *adj.*, (min.) specular. ⊙*Science —*; the science of mirror-making.

spéculat-eur, *n.m.*, -**rice**, *n.f.*, speculator; ⊙observer of the stars; ⊙(unlit.) sentry, scout.

spéculati-f. -ve, *adj.*, speculative.

spéculatif, *n.m.*, speculative man, speculative mind.

spéculation, *n.f.*, speculation.

spéculativement, *adv.*, in a speculative manner.

spéculer, *v.n.*, to speculate.

⊙**spéculer**, *v.a.*, to observe the stars.

speculum (spé-cu-lom), *n.m.* (—), (surg.) speculum.

⊙**spée**, *n.f. V.* **cépée**.

spencer (spin-sèr), *n.m.* (—s), spencer.

spergule, *n.f.*, (bot.) spurrey.

spermaceti (-céti), *n.m.* (n.p.), spermaceti, sperm.

spermatique. *adj.*, spermatic.

spermatocèle, *n.f.*, (med.) spermatocele.

spermatologie, *n.f.*, (med.) spermatology.

sperme, *n.m.*, sperm. — *de baleine, blanc de baleine;* spermaceti.

spermophile, *n.m.*, ground squirrel.

sphacèle, *n.m.*, (med.) sphacelus.

sphacélé, **-e**, *adj.*, sphacelated.

sphénoïdal, **-e**, *adj.*, sphenoidal.

sphénoïde, *n.m.* and *adj.*, (anat.) sphenoid, sphenoidal.

sphère, *n.f.*, (geom.) sphere, globe; circle, orb, orbit. *Sortir de sa* —; to go out of one's sphere. *Étude de la* —; use of the globes.

sphéricité, *n.f.*, sphericity, sphericalness.

sphérique, *adj.*, spherical, globose. *Triangle* —; curvilinear triangle.

sphériquement, *adv.*, spherically.

sphériste, *n.m.*, (antiq.) one who taught ball playing.

sphéristère, *n.m.*, (antiq.) ball playing ground.

sphéristique, *n.f.*, (antiq.) the art of ball playing.

sphéroïdal, **-e**, *adj.*, spheroidal.

sphéroïde, *n.m.*, (geom.) spheroid.

sphéromètre, *n.m.*, spherometer.

sphincter (-tèr), *n.m.*, (anat.) sphincter.

sphinx (sfìnks), *n.m.*, sphinx; (ent.) sphinx, hawk-moth.

sphragistique, *n.f.*, sphragistics.

spic, *n.m.*, (bot.) spica.

spica, *n.m.*, (surg.) spica-bandage.

spicanard, *n.m.*, (bot.) spikenard.

spicilège, *n.m.*, collection of writings that had not been printed; miscellanea.

spigélie, *n.f.*, (bot.) worm-grass.

spina-bifida, *n.f.* (*n.p.*), (med.) rachitis, rickets.

spinal, **-e**, *adj.*, spinal.

spina-ventosa, *n.m.* (*n.p.*), (med.) spinaventosa.

spinelle, *n.m.*, spinel, spinelle.

spinifère, *n.m.*, spiniferous.

spinosisme, *n.m.*, Spinozism.

spinosiste, *n.m.*, Spinozist.

spiral, **-e**, *adj.*, spiral.

spiral, *n.m.*, (horl.) spiral spring.

spirale, *n.f.*, (geom.) spiral; spire; (conch.) turban. *En* —; spirally.

⊙**spiralement** (-ral-màn), *adv.*, in a spiral form, spirally.

spiration, *n.f.*, (theol.) spiration.

spire, *n.f.*, (ancient arch.) spire; (geom.) helix, revolution of the helix.

spirée, *n.f.*, (bot.) spiraea (genus). — *ulmaire*, or *reine-des-prés;* spiraea ulmaria, queen of the meadow. — *filipendule;* dropwort.

spirite, *n.m.*, spirit-rapper, spiritualist.

spiritisme, *n.m.*, the tenets of the spirit-rapper, spiritualism.

spiritualisation, *n.f.*, (chem.) spiritualisation.

spiritualiser, *v.a.*, to spiritualize.

spiritualisme, *n.m.*, spiritualism.

spiritualiste, *n.m.f.* and *adj.*, spiritualist.

spiritualité, *n.f.*, spirituality.

spirituel, *n.m.*, spirituality (not temporality —*opposé de temporel*); (rel.) spiritual man.

spirituel, **-le**, *adj.*, spiritual (incorporeal —*incorporel*); mental, intellectual; witty, ingenious, intelligent. *Un homme fort* —; a very ingenious, witty man. *Une réponse* —*le;* a witty answer.

spirituellement (-èl-màn), *adv.*, spiritually, ingeniously, wittily.

spiritueux, **-se**, *adj.*, spirituous.

spiritueux, *n.m.*, spirit, ardent spirit.

splanchnique, *adj.*, (anat.) splanchnic.

splanchnologie (splàn-kno-), *n.f.*, (anat.) splanchnology.

spleen (splì-n), *n.m.*, spleen, melancholy.

splénalgie, *n.f.*, spleenalgy.

splendeur, *n.f.*, splendour, brightness, lustre; brilliancy, magnificence, pomp.

splendide, *adj.*, splendid, sumptuous, magnificent.

splendidement (-dìd-màn), *adv.*, splendidly, sumptuously, magnificently.

splénétique, *adj.*, splenetic.

splénique, *adj.*, (anat.) splenic.

spode, *n.m.*, (chem.) old name of the oxide of zinc.

spoliat-eur, *n.m.*, **-rice**, *n.f.*, spoiler, despoiler.

spoliation, *n.f.*, spoliation.

spolier, *v.a.*, to spoliate, to despoil.

spondaïque, *n.m.* and *adj.*, spondaic.

spondée, *n.m.*, spondee.

spondyle, *n.m.*, (anat.) spondyl, spondyle; (conch.) spondylus.

spondylite, *n.f.*, (med.) inflammation of the vertebrae.

spongieu-x, **-se**, *adj.*, spongy; spongious.

spongiosité, *n.f.*, sponginess.

spongite, *n.f.*, (min.) spongite.

spontané, **-e**, *adj.*, spontaneous; voluntary.

spontanéité, *n.f.*, spontaneity, spontaneousness, voluntariness.

spontanément, *adv.*, spontaneously, of one's own accord, voluntarily.

sponton, *n.m.* *V.* **esponton**.

sporadique, *adj.*, (med.) sporadic.

spore, *n.f.*, (bot.) spore, sporule.

sport, *n.m.* (—*s*), sport.

sportule, *n.f.*, ⊙ bribe given to a judge; (Roman antiq.) little basket; distribution of food or money to clients.

sporule, *n.f.*, (bot.) sporule, spore.

spumeu-x, **-se**, *adj.*, spumous, foamy.

spumosité, *n.f.*, frothiness.

sputation, *n.f.*, (med.) sputation, expectoration.

squale (skooal), *n.m.*, (ich.) dog-fish.

⊙**squalide** (skooa-lid), *adj.*, filthy, squalid; thin, lean.

squammeu-x, **-se** (skooa-), *adj.*, squamous, scaly.

square (skooèr), *n.m.* (—*s*), square (public place—*place publique*).

squelette, *n.m.*, skeleton; carcass (of a ship—*de vaisseau*). *C'est un* —, *c'est un vrai* — (pers.); he, she, is a living skeleton.

***squille**, *n.f.*, squill, crustaceous animal of the genus squilla.

squinancie. *V.* **esquinancie**.

squine, *n.f.*, (bot.) China-root.

squirre, or **squirrhe** (skìr), *n.m.*, (med.) scirrhus.

squirreu-x, **-se**, or **squirrheux**, *adj.*, scirrhous.

S.S., initial letters of *Sa Sainteté*, His Holiness, title of the Pope.

S.S., p.p., abbreviations of *Saints Pères;* Holy Fathers.

st! *int.*, here, come here!

stabat, *n.m.* (—), (c. rel.) Stabat Mater, a Latin hymn set to music and performed in Roman Catholic Churches during the Holy Week.

stabilité, *n.f.*, stability, stableness, consistence, firmness, solidity; durability, steadfastness.

stable, *adj.*, stable, solid, durable, lasting, permanent; steadfast.

stade, *n.m.*, (antiq.) stadium, stade; (med.) stage, period.

stage, *n.m.*, period between the admission as licentiate in law and the call to the bar; stay which it was necessary for a new canon to make, in order to enable him to enjoy the

17

advantages of his prebend. *Faire son* — ; to go through one's *stage*.

stagiaire, *n.* and *adj. m.*, licentiate in law going through his *stage*. *Avocat* —; licentiate in law not admitted to the bar.

stagnant, -e, *adj.*, stagnant, standing.

stagnation, *n.f.*, stagnation, stagnancy.

*stagnon, *n.m.* *V.* estagnon.

stagirite, *n.m.*, stagyrite.

stalactite, *n.f.*, (min.) stalactite.

stalagmite, *n.f.*, (min.) stalagmite.

stalle, *n.f.*, stall.

stamenais, *n.m.pl.*, (nav.) lower futtocks.

stance, *n.f.*, stanza.

stangue (stăn-g), *n.f.*, (her.) shank of an anchor.

stannifère, *adj.*, stanniferous, tinny. *Terrain* — ; tin-ground. *Veine* — ; tin-floor.

staphisaigre, *n.f.*, (bot.) stavesacre, licebane, lousewort.

staphylin, *n.m.*, (ent.) staphylinus.

staphylôme, *n.m.*, (med.) staphyloma, staphylosis.

staroste, *n.m.*, staroste (Polish noble— *noble polonais*).

starostie (-tî), *n.f.*, starosty (fief granted by th' King of Poland—*fief accordé par les rois de Pologne*).

stase, *n.f.*, (med.) arrest, stagnation.

stater, *or* **statère**, *n.m.* (—s), (antiq.) stater.

statère, *n.f.* (—s), (antiq.) statera (Rom. balance).

stathouder (-dèr), *n.m.*, stadtholder.

stathoudérat, *n.m.*, stadtholdership, stadtholderate.

statice, *n.f.*, (bot.) sea-lavender.

station, *n.f.*, action of standing; manner of standing, stay; station (short stay—*court séjour*); stoppage; stand (of public coaches— *de voitures publiques*); station. *Il n'y a point de voitures à la* — ; there are no coaches on the stand. *Chef de* — (railways); station-master.

stationnaire, *adj.*, stationary.

stationnaire, *n.m.*, (nav.) guard-ship.

stationnale, *adj.f.*, stational (of churches —*d'églises*).

stationnement (-sio-n-măn), *n.m.*, stoppage; standing (of coaches—*de voitures*).

stationner, *v.n.*, to stand (of coaches—*des voitures*).

statique, *n.f.*, statics.

statisticien (-si-in), *n.m.*, statistician.

statistique, *n.f.*, statistics.

statuaire, *n.m.*, (pers.) statuary.

statuaire, *adj.*, statuary.

statuaire, *n.f.*, statuary (art).

statue, *n.f.*, statue; (Bibl.) pillar.

statuer, *v.a.*, to decree, to resolve, to ordain, to enact.

statuette, *n.f.*, small statue, statuette.

statu quo *n.m.* (*n.p.*), statu quo. *In* —; in statu quo.

stature, *n.f.*, stature.

statut, *n.m.*, statute.

statutaire, *adj.*, statutable, conformable to statute.

steamer (sti-meur), *n.m.* (—s), steamer.

stéarine, *n.f.*, (chem.) stearine.

stéarique, *adj.*, (chem.) stearic.

stéatite, *n.f.*, (min.) steatite.

stéatocèle, *n.f.*, (med.) steatocele.

stéatôme, *n.m.*, (med.) steatoma.

steeple-chase, *n.m.* (— —s), steeple-chase.

stéganographe, *n.m.*, steganographist.

stéganographie, *n.f.*, steganography.

stéganographique, *adj.*, steganographic.

stèle, *n.f.*, (arch.) stela.

stellaire, *n.f.*, (bot.) stitchwort.

stellaire, *adj.*, (astron.) stellar, stellary.

stellionat, *n.m.*, stellionate.

stellionataire, *n.m.*, (jur.) person guilty of stellionate.

sténographe, *n.m.*, stenographer, shorthand writer; reporter. — *des chambres*; parliamentary reporter.

sténographie, *n.f.*, stenography, shorthand.

sténographier, *v.a.*, to write in short-hand, to take down in short-hand, to report.

sténographique, *adj.*, stenographic, stenographical.

sténographiquement, *adv.*, stenographically.

stentor, *n.m.*, stentor.

steppe, *n.m.*, or *f.*, steppe.

stercoraire, *adj.*, stercoracecus.

stère, *n.m.*, (French measure) stère, cubic mètre (35,3174 cubic feet).

stéréobate, *n.m.*, (arch.) stereobate.

stéréographie, *n.f.*, stereography.

stéréographique, *adj.*, stereographic, stereographical.

stéréométrie, *n.f.*, (geom.) stereometry.

stéréoscope, *n.m.*, stereoscope.

stéréotomie, *n.f.*, (geom.) stereotomy.

stéréotypage, *n.m.*, stereotyping.

stéréotype, *adj.*, stereotype.

stéréotyper, *v.a.*, to stereotype.

stéréotypeur, *n.m.*, stereotyper.

stéréotypie, *n.f.*, stereotypography; stereotype printing; stereotype printing-office.

stérile, *adj.*, sterile, barren, unfruitful. *Année* —; year of scarcity. *Ouvrage* —; dry work. *Gloire* —; empty glory. *Vache* —; farrow cow.

stérilement, *adv.*, barrenly, unfruitfully.

stériliser, *v.a.*, to make, to render sterile.

stérilité, *n.f.*, sterility, barrenness, unfruitfulness. — *de nouvelles*; scarcity of news.

sterling, *n.* and *adj.m.* *invariable*, sterling. *Monnaie* —; sterling. *Livre* —; pound sterling.

sterne, *n.m.*, (orni.) tern, black tern.

sternum (-nom), *n.m.* (—), (anat.) sternum, breast-bone.

sternutatoire, *n.m.* and *adj.*, sternutatory, sternutative.

stertoreu-x, -se, *adj.*, (med.) stertorous.

stéthoscope, *n.m.*, (med.) stethoscope.

stibié, -e, *adj.*, (pharm.) stibial, antimonial, stibiated.

stigmate, *n.m.*, scar, stigma, brand, mark of infamy; mark, spot, trace, stain; (ent.) spiracle; (bot.) stigma; *pl.*, (theol.) stigmata. — *flétrissant*; mark of infamy, stigma of infamy. *Porter les* —*s de la petite vérole*; to be pockmarked. *En porter encore les* —*s*; to have just been publicly humiliated.

stigmatiser, *v.a.*, to brand (with a hot iron—*avec un fer chaud*); to stigmatize, to brand.

stil de grain, *n.m.*, (paint.) a kind of yellow colour.

stillation, *n.f.*, (phys.) action of dropping.

stimulant, -e, *adj.*, stimulating, stimulant.

stimulant, *n.m.*, stimulant, stimulus.

stimulation, *n.f.*, stimulation.

stimuler, *v.a.*, to stimulate, to excite, to rouse.

stimulus, *n.m.*, (med.) stimulus.

stipe, *n.f.*, (bot.) feather-grass, stipa; ⊙ a tax on leases.

stipe, *n.m.*, (bot.) stipe; caudex.

stipelle, *n.f.*, (bot.) stipel.

stipendiaire, *adj.*, stipendiary, hired.

stipendié, *n.m.*, stipendiary.

stipendier, *v.a.*, to keep in pay, to stipend. — *des troupes*; to keep troops in pay.

stipulacé, -e, *adj.*, (bot.) stipulaceous.

stipulant, -e, *adj.*, (jur.) stipulating.

stipulation, *n.f.*, (jur.) stipulation; (bot.) stipulation.

stipule. *n.f.*, (bot.) stipula, stipule.

stipuler, *v.a.*, (jur.) to stipulate, to covenant, to contract.

stock, *n.m.* (—), (com.) stock.

stockfisch, *n.m.* (*n.p.*), stockfish.

stoff, *n.m.*, stuff (cotton or woollen—*de coton ou de laine*).

stoïcien, -ne (in, -ĕ-n), *n.* and *adj.*, stoic; stoical.

stoïcisme, *n.m.*, stoicism, stoicalness.

stoïcité, *n.f.*, stoicism, stoicalness.

stoïque, *n.m.f.* and *adj.*, stoic; stoical.

stoïquement (-ik-mān), *adv.*, stoically.

stokfiche, *n.m.* *V.* **stockfisch**.

stole, *n.f.*, (antiq.) stola.

stomacal, -e, *adj.*, stomachic.

stomachique, *n.m.* and *adj.*, (med.) stomachic; (anat.) of the stomach, pertaining to the stomach.

stomate, *n.m.*, (bot.) stomatum.

stopper, *v.a.* and *n.*, to stop a railway train, a steamboat, an engine.

storax (-aks), *n.m.*, (bot., pharm.) storax.

store, *n.m.*, spring-roller blind, blind. *Lever les—s;* to pull up the blinds. *Baisser les —s;* to let the blinds down.

strabisme, *n.m.*, (med.) strabism, strabismus; squinting.

stramonium, *n.m.*, (bot.) stramony, thornapple, stramonium.

strangulation, *n.f.*, strangulation.

Θ**stranguler**, *v.a.* *V.* **étrangler**.

strangurie, *n.f.*, (med.) strangury.

strapasser, *v.a.*, Θ to drub, to bang, to thrash; (paint.) (l.u.) to paint hastily.

strapassonner, *v.a.*, (paint.) *V.* **strapasser**.

strapontin, *n.m.*, bracket-seat (of carriages —*de voitures*).

stras (strās), *n.m.*, strass, paste (of jewels—*joaillerie*).

strasse, *n.f.*, floss-silk.

stratagème, *n.m.*, stratagem.

strate, *n.f.*, (geol.) stratum.

stratège, *n.m.*, (Grec. antiq.) stratege, strategus.

stratégie, *n.f.*, strategy.

stratégique, *adj.*, strategic, strategical.

stratégiste, *n.m.*, strategist.

stratègue. *V.* **stratège**.

stratification, *n.f.*, stratification.

stratifier, *v.a.*, to stratify.

stratocratie (-ci), *n.f.*, stratocracy.

stratographie, *n.f.*, stratography.

strélitz, *n.m.*, strelitz.

strette, *n.f.*, (mus.) a part of a fugue or fuga; the termination of a lively tune.

stribord, *n.m.*, (nav.) *V.* **tribord**.

strict (strikt), **-e**, *adj.*, strict, precise, rigid, severe, rigorous.

strictement, *adv.*, strictly, precisely, rigidly, severely, rigorously.

stricture, *n.f.*, (med.) (l.u.) stricture.

strident, -e, *adj.*, jarring, screeching, shrill. *Voix —e;* shrill voice.

strideur, *n.f.*, harshness, creaking (of sound—*du son*).

strié, -e, *adj.*, (min., arch., natural hist.) striate, striated.

strie, *n.f.*, (natural hist.) striæ; (arch.) strigæ, fillets, flutings.

strige. *n.f.*, or **stryge**, *n.m.*, vampire, ghost.

strigile, *n.m.*, (antiq.) strigil.

strigueu-x, -se (-gheú,-z), *adj.*, (bot.) strigous, strigose.

striures, *n.f.pl.* *V.* **strie**.

strobile, *n.m.* (bot.), *V.* **cône** (bot.).

strophe, *n.f.*, strophe.

structure. *n.f.*, structure.

strumeu-x, -se, *adj.*, strumous.

strychnine (strik-), *n.f.*, (med.) strychnine, strychnia.

strychnos (stri-knôs), *n.m.*, (bot.) strychnos.

stryge, *n.m.* *V.* **strige**.

stuc. *n.m.*, stucco.

stucateur, *n.m.*, worker in stucco.

studieusement (-eûz-mān), *adv.*, studiously.

studieu-x, -se, *adj.*, studious.

stupéfacti-f. **-ve**, *adj.*, (med.) stupefactive.

stupéfaction, *n.f.*, (med.) stupefaction; stupefaction, great astonishment.

stupéfait. -e, *adj.*, stupified, astonished.

stupéfiant, -e, *adj.*, (med.) stupefactive; stupifying.

stupéfiant, *n.m.*, (med.) narcotic.

stupéfier. *v.a.*, (med.) to stupefy; to stupefy, to astonish.

stupeur, *n.f.*, (med.) stupor; stupor, astonishment.

stupide, *n.m.f.* and *adj.*, stupid person, stupid.

stupidement (-pid-mān), *adv.*, stupidly.

stupidité, *n.f.*, stupidity, stupidness; stupid thing, piece of stupidity.

stupre, *n.m.*, stupration.

stygmate, *n.m.* *V.* **stigmate**.

style, *n.m.*, (antiq.) style (instrument for writing—*pointe à écrire*); style (of writing—*d'écrivain*); tone, manner, strain; (fine arts) style; (chronology) style; (bot.) style. — *décousu;* unconnected style. — *badin;* jocular style. — *fleuri;* florid style. — *coulant;* fluent style. — *soutenu;* elevated, lofty, style. — *de pratique;* law terms. *Voilà bien son —;* that is just his way, that is just like him.

styler, *v.a.*, to train, to bring up, to use, to accustom.

stylet, *n.m.*, stiletto; (surg.) probe, stylet.

styliforme, *adj.*, (bot.) styliform.

stylite, *n.m.* and *adj.*, (rel. hist.) stylite.

stylobate, *n.m.*, (arch.) stylobate.

styloïde, *adj.*, (anat.) styloid.

styptique, *n.m.* and *adj.*, (med.) styptic, styptical.

styrax, *n.m.*, (bot., pharm.) storax.

su, *n.m.*, knowledge. *Au vu et au — de tout le monde;* as everybody knows.

su, *part.* (of Savoir), known.

suaire, *n.m.*, winding-sheet, shroud.

suant, -e, *adj.*, sweating, in a sweat; perspiring.

suave, *adj.*, sweet; agreeable, pleasant; fragrant, odoriferous.

suavement (-av-mān), *adj.*, sweetly, agreeably, pleasantly.

suavité, *n.f.*, suavity; sweetness, fragrance, odoriferousness; pleasantness, agreeableness.

subalterne, *n.m.* and *adj.*, subaltern, subordinate, inferior.

subalternité, *n.f.*, subalternation.

subdélégation, *n.f.*, subdelegation.

subdélégué (-ghé), *n.m.*, subdelegate.

subdéléguer (-ghé), *v.a.*, to subdelegate.

subdiviser, *v.a.*, to subdivide.

se **subdiviser**, *v.r.*, to subdivide, to be subdivided.

subdivision, *n.f.*, subdivision.

subéreu-x, -se, *adj.*, (bot.) suberous, corky.

subérique, *adj.*, suberic.

Θ**subhastation**, *n.f.*, (jur.) subhastation.

subintrant, -e, *adj.*, (med.) beginning before the other is over (of attacks of fever—*d'accès de fièvre*).

subir, *v.a.*, to undergo, to suffer. to submit, to sustain, to support. — *son sort;* to submit to one's fate. — *la question;* to undergo the torture. — *un examen;* to pass an examination, to undergo an examination.

subit, *-e*, *adj.*, sudden, unexpected.

subitement (-bit-măn), *adv.*, suddenly, on a sudden, all of a sudden, unexpectedly.

subito, *adv.*, suddenly, on a sudden, all of a sudden.

subjecti-f, *-ve*, *adj.*, subjective.

subjectivement (-tiv-măn), *adv.*, subjectively.

subjectivité, *n.f.*, (philos.) subjectivity.

subjonctif, *n.m.*, (gram.) subjunctive.

subjugation, *n.f.*, subjugation.

subjuguer (-ghé), *v.a.*, to subjugate, to subdue, to subject, to bring under the dominion of, to bring under subjection, to master, to get the better of, to overcome.

subjugueur, *n.m.*, subduer.

sublimable, *adj.*, (chem.) sublimable.

sublimation, *n.f.*, (chem.) sublimation, subliming.

sublimatoire, *n.m.*, (chem.) subliming pot.

sublime, *n.m.* and *adj.*, sublime, sublimity, sublimeness; sublime.

sublimé, *n.m.*, (chem.) sublimate.

sublimement, *adv.*, sublimely.

sublimer, *v.a.*, (chem.) to sublimate.

sublimité, *n.f.*, sublimity, sublimeness.

sublingual, *-e* (-gooal), *adj.*, (anat.) sublingual.

sublunaire, *adj.*, sublunar, sublunary.

submerger, *v.a.*, to submerge, to drown.

submersible, *adj.*, that can be submerged; (bot.) submerse.

submersion, *n.f.*, submersion.

subodorer, *v.a.*, to scent at a distance.

subordination, *n.f.*, subordination.

subordonnément, *adv.*, subordinately.

subordonner, *v.a.*, to subordinate.

⊙**subornateur**, *n.m.*, V. **suborneur**.

subornation, *n.f.*, subornation, suborning; (jur.) embracer (of juries—*de jurés*).

suborner, *v.a.*, to suborn, to bribe, to tamper with; (jur.) to embrace (a jury—*un jury*).

suborneu-r, *n.m.*, *-se*, *n.f.*, suborner, briber; (jur.) embracer (of juries—*de jurés*).

suborneu-r, *-se*, *adj.*, of subornation.

subrécargue (-kar-g), *n.m.*, (com., nav.) supercargo.

subrécot, *n.m.*, after-reckoning.

subreptice, *adj.*, subreptitious, surreptitious.

subrepticement (-tis-măn), *adv.*, subreptitiously.

subreption, *n.f.*, subreption.

subrogation, *n.f.*, (jur.) subrogation.

subrogatoire, *adj.*, of a deed of subrogation.

subrogé, *-e*, *adj.*, surrogated. — *tuteur:* person appointed to watch over the conduct of a guardian and to protect the interests of the ward.

subroger, *v.a.*, (jur.) to surrogate.

subséquemment (-ka-măn), *adv.*, subsequently.

subséquent, *-e*, *adj.*, subsequent.

subside, *n.m.*, subsidy; *pl.*, supplies (of the state—*de l'État*).

subsidiaire, *adj.*, subsidiary, auxiliary.

subsidiairement (-dièr-măn), *adv.*, further, also, likewise; in a subsidiary manner.

subsistance, *n.f.*, subsistence, sustenance, maintenance, support.

subsistant, *-e*, *adj.*, subsisting.

subsister, *v.n.*, to subsist, to stand, to continue, to be extant, to have existence; to be in

force; to subsist, to live. *J'ai de la peine à — ;* I can hardly get a livelihood.

substance, *n.f.*, substance. *En — ;* summarily, in substance.

substantiel, *-le*, *adj.*, substantial.

substantiellement (-sièl-măn), *adv.*, (theol.) substantially.

substantif, *n.m.* and *adj.*, (gram.) substantive.

substantive, *adj.f.*, (dy.) substantive. *Couleur — ;* substantive colour.

substantivement (-tiv-măn), *adv.*, substantively.

substituer, *v.a.*, to substitute; (jur.) to entail; (jur.) to appoint. — *un mot à un autre;* to substitute one word for another.

se **substituer**, *v.r.*, to substitute one's self; to supersede.

substitut, *n.m.*, substitute, deputy.

substitution, *n.f.*, substitution; (jur.) entail, entailment; (jur.) estate in tail.

substratum (-tom), *n.m.* (*n.p.*), (philos.) substratum.

substruction, *n.f.*, (arch.) substructure.

subterfuge, *n.m.*, subterfuge, evasion, shift.

subtil, *-e*, *adj.*, subtile, thin, fine; acute, keen, sharp, quick, sagacious; ready, dexterous; cunning, smart, shrewd, artful, crafty.

subtilement (-til-măn), *adv.*, subtilely, artfully, cunningly, acutely, sharply, smartly.

subtilisation, *n.f.*, (chem.) subtilization.

subtiliser, *v.a.*, to subtilize; (fam.) to cheat, to take in, to deceive.

subtiliser, *v.n.*, to subtilize.

subtilité, *n.f.*, subtileness, subtility; fineness, piercingness; penetration, refinement, acuteness; subtleness, expertness, adroitness, shrewdness; cunning, artfulness, craftiness. *La — des sens;* the acuteness of the senses. — *d'esprit;* sharpness of the understanding.

subulé, *-e*, *adj.*, (bot.) subulate, awl-shaped.

suburbain, *-e* (-bĭn, bè-n), *adj.*, suburban.

suburbicaire, *adj.*, (Roman antiq.) suburbicarian, suburbicary; (c. rel.) within the diocese of Rome.

subvenir, *v.n.*, to relieve, to help, to assist; to supply, to provide. — *aux besoins de quelqu'un;* to provide for any one's wants.

subvention, *n.f.*, supply, subsidy, grant; aid, help.

subventionner, *v.a.*, to grant a relief (in public money—*sur les fonds publics*), to subsidize.

subversi-f, *-ve* (-vèr-), *adj.*, subversive.

subversion (-vèr-), *n.f.*, subversion, ruin, overthrow.

subvertir (-vèr-), *v.a.*, to subvert, to destroy, to overthrow.

suc, *n.m.*, juice, essence, quintessence. — *gastrique;* gastric juice.

succédané, *n.m.*, (med.) succedaneum.

succédané, *-e*, *adj.*, (med.) of a succedaneum.

succéder, *v.n.*, to succeed, to follow; to prosper. *La nuit succède au jour;* night follows day. — *à quelqu'un;* to succeed any one. — *à un royaume;* to succeed to a kingdom. *Tout lui succède;* he, she, is successful in everything.

se **succéder**, *v.r.*, to succeed one another, to follow one another.

succès, *n.m.*, success. — *de circonstance;* accidental success. — *d'estime;* quiet success.

successeur (suk-sè-), *n.m.*, successor.

successibilité (suk-sè-), *n.f.*, (jur.) right of succession.

successible (suk-sè-), *adj.*, (jur.) heritable.

successi-f, *-ve* (suk-sè-), *adj.*, successive, (jur.) in succession.

succession (suk-sè-), *n.f.*, succession, inheritance, heritage; series. *Renoncer à une — ;*

) give up one's right to a succession. *Par —
de temps;* in process of time. *Droit d'administrer la —* (jur.); letters of administration.
Recueillir une —; to acquire an inheritance, to
have an estate left one, to have property left
one, to come into property.

successivement (suk-sè-siv-mān), *adv.*,
successively, in succession.

succin (suk-sin), *n.m.*, yellow amber.

succinct, -e (suk-sin, -t), *adj.*, succinct, concise, brief.

succinctement (suk-sint-mān), *adv.*, succinctly, briefly, concisely.

succion (suk-si-), *n.f.*, suction, sucking.

succomber, *v.n.*, to sink, to fall, to fall
down; to yield, to succumb, to be overcome, to
fail, to be worsted, to get the worst of it; to
die, to perish. — *à la douleur;* to be overcome
with grief. — *à la tentation;* to yield to temptation.

succube, *n.m.*, succubus.

succulent, -e, *adj.*, succulent, juicy, nutritious.

succursale, *n.* and *adj.f.*, (eccl.) chapel
of ease, parochial chapel; branch establishment, branch; additional.

succursaliste, *n.m.*, curate of a chapel of
ease.

sucement (sus-mān), *n.m.*, sucking, suck.

sucer, *v.a.*, to suck, to suck, to imbibe;
to suck out; to suck up; to draw, to drain.

sucet, *n.m.*, (ich.) sucking-fish, sucker,
remora; (orni.) common wren.

suceur, *n.m.*, person that sucked wounds to
cure them; (zool.) suctorian.

suçoir, *n.m.*, sucker; (ent.) proboscis.

suçon, *n.m.*, spot made by sucking.

suçoter, *v.a.*, to suck over and over, to suck
gradually, to suck at. — *un sucre d'orge;* to
suck a stick of barley-sugar.

sucre, *n.m.*, sugar. — *brut;* raw sugar,
brown sugar. — *pilé;* powdered sugar, ground
sugar. — *raffiné;* refined sugar, lump sugar,
loaf sugar. — *d'orge;* barley-sugar. *Pain de
—; sugar loaf. — brut;* moist sugar. — *en pain;*
loaf sugar. *Être tout — et tout miel;* to be all
honey.

sucré, -e, *part.*, sugared, sweet, luscious; demure, prim. *Air —;* prim air.

sucrer, *v.a.*, to sugar, to sweeten, to put
sugar in.

sucrerie, *n.f.*, sugar-house sugar-works,
sugar-refinery; sweetmeat; sweet thing.

sucrier, *n.m.*, sugar-bowl, sugar-basin;
sugar-maker.

sucr-ier, ière, *adj.*, sugar, of sugar. *Industrie — ère;* sugar-making, sugar trade.

sucrin, *adj.*, sugary (melons).

sud (sud), *n.m.*, South; south wind, souther.
Du —; southern. *Vers le —;* southward. —
-est; south-east.

sud, *adj.*, south, southerly (of the wind—
du vent).

sudation, *n.f.*, (med.) sudation.

sudatoire, *adj.*, sudatory.

sudiste, *n.m.* and *adj.*, said of the Southern
Confederate States during the American war of
secession.

sudorifère, *adj.*, (anat.) perspirative, perspiratory; (med.) sudorific.

sudorifique, *n.m.* and *adj.*, (med.) sudorific.

sud-ouest (sud-ooèst), *n.m.*, south-west.

suédois, -e, *n.* and *adj.*, Swede; Swedish.

suée, *n.f.*, (fam., pop.) sudden fright, sudden fear.

suer, *v.n.*, to sweat, to be in a sweat, to perspire; to toil, to drudge. — *à grosses gouttes;*

to have the sweat pouring down one in large
drops. *Faire — le tabac;* to heat tobacco.

suer, *v.a.*, to sweat. — *sang et eau;* to toil
and moil.

suerie (sû-rî), *n.f.*, drying-place (for tobacco
—*pour le tabac*).

suette, *n.f.*, sweating sickness, bloody sweat.

sueur, *n.f.*, sweat, perspiration; sweating;
pl., labour, toil, pains. — *rentrée* (med.); suppressed perspiration. *À la — de;* by the sweat
of.

suffètes, *n.m.*, (antiq.) Suffetes (Carthaginian magistrates—*magis'rats carthaginois*).

suffire (suffisant, suffi), *v.n.*, to suffice, to be
sufficient, to be enough; to be adequate. *Le
peu que j'ai me suffit;* the little I have is sufficient for me. *Qu'il vous suffise que;* let it suffice
you that. *Il suffit que vous le disiez pour que je
le croie;* your saying so is sufficient for me to
believe it. *Suffit, cela suffit;* enough, that's
enough. *A chaque jour suffit sa peine;* sufficient
for the day is the evil thereof.

se**suffire**, *v.r.*, to support one's self, to keep
one's self; to be sufficient in one's self.

suffisamment (-za-mān), *adv.*, sufficiently,
enough.

suffisance, *n.f.*, sufficiency, adequacy;
⊙ability; conceit, pride, presumption; self-
sufficiency. *Avoir — de vivres;* to have provisions enough. *A —, en —;* sufficiently,
enough. *Un air de —;* a self-conceited air.

suffisant, -e, *adj.*, sufficient, enough; consequential, conceited, self-sufficient.

suffisant, *n.m.*, **-e**, *n.f.*, self-conceited person.

suffixe, *n.m.*, (gram.) suffix.

suffocant, -e, *adj.*, suffocating, choking,
stifling.

suffocation, *n.f.*, suffocation, choking,
stifling.

suffoquer, *v.a.*, to suffocate, to stifle, to
choke.

suffoquer, *v.n.*, to suffocate, to stifle, to
choke; to burst (with anger—*de colère*).

suffragant, *n.* and *adj.m.*, suffragan.

suffrage, *n.m.*, suffrage, vote; approbation,
commendation. — *universel;* manhood suffrage.

suffumigation, *n.f.*, (med.) suffumigation.

suffusion, *n.f.*, (med.) suffusion.

suggérer (sug-jé-), *v.a.*, to suggest, to hint,
to intimate.

suggestion (sug-jes-ti-on), *n.f.*, (b.s.) suggestion, hint, instigation.

suicide, *n.m.*, suicide, self-murder; (pers.)
suicide, self-murderer; (jur.) (pers.) felo de se.

suicidé, *n.m.*, **-e**, *n.f.*, self-murderer.

se**suicider**, *v.r.*, to commit suicide, to make
away with one's self.

suie, *n.f.*, soot.

suif, *n.m.*, tallow; candle-grease; (nav.) coat,
stuff. *Donner un — à quelqu'un* (pop.); to blow
up any one. *Donner un — à un vaisseau* (nav.);
to pay a ship.

suiffer, *v.a.*, to tallow; (nav.) to pay a ship.

sui generis, *adj.*, sui generis, of its own
particular kind.

suint, *n.m.*, grease (of wool-bearing animals
—*des bêtes à laine*).

suintement (suint-mān), *n.m.*, oozing, ooze.

suinter, *v.n.*, to ooze, to leak.

suisse, *n.m.*, Swiss; porter (of a mansion—
d'une grande maison); beadle (of a church—
d'église); (mam.) ground squirrel.

suissesse, *n.f.*, Swiss woman.

suite, *n.f.*, rest; retinue, train, attendance;
attendants; sequel; continuation; series, succession; connection, order; set; consequence,
result. *Laisser entrer les premiers et fermer la
porte à la —;* to allow the first to enter and to

shut the doors on the others, on the rest. — *de médailles;* set of medals. *Cela peut avoir de fâcheuses* —*s;* that may be attended with disagreeable consequences. *Sans* —; unconnected. *De* —; one after another. *Tout de* —: immediately, at once. *Et ainsi de* —; and so forth, and so on.

suites, *n.f.pl.,* (hunt.) testicles of the wild boar.

suivant. *prep.,* according to, agreeably to; in the opinion of.

suivant que, *conj.,* as, according as.

suivant, -e, *adj.,* next, following, succeeding, subsequent, ensuing.

suivant, *n.m.,* **-e,** *n.f.,* follower, attendant: near relation. —*e;* waiting-maid; (thea.) chambermaid.

suiver, *v.a.,* to tallow. — *un vaisseau* (nav.); to pay a ship. *V.* **suiffer,** which is more used.

suivi, -e, *part.,* followed; connected; consistent. *Discours bien* —; coherent discourse.

suivre (suivant, suivi), *v.a.,* to follow, to go after, to come after, to go next, to be next, to come next; to pursue; to attend, to go with, to accompany; to attend; to follow; to observe; (nav.) to run along (the coast—*la côte*); to give way to, to indulge. — *de près,* — *de loin;* to follow close, to follow at a distance. — *son chemin;* to go one's way. *L'envie suit la prospérité;* envy attends prosperity. — *le barreau;* to follow the law. — *la mode;* to follow the fashion. — *sa pointe;* to pursue one's end.

se suivre, *v.r.,* to follow each other, to succeed each other; to be connected.

suivre, *v.n.,* to follow, to go after, to come after; to pay attention; to attend.

sujet, -te, *n.* and *adj.,* subject; subject, subjected, amenable, liable, exposed; apt, addicted, inclined. — *aux lois;* amenable to the laws. — *à de grandes maladies;* subject to severe diseases. — *à caution;* not to be trusted, not trustworthy, suspicious.

sujet, *n.m.,* subject; person, individual; cause, reason; matter, motive, occasion, ground, account; theme, argument, topic; (hort.) stock. *J'ai* — *de me plaindre;* I have reason to complain. *S'éloigner de son* —; to wander from one's subject. *Mauvais* —; bad fellow, worthless fellow.

sujétion, *n.f.,* subjection, dependence, constraint.

sulfate, *n.m.,* (chem.) sulphate.

sulfaté, -e, *adj.,* (chem.) sulphatic.

sulfhydrate, *n.m.,* (chem.) hydrosulphate.

sulfhydrique, *adj.,* (chem.) hydrosulphuric.

sulfite, *n.m.,* (chem.) sulphite.

sulfuration, *n.f.,* (chem.) sulphuration.

sulfure, *n.m.,* (chem.) sulphuret.

sulfuré, -e, *adj.,* (chem.) sulphuretted.

sulfureu-x, -se, *adj.,* sulphurous, sulphureous, sulphury.

sulfurique. *adj.,* (chem.) sulphuric.

sultan, *n.m.,* sultan; scent-satchel, scent-basket.

sultane. *n.f.,* sultana, sultaness; Turkish man-of-war.

sultanin. *n.m.,* sultanin (Turkish coin—*pièce de monnaie turque*).

sumac, *n.m.,* sumac-tree; sumac, sumach.

sunnite. *n.m.,* sunnite, orthodox Mahometan. *V.* **schiite.**

super (su-pé), *v.n.,* (nav.) to be stopped up.

superbe (-pèrb), *n.m.* and *adj.,* (Bibl.) proud, haughty man; proud, arrogant; superb, splendid; gorgeous; lofty; supercilious, vainglorious. *Dieu résiste au* — : God resisteth the proud. *Un* — *tableau;* a splendid painting. *Un dîner* —; a splendid dinner. *Meubles* —*s;* splendid furniture.

superbe (-pèrb), *n.f.,* arrogance, haughtiness, vainglory.

superbement (-pèr-), *adv.,* proudly, arrogantly; sumptuously, splendidly; loftily.

supercherie (-pèr-), *n.f.,* deceit, fraud, trickery.

superfétation (-pèr-), *n.f.,* superfetation; superfluity.

superficie (-pèr-). *n.f.,* superficies, surface; area.

superficiel, -le (-pèr-), *adj.,* superficial, shallow. *Homme* —: superficial man.

superficiellement (su-pèr-fi-si-èl-màn), *adv.,* superficially.

superfin. -e (-pèr-), *adj.,* superfine.

superfin (-pèr-). *n.m.,* superfine quality.

superflu, -e (-pèr-), *adj.,* superfluous.

superflu (-pèr-), *n.m.,* superfluity, superfluousness.

superfluité (-pèr-), *n.f.,* superfluity; superfluousness.

supérieur. -e, *n.* and *adj.,* superior, upper.

supérieurement (-eur-màn), *adv.,* in a superior manner, in a superior degree, superlatively well.

supériorité, *n.f.,* superiority.

superlati-f, -ve (-pèr-), *adj.,* (gram.) superlative.

superlatif (-pèr-), *n.m.,* superlative. *Au* —; superlatively; (gram.) in the superlative. *Cet homme est bête au* —; that man is superlatively stupid.

superlativement (su-pèr-la-tiv-màn), *adv.,* superlatively.

superposer (-pèr-), *v.a.,* to superpose.

superposition (-pèr-), *n.f.,* superposition.

superpurgation (-pèr-), *n.f.,* superpurgation.

superséder (-pèr-), *v.n.,* (jur.) to postpone, to put off.

superstitieusement (su-pèrs-ti-si-euz-màn), *adv.,* superstitiously.

superstitieu-x, -se (-pèrs-ti-si-), *adj.,* superstitious; overnice.

superstition (-pèrs-ti-si-), *n.f.,* superstition; overnicety.

superstructure (-pèr-), *n.f.,* superstructure.

supersubstantiel. -le (-pèr-), *adj.,* supersubstantial.

supin, *n.m.,* (gram.) supine.

supinateur, *n.m.,* (anat.) supinator.

supination, *n.f.,* supination.

supplantation, *n.f.,* supplantation.

supplanter, *v.a.,* to supplant; to oust.

suppléance, *n.f.,* replacing, the acting as a substitute of another; the functions of a substitute.

suppléant, n.m., **-e,** *n.f.,* substitute.

suppléer, *v.a.,* to supply, to fill up, to make up (what is deficient—*ce qui manque*); to supply the place of.

suppléer, *v.n.,* to make up the deficiency; to supply the place. *La valeur supplée au nombre;* valour makes up for deficiency of number.

supplément. *n.m.,* supplement, addition; additional price.

supplémentaire, *adj.,* supplementary, additional.

suppléti-f, -ve, *adj.,* suppletory.

suppliant, -e, *n.* and *adj.,* suppliant, supplicant; supplicating.

supplication, *n.f.,* supplication, entreaty, humble petition.

supplice, *n.m.,* corporal punishment; torment, pain, anguish. *Être au* —; to be upon the rack. *Dernier* —; capital punishment.

supplicié, *n.m.,* criminal executed.

supplicier, v.a., to put to death, to execute.

supplier, v.a., to beseech, to entreat, to supplicate.

supplique, n.f., petition, supplication, prayer.

support, n.m., support, prop; assistance; rest; fulcrum; (carp.) strut; (her.) supporter; (arch.) pillar.

supportable, adj., supportable, bearable.

supportablement, adv., tolerably.

supporter, v.a., to support, to sustain, to uphold; to endure; to suffer, to tolerate, to bear with.

se **supporter**, v.r., to be supported; to be borne; to be suffered; to bear one another.

supposable, adj., supposable.

supposé, -e, part., supposed; suppositious, pretended, counterfeit. *Supposé qu'il y consente;* suppose he consents to it.

supposer, v.a., to suppose, to grant, to infer, to put the supposition; to conjecture. — *un testament;* to forge a will. — *un enfant;* to substitute a child, to palm a child upon.

suppositi-f, -ve, adj., suppositive.

supposition, n.f., supposition. — *d'enfant;* substitution, palming of a child.

suppositoire, n.m., (med.) suppository.

suppôt, n.m., agent, instrument, tool; (b.s.) abettor; imp (of the devil—*du diable*).

suppression, n.f., suppression.

supprimer, v.a., to suppress, to pass over in silence; to put down, to abolish, to take off. — *des impôts;* to take off taxes. — *une loi;* to abolish a law.

suppurati-f, -ve, adj., (med.) suppurative.

suppuratif, n.m., (med.) suppurative.

suppuration, n.f., suppuration.

suppurer, v.n., to suppurate.

supputation, n.f., computation, calculation, supputation.

supputer, v.a., to calculate, to compute, to reckon, to suppute.

suprématie (-ci), n.f., supremacy.

suprême, adj., supreme, last. *À l'heure* —; at the last hour (death—*mort*).

suprêmement, adv., supremely.

sur, prep., upon, on, over; by; in; about; towards; above; on account of, respecting, concerning; out of. *Compter* —; to rely on, to make sure of. — *un vaisseau;* on board a ship. *Il l'a mis — son testament;* he has put him in his will. *N'avoir pas d'argent—soi;* to have no money about one's self. — *le soir;* towards the evening. — *la brune;* about dusk. — *la fin de la semaine;* towards the end of the week. — *ma parole;* upon my word. *Il s'excusa — son âge;* he excused himself on account of his age. *Il prend trop — lui;* he undertakes too much. — *-le-champ;* immediately. — *ces entrefaites;* in the meantime. *Dix — quinze;* ten out of fifteen. — *toute chose,* — *toutes choses;* above all, above all things. ⊙ — *et tant moins;* in deduction. — *le tout;* upon the whole. — *le tout* (her.); over all.

sur, -e, adj., sour.

sûr, -e, adj., sure, certain; safe, secure; trustworthy. *Je suis — de vous;* I can depend on you. *Il est — de son fait;* he is sure of success. *Les chemins sont —s;* the roads are safe. *Le temps n'est pas —;* the weather is not certain. *Il est en lieu —;* he is in a place of safety, he is out of harm's way. *C'est un ami —;* he is a trusty friend. *Ce port est —;* this port is safe. *À coup —, pour —;* surely, for certain, for sure. — *comme père et mère;* as sure as a gun.

surabondamment (-da-màn), adv., superabundantly.

surabondance, n.f., superabundance.

surabondant, -e, adj., superabundant.

surabonder, v.n., to superabound.

suracheter (-ash-té), v.a., to overpay.

suraigu, -ë, adj., (mus.) very high.

surajoutement (-joot-màn), n.m., superaddition.

surajouter, v.a., to superadd.

sural, -e, adj., (anat.) sural.

sur-aller, v.n., (hunt.) to go over a track silently (of a dog—*du limier*).

*****sur-andouiller**, n.m. (— —s), (hunt.) sur-antler.

surannation (-an-na-), n.f., expiration.

suranné, -e (-ra-né), part., expired; superannuated, grown out of date; antiquated. *Beauté—e;* antiquated beauty.

suranner (-ra-né), v.n., to be past one year's date, to expire. [Little used, *V.* **périmer**.]

sur-arbitre, n.m. (— —s), umpire who decides between two other umpires.

surard, adj., of elder-flower. *Vinaigre* —; elder-flower vinegar.

surate, n.f., name of the chapters of the Koran.

surbaissé, -e, adj., (arch.) surbased (of vaults—*arches*).

surbaissement (-bès-màn), n.m., (arch.) surbasement.

surbaisser, v.a., (arch.) to make elliptic.

surbande, n.f., (surg.) bandage placed over a compress.

surcens (-sans), n.m., (feudalism—*féodalité*) lord's rent.

surcharge, n.f., additional burden; overloading; word written over another.

surcharger, v.a., to overload, to overburden, to overcharge; to write over words. — *de travail;* to overtask. — *d'impôts;* to overtax.

surchauffer, v.a., to overheat.

surchauffure, n.f., (metal.) overheating.

surcomposé, -e, adj., (gram.) double compound.

surcomposé, n.m., (chem.) double compound.

surcouper, v.a., to trump over (at cards—*aux cartes*).

surcroissance, n.f., preternatural growth.

surcroît, n.m., superaddition, increase. *Pour — de malheur;* to make it worse, to complete the misfortune.

surcroître, v.n., to grow out.

*****surcroître**, v.a., to increase beyond measure.

surdemande, n.f., immoderate demand.

surdent, n.f., irregular tooth; wolf-tooth (of horses—*des chevaux*).

surdité, n.f., deafness, surdity.

surdoré, -e, part., double-gilt.

surdorer, v.a., to double-gild.

surdos, n.m., loin-strap (of a horse—*d'un cheval*).

sureau, n.m., elder, elder-tree.

surélever, v.a., to increase the height; to make higher.

surelle, n.f., (bot.) sorrel, little wood-sorrel.

sûrement (sur-màn), adv., surely, certainly; safely, securely.

suréminent, -e, adj., pre-eminent.

surémission, n.f., (fin.) over-issue.

surenchère, n.f., outbidding, higher bid.

surenchérir, v.n., to outbid, to bid higher.

surenchérisseur, n.m., outbidder.

surérogation, n.f., supererogation.

surérogatoire, adj., supererogatory.

surestarie (-rès-), n.f., (nav., com.) detention of a vessel in a port beyond the time appointed for departure. *Indemnité pour* —; demurrage.

surestimation, n.f., over-estimate.

suret. -te. *adj.*, sourish.

sûreté (sur-té), *n.f.*, safety, surety, security; sureness, warranty. *Être en lieu de* — ; to be out of harm's way, to be in good custody, in safe keeping. *Mettre un homme en* — ; to place a man in safety, in safe keeping.

surévaluation, *n.f.*, overvaluation, over-estimate.

surévaluer, *v.a.*, to overvalue, to over-estimate.

surexcitation, *n.f.*, excessive excitement.

surexciter, *v.a.*, to excite excessively.

surface, *n.f.*, surface.

surfaire, *v.a.*, to overcharge, to ask too much.

surfaix. *n.m.*, surcingle.

surfleurir. *v.n.*, (bot.) to blow again.

surgeon (-jon), *n.m.*, (hort.) sucker, shoot; ⊙descendant. ⊙ — *d'eau* : natural little jet of water issuing from the earth, &c.

surgir, *v.n.*, to come to land, to land ; to reach (port) ; to arise, to spring up ; to rise into notice. — *au port* ; to come into port. *Faire* — ; to give rise to.

surhaussement (-hôs-mãn), *n.m.*, raising, making higher ; raising (of prices—*de prix*).

surhausser, *v.a.*, (arch.) to raise ; to raise the price too high.

surhumain, -e (-mĭn, -mè-n), *adj.*, super-human.

surintendance, *n.f.*, superintendence.

surintendant, *n.m.*, superintendent.

surintendante, *n.f.*, superintendent's lady; lady superintendent.

surjalé, *part.*, (nav.) foul (of anchors—*des ancres*).

surjaler, *or* **surjauler,** *v.n.*, (nav.) to foul (of anchors—*des ancres*).

surjaler, *or* **surjauler,** *v.a.*, (nav.) to raise the anchor to clear its stock.

surjet, *n.m.*, (of seams—*couture*) whip, overcasting.

surjeter, *v.a.*, to whip, to overcast (seams —*couture*).

surlendemain (-land-mĭn), *n.m.*, two days after ; third day.

surlonge, *n.f.*, sirloin (of beef—*de bœuf*).

surlunaire, *adj.*, superlunar, superlunary.

surmener, *v.a.*, to jade, to overdrive, to override (horses—*des chevaux*).

surmesure, *n.f.*, over-measure.

surmeule, *n.f.*, runner-stone (of a mill—*de moulin*).

surmontable, *adj.*, surmountable, super-able.

surmonter, *v.a.*, to surmount ; to overcome, to conquer, to subdue ; to outdo, to surpass ; to rise above (of fluids—*fluides*). *Il a surmonté tous les obstacles* ; he has surmounted every obstacle. — *sa colère* ; to subdue one's anger.

surmonter, *v.n.*, to rise above (of fluids—*fluides*).

surmoule, *n.m.*, cast taken on one of plaster.

surmouler, *v.a.*, to make a cast on a figure or ornament.

surmoût, *n.m.*, new wort (of wine—*vin*).

surmulet, *n.m.*, (ich.)surmullet,gray mullet.

surmulot, *n.m.*, surmulot, Norway rat.

surnager, *v.n.*, to float on the surface ; to survive.

⊙**surnaître,** *v.n.*, to grow upon.

surnaturalité, *n.f.*, (theol.) supernatural-ness.

surnaturel, -le *adj.*, supernatural, preter-natural.

surnaturel, *n.m.*, supernatural.

surnaturellement (-rèl-mãn), *adv.*, super-naturally, preternaturally.

surnom (-non), *n.m.*, surname, cognomen.

surnommer, *v.a.*, to surname.

surnuméraire, *n.m.* and *adj.*, superne-merary.

surnumérariat, *n.m.*, time one serves as a supernumerary.

suron, *n.m.*, seroon ; (bot.) earth-nut.

suros (-rô), *n.m.*, (vet.) splint.

suroxydation, *n.f.*, (chem.) peroxidizing.

suroxyde, *n.m.*, (chem.) peroxide.

suroxyder, *v.a.*, (chem.) to peroxidize.

suroxygéné, -e, *adj.*, (chem.) overloaded with oxygen.

surpasser, *v.a.*, to surpass, to exceed, to go beyond, to excel, to surmount, to outdo ; to astonish, to overweigh. *Il les surpasse en science* ; he excels them in knowledge.

surpayer, *v.a.*, to overpay.

surpeau, *n.f.*,(l.u.)epidermis. *L'épiderme*

surplis, *n.m.*, surplice.

surplomb (-plon), *n.m.*, overhanging (of buildings—*de bâtiments*). *Ce mur est en* — ; this wall hangs over.

surplomber, *v.n.*,to hang over,to overhang.

surplus, *n.m.*, surplus. *Au* — ; besides, in addition to which.

surprenant, -e, *adj.*, surprising, astonish-ing.

surprendre, *v.a.*, to surprise, to take by surprise, to overtake ; to deceive, to catch ; to astonish, to amaze. — *une ville* : to take a town by surprise. *La nuit nous surprit* ; night over-took us. *La pluie me surprit* ; I was caught in the rain.

se **surprendre,** *v.r.*, to surprise one's self : to catch one's self.

surprise, *n.f.*, surprise ; amazement ; deceit. *Ménager une* — *à quelqu'un* ; to prepare a sur-prise for any one. *Revenir de sa* — ; to recover from one's surprise.

surrénal, -e, *adj.*, (anat.) suprarenal.

sursaturation, *n.f.*, supersaturation.

sursaturer, *v.a.*, to supersaturate.

sursaut, *n.m.*, start. *S'éveiller en* — ; to start up out of one's sleep.

surséance, *n.f.*, suspension.

sursel, *n.m.*, (chem.) supersalt.

sursemer, *v.a.*, to sow over again.

surseoir (sursoyant, sursis), *v.a.* and *n.*, to suspend, to delay, to respite.

sursis, *n.m.*, delay, respite, reprieve.

sursolide. *n.m.* and *adj.*, (alg.) sursolid.

surtare, *n.f.*, (com.) supertare.

surtaux, *n.m.*, excessive taxation.

surtaxe, *n.f.*, surcharge, additional tax.

surtaxer, *v.a.*, to overtax, to overassess.

surtout, *adv.*, above all, especially.

surtout, *n.m.*, surtout (coat—*pardessus*); light cart ; épergne.

*****surveillance.** *n.f.*, superintendence, in-spection, supervision.

*****surveillant, -e,** *n.* and *adj.*, inspector, overseer, superintendent ; attendant ; vigilant.

*****surveille,** *n.f.*, two days before.

*****surveiller,** *v.a.*, to superintend, to inspect, to look after, to watch, to have an eye upon.

survenance, *n.f.*, (jur.) unexpected birth of children after the time of a donation.

survenant, -e, *n.* and *adj.*, (jur.) child born unexpectedly after the time of a donation ; new-comer.

survendre, *v.a.* and *n.*, to overcharge.

survenir, *v.n.*, to supervene, to come on, to happen unexpectedly, to come unexpectedly.

survente. *n.f.*, overcharge.

surventer, *v.n.*, (nav.) to blow hard.

survider, *v.a.*, to lighten (anything that is too full—*ce qui est trop plein*).

survie, *n.f.*, survivorship, survival.

survivance, *n.f.*, reversion (of offices—*de charges*).

survivancier, *n.m.*, reversioner (of offices—*de charges*).

survivant, -e, *n.* and *adj.*, survivor ; surviving.

survivre, *v.n.*, to survive, to outlive. — *à son père ;* to outlive one's father.

se **survivre**, *v.r.*, to live again. — *à soi-même ;* to lose one's natural faculties. — *dans ses enfants ;* to live again in one's children.

sus, *prep.*, (l.u.) upon. *Courir — à quelqu'un ;* to fall upon, to attack, any one. *En — ;* over and above.

sus, *int.*, come ! cheer up !

susceptibilité, *n.f.*, susceptibility, irritability, touchiness, irascibility.

susceptible, *adj.*, susceptible, irascible, easily offended, touchy. *Elle est trop — ;* she takes offence too easily.

susception, *n.f.*, taking of holy orders; (c.rel.) reception (of the crown, of the cross—*de la couronne, de la croix*).

⊙suscitation, *n.f.*, instigation, (ant.) suscitation.

susciter, *v.a.*, to raise, to raise up, to create, to give rise to, to give birth to, to raise against, to stir up.

suscription, *n.f.*, superscription, direction, address.

susdénommé, -e, *adj.*, herein before mentioned.

susdit, -e, *adj.*, aforesaid.

susénoncé. -e, *adj.*, above-mentioned.

susmentionné, -e, *adj.*, (jur.) above-mentioned.

susnommé, -e, *adj.*, above-named.

suspect, -e (-pèk, -t), *adj.*, suspected, suspicious. *Cela m'est — ;* that appears suspicious to me.

suspecter, *v.a.*, to suspect.

suspendre, *v.a.*, to suspend, to hang, to hang up ; to stop, to delay. — *son travail ;* to lay aside one's work.

se **suspendre**, *v.r.*, to suspend one's self.

suspens, *adj.*, (eccl.) suspended. *Prêtre — ;* suspended, inhibited priest. *En — ;* in suspense.

suspense, *n.f.*, (eccl.) suspension, inhibition.

suspenseur, *adj.*, (anat.) suspensory.

suspensi-f, -ve, *adj.*, (jur.) being a bar to subsequent proceedings.

suspension, *n.f.*, suspension, interruption, discontinuance.

suspensoir, *or* **suspensoire**. *n.m.*, (surg.) suspensory bandage, suspensor.

suspicion. *n.f.*, (jur.) suspicion.

sustentation, *n.f.*, sustentation, sustenance.

sustenter, *v.a.*, to sustain, to support, to maintain.

se **sustenter**, *v.n.*, to maintain one's self, to support one's self.

susurration (su-sur-ra-), *n.f.*, susurration, whispering.

⊙susurrer (su-sur-ré), *v.n.*, to murmur softly, to whisper. *V.* **chuchoter**.

suttee, *or* **suttie**. *n.f.* (—), suttee.

suture, *n.f.*, (anat.) suture ; (bot.) seam : joint.

suzerain, -e (suz-rin, -rè-n), *n.* and *adj.*, suzerain, lord paramount ; paramount.

suzeraineté (suz-rè-n-té), *n.f.*, suzerainty ; seigniory.

svelte, *adj.*, light, slender, slim ; elegant.

sybarite, *n.m.* and *adj.*, Sybarite ; Sybaritical, Sybaritic.

sycomore, *n.m.*, (bot.) sycamore.

sycophante, *n.m.*, sycophant, knave, rogue.

syllabaire (sil-la-), *n.m.*, spelling-book.

syllabe (sil-lab), *n.f.*, syllable.

syllabique (sil-la-), *adj.*, syllabic. syllabical.

syllabiquement (sil-la-), *adv.*, syllabically.

syllabisation (sil-la-), *n.f.*, syllabication.

syllabus (sil-la-), *n.m.* (—). (c.rel.) syllabus.

syllepse (sil-lèps), *n.f.*, (gram.) syllepsis; substitution.

syllogisme (sil-lo-), *n.m.*, syllogism.

syllogistique (sil-lo-), *adj.*, syllogistic, syllogistical.

sylph-e, *n.m.*, **-ide**, *n.f.*, sylph.

sylvain, *n.m.*, sylvan ; (min.) sylvanite.

sylvatique, *adj.*, sylvatic.

sylves, *n.f.pl.*, sylva, collection of poetical works.

sylvestre, *adj.*, wild, growing in woods (of plants—*plantes*).

sylviculture, *n.f.*, cultivation of forests.

sylvie. *n.f.*, (orni.) sylvia.

symbole, *n.m.*, symbol ; creed. — *des Apôtres ;* Apostles' creed.

symbolique, *adj.*, symbolic, symbolical, typical.

symboliser, *v.n.*, to symbolize.

symbolisme. *n.m.*, (philos.) state of a language in which ideas and dogmas are expressed by symbols.

symétrie, *n.f.*, symmetry.

symétrique, *adj.*, symmetrical.

symétriquement (-trik-mân), *adv.*, symmetrically.

symétriser, *v.n.*, to be in symmetry.

sympathie, *n.f.*, sympathy, fellow-feeling.

sympathique, *adj.*, sympathetic, sympathetical.

sympathiser, *v.n.*, to sympathize.

symphonie, *n.f.*, symphony.

symphoniste, *n.m.*, symphonist.

symphyse, *n.f.*, (anat.) symphysis.

symposiaque, *adj.*, symposiac.

symptomatique, *adj.*, symptomatic, symptomatical.

symptomatologie, *n.f.*, symptomatology.

symptôme, *n.m.*, symptom, indication, sign, token.

synagogue (-gog), *n.f.*, synagogue.

synalèphe, *n.f.*, (gram.) synalepha, synaloepha.

synallagmatique, *adj.*, (jur.) (of a contract—*d'un contrat*) synallagamatic, reciprocal.

synanthéré, -e, *adj.*, (bot.) synantherous.

synanthérées, *n.f.pl.*, (bot.) compositæ.

synanthérie, *n.f. V.* **syngénésie**.

synarthrose, *n.f.*, (anat.) synarthrosis.

syncelle, *n.m.*, in the ancient Greek Church an official to watch over the Patriarch.

synchondrose (-kon-), *n.f.*, (anat.) synchondrosis.

synchrone (-krô-n), *adj.*, (phys.) synchronical.

synchronique, *adj.*, (hist.) synchronical.

synchronisme, *n.m.*, synchronism.

synchyse (-kiz), *n.f.*, (gram.) synchysis.

syncope, *n.f.*, (med.) syncope, swoon, fainting fit ; (mus.) syncopation, syncope ; (gram.) syncope.

syncopé, -e, *adj.*, syncopated.

syncoper, *v.n.*, (gram., mus.) to syncopate.

syncrétisme, *n.m.*, syncretism.

syndérèse, *n.f.*, (rel.) remorse.

syndic, *n.m.*, syndic, trustee, assignee. *d'office ;* official assignee.

syndical, *adj.*, pertaining to a syndic.

syndicat, *n.m.*, syndicate.

synecdoche, *or* **synecdoque**, *n.f.*, (rhet.) synecdoche.

synérèse, *n.f.*, (gram.) synæresis.

synévrose, *n.f.*, (anat.) synneurosis.

syngénésie, *n.f.*, (bot.) syngenesia.

syngnathe, *n.m.*, (ich.) syngnathus, horn-fish. sea-needle.

synodal, -e, *adj.*, synodic, synodal.

synodalement (-dal-mân), *adv.*, synodically.

synode. *n.m.*, synod.

17*

synodique, *adj.*, synodic, synodical.
synonyme, *n.m.* and *adj.*, synonym, synonymous.
synonymie, *n.f.*, synonymy.
synonymique, *adj.*, pertaining, relating to synonymy.
synopse, *n.f.*, synopsis of the Gospel.
synoptique, *adj.*, synoptic, synoptical.
synoque, *n.f.*, synocha, synochus.
synovial, **-e**, *adj.*, (anat.) synovial.
synovie, *n.f.*, (anat.) synovia.
syntaxe, *n.f.*, syntax.
syntaxique, *adj.*, syntactic, syntactical.
synthèse, *n.f.*, synthesis, composition.
synthétique, *adj.*, synthetic, synthetical.
synthétiquement, *adv.*, synthetically.
syphilis (-liss), *n.f.*, syphilis.
syphilitique, *adj.*, syphilitic.
syphon, *n.m.* V. **siphon**.
syriaque, *n.m.* and *adj.*, Syriac.
syrien, **-ne** (-ri-in, -è-n), *n.* and *adj.*, Syrian.
syringa, *n.m.*, (bot.) syringa, lilac.
syringotome, *n.m.*, (surg.) an instrument to perform syringotomy.
syringotomie, *n.f.*, (surg.) syringotomy.
syrop. V. **sirop**.
syrtes, *n.f.pl.*, syrt, quicksands.
systaltique, *adj.*, (physiology) systaltic.
systématique, *adj.*, systematic, systematical.
systématiquement (-tik-mān), *adv.*, systematically.
systématiser, *v.a.*, to systematize.
système, *n.m.*, system.
systole, *n.f.*, (anat., gram.) systole.
systolique, *adj.*, systolic.
systyle, *n.m.* and *adj.*, (arch.) systyle.
syzygie, *n.f.*, (astron.) syzygy.

T

t, *n.m.*, the twentieth letter of the alphabet, t. [T is put for the sake of euphony between a verb ending with a vowel and the pronouns *il, elle, on*; ex.: *Aime-t-il?* does he love?]
t', contraction of *te* and *toi*.
ta, *possessive adj.f.*, thy. V. **ton**.
tabac (-ba), *n.m.*, tobacco, snuff. *Carotte de —*; roll of tobacco. *— en carotte*; pig-tail tobacco. *Débitant de —*; tobacconist, dealer in snuff and tobacco. *Marchand de —*; tobacconist. *— à chiquer*; chewing tobacco.
tabagie, *n.f.*, smoking-house, smoking-room; ⊙ tobacco box.
tabarin, *n.m.*, merry-andrew.
tabarinage, *n.m.*, buffoonery.
tabatière (-tièr), *n.f.*, snuff-box.
⊙**tabellion**, *n.m.*, tabellion.
⊙**tabellionage**, *n.m.*, tabellion's business.
tabernacle, *n.m.*, tent, tabernacle.
tabide, *adj.*, tabid, tabetic.
tabis, *n.m.*, tabby, waved silk.
tabiser, *v.a.*, to tabby.
tablature, *n.f.*, (mus.) tablature. *Donner de la — à quelqu'un*; to cause any one embarrassment, trouble.
table, *n.f.*, table; board (food—*nourriture*); table, index (of a book—*d'un livre*); (nav.) mess (of officers—*d'officiers*); slab (of stone—*de pierre*); (anat.) table; (of jewellery—*joaillerie*) table; *pl.*, men (at backgammon—*trictrac*). *— à jouer*; card-table. *— à manger*; dining-table. *— de nuit*; night-table. *— à ouvrage*; work-table. *— de cuisine*; kitchen-dresser. *Se mettre à —*; to sit at table. *Tenir —*; to keep a table, to sit long at table. *Tenir bonne —*; to keep a good table. *Donner la — à quelqu'un*; to board any one. *La — du commun*; the ser-

vants' table. *Courir les —s*; to sponge for a dinner. *— s astronomiques*; astronomical tables. *— pythagorique*, *— de Pythagore*; multiplication-table. *— d'harmonie*; sounding-board.
tableau, *n.m.*, painting, picture; (nav.) breast-work; list, roll, table; panel (of juries *—des jurés*) (paint.) painting, piece. *— de chevalet*; easel-piece. *—x vivants*; tableaux vivants. *Encadrer un —*; to frame a picture. *Former un —* (jur.); to array a panel.
tabler, *v.n.*, to place one's men (trick-track). *Vous pouvez — là-dessus*; you may depend upon it.
tableti-er, *n.m.*, **-ère**, *n.f.*, (-blě-tié, -blě-tiè-r), dealer in fancy turnery.
tablette (-blèt), *n.f.*, shelf; tablet; (nav.) rising-staff; (arch.) table; cake (of chocolate, &c.—*de chocolat, &c.*); (pharm.) lozenge; *pl.*, note-book. *— de chocolat*; cake of chocolate. *Rayez cela de vos —s*; do not depend upon that. *Vous êtes sur mes —s*; I have you in my books.
tabletterie (-blě-trî), *n.f.*, fancy turnery trade.
tablier, *n.m.*, apron; (of carriages, of docks, of basins—*de voitures, de docks, de bassins*) apron; floor, platform (of a bridge—*d'un pont*); (fort.) platform.
tabloin, *n.m.*, (artil.) wooden platform.
tabouret, *n.m.*, stool; foot-stool; (bot.) shepherd's-pouch.
tac, *n.m.*, (vet.) rot.
tacaud, *n.m.*, (ich.) whiting-pout.
tacet (-sèt), *n.m.*, (mus.) tace, tacet. *Il a gardé le —*; he kept silent.
tache, *n.f.*, spot, stain, blot, speck; speckle, blemish. *— de rousseur*; freckle. *Avoir des —s de rousseur*; to be freckled. *C'est une — à son honneur*; it is a blot on his escutcheon.
tâche, *n.f.*, task; task-work; job. *À la —*; by the task, by the job, by the piece. *Travailler à la —, être à la —*; to work by the task, by the piece. *Prendre à — de faire une chose*; to make it one's business to do a thing. *Ouvrier à la —*; jobber.
tacher, *v.a.*, to stain; to spot; to taint; to tarnish; to blemish.
se tacher, *v.r.*, to soil one's self; to soil.
tâcher, *v.n.*, to try, to endeavour, to do one's endeavour, to strive. *Il tâche de me nuire*; he tries to harm me. *Pardonnez-lui, il n'y tâchait pas* (iron.); pardon him, he did not intend it.
tâcheron, *n.m.*, (tech.) jobber.
tacheté, **-e**, *part.*, spotted, speckled.
tacheter (tash-té), *v.a.*, to speckle, to mark with spots.
tachygraphe, *n.m.*, tachygrapher, shorthand-writer.
tachygraphie, *n.f.*, tachygraphy, shorthand-writing.
tachygraphique, *adj.*, tachygraphic.
tacite, *adj.*, tacit, implied. *— réconduction* (jur.); continuing to hold premises after the expiration of a lease, on the same conditions, but without actually renewing the lease.
tacitement (-sit-man), *adv.*, tacitly, impliedly.
taciturne, *adj.*, taciturn.
taciturnité, *n.f.*, taciturnity.
tact (takt), *n.m.*, feeling, touch; tact.
tac tac, onomatopœia, ticktack.
tacticien (-si-in), *n.m.*, tactician.
tactile, *adj.*, tactile.
tactilité, *n.f.*, tactility, tangibility.
taction, *n.f.*, taction, touch.
tactique, *n.f.* and *adj.*, tactics; tactical.
tadorne, *n.m.*, (orni.) sheldrake, shelldrake, shieldrake.

tael, n m., tael, in China, a denomination of money worth nearly 7 shil. English.

tænia, n.m. V. **ténia**.

taffetas (taf-tâ), n.m., taffeta; lustring. — *d'Angleterre;* court-plaster.

tafia, n.m., tafia (rum).

taïaut, or **tayaut**, n.m., (hunt.) tally-ho.

taïcoun. n.m. (—s), Tycoon.

taie, n.f., pillow-case; (med.) film, speck. — *d'oreiller;* pillow-case.

⊙***taillable**, n.m. and adj., person who pays taille: liable to the taille (tax—*impôt*).

*****taillade**. n.f., slash, gash, cut.

*****taillader**, v.a., to slash, to cut, to gash. *Des manches tailladées;* slashed sleeves.

*****taillanderie**. n.f., edge-tool trade; edge-tools.

*****taillandier**, n.m., edge-tool maker.

*****taillant**, n.m., edge (of edge-tools—*d'instruments tranchants*).

*****taille**, n.f., cutting, cut; edge of a sword; size, height, stature; shape, waist (of a person —*d'une personne;* tally-stick; (hort.) pruning; (surg.) cystotome; (mus.) tenor part; (feudalism—*féodalité*) taille (villain-tax—*impôt*); tax; subsidy; deal (at cards—*aux cartes*); (mus.) tenor. *Frapper d'estoc et de* —; to cut and thrust. *La* — *des arbres;* the pruning of trees. *La* — *d'un habit;* the cut of a coat. *La* — *des pierres;* the cutting of stones. *Pierre de* —; free-stone. *Il est de ma* —; he is of my size. --*douce* (—s —s); (engr.) copper-plate. *Haute-* — (mus.); upper-tenor. *Basse-*— (mus.); bass.

*****taillé**, **-e**, part., cut, carved, trimmed. *Être bien* —; to be well-shaped.

*****taille-crayon**, n.m. (— —s), pencil-pointer.

*****taille-mèche**, n.m. (— —s), wick-cutter.

*****taille-mer**, n.m. (—), (nav.) cut-water.

*****taille-plume**, n.m. (— —s), pen-cutter.

*****tailler**, v.a., to cut, to cut out; to carve; to hew; to trim, to prune; to make, to mend (pens—*les plumes*). — *un diamant;* to cut a diamond. — *des arbres;* to prune trees. — *un habit;* to cut out a coat. — *des plumes;* to make pens. — *en pièces une armée;* to cut an army to pieces.

*****tailler**, v.n., to cut (shape—*forme*). *Il peut* — *en plein drap;* he has everything at his command.

*****tailleresse**, n.f., (coin.) workwoman who formerly reduced the coined pieces to the regulation weight.

*****tailleur**, n.m., tailor; cutter; hewer; banker (at faro—*au pharaon*). — *de pierre;* stone-cutter. — *d'habits;* tailor. *Garçon* —; journeyman tailor.

*****tailleuse**. n.f., cutter out (dress-making—*de couturière*).

*****taillis**, n.m. and adj., copse, coppice, underwood; cut. *Bois* —; copse.

*****tailloir**, n.m., trencher; (arch.) abacus.

*****taillon**. n.m., a tax with which the police was paid.

tain, n.m., foil, tin-foil.

taire (taisant, tu), v.a., to say nothing of; to pass over in silence; to conceal, to suppress. *se* **taire**, v.r., to hold one's tongue, to be silent, to remain silent. *Taisez-vous;* hold your tongue, tongues. *Faire taire;* to silence.

taisson, n.m., (mam.) badger; (ich.) a Chili boneless fish.

talapoin, n.m., talapoin, telapoin; (mam.) talapoin.

talc. n.m., talc, isinglass-stone.

talcique. adj., (min.) talcky.

taled (-lèd), n.m., taled, veil worn by the Jews in their synagogues.

talent, n.m., talent, power, ability, attainments; talented person; (antiq.) talent. *Avoir du* — *pour;* to have a talent for.

⊙**taler**, n.m. V. **thaler**.

talion, n.m., retaliation, talio. *Loi du* — ; law of retaliation, lex talionis.

talisman, n.m., talisman.

talismanique, adj., talismanic.

talle, n.f., (hort.) sucker.

taller, v.n., (hort.) to throw out suckers.

tallipot, n.m., (bot.) tallipot-palm.

talmouse, n.f., cheese-cake; (pop.) slap in the face; blow with the fist.

talmud (-mud), n.m., Talmud.

talmudique, adj., Talmudical.

talmudiste, n.m., Talmudist.

taloche, n.f., thump on the head.

talon, n.m., heel; stock (at cards—*aux cartes*); heel (of shoes, razors—*de chaussures, de rasoirs*); (nav.) sole (of a rudder—*du gouvernail*); shoulder (of a sword—*d'épée*); (arch.) ogee; voucher (of receipts, checks, &c.—*de reçus, de chèques, &c.*). *Marcher sur les* —s *de quelqu'un;* to tread upon any one's heels.

talonner, v.a., to be close at the heels of; to pursue close; to press, to urge.

talonner, v.n., (nav.) to touch the ground.

talonnières, n.f. pl., (myth.) talaria, Mercury's heel wings.

talus, n.m., slope, declivity; (arch., fort.) talus.

taluter, v.a., (arch.) to slope.

tamandua, n.m., (mam.) a species of ant-eaters.

tamanoir, n.m., (mam.) a species of larger ant-eaters.

tamarin. n.m., tamarind; tamarind-tree; (mam.) tamarin.

tamarinier, n.m., tamarind, tamarind-tree, Indian acacia.

tamaris, **tamarisc**, or **tamarix**, n.m., (bot.) tamarisk.

tambour, n.m., drum; drummer; (horl.) barrel; (mec.) drum, barrel, tympan; (arch.) drum; embroidery-frame; (anat.) tympanum; paddle-box (of steamboats—*de bateaux à vapeur*). --*major* (—s —s), --*maître*(—s—s); drum-major. *Mener quelqu'un* — *battant;* to carry it with a high hand over any one, to beat any one out and out. — *de basque;* tambourine. — *voilé;* muffled drum.

tambourin, n.m., tambourine, tabour; timbrel; player on the tambourine.

tambourinage, n.m., drumming.

tambouriner, v.n., to drum, to beat the drum.

tambouriner, v.a., to advertise, to cry by the town drummer.

tambourineur, n.m., (b.s.) drummer.

taminier, n.m., (bot.) Indian acacia, black briony.

tamis, n.m., sieve. *Passer au* —; to sift.

tamisage, n.m., sifting.

*****tamisaille**, or **tamise**, n.f., (nav.) sweep of the tiller.

tamiser, v.a., to sift.

tamiser, v.n., (nav.) to shake.

tamiseur, n.m., sifter (in a glass-manufactory—*de manufacture de verre*).

tamisier, n.m., sieve-maker.

tampe, n.f., wedge (used in the manufacture of cloth—*dans la fabrication du drap*).

tamper, v.a., to fix the wedge on the friezing-table (in cloth manufacture—*dans la fabrication du drap*).

tampon, n.m., plug; stopper, pad; (artil.) tompion; (tech.) buffer.

tamponnement, n.m., plugging.

tamponner, v.a., to plug.

tam-tam, *n.m.* (— —*s*), tamtam (kind of drum—*espèce de tambour*).

tan, *n.m.*, tan (before it is used—*avant l'emploi*); tanner's bark. *Gros —;* coarse bark.

tanaisie, *n.f.*, (bot.) tansy.

tancer, *v.a.*, torebuke, to taunt, to reprimand.

tanche, *n.f.*, (ich.) tench.

tandis que (-di-), *conj.*, whilst; while; whereas.

tandour, *n.m.* (—*s*), in Greece, Turkey, and Armenia a square or round table under which is placed a pan full of embers, around which people sit to warm themselves.

tangage, *n.m.*, (nav.) pitching (of ships—*des vaisseaux*).

tangara, *n.m.*, (orni.) tanagra.

tangence, *n.f.*, (geom.) tangency.

tangent, -e, *adj.*, (geom.) tangential.

tangente, *n.f.*, (geom.) tangent.

tangibilité, *n.f.*, tangibility, tangibleness.

tangible, *adj.*, tangible.

tangon, *n.m.*, (nav.) fore-sail boom.

tanguer (-ghé), *v.n.*, (nav.) to pitch, to heave and set. *Il tangue sous voiles;* she heaves and sets (of a ship—*d'un vaisseau*).

tanière, *n.f.*, den (of wild beasts—*de bêtes sauvages*).

tanin, *n.m.*, (chem.) tannin.

tannage, *n.m.*, tanning.

tannant, -e, *adj.*, tanning, having the power of tanning; (pop.) tiresome, irksome. *Une substance —e;* a tanning substance. *Un homme —;* a bore. *Une occupation —e;* an irksome work.

tanne, *n.f.*, (med.) comedo, grub.

tanné, *n.m.*, tan-colour.

tanné, -e, *adj.*, tan-coloured.

tannée, *n.f.*, tan (after it is used—*après l'emploi*); waste tan; tanner's bark.

tanner, *v.a.*, to tan; (pop.) to vex, to tease, to annoy.

tannerie (ta-n-rî), *n.f.*, tan-yard.

tanneur, *n.m.*, tanner.

⊙**tannin**, *n.m. V.* **tanin**.

tant, *adv.*, so much; so many; as much; both; to such a degree; so; so far; so long; as far; as long. *— soit peu;* ever so little. *Tous — que nous sommes;* every one of us. *Nous sommes — à —;* we are even (at play—*au jeu*). *— petits que grands;* both small and great. *— pour vous que pour lui;* as much for you as for him. *— il était abusé;* so much was he deceived. *— il est vrai;* so true it is. *— le monde est crédule;* so credulous is the world. *— que;* as long as. *— que je vivrai;* as long as I live. *— mieux;* so much the better. *— pis;* so much the worse. *— s'en faut que;* so far from. *— il y a que;* at all events, however. *Si — est que je le puisse;* if I can. *—de monde;* so many people.

tantale, *n.m.*, Tantalus. *Supplice de —;* tantalism.

tante, *n.f.*, aunt. *Grand'—;* great aunt.

tantet, *n.m.*, the least bit, the least drop.

tantinet, *n.m.*, the least bit, the least drop.

tantôt, *adv.*, presently, by and by, soon, anon: a little while ago; just now; sometimes. *Je finirai cela —;* I shall finish that by and by. *Il est — nuit;* it will soon be night. *Il se porte — bien, — mal;* sometimes he is well, sometimes he is ill.

taon (tān), *n.m.*, (ent.) ox-fly, breeze, gad-fly.

⊙**tapabor**, *n.m.*, a kind of cap with sides that can be turned down.

tapage, *n.m.*, noise, uproar, row, racket, piece of work.

tapageur, *n.m.*, noisy fellow, blusterer.

tape, *n.f.*, rap, slap, tap, thump; (nav.) tompion.

tapecu (tap-ku), *n.m.*, swing-gate; (nav.) ring-tail, ring-sail; carriage that jolts.

tapée, *n.f.*, (pop.) a lot, a large number.

taper, *v.a.*, to strike, to hit, to slap; to frizzle (the hair—*les cheveux*); (paint.) to sketch freely; (nav.) to put a tompion in (a gun—*à un canon*).

taper, *v.n.*, to strike, to hit; to stamp; to strum (musical instruments—*instruments de musique*). *— du pied;* to stamp with one's foot.

en **tapinois**, *adv.*, stealthily, clandestinely, slily.

tapioca, *or* **tapioka**, *n.m.*, tapioca.

se **tapir**, *v.r.*, to squat, to squat down, to crouch.

tapir, *n.m.*, (mam.) tapir.

tapis, *n.m.*, carpet, rug; tapis, cover (for tables—*de table*). *Mettre sur le —;* to bring on the tapis. *Amuser le —;* to beat about the bush.

tapisser, *v.a.*, to hang with tapestry; to deck, to adorn.

tapisserie (-pî-srî), *n.f.*, tapestry, hangings; upholstery.

tapissier, *n.m.*, upholsterer, tapestry-worker.

tapissière, *n.f.*, upholsterer, tapestry-worker; tilted cart.

tapon, *n.m.*, (fam.) bundle (of clothes—*de vêtements, &c.*).

tapoter, *v.a.*, to pat, to tap.

tapure, *n.f.*, frizzling (of hair—*des cheveux*).

taquer, *v.a.*, (print.) to plane, to plane down.

taquet, *n.m.*, (nav.) whelp (of the capstern — *du cabestan*); (nav.) kevel, cleat; (joiner's work—*menuiserie*) angle-block.

taquin, -e, *n.* and *adj.*, teaser, torment (pers.); teasing.

taquinement (-ki-n-măn), *adv.*, (l.u.) teasingly.

taquiner, *v n.*, to tease, to plague.

taquinerie (-ki-n-rî), *n.f.*, teasing.

taquoir, *n.m.*, (print.) planer.

tarabuster, *v.a.*, to pester, to plague, to tease, to bother.

tarare, *n.m.*, (agri.) winnowing-machine.

tarare! *int.*, pshaw! fiddlestick! *— -ponpon!* (l.u.) brag!

taraud, *n.m.*, (tech.) tap-borer.

taraudage, *n.m.*, tapping (screws, nuts—*de vis, d'écrous*).

tarauder, *v.a.*, (tech.) to tap (screws, nuts —*vis, écrous*).

tard, *n.,adj.* and *adv.*, late; late hour. *Trop —;* too late. *Au plus —;* at the latest. *Tôt ou —;* sooner or later. *Il est —;* it is late. *Il se fait —;* it is getting late. *Il vaut mieux — que jamais;* better late than never.

tarder, *v.n.*, to delay, to put off, to stay, to tarry; to loiter, to dally; to be long. *Que tardons-nous?* what do we stay for? *Il me tarde de le faire;* I long to do it. *Il ne tardera pas à venir;* it will not be long before he comes.

tardi-f, -ve, *adj.*, tardy, late, slow; backward. *Fruits —s;* late fruits.

tardigrade, *adj.*, tardigradous.

tardigrades, *n.m.pl.*, tardigrades; also infusoria which, like the rotifier, can be revived after being dried.

tardivement (-div-măn), *adv.*, tardily, slowly.

tardiveté (-div-té), *n.f.*, (hort.) lateness.

tare, *n.f.*, (com.) tare, waste; blemish, defect, fault, imperfection.

taré, -e, *adj.*, injured, damaged, spoiled; of bad character.

tarentelle, *n.f.*, tarentella, an Italian dance.

tarentisme, *n.m.*, tarentism.

tarentule, *n.f.*, (ent.) tarentula.

tarer, *v.a.*, to injure, to damage, to hurt; (com.) to tare.

se **tarer**, *v.r.*, to spoil (of a thing—*des choses*).

targe, *n.f.*, target (shield—*bouclier*).

targette, *n.f.*, flat bolt.

se targuer (-ghé), *v.r.*, to be proud of, to boast of, to brag of.

targum (-gom), *n.m.* (—), targum.

tari, *n.m.* (—), a liquor extracted from the palm and cocoa trees.

tarier, *n.m.*, (orni.) white bustard, whinchat.

tarière, *n.f.*, wimble, auger; (ent.) terebra.

tarif, *n.m.*, tariff, rate of prices.

tarifer, *v.a.*, to tariff.

tarin, *n.m.*, (orni.) tarin.

tarir, *v.a.*, to drain, to dry up, to exhaust.

se tarir, *v.r.*, to dry up.

tarir, *v.n.*, to be drained; to dry up.

tarissable, *adj.* that can be drained or dried up; exhaustible.

tarissement (-ris-mān), *n.m.*, being dried up.

tarlatane, *n.f.*, a kind of muslin.

taroté, -e, *adj.*, checkered (of cards—*cartes*). *Des cartes —es;* cards checkered on the back.

tarots (-rô), *n.m.pl.*, checkered playing-cards.

taroupe, *n.f.*, hair growing between the eye-brows.

tarpéienne, *adj.f.*, Tarpeian, only used in *Roche —;* Tarpeian rock.

tarse, *n.m.*, tarse, tarsus.

tarsien, -ne (-si-in, -si-è-n), *adj.*, tarsal.

tarsier, *n.m.*, (mam.) tarsier.

tartan *n.m.*, tartan.

tartane, *n.f.*, (nav.) tartan.

tartare, *n.m.*, Tartar; at Constantinople, couriers employed by the Porte and European Ambassadors; (myth.) hell.

tartareu-x, -se, *adj.*, tartareous.

tartarin, *n.m.*, Barbary ape.

tartarique, *adj.*, tartaric. *V.* **tartrique**.

tarte, *n.f.*, (cook.) tart.

tartelette, *n.f.*, little tart.

tartine, *n.f.*, slice of bread spread with butter, preserves, &c.; (fig.) long, tedious, uninstructive speech or newspaper article.

tartrate, *n.m.*, (chem.) tartrate.

tartre, *n.m.*, (chem.) tartar.

tartrique, *adj.*, (chem.) tartaric.

tartufe, *n.m.*, tartuffe, hypocrite.

tartuferie (-tu-fri), *n.f.*, hypocrisy.

tas, *n.m.*, heap, pile; lot, set (of persons—*de personnes*); hand-anvil; (agri.) shock. *Mettre en —;* to put in a heap. — *de pierres;* heap of stones. *Un — de filous;* a set of sharpers.

tasse, *n.f.*, cup.

tasseau, *n.m.*, (arch.) hammer-beam, tassel.

tassée, *n.m.*, cupful.

tassement (tâs-mān), *n.m.*, (arch.) settling, sinking.

tasser, *v.a.*, to heap up, to pile up; to ram, to beat down.

se tasser, *v.r.*, (arch.) to sink, to settle.

tasser, *v.n.*, (arch.) to settle; to sink; (hort.) to grow thick.

tassette, *n.m.*, tasses, tassets (of armour—*d'armure*).

tâte-poule, *n.m.* (—), (pop.) molly-cot; molly.

tâter, *v.a.* and *n.*, to feel; to try, to taste; to sound. — *le pouls;* to feel the pulse. — *de quelque chose;* to taste any thing.

se tâter, *v.r.*, to examine one another, to examine one's self.

tâteu-r, *n.m.*, **-se**, *n.f.*, irresolute person.

tâte-vin, *n.m.* (—), wine-taster (instrument).

*tatillon, *n.m.*, **-ne**, *n.f.*, meddler, busy-body.

*tatillonnage, *n.m.*, meddling, intermeddling.

*tatillonner, *v.n.*, to meddle, to intermeddle.

tâtonnement (-to-n-mān), *n.m.*, feeling one's way, groping.

tâtonner, *v.n.*, to feel one's way, to grope.

tâtonneu-r, *n.m.*, **-se**, *n.f.*, groper.

à tâtons, *adv.*, feeling one's way, groping; in seeking one's way.

tatou, *n.m.*, (mam.) armadillo, tatou, dasypus.

tatouage, *n.m.*, tattooing.

tatouer, *v.a.*, to tattoo.

tattersall, *n.m.* (*n.p.*), tattersall.

taudion, *n.m.*, (pop.). *V.* **taudis**.

taudis, *n.m.*, dirty place, dirty lodging, hole, hovel.

taupe, *n.f.*, (mam.) mole; (vet.) ○ pollevil; (med.) ⊙ wen, *V.* **loupe**; (pers.) cunning fox.

*taupe-grillon, *n.m.* (—*s* —*s*), (ent.) molecricket.

taupier, *n.m.*, mole-catcher.

taupière, *n.m.*, mole-trap.

taupinière, *n.f.*, mole-hill; little hut.

taupins (francs), *n.m.pl.*, the name of a French militia in King Charles VII.'s reign.

taure, *n.f.*, heifer.

tauréador, *n.m.* (—*s*). *V.* **toréador**.

taureau, *n.m.*, bull; (astron.) Taurus. — *sauvage;* wild bull. *Un combat de —x;* a bullfight.

tauricorne, *adj.*, tauricornous.

taurobole, *n.m.*, (antiq.) sacrifice of a bull offered to Cybele; the altar on which this sacrifice was made.

tautochrone (-krô-n), *adj.*, tautochronous.

tautochronisme (-kro-), *n.m.*, tautochronism.

tautogramme, *n.m.*, a poem every word of which begins with the same letter.

tautologie, *n.f.*, tautology.

tautologique, *adj.*, tautological.

taux, *n.m.*, price, rate; assessment.

tavaïolle, *n.f.*, chrisom-cloth; cloth for consecrated bread; anti-macassar.

taveler (ta-vlé), *v.a.*, to spot, to speckle.

tavelure (ta-vlur), *n.f.*, spots, speckles.

taverne, *n.f.*, tavern, pot-house.

taverni-er, *n.m.*, **-ère**, *n.f.*, tavern-keeper.

taxateur, *n.m.*, (jur.) taxer; letter-taxer.

taxation, *n.f.*, taxation; fixing of prices.

taxe, *n.f.*, assize, price, price fixed; tax, assessment, impost, toll.

taxer, *v.a.*, to rate, to fix the price of; to assess; to tax, to lay a tax upon; to charge, to accuse. *On le taxa d'avarice;* they taxed him with avarice.

se taxer, *v.r.*, to tax one's self.

taxiarque, *n.m.*, (antiq.) commander of an army corps, a brigadier.

taxidermie, *n.f.*, taxidermy.

taxis, *n.f.*, (surg.) pressure exerted with the hand to reduce a hernia.

tayaut, *n.m.* (hunt.). *V.* **taïaut**.

tayon, *n.m.*, staddle about 9 years old (forestry—*eaux et forêts*).

tchèque, *n.m.*, (philology) Tzechish (language—*langue*).

té, *n.m.*, (fort.) mines having the shape of a T, to blow up an enemy's fortification.

te, *pron.*, thee, to thee, you, to you. *Il — loue;* he praises thee, you. — *voilà;* there you are.

technique (tèk-nik), *adj.*, technical.

technique (tèk-nik), *n.f.*, technics.

technique (tèk-nik), *n.m.*, (arts) material execution, make, style.

techniquement (tèk-nik-mān), *adv.*, technically.

technologie (tèk-no-), *n.f.*, technology.

technologique (tèk-no-), *adj.*, technological.

teck, *or* **tek**, *n.m.*, (bot.) teak, teak-wood.

te deum (té-dé-om), *n.m.* (—), Te Deum.

tégument, *n.m.*, tegument ; (anat.) integument.

*tegignasse, *n.f.* *V.* **tignasse**.

*teigne. *n.f.*, (med.) ringworm of the scalp, trichonosis tonsurans, tinea capitis ; (ent.) moth ; (vet.) thrush.

*teigneu-x, -se, *n.* and *adj.*, person suffering with ringworm of the scalp ; pertaining, relating to ringworm of the scalp.

*teillage, *n.m.* *V.* **tillage**.

*teille, *n.f.* *V.* **tille**.

*teiller, *v.a.* *V.* **tiller**.

*teilleur, *n.m.*, -se, *n.f.*, (agri.) *V.* **tilleur**.

teindre (*teignant, teint), *v.a.*, to dye, to tinge, to stain.

teint, *n.m.*, (dy.) dye, colour ; tincture ; complexion.

teinte, *n.f.*, (paint.) tint ; tincture ; shade, dye. *Demi- — (—s —s)* ; mezzotinto.

teinter, *v.a.*, (paint.) to tint.

teinture, *n.f.*, dye, dyeing ; (pharm.) tincture ; (fig.) superficial knowledge, smattering.

teinturerie (-tur-rî), *n.f.*, dye-shop ; dye-works.

teinturi-er, *n.m.*, -ère, *n.f.*, dyer.

tel, -le, *adj.*, such, like ; similar ; such an one. — *maître,* — *valet ;* like master, like man. *M. un —;* Mr. such an one. *J'irai dans —le ville à —le époque ;* I shall go to such a town at such a time. — *quel ;* such as it is.

télamons, *n.m.pl.*, (arch.) telamones.

télégramme, *n.m.*, telegram.

télégraphe, *n.m.*, telegraph. — *électrique ;* electric telegraph.

télégraphie, *n.f.*, telegraphy.

télégraphier, *v.a.*, to telegraph.

télégraphique, *adj.*, telegraphic.

télescope, *n.m.*, telescope.

télescopique, *adj.*, telescopic.

tellement (tèl-màn), *adv.*, so, in such a manner ; so much ; so far. — *que ;* so that. — *quellement ;* indifferently, so-so.

tellière, *n.f.*, foolscap paper.

tellure, *n.m.*, (chem.) tellurium.

tellurique, *adj.*, (chem.) telluric.

téméraire, *n.m.f.* and *adj.*, rash person ; rash, fool-hardy. *Un coup —;* a rash enterprise. *Jugement —;* rash judgment.

témérairement (-rèr-màn), *adv.*, rashly.

témérité, *n.f.*, temerity, rashness.

*témoignage, *n.m.*, testimony, evidence ; testimonial ; witness. *Rendre — à la vérité de ;* to bear witness to the truth of. *Appeler en —;* to call to witness. *En — de quoi ;* in witness whereof.

*témoigner. *v.a.*, to testify ; to show. — *du chagrin ;* to show sorrow. — *de l'amitié ;* to testify friendship.

*témoigner, *v.n.*, to testify ; to witness, to bear witness.

témoin, *n.m.*, witness, evidence ; testimony ; proof ; mark ; second (in duels). — *auriculaire ;* ear-witness. — *à charge ;* witness, evidence, for the prosecution. — *à décharge ;* witness, evidence, for the prisoner. — *oculaire :* eye-witness. *Prendre à —;* to call to witness.

tempe, *n.f.*, (anat.) temple.

tempérament, *n.m.*, constitution, temperament ; temper ; medium. *Un — ruiné ;* a broken constitution.

tempérance, *n.f.*, temperance, sobriety.

tempérant. -e, *adj.*, temperate, sober ; (med.) sedative.

tempérant, *n.m.*, temperate man ; (med.) sedative.

température, *n.f.*, temperature.

tempéré, *n.m.*, temperate, temperature ; (rhet.) middle style.

tempéré, -e, *adj.*, temperate, mild ; mixed (governments) ; (rhet.) middle.

tempérer, *v.a.*, to temper, to allay, to mollify.

tempête, *n.f.*, tempest, storm.

tempêter, *v.n.*, to storm, to bluster.

tempétueu-x, -se, *adj.*, tempestuous, boisterous.

temple, *n.m.*, temple.

templier, *n.m.*, templar, knight-templar.

temporaire, *adj.*, temporary.

temporairement, *adv.*, temporarily.

temporal, -e, *adj.*, (anat.) temporal.

⊙**temporalité**, *n.f.*, temporality. °

temporel, -le, *adj.*, temporal.

temporel, *n.m.*, (ecc.) temporalities ; (pol.) temporal power.

temporellement (-rèl-màn), *adv.*, temporally.

temporisateur, -rice, *n.* and *adj.*, procrastinator, temporizer ; procrastinating, temporizing.

temporisation, *n.f.*, temporizing, procrastination.

temporisement, *n.m.*, (l.u.) procrastination, delay.

temporiser, *v.n.*, to temporize, to delay, to procrastinate.

temporiseur, *n.m.*, (l.u.). *V.* **temporisateur**.

temps (tàn), *n.m.*, time, while, period, term ; leisure ; season ; weather ; (gram.) tense ; (mus.) time-stroke. *Passer son — à étudier ;* to spend one's time in study. *Il a fait son —;* he has had his day, he has served his time. *Du —; d'Auguste ;* in the time of Augustus. *Dans le —;* formerly, of yore. *Avec le —;* in time, in course of time. *En même —;* at the same time. *À —;* in time. *De — en —;* from time to time, now and then. *De tout —;* at all times. *À quelque — de là ;* some time after. *S'accommoder au —;* to comply with the times. *Tuer le —;* to kill time. *Le — perdu ne se retrouve point ;* lost time is never found again. *En — et lieu ;* in proper time and place. *Prendre bien son —;* to choose one's time well. *Quel — fait-il ?* what sort of weather is it ? *Il fait beau —;* it is fine weather. *Gros —* (nav.) ; stormy weather, foul weather. *Mauvais —;* bad weather. *— fait ;* settled weather.

tenable, *adj.*, tenable.

tenace, *adj.*, tenacious, adhesive, sticky ; niggardly, stingy ; retentive (of the memory— *de la mémoire*).

ténacité, *n.f.*, tenacity, tenaciousness, adhesiveness ; retentiveness (of the memory—*de la mémoire*) ; stinginess, niggardliness.

*tenaille, *n.f.*, (fort.) tenaille ; pincers, nippers, pinchers, tongs.

*tenailler, *v.a.*, to torture with red-hot tongs ; (fig.) to torture, to torment.

*tenaillon, *n.m.*, (fort.) tenaillon.

tenance, *n.f.*, (feudalism—*féodalité*)tenancy.

tenanci-er, *n.m.*, -ère. *n.f.*, (feudalism— *féodalité*) holder, sub-tenant.

tenant, *n.m.*, (at a tournament—*dans les tournois*) challenger ; supporter of an opinion ; defender of any one ; person who frequents a house and acts like the master in it. *Les —s et aboutissants ;* the adjacent lands, houses, &c. ; (fig.) details, particulars, circumstances.

tenant, -e, *adj.*, seldom used but in the expression : *séance —e ;* before the meeting separates.

ténare, *n.m.*, (poet.?) Tænarus, the pagans'? hell.

tendance, *n.f.*, tendency.

tendant, -e, *adj.,* tending.

tendelet (tan-dlè), *n.m.,* (nav.) awning, canopy ; (arch.) tilt.

tender (tin-dèr), *n.m.,* (railways¿) tender.

tendeur, *n.m.,* hanger (of tapestry—*de tapisserie*); spreader, layer (of snares—*de pièges*).

tendineu-x, -se, *adj.,* tendinous.

tendon, *n.m.,* (anat.) tendon, sinew.

tendre, *adj.,* tender, soft; delicate, fond, affectionate, loving; new (of bread—*du pain*). *Du pain* —; new bread. *Avoir le cœur* —; to be tender-hearted. *Regarder quelqu'un d'un air* —; to look at any one tenderly. *Un métal* —; a soft metal. *Couleur* —; delicate colour.

tendre, *n.m.,* (fam.) tenderness, affection.

tendre, *v.a.,* to bend, to stretch, to spread, to lay; to strain; to set; to hold out; to pitch (tents—*des tentes*); to hang (tapestry—*tapisserie*). — *un arc;* to bend a bow. — *une souricière;* to set a mouse-trap. — *un lit;* to put up a bed. *Il me tendit la main;* he stretched out his hand to me. — *la joue;* to hold out the cheek. — *les bras à quelqu'un;* to lend any one a helping hand. — *une tente;* to pitch a tent.

tendre, *v.n.,* to lead to; to tend; to conduce; to hang tapestry, &c. *Où tend ce chemin?* where does that road lead to?

tendrement, *adv.,* tenderly, affectionately.

tendresse, *n.f.,* tenderness, love, fondness; *pl.,* tender caresses. — *extravagante;* extravagant fondness, dotage.

tendreté, *n.f.,* (l.u.) tenderness (of fruit or meat, &c.—*des fruits, de la viande, &c.*).

tendron, *n.m.,* shoot (of plants—*des plantes*); gristle; (fam.) young girl.

tendu, -e, *part.,* bent; tight, stiff; strained. *Style* —; stiff style.

ténèbres, *n.f.pl.,* darkness, night, gloom; (c.rel.) tenebræ.

ténébreusement (-eûz-măn), *adv.,* in darkness; in a gloomy manner.

ténébreu-x, -se, *adj.,* dark, tenebrous, gloomy, obscure, overcast, melancholy; underhand.

tènement (tè-n-măn), *n.m.,* (feudalism—*féodalité*) tenement.

ténesme, *n.m.,* (med.) tenesmus.

tenettes, *n.f.pl.,* (surg.) lithotomy forceps, extractor.

teneur, *n.f.,* terms, text; purport.

teneur de livres, *n.m.,* book-keeper.

tenez! *int. V.* **tiens.**

ténia, *n.m.,* tænia, tape-worm.

tenir (tenant, tenu), *v.a.,* to hold, to have hold of, to have; to contain; to possess, to be possessed of, to occupy; to take up, to keep; to perform (promises—*promesses*); to account, to look upon, to consider, to think. *Tenez, voilà ce que je vous dois;* here, there is what I owe you. — *la vie de quelqu'un;* to be the child of any one; to have been preserved from death by any one. *Vous tenez trop de place;* you take up too much room. — *une maison;* to keep a house. — *boutique;* to keep a shop. — *le lit;* to keep one's bed. — *le large* (nav.); to navigate on the high seas. — *la mer* (nav.); to keep the sea; to navigate on the high seas; to be sea-worthy. — *la campagne* (milit.); to have taken the field. — *la tête droite;* to hold up one's head. — *les yeux baissés;* to keep one's eyes down. *Cela m'a tenu plus que je ne pensais;* that detained me longer than I thought. *Je tiens cela pour certain;* I hold that for a certainty. *Je le tiens honnête homme, je le tiens pour honnête homme;* I look upon him as an honest man. *Voilà la conduite qu'il tient;* such is the way in which he behaves. — *sa parole;* to keep one's word. *Cessez de* — *ce langage;* cease to hold this language, to speak in such a

manner. *Il tient table ouverte;* he keeps open house. — *les livres en partie double;* to keep books by double entry. — *la caisse;* to be a cashier. — *registre de quelque chose;* to keep an account of any thing. *Je tiendrai compte de cela;* I shall take that into consideration. — *quelqu'un à distance;* to keep any one at a distance. — *quelque chose dans la main;* to hold any thing in one's hand. *Faire* — *des lettres à quelqu'un;* to forward letters to any one. — *lieu de;* to be instead of. *Il m'a tenu lieu de père;* he has been like a father to me.

se tenir, *v.r.,* to hold, to hold on, to hold fast, to cling, to adhere, to stick; to keep, to stay; to keep one's self; to be; to stand, to lie; to remain; to be held; to sit; to think one's self, to consider one's self; to contain one's self, to refrain. *Il se tint à une branche;* he laid hold of a branch. *Je n'y tiens;* I stand (at cards—*aux cartes*). *S'en tenir;* to rely on, to adhere to. *Je m'en tiens à votre avis;* I stick to your advice. — *mal à cheval;* not to sit well on horseback. *Tenez-vous là;* stay there. — *en embuscade;* to lie in ambush. — *sur ses gardes;* to stand upon one's guard. *Tenez-vous en repos;* be quiet. — *à ne rien faire;* to stand doing nothing. — *les bras croisés;* to sit with one's arms crossed. — *à genoux;* to be, to remain, upon one's knees. — *debout;* to stand up. — *droit;* to stand straight.

tenir, *v.n.,* to hold, to hold fast; to be contiguous; to hang; to adhere, to stick; to be held (of fairs, markets, assemblies—*de foires, de marchés, d'assemblées, &c.*); to take after; to be of the nature; to keep together, to remain; to withstand, to resist; (milit.) to hold out; to subsist; to be connected with; to be desirous; to proceed, to result. — *bon;* to hold out, to stick fast. *Il tient à le faire;* he is anxious to do it. *Il ne tient pas à moi qu'elle ne vienne pas;* it is not my fault that she does not come. *Qu'à cela ne tienne;* never mind, that makes no difference. *La vie ne tient qu'à un fil;* life hangs but on a thread. *S'il ne tient qu'à cela;* if that is all. *À quoi tient-il que?* how is it that? *Il tient de son père;* he takes after his father. *Ce clou ne tient pas;* this nail does not hold. *Je n'y tiens plus;* I cannot stand it any longer. *Il vaut mieux* — *que courir* (prov.); a bird in the hand is better than two in the bush.

tenon, *n.m.,* tenon; bolt (of fire-arms—*d'armes à feu*); nut (of an anchor—*d'une ancre*).

ténor, *n.m.* (—*s*), (mus.) tenor.

ténotomie, *n.f.,* (surg.) tenotomy.

tensi-f, -ve, *adj.,* tense.

tension, *n.f.,* tension. — *d'esprit;* intense application of mind.

tenson, *n.f.,* (ancient poet.) troubadours' poetry, tenzon.

tentacule, *n.m.* (ent.) tentacle, feeler.

tentant, -e, *adj.,* tempting.

tentat-eur, *n.m.,* **-rice,** *n.f.,* tempter.

tentation. *n.f.,* temptation. *Il résista à la* —; he resisted the temptation.

tentative, *n.f.,* attempt, trial, endeavour.

tente, *n.f.,* tent, pavilion.

tenter, *v.a.,* to attempt, to try, to tempt.

tenture, *n.f.,* tapestry, hangings.

tenu, -e, *part.,* held, kept; bound, obliged; reputed, considered. *Je ne suis pas* — *à cela;* I am not bound to that. *À l'impossible nul n'est* —; there's no flying without wings.

ténu, -e, *adj.,* tenuous.

tenue, *n.f.,* holding (of assemblies—*d'assemblées*); session; attitude (of a person on horseback—*d'une personne à cheval*); dress; deportment, carriage, bearing, address; appearance (of troops—*de troupes*); keeping (of books—*de livres*); (mus.) holding-note; (nav.) anchor-hold; holding (of the pen—*de la plume*); steadiness (of a thing—*d'une chose*). *Tout d'une* —; contiguous (of lands—*de pièces de terre*). *Grande* — (milit.); full dress. *Petite* — (milit.); undress. — *des livres*; book-keeping.

ténuirostres, *n.m.pl.*, (orni.) tenuirostres.

ténuité, *n.f.*, tenuity.

tenure, *n.f.*, tenure.

téorbe, *n.m.*, (mus.) theorbo. archlute.

tépide, *adj.*, (l.u.). V. **tiède**.

tépidité, *n.f.*, (l.u.). V. **tiédeur**.

ter (tèr), *adv.*, third house of the same number; (mus.) three times.

tératologie, *n.f.*, (physiology) teratology.

tercer. *or* **terser** (tèr-), *v.a.*, to dress vines a third time.

tercet (tèr-sè), *n.m.*, tiercet (poet.).

térébenthine, *n.f.*, turpentine.

térébinthacées, *n.f.pl.*, (bot.) the turpentine-tree tribe.

térébinthe, *n.m.*, (bot.) turpentine-tree.

térébrant, *adj.*, (med.) keen, lancinating pain; (mol.) terebrating.

térébrants, *n.m.pl.*, (ent.) terebrantia.

térébration, *n.f.*, terebration.

tergiversation, *n.f.*, tergiversation, shift, evasion.

tergiverser, *v.n.*, to tergiversate, to shift, to practise evasion.

terme (tèrm), *n.m.*, term; termination; bound, end, limit; time; quarter's-rent, quarter-day; boundary; word, expression; *pl.*, state, condition. *Toucher au* —; to draw near the term. *Payer son* —; to pay one's rent. *Parler en* —*s choisis;* to make use of choice words.

termès, *n.m.* V. **termite**.

terminaison, *n.f.*, termination, end, ending.

terminal. **-e**, *adj.*, (bot.) terminal.

terminati-f, **-ve**, *adj.*, (gram.) terminational.

terminer (tèr-), *v.a.*, to terminate, to end, to bound, to limit, to put an end to, to conclude, to bring to a close.

se **terminer**, *v.r.*, to end, to come to an end, to terminate, to be bounded; to conclude, to come to a conclusion.

terminologie, *n.f.*, terminology.

termite, *or* **termès**, *n.m.*, (ent.) white ant; termes, (pl.) termites.

ternaire (tèr-nèr), *adj.*, ternary.

terne (tèr-n), *adj.*, tarnished, dull; wan, tame, spiritless.

terne (tèr-n), *n.m.*, two threes (at dice—*aux dés*); trey (in the lottery—*à la loterie*).

terné, **-e** (tèr-), *adj.*, (bot.) ternate.

ternir, *v.a.*, to tarnish, to dull; to deaden; to sully; to stain. — *des couleurs;* to deaden the colours. — *sa gloire;* to tarnish one's glory.

se **ternir**, *v.r.*, to tarnish, to grow dull, to be sullied; to fade (of colours—*des couleurs*).

ternissure, *n.f.*, tarnishing, dullness.

terrage, *n.m.*, claying (of sugar—*du sucre*); (feudalism—*féodalité*) lord's right to take certain products of a tenant's lands.

terrain, *n.m.*, ground; ground-plot; piece of ground. *Gagner du* —; to gain ground.

terral, *n.m.*, (nav.) wind coming from land.

terraqué, **-e** (-ké), *adj.*, terraqueous.

terrasse, *n.f.*, terrace; (paint.) fore-ground.

terrassement (-ras-màn), *n.m.*..earth-work.

terrasser, *v.a.*, to fill in walls behind with earth-work; to throw on the ground; to fell, to throw down; to knock down; to confound, to throw into consternation.

terrasseu-x, **-se**, *adj.*, earthy (of marble, stones—*du marbre, des pierres*).

terrassier, *n.m.*, digger, excavator, navvie.

terre, *n.f.*, earth, land, ground, mould; dominion, territory, grounds, estate. *Cultiver la* —; to till the ground. — *ferme;* dry-land, terra firma. *Se coucher à* —; to lie flat on the ground. *Jeter un homme à* —; to throw a man on the ground. — *à foulon;* fuller's earth. — *à potier;* potter's earth. *Vaisselle de* —; earthenware. *Mettre pied à* —; to alight. *Mettre à* —; to put down; (nav.) to land. *Perdre* —; to lose sight of land; to get out of one's depth (in swimming—*en nageant*). *Aller à* —; to have no elevated ideas, to grovel on the earth; (man.) to passage low; (nav.) to sail along the coast. — *franche;* vegetable mould. — *à porcelaine;* china clay. *Par* —; on the ground, on the floor; by land. *À* —; on the ground, on the floor. *Tomber par* —, *tomber à* —; to fall down. *Aller par* —; to go by land.

terreau, *n.m.*, (gard.) vegetable mould; mould, compost.

terre d'ombre, *n.f.* V. **ombre**.

terre-mérite, *n.f.* (n.p.), turmeric in powder.

terre-neuve, *n.m.* (—), Newfoundland dog.

terre-neuvier, *n.m.* (— —*s*), (nav.)banker; Newfoundland fisher; Newfoundland dog.

terre-noix, *n.f.* (—), (bot.) pig-nut, earth-nut, ground-nut.

terre-plein, *n.m.* (— —*s*), (fort.) terre-plein; platform.

terrer, *v.a.*, (gard.) to renew the mould of; to clay (sugar—*le sucre*).

se **terrer**, *v.r.*, to earth, to burrow.

terrer, *v.n.*, to burrow.

terrestre, *adj.*, terrestrial, earthly.

terrette, *n.f.*, ground-ivy.

terreur (tè-reur), *n.f.*, terror, trepidation, awe, dread. *Temps de la* —; (French hist.) Reign of Terror.

terreu-x, **-se**, *adj.*, terreous, earthy; dirty; dull (of colours—*des couleurs*); cadaverous (of the countenance—*du visage*). *Avoir le visage* —; to have a cadaverous-looking face.

terrible (tè-ribl), *adj.*, terrible, dreadful, awful; wild (of children—*des enfants*).

terriblement (tè-ri-), *adv.*, terribly, dreadfully, awfully; with a vengeance.

terrien (tè-ri-in), *n.m.*, **-ne** (tè-ri-è-n), *n.f.*, landholder; ⊙ prince possessing large dominions.

terrien, **-ne** (tè-ri-in, -è-n), *adj.*, of him who possesses land; ⊙ earthly.

terrier (tè-rié), *n.m.*, terrier (hole—*trou*), burrow, hole; terrier (dog—*chien*); (feudalism —*féodalité*) terrier.

terrier (tè-rié), *adj.m.*, only used in the expression: *papier* —; terrier (feudalism—*féodalité*).

terrifier (tèr-ri-), *v.a.*, to terrify.

terrine (tè-ri-n), *n.f.*, earthen-pan; (cook.) dish (ragout).

terrinée (tè-ri-), *n.f.*, panful.

terrir (tè-rir), *v.n.*, to lay eggs in earth or sand (of the tortoise—*de la tortue*); (nav.) to land.

territoire (tè-ri-toar), *n.m.*, territory; jurisdiction.

territorial, **-e** (tè-ri-), *adj.*, territorial.

terroir (tè-rόar), *n.m.*, soil, ground.

terroriser (tèr-ro-), *v.a.*, to govern by terror.

terrorisme (tèr-ro-), *n.m.*, terrorism.

terroriste (tèr-ro-), *n.m.*, terrorist.

terser (tèr-), *v.a.* V. **tercer**.

tertiaire (tèr-siè-r), *adj.*, (geol., med.) tertiary.

tertio (tèr-siö), *adv.*, thirdly.

tertre (tèr-), *n.m.*, hillock, rising ground.

tes (tè), *possessive adj.pl.*, thy. V. **ton**.

tessère (tè-), *n.f.*, (antiq.) square tablet used as token, tally, ticket, etc.; watchword.

tesson (tè-), *or* **têt** (tè), *n.m.*, fragment of broken glass or earthenware.

test (tèst), *n.m.*, (English hist.) test.

test (tèst), *or* **têt** (tè), *n.m.*, (zool.) shell.

testacé (tès-), *n.m.*, shelled animal, testacean.

testacé, -e. (tès-), *adj.*, testaceous.

testament (tès-), *n.m.*, Testament ; testament, will, last will and testament. *Ancien —* ; Old Testament. *Nouveau —* ; New Testament. *Faire son —* ; to make one's will.

testamentaire (tès-), *adj.*, testamentary.

⊙**testat** (tès-tat), *adj.*, testate.

testat-eur, *n.m.*, **-rice,** *n.f.*, (tès-), testator, testatrix.

tester (tès-), *v.n.*, to make one's will. *Mourir sans —* ; to die intestate.

testicule (tès-), *n.m.*, testicle.

testif (tès-), *n.m.*, camel's hair.

testimonial, -e (tès-), *adj.*, testifying.

⊙**teston** (tès-), *n.m.*, a silver coin formerly used in France.

⊙**testonner** (tès-), *v.a.*, to comb, and dress the hair.

têt (tè), *or* **test** (tèst), *n.m.*, (chem., metal.) test, cupel.

⊙**têt** (tè), *n.m.*, (anat.) the skull.

tétanique, *adj.*, (med.) tetanic.

tétanos (-nos), *n.m.*, (med.) tetanus ; lock-jaw.

têtard, *n.m.*, tadpole ; pole-socket (of carriages—*de voitures*) ; (ich.) bull-head, miller's thumb.

tetasses (té-), *n.f.pl.*, (triv.) flabby and hanging-down breasts.

tête, *n.f.*, head ; brains, sense, judgment ; presence of mind, self-possession ; hair, head of hair ; horns (of stags—*de cerfs*) ; front, head (of a bridge—*de pont*) ; top (of things—*des choses*) ; (milit.) van, vanguard ; court-card (of playing-cards—*de cartes à jouer*) ; (bot.) capitulum. —*de Méduse* ; Medusa's head ; (fig.) anything producing terror, anything horrible. *Mal de —* ; headache. *Signe de —* ; nod. *Payer tant par —* ; to pay so much a head, a piece. *Aller la — levée* ; to carry one's head high. *Donner — baissée contre* ; to run full butt at. *Avoir la — fêlée* ; to be crack-brained. *Avoir des affaires par-dessus la —* ; to be over head and ears in business. *Avoir de la —* ; to have presence of mind, to be resolute. *Crier à tue —* ; to bawl out loud. *— baissée* ; headlong. *— pelée, chauve* ; bald head. *Cela lui met martel en —* ; that worries him to death. *La — me fend* ; my head is ready to split. *La — me tourne* ; my head is giddy. *La — lui a tourné* ; he has lost his senses. *Il ne sait où donner de la —* ; he does not know which way to turn. *Autant de —s, autant d'opinions* ; so many men, so many minds. *Il y va de votre —* ; your life is at stake. *Vous en répondrez sur votre —* ; your head will answer for it. *Il est homme de —* ; he has a good head. *Il a la — dure* ; he has a thick head, he is dull of understanding. *C'est une mauvaise —* ; he is an obstinate fellow. *Avoir une chose en —* ; to have a thing in one's head, to be bent upon a thing. *Perdre la —* ; to lose one's head, to lose one's self-possession ; to lose one's wits, to be crazy. *Agir de —* ; to act with prudence. *Faire à sa —* ; to have one's own way, to follow one's own bent. *Avoir la — chaude* ; to be hot-headed. *Tenir à quelqu'un* ; to cope with any one. *Tourner la — à quelqu'un* ; to turn any one's head, brain. *De la — aux pieds* ; from head to foot ; from top to toe. *Faire un signe de —* ; to nod. *— de mort* ; death's head. *En —* ; in one's head ; in front, ahead. *— d'âne* (ich.) ; miller's thumb, bull-head. cottus.

tête-à-tête, *n.m.* (—), tête-à-tête, private conversation, face to face.

tête-bleu! *int.*, zounds !

teter (té-), *or* **téter,** *v.a.*, to suck milk from persons or animals.

teter (té-), *or* **téter,** *v.n.*, to suck. *Donner à — à* ; to give suck to, to suckle.

têtière (-ti-è-r), *n.f.*, infant's cap ; head-stall (of a bridle—*d'une bride*).

tetin (té-), *n.m.*, nipple, teat ; ⊙bosom.

tetine (té-), *n.f.*, (cook.) udder ; dent made by a shot on a cuirass.

teton (té-), *n.m.*, teat, breast (of a woman—*de femme*). *Bouton du —* ; pap, nipple.

tetonnière (té-), *n.f.*, band to support the breast of a woman ; (l.ex.) full-breasted woman.

tétra, a prefix from Gr. τετρα.

tétracorde, *n.m.*, tetrachord.

tétradrachme, *n.m.* and *f.*, (antiq.) tetradrachm.

tétradynamie, *n.f.*, (bot.) tetradynamia.

tétraèdre, *n.m.*, (geom.) tetrahedron.

tétragone, *n.m.* and *adj.*, (geom.) tetragon ; tetragonal.

tétralogie, *n.f.*, (antiq.) tetralogy.

tétramètre, *n.m.*, tetrameter.

tétrandrie, *n.f.*, (bot.) tetrandria.

tétrapétale, -e, *adj.*, (bot.) tetrapetalous.

tétraphylle, *adj.*, (bot.) tetraphyllous.

tétrarcat, *or* **tétrarchat,** *n.m.*, tetrarchate.

tétrarchie, *n.f.*, tetrarchy.

tétrarque, *n.m.*, tetrarch.

tétras (-trâs), *n.m.*, (orni.) grouse.

tétrastyle, *n.m.*, (arch.) tetrastyle.

tétrasyllabe, *n.m.*, (gram.) quadrisyllable.

tetto (tèt), *n.f.*, teat, dug (of animals—*des animaux*).

tette-chèvre (tèt-), *n.m.* (— —s), (orni.) goat-sucker, fern-owl.

têtu, -e, *adj.*, headstrong, wilful, stubborn, obstinate.

têtu, *n.m.*, (tech.) granite hammer.

teutonique, *adj.*, Teutonic.

texte (tèkst), *n.m.*, text ; (jur.) purview ; passage (of Scripture—*de l'Écriture sainte*). *Petit —* (print.) ; brevier. *Gros —* (print.) ; two-line brevier. *Revenir à son —* ; to return to the point. *Restituer un —* ; to restore a text. *Livre de —* ; text-book.

textile (tèks-til), *n.m.* and *adj.*, textile fabric ; textile.

textuaire (tèks-tu-è-r), *n.m.*, book containing the text without comment.

textuel, -le (tèks-tu-èl), *adj.*, textual.

textuellement (tèks-tu-èi-mán), *adv.*, conformably to the text, word for word, verbatim.

texture (tèks-tur), *n.f.*, weaving, texture ; connection, texture.

thalame, *n.m.*, (bot.) thalamus.

thaler (-lèr), *n.m.*, dollar (German coin—*pièce de monnaie allemande*).

thallium, *n.m.* (n.p.), (chem.) a recently discovered metal.

thalweg, *n.m.* (—s), (geog.) thalweg, line followed by the waters of a valley ; middle line of a river.

thane, *n.m.*, thane (Saxon or Danish baron—*baron saxon ou danois*).

thapsie, *n.f.*, (bot.) deadly carrot.

thaumaturge, *n.m.* and *adj.*, thaumaturgus ; thaumaturgic, thaumaturgical.

thaumaturgie, *n.f.*, thaumaturgy.

thé, *n.m.*, tea ; tea-party ; (bot.) tea-tree. *Boîte à —* ; tea-caddy, tea-canister. *Cabaret à —, service à —* ; tea-things, set of tea-things, tea-service, tea-equipage.

théatin, *n.m.*, theatin (monk—*moine*).

théâtral, -e, *adj.*, theatric, theatrical.

théâtralement, *adv.*, theatrically.

théâtre, *n.m.*, theatre, playhouse; stage; plays (collection); theatre (scene, place of action—*lieu d'une action*); scene. *Monter sur le* —; to appear upon the stage, to act, to tread the boards. *Changement de* —; change of scenery. *Coup de* —; unexpected event, striking event; (fam.) clap-trap. *— de la guerre*; seat of war. *— de Corneille*; Corneille's plays. *Roi de* —; shadow of a king. *Accommoder un sujet au* —; to adapt a subject to the stage.

thébaïde, *n.f.*, Egyptian desert into which pious Christian hermits had retired; (fig.) a lonely, deserted place.

thébain, *n.m.*, Theban.

théière, *n.f.*, tea-pot.

théiforme,*adj.*,prepared like tea (infusions).

théisme, *n.m.*, theism.

théiste, *n.m.*, theist.

thème, *n.m.*, topic, subject, theme; (mus.) theme; (astrol.) scheme; theme, exercise (in schools—*aux écoles*).

thémis, *n.f.*, Themis, (poet., st. e.) justice.

théocratie (-ci), *n.f.*, theocracy.

théocratique, *adj.*, theocratic, theocratical.

théocratiquement (-tik-mān), *adv.*, theocratically.

théodicée, *n.f.*, theodicy.

théodolite, *n.m.*, (math.) theodolite.

théodosien, *adj.*, used only in: *code* —; the code of laws published in the reign of the Emperor Theodosius II.

théogonie, *n.f.*, theogony.

théogonique, *adj.*, relating, pertaining to, theogony.

théologal, *n.m.*, a canon, lecturer on divinity in a chapter.

théologal, -e, *adj.*, theologic, theological, cardinal.

théologale, *n.f.*, office of a theologal.

théologie, *n.f.*, theology, divinity. *Docteur en* —; doctor of divinity.

théologien (-ji-in), *n.m.*, theologian, divine, theologist.

théologique, *adj.*, theologic, theological.

théologiquement (-jik-mān), *adv.*, theologically.

théophilanthrope, *n.m.*, theophilanthropist.

théophilanthropie, *n.f.*, theophilanthropism.

théorbe, *n.m.* V. **téorbe**.

théorème, *n.m.*, theorem.

théoricien (-si-in), *n.m.*, theorist.

théorie, *n.f.*, theory; speculation.

théorique, *adj.*, theoretic, theoretical.

théoriquement (-rik-mān), *adv.*, theoretically.

théoriser, *v.a.*, to theorize.

théoriste, *n.m.*, theorist.

théosophe, *n.m.*, theosophist.

théosophie, *n.f.*, theosophy.

thérapeutes, *n.m.pl.*, (religious order—*ordre religieux*) Therapeutics.

thérapeutique, *adj.*, of the Therapeutics.

thérapeutique, *n.f.*, (med.) therapeutics.

thériacal, -e, *adj.*, (pharm.) theriac, theriacal.

thériaque, *n.f.*, (pharm.) theriac.

thermal. -e (tèr-), *adj.*, thermal. *Eaux* —*es*; warm mineral waters.

thermantique (tèr-), *n.m.* and *adj.*, (med.) stimulant.

thermes (tèrm), *n.m.pl.*, thermal baths; (Roman antiq.) thermæ.

thermidor (tèr-), *n.m.*, Thermidor, eleventh month of the calendar of the first French republic, from July 19th to August 17th.

thermidorien, -ne (tèr-), *n.* and *adj.*, name

given to the party which overthrew Robespierre on the 9th of thermidor, of the year II. of the French republic (July 27th, 1794).

thermo-manomètre (tèr-), *n.m.*, (of steam-engines—*de machine à vapeur*) thermometer-gauge.

thermomètre (tèr-), *n.m.*, thermometer.

thermométrique (tèr-), *adj.*, thermometric.

thermoscope (tèr-), *n.m.*, (phys.) thermoscope.

thermostat (tèr-), *n.m.*, (phys.) thermostat.

thésauriser, *v.n.*, to treasure up, to hoard up, to heap up treasure.

thésauriseu-r, *n.m.*, **-se**, *n.f.*, hoarder.

thèse, *n.f.*, thesis, theme; disputation, argument, discussion; the printed sheet containing the thesis. *Vous sortez de la* —; you are wandering from the question. *Soutenir — pour quelqu'un*; to side with any one. *Il voulut soutenir sa* —; he resolved to maintain his assertion. *Cela change la* —; that is another affair, that alters the matter.

thesmophories, *n.f.pl.*, (antiq.) Thesmophoria.

thesmothète, *n.m.*, (Grec. antiq.) thesmothete.

théurgie, *n.f.*, theurgy.

théurgique, *adj.*, theurgic, theurgical.

thibaude, *n.f.*, hair-cloth, cow-hair cloth.

thlaspi, *n.m.*, (bot.) thlaspi.

thon, *n.m.*, (ich.) tunny, tunny-fish, Spanish mackerel.

thoracique, *or*⊙**thorachique**, *n.m.* and *adj.*, (med.) pectoral, bechic; thoracic. *Canal* —; thoracic duct.

thorax (-raks), *n.m.*, (anat.) thorax, chest.

thridace, *n.f.*, (pharm.) lactucarium.

thrombus (-bus), *n.m.*, (surg.) thrombus.

thuia, *n.m.*, (bot.) thuja, tree of life.

thuriféraire, *n.m.*, (c. rel.) censer-bearer.

thurifère, *n.m.*, (bot.) thuriferous.

thuya, *n.m.* V. **thuia**.

thyade, *n.f.*, (antiq.) Bacchant.

thym (tin), *n.m.*, (bot.) thyme.

thymus, *n.m.* (—), (anat.) thymus.

thyroïde, *adj.*, (anat.) thyroid.

thyrse, *n.m.*, (antiq.) thyrsus; (bot.) thyrsus, thyrse.

tiare (tiar), *n.f.*, tiara.

tibia, *n.m.*, (anat.) tibia, shin, shin-bone.

tibial, -e, *adj.*, (anat.) tibial.

tibio-tarsien, -ne (-si-in, -è-n), *adj.*, (anat.) tibio-tarsal.

tic, *n.m.*, bad, ridiculous habit such as biting one's nails &c.; (vet.) crib-biting; bad habits of cattle; (med.) tic. *— douloureux*; tic douloureux, facial neuralgia.

tic tac, *n.m.*, ticktack; pit-pat.

tiède, *adj.*, lukewarm, tepid; indifferent.

tièdement (tiè-mān), *adv.*, coldly, with indifference; lukewarmly.

tiédeur, *n.f.*, lukewarmness, tepidity; coldness, indifference.

tiédir, *v.n.*, to cool, to grow lukewarm, to become lukewarm; to grow cool, to become cool.

tien, -ne (ti-in,-è-n), *pron.*, thine, yours.

tien, *n.m.*, thine, thy own, yours, your own. *Les* —*s*; thy people, thy relations and friends.

tiens, *n.m.*, only used in the expression: *Un* — *vaut mieux que deux tu l'auras* (prov.); a bird in the hand is better than two in the bush.

tiens! tenez! *int.*, expressing astonishment, or to call the attention of the hearer; look! look here! look there! hold! now then! there!

tierce (tièrs), *n.f.*, third (of time—*temps*);

(mus.) third, tierce;tierce(at cards—*aux cartes*) ; (fenc.) tiers; (print.) press-revise. — *majeure* (mus.); major third. — *mineure* (mus.); minor third.

tiercelet (tièr-slè), *n.m.*, (hawking—*fauconnerie*) tercel, tiercel, tiercelet, tarsel.

tiercement (tièrs-mǎn), *n.m.*, (thea.) enhancing the price of places by a third part; ☉(jur.) outbidding by one third a price offered ; (milit.) numbering and placing the companies in every battalion according to the rank of seniority of the captains.

tiercer (tièrsé), *v.a.* and *n.*, (thea.) to enhance the price of places by a third part; ☉(jur.) to outbid by one third a price offered; (agri.) to plough a third time, *V.* **tercer**; (milit.) to number and place the companies in every battalion according to the rank of seniority of the captains.

tierceron (tièr-), *n.m.*, (arch.) tierceron.

tierçon (tièr-), *n.m.*, a measure.

tier-s, -ce (tièr, tièrs), *adj.*, third, of a third person. *Le — état ;* the people, the commons. *Fièvre —ce ;* tertian ague. *Main —ce ;* hands of a third person. — *parti ;* third party.

tiers, *n.m.*, third, third person; third part. *Le — et le quart ;* every body, all the world.

tiers-point, *n.m.* (— —s), (arch.) tierce-point.

tige, *n.f.*, trunk, stem, body; stalk; leg (of a boot—*de botte*); shank (of a candlestick—*de chandelier*); stock, head (of a family—*d'une famille*); `shank (of an anchor—*d'une ancre*); straw (of corn—*de blé*); tail (of a valve—*de soupape*); (tech.) rod. *Arbres à haute — ;* tall trees. *Arbres à basse — ;* dwarf trees.

tigette, *n.f.*, (arch.) honeysuckle ornament (at the springing of a volute—*où commencent les volutes*).

*tignasse, *n.f.*, (fam., pop.) old wig.

*tignon, *n.m.*, roll of hair twisted behind the head. *V.* **chignon**.

*tignonner, *v.a.*, to curl the hair behind the head (of women—*des femmes*).

*se tignonner, *v.r.*, to seize each other by the hair behind, to pull caps.

tigre, *n.m.*, (mam.) tiger; (ich.) square fish; (conch.) tiger-shell; groom ; (ent.) tiger-beetle.

tigre, *adj.*, spotted (like a tiger—*comme un tigre*).

tigré, -e, *adj.*, spotted, speckled.

tigresse, *n.f.*, (mam.) tigress.

tilbury, *n.m.*, tilbury (carriage).

tiliacées, *n.f.pl.*, (bot.) tiliaceæ.

*tillac, *n.m.*, (nav.) deck (of merchant ships —*de vaisseau marchand*). *Franc — ;* deck.

*tillage, or teillage, *n.m.*, (agri.) stripping (hemp—*le chanvre*).

*tille, or teille, *n.f.*, bast of the lime-tree ; cabin (of an undecked vessel—*d'un navire sans pont*); axe-hammer; hemp-harl.

*tiller, or teiller, *v.a.*, (agri.) to peel, to strip (hemp—*le chanvre*).

*tilleul, *n.m.*, (bot.) linden-tree, lime-tree.

*tilleu-r, *n.m.*, -se, *n.f.*, or teilleu-r, -se, (agri.) stripper (of hemp—*de chanvre*).

timar, *n.m.* (—s), profit of a *timariot*, which see below.

timariot, *n.m.*, Turkish soldier who received a sum of money to keep himself and a number of militia-men.

timbale, *n.f.*, kettle-drum ; (mus.) timbal ; cup (of metal—*métallique*); battledore.

timbalier, *n.m.*, kettle-drummer.

timbrage, *n.m.*, stamping of the paper used for deeds, bills of exchange, &c., with a government stamp.

timbre, *n.m.*, bell, clock-bell ; ring, sound (of a bell—*d'une cloche*); thrill, tone, voice ;

stamp (on paper—*sur le papier*); (her.) helmet; (horl.) bell ; (post-office—*de la poste*) post-mark ; head, brains. — *de la voix ;* tone of the voice. *Sa voix a un — argentin ;* he has a silver-toned voice. *Il a le — fêlé ;* he is crack-brained, he is cracked.

timbré, -e, *part.*, stamped. *Papier — ;* stamped paper. *Esprit, cerveau — ;* crackbrained person. *Il est — ;* he is cracked.

timbre-poste, *n.m.* (—s —), postage-stamp.

timbrer, *v.a.*, to stamp (paper, parchment —*le papier, le parchemin*); (her.) to crest.

timbreur, *n.m.*, stamper, person that stamps the paper used for law-business.

timide, *adj.*, timid, bashful, timorous, shy.

timidement (-mid-mǎn), *adv.*, timidly, bashfully; timorously; shyly.

timidité, *n.f.*, timidity, timorousness, fearfulness, shyness.

timon, *n.m.*, pole (of a coach—*de voiture*); beam (of a plough—*de charrue*); (nav.) helm, tiller (of a rudder—*de gouvernail*); helm, direction, government ; (tech.) draught-bar. *Tenir le — ;* to be at the helm.

timonerie (-mo-n-rî), *n.f.*, (nav.) steerage.

timonier, *n.m.*, wheeler, wheel-horse; (nav.) steersman, helmsman.

timoré, -e, *adj.*, timorous, fearful, scrupulous.

tin, *n.m.*, (nav.) block of wood.

tincal, *n.m.*, (chem.) tinkal.

tinctorial, -e, *adj.*, tinctorial.

tine, *n.f.*, tub, water-cask.

tinet, *n.m.*, gambrel (of butchers—*de boucher*).

tinette, *n.f.*, half a tub, kit (of butter—*de beurre*).

tintamarre, *n.m.*, hubbub, uproar, clutter.

☉tintamarrer, *v.n.*, (pop.) to clutter, to make an uproar.

tintement (tint-mǎn), *n.m.*, ringing sound, tinkling; toll, tolling. — *funèbre ;* funeral toll, knell. — *d'oreilles ;* tingling in the ears.

tintenague (tint-nag), *n.f. V.* **toutenague**.

tinter, *v.a.*, to toll, to ring, to ring for; (nav.) to put upon the stocks, to prop, to support.

tinter, *v.n.*, to toll, to ring ; to tinkle, to jingle; to ring, to tingle. *Les oreilles me tintent ;* my ears tingle.

tintin, *n.m.*, jingling (of bells, glasses—*des cloches, des verres*).

tintouin, *n.m.*, tingling (in one's ear—*dans les oreilles*); anxiety, uneasiness. *Avoir du — ;* to be upon thorns.

tique, *n.f.*, (ent.) tick.

tiquer, *v.n.*, (of horses—*des chevaux*) to have bad habits, such as crib-biting, &c.

tiqueté, -e (tik-té), *adj.*, variegated, speckled, spotted.

tiqueu-r, -se, *adj.*, crib-biter (of horses—*des chevaux*).

tir, *n.m.*, shooting, firing; shooting-gallery, shooting-ground. — *à la cible ;* target-shooting. *Chasse au —* (hunt.); shooting. *Justesse du — ;* trueness of the aim.

tirade, *n.f.*, tirade; (mus., thea.) tirade; passage of prose or verse. *Tout d'une — ;* all at one time.

tirage, *n.m.*, draught; towing (of boats—*de bateaux*); towing-path; drawing (of a lottery —*d'une loterie*); (print.) working, working off, pulling, printing; winding-off (of silk—*de la soie*).

*tiraillement, *n.m.*, plucking, pulling, hauling about, twitching, twinge. — *d'estomac ;* pain in the stomach.

*tirailler, *v.a.*, to pull, to haul about, to tug, to twitch ; to tease, to plague, to bother.

*se tirailler, *v.r.*, to pull one another about.

*tirailler, *v.n.*, to shoot badly; (milit.) to skirmish.

*tiraillerie, *n.f.*, (milit.) desultory, disorderly, aimless firing.

*tirailleur, *n.m.*, (milit.) sharp-shooter; skirmisher.

tirant, *n.m.*, string (of purses—*de bourse*); boot-strap; cramp, cramp-iron; (carp.) collar; iron-bar, bolt, holdfast; (cook.) white leather; string of parchment; brace (of a drum—*de tambour*); ship's gauge, ship's draught. — *d'eau* ; (nav.) gauge, sea-gauge, ship's draught.

tirasse, *n.f.*, (hunt.) draw-net.

tirasser, *v.a.* and *n.*, (hunt.) to catch with a draw-net, to take with a draw-net; to set a draw-net, to lay a draw-net.

tire, *n.f.*, quick jerk of the wing. *Tout d'une* —; at a stretch. *Voleur à la* —; pickpocket.

tiré, -e, *adj.*, drawn.

tiré, *n.m.*, (hunt.) shooting; (com.) drawee (of bills—*de lettres de change*).

tire-balle, *n.m.* (——*s*), (surg.) forceps; (milit.) worm-screw.

tire-botte, *n.m.* (——*s*), boot-hook; boot-jack.

tire-bouchon, *n.m.* (——*s*), cork-screw; ringlet of hair—*de cheveux*).

tire-bourre, *n.m.* (——*s*), worm, worm-screw (to unload a gun—*pour décharger un fusil*).

tire-bouton, *n.m.* (——*s*), button-hook.

tire-clou, *n.m.* (——*s*), nail-drawer; (tech.) claw-hammer; slater's hammer.

à tire-d'aile, *adv.*, quick jerk of the wings. *Voler à* —; to fly as quickly as possible.

tire-étoupe, *n.m.* (—), (tech.) worm.

tire-fond, *n.m.* (—), turrel.

⊙**tire-laisse**, *n.m.* (—), (fam.) sudden disappointment.

à tire-larigot, *adv.*, only used in : *boire à* —; to drink hard, to drink like a fish.

* **tire-ligne**, *n.m.* (——*s*), drawing-pen.

tirelire, *n.f.*, money-box.

⊙**tirelire**, *n.m.*, song, carol (of the lark).

⊙**tirelirer**, *v.n.*, to sing like a lark.

tire-moelle, *n.m.* (—), marrow-spoon.

tire-pied, *n.m.* (——*s*), shoemaker's stirrup.

tire-plomb, *n.m.* (—), glazier's lead-flatting mill ; glazier's vice.

tire-point, or **tire-pointe** *n.m.* (—), pricker used in stitching.

tirer, *v.a.*, to draw, to pull, to give a pull; to take, to take out, to pull out ; to get, to extract, to collect; to fire, to shoot, to fire at, to shoot at; to trace, to delineate; to receive, to reap, to recover; to extricate, to free from; to conclude, to infer, to deduce; to draw on, to put on; to draw up; to draw down ; (print.) to work, to work off, to pull, to print, to pull off; (nav.) to draw; to tighten (a rope—*une corde*); to tap (liquors—*liqueurs*); to stretch (linen—*linge*); to cast (a nativity—*un horoscope*) ; to draw (a bill—*une lettre de change*); to take out (a tooth—*une dent*). — *en arrière;* to pull back. — *de l'eau;* to draw water. — *dedans;* to pull in. — *en haut;* to pull up. — *en bas;* to pull down. — *les oreilles à quelqu'un;* to pull any one's ears. — *la langue;* to put out one's tongue. *Faire*— *l'épée à quelqu'un;* to make any one draw his sword. *Il se fait*—*l'oreille;* he requires great entreaty. — *ses bottes;* to pull off one's boots. — *de l'argent de sa poche;* to pull money out of one's pocket. — *pied ou aile d'une chose;* to reap some benefit from a thing by hook or by crook. *Il tire beaucoup de la cour;* he gets a great deal by the court. — *parti de;* to make use of, to turn to account. — *satisfaction d'une injure;* to obtain satisfaction for an injury. — *vengeance;* to be revenged. — *vanité d'une chose;* to take a pride in a thing. — *avantage d'une chose;* to

derive advantage from a thing. — *la racine carrée, la racine cubique d'un nombre;* to extract the square, the cubic root of a number. — *le suc des herbes;* to extract the juice of herbs. — *une conséquence;* to draw an inference. — *une corde;* to tighten a cord. — *quelqu'un à quatre chevaux;* to draw and quarter any one, to tear any one to pieces. — *ses chausses,* — *ses guêtres;* (fam., pop.) to cut one's stick, to scamper off. — *une vache;* to milk a cow. — *les rideaux;* to open the curtains; to close, to pull the curtains to. — *l'or;* to wire-draw gold. — *une affaire en longueur;* to protract a piece of business. — *une allée au cordeau;* to make a walk in a straight line. *On l'a tiré en cire;* they have taken him off in wax. — *des estampes;* to pull prints. — *un fusil;* to shoot a gun. — *un coup de canon;* to fire a gun. — *des fusées;* to let off rockets. — *un oiseau;* to shoot at a bird. — *une estocade* (fenc.); to make a pass. se**tirer**, *v.r.*, to extricate one's self ; to get out, to get through; to recover (from illness—*de maladie*). — *d'affaire sain et sauf;* to escape safe and sound, to get off scot free.

tirer, *v.n.*, to draw ; to go, to make for; to shoot; to tend, to border, to verge; to fire. — *sur;* to incline to. *Cette pierre tire sur le vert;* that stone is greenish.

tire-racine, *n.m.* (—), stump-forceps (of a dentist—*de dentiste*).

tiret, *n.m.*, slip of parchment; hyphen.

tiretaine (tir-tè-n), *n.f.*, linsey-woolsey.

tire-tête, *n.m.* (——*s*), instrument used in obstetrical operations.

tireu-r, *n.m.*, **-se**, *n.f.*, one who draws, drawer ; marksman, shot (pers.); rifleman, sharp-shooter; drawer (of a bill of exchange —*d'une lettre de change*). — *d'or;* gold wire-drawer. ⊙ — *d'armes;* fencing-master. —*se de cartes;* fortune-teller. *C'est un bon* —; he is a good shot.

*tire-veille, *n.f.* (—), (nav.) ladder-rope; man-rope. — *de l'échelle hors le bord;* man-ropes of the sides. — *de cabestan;* swifter.

tiroir, *n.m.*, drawer (of a table, &c.—*de table, &c.*); (milit.) middle rank; (tech.) slide, slide-box. *Pièce à* — (thea.) ; comedy of episodes.

tironien, -ne (-in, -è-n), *adj.*, (antiq.) Tironian. *Abréviation* —*ne;* Tironian note.

tisane, *n.f.*, (med.) diet-drink.

tisard, *n.m.*, door (of an oven—*de four*).

tison, *n.m.*, brand, fire-brand.

tisonné, *adj.m.*, only used in : *gris* — (of horses—*des chevaux*) ; marked with black spots.

tisonner, *v.n.*, to stir the fire, to poke the fire.

tisonneu-r, *n.m.*, **-se**, *n.f.*, person who is fond of poking the fire.

tisonnier, *n.m.*, poker; blacksmith's poker.

tissage, *n.m.*, weaving; texture.

tisser, *v.a.*, to weave.

tisserand (tis-rân), *n.m.*, weaver.

tisseranderie (tis-ran-drî), *n.f.*, weaving business.

tissu, -e, *past part.* (of ⊙ *tistre*), woven. *Des jours* — *d'or et de soie;* happy days.

tissu, *n.m.*, texture, textile fabric, contexture; tissue. — *de mensonges;* tissue of lies. — *d'argent;* silver tissue. — *d'or;* golden tissue. — *métallique;* gauze wire, gauze wirework. — *réticulaire* (anat.) reticular body.

tissure, *n.f.*, tissue, texture, web, weaving. — *d'un discours;* contexture of a discourse.

tissutier (-tié), *n.m.*, weaver (of silk textures—*de soieries*).

⊙**tistre**, *v.a.*, to weave.

titan, *n.m.*, (myth.) Titan.

titane, *n.m.*, or **titanium** (-om), *n.m.*, (chem.) titanium.

titanique, *adj.*, (myth.) pertaining, relating to Titan.

tithymale, *n.m.* (bot.) tithymal.

titillant, **-e** (-til-lân, -t), *adj.*, titillating; tickling.

titillation (-til-la-), *n.f.*, titillation, tickling; slight agitation.

titiller (-til-lé), *v.n.* and *a.*, to titillate, to tickle.

titre, *n.m.*, title; right; standard (of coin—*des monnaies*); (jur.) title, title-deed, deed, indenture. *Donner un — à;* to entitle to. *À — de;* by right of, in virtue of.

titré, **-e**, *adj.*, titled; to which a title is attached (of estates—*des domaines*).

titrer, *v.a.*, to give a title, to title.

titrier, *n.m.*, forger of titles (l.u.); curator of the deeds (in monastic establishments—*dans les monastères*).

titubant, **-e**, *adj.*, staggering.

titubation, *n.f.*, titubation.

tituber, *v.n.*, to stagger.

titulaire, *n.m.f.* and *adj.*, titular, titulary, incumbent.

toast, or **toste** (tost). *n.m.*, toast, health. *Porter, donner, un —;* to drink a health, to give a toast.

toaster (tos-té), *v.a.* *V.* **toster**.

toc ! *int.*, and *onomatopœia*, a rap, a knock, at a door, or some other similar noise.

tocane, *n.f.*, unpressed wine.

tocsin, *n.m.*, tocsin, alarm-bell. *Sonner le — sur quelqu'un;* to raise a hue and cry after one.

todier, *n.m.*, (orni.) tody.

toge, *n.f.*, (Rom. antiq.) toga.

tohu-bohu, *n.m.* (—), (from Hebrew—*de l'hébreu*) chaos; (fig.) confusion, uproar, disorder.

toi, *pron.*, thee, thyself, thou, you, yourself. *C'est —;* it is thou, you.

toile, *n.f.*, cloth, linen-cloth; (thea.) curtain; canvas (for painting—*pour peindre*); canvas. sail ; (paint.) painting, picture, piece; web (of a spider—*d'araignée*); *pl.*, (hunt.) toils. — *à sac;* sack-cloth. — *écrue;* brown holland. — *ouvrée;* huckaback. —*s de sabords;* port-sails. — *de dunette;* canvas-covering for the poop. — *d'or;* gold-cloth. — *cirée;* oil-cloth. — *peinte;* printed calico. — *d'araignée;* cobweb. *Blanchisseur de —s;* bleacher. *Marchand de —s;* linendraper. — *de Pénélope;* Penelope's web. *La — est levée* (thea.); the curtain is drawn up. *La — tombe* (thea.); the curtain falls. *Derrière la —* (thea.); behind the curtain.

toilerie (toal-rî), *n.f.*, linen-cloth trade, linen drapery.

toilette, *n.f.*, toilet; toilet, dress; dressing-table; trimming (of horses—*des chevaux*). *Revendeuse à la —;* old-clothes woman, dealer in ladies' left-off wearing apparel. *Grande —;* full dress. *Cabinet de —;* dressing-closet, dressing-room. *Il fait sa —;* he is dressing.

toili-er, *n.m.*, **-ère**, *n.f.*, dealer in linen; linen-cloth maker, cotton-cloth maker.

toise, *n.f.*, toise (6·39459 feet); fathom. *On ne mesure pas les hommes à la —;* men ought not to be estimated by their size. *Mesurer les autres à sa —;* to measure others by one's own standard.

toisé, *n.m.*, measuring; (math.) mensuration.

toiser, *v.a.*, to measure; to eye from head to foot; to terminate, to conclude. — *un soldat;* to take the height of a soldier. — *quelqu'un;* to measure any one. *Cela est toisé* (pop.); that is done for.

toiseur, *n.m.*, measurer.

toison, *n.f.*, fleece, — *d'or;* golden fleece.

L'ordre de la — d'or; the order of the golden fleece.

toit, *n.m.*, roof, top (of a house—*de maison*); top (of a mine—*de mine*); dwelling. — *à cochons:* hog-sty, pig-sty. — *à deux croupes* (arch.); compass roof, span roof. *Dire quelque chose sur les —s;* to proclaim anything from the house-top.

toiture, *n.m.*, roofing.

tokai, or **tokay**, *n.m.*, Tokay wine.

tôle, *n.f.*, sheet-iron; (metal.) plate, sheet.

tolérable, *adj.*, tolerable, bearing, supportable; tolerable, middling, passable.

tolérablement, *adv.*, tolerably, supportably; tolerably, passably, middlingly.

tolérance, *n.f.*, tolerance, toleration; (jur.) sufferance; (coin.) deduction, allowance.

tolérant, **-e**, *adj.*, tolerant.

tolérantisme, *n.m.*, (theol.)too great toleration.

tolérer, *v.a.*, to tolerate, to suffer, to allow, to allow of; to wink at.

tôlerie (tôl-rî), *n.f.*, sheet-iron manufactory; (metal.) flatting-mills; sheet-iron goods.

tolet, *n.m.*, (nav.) thole.

toletière (tol-tièr), *n.f.*, (nav.) rowlock.

tollé, *n.m.*, hue and cry. *Crier — sur quelqu'un;* to raise a hue and cry against any one.

tomahawk, *n.m.*, tomahawk.

tomaison, *n.f.*, numbering, number, of a volume.

toman, *n.m.* (—s), toman, tomaun, a Persian gold coin varying in value from 12s. to £1 15s. st.

tomate, *n.f.*, (bot.) tomato, love-apple.

tombac, *n.m.*, (metal.) tombac.

tombal, **-e**, *adj.*, (archæology) only used in: *pierre —e;* tomb-stone.

tombant, **-e**, *adj.*, falling down, flowing.

tombe, *n.f.*, tomb, grave, tombstone, headstone, gravestone. *Descendre dans la —;* to die, to sink into the grave. *Être sur le bord de la —;* to be on the brink of the grave.

tombeau, *n.m.*, tomb, grave; tombstone; sepulchre, death. *Mettre au —;* to bring down to the grave.

tombée, *n.f.*, fall of day. *À la — de la nuit;* at night-fall.

tombelier, *n.m.*, carter.

tomber, *v.n.*, to fall, to fall down; to tumble, to tumble down; to drop, to drop down; to sink, to sink down; to break in, to come, to light, to hit on; to come down, to sink, to decay, to fall away, to dwindle, to droop, to come out; to abate, to die away; (nav.) to sag; to hang, to incline. *Il est tombé de cheval;* he fell off his horse. — *à terre,* — *par terre;* to fall down. *Le brouillard tombe;* the fog falls. — *malade;* to fall sick. — *de faiblesse;* to drop down from weakness. — *d'inanition;* to be ready to faint for want of food. — *en apoplexie;* to fall down in a fit of apoplexy. — *du haut mal;* to have the falling sickness. — *raide mort;* to fall down dead. *Se laisser —;* to get a fall. — *en enfance;* to become childish. — *dans les bras de quelqu'un;* to fall into any one's arms. — *d'accord;* to agree. — *de son haut,* — *des nues;* to be extremely amazed. *Les bras m'en tombèrent;* I let my arms drop with surprise. *Le sort est tombé sur lui;* the lot has fallen upon him. *Cela m'est tombé entre les mains;* that fell into my hands. *Le jour tombe;* the day is closing. — *sous le vent* (nav.); to fall to leeward. — *de fièvre en chaud mal,* — *de la poêle dans la braise;* to jump out of the frying-pan into the fire.

tombereau (ton-brô), *n.m.*, tumbrel, dung-cart.

tombola, *n.f.*, tombola (game and lottery—*sorte de loterie*).

tome, *n.m.*, volume, book, tome. *Faire le second — de quelqu'un;* to resemble any one, to be any one's counterpart.

tomenteu-x, -se, *adj.*, (bot., zool., anat.) tomentous, tomentose, downy.

ton, *m.*, **ta**, *f.*, **tes**, *pl.m.f.*, *possessive adj.*, thy, your. *— frère, ta sœur et tes cousins;* thy brother, sister, and cousins. *— âme;* thy soul. [*Ton* is used for the *f.* before a vowel or silent *h.*]

ton, *n.m.*, tone; tune; voice, accent; manner, strain, style, taste. *— aigre;* shrill tone. *— doux;* soft, sweet tone. *— de déclamateur;* declamatory tone. *Donner le —;* to give the tone, to lead the fashion; (mus.) to pitch, to tone. *Parler d'un —fier;* to speak haughtily. *Parler d'un — de maître;* to speak in a magisterial manner. *Le prendre sur un —;* to assume airs. *Le prendre sur un — de fierté;* to take a high tone. *Changer de —;* to sing to another tune, to change one's tone. *Il donne le — à la conversation;* he takes the lead in conversation. *C'est le — qui fait la musique;* it is the manner which shows the intention.

tonalité, *n.f.*, (mus.) tonality.

tonarion, *n.m.*, (antiq.) a flute with which the tone was given to orators.

tondaison, *n.f.* V. **tonte**.

tondeu-r, *n.m.*, **-se**, *n.f.*, shearer, clipper. *— de draps;* shearman, clothworker.

tondeuse, *n.f.*, shearing-machine.

tondre, *v.a.*, to shear, to clip, to crop; to shave, to trim. *— les brebis;* to shear the sheep. *— du drap;* to shear cloth. *— une haie;* to clip a hedge. *— sur un œuf;* to skin a flint.

tondu, -e, *part.*, shorn. *Il n'y avait que trois —s et un pelé;* there was nothing but ragtag and bobtail.

tonicité, *n.f.*, (med.) tonic condition of the body or of any of its parts.

tonique, *adj.*, (med., mus., gram.) tonic.

tonique, *n.m.*, (med.) tonic.

tonique, *n.f.*, (mus.) tonic, key-note, key.

⊙**tonisme**, *n.m.* V. **tonicité**.

tonlieu, *n.m.*, toll paid for standing in a market.

tonnage, *n.m.*, tonnage.

tonnant, -e, *adj.*, thundering. *Jupiter —* (myth.); Jupiter the thunderer.

tonne, *n.f.*, tun (wooden vessel—*tonneau*); (conch.) spotted tun; (nav.) can-buoy; ton (20 cwts.=1000 kil.).

tonneau, *n.m.*, tun (wooden vessel—*vaisseau de bois*); cask; tun (measure—*mesure*); (nav.) ton (1000 kil.; 1 mètre cube). *Enfoncer un —;* to stave a cask. *Mettre un — en perce;* to broach a cask. *— percé;* leaky cask; spendthrift.

tonneler (to-n-lé), *v.a.*, (hunt.) to tunnel.

tonnelet (to-n-lè), *n.m.*, small cask, keg.

tonneleur (to-n-leur), *n.m.*, (hunt.) tunneler, one who takes partridges with a tunnel-net.

tonnelier, *n.m.*, cooper.

tonnelle, *n.f.*, (hunt.) tunnel-net, for catching partridges; arbour, green arbour; (arch.) semi-circular, waggon-headed vault.

tonnellerie (to-nèl-ri), *n.f.*, cooperage; cooper's trade; (nav.) cooper's shed.

tonner, *v.n.*, to thunder; to inveigh; to exclaim. *Il tonne;* it thunders.

tonnerre, *n.m.*, thunder, thunderbolt; thundering noise. *Coup de —, éclat de —;* clap of thunder, peal of thunder.

tonsille, *n.f.*, (l.u.) (anat.) tonsil. V. **amygdale**.

tonsure, *n.f.*, tonsure.

tonsuré, *n.m.*, person who has received the tonsure.

tonsurer, *v.a.*, to give the tonsure to.

tonte, *n.f.*, shearing, sheep-shearing; shearing-time.

tontine, *n.f.*, tontine.

tontini-er, *n.m.*, **-ère**, *n.f.*, sharer of a tontine.

tontisse, *adj.*, of shearings of woollen cloth.

tontisse, *n.f.*, hangings coated with the shearings of cloth. *Papier- —;* hanging-paper coated with the shearings of cloth.

tonture, *n.f.*, shearing (of leaves, grass—*de feuilles, d'herbe, &c.*); shearings, clippings, flock (of cloth—*de drap*); (nav.) sheer. *— de drap;* flock. *— des ponts;* sheer of a ship's decks.

topaze, *n.f.*, topaz.

toper, *v.n.*, to stake as much as one's adversary, to agree. *Je tope à cela;* I agree to that. *Tope et tingue! done!* agreed! *Tope et tingue;* dice game.

tophacé, -e, *adj.*, (med.) gouty.

tophus (-fus), *n.m.*, (med.) tophus.

topinambour, *n.m.*, Jerusalem-artichoke.

topique, *adj.*, (med.) topic, topical.

topique, *n.m.*, (rhet., med.) topic.

topique, *n.f.*, (rhet.) the art of finding topics, arguments, &c.

topiques, *n.m.pl.*, (antiq.) treatise on topics, arguments, &c.

topographe, *n.m.*, topographer.

topographie, *n.f.*, topography.

topographique, *adj.*, topographical.

toquade, *n.f.*, (fam., pop.) infatuation, oddity.

toque, *n.f.*, flat cap (plaited all round—*plissée tout autour*).

toquer, *v.a.*, (l.u.) to offend; to hit, to knock; (pop.) to craze.

toquet, *n.m.*, toquet (head-dress—*coiffure*).

torche, *n.f.*, torch, link.

torche-cul, *n.m.* (— —s), (l.ex.) paper or linen to wipe one's self; (fig.) a worthless writing, trash.

torche-nez, *n.m.* (—), (man.) twitch.

torche-pot, *n.m.* (—), (orni.) nut-hatch.

torcher, *v.a.*, to wipe; to work badly; to beat.

se **torcher**, *v.r.*, to be wiped; to wipe one's self; (triv.) to fight.

torchère, *n.f.*, torch, cresset, tall candelabrum.

torchis, *n.m.*, mud, loam. *Mur de —;* mud-wall.

torchon, *n.m.*, dish-cloth, dish-clout; house-cloth, duster.

torcol, *n.m.*, (orni.) wry-neck.

tordage, *n.m.*, twisting.

tordeu-r, *n.m.*, **-se**, *n.f.*, twister; throwster (of silk—*de soie*).

tord-nez, *n.m.* (—), (man.) twitch (for horses—*pour chevaux*).

tordre, *v.a.*, to twist, to wring, to wring out; to contort, to disfigure; to throw (silk—*la soie*). *— la bouche;* to twist one's mouth. *Il ne fait que — et avaler;* he gives but one twist, and down it goes.

se **tordre**, *v.r.*, to twist; to writhe.

tore, *n.m.*, (arch., bot.) torus, tore.

toréador, *n.m.* (—s), matadore.

toreutique, *n.f.*, (antiq.) the art of chasing, engraving, on metals and ivory.

torisme, *n.m.* V. **torysme**.

*****tormentille**, *n.f.*, (bot.) tormentil, septfoil.

torminal, -e, *adj.*, (med.) causing gripes.

toron, *n.m.*, strand (of a rope—*d'une corde*); (arch.) torus.

torpeur, *n.f.*, torpor, torpidity, torpidness.

*****torpille**, *n.f.*, (ich.) torpedo, cramp-fish.

torquer, *v.a.*, to twist tobacco into a roll.

⊙**torquet**, *n.m.*, (pop.) snare. *Donner un —, donner le — à quelqu'un;* to humbug any one, to take any one in. *Donner dans le —;* to fall into the snare, to be taken in.

torquette, *n.f.*, a wicker-basket used to

carry sea-fish; quantity of sea-fish thus carried; fowl *or* game wicker-basket.

torréfaction (tor-ré-), *n.f.*, torrefaction.

torréfier (tor-ré), *v.a.*, to torrefy.

torrent (tor-rän), *n.m.*, torrent, stream; flood (of tears—*de larmes*); flow (of words—*de paroles*).

torrentueu-x, **-se** (tor-ran-), *adj.*, that flows like a torrent; torrent-like.

torride (tor-rid), *adj.*, torrid.

tors, **-e**, *adj.*, twisted, wry, crooked; wreathed. *Jambes —es;* crooked legs. *Bouche —e;* wry mouth.

torsade, *n.f.*, twisted fringe; bullion of epaulets.

torse, *n.m.*, trunk of a person; (sculpt., paint.) torso, trunk.

torser, *v.a.*, to twist the shaft of a column.

torsil, **-e**, *adj.*, (bot.) twisted, contorted.

torsion. *n.f.*, torsion; tortuousness.

tort, *n.m.*, wrong, harm, injury, hurt, prejudice, detriment. *Faire — à quelqu'un;* to wrong any one. *Réparer le — qu'on a fait;* to repair the wrong one has done. *Se faire —;* to injure one's self. *Avoir —;* to be wrong, to be in the wrong. *Donner — à quelqu'un;* to decide against any one. *À —;* wrong, wrongly, wrongfully, injuriously. *Il parle à — et à travers;* he speaks at random. *À — et à droit,* at random. *À — ou à droit, à — ou à raison;* rightly or wrongly.

ⓞ**torte**, *adj.*, a feminine form of *tors*, which see.

tortelle, *n.f.*, hedge-mustard. *V.* **vélar**.

torticolis, *n.m.*, wry-neck, stiff neck; hypocrite, canter.

tortil. *n.m.*, (her.) a baron's wreath.

*****tortillage**, *n.m.*, rigmarole, embarrassed language.

*****tortille**, *or* **tortillère**. *n.f.*, serpentine walk.

*****tortillé**, **-e**, *adj.*, twisted, wreathed.

*****tortillement**, *n.m.*, twisting, twist; wrench; shifting, shuffling.

*****tortiller**, *v.a.*, to twist, to wriggle.

se tortiller. *v.r.*, to wriggle, to writhe.

*****tortiller**, *v.n.*, to wriggle, to shuffle.

*****tortillère**, *n.f.* *V.* **tortille**.

ⓞ*****tortillon**, *n.m.*, sort of girl's cap; country servant-girl.

tortionnaire (tor-sio-), *n.m.* and *adj.*, ⓞexecutioner; (jur.) wrongful.

tortionnairement (tor-sio-nèr-män), *adv.*, (jur.) wrongfully.

ⓞ**tortionner** (tor-sio-), *v.a.*, to strain a text, a passage of an author. *V.* **torturer**.

tortis, *n.m.*, twist (of threads—*de fils*); ⓞwreath, garland; (her.) circle of pearls round a baron's coronet.

tortu, **-e**, *adj.*, crooked, tortuous, bandy. *Jambes —es;* crooked legs.

tortue, *n.f.*, tortoise, turtle; transport-ship; (Rom. antiq.) testudo. *Marcher à pas de —;* to walk at a snail's pace.

tortuer, *v.a.*, to make crooked.

se tortuer, *v.r.*, to grow crooked.

tortueusement (-eûz-män), *adv.*, crookedly.

tortueu-x, **-se**, *adj.*, tortuous, winding, bending in and out; artful, crafty. *Une conduite—se;* disingenuous, shuffling, conduct.

tortuosité, *n.f.*, (l.u.) tortuosity, crookedness.

torture, *n.f.*, torture, rack, pain. *Mettre à la —;* to put to the rack.

torturer, *v.a.*, to torture, to put to the rack. *— un texte, un passage;* to strain a text, a part of a book, a writing.

tory, *n.m.* and *adj.*, Tory.

torysme, *n.m.*, Toryism.

toscan, **-e**, *n.* and *adj.*, Tuscan.

toste, *n.m.* *V.* **toast**.

toster, *v.a.* and *n.*, to toast, to give, to propose, a toast, to drink health.

tôt, *adv.*, soon, shortly. *Trop —;* too soon. *— ou tard;* sooner or later. *Au plus —;* at soonest, as soon as possible.

total, **-e**, *adj.*, total, whole, entire, utter, universal.

total, *n.m.*, whole, whole sum, total, sum total. *Au —, en —;* upon the whole, taken all in all, when all comes to all.

totalement (-tal-män), *adv.*, totally, wholly, entirely, utterly.

totaliser, *v.a.*, to form a total of.

totalité, *n.f.*, totality, whole. *En —;* the whole.

toton, *n.m.*, teetotum.

touage, *n.m.*, (nav.) towage, towing; warping.

*****touaille**, *n.f.*, round towel.

touc, *or* **toug**, *n.m.* (—s), the pike and horse's tail attached to it which, among the Turks, is borne as a standard before the grand vizier, pachas, and sangiacs.

toucan, *n.m.*, (orni., astron.) toucan.

touchant, **-e**, *adj.*, touching, moving, affecting.

touchant, *n.m.*, what is touching, moving, affecting.

touchant, *prep.*, concerning, respecting, touching, about, with respect to.

ⓞ**touchante**, *n.f.* (geom.). *V.* **tangente**.

touchau, *or* **touchaud**, *n.m.*, touch-needle.

touche, *n.f.*, touch; trial; (paint.) stroke, touch; fret (of violins, guitars, &c.—*de violon, de guitare, &c.*); key (of a piano, organ, harpsichord—*de piano, d'orgue, de clavecin*); (print.) inking the form. *Pierre de —;* touch-stone. *L'adversité est la pierre de — l'amitié;* adversity is the touch-stone of friendship.

touché, **-e**, *part.*, touched, affected. *Pièce —e, pièce jouée* (chess—*échecs*); *dame —e, dame jouée* (draughts, backgammon—*dames, tricirac*); if you touch your man or piece you must play it.

toucher, *v.a.*, to touch, to handle, to feel, to finger; to assay, to try (precious metals—*les métaux précieux*); to receive (money—*de l'argent*); to beat, to whip, to strike (animals —*des animaux*); (mus.) to play (the lyre, the organ, the harpsichord, the piano—*la lyre, l'orgue, le clavecin, le piano*); to express, to convey; (print.) to ink; to paint, to draw, to depict; to touch on, to allude to; to move, to affect; to concern, to regard; to interest, to inspire interest in. *— le piano;* to play the piano. *— les aiguilles d'un compas;* to touch the needles of a compass with a magnet. *— un ulcère* (surg.); to touch an ulcer with caustic. *— ses appointements;* to receive one's salary. *Ce poète touche bien les passions;* that poet expresses the passions very well. *Cela ne me touche point;* that does not concern me. *— la grosse corde;* to touch upon the main point of an affair. *Se laisser — par les larmes de quelqu'un;* to be affected, to be moved, by any one's tears.

se toucher, *v.r.*, to touch, to touch one another, each other.

toucher, *v.n.*, to touch; to reach; to take away; to play a musical instrument; to draw near, to approach; to change, to alter; to concern, to regard, to interest; to be affected, to be moved; to drive, to drive on; (man.) to whip; to be related, to be akin; to be like; (nav.) to touch; (nav.) to ground; (nav.) to strike. *Sa maison touche à la mienne;* his house is next to mine. *— à une île* (nav.); to touch at an island. *Touchez, cocher, allons plus vite :* drive on, coachman, let us go faster. *J'y touche de la main :* I reach it with my hand. — *à un certain temps ;* to be very near a particular time. *Il n'osa — à la religion ;* he dared not meddle with religion. *Il y a touché ;* he had a hand in it. — *de près à quelqu'un ;* to be nearly related to one. *N'avoir pas l'air d'y —;* to look as if butter would not melt in one's mouth.

toucher, *n.m.,* touch, feeling ; touch (manner of playing an instrument—*manière de jouer d'un instrument*).

toucheur, *n.m.,* cattle drover.

tou-coï, *int.,* (hunt.) lie down ! down !

toue, *n.f.,* ferry-boat.

touée, *n.f.,* (nav.) towage. *Amarre de —;* towline.

touer, *v.a.,* (nav.) to tow, to warp.

se **touer,** *v.r.,* (nav.) to haul herself ahead.

toueur, *n.m.,* towing-boat (on rivers—*sur les rivières*).

touffe, *n.f.,* tuft, bunch, cluster, clump; wisp (of straw, hay—*de paille, de foin*). — *de cheveux ;* tuft of hair. — *d'arbres ;* cluster of trees.

touffeur, *n.f.,* (fam.) stifling heat.

touffu, -e, *adj.,* tufted, bushy, branchy.

toug, *n.m.* *V.* **touc.**

toujours, *adv.,* always, for ever, ever, evermore ; still ; nevertheless, at least. *Est-il — à Paris ?* is he still in Paris ? *Se dire adieu pour —;* to bid each other adieu for ever.

toupet, *n.m.,* tuft of hair ; forelock ; Brutus, front hair sticking up ; presumption, brass, effrontery. *Avoir du —;* to have presumption, brass. *Se prendre au —;* to take each other by the hair.

toupie, *n.f.,* spinning-top, peg-top ; humming-top ; top. — *d'Allemagne ;* humming-top. *Faire aller une —;* to spin a top.

*****toupiller,** *v.n.,* (fam.) to do nothing but run up and down in a house.

*****toupillon,** *n.m.,* little tuft of hair ; waste branch (of an orange-tree—*d'oranger*).

tour, *n.f.,* tower ; rook, castle (at chess—*aux échecs*).

tour, *n.m.,* turn, going round, winding ; revolution ; turn ; circumference, circuit ; trick ; feat ; order ; lathe ; turning-box ; tour, trip; valance (of beds—*de lit*) ; turn (act—*action*) ; tour (of hair—*de cheveux*). *Faire le — de ;* to go round. *En un — de main ;* in the twinkling of an eye. *Faire un — de jardin ;* to take a turn round the garden. *Cet arbre a dix pieds de —;* that tree is ten feet in circumference. *—s de gobelets ;* juggler's tricks, legerdemain. *Vous aurez votre —;* you will have your turn. *Faire, jouer, un mauvais — à quelqu'un ;* to serve any one a trick, to play any one a nasty trick. *Chacun à son —;* every one in his turn. *— à —;* by turns. *— en l'air ;* mandrel-lathe. *Fait au —;* made with a lathe, turned ; extremely well made. *À — de rôle ;* in turn, in succession.

*****touraille,** *n.f.,* malt kiln.

touranien, -ne (-ni-in, -ni-è-n), *adj.,* applied as a general appellation to the peoples that inhabit between the Caspian Sea and the Sea of Japan ; also to their languages.

tourbe, *n.f.,* turf, peat ; mob, vulgar herd.

tourbeu-x, -se, *adj.,* turfy, peaty.

tourbière, *n.f.,* peat-bog, peat-moss.

*****tourbillon,** *n.m.,* whirlwind, vortex ; whirlpool ; eddy ; tourbillon (fire-work—*pièce d'artifice*).

*****tourbillonnement,** *n.m.,* whirling.

*****tourbillonner,** *v.n.,* to eddy, to whirl, to wind.

tourd, *n.m.,* (ich.) sea fish of the genus Jabrax.

tourd, *n.m.,* or **tourdelle,** *n.f.,* (orni.) field-fare.

*****tourdille,** *adj.,* dirty (of grey—*du gris*).

tourelle, *n.f.,* turret.

touret, *n.m.,* wheel (of a lathe—*de tour*); reel.

tourie, *n.f.,* large stoneware bottle protected by wicker-work, a kind of carboy.

tourière, *n.f.,* nun who attends to the turning-box in a nunnery.

*****tourillon,** *n.m.,* trunnion ; spindle (of a gate —*d'une grille*) ; axle ; axle-tree, arbor.

touriste, *n.m.,* tourist.

tourlourou, *n.m.,* (pop.) foot-soldier.

tourmaline, *n.f.,* tourmalin, turmalin.

tourment, *n.m.,* torment, torture ; anguish, pain ; plague, scourge, vexation.

tourmentant, -e, *adj.,* tormenting, troublesome.

tourmente, *n.f.,* tempest, storm, foul weather ; (fig.) disturbance.

tourmenter, *v.a.,* to torment, to torture, to rack ; to grieve, to vex, to trouble, to plague ; to harass, to annoy, to pester ; to jolt ; to strain (a ship—*un vaisseau*). *Son procès le tourmente ;* his lawsuit plagues him. *Que cela ne vous tourmente point ;* do not let that make you uneasy.

se **tourmenter,** *v.r.,* to toss, to tumble ; to torment one's self, to labour very hard ; to be uneasy, to fret ; (of wood—*du bois*) to warp ; to be restless, agitated (of horses—*du cheval*).

tourmenteu-x, -se, *adj.,* (nav.,l.u.)stormy (of regions—*de parages*).

tourmentin, *n.m.,* (nav.) storm-jib.

*****tournailler,** *v.n.,* (fam.) to turn, to go round and round one place ; to prowl about one place.

tournant, *n.m.,* turn, turning ; turning-space (for a carriage—*de voiture*); whirlpool, vortex ; indirect means. *Au — de la rue ;* at the corner of the street.

tournant, -e, *adj.,* turning. *Pont —;* revolving, swing-bridge. *Mouvement —* (milit.); turning, out-flanking of an enemy's position, troops.

tourné, -e, *part.,* turned ; awry. *Avoir l'esprit mal —;* to be cross-grained.

tourne-à-gauche, *n.m.* (—), (tech.) wrench.

⊙**tournebride,** *n.m.,* tavern, inn (near a mansion in the country—*près d'un château*).

tournebroche, *n.m.,* jack, kitchen-jack, roasting-jack ; turnspit (of persons, of dogs— *des personnes, des chiens*).

tournée, *n.f.,* circuit, progress, visit ; round, turn, walk ; journey. *Faire sa —:* to make one's round. *Il est en —:* he is on his rounds ; he is gone circuit (of judges, barristers—*de juges, d'avocats*).

tourne-gants, *n.m.* (—), glove-stick.

⊙**tournelle,** *n.f.,* small tower ; Tournelle, chamber of the Parliament of Paris.

⊙**tournemain.** *n.m.,* trice, twinkling, instant. *En un —;* in a trice, in a twinkling. *V. tour de main* under **tour.**

tournement, *n.m.,* turning, whirling. *— de tête ;* swimming in the head, giddiness.

*****tourne-oreille,** *n.m.* (—), (agri.) turning mouldboard.

tourne-pierre, *n.m.* (— —s), (orni.) turnstone.

tourner, *v.a.,* to turn, to turn round, to wind round, to revolve, to move round, to twirl, to twirl round ; to do, to translate ; to construe, to interpret ; to turn off ; to turn up. — *une broche ;* to turn a spit. — *le dos à quelqu'un :* to turn one's back on any one. — *ses souliers :* to wear one's shoes on one side. — *une personne à son gré ;* to manage any one as one likes, to wind any one round one's little finger. — *tout* en bien; to put a good construction upon everything. — une chose en raillerie; to make a jest of a thing. — du latin en français; to turn Latin into French. Il tourne bien un vers; he can turn a verse very well.

setourner, v.r., to turn; to turn round, to turn about; to turn, to change, to become changed. Le temps se tourne au beau; the weather is changing to fair.

tourner, v.n., to turn, to turn round, to wheel, to revolve, to tack about; to turn out; to change; to colour, to ripen; to turn up (of cards—aux cartes); to spoil (of liquids—des liquides). — vers; to turn towards. Le vent a tourné; the wind has shifted. Il tourne comme une girouette; he turns like a weather-cock. La tête me tourne; my head is giddy. La tête lui a tourné; he has lost his senses. — autour du pot; to beat about the bush. — du côté de quelqu'un; to go over to any one. Il ne sait plus de quel côté — ; he does not know which way to turn. Cela tournera mal; that will come to no good. La chance a tourné; the tables are turned.

tournesol, n.m., (bot.) turnsol, girasole; dyer's croton.

tournette, n.f., squirrel's cage; cotton winder (of candle-makers—de chandeliers); (l.u.) skein-holder.

tourneur, n.m., turner.

tourne-vent, n.m. (—), cowl (on chimneys —de cheminée).

tournevire, n.f., (nav.) voyol, viol. Garcettes de —; nippers. Œillets de—; eyes of the voyol.

tournevis (-viss), n.m., turn-screw, screw-driver.

tourniquet, n.m., turnstile, turnpike; (carp.) screw-jack; sash-pulley; (nav.) roller; (surg.) tourniquet; swivel.

tournis, n.m., (vet.) sturdy, turnsick, staggers.

tournoi, n.m., tournament.

tournoiement, or **tournoîment** (-noa-mān), n.m., turning round, wheeling round; (vet.) sturdy, turnsick, staggers. Un — de tête; a swimming in the head.

tournois, adj., of Tours. Livre — ; livre, Tours currency, worth about 10 pence.

tournoyer, v.n., to turn round and round, to wheel round, to wind; to beat about the bush.

tournure, n.f., figure, shape; tournure, bustle (part of a lady's dress—partie d'un vétement de femme); turn, direction; cast; appearance; turn (of mind, style—d'esprit, de style). Avoir bonne — ; to be a good figure, to have a good figure. Avoir mauvaise — ; to be a bad figure, to have a bad figure.

tourte, n.f., tart, fruit-pie; pie.

tourteau, n.m., (agri.) oil-cake; ⊙a cake; hermit-crab.

tourtereau, n.m., young turtle-dove.

tourterelle, n.f., turtle, turtle-dove.

tourtière (-ti-èr), n.f., tart-dish.

⊙**tourtre**, n.f., stock-dove.

tous, adj.m.pl., **toutes**, adj.f.pl. V. **tout**.

touselle, n.f., (agri.) lammas wheat.

toussaint, n.f., All Saint's-day.

tousser, v.n., to cough; to hem.

tousserie, n.f., (fam.) habitual coughing.

tousseu-r, n.m.,-**se**, n.f., cougher.

tout, -e, adj., all, whole, each, any; every. — le monde; all the world, every body. — e la famille; all the family. Tous mes livres; all my books. —es les fois que; as often as. Courir à —es jambes; to run full speed. C'est — un: it is all the same. — homme qui; any man who. Tous les jours; every day. — le jour; the whole day.

tout, n.m. (touts), whole, all; every one:

every thing. Il veut — avoir; he wants to have all. Est-ce là — ? is that all? Aves-vous — dit? have you said all? — bien considéré; all things being well considered. Il est propre à — ; he is fit for any thing. Du—; not at all. Il n'aura rien du — ; he shall have nothing at all. En — ; in all, upon the whole. Voilà — ; that is all. C'est — ; that is all. Par-dessus — ; above all. Point du — ; not at all. Plusieurs touts distincts; several distinct wholes.

tout, adv., wholly, entirely, quite, completely, thoroughly; all, for all; although, though, however. Je suis — à vous; I am quite at your service. Il est — malade; he is ill all over. — à fait; quite, wholly, entirely. — malades qu'ils sont; ill as they are. —es malades qu'elles sont; ill as they are. Des femmes — éplorées; women all in tears. — nu; stark naked. Ces fleurs sont — es fraîches; these flowers are quite fresh. —e femme qu'elle est; though she is a woman. — es bonnes qu'elles sont; however good they may be. — prêt; quite ready. Parler — haut; to speak aloud. — comme vous voudrez; just as you please. — le long de la rivière; all along the river. — beau; softly. — de go; bluntly. — de bon; in earnest. — à coup; suddenly. — d'un coup; all on a sudden. — au moins; at the least. — au plus; at the most. — à l'heure; just now. [Tout, adv., coming before an adjective or past participle beginning with a consonant, and qualifying a feminine noun or pronoun, is changed into toute; and into toutes, if the noun or pronoun is in the plural.]

tout à fait, adv., quite, wholly, entirely.

toute-bonne, n.f. (—s —s), (bot.) clary, all good; a sort of pear.

toute-épice, n.f. (—s —s), allspice.

toutefois, (toot-foa), adv., yet, nevertheless, however, still.

toutenague (toot-nag), or **tintenague**, n.f., (metal.) tutenag.

tout-ensemble, n.m. (—), (arts) whole, ensemble.

toute-présence, n.f. (n.p.), omnipresence, ubiquity.

toute-puissance, n.f. (n.p.), omnipotence, almighty power.

toute-saine, n.f. (—s —s), (bot.) tutisan.

toute-science, n.f. (n.p.), omniscience.

toute-table, or **toutes-tables**, n.m., tables (backgammon—sorte de revertier).

tou-tou, n.m. (— —s), bow-wow, dog.

tout-ou-rien, n.m. (—), (horl.) all or nothing.

tout-puissant, adj.m., **toute-puissante**, adj.f., Almighty, Omnipotent, all-powerful.

tout-puissant, n.m. (n.p.), Omnipotent, Almighty.

toux, n.f., cough, coughing. — opiniâtre; obstinate cough. — qui sent le sapin; church-yard cough. Quinte de — ; fit of coughing.

toxicodendron, n.m., (bot.) toxicodendron.

toxicologie, n.f., toxicology.

toxique, n.m. and adj., (med.) poison; poisonous.

traban, n.m., soldier armed with a halberd and employed in a special duty.

trabée, n.f., (Roman antiq.) trabea.

⊙**trac**, n.m., track, trace (of animals—d'animal); pace of horses, mules.

traçant, -e, adj., (bot.) running (of roots— des racines).

tracas, n.m., bustle, confusion, disorder; splutter. — des affaires; bustle of business. — du monde; bustle of the world.

tracasser, v.n., to bustle, to be busy, to be full of bustle; to meddle.

tracasser, *v.a.*, to plague, to trouble, to vex, to pester, to annoy.

tracasserie (-ka-srî), *n.f.*, cavil, chicane; quarrel; bickering, broil; pester, bother, plague.

tracassi-er, -ère, *n.* and *adj.*, chicaner, caviller; troublesome person, mischief-maker; pesterer; shuffling, cavilling; mischief-making; pestering, bothering.

trace, *n.f.*, trace, track, step, footstep, print (of the foot—*du pied*); sign, mark, impression, vestige; outline, sketch; (hunt.) trail; slot (of deer—*du cerf*).

tracé, *n.m.*, laying out (of ground—*d'un terrain*); outline, sketch; direction, line; draught.

tracement (tras-màn), *n.m.*, laying out (of grounds, roads—*des terrains, des routes*).

tracer, *v.a.*, to draw, to trace, to draw out, to trace out, to make out, to sketch; to lay out (grounds, roads—*des terrains, des routes*).

tracer, *v.n.*, (of trees—*des arbres*) to spread their roots; to run out.

trachée, *n.f.*, (ent., bot.) spiral vessel, trachea.

trachée-artère, *n.f.*, (−s −s) (anat.) trachea, windpipe.

trachéite, *n.f.*, (med.) trachitis.

trachéotomie, *n.f.*, (surg.) tracheotomy.

trachyte, *n.m.*, (min.) trachyte.

traçoir, *n.m.*, tracer.

traction, *n.f.*, traction; thrust (of suspension-bridges—*de ponts suspendus*).

traditeur, *n.m.*, (ecc. hist.) traditor.

tradition, *n.f.*, tradition; delivery.

traditionnaire, *n.m.*, traditionary.

traditionnel, -le, *adj.*, traditional, traditionary, traditive.

traditionnellement (-nèl-màn), *adv.*, traditionally.

traducteur, *n.m.*, translator.

traduction, *n.f.*, translation.

traduire (traduisant, traduit). *v.a.*, to translate, to interpret, to construe, to render; (jur.) to remove, to arraign, to indict. — *facilement, à livre ouvert;* to translate easily, at sight.

traduisible, *adj.*, translatable.

trafic, *n.m.*, traffic, trading. *Faire — de;* to make a trade of, to deal in. *Il fait — de toute sorte de marchandises;* he traffics in all sorts of goods.

trafiquant, *n.m.*, trafficker.

trafiquer, *v.n.*, to traffic, to trade, to deal.

tragacanthe, *n.f.*, (bot.) tragacanth.

tragédie, *n.f.*, tragedy.

tragédien, *n.m.*, **-ne**, *n.f.* (-in, -è-n), tragedian.

tragi-comédie, *n.f.*, tragi-comedy.

tragi-comique, *adj.*, tragi-comic, tragi-comical.

tragique, *adj.*, tragic, tragical.

tragique, *n.m.*, tragedy; tragedian; tragic writer; tragicalness. *Prendre une chose au —;* to take a thing too seriously. *Tourner au —;* to assume a tragical appearance.

tragiquement (-jik-màn), *adv.*, tragically.

trahir, *v.a.*, to betray, to disclose, to discover; to be false to, to deceive; to disappoint. — *sa patrie;* to betray one's country. — *le secret de quelqu'un;* to divulge, to betray, any one's secret.

se **trahir**, *v.r.*, to betray one's self; to betray one another.

trahison, *n.f.*, treachery, treacherousness; treason.

*****traille**, *n.f.*, ferry-boat (of a large size—*de grande dimension*).

train, *n.m.*, pace, rate; train, suite, attendants; way, manner; noise, dust; carriage, skele-

ton (of carriages—*de voiture*); quarters (of a horse—*du cheval*); train (of boats—*de bateaux*); (print.) carriage; raft; (railways) train; (railways) truck. — *d'artillerie;* train of artillery. — *de presse* (print.); carriage. — *de bois;* raft of wood. — *direct;* through train. — *omnibus;* slow train. — *mixte;* mixed train. — *express;* express train. — *-poste* (−s −); mail-train. — *d'aller;* down train. — *de marchandises;* goods train. — *de plaisir;* excursion train. — *de retour;* up train. — *de grande vitesse;* fast train. — *de petite vitesse;* goods train. — *de voyageurs;* passenger-train. *Mise en —* (print.); making ready. *Aller grand —;* to go at a great rate, to go very fast. *Le cocher nous a menés bon —;* the coachman drove us very fast. *Faire du —,* to make a noise. *L'affaire est en bon —;* the business is in a fair way. *Mettre quelqu'un en — de faire une chose;* to put any one in the way of doing a thing. *Tel était notre—de vie;* such was our way of living. *Il va toujours son —;* he goes on in his old way. *Être en —;* to be in good spirits, to be in the mood. *Va —dont il y va;* at the rate he goes on. *Fort en —;* in high spirits. *Se mettre en — de faire une chose;* to set one's self about a thing. *Tout d'un —;* all together.

trainage, *n.m.*, sledging, sleighing.

trainant, -e, *adj.*, dragging, trailing. *Drapeaux —s;* trailing colours. *Style —;* heavy style. *Voix —e;* drawling voice.

trainard, *n.m.*, loiterer, straggler.

trainasse, *n.f.*, (bot.) florin; knot-grass.

trainasser, *v.a.* and *n.*, (fam.) to draw out, to spin out, to be dilatory about; to be dilatory, to linger.

traine, *n.f.*, being dragged. *Bateau à la —;* boat in tow at the stern of a ship. *Perdreaux en —;* young partridges that cannot fly.

traineau, *n.m.*, sledge, sled, sleigh; trammel, drag-net, draw-net.

traine-buissons, *n.m.*, (orni.) hedge-sparrow.

trainée, *n.f.*, train (of gunpowder—*de poudre*); trail (long line of anything spilt—*ligne faite par quelque chose de répandu*); (hunt.) track; street-walker, trollop.

traine-malheur, *n.m.* (—), wretch.

traine-potence, *n.m.* (—), hang-gallows-fellow, Newgate-bird, gaol-bird, gallows-bird.

trainer, *v.a.*, to draw, to drag, to drag along, to trail; to put off, to spin out, to draw out, to protract, to lengthen; to drawl. — *un homme en prison;* to drag a man off to prison. *Il traine la jambe;* he drags his leg. *Cet oiseau traine l'aile;* that bird hangs its wing. — *ses paroles;* to draw out one's words. — *les choses en longueur;* to protract things. — *dans la boue;* to draggle; to defame.

se **trainer**, *v.r.*, to crawl, to creep along; to lag, to lag behind, to drag one's self along.

trainer, *v.n.*, to trail, to drag, to lag; to droop; to lie about; to languish, to linger; to be spun out, to be protracted, to be drawn out, to be lengthened; to be found. *Votre robe traine;* your gown sweeps the ground, drags along the ground. *Il y a longtemps qu'il traine;* he has been in a lingering state for a long time. *Cela traine dans tous les livres;* that is found in every book.

traineur, *n.m.*, straggler, lagger; poacher who catches game with a trammel; (nav.) ship in the rear. — *d'épée,* — *de sabre,* idle fellow, that carries a sword, sword dangler.

traire (trayant, trait), *v.a.* to milk.

trait, -e, *part.,* milked; (of precious metals —*des métaux précieux*) wire-drawn.

trait, *n.m.,* arrow, dart, bolt, shaft, thunderbolt; stroke, hit, trait; trace (of harness—*harnais*); leash (for dogs—*de limier*); turn (of the scale—*de la balance*); draught, gulp; dash (of the pen—*de plume*); (paint.) touch; kerf (of a saw—*de scie*); feature, lineament (of one's face—*du visage*); act; prime move (at chess, draughts —*aux échecs, aux dames*); (c.rel.) tract; gold or silver-wire. *Décocher, lancer un* —; to shoot, to let fly an arrow. *Lancer un trait;* to shoot a dart. *Il partit comme un* —; he darted off as swift as an arrow. —*s de l'Amour;* shafts of Love. — *piquant;* smart hit. — *de satire;* satirical stroke. *Chacun me lança son* —; every one had a fling at me. —*s de l'envie;* shafts of envy. *Avaler tout d'un* —; to swallow at one draught. *Boire à longs* —*s;* to quaff. *Goûter un plaisir à longs* —*s;* to relish a pleasure. *Copier* — *pour* —; to copy stroke for stroke. — *d'esprit;* witticism, flash of wit. *Cheval de* —; draught-horse. *Boutons de* —; gold or silver-wire buttons.

traitable, *adj.,* tractable, manageable; (metal.) ductile, pliant, soft, malleable.

traitant, *n.m.,* farmer of the public revenues; contractor.

traite, *n.f.,* stage, journey; trade, trading on the African coast; milking; draft, bill; (com.) banking; exportation ⊙ custom duty; ⊙ (coin.) defalcation on the intrinsic value of coins. *Je m'y rendis tout d'une* —; I made but one stage of it. — *des nègres,* — *des noirs;* slave-trade. *Bâtiment de* —; slaver, slave-ship. *Faire la* —; to carry on the slave-trade; to trade with the coast of Africa.

traité, *n.m.,* treatise, tract, dissertation; treaty; agreement. — *de paix;* treaty of peace. — *de commerce;* commercial treaty.

traitement (trèt-mān), *n.m.,* treatment; reception, entertainment; usage; entertainment (to ambassadors or envoys—*d'ambassadeurs, d'envoyés, &c.*); salary, emoluments of a place; (med., chem.) treatment; (nav.) full pay. *Mauvais* —*s;* ill-usage, ill-treatment.

traiter, *v.a.,* to treat; to discuss, to handle, to discourse on; to use, to behave to; to negotiate, to treat for, to be in treaty for; to treat of; to entertain, to board; to execute, to do; (med., chem.) to treat. *Il m'a traité en frère;* he treated me like a brother. — *quelqu'un avec honneur;* to show any one great honour. — *de haut en bas;* to treat with contempt. *Il l'a traité de fat;* he called him a fop. — *quelqu'un de Turc à More;* to treat any one like a Turk.

se traiter, *v.r.,* to be treated; to treat one's self; to treat one another.

traiter, *v.n.,* to treat, to discuss; to negotiate, to be in negotiation for; to come to terms; to entertain, to treat; to keep an ordinary; to keep a boarding-house. — *d'une matière;* to treat of a matter. *Partir pour aller* —*de la paix;* to set out for the purpose of negotiating a peace. — *à tant par tête;* to board people at so much a head; to board people at so much a head.

traiteur, *n.m.,* eating-house keeper; Louisiana trader.

traître, -sse, *n.* and *adj.,* traitor, treacherous man; traitress, treacherous woman; treacherous, false, perfidious; traitorous. *Les chats sont* —*s;* cats are treacherous. *Âme traîtresse;* perfidious man or woman.

traîtreusement (-eûz-mān), *adv.,* traitorously, treacherously.

trajectoire, *n.f.,* (ballistics—*balistique*) trajectory.

trajet, *n.m.,* passage, voyage, journey;

(surg.) course. — *d'une plaie;* direction of a wound.

*tramail, or **trémail,** *n.m.,* trammel, drag-net.

trame, *n.f.,* waft, woof; plot; course, progress. *La* — *de sa vie;* the course of his life. *Ourdir une* —; to lay a plot.

tramer, *v.a.,* to weave; to plot, to brew, to contrive, to hatch. — *une étoffe de soie;* to weave a stuff with a silk woof. — *une conspiration;* to hatch a plot.

se tramer, *v.r.,* to be woven; to be hatched, plotted; to be in course of being hatched, plotted.

⊙tramontain, -e (-tin, -tè-n), *adj.,* tramontane, lying beyond the mountains.

tramontane, *n.f.,* tramontane, North wind; North; North star (in the Mediterranean—*dans la Méditerranée*). *Perdre la* —; to be at a loss what to do, to be at one's wit's end.

tramway, *n.m.* (-*s*), tram-way, tram-road.

tranchant, -e, *adj.,* sharp, cutting; peremptory, decisive. *Épée* —*e;* sharp sword. *C'est un homme* —; he is a peremptory man. *Écuyer* —; gentleman-carver. *Couleurs* —*es;* strong, glaring colours.

tranchant, *n.m.,* edge (of cutting instruments—*d'instruments coupants*); web (of coulters —*de coutre*). *Épée à deux* —*s;* two-edged sword.

tranche, *n.f.,* slice, chop, collop, steak; (of a book—*de livre*) edge; (arith.) period, set. *Livre doré sur* —*s;* book with gilt edges. — *de lard;* rasher of bacon.

tranchée, *n.f.,* trench, drain; *pl.,* throes, pains (of a woman in labour—*d'une femme en travail*); cut, cutting, excavation; *pl.,* gripes, griping. *Avoir des* —*s;* to be griped. —*s rouges* (vet.); gripes (of horses—*du cheval*).

tranchefile (transh-fil), *n.f.,* (book-bind.) headband; bar (in a shoe—*de soulier*); cross-chain of a bridle; little chain (about a bit—*de mors*).

tranchelard (transh-lār), *n.m.,* larding-knife.

*tranche-montagne, *n.m.* (— —*s*), hector, bully, swaggerer.

trancher, *v.a.,* to cut, to cut off; to decide, to determine, to settle. — *la tête à quelqu'un;* to cut off any one's head. *Ceci tranche la difficulté;* this removes the obstacle. — *le mot;* to say the word, to speak out.

trancher, *v.n.,* to decide, to determine, to resolve, to set up for, to affect; to cut; (of colours—*des couleurs*) to glare, to show. — *court;* to cut short. — *net;* to tell one's mind plainly. — *du grand seigneur;* to give one's self the airs of a lord. — *du philosophe;* to set up for a philosopher. — *du petit-maître;* to affect the beau. *Ce couteau tranche comme un rasoir;* this knife cuts like a razor.

tranchet, *n.m.,* shoemaker's knife; paring-knife; shank (of chisels—*de ciseau*).

tranchoir, *n.m.,* trencher, plate.

tranquille, *adj.,* quiet, calm, still, tranquil, peaceful; easy (in mind—*d'esprit*). *Tenez-vous* —; be quiet. *Séjour* —; tranquil abode.

tranquillement (-kil-mān), *adv.,* tranquilly, quietly, peaceably, calmly, sedately.

tranquillisant, -e, *adj.,* tranquillizing.

tranquilliser, *v.a.,* to tranquillize, to make easy, to still, to quiet.

se tranquilliser, *v.r.,* to grow tranquil, easy; to become tranquil, to be tranquillized.

tranquillité, *n.f.,* tranquillity, tranquilness, calmness.

trans, a prefix from Lat. *trans.*

transaction (-zak-ci-), *n.f.,* transaction, compromise.

transalpin, -e (-zal-pin, -pi-n), *adj.,* lying beyond the Alps, transalpine.

transatlantique, *adj.*, transatlantic.

transbordement, *n.m.*, trans-shipment.

transborder, *v.a.*, to trans-ship.

transcendance, *n.f.*, transcendency.

transcendant, -e, *adj.*, transcendent.

transcendantal, -e, *adj.*, (philos.) transcendental.

transcripteur, *n.m.*, transcriber.

transcription, *n.f.*, transcription, copy.

transcrire, *v.a.*, to transcribe, to copy.

transe, *n.f.*, affright, fright. *Être dans des —s;* to be in fear.

transept, *n.m.*, (arch.) transept.

transférable, *adj.*, transferable; (com.) endorsable.

transférement, *n.m.*, removal, conveying (of convicts—*de condamnés*).

transférer, *v.a.*, to transfer, to transport, to convey; to translate (bishops—*un évêque*); to remove; to put off; to make over; to postpone. *— son droit;* to make over one's right. *— une fête;* to postpone a fête.

transfert, *n.m.*, transfer.

transfiguration, *n.f.*, transfiguration.

transfigurer, *v.a.*, to transfigure.

se **transfigurer**, *v.r.*, to be transfigured.

transfilage, *n.m.*, (nav.) marling.

transfiler, *v.a.*, (nav.) to marl.

transformation, *n.f.*, transformation, transmutation.

transformer, *v.a.*, to transform, to transmute.

se **transformer**, *v.r.*, to transform, to be transformed, to be transmuted.

transfuge, *n.m.*, (milit.) deserter; fugitive, turncoat.

transfuser, *v.a.*, to transfuse.

transfusion, *n.f.*, transfusion.

transgresser, *v.a.*, to transgress, to trespass against, to violate.

transgresseur, *n.m.*, transgressor.

transgression, *n.f.*, transgression, violation.

transi, -e, *part.*, chilled, benumbed. *— de froid;* chilled with cold. *Un amoureux —;* a bashful lover.

transiger (-zi-jé), *v.n.*, to compound, to come to terms.

transir, *v.a.*, to chill, to benumb; to overcome with fear of affliction.

transir, *v.n.*, to be chilled (with cold—*de froid*); to be overcome with fear or affliction.

transissement (-sis-màn), *n.m.*, (l.u.) chill, numbness.

transit (tran-zit), *n.m.*, transit.

transiti-f, -ve (tran-zi-), *adj.*, transitive. *Verbe —;* transitive verb.

transition (tran-zi-), *n.f.*, transition.

transitoire (tran-zi-), *adj.*, transitory, transient.

○**translater**, *v.a.*, to translate.

○**translateur**, *n.m.*, translator.

translati-f, -ve, *adj.*, (jur.) transfering.

translation, *n.f.*, translation (of bishops—*d'évêque*); removal; postponement (of a ceremony —*d'une cérémonie*); (jur.) transfer; ○translation.

translucide, *adj.*, translucid.

translucidité, *n.f.*, translucency.

transmarin, -e (-rin, -ri-n), *adj.*, transmarine.

transmettre, *v.a.*, to transmit, to convey; to forward; to send on; to transfer, to make over. *— son nom à la postérité;* to transmit one's name to posterity.

transmigrant, -e, *adj.*, (zool.) migratory.

transmigration, *n.f.*, transmigration.

transmissibilité, *n.f.*, transmissibility.

transmissible, *adj.*, transmissible, transferable.

transmission, *n.f.*, transmission.

transmuable, *adj.*, transmutable.

transmuer, *v.a.*, to transmute.

transmutabilité, *n.f.*, transmutability.

transmutation, *n.f.*, transmutation.

transparence, *n.f.*, transparency.

transparent, -e, *adj.*, transparent.

transparent, *n.m.*, (paint.) transparency; lines (for writing straight—*pour écrire droit*).

transpercer, *v.a.*, to transpierce, to pierce through and through, to run through.

transpirable, *adj.*, (l.u.) perspirable.

transpiration, *n.f.*, perspiration, transpiration.

transpirer, *v.n.*, to perspire, to exhale; to transpire.

○**transplantateur**, *n.m.*, (gard.) transplanter.

transplantation, *n.f.*, transplantation.

○**transplantement**, *n.m.* *V.* **transplantation.**

transplanter, *v.a.*, to transplant.

transplanteur, *n.m.*, (hort.) (pers.) transplanter.

transplantoir, *n.m.*, transplanter (instrument).

transport, *n.m.*, carriage; conveyance, transport; transfer, assignment; rapture, ecstacy, delirium; (nav.) transport-ship, transport. *Vaisseau de —;* transport-ship. *— de joie;* transport of joy. *— au cerveau;* delirium, deliriousness. *Commerce de —;* carrying-trade. *Frais de —* (com.); carriage.

transportable, *adj.*, that may be conveyed.

transportation, *n.f.*, transportation, banishment.

transporté, -e, *n.* and *adj.*, one who has been banished; transported, rapt.

transporter, *v.a.*, to convey, to transport; to transfer; to make over; to transport, to banish; to enrapture. *— une créance;* to transfer a debt. *La joie l'a tout transporté;* he is quite transported with joy.

se **transporter**, *v.r.*, to go, to repair. *— sur les lieux;* to go to the place.

○**transposable**, *adj.*, transposable.

transposer, *v.a.*, to transpose.

transpositeur, *adj.m.*, only used in: *piano, instrument —:* transposing piano, instrument.

transpositi-f, -ve, *adj.*, transpositive.

transposition, *n.f.*, transposition.

transrhénan, -e, *adj.*, of beyond the Rhine.

transsubstantiation (-stàn-ci-a-cion), *n.f.*, transsubstantiation.

transsubstantier (-stàn-cié), *v.a.*, to transsubstantiate.

transsudation, *n.f.*, transudation.

transsuder, *v.n.*, to transude.

transvasation, *n.f.*, decanting, transfusion.

transvasement, *n.m.*, decantation, transfusion.

transvaser, *v.a.*, to decant, to transfuse.

transversal, -e, *adj.*, transversal, transverse.

transversalement (-sal-màn), *adv.*, transversely.

transverse, *adj.*, transversal, transverse.

trantran, *n.m.*, (fam.) routine, course of certain things; knack (in treating certain things—*en tra'tant de certaines choses*). *Savoir le —;* to be an old stager. *Savoir le — du palais* (fam.); to be up to the ways of the law courts.

trapèze, *n.m.*, (geom.) trapezium; (anat.) trapezium (bone—*os*); trapezius (muscle). [In the language of anatomy this word is also used adjectively: *os —;* trapezium; *muscle —;* trapezius.]

trapéziforme, *adj.*, trapeziform.

trapézoïde. *n.m. and adj.*, (geom.) trapezoid; (anat.) trapezoidal.

trapp, *n.m.*, (geol., min.) trap.

trappe, *n.f.*, trap-door; trap, pitfall. *Tendre une — ;* to lay a trap.

trappeur, *n.m.*, trapper.

trappiste, *n.m.*, Trappist.

trapu, -e, *adj.*, squat, dumpy, thick-set.

traque, *n.f.*, (hunt.) beating for game.

traquenard (trak-nar), *n.m.*, rocking-pace (of a horse—*du cheval*); trap (for noxious animals—*pour les animaux nuisibles*).

traquer, *v.a.*, (hunt.) to beat a wood for game; to enclose; to encircle; to ferret out; to surround, to hem in. — *un bois;* to enclose a wood. — *des voleurs;* to surround thieves.

traquet, *n.m.*, trap (for fetid animals—*pour les bêtes puantes*); (orni.) stone-chatter; millclapper. *Donner dans le — ;* to be entrapped.

traqueur, *n.m.*,(hunt.) huntsman who beats a wood, who encloses game.

trass, *n.m.*, (min.) trass.

traumaticine, *n.f.*, (med.) pigment of gutta-percha.

traumatique, *adj.*, traumatic.

*****travail,** *n.m.* (*travaux*), labour, work, toil; piece of work; employment; study; travail. *Travaux;* works; workmanship. *Vivre de son — ;* to live by one's labour. *À force de — ;* by dint of labour. *Se mettre au — ;* to set to work. — *d'enfant ;* child-birth, labour, travail. *Travaux forcés;* penal servitude with *or* without transportation.

*****travail,** *n.m.* (*travails*), trave, travis, brake for the shoeing of refractory horses; reports of Ministers to the Head of the State, of heads of departments to Ministers.

*****travailler,** *v.n.*, to labour, to work; (of wine—*du vin*) to ferment; to study; to make it one's study; to endeavour; to digest with difficulty (of the stomach—*de l'estomac*); (of a ship—*d'un vaisseau*) to be strained. — *à l'aiguille;* to work with the needle. *Ce bois travaille;* that wood is warping. *Ce mur travaille;* that wall is chinking.

*****travailler,** *v.a.*, to work, to work at, to labour; to do with care; to fashion; to work up; to cultivate, to improve (ground—*un champ*); to exercise, to overwork (a horse—*un cheval*); to torment. *Un cheval trop travaillé;* a horse overworked.

*****se travailler,** *v.r.*, to torment one's self; to make one's self uneasy; to torment each other; to work up; to endeavour.

*****travailleu-r, -se,** *n. and adj.*, workman; labourer, artisan; industrious, hard-working man; industrious, laborious woman; laborious, industrious, hard-working.

travée, *n.f.*, (arch.) bay; truss (of bridges—*de ponts*). — *de balustres;* balustrade.

travers, *n.m.*, breadth; whim, caprice, oddity, eccentricity. *À — ;* athwart, through, across. *Au — de;* through. *Au — du corps;* through the body. *À — les bois;* across the woods. *À — champs;* across the fields. *Parler à tort et à — ;* to talk at random. *De — ;* awry, crooked; askew, cross, wrong. *Marcher de — ;* to walk crooked. *Regarder quelqu'un de — ;* to look black at any one. *Il prend tout de — ;* he takes every thing wrong. *Avoir l'esprit de — ;* to be of a cross-grained temper. *En — ;* across, cross-wise.

traverse, *n.f.*, cross-bar; (carp.) cross-beamgirder; (railways) sleeper; (fort.) traverse; misfortune. *À la — ;* (obstacle) in the way. *Se jeter, venir, à la — ;* to place one's self in the way.

traversée, *n.f.*, (nav.) passage, voyage,

traverser, *v.a.*, to cross, to go *or* pass over, to travel over, to travel through; to lie across; to traverse, to get over; to go across; to run through with a sword; to penetrate, to go, to run through; to thwart, to disturb, to vex. — *une rivière à la nage;* to swim over a river. — *l'ancre* (nav.); to stow the anchor. — *les voiles* (nav.); to flat in the sails. — *un projet;* to thwart a project.

*****se traverser,** *v.r.*, to be crossed; to cross each other; to thwart each other; (man.) to traverse.

traversi-er, -ère, *adj.*, cross, that goes across.

traversin, *n.m.*, bolster; (carp., nav.) cross beam.

traversine, *n.f.*, (arch.) sleeper, transom.

travertin, *n.m.*, travertin.

travesti, -e, *adj.*, disguised, travestied. — *en paysan;* disguised as a peasant.

travestir, *v.a.*, to disguise, to travesty.

*****se travestir,** *v.r.*, to disguise one's self.

travestissement(-tis-màn), *n.m.*, disguise, travesty.

trayon, *n.m.*, dug, teat (of cows, goats, &c.—*de vaches, &c.*).

trébellianique, *or* **trébellienne,** *adj.*, (antiq., Roman jur.) only used in: *quarte — ;* the fourth part of a succession which the heir had a right to receive by giving up the rest.

trébuchant, -e, *adj.*, (coin.) of weight, of full weight; stumbling.

trébuchant, *n.m.*, (coin.) full weight.

trébuchement (-bush-man), *n.m.*, (l.u.) stumbling.

trébucher, *v.n.*, to stumble, to slip, to trip, to err; to weigh down.

trébuchet, *n.m.*, assay-balance; bird-trap. *Prendre quelqu'un au — ;* to entrap any one.

tréfiler, *v.a.*, to draw wire.

tréfilerie (-fil-rî), *n.f.*, wire-drawing mill.

tréfileur, *n.m.*, wire-drawer.

trèfle, *n.m.*, (bot.) trefoil, clover; clubs (at cards—*cartes*); (arch.) trefoil.

tréfoncier, *n.m.*, owner of a wood subject to certain dues.

tréfonds, *or* **très-fonds**(-fon), *n.m.*, subsoil. *Savoir, le fond et le — d'une affaire;* to be thoroughly acquainted with an affair.

*****treillage,** *n.m.*, trellis, lattice; treillage (of gardens—*de jardin*); fence.

*****treillageur,** *n.m.*, lattice-maker, trellismaker.

*****treille,** *n.f.*, vine-arbour. *Le jus de la — ;* the juice of the grape.

*****treillis,** *n.m.*, trellis, lattice; lattice-work; glazed calico; sack-cloth.

*****treillissé, -e** *adj.*, trellised, latticed.

*****treillisser,** *v.a.*, to trellis, to lattice.

treize, *n.m. and adj.*, thirteen, thirteenth.

treizième. *n.m.f. and adj.*, thirteenth.

treizièmement (trè-zièm-màn), *adv.*, thirteenthly.

tréma, *n.m. and adj. invariable*, diæresis; with a diæresis.

trémail. *n.m. V.* **tramail.**

tremblaie. *n.f.*, grove of aspens.

tremblant, -e, *adj.*, trembling, quaking, tremulous, shivering, quivering.

tremble, *n.m.*, (bot.) aspen.

tremblé, *n.m.*, (print.) waved rule.

tremblé, -e *adj.*, waved (of lines—*des lignes*); shaking (or writing—*de l'écriture*). *Écriture —e;* shaking handwriting.

tremblée, *n.f.*, (vet.) thwarter.

tremblement, *n.m.*, trembling, quaking, trepidation, shaking, shivering, tremor; (mus.) shake. — *de nerfs;* nervous shivering. — *de terre;* earthquake.

trembler. *v.n.*, to tremble, to shake, to shiver; to quake, to fear. — *de froid;* to shiver with cold. *La main lui tremble ;* his hand shakes.

trembleu-r, *n.m.,* **-se,** *n.f.,* trembler, quaker.

tremblotant, -e, *adj.,* trembling (of sound —*du son*) ; shivering, quivering.

trembloter, *v.n.,* to tremble (of sound—*du son*) ; to quiver, to shiver.

trémie, *n.f.,* hopper, mill-hopper.

trémière, *adj. f.,* only used in : *rose —* ; holly-hock, rose-mallow.

tremolo (tré-), *n.m.* (—), (mus.) tremo'o.

trémoussement (-moos-män), *n.m.,* fluttering ; frisking.

trémousser, *v.n.,* to flutter.

se trémousser, *v.r.,* to flutter about, to frisk ; to bestir one's self.

trémoussoir, *n.m.,* gymnastic apparatus for taking exercise in one's room.

trempage, *n.m.,* steeping ; (print.) wetting.

trempe, *n.m.,* temper (of steel—*de l'acier*) ; constitution ; character, stamp, quality ; (print.) wetting. *Donner la — au fer ;* to temper iron. *Ce sont des gens de la même — ;* they are people of the same stamp.

trempé, -e, *part.,* soaked, wet ; tempered (of iron and steel—*du fer et de l'acier*). *Il est tout — ;* he is wet to the skin. *Du vin — ;* diluted wine.

tremper, *v.a.,* to dip, to soak, to steep, to drench, to wet, to temper (iron and steel—*le fer et l'acier*) ; to dilute (wine—*du vin*) ; (print.) to wet (paper—*le papier*) ; to imbrue. *— la soupe ;* to pour the soup on the bread. *— ses mains dans le sang ;* to imbrue one's hands in blood.

tremper, *v.n.,* to soak, to be steeped ; to be implicated. *— dans un crime ;* to be concerned in a crime.

tremperie (tran-pri), *n.f.,* (print.) wetting-room, sink.

tremplin, *n.m.,* springing-board.

trentain, *n.m.,* thirty all (at tennis—*à la paume*).

trentaine, *n.f.,* about thirty ; age of thirty. *Il a passé la — ;* he is passed thirty.

trente, *n.m. and adj.,* thirty, thirtieth.

trentenaire, *adj.,* of thirty years' duration.

trentième (-tièm), *n.m.f. and adj.,* thirtieth.

tréou, *n.m.,* (nav.) lug-sail.

trépan, *n.m.,* (surg.) trepan (instrument) ; trepanning.

trépanation, *n.f.,* (surg.) trepanning.

trépaner, *v.a.,* (surg.) to trepan.

trépang, *n.m.,* (zool.) trepang.

trépas, *n.m.,* (poet.) decease, death.

trépassé, *n.m.,* dead person. *Les —s ;* the dead.

trépassement (-pâs-män), *n.m.,* death.

trépasser, *v.n.,* to die, to depart this life.

trépidation, *n.f.,* trepidation, trembling, tremor ; (ancient astron.) trepidation, libration ; slight shock of earthquake.

trépied, *n.m.,* trivet ; tripod.

***trépignement,** *n.m.,* stamping.

***trépigner,** *v.n.,* to stamp. *Il trépigne de colère ;* he stamps with passion.

trépointe, *n.f.,* welt (of a shoe—*de chaussure*).

très, *adv.,* very ; most ; very much. *— bon ;* very good. *— agité ;* very much agitated.

tré-sept (-sèt), *n.m.* (n.p.), a card game.

très-fonds, *n.m.* (—). *V.* **tréfonds.**

trésor, *n.m.,* treasure ; treasury ; record-office ; (c. rel.) relics and ornaments. *Amasser des —s ;* to heap up treasures. *Les —s de la science ;* the treasures of science.

trésorerie (-zor-rî), *n.f.,* treasury.

trésorier, *n.m.,* treasurer ; (milit.) pay-master.

trésorière, *n.f.,* treasurer.

***tressaillement,** *n.m.,* start, starting.

***tressaillir** (tressaillant, tressailli), *v.n.* to start, to leap, to tremble, to give a start. *— de peur ;* to start with fear. *— de joie ;* to leap for joy.

tresse, *n.f.,* tress, plait.

tresser, *v.a.,* to weave, to interweave, to plait, to form into tresses. *— des cheveux ;* to braid hair.

tresseu-r, *n.m.,* **-se,** *n.f.,* plaiter.

tróteau, *n.m.,* trestle. *—x ;* stage of a mountebank. *Monter sur les —x ;* to make a mountebank of one's self.

***treuil,** *n.m.,* windlass ; hand-winch ; (mec.) wheel and axle.

trêve, *n.f.,* truce. *— de compliments ;* a truce with all compliments.

trévire, *n.f.,* (nav.) parbuckle.

tri, a prefix from Lat. *tri,* and Gr. τρι.

tri, *n.m.,* "tri" (card game—*jeu de cartes*) ; sorting ; trick (whist).

triade, *n.f.,* triad.

triage, *n.m.,* choosing, picking, sorting.

triaires, *n.m.pl.,* (antiq.) veteran Roman soldiers who formed the third rank from the front when in order of battle.

triandre, *adj.,* (bot.) triandrous.

triandrie, *n.f.,* (bot.) triandria.

triangle, *n.m.,* (geom., astron., mus.) triangle ; (nav.) triangular hanging stage (for caulking, &c.—*pour calfater, &c.*).

triangulaire, *adj.,* triangular.

triangulairement, *adv.,* triangularly.

triangulation, *n.f.,* triangulation ; trigonometrical survey.

triangulé, -e, *adj.,* triangled.

trias, *n.m.,* (geol.) trias.

triasique, *adj.,* (geol.) triassic.

tribade, *n.f.,* (l.ex.) shameless, unnatural woman.

tribord, *n.m.,* (nav.) starboard, starboard-watch. *— tout !* (nav.) hard a starboard !

tribordais, *n.m.,* (nav.) starboard-watch.

tribouiet, *n.m.,* (gold.) triblet.

tribraque, *n.m.,* tribrach.

tribu, *n.f.,* tribe.

tribulation, *n.f.,* tribulation.

tribun, *n.m.,* tribune.

tribunal, *n.m.,* tribunal, judgment-seat ; court of justice.

tribunat, *n.m.,* tribuneship ; tribunate.

tribune, *n.f.,* tribune (rostrum) ; gallery.

tribunitien, -ne (-ci-in, -ci-è-n), *adj.,* tribunitial.

tribut, *n.m.,* tribute. *Payer le — à la nature ;* to pay the debt of nature.

tributaire, *n.m. and adj.,* tributary.

triceps (-sèps), *n.m. and adj.,* (anat.) triceps.

tricher, *v.a.* and *n.,* (fam.) to cheat ; to trick (at play—*au jeu*).

tricherie (tri-shri), *n.f.,* cheat, cheating, trick, trickery (at play—*au jeu*).

tricheu-r, *n.m.,* **-se,** *n.f.,* cheat, trickster.

trichine (-ki-n), *n.f.,* thread-worm, trichina spiralis (of the pig—*du cochon*).

triclinium, *n.m.,* (antiq.) triclinium.

tricoises, *n.f. pl.,* farrier's pincers.

tricolor, *n.m.,* (bot.) three-coloured amaranth.

tricolore, *adj.,* tricoloured.

tricorne, *n.m.,* three-cornered hat.

tricot, *n.m.,* cudgel ; knitting ; knitted vest.

tricotage, *n.m.,* knitting.

tricoter, *v.a.* and *n.,* to knit ; to make lace.

⊙**tricotets,** *n.m.pl.,* an obsolete dance.

tricoteu-r, *n.m.,* **-se,** *n.f.,* knitter. (French hist.) *—ses ;* women who, during the French revolution, attended political assemblies, &c.

trictrac, *n.m.*, trick-track, backgammon; trick-track-board, backgammon-board.

tricycle, *n.m.*, a three-wheeled carriage.

tride, *adj.*, (man.) swift.

trident, *n.m.*, trident; fish-gig.

tridenté, **-e**, *adj.*, (bot.) tridented; trident-pointed.

tridi, *n.m.*, tridi, third day of the decade in the calendar of the first French republic.

triduo, *n.m.* (—*s*), (c.rel.) religious exercises which last three days.

trièdre, *adj.*, (geom.) trihedral.

triennal, **-e** (-è-n-nal), *adj.*, triennial.

triennalité (-è-n-na-), *n.f.*, term of three years.

triennat (-è-n-na), *n.m.*, space of three years.

trier, *v.a.*, to pick, to pick out, to cull, to sort.

triérarchie, *n.f.*, (antiq.) trierarchy.

triérarque, *n.m.*, (antiq.) trierarch.

trieu-r, *n.m.*, **-se**, *n.f.*, sorter.

trifide, *adj.*, (bot.) trifid.

triflore, *adj.*, (bot.) three-flowered.

triforium (-om), *n.m.*, (arch.) triforium, blind story.

trigamie, *n.f.*, trigamy.

trigaud, **-e**, *adj.*, (fam.) shuffling, cunning, crafty.

trigauder. *v.n.*, (fam.) to shuffle.

trigauderie (-gô-dri), *n.f.*, (fam.) shuffling trick; artful trick.

trigle, *n.f.*, (ich.) gurnard.

triglyphe, *n.m.*, (arch.) triglyph.

trigone, *n.m.*, trigon.

trigonométrie, *n.f.*, trigonometry.

trigonométrique, *adj.*, trigonometrical.

trigonométriquement, *adv.*, trigonometrically.

tril, *n.m.*, (mus.). *V.* **trille**.

trilatéral, **-e**, *adj.*, trilateral.

trilatère, *n.m.*, (l.u.). *V.* **triangle**.

***trille**, *or* **tril**, *n.m.*, (mus.) quaver, trill.

***triller**, *v.a.*, (mus.) to shake, to trill.

trillion, *n.m.*, one billion.

trilobé, **-e**, *adj.*, (bot.) trilobate.

triloculaire, *adj.*, (bot.) trilocular.

trilogie, *n.f.*, trilogy.

trimbaler, *v.a.*, to trail, to drag about.

trimer, *v.n.*, to run up and down; to trudge.

trimestre, *n.m.*, quarter of a year; quarter's money; three months.

trimestriel, **-le**, *adj.*, quarterly.

trimètre. *n.m.*, trimeter.

trin, *or* **trine**, *adj. m.*, trine. —*'aspect*; (astron.) trine aspect.

tringa, *n.m.*, (orni.) tringa.

tringle, *n.f.*, curtain-rod; (arch.) tringle; rod.

tringler, *v.a.*, (carp.) to line out.

trinitaire, *n.m.*, Trinitarian.

trinité, *n.f.*, trinity; Trinity Sunday.

trinôme, *n.m.*, (alg.) trinomial.

trinquart, *n.m.*, small fishing-boat.

trinquer, *v.n.*, to touch glasses in drinking.

trinquet, *n.m.*, (nav.) fore-mast (in a lateen vessel—*d'un vaisseau à voiles latines*).

trinquette, *n.f.*, (nav.) storm-jib.

trio, *n. m.* (—*s*), trio; triplet.

triolet, *n.m.* (poet.) triolet; (mus.) triplet.

triomphal, **-e**, *adj.*, triumphal.

triomphalement(-fal-mân),*adv.*,triumphantly

triomphant. **-e**, *adj.*, triumphant.

triomphateur, *n.m.*, triumpher.

triomphe, *n.m.*, triumph.

triomphe, *n.f.*, (card game—*jeu de cartes*) triumph.

triompher, *v.n.*, to triumph. — *de ses passions*: to triumph over one's passions.

***tripaille**, *n.f.*, garbage.

tripan, *n.m.* *V.* **trépang**.

tripartite, *adj.*, tripartite.

tripe, *n.f.*, tripe; imitation velvet, velveteen.

tripe-madame, *n.f.* (—). *V.* **triquemadame**.

triperie (tri-pri), *n.f.*, tripe-house, tripe-shop.

tripette, *n.f.*, small tripe. *Il ne vaut pas* —; he is not worth a straw.

triphtongue (-tong), *n.f.*, (gram.) triphthong.

triphylle, *adj.*, (bot.) triphyllous.

tripi-er, *n.m.*, **-ère**, *n.f.*, dealer in tripe.

tripier, *adj.*, (hawking—*fauconnerie*) untamable.

triple. *n.m.* and *adj.*, treble; triple. threefold, treble.

triplement, *adv.*, trebly.

triplement, *n.m.*, trebling.

tripler, *v.a.* and *n.*, to treble, to triple.

triplicata, *n.m.*, triplicate.

triplicité, *n.f.*, triplicity, trebleness.

tripoli, *n.m.*, tripoli; rotten-stone.

tripolir, *v.a.*, to polish with rotten-stone.

tripot, *n.m.*, gaming-house; bad house.

tripotage, *n.m.*, medley, jumble; mishmash; jobbing; underhand dealing; gossiping story.

tripotée, *n.f.*, (pop.) a beating, a drubbing.

tripoter, *v.a.* and *n.*, (fam.) to plot; to hatch, to brew mischief; to make a medley; to act in an underhand manner.

tripoti-er, *n.m.*, **-ère**, *n.f.* (-tié, -tièr), low intriguer.

triptote, *n.m.*, (gram.) triptote.

triptyque, *n.m.*, (paint.) triptych.

trique, *n.f.*, cudgel; stick.

triqueballe, *n.m.* or *f.*, (artil.) truck.

trique-madame, *n.f.* (—), (bot.) white stone-crop.

triquet, *n.m.*, tennis-bat.

***trirègne**, *n.m.*, tiara of the pope.

trirème, *n.f.*, trireme.

trisaïeul, *n.m.*, great-great-grandfather.

trisaïeule, *n.f.*, great-great-grandmother.

trisection, *n.f.*, trisection.

trismégiste, *n.m.*, (print.) two-line double pica.

trismégiste, *adj.m.*, (Grec. antiq.) surname given by the ancient Greeks to Hermes the Egyptian Mercury.

trismus, *n.m.*, (med.) trismus, lock-jaw.

trissement (tris-mân), *n.m.*, cry of swallows.

trissyllabe, *n.m.* and *adj.*, trisyllable; trisyllabic.

triste, *adj.*, sorrowful, sad; melancholy; dull; dark, gloomy; poor, sorry. *Une* — *nouvelle;* a sad piece of news. *Un* — *spectacle;* a sad spectacle. *Faire un* — *repas;* to make a sorry meal. *Le temps est* —; the weather is dull.

tristement, *adv.*, in a melancholy manner, sadly, sorrowfully, sorrily, poorly; dully. *les* **tristes**, *n.m.pl.*, Ovid's Tristia.

tristesse, *n.f.*, sadness, melancholy, dreariness, dulness.

triton, *n.m.*, Triton, sea-god; (mus.) tritone.

tritoxyde, *n.m.*, (chem.) tritoxide.

triturable, *adj.*, triturable.

trituration, *n.f.*, trituration.

triturer, *v.a.*, to triturate.

triumvir (-om-vir), *n.m.* (—*s*), triumvir.

triumviral, **-e**, *adj.*, pertaining to the triumvirs.

triumvirat, *n.m.*, triumvirate.

trivalve, *adj.*, (bot.) trivalvular.

trivelin, *n.m.*, (l.u.) buffoon.

trivelinade, *n.f.*, (l.u.) buffoonery.

triviaire, *adj.*, only used in: *carrefour* —; a place where three roads end.

trivial, **-e**, *adj.*, trivial, trite, vulgar.

trivialement (-mân), *adv.*, trivially, vulgarly.

trivialité, *n.f.*, triviality, trivialness, commonness.

trivium (-vio-m), *n.m.* (n.p.),trivi·um.

troc (trok), *n.m.*, truck, chop, exchange.

trocart, *or* **trois-quarts**, *n.m.*, (surg.) trocar.

trochaïque (-ka-ik), *n.m.* and *adj.*, trochaic.

trochanter (-kan-tèr), *n.m.*, (anat.) trochanter.

trochée (-shé), *n.f.*, (agri.) brushwood.

trochée (-shé), *n.m*, (poet.) trochee.

troches (trosh), *n.m.pl.*, (hunt.) fumet.

trochet (-shè), *n.m.*, cluster (of fruit or flowers—*de fruits, de fleurs*).

trochile (-kil), *n.m.*, (arch.) trochilus; (orni.) trochilus.

trochisque (-shisk), *n.m.*, (pharm.) troche, troschiso, trochiscus.

trochure (-shur), *n.f.*, (hunt.) cluster of horns, trochings, surantler.

troène, *n.m.*, (bot.) privet.

troglodyte, *n.m.*, troglodyte; (mam.) chimpanzee; (orni.) wren.

*__trogne__, *n.f.*, full face, phiz. — *enluminée*; large red face.

*__trognon__, *n.m.*, core (of a pear or apple—*de poire, de pomme*); stump (of a cabbage—*de chou*). *Un petit* — (pop.); a pretty little girl.

trois, *n.m.* and *adj.*, three; third. *Règle de* —; rule of three.

troisième, *n.m.f.*, and *adj.*, third.

troisième, *n.m.*, pupil of the 3rd form in a public school; third story, third floor of houses.

troisième, *n.f.*, third class of a college.

troisièmement (troa-zièm-mân), *adv.*, thirdly.

trois-mâts, *n.m.* (—), (nav.) three-master.

trois-quarts, *n.m.*, (—). *V.* **trocart**.

trois-six, *n.m.* (—), (com.) brandy *or* alcohol (36 deg.).

trôle, *n.f.*, used only in: *ouvrier à la* —; furniture hawker.

trôler, *v.a.* and *n.*, to lead somebody about; to stroll about, to ramble, to rove, to tramp about.

trolle, *n.f.*, (hunt.) trolling.

trolle, *n.m.*, (bot.) globe-flower, trollius.

trombe, *n.f.*, (phys.) water-spout.

tromblon, *n.m.*, blunderbuss (fire-arm—*arme à feu*).

trombone, *n.m.*, (mus.) trombone.

tromboniste, *n.m.*, trombonist, trombone-player.

trompe, *n.f.*, horn, trumpet; probos·is, trunks (of elephants, of insects—*d'éléphants, d'insectes*); (arch.) overhanging; Jew's-harp. —*s de fallope* (anat.); Fallopian tubes.

trompe-l'œil, *n.m.* (—), (paint.) still life deception.

tromper, *v.a.*, to deceive, to cheat, to delude, to beguile, to take in; to impose on; to elude. — *la loi*; to elude the law.

se tromper, *v.r.*, to be mistaken, to mistake, to make a mistake; to deceive one's self, to be deceived. *Vous vous trompez*; you are mistaken.

tromperie (trôn-pri), *n.f.*, deception, cheating, deceit, imposition.

trompeter, *v.n.*, to publish by sound of trumpet; to blab out, to publish; (of the eagle — *de l'aigle*) to scream.

trompeteur, *n.m.*, (anat.) buccinator.

trompette, *n.f.*, (mus.) trumpet; (fig.) trumpeter, person who divulges all he knows; (conch.) trumpet-shell. — *parlante* (l.u.); speaking-trumpet. *V.* **porte-voix**. — *marine*; one-stringed violoncello. *Sonner de la* —; to blow the trumpet.

trompette, *n.m.*, trumpeter, trumpet.

trompeu-r, **-se**, *n.* and *adj.*, deceiver, cheat; deluder, betrayer; deceitful, delusive, fallacious, beguiling, designing, cheating, false.

*__trompillon__, *n.m.*, (arch.) small pendentive.

tronc (tron), *n.m.*, trunk, stem, stump; stock; poor's box, charity box; (arch.) broken shaft (of a column, pillar—*d'une colonne, d'un pilier*); (geom.) frustrum.

tronchet, *n.m.*, cooper's block.

tronçon, *n.m.*, broken piece, fragment, stump; portion, piece of a line of railway.

tronçonner, *v.a.*, to truncate, to lop, to cut into long pieces, to cut up.

trône, *n.m.*, throne.

trôner, *v.n.*, to sit on a throne; (fig.) to lord over.

tronquer, *v.a.*, to mutilate, to truncate, to detruncate; to garble, to mangle (book—*livre*).

trop, *adv.*, too much, too many, too, over. *Par* —; too much. *Pas* — *bon*; not very good. — *peu*; too little. *De* —; too much, too many, over. — *de peine*; too much trouble. *~ cuit*; over-done.

trop, *n.m.*, excess, exuberance.

trope, *n.m.*, (rhet.) trope.

trophée, *n.m.*, trophy. *Faire* — *d'une chose*; to glory in a thing.

tropical, **-e** *adj.*, tropic, tropical. *Plante* —*e*, tropical plant.

tropique, *n.m.*, and *adj.*, tropic; tropical; (bot.) ☉ diurnal. *Année* —; tropical year. *Plante* ☉ —; diurnal plant.

tropologique, *adj.*, tropological.

trop-plein, *n.m.* (——*s*), overflow; overplus.

troquer, *v.a.*, to truck, to barter, to exchange, to chop and change. — *son cheval borgne contre un aveugle*; to change for the worse.

troqueu-r, *n.m.*, **-se**, *n.f.*, barterer, trucker.

trot, *n.m.*, trot (of horses—*des chevaux*).

trotte, *n.f.*, trot, run, way, walk.

trotte-chemin, *n.m.* (—), (orni.) *V.* **traquet**.

trotte-menu, *adj.*, slow-trotting.

trotter, *v.n.*, to trot; to trot about, to run about, to go about. *Cette idée me trotte dans la tête*; this idea is running in my head, this idea keeps running in my head.

trotter, *v.a.*, (man.) to cause to trot. — *un cheval*; to trot out a horse.

trotterie (tro-tri), *n.f.*, excursion, jaunt, trip.

trotteur, *n.m.*, trotter.

☉**trotti-er**, **-ère**, *adj.*, fond of walking.

trottin, *n.m.*, errand-boy; ☉page. *Aller chercher les pardons de Saint* —; to take a walk instead of going to church.

trottiner, *v.n.*, to go a jog trot.

trottoir, *n.m.*, foot-path, footway, foot-pavement (of streets—*de la rue*).

trou, *n.m.*, hole, gap, orifice, mouth; (anat.) foramen, orifice; hazard (at tennis—*à la paume*). *Boucher un* —; to stop a hole. *Boire comme un* —; to drink like a fish. *N'avoir rien vu que par le* — *d'une bouteille*; to have seen nothing of the world.

troubadour, *n.m.*, troubadour.

troublant, **-e**, *adj.*, disturbing, troubling.

trouble, *adj.*, thick, muddy, troubled; dull, cloudy, overcast, dim. *Avoir la vue* —; to be dim-sighted.

trouble, *n.m.*, confusion, disorder, disturb-

ance; dispute, quarrel; *pl.*, troubles, broils, commotions. **—s civils**; civil broils. *Exciter des —s dans un État*; to raise commotions in a state.

trouble, *or* **truble**, *n.f.*, hoop-net (for fishing—*à pêcher*).

troubleau, *n.m.*, small hoop-net for fishing.

trouble-fête, *n.m.* (—), mar-joy, troublesome guest.

troubler, *v.a.*, to trouble, to make thick, to make muddy; to muddle, to turn; to disturb, to disorder, to confound, to agitate, to perplex, to disconcert; to put to trouble; to interrupt; to destroy the harmony of; to ruffle, to annoy, to discompose, to confuse; to dim, to dull. — *le repos public*; to disturb the public peace. *La peur lui trouble la raison;* fear confuses his understanding. — *quelqu'un;* to put anyone out.

se troubler, *v.r.*, to grow thick, to become thick, to grow muddy, to become muddy, to grow turbid, to become turbid; to turn, to sour, to become sour, to turn sour; to be confused, to be disconcerted, to become agitated; to become foggy, to be foggy, to become overcast, to get overcast, cloudy; to become confused, dim. *Sa mémoire se trouble;* his memory is getting confused.

trouée, *n.f.*, opening, gap; large hole.

trouer, *v.a.*, to bore, to perforate, to make a hole in; (tech.) to hole.

se trouer, *v.r.*, to have a hole.

trou-madame, *n.m.* (—s —), bagatelle, pigeon-holes (game—*jeu*).

troupe, *n.f.*, troop, band, company, crew, gang, set; crowd (of children—*d'enfants*); flock; *pl.*, troops, forces. *Aller en —;* to flock together. **—s de terre;** land-forces.

troupeau, *n.m.*, flock, herd, drove. **— de moutons;** flock of sheep. **— de gros bétail;** drove of cattle.

troupier, *n.m.*, soldier, trooper. *Vieux —;* old campaigner.

trousse, *n.f.*, bundle, truss; (surg.) case of instruments; case (of a barber—*de barbier*); ☉**quiver.** *Être aux —s de l'ennemi;* to be upon the enemy's heels.

troussé, -e, *adj.*, tucked up. *Cheval bien —;* well-set horse. *Compliment bien —;* well turned compliment.

trousseau, *n.m.*, bunch (of keys—*de clefs*); ☉small sheaf of arrows; trousseau (of a lady about to be married—*de mariée*); out-fit (of nuns, school-boarders, &c.—*de religieuses, de pensionnaires, &c.*); (anat.) fasciculus.

trousse-col, *n.m.* (— —s). *V.* **torcol.**

trousse-étriers, *n.m.* (—). stirrup-leather.

trousse-galant, *n.m.* (*n.p.*), (fam.) cholera.

trousse-pète, *n.f.* (—), (pop.) hussy, jade.

trousse-queue, *n.m.* (—), (man.) tail-case.

troussequin, *n.m.*, cantel, cantle (of a saddle—*de selle*).

trousser, *v.a.*, to tie up, to tuck up, to turn up, to pin up; to truss; to dispatch (business —*une affaire*); to hasten. **— ses jupes;** to tuck up one's petticoats. **— un poulet;** to truss a chicken.

se trousser, *v.r.*, to tuck up one's clothes.

troussis, *n.m.*, part tucked up.

trouvable, *adj.*, that can be found.

***trouvaille**, *n.f.*, thing found by chance, godsend, windfall.

trouvé, -e, *part.*, found. *Bien —;* felicitous, happy (of words—*de mots*). *Enfant —;* foundling. *Croire avoir trouvé la pie au nid;* to have found a mare's nest.

trouver, *v.a.*, to find, to find out, to discover, to detect; to meet with, to meet, to light on, to come across; to like; to think, to dream, to judge. *Comment le trouvez-vous?* how do you

like it? *Je lui trouve bon visage;* I think he looks well. **— à dire, à redire;** to find fault with. **— bon;** to approve, to think fit. *Où avez-vous trouvé cela?* what made you think of that? what put that in your head?

se trouver, *v.r.*, to find one's self; to be present, to be, to be by; to feel, to feel one's self, to prove, to turn out; to happen, to chance, to chance to be. *Il s'est trouvé à cette action;* he was at that action. **— mal;** to faint away. **— bien;** to be well.

trouvère. *or* ☉**trouveur**, *n.m.*, Trouvère, name of old poets of the North of France.

truand, *n.m.*, **-e,** *n.f.*, (pop.) (l.u.) vagrant.

***truandaille**, *n.f.*, (pop.) (l.u.) vagrants, beggars.

truander, *v.n.*, (pop.) (l.u.) to beg, to mump.

truanderie (-an-drī), *n.m.*, (pop.) (l.u.) mumping, begging, vagrancy.

truble, *n.f.* *V.* **trouble.**

truc, *n.m.*, (thea.) machinery; (pop.) knack, dodge. *Il a le —;* he has a knack to do it, he is up to it. *V.* **truck.**

trucheman (trush-män), *n.m., or* **truchement**, *n.m.*, interpreter; dragoman, drogman.

☉**trucher**, *v.n.*, (pop.) to beg from laziness.

☉**trucheu-r**, *n.m.*, **-se,** *n.f.*, (pop.) beggar.

truck, *or* **truc**, *n.m.*, (railways) truck.

truelle, *n.f.*, trowel; fish-slice, fish-trowel.

truellée, *n.f.*, trowelful.

truffe, *n.f.*, (bot.) truffle.

truffer, *v.a.*, to stuff with truffles.

truffière, *n.f.*, truffle-ground.

truffier, *n.m.*, (bot.) privet.

truie, *n.f.*, (mam.) sow.

truisme, *n.m.*, truism.

truite, *n.f.*, (ich.) trout. **— saumonée;** salmon trout. *Vivier à —s;* trout stream.

truité, -e, *adj.*, spotted (porcelain); trout-coloured (of dogs and horses—*des chiens et des chevaux*). *Fonte —e* (metal.); pig-iron spotted white and grey.

trullisation, *n.f.*, (arch.) trowelling.

trumeau, *n.m.*, (arch.) pier; pier-glass; leg of beef.

trusquin, *n.m.* *V.* **troussequin.**

tsar, *n.m.* *V.* **czar.**

tsarien, tsarine, tsarowitz. *V.* **czarien, czarine, czarowitz.**

tu, *pron.*, thou, you. **— es;** thou art, you are.

tuable, *adj.*, fit to be killed.

tuage, *n.m.*, killing, slaughter (of an animal).

tuant, -e, *adj.*, killing, toilsome, tiresome, laborious, tedious. *C'est un homme —;* he is a regular bore.

tu-autem (-ô-tèm), *n.m.* (*n.p.*), main thing, difficulty, rub.

tube, *n.m.*, tube, pipe; (anat.) duct; (bot.) tube; (zool.) duct, tube.

tuber, *v.a.*, to tube.

tubercule, *n.m.*, (bot., med.) tubercle.

tuberculé, -e, *adj.*, (med.) tuberculate, tubercled.

tuberculeu-x, -se, *adj.*, tubercular, tuberculous; (bot.) tubercular, tuberculous, grained; (med.) tubercled, tubercular, tuberculous.

tuberculisation, *n.f.*, (med.) formation and growth of tubercles.

tubéreu-x, -se, *adj.*, (bot.) tubercus.

tubéreuse, *n.f.*, (bot.) tuberose.

tubérifère, *adj.*, tuberiferous.

tubérosité, *n.f.*, (anat.) tuberosity.

tubiforme, *adj.*, tubeform, tubiform.

tubulaire, *adj.*, tubular.

tubule, *n.m.*, small tube, tubule.

tubulé, -e, *adj.*, tubular, tubulated, tubulous.

tubuleu-x, -se, *adj.*, tubulated, tubulous.

18

tubulure, *n.f.,* (chem.) tuoulature ; (bot.) small tube, tubule.

tudesque, *n.m.* and *adj.,* Teutonic, Germanic (language—*langue*) ; inelegant, rough, coarse.

tudieu, *int.,* zounds !

tue-chien, *n.m.* (— —s), (bot.) meadow saffron, dog's bane, colchicum.

tuer, *v.a.,* to kill, to slay, to slaughter, to butcher ; to kill, to tire to death ; to while away. — *des bœufs ;* to slaughter oxen. — *le temps ;* to kill time.

se **tuer,** *v.r.,* to kill one's self, to make away with one's self, to commit suicide. — *de peine ;* to work one's self to death.

tuer, *v.n.,* to kill.

tuerie (tü-rï), *n.f.,* slaughter, massacre, butchery, carnage ; slaughter-house.

à **tue-tête,** *adv.,* (of shouting and quarrelling—*de cris et de querelles*) with all one's might, as loud as one can.

tueur, *n.m.,* killer, slayer. — *de gens ;* bully, braggadocio.

tuf, *n.m.,* (min.) tuf, tufa.

tufacé, -e, *adj.,* (min.) tufaceous.

tuffeau, *n.m.,* tuf, tufa.

tufi-er, -ère, *adj.,* of the nature of tuf *or* tufa.

tuile, *n.f.,* tile. — *faîtière ;* crest-tile ; ridge-tile. — *en S ;* pantile. — *de Guienne,* gutter-tile. — *vernissée ;* glazed tile.

tuileau, *n.m.,* broken tile.

tuilerie (tuil-rï), *n.f.,* tile-works, tile-fields. *Les —s ;* Tuileries, a palace in Paris.

tuilier, *n.m.,* tile-maker.

tulipe, *n.f.,* (bot.) tulip.

tulipier, *n.m.,* (bot.) tulip-tree.

tulle, *n.m.,* tulle.

tulliste, *n.m.f.,* tulle-maker.

tuméfaction, *n.f.,* (med.) tumefaction.

tuméfier, *v.a.,* (med., surg.) to tumefy.

se **tuméfier,** *v.r.,* (med., surg.) to tumefy.

tumeur, *n.f.,* tumor ; *pl.,* (vet.) warbles.

tumulaire, *adj.,* pertaining to a tomb. *Pierre — ;* tombstone.

tumulte, *n.m.,* tumult, uproar, riot, hubbub.

tumultuaire, *adj.,* tumultuous, tumultuary ; against the law.

tumultuairement (-èr-män), *adv.,* tumultuarily.

tumultueusement (-euz-män), *adv.,* tumultuously.

tumultueu-x, -se, *adj.,* tumultuous, riotous.

tumulus (-lus), *n.m.,* tumulus, barrow (burial-place—*sépulture*).

tungstène, *n.m.* (*n.p.*), (chem.) tungsten.

tunique, *n.f.,* tunic ; (bot.) tunic ; (anat.) tunic, coat, film ; wall, coat (of the stomach—*de l'estomac*) ; tunic (of the eye—*de l'œil*).

tuniqué, -e, *adj.,* (bot.) tunicated.

tunnel, *n.m.,* tunnel.

tuorbe, *n.m.* *V.* **téorbe.**

turban, *n.m.,* turban. *Prendre le — ;* to turn Mahometan.

Ⓣ **turbe,** *n.f.,* (jur.) public inquest to determine the ways and customs, the unwritten law, of a place.

turbine, *n.f.,* (mec.) turbine.

turbiné, -e, *adj.,* turbinate, turbinated.

turbinite, *n.f.,* (conch.) turbinite, turbite.

turbith, *n.m.,* (pharm.) turbith, turpeth ; — *minéral ;* turpeth-mineral, subsulphate of mercury.

turbot, *n.m.,* (ich.) turbot.

turbotière (ti-è-r), *n.f.,* turbot-kettle.

turbotin, *n.m.,* (ich.) young turbot.

turbulemment (-la-män), *adv.,* turbulently.

turbulence, *n.f.,* turbulence, turbulency.

turbulent, -e, *adj.,* turbulent, noisy ; rude, wild (of children—*des enfants*).

turc, *n.m.,* Turk ; wood-worm. *Se faire — ;* to turn Turk.

tur-c,-que, *adj.,* Turkish.

turcie, *n.f.,* (l.u.) dike, embankment.

turcisme, *n.m.,* Turcism.

turco, *n.m.* (—s), turco; soldier of the native Algerian troops in French service.

turelure (tur-lur), *n.f.,* tol de rol, words used as chorus at the conclusion of a song. *C'est toujours la même — ;* it is always the same thing over and over again.

turf, *n.m.* (*n.p.*), turf.

turgescence, *n.f.,* turgescence, turgescency, turgidness.

turgescent, -e, *adj.,* turgid, turgescent.

turlupin, *n.m.,* maker of bad conundrums, *or* jokes.

turlupinade, *n.f.,* sorry jesting ; bad conundrum, bad joke.

turlupiner, *v.n.,* to make bad conundrums, *or* jokes.

turlupiner, *v.a.,* to laugh at, to turn into ridicule, to jeer.

turlurette, *n.f.,* an obsolete guitar in use in the 14th century.

turlut, *n.m.,* (orni.) titlark.

turlututu! *int.,* hush ! hush !

turlututu, *n.m.,* reed-pipe.

turneps (-nèps), *n.m.,* field-turnip.

turpitude, *n.f.,* turpitude, baseness, vileness.

turque, *n.f.,* Turkish woman.

turquette, *n.f.* (bot.) rupture-wort.

turquin, *adj.,* dark (of blue—*du bleu*).

turquoise, *n.f.,* turkois, turquoise.

tussilage, *n.m.,* (bot.) colt's-foot, horse-foot.

tutélaire, *adj.,* tutelary, guardian.

tutelle, *n.f.,* (jur.) tutelage, guardianship, protectorship ; committeeship (of lunatics—*des fous*). *Enfants en — ;* children under the care of a guardian.

tut-eur, *n.m.,* **-rice,** *n.f.,* (jur.) guardian ; protector ; committee (of lunatics—*des fous*) ; (hort.) prop.

tutie (-tï), *n.f.,* (chem.) tutty.

tutoiement, *or* **tutoîment** (-toa-män), *n.m.,* theeing and thouing, saying thou and thee.

tutoyer, *v.a.,* to thee and thou.

se **tutoyer,** *v.r.,* to thee and thou each other ; to say thou and thee to each other.

tutrice, *n.f.* *V.* **tuteur.**

tuyau, *n.m.,* pipe, tube, tunnel, funnel ; barrel (of a quill—*de plume d'oie*) ; stalk (of corn —*de blé*) ; stalk, stem (of feathers—*de plumes*) ; nozzle (of bellows, of candlesticks—*de soufflets, de chandeliers*) ; shank (of tobacco-pipes—*de pipes*) ; goffering of frills, &c. — *aspirant ;* suction-pipe. — *atmosphérique ;* vacuum-pipe. — *de conduite ;* delivery-pipe. — *de dégagement de la vapeur ;* waste steam-pipe. — *d'embranchement ;* branch-pipe. — *de trop-plein ;* waste-pipe. — *de la cheminée ;* flue of the chimney.

tuyauter, *v.a.,* to goffer (frills, linen &c. —*du linge, &c.*).

tuyauterie (tui-io-trï), *n.f.,* system of pipes ; pipe-store ; pipe-trade.

tuyère (tu-iè-r), *n.f.,* tue-iron ; tewel ; blast-pipe.

tympan, *n.m.,* (anat.) tympanum ; drum of the ear ; (print., arch., mec.) tympan ; spandrel (of bridges—*de ponts*).

tympaniser, *v.a.,* (fam.) to run down, to inveigh against, to decry.

tympanite, *n.f.,* tympanite, tympany ; wind (in horses—*chez les chevaux*).

tympanon, *n.m.*, (mus.) dulcimer.
type, *n.m.*, type; symbol; (astron.) plan
drawing; (print.) type.
typha, *n.m.*, (bot.) reed-mace, Indian grass.
typhcïde, *adj.*, (med.) typhoid, typhus.
typhon, *n.m.*, (phys.) water-spout; typhoon.
typhus (-fus), *n.m.*, (med.) typhus, typhus
fever, camp-fever, gaol-fever.
typique, *adj.*, typic, typical, emblematic,
emblematical, symbolical.
typographe, *n.m.*, typographer, printer.
typographie, *n.f.*, typography; printing;
printing-office.
typographique, *adj.*, typographical.
typographiquement (-fik-mân), *adv.*,
typographically.
tyran, *n.m.*, tyrant.
tyranneau (-ra-nô), *n.m.*, petty tyrant.
tyrannicide (-ra-ni-), *n.m.*, tyrannicide.
tyrannie (-ra-nî), *n.f.*, tyranny.
tyrannique, *adj.*, tyrannic, tyrannical.
tyranniquement (-ra-nik-mân), *adv.*,
tyrannically.
tyranniser (-ra-ni-), *v.a.*, to tyrannize over,
to play the tyrant over, to oppress.
tyrolienne, *n.f.*, mountain song; dance *or*
waltz popular in the Tyrol.
tzar, *n.m.* *V.* **czar.**

U

u, *n.m.*, the twenty-first letter of the alphabet, u.
ubiquiste (-kuist), *n.m.*, (ecc. hist.)
Ubiquist.
ubiquitaire (-kui-), *n.m.*, (ecc. hist.) Ubi-
quitarian, Ubiquitary.
ubiquité (-kui-), *n.f.*, ubiquity.
udomètre, *n.m.*, (phys.) udometer, pluviameter, rain-gauge.
uhlan, *n.m.* (—s), German lancer.
ukase, *n.m.*, ukase, edict of the Emperor of
Russia.
ulcération, *v.f.*, (med.) ulceration.
ulcère, *n.m.*, ulcer.
ulcéré, **-e**, *part.*, (med.) ulcerated; (fig.)
embittered, full of deep resentment (of the
heart—*du cœur*); gangrened (conscience).
ulcérer, *v.a.*, to ulcerate; (fig.) to exasperate, to embitter, to provoke.
s'ulcérer, *v.r.*, (med.) to ulcerate, to exulcerate.
ulcéreu-x, -se, *adj.*, (med.) ulcerous.
uléma, *n.m.* (—s), ulema, in Turkey a doctor
of law.
uligineu-x, -se, *adj.*, (bot.) uliginous.
ulmaire, *n.f.*, (bot.) common meadow-sweet.
ulmine, *n.f.*, (chem.) ulmine.
ulmique, *adj.*, (chem.) ulmic. *Acide* —;
ulmic acid.
ultérieur, -e, *adj.*, ulterior, subsequent;
further.
ultérieurement (-eur-mân), *adv.*, subsequently, later, beyond.
ultimatum (-to-m), *n.m.* (—s), ultimatum.
ultra, *n.m.* (—s), ultra, person of violent
opinions.
ultra-mondain, -e (-dîn, -dè-n), *adj.*,
ultramondane, ultramundane.
ultramontain, -e (tîn,-tè-n), *n.* and *adj.*,
ultramontanist; ultramontane; tramontane.
ultramontanisme, *n.m.*, ultramontanism.
ultrazodiacal, *adj.*, (astron.) applied to
those planets, the orbit of which is not limited
to the width of the zodiac.
umble, *n.m.*, (ich.) umber, char.
un, *n.m.*, one; unit.

un, -e, *pron.*, one. — *pour cent;* one per
cent. *L'*— *vaut l'autre;* one is as good as the
other. *L'*— *après l'autre;* one after another.
Les —*s disent oui, les autres disent non;* some
say yes, the others say no. *L'*— *ou l'autre;*
either, the one or the other. *L'un et l'autre;*
both. *Les* —*s et les autres;* all, all together.
Ni l'— *ni l'autre;* neither the one nor the other,
neither. *L'*— *portant l'autre;* one with another.
En donner d'—*e à quelqu'un;* to take any one in.
un, -e, *art.*, a, an, any.
un, -e, *adj.*, one. *C'est tout* —; it is all one.
Sur les —*e heure;* about one o'clock.
unanime, *adj.*, unanimous.
unanimement (-nim-mân). *adv.*, unanimously.
unanimité, *n.f.*, unanimity.
unau, *n.m.*, (mam.) sloth.
unciale (ôn-), *adj.f.* *V.* **onciale.**
unguis (on-gu-iss), *n.m.*, (anat.) unguis.
uni, -e, *adj.*, united; smooth, even, level;
plain, simple, unaffected; uniform. *Chemin*
—; level road. *Du linge* —; plain linen. ⊙*A*
l'—, *adv.*, level.
unicorne, *n.m.*, unicorn; rhinoceros; sea-
unicorn, narwhal, narwal.
unième, *adj.*, first. [Only used in *vingt et*
—, *trente et* —, *&c.;* 21st, 31st, &c.]
unièmement (-èm-mân), *adv.*, firstly.
[Only used when preceded by 20, 30, 40, &c.]
unification, *n.f.*, uniting several things
into one; making one; amalgamation.
unifier, *v.a.*, to unite several things into
one; to amalgamate, to unite.
uniflore, *adj.*, (bot.) uniflorous.
uniforme, *adj.*, uniform.
uniforme, *n.m.*, uniform; uniform, regimentals. *Quitter l'*—; to quit the service.
uniformément, *adv.*, uniformly.
uniformité, *n.f.*, uniformity.
unilatéral, *adj.*, (bot.) unilateral; (of contracts—*des contrats*) binding on one party only.
uniloculaire, *adj.*, (bot.) unilocular.
uniment, *adv.*, evenly, even, smoothly;
plainly, simply.
uninominal, -e, *adj.*, of one name.
union, *n.f.*, union, conjunction; concord,
agreement, harmony; (jur.) deed of agreement;
(jur.) concurrence.
unipare, *adj.*, uniparous.
unipersonnel, -le, *adj.*, (gram.) uniper-
sonal.
unique, *adj.*, only, sole; single, unique.
Fils —; only son.
uniquement (u-nik-mân), *adv.*, only,
solely; above the rest.
unir, *v.a.*, to unite, to join, to combine; to
smooth, to level, to plane, to make smooth; to
pair.
s'unir, *v.r.*, to unite, to be united, to join together, to coalesce.
unisexué, -e (-ni-cèksué), *or* **unisexuel,**
-le (-ni-cèksu-èl), *adj.*, (bot.) unisexual.
unisson, *n.m.*, (mus.) unison, keeping.
Deux cordes à l'—; two strings in unison.
unitaire, *n.m.f.* and *adj.*, Unitarian.
unitarisme, *n.m.*, unitarianism.
unité, *n.f.*, unity, unit; unity, concord,
agreement.
uniti-f, -ve, *adj.*, (theol.) of pure love.
univalve, *adj.*, (bot., conch.) univalve,
univalvular.
univers, *n.m.*, universe.
universaliser, *v.a.*, to make universal.
universalité, *n.f.*, universality, generality.
universaux, *n.m.*, Plural of **universel,**
noun, which see.
universel, -le, *adj.*, universal, residuary (of
legatees—*de légataires*).

aniversel, *n.m.* (*universaux*), (log.) predicable, universal.

universellement (-sèl-mān), *adv.*, universally.

universitaire, *adj.*, of *or* belonging to the university.

université, *n.f.*, university.

univocation, *n.f.*, univocation.

univoque, *adj.*, univocal.

upas (u-pâs), *n.m.*, (bot.) poison-tree, bohun upas.

urane, *or* **uranium** (-nio-m), *n.f.*, (min.) uranite, uranium.

uranographie, *n.f.*, uranography.

uranographique, *adj.*, uranographic, uranographical.

uranoscope, *n.m.*, (ich.) uranoscopus.

uranus (-nus), *n.m.*, (astron.) Uranus, Georgium Sidus.

urate, *n.m.*, (chem.) urate.

urbain, **-e**, (-bin, -bè-n), *adj.*, urban.

urbanité, *n.f.*, urbanity.

urcéolé, **-e**, *adj..* (bot.) urceolate.

ure, aurochs, *or* **urus**, *n.m.*, (mam.) v. e, ure-ox, urus.

urédo, *n.m.*, (bot.) uredo.

urée, *n.f.*, (chem.) urea.

uretère, *n.m..* (anat.) ureter.

urètre, *or* **urèthre**, *n.m.*, (anat.) urethra.

urgence, *n.f.*, urgency.

urgent, -e, *adj.*, urgent, cogent, pressing.

urinaire, *adj.*, urinary.

urinal, *n.m.*, urinal.

urine, *n.f.*, urine, chamber-lye; stale (of animals—*des animaux*).

uriner, *v.n.*, to urine, to make water; to stale (of animals—*des animaux*).

urineu-x, -se, *adj.*, urinous.

urinoir, *n.m.*, urinary, urinal.

urique, *adj.*, (chem.) uric.

urne, *n.f.*, urn ; ballot-box.

ursuline, *n.f.*, Ursuline nun, Ursuline.

urticaire, *n.f.*, (med.) urticaria, nettle-rash.

urtication, *n.f.*, (surg.) urtication.

urticées, *n.f.pl.*, (bot.) nettle tribe.

urus, *n.m.* V. **ure**.

us, *n.m.* (n.p.), used only in : *un savant en* —; a learned man who claims profound knowledge of dead languages, especially Latin.

us (us), *n.m.pl.* (*n.s.*), usage, use. *Les — et coutumes ;* the ways and customs.

usage, *n.m.*, custom, practice, use, usage; wear (of clothes—*des vêtements*); *pl.*, churchbooks. *L'— le veut ainsi ;* custom will have it so. *Cela est hors d'— ;* that's out of use. *Mettre une chose en — ;* to use a thing. *Hors d'— ;* obsolete.

usager, *n.m.*, (jur.) commoner.

usance, *n.f.*, (com.) usance.

usante, *adj.f.*, (jur.) (of spinsters—*fille majeure*) making use of, using.

usé, -e, *adj.*, worn out, threadbare. *Conte — ;* stale story.

user, *v.n.*, to use, to make use of. — *de violence ;* to use violence. — *de douceur ;* to use gentle means. *En — bien avec quelqu'un :* to use any one well. *En — mal avec quelqu'un ;* to use any one ill.

user, *v.a.*, to use, to consume; to wear out, to wear off; to use up, to spend, to waste; to wear away ; — (surg.) to eat off, to consume. — *des souliers ;* to wear out shoes.

s'user, *v.r.*, to wear out; to be worn out, to be used, to be consumed; to waste, to decay; to be spent.

user, *n.m.*. wear, service. *Ce drap est d'un bon — ;* this cloth wears well.

usine, *n.f.*, works, manufactory.

usité, -e, *adj.*, usual; used, in use. *Ce mot n'est guère — ;* that word is seldom used.

usquebac (us-kè-bak), *n.m.*, usquebaugh (spirits—*spiritueux*).

ustensile, *n.m.*, utensil; tool, implement. —*s de cuisine ;* kitchen utensils.

ustion (u-sti-on), *n.f.*, ustion.

nsucapion, *n.f.*, (Rom. jur.) usucaption.

usuel, -le, *adj.*, usual, customary.

asuellement (-èl-mān), *adv.*, usually, customarily.

usufructuaire, *adj.*, (jur.) of use.

usufruit, *n.m.*, (jur.) usufruct, use.

usufruiti-er, *n.m.*, **-ère**, *n.f.* (-tié, -tiè-r), usufructuary, beneficial occupant.

usufruit-ier, -ière, *adj.*, (jur.) to be performed by the usufructuary (of repairs—*réparations*).

usuraire, *adj.*, usurious.

usurairement (-rèr-mān), *adv.*, usuriously.

usure, *n.f*, usury, unlawful interest; wearing, wear, wear and tear. *Prêter à — ;* to lend upon usury. *Rendre avec — ;* to return with interest.

usuri-er (rié), *n.m.*, **-ère** (-riè-r), *n.f.*, usurer.

usurpat-eur, *n.m.*, **-rice**, *n.f.*, usurper.

usurpation, *n.f.*, usurpation.

usurper, *v.a.* and *n.*, to usurp; to encroach.

ut (ut), *n.m.*, (mus.) ut. do, c.

utérin, -e, *adj.*, (med.) uterine; (jur.) uterine, by the mother's side.

utérins, *n.m.pl.*, (jur.) brothers of the half blood,by the same venter ; brothers and sisters of the half blood,by the same venter.

utérus (-rus), *n.m.*, womb, matrix, uterus.

utile, *adj.*, useful, of use, advantageous, beneficial, profitable, serviceable; subservient.

utile, *n.m.*, utility, useful. *Joindre l'— à l'agréable ;* to combine utility and pleasure.

utilement (u-til-mān), *adv.*, usefully, profitably, beneficially.

utiliser, *v.a.*, to find use for, to turn to account, to make use of, to avail one's self of.

utilitaire, *n.m.* and *adj.*, utilitarian.

utilité, *n.f.*, utility, use, usefulness, benefit, profit, service, purpose ; (thea.) utility (actor —*acteur*). *But d'— ;* purpose, useful end.

utopie, *n.f.*, utopia.

utopiste, *n.m.* and *adj.*, utopist; utopian.

utricule, *n.m.*, utricle.

utriculé, -e, *adj.*, utricular.

uvée, *n.f.*, (anat.) uvea.

uvulaire, *adj.*, (anat.) uvular.

V

v, *n.m.*, the twenty-second letter of the alphabet, v.

v. (initial letter of *voir*, to see), V., vide.

va, imperative of *aller*, to go. — *pour cela ;* I consent to it ; done, agreed.

va, *n.m.*, va (at basset, faro—*à la bassette, au pharaon*).

vacance, *n.f.*, vacancy ; *pl.*, vacation, holidays ; recess (of parliament—*du parlement*).

vacant, -e, *adj.*, vacant, unfilled, unoccupied ; (jur.) in abeyance.

vacarme, *n.m.*, hubbub, tumult, uproar. *Faire du — ;* to make an uproar.

vacation, *n.f.*, attendance, sitting (of public officers—*d'officiers publics*) ; day's sale (of auctions—*d'enchères publiques*) ; vacation (of courts—*de tribunaux*) ; ⊙trade, profession. — *avenante :* in case of a vacancy.

vaccin, *n.m.*, (med.) vaccine matter.

vaccinable, *adj.*, that may be vaccinated.

vaccinateur, *n.m.*, vaccinator.

vaccination, *n.f.*, vaccination.

vaccine, *n.f.*, vaccinia, cow small-pox, cow-pox ; vaccination.

vacciner, *v.a.*, to vaccinate.

vache, *n.f.*, (mam.) cow; cow-hide (prepared for use—*corroyée*). *Étable à —s*; cow-house. — *à lait*; milk cow, milch cow, dairy cow. *Manger de la — enragée*; to endure great hardships. *Le plancher des —s*; dry land, terra firma.

vach-er, *n.m.*, **-ère**, *n.f.*, cowherd, cowkeeper, neat-herd.

vacherie (va-shrî), *n.f.*, cow-house.

vacillant, -e (-sil-lân, -t), *adj.*, vacillating; wavering, uncertain, undecided; (bot.) versatile.

vacillation (-sil-la-), *n.f.*, vacillation; wavering.

vaciller (-sil-lé), *v.n.*, to vacillate; to waver; to reel, to stagger.

vacuité, *n.f.*, vacuity.

vade, *n.f.*, vade, stake (at play—*au jeu*).

vademanque, *n.f.*, (banking) decrease of the money in reserve.

vade-mecum (va-dé-mé-ko-m), *n.m.* (—), vade-mecum.

va-et-vient, *n.m.* (—), (mec.) reciprocating motion, see-saw motion; small ferry-boat; pass-rope, traversing gear.

vagabond, -e, *n.* and *adj.*, vagabond, vagrant; wandering.

vagabondage, *n.m.*, vagrancy; roguery.

vagabonder, or ⊙**vagabonner**, *v.n.*, to be a vagabond, to wander, to roam, to tramp about.

vagin, *n.m.*, (anat.) vagina.

vaginal, -e, *adj.*, (anat.) vaginal.

vagir, *v.n.*, (of infants—*des petits enfants*) to wail, to mewl.

vagissant, *adj.*, mewling, wailing.

vagissement, *n.m.*, crying, wailing, mewling (of infants—*des petits enfants*).

vague (vag), *n.f.*, wave, billow, surge.

vague, *adj.*, vague, indeterminate, loose, uncertain. *Terres —s*; waste-land.

vague, *n.m.*, vagueness, looseness; uncertainty; space, empty space, emptiness.

vaguement (vag-mân), *adv.*, vaguely.

vaguemestre (vag-mès-tr), *n.m.*, (milit.) master of the waggons, baggage-master.

vaguer (va-ghé), *v.n.*, to ramble, to rove, to range about, to wander, to stray, to straggle.

vaigrage, *n.m.*, (nav.) ceiling, foot-waling.

vaigre, *n.f.*, (nav.) ceiling, foot-waling.

*****vaillamment** (va-ia-mân), *adv.*, valiantly, valorously, courageously, stoutly.

*****vaillance**, *n.f.*, valiance, valour, courage, bravery.

*****vaillant, -e**, *adj.*, valiant, valorous, brave, courageous. *Il est — comme l'épée qu'il porte*; he is steel to the backbone.

*****vaillant**, *n.m.*, all a man is worth, one's substance.

*****vaillant**, *adv.*, worth, value. *N'avoir pas un sou —*; not to be worth a penny (of a person—*des personnes*). *Il n'a rien —*; he is penniless. *Il a dix mille écus —*; he is worth 30,000 francs.

⊙*****vaillantise**, *n.f.*, (fam.) valiantness, prowess, valorous feat.

vain, -e (vin, vè-n), *adj.*, vain, fruitless, ineffectual, unprofitable; empty, shadowy, foolish, trifling, frivolous; vainglorious, presumptuous, self-conceited. *En —*; vainly, in vain, to no purpose. *Prendre le nom du Seigneur en —*; to take the name of God in vain. *Homme —*; vain, conceited man.

vaincre (vainquant, vaincu), *v.a.*, to vanquish, to conquer; to overcome, to defeat, to get the better of; to outdo, to surpass, to excel. *Se laisser —*; to give way to. *Se laisser — à la pitié*; to be moved to pity.

se **vaincre**, *v.r.*, to conquer one's self; to conquer one's passions.

vaincu, *n.m.*, conquered, vanquished.

vainement (vè-n-mân), *adv.*, vainly, in vain, fruitlessly; to no purpose.

vainqueur, *n.m.* and *adj.*, vanquisher, conqueror, subduer, victor, overcomer; conquering, victorious, triumphant.

vair, *n.m.*, (her.) vair.

vairé, -e, *adj.*, (her.) vairy.

vairon, *adj.*, silver-eyed (of horses—*du cheval*); (pers.) odd-eyed.

vairon, *n.m.*, (ich.) minnow.

vaisseau, *n.m.*, ship, vessel; structure (inside of a building—*intérieur d'un édifice*); (anat.) vessel, tube; (bot.) duct; pl., (nav.) shipping. — *d'approvisionnement*; victualling-ship. — *marchand*; merchantman. — *de guerre*; man of war. — *à deux ponts*; two-decker. — *de la marine royale*; His, Her, Majesty's ship. — *frégate*; frigate-built ship. — *de compagnie* (nav.); good company keeper. — *armé en guerre*; armed ship.

vaisselle, *n.f.*, plates and dishes; plate (of gold or silver—*d'or ou d'argent*). — *de terre*; earthenware. — *d'or*; gold plate. — *d'argent*; silver plate. — *ciselée*; carved plate. — *plate* (of gold or silver—*d'or ou d'argent*); plate.

val, *n.m.*, valley, vale. *Par monts et par vaux*; up hill and down dale.

valable, *adj.*, valid.

valablement, *adv.*, validly.

valenciennes, *n.f.*, valenciennes (lace).

valériane, *n.f.*, (bot.) valerian.

valet, *n.m.*, footman, valet; knave (at cards —*cartes*) door-weight; hold-fast (of a joiner—*de menuisier*); support (of a looking-glass—*de miroir*). — *de pied*; footman. *Faire le bon —*; to be officious. *Maître —* (agri.); headman. — *de ferme*; farmer's man. — *de chiens*; whipper-in.

valetage (val-taj), *n.m.*, duty of a valet.

*****valetaille** (val-tâ-i), *n.f.*, pack of men-servants, footmen.

valet-à-patin, *n.m.* (—*s* —), (surg.), forceps to perform ligatures.

valeter (val-té), *v.n.*, to cringe, to dance attendance, to fawn.

valétudinaire, *n.m.f.* and *adj.*, valetudinary, valetudinarian.

valeur, *n.f.*, value, worth, consideration; import, meaning; pl., (com.) bills, paper; valour, bravery, courage, gallantry. *Être en —*; to bear a good price. *Être de nulle —*; to be of no value, to be valueless. *Abaisser la —*; to depreciate. *Mettre en —*; to improve land.

valeureusement (-reûz-mân), *adv.*, valiantly, valorously, bravely, courageously.

valeureu-x, -se, *adj.*, valiant, valorous, brave, courageous, gallant.

validation, *n.f.*, (jur.) validation, rendering valid.

validé, *n.f.* (*n.p.*), the title of the Sultan's mother.

valide, *n.m.* and *adj.*, person in health; valid, good; healthy, in health.

validement (-lid-mân), *adv.*, (jur.) validly.

valider, *v.a.*, to validate, to confirm, to make valid.

validité, *n.f.*, validity, validness.

valise, *n.f.*, valise, portmanteau.

valisnère, or **valisnérie**, *n.f.*, (bot.) frogbit.

valkyrie, *n.f.* (—*s*), (Scandinavian myth.) valkyriur, goddess.

vallaire, *adj.*, (antiq.) vallary, vallar. *Couronne —*; vallar crown.

vallée, *n.f.*, valley, vale. *La —*; name of a poultry and game market in Paris.

vallon, *n.m.*, dale.

valoir (valant, valu), *v.n.*, to be worth, to be as good as, to be equal to; to yield, to bring. — *mieux;* to be better, to be preferable. *Il vaut mieux ne pas y aller;* it is better not to go there. *Cela ne vaut rien;* that is good for nothing. *Cet habit ne vaut plus rien;* this coat is quite worn out. *Cela ne vaut pas la peine d'y penser;* that is not worth the trouble of thinking of. *Il ne vaut pas la peine qu'on lui réponde;* he is not worth answering. *Vous ne faites rien qui vaille;* nothing you do is worth anything. *Chaque chose vaut son prix;* everything is good for something. *Cela vaut son pesant d'or;* that is worth its weight in gold. *Faire — une terre;* to improve an estate. *Faire — son argent;* to turn one's money to account. *Faire — son talent;* to turn one's talent to account. *Faire — sa marchandise;* to set off one's goods. *Il fait bien — ce qu'il sait;* he makes the best of his knowledge. *Faire — son droit;* to prosecute one's right. *Se faire —;* to push one's self forward. *Cela vaut fait;* that's as good as done. *Vaille que vaille;* at all events, for better or worse. *Que lui a valu son ambition?* What has his ambition brought to him ?

ad valorem, *adj.*, (com.) ad valorem.

valse, *n.f.*, waltz. — *à deux temps;* waltz in common time, in double time. — *à trois temps;* waltz in triple time.

valser, *v.n.*, to waltz.

valseu-r, *n.m.*, **-se**, *n.f.*, waltzer.

value, *n.f.*, value. *Plus- —;* superior value. *Moins- —;* inferior value.

valvaire, *adj.*, (bot.) valvate.

valve, *n.f.*, valve; (tech.) clack-door.

valvé, **-e**, *adj.*, (bot.) valved, valvate.

valvule, *n.f.*, (anat.) valvlet, valvula.

vampire, *n.m.*, vampire.

van, *n.m.*, (agri.) fan, van.

vandale, *n.m.* and *adj.*, Vandal; vandalic.

vandalisme, *n.m.*, vandalism.

vandoise, *n.f.*, (ich.) dart; dace.

*vanille, *n.f.*, (bot.) vanilla, vanilla-tree; (bot.) vanilla (fruit).

*vanillier, *n.m.*, (bot.) vanilla-tree, vanilla.

vanité, *n.f.*, vanity, self-conceit, self-conceitedness. *Que vous avez de —!* how full of vanity you are! *Faire — d'une chose;* to be proud of a thing.

vaniteu-x, **-se**, *adj.*, absurdly vain.

vannage, *n.m.*, (agri.) winnowing; (hydraul.) system of water-gates in a dam, &c.

vanne, *n.f.*, water-gate, sluice, paddle-door.

vanneau, *n.m.*, (orni.) lapwing, pewet, plover.

vanner, *v.a.*, to winnow, to eventilate, to fan, to sift; (hydraul.) to make, to place water-gates in dams, &c.

vannerie (va-n-rî), *n.f.*, basket-trade; basket-work.

vannette, *n.f.*, server, flat basket to give horses their corn.

vanneur, *n.m.*, winnower.

vannier, *n.m.*, basket-maker.

*vantail, *n.m.*, leaf of a folding-door; window-shutter; lock-gate.

vantard, **-e**. *n.* and *adj.*, boaster, bragger, braggart; boasting, boastful; bragging.

vantardise, *n.f.*, (fam.) habitual boasting, bragging.

vanter, *v.a.*, to vaunt, to cry up, to praise up, to extol.

se **vanter**, *v.r.*, to boast, to vaunt, to brag; to praise one's self; to plume one's self. *Il n'y a pas de quoi —;* there is nothing to brag of.

vanterie (vân-trî), *n.f.*, boasting, bragging, vaunting; brag, boast.

⊙**vanteur**, *n.m. V.* **vantard**.

va-nu-pieds, *n.m.* and *f.*(—), tatterdemalion, ragged rascal.

vapeur, *n.f.*, vapour, fume, steam. damp. exhalation; *pl.*, vapours, hysterics. *Bateau à —;* steam-boat, steamer. *Chaudière à —;* steam-boiler. *Machine à —;* steam-engine. *Registre de —;* throttle-valve (of a steam-engine—*de machine à vapeur*). *En —;* with the steam on. *Mettre en —;* to put the steam on.

vapeur, *n.m.*, (fam.) steamer.

vaporeu-x, **-se**, *adj.*, vapourous, vapourish; (paint.) aerial.

vaporisation, *n.f.*, vaporization.

vaporiser, *v.a.*, to vaporize.

se **vaporiser**, *v.r.*, to vaporize, to be vaporized.

vaquer (va-ké), *v.n.*, to be vacant, void, empty; to be in vacation-time, not to sit; to attend, to devote one's self to. *Il vaque à ses affaires;* he is attending to his business.

*varaigne, *n.f.*, tide-sluice (of salt marshes —*de marais salants*).

varaire, *n.f.*, (bot.) white hellebore.

varangue (-râng), *n.f.*, (nav.) floor-timbers of a ship. — *plate ou de fond;* flat floor-timber. — *fort acculée;* rising floor-timber amidship.

vare, *n.f.*, Spanish measure of length, about a yard.

varec, or **varech**, *n.m.*, (bot.) varec, wrack, sea-wrack; (jur.) things washed upon the shore by the sea, and the right to appropriate them; sunken ship.

varenne, *n.f.*, waste-land; (hunt.) ⊙ Royal preserve.

vareuse, *n.f.*, pea-jacket.

variabilité, *n.f.*, variableness, variability, changeableness; (alg.) variability.

variable, *adj.*, variable, changeable, fickle, unsettled, unsteady. *La fortune est —;* fortune is fickle. *Pouls —;* changeable pulse.

variable, *n.m.*, variable. *Le baromètre est au —;* the barometer is at variable.

variant, **-e**, *adj.*, (l.u.) variable, fickle.

variante, *n.f.*, different reading; alteration, difference, in different editions of a book, writing, &c.

variation, *n.f.*, variation, variety, change, changeableness; alteration.

varice, *n.f.*, (med.) varix, varicose vein.

varicelle, *n.f.*, (med.) varicella, swine-pox.

varicocèle, *n.f.*, (med.) varicocele.

varier, *v.a.*, to vary, to variegate, to diversify. — *la phrase;* to say the same thing in other words.

varier, *v.n.*, to vary, to change, to be changeable; to disagree, to be at variance; to be fickle.

variété, *n.f.*, variety, diversity, change; *pl.*, miscellanea.

ne **varietur** (né varié-tur), *adv.*, (jur.) in order that no change may be made.

variole, *n.f.*, small-pox, variola.

varioleu-x, **-se**, *adj.* and *n.*, a person suffering from small-pox.

variolique, *adj.*, (med.), variolous, variolar, variolic.

variolite, *n.f.*, (min.) variolite.

varioloïde, *n.f.*, (med.) varioloid, chicken-pox.

variorum, *n.m.* and *adj.* (—), variorum.

variqueu-x, **-se**, *adj.*, varicose, varicous.

⊙**varlet**, *n.m.*, varlet, page.

varlope, *n.f.*, jointer, jointing-plane.

vasculaire, or (l.u.) **vasculeu-x**, **-se**, *adj.*, (anat.) vascular.

vase, *n.m.*, vase, vessel, urn. — *s antiques;* antique vases. —*s étrusques;* Etruscan vases. —*s cinéraires;* funeral urns. — *de nuit;* chamber utensil.

vase, *n.f.*, slime, mud, mire.

vaseu-x, -se, *adj.*, slimy, muddy, miry.

vasistas (-tâs), *n.m.*, casement-window ; hatch-door ; blind (of a carriage—*de voiture*).

vasque. *n.f.*, basin (of a fountain—*de fontaine*).

vassal, *n.m.*, vassal.

vassalité, *n.f.*, vassalage ; land held by vassals.

vasselage (vas-laj), *n.m.*, vassalage.

vaste, *adj.*, vast, vasty, great, spacious, extensive. — *pays* ; vast country. *De —s desseins* ; great designs. *Un lieu —* ; a vast place.

vastement, *adv.*, vastly.

vatican, *n.m.*, Vatican, the Palace of the Pope.

va-tout, *n.m.* (—), staking all one has (at cards—*aux cartes*).

à vau-de-route, *adv.*, à **vau-l'eau** *adv. V.* à **vau-l'eau.**

vaudeville (vôd-vil), *n.m.*, (thea.) vaudevil ; ballad.

vaudevilliste, *n.m.*, vaudevil-writer ; ballad-writer.

vaudois, *n.m.*, Vaudois.

vaurien (-in), *n.m.*, good-for-nothing wretch, worthless fellow, scamp.

vautour, *n.m.*, (orni.) vulture.

vautrait, *n.m.*, (hunt.) equipage for wild boar-hunting.

se **vautrer**, *v.r.*, to wallow, to spread one's self out.

7avasseur, *n.m.*, vavasor, vassal of a vassal.

vayvode, *n.m.* (—s), waiwode, waywode.

veau, *n.m.*, calf ; calf's leather ; veal ; lazy fellow. *Chair de —* ; veal. *Longe de —* ; loin of veal. *Rouelle de —* ; fillet of veal. *Des pieds de —* ; calves' feet. *Eau de —* ; veal broth.

vecteur, *adj.*, (astron.) vector. *Rayon —* ; radius vector.

véda, *n.m.*, Veda, sacred books of the Hindoos.

védasse, *n.f.*, (dy.) weed-ashes.

vedette, *n.f.*, scout, vedette ; watch-box. *Écrire quelque chose en —* ; to write anything in a line by itself. *Mettre en —* ; to place on vedette.

védique, *adj.*, of, relating to, the Veda.

végétable, *adj.*, vegetable.

végétal, *n.m.*, vegetable.

végétal, -e, *adj.*, vegetable.

végétalité, *n.f.*, vegetability.

végétant, -e, *adj.*, vegetating.

végétati-f, -ve, *adj.*, vegetative.

végétation, *n.f.*, vegetation.

végéter, *v.n.*, to vegetate. *Il ne fait plus que —* ; he merely vegetates.

véhémence, *n.f.*, vehemence, vehemency, impetuosity.

véhément, -e, *adj.*, vehement, impetuous, hot, passionate. *Naturel —*, hot temper. *Orateur —* ; vehement orator, impassioned orator.

véhémentement, *adv.*, ⊙(jur.) strongly ; (fam., fig.) vehemently.

véhicule, *n.m.*, vehicle.

vehme, *n.f.* (n.p.), Vehmic Court.

vehmique, *adj.*, Vehmic.

*****veille**, *n.f.*, watch, watching, sitting up ; eve, vigil, day before ; point, verge. *Être à la — de* ; to be on the point of. *Entre la — et le sommeil* : between sleeping and waking.

*****veillée**, *n.f.*. sitting up to work in company ; night attendance (upon a sick person—*d'un malade*).

*****veiller**, *v.n.*, to watch, to sit up, to wake, to be awake, to lie awake ; to be on the watch ; to attend, to take care, to see. — *au salut de l'état* ; to watch over the safety of the state. — *sur soi même* ; to be upon one's guard. *Faire —* ; to keep any one up, to prevent any one from going to bed.

*****veiller**, *v.a.*, to watch over, to look after, to sit up with. — *un malade* ; to sit up with a sick person.

*****veilles**, *n.f.pl.*, lucubrations, night-studies, night-watches.

*****veilleur**, *n.m.*, watcher (one who sits up with a dead person—*de morts*) ; night-watchman.

*****veilleuse**, *n.f.*, night-lamp ; float-light.

*****veillotte**, *n.f.*, cock (of hay—*de foin*) ; (bot.) meadow-saffron.

veinage, *n.m.*, (paint.) veining.

veine, *n.f.*, (anat., geol., min.) vein ; (of marble or wood—*du marbre, du bois*) vein ; (geol.) seam ; under-ground spring of water ; (fig.) vein. *Je suis en —* ; my hand is in. *En — de* ; in the vein for, in the humour for. *Bonne —* ; good run (at play—*au jeu*).

veiné, -e, *adj.*, veiny, veined.

veiner, *v.a.*, (paint.) to vein.

veineu-x, -se, *adj.*, veined, veiny ; (anat.) venous, venal.

veinule, *n.f.*, (anat.) small vein.

vélar, *n.m.*, hedge-mustard, hedge-garlic.

vélarium (-rio-m), *n.m.* (—s), (Rom. antiq.) awning stretched above the theatre to keep off the sun.

vélaut ! *int.*, (hunt.) tally-ho.

velche, *n.m.*, Goth (ignorant person—*ignorant*).

vêler, *v.a.*, (of cows—*des vaches*) to calve.

vélin, *n.m.*, vellum.

vélite, *n.m.*, (Rom. antiq.) light-armed soldier, skirmisher.

velléité (vèl-lé-), *n.f.*, velleity, slight desire.

⊙**véloce**, *adj.*, (astron.) swift.

vélocipède, *n.m.*, bicycle.

vélocité, *n.f.*, velocity, swiftness, rapidity, speed.

velours, *n.m.*, velvet. — *ras* ; short-nap velvet. — *façonné* ; figured velvet. — *de soie* ; silk velvet. — *de coton* ; cotton velvet. — *à côtes* ; corduroy. — *de coton croisé* ; velveteen.

velouté, -e, *n.m.*, velveting, flock surface ; (bot.) velvet ; (med.) ⊙ mucous membrane.

velouté, -e, *adj.*, velvet, velvety ; cut in imitation of velvet ; velvet-like.

veloutier (-tié), *n.m.*, velvet-worker.

veltage, *n.m.*, measuring liquids by the velte.

velte, *n.f.*, an obsolete measure of capacity, about 7 quarts English ; a sort of gauge to measure the capacity of casks.

velter, *v.a.*, to measure liquids by the velte.

velteur, *n.m.*, gauger ; one who measures by the velte.

velu, -e, *adj.*, hairy (not applied to the head or beard—*ne se dit pas par rapport aux cheveux ou à la barbe*), shaggy.

velvote, *n.f.*, (bot.) spurious toad-flax.

venaison, *n.f.*, venison.

vénal, -e, *adj.*, venal, mercenary.

vénalement (-nal-mân), *adv.*, in a venal, mercenary manner.

vénalité, *n.f.*, venality.

venant, *n.m.* and *adj.*, comer ; coming. *A tout —* ; to the first comer.

vendable, *adj.*, salable, vendible.

vendange, *n.f.*, vintage. *Faire —* ; to gather the grapes ; to make a good thing of, to profit by.

vendanger, *v.a.* and *n.*, to gather grapes ; to vintage ; (fig.) to make illicit profits ; to ravage, to spoil, to devastate.

vendangeu-r, *n.m.*, **-se**, *n.f.*, vintager, grape-gatherer.

vendémiaire, *n.m.*, Vendémiaire, the first month of the calendar of the first French republic, from September 22nd or 23rd to October 21st or 22nd.

venderesse (văn-drès), *n.f.*, (jur.) vendor.

vendetta, *n.f.* (—*s*). vendetta, vengeance.

vendeu-r, *n.m.*, **-se,** *n.f.*, seller, vendor. — *d'orviétan;* quack.

vendication, *n.f.* *V.* **revendication.**

vendiquer, *v.a.* *V.* **revendiquer.**

⊙**vendition,** *n.f.*, (jur.) sale.

vendre, *v.a.* and *n.*, to sell, to vend, to sell out; to betray. — *cher;* to sell dear. — *à bon marché;* to sell cheap. — *argent comptant;* to sell for ready money.

se **vendre.** *v.r.*, to sell one's self; to sell, to go off (of a thing—*des choses*).

vendredi, *n.m.*, Friday. *Le —saint;* Good-Friday.

vené, -e. *adj.*, high (of meat—*de la viande*)

⊙**vénéfice.** *n.m.*, (jur.) poisoning by malefice.

⊙**venelle,** *n.f.*. small street. [Only used in the popular expression : *Enfiler la —;* to run away.]

vénéneu-x, -se. *adj.*, venomous, poisonous (of plants only—*des plantes seulement*).

vener, *v.a.*, to run domestic animals, in order to make their flesh tender. *Faire — de la viande;* to keep meat until it gets high.

vénérable, *adj.*, venerable, reverend.

vénérablement, *adv.*, venerably, reverently.

vénération. *n.f.*, veneration. *Sa mémoire est en —;* his memory is held in veneration.

vénérer. *v.a.*, to venerate, to reverence.

vénerie (vé-n-ri), *n.f.*, venery, hunting; hunting-train.

vénérien, -ne (-in, -è-n), *adj.*, venereal.

venette, *n.f.*, (pop.) fright. *Avoir la —;* to be in a fright. *Donner la —;* to frighten.

veneur, *n.m.*, huntsman (servant—*serviteur*). *Grand —;* first huntsman of the Royal hunting-train.

venez-y-voir, *n.m.* (—). (fam., iron.) a trifle.

vengeance (-jans), *n.f.*, vengeance, revenge. *Assouvir sa —;* to glut one's vengeance. *Tirer — d'un affront;* to be revenged for an affront. *Esprit de —;* revengefulness.

venger, *v.a.*, to revenge, to avenge, to take revenge for, to resent. — *une injure;* to revenge an injury.

se **venger,** *v.r.*, to revenge one's self, to avenge one's self; to be revenged. — *de quelqu'un;* to be revenged on any one.

venge-ur, -resse, *n.* and *adj.*, avenger, revenger; revengeful, avenging.

veniat (vé-ni-at), *n.m.* (—), (jur.) summons to an inferior magistrate to attend his superior.

véniel. -le. *adj.*, venial.

véniellement (-nièl-măn), *adv.*, venially.

veni-mecum (vé-ni-mé-co-m), *n.m.* (—). *V.* **vade-mecum.**

venimeu-x, -se. *adj.*, communicating poison, venomous (of animals—*des animaux seulement*); poisonous.

venin, *n.m.*, venom, poison, venomousness. *Morte la bête, mort le —;* dead men don't bite. *Il a jeté tout son —;* he has vented all his spite.

venir (venant, venu), *v.n.*, to come, to be coming; to come along, to arrive; to chance. to fall out, to occur, to happen; to be descended; to grow, to grow up, to thrive (of plants—*des plantes*); to issue, to run, to flow; to emanate, to proceed, to arise, to derive; to reach. *Je le vois —;* I see him coming. *Le voilà qui rient;* there he comes. *Venez ici;* come here. *Voulez-vous — avec nous à Londres?* will you go with us to London? *Faire —;* to send for. *Faire — le médecin;* to send for the doctor. *Il va et vient;* he goes in and out. *Il s'en est allé comme il est venu;* he has had his labour for his pains. *Je ne ferai qu'aller et —;* I will not stay, I shall

be back again directly. *En — aux extrémités;* to come to extremities. *Il en vint jusqu'à le menacer;* he went so far as to threaten him. · *Il en faut — là;* we must come to that at last. *Si ma lettre venait à se perdre;* if my letter should happen to be lost. *Tout lui vient à souhait;* everything succeeds according to his wishes. *Cette nouvelle est venue jusqu'à moi;* that news reached even me. *Il me vint une pensée;* a thought came into my head. *D'où vient-il que?* how is it that? *D'où vient cela?* what is the cause of that? *Quand il vint à parler de;* when he came to speak of. — *au monde;* to come into the world. — *de;* to come from; (followed by an infinitive—*devant un infinitif*) to have just. *Je viens de le quitter;* I have just left him. *Il vient de partir;* he has but just gone. *Il vient d'arriver;* he has just arrived. *Cet arbre vient bien;* that tree thrives well. *Viens donc, venez donc;* come away, come along. *Où voulez-vous en —?* what are you aiming, driving, at? *D'où venez-vous?* where do you come from? where were you brought up? *Il faut le voir —;* we must first see what his intentions are. *Temps à —;* future time.

venir, *n.m.*, coming.

vent, *n.m.*; wind, gale; flatulence; breath; (hunt.) scent; vanity, emptiness; (artil.) windage. *Un souffle de —;* a puff of wind. *Un — coulis;* wind that comes through a chink or hole. *Il fait du —;* it is windy. *Être à l'abri du —;* to be sheltered from the wind. *Jeter la plume au —;* to allow chance to decide. *Autant en emporte le —;* all that is idle talk. — *fait;* settled wind. *Au —;* to the wind; (nav.) to the windward. *Sous le —* (nav.); leeward. *— de terre;* land breeze. — *de mer;* sea breeze. *Avoir — et marée;* to have both wind and tide. *Avoir le dessus du —* (nav.); to have the weather-gauge; to have the upper hand of one. *Avoir des —s;* to be troubled with flatulence. *Lâcher un —;* to break wind. *Tout cela n'est que du —;* all that signifies nothing. *Si le — le permet;* weather permitting. *Filer — arrière* (nav.); to sail before the wind. — *frais;* fresh gale. *Gros coup de —;* strong gale. *Être logé aux quatre —s;* to be exposed to every wind that blows. *Avoir le — contraire;* to have the wind against one. *Flotter au gré du —;* to float in the wind. *Iles du —* (geog.); Windward Islands.

*****ventail,** *n.m.*, (her.) ventail (of a helmet— *de casque*).

vente, *n.f.*, sale; felling (of timber—*eaux et forêts*); ⊙ public place for selling; (forestry— *eaux et forêts*) part of a forest where trees have been felled; *pl.*, (feudalism—*féodalité*) a tax on the sales of heritages; a branch association of the Carbonari. *En —;* for sale. *Mettre en —;* to offer for sale. — *aux enchères;* auction. *Marchandise de —;* goods that go off well. *Asseoir les —s;* to mark the trees that are to be felled. *Lods et —s;* tax on the sale of heritages (feudalism—*féodalité*).

ventelle, *n.f.*, paddle-valve (of lock-gates— *d'écluses*).

venter. *v.n.imp.*, to blow (of the wind—*du vent*). *Il vente:* the wind blows, it is windy.

venteu-x, -se. *adj.*, windy, flatulent.

ventilateur, *n.m.*, ventilator; (phys.) air-exhauster.

ventilation, *n.f.*, ventilation; (jur.) estimation at a relative value.

ventiler, *v.a.*, to ventilate; (jur.) to estimate at a relative value; ⊙to discuss, to moot.

ventolier, *n.m.*, (hawking—*fauconnerie*) bird that flies well against the wind.

ventôse, *n.m.*, Ventose, the sixth month of the calendar of the first French republic, from February 19th or 20th to March 20th.

ventosité, *n.f.*, flatulency, ventosity.

ventouse, *n.f.*, cupping-glass; ventilator; (arch.) ventiduct; *pl.*, cupping-glasses. *Appliquer les —s*; to cup.

ventouser, *v.a.*, to cup.

ventouseur, *n.m.*, cupper.

ventral, -e, *adj.*, ventral.

ventre, *n.m.*, belly, stomach, womb. — *à terre*; at full speed. *Le bas—* (anat.); the abdomen. *J'ai mal au — ;* my belly aches. *Remettre le cœur au — à quelqu'un*; to give any one fresh courage.

ventrebleu! *int.*, zounds!

ventrée,*n f.*,litter(of animals—*des animaux*).

ventricule, *n.m.*, ventricle.

ventrière, *n.f.*, girth (of a horse—*d'un cheval*); (carp.) purlin.

ventriloque, *n.m.* and *adj.*, ventriloquist; ventriloquous.

ventriloquie, *n.f.*, ventriloquy, ventriloquism.

*se **ventrouiller**, *v.r.*, to wallow in the mire, in the mud.

ventru, -e, *adj.*, big-bellied, corpulent.

venu, -e, *part.*, come. *Le bien — ;* welcome. *Le dernier — ;* the last comer. *Nouveau — ;* new-comer (*m.s.*). *Des nouveaux —s ;* new-comers (*m.pl.*). *Une nouvelle — e;* a new-comer (*f.s.*). *Des nouvelles — es ;* new-comers (*f.pl.*).

venue, *n.f.*, coming, arrival, growth. *Allées et —s ;* coming and going.

⊙**vénule**, *n.f.* V. **veinule**.

vénus (-nus), *n.f.*, (astron., myth.) Venus; ⊙(chem.) copper.

⊙**vénuste**, *adj.*, beautiful, handsome.

vénusté, *n.f.*, (l.u.) handsomeness.

⊙**vêpre**, *n.m.*, vesper, evening.

vêpres, *n.f.pl.*, vespers.

ver (vèr), *n.m.*,worm,maggot; moth ; mite. — *luisant;* glowworm. — *de fumier;* muckworm. — *à soie;* silk-worm. — *rongeur;* never-dying worm. — *de fromage;* cheese-mite. — *solitaire;* tape-worm. — *de terre;* earth-worm.

véracité, *n.f.*, veracity.

véranda, *n.f.*, verandah.

vératre, *n.m.*, (bot.) veratrum.

vératrine, *n.f.*, (chem.) veratria, veratrine.

verbal, -e, *adj.*, verbal. *Promesse —e ;* promise by word of mouth.

verbalement (-bal-män), *adv.*, verbally, by word of mouth.

verbaliser, *v.n.*, to draw up a written statement; to state facts.

verbe, *n.m.*, (gram.)verb; voice; (theol.)the Word.

verbénacées, *n.f.pl.*, (bot.) verbenaceæ.

verbération, *n.f.*, verberation.

verbeu-x, -se, *adj.*, verbose, prolix.

verbiage, *n.m.*, verbiage.

verbiager, *v.n.*, to be verbose.

verbiageu-r, *n.m.*, **-se**, *n.f.*, verbose talker.

verbosité, *n.f.*, verbosity.

ver-coquin, *n.m.* (—*s* —*s*), (ent.) vine-grub ; (vet.) staggers ; caprice, whim.

verd, *adj.* V. **vert**.

verdâtre, *adj.*, greenish.

verdée, *n.f.*, white wine of Tuscany.

verdelet, -te. *adj.*, tart (of wine—*du vin*), vigorous (of old people—*des vieillards*).

verderie, *n.f.*, verderer's range; verderer's jurisdiction.

verdet, *n.m.*, verdigris.

verdeur, *n.f.*, greenness, viridity, sap ; tartness, harshness (of wine—*du vin*); acrimony ; (of old people—*des vieillards*) vigour, freshness.

verdict (-dikt), *n.m.*, (jur.) verdict, finding. *Rendre un — ;* to deliver in a verdict.

verdier, *n.m.*, verderer, verderor ; (orni.) greenfinch, green-linnet.

verdir, *v.a.* and *n.*, to paint green ; to grow green, to become green; to get covered with verdigris (of copper—*du cuivre*).

verdoyant, -e, *adj.*, verdant, green.

verdoyer, *v.n.*, to be verdant, to become green.

verdure, *n.f.*, verdure, greenness, green ; pot-herbs.

verdurier,*n.m.*, salad-purveyor to the Royal household.

véreu-x, -se, *adj.*, worm-eaten, maggoty, full of maggots, rotten ; suspicious, suspected of a concealed vice or defect; (com.) (of bills— *de dettes, de créances*) insecure, unsafe.

verge, *n.f.*, rod; shank (of an anchor—*d'an-cre*); handle (of a whip—*d'un fouet*); *pl.*, rod, birch. *Cet enfant craint les —s ;* that child fears the rod. *Donner des —s pour se faire fouetter ;* to give a rod to beat one's self.

vergé, -e, *adj.*, (of paper—*du papier*) laid ; (of textile fabrics—*des tissus*) streaky.

vergée, *n.f.*, about a rood.

verger, *v.a.*, to measure by the rod.

verger, *n.m.*, fruit-garden, orchard.

vergeté, -e, *part.*, beaten (cleaned with a cane—*nettoyé avec une baguette*); streaked(of skin —*de la peau*).

vergeter, *v.a.*, to beat (to clean with a cane —*nettoyer avec une vergette*).

vergetier (-tié), *n.m.*, brushmaker.

vergette, *n.f.*, brush, clothes-brush (generally used in the plural); hoops (of a drum—*de tambour*).

vergeure (-jur), *n.f.*, wire-mark (of paper— *du papier*).

verglas, *n.m.*, glazed frost.

vergne, *n.m.*, alder-tree.

vergogne, *n.f.*, shame.

vergue (vèrg), *n.f.*, (nav.) yard. *Grande — ;* main-yard.

véricle, *n.f.*, paste, imitation of precious stones.

véridicité, *n.f.*, veracity, credibility.

véridique, *adj.*, veracious.

véridiquement, *adv.*, veraciously, truthfully.

vérificateur, *n.m.*, verifier, examiner (of work—*de travaux*) ; auditor (of accounts—*de comptes*).

vérification, *n.f.*, verification, examining, auditing.

vérifier, *v.a.*, to inspect, to examine. to verify; to try (weights, measures—*poids et mesures*); to audit.

vérin, *n.m.*, screw-jack.

vérine, *n.f.*, best American tobacco ; (nav.) binnacle-lamp.

véritable, *adj.*, true, genuine, real, staunch. *Un — ami ;* a true friend.

véritablement, *adv.*, truly, really, in reality, indeed, in truth.

vérité, *n.f.*, truth, verity. *Dire la — ;* to speak the truth. *En — ;* indeed, truly. *A la — ;* indeed ; it is true ; I confess.

verjus, *n.m.*, verjuice ; sour grapes.

verjuté, -e, *adj.*, sharp, tart.

vermeil, -le, *adj.*, vermilion, ruby, ruddy, rosy, coral. *Teint — ;* rosy complexion.

vermeil, *n.m.*, silver-guilt.

vermicel, *or* **vermicelle**, *n.m.*, vermicelli.

vermicelier, *n.m.*, vermicelli manufacturer.

vermiculaire, *adj.*, vermicular, worm shaped ; (anat.) vermiform.

vermiculaire, *n.f.*, (bot.) stone-crop.

vermiculé, -e, *adj.*, (arch.) vermicular, vermiculated.

vermiculures, *n.f.pl.*, (arch.) vermiculated work.

vermiforme, *adj.*, worm-shaped ; (anat.) vermiform.

18 *

vermifuge, *n.m.*, (med.) vermifuge.

*****vermiller**, *v.n.*, (hunt.) (of boars)to scratch for worms. &c.

*****vermillon**, *n.m.*, vermilion.

*****vermillonner**, *v.a.*, to vermilion; to paint in red.

vermine, *n.f.*, vermin.

vermineu-x, -se, *adj.*, (med.) caused by worms.

vermisseau, *n.m.*, vermicule, grub.

se **vermouler**, *v.r.*, to be worm-eaten.

vermoulu, -e, *adj.*, worm-eaten.

vermoulure, *n.f.*, worm-hole, rotteuness in wood.

vermout, *n.m.*, bitters (wine and wormwood —*vin absinthé*).

vernaille, *n.f.*, (min.) telesia.

vernal, -e, *adj.*, vernal, spring.

vernation, *n.f.*, (bot.) vernation, foliation.

verne, *n.m.*, (bot.). *V.* **vergne**.

vernier, *n.m.*, vernier, sliding-rule.

vernir, *v.a.*, to varnish; to glaze; to japan.

vernis, *n.m.*, varnish, polish, glaze, glazing. *Donner un — à;* to polish, to set off.

vernissage, *n.m.*, varnishing; glazing.

vernisser, *v.a.*, to varnish, to glaze, to japan.

vernisseur, *n.m.*, varnisher.

vernissure, *n.f.*, the application of varnish, or of glazing on anything.

vérole, *n.f.*, pox. *La petite —;* the small-pox. *Grain de petite —;* pock. *Petite —* **vo-lante;** chicken-pox. [Without the adjective *petite*, this word is a low expression to be avoided, it means syphilis.]

vérolé, -e, *n.* and *adj.*, (l.ex.) one suffering from syphilis.

vérolique, *adj.*, (med.) syphilitic.

véron, *n.m. V.* **vairon**.

véronique, *n.f.*, (bot.) veronica, speedwell.

*****verraille**, *n.f.*, small objects made of glass.

verrat, *n.m.*, boar.

verre, *n.m.*, glass. *— à boire;* drinking glass. *Choquer les —s;* to touch glasses. *— grossissant;* magnifying-glass. *— ardent;* burning-glass. *Grand —;* tumbler. *— à pied;* wine-glass.

`**verrée**. *n.f.*, glassful.

verrerie (vér-rî), *n.f.*, glass-works; glass-making; glass-wares.

verrier, *n.m.*, glass-maker, glassman, glass-blower; dealer in glass-wares; glass-basket.

verrière, *n.f.*, glass-stand; church painted window.

verrine, *or* **verrière**, *n.f.*, glazed box; picture frame.

verroterie (vè-ro-trî),*n.f.*, glass-ware; glass trinket; glass beads.

verrou, *n.m.*, bolt. *Fermer une porte au —;* to bolt a door. *S'enfermer au —;* to bolt one's self in.

*****verrouiller**, *v.a.*, to bolt, to bar.

*****se* **verrouiller**, *v.r.*, to bolt one's self in.

verrucaire, *n.f.*, (bot.) wartwort.

verrue, *n.f.*, wart.

verruqueu-x, -se, *adj.*, warty; wart-like; (med.) tubercled.

vers (vèr), *n.m.*, verse. *Faire des —;* to write verses.

vers, *prep.*, towards, about, to. *Tournez-vous — moi;* turn towards me. *— les quatre heures;* about four o'clock.

versant, -e, *adj.*, liable to be overturned (of carriages—*des voitures*).

versant, *n.m.*, declivity, side (of mountains —*des montagnes*).

versatile, *adj.*, versatile, variable, change-able.

versatilité, *n.f.*, versatility, variableness.

verse, *adj.*, (geom.) versed. *Sinus —;* versed sine.

à **verse**. *adv.*, (of raining—*de la pluie*) very fast, as fast as it can pour.

versé, -e, *adj.*, versed, skilled, conversant.

verseau, *n.m.*, (astron.) Aquarius.

versement, *n.m.*, payment; deposit. — *partiel;* instalment.

verser, *v.a.*, to pour, to pour out; to shed, to spill; to lodge, to deposit (money—*de l'argent*); to overturn, to upset. *— du vin dans un verre;* to pour wine into a glass. *— des larmes;* to shed tears.

verser, *v.n.*, to overturn, to upset, to be overturned, to overset (of vehicles—*des voitures*); to be laid, to be beaten down (of standing corn—*du blé sur pied*).

verset, *n.m.*, (Bibl.) verse.

versicules, *or* **versiculets**, *n.m. pl.*(fam., jest.) little verses.

versificateur, *n.m.*, versifier.

versification, *n.f.*, versification.

versifier, *v.n.*, to versify, to make verses.

versifier, *v.a.*, to turn into verses.

se **versifier**, *v.r.*, to be versified, to be put into verse.

version, *n.f.*, version, translation.

verso, *n.m.* (—*s*), back (of a leaf—*d'une feuille*); (print.) reverse, even, left-hand page.

versoir, *n.m.*, mould-board (of a plough—*de charrue*).

verste,*n.f.*, verst, Russian measure of length about 1166 yards.

vert, -e. *adj.*, green; sharp, harsh (of things —*des choses*); tart (of wine—*du vin*); raw (of hides—*des peaux*); vigorous, robust (of old age —*des vieillards*); resolute. *Bois —;* greenwood. *Morue —e;* salt fish that has not been yet dried. *Cuir —;* raw leather. *Fruit —;* green fruit. *Du vin —;* tart wine. *La —e jeunesse;* youthful years. *Une —e vieillesse;* a vigorous old age. *Une —e réponse;* a sharp answer.

vert, *n.m.*, green, green colour; grass, green meat; tartness (of wine—*du vin*). *— de mer;* sea-green. *Employer le — et le sec;* to leave no stone unturned. *Mettre des chevaux au —;* to turn horses out to grass.

vert-de-gris, *n.m.* (*n.p.*), verdigris.

vertébral, -e, *adj.*, vertebral.

vertèbre, *n.f.*, vertebra.

vertébré, -e, *adj.*, vertebral, vertebrate, vertebrated.

vertébré, *n.m.*, (zool.) vertebral, vertebrate. *Les —s;* vertebrates, vertebrata.

vertement, *adv.*, vigorously, briskly, sharply; harshly.

vertical, -e, *adj.*, vertical.

verticalement (-kal-mân), *adv.*, vertically.

verticalité, *n.f.*, verticalness.

*****verticille**, *n.m.*, (bot.) verticil; whorl.

*****verticillé, -e**, *adj.*, (bot.) verticillate.

verticité, *n.f.*, verticity (of the sea compass —*de la boussole*).

vertige, *n.m.*, dizziness, giddiness, vertigo, swimming in the head; (vet.) staggers.

vertigineu-x,-se,*adj.*, subject to giddiness.

vertigo, *n.m.*(—*s*), maggot, whim, crotchet; (vet.) staggers.

vertu, *n.f.*, virtue, virtuousness; property, faculty. *Faire de nécessité —;* to make a virtue of necessity. *En — de;* by virtue of, in pursuance of.

⊙**vertubleu! vertuchou!** *int.*, bless my heart!

vertueusement (-éûz-mân), *adv.*, virtuously.

vertueu-x, -se, *adj.*, virtuous.

⊙**vertugadin**, *n.m.*, farthingale.

verve, *n.f.*, warmth, heat of fancy; animation, liveliness; (l.u.) fancy, whim, crotchet. *Avoir de la —;* to be sprightly, spirited.

verveine, *n.f.*, (bot.) vervain.

vervelle. *n.f.*, (falconry—*fauconnerie*) varvel.

verveux, *n.m.*, hoop-net (for fishing—*pour la pêche*).

vésanie, *n.f.*, (med.) madness, insanity.

vesce, *n.f.*, (bot.) vetch.

vésical, -e, *adj.*, vesical.

vésicant, -e, *adj.*, causing blisters, vesicatory.

vésication, *n.f.*, (med.) vesication.

vésicatoire, *n.m.* and *adj.*, blister, vesicatory; blistering. *Un emplâtre —*; a blistering plaster. a blister. *Un —*; a blister.

vésiculaire, *adj.*, vesicular.

vésicule, *n.f.*, vesicle, bladder.

vésiculeu-x, -se, *adj.*, vesiculate, bladdery.

vesou, *n.m.*, juice of sugar-canes.

vespasienne (-zi-èn), *n.f.*, urinary.

vesper (vès-pèr), *n.m.*, (astron.) Vesper, Venus.

⊙**vespérie** (vès-), *n.f.*, the last thesis that a licentiate had to sustain to obtain his doctor's degree; a severe scolding.

⊙**vespériser.** *v.a.*, to scold, to reprimand.

vespétro, *n.m.*, a stomachic ratafia, a cordial.

vesse, *n.f.*, (l. ex.) fizzling.

vesse-de-loup, *n.f.* (—*s* —), (bot.) puff-ball.

vesser. *v.n.*, (l. ex.) to fizzle.

vesseu-r, *n.m.*, **-se,** *n.f.*, (l. ex.) one who fizzles; a coward.

vessie, *n.f.*, bladder; blister; (ich.) bladder. *Faire venir des —s*; to blister.

vessigon, *n.m.*, (vet.) vessicnon, wind-gall.

vesta, *n.f.*, (astron.) Vesta.

vestale, *n.f.*, vestal.

veste, *n.f.*, round jacket.

vestiaire (-ti-èr), *n.m.*, vestiary; robing-room; dressing-room; cloak-room; charity clothing-club; expense of clothing in convents.

vestibule, *n.m.*, vestibule, lobby.

vestige, *n.m.*, footstep, track; vestige.

veston. *n.m.*, a kind of vest. jacket.

vésuvien, -ne, *adj.*, Vesuvian.

vêtement (vêt-mān), *n.m.*, garment; garb; *pl.*, dress, clothes, raiment, wearing apparel.

vétéran, *n.m.*, veteran; pupil who stays a second year in the same class (at school—*au collège*).

vétérance, *n.f.*, quality of a veteran.

vétérinaire, *n.m.* and *adj.*, veterinary surgeon; veterinary.

*****vétillard, -e.** *V.* **vétilleur.**

*****vétille,** *n.f.*, trifle.

*****vétiller,** *v.n.*, to trifle, to stand upon trifles.

*****vétilleu-r,** *n.m.*, **-se,** *n.f.*, one who stands upon trifles, trifler.

*****vétilleu-x, -se,** *adj.*, standing upon trifles (of a person—*des personnes*); that requires great care (of a thing—*des choses*).

vêtir (vêtant, vêtu), *v.a.*, to clothe, to vest, to array.

se **vêtir,** *v.r.*, to put on one's clothes, to dress one's self.

vétiver (-vèr), *n.m.*, (bot.) whorl-flowered bent-grass.

veto (vé-tô), *n.m.* (*n.p.*), veto.

vêtu, -e, *part.*, dressed, clothed, clad, arrayed. *Mal —*; ill-dressed. *— de blanc*; dressed in white.

vêture, *n.f.*, taking the habit *or* the veil among friars and nuns. [*Prise d'habit* is more frequently used.]

vétusté, *n.f.*, oldness, decay.

vétyver (-vèr), *n.m.* *V.* **vétiver.**

veu-f, -ve, *n.* and *adj.*, widower; widow; widowed. *Cette église est —ve de son évêque*; this church is deprived of its bishop. *Église —ve*;

a church which was once, but is no longer, a cathedral church.

veule, *adj.*, (gard.) too light (of earth—*de la terre*); long, small and weak (branches); (pers.) ⊙weak, powerless.

veuvage, *n.m.*, widowhood.

veuve, *n.f.*, widow; (bot.) tulip streaked white and violet; (orni) widow-bird, whidah-finch, vidua.

vexant, -e, *adj.*, vexing, provoking.

vexateur, *n.m.*, he who annoys, provokes.

vexation, *n.f.*, vexation, molestation.

vexatoire, *adj.*, vexatious.

vexer, *v.a.*, to vex, to plague, to molest.

vexillaire, *n.m.*, (Rom. antiq.) vexillary, standard-bearer; veteran soldier serving his last four years.

vexillaire, *adj.*, (nav.) of signals made by means of flags; (bot.) having the shape of a flag.

viabilité, *n.f.*, (med., jur.) viability (of infants—*des nouveau-nés*); condition of the roads of a country.

viable, *adj.*, viable.

viaduc, *n.m.*, viaduct.

viag-er, -ère, *adj.*, for life, during life. *Rente —ère*; life-annuity.

viager, *n.m.*, (fin.) life-interest.

viande, *n.f.*, meat, viand. *— de boucherie*; butcher's meat *Menue —*; fowl and game. *— blanche*; white meat. *— noire*; brown meat (game—*gibier*). *Un mangeur de —s apprêtées*; a lazy fellow, a sponger.

viander, *v.n.*, (hunt.) to graze (of fallow beasts—*des fauves*).

viandis. *n.m.*, pasture, grazing (of fallow beasts—*des fauves*).

viatique, *n.m.*, Viaticum.

vibord, *n.m.*, (nav.) waist (of a ship—*d'un vaisseau*).

vibrant, -e, *adj.*, vibrating.

vibration, *n.f.*, vibration.

vibratoire, *adj.*, vibratory.

vibrer, *v.n.*, to vibrate.

vibrion, *n.m.*, (zool.) vibrio.

vicaire, *n.m.*, vicar (delegate—*délégué*); curate of a parish. *Le — de Jésus-Christ*; the Pope. *Cardinal —*; the Cardinal whom the Pope appointed to the ecclesiastical supervision of the city of Rome.

vicairie, *n.f.*, *or* **vicariat,** *n.m.*, curacy, curateship.

vicarial, -e, *adj.*, of a curate.

vicarier, *v.n.*, to officiate as a curate.

vice, *n.m.*, vice, fault; blemish, defect, imperfection. *Pauvreté n'est pas —*; poverty is no crime.

vice, Latin particle, vice, instead of. [Only used in French in composition with nouns.]

vice-amiral, *n.m.* (— *-amiraux*), vice-admiral; second ship of a fleet.

vice-amirauté, *n.f.*(— *-s*), vice-admiralty.

*****vice-bailli,** *n.m.* (— *-s*), vice-bailiff.

vice-chancelier, *n.m.* (— *-s*), vice-chancellor.

vice-consul. *n.m.* (— *-s*), vice-consul.

vice-consulat, *n.m.* (— *-s*), vice-consulship.

vice-gérant, *n.m.* (— *-s*), vicegerent, deputy manager.

vice-gérent, *n.m.* (— *-s*), vicegerent.

vice-légat, *n.m.* (— *-s*), vice-legate.

vice-légation, *n.f.* (— *-s*), vice-legateship.

vicennal, -e, *adj.*, vicennial, of twenty years.

vice-présidence, *n.f.* (— *-s*), vice-presidency.

vice-président, *n.m.*(— *-s*), vice-president.

vice-reine, *n.f.* (— *-s*), vice-queen.

vice-roi, *n.m.* (— —s), viceroy.

vice-royauté, *n.f.* (— —s), viceroyalty, viceroyship.

vice-sénéchal, *n.m.* (— -sénéchaux), deputy-seneschal.

vice versa, *adv.*, vice versa.

vicié, -e, *adj.*, vitiated, depraved, corrupted; foul (air).

vicier, *v.a.*, to vitiate, to taint, to corrupt.

vicieusement (-euz-mān), *adv.*, viciously.

vicieu-x, -se, *adj.*, vicious, faulty, defective.

vicinal, -e, *adj.*, (of roads—*routes*) parish, parochial.

vicinalité, *n.f.*, condition of the roads of a parish.

vicissitude, *n.f.*, vicissitude, revolution, change.

vicomte, *n.m.*, viscount.

vicomté, *n.f.*, viscountship; viscounty.

vicomtesse, *n.f.*, viscountess.

victimaire, *n.m.*, (antiq.) an assistant at sacrifices.

victime, *n.f.*, victim, sufferer. *Être — de*; to be a sufferer by. *Mourir — de*; to die a victim to.

victimer, *v.a.*, to victimize; to sacrifice; to ridicule; to make a laughing-stock of.

victoire, *n.f.*, victory, conquest. *Remporter la —*; to gain the victory.

victorieuse, *n.f.*, (bot.) a variety of anemone.

victorieusement (-euz-mān), *adv.*, victoriously, triumphantly.

victorieu-x, -se, *adj.*, victorious, triumphant.

victorioux, *n.m.*, (bot.) a variety of carnation.

*__victuaille__, *n.f.*, (l.u.) provisions; *pl.*, (nav.) ⊙stores, victuals, eatables. *V.* **vivres**.

⊙*__victuailleur__, *n.m.*, (nav.) victualler, victualling-agent.

vidame, *n.m.*, (feudalism—*féodalité*)vidame.

vidamé, *n.m.*, *or* **vidamie**, *n.f.*, dignity of a vidame.

vidange, *n.f.*, clearing, emptying, removing; night-work (of cess-pools—*de fosses*); *pl.*, night-soil; (med.) lochia.

vidangeur, *n.m.*, night-man.

vide, *adj.*, empty, void, devoid, vacant, vacuous; (mus.) open. *Corde à —*; open string.

vide, *n.m.*, void, gap, chasm, hole; vacuum, emptiness, blank. *À —*; empty.

vidé, -e, *part.*, emptied, empty.

*__vide-bouteille__, *n.m.* (— —s), country-box (house—*maison*).

vide-poches, *n.m.* (—), lady's work-table.

vider, *v.a.*, to empty; to vacate; to decide, to end; to settle; to draw (poultry—*la volaille*); to gut (fish—*le poisson*); to drain. *— un étang*; to drain a pond. *— une clef*; to bore a key. *— du drap*; to pink cloth. *— un procès*; to determine a lawsuit. *— un différend*; to settle a dispute. *— ses comptes*; to make up one's accounts. *— les lieux, une province, &c.*; to leave, to be driven from, a place, a province, &c., by force.

se **vider**, *v.r.*, to be emptied; to empty itself (of a thing—*des choses*); to be settled, to be adjusted.

vidimer, *v.a.*, (jur.) to collate the copy of a document with the original, and certify the former.

⊙**vidimus**, *n.m.*, the certifying the copy of a document as conforming to the original.

vidrecome, *n.m.*, (l.u.) tumbler, large drinking-glass.

viduité, *n.f.*, widowhood.

vie, *n.f.*, life, lifetime; livelihood, living; food, subsistence; way of living, course of life; spirit, animation. *Rendre la — a quelqu'un*; to

restore life to any one. *Être en —*; to be alive. *Il y va de la —*; it is a case of life and death. *Demander la —*; to beg for life. *Je n'ai rien vu de pareil de ma —*; I never saw anything like it in all my life. *Gagner sa —*; to get one's livelihood. *Mendier sa —*; to beg one's bread. *Faire bonne —*; to lead a merry life. *Faire — qui dure*; to lead a sober life. *Mener une — heureuse*; to lead a happy life. *Train de —*; way of living. *Tourmenter sa —*; to bestir one's self. *Faire — de garçon*; to live like a bachelor. *Mener une — réglée*; to live a regular life. *C'est ma —*; it is my very life. *Telle —, telle fin*; people die as they live. *Il a écrit lui-même sa —*; he has written his own life. *À la — et à la mort*; in life and death. *Une pension à —*; a pension for life. *Sa — durant*; during his life. *Prodiguer sa —*; to throw away one's life.

vidase, *n.m.*, (l.ex.) (pers.) puppy, jackanapes.

*__vieil__. *adj.* *V.* **vieux**.

*__vieillard__, *n.m.*, old man.

*__vieille__, *adj.* *V.* **vieux**.

*__vieille__, *n.f.*, old woman.

*__vieillement__, *adv.*, in an old way, manner, in an old-man-like manner.

*__vieillerie__, *n.f.*, old things; old clothes, old goods, old stuff, old lumber, rubbish.

*__vieillesse__, *n.f.*, old age; oldness. *Elle est morte de —*; she died of old age.

*__vieillir__, *v.n.*, to grow old; to get old; to look old; to become obsolete (of words—*des mots*).

*__vieillir__, *v.a.*, to make old; to make look old.

se **vieillir**, *v.r.*, to make one's self look old; to give one's self as older than one actually is.

*__vieillissant, -e__, *adj.*, growing old.

*__vieillissement__ (-is-mān), *n.m.*, growing old.

*__vieillot, -te__, *adj.*, oldish.

vielle, *n.f.*, hurdy-gurdy. *Il est du bois dont on fait les —s*; he is of a pliant temper.

vieller, *v.n.*, to play upon the hurdy-gurdy; (pop.) ⊙to stand trifling.

vielleu-r, *n.m.*, **-se**, *n.f.*, player on the hurdy-gurdy.

vierge, *n.f.*, virgin, maid; (astron.) Virgo.

vierge, *adj.*, virgin, virginal, maiden; pure. *Métaux —s*; native *or* virgin metals. *Forêt —*; primeval, untrodden, virgin forest.

vieux, vieil, *adj.m.*, **vieille**, *f.*, old; aged, advanced in years; ancient, venerable. *Un vieux soldat*; an old soldier. *Un vieil arbre*; an old tree. *Un vieil harpagon*; an old miser. *Une vieille femme*; an old woman. [*Vieil* may be used instead of *vieux* before a vowel or a silent *h*.]

vieux, *n.m.*, old man.

vieux. *n.m.*, anything that is old, especially clothes, shoes, &c.

vi-f, -ve, *adj.*, alive, live, living; quick; lively, brisk, sprightly, smart, animated, fiery, mettlesome, ardent, eager, hasty, keen, alert, nimble; sharp, violent (of pain—*des douleurs*); vivid, bright (of colours—*des couleurs*). *Cheval —*; mettlesome horse. *Des yeux —s*; sparkling eyes. *Couleur —ve*; bright colour. *Un froid —*: a piercing cold. *Une —ve douleur*; a violent pain. *Eau —ve*; spring-water. *Chaux —ve*; quicklime. *Haie —ve*; quickset hedge. *De —ve voix*; by word of mouth. *Mort ou —*: dead or alive.

vif, *n.m.*, quick; (jur.) person living; shaft (of a column—*de colonne*). *Être touché au —*; to be touched to the quick.

vif-argent, *n.m.* (*n.p.*), quicksilver.

vigie, *n.f.*, (nav.) look-out; look-out man; lurking rock; (railways) seat placed on the top of guards' vans. *Être en —* (nav.); to be on the look-out.

vigilamment (-la-män), *adv.*, vigilantly, watchfully.

vigilance, *n.f.*, vigilance, watchfulness.

vigilant, -e, *adj.*, vigilant, watchful.

vigile, *n.f.*, vigil, eve.

*****vigne,** *n.f.*, vine; vineyard. *— sauvage;* wild vine. *— vierge;* wild-grape. *— blanche;* white briony. *— de Judée;* woody nightshade, bitter-sweet. *Être dans les —s du Seigneur;* to be in one's cups, to be half-seas-over.

*****vigneau,** *n.m.* V. **vignot.**

*****vigneron,** *n.m.,* **-ne,** *n.f.,* vine-dresser.

*****vignette,** *n.f.,* (engr.) vignette.

*****vignoble,** *n.m.,* vineyard. *Propriétaire de —s;* wine-grower.

*****vignoble,** *adj.,*wine-growing.

*****vignot,** *or* **vigneau,** *n.m.,* periwinkle.

*****vigogne,** *n.m.,* hat made of vicugna wool.

*****vigogne,** *n.f.,* vicugna, vicunga, vicuña, vicuna.

vigoureusement (-reûz-mān), *adv.,* vigorously, stoutly, forcibly.

vigoureu-x, -se, *adj.,* vigorous, stout, hardy, lusty, forcible, energetic.

viguerie, *n.f.,* provostship (in Languedoc, Provence).

vigueur, *n.f.,* vigour, strength, force; power, sturdiness; energy, spirit. *Mettre en —;* to put in force. *— d'esprit;* strength of mind.

viguier, *n.m.,* provost (Languedoc, Provence).

vil, -e, *adj.,* vile, base, mean, despicable, low, wretched. *À — prix;* very cheap.

vilain, *n.m.,* (feudalism—*féodalité*) villain, villein, villan; niggard; blackguard. *Oignez — il vous poindra, poignez — il vous oindra;* a bad man will return evil for good.

vilain, -e (-lîn, -lè-n), *adj.,* ugly, vile, villainous, pitiful, miserable, unhandsome; shabby, worthless, nasty, filthy, slovenly, wicked; sordid, wretched, infamous, scandalous. *Il m'a joué un — tour;* he has played me a nasty trick. *— temps;* bad weather. *Il fait —;* it is nasty weather.

vilain (-lîn), *n.m.,* **-e** (-lè-n) *n.f.,* (fam.) naughty boy, naughty girl.

vilainement (-lè-n-mān), *adv.,* uglily; basely, nastily, shamefully, scandalously, unworthily, villainously, wretchedly, naughtily, sordidly, improperly, deplorably.

vilayet, *n.m.,*vilayet,largeTurkish province.

vilebrequin (vil-brè-kin), *n.m.,* centre-bit, wimble.

vilement (vil-mān), *adv.,* vilely, basely, meanly, abjectly, contemptibly.

vilenie (vil-nî), *n.f.,* filth, nastiness, foulness, dirt; sordid avarice, niggardliness; trash, unwholesome food; mean, base, vile action; *pl.,* offensive words; filthiness, obscenity.

vileté (vil-té), *or* **vilité,** *n.f.,* cheapness, low price; unimportance.

vilipender, *v.a.,* to villify, to despise, to cry down; to undervalue.

vilité, *n.f.* V. **vileté.**

villa, *n.f.,* villa.

villace, *n.f.,* (fam., l.u.) large ill-built and thinly-peopled city.

village, *n.m.,* village. *Des gens de —;* country-folks. *Il est bien de son —;* he knows nothing of what is going on in the world.

villageois (-joâ), *n.m.,* **-e** (-joaz), *n.f.,* villager.

villanelle, *n.f.,* pastoral poetry; a dancing tune.

ville, *n.f.,* town, city. *— de commerce;* commercial town. *— maritime;* sea-port town.

Corps de —; corporation, town-council. *Être en —;* to be out (not at home—*être sorti*). *Il est allé dîner en —;* he has gone out to dine. *Être à la —;* to be in town.

villégiature, *n.f.,* sojourn in the country.

villette, *n.f.,* (fam.) little town.

villeu-x -se, *adj.,* (bot.) villous, villose.

villosité, *n.f.,* (bot.) villosity.

vimaire, *n.f.,* damage caused to forests by storms.

vin, *n.m.,* wine. *— mousseux;* sparkling wine. *— non mousseux;* still wine. *Du — éventé;* dead wine. *— de Bordeaux;* claret. *Du — paillet;* pale wine. *— du Rhin;* Rhenish wine. *— de deux feuilles;* wine two years old. *— qui a beaucoup de corps;* strong-bodied wine. *Un doigt de —;* a drop of wine. *Tremper son —;* to dilute one's wine. *Il est en pointe de —;* he has had a drop too much. *Être pris de —;* to be the worse for liquor. *Être entre deux —s;* to be half-seas-over. *Cuver son —;* to sleep one's self sober. *Un sac à —;* a drunken sot. *Il a le — mauvais;* he is quarrelsome in his liquor.

vinage, *n.m.,* putting alcohol into wine.

vinaigre, *n.m.,* vinegar.

vinaigré, -e, *adj.,* seasoned with vinegar.

vinaigrer, *v.a.,* to season with vinegar.

vinaigrerie, *n.f.,* vinegar manufactory.

vinaigrette, *n.f.,* vinegar sauce; meat seasoned with vinegar; Bath chair.

vinaigrier, *n.m.,* vinegar merchant; vinegar cruet; (bot.) sumac-tree,

vinaire, *adj.,* for wine. *Vaisseaux —s;* wine vessels.

vindas (-dâs), *n.m.,*(tech.) windlass.

vindicati-f,-ve,,*adj.,*vindictive,revengeful.

vindicte, *n.f.,* (jur.) prosecution of crime. *La — publique;* prosecution by the public prosecutor.

vinée, *n.f.,* crop of wine, vintage.

viner, *v.a.,* to put alcohol into wine.

vinetier (vi-n-tié), *or* **vinettier** (-nè-tié), *n.m.,* barberry-tree.

vineu-x, -se, *adj.,* vinous; winy, wine-coloured.

vingt (vîn), *n.m.* and *adj.,* twenty, score; twentieth. *Quatre-vingts hommes;* eighty men. *Quatre-vingt-six bœufs;* eighty-six oxen. [*Vingt* takes an *s* when preceded and multiplied by another number, but remains invariable when it is followed by another number.]

vingtaine (vin-tè-n), *n.f.,* a score, about twenty.

vingt et un, *n.m.* (n.p.), vingt-un (card game—*jeu de cartes*).

vingtième (vin-ti-èm), *n.m.* and *adj.,* twentieth.

vinicole, *adj.,* wine-growing.

vinification, *n.f.,* wine-making.

viol, *n.m.,* rape, violation.

violacé, -e, *adj.,* violaceous; (med.) purple.

violacées, *or* **violariées,** *n.f.pl.,* (bot.) violaceæ.

violat, *adj.,* of violets.

violat-eur, *n.m.,* **-rice,** *n.f.,* violator, infringer.

violation, *n.f.,* violation, transgression, breach.

violâtre, *adj.,* inclining to a violet-colour.

viole, *n.f.,* (mus.) tenor violin; viol.

violement (viol-mān), *n.m.,* (l.u.)violation, infringement, infraction; rape.

violemment (-la-mān), *adv.,* violently.

violence, *n.f.,* violence; (jur.) force. *Faire — à quelqu'un;* to offer violence to any one.

violent, -e, *adj.,* violent; strong (of suspicion—*des soupçons*). *Douleur —e;* violent pain. *Mort —e;* violent death.

violenter, *v.a.*, to force, to offer viole*n*ce to.

violer, *v.a.*, to violate, to ravish, to break, to infringe, to transgress. — *sa foi* ; to break one's faith. — *le droit des gens* ; to break the law of nations.

violet, *n.m.*, violet-colour.

violet, -te, *adj.*, violet-coloured.

violette, *n.f.*, (bot.) violet. — *tricolore* ; heart's-ease, pansy. — *de la chandeleur* ; snow-drop.

violier, *n.m.*, wall-flower.

violiste, *n.m.*, violist.

violon, *n.m.*, violin, fiddle ; violinist, violin-player, fiddler ; cage, round-house, lock-up (prison). *Mettre quelqu'un au* — ; to put any one in the cage. *Il a payé les* —*s* ; he paid the piper. *Jouer du* — ; to play on the violin.

violoncelle, *n.m.*, violoncello.

violoncelliste, *n.m.*, violoncellist.

violoniste, *n.m.*, violinist.

viorne, *n.f.*, (bot.) viburnum.

vipère, *n.f.*, viper, adder.

vipereau, *n.m.*, young viper.

vipérin, -e (-rin, -ri-n), *adj.*, viperine.

vipérine (-ri-n), *n.f.*, (bot.) viper's-bugloss.

virago, *n.f.*, virago.

virelai, *n.m.*, virelay, ancient French poem of two rhymes.

virement (vir-mān), *n.m.*, turning ; (nav.) veering, tacking about ; (fin.) clearing. — *d'eau* ; (nav.) turn of the tide.

virer, *v.n.* and *a.*, to turn, to turn about ; (nav.) to tack ; to heave. — *de bord* (nav.) ; to tack about.

vireu-x, -se, *adj.*, of poison.

virevau, or **vireveau** (vir-vō), *n.m.*, (nav.) winch.

virevaude, *n.f.* V. **vire-vire.**

virevent (vir-vān), *n.m.*, (orni.) king-fisher.

vire-vire, *n.f.* (—), (nav.) whirlpool.

virevolte, *n.f.*, (man.) volt right and left.

⊙**virevousse**, or **virevouste**, *n.f.*, (fig.) prevarication, shuffling, shifting.

virginal, -e, *adj.*, virginal, maidenly.

virginalement, *adv.*, maidenly, in a maiden-like manner.

virginité, *n.f.*, virginity, maidenhead.

virgouleuse, *n.f.*, a sort of winter pear.

virgule, *n.f.*, (gram.) comma ; (horl.) hook escapement. *Point et* — ; semicolon.

viril, -e, *adj.*, male, virile, manly. *Âge* — ; age of manhood.

virilement (-ril-mān), *adv.*, manfully, manly, like a man.

virilité, *n.f.*, virility, manhood, vigour, force.

virole, *n.f.*, ferrule.

virolé, -e, *adj.*, (her.) virole.

virtualité, *n.f.*, virtuality, potentiality.

virtuel, -le, *adj.*, virtual, potential.

virtuellement (-èl-mān), *adv.*, virtually, potentially.

virtuose, *n.m.f.*, virtuoso.

virulence, *n.f.*, virulence, virulency.

virulent, -e, *adj.*, virulent.

virus (-rus), *n.m.*, virus.

vis (vis), *n.f.*, screw.

visa, *n.m.* (—), visa, signature (on passports, &c.—*de passeports, &c.*).

visage, *n.m.*, face, visage ; countenance, aspect, look, air. — *pâle* ; pale face. *Faire bon* — *à quelqu'un* ; to look pleasantly at any one. *Se composer le* — ; to compose one's countenance. *Changer de* — ; to change countenance ; to have one's face at command. *Trouver* — *de bois* ; to find the door shut, to find nobody at home.

vis-à-vis, *adv.*, opposite, in juxtaposition.

vis-à-vis (vi-za-vi), *n.m.* (—), vis-a-vis (in dancing—*terme de danse*) ; vis-a-vis(carriage—*voiture*) ; person seated opposite one at table.

vis-à-vis, *prep.*, opposite, over-against, over the way ; towards, relatively. — *de l'église* ; opposite the church.

viscéral, -e (vis-sé-), *adj.*, visceral.

viscère (vis-sèr), *n.f.*, (anat.) viscus. —*s* ; viscera.

viscosité, *n.f.*, viscosity, viscidity, viscousness ; clamminess.

visée, *n.f.*, aim ; end ; design.

viser, *v.n.*, to aim, to take aim ; to aspire, to endeavour. *Il visait à ce but* ; he aimed at that mark.

viser, *v.a.*, to aim at, to take aim at ; to sign (passports, &c.—*passeports, &c.*). *Faire* — *un passeport* ; to get a passport signed.

vishnou (vis-noo), *n.m.*, Vishnu, name of one of the Hindoo deities.

visibilité, *n.f.*, visibility, visibleness.

visible, *adj.*, visible, evident, manifest, obvious.

visiblement, *adv.*, visibly, evidently, manifestly, obviously.

visière, *n.f.*, visor (of a helmet—*de casque*) ; foresight (of fire-arms—*d'armes à feu*) ; shade (for the eyes—*pour les yeux*) ; peak (of caps, &c.—*de casquettes, &c.*) ; (fam.) eyesight. *Rompre en* — *à quelqu'un* ; to break one's lance in any one's face ; to attack any one to his face. *Elle lui a donné dans la* — ; he was smitten with her.

visigoth (-gô), *n.m.*, Visigoth ; barbarian, Goth.

vision, *n.f.*, vision, sight, phantom, chimera, fancy.

visionnaire, *n.m.f.* and *adj.*, a visionary, a dreamer ; visionary.

visir, *n.m.* V. **vizir.**

visirat, *n.m.* V. **vizirat.**

visitandine, *n.f.*, Visitandine, nun of the Order of the Visitation.

visitation, *n.f.*, visitation. *L'ordre de la* — ; the Order of the Visitation.

visite, *n.f.*, visit ; call ; visiting ; visitation ; examination. *Aller en* — ; to go visiting. *Faire* —, *rendre* —, *à quelqu'un* ; to make a call upon any one, to pay any one a visit. *Rendre sa* — *à quelqu'un* ; to return any one a visit. *Faire la* — *des caves* ; to search the cellars. *Droit de* — ; right of search.

visiter, *v.a.* and *n.*, to visit ; to make a visit, a visitation ; to search, to examine, to inspect, to look. — *un vaisseau*, to search a ship.

visiteu-r, *n.m.*, **-se**, *n.f.*, visitor ; searcher ; land-waiter.

vison, *n.m.*, American marten.

vison-visu, *adv.*, opposite one another.

visorium (-om), *n.m.*, (print.) copy-holder, catch, jigger.

visqueu-x, -se, *adj.*, viscous, slimy, clammy, sticky.

vissage, *n.m.*, screwing.

visser, *v.a.*, to screw, to screw on ; to screw up, to screw down.

se visser, *v.r.*, to screw, to screw on ; to screw up, to screw down.

visuel, -le, *adj.*, visual.

vital, -e, *adj.*, vital ; essential.

vitalement (-tal-mān), *adv.*, vitally ; essentially.

vitalisme, *n.m.*, doctrine of the *vitaliste*.

vitaliste, *n.m.* and *adj.*, name given to physicians who account for the phenomena of life by referring them to a vital principle.

vitalité, *n.f.*, vitality.

vitchoura, *n.m.* (—*s*), fur greatcoat.

vite, *adj.*, swift, quick, fleet, speedy, rapid. *Pouls* — ; quick pulse. — *comme le vent* ; as fleet as the wind.

vite, *adv.*, quick, quickly, fast, speedily; rapidly; expeditiously. *Allez —;* go quickly. *Aller — en besogne;* to be quick at work. *—! quick! —!—!* quick! make haste!

vitelotte (vi-tlot), *n.f.,* kidney potato.

vitement (vit-mǎn), *adv.,* quickly, speedily.

vitesse, *n.f.,* swiftness, speed, celerity, quickness, rapidity. *À la — de;* at a speed of, at the rate of. *Gagner quelqu'un de —;* to outstrip, to outrun, any one. *À grande —;* at full speed. *Train de grande —* (railways); express, express train. *Train de petite —;* goods train.

vitex, *n.m.,* (bot.) vitex, chaste-tree.

viticole, *adj.,* relating, pertaining to vine culture.

viticulture, *n.f.,* culture of the vine.

vitrage, *n.m.,* glazing; glass windows; glass partition.

vitrail, *n.m.,* glass windows (of a church— *d'église*).

vitre, *n.f.,* window-glass; pane of glass; window. *Casser les —s;* to breakthe windows; to speak boldly, to speak out one's mind.

vitré, -e, *adj.,* glazed; (of doors—*des portes*) glass; (anat.) vitreous. *Porte —e;* glass door.

vitrer, *v.a.,* to furnish with glass windows, to glaze.

vitrerie, *n.f.,* glaziery, glazier's work.

vitrescibilité, *n.f.,* vitrescence.

vitrescible, *adj.,* vitrifiable, vitrescible.

vitreu-x, -se, *adj.,* vitreous.

vitri-er, *n.m.,* **-ère**, *n.f.,* glazier; glazier's wife.

vitrifiable, *adj.,* vitrifiable.

vitrification, *n.f.,* vitrification.

vitrifier, *v.a.,* to vitrify.

se **vitrifier**, *v.r.,* to vitrify.

vitrine, *n.f.,* shop-window; glass case in museums, etc.

vitriol, *n.m.;* vitriol.

vitriolé, -e, *adj.,* vitriolated.

vitriolique, *adj.,* vitriolic.

vitriolisation, *n.f.,* vitriolation.

G **vitupère**, *n.m.,* blame.

vitupérer, *v.a.,* to vituperate, to reprimand.

vivace, *adj.,* long-lived, perennial. *Plantes —s;* perennial plants, perennials.

vivacité, *n.f.,* vivacity, vivaciousness, liveliness, sprightliness, briskness; ardour, vividness.

vivandi-er, *n.m.,* **-ère**, *n.f.,* sutler.

vivant, -e, *adj.,* living, alive; quick. *Langue —e;* living language. *Rue —e;* lively street.

vivant, *n.m.,* person living, person alive; determined character; life, lifetime. *De son —;* in his lifetime. *Du — de son frère;* when his brother was alive. *Un bon —;* a jolly companion.

vivat (-vat), *int.,* hurra! huzza!

vivat (-vat), *n.m.* (—s), hurra, huzza. *Crier —;* to cheer, to hurra.

vive, *n.f.,* (ich.) viver, weever.

⊙ **vive-la-joie**, *n.m.* (—), jolly, merry companion.

vivement (viv-mǎn), *adv.,* quickly, briskly, sharply, smartly, vigorously, eagerly, keenly, deeply; angrily; poignantly; acutely; spiritedly; with animation.

viveur, *n.m.,* high liver, free liver.

vivier, *n.m.,* fish-pond.

vivifiant. -e, *adj.,* vivifying, quickening.

vivification, *n.f.,* vivification; revival.

vivifier, *v.a.,* to vivify, to quicken; to give life to, to enliven, to animate.

vivifique, *adj.,* (l.u.) vivifying. *V.* **vivifiant.**

vivipare, *adj.,* viviparous.

vivisection, *n.f.,* vivisection.

vivoter, *v.n.,* to live poorly; to live from

hand to mouth, to make just shift to live. to rub on.

vivre (vivant, vécu), *v.n.,* to live, to be living, to be alive; to subsist, to be maintained. *Il vit mal;* he lives badly. *Il vit mal avec son frère;* he is on bad terms with his brother. *Il vit aux dépens d'autrui;* he lives at other people's expense. *Il fait cher — à Londres;* it is dear living in London. *Faire —;* to feed, to keep alive, to maintain. *— de son travail;* to live by one's labour. *— d'industrie, — d'invention;* (b.s.) to live by one's wits. *— d'espérance;* to live in hope. *Il faut que tout le monde vive;* every body must live. *— en prince;* to live like a prince. *Savoir —;* to be a person of good manners. *Il ne sait pas —;* he has no manners. *Apprendre à —;* to learn manners. *Vive le roi!* long live the king! *Vivent les ministres!* long live the ministers!

vivre, *n.m.,* living, board, food; *pl.,* provisions, victuals. *Couper les —s à quelqu'un;* to cut off any one's bread. *Agents des —s* (nav.); agent-victualler. *Bureau des —s;* victualling-office.

vivres-pain, *n.m.pl.* (n.s.), (milit., nav.) bread-store.

vivres-viande, *n.m.pl.* (n.s.), (milit., nav.) meat-store.

vizir, *n.m.,* vizier.

vizirat, or **viziriat**, *n.m.,* vizierate, viziership.

vocable, *n.m.,* vocable, word, term, name.

vocabulaire, *n.m.,* vocabulary.

vocabuliste, *n.m.,* (l.u.) author of a vocabulary.

vocal, *n.m.,* **-e**, *n.f.,* (ecc.) vocal (voter—*votant*).

vocal, -e, *adj.,* vocal.

vocalement (-kal-mǎn), *adv.,* (l.u.) vocally, orally.

vocalisation, *n.f.,* vocalization.

vocalise, *n.f.,* piece of music for exercising the voice.

vocaliser, *v.n.,* (mus.) to vocalize, to execute upon a vowel.

vocatif, *n.m.,* (gram.) vocative.

vocation, *n.f.,* vocation, calling, call; inclination; destination, talent. *Suivre sa —;* to follow one's vocation.

vociférat-eur, *n.m.,* **-rice**, *n.f.,* one who vociferates.

vociférations, *n.f.pl.,* vociferations.

vociférer, *v.a.* and *n.,* to vociferate, to cry out.

vœu, *n.m.,* vow; votive offering; vote, suffrage; prayer, wish, desire; *pl.,* vows (religious ceremony—*cérémonie religieuse*). *Faire —; de jeûner;* to make a vow of abstinence. *Faire des —x pour quelqu'un;* to offer up prayers for any one.

vogue (vog), *n.f.,* (nav.) ⊙ momentum, rate of motion imparted to a ship by rowing; (fig.) vogue, fashion, credit, reputation. *Avoir de la —;* to be in vogue, in fashion. *Mettre en —;* to bring into vogue, into fashion.

voguer (-ghé), *v.n.,* (nav.) to impel a boat, &c., to row; to ride, to sail; to row (l.u.). *V.* **ramer, nager.** *Vogue la galère!* come what may!

⊙ **vogueur** (-gheur), *n.m.,* rower.

voici, *prep.,* see here, behold, here is, here are, this is, these are. *— mon livre, voilà le vôtre;* here is my book, there is yours. *En — bien d'une autre;* this is still more singular. *Me —, le voilà;* here I am, there he is. *Monsieur que —;* this gentleman. *Le — qui vient;* here he comes. *Nous y —;* here we are. *— venir le printemps;* spring is coming.

voie, *n.f.,* way, ...: '; path; breadth

between the wheels of carriages ; (hunt.) track (of deer, boars—*du cerf, du sanglier*); conveyance, means of conveyance ; load (of wood, stone, sand—*de bois, de pierre, de sable*); means ; (nav.) leak ; (railways) gauge, permanent way, four-foot way; (chem.) process. *Il est toujours par — et par chemin ;* he is always rambling about. *La — lactée ;* the Milky Way. *— d'eau ;* two pailfuls of water; (nav.) leak. *Faire une — d'eau* (nav.); to spring a leak. *Boucher une — d'eau ;* to stop a leak. *—s de fait* (jur.); assault. *En venir aux —s de fait ;* to come to blows. *— ferrée ;* railway, railroad. *— de garage, — d'évitement* (railways) ; siding, shunting-line.

voilà, *prep.,* see there, behold, that is, those are, there is, there are. *— l'homme ;* that is the man. *Le — ;* there he is. *Ah! vous — ;* oh! there you are. *— qui va bien ;* that is getting on well now. *Le — qui arrive ;* there he comes. *— qu'on m'appelle ;* I am called. *Comme la — triste ! how sad she is ! Comme vous — fait !* what a strange figure you cut ! what a pickle you are in ! *— ce que c'est ;* that is what it is. *— tout ;* that is all. *En — assez ;* that is enough.

voile, *n.m.,* veil ; cover, mask, disguise ; cloak, colour, show, pretence. *Avoir un — devant les yeux ;* to have a mist before one's eyes.

voilé, -e, *adj.,* (nav.) provided with sails, rigged.

voile, *n.f.,* (nav.) sail ; (fig.) sail, ship. *La — de misaine ;* the foresail. *La — d'artimon ;* the mizzen. *Forcer de —s ;* to crowd sail. *Aller à —s et à rames ;* to go with the sails and oars. *Déployer les —s ;* to unfurl the sails. *A pleines —s* (nav.); with full sail ; (fig.) willingly, heartily. *Faire — ;* to sail. *Caler la — ;* to strike sail. *Mettre à la — ;* to set sail.

voiler, *v.a.,* to veil, to cover ; to cloak, to colour, to blind, to disguise ; to conceal. *se* **voiler**, *v.r.,* to wear a veil ; to be veiled, concealed, covered.

voilerie (voal-rî), *n.f.,* (nav.) sail-loft ; sail-making.

voilier. *n.m.,* sail-maker ; sailer (ship—*vaisseau*). *Un bon — ;* a fast sailer.

voilure. *n.f.,* set of sails ; trim of the sails.

voir (voyant, vu), *v.a.,* to see ; to look at, to behold, to observe, to view; to inspect, to superintend ; to keep company with ; to be on visiting terms with, to frequent the society of. *Je l'ai vu de mes propres yeux ;* I have seen it with my own eyes. *Il veut tout — par lui-même ;* he insists on seeing everything with his own eyes. *Que vois-je ! — quelque chose en songe ;* to see anything in a dream. *Faire — ;* to show, to let see. *On n'a jamais rien vu de pareil ;* the like was never seen before. *Vit-on jamais rien d'égal ?* was anything like it ever seen ? *Voyez ce tableau ;* look at that picture. *Faire — du pays à quelqu'un ;* to lead any one a dance. *Il ne voit personne ;* he sees no company. *Se faire — ;* to appear, to show one's self.

se **voir**, *v.r.,* to see one's self ; to see one another ; to visit one another ; to be, to find one's self. *Ils ne se voient point ;* they do not visit one another.

voir, *v.n.,* to see ; to have one's sight ; to superintend ; to inspect, to look, to look out. *Je vois bien quelle est son intention ;* I see plainly what is his intention. *Je ne vois point à quoi cela peut servir ;* I don't see what can be the use of that. *Je lui ferai bien — à qui il s'adresse ;* I'll show him what sort of a person he has to do with. *— clair ;* to see clearly. *Ne — goutte ;* not to see a bit, not to see in the least. *Voyons ! let us see ! Ma maison voit sur un jardin ;* my house looks into a garden.

voire. *adv.,* even ; ☉indeed, truly.

voirie, *n.f.,* commission of public ways ; common sewer.

voisin, -e, *adj.,* neighbouring, bordering, adjacent, next ; next door. *La maison —e ;* the next house.

voisin, *n.m., -e, n.f.,* neighbour. *Être —s ;* to be next-door neighbours.

voisinage, *n.m.,* neighbourhood ; vicinity ; proximity ; neighbours ; (jur.) venue, visne.

voisiner, *v.n.,* to visit one's neighbours ; to go to see a neighbour.

voiturage, *n.m.,* conveying, transporting, carriage of goods in cars, carts, vans, &c.

voiture, *n.f.,* carriage ; coach ; conveyance, vehicle ; fare ; load. *— publique ;* stage-coach. *— à deux chevaux ;* coach and pair. *— de louage ;* job-coach, hired coach. *Bureau de la —:* coach-office. *Place de —s ;* coach-stand. *Descendre de —;* to alight from a coach. *Se promener en —, aller en — ;* to ride in a carriage. *— de place ;* hackney-coach. *— de remise ;* hired carriage livery coach.

voiturer, *v.a.,* to carry, to convey, to transport, to cart.

voiturier, *n.m.,* carrier ; waggoner ; driver.

voiturin, *n.m.,* driver and owner of a carriage usually lent on hire ; the carriage so hired.

voix, *n.f.,* voice ; vote, suffrage ; opinion, judgment ; singer. *— grêle ;* faint voice. *— de tête ;* falsetto. *Faire la petite — ;* to speak small. *— aiguë ;* shrill voice. *De vive — ;* by word of mouth, orally. *Aller aux — ;* to put to the vote, to divide. *Donner sa — ;* to give one's vote. *À l'unanimité des — ;* without a dissentient voice.

vol, *n.m.,* robbery, theft, robbing ; larceny ; stolen goods. *— de nuit avec effraction dans une maison habitée ;* burglary. *— de grand chemin ;* highway robbery. *On l'a trouvé saisi du — ;* they found the stolen goods upon him.

vol, *n.m.,* flying ; flight, soaring ; flock ; cast (of hawks). *Prendre un — trop haut ;* to soar too high. *A — d'oiseau ;* as the crow flies.

volable, *adj.,* liable to be stolen.

volage, *adj.,* fickle, volatile, inconstant, unsteady. *La jeunesse est — ;* youth is inconstant.

**volaille, *n.f.,* poultry, fowls. *Marchand de — ;* poulterer.

**volailler, *n.m.,* poulterer ; poultry-yard.

volant, -e, *adj.,* flying, volatile ; (of paper—*papier*) loose ; (nav.) travelling ; (paint.) floating (of drapery—*draperie*).

volant. *n.m.,* shuttle-cock ; flounce (of a dress—*de robe*) ; fly-wheel (of machinery—*de machine*); sail (of a wind-mill—*de moulin*). *Jouer au — ;* to play at battle-door and shuttle-cock.

volatil, -e, *adj.,* volatile ; airy, light.

volatile, *n.m.f.,* and *adj.,* winged animal ; winged.

volatilisation, *n.f.,* volatilization.

volatiliser, *v.a.,* to volatilize. *se* **volatiliser**, *v.r.,* to volatilize.

volatilité, *n.f.,* volatility, volatileness.

**volatille, *n.f.,* (fam.) small birds for the table.

vol-au-vent, *n.m.* (—), (cook.) vol-au-vent.

volcan, *n.m.,* volcano.

volcanique, *adj.,* volcanic.

volcanisé, -e, *adj.,* volcanized.

volcanisme, *n.m.,* volcanicity.

vole, *n.f.,* vole (at cards—*aux cartes*).

volée, *n.f.,* flight (of birds—*d'oiseau*) ; flock ; covey, bevy, brood ; rank ; discharge (of one gun—*d'un canon*) ; volley (of guns—*de canons*); shower (of blows—*de coups*) ; peal (of bells—*de cloches*) ; swing-tree (of a coach—*de voiture*) : drubbing, thrashing. *Il a pris sa — ;* he has taken wings. *Tirer à toute — ;* to fire a random

ьhot. *Sonner à toute* — ; to ring a full peal. *Une* — *de coups de bâton* ; a shower of blows. *Étre de la première* — ; to be of the first water. *Donner une* — *à quelqu'un* ; to give any one a drubbing. *A la* — ; flying, in the air; at random, rashly, inconsiderately.

voler. *v.n.,* to fly, to fly about. to take wings, to soar, to be upon the wing. *Le temps vole* ; time flies. — *en éclats* ; to fly into pieces.

voler. *v.a..* (hawking—*fauconnerie*) to chase ; to fly at, to fly.

voler. *v.a.,* to steal, to rob; to plunder. — *la bourse de quelqu'un* : to steal any one's purse. — *de l'argent* ; to steal money. *Il ne l'a pas volé* ; he richly deserves it, he is served quite right.

voler. *v.n.,* to steal. to rob. — *sur le grand chemin* ; to rob on the high-way.

⊙**volereau** (vol-rô), *n.m.,* young thief, pilferer.

volerie (vol-rî), *n.f.,* robbery ; robbing, pilfering ; (falconry—*fauconnerie*) flying.

volet, *n.m.,* window-shutter; pigeon-house ; dove-cot ; ledge (of a pigeon-house—*de colombier*) ; (bot.) water-lily.

voleter (vol-té), *v.n.,* to flutter.

volette, *n.f.,* small hurdle.

voleu-r, *n.m.,* **-se,** *n.f.,* thief, robber. — *de grand chemin* ; highway-man. *Au* — *!* stop thief ! *Crier au* — ; to cry out, stop thief !

volière, *n.f..* aviary, pigeon-house, large birdcage.

volige, *n.f.,* (carp.) thin deal, batten.

volition, *n.f.,* volition.

volontaire, *n.m.f.* and *adj.,* obstinate, headstrong person ; voluntary ; obstinate, wilful, heady, headstrong.

volontaire, *n.m.,* volunteer. — *d'un an* ; in the French army a man who, by enlisting for one year and paying a certain sum, frees himself from certain military obligations.

volontairement (-tèr-mān), *adv.,* voluntarily, willingly, wilfully.

volontariat, *n.m.,* (milit.) condition of the volunteer; volunteering.

volonté, *n.f.,* will ; *pl.,* whims, fancies, caprices. *La bonne* — *est réputée pour le fait* ; the will is as good as the deed. *Tout plie sous sa* — ; every thing yields to his will. *Il aime à faire ses* —*s* ; he likes to have his own will. *Dernières* —*s* ; last will and testament. *Bonne* — ; good-will, readiness, willingness. *Mauvaise* —; ill-will, unwillingness. *A* — ; at pleasure, at will.

volontiers (-tié), *adv.,* willingly, readily.

volsque, *n.m.f.* and *adj.,* Volscian.

voltaïque, *adj.,* voltaic. *Pile* — ; voltaic pile.

voltairien, *n.m.,* **-ne.** *n.f..* a partisan of Voltaire's philosophy, ideas, and opinions.

voltaïsme. *n.m.,* voltaism.

volte, *n.f.,* (fenc., man.) volt.

volte-face, *n.f.* (—), turning of the head, turning round. *Faire* — (milit.); to face about.

volter. *v.n.,* (fenc.) to make a volt.

voltige, *n.f.,* slack-rope ; dancing on the slack-rope ; tumbling ; (man.) vaulting.

voltigeant, **-e** (-jan, -t), *adj.,* fluttering, flickering.

voltigement (-tij-mān), *n.m.,* tumbling, flutter; vaulting on a slack-rope.

voltiger. *v.n.,* to flutter. to vault on a slack rope or on a horse; to tumble ; to hover.

voltigeur. *n.m..* vaulter, voltigeur, tumbler, leaper ; (milit.) voltigeur.

volubile. *adj.,* (bot.) voluble, volubilate.

volubilis, *n.m.,* (bot.) convolvulus.

volubilité, *n.f.,* volubility. — *de langue* ; volubility.

voluble, *adj.,* (bot.) volubile, volubilate ; voluble, fluent, quick (of speech—*de langue*).

volume, *n.m.,* volume; bulk, size, mass, compass. *Un livre en six* —*s* ; a book in six volumes.

volumineu-x,-se, *adj.,* voluminous, bulky, large, considerable.

volupté, *n.f.,* voluptuousness; pleasure. *Il y a de la* — *à boire quand on a soif* ; it is a pleasure to drink when one is thirsty.

voluptuaire, *adj.,* (jur.) of expenses on ornamental repairs.

voluptueusement (-eûz-mān).*adv.,*voluptuously.

voluptueu-x. -se, *n.* and *adj.,* voluptuous person; voluptuous.

volute. *n.f.,* (arch.) volute ; (conch.) voluta.

voluter, *v.a.,* to wind silk-thread ; (arch.) to make volutes.

volva, *or* **volve.** *n.f.,* (bot.) volva. wrapper.

volvé. **-e,** *adj.,* (bot.) having a volva.

⊙**volvulus** (-lus), *n.m.,* (med.) ileus.

vomer (vomèr), *n.m.,* (anat.) os vomer.

vomique, *n.f.,* (med.) vomica.

vomique, *adj.,* vomic. *Noix* —; vomic-nut ; nux vomica.

vomiquier, *n.m.,* (bot.) strychnos nux vomica, nux vomica tree.

vomir, *v.a.* and *n.,* to vomit, to bring up, to throw up; to vomit forth. *Avoir envie de* — ; to feel an inclination to vomit, to feel sick. *Faire des efforts pour* — ; to retch. — *des injures* ; te vomit out abuse.

vomissement (-mis-mān), *n.m.,* vomiting.

vomiti-f, -ve, *adj.,* vomitive, vomitory.

vomitif. *n.m.,* vomitory, vomit, emetic.

vomitoire, *n.m.,* (med.) ⊙emetic ; (antiq.) vomitory, large doors of the Roman theatres.

vorace. *adj.,* voracious, ravenous.

voracement (-ras-mān), *adv.,* voraciously, ravenously.

voracité, *n.f.,* voracity, ravenousness.

vos, *possessive adj.pl.,* your. *V.* **votre.**

votant, *n.m.,* voter.

votant, -e, *adj.,* voting, that has a vote.

votation, *n.f.,* voting.

vote, *n.m.,* vote, voice, suffrage.

voter, *v.n.,* to vote.

voter, *v.a.,* to vote.

voti-f, -ve, *adj.,* votive, votary.

votre, *possessive adj.m.f.,* **vos,** *pl.,* your. — *serviteur* ; your servant. *Vos parents* ; your relations.

le **vôtre,** *possessive pron. m.,* **la vôtre.** *f.,* **les vôtres,** *pl.m.f.,* yours. *Il a pris ses livres et les* —*s* ; he has taken his books and yours.

le **vôtre,** *n.m.,* your own, yours; *pl.,* your relations, friends, &c. ; your pranks, tricks. *Je suis des* —*s* ; I am one of your party. *Vous avez fait des* —*s* ; you have played your pranks.

vouer, *v.a.,* to vow, to devote, to dedicate, to consecrate.

se **vouer,** *v.r.,* to dedicate one's self, to apply one's self, to devote one's self.

vouge, *n.m.,* boar-spear.

vouloir (voulant, voulu), *v.a.,* to will, to be willing, to be pleased, to intend, to wish, to require; to consent ; to want ; to admit, to grant. *Je le veux ainsi* ; I will have it so. *Il veut que vous obéissiez* ; he will have you obey. *Je ne veux pas* ; I won't. *Que voulez-vous?* what do you want? *Il ne sait ce qu'il veut* ; he does not know his own mind. *Dieu le veut* ; God wills it. *Dieu le veuille!* God grant it ! *Ce que femme veut, Dieu le veut* ; a woman must have her way. *Il veut que cela soit* ; he will have it so. — *du bien à quelqu'un* ; to wish any one well. *Je vous veux du bien* ; I am your well-wisher. — *du mal à quelqu'un* ; to wish any one harm. *En — à quelqu'un* ; to bear any one ill-will. *Elle m'en veut du mal* ; she bears me a grudge for it. *Il en voulait à l'argent;* he had an inkling for the money. *Il nous demanda ce que nous lui voulions* ; he asked us what we wanted of him. *À qui en veut-il?* of whom, of what, has he to complain ? *Que veut dire cet homme!* what does that man mean? *Que veut dire cela!* what does that mean ? *Que veut dire ce mot!* what is the meaning of this word ? *Si vous le voulez, il le voudra aussi;* if you consent to it, he will do so too. *Oui, je le veux bien;* yes, I consent to it. *Je veux que vous sachiez;* I wish you to know. *Veuillez me dire;* please tell me.

vouloir, *n.m.*, will. *Bon —;* good-will. *Mauvais —;* ill-will.

vous, *personal pron.*, you, ye. — *dites;* you say. *De — à moi;* between you and me.

voussoau, or **voussoir**,*n.m.*,(arch.) wedge; archstone, voussoir.

voussure, *n.f.*, (arch.) curve, elevation of an arch.

voûte, *n.f.*, vault, arch.; *pl.*, vaulting. — *surbaissée;* surbased vault. *La clef de —;* the keystone. — *imparfaite;* diminished arch. — *oblique;* skew arch. — *d'arête;* groined vault. — *de décharge;* relieving vault. *La — du ciel;* the canopy of heaven.

voûter, *v.a.*, to vault, to arch. — *un fer à cheval,* to hollow a horseshoe.

se**voûter**, *v.r.*, to arch, to vault; (pers.) to be bent.

voyage, *n.m.*, voyage, journey, travel, trip; *pl.*, travels. — *de long cours* (nav.); long voyage. — *d'aller* (nav.); outward voyage. — *de retour* (nav.); return voyage. *Faire un —;* to go, to take, a journey. *Faire un petit —;* to take a trip. *Bon — et prompt retour;* a good journey and quick return. *Êtrs en —;* to be upon a journey, to be abroad.

voyager, *v.n.*, to travel, to voyage. — *à pied;* to travel on foot. — *à cheval;* to travel on horseback.

voyageu-r, *n.m.*, -se, *n.f.*, traveller; passenger. *Commis voyageur* (com.); commercial traveller, traveller. *Oiseau voyageur;* migratory bird.

voyant, -e, *adj.*, gaudy, showy (of colours—*des couleurs*); person who can see, who is not blind.

voyant, *n.m.*, (Bibl.) seer, prophet.

voyelle, *n.f.*, (gram.) vowel.

voyer, *n.* and *adj.m.*, surveyor of roads; relating, pertaining to roads.

voyou, *n.m.*, (pop.) dirty street boy, blackguard boy.

vrac, vrague, or **vraque**, *n.m.*, (nav.) disorder. *En —,* pell-mell. *Charger en —* (nav.) ; to lade with a loose cargo.

vrai, -e, *adj.*, true, real, right, genuine; proper; fit; natural, arrant; very. *Il est — que je l'ai dit;* it is true I said so. *Est-il que vous l'ayez dit?* is it true you have said it ? *Toujours est-il —;* it is nevertheless true. *Un — savant;* a thorough scholar. *Un — coquin;* an arrant knave.

vrai, *n.m.*, truth. *À dire —, à — dire;* to speak the truth. *Cela sort du —;* that is going from the truth, that is out of character. *Au —;* in truth, truly.

vrai, *adv.*, in truth, truly.

vraiment, *adv.*, truly, indeed ; verily, in truth, forsooth ! *Oui, vraiment;* yes, indeed.

vraisemblable (-san-), *n.m.* and *adj.*, probability, likelihood; likely, probably.

vraisemblablement (-san-), *adv.*, likely, probably.

vraisemblance (-san-), *n.f.*, probability, likelihood. *Cela pèhe contre la —;* that is contrary to probability.

vraque, *n.m.* V. **vrac**.

*****vrille**, *n.f.*, gimlet ; wimble, borer, piercer ; (bot.) clasper, tendril.

*****vriller**, *v.a.* and *n.*, to bore, to make holes with a gimlet ; (fig.) to ascend spirally (of fireworks—*de pièces d'artifice*).

*****vrillerie**, *n.f.*, gimlet-making.

*****vrillier**, *n.m.*, gimlet-maker.

*****vrillon**, *n.m.*, small wimble.

vu, *prep.*, seeing, considering. — *son âge;* considering his age.

vu que, *conj.*, seeing that, since.

vu, *n.m.*, sight, examination, inspection; (jur.) introductory part. *Au — et au su de tout le monde;* in the sight of the whole world, with the knowledge of everybody.

vue, *n.f.*, sight, eyesight ; eyes ; view, survey, inspection; prospect; light, window; design. *Il a perdu la —;* he has lost his sight. *Avoir la — bonne;* to have good eyes. *Avoir la — courte;* to be short-sighted. *Avoir la — basse;* to be near-sighted. *Jeter la — sur un objet;* to cast one's eye upon an object. *Baisser la —;* to look down. *Donner dans la —;* to strike upon the eyes, to catch one's eye. *Cette fille lui a donné dans la —;* that girl has caught his eye. *À perte de —;* farther than the eye can reach; at random. *Des compliments à perte de —;* long-winded compliments. *Perdre de — une chose;* to lose sight of a thing. *À —;* at sight. *Garder un prisonnier à —;* not to let a prisoner out of sight. *À — d'œil;* by the eye, visibly. *Avoir la — sur quelqu'un;* to keep a watch over any one. *À dix jours de —;* ten days after sight. *Une — de côté;* a side view. *Un plan à — d'oiseau;* a birdseye view. *Cette maison a une belle —;* that house has a fine view. *Son appartement a — sur la rivière;* his apartment looks over the river. *Dans la — de;* with a view of. *Il a de grandes —s;* he aims at great things. *Je l'ai fait dans cette —;* I did it with that view. *Avoir une chose en —;* to have a thing in one's eye.

vulcanien, -ne (ni-in, -ni-è-n), *adj.*, (geol.) plutonian, vulcanian.

vulcanisation, *n.f.*, vulcanization.

vulcanisé, *adj.*, vulcanized.

vulcaniser, *v.a.*, to vulcanize.

vulgaire, *n.m.* and *adj.*, vulgar, common people ; vulgar, common.

vulgairement (-ghèr-màn), *adv.*, vulgarly, commonly.

vulgarisateur, *n.m.*, one who has talent to diffuse scientific knowledge among the people.

vulgarisation, *n.f.*, vulgarizing, diffusing knowledge among the people.

vulgariser, *v.a.*, to vulgarize, to diffuse knowledge, science.

se**vulgariser**, *v.r.*, to be, to become vulgarized, generally known (of knowledge—*des sciences, &c.*).

vulgarité, *n.f.*, vulgarity, commonness, trivialness.

vulgate, *n.f.*, vulgate.

vulnérable, *adj.*, vulnerable.

vulnéraire, *n.m.* and *adj.*, (pharm.) vulnerary.

vulnéraire, *n.f.*, (bot.) kidney-vetch, woundwort.

vulpin, *n.m.*, (bot.) foxtail.

vultueu-x, -se, *adj.*, (med.) red and swelled (of the face—*du visage*).

vulve, *n.f.*, (anat.) vulva.

W

w (double vé), *n.m.* (this letter does not belong to the French alphabet, and is used in foreign words only), w.

wagon (va-gon), *n.m.*, railway-carriage.

walhalla, *n.m.* (*n.p.*), Odin's paradise.

walkyrie, *n.f.* (—s). *V.* **valkyrie**.

wallon, *n.m.*, **-ne**, *n.f.*, Walloon.

wallon, *n.m.*, Walloon (language—*langue*).

warrant, *n.m.*, warrant.

watergang, *or* **watregan**, *n.m.*, small canal; ditch with *or* without water (in Flanders and in the Netherlands—*en Flandre et dans les Pays-Bas*).

whig (ooig), *n.m.*, Whig.

whiskey (ooiski), *n.m.*, whisky (spirit—*spiritueux*).

whist, *n.m.*, whist.

wisk, *n.m.* *V.* **whist**.

wiskey, *n.m.* *V.* **whiskey**.

wiski (ooiski), *n.m.*, whisky, whiskey (gig —*cabriolet léger*).

wolfram (vol-fram), *n.m.*, (min.) wolfram.

wombat, *n.m.*, (mam.) wombat.

X

x (iks), *n.m.*, the twenty-third letter of the alphabet, x.

xbre (ab. of *décembre*). Dec.

xénélasie (ksé-), *n.f.*, (Grec. antiq.) exclusion of foreigners from a town.

xérasie (ksé-), *n.f.*, (med.) xerasia, alopecia.

xérophagie (ksé-), *n.f.*, xerophagy.

xérophtalmie (ksé-), *n.f.*, xerophthalmy.

xiphias (ksi-fias), *n.m.*, (ich., astron.) xiphias.

xiphoïde (ksi-), *adj.*, (anat.) xiphoid, ensiform.

xylographe (ksi-), *n.m.*, xylographer, wood-engraver.

xylographie (ksi-), *n.f.*, xylography, wood-engraving.

xylographique (ksi-), *adj.*, xylographic, of wood-engraving.

xylophage (ksi-) *n.m.* and *adj.*, (ent.) xylophagan; xylophagous.

xyste (ksist) *n.m.*, (antiq.) xyst, xystos.

Y

y (i-grèk), *n.m.*, the twenty-fourth letter of the alphabet, y.

y, *adv.*, there, thither; within, at home. *Je l'y ai vu;* I saw him there. *Allez-y;* go there. *Voulez-vous y aller?* will you go there? *Monsieur A. y est-il?* is Mr. A. within, at home? *Oui, il y est;* yes, he is at home.

y, *personal pron.*, by it, by them; for it, for them; in it, in them; at it, at them; to him, to her, to it, to them. *Il n'y est pas propre;* he is not fit for it. *Il n'y gagnera rien;* he will get nothing by it. *Ne vous y fiez pas;* don't trust to him. *Sans y penser;* without thinking of it.

yacht (iak), *n.m.*, yacht.

yankee (-ki), *n.m.*, Yankee.

yard (iard), *n.m.*, yard (measure—*mesure*).

yatagan, *n.m.*, yataghan.

yèble, *n.m.* *V.* **hièble**.

yénite, *n.f.*, (min.) yenite.

yeuse, *n.f.*, ilex, holm, evergreen oak.

yeux, *n.m.pl.*, eyes (*plur.* of **œil**, which see).

yole, *n.f.*, (nav.) yawl.

ypréau, *n.m.*, Ypres-elm.

ysard, *n.m.* *V.* **isard**.

yucca, *n.m.* (bot.) yucca.

Z

z (zèd), *n.m.*, the twenty-fifth letter of the alphabet, z.

zagaie, *n.f.*, assegai, the African tribes' javelin.

zaïm, *n.m.*, zaïm (Turkish soldier—*soldat turc*).

zain, *adj.*, whole-coloured (of horses—*des chevaux*).

zani, *n.m.*, zany.

zèbre, *n.m.*, zebra.

zébré, **-e**, *adj.*, striped like the zebra.

zébrure, *n.f.*, stripes like the zebra's.

zébu, *n.m.*, (mam.) zebu.

zédoaire, *n.f.*, (bot.) zedoary.

zée, *n.m.*, (ich.) zeus.

zélat-eur, *n.m.*, **-rice**, *n.f.*, zealous person.

zèle, *n.m.*, zeal. *Avoir du — pour, à;* to be zealous in. *Avoir peu de —;* not to be zealous, to be lukewarm.

zélé, **-e**, *adj.*, zealous.

zend (zind), *n.m.*, (*n.p.*) Zend; religious doctrine of Zoroaster.

zend, **-e** (zind), *adj.*, relating to Zend.

zend-avesta (zind-), *n.m.* (*n.p.*), Zendavesta (sacred book of the Guebers or Parsees—*livres sacrés des anciens Perses*).

zénith (-nit), *n.m.*, (astron.) zenith.

zénonique, *adj.*, Zenonic.

zénonisme, *n.m.*, Zenonism.

zéolithe, *n.m.*, zeolite.

zéphire, *or* **zéphyr**, *n.m.*, zephyr.

zéro, *n.m.*, nought; cipher; zero (of the thermometer—*du thermomètre*). *À —;* at zero. *Au-dessous de —;* below zero. *C'est un —;* he is a mere cipher.

zest (zèst), *n.m.*, only used in the proverbial and familiar expression: *Entre le zist et le —;* pretty well, so-so; (of persons—*des personnes*) undecided, wavering.

zest (zèst), *int.*, pshaw! nonsense! presto!

zeste (zèst), *n.m.*, zest (of a lemon, orange, walnut—*de citron, d'orange, de noix*); straw, fig. nothing. *Cela ne vaut pas un —;* it is not worth a straw.

zététique, *n.f.* and *adj.*, zetetic method; zetetic.

zeugme, *n.m.*, (rhet.) zeugma.

zézaiement, *n.m.*, bad pronunciation which consists in giving to *g* or *j* the soft sound of *z*.

zézayer, *v.n.*, to pronounce *g* or *j* like *z*.

zibeline *n.f.*, sable.

zigzag (zig-zag), *n.m.*, zigzag; crankle. *Faire des —s;* to reel about. *Aller en —;* to zigzag.

zinc, *n.m.*, zinc.

zincographe, *n.m.*, zincographer.

zincographie, *n.f.*, zincography.

zincographique, *adj.*, zincographic, zincographical.

zingari, *n.m.* (—s), Gipsy.

zinguer (-ghé), *v.a.*, to cover with zinc; to lay with zinc.

zingueur (-gheur), *n.m.*, zinc-worker.

zinzolin, *n.m.*, red violet.

zircon, *n.m.*, (min.) zircon.

zirconium, *n.m.*, (chem.) zirconium.

zist (zist), *n.m.* *V.* **zest**.

zizanie, *n.f.*, (bot.) ⊙tare, darnel-grass, drank-grass; (fig.) division, dissension, variance. *Semer la —;* to sow dissension.

zizi, *n.m.*, (orni.) cirl-bunting.

zodiacal, **-e**, *adj.*, zodiacal.

W
X
Y
Z

zodiaque, *n.m.*, zodiac.

zoïle, *n.m.* (—*s*), Zoïlus; (fig.) a zoïlean critic.

zona,*or* **zoster** (-tè-r),*n.m.*, (med.) shingles.

zone, *n.f.*, zone. — *glaciale;* frigid zone. — *tempérée;* temperate zone. — *torride;*·torrid zone.

zoné, -e, *adj.*, zoned.

zoographe, *n.m* , zoographer.

zoographie, *n.f.*, zoography.

zoolâtrie, *n.f.*, zoolatry.

zoolithe, *n.m.*, zoolite.

zoologie, *n.f.*, zoology.

zoologique, *adj.*, zoologic. zoological.

zoologiste, *n.m.*, zoologist.

zoologue, *n.m.*, *V.* **zoologiste.**

zoonomie, *n.f.*, zoonomy.

zoophage, *n.m.* and *adj.*, zoophagon; zoophagous.

zoophore, *n.m* , (arch.) zoophorus.

zoophyte, *n.m.*, zoophyte.

zoophytologie, *n.f.*, zoophytology.

zootomie, *n.f.*, zootomy.

zootomiste, *n.m.*, zootomist.

zoster, *n.m.* *V.* **zona.**

zostère, *n.f.*, (bot.) wračk-grass, sea-weeds.

zouave, *n.m.*, zouave, soldier in a regiment of zouaves, a French infantry corps employed in Algeria.

zygène, *n.f.*, (ich.) hammer-headed shark.

zygoma, *n.m.*, (anat.) zygoma.

zygomatique, *adj.*, (anat.) zygomatic.

zymique *adj.*, (chem.) zumic, zymic.

zymologie, *n.f.*, zumology, zymology.

zymologiste, *n.m.*, zumologist, zymologist.

zymome. *n.m* , (chem.) zimome.

zymosimètre, *n.m.*, zumometer, zumosimeter, zymometer, zymosimeter.

zymotechnie (-tèk-), *n.f.*, zumology. zymology.

zymotique. *adj.*. (med.) zymotic.

VOCABULARY

OF

PROPER NAMES,

INCLUDING THOSE OF

HISTORY AND MYTHOLOGY.

A

Aaron (aarŏn). *n.m.*, Aaron
Abdias (abdiâs), *n.m.*, Obadiah
Abdolonyme, *n.m.*, Abdalonimus
Abel, *n.m.*, Abel
Abias (abiâs), *n.m.*, Abia
Abigaïl, *n.f.*, Abigail
Abner (abnèr), *n.m.*, Abner
Abraham, *n.m.*, Abraham
Absalon, *n.m.*, Absalom
Absyrte, *n.m.*, Absyrtus
Acaste, *n.m.*, Acastus
Aceste, *n.m.*, Acestes
Achab (akab), *n.m.*, Ahab
Achate (akat),*n.m.*, Achates
Achille(ashil),*n.m.*, Achilles
Achmet (akmè), *n.m.*, Achmet
Acidalie, *n.f.*, Acidalia
Acrise, *n.m.*, Acrisius
Actéon. *n.m.*, Actæon
Ada, *n.f.*, Adah
Adam (adăn), *n.m.*, Adam
Adélaïde (adé-la-ï-d), *n.f.*, Adelaïde
Adèle, *n.f.*, Adela
Adeline (adli-n), *n.f.*, Adeline
Admète, *n.m.*, Admetus
Adolphe, *n.m.*, Adolphus
Adonis (-nîs), *n.m.*, Adonis
Adraste,*n.m.*, Adrastus
Adrastée, *n.f.*, Adrastia
Adrien(adriin),*n.m.*,Adrian
Agamemnon, *n.m.*, Agamemnon
Agar. *n.f.*, Hagar
Agathe. *n.f.*, Agatha
Agathocle,*n.m.*,Agathocles
Agésilas (-lâs), *n.m.*, Agesilaus
Aggée, *n m.*, Haggai
Agis (ajis), *n.m.*, Agis
Aglaé, *n.f.*, Aglaia
*Agnès** (-ès), *n.f.*, Agnès
Agricola, *n.m.*, Agricola
Agrippine, *n.f.*, Agrippina
Aimée, *n.f.*, Amy
Alain, *n.m.*, Allen
Alaric, *n.m.*, Alaric
l'Albane, *n.m.*, Albano
Albert. *n.m.*, Albert

Alcée. *n.m.*, Alcæus
Alceste, *n.m.*, Alcestis
Alcibiade, *n.m.*, Alcibiades
Alcide, *n.m.*, Alcides
Alcinoüs, *n.m.*, Alcinous
Alcmène,*n.f.*, Alcmena
Alecton. *n.f.*, Alecto
Alexandre (alèksăndr), *n.m.*, Alexander
Alfred (-frèd), *n.m.*, Alfred
Algernon, *n.m.*, Algernon
Alice, *n.f.*, Alice
Alithée, *n.f.*, Alithea
Alphée, *n.m.*, Alpheus
Alphonse, *n.m.*, Alphonso
Althée, *n.f.*, Althæa
Aluin, *n.m.*, Alwin
Alyatte. *n.m.*, Alyattes
Amalasonte, *n.f.*, Amalasontha
Amalec. *n.m.*, Amalek
Amalthée, *n.f.*, Amalthæa
Aman, *n.m.*, Haman
Amazias (-ziâs), *n.m.*, Amaziah
Ambroise, *n.m.*, Ambrose
Amédée, *n.m.*, Amedeus
Amélie, *n.f.*, Amelia
Améric Vespuce. *n.m.*, Americus Vesputius
Ammien (amiin), *n.m.*, Ammianus
Amos (amôs), *n.m.*, Amos
Amphitryon,*n.m.*, Amphitryon
Amurat, *n.m.*, Amurath
Anacharsis (-karsis), *n.m.*, Anacharsis
Anacréon, *n.m.*, Anacreon
Anastase,*n.m.*, Anastasius
Anaxagore, *n.m.*, Anaxagoras
Anaxarque, *n.m.*, Anaxarchus
Anaximandre, *n.m.*, Anaximander
Anchise,*n.m.*, Anchises
André, *n.m.*, Andrew
Androgée,*n.m.*, Androgeus
Andromaque, *n.f.*, Andromache
Andromède, *n.f.*, Andromeda
Andronique, *n.m.*, Andronicus

Ange, *n.m.*, Angelus
Anna, *n.f.*, Hannah
Anne, *n.f.*,Anne. Anna
Annette, *n.f.*, Nancy
Annibal, *n.m.*, Hannibal, Annibal
Anselme. *n.m.*, Anselmo
Antée. *n.m.*,Antæus
Anthée, *n.m.*, Antheas
Antigone, *n.m.*, Antigonus
Antigone, *n.f.*, Antigone
Antiloque.*n.m.*, Antilochus
Antiochus (-tiokus), *n.m.*, Antiochus
Antipater(-tèr),*n.m.*,Antipater
Antisthène *n.m.*, Antisthenes
Antoine, *n.m.*, Anthony. Antony. *Marc* —; Marc Antony
Antoinette,*n.f.*,Antoinette
Antonia, *n.f.*, Antonia
Antonin, *n.m.*, Antoninus
Antonine, *n.f.*, Antonina
Anytus (-tûs),*n.m.*, Anytus
Aod *or* **Ahod**, *n.m.*, Ehud
Apelle (apèl), *n.m.*, Apelles
Apollodore, *n.m.*, Apollodorus
Apollon, *n.m.*, Apollo
Appien(apiin),*n.m.*,Appian
Apulée, *n.m.*, Apuleius
Aquin. *n.m.*, Aquinas
Arabelle, *n.f.*, Arabella
Arachné, *n.f.*, Arachne
Arbace, *n.m.*, Arbaces
Arcade. *n.m.*, Arcadius
Arcésilas (-lâs),*n.m.*,Arcesilaus
Archambaud (-bô), *n.m.*, Archibald
Archélaüs (-kéla-ûs), *n.m.*, Archelaus
Archidamus (-mûs), *n.m.*, Archidamus
Archiloque, *n.m.*, Archilochus
Archimède, *n.m.*, Archimedes
Aréthuse, *n.f.*, Arethusa
Argée. *n.m.*, Argæus
Argus (-gûs), *n.m.*, Argus
Ariane, *n.f.*, Ariadne
Aricie, *n.f.*, Aricia

Aridée, *n.m.*, Arridæus

Arie, *n.f.*, Aria

l'Arioste, *.n.m.*, Ariosto

Arioviste *n.m.*, Ariovistus

Aristarque, *n.m.*, Aristarchus

Aristée, *n.m.*, Aristeus

Aristide, *n.m.* Aristides

Aristippe, *n.m.* Aristippus

Aristobule, *n.m.*, Aristobulus

Aristodème, *n.m.*, Aristodemus

Aristogiton, *n.m.*, Aristogiton

Aristomène, *n.m.*, Aristomenes

Aristophane, *n.m.*, Aristophanes

Aristote, *n.m.*, Aristotle

Aristoxène, *n.m.*, Aristoxenus

Arminius (-ûs), *n.m.*, Arminius

Arnaud, *n.m.*, Arnold

Arnobe, *n.m.*, Arnobius

Arrhidée, *n.m.*, Arrhidæus

Arrien (ariin), *n.m.*, Arrian

Arsace (arza-s), *n.m.*, Arsaces

Arsène, *n.m.*, Arsenius

Artaban, *n.m.*, Artabanus

Artabaze, *n.m.*, Artabazus

Artaxerce (-gzer-s), *n.m.*, Artaxerxes. — *Longue-Main;* Artaxerxes Longimanus

Artémidore, *n.m.*, Artemidorus

Artémise, *n.f.*, Artemisia

Arthur, *n.m.*, Arthur

*Ascagne, *n.m.*, Ascanius

Asclépiade, *n.m.*, Asclepiades

Asmodée, *n.m.*, Asmodeus

Aspasie, *n.f.*, Aspasia

Asser (a-cè-r), *n.m.*, Asher

Assuérus (-rûs), *n.m.*, Ahasuerus

Astrée, *n.f.*, Astræa

Astyage, *n.m.*, Astyages

Atalante, *n.f.*, Atalanta

Athalie, *n.f.*, Athaliah

Athanase, *n.m.*, Athanasius

Athelstan, *n.m.*, Athelstane

Athénodore, *n.m.*, Athenodorus

Atlas, *n.m.*, Atlas

Atrée, *n.m.*, Atreus

Atride, *n.m.*, Atrides

Attale, *n.m.*, Attalus

Atticus (-kûs), *n.m.*, Atticus

Augias (ôjiâs), *n.m.*, Augeas

Auguste, *n.m.*, Augustus

Augustin, *n.m.*, Austin *Saint* — *;* Saint Augustin

Augustule, *n.m.*, Augustulus

Aulu-Gelle, *n.m.*, Aulus-Gellius

Aurèle, *n.m.*, Aurelius. *Marc* — *;* Marcus Aurelius

Aurélie, *n.f.*, Aurelia

Aurélien (-liin), *n.m.*, Aurelian

Aurélius (-liûs), *n.m.*, Aurelius

Aurore, *n.f.*, Aurora

Ausone, *n.m.*, Ausonius

Aventin, *n.m.*, Aventine

Avicenne, *n.m.*, Avicenna

Azarias, *n.m.*, Azariah

B

Babet, *n.f.*, *V.* **Elizabeth**

*Bailleul, *n.m.*, Baliol

Bajazet, *n.m.*, Bajazeth

Bala, *n.f.*, Bilha

Balthazar, *n.m.*, Balthazar, Belshazzar

Baptiste (batist), *n.m.*, Baptist

Barabbas (-bâs), *n.m.*, Barabbas

Barbe, *n.f.*, Barbara

Barberousse, *n.m.*, Barbarossa

Bardesane, *n.m.*, Bardesanes

Barnabé, *n.m.*, Barnaby

Barthélemi (-télmi), *n.m.*, Bartholomew

Barthole, *n.m.*, Bartolo

Basile, *n.m.*, Basil

Basilide, *n.m.*, Basilides

Batnuel, *n.m.*, Bethuel

Baudouin, *n.m.*, Baldwin

Béatrice, *n.f.*, Beatrice

Béatrix, *n.f.*, Beatrix

Bède, *n.m.*, Beda

Bélisaire, *n.m.*, Belisarius

Bellone, *n.f.*, Bellona

Bellovèse, *n.m.*, Bellovesus

Belzébuth, *n.m.*, Beelzebub

Bénédict (-dict), *n.m.*, Benedict

Bénédicte, *n.f.*, Benedicta

Benjamin (bin-), *n.m.*, Benjamin

Benoît, *n.m.*, Benedict

Benoîte, *n.f.*, Benedicta

Benserade (bìnsrad), *n.m.*, Benserade

Bérenger, *n.m.*, Berengarius

Bérénice, *n.f.*, Berenice, Beronice

Bernard, *n.m.*, Bernard

Bernardin, *n.m.*, Bernardine

Berthe, *n.f.*, Bertha

Bertrand, *n.m.*, Bertram

Bethsabé, *n.f.*, Bathsheba

Bèze, *n.m.*, Beza

Blaise, *n.m.*, Blase

Blanche, *n.f.*, Blanch

Boccace, *n.m.*, Boccacio

Boèce, *n.m.*, Boethius

Boleslas (-lâs), *n.m.*, Boleslaus

Bonaventure, *n.m.*, Bonadventure

Boniface, *n.m.*, Boniface

Bonne, *n.f.*, Bona

Booz (boôz), *n.m.*, Boaz

Borée, *n.m.*, Boreas

Briarée, *n.m.*, Briareus

Brigitte, *n.f.*, Bridget

Britannicus (-kûs), *n.m.*, Brittanicus

Broglie (bro-li), *n.m.*, Broglio

Brutus (-tûs), *n.m.*, Brutus

Buddée, *n.m.*, Buddæus

Burrhus (bur-rûs) *n.m.*, Burrhus

C

Cadmus (-mûs), *n.m.*, Cadmus

Caïn, *n.m.*, Cain

Caïnan, *n.m.*, Cainan

Caïphe, *n.m.*, Caiaphas

Caïus (ka-iûs), *n.m.*, Caius

Calchas (-kâs), *n.m.*, Calchas

Caligula, *n.m.*, Caligula

Caliste, *n.m.*, Calistus

Callicrate (kal-li-), *n.m.*, Callicrates

Callimaque, *n.m.*, Callimachus

Calliope, *n.f.*, Calliope

Callisthène, *n.m.*, Callisthenes

Calpurnie, *n.f.*, Calpurnia

Calvin, *n.m.*, Calvin

Calypso, *n.f.*, Calypso

Cambyse, *n.m.*, Cambyses

*Camille, *n.m.*, Camillus

*Camille, *n.f.*, Camilla

Candaule, *n.m.*, Candaules

Canut, *n.m.*, Canute. — *le Hardi;* Hardicanute

Capitolin, *n.m.*, Capitolinus

Caractacus (-kûs), *n.m.*, Caractacus

Carbon, *n.m.*, Carbo

Carin, *n.m.*, Carinus

Carnéade, *n.m.*, Carneades

Caroline, *n.f.*, Caroline

Casimir, *n.m.*, Casimir

Cassandre, *n.m.*, Cassander

Cassandre, *n.f.*, Cassandra

Cassius (-ûs), *n.m.*, Cassius

Catherine (ka-tri-n), *n.f.*, Catharine

Catilina, *n.m.*, Catilina, Catiline

Caton, *n.m.*, Cato

Catulle, *n.m.*, Catullus

Cécile, *n.f.*, Cecilia

Célestin, *n.m.*, Celestine

Célie, *n.f.*, Celia

Celse, *n.m.*, Celsus

Céphale, *n.m.*, Cephalus

Cépion, *n.m.*, Cæpio

Cerbère, *n.m.*, Cerberus

Cérès (-rès), *n.f.*, Ceres

Cérinthe, *n.m.*, Cerinthus

César, *n.m.*, Cæsar

Chabrias (-âs), *n.m.*, Chabrias

Cham (kam), *n.m.*, Ham

Charès (karès), *n.m.*, Chares

*Charlemagne, *n.m.*, Charlemagne

Charles, *n.m.*, Charles. — *Quint;* Charles the Fifth (of Spain—*d'Espagne*). — *le Téméraire;* Charles the Bold

Charlot, *n.m.*, Charly

Charlotte, *n.f.*, Charlotte

Charon (kâron), *n.m.*, Charon

Chloé, *n.f.*, Chloe

Chosroès (kos-ro-ès), *n.m.*, Chosroes

Chrétien (krétiin), *n.m.*, Christian

le **Christ** (krist), *n.m.*, Christ

Christiana, *n.f.*, Christiana

Christine (kris-), *n.f.,* Christina
Christophe (kris-), *n m.,* Christopher
Chryséis (krizéis), *n.f.,* Chryseis
Chrysès (krizès), *n.m.,* Chryses
Chrysippe (krizip), *n.m.,* Chrysippus
Chrysostôme (kri-), *n.m.,* Chrysostom
Cicéron, *n.m.,* Cicero
les **Cimbres,** *n.m.,* the Cimbri
Cimon, *n.m.,* Cimon
Cincinnatus (-ci-n-na-tûs), *n.m.,* Cincinnatus
Circé, *n.f.,* Circe
Clara, *or* **Claire,** *n.f.,*Clara
Clarisse, *n.f.,* Clarissa
Claude, *n.m.,* Claudius
Claude, *n.f.,* Claudia
Claudie, *n.f.,* Claudia
Claudien (-diin), *n.m.,* Claudian
Cléanthe, *n.m.,* Cleanthes
Cléarque, *n.m.,* Clearchus
Clélie, *n.f.,* Clœlia
Clément, *n.m.,* Clement
Clémentine, *n.f.,* Clementina
Cléobule, *n.m.,* Cleobulus
Cléombrote, *n.m.,* Cleombrotus
Cléomène, *n.m.,*Cleomenes
Cléo pâtre, *n.f.,* Cleopatra
Clio, *n.f.,* Clio
Cloanthe, *n.m.,* Cloanthus
Clotaire, *n.m.,* Clotharius
Clotho, *n.f.,* Clotho
Clotilde, *n.f.,* Clotilda
Clovis (-vis), *n.m.,* Clovis
Clytemnestre (klitèm-nèstr), *n.f.,* Clytemnestra
Codrus (kodrûs), *n.m.,* Codrus
Collatin, *n.m.,* Collatinus
Colomb (kolon), *n.m.,* Columbus
Columelle, *n.m.,* Columella
Côme, *n.m. V.* **Cosme.**
Commode, *n.m.,* Commodus
Comnène (komnè-n), *n.m.,* Comnenus
*****Condillac,** *n.m.,* Condillac
Confucius (-ûs), *n.m.,* Confucius
Conrad (-rad), *n.m.,* Conrad
Constance, *n.m.,* Constantius
Constance, *n.f.,* Constance
Constantin, *n.m.,* Constantinus
Copernic, *n.m.,* Copernicus
Corbulon, *n.m.,* Corbulo
Coré, *n.m.,* Korah
Corinne, *n.f.,* Corinna
Coriolan, *n.m.,* Coriolanus
*****Corneille,** *n.m.,* Cornelius
Cornélie, *n.f.,* Cornelia
Cornélius (-ûs), *n.m.,* Cornelius
le **Corrège,** *n.m.,* Correggio
Cosme (kô-m),*n.m.,* Cosmus
Cratère, *n.m.,* Craterus
Créon, *n.m.,* Creon
Crépin, *n.m.,* Crispin
Crésus (-zus), *n.m.,* Crœsus

Créuse, *n.f.,* Creusa
Cupidon, *n.m.,* Cupid
les **Curiaces,** *n.m.,* the Curiatii
Curion, *n.m.,* Curio
Cyaxare, *n.m.,* Cyaxares
Cybèle, *n.f.,* Cybela
les **Cyclopes,** *n.m.pl.,*Cyclopes
Cynégire, *n.m.,* Cynegirus
Cyprien (sipriin), *n.m.,* Cyprianus
*****Cyrille,** *n.m.,* Cyrillus
Cyrus (-rûs), *n.m.,* Cyrus
Cythórée, *n.f.,* Cytheræa

D

Damascène, *n.m.,* Damascene
Damase, *n.m.,* Damasus
Damoclès (-clès), *n.m.,* Damocles
Danaüs (-us), *n.m.,* Danaus
Daniel, *n.m.,* Daniel
le **Dante,** *n.m.,* Dante
Daphné, *n.f.,* Daphne
Daphnis (-nis), *n.m.,* Daphnis
Darius (-ûs), *n.m.,* Darius
— *Codoman;* Darius Codomanus
Datame, *n.m.,* Datames
David (-vid), *n.m.,* David
Débora, *n.f.,* Deborah
Dèce, *n.m.,* Decius
Dédale, *n.m.,* Dædalus
Deidamie, *n.f.,* Deidamia
Déiphobe, *n.m.,* Deiphobus
Déjanire, *n.f.,* Dejanira
Délie, *n f.,* Delia
Démade, *n.m.,* Demades
Démarate, *n.m.,* Demaratus
Démétrius (-ûs), *n.m.,* Demetrius
Démocède, *n.m.,* Democoedes
Démocrate, *n.m.,* Democrates
Démocrite, *n.m.,* Democritus
Démosthène,.*n.m.,* Demosthenes
Denis, *n.m.,* Dionysius; Denis. — *l'Ancien;* Dionysius the elder. — *le Jeune;* Dionysius the younger
Descartes (dèkart), *n.m.,* Descartes
Diane, *n.f.,* Diana
Dicéarque, *n.m.,* Dicæarchus
Didon, *n.f.,* Dido
Dioclétien (-siin),*n.m.,*Diocletianus
Diodore, *n.m.,* Diodorus. — *de Sicile;* Diodorus Siculus
Diogène, *n.m.* Diogenes. — *Laerce;* Diogenes Laertius
Diomède, *n.m.,* Diomedes
Dion, *n.m.,* Dion
Diophante, *n.m.,* Diophantus
Dioscoride, *n.m.,* Dioscorides
Dominique, *n.m.,* Dominic
le **Dominiquin,** *n.m.,* Dominichino

Domitien (-siiif), *n.m.,* Domitianus
Donat. *n.m.,* Donatus
Dorothée, *n.f.,* Dorothea
Dracon. *n.m.,* Draco
*****Drusille,** *n.f.,* Drusilla
Dulcinée, *n.f.,* Dulcinea

E

Éaque. *n.m.,* Æacus
Edmond, *n.m.,* Edmund. — *côte de fer;* Edmund Iron, side
Édouard, *n.m.,* Edward
Égée, *n.m.,* Ægeus
Égéon, *n.m.* Ægæon
Égérie, *n.f.,* Egeria
Égialée, *n.f.,* Ægialeus
Égisthe, *n.m.,* Ægisthus
Égló, *n.f.,* Ægle
Égyptus (-tûs), *n.m.,* Ægyptus
Électre, *n.f.,* Electra
Éléonore, *n.f.,* Eleanor
Éliacim, *n.m.,* Eliakim
Élie, *n.m.,* Elias, Eliah
Élien (éliin), *n.m.,* Ælianus
Élisabeth, *n.f.,* Elizabeth
Élise, *n.f.,* Eliza
Élisée, *n.m.,* Elisha
Émeri, *n.m.,* Emery
Émile, *n.m.,*.Æmilius. *Paul* —; Paulus Æmilius
Émilie, *n.f.,* Emily
Émilien(-liin),*n.m.,*Æmilianus
Emma (èm-ma), *n.f.,* Emma
Emmanuel (è-m-manuèl), *n.m.,* Emmanuel
Encelade, *n.m.,* Enceladus
Endymion, *n.m.,* Endymion
Énée, *n.m.,* Æneas
Énoch, *n.m.,* Enoch
Éole, *n.m.,* Æolus
Épaminondas (-dàs), *n.m.,* Epaminondas
Épicharme (-karm), *n.m.,* Epicharmus
Épictète, *n.m.,* Epictetus
Épicure, *n.m.,* Epicurus
les **Épigones,** *n.m.,* the Epigoni
Épiménide, *n.m.,* Epimenides
Épiphane,.*n.m.,*Epiphanius
Érasme, *n.m.,* Erasmus
Éraste, *n.m.,* Erastus
Érato. *n.f.,* Erato
Ératosthène, *n.m.,* Eratosthenes
Ératostrate, *n.m.,* Eratostratus
Érèbe, *n.m.,* Erebus
Ernest, *n.m.,* Ernest
Érostrate, *n m.,* Erostratus
Ésaü, *n.m.,* Esau

Eschine (ès-shĭ-n), *n.m.*, Æschines

Eschyle (ès-shĭl), *n.m.*, Æschylus

Esculape. *n.m.*, Æsculapius

Esdras (-drâs), *n.m.*, Esdras

Éson, *n.m.*, Æson

Ésope. *n.m.*, Æsop

Esron. *n.m.*, Esrom

Esther (èstèr), *n.f.*, Esther

Étéocle, *n.m.*, Eteocles

Étienne (étiè-n), *n.m.*, Stephen

Euclide, *n.m.*, Euclid

Eudoxie, *n.f.*, Eudoxia

Eugène, *n.m.*, Eugenius

Eugénie, *n.f.*, Eugenia

Eumée, *n.m.*, Eunæus

Eumène. *n.m.*, Eumenes

Euripide, *n.m.*, Euripides

Europe, *n.f.*, Europa

Euryale, *n.m.*, Euryalus

Eurybate, *n.m.*, Eurybates

Eurydice, *n.f.*, Eurydice

Eurypyle, *n.m.*, Eurypylus

Eurysthée, *n.m.*, Eurystheus

Eusèbe, *n.m.*, Eusebius

Eustache. *n.m.*, Eustace

Eustathe, *n.m.*, Eustathius

Eutrope, *n.m.*, Eutropius

Évandre. *n.m.*, Evander

Ève. *n.f.*, Eve

Ézéchias (-kiâs), *n.m.*, Hezekiah. Ezechias

Ézéchiel (-kièl), *n.m.*, Ezekiel

F

Fabien(-biin),*n.m.*,Fabian

Fabius(-ûs) *n.m.*, Fabius

Fabricius (-ûs), *n.m.*, Fabricius

Fallope. *n.m.*, Fallopio

Fanchon, *n.f.*, Fanny

Faunus, *n.m.*, Faunus

Faust (fòst), *n.m.*, Faustus, Faust

Faustine, *n.f.*, Faustina

Félicie. *n.f.*, Felicia

Félicité, *n.f.*, Felicity

Félix (-liks), *n.m.*, Felix

Ferdinand, *n.m.*, Ferdinand

Festus (-tûs), *n.m.*, Festus

Fiesque, *n.m.*, Fiesco

Firouz, *n.m.* *V.* Pórosès

Flavien (-viin), *n.m.*, Flavian

Flore, *n.f.*, Flora

Florence, *n.f.*, Florence

Fortune, *n.f.*, Fortuna

Fortuné, *n.m.*, Fortunatus

Foulque, *n.m.*, Fulk

François, *n.m.*, Francis

Françoise, *n.f.*, Frances

Frédéric, *n.m.*, Frederick

Frontin, *n.m.*, Frontinus

Fulvie, *n.f.*, Fulvia

G

Gabriel, *n.m.*, Gabriel

Gabrielle. *n.f.*, Gabriella

Galatée, *n.f.*, Galatea

Galère, *n.m.*, Galerius

Galien (-liin),*n.m.*, Galen

Galilée. *n.m.*, Galileo

Gallien (-liin), *n.m.*, Gallienus

Ganymède *n.m*,Ganymede

Gaspard, *n.m.*, Jasper

Gauthier, *n.m.*, Walter

Gédéon, *n.m.*, Gideon

Gélon, *n.m.*, Gelo, Gelon

Genséric, *n.m.*, Genseric

Geoffroy (jofroa),*n.m.*, Geffery, Geffrey

George (jorj), *n.m.*, George

Georgette (jorjèt), *n.f.*, Georgetta

Georgine (jorji-n), *n.f.*, Georgina

les **Gépides**, *n.m.*, Gepidæ

Gertrude, *n.f.*, Gertrude

Gervais, *n.m.*, Gervase

Géryon. *n.m.*, Geryon, Geryones

Gilbert, *n.m.*, Gilbert

Gilles (jil), *n.m.*, Giles

Glycère, *n.f.*, Glycera

Godefroy (godfroa), *n.m.*, Godfrey

Goliath, *n.m.*, Goliath, Goliah

Gondebaud(gondbô),*n.m.*, Gondebald

Gordien (-diin), *n.m.*, Gordian

Gorgias (-âs), *n.m.*, Gorgias

Gracchus (grakûs), *n.m.*, Gracchus

les **Gracques** (grak),*n.m.*,the Gracchi

Gratien (-siin), *n.m.*, Gratian

Grégoire, *n.m.*, Gregory

***Guillaume** (ghi-iô-m), *n.m.*,William. — *le conquérant ;* William the Conqueror. — *le Roux :* William Rufus

***Guillot** (ghi-io), *n.m.*, Bill, Billy

Gustave, *n.m.*, Gustavus

Guy (ghi), *n.m.*, Guy

Gygès (jijè), *n.m.*, Gyges

Gylippe, *n.m.*, Gylippus

H

Habacuc. *n.m.*, Habakkuk

Haggée. *n.m.*, Haggai

Hannon. *n.m.*, Hanno

†**Hardi Canut**, *n.m.*, Hardicanute

†**Harold**, *n.m.*, Harold

Harpale. *n.m.*, Harpalus

Harpocrate, *n.m.*, Harpocrates

Hébé. *n.f.*, Hebe

Hécate, *n.f.*. Hecate

Hector. *n.m.*, Hector

Hécube, *n.f.*, Hecuba

Hégésippe, *n.m.*, Hegesippus

Helcias (-âs), *n.m.*, Helkiah

Hélène, *n.f.*, Helen

Héliodore.*n.m.*,Heliodorus

Héliogabale,*n.m.*,Heliogabalus

Héloïse, *n.f.*, Eloisa

Hénoch (énok), *n.m.* *V.* Enoch

†**Henri**, *n.m.*, Henry. [Henri in familiar style has the *h* mute.]

Henriette, *n.f.*, Henrietta, Harriet

Héraclide.*n.m.*, Heraclides

Héraclite. *n.m.*, Heraclitus

Hercule. *n.m.*, Hercules

Hermione, *n.f.*, Hermione

Hermocrate, *n.m.*,Hermocrates

Hermodore, *n.m.*, Hermodorus

Hermogène, *n.m.*, Hermogenes

Hermotime, *n.m.*, Hermotimus

Hérode, *n.m.*, Herod

Hérodien (-diin), *n.m.*, Herodianus

Hérodote, *n.m.*,Herodotus

Hersilie. *n.f*, Hersilia

Hésiode, *n.m.*, Hesiod

Hespérus (-rûs), *n.m.*, Hesperus

Hiéron, *n.m.*, Hiero

Hilaire, *n.m.*, Hilary

Himilcon, *n.m.*, Himilco

Hipparque, *n.m.*, Hipparchus

Hippias (-âs),*n.m.*, Hippias

Hippocrate, *n.m.*, Hippocrates

Hippodamie, *n.f.*, Hippodamia

Hippolyte, *n.f.*, Hippolyta

Hippolyte.*n.m.*,Hippolytus

Hippomène. *n.m.*, Hippomenes

Hircan, *n.m.*, Hyrcanus

Homère, *n.m.*, Homer

†**Homfroi**, *n.m.*, Humphrey

Horace,*n.m.*, Horatio ; Horace

les **Horaces**, the Horatii

Hortense, *n.f.*, Hortensia

†**Hugues** (hug). *n.m.*, Hugh

Hunyade, *n.m.*, Huniades

Hyacinthe, *n.m.*, Hyacinthus

Hymen, Hyménée, *n.m.*, Hymen, Hymenæus

Hypéride, *n.m.*, Hyperides

Hypérion. *n.m.*, Hyperion

Hypermnestre, *n.f.*, Hypermnestra

Hystaspe, *n.m.*, Hystaspes

I

Ibrahim (-him), *n.m.*, Ibrahim

Icare. *n.m.*, Icarus

Idoménée,*n.m.*,Idomeneus

***Ignace**. *n.m.*, Ignatius

Inachus (-kus), *n.m.*, Inachus

Ilionée, *n.m.*, Ilioneus

Ilus, *n.m.*, Ilus

Iphicrate, *n.m.*, Iphicrates

Iphigénie, *n.f.*, Iphigenia

Irène, *n.f.*, Irene

Irénée, *n.m.*, Irenæus

Iris (irîs), *n.f.*, Iris

Isaac (izaak), *n.m.*, Isaac

Isabelle,*n.f.*, Isabella

Isaïe, *n.m.*, Isaiah

Isidore, *n.m.*, Isidore. Isidorus

Isis (izìs), *n.f.*, Isis
Ismaël. *n.m.*, Ishmael
Isocrate, *n.m.*, Isocrates
Israël (izraèl), *n.m.*, Israel
Iule, *n.m.*, Iulus
Ixion, *n.m.*, Ixion

J

Jacob, *n.m.*, Jacob
Jacques (jâk), *n.m.*, James
Jamblique, *n.m.*, Iamblichus
Jansénius (-ûs), *n.m.*, Jansenius
Janus (janûs), *n.m.*, Janus
Jean (jan), *n.m.*, John. — *sans Terre;* John Lackland
Jeanne (jâ-n), *n.f.*, Jane, Joan. — *d'Arc;* Joan of Arc
Jeannette (ja-nèt), *n.f.*, Jenny
Jéchonias (jékoniâs), *n.m.*, Jechoniah
Jenny, *n.f.*, Jenny
Jephté, *n.m.*, Jephthah
Jérémie, *n.m.*, Jeremy, Jeremiah
Jérôme, *n.m.*, Jerome
Jessé, *n.m.*, Jesse
Jésus (jézu), *n.m.*, Jesus
Jésus-Christ (jézu kri), *n.m.*, Jesus Christ
Joachaz (joakâz), *n.m.*, Jehohaz
Joachim (-ki-m), *n.m.*, Joachim
Joad, *or* **Joiada**, *n.m.*, Jehoida
Jocaste, *n.f.*, Jocasta
Joel, *n.m.*, Joel
Jonas (-nâs), *n.m.*, Jonah
Jonathas (-tâs), *n.m.*, Jonathan
Joram, *n.m.*, Jehoram
Josaphat, *n.m.*, Jehoshaphat
Joseph, *n.m.*, Joseph
Josèphe (Flavien), *n.m.*, Josephus (Flavius)
Josias (-âs), *n.m.*, Josiah
Josué, *n.m.*, Joshua
Jovien (-viin), *n.m.*, Jovianus
Jovin, *n.m.*, Jovinus
Jovinien (-niin), *n.m.*, Jovinian
Juan, *n.m.*, Juan
Juda, *n.m.*, Judah
Judas, *n.m.*, Judas (the apostle). — *Iscariote;* Judas Iscariot
Jude, *n.m.*, Judas
Jules, *n.m.*, Julius
Julie, *n.f.*, Julia
Julien (-liin). *n.m.*, Julian
Julienne, *n.f.*, Juliana
Juliette, *n.f.*, Juliet
Junie, *n.f.*, Junia
Junius (-ûs), *n.m.*, Junius
Junon, *n.f.*, Juno
Jupiter (-tèr), *n.m.*, Jupiter. — *Férétrien;* Jupiter Feretrius. — *Olympien;* Jupiter Olympius. — *Tonnant;* Jupiter the Thunderer
Juste, *n.m.*, Justus
Justine, *n.f.*, Justina

Justinien (-niin), *n.m.*, Justinian
Juturne, *n.f.*, Juturna
Juvénal, *n.m.*, Juvenal

L

Lactance, *n.m.*, Lactantius
Ladislas (-lâs), Ladislaus
Laerce, *n.m.* V. **Diogène**
Laërte, *n.m.*, Laertes
Lamachus (-kûs), *n.m.*, Lamachus
Lancelot (lanslô), *n.m.*, Launcelot
Laodamie, *n.f.*, Laodamia
les **Lapithes**, *n.m.*, Lapithæ
Latone, *n.f.*, Latona
Laure, *n.f.*, Laura
Laurent, *n.m.*, Laurence
Lavater (-tèr), *n.m.*, Lavater
Lavinie, *n.f.*, Lavinia
Lazare, *n.m.*, Lazarus
Léandre, *n.m.*, Leander
Léon, *n.m.*, Leon, Leo
Léonard, *n.m.*, Leonard
Léonat, *n.m.*, Leonatus
Léonidas (-dâs), *n.m.*, Leonidas
Léonore, *n.f.*, Leonora
Léopold (-pold), *n.m.*, Leopold
Léosthène, *n.m.*, Leosthenes
Lépide, *n.m.*, Lepidus
Leptine, *n.m.*, Leptines
Leucippe, *n.m.*, Leucippus
Leucothoé, *n.f.*, Leucothoe
Lévi, *n.m.*, Levy
Libère, *n.m.*, Liberius
Libitine, *n.f.*, Libitina
Linné, *n.m.*, Linnæus
Lipse, *n.m.*, Lipsius
Lisette, *n.f.*, Assy
Livie, *n.f.*, Livia
Longin, *n.m.*, Longinus
Lothaire, *n.m.*, Lotharius, Lothario
Louis, *n.m.*, Lewis
Louise, *n.f.*, Louisa
Luc, *n.m.*, Luke
Lucain, *n.m.*, Lucan
Lucie, *n.f.*, Lucy
Lucien (-siin), *n.m.*, Lucian
Lucifer (-fèr), *n.m.*, Lucifer
Lucine, *n.f.*, Lucina
Lucius (-ûs), *n.m.*, Lucius
Lucrèce, *n.m.*, Lucretius
Lucrèce, *n.f.*, Lucretia
Lucullus (-lûs), *n.m.*, Lucullus
Luther (-tèr), *n.m.*, Luther
Lycomède, *n.m.*, Lycomedes
Lycurgue (-kurg), *n.m.*, Lycurgus
Lydie, *n.f.*, Lydia
Lyncée, *n.m.*, Lynceus
Lysandre, *n.m.*, Lysander
Lysimaque, *n.m.*, Lysimachus
Lysippe, *n.m.*, Lysippus

M

Macaire, *n.m.*, Macarius
Machabée (makabé), *n.m.*, Maccabeus
les **Machabées**, *n.m.*, Maccabees
Macrin, *n.m.*, Macrinus
Macrobe, *n.m.*, Macrobius
Madeleine (mad-lè-n), *n.f.*, Magdelen
Madelon (madlon), *n.f.*, Maudlin
Magnence, *n.m.*, Magnentius
Magon, *n.m.*, Mago
Mahomet, *n.m.*, Mahomet, Mahommed
Mainfroi, *n.m.*, Manfred
Majorien (-riin), *n.m.*, Majorian
Malachie, *n.m.*, Malachi
Mammée (mam-mé), *n.f.*, Mammea
Manassé, *n.m.*, Manasseh, Manasses
Manéthon, *n.m.*, Manetho
Marc, *n.m.*, Mark
Marc-Aurèle, *n.m.*, Marcus-Aurelius
Marcellin (-cèl-lin), *n.m.*, Marcellinus
Marcellus (-cèl-lûs), *n.m.*, Marcellus
Marcien (-siin), *n.m.*, Marcianus
Mardochée, *n.m.*, Mordecai
Margot, *n.f.*, Marget
Marguerite (-grit), *n.f.*, Margaret
Maria, *n.f.*, Maria
Marianne, *n.f.*, Marianne
Marie, *n.f.*, Mary
Marius (-ûs), *n.m.*, Marius
Mars, *n.m.*, Mars
Marthe, *n.f.*, Martha
Martin, *n.m.*, Martin
Mathan, *n.m.*, Matthan
Mathilde, *n.f.*, Matilda
Mathusaël, *n.m.*, Methusael
Mathusalem (-lò m), *n.m.*, Methuselah
Matthias, *n.m.*, Matthias
Matthieu, *n.m.*, Matthew
Maurice, *n.m.*, Maurice, Morice
Mausole, *n.m.*, Mausolus
Maviaël, *n.m.*, Mehujael
Maxence, *n.m.*, Maxentius
Maxime, *n.m.*, Maximus
Maximien (-miin), *n.m.*, Maximianus
Maximilien (-liin), *n.m.*, Maximilian
Mécène, *n.m.*, Mecænas
Mécistée, *n.m.*, Mecisteus
Médée, *n.f.*, Medea
Méduse, *n.f.*, Medusa
Mégère, *n.f.*, Megæra
Mélampe, *n.m.*, Melampus
Melcha (mèlka), *n.f.*, Mileah
Melchisédech (mèlkizédèk), *n.m.*, Melchizedech
Méléagre, *n.m.*, Meleager
Mélicerte, *n.m.*, Melicerta
Mélisse, *n.f.*, Melissa
Ménandre, *n.m.*, Menander
Ménèce, *n.m.*, Menœtius

Ménélas (-lâs), *n.m.*, Menelaus

Ménippe, *n.m.*, Menippus

Mentor (mintor),*n.m.*, Mentor

Mercure. *n.m.*, Mercury

Messaline, *n.f.*, Messaline

Métastase,*n.m.*,Metastasio

Michaud, *n.m.*, Mike

Michée, *n.m.*, Micah

Michel, *n.m.*, Michael

Michel-Ange (mikèl-ânj), *n.m.*, Michael-Angelo

Milon, *n.m.*, Milo

Miltiade, *n.m.*, Miltiades

Minerve, *n.f.*, Minerva

Minos (minôs), *n.m.*, Minos

Minotaure, *n.m.*, Minotaurus

Misithée, *n.m.*, Misitheus

Mithridate, *n.m.*, Mithridates

Mohammed, *n.m.*,Mohammed, Mahomet

Moïse, *n.m.*, Moses

Monime, *n.f.*, Monima

Morphée, *n.m.*, Morpheus

Mucien, *n.m.*, Mucianus

Myrtée, *n.f.*, Myrtea

Myrtile, *n.m.*, Myrtilus

N

Nabuchodonosor, (-ko-), *n.m.*, Nebuchadnezzar

Nannette, *n.f.*, Nancy

Napoléon, *n.m.*, Napoleon

Narcisse, *n.m.*, Narcissus

Nathaniel, *n m.*,Nathaniel

Néarque, *n.m.*, Nearchus

Néhémie, *n.m.*, Nehemiah

Néléo, *n.m.*, Neleus

Némésis (-zîs), *n.f.*, Nemesis

Néoptolème, *n.m.*, Neoptolèmus

Neptune, *n.m.*, Neptune

Nérée, *n.m.*, Nereus

Néron. *n.m.*, Nero

Nicéphore, *n.m.*, Nicephorus

Nicias (-âs), *n.m.*, Nicias

Nicodème, *n.m.*, Nicodemus

Nicolas, *n.m.*, Nicholas

Nicomède, *n.m.*, Nicomedes

Ninon, *n.f.*, Nino

Niobé, *n.f.*, Niobe

Noé, *n.m.*, Noah

Noël, *n.m.*, Noel

Noéma. *n.f.*, Naamah

Noémi. *n.f.*, Naomi

Numérien (-riin), *n.m.*,Numerian

O

Océan, *n.m.*, (myth.) Oceanus

Ochozias (okoziâs), *n.m.*, Ahaziah

Octave, *n.m*, Octavius

Octavie, *n.f.*, Octavia

Octavien (-viin), *n.m.*, Octavianus

Odin, *n.m.*, Odin, Woden

Odoacre, *n.m.*, Odoacer

Œdipe (édip),*n.m.*, Œdipus

Œnée, *n.m.*, Œneus

Olivie, *n.f.*, Olivia

Olivier, *n.m.*, Oliver

Olympe, *n.f.*, Olympia

Olympiodore, *n.m.*, Olympiodorus

Omphale, *n.f.*, Omphale

Onésime, *n.m.*,Onesimus

Onomacrite,*n.m.*,Onomacritus

Onomarque, *n.m.*, Onomarchus

Ophélie, *n.f.*, Ophelia

Oppien (opiin), *n.m.*, Oppian

Oreste, *n.m.*, Orestes

Origène, *n.m.*, Origen

Orion, *n.m.*, Orion

Orithyie, *n.f.*, Orithyia

Oronte, *n.m.*, Orontes

Orose, *n.m.*, Orosius

Orphée, *n.m.*, Orpheus

Osée. *n.m.*, Hosea

Osiris (-ris), *n.m.*, Osiris

Othon, *n.m.*, Otho

Ovide, *n.m.*, Ovid

P

Palamède,*n.m.*,Palamedes

Palémon. *n.m.*, Palæmon

Paléologue (-log), *n.m.*, Palæologus

Palinure.*n.m.*, Palinurus

Pallas, *n.f.*, Pallas

Pandore, *n.f.*, Pandora

Panthée, *n.m.*, Pantheus

Paolo (Fra), *n.m.*, Paul of Venice

Papinien (-niin), *n.m.*, Papinian

Paracelse, *n.m.*,Paracelsus

Pâris (-ris), *n.m.*, Paris

Parménide, *n.m.*, Parmenides

Parménion,*n.m.*.Parmenio

les **Parques**, *n.f.*, the Parcæ, the Fates

Patrice, *n.m.*, Patrick

Patrocle,*n.m.*, Patroclus

Paul (pol), *n.m.*, Paul

Pauline, *n.f.*, Paulina

Pausanias (-âs), *n.m.*, Pausanias

Pégase, *n.m.*, Pegasus

Pélage, *n.m.*, Pelagius

Pélée. *n.m.*, Peleus

Pélopidas (-dâs), *n.m.*, Pelopidas

Pénélope, *n.f.*, Penelope

Penthée, *n.m.*, Pentheus

Penthésilée, *n.f.*, Penthesilea

Pépin, *n.m.*, Pepin

Périandre, *n.m.*, Periander

Périclès (-klès), *n.m.*, Pericles

Pérosès (-zès), *or* **Firouz**, *n.m.*, Perozes, Firouz

Perse. *n.m.*, Persius

Persée, *n.m.*, Perseus

Pétrarque, *n.m.*, Petrarch

Pétrone, *n.m.*, Petronius

Pharaon, *n.m.*, Pharaoh

Pharasmane. *n.m.*, Pharasmanes

Pharnabaze, *n.*, Pharnabazus

Pharnace, *n.m.*, Pharnaces

Phébé, *n.f.*, Phœbe

Phébus (-bûs), *n.m.*, Phœbus

Phédon, *n.m.*, Phædon

Phèdre, *n.m.*, Phædrus

Phèdre, *n.f.*, Phædra

Phidias (-diâs), *n.m.*, Phidias

Philadelphe, *n.m.*, Philadelphus

Philippe, *n.m.*, Philip. — *le Bel;* Philip the Fair (of France). — *le Beau;* Philip the Handsome (of Spain—*d'Espagne*)

Philocrate, *n.m.*, Philocrates

Philoctète, *n.m.*, Philoctetes

Philologue (-log), *n.m.*, Philologus

Philomèle, *n.f.*, Philomela

Philomèle, *n.m.*, Philomelus

Phinée, *n.m.*, Phineus

Phocion, *n.m.*, Phocion

Phryné, *n.f.*, Phryne

Phylée,*n.m.*, Phyleus

Pie, *n.m.*, Pius

Pierre, *n.m.*, Peter

Pilate, *n.m.*, Pilate. *Ponce* —; Pontius Pilate

Pindare, *n.m.*, Pindarus

Pisandre, *n.m.*, Pisander

Pisistrate,*n.m.*,Pisistratus

Pison. *n.m.*, Piso

Pitthée, *n.m.*, Pittheus

Placidie, *n.f.*, Placidia

Plancine, *n.f.*, Plancina

Plantagenet(-tajnè),*n.m.*, Plantagenet

Platon, *n.m.*, Plato

Plaute, *n.m.*, Plautus

Plautien, (-siin), *n.m.*, Plautian

Pline, *n.m.*, Pliny. — *l'Ancien;* Pliny the Elder. — *le Jeune;* Pliny the Younger

Plutarque, *n.m.*, Plutarch

Pluton, *n.m.*, Pluto

Podalire, *n.m.*, Podalirius

Politien (-siin), *n.m.*, Politiano

Pollion, *n.m.*, Pollio

Polybe, *n.m.*, Polybius

Polycarpe, *n.m.*, Polycarp

Polyclète, *n.m.*, Polycletus

Polycrate, *n.m.*,Polycrates

Polydore, *n.m.*, Polydorus

Polymnie (-lim-nî), *n.f.*, Polymnia

Polynice, *n.m.*, Polynices

Polyphème,*n.m.*,Polyphemus

Polyxène, *n.f.*. Polyxena

Pomone, *n.f.*, Pomona

Pompée, *n.m.*, Pompéy

Pompéius, *n.m.*, Pompeius

Pompilius (-ûs), *n.m.*, Pompilius

Ponce, *n.m.*, Pontius

Poppée, *n.f.*, Poppæa

Porcie, *n.f.*, Porcia, Portia

Porphyre, *n.m.*, Porphyry

Porus (pórus), n.m., Porus
Praxitèle. n.m., Praxiteles
Priam (-am), n.m., Priamus
Priape. n.m., Priapus
Priscien (pri-siin), n.m.,
Priscian
Priscille. n.f., Priscilla
Priscillien (-liin), n.m..
Priscillian
Procope, n.m., Procopius
Procuste, or Procruste,
n.m., Procrustes
Prométhée, n.m., Prome-
theus
Properce, n.m., Propertius
Proserpine, n.f., Proser-
pina
Protée, n.m., Proteus
Protésilas (-lâs), n.m.,
Protesilaus
Protogène, n.m., Proto-
genes
Prudence.n.m., Prudentius
Psamménit, n.m., Psam-
menitus
Psammétique, n.m., Psam-
metichus
Psyché, n.f., Psyche
Ptolémée, n.m., Ptolemy
Pulchérie (-kéri),n.f., Pul-
cheria
Pupien (-piin), n.m., Pupie-
nus
Putiphar, n.m., Potiphar
Pylade, n.m., Pylades
Pyrame, n.m., Pyramus
Pyrrhon (pir-ron), n.m.,
Pyrrho
Pyrrhus, (pir-rûs), n.m.,
Pyrrhus
Pythagore, n.m., Pytha-
goras
Pythée, n.m., Pytheas

Q

Quichotte (ki-shot), n.m.,
Quixote
Quinte-Curce (kuint-kurs),
n.m., Quintus-Curtius
Quintilien (kuintiliin),
n.m., Quintilian

R

Rachel, n.f., Rachel
Radegonde (radgond),n.f.,
Radegund
Rahab, n.f., Rachab
Randolphe, n.m., Ran-
dolph, Randal
Raoul, n.m., Ralph
Raphaël, n.m., Raphael
Renaud, n.m., Reynold
Rhadamanthe, n.m., Rha-
damanthus
Rhadamiste, n.m., Rhada-
mistus
Rhée, n.f., Rhea
Rhésus, n.m., Rhesus
Richard, n.m., Richard
Robert, n.m., Robert
Roboam (-am), n.m., Reho-
boam
Rodolphe, n.m., Rodolph

Roger, n.m., Roger
Roland, n.m., Rowland, Ro-
lando
Romain, n.m., Romanus
Roméo, n.m., Romeo
Romulus (lûs-),n.m.,Romu-
lus
Rosalie, n.f., Rosaline
Rose, n.f., Rose, Rosa
Rosemonde (rôz-mond),
n.f., Rosamund
Roxane, n.f., Roxana
Ruben (-bin), n.m., Reuben
Rufin, n.m., Rufinus

S

Sabine, n.f., Sabina
Salluste. n.m., Sallust
Salmonée,n.m.,Salmoneus
Salomon, n.m., Solomon
Salvien (-viin), n.m., Sal-
vian
Samson (sanson), n.m.,
Samson, Sampson
Samuel, n.m., Samuel
Sapho, n.f., Sapho, Sappho
Sara, n.f., Sarah
Sardanapale, n.m., Sarda-
napalus
Satan, n.m., Satan
Saturne, n.m., Saturn
Saturnin, n.m., Saturninus
Saül, n.m., Saul
Saumaise, n.m., Salmasius
Scipion, n.m., Scipio. --
l'Africain; Scipio Africanus.
—l'Asiatique; Scipio Asiaticus
Sébastien (-tiin), n.m., Se-
bastien
Sédécias (-âs), n.m., Zede-
kiah
Séjan, n.m., Sejanus
Sélène, n.f., Diana ; Selene
Sem (sè-m), n.f., Shem
Sémélé, n.f., Semele
Sémiramis(-mis),n.f.,Semi-
ramis
Sénèque, n.m., Seneca
Séphora, n.f., Zipporah
Septime, n.m., Septimius
Sergeste, n.m., Sergestus
Sertorius (-ûs), n.m., Ser-
torius
Sésostris (-tris), n.m., Sesos-
tris
Sévère, n.m., Severus
Sforce, n.m., Sforza
Sichée, n.m., Sichaeus
Sigismond, n.m., Sigis-
mund
Silène, n.m., Silenus
Silvain. n.m. V. Sylvain
Silvestre, n.m., Silvester
Siméon, n.m., Simeon
Simon, n.m., Simon
Simonide, n.m., Simonides
Sisyphe, n.m., Sisyphus
Sixte, n.m., Sextus. —
Quint; Sixtus the Fifth
Sminthée, n.m., Smintheus
Socrate, n.m., Socrates
Solon, n.m., Solon
Sophie, n.f., Sophia
Sophocle, n.m., Sophocles
Sophonisbe, n.f., Sophon-
isba
Sophronie, n.f., Sophronia

Sosthène, n.m.. Sosthenes
Stace, n.m., Statius
Stanislas (-lâs), n.m.,
Stanislaus
Stésichore (-kor), n.m.,
Stesichorus
Stilicon, n.m., Stilicho
Stobée, n.m., Stobaeus
Strabon, n.m., Strabo
Suénon, n.m., Sweyn
Suétone, n.m., Suetonius
Sulpice, n.m., Sulpitius
Susanne, n.f., Susan,
Susannah
Sylla (sil-la), n.m., Sylla
Sylvain, n.m., Sylvan.
Sylvanus
Symmaque(sim-mak),n.m..
Symmachus
Syphax (sifaks), n.m.,
Syphax

T

Tacite, n.m., Tacitus
Tamerlan, n.m., Tamer-
lane
Tantale, n.m.. Tantalus
Tarquin, n.m., Tarquinius
Tarquinie, n.f.. Tarquinia
le Tasse, n.m., Tasso
Tatius (ta-sius), n.m.,
Tatius
Taxile, n.m., Taxilus
Télégone, n.m., Telegonus
Télémaque, n.m., Tele-
machus
Télèphe, n.m., Telephus
Térée, n.m., Tereus
Térence, n.m., Terence
Terpandre, n.m., Terpan-
der
Terpsichore (-kor), n.f.,
Terpsichore
Tertullien (-liin), n.m., Ter-
tullian
Thaïs (ta-îs), n.f., Thais
Thalès (-lès), n.m., Thales
Thalie, n.f., Thalia
Thamar, n.f., Tamar
Thémis (-mis), n.f., Themis
Thémistocle, n.m.,Themis-
tocles
Théocrite, n.m., Theocritus
Théodat, n.m., Theodatus
Théodora, n.f., Theodora
Théodore, n.m., Theodorus
Théodoret, n.m., Theodo-
retus
Théodoric, n.m., Theodoric
Théodose, n.m., Theodosius
Théodosie, n.f., Theodo-ia
Théon, n.m., Theon
Théophane, n.m., Theo-
phanes
Théophile, n.m., Theo-
philus
Théophraste, n.m., Theo-
phrastus
Théopompe, n.m., Theo-
pompus
Théramène, n.m., Thera-
menes
Thérèse. n.f.. Theresa
Thersite, n.m.. Thersites
Thésée, n.m., Theseus
Thespis (-pis), n.m., Thespis
Thétis (-tis), n.f., Thetis

Thibaut, *n.m.*, Theobald
Thomas, *n.m.*, Thomas
Thomassine, *n.f.*, Thomassin
Thrasybule, *n.m.*, Thrasybulus
Thrasymède. *n.m.*, Thrasymedes
Thucydide. *n.m.*, Thucydides
Thyeste. *n.m.*, Thyestes
Tibère. *n.m.*, Tiberius
Tibulle. *n.m.*, Tibullus
Tigrane, *n.m.*, Tigranes
Timagène. *n.m.*, Timagenes
Timarque. *n.m.*, Timarchus
Timée. *n.m.*, Timæus
Timocrate, *n.m.*, Timocrates
Timoléon. *n.m.*, Timoleon
Timophane, *n.m.*, Timophanes
Timothée, *n.m.*, Timothy, Timotheus
Tiridate, *n.m.*, Tiridates
Tite, *n.m.*, Titus
Tite-Live, *n.m.*, Livy
Tithon, *n.m.*, Tithonus
le **Titien** (-siin), *n.m.*, Titian
Titus (-tûs), *n.m.*, Titus
Tobie, *n.m.*, Tobias
Trajan, *n m.*, Trajan
Tribonien (-niin), *n.m.*, Tribonian
Triptolème, *n.m.*, Triptolemus
le **Trissin**, *n.m.*, Trissino
Trogue-Pompée (trog-), *n.m.*, Trogus-Pompeius.
Troïlus, *n.m.*, Troilus
Tubalcain, *n.m.*, Tubal-Cain
Tullie (tul-lî), *n.f.*, Tullia
Tullius (tul-liûs), *n.m.*, Tullius
Turenne (turè-n), *n.m.*, Turenne

Tydée, *n.m.*, Tydeus
Tyndare, *n.m.*, Tyndareus
Typhée. *n.m.*, Typhœus
Typhon, *n.m.*, Typhonis
Tyrtée, *n.m.*, Tyrtæus

U

Ulphilas (-lâs), *n.m.*, Ulphilas
Ulpien(-piin),*n.m.*,Ulpian
Ulysse. *n.m.*, Ulysses
Uranie. *n.f.*, Urania
Urbain. *n.m.*, Urban
Urie. *n.m.*, Uriah
Ursule, *n.f.*, Ursula

V

Valentin, *n.m.*, Valentine
Valentine, *n.f.*, Valentine
Valentinien (-niin), *n.m.*, Valentinian
Valère. *n.m.*, Valerius
Valérie, *n.f.*, Valeria
Valérien (-riin), *n.m.*, Valerian
Varron, *n.m.*, Varro
Vatace, *n.m.*, Vataces
Vénus (-nûs), *n.f.*, Venus
Véronique. *n.f.*, Veronica
Vertumne (-tum-n), *n.m.*, Vertumnus
Vespasien(-ziin),*n.m.*,Vespasian
Véturie, *n.f.*, Veturia
Victoire, *n.f.*, Victoria
Victoria, *n.f.*, Victoria
Victorin, *n.m.*, Victorinus
Victorine, *n.f.*, Victorine
Vigilance,*n.m.*, Vigilantius
Vincent, *n.m.*, Vincent
Virgile, *n.m.*, Virgil

Virginie, *n.f.*, Virginia
Viriathe, *n.m.*, Viriathus
Vitruve. *n.m*, Vitruvius
Vivien (-viin), *n.m.*, Vivian
Vulcain, *n m.*, Vulcan

W

Wilhelmine, *n.f.*, Wilhelmina
Winifred, *n.m.*, Winifred

X

Xanthippe,*n.m.*,Xantippus
Xanthippe, *n.f.*, Xantippe
Xénocrate, *n.m.*, Xenocrates
Xénophane, *n.m.*, Xenophanes
Xénophon, *n.m.*, Xenophon
Xerxès (gzèrcès). *n.m.*, Xerxes
Ximénès (gzim-nès), *n.m.*, Ximenes

Z

Zacharie (zakarî), *n.m.*, Zacariah
Zachée, *n.m.*, Zaccheus
Zénobie, *n.f.*, Zenobia
Zénon, *n.m.*, Zeno
Zéphire, *n.m.*, Zephyr, Zephyrus
Zeuxis (-ksîs), *n.m.*, Zeuxis
Zoïle, *n.m.*, Zoilus
Zopyre, *n.m.*, Zopyrus
Zoroastre, *n.m.*, Zoroaster
Zorobabel, *n.m.*, Zerubbabel
Zosime, *n.m.*, Zosimus

VOCABULARY

OF

ANCIENT AND MODERN

GEOGRAPHICAL NAMES.

A

Abdère, *n.f.*, Abdera
l'Abruzze, *n.f.*, Abruzzo
les **Abruzzes**, *n.f.*, the Abruzzi
Abyssinie, *n.f.*, Abyssinia
Acadie, *n.f.*, Acadia
Acarnanie, *n.f.*, Acarnania
Achaïe (aka-ï), *n.f.*, Achaia
l'Achéron, *n.m.*, the Acheron
les **Açores**, *n.f. pl.*, the Azores
Acre, *or* **St-Jean d'Acre**, *n.m.*, Acre
Actium (aksiom), *n.m.*, Actium
Adriatique, *n.f.*, Adriatic
Afghanistan, *n.m.*, Afghanistan
Afrique, *n.f.*, Africa
Agen (ajin), *n.m.*, Agen
Agrigente, *n.m.*, Agrigentum
Aigle (Cap de l'), *n.m.*, Eagle-Point
Ain (in), *n.m.*, Ain
Aisne, *n.f.*, Aisne
Aix-la-Chapelle, *n.f.*, Aix-la-Chapelle, Aachen
Alabama, *n.m.*, Alabama
Albanie, *n.f.*, Albania
Albe, *n.f.*, Alba, Alva
Albion, *n.f.*, Albion
Aléoutiennes (îles), *n.f.pl.*, the Aleutian Islands
Alep, *n.m.*, Aleppo
Alexandrette, *n.f.*, Alexandretta
Alexandrie, *n.f.*, Alexandria
Algarve, *n.f.*, Algarva
Alger, *n.m.*, Algiers
Algérie, *n.f.*, Algeria
Alicante, *n.f.*, Alicant
Allegany (les Monts), *n.m.*, the Alleghany mountains
*Allemagne, *n.f.*, Germany
Alpes, *n.f.pl.*, Alps. *Basses-—;* Lower Alps. *Hautes-—;* Upper Alps
Alphée, *n.m.*, Alpheus
Alsace (alza-s), *n.f.*, Alsace
Amarapoura, *or* **Umerapoura**, *n.m.*, Amarapoora
Amazones (fleuve des), *n.m.*, the Amazon river, Maranon
Ambracie, *n.f.*, Ambracia

Amérique, *n.f.*, America. *États Unis d'—;* United States of America
Amiens (amiïn), *n.m.*, Amiens
Amirauté (îles de l') *n.f.*, Admiralty Islands
Amis (îles des), *n.f.*, Friendly Islands
Anatolie, *n.f.*, Anatolia
Ancône, *n.f.*, Ancona
Andalousie, *n.f.*, Andalusia
Andorre, *n.m.*, Andorra
Andrinople, *n.f.*, Adrianople
Angermanie, *n.f.*, Angermanland
Angers, *n.m.*, Angers, Angiers
Angleterre, *n.f.*, England
*l'Anguille, *n.f.*, Snake's Island
Anse, *n.f.*, *V.* **Hanse**
Anséatiques (Villes), *n.f. V.* **Hanséatiques**
Antigoa, *n.f.*, Antigua
*Antilles, *n.f.*, West Indies
Antioche, *n.f.*, Antioch
Anvers (anvèrs), *n.m.*, Antwerp
Aorne, *n.m.*, Aornus
Aoude, *n.m.*, Oude
Apennins, *n.m.pl.*, Apennines
Appenzell (apinzèl), *n.m.*, Appenzell
Apulie, *n.f.*, Apulia
Aquilée, *n.f.*, Aquilea
Aquitaine, *n.f.*, Aquitaine
Arabie, *n.f.*, Arabia. *—Heureuse;* Arabia Felix. *— Déserte;* Arabia Deserta. *— Pétrée;* Arabia Petræa
Aragon, *n.m.*, Aragon
Arbèles, *n.f.*, Arbela
Arcadie, *n.f.*, Arcadia
Archangel (arkanjèl), *n.m.*, Archangel
Archipel, *n.m.*, Archipelago
Ardennes (ardè-n), *n.f.*, Ardennes
Arginuses, *n.f.pl.*, Arginusæ
Argolide, *n.f.*, Argolis
Argovie, *n.f.*, Aargau
Arkansas (-sâs), *n.m.*, Arkansas

Arménie, *n.f.*, Armenia
Armorique, *n.f.*, Armorica
Asie, *n.m.*, Asia. *— Mineure;* Asia Minor
Assyrie, *n.f.*, Assyria
Astracan, *n.m.*, Astrakhan
Asturies, *n.f.pl.*, Asturias
Athènes, *n.f.*, Athens
Athos (atôs), *n.m.*, Athos
Atlas (-lâs), *n.m.*, Atlas
Attique, *n.f.*, Attica
Aube (ôb), *n.f.*, Aube
Auch (osh), *n.m.*, Auch
Aude (ôd), *n.f.*, Aude
Augsbourg, *n.m.*, Augsburg
Aulide, *n.f.*, Aulis
*Aurigny, *n.m.*, Alderney
Austerlitz (ôsterlits), *n.m.*, Austerlitz
Australasie, *n.f.*, Australasia
Australie, *n.f.*, Australia
Austrasie, *n.f.*, Austrasia
Autriche, *n.f.*, Austria
Auxerre (ô-sèr), *n.m.*, Auxerre
Auxonne (ô-so-n), *n.m.*, Auxonne
Aventin, *n.m.*, Aventine
Averne, *n.m.*, Averno
Azincourt, *n.m.*, Agincourt
Azof, *n.*, Azov. *La mer d'—;* the Sea of Azov

B

Babylone, *n.f.*, Babylon
Babylonie, *n.f.*, Babylonia
Bactres, *n.m.*, Balkh
Bactriane, *n.f.*, Bactriana
Bade, *n.f.*, Baden
Baffin (Baie de), *n.f.*, Baffin's Bay
Bagdad (-dad), *n.m.*, Bagdad
Bahama (îles), *n.f.*, Bahama Islands
Bahia, *n.m.*, Bahia
Bâle, *n.f.*, Basle, Basel
Baltique, *n.f.*, Baltic
Barbade, *n.f.*, Barbadoes
Barbaresques (États), *n.m.*, Barbary States
Barbarie, *n.f.*, Barbary

Barboude, n.f., Barbuda
Barcelone, n.f., Barcelona
Barcelonnette, n.f., Barcelonnette
Basan, n.m., Bashan
Bassora, n., Bassora
Batavia, n.f., Batavia (capital of Java)
Batavie, n.f., Batavia (Holland)
Bavière, n.f., Bavaria
Bayonne (ba-io-n), n.f., Bayonne
Belgique. n.f., Belgium
Béloutchistan, n.m., Beloochistan
Bénarès (-rès), n.m., Benares
Bencoulen (bankoulè-n), n.m., Bencoolen
Bender (bindèr), n.m., Bender
Bénévent, n.m., Benevento
Bengale (bingal), n.m., Bengal
Béotie, n.f., Beotia
Bergamasque, n.m., Bergamasco
Bergame, n.f., Bergamo
Berg-op-zoom, n., Bergen-op-zoom
Berks (Comté de), n., Berkshire
Berlin, n.m., Berlin
Bermudes (îles), n.f., the Bermudas
Bernbourg, n.m., Bernburg
Berne, n.f., Bern
Bersabée, n.f., Beersheba
Bessarabie, n.f., Bessarabia
Béthanie, n.f., Bethany
Bethléem (bètlé-èm), n.f., Bethlehem
Bétique, n.f., Bætica
Bcydjapour, n., Bejapoor
Birman (Empire), n.m., Burmah
Biscaye, n.f., Biscay. La mer de —; the Bay of Biscay. V. Gascogne
Bithynie, n.f., Bithynia
Blenheim (blè-nèm), n.m., Blenheim
Bohème, n.f., Bohemia
*Bologne, n.f., Bologna
Bolonais, n.m., Bolognese
Bone, n.f., Bona
Bordeaux (-dô), n.m., Bordeaux
Borysthène, n.m., Borysthenes
Bosnie, n.f., Bosnia
Bosphore, n.m., Bosphorus
Botnie, n.f., Bothnia
Bougie, n.f., Bugia
Boukharest, Bucharest (-rèst), n.m., Bucharest
Boukharie, n.f., Bukaria
*Boulogne, n., Boulogne
*Bourgogne, n.f., Burgundy
Brabant, n.m., Brabant
Bragance, n.f., Braganza
Brahmapoutra, n.m., Brahmapootra
Brandebourg (brand-bour, n.m., Brandenburg
Brême, n.m., Bremen
Brésil, n.m., Brazil

*Bretagne, n.f., Brittany (France). Grande —; Great Britain
Brindes, n.m., Brindisi
Britanniques (îles), n.f., British Isles
Brousse, n.m., Brousse
Brunswick (bronsvick), n.m., Brunswick
Bruxelles (brussèl), n.f., Brussels
Bucharie (bukari), n.f., V. Boukharie
Bude, n., Buda
Buénos-Ayres (buénozèr), n.m., Buenos Ayres
Bulgarie, n.f., Bulgaria
Byzance, n.f., Byzantium

C

Caboul, n.m. V. Kaboul
Cachemire (kashmir), n.f., Cashmere
Cadix, n.f., Cadiz
la Cadmée, n.f., Cadmea
Caen (kan), n.m., Caen
Cafrerie, n.f., Kaffraria
le Caire, n.m., Cairo
Calabre, n.f., Calabria
Calais (kalè), n.m., Calais. Pas-de- —; Straits of Dover
Calédonie, n.f., Caledonia
Calicut (-kut), n., Calicut
Californie, n.f., California. Basse- —, Vieille- —; Lower or Old California. Haute- —, Nou-velle- —; Upper California
Calvados (-dos), n.m., Calvados
Calvaire, n.m., Calvary
Cambaye (kambè), n., Cambay
Camboge, n.f., Camboja
*Campagne de Rome, n.f., Campagna Romana
Campanie, n.f., Campania
Campêche, n.f., Campeche, Campeachy
Canada, n.m., Canada. Bas- —; Lower Canada. Haut- —; Upper Canada
Canarie (la Grande), n.f., Grand Canary
Candie (île de), n.f., Candia
Canée, n.f., Canea
Cannes, n.f., Cannæ (in Italy —en Italie). Cannes (France)
Cantorbéry, n.m., Canterbury
Cap, n.m., Cape. —de Bonne Espérance; Cape of Good Hope
Capharnaüm (-na-om), n.m., Capernaum
Capoue, n.f., Capua
Cappadoce, n.f., Cappadocia
Caracas (-câs), n., Caracas
Caraïbes (îles), n.f., Leeward and Windward Islands
Caramanie, n.f., Kerman (Persia)
Carélia, n.f., Carelia
Carie, n.f., Caria
Carinthie, n.f., Carinthia
Carmanie, n.f., Carmania
Carniole, n.f., Carniola
Caroline, n.f., Carolina

Carpathes (Monts), n.m., Carpathian Mountains
Carthage, n.f., Carthage
Carthagène, n.f., Carthagena
Caspienne (Mer), n.f., Caspian Sea
Castalie, n.f., Castalia
*Castille, n.f., Castile
*Catalogne, n.f., Catalonia
Catane, n.f., Catana
Caucase, n.m., Caucasus
Cayenne (ka-iè-n), n.f., Cayenne
Célésyrie (sélé-si-rî), n.f., Coelesyria
Céphalonie, n.f., Cephalonia
*Cerdagne, n.f., Cerdagna
Césarée, n.f., Cæsarea
Cévennes (sé-vè-n), n.f., Cevennes
Ceylan, n.m., Ceylon
Chalcédoine (kal-), n.f., Chalcedon, Chalcedonia
Chalcis (kalsis), n., Chalcis
Chaldée (kal-), n.f., Chaldea
Chambéry, n.m., Chambery
*Champagne, n.f., Champagne
Chanaan (kana-an), n.m., Canaan
Chaonie (ka-)- n.f., Chaonia
Charlottenburg (charlotinboor), n.m., Charlottenburg
Charybde (karibd), n.m., Charybdis
Cher (shèr), n.m., Cher
Cherbourg, n.m., Cherbourg
Chéronée (ké-), n., Chæronea
Chersonèse (kèr-), n.f., Chersonese
Chili, n.m., Chili
Chine, n.f., China
Chios (kiós), n.f., Chios
Chypre, n.f., Cyprus
Cilicie, n.f., Cilicia
Circassie, n.f., Circassia
Cithéron, n.m., Cithæron
Coblentz (koblâns), n., Coblentz
Cobourg, n.m., Coburg
Cochinchine, n.f., Cochin China
Cocyte, n.m., Cocytus
Coimbre, n.f., Coimbra
Colchide (-kid), n.f., Colchis
*Cologne, n.f., Cologne
Colombie, n.f., Columbia
Colonnes d'Hercule, n.f., Hercules' Pillars
Compostelle, n.f., Compostella
Connecticut (-cut), n.m., Connecticut
Constantine, n.f., Constantine
Constantinople, n.f., Constantinople
Copenhague (kopè-nag), n.f., Copenhagen
Corcyre, n.f., Coreyra
*Cordillères, n.f.pl., Cordilleras
Cordoue, n.f., Cordova

Corée, n.f., Corea

Corfou. n.f., Corfu

Corinthe. n.f., Corinth

*Cornouailles. n.m.. Cornwall. La pointe de — ; Land's End

la***Corogne**. n.f.. Corunna

Coronée, n.. Coronea

Corse, n.f., Corsica

Cortone. n.f , Cortona

Côte d'Or, n.f., Côte d'or (France)

Côte d'Or. n.f. Gold Coast (in Africa—en Afrique)

Courlande, n.f., Courland

Cracovie. n.f., Cracow

Crémone. n.f., Cremona

Crète, n.f., Crete

Crimée, n.f., Crimea

Croatie, n.f., Croatia

Cuba. n.f.. Cuba

Cume. n.f.. Cuma

Cumes, n.f., Cumæ

Curaçao, n.f.. Curacoa

Cynthe. n.m.. Cynthus

Cynurie, n.f., Cynuria

Cyrénaïque, n.f., Cyrenaica

Cythère, n.f., Cythera

D

Dacie, n.f., Dacia

Dalécarlie, n.f., Dalecarlia

Dalmatie, n.f.. Dalmatia

Damas (-mâs), n.f., Damascus

Damiette, n.f.. Damietta

Danemark (da-n-mark), n.m.. Denmark

Dantzick, n.m.. Danzig

Danube, n.m.. Danube

Dardanelles, n.f., Dardanelles

Dardanie. n.f.. Dardania

Darien (dariin), n.m., Darien

Daunie, n.f., Daunia

Dauphiné, n.m.. Dauphiny

Davis (le Détroit de), n.m , Davis' Strait

Décan, n.m., Deccan

Décélie. n.f., Decelium

Dekhan, n.m.. V. Décan

Delaware. n.f.. Delaware

Delphes, n.f., Delphi

Dents (Côte des), n.f., Ivory Coast

Devon (Comté de), n.m., Devonshire

Diémen (diémè-n) (Terre de Van), n.f.. Van Diemen's Land

Djaguernat, n., Juggernauth

Djihoun. n.m..Jihoon,Oxus, Amoo

Dniéper, n.m.. Dnieper

Dniester. n.m.. Dniester

la **Dominique**, n.f., Dominica

*Dordogne, n.f.. Dordogne

Doride, n.f., Doris.

Dorvlée n.f., Dorylæum

Doubs (doo), n.m., Doubs

Douvres. n.m.. Dover

Dresde. n.f., Dresden

Dunkerque, n.m., Dunkirk

E

Èbre, n.m., Ebro

Ecbatane, n.f., Ecbatana

l'**Écluse**. n.f., Sluys

Écosse. n.f., Scotland. Nouvelle — ; Nova Scotia

Éden (édè-n), n.m., Eden

Édesse, n.f., Edessa

Édimbourg, n.m. or f., Edinburgh

Égine, n.f.. Ægina

Égypte, n.f.. Egypt. Basse- — ; Lower Egypt. Haute- — ; Upper Egypt. Moyenne- — ; Middle Egypt

Élatée, n.f., Elatea

Elbe (île d'), n.f., Island of Elba

Elbe, n.m., Elbe

Éleusis (-zîs), n.f., Eleusis

Élide, n.f., Elis (country—contrée)

Élis (élîs), n.f , Elis (capital —ville)

Elseneur, n.f., Elsinore

Émathie, n.f., Æmathia

Émèse, n.f., Emesa

Emmaüs (èm-ma-ûs), n.m., Emmaus

Éolie, n.f., Eolia

Éphèse, n.f., Ephesus

Épices (îles aux), n.f., Spice Islands

Épidamne (-dam-n), n.m., Epidamnus, Dyrrachium

Épidaure, n.f., Epidaurus

Épire, n.f., Epirus

l'**Équateur** (République de), n.f.. Ecuador

Érétrie, n.f., Eretria

Érié (le Lac), n.m., Lake Erie

Escaut, n.m., Scheldt

Esclave (Lac de l'), n.m , Slave Lake

Esclaves (Côte des), n.f., Slave Coast

Esclavonie, n.f , Sclavonia

*Espagne. n.f., Spain

Estramadure, n.f., Estramadura

États-Unis, n.m., United States

Éthiopie. n.f.. Ethiopia

Etna, n.m., Étna

Étolie. n.f., Etolia

Étrurie, n.f., Etruria

Eubée, n.f., Eubœa

Euphrate. n.m., Euphrates

Euripe, n.m., Euripus

Europe, n.f., Europe

F

Fer (fèr), (île de), n.f., Ferro

Fernambouc, n.m., V. Pernambouc

Féroé (îles), n.f., Fero Islands

Ferrare, n.f., Ferrara

Fez (fèz), n.f., Fez

Figuières (fighièr), n f., Figueras

Finistère (Cap), n.m.. Land's End (in England—en Angleterre); Cape Finisterra (in Spain—en Espagne)

Finistère (Département du), n.m.. Department of Finistère (France)

Finlande, n.f.. Finland

Fionie, n.f., Fuhnen, Funen, Fyen

Flandre, n.f..Flanders

Flessingue (flè-sing), n.m., Flushing

Florence. n.f..Florence

Floride. n.f., Florida

Fontarabie, n.f., Fontarabia

Forêt-Noire, n.f., Black Forest

Formose, n.f., Formosa

Forth (Golfe du), n.m., Frith of Forth

France, n.f., France. L'Ile de — ; The Isle of France, Mauritius

Francfort, n.m., Frankfort

Franconie, n.f., Franconia

Fribourg, n.m., Fribourg (Switz.)

Frioul. n.m.. Friuli

Frise, n.f., Friesland

G

Gabaon, n.m., Gibeon

Gadès, n., Gades (Cadiz)

Gaëte, n.f., Gaeta

Galaad, n.m., Gilead

Galatie, n.f., Galatia

Galgala, n.m., Gilgal

Galice, n.f., Galicia (in Spain—en Espagne).

Galicie, n.f., Galicia (in Austria—en Autriche)

Galilée, n.f., Galilæa

Galles (Pays de), n.m.. Wales. La Nouvelle - — ; New South Wales

Gambie, n.f., Gambia

Gand. n.m., Ghent

Gange, n.m., Ganges

*Gascogne, n.f., Gascony. Le Golfe de —; the Bay of Biscay

Gaule, n.f., Gaul

Géants (Chaussée des), n.f., Giant's Causeway

Gédrosie, n.f., Mekran

Gènes, n.f., Genoa

Genève, n.f.. Geneva

Géorgie, n.f., Georgia

Germanie. n.f., Germany (ancient—ancienne)

Gessen (jècè-n), n.. Goshen

Ghattes, n.f.pl., Ghauts

Girone, n.f., Gerona

Glasgow. n.m., Glasgow

Gnesne, n f., Gnesen

Gœttingue (gheutin-g), n.m., Gottingen

Golconde, n.f., Golconda

Gothembourg (gotanbour), n.m., Gottenburg

Gothie. n.f., Gothland

Gottingue, n.m. V.
Gœttingue

Goudelour (goodloor),n.m. V. **Kaddalor**

Goudjerate. *n.m.* *V.* **Guzzerat**

Graines (Côte des), *n.f.,* Grain Coast

Grampians (Monts), *n.m.,* Grampian Mountains

Granique, *n.m.,* Granicus

Grèce, *n.f.,* Greece

Grenade, *n.f.,* Granada

Grœnland (gro-inlan), *n.m.* Greenland

Groningue (-ning), **Grœningen,** *n.m.,* Groningen

Guadalquivir (gooadal-kivir), *n.m.,* Guadalquivir

Guadeloupe (gooadloop), *n.f.,* Guadaloupe

Guadiana (gooa-), *n.f.,* Guadiana

Guatémala (gooa-), *n.m.,* Guatemala

Gueldre (ghèldr), *n.f.,* Guelders

Guernesey. *f.m.,* Guernsey

Guyane (ghia-n), *n.f.,* Guiana.

Guinée. *n.f.,* Guinea

Guyenne, *n.f.,* Guienne

Guzzerat, *n.m.,* Guzerat

H

†**Haarlem,** *n.m.* *V.* **Harlem**

†**Habsbourg,** *n.m.,* Habsburg

†**Hainaut,** *n.m.,* Hainault

Haïti, *n.f.,* Hayti

Halicarnasse, *n.f.,* Halicarnassus

†**Hambourg,** *m.,* Hamburg

†**Hanovre,** *n.m.,* Hanover

†**Hanse,** *n.f.,* Hanse-Towns

†**Hanséatiques** (Villes), *n.f.,* Hanse-Towns

†**Harburg,** *n.m.,* Harburg

†**Harlem** (-lè-m), *n.m.,* Harlem, Haarlem

la†**Havane,** *n.f.,* Havanna

le†**Havre,** *n.m.,* Havre

Hawaii, *n.m.,* Hawaii, Owhyhee

la†**Haye** (hè), *n.f.,* the Hague

les **Hébrides,** *n.f.,* Hebrides

Hélicon. *n.m.,* Helicon

Héliopolis (-lis), *n.f.,* Heliopolis

Hellespont, *n.m.,* Hellespont

Helvétie, *n.f.,* Helvetia

Héraclée, *n.f.,* Heraclea

Hérault (êrô),*n.m.,* Herault

Herculanum (-nom), *n.m.,* Herculaneum

Hespérie, *n.f.,* Hesperia

Hibernie. *n.f.,* Hibernia

Hindoustan, *n.m.,* Hindostan

†**Hollande** *n.f.,* Holland

†**Hombourg,** *r.m.,* Hombourg

†**Hoagrie.** *n.f.,* Hungary

Huningue (unin-g), *n.m.,* Huningen

Hydaspe, *n.m.,* Hydaspes (Jeloum)

Hydraote, *n.m.,* Hydraotes (Ravee)

Hyphase. *n.m.,* Hyphasis (Bevas. Sutlej ?)

Hyrcanie. *n.f.,* Hyrcania

I

Ibérie, *n.f.,* Iberia

Icarie, *n.f.,* Icaria

Icarienne (Mer), *n.f.,* Icarian Sea

Idalie. *n.f.,* Idalia

Idumée, *n.f.,* Idumea

Iéna. *n.m.,* Jena

Ile, *n.f.,* Island. —s *du Vent;* Windward Islands. —s *sous le Vent;* Leeward Islands

Ile-de-France, *n.f.,* Isle of France

Ilion, *n.m.,* Ilium (Troy)

Illinois (il-linoâ), *n.m.,* Illinois

Illyrie (il-lirî), *n.f.,* Illyria

Inde, *n.f.,* India. —s *Occidentales;* West Indies. —s *Orientales;* East Indies

Indiana, *n.m.,* Indiana

Indostan, *n.m.* *V.* **Hindoustan**

Ingrie, *n.f.,* Ingria

Ionie, *n.f.,* Ionia

Ioniennes (îles), *n.f.pl.,* the Ionian Isles

Irlande, *n.f.,* Ireland

Isaurie, *n.f.,* Isauria

Islande, *n.f.,* Iceland

Istrie, *n.f.,* Istria

Italie. *n.f.,* Italy

Ithaque, *n.f.,* Ithaca

Ivoire (Côte d'), *n.f.,* Ivory Coast

Ivrée, *n.f.,* Ivrea

J

Jagernaut, *n.m.* *V.* **Djaguernat**

Jamaïque, *n.f.,* Jamaica

Japon, *n.m.,* Japan

Jéricho (jériko),*n.f.,* Jericho

Jersey (jerzè), *n.f.,* Jersey

Jérusalem (-lè-m), *n.f.,* Jerusalem

Jourdain, *n.m.,* Jordan

Judée, *n.f.,* Judæa

K

Kaboul, *n.m.,* Cabool, Cabul

Kachgar, *n.m.,* Cashgar

Kaddalor. *n.m.,* Cuddalore

Kamtchatka (kamtchatka), *n.m.,* Kamtschatka

Karnatic. *n.m.,* Carnatic

Kécho, *n..* Kachao

Kent (kànt), *n.m.,* Kent

Kouriles. *n.f.pl.,* Kuriles

Krapacks (Monts), *n.m.,* Carpathian Mountains

L

Lacédémone, *n.f.,* Lacedæmon

Lacknau, *n.m.* *V.* **Luknow**

Laconie. *n.f.,* Laconia

Lahore. *n.m.,* Lahore

Lamia. *n.f.,* Lamia

Lampsaque, *n.f.,* Lampsacus

Lancastre. *n.m.,* Lancaster

Laodicée, *n.f.,* Laodicea

Laon (lan), *n.m.,* Laon

Laponie, *n.f.,* Lapland

Laquedives (lakdiv) (îles) *n.f.,* Laccadives, Laccadive Islands

Larisse, *n.f.,* Larissa

Larrons (îles des), *or* **Mariannes** (îles), *n.f.,* Ladrone Islands, Mariana Islands

Latium (-ci- o-m), *n.m.,* Latium

Leinster (linstèr), *n.m.,* Leinster

Leipsick (lèpsik), *n.m.,* Leipsic, Leipzig

Lemnos (lèm-nôs), *n.f.,* Lemnos

Lépante, *n.f.,* Lepanto

Lerme, *n.f.,* Lerma

Lerne, *n.m.,* Lerna

Leuctres, *n.f.,* Leuctra

Levant, *n.m.,* Levant

Leyde, *n.f.,* Leyden

Liban, *n.m.,* Lebanon

Liburnie, *n.f.,* Liburnia

Libye, *n.f.,* Libya

Liège, *n.m.,* Liège

Ligurie, *n.f.,* Liguria

Lille, *n.f.,* Lille

Limbourg, *n.m.,* Limbourg (Holl.); Limbourg (Belg.)

Limousin, *n.m.,* Limousin

Lisbonne, *n.f.,* Lisbon

Lithuanie, *n.f.,* Lithuania

Livadie, *n.f.,* Livadia

Livonie, *n.f.,* Livonia

Livourne, *n.m.,* Leghorn

Locride, *n.f.,* Locris

Lombardie, *n.f.,* Lombardy

Londres, *n.m.,* London

Lorette, *n.f.,* Loretto

Lorraine, *n.f.,* Lorraine

Louisbourg, *n.m.,* Louisburg

Louisiane, *n.f.,* Louisiana

Lucanie, *n.f.,* Lucania

Lucayes (lukê),*n.f.,* Bahama Islands

Luçon, *n.f.,* Luzon

Lucques, *n.f.,* Lucca

Luknow, *n.m.,* Lucknow

Lunebourg, *n.m.,* Luneburg

Lusace. *n.f.,* Lusatia

Lusitanie. *n.f.,* Lusitania

Lutzen (-zè-n), *n.m.,* Lutzen

Luxembourg, *n.m.,* Luxembourg. Luxembourg

Lycaonie, *n.f.,* Lycaonia

Lycie, *n.f.,* Lycia

Lydie, *n.f.,* Lydia

Lyon, *n.m.,* Lyons

Lysimachie, *n.f.,* Lysimachia

M

Macédoine. *n.f.,* Macedonia

Madère. *n.f.,* Madeira

Madras (-dràs),*n.m.,* Madras

Madrid (-dri), Madrid

Maëstricht (maèstrik),*n.m.,* Maastricht

Magdebourg, *n.m.,* Magdeburg

Magellan (Détroit de), *n.m.,* Straits of Magellan

Mahrattes, *n.m.,* Mahrattas

Maine, n.m., Maine
Maissour. n.m., Mysore
Majorque, n.f., Majorca
Malines, n.f., Mechlin
Malouines (îles), n.f., Falkland Islands
Malte, n.f., Malta
la Manche, n.f., the British Channel
*Manille, n.f., Manila
Mantinée, n.f., Mantinea
Mantoue. n.f., Mantua
Maragnon, n.m., Maranon, Amazon
Marengo (marengo), n.m., Marengo
la Marguerite (-ghèrit) n.f., Margarita
Mariannes (îles), n.f., Mariana Islands. V. Larrons
Marienbourg (mariin-booi), n.f., Marienburg
Marmara (la Mer de), n.f., the Sea of Marmora
Maroc. n.m., Morocco
Marquises (îles), n.f.pl., Marquesas
*Marseille, n.f., Marseilles
la Martinique, n.f., Martinique
Massachussets, n.m., Massachusetts
Maurice (l'île), n.f., Mauritius. V. France
Mauritanie n.f., Mauritania
Mayence (ma-ian-s), n.f., Mentz, Maintz
Mayenne (ma-iè-n), n.f., the Mayenne
Mecklembourg (méklin-boor), n.m., Mecklenburg
la Mecque, n.f., Mecca
Médine. n.f., Medina
Méditerranée, n.f., Mediterranean
Mégare, n.f., Megara
Mégaride, n.f., Megaris
Mélinde, n.f., Melinda
Memphis, n.f., Memphis
Méonie, n.f., Mæonia
Mésie. n.f., Mœsia
Mésopotamie, n.f., Meso-potamia
Messénie, n.f., Messenia
Messine, n.f., Messina. Phare de —; Straits of Messina
Metz (mès), n.m., Metz
Meuse, n.f., the Meuse, the Maas
Mexico, n.m., Mexico (town —ville)
Mexique, n.m., Mexico (country—contrée)
Michigan (Lac), n.m., Lake Michigan
Middelbourg, n.m., Middleburg
Milan, n.m., Milan
Milanais, n.m., Milanese
Milet, n.m., Miletus
Mingrélie, n.f., Mingrelia
Minorque, n.f., Minorca
Minturnes, n.f., Minturnæ
Mississippi, n.m., Mississippi
Missouri, n.m., Missouri
Modène, n.f., Modena
Mœsie (mézl), n.f. V.Mésie
Mogador, n.m., Mogador

Moka, n.f., Mocha, Mokha
Moldavie. n.f., Moldavia
Moluques, n.f.pl., Moluccas
Mongolie, n.f., Mongolia
Moravie, n.f., Moravia
Morée, n.f., Morea
Morlaquie, n.f., Morlachia
Moscou, n.m., Moscow
Moscovie, n.f., Muscovy, Russia
Moskova, or Moskva, n.f., Moskva
Mossoul. n.f., Mosul
Mozambique, n.m., Mozam-bique
Munich (munik), n.m., Munich
Munster (monstèr), n.m., Munster
Munychie, n.f., Munychia
Murcie, n.f., Murcia
Mycènes, n.f., Mycenæ
Mysie, n.f., Mysia

N

Nankin, n.m., Nankin
Nantes, n.f., Nantes
Naples, n.f., Naples
Nassau, n.m., Nassau
Naupacte, n., Naupactus
Nauplie, n.f., Nauplia
Navarin. n.m., Navarino
Navigateurs (Archipel des), n.m., Navigators' Islands
Naxos (naksôs), n.f., Naxos
Néerlande, n.f., Nether-lands
Négrepont, n.f., Negropont
Népal, or Népaul, n.m., Nepaul
Neustrie, n.f., Neustria
New-York (neu-iork), n.m., New-York
Nicomédie, n.f., Nicomedia
Nicosie, n.f., Nicosia
Niémen (niémè-n), n.m., Niemen
Niger (nijèr), n.m., Niger
Nigritie, n.f., Nigritia, Central Africa
Nil, n.m., Nile
Nimègue (nimè-g), n.m., Nimeguen
Nimes, n.f., Nismes
Ninive, n.f., Niniveh
*Noailles, n.m., Noailles
Norique, n.f., Noricum
Normandie, n.f., Nor-mandy
Norvège, or Norwège, n.f., Norway
Nouvelle-Zemble, n.f., Nova Zembla
Nubie, n.f., Nubia
Numance, n.f., Numantia
Numidie, n.f., Numidia
Nuremberg. n.m., Nurem-berg

O

Océan, n.m., Ocean
Océanie, n.f., Oceania
Oder (odèr). n.m., Oder
Œchalie (ékali), n.f., Œchalia
Ohio, n.m., Ohio

Oldenbourg (oldinboor), n.m., Oldenburg
Olympe, n.m., Olympus
Olympie, n.f., Olympia
Olynthe, n.f., Olynthus
St-Omer (sintomèr), n.m., St. Omer
Oporto, n.m., Oporto
Orcades, n.f.pl., Orkneys
Orchomène (-ko-),n.m., Or-chomenus
Orégon, n.m., Oregon
Orenbourg(orinbour),n.m., Orenburg
Orénoque, n.m., Orinoco
Orléans. n.m. or f., Orleans
Osnabruck, n.m., Osna-bruck
Ostende, n.m., Ostend
Ostie, n.f., Ostia
Ostrasie, n.f. V. Aus-trasie
Otahiti, n.f. V. Taïti
Otrante, n.m., Otranto
Oudjein, n., Oojein
Ouessant, n.m., Ushant
Oural, n.m., Ural

P

Pactole, n.m., Pactolus
Padoue, n.f., Padua
Palatinat, n.m., Palatinate
Palerme, n.f., Palermo
Palestine, n.f., Palestrina
Palmyre, n.f., Palmyra
Palos (païôs), n.m., Palos
Pampelune (panbiu-n),n.f., Pampeluna
Pamphylie, n.f., Pamphylia
Panama, n.f., Panama
Pannonie, n.f., Pannonia
Paphlagonie, n.f., Pa-phlagonia
Papouasie, n.f., Papua
Paraguay (-ghè), n.m., Paraguay
Paris (pari), n.m., Paris
Parme, n.f., Parma
Parnasse, n.m., Parnassus
Paros (-rôs), n.f., Paros
Parthie, n.f., Parthia
Patagonie, n.f., Patagonia
Pathmos (-môs), n.f., Pat-mos
Patras (patrâs),n.m., Patras
Pausilippe, n.m., Pau-silippo
Pavie, n.f., Pavia
Pays-bas, n.m., Netherlands
Pégou, n.m., Pegu
Pékin, n.m., Pekin, Peking
Péloponèse, n.f., Pelopon-nesus
Pensylvanie (pin-), n.f., Pennsylvania
Penthièvre (pin-), n., Pen-thievre
Péonie, n.f., Pæonia
Pergame, n.f., Pergamos
Périnthe, n., Perinthus
Permesse, n.m., Permessus
Pernambouc, n.m., Per-nambuco
Pérou, n.m., Peru
Pérouse, n.f., Perugia
Perse. n.f., Persia
Perside, n.f., Persis, Fars, Farsistar

Persique (Golfe), *n.m.*, Persian Gulf
St. Pétersbourg, *n.m.*, St. Petersburg
Pharos (farôs), *n.f.*, Pharos
Pharsale, *n.f.*, Pharsalia
Phase, *n.m.*, Phasis
Phénicie, *n.f.*, Phœnicia
Phères, *n.m.*, Pheræ
Phigalie, *n.*, Phigalea
Philadelphie, *n.f.*, Philadelphia
Philippes, *n.f.*, Philippi
Philippines (îles), *n.f.*, Philippine Islands
Philipsbourg, *n.m.*, Philipsburg
Phocée, *n.f.*, Phocæa
Phocide, *n.f.*, Phocis
Phrygie, *n.f.*, Phrygia
Phthie (ftî), *n.f.*, Phthia
Phthiotide (ftiotid), *n.f.*, Phthiotis
Picardie, *n.f.*, Picardy
Piémont, *n.m.*, Piedmont
Piérie, *n.f.*, Pieria
Pinde, *n.m.*, Pindus
Pirée, *n.f.*, Piræus
Pise, *n.f.*, Pisa
Pisidie, *n.f.*, Pisidia
Plaisance, *n.f.*, Placencia
Platée, *n.f.*, Platææ
Podolie, *n.f.*, Podolia
Poitiers (poatié), *n.m.*, Poitiers
Polésie, *n.f.*, Polesia
Pologne. *n.f.*, Poland
Polynésie *n.f.*, Polynesia
Poméranie, *n.f.*, Pomerania
Pomérellie, *n.f.*, Minor Pomerania
Pompéïes (ponpèis), *n.f.*, Pompeii
Pondichéry, *n.m.*, Pondicherry
Pont, *n.m.*, Pontus
Pont-Euxin. *n.m.*, Euxine
Pontins (Marais), *n.m.*, Pontine Marshes
Porto, *n.m.*, Porto, Oporto
Potsdam (-dam), *n.m.*, Potsdam
Poury, *n.m.* V. Djaguernat
Préneste, *n.f.*, Præneste
Presbourg, *n.f.*, Presburg
Propontide,*n.f.*,Propontis
Prusse, *n.f.*, Prussia
Ptolémais (-ma-is), *n.f.*, Ptolemais
Pyrénées, *n.f.pl.*, Pyrenees. *Basses— —;* Lower Pyrenees. *Hautes— —;* Upper Pyrenees

Q

Québec (kébèk), *n.m.*, Quebec
Quiberon (kibron), *n.m.*, Quiberon
Quimper (kinpèr), *n.m*, Quimper

R

Raguse, *n.f.*, Raguse
Rangoun (-goo-n), *n.m.*, Rangoon

Ratisbonne, *n.f.*, Ratisbon
Ravenne, *n.f.*, Ravenna
Reims, *or* **Rheims** (-rins), *n.m.*, Rheims
Rhétie, *n.f.*, Rhætia
Rhin, *n.m.*, Rhine
Rhodes (rod), *n.f.*, Rhodes
Rhône, *n.m.*. Rhone
Riphées (Monts), *n.m.*, Rhiphæi, Rhipæi Mountains
la **Rochelle**, *n.f.*, Rochelle
Rocheux (Monts), *n.m.*, Rocky Mountains
*****Romagne**, *n.f.*, Romagna
Rome, *n.f.*, Rome
Rosette, *n.f.*, Rosetta
Rotterdam (roterdam), *n.m.*, Rotterdam
Rouen (roo-ân),*n.m.*, Rouen
Roumanie,*n.f.*, Roumania
Roumélie, *n.f.*, Roumelia
Roveredo, *n.m.*, Roveredo
Roxburgh,*n.m.*, Roxburgh
Rubicon, *n.m.*, Rubicon
Russie, *n.f.*, Russia. *La — d'Asie ;* Russia in Asia. *La— d'Europe;* Russia in Europe.

S

Saba, *n.f.*, Saba; Sheba
Sabine, *n.f.*, Sabina
Sagonte, *n.f.*, Saguntum
Sahara, *n.m.*, Sahara
Saigon, *n.m.*, Saigon
Saint-Domingue (île de), *n.f.*, San Domingo
Salamanque, *n.f.*, Salamanca
Salamine, *n.f.*, Salamina, Salamis
Salapie, *n.f.*, Salapia
Salerne, *n.f.*, Salerno
Salone, *n.f.*, Salona
Salonique, *n.f.*, Salonica
Saltburn, *n.m.*, Saltburn
Salzbourg, *n.m.*, Salzburg
Samara, *n.f.*, Samara
Samarie, *n.f.*, Samaria
Samogitie, *n.f.*, Samogitia
Samos (-môs), *n.f.*, Samos
Samosate, *n.f.*, Samosata
Samothrace, *n.f.*, Samothracia
Sana, *n.m.*, Sana
Santander (-dèr), *n.m.*, Santander
Saône (sô-n), *n.f.*, Saone
Saragosse, *n.f.*, Saragossa
*****Sardaigne**, *n.f.*, Sardinia
Sardes,*n.f.*, Sardis
Sarepta, *n.f.*, Sarepta
Sarmatie, *n.f.*, Sarmatia
Sarthe, *n.f.*, Sarthe
Saumur,*n.f.*, Saumur
Savoie, *n.f.*, Savoy
Saxe, *n.f.*, Saxony
Scamandro, *n.m.*,Scamander
Scandinavie, *n.f.*, Scandinavia
Scarborough, *n.m.*, Scarborough
Schaffhouse (shafoo-z), *n.f.*, Schaffhausen
Schwarzbourg (shvarzboor), *n.m.*, Schwarzburg
Sclavonie, *or* **Slavonie**, *n.f.*, Sclavonia

Scutari, *n.m.*, Scutari
Scylla, *n.f.*, Scylla
Scythie, *n.f.*, Scythia
Sébastopol, *or* **Sévastopol**, *n.m.*, Sebastopol
Ségovie, *n.f.*, Segovia
Seine (sè-n), *n.f.*, Seine
Séleucide, *n.f.*, Seleucis
Séleucie, *n.f.*, Seleucia
Sellasie, *n.f.*, Sellasia
Selymbrie, *n.f.*, Selymbria
Sénégal, *n.m.*, Senegal
Sénégambie, *n.f.*, Senegambia
Sens (sâns), *n.m.*, Sens
Servie, *n.f.*, Servia
Severn, *n.f.*, Severn
Séville, *n.f.*, Sevilla
Siam (si-am), *n.m.*, Siam
Sibérie, *n.f.*, Siberia
Sichem (sishè-m), *n.f.*, Shechem
Sicile, *n.f.*, Sicily
Sicyone, *n.f.*, Sicyon
Sienne (siè-n). *n.f.*, Sienna
Silésie, *n.f.*, Silesia
Siloé, *n.f.*, Siloah
Siloh, *n.m.*, Shiloh
Sinaï, *n.m.*, Sinai
Sindhy, *n.f.*, Sinde
Singapour, *m.*, Singapore
Smyrne, *n.f.*, Smyrna
Société (îles de la), *n.f.*, Society Islands
Sodome, *n.f.*, Sodom
Sogdiane, *n.f.*, Sogdiana
Solfatare, *n.f.*, Solfatara
Sonde (Archipel de la), *n.m.*, Sunda Isles
Sorlingues (-lin-g) (îles), *n.f.*, Scilly Isles
Souabe, *n.f.*, Suabia
Sparte, *n.f.*, Sparta
Spire, *n.m.*, Speyer, Spires
Spitzberg, *n.m.*, Spitzbergen
Stagire, *n.f.*, Stagira
Steinkerque, *or* **Steenkerke**, *n.m.*, Steenkerque
Strasbourg, *n.m.*, Strasburg, Strasbourg
Stuttgard,*n.m.*, Stuttgart
Styrie,*n.f.*, Styria
Suède, *n.f.*, Sweden
Suisse, *n..f*, Switzerland
Sund (sond), *n.m.*, Sound
Surate, *n.f.*, Surat
Suse, *n.f.*, Susa
Susiane, *n.f.*, Susiana
Sybaris (-ris), *n.f.*, Sybaris
Syracuse, *n..f*, Syracusæ
Syrie, *n.f.*, Syria

T

Tabago, *n.f.*, Tobago
Tage, *n.m.*, Tagus
Taïti, *n.f.*, Otaheite, Tahiti
Tamise, *n.f.*, Thames
Tanger, *n.m.*, Tangier
Tarente, *n.f.*, Taranto
Tarragone, *n.f.*,Tarragona
Tarse, *n.f.*, Tarsus
Tartarie, *n.f.*, Tartary
Tauride, *n.f.*, Taurida
Tauris (tôris), *n.f.*, Tabreez, Tabriz
Taurus (tôrûs),*n.m.*, Taurus
Taxila, *n.f.*, Taxila

Tégée, n.f., Tegea
Ténare, n.m., Tænarus
Ténériffe, n.f., Teneriffe
Tennessée, n.m., Tennessee
Terceire, n.f., Terceira
Terracine, n.f., Terracina
Terre de Feu, n.f., Terra del Fuego
Terre de Van Diémen, n.f., Van Diemen's Land, Tasmania
Terre-Ferme, n.f., Terra-Firma
Terre-Neuve, n.f., Newfoundland
Terre-Sainte, n.f., Holy Land
Tessin, n.m., Tessin; Ticino
Texas (tèksàs), n.m., Texas
Thébaïde, n.f., Thebaid
Thèbes, n.f., Thebes
Thermopyles, n.m., Thermopylæ
Thespies, n.m., Thespiæ
Thessalie, n.f., Thessaly
Thessalonique, n.f., Thessalonica
Thibet, n.m., Thibet
Thurgovie, n.f., Thurgau
Thuringe, n.f., Thuringia
Tibet, n.m. V. Thibet
Tibre, n.m., Tiber
Tigre, n.m., Tigris
Tilsitt (tilsit), n.m., Tilsit
Tolède, n.f., Toledo
Tonkin, Tonquin, or Tong King n.m., Tonquin
Tortose n.f., Tortosa
Toscane, n.f., Tuscany
Transylvanie, n.f., Transylvania
Travnik, n.m., Travinik
Trébie, n.f., Trebia
Trébizonde, n.f., Trebizond
Trente, n.f., Trent
Trèves, n.m., Treves, Trier
Trévise, n.f., Treviso
Trieste, n.f. or m., Triest
Trinité, n.f., la Trinité, Trinidad

Trinquemale, or Trincomaly, n.m., Trincomalee
Triphylie, n.f., Triphylia
Troade, n.f., Troas, Troad
Troie, n.f., Troja, Troia
Troyes (troâ), n.f., Troyes
Tunis (-nîs), n.f., Tunis
Turcomanie, n.f., Turkomania
Turquie, n.f., Turkey
Tyr, n.f., Tyros, Tyrus
Tyrol, n.m., Tyrol
Tyrone, n.m., Tyrone

U

Ukraine, n.f., Ukraine, Ukraina
Umerapoura, n.m. V. Amarapoura
Urbin, n.m., Urbino
Utique, n.f., Utica
Utrecht (utrèk), n.m. Utrecht

V

Valachie (-kî), n.f., Walachia
Valence, n.f., Valencia
Valette, n.f., Valetta
Valladolid (-lid), n.m., Valladolid
Valteline, n.f., Valtellina
Van Diémen (Terre de), n.f., Van Diemen's Land, Tasmania
Varsovie, n.f., Warsaw
Vendée, n.f., Vendée
Vénétie, n.f., Venetia
Venise, n.f., Venice
Vénosa, n.f., Venosa
*Vermeille (Mer), n.f., Gulf of California
Vérone, n.f., Verona
*Versailles (vèr-), n m, Versailles

Vésuve, n.m., Vesuvius
Viborg, or Wiborg, n.m., Viborg, Wiborg
Vicence, n.f., Vicenza
Vienne (viè-n), n.f., Vienna (in Austria—Autriche); Vienne (France)
Virginie, n.f., Virginia
Vistule, n.f., Vistula
Vitoria, n.f., Vitoria
Volterra, n.f., Volterra
Vosges, n.f., Vosges

W

Westphalie (vès-fa-lî), n.f., Westphalia
Wettin, n.m., Wettin
Wiborg, n.m. V. Viborg
Wight (waite) (île de), n.f., Isle of Wight
Wurtemberg (vurtinbèr). n.m., Wurtemberg
Wurtzbourg, n.m., Wurzburg

X

Xanthe, n.m., Xanthus
Xérès, or Kérez (gzérès), n.m., Xeres

Y

Yémen (iémè-n), n.m., Yemen
York, n.m., York

Z

Zélande, n.f., Zealand
Zurich (------) n.m. Zurich

TABLE OF FRENCH COINS, MEASURES, AND WEIGHTS,
REDUCED TO UNITED STATES MONEY, MEASURES, AND WEIGHTS.

Francs, Centimes.	Dollars, Cents.	Francs, Centimes.	Dollars, Cents.	Francs, Centimes.	Dollars, Cents.
Fr. c.	$ c.	Fr. c.	$ c.	Fr. c.	$ c.
0 05	0 01	5 00	1 00	13 00	2 60
0 10	0 02	6 00	1 20	14 00	2 80
0 25	0 05	7 00	1 40	15 00	3 00
0 50	0 10	8 00	1 60	16 00	3 20
1 00	0 20	9 00	1 80	17 00	3 40
2 00	0 40	10 00	2 00	18 00	3 60
3 00	0 60	11 00	2 20	19 00	3 80
4 00	0 80	12 00	2 40	20 00	4 00

SUPERFICIAL MEASURE.
Are (100 square mètres) ... 0·098845 rood
Hectare (10,000 square mètres) ... 2·471143 acres.
Centiare (1 square mètre) ... 1·196033 sq.yd.

SOLID MEASURE.
Stère (1 cubic mètre) ... { 1·31 cubic yard or 35 cubic feet, 547 cubic inches.
Décastère (10 stères) .. 13·1 cubic yards.
Décistère(10th of a stère) { 3 cubic ft. 918·7 cubic inches.

WEIGHTS.
Gramme (weight of 1 cubic centimètre of water in its state of maximum density, or 39¼ Fahr., or 4 degrees centigrade) ... } 15·4325 grains troy.
Décagramme (10 grammes).. 6·43 dwt.
Hectogram. (100 grammes) { 3·527 oz. avoir. 3·216 oz. troy.
Kilogram. (1,000 grammes) { 2·2055 lb. avoir. or 2·6803 lb. troy.
Quintal métrique(100kilogs.)220·548 lb.
Millier, tonneau de mer (1,000 kilogrammes) .... } 19 cwt. 12 oz.5 dwt.
Décigram. (10th of 1 gram.) 1·5432 grain.
Centigram. (100th do.) 0·15432 grain.
Milligramme (1000th do.) 0·015432 grain.

ITINERARY MEASURE.
Mètre (ten millionth part of the arc of a meridian between the pole and the equator) .... } 3·2808992 feet.
Décamètre (10 mètres) .... 32·808992 feet.
Kilomètre (1,000 mètres) ......1093·633 yards.
Myriamètre (10,000 mètres) ... 6·2138 miles.

LONG MEASURE.
Décimètre (10th of a mètre)...3·937079 inches.
Centimètre (100th of a mètre)...0·393708 inch.
Millimètre (1,000th of a mètre)...0·03937 inch.

MEASURE OF CAPACITY (Liquid).
Centilitre (100th of a litre) 0·0211 pints.
Décilitre (10th of a litre) ... 0·2113 pints.
Litre (1 cubic décimètre) ... 1·0567 quarts.
Décalitre (10 litres) .... 2·6417 gallons.
Hectolitre (100 litres).........{ 26·4177 gallons or 2·8377 bushels.
Kilolitre (1 cubic mètre) ... 264·177 bushels.

THERMOMETER.
0° Centigrade Melting ice ... 32° Fahr'nh't.
100° do. Boiling water.. 212° do.
0° Réaumur Melting ice ... 32° do.
80° do. Boiling water.. 212° do.

TABLE OF UNITED STATES COINS, MEASURES, AND WEIGHTS,
REDUCED TO FRENCH COIN, MEASURES, AND WEIGHTS.

Dollars.	Francs.	Cents.	Francs. Centims		Feet.	Inches.
					Mètres.	Centimètres
1	5	1	0 05	1	0·30479449	2·539954
2	10	2	0 10	2	0·60953898	5·079908
3	15	3	0 15	3	0·91438348	7·619862
4	20	4	0 20	4	1·21917796	10·159816
5	25	5	0 25	5	1·52397245	12·699770
6	30	6	0 30	6	1·82876694	15·239724
7	35	7	0 35	7	2·13356143	17·779678
8	40	8	0 40	8	2·43836592	20·319632
9	45	9	0 45	9	2·74315041	22·859586
10	50	10	0 50	10	3·0479449	25·399540
20	100	20	1 00	11	3·3527394	27·939494
30	150	30	1 50	12	3·6575338	30·479448
40	200	40	2 00			
50	250	50	2 50			
60	300	60	3 00		One dollar is worth	
70	350	70	3 50		really 5.1813 francs.	
80	400	80	4 00			
90	450	90	4 50			
100	500	100	5 00			

TROY WEIGHT.
Grain = 0·064798 grammes.
Pennyweight = 1·55517 „
Ounce = 31·1035 „
Pound = 0·373242 kilogrammes.

LONG MEASURE.
					Mètres.
3 feet	(yard)			=	0·914383
Fathom	(2	yards)		=	1·828766
Pole	(5½	„	)	=	5·02911
Furlong	(220	„	)	=	201·16437
Mile	(1760	„	)	=	1609·3149

SUPERFICIAL MEASURE.
Square inch = 6·451366 centimètres carrés.
„ foot = 0·0929 mètres carrés.
„ yard = 0·836097 „
Rod .... = 25·291939 „
Rood (1,210 square yards) = 10·116775 ares.
Acre (4,840 „) = 40·4671 „
Square mile „ = 2·588881 kilomètres carrés.

SOLID MEASURE.
Cubic inch = 16·386176 centimètres cubes.
„ foot = 0·028214 mètre cube.
„ yard = 0·764502 „

AVOIRDUPOIS WEIGHT.
Dram ... ... = 1·17718 grammes.
Ounce ... ... = 28·3495 „
Pound... ... = 0·4535926 kilogrammes.
Quarter ... = 12·6956 „
Hundredweight = 50·802 „
Ton ... ... = 1016·048 „

MEASURE OF CAPACITY.
Pint (liquid) ... ... = 0·4731 litres.
Quart „ ... ... = 0·946° „
Gallon „ ... ... = 3·7852 „
Peck (dry) ... ... = 8·810 „
Bushel „ ... ... = 35·240 „
United States wine gallon = 231 cubic inches.

The Classic
French Dictionary

❦

ENGLISH-FRENCH
DIVISION

For the explanation of the Abbreviations used in the English-French Division, see Pages xxiv., xxv.

— Indicates the repetition of the English word.

Words in parentheses serve to complete the sense of those words that precede or follow them. They are given in French and in English.

When two or more French nouns of the same gender follow; their gender is indicated after the last noun only.

The pronunciation of English words is indicated, in the English-French Division, in the same manner as that of French words in the French-English division, and represented in *all* cases by means of the French spelling, with the exception of:

1st, *th* hard, which is expressed by (th);
2nd, *th* soft ,, ,, (th);
3rd, *g*, when hard before *e, i,* or *y*, by (gʰ).

⊙ Indicates obsolete French words.

(ant.) Indicates obsolete English words.

GENERAL ENGLISH-FRENCH
DICTIONARY.

a, première lettre de l'alphabet, a;(mus.)la, *m.*
a (é). *indefinite art.*, un, *m.*, une, *f.* Three —
day; *trois par jour.* — shilling — pound; *un
schelling la livre.*
   aback, *aav.*, (nav.) sur le mât; coiffé. To
lay a sail — ; (nav.) *coiffer une voile.*
   abacus (-keuss),*n.,* (arch., math.)abaque, *m.*
   abaft, *adv.*, (nav.) à l'arrière, en arrière.
   abaft, *prep.*, (nav.) en arrière de; arrière.
   abaisance, *n.* *V.* **obeisance.**
   abandon (a-ba'n'do'n), *v.a.*, abandonner,
délaisser, quitter.
   abandoner (-ba'n'do'n'eur), *n.*, personne qui
abandonne, *f.*
   abandoning (-ba'n'do' n'igne), *n.*, abandon, *m.*
   abandonment (-ba'n'do'n'mè-nte), *n.*,
abandon, délaissement; laisser aller, *m.*
   abase (-béss), *v.a.*, abaisser, avilir, ravaler.
   abasement (-béss-mè-nte), *n.*, abaissement,
avilissement, ravalement, *m.*
   abash (abashe), *v.a.*, déconcerter, intimider,
interdire, confondre.
   abashment, *n.*, confusion, *f.*
   abate, *v.a.*, rabattre; diminuer.
   abate (-béte), *v.n.*, diminuer, baisser, s'affaiblir, s'arrêter.
   abatement (-bét'mè-nte), *n.*, diminution, *f.*; rabais, *m.*, réduction; remise, *f.*
   abater *n.*, personne qui diminue, qui fait
un rabais; chose qui diminue, qui affaiblit, *f.*
   abating (-bét'igne), *n.*, diminution, remise, *f.*; rabais, *m.*
   abature (-tiour), *n.*, (hunt.) abattures, *f.pl.*
   abb, *n.*, chaîne de tisserand, *f.*
   abbacy, *n.*, dignité d'abbé, *f.*
   abbatical, *or* **abbatial** (-shial), *adj.*,
abbatial.
   abbe (-bé), *n.*, abbé, *m.*
   abbess, *n.*, abbesse, *f.*
   abbey, *n.*, abbaye, *f.*
   abbot, *n.*, abbé, *m.*
   abbotship, *n.*, dignité d'abbé, fonctions
d'abbé, d'abbesse, *f.*
   abbreviate (ab-bri-vié-te), *v.a.*, abréger;
raccourcir.
   abbreviation, *n.*, abréviation, *f.*
   abbreviator (-teur), *n.*, abréviateur, *m.*
   abbreviatory (-via-teuri), *adj.*, qui abrège,
abréviatif.
   abbreviature (-via-tioure), *n.*, abrégé, *m.*
   a b c, *n.*, a b c, a b c d (alphabet), *m.*
   abdicate (-kéte), *v.a.* and *n.*, abdiquer.
   abdication (-ké-), *n.*, abdication, *f.*
   abdicative, *adj.*, qui fait abdiquer.
   abdomen, *n.*, (anat.) abdomen; bas-
ventre, *m.*

   abdominal, *or* **abdominous** (-neusse),
adj., abdominal.
   abduce (-diouce), *v.a.*, retirer, détourner,
enlever.
   abducent (-diou-cè-nte). *adj.*, (anat.) abducteur.
   abduction (-deuk-), *n.*, action de mouvoir,
de porter d'un point à un autre, *f.* ; (jur.)
enlèvement, *m.*
   abductor (-deuk-teur), *n.*, (anat.) abducteur, *m.*
   abecedarian (é-bi-ci-da-ri-a-n), *n.*, abécédaire, *m.*
   abecedary (é-bi-ci-dé-ri), *adj.*, abécédaire.
   abed, *adv.*, au lit, couché.
   aberrance, *or* **aberrancy** (-bèr-ra-nse, -ci),
n., égarement, *m.*, aberration, *f.*
   aberrant, *adj.*, égaré.
   aberration (-bèr-ré-), *n.*, aberration, *f.*;
éloignement, *m.*
   abet (-bète), *v.a*, soutenir, encourager,
appuyer; exciter, soutenir.
   abetment (-bèt'mè-nte), *n.*, appui, encouragement, *m.*
   abeter, *or* **abettor** (-teur), *n.*, fauteur,
instigateur, *m.*
   abeyance, *n.*, (jur.) vacance; attente, *f.*
   abhor, *v.a.*, abhorrer, avoir en horreur.
   abhorrence (-rè-nce), *n.*, horreur, *f.*
   abhorrent (-rè-nte), *adj* , avec horreur, en
horreur; incompatible, contraire.
   abhorrently, *adv.*, avec horreur.
   abhorrer (-reur), *n.*, personne qui abhorre, *f.*
   abide (-baïde), *v.a.*, attendre; supporter,
subir, souffrir.
   abide, *v.n.*, demeurer; rester, souffrir. To—
by ; *s'en tenir à.*
   abider (-baïdeur), *n.*, personne qui demeure. *f.*
   aoiding (-baïdigne), *n.*, séjour, *m.*; demeure, *f.*
   abigail, *n.*, suivante, soubrette, *f.*; femme
de chambre.
   ability, *n.*, capacité, portée, *f.*; pouvoir,
talent, *m.*, habileté, *f.*
   abintestate (-bi-n-tès-tète), *adv.*, (jur.) ab
intestat.
   abject, *adj.*, abject, bas, vil.
   abject, *n.*, un homme abject, un misérable, *m.*
   abjectedness, *n.*, abjection, *f.*
   abjection (-sheune), *n.*, abjection, *f.*
   abjectly, *adv.*, d'une manière abjecte.
   abjectness, *n.*, abjection, *f.*
   abjuration (-jiou-ré-), *n.*, abjuration, *f.*
   abjure (-jiour), *v.a.*, abjurer, renoncer.
   abjurer (-jiour'eur), *n.*, personne qui
abjure, *f.*

ablactate (-téte), *v.a.*, sevrer.

ablaqueation (-koui-é-), *n.*, (hort.) déchaussement,*m.*

ablation (-blé-), *n.*, enlèvement, *m.*; soustraction, *f.*

ablative, *adj.*, qui enlève; (gram.) de l'ablatif.

ablative, *n.*, (gram.) ablatif, *m.*

able (éb'l), *adj.*, capable; habile; robuste.

To be — to; *pouvoir*; *être à même de*; *être en état de.* He is — to do it; *il peut le faire.*

able-bodied (éb'l-bodide), *adj.*, fort, robuste, vigoureux; (nav.) habile.

ablen (-blène), *or* **ablet** (-blète), *n.*, (ich.) able, *m.*, ablette,*f.*

ableness (éb'l-nèsse), *n.*, pouvoir, *m.*; habileté, *f.*

abluent (-bliou-), *adj.*, qui nettoie, détersif.

ablution (-bliou-), *n.*, ablution, *f.*

ably (ébli), *adv.*, habilement, adroitement.

abnegation (-ni-ghé-), *n.*, abnégation, renonciation,*f.*

abnegator (-ni-ghé-teur), *n.*, personne qui nie,*f.*

abnodation (-dé-), *n.*, (hort.) enlèvement des nœuds, *m.*

abnormal, *adj.*, anormal, irrégulier, difforme.

aboard (abôrde), *adv.*, (nav.) à bord.

abode,*v.a.* and *n.*,augurer,présager; augurer.

abode (abôde), *n.*, séjour, *m.*, demeure, *f.*

abodement, *n.*, pressentiment, présage, *m.*

aboding (abôdigne), *n.*, pressentiment, présage, *m.*

abolish, *v.a.*, abolir; détruire.

abolishable, *adj.*, abolissable.

abolisher, *n.*, personne qui abolit, *f.*

abolishment, *n.*, abolissement, *m.*

abolition, *n.*, abolition, *f.*

abolitionist, *n.*, abolitionniste, partisan de l'abolition de l'esclavage, *m.*

abominable, *adj.*, abominable, infâme.

abominableness, *n.*, abomination,*f.*

abominably, *adv.*, abominablement.

abominate (-mi-néte), *v.a.*, avoir en abomination.

abomination, *n.*, abomination,*f.*

aboriginal (-bô-rid'ji-), *adj.*, aborigène, primitif.

aborigines (-nize), *n.pl.*, aborigènes, *m.pl.*

abortion, *n.*, avorton; avortement, *m.*

abortive, *adj.*, abortif; avorté.

abortively, *adv.*, en avorton; avant terme.

abortiveness, *n.*, état d'avorton; avortement, *m.*

abound (-baou-n-de), *v.n.*, abonder.

abounding (-digne), *adj.*, abondant.

abounding, *n.*, accroissement, *m.*

about, *adv.*, autour, tout autour, à l'entour; à la ronde; çà et là; environ; sur le point de. To be — to; *être sur le point de.* All —; *partout.*

about (ébaoute), *prep.*, autour de; auprès de; touchant, au sujet de; sur; vers; dans; par. To set — anything; *se mettre à quelque chose.* — the streets; *par les rues.* — two o'clock; *vers les deux heures.* I have no money — me; *je n'ai pas d'argent sur moi.* To be — any thing; *être occupé à quelque chose.*

above, *prep.*, au-dessus de; au-delà de; plus de; (nav.) en amont de.

above, *adv.*, en haut; là-haut; au-dessus; ci-dessus. — all; surtout. — board; ouvertement, franchement. — ground; en vie.

abrade (-bréde), *v.a.*, user par le frottement; produire une abrasion; faire une écorchure, écorcher.

abraham, *or* **abram**, *n.*, fourbe fieffé, *m.* To sham — ; *jouer l'innocence patriarcale.*

abrasion (ab'ré-jeune), *n.*, action d'enlever par le frottement, *f.*; (med.) abrasion, *f.*

abreast (-brèste), *adv.*, de front; à côté l'un de l'autre; vis-à-vis; (nav.) par le travers.

abridge, *v.a.*, abréger; retrancher, réduire.

abridger (-jeur), *n.*, personne qui abrège,*f.*; abréviateur, *m.*

abridgment (-brid-je-), *n.*, abrégé, *m.*, réduction, *f.*

abroach (-brôt-she), *adv.*, en perce; (fig.) en avant, en train.

abroad (abrôde), *adv.*, dehors; à l'étranger; au large.

abrogate (a-brô-ghéte), *v.a.*, abroger.

abrogation, *n.*, abrogation,*f.*

abrupt, *adj.*, brusque, brisé; saccadé; abrupt, escarpé.

abrupt, *adv.*, soudain, abruptement.

abrupt (-breup-te), *n.*, précipice, *m.*

abruption, *n.*, rupture,*f.*

abruptly, *adv.*, brusquement, avec précipitation.

abruptness,*n.*, brusquerie, précipitation,*f.*

abscess, *n.*, abcès, *m.*

abscind, *v.a.*, retrancher.

absciss, *or* **abscissa**, *n.*, (geom.) abscisse,*f.*

abscission (-jeune), *n.*, amputation,*f.*

abscond (-ko'nde),*v.n.*, se cacher; s'enfuir; se soustraire aux poursuites de la justice.

abscondedly,*adv.*, en cachette.

absconder (-deur), *n.*, personne qui se cache; personne qui se soustrait aux poursuites de la justice, *f.*

absconding, *n.*, action de se cacher; action de se soustraire aux poursuites de la justice,*f.*

absence (-sè-n-e), *n.*, absence; absence d'esprit, distraction,*f.*

absent, *adj.*, absent; distrait.

absent, *v.a.*, éloigner. To — one's self; *s'absenter.*

absentee (-ti), *n.*, absent, *m.*

absenteeism (-ti-izme),*n.*, absentéisme, *m.*

absenter, *n.*, absent (de son poste), *m.*

absinthiated (-thié-), *adj.*, absinthé.

absis, *n.* V. **apsis.**

absist, *v.n.*, se désister.

absolute (-liou-te), *adj.*, absolu; vrai; parfait; pur et simple.

absolutely, *adv.*, absolument.

absoluteness, *n.*, pouvoir absolu; arbitraire, *m.*

absolution, *n.*, absolution; (rel.) absoute,*f.*

absolutory, *adj.*, absolutoire.

absolve (-zolve), *v.a.*, absoudre, délier.

absonant, *adj.*, en contradiction.

absorb, *v.a.*, absorber; engloutir.

absorbability, *n.*, faculté d'absorber,*f.*

absorbable, *adj.*, (chem.) qui peut être absorbé.

absorbent, *n.*, absorbant, *m.*

absorbent, *adj.*, absorbant.

absorption, *n.*, absorption; extinction,*f.*

absorptive, *adj.*, qui a la faculté d'absorber; (chem.) absorbant.

abstain (-tè-ne), *v.n.*, s'abstenir.

abstaining, *n.*, abstinence,*f.*

abstemious (-mieusse),*adj.*, abstème, sobre.

abstemiously, *adv.*, sobrement; avec abstinence.

abstemiousness, *n.*, abstinence, modération; sobriété,*f.*

abstention (-tè'n-), *n.*, abstinence, privation, abstention,*f.*

absterge (-teurd'je),*v.a.*,(surg.) absterger; nettoyer.

abstergent, *n.*, abstergent, *m.*

abstergent, *adj.*, abstergent, abstersif.

abstersion (-teur), *n.*, (med.) abstersion,*f.*

abstersive, *adj.*, abstersif, abstergent.

abstinence, *or* **abstinency**, *n.*, abstinence,*f.*

abstinent, *adj.*, abstinent, sobre.

abstinently, *adv.*, avec abstinence.

abstract, *v.a.*, abstraire, extraire, soustraire, dérober.

abstract, *adj.*, abstrait.

abstract, *n.*, résumé, *m.*; analyse, *f.*; extrait, *m.*

abstractedly (-tèd'-), *adv.*, d'une manière abstraite; par abstraction.

abstractedness, *n.*, caractère abstrait, *m.*

abstracter (-teur), *n.*, auteur d'un résumé, *m.*

abstraction, *n.*, abstraction; distraction,*f.*

abstractive, *adj.*, abstractif; extrait.

abstractly, *adv.*, abstractivement.

abstractness, *n.*, abstraction, *f.*; caractère abstrait, *m.*

abstruse (-strouss), *adj.*, caché; abstrus, abstrait.

abstrusely, *adv.*, d'une manière abstruse, abstraitement.

abstruseness, *n.*, qualité abstruse,*f.*

absurd (-seurde), *adj.*, absurde.

absurdity, *n.*, absurdité, *f.*

absurdly, *adv.*, absurdement.

absurdness, *n.*, absurdité, *f.*

abundance (-beune-), *n.*, abondance; prospérité; quantité, *f.*

abundant, *adj.*, abondant.

abundantly, *adv.*, abondamment; largement.

abuse, *v.a.*, abuser de; médire de; dire des sottises à, injurier, dire des injures à, maltraiter; tromper.

abuse (-biouze), *n.*, abus, *m.*; sottises, injures, *f.pl.*

abuser, *n.*, abuseur, *m*; personne qui dit des injures, des sottises, *f.*

abusive, *adj.*, injurieux; abusif.

abusively, *adj.*, injurieusement, abusivement.

abusiveness, *n.*, langage injurieux, *m.*

abut (-beute), *v.n.*, aboutir; s'embrancher.

abutment, *n.*, but, *m.*; borne; contre-fiche; (of a bridge—*de pont*) culée, *f.*

abutment-pier (-pieurre), *n.*, pile-culée, *f.*

abutting, *n.*, embranchement (of a road—*de route*), *m.*

abyss, *n.*, abîme, *m.*

acacia (-shia), *n.*, acacia, *m.* Indian —; *tamarinier*, *m.* Common — ; *acacia vulgaire.* Bastard — ; *robinier*, *m.*

academic (-dé-), *n.*, académicien de l'école de Platon, *m.*

academic, *or* **academical**, *adj.*, académique, universitaire, classique.

academically, *adv.*, académiquement.

academician (-di-), *n.*, académicien, *m.*

academism, *n.*, système académique de Platon, *m.*

academist, *n.*, académicien; philosophe académique, *m.*

academy (-di-), *n.*, académie; pension, institution, *f.*, pensionnat, *m.*

acajou, *n.*, (bot.) acajou, *m.*

acantha (-tha), *n.*, (bot.) acanthe, branche-ursine, *f.*

acanthine (-thine), *adj.*, fait d'épine.

acanthus (-theusse), *n.*, (bot., arch.) acanthe, *f.*

accede (-cîde), *v.n.*, accéder, consentir.

accelerate (-leu-rête), *v.a.*, accélérer, hâter.

acceleration (-ré-), *n.*, accélération, *f.*

accelerative, *adj.*, accélérateur.

acceleratory (-leu-ra-teuri),*adj.*, accélérant.

accendibility, *n.*, (chem.) inflammabilité, *f.*

accendible, *adj.*, (chem.) inflammable.

accension, *n.*, (chem.) inflammation, *f.*

accent, *n.*, accent; parler, *m.*

accent, *v.a.*, accentuer; articuler.

accenting, *n.*, manière d'accentuer; accentuation, *f.*

accentuate (-tiouéte), *v.a.*, accentuer.

accentuation, *n.*, accentuation, *f.*

accept, *v.a.*, accepter, agréer, accueillir; comprendre, entendre.

acceptable, *adj.*, acceptable, agréable.

acceptableness, *n.*, qualité d'être acceptable, *f.*; bon accueil, droit au bon accueil, *m.*

acceptably, *adv.*, agréablement.

acceptance, *n.*, acceptation, *f.*; accueil, *m.* Worth — ; *qui vaut la peine d'être accepté.* To beg any one's — of anything ; *prier quelqu'un d'accepter quelque chose.* To cancel an — ; (com.) *annuler une acceptation.* To furnish with an — ; *revêtir d'une acceptation.* To leave for — ; *laisser à l'acceptation.* To refuse — ; *refuser à l'acceptation.* To present for — ; *présenter à l'acceptation.* To send out for — ; *envoyer à l'acceptation.*

acceptation (-té-), *n.*, accueil, *m.*; (gram.) acception, *f.*

accepter (-teur), *n.*, personne qui accepte, *f.*; (com.) accepteur, *m.*

acception, *n.*, (gram.) acception.

access, *n.*, accès, abord, *m.*

accessary. *V.* accessory.

accessible, *adj.*, accessible.

accession, *n.*, accession, acquisition, *f.*; accroissement; avènement, *m.*

accessional, *adj.*, additionnel.

accessorial, *adj.*, de complicité.

accessorily, *adv.*, accessoirement.

accessoriness, *n.*, état accessoire, *m.*

accessory, *adj.*, accessoire.

accessory, *n.*, accessoire, promoteur, complice, *m.*

accidence,*n.*,rudiments de grammaire,*m.pl.*

accident, *n.*,accident; incident; sinistre, *m.*

accidental, *adj.*, accidentel, fortuit, casuel.

accidental, *n.* accident.

accidentally, *adv.*, accidentellement, fortuitement, par accident, casuellement.

accidentalness, *n.*, qualité de ce qui est accidentel, *f.*

accoite (-saîte), *v.a.*, citer, assembler, convoquer, appeler.

acclaim, *n.*, acclamation,*f.*

acclaim, *v.a.*, acclamer.

acclamation (-mé-), *n.*, acclamation,*f.*

acclamatory, *adj.*, d'acclamation, d'applaudissement.

acclimated, *adj.*, acclimaté.

acclimation (-mé-), *n.*, acclimatement, *m.*; acclimatation,*f.*

acclivity, *n.*, montée, pente, élévation, rampe,*f.*

acclivous (-veusse), *adj.*,en pente, montant.

accolade, *n.*, accolade,*f.*

accommodable, *adj.*, accommodable.

accommodate (-déte), *v.a.*, accommoder, ajuster; disposer; loger; obliger, servir.

accommodated, *adj.*, accommodé.

accommodately, *adv.*, convenablement.

accommodating, *adj.*, accommodant; flexible.

accommodation,*n.*,adaptation,*f.*; accommodement, *m.*; convenance, *f.*; logement, *m.*; (com.) facilités, *f.pl.* — bill ; *billet de complaisance.* To be engaged in — bills ; *faire des billets de complaisance.*

accommodator (-teur), *n.*, personne qui accommode, *f.*

accompaniment, *n.*, accompagnement, *m.*

accompanist, *n.*, (mus.) accompagnateur, *m.*, accompagnatrice, *f.*

accompany, *v.a.*, accompagner.

accomplice, *n.*, complice, *m.f.*

accomplish, *v.a.*, accomplir; former; perfectionner; remplir.

accomplished (-plish'te), *adj.*, accompli, parfait.

accomplisher (-sheur), *n.*, personne qui accomplit, *f.*

accomplishment, *n.*, accomplissement; talent, art d'agrément, *m.*

accompt. *V.* **account**.

accord, *n.*, accord, consentement, *m.*

accord, *v.a.*, accorder; ajuster.

accord, *v.n.*, s'accorder.

accordance, *n.*, accord, *m.*; conformité, *f.*

accordant, *adj.*, d'accord.

according, *adj.*, conforme.

according as, *conj.*, selon que, suivant que.

according to, *prep.*, selon, suivant, conformément à.

accordingly, *adv.*, en conséquence.

accost, *v.a.*, accoster, aborder.

accostable, *adj.*, abordable.

accoucheur, *n.*, accoucheur, *m.*

account (-caou-n-te), *n.*, compte; récit, exposé, *m.*, relation, nouvelle; importance; considération; raison; histoire; description, *f.*; motif, sujet; poids, *m.*; (com.) facture, *f.* Old —; *ancien compte.* Current —; *compte courant.* Outstanding —; *compte non soldé.* — agreed upon; *arrêté de compte.* Overdrawn —; *compte découvert.* Bank —; *compte de banque.* Cash —; *compte de caisse.* Stock —; *compte de capital.* Statement of an —; *situation d'un compte.* Abstract of an —; *relevé de compte.* In —with; *en compte avec.* As per — rendered; *suivant compte remis.* On — of; *pour le compte de.* Or. — and risk of; *aux risques et pour le compte de.* On joint —; *de compte en participation.* Per —; *suivant compte.* To appear in any one's —; *figurer sur le compte de quelqu'un.* To audit an —; *vérifier un compte.* To balance an —; *balancer un compte.* To carry to —; *porter en compte.* To close an —; *clore un compte.* To compare —; *confronter un compte.* To deliver an —; *remettre un compte.* To have a current — with; *être en compte courant avec.* To keep —s; *tenir des livres.* To make out any one's —; *établir le compte de quelqu'un.* To make up an —; *balancer un compte.* To note an —; *pointer un compte.* To open an —; *ouvrir un compte.* To pass to —; *passer en compte.* Short —s make long friends; *les bons comptes font les bons amis.* On — of; *à cause de.* On your —; *par égard pour vous.* To turn anything to —; *mettre quelque chose à profit.* To make — of; *faire cas, de.* To make no — of; *ne faire aucun cas de.* The —s from China; *les nouvelles de la Chine.*

account, *v.a.*, compter; estimer, regarder comme.

account, *v.n.*, (-caou-n-te), *v.n.*, rendre compte; expliquer; répondre de. — for; *expliquer.*

accountability, *n.*, obligation de rendre compte; responsabilité, *f.*

accountable, *adj.*, responsable, comptable.

accountableness, *n.*, responsabilité, *f.*

accountant, *n.*, comptable; teneur de livres, *m.*

account-book (-bouke), *n.*, livre de comptes, *m.*

accouple (ac-keu-p'l), *v.a.*, accoupler.

accoutre (-teur), *v.a.*, équiper; accoutrer.

accoutrement, *n.*, accoutrement, *m.*

accredit, *v.a.*, croire; accréditer.

accreditation (-té). *V.* **credence**.

accredited, *adj.*, accrédité.

accretion, *n.*, accroissement, *m.*

accretive, *adj.*, croissant.

accrimination (-né-), *n.*, incrimination, *f.*

accrue (-crou-), *v.n.*, s'accroître; provenir, résulter.

accubation (-kiou-bé-), *n.*, posture à demi couchée, *f.*

accumbency (-keu-m-), *n.*, état de celui qui est à demi couché, *m.*

accumbent, *adj.*, couché à demi.

accumulate, *v.a.*, accumuler, entasser.

accumulate (aʊ-kiou-miou-léte), *v.n.*, s'accumuler, s'amonceler.

accumulate, *adj.*, accumulé.

accumulation, *n.*, accumulation, *f.*; amoncellement; (jur.) cumul, *m.*

accumulative, *adj.*, qui accumule.

accumulatively, *adv.*, cumulativement.

accumulator (-lé-teur) *n.*, accumulateur, *m.*, accumulatrice, *f.*

accuracy (-kiou-), *n.*, exactitude, justesse, *f.*

accurate (-kiou-réte), *adj.*, exact; juste.

accurately, *adv.*, exactement.

accurateness, *n.*, exactitude, justesse, *f.*

accurse (-keurse), *v.a.*, maudire.

accursed (-keurste), *adj.*, maudit.

accusable (-kiou-za-b'l), *adj.*, accusable.

accusation (-zé-), *n.*, accusation, *f.*

accusative, *n.*, (gram.) accusatif, *m.*

accusative. *adj.*, (gram.) de l'accusatif.

accusatively, *adv.*, (gram.) comme accusatif.

accusatory (-teuri), *adj.*, accusatoire.

accuse (-kiouze), *v.a.*, accuser.

accuser, *n.*, accusateur, *m.*, accusatrice, *f.*

accustom (-keus-teume), *v.a.*, accoutumer. To — one's self; *s'accoutumer.*

accustomable, *adj.*, (l.u.) habituel.

accustomably, *adv.*, (l.u.) habituellement.

accustomarily, *adv.*, (l.u.) ordinairement.

accustomary, *adj.*, (l.u.) ordinaire.

ace (éce), *n.*, (cards—*cartes*) as; (fig.) point; iota, *m.*

acephalous (-céf-al-eusse), *adj.*, (zool.) acéphale.

acerbate (-seur-béte), *v.a.*, rendre acerbe.

acerbity, *n.*, acerbité, aigreur; dureté, *f.*

acerous (-seu-reusse), *adj.*, acéré.

acescency, *n.*, acescence, *f.*

acescent, *adj.*, acescent.

acetabulum (a-ci-té-biou-leume), *n.*, (anat.) cavité cotyloïde, *f.*

acetate (-ci-té-te), *n.*, (chem.) acétate, *m.*

acetic, *adj.*, (chem.) acétique.

acetite, *n.*, (chem. ant.) acétate, *m.*

acetous, *adj.*, (chem.) acéteux.

ache (éke), *n.*, mal, *m.*, douleur, *f.* Head—; *mal de tête, mal à la tête.* Tooth—; *mal de dents, mal aux dents.* To have a head—; *avoir mal à la tête, avoir un mal de tête.*

ache (éke), *v.n.*, faire mal; souffrir.

achievable, *adj.*, exécutable.

achieve (a-tshive), *v.a.*, exécuter, accomplir.

achievement, *n.*, exploit, fait d'armes, *m.*; œuvre, production, *f.*; (her.) écusson, *m.*, armoiries, *f.pl.*

achiever, *n.*, auteur d'un exploit, *m.*; celui qui accomplit une œuvre, *f.*

aching (ékigne), *n.*, douleur, souffrance, *f.*

achor (ékor), *n.*, (med.) croûte de lait, teigne, *f.*

achromatic (-krô-), *adj.*, (opt.) achromatique.

acid, *adj.*, acide.

acid, *n.*, acide, *m.*

acidity, *n.*, acidité, *f.*

acidulate (-diou-léte), *v.a.*, aciduler.

acidulous (-leusse), *adj.*, acidule.

acinose (-nôss), or **acinous** (-neusse), *adj.*, granulaire, granulé.

acknowledge (ak-no-lèdje), *v.a.*, reconnaître; répondre à; avouer, confesser, convenir; accuser réception.

acknowledgment (-lèdj'), *n.*, reconnaissance, *f.*, aveu, *m.*, excuse, *f.* ; tribut ; accusé de réception, *m.*

acme (-mi), *n.*, (med.) acmé ; (fig.) apogée ; comble, *m.*

acolothist (-thiste), *or* **acolyte** (-laïte), *n.*, acolyte, *m.*

aconite (-naïte), *n.*, aconit, *m.*

acorn, *n.*, gland, *m.* ; (nav.) pomme de girouette, *f.* ; (conch.) gland de mer, *m.*

acorned (-cō'n'de), *adj.*, chargé de glands.

acotyledon (-ti-li-done), *n.*, (bot.) acotylédone, *f.*

acotyledonous, *adj.*, (bot.) acotylédone.

acoustic, *adj.*, acoustique.

acoustics (-eaous-), *n.*, acoustique, *f.*

acquaint (ac-coué-nte), *v.a.*, informer ; avertir ; faire savoir. To make any one —ed with any thing ; *faire connaître quelque chose à quelqu'un.* To get —ed with any one ; *faire la connaissance de quelqu'un.* To be —ed with ; *connaître.* To be intimately —ed with any one ; *être lié avec quelqu'un.*

acquaintance, *n.*, connaissance, *f.* To have a great many —s ; *avoir beaucoup de connaissances.* To make — with any one ; *faire connaissance avec quelqu'un.*

acquest (ac-couèste), *n.*, acquisition ; conquête, *f.*

acquiesce (ac-koui-èsse), *v.n.*, acquiescer ; adhérer ; accéder.

acquiescence, *or* **acquiescency**, *n.*, acquiescement, *m.*

acquiescent, *adj.*, disposé à acquiescer.

acquirability (ac-kouaeur-a-), *n.*, faculté d'acquérir, *f.*

acquirable, *adj.*, qui peut être acquis.

acquire (ac-kouaeur), *v.a.*, acquérir ; obtenir ; apprendre.

acquirement, *n.*, acquis, *m.* ; acquisition ; instruction, connaissance, *f.*, talent, *m.*

acquirer, *n.*, acquéreur, *m.*, acquéreuse, *f.*

acquisition (ac-koui-zi-), *n.*, acquisition ; connaissance, *f.*

acquisitive, *adj.*, qui est acquis.

acquit (ac-kouite), *v.a.*, acquitter, absoudre, décharger. To — one's self of ; *s'acquitter de.*

acquittal, *n.*, acquittement, *m.*

acquittance, *n.*, acquittement, *m.*, quittance, *f.* ; (com.) acquit, *m.*

acre (é-keur), *n.*, arpent, *m.*, acre, *f.* — fight ; *combat en champ clos, m.*

acrid, *adj.*, âcre.

acridness, *n.*, âcreté, *f.*

acrimonious, *adj.*, acrimonieux, âcre.

acrimoniously, *adv.*, avec aigreur, avec acrimonie.

acrimony, *n.*, acrimonie, âcreté, aigreur, *f.*

acritude (-tioude), *n.*, âcreté, *f.*

acrospire (-paeur), *n.*, germe, *m.*, semence, *f.*

across, *adv.*, à travers ; au travers de ; par.

acrostic, *n.*, acrostiche, *m.*

acrostic, *adj.*, acrostiche.

act, *n.*, action, *f.*, fait, acte, trait, *m.* In the — ; *sur le fait.* In the very — ; *sur le fait même, en flagrant délit.*

act, *v.a.*, représenter, jouer ; feindre.

act, *v.n.*, agir ; se conduire ; opérer ; influer.

acting, *n.*, action, *f.* ; (thea.) jeu, *m.*

acting, *adj.*, qui agit ; (tech.) à effet.

action, *n.*, action, *f.* ; fait, événement ; (jur.) procès ; combat, *m.*, affaire, bataille, *f.* To carry into — ; *mettre en action.* Naval — ; *combat naval.*

actionable, *adj.*, que l'on peut poursuivre judiciairement.

actionably, *adv.*, d'une manière sujette à procès.

active, *adj.*, actif ; agile, ingambe.

actively, *adv.*, activement, agilement.

activeness, *n.*, activité, *f.*

activity, *n.*, activité, agilité, *f.*

actor, *n.*, acteur, comédien, *m.*

actress, *n.*, actrice, comédienne, *f.*

actual (act-iou-al), *adj.*, réel, effectif, véritable, actuel.

actuality, *n.*, réalité, actualité, *f.*

actually, *adv.*, réellement, positivement, véritablement.

actualness, *n.*, réalité, *f.*

actuary (act-iou-), *n.*, secrétaire, *m.*

actuate (-tiou-ête), *v.a.*, mettre en action, mouvoir, pousser, animer, guider, inciter.

aculeate (-kiou-li-éte), *or* **aculeated** (-kiou-li-étède), *adj.*, (bot.) pourvu de piquants, d'épines, d'aiguillons ; (zool.) pourvu d'un aiguillon, d'un dard, de piquants.

acumen (-kiou-mène), *n.* subtilité d'esprit, finesse, *f.*

acuminate, *v.n.*, s'élever en cône ; se terminer en pointe.

acuminate (-kiou-mi-néte), *adj.*, aigu, subtil ; (bot.) acuminé.

acuminated, *adj.*, (bot.) acuminé ; terminé en pointe.

acumination, *n.* pointe aiguë ; finesse, *f.*

acupuncture (-kiou-peu-nkt-iour), *n.*, (surg.) acuponcture, *f.*

acus (-keusse), *n.*, (ich.) aiguille, *f.*

acute (-kioute), *adj.*, aigu ; fin ; poignant ; pénétrant.

acutely, *adv.*, d'une manière aiguë, finement, subtilement.

acuteness (-kiout'nèsse), *n.*, état aigu, *m.*, force, intensité, finesse, *f.*

adacted (-téde), *part.*, forcé.

adage (-dèdje), *n.*, adage, *m.*

adagial, *adj.*, (ant.) passé en adage.

adagio (-dadjiô), *n.*, (mus.) adagio, *m.*

adamant, *n.*, diamant, *m.*

adamantean (-ti-an), *adj.*, dur comme le diamant.

adamantine, *adj.*, de diamant ; (min.) adamantin.

adapt, *v.a.*, adapter, approprier.

adaptable, *adj.*, que l'on peut adapter.

adaptation (-dap-té-), *n.*, adaptation, *f.*

adapted, *part.*, propre à ; adapté.

adapter, *n.*, celui, celle qui adapte.

adaptibility, *n.*, faculté d'être adapté, *f.*

adays, *adv.*, aujourd'hui. Now — ; *de nos jours.*

add, *v.a.*, ajouter, joindre ; adjoindre ; additionner.

addable. *V.* **addible**.

adder, *n.*, vipère, *f.*

adderlike (ad-deur-laïke), *adj.*, en serpent.

adder's-tongue, *n.*, (bot.) langue de serpent, *f.*

adder's-wort, *n.*, (bot.) vipérine, *f.*

addibility, *n.*, qualité de ce qui peut être ajouté, *f.*

addible, *or* **addable**. *adj.*, qui peut être ajouté.

addict, *v.a.*, consacrer, dévouer. To — one's self ; *s'adonner, se consacrer, se livrer.* To be —ed ; *s'adonner.*

addictedness, *or* **addiction**, *n.*, dévouement ; goût, *m.*, disposition, *f.*

addition (ad-di-), *n.*, addition, *f.*, surcroît ; accroissement, *m.*

additional, *adj.*, additionnel, de plus.

additionally, *adv.*, par addition.

additory, *adj.*, qui a la faculté d'ajouter.

addle, *n.*, tartre (from wine—*du vin*).

addle, *adj.*, couvi ; trouble ; (fig.) stérile.

addle, *v.a.*, rendre couvi ; troubler.

addled, *part.*, couvi, trouble ; (fig.) stérile.

addle-headed (-hè-dède), **addle-pated** (-pé-tède), *adj.*, à caboche trouble.

address, v.a., adresser ; s'adresser à ; parler à, adresser la parole à.

, **address**, n., adresse, f., discours ; port, m., tenue, f. To pay one's —es to ; faire la cour à, rechercher en mariage. Of good — ; de bonne tenue, de bonne tournure, à l'air distingué, ayant l'air comme il faut.

adresser ad-drès-seur), n., pétitionnaire, m.

adduce (-diouce), v.a., présenter, alléguer ; apporter.

adducent, adj., (anat.) adducteur.

adducible, adj., qui peut être allégué.

adduction (-deuk-), n., citation ; (philos.) adduction, f.

adductive, adj., adducteur.

adductor (-deuk-), n., (anat.) adducteur, m.

ademption, n., (jur.) ademption, f.

adept, adj., d'adepte.

adept, n., adepte, m.f.

adequacy (-di-koua-), n., juste proportion ; suffisance, f.

adequate (-di-kouéte), adj., proportionné, égal ; suffisant.

adequately, adv., en juste proportion, justement, suffisamment.

adequateness, n., juste proportion, égalité, f.

adhere (ad-îre), v.n., adhérer, s'attacher, se fier, s'en tenir à.

adherence, n., adhérence, f.

adherent, n., adhérent, partisan, dépendant, m.

adherently, adv., d'une manière adhérente.

adherer, n., partisan, adhérent, m.

adhesion (-di-jeune), n., adhésion, adhérence, f.

adhesive (-di-cive), adj., qui adhère ; (med.) adhésif.

adhesively, adv., par adhérence.

adhesiveness, n., adhérence, adhésion, f.

adhortatory, adj., renfermant une exhortation, exhortatoire, f.

adiantum (-teume), n., (bot.) adiante, f.

adiaphorous (-di-a-fo-reusse), adj., indifférent, neutre.

adieu, adv., adieu.

adieu (-diou), n., adieu, m. To bid any one — ; faire ses adieux à quelqu'un.

ad infinitum (-teume), adv., à l'infini

ad interim, adv., par intérim.

adipocere (-cîre), n., adipocire, f.

adipose (-pòss), or **adipous** (-peusse), adj., adipeux.

adit, n., (mines) entrée ; galerie d'écoulement, f.

adjacency, n., contiguité, f., voisinage, m.

adjacent, adj., adjacent ; contigu.

adjacent, n., (l.u.) voisin, m.

adject, v.a., (l.u.) ajouter.

adjection, n., (l.u.) addition, f.

adjectitious (-ti-sheusse), adj., ajouté.

adjective, n., adjectif, m.

adjective, adj., (dy.) adjective. — colour ; couleur adjective, f.

adjectively, adv., adjectivement.

adjoin (-joine), v.a., joindre, adjoindre, toucher.

adjoin, v.n., être attenant ; se joindre.

adjourn (-jeurn), v.a., ajourner, différer.

adjourn, v.n., s'ajourner.

adjournment, n., ajournement, m.

adjudge (-jeudje), v.a., adjuger ; juger, condamner.

adjudgment, n., jugement, m., décision, f.

adjudicate, v.a., juger.

adjudicate (-jiou-di-kéte), v.a., adjuger.

adjudication, n., jugement, m.; décision, f.; arrêt, m.

adjudicator (-teur), n., juge, m.

adjunct, adj., joint, adjoint, secondaire.

adjunct (ad-jeu'n'kte), n., accessoire ; adjoint, m.

adjunction, n., adjonction, addition, f.

adjunctive, adj., qui joint.

adjunctive, n., chose jointe, f.

adjunctively, adj., d'une manière jointe, par addition, par adjonction.

adjuration (-jiou-ré-), n., appel sacré, m., adjuration, f.

adjure (-jioure), v.a., adjurer.

adjurer, n., personne qui adjure, f.

adjust (-jeuste), v.a., ajuster, régler, arranger.

adjuster, n., personne qui ajuste, f.

adjustment, n., ajustement, accord, arrangement, m. Amicable — ; arrangement à l'amiable.

adjutancy, n., (milit.) fonctions d'adjudant, f.pl. ; ordre, m., classification, f.

adjutant (-jiou-) n., (milit.) adjudant ; second, m.

adjutor, n., (l.u.) aide, m.

adjuvant (-jiou-), adj., aidant.

adjuvant, n., aide f. ; (pharm.) adjuvant, m.

admeasure (-mè-jeur), v.a., mesurer ; régler.

admeasurement, n., mesurage, m. ; dimension, f. ; règlement, m.

admeasurer, n., mesureur, m.

admensuration, n. V. **admeasurement**.

adminicular (-kiou-leur), adj., qui aide, qui sert d'aide.

administer, v.a., administrer ; régir ; donner ; fournir.

administer (-teur), v.a., subvenir, pourvoir.

administrate (-tréte), v.a., administrer ; régir ; donner.

administration, n., administration, f., gouvernement, m.

administrative, adj., administratif.

administratively, adv., administrativement.

administrator, n., administrateur, régent, m.

administratorship, n., fonctions d'administrateur, f.(p'., administration, f.

administratrix, n., administratrice, f.

admirable, adj., admirable.

admirableness, n., excellence, f.

admirably, adv., admirablement, à ravir.

admiral, n., amiral, m. Rear—; contreamiral. Vice— ; vice-amiral.

admiral, adj., amiral.

admiralship, n., dignité d'amiral, f., amiralat, m.

admiralty, n., amirauté, f. Board of —; conseil d'amirauté, m.

admiration (-ré-), n., admiration, f.; étonnement, m.

admire, v.a., admirer.

admire (-maeur), v.n., s'étonner.

admirer, n., admirateur, m., admiratrice, f.

admiringly, adv., avec admiration.

admissibility, n., admissibilité, f.

admissible, adj., admissible.

admissibly, adv., d'une manière admissible.

admission, n., réception, admission, entrée, f. ; accès, m.

admit, v.a., admettre ; laisser entrer.

admittable, adj., admissible.

admittance, n., accès, m. ; admission, entrée, f.

admitter (-teur), n., personne qui admet, f.

admix, v.a., mêler, mélanger.

admixtion, n., action de mélanger, f.

admixture, n. mélange, m.

admonish, v.a., avertir ; exhorter.

admonisher, *n.*, personne qui avertit, *f.*

admonishment, *n.*, admonition, *f.*; avertissement, *m.*

admonition, *n.*, avertissement, avis, *m.*; admonition, *f.*

admonitioner (-neur), *n.* conseiller, conseilleur, donneur d'avis, *m.*

admonitive, *adj.*, d'avertissement.

admonitor (-teur), *n.*, moniteur, conseiller, *m.*

admonitory, *adj.*, d'avertissement.

ado (-dou), *n.*, fracas, tintamarre, *m.*; peine ; affaire, *f.*; façons, cérémonies, *f.pl.* Without any more —; *sans plus de façons.*

adolescence, *or* **adolescency**, *n.*, adolescence, *f*

adolescent, *n.*, adolescent, *m.*

adolescent, *adj.*, adolescent.

adopt, *v.a.*, adopter.

adopted, *adj.*, adoptif, adopté.

adoptedly, *adv.*, par adoption.

adopter, *n.*, personne qui adopte, *f.*, adoptant, *m.*

adoption, *n.*, adoption, *f.*

adoptive, *adj.*, adoptif, adopté.

adoptive, *n.*, adopté, *m.*, adoptée, *f.*; chose adoptée, *f.*

adorable, *adj.*, adorable.

adorableness, *n.*, qualité adorable, *f.*

adorably, *adv.*, d'une manière adorable.

adoration (-ré-), *n.*, adoration, *f.*

adore, *v.a.*, adorer.

adorer, *n.*, adorateur, *m.*, adoratrice, *f.*

adorn, *v.a.*, orner; parer. To — one's self; *se parer.*

adornment, *n.*, ornement, *m.*, parure, *f.*

adown (-daoune), *adv.*, en bas à terre, par terre.

adown, *prep.*, en bas de.

adrift, *adv.*, (nav.) en dérive, à l'abandon.

adroit (-droite), *adj.*, adroit.

adroitly, *adv.*, adroitement.

adroitness, *n.*, adresse, *f.*

adry (-dra'ye), *adj.*, altéré.

adscititious (-sheusse), *adj.*, étranger, emprunté.

adstringent. *V.* astringent.

adulate (-diou-léte), *v.a.*, aduler.

adulation, *n.*, adulation, *f.*

adulator, *n.* adulateur, *m.*, adulatrice, *f.*

adulatory, *adj.*, adulateur.

adult, *adj.*, adulte.

adult (-deulte), *n.*, adulte, *m.f.*

adulterant, *n.*, la personne, la chose qui frelate.

adulterate (-deul-teur-éte), *v.a.*, frelater, falsifier, adultérer, sophistiquer.

adulterate, *adj.*, adultère; frelaté, falsifié, faux.

adulterately, *adv.*, d'une manière falsifiée.

adulterateness, *n.*, falsification, *f.*

adulteration, *n.*, falsification, frelaterie, sophistication, *f.*

adulterer (-deul-teur-eur), *n.*, adultère, *m.*

adulteress (-deul-teur-èsse), *n.*, adultère, femme adultère, *f.*

adulterine, *adj.*, adultérin; falsifié.

adulterous (-deul-teur-eusse), *adj.*, adultère; impur.

adulterously, *adv.*, par l'adultère.

adultery (adeul-teur), *n.*, adultère, *m.*

adultness (adeult-nèsse), *n.*, état adulte, *m.*

adumbrant, *adj.*, ébauché, esquissé.

adumbrate (-deu'm'bréte), *v.a.*, ébaucher : esquisser.

adumbration, *n.*, ébauche, esquisse, *f*

aduncity (-deu'n'-), *n.*, courbure, *f.*

aduncous (-keusse), *adj.*, crochu.

adust (-deuste), *adj.*, brûlé; (med.) aduste.

adustion, *n.*, (surg.) adustion; cautérisation, *f.*

advance, *v.a.*, avancer, faire avancer, élever; (com.) hausser.

advance, *v.n.*, s'avancer, avancer, se porter en avant.

advance, *n.*, avancement, progrès, *m.*; (com.) hausse, *f.*; avance, *f.*; (com.) avances, *f.pl.* On the —; (com.) *en hausse.* In —; *en avant; d'avance.* To make —s ; *faire des avances.* To pay in —; *payer d'avance.*

advance-guard (-gârde), *n.*, (milit.) garde avancée, *f.*

advance-money, *n.*, avance, *f.*

advanced, *part.*, avancé.

advancement, *n.*, avancement, *m.*

advancer (-seur), *n.*, personne qui avance ; promoteur.

advancive, *adj.*, tendant à avancer.

advantage (-tèdge), *n.*, avantage; profit, intérêt, *m.* To take — of; *profiter de, tirer profit de.* To take an — of any one's kindness; *abuser de la bonté de quelqu'un.* To the best —; *au plus grand avantage.* To any one's best —; *au mieux des intérêts de quelqu'un.*

advantage, *v.a.*, avantager.

advantageable (-tèdj'ab'l), *adj.*, (l.u.) avantageux.

advantaged (-tèdj'de), *part.*, avantagé.

advantage-ground (-graounde), *n.*, terrain avantageux, avantage, *m.*

advantageous (-té-djeusse), *adj.*, avantageux.

advantageously, *adv.*, avantageusement.

advantageousness, *n.*, avantage, *m.*

advene (-vine), *v.n.*, survenir, advenir.

advent (-vè'n'te), *n.*, venue, *f.*; Avent, *m.*

adventitious (-vè-n-ti-sheusse), *adj.*, adventice, accidentel.

adventitiously, *adv.*, d'une manière adventice.

adventive, *adj.*, adventice.

adventual (-tioual), *adj.*, de l'Avent.

adventure, *n.*, aventure, *f.*, hasard, *m.* At all —s ; *à tout hasard.*

adventure (-tioure), *v.a.*, aventurer, risquer, hasarder.

adventure, *v.n.*, s'aventurer, se hasarder, se risquer.

adventurer (-tiour-eur), *n.*, aventurier, *m.*, aventurière, *f.*

adventuresome, *adj.*, aventurier, aventureux.

adventuresomeness, *n.*, esprit aventurier, *m.*

adventurine, *n.*, (min.) aventurine, *f.*

adventurous, *adj.*, aventureux.

adventurously, *adv.*, aventureusement.

adventurousness, *n.*, esprit aventureux, caractère aventureux, *m.*

adverb (-veurbe), *n.*, adverbe, *m.*

adverbial, *adj.*, adverbial.

adverbially, *adv.*, adverbialement.

adversary, *n.*, adversaire, *m.*

adversative, *adj.*, adversatif.

adverse (-veurse), *adj.*, adverse, contraire, opposé.

adversely, *adv.*, d'une manière opposée.

adverseness, *n.*, opposition ; hostilité, *f.*

adversity, *n.*, adversité, *f.*

advert (-veurte), *v.n.*, faire allusion à ; considérer, mentionner.

advertence, *or* **advertency**, *n.*, attention, *f.*

advertise (-veur-taïze), *v.a.*, avertir, annoncer, afficher, publier.

advertisement (-veur-tize-), *n.*, avis, avertissement, *m.*; annonce, *f.*

advertiser (-veur-taïzeur), *n.*, personne qui fait des annonces; feuille d'annonces, *f.*

advice (-vaïce), *n.*, avis, conseil, *m.* To take —; *prendre conseil.* To give — of; *donner avis de.* Letter of —; (com.) *lettre d'avis.*

advice-boat (-bôte), *n.*, aviso, *m.*

advisable, *adj.*, judicieux, convenable.

advisableness, *n.*, utilité, convenance, *f.*

advise (-vaïze),*v.a.*, conseiller; donner avis de. To keep any one constantly advised of; *tenir quelqu'un au courant de.*

advised (-vaïz'de), *adj.*, avisé; mûri. Ill- —; *mal avisé.* Well- —; *bien avisé.*

advisedly (-vaïzèd'li), *adv.*, attentivement, judicieusement, prudemment.

advisedness (-vaï-zèd'nèsse), *n.*, sagesse, prudence,*f.*

adviser, *n.*, conseiller, *m.*

advocacy, *n.*, défense, intercession, *f.*

advocate (-vô-kéte),*n.*, avocat, défenseur,*m.*

advocate, *v.a.*, soutenir, défendre.

advocation, *n.*, défense, intervention, *f.*; soutien, *m.*

advoutrer (-vaou-treur),*n.*, adultère, *m.*

advoutress, *n.*, adultère,*f.*

advoutry, *n.*, adultère, *m.*

advowee (-vaou-î), *n.*, patron, *m.*

advowson, *n.*, patronage,*m.*

adynamic, *adj.*, (med.) adynamique.

adynamy, *n.*, (med.) adynamie,*f.*

adze, *n.*, erminette; doloire,*f.*

ægis (idjisse), *n.*, égide,*f.*

æglogue (igl'oghe), *n.*, églogue,*f.*

ægophony (igo-), *n.*, (med.) égophonie, voix chevrotante,*f.*

ænigma. *V.* **enigma.**

aerate (-euréte), *v.a.*, (chem.) aérer.

aerial (é-i-ri-al), *adj.*, aérien, d'air.

aerie, *or* **aery** (iri), *n.*, aire,*f.*

aeriform (é-eur-i-), *adj.*, aériforme.

aerify (é-eur-i-fa'ye), *v.a.*, remplir d'air.

aerography, *n.*, aérographie,*f.*

aerolite, *or* **aerolith**, *n.*, aérolithe, *m.*

aerological, *adj.*, aérologique.

aerologist, *n.*, savant dans l'aérologie, *m.*

aerology, *n.*, aérologie,*f.*

aerometer (é-eur-o-miteur),*n.*,aéromètre,*m.*

aerometry, *n.*, aérométrie,*f.*

aeronaut (é-eur-ô-), *n.*, aéronaute, *m.f.*

aeronautic, *adj.*, aérostatique.

aeronautics,*n.pl.*, science de l'aéronaute,*f.*

aeronautism, *n.*, art de l'aéronaute, *m.*

aerostat, *n.*, aérostat, *m.*

aerostatic, *adj.*, aérostatique.

aerostatics, *n.pl.*, art aérostatique, *m.*

aerostation, *n.*, aérostation,*f.*

æruginous(i-rioud'jineusse),*adj.*,érugineux.

æsthetic, *or* **æsthetical**, *adj.*, esthétique.

æsthetics (is-thè-), *n.pl.*, esthétique,*f.*

ætiology, *or* **etiology** (i-tio-lod'ji), *n.*, (med.) étiologie,*f.*

ætites (î-taï-tize), *n.*, aétite, pierre d'aigle,*f.*

afar, *adv.*, de loin, loin, au loin.

affability, *n.*, affabilité,*f.*

affable, *adj.*, affable, doux.

affableness, *n.*, affabilité,*f.*

affably, *adv.*, affablement.

affair. *n.*, affaire, *f.* Mercantile —s; *les affaires de commerce, le commerce.* As —s stand; *au point où en sont les affaires.* To liquidate, to wind up, one's —s; *liquider ses affaires.*

affect (af-fècte), *v.a.*, affecter; intéresser; toucher; aimer.

affectation (-fec-té), *n.*, affectation,*f.*

affected, *adj.*, disposé; affecté; précieux.

affectedly, *adv.*, d'une manière affectée.

affectedness, *n.*, affectation,*f.*

affecter, *n.*, personne qui affecte,*f.*

affecting, *adj.*, touchant.

affectingly (-tigne-), *adv.*, d'une manière touchante.

affection,*n.*, affection; inclination,*f.*; penchant,*m.*; maladie, *f.*

affectionate (-sheunéte), *adj.*, affectueux, affectionné.

affectionately, *adv.*,affectueusement, avec affection. affectionnément.

affectionateness, *n.*, affection,*f.*, caractère affectueux, *m.*

affectioned (-sheu-n-de), *adj.*, disposé; affectionné; (ant.) affecté.

affectuous (-tiou-eusse), *adj.*, (ant.) passionné.

affiance (af-fa'ya-n-se), *n.*,fiançailles, *f.pl.*; confiance; confiance en Dieu,*f.*

affiance,*v.a.*, fiancer; accorder sa confiance.

affianced (af-fa'ya'nste), *part.*, fiancé.

affiancer, *n.*, personne qui fiance,*f.*

affidavit, *n.*, déclaration écrite et affirmée par serment, *m.*

affiliate (af-fil-i-éte), *v.a.*, affilier; adopter (comme fils).

affiliation, *n.*, affiliation; adoption (comme fils),*f.*

affinage (-néd'je), *n.*, (metal.) affinage, *m.*

affinity, *n.*, affinité, alliance,*f.*

affirm, *v.a.*, affirmer; confirmer.

affirm (af-feurme), *v.n.*, affirmer.

affirmable, *adj.*, qu'on peut affirmer.

affirmance, *n.*, (l.u.) affirmation,*f.*

affirmant, *n.*, personne qui affirme,*f.*

affirmation (-mé-), *n.*, affirmation; confirmation,*f.*

affirmative (-ma-), *adj.*, affirmatif.

affirmative, *n.*, affirmative,*f.* To reply in the —; *répondre affirmativement.*

affirmatively, *adv.*, affirmativement.

affirmer, *n.*, personne qui affirme,*f.*

affix,*v.a.*, apposer; ajouter; fixer.

affix, *n.*, affixe, *m.*

affixture (-tioure), *n.*, chose attachée,*f.*

afflation (-flé-), *n.*, action de souffler,*f.*

afflatus (-flé-teusse), *n.*, souffle, *m.*, haleine,*f.*

afflict, *v.a.*, affliger.

afflictedness (-tèd-nèsse),*n.*,douleur, affliction,*f.*

afflicter, *n.*, personne qui afflige,*f.*

afflicting, *adj.*, affligeant, chagrinant.

affliction, *n.*, affliction,*f.*

afflictive, *adj.*, affligeant.

afflictively, *adv.*, d'une manière affligeante.

affluence (af-flou-è-nse), *n.*, abondance, opulence, affluence,*f.*

affluent, *adj.*, abondant; opulent, riche.

affluentness, *n.*, abondance, opulence, *f.*

afflux (af-fieuxe), *n.*, (med.) afflux, *m.*

affluxion, *n.*, (med.) afflux, *m.*

afford, *v.a.*, donner; fournir; offrir; avoir le moyen, les moyens. I cannot — it; *mes moyens ne me le permettent pas, je n'en ai pas les moyens.*

afforest, *v.a.*, convertir en forêt.

afforestation. *n.*, conversion en forêt, *f.*

affranchise (af-fra-n-tchaïze), *v.a.*, affranchir.

affranchisement. *n.*, affranchissement, *m.*

affray, *n.*, querelle, échauffourée, rixe, batterie,*f.*

affright (af-fraïte), *v.a.*, effrayer.

affright, *n.*, effroi, *m.*, épouvante,*f.*

affrightedly, *adv.*, avec effroi, avec épouvante.

affrightment, *n.*, (l.u.) effroi, *m.*

affront (af-freu'nte), *v.a.*, (ant.) rencontrer; affronter; offenser, insulter.

affront, *n.*, affront, *m.*, insulte; (ant.) rencontre, *f.* To put an — on any one; *faire un affront à quelqu'un.* To brook an —; *digérer un affront.* To pocket an —; *boire, avaler un affront.*

affronter, *n.*, offenseur, *m.*

affronting. *adj*., offensant, choquant.

affrontiveness, *n*., caractère offensant, caractère choquant, *m*.

affuse (af-fiouze), *v.a*., verser sur.

affusion (af-fiou-jeune), *n*., action de verser; (pharm.) affusion, *f*.

afield (-filde), *adv*., au champ,en campagne.

afire (-faeur), *adv*., en feu.

afiat, *adv*., à plat.

afloat (-flôte),*adv*., (nav.)à flot; sur l'eau; en train. To set a ship —; *mettre un vaisseau à flot*.

afoot (-foute), *adv*., à pied; sur pied.

afore, *prep*., devant, avant.

afore, *adv*., auparavant; en avant; sur le devant.

aforegoing (-goïgne), *adj*., précédent.

aforehand, *adv*., par avance.

aforementioned (-mèn-sheun'de), *adj*., mentionné plus haut, précité.

aforenamed (-né-m'de), *adj*., susnommé.

aforesaid, *adj*., susdit.

aforethought (-thôte), *adj*., prémédité.

aforetime (-taïme), *adv*., autrefois.

a fortiori (-ti-ô-), *adv*., à plus forte raison, à fortiori.

afraid (-fréde), *adj*., effrayé, craintif, qui a peur. To be — of anything; *avoir peur de quelque chose*.

afresh (-frè-she), *adv*., de nouveau, encore.

afric, *or* **african**, *adj*., Africain, d'Afrique.

african (-ca-n), *n*., Africain, *m*., Africaine, *f*.

afront (a-freu'nte), *adv*., en face.

aft, *adj*., (nav.) arrière, de l'arrière. Fore and —; (nav.) *en avant et en arrière*.

after, *adv*., après; suivant.

after, *prep*., après; après que; selon; sur; d'après.

after (-teur), *adj*., ultérieur, futur; arrière (nav.) d'arrière.

after-ages (-éd'jize), *n.pl*., siècles futurs, *m.pl*.; postérité, *f*.

after-all (-ôl), *adv*., après tout; enfin.

after-birth (-beurth), *n*., arrière-faix; (med.) placenta, délivre, *m*., secondines, *f.pl*.

after-clap, *n*., coup inattendu, *m*.

after-cost, *n*., frais ultérieurs, *m.pl*.

after-crop, *n*., seconde récolte, *f*.

after-days, *n.pl*., jours à venir, *m.pl*.

after-dinner, *n*., après-dîner, après-dîné, *m*., ⊙après-dînée, *f*.

after-dream (-drîme), *n*., rêverie, *f*.

after-fortune (-tioune), *n*., destinée ultérieure, *f*.

after-game (-ghéme), *n*., revanche.

after-grass, *n*., regain, *m*.

after-growth (-grôth), *n*., regain, *m*.

after-guard (-gârde), *n*., (nav.) surveillant de l'arrière, *m*.

after-hope (-hôpe). *n*., espérance future, *f*.

after-hours (-aeurze), *n.pl*., heures en sus, *f.pl*.

after-life (-laïfe), *n*., vie ultérieure, *f*.; avenir, *m*.

after-love, *n*., second amour, *m*.

aftermath (-math), *n*., regain, *m*.

afternoon (-noune), *n*., après-midi, *m.f*.; après-dîner, *m*.

after-pains (-pè'nze), *n.pl*., douleurs qui suivent l'accouchement; (med.) tranchées, *f.pl*.

after-part (-pârte), *n*., dernière partie, *f*.

after-piece (-pîce), *n*., (thea.) petite pièce, *f*.

after-sail (-séle),*n*.,(nav.)voile de l'arrière,*f*.

after-state (-stéte), *n*., état futur. *m*.

after-sting (-stigne), *n*., nouvelle piqûre,*f*.

after-storm, *n*., tempête nouvelle, *f*.

after-supper (-seup-peur),*n*., après-souper, après-soupé, *m*., après-soupée, *f*.

after-swarm (-swôrme), *n*., arrière-essaim, *m*.

after-taste (-'éste), *n*., arrière-goût, dé boire. *m*.

after-thought (-thôte), *n*., pensée ultérieure,*f*.

after-times (-taïm'ze), *n.pl*., temps à venir, *m.pl*.

after-tossing (to-cigne, *n*., (nav.)agitation de la mer après une tempête, *f*.; clapotage, *m*.

after-touch (-teut'she), *n*., (paint.) retouche, *f*.

afterward (-weurd), *or* **afterwards** (-weurdze), *adv*., ensuite, puis, plus tard.

after-wise (-waïze), *adj*., sage après coup.

after-wit (-wite), *n*., esprit tardif, *m*.; sagesse après coup, *f*.

aga, *n*., aga. *m*.

again (-ghéne), *adv*., encore; encore une fois, de nouveau. As much —; *encore autant*.

against (-ghé'nste), *prep*., contre; vis-à-vis; sur; vers, près de.

agami, *n*., (orni.) agami, *m*.

agamous (-meusse), *adj*., (bot.) agame.

agape (-ghépe), *adv*., la bouche béante.

agape (-pi), *n*. (*agape*), (theol.) agape, *f*.

agaric, *n*., (bot.) agaric, *m*.

agate (-ghéte), *n*., agate, *f*.

agaty (-ghé-). *adj*., de la nature de l'agate.

agave (-vi), *n*., (bot.) agavé, *m*.

age (édje), *n*., âge; siècle, *m*. Brazen —; *âge d'airain*. Golden —; *âge d'or*. Silver —; *âge d'argent*. Mi ldle —s; *moyen âge*. Dark -s; *siècles de ténèbres*. — of discretion; *âge de raison*. To be of —; *être majeur*. To be of an — to; *être d'âge à*. To look one's —; *paraître son âge*.

aged (é-djéde), *adj*., âgé.

agedly, *adv*., en vieillard.

agency, *n*., agence; maison de commission; action, entremise, influence, *f*.

agent (édjè-n-te), *n*., agent; homme d'affaires, *m*.

agglomerate, *v.a*., agglomérer.

agglomerate (-meur-éte), *v.n*., s'agglomérer.

agglomerated, *adj*., (bot.) agglomère.

agglomeration (-meur é-), *n*., agglomération, *f*.

agglutinant, *n*., agglutinant, *m*.

agglutinant (-gliou-). *adj*., agglutinant.

agglutinate (-gliou-ti-néte), *v.a*., agglutiner.

agglutination (-gliou-ti-né-), *n*., agglutination, *f*.

agglutinative (-gliou-ti-né-), *adj*., agglutinatif.

aggrandize (-daïze), *v.a*., agrandir.

aggrandizement, *n*., agrandissement, *m*.

aggrandizer, *n*., personne qui agrandit, *f*.

aggravate (-véte), *v.a*., aggraver; provoquer.

aggravation,*n*.,aggravation; circonstance aggravante, *f*.

aggregate, *v.a*., réunir, rassembler.

aggregate, *adj*., rassemblé, réuni; agrégé.

aggregate (-gri-ghéte), *n*., agrégation, masse, *f*.; total *m*.; somme totale, *f*.; agrégat, *m*.

aggregately,*adv*.,en masse,collectivement.

aggregation, *n*., agrégation, réunion, *f*.; assemblage, *m*.

aggregative, *adj*., agrégatif.

aggregator, *n*., collecteur en masse, *m*.

aggress, *v.n*., attaquer.

aggression, *n*., agression, attaque. *f*.

aggressive, *adj*., offensif, hostile; agressif.

aggressor, *n*., agresseur, *m*.

aggrievance. *V*. **grievance**.

aggrieve (ag-grîve), *v.a*., affliger; blesser, léser, offenser.

aggroup, *v a*., (paint.) grouper, agrouper.

aghast, *adj.*, frappé d'effroi; épouvanté, ébahi.

agile (adjile), *adj.*, agile, leste.

agileness, *n.*, agilité, légèreté, *f.*

agility, *n.*, agilité, légèreté, *f.*

agio (édji-ô), *n.*, change; agio, *m.*

agitable, *adj.*, que l'on peut agiter.

agitate (adjitéte), *v.a.*, agiter.

agitation, *n.*, agitation, *f.*; trouble, *m.*; discussion, *f.* To be in —; (of persons—*des personnes*) *avoir de l'agitation;* (of things—*des choses*) *être en question, être sur le tapis.*

agitator (-teur), *n.*, agitateur; meneur, *m.*

aglet, or **aiglet**, *n.*, aiguillette, *f.*; (bot.) onglet, *m.*

agnail (ag-néle), *n.*, envie, *f.*; panaris, *m.*

agnate (ag-néte), *n.*, agnat, *m.*

agnate, *adj.*, d'agnat, agnatique.

agnatic (ag-nat-), *adj.*, agnatique.

agnation (-ag-né-), *n.*, agnation, *f.*

agnize (ag-naïze), *v.a.*, (ant.) reconnaître.

agnomen (ag-nô-mè-n), *n.*, surnom, *m.*

agnomination (ag-no-mi-né-), *n.*, surnom, *m.*

ago, *adv.*, il y a. Long —; *il y a longtemps.* A long while —; *il y a bien longtemps.*

agog, *adv.*, avec feu. To be all —; *avoir la tête montée.*

agoing (-gôïgne), *adv.*, en train, en action.

agon (égône), *n.*, (antiq.) agone, *m.*

agone, *adv.*, (ant.) passé.

agonize, *v.n.*, souffrir l'agonie.

agonize (ag-ô-naïze), *v.a.*, torturer, faire souffrir.

agonized (ag-ô-naïz'de), *adj.*, (of persons—*des personnes*) qui souffre l'agonie; (of things —*des choses*) poignant.

agonizing (ag-ô-naïz-igne), *adj.*, qui fait souffrir; qui torture; le plus cruel.

agonizingly, *adv.*, avec angoisse.

agony, *n.*, agonie; douleur, angoisse, *f.*

agouti, *n.*, (mam.) agouti, *m.*

agrammatist, *n.*, (ant.) personne illettrée, *f.*

agrarian, *adj.*, agraire, agricole, d'agriculture.

agree, *v.n.*, s'accorder; convenir; se convenir; être d'accord.

agree, *v.a.*, accorder, mettre d'accord.

agreeable, *adj.*, agréable; conforme.

agreeableness, *n.*, agrément, *m.*; conformité, *f.*

agreeably, *adv.*, agréablement; conformément.

agreed, *adj.*, convenu, d'accord.

agreement, *n.*, accord; rapport, *m.*; convention; bonne intelligence; conformité, *f.*

agrestic, or **agrestical** (-grès-), *adj.*, agreste.

agricultor (-keult-eur), *n.*, agriculteur, *m.*

agricultural, *adj.*, agricole, d'agriculture.

agriculture (-keult-iour), *n.*, agriculture, *f.*

agriculturist, *n.*, agriculteur, agronome, *m.*

agrimony, *n.*, (bot.) aigremoine, *f.*

agriot, *n.*, griotte, *f.*

aground (-graou-n'de), *adj.*, (nav.) échoué; à terre. To run —; *échouer, mettre à la côte.*

ague (é-ghiou), *n.*, fièvre, fièvre intermittente, *f.*

ague-fit, *n.*, accès de fièvre intermittente, *m.*

ague-proof, *adj.*, à l'épreuve de la fièvre intermittente.

ague-spell, *n.*, charme fébrifuge, *m.*

ague-struck (-streuke), *adj.*, atteint de fièvre intermittente.

ague-tree (-trî), *n.*, (bot.) sassafras, *m.*

aguish (é-ghiou-ishe), *adj.*, fièvreux; ardent.

aguishness, *n.*, état fébrile, *m.*

ah! *int.*, ah! hélas!

aha! *int.*, aha!

ahead (-hède), *adv.*, (nav.) en avant, de-

vant; à la tête, en tête. To get — of (nav.); *gagner l'avant de;* (fig.) *devancer.*

ahigh (a-ha-ye), *adv.*, (ant.) en haut.

ahoy! (a-hoï), *int.*, (nav.) he!

ahull (-heul), *adv.*, (nav.) à mâts et à cordes.

ahungry, *adj.*, (ant.) tourmenté par la faim.

ai (é-i), *n.*, (mam.) aï, *m.*

aid, *v.a.*, aider; secourir. To — each other; *s'entr'aider.*

aid, *n.*, aide, *f.*; secours, *m.* With the — of; *à l'aide de.* To come to any one's —; *venir à l'aide de quelqu'un, venir en aide à quelqu'un.*

aidance (éd-anse), *n.*, (ant.) aide, *f.*

aidant (éd-ante), *adj.*, (ant.) qui aide.

aide-de-camp, *n.*, aide de camp, *m.*

aider, *n.*, aide, *m.f.*

aidless, *adj.*, sans secours.

aigremore (égheur-), *n.*, aigremore, *m.*

aiglet, *n.*, (her.) aiglon, *m.*

aigret, or **aigrette**, *n.*, aigrette, *f.*

aigulet (é-ghiou-lette), *n.*, aiguillette, *f.*

ail (éle), *v.a.*, avoir, faire mal. What —s you? *qu'avez-vous? qu'est-ce qui vous fait mal?* Nothing —s me; *je n'ai rien.*

ail, *n.*, mal, *m.*; indisposition, *f.*

ailing (él-igne), *adj.*, souffrant.

ailment, *n.*, mal, *m.*; incommodité, *f.*

aim, *v.a.*, viser; ajuster, diriger.

aim, *v.n.*, viser, aspirer.

aim (éme), *n.*, visée, *f.*; but; point de mire, *m.* To take— at; *viser; coucher en joue.* To miss one's—; *manquer son coup.*

air, *n.*, air, *m.*, mine, apparence, *f.*; vent, *m.* To build castles in the —; *faire des châteaux en Espagne.* To give one's self —s; *se donner des airs.* To give one's self an — of; *se donner un air de.* To let the —into a room; *donner de l'air à une chambre.* To take the —; *prendre l'air.* In the —; *en l'air.* Foul —; *air vicié.* Confined —; *air renfermé.* Downcast —; *air abattu.*

air, *v.a.*, aérer; mettre à l'air; ressuyer. This linen must be —ed; *il faut mettre ce linge à l'air.*

air-balloon (bal-loune), *n.*, ballon aérostatique, *m.*

air-bladder (-blad-deur), *n.*, vessie pleine d'air; (ich.) vessie aérienne, vessie natatoire, *f.*

air-braving (-brév-igne), *adj.*, qui brave les vents.

air-built (-bîlte), *adj.*, bâti en l'air, chimérique.

air-cell, *n.*, (bot.) cellule aérienne, *f.*

air-cushion (-coush-eune), *n.*, coussin à air, *m.*

air-drawn (-drône), *adj.*, imaginaire.

airer (aireur), *n.*, personne qui expose à l'air, *f.*

air-exhauster, *n.*, (phys.) ventilateur, *m.*

air-gun (-gheune), *n.*, fusil à vent, *m.*

air-holder, *n.*, tube à air, *m.*

air-hole, *n.*, soupirail; évent (of a furnace— *de fourneau*), *m.*

airily, *adv.*, légèrement.

airiness, *n.*, exposition à l'air; légèreté, *f.*

airing (air-igne), *n.*, aérage, *m.*; promenade, *f.* To take an —; *prendre l'air, faire une promenade.*

air-jacket (-djak-ète), *n.*, ceinture de natation, ceinture à air, *f.*

air-lamp, *n.*, lampe à courant d'air, *f.*

airless, *adj.*, privé d'air.

airling (-ligne), *n.*, éventé, *m.*; tête à l'évent, *f.*

air-mattress, *n.*, matelas à air, *m.*

air-passages (-pass'édjize), *n.*, voies aériennes, *f.pl.*

air-poise (-poïze), *n.*, aéromètre, *m.*

air-pump (-peu'mpe), *n.*, machine pneumatique, pompe à air, *f.*

air-shaft, *n.*, (tech.) puits d'aérage, *m.*

air-stirring (-steur'rigne), *adj.*, qui bat l'air.

air-stove (-stôve). *n.*, calorifère, *m.*

air-thread (-thrède), *n.*, fil de la vierge, *m.*

air-tight (-taïte), *adj.*, imperméable à l'air.

air-tightness, *n.*, imperméabilité à l'air, *f.*

air-trap, *n.*, machine à ventiler, *f.*, ventilateur, *m.*

air-tubes (-tioub'ze), *n.*, conduits aériens, *m.pl.*

air-valve, *n.*, soupape à air, *f.*

air-vessel (-vès's'l), *n.*, (bot.) vaisseau aérien; (tech.) réservoir d'air, *m.*

airy, *adj.*, aérien; ouvert à l'air, aéré; léger, gai.

airy-flying (-fla-ïgne), *adj.*, qui vole comme l'air.

airy-light (-laïte), *adj.*, léger comme l'air.

aisle (aïle), *n.*, (of a church—*d'église*) aile, nef latérale, *f.*, bas coté, *m.*

ajar (adjàr), *adj.*, entr'ouvert, entre-bâillé.

akimbo (-ki-m'bô), *adv.*, appuyé sur la hanche. With one's arms — ; *les poings sur les hanches.*

akin (-kine), *adj.*, allié; parent.

alabaster (-teur), *n.*, albâtre, *m.*

alabaster, *adj.*, d'albâtre.

alack ! *int.*, hélas !

alackaday ! *int.*, hélas !

alacrity, *n.*, vivacité, ardeur, *f.*, empressement, *m.*

alamode (-môde), *adv.*, à la mode.

alarm, *n.*, alarme, *f.*; (horl.) réveille-matin, *m.*

alarm, *v.a.*, alarmer, effrayer.

alarm-bell, *n.*, cloche d'alarme, *f.*, tocsin, *m.*

alarm-clock, *n.*, réveille-matin, *m.*

alarming, *adj.*, alarmant.

alarmingly, *adv.*, d'une manière alarmante.

alarmist, *n.*, alarmiste, *m.*

alarum (-la-reume, -lê-), *n.* *V.* **alarm**.

alas ! *int.*, hélas !

alate (é-léte), *adv.*, (ant.) dernièrement.

alate (él'éte, or **alated** (él'étède), *adj.*, ailé.

alaternus (-teur-neusse), *n.*, (bot.) alaterne, *m.*

alb, *n.*, aube (priest's vestment—*vêtement d'ecclésiastique*), *f.*

albatross, *n.*, (orni.) albatros, *m.*

albeit (ôl-bi-ite), *adv.*, quoique.

albescent (al-bès-sè-nte), *adj.*, blanchissant.

albino, *n.*, albinos; ⊙nègre-blanc, *m.*

albugineous (-bioud'ji-n'i-eusse), *adj.*, albuginé, albugineux.

albugo (-biou-gô), *n.*, (med.) albugo, *m.*

album, *n.*, album, *m.*

albumen (-biou-), *n.*, albumine, *f.*

albuminous (-neusse), *adj.*, albumineux.

alburnum (-beur-neume), *n.*, (bot.) aubier, *m.*

alcaic (-ké-îke), *adj.*, alcaïque.

alcaic, *n.*, alcaïque, *m.*

alcaid (-kéde), *n.*, (of Morocco, Spain—*au Maroc, en Espagne*) alcade.

alchemic, *or* **alchemical** (-ké-), *adj.*, alchimique.

alchemically, *adv.*, par un procédé alchimique.

alchemist (-ké-), *n.*, alchimiste, *m.*

alchemistic, *or* **alchemistical**, *adj.*, d'alchimiste, alchimique.

alchemy (-ké-), *n.*, alchimie, *f.*

alcohol (cô-), *n.*, alcool, *m.*

alcoholic, *adj.*, alcoolique.

alcoholization (-zé-), *n.*, alcoolisation, *f.*

alcoholize (-laïze), *v.a.*, alcooliser.

alcoholmeter, *or* **alcohometer** (-mi-teur), *n.*, alcoolomètre, *m.*

alcoran, *n.* *V.* **alkoran**, **koran**.

alcove, *n.*, alcôve; niche; (gard.) loge, *f.*; pavillon, *m.*

alder (ôl-deur), *n.*, (bot.) aune, *m.*

alderman (ôl-deur-mane), *n.*, alderman, *m.*

aldermanly, *adj.*, d'alderman.

alder-plot (-plote), *n.*, aunaie, *f.*

ale (éle), *n.*, ale, *f.*

ale-bench (-bè-nshe), *n.*, banc de cabaret, *m.*

ale-brewer (-brou-eur), *n.*, brasseur d'ale, *m.*

ale-conner (-con-neur), *n.*, inspecteur de mesures pour les liquides, *m.*

alecost (éle-), *n.* *V.* **tansy**.

alee (ali), *adv.*, (nav.) sous le vent.

ale-gar (éli-gheur), *n.*, vinaigre d'ale, *m.*

ale-hoof (-houfe), *n.*, (bot.) lierre terrestre, *m.*

ale-house (-haouce), *n.*, cabaret où l'on débite de l'ale, *m.*

ale-knight (naïte), *n.*, (ant.) pilier de cabaret, *m.*

alembic, *n.*, alambic, *m.*

alength, *adv.*, (ant.) tout de son long.

alert (-leurte), *adj.*, alerte, vigilant, vif.

alertness, *n.*, activité, vigilance, *f.*

ale-shot, *n.*, écot de cabaret, *m.*

ale-stake (él-stéke), *n.*, bouchon de cabaret, *m.*

ale-taster (-tésteur), *n.*, inspecteur des boissons, dégustateur, *m.*

ale-washed (-wosht), *adj.*, trempé, imbibé d'ale.

ale-wife (-waïfe), *n.*, cabaretière, *f.*

alexandrian, *adj.*, alexandrien, d'Alexandrie.

alexandrian, *or* **alexandrine**, *n.*, alexandrin, *m.*

alga (algha), *n.* (*algæ*), (bot.) algue, *f.*

algaly, *n.*, (surg.) algalie, *f.*

algazel, *n.*, gazelle, *f.*

algebra (al-dji-), *n.*, algèbre, *f.*

algebraic (-bré-ik), *or* **algebraical** (bré-i-), *adj.*, algébrique.

algebraically, *adv.*, algébriquement.

algebraist (-bré-iste), *n.*, algébriste, *m.*

algid, *adj.*, (ant.) froid, glacé.

algidity, *n.*, (ant.) froid, *m.*

algific, *adj.*, (ant.) refroidissant.

algor, *n.*, (med.) (ant.) froid extrême, *m.*

algorithm (-gô-rith'm), *n.*, (math.) algorithme, *m.*

algous (-gheusse), *adj.*, qui a rapport aux algues.

alguazil, *n.*, alguazil, *m.*

alias (é-li-), *adv.*, dit, autrement dit.

alibi, *n.*, (jur.) alibi, *m.*

alible, *adj.*, (ant.) (med.) alibile.

alien (éliène), *adj.*, étranger; éloigné.

alien, *n.*, étranger, *m.*, étrangère, *f.*

alienability (éliè-), *n.*, aliénabilité, capacité d'être aliéné, *f.*

alienable, *adj.*, aliénable.

alienate, *v.a.*, aliéner, éloigner.

alienate, *adj.*, étranger.

alienation (-né-), *n.*, aliénation, *f.*; éloignement, *m.* Mental — ; *aliénation mentale.*

alienator, *n.*, aliénateur, *m.*, aliénatrice, *f.*

alienee, *n.*, aliénataire, *m.f.*

alight, *adj.*, allumé.

alight (-laïte), *v.n.*, descendre ; mettre pied à terre; s'abattre.

align, *v.a.* *V.* **align**.

alike, *adv.*, également ; de même ; à la fois.

alike (-laïke), *adj.*, semblable, pareil; ressemblant.

aliment, *n.*, aliment, *m.*

alimental, *adj.*, alimentaire.

alimentally, *adv.*, de manière à servir d'aliment.

alimentariness, *n.*, qualité alimentaire, *f.*

alimentary, *adj.*, alimentaire.

alimentation (-té-), *n.*, alimentation, *f.*

alimony, *adj.*, pension alimentaire, *f.*

aliquant (-kwa-n-te), *adj.*, aliquante.
aliquot (-kwote), *adj.*, aliquote.
alish (é-), *adj.*, sentant l'ale ; d'ale.
alive (-laïve), *adj.*, en vie, vivant ; vif, sensible ; animé. While — ; *de son vivant.* Dead or — ; *mort ou vif.* More dead than — ; *plus mort que vif.*
alkalescency, *n.*, (chem.) alcalescence. *f.*
alkalescent, *adj.*, alcalescent.
alkali. *n.*, alcali, *m.*
alkalify (-fa'ye), *v.n.*, rendre alcalin ; alcaliser.
alkalimeter (-miteur), *n.*, (chem.) alcalimètre, *m.*
alkaline, *adj.*, alcalin.
alkaline (-laïne), *n.*, substance alcaline, *f.*
alkalization (-laï-zé-), *n.*, (ant.) alcalisation. *f.*
alkalize (-laïze), *v.a.*, alcaliser.
alkanet (-nète), *n.*, (bot.) orcanète, *f.*
alkoran (-kôra-n), *n.*, alkoran, coran, *m.*
all (ôl), *adj.*, tout, tous. — of you ; *vous tous.* That is — ; *voilà tout, c'est tout.* It is — the same ; *c'est tout de même.* One and — ; *tous sans exception.* Above — ; *surtout, par-dessus tout.*
all, *adv.*, tout, entièrement, souverainement. Not at — ; *point du tout.* — at once ; *tout d'un coup.* Nothing at — ; *rien du tout.*
all. *n.*, tout, *m.*, *pl.*, touts.
all-abhorred (-ab-hord), *adj.*, abhorré de tous.
all-admiring (-maeur-), *adj.*, tout dans l'admiration.
allantois (al-la-n-toïsse), *n.*, (anat.) allantoïde, *f.*
allay, *v.a.*, apaiser, soulager, adoucir, calmer.
allay, *n.*, affaiblissement, *m.*
allayer (al-lé-eur), *n.*, personne qui tempère, qui soulage, qui calme, *f.* ; calmant, soulagement, *m.*
allayment, *n.*, (ant.) adoucissement, *m.*
all-beauteous (-biouti-eusse), *adj.*, souverainement beau.
all-bountiful (-baoun-tifoul), *adj.*, infiniment bon.
all-cheering (-tshîrigne), *adj.*, qui réjouit tout.
all-complying (-ko-m-plaïgne), *adj.*, qui se prête à tout.
all-dreaded (-drèdède), *adj.*, redouté de tous.
all-efficient (-shi-è-nte), *adj.*, tout efficace.
allegation (al-li-ghé-), *n.*, allégation, *f.*
allege (al-lèdje), *v.a.*, alléguer.
allegeable, *adj.*, qu'on peut alléguer.
alleger, *n.*, celui, celle qui allègue.
allegiance (al-lîd-jia-nce), *n.*, fidélité ; obéissance, *f.* Oath of — ; *serment de fidélité ;* (English hist.) *serment d'allégeance, m.*
allegoric, or **allegorical**, *adj.*, allégorique.
allegorically, *adv.*, allégoriquement.
allegoricalness (al-li-), *n.*, qualité de ce qui est allégorique, *f.*
allegorist, *n.*, allégoriseur ; allégoriste, *m.*
allegorize, *v.a.*, allégoriser.
allegorize (-raïze), *v.n.*, faire des allégories.
allegorizing, *adj.*, qui fait des allégories, qui aime les allégories.
allegory (al-li-), *n.*, allégorie, *f.*
allegro (al-li-), *adv.*, (mus.) allegro.
all-eloquent (-èlôkouè-n-te), *adj.*, tout éloquent.
alleluiah (al-li-liou-ya), *n.*, alléluia, *m.*
all-enduring (-è-n-diourigne), *adj.*, résigné, qui endure tout.
alleviate (al-ll-vié-te), *v.a.*, alléger, soulager, adoucir.
alleviation. *n.*, allégement, adoucissement, soulagement. *m.*

alley (al-li). *n.*, ruelle, allée, *f.* Blind — ; *impasse, f.*
all-fours (ôl-fôrze), *n.*, (cards—*aux cartes*) impériale, *f.* To go on — ; *marcher à quatre pattes.*
all-giver (-ghiveur), *n.*, dispensateur de tous les biens, *m.*
all-good, *adj.*, souverainement bon.
all-good (ôl-goude), *n.*, (bot.) chenopode, épinard sauvage, *m.*
all-hail! (-héle), *int.*, salut !
all-hallows (ôl-hal-lôze), *n.*, La Toussaint, *f.* — -tide ; *époque de la Toussaint, f.*
all-happy, *adj.*, bienheureux.
all-heal (-hîle), *n.*, (bot.) berce, branche-ursine bâtarde, *f.*
alliaceous (al-lié-shi-eusse), *adj.*, (bot.) alliacé.
alliance (al-la-ia-nce), *n.*, alliance, *f.*
alligate (al-li-ghéte), *v.a.*, lier.
alligation, *n.*, action de lier ; (arith.) règle d'alliage, *f.*
alligator (al-ll-ghé-teur), *n.*, crocodile d'Amérique, alligator, *m.*
align (al-laïne), *v.a.*, aligner.
alignment, *n.*, alignement, *m.*
allision (al-li-jeune), *n.*, heurt, choc, *m.*
alliteration (al-li-teuré-), *n.*, (rhet.) allitération, *f.*
alliterative (al-li-teura-), *adj.*, qui a rapport à l'allitération, *f.*
all-judging (-djeud'jigne), *adj.*, juge suprême.
all-just (-djeuste), *adj.*, qui est tout justice.
all-kind (-kaï-n-de), *adj.*, tout de bonté ; extrêmement bon.
all-knowing (-nôïgne), *adj.*, de science infinie, omniscient.
all-loving, *adj.*, dont l'amour est infini.
allocate (al-lôkéte), *v.a.*, allouer.
allocation, *n.*, allocation ; disposition, *f.*, arrangement, *m.*
allocution (al-lô-kiou-), *n.*, allocution. *f.*
allodial (al-lô-), *adj.*, allodial.
allodium (al-lô-dieume), *n.*, (feudalism—*féodalité*) franc-alleu, *m.*
allonge (al-leu'n-je), *n.*, (fenc.) botte, *f.*
allonge, *v.a.*, (fenc.) allonger.
alloo. *V.* halloo.
alloquy (al-lô-kwi), *n.*, (ant.) discours, *m.*
allot (al-lote), *v.a.*, assigner en partage, donner, départir, répartir, accorder ; ⊙(jur.) allotir.
allotment, *n.*, partage, lot ; décret, *m.* ; distribution, répartition, *f.*
allottery, *n.*, (ant.). *V.* allotment.
allow (al-laou), *v.a.*, permettre ; donner ; allouer, approuver, avouer ; souffrir. I will not — it ; *Je ne le souffrirai pas.* — me ; *permettez-moi.*
allowable. *adj.*, légitime, juste, permis.
allowableness, *n.*, qualité de ce qui est permis ; légitimité, *f.*
allowance. *n.*, allocation, pension ; gratification ; ration ; (com.) remise, réduction, *f.* Short — ; *ration réduite, ration diminuée.* Trade — ; (com.) *remise, réduction.* To be on short — ; *être rationné.* To make — for ; *avoir de l'indulgence pour ; avoir égard à, tenir compte de.* To put on short — ; *rationner.*
allowance, *v.a.*, mettre à la ration, rationner.
alloy (al-lo-i), *n.*, alliage, *m.*
alloy, *v.a.*, (metal.) allier ; altérer, diminuer. flétrir.
alloyage (al-lo-yèdge), *n.*, (metal.) alliage. *m.*
all-powerful (-paoueurfoul), *adj.*, tout-puissant.

all-saints'-day (-sé-ntse-), n., jour de la Toussaint, m.

all-souls'-day (-sôlze-), n., jour des morts, m.

all-spice (-spaîce), n., (bot.) piment, m.

all-sufficient (-seuf-fi-shiè-n-te), adj., suffisant.

allude (al-lioude), v.a., faire allusion ; avoir trait ; vouloir parler, vouloir dire.

alluminor (al-liou-), n., enlumineur, m.

allure (al-lioure), v.a., amorcer, attirer séduire.

allurement, n., ' amorce, séduction, f. ; attrait, m.

allurer, n., séducteur, flatteur, m.

alluring, adj., entraînant, attrayant, séduisant.

alluringly, adv., d'une manière séduisante, attrayante, entraînante.

alluringness, n., entraînement, m. ; séduction, f.

allusion (al-liou-jeune), n., allusion ; comparaison ; figure, f.

allusive, adj., qui fait allusion ; figuré.

allusively, adv., par allusion.

allusiveness, n., qualité de renfermer une allusion, f.

alluvia (al-liou-), n.pl., terres d'alluvion, f.pl., alluvion, f.

alluvial, adj., d'alluvion, alluvial.

alluvious (al-liou-vi-eusse), adj. (ant.) V. **alluvial**.

alluvium (al-liou-vieume), n., alluvion, f., atterrissement, m.

all-wise (-waîze), adj., d'une sagesse infinie.

all-worshipped (-shipte), adj., adoré de tous.

all-worthy (-weurthi), adj., infiniment digne.

ally, v.a., allier, unir. To — one's self ; s'allier.

ally (al-laï), n., allié, m.

almagist (-djiste), n., almageste, m.

almanac (ôl-ma-nake), n., almanach, m.

almightiness (ôl-maï-ti-nèsse), n., toutepuissance, omnipotence, f.

almighty (ôl-maï-ti), adj., tout-puissant, omnipotent.

almighty, n., Tout-Puissant, m.

almond (â-meu-n-de), n., amande, f. Burnt —; praline, amande pralinée, f. Milk of —s; lait d'amandes, m. Bitter —; amande amère. Sweet —; amande douce. African —; amande d'Afrique, f. Italian —; amande d'Italie. Shelled —s; amandes cassées. Oil of —s; huile d'amandes, f. — paste; pâte d'amande, f. — soap; savon d'amande, m.

almond-flower (-flaoueur), n., fleur d'amande, f.

almond-tree (-trî), n., amandier, m.

almoner (-neur), n., aumônier, m.

almonry (-meun'ri), n., aumônerie, f.

almost (ôl-môste), adv., presque.

alms (â'mze), n., aumône, f.

alms-box, n., tronc des aumônes, m.

almsdeed, n. (-dide), œuvre de charité, f.

alms-giving (-ghi-), n., aumônes, f.pl.

alms-house (-haouce), n., maison de charité, f ; hospice pour les pauvres, m.

alms-man, n., homme qui vit d'aumônes, m.

alnage (al-nèdje), n., aunage, m.

alnight (al-naïte), n., (ant.) veilleuse, f.

aloe, (-lô), n., (bot.) aloès, m.

aloes (-lôze), n., (med.) aloès, m.

aloes-wood (-woude), n., bois d'aloès, m.

aloetic (-ètic), or **aloetical** (-ètical), adj., aloétique.

aloetic, n., médicament aloétique, m.

aloft, adv., en haut, haut, en l'air.

aloft, prep., au-dessus de.

alone (-lône), adj., seul ; unique. To let —;

laisser, laisser de côté, laisser là. Let me —; laissez-moi tranquille.

along, adv., le long, le long de. Come —; venez donc. All —; tout le temps; tout le long de; tout le long du chemin.

aloof (-loufe), adv., loin ; au loin ; éloigné ; (nav.) au lof. To keep —; se tenir à l'écart.

alosa (-lô-ça), n., (ich.) alose, f.

aloud (-laoude), adv., haut ; à haute voix ; à grand bruit.

alpaca, n., alpaga, m.

alpha, n., alpha (of the Grecian alphabet —de l'alphabet Grec); alpha, commencement, principe, m.

alphabet, n., alphabet ; (com.) répertoire alphabétique, m.

alphabet, v.a., classer par ordre alphabétique.

alphabetic, or **alphabetical**, adj., alphabétique.

alphabetically, adv., alphabétiquement.

alpine, adj., alpin ; des Alpes, alpestre.

already (ôl-rè-), adv., déjà.

also (ôl-sô), adv., aussi.

altar (-teur), n., autel, m.

altar-cloth (-clôth), n., nappe d'autel, f.

altar-piece (-pîce), n., tableau d'autel, m.

altarwise (-waîze), adj., en forme d'autel.

alter, v.a., changer; altérer.

alter (ôl-teur), v.n., changer, se changer.

alterable, adj., changeant.

alterableness, n., nature changeante, f.

alterably, adv., de manière à pouvoir être changé.

alterant, adj., changeant, qui peut changer.

alteration (-teuré-), n., changement, m. To require —; demander du changement.

alterative (-teura-), adj., (med.) altérant.

alterative, n., (med.) altérant, m.

altercation (-ôl-teur-ké-) n., altercation, f.

altern (ôl-teurne), adj., (ant.) alternatif; alterne.

alternate, adj., alterne, alternant.

alternate, n., alternative (succession), f.

alternate (ôl-teur-néte), v.a., alterner, faire alterner.

alternate, v.n., alterner.

alternately, adv., alternativement, tour à tour.

alternateness, n., alternat, m.

alternation, n., alternative ; (geol.) alternance, f.

alternative, adj., alternatif, alternant.

alternative (ôl-teur-né-), n., alternative, f.; choix, m.

alternatively, adv., de manière à offrir une alternative.

although (ôl-thô), conj., bien que, quoique.

altiloquence (-lo-kwè-n-se), n., (ant.) discours pompeux, m.

altitude (-tioude), n., élévation, hauteur, altitude, f.

altivolant (-vo-la-n'te), adj., (ant.) dont le vol est élevé.

altogether (ôl-tou-ghè-theur), adv., tout à fait, entièrement.

alto-relievo (-tô-ri-li-vo), n., plein, haut relief, m.

aludel (-liou-) n., (chem.) aludel, m.

alum (-leume), n., alun, m. Rock —; alun de roche.

alum, v.a., aluner.

alumed (-leum'de), adj., aluné.

alumina, or **alumine** (-liou-) n., (min.) alumine, f.

aluming (-leumigne), n., (dy.) alunage, m.

aluminous (-liou-mi-neusse), adj., alumineux.

alumish (-leu-mishe), adj., de la nature de l'alun, ressemblant à l'alun.

alum-making (-mé-kigne),n., alunation,f.
alum-pit, n., alunière,f.
alum-water (-wŏ-teur), n., eau alumíneuse,f.
alum-works (-weurkse),n., fabrique d'alun.
alveole (-vi-oli), or **alveolus** (-vi-oleusse) n. (alveoli) (anat.) alvéole, m.
always (ōlwéze), adv., toujours.
amability, n., amabilité,f.
amain (-méne), adv., vigoureusement, avec force; (nav.) tout de suite; (nav.) amène !
amalgam (-game), n., amalgame, m.
amalgamable, adj., qui peut s'amalgamer.
amalgamate (-méte), v.a., amalgamer.
amalgamate, v.n., s'amalgamer.
amalgamation (-ga-mé-), n., amalgamation,f.; amalgame, m,
amanuensis (-niou-è-n), n. (amanuenses) secrétaire, copiste, m.
amaranth (-ra-nth), or **amaranthus** (-ra-ntheusse), n., amarante, f.
amaranthine (-ra-n-thíne), adj., d'amarante.
amaryllis, n., (bot.) amaryllis, f.
amass, v.a., amasser, entasser.
amateur (-tioure), n., amateur, m.
amatorial (-tŏ-), adj., d'amour; amoureux.
amatorially, adv., amoureusement.
amatory (-to-), adj., d'amour; amoureux.
amaurosis, n., (med.)goutte sereine, amaurose,f.
amaze (-méze), v.a., surprendre, étonner, frapper d'étonnement.
amaze, n., étonnement; effroi, m.
amazed (-méz'de), part., surpris; dans l'étonnement.
amazedly (-mézèdli), adv., avec étonnement.
amazedness (-mézèd'nèsse), n., étonnement, m.
amazement, n., étonnement, effroi, 'm.
amazing, adj., étonnant.
amazingly, adv., étonnamment.
amazon, n., amazone,f.
amazonia, (myth., lit.) pays des amazones, m.
amazonian (-zŏ-), adj., d'amazone.
ambages (a-m-bé-d'jize), n.pl., ambages, f.pl., détours, m.pl.
ambassador (-deur), n., ambassadeur, m.
ambassadress(-drèsse),n.,ambassadrice,f.
amber, n., ambre, m.
amber (-beur), adj., d'ambre.
amber, v.a., ambrer.
amber-coloured (-keu-leurde), adj., de couleur ambrée.
amber-drink, n., boisson de couleur ambrée, f.
ambergris (-grisse), n., ambre gris, m.
amber-seed (-síde), n., graine musquée, ambrette,f.
ambidexter (-teur), n., ambidextre, m,f.
ambidextrous(-treusse), adj., ambidextre.
ambidextrousness (-treuss'nèsse), n., faculté de se servir des deux mains avec une égale facilité;duplicité, f.; double jeu, m.
ambient, adj., ambiant.
ambigu (-ghiou), m., ambigu, m.
ambiguity, n., ambiguïté; équivoque, f.
ambiguous (-ghiou-eusse), adj., ambigu, équivoque, douteux.
ambiguously, adv., ambigument.
ambiguousness, n., ambiguïté,f.
ambit, n., contour, m.
ambition, n., ambition, f.
ambitious (-sheusse), adj., ambitieux.
ambitiously, adv., ambitieusement
ambitiousness, n., caractèreambitieux, m.
amble, v.n., aller l'amble. To make a horse — ; mettre un cheval à l'amble

amble, v.n., faire aller l'amble à.
amble, n., amble,m.
ambler (-bleur), n., haquenée, f.; cheval qui va l'amble, m.
ambling, adj., à l'amble.
amblingly, adv., à l'amble.
ambrosia (-brŏ-jia), n., ambroisie, f.
ambrosial, adj., d'ambroisie, délicieux, doux.
ambrosian (-brŏ-ji-), adj., d'ambroisie; ambroisien, de Saint Ambroise.
ambs-ace (é'mz'éce), n., bezet, ambesas, m.
ambulance n. (-biou-), hôpital militaire, m.; ambulance, f.
ambulant (-biou-), adj., ambulant.
ambulatory, adj., ambulatoire.
ambury (-biou-), n., (vet.) furoncle, m.
ambuscade (-beus-kéde), n., embuscade, f. To lay an — for; dresser une embuscade à. To fall into an — ; tomber dans une embuscade.
ambuscade, v.a., embusquer, mettre en embuscade.
ambush (-boushe), n., (b.s.) embûche; (milit.) embuscade,f.
ambush, v.a., embusquer.
ambush, v.n., s'embusquer.
ambushment, n., (ant.) embûche,f.
ameer (-mieur), or **amir**, n., Émir, m.
ameliorate (-mi-lieu-réte),v.a., améliorer, perfectionner.
ameliorate,v.n., s'améliorer, se perfectionner.
amelioration, n., amélioration,f.; perfectionnement, m.
amen.(é-mè-ne), adv., amen.
amenable (-mi-), adj., responsable; justiciable, soumis, sujet.
amend, v.a., amender, corriger; réparer.
amend, v.n., s'amender, s'améliorer, se corriger.
amendable (-dab'l), adj., amendable.
amendatory (-to-), adj., qui amende, qui corrige.
amender, n., personne qui amende, chose qui amende, f.; correctif, m.
amendment, n., amendement, changement, m.
amends (mè-n-dze),n., dédommagement, m.; compensation; réparation,f. To make — for; dédommager de.
amenity (-mè-), n., aménité,f.
amentaceæ, n.pl.,(bot.) amentacées, f.pl.
amerce (-meurse), v.a., mettre à l'amende.
amercer, n.,personne qui met à l'amende,f.
american,adj., américain.
american,n., Américain, m., Américaine, f.
american, n., (print.) américaine, f.
americanism, n., patriotisme américain; idiotisme américain, m.
americanize (-naïze), v.a., naturaliser Américain.
amethyst (-mé-thiste), n., améthyste, f.
amethystine (-taïne), adj., de la nature de l'amethyste; fait d'améthyste.
amiability (é-mia-), n., amabilité, f.
amiable, adj., aimable; attrayant.
amiableness, n., amabilité, f.
amiably, adv., avec amabilité.
amianth (-a-nth),or **amianthus**(-theusse), n., (min.) amiante, m.
amicable, adj., amical; amiable.
amicableness, n., état amical, m.
amicably, adv.,amicalement;amiablement, à l'amiable.
amice (-misse), or **amict** (-mikte), n., amict, m.
amid, or **amidst**, prep.,au milieu de.
amidships (-jí-), adv., (nav.) par le travers.
amiss, adj., mauvais.
amiss, adv., mal. To do — ; malfaire.

amity, *n.*, amitié, *f.*

ammi, *n.*, (bot.) ammi, sison, *m.*

ammonia (am-mô-), *n.*, ammoniaque, *m.f.*

ammoniac, *or* ammoniacum (-keume), *n.*, gomme ammoniaque, *f.*

ammoniac. *or* ammoniacal, *adj.*, ammoniac, ammoniacal.

ammunition (am-miou-), *n.*, munitions de guerre, *f.pl.*

amnesty, *n.*, amnistie, *f.*

amomum (mô-meume), *n.*, (bot.)amome, *m.*

among (-meu-n'g), amongst (-meu-n'gst), *prep.*, entre, parmi ; avec, au milieu de.

amorist, *or* amoroso (-rô-çô), *n.*, (ant.) galant, amoureux, *m.*

amorous (-reusse), *adj.*, amoureux.

amorously, *adv.*, amoureusement.

amorousness. *n.*, galanterie, *f.*

amorphous (-feusse), *adj.*, amorphe.

amort (-morte), *adj.*, mort ; abattu.

amortization (-taïzé-),*n.*,amortissement,*m.*

amortize (-taïze), *v.a.*, affaiblir ; amortir.

amortizement, *n.*, amortissement, *m.*

amount, *v.n.*, se monter, monter, revenir à, s'élever.

amount (-maou-n'te), *n.*, montant, total, *m.* ; quantité, *f.*

amour, *n.*, amours (intrigue), *f.pl.*

amove (-mouve), *v.n.*, ôter, éloigner.

amphibia, *n.pl.*, amphibies, *m.pl.*

amphibial, *n.*, amphibie, *m.*

amphibious (-bieusse), *adj.*, amphibie.

amphibiousness, *n.*, nature amphibie, *f.*

amphibological (-lod'ji-), *adj.*, amphibologique.

amphibologically, *adv.*, amphibologiquement

amphibology, *n.*, amphibologie, *f.*

amphibrach (-brake), *n.*, amphibraque, *m.*

amphictyonic (-ti-o-), *adj.*, amphictyonique.

amphictyons (-ti-o-n-ze), *n.pl.*, amphictyons, *m.pl.*

amphisciaus (-fis-si-a-n-ze *or* amphiscii (-fis-si-a-ye),*m.pl.*,(geog.)amphisciens,*m.pl.*

amphitheatral (-thi-),.*adj.* en amphithéâtre.

amphitheatre (-thi-a-teur), *n.*,amphithéâtre, *m.*

amphitheatrical, *adj.*, amphithéâtral.

ample, *adj.*, ample, large.

ampleness, *n.*, ampleur, grandeur, *f.*

ampliation (-pli-é-), *n.*, (Rom. antiq.) ajournement d'un jugement criminel, *m.* ; (l.u.) amplification, prolixité, *f.*

amplification (-ké-), *n.*, amplification, *f.*

amplifier (fa-ieur), *n.*, amplificateur, *m.*

amplify (-fa'ye), *v.a.*, agrandir, amplifier, augmenter.

amplitude (-tioude), *n.*, amplitude, étendue,*f.*

amply, *adv.*, amplement.

ampulla (-peul-la), *n.*, (bot.) ampoule, *f.*

amputate (-piou-téte), *v.a.*, amputer.

amputation, *n.*,amputation,*f.* To perform an — ; *faire une amputation.*

amulet (-mioulète), *n.*, amulette, *f.*

amuse (-miouze), *v.a.*, amuser, divertir, récréer, distraire. To be —d ; *s'amuser.*

amusement, *n.*, amusement, divertissement. *m.* ; distraction,*f.*

amuser. *n.*, amuseur, *m.*

amusing, *adj.*, amusant.

amusingly, *adv.*, d'une manière amusante.

amusive, *adj.*, amusant, agréable.

amusively, *adv.*, agréablement.

amygdalate (-da-léte), *adj.*, faitd'amandes.

amygdalate, *n.*, amandé, *m.*

amygdaloid (-loïde), *n.*, (min.) amygdaloïde,*f.*

amylaceous (-lé-shi-eusse), *adj.*, amylacé.

an, *art.*, un, *m.*, une, *f.*

an, *conj.*, (ant.) si.

anabaptism (-bap-tiz'me), *n.*, anabaptisme, *m.*

anabaptist. *n.*, anabaptiste, *m.f.*

anabaptistic. *or* anabaptistical, *adj.*, des anabaptistes.

anabaptistically, *adv.*, en anabaptiste.

anabaptistry, *n.*, anabaptisme, *m.*

anabaptize (-bap-taïze), *v.a.*, (ant.) rebaptiser.

anacardium (-câr-dieume), *n.*, (bot.) anacarde, *m.*

anachoret (-kô-rète), *or* anachorite (-kô-raïte), *n. V.* anchoret.

anachronism, *n.*, anachronisme, *m.*

anachronistic, *adj.*, qui contient un anachronisme.

anacoluthon (-liou-tho-n), *n.*, (gram.) anacoluthe, *f.*

anacreontic (-cri-o-n-), *adj.*, anacréontique.

anacreontic, *n.*, poème anacréontique, *m.*

anagogical (-god'ji-), *adj.*, (theol.) anagogique.

anagram, *n.*, anagramme, *f.*

anagrammatic, *or* anagrammatical, *adj.*, d'anagramme.

anagrammatically,*adv.*,par anagramme.

anagrammatist, *n.*, anagrammatiste, *m.*

anagrammatize, *v.n.*, anagrammatiser.

analecta, *or* analects (-lèkta, -lèktse), *n.*, *pl.*, analectes, *m.pl.*

analemma, *n.*, (astron.) analemme, *m.*

analeptic, *adj.*, analeptique.

analeptic, *n.*, analeptique, *m.*

analogical (-lod'ji-), *adj.*, analogique.

analogically, *adv.*, analogiquement.

analogicalness, *n.*, qualité d'avoir de l'analogie,*f.*

analogism (-lod'jiz'me), *n.*, analogisme, *m.*

analogist, *n.*, personne qui fait des analogies,*f.*

analogize (-lod'jaïze), *v.a.*, expliquer analogiquement.

analogous (-logheusse), *adj.*, analogue.

analogously, *adv.*, d'une manière analogue.

analogy (-lod'ji), *n.*, analogie, *f.* By— ; *par analogie.*

analysis, *n.*, analyse, *f.*

analyst, *n.*, analyste, *m.*

analytic, *or* analytical, *adj.*, analytique, raisonné.

analytically, *adv.*, analytiquement.

analytics, *n.*, art de l'analyse, *m.*

analyze (-laïze), *v.a.*, analyser, faire l'analyse de.

analyzer, *n.*, analyste; agent de décomposition, *m.*

anamorphosis (-cisse), *n.*, anamorphose,*f.*

ananas, *or* ananassa, *n.*, ananas, *m.*

anapæst, *or* anapest, *n.*, anapeste, *m.*

anapestic, *adj.*, anapestique.

anapestic, *n.*, mesure anapestique, *f.*

anaphora, *n.*, (rhet.) anaphore, *f.*

anarchic, *or* anarchical (-kik, -ki-kal), *adj.*, anarchique.

anarchist, *n.*, anarchiste, *m.f.*

anarchy (-ki), *n.*, anarchie,*f.*

anasarca (-câr-), *n.*, (med.) anasarque, *f.*

anasarcous (-câr-keusse), *adj.*, qui a rapport à l'anasarque.

anastomosis (-tô-mo-cisse), *n.*, (anat.) anastomose,*f.*

anastomotic (-to-mô-), *adj.*, (anat.) anastomotique.

anastrophe, *or* anastrophy (-tro-fi, -tro-fi), *n.*,(gram.) anastrophe, *f.*

anathema (-nath-é-), *n.*, anathème, *m.*

anathematical, *adj.*, d'anathème.

anathematically, *adv.*, en forme d'anathème.

anathematization (-nath-é-matizé-), *n.*, action d'anathématiser, *f.*

anathematize (-nath-é-ma-taïze), *v.a.*, anathématiser, frapper d'anathème.

anathematized (-nath-é-ma-taïz'de), *adj.*, anathème.

anatomical, *adj.*, anatomique.

anatomically, *adv.*, anatomiquement.

anatomist (-to-), *n.*, anatomiste, *m.*

anatomize (-to-maïze), *v.a.*, anatomiser. ·

anatomy (-to-), *n.*, anatomie, *f.*

ancestor (-cès-teur), *n.*, ancêtre.

ancestors (-cès-teurze), *n.pl.*, ancêtres, aïeux. *m. pl.*

ancestral, *adj.*, d'ancêtres, de mes, de tes, de ses, &c., ancêtres.

ancestry, *n.*, ancêtres, *m.pl.*

anchor (-keur), *n.*, ancre, *f.* Best bower —; *seconde ancre.* Bower —; *ancre de poste.* Ebb —; *ancre de jusant.* Flood —; *ancre de flot.* Foul —; *ancre surjalée.* Kedge —; *ancre à empenneler.* Sea —; *ancre du large.* Sheet- —; *maîtresse ancre, ancre de miséricorde;* (fig.) *ancre de salut, planche de salut, f.* Shore —; *ancre de terre.* Small bower —; *ancre d'affourche.* Spare —; *ancre de rechange.* Stream —; *ancre de touée.*

anchor, *v.n.*, m'ouiller, ⊙s'ancrer, ⊙ancrer.

anchor, *v.a.*, mouiller, ⊙ancrer.

anchorage (-keur-édje), *n.*, mouillage, ancrage : droit d'ancrage, *m.*

anchored (-keur'de), *adj.*, mouillé, ancré.

anchoret (-keu-rète), *or* **anchorite** (-keu-raïte), *n.*, anachorète, ermite, *m.*

anchor-ground (-graounde), *n.*, (nav.) mouillage, *m.*

anchor-hold, *n.*, (nav.) tenue, *f.*

anchoring, *n.*, (nav.) mouillage, ancrage, *m.*

anchoring-ground, *n.*, mouillage, *m.*

anchoring-place (-keurigne-plèce), *n.*, mouillage, *m.*

anchor-stock, *n.*, (nav.) jas d'ancre, *m.*

anchovy (-a-n-tshô-), *n.*, anchois, *m.*

anchylosis (-ĸi-lô-cisse), *n.*, (med.) ankylose, *f.*

ancient (é'n'shi-è-nte), *n.*, ancien ; (milit.) drapeau ; (nav.) pavillon, *m.*

ancient, *adj.*, ancien, antique.

anciently, *adv.*, anciennement.

ancientness, *n.*, ancienneté, *f.*

ancientry, *n.*, ancienneté (of a family— *d'une famille*), *f.*

and, *conj.*, et. Better — better; *de mieux en mieux.* Carriage — pair; *voiture à deux chevaux, f.*

andante, *n.*, (mus.) andante, *m.*

andean (-di-), *adj.*, des Andes.

andiron (a-n-daï-eurn), *n.*, chenet, *m.*

androgynal (-drod'ji-), *or* **androgynous** (-drod'ji-neusse), *adj.*, (bot.) androgyne ; (zool.) hermaphrodite.

androgyne (-drod'jini), *n.*, androgyne, hermaphrodite, *m.*

anecdote (-dôte), *n.*, anecdote, *f.*

anecdotical (-do-), *adj.*, anecdotique.

anemometer (-ni-mo-mi-teur), *n.*, anémomètre, *m.*

anemone, *or* **anemony** (-mô-ni), *n.*, anémone, *f.*

anemone-root, *n.*, patte, griffe d'anémone, *f.*

anemoscope (-né-mo-scôpe), *n.*, anémoscope, *m.*, girouette, *f.*

anent, *prep.*, concernant, touchant, sur.

an-end, *adj.*, (nav.) debout, guindé.

anet, *n.*, (bot.) fenouil puant, *m.*

aneurism (-iou-), *n.*, anévrisme, *m.*

aneurismal, *adj.*, anévrismal.

anew (-niou), *adv.*, de nouveau.

anfractuosity (-tion-), *n.*, anfractuosité, *f.*

anfractuous (-tiou-eusse), *adj.*, anfractueux.

anfractuousness, *n.*, anfractuosité, *f.*

angel (é-n-d'jèle), *n.*, ange, *m.*

angel-fish, *n.*, angelot, ange de mer, *m.*

angelic, *or* **angelical**, *adj.*, angélique.

angelica, *n.*, angélique, *f.*

angelically, *adv.*, angéliquement.

angelicalness, *n.*, nature angélique, *f.*

angelot (a-n-d'jèlote), *n.*, angelot, *m.*

angel-shot, *n.*, (nav.) boulet ramé, *m.*

angelus, *n.*, angélus, *m.*

angel-water (-wô-teur) *n.*, eau de Portugal, *f.*

angel-worship (-weur-), *n.*, culte des anges, *m.*

anger (ain'gheur), *n.*, colère, *f.* ; courroux, *m.* To provoke any one to —; *exciter la colère de quelqu'un.*

anger, *v.a.*, fâcher, irriter, provoquer, mettre en colère.

angerly, *adj.*, en colère, irrité.

angerly, *adv.*, avec colère.

angina (a-nd'jaïna), *n.*, (med.) angine, *f.*

angiography (a-nd'jio-), *n.*, (anat.) angiographie, *f.*

angiology, *n.*, angiologie, *f.*

angiospermous (a-nd'jio-speurmeusse), *adj.*, (bot.) angiosperme.

angle (a'n-g'l), *n.*, angle ; coin, *m.*

angle, *v.n.*, pêcher à la ligne.

angled (a'n-g'l'de), *adj.*, à angles. Acute —; *acutangle.* Eight— ; *octogone.* Five— ; *pentagone.* Four—; *quadrangulaire.* Many— ; *polygone.* Nine—; *ennéagone.* Obtuse —; *obtusangle.* Right— ; *rectangulaire.* Seven— ; *heptagone.* Six— ; *hexagone.* Ten— ; *décagone.* Twelve— ; *dodécagone.*

angler, *n.*, pêcheur à la ligne, *m.* ; (ich.) baudroie, *f.*

anglican, *adj.*, anglican.

anglican, *n.*, anglican, *m.*, anglicane, *f.*

anglicism, *n.*, anglicisme, *m.*

anglicize (-çaïze), *v.a.*, rendre anglais.

angling, *n.*, pêche à la ligne, *f.*

anglo-saxon, *adj.*, anglo-saxon.

anglo-saxon, *n.*, Anglo-saxon, *m.*

angrily, *adv.*, avec colère.

angry, *adj.*, fâché, en colère, irrité, furieux, courroucé. To be — with any one ; *être en colère contre quelqu'un.* To get — ; *se fâcher : se mettre en colère.*

anguish (-gouishe), *n.*, angoisse, *f.*

angular (-ghiou-leur), *adj.*, angulaire.

angularity, *n.*, état angulaire, *m.*

angularly, *adv.*, angulairement.

angulated (-ghiou-lé-tède), *adj.*, (ant.) angulé.

angulous (-ghiou-leusse), *adj.*, (ant.) anguleux.

anight (-naïte), *or* **anights** (-naïtse), (ant.) *adv.*, de nuit, la nuit.

anil, *n.*, (bot.) anil, *m.*

anile (-naïle), *adj.*, de vieille femme.

anileness (-naïl-), *or* **anility** (-ni-li-), *n.*, radotage, *m.*

animadversion (-veur-), *n.*, animadversion, *f.*

animadvert (-veurte), *v.n.*, exercer son animadversion ; critiquer, censurer.

animadverter (-veur-), *n.*, censeur, frondeur, *m.*

animal, *n.*, animal, *m.*

animal, *adj.*, animal.

animalcular (-kiou-leur), *or* **animalculine** (-kiouline), *adj.*, des animalcules.

animalcule (-kioule), *n.* (*animalcula*), animalcule, *m.*

animalish, *adj.*, d'animal.

animality, *n.*, animalité, *f.*
animalization (-li-zé-), *n.*, animalisation, *f.*
animalize (-laïze), *v.a.*, animaliser.
animally, *adv.*, en animal.
animate (-méte), *v.a.*, animer ; ranimer.
animate, *adj.*, animé.
animated, *adj.*, animé.
animating, *adj.*, qui anime, qui ranime.
animatingly, *adv.*, d'une manière propre à animer.
animation, *n.*, animation, vivacité, chaleur, *f.* Suspended — ; asphyxie, *f.*
animative, *adj.*, capable d'animer, animateur.
animator (-méteur), *n.*, personne qui anime, chose qui anime, *f.*
animetta, *n.*, (c.rel.) voile du calice, *m.*
animosity, *n.*, animosité, *f.*
animus, *n.*, animosité, *f.*; but, *m.*, intention, *f.*; esprit, esprit de, *m.*
anise (-nice), *n.*, anis, m.
anise-seed (-nis-side), *n.*, (bot.) graine d'anis. *f.*; anis, *m.*
anise-seed-tree (-tri), *n.*, badiane, *f.*
ankle (a'n-k'l), *n.*, cheville du pied, *f.*
ankle-bone (-bône), *n.*, astragale, *m.*
ankled (a-n-k'lde), *adj.*, pourvu de chevilles
ankle-joint (-djoï'n'te), *n.*, cou-de-pied, *m.*
annalist, *n.*, annaliste, *m.*
annals, *n.pl.*, annales, *f.pl.*, fastes, *m.pl.*, histoire, *f.*
annats, *n.pl.*, annate, *f.*
anneal (-nîle), *v.a.*, recuire.
annelides (-nè-li-dize), *n.pl.*, annélides, *m.pl.*
annex, *v.a.*, annexer, joindre.
annex, *v.n.*, se joindre.
annex, *n.*, annexe, *f.*
annexation (-nèk-sé-), *n.*, annexion, jonction, *f.*
annexed (-nèkste), *adj.*, ci-joint ; annexé.
annihilable (an-naï-hi-la'-b'l), *adj.*, qui peut être anéanti, qui peut être anihilé.
annihilate (-naï-hi-léte), *v.a.*, anéantir, détruire, annihiler.
annihilating, *n.*, anéantissement, *m.* ; annihilation, *f.*
annihilation, *n.*, anéantissement, *m.*, annihilation, *f.*
anniversarily (-veur-), *adv.*, par anniversaire.
anniversary (-veur-), *n.*, anniversaire, *m.*
anniversary, *adj.*, anniversaire.
anno domini. latin ex., l'an du Seigneur.
annomination (-mi-né-), *n.*, annomination; allitération, *f.*
annotate (-no-téte), *v.a.*, annoter.
annotation, *n.*, annotation, *f.*
annotationist, *n.*, (l.u.) annotateur.
annotator (-no-té-teur), *n.*, annotateur, *m.*
announce (-naou-nse), *v.a.*, annoncer.
announcement, *n.*, annonce, *f.*, avis, *m.*
announcer, *n.*, personne qui annonce une nouvelle, *f.*
annoy (a-n-no-ye), *v.a.*, incommoder, ennuyer, molester, contrarier, être désagréable à.
annoy, or annoyance, *n.*, incommodité ; contrariété, *f.*; ennui, *m.*
annoyer, *n.*, personne qui ennuie, qui tourmente, qui contrarie, qui incommode, *f.*, taquin, *m.*, taquine, *f.*
annoying, *adj.*, ennuyant, contrariant, tourmentant.
annual (-niou-), *adj.*, annuel.
annual, *n.*, annuaire, *m.* ; (bot.) plante annuelle, *f.*
annually, *adv.*, annuellement.
annuary (-niou-), *adj.*, (ant.) annuel.
annuitant (-niou-i-), *n.*, rentier ; détenteur d'annuité, détenteur d'une rente annuelle, *m.*
annuity (-niou-i-), *n.*, rente annuelle, annuité, *f.* Life — ; rente viagère.. Contingent — ;

rente viagère. Consolidated annuities; rentes consolidées, *f.pl.* Interminable — ; rente perpétuelle. Long — ; annuité à long terme. Reduced — ; rente réduite. Terminable — ; annuité. Government —; rente sur l'État. Writ of — ; bref d'annuité, *m.* To buy up an — ; amortir une rente. To redeem an — ; racheter une rente. To settle an — on ; constituer une rente à.
annul (an-neul), *v.a.*, annuler.
annular (-niou-leur), or annulary (-niou-), *adj.*, annulaire.
annulate (an-niou-léte), *adj.*, annelé.
annulated (an-niou-lé-tède), *adj.*, annelé.
annulet (an-niou-lète), *n.*, annelet, *m.* : (arch.) armilles, *f.pl.*
annulment (an-neul-), *n.*, annulation, *f.*
annum (an-neume), *n.*, an, *m.* Per —; par an.
annunciation (an-neu-n-ci-é-), *n.*, annonce, promulgation, *f.* ; avis, *m.* ; annonciation, *f.*
anodyne (-no-daïne), *adj.*, anodin.
anodyne, *n.*, remède anodin ; calmant, *m.* ?
anoint (-noï-n'te), *v.a.*, oindre.
anointed, *adj.*, oint.
anointed, *n.*, oint, *m.* The Lord's — ; l'oint du Seigneur.
anointer, *n.*, personne qui oint, qui sacre, *f.*
anointing, *n.*, onction, *f.*
anointment, *n.*, onction, *f.*
anomalistic, or anomalistical, *adj.*, (astron.) anomalistique.
anomalous (-leusse), *adj.*, anomal, irrégulier, anormal.
anomalously, *adv.*, irrégulièrement.
anomaly, *n.*, irrégularité, anomalie, *f.*
anomia, *n.*, (conch.) anomie, *f.*
anon (-none), *adv.*, tout à l'heure ; tantôt.
anonymous (-meusse), *adj.*, anonyme.
anonymously, *adv.*, anonymement ; en gardant l'anonyme.
anorexy, *n.*, (med.) anorexie, *f.*
anormal, *adj.*, anormal.
another (a-n'eutheur), *adj.*, un autre, encore un. One — ; l'un l'autre ; les uns les autres. One with — ; l'un dans l'autre, l'un portant l'autre.
ansated (-sé-tède), *adj.*, (ant.) qui a des anses
anserine (-seuraïne), *adj.*, d'oie.
answer (-seur), *v.a.*, répondre ; répondre à ; satisfaire.
answer, *v.n.*, répondre ; (b.s.) raisonner, faire le raisonneur ; réussir. That did not — ; cela n'a pas réussi.
answer, *n.*, réponse, *f.* ; (b.s.) raisonnement, *m.* In — to your letter; en réponse à votre lettre. No —s ! point de raisonnements !
answerable, *adj.*, susceptible de réponse ; conforme ; responsable.
answerableness, *n.*, convenance; conformité, *f.*
answerably, *adv.*, convenablement.
answerer, *n.*, personne qui répond, *f.*; répondant, *m.*
answering, *adj.*, qui répond à ; correspondant.
ant (an-n'te), *n.*, fourmi, *f.*
ant-eater (-îteur), *n.*, (mam.) fourmilier, *m.*
ant-hill, *n.*, fourmilière, *f.*
antagonism (-go-niz'me), *n.*, contestation, lutte, opposition, *f.*, antagonisme, *m.*
antagonist, *n.*, antagoniste, *m.*
antagonist, *adj.*, (anat.) antagoniste.
antagonize (-go-naïze), *v.n.*, lutter, combattre, opposer.
antanaclasis (-clé-cisse), *n.*, (rhet.) antanaclase, *f.*
antarctic (-târk-), *adj.*, antarctique.
ante-act (-ti-), *n.*, acte antérieur, *m.*
antecedence (-tè-ci-), *n.*, antécédence, *f.*
antecedent, *adj.*, antécédent.
antecedent, *n.*, antécédent, *m.*

antecedently. adv., antecédemment.

ante-chamber (-ti-tshé'm'beur), n., antichambre. f.

ante-chapel (-ti-tshap'l), n., avant-corps de chapelle, m.

antecians (-ti-shi-), n.pl., antéciens, m.pl.

antecursor (-ti-keur-seur), n., (antiq.) éclaireur: avantcoureur, m.

antedate (-ti-déte), n., antidate, f.

antedate. v.a., antidater.

antediluvial, or **antediluvian** (-ti-di-liou-). adj., antédiluvien.

antediluvian. n., qui existait avant le déluge.

antelope (-ti-lô-), n., antilope, f.

antemeridian (-ti-mé-), adj., avant midi.

antemundane (-ti-meu-n'déne), adj., avant la création du monde.

antenna (-tèn-na), n.(antennæ), antenne, f.

antenumber (-ti-neu-m'beur), n., nombre antécédent m.

antenuptial (-ti-neup-shial), adj., d'avant le mariage.

antepaschal (-ti-pâs-kal), adj., d'avant Pâques.

antepenult (-ti-pi-neulte), or **antepenultima** (-ti-pi-neul-), n., antépénultième, f.

antepenultimate (-méte), n. and adj., antépénultième.

ante-position (a'n-ti-). n., (gram.) inversion, f.

anterior (-ti-rieur), adj., antérieur.

anteriority, n., antériorité, f.

ante-room (-ti-roume), n., antichambre, f.; vestibule m.

ante-saloon (-ti-sa-loune), n., antichambre de salon, f.

anthem (-thème), n., antienne, f.

anther (-theur), n., (bot.) anthère, f.

anthological (-tho-lod'ji-), adj., d'anthologie.

anthology (-tho-lod'ji), n., anthologie, f.

anthony's fire (-thôniz' faïeur), n., (med.) feu de Saint Antoine (l.u.), érésipèle, m.

anthracite (-thra-), n.,(min.) anthracite,m.

anthrax (-thrakse), n., (med.) anthrax, charbon, m.

anthropological (-thro-po-lod'ji-), adj., anthropologique.

anthropologist, n., versé en anthropologie.

anthropology, n., anthropologie, f.

anthropomorphism (-thrô-pô-), n., anthropomorphisme, m.

anthropomorphous (-feusse),adj.,anthropomorphe.

anthropophaginian (-fa'dji-), n., anthropophage, m.f.

anthropophagous (-gheusse), adj., anthropophage.

anthropophagus (-gheusse), n. (anthropophagi) anthropophage, m.f.

anthropophagy. n., anthropophagie, f.

antic, n. bouffon m. : bouffonnerie, f.

antic. adj., grotesque, étrange, drôle.

antichrist n., antéchrist, m.

antichristian, adj., antichrétien.

antichristian, n., ennemi du christianisme, m.

antichristianity, n., antichristianisme, m.

anticipate (-péte), v.a., anticiper, prévenir; s'attendre à; devancer; se proposer, compter.

anticipated, adj., prématuré, anticipé.

anticipation, n., anticipation, attente, f.; avant-goût, m.

anticipator, n., personne qui anticipe, f.

anticipatory, adj., par anticipation.

anti-climax (-claï-), n., (rhet.) gradation renversée, f.

anticly, adv., grotesquement, étrangement, drôlement.

anti-constitutional (-sti-tiou-), adj., anti-constitutionnel.

anti-convulsive (-veul-),adj ,contre les convulsions.

anti-courtier (-kôr-tieur), n., ennemi de la cour, m.

anti-democratic. or **anti-democratical** (-mô-), adj., contraire à la démocratie.

antidotal (-dô-), adj., bon contre le poison.

antidotary, adj., qui sert d'antidote.

antidotary, n., recueil d'antidotes, antidotaire, m.

antidote (-dôte), n., antidote, m.

antidote, v.a., (ant.) fournir des antidotes. ?

antidotical, adj., qui sert d'antidote.

antidotically, adv., comme antidote.

anti-episcopal, adj., opposé à l'épiscopat, contre l'épiscopat.

anti-evangelical (-i-va-n'd'jè-), adj., anti-évangélique

anti-febrile, adj., antifébrile, fébrifuge.

anti-febrile. n., fébrifuge, m.

antilogy (-lod'ji), n., (ant.) antilogie, f.

antiloimic (-loi-), adj., (med.) contre la peste, antipestilentiel.

anti-ministerial (-nis-ti-), adj., opposé au ministère.

anti-ministerialist, n., personne opposée au ministère, f.

anti-monarchic, or **anti-monarchical** (-kik.-kikal). adj., antimonarchique.

anti-monarchicalness, n., caractère antimonarchique, m.

antimonial (-mô-), adj., antimonial, antimonié.

antimony. n., antimoine, m.

antinomy. n., antinomie, f.

anti-papal (-pé-), adj, opposé au papisme.

anti-pathetic,or **anti-pathetical** (-thè-), adj., antipathique

anti-pathetically, adv., avec antipathie.

anti-patheticalness, n., caractère d'antipathie, m.

antipathy (-thi), n., antipathie, f.

anti-patriotic (-pé-), adj., anti-patriotique.

anti-peristaltic, adj., antipéristaltique.

anti-pestilential, adj., antipestilentiel.

anti-philosophical, adj., antiphilosophique.

antiphonary (-fo-), n., antiphonaire, m.

antiphrasis (-cisse), n., antiphrase, f.

antipodal (-po-), adj., des antipodes.

antipode (-pôde), n., antipode, m.

anti-pope (-pôpe), n., antipape, m.

antiquarian (-kwé-), adj., antique.

antiquarian (-kwé-), or **antiquary** (-kwa-). n., antiquaire, m.

antiquarianism (-kwé-), n., passion pour les antiquités, f.

antiquate (-kwéte), v.a., vieillir, faire tomber en désuétude; (jur.) abroger.

antiquated, adj., vieilli, antique; suranné.

antiquatedness, n., état de ce qui est tombé en désuétude, m.

antique, n., antique, antiquité; (print.' normande, f.

antique, adj., ancien, antique.

antiqueness, n., ancienneté, antiquité, f.

antiquity (-kwi-), n., antiquité, f.

anti-revolutionary (-vo-liou-), adj., anti-révolutionnaire.

anti-revolutionist, n., antirévolutionnaire, m.

antiscians (-shi-a-nze). or **antiscii** (-shi-a've), n.pl., antisciens. m.pl.

antiscorbutic. or **antiscorbutical** (-biou-), adj., antiscorbutique.

antiscorbutic, n., (med.) antiscorbutique. m.

antiseptic, adj., (med.) antiseptique.

antiseptic. *n.*, antiseptique, *m.*
anti-social (-sô-shial), *adj.*, antisocial.
antispasmodic, *adj.*, antispasmodique.
antispasmodic, *n.*, antispasmodique, *m.*
antistrophe (-fi), *n.*, antistrophe, *f.*
antisyphilitic, *adj.*, antisyphilitique.
antithesis (-thê-cisse), *n.*, antithèse, *f.*
antithetic, *or* **antithetical** (-tho-), *adj.*, antithétique.
antitype (-taïpe), *n.*, type, *m.*
anti-venereal (-vè-ni-ri-),*adj.*,antivénérien.
antler, *n.*, andouiller, *m.*
antlered (-leurde), *adj.*, à andouillers.
antonomasia (-mé-jia), *n.*, (rhet.) antonomase,*f.*
antre (-teur), *n.*, (ant.) antre, *m.*
anus (é-neusse), *n.*, (anat.) anus, *m.*
anvil, *n.*, enclume, *f.* ; (fig.) métier, *m.* Upon the — ; *sur le métier.*
anvil-block, *n.*, billot d'enclume, *m.*
anxiety (c'ng-zaï-èti),*n.*,anxiété,inquiétude, sollicitude,*f.*
anxious (a'nk-shi-eusse), *adj.*, inquiet ; désireux, curieux. To be — to ; *désirer beaucoup de, tenir à.*
anxiously, *adv.*, avec inquiétude ; avec sollicitude, avec impatience, avec anxiété.
anxiousness, *n.*, anxiété ; inquiétude, sollicitude, *f.*
any (è-ni), *adj.*, quelque ; tout; du, de la, de l', des; de ; en. In — wise ; *de quelque manière que ce soit.* — thing — *quoi que ce soit.* — one ; *qui que ce soit, quelqu'un.* — man ; *tout homme.* Have you — wine? *avez-vous du vin?* Have you — ? *en avez-vous?* I do not know — of your judges ; *je ne connais aucun de vos juges.* Scarcely — ; *presque pas.* — further; *plus loin.*
aorist (è-oriste), *n.*, (gram.) aoriste, *m.*
aorta (é-or-), *n.*, (anat.) aorte, *f.*
aortal, *or* **aortic**, *adj.*, aortique.
apace (-péce), *adv.*, vite; à grands pas.
apart (-pârte), *adv.*, à part, de côté, en dehors.
apartment (-pârt'), *n.*, chambre; pièce d'un appartement, *f.* A suite of —s; *un appartement, m.*
apathetic (-thè-), *adj.*, apathique.
apathy (-thi), *n.*, apathie, *f.*
ape (épe), *n.*, singe, *m.*
ape, *v.a.*, singer.
apeak (-pîke), *adv.*, (nav.) à pic.
apennine (-pèn-naine), *adj.*, des Apennins.
aperient (-pi-), *n.* and *adj.*, apéritif, *m.*
aperitive (-pè-), *adj.*, apéritif.
apertion (-peur-), *n.* ouverture, fente,*f.*
apertly (-peur-), *adv.*, ouvertement.
aperture (-peur-tioure), *n.*, ouverture, *f.*; orifice, *m.*
apetalous (-pè-ta-leusse), *adj.*, (bot.) apétale, *f.*
apex (é-peks), *n.*. (*apices, apexes*), sommet; cimier (of a helmet—*de casque*), *m.*
aphæresis, *or* **apheresis** (-fi-ri-cisse), *n.*, (gram.) aphérèse,*f.*
aphelion (-fi-), *n.*, aphélie, *m.*
aphonia, *or* **aphony** (-fô-), *n.*, aphonie, *f.*
aphorism, *n.*, aphorisme, *m.*
aphoristic, *or* **aphoristical**,*adj.*, aphoristique.
aphoristically, *adv.*, par aphorisme.
aphrodisiac, *or* **aphrodisiacal**, *adj.*, aphrodisiaque.
aphrodisiac, *n.*, aphrodisiaque, *m.*
aphrodita, *or* **aphrodite** (-daïta, -daïte), *n.*, magnésite, (pop.) écume de mer,*f.*
aphthæ (-thi), *n.pl.*, (med.) aphtes, *m.pl.*
aphyllous (-fil-leusse), *adj.*, aphylle.
apiary (é-pi-), *n.*, rucher, *m.*
apiece (-pîce), *adv.*, la pièce ; chacun.
apish (é-), *adj.*, badin, bouffon ; de singe.
apishly, *adv.*, en singe, en badin.

apishness, *n.*, bouffonnerie, singerie,*f.*
apitpat, *adv.*, avec palpitation.
apocalypse, *n.*, apocalypse,*f.*
apocalyptic, *or* **apocalyptical**, *adj.*, apocalyptique.
apocalyptically, *adv.*, d'une manière apocalyptique.
apocope (-pi), *n.*, (gram.) apocope, *f.*
apocrypha, *n.*, les apocryphes, les livres apocryphes, *m.pl.*
apocryphal, *adj.*, apocryphe.
apocynum (-neume), *n.*, (bot.) apocyn, *m.*
apodal, *adj.*, (ich.) apode.
apode (-pôde), *n.* (*apodes, apoda*), (zool.) apode.
apodictic, *or* **apodictical**, *adj.*, apodictique.
apodictically, *adv.*, d'une manière apodictique.
apogee (-pod'ji), *n.*, apogée, *m.*
apologetic, *or* **apologetical** (-lod'jè-), *adj.*, apologétique.
apologetically, *adv.*,d'une manière apologétique.
apologist (-lod'jiste), *n.*, apologiste, *m.*
apologize (-lod'jaïze), *v.n.*, faire une apologie; s'excuser, faire des excuses. To — for any one ; *faire des excuses pour quelqu'un.*
apologue, *n.*, apologue, *m.*
apology (-lod'ji), *n.*, apologie ; excuse,*f.*
aponeurosis (-niou-rô-cisse), *n.*, (anat.) aponévrose, *f.*
apophthegm (-po-thème), *n.* V. **apothegm.**
apoplectic, *or* **apoplectical** (-pô-plèk-), *adj.*, apoplectique.
apoplexy (-pô-), *n.*, apoplexie, *f.* To fall down in a fit of — ; *tomber en apoplexie.* To be seized with — ; *être frappé d'apoplexie.*
aport (a-porte), *adv.*, (nav.) bâbord.
apostasy (-ci), *n.*, apostasie, *f.*
apostate (-téte), *n.*, apostat, *m.*
apostate, *adj.*, apostat, d'apostat.
apostatical, *adj.*, apostat.
apostatize (-taïze), *v. i.*, apostasier, renier.
apostema, *or* **aposteme** (-sti-ma, -stime), *n.*, abcès, ⊙ apostème, ⊙ apostume, *m.*
apostemation (-ti-mé-),*n.*,(med.)formation d'un ⊙apostème,*f.*, d'un abcès, *m.*
apostematous (-tèm-ateusse), *adj.*, d'apostème, de la nature de ⊙l'apostème, de l'abcès.
a posteriori (-pôs-ti-riô-), *adv.*, a posteriori.
apostle (a-pos-s'l), *n.*, apôtre, *m.* The acts of the —s ; *les actes des apôtres.*
apostleship, *n.*, apostolat, *m.*
apostolic, *or* **apostolical**, *adj.*, apostolique. — creed ; *symbole des apôtres.*
apostolically, *adv.*, apostoliquement.
apostolicalness, *n.*, caractère apostolique, *m.*
apostrophe (-fi), *n.*, apostrophe, *f.*
apostrophic, *adj.*, (rhet.) en forme d'apostrophe ; (gram.) avec l'apostrophe.
apostrophize (-faïze), *v.a.*, apostropher.
apothecary (-po-thè-). *n.*, apothicaire (l.u.), pharmacien, *m.*
apothegm, *or* **apothem** (-thème), *n.*, apophthegme, *m.*
apothegmatical, *adj.*, en forme d'apophtegme.
apothegmatize (-thèg-ma-taïze), *v.n.*, parler par apophtegmes.
apotheosis (-thi-o-cisse), *n.*, apothéose, *f.*
apozem (-zème), *n.*, apozème, *m.*
apozemical, *adj.*, d'apozème.
appal, *v.a.*, épouvanter, terrifier.
appalling, *adj.*, effrayant, épouvantable terrifiant.
appalment, *n.*, (ant.) frayeur. épouvante, terreur. *f.*

appanage (-nèd'je), *n.*, apanage, *m.*
apparatus (-ré-teusse), *n.*, appareil, *m.*
apparel, *v.a.*, vêtir ; (nav.) équiper.
apparel, *n.*, habit, vêtement ; habillement, appareil ; (nav.) équipement, *m.* Wearing —; *habits, m.pl., hardes, f.pl.*
apparent (-pé-), *adj.*, apparent, évident, clair, manifeste. Heir —; *héritier présomptif.*
apparently, *adv.*, évidemment, en apparence, apparemment.
apparition, *n.*, apparition, *f.*
apparitor (-teur), *n.*, appariteur, *m.*
appeach, *v.a.* (ant.) *V.* **impeach**.
appeal (-pîle), *v.a.*, évoquer à un tribunal supérieur.
appeal, *v.n.*, appeler, en appeler.
appeal, *n.*, appel, *m.* Court of —; *cour d'appel.* To lodge an —; *interjeter appel.*
appealable, *adj.*, sujet à appel.
appealant, *n.*, (ant.) (jur.) appelant, *m.*
appear (ap-pîre), *v.n.*, paraître ; apparaître ; se montrer, comparaître, se présenter. It would —; *il paraîtrait.* To — against any one; (jur.) *se présenter contre quelqu'un ; se porter partie contre quelqu'un.*
appear, *n.*, (ant.) apparence, apparition, *f.*
appearance, *n.*, apparition, apparence, figure, *f.*; air, aspect, extérieur, *m.* ; (persp.) perspective ; (jur.) comparution, *f.* To save —s; *sauver les apparences.* For the sake of —; *pour sauver les apparences.* There is every —; *il y a toute apparence.* To all —s; *selon toute apparence.* To judge by —s ; *à en juger d'après les apparences.* To make one's —; *faire son apparition ; faire son entrée ;* (jur.) *comparaître.* To make one's first —; (thea.) *faire son début, débuter.*
appeasable (ap-pîzab'l), *adj.*, qu'on peut apaiser.
appeasableness, *n.*, possibilité d'être apaisé, *f.*
appease (ap-pîze), *v.a.*, apaiser.
appeasement, *n.*, apaisement, *m.*, action d'apaiser, *f.*
appeaser, *n.*, pacificateur, *m.*
appeasing, *adj.*, qui apaise.
appeasive, *adj.*, qui apaise.
appellant (ap-pèl-la'nte),*n.*,(jur.) appelant, provocateur, *m.*
appellant, *adj.*, appelant ; en appel.
appellate (-ap-pèl-léte), *adj.*, d'appel.
appellate, *n.*, (ant.) intimé ; accusé, *m.*
appellation (ap-pèl-lé-), *n.*, nom, *m.* ; qualification, appellation, *f.*
appellative, *adj.*, appellatif.
appellative, *n.*, (gram.) nom commun, *m.*
appellatively, *adv.*, au moyen d'un nom commun.
appellatory, *adj.*, d'appel.
appellee (ap-pèl-li), *n.*, (jur.) intimé, *m.*, intimée, *f.*
appellor (ap-pèl-lor), *n.*, (jur.) appelant, *m.*, appelante, *f.*
append (ap-pè-n-d), *v.a.*, apposer, annexer, attacher.
appendage (ap-pè-n-dèd'je), *n.*, accessoire, appendice, *m.*
appendant, *adj.*, dépendant, accessoire.
appendix (*appendices, appendixes*), *n.*, appendice, *m.*
apperception (ap-peur-cèp-), *n.*, (philos.) perception, *f.*
appertain (ap-peur-téne), *v.n.*, appartenir.
appertenance (ap-peur-te-), *n.*, appartenance, *f.*
appetence (ap-pi-tè-n-se), *or* **appetency** (ap-pi-tè-n-ci), *n.*, appétence,envie, *f.*
appetent (ap-pi-tè-n-te), *adj.*, avide.
appetibility (ap-pi-), *n.*, (ant.) qualité d'être désirable, *f.*

appetible, *adj.*, (ant.) désirable.
appetite (ap-pi-taïte), *n.*, appétit ; (fig.) penchant, *m.*, soif, *f.* A good — to you; *bon appétit.* Ravenous —; *appétit de cheval.* To get an —; *gagner de l'appétit.* To have an —; *avoir de l'appétit.* To have a good —; *avoir bon appétit.*
appetizer (ap-pi-taïzeur), *n.*, chose qui excite l'appétit, *f.*
applauder, *n.*, applaudisseur, *m.*
applause, *n.*, applaudissement, *m.*, applaudissements, *m.pl.*
applaud (ap-plô-de), *v.a.*, applaudir, applaudir à.
apple (ap-p'l), *n.*, pomme, *f.* Apple of the eye ; *pupille, prunelle, f.* Crab- —; *pomme sauvage.* Pine- —; *ananas, m.* Oak- —; *noix de galle, f.* ; *pomme de chêne.* — of love, love- —; *pomme d'amour, tomate, f.* Fir- —; *pomme de pin.* Baking —; *pomme à cuire.* Adam's —; *pomme d'Adam ; citron, m.*
apple-core, *n.*, trognon de pomme, *m.*
apple-grove (-grôve), *n.*, pommeraie, *f.*
apple-loft, *n.*, fruiterie, *f.*
apple-peel (-pîle), *n.*, pelure de pomme, *f.*
apple-puff (-peuf), *n.*, (cook) chausson, *m.*
apple-sauce (-sô-ce), *n.*, marmelade de pommes, *f.*
apple-tree (-trî), *n.*, pommier, *m.*
apple-woman (-wou-ma-ne), *n.*, marchande de pommes.
appliance (ap-pla'ya-n-ce), *n.*, action, condition, *f.*; moyen ; remède, *m.*
applicability (ap-pli-), *n.*, possibilité d'appliquer, *f.*
applicable (ap-pli-cab'l), *adj.*, applicable.
applicableness, *n.* *V.* **applicability**.
applicably,*adv.*, de manière à pouvoir être appliqué.
applicant, *n.*, postulant ; (jur.) demandeur, *m.* ; postulante ; (jur.) demanderesse, *f.*
applicate (ap-pli-kéte), *adj.*, (math.) concret ; nombré.
application (ap-pli-ké-), *n.*, application, *f.*; usage, emploi, *m.* ; sollicitation, demande, *f.* To make — to; *s'adresser à.*
applicative (ap-pli-), *or* **applicatory** (ap-pli-ca-teuri), *adj.*, qui applique.
apply (ap-pla'ye), *v.a.*, appliquer ; adresser ; porter ; (arith.) diviser.
apply, *v.n.*, s'appliquer, s'adresser.
appoint (ap-po-nte), *v.a.*, nommer ; établir ; arrêter, désigner, fixer, indiquer ; ordonner à.
appoint, *v.n.*, arrêter
appoint. *n.*, (com.) appoint.
appointable, *adj.*, qui peut être nommé.
appointed (-tède), *part.*, nommé, établi, arrêté, désigné, fixé, indiqué ; fourni (of troops —*des troupes*).
appointee (-tî), *n.*, fonctionnaire nommé, *m.*
appointer (-teur), *n.*, personne qui indique, qui nomme, qui ordonne, *f.*
appointment, *n.*, rendez-vous ; ordre, *m.* ; appointments, *m. pl.* ; décret, arrêt ; établissement ; emploi, *m.*, charge ; nomination, *f.* To make an — with any one; *donner un rendez-vous à quelqu'un.*
apportion (ap-pôr-), *v.a.*, proportionner, répartir.
apportioner (-eur), *n.*, répartiteur, *m.*
apportionment, *n.*, répartition, *f.*, partage, *m.*
appose, *v.a.*, (ant.) interroger ; apposer.
apposer, *n.*, interrogateur, *m.*
apposite, *adj.*, à propos, applicable ; convenable, bien placé.
appositely, *adv.*, convenablement, justement.
appositeness, *n.*, convenance ; justesse, *f.*

apposition, *n.*, apposition, *f.*
appraise (ap-préze), *v.a.*, priser, évaluer.
appraisement, *n.*, prisée, évaluation, estimation, *f.*
appraiser (-zeur), *n.*, estimateur, commissaire-priseur, *m.*
appreciable (ap-pri-shiab'l), *adj.*, appréciable.
appreciate (ap-pri-shiéte), *v.a.*, apprécier, estimer.
appreciation (ap-pri-shié-), *n.*, appréciation, *f.*
apprehend (ap-pri-hè-nde), *v.a.*, prendre; appréhender; embrasser; comprendre; présumer.
apprehender, *n.*, personne qui arrête, *f.*; penseur, *m.*
apprehensible, *adj.*, appréhensible.
apprehension (ap-pri-hè-n-), *n.*, appréhension; conception; arrestation; crainte, *f.*
apprehensive, *adj.*, intelligent, prompt à saisir; appréhensif, inquiet, alarmé.
apprehensively, *adv.*, avec intelligence; avec crainte.
apprehensiveness, *n.*, appréhension; intelligence, *f.*
apprentice (ap-prè-n-), *n.*, apprenti; (of lawyers—*d'hommes de loi*) clerc; (of medical men—*de médecins*) élève; (nav.) novice, *m.* To put — to a shoemaker; *mettre en apprentissage chez un cordonnier.*
apprentice, *v.a.*, mettre en apprentissage.
apprenticeship, *n.*, apprentissage, *m.*
apprise (ap-praïze), *v.a.*, apprendre, informer, donner avis à; prévenir.
apprize (ap-praïze), *v.a.*, priser, évaluer.
apprizement, *n.* (ant.). *V.* **appraisement.**
apprizer, *n.* (ant.). *V.* **appraiser.**
approach (ap-prôt-she), *n.*, approche, *f.*; accès; pas; rapprochement, *m.*; (math.) approximation, *f.* On his —, on her —; *à son approche.* An — towards; *un pas vers; un rapprochement vers.*
approach, *v.a.*, approcher, s'approcher de, aborder.
approach, *v.n.*, approcher, s'approcher.
approachable, *adj.*, abordable, accessible.
approacher (ap-prôt'sheur), *n.*, personne qui approche, *f.*
approaching, *adj.*, dont on s'approche; approchant.
approaching, *n.*, (hort.) greffe par approche, *f.*
approachment, *n.*, (ant.) approche, *f.*
approbation (ap-prô-bé), *n.*, approbation, *f.*
appropriable (ap-prô-priab'l), *adj.*, qui peut être approprié.
appropriate (ap-prô-pri-éte), *adj.*, approprié, propre, qui convient, convenable.
appropriate, *v.a.*, approprier; s'approprier; destiner, réserver.
appropriately, *adv.*, d'une manière propre; à juste titre; proprement.
appropriateness, *n.*, convenance particulière, *f.*
appropriation (ap-prô-prié-), *n.*, application, destination; appropriation; (jur.) propriété, *f.*; emploi, *m.*
appropriator (ap-prô-pri-é-teur), *n.*, personne qui emploie quelque chose à son usage, *f.*
approvable (ap-prou-vab'l), *adj.*, digne d'approbation; estimable.
approval, *n.*, approbation, *f.*
approve (ap-prouve), *v.a.*, approuver, confirmer.
approved (ap-prouv'de), *adj.*, approuvé.
approver (ap-prou-veur), *n.* approba-

teur, *m.*, approbatrice, *f.*; (jur.) (ant.) témoin révélateur de ses complices, *m.*
approving (ap-prou-vigne), *adj.*, approbateur.
approvingly, *adv.*, avec approbation.
approximate (ap-prok-si-méte), *v.a.*, rapprocher.
approximate, *v.n.*, se rapprocher; approcher.
approximation (ap-prok-si-mé-), *n.*, approximation, *f.*; rapprochement, *m.*
approximative, *adj.*, approximatif.
appui (ap-poui), *n.*, (milit.) point d'appui, *m.*
appulse (ap-peulse), *n.*, choc, *m.*; rencontre, approche, *f.*
appurtenance (ap-peur-te-), *n.*, appartenance, *f.*
appurtenant, *adj.*, appartenant.
apricot (-cote), *n.*, abricot, *m.*
april (é-pril), *n.*, Avril, *m.*
april-fool (-foule), *n.*, personne à qui on a donné un poisson d'avril, *f.* To be made an —; *recevoir un poisson d'avril.*
apron (é-preune), *n.*, tablier; (artil.) couvre-lumière; (nav.) éperon, *m.*
apron-man (-ma-ne), *n.*, ouvrier, *m.*
apsis, *n.*, (arch., rel.) abside, *f.*; (astron.) apside, *f.*
apt, *adj.*, sujet; enclin; propre, convenable. To be — to; *être porté à, être disposé à.*
apt, *v.a.*, adapter, disposer.
aptate (ap-téte), *v.a.*, adapter, ajuster.
aptera (-teu-), *or* **apterans** (-teura'n'ze), *n.pl.*, (ent.) aptères, *m.pl.*
apterous (ap-teureusse), *adj.*, aptère.
aptitude (-tioude), *n.*, aptitude, disposition, *f.*
aptly, *adv.*, àpropos; justement, convenablement.
aptness (-nèsse), *n.*, disposition, convenance, aptitude, *f.*
aptote (-tôte), *n.*, (gram.) nom indéclinable, *m.*
apyrous (a-païreusse), *adj.*, apyre, infusible.
aqua (é-kwa), *n.*, eau, *f.*
aqua-fortis (é-kwa-), *n.*, eau-forte, *f.*
aqua-marina (é-kwa-), *n.*, aigue-marine, *f.*
aqua-regia (é-kwa-rid'jia-), *n.*, eau régale, *f.*
aquarelle, *n.*, aquarelle, *f.*
aquarium (-rieume), *n.*, aquarium, *m.*
aquarius (-rieusse), *n.*, (astron.) Verseau.
aquatic, *or* **aquatical**, *adj.*, aquatique.
aquatic, *n.*, plante aquatique, *f.*
aqua-tint (é-kwa-ti-n-te), *or* **aqua-tinta** (é-kwa-ti-n-ta), *n.*, (engr) aqua-tinta, *f.*
aqua-vitæ (é-kwa-vaïti), *n.*, spirit-deux à la première distillation, *m.*
aqueduct (a-kwi-deuct), *n.*, aqueduc, *m.*
aqueous (é-kwi-eusse), *adj.*, aqueux.
aqueousness, *n.*, aquosité, *f.*
aquiline (a-kwi-laïne), *adj.*, aquilin, d'aigle
aquilon (a-kwi-lone), *n.*, aquilon, *m.*
aquose (a-kwôss), *adj.*, aqueux.
aquosity (a-kwociti), *n.*, aquosité, *f.*
arab, *n.*, Arabe, *m.f.*
arabe, *adj.*, arabe.
arabesque, *adj.*, arabesque.
arabesque, *n.*, arabesque, *f.*
arabian (a-ré-bia-n), *n.*, Arabe, *m.f.*
arabian, *adj.*, arabe; (geog.) arabique.
arabic, *adj.*, arabe, arabique.
arabic, *n.*, arabe (language—*langue*), *m.*
arable, *adj.*, arable, labourable.
arachnoid (-rak-noïde), *n.*, arachnoïde, *f.*
araneose (ré-ni-eusse), *or* **araneose** (ré-ni-ôss), *adj.*, d'araignée.
arbalist (âr-), *n.*, arbalète, *f.*
arbiter (âr-), *n.*, arbitre, *m.*
arbitrament (âr-), *n.*, arbitrage, *m.*

arbitrarily, *adv.*, arbitrairement.
arbitrariness (-nèsse), *n.*, arbitraire, *m*
arbitrary, *adj.*, arbitraire.
arbitrate (âr-bi-tréte), *v.a.*, arbitrer, décider.
arbitrate, *v.n.*, arbitrer, décider.
arbitration (âr-bi-tré-), *n.*, arbitrage, *m.*; décision, *f.* By —; *par arbitrage; arbitralement.*
arbitration-bond (-bo-n'd), *n.*, (jur.) compromis, *m.*
arbitrator (âr-bi-tré-teur), *n.*, arbitre, *m.*
arbitrement (âr-bi-tri-), *n.*, décision, *f.*; jugement; (philos.) arbitre, *m.*
arbitress (âr-bi-trèsse), *n.*, arbitre, *m.*
arbor, *n.*, (bot., tech.) arbre, *m.*
arboreous (âr-bō-ri-eusse), *or* **arborous** (âr-bo-reusse), *adj.*, d'arbre; (bot.) arborescent.
arborescence, *n.*, arborescence, *f.*
arborescent (âr-bo-rès-sè-nte), *adj.*, arborescent.
arboret (âr-bo-rète), *n.*, arbrisseau, arbuste, *m.*
arboriculture (âr-bo-ri-keul-tioure), *n.*, arboriculture, culture des arbres, *f.*
arborization (âr-bo-ri-zé-), *n.*, arborisation, *f.*
arborize (âr-bo-raïze), *v.a.*, arboriser.
arbour (âr-beur), *n.*, berceau de verdure, *m.*
arbute (âr-bioute), *or* **arbutus** (âr-biouteusse), *n.*, (bot.) arbousier, *m.*
arbutean (âr-biou-ti-a'n), *adj.*, (bot.) d'arbousier.
arbute-berry, *n.*, (bot.) arbouse, *f.*
arc, *n.*, arc, *m.*
arcade (âr-kéde), *n.*, arcade, *f.*
arcadian (âr-ké-di-a'n), *adj.*, arcadien.
arcanum (âr-ké-neume), *n.*, arcane, secret, mystère, *m.*
arc-boutant, *n.*, arc-boutant, *m.*
arch (ârt'she), *n.*, arche, *f.*; arc, cintre, *m.*; voûte, *f.* Triumphal —; *arc de triomphe.*
arch, *v.a.*, voûter; cintrer, arquer.
arch, *adj.*, fin; malin.
archæologic (âr-ki-olod'jik), *adj.*, archéologique.
archæology (âr-ki-olod'ji), *or* **archaiology** (âr-ké), *n.*, archéologie, *f.*
archaism (âr-ké-izme), *n.*, archaïsme, *m.*
archangel (âr-ké-nd'jèle), *n.*, archange, *m.*
archangelic, *adj.*, archangélique, de l'archange.
archbeacon (ârt'sh-bîk'n), *n.*, fanal principal, *m.*
archbishop (ârt'sh-bi-sheupe), *n.*, archevêque, *m.*
archbishopric, *n.*, archevêché, *m.*
archdeacon (ârt'sh-dîk'n), *n.*, archidiacre, *m.*
archdeaconry, *n.*, archidiaconat, *m.*
archduchess (ârt'sh-deut'shèsse), *n.*, archiduchesse, *f.*
archduchy (-deutshi), *n.*, archiduché, *m.*
archduke (-diouke), *n.*, archiduc, *m.*
archdukedom, *n.*, archiduché, *m.*
arched (ârt'shte), *adj.*, voûté, cintré, arqué.
archer (ârt'sh'eur), *n.*, archer; (astron.) sagittaire, *m.*
archery, *n.*, l'art de tirer de l'arc, *m.*
arches-court (ârt'shize-côrte), *n.*, cour des arches, *f.*
archetypal (âr-ki-taï-pal), *adj.*, archétype.
archetype (âr-ki-taïpe), *n.*, archétype, *m.*
arch-fiend (ârt'sh-fîn'de), *n.*, démon, *m.*
arch-foe (-fô), *n.*, grand ennemi, ennemi juré, *m.*
arch-head (art sh-hède), *n.*, (arch.) tête de voûte, *f.*
arch-heresy (ârt'sh-hè-ri-ci), *n.*, hérésie principale, *f.*
arch-heretic (-hè-ri-), *n.*, hérétique, *m. f.*

arch-hypocrite (-po-), *n.*, hypocrite, *m.*
archical (ar-ki-), *adj.*, principal.
archidiaconal (âr-ki-di-ako-), *adj.*, d'arc i-diacre.
archiepiscopacy (âr-ki-i-pis-ko-), *n.*, arc i-épiscopat, *m.*
archiepiscopal, *adj.*, archiépiscopal.
arching (ârt'shigne), *n.*, arche, voûte, *f.*
archipelago (âr-ki-), *n.*, archipel, *m.*
architect (âr-ki-), *n.*, architecte; (fig.) artisan, *m.*
architectonic, *adj.*, architectonique.
architectural (-tiou-), *adj.*, architectural.
architecture (âr-ki-tèk-tioure), *n.*, architecture, *f.*
architrave (ârki-tréve), *n.*, architrave, *f.*
archival (-kaï-), *adj.*, d'archives, des archives.
archivault (ki-vôlte), *or* **archivolt** (-ki-volte), *n.*, (arch.) archivolte, *f.*
archives (-kaïv'ze), *n.pl.*, archives, *f.pl.*
archivist (-kiviste), *n.*, archiviste, *m.*
archlike (ârt'sh-laike), *adj.*, en arche, en voûte; voûté.
archlute (ârt'sh-lioute), *n.*, téorbe, théorbe, tuorbe, *m.*
archly (ârt'shli), *adv.*, avec malice, malicieusement.
archness (ârt'shnèsse), *n.*, malice, *f.*
archon (âr-ko'n), *n.*, archonte, *m.*
arch-priest (ârt'sh-priste), *n.*, archiprêtre, *m.*
arch-primate (-praï-méte), *n.*, grand primat, *m.*
arch-prophet, *n.*, grand prophète, *m.*
arch-stone (-stône), *n.*, (arch.) voussoir, *m.*
arch-traitor (-teur), *n.*, traître insigne, *m.*
arch-villain (-vil-la-n), *n.*, grand misérable, *m.*
arch-villainy, *n.*, profonde scélératesse, *f.*
archwise (ârt'shwaïze), *adv.*, en forme de voûte, en forme d'arche.
arctic (ârk-tike), *adj.*, arctique.
arcuate (âr-kiou-éte), *adj.*, en forme d'arc.
ardency, *n.*, ardeur, *f.*
ardent, *adj.*, ardent, brûlant.
ardently, *adv.*, ardemment.
ardour (-deur), *n.*, ardeur, *f.*
arduous (-diou-eusse), *adj.*, ardu, rude, pénible.
arduousness, *n.*, difficulté, *f.*
area (ê-ri-a), *n.*, aire, étendue enceinte, surface, superficie, *f.*
areal (è-ri-al), *adj.*, de superficie.
arefaction (ar-i-), *n.*, aréfaction, *f.*
arefy (-ri-fa'ye), *v.a.*, dessécher.
arena (-ri-), *n.*, arène; (med.) gravelle, *f.*
arenaceous (-ri-né-shi-eusse), *adj.*, arénacé.
arenation (-ri-né-), *n.*, arénation, *f.*
arenose (-ri-nôss), *adj.*, aréneux, sablonneux.
areola (-ri-ô-), **areole** (-ri-ôle), *n.*, (anat., med.) aréole, *f.*
areometer (-ri-o'mi-teur), *n.*, aréomètre, *m.*
areometry, *n.*, art de mesurer la gravité spécifique des fluides, *m.*
areopagite (-ri-op-ad'jaïte), *n.*, aréopagite, *m.*
areopagus (-ri-o-pa-gheusse), *n.*, aréopage, *m.*
areostyle (-ri-ostaïle), *n.*, aréostyle, *m.*
argal, *n.*, tartre brut, *m.*
argemone (ard'ji-mô-ni), *n.*, (bot.) argemone, *f.*, pavot épineux, *m.*
argent (ard'j'è-n'te), *adj.*, d'argent, argenté.
argent, *n.*, (her.) argent, *m.*
argental, *adj.*, d'argent.
argentate (-téte), *n.*, (chem.) azotate d'argent, *m.*
argentation (-té-), *n.*, argenture, *f.*

argentiferous (-ti-feureusse), *adj.*, argentifère.

argentine, (-taïne), *n.*, (bot., ich.) argentine, *f.*

argentine, *adj.*, argentin.

argil (ârd'jile), *n.*, argile, *f.*

argil (ârd'jile), *n.*, (orni.) cigogne à sac, *f.* ; marabout, *m.*

argillaceous (ârdjil-lé-shieusse), *adj.*, argilacé.

argilliferous (ârd-jil-li-feu-reusse), *adj.*, argilifère.

argonaut (-go-), *n.*, argonaute, *m.*

argosy (-go-ci),*n.*,(nav.) vaisseau marchand, *m.* ; caraque, *f*

argue (-ghiou), *v.n.*, argumenter, raisonner, arguer, soutenir.

argue, *v.a.*, discuter ; annoncer.

arguer (-ghiou-eur), *n* argumentateur, logicien,disputant, *m.*

argument (-ghiou-), *n.*, argument, *m.* ; thèse, *f.*

argumental, *adj.*, d'argument.

argumentation(-té-),*n.*,argumentation,*f.*

argumentative, *adj.*, de raisonnement, d'argumentation ; disposé à argumenter.

argumentatively, *adv.*, par argument, comme argument.

argus (-gheusse), *n.*, àrgus, *m.*

argute (-ghioute), *adj.*, (ant.) fin, subtil.

arian, *adj.*, arien.

arian (a-ria-n), *n.*, arien, *m.*, arienne, *f.*

arianism, *n.*, arianisme, *m.*

arid, *adj.*, aride.

aridity, *n.*, aridité, *f.*

aridness (-nèsse), *n.* *V.* **aridity**.

aries (éri-îze), *n.*, (astron.) Bélier, *m.*

arietta (ariêt-ta), *n.*, ariette, *f.*

aright (araïte), *adv.*, droitement ; bien.

arise (araïze), *v.n.*, se lever, s'élever ; se soulever, surgir.

aristarch, *n.*, aristarque, *m.*

aristocracy, *n.*, aristocratie, *f.*

aristocrat, *n.*, aristocrate, *m.f.*

aristocratic, *or* **aristocratical**, *adj.*, aristocratique.

aristocratically,*adv.*,aristocratiquement.

aristocraticalness, *n.*, caractère aristocratique, *m.*

aristotelian (-ti-), *adj.*, aristotélicien.

aristotelian, *n.*, aristotélicien, *m.*, aristotélicienne, *f.*

aristotelianism, *n.*, aristotélisme, *m.*

arithmetic (-rith-mi-), *n.*, arithmétique, *f.*

arithmetical, *adj.*, arithmétique.

arithmetically, *adv.*, arithmétiquement.

arithmetician (arith-mi-ti-sha'n), *n.*, arithméticien, *m.*

ark, *n.*, coffret, *m.* Noah's —; *l'arche de Noé, f.* The — of the covenant, the — of the Lord; *l'arche d'alliance, l'arche du Seigneur, f.*

arm, *n.*, bras ; (horl.) levier, *m.* With —s folded ; *les bras croisés* With open —s ; *à bras ouverts.* — in —; *bras dessus, bras dessous.*

arm, *v.a.*, armer, donner, prendre des armes.

arm, *v.n.*, s'armer, armer.

armada. *n.*, flotte, armada, *f.*

armadilla, *n.*, armadille, *f.*

armadillo, *n.*, (mam.) tatou, *m.*

armament. *n.*, armement, *m.*

arm-chair (ârm-tchère), *n.*, fauteuil, *m.*

armed (ârm'de), *adj.*, armé.

armful (-foule), *n.*, brassée, *f.*

armhole (-hôle), *n.*, aisselle ; emmanchure, entournure, *f.*

armillary, *adj.*, armillaire.

armistice, *n.*, armistice, *m.*

armless (-lèsse), *adj.*, sans bras.

armlet (-lète), *n.*, brassard, bracelet, *m.*

armorial (-mô-), *adj.*, armorial.

armorist (ârmeuiste),*n.*,(ant.) armoriste,*m.*

armour (-meur), *n.*, armure, *f.* ; armement, *m.*

armourer (âr-meureûr),*n.*, armurier, *m.*

armoury, *or* **armory** (-meuri), *n.*, arsenal, *m.* ; salle d'armes ; armure, *f.*

armpit (-pite), *n.*, aisselle, *f.*

arms (ârm'ze), *n.pl.*, armes ; (her.) armes, armoiries,*f.pl.* Man at—; *homme d'armes, m.* Passage of —; *pas d'armes, m.* Defensive —; *armes défensives.* Offensive —; *armes offensives.* Irregular—; (her.) *armes fausses,armes à enquerre.* By force of —; *par la force des armes.* To beat to —; (milit.) *battre le rappel, battre la générale.* To take up —; *prendre les armes.* Ground—; (milit.)*reposez vos armes.* Shoulder —; (milit.) *portez armes.*

army, *n.*, armée ; (fig.) multitude, *f.* To enter the —; *entrer dans l'armée.*

arnica *n.*, arnique,*f.* ; arnica, *m.*

arnotto, *n.*, (bot.) rocou, rocouyer ; (dy.) rocou, *m.*

arnuts (-neutse), *n.*, avoine cultivée, *f.*

aromatic, *or* **aromatical** (-ro-), *adj.*, aromatique.

aromatic (-ro-), *n.*, aromate, *m.*

aromatization (-ro-matizé-), *n.*, aromatisation, *f.*

aromatize (-rô-mataïze), *v.a.*, aromatiser.

aromatous (-rô-mateusse), *adj.*, aromatique.

around (-raou'nde), *prep.*, autour de, à l'entour de.

around. *adv.*, autour, à l'entour, à la ronde.

arouse (-raouze), *v.a.*, soulever, réveiller, éveiller, exciter, animer.

arow (arô), *adv.*, en rang, l'un après l'autre.

aroynt (arô-ï-n'te), *adv.*, (ant.) va-t-en ; loin d'ici.

arpeggio (-pèd'ji-ô), *n.*, (mus.) arpège, *m.*

arquebusade (-kwi-beu-céde), *n.*, arquebusade; (pharm.) eau d'arquebusade, *f.*

arquebuse (-kwi-beusse), *n.*, arquebuse, *f.*

arquebusier (ârkwi-beu-cir), *n.*, arquebusier, *m.*

arrack,*n.*, arack, rack, *m.*

arraign (ar-réne), *v.a.*, traduire en justice, accuser.

arraignment (-rén'-), *n.*, mise en accusation ; accusation,*f.*

arrange (-ré-n'je), *v.a.*, arranger, ranger.

arrangement, *n.*, arrangement ; agencement, accommodement, *m.* ; disposition, *f.*

arranger (-ré-n'jeur), *n.*, arrangeur; meneur, *m.*

arrant, *adj.*, vrai, insigne, grand, fieffé, déterminé.

arrantly, *adv.*, notoirement; impudemment.

array, *n.*, ordre, *m.*; revue; suite, *f.*; appareil, *m.*; atours, *m.pl.* ; (jur.) liste des douze jurés, *f.* In battle- —; *en ordre de bataille.*

array, *v.a.*, déployer, ranger ; revêtir ; (jur.) dresser.

arrear (ar-rire), *n.*, arriéré, *m.* —s; *arréra-ges, m.pl.* In —; *en arrière, arriéré.* To pay up one's —s ; *payer son arriéré.*

arrect (ar-rèkte), *adj.*,(ant.) dressé ; attentif.

arrest (ar-rèste), *n.*, empêchement ; arrêt, *m.*; arrestation, prise de corps,*f.*

arrest, *v.a.*, arrêter, saisir ; fixer, suspendre.

arrestation (-rès-té-), *n.*, arrestation,*f.*

arrival (ar-raï-), *n.*, arrivée, *f.* ; arrivage, *m.*

arrive (ar-raïve), *v.n.*, arriver ; parvenir.

arrogance, *or* **arrogancy** (-ro-), *n.*, arrogance,*f.*

arrogant (-ro-), *adj.*, arrogant.

arrogantly, *adv.*, arrogamment.

arrogate (-ro-ghéte), *v.a.*, s'arroger.

arrogation (-ro-ghé-), *n.*, prétention arrogante, *f.*

arrow (ar-rô), *n.*, flèche, *f.*; trait, *n.* Shower of —s; grêle de flèches, *f.*

arrow-head (-hède), *n.*, tête de flèche; (bot.) sagittaire, fléchière, *f.*

arrow-maker (-mék-eur), *n.*, fléchier, *m.*

arrow-root (-route), *n.*, arrow-root, *m.*; herbe à la flèche, *f.*

arrow-shaped (-ro-shépte), *adj.*, sagitté.

arrowy (ar-ro-i), *adj*, de flèche, en flèche.

arse, *n.*, (l.ex.) cul, derrière, *m.*

arsenal (-si-), *n.*, arsenal, *m.*

arseniate (-sï-niéte), *n.*, arséniate, *m.*

arsenic (-sè-nike), *n.*, arsenic, *m.*

arsenical (-sè-), *adj.*, arsenical.

arsenicate (-sè-ni-kéte), *v.a.*, combiner avec l'arsenic.

arsenite (-sè-naïte), *n.*, arsénite, *m.*

arson (-so'n), *n.*, incendie par malveillance, *m.*

art (ârte), *n.*, art; artifice, *m.*; adresse, *f.* Black —; magie noire, *f.* The fine —s; les beaux-arts, *m.pl.*

arterial (-tî-), *adj.*, (anat.) artériel.

arteriology (âr-tî-riolod'ji), *n.*, artériologie, *f.*

artery (âr-teuri), *n.*, artère, *f.*

artesian (ar-tîzia'n), *adj.*, artésien.

artful (ârt'foul), *adj.*, rusé, fin ; fait avec art; (b.s.) artificieux.

artfully (-foul-li), *adv.*, avec artifice, artificieusement, avec finesse ; artistement.

artfulness (art'foulnèsse), *n.*, ruse, finesse, *f.*; art, *m.* ; habileté, *f.*

arthritic, *or* **arthritical** (arthri-), *adj.*, arthritique.

arthrosis (ârthrô-cisse), *n.*, (anat.) articulation, *f.*

artichoke (ârtit'shôke), *n.*, artichaut, *m.*

article (âr-t'k'l), *n.*, article ; objet, *m.* Definite —; (gram.) article défini.

article, *v.a.*, engager par contrat; mettre chez un avoué, comme clerc, chez un médecin, comme élève.

articled (artik'lde), *adj.*, rédigé en articles ; lié, obligé, engagé par contrat écrit.

articular (ar-ti-kiou-leur), *adj.*, articulaire.

articulate (ar ti-kiou-léte), *adj.*, articulé.

articulate, *v.a.*, articuler; traiter.

articulate, *v.n.*, articuler.

articulately, *adv.*, distinctement; article par article.

articulateness, *n.*, qualité de ce qui est articulé, *f.*

articulation (ar-ti-kiou-lé) *n.*, articulation, *f.*; article, *m.*

artifice, *n.*, artifice, *m.*

artificer (-seur), *n.*, artisan ; artiste, *m.*

artificial (-shial), *adj.*, artificiel; adroit, habile.

artificiality, *n.*, état artificiel, *m.*

artificially, *adv.*, artificiellement; artistement.

artificialness, *n.*, état artificiel, *m.*

artillerist (-til-leurist), *n.*, artilleur, *m.*

artillery (-lri), *n.*, artillerie, *f.* Horse-—; artillerie à cheval. Field-—; artillerie de campagne.

artillery-man, *n.*, artilleur, *m.*

artisan (-za-n), *n.*, artisan, ouvrier, *m.*

artist, *n.*, artiste, *m.*

artistic, *or* **artistical**, *adj.*, artistique.

artistically, *adv.*, artistement; avec art.

artless, *adj.*, ingénu, simple, naïf; sans art.

artlessly, *adv.*, ingénument, simplement, sans art.

artlessness, *n.*, naturel, *m.*; naïveté, *f.*

arts-man, *n.*, (ant.) savant, *m.*

arum (é-reume), *n.*, arum, *m.*

arundelian (-reu'n-dî-lia-n), *adj.*; de la collection de marbres grecs d'Arundel.

arundineous (reu'n-di-ni-eusse), *adj.*, convert de roseaux.

aruspex (-reus-pèkse), *or* **aruspice** (-reus-), *n.* (aruspices), aruspice, *m.*

as (âce), *n.*, (Rom. antiq.) as, *m.*; (arith.) entier, nombre entier, *m.*

as (aze), *conj.*, comme, ainsi que, selon que, suivant que; à mesure que; en. — much —; autant que. — ...— ; aussi ... que. — great —; aussi grand que. Rich — she is; toute riche qu'elle est. — for; quant à. — he advanced; à mesure qu'il avançait. She was dressed — a page; elle était habillée en page.

asafœtida, *or* **asafetida** (a-ça-), *n.*, assa fœtida, *f.* V. **assafœtida**.

asarum (-ça-reume), *n.*, asaret, cabaret, *n.*

asbestos (-bès-tosse), *or* **asbestus** (-bès-tcusse), *n.*, asbeste, *m.*

ascend, *v.n.*, monter, remonter, s'élever.

ascend, *v.a.*, monter; remonter (a river— un fleuve).

ascendable (as-cè-n'dab'l), *adj.*, où l'on peut monter.

ascendant, *n.*, ascendant, *m.* ; supériorité, *f.*

ascendant (-da'nte), *adj.*, ascendant.

ascendency (-dè-nsi), *n.*, ascendant, *m.* ; supériorité, *f.*

ascending (-digne), *adj.*, ascendant.

ascension (as-cè-n-sheune), *n.*, ascension, *f.*

ascensional, *adj.*, ascensionnel.

ascension-day, *n.*, jour de l'Ascension, *m.*

ascent (as-cè-n'te), *n.*, ascension ; hauteur, élévation, montée, pente, inclinaison, *f.*; coteau, *m.*

ascertain (as-ceur-téne), *v.a.*, assurer; s'assurer; s'assurer de; constater; vérifier; fixer.

ascertainer (-té-neur) *n.*, personne qui constate, qui détermine, *f.*

ascertainment, *n.*, fixation, vérification, *f.*

ascetic, *adj.*, ascétique.

ascetic (as-sè-tike), *n.*, ascète, ascétique, *m.*

asceticism, *n.*, ascétisme, *m.*

ascians (as-sia-nze), *or* **ascii** (as-si-a'ye), *n.*, asciens, *m.pl.*

ascites (as-saï-tîze), *n.*, (med.) ascite. *f.*

ascitic, *or* **ascitical** (as-si-), *adj.*, ascitique, ascite.

ascititious (as-si-ti-shieusse), *adj.*, additionnel.

asclepiad (-kli-), *n.*, (poet.) asclépiade, *m.*

ascribable (-craï-), *adj.*, que l'on peut attribuer; imputable.

ascribe (-craïbe), *v.a.*, attribuer ; imputer.

ascription, *n.*, imputation, *f.*

ash, *n.*, (bot.) frêne, *m.*

ash, *adj.*, de frêne.

ashamed (-shè-m'de), *adj.*, honteux, confus.

ash-coloured (ashe-keuleurde), *adj.*, cendré.

ashen (a-shène), *adj.*, de frêne.

ashes (ashize), *n.pl.*, cendre, *f.*; cendres, *f.pl.*

ash-fire (-faïeur), *n.*, feu couvert, *m.*

ashlar, *n.*, moellon, libage, *m.*

ashore (-shore), *adv.*, à terre; (of a ship— d'un vaisseau) échoué.

ash-pit, *n.*, cendrier, *m.*

ash-wednesday (-wè-n'z'dè), *n.*, mercredi des cendres, *m.*

ashy, *adj.*, cendré; terreux.

ashy-pale (-péle), *adj.*, pâle comme la mort.

asian (é-shia'n), *adj.*, asiatique, d'Asie.

asiatic (ê-shia-tike), *adj.*, asiatique.

asiaticism, *n.*, orientalisme, *m.*

aside (-çaïde), *adv.*, de côté; à part; à l'écart.

asinego (a-ci-ni-gô), *n.*, (pers.) âne, sot, *m.*

asinine (a-ci-naïne, *adj.*, d'âne.

ask (âske), *v.a.*, demander; inviter; s'informer. To — after any one's health; *demander des nouvelles de la santé de quelqu'un.* To — a question; *faire unc question.*

askance, or **askant**, *adv.*, de travers; de côté, obliquement.

asker (âsk-eur), *n.*, demandeur, questionneur, *m.*; demandeuse, questionneuse, *f.*

askew (a-skiou), *adv.*, de travers.

aslant, *adv.*, obliquement, de biais, de côté.

asleep (a-slipe), *adv.*, endormi.

aslope (a-slôpe), *adv.*, en pente.

asp, or **aspic**, *n.*, aspic, *m.*

asparagus (-gheusse), *n.*, asperge, *f.* Bundle of — ; *botte d'asperges, f.*

aspect '-pèkte), *n.*, aspect, regard, *m.*

aspect, *v.a.*, (ant.) regarder, contempler.

aspen (-pène), *n.*, (bot.) tremble, *m.*

aspen-grove (-grôve), *n.*, tremblaie, *f.*

aspen-tree (-tri), *n.*, tremble, *m.*

asper (as-peur), *adj.*, âpre, rude.

asper (as-peur), *n.*, (gram.) esprit rude, *m.*; (Turkish coin—*monnaie turque*) aspre, *m.*

asperate (as-peur-éte), *v.a.*, (ant.) rendre rude, rugueux.

asperity (-pè-), *n.*, aspérité, âpreté, *f.*

asperse (as-peurse), *v.a.*, diffamer, noircir; vilipender.

asperser (-seur), *n.*, calomniateur, *m.*

aspersion (-peur-), *n.*, aspersion; diffamation, calomnie, *f.*

asphalte, or **asphaltum** (-teume), *n.*, asphalte, *m.*

asphaltic, *adj.*, d'asphalte.

asphaltite (-taïte), *adj.*, d'asphalte; asphaltite.

asphyxia, or **asphyxy**, *n.*, (med.) asphyxie, *f.*

aspic, *n.*, (erpetol., bot.) aspic, *m.*; (artil.) ⊙coulevrine, *f.*

aspirant (-païeur-, *ou* -pi-), *n.*, aspirant, *m.*, aspirante, *f.*

aspirate, *adj.*, aspiré.

aspirate (-réte), *v.a.*, aspirer.

aspirate, *v.n.*, s'aspirer.

aspirate, *n.*, (gram.) aspirée, *f.*; esprit rude, *m.*

aspiration (-ré-), *n.*, aspiration, *f.*; élan, *m.*

aspire, *v.n.*, aspirer.

aspire (as-païeur), *v.n.*, aspirer à.

aspirer (as-païeur-eur), *n.*, aspirant, *m.*

aspiring, *n.*, aspiration, *f.*; désir, *m.*

aspiring (as-païeur-igne), *adj.*, ambitieux.

asquint, *adv.*, de travers; en louchant.

ass, *n.*, âne, *m.* She- —; *ânesse, f.* Young —; *ânon, m.*

assafœtida, *n.*, assa fœtida, *f.*

assail (as-séle), *v.a.*, assaillir, attaquer.

assailable (-lab'l), *adj.*, attaquable.

assailant (-la-n'te), *n.*, assaillant, *m.*

assailer (-leur), *n.*, assaillant *m.*

assailment (-mè-n'te), *n.*, attaque, *f.*

assart (as-sarte), *n.*, (ant.) essartement; arbre essarté, *m.*

assart, *v.a.*, essarter.

assassin (-cine), *n.*, assassin, *m.*

assassinate (-néte), *v.a.*, assassiner.

assassinating (-nétigne), *adj.*, d'assassinat; assassinant.

assassination (-né-). *n.*, assassinat, *m.*

assassinator (-né-teur), *n.*, assassin, *m.*

assassin-like (-laïke), *adj.*, d'assassin.

assault (as-sôlte), *n.*, assaut, *m.*; attaque, *f.*; (jur.) voies de fait, *f.pl.* Brought up for —; *traduit en police correctionelle pour voies de fait.*

assault, *v.a.*, assaillir, attaquer; (jur.) commettre des voies de fait.

assaultable (-tab'l), *adj.*, attaquable.

assaulter (-teur), *n.* *V.* **assailant.**

assay, *n.*, essai, *m.*; épreuve, *f.*

assay, *v.a.*, essayer.

assay, *v.n.*, essayer; tenter.

assay-balance (-la-n'ce), *n.*, trébuchet, *m.*; balance d'essayeur, *f.*

assayer (as-sé-eur), *n.*, essayeur, *m.*

assay-master, *n.*, maître-essayeur, *m.*

assemblage (-sè-m'bléd'je), *n.*, assemblage, *m.*; assemblée, *f.*

assemble (-sè-m'b'l), *v.a.*, assembler, réunir.

assemble, *v.n.*, s'assembler, se réunir.

assembler (-bleur), *n.*, personne qui rassemble, *f.*; meneur, *m.*

assembly, *n.*, assemblée, réunion, *f.* To meet in — ; *se réunir en assemblée publique.*

assembly-room (-roume), *n.*, salle d'assemblée, *f.*

assent (as-sè-n'te), *n.*, assentiment, *m.*

assent, *v.n.*, donner son assentiment, approuver, assentir, consentir.

assenter (-teur), *n.*, approbateur, *m.*, approbatrice, *f.*

assentingly (-tigneli), *adv.*, avec approbation.

assentment, *n.*, (ant.) assentiment, *m.*

assert (-seurte), *v.a.*, avancer; soutenir; prononcer, affirmer, proclamer, revendiquer.

assertion, *n.*, assertion, revendication, *f.*

assertive, *adj.*, (ant.) assertif.

assertor (-teur), *n.*, défenseur, *m.*, celui qui affirme, *m.*

assertory, *adj.*, affirmatif.

assess, *v.a.*, taxer, imposer.

assessable, *adj.*, imposable.

assessed (as-sès-ste), *part.*, taxé, imposé, fixé, déterminé.

assessionary (-sheunari), *adj.*, assessorial.

assessment, *n.*, cote, imposition, *f.*

assessor (-seur), *n.*, fonctionnaire chargé d'asseoir les impôts, *m.*

assets (as-sètse), *n.*, actif, *m.* — and debts; *actif et passif, m.*

assever (as-sèv-eur), or **asseverate** (as-sèv-euréte), *v.a.*, affirmer solennellement.

asseveration (-ré-), *n.*, affirmation solennelle, *f.*

assiduity (-diou-i-), *n.*, assiduité, *f.*

assiduous (-diou-eusse), *adj.*, assidu.

assiduously, *adv.*, assidûment.

assign (as-saïne), *n.*, (jur.) ayant droit, ayant cause, *m.*

assign, *v.a.*, assigner; déterminer; transférer.

assignable (-nab'l), *adj.*, assignable; (jur.) transférable; qu'on détermine.

assignation (as-sig-né-), *n.*, assignation, *f.*; rendezvous d'amour, *m.*

assignee (as-saï-ni), *n.*, syndic; cessionnaire; mandataire, *m.* Official — ; *syndic provisoire.*

assigner (-neur), *n.*, personne qui assigne, *f.*

assignment (as-saï-n-mè-n'te), *n.*, transport, *m.*; cession de biens; allocation, *f.*

assignor (-neur), *n.*, (jur.) cédant, *m.*

assimilable, *adj.*, assimilable.

assimilate (-léte), *v.a.*, assimiler, s'assimiler.

assimilation (-lé-), *n.*, assimilation, *f.*

assist, *v.a.*, assister; secourir, aider.

assistance, *n.*, assistance, aide, *f.*

assistant, *n.*, aide; assistant; appui, *m.*

assistant, *adj.*, qui aide; auxiliaire.

assister (-teur), *n.*, aide, *m.f.*, personne qui assiste, qui aide, *f.*

assize (as-saïze), or **assizes** (-saïzize), *n.*, assises, *f.pl.*; tarif, *m.*, taxe, *f.* Court of assizes; *cour d'assises, f.* Assize of bread; *taxe du pain.*

assize, *v.a.*, taxer, imposer; fixer le prix des denrées.

assizes (-zeur), *n.*, inspecteur des poids et mesures, *m.*

associability (as-sô-shia-), *n.*, sociabilité, *f.*

associable (-shiab'l), *adj.*, sociable.

associate (-shi-éte), *n.*, associé, *m.*, associée, *f.*; collègue; compagnon, *m.*, compagne, *f.*

associate, *v.a.*, associer.

associate, *v.n.*, s'associer.

association (-cié-), *n.*, association, *f.*

assonance (as-so-na'nce), *n.* (rhet.) assonance, *f.*

assonant, *adj.*, assonant.

assort (as-sorte), *v.a.*, assortir.

assortment, *n.*, assortiment; assemblage, *m.*

assuage (as-swéd'je), *v.a.*, adoucir, apaiser.

assuagement, *n.*, adoucissement, *m.*

assuasive (as-swé-cive), *adj.*, soulageant; adoucissant.

assume (as-sioume), *v.a.*, prendre sur soi; assumer (*une responsabilité*—responsibility); prendre; supposer; prétendre; se permettre, se donner.

assume, *v.n.*, être arrogant; s'en faire accroire.

assumer (-meur), *n.*, arrogant, présomptueux, *m.*

assuming (-migne), *adj.*, arrogant, prétentieux; ambitieux.

assumpsit (as-seu-m-site), *n.*, (jur.) promesse verbale, *f.*

assumption (as-seu-m-sheune), *n.*, (rel.) assomption; présomption; prétention; supposition, *f.*

assumptive (as-seu-m-tive), *adj.*, qu'on peut prendre; (log.) assomptif.

assurance (a-shiou-ra'nce), *n.*, assurance, *f.*

assure (a-shiour), *v.a.*, assurer.

assuredly, *adv.*, assurément.

assuredness, *n.*, certitude, *f.*

assurer (-reur), *n.*, assureur, *m.*

asteism (asti-iz'me), *n.*, (rhet.) ironie, *f.*

aster (-teur), *n.*, (bot.) aster, *m.*

asterias (-tî-), *n.*, astérie, *f.*

asteriated (as-tî-ri-étède), *adj.*, étoilé.

asteriatite (as-tî-rié-taïte), *n.*, astérie pétrifiée, *f.*

asterisk (-teuriske), *n.*, astérisque, *m.*

asterism (as-teu-riz'me), *n.*, astérisme, *m.*

astern (as-teurne), *adv.*, (nav.) à l'arrière, en poupe.

asthma (ast-ma), *n.*, asthme, *m.*

asthmatic, *adj.*, asthmatique.

astonish, *v.a.*, étonner.

astonishing (-shigne), *adj.*, étonnant.

astonishingly (-shigne-li), *adv.*, étonnamment.

astonishingness (-shigne-nèsse), *n.*, caractère étonnant, *m.*

astonishment, *n.*, étonnement, *m.* To strike with —; *frapper d'étonnement.* To recover from one's —; *revenir de son étonnement.* To the — of all; *à l'étonnement de tous.*

astound (as-ta-ou'nde), *v.a.*, étonner, abasourdir, étourdir.

astraddle, *adv.*, à califourchon.

astræa, *or* **astrea** (astri-a), *n.*, astrée, *f.*

astragal, *n.*, (arch.) astragale, *m.*

astragalus (-leusse) *n.*; (anat., bot.) astragale, *m.*

astral, *adj.*, astral.

astray, *adv.*, de travers; égaré. To go —; *s'égarer.* To lead —; *égarer.*

astrea, *n.* V. **astræa**.

astrict (-trikte), *v.a.*, resserrer, comprimer.

astriction (as-trik-sheune), *n.*, contrainte; (med.) constriction; (surg.) compression, *f.*

astride (astraïde), *adv.*, à califourchon; avec les jambes écartées.

astringe (-tri-nd'je), *v.a.*, resserrer.

astringency (-tri-n-), *n.*, qualité astringente, *f.*, caractère astringent, *m.*

astringent, *adj.*, astringent.

astringent (-tri-n-), *n.*, astringent, *m.*

astrography, *n.*, description des astres, *f.*

astrolabe (-tro-lèbe), *n.*, astrolabe, *m.*

astrologer (-lod'jeur), *n.*, astrologue, *m.*

astrologic, *or* **astrological** (-lod'jik, -lod-jical), *adj.*, astrologique.

astrologically, *adv.*, par l'astrologie.

astrologize (-lod'jaize), *v.n.*, pratiquer l'astrologie.

astrology (-lod'ji), *n.*, astrologie, *f.*

astronomer (-no-meur), *n.*, astronome, *m.*

astronomic, **astronomical** (as-tro-no-), *adj.*, astronomique.

astronomically (as-tro-no-), *adv.*, astronomiquement.

astronomy (as-tro-nô-), *n.*, astronomie, *f.*

astrut (a-streute), *adv.*, en se rengorgeant.

astute (as-tioute), *adj.*, fin, pénétrant.

asunder (a-ceu-n'deur), *adv.*, séparé, séparément, éloigné l'un de l'autre.

asylum (a-çaï-leume), *n.*, asile, ☉asyle, *m.* Lunatic —; *maison d'aliénés, f.*

asymptote (a-ci-m'tôte), *n.*, (geom.) asymptote, *f.*

asymptotical, *adj.*, asymptotique,

at, *prep.*, à, dans; en; après. — peace; *en paix.* — war; *en guerre.* They are all — me; *ils sont tous après moi.* To be hard — it; *travailler ferme.* — home; *chez soi.* —...'s; *chez.* — my brother's; *chez mon frère.* — London; *à Londres.* — his request; *sur sa demande.* To be — any thing; *être occupé à quelque chose.*

ataghan (-ga'n), *n.*, yatagan, *m.*

ataraxy (-a), *n.*, (ant.) ataraxie, *f.*

ataxia, *or* **ataxy**, *n.*, (ant.) ataxie, *f.*

ataxic, *adj.*, ataxique.

athanasian (ath-a-né-shia'n), *adj.*, de Saint Athanase. — creed; *symbole de Saint Athanase, m.*

atheism (é-thi-iz'me), *n.*, athéisme, *m.*

atheist (é-thi-iste), *n.*, athée, *m.*

atheist, **atheistic**, *or* **atheistical**, *adj.*, athée, d'athée.

atheistically, *adv.*, en athée.

athenæum, *or* **atheneum** (ath-i-nî-eume), *n.* (*athenæa, -nea*), Athénée, *m.*

athenian (a-thî-ni-a'n), *adj.*, Athénien.

athenian, *n.*, Athénien, *m.*, Athénienne, *f.*

athirst (atheurste), *adj.*, altéré, qui a soif.

athlete (ath-lîte), *n.* (*athletæ*), athlète, *m.*

athletic (ath-lè-tike), *adj.*, athlétique, robuste, fort.

athwart, *adv.*, de travers; à la traverse.

athwart (a-thwŏrte), *prep.*, à travers; à l'encontre; (nav.) en travers de, par le travers de.

atilt, *adv.*, en champ clos.

atlantean, *or* **atlantian** (at-la-n-tia-n), *adj.*, de l'Atlantide; d'Atlas.

atlantes (at-la-n-tize), *n.pl.*, (arch.) atlante, *m.*

atlantic, *adj.*, atlantique.

atlantic (at-la-n-), *n.*, Atlantique, *f.*

atlas, *n.*, (geog., anat.) atlas, *m.*

atmosphere (-fire), *n.*, atmosphère, *f.*

atmospheric, *or* **atmospherical** (-fè-), *adj.*, atmosphérique.

atom (a-teume), *n.*, atome, *m.*

atomic, *or* **atomical**, *adj.*, atomique.

atom-like (-laike), *adj.*, comme un atome.

atone, *v.a.*, expier; racheter.

atone (-tône), *v.n.*, expier, apaiser.

atonement, *n.*, expiation, *f.*

atoner (-neur), *n.*, personne qui expie, *f.*

atonic (-to-nike), *adj.*, atonique.

atony (-to-ni), *n.*, (med.) faiblesse, atonie, *f.*

atop (atope), *adv.*, en haut, au sommet.

atrabilarian (-lé-ria-n), *or* **atrabilarious** (-lé-ri-eusse), *adj.*, atrabilaire.

atrabiliariousness (-ló-ri-eusse-nèsse), _n._, humeur atrabilaire, _f._
atrabilis, _n._, (med.) atrabile. _f._
atramental (-mè-n-), _or_ **atramentous** (mèn'teusse), _adj._, noir.
atrip (atripe), _adv._, (nav.) dérapé.
atrocious (-trô-shieusse), _adj._, atroce.
atrociously, _adv._, atrocement.
atrociousness, _n._, atrocité, _f._
atrocity (atro-ci-), _n._, atrocité, _f._
atrophy (-tro-), _n._, (med.) atrophie, consomption, _f._
attach (at-tat'she), _v.a._, attacher, lier; arrêter; (jur.) mettre opposition à, contraindre, saisir.
attachable (at-tat'shab'l), _adj._, (jur.) saisissable.
attachment, _n._, attachement, _m._; (jur.) opposition, contrainte, saisie, _f._
attack, _n._, attaque, _f._; accès, _m._
attack, _v.a._, attaquer.
attacker (-keur), _n._, attaquant, _m._
attain (at-té-n), _v.a._, atteindre, parvenir à.
attainable (-nab'l), _adj._, qu'on peut atteindre.
attainableness, _n._, possibilité d'atteindre, _f._
attainder (-té-n-deur), _n._, atteinte; (jur.) sentence de mort rendue contre une personne déclarée coupable de haute trahison ou de félonie, _f._; jugement rendu contre une personne déclarée coupable de haute trahison ou de félonie, et entraînant la confiscation des biens et la mort civile, _m._
attainment (-té-n-), _n._, acquisition; portée; possession, connaissance, _f._; talent, _m._
attaint (-té-nte), _n._, tache; (man.) atteinte; (jur.) poursuite dirigée contre un jury pour faux verdict, _f._
attaint, _v.a._, atteindre, entacher; vicier; frapper de mort civile; dégrader, déshonorer; (ant.) déclarer faux le verdict d'un jury.
attainture (-t-én-tioure), _n._, note d'infamie, _f._
attemper (-tè-m-peur), _v.a._, tempérer, adoucir, régulariser, convenir.
attempt (at-tè-m'te), _n._, essai, effort, _m._; entreprise, _f._; (jur.) attentat, _m._, tentative, _f._ An — on any one's life; _un attentat contre la vie de quelqu'un._
attempt, _v.a._, entreprendre, essayer; attenter à; (jur.) faire une tentative de.
attemptable (-tab'l), _adj._, attaquable; qui peut être essayé, tenté.
attempter (-teur), _n._, personne qui essaie, _f._; (b.s.) agresseur, _m._
attend (at-tè-n'de), _v.a._, faire attention à; s'occuper de; soigner un malade; suivre des leçons; écouter, accompagner; servir; attendre.
attend, _v.n._, faire attention, écouter; assister, être présent; servir; accompagner; observer; avoir égard; veiller, vaquer, avoir soin; s'appliquer.
attendance (at-tè-n'da-nce), _n._, attention, _f._; service, _m._; assiduité; présence, _f._; soins pour un malade, _m.pl._
attendant (-da-n'te), _adj._, qui suit, qui accompagne.
attendant, _n._, assistant; compagnon, _m._, compagne, _f._; serviteur, domestique, _m._; personne de la suite, _f._ —s; _escorte_, _f._
attent (at-tè-n'te), _adj._, (ant.) attentif.
attention (at-tè-n-), _n._, attention, _f._ To pay —; _faire attention._
attentive, _adj._, attentif, soigneux.
attentively, _adv._, attentivement.
attentiveness, _n._, attention, _f._
attenuant (at-tè-niou-a-nte), _adj._, atténuant.
attenuant, _n._, ☉atténuant, _m._

attenuate (at-tè-niou-éte), _adj._, atténué.
attenuate, _v.a._, atténuer, amoindrir, diminuer.
attenuated (-tède), _adj._, atténué.
attenuation (-niou-é-), _n._, atténuation, diminution, _f._; amoindrissement, _m._
attermining (at-teur-mi-nigne), _n._, (jur.) atermoiement, _m._
attest (at-tèste), _v.a._, attester, témoigner.
attestation (-tès-té), _n._, attestation, _f._; témoignage, _m._
attestor (-teur), _n._, personne qui atteste, _f._
attic, _adj._, attique.
attic (at-tike), _n._, Athénien, _m._, Athénienne, _f._; attique, auteur attique, _m._
attic, _n._, (arch.) attique, _m._, mansarde, _f._
atticism, _n._, atticisme, _m._
atticize (at-ti-çaize), _v.a._, donner une forme attique à.
atticize, _v.n._, employer l'atticisme.
attire (at-taeur), _n._, vêtement, _m._; parure, _f._
attire, _v.a._, vêtir, parer.
attirer (at-taeureur), _n._, personne qui habille, qui pare, _f._
attitude (at-ti-tioude), _n._, attitude, pose, _f._
attollent, _adj._, élevant; (anat.) élévateur.
attollent, _n._, (anat.) élévateur, _m._
attorney (at-teur-ni), _n._, procureur, avoué, fondé de pouvoir, _m._ Power of —; procuration, _f._; _pouvoir_, _m._ —general; _procureur général._
attorneyship, _n._, fonctions d'avoué, _f.pl._
attract (at-trakte), _v.a._, attirer.
attractability, _n._, propriété d'être attiré, _f._
attractable, _adj._, attirable.
attractile, _adj._, attracteur.
attractingly (at-trac-tigne-li), _adv._, par attraction.
attraction (-trak-sheune), _n._, attraction, _f._; attrait, _m._
attractive, _adj._, attrayant, attractif.
attractively, _adv._, d'une manière attrayante.
attributable (-biou-t-ab'l), _adj._, attribuable, qui peut être attribué; imputable.
attribute (-n, attribut, _m._; qualité, _f._
attribute (-bioute), _v.a._, attribuer, imputer.
attribution (-biou-sheune), _n._, attribution, _f._, éloge, _m._
attributive, _adj._, qui attribue; attributif.
attributive, _n._, (gram.) attributif, _m._
attrite (at-traïte), _adj._, frotté.
attriteness, _n._, état de ce qui est usé par le frottement, _m._
attrition (at-tri-sheune), _n._, attrition, trituration, _f._
attune (at-tiou-ne), _v.a._, accorder, tirer des accords de.
aubin (ô-bine), _n._, aubin, _m._
auburn (ô-beurne), _adj._, châtain.
auction (ôk-sheune), _n._, encan, _m._; enchère, _f._; enchères, _f.pl._; vente à l'encan, _f._ Sale by —; _vente aux enchères, à l'encan._ To sell by —; _vendre aux enchères, vendre à l'encan._
auctionary (ôk-sheuna-ri), _adj._, des enchères; de commissaire-priseur.
auctioneer (ôk-sheunîre), _n._, commissaire-priseur, _m._
auctioneer, _v.a._, vendre aux enchères.
audacious (ô-dé-shieusse), _adj._, audacieux.
audaciously, _adv._, audacieusement.
audaciousness, _n._, audace, _f._
audacity (ô-da-ci-), _n._, audace, _f._
audible (ô-dib'l), _adj._, qu'on peut entendre.
audibleness, _n._, faculté de produire un son, de se faire entendre, _f._
audibly, _adv._, de manière à être entendu.
audience (ô-di-è-nce), _n._, audience, _f._; auditoire, _m._
audience-chamber (-tshé-m'beur), _n._, salle d'audience, _f._

20

audit (ŏ-dite), *n.*, audition, *f.*

audit, *v.a.*, apurer, vérifier des comptes.

audit-house (-haouce), *n.*, sacristie (of a cathedral—*de cathédrale*), *f.*

auditor, *n.*, auditeur, vérificateur, *m.*

auditorship, *n.*, charge d'auditeur, *f.*

auditory, *n.*, auditoire, *m.*

auditory, *adj.*, auditif.

auditress, *n.*, femme qui écoute, *f.*

auf (ŏfe), *n.*, (ant.) sot, benêt, *m.*

augean (ŏdji-a-n), *adj.*, d'Augias.

auger (ŏ-gheur), *n.*, (tech.) tarière ; mèche, *f.*

aught (ŏte), *n.*, quelque chose ; quoi que ce soit ; rien, tout.

augment (ŏg-mè-n-te), *n.*, accroissement ; (gram.) augment, *m.*

augment, *v.a.*, augmenter.

augment, *v.n.*, augmenter, s'augmenter.

augmentation (ŏg-mè-n-té-sheune), *n.*, augmentation, *f.*

augmentative (ŏg-mè-n-ta-), *adj.*, augmentatif.

augur (ŏgheur), *n.*, augure, devin, *m.*

augur, *v.n.*, augurer.

augural (-ghiou-), *adj.*, augural.

auguration (-ghiou-ré-sheune), *n.*, (ant.) divination par les augures, *f.*

augurial (-ghiou-), *adj.*, des augures.

augurship (-gheur-), *n.*, charge d'augure, *f.*

augury (-ghiou-), *n.*, divination par les augures, *f.* ; augure, présage, *m.*

august, *adj.*, auguste.

august (-gheuste), *n.*, août, *m.*

augustan (-gheusta-n), *adj.*, d'Auguste ; d'Augsbourg.

augustin (-gheusti-ne), *n.*, augustin, *m.*

augustness, *n.*, caractère auguste, *m.*

aulic, *adj.*, aulique.

aunt (ân-n-t), *n.*, tante, *f.* Great — ; *grand'tante.*

aura, *n.*, exhalaison, *f.*

aurate (-réte), *n.*, aurate, *m.*

aurated (-ré-tède), *adj.*, qui ressemble à l'or.

aurelia (-ré-), *n.*, chrysalide, nymphe, *f.*

auricle (-rik'l), *n.*, auricule, *f.* ; pavillon de l'oreille, *m.* ; (of the heart—*du cœur*) oreillette, *f.*

auricular, *adj.*, auriculaire.

auricularly, *adv.*, à l'oreille ; secrètement.

auriferous (-fé-reuss), *adj.*, aurifère.

aurist, *n.*, médecin pour les maladies de l'oreille, *m.*

aurora, *n.*, aurore, *f.* — Borealis ; *aurore boréale.*

auroral, *adj.*, d'aurore.

auscultate (-keul-téte), *v.a.*, (med.) ausculter.

auscultation (-keul-té-sheune), *n.*, auscultation, *f.*

auspicate (-kéte), *v.a.*, présager.

auspice, *n.*, auspice, *m.* Under the —s of ; *sous les auspices de.*

auspicious (-shieusse), *adj.*, de bon augure, propice, favorable.

auspiciously, *adv.*, sous de bons auspices, favorablement.

auspiciousness, *n.*, heureux auspices, *m.pl.*

auster (-teur), *n.*, auster, autan, *m.*

austere (-tire), *adj.*, austère, âpre.

austerely, *adv.*, austèrement.

austereness, *n.*, austérité ; âpreté (of taste —*au goût*), *f.*

austerity, *n.*, austérité ; âpreté (of taste— *au goût*), *f.*

austin (-ti'ne), *adj.*, augustin.

austral, *adj.*, austral.

australian (-li-a'n), *adj.*, australien.

austrian, *adj.*, autrichien.

austrian, *n.*, Autrichien, *m.*, Autrichienne, *f.*

authentic, *or* **authentical** (-thè'n'), *adj.*, authentique.

authentically, *adv.*, authentiquement.

authenticate, *v.a.*, constater ; légaliser.

authentication, *n.*, authenticité ; (jur.) légalisation, *f.*

authenticity, *n.*, authenticité, *f.*

author (-thor), *n.*, auteur, *m.* ; cause, *f.*

authoress, *n.*, auteur, *m.* ; femme auteur, *f.*

authoritative, *adj.*, qui a de l'autorité ; plein d'autorité, impérieux.

authoritatively, *adv.*, avec autorité.

authoritativeness, *n.*, autorité, *f.* ; air d'autorité, *m.*

authority (-tho-), *n.*, autorité, *f.*

authorization (-zé-), *n.*, autorisation, *f.*

authorize (-raï-ze), *v.a.*, autoriser.

authorship, *n.*, profession d'auteur, qualité d'auteur, *f.*

autocracy, *n.*, autocratie, *f.*

autocrat, *n.*, autocrate, *m.*

autocratic, *or* **autocratical**, *adj.*, autocratique.

autocratrix, *or* **autocratrice**, *n.*, autocratrice, *f.*

auto-da-fe, *n.*, autodafé, *m.*

autograph, *n.*, autographe, *m.*

autograph, *v.a.*, autographier.

autographic, *or* **autographical**, *adj.*, autographe, autographique.

autography, *n.*, autographie, *f.*

automatic, *or* **automatical**, *adj.*, automatique.

automaton (-to'n), *n.* (*automata, automatons*), automate, *m.*

automatous (-teusse), *adj.*, (ant.) automatique.

autopsy, *n.*, autopsie, *f.*

autumn (-teume), *n.*, automne, *m. f.*

autumnal (-teum-nal), *adj.*, automnal, d'automne.

autumnal, *n.*, plante automnale, *f.*

auxiliary, *adj.*, auxiliaire.

auxiliary (ŏg-zi-), *n.*, auxiliaire, *m.*

avail, *n.*, avantage, *m.* ; utilité, *f.* To be of no — ; *ne servir de rien, ne servir à rien.*

avail, *v.n.*, servir. That —s nothing ; *cela ne sert à rien.*

avail, *v.a.*, profiter à, servir à. To — one's self of ; *profiter de, se prévaloir de.*

available (-lab'l), *adj.*, utile, profitable.

availableness, *n.*, utilité ; efficacité, *f.*

availably, *adv.*, utilement, avec profit.

avalanche, *or* **avalange**, *n.*, avalanche, *f.*

avarice, *n.*, avarice, *f.*

avaricious (-shieusse), *adj.*, avare, avaricieux.

avariciously, *adv.*, avec avarice, avaricieusement.

avariciousness, *n.*, avarice, *f.*

avast, *int.*, (nav.) tiens bon.

avaunt, *int.*, loin d'ici ! arrière !

ave, *n.*, avé, *m.* — Maria ; *avé Maria.*

avenage (-nédje), *n.*, avénage, *m.*

avenge (-vè'n'dje), *v.a.*, venger. To — one's self ; *se venger.*

avengement, *n.*, vengeance, *f.*

avenger (-vè'n'djeur), *n.*, vengeur, *m.*, vengeresse, *f.*

avengeress, *n.*, vengeresse, *f.*

avenging, *adj.*, vengeur.

avens, *n.*, (bot.) benoîte, *f.*

aventure (-vè-nt-shioure), *n.*, (ant.) accident, *m.*

avenue (-vi-niou), *n.*, avenue, *f.*

aver (-veur), *v.a.*, affirmer, avérer.

average, *n.*, prix moyen ; terme moyen, *m.* ; mercuriale des grains ; (com., nav.) avarie, *f.* Petty —s ; *menues avaries.* General —s ; *avaries communes.* Weekly —s ; (of corn—*des grains*).

mercuriale hebdomadaire. Statement of —s;
règlement d'avaries, m. Free of —; *franc d'avarie.* On an —; *en moyenne.* To make good an —;
indemniser d'une avarie. To state the —s; *régler
les avaries.*

average (-édje), *adj.*, commun; moyen.
— prices of corn ; *mercuriale, f.*

average, *v.a.*, calculer, prendre le terme
moyen.

average, *v.n.*, revenir, terme moyen, à.

averment (-veur-mè-nte), *n.*, affirmation, *f.*

averruncate (-veur-reu'n-kéte), *v.a.*, déraciner.

averse (-veurse), *adj.*, opposé, défavorable,
éloigné, qui a de l'éloignement, ennemi. To be
— to; *avoir de l'éloignement pour, avoir de l'aversion pour, être peu disposé à.*

aversely, *adv.*, à regret.

averseness, *n.*, répugnance, aversion, *f.*;
éloignement, *m.*

aversion, *n.*, aversion, *f.*; éloignement, *m.*

avert, *v.a.*, détourner, éloigner, écarter.

avert (-veurte), *v.n.*, détourner.

aviary, *n.*, volière, *f.*

avidity, *n.*, avidité, *f.*

avocation (-vo-ké-sheune), *n.*, dérangement
momentané, *m.*; occupation; occupation acci-
dentelle, *f.*

avoid, *v.a.*, éviter, fuir.

avoid (-voïde), *v.n.*, se retirer.

avoidable, *adj.*, qu'on peut éviter, évitable.

avoidance, *n.*, action d'éviter, *f.*; vacance,
f.; annulation, *f.*; écoulement, *m.*

avoider, *n.*, personne qui évite, *f.*

avoidless (-voïd'), *adj.*, inévitable, inéluctable.

avoirdupois, *n.*, (com.) avoir du poids, *m.*

avouch (-va-outshe), *v.a.*, affirmer, déclarer.

avouchment, *n.*, (ant.) déclaration, *f.*

avow (-va-ou), *v.a.*, avouer, déclarer.

avowable, *adj.*, qu'on peut avouer.

avowal, *n.*, aveu, *m.*

avowedly, *adv.*, d'une manière avouée;
ouvertement.

avower, *n.*, personne qui avoue, *f.*

avowry, *n.*, (jur.) aveu, *m.*

avulsion (-veul-sheune), *n.*, avulsion, *f.*;
arrachement, *m.*

awaft, *adv.*, (nav.) en berne.

await, *v.a.*, attendre.

awake, *v.a.*, éveiller, réveiller.

awake (-wéke), *v.n.*, s'éveiller, se réveiller.

awake, *adj.*, éveillé, vigilant.

awaken, *v.a.*, éveiller, réveiller.

awakened, *adj.*, éveillé.

awakener, *n.*, personne qui réveille, *f.*

awakening (-wékenigne), *n.*, réveil, *m.*

awaking, *n.*, réveil, *m.*

award, *v.a.*, décerner, adjuger.

award, *v.n.*, décréter.

award, *n.*, arrêt, décret, jugement, jugement arbitral, *m.*, sentence, *f.*

aware (-wére), *adj.*, qui sait; instruit. To
be — of; *savoir, connaître, être instruit de,
s'apercevoir de.*

away (-wè), *adv.*, absent; loin, au loin. To
go —; *s'en aller.* To fly —; *s'envoler.* To send
—; *renvoyer.* To give —; *donner.* To take —;
enlever. He is —; *il est absent.*

away! *int.*, en avant! arrière! loin de moi!
loin d'ici!

awe (ô), *n.*, terreur, crainte, *f.*; effroi,
respect, *m.* To fill with —; *remplir de terreur.*
To strike with —; *frapper de terreur.*

awe, *v.a.*, imprimer le respect à; tenir en
respect; imprimer la terreur à; imposer à.

aweather (-wétheur), *adv.*, (nav.) au vent.

aweigh (a-wé), *adv.*, (nav.) pendant.

awe-struck (ô-streuke), *adj.*, frappé de
terreur.

awful, *adj.*, qui inspire la terreur; solennel,
redoutable; imposant.

awfully, *adv.*, d'une manière qui inspire la
terreur; terriblement; avec respect; excessivement.

awfulness, *n.*, crainte, terreur, *f.*; caractère
terrible. *m.*

awhile (-waïle), *adv.*, pendant quelque
temps; un instant.

awkward (ôk-weurde), *adj.*, maladroit,
gauche, embarrassant.

awkwardly, *adv.*, gauchement, maladroitement, d'une manière embarrassante.

awkwardness, *n.*, gaucherie, maladresse,
f.; embarras, *m.*

awl (ôl), *n.*, alène, *f.*; poinçon, *m.*

awless, *adj.*, sans crainte; qui n'inspire
aucune crainte.

awl-shaped (-shépte), *adj.*, en alène;
subulé.

awn, *n.*, (bot.) barbe, arête, *f.*

awned, *adj.*, épié, monté en épi.

awning, *n.*, tente, banne, *f.*

awry, *adv.*, de travers, de côté.

axal, *adj.*, de l'axe.

axe, *n.*, hache, *f.*

axial, *adj.*, de l'axe.

axil, or **axilla**, *n.*, (anat., bot.) aisselle, *f.*

axillary, *adj.*, axillaire.

axiom, *n.*, axiome, *m.*

axiomatic, or **axiomatical**, *adj.*,
d'axiome.

axis, *n.* (axes), axe, *m.*

axle, or **axle-tree** (ax'l-tri), *n.*, essieu, *m.*

ay, or **aye**, *adv.*, oui; (nav.) bon quart!

aye, *adv.*, à jamais, pour toujours.

aye, *n.* (ayes), affirmation, *f.*, oui; celui qui
vote affirmativement; vote pour, *m.*

azarole, *n.*, (bot.) azerole, *f.*

azimuth, *n.*, (astron.) azimut, *m.*

azote, *n.*, (chem.) azote, *m.*

azotic, *adj.*, azotique.

azure, *adj.*, d'azur.

azure (ajiour), *n.*, azur, *m.*

azure, *v.a.*, azurer.

azured (ajiour'de), *adj.*, azuré.

azure-stone (-stône), *n.*, pierre d'azur, *f.*
lapis lazuli, *m.*

azurite (ajiouraïte), *n.*, (min.) lazulite, *f.*

azyme, *n.*, (ant.) pain azyme, *m.*

azymites (-maït'se), *n.pl.*, Azymites, *m.*

azymous (-meusse), *adj.*, azyme.

B

b, *n.*, seconde lettre de l'alphabet, b, *m.*;
(mus.) si, *m.*

baa (bà), *v.n.*, bêler.

baa, *n.*, bêlement, *m.*

baal, *n.*, Baal, *m.*

babble, *v.a.*, babiller, gazouiller.

babble, *n.*, babil, *m.*

babblement, *n.*, (ant.) babil, babillement, *m.*

babbler, *n.*, babillard, *m.*, babillarde, *f.*

babbling, *n.*, babil, babillage, *m.*

babbling, *adj.*, babillard.

babe (bébe), *n.*, enfant nouveau-né, petit
enfant, poupon, *m.*, pouponne, *f.*

babel (bé-), *n.*, Babel, *f.* Tower of —; *tour
de Babel, m.*

babery (bé-biri). *n.*, babiole, *f.*

babish (bé-), *adj.*, (ant.) enfantin, de petit
enfant.

babishly, *adv.*, (ant.) en enfant.

baboon (ba-boune), *n.*, babouin, *m.*

baby (bé-bi), *n.*, enfant nouveau-né, petit
enfant, poupon, *m.*, poupée, poupée, *f.*

baby, *v.a.*, traiter en petit enfant.

babyhood (bé-bi-houde), *n.*, bas âge, *f.*

babyish (bé-bi-ish), *adj.*, enfantin, de petit enfant.

babylonian, *or* **babylonish**, *adj.*, babylonien; de Babel.

babylonian, *n.*, Babylonien, *m.*, Babylonienne, *f.*; (ant.) astrologue. *m.*

babylonic, *or* **babylonical**, *adj.*, babylonien, de Babylone.

baccalaureate. *n.*, baccalauréat, *m.*

bacchanal, *adj.*, ivre; d'orgie, de débauche.

bacchanal (bak-ka-), *or* **bacchanalian** (bak-ka-na-lia'n), *n.*, ivrogne, *m.*, ivrognesse, *f.*

bacchanalia, *or* **bacchanals**. *n.pl.*, bacchanales.

bacchanalian, *adj.*, bachique.

bacchanals, *n.pl.* V. **bacchanalia**.

bacchant. *n.*, prêtre de Bacchus, *m.*

bacchante, *n.*, bacchante, *f.*

bacchic (bak-kik), *or* **bacchical** (-kikal), *adj.*, bachique.

bacciferous (bak-si-feureusse), *adj.*, baccifère.

bachelor (bat'sheu-leur), *n.*, célibataire, garçon, bachelier, *m.*

bachelorship, *n.*, célibat; baccalauréat, *m.*

back, *adv.*, en arrière; de retour. To call —; rappeler. To come —; revenir. To give —; rendre. To send —; renvoyer. To go —; retourner. To come —; revenir. A few years —; il y a de cela quelques années.

back. *n.*, dos; derrière, *m.*; reins, *m.pl.* — of a chair; dos, dossier de chaise, *m.* — of the head; derrière de la tête. — of the stage; fond de théatre. *m.* — of a chimney; fond de cheminée. *m.* — of a house; derrière d'une maison. — to —; dos à dos. Behind one's —; derrière le dos. To break any one's —; casser les reins à quelqu'un. To turn one's — on any one; tourner le dos à quelqu'un. At the —; au dos de; derrière.

back, *v.a.*, faire reculer; soutenir, appuyer; parier pour; (nav.) coiffer; viser (a warrant—un mandat d'arrêt).

back. *v.n.*, reculer; (nav.) scier à culer.

backbite (-baïte), *v.a.*, médire; calomnier.

backbiter (-baïteur), *n.*, médisant, détracteur, *m.*

backbiting (-baïtigne), *n.*, médisance, calomnie, détraction, *f.*

backbitingly, *adv.*, avec médisance.

backboard (-bôrde), *n.*, (nav.) dossier, *m.*

backbone (-bône), *n.*, épine du dos, *f.*

backdoor (-dore), *n.*, porte de derrière, *f.*

backed (bak'te), *adj.*, à dos; à dossier.

backfriend (-frè-nde), *n.*, ennemi secret, 'auxami, *m.*

back-gammon (-gam-meune), *n.*, trictrac, toute-table, *m.*

background (-gra-ou'n'de), *n.*, terrain de derrière; fond; (paint.) arrière-plan, fond, *m.*

back-handed, *adj.*, donné avec le revers de la main.

back-handed, (-ha-ndède), *adv.*, avec le revers de la main.

backroom (-roume), *n.*, chambre de derrière, *f.*

backside (-saïde), *n.*, derrière, *m.*

backsight (-saïte), *n.*, (of firearms—d'armes à feu), hausse, *f.*

back-slide (-slaïde), *v.n.*, apostasier.

back-slider (-deur), *n.*, apostat; infidèle, *m.*

back-sliding (-digne), *n.*, infidélité, tergiversation, *f.*

backstairs (-stèrze), *n.*, escalier dérobé, *m.*

backsword (-sôrde), *n.*, sabre, *m.*

backward (-worde), *adj.*, arriéré, en retard, en arrière, lent, tardif.

backward, *adv.*, à reculons; à la renverse; à rebours; en arrière. To fall —; tomber à la renverse. To walk — and forward; se promener en long et en large.

backwardly, *adv.*, en arrière, à contre-cœur.

backwardness (-nèsse), *n.*, état arriéré, *m.*; répugnance, *f.*

backwards (-wordze), *adv.* V. **backward**.

backwood (-woude), *n.*, arrière-bois, *m.*

backwound (-wou-n'de), *v.a.*, blesser par derrière.

bacon (bè-k'n), *n.*, lard, *m.* Rasher of —; tranche de lard; barde, *f.* Flitch of —; flèche de lard, *f.*

bacule (bakioule), *n.*, (fort.) herse, *f.*

bad (bade), *adj.*, méchant; mauvais; (of health—de la santé) malade. That is too —; c'est trop fort..

badge, *n.*, plaque, marque, *f.*; signe, symbole, *m.*

badge, *v.a.*, marquer.

badgeless (-lèsse), *adj.*, sans plaque; sans marque.

badger (-jeur), *n.*, blaireau, *m.*

badger-legged (-lèg'de), *adj.*, à jambes de blaireau.

badiane, *or* **bandian** (ba'n'dia'n), *n.*, (bot.) badiane, *f.*

badigeon (-did'jeune), *n.*, badigeon, *m.*

badly, *adv.*, mal; grandement. — dressed; mal mis. To want —; avoir grandement besoin de.

badness (-nèsse), *n.*, méchanceté; mauvaise qualité, *f.*; mauvais état, *m.*

baffle (baf-f'l), *v.a.*, confondre, déjouer; bafouer.

baffle, *n.*, défaite, *f.*

baffler (-fl'eur), *n.*, personne qui déjoue, qui confond, *f.*

bag, *n.*, sac, cabas, *m.*; bourse (for the hair —à cheveux); outre, poche, *f.* Carpet-—; sac de nuit, *m.*

bag, *v.a.*, ensacher, mettre en sacs; gonfler comme un sac; (at billiards—au billard) blouser; (of game—du gibier) tuer.

bag, *v.n.*, faire le sac; être gonflé comme un sac.

bagatelle, *n.*, bagatelle, *f.*, joujou; billard de dame, *m.*

bagful (-foule), *n.*, sachée, *f.*

baggage (baghé'dje), *n.*, bagage, *m.*; (jest.) coquine, prostituée, *f.*

bagging (baghigne), *n.*, toile à sac, *f.*

bagnio (ba-niô), *n.*, maison de bains; maison de prostitution, *f.*; quartier des esclaves, *m.*

bagpipe (-païpe), *n.*, cornemuse, musette, *f.*

bagpipe, *v.a.*, (nav.) masquer, coiffer.

bagpiper (-païpeur), *n.*, joueur de cornemuse, *m.*

baguette (baghète), *n.*; (arch.) baguette, *f.*

bail (bèle), *n.*, caution, *f.*; cautionnement, *m.* On—; sous caution. To put in —; fournir caution.

bail, *v.a.*, cautionner.

bailable (bélab'l), *adj.*, qui peut être admis à fournir caution.

bail-bond (-bo'nde), *n.*, cautionnement, *m.*

bailee (bél-i), *n.*, dépositaire. *m.f.*

bailer, *or* **bailor** (bél-eur), *n.*, déposant, *m.*; caution, *f.*

bailiff (bé-life), *n.*, bailli; huissier, garde du commerce, *m.*

bailiwick (bél'i-wike), *n.*, bailliage, *m.*

bailment, *n.*, dépôt, nantissement, *m.*

bait, *v.a.*, rafraîchir; amorcer; faire combattre; harceler.

bait (bète), *v.n.*, se restorer, se rafraîchir; battre des ailes.

bait. *n.*, amorce, *f.*; appât, *m.* White-—; able. *m.*, ablette, *f.*

baiting (-tigne), *n.*, combat (of animals—*d'animaux*). *m.* Bull- ; *combat de taureaux*.

baize (béze), *n.*, drap de billard, *m.*.serge, *f.*

bake (béke), *v.a.*, cuire au four, faire cuire au four.

bakehouse (-baouce), *n.*, fournil, *m.*

baker (bék-eur), *n.*, boulanger, *m.* —'s shop, —'s trade ; *boulangerie, f.*

baker-legged (-lèg'de) *adj.*, bancal.

bakery (bék-euri), *n.*, boulangerie, *f.*

baking (bék'igne), *n.*, cuisson ; (things baked —*contenu du four*) fournée, *f.*

balance (-la'nce), *n.*, balance, *f.* ; équilibre, contrepoids ; (horl.) balancier, *m.* — of an account ; *solde d'un compte, m.* To turn the — ; *faire pencher la balance.* To lose one's —; *perdre l'équilibre.* To strike a — ; (com.) *établir une balance.*

balance, *v.a.*, balancer ; pondérer.

balance, *v.n.*, se balancer ; (fig.) balancer.

balance-beam (-bîme), *n.*, (tech.) balancier, *m.*

balance-maker (-mék-eur), *n.*, fabricant de balances, *m.*

balancer (-ceur), *n.*, personne qui balance, *f.* ; peseur, *m.*

balance-sheet (-shîte),*n.*,(com.)balance,*f.*; bilan, *m.*

balance-weight (-wéte), *n.*, poids de balance ; contrepoids, *m.*

balancing (-cigne), *n.*, balancement, *m.*

balcony (-kô-), *n.*, balcon, *m.*

bald (bôld), *adj.*, chauve ; (fig.) nu.

baldachin (bôld'akine), *n.*, baldaquin, *m.*

balderdash (bôldeurdashe), *n.*, galimatias ; phébus, *m.*

bald-head (-hède), *n.*, tête chauve,*f.*

baldly, *adv.*, nûment.

baldness (-nèsse), *n.*, calvitie ; (fig.) platitude, *f.*

baldpate (-péte), *n.*, tête chauve, *f.*

baldpated (-pétède), *adj.*, à tête chauve.

baldrick, or **baldric** (bôld'rike), *n.*, baudrier, ceinturon, *m.* ; ceinture, *f.*

bale (béle), *n.*,(com.) balle,*f.*, ballot, colis, *m.*

bale, *v.a.*, emballer ; (nav.) vider l'eau avec l'escope.

balearic (-lî-), *adj.*, des îles Baléares.

baleful (bélefoule), *adj.*, malheureux, funeste.

balk (bôke), *n.*, désappointement, *m.*

balk, *v.a.*, frustrer ; entraver.

ball (bôl), *n.*, boule ; (of snow—*de neige*) boule, pelote ; (of a musket—*de fusil*) balle, *f.*; (of cannon—*de canon*) boulet, *m.* ; (at billiards —*au billard*) bille ; (cook.) boulette,*f.* ; (for playing—*à jouer*) balle, *f.* — of the eye ; globe, *m.* ; *prunelle, pupille, f.* — of thread ; peloton de *fil, m.*

ball, *v.n.*, (of snow—*de la neige*) . se peloter.

ball, *n.*, (entertainment—*danse*) bal, *m.* Fancy — ; *bal costumé.*

ballad (bal-lade), *n.*, ballade ; romance, *f.*

ballad, *v.n.*, chanter des ballades ; faire des ballades.

ballad-maker (-mék-eur), *n.*, faiseur de ballades, *m.*

ballad-monger (-meu'ngheur), *n.*, marchand de ballades, *m.*

ballad-writer (-raïteur), *n.*, auteur de ballades, *m.*

ballast (bal-laste), *n.*, (nav.) lest, *m.* ; (railways) ballast, *m.*

ballast. *v.a.*, lester.

ballasting (-tigne), *n.*, (engineering—*terme d'ingénieur*) ensablement, empierrement; (nav.) lestage, *m.*

ballast-lighter (-laï-teur), *n.*, bateau lesteur, *m.*

ballet (bal-lè), *n.*, ballet, *m.*

ballet-master (-mâs-teur), *n.*,directeur des ballets, *m.*

balling (bôl-ligne), *n.*, (metal.) ballage, réchauffage. *m.*

ballista (bal-lis-), *n.*, baliste, *f.*

ballistic (bal-lis-tike), *adj.*, qui a rapport à la balistique.

ballistics (bal-lis-tikse), *n.pl.*, balistique,*f.* sing.

balloon (ba-loune), *n.*, ballon, *m.*

ballot (bal-lote), *n.*, boule, *f.*; bulletin, *m.* By —; *au scrutin secret.*

ballot, *v.n.*, voter au scrutin.

ballot-box, *n.*, urne du scrutin, *f.*

balloting (-tigne), *n.*, scrutin, *m.*

balm (bâme), *n.*, baume, *m.* ; (bot.) mélisse,*f.*

balm, *v.a.*, parfumer ; servir de bau:ne à.

balm-mint (-mi-n'te), *n.*, mélisse, citronnelle, *f.*

balmy (bâm'i), *adj.*, balsamique ; embaumé, parfumé.

balneary (-ni-), *n.*, (ant.) salle de bain; *f.*

balneation (-ni-é-), *n.*, (ant.) action de baigner *f.*

balneatory (-ni-a-to-), *adj.*, de bain.

balsam (bôl-çame), *n.*, baume, *m.* ; balsamine, *f.*

balsamic (bal-). *n.*, balsamique, *m.*

balsamic, or **balsamical,***adj.*, balsamique.

balsamine (bôl-ça-), *n.*, balsamine, *f.*

balsam-tree (-trî), *n.*, balsamier, baumier, *m.*

baluster (ba-leus-teur), *n.*, rampe (of a staircase—*d'escalier*), *f.* ; (arch.) balustre, *m.*

balustered (-teurde), *adj.*, à balustres.

balustrade (-trède), *n.*, balustrade, *f.*

bamboo (ba-m'bou), *n.*, bambou, *m.*

bamboozle (-bou'z'l), *v.a.*, embrouiller, tromper.

bamboozler (-z'leur), *n.*, embrouilleur, trompeur, *m.*

ban (ba-n), *n.*, ban, *m.* ; interdiction ; malédiction.

ban. *v.a.*, anathématiser, maudire.

ban, *v.n.*, proférer des malédictions.

banana (ba-nâ-na), *n.*, (bot.) banane, *f.*

banana-tree (-trî), *n.*, bananier, *m.*

banco (bân-kô), *adj.*, (com.) banco, de banque.

band (ba-n'de), *n.*, bande ; troupe,*f.* ; lien ; rabat, *m.*

band. *v.a.*, bander ; liguer.

band, *v.n.*, se liguer.

bandage (ba-n'dédje), *n.*, bandeau ; (surg.) bandage, *m.*

bandage-maker (-mék-eur), *n.*, bandagiste, *m.*

bandana, or **bandanna** (ba-n'-), *n.*, indienne, *f.*

bandbox (ba'nd'-), *n.*, carton, *m.*

bandelet. or **bandlet** (ba'nd-lète), *n.*, bandelette, *f.*

bandian, *n.* V. **badiane**.

bandit (bân'dîte), *n.* (*banditti*), bandit, *m.*

bandog (ban'doghe), *n.*, chien d'attache, *m.*

bandoleer (ban'do-lîre), *n.*, bandoulière,*f.*

bandrol (ban'drôle), *n.*, banderole,*f.*

bandy (ban'di), *n.*, crosse (to play, to strike, a ball—*pour jouer à la balle*),*f.*

bandy, *v.a.*, renvoyer (a ball—*une balle*); ballotter ; se renvoyer.

bandy, *v.n.*, se mesurer, rivaliser ; se disputer.

bandy, *adj.*, tortu.

bandy-legged (-lèg'de), *adj.*, bancal.

bane (béne), *n.*, poison ; fléau, *m.* ; ruine,*f.*

bane. *v.a.*, (l.u.) empoisonner.

baneberry, *n.*, herbe de saint-Christophe. *f.* (*actæa spicata*).

baneful (-foule), *adj.*, empoisonné, funeste, mortel.

banefulness (-nèsse), *n.*, chose fatale, destructive, *f.*

bang (ban'ghe), *n.*, coup, *m.*

bang, *v.a.*, rosser, étriller.

bang! *int.*, pan!

banging (-ghigne), *n.*, roulée, volée. *f.*

bangle (bäng'g'l), *v.a.*, (ant.) gaspiller.

banian (ban'i-a-n), *n.*, banian, *m.*

banian-tree (-tri), *n.*, figuier d'Adam, figuier des Banians, *m.*

banish (ban'ishe), *v.a.*, bannir.

banisher (-sheur), *n.*, proscripteur, *m.*

banishment, *n.*, bannissement, *m.*, proscription, *f.*

banistor (-teur), *n.* *V.* **baluster.**

bank (bän'k), *n.*, terrasse ; rive, *f.* ; rivage, bord ; banc de sable, de gazon, *m.*

bank, *v.a.*, terrasser, encaisser.

bank (bän'k), *n.*, (com.) banque, *f.* Branch —; *succursale de banque.* Savings— ; *caisse d'épargne, f.* Joint-stock — ; *banque par actions, en commandite.*

bank, *v.a.*, déposer dans une banque.

bank (with), *v.n.*, avoir pour banquier.

bank-account (ak-kaou'nte), *n.*, compte de banque, *m.*

bank-book (-bouke), *n.*, carnet de banque, *m.*

bank-clerk (-clärke), *n.*, commis de banque, *m.*

banker (-keur), *n.*, banquier, *m.*

banker, *n.*, (nav.) terre-neuvier, *m.*

bank-holiday, *n.*, fête légale, *f.*

banking (bänk'igne), *n.*, banque, *f.* — establishment ; *établissement de banque, m.*

bank-note (-nôte), *n.*, billet de banque, *m.*

bank-porter (-por-teur), *n.*, garçon de banque, *m.*

bank-post bill (-pôste-), *n.*, mandat de la banque, *m.*

bankrupt (bänk'reupte), *n.*, banqueroutier, *m.*, banqueroutière, *f.* ; failli, *m.*, faillie, *f.* Fraudulent— ; *banqueroutier frauduleux.* To be. to become, a— ; *faire banqueroute.* —'s certificate ; *concordat, m.*

bankrupt, *adj.*, en faillite, en banqueroute; ruiné.

bankrupt, *v.a.*, mettre en faillite.

bankruptcy (bänk'reup'ci), *n.*, banqueroute, faillite, *f.* Court of —; *cour des faillites, f.*

bank-stock, *n.*, actions de banque, *f.pl.*

banner (ba'n'neur), *n.*, bannière, *f.* ; étendard, *m.*

bannered (ba'n'neurde), *adj.*, portant ses bannières ; pavoisé.

banneret (ba'n'neurète), *n.*, banneret, *m.*

banerol (ba'n'neurôle), *n.* *V.* **bandrol.**

bannock, *n.*, gâteau d'avoine, *m.*

banns (ba'n'ze), *n.pl.*, ban de mariage, *m.*, publication de mariage, *f.*

banquet (bän'kwète), *n.*, banquet, festin, *m.* ; (fort.) *V.* **banquette.**

banquet, *v.a.*, donner un banquet à.

banquet, *v.n.*, banqueter, festiner.

banqueter (ban'kwèteur), *n.*, amateur de banquets, *m.*

banqueting (-tigne), *n.*, banquet, *m.*

banqueting-house (-haouce), *n.*, maison de banquet, *f.*

banqueting-room (-roume), *n.*, salle de banquet, *f.*

banquette (bän'kète), *n.*, (fort.) banquette, *f.*

banter (ban'teur), *n.*, plaisanterie, *f.*

banter, *v.a.*, plaisanter, railler.

banterer (ban'teureur), *n.*, railleur, *m.*, railleuse, *f.*

bantering (ba'n'teurigne), *n.*, raillerie, *f.*

bantering, *adj.*, railleur.

bantling (ba'n'tlígne), *n.*, poupon, *m.*

banyan, *n.* *V.* **banian.**

baptism (bap'tiz'm), *n.*, baptême, *m.* Certificate of — ; *extrait de baptême, m.*

baptismal (bap'tiz-), *adj.*, baptismal, de baptême.

baptist (bap'tiste), *n.*, baptiste, *m.*

baptistery (bap-tis-tèri), *n.*, baptistère, *m.*

baptistic, *or* **baptistical** (bap'tis-), *adj.*, du baptême.

baptize (bap'taïze), *v.a.*, baptiser.

baptizer (bap-taizeur), *n.*, personne qui baptise, *f.*

bar, *n.*, barre, *f.* ; barreau ; obstacle ; (of public houses—*de cabarets, d'hôtels, &c.*) comptoir, *m.*

bar, *v.a.*, barrer ; empêcher ; (jur.) interrompre.

barb, *n.*, barbe, *f.* ; pointe, dent (of a fish-hook, of an arrow—*d'un hameçon, d'une flèche*), *f.*

barb, *n.*, cheval de Barbarie ; barbe, *m.*

barb, *v.a.*, barder (a horse—*un cheval*) ; faire des dents à un hameçon, à une flèche.

barbacan (bar-ba-ca'n), *n.*, barbacane, *f.*

barbarian, *adj.*, barbare.

barbarian (bar-bé-ria'n), *n.*, barbare, *m.f.*

barbaric, *adj.*, barbare, des barbares.

barbarism (bär-ba-), *n.*, barbarie, *f.* ; (gram.) barbarisme, *m.*

barbarity, *n.*, barbarie, *f.*

barbarize (bär-ba-raïze), *v.a.*, rendre barbare.

barbarous (bär-bareusse), *adj.*, barbare.

barbarousness (-nèsse), *n.*, barbarie, *f.*

barbary, *n.*, cheval barbe, *m.*

barbate (bär-béte), *or* **barbated** (bär-bétède), *adj.*, barbelé ; (bot.) barbé, barbu.

barbecue (bär-bi-kiou), *v.a.*, faire cuire un animal tout entier.

barbecue, *n.*, animal rôti entier, *m.*

barbed (bärb'de), *adj.*, barbelé ; bardé.

barbel (bär-b'l), *n.*, (ich.) barbeau, *m.* ; (vet.) barbillons, *m.pl.*

barber (bär-beur), *n.*, barbier, *m.*

barber, *v.a.*, barbifier.

barber-monger (-meu'n-gheur), *n.*, petit-maître, *m.*

barber-surgeon (-seur'd'jeune), *n.*, chirurgien-barbier, *m.*

barbican (bär-bi-ca-n), *n.* *V.* **barbacan.**

barbles (bär-b'lze), *n.*, (vet.) barbillons, *m.pl.*

barcarolle, *n.*, barcarolle, *f.*

bard, *n.*, barde, *m.*

bardic, *adj.*, de barde.

bardish, *adj.*, de barde.

bardism, *n.*, science des bardes, *f.*

bare (bére), *adj.*, nu ; seul ; simple.

bare, *v.a.*, découvrir ; dépouiller ; mettre à nu.

bareback, *adv.*, à dos nu ; à nu ; à poil.

barebone (-bône), *n.*, corps décharné, *m.*

barefaced (-fés'te), *adj.*, à visage découvert ; effronté.

barefacedly (-fés'tli), *adv.*, ouvertement ; effrontément.

barefacedness (-fés't'nèsse), *n.*, effronterie, *f.*

barefoot (-foute), *adj.*, nu-pieds ; pieds nus.

baregnawn (-nône), *adj.*, rongé au vif.

bareheaded (-hè-dède), *adj.*, nu-tête, tête nue.

barelegged (-lèg'de), *adj.*, nu-jambes.

barely (bér'li), *adv.*, à peine ; simplement ; seulement ; pauvrement, chétivement.

bareness (bér'nèsse), *n.*, nudité, *f.* ; pauvreté, misère, *f.*, dénûment, *m.* ; stérilité, *f.*

bargain (bär-ghi-n), *n.*, marché ; accord, contrat, *m.* To make a good — ; *faire un bon marché; acheter quelque chose à bon marché.* It is a — ; *tope! j'y consens ; voilà qui est fait.* It is no — ; *marché nul.* To strike a — ; *faire un marché.* Into the — ; *par-dessus le marché.* To get the best of the — ; *avoir la meilleure part.*

bargain, *v.a.*, marchander ; faire marché.

bargainee (-ni), *n.*, (jur.) acquéreur, *m.*

bargainer (-neur), *n.*, vendeur, *m.*

barge (bârdje), *n.*, barque, *f.* ; bateau, *m.* ; (nav.) canot de parade, *m.*

bargeman (-mane), *n.*, batelier, canotier, *m.*

bargemaster (-mâsteur), *n.*, patron de barque, *m.*

barilla (-ril'la), *n.*, (bot., chém.) barille, soude, *f.*

bark (bârke), *n.*, écorce, *f.* ; (pharm.) quinquina, *m*

bark, *v.a.*, écorcer, enlever l'écorce à un arbre.

bark, *v.n.*, aboyer.

bark, *n.*, barque, *f.*

barkbared (-bér'de), *adj.*, écorcé.

barked (bârk'te), *adj.*, écorcé.

barker (-keur), *n.*, aboyeur ; celui qui écorce les arbres, *m.*

barking (bârk'igne), *n.*, aboiement, *m.*

barking, *n.*, (hort.) décortication, *f.*

barkless (-lèsse), *adj.*, sans écorce.

bark-mill, *n.*, moulin à tan, *m.*

barky, *adj.*, d'écorce.

barley (bâr-li), *n.*, orge, *f.* Peeled, hulled — ; *orge mondé*, *m.* Pearl — ; *orge perlé*, *m.* Malted — ; *orge maltée*, *f.* —-water ; *eau d'orge*, *f.* —-sugar ; *sucre d'orge*, *m.*

barm (bârme), *n.*, levure, *f.*

barmaid (-méde), *n.*, fille de comptoir (in a public house—*dans un cabaret, un hôtel, &c.*).

barman (-mane), *n.*, garçon de comptoir (in a public house—*dans un cabaret, un hôtel, &c.*).

barmy, *adj.*, qui contient de la levure.

barn (bârne), *n.*, grange, *f.*

barn, *v.a.*, engranger.

barnacle (bâr-na'k'l), *n.*, (orni.) barnache, barnacle, *f.* ; (mol.) cirripède, *m.* ; (mol.) anatife, poussepieds, *m.* ; (pl.) (vet.) morailles, *f.pl.*

barometer (-mi-teur), *n.*, baromètre, *m.*

barometric, *or* **barometrical** (-ro-mè-), *adj.*, barométrique.

baron (bar'eu'n), *n.*, baron ; (jur.) mari, *m.* ; (her.) armes mi-parties, *f.pl.* — of beef (cook.); *aloyau*, *m.*

baronage (bar'eu'n'adje), *n.*, baronnage, *m.* ; dignité de baron, *f.* ; baronnie ; contribution prélevée sur les barons, *f.*

baroness (bar'eun'èsse), *n.*, baronne, *f.*

baronet (bar'o'n'ète), *n.*, baronnet, *m.*

baronetage (bar'o-n'ètadje), *n.*, corps des baronnets, *m.*

baronetcy (bar'o-nèt'ci), *n.*, dignité de baronnet, *f.*

baronial (-rô-), *adj.*, baronnial ; de baron.

barony. *n.*, baronnie, *f.*

barouche, *n.*, barouche, *f.*

barracan (bar-ra-ka-n), *n.*, bouracan, *m.*

barrack (bar-rake), *n.*, caserne, *f.*

barrator (bar-ra-teur), *n.*, (jur.) personne qui incite aux procès, *f.* ; (nav.) marin coupable de baraterie, *m.*

barratrous (-treusse), *adj.*, (nav.) entaché de baraterie.

barratrously, *adv.*, avec, de, par, baraterie, *f.*

barratry, *n.*, excitation aux procès ; (nav.) baraterie, *f.*

barrel (bar-rèle). *n.*, baril ; canon de fusil ; fût ; barillet, *m.* ; fusée, *f.* — of the capstern ; (nav.) *mèche du cabestan, f.* — of a gun ; *canon de fusil*, *m.* — of a drum ; *fût de tambour*, *m.* Watch — ; *barillet de montre*, *m.* — of a pump ; *corps de pompe*, *m.*

barrel, *v.a.*, embariller ; (of roads—*des routes*) arrondir en dos d'âne, bomber.

barrel-bellied (-bèl'lide), *adj.*, gros comme une barrique.

barren (bar-rène), *adj.*, stérile.

barrenly, *adv.*, stérilement.

barrenness (bar-rè-n-nèsse), *n.*, stérilité, *f.*

barricade (-kéde), *n.*, barricade ; (nav.) batayole, *f.*

barricade, *v.a.*, barricader ; (nav.) bastinguer.

barricading (-digne), *n.*, action de barricader, *f.* ; (nav.) bastingage, *m.*

barrier (bar-ri-eur), *n.*, barrière ; limite, *f.*

barrister (bar-ris-teur), *n.*, avocat, *m.*

barrow (bar-rô), *n.*, brouette, *f.* Hand- — ; *brancard*, *m.* ; *civière*, *f.* ; (ant.) pourceau, porc, *m.* ; (mines) amas de décombres, *m.* ; bois, bosquet, *m.* ; (antiq.) tumulus, *m.*

barrowman (-mane), *n.*, brouettier, *m.*

barse (bârse), *n.*, (ich.) perche commune, *f.*

barter (-teur), *n.*, échange, troc, trafic, *m.*

barter, *v.a.* and *n.*, troquer, échanger, trafiquer.

barterer (-teureur), *n.*, trafiquant, *m.*

bartizan (bâr-ti-za-n), *n.*, (arch.) galerie en saillie, *f.*

baryta (ba-raï-ta), *or* **baryte** (bar'aïte), *n.*, (min.) baryte, *f.*

barytone (-tô-ne), *n.*, baryton, *m.*

barytone, *adj.*, (mus.) de baryton.

bascule-bridge (-kioule-), *n.*, pont-levis ; pont à bascule, *m.*

base (béce), *adj.*, vil, bas, infâme, indigne, méprisable ; illégitime ; de mauvais aloi; (of all metals, except gold and silver—*des métaux*, *excepté l'or et l'argent*) non précieux. — -born ; *bâtard ; de basse naissance.*

base (béce), *n.*, base, *f.* ; fondement ; (arch.) soubassement, *m.* ; (mus.) basse, *f.* ; (game—*jeu*) barres, *f.pl.* ; (of roads—*des routes*) encaissement ; (tech.) fond, *m.* ; — of a pedestal ; *socle de piédestal*, *m.* — of a bed ; *soubassement de lit.*

base, *v.a.*, baser, asseoir.

baseless (-lèsse), *adj.*, sans base, sans fondement.

basely, *adv.*, bassement, lâchement, vilainement, honteusement, vilement.

basement (-mè-nte), *n.*, fondation, *f.* ; (arch.) soubassement, *m.*

baseness (-nèsse), *n.*, bassesse, lâcheté ; illégitimité, *f.* ; altération, mauvaise qualité (of metals—*d'un métal*), *f.* ; gravité (of sound—*du son*), *f.*

bash (bashe), *v.n.*, (ant.) rougir, avoir honte, être honteux.

bashaw (-shô), *n.*, bacha, pacha, *m.*

bashful (-foule), *adj.*, timide, modeste, honteux.

bashfully, *adv.*, timidement, modestement, avec timidité, avec modestie.

bashfulness (-nèsse), *n.*, timidité, pudeur, modestie, mauvaise honte, *f.*

bashless (-lèsse). *adj.*, éhonté, déhonté, sans honte, sans vergogne.

basic (bé-cike), *n.*, *adj.*, (chem.) basique.

basil (baz'îl). *n.*, biseau ; (bot.) basilic, *m.*

basil (baz'il), *or* **basan** (baz'a'n), *n.*, basane, *f.*

basil, *v.a.*, tailler en biseau.

basilar (béss'i-lâr), *or* **basiliary** (béss'i-lari), *adj.*, basilaire.

basilic, *or* **basilica**, *n.*, (arch., anat.) basilique, *f.*

basilic, *or* **basilical**, *adj.*, (anat.) basilique ; (arch.) d'une basilique.

basilicon (-ko-n), *n.*, (pharm.) basilicon, basilicum, *m.*

basilisk (-ske), *n.*, basilic, *m.*

basin (bèss'n), *n.*, bassin; réservoir; bol, *m*; cuvette; (nav.) darse, darce (in the Mediterranean—*dans la Méditerranée*), *f.* Holy-water —; *bénítier*, *m.* Wash-hand— ; *cuvette*, *f.*

basis (bè-cisse), *n.* (*bases*), base, *f.*; fondement. *m.*

bask (baske). *v.a.*, chauffer au soleil.

bask. *v.n.*, se chauffer. To — in the sun; *se chauffer au soleil.*

basket (bas-kète), *n.*, corbeille, *f.*; panier, *m.*; impériale de diligence, *f.* Fruit— ; *corbeille à fruits, f.* Table- —; *manne, f.* Back- —; *hotte, f.* Hand- —; *panier, m.* Little —; *corbillon, m.* — full; *panier plein, m.*; *panerée* (*fruits*), *f.* — handle; *anse de panier, f.* — -hilt; *garde en coquille, f.* —-hilted; *en coquille.* —-maker; *vannier, m.* —-rod; *osier, m.* — -woman; *porteuse, f.* — -work; *vannerie, f.*; *clayonnage, m.*

bason (bèss'n), *n.* *V.* **basin.**

bas-relief, bass-relief (bass'rèlfe), *or* **basso-relievo** (bass-rèll-vo), *n.*, bas-relief, *m.*

bass (bèsse), *n.*, (mus.) basse, clef de fa, *f.*; (musical instrument—*instrument de musique*) basse, *f.*, violoncelle, *m.*; (mus.) basse -taille, *f.* — viol; (mus.) *basse de viole, f.* Thorough- —; *basse continue, f.* Double— ; (mus.); *contrebasse, f.* — of an organ; *jeu de bourdon, m.*

bass (basse), *n.*, natte, *f.* (bot.) tilleul d'Amérique, *m.*

bass (bèsse), *v.a.*, gronder; bruire sourdement, murmurer.

basset (bas'sète), *n.*, bassette (card game—*jeu de cartes*), *f.*

bassock, *n.*, natte, *f.*

bassoon (bas'soune), *n.*, basson, *m.*

bassoonist, *n.*, basson (pers.), *m.*

basso-relievo, bass-relief, *n.* *V.* **bas-relief.**

bast. *n.*, teille, tille, *f.*; agenouilloir, *m.*

bastard (bas'teurde), *n.*, bâtard; faux.

bastard, *n.*, bâtard, *m.*, bâtarde, *f.*; (jur.) enfant naturel, *m.*

bastardism (-teurdiz'me), *n.*, (ant.) bâtardise, *f.*

bastardize (-daïze), *v.a.*, déclarer bâtard.

bastardly, *adv.*, (ant.) en bâtard.

bastardy, *n.*, bâtardise, *f.*

baste (bèste), *v.a.*, bâtonner; arroser la viande qui rôtit; (needle-work—*ouvrage à l'aiguille*), faufiler, bâtir.

bastinade, *or* **bastinado** (-néde, -nédô), *n.*, bastonnade, *f.*

bastinade, *or* **bastinado**, *v.a.*, bâtonner, donner la bastonnade à.

basting (bés'tigne), *n.*, bastonnade. *f.*; arrosement de la viande qui rôtit, *m.*,(needle-work —*ouvrage à l'aiguille*) faufilure, *f.*

bastion (bas'ti-o-n), *n.*, bastion, *m.*; demilune, *f.*

basto, *n.*, baste (hombre, quadrille), *m.*

bat (bate), *n.*, bâton, *m.*; crosse; (mam.) chauve-souris, *f.*

bat, *v.n.*, jouer du bâton.

batatas (baté-tass), *n.*, (bot.) patate. *f.*

batavian, *adj.*, batave.

batavian (-té-vi-a-n), *n.*, Batave, *m.f.*

batch (bat'she), *n.*, fournée, *f.*

bate, *n.*, débat, *m.*; dispute, *f.*

bate (béte), *v.a.*, rabattre, rabaisser, diminuer; ôter, retrancher; excepter; faire remise de. He will not — an inch of it; *il n'en veut point démordre.*

bate. *v.n.*, diminuer; rabattre; (hawking—*fauconnerie*) battre des ailes.

bath (bâth), *n.*, bain, *m.*; baignoire. *f.* —-keeper; *baigneur, m.* Dry —; *étuve, f.* Hot —; *bain chaud. m.* Medicated —; *bain médicamenteux, m.* Warm —; *bain chaud, m.* Tepid

—; *bain tempéré, m.* Hip- —; *bain de siège, demi-bain, m.* Slipper- —; *sabot, m.* Hot air —; *étuve sèche, f.* Shower- —; *douche, douche en arrosoir, f.* — -room; *salle de bain. f.* The Order of the —; *l'Ordre du Bain, m.*

bathe (béthe), *v.a.*, baigner, arroser, tremper, mouiller; bassiner, étuver. To — a wound; *bassiner une plaie.*

bathe, *v.n.*, se baigner.

bather (bétheur). *n.*, baigneur, *m.*, baigneuse, *f.*

bathing (béthigne), *n.*, action de baigner, de se baigner, *f.*; bain, *m.* Sea- —; *bains de mer, m.pl.* River- —; *bains de rivière, m.pl.* — -dress. — -gown, *peignoir, m.* —-establishment; *établissement de bains, m.* — -tub; *baignoire, f.* — -room; *salle de bain, f.* — -machine; *voiture de bain, f.*

bathos (béthoss), *n.*, pathos, *m.*

bating (bétigne), *prep.*, excepté, hormis. — a few; *hormis quelques-uns, à quelques-uns près.* — mistakes; *sauf erreur.*

batlet (bat'lète), *n.*, battoir, *m.*

baton (bat'on), *n.*, bâton, tricot, *m.*, trique, *f.*, gourdin, *m.*; baguette, *f.*

batoon (ba-toune), *n.*, bâton; tricot, gourdin, *m.*; trique; massue; baguette, *f.*

batrachia, *or* **batrachians** (-tré-kia, -kia-nze), *n.*, batraciens, *m.*

batrachian (-tré-kia-n), *adj.*, des batraciens.

battalia (bat-té-lia), *n.*, ordre de bataille, *m.*

battalion (bat-ta-lieune), *n.*, bataillon, *m.*

battalous (bat-ta-leusse), *adj.*, (ant.) belliqueux, guerrier, martial; batailleur.

batten, *v.a.*, (ant.) engraisser, fertiliser.

batten (bat't'n), *v.n.*, (ant.) s'engraisser; (carp.) construire en volige.

batten, *n.*, (ant.) volige, *f.*; battant, *m.*; chasse de tisserand, *f.*; chevron, *m.*; latte; (nav.) latte, *f.* —s of the hatches; *lattes des écoutilles, f.pl.*

batter (bat'teur), *n.*, pâte de farine détrempée pour faire des crêpes, des beignets à l'anglaise, *f.*

batter, *v.a.*, battre en brèche; battre; délabrer; ébranler; écraser; démolir. To — with ordnance; *battre à coups de canon, canonner.* To — in breach; *battre en brèche.* To — down; *abattre, renverser, battre en ruine.*

battered (bat'teurde), *adj.*, battu en brèche, battu; délabré; (print.) mauvais.

batterer, *n.*, abatteur; batteur, *m.*

battering (bat'teurigne), *n.*, (milit.) action de battre en brèche, *f.* — -piece; *pièce de batterie, pièce de siège, f.* — -ram; *bélier, m.* — -train; *artillerie de siège, f.*

battery (bat'teuri), *n.*, batterie; action de battre en brèche, *f.*; (jur.) voies de fait, *f.pl.*; (phys.) batterie, *f.* Galvanic —; *pile galvanique, f.*

batting (bat'tigne), *n.*, jeu de crosse, *m.*

battish (bat'ishe), *adj.*. de chauve-souris.

battle (bat't'l), *n.*, bataille, *f.*; combat, *m.*

battle, *v.a.*, se battre; combattre; batailler.

battle-axe (-axe). *n.*, hache d'armes, *f.*

battledore (bat't'ldore), *n.*, battoir, *m.*; raquette, *f.*

battlement (bat't'l-mè-nte), *n.*, créneau, *m.*

batton (bat't'n), *n.*, (ant.), *V.* **batten.**

batty, *adj.*, *V.* **battish.**

bauble (bô-b'l), *n.*, *V.* **bawble.**

bavaroy, *n.*, polonaise (frock-coat—*redingote*), *f.*

bavin (-vi-n), *n.*, bourrée, fascine, *f.*; cotret, *m.*; javelle (of vine branches—*de sarment de vigne*), *f.*

bawble, *or* **bauble** (bô-b'l), *n.*, babiole, bagatelle, *f.*; colifichet, *m.*; breloque, *f.* Fool's — ; *marotte de fou, f.*

bawbling (bô-bligne), *adj.*, (ant.) mesquin, de nulle valeur, qui n'est qu'une babiole.

bawcock (bô-koke), *n.*, (ant.) godelureau, *m.*

bawdrick (bô-drike), *n.* *V.* **baldric.**

bawl (bôl), *v.n.*, crier, brailler.

bawl, *v.a.*, crier.

bawler (bôl-eur), *n.*, crieur, *m.*, crieuse, *f.*; brailleur, *m.*, brailleuse, *f.*; criailleur, *m.*,criailleuse, *f.*; braillard, *m.*, braillarde, *f.*

bawling (bôl-igne), *n.*, cri. *m.*; cris, *m.pl.*; crierie, criaillerie, clabauderie, *f.*

bawn (bô-n), *n.*, (ant.) enclos, *m.*

bay, *n.*, baie. *f.*; écluse, *f.*; (arch.) travée, *f.*; abois, *m.pl.*; (bot.) laurier, laurier femelle, *m.* — of joists ; *travée, f.* —-window ; *fenêtre en saillie. f.* The stag stands at — ; *le cerf est aux abois.* To keep any one at — ; *mettre quelqu'un aux abois.* Small — ; *anse, f.* —-berry ; *baie de laurier, f.* —-cherry; *laurier-cerise, m.* —-tree ; *laurier, m.*

bay, *adj.*, bai. Light — ; *bai clair.* Dark —; *bai brun.* Chestnut —; *bai châtain.* Gilded — ; *bai fauve.*

bay, *v.n.*, aboyer.

bayard (bé-arde), *n.*, bai, cheval bai ; cheval aveugle, *m.*

bayardly (bé-ardly), *adj.*, aveugle ; stupide.

bayed (bé-de), *adj.*, (mas.) à ouvertures, à intervalles, à baies.

bayonet, *n.*, baïonnette, *f.*

bayonet, *v.a.*, tuer, blesser avec une baïonnette.

bazaar, *or* **bazar** (bazâre), *n.*, bazar.

bdellium (dèl'lieume), *n.*, bdellium, *m.*

be (bi), *v.n.* (preterit, Was ; past part., Been), être, exister ; devoir, falloir. The title is to descend to his heir ; *le titre doit passer à son héritier.* To — very well; *se porter très bien.* What is the matter? *qu'est-ce qu'il y a? qu'y a-t-il?* To — out (to be mistaken); *se tromper.* To — right; *avoir raison.* To — wrong ; *avoir tort.* That is nothing to me; *cela ne me regarde pas; cela ne me fait rien.* To — a witness; *servir de témoin.* To — better; *valoir mieux; se porter mieux.* It is no matter; *il n'importe, n'importe.* Nobody is to know it ; *personne ne doit le savoir ; il faut que personne ne le sache.* To — cold, warm, thirsty, hungry ; *avoir froid, chaud, soif, faim.* It is warm, cold, fine; *il fait chaud, froid, beau.* To — twenty, thirty years old ; *avoir vingt ans, trente ans.* There to — ; *y avoir ; être.* There is ; *il y a ; il est.* There are; *il y a ; il est.* If it were not for; *sans.* — that as it may; *quoi qu'il en soit.* As it were; *pour ainsi dire.*

beach (bitshe), *n.*, rivage; (of a river—*d'une rivière*) bord, *m.*, rive, *f.*

beacon (bî'k'n), *n.*, balise, *f.*; fanal, phare, *m.*

beacon, *v.a.*, allumer.

beaconage (—édje), *n.*, droit de balise, *m.*

beaconed (bî'k'n'de), *adj.*, surmonté d'un fanal, surmonté d'un phare ; à fanal, à phare.

bead (bîde), *n.*, grain de chapelet, de bracelet, de collier ; chapelet, rosairè, *m.* ; perle, *f.* ; bulle, *f.* ; globule, *m.* To thread —s ; *enfiler des perles.* To say over one's —s, to tell one's —s; *dire son chapelet.* Steel —s; *grains d'acier, m.pl.*

bead, *v.n.*, perler, former des globules.

beadle (bîd'l), *n.*, bedeau ; huissier ; huissier audiencier ; sergent de ville, *m.*

bead-maker (—mék'eur), *n.*, fabricant de perles, de grains de perles, *m.* ; patenôtrier, *m.*

beadroll (—rôl), *n.*, liste de ceux pour qui les prêtres doivent prier, *f.*

beadsman, *or* **bedesman** (bidz'ma'n), *n.*, homme voué à la prière ; homme qui intercède par la prière ; moine, *m.*

beadswoman (bidz'wouma'n), *n.*, femme vouée à la prière ; femme qui intercède par la prière, *f.*

beadtree (-trî), *n.*, (bot.) azédarac, *m.*

beagle (bi'g'l), *n.*, chien basset, *m.*

beak (bîke), *n.*, bec, *m.*

beak, *v.a.*, saisir avec le bec.

beaker, *n.*, gobelet, *m.* ; coupe, *f.*

beak-iron (-aï'eur'ne), *n.*, bigorne, *f.*

beam (bîme), *n.*, (of timber—*charpente*) poutre, *f.* ; (of light—*de lumière*) rayon ; (of a plough, a carriage—*de charrue, de voiture*) timon; (of scales—*de balances*) fléau ; (nav.) bau, *m.*

beam, *v.n.*, rayonner.

beam, *v.a.*, lancer, darder des rayons.

beam-ends (-è'nd'ze), *n.pl.*, (nav.) côté, *m.*

beaming, *n.*, rayonnement, *m.*

beamless, *adj.*, sans rayon, sans éclat.

beam-tree (-trî),*n.*, alisier blanc, alisier commun, alouchier, *m.*

beamy, *adj.*, rayonnant, brillant ; massif.

bean (bîne), *n.*, fève, *f.* French — ; *haricot vert, m.*

bear (bère), *n.*, ours, *m.*, ourse, *f.* ; (at the Exchange—*terme de bourse*) joueur à la baisse, batssier, *m.*

bear, *v.a.* (preterit, Bore ; past part., Born), porter ; soutenir ; supporter, souffrir; essuyer; avoir ; tenir; faire ; garder. — away; *remporter.* — down; *entraîner; renverser.* — out; *maintenir; justifier; avancer.* — company; *tenir compagnie.* — sway ; *dominer, régner.* — the charges ; *payer les frais.* To — fruit ; *porter fruit.* To — interest ; (com.) *porter intérêt.* To be born; *naître.* To be borne; *être porté, supporté, soutenu.*

bear, *v.n.*, souffrir; rapporter, être fertile : porter; se porter ; peser.

bear-baiting (-bêt'-), *n.*, combat d'ours, *m.*

bear-berry (-, (bot.) raisin d'ours, *m.*

bear-bind (-baï'n'de), *n.*, (bot.) liseron des haies, *m.*

beard (bîrde), *n.*, barbe; (of an arrow—*de flèche*) dent, *f.* To do, to say anything to any one's — ; *dire, faire quelque chose à la barbe de quelqu'un.*

beard, *v.a.*, braver, faire quelque chose à la barbe de quelqu'un.

bearded, *adj.*, barbu ; barbelé.

beardless, *adj.*, sans barbe; imberbe, qui n'a point de barbe. — boy; *blanc bec, m.*

beardlessness, *n.*, défaut de barbe, manque de barbe, *m.*

bearer, *n.*, porteur, *m.*, porteuse, *f.* —s of a tree ; *crochets d'arbre, m.pl.*

bear-garden (-gârd'n), *n.*, arène où les dogues se battent avec les ours, *f.* ; endroit où tout est en désordre, *m.* ; pétaudière, *f.*

bearherd (-heurde), *n.*, meneur d'ours, *m.*

bearing, *n.*, rapport; maintien ; *m.*,conduite, *f.*, (nav.) gisement, *m.* ; hauteur, situation, *f.* ; (her.) armes, armoiries, *f.pl.* — out; (arch.) saillie, avance, *f.*

bearing-block, *n.*, (tech.) support, *m.*

bearing-cloth (-clôth), *n.*, robe baptismale, *f.*

bearing-neck (-nèke), *n.*, tourillon, *m.*

bearing-rein (-rêne), *n.*, rêne, *f.*

bearing-surface (-seur-féce), *n.*, point d'appui, *m.*

bearing-wall (-wôl), *n.*, mur de refend, *m.*

bearish, *adj.*, d'ours.

bearlike (-laïke), *adj.*, qui tient de l'ours, semblable à un ours.

bear's-ear, *n.*, (bot.) oreille d'ours, *f.*

bear's-whortle-berry, *n.*, (bot.) raisin d'ours, *m.*

beast (bîste), *n.*, bête; (card game—*jeu de cartes*) bête, *f.* ; (of a person—*d'une personne*) animal, *m.*, bête, bête brute, *f.* Wild —; *bête sauvage, f.* — of burden; *bête de somme, f.* — of chase; *bête de chasse, f.*

20 *

beastliness, *n.*, brutalité; saleté, saloperie, obscénité, *f.*

beastly, *adj.*, bestial; sale, vilain, malpropre.

beat (bite), *n.*, battement; son, *m.*; station, ronde (of policemen—*de police*), *f.*; (hunt.) lieu où se fait une battue, *m.* — of the drum; *batterie de tambour, f.*

beat, *v.a.* (preterit, Beat; past part., Beaten), battre; frapper; piler, broyer; l'emporter sur. To — down; *abattre; diminuer.* To — back; *repousser.* To — in; *faire entrer de force.* To — any one hollow, to — any one all to nothing; *lattre quelqu'un à plate couture.* To — away; *éloigner, écarter.* To — black and blue; *meurtrir.*

beat, *v.n.*, battre; être agité. To — up for soldiers; *recruter des soldats.* To — about; (nav.) *louvoyer.* To — up to windward; *courir des bordées.* — against; *battre, se briser, se froisser.*

beater, *n.*, batteur, *m.*; (instrument) batte, *f.*; (print.) balle, *f.*; (tech.) fouloir, *m.*

beatific, or **beatifical** (bi-a-), *adj.*, béatifique.

beatifically, *adv.*, d'une manière béatifique.

beatification (-fi-ké-), *n.*, béatification, *f.*

beatify (-fa'ye), *v.a.*, béatifier.

beating (bit'igne), *n.*, batterie; bourrade; volée, rossée, *f.*; coups, *m.pl.*

beatitude (béati-tioude), *n.*, béatitude, félicité, *f.*

beau, *n.*, dam'oiseau; ⊙plumet (military beau—*militaire*); petit-maître; amant; futur, *m.*

beauish (beau-ishe), *adj.*, pimpant, fat.

beauteous (biou-té-euse), *adj.*, beau.

beauteously, *adv.*, avec beauté.

beauteousness, *n.*, beauté; bonne grâce, *f.*

beautifier (-fa'i'eur), *n.*, personne, chose qui embellit, *f.*

beautiful (-foul), *adj.*, beau, superbe.

beautifully, *adv.*, avec beauté, admirablement, d'une belle manière; parfaitement bien.

beautifulness, *n.*, beauté, *f.*

beautify (-fa'ye), *v.a.*, embellir, orner.

beautify, *v.n.*, s'embellir.

beauty (biouté), *n.*, beauté, *f.*; charme, *m.*

beauty-spot, *n.*, mouche, *f.*; grain de beauté, *m.*

beauty-wash (-woshe), or **beauty-water** (-wôteur), *n.*, eau de beauté, *f.*

beaver (bi'veur), *n.*, castor; chapeau de castor, *m.*; visière (of a helmet—*de casque*), *f.*

beavered (-veurde), *adj.*, coiffé d'un chapeau.

becafico (béc-a-fi-cô), *n.*, (orni.) becfigue, *m.*

becalm (bi-câme), *v.a.*, apaiser, calmer; (nav.) abriter, abrier. To be becalmed; (nav.) *être abrité, être pris de calme.*

because (bicôze), *conj.*, parce que, à cause que, de ce que. — of; à cause de.

bechance (bi-tshâ'nse), *v.n.*, arriver, avenir, advenir.

bechance, *adv.*, par accident.

becharm (bi-tshârme), *v.a.*, charmer, ensorceler.

bechic (bi'kike), *n.*, (med.) béchique.

beck, *n.*, signe (of the hand, of the head—*de main, de tête*), *m.*

beck (bèke), or **beckon** (bèk'k'n). *v.n.*, faire signe (of the hand, of the head—*de la main, de la tête*); faire signe, inviter.

beckon, *v.a.*, faire signe à (of the hand, of the head—*de la main, de la tête*).

beckon, *n.*, signe (of the finger, of the hand —*du doigt, de la main*), *m.*

becloud (bi-claoude), *v.a.*, couvrir d'un nuage, couvrir de nuages.

become (bi-keume), *v.n.* (preterit, Became; past part., Become), devenir. What will — of me? *que deviendrai-je?*

become, *v.n.*, aller bien à, seoir à, convenir à, être propre à. To — ill; *convenir mal, peu.*

becoming, *adj.*, avenant, séant, bienséant, convenable, qui sied bien, qui va bien.

becomingly (bi-), *adv.*, avec bienséance, convenablement.

becomingness, *n.*, convenance; bienséance, *f.*

bed (bède), *v.a.*, coucher, mettre au lit; coucher avec; loger, fixer.

bed, *v.n.*, coucher, se coucher.

bed, *n.*, lit. *m.*; couche, *f.* —of a river; *lit de rivière.* Feather- —; *lit de plume.* State- —; *lit de parade.* Folding- —; *lit brisé, lit de sangle.* Tent- —; *lit à tombeau.* Press- —; *lit en forme d'armoire.* Four-post —; *lit à quenouilles.* — of a ship; (nav.) *souille, f.* — of a gun; coussin de mire, *m.* —; (gard.) *massif, carreau, m.,* couche, planche, plate-bande, *f.*

bedabble (bi-dab'b'l), *v.a.*, éclabousser, asperger.

bedaggle (bi-dag-g'l), *v.a.*, crotter.

bedarken (bi-dâr-kè-n), *v.a.*, assombrir, obscurcir.

bedash (bi-), *v.a.*, éclabousser, arroser, mouiller.

bedaub (bi-), *v.a.*, souiller, salir; barbouiller.

bedazzle (bi-daz'z'l), *v.a.*, éblouir.

bed-bolt (-bôlte), *n.*, boulon qui traverse l'affût d'un canon, *m.*

bedchamber (-tshé-m-beur), *n.*, chambre à coucher, *f.*

bedclothes, *n.*, couvertures, *f.pl.*; draps, *m.pl.*

bedding (bèd'digne), *n.*, literie, *f.*, coucher, *m.*

bedeck (bi-dèke), *v.a.*, orner, parer, décorer.

bedehouse (bid'haouce), *n.*, hospice, *m.*

bedel (bi-dèle), *n.*, appariteur, *m.*

bedelry, *n.*, fonctions d'appariteur, de massier, *f.pl.*

bedesman, *n.* V. **beadsman**.

bedevil (bi-dev'v'l), *v.a.*, faire endiabler; lutiner.

bedew (bi-diou), *v.a.*, arroser, mouill'er.

bedewer, *n.*, chose qui mouille, *f.*

bedewy, *adj.*, (ant.) humide de rosée.

bedfellow (-fèl-lô), *n.*, camarade de lit, coucheur, *m.*; compagne de lit, coucheuse, *f.*

bedframe (-fréme), *n.*, bois de lit, *m.*

bedhangings (-hain-n'ghign'ze), *n.pl.*, tour de lit, *m.*; tenture de lit, *f.*

bedight (bé-daïte), *v.a.*, (ant.) décorer, parer, orner.

bedim (bi-dime), *v.a.*, obscurcir, rembrunir.

bedismal (bi-diz'-), *v.a.*, (ant.) attrister.

bedizen (bedaï-zène, ou bedizène), *v.a.*, (l.ex.) parer, orner.

bedlam, *n.*, Bedlam (hôpital des fous), *m.*; petites maisons, *f.pl.*; fou, *m.*, folle, *f.*

bedlamite (-lam'aïte), *n.*, fou, *m.*, folle, *f.*

bedlamlike (-laike), *adv.*, en fou, en insensé, comme un fou, comme une folle.

bedmaker (-mék'-), *n.*, personne qui fait le lit, chambrière, *f.*

bedmoulding (-môld-igne), *n.*, (arch.) filet, *m.*

bedpost (-pôste), *n.*, colonne de lit, quenouille de lit, *f.*

bedpresser (-près'-), *n.*, dormeur, *m.*, dormeuse, *f.*

bedraggle (bi-drag'g'l), *v.a.*, crotter (the extremity of a dress—*le bas de la robe*).

bedrench (bi-drè'nshe), *v.a.*, tremper, abreuver.

bedrid (bèd'ride), or **bedridden** (-rid'd'n), *adj.*, grabataire, alité.

bedroom (bèd'roume), *n.*, chambre à coucher, *f.*

bedrop (bi-drope), *v.a.*, arroser, mouiller, tacheter, semer, parsemer.

bedscrew (bèd'scrou), *n.*, écrou de lit *m.*, vis de lit, *f.*

bedside (bèd'saïde), *n.*, ruelle, *f.* ; bord du lit, *m.*

bedstead (-stède), *n.*, bois de lit, lit, *m.*

bedstraw (-strô), *n.*, paillasse, *f.* ; (bot.) caille-lait ; gaillet, *m.*

bedswerver (-sweurv'eur), *n.*, époux infidèle, *m.*, épouse infidèle, *f.*

bedtime (-taïme), *n.*, heure de se coucher, *f.* ; temps de se coucher, *m.*

bedung (bi-dun'n'ghe), *v.a.*, engraisser avec du fumier, fumer.

bedward (bèd'worde), *adv.*, vers le lit.

bedwarf (bi-dwôrfe), *v.a.*, rapetisser.

bedye (bi-da'ye), *v.a.*, teindre.

bee (bi), *n.*, abeille ; mouche à miel, *f.* Bull---- ; *taon, m.* Hive---- ; *abeille domestique, de ruche.* Humble---- ; *bourdon, m.* Queen---- ; *reine abeille, mère abeille, f.* To ring ----s ; *carillonner les abeilles.* Swarm of ----s ; *essaim d'abeilles, m.*

bee-board (-bôrde), *n.*, tablette à ruches, *f.*

bee-bread (-brède), *n.*, pain d'abeilles, *m.*

beech, beech-tree (bitshe-trî), *n.*, (bot.) hêtre, fouteau, fayard, *m.* Plantation of ----s ; *foutelaie, f.*

beech-martin (-tine), *n.*, (mam.) fouine, *f.*

beechmast, *or* **beechnut** (-maste, -neute), *n.*, (bot.) faîne, *f.*

beechoil (-oïle), *n.*, huile de faîne, *f.*

bee-eater (bi-ît'eur), *n.*, (orni.) guêpier, *m.*

beef (bîfe), *n.*, (*beeves*) bœuf, *m.*

beef-eater (-ît'eur), *n.*, mangeur de bœuf ; bœuf (stout man---- *homme corpulent*) ; (orni.) pique-bœuf ; soldat aux gardes de la Tour de Londres, *m.*

bee-flower (-flaou-eur), *n.*, (bot.) orchis, *m.*

beefsteak (bîfe-stèke), *n.*, bifteck, *m.*

beefwitted (-wit'tède), *adj.*, (ant.) lourd comme un bœuf.

bee-garden (-gârd'n), *n.*, rucher, *m.*

bee-house (-haouce), *n.*, rucher, *m.*

beelike (-laïke), *adj.*, d'abeille, comme les abeilles.

bee-master (-mâs'teur), *n.*, éleveur d'abeilles, *m.*

beer (bîre), *n.*, bière, *f.*

beer-engine (-èn-djine), *n.*, pompe à bière, *f.*

beerhouse (-haouce), *n.*, taverne (où l'on ne vend que de la bière), *f.*

beershop (-shope), *n.*, débit, *m.*, boutique de bière, *f.*

beet (bîte), *n.*, (bot.) bette, betterave, *f.*

beet-chard (-tshârde), *n.*, (bot.) carde poirée, *f.*

beetle (bî't'tl), *n.*, battoir (laundress's---- *de blanchisseuse*), *m.* ; hie, demoiselle (pavior's---- *de paveur*), *f.* ; mouton (of a pile-driver---- *d'une sonnette*), *m.* ; (ent.) scarabée, escarbot, *m.* Horn---- ; stag---- ; *cerf-volant, m.*

beetle, *v.n.*, surplomber.

beetle-browed (-braoude), *adj.*, à sourcils épais.

beetle-head (-hède), *n.*, souche, bûche, ganache, *f.*

beetle-stock, *n.*, (tech.) manche de mail, de mailloche, *m.*

beetradish (bîte-rad'ishe), **beetrave** (-réve), *or* **beetroot** (-route), *n.*, (bot.) betterave, *f.*

befall (bi-fôl), *v.a.* and *n.* (preterit, Befell ; past part., Befallen), arriver à, survenir à ; échoir.

befeathered (bi-fè-*theur*'de), *adj.*, emplumé, couvert de plumes.

befiddled (bi-fid'd'lde), *adj.*, fou du violon.

befit (bi-fite), *v a.*, convenir à.

befoam (bi-fôme), *v.a.*, couvrir d'écume.

befool (bi-foule), *v.a.*, duper, tromper.

before (bi-), *prep.*, (of time---- *de temps*) avant; (of place---- *de lieu*) devant ; par devant ; (jur.) par-devant.

before, *adv.*, (of time---- *de temps*) auparavant, avant ; (of place---- *de lieu*) en avant.

before, *conj.*, avant que ; plutôt que.

beforehand (-hain'n'de), *adv.*, par avance, d'avance.

beforetime (-taïme), *adv.*, autrefois.

befortune (bi-fôrt-ioune), *v.a.*, (ant.) arriver à, survenir à.

befoul (bi-faoule), *v.a.*, salir, souiller.

befriend (bi-frè'nde), *v.a.*, favoriser ; être l'ami de.

befringe (bi-fri'n'je), *v.a.*, franger.

beg (bèghe), *v.a.*, mendier ; demander, prier.

beg, *v.n.*, mendier. To ---- of ; *prier.*

begass (bi-gasse), *n.*, bagasse, bagace, *f.*

beget (bi-ghète), *v.a.* (preterit, Begot ; past part., Begotten), engendrer ; produire ; causer.

begetter, *n.*, auteur, producteur, *m.*

beggable (bèg-gab'l), *adj.*, à demander.

beggar (bèg-gheur), *n.*, mendiant, *m.*, mendiante, *f.* ; gueux, *m.*

beggar, *v.a.*, réduire à la mendicité ; rendre impossible, rendre impuissant.

beggar-girl (-gheur'l), *or* **beggar-maid** (-méde), *n.*, jeune mendiante, *f.*

beggarliness, *n.*, gueuserie, pauvreté, misère, *f.*

beggarly, *adj.*, chétif, pauvre, misérable.

beggarly, *adv.*, misérablement, chétivement.

beggar-man (-ma'n), *n.*, mendiant, *m.*

beggar-woman (-woum'a'n), *n.*, mendiante, *f.*

beggary, *n.*, mendicité, misère, *f.*

begin (bi-ghi'n), *v.a.* (preterit, Began ; past part., Begun), commencer.

begin, *v.n.*, commencer. ----afresh ; recommencer, se renouveler.

beginner, *n.*, commençant, *m.*, commençante, *f.* ; débutant, *m.*, débutante, *f.*

beginning (bi-ghin'), *n.*, commencement, *m.*

begird (bi-gheurde), *or* **begirt** (ant.), *v.a.*, ceindre, enceindre ; entourer ; cerner.

begnaw (bi-nô), *v.a.*, ronger.

begone (bi-), *int.*, va-t'en ! allez-vous-en ! retire-toi ! retirez-vous ! loin d'ici !

begotten (bi-got'tène). *V.* **beget.**

begrease (bi-grize), *v.a.*, graisser.

begrime (bi-graïme), *v.a.*, barbouiller, souiller.

begrudge (bi-greud'je), *v.a.*, envier à ; refuser à ; plaindre, se palindre.

beguile (bi-gaïle), *v.a.*, décevoir ; abuser ; surprendre ; tromper ; faire oublier à.

beguiler, *n.*, trompeur, *m.*, trompeuse, *f.*

beguin (bé-ghine), *n.*, béguin, frère convers de l'ordre de saint François ; béguin (for an infant---- *de petit enfant*) ; béguard, béguin, *m.*

beguine (bé-ghine), *n.*, béguine ; dévote minutieuse, *f.*

behalf (bi-hâfe), *n.*, faveur ; part, *f.* ; (com.) profit, *m.* On his ---- ; *de sa part.* In ---- of ; *en faveur de* ; (com.) *au profit de.* On ---- of ; *au nom de.*

behave, *v.n.*, se comporter, se conduire.

behave (bi-héve), *v.a.*, comporter, conduire. To ---- one's self ; *se comporter, se conduire.*

behaviour (bi-hév'ieur), *n.*, conduite, tenue, contenance, manière d'être, *f.* ; manières, *f.pl.*

behead (bi-hède), *v.a.*, décapiter, décoller.

beheading (-), *n.*, décapitation ; (of St.John the Baptist---- *de saint Jean-Baptiste*) décollation, *f.*

behemoth (bi-hi-moth), *n.*, béhémoth, *m.*

behest (bi-hèste), *n.*, commandement, *m.*

behind, *prep.*, derrière ; après ; en retard.

behind (bi-haï'n'de), *adv.*, derrière, par derrière, en arrière.

behindhand, *adj.*, en arrière, en retard; en reste; tardif.

behold (bi-hôl'de), *v.a.*, (*preterit.* and *past part.* Beheld), voir, regarder; contempler.

behold! *int.*, vois! voyez! voici! voilà! tenez!

beholden (-dène), *adj.*, redevable, obligé.

beholder, *n.*, spectateur, *m.*

behoof (bi-houfe), *n.*, avantage, *m.*; faveur, *f.*

behoofed (-houf'te), *adj.*, à sabot.

be'loove, or **behove** (bi-houve), *v.n.imp.*, convenir, falloir.

behowl (bi-haoule), *v.n.*, hurler après.

being (bi-igne), *n.*, être, *m.*; existence, *f.*

being, *pres. part.* (of to be), étant. The time —; *le temps présent, m.*

being-place (-pléce), (ant.) *n.*, existence, *f.*

beiram, *n.*, (Mahom. rel.) beiram, bairam, *m.*

bejade (bi-d'jéde), *v.a.*, harasser; surmener.

beknave (bi-néve), *v.a.*, traiter de coquin.

belabour (bi-lé'beur), *v.a.*, rosser, battre.

belace, (bi-léce), *v.a.*, (ant.) tresser; galonner; donner les étrivières à.

belated (bi-lét'éde), *adj.*, attardé, anuité, surpris par la nuit.

belay (bi-), *v.a.*, intercepter le passage de, arrêter, entraver; (nav.) amarrer.

belch (bèlshe), *n.*, rot (l.ex.), *m.*

belch, *v.a.*, vomir. To — out blasphemies; *vomir des blasphèmes.*

belch, *v.n.*, roter (l.ex.); vomir.

belcher, *n.*, roteur, *m.* (l.ex.).

beldam, *n.*, sorcière; vieille, *f.*

beleaguer (bi-lî-gheur), *v.a.*, assiéger.

beleaguerer, *n.*, assiégeant, *m.*

belee (bi-lî), *v.a.*, (nav.) abrier; dérober le vent à.

beleper (bi-lèp-), *v.a.*, infecter de la lèpre.

belfry, *n.*, clocher; beffroi; (nav.) montant de cloche, *m.*

belgian (-d'jt-a'n), *adj.*, belge.

belgian, *n.*, Belge, *m.f.*

belie (bi-la'ye), *v.a.*, contrefaire; calomnier; démentir.

belief (bi-life), *n.*, foi, créance, croyance, *f.*; credo, *m.* Light of —; *crédule.* Hard of —; *incrédule.* Past —; *incroyable.* To the best of one's —; *autant qu'on le sache.*

believable, *adj.*, croyable, probable.

believe (bi-live), *v.n.*, croire. To — in God; *croire en Dieu.* I — so; *je crois que oui; je le crois.* I — not; *je crois que non; je ne le crois pas.*

believe, *v.a.*, croire. I — you; *je vous crois.* If you are to be believed; *à vous en croire.*

believer, *n.*, croyant, *m.*, croyante, *f.*; fidèle, *m.f.*

believingly, *adv.*, avec foi.

belike (bi-laïke), *adv.*, apparemment, peut-être.

belime (bi-laïme), *v.a.*, engluer.

bell, *n.*, cloche, clochette, *f.*; grelot, *m.*; sonnette, *f.*; (arch.) vase, *m.*, corbeille, *f.*; (horl.) timbre, *m.* Chime of —s; *carillon, m.* — of a trumpet; *pavillon de trompette, m.* — of a flower; (bot.) *calice d'une fleur, m.* To ring the —; *sonner.*

bell, *v.n.*, fleurir en forme de grelot, de cloche; (hunt.) réer, raire.

belladonna, *n.*, (bot.) belladone, belle-dame, *f.*

belle, *n.*, belle, *f.*

belled (bèl'de), *adj.*, à clochette, à grelot; (hawking-*fauconnerie*) grilleté.

belles-lettres, *n.*, belles-lettres, *f.pl.*

bell-fashioned (-fasheu'n'de), *adj.*, en cloche.

bellflower (-flaou'eur), *n.*, (bot.) campanule, clochette, *f.*

bellfounder (-faoun'deur), *n.*, fondeur de cloches, *m.*

bell-foundery, *n.*, fonderie de cloches, *f.*

bell-gable (-ghé'b'l), *n.*, (arch.) clocheton en forme de pignon, *m.*

bell-glass (-glâce), *n.*, cloche de jardin, *f.*

bellhanger (-haïn'gh'eur), *n.*, poseur de sonnettes, *m.*

bellied (bèl'lide), *adj.*, à ventre. Big—; *à gros ventre, ventru.*

belligerent (bèl-li'd'jère'n'te), *adj.*, belligérant.

belligerent, *n.*, belligérant, *m.*

belliing, *n.*, (hunt.) bramement, *m.*

belling, *adj.*, (of hops—*du houblon*) qui croît en forme de cloche.

bellman, *n.*, homme à la cloche; crieur public, *m.*

bellmetal, *n.*, métal de cloche, *m.*

bell-mouth (-maouth), *n.*, (tech.) évasement, *m.*

bell-mouthed (-maouth'de), *adj.*, (tech.) évasé.

bellow (bèl-lô), *v.n.*, beugler, mugir; gronder.

bellows (bèl-loze), *n.pl.*, soufflet, *m.sing.*

bellpull (-poule), *n.*, cordon de sonnette, *m.*

bellringer (-rign'eur), *n.*, sonneur, *m.*

bellrope (-rôpe), *n.*, corde de cloche, *f.*; cordon de sonnette, *m.*

bell-shaped (-shép'te), *adj.*, en cloche.

belltower (-taoueur), *n.*, beffroi, clocher, *m.*

bellturret (-teur'rète), *n.*, (arch.) clocheton, *m.*

bellwether (-wètheur), *n.*, sonnailler, *m.*

belly, *n.*, ventre, *m.* — of a lute; *table de luth, f.*

belly, *v.n.*, bomber, faire ventre, pousser en dehors; se gonfler.

belly-ache (-éke), *n.*, mal au ventre, *m.*

belly-band, *n.*, sous-ventrière, *f.*

belly-bound (-baou'n'de), *adj.*, constipé.

belly-cheer (-tshîre), *n.*, (ant.) bonne chère, *f.*

belly-ful (-foule), *n.*, soûl, *m.* I had my — of it; *j'en ai eu tout mon soûl.*

belly-god, *n.*, (ant.) glouton, *m.*

belly-pinched (-pi'n'shte), *adj.*, (ant.) affamé.

belly-slave (-sléve), *n.*, (ant.) esclave de son ventre, *m.*

belly-timber, *n.*, (pop.) nourriture, *f.*, vivres, *m.pl.*

belong (bi-lôn'ghe), *v.n.*, appartenir, être à.

beloved (bi-leuv'd, *ou* -leuvède), *adj.*, chéri, bien-aimé, favori.

below, *prep.*, sous, en dessous de; après, depuis; (nav.) en aval de.

below (bi-lô), *adv.*, au-dessous, en bas; ici-bas.

belt, *n.*, ceinturon, baudrier, *m.*

belt, *v.a.*, attacher, ceindre.

belting, *n.*, ceinture, *f.*

belting-course (-côrse), *n.*, (arch.) chaîne, *f.*

belt-maker (-mék-eur), *n.*, ceinturier, *m.*

belt-strap, *n.*, allonge de ceinturon; bélière, *f.*

belvedere (-vè-dîre), *n.*, belvédère, *m.*

bemad (bi-made), *v.a.*, rendre fou.

bemask (bi-mâske), *v.a.*, masquer.

bemaul (bi-môle), *v.a.*, (ant.) rosser, maltraiter.

bemire (bi-maeur), *v.a.*, embourber, crotter.

bemoan (bi-mône), *v.a.*, plaindre, lamenter.

bemoaner, *n.*, faiseur de lamentations, *m.*

bemock (bi-moke), *v.n.* and *a.*, (ant.) se moquer; se moquer de.

bemoil (be-moïle), *v.a.*, (ant.) embouer.

bemoisten (bi-moïs'n), *v.n.,* humecter, rendre moite; rendre humide.

bemol (bi-), *n.,* (mus.) bémol, *m.*

bench (bè'n'she), *n.,* banc, *m.*; banquette, *f.*; (tech.) établi. *m.*; banc, siège, tribunal, *m.,* cour de justice, *f.* Court of King's —, of Queen's —; *cour du Banc du roi, de la reine.* — of a canal; *berme, f.* To play to empty —es; (thea.) *jouer devant les banquettes, jouer pour les banquettes.*

bench, *v.a.,* garnir de bancs; placer sur un banc.

bencher, *n.,* juge; avocat du premier rang, *m.*

bend (bè'n'de), *v.a.* (*preterit.* and *past part.,* Bent.), plier; courber, faire plier; incliner, tendre, bander; fléchir; appliquer, diriger; (nav.) nouer. To — one's brows; *froncer le sourcil, rider le front.* To — one's endeavours; *appliquer ses efforts.* To — one's knee; *fléchir le genou.* To — a sail; (nav.) *enverguer une voile.* To — a cable; *étalinguer un câble.* On bended knees; *à genoux.*

bend, *v.n.,* plier, ployer; se courber, être courbé; se pencher, s'incliner; s'appliquer; tourner; fléchir.

bend, *n.,* courbure; inclinaison, *f.*; pli, détour, *m.*; coude, *m.*; (nav.) nœud, *m.*; (her.) bande, *f.*

bender, *n.,* personne qui courbe, *f.*

bending, *adj.,* courbé, incliné, penchant, penché.

bendy, *n.,* (her.) bande, *f.*

beneath (bi-nîth), *prep.,* sous; au-dessous de.

beneath, *adv.,* dessous, au-dessous, en bas.

benedictine (bè'n'idictine), *n.,* bénédictin, *m.,* bénédictine, *f.*

benedictine, *adj.,* de l'ordre de saint Benoît; bénédictin.

benediction (bè'n'i-), *n.,* bénédiction, *f.*; bénédicité, *m.*

benefaction (bè'n'i-), *n.,* don, bienfait. *m.,* œuvre de bienfaisance, *f.*; grâce, faveur *f.*

benefactor (bè'n'i-), *n.,* bienfaiteur, *m.*

benefactress (bè'n'i-), *n.,* bienfaitrice, *f.*

benefice (bè'n'i-), *n.,* bénéfice, *m.*

beneficed (bè'n'i-fiste), *adj.,* qui a un bénéfice.

beneficence (bè-nèf'i-), *n.,* bienfaisance, *f.*

beneficent, *adj.,* bienfaisant.

beneficently, *adv.,* avec bienfaisance.

beneficial (bè'n'i-fish'al), *adj.,* bienfaisant, salutaire; avantageux, utile; (jur.) qui a droit au bénéfice.

beneficially, *adv.,* salutairement, avantageusement, utilement.

beneficialness, *n.,* avantage, profit, *m.*; utilité, *f.*

beneficiary (bè'n'i-fish'iari), *n.,* bénéficier; (feudalism—*féodalité*) feudataire, *m.*

beneficiary, *adj.,* (feud.—*féodal.*) qui relève d'un seigneur; de feudataire.

beneficient (bèn'i-fish'è'n'te), *adj*, bienfaisant.

benefit (bè'n'i-fite), *n.,* bienfait; service; bénéfice; profit, avantage, *m.*; (thea.) représentation à bénéfice, *f.*

benefit, *v.a.,* avoir du bénéfice, tirer du profit, profiter; faire du bien.

benefit, *v.n.,* profiter.

benefit-night (-naïte), *n.,* (thea.) représentation à bénéfice, *f.*

benefit-society (-so-ça'yiti), *n.,* société de secours mutuels, *f.*

benevolence (bi-nèv'o-), *n.,* bienveillance, bonté, bienfaisance, *f.*; don gratuit, *m.*

benevolent. *adj.,* bienveillant, bienfaisant; *f* iest.; bénévole.

benevolently, *adv.,* avec bienveillance, avec bienfaisance, bénévolement.

bengalee (bè'n'gali), *n.,* bengali, dialecte du Bengale, *m.*

bengalese (-lîze), *n.,* natif du Bengale, *m.*

bengaly, *n.,* (orni.) bengali, *m.*

benight (bi-naïte), *v.a.,* obscurcir.

benighted (-tède), *adj.,* anuité; couvert de ténèbres; ignorant.

benign (bi-naïne), *adj.,* bénin, bienfaisant, généreux.

benignant (bi-nig-na'nte), *adj.,* bon, gracieux, bienveillant.

benignity (bi-nig'niti), *n.,* bénignité, douceur, *f.*

benignly (bi-naï'n'li), *adv.,* bénignement.

benison (bè'n'i-ceune), *n.,* (ant.) bénédiction, *f.*

benjamin (bè'n'djamine), *n.,* benjoin, *m.,* assa dulcis, *f.*

bennet (bè'n'nète), *n.,* (bot.) benoîte; galiote, *f.*

bent, *n.,* pli; penchant, *m.*; pente; courbure, *f.*

bent (bè'n'te), *past part.* (of to bend), courbé, plié. — on; *décidé à; appliqué à.*

bentgrass. *n.,* (bot.) agrostide, *f.*

benumb (bi-neume), *v.a.,* engourdir; glacer.

benumbedness (bi-neum'èdnèsse), *or* **benumbing,** *n.,* engourdissement, *m.*

benzoic (bè'n'zöïke), *adj.,* (chem.) benzoïque.

benzoin (-zoïne), *n.* *V.* **benjamin.**

bepaint (bi-pé'n'te), *v.a.,* peindre; barbouiller, peinturer.

bepepper (bi-pèp'peur), *v.a.,* poivrer.

bepinch (bi-pi'n'she), *v.a.,* pincer.

beplaster (bi-plâsteur), *v.a.,* (fam.) plâtrer.

beplume (bi-plioume), *v.a.,* (fam.) emplumer.

bepowder (bi-paoudeur), *v.a.,* (fam.) poudrer.

bepraise (bi-préze), *v.a.,* louanger.

bequeathe (bi-kwîthe), *v.a.,* léguer, laisser

bequeather, *n.,* testateur, *m.,* testatrice, *f.*

bequeathment, *n.,* (ant.) legs, *m.*; action de léguer, *f.*

bequest (bi-kwèste), *n.,* legs, héritage, *m.*

berate (bi-rête), *v.a.,* insulter; vilipender.

berattle (bi-rat't'l) *v.a.,* remplir de bruit.

beray (bi-), *v.a.,* (ant.) souiller, salir.

berberry (beur-), *n.,* (bot.) épine-vinette, *f.*

bereave (bi-rîve), *v.a.,* dépouiller, priver.

bereavement, *n.,* privation (by death—*par suite de mort*), *f.*

berenice's hair (bè-ri-naïciz'hère), *n.,* (astron.) chevelure de Bérénice, *f.*

bergamot (beur-ga-mote), *n.,* bergamote, *f.*

berhyme (bi-raïme), *v.a.,* rimer.

berlin (beur-line, *ou* bèr-), *n.,* berline (carriage —*voiture*), *f.*

berme (beurme), *n.,* berme, *f.*

bernardine (beur-), *adj.,* de saint Bernard, des Bernardins.

berogue (bi-rôghe), (ant.) *v.a.,* traiter de fripon.

berry, *n.,* grain, *m.*; baie, *f.*

berry, *v.n.,* (bot.) porter des baies.

berry-bearing (-bèr'igne), *adj.,* (bot.) baccifère.

berth (beurth), *n.,* (nav.) cabine, *f.*; (nav.) poste, évitage, *m.*

beryl (bèr'ile), *n.,* (min.) béryl, *n.*

berylline (-laïne), *adj.,* de béryl.

bescrawl (bi-scröl), *v.a.,* (ant.) barbouiller (of writing—*de l'écriture*).

bescribble (bi-), *v.a.,* (ant.) barbouiller (of writing—*de l'écriture*).

beseech (bi-cîtshe), *v.a.* (*preterit.* and *past part.,* Besought), supplier, conjurer, implorer.

beseecher, n., suppliant, m.. suppliante, f.
beseeching, n., supplication, f.
beseem (bi-cîme), v.n., convenir à, seoir à.
beseemly, adj., convenable, bienséant.
beset (bi-cète), v.a., (preterit. and past part., Beset), assiéger, obséder; entourer, assiéger; embarasser.
besetting, adj., habituel.
beshrew (bi-shrou), v.a., maudire.
beside (bi-caïde), or **besides** (-caïd'ze), prep., à côté de, auprès de; outre; hors, hors de; hormis, excepté. To be — one's self; être hors de soi.
beside, or **besides**, adv., d'ailleurs, en outre, encore; hors de là; au delà.
beside that (-thate), conj., outre que.
besiege (bi-cî'dje), v.a., assiéger.
besieged (bi-cî'dj'd), n., assiégé, m.
besieger, n., assiégeant, m.
besieging, n., action d'assiéger, f.; siège, m.
besieging, adj., de siège.
beslubber (bi-sleub'beur), v.a., couvrir de bave.
besmear (bi-smîre), v.a., barbouiller, salir; enduire.
besmirch (bi-smeurt'she), v.a., (ant.) souiller, salir.
besmoke (bi-smôke),v.a., enfumer, noircir.
besmut (bi-smeute), v.a., noircir avec de la suie.
besnuff (bi-sneufe), v.a., barbouiller de tabac.
besom (bi-zeume), n., balai, m.
besom, v.a., balayer.
besort (bi-sorte), v.a., (ant.) convenir à, aller bien à.
besot (bi-cote), v.a., assoter; abrutir, rendre stupide.
besotted (bi-çot'tède), past part., infatué; stupéfié; abruti.
besottedly (bi-çot'tèd-), adv., sottement, stupidement.
besottedness, n., abrutissement, m.
besought (bè-çôte), V. **beseech**.
bespangle (bi-spa'n'g'l), v.a., orner de paillettes; parsemer.
bespatter (bi-), v.a., éclabousser, couvrir de boue; asperger; noircir, diffamer, flétrir.
bespawl (bi-spôl), v.a., (ant.) cracher sur.
bespeak (bi-spîke), v.a. (preterit., Bespoke; past part., Bespoken), commander, faire faire; retenir; prévenir; discourir; parler à, s'adresser à. To — a place; retenir une place. To — a coat; commander, faire faire un habit.
bespeaker, n., celui qui commande, qui fait faire, m.
bespeckle (bi-spèc'k'l), v.a., tacheter, marqueter, moucheter.
bespice (bi-spaïce), v.a., épicer; assaisonner.
bespot (bi-spote), v.a., tacher, salir, souiller, crotter.
bespread (bi-sprède), v.a., tendre, étendre; semer; couvrir.
besprent (bi-sprè'n'te), adj., (ant.) arrosé; semé; couvert.
besprinkle (bi-spri'n'k'l), v.a., arroser, parsemer.
besprinkler, n., personne qui arrose, f.
bespurt (bi-speurte), v.a., asperger.
besputter (bi-speut'-), v.a., cracher sur, couvrir de crachats.
best (bèste), adj., meilleur, le meilleur, le mieux. To do one's —; faire tout son possible; faire de son mieux. To act for the —; faire, agir pour le mieux. To the — of my remembrance; autant que je puis m'en souvenir. The — of it is that; le meilleur est que. At — ; au mieux, tout au mieux; au plus, tout au plus. For the — ; pour le mieux, au mieux. To have the — of it; avoir le dessus. To make the — of;

best, adv., mieux, le mieux; plus. To strive who shall do — ; faire à qui mieux mieux. One had — ; mieux vaudrait.
bestain (bi-stène), v.a., tacher.
bestead (bi-stède), v.a., (ant.) profiter à, servir à.
bestial (bèst'ial), adj., bestial, de bête.
bestiality, n., bestialité, f.
bestialize (bèst'ial'aïze), v.a., abrutir.
bestially, adv., bestialement.
bestiarius (bèstiarieusse), n., (Rom. antiq.) bestiaire, m.
bestick (bi-), v.a., fixer sur...au moyen de pointes, de clous.
bestir (bi-steur), v.a., remuer. To — one's self ; se remuer.
bestow (bi-stô), v.a., donner; appliquer; dispenser; accorder; conférer; employer, consacrer. To — a kindness on any one ; faire une faveur, rendre un bon office à quelqu'un.
bestowal, n., action d'accorder, de donner, f.
bestower, n., dispensateur, m., dispensatrice, f.
bestowing, n., donation, f.; don. m.
bestraddle (bi-), v.a., enfourcher.
bestraught (bi-strâote), adj., (ant.) insensé, égaré, aliéné, fou, hors de soi.
bestrew (bi-strou), v.a., joncher.
bestride (bi-straïde), v.a., monter (a horse —un cheval); enjamber, enfourcher.
bestud (bi-steude), v.a., orner de clous.
bet (bète), n., pari, m.; gageure, f.
bet, v.a., parier, gager, faire un pari, faire une gageure.
betag, v.a., galonner.
betake (bi-téke), v.a. (preterit., Betook; past part., Betaken). To — one's self ; se livrer, se mettre, s'adonner, se retirer. To — one's self to one's study ; se retirer dans son cabinet. To — one's self to one's heels ; se sauver, s'enfuir. To — one's self to one's studies ; se livrer à ses études.
bethink (bi-thi'n'k), v.n. (preterit. and past part., Bethought), ruminer; s'aviser, réfléchir.
bethink, v.a., se rappeler, se ressouvenir.
bethlehem (bèth-lî'ème), n., hospice pour les aliénés, m. V. **bedlam**.
bethlemite (bèth-lè'm'aïte), n., (geog.) Bethléhémite, m.f.; habitant de Bedlam, m., habitante de Bedlam, f. V. **bedlam**.
bethral (bi-thrôl),v.a.,(ant.)rendre esclave; asservir.
bethump (bi-theu'm'p), v.a., rosser, étriller, assommer.
betide (bi-taïde), v.a., arriver à, advenir à ; prédire, annoncer.
betide, v.n., arriver, advenir.
betime (bi-taïme), or **betimes** (bi-taï'mze), adv., de bonne heure.
betoken (bi-tô'k'n),v.a.,indiquer; annoncer, dénoter.
beton (bi-teune), n., béton, m.
betony (bèt'o'ni), n., (bot.) bétoine, f.
betoss (bi-), v.a., ballotter; berner.
betray (bi-tré), v.a., trahir; livrer; laisser; abandonner.
betrayer, n., traître, m., traîtresse, f. ; chose qui trahit, f.
betrim (bi-trime), v.a., parer, orner, décorer, embellir.
betroth (bi-troth), v.a., fiancer, accorder.
betrothed (bi-trothte), n., fiancé, accordé, m.; fiancée, accordée, f.
betrothed, adj., fiancé, accordé.
betrothing, or **betrothment**, n., fiançailles, (pop.) accordailles, f.pl.
betrust (bi-treuste), v.a., (ant.) confier, placer entre les mains.

tirer tout ce qu'on peut de; tirer le meilleur parti de.

betrustment, *n.*, confiance, *f.*; dépôt, *m.*; chose confiée, *f.*

better (bèt'teur), *adj.*, meilleur. — and —; *de mieux en mieux.* For the —; *en mieux.* To be —; *se trouver mieux, se rétablir; valoir mieux.* To grow —; *devenir meilleur; se porter mieux, se rétablir.* The — the day, the — the deed; *bon jour, bonne œuvre.* To get the — of; *prendre le dessus de; avoir le dessus de; l'emporter sur; venir à bout de; se rétablir de.*

better, *adv.*, mieux. To be —; *valoir mieux.* So much the —! *tant mieux!* — and —; *de mieux en mieux.* To be —; *valoir mieux, se porter mieux, être mieux.* To get —; *aller mieux, se porter mieux.* I had —; *je ferais mieux.* To think — (reflect); *se raviser.* I like her the — for it; *je l'en aime davantage.* The more I know you, the — I like you; *plus je vous connais, plus je vous aime.*

better, *n.*, supérieur, *m.* One's elders and —s; *gens qui valent mieux que soi.*

better, *v.a.*, améliorer, avancer.

bettering-house (-haouce), *n.*, maison de correction, *f.*

betting (bèt-tigne), *n.*, pari (action), *m.*

bettor (bèt-tor), *n.*, parieur; joueur, *m.*

betty (bèt'ti), *n.*, monseigneur (instrument), *m.*

betumbled (bi-teu'm'b'lde), *adj.*, en désordre.

between (bi-twine), *prep.*, entre. — us; *entre nous.* — wind and water; *à fleur d'eau.*

between, *n.*, intervalle, *m.*

betwixt (bi-), *prep.*, entre. — and between; *entre les deux.*

bevel (bè-vèl), *n.*, (tech.) fausse équerre, *f.*

bevel, *adj.*, de biais ; en biseau.

bevel, *v.a.*, équarrir, tailler en biseau.

bevel, *v.n.*, aller en biais, biaiser; (mines) diriger.

bevelling, *n.*, manière de couper le bois en biais, *f.*; biseau, *m.*

bevelling, *adj.*, de biais.

beverage (bèv'eur'édge), *n.*, breuvage, *m.*; boisson, *f.*

bevil. *V.* **bevel.**

bevy (bè-vi), *n.*, volée; troupe, bande, *f.* — of partridges; *compagnie de perdrix, f.* — of quails; *volée de cailles, f.* — of animals; *troupe d'animaux, f.* — of roebucks; *troupe de chevreuils, f.*

bewail (bi-wêle), *v.a.*, regretter, pleurer.

bewail, *v.n.*, se lamenter.

bewailer, *n.*, personne qui pleure, qui déplore, *f.*

bewailing, *n.*, lamentation, *f.*

beware (bi-wére), *v.n.*, se garder, prendre garde.

beweep (bi-wîpe), *v.a.* and *n.*, pleurer.

bewet (bi-wète), *v.a.*, humecter.

bewhisker (bi-), *v.a.*, parer de favoris.

bewilder (bi-), *v.a.*, égarer, embrouiller, embarrasser, dérouter; transporter, ravir.

bewitch (bi-wit'she), *v.a.*, ensorceler; enchanter.

bewitcher, *n.*, ensorceleur, *m.*, ensorceleuse, *f.*

bewitchery, *n.*, ensorcellement, *m.*

bewitchful (-foule), *adj.*, (ant.) ravissant, enchanteur.

bewitching, *adj.*, enchanteur, séduisant.

bewitchingly, *adv.*, d'une manière séduisante.

bewray (bi-ré), *v.a.*, déceler; tromper; trahir.

bewrayer (bi-râ'y'eur), *n.*, (ant.) traître, *m.*, traîtresse, *f.*

bey, *n.*, bey, *m.*

beyond (bi-yon'dé), *prep.*, delà, par delà, au-delà de; au dessus de; outre; hors de. — measure; *outre mesure, démesurément.* To be — reach; *être hors de la portée de.*

beyond, *adv.*, là-bas.

bezant (bi-zan't), *n.*, (Rom. antiq., her.) besant, *m.*

bezantler (bi-zan't'-), *n.*, (hunt.) second andouiller, *m.*

bezel (bè-zèl), *or* **bezil**, *n.*, chaton (of a ring —de bague), *m.*

bezoar (bi-zôre), *n.*, bézoard, *m.*

bia, *n.*, cauris, coris, *m.*

biangulate (-ghiou-léte), **biangulated** (-ghiou-létède), *or* **biangulous** (-ghiou-leusse), *adj.*, à deux angles.

bias (baï'ass), *n.* (biasses), biais, *m.*; pente, *f.*, penchant; but; préjugé, *m.*

bias, *v.a.*, incliner, faire pencher; prévenir; influencer, porter à; diriger.

bias, *adj.*, de biais, de travers.

bias, *adv.*, de biais, de travers.

bias-drawing (-drô'-), *n.*, prévention, partialité, *f.*

bib, *n.*, bavette, *f.*

bib, *v.a.*, buvoter.

bibacious (baï-bé-sheusse),*adj.*, qui s'adonne beaucoup à boire, qui aime à boire.

bibber (bib'-), *n.*, biberon, *m.*, biberonne, *f.*

bible (baï'b'l), *n.*, bible, *f.*

bibler (bib'leur), *n.*, biberon, *m.*, biberonne, *f.*

biblical (bi-), *adj.*, biblique.

bibliographer, *n.*, bibliographe, *m.*

bibliographic, *or* **bibliographical**, *adj.*, bibliographique.

bibliography, *n.*, bibliographie, *f.*

bibliomania (-mé-), *n.*, bibliomanie, *f.*

bibliomaniac (-mé-), *n.*, bibliomane, *m.*

bibliophilist (-fi-), *n.*, bibliophile, *m.*

bibliopole (-pôle), *n.*, libraire, *m.*

b'blist, *n.*, celui, celle dont la seule règle est la Bible.

bibulous (-biou-leusse), *adj.*, spongieux.

bice, *or* **bise** (baïce), *n.*, (paint.) bleu pâle; vert pâle, *m.*

biceps (baï-), *n.*, (anat.) biceps, *m.*

bicker (bik'-), *v.n.*, se quereller, disputer, contester, se picoter, se chamailler.

bickerer, *n.*, querelleur, *m.*

bickering, *n.*, picoterie; querelle, *f.*

bickern (bik'èrne), *n.*, bec, *m.*; bigorne, *f.*, enclume à deux cornes, *f.*

bicorn (baï-), *adj.*, (ant.). *V.* **bicornous.**

bicornous (baï-cor'neusse), *adj.*, à deux cornes, bicorne, *m.*

bicorporal (baï-), *adj.*, à deux corps.

bid, *v.a.*, offrir; ordonner; (at auctions—*aux enchères*) enchérir; dire; convier, inviter.

bid, *n.*, enchère, *f.*

bidder, *n.*, enchérisseur, *m.*

bidding, *n.*, commandement, ordre, *m.*; (at auctions—*aux enchères*) enchère, *f.*

bide (baïde), *v.a.*, endurer, souffrir; attendre.

bide, *v.n.*, demeurer, rester.

bidental, **bidentate**, *or* **bidentated** (baï-dè'n-, -téte, -tétède), *adj.*, à deux dents, bidenté.

bidet (bi-dète), *n.*, bidet (horse—*cheval*); bidet (furniture—*meuble*), *m.*

biding (baïd'-), *n.*, (ant.) demeure, *f.*; séjour, *m.*

bidon (bid'eune), *n.*, bidon, *m.*

biennial (baï'è'n-ni-), *adj.*, biennal, de deux ans; (bot.) bisannuel.

biennially, *adv.*, tous les deux ans, de deux ans en deux ans.

bier (bieur), *n.*, bière, *f.*, cercueil, *m.*; civière, *f.*; brancard, *m.*

biferous (bif'é-reusse), *adj.*, qui produit deux fois par an.

bifid (baï-fide), *or* **bifidated** (bif'idé'ède), *adj.*, bifide.

bifold (baï-fôlde), adj., double.
bifurcate (baï-feur-kéte), or **bifurcated** tède), adj., bifurqué.
bifurcation, n., bifurcation, f.
big, adj., gros; superbe, fier; grand; plein; (of women—des femmes) enceinte, grosse; (of animals—des animaux) pleine.
bigamist, n., bigame, m.f.
bigamy, n., bigamie, f.
bigly, adv., fièrement, superbement.
bigness (big'nèsse), n., grosseur, grandeur, f.
bigot (big'ote), n., bigot, cagot, m.; bigote, cagote, f.
bigot, adj., (ant.). V. **bigoted**.
bigoted (big'ot'ède), adj., bigot, cagot.
bigotedly, adv., avec bigoterie; en bigot.
bigotry, n., bigoterie, cagoterie, f.
bilander, n., (nav.) bélandre, f.
bilateral (baï-), adj., bilatéral.
bilberry, n., (bot.) airelle; myrtille, f.
bilbo, n. (bilboes), rapière, f.; pl., (nav.) fers, m.pl.
bile (baïle), n., bile, f.
bile-duct (-deucte), n., conduit, canal cholédoque, m.
bilge (bild'je), n., (nav.) sentine (of a ship—d'un vaisseau), f. — -water; eau de la cale, f.
bilge, v.n., (nav.) faire une voie d'eau à fond de cale.
biliary (bil'iari), adj., biliaire.
bilious, adj., bilieux.
bilk, v.a., flouer.
bill, n., bec d'oiseau, m.; hache, f.
bill, v.n., se becqueter.
bill, v.a., afficher.
bill, n., note, f.; mémoire, compte, m., facture, f.; billet, effet, m.; compte, (at dining-rooms—au restaurant) carte à payer, addition, f.; (of parliament—du parlement) bill, projet de loi, m. Hand-—; affiché, f., placard, m. Stick no —s! défense d'afficher! Exchequer-—; bon du trésor, m. To discount a —; escompter un billet. Tradesman's —; mémoire de fournisseur. To make a — payable to ; passer un effet à l'ordre de; faire un billet à l'ordre de. To honour a — ; faire honneur à, payer, un billet. To dishonour a —; ne pas faire honneur à, ne pas payer, un billet. To be able to bearer; billet au porteur. To take up a —; acquitter un billet, payer un billet. The expiration of a —; l'échéance d'un effet, f. To provide for the payment of a —; faire les fonds d'un effet.
bill-broker (brô-), n., courtier de change, m.
bill-brokerage (-édje), n., courtage de change, m.
billet (bil'lète), n., bûche m; (her.) billette, f.; billet; billet de logement, m.
billet, v.a., délivrer des billets de logement à, loger.
billet-doux (bil'lè-), n. (billets-doux), billet doux, m.
billiard (bil'ieurde), adj., de billard.
billiard-room (-roume), n., salle de billard, f.
billiards (bil'ieurdze), n.pl., billard, m.sing. To play a game at — ; faire une partie de billard.
billiard-table (-tè'b'l), n., billard, m.; table de billard, f.
billingsgate (bil'ligne'z'ghéte), n., langage de la halle, m.
billion (bil'ieu'ne), n., trillion, m.
billow (bil'lô), n., flot, m.; vague, f.
billow, v.n., s'élever en vagues, ondoyer.
billowy (bil-lô-i), adj., houleux.
billsticker n., afficheur, m.
bilobate, or **bilobated** (baï-lô-béte, -tède), adj., bilobé.
bilobed (baï-lôb'de), adj. V. **bilobate**.
bilocular (baï-), adj., (bot.) biloculaire.

bimanous (-neusse), adj., bimane.
bin (bine), n., huche, f.
binary, adj. binaire.
binary (baï-), n., (arith.) nombre binaire, m.
bind (baï'n'de), v.a., lier; obliger; resserrer; ceindre, border. To — a book; relier un livre. To — a carpet; border un tapis. To be bound over; (jur.) être tenu de comparaître.
bind, v.n., se lier.
binder, n., lieur; relieur, m.
bindery (baï'n'deuri), n., atelier de relieur, m.
binding, n., reliure, f.; bandeau, m.
binding, adj., obligatoire; (jur.) commissoire.
bindweed (baï'n'd'wîde), n., (bot.) liseron, m., liane, f.
binnacle, n., (nav.) habitacle, m.
binocle, n., binocle, m.
binocular (baï-), adj., binoculaire.
binomial (baï-nô-), adj., (alg.) binôme.
biographer (baï'og'graf'-), n., biographe, m.
biographic, or **biographical** (baï'o-), adj., biographique.
biography (baï'o-), n., biographie, f.
bipartient (baï-pâr-shè'nte), adj., qui divise en deux.
bipartite (bip'ar-taïte), adj., divisé en deux.
biped (baï-pède), n., bipède, m.
bipedal (bi-pi-), adj., bipède; bipédal.
biquadratic (baï-kwo-), adj., (alg.) biquadratique.
birch (beurtshe), n., bouleau, m.; verge, f ; verges, f.pl.
birchen (beurtshène), adj., de bouleau.
birch-tree (-trî), n., bouleau, m.
bird (beurde), n., oiseau, m. A little — told me; mon petit doigt me l'a dit. To kill two —s with one stone; faire d'une pierre deux coups.
bird, v.n., oiseler.
birdcall (-côl), n., appeau, pipeau, m.
bird-catcher, n., oiseleur, m.
bird-eyed (-aye'de), adj., à œil d'oiseau.
bird-fancier, n., amateur d'oiseaux, m.
birdlike (-laïke), adj., comme un oiseau.
birdlime (-laïme), n., glu, f.
birdman, n., oiseleur, m.
bird-organ, n., serinette, f.
birdseye (beurd'z'a'ye), adj., à vue d'oiseau.
birdsfoot (-foute), n., (bot.) ornithope; pied d'oiseau, m.
birdsnest, n., nid d'oiseau, m.; (bot.) carotte sauvage, f.
birdsnest, v.a., dénicher des oiseaux.
birdwitted (-tède), adj., à tête de linotte.
birth (beurth), n., naissance, f.; couche, f., enfantement, m.; (nav.) évitée, f., évitage, m.
birthday, n., jour de naissance, m.
birthplace (-plèce), n., lieu natal, m.
birthright (-raïte), n., droit d'aînesse, droit d'aînesse, m.
bis, adv., bis.
biscuit (bis'kite), n., biscuit, m.
bise, n. V. **bice**.
bisect (baï-cèkte), v.a., diviser en deux parties égales.
bisection (baï-), n., bissection, f.
bisexual (baï-), adj., bissexuel.
bishop (bish'eupe), n., évêque; (at chess—aux échecs) fou; bishop, bischop, bichoff, bischof (drink—liqueur), m.
bishop, v.a., confirmer.
bishopdom (-deume), n., (ant.) épiscopat, m.
bishop-like (-laïke), adj., d'évêque.
bishoply, adj., épiscopal.
bishopric, n., évêché, m.
bishops-wort (-weurte), n., ammi, m.
bisk, n., bisque, f.; coulis, m.
bismuth (biz'meuth), n., bismuth, m.
bissextile, n., année bissextile, f.
bissextile, adj., bissextil.
bistort (-teurte), n., bistorte, f.

bistoury (bis-teuri), *n.*, bistouri, *m.*

bistre (bisteur), *n.*, bistre, *f.*

bit, *n.*, morceau, *m.*; pièce, *f.*; brin, bout; peu, *m.*; (nav.) bitte, *f.*; (man.) mors, frein, *m.* Not a —; *pas un brin, pas le moins du monde.*

bit, *v.a.*, emboucher; (nav.) bitter.

bitch, *n.*, chienne, *f.*

bite (baïte), *n.*, morsure; piqûre; (fig.) attrape, *f.*; (fig.) attrapoire, *f.*; (print.) larron, *m.*

bite, *v.a.* (*preterit*, Bit; *past part.*, Bit, Bitten), mordre; ronger; attraper, duper. — off; *emporter en mordant.*

biter, *n.*, personne qui mord, *f.*; (fig.) trompeur, *m.*

biting, *adj.*, mordant, piquant.

biting, *n.*, morsure, *f.*

bitingly, *adv.*, d'une manière mordante, d'une manière piquante.

bitless (bit'lèsse), *adj.*, sans mors.

bittacle, *n.* V. **binnacle**.

bitter, *adj.*, amer, aigre, acharné.

bitter, *n.*, amer, *m.*; amertume, *f.*

bitterish, *adj.*, un peu amer.

bitterishness, *n.*, amertume modérée, *f.*

bitterly, *adv.*, avec amertume; amèrement.

bittern (bit'teurne), *n.*, (orni.) butor, *m.*; (chem.) eau mère, *f.*

bitterness, *n.*, amertume, *f.*

bitumen (bi-tiou-mène), *n.*, bitume, *m.*

bituminate (-néte), *v.a.*, bituminer.

bituminous (-neusse), *adj.*, bitumineux.

bivalve, bivalvular, *or* **bivalvous** (baï-, -lar, -veusse), *adj.*, bivalve.

bivouac, *n.*, bivouac, *m.*

bivouac, *v.n.*, bivouaquer.

bizantine (-taïne), *n.*, don royal à l'occasion d'une fête, *m.*

blab, *n.*, bavard, jaseur, *m.*; bavarde, jaseuse, *f.*; rapporteur, *m.*, rapporteuse, *f.*

blab, *v.a.*, jaser de, bavarder de.

blab, *v.n.*, jaser, bavarder.

black, *v.a.*, noircir.

black, *n.*, noir, *m.* Ivory —; *noir d'ivoire.* Lamp —; *noir de fumée.* Dressed in —; *habillé de noir.* The —s; *les noirs, les nègres.*

black, *adj.*, noir. To look — at any one; *regarder quelqu'un de travers.*

blackamoor (-mour), *n.*, moricaud, *m.*, moricaude, *f.*

blackball (-bôle), *n.*, cirage en boule, *m.*; boule noire, *f.*

blackball, *v.a.*, noircir, injurier; rejeter (by a vote—*au scrutin*).

blackberry, *n.*, mûre sauvage, *f.*

blackbird (-beurde), *n.*, merle, *m.*

blacken (blak'n), *v.a.* and *n.*, noircir.

blackguard (blag'gârde), *n.*, polisson, galopin, vaurien, goujat, *m.*

blackguard, *adj.*, polisson de; galopin de.

blackguardism, *n.*, polissonnerie, *f.*

blacking, *n.*, (for shoes, &c.—*pour chaussures*) cirage, *m.*

blackish, *adj.*, noirâtre.

blackleg (-lèghe), *n.*, escroc (in gambling—*au jeu*).

blackly, *adv.*, avec noirceur.

black-mail (-méle) *n.*, redevance en blé, ou en bœufs, *f.*; tribut payé à des bandes de voleurs, *m.*; (fig.) fraude, extorsion, exaction, *f.*

blackness, *n.*, noirceur, *f.*

blacksmith (-smith), *n.*, forgeron, *m.*

blacky-top, *n.*, (orni.) traquet, *m.*

bladder, *n.*, vessie, vésicule, *f.*

bladdered (-deurde), *adj.*, gonflé, enflé.

bladdery, *adj.*, vésiculaire; vésiculeux.

blade (blède), *n.*, lame (of cutting instruments—*d'instruments tranchants*), *f.*; brin (of grass—*d'herbe*); plat (of an oar—*d'aviron*); gaillard, compagnon, *m.* Jolly —; *joyeux compagnon,*

blade, *v.a.*, garnir d'une lame.

bladebone (-bône), *n.*, omoplate, *f.*

bladed (-'ède), *adj.*, lamelleux; (min.) lamellé.

blain (bléne), *n.*, tumeur, *f.*

blamable (blèm'-), *adj.*, blâmable.

blamableness, *n.*, faute, *f.*

blame (bléme), *n.*, blâme, *m.*; faute, *f.*

blame, *v.a.*, blâmer, reprendre.

blameful (-foule), *adj.*, coupable, blâmable.

blameless, *n.*, irrépréhensible, irréprochable.

blamelessly, *adv.*, irréprochablement.

blamelessness, *n.*, innocence, *f.*

blamer, *n.*, désapprobateur, *m.*

blameworthy (-weurthi), *adj.*, digne de blâme.

blanch, *v.a.*, blanchir; peler (kernelled fruits—*des fruits à amandes*); pâlir; faire pâlir.

blanch, *v.n.*, pâlir; faiblir; tergiverser.

blanching, *n.*, blanchiment, *m.*

blanc-mange, *n.*, blanc-manger, *m.*

bland (bla'n'de), *adj.*, doux, aimable.

blandiloquence (-kwè'n'ce), *n.*, doux parler, langage caressant, *m.*

blandish, *v.a.*, caresser, flatter.

blandishing, *or* **blandishment**, *n.*, caresse, *f.*; attrait, *m.*

blank, *adj.*, blanc, en blanc; (fig.) pâle; confus; (arch.) faux; (of cartridges—*de cartouches*) sans balle.

blank, *n.*, blanc; (of lotteries) billet blanc, billet perdant; (fig.) vide, *m.*, lacune, *f.*

blank, *v.a.*, laisser vide, laisser en blanc; faire pâlir, pâlir; confondre; annuler.

blanket (ba'nk'ète), *n.*, couverture, *f.*; (print.) blanchet, *m.*

blanket, *v.a.*, envelopper avec une couverture.

blanketeer (-ieur), *n.*, berneur, *m.*

blankly, *adv.*, avec confusion.

blankness, *n.*, blancheur, pâleur, *f.*

blare (blére), *v.n.*, (of candles—*des chandelles*) fondre, couler.

blarney, *v.a.*, encenser, enjôler, flagorner.

blarney, *n.*, eau bénite de cour, flagornerie, *f.*

blaspheme (-fîme), *v.a.* and *n.*, blasphémer.

blasphemer, *n.*, blasphémateur, *m.*

blasphemous (-fi-meusse), *adj.*, blasphématoire.

blasphemously, *adv.*, avec blasphème.

blasphemy (-fi-), *n.*, blasphème, *m.*

blast, *n.*, souffle; vent, coup de vent; vent pestilentiel; son d'un instrument à vent, *m.*; explosion, *f.*

blast, *v.a.*, flétrir; brûler; détruire, ruiner; (mines) faire sauter.

blast-engine, *n.*, machine soufflante, *f.*

blaster, *n.*, destructeur, détracteur, *m.*

blast-furnace (-feur-néce), *n.*, haut fourneau, *m.*

blasting, *adj.*, destructeur.

blasting, *n.*, (mines) sautage, *m.*

blastpipe (-païpe), *n.*, tuyau d'échappement de la vapeur, *m.*

blay, *n.*, (ich.) able, *m.*, ablette, *f.*

blaze (bléze), *n.*, flamme; lumière, *f.*; feu; éclat, *m.*; (man.) étoile, *f.*

blaze, *v.n.*, être en flammes; flamber, brûler.

blaze, *v.a.*, faire briller; faire connaître, publier.

blazing, *adj.*, flamboyant; brillant.

blazon (blé-z'n), *n.*, blason, *m.*; révélation, divulgation, *f.*

blazon, *v.a.*, blasonner; faire briller; proclamer, publier.

bleach (blîtshe), *v.a.*, rendre blanc, blanchir; pâlir.

bleach, *v.n.*, blanchir.

bleacher, *n.*, blanchisseur (of linen-cloth—*de toiles*), *m.*

bleaching, *n.*, blanchiment, *m.*
bleaching-liquid (-lik'wide), *n.*, eau de javelle, *f.*
bleach-works (-weurkse), *n.*, blanchisserie, *f.*
bleak (blîke), *adj.*, froid ; glacial.
bleakish, *adj.*, presque glacial.
bleakly, *adv.*, froidement.
bleakness, *n.*, froidure, *f.* ; froid glacial, *m.*
bleaky, *adj.* (ant.). *V.* **bleak**.
blear (blîre), *adj.*, chassieux. — -eyed ; *chassieux.*
blear, *v.a.*, rendre chassieux ; (fig.) troubler.
blearedness (blîr'èd'-), *n.*, chassie, *f.*
bleat (blîte), *v.n.*, bêler.
bleat, *n.*, bêlement, *m.*
bleating, *adj.*, bêlant.
bleating, *m.*, bêlement, *m.*
bleb (blèbe), *n.*, globule, *m.*
blebby, *adj.*, globuleux.
bleed (blîde), *v.n.* (*preterit and past part.*, Bled), saigner.
bleed, *v.a.*, saigner.
bleeding, *n.*, saignement, *m.* ; (surg.) saignée, *f.*
blemish (blè'-), *v.a.*, flétrir, ternir.
blemish, *n.*, flétrissure, tache, *f.* ; défaut, *m.*
blend (blè'n'de), *v.a.*, fondre, mêler, mélanger.
blend, *v.n.*, se fondre. To — with ; *se confondre avec, se mêler avec.*
blende, *n.*, (min.) blende, *f.*
blending, *n.*, fusion, *f.* ; mélange, *m.*
blennorrhœa, *n.*, (med.) blennorrhée, *f.*
bless, *v.a.*, bénir ; charmer.
blessed (blèste), *adj.*, béni ; bienheureux.
blessedly (blèss'èd'ii), *adv.*, heureusement.
blessedness (blèss'èd'-), *n.*, béatitude, félicité, *f.*
blesser, *n.*, personne qui bénit, *f.*
blessing, *n.*, bénédiction, *f.* ; bonheur, *m.*
blest, *adj.* *V.* **blessed**.
blight (blaïte), *v.a.*, (of the wind—*du vent*) flétrir ; (of the sun—*du soleil*), brouir ; (fig.) frustrer, détruire.
blight, *n.*, (of flowers and fruit—*des fleurs et des fruits*) brouissure ; (of corn—*du blé*) nielle ; (fig.) flétrissure, tache, *f.*
blind (blaï'n'de), *adj.*, aveugle ; obscur. — of one eye ; *borgne.* Stone—; *complètement aveugle.*
blind, *n.*, (fort.) blinde, *f.* ; store, *m.* ; jalousie, *f.* ; (fig.) voile, *m.* Venetian — ; *jalousie.*
blind, *v.a.*, aveugler ; bander les yeux à.
blindfold (-fôlde), *v.a.*, bander les yeux à.
blindfold, *adj.*, qui a les yeux bandés ; les yeux bandés ; (fig.) aveugle.
blindly, *adv.*, aveuglément.
blindman's-buff (blaï'n'd'ma'n'z'beufe), *n.*, colin-maillard, *m.*
blindness, *n.*, cécité, *f.* ; aveuglement, *m.*
blindside (-saïde), *n.*, côté faible, *m.*
blink (bli'n'ke), *v.n.*, cligner, clignoter.
blink, *n.*, clignement ; clignotement, *m.*
blinkard (bli'n'k'arde), *n.*, personne qui clignote, *f.*
blinker, *n.*, personne qui cligne des yeux ; visière, *f.* ; bandeau, *m.* ; (for horses—*pour les chevaux*) œillère, *f.*
bliss, *n.*, félicité, *f.* ; bonheur, *m.*
blissful (-foule), *adj.*, bienheureux.
blissfully, *adv.*, dans la félicité ; heureusement.
blissfulness, *n.*, félicité, béatitude, *f.*
blister, *n.*, ampoule, cloche, bulle, vessie, *f.* ; (med.) vésicatoire, *m.*
blister, *v.a.*, appliquer un vésicatoire ; faire venir des ampoules.
blister, *v.n.*, s'élever en forme de vessie ; se couvrir d'ampoules.

blister-fly (-fla'ye), *n.*, mouche à vésicatoire, cantharide, *f.*
blite (blaïte), *n.*, (bot.) blette, blète, *f.*
blithe (blaïthe), *adj.*, gai, joyeux.
blithely, *adv.*, joyeusement.
blithesome (blaïth'œume), *adj.*, gai, joyeux.
blithesomeness, *n.*, gaîté, *f.*
bloat (blôte), *v.a.*, gonfler, bouffir.
bloat, *v.n.*, bouffir, s'enfler.
bloated (blôt'ède), *adj.*, bouffi, gonflé ; (fig.) considérable, immense.
bloatedness, *n.*, bouffissure, *f.*
bloater, *n.*, hareng, *m.*
blobber, *n.*, bulle, *f.*
blobber-lip, *n.*, grosse lèvre, *f.*
blobber-lipped (-lipte), *adj.*, lippu.
block, *n.*, bloc, billot, *m.* ; forme (of a hat—*de chapeau*), *f.* ; (nav.) poulie, *f.* ; (print.) encrier, *m.* Stumbling — ; *pierre d'achoppement, f.*
block, *v.a.*, bloquer. — up : *fermer.*
blockade (blok'éde), *n.*, blocus, *m.*
blockade, *v.a.*, bloquer, faire le blocus de.
blockhead (-hède), *n.*, ganache, *f.* ; imbécile, *m.f.* ; sot, *m.*
blockheaded, *adj.*, sot, stupide.
blockishly, *adv.*, stupidement.
blockishness, *n.*, stupidité, *f.*
blocklike (-laïke), *adj.*, comme un imbécile.
blood (bleude), *n.*, sang, *m.* ; (fig.) parenté, *f.* ; tempérament, *m.* ; (man.) race, *f.* That makes one's — run cold ; *cela glace le sang.*
blood, *v.a.*, saigner ; ensanglanter.
blood-coloured (-keul'leur'de), *adj.*, couleur de sang.
blood-guiltiness (-ghil-), *n.*, crime de meurtre, *m.*
bloodheat (-hite), *n.*, chaleur du sang, *f.*
blood-horse, *n.*, cheval de race, *m.*
bloodhound (-haou'n'de), *n.*, limier, *m.*
bloodily, *adv.*, d'une manière sanglante ; d'une manière sanguinaire.
bloodiness, *n.*, disposition sanguinaire, *f.* ; état sanglant, *m.*
bloodless, *adj.*, qui n'a point de sang ; pâle, inanimé.
bloodlet (-lète), *v.a.*, phlébotomiser, saigner.
bloodletter, *n.*, phlébotomiste, *m.*
bloodletting, *n.*, phlébotomie, saignée, *f.*
bloodshed (-shède), *n.*, effusion de sang, *f.* ; sang répandu, *m.*
bloodshedder, *n.*, meurtrier, *m.*
bloodshedding, *n.*, effusion de sang, *f.*
bloodshot (-shote), *adj.*, rouge ; (of the eyes—*des yeux*) éraillé, injecté de sang.
blood-stone (-stône), *n.*, sanguine, *f.* ; jaspe sanguin, *m.*
bloodsucker (-souk'-), *n.*, suceur de sang ; buveur de sang, *m.*
bloodthirstiness (-theurs'-), *n.*, soif de sang, *f.*
bloodthirsty, *adj.*, sanguinaire.
bloodvessel, *n.*, vaisseau sanguin, *m.*
blood-wood (-woude), *n.*, bois de campêche, *m.*
bloodwort (-weurte), *n.*, (bot.) sanguinaire, *f.*
bloody, *adj.*, de sang, sanglant, sanguinaire.
bloody, *v.a.*, ensanglanter.
bloom (-bloume), *n.*, fleur ; (metal.) loupe, *f.* In — ; *en fleur.*
bloom, *v.n.*, fleurir ; être éclatant.
bloomingly, *adv.*, d'une manière florissante.
bloomy, *adj.*, fleuri, fleurissant.
blossom (blos'seume), *n.*, fleur, *f.*
blossom, *v.n.*, fleurir, être en fleur.
blossomy, *adj.*, couvert de fleurs.
blot (blote), *n.*, tache ; effacure, *f.* ; (of ink—*d'encre*), pâté, *m.*, tache, *f.*
blot, *v.a.*, tacher, noircir ; of ink—*d'encre*)

faire un pâté sur ; effacer ; souiller. To — out; *rayer, effacer.*

blot, *v.n.*, (of paper—*du papier*) boire.

blotch, *n.*, pustule, *f.*

blotch, *v.a.*, couvrir de pustules.

blote (blôte), *v.a.*, (ant.) (of herrings—*des harengs*) fumer à moitié.

blotting (blot'-), *adj.*, qui fait des taches ; (of paper—*du papier*) qui boit.

blotting-case (-kéce), *n.*, buvard, *m.*

blotting-paper (-pé-peur), *n.*, papier brouillard, *m.*

blow, *n.*, coup, *m.* A — with a stick ; *un coup de bâton.* To deal any one a — ; *porter un coup à quelqu'un.* Without striking a — ; *sans coup férir.* To come to —s ; *en venir aux mains.*

blow, *v.n.* (preterit, Blew ; *past part.*, Blown), souffler ; faire, y avoir du vent ; (of wind-instruments—*des instruments à vent*) sonner ; (of flowers—*des fleurs*) s'épanouir. To — ; *passer, se dissiper.* To — up (by gunpowder—*par la poudre*) ; *sauter ; éclater.* The wind —s, it —s ; *il fait du vent.*

blow, *v.a.*, chasser ; souffler ; (of wind-instruments—*des instruments à vent*) sonner ; (of flies—*des mouches*) couvrir de piqûres, couvrir d'œufs. To — away ; *chasser ; dissiper.* To — down ; *renverser (par le vent).* To — out ; *souffler, éteindre (une lumière) ; faire sauter (la cervelle).* To — out one's brains ; *se faire sauter, se brûler la cervelle.* To — up ; *souffler en l'air ; faire sauter (par la poudre).* To — any one up ; *faire une scène à quelqu'un ; donner un savon à quelqu'un.*

blow, *n.*,fleur, *f.*,bouton de fleur, *m.* ; (nav.) grain, *m.*

blower, *n.*, souffleur, *m.*, souffleuse, *f.* ; rideau de cheminée, *m.*

blowfly (-fla'ye), *n.*, mouche à viande, *f.*

blowing, *n.*, action de souffler, *f.* ; souffle ; soufflage ; (of wind-instruments—*d'instruments à vent*) son, *m.*

blowpipe (-païpe), *n.*, chalumeau, *m.*

blowze (blaouze), *n.*, grosse joufflue à teint hâlé, *f.*

blowzy, *adj.*, haut en couleur.

blubber (bleub'beur), *n.*, lard de baleine, *m.*; ortie de mer, *f.*

blubber, *v.n.*, pleurer comme un veau.

blubber, *v.n.*, gonfler à force de pleurer.

bludgeon (bleud'jeune), *n.*, assommoir, *m.* ; trique, *f.*

blue, *adj.*, bleu, azur. He looked — at it ; *il y a fait la grimace.*

blue (blou), *n.*, bleu, azur, *m.* Prussian — ; *bleu de Prusse.* Sky — ; *bleu de ciel.*

blue, *v.a.*, bleuir ; (dy.) mettre en bleu.

bluebell, *n.*, jacinthe des prés, *f.*

bluebottle (-bot-t'l), *n.*, (bot.) bluet, *m.* ; (ent.) mouche à viande, *f.*

blue-devils (-dèv'lze),*n.pl.*, maladie noire,*f.*

bluely, *adv.*, d'une couleur bleue.

blueness (-nèsse), *n.*, couleur bleue, *f.*

bluestocking, *n.*, bas bleu, *m.*, femme auteur, *f.*

bluff (bleufe), *adj.*, gros ; rude ; criard, colère, violent.

bluff, *n.*, (nav.) accore, *m.*, falaise, *f.*

bluffness (-nèsse), *n.*, bouffissure ; (fig.) rudesse, *f.*

bluish (blou-ishe), *adj.*, bleuâtre.

bluishness (-nèsse), *n.*, couleur bleuâtre, teinte bleuâtre, *f.*

blunder (bleu'n'-), *n.*, bévue, grosse faute, *f.*

blunder, *v.n.*, faire une bévue.

blunder, *v.n.*, embrouiller. — a thing out; *lâcher quelque chose.*

blunderbuss (-beusse), *n.*, espingole, *f.*

blunderer, *n.*, faiseur de bévues, *m.*, faiseuse de bévues, *f.* ; maladroit, *m.*, maladroite, *f.*

blunder-head (-hède), *n.*, brouillon, *m.*, brouillonne, *f.*

blundering, *adj.*, qui fait des bévues ; étourdi.

blunderingly, *adv.*, par bévue.

blunt (bleu'n'te), *adj.*, émoussé ; brusque, grossier.

blunt, *v.a.*, émousser ; (fig.) adoucir.

bluntly, *adv.*, brusquement, crûment.

bluntness (-nèsse), *n.*, état émoussé, *m.* ; brusquerie, *f.*

blur (bleur), *n.*, tache, *f.*

blur, *v.a.*, tacher, barbouiller ; souiller.

blurt (bleurte),*v.a.*, jeter, dire à l'étourdie, laisser échapper (words—*paroles*).

blush (bleushe), *v.n.*, rougir.

blush, *n.*, rougeur, *f.* The —es came into her face ; *la rougeur lui monta au visage.*

blushful (-foule), *adj.*, qui rougit.

blushing, *adj.*, rougissant ; qui rougit.

blushless (-lèsse), *adj.*, qui ne rougit point; effronté.

blushy, *adj.*, rougeâtre.

bluster (bleus'teur), *v.n.*, faire du fracas, tempêter, crier.

bluster, *n.*, fracas, bruit, tapage, *m.* ; fanfaronnade, *f.*

blusterer, *n.*, fanfaron, rodomont, tapageur, *m.*

blustering, *adj.*, fanfaron.

blusterous (-eusse), *adj.*, (ant.) orageux ; fanfaron ; tapageur.

boa, *n.*, (zool.) boa ; (fur—*fourrure*) boa, *m.*

boa-constrictor (-con'stric-teur), *n.*, boa, boa constricteur, devin, *m.*

boar (bôre), *n.*, verrat, *m.* Wild— ; *sanglier, m.*

boar, *v.n.*, (man.) porter le nez au vent (of the horse—*du cheval*).

board (bôrde), *n.*, planche ; (aliments) table, pension, nourriture, *f.*; (print.) carton ; (bookbind.) plat ; (nav.) bord, *m.*

board, *v.a.*, planchéier ; (nav.) aborder ; nourrir, mettre en pension.

board, *v.n.*, être, se mettre en pension.

boarder, *n.*, pensionnaire ; interne, pensionnaire (at school, &c.—*de maison d'éducation*), *m.f.* ; marin qui va à l'abordage, *m.*

boarding, *n.*, action de planchéier ; action de recevoir des pensionnaires ; pension, *f.* ; (nav.) abordage, *m.*

boarding-house (-haouce), *n.*, pension bourgeoise, *f.*

boarding-pike (-païke), *n.*, (nav.) pique d'abordage, *f.*

boarding-school (-skoule), *n.*, pension, institution, *f.* ; pensionnat, *m.*

board-wages (-wé'djze), *n.pl.*, gages pour frais de nourriture, *m.pl.*

boar-hunt (-heu'n'te), *n.*, chasse aux sangliers, *f.*

boarish (bôr'ishe), *adj.*, de sanglier.

boar-spear (-spire), *n.*, (hunt.) épieu, *m.*

boast (bôste), *v.a.*, se vanter de ; (mas., sculpt.) ébaucher.

boast, *v.n.*, se vanter, se glorifier a — of ; *se vanter de, se faire gloire de.*

boaster, *n.*, vantard ; (mas., sculpt.) ébauchoir, *m.*

boastful (-foulè), *adj.*, vantard ; arrogant.

boasting, *n.*, vanterie, jactance,*f.*

boastingly, *adv.*, avec vanterie.

boasting-tool (-toule), *n.*, (mas., sculpt.) ébauchoir, *m.*

boat (bôte), *n.*, bateau, canot, *m.*

boat, *v.a.*, transporter par bateau.

boatbuilder (-bild'eur), *n.*, constructeur de bateaux, *m.*

boat-hook (-houke), *n.*, gaffe, *f.*

boat-house (-haouce), *n.*, hangar à bateaux, *m.*

boat-load (-lôde), *n.*, batelée, *f.*

boatman, *or* **boatsman** (bôt'man, bôt's-ma'n), *n.*, batelier, *m.*

boat-oar (-ôre), *n.*, rame, *f.* ; aviron, *m.*

boat-rope (-rôpe), *n.*, câbleau, câblot, *m.*

boatsman, *n.*, *V.* **boatman**.

boatswain (-swéne, bôs'n), *n.*, (nav.) maître d'équipage, *m.* —'s mate ; *contre-maître, m.*

boatwise (-waïze), *adv.*, comme un bateau.

bob, *n.*, pendant, *m.* ; (wig) perruque à nœuds ; lentille (of a pendulum—*de balancier*), *f.* ; (blow) coup, *m.*, tape, *f.* ; (of a stanza—*d'un couplet*) refrain, *m.*

bob, *v.a.*, écourter (the tail—*la queue*) ; balancer ; bafouer ; taper.

bob, *v.n.*, heurter ; pendiller.

bobbin (bob'bine), *n.*, bobine, *f.*

bobbin-work (-weurke), *n.*, ouvrage fait à la bobine, *m.*

bobtail (-téle), *n.*, queue écourtée ; canaille, *f.*

bobtailed (-tél'de), *adj.*, à queue écourtée.

bobwig. *n.*, perruque à nœuds, *f.*

bocasine (boc'a-cine), *n.*, (com.) bocassin, boucassin, *m.*

bode (bôde), *v.a.*, présager.

bode well, ill, *v.n.*, être de bon augure, de mauvais augure.

bodice (bod'ice), *n.*, corset ; corsage, *m.*

bodied (bod'ide), *adj.*, à corps.

bodiless (-lèsse), *adj.*, sans corps ; incorporel.

bodily, *adj.*, corporel, matériel.

bodily, *adv.*, corporellement.

boding (bôd'igne), *adj.*, qui a le pressentiment de l'avenir.

boding, *n.*, présage, *m.*

bodkin (bod'kine), *n.*, poinçon ; passelacet, *m.* ; (print.) pointe, *f.*

body, *n.*, corps ; (geom.) solide ; (principal thing) fond ; (centre) cœur, centre, *m.* ; (jur.) personne, *f.* Dead — ; *corps mort* ; *cadavre, m.* Some— ; *quelqu'un.* Any— ; *quelqu'un, tout le monde.* No— ; *personne.* Every— ; *tout le monde.* In a — ; *en corps.* Any — ; *personne.*

body, *v.a.*, corporifier.

body-clothes (-cloze), *n.pl.*, (for a horse—*pour un cheval*) housse, *f. sing.*

body-guard, *n.*, garde du corps, *f.*

bog, *n.*, marais, *m.*

bog, *v.a.*, embourber.

bogbean (-bine), *n.*, (bot.) ménianthe trifolié, trèfle d'eau, *m.*

boggle (bog'g'l), *v.n.*, hésiter ; dissimuler.

boggler, *n.*, couard ; barguigneur, *m.*, barguigneuse, *f.*

boggy (bog'ghi), *adj.*, marécageux.

bog-trotter, *n.*, habitant d'un pays marécageux, *m.*

bohea (bô-hî), *n.*, thé bohé, *m.*

boil (bo-île), *v.a.*, faire bouillir.

boil, *v.n.*, bouillir. To — away ; *ébouillir.* To — fast ; *bouillir à gros bouillons.* To — to rags ; *pourrir à force de cuire.*

boil, *n.*, (med.) furoncle ; clou, *m.*

boiler, *n.*, (pers.) bouilleur, *m.* ; (thing—*chose*) bouilloire ; chaudière, *f.*, bouilleur (of a steam-engine—*de machine à vapeur*), *m.*

boiler-tube (-tioube), *n.*, (mec.) tube de bouilleur, *m.*

boilery, *n.*, bouillerie, *f.*

boiling, *n.*, bouillonnement, *m.* ; ébullition, *f.*

boiling, *adj.*, bouillant ; en ébullition.

boisterous (bo-is'teur'eusse), *adj.*, orageux ; violent, impétueux ; vif ; bruyant.

boisterously, *adv.*, impétueusement, violemment, bruyamment.

boisterousness, *n.*, impétuosité ; turbulence. *f.*

bolary, *adj.*, bolaire.

bold (bôlde), *adj.*, hardi ; audacieux, téméraire. To make — to ; *prendre la liberté de.*

bolden, *v.a.*, (ant.) rendre hardi, enhardir.

boldly, *adv.*, hardiment.

boldness, *n.*, hardiesse, audace, *f.*

bole (bôle), *n.*, bol, *m.*, terre bolaire, *f.* ; mesure de six boisseaux, *f.* Armenian — ; *bol d'Arménie.*

bolis (bô-lisse), *n.* (*bolides*) bolide, *m.*, (nav.) sonde, *f.* ; plomb, fil à plomb, contrepoids, *m.*

boll (bôl), *n.*, (bot.) balle, *f.*

boll, *v.n.*, monter en graine.

bollard (bol'larde), *n.*, (nav.) corps mort, *m.*

bolster (bôl-), *n.*, traversin ; coussin ; (arch.) couchis ; (nav.) coussin de ferrure, *m.*

bolster, *v.a.*, mettre un traversin sous ; (fig.) appuyer, soutenir.

bolsterer, *n.*, défenseur, appui, *m.*

bolstering, *n.*, appui, *m.*

bolt (bôlte), *n.*, verrou ; pène ; bluteau, blutoir, *m.* ; cheville, *f.* ; (fig.) trait, *m.* To draw a — ; *tirer un verrou.*

bolt, *v.a.*, verrouiller ; fermer au verrou ; (to sift—*tamiser*) bluter ; sasser ; (to swallow—*avaler*) avaler d'un seul morceau. To — in ; *enfermer au verrou.* To — one's self in ; *s'enfermer au verrou.* To — any one out ; *mettre le verrou contre quelqu'un.*

bolt, *v.n.*, se lancer ; prendre la clef des champs ; (of a horse—*du cheval*) s'emporter. To — in ; *entrer brusquement.* To — out ; *sortir brusquement.*

bolter, *n.*, bluteau, sas, *m.*

bolting. *n.*, action de fermer au verrou, *f.* ; blutage, *m.*

bolting-cloth (-clôth), *n.*, étamine, *f.*

bolting-house (-haouce), *n.*, bluterie, *f.*

bolting-hutch (-heutshe), *n.*, huche à bluter, *f.*

bolting-mill, *n.*, bluteau mécanique ; blutoir, *m.*

bolt-rope (-rôpe), *n.*, (nav.) ralingue, *f.*

bolus (bô-leusse), *n.*, (pharm.) bolus, bol, *m.*

bomb (beume), *n.*, bombe, *f.* ; bruit éclatant, *m.*

bomb, *v.n.*, retentir, résonner.

bombard (beu'm'bârde), *n.*, bombardement, *m.*

bombard. *v.a.*, bombarder.

bombardier (-bardieur), *n.*, bombardier, *m.*

bombardment (-bârd'-), *n.*, bombardement, *m.*

bombardo (beu'm'bârdo), *n.*, (mus.) bombarde, *f.*

bombast (beu'm'bâste, *ou* bo'm'-), *n.*, boursouflage, *m.* ; enflure, *f.*

bombast, *adj.*, ampoulé, boursouflé.

bombast, *v.a.*, enfler.

bombastic, *adj.*, enflé, ampoulé.

bombastry, *n.*, enflure, *f.* ; boursouflage, *m.*

bombazine (beu'm'ba-zine), *n.*, alépine, *f.*

bombketch (-kètshe), *or* **bomb-vessel** (-vès's'l), *n.*, galiote à bombes, *f.*

bomb-proof (-proufe), *adj.*, à l'épreuve de la bombe.

bona-fide (bô'na-faï-di), *adj.*, sérieux et de bonne foi.

bona-fide, *adv.*, sérieusement et de bonne foi.

bond (bo'n'de), *n.*, lien ; engagement, *m.* ; (carp.) assemblage, *m.* ; (jur., fin.) obligation, *f.* ; (fin.) bon, *m.* ; (of the customs—*de la douane*) entrepôt, *m.* Matrimonial — ; *lien conjugal.* To enter into a —; (jur. *passer une obligation.* In —; (of the customs—*de la douane*) à l'entrepôt.

bond, *v.a.*, (of the customs—*de la douane*)

entreposer. —ed goods; *marchandise entreposée,* f. sing.

bondage (bo'n'd'édje), *n.,* esclavage, *m.;* servitude, *f.*

bonder, *n.,* (of the customs—*de la douane*) entrepositaire, *m.f.*

bond-holder (-hôld'-), *n.,* porteur de bon, détenteur de bon, *m.*

bonding, *n.,* (of the customs—*de la douane*) entreposage, *m.*

bondman (-ma'n), *n.* (*bondmen*), serf, esclave, *m.*

bondservant (-seur-), *n.,* esclave, *m.f.*

bondservice (-seur-), *n.,* esclavage, *m.*

bondslave (-sléve), *n.,* esclave, *m.f.*

bondsman (bo'n'dz'ma'n), *n.* (*bondsmen*), (jur.) caution, *f.*

bond-stone (-stône), *n.,* (mas.) boutisse, *f.*

bondwoman (-wou'm'a'n), *n.,* esclave, *f.*

bone (bône), *n.,* os, *m.;* (of fish—*de poisson*) arête, *f.* —s; *ossements, m.pl.; restes mortels, m.pl.* —of contention; *pomme de discorde, f.* He makes no —s about that; *il ne se fait pas scrupule de le faire.* To have a.— to pick with any one; *avoir quelque chose à démêler avec quelqu'un.*

bone, *v.a.,* désosser.

bone-ache (-éke), douleurs ostéocopes, *f.pl.*

boneblack, *n.,* charbon, noir animal, *m.*

boned (bô'n'de), *past part.,* désossé; à os; pourvu d'os. High-—; *à os saillants.* Large-—; *ossu.*

bone-earth, *n.,* phosphate de chaux; charbon animal, *m.*

boneless, *adj.,* sans os.

bonfire (bo'n'faïeur), *n.,* feu de joie, *m.*

bon-mot, *n.,* bon mot, *m.*

bonnet (bo'n'nète), *n.,* chapeau (woman's—*de femme*), *m.;* (fort., nav.) bonnette, *f.*

bonnet, *v.n.,* (ant.) ôter le chapeau.

bonnet-box, *n.,* carton à chapeau, *m.*

bonneted (-nèt'ède), *adj.,* coiffé d'un chapeau.

bonnibel, *n.,* (ant.) belle fille, *f.*

bonnilass, *n.,* belle fille, *f.*

bonnily, *adv.,* gentiment; gaiement.

bonniness, *n.,* gentillesse, *f.*

bonny, *adj.,* gentil, joli, joyeux, gai.

bonny-clabber, *n.,* lait de beurre aigre; lait tourné, petit-lait, *m.*

bonum magnum, *n.,* (bot.) prune royale, *f.*

bonus (bo-neusse), *n.,* boni; don gratuit, *m.*

bony (bô-ni), *adj.,* osseux; fort.

bony-joint (-djoï'n'te), *n.,* (anat.) phalange, *f.*

booby (bou-bi), *n.,* nigaud, *m.,* nigaude, *f.;* (orni.) fou, *m.,* boubie, *f.*

boobyish, *adj.,* nigaud.

book (bouke), *v.a.,* enregistrer, inscrire.

book, *n.,* livre; cahier, *m.* Note —; *carnet, m.* Depositor's — (at a savings-bank—*caisse d'épargne*); *livret, m.* Day- —; (com.) *journal, m.* To be in any one's good —s; *être bien dans les papiers de quelqu'un.* To turn over the leaves of a —; *feuilleter un livre.* Old —; *vieux livre, bouquin, m.*

bookbinder (bouk'baï'n'd'-), *n.,* relieur, *m.*

bookbinding, *n.,* reliure, *f.*

bookcase (-kéce), *n.,* bibliothèque, *f.;* corps de bibliothèque, *m.*

bookful (-foule), *adj.,* érudit.

booking, *n.,* enregistrement (of parcels, &c.—*de paquets, &c.*), *m.*

booking-office, *n.,* bureau (of public conveyances, railways, &c.—*de voitures publiques, chemins de fer, &c.*), *m.*

bookish, *adj.,* studieux, attaché aux livres.

bookkeeper (bouk'kip'-), *n.,* teneur de livres, *m.*

bookkeeping, *n.,* comptabilité, tenue des livres, *f.*

booklearned (-leur'n'ède), *adj.,* savant.

booklearning, *n.,* savoir puisé dans les livres, *m.*

bookmaker (-mék'eur), *n.,* faiseur de livres.

bookmaking, *n.,* fabrication de livres, *f.*

bookman (-ma'n), *n.,* savant, *m.*

bookmate (-méte), *n.,* camarade d'études, *m.*

bookseller (-sèll'-), *n.,* libraire, *m.* Second-hand —; *marchand de livres d'occasion, bouquiniste, m.*

bookselling, *n.,* profession de libraire, *f.*

bookstall (-stôl), *n.,* étalage de livres, *m.*

bookworm (-weurme), *n.,* dévoreur de livres; (ent.) lépisme, ciron, *m.*

boom (boume), *n.,* (nav.) boute-hors, arc-boutant, *m.*

booming (boum'-), *n.,* bruit retentissant, *m.*

boon (boune), *n.,* bienfait, don, *m.;* faveur, *f.*

boon, *adj.,* bon, gai, joyeux.

boor (bour), *n.,* paysan, rustre, *m.*

boorish, *adj.,* rustre, grossier.

boorishly, *adv.,* grossièrement.

boorishness, *n.,* rusticité, grossièreté, *f.*

boose (bouze), *v.n.,* boire à l'excès. V. **bouse.**

boot (boute), *v.a.,* servir à; profiter à; botter.

boot, *n.,* profit, avantage; butin, *m.* To —; *en sus, par-dessus le marché.*

boot, *n.,* (of men—*d'homme*) botte; (of women—*de femme*) bottine, *f.;* (of women and children—*de femme et d'enfant*) brodequin, *m.;* (of a carriage—*de voiture*) coffre, *m.,* cave, *f.* Half- —s; *bottines.* Blucher —s; *souliers-bottes, m.* Top—s; *bottes à revers.* Hessian —s; *bottes à l'écuyère.* Wellington —s; *bottes.* Dress- —s; *bottes fines.*

booted (bout'ède), *part.,* botté.

booth (bouth), *n.,* baraque, *f.*

boothooks (-houkse), *n.,* tirants, *m.*

boot-hose (-hôze), *n.,* houseaux, *m.pl.*

bootjack, *n.,* tire-botte (pour ôter les bottes), *m.*

boot-last (-lâste), *n.* V. **boot-tree.**

bootleg (-lèghe), *n.,* tige de botte, *f.*

bootless (-lèsse), *adj.,* inutile, vain.

bootlessly, *adv.,* inutilement; vainement.

boot-tree (-trî), *n.,* embauchoir, *m.*

booty, *n.,* butin, *m.*

bo-peep (-pîpe), *n.,* cligne-musette, *f.,* cache-cache, *m.*

borage (bor'adge), *n.,* (bot.) bourrache, *f.*

borax, *n.,* borax, *m.*

border, *n.,* bord, *m.;* bordure; (of a country—*d'un pays*) frontière, *f.*

border, *v.a.,* border, confiner.

border, *v.n.,* confiner; toucher.

borderer, *n.,* habitant de la frontière, *m.*

bore, *v.a.,* percer, forer; sonder; (fig.) ennuyer, importuner, scier le dos à.

bore, *v.n.,* percer; (man.) porter le nez au vent.

bore, *n.,* trou; calibre; foret; (fig.) (per.) ennuyeux, cauchemar; (of things—*des choses*) ennui, *m.,* corvée, *f.;* (nav.) raz de marée, *m.*

boreal (bô-ri-al), *adj.,* boréal.

boreas (bô-ri-asse), *n.,* Borée, *m.*

borer, *n.,* ouvrier qui fore; (instrument) percoir, *m.,* vrille, *f.;* (ent.) perce-bois, *m.*

bergee (bor'dji), *n.,* (nav.) cornette, *f.*

boring, *n.,* sondage, forage, *m.*

born, *past part.,* né; de naissance. Low—; *de basse naissance.* V. **bear.**

borne, *past part.* V. **bear.**

boron (bô-ro'n), *n.,* (chem.) bore, *m.*

borough (beur'ô), *n.,* bourg, *m.*

borrow (bor'ô), *v.a.,* emprunter.

borrower, *n.,* emprunteur, *m.*

boscage (bos'kédje), *n.*, bocage, *m.*

bosky, *adj.*, boisé.

bosom (bouz'eume, bou'zeume), *n.*, sein; (fig.) cœur, *m.*, intimité, *f.* — friend; *ami de cœur, m.* In the —; *au sein de.*

bosom, *v.a.*, renfermer dans son sein.

boss, *n.*, bosse, bossette, *f.*

bossage (bos'sadje), *n.*, bossage, *m.*

botanic, *or* **botanical**, *adj.*, botanique.

botanically, *adv.*, conformément à la botanique.

botanist, *n.*, botaniste, *m.f.*

botanize (-naïze), *v.n.*, botaniser.

botany, *n.*, botanique, *f.*

botch, *n.*, pustule, *f.*; (fig.) ravaudage, replâtrage, bousillage, *m.*

botch, *v.a.*, rapetasser, ravauder; replâtrer.

botcher, *n.*, ravaudeur, *m.*, ravaudeuse, *f.*

botching, *n.*, ravaudage, *m.*

botchy, *adj.*, de pièces et de morceaux; tacheté.

both (bôth), *adj.*, l'un et l'autre; les deux; tous les deux; tous deux. — of us; *nous deux.* — sides; *les deux côtés.*

both, *adv.*, tant. — ... and ...; *et* ... *et* ...; *tant* ... *que* — ... you and I; *et vous et moi.* — for you and him; *tant pour vous que pour lui.*

bother (both'eur), *v.a.*, ennuyer; tracasser.

bother, *or* **botheration** (-ré-), *n.*, ennui, *m.*

bottle (bot't'l), *n.*, bouteille, *f.*; flacon, *m.*; (of hay—*de foin*) bottle, *f.*

bottle, *v.a.*, mettre en bouteille.

bottle-companion (-co'm'pa'n'ieune), *n.*, camarade de bouteille, *m.*

bottled (bot't'lde), *part.*, en bouteille; (fig.) ventru.

bottle-flower (-flaou'eur), *n.*, bluet, *m.*

bottle-friend (-frè'n'de), *n.*, ami de bouteille, *m.*

bottle-gourd, *n.*, gourde, *f.*

bottle-nose, *n.*, gros nez, *m.*

bottle-nosed (-noz'de), *adj.*, à gros nez.

bottle-rack, *n.*, planche à bouteilles, *f.*

bottle-tit, *n.*, (orni.) mésange à longue queue, *f.*

bottling, *n.*, mise en bouteilles, *f.*

bottom (bot'teume), *n.*, fond; bas; bout, *m.*; base (dale—*fond*) vallée; (nav.) carène, *f.*; (nav.) navire, bâtiment, *m.*; (fig.) borne, limite, *f.* From top to —; *de haut en bas; de fond en comble.*

bottom, *v.a.*, mettre un fond à; asseoir, baser.

bottom, *v.n.*, se fonder; être assis.

bottomed (bot'teu'm'de), *adj.*, à fond. Flat- —; *à fond plat.*

bottomless (-lèsse), *adj.*, sans fond.

bottomry, *n.*, (nav.) contrat à la grosse aventure; prêt à la grosse aventure, *m.*

boudoir, *n.*, boudoir, *m.*

bough (baou), *n.*, branche, *f.*

bought (bôte), *n.*, contour, *m.*

bought, *preterit and past part.* V. **buy.**

bougie, *n.*, (surg.) bougie, *f.*

boultin (bôl'ti'n), *n.*, (arch.) quart de rond, *m.*

bounce (baou'n'ce), *v.a.*, éclater; sauter avec grand bruit; faire le tapageur; faire le matamore; se vanter.

bounce, *n.*, éclat, *m.*; hâblerie, vanterie, *f.*

bouncer, *n.*, fanfaron; hâbleur, menteur, *m.*

bouncingly, *adv.*, en fanfaron; en menteur.

bound (ba'ou'n'de), *preterit* and *past part.* V. **bind.**

bound, *adj.*, (nav.) destiné, allant. Where are you — to? *où allez-vous; où va le navire?* Homeward- —; *en retour.*

bound, *n.*, borne; limite, *f.*; (jump—*saut*) bond, *m.*

bound, *v.a.*, borner, limiter.

bound, *v.n.*, bondir.

boundary, *n.*, limite, borne, *f.*

bounden (-dène), *adj.*, obligatoire, impérieux.

boundless (-lèsse), *adj.*, sans bornes; illimité.

boundlessness (-nèsse), *n.*, étendue infinie, infinité, *f.*

bounteous (baou'n'ti'eusse), *adj.*, libéral, généreux; bienfaisant.

bounteously, *adv.*, libéralement, généreusement.

bounteousness (-nèsse), *n.*, libéralité, munificence, générosité, *f.*

bountiful (-foule), *adj.*, généreux, libéral.

bountifully, *adv.*, généreusement; avec bienfaisance.

bountifulness (-nèsse), *n.*, générosité, libéralité, *f.*

bounty, *n.*, bienfaisance, largesse, libéralité, gratification, *f.*; don, *m.*

bouquet, *n.*, bouquet, *m.*

bourgeois, *n.*, (print.) gaillarde, *f.*

bourgeon (beur'djeune), *v.n.*, bourgeonner

bourn (bourne), *n.*, limite, *f.*

bouse (bouze), *v.n.*, boire à l'excès.

bousy (bouzi), *adj.*, gris, ivre.

bout (baoute), *n.*, coup, *m.*; partie de plaisir, *f.* To have a — of it; *s'en donner.* At one —; *d'un seul coup.*

bovine (bôvaïne), *adj.*, bovine.

bow (baou), *v.a.*, courber; plier, fléchir, incliner.

bow, *v.n.*, plier; se courber; s'incliner.

bow, *n.*, salut, *m.*; (b.s.) courbette, *f.*; (nav.) avant (of a ship—*de vaisseau*), *m.*

bow (bô), *n.*, arc; (of a violin—*de violon*) archet; (math.) demi-cercle, *m.*; (of a saddle —*de selle*) arçon; (of ribbons—*de rubans*) nœud, *m.*

bowel (baou-èl), *v.a.*, éventrer, enlever les entrailles à.

bowels (-èlze), *n.*, entrailles, *f.pl.*; intestins, boyaux, *m.pl.*

bower (baou'eur), *n.*, berceau de verdure, bosquet, *m.*; retraite, *f.*; (nav.) ancre de poste, *f.*

bower, *v.a.*, enfermer dans un berceau de verdure; loger.

bowery, *adj.*, pourvu de berceaux de verdure; en charmille, en berceau; touffu, ombragé.

bowl (bôle), *n.*, bol, bassin; (of a spoon—*de cuiller*) cuilleron; (of a pipe—*de pipe*) fourneau, *m.*; (spherical body—*sphère*) boule, *f.*

bowl, *v.a.*, faire rouler (a bowl, a ball—*une boule, une balle*).

bowlder (bôl'deur), *n.*, caillou rond, *m.*; roche arrondie, *f.*

bowlegged (bô-lèg'de), *adj.*, à jambes en manches de veste.

bowler (bôl'eur, baôul'eur), *n.*, joueur de boule, *m.*

bowline (bô-laïne), *n.*, (nav.) bouline, *f.*

bowling, *n.*, jeu de boule, *m.*

bowling-green (-grîne), *n.*, jeu de boule, *m.*

bowman (-ma'n), *n.*, archer, *m.*; (nav.) brigadier, *m.*

bownet (bô-nète), *n.*, nasse de pêcheur, *f.*

bowse (baouce), *v.a.*, (nav.) haler.

bowshot (bô-shote), *n.*, portée de trait, *f.*

bowsprit (bô-sprite), *n.*, (nav.) beaupré, *m.*

bowstring (bô-strigne), *n.*, corde d'arc, *f.*; cordon (to strangle—*pour étrangler*), *m.*

box, *n.*, (for the poor—*pour les pauvres*) tronc, *m.*; boîte, malle, caisse; (thea.) loge, *f.*; (bot.) buis; (print.) cassetin, *m.* Coach- — siège de cocher, *m.* — on the ear; *soufflet, m.* Christmas-—; *étrennes, f.pl.* Strong- —; *coffre-fort, m.*

box, *v.n.*, boxer, se boxer.

box 631 **bra**

box, r.a., enfermer dans une boîte; souffleter.
boxen (bok's'n), adj., de buis.
boxer, n., boxeur, m.
boxkeeper (-kîp'eur), n., (thea.) ouvreur de loges, m., ouvreuse de loges, f.
boxmaker (-mék'eur), n., layetier, m.
box-tree (-tri), n., buis, m.
boy (bo-i), n., garçon, petit garçon, enfant, m.
boyar (bo-yâr), n., boyard, boïard, m.
boyhood (-houde), n., enfance (de l'enfant mâle), f.
boyish (bo-i-ishe), adj., puéril; d'enfant, enfantin.
boyishly, adv., puérilement; en enfant.
boyishness, n., enfantillage, m.; puérilité, f.
brace (bréce), v.a., lier, serrer, attacher; (nav.) brasser.
brace, n., couple, paire, f.; (arch.) tirant, m.; (carp.) ancre; (mus., print.) accolade, f.; (nav.) bras (of a yard—de vergue), m.; (of a conch—d'un carrosse) soupente, f. —s; bretelles, f.pl.
bracelet (bréss'lète), n., bracelet, m.
bracer, n., bandage, m.
brach (brake), n., chien de chasse, m.; chienne de chasse, f.
brachial (brak'ial, bré-ki-al), adj., brachial.
bracing (brécigne), adj., fortifiant, salutaire.
bracket (brakète), n., (print.) crochet; (arch.) tasseau, m.; console, f.
brackish (brak'ishe), adj., saumâtre.
brackishness (-nèsse), n., goût saumâtre, m.
brad (brade), n., clou sans tête, m.
bradawl (brad'ôl), n., poinçon effilé, m.
brag, v.n., se vanter.
brag, n., fanfaronnade, vanterie, f.
braggadocio (brag'ga-dô-shi-ô), n., bravache; fanfaron, m.
braggart (brag'garte), adj., fanfaron, vantard.
braggart, or **bragger** (brag'gheur) n., vantard, fanfaron, m.
bragging (brag'ghigne), n., vanterie, forfanterie, f.
braggingly, adv., en fanfaron.
brahmin (brâ'mi'n), n., brame; brahmane, m.
brahminee (-nî), or **brahminess** (-nèsse), n., bramine, f.
brahminical, adj., brahmanique.
brahminism, n., brahmanisme, m.
braid (bréde), n., tresse, f.
braid, v.a., tresser.
brails (brél'z), n.pl., (nav.) cargue, f.
brail-up (-eupe), v.a., (nav.) carguer.
brain (bréne), n., cerveau, m.; cervelle, f. To puzzle one's —s; se creuser la cervelle. To blow one's —s out; se faire sauter, se brûler la cervelle.
brain, v.a., faire sauter, brûler la cervelle à.
brainish (brén'ishe), adj., insensé; à tête chaude.
brainless (-lesse), adj., sans cervelle; à cerveau vide.
brainsick, adj., à cerveau malade.
brainsickly, adv., en cerveau malade.
brainsickness (-nèsse), n., folie, f.; état d'un écervelé, m., étourderie, indiscrétion, f.
brake (bréke), n., fougère; fougeraie, ronceraie, f.; (agri.) casse-motte, m.; (hydr.) brimbale, f.; (man.) bridon; (tech.) frein, m.; (for kneading—pour pétrir) huche au pain, f., pétrin, m.; (for curriers—de corroyeurs) brisoir, m.
braky, adj., épineux.
bramble (bra'm'b'l), n., ronce, f.
bramin, &c. V. **brahmin**, &c.
bran (bra'n), n., son, m.
branch (bra'n'she), v.n., pousser des branches. To — off; se ramifier: (of roads—des routes) s'embrancher; se bifurquer.
branch, v.a., diviser en branches.
branch, n., branche; (of public establish-ment—d'établissements publics) succursale, f.; (railways) embranchement, m.
branchiness (-nèsse), n., état branchu, m.
branchless (-lèsse), adj., sans branches; ébranché.
branchy, adj., branchu.
brand (bra'n'de), n., brandon, tison, m.; flétrissure, marque, f.
brand, v.a., flétrir.
branding-iron, n., fer à marquer, m.
brand-iron (-a'i'eurne), n., fer à marquer; trois-pieds, m.
brandish (-dishe), v.a., brandir.
brandisher, n., personne qui brandit, f.
brandy, n., eau-de-vie, f.
brangle (bra'n'g'l), n., disputaillerie, f.
brangle, v.n., disputailler.
brank-ursine (-eur'saïne), n., branche-ursine, branc-ursine, berce, acanthe, f.
branny, adj., de son.
brasier (bré-jeur), n., dinandier; cuyvier en cuivre jaune; braisier (coal-pan—bassin à braise), m.
brass (brâce), n., airain, cuivre jaune, laiton; toupet (effronterie), m.
brass, v.a., couvrir de laiton.
brass-foil (-fo-il), n., cuivre battu, m.
brass-founder (-faou'n'deur), n., fondeur de cuivre, m.
brass-foundry, n., fonderie de cuivre, f.
brassiness (-nèsse), n., ressemblance avec le cuivre, f.
brass-visaged (-viz'adj'de), adj., à front d'airain, effronté.
brass-wares (-wér'ze), n.pl., dinanderie, f.
brass-wire (-wa'eur), fil de laiton, m.
brass-work, n., objet, ouvrage de cuivre, m.
brass-works (-weurkse), n.pl., usine à cuivre, f.
brassy, adj., d'airain.
brat (brate), n., marmot, m., marmotte, f.
bravado (-vâdô), n., bravade, f.
brave (brévo), adj., brave; vaillant.
brave, n., bravache, fanfaron, m.
brave, v.a., braver.
bravely, adv., courageusement, bravement.
bravery, n., bravoure, f.
bravo (brâ-vô, bré-vô), n., bravo, assassin, m.
bravo! int., bravo!
bravura (bra-viou-ra), n., (mus.) air de bravoure, m.
brawl (brôl), n., clabauderie, dispute, f.
brawl, v.n., brailler, clabauder, disputer.
brawler, n., clabaudeur; braillard, m., braillarde, f.; brailleur, m., brailleuse, f.
brawling, n., clabauderie, criaillerie, f.
brawlingly, adv., en clabaudant, en braillant.
brawn (brô'n), n., sanglier, m.; chair de sanglier, f., bras, m.; partie charnue, f.
brawner, n., sanglier, m.
brawniness (-nèsse), n., état musculeux, m., force, f.
brawny, adj., charnu, musculeux, robuste.
bray (bré), v.a., broyer.
bray, v.n., braire.
bray, or **braying** (bré-igne), n., braiment, m.
brayer (bré-eur), n., braillard, m.
braze (bréze), v.a., travailler en airain; braser; endurcir.
brazen (bré-z'n), adj., d'airain.
brazen, v.n., montrer un front d'airain. To — it out; payer d'effronterie.
brazen-face (-féce), n., front d'airain; effronté, m., effrontée, f.
brazen-faced (-féss'te), adj., à front d'airain.
brazenness (bré-z'n'nèsse), n., qualité propre à l'airain; impudence, effronterie, f.

brazil, or **brazil-wood** (bra-zil-wo ude), n., brésillet; bois du Brésil, m.

brazilian, adj., brésilien.

brazil-nut (-neute), n., noix du Brésil; amande de l' Amazone, f.

breach (britshe), n., brèche; rupture; violation, infraction, f.

bread (brède), n., pain, m. Daily — ; pain quotidien. New — ; pain frais. Stale — ; pain rassis. To take the — out of one's mouth ; voler le pain de la bouche à quelqu'un. To be in want of — ; manquer de pain. On — and water ; au pain et à l'eau.

breadless adj., sans pain.

bread-room (-roume), n., (nav.) soute au pain, f.

breadth (brèd'th), n., largeur, f.; (of stuffs —des étoffes) lé, m.

bread-tree (-trî), n., jaquier; arbre à pain, m.

break (brèke), v.a.(preterit, Broke ; past part., Broken), rompre ; casser ; briser ; violer, enfreindre ; faire faire faillite à ; ruiner. To — open a door ; enfoncer une porte. To — open a letter ; décacheter une lettre. To — off ; rompre, interrompre. To— up; démolir ; dissoudre. To — through; se frayer un passage à travers. To — in a horse; rompre un cheval. To — any one of a bad habit; faire perdre à quelqu'un une mauvaise habitude. To — any one's heart ; briser le cœur à quelqu'un. To — one's oath; violer, fausser son serment.

break, v.n., rompre, se rompre, casser, se casser, briser, se briser; éclater; (com.) faire faillite ; (of daybreak—du jour) poindre; (of an abscès—d'un abcès) percer. To — in; envahir, pénétrer, s'introduire. To — up; (of an assembly —d'une assemblée) se séparer ; (of schools, &c.— d'écoles, &c.) entrer en vacances; (of cold—du froid) s'adoucir; (of fine weather—du beau temps) ce gâter. To — out; éclater ; (of diseases— des maladies) se déclarer. To — off ; rompre, cesser. To —.down ; (of carriages—des voitures) verser; (of horses—des chevaux) s'abbattre; (of orators, &c.—d'orateurs, &c.) rester court, s'arrêter tout court.

break, n., percée, trouée; (fig.) interruption, f.; print.) alinéa, m.; (man.) voiture pour dresser les chevaux, f. — of day ; point du jour, m. ; pointe du jour, f.

breakage (-édje), n., (com.) casse, f.

breaker, n., infracteur ; briseur, m., briseuse, f.; violateur, m., violatrice, f.

breakfast (brèk'feuste), n., déjeuner, m.

breakfast, v.n., déjeuner.

break-iron (-aï'eurne), n., enclume, f.

breakneck (-nèke), n., casse-cou, m.; chute à se casser le cou, f.

breakshare (-shére), n., (vet.) cours de ventre, m.

break-stone (-stône), n., (bot.) saxifrage, f.

breakwater (-wôteur), n., (of bridges—de ponts) avant-bec; arrière-bec ; (of harbours—de ports) brise-lames, m. ; digne, f. ; rempart, m.

bream (brîme), n., (ich.) brème, f.

bream, v.a., (nav.) chauffer (a ship—un vaisseau).

breast (brèste), n., poitrine, f.; sein; (nav.) flanc ; (of a horse—du cheval) poitrail, m.

breastthigh (-lia'ye), adj., à hauteur d'appui.

breastplate (-plète), n., cuirasse, f.

breastwork (-veurke), n., parapet; (nav.) fronteau, m.

breath (brèth), n., haleine, f; souffle, m. To be out of — ; être hors d'haleine, être essouflé. To get out of — ; se mettre hors d'haleine ; perdre haleine. Last ; dernier soupir, m.

breathe (brithe), v.n., respirer, souffler. To— one's last ; rendre le dernier soupir.

breather, n., personne qui respire, f.

breathing, adj., qui respire ; pour respirer.

breathing-time (-taime), n., temps de respirer, m.

breathless (brèth'lèsse), adj., essouflé ; haletant ; inanimé.

bred (brède), past part. (of to breed), élevé. Ill— ; mal élevé.

breech (brit'she), n., derrière, m.; (of firearms—d'armes à feu) culasse, f.

breech, v.a., mettre en culotte; fesser; mettre une culasse à.

breeches (brit'shize), n.pl., culotte, f.sing.

breed (brîde), v.a. (preterit and past part., Bred), enfanter, engendrer; élever.

breed, v.n., s'engendrer; multiplier.

breed, n., race; couvée, f.

breeder, n., mère, f. ; éleveur, m.

breeding. n., génération, éducation, f. Good— ; politesse, f.

breeze (brîze), n., brise, f.; vent, m.

breezy, adj., rafraîchi par la brise.

brethren (breth'rène), n. (pl. of brother), frères (of the same society—de la même société), m.pl.

breve (brîve), n., (mus.) brève, f.

brevet (brî'vète, brèv'ète), adj., (milit.) à brevet.

brevet, n., brevet, m.

breviary (briv'ia-ri), n., bréviaire ; abrégé, m.

breviate (brî'vi-éte), n., extrait, abrége, m.

breviature (brîv'ia-tioure), n., abréviation, f.

brevier (bri-vieur), n., (print.) petit texte, m.

brevity (brèv'iti), n., brièveté ; concision, f.

brew (brou), v.a., brasser ; mêler ; (fig.) tramer.

brew, v.n., faire de la bière; (fig.) se préparer, se tramer, couver.

brewer, n., brasseur, m.

brewery, n., brasserie, f.

brewhouse (-haouce), n., brasserie, f.

brewing, n., brassage. m.

briar (braï'ar), n. V. **brier.**

bribe (braïbe), n., présent (given to corrupt —fait dans le but de corrompre); prix; appât, m.

bribe, v.a., gagner, corrompre; suborner.

briber, n., suborneur, corrupteur, m., corruptrice, f.

bribery, n., corruption, séduction; concussion, f.

brick (brike), n., brique, f.

brick, v.a., bâtir de briques, briqueter.

brickbat (-bate), n., morceau de brique, m.

brickdust (-deuste), n., poussière de briques, f.

bricklayer (-lé-eur), n., maçon en briques, maçon, m.

brickmaker (-mék'eur), n., briquetier, m.

brickwork (-weurk), n., briquetage, m.

bricky, adj., (ant.) plein de briques ; formé de briques ; convenable pour les briques.

bridal (braï-), n., fête nuptiale, f.

bridal, adj., nuptial, de noce.

bride (braïde), n., nouvelle mariée ; épousée; fiancée, f.

bridebed (-bède), n., lit nuptial, m.

bridecake (-kéke), n., gâteau de noces. m.

bridegroom - (-groume), n., épousé, marié, m.

bridemaid. or **bridesmaid** (-méde). n., amie de noce; demoiselle d'honneur (at a wedding—à une noce), f.

brideman, or **bridesman,** n., ami de noce; garçon d'honneur (at a wedding—à une noce), m.

bridewell (braïd'wèle), n., maison de correction, f.

bridge, n., pont; (of stringed instruments —d i struments à cordes) chevalet; (of the nose

—*du nez*) dos ; (of a comb—*d'un peigne*) champ, *m.* ; (of a gun-carriage—*d'affût de canon*) hausse, *f.*

bridge, *v.a.*, construire un pont sur.

bridle (braï'd'l), *n.*, bride, *f.*; (fig.) frein, *m.*

bridle, *v.a.*, brider ; (fig.) mettre un frein à.

bridle, *v.n.*, redresser la tête. To — up ; *se redresser.*

bridoon (braï-doune), *n.*, (man.) filet, bridon, *m.*

brief (brîfe), *adj.*, bref, court.

brief, *n.*, bref; abrégé; (of barristers—*d'avocats*) cause, *f.*

briefless, *adj.*, (of barristers—*d'avocats*) sans causes.

briefly, *adv.*, brièvement; en peu de mots.

briefness, *n.*, brièveté, *f.*

brier (braï'eur), *n.*, ronce, *f.*; églantier, *m.*

briery, *adj.*, plein de ronces.

brig, *n.*, (nav.) brig, brick, *m.*

brigade (-ghéde), *n.*, brigade, *f.*

brigade, *v.a.*, former en brigades.

brigadier (brig-a-dîre), *n.*, . général de brigade, *m.*

brigand (brig'a'n'de), *n.*, brigand, *m.*

brigandage (-'d'édje), *n.*, brigandage, *m.*

brigantine(brig-a'n'-tîne), *n.*, brigantin, *m.*; brigantine, *f.*

bright (braïte), *adj.*, brillant, clair, éclatant.

brighten (braït'n), *v.a.*, . faire briller ; répandre de l'éclat sur. To — up; *éclaircir*; (fig.) *égayer.*

brighten, *v.n.*, s'éclaircir. To — up; (of the face—*du visage*) rayonner ; (of the weather—*du temps*) *s'éclaircir.*

brightly, *adv.*, d'une manière brillante ; brillamment.

brightness, *n.*, brillant, éclat, *m.*; (fig.) joie, *f.*

brilliance, or **brilliancy**, *n.*, . brillant, lustre, éclat, *m.*

brilliant, *adj.*, brillant, éclatant.

brilliant, *n.*, brillant (diamond—*diamant*), *m.*

brilliantly, *adv.*, brillamment.

brilliantness, *n.*, brillant, lustre, éclat, *m.*

brills (brilze), *n.*, cils (of the horse—*du cheval*), *m.pl.*

brim (brime), *n.*, bord, *m.*

brim, *v.a.* and *n.*, remplir jusqu'au bord; être plein jusqu'au bord.

brimful (-foule), *adj.*, plein jusqu'au bord; tout plein.

brimless, *adj.*, sans bords.

brimmer, *n.*, rasade, *f.*; rouge bord, *m.*

brimstone (bri'm'stône), *n.*, soufre, *m.*

brimstony, *adj.*, sulfureux.

brinded (bri'n'dède), *adj.*, tavelé.

brindle (bri'n'd'l), *n.*, tavelure, *f.*

brindled (-d'lde), *adj.*, tavelé.

brine (braïne), *n.*, saumure, *f.*

brine, *v.a.*, mettre dans la saumure, salér.

bring (brigne), *v.a.*, (*preterit* and *past part.*, Brought), apporter; amener; conduire; porter; transporter; réduire. To — about; *amener, venir à bout de.* To — away; *emporter, emmener.* To — back; *rapporter, ramener.* To — down; *descendre, amener en bas; abattre; humilier ; diminuer.* To — forth; *produire; mettre au monde; mettre bas.* To — forward; *faire avancer.* To — in; *faire entrer, introduire.* To — on; *amener, occasionner.* To — out; *sortir, faire sortir ; faire paraître, publier ; représenter sur la scène.* To — over; *transporter; faire passer ; convertir, attirer.* To — under; *soumettre ; assujettir.* To — up; *nourrir ; élever ; monter ; vomir.* To — upon; *attirer.* To — to; *faire reprendre connaissance à ;* (nav.) *amener.* To — close to; *approcher.* To — into fashion; *met-*

tre à la mode. To - into question ; *mettre en question.* To — into trouble; *engager dans de mauvaises affaires.* To — to bed; *accoucher.* To — to pass; *exécuter, effectuer.* To — to perfection; *perfectionner.* To — together; *assembler ; réconcilier, raccommoder.* To — word of ; *apporter la nouvelle de.*

bringer, *n.*, personne qui apporte, *f.*; porteur, *m.*

brinish (braïnishe), *adj.*, saumâtre, salé; amer.

brink (bri'n'ke), *n.*, bord, *m.* The — of a precipice; *le bord d'un précipice.* On the — of ruin; *sur le penchant de la ruine.*

briny (braï-), *adj.*, saumâtre, salé ; amer.

brisk, *adj.*, vif ; piquant ; animé, éveillé.

brisk, *v.a.*, animer. To — up; *animer ; s'animer; se tenir droit; prendre une attitude hardie.*

brisket (-kète), *n.*, poitrine (butcher's meat —*viande de boucherie*), *f.*

briskly, *adv.*, vivement.

briskness, *n.*, vivacité, *f.*

bristle (bris's'l), *n.*, (of pigs, boars—*du cochon, du sanglier*) soie, *f.*; poil raide, *m.*

bristle, *v.a.* and *n.*, hérisser ; se hérisser ; se raidir.

bristly, *adj.*, (of pigs. boars—*du cochon, du sanglier*) qui a des soies ; hérissé.

britannic, *adj.*, britannique.

brite, or **bright** (braïte), *v.n.*, s'égrener (of wheat, barley, &c.—*des grains sur pied*).

british, *adj.*, britannique ; anglais.

brittle (brit't'l), *adj.*, fragile ; cassant.

brittleness, *n.*, fragilité, *f.*

broach (brót'she), *n.*, broche (for roasting — *à rôtir*), *f.*

broach, *v.a.*, embrocher ; (a cask—*un tonneau*) mettre en perce ; émettre, communiquer. To — to ; (nav.) *se coiffer ; faire chapelle.*

broacher, *n.*, broche (for roasting—*à rôtir*), *f.*; auteur, *m.*; personne qui émet, publie la première; *f.*

broad (brôde), *adj.*, large, grand ; (fig.) grossier, hardi ; (accent) bien prononcé. — awake ; *bien éveillé.* — daylight ; *grand jour.*

broad-brimmed (-bri'm'de), *adj.*, 'à large bord.

broadcast, *adj.*, (agri.) à la volée ; (fig.) au hasard.

broadcast, *n.*, (agri.) semis à la volée, *m.*

broaden (brô'd'n), *v.n.*, s'élargir.

broadish, *adj.*, un peu large, assez large.

broadly, *adj.*, largement.

broadness, *n.*, largeur; (fig.) grossièreté, *f.*

broadside (-saïde), *n.*, (nav.) bordée, *f.*; (nav.) côté, bord ; (print.) in-plano, *m.*

broadsword (-sôrde), *n.*, sabre, *m.*

broadwise (-waïze), *adv.*, en largeur.

brocade (-kéde), *n.*, brocart, *m.*

brocaded (-dède), *adj.*, de brocart ; vêtu de brocart.

brocage, or **brokage** (brô'kédje), *n.*, courtage, *m.*

brocket (brok'ète), *n.*, jeune cerf, daguet, *m.*

brogue (brôghe), *n.*, accent très fortement prononcé, *m.*; (Scotch Highlander's shoe— *soulier des montagnards écossais*) brogue, *f.*

broil (broïle), *n.*, discussion, dispute ; querelle, *f.*; tumulte, *m.*

broil, *v.a.*, griller.

broil, *v.n.*, griller, se griller.

broiler, *n.*, gril ; (fig.) perturbateur, *m.*, perturbatrice, *f.*

broken (brô'k'n), *adj.*, cassé, brisé ; navré ; dissous; dispersé ; décousu ; baragouiné.

broken-backed (-bak'te), *adj.*, qui a le dos rompu; qui a les reins cassés.

broken-hearted (-hârt'ède), *adj.*, qui a le

cœur brisé, qui a le cœur navré. To die —;
mourir de chagrin.

brokenly, *adv.*, par morceaux.

broken-winded (-wi'n'dède), *adj.*, (vet.)
poussif.

broker (brô-), *n.*, courtier; fripier, *m.*

brokerage (-édje), *n.*, courtage, *m.*

brome, *or* **bromine** (brôme, -maïne) *n.*,
brome, *m.*

bronchi, **bronchia**, *or* **bronchiœ** (-ki,
-ki-a, -ki-i), *n.pl.*, bronches, *f.pl.*

bronchial, *or* **bronchic** (-kial, -kike), *adj.*,
bronchique.

bronchitis (-kaï-tisse), *n.*, bronchite, *f.*;
catarrhe pulmonaire, *m.*

bronchotomy (-ko-), *n.* bronchotomie, *f.*

bronze, *n.*, bronze, *m.*

bronze, *v.a.*, bronzer; durcir comme l'airain.

brooch (brô'tshe), *n.*, (jewel—*bijou*) broche,
f.; (paint.) camaïeu, *m.*

brood (broude), *v.a.*, couver; (fig.) nourrir.

brood, *v.n.*, couver; se couver; se préparer.
To — over; *méditer sur.*

brood, *n.*, couvée, engeance, race, *f.*

brook (brouke), *n.*, ruisseau, *m.*

brook, *v.a.*, souffrir, avaler, digérer, boire.

brooklet (-lète), *n.*, petit ruisseau, *m.*

broom (broume), *n.*, balai; (bot.) genêt, *m.*

broomrape (-rôpe), *n.*, (bot.) orobanche;
clandestine, *f.*

broomstaff, *or* **broomstick** (-stâfe), *n.*,
manche à balai, *m.*

broomy, *adj.*, rempli de genêts.

broth (brôth), *n.*, bouillon. *m.* Black —;
brouet noir, m.

brother (breutheur), *n.*, frère, *m.* — Inlaw; *beau-frère.* Foster —; *frère de lait.*
Elder —; *frère aîné.* Younger —; *frère cadet.*
—s (of the same family—*de la même famille*)
frères. *V.* **brethren.**

brotherhood (-houde), *n.*, fraternité;
confrérie, *f.*

brotherless, *adj.*, sans frère.

brotherlike (-laïke), *adj.*, en frère;
fraternel.

brotherly, *adj.*, fraternel.

brotherly, *adv.*, fraternellement.

brought (brôte), *preterit* and *past part.* *V.*
bring.

brow (braou), *n.*, sourcil; front, *m.*

browbeat (-bîte), *v.a.*, mater, déconcerter
(by arrogance—*par un langage arrogant*).

browbeaten, *past part.*, maté, déconcerté.

browbeating, *n.*, langage arrogant, *m.*;
arrogance, *f.*; action de mater, *f.*

browbound (-baou'nde), *adj.*, couronné.

brown (braoune), *adj.*, brun; sombre, rembruni. — bread; *pain bis.* — paper; *papier
gris.* — sugar; *cassonade.*

brown, *n.*, brun; (cook.) rissolé, *m.*

brown, *v.a.*, brunir; (cook.) rissoler.

brown, *v.n.*, brunir, se brunir.

brownish, *adj.*, brunâtre.

brownness, *n.*, couleur brune, *f.*

browse (braouze), *v.a.* and *n.*, brouter.

browsewood (-woude), *n.*, brout, *m.*

bruise (brouze), *v.a.*, meurtrir; écraser,
piler.

bruise, *n.*, meurtrissure, *f.*

bruit (broute), *v.a.*, ébruiter.

brumal (brou-), *adj.*, d'hiver, brumal.

brunette (brou-), *n.*, brune, brunette. *f.*

brunt (brun'te), *n.*, choc; fort, *m.*; violence,
fureur, *f.*

brush (breushe), *n.*, brosse, *f.*; balai; pinceau; (fig) coups, *m.*, batterie, *f.*; escarmouche, *f.*; queue (of a fox—*de renard*), *f.*

brush, *v.a.*, brosser; effleurer, raser.

brusher, *n.*, personne qui brosse, *f.*

brushing, *n.*, action de brosser, *f.*; petite

tape, *f.*; allure légère et rapide, *f.*; action
d'effleurer, *f.*

brushmaker (-mék'-), *n.*, brossier, *m.*

brushwood (-woude), *n.*, broussailles. *f.pl.*

brushy, *adj.*, comme une brosse; rude.

brustle (breus's'l), *v.n.*, (ant.) pétiller,
craquer.

brutal (brou-), *adj.*, brutal, cruel.

brutality, *n.*, brutalité, cruauté.

brutalize (-aïze), *v.a.*, abrutir.

brutalize, *v.n.*, s'abrutir.

brutally, *adv.*, brutalement.

brute (broute), *n.*, brute, bête, *f.*; brutal, *m.*

brute, *adj.*, insensible; (of animals—*des
animaux*) sauvage.

brutify (-fa'ye), *v.a.*, abrutir.

brutish (brout'-), *adj.*, brut; abruti, de brute,
brutal.

brutishly, *adv.*, brutalement; comme une
brute, en brute.

brutishness, *n.*, brutalité, *f.*

brutism, *n.*, (ant.) caractère de la brute;
abrutissement, *m.*

bryony (braï'o-), *n.*, (bot.) bryone, couleuvrée, *f.*

bubble (beub'b'l), *n.*, bulle d'air; (fig.)
entreprise illusoire, vaine chimère, *f.*

bubble, *v.a.*, duper.

bubble, *v.n.*, bouillonner. To — up; *bouillonner.*

bubbler, *n.*, trompeur, *m.*

bubbling, *n.*, bouillonnement; (fig.) murmure, *m.*

bubo (biou-), *n.*, (med.) bubon, *m.*

buccaneer (beuk-ka-nîre), *n.*, boucanier, *m.*

buck (beuke), *n.*, lessive, *f.*; daim; bouc;
bélier; mâle (of the hare, of the rabbit—*du
lièvre et du lapin*), *m.*; (fig.) élégant, gaillard, *m.*

buck, *v.a.*, lessiver, laver.

buck, *v.n.*, (man.) faire le saut de mouton.

buckbasket (-kète), *n.*, panier au linge
sale, *m.*

buckbean (-bîne), *n.* *V.* **bogbean.**

bucker, *n.*, (man.) marsouin, *m.*

bucket (-kète), *n.*, seau, *m.*

bucking, *n.*, lessive, *f.*

bucking-cloth (-clôth), *n.*, charrier, *m.*

bucking-tub (-teube), *n.*, cuvier, *m.*

buckle (beuk'k'l), *n.*, boucle, *f.*

buckle, *v.a.*, boucler, attacher, agrafer.

buckle, *v.n.*, plier, se plier, se courber; se
boucler; s'attacher avec une boucle. To — to;
s'appliquer.

buckler (beuk'-), *n.*, bouclier, *m.*

buckler, *v.a.*, défendre; soutenir.

buckram (beuk'-), *n.*, bougran, *m.*

buckwheat (beuk'hwîte), *n.*, sarrasin, blé
noir, *m.*

bucolic (biou-), *adj.*, bucolique.

bucolic, *n.*, (poème) bucolique, *f.*; (poète)
bucoliaste, *m.*

bud (beude), *n.*, bourgeon, bouton. *m.*

bud, *v.n.*, bourgeonner; s'épanouir; fleurir;
germer, boutonner.

bud, *v.a.*, écussonner, greffer.

budding, *n.*, bourgeonnement; germe, *m.*;
greffe en écusson, *f.*

buddle (beud'd'l) *n.*, (metal.) caisse à laver.

buddle, *v.a.*, (metal.) laver.

budge (beudje), *v.n.*, bouger, bouger de.

budge, *n.*, peau d'agneau, *f.*

budget (beud'jète), *n.*, budget; sac. *m.*

budlet (beud'let), *n.*, petit bouton, petit
bourgeon, *m.*

buff (beufe), *n.*, buffle (skin—*peau*), *m.*;
couleur chamois; (med.) couenne, *f.*

buff, *adj.*, de peau de buffle; de couleur
chamois.

buffalo (beuf'fa-lô), *n.*, buffle, *m.*

buffalo-snake (-snéke), *n.*, boa, boa constricteur, devin, *m.*

buffer (beuf'-), *n.*, tampon, *m.*

buffet (beuf'fète), *n.*, soufflet, coup de poing, *m.*

buffet, *v.n.*, se battre à coups de poing; boxer.

buffet, *v.a.*, frapper à coups de poing, battre; assaillir; étouffer le son (of bells—*de cloches*).

buffet (beuf'fète, *ou* beuf'fé), *n.*, buffet, *m.*

buffle (beuf'f'l), *v.n.*, (ant.) être embarrassé.

buffle-headed (-hèdède), *adj.*, stupide.

buffoon (beuf'foune), *n.*, bouffon, *m.*

buffoon, *v.a.*, bafouer.

buffoonery, *n.*, bouffonnerie, *f.*

buffy, *adj.*, (med.) de couenne; couenneux.

bug (beughe), *n.*, punaise, *f.* May-—; *hanneton, m.*

bugbear (-bòre), *n.*, épouvantail; loup-garou, *m.*

buggy (beug'ghi), *adj.*, plein de punaises.

bugle (bioug'l), *n*, perle de Venise; (bot.) bugle, *f.*

bugle. *or* **bugle-horn**, *n.*, cor de chasse, *m.*

bugle-weed (-wîde), *n.*, (bot.) marrube, *m.*

bugloss (biou-), *n.*, buglose, *f.*

build (bilde), *v.a.* (*preterit* and *past part.*, Built), bâtir; construire; édifier. — on; *compter sur.*

build, *v.n.*, bâtir.

builder, *n.*, constructeur, entrepreneur de bâtiments, *m.*

building, *n.*, construction, structure, *f.*; édifice, monument; bâtiment, *m.*

bulb (beulbe), *n.*, (anat.) bulbe, *m.*; (bot.) bulbe, *f.*

bulbous, *adj.*, bulbeux.

bulge (beul'dje), *n.*, ventre, *m.*; (nav.) fond le cale, *m.*, sentine, *f.*

bulge, *v.n.*, faire ventre, bomber.

bulimy (biou-), *n.*, boulimie, *f.*

bulk (beulke), *n.*, volume, *m.*; grosseur, masse; grandeur, *f.*

bulkhead (beulk'hède), *n.*, (nav.) cloison étanche, *f.*

bulkiness, *n.*, grosseur, *f.*; volume, *m.*

bulky, *adj.*, gros, volumineux.

bull (boule), *n.*, taureau, *m.*; (of the pope—*du pape*) bulle; (blunder—*erreur*) bêtise, boulette, bévue, *f.*; (at the exchange—*à la bourse*) joueur à la hausse, haussier, *m.*

bulla (boul'la), *n.*, (med.) bulle, ampoule, cloche, *f.*

bullace (boul'léce), *n.*, (bot.) prunelle, *f.*; prunellier, *m.*

bullace-tree (-trî), *n.*, prunellier, *m.*

bull-baiting (-bét'-), *n.*, combat de taureaux avec des chiens, *m.*

bull-beggar (-bèg-gheur), *n.*, croquemitaine, *m.*

bull-dog, *n.*, dogue, *m.*

bullen (beul'lène), *n.*, chènevotte, *f.*

bullen-nail (-néle), *n.*, clou de tapissier, *m.*

bullet (boul'lète), *n.*, (for small fire-arms—*d'armes à feu portatives*) balle, *f.*

bulletin (boul'li-tîne), *n.*, bulletin, *m.*

bull-fight (-faïte), *n.*, combat de taureaux avec des hommes, *m.*

bull-finch (-fi'n'she), *n.*, bouvreuil, *m.*

bull-fly, *or* **bull-bee** (-fla'ye,-bî), *n.*, taon, *m.*

bull-head (-hède), *n.*, grosse bête, *f.*; (ich.) cotte. chabot, cabot, *m.*; têtard, *m.*

bullion (boul'ieune), *n.*, lingot, *m.*; matières d'or et d'argent, *f.pl.*

bullion-office, *n.*, (com.) bureau pour l'achat des matières d'or et d'argent, *m.*

bullish (boull'-), *adj.*, ridicule, saugrenu.

bullock (boul'-), *n.*, bœuf, *m.* Young —; *bouvillon, m.*

bully (boul'-), *n.*, fier-à-bras, matamore, fendant, *m.*

bully, *v.a.*, rudoyer, maltraiter, malmener; intimider.

bully, *v.n.*, faire le fendant, le fier-à-bras, le matamore.

bulrush (boul'reushe), *n.*, jonc, *m.*

bulwark (boul'weurke), *n.*, boulevard, rempart, *m.*

bulwark, *v.a.*, fortifier par des boulevards.

bum (beume), *n.*, derrière, *m.*

bum-bailiff (-bé-), *n.*, (triv.) pousse-cul (pop.), *m.*

bumble-bee (beu'm'b'l-bî), *n.*, bourdon, *m.*

bumboat (-bôte),*n.*,bateau de provisions, *m.*

bumkin (beu'm'-), *n.*, (nav.) arc-boutant,*m.*

bump (beu'm'pe), *n.*, bosse, *f.*; coup, *m.*

bump, *v.a.*, frapper.

bumper, *n.*, rasade, *f.*; rouge bord, *m.*

bumpkin (beu'm'p'-), *n.*, rustre, *m.*, rustaud, *m.*, rustaude, *f.*

bunch (beu'n'she),*n.*,(of keys—*de clefs*) trousseau; (things tied together—*de choses liées ensemble*) botte, grappe,*f.*,bouquet, *m.*; (on the back—*sur le dos*) bosse; (agri.) javelle,*f.* — of onions; *botte d'oignons.* — of grapes; *grappe de raisin.*

bunch, *v.n.*, faire bosse.

bunch, *v.a.*, lier en botte, en bouquet.

bunchbacked (-bak'te), *adj.*, bossu.

bunchy, *adj.*, touffu.

bundle (beu'n'd'l), *n.*, paquet; faisceau, *m.*; botte; (agri.) javelle, *f.* — of asparagus; *botte d'asperges.*

bundle, *v.a.*, empaqueter. To — out; *mettre à la porte.*

bung (beu'n'ghe), *n.*, bondon; (artil.) tampon, *m.* —-borer; *bondonnière, f.*

bung, *v.a.*, bondonner, boucher.

bunghole (-hôle), *n.*, bonde, *f.*

bungle (beu'n'g'l), *n.*,bousillage, *m.*; bévue,*f.*

bungle, *v.a.*, saveter, gâter, massacrer.

bungle, *v.n.*, s'y prendre de travers.

bungler, *n.*, maladroit, savetier, *m.*

bungling, *adj.*, maladroit.

bunglingly, *adv.*, en savetier, maladroitement, absurdement, inhabilement.

bunion (beu'n'io'n), *n.*, oignon (on the foot—*au pied*), *m.*

bunt (beu'n'te), *n.*, (nav.) fond de voile, *m.*

bunt, *v.n.*, (nav.) s'enfler.

bunting (-), *n.*, étamine, *f.*; (orni.) bruant, *m.*

buoy (buoï), *n.*, (nav.) bouée, *f.*

buoy, *v.a.*, soutenir sur l'eau. To — up; *soutenir sur l'eau;* (fig.) *soutenir, ranimer.*

buoyance, *or* **buoyancy** (bo'y'a'n'ce, -cî), *n.*, faculté de surnager; légèreté, *f.*; élan, *m.*; fermeté,*f.*

buoyant, *adj.*, léger, flottant, élastique, ferme.

bur (beur), *n.*, (of a spear—*de lance, d'épieu*) arrêt; (bot.) glouteron, *m.*

burbot (beur'bote), *n.*, (ich.) lotte commune, *f.*

burden (beur'd'n), *n.*, fardeau, *m.*; charge, *f.*; (nav.) port, *m.* Beast of —; *bête de somme, f.* — of a song; *refrain, m.*

burden, *v.a.*, imposer un fardeau à; charger; opprimer.

burdensome (-seume), *adj.*, onéreux; lourd; ennuyeux.

burdock (beur-), *n.*, (bot.) bardane, *f.*; glouteron, *m.*

bureau (biou-), *n.*, bureau, *m.*

burgamot (beur-), *n.* *V.* **bergamot**.

burgess (beur'djèce), *n.*, bourgeois, habitant, *m.*

burgh (beurghe), *n.*, bourg, *m.*

burgher (beurgh'-), *n.*, bourgeois; citoyen, *m.*

burghership, *n.*, droit de bourgeoisie, *m.*

burglar (beurg'leur), *n.*, auteur de vol de nuit avec effraction dans une maison habitée, *m.*

burglarious, *adj.*, de vol de nuit avec effraction dans une maison habitée.

burglariously, *adv.*, la nuit avec effraction et dans une maison habitée.

burglary (beurg'leuri), *n.*, vol de nuit avec effraction dans une maison habitée, *m.*

burgomaster (beur'go-mas-teur), *n.*, bourgmestre, *m.*

burial (bè-), *n.*, enterrement: ensevelissement, *m.*; sépulture, *f.* Christian —; *sépulture ecclésiastique.*

burial-ground (-graou'n'de), *n.*, cimetière, *m.*

burier (bè-ri-eur), *n.*, fossoyeur, *n.*

burin (biou-ri'n), *n.*, burin, *m.*

burl (beurl), *v.a.*, épinceter (woollen cloth — *du drap*).

burlesque (beur-), *adj.*, burlesque.

burlesque, *n.*, burlesque, *m.*

burlesque, *v.a.*, rendre burlesque.

burlesquer, *n.*, personne qui fait du burlesque, *f.*

burletta (beur-), *n.*, vaudeville, *m.*

burliness (beur-), *n.*, grosseur ; haute taille ; fanfaronnade, *f.*

burly (beur-), *adj.*, gros et grand ; bruyant.

burn (beurne), *n.*, brûlure ; cuite (of bricks — *de briques*), *f.*

burn, *v.a.* (*preterit* and *past part.*, Burnt, Burned), brûler ; (tech.) cuire. To — down; *brûler*. To — down to the ground: *brûler de fond en comble.* To — up; *brûler entièrement.*

burn, *v.n.*, brûler. To — out; *se consumer.*

burner, *n.*, brûleur ; (of a lamp — *de lampe*) bec, *m.*

burning, *n.*, brûlure, *f.*; incendie, *m.*

burning, *adj.*, en feu ; brûlant.

burning-glass (-glâce), *n.*, verre ardent, *m.*, lentille, *f.*

burnish (beur-), *v.a.*, brunir, polir.

burnish, *v.n.*, devenir brillant.

burnisher, *n.*, (pers.) brunisseur, *m*, brunisseuse, *f.*; (tool — *outil*) brunissoir, *m.*

burnt. *V.* **burn**.

burnt-offering (beurn't'of-feur'-), *n.*, holocauste, *m.*

burr (beure), *n.*, lobe (of the ear — *de l'oreille*); ris de veau, *m.*

burrel-shot (beur'rèl-shote), *n.*, mitraille, *f.*

burrow (beur'rô), *n.*, terrier, clapier, *m.*

burrow, *v.n.*, terrer, se terrer.

bursar (beur-), *n.*, économe (of a college — *de collège*); boursier, *m.*

bursarship, *n.*, économat, *m.*

burst (beurste), *n.*, fracas, éclat, *m.*

burst. *v.a.* (*preterit* and *past part.*, Burst), crever ; faire éclater ; fendre ; rompre, briser.

burst, *v.n.*, crever, éclater ; se fendre; faire explosion. To — into tears ; *fondre en larmes.* To — out into; *éclater en.*

burt (beurte), *n.*, turbot, *m.*

burthen (beur'th'n), *n.* *V.* **burden**.

bury (bèr'ré), *v.a.*, enterrer ; ensevelir.

'bus (beuce), *abréviation de* omnibus.

bush (boushe), *n.*, buisson ; (sign-board — *enseigne*) bouchon, *m.*; (hunt.) queue de renard, *f.*

bush, *v.n.*, devenir touffu.

bushel (boush'èl), *n.*, boisseau, *m.*

bushiness (boush'-), *n.*, qualité de ce qui est touffu, *f.*

bushy (boushi), *adj.*, buissonneux ; touffu.

busiless (biz'i-), *adj.*, sans occupation ; à loisir.

busily, *adv.*, activement ; avec empressement.

business (biz'-), *n.*, affaire, occupation, besogne, *f.* état, métier, *m.*; affaires, *f.pl.*; com-

merce; fonds, fonds de commerce, *m.*; (of a banker — *de banquier*) clientèle, *f.* Extensive —; *affaires considérables.* Line of —; *genre de commerce, m.* Run of —; *courant d'affaires, m.* In —; *dans les affaires ; dans le commerce.* On —; *pour affaire.* To attend to one's —; *soigner ses affaires; être à ses affaires.* To be in — for one's self; *être établi pour son compte.* To buy a —; *acheter un fonds.* To do —; *faire des affaires.* To do a great deal of —; *faire de bonnes affaires.* To give up —; *se retirer des affaires.* To give up one's —; *céder son fonds.* To put to —; *mettre dans les affaires.* To retire from —; *se retirer des affaires.* To settle a —; *arranger une affaire.* To send any one about his —; *envoyer promener quelqu'un.* Go about your —; *allez vous promener.* What — is that of yours? *est-ce que cela vous regarde?* You have done a fine piece of — indeed! *Vous avez fait là une belle équipée!*

business-like (-laïke), *adj.*, d'affaires, propre aux affaires.

busk (beuske), *n.*, busc. *m.*

buskin (beus'-), *n.f.*, cothurne, brodequin, *m.*

buskined (beus'ki'n'de), *adj.*, en brodequins ; en cothurnes ; tragique.

buss (beuce), *n.*, (triv.) baiser, *m.*

buss, *v.a.*, (triv.) embrasser, baiser.

bust (beuste), *n.*, buste, *m.*; bosse, *f.*

bustard (beus'-), *n.*, outarde, *f.*

bustle (beus's'l), *n.*, mouvement ; tumulte, bruit, *m.*

bustle. *v.n.*, se donner du mouvement ; se hâter ; tracasser.

bustler, *n.*, personne qui se donne du mouvement, *f.*

bustling, *adj.*, actif, affairé ; empressé ; remuant, bruyant.

busy (biz'zi), *adj.*, affairé, occupé ; actif; en mouvement ; agité.

busy, *v.a.*, occuper. To — one's self about — ; *s'occuper de.*

busy-body, *n.*, officieux, *m.*, officieuse, *f.*

but (beute), *conj.*, mais, qui ne. There is not one of them — knows it; *il n'y en a pas un qui ne le sache.* — that; *sans que.* Not — that; *non que.*

but, *adv.*, excepté; ne . . . que; moins; seulement; si ce n'est que ; ne fût-ce que. — for; *sans.* I should have died, — for him ; *sans lui, je serais mort.* The last — one; *l'avant-dernier.* There is — you who ; *il n'y a que vous qui.*

but, *n.* *V.* **butt**.

butcher (bout'sh'eur), *n.*, boucher, *m.* —'s boy; *garçon boucher, m.* Journey-man —; *étalier, m.*

butcher, *v.a.*, égorger, massacrer.

butcherliness, *n.*, cruauté, *f.*

butcherly, *adj.*, cruel, barbare.

butchery, *n.*, boucherie, *f.*

butler (beut'-), *n.*, sommelier, *m.*

butment (beut'-), *n.*, contrefort, contre-boutant, *m.*

butt (beute), *n.*, bout ; coup de tête (d'animal), *m.*; (fig.) but, point de mire, *m.*, cible, *f.*; (nav.) butte, tête de bordage ; (cask — *tonneau*) pipe, *f.*; (pers.) plastron, *m.*

butt, *v.n.*, cosser.

butt-end (beut'-è'n'de), *n.*, gros bout, *m.* : (of a gun — *de fusil, pistolet, &c.*) crosse, *f.*

butter (beut'-), *n.*, beurre, *m.*

butter, *v.a.*, beurrer ; augmenter les enjeux.

butter-boat (-bôte), *n.*, beurrier, *m.*.

butter-cup (-keupe), *n.*, (bot.) bouton d'or, *m.*

butter-dairy, *n.*, beurrerie, *f.*

butter-dish. *n.* *V.* **butter-boat**.

butter-fly (-fla'ye), *n.*, papillon, *m.*

butter-man (-ma'n), *n.*, beurrier, marchand de beurre, *m.*

butter-milk, n., lait de beurre, petit-lait, m.
butter-pear (-père), n., (bot.) beurré, m.
butter-wife, or **butter-woman** (-waïfe, -wouma'n), n., beurrière, marchande de beurre, f.
butter-wort (-weurte), n., (bot.) grassette, f.
buttery (beut'teur'i), adj., de beurre; butyreux.
buttock (beut'-), n., fesse, f.; (of an ox—d'un bœuf) cimier, m.
button (beut't'n), n., bouton, m
button, v.a., boutonner.
button, v.n., se boutonner.
button-hole (-hôle), n., boutonnière, f.
button-maker (-mék'eur), n., boutonnier, m.
buttress (beut'trèce), n., arc-boutant, m.
buttress, v.a., arc-bouter.
buxom (beuk'seume), adj., beau; enjoué, gai, folâtre.
buxomly, adv., gaiement, joyeusement, gaillardement.
buxomness, n., gaillardise, f.
buy (ba'ye), v.a. (preterit and past part., Bought), acheter. To — off; racheter. To — up; accaparer.
buy, v.n., acheter.
buyer, n., acheteur, m.
buzz (beuze), v.a., chuchoter, dire tout bas.
buzz, n., bourdonnement, m.
buzz, v.n., bourdonner.
buzzard (beuz'zarde), n., busard, m.; buse, f.
buzzer, n., chuchoteur, m., chuchoteuse, f.
by (ba'ye), prep., près de; auprès de; à côté de; par; de; à; d'après; en. He was — me; il était près de moi, à côté de moi. — that means; par ce moyen. Loved — all; aimé de tous. One —one; un à un. — what you say; d'après ce que vous dites. — doing that; en faisant cela. — that time; d'ici là. Money — one; de l'argent par devers soi. — one's self; tout seul.
by, adv., près; là, par là; passé. To be standing—; être là. Close—; tout près.
by, or **bye,** n., ce qui n'occupe l'attention qu'indirectement. By the —; en passant.
by and by, adv., tout à l'heure.
by-by, n., dodo, m.
bye (ba'ye), n., demeure, f.
bygone, adj., passé; qui n'est plus.
by-lane (-léne), n., ruelle écartée, f.; sentier, chemin détourné; chemin de traverse, m.
by-law (-lô), n., loi particulière, loi réglementaire, loi locale, f.; règlement, m.
by-name (-néme), n., sobriquet, m.
by-name, v.a., donner un sobriquet à.
by-stander, n., personne présente, f.; spectateur, m., spectatrice, f.
byway (-wé), n., chemin détourné, obscur, écarté, m.
byword (-weurde), n., dicton, proverbe, m.
byzantian (biz'a'n'shi'a'n), or **byzantine** (-taïne), adj., byzantin.

C

C, troisième lettre de l'alphabet, c, m.; (mus.) ut, do, m.; (mus.) clef d'ut, f.
cab, n., cabriolet; fiacre, m.
cabal n., cabale, f.
cabal, v.n., cabaler.
cabala, n., cabale, f.
cabalism, n., science de cabale, f.
cabalist, n., cabaliste, m.
cabalistic, or **cabalistical,** adj., cabalistique.
caballer, n., cabaleur, m.
cabbage (-bédje), n., chou, m.; (material

kept by tailors, &c.—étoffe gardée par le tailleur, &c.) gratte, f. Turnip-—; chou-navet. Savoy—; chou frisé.
cabbage, v.a., gratter (to keep material—garder de l'étoffe).
cabbage, v.n., (hort.) pommer.
cabbage-head (-hède), n., pomme de chou, f.
cabbage-sprout (-spraoute), n., chou cavalier, m.
cabbage-stalk (-stôke), n., tige de chou, f.
cabbage-stump (-steu'm'pe), n., trognon de chou, m.
cabbage-tree (-trî), n., arec d'Amérique; chou palmiste, m.
cabin (-bine), n., cabane; (nav.) chambre, cabine, f.
cabin, v.n., vivre dans une cabane.
cabin, v.a., enfermer dans une cabane.
cabin-boy (-bo-i), n., (nav.) mousse, m.
cabinet (-nète), n., cabinet, m.
cabinet-council (-caou'n'-), n., conseil des ministres, m.
cabinet-maker (-mék'-), n., ébéniste, m.
cable (ké'b'l), n., câble, m.
cable, v.a., (arch.) orner (with cables- de cannelures).
cablet (ké-blète), n., (nav.) câbleau, m.
caboose (ca-bouce), n., (nav.) fourneaux, m.pl., cuisine, f.
cabriolet (-lè), n., cabriolet, m.
cacao (ké-kô), n., (bot.) cacao; cacaoyer, cacaotier, m.
cacao-pod (-pode), n., (bot.) cabosse, f.
cachectic, or **cachectical** (-kèk-), adj., (med.) cachectique.
cachexy (-kèk-si), n., (med.) cachexie, f.
cachinnation (cak'i'n'né-), n., (ant.) rire excessif; éclat de rire, m.
cack, v.n., faire caca.
cackle (cak'k'l), n., caquet, m.
cackle, v.n., caqueter, crételer.
cackler, n., poule qui caquette; oie qui caquette, f.; caqueteur, m., caqueteuse, f.
cackling, n., caquetage, m.
cacochymical (-ki'm'-), adj., (med.) cacochyme.
cacochymy (kak'o-ki'm-i), n., (med.) cacochymie, f.
cacophony, n., cacophonie, f.
cactus (-teusse), n., cactus, m.
cadaverous (-èr-), adj., cadavéreux.
caddis (cad'dice), n., cadis, m.; charpie, f.
caddy, n., boîte à thé, f.
cade (kéde), adj., doux; apprivoisé.
cade (kéde), n., caque, f.
cade (kéde), v.a., élever à la main.
cadence, or **cadency** (ké-dò'n'ce, -ci), n., cadence; chute, f.
cadence, v.a., cadencer.
cadet (-dète), n., cadet, m.
cadger, n., regrattier, m.
cadmean (-mi-), or **cadmian,** adj., cadméen.
caduceus (-diou-sheusse), n., caducée, f.
caducity (-diou-), n., caducité, f.
cæsura (si-ziou'-), n., césure, f.
cag, n. V. **keg.**
cage (kédje), n., cage, f.; (prison) violon, m.
cage, v.a., encager; mettre au violon.
caisson (ké'çô'n), n., (arch., milit.) caisson, m.
caitiff (ké-), n., misérable, pendard, m.
cajole (ca'djôle), v.a., cajoler.
cajoler, n., cajoleur, m., cajoleuse, f.
cajolery, n., cajolerie, f.
cake (kéke), n., gâteau; (agri.) tourteau; (of wax, &c.—de cire, &c.) pain, m.; (metal.) rosette, f. Twelfth —; gâteau des rois.

cake, *v.n.*, se lier, se coller.
calabash, *n.*, (bot.) calebasse, *f.*
calamine (-maïne), *n.*, calamine, *f.*
calamitous, *adj.*, calamiteux, désastreux, affreux.
calamitously, *adv.*, désastreusement.
calamitousness, *n.*, état de calamité, *m.*
calamity, *n.*, calamité, *f.*
calamus, *n.*, roseau, *m.*
calash, *n.*, calèche, *f.*
calcarate (-réte), *adj.*, (bot.) éperonné
calcareous (-ké-ri-), *adj.*, calcaire.
calceated (-si-étède), *adj.*, chaussé.
calciform, *adj.*, semblable à la chaux.
calcinate (-néte), *v.a.*, *V.* **calcine**.
calcination (-né-), *n.*, calcination, *f.*
calcine (-saïne), *v.a.*, calciner.
calcine, *v.n.*, se calciner.
calc-spar (-spâr), *n.*, spath calcaire, *m.*
calculable (-kiou-), *adj.*, calculable.
calculate (-léte), *v.a.*, calculer; adapter.
calculate, *v.n.*, calculer, compter.
calculation (-lé-), *n.*, calcul, *m.*
calculative (-lé-), *adj.*, de calcul.
calculator (-lé-teur), *n.*, calculateur, *m.*
calculatory, *adj.*, qui a rapport au calcul.
calculose, *or* **calculous** (-kiou-lôss, -leusse), *adj.*, calculeux.
calculus (-leusse), *n.*, (math., méd.) calcul, *m.*
caldron (côl'dreu'ne), *n.*, chaudron, *m.*; chaudière, *f.*
caledonian (-li-dô-), *adj.*, calédonien.
caledonian, *n.*, Calédonien, *m.*, Calédonienne, *f.*
calefacient (-lifé-shè'n'te), *adj.*, chauffant.
calefaction (-l'i-fac-), *n.*, caléfaction, *f.*
calefactive, *or* **calefactory** (cal-i-,-teuri), *adj.*, qui chauffe.
calefy (cal-i-fa'ye), *v.n.*, s'échauffer.
calefy, *v.a.*, chauffer; échauffer.
calendar (cal-è'n'-), *n.*, calendrier, *m.*; (jur.) liste des accusés d'une session de la cour d'assises, *f.*
calender, *n.*, cylindre, *m.*; calandre, *f.*
calender, *v.a.*, cylindrer, calandrer.
calendering, *n.*, calandrage, *m.*
calends (cal-è'n'd'ze), *n.pl.*, calendes. *f.pl.*
calf (kâfe), *n.* (*calves*), veau; (of the deer—*des fauves*) faon; (of the leg—*de la jambe*) mollet, gras, *m.* Fatted — ; *veau gras.*
caliber, *or* **calibre** (cal'i-beur), *n.*, calibre; (tech.) compas d'épaisseur, *m.*
calice (cal'ice), *n.* *V.* **chalice**.
calico, *n.*, calicot, *m.* Printed — ; *indienne*, *f.*
calico-printer, *n.*, imprimeur d'indiennes, imprimeur de toiles peintes, *m.*
calid, *adj.*, (ant.) chaud ; brûlant.
calidity, *n.*, (ant.) chaleur, *f.*
calif, *n.* *V.* **caliph**.
califate, *n.* *V.* **caliphate**.
caligation (-ghé-), *n.*, obscurcissement de la vue, *m.*
caliginous (-dji-), *adj.*, obscur, sombre.
caligraphic, *adj.* *V.* **calligraphic**.
caligraphy, *n.* *V.* **calligraphy**.
caliph (ké'life), *n.*, calife, *m.*
caliphate (-'éte), *n.*, califat, *m.*
calk (kôke), *v.a.*, calfater.
calker, *n.*, calfat, *m.*
calkin, *n.*, calfat, *m.*
calking-iron (-ai'eurne), *n.*, calfait, *m.*
call (kôl), *n.*, appel, *m.*; ordres, *m.pl.*; demande, *f.*; (nav.) sifflet, *m.*; visite, *f.* Bird-— ; *appeau, pipeau, m.* To give any one a —; *faire une visite à quelqu'un; passer chez quelqu'un.* At any one's —; *aux ordres de tout le monde.* Within—; *à portée de voix.*
call, *v.n.*, appeler, crier. To — on any one, *et any one's house; passer chez quelqu'un.*

call, *v.a.*, appeler ; invoquer, nommer. To — a coach ; *faire venir, faire avancer une voiture.* To — again, to — back; *rappeler.* To — aside; *prendre à part.* To — for ; *appeler, demander.* To — to order ; *rappeler à l'ordre.* To — to mind ; *se rappeler.* To — in ; *faire rentrer.* To — in a doctor ; *faire venir un médecin.* To — in money ; *retirer de la monnaie de la circulation.* To — out ; *appeler ; appeler en duel.* To — up ; *faire monter ; réveiller, faire lever ; évoquer.* To — off ; *appeler, rappeler.* To — together ; *assembler, réunir.*
call-boy (bo-i), *n.*, (thea.) avertisseur, *m.*
calligraphic, *or* **calligraphical**, *adj.*, calligraphique.
calligraphy, *n.*, calligraphie, *f.*
calling, *n.*, appellation ; profession, vocation, *f.* ; métier, *m.*
callosity (cal-loss'iti), *n.*, callosité, *f.*, cal, calus, *m.*
callous, *adj.*, calleux ; endurci, insensible.
callously, *adv.*, d'une manière calleuse ; avec insensibilité.
callousness, *n.*, callosité ; insensibilité, *f.*
callow (-lô), *adj.*, sans plume.
callus, *n.*, cal, calus, *m.* ; callosité, *f.*
calm (kâme), *n.*, calme, *m.*
calm, *adj.*, calme.
calm, *v.a.*, calmer.
calmer, *n.*, personne qui calme, *f.*; calmant, *m.*
calmly, *adv.*, avec calme ; tranquillement.
calmness, *n.*, calme, *m.*
calomel, *n.*, calomel, *m.*
caloric, *adj.*, calorique, *m.*
caloric, *adj.*, de calorique.
calorific, *adj.*, calorifique.
caltrop, *n.*, (bot.) herse, croix de Malte ; (milit.) chausse-trape, *f.*
calumba (-leu'm'-), *n.*, (bot.) colombo, *m.*
calumet (cal'iou-mète), *n.*, calumet, *m.*
calumniate (-leu'm'niéte), *v.a.* and *n.*, calomnier.
calumniation (-ni-é-), *n.*, calomnie, *f.*
calumniator (-teur), *n.*, calomniateur, *m.*
calumniatory, *or* **calumnious**, *adj.*, calomnieux.
calumniously, *adv.*, calomnieusement.
calumniousness, *n.*, caractère calomnieux, *m.*
calumny (cal'eu'm'ni), *n.*, calomnie, *f.*
calvary, *n.*, calvaire, *m.*
calve (kâve), *v.n.*, vêler.
calvinism, *n.*, calvinisme, *m.*
calvinist, *n.*, calviniste, *m.f.*
calvinistic, *or* **calvinistical**, *adj.*, calviniste.
calvish (kâv'ishe), *adj.*, de veau ; comme un veau.
calx, *n.* (*calces, calxes*), chaux, *f.*
camaieu (ka-mé-yô), *n.* *V.* **cameo**.
camber, *v.a.*, cambrer.
camber, *n.*, cambre, cambrure, *f.*
cambering, *adj.*, cambré.
cambist, *n.*, agent de change, ⊙ cambiste, *m.*
cambric (ké'm'-), *n.*, batiste, *f.*
came (kéme), *v.n.* *V.* **come**.
came (kéme), *n.*, plomb de vitrier, *m.*
camel (cam'èl), *n.*, chameau, *m.*, chamelle, *f.*
camel-backed (-bak'te), *adj.*, à dos de chameau.
camel-driver (-draïv'-), *n.*, chamelier, *m.*
cameleon, *or* **cameleon-mineral** (-mi-li-), *n.*, (chem.) caméléon minéral, permanganate de potasse, *m.*
camelopard (-pârde), *n.*, girafe, *f.*, ⊙ camélopard, caméléopard, *m.*
camel's hair (-el'z'hère), *n.*, poil de chameau, *m.*
cameo (ca'm'i-ô), *n.*, camaïeu, camée, *m.*

camera-lucida (-'l-ra-liou-), *n.*, chambre claire, *f.*

camera-obscura (-'l-ra-ob-sklou-), *n.*, chambre obscure, *f.*

camerated (ca'm'i-ré-tède), *adj.*, voûté.

cameration (ca'm'i-ré-), *n.*, courbure, voûte, *f.*

camisade, *or* **camisado** ('-i-cé-), *n.*, attaque de nuit, *f.*

camlet, *n.*, camelot, *m.*

camomile (-maïle), *n.* *V.* **chamomile**.

camp (ca'm'pe), *n.*, camp, *m.* To pitch a —; *asseoir un camp.* To break up a —; *lever un camp.*

camp, *v.a.* and *n.*, camper.

campaign (ca'm'péne), *n.*, campagne, *f.*

campaign, *v.n.*, (milit.) faire campagne.

campaigner, *n.*, vieux soldat, vétéran, *m.*

campanile (-nîle), *n.*, campanile, *m.*, campanille, *f.*

campanula (-niou-), *n.*, campanule, *f.*

campanulate, *adj.*, (bot.) campanulé, en cloche.

campeachy wood (-pi-tshi woude), *n.* *V.* **logwood**.

camphire, *or* **camphor** (-feur), *n.*, camphre, *m.*

camphorate, *or* **camphorated** (-feur'éte. -étède), *adj.*, camphré.

can (cane), *n.*, burette, *f.* ; bidon, *m.*

can (cane), *v.n.* (preterit and conditional, Could), pouvoir, savoir. I — do it ; *je peux le faire.* That — not be; *cela ne peut pas être; cela ne se peut pas.* He — read ; *il sait lire.*

canal, *n.*, canal, *m.*

canaliculate, *or* **canaliculated** (-kiou-léte, -létède), *adj.*, cannelé.

canary (-né-), *n.*, vin des Canaries ; (orni.) serin, *m.*

canary-bird (-beurde), *n.*, serin, *m.* Cock- — ; *serin, m.* Hen- — ; *serine, f.*

canary-grass (-grâce), *n.*, alpiste ; blé des Canaries, *m.*

canary-seed (-sîde), *n.*, graine des Canaries, *f.*

cancel, *v.a.*, annuler ; résilier ; effacer, biffer, rayer ; (jur.)⊙ canceller.

cancel, *n.*, (print.) feuillet refait, *m.*

cancellated (-létède), *adj.*, rayé; cellulaire.

cancellation (-lé-), *n.*, cancellation, *f.*

cancer, *n.*, cancer, *m.*

cancerate (-ceur'éte), *v.n.*, devenir cancer ; s'ulcérer.

canceration (-ceur'é-), *n.*, ulcération cancéreuse, *f.*

cancerous, *adj.*, cancéreux.

cancerousness, *n.*, état cancéreux, *m.*

cancrine (-craïne), *adj.*, de cancre, de crabe.

candelabrum (-lé-breu'me), *n.* (candelabra), candélabre, *m.*

candent (-dè'n'te), *adj.*, blanc de feu.

candid, *adj.*, blanc (l.u.) ; candide, franc.

candidate (-déte), *n.*, candidat, aspirant, *m.*

candidly, *adv.*, candidement, franchement.

candidness, *n.*, candeur, franchise, *f.*

candied (ca'n'dide), *adj.*, candi.

candle (ca'n'd'l), *n.*, chandelle ; lumière, *f.* Wax — ; *bougie, f.* Mould — ; *chandelle moulée.* Dipped — ; *chandelle plongée.*

candle-end (-è'n'de), *n.*, bout de chandelle, *m.* ; *pl.*, débris, brins, fragments

candle-grease (-grîce), *n.*, suif, *m.*

candle-light (-laïte), *n.*, lumière de la chandelle, *f.* By — ; *à la lumière, à la lumière de la chandelle.*

candlemas (-meusse), *n.*, la Chandeleur, *f.*

candle-stick (-stîke), *n.*, chandelier, *m.*

candle-stuff (-steufe), *n.*, suif, *m.*

candle-waster (-wést'-), *n.*, étudiant qui travaille beaucoup; prodigue, *m.*

candle-wick, *n.*, mèche de chandelle, *f.*

candor (-deur), *n.*, candeur, franchise, *f.*

candy, *v.a.*, faire candir.

candy, *v.n.*, se candir, se cristalliser.

candy, *n.*, candi, *m.*

cane (kéne), *n.*, canne, *f.* ; jonc, *m.*

cane, *v.a.*, donner des coups de canne à.

cane-mill, *n.*, moulin à sucre, *m.*; sucrerie, *f.*

canescent (-nès-cè'n'te), *adj.*, blanchissant, blanchâtre, tirant sur le blanc.

canetrash (-trashe), *n.*, bagasse, *f.*

cane-work (-weurke), *n.*, objet, ouvrage de canne, *f.*

canicula, *or* **canicule** (-nik'iou-), *n.*, (astron.) canicule, *f.*

canicular, *adj.*, caniculaire.

canine (-naïne), *adj.*, canin, de chien.

caning (ké-), *n.*, coups de canne, *m.pl.*

canister, *n.*, boîte de fer blanc, *f.*

canister-shot (-shote), *n.*, mitraille ; boîte à balles, *f.*

canker (kang'keur), *n.*, ver rongeur; (fig., med.) chancre ; (bot.) gratte-cul, *m.*

canker, *v.a.*, ronger ; corrompre.

canker, *v.n.*, se ronger ; se gangrener.

canker-bit (-bite), *adj.*, gangréné.

cankered (-keurde), *adj.*, rongé, gangréné ; hargneux.

canker-fly (-fla'ye), *n.*, ver rongeur des fruits, *m.*

cankerous, *adj.*, chancreux; rongeant.

canker-worm (kang'keur-weurme), *n.*, ver rongeur, *m.*

cannibal (ca'n'ni-bal), *n.*, cannibale, anthropophage, *m.f.*

cannibalism, *n.*, cannibalisme, *m.* ; anthropophagie, *f.*

cannibally, *adv.*, en cannibale.

cannon (ca'n'no'n), *n.*, (artil., print.) canon.

cannonade (-éde), *n.*, canonnade, *f.*

cannonade, *v.a.*, canonner.

cannonade, *v.n.*, se canonner.

cannon-ball (-bôl), *n.*, boulet de canon, *m.*

cannoneer, *or* **cannonier** (-îre), *n.*, canonnier, *m.*

cannon-proof (-proufe), *adj.*, à l'épreuve du canon.

cannon-shot (-shote), *n.*, boulet de canon, *m.* ; portée de canon, *f.* Within — ; *à portée de canon.*

cannular (-'niou-), *adj.*, tubuleux.

canoe (-nou), *n.*, canot, *m.* ; pirogue, *f.*

canon (ca'n'o'n), *n.*, (ecc.) canon; chanoine, *m.* ; (at billiards—au billard) carambolage, *m.*

canon, *v.n.*, (at billiards—au billard) caramboler.

canoness, *n.*, chanoinesse, *f.*

canonical, *adj.*, canonique.

canonically, *adv.*, canoniquement.

canonicalness, *n.*, canonicité, *f.*

canonicals (-calze), *n.pl.*, (ecc.) costume de cérémonie, *m.*

canonicate (-kéte), *n.*, canonicat, *m.*

canonist, *n.*, canoniste, *m.*

canonistic, *adj.*, de canoniste.

canonization (-aïzé-), *n.*, canonisation, *f.*

canonize (-naïze), *v.a.*, canoniser.

canon-law (-lô), *n.*, droit canon, *m.*

canonry, *or* **canonship**, *n.*, canonicat, *m.*

canopy, *n.*, dais ; pavillon ; (arch.) baldaquin, *m.*

canopy, *v.a.*, couvrir d'un dais.

cant (ka'n'te), *n.*, jargon, *m.* ; afféterie; cafarderie, *f.* ; langage hypocrite, *m.*

cant, *v.n.*, parler avec afféterie, avec cafarderie; nasiller.

cant, *v.a.*, pousser, jeter; (arch.) chanfreiner; (nav.) rouler; incliner.

cantaliver, *n.* *V.* **cantilever**.

cantaloupe(-loupe),n.,(hort.)cantaloup, m.
cantata (-tâ-), n., cantate, f.
canteen (-tîne), n., (milit.) cantine, f.
canter, n., hypocrite, m.f.; cafard, m.,
cafarde, f.; galop de chasse; petit galop, m.
canter, v.n., aller au petit galop.
cantharis (-tha-), n. (cantharides), cantharide, f.
canticle (-ti'k'l), n., cantique, m.
cantilate (-léte), v.a., chantonner.
canting, adj., affété, cafard; (her.) parlant.
cantingly, adv., avec afféterie, avec cafarderie.
cantle (ka'n't'l), v.a., diviser, morceler.
canto (-tô), n., chant, m.
canton, n., canton, m.
canton, v.a., diviser en cantons; (milit.)
cantonner.
cantonize (-aïze), v.a., diviser en cantons.
cantonment, n., cantonnement, m.
canula (-'iou-), n., (surg.) canule, f.
canvas (-'vace), n., canevas, m.; toile, f.
canvass (-'vace), n., brigue; sollicitation
de suffrages, f.
canvass, v.a., agiter, débattre, discuter.
canvass, v.n., briguer; solliciter des suffrages.
canvasser, n., brigueur; solliciteur de suffrages, m.
cany (ké-ni), adj., de canne, de jonc.
canzonet (-nète), n., chansonnette, f.
caoutchouc (-'tshouke), n., caoutchouc, m.
cap, n., (woman's—de femme) bonnet, m.;
(man's—d'homme) casquette; (of a cardinal—de
cardinal) barrette, f.; (of a bell—de cloche) chapeau; (nav.) chouquet; (horl.)recouvrement, m.
cap, v.n., coiffer, couronner.
capability (ké-), n., capacité, f.
capable (ké-pa'b'l), adj., capable, susceptible.
capableness, n., capacité, f.
capacious (-pé-sheusse), adj., ample, vaste,
étendu; grand.
capaciousness, n., capacité; étendue, f.
capacitate (-téte), v.a., rendre capable.
capacity, n., capacité; (employment—
emploi) qualité, f.
cap-a-pie (-pî), adv., de pied en cap.
caparison (-ceune), n., caparaçon, m.
caparison, v.a., caparaçonner.
cape (képe), n., collet, m.; pèlerine, f.;
(geog.) cap, m.
caper (ké-), n., cabriole, f.; entrechat, m.;
(bot.) câpre, f.
caper, v.n., cabrioler.
caper-bush (-boushe), n., câprier, m.
caperer, n., cabrioleur, m.
capias (ké-), n., (jur.) mandat d'arrêt, mandat d'amener, m.
capillaceous (-lé-sheusse), adj., capillaire.
capillaire, n., sirop de capillaire, m.
capillariness, or **capillarity**, n., capillarité, f.
capillary, adj., capillaire.
capital,n.,(com., fin.) capital; (arch.)chapi-
teau, m.; (town—ville) capitale, f.; (com.) fonds
social, m.;(print.,writing)majuscule, capitale, f.
capital, adj., capital, excellent.
capitalist, n., capitaliste, m.
capitally, adv., d'un crime capital; pour
crime capital; parfaitement.
capitation (-té-), n., dénombrement, m.;
capitation, f.
capitol (-tôle), n., capitole, m.
capitolian, or **capitoline** (-tô-li-a'n,
-laïne), adj., capitolin.
capitular, or **capitulary** (-pit'iou-), n.,
capitulaire, m.
capitularly, adv., capitulairement.
capitulate (-pit'iou-léte), v.n., capituler.

capitulation (-pit'iou-lé-), n., capitulation, f.
capon (ké'p'n), n., chapon, m.
capon, v.a., chaponner.
caponniere (-nîre), n., caponnière, f.
capped (cap'te), adj., coiffé; couronné;
(horl.) à recouvrement.
caprice (-price), n., caprice, m.
capricious (-prish'eusse), adj., capricieux.
capriciously, adv., capricieusement.
capriciousness, n., caractère capricieux,
m.; humeur capricieuse, f.
capricorn (-côrne), n., capricorne, m.
capriform, or **caprine** (cap'raïne), adj.,
en chèvre; lascif.
capsize (-saïze), v.a., chavirer.
capsize, v.n., (nav.) chavirer.
capstan, n., cabestan, m.
capsular, or **capsulary** (-siou-), adj.,
capsulaire.
capsulate (-siou-léte), or **capsulated**
(-siou-létède), adj., enfermé dans une capsule.
captain (kap'ti'n), n., capitaine, m. Post—;
(nav.) capitaine de vaisseau.
captaincy, n., capitainerie, f.
captainship, n., grade de capitaine, m.;
capitainerie, f.
captation (-té-), n., (ant.) capture; (courtship—assiduités auprès d'une femme) cour, f.
captious (-sheusse), adj., captieux; susceptible.
captiously, adv, captieusement.
captiousness, n., disposition à la critique,
susceptibilité, f.
captivate (-véte), v.a., captiver; capter;
assujettir.
captivation (-vé-), n., assujettissement, m.
captive, n., captif, m., captive, f.
captive, adj., captif; de captif.
captive, v.a., captiver.
captivity, n., captivité, f.
captor (-teur), n., capteur; preneur, m.
capture (capt'ioure), n., capture; prise, f.
capture, v.a., capturer.
capuchin (cap'iou-shïne), n., capucin, m.,
capucine; mante à capuchon (woman's—de
femme), f.
car (câre), n., char, chariot, m.; (of a balloon
—de ballon) nacelle, f.
carabine (-baïne), or **carbine** (câr-baïne),
n., carabine, f.; mousqueton, m.
carabineer (-nîre), n., carabinier, m.
caracole (-côle), n., caracole, f.
caracole, v.n., (man.) caracoler.
caramel, n., caramel, m.
caranna, n., caragne, gomme caragne, f.
carat (-ate), n., carat, m.
caravan (-va'n), n., caravane, f.
caravansary (-va'n'sa-), or **caravansera**
(-va'n'sè-). n., caravansérail, m.
caravel, or **carvel** (câr-), n., caravelle, f.
caraway (-wé), n., carvi, cumin des prés, m.
carbon (câr-bo'n), n., (chem.) carbone, m.
carbonate (-éte), n., carbonate, m.
carbonic (-), adj., carbonique.
carbonization (-aïzé-), n., carbonisation, f.
carbonize (-'aïze), v.a., carboniser.
carbuncle (câr-bung'k'l), n., escarboucle, f.;
(med.) charbon, m.
carbuncled (-k'lde), adj., garni d'escar-
boucles; (of the nose—du nez) bourgeonné.
carbuncular (-kiou-), adj., d'escarboucle;
rouge.
carburet (câr-biou-rète), n., (chem.) carbure, m.
carcanet (câr-ca-nète), n., carcan, collier de
pierreries, m.
carcase or **carcass** (câr-), n., carcasse, f.
carcinoma (câr-ci-nô-), n., carcinome, cancer, m.

card (cârde), n., carte, f.
card, v.a., carder.
cardamine (câr-da-maïne), n., (bot.) cardamine, f.
cardamom (câr-da-meume), n., (bot.) cardamome, m.
card-case (-kéce), n., étui à cartes, m.
carder (cârd'-), n., cardeur, m., cardeuse, f.
cardiac, adj., cardiaque.
cardiac, n., (med.) cardiaque, m.
cardiacal (câr-), adj., fortifiant.
cardialgy (câr-di-al-djï), n., cardialgie, f.
cardinal (câr-), n., cardinal, m.
cardinal, adj., cardinal.
cardinalate (-éte), or **cardinalship**, n., cardinalat, m.
cardmaker (-mék'-), n., cartier, m.
card-paper (-pé-peur), n., carton fin, m.
card-rack (-rack), n., porte-cartes, m.
card-room (-roume), n., salon de jeu, m.
card-table (-téb'l), n., table de jeu, f.
care (kére), n., soin ; souci, m. ; sollicitude ; attention, f. To take — of ; prendre soin de. To take — to ; prendre garde à : avoir soin de.
care, v.n., se soucier. s'inquiéter.
care-crazed (-créz'de), adj., accablé de soucis.
careen (-rîne), n., (nav.) carène, f.
careen, v.a., (nav.) mettre en carène, caréner, abattre.
careen, v.n., (nav.) donner à la bande.
careening, n., carénage, m.
career (-rieur), n., carrière, f.
career, v.n., courir rapidement ; s'élancer.
careful (kér'foule), adj., soigneux, attentif ; plein de soucis, soucieux.
carefully, adv., soigneusement, attentivement.
carefulness, n., attention, f.; soin ; souci, m.
careless, adj., sans souci ; insouciant, nonchalant, négligent.
carelessly, adv., sans souci, avec insouciance, nonchalamment, négligemment.
carelessness, n.,insouciance, nonchalance, négligence, f.
caress (-rèce), n., caresse, f.
caress, v.a., caresser.
caret (ké'rète), n., renvoi, m.
careworn (-wôrne), adj., usé par les soucis.
cargo (cârgô), n., cargaison, f.; chargement, m.
caribou, n., caribou, m.
caricature (-tioure), n., caricature, charge, f.
caricature, v.a., caricaturer.
caricaturist (-tiouriste), n., caricaturiste, m.
caries (ké-ri-ize), n., carie, f.
carillon (ca-rïl-leune), n., petite cloche, f.; (mus.) carillon, m.
carious (ké-), adj., carié.
carman (câr-ma'n), n., (carmen) charretier, m.
carlings (câr-lign'ze), n.pl., (nav.) carlingue, f.
carmelite (câr-mèl-aïte), adj., de carme, de carmélite.
carmelite, n., carme, m. —nun ; carmélite, f.
carminativo, adj., carminatif.
carminative, n., carminatif, m.
carmine (câr-maïne), n., carmin, m.
carnage (câr-nédje), n., carnage, m.
carnal (câr-), adj., charnel.
carnally, adv., charnellement.
carnation (-né-), n., carnation, f.; (bot.) œillet girofle, œillet des fleuristes, m.
carnation-colour (-keul'leur), n., incarnat, m.
carneous (câr-ni-eusse), adj., charnu.
carney (câr-), n., (vet.) maladie de la bouche (of horses—des chevaux), f.

carnification (câr-ni-fi-ké-), n., carnification, f.
carnify (câr-ni-fa'ye), v.n., se carnifier.
carnival (câr-), n., carnaval, m.
carnivorous, adj., carnivore.
carnosity (-noss'i-), n., carnosité, f.
carny (câr-), v.n., pateliner.
carnying, adj., patelin.
carob, n., (bot.) (tree—arbre) caroubier, (fruit) caroube, carouge, m.
carol, n., chanson, f.; chant, m. Christmas — chant de Noël.
carol, v.a., chanter.
carol (car'ol), v.n., chanter ; (of the lark—de l'alouette) grisoller.
carotid, n., (anat.) carotide, f.
carotid, adj., (anat.) carotide, carotidien
carousal (-zal), n., carrousel, m.
carouse (ca-rou-ze), v.n., boire copieusement riboter.
carouser, n., grand buveur, riboteur, m.
carp (cârpe), n., (ich.) carpe, f.
carp (cârpe), v.a. and n., blâmer ; gloser. To — at ; gloser sur.
carpenter (câr-pè'n'-), n., charpentier, menuisier, m.
carpentry, n., charpenterie, menuiserie, f.
carper, n., gloseur, m., gloseuse, f.
carpet (câr-pète), n., tapis, m.
carpet, v.a., garnir de tapis ; (fig.) tapisser.
carpet-bag (-baghe), n., sac de nuit, m.
carping (cârp'-), adj., glose, censure, critique, f.
carriage (car'ridje), n., voiture, f.; équipage ; (of parcels—de paquets) port ; of the body—de la personne) port, maintien, m. ; tenue, f. ; (of cannon—de canon) affût, m. ; (com.) frais de transport, m.pl. To keep one's — ; avoir équipage ; tenir équipage. Gentleman's — ; voiture de maître. — and pair, and four ; voiture à deux chevaux, à quatre chevaux. — paid ; port payé.
carrier (car'rieur), n., porteur ; voiturier, m.
carrion (-'ri-o'n), n., charogne, f.
carrion, adj., de charogne.
carrot (car'rote), n., carotte, f.
carrotiness, n., couleur rousse, f.
carroty, adj., couleur de carotte ; roux.
carry, v.a., porter ; mener ; entraîner ; emporter ; rapporter ; (arith.) retenir. To — it high ; le prendre sur un haut ton. To — about ; porter à droite et à gauche ; porter partout ; riener à droite et à gauche ; mener partout. to — away ; emporter ; enlever ; emmener ; entraîner par persuasion. To — back ; reporter. To — down ; descendre. To — forward ; (com.) reporter. To — forth ; sortir. To — in ; rentrer. To — off ; emporter ; remporter ; enlever. To — on ; pousser ; poursuivre ; continuer ; exercer. To — out ; porter dehors ; développer. To — over to ; faire passer à. To — up ; porter en haut ; monter. To — it over any one ; l'emporter sur quelqu'un. — the day ; remporter la victoire. — to and fro ; porter çà et là.
carry, v.n., (artil.) porter ; (man.) porter, porter la tête.
cart (cârte), n., charrette, f.; chariot ; (milit.) fourgon, m.
cart (cârte), v.a., charrier, charroyer, voiturer.
cartage (cârt'édje), n., charriage, charroi, transport, m.
carte (cârte), n., carte, f. ; menu, m.
carte-blanche (cârte-), n., carte blanche, f.
cartel, n., cartel, m.
cartel-ship (-shipe), n., cartel, bâtiment parlementaire, m.
carter, n., charretier, roulier, m.
cartesian (-tï-), adj., cartésien.
cartesian, n., cartésien, m.

21

cartesianism, *n.*, cartésianisme, *m.*

carthaginian, *adj.*, carthaginois.

carthaginian (câr-tha-dji-), *n.*, Carthaginois, *m.*, Carthaginoise, *f.*

carthamus (câr-tha-), *n.*, (bot.) carthame, *m.*

carthusian (-thiou'ja'n), *n.*, chartreux.

cartilage (câr-ti-lédje), *n.*, cartilage, *m.*

cartilaginous (câr-ti-ladj'i), *adj.*, cartilagineux.

cart-load (-lôde), *n.*, charretée, *f.*

cartoon (-toune), *n.*, carton, *m.*

cartouch, *n.*, (artil.) boîte à mitraille, *f.*; (arch.) cartouche, *m.*; (milit.) giberne, *f.*

cartridge (câr-), *n.*, cartouche; (of cannon —*de canon*) gargousse, *f.*

cartridge-box, *n.*, giberne, *f.*

cartrut (-reute), *n.*, ornière, *f.*

cart-shed (-shède), *n.*, hangar, *m.*

cartwright (-raïte), *n.*, charron, *m.*

caruncle (-'ung'k'l), *n.*, caroncule, *f.*

carve (cârve), *v.a.* and *n.*, tailler; graver; couper; ciseler; (meat—*la viande*) découper; sculpter.

carver, *n.*, personne qui découpe, *f.*; écuyer tranchant; (sculpt.) sculpteur, *m.*

carving, *n.*, action de découper; (sculpt.) sculpture, *f.*

caryatides, *n.*, *pl.*, cariatide, caryatide, *f.*

cascade (-kéde), *n.*, cascade, *f.*

case (kéce), *n.*, étui, *m.*; enveloppe; (for packing—*à empaqueter*) caisse; (print.) casse; (of a watch—*de montre*) boîte, *f.*; cas, état; (gram., math., med.) cas, *m.*; (jur.) cause, *f.* In that —; *dans ce cas, en ce cas.* In —; *au cas que; en cas que: dans le cas où.* Should the — occur; *le cas échéant.*

case, *v.a.*, mettre dans un étui; enfermer; envelopper.

casemate (késs'méte). *n.*, casemate, *f.*

casement (késs'-), *n.*, fenêtre; croisée, *f.*

cash (cashe), *n.*, argent, numéraire, *m.*; espèces, *f.pl.*

cash, *v.a.*, (com.) convertir en espèces; escompter; recevoir; toucher.

cash-account (-ac-cou'n'te), *n.*, compte de caisse, *m.*

cash-book (-bouke), *n.*, livre de caisse, *m.*

cash-box, *n.*, cassette; (com.) caisse, *f.*

cashew-nut (ca-shou-neute), *n.*, noix d'acajou, pomme d'acajou, *f.*

cashew-tree (-trî), *n.*, (bot.) anacardier, *m.*

cashier (-shîre), *n.*, caissier, *m.*

cashier, *v.a.*, (milit.) casser.

cashmere (-mîre), *n.*, cachemire, *m.*

cashoo (-shou), *n.*, cachou, *m.*

casing (-késs'-), *n.*, (carp.) revêtement; chambranle; entourage, *m.*

cask (câske), *n.*, baril, *m.*; barrique, *f.*; tonneau, *m.*

cask, *v.a.*, mettre en baril, en tonneau.

casket (câskète), *n.*, cassette, *f.*; écrin, *m.*

casque, or **cask** (câske), *n.*, casque, *m.*

cassation (-sé'-), *n.*, cassation, *f.*

cassava (-sé-, *ou* -sa-), *n.*, cassave, *f.*

cassia (cash'shi-a), *n.*, casse, *f.*

cassock (-késs'-), *n.*, soutane, *f.*

cast (câste), *v.a.* (*preterit* and *past part.*, Cast), jeter; lancer; condamner; (metal.) couler; (of trees and animals—*d'arbres et d'animaux*) dépouiller; (reptiles) changer (skin —*de peau*); (thea.) distribuer. To — about; *jeter de tous côtés.* To — aside; *jeter à l'écart.* To — away; *jeter.* To — down; *affliger; abattre; décourager; baisser.* To — forth; *exhaler.* To — headlong; *précipiter.* To — off; *rejeter, repousser, abandonner.* To — out; *chasser.* To — up; *additionner, faire l'addition de; vomir.* To—anchor; *jeter l'ancre.*

cast, *v.n.*, se jeter; s'écouler; (nav.) abattre.

cast, *n.*, jet; coup; moule, *m.*; (metal.) fonte; (thea.) distribution; (fig.) nuance, *f.* To have a — in the eye; *loucher.*

castanet, *n.*, castagnette, *f.*

castellan, *n.*, châtelain, *m.*

caster (câst'eur), *n.*, personne qui jette, *f.*; calculateur, *m.*; roulette (of furniture—*de meuble*), *f.*

castigate (-ghéte), *v.a.*, châtier.

castigation (-ghé-), *n.*, châtiment, *m.*; discipline, *f.*

castigator (-ghéteur), *n.*, personne qui punit, *f.*

castigatory, *adj.*, qui punit.

casting (câst'-), *n.*, fonte, *f.*; moulage; calcul, *m.*; (nav.) abatée, *f.*

castle (câs's'l), *n.*, château, *m.*; (at chess—*aux échecs*) tour, *f.*

castle, *v.a.*, (at chess—*aux échecs*) roquer.

castled (câs's'lde), *adj.*, chargé de châteaux.

castor, *n.*, (mam., astron.) castor; chapeau de castor, *m.*

castorine (-raïne), *n.*, castorine, *f.*

castor-oil (câs'tor-oïle), *n.*, huile de ricin, *f.*

castrametation (-mi-té-), *n.*, castramétation, *f.*

castrate (-tréte), *v.a.*, châtrer.

castration (-tré-), *n.*, castration, *f.*

castrato (-trâ-tô), *n.*, castrat, *m.*

casual (caj'iou-), *adj.*, fortuit, accidentel, casuel.

casually, *adv.*, fortuitement, accidentellement.

casualness, or **casualty** (caj'iou-), *n.*, hasard, cas fortuit, *m.*

casuist (ca-jiou-), *n.*, casuiste, *m.*

casuist, *v.n.*, faire le casuiste.

casuistic, or **casuistical**, *adj.*, de casuiste.

casuistically, *adv.*, en casuiste.

casuistry, *n.*, science du casuiste, *f.*

cat (câte), *n.*, chat, *m.*, chatte, *f.*; (milit., nav.) fouet; (nav.) capon (of a ship—*de vaisseau*), *m.*

catachresis (-kri-cisse), *n.*, (rhet.) catachrèse, *f.*

catachrestical (-krèss-), *adj.*, de catachrèse.

catachrestically, *adv.*, par catachrèse.

cataclysm, *n.*, cataclysme, *m.*

catacomb (-coume), *n.*, catacombes, *f.pl.*

catacoustics, *n.pl.*, catacoustique, *f.sing.*

catadioptric, or **catadioptrical**, *adj.*, catadioptrique.

catafalco, *n.*, catafalque, *m.*

catalepsy, *n.*, catalepsie, *f.*

cataleptic, *adj.*, cataleptique.

catalogue, *n.*, catalogue, *m.*

catamenia (-mî-), *n.*, flux menstruel, *m.*, règles, *f.pl.*

catapasm, *n.*, mélange de poudres pour saupoudrer le corps, *m.*

catapult (-peulte), *n.*, catapulte, *f.*

cataract, *n.*, cataracte, *f.* The —s of the Nile; *les cataractes du Nil.* To couch a —; (med.) *abaisser une cataracte.*

catarrh (ka-târ), *n.*, catarrhe, *m.*

catarrhal, *adj.*, catarrhal.

catastrophe (-fi), *n.*, catastrophe, *f.* (thea.) dénoûment, *m.*

catcall (-kôl), *n.*, (thea.) sifflet, *m.*

catch, *n.*, prise; (fig.) belle affaire, attrape, *f.*; crampon (of a door—*de porte*) anneau; (of a latch—*d'un loquet*) mentonnet; (mus.) air à reprises; (print.) visorium, *m.*

catch, *v.a.*, (*preterit* and *past part.*, Caught), attraper; prendre; saisir; surprendre. — at; *s'empresser de saisir.* — cold; *s'enrhumer.* — up; *saisir; relever; rattraper, atteindre.* To — any one crying; *surprendre quelqu'un à pleurer.*

He is gone, but I shall — him up; *il est parti, mais je le rattraperai.*

catch, *v.n.,* s'accrocher, s'engager.

catcher, *n.,* attrapeur, *m.,* attrapeuse, *f.*

catchfly (-fla'ye), *n.,* (bot.) silène, *f.,* attrape-mouche, *m.*

catching, *adj.,* qui saisit; contagieux. To be —; *être contagieux.*

catchpenny (-pèn'ni), *n.,* moyen d'attraper de l'argent, *m.*

catchword (-weurde), *n.,* (print.) réclame, *f.*

catechism (cat'i-kiz'm), *n.,* catéchisme, *m.*

catechist (-kiste), *n.,* catéchiste, *m.*

catechistical (-kis'-), *adj.,* de catéchiste; de catéchisme.

catechize (cat'i-kaïze), *v.a.,* catéchiser; interroger.

catechizer (-kaïz'-), *n.,* catéchiste, *m.*

catechumen (-kiou-mène), *n.,* catéchumène, *m.f.*

categorical (cat'i-), *adj.,* catégorique.

categorically, *adv.,* catégoriquement.

category (cat'i-), *n.,* catégorie, *f.*

catenarian (cat'i-né-), *adj.,* en chaîne, comme une chaîne.

catenate (cat'i-néte), *v.a.,* enchaîner, lier.

catenation (-né-), *n.,* enchaînement, *m.*

cater (ké-), *v.n.,* pourvoir à.

cater, *n.,* (at cards—*aux cartes*) quatre, *m*

caterer, *n.,* pourvoyeur, *m.*

cateress (ca-), *n.,* pourvoyeuse, *f.*

caterpillar, *n.,* chenille, *f.*

caterwaul, *v.n.,* (of the cat—*du chat*) appeler; miauler; (fig.) faire une musique de chat.

caterwauling, *n.,* sabbat des chats, *m.*

catfish (-fishe), *n.,* (ich.) loup de mer, *m.,* (*anarhicas lupus*).

catgut (-gheute), *n.,* corde à boyau, *f.,* — ; scraper; *racleur, m.*

cathartic (-thâr-), *adj.,* cathartique.

cathartic, *n.,* cathartique, *m.*

catharticalness, *n.,* qualité cathartique, *f.*

cathead (cat'hède), *n.,* (nav.) bossoir, *m.*

cathedral (-thi-), *n.,* cathédrale, *f.*

catheter (cath-), *n.,* cathéter, *m.*

cat-hole (-hôle), *n.,* chatière, *f.*

catholic (cath-), *adj.,* catholique.

catholic, *n.,* catholique, *m.f.*

catholicism, *n.,* catholicisme, *m.*

catholicity, *n.,* catholicité, *f.*

catholicly, *adv.,* catholiquement; universellement.

catholicness, *n.,* universalité, *f.*

catholicon (ca-tho-), *n.,* électuaire purgatif, catholicon, *m.*

catkin (cat'kine), *n.,* (bot.) chaton, *m.*

catling, *n.,* corde à violon, *f.*

catmint (cat'mi'n'te), *n.,* (bot.) cataire, chataire, herbe aux chats, *f.*

cat-o-nine-tails (-naéne't'elze), *n.,* fouet à neuf lanières, *m.*

catoptric, or **catoptrical**, *adj.,* catoptrique.

catoptrics (-trikse), *n.pl.,* catoptrique, *f. sing.*

cat's-eye (-a'ye), *n.,* (min.) œil-de-chat, *m.*

cat's-foot (-foute), *n.,* (bot.) pied-de-chat, lierre terrestre, *m.*

cat-skin, *n.,* peau de chat, *f.*

cat's-paw (-pô), *n.,* patte de chat, *f.* To be any one's —; *tirer les marrons du feu pour quelqu'un.*

cat's-pur (-peur), *n.,* (med.) frémissement cataire, *m.*

cat's-tail (-téle), *n.,* (bot.) massette, *f.*

catsup (cat'seupe), *n.,* sauce piquante faite de champignons, *f.*

cat-thyme (-taïme), *n.,* marum, *m.;* germandrée maritime, *f.*

cattle. *n.,* bétail, *m.;* bestiaux, *m.pl.* Black — ; *gros bétail.*

cattle show (-shô), *n.,* exposition de bétail, *f.*

cat-tribe (cat'traïbe), *n.sing.,* (zool.) félins, *m.pl.*

caudex, *n.* (*caudices*), caudex, *m.*

caudine, *adj.,* caudine. — forks; *fourches caudines, f.pl.*

caudle, *n.,* brouet, chaudeau, *m.*

caudle, *v.a.,* faire du brouet de.

caught (côte). *V.* **catch**.

caul, *n.,* coiffe de réseau; coiffe d'enfant, *f.*

cauliflower (col'li-flaou'eur), *n.,* chou-fleur, *m.*

cauline (cô-laïne), *adj.,* (bot.) caulinaire.

causable, *adj.,* qui peut être causé.

causal, *adj.,* causal.

causality, *n.,* causalité, *f.*

causally, *adv.,* suivant l'ordre des causes.

causative, *adj.,* causatif.

cause (cô-ze), *n.,* cause, *f.*

cause, *v.a.,* causer; occasioner. To — sorrow; *donner du chagrin.* To — to be punished; *faire punir.*

causeless, *adj.,* sans cause.

causelessly, *adv.,* sans cause.

causer, *n.,* cause, *f.*

causeway (-wé), *n.,* chaussée; digue, jetée, *f.*

caustic, *adj.,* caustique.

caustic, *n.,* caustique, *m.* Lunar — ; *pierre infernale, f.*

cautelous (-tî-), *adj.,* (ant.) prudent; cauteleux, rusé, fin.

cautelously, *adv.,* cauteleusement, prudemment.

cauterization (-tèr'aï-zé-), *n.,* cautérisation, *f.*

cauterize (-tèr'aïze), *v.a.,* cautériser.

cauterizing, *n.,* cautérisation, *f.*

cautery (-tèr'i), *n.,* cautère, *m.*

caution (cô'sheune), *n.,* avis, *m.;* précaution; garantie, *f.*

caution, *v.a.,* précautionner; avertir, aviser.

cautionary, *adj.,* d'avertissement, de prévoyance, de précaution.

cautious (cô'sheusse), *adj.,* précautionné, circonspect, prudent.

cautiously, *adv.,* avec précaution, prudemment.

cautiousness, *n.,* prévoyance, circonspection, *f.*

cavalcade (-kéde), *n.,* cavalcade, *f.*

cavalier (-lire), *n.,* cavalier, *m.*

cavalier, *adj.,* vaillant, courageux; cavalier, *m.*

cavalierly, *adv.,* cavalièrement.

cavalry, *n.,* cavalerie, *f.*

cavatina (-tî-), *n.,* cavatine, *f.*

cavation (-vé-), *n.,* (ant.) (arch.) excavation, *f.*

cave (kéve), *n.,* caverne, *f.;* antre, *m.*

cave, *v.a.,* creuser.

cave, *v.n.,* habiter une caverne.

cavern (cav'eurne), *n.,* caverne.

cavernous, *adj.,* caverneux.

cavesson (cav'ès'seune), *n.,* (man.) caveçon, *m.*

caviare (-ére), *n.,* caviar, *m.*

cavil, *n.,* pointillerie; chicane, *f.*

cavil, *v.n.,* pointiller; chicaner.

cavil, *v.a.,* (ant.) contester.

caviller, *n.,* chicanier, chicaneur, *m.*

cavillingly, *adv.,* par pointillerie, par des chicanes.

cavillous, *adj.,* chicanier.

cavillously, *adv.,* par pointillerie.

cavity, *n.,* cavité, *f.*

caw (cô), *v.n.,* croasser.

cease (cîce), *v.n.,* cesser, discontinuer.

cease, *v.a.,* cesser, faire cesser.

ceaseless, *adj.*, incessant, continuel.
ceaselessly, *adv.*, sans cesse.
ceasing, *n.*, cessation, *f.*
cecity (cè-ci-, *ou* ci-ci), *n.*, cécité, *f.*
cedar (ci-), *n.*, cèdre, *m.*
cede (cide), *v.a.* and *n.*, céder.
cedilla (ci-), *n.*, (gram.) cédille, *f.*
cedrate (ci-drète), *n.*, cédrat, *m.*
cedrine (ci-), *adj.*, de cèdre.
cedry (ci-), *adj.*, de la couleur du cèdre.
ceil (cile), *v.a.*, plafonner.
ceiling, *n.*, plafond ; plafonnage, *m.*
celebrate (cèl'i-brète), *v.a.*, célébrer.
celebrated (-tède), *past part.*, célébré ; célèbre, *adj.*
celebration (-bré-), *n.*, célébration ; louange, *f.* ; éloge, *m.*
celebrator (-teur), *n.*, panégyriste, *m.*
celebrity (ci-lèb'-), *n.*, célébrité, *f.*
celerity (ci-lèr'-), *n.*, célérité, *f.*
celery (cèl'i-), *n.*, céleri, *m.* Bundle of —; *botte de céleri, f.*
celestial (ci-lès-), *adj.*, céleste.
celestial, *n.*, habitant du ciel, *m.*. The —s ; *les habitants du céleste empire, les Chinois.*
celestially, *adv.*, d'une manière céleste.
celiac (ci-), *adj.*, (anat.) céliaque.
celibacy (cèl'-), *n.*, célibat, *f.*
cell (cèle), *n.*, cellule, *f.* ; compartiment, *m.*
cellar (cèl'lar), *n.*, cave, *f.*
cellarage (-édje), *n.*, caves, *f.pl.*
cellaret (-rète), *n.*, cave à liqueurs, *f.*
cellarist, *n.*, cellérier, *m.*, cellérière, *f.*
cellular (cèl'liou-), *adj.*, cellulaire.
celt (kelte), *n.*, Celte, *m.f.*
celtic, *adj.*, celtique.
cement (cèm'-), *n.* ciment, mastic ; cément, *m.*
cement, *v.a.*, cimenter ; cémenter.
cementation (-té-), *n.*, cémentation, *f.*
cemetery (cèm'i-tèr'i), *n.*, cimetière, *m.*
cenatory (cèn'a-teuri), *adj.*, du souper.
cenobite (cèn'o-baïte), *n.*, cénobite, *m.*
cenobitic, *or* **cenobitical**, *adj.*, (ant.) cénobitique.
cenotaph (cèn'-), *n.*, cénotaphe, *m.*
cerse, *n.*, (ant.) impôt, *m.* ; taxe, *f.*
cense (cèn'se), *v.a.*, encenser.
censer (cè'n'-), *n.*, encensoir, *m.*
censor (cè'n'-seur), *n.*, censeur, *m.*
censorial, *or* **censorian** (-sô-), *adj.*, censorial.
censorious (-sô-), *adj.*, de censeur ; critique
censoriously, *adv.*, en censeur.
censoriousness, *n.*, disposition à la censure, *f.*
censorship (-seur-), *n.*, fonctions de censeur, *f.pl.* ; censure, *f.*
censurable (cè'n'shiou-), *adj.*, censurable blâmable.
censurably, *adv.*, d'une manière censurable.
censure (cè'n'shioure), *n.*, censure, critique, *f.*, blâme, *m.*
censure, *v.a.*, censurer, critiquer, blâmer.
censurer, *n.*, censeur ; critique, *m.*
census (cè'n'-), *n.*, recensement, dénombrement, *m.*
cent (cè'n'te), *n.*, cent, *m.* Ten per —; *dix pour cent.*
centaur (cè'n'-), *n.*, centaure, *m.*
centaury (cè'n'-), *n.*, (bot.) centaurée, *f.*
centenary (cè'n'ti-né-), *adj.*, centenaire.
centennial (cè'n'tè'n'-), *adj.*, séculaire.
centesimal (cè'n'tèss'-), *adj.*, centésimal.
centesimal, *n.*, chiffre centésimal, *m.*
centigrade (cè'n'ti-gréde), *adj.*, centigrade.
centigramme (cè'n'ti-),*n.*, centigramme,*m.*
centime (cè'n'tîme), *n.*, centime, *m.*

centimeter, *or* **centimetre** (cè'n'tim'i-teur), *n.*, centimètre, *m.*
centiped (cè'n'ti-pède), *n.*, (ent.) scolopendre, *f.* ; mille-pieds, *m.*
cento (cè'n'tô), *n.*, centon, *m.*
central (cè'n'-), *adj.*, central.
centrality, *n.*, état central; *m.*; position centrale, *f.*
centralization (-tral'aïzé-), *n.*, centralisation, *f.*
centralize (-'aïze) *v.a.*, centraliser.
centrally, *adv.*, d'une manière centrale.
centre (cè'n'teur), *n.*, centre, *m.*
centre, *v.a.*, placer au centre ; concentrer.
centre, *v.n.*, faire centre ; se concentrer.
centric, *or* **centrical** (cè'n'-), *adj.*, central, placé au milieu.
centrically, *adv.*, dans une position centrale.
centricalness, *n.*, position centrale, *f.*
centrifugal (-trif'iou-), *adj.*, centrifuge.
centripetal (-trip'i-), *adj.*, centripète.
centumvir (cè'n'-teu'm'veur), *n.* (*centumviri*), centumvir, *m.*
centumvirate (-vi-réte), *n.*, centumvirat,*m.*
centuple (-tiou-p'l), *adj.*, centuple.
centuple, *v.a.*, centupler.
centuplicate (-tiou'pli-kéte),*v.a.*, centupler.
centuriate (-tiou'ri'-éte), *v.a.*, (ant.) diviser par centuries.
centurion(cè'n'tiou-ri-eune),*n.*, centurion. *m.*
century (cè'n'tiou-),*n.*,siècle, *m.* ; centurie,*f.*
cephalalgy (-dji), *n.*, céphalalgie, *f.*
cephalic (ci-), *adj.*, céphalique.
cerate (ci-réte), *n.*, cérat, *m.*
cere (cîre), *v.a.*, cirer ; enduire de cire.
cereal (cî'ri-), *adj.*, céréale.
cerebellum (cèr'i-bèl'leume), *n.*, (anat.) cervelet, *m.*
cerebral (cèr'i-), *adj.*, cérébral.
cerecloth (cîr'clôth), *n.*, toile d'embaumement, *f.*
cerement (cîrè-), *n.*, suaire d'embaumement, *m.*
ceremonial (cèr'i-mô-), *adj.*, de cérémonie.
ceremonial, *n.*, cérémonie, *f.* ; cérémonial, *m.*
ceremonially, *adv.*, suivant les cérémonies.
ceremonious, *adj.*, de cérémonie, cérémonieux.
ceremoniously, *adv.*, avec cérémonie.
ceremoniousness, *n.*, manières cérémonieuses, *f.pl.*
ceremony (cèr'i-mo-), *n.*, cérémonie ; façon, *f.* ; cérémonial, *m.* Without — ; *sans façon, sans cérémonie.*
certain (ceur'ti'n), *adj.*, certain.
certainly, *adv.*, certainement.
certainty, *n.*, certitude ; chose certaine, *f.*
certificate (cèr-tif'i-kéte), *n.*, certificat ; (of a bankrupt—*d'un failli*) concordat, *m.*
certifier, *n.*, certificateur, *m.*
certify (ceur-ti-fa'ye),*v.a.*, certifier, déclarer.
certitude (ceur-ti-tioude), *n.*, certitude, *f*
cerulean (ci-rou-li-), *adj.*, bleu.
ceruleous, *adj.*, (ant.). V. **cerulean.**
cerumen (ci-rou-mè'ne), *n.*, cérumen,.*m.*
ceruminous, *adj.*, cérumineux.
ceruse (ci-rouce), *n.*, céruse, *f.* ; blanc de céruse. *m.*
cervical (ceur-), *adj.*, (anat.) cervical.
cesarean (ci-za-ri-), *adj.*, (surg.) césarienne.
cespitous (cèss'pi-), *adj.*, de gazon.
cessation (cès'sé-), *n.*, cessation, *f.*
cessibility, *n.*, qualité de ce qui cède, de ce qui ne résiste pas, *f.*
cessible, *adj.*, qui cède facilement, qui ne résiste pas.
cession (cèsh'eune), *n.*, action de céder, cession, *f.*

cessionary. *adj.*, cessionnaire.
casspool (cèss'poule), *n.*, puisard, *m.*; fosse d'aisances, *f.*
cestus (cès-), *n.*, ceste, *m.*
cesure (cî-jeur), *n.* *V.* **cæsura.**
cetacean (ci-té-sha'n), *n.*, (zool.) cétacé, *m.*
cetaceous (-sheusse), *adj.*, cétacé.
chad (shade), *n.*, alose, *f.*
chafe (tshéfe), *n.*, irritation, *f.*; courroux, *m.*
chafe, *v.a.*, chauffer; courroucer, irriter.
chafe, *v.n.*, s'érailler, s'irriter; s'enflammer.
chafer, *n.*, personne qui s'irrite, *f.*; (ent.) hanneton, *m.*
chafery, *n.*, chaufferie, *f.*
chaff (tshafe), *n.*, menue paille. *f.*
chaffer, *v.n.*, barguigner, marchander.
chafferer, *n.*, barguigneur, *m.*
chaffinch (tshaf'fi'n'she),*n.*,(orni.)pinson,*m.*
chafing (tshéf'-), *n.*, action d'échauffer, *f.*; échauffement,.*m.* ; irritation, *f.*
chafing-dish (-dishe),*n.*, réchaud, *m.*
chafing-pan (-pane), *n.*, chaufferette, *f.*
chagreen (sha-grîne), *n.*, chagrin ; *m.*, peau de chagrin, *f.*
chagrin (sha-grîne), *n.*, chagrin; dépit,*m.*
chagrin, *v.a.*, chagriner, vexer.
chain (tshéne), *n.*, chaine, *f.* (surveying-lever des plans) Gunter's chain; chaine d'arpentage.
chain, *v.a.*, enchaîner.
chainshot (-shote), *n.*, boulets ramés, *m.pl.*, ange, *m.*
chair (tshére), *n.*, chaise, *f.*; siège, *m.*; (of a professor—de professeur) chaire, *f.*; (of the chairman or president of an assembly—d'un président d'assemblée) fauteuil, *m.* Arm— ; fauteuil Sedan— ; chaise à porteurs. Easy— ; bergère, *f.* To be in the —; occuper le fauteuil.
chair-maker (-mék'-), *n.*, fabricant de chaises, *m.*
chairman (-ma'n), *n.*, porteur de chaise; (of an assembly—d'une assemblée) président, *m.*
chair-mendor (-mè'n'd-), *n.*, rempailleur, *m.*, rempailleuse, *f.*
chaise (shéze), *n.*, chaise, *f.* Post-—; chaise de poste.
chalcographer (kal-), *n.*, chalcographe, *m.*
chalcography, *n.*, chalcographie, *f.*
chaldron (tshôl-), *n.*, mesure de trente-six boisseaux, *f.* ; poids de 2,500 livres,*m.*, (for coal —pour la houille).
chalice (tshal'-), *n.*, calice, *m.*, coupe,*f.*
chaliced (tshal'iste), *adj.*, à calice.
chalk (tshôke), *n.*, craie, *f.*; (for drawing—à dessin) pastel, crayon, *m.*
chalk, *v.a.*, blanchiravecdela craie; marquer avec de la craie ; tracer.
chalkiness, *n.*, nature de la craie. *f.*
chalk-pit (-pite), *n.*, carrière de craie, *f.*
chalk-stone (-stône), *n.*, pierre à chaux,*f.*; (med.) calcul arthritique, *m.*
chalky, *adj.*, de craie, crayeux.
challenge (tshal'lè'n'dje), *n.*, cartel ; défi, *m.* ; prétention ; (jur.) récusation, *f.* ; (milit.) qui-vive, *m.*
challenge, *v.a.*, défier; provoquer ; réclamer ; (jur.) récuser ; sommer ; (milit.) reconnaître.
challenger, *n.*, auteur d'un cartel, *m.*; personne qui jette un défi ; (jur.) personne qui récuse un juré, un jury.*f.*
chalybeate (ka-lib'i-éte), *adj.*, ferrugineux.
chalybeate, *n.*, eau ferrugineuse, *f.*
chamade (sha-méde), *n.*,(milit.) chamade,*f.*
chamber (tshé'm'-), *n.*, chambre; (of the nose—du nez) fosse, *f.*; (of a mine—de mine) fourneau, *m.* ; (artil.) chambre, âme,*f.*
chamber, *v.a.*, enfermer dans une chambre.
chamberer, *n.*,homme à intrigues, galant. *m.*

chamberlain (tshé'm'beur-line), *n.*, chambellan ; trésorier, *m.*
chamberlainship, *n.*, dignité de chambellan,*f.*
chamber-maid (-méde), *n.*, femme de chambre ; fille de chambre, fille de service.*f.*
chamber-pot (-pote), *n.*, pot de chambre,*m.*
chameleon (ka-mi-li-),*n.*,(zool.)caméléon,*m.*
chameleonize (-'aïze), *v.a.*, changer de couleurs comme le caméléon.
chamfer, or chamfret(tsha'm-, -frète), *n.*, (arch.) chanfrein, *m.*
chamfer,*v.a.*, (arch.) tailler en chanfrein, chanfreiner.
chamois (sham'mé, ou sha-moi), *n.*, chamois, *m.*
chamois leather (-lètheur), *n.*, chamois, *m.*, peau de chamois, *f.*
chamomile (ca-mô-maïle), *n.*, (bot.) camomille, *f.*
champ (tsha'm'pe), *v.a.*, ronger, mâcher.
champ, *v.n.*, ronger son frein.
champagne (sha'm'péne), *n.*, vin de Champagne, *m.*
champaign (sha'm'péne,.*n.*, campagne,*f.*
champaign, *adj.*, de campagne.
champignon (-pi'n'ieune), *n.*, champignon, *m.*
champion (tsha'm'pi'eune), *n.*, champion, *m.*
champion, *v.a.*, défier au combat.
chance (tshā'n'ce), *n.*, chance, *f.*; hasard, sort; (jur.) cas fortuit, *m.*
chance, *v.n.*, arriver par hasard, venir à.
chance, *adj.*, du hasard, par hasard, de hasard.
chanceable (-'sab'l), *adj.*, accidentel.
chancel (tshā'n'cèle), *n.*, sanctuaire, *m.*
chancellor (tshā'n'cèl'leur), *n.*, chancelier, *m.* Lord- —; grand chancelier, *m.*
chancellorship,*n.*,charge dechancelier,*f.*
chancemedley (-mèd'li), *n.*,(jur.) homicide commis involontairement en se défendant.
chancery (tshā'n'cè-), *n.*, cour de la chancellerie, *f.*
chancre (shangk'eur), *n.*, chancre, *m.*
chancrous (shangk'reusse),*adj.*,chancreux.
chandelier (sha'n'di-lîre), *n.*, lustre, *m.*
chandler (tsha'n'dleur), *n.*, chandelier ; fabricant de chandelles ; petit épicier, *m.*
chandlery, *n.*, petite épicerie,*f.*; regrat, *m.*
change (tshé'n'dje), *n.*, changement, *m.* (abbreviation of exchange, building—édifice) bourse; (out of money—d'argent) monnaie, *f.*, appoint, *m.* I have no —; je n'ai pas de monnaie. A — of linen ; du linge blanc.
change, *v.a.*, changer.
change, *v.n.*, changer; (of the moon—de la lune) se renouveler.
changeable (-'djab'l), *adj.*, changeant, variable.
changeableness, *n.*, caractère variable,*m.*; inconstance; mobilité, *f.*
changeably, *adv.*, inconstamment.
changeful (-foule), *adj.*, inconstant, changeant.
changeling, *n.*, esprit changeant; enfant substitué, *m.*
changer, *n.*, changeur, *m.*
channel (tsha'n'nèle), *n.*, canal, *m.*; (fig.) voie,*f.* The British — ; la Manche,*f.*
channel, *v.a.*, creuser; sillonner.
chant (tsha'n'te), *n.*, chant; plain-chant, *m.*
chant, *v.a.*, chanter.
chant, *v.n.*, chanter; chanter le plain-chant.
chanter, *n.*, chanteur; chantre, *m.*
chanticleer (-ti-clîre), *n.*, réveille-matin (le coq); chantre du jour, *m.*
chanting, *n.*, chant; plain-chant, *m.*
chantress (-trèce), *n.*, chanteuse,*f.*

chaos (ké-oss), *n.* chaos, *m.*

chaotic (ké-), *adj.*, chaotique, de chaos.

chaotically, *adv.*, comme le chaos, en chaos, dans un chaos.

chap (tshape, *ou* tshope),*n.*, homme, garçon, gars, *m.* ; (on the hands, &c.—*aux mains, &c.*) gerçure, crevasse, *f.* Bad — ; *mauvais garnement, m.*

chap, *v.a.*, gercer.

chap, *v.n.*, gercer, se gercer.

chape (tshépe), *n.*, chape, bouterolle, *f.*

chapel (tshap'l), *n.*, chapelle, *f.* ; (print.) atelier, *m.* — of ease ; *église succursale, f.*

chapeless (tshép'lèsse),*adj.*, sans bouterolle.

chaperon (tshap'èr'eune), *n.*, chaperon, *m.*

chaperon, *v.a.*, chaperonner.

chapfallen (tshop'fôl'n), *adj.*, à mâchoire tombante ; l'oreille basse.

chaplain (tshap'line), *n.*, chapelain ; aumônier, *m.*

chaplaincy, *or* **chaplainship**, *n.*, chapellenie,*f.* ; fonctions d'aumônier, *f.pl.*

chapless (tshop'lèsse), *adj.*, aux mâchoires décharnées.

chaplet (tshap'lète), *n.*, chapelet, *m.* ; guirlande ; (of a peacock—*du paon*) aigrette, *f.*

chappy (tshap'-, *ou* tshop'-), *adj.*, plein de gerçures.

chaps (tshopse), *n.*, gueule ; mâchoires ; mâchoires d'étau, *f.*

chapter (tshap'-), *n.*, chapitre. *m.* ; lettre capitulaire, *f.*

chapter, *v.a.*, chapitrer.

chapter-house (-haouce), *n.*,chapitre, *m.*

char (tshâr), *v.a.*, réduire en charbon, carboniser ; purifier (by heat—*par la chaleur*).

char, *or* **chare** (tshar), *v.n.*, aller en journée.

char, *or* **chare** (tshar), *n.*, ouvrage fait à la journée, *m.*

char (tshar), *n.*, (ich.) ombre, *m.*

character (kar'ak-teur), *n.*, caractère ; (thea.)rôle ; personnage ; genre, *m.* ; renommée, réputation, moralité, *f.* ; certificat de moralité, *m.* He is quite a — ; *c'est un vrai original.* A man of bad — ; *un homme de mauvaise réputation.* I do not like books of that — ; *je n'aime pas les livres de ce genre.* What —s does he play? *quels rôles joue-t-il ?* To go for a — (of servants, &c.—*des domestiques*) ; *aller aux informations.* In — ; *dans le vrai ; à sa place.*

character, *v.a.*, inscrire ; écrire, décrire, graver.

characteristic, *or* **characteristical**, *adj.*, caractéristique.

characteristic, *n.*, trait caractéristique, *m.*; (gram., math.) caractéristique, *f.*

characteristically, *adv.*, d'une manière caractéristique.

characteristicalness, *n.*, qualité caractéristique, *f.*

characterize (-'aïze), *v.a.*, caractériser.

characterless, *adj.*, sans caractère.

charade (sha-réde), *n.*, charade, *f.*

charcoal (tshâr'côle), *n.*, charbon de bois ; (chem.) carbone, *m.*

chard (tshârde), *n.*, carde, *f.*

charge (tshârdje), *n.*, charge, *f.* ; fardeau ; (of a judge—*d'un juge*) résumé ; (jur.) chef d'accusation, *m.*, accusation, *f.* ; (milit., vet.) charge, *f.* ; (of a bishop—*d'un évêque*) mandement, *m.* ; (protection) garde, *f.* ; dépôt, objet confié aux soins de ; (price—*prix*) prix, *m.* —s ; *frais, dépens, m.pl.* To give any one in — ; *faire arrêter quelqu'un.*

charge, *v.a.*, charger ; accuser ; faire payer ; adjurer ; (of taxes—*d'impôts*) grever.

charge, *v.n.*, (milit.) charger.

chargeable, *adj.*, à charge ; accusable ; imputable ; imposé, grevé.

chargeableness, *n.*, cherté, haut prix.

chargeably, *adv.*, à grands frais.

charger, *n.*, grand plat ; cheval de bataille, *m.*

charily (tshé'rili), *adv.*, avec précaution ; frugalement ; chichement.

chariness (tshé-), *n.*, précaution, prudence ; mesquinerie, *f.*

chariot (tshar'i-ote), *n.*, coupé, *m.* ; (antiq.) char, *m.*

charioteer (-'ïre), *n.*, conducteur de chariot ; (astron.) cocher, charretier, *m.*

charitable (tshar'i-ta'b'l), *adj.*, charitable.

charitably, *adv.*, charitablement.

charity, *n.*, charité, *f.*

charlatan (tshâr-), *n.*, charlatan, *m.*

charlatanic, *or* **charlatanical**, *adj.*, charlatanesque.

charlatanism, *or* **charlatanry**, *n.*, charlatanerie, *f.* ; charlatanisme, *m.*

charles's-wain (tshârlz'iz'wéne), *n.*, (astron.) chariot, *m.*, grande ourse, *f.*

charm (tshârme), *n.*, charme, *m.*

charm, *v.a.*, charmer.

charmer, *n.*, enchanteur, *m.*, enchanteresse, *f.* ; charmeur, *m.*, charmeuse, *f.*

charming, *adj.*, enchanteur ; charmant ; joli.

charmingly,*adv.*, d'une manière charmante.

charmingness, *n.*, charme, *m.*

charnel (tshâr'nèle), *adj.*, de charnier.

charnel-house (-haouce), *n.*, charnier, *m.*

chart (tshârte), *n.*, carte de géographie ; carte marine, *f.*

charter (tshar'-), *n.*, ⊙charte ; charte, *f.*

charter,*v.a.*,instituer par une charte ; (com., nav.) fréter, affréter, noliser (in the Mediterranean—*dans la Méditerranée*).

charter-party (-pâr-), *n.*, charte partie, *f.*

char-woman (tshar-woum'a'n), *n.*, femme de journée, femme de ménage, *f.*

chary (tshér'-), *adj.*, prudent ; économe ; chiche.

chase (tshéce), *n.*, chasse ; poursuite ; (of cannon—*de canon*) volée, *f.* ; (print.) châssis, *m.*

chase, *n.a.*, chasser ; (metal.) ciseler.

chaser, *n.*, chasseur ; (metal.) ciseleur, *m.*

chasm (kaz'm), *n.*, brèche, *f.* ; vide, abîme, *m.*

chaste (tshéste), *adj.*, chaste, pudique.

chastely, *adv.*, chastement, pudiquement.

chasten (tshés's'n), *v.a.*, châtier ; réprimer ; purifier.

chastener (tshés's'-neur), *n.*, celui qui châtie, *m.*

chasteness (tshést'-), *n.*, pureté de langage, de style, *f.*

chastening. *n.*, châtiment, *m.*

chastise (tshas'taïze), *v.a.*, châtier.

chastisement, *n.*, châtiment, *m.*

chastiser, *n.*, personne qui châtie, *m.*

chastity (tshas'-), *n.*, chasteté, pureté, *f.*

chasuble (shaz'iou-b'l), *n.*, chasuble, *f.*

chat (tshate), *n.*, causerie, *f.* ; (orni.) traquet, *m.*

chat, *v.n.*, causer ; jaser.

chatellany (châ'tèl'-), *n.*, châtellenie, *f.*

chatoyant (sha-to'ya'nte),*adj.*, chatoyant.

chatoyment (sha-toi'-), *n.*, chatoiement, chatoîment, *m.*

chattel (tshat't'l), *n.*, biens, effets, *m.pl.*

chatter (tshat'-), *v.n.*, jaser ; (of the teeth—*des dents*) claquer.

chatter-box (-bokse), *n.*, babillard, *m.*, babillarde, *f.*

chatterer, *n.*, jaseur, babillard, *m.*

chattering,*n.*,jaserie,*f.* ; babil,caquetage,*m.*

chatty (tshat'-), *adj.*, causeur.

chatwood (tshat'woude), *n.*, fagot de broussailles, *m.*

chaw (tshô), *v.a.*, mâcher.

chawâron (tshŏ-), *n.,* entrailles, *f.pl.*

cheap (tshîpe), *adj.,,* à bon marché ; économique.

cheapen, *v.a.,* marchander ; diminuer la valeur de.

cheapener, *n.,* personne qui marchande, *f.*

cheaply, *adv.,* à bon marché ; économiquement.

cheapness, *n.,* bon marché, *m.*

cheat (tshîte), *n.,* (thing—*chose*) fourberie, tromperie, *f.;* (pers.) fourbe, *m.,* trompeur, *m.,* trompeuse, *f.,* tricheur, *m.,* tricheuse, *f.*

cheat, *v.a.,* tromper, tricher.

cheater, *n.,* fourbe, *m.f.;* tricheur, *m.,* tricheuse, *f.*

cheating, *n.,* fourberie ; tromperie, tricherie, *f.*

check (tshèke), *v.a.,* faire éprouver un échec à ; contenir, arrêter ; reprendre ; vérifier ; (at chess—*aux échecs*) faire échec à.

check (tshèke), *n.,* échec, *m.;* réprimande ; (thea.) contremarque, *f.* ; (com.) mandat, bon, chèque, *m.* ; toile de coton rayée, *f.;* (at chess—*aux échecs*) échec, *m.*

check-book (-bouke), *n.,* livre de mandats, *m.*

checker, *v.a.,* marqueter; diaprer; tacheter.

checker-work (-weurke), *n.,* marqueterie, *f.*

checkmate (-méte), *n.,* échec et mat, *m.*

checkmate, *v.a.,* faire échec et mat à ; mater.

checkstring (-strigne), *n.,* cordon de communication avec le cocher d'une voiture, *m.*

check-taker (-té-), *n.,* receveur de contremarques, *m.*

cheek (tshîke), *n.,* joue ; (of a press—*de presse*) jumelle ; (of scales—*de balance*) chasse, *f.*

cheek-bone (-bône), *n.,* os malaire ; os de la pommette, *m.*

cheer (tshîre), *n.,* chère ; acclamation, *f.;* applaudissement, *m.;* gaieté ; consolation, *f.;* vivat, *m.*

cheer, *v.a.,* égayer, réjouir ; animer ; applaudir.

cheer, *v.n.,* se réjouir ; crier vivat. To — up ; *se ranimer ; s'égayer.*

cheerer, *n.,* personne qui crie vivat ; personne qui répand la joie, *f.;* applaudisseur, *m.*

cheerful (-foule), *adj.,* joyeux, gai.

cheerfully, *adv.,* gaiement, gaîment, joyeusement.

cheerfulness, *n.,* gaieté, gaîté, *f.*

cheerily, *adj.,* gaiement, gaîment.

cheering, *n.,* consolation, *f.;* applaudissement, *m.*

cheering, *adj.,* consolant, réjouissant, encourageant.

cheerless, *adj.,* triste.

cheerly, *adv.,* gaiement, gaîment.

cheery, *adj.,* gai.

cheese (tshîze), *n.,* fromage, *m.*

cheesemonger (-meun'gh'eur), *n.,* marchand de fromage.

cheese-paring (-pér'-), *n.,* pelure de fromage, *f.*

cheese-rennet (-rè'n'nète), *n.,*(bot.) gaillet, caille-lait blanc, *m.*

cheesy (tshîzi), *adj.,* fromageux, caséeux.

chemical (kè'm'-), *adj.,* chimique.

chemically, *adv.,* chimiquement.

chemise (shi-mîze), *n.,* chemise, *f.*

chemist (kè'm'-), *n.,* chimiste; pharmacien, *m.*

chemistry (kè'm'-, *ou* ki'm'-), *n.,* chimie, *f.*

cheque (tshèke), *n.,* (com.) bon, mandat, chèque, *m.*

chequer (tshèk'-), *n.,* mosaïque, *f.;* tré-

sorerie. *f.,* trésor, *m.;* *abréviation de* exchequer, *trésor public.*

cherish (tshèr'-), *v.a.,* chérir ; nourrir.

cherry (tshèr'-), *n.,* cerise, *f.*

cherry, *adj.,* de cerise, rouge comme la cerise.

cherry-cheeked (-tshîk'te), *adj.,* aux joues vermeilles.

cherry-laurel (-lô-), *n.,* laurier-cerise, *m.*

cherry-stone (-stône), *n.,* noyau de cerise, *m.*

cherry-tree (-trî), *n.,* cerisier, *m.*

cherub (tshèr'eube), *n.* (*cherubs, cherubim*), chérubin, *m.*

cherubic, *or* **cherubical** (tshè-roub'), *adj.,* de chérubin.

cherubin (tshèr'iou-bine), *adj.,* angélique.

cherubin, *n.,* (*cherubim*). *V.* **cherub.**

chervil (tsheur'-), *n.,* cerfeuil, *m.*

chess (tshèsse). *n.,* échecs, *m.pl.*

chess-board (-bôrde), *n.,* échiquier, *m.*

chess-man (-ma'n), *n.,* pièce, *f.*

chessom (tshè's'-), *n.,* terre franche, terre végétale, *f.*

chess-player (-plé-eur), *n.,* joueur d'échecs, *m.*

chest (tshèste), *n.,* caisse, *f.,* coffre, *m.;* (of the body—*du corps*) poitrine, *f.;* (of a horse—*du cheval*) poitrail, *m.;* (milit.) caisson, *m.*

chest, *v.a.,* encoffrer, mettre dans un coffre.

chest-founder, *or* **chest-foundering** (-faou'n'd'-), *n.,* (vet.) courbature ; phtisie pulmonaire, *f.*

chest-foundered (-faou'n'd'eurde), *adj.,* (vet.) courbatu ; phtisique.

chestnut (-neute), *n.,* châtaigne, *f.;* marron, *m.*

chestnut, *adj.,* châtain ; (of horses—*du cheval*) alezan.

chestnut-tree (-trî), *n.,* châtaignier, marronnier, *m.*

cheval-glass (shèv'al-glâce), *n.,* psyché, *f.*

chevalier (-lîre), *n.,* chevalier, cavalier, *m.*

chevaux-de-frise (shèv'ô-dè-frîze), *n.pl.,* (fort.) chevaux de frise, *m.pl.* ; [*sing.* (l.u.) cheval de frise, *m.*]

chew (tshiou), *v.a.,* mâcher ; ruminer. To — tobacco ; *chiquer.*

chewer, *n.,* mâcheur, *m.*

chewing, *n.,* mastication, *f.*

chicane (tshi-kéne), *n.,* chicane, *f.*

chicane, *v.n.,* chicaner.

chicaner, *n.,* chicaneur, *m.,* chicaneuse, *f.*

chicanery. *n.,* chicanerie, chicane, *f.*

chick (tshike), *n.,* poussin, poulet, *m.,* poulette, *f.*

chicken (tshick'ène), *n.,* poulet, *m.*

chicken-hearted (-hârtède), *adj.,* au cœur de poule ; timide.

chicken-pox (-pokse), *n.,* petite vérole volante, *f.*

chickling, *n.,* poussin, *m.*

chickpea (-pî), *n.,* pois chiche, *m.*

chickweed (-wîde), *n.,* morgeline, *f.,* mouron desoiseaux, *m.*

chicory (tshik'-), *n.,* chicorée, *f.*

chide (tshaïde), *v.a.,* gronder, blâmer.

chide, *v.n.,* gronder.

chider. *n.,* grondeur, *m.,* grondeuse, *f.*

chiding, *n.,* gronderie, *f.*

chidingly, *adv.,* en grondant.

chief (tshîfe), *n.,* chef, *m.;* partie principale, *f.;* (com.) associé principal, *m.*

chief, *adj.,* principal ; en chef.

chiefless, *adj.,* sans chef.

chiefly, *adv.,* surtout ; principalement.

chieftain (-tine), *n.,* chef, *m.*

chiffonnier (shif-fo'n'îre), *n.,* chiffonnier (furniture—*meuble*), *m.*

chilblain (tshil'blène), *n.,* engelure, *f.*

child (tshaïlde), n. (*children*), enfant, m.f. Good —; *enfant sage*. Naughty —; *enfant méchant*. To be a good —; *être sage*. To be a naughty —; *être méchant*. To be with —; *être enceinte, être grosse*.

child-bearing (-bèr'-), n., travail d'enfant, m.

childbed (-bède), n., couches, f.pl.

childbirth (-beurth), n., enfantement, m.; couches, f.pl.

childe (tshaïlde), n., chevalier,'m.

childhood (-houde), n., enfance, f.

childish, adj., enfant, puéril, enfantin.

childishly, adv., puérilement.

childishness, n., puérilité, f.; enfantillage, m.; seconde enfance, f.

childless, adj., sans enfant.

childlike (-laïke), adj., comme un enfant, enfantin, puérile.

children, n.pl. V. **child**.

chili (tshili), n., poivre de Guinée, m.

chill (tshile), n., froid, m.; glace, f.

chill, adj., froid; glacé.

chill, v.a., refroidir; glacer.

chilliness, or **chillness**, n., froid; (med.) drissonnement, m.

chillness, n. V. **chilliness**.

chilly, adj., (pers.) frileux; (of things—*des choses*) un peu froid.

chiltern hundreds (tshiltèrne hun'n'-dredze), n., commune de Chiltern, f. To accept the —; *donner sa démission de membre de la Chambre des Communes*.

chime (tshaïme), n., carillon; son harmonieux, m.

chime, v.n., carillonner.

chime, v.n., accorder; battre la cloche pour carillonner.

chimer, n., carillonneur, m.

chimera (ki-mi-), n., chimère, f.

chimerical (ki-mèr'i-), adj., chimérique.

chimerically, adv., chimériquement.

chimney (tshim'ni), n., cheminée, f.

chimney-corner (-cor-neur), n., coin du feu, m.

chimney-draught (-drâfte), n., tirage de cheminée, m.

chimney-flue (-flou), n., tuyau de cheminée, m.

chimney-piece (-pîce), n., cheminée, f.; chambranle de cheminée, m.

chimney-pot (-pote), n., mitre de cheminée, f.

chimney-stack, n., corps de cheminée, m.

chimney-sweep, or **chimney-sweeper** (-swipe,'eur), n., ramoneur, m.

chin (tshi'n), n., menton, m.

china (tshaï-), n, porcelaine, f.

chincough (-kôf), n., coqueluche, f.

chine (tshaïne), n., (anat.) échine; (cook.) échinée, f.

chine, v.a, couper l'échine de.

chinese (tshaï-nîze), adj., chinois.

chinese, n., Chinois, m., Chinoise, f.; (language—*langue*) chinois, m.

chink (tshi'n'ke), n., crevasse,fente.lézarde,f.

chink, v.a., crevasser, faire crevasser; faire sonner.

chink, v.n., se fendiller, se crevasser; (of metallic substances—*des métaux*) sonner.

chinky, adj., crevassé.

chintz (tshi'n'tse), n., indienne; perse, toile peinte, f.

chip (tshipe), n., copeau, fragment, éclat. m.

chip, v.a., couper, tailler; chapeler (bread—*du pain*).

chip, v.n., éclater; s'éclater.

chipping, n., fragment, éclat, m.; (of bread—*de pain*) chapelure, f.

chiragra (kaï-ré-), n., (med.) chiragre, f.

chirology (ki-rol-o-dji), n, chirologie, f.

chiromancy (ki-), n., chiromancie, f.

chiroplast (ki-), n., (piano) guide-main, m.

chirp (tsheurpe), n., gazouillement, ramage; (of some insects—*d'insectes*) cri, m.

chirp, v.n., gazouiller; (of some insects—*d'insectes*) crier.

chirper, n., oiseau qui gazouille, m.; personne qui gazouille; personne joyeuse, f.

chirping, n., gazouillement, ramage; (of some insects—*d'insectes*) cri, m.

chirurgeon (ki-reur-dj'-), n., (ant.) V. surgeon.

chisel (tshiz'èl), n., ciseau, m.

chisel, v.a., ciseler.

chit (tshite), n., germe; (fig.) marmot, petit enfant, m.

chit, v.n., germer.

chitchat (tshit'shate), n., babil, caquet, m., causerie, f.

chitterlings (tshit'tèr-lign'ze), n.pl., tripes, andouilles, f.pl.

chitty (tshit'-), adj., (ant.) enfantin, puéril.

chivalric, or **chivalrous** (shiv'-), adj., chevaleresque; de chevalerie.

chivalry, n., chevalerie, f.

chlorate (klô-réte), n., chlorate,m.

chloride (-ride), n., chlorure, m.

chlorine (-rine), n., chlore, m.

chlorosis (klo-rô-zice), n.,chlorose,f.; pâles couleurs, f.pl.

choak (tshôke), v.a. V. **choke**.

chocolate (tshok'o-léte), n., chocolat, m.—pot; *chocolatière*, f. — -stick; *moussoir*, m.

choice (tshoïce), n., choix; objet de son choix, m.

choice, adj., rare, choisi; d'élite; recherché.

choiceless, adj., qui n'a pas de choix.

choicely, adv., avec choix; avec grand soin.

choiceness, n., valeur; qualité recherchée, f.

choir (kwa'eur), n., chœur, m.

choke (tshôke), n., foin d'artichaut, m.

choke, v.a., étouffer, suffoquer.

choke-damp (-da'm'pe),n., air vicié;(mines) gaz étouffant, m.

choke-pear (-père), n., poire d'angoisse, f.

choking, n., étouffement, m.; suffocation, f.

choky, adj, étouffant, suffoquant.

choler (kol'ère), n., bile; colère, f.

cholera (kol'i-), n., (med.) choléra, m. — -morbus; *choléra-morbus*.

choleric (kol'èr'-), adj., cholérique, bilieux; de colère.

cholericness,n.,emportement, m. ; colère,f

cholerine (kol'èr'-), n., cholérine, f.; faux choléra, m.

choose (tshouze), v.a. (*preterit*, Chose; *past part.*, Chosen), choisir; élire; préférer; vouloir. I — to do it; *il me plaît de le faire*.

chooser, n., personne qui choisit, f.

chop (tshope), n., tranche; (tech.) mâchoire, f. —-s (of an animal—*d'animal*); gueule, f. Mutton —; *côtelette de mouton*, f.

chop, v.a., couper; hacher; trafiquer,troquer, échanger. To — off; *trancher, couper*. To — up; *hacher*.

chop, v.n., trafiquer, troquer; (nav.) (of the wind—*du vent*) jouer; (of the sea—*de la mer*) clapoter.

chop-fallen (-fôl'n), adj., à mâchoire tombante; l'oreille basse.

chop-house (-haouce), n., café restaurant,m.

chopper, n., couperet, m., hachette, f.

chopping, n., coupe, action de couper, f.; (nav.) clapotage, m.

chopping-knife (-naïfe), n., couperet, m., hachette, f.

choppy, adj., crevassé.

choral (kô-), adj., en chœur, de chœur.

chord (corde), *n.*, corde, *f.* ; (mus.) accord, *m.*

chord, *v.a.*, accorder un instrument à cordes.

chorion (kô-), *n.*, (anat.) chorion, *m.*

chorister (kor'-), *n.*, chantre, choriste, *m.*

chorography (ko-), *n.*, chorographie, *f.*

chorus (kō-reusse), *n.*, chœur, *m.*

chose, chosen (tshōze, -z'n). *V.* **choose**

chrism (kriz'm), *n.*, chrême, *m.*

christ (kraïste), *n.*, le Christ, *m.*   Jesus —; *Jésus Christ.*

   christen (kris's'n), *v.a.*, baptiser.

   christendom (kris's'n'deume), *n.*, chrétienté, *f.*

   chrisƚening, *n.*, baptême, *m.*

   christian (krist'-), *adj.*, chrétien.

   christian, *n.*, chrétien, *m.*, chrétienne, *f.*

   christianism (kris'ti-).*n.*,christianisme, *m.*, doctrine chrétienne ; chrétienté, *f.*

   christianity, *n.*, religion chrétienne, *f.*, christianisme. *m.*

   christianize (-'aïze), *v.a.*, christianiser.

   christianly, *adj.*, chrétien.

   christianly, *adv.*, chrétiennement.

   christian name (-néme), *n.*, nom de baptême, *m.*

   christmas (kris'meusse), *n.*, Noël, *m.*

   christmas-box, (-bokse), *n.*, étrennes, *f.pl.*

chromatic (kro-), *adj.*, chromatique.

chronic, *or* **chronical** (kro-), *adj.*, chronique.

chronicle (kro'n'-), *n.*, chronique, *f.*

chronicle, *v.a.*, faire la chronique de.

chronicler, *n.*, chroniqueur, *m.*

chronologer, *or* **chronologist** (-djeur, -djiste), *n.*, chronologiste, *m.*

chronologic, *or* **chronological** (kro'n'o-lodjik, -cal), *adj.*, chronologique.

chronologically, *adv.*, chronologiquement.

chronology, *n.*, chronologie, *f.*

chronometer (kro-no'm'i-), *n.*, chronomètre, *m.* ; montre marine, *f.*

chrysalis (kriss'-), *n.* (*chrysalides*), chrysalide, *f.*

chrysolite (kriss'o-laïte), *n.*, chrysolithe, *f.*

chub (tsheube), *n.*, (ich.) chabot ; meunier, *m.*

chubbed (tsheub'de), *adj.*, à grosse tête.

chubby (tsheub'bi), *adj.*, joufflu ; (of the hands—*des mains*) potelé.

chuck (tsheuke), *n.*, gloussement, *m.* ; (term of endearment—*terme d'affection*) poulet, *m.*, poulette, *f.*

chuck (tsheuke), *v.n.*, (of the cock—*du coq*) appeler ; (of the hen—*de la poule*) glousser.

chuck, *v.a.*, donner des petits coups à ; jeter.

chuck-farthing (-fàr-*thigne*), *n.*, fossette, *f.*

chuckle (tsheuk'k'l), *v.n.*, rire.

chuckle, *v.a.*, (of the hen—*de la poule*) appeler, glousser ; caresser.

chuff (tsheufe), *n.*, butor, gros rustre, *m.*

chuffily, *adv.*, en butor, grossièrement.

chuffiness, *n.*, grossièreté, rusticité, *f.*

chuffy, *adj.*, grossier, rustique.

chum (tsheume),*m.*,camarade de chambre,*m.*

chump (tsheu'm'pe), *n.*, tronçon de bois, *m.*

church (tsheurtshe), *n.*, église, *f.* ; (for protestants in catholic countries—*de protestants dans les pays catholiques*) temple, *m.*

church,*v.a.*, célébrer l'office des relevailles.

churching, *n.*, relevailles, *f.pl.*

churchman (-ma'n), *n.*, homme d'église ; partisan de la religion dominante, *m.*

church-rate (-réte), *or* **church-tax** (-takse), *n.*, taxe pour l'entretien de l'église, *f.*

church-warden (-wôr-d'n), *n.*, marguillier, *m.*

churchyard (-yârde), *n.*, cimetière, *m.*

churl (tsheurle),*n.*,paysan, rustre, manant,*m.*

churlish, *adj.*, grossier, rude, dur.

---

churlishly, *adv.*, grossièrement ; rudement, durement.

churlishness, *n.*, grossièreté, dureté,*f.*

churn (tsheurne), *n.*, baratte, *f.*

churn, *v.a.*, baratter, battre.

chyle (kaïle), *n.*, chyle, *m.*

chylifaction (kaïl'i-fak-),*n.*, chylification,*f.*

chyme (kaïne), *n.*, chyme, *m.*

chymist (kim'-). *V.* **chemist**.

cicatrice, *or* **cicatrix**, *n.* (*cicatrices*), cicatrice, *f.*

cicatrize (-traïze), *v.a.* and *n.*, cicatriser ; se cicatriser.

cicerone (tshī-tshi-rō-ni), *n.*, cicérone, *m.*

cicisbeo (tshī-tshis'bē'-o), *n.*, sigisbée, ⊙cicisbée, *m.*

cider (çaï-), *n.*, cidre, *n.* Strong —; *gros cidre.*

ciderist, *n.*, faiseur de cidre, *m.*

cider-kin (-kine), *n.*, petit cidre, *m.*

ciliated (-'ède), *adj.*, (bot.) cilié.

cimeter (sim'i-ƚeur), *n.*, cimeterre, *m.*

cincture (çi'nkt'ieur), *n.*, ceinture, *f.*

cinder, *n.*, cendre ; (of coal—*de houille*) escarbille, *f.*

cinerary (-'i-ré-), *adj.*, cinéraire.

cineration (-'i-ré-), *n.*, cinération,*f.*

cinnabar, *n.*, cinabre, *m.*

cinnamon, *n.*, cannelle, *f.*

cinque (cign'ke), *n.*, (at cards—*aux cartes*) cinq, *m.*

cinque-foil (-foïl), *n.*, quintefeuille ; potentille, *f.*

cinque-ports (-pôrtoe), *n.pl.*, cinq ports, *m.pl.* Warden of the —; *gouverneur des cinq ports, m.*

cinque-spotted (-tède), *adj.*, à cinq taches.

cion (çaï'-), *n.*, (bot.) scion, *m.* ; (ant.) (annat.) luette, *f.*

cipher (saï-), *n.*, chiffre ; zéro ; (fig.) homme nul, *m.*

cipher, *v.a.*, chiffrer ; écrire en chiffre.

cipher, *v.n.*, (pop.) chiffrer ; calculer.

ciphering, *n.*, calcul, *m.* ; arithmétique, *f.*

ciphering-book (-bouke), *n.*, cahier d'arithmétique, *m.*

circean (-ci-), *adj.*, de Circée.

circinate (-néte), *v.a.*, tourner en cercle.

circination (-né-), *n.*, mouvement circulaire, *m.*

circle (ceur'k'l), *n.*, cercle, *m.*

circle, *v.a.*, entourer ; environner.

circle, *v.n.*, former un cercle ; faire le tour.

circled (-k'lde), *adj.*, circulaire, en cercle.

circlet (-clète), *n.*, petit cercle, anneau, *m.*

circling, *adj.*, circulaire, tournoyant ; environnant.

circuit (ceur-kite), *n.*, circuit ; tour, *m.* ; (of the judges—*des juges*) tournée, *f.* On the —; *en tournée.*

circuit, *v.n.*, faire un circuit.

circuit, *v.a.*, faire le tour de.

circuitous (ceur-kiou-i-), *adj.*, détourné.

circuitously, *adv.*, d'une manière détournée.

circuity (ceur-kiou-i-), *n.*, circuit, *m.* ; (of words—*de paroles*) circonlocution, *f.*, détours, *m.pl.*

circular (ceur-kiou-), *adj.*, circulaire ; (of bills of exchange—*de lettres de change*) indirect.

circular, *n.*, circulaire, *f.*

circularity, *n.*, forme circulaire,*f.*

circularly, *adv.*, circulairement ; par circulation.

circulate,*n.*, (math.) fraction périodique, *f.*

circulate, *v.a.*, mettre en circulation.

circulate, *v.n.*, circuler.

circulation (-lā-), *n.*, circulation,*f.*

circulatory (-teu-ri), *adj.*, circulaire ; circulatoire.

circumambient, *adj.*, environnant; ambiant.

circumcise (-saïze), *v.a.*, circoncire.

circumcision (-keu'm'si-jeune), *n.*, circoncision, *f.*

circumference (ceur-keu'm'fèr'-), *n.*, circonférence, *f.*

circumferentor (-teur), *n.*, boussole, *f.*

circumflex (-flèkse), *adj.*, circonflexe.

circumflex, *n.*, (gram.) circonflexe, accent circonflexe, *m.*

circumfluent, *or* **circumfluous** (-fli-ou-), *adj.*, qui coule autour; environnant.

circumfuse (-fiouze), *v.a.*, répandre autour; disperser.

circumfusion (-fiou-jeune), *n.*, action de répandre; expansion, *f.*

circumjacent (-keu'm'djé-), *adj.*, circonvoisin.

circumligation (-ghé-), *n.*, action de lier, *f.*; lien, *m.*

circumlocution (-kiou-), *n.*, circonlocution, *f.*

circummured (-miourde), *adj.*, entouré de murs.

circumnavigate, *v.a.*, naviguer autour de, faire le tour de.

circumnavigation (-ghé-), *n.*, circumnavigation, *f.*

circumscribe (-scraïbe), *v.a.*, circonscrire.

circumscription, *n.*, circonscription, *f.*

circumscriptive, *adj.*, circonscrit.

circumscriptively, *adv.*, d'une manière circonscrite.

circumspect, *adj.*, circonspect.

circumspection, *n.*, circonspection, *f.*

circumspective, *adj.*, circonspect.

circumspectly, *adv.*, avec circonspection.

circumstance, *n.*, circonstance. — s; moyens, *m.pl.*; position, *f.*

circumstance, *v.a.*, placer. As I was —d; dans la position où je me trouvais.

circumstantial (-stan'shal), *adj.*, des circonstances; circonstancié, minutieux.

circumstantially, *adv.*, suivant les circonstances.

circumstantiate (-shi-éte), *v.a.*, circonstancier.

circumvallation (-val'lé-), *n.*, circonvallation, *f.*

circumvent (-vè'n'te), *v.a.*, circonvenir.

circumvention, *n.*, circonvention, *f.*

circumvest (-vèste), *v.a.*, envelopper.

circumvolution (-liou-), *n.*, circonvolution, *f.*

circumvolve, *v.a.*, tourner autour.

circus (ceur-keusse), *n.*, cirque, *m.*

cisalpine (ciss'al-païne), *adj.*, cisalpin.

cist, *n.*, ciste; boîte, caisse, *f.*; sac, *m.*

cistern (-teurne), *n.*, citerne; fontaine; (of barometers—de baromètres) cuvette, *f.*; (of pumps and steam-engines—des pompes et des machines à vapeur) réservoir, *m.*

cit, *n.*, bon bourgeois.

citadel, *n.*, citadelle, *f.*

citation (-té-), *n.*, citation, *f.*

cite (caïte), *v.a.*, citer; astreindre.

citer, *n.*, personne qui fait une citation, *f.*; citateur, *m.*

citicism, *n.*, manières bourgeoises, *f.pl.*

citizen (cit'i-z'n), *n.*, citoyen; habitant, *m.*; habitante, *f.*

citizenship, *n.*, droit de cité, *m.*

citrine (-raïne), *adj.*, citrin.

citron (-reune), *n.*, citron, *m.* — -tree; citronnier, *m.*

citrul (-reule), *n.*, citrouille, *f.*, potiron, *m.*

city, *n.*, ville; cité, *f.*

civet (-'ète), *n.*, civette, *f.*

civic, *adj.*, civique.

civil, *adj.*, civil, municipal; honnête, poli.

civilian, *n.*, légiste en droit civil; étudiant en droit civil; bourgeois, *m.*

civility, *n.*, civilité, honnêteté, politesse, *f.*

civilization (-aïzé-), *n.*, civilisation, *f.*

civilize (-aïze), *v.a.*, civiliser.

civilizer, *n.*, civilisateur, *m.*, civilisatrice, *f.*

civilly, *adv.*, civilement, honnêtement, poliment.

clack, *n.*, caquet; (of a mill—de moulin) cliquet, claquet, *m.*

clack, *v.a.*, caqueter; (of a mill—d'un moulin) cliqueter.

clacking, *n.*, caquetage, *m.*

clad. *V.* **clothe**.

claim (cléme), *n.*, demande, prétention, *f.*; droit, *m.*; (jur.) réclamation, *f.* To lay — to; prétendre à, avoir des droits à.

claim, *v.a.*, demander; réclamer; prétendre à.

claimable, *adj.*, qu'on peut réclamer.

claimant (clém'-), *n.*, personne qui a des prétentions, *f.*; prétendant, *m.*

claimer, *n.* *V.* **claimant**.

clamber (cla'm'-eur), *v.n.*, grimper.

clamminess, *n.*, viscosité, *f.*

clammy, *adj.*, visqueux, gluant; pâteux; humide, moite.

clamorous, *adj.*, bruyant; criard.

clamorously, *adv.*, bruyamment.

clamour (clam'eur), *n.*, clameur, *f.*; bruit, *m.*

clamour, *v.n.*, crier. To — against; crier contre, se récrier contre.

clamp, *n.*, crampon, *m.*; (carp.) emboîture, *f.*

clamp, *v.a.*, (carp.) emboîter.

clan (cla'n), *n.*, clan, *m.*; troupe, *f.*

clandestine, *adj.*, clandestin.

clandestinely, *adv.*, clandestinement.

clandestineness, *n.*, clandestinité, *f.*

clang, *n.*, cliquetis, *m.*

clang, *v.a.* and *n.*, faire résonner; résonner.

clangous, *adj.*, aigu.

clank, *n.*, cliquetis, *m.*

clank, *v.a.*, faire résonner.

clansman (cla'n'z'ma'n), *n.*, membre d'un clan, *m.*

clap, *n.*, coup; battement de mains; (of thunder—du tonnerre) coup, *m.*

clap, *v.a.*, frapper, battre (the hands, the wings—des mains, des ailes); applaudir; claquer; flanquer, fourrer, mettre.

clap, *v.n.*, faire résonner en frappant; commencer avec empressement ou vigueur; claquer des mains, battre des mains.

clapper, *n.*, claqueur; (of a bell—de cloche) battant; (of a mill—de moulin) claquet, *m.*

clapper-claw (-clô), *v.a.*, se battre du bec et des ongles; (fig.) donner des coups de langue à; gronder; injurier, vilipender.

clare-obscure (clér'obs-kioure), *or* **claro-obscure** (clâ-), *n.*, (paint.) clair-obscur, *m.*

claret (-'ète), *n.*, vin de Bordeaux, *m.*

clarification (-ké-), *n.*, clarification, *f.*

clarify (-fa'ye), *v.n.*, se clarifier.

clarify, *v.a.*, clarifier.

clarion, *n.*, clairon, *m.*

clary (clé-), *n.*, (bot.) orvale, toute-bonne, *f.*

clash, *n.*, fracas, coup, choc, *m.*

clash, *v.n.*, résonner, s'entre-choquer; être aux prises; être en opposition; être contraire.

clash, *v.a.*, faire résonner en frappant.

clasp, *n.*, fermoir, *m.*; agrafe, *f.*; (of necklaces and bracelets—de colliers et de bracelets) cadenas, *m.*

clasp, *v.a.*, fermer avec un fermoir; agrafer; cadenasser; serrer; enlacer. To — any one round the neck; sauter au cou de quelqu'un. To — one's hands; joindre les mains.

clasper, *n.*, (bot.) vrille, *f.*

class, *n.*, classe, *f.* — -room; classe.

class, *v.a.*, classer.

classic, *n.*, classique, *m.*

classic, *or* **classical**, *adj.*, classique.

classically, *adv.*, d'une manière classique.

classific, *adj.*, par classes.

classification (-ké-), *n.*, classification, *f.*

classify (-fa'ye), *v.a.*, classifier.

clatter, *n.*, bruit, tapage, *m.*

clatter, *v.n.*, faire du bruit ; claquer ; résonner.

clatterer, *n.*, tapageur ; babillard, *m.*

clattering, *n.*, bruit, *m.*

clause (clôze), *n.*, clause, *f.* ; (gram.)membre de phrase, *m.*, proposition, *f.*

claustral, *adj.*, claustral.

clavate (clé-véte), *adj.*, (bot.) claviforme.

clavation (clé-vé-), *n.*, (anat.) gomphose, *f.*

clavicle (-'k'l), *n.*, (anat.) clavicule, *f.*

clavus, *n.*, (bot.) ergot (disease of rye, &c. —*maladie des céréales*) ; (med.) cor (on the feet— *aux pieds*), *m.*

claw (clô), *n.*, griffe, *f.* ; (bot., zool.) ongle, *m.* ; (of crustaceous animals—*des crustacés*) pince, *f.*

claw, *v.a.*, tirer, déchirer avec les griffes ; mettre en pièces, déchirer ; railler, gronder ; (ant.) flatter ; gratter, chatouiller ; (nav.) faire, courir des bordées, louvoyer ; (pop.) se sauver, s'échapper.

clawed (clô'd), *adj.*, armé de griffes.

clawless, *adj.*, sans griffe.

clay (clè), *n.*, argile ; boue, terre glaise, glaise, *f.* Baked —; *terre cuite.*

clay, *v.a.*, (agri.) marner.

clay-cold (-côlde), *adj.*, froid comme l'argile ; sans vie, mort.

clayey (clè-i), *adj.*, argileux.

claying (clè-igne), *n.*, (sugar-making— *fabrication du sucre*) terrage, *m.* ; (mas.) corroi, *m.*

claying-house (-haouce), *n.*, étuve à sucre, *f.*

clay-marl, *n.*, marne argileuse, *f.*

claymore, *n.*, claymore, *f.*, grande et large épée des Ecossais.

clay-pit, *n.*, argilière, marnière, *f.*

clay-slate (-sléte), *n.*, schiste argileux, *m.*

clean (cline), *adj.*, propre ; (of shoes—*de la chaussure*) ciré ; (of linen—*du linge*) blanc ; (print.) (of proofs—*d'épreuves*) peu chargé ; (fig.) adroit ; net.

clean, *adv.*, entièrement, tout à fait.

clean, *v.a.*, nettoyer ; (sewers, canals, &c.— *égouts, canaux, &c.*) curer ; (of shoes—*les chaussures*) décrotter, cirer ; (chem.) décaper ; (manu.) dégraisser.

cleaning, *n.*, nettoyage ; (of sewers, canals, &c.—*d'égouts, de canaux, &c.*) curage ; (manu.) dégraissage ; (chem.) décapage, *m.*

cleanliness, *n.*, propreté ; netteté, *f.*

cleanly, *adj.*; propre.

cleanly, *adv.*, proprement.

cleanness, *n.*, propreté ; (fig.) netteté, justesse, *f.*

cleanse (clè'n'ze), *v.a.*, nettoyer ; laver; (sewers, canals, &c.—*les égouts, les canaux, &c.*) curer ; (fig.) purifier. To — the blood ; *purifier le sang.*

cleanser, *n.*, chose qui nettoie ; *f.*, (of sewers, canals, &c.—*d'égouts, de canaux, &c.*) cureur ; (med.) abstergent, *m.*

cleansing, *n.*, nettoyage, *m.* ; (fig.) purification, *f.* ; (of sewers, canals, &c.—*d'égouts, de canaux, &c.*) curement, *m.*

clear (clîre), *n.*, (arch.) net ; dans œuvre, *m.*

clear, *adj.*, clair ; net ; innocent ; sans tache ; (arch.) dans œuvre. — of ; *exempt de.* To keep — of ; *ne pas se heurter contre, ne pas s'approcher ; se tenir à distance, éloigné de.*

clear, *adv.*, clair ; net.

clear, *v.a.*, éclaircir ; clarifier ; faire évacuer ;

---

gagner ; (agri.) défricher ; (nav.) parer, dégager. To — a hedge; *franchir une haie.* To — the customs; *acquitter les droits de la douane.* To — from ; *dégager de ; débarrasser de.* To — of ; *purger de ; acquitter de.* To — a good deal of money ; *gagner beaucoup d'argent.* To — the table ; *desservir.* To — up one's brow ; *se dérider le front.* To — for action ; (nav.) *faire branle-bas de combat.*

clear, *v.n.*, (of the weather—*du temps*) s'éclaircir, se rasséréner ; se dissiper. To — up; (of the weather—*du temps*) s'éclaircir ; se rasséréner ; (fig.) s'éclaircir, se débrouiller. To — away; *desservir.*

clearance, *n.*, dégagement ; (nav.) congé, *m.*

clear-headed (-hèdède), *adj.*, qui a l'esprit clair ; à l'esprit clair.

clearly, *adv.*, avec clarté, clairement.

clearness, *n.*, clarté ; netteté ; pureté, *f.*

clear-sighted (-saït'ède), *adj.*, clairvoyant.

clear-sightedness, *n.*, clairvoyance, *f.*

clear-starch (-stärtshe), *v.a.*, blanchir à neuf ; empeser.

clear-starcher, *n.*, blanchisseur de fin, *m.*, blanchisseuse de fin, *f.*

cleat (clîte), *n.*, (nav.) taquet, *m.*

cleavage (clîv'édje), *n.*, action de fendre ; (min.) fente, *f.*

cleave (clîve), *v.n.*, se coller, s'attacher, s'unir.

cleave, *v.a. and n.* (*preterit*, Clove, Cleft ; *past part.*, Cloven, Cleft), fendre, diviser ; se fendre.

cleaver, *n.*, (pers.) fendeur ; (thing—*chose*) fendoir, *m.*

cleavers (clî-veurze), *n.*, (bot.) gaillet, caille-lait, grateron, *m.*

clef (clèfe), *n.*, (mus.) clef, clé, *f.*

cleft (clèfte), *n.*, fente ; ouverture, *f.*

clemency (clè'm'è'n'-), *n.*, clémence ; (of the weather—*du temps*) douceur, *f.*

clement (clè'm'ên'te), *adj.*, doux, clément.

clepsydra (clèp'-;, *n.*, clepsydre, *f.*

clergy (cleur'dji), *n.*, clergé, *m.*

clergyman, *n.*, ecclésiastique, *m.*

clerical (clèr'-), *adj.*, clérical.

clerically, *adv.*, cléricalement.

clerk (clârke, *ou* cleurke). *n.*, (of lawyers and churches—*d'hommes de loi, d'église*) clerc ; (com.) commis ; (in public offices—*d'administration publique*) employé, *m.*

clerkship, *n.*, cléricature ; place de clerc, place de commis, *f.*

clever (clèv'-), *adj.*, adroit, habile.

cleverly, *adv.*, habilement, adroitement.

cleverness, *n.*, habileté, adresse, *f.*

clew (cliou), *n.*, peloton de fil ; peloton ; fil, guide ; (nav.) point de voile, *m.*

clew (cliou). *v.a.*, (nav.) carguer.

click, *v.n.*, faire tic tac ; (print.) mettre en pages.

clicker, *n.*, commis qui invite les passants à entrer ; (print.) metteur en pages, *m.* ; (man.) cheval qui forge, *m.*

clicking, *n.*, (print.) mise en pages, *f.*

client (cla'yè'n'te), *n.*, client, *m.* ; cliente, *f.* —s ; *clientèle, f.*

cliented, *adj.*, ayant des clients.

clientship, *n.*, état de client, *m.* ; dépendance, *f.*

cliff, *n.*, falaise, *f.* ; rocher, *m.* ; (ant.) (mus.) clef, *f.*

cliffy, *adj.*, à falaises ; rocailleux.

climacteric, *or* **climacterical** (-tèr'-), *adj.*, climatérique.

climacteric, *n.*, climatérique, *f.*

climate (claï-), *n.*, climat, *m.*

climax (claï-), *n.*, climax (l.u.), *m.* ; gradation, *f.*

climb (claïme), *v.a.*, grimper; monter; gravir.

climb, *v.a.*, escalader. gravir. monter.

climber, *n.*, personne qui grimpe; (bot.) plante grimpante, *f.*; (orni.) grimpeur, *m.*

clime (claïme), *n.*, climat; pays. *m.*

clinch (cli'n'she), *n.*, mot à deux ententes, *m.*; bonne repartie, *f.*; crampon, *m.*; (nav.) étalingure, *f.*

clinch, *v.a.*, tenir à main fermée; fermer le poing; river; (nav.) étalinguer.

clincher, *n.*, crampon, *m.*; (fig.) bonne repartie; personne qui fait une bonne repartie, *f.*

cling (cligne), *v.n.* (*preterit* and *past part.*, Clung), se cramponner, s'attacher, se tenir, s'accrocher.

cling-stone (-stône), *n.*, pavie, *m.*

clingy, *adj.*, qui s'attache, qui s'accroche.

clinic, *n.*, malade alité, *m.*, malade alitée, *f.*

clinical, *adj.*, (med.) clinique; (theol.) converti au lit de la mort.

clinically, *adv.*, d'une manière clinique.

clink (cli'ngk), *n.*, tintement, cliquetis, *m.*

clink *v.n.*, tinter; résonner.

clink, *v.a.*, tinter; faire résonner.

clip, *v.a.*, couper (with scissors—*avec des ciseaux*); rogner; (dogs and horses—*des chiens et des chevaux*) tondre.

clipper, *n.*, rogneur, *m.*, rogneuse, *f.*; (nav.) fin voilier, *m.*

clipping, *n.*, action de rogner; rognure, *f.*

cloak (clôke), *n.*, manteau; (fig.) masque, *m.*

cloak, *v.a.*, couvrir d'un manteau; (fig.) masquer.

cloakedly, *adv.*, sous le manteau, en cachette.

clock, *n.*, horloge; pendule, *f.*; (of stockings —*de bas*) coin, *m.* Eight-day —; *pendule, horloge qui marche huit jours.* What o'— is it? *quelle heure est-il?* It is one o'—; *il est une heure.* Ornamental —; *pendule.*

clock-maker (-mék'-), *n.*, horloger, *m.*

clock-work (-weurke), *n.*, (horl.) mouvement, *m.*; (fig.) travail régulier, bien ajusté, *m.*; régularité, *f.*

clod, *n.*, motte de terre, *f.*; grumeau, caillot, *m.*

clod, *v.n.*, se cailler, se coaguler, se grumeler.

clod *v.n.*, lancer des mottes de terre contre.

cloddy, *adj.*, plein de mottes; grumeleux.

clodhopper, *n.*, rustre, rustaud, *m.*

clodpate, *n.*, claude, lourdaud, sot, imbécile, *m.*

clodpated (-pét'ède), *adj.*, claude; lourd, hébété.

clodpoll (clod'pol), *n.*, claude, lourdaud, sot, imbécile, *m.*

clog, *n.*, (for an animal—*d'animal*) entraves, *f.pl.*; (for the foot—*chaussure*) socque; (fig.) empêchement, embarras, *m.*

clog, *v.a.*, (animal) entraver; (fig.) entraver, embarrasser.

clog, *v.n.*, s'embarrasser; s'attacher.

cloggy (-ghi), *adj.*, embarrassant; pesant.

cloister (clôis'-), *n.*, cloître, *m.*

cloister, *v.a.*, cloîtrer.

close (clôce), *n.*, clos, enclos, *m.*

close (clôce), *adj.*, clos, bien fermé; compact, étroit; (avaricious, tight—*avare, tendu*) serré; (of the weather—*du temps*) lourd; (of the air—*de l'air*) renfermé; (fig.) mystérieux; discret; attentif, appliqué. — to; *près de.* In — confinement; *au secret.*

close (clôce), *adv.*, serré, de près. — by; *tout près.*

close (clôze), *v.a.*, clore, fermer; terminer; conclure; serrer. To — in; *clore.* To — up; *fermer.*

close (clôze), *v.n.*, se fermer; clore; finir; (milit.) en venir aux mains; (of a wound—*d'une blessure*) se fermer. se cicatriser. To — with; *se rangement par, terminer avec:* (to come to an arrangement—*en venir à un arrangement*) *s'arranger avec.* To — upon; *s'arrêter à, se déterminer à.*

close (clôze). *n.*, fin; clôture; prise (in wrestling—*à la lutte*); *f.*

closely (clôss'li), *adv.*, serré; de près; étroitement; secrètement; strictement.

closeness (clôss'-), *n.*, manière serrée, *f.*; état serré, *m.*; compacité, *f.*; (of the weather —*du temps*) état lourd; air renfermé, *m.*; (fig.) connexion; avarice; discrétion, *f.*

closer (clôz'-), *n.*, ouvrier qui met la dernière main, *m.*

closestool (clôss'stoule), *n.*, chaise percée. *f.*

closet (kloz'ète), *n.*, cabinet; boudoir, *m.*; grande armoire, *f.*

closet (kloz'ète), *v.a.*, enfermer dans un cabinet.

closh, *n.*, (vet.) solbature, *f.*

closing (clôz'-), *n.*, clôture; fin, conclusion, *f.*

closure (clô'jeur), *n.*, clôture, fermeture, *f.*; enclos, *m.*; enceinte, *f.*

clot, *n.*, grumeau; caillot, *m.*

clot, *v.n.*, se cailler; se grumeler.

cloth (clôth), *n.*, (woollen, gold or silver tissue—*tissu d'or, d'argent, de laine*) drap, *m.*; (linen tissue—*tissu de toile*) toile, *f.*; (cotton tissue—*tissu de coton*) calicot, coton, *m.*; (cover for a table—*de table*) tapis, *m.* Table —; *nappe, f.*

clothe (clôthe), *v.a.* (*preterit* and *past part.*, Clad, Clothed), vêtir, revêtir, habiller.

clothes (clôze), *n.*, hardes, *f.pl.*; habits, *m.pl.* Bed —; *draps (m.pl.) et couvertures, f.pl.*

clothier (clôthieur), *n.*, drapier, tailleur, marchand de confection, d'habits tout faits. *m.*

clothing (clôth'-), *n.*, vêtement, habillement, *m.*

clotter, *v.n.*, (ant.) se grumeler; se cailler.

clotty, *adj.*, grumeleux.

cloud (claoude), *n.*, nuage, *m.*; nue; (fig.) nuée, *f.*

cloud, *v.a.*, couvrir de nuages; obscurcir.

cloud, *v.n.*, se couvrir de nuages; se couvrir, s'obscurcir.

cloudcapt, *adj.*, couvert de nuages; s'élevant jusqu'aux nues; extrêmement haut.

cloud-compelling, *adj.*, qui amasse des nuages.

cloudily, *adv.*, avec des nuages; (fig.) obscurément.

cloudiness, *n.*, état nuageux, *m.*; (fig.) tristesse, *f.*

cloudless, *adj.*, sans nuage.

cloudy, *adj.*, nébuleux; ténébreux, sombre.

clout (claoute), *n.*, torchon; chiffon. *m.*; (thump—*coup*) tape, *f.*; (nail—*clou*) clou à tête plate, *m.*; pièce pour raccommoder, *f.* — for children; *lange. m., couche,* ⊙ *braie, f.*

clout, *v.a.*, rapetasser; taper; garnir, de clous.

clouterly, *adj.*, grossier; épais.

clove (clôve), *n.*, clou de girofle, *m.* — of garlic; *gousse d'ail, f.*

clovebark (-bârke), *n.*, cannelle giroflée, *f.*

cloven (clô'v'n), *adj.*, fendu; fourchu.

cloven-footed, or **cloven-hoofed** (-foutède, -houf'te), *adj.*, qui a le pied fendu, fourchu.

clover (clô-), *n.*, trèfle. *m.* In —; *dans l'abondance; à gogo.*

clovered (clô-veurde), *adj.*, couvert de trèfle.

clove-stalk (-stôke), *n.*, griffe de girofle, *f.*

clown (claoune), *n.*, bouffon, paillasse; manant. *m.*

clownish, *adj.*, de paysan; rustre, grossier.

clownishly, *adv.*, en manant.

clownishness, *n.*, rusticité; gaucherie; grossièreté, *f.*

cloy (clo'ye), *v.a.*, rassasier; affadir.

cloyless. *adj.*, qui ne rassasie pas.

cloyment, *n.*, affadissement, *m.*

club (cleube), *n.*, massue; (assembly—*assemblée*) réunion, *f.*, cercle, club, *m.*; cotisation, *f.*; (at cards—*aux cartes*) trèfle, *m.*

club, *v.a.*, cotiser, réunir; renverser.

club, *v.n.*, se réunir, se cotiser.

club-foot (-foute), *n.*, pied bot, *m.*

club-headed (-hèdède), *adj.*, à grosse tête, stupide, bête.

club-law (-lō), *n.*, loi du plus fort, *f.*

cluck (cleuke), *v.n.*, (of the hen—*de la poule*) glousser.

cluck (cleuke), *v.a.*, appeler (of the hen—*de la poule*).

clue (cliou), *n.* *V.* **clew.**

clue, *v.a.* *V.* **clew.**

clump (cleu'm'pe), *n.*, gros bloc; (fig.) groupe, *m.* — of trees; *groupe d'arbres, m.*

clumsily (cleu'm'-), *adv.*, gauchement, maladroitement; grossièrement.

clumsiness, *n.*, gaucherie, maladresse, *f.*

clumsy, *adj.*, grossier; gauche; maladroit, rude.

cluster (cleus'-), *n.*, grappe, *f.*; groupe; amas, *m.*

cluster, *v.n.*, croître en grappes; s'amasser; se grouper.

cluster, *v.a.*, réunir en grappe; amasser.

clustery, *adj.*, en grappe.

clutch (cleutshe), *v.a.*, saisir, empoigner, serrer.

clutch, *n.*, griffe, *f.*

clutter (cleut'-), *n.*, amas confus, vacarme, *m.*

clutter, *v.a.*, remplir en confusion, sans ordre.

coach (côtshe), *n.*, voiture, *f.*; carrosse, *m.*; (nav.) chambre de conseil, *f.*

coach, *v.a.*, voiturer.

coach, *v.n.*, aller en voiture.

coach-box (-bokse), *n.*, siège du cocher, *m.*

coach-hire (-haeur), *n.*, prix de louage d'une voiture, *m.*

coach-maker (-mék'-), *n.*, carrossier, *m.*

coachman (-ma'n), *n.*, cocher, *m.*

coach-office. *n.*, bureau de voitures, bureau de la diligence, *m.* To be left at the —; *bureau restant.*

coach-stand (-sta'n'de), *n.*, place de fiacres, *f.*

coact, *v.n.*, (ant.) agir de concert.

coaction, *n.*, coaction, *f.*

coactive, *adj.*, coactif.

coactively, *adv.*, d'une manière coactive.

coadjument (-ad'jiou-), *n.*, assistance mutuelle, *f.*

coadjutant (-ad'-jiou-), *adj.*, qui aide.

coadjutor (-ad-jou-teur), *n.*, coadjuteur, adjoint, collègue, *m.*

coadventurer (cô-ad-vè'n'tiour-), *n.*, compagnon d'aventure, *m.*

coagent (-é'djè'n'te), *n.*, coopérateur, *m.*

coagulable (-agh'iou-), *adj.*, qui se coagule.

coagulate, *v.a.* and *n.*, coaguler; se coaguler.

coagulation, *n.*, coagulation, *f.*

coagulative, *adj.*, coagulant.

coal (côl), *n.*, charbon de terre, *m.*; houille, *f.* To carry —s to Newcastle; *porter de l'eau à la rivière.*

coal-bed (-bède), *n.*, couche de houille, *f.*

coal-black, *adj.*, noir comme du charbon.

coal-box (-bokse), *n.*, boîte à charbon de terre.

coal-cinders (-ci'n'deurze), *n.pl.*, escarbille, *f.* *sing.*

coal-drawing (-drô-), *n.*, extraction de la houille, *f.*

coal-dross, *n.*, poussier de charbon, fraisil, *m.*

coalery (-èr'-), *n.*, houillère, *f.*

coalesce (-lèce), *v.n.*, s'unir, se confondre.

coalescence (-lès'cè'n'ce), *n.*, union, coalition.

coal-field (-filde), *n.*, terrain houiller, *m.*

coal-heaver (-hîv'-), *n.*, porteur de charbon de terre, *m.*

coal-hole (-hôl), *n.*, (nav.) charbonnier, *m.*

coal-hood (-houde), *n.*, (orni.) bouvreuil, *m.*

coalition (cô-a-lish'eune), *n.*, coalition, *f.*

coal-master (-mâs'-), *n.*, exploitant de houillère, *m.*

coal-measure (-mèj'eur), *n.*, (min.) gisement houiller, *m.*; formation houillère, *f.*

coal-merchant (-meur'tsha'n'te), *n.*, marchand de charbon de terre, *m.*

coal-mine (-maïne), *n.*, mine de houille, *f.*

coal-miner *n.*, houilleur, *m.*

coal-scuttle (-skeut't'l), *n.*, seau, panier, *m.*, boîte, *f.*, à charbon.

coal-stone (-stône), *n.*, anthracite, *m.*

coal-wharf (- wôrfe), *n.*, dépôt de houille, *m.*

coal-whipper (-hwip'-), *n.*, déchargeur de houille, *m.*

coal-work (-weurke), *n.*, houillère, *f.*

coaly, *adj.*, houilleux.

coaptation (cô-ap-té-)', *n.*, adaptation, *f.*; arrangement, *m.*; (surg.) coaptation, *f.*

coarct, *or* **coarctate** (cô-ârcte, -téte), *v.a.*, (ant.) resserrer, rétrécir.

coarctation (-té-), *n.*, (ant.) coarctation, *f.*

coarse (côrse), *adj.*, gros, grossier.

coarsely, *adv.*, grossièrement.

coarseness, *n.*, grossièreté, *f.*

coast (côste), *n.*, côte, plage, *f.*; rivage, littoral, *m.*

coast, *v.n.*, suivre la côte; caboter, ranger la côte.

coast, *v.a.*, côtoyer.

coaster, *n.*, cabotier, *m.*

coast-guard (-gârde), *n.*, garde-côte, *m.*

coasting, *n.*, cabotage, *m.*

coat (côte), *n.*, habit, *m.*; (mas., paint.) couche; (of serpents—*des serpents*) peau; (of some animals—*de quelques animaux*) robe, *f.*; (her.) écusson, *m.*, cotte, *f.*; (anat.) paroi, *m.*; (nav.) braie, *f.*, suif, *m.* Frock—; *redingote, f.* Tail—, dress—; *habit.* Great—; *pardessus, paletot, m.*

coat, *v.a.*, habiller; revêtir; enduire.

coating, *n.*, étoffe pour habits, *f.*; revêtement, enduit, *m.*; couche, *f.*

coax (côkse), *v.a.*, amadouer, cajoler, enjôler.

coaxer, *n.*, cajoleur, enjôleur, amadoueur, *m.*

cob, *n.*, pince-maille, *m.*; balle (of maize—*du maïs*); (for feeding fowls—*pour la volaille*) boulette; (orni.) mouette, *f.*; (man.) petit cheval entier.

cobail (-béle), *n.*, cofidéjusseur, *m.*

cobalt (cô-bâlte), *n.*, cobalt, *m.*

cobble (cob'b'l), *v.a.*, saveter.

cobbler, *n.*, savetier, *m.*

cobbles, *or* **cobcoals** (cob'b'lze, -côlze), *n.*, houille de moyenne grosseur, *f.*

cobweb (-wèbe), *n.*, toile d'araignée, *f.*

cocalon (cô-), *n.*, gros cocon d'une faible texture, *m.*

coccyx (cok'sikse), *n.*, coccyx, *m.*

cochineal (cotsh'i-nîle), *n.*, cochenille, *f.*

cochlea (cok'li-a), *n.*, (anat.) limaçon de l'oreille, *m.*; vis, *f.*

cochleariform, *or* **cochleary** (cok'li-èr'-), cok'li-a-), *adj.*, en forme de vis; en spirale.

cock, *n.*, coq; (of small birds—*des petits oiseaux*) mâle; (tap—*de fontaine, tuyau, &c.*) robinet; (of fire-arms—*d'armes à feu*) chien; (of hats —*de chapeaux*) retroussis; (of dials—*de cadrans*) style, *m.*; (of a balance—*de balance*) aiguille; (of hay—*de foin*) meule, *f.*

cock, *v.a.*, dresser, retrousser ; (fire-arms—*d'armes à feu*) armer ; (hay—*du foin*) mettre en meule.

cockade (-éde), *n.*, cocarde, *f.* ; signe, emblème, *m.*

cock-a-doodle-doo (-é-dou'd'l'dou), *n.*, coquerico, *m.*

cockatoo (-é-tou), *n.*, kakatoès ; cacatois, *m.*

cockatrice (-traïce), *n.*, cocatrix, *m.*

cockboat (-bôte), *n.*, petit bateau, coquet, *m.*

cockbrained (-bré'n'de), *adj.*, étourdi, écervelé.

cock-chafer (-tshéf'-), *n.*, hanneton, *m.*

cock-crow (-crô), *n.*, chant du coq, *m.*

cocked (cok'te). *adj.*, (of hats—*de chapeaux*) à cornes ; (of fire-arms—*d'armes à feu*) armé.

cocker, *v.a.*, (ant.) choyer, dorloter.

cocket (-ète), *n.*, acquit de la douane ; cachet de la douane, *m.*

cockfight, *or* **cockfighting** (-faïte, -faït'-), *n.*, combat de coqs, *m.* ; joute de coqs, *f.*

cock-horse, *n.*, dada, *m.*

cockle (cok'k'l), *n.*, (conch.) bucarde, *m.*, coque, *f.* ; (bot.) agrostide, *f.* ; (of corn—*du blé*) nielle, *f.*

cockle, *v.a.* and *n.*, recoquiller ; se recoquiller ; (of the sea—*de la mer*) moutonner.

cockled (cok'k'lde), *adj.*, à coquille.

cockle-stairs (-stérze), *n.*, escalier à vis, *m.*

cockloft, *n.*, grenier, galetas, *m.*

cockmatch, *n.*, joute de coqs, *f.*

cockney (-ni), *n.*, badaud de Londres, *m.*

cockpit, *n.*, arène des combats de coqs, *f.* ; (nav.) poste des malades, *m.*

cockroach (-rôtshè), *n.*, blatte, *f.*

cocks-comb (coks'kôme), *n.*, crête de coq ; (bot.) célosie à crête ; crête-de-coq, amarante des jardiniers, *f.* ; (pers.) fat, freluquet, *m.*

cockshead (coks'hède), *n.*, (bot.) centaurée noire, *f.* ; plantain, *m.*

cocksure (-shioure), *adj.*, sûr et certain.

cockswain (cok'swéne, *ou* cok's'n), *n.*, patron de chaloupe, *m.*

cock-throttled (-throt't'l'de), *adj.*, au cou de cygne.

cocoa (cô'cô), *n.*, coco ; cocotier, *m.* ; cacao en poudre, cacao, *m.* [*V.* **cacao**, au lieu duquel *cocoa* est généralement employé.]

cocoa-nut (cô-cô-neute), *n.*, coco, *m.* ; noix de coco, *f.*

cocoon (co-coune), *n.*, cocon, *m.*

coction (cok'-), *n.*, coction, *f.*

cod (code), *n.*, (ich.) morue ; (pod—*gousse*) cosse ; (anat.) scrotum, *m.*, bourses, *f.pl.* — *fish ; morue, f.*

coddle, *v.a.*, mitonner ; dorloter, choyer.

code (côde), *n.*, code, *m.*

codicil, *n.*, codicille, *m.*

codlin, *or* **codling**, *n.*, pomme à cuire ; pomme cuite, *f.*

codling, *n.*, (ich.) jeune morue, *f.*

cod-piece (-pîce), *n.*, languette, *f.*

coefficacy (-cô-èf'-). *n.*, efficacité égale, *f.*

coefficiency (cô-èf-fish'è'n-), *n.*, coopération, *f.*

coefficient, *n.*, coefficient, *m.*

coemption, *n.*, coemption, *f.*

coengage (-è'n-ghédje), *v.a.*, engager conjointement.

coenjoy (-è'n'djoï), *v.a.*, jouir conjointement de.

coequal (-i-kwôl), *adj.*, égal, coégal.

coequality (-i-kwôl'-), *n.*, égalité, coégalité, *f.*

coerce (cô-eurce), *v.a.*, forcer, contraindre.

coercible, *adj.*, qui peut être contraint.

coercion (cô-eur-), *n.*, coercition, coërcion, *f.*

coercive. *adj.*, coercif, coercitif.

coercively, *adv.*, par coercition.

coessential (cô-ès'sè'n-shal), *adj.*, de la même nature.

coessentiality, *n.*, participation à la même essence, *f.*

coessentially, *adv.*, avec participation à la même essence.

coeternal (cô-i-teur-), *adj.*, coéternel.

coeternally, *adv.*, de toute éternité.

coeternity, *n.*, coéternité, *f.*

coeval (cô-i-), *adj.*, contemporain, du même âge.

coexist, *v.n.*, coexister.

coexistence, *n.*, coexistence, *f.*

coexistent, *or* **coexisting**, *adj.*, coexistant.

coffee (cof-fi), *n.*, café, *m.*

coffee-berry (-bèr'-), *n.*, grain de café, *m.*

coffee-house (-haouce), *n.*, café, *m.*

coffee-plantation (-pla'n'té-), caféière, *f.*

coffee-pot (-pote), *n.*, cafetière, *f.*

coffee-room (-roume), *n.*, salon d'hôtel, *m.*

coffee-tree (-tri), *n.*, caféier, cafier, *m.*

coffer, *n.*, coffre, coffret, *m.* ; caisse, cassette, *f.*

coffer, *v.a.*, encoffrer.

coffin, *n.*, cercueil, *m.* ; bière, *f.*

coffin, *v.a.*, enfermer dans un cercueil.

cog, *n.*, dent, *f.* ; cran, *m.* — -wheel ; *roue dentée, f.*

cog, *v.a.*, cajoler ; enjôler ; (dice—*dés*) piper ; (tech.) garnir de dents.

cog, *v.n.*, cajoler, enjôler.

cogency (cô-djè'n-), *n.*, force, *f.*

cogent. *adj.*, puissant, fort.

cogently, *adv.*, avec force.

cogger (cog-gheur), *n.*, cajoleur, *m.*, cajoleuse, *f.*

cogitate (codj'i-téte), *v.n.*, penser, ruminer.

cogitation, *n.*, réflexion, pensée, méditation, *f.*

cogitative, *adj.*, pensif, réfléchi.

cognate (cog-néte), *adj.*, de la même famille ; analogue, cognat.

cognation, *n.*, analogie ; parenté ; (jur.) cognation, *f.*

cognition (cog-nish'eune), *n.*, connaissance ; cognition, *f.*

cognitive. *adj.*, cognitif.

cognizable (cog-), *adj.*, (jur.) du ressort ; de la compétence.

cognizance (cog-), *n.*, marque, *f.* ; insigne, *m.* ; connaissance ; (jur.) juridiction, compétence, *f.*

cognizant (cog-), *adj.*, instruit ; (jur.) compétent.

cognizee (cog-ni-zî, *ou* co'n'i-), *n.*, (jur.) personne à la requête de laquelle une obligation est consentie, *f.* ; demandeur, *m.*

cognizor (cog-ni-zeur, *ou* co'n'i-), *n.*, (jur.) auteur d'une obligation ; défendeur, *m.*

cognomen (cog-nô-mène), *n.*, surnom, *m.*

cognominal, *adj.*, de surnom, homonyme.

cohabit (cô-), *v.n.*, cohabiter.

cohabitation (-té-), *n.*, cohabitation, habitation avec un autre, *f.*

coheir (cô-ère), *n.*, cohéritier, *m.*

coheiress. *n.*, cohéritière, *f.*

cohere (cô-hire), *v.n.*, adhérer ; convenir.

coherence, *or* **coherency**, *n.*, cohésion, cohérence, *f.*

coherent, *adj.*, conséquent ; cohérent, adhérent.

coherently, *adv.*, d'une manière cohérente.

cohesibility (cô-hi-), *n.*, tendance à la cohésion, *f.*

cohesible, *adj.*, susceptible de cohésion.

cohesion (cô-hi-jeune), *n.*, cohésion, *f.*

cohesive (-cive), *adj.*, qui peut adhérer ; gluant.

cohesiveness, *n.*, cohésion, *f.*

cohobate (cô-), *v.n.*, cohober.

cohobation, *n.*, cohobation, *f.*

cohort (cô-), *n.*, cohorte, *f.*

coif (coïfe), v.a., coiffe, calotte, f.

coif, n., coiffer.

coil (coïl), n., (of serpents—des serpents) repli, m.; (nav.) glène, f.

coil, v.a., replier, rouler; (nav.) gléner, lever, rouer.

coil, v.n., se replier.

coin, n., encoignure ; (money—argent) monnaie ; pièce de monnaie, f. ; coin, m.

coin, v.a., monnayer ; (b.s.) forger. To — words ; faire, forger des mots.

coinage (coï'n'édje), n., monnayage, m., monnaie, f.

coincide (cô-i'n-çaïde), v.n., s'accorder, coïncider.

coincidence, or **coincidency** (cô-i'n-ci-), n., coïncidence ; rencontre, f. ; accord, m.

coincident, adj., coïncident ; d'accord.

coiner (coï'n-), n., monnayeur ; (b.s.) faux monnayeur, m.

coining-press (-prèce), n., balancier monétaire, m.

coit, n. V. **quoit**.

coition (co-ish'eune), n., coït, m. ; conjonction, copulation, f.

coke (côke), n., coke, m.

coke-burner (-beurn'-), n., ouvrier qui veille à la production du coke, m.

colander, n., passoire, f.

colchicum (-tshi-keume), n., colchique, m.

colcothar (-thar), n., colcotar, m.

cold (côlde), adj., froid. To be — ; avoir froid. To grow — ; se refroidir.

cold, n., froid ; (illness—maladie) rhume, m.

coldly, adv., froidement.

coldness, n., froid m. ; froideur, f.

cole; or **colewort** (côl,-weurte), n., chou,m.

coleoptera, or **coleopterans** (cô-li-op-teur-a, -a'n'ze), n.pl., coléoptères, m.

colessee (cô-lès-sî), n., (jur.) copreneur, m.

colic, n., colique, f.

coliseum (-si-eume), n. V. **colosseum**.

collapse (col'lapse), v.n., s'affaisser; tomber ensemble.

collapse, n., rapprochement ; (med.) collapsus, m.

collapsion, n., affaissement, m.

collar (col'leur), n., collier; (of a shirt—de chemise) col ; (of a coat, a dress—d'un habit, d'une robe) collet, m. ; (for ladies—pour dames) collerette: (arch.) ceinture, f.

collar, v.a., colleter, saisir, prendre au collet ; (cook.) rouler ; mettre un collier à.

collar-bone (-bône), n., (anat.) clavicule, f.

collar-pin (-pine), n., bouton à clavette, m.

collate (col'léte), v.a., collationner ; conférer ; comparer.

collateral (-lat'eur-), n., (jur.) collatéral, m.

collateral, adj., collatéral ; côte à côte ; indirect.

collaterally, adv., en ligne collatérale ; indirectement, côte à côte.

collation (-'lé-), n., collation ; comparaison, f.

collator (-'lé-teur), n., celui qui compare ; collateur, m.

colleague (-'lîghe), n., collègue, m.

colleague, v.a., unir.

collect (col'lècte), n., collecte ; quête, f.

collect, v.a., recueillir ; ramasser, rassembler. To — one's self; se recueillir.

collect, v.n., s'amasser.

collectaneous (col'lèc'té-ni-), adj., recueilli, amassé.

collected (-'ède), adj., réuni ; calme, tranquille.

collection, n., assemblage, rassemblement. m. ; collection ; collecte, quête, f.

collective, adj., collectif.

collectively, adv., collectivement.

collector (-teur), n., personne qui fait une

collection, f.; (of taxes—des impôts) percepteur ; compilateur, m.

college (col'lèdje), n., collège, m. — of physicians ; faculté de médecine, f.

collegial (col-li'djial), adj., collégial.

collegian (-djia'n), n., collégien, m.

collegiate (-djiéte), adj., contenant un collège ; de collège ; collégial.

collet (col'lète), n., (tech.) collet, m.

collier (col'lieur), n., houilleur ; (nav.) charbonnier, m.

colliery, n., houillère, f.

colligate (col'li-ghéte), v.a., (ant.) lier ensemble.

colliquament (col'li-kwa-), n., (ant.) masse fondue, f. ; jaune (m.), partie fœtale de l'œuf, f.; commencement de l'embryon, m.

colliquant (-kwa'n'te), adj., (ant.) fondant.

colliquate (-kwéte),v.a. and n.,(ant.) fondre; se fondre ; se dissoudre.

colliquation (-kwé-), n., fusion, liquéfaction.

colliquative (-kwa-), adj., colliquatif.

colliquefaction (-kwi-), n., liquéfaction simultanée de plusieurs substances, f.

collision (-lijeune), n., collision, f. ; choc, m.

collocate (col'lo-kéte), v.a., placer ; (jur.) colloquer.

collocation (-ké-), n., placement, m. ; place, f.

collocution (-kiou-), n., (ant.) conversation, conférence, f.

collop (col'lope), n., tranche de viande, f.

colloquial (-'lô'kwi-al), adj., dialogué, de conversation.

colloquy (col-lô-kwi), n., colloque, entretien, m.

collude (col-lioude), v.n., ⊙colluder.

collusion (col'liou'jeune), n., collusion, f.

collusive (col'liou'cive), adj., collusoire.

collusively, adv., collusoirement.

colly, n., suie, f.

colly, v.a., noircir, barbouiller avec de la suie.

collyrium (-eume), n., collyre, m.

colocynth (-ci'n'th), n., (bot.) coloquinte, f.

colon (cô-), n., (anat.) colon, m. ; (gram.) deux points, m.pl.

colonel (keur'nèle), n., colonel, m.

colonelcy, or **colonelship** (keur-), n., grade de colonel, m.

colonial, adj., colonial.

colonist, n., colon, m.

colonization (-naï-zé-), n., colonisation, f.

colonize (-naïze), v.a., coloniser.

colonnade (-néde), n., colonnade, f.

colony, n., colonie, f.

colophony, n., colophane, f.

coloquintida (-kwi'n'-), n., coloquinte, f.

colorate, adj., (ant.) coloré ; teint.

colossal, adj., colossal.

colosseum (-'si-eume), n., Colisée, m.

colossus (-ceusse), n. (colossi, colossuses), colosse, m.

colour (keul'leur), n., couleur ; (fig.) ombre, apparence, f. ; (house-painting—peinture en bâtiments) badigeon, m. —s ; (milit.) drapeau, m. ; (nav.) pavillon, m.

colour, v.a., colorer ; colorier ; enluminer; badigeonner ; nuancer.

colour, v.n., (of persons—des personnes) rougir ; (of things—des choses) se colorer.

colourable, adj., plausible.

coloured (keul'leurde), adj., coloré, colorié, enluminé ; nuancé.

colouring, n., coloris, m.; couleur, f.; badigeonnage, m.

colourist, n., coloriste, m.

colourless, adj., sans couleur.

colt (côlte), n., poulain, m. —sfoot; pas-d'âne, m. —s-tooth ; dent imparfaite ou surperflue chez le *cheval*, *f.*; (fig.) (l.u.) *amour des plaisirs de la jeunesse*, *m.*

columbine (col'eu'm'baïne), *adj.*, de pigeon; gorge-de-pigeon.

columbine, *n.*, (thea.) Colombine ; (bot.) colombine, églantine, *f.*

columbo, *n.* *V.* **calumba.**

column (col'leume), *n.*, colonne, *f.*

columnar (kol'leu'm'-neur),*adj.*, en colonne.

colure (-lioure), *n.*, colure, *m.*

coma (cô-), *n..* (med.) coma, assoupissement, *m.*; (astron.) chevelure,*f.*

comate (cô-méte), *n.*, compagnon, camarade, *m.*

comatose, *or* **comatous** (-tôss, -teusse), *adj.*, comateux.

comb (côme), *n..* peigne, *m.* ; (of a cock—*de coq*) crête,*f.* ; (of honey—*de miel*) rayon, *m.*

comb, *v.a.*, peigner ; (a horse—*un cheval*) étriller.

combat (keu'm'-, *ou* co'm'-), *n.*, combat, *m.*

combat, *v.a.* and *n.*, combattre.

combatant, *n.*, combattant, *m.*

comber (côm'eur), *n.*, peigneur, *m.*

combination (-baï-né-), *n.*, combinaison; union, association, cabale, ligue,*f.*

combine (-baïne),*v.a.*, combiner ; réunir.

combine, *v.n.*, se combiner, se réunir, se coaliser, se liguer.

combless (côm'lèce), *adj.*, sans crête.

comb-maker (-mék'-), *n.*, peignier, *m.*

combustible (-beus'-), *adj.*, combustible.

combustibleness, *n.*, combustibilité, *f.*

combustion (-beust'ieune), *n.*, combustion; conflagration,*f.* ; (fig.) tumulte, désordre, *m.*

come (keume), *v.n.* (preterit, Came; *past part.*, Come), venir. To — after ; *venir après* ; *suivre; venir chercher.* To — again ; *venir de nouveau; revenir.* To — away ; *partir ; venir.* To — back; *revenir.* To — by; *venir par ; passer par ; entrer en possession de.* To — down ; *descendre.* To — for; *venir pour; venir chercher.* To — forward ; *s'avancer : se présenter.* To — in; *entrer ; arriver ;* (of the tide—*de la marée*) *monter.* To — in again; *rentrer.* To — off; *se détacher, s'enlever ; se dégager de.* To — out ; *sortir ; se déclarer ;* (of the hair—*des cheveux*) *tomber ;* (of the stars—*des astres*) *se montrer, paraître ;* (of stains—*des taches*) *s'effacer, disparaître.* To — out again; *ressortir.* To — out with; *lâcher ; lurrer.* To — round; *venir ; arriver ;* (of health —*de la santé*) *se remettre, se rétablir.* To —.to ; *se remettre, recouvrer ses sens.* To — together; *venir ensemble;* To — up; *monter; s'élever.* To — up with ; *atteindre.*

comedian (-mí-), *n.*, comédien, *m.*, comédienne,*f.*; comique, *m.*

comedy, *n.*, comédie, *f.*

comeliness (keu'm'-), *n.*, beauté, *f.*; agréments, *m.pl.*

comely, *adj.*, avenant ; beau ; bienséant.

comely, *adv.*, avec convenance.

come-off (keum'ôfe), *n.*, défaite, *f.*; fauxfuyant, *m.*

comer (keum'eur), *n.*, venant ; venu, *m.*, venue, *f.*

comet (com'ète), *n.*, comète,*f.*

cometary, *or* **cometic**, *adj.*, cométaire.

comfit (keu'm'-), *n.*, dragée,*f.*

comfort (keum'feurte), *n.*, aisance, aise,*f.*; bien-être ; agrément; soulagement, *m.* ; consolation. *f.*

comfort, *v.a.*, conforter, soulager ; consoler ; encourager.

comfortable, *adj.*, (pers.) à son aise ; rassis, posé ; (of things—*des choses*) agréable, bon, confortable.

comfortably, *adv.*,à son aise, agréablement, avec aisance, confortablement.

comforter (keum'feurt'eur), *n.*, consolateur ,

m., consolatrice, *f.* ; (kerchief—*cravate*) cachenez de laine, *m.*

comfortless,*adj.*, sans agrément ; sans consolation : désolé, triste.

comfrey (keum'fri), *n.*, (bot.) consoude, grande consoude,*f.*

comic. *or* **comical**, *adj.*, comique, drôle.

comically, *adv.*, comiquement, *m.*

comicalness, *n.*, caractère comique, *m.*

coming (keum'-), *n.*, venue ; arrivée,*f.*

coming, *adj.*, qui arrive, qui vient ; arrivant. — in ; *revenu, m.*

comma (com'ma), *n.*, virgule, *f.*; (mus.) comma, *m.*

command (com'mâ'n'de), *n.*, commandement; pouvoir, *m.*

command, *v.a.*, commander; avoir à sa disposition ; posséder.

commander, *n.*, commandant ; commandeur, *m.*

commanding. *adj.*, commandant ; imposant.

commandingly, *adv.*, d'une manière imposante.

commandment, *n.*, commandement, *m.*

commaterial (-tï-), *adj.*, (ant.) de la même matière.

commateriality, *n.*, (ant.) identité de matière,*f.*

commemorable (-mèm'-), *adj.*, notable, mémorable.

commemorate, *v.a.*, célébrer, solenniser ; commémorer.

commemoration (-ré-), *n.*, souvenir, *m.* ; commémoration ; solennisation,*f.*

commemorative, *or* **commemoratory**, (-teuri), *adj.*, commémoratif.

commence (com'mè'n'ce),*v.a.*, commencer; débuter comme.

commence, *v.n.*, commencer.

commencement, *n.*, commencement ; début, *m.*

commend (com'mè'n'de), *v.a.*, louer ; recommander ; commettre.

commendable, *adj.*, louable ; recommandable.

commendably,*adv.*, d'une manière louable.

commendam, *n.*, (ecc.) commende, *f.* ; bénéfice par intérim, *m.*

commendatary, *n.*, ecclésiastique commendataire, *m.*

commendation (-dé-sheune), *n.*, éloge, *m.* ; louange,*f.*

commendatory (-teuri), *adj.*, de recommandation; d'éloges ; commendataire.

commender, *n.*, panégyriste, *m.*

commensurability (-mè'n'siou-), *n.*, commensurabilité,*f.*

commensurable, *adj.*, commensurable.

commensurate, *adj.*, réductible à une mesure commune ; proportionné, égal ; (of measure,of space—*de mesure, d'étendue*) commensurable.

commensurate, *v.a.*, réduire à une mesure commune ; proportionner ; mesurer.

commensurately, *adv.*, proportionnellement.

comment, *n.*, commentaire, *m.*

comment, *or* **commentate**, *v.n.*, commenter.

commentary, *n.*, commentaire, *m.*

commentator (-té-teur), *n.*, commentateur, *m.*

commenter, *n.*, annotateur, *m.*

commentitious (-tish'eusse), *adj.*, d'interprétation.

commerce (-'meurce), *n.*, commerce, *m.*, échange, *m.*

commerce, *v.n.*, (ant.) entretenir des rapports, un commerce, des liaisons.

commercial (-'meur'shal), *adj.*, commercial, commerçant.

commercially, *adv.*, commercialement.

commigrate, *v.n.*, émigrer avec un autre.

commination (-né-), *n.*, menace; (rhet.) commination, *f.*

comminatory (-teuri), *adj.*, comminatoire, menaçant.

commingle (-mign'g'l), *v.a.*, mêler ensemble; mêler.

commingle, *v.n.*, se mêler ensemble; se mêler.

comminuible (-mi'n'lou-i-), *adj.*, qui peut être réduit en poudre.

comminute (-nioute), *v.a.*, réduire en petits fragments.

comminution (-niou-), *n.*, comminution, *f.*

commiserable (-miz'eur'-), *adj.*, digne de commisération.

commiserate (-miz'eur-), *v.a.*, avoir de la commisération pour; plaindre, avoir compassion.

commiseration (-miz'eur'é-), *n.*, commisération, *f.*

commiserator (-teur), *n.*, personne qui a de la commisération, *f.*

commissariat (-cé-ri-ate), *n.*, commissariat, *m.*; commissaires des vivres, *m.pl.*

commissary, *n.*, commissaire, *m.*

commissaryship, *n.*, commissariat, *m.*

commission (-mish'eune), *n.*, commission, *f.*; (milit.) brevet; (jur.) mandat, *m.* — of a crime; *perpétration d'un crime, f.*

commission, *v.a.*, charger, commissionner, autoriser.

commissioner (-mish'eu'n'eur), *n.*, commissaire, commissionnaire, *m.*

commissure (-mish'ioure), *n.*, (anat.) commissure, *f.*

commit, *v.a.*, commettre; livrer, entraîner; mettre; envoyer en prison. To — one's self; *se commettre; se compromettre.*

commitment, *n.*, perpétration, *f.*; emprisonnement; mandat de dépôt, *m.*

committee (-mit'tî), *n.*, comité, *m.*; (in parliament—*de parlement*) commission, *f.*

committer, *n.*, auteur, *m.*

commode (com'môde), *n.*, ancienne coiffure de femme; commode, *f.*; buffet à étagère, *m.*

. **commodious** (-mô-), *adj.*, commode; utile.

commodiously (-mô-), *adv.*, commodément; utilement.

commodiousness (-mô-), *n.*, commodité, *f.*; avantage, *m.*

commodity, *n.*, commodité; marchandise, denrée, *f.*; profit, avantage, *m.*

commodore (-dôre), *n.*, commodore; bâtiment convoyeur, *m.*

common, *adj.*, commun; ordinaire; vulgaire; simple. — people; *menu peuple.* — soldier; *simple soldat.*

common, *n.*, commune, *f.*; communal, *m.*, (jur.) vaine pâture, *f.*

common, *v.n.*, vivre en commun.

commonable, *adj.*, du domaine public; pour lequel le droit de vaine pâture est admis.

commonage (-édje), *n.*, droit d'envoyer paître dans les communaux; usage; droit d'usage, *m.*

commonalty, *n.*, bourgeoisie, *f.*

commoner, *n.*, membre de la Chambre des Communes; bourgeois; (b.s.) roturier, *m.*; personne qui jouit du droit d'usage, du droit de vaine pâture, *f.*

commonition, *n.*, (ant.) avertissement, *m.*

commonly, *adv.*, ordinairement.

commonness, *n.*, participation (l.u.); généralité, fréquence, *f.*

common-place (-pléce), *adj.*, banal.

common-place, *n.*, lieu commun; resumé, *m.*; note, *f.*

common-place, *v.a.*, résumer, rendre en peu de mots.

commons (-meu'n'ze), *n.*, ordinaire, *m.* table, nourriture en commun, *f.*; Chambre des Communes; bourgeoisie, *f.*

commonweal (-wîle), *n.*, bien public, *m.*

commonwealth (-wèlth), *n.*, chose publique, république, *f.*; état, gouvernement, *m.*

commotion (-mô-), *n.*, commotion, *f.*

commune (-mioune), *v.n.*, conférer, parler; converser.

communicable (-miou-), *adj.*, communicable; qu'on peut communiquer.

communicant (-miou-), *n.*, communiant, *m.*, communiante, *f.*

communicate (-miou-), *v.a.*, communiquer, faire connaître.

communicate, *v.n.*, communiquer; se communiquer; communier; correspondre.

communication (-miou-ni-ké-), *n.*, communication, *f.*

communicative, *adj.*, communicatif.

communicativeness, *n.*, caractère communicatif, *m.*

communion (-miou'n'ieune), *n.*, communion, *f.*; commerce, *m.*; relations, *f.pl.*

communion-service (-seur-), *n.*, office du saint sacrement, *m.*

community (-miou-), *n.*, communauté, *f.*

commutability (-miou-), *n.*, qualité de ce qui peut être échangé, *f.*

commutable (-miou-), *adj.*, qui peut être échangé; (jur.) commuable.

commutation (-miou-té-), *n.*, commutation, *f.*; échange, *m.*

commutative (-miou-té-), *adj.*, commutatif.

commute (-mioute), *v.n.*, commuer, changer.

commutual (-miout'iou-), *adj.*, mutuel, réciproque.

compact, *n.*, pacte; contrat, *m.*; convention, *f.*

compact, *adj.*, compact; serré; lié; uni.

compact, *v.a.*, rendre compact; unir.

compactly, *adv.*, d'une manière serrée; brièvement.

compactness, *n.*, caractère compact, *m.*; compacité, *f.*

companion, *n.*, compagnon, *m.*, compagne, *f.*; camarade, *m. f.*; (to a lady—*d'une dame*) dame de compagnie, demoiselle de compagnie, *f.*

companionable, *adj.*, sociable; d'un commerce facile.

companionably, *adv.*, sociablement.

companionship, *n.*, camaraderie; société, *f.*

company, *n.*, compagnie; société, *f.*; monde, *m.*; (of actors—*d'acteurs*) troupe, *f.*; (nav.) équipage, *m.* Joint-stock —; *société par actions, société anonyme.* We have — to-day; *nous avons du monde aujourd'hui.*

comparable, *adj.*, comparable.

comparates (-rètse), *n.*, (log.) objets comparés, *m.pl.*

comparative, *adj.*, comparatif; du comparatif.

comparative, *n.*, comparatif, *m.*

comparatively, *adv.*, comparativement.

compare (-père), *v.a.*, comparer; confronter.

comparison (-ceune), *n.*, comparaison, *f.*

compartiment, *n.*, compartiment, *m.*, division, *f.*

compartition(-tish'eune), *n.*, répartition, *f.*

compartment, *n.*, subdivision d'un bâtiment; partie d'un terrain, d'un dessin, *f.*

compass (keu'm'-), *n.*, enceinte, *f.*; cercle,

m.; (fig.) sphère, étendue, *f.*; (nav.) compas de route, *m.*, boussole, *f.*

compass (keu'm'-), *v.a.*, faire le tour de; environner; assiéger; venir à bout de.

compasses (keu'm'pass'ize), *n.pl.*, compas, *m. sing.*

compassion (co'm'pash'eune), *n.*, compassion, *f.*

compassionate, *adj.*, compatissant.

compassionate, *v.a.*, compatir à; avoir pitié de.

compassionately, *adv.*, avec pitié.

compaternity, *n.*, compérage, *m.*

compatibility, *n.*, compatibilité, *f.*

compatible, *adj.*, compatible.

compatibleness, *n.*, compatibilité, *f.*

compatibly, *adv.*, d'une manière compatible.

compatriot (-pé-), *n.*, compatriote, *m.f.*

compeer (-pîre), *n.*, compagnon, *m.*, compagne, *f.*; confrère, *m.*

compeer, *v.a.*, égaler; aller de pair avec.

compel (-pèle), *v.a.*, contraindre; forcer; obliger.

compellable (-pèl'lab'l), *adj.*, contraignable; qu'on peut forcer.

compellably, *adv.*, par force.

compellation (-lé-), *n.*, apostrophe; invocation, *f.*

compeller, *n.*, personne qui contraint, *f.*

compend, *n.*, abrégé, épitomé, *m.*

compendious, *adj.*, (ant.) raccourci, abrégé.

compendiously, *adv.*, brièvement, en abrégé, en raccourci, compendieux.

compendiousness, *n.*, brièveté, concision, *f.*

compendium (-pè'n'di-eume), *n.*, compendium, abrégé, précis, *m.*

compensable, *adj.*, (ant.) compensable.

compensate (-séte), *v.a.*, compenser; dédommager.

compensate, *v.n.*, se compenser.

compensation (-sé-), *n.*, compensation, *f.*

compensative, *or* **compensatory** (-teuri), *adj.*, compensatoire.

compete (-pîte), *v.n.*, concourir; rivaliser.

competence, *or* **competency** (-pi-), *n.*, capacité, aptitude; (jur.) compétence; (fortune) aisance, *f.*

competent (-pi-), *adj.*, compétent; raisonnable; suffisant; convenable.

competently, *adv.*, convenablement; suffisamment; raisonnablement.

competition (-pi-cish'-), *n.*, concurrence, *f.*; concours, *m.*

competitor (-teur), *n.*, compétiteur; concurrent, *m.*

compilation (-paï-lé-), *n.*, compilation, *f.*

compile (-païle), *v.a.*, compiler.

compiler, *n.*, compilateur, *m.*

complacence, *or* **complacency** (-plé-), *n.*, plaisir, *m.*; satisfaction; complaisance, *f.*

complacent (-plé-), *adj.*, de complaisance.

complacently, *adv.*, avec complaisance.

complain (-plé'ne), *v.n.*, se plaindre.

complainant, *n.*, plaignant, *m.*, plaignante, *f.*

complainer, *n.*, personne qui se plaint, *f.*

complaint (-plé'n'te), *n.*, plainte; (illness = mal) maladie, *f.*

complaisance (-za'n'ce), *n.*, complaisance, *f.*

complaisant, *adj.*, complaisant.

complaisantly, *adv.*, complaisamment.

complement (-pli-), *n.*, complément, *m.*

complemental, *adj.*, complémentaire.

complete (-plîte), *adj.*, complet, achevé; accompli.

complete, *v.a.*, compléter, achever; accomplir.

completely, *adv.*, complètement.

completement (-plit'-), *n.*, (ant.) complétement, *m.*; perfection, *f.*

completeness (-plît'-), *n.*, caractère complet, *m.*; perfection, *f.*

completion (-plî-), *n.*, achèvement, accomplissement, *m.*, perfection, *f.*

completory (-plî-), *adj.*, qui accomplit.

completory, *n.*, (rel.) complies, *f.pl.*

complex (-plèkse), *adj.*, complexe, compliqué.

complexedness, *n.*, complication, *f.*

complexion (-plèk'sheune), *n.*, teint, *m.*; couleur, *f.*; (med.) tempérament, *m.*; complexion, *f.*

complexional, *adj.*, de tempérament.

complexionally, *adv.*, par le tempérament.

complexity, *or* **complexness** (-plèks'-), *n.*, complexité, *f.*

complexly, *adv.*, d'une manière complexe; en général.

compliance (-plaï'-), *n.*, consentement, *m.*; complaisance; condescendance, *f.*

compliant, *adj.*, soumis; complaisant.

compliantly, *adv.*, avec complaisance.

complicate (-pli-), *adj.*, compliqué.

complicate, *v.a.*, compliquer; unir; embrouiller; composer.

complication (-pli-ké-), *n.*, complication, *f.*

complier (-plaï'eur), *n.*, complaisant, *m.*

compliment, *n.*, compliment; présent, cadeau, *m.*

compliment, *v.a.*, complimenter; faire présent, faire cadeau.

complimental, *adj.*, de compliments.

complimentally, *adv.*, avec des compliments.

complimentary, *adj.*, complimenteur; flatteur.

complimenter, *n.*, complimenteur, *m.*, complimenteuse, *f.*

complin (-pline), *or* **compline** (-pline), *n.*, complies, *f.pl.*

complot (-plote), *n.*, complot, *m.*

comply (-pla'ye), *v.n.*, acquiescer; se soumettre; se conformer; s'accommoder, se plier; se rendre, adhérer.

component (-pô-), *adj.*, constituant.

component, *n.*, composé; constituant, *m.*

comport (-pôrte), *n.*, (ant.) conduite; manière d'agir, *f.*

comport, *v.n.*, s'accorder; convenir. To — with; *supporter.*

comport, *v.a.*, souffrir, endurer. To — one's self; *se comporter.*

comportable, *adj.*, conséquent.

comportment, *n.*, (ant.) conduite, *f.*

compos mentis (-mè'n'-), *adj.*, (jur.) sain d'esprit.

compose (-pôze), *v.a.*, composer; écrire; calmer; apaiser. To — one's self; *se calmer, se remettre.*

composed (-pôz'de), *adj.*, tranquille, apaisé.

composedly (-pôz'èdli), *adv.*, tranquillement, avec calme.

composedness (-pôz'èd'-), *n.*, calme, *m.*; tranquillité, *f.*

composer (-pôz'-), *n.*, personne qui calme, *f.*; auteur; compositeur, *m.*

composing (-pôz'-), *adj.*, (pharm.) calmant; (print.) à composer.

composing-stick, *n.*, (print.) composteur, *m.*

composite (-pôz'aïte), *adj.*, composite; composé.

composition (-zish'-), *n.*, composition, *f.*; (com.) atermoiement, atermoîment; arrangement, *m.*; (jur.) transaction, *f.*

compositor (-pôz'i-teur), *n.*, compositeur, *m.*

compost (-pôste), *n.*, compost, engrais, *m.*
compost, *v.a.*, composter.
composure (-pô-jeur), *n.*, calme, *m.*; tranquillité; (i.u.) composition, *f.*
compotation (-té-), *n.*, libation, *f.*
compound (-paou'n'de), *n.*, composé, *m.*
compound, *adj.*, composé.
compound, *v.a.*, composer ; entrer en composition pour, venir à composition pour ; mêler.
compound, *v.n.*, s'arranger ; entrer en arrangement ; venir à composition.
compoundable, *adj.*, qui peut être composé.
compounder, *n.*, personne qui mélange, *f.* ; auteur de transactions ; arbitre, entremetteur, *m.*
comprehend (-pri-hè'n'de), *v.a.*, comprendre ; renfermer.
comprehensible (-pri-), *adj.*, compréhensible ; saisissable.
comprehensibly, *adv.*, intelligiblement.
comprehension (-pri-), *n.*, action de comprendre ; compréhension, *f.*
comprehensive (-pri-), *adj.*, étendu, vaste ; compréhensif.
comprehensively, *adv.*, avec une grande étendue.
comprehensiveness, *n.*, étendue, *f.* ; richesse (of ideas—*d'idées*), *f.pl.* ; (philos.) compréhensivité, *f.*
compress (-prèce), *n.*, compresse, *f.*
compress (-prèce), *v.a.*, resserrer, comprimer.
compressibility (-prèce), *n.*, compressibilité, *f.*
compressible, *adj.*, compressible.
compression (-prèsh'-), *n.*, compression ; concision, *f.* ; refoulement, *m.*
compressive, *adj.*, compressif.
comprisal (-praï-zal), *n.*, chose qui comprend, qui renferme, *f.*
comprise (-praïze), *v.a.*, contenir, renfermer, comprendre.
compromise (-maïze), *n.*, compromis, *m.* ; transaction, *f.*
compromise, *v.a.*, arranger, compromettre.
compromise, *v.a.*, transiger.
compromiser, *n.*, personne qui fait un compromis, *f.*
comptrol (co'n'trôl), *n.* V. **control**.
compulsatively (-peul-), *adv.*, par force, par contrainte.
compulsatory (-peul-sa-teuri), *adj.*, impératif, forcé, obligatoire.
compulsion (-peul-), *n.*, contrainte, *f.*
compulsive (-peul-), *adj.*, par contrainte, forcé, obligatoire.
compulsively, *adv.*, par force.
compulsiveness, *n.*, contrainte, *f.*
compulsorily (-peul-), *adv.*, par force.
compulsory (-peul-), *adj.*, obligatoire.
compunction (-peungk'sheune), *n.*, componction, *f.* ; vif remords, *m.*
compunctious (-peungk'sheusse), *adj.*, de remords cuisant.
compunctive, *adj.*, (ant.) qui donne du remords.
computable (-piout'-), *adj.*, qui peut être compté, computé, supputé.
computation (-piou-té-), *n.*, supputation, *f.* ; compte, calcul, *m.*
compute (-pioute), *v.a.*, calculer ; supputer ; compter.
computer, *n.*, calculateur, *m.*
comrade (-réde), *n.*, camarade, *m.*
con, *n.*, contre, *m.*
con, *v.a.*, savoir ; répéter ; repasser, relire.
conatus (-né-), *n.*, (phys.) tendance d'un corps en mouvement vers un point donné, *f.* ; effort, *m.*
concamerate (-cam'eu réte), *v.a.*, voûter.

concameration (-ré-), *n.*, voûte arche, *f.*
concatenate (-cat'i-), *v.a.*, enchaîner, lier.
concatenation (-né-), *n.*, enchaînement, *m.* ; (rhet.) concaténation, *f.*
concave (congn'kéve), *adj.*, concave ; creux.
concaveness (-kév'-), *or* **concavity** (-cav'i-), *n.*, concavité, *f.*
concavo-concave (-kévo- -kéve), *adj.*, concavo-concave.
concavo-convex (-ké'vo-), *adj.*, concavo-convexe.
conceal (-cîle), *v.a.*, cacher ; céler, celer; taire.
concealable, *adj.*, qui peut être caché.
concealedness (-cîl'èd'-), *n.*, secret, *m.*
concealer, *n.*, receleur ; (jur.) non-révélateur, *m.*
concealment, *n.*, action de cacher, *f.* ; abri, *m.* ; retraite, *f.* ; (jur.) recèlement, *m.*
concede (-cîde), *v.a.*, concéder.
concede, *v.n.*, faire des concessions.
conceit (-cîte), *n.*, imagination, vaine imagination ; idée plaisante; suffisance, *f.*
conceit, *v.a.*, s'imaginer, se figurer.
conceited, *adj.*, suffisant ; vain.
conceitedly, *adv.*, avec suffisance ; avec vanité.
conceitedness, *n.*, vanité, suffisance, *f.*
conceivable (-cîv'-), *adj.*, concevable.
conceivableness, *n.*, qualité de ce qui est concevable, *f.*
conceivably, *adv.*, d'une manière concevable.
conceive (-cîve), *v.a.*, concevoir ; imaginer ; croire.
conceive, *v.n.*, concevoir.
concent, *n.*, harmonie, *f.*
concentrate, *v.a.*, concentrer.
concentrate, *v.n.*, se concentrer; concentrer.
concentration (-tré-), *n.*, concentration, *f.*
concentre (-cè'n'teur), *v.a.*, concentrer ; réunir en un centre.
concentre, *v.n.*, se concentrer.
concentric, *or* **concentrical**, *adj.*, concentrique.
conceptible, *adj.*, (ant.) concevable.
conception (-cèp'-), *n.*, conception ; idée, notion, *f.* ; projet, dessein, *m.*
conceptious (-sheusse), *adj.*, (ant.) fécond ; enceinte ; (animal) pleine.
concern (-ceurne), *n.*, affaire, *f.* ; intérêt ; soin, souci, chagrin, *m.*
concern, *v.a.*, concerner ; intéresser ; inquiéter. — To — one's self about ; *s'intéresser à* ; *s'occuper de* ; *s'inquiéter de*.
concernedly (-ceurn'èd-), *adv.*, avec intérêt, avec empressement.
concerning, *prep.*, touchant, concernant.
concernment, *n.*, intérêt, *m.* ; affaire ; influence ; émotion, *f.*
concert (-ceurte), *v.a. and n.*, concerter ; ajuster ; composer ; se concerter.
concert, *n.*, concert ; (fig.) unisson, *m.*
concertation (-té-), *n.*, (ant.) dispute, *f.* ; débat, *m.*
concerto (-ceur-), *n.*, (mus.) concerto, *m.*
concession (-cèsh'-), *n.*, concession, *f.* ; aveu, *m.*
concessionary, *adj.*, par concession.
concessive (-cès'sive), *adj.*, qui implique concession.
concessively, *adv.*, par concession.
conch (congn'ke), *n.*, conque ; coquille, *f.*
concha (-ka), *n.*, (anat.) conque, *f.*
conchiferous (-kif'eur'-), *adj.*, conchifère.
conchite (-kaïte), *n.*, conchite, *f.*
conchoid (-koïde), *n.*, (geom.) conchoïde, *f.*
conchologist (-kol'-), *n.*, conchyliologiste, *m.*
conchology (-kol'-), *n.*, conchyliologie, *f.*

conchylious (-kil'-), *adj.*, de coquillage.
conciliable, *adj.*, (ant.) conciliatoire.
conciliate, *v.a.*, concilier.
conciliation (-cil-i-é-), *n.*, conciliation, *f.*
conciliator (-é-teur), *n.*, conciliateur, *m.*, conciliatrice, *f.*
conciliatory (-teuri), *adj.*, conciliant, conciliatoire.
concise (-çaîce), *adj.*, concis.
concisely, *adv.*, avec concision.
conciseness, *n.*, concision, *f.*
concision (-cij'eune), *n.*, coupure ; circoncision, *f.*
conclave (congn'cléve), *n.*, conclave, *m.*, assemblée, *f.*
conclude (-clioude),*v.a.*, conclure ; terminer, finir ; considérer comme.
conclude, *v.n.*, conclure ; se terminer, finir.
concludent, *adj.*, (ant.) concluant.
concluder, *n.*, personne qui conclut, *f.*
concluding, *adj.*, final, dernier.
conclusion (-cliou'jeune), *n.*, conclusion ; fin, *f.*
conclusive (-cliou-cive), *adj.*, concluant, final, décisif, conclusif.
conclusively, *adv.*, d'une manière concluante, décisive.
conclusiveness,*n.*, caractère concluant, *m.*
concoagulate (-cô-agh'iou-), *v.a.*, coaguler ensemble.
concoagulation (-lé'-), *n.*, coagulation de différents corps en une seule masse, *f.*
concoct, *v.a.*, digérer ; mûrir.
concoction, *n.*, coction, concoction ; élaboration, *f.*
concoctive, *adj.*, concocteur.
concomitance, *or* **concomitancy**, *n.*, concomitance, *f.*
concomitant, *adj.*, concomitant, qui accompagne.
concomitantly, *adv.*, par concomitance.
concord, *n.*, concorde ; harmonie, *f.* ; accord, *m.* ; (mus.) consonance ; (gram.) concordance, *f.*
concord, *v.n.*, (ant.) s'unir, concorder, s'accorder.
concordance, *n.*, concordance, *f.* ; index de l'Écriture sainte, *m.*
concordancy, *n.*, concordance, *f.*, accord, *m.*
concordant, *adj.*, d'accord ; concordant.
concordat, *n.*, concordat, *m.*
concorporal, *adj.*, (ant.) du même corps.
concorporate,*v.n.*, se réunir en un seul corps.
concorporation (-ré-), *n.*, incorporation ; réunion en un seul corps, *f.*
concourse (congn'côrse), *n.*, concours, *m.* ; affluence ; réunion, *f.*
concrement (-cri-), *n.*, concrétion, union, *f.*
concrescence (-crès'-), *n.*, concrétion, *f.*
concrete (-crite), *adj.*, concret, corps concret ; (mas.) béton, *m.*
concrete, *adj.*, nombré, concret ; figé.
concrete,*v.n.*, devenir concret ; se coaguler ; se solidifier.
concrete, *v.a.*, rendre concret ; solidifier.
concretely, *adv.*, d'une manière concrète.
concreteness, *n.*, état concret, *m.*
concretion (-cri-), *n.*, concrétion, *f.*
concretive, *adj.*, coagulant.
concubinage (-kiou-bi-nédge), *n.*, concubinage, *m.*
concubine (congn'kiou-baîne), *n.*, concubine, *f.*
concupiscence (-kiou-), *n.*, concupiscence, *f.*
concupiscent, *adj.*, lascif, libidineux.
concupiscible, *adj.*, concupiscible.
concur (-keur), *v.n.*, concorder, s'accorder ; concourir.

concurrence (-keur-),*n.*, concours ; assentiment, *m.*
concurrent, *n.*, chose qui concourt, *f.*
concurrent. *adj.*, qui concourt. qui réunit.
concurrently, *adv.*, concurremment.
concussion (-keush'-), *n.*, secousse, *f.* ; ébranlement, *m.*
concussive (-keus'-), *adj.*, qui ébranle.
condemn (-dème), *v.a.*, condamner.
condemnable (-dèm-na-), *adj.*, condamnable.
condemnation (-dèm-né-), *n.*, condamnation, *f.*
condemnatory (-dèm'na-teuri), *adj.*, condamnatoire.
condemner (-dèm-neur), *n* , personne qui condamne, *f.*
condensable, *adj.*, condensable.
condensation (-sé-), *n.*, condensation, *f.*
condense, *v.a.*, condenser.
condense, *v.n.*, se condenser, se resserrer.
condenser, *n.*, (phys.) condensateur ; (mec.) condenseur. *m.*
condensing, *n.*, condensation, *f.*
condensing-engine (-è'n'djine), *n.*, machine à condenseur, *f.*
condensing-jet (-djète), *n.*, jet d'eau froide, *m.*
condensity, *n.*, condensation ; densité, *f.*
condescend, *v.n.*, condescendre, daigner ; se soumettre.
condescendence, **condescendency** (ant.), *n.*, condescendance, *f.*
condescendingly, *adv.*, par condescendance.
condescension (-di-),*n.*,condescendance,*f.*; acte de condescendance, *m.*
condign (-daîne),*adj.*, proportionné ; mérité, juste.
condignly, *adv.*, justement.
condiment, *n.*, assaisonnement, *m.*
condisciple (-dis-çaî-), *n.*, condisciple, *m.*
condition (-dish'-), *n.*, condition, *f.*; état, *m.*
condition, *v.n. and a.*, faire des conditions. stipuler.
conditional (-dish'eu'n'-), *adj.*, conditionnel.
conditional, *n.*, (ant.) restriction, *f.* ; (gram.) conditionnel, *m.*
conditionally, *adv.*, conditionnellement.
conditioned (-dish'eu'n'de), *adj.*, conditionné ; de condition, de rang.
condole (-dôle), *v.n. and a.*, partager la douleur. To—with; *faire ses compliments de condoléance à.*
condolement, *n.*, affliction, *f.*
condolence, *n.*, condoléance, *f.*
condoler, *n.*, personne qui fait des compliments de condoléance, *f.*
condor, *n.*, condor, *m.*
conduce (-diouce), *v.n.*, contribuer ; servir ; conduire.
conducible, *adj.*, utile ; avantageux ; qui contribue.
conducibleness, *n.*, utilité, *f.*
conducive (-diou-cive), *adj.*, utile ; avantageux, propre ; qui contribue.
conduciveness, *n.*, utilité ; propriété de conduire, de contribuer, *f.*
conduct (-deucte), *n.*, conduite ; direction, *f.* ; guide, *m.*
conduct, *v.a. and n.*, conduire ; diriger.
conductor (-deuct'eur), *n.*, personne qui conduit, *f.* ; directeur ; guide ; (of an omnibus —*d'omnibus*) conducteur, *m.*
conductress, *n.*, conductrice, *f.*
conduit (-dwite), *n.*, conduit, *m.*
condyle (-dil), *n.*, (anat.) condyle, *m.*
condyloma (-dil'-), *n.* (*condylomata*), condylome, *m.*

cone (cône), *n.*, (math.) cône ; (bot.) cône, strobile, *m.*

coney (cô-), *n.* *V.* **cony.**

coney-wool, *n.* *V.* **cony-wool.**

confabulate (-fab'iou-), *v.n.*, confabuler.

confabulation (-fab'iou-lé-), *n.*, confabulation, *f.*

confect, *or* **confection** (-fèk-), *n.*, confection ; confiture, *f.*

confectioner (-eur), *n.*, confiseur, *m.*

confectionery (-euri), *n.*, confiserie (*f.*) ; magasin (*m.*), fabrique (*f.*), de bonbons (*m.pl.*), de sucreries (*f.pl.*) ; bonbons (*m.pl.*), sucreries (*f.pl.*).

confederacy (-fèd'èr'-), *n.*, confédération ; ligue ; (jur.) association illégale, *f.*

confederate (-fèd'èr'-), *v.a.*, confédérer.

confederate, *v.n.*, se confédérer.

confederate, *adj.*, confédéré ; de confédéré, ligué, allié.

confederate, *n.*, allié ; complice, *m.*

confederation (-fèd'èr'é-), *n.*, fédération, confédération, *f.*

confer (-feur), *v.a.*, conférer ; accorder.

confer, *v.n.*, conférer.

conference (-fèr-), *n.*, conférence, *f.*

conferrer (-feur'-), *n.*, personne qui confère ; personne qui accorde, *f.*

conferva (-feur-), *n.*, (bot.) conferve, *f.*

confess (-fèce), *v.a.*, confesser ; avouer ; reconnaître.

confess, *v.n.*, se confesser.

confessedly (-fèss'èd-), *adv.*, de son aveu ; de l'aveu de tout le monde.

confession (-fèsh'-), *n.*, confession, *f.* ; aveu, *m.* To go to —; *aller à confesse.*

confessional, *n.*, confessionnal, *m.*

confessor (-ceur), *n.*, confesseur, *m.*

confest (-fèste), *adj.*, reconnu, avoué.

confidant (-fi-), *n.*, confident, *m.*

confidante, *n.*, confidente, *f.*

confide (-faïde), *v.n.*, se confier ; se fier.

confide, *v.a.*, confier.

confidence (-fi-), *n.*, confiance ; confidence ; hardiesse, *f.*

confident, *n.*, confident, *m.*, confidente, *f.*

confident, *adj.*, confiant ; certain ; assuré.

confidential, *adj.*, de confiance ; confidentiel.

confidentially, *adv.*, de confiance; confidentiellement.

confidently, *adv.*, avec confiance.

confidentness, *n.*, hardiesse ; confiance, *f.*

configuration (-figh'iou-ré-), *n.*, configuration, *f.*

confinable (-faï'n'-), *adj.*, que l'on peut limiter.

confine (-faïne), *n.*, confin, bord, *m.* ; limite, *f.*

confine, *v.n.*, confiner à, avec.

confine, *v.a.*, confiner, enfermer; retenir, limiter, borner.

confineless (-faï'n'-), *adj.*, illimité.

confinement (-faï'n'-), *n.*, confinement ; emprisonnement, *m.* ; (milit.) arrêts, *m.pl.* ; (of women—*des femmes*) couches, *f.pl.*

confiner (-faï'n'-), *n.*, personne qui retient, qui limite, *f.* ; habitant de la frontière ; proche voisin, *m.*

confinity, *n.*, proximité ; contiguïté, *f.*

confirm (-feurme), *v.a.*, confirmer ; fortifier.

confirmable, *adj.*, qui peut être confirmé.

confirmation, *n.*, confirmation, *f.* ; affermissement, *m.*

confirmatory, *adj.*, qui confirme ; en confirmation.

confirmed (-feurm'de), *adj.*, invétéré, fieffé.

confirmedness (-feurm'èd'-), *n.*, caractère invétéré, *m.*

confirmer, *n.*, personne qui confirme, *f.*

confiscable, *adj.*, confiscable.

confiscate, *v.a.*, confisquer.

confiscation (-ké-), *n.*, confiscation, *f.*

confiscator (-ké-teur), *n.*, auteur de confiscation, *m.*

confiscatory, *adj.*, de confiscation.

confiteor, *n.*, confiteor, *m.*

confiture (-tioure), *n.*, (ant.) confiture, *f.*)

confix, *v.a.*, (ant.) fixer.

conflagrant (-flé-), *adj.*, embrasé.

conflagration (-gré-), *n.*, conflagration, *f.* ; embrasement ; incendie, *m.*

conflation (-flé-), *n.*, (l.u.) action de souffler ensemble, *f.*

conflict, *n.*, conflit, *m.* ; lutte, *f.*

conflict, *v.n.*, s'entre-choquer ; lutter.

confluence (-flou-), *n.*, confluent, *m.* ; affluence, *f.* ; concours, *m.*

confluent, *adj.*, confluent.

conflux (-fleukse), *n.*, affluence, *f.* ; concours, *m.*

conform, *adj.*, (ant.) conforme.

conform, *v.a.*, conformer.

conform, *v.n.*, se conformer.

conformable, *adj.*, conforme.

conformably, *adv.*, conformément.

conformation (-mé-), *n.*, conformation; conformité, *f.*

conformist, *n.*, conformiste, *m.*

conformity, *n.*, conformité, *f.*

confound (-faou'n'dé), *v.a.*, confondre ; renverser ; embarrasser ; rendre confus ; troubler.

confounded (-faou'n'd'ède), *part.*, a'ji., confondu ; maudit, vilain.

confoundedly, *adv.*, terriblement, furieusement.

confoundedness, *n.*, confusion, *f.* ; embarras, *m.*

confounder, *n.*, personne qui confond ; chose qui confond, *f.* ; destructeur, *m.*

confraternity (-teur-), *n.*, confrérie, *f.*

confrication (-ké-), *n.*, frottement, *m.*

confrier (-fraï'eur), *n.*, confrère, membre d'une confrérie, *m.*

confront (-freu'n'te), *v.a.*, confronter ; affronter ; attaquer de front.

confrontation (-freu'n'té-), *n.*, confrontation, *f.*

confuse (-fiouze), *v.a.*, mettre la confusion dans ; rendre confus, déconcerter ; embrouiller ; confondre.

confusedly (-fiouz'dli), *adv.*, confusément.

confusedness (-fiouz'èd'-), *n.*, confusion, *f.*

confusion (-fiou-jeune), *n.*, confusion ; ruine, *f.* ; embarras, *m.*

confutable (-fiou-), *adj.*, qui peut être réfuté.

confutant, *n.*, réfutateur, *m.*

confutation, *n.*, réfutation, *f.*

confute, *v.a.*, réfuter, confuter.

confuter, *n.*, réfutateur, *m.*

conge (-dji), *v.n.*, prendre congé.

conge, *n.*, congé, adieu ; salut, *m.*

congeal (-djîle), *v.a.*, congeler.

congeal, *v.n.*, se congeler.

congealable, *adj.*, congelable.

congealment, *n.*, congélation, *f.*

congelation (-dji-lé-), *n.*, congélation, *f.*

congener (-djî-neur), *n.*, ayant une origine commune.

congenerous, *adj.*, congénère.

congenerousness, *n.*, (ant.) nature congénère, *f.*

congenial (-djî-), *adj.*, de la même nature ; sympathique, conforme.

congeniality, *or* **congenialness**, *n.*, affinité, conformité, *f.*

congenital (-djè'n'-), *adj.*, naturel ; (med.) congénital.

congenite (-djò'n'-), *adj.*, né en même temps.

conger (co'n'gh'eur), *n.*, congre, *m.*; anguille de mer, *f.*

congeries (-djî-ri-ize),*n .s.* and *pl.*, masse informe, *f.*; amas, *m.*

congest (-djeste), *v.a.*, amasser, entasser, amonceler.

congest'on (-djèst'ieune), *n.*, amas, *m.*; (med.) congestion,*f.*

conglobate (-glô-), *v.a.*, former en globe, englober.

conglobate, *adj.*, conglobé; en forme de globe.

conglobe (-glôbe), *v.a.* and *n.*, (ant.) conglober; se conglober.

conglobulate (-glob'iou-), *v.n.*, (of animals —*des animaux*) se pelotonner; (of fluids—*des fluides*) se réunir en globules.

conglomerate (-glom'eur'-), *v a.*, conglomerer.

conglomerate, *adj.*, congloméré.

conglomeration (-eur'é-), *n.*, conglomération,*f.*

conglutinate (-gliou-), *v.a.*, conglutiner.

conglutinate. *v.n.*, s'unir par conglutination.

conglutination, *n.*, conglutination; fusion,*f.*

conglutinative. *adj.*, conglutinatif.

congratulate (-grat'iou-), *v.a.*, féliciter, complimenter.

congratulation (-lé-), *n.*, félicitation, congratulation (l.u.),*f.*

congratulator (-lé-teur), *n.*, personne qui félicite,*f.*

congratulatory, *adj.*, de félicitation.

congreet (-grîte), *v.n.*, se saluer réciproquement.

congregate (-grî-), *v.a.*, rassembler.

congregate, *v.n.*, se rassembler.

congregate, *adj.*, compact.

congregation (-gri-ghé-), *n.*, congrégation; (in a church—*à l'église*) assemblée; (of things— *des choses*) agrégation, *f.*, amas, *m.*

congregational, *adj.*, de la congrégation; de l'assemblée.

congress (cong-grèce), *n.*, congrès, *m.*; rencontre,*f.*

congrue (-griou), *v.n.*, (ant.) s'accorder; se rapporter.

congruence, *or* **congruency** (-grou-), *n.*, convenance,*f.*

congruent, *adj.*, convenable, congru; conforme.

congruity (-grou-), *n.*, convenance, conformité congruité,*f.*

congruous, *adj.*, convenable, conforme; congru.

congruously, *adv.*, ⊙ congrûment; convenablement.

conic, *or* **conical**, *adj.*, conique.

conically, *adv.*, en forme de cône.

conicalness, *n.*, forme conique.*f.*

conics, *n.pl.*,(geom.) sections coniques,*f.pl.*

coniferous (-'eur'-), *adj.*, conifère.

conjectural (-djèkt'iou-), *adj.*, conjectural, de conjecture.

conjecturally, *adv.*, conjecturalement.

conjecture (-djèkt'ioure), *v.a.* and *n.*, conjecturer.

conjecture, *n.*, conjecture,*f.*

conjecturer, *n.*, faiseur de conjectures, *m.*

conjoin (-djoïne),*v.a.*, joindre, conjoindre; adjoindre.

conjoin, *v.n.*, se joindre.

conjoint (-djoï'n'te), *adj.*, lié; (mus.) uni, conjoint.

conjointly, *adv.*, conjointement.

conjugal (-djiou-), *adj.*, conjugal, matrimonial.

conjugally, *adv.*, conjugalement.

conjugate (-djiou-), *v.a.*, conjuguer.

conjugation, *n.*, conjugaison,*f.*

conjunct (-djeu'n'kte), *adj.*, réuni.

conjunction, *n.*, union, conjonction,*f.*

conjunctiva (-djeu'n'k'-), *n.*, (anat.) conjonctive,*f.*

conjunctive. *adj.*, uni; conjonctif.

conjunctively, *adj.*, conjointement.

conjunctiveness. *n.*,propriété de joindre.*f.*

conjunctly. *adv.*, conjointement.

conjuncture (-djeu'n'kt'ioure), *n.*, conjoncture; rencontre,*f.*

conjuration (keu'n'djiou-ré-), *n.*, conjuration; adjuration; sorcellerie. *f.*

conjure (co'n'-djioure), *v.a.*, conjurer.

conjure (keu'n'djeur), *v.a.*, ensorceler, évoquer; faire venir par la sorcellerie.

conjure (keun'djeur), *v.n.*, faire de la sorcellerie.

conjurer (keu'n'djeur-eur), *n.*, sorcier, *m.*; sorcière, *f.*; physicien, *m.*; (jest.) habile homme.

conjurer (ko'n'-djiour'-eur) *n.*, celui qui conjure, qui implore, qui enjoint solennellement.

conjuror (ko'n-djiour'-eur), *n.*, (jur.) celui qui est lié avec d'autres par un serment.

connascence, *or* **connascency**, *n.*, naissance commune,*f.*

connate (co'n-néte), *adj.*, né en même temps; (bot.) conné.

connatural (-nat'iou-), *adj.*, qui naît en même temps; de même nature; en rapport naturel.

connaturally, *adv.*, par la nature.

connect (co'n-nèkte), *v.a.*, lier, attacher, allier.

connect,*v.n.*, se lier.

connection, *n.* *V.* **connexion**.

connective, *n.*, (gram.) liaison,*f.*; (bot.) connectif, *m.*

connective. *adj.*, de liaison.

connectively. *adv.*, ensemble.

conner. *n.*, vérificateur de mesures, *m.*

connexion, *or* **connection**. *n.*, liaison; connexion,*f.*; rapport, *m.*; relations,*f.pl.*

connivance, *or* **connivency** (-nai-), *n.*, connivence,*f.*

connive (-naïve), *v.n.*, conniver.

connivency, *n.* *V.* **connivance**.

conniver (-naïv'-), *n.*, personne qui connive,*f.*

connoisseur (ko'n'-nès'cioure), *n.*, connaisseur, *m.*

connubial (-niou-), *adj.*, du mariage; conjugal.

conoid (cô-noïde), *n.*, conoïde, *m.*

conoidal, conoidic, *or* **conoidical** (-noïd'-), *adj.*, conoïde, conoïdal.

conquer (co'n'keur, *ou* -'kweur), *v.a.*, vaincre, dompter; conquérir.

conquer, *v.n.*, vaincre.

conquerable, *adj.*, à vaincre; domptable.

conqueress, *n.*, conquérante. *f.*

conqueror (-keur'eur), *n.*, vainqueur; conquérant, *m.*

conquest (co'ng'kwèste), *n.*, conquête; victoire,*f.*

consanguineal, *or* **consanguineous** (-sa'n'gwi'n'i-), *adj.*, de même sang.

consanguinity, *n.*, consanguinité, parenté,*f.*

conscience (co'n'shè'n'se), *n.*,conscience,*f.*

conscientious (-shi'è'n'sheusse), *adj.*, consciencieux.

conscientiously, *adv.*, consciencieusement.

conscientiousness, *n.*, conscience, *f.*
conscionable (-sheu'n'-), *adj.*, raisonnable; juste.
conscionableness, *n.*, équité, justice, *f.*
conscionably, *adv.*, avec conscience; raisonnablement.
conscious (co'n'sheusse), *adj.*, conscient, qui a conscience de; qui a sa connaissance; dont on a conscience. To be —; *avoir sa connaissance.* To be — of: *avoir conscience de; savoir.*
consciously, *adv.*, sciemment, avec conscience de soi-même.
consciousness, *n.*, sentiment intérieur, *m.*; conscience, *f.*
conscript (-scripte). *adj.*, conscrit.
conscript, *n.*, conscrit, *m.*
conscription, *n.*, conscription, *f.*; enrôlement, *m.*
consecrate (-si-). *v.a.*, consacrer; (a churchyard—*un cimetière*) bénir; (a bishop, a king—*un évêque, un roi*) sacrer.
consecration (-cré-), *n.*, consécration; canonisation, *f.*, (of a king, a bishop—*d'un roi, d'un évêque*) sacre, *m.*
consecrator (-si-cré-teur), *n.*, consécrateur, consacrant, *m.*
consecratory, *adj.*, de consécration; sacramental, sacramentel.
consectary, *adj.*, conséquent.
consectary, *n.*, consequence, induction, déduction, *f.*, corollaire, *m.*
consecution (-si-kiou-), *n.*, succession, *f.*
consecutive (-sèk'iou-), *adj.*, consécutif, qui suit.
consecutively, *adv.*, consécutivement.
consent, *n.*, consentement; accord, *m.*
consent, *v.n.*, consentir.
consentaneous (-té-ni-), *adj.*, conforme.
consentaneously, *adv.*, conformément, d'accord.
consentaneousness, *n.*, accord, *m.*; conformité, *f.*
consenter, *n.*, personne qui consent, *f.*
consentient (-sè'n'-shè'n'te), *adj.*, du même sentiment; unanime.
consequence (-sè-kwè'n'se), *n.*, conséquence, suite; importance, *f.* In —; *en conséquence.* Of no —; *de nulle importance.*
consequent (-si-), *n.*, suite, *f.*; (log.- math.) conséquent, *m.*
consequent, *adj.*, conséquent.
consequential (-kwè'n'shal), *adj.*, conséquent; logique; (b.s.) suffisant.
consequentially, *adv.*, conséquemment; avec suite; (b.s.) avec suffisance.
consequentialness, *n.*, justesse de raisonnement; (b.s.) suffisance, *f.*
consequently, *adv.*, conséquemment; par conséquent.
conservable (-seur-), *adj.*, qui peut être conservé.
conservation (-seur-vé-), *n.*, conservation, *f.*
conservative (-seur-), *adj.*, conservateur.
conservator (-seur-vé-teur), *n.*, conservateur, *m.*, conservatrice, *f.*
conservatory (-seur-va-teuri), *n.*, conservatoire; magasin; dépôt, *m.*; (hort.) serre, *f.*
conservatory, *adj.*, conservateur.
conserve (-seurve), *n.*, conserve, *f.*
conserve, *v.a.*, conserver; confire.
conserver, *n.*, conservateur, *m.*, conservatrice, *f.*; personne qui fait des conserves, *f.*
consider, *v.a.*, considérer; reconnaître.
consider, *v.n.*, considérer. To — of; *réfléchir à.*
considerable (-sid'eur'-), *adj.*, considérable; grand.
considerableness, *n.*, importance; grandeur, *f.*

considerably, *adv.*, considérablement.
considerate (-sid'eur'-), *adj.*, réfléchi, modéré; indulgent; attentif.
considerately, *adv.*, d'une manière réfléchie; avec modération, avec indulgence; avec attention.
considerateness, *n.*, caractère réfléchi, *m.*; attention, *f.*
consideration, *n.*, considération, *f.*; examen; égard, *m.*
considerer, *n.*, penseur, *m.*
considering, *prep.*, considérant; eu égard à; vu, attendu.
consign (-saïne), *v.a.*, consigner; livrer, confier.
consignation (-sig-né-), *n.*, (ant.) consignation, *f.*
consignee (-si-ni), *n.*, (com.) consignataire, *m.f.*
consigner (-saï'n'eur), *or* **consignor** (-si-nor), *n.*, consignateur, *m.*
consignification (-sig-ni-fi-ké-), *n.*, signification relative, *f.*
consignment (-saï'n'-), *n.*, consignation; lettre de consignation, *f.*
consist, *v.n.*, consister, exister. To — in; *consister en, consister à.* To — of; *consister en, consister dans, se composer de.* To — with; *se maintenir, exister.* [*Consister* requires the preposition *à* before a verb; the preposition *dans* before a noun taken in a limited sense; and the preposition *en* in any other case.]
consistence, *or* **consistency**, *n.*, consistance, *f.*
consistent, *adj.*, solide; conséquent.
consistently, *adv.*, d'une manière conséquente.
consistorial, *or* **consistorian** (-tô-), *adj.*, consistorial.
consistory (-teuri), *n.*, consistoire, *m.*
consociate (-sô-shi-), *n.*, associé, *m.*
consociate, *v.a.*, associer.
consociation (-sô-shi-é-), *n.*, association, *f.*
consolable (-sô-la'b'l), *adj.*, consolable.
consolation (-so-lé-), *v.a.*, consolation, *f.*
consolatory (-sol'a-teuri), *adj.*, consolant; (l.u.) consolatif.
console (-sôle), *n.*, console, *f.*
console (-sôle), *v.a.*, consoler.
consoler (-sôl'-), *n.*, consolateur, *m.*, consolatrice, *f.*
consolidate, *v.a.*, consolider.
consolidate, *v.n.*, se consolider.
consolidation (-dé-), *n.*, consolidation, *f.*
consols (-solze), *n.pl.*, consolidés; fonds publics, *m.pl.*; rentes consolidées, *f.pl.*
consonance, *or* **consonancy**, *n.*, consonance, *f.*; accord, *m.*
consonant, *adj.*, consonant; conforme.
consonant. *n.*, (gram.) consonne, *f.*
consonantly, *adv.*, d'accord.
consonantness, *n.*, accord, *m.*
consonous, *adj.*, à l'unisson.
consort, *n.*, compagnon, *m.*, compagne, *f.*; époux, *m.*, épouse, *f.*
consort, *v.a.*, unir; marier.
consort, *v.n.*, s'associer; s'unir. To — with; *être le compagnon de.*
consound (-saou'n'de), *n.*, (bot.) consoude, *f.*
conspicuous (-spik'iou-), *adj.*, en vue; en évidence; bien visible; remarquable, éminent.
conspicuously, *adv.*, évidemment; visiblement; éminemment.
conspicuousness, *n.*, visibilité; renommée, *f.*; caractère remarquable, *m.*
conspiracy, *n.*, conspiration; association illégale, *f.*
conspirant (-spaeur'-), *adj.*, (ant.) conjuré.
conspiration (-spi-ré-), *n.*, conspiration, *f.*

conspirator (-spir-a-teur), *n.*, conspirateur; conjuré, *m.*

conspire (-spaeur), *v.n.*, conspirer.

conspire, *v.a.*, conspirer, comploter.

conspirer, *n.*, conjuré, *m.*

conspiringly, *adv.*, par conspiration.

constable (keu'n'-), *n.*, connétable; constable, officier de paix, *m.*

constancy, *n.*, stabilité; constance; fermeté, *f.*

constant, *adj.*; stable; constant; fidèle.

constantly, *adv.*, constamment; invariablement.

constellation (-stèl-lé-),*n.*, constellation,*f.*

consternation (-steur-né-), *n.*, consternation,*f.*

constipate, *v.a.*, serrer; constiper.

constipation, *n.*, resserrement, *m.*; constipation,*f.*

constituency (-stit'iou-), *n.*, collège électoral, *m.*

constituent, *n.*, personne qui constitue; chose qui constitue; partie constituante, *f.*; auteur; commettant, *m.*

constituent, *adj.*, constituant.

constitute (-tioute), *v.a.*, constituer.

constituter, *n.*, personne, chose qui constitue,*f.*

constitution (-tiou-), *n.*, constitution; complexion, *f.*; tempérament, *m.*

constitutional, *adj.*, constitutionnel.

constitutionalist, *n.*, constitutionnel, *m.*

constitutionality,*n.*,constitutionnalité, *f.*

constitutionally, *adv.*, par tempérament; constitutionnellement.

constitutionist, *n.*, constitutionnel zélé, *m.*

constitutive (-tiou-), *adj.*, constitutif.

constrain (stréne). *v.a.*, contraindre; forcer; retenir, comprimer; enfermer, astreindre.

constrainable, *adj.*, sujet à être contraint; contraignable.

constrainer, *n.*, personne qui contraint, *f.*

constraint, *n.*, contrainte; gêne, *f.*

constrict, *v.a.*, resserrer.

constriction, *n.*, constriction, *f.*; (med.) rétrécissement, *m.*

constrictor (-teur), *n.*, (anat.) constricteur; boa, boa constricteur, *m.*

constringe (-stri'n'dje), *v.a.*, resserrer, contracter.

constringent (-stri'n'djè'n'te), *adj.*, constringent, qui resserre.

construct (-streukte), *v.a.*, construire, bâtir; dresser.

constructer, *n.*, constructeur, *m.*

construction, *n.*, construction; interprétation,*f.*

constructive, *adj.*, par interprétation, par induction.

constructively, *adv.*, par interprétation, par induction.

construe (-strou), *v.a.*, traduire; expliquer; interpréter; construire.

constuprate (-stiou-), *v.a.*, violer; débaucher.

constupration (-stiou-pré-), *n.*, viol, *m.*

consubsist (-seub'-', *v.n.*, subsister ensemble.

consubstantial (-seub-sta'n'shal), *adj.*, consubstantiel.

consubstantialist,*n.*, personne qui croit à la consubstantiation,*f.*

consubstantiality, *n.*, consubstantialité,*f.*

consubstantially, *adv.*, consubstantiellement.

consubstantiate (-shi-éte), *v.a.*, unir en une seule et même substance.

consubstantiate, *v.n.*, professer la consubstantiation.

consubstantiation (-shi-é-), *n.*, consubstantiation; impanation, *f.*

consuetude (-swi-tioude), *n.*, coutume, habitude,*f.*

consul (-seul), *n.*, consul, *m.*

consular, *adj.*, consulaire.

consulate, *or* **consulship**, *n.*, consulat, *m.*

consult (-seulte), *v.a.*, consulter.

consult, *v.n.*, délibérer.

consult, *n.*, (ant.) consultation; résolution, *f.*; conseil, *m.*

consultation (-té-), *n.*, consultation; délibération,*f.*

consulter, *n.*, personne qui consulte, *f.*; consultant, *m.*

consumable (-sioum'-), *adj.*, qui peut être consumé; qui peut être consommé.

consume (-sioume), *v.a.*, consumer; consommer.

consume, *v.n.*, se consumer.

consumer, *n.*, personne, chose qui consume, *f.*; consommateur, *m.*

consummate (-seu'm'-), *v.a.*, consommer.

consummate, *adj.*, consommé; parfait, complet.

consummation (-seu'm'-mé-), *n.*, consommation; fin,*f.*; but, *m.*

consumption (-seu'm'-), *n.*, consomption, action de consumer; consommation; (med.) consomption, maladie de poitrine,*f.*

consumptive (-seu'm'-tive), *adj.*, qui consume; (med.) de consomption, poitrinaire. To become —, *tomber en consomption.*

consumptiveness, *n.*, tendance à la consomption,*f.*

contact, *n.*, contact; rapport, *m.*

contagion (-té-djeune), *n.*, contagion, *f.*

contagious (-té-djeusse), *adj.*, contagieux.

contagiousness, *n.*, caractère contagieux, *m.*

contain (-téne), *v.a.*, contenir; réprimer; retenir.

containable, *adj.*, qui peut être contenu.

container, *n.*, chose qui contient,*f.*; contenant, *m.*

contaminate, *v.a.*, souiller; contaminer.

contamination (-né-), *n.*, souillure; contamination,*f.*

contemn (-tème), *v.a.*, mépriser, dédaigner.

contemner (-tè'm'neur), *n.*, contempteur,*m.*

contemper, *v.a.*, tempérer.

contemperament, *n.*, tempérament, *m.*; modification,*f.*

contemplate, *v.a.*, contempler; méditer, projeter.

contemplate, *v.n.*, contempler.

contemplation (-plé-), *n.*, contemplation; pensée,*f.*; projet, *m.*

contemplative (-plé-), *adj.*, contemplatif.

contemplatively, *adv.*, contemplativement.

contemplator (-plé-teur), *n.*, contemplateur, *m.*, contemplatrice,*f.*

contemporaneity (-ni-iti), *n.*, contemporanéité,*f.*

contemporaneous (-ré-ni-), *adj.*, contemporain.

contemporary, *adj.*, contemporain.

contemporary, *n.*, contemporain, *m.*, contemporaine, *f.*; (of newspapers—*des journaux*) confrère, *m.*

contempt (-tè'm'te), *n.*, mépris, *m.* — of court; *offense à la cour, f.* To feel — for; *avoir du mépris pour.* To fall into — ; *tomber dans le mépris.*

contemptible (-tè'm'ti-b'l), *adj.*, méprisable; chétif.

contemptibleness, *n.*, caractère méprisable, *m.*

contemptibly, *adv.*, d'une manière méprisable ; avec mépris.

contemptuous (-tè'm't'iou-eusse), *adj.*, méprisant.

contemptuously, *adv.*, avec mépris.

contemptuousness, *n.*, caractère méprisant ; mépris, *m.*

contend. *v.n.*, lutter, combattre ; contester, soutenir. To — for ; *combattre pour ; se disputer.*

contend, *v.a.*, disputer.

contender, *n.*, contendant, *m.*

contending, *adj.*, contendant ; en lutte ; opposé, rival.

contenement (-tè'n'i-), *n.*, dépendances d'une maison, d'une terre, d'une ferme, &c., donnée en location, *f.pl.*

content, *n.*, contentement, *m.*

content, *adj.*, content, satisfait.

content, *v.a.*, contenter, satisfaire.

contented (-tè'n'tède), *adj.*, satisfait, content.

contentedly, *adv.*, avec contentement ; patiemment.

contentedness, *n.*, contentement, *m.*

contention, *n.*, contention, dispute, lutte, *f.*

contentious (-tè'n'sheusse), *adj.*, contentieux.

contentiously, *adv.*, contentieusement.

contentiousness, *n.*, disposition contentieuse, *f.*

contentless. *adj.*, mécontent.

contentment, *n.*, contentement, *m.*

contents. *n.pl.*, contenu, *m. sing.*

conterminate (-teur-), *adj.*, qui a les mêmes bornes.

conterminous (-teur-), *adj.*, contigu.

contest, *n.*, contestation, lutte, *f.* ; débat, *m.*

contest, *v.a.*, contester, disputer.

contest, *v.n.*, contester, disputer, lutter.

contestable, *adj.*, contestable.

contestableness, *n.*, (ant.) caractère contestable, *m.*

context, *n.*, contexte, *m.*

contextual, *adj.*, de contexture.

contexture (-tèkst'ioure), *n.*, contexture ; suite, série, *f.* ; tissu ; (fig.) enchaînement, *m.*

contignation (-tig'né-), *n.*, assemblage de poutres, *m.*

contiguity (-ghiou-i-), *n.f.*, contiguïté. *f.*

contiguous (-tigh'iou-eusse), *adj.*, contigu.

contiguously, *adv.*, tout près, contigu.

contiguousness, *n.*, contiguïté, *f.*

continence, *or* **continency**, *n.*, continence ; chasteté, *f.*

continent, *adj.*, continent ; modéré ; chaste.

continent, *n.*, (geog.) continent, *m.*

continental, *adj.*, continental.

contingence, *or* **contingency** (-ti'n'djè'n'ce, -'djè'n'-), *n.*, contingence, éventualité, *f.* ; cas imprévu, *m.*

contingent (-ti'n'djè'n'te), *n.*, contingent ; événement fortuit, *m.*

contingent, *adj.*, contingent, éventuel.

contingently, *adv.*, fortuitement.

contingentness, *n.*, contingence, *f.*

continual (-ti'n'iou-al), *adj.*, continuel ; continu.

continually, *adv.*, continuellement ; continûment.

continuance (-ti'n'iou-), *n.*, continuation ; continuité ; durée, *f.* ; séjour, *m.*

continuate (-ti'n'iou-), *adj.*, continu ; continuel.

continuation (-ti'n'iou-é-), *n.*, continuation ; continuité, *f.*

continuator (-ti'n'iou-é-teur), *n.*, continuateur, *m.*

continue (-ti'n'iou), *v.a.*, continuer ; prolonger ; conserver.

continue, *v.n.*, continuer ; demeurer, rester.

continuedly (-ti'n'iou'-Jû), *adv.*, continûment.

continuer, *n.*, personne qui persévère ; chose qui continue, *f.* ; continuateur, *m.*

continuity (-niou-i-ti), *n.*, continuité, *f.*

continuous (-ti'n'iou-eusse), *adj.*, continu.

contort. *v.a.*, tordre.

contorted (-tort'ède), *adj.*, tordu ; tors ; (bot.) tortile.

contortion (-sheune), *n.*, contorsion ; (med.) luxation, *f.*

contour, *n.*, contour, *m.*

contraband, *adj.*, de contrebande.

contraband, *n.*, contrebande, *f.*

contract, *v.a.*, contracter ; abréger ; resserrer ; rétrécir.

contract, *v.n.*, se contracter. To — for ; *traiter pour.*

contract, *n.*, contrat ; pacte, *m.*; (for public works—*de travaux publics*) adjudication, soumission, *f.*

contractedness (-tract'èd-), *n.*, caractère borné, *m.* ; brièveté, *f.*

contractibility, *n.*, contractilité, faculté de se contracter ; force contractive, *f.*

contractible, *adj.*, contractile, susceptible de contraction.

contractibleness, *n. V.* **contractibility**.

contractile, *adj.*, contractile.

contractility, *n.*, force contractive, contractilité, *f.*

contraction, *n.*, contraction, *f.* ; rétrécissement ; raccourcissement, *m.* ; (math.) abréviation, *f.*

contractor (-teur), *n.*, contractant, *m.*, contractante, *f.* ; entrepreneur ; (for the army, navy —*de l'armée, de la marine*) fournisseur, *m.*

contradict, *v.a.*, contredire.

contradicter, *n.*, contradicteur, *m.*

contradiction, *n.*, contradiction, *f.*

contradictious (-dik'sheusse), *adj.*, contradictoire ; plein de contradictions.

contradictiousness, *n.*, contradiction, *f.*; esprit de contradiction, *m.*

contradictorily, *adv.*, contradictoirement.

contradictoriness, *n.*, caractère contradictoire, *m.*

contradictory, *adj.*, contradictoire.

contradistinct, *adj.*, (ant.) distinct.

contradistinction, *n.*, opposition, *f.* ; contraste, *m.*

contradistinctive, *adj.*, (ant.) qui marque une distinction tranchée.

contradistinguish (-tign'gwish), *v.a.*, distinguer.

contra-fissure (-fish'ioure), *n.*, contre-fissure ; contrefente, *f.*

contra-indicate. *v.a.*, contre-indiquer.

contra-indicant, *or* **contra-indication** (-ké-), *n.*, contre-indication, *f.*

contralto, *n.*, (mus.) contralto, *m.*

contra-mure (-mioure), *n.*, (fort.) contremur, *m.*

contranitency (-naï-), *n.*, (ant.) résistance ; réaction, *f.*

contra-position (-po-zi-), *n.*, contre-position, *f.*

contra-regularity (-règh'iou-), *n.*, opposition à la règle ; irrégularité, *f.*

contraries (-rize), *n.pl.*, contraires, *m.pl.*

contrariety (-tra-raï-è-), *n.*, opposition ; contradiction ; contrariété, *f.*

contrarily, *adv.*, contrairement ; en sens contraire.

contrariness, *n.*, contrariété, *f.*

contrarious (-tré-), *adj.*, contraire ; difficile.

contrariously. *adv.*, contrairement.

contrariwise (-waize), *adv.*, au contraire.

contrary, *n.*, contraire, *m.*
contrary, *adj.*, contraire, opposé.
contrast (-tràste), *n.*, contraste, *m.*
contrast, *v.a.*, contraster ; mettre en contraste.
contrate-wheel (-hwile), *n.*, (horl.) roue de rencontre, *f.*
contravaliation (-val-lé-), *n.*, (fort.) contrevallation, *f.*
contravene (-vine), *v.a.*, contrevenir.
contravener, *n.*, contrevenant, *m.*, contrevenante, *f.*
contravention, *n.*, contravention, *f.*
contributary (-trib'iou-), *adj.*, tributaire.
contribute (-trib'ioute), *v.a.* and *n.*, contribuer.
contribution (-biou-), *n.*, contribution ; (com.) assurance mutuelle, *f.*
contributive (-trib'iou-), *adj.*, qui contribue.
contributor (-trib'iou-teur), *n.*, personne qui contribue, *f.* ; collaborateur, *m.*
contrite (-traite), *adj.*, contrit.
contritely, *adv.*, avec contrition.
contriteness, *n.*, contrition, *f.*
contrition (-trish'-), *n.*, contrition, *f.*
contrivable (-traïv'-), *adj.*, à arranger, à combiner.
contrivance (-traïv'-), *n.*, invention ; combinaison, *f.*
contrive (-traïve), *v.a.*, inventer ; trouver, combiner ; imaginer.
contrive, *v.n.*, s'arranger.
contriver, *n.*, inventeur, *m.*, inventrice, *f.* ; combinateur, *m.*, combinatrice, *f.*
control (-trôl), *n.*, contrôle, *m.* ; influence, autorité, *f.*
control, *v.a.*, contrôler ; exercer de l'empire sur, gouverner.
controllable (-trôl'la-b'l), *adj.*, sujet à contrôle ; soumis.
controller, *n.*, contrôleur, *m.*
controllership, *n.*, charge de contrôleur, *f.*
controlment, *n.* *V.* **control**.
controversial (-veur-shal), *adj.*, de controverse ; polémique.
controversialist, *n.*, controversiste, *m.*
controversy (-veur-), *n.*, controverse ; polémique, *f.* ; différend, *m.*
controvert (-veurte), *v.a.*, controverser, mettre en controverse.
controvertible, *adj.*, controversable.
controvertist, *n.*, controversiste, *m.*
contumacious (-tiou-mé-sheusse), *adj.*, obstiné ; opiniâtre ; pervers.
contumaciously, *adv.*, avec obstination ; opiniâtrément.
contumaciousness, *n.*, opiniâtreté ; perversité, *f.*
contumacy (-tion-), *n.*, obstination ; opiniâtreté ; (jur.) contumace ; désobéissance, *f.*
contumelious (-tiou-mi-), *adj.*, injurieux, outrageant.
contumeliously, *adv.*, injurieusement, outrageusement
contumeliousness, *n.*, injure, *f.* ; mépris, *m.*
contumely (-tiou-mè-), *n.*, injure, *f.* ; outrage, mépris, *m.*
contuse (-tiouze), *v.a.*, contusionner.
contusion (-tiou-jeune), *n.*, contusion, meurtrissure, *f.*
conundrum (-neu'n'-dreume), *n.*, énigme, *f.* ; argutie, *f.* ; quolibet, *m.* ; turlupinade, *f.*
convalescence, *or* **convalescency** (-lès'-), *n.*, convalescence, *f.*
convalescent, *adj.*, convalescent.
convalescent, *n.*, convalescent, *m.*, convalescente, *f.*

convallaria (-val-lé-), *n.*, (bot.) convallaire, *f.* ; muguet, lis de mai, lis des vallées, *m.*
convenable (-vi'n'-), *adj.*, qui peut être convoqué.
convene (-vîne), *v.a.*, convoquer ; réunir, assembler.
convene, *v.n.*, s'assembler.
convener (-vi'n'-), *n.*, personne qui convoque, *f.*
convenience, *or* **conveniency** (-vi'n'-), *n.*, commodité, *f.*
convenient (-vi'n'-), *adj.*, commode, convenable.
conveniently, *adv.*, commodément, convenablement.
convent, *n.*, couvent, *m.*
conventicle (-tik'l), *n.*, conciliabule, *m.*
conventicler, *n.*, personne qui fréquente les conciliabules, *f.*
convention, *n.*, convention ; assemblée, *f.*
conventional, *adj.*, conventionnel.
conventionalism, *n.*, ce qui est conventionnel.
conventionality, *n.*, qualité de ce qui est conventionnel, *f.*
conventionary, *adj.*, réglé par convention.
conventioner, *n.*, membre d'une convention, *m.*
conventual (-vè'n't'iou-), *n.*, conventuel ; religieux, *m.*, religieuse, *f.*
conventual, *adj.*, conventuel.
conventually, *adv.*, conventuellement.
converge (-veurdje), *v.n.*, converger.
convergence, *or* **convergency** (-veurdjè'n'ce, -ci), *n.*, convergence, *f.*
convergent, *or* **converging** (-veurdj'-), *adj.*, convergent.
conversable (-veur'sa-b'l), *adj.*, agréable dans la conversation ; de bonne conversation.
conversableness, *n.*, qualité d'une personne agréable dans la conversation, amabilité ; sociabilité, *f.*
conversably, *adv.*, d'une manière propre à la conversation.
conversant (-vèr-, *ou* -veur-), *adj.*, familier ; familiarisé. — with ; versé dans.
conversation (-sé-), *n.*, conversation, *f.* ; entretien ; commerce, *m.*
conversazione (-vèr-sât'zi-ô'né), *n.*, assemblée littéraire, *f.*
converse (-veurse), *v.n.*, converser, s'entretenir ; fréquenter.
converse, *n.*, commerce, *m.* ; relations, *f.pl.* ; entretien, *m.*, conversation ; (log.) converse ; (math.) inverse, *f.*
converse, *adj.*, (math.) réciproque, inverse.
conversely, *adv.*, (log.) réciproquement.
conversion (-veur-), *n.*, conversion ; (jur.) appropriation, *f.*
conversive (-veur-), *adj.*, (ant.) communicatif ; sociable.
convert (-vèrte), *n.*, converti, *m.*, convertie, *f.*
convert (-veurte), *v.a.*, convertir ; transformer ; faire servir.
convert, *v.n.*, se convertir.
converter (-veurt'-), *n.*, convertisseur, *m.*
convertibility, *or* **convertibleness** (-veurt'-), *n.*, convertibilité, *f.*
convertible, *adj.*, convertible ; (fin.) convertissable, conversible.
convertibly, *adv.*, réciproquement.
convex, *adj.*, convexe.
convex, *n.*, corps convexe, *m.* ; convexité, *f.*
convexed (-vèkste), *adj.*, convexe.
convexedly (-vèks'èd'-), *adv.*, de forme convexe.
convexity, *n.*, convexité, *f.* ; (of roads—*des routes*) bombement, *m.*

convexly, *adv.*, de forme convexe; convexe.

convexness, *n.*, convexité, *f.*

convexo-concave (-kéve), *adj.*, convexo-concave.

convexo-convex, *adj.*, convexo-convexe.

convey (-vè),*v.a.*, transporter; porter; présenter; rendre, exprimer; (jur.) faire transport de. To — away; *emporter.*

conveyable (-vè-a'b'l), *adj.*, transportable; qui peut être transféré.

conveyance (-vè-a'n'ce), *n.*, transport; passage, *m.*; voie; voiture,*f.*; moyen de transport, *m.*; (jur.) translation de propriété,*f.*; (jur.) acte translatif de propriété, *m.*

conveyancer, *n.*, notaire qui dresse les actes translatifs de propriété; notaire, *m.*

conveyancing, *n.*, action de dresser des actes translatifs de propriété,*f.*; notariat, *m.*

conveyer (-vè-eur), *n.*, personne qui transporte, qui transmet,*f.*; porteur, voiturier, *m.*

convict, *v.a.*, condamner, déclarer coupable; convaincre.

convict (-vik'te), *n.*, condamné, *m.*, condamnée. *f.*; criminel; forçat, *m.*

convict-keeper (-kip'-peur), *n.*, gardechiourme, *m.*

conviction, *n.*, conviction; (jur.) condamnation,*f.*

convictive, *adj.*, convaincant.

convince, *v.a.*, convaincre, persuader.

convincement (-vi'n's'mè'n'te), *n.*, conviction, *f.*

convincible, *adj.*, incontestable, certain.

convincing, *adj.*, convaincant.

convincingly, *adv.*, d'une manière convaincante.

convincingness (-cign'nèce), *n.*, caractère convaincant, *m.*

convivial, *adj.*, (ant.) de fête; sociable; joyeux.

conviviality, *n.*, sociabilité, *f.*

convocate, *v.a.*, convoquer; assembler.

convocation (-kè-), *n.*, convocation; assemblée,*f.*

convoke (-vôke), *v.a.*, convoquer, assembler.

convolute, *or* **convoluted** (-lioute, -ède) *adj.*, convoluté.

convolution (-liou-), *n.*, contournement, *m.*, circonvolution,*f.*

convolve, *v.a.*, rouler, enrouler.

convolvulus (-vol-viou-), *n.* (*convolvuli*), belle de jour, *f.*; liseron, *m.*

convoy (-voï-), *v.a.*, convoyer.

convoy, *n.*, convoi, *m.*; escorte, *f.* — ship; *bâtiment convoyeur, bâtiment d'escorte, m.*

convulse (-veulse), *v.a.*, jeter dans des convulsions; ébranler; bouleverser.

convulsion (-veul-sheune), *n.*, convulsion, *f.*; mouvement convulsif, *m.* To be taken with —s; *tomber en convulsion.* Fit of —s; *accès de convulsion, m.*

convulsive, *adj.*, convulsif.

convulsively, *adv.*, convulsivement.

cony (-keu-, *ou* cô-), *n.*, lapin, *m.*; (fig.) niais, *m.*

cony-wool (-woule), *n.*, poil de lapin, *m.*

coo (coû), *v.n.*, roucouler.

cooing (coû-igne), *n.*, roucoulement, *m.*

cook, *n.*, cuisinier, *m.*; cuisinière, *f.*; (nav.) coq. *m.* Man- —; *cuisinier.* Woman- —; *cuisinière.* —shop; *restaurant, m.*; *rôtisserie. f.*

cook (couke), *v.n.*, cuire; faire la cuisine, cuisiner.

cook, *v. a.*. faire cuire; apprêter.

cookery (-'eur'i), *n.* cuisine (art), *f.*

cookery-book (-bouke), *n.*, livre de cuisine, *m.*

cool (coûl), *adj.*, froid; frais.

cool, *n.*, frais, *m.* In the —; *au frais.*

cool, *v.a.*, rafraîchir; refroidir.

cool, *v.n.*, se refroidir; refroidir.

cooler, *n.*, rafraîchissoir, réfrigérant; (med.) rafraîchissant, *m.*

coolie (coû-li), *n.*, coolis, *m.*

cooling, *adj.*, rafraîchissant, calmant.

coolish, *adj.*, un peu frais.

coolly, *adv.*, fraîchement, froidement; de sang-froid.

coolness, *n.*, fraîcheur; froideur,*f.*; refroidissement; sang-froid, *m.*

coom (coume), *n.*, suie,*f.*; cambouis, *m.*

coop (coupe), *n.*, mue,*f.*

coop, *v.a.*, enfermer dans une mue; enfermer étroitement.

coopee (cou-pî), *n.*, (dance—*danse*) coupé, *m.*

cooper (ooup'-), *n.*, tonnelier, *m.*

cooperage (-'édje), *n.*, tonnellerie,*f.*

co-operate (-cô-), *v.n.*, coopérer, concourir.

co-operation (cô-op'eur-é-), *n.*, coopération,*f.*

co-operative, *adj.*, coopérant.

co-operator (-teur), *n.*, coopérateur, *m.*

co-ordinate (cô-), *adj.*, du même rang; égal; (math.) coordonné.

co-ordinately, *adv.*, également; au même degré.

co-ordinateness, *n.*, égalité de rang. *f.*

co-ordinates (cô-or-di-nétse), *n.pl.*, (math.) coordonnées,*f.pl.*

co-ordination (-né-)*, n.*, égalité de rang; coordination,*f.*

coot (coute), *n.*, poule d'eau, foulque,*f.*

copaiba (-pî-), *or* **copivi**, *n.*, copahu, baume de copahu, *m.*

copal (cô-), *n.*, copal, *m.*

coparcenary, *or* **coparceny** (côpâr-cè-), *n.*, (jur.) indivis, *m.*; part d'un propriétaire par indivis,*f.*

coparcener (cô-pâr-cè-), *n.*, (jur.) propriétaire indivis, *m.*, propriétaire indivise,*f.*

copartner (cô-pârt'-), *n.*, associé, coassocié, *m.*

copartnership, *or* **co-partnery** (côpârt'-), *n.*, égalité de part; société en nom collectif,*f.*

copatain (cô-pa-téne), *adj.*, (ant.) élevé en cône.

copayva (-pê-), *n.* *V.* **copaiba**.

cope (cône), *n.*, coiffe; (sacerdotal vestment —*ornement sacerdotal*) chape; (arch.) chape; voûte,*f.*

cope, *v.a.*, couvrir (as with a cope—*comme d'une coiffe*).

cope, *v.n.*, opposer; résister; lutter. To — with; *tenir tête à; lutter contre; rivaliser avec.*

copernican, *adj.*, copernicien.

copier, *or* **copyist** (cop'i-, cop'i-iste), *n.*, copiste, *m.*

coping (cô'-), *n.*, (of a building—*d'un bâtiment*) faîte; (of a wall—*d'un mur*) couronnement, *m.*

copious (cô'-), *adj.*, abondant; copieux; riche.

copiously, *adv.*, copieusement, abondamment; richement.

copiousness, *n.*, abondance, richesse,*f.*

copped (copte), *adj.*, qui s'élève en pointe.

coppel (cop-), *n.* *V.* **cupel**.

copper (cop-), *adj.*, de cuivre.

copper, *n.*, cuivre, *m.*; (boiler—*chaudron*) chaudière, *f.*; (small boiler—*petite chaudière*) chaudron, *m.*

copper, *v.a.*, cuivrer; (vessels—*vaisseaux*) doubler en cuivre.

copperas (cop'peur-ace), *n.*, couperose,*f.*

copper-bottomed (bot'teu'm'de), *adj.*, doublé en cuivre.

copper-coloured (-keul'leurde), *'adj.*, cuivré.

copper-fastened (-fàs's'n'de), *adj.*, chevillé en cuivre.

copper-plate, *n.*, planche de cuivre; taille-douce, *f.*

copper-smith (-smith), *n.*, chaudronnier, *m.*

copper-wire (-waeur), *n.*, fil de cuivre, fil de laiton, *m.*

copper-work (-weurke), *n.*, usine à cuivre, *f.*

coppery (cop'peur'i), *adj.*, cuivreux.

coppice, *or* **copse**, *n.*, taillis, *m.*

coppled (cop'p'lde), *adj.*, qui s'élève en pointe; coniq e.

copse, *v.a.*, conserver en taillis.

copse, *n. V.* **coppice**.

copt, *n.*. Cophte, Copte, *m.*

coptic, *n.*, (language—*langue*)cophte, copte, *m.*

coptic, *adj.*, cophte, copte.

copula (cop'lou-), *n.*, (log.) copule, *f.*

copulate (cop'iou-léte) *v.n.*, s'accoupler.

copulation (-lé-), *n.*, copulation, *f.*

copulative, *adj.*, (gram.) copulatif.

copulative, *n.*, (gram.) copulative, *f.*

copy, *n.*, copie, *f.*; (model for writing—*modèle d'écriture*) exemple; (of printed books—*de livres imprimés*) exemplaire, *m.*; (jur.) expédition, grosse, *f.*; (for drawing—*de dessin*) modèle, *m.*

copy, *v.a.*, copier.

copy-book (-bouke), *n.*, cahier; manuscrit, *m.*

copyhold (-hôlde), *n.*, tenure en vertu de copie du rôle de la cour seigneuriale, *f.*

copyholder, *n.*, tenancier par *copyhold*, *m.*

copying-press (copi'-ign'-prèce), *n.*, presse à copier, *f.*

copyist, *n. V.* **copier**.

copyright (-raïte), *n.*, droit d'auteur, *m.*; propriété littéraire, *f.*

coquet (co-kète), *v.a.*, faire le coquet avec; faire la coquette avec; (l.u.) coqueter.

coquet, *v.n.*, faire le coquet; faire la coquette — ; *coquet*, *m.*

coquet, *or* **coquette**, *n.*, coquette, *f.* Male — ; *coquet*, *m.*

coquetry (co-kèt'ri), *n.*, coquetterie, *f.*

coquettish, *adj.*, de coquette, en coquette.

coral, *n.*, corail; (rattle—*jouet*) hochet de corail, *m.* —-reef; *banc de corail*, *m.* — -wort; (bot.) *clandestine*, *f.*

coral, *adj.*, de corail.

coralline (cor-al-laïne), *n.*, coralline, *f.*

corbeil (-bîle), *n.*, (fort.) corbeille, *f.*

corbel, *n.*, (arch.) corbeau, *m.*; niche, *f.*

cord, *n.*, corde, *f.*; lien; cordon, *m.*

cord, *v.a.*, corder.

cordage (-'édje), *n.*, cordes, *f.pl.*; (nav.) cordage, *m.* — of a canon; *comblan*, *comblau*, *combleau*, *m.*

cordate, *or* **cordated** (-dé'-), *adj.*, en cœur, ayant la forme d'un cœur.

corded (-'ède), *adj.*, de corde; cordé.

cordelier (-dè-lire), *n.*, cordelier, *m.*

cordial, *adj.*, cordial.

cordial, *n.*, cordial, *m.*; liqueur, *f.*

cordiality, *n.*, cordialité, *f.*

cordially, *adv.*, cordialement.

cord-maker (-mék'-), *n.*, cordier, *m.*

cordon (-deune), *n.*, (arch., fort., milit.) cordon, *m.*

corduroy (-diou-roï), *n.*, velours à côtes, *m.*

cord-wood (-woude), *n.*. bois cordé, *m.*

core (côre), *n.*, cœur, *m.*; (of fruit) trognon, cœur; (of an abscess—*d'un abcès*) bourbillon, *m.*

cored (côr'd), *adj.*, (herrings—*harengs*) salé et préparé pour être séché.

coriander (cô-), *n.*, (bot.) coriandre, *f.*

corinthian (-thi-), *adj.*, corinthien; de Corinthe.

co-rival (cô-raï-), *n.*, rival; compétiteur, *m.*

co-rivalry, *or* **co-rivalship** (cô-raï-), *n.*, rivalité, *f.*

cork, *n.*, liège; bouchon, *m.*

cork, *v.a.*, boucher.

corkscrew (-scru), *n.*, tire-bouchon, *m.*

corky, *adj.*, de liège.

cormorant, *n.*, (orni.) cormoran; glouton, *m.*

corn (côi'n), *n.*, blé; grain, froment, *m.*; céréales, *f.pl.*; (on the foot—*au pied*) cor, *m.* Indian — ; *maïs*, *m.* Ear of —; *épi de blé*, *m.*

corn, *v.a.*, saler; grener.

cornchandler (-tsha'n'd'-), *n.*, blatier; marchand de blé, *m.*

corn-crops, *n.*, céréales, *f.pl.*

corncutter (-keut'-), *n.*, pédicure, *m.*

corn-dealer (-dil'-), *n.*, marchand de blé, *m.*

corn-drill, *n.*, (agri.) semoir, *m.*

cornea (-ni-), *n.*, (anat.) cornée, *f.*

corned-beef (cor'n'de-bife), *n.*, bœuf salé, *m.*

cornel-tree (-tri), *n.*, cornouiller, *m.*

cornelian (-ni-), *n.*, cornaline, *f.*

cornelian-tree (-tri), *n.*, cornouiller, *m.*

corneous (-ni-), *adj.*, corné.

corner, *n.*, coin, *m.*; encoignure; extrémité; (tech.) cornière, *f.* —-stone; *pierre angulaire*, *f.*

cornerwise (-waize), *adv.*, diagonalement.

cornet (-nète), *n.*, (mus., conch.) cornet; (milit.) porte-étendard, *m.*; (vet.) couronne, *f.*; (of paper—*de papier*) cornet, *m.*

corn-factor (-teur), *n.*, facteur en blé, *m.*

cornfield (-filde), *n.*, champ de blé, *m.*

cornflag, *n.*, (bot.) glaïeul, *m.*

cornice (-nice), *n.*, corniche; *f.*

cornicle (-ni'k'l), *n.*, cornichon, *m.*; cornicule, *f.*

cornific, *adj.*, qui produit des cornes.

cornish, *adj.*, de Cornouailles.

cornist, *n.*. corniste, *m.*

corn-laws (-lôze), *n.pl.*, lois des céréales, *f. pl.*

corn-merchant (-tsha'n'te), *n.*, négociant en blé, *m.*

corn-pipe (-païpe), *n.*, chalumeau de paille, *m.*

corn-sheaf (-shife), *n.*, gerbe de blé, *f.*

corn-stack, *n.*. meule de blé, *m.*

corn-stalk (-stôke), *n.*, épi de blé, *m.*

cornucopia (-niou-cô-), *n.*, corne d'abondance, *f.*

corny, *adj.*, de corne; de grains.

corolla, *n.*, (bot.) corolle, *f.*

corollary, *n.*, corollaire, *m.*

corona (-rô-), *n.*, couronne, *f.*; (arch.) larmier, *m.*; (anat., astron., bot.) couronne, *f.*

coronal, *n.*, couronne, guirlande; (anat.) suture coronale, *f.*

coronal, *adj.*, (anat.) coronal.

coronary, *adj.*, de couronne; coronaire.

coronation (-né-), *n.*, couronnement, sacre, *m.*

coroner, *n.*, coroner, *m.*

coronet (-nète), *n.*, couronne, *f.*

corporal, *n.*, (nav.) caporal; (of infantry—*d'infanterie*) caporal; (of cavalry—*de cavalerie*) brigadier, *m.*

corporal, *adj.*, corporel.

corporale (-rél), *n.*, (c.rel) corporal, *m.*

corporality, *n.*, corporalité, matérialité, *f.*

corporally, *adv.*, corporellement; de corps.

corporate, *adj.*, érigé en corporation; de corporation.

corporation (-ré-), *n.*, corporation, communauté, société, *f.*; (of a town—*d'une ville*) conseil municipal, *m.*

corporeal (-pô-ri-), *adj.*, corporel, matériel.

corporeally, *adv.*, corporellement, matériellement.

corporeity (-pô-rî-i-), *n.*, corporéité, *f.*

corporeous (-pô-ri-), *adj.*, (ant.) *V.* **corporeal**.

corporify (-fa'ye), *v.a.*, (ant.) corporifier.

corposant (-za'n'te), *n.*, (nav.) feu Saint-Elme, *m.*

corps (côr; *pl.* côrze), *n.*, corps, *m.*

corpse (corpse), *n.*, cadavre; corps mort, *m.*

corpulence, *or* **corpulency** (-piou-), *n.*, corpulence, *f.* ; embonpoint, *m.*

corpulent (-piou-), *adj.*, corpulent; replet, gras.

corpus-christi (-peusse-kris-ta'ye), *n.*, (c.rel.) la Fête-Dieu, *f.*

corpuscle (peus's'l), *n.*, corpuscule, *m.*

corpuscular (-peus'kiou-), *or* **corpuscularian** (-peus'kiou-lé-),*adj.*, corpusculaire.

corpuscularian (-peus'kiou-lé-),*n.*, corpusculiste, *m.*

corradiation (-ré-di-é-), *n.*, union de rayons en un point, *f.*

correct, *adj.*, correct; exact, juste.

correct, *v.a.*, corriger.

correction,.*n.*, correction, *f.*

corrective, *adj.*, de correction; correctif.

corrective, *n.*, correctif, *m.*

correctly, *adv.*, correctement, exactement.

correctness, *n.*, exactitude, justesse, *f.*

corrector (-teur), *n.*, correcteur, *m.*.

correlate (-ri-léte), *v.n.*, être corrélatif.

correlation (-ri-lé-), *n.*, corrélation, *f.*

correlative (-rèl-è-), *adj.*, corrélatif.

correlative. *n.*, corrélatif, *m.*

correlatively, *adv.*, par corrélation.

correlativeness, *n.*,caractère corrélatif, *m.*

correspond, *v.n.*, correspondre; se correspondre; se rapporter; s'accorder.

correspondence, *or* **correspondency**, *n.*, correspondance, *f.*; rapport, *m.*; relations, *f.pl.*

correspondent, *adj.*, correspondant, conforme.

correspondent, *n.*, correspondant, *m.*

correspondently, *adv.*, d'une manière correspondante.

corresponding, *adj.*, correspondant.

corresponsive, *adj.*, correspondant.

corridor (-dôr), *n.*, corridor; (fort.) chemin couvert, *m.*

corrigible (-ri-dji-b'l), *adj.*, corrigible; digne de correction.

corrigibleness, *n.*, caractère corrigible, *m.*

corrival, *n.* *V.* **co-rival**.

corrivalry, *n.*. *V.* **co-rivalry**.

corroborant, *adj.*, (pharm.) corroborant.

corroborant, *n.*, (pharm.) corroborant, *m.*

corroborate, *v.a.*, corroborer, fortifier, confirmer.

corroboration (-ré-), *n.*, corroboration; confirmation, *f.*

corroborative, *adj.*, corroboratif.

corroborative, *n.*, (pharm.)corroborant, *m.*

corrode (-rôde), *v.a.*, corroder, ronger.

corrodent, *adj.*, corrodant.

corrodibility, *or* **corrosibility** (-ci-), *n.*, qualité de ce qui peut être corrodé, *f.*

corrodible, *or* **corrosible** (-ci-), *adj.*, qui peut être corrodé.

corrosion (-rô-jeune), *n.*, corrosion; (fig.) destruction, *f.*

corrosive (-rô-cive), *adj.*, corrosif; (fig.) rongeur.

corrosive, *n.*, corrosif; (fig.) souci rongeur, *m.*

corrosively, *adv.*, comme un corrosif.

corrosiveness, *n.*, nature corrosive, *f.*

corrugant (-riou-),*adj.*, qui ride, qui plisse.

corrugate, *v.a.*, rider, plisser.

corrugation (-riou-ghé-), *n.*, corrugation, *f.*; plissement, *m.*

corrupt (cor-reupte), *v.a.*, corrompre.

corrupt, *v.n.*, se corrompre.

corrupt, *adj.*, corrompu.

corrupter, *n.*. corrupteur,*m.*, corruptrice,*f.*

corruptibility, *n.*, corruptibilité; corruption,*f.*

corruptible,*adj.*, corruptible.

corruptibleness, *n.*, corruptibilité, *f.*

corruptibly, *adv.*, d'une manière corruptible.

corrupting *adj.*, corrupteur.

corruption, *n.*, corruption,*f.*

corruptive (cor-reup'-), *adj.*, corrupteur; (l.u.) corruptif.

corruptless, *adj.*, incorruptible.

corruptly, *adv.*, par la corruption; par corruption.

corruptness, *n.*, corruption,*f.*

corruptress, *n.*, corruptrice,*f.*

corsair, *n.*, corsaire, *m.*

corse. *n.*, cadavre, corps,*m.*

corselet (cors'lète), *n.*, corselet, *m.*

corselet, *v.a.*, revêtir d'un corselet.

corset (-sète), *n.*, corset, *m.*

corset-maker (-mék'-), *n.*,fabricant de corsets, *m.* ; marchande de corsets,*f.*

corsican, *adj.*, corse; de Corse.

cortes (-tize), *n.pl.*,cortès, *f.pl.*

cortical,*adj.*, cortical.

corundum (co-reu'n'deume), *n.*, corindon, *m.*

coruscant (-reus'-), *adj.*, scintillant.

coruscate, *v.n.*, scintiller.

coruscation (-eus'ké-), *n.*, coruscation,*f.*

corvette, *n.*, corvette,*f.*

corymb, *n.*, (bot.) corymbe, *m.*

co-secant (cô-cî-), *n.*, (geom.) cosécante,*f.*

cosey (cô-ci), *adj.*, commode et petit; chaud, confortable; sociable; causeur.

cosily (cô-ci-), *adv.*, à l'aise; agréablement.

cosine (co-çaïne), *n.*, (geom.) cosinus, *m.*

cos-lettuce (-lèt'tiss), *n.*, laitue romaine,*f.*

cosmetic (coz'-), *adj.*, cosmétique.

cosmetic, *n.*, cosmétique, *m.*

cosmic, *or* **cosmical** (coz'-),*adj.*, cosmique.

cosmically, *adv.*, cosmiquement.

cosmogony (coz'-). *n.*, cosmogonie,*f.*

cosmographer (coz'-). *n.*, cosmographe, *m.*

cosmographic, *or* **cosmographical**, *adj.*, cosmographique.

cosmographically, *adv.*, d'une manière cosmographique.

cosmography (coz'-), *n.*, cosmographie,*f.*

cosmological (coz'-), *adj.*, cosmologique.

cosmologist, *n.*, cosmologiste, cosmologue, *m.*

cosmology (coz'-), *n.*, cosmologie, *f.*

cosmopolitan (coz'-), *or* **cosmopolite** (coz'mop-o-laïte), *n.*, cosmopolite, *m.*

cosmorama (coz'mo-râ-), *n.*, cosmorama,*m.*

cosset (cos'sète), *n.*, agneau favori; agneau privé; favori, *m.*, favorite,*f.*

cost, *n.*, prix; frais, *m.*; dépense, *f.*; (com.) coût; dépens, *m.pl.* —s; (jur.) dépens; *m.pl.* — price; *prix coûtant.* To one's —; *à ses dépens.* To carry —s; (jur.) *entraîner les dépens.*

cost, *v.n.* (preterit and past part., Cost), coûter.

costal, *adj.*, (anat.) costal.

costardmonger, *or* **costermonger** (cos-'teur-meu'n'gh'eur), *n.*, marchand ambulant de pommes et d'autres fruits, *m.*

costive, *adj.*, constipé.

costiveness, *n.*, constipation, *f.*

costless, *adj.*, qui ne coûte rien, sans frais.

costliness, *n.*, haut prix, *m.* ; dépense ; somptuosité ; opulence,*f.*

costly, *adj.*, coûteux, de prix ; somptueux ; opulent ; de luxe.

costmary, *n.*, (bot.) balsamite, balsamite odorante,*f.*

costume (-tioume), *n.*, costume, *m.*

cosurety (cô-shour'-), *n.*, (jur.) coûdéjusseur, *m.*

cosy (cô-zi), adj., petit et commode, &c. V. **cosey**.

cot, n., cabane ; chaumière, f. ; (for sheep—de moutons) parc ; (bed—lit) petit lit, lit d'enfant ; lit volant ; (nav.) lit de bord, m.

co-tangent (cô-ta'n'-djè'n'te), n., cotangente, f.

cotemporary (cô-). V. **contemporary** (cô-).

cotenant (cô-tè'n'-), n., tenancier avec un autre, m. ; colocataire m.,f.

coterie (cô-tô-ri), n., coterie, f.

cothurnate, or **cothurnated** (-theur'-), adj., cothurné.

coticular (-tik'iou-), adj., de pierre à aiguiser.

cotquean (cot'kwîne), n., homme qui s'occupe du ménage, m.

cotswold (cots'wôlde), n., parc (of sheep—de moutons) en pleine campagne, m.

cottage (cot'tédje), n., chaumière, cabane, f.

cottager, n., paysan, m., paysanne,f.

cotter (cot'-), or **cottier** (cot'tieur), n., paysan, m., paysanne ; (tech.) clavette, f.

cotton (cot't'n), n., coton ; calicot ; fil d'Écosse, m. Darning—; coton plat. Sewing—; fil d'Écosse, coton à coudre. Knitting—; coton à tricoter. Ball of —; pelote de coton, f. Reel of —; bobine de coton, f.

cotton, v.n., cotonner ; se cotonner ; (fig.) corder.

cotton-check (-tshèke), n., cotonnade, f.

cotton-cloth (-clôth), n., toile de coton, f., calicot, m.

cotton-cord, n., ganse de coton, f.

cotton-fabric, n., tissu de coton, calicot, m.

cotton-factory (-teu'ri), n., filature de coton, f.

cotton-gin (-djine), n., machine à égrener le coton, f.

cotton-jenny (-djè'n'ni), n., métier à filer le coton, m.

cotton-mill, n., moulin à coton, m. ; filature de coton, f.

cotton-plant, **cotton-shrub** (-shreube), or **cotton-tree** (-trî), n., cotonnier, m.

cotton-wool (-woule), n., ouate, f.

cotton-yarn (-yârne), n., fil de coton, m.

cotyledon (-li-deune), n., (bot., anat.) cotylédon, m.

cotyledonous, adj., cotylédoné.

couch (caoutshe), n., couche, f. ; lit de repos ; canapé, m.

couch, v.n., coucher ; se coucher ; (surg.) abaisser la cataracte.

couch, v.a., coucher ; étendre ; rédiger ; cacher ; (surg.) abaisser la cataracte.

couchant, adj., couché, accroupi ; (her.) couché.

coucher, n., oculiste, m.

couchgrass (-grâce), n., chiendent, m.

cough (cofe), n., toux, f. Hooping—; coqueluche, f.

cough, v.n., tousser.

cough, v.a., expectorer.

cougher, n., tousseur, m., tousseuse, f.

could (coude). V. **can** (verb).

coulter (côl'-), n., coutre, m.

council (caou'n'-), n., conseil ; concile, m.

council-board (-bôrde), n., séance du conseil, f.

councillor (-'leur), n., conseiller, m.

counsel (-sèle), n., conseil, avis, m. ; défenseurs, avocats d'une partie, m.pl.

counsel, v.a., conseiller.

counsellable, adj., disposé à recevoir des conseils.

counsellor (-sèl'leur), n., conseil, avocat, m.

counsellorship, n., fonctions de conseil, d'avocat, f.pl.

count (caou'n'te), n., calcul ; compte, m. ; (jur.) charge, f.; (jur.) chef ; (title—titre) comte, m.

count. v.a., compter.

countenance (caou'n'tè'n'-), n., figure, mine, physionomie ; contenance, f. ; air, m.; (fig.) faveur, f. ; appui, m. The knight of the rueful —; le chevalier de la triste figure. To be out of —; perdre contenance. To keep one's — ; garder son sérieux. The light of his —; (biblically—biblique) la lumière de son visage. To look any one out of — ; faire baisser les yeux à quelqu'un. To give — to ; favoriser, encourager. To change —; changer de visage.

countenance, v.a., appuyer, encourager, favoriser.

counter, n., calculateur ; (at cards—aux cartes) jeton ; (of a shop—d'un magasin) comptoir, m. ; (mus.) haute-contre, f.

counter, adv., contre, à l'encontre.

counteract (caou'n'teur'acte), v.a., compenser ; détruire ; contrarier ; déjouer ; neutraliser.

counteraction, n., action contraire, f.

counter-alley, n., contre-allée, f.

counter-attraction, n., attraction opposée, f.

counterbalance, n., contrepoids, m.

counterbalance, v.a., contre-balancer.

counter-bass (-béce), n., (mus.) contre-basse, f.

counterbond, n., (jur.) sous-garantie donnée au garant, f.

counterbuff (-beufe), v.a., rendre un coup; arrêter, faire reculer par un coup.

counterbuff, n., coup rendu, m.

counterchange (-tshè'n'dje), n., contre-échange, m.

countercharm (-tshârme), n., contre-charme, m.

countercheck (-tshèke), n., force opposée, f.

countercheck, v.a., opposer.

counter-current (-keur'-), adj., qui prend une direction contraire.

counter-current, n., contre-courant, m.

counter-drain (-dréne), n., contre-fossé, m.

counterdraw (-drô), v.a., calquer.

counterdrawing (-drô-igne), n., calque, m.

counter-evidence, n., déposition contradictoire, f.

counterfeit (-fite), n., contrefaçon ; imitation, f. ; imposteur, m.

counterfeit, adj., contrefait, feint, simulé, faux.

counterfeit, v.a., contrefaire ; imiter ; feindre.

counterfeit, v.n., feindre.

counterfeiter, n., contrefacteur ; imitateur ; faussaire, m.

counterfeitly, adv., par contrefaçon ; en faisant semblant.

counter-ferment (-feur-), n., ferment contre ferment, m.

counter-fissure. V. **contra-fissure**.

counterfort (-fôrte), n., contre-boutant ; contrefort, m.

counter-fugue (-fioughe), n., (mus.) contre-fugue, f.

counterguard (-gârde), n., (fort.) contre-garde, f.

counter-indication (-ké-), n., contre-indication, f.

counter-lath (-lâth), n., (carp.) contre-latte, f.

counter-lath, v.a., (carp.) contre-latter.

counterlight (-laïte), n., (paint.) contre-jour, m.

countermand, n., contre-ordre, m.

countermand, v.a., contremander.

counter-march (-mârtshe), n., (milit.) contremarche, f. ·

counter-march, *v.n.*, (milit.) exécuter une contremarche.

countermark (-mârke), *n.*, contremarque, *f.*

countermark, *v.a.*, contremarquer.

countermine (-maine), *n.*, contre-mine, *f.*

countermine, *v.a.*, contre-miner; (fig.) opposer.

counter-motion (-mô-), *n.*, mouvement opposé, *m.*

countermovement (-mouv'-), *n.*, (milit.) contremarche, *f.*

countermure (-mioure), *n.*, contre-mur, *m.*

countermure, *v.a.*, contre-murer.

counter-natural (-nat'iou-), *adj.*, contre nature.

counter-negociation, *n.*, négociation contraire, *f.*

counterpace (-péce), *n.*, mesure opposée, *f.*

counterpane (-péne), *n.*, courtepointe, *f.*

counterpart (-pârte), *n.*, contre-partie, *f.*; pendant; (jur.) (of deeds, &c.—*de titres*, &c.) double, duplicata, *m.*; (mus.) contre-partie, *f.*

counter-petition (-pi-), *n.*, pétition opposée, *f.*

counterplea (-plî), *n.*, (jur.) conclusions du demandeur contre l'intervenant dans une instance, *f.pl.*

counterplot, *v.n.*, contre-ruse, (t.u.) *f.*

counterplot, *v.a.*, combattre par une contre-ruse.

counterpoint (-pwaï'n'te), *n.*, (mus.) contrepoint, *m.*

counterpoise (-poïze), *n.*, contrepoids, *m.*

counterpoise, *v.a.*, contre-balancer.

counterpoison (-pwaï-z'n), *n.*, contre-poison, *m.*

counterpressure (-prèsh'eur), *n.*, force contraire, *f.*

counterproject (-prodj'ècte), *n.*, contre-projet, *m.*

counterproof (-proufe), *n.*, contre-épreuve, *f.*

counterprove (-prouve), *v.a.*, contre-épreuver.

counter-revolution (-liou-), *n*, contre-révolution, *f.*

counter-revolutionary, *adj.*, contre-révolutionnaire.

counter-revolutionist, *n.*, contre-révolutionnaire, *m.*, *f.*

counterroll (-rôle), *n.*, (jur.) contrôle, *m.*

counterscarp (-scârpe), *n.*, (fort.) contrescarpe, *f.*

counterscarp, *v.a.*, (fort.) contrescarper.

counter-scuffle (-skeuf'f'l), *n.*, bagarre opposée à une autre, *f.*

counterseal (-sîl), *v.a.*, contre-sceller.

counter-security (-sèkiou-), *n.*, (jur.) sous-garantie donnée au garant, *f.*

countersign (-saine), *v.a.*, contresigner.

countersign, *n.*, (milit.) mot de ralliement, *m.*

counter-signature (-sig-na-tioure), *n.*, contreseing, *m.*

counter-statement (-stéte'-), *n.*, assertion contraire, *f.*

counter-statute (-stat'ioute), *n.*, statut contraire, *m.*

counter-struggle (-streug'g'l), *n.*, lutte en sens contraire, *f.*

countersway (-swè-), *n.*, influence opposée, *f.*

countertally, *n.*, (com.) contre-taille, *f.*

countertaste (-téste), *n.*, faux goût, *m.*

countertenor (-tè'n'-), *n.*, (mus.) haute-contre, *f.*

countertide (-taïde), *n.*, retour de marée, *m.*

countertime (-taïme), *n.*, résistance, opposition, *f.*

countervail (-véle), *n.*, équivalence, *f.*

countervail, *v.a.*, contre-balancer; compenser de.

counterview (-viou), *n.*, contraste, *m.*

counterwheel (-hwil), *v.a. and n.*, (milit.) commander, exécuter une conversion en arrière.

counterwork (-weurke), *v.a.*, contreminer; confondre.

countess (caou'n't'-), *n.*, comtesse, *f.*

counting-house (-haouce), *n.*, bureau, *m.*

countless, *adj.*, innombrable.

countrified (keu'n'tré-faïde), *adj.*, provincial; campagnard; agreste, champêtre.

country (keu'n'tré), *n.*, patrie; contrée, *f.*; pays, *m.*; campagne, *f.* To love one's —; *aimer sa patrie.* To live in the —; *demeurer à la campagne.*

country-box, *n.*, pied-à-terre à la campagne, *m.*

country-house (-haouce), *n.*, maison de campagne, *f.*

country-man (-ma'n), *n.*, habitant d'un pays; compatriote; paysan, campagnard, homme de la campagne, *m.* What — are you ? *de quel pays êtes-vous?* Fellow- —; *compatriote.*

country-seat (-sîte), *n.*, campagne; maison de campagne, *f.*; château, *m.*

county (caou'n'-), *n.*, comté, *m.*

coupee (-pî), *n.*, (dance—*danse*) coupé, *m.*

couple (keup'p'l), *n.*, couple, *f.*; (a male and female—*mari et femme; mâle et femelle*) couple, *m.*; (carp.) moise, *f.*

couple, *v.n.*, s'accoupler.

couple, *v.a.*, coupler, accoupler, joindre.

coupler, *n.*, doublette, *f.* (of organs—*d'orgues*).

couplet (keup'lète), *n.*, couplet, distique, *m.*

courage (keur'édje), *n.*, courage, *m.*

courageous (keur'ré djeusse), *adj.*, courageux.

courageously, *adv.*, courageusement.

courageousness, *n.*, courage, *m.*

courier (cou'rieur), *n.*, courrier, *m.*

course (côrse), *n.*, cours, *m.*; course, carrière, *f.*; (of life—*de vie*) genre; (at a meal—*à un repas*) service; (duration—*durée*) courant, *m.*; (for races—*de courses*) arène, *f.*, terrain de course; (for horse-races—*de chevaux de course*) hippodrome, *m.*; (mas.) assise, *f.*; (geol.) filon, *m.*; (nav.) route, *f.* —s; (med.) *règles, f.pl.* In due —; *en ordre, en son temps, en temps utile.* In the — of; *dans le cours de,* (of time—*du temps*) *dans le courant de.* Of —; *naturellement;* (jur.) *de droit.* That is a matter of —; *cela va sans dire.* To take its —; *prendre son cours.* Water- —; *lit de rivière; cours d'eau, m.*

course, *v.a.*, courir; faire courir, parcourir.

course, *v.n.*, courir.

courser, *n.*, coureur, coursier, *m.*

court (côrte), *n.*, cour, *f.*; tribunal, *m.*; (small street—*petite rue*) ruelle, *f.* Criminal —; *cour de justice criminelle.* To go to —; *aller à la cour.* To pay one's — to; *faire sa cour à.* In open —; *en plein tribunal.*

court, *v.a.*, faire la cour à; courtiser; fêter; solliciter; rechercher.

court-bred (-brède), *adj.*, élevé à la cour.

courteous (keur-tè-, *ou* kôrtieusse), *adj.*, courtois; poli.

courteously, *adv.*, courtoisement; poliment.

courteousness, *n.*, courtoisie; politesse, *f.*

courter, *n.*, amant, *m.*

courtesy (keur-tè-ci), *n.*, courtoisie; politesse; (of women—*des femmes*) révérence, *f.*

courtesy, *v.n.*, faire une révérence.

courtezan (keur-tè-zâne), *n.*, courtisane, *f.*

courtier (côrt'ieur), *n.*, courtisan, *m.*

courtlike (côrt'laïke), *adj.*, de cour; poli; élégant.

courtliness (côrt'-), *n.*, esprit de la cour, *m.*; politesse, *f.*

courtly, *adj.*, de cour; poli, galant.

courtly, *adv.*, dans le ton de la cour ; poliment, avec grâce.

court-martial (-mârsh'al), *n.*, conseil de guerre, *m.*

court-plaster (-plâs'-) *n.*, taffetas d'Angleterre, *m.*

courtship, *n.*, assiduités auprès d'une femme, *f.pl.*, cour, *f.*

cousin (keuz'z'n), *n.*, cousin, *m.*, cousine, *f.*

cove (côve), *n.*, (geog.) anse, *f.*

cove, *v.a.*, voûter.

covenant (keuv'è-), *n.*, convention, *f.* ; (English hist.) covenant, *m.*

covenant, *v.n.*, stipuler.

covenant, *v.a.*, accorder par contrat.

covenantee, *n.*, (jur.) créancier, *m.*, créancière, *f.*

covenanter, *n.*, partie contractante, *f.* ; (jur.) débiteur, *m.*, débitrice, *f.* ; (English hist.) covenantaire, *m.*

cover (keuv'-), *v.a.*, couvrir ; cacher ; (of birds—*des oiseaux*) couver.

cover, *n.*, couverture; (of a dish, a plate—*de plat, d'assiette*) cloche; (of a letter, a parcel—*de lettre, de paquet*) enveloppe; (of a chair, &c.—*de chaise, &c.*) housse, *f.* ; (of a pot, a saucepan—*de pot, de casserole*) couvercle; (bot.) involucre; (fig.) voile, *m.*

covering, *n.*, couverture, enveloppe, *f.*

coverlet (keuv'eur'lète), *n.*, couvre-pied, *m.*

covert (keuv'eurte), *n.*, couvert, abri ; gîte, *m.* ; tanière, *f.*

covert, *adj.*, couvert ; caché ; insidieux ; (jur.) en puissance de mari.

covertly, *adv.*, secrètement.

coverture (keuv'eurt'ioure), *n.*, abri ; (jur.) état de la femme en puissance de mari, *m.*

covert-way (-wé), *n.*, (fort.) chemin couvert, *m.*

covet (keuv'ète), *v.a.*, convoiter ; ambitionner ; désirer ardemment.

covetable, *adj.*, convoitable.

covetous, *adj.*, avide, avare, cupide, convoiteux.

covetously, *adv.*, avec convoitise ; avidement.

covetousness, *n.*, convoitise, avarice ; cupidité, avidité, *f.*

covey (keuv'è), *n.*, (of birds of the same nest —*d'une nichée*) couvée ; (of birds—*d'oiseaux*) volée, *f.*

coving (côv'-), *n.*, voussure, *f.*

cow (cao), *n.*, vache, *f.* Milch —; *vache laitière, vache à lait.*

cow, *v.a.*, intimider; dompter ; accabler.

coward (caou'eurde), *n.*, couard, poltron, *m.*, poltronne, *f.* ; lâche, *m.*

cowardice, *n.*, couardise, poltronnerie, lâcheté, *f.*

cowardliness, *n.*, couardise, lâcheté, *f.*

cowardly, *adj.*, couard, lâche, poltron.

cowardly, *adv.*, couardement, lâchement.

cowbane, *n.*, (bot.) cicutaire aquatique, *f.*

cow-berry (-bèr'-), *n.*, (bot.) airelle, canneberge, *f.*

cow-boy (-boï), *n.*, jeune vacher ; gardeur de vaches, *m.*

cow-catcher (-catsh'-), *m.*, (railways) chasse-pierres, *m.*

cowdung (-deu'n'gne), *n.*, bouse de vache, *f.*

cower, *v.n.*, s'accroupir, se blottir ; s'affaisser.

cow-grass (-grâce), *n.*, (bot.) trèfle des prés, *m.*

cow-herd, *n.*, vacher, *m.*, vachère, *f.*

cow-keeper (-kip'-), *n.*, vacher, *m.*, vachère, *f.* ; nourrisseur, *m.*

cowl (caoul), *n.*, capuce ; capuchon, *m.*

cow-leech (-lîtshe), *n.*, vétérinaire pour les vaches, *m.*

cowparsnip (-pârs'-), *n.*, (bot.) berce ; branche-ursine bâtarde, *f.*

cow-pen (-pène), *n.*, parc aux vaches, *m.*

cow-pox, *n.*, (med.) vaccine, *f.*

cow-shot, *n.*, (orni.) ramier, pigeon ramier, *m.*

cowslip, *n.*, (bot.) primevère. *f.*

cows-lungwort (caoz'leu'n'gn'wcurte), *n.*, (bot.) bouillon-blanc, *m.*

cow-tree (-trî), *n.*, arbre à la vache, *m.* (*galactodendron utile*).

cow-weed (-wîde), *n.*, cerfeuil sauvage, *m.*

cow-wheat (-hwîte), *n.*, (bot.) mélampyre, blé de vache, *m.* ; queue-de-renard, *f.*

coxcomb (-côme), *n.*, fat, petit-maître, *m.* ; (bot.) célosie, *f.*, passe-velours, *m.*, amarante, *f.*

coxcombry (-côm'ri), *n.*, fatuité, *f.*

coxcomical, *adj.*, fat ; (of things—*des choses*) de fat.

coy (coï), *adj.*, modeste ; timide ; réservé.

coy, *v.n.*, être réservé ; se comporter avec modestie, avec timidité.

coyly, *adv.*, modestement, timidement ; avec réserve.

coyness, *n.*, modestie, timidité, réserve, *f.*

coz (keuze), *abréviation de cousin, m., cousine, f.*

cozen (keuz'z'n), *v.a.*, duper, tromper.

cozenage (-édje), *n.*, fourberie, tromperie, *f.*

cozener, *n.*, fourbe, trompeur, *m.*

crab, *n.*, crabe, cancre, *m.* ; écrevisse de mer ; (bot.) pomme sauvage, *f.* ; (astron.) cancer, *m.*, écrevisse, *f.* ; (nav.) cabestan volant ; (of men—*des hommes*) loup-garou, *m.* ; (of women —*des femmes*) pie-grièche, *f.*

crab-apple (-ap'p'l), *n.*, pomme sauvage, *f.*

crabbed (crab'éde), *adj.*, acariâtre ; dur, bourru. — look ; *mine rechignée.*

crabbedly (-'èd'-), *adv.*, d'une manière bourrue.

crabbedness (-'èd'-), *n.*, humeur acariâtre ; âpreté, rudesse, *f.*

crabber, *n.*, rat d'eau, *m.*

crab-fish, *n.*, crabe, *m.* ; écrevisse de mer, *f.*

crab-tree (-trî), *n.*, pommier sauvage, *m.*

crack, *n.*, (action) craquement, *m.* ; fente ; (in glass—*dans le verre*) fêlure, *f.* ; (pers.) hâbleur, *m.*, hâbleuse, *f.* ; hâblerie ; (tech.) fissure, lézarde, *f.* In a —; *en un clin d'œil.*

crack, *v.a.*, fêler, faire fêler ; gercer ; fendre ; (nuts, &c.—*noix, &c.*) casser ; (a whip—*un fouet*) faire claquer ; (a bottle of wine—*bouteille de vin*) faire sauter ; (a joke—*plaisanterie*) dire, faire ; (fig.) rompre, briser.

crack, *v.n.*, craquer, se fendre ; (of the ground, the skin—*de la terre, de la peau*) se gercer ; (of a whip—*d'un fouet*) claquer ; (of glass, pottery-wares—*de verrerie, poterie, &c.*) se fêler ; (fig.) rompre.

crack-brained (-bré'n'de), *adj.*, timbré.

cracked (crak'te), *adj.*, fendu, fêlé ; (fig.) timbré.

cracker, *n.*, vantard, craqueur ; (firework—*pièce d'artifice*) pétard, *m.*

crackle (crak'k'l), *v.a.*, pétiller, craqueter.

cracknel (-nèle), *n.*, craquelin, *m.*

cradle (kré'd'l), *n.*, berceau, *m.*

cradle, *v.a.*, coucher dans un berceau.

cradle-cap, *n.*, croûte de lait (of children—*des enfants*), *f.*

craft (crâfte), *n.*, (trade—*profession*) métier, *m.* ; (cunning—*fourbe*) ruse ; (nav.) embarcation, *f.*

craftily, *adv.*, artificieusement, avec ruse.

craftiness, *n.*, artifice, *m.* ; ruse, astuce, *f.*

craftsman (crâfts'ma'n), *n.*, artisan, *m.*

craftsmaster (-mâs-), *n.*, maître en son art, *m.*

crafty, *adj.*, artificieux ; rusé, astucieux.

crag, *n.*, rocher escarpé ; roc ; (of meat—*viande*) bout saigneux, *m.*

r **cragged** (crag'ghède), *adj.*, rocailleux ;
escarpe.

craggedness, *or* **cragginess** (crag'ghèd'-,
-'ghi-), *n.*, état rocailleux, *m.*

craggy (crag'ghi), *adj.*, rocailleux.

cram (crame), *v.a.*, fourrer, remplir ; bourrer,
farcir. To — poultry ; *gaver de la volaille.*

cram (crame), *v.n.*, se bourrer, se gaver.

crambo (cra'm'bô), *n.*, bout rimé ; jeu des
bouts rimés, *m.*

cramp (cra'm'pe), *n.*, crampe, *f.*, (tech.)
crampon, *m.* ; (fig.) gêne, entrave, *f.*

cramp, *v.a.*, tourmenter par la crampe ;
(fig.) gêner, entraver, restreindre ; (tech.)
cramponner. To — in ; *sceller, cramponner.*
To — out ; *arracher.*

cramp, *adj.*, difficile, fantastique.

cramp-fish, *n.*, torpille, *f.*

cramp-iron (-aï'eur'n), *n.*, crampon, *m.*

crampit (cra'm'pite), *n.*, bouterolle, *f.*

cranage (cré-nédje), *n.*, droit de grue. *m.*

cranberry (cra'n'bèr'-), *n.*, (bot.) airelle,
canneberge, *f.*

cranch (cra'n'she), *v.a.*, broyer avec les
dents, croquer.

crane, *n.*, (orni., tech.) grue, *f.* ; (hydr.)
siphon, *m.*

cranesbill (cré'n'z'-), *n.*, bec-de-grue, *m.*

craniological (cré-ni-o-lodj'-), *adj.*, craniologique.

craniologist (-djiste), *n.*, craniologiste, *m.*

craniology (-dji), *n.*, craniologie, *f.*

craniometry (-èt'-), *n.*, craniométrie, *f.*

cranioscopy, *n.*, cranioscopie, *f.*

cranium (cré-ni-eume), *n.*, (anat.) crâne, *m.*

crank (cra'n'gn'ke), *n.*, détour ; jeu de mots ;
(tech.) cran, *m.* ; manivelle, *f.*

crank, *adj.*, vif, gaillard, dispos, éveillé ;
(nav.) qui a le côté faible.

crankle (cra'n'k'l), *v.n.*, sortir et rentrer ;
aller en zigzag.

crankle, *v.a.*, couper en zigzag.

crankle, *n.*, détour ; zigzag, *m.*

crannied (cra'n'ide), *adj.*, crevassé, gercé.

cranny, *n.*, crevasse, fente, *f.* ; trou, *m.*

crape, *n.*, crêpe, *m.*

crape, *v.a.*, crêper.

crapulous (crap'iou-), *adj.*, crapuleux.

crash, *n.*, fracas ; craquement, *m.*

crash, *v.n.*, faire un grand fracas.

crasis (cré-ciss), *n.*, (gram.) crase, *f.*

crass, *adj.*, épais.

crassitude (cras'si-tioude), *n.*, épaisseur, *f.*

crate (créte), *n.*, caisse à claire-voie, *f.* ;
panier à verrerie, *m.*

crater (cré-), *n.*, cratère, *m.*

craunch (cra'n'she), *or* **crunch** (creu'n'she),
v.a., croquer.

cravat, *n.*, cravate, *f.*

crave, *v.a.*, solliciter ; implorer ; demander.

craven (cré'v'n), *adj.*, de lâche ; poltron,
lâche.

craven, *n.*, lâche, poltron, *m.*

craven, *v.a.*, rendre lâche.

craver (crév'-), *n.*, demandeur, solliciteur, *m.*

craving, *n.*, désir ardent, besoin impérieux, *m.*

craw (crô), *n.*, jabot (of a bird—*d'oiseau*), *m.*

crawfish (crô-), *or* **crayfish** (crè-), *n.*, écrevisse, *f.* Sea — ; *langouste, f.*

crawl (crôl), *v.n.*, ramper ; se traîner ; avoir
la chair de poule. My flesh —s ; *j'ai la chair
de poule.*

crawler, *n.*, reptile, *m.*

crayon (cré-eune), *n.*, crayon de pastel ;
pastel, *m.*

crayon, *v.a.*, dessiner au pastel ; crayonner.

craze, *v.a.*, briser ; broyer ; frapper de
folie ; déranger le cerveau.

crazedness (cré-zèd'-), *n.*, caducité ; **aliéna-**
tion mentale, *f.*

craziness (cré-), *n.*, caducité ; démence, *f.*

crazy (cré-zi), *adj.*, cadue ; infirme ; fou.

creak (crike), *v.n.*, crier ; (of the crane—*de
la grue*) glapir.

creaking (crîk-), *n.*, cri, *m.*

cream (crime), *n.*, crème. *f.* — -cheese ;
fromage à la crème, m. Whipped — ; *crème
fouettée.*

cream, *v.a.*, écrémer.

cream, *v.n.*, crémer.

cream-coloured (-keul'leurde), *adj.*, couleur café au lait, isabelle.

creamy, *adj.*, crémeux ; de crème.

crease (cri-ce), *n.*, pli ; faux pli, *m.*

crease, *v.a.*, faire des plis à ; faire des faux
plis à ; chiffonner.

creasote (cri-a-çôte), *n.*, créosote, *f.*

creat (cri-ate), *n.*, (man.) créat, *m.*

create (cri-éte), *v.a.*, créer ; faire naître ;
causer ; constituer.

creation, *n.*, création ; nature, espèce, *f.*

creative, *adj.*, créateur.

creator (-teur), *n.*, créateur, *m.*

creature (crit'ioure), *n.*, créature, *f.* ; être, *m.*

credence (cri-), *n.*, créance ; croyance, *f.*
To give — to ; *ajouter foi à.*

credenda (cri-dè'n'-), *n.pl.*, articles de
foi, *m.pl.*

credent (cri-), *adj.*, crédule.

credentials (cri-dè'n'shalze), *n.*, lettres de
créance, *f.pl.*

credibility (crèd'-), *n.*, véridicité ; crédibilité, *f.*

credible (crèd'i-b'l), *adj.*, croyable.

credibleness, *n.*, crédibilité, *f.*

credibly (crèd'-), *adv.*, d'une manière digne de foi.

credit (crèd'ite), *n.*, croyance, foi, *f.* ; honneur ; crédit, *m.*, influence, *f.* ; (com.) crédit, *m.*
To give — to ; *faire crédit.* To do — to ; *faire
honneur à.* Worthy of — ; *digne de foi.* On — ;
à crédit.

credit, *v.a.*, ajouter foi à ; croire à ; faire
honneur à ; (com.) donner à crédit, faire crédit
de ; (book-keeping—*comptabilité*) créditer.

creditable, *adj.*, honorable ; estimable.

creditableness, *n.*, estime, *f.*

creditably, *adv.*, honorablement.

creditor (-teur), *n.*, créancier, *m.*, créancière, *f.* ; (book-keeping—*comptabilité*) crédit,
avoir, *m.*

credulity (crè-diou-), *n.*, crédulité, *f.*

credulous, *adj.*, crédule.

credulousness, *n.*, crédulité, *f.*

creed (cride), *n.*, credo, *m.* ; croyance,
foi, *f.* ; symbole, *m.* ; profession de foi, *f.* The
Apostles' — ; *le symbole des Apôtres.*

creek (crike), *n.*, (geog.) crique, anse, *f.*

creek, *v.a.*, craquer.

creeky, *adj.*, plein de criques ; sinueux.

creep (cripe), *v.n.*, (*preterit and past part.,*
Crept), se traîner, ramper ; se glisser. To — in ;
se glisser dans ; s'insinuer dans. To — on ;
s'avancer peu à peu ; s'avancer en rampant. To —
out ; *sortir en rampant ; sortir à l'improviste ;*
s'esquiver.

creeper, *n.*, reptile ; (orni.) grimpereau, *m.* ;
(bot.) plante grimpante, *f.*

creephole (crip'hôl), *n.*, trou, *m.* ; (fig.)
échappatoire, *f.*, faux-fuyant, *m.*

creepingly, *adv.*, en rampant ; lentement.

cremation (cri-mé-), *n.*, crémation (of the
dead—*des morts*), *f.*

crenate, *or* **crenated** (cri-néte, -'ède),
adj., entaillé ; échancré.

crenature (crè'n'a-tioure), *n.*, crénelure, *f.*

crenellated (crè'n'lé-tède), *adj.*, crénelé.

crenelled (crè'n'èlde), *adj.*, entaillé, échancré.

creole (cri-ôl), *n.*, créole. *m.f.*

22

creosote (cri-o-çote), *n.* *V.* **creasote**.

crepitate (crèp'-), *v.n.*, décrépiter, crépiter.

crepitation (crèp'i-té-), *n.*, décrépitation, crépitation, *f.*

crepuscle (cri-peus's'l), *or* **crepuscule** (cri-peus'kioul), *n.*, (ant.) crépuscule, *m.*

crescendo (crès'cè'n'dô), *adv.*, (mus.) crescendo.

crescent (crès'-), *n.*, croissant, *m.*

crescent, *or* **crescive**, *adj.*, croissant.

cress (crèce), *n.*, cresson, *m.*   Water—; *cresson de fontaine.*

cresset (crès'sète), *n.*, feu de fanal; flambeau, *m.*; torche, *f.*

crest (crèste), *n.*, (of a cock—*d'un coq*) crête; (orni.) huppe ; (of a peacock—*de paon*) aigrette, *f.*; (of a helmet—*de casque*; her.) cimier, *m.*; (anat., fig.) crête, *f.*

crest, *v.a.*, orner d'un cimier.

crested (-ède), *adj.*, orné d'un cimier; à crête; huppé; à aigrette.

crestfallen (-fôln), *adj.*, abattu, penaud.

crestless, *adj.*, sans crête; sans cimier.

cretaceous (cri-té-sheusse), *adj.*, crétacé.

cretin (cri-), *n.*, crétin, *m.*

cretinism, *n.*, crétinisme, *m.*

crevice (crèv'iss), *n.*, crevasse, *f.*

crew (crou), *n.*, bande, *f.*; (nav.) équipage, *m.*

crewel (crou'èl), *n.*, laine à border, *f.*

crib, *n.*, berceau, lit d'enfant, *m.*; (in a cowhouse—*d'étable*) crèche, mangeoire, *f.*

crib, *v.a.*, piller, chiper.

crick, *n.*, douleur spasmodique; crampe, *f.*

cricket (crik'ète), *n.*, (ent.) grillon, criquet; (stool—*siège*) tabouret, *m.* ;(game—*jeu*) crosse, *f.*

crier (craï'eur), *n.*, crieur ; (of a court—*d'un tribunal*) huissier, *m.*

crime (craïme), *n.*, crime, *m.* Heinous —; *forfait, m., crime énorme.* To charge with a —; *accuser d'un crime.*

crimeful (-foule), *adj.*, criminel.

crimeless, *adj.*, exempt de crime, innocent.

criminal (crim'-), *adj.*, criminel.

criminal, *n.*, criminel, *m.*

criminally, *adv.*, criminellement.

criminalness, *n.*, culpabilité, criminalité, *f.*

criminate, *v.a.*, incriminer.

crimination (-né-), *n.*, incrimination, accusation.

criminative (-né-), *or* **criminatory** (-néteu'ri), *adj.*, accusatoire.

crimp, *n.*, commissionnaire pour la vente de la houille ; (for the army, navy—*pour l'armée, la marine*) racoleur, *m.*

crimp, *v.a.*, gaufrer; friser, boucler.

crimple (cri'm'p'l), *v.a.*, plisser.

crimson (cri'm'z'n), *adj.*, cramoisi ; rouge, incarnat.

crimson, *n.*, cramoisi ; rouge, incarnat, *m.*

crimson, *v.a.*, teindre en cramoisi.

crimson, *v.n.*, se teindre en cramoisi ; rougir.

cringe (cri'n'dje), *n.*, courbette ; basse servilité, *f.*

cringe, *v.a.*, contracter, froncer.

cringe, *v.n.*, faire des courbettes ; ramper. To — to : *faire le chien couchant auprès de.*

cringle (cri'n'g'l), *n.*, osier pour assujettir une porte, *m.*; (nav.) branche de bouline, *f.*

crinigerous (cri-nidj'èr'-), *adj.*, velu; couvert de poil.

crinkle (crign'k'l), *v.n.*, serpenter; aller en zigzag.

crinkle, *v.a.*, former en zigzag.

crinosity (cri-nôss'-), *n.*, abondance de poil, *f.*

cripple (crip'p'l), *n.*, boiteux, *m.*, boiteuse, *f.*; estropié, *m.*

cripple, *adj.*, boiteux, estropié.

cripple, *v.a.*, estropier : mettre hors de combat ; (nav.) causer des avaries à.

crippleness, *n.*, état d'une personne estropiée, *m.*

crisis (craï-ciss), *n.* (*crises*), crise, *f.*

crisp, *adj.*, fragile, friable ; croquant ; (hair—*des cheveux*) crépu, crispé ; (of hair—*des cheveux*) frisé, bouclé.

crisp, *v.a.*, friser, boucler ; (stuffs—*étoffes*) crêper ; (fig.) faire serpenter.

crisping, *n.*, action de friser, de boucler, *f.*

crisping-iron (-aï'eur'n), *or* **crisping-pin** (-pine), *n.*, fer à friser, *m.*

crispness, *n.*, fragilité ; qualité de ce qui est croquant, sec, cassant, *f.* ; état de ce qui est frisé, *m.* ; frisure, *f.*

crispy, *adj.*, frisé ; croquant, sec, cassant.

criterion (cri-ti-ri-eunc), *n.*, épreuve, *f.* ; criterium, *m.*

critic, *n.*, critique, *m.*

critical, *adj.*, de la critique ; critique ; délicat. — affair ; *affaire délicate, f.*

critically, *adv.*, d'une manière critique ; de crise.

criticalness, *n.*, caractère critique, *m.*

criticism (-ciz'm), *n.*, critique, censure, *f.*

criticize (-çaïze), *v.a.*, critiquer, faire la critique de.

criticize, *v.n.*, faire de la critique.

critique (-tike), *n.*, observation critique ; critique, *f.*

croak (crôke), *n.*, (of frogs—*des grenouilles*) coassement ; (of rooks—*des corbeaux*) croassement, *m.*

croak, *v.n.*, (of frogs—*des grenouilles*) coasser ; (of rooks—*des corbeaux*) croasser ; (fig.) gronder, grogner.

croaker (crôk'), *n.*, grognon ; faiseur de jérémiades, *m.*

croaking, *n.* *V.* **croak** (noun).

croceous (crô-sheusse), *adj.*, safrané.

crock (croke), *n.*, pot de terre, *m* ; suie, *f.* ; noir de fumée, *m.*

crockery (crok'eur'i), *or* **crockery-ware** (-wére), *n.*, faïence, *f.*

crocodile (-dail, *ou* -dil), *n.*, crocodile, *m.*

crocus (crô-), *n.*, safran, crocus, *m.*

croft, *n.*, petit clos, *m.*

croisade, *n.* *V.* **crusade**.

crone (crône), *n.*, vieille brebis ; vieille femme, *f.*

cronet (crô-nète), *n.*) couronne, *f.*

crony (crô-), *n.*, vieux ami ; compère, *m.*

crook (crouke), *n.*, courbure ; (of a shepherd —*de berger*) houlette, *f.* ; (fig.) détour, *m.*

crook, *v.a.*, courber, tortuer ; plier.

crook-back, *n.*, bossu, *m.*, bossue, *f.*

crook-backed (-bak'te), *adj.*, à dos voûté ; voûté ; bossu.

crooked (crouk'ède), *adj.*, courbe ; courbé ; tortueux ; crochu ; (fig.) pervers ; tortu ; travers.

crookedly, *adv.*, tortueusement.

crookedness, *n.*, courbure, *f.* ; état tortu ; (fig.) travers, *m.*, perversité, *f.*

crook-kneed (-nide), *adj.*, bancal, cagneux.

crook-legged (-lèg'de), *adj.*, bancal, qui a les jambes cagneuses, tortues. To be —; *avoir les jambes cagneuses, tortues, être bancal.*

crook-neck (-nèke), *n.*, (bot.) gourde ; calebasse, *f.*

crook-shouldered (-shôl'deur'de), *adj.*, qui a une épaule plus haute que l'autre.

crop, *n.*, (of a bird—*d'oiseau*) jabot, *m.* ; (agri. hort.) récolte, *f.*

crop, *v.a.*, cueillir ; récolter ; moissonner faucher ; couper le bout ; (horses—*des chevaux*) écourter ; (of animals—*des animaux*) brouter.

crop, *v.n.*, donner une récolte.

crop-ear (îre), *n.*, cheval essorillé, cheval bretaudé, *m.*

cropper, *n.*, pigeon à grosse gorge, *m.*

cropping, *n.*, action de couper; mutilation ; (of animals—*des animaux*) action de brouter ; (agri.) exploitation d'un champ, *f.*

crosier (crô-jeur), *n.*, crosse (of a bishop—*d'évêque*), *f.*

croslet (cros'lète), *n.*, (her.) croisette, *f.*

cross, *n.*, croix, *f.*; (of roads, streets—*de routes, de rues*) carrefour, *m.*; (fig.) revers, *m.*, traverse, *f.*

cross, *adj.*, oblique; en travers; de travers; fâcheux, contraire; bourru; méchant, de mauvaise humeur. — woman; *femme de mauvaise humeur*, *f.* — answer; *réponse de travers*, *f.*

cross, *v.a.*, croiser ; faire le signe de la croix sur; faire une croix sur; (fig.) franchir, traverser; contrarier, contre-carrer. To — out; *effacer*, *rayer*. To — over; *traverser*. To — a threshhold; *franchir un seuil*.

cross, *v.n.*, être en travers; traverser.

cross, *prep.*, à travers.

cross-armed (-àrm'de), *adj.*, qui a les bras croisés; (bot.) à paires croisées; opposé, croisé.

cross-arrow, *n.*, flèche d'arbalète, *f.*, carreau, *m.*

crossbar (-bâr), *n.*, (carp.) traverse, *f.*

crossbar-shot, *n.*, (artil.) boulet ramé, ange, *m.*

cross-battery, *n.*, (milit.) contre-batterie, *f.*

cross-beam (-bîme), *n.*, (carp.) traverse, *f.*, traversin, *m.*, solive croisée, *f.*; (nav.) traversin, *m.*

cross-bearer (-bèr'-), *n.*, porte-croix. *m.*

cross-berry (-bèr'-), *n.*, (bot.) camarine, *f.*

cross-bite (-baïte), *n.*, tromperie, fourberie, *f.*

cross-bite, *v.a.*, tromper, duper.

crossbow (-bô), *n.*, arbalète, *f.*

crossbow-man (-ma'n), *n.*, arbalétrier, *m.*

cross-breed (-bride), *n.*, race croisée, *f.*

cross-breeding, *n.*, croisement, *m.*

crossbun (-beune), *n.*, baba marqué d'une croix, *m.*

cross-cut (-keute), *v.a.*, couper en travers.

crosscut-saw (-sô), *n.*, scie à deux mains, *f.*

cross-examination (-né-), *n.*, (jur.) interrogatoire contradictoire, *m.*

cross-examine (-ègz'am'ine), *v.a.*, (jur.) interroger contradictoirement.

cross-flow (-flô), *v.n.*, couler dans une direction opposée.

cross-framing (-frô'm'-), *n.*, (carp.) traverse, *f.*

crossgrained (-grê'n'de), *adj.*, (of wood—*de bois*) dont la veine est à rebours; (fig.) rebours, revêche. To be —; *avoir l'esprit mal tourné; être acariâtre.*

cross-hands (-ha'n'dze), *n.*, (dancing—*danse*) chaîne anglaise, *f.*

cross-hatch (hat'she), *v.a.*, (engr.) contrehacher.

cross-hatching, *n.*, (engr.) contrehachure, *f.*

crossing, *n.*, passage pour les piétons sur une route, dans une rue, &c.; signe de croix; (railways) croisement; passage à niveau, *m.*; (of animals—*des animaux*) croisement; (fig.) travers, *m.*

crossjack (-djak), *n.*, (nav.) voile carrée, *f.*

cross-legged (-lèg'de), *adj.*, qui a les jambes croisées.

cross-like (⁓e), *adj.*, (bot.) cruciforme; en croix; (surg.) crucial.

crossly, *adv.*, en travers; (fig.) malheureusement; mal; de travers; avec mauvaise humeur.

crossness, *n.*, travers, *m.*; mauvaise humeur, méchanceté, *f.*

cross-pawl (-pôl), *n.*, (nav.) lisse, *f.*

crosspiece (-pîce), *n.*, (carp.) entretoise ; traverse, *f.*

cross-post (-pôste), *n.*, service de correspondance des postes, *m.*

cross-purpose (peur'poss), *n.*, système contraire, but contraire, *m.*, opposition, contradiction, *f.*; contresens: malentendu, *m.*; énigme, *f.* . To be at cross-purposes; *se contrecarrer.*

cross-question (-kwèst'ieune), *v.a.*, interroger contradictoirement.

crossroad (-rôde), *n.*, chemin de traverse, *m.*

cross-shaped (-shê'p'te), *adj.*, en forme de croix; cruciforme.

cross-wind (-wi'n'de), *n.*, vent contraire, *m.*

cross-wise (-waîze), *adv.*, en croix; en forme de croix; en travers ; en sautoir.

crotchet (crotsh'ète), *n.*, (mas.) étai, *m.*; (mus.) noire, *f.*; (surg.) crochet, *m.*; (idea—*idée*) lubie, marotte, *f.*

crotcheted (-èt'éde), *adj.*, (mus.) mesuré.

crotchety (-èt'i), *adj.*, sujet aux lubies.

crouch (craoutshe), *v.n.*, se tapir; se blottir; (fig.) ramper, s'abaisser, faire le chien couchant.

croup, *n.*, (of animals—*des animaux*) croupe, *f.*; (of birds—*des oiseaux*) croupion, *m.*; (med.) croup, *m.*

croupade, *n.*, croupade, *f.*

crow (crô), *n.*, (orni.) corbeau, *m.*; corneille, *f.*; levier de fer; chant du coq, *m.*

crow, *v.n.* (preterit, Crew, Crowed; past part., Crowed), chanter. To — over; *chanter victoire sur.*

crow-bar (-bâr), *n.*, pince (iron-lever—*levier de fer*), *f.*

crowd (craoude), *n.*, foule, *f.*

crowd, *v.a.*, presser; serrer. To — with ; *remplir de.* — sail; (nav.) *forcer de voiles.*

crowd, *v.n.*, affluer; se presser; se présenter en foule.

crowfoot (-foute), *n.*, (milit.) chausse-trape; (bot.) renoncule; (nav.) araignée, *f.*

crow-keeper (-kîp'-), *n.*, épouvantail, *m.*

crown (craoune), *n.*, couronne, *f.*; sommet; (piece of money—*monnaie*) écu, *m.*, couronne, *f.*; (nav.) collet, *m.*; (of a hat—*d'un chapeau*) calotte; (of a stag—*du cerf*) couronnure, *f.*; sommet (of the head—*de la tête*); accomplissement, *m.*

crown, *v.a.*, couronner; (at draughts—*aux dames*) damer.

crownland (-la'n'de), *n.*, domaine de la couronne, *m.*

crown-side (-saïde), *n.*, (jur.) cour criminelle, *f.*

crown-wheel (-hwîl), *n.*, (horl.) roue de champ, *f.*

crown-work (-weurke), *n.*, (fort.) ouvrage à couronne, *m.*

croyn (croïne), *v.n.*, (hunt.) réer, raire.

cruchet (creutsh'ète), *n.*, (orni.) ramier, *m.*

crucial (crou-shi-), *adj.*, crucial, en croix.

crucible (crou-ci-b'l), *n.*, creuset, *m.*

cruciferous (crou-cif-eur-), *adj.*, crucifère.

crucifier (crou-ci-fai'eur), *n.*, celui qui crucifie, *m.*

crucifix (crou-ci-fikse), *n.*, crucifix, *m.*

crucifixion (-fik'sheune), *n.*, crucifiement, crucifiment, *m.*; crucifixion, *f.*

cruciform, *adj.*, cruciforme.

crucify (-fa'ye), *v.a.*, crucifier.

crude (croude), *adj.*, cru.

crudely, *adv.*, crûment.

crudeness, *n.*, crudité, *f.*

crudity, *n.*, crudité, *f.*; (med.) substance non digérée, *f.*

cruel (crou'èl), *adj.*, cruel.

cruelly, *adv.*, cruellement.

cruelness, *n.*, cruauté, *f.*

cruelty, *n.*, cruauté, *f.*
cruet (crou'ète), *n.*, vinaigrier, huilier, *m.*
cruet-stand (-sta'n'd), *n.*, huilier; porte-huilier, *m.*
cruise (crouze), *n.*, croisière, course, *f.*
cruise, *v.n.*, croiser; faire la course.
cruiser, *n.*, croiseur, *m.*
crum. or **crumb** (creume), *n.*, mie; miette, *f.*
crumble (creu'm'b'l), *v.a.*, émietter; émier: broyer; réduire en poussière.
crumble, *v.n.*, s'émier; s'émietter; tomber en poussière.
crummy, *adj.*, plein de mie.
crump (creu'm'pe), *adj.*, courbé, crochu.
crumpet (creu'm'pète), *n.*, gâteau à la farine, *m.*
crumple (creu'm'p'l), *v.a.*, rider; chiffonner: froisser.
crumple, *v.n.*, se rider, se chiffonner.
crumpling, *n.*, pomme ratatinée, *f.*
crunch (creu'n'she), *v.a.* V. **craunch**.
cruor (crou-eur), *n.*, cruor; caillot, *m.*
crupper (creup'-), *n.*, croupe; croupière, *f.*
crural (crou'-), *adj.*, crural.
crusade (crou-céde), *n.*, croisade, *f.*
crusader, *n.*, croisé, *m.*
cruset (crou-cète), *n.*, creuset, *m.*
crush (creushe), *n.*, écrasement, choc, *m.*
crush, *v.a.*, écraser; détruire.
crushing, *n.*, broiement, broîment, ecrasement, *m.*
crushing-machine (-ma-shîne), *n.*, machine à broyer, *f.*; (metal.) bocard, *m.*
crust (creuste), *n.*, croûte, *f.*
crust, *v.a.*, encroûter; couvrir d'une croûte.
crust, *v.n.*, s'encroûter.
crustacea (creus-té-shi-a), *n.pl.*, crustacés, *m.pl.*
crustaceous (-té-sheusse), *adj.*, crustacé.
crustily, *adv.*, d'une manière morose, d'une manière hargneuse.
crustiness, *n.*, qualité de ce qui a de la croûte; (fig.) humeur hargneuse, *f.*
crusty, *adj.*, qui a beaucoup de croûte; hargneux, morose.
crutch (creutshe), *n.*, béquille, *f.*
crutch, *v.a.*, soutenir avec des béquilles.
cry (cra'ye), *n.*, cri, *m.*; (pack of hounds—*chiens de chasse*) meute, *f.*
cry, *v.n.*, crier; (to weep—*verser des larmes*) pleurer. To — aloud; *élever la voix*. To — out; *s'écrier*; crier; se récrier. To — to; *réclamer*, *invoquer*.
cry, *v.a.*, crier. To — down; *décrier*. To — out; *crier très fort*. To — up; *exalter*, *prôner*; *vanter*.
crying, *n.*, cri, *m.*, (weeping—*verser des larmes*) action de pleurer, *f.*, pleurs, *m.pl.*
crying, *adj.*, criant.
crypt (cripte), *n.*, crypte, *f.*
cryptic, or **cryptical**, *adj.*, secret, occulte.
cryptically, *adv.*, secrètement.
cryptogam, *n.*, (bot.) cryptogame, *f.*
cryptogamous, *adj.*, (bot.) cryptogame.
cryptography, *n.*, cryptographie, stéganographie, *f.*
crystal, *n.*, cristal, *m.*
crystal, *adj.*, de cristal.
crystalline (-laïne, *ou* -line), *adj.*, cristallin. — lens; *cristallin* (of the eye—*de l'œil*), *m.*
crystallization (-laï-zé-), *n.*, cristallisation, *f.*
crystallize (-laïze), *v.a.*, cristalliser.
crystallize, *v.n.*, se cristalliser.
cub (keube), *n.*, petit; (of a bear—*de l'ours*) ourson; (of a lion—*du lion*) lionceau; (of a fox—*du renard*) renardeau, *m.* An unlicked —; *un ours mal léché*.
cub, *v.n.*, mettre bas.

cubature (kiou-ba-tioure), *n.*, cubature, (l.u.) cubation, *f.*, cubage, *m.*
cube (kioube), *n.*, cube, *m.* — root; *racine cubique*, *f.*
cube, *v.a.*, cuber.
cubeb (kiou-bèbe), *n.*, cubèbe, *m.*
cubic, or **cubical** (kiou-), *adj.*, cubique, cube.
cubiform, *adj.*, cubique, en cube.
cubit (kiou-), *n.*, (anat.) cubitus, *m*; (measure —*mesure*) coudée, *f.*
cubital, *adj.*, cubital.
cucking-stool (keuk'ign'stoul), *n.*, (jur.) sellette de correction, *f.*
cuckold (keuk'-), *n.*, cocu, cornard, *m.*
cuckold, *v.a.*, faire cocu.
cuckoldom (-deume), *n.*, cocuage, *m.*
cuckoo (couk'ou), *n.*, coucou, *m.*
cucullate, or **cucullated** (kiou-keul-léte, -ède), *adj.*, encapuchonné.
cucumber (kiou-keu'm'-), *n.*, concombre, *m.*
cucurbitaceous (kiou-keur-bi-té-sheusse), *adj.*, cucurbitacé.
cucurbite (kiou-keur-), *n.*, cucurbite, *f.*
cud (keude), *n.*, aliments contenus dans le premier estomac des ruminants, *m.pl.*; panse (of ruminants—*des ruminants*); chique de tabac, *f.*
cudbear (-bère), *n.*, couleur violette; prune de Monsieur, *f.*
cuddle (keud'd'l), *v.a.*, embrasser étroitement.
cuddle, *v.n.*, se blottir; s'embrasser étroitement, s'étreindre.
cuddy (keud'-), *n.*, (nav.) cuisine, *f.*; (ich.) charbonnier, *m.*
cudgel (keud'djèl), *n.*, gourdin; bâton, *m.*
cudgel, *v.a.*, bâtonner.
cudgel-proof (-proufe), *adj.*, à l'épreuve du gourdin.
cue (kiou), *n.*, queue de billard; (thea.) réplique, *f.*; (fig.) avis, mot, *m.*, instruction; (fig.) veine, *f.*
cue, *v.a.*, tresser en queue.
cuff (keuf), *v.a.*, souffleter; donner des coups de patte à.
cuff, *n.*, coup de poing; coup de patte, *m.*; taloche, *f.*; (of a coat, &c.—*d'un habit, &c.*) parement; (of a gown—*d'une robe*) poignet, *m.*; manchette, *f.*
cuirass (kwi-), *n.*, cuirasse, *f.*
cuirassier (kwi-ras'sire), *n.*, cuirassier, *m.*
cuish, or **cuisse** (kwice), *n.*, cuissard, *m.*
culinary (kiou-), *adj.*, de cuisine; culinaire.
cull (keul), *v.a.*, recueillir, cueillir, choisir.
cullender, *n.*, couloire, passoire, *f.*
culler (keul'-), *n.*, personne qui choisit, *f.*
cullion (keul'ieune), *n.*, drôle; nigaud; (bot.) orchis, *m.*
cullionly, *adj.*, de drôle; vilement.
cully (keul'-), *n.*, dupe, *f.*
cully, *v.a.*, duper.
culm (keulme), *n.*, (bot.) chaume, *m.*; (min.) houille sèche, *f.*
culminate (keul-), *v.n.*, (astron.) culminer.
culmination (-né-), *n.*, (astron.) culmination, *f.*
culpability (keul-), *n.*, culpabilité, *f.*
culpable, *adj.*, coupable.
culpableness, *n.*, culpabilité, *f.*
culpably, *adv.*, coupablement, d'une manière coupable.
culprit (keul'-), *n.*, accusé, *m.*, accusée, *f.*; criminel, *m.*, criminelle, *f.*
culter (keul'-), *n.*, soc, coutre, *m.*
cultivate (keul'-), *v.a.*, cultiver.
cultivation (-vé-), *n.*, culture, *f.*
cultivator (-vé-teur), *n.*, cultivateur, *m.*
culture (keult'ioure), *n.*, culture, *f.*
culture, *v.a.*, cultiver.

culver (keul-), *n.*, pigeon ramier, *m.*

culverin (keul-veur'ine), *n.*, couleuvrine, *f.*

culvert (keul-veurt), *n.*, rigole, *f.*; petit aqueduc, *m.*

cumber (keu'm'-), *n.*, embarras, obstacle, *m.*

cumber, *v.a.*, embarrasser; encombrer.

cumbersome (-seume), *adj.*, embarrassant; gênant.

cumbersomely, *adv.*, d'une manière embarrassante.

cumbersomeness, *n.*, embarras, fardeau, *m.*

cumbrance, *n.*, embarras, fardeau, *m.*

cumbrous, *adj.*, embarrassant, gênant, accablant, à charge.

cumin (keu'm'ine), *n.*, (bot.) cumin, *m.*

cumulate (kiou-miou-), *v.a.*, cumuler.

cumulation (-lé-), *n.*, cumulation, *f.*

cuneal (kiou-ni-), *adj.*, en coin; cunéaire.

cuneate, *or* **cuneated** (-ède), *adj.*, en coin, cunéaire.

cuneiform (kiou-ni-i-), *or* **cuniform** (kiou-ni-), *adj.*, cunéiforme.

cunning (keu'n'-), *n.*, finesse; adresse; ruse, *f.*

cunning, *adj.*, fin, rusé, adroit.

cunningly, *adv.*, avec finesse; avec artifice; adroitement; par ruse.

cunning-man (-ma'n), *n.*, devin; sorcier, *m.*

cunningness, *n.*, ruse, finesse, *f.*

cup (keupe), *n.*, tasse, coupe, *f.*; (bot.) calice, *m.* In one's —s; *dans les vignes du Seigneur.*

cup, *v.a.*, ventouser.

cupbearer (-bèr'-), *n.*, échanson, *m.*

cupboard (-bôrde), *n.*, armoire, *f.*; buffet, *m.*

cupel (kiou-), *n.*, (chem.) coupelle, *f.*

cupellation (kiou-pèl-lé-), *n.*, coupellation, *f.*

cupidity (kiou-), *n.*, cupidité, *f.*

cupola (kiou-), *n.*, coupole, *f.*

cupper (keup'-), *n.*, ventouseur, *m.*

cupping, *n.*, application de ventouses, *f.*

cupping-glass (-glâce), *n.*, ventouse, *f.*

cupreous (kiou-pri-), *adj.*, cuivreux.

cupulate (kiou-piou-), *adj.*, (bot.) muni d'une cupule, cupulé.

cupule (kiou-pioul), *n.*, (bot.) cupule, *f.*

cur (keur), *n.*, mauvais chien, chien hargneux, *m.*

curable (kiou-ra-b'l), *adj.*, guérissable, curable.

curableness, *n.*, curabilité, *f.*

curacoa (kiou-ra-cô), *n.*, curaçao (liqueur), *m.*

curacy (kiou-), *n.*, vicariat, *m.*

curate (kiou-), *n.*, vicaire; pasteur, *m.*

curative (kiou-ré-), *adj.*, curatif.

curator (kiou-ré-teur), *n.*, curateur, administrateur, *m.*

curb (keurbe), *n.*, (man.) gourmette, *f.*; (fig.) frein, *m.*; (of a well—*de puits*) margelle; (of a foot pavement—*de trottoir*) bordure; (vet.) tare, *f.*

curb, *v.a.*, (man.) gourmer; (fig.) réprimer, brider.

curb-stone (-'stône), *n.*, (of a foot pavement —*de trottoir*) bordure, *f.*

curculio (keur-kiou-), *n.*, (ent.) charançon, *m.*

curcuma (keur-kiou-), *n.*, (bot.) curcuma, *m.*

curd (keurde), *n.*, lait caillé, *m.*

curd, *v.a.*, cailler, figer.

curdle (keur d'l), *v.a.*, cailler; figer.

curdle, *v.n.*, se cailler, se coaguler, se figer.

curdy, *adj.*, caillé.

cure (kioure), *n.*, guérison; cure, *f.*; remède, *m.* — of souls; *charge d'âmes, f.*

cure, *v.a.*, guérir; (meat, &c.—*viande, &c.*) mariner, saler.

cureless, *adj.*, incurable.

curer, *n.*, guérisseur; (of meat, &c.—*viande, &c.*) saleur, *m.*

curfew (keur-fiou), *n.*, couvre-feu, *m.*

curfew-bell, *n.*, couvre-feu, *m.*

curiosity (kiou-ri- os'-), *n.*, curiosité, *f.*

curious (kiou-), *adj.*, curieux; exact; délicat.

curiously, *adv.*, curieusement.

curl (keurl), *n.*, boucle, *f.* —s; *frisure, f.*

curl, *v.a.*, boucler; friser; (fig.) faire onduler.

curl, *v.n.*, friser, boucler; (of the serpent—*du serpent*) se replier, s'entortiller; (of the vine —*de la vigne*) s'entrelacer.

curled (keur'l'de), *adj.*, (bot.) crispé, crépu.

curlew (keur-liou), *n.*, (orni.) courlieu, courlis, *m.*

curliness (keurl'-), *n.*, frisure, *f.*

curling, *n.*, frisure, *f.*

curling-irons (-ai'eurn'z), *or* **curling-tongs** (-to'n'gze), *n.pl.*, fer à friser, *m.sing.*

curl-paper, *n.*, papillote (for the hair— *pour les cheveux*), *f.*

curly, *adj.*, frisé; bouclé; (fig.) qui ondule.

curmudgeon (keur-meud'jeune), *n.*, grognon; ladre, *m.*

curmudgeonly, *adv.*, en ladre, de ladre.

currant (keur'ra'n'te), *n.*, groseille, *f.* Dried —s; *raisin de Corinthe, m.* Black —; cassis, *m.* Red —; *groseille rouge, f.* White —; *groseille blanche, f.*

currant-bush (-boushe), *n.*, groseiller, *m.*

currency (keur-rè'n'-), _ (of money—*des monnaies*) cours, *m.*, circulation, *f.*; (fig.) cours, crédit, *m.*, vogue, *f.* Legal —; *monnaie légale, f.* Paper —; *circulation de papier-monnaie. f.* To give — to; *donner cours à.*

current, *adj.*, courant; *ce.*; admis, reçu.

current, *n.*, courant d'eau; durant; cours; entraînement, *m.*

current, *v.a.*, incliner pour faciliter l'écoulement des eaux.

currently, *adv.*, continuellement; avec un mouvement continuel; couramment.

curricle (keur'ri-k'l), *n.*, cabriolet à pompe, *m.*

currier (keur-ri-eur), *n.*, corroyeur, *m.*

currish (keur-rishe), *adj.*, comme un chien; hargneux.

currishly, *adv.*, d'une manière hargneuse.

curry (keur-ri), *v.a.*, corroyer; (a horse—*un cheval*) étriller. To — favour with; *s'insinuer dans les bonnes grâces de.*

curry-comb (-côme), *n.*, étrille, *f.*

curse (keurse), *n.*, malédiction, *f.*

curse, *v.a.*, maudire.

curse, *v.n.*, proférer des malédictions.

cursed (keurs'ède), *adj.*, maudit, exécrable.

cursedly, *adv.*, abominablement; terriblement.

cursedness, *n.*, noirceur, *f.*

curship (keur-), *n.*, nature hargneuse, *f.*

cursitor (keur-si-teur), *n.*, greffier de la Cour de Chancellerie, *m.* [Cour suprême d'Angleterre, dont les attributions ont un certain rapport avec celles de la Cour de Cassation en France.]

cursorily (keur-), *adv.*, rapidement; à la hâte.

cursoriness (keur-), *n.*, rapidité, *f.*

cursory (keur-), *adj.*, rapide, léger, superficiel.

curst (keurste), *adj.*, (ant.) revêche, bourru; grossier, insolent.

curt (keurte), *adj.*, court, bref; sec.

curtail (keur-téle), *v.a.*, retrancher; réduire; écourter. To — of; *priver de.*

curtailment, *n.*, réduction, *f.*; retranchement, *m.*

curtain (keur-tine), *n.*, rideau, *m.*; (fort.) courtine, *f.*; (thea.) rideau, *m.*, toile, *f.* — -rod; *tringle, f.*

curtain, *v.a.*, garnir de rideaux ; (fig.) envelopper.

curtain-arm (-arme), *or* **curtain-band** (-ba'n'd), *n.*, embrasse, *f.*

curtsy (keurt'-), *n. V.* **courtesy.**

curvated (keur-vé-tède), *adj.*, courbé.

curvation (keur-vé-), *n.*, courbure, *f.*

curvature (keur-va-tioure), *n.*, courbure, *f.*

curve (keurve), *adj.*, courbe.

curve, *n.*, (geom.) courbe, *f.*

curve, *v.a.*, courber ; cintrer.

curvet (keur-vète), *v.n.*, (man.) faire des courbettes ; sauter, gambader.

curvet, *n.*, (man.) courbette, *f.*

curvilineal, *or* **curvilinear** (keur-), *adj.*, curviligne.

cushion (coush'eune), *n.*, coussin ; (of a steam engine—*de machine à vapeur*) matelas ; (of a pump—*de pompe*) coussinet, *m.*

cushion, *v.a.*, asseoir sur un coussin.

cushioned (coush'eu'n'de), *adj.*, placé sur un coussin.

cusp (keuspe), *n.*, corne du croissant, *f.* ; (arch.) lobe, *m.*

cuspated (keus-pét'ède), *or* **cuspidal** (keus'-), *adj.*, (ant.) terminé en pointe.

cuspidated (keus'pi-dét'ède), *adj.*, terminé en pointe.

custard (keus-), *n.*, crème cuite au four, *f.* ; flan, *m.*

custody (keus'-), *n.*, garde ; arrestation, *f.* To give any one into — ; *faire arrêter quelqu'un.* To commit to one's — ; *confier à la garde de quelqu'un.* In — ; *en état d'arrestation.*

custom (keus'-), *n.*, coutume, habitude ; douane ; (of a shop—*d'un magasin*) pratique, *f.*, chalands, *m.pl.*, ☉chalandise, *f.*

customable (keus'to'm'a-b'l), *adj.*, habituel ; accoutumé.

customableness, *n.*, fréquence, *f.*

customably, *adv.*, de coutume ; par habitude, habituellement.

customarily (keus'-), *adv.*, ordinairement, d'habitude.

customariness, *n.*, habitude, fréquence, *f.*

customary (keus'-), *adj.*, ordinaire ; coutumier ; d'usage.

custom-duty (-diou-), *n.*, droit de douane, *m.*

customed (keus-teu'm'de), *adj.*, accoutumé ; achalandé.

customer (keus'-), *n.*, chaland, *m.* ; pratique, *f.*

custom-house (-haouce), *n.*, douane, *f.*

cut (keute), *n.*, (with a sharp instrument—*avec un instrument tranchant, aigu*) coup ; (piece cut off—*partie coupée*) morceau, *m.* ; (place cut open—*endroit coupé*) coupure ; (of clothes—*des vêtements*) coupe ; (engr.) gravure ; (at cards—*aux cartes*) coupe ; (channel—*canal*) coupure, dérivation, *f.* ; (words—*mots, paroles*), ironie incisive, *f.*, reproche vif, mot piquant, *m.* ; (short way—*de chemin*) traverse, le plus court, au plus court.

cut, *v.a.* (preterit and past part., Cut), couper ; tailler ; trancher. To — one's teeth ; *faire ses dents.* To — a figure ; *faire figure.* To — a loaf ; *entamer un pain.* To — down ; *abattre.* To — off ; *supprimer ; retrancher ; extirper ; élider ; séparer.* To — small ; *hacher ; rapetisser.* To — short ; *interrompre ; abréger.* To — to the heart ; *fâcher ; faire enrager.* To — up ; *ouvrir ; couper ; trancher ; disséquer ; déchirer.* To — asunder ; *déchirer ; couper ; briser.* To — down ; *couper ; scier ; dépendre.* To — off ; *couper ; trancher ; tailler ; priver ; retrancher ; empêcher.* To — out ; *tailler ; couper.*

cut, *v.n.*, couper, se couper.

cutaneous (kiou-té-ni-), *adj.*, cutané.

cutch (keutshe), *n.*, cachou ; frai d'huître, *m.*

cuticle (kiou-ti-k'l), *n.*, cuticule, *f.* ; épiderme, *m.*

cuticular (kiou-tik'iou-), *adj.*, cutané.

cutlass (keut'-), *n.*, coutelas, *m.*

cutler (keut'-), *n.*, coutelier, *m.*

cutlery, *n.*, coutellerie, *f.*

cutlet (keut'-), *n.*, côtelette de veau, *f.*

cutpurse (-peurse), *n.*, coupeur de bourse, *m.*

cutter (keut'-), *n.*, coupeur ; (nav.) canot, cutter ; (tech.) taillant, *m.*

cutthroat (-thrôte), *n.*, coupe-jarret, *m.* — place ; *coupe-gorge, m.*

cutting (keut'-), *n.*, incision ; (of wood, of cards—*de bois, de cartes*) coupe ; (hort.) bouture, *f.*

cutting, *adj.*, incisif ; piquant ; poignant.

cutting-engine (-è'n'djine), *n.*, machine à diviser, *f.*

cutting-knife (-naïfe), *n.*, (print.) coupoir, *m.*

cutting-out-machine (-aoute-ma-shine), *n.*, (coin.) emporte-pièce, *m.*

cutting-press (-prèce), *n.*, (bookbind.) rognoir, *m.*

cuttle, *or* **cuttle-fish** (keut't'l, -fishe), *n.*, (mol.) sèche, seiche, *f.*

cuttle-bone, *n.*, (conch.) os de sèche, *m.*

cut-water (-wôteur), *n.*, (engineering—*terme d'ingénieur*) avant-bec ; arrière-bec ; (orni.) coupeur d'eau, bec-en-ciseaux ; (nav.) taille-mer. *m.*

cycle (caï'k'l), *n.*, cycle, *m.* — of the sun ; *cycle solaire.* — of the moon ; *cycle lunaire.*

cycloid (caï-cloïde), *n.*, cycloïde, *f.*

cyclop (caï-), *n.*, cyclope, *m.*

cyclopædia (caï-klo-pî-), *n.*, encyclopédie, *f.*

cyclopean (caï-clo-pî-), *adj.*, cyclopéen.

cyclopic (caï-), *adj.*, de cyclope ; cyclopéen.

cygnet (-), *n.*, jeune cygne, *m.*

cylinder (ci-), *n.*, cylindre ; (of a pump—*de pompe*) corps de pompe, *m.*

cylindraceous (ci-li'n'dré-sheusse), *adj.*, (l.u.) cylindracé.

cylindric, *or* **cylindrical** (ci-li'n'-), *adj.*, cylindrique.

cymatium (si-mé-shi-eume), *n.*, (arch.) cymaise, *f.*

cymbal (si'm'-), *n.*, cymbale, *f.*

cymbal-player (-plè'-), *n.*, cymbalier, *m.*

cynanche (si-na'n'-ki), *n.*, (med.) esquinancie, *f.*

cynic, *n.*, cynique, *m.*

cynic, *or* **cynical** (-), *adj.*, sévère ; austère ; cynique.

cynically, *adj.*, cyniquement, d'une manière cynique.

cynicalness (-), *n.*, cynisme, *m.*

cynicism (-ciz'm), *n.*, cynisme, *m.*

cynosure (caï-no-shioure, *ou* ci-), *n.*, cynosure, *f.*

cyperus (caïp'èr'-), *n.*, (bot.) souchet, *m.*

cypress, *or* **cypress-tree** (caï-prèce, -trî), *n.*, cyprès, *m.*

cypress-wood (-woude), *n.*, cyprès, bois de cyprès, *m.*

cyst, *or* **cystis** (ciste, *ou* -tiss), *n.*, (surg.) kyste, *m.*

cystitis (cis-taï-tiss), *n.*, (med.) cystite, *f.*

cystotomy (cis'to-), *n.*, cystotomie, *f.*

cytisus (-ciouss), *n.*, (bot.) cytise ; faux ébénier, *m.*

czar (zâr), *n.*, czar, *m.*

czarina (-rî-), *n.*, czarine, *f.*

czarish, *adj.*, de czar.

czarowitz (zar'o-vitse), *n.*, czarowitz, *m.*

D

d, quatrième lettre de l'alphabet, d, *m.* ; (mus.) ré, *m.*

dab, *n.*, coup léger, *m.* ; éclaboussure, tache,

f. ; petit morceau, *m.* ; (ich.) limande, *f.* To be

— at; *avoir le chic de.*

dab, *v.a.,* dauber; toucher légèrement; éponger à petits coups.

dabble (dab'b'l), *v.a.,* barbouiller, souiller.

dabble, *v.n.,* barboter, patauger. To — in; *se mêler de.*

dabbler, *n.,* barboteur; bousilleur; barbouilleur, *m.*

dabchick (-tshik), *n.,* plongeon, *m.*

dabster, *n.,* malin ; passé maître, *m.*

dace, *n.,* (ich.) vandoise, *f.*

dactyle, *n.,* dactyle, *m.*

dactylic, *n.,* dactylique.

dad, *or* **daddy,** *n.,* papa, *m.*

dado (dâ-dô), *n.,* (arch.) dé; fût vertical, *m.*

daffodil, *n.,* asphodèle, narcisse des prés,*m.*

dag, *n.,* (ant.) dague,*f.*

dagger (dag'gheur), *n.,* poignard, *m.*; (print.) croix, *f.* At —s drawn ; *à couteaux tirés.*

daggers-drawing (-'gheurz'drô'-), *n.,* tirer les poignards du fourreau; mettre l'épée à la main; mettre flamberge au vent. At —; *au moment de se battre, près d'en venir aux mains.*

daggle (dag'g'l), *v.n.,* se crotter; se traîner dans la boue.

daggle, *v.a.,* crotter ; traîner dans la boue.

daggle-tail (-téle), *adj.,* crotté jusqu'à l'échine.

dagon (dé-), *n.,* Dagon, *m.*

daguerreotype (-taïpe), *n.,* daguerréotype, *m.*

dahlia (dâ-), *n.,* (bot.) dahlia, *m.*

daily (dè-lè), *adj.,* journalier, quotidien ; astron.) diurne.

daily, *adv.,* quotidiennement, journellement, tous les jours.

daintily (dé'n'-), *adv.,* avec délicatesse ; avec friandise.

daintiness, *n.,* friandise; délicatesse,*f.*

dainty, *n.,* délicatesse, friandise,*f.*

dainty (dé'n'-), *adj.,*friand, délicat; difficile.

dairy (dè-ré), *n.,* laiterie,*f.*

dairy-farm (-fârme), *n.,* laiterie en gros ; *ferme pour l'exploitation du lait de vache,f.*

dairyist (-ri-iste), *n.,* laitier, crémier, *m.*

dairy-maid (-méde), *n.,* fille de laiterie,*f.*

dairy-man (-ma'n), *n.,* garçon de laiterie; laitier, crémier, *m.*

dairy-room (-roume), *n.,* laiterie (lieu où l'on tient le lait), *f.*

dairy-woman (-woum'a'n), *n.,* laitière, crémière, *f.*

daisy (dè-zé), *n.,* marguerite, pâquerette,*f.*

daisy-cutter (-cut'-), *n.*; (man.) cheval qui rase le tapis, *m.*

daisy-rake (-réke), *n.,* râteau à gazon, *m.*

dale, *n.,* vallon, *m.* ; vallée, *f.* Up hill and down —; *par monts et par vaux.*

dalliance (dal'li-), *n.,* folâtrerie, *f.*; badinage, *m.* ; caresses,*f.pl.*; délai, *m.*

dallier (dal'li-), *n.,* folâtre, *m.*; personne légère, *f.*

dally (dal'li), *v.n.,* tarder; s'amuser; badiner ; folâtrer.

dam (dame), *n.,* (of animals—*des animaux*) mère ; (at draughts—*aux dames*) dame damée, dame ; (of a canal—*de canal*) dame, *f.*; (of a river—*de rivière*) barrage, *m.*; digue,*f.*

dam, *v.n.,* diguer, contenir ; (fig.) arrêter.

damage (dam'édje), *n.,* dommage; tort, *m.* ; (nav.) avarie, *f.* —s; (jur.) *dommayes-intérêts, dommages et intérêts, m.pl.*

damage, *v.a.,* endommager; avarier.

damage, *v.a.,* s'endommager.

damageable (-'édj'a-b'l), *adj.,* susceptible de s'endommager.

damascene (-'cine), *n.,* prune de damas,*f.*

damask, *n.,* damas, *m.*

damask, *v.a.,* damasser.

---

damaskeen (-'kîne), *v.a.,* damasquiner.

damaskeening, *n.,* (art) damasquinerie; (ornament—*ornement*) damasquinure,*f.*

damasking, *n.,* damassure,*f.*

damask-worker, *n.,* damasseur, *m.*

dame (déme), *n.,* dame ; mère,*f.*

damn (da'm), *v.a.,* damner ; désapprouver; siffler (as a mark of disapprobation—*en signe de désapprobation*).

damnable (da'm'na'b'l),*adj.,* damnable.

damnably, *adv.,* damnablement.

damnation (da'm'né-), *n.,* damnation,*f.*

damnatory (da'm'na-teuri), *adj.,* qui condamne.

damned (da'm'de, *ou* da'm'nède), *adj.,* damné; (l.ex.) maudit.

damnify (da'm'ni-fa'ye), *v.a.,* (ant.) nuire à.

damp (da'm'pe), *n.,* humidité, vapeur ; (fig.) tristesse, *f.,* abattement, *m.*

damp, *adj.,* humide ; (fig.) triste, abattu.

damp, *v.a.,* rendre humide ; (fig.) décourager, ralentir, obscurcir, refroidir.

damper, *n.,* éteignoir ; (piano) étouffoir , *m.,* pédale douce, sourdine,*f.* ; (of a chimney—*de cheminée*) registre, *m.*

dampish, *adj.,* un peu humide.

dampness, *n.,* humidité, moiteur,*f.*

dampy, *adj.,* humide; (fig.) triste, abattu.

damsel (da'm'zèl), *n.,* jeune fille,*f.*

damson (da'm'z'n), *n.,* prune de damas,*f.*

damson-tree (-trî), *n.,* prunier de damas, *m.*

dance (da'n'se), *n.,* danse, *f.* To lead the —; *mener la danse.*

dance, *v.n.,* danser ; agiter. — attendance ; *faire le pied de grue.*

dance, *v.a.,* danser ; faire danser.

dancer, *n.,* danseur, *m.,* danseuse,*f.*

dancing, *n.,* danse,*f.*

dancing, *adj.,* de danse. — -master; *maître de danse, m.* — -room; *salle de danse, f.*

dandelion (da'n'dé-laï'one), *n.,* (bot.) dent-de-lion,*f.*; pissenlit, *m.*

dandle (da'n'd'l), *v.a.,* dorloter; bercer.

dandruff (da'n'dreufe),*n.,* dartre farineuse,*f.*

dandy, *n.,* dandy, élégant, petit-maître, *m.*

dandy, *adj.,* de dandy ; élégant.

dane, *n.,* Danois, *m.,* Danoise, *f.*

danewort (-weurte), *n.,* hièble, *f.*

danger (dé'n'djeur), *n.,* danger, *m.*

dangerous, *adj.,* dangereux.

dangerously, *adv.,* dangereusement.

dangle (da'n'g'g'l), *v.n.,* pendiller.

dangler, *n.,* damoiseau, dameret, *m.*

danish (dé'n'-), *adj.,* (ant.) danois.

danish, *n.,* Danois (language—*langue*), *m.*

dank, *adj.,* (ant.) moite, humide.

dank, *n.,* humidité,*f.*

dankish, (ant.) *adj.,* humide.

dankishness, *n.,* humidité,*f.*

dapper, *adj.,* éveillé ; leste.

dapperling, *n.,* nain, petit bonhomme, *m.*

dapple (dap'p'l), *adj.,* pommelé, truité. — gray ; *gris pommelé, m.*

dapple, *v.a.,* tacheter.

dare, *n.,* défi, *m.*

dare, *v.n.,* (preterit, Durst), oser.

dare, *v.a.,* défier ; braver ; affronter.

daring, *adj.,* audacieux, hardi.

daringly, *adv.,*audacieusement, hardiment.

daringness, *n.,* hardiesse, *f.*

dark (dârke), *n.,* ténèbres,*f. pl.*; obscurité,*f.*

dark, *adj.,* obscur, sombre; noir. — lantern ; *lanterne sourde.* To be — ; *faire sombre ; faire nuit.* The — ages ; *l'âge des ténèbres, m.*

darken (dâr'k'n),*v.a.,* obscurcir, assombrir; (the complexion—*le teint*) brunir.

darkening, *n.,* obscurcissement, *m.*

darkish, *adj.,* un peu sombre ; noirâtre.

darkling, *adj.,* (ant.) dans l'obscurité.

darkly, *adv.,* obscurément.

darkness, n., obscurité; f. ;ténèbres, f. pl.
darksome (-seume), adj., sombre.
darling (dâr-), n., favori, m., favorite, f.;
mignon, m., mignonne, f.; bien-aimé, m.,
bien-aimée, f.
darling, adj., chéri, favori, bien-aimé.
darn (dârne), n., reprise, f.
darn, v.a., repriser; faire des reprises à,
ravauder.
darnel (dâr-), n., ivraie, f.
dart (dârte), n., dard; trait, m.
dart, v.a., darder; lancer.
dart, v.n., se lancer.
dash, n., choc; coup; (with a pen—*de la
plume*) trait, m.; (small quantity—*légère apparence*) teinte, f. To cut a —; *mener grand
train*.
dash, v.a., frapper; écraser, heurter, briser;
(fig.) détruire. To — against; *heurter contre*.
To — away; *jeter*. To — in pieces; *briser en
morceaux*. To — down; *précipiter, renverser*.
To — out; *effacer; faire sauter*.
dash, v.n., se heurter, se briser; se précipiter.
dashing, adj., fougueux; brillant, superbe.
dastard, n., lâche, m. f.; poltron, m., poltronne, f.
dastard, adj., lâche; poltron.
dastardize (-'aïze), v.a., effrayer, faire
peur à.
dastardliness, n., poltronnerie, lâcheté, f.
dastardly, adj., lâche; poltron.
dastardy, n., (ant.) lâcheté, poltronnerie, f.
data (dé-), n.pl., données, f.pl.
date, n., date, f.; (of money—*des monnaies*)
millésime, m.; (bot.) datte, f.
date, v.a. and n., dater; dater de.
dateless, adj., sans date.
date-tree (-trî). n., dattier, m.
dative (dé-), adj., datif.
dative (dé-), n., datif, m.
datum (dé-teume), n. (data), donnée, f.;
(mes.) repère, m.
daub (dôbe), v.a., barbouiller; enduire;
(fig.) colorer.
daub, n., barbouillage, m.; (paint.) croûte, f.
dauber, n., barbouilleur, m.
dauby, adj., gluant, visqueux.
daughter (dô'teur), n., fille, f. — -in-law;
belle-fille, bru, f. Step— ; belle-fille, f. Grand-
— ; petite-fille, f.
daughterly, adj., filial.
daunt (dâ'nte, ou dô'nte), v.a., dompter,
intimider.
dauntless, adj., indomptable, intrépide.
dauntlessness, n., indomptabilité, intrépidité, f.
dauphin (dô-fine), n., Dauphin, m.
dauphiness, n., Dauphine, f.
davit (dé-vite), n., (nav.) davier, m.
dawdle (dô'd'l), v.n., lambiner, muser.
dawdler, n., lambin, musard, m.
dawdling, adj., langoureux.
dawn (dô'ne), n., aube, aurore, f.; point
du jour, m.; pointe du jour, f.
dawn, v.n., poindre.
day (dè), n., jour, m.; journée, f. To- —;
aujourd'hui. — before yesterday; avant-hier.
— after to-morrow; après-demain. Every —;
tous les jours. All — ; tout le jour ; toute la
journée. The — after; le lendemain. This
— ; aujourd'hui ; ce jour. From this — ;
dès aujourd'hui. Broad — ; plein jour. Every
two —s, every other — ; tous les deux jours. In
our —s ; de nos jours. Good — ; bonjour.
daybook (-bouke), n., (com.) journal; livre
journal, m.
daybreak (-brèke), n., point du jour, m.;
pointe du jour; aurore, f.
daylight (-laïte), n., jour, m., lumière du

jour f.   Broad — ; grand jour. By — ; de jour.
In broad — ; au grand jour, en plein jour.
dayly. V. **daily**.
dayspring, n., jour naissant, m.; aurore, f.
day's-work (dé'z'weurke), n., ouvrage d'un
jour, m.; journée, f.
daytime (-taïme), n., (from sunrise to sun-
set—*depuis le lever jusqu'au coucher du soleil*)
jour, m.; journée, f. In the —; pendant le
jour, pendant la journée.
day-wearied (-wî-ride), adj., fatigué de sa
journée.
daze, n., pierre brillante, f.
dazzle (daz'z'l), v.a., éblouir.
dazzle, v.n., (l.u.) être ébloui.
dazzling, n., éblouissement, m.
dazzling, adj., éblouissant.
dazzlingly, adv., d'une manière éblouis-
sante.
deacon (dî'k'n), n., diacre, m.
deaconess (dî'kn'èce), n., diaconesse, f.
deaconry (dî'kn-ri), or **deaconship**
(dî'k'n-), n., diaconat, m.
dead (dède), adj., mort; inanimé; (of liquor
—*des liqueurs*) éventé; (of fire—*du feu*) sans flamme; (of sound—*du son*) sourd. — coal; charbon
éteint. — sleep; profond sommeil. — time
of the night; silence de la nuit. — time of the
year; morte-saison. — wall; muraille isolée.
— calm; calme plat. Money lying —; de l'argent qui dort. To drop down —; tomber mort.
dead, n., (of the winter—*de l'hiver*) cœur,
fort; (of the night—*de la nuit*) milieu, m.
deaden (dèd'd'n), v.a., amortir (liquor—*des
liqueurs*) éventer; (gold and silver—*de l'or, de
l'argent*) matir, amatir.
deadliness, n., caractère mortel, m.
deadly, adj., mortel.
deadly, adv., mortellement.
deadness, n., mort, f.; (fig.) engourdissement, m., stagnation, f.
deaf (dèfe), adj., sourd; (fig.) insensible.
deafen (dèf'f'n), v.a., rendre sourd; assourdir; étourdir.
deafening, adj., assourdissant.
deafly (dèf'li), adv., (of hearing—*de l'ouïe*)
mal, imparfaitement.
deafness (dèf'-), n., surdité, f.
deal (dîl), n., quantité; (at cards—*aux cartes*)
donne, f.; (wood—*bois*) bois blanc, sapin, bois
de sapin, m. A great —, a good —; beaucoup.
deal, v.a., distribuer; répartir; (at cards—
aux cartes) donner; (blows—*coups*) porter.
deal, v.n., agir, traiter, en user. To — by
any one; traiter quelqu'un, en user à l'égard de
quelqu'un. To — with any one; en user avec
quelqu'un; (com.) donner sa pratique à quelqu'un,
se servir chez quelqu'un.
dealer, n., marchand, m.; (at cards—*aux
cartes*) personne qui donne, f.
dealing, n., conduite, f.; procédé, m.;
affaire, f.
deambulation (di-a'm'biou-lé-), n., (ant.)
promenade, (l.u.) déambulation, f.
deambulatory, adj., (ant.) déambulatoire
(l.u.).
deambulatory, n., (ant.) promenade
(lieu), f.
dean (dîne), n., doyen, m.
deanery (dî'n'euri), or **deanship** (dî'n'-),
n., doyenné, m.
dear (dîre), n., cher; cher ami, m.; chère,
chère amie, bonne, f.
dear! int., mon Dieu! Oh — me! mon Dieu!
dear, adj., cher; chéri; précieux.
dear, adv., cher; beaucoup.
dear-bought (-bôte), adj., acheté cher.
dearly, adv., chèrement; tendrement.
dearness, n., cherté; tendresse, f.
dearth (deurth), n., disette, f.

death (dèth), n., mort, f. ; trépas ; décès, m.
death-bed (-bède), n., lit de mort, m. On one's — ; à son lit de mort ; au lit de la mort.
death-bell, n., cloche funèbre, f. ; glas funèbre, m.
death-blow (-blô), n., coup de mort ; coup mortel, m.
death-boding (-bod'-), adj., qui présage la mort.
death-darting (-dàrt'-), adj., qui lance la mort ; meurtrier.
death-doing (-dou'-), adj., destructif.
death-doing, n., destruction, f.
deathful (-foule), adj., (ant.) mortel ; meurtrier.
death-hunter (-heu'n't'-), n., croque-mort, m.
deathless, adj., immortel.
deathlike (-laïke), adj., semblable à la mort.
death-note (-nôte), n., son de mort, m.
death-psalm (-sâme), n., psaume des morts, m.
death-rattle (-rat't'l), n., râle de la mort, râle de l'agonie, râle, m.
death's-door (dèths'dôre), n., porte du tombeau, f. At — ; à deux doigts de la mort.
death-shadowed (-shad'ôde), adj., couvert des ombres de la mort.
death's-head (dèths'hède), n., tête de mort, f.
death-shot (-shote), n., coup mortel, m.
death-struggles (-streug'g'lze), n.pl., agonie, dernière lutte de la nature contre la mort, f.sing.
death-warrant (-wor'ra'n'te), n., ordre d'exécution d'un condamné à mort, m.
deathwatch (-wôtshe), n., (ent.) horloge de la mort, f.
debar (dèbâr), v.a., exclure ; priver.
debark (dèbàrke), v.a., débarquer.
debase (dèbéce), v.a., avilir ; abaisser ; ravaler ; (chem.) dénaturer.
debasement (-bèss'-), n., abaissement, avilissement, m. ; (chem.) dénaturation, f.
debaser (-bèss'-),n.,personne qui abaisse,qui avilit, f.
debasing (-bess'-), adj., avilissant.
debatable (dè-bét'a-b'l), adj., contestable.
debate (dèbéte), n., débat, m. ; discussion, f.
debate, v.a., débattre, discuter, disputer.
debate, v.n., discuter ; délibérer.
debater, n., personne qui discute, f.; disputeur, m.
debauch (dè-bôtsh), n., débauche, f.
debauch, v.a., débaucher, corrompre.
debauchedly (dè-bôtsh'èd-), adv., dans la débauche.
debauchee (dèb-ô-shî), n., libertin, débauché, m.
debaucher (dè-bôtsh'-), n., débaucheur, m., débaucheuse, f.
debauchery (dè-bôtsheur'i), n.,débauche, f.
debenture (dè-bè'n't'ioure), n., reconnaissance d'une dette, f.; (at the customs—douanes) certificat de prime, m.
debile (dib'-). adj.,(ant.) débile.
debilitate (di-), v.a., débiliter, affaiblir.
debilitation (-li-té-), n., débilitation, f.; affaiblissement, m.
debility. n., débilité ; faiblesse, f.
debit (dèb'ite), n., débet, débit, m. To carry to any one's — ; porter au débit de quelqu'un.
debit, v.a., débiter.
debonair (dèb'o-nére), adj., débonnaire.
debonairly, adv., débonnairement.
debouch (dè-boushe), v.n., déboucher.
debt (dète), n., dette ; obligation ; créance, f. —s ; dettes, f.pl.: passif, m. sing. Bad —; mauvaise créance. Floating —; dette courante; (fin.)

dette flottante. Large — ; grosse dette. National — ; dette publique. Outstanding — ; créance courante, créance à recouvrer. Passive — ; dette passive. Privileged — ; créance privilégiée. — due ; créance exigible. To admit a — ; reconnaitre une dette. To be in — to any one; devoir à quelqu'un. To contract a — ; contracter une dette. To discharge a — ; acquitter une dette. To prove a — ; produire ses titres de créance. To recover a — ; recouvrer une créance. Deeply in — ; accablé de dettes.
debted (dèt'tède), adj., endetté.
debtee (dèt'i), n., (jur.) créancier, m.
debtor (dèt'teur), n., débiteur, m., débitrice, f.
decade (di-kéde). n., dizaine ; décade, f.
decadence, or decadency (dèk-a-dé-), n., décadence, f.
decagon (dèk'-), n., (geom.) décagone, m.
decagram (dèk'-), n., décagramme, m.
decahedron (dèk'a-hî-), n., décaèdre, m.
decalitre (-li-teur), n., décalitre, m.
decalogue (dèk'a-loghe), n., décalogue, m.
decameron, n., décaméron, m.
decamp (dè-ca'm'pe), v.n., (milit.) décamper ; déguerpir.
decampment, n.. décampement, m.
decangular (dèk'a'n'-ghiou-), adj., décagone.
decant (dè-), v.a., décanter, transvaser, verser.
decanter, n., carafe, f.
decapitate (dè-), v.a., décapiter.
decapitation (-'i-té-), n., décapitation, f.
decastich (dèk'a-stike), n., dizain, m.
decastyle (dèk'a-staile), n., décastyle, m.
decay (di-ké), n., décadence ; ruine, f.; délabrement, dépérissement, m. To sink to —; tomber en ruine, en décadence.
decay, v.n., tomber en décadence, se délabrer, se perdre ; dépérir.
decay, v.n., faire dépérir ; gâter, ruiner.
decease (di-cice), n., décès, m.; mort, f.
decease, v.n., décéder ; mourir.
deceased (di-ciste), adj., décédé; mort.
deceased, n., défunt, m., défunte, f.
deceit (dè-cîte), n., déception ; supercherie, tromperie, ruse; (jur.) fraude, f.
deceitful (-foule), adj., trompeur ;(of things —des choses) décevant.
deceitfully, adv., frauduleusement
deceitfulness, n., caractère trompeur, m. ; tromperie, f.
deceitless, adj., sans tromperie.
deceivable (dè-civ'a-b'l), adj., facile à tromper ; trompeur ; illusoire ; décevant.
deceive (dè-cîve), v.a., décevoir ; tromper.
deceiver, n., trompeur, m., trompeuse, f.
december (di-cè'm'beur), n., décembre, m.
decemvirate, n.. décemvirat, m.
decency (di-cè'n'-), n., bienséance ; décence, f.
decennial (dè-), adj., décennal.
decent (dî-), adj., bienséant, décent, honnête.
decently, adv., décemment ; convenablement, modérément.
deceptible (dè-), adj., décevable.
deception (dè-), n., tromperie, fraude, f.
deceptious (dè-cèp'sheusse), adj., trompeur, qui tend à tromper, décevant.
deceptive (dè-cèp'-), adj., décevant.
decerptible (dè-ceurp'ti-b'l), adj.,(ant.) qui peut être emporté.
decerption (dè-ceurp'-), n., excision, f.
decharm (dè-tshârme), v.a., désenchanter.
decide (dè-çaïde), v.a., décider ; décider de.
decide. v.n., décider ; se décider.
decided (-'ède), adj., décidé.

22 *

decidedly, *adv.*, décidément; à une manière décidée.

decider (dè-caïd'eur), *n.*, arbitre, juge, *m.*

deciduous (dè-cid'iou-), *adj.*, (bot.) décidu.

decigram, *n.*, décigramme, *m.*

decilitre (dè-ci-li-teur), *n.*, décilitre, *m.*

decimal, *adj.*, décimal; dixième.

decimal, *n.*, décimale, fraction décimale, *f.*; dixième, *m.*

decimate, *v.a.*, décimer; dîmer.

decimation (-mé-), *n.*, décimation, *f.*

decipher (dè-çaï'-), *v.a.*, déchiffrer.

decipherer, *n.*, déchiffreur, *m.*

decision (dè-ci-jeune), *n.*, décision; issue, *f.*

decisive (dè-çaï-cive), *adj.*, décisif; tranchant.

decisively, *adv.*, décisivement.

decisiveness, *n.*, caractère décisif, *m.*

deck (dèke), *n.*, (nav.) pont; (of merchant ships—*de vaisseaux marchands*) tillac, *m.* Lower —; *franc tillac.* Quarter- —; *gaillard d'arrière, m.* Fore— —; *gaillard d'avant, m.*

deck (dèke), *v.a.*, parer; orner; embellir.

decker, *n.*, personne qui pare, *f.*; vaisseau ponté, *m.* Three- —; *vaisseau à trois ponts, m.*

declaim (dè-cléme), *v.a.* and *n.*, déclamer, haranguer.

declaimer, *n.*, déclamateur, *m.*

declamation (dèk-la-mé-), *n.*, déclamation, *f.*; discours public, *m.*

declamatory (-ma-), *adj.*, déclamatoire; de déclamation.

declarable (dè-clér-a-b'l), *adj.*, qu'on peut déclarer; qui peut être prouvé.

declaration (dèk-la-ré-), *n.*, déclaration; manifestation, *f.*

declarative (dè-clar-a-), *adj.*, qui déclare, qui annonce; (jur.) déclaratif.

declaratorily (dè-clar-a-), *adv.*, par déclaration.

declaratory (dè-clar-a-), *adj.*, énonciatif; déclaratoire; déclaratif.

declare (dè-clére), *v.a.*, déclarer; annoncer, qualifier.

declare, *v.n.*, se déclarer, se prononcer.

declaredly (dè-clér'èd-), *adv.*, formellement.

declarement, *n.*, déclaration, *f.*

declarer, *n.*, personne qui annonce, *f.*

declension (dè-clè'n'-), *n.*, (gram.) déclinaison; décadence, *f.*; abattement, *m.*

declinable (dè-claï'n'a-b'l), *adj.*, déclinable.

declination (dèk-li-né-), *n.*, déclin, *m.*; descente; décadence; (gram.) déclinaison, *f.*

declinatory (dè-cli'n'a-teuri), *adj.*, déclinatoire.

decline (dè-claïne), *n.*, déclin, *m.*; décadence; (med.) maladie de langueur, *f.*

decline, *v.a.*, pencher, incliner; refuser; éviter; (gram.) décliner.

decline, *v.n.*, pencher; décliner (of price—*des prix*) baisser. To — from; *dévier de.*

declivity, *n.*, pente, *f.*; penchant, *m.*

declivous (dè-claï-), *adj.*, en pente; déclive.

decoct, *v.a.*, faire bouillir.

decoctible (-i-b'l), *adj.*, (ant.) qui peut être bouilli.

decoction, *n.*, action de bouillir; décoction, *f.*

decollate, *v.a.*, décoller.

decollation (-lé-), *n.*, décollation, *f.*

decoloration (dè-keul-eur'é-), *n.*, décoloration, *f.*

decolour (dè-keul-eur), *or* **decolorate** (dè-keul'eur'éte), *v.a.*, décolorer.

decomplex (dî-co'm'-), *adj.*, composé d'idées complexes.

decompose (dî-co'm'poze), *v.a.*, décomposer.

decomposition (dî-co'm'po-zish'eune), *n.*, décomposition, *f.*

decompound (dî-co'm'paou'n'de), *v.a.*, décomposer.

decorate (dèk'-), *v.a.*, décorer, orner, embellir.

decoration (-ré-), *n.*, décoration, *f.*; ornement, embellissement, *m.*

decorative (-ré-), *adj.*, de décoration, décoratif.

decorator (-ré-teur), *n.*, décorateur, *m.*

decorous (di-cô- *ou* dèk'o-), *adj.*, bienséant, convenable.

decorously, *adv.*, convenablement; avec bienséance.

decorticate, *v.a.*, décortiquer.

decortication (-ké-), *n.*, décortication, *f.*

decorum (-cô-reume), *n.*, bienséance, convenance, *f.*; décorum, *m.*

decoy (dè-co'ye), *v.a.*, leurrer, attirer, amorcer.

decoy, *n.*, leurre, *m.* — -duck; *oiseau de leurre, m.*

decrease (dè-crîce), *n.*, décroissement, *m.*; diminution; (of water—*des eaux*) décrue, *f.*; (of the moon—*de la lune*) décours, *m.*

decrease, *v.n.*, diminuer; décroître.

decrease, *v.a.*, faire décroître, diminuer.

decree (dè-cri), *n.*, décret, arrêt.

decree, *v.a.*, décréter; ordonner; arrêter.

decrement (dèc'ri-), *n.*, décroissement, *m.*

decrepit (dè-crèp'ite), *adj.*, décrépit.

decrepitate (dè-crèp'-), *v.a.*, calciner une substance qui décrépite.

decrepitate (dè-crèp'-), *v.n.*, crépiter, décrépiter.

decrepitation (-té-), *n.*, crépitation, décrépitation, *f.*

decrepitness (dè-crèp'-), *or* **decrepitude** (dè-crèp'i-tioude), *n.*, décrépitude, *f.*

decrescent (dè-crès'-), *adj.*, qui décroît; qui diminue.

decretal (-cri-), *adj.*, décrétal.

decretal, *n.*, décrétale, *f.*; recueil de décrétales, *m.*

decretorily (dèc'ri-teuri-), *adv.*, péremptoirement.

decretory (dèc'ri-teuri), *adj.*, décrété; décisif.

decrial (dè-cri-), *n.*, décri, *m.*

decry (dè-cra'ye), *v.a.*, décrier.

decumbent (dè-keu'm'-), *adj.*, décombant.

decuple (dèk'iou-p'l), *adj.*, décuple.

decurion (dè-kiou-), *n.*, décurion, *m.*

decursion (dè-keur-), *n.*, (ant.) course; chute, *f.*

decurtation (dèk'eur-té-), *n.*, (ant.) raccourcissement, *m.*

decussate (dè-keus'-), *or* **decussated** (-tède), *adj.*, (bot.) décussatif; (conch.) strié en croix.

decussation (-sé-), *n.*, décussation, *f.*

dedecorate (dè-dèc'-), *v.a.*, (ant.) déshonorer.

dedecorous (dè-dèk-), *adj.*, déshonorant.

dedicate (dèd-), *v.a.*, dédier; dévouer.

dedicate, *adj.*, dédié.

dedication (-ké-), *n.*, dédicace, *f.*

dedicator (-ké-teur), *n.*, personne qui fait une dédicace, *f.*

dedicatory (-ké-teuri), *adj.*, dédicatoire.

dedition (dè-dish'eune), *n.*, (ant.) reddition, *f.*

deduce (dè-diouce), *v.a.*, déduire, inférer.

deducement, *n.*, déduction, *f.*

deducible (-ci-b'l), *adj.*, qu'on peut déduire.

deducive (-ci-), *adj.*, qui déduit.

deduct (dè-deukte), *v.a.*, déduire, rabattre.

deduction, *n.*, déduction; conséquence; (com.) remise, *f.*

deductive, *adj.*, conséquent.

deductively, *adv.*, par déduction.

deed (dîde), n., action, f.; acte; fait; acte sous seing privé, m.
deedless, adj., sans action.
deem (dîme), v.a., juger; penser.
deep (dîpe), n., mer, f.; abîme, m.
deep (dîpe), adj., profond; (fig.) grand, extrême; (of colour—des couleurs) foncé; (at play—du jeu) gros; (of sound—du son) grave; (b.s.) rusé. This well is thirty feet —; ce puits a trente pieds de profondeur. — mourning; grand deuil.
deepen (dîp'p'n), v.a., approfondir; rembrunir; (colour—couleur) rendre plus foncé; (sound—son) rendre plus grave.
deepen, v.n., devenir plus profond.
deep-fetched (-fètsh'te), adj., profond.
deeply, adv., profondément; (of colour—couleur) fortement; (of sound—de son) gravement; (b.s.) avec ruse.
deepness, n., profondeur; (b.s.) ruse, f.
deer (dîre), n., daim, m., daine, f.; bête fauve, f.; cerf, m. Fallow —; daim. Red —; cerf commun.
deer-slayer (-slè-eur), n., tueur de bêtes fauves, tueur de cerfs, m.
deer-stalker (-stôk'-), n., chasseur à la bête fauve à l'affût.
deer-stalking, n., chasse à la bête fauve à l'affût.
deer-stealer (-stîl'-), n., voleur de bêtes fauves, voleur de cerfs, m.; (jur.) auteur d'un enlèvement de bêtes fauves, m.
deface (dè-), v.a., défigurer; effacer; dégrader, détériorer.
defacement, n., dégradation; détérioration; action d'effacer, f.
defacer, n., personne qui dégrade, qui détériore, qui efface, f.; destructeur, m.
defalcate (dè-), v.a., défalquer; retrancher.
defalcation (dè-fal-ké-), n., défalcation, diminution, f.
defamation (dèf-a-mé-), n., diffamation, f.
defamatory (-teuri), adj., diffamatoire.
defame (dè-), v.a., diffamer.
defamer, n., diffamateur, m.
defatigate (dè-), v.a., (ant.) fatiguer, lasser.
default (dè-fôlte), n., défaut, m. In — of; à défaut de. To suffer —; (jur.) faire défaut.
default, v.a., (jur.) donner défaut contre, juger par défaut; (ant.) manquer à.
default, v.n., (jur.) faire défaut, ne pas comparaître.
defaulter (-fôlt'-), n., délinquant, m., délinquante, f.; (jur.) défaillant, m., défaillant, personne qui ne remplit pas ses engagements, f.
defeasance (dè-fî-za'n'ce), n., (jur.) abrogation; contre-lettre, f.
defeasible (dè-fîz'i-b'l), adj., annulable.
defeat (dè-fîte), n., défaite; déroute, f.
defeat, v.a., défaire, mettre en déroute, vaincre; (fig.) annuler, repousser, déjouer.
defecate (dèf'i-kéte), v.a., déféquer.
defecation, n., défécation, f.
defect (dè-fècte), n., défaut, vice, m.; défectuosité, f.
defectibility, n., (ant.) défaut, m.
defectible (-i-b'l), adj., défectueux.
defection (dè-fèk-), n., défection; apostasie; révolte, f.
defective (dè-fèc-), adj., qui a un défaut; défectueux, défectif; en défaut, fautif.
defectively, adv., défectueusement.
defectiveness, n., état vicieux, m.; défectuosité, f.
defence (dè-), n., défense, f.
defenceless, adj., sans défense.
defend (dè-), v.a., défendre, interdire.
defendable (-a-b'l), adj., qui peut se justifier; tenable.

defendant, n., défendeur, m., défenderesse, f.; intimé, m., intimée, f.
defender, n., défenseur, m.
defensible (-si-b'l), adj., défendable; qui peut être défendu; qui peut se justifier.
defensive, adj., défensif.
defensive, n., défensive, f.
defensively, adv., sur la défensive; pour la défense.
defer (dè-feur), v.a., différer, remettre, renvoyer.
defer (dè-feur), v.n., différer; (submit—se soumettre) déférer. To — to any one; déférer à quelqu'un.
deference (dèf'èr-), n., déférence, f.
deferent (dèf'èr-), adj., qui transporte; (anat.) déférent.
deferent, n., véhicule; (anat.) canal, m.
deferential (dèf'i-rè'n'shal), adj., de déférence; respectueux.
defiance (dè-faï'-), n., défi, m.
deficience, or **deficiency** (dè-fish'-), n., manque, défaut, m.; insuffisance, f.; déficit, m.
deficient (dè-fish'-), adj., défectueux; insuffisant, faible.
deficit (dèf-), n., déficit, m.
defier (dè-faï-), n., personne qui défie, f.
defile (dè-faïl), n., défilé, m.
defile (dè-faïl), v.a., souiller; déshonorer, corrompre.
defile, v.n., défiler.
defilement (dè-faïl), n., action de souiller; souillure, f.; (fort.) défilement, m.
defiler, n., corrupteur, m., corruptrice, f.; ravisseur, m.
definable (dè-faï'n'-), adj., qui peut être déterminé; définissable.
define (dè-faine), v.a., définir; déterminer.
definer, n., personne qui définit, f.
definite (dèf'i-nite), adj., défini; déterminé.
definite, n., défini, m.
definitely, adv., d'une manière déterminée.
definiteness, n., caractère déterminé, m.
definition (dèf'i-nish'eune), n., définition, f.
definitive (dè-fi'n'i-tive), adj., définitif.
definitive, n., (gram.) déterminatif, m.
definitively, adv., définitivement, en définitive.
definitiveness, n., caractère définitif, m.
deflagrability (di-flé-gra-), n., combustibilité, f.
deflagrable (di-flé-gra-b'l, or dèf'la-), adj., combustible.
deflagrate (dèf-la-), v.a., (chem.) brûler avec flamme.
deflagration (-gré-), n., déflagration, f.
deflect (dè-flècte), v.a. and n., dévier.
deflection, n., déviation, f.
defloration (dèf'lo-ré-), n., défloration; (fig.) essence, crème, f.
deflour (dè-flaeur), v.a., déflorer; (fig.) flétrir.
deflourer, n., celui qui déflore, m.
defluous (dèf'liou-), adj., (l.u.) découlant.
defluxion (dè-fleuk'sheune), n., écoulement, m.
deforce (dè-fôrce), v.a., (jur.) détenir à titre précaire.
deforcement, n., (jur.) possession précaire, f.
deforciant (dè-fôr-shi-), n., (jur.) détenteur à titre précaire, m.
deform (dè-), adj., difforme.
deform, v.a., déformer, défigurer, enlaidir.
deformation (dè-form'é-), n., déformation, f.; défigurement, m.
deformedly (dè-form'èd'-), adv., d'une manière difforme.
deformedness (dè-form'èd'-), or **deformity**, n., difformité; laideur, f.

defraud (dĕ-frŏde), *v.a.*, frauder, frustrer.
defrauder, *n.*, fraudeur, *m.*, fraudeuse, *f.*
defray (di-frĕ), *v.a.*, défrayer ; payer.
defrayer (di-frĕ-eur), *n.*, défrayeur, *m.*
defrayment, *n.*, défrai, *m.*
deft (dĕf'te), *adj.*, (ant.) adroit ; leste.
deftly, *adv.*, (ant.) adroitement.
defunct (dĕ-feu'n'cte), *adj.*, défunt, trépassé.
defunct, *n.*, défunt, *m.*, défunte, *f.*
defunction, *n.*, (ant.) mort, *f.* ; décès, *m.*
defy (dĕ-fa'ye), *n.*, défi, *m.*
defy, *v.a.*, défier.
defyer, *n.* *V.* **defier.**
degeneracy (dĕ-djè'n'èr'-), *n.*, dégénération, *f.* ; abâtardissement, *m.*
degenerate (dĕ-djò'n'èr'-), *adj.*, dégénéré, abâtardi.
degenerate, *v.n.*, dégénérer, s'abâtardir.
degenerately, *adv.*, avec dégénération.
degenerateness, *or* **degeneration**, *n.*, dégénération, *f.* ; abâtardissement, *m.*
degenerous, *adj.*, dégénéré ; bas, vil, misérable ; indigne.
deglutinate (dĕ-glou'-), *v.a.*, décoller.
deglutition (dĕg-lou-tish'eune), *n.*, déglutition, *f.*
degradation (dĕg-ra-dé-), *n.*, dégradation, *f.* ; avilissement, *m.*
degrade (dĕ-), *v.a.*, dégrader ; avilir.
degraded (-ède), *adj.*, dégradé.
degrading, *adj.*, dégradant.
degradingly, *adv.*, d'une manière dégradante.
degree (dĕ-grî), *n.*, degré ; rang, *m.* ; qualité, condition, *f.*
degustation (dĕ-gheus-té-), *n.*, (ant.) dégustation, *f.*
dehisce (dĕ-hice), *v.n.*, (bot.) s'ouvrir ; être déhiscent.
dehiscence, *n.*, (bot.) déhiscence, *f.*
dehiscent, *adj.*, (bot.) déhiscent.
dehort (dĕ-), *v.a.*, dissuader, déconseiller.
dehortation (-hort'é-), *n.*, dissuasion, *f.*
dehortative, *or* **dehortatory**, *adj.*, qui dissuade.
dehorter, *n.*, personne qui dissuade, *f.*
deicide (dî-i-çaïde), *n.*, déicide, *m.*
deification (dĕ-i-fi-ké-), *n.*, déification, *f.*
deiform (dî-i-), *adj.*, divin.
deify (dî-i-fa'ye), *v.a.*, déifier, diviniser.
deign (déne), *v.n.*, daigner.
deign, *v.a.*, daigner, accorder.
deism (dî-iz'm), *n.*, déisme, *m.*
deist (dî-iste), *n.*, déiste, *m.*
deistic, *or* **deistical** (dĕ-is-), *adj.*, déiste.
deity (dî-i-), *n.*, divinité ; (myth.) déité, *f.*
deject (dĕ-djècte), *adj.*, abattu.
deject, *v.a.*, abaisser ; abattre ; affliger.
dejected, *adj.*, abattu.
dejectedly, *adv.*, dans l'abattement ; tristement.
dejectedness, *n.*, abattement, *m.*
dejection, *n.*, abattement, *m.* ; (med.) défécation, *f.*
dejecture (-'loure), *n.sing.*, (med.) évacuations alvines, *f.pl.*
delapse (dĕ-lapse), *v.n.*, tomber.
delate (dĕ-léte), *v.a.*, accuser ; dénoncer.
delation (dĕ-lé-), *n.*, accusation, délation, *f.*
delator (dĕ-lé-teur), *n.*, (ant.) accusateur, délateur, *m.*
delay (di-lè), *n.*, délai, retardement, *m.*
delay, *v.a.*, différer, remettre, retarder.
delayer (di-lè-eur), *n.*, temporiseur, temporisateur, *m.*
dele (dî-li), *v.a.*, (print.) deleatur, *m.*
delectable (dĕ-lèc-ta-b'l), *adj.*, délectable.
delectableness, *n.*, délectation, *f.*
delectably, *adv.*, délectablement.
delectation (-té-), *n.*, délectation, *f.*

delegate (dĕl'î-), *adj.*, délégué.
delegate (dĕl'î-), *n.*, délégué, *m.*
delegate (dĕl'-i-), *v.a.*, déléguer.
delegation (dĕl-i-ghé-), *n.*, délégation, *f.*
delegator, *n.*, (jur.) délégant, délégateur *m.*, délégatrice, *f.*
deleterious (dĕl-i-tî-), *adj.*, délétère, nuisible.
deletion (dĕ-lî-), *n.*, rature, *f.* ; grattage, *m.*
deletory (dĕl-i-teuri), *n.*, chose qui efface, *f.*
delf, **delft**, *or* **delft-ware** (-wére), *n.*, faïence de Delft, *f.*
deliberate (dĕ-lib'èr'-) *adj.*, délibéré ; mûri avisé.
deliberate, *v.n.*, délibérer.
deliberately, *adv.*, mûrement ; de propos délibéré ; à dessein.
deliberateness, *n.*, délibération, *f.*
deliberation (-èr'é-), *n.*, délibération, *f.*
deliberative (-èr-a-), *adj.*, délibérant, délibératif.
deliberatively, *adv.*, par délibération.
delicacy (dĕl-i-), *n.*, délicatesse, *f.*
delicate (dĕl-i-), *adj.*, délicat.
delicately, *adv.*, délicatement.
delicateness, *n.*, délicatesse, *f.*
delicious (dĕ-lish'eusse), *adj.*, délicieux.
deliciously, *adv.*, délicieusement.
deliciousness, *n.*, délices, *f.pl.*, charme, *m.*
delight (dĕ-lâite), *n.*, délices, *f.pl.*, délice ; plaisir, *m.*
delight, *v.a.*, plaire à ; faire les délices de.
delight, *v.n.* To — in ; *faire ses délices de ; se plaire à.* To — to ; *être enchanté de.*
delightful (-foule), *adj.*, délicieux, charmant.
delightfully, *adv.*, délicieusement, à ravir.
delightfulness, *n.*, charme, *m.* ; délices, *f.pl.*
delightless, *adj.*, sans charme.
delightsome (-seume), *adj.*, agréable, délicieux.
delightsomely, *adv.*, agréablement.
delightsomeness, *n.*, agrément, *m.*
delineament (dĕ-li'n'i-), *n.*, délinéation, *f.*
delineate (dĕ-li'n'i-), *v.a.*, faire la délinéation de ; tracer, décrire ; peindre.
delineation (dĕ-li'n'i-é-), *n.*, délinéation, esquisse ; (fig.) peinture, description, *f.*
delineator (dĕ-li'n'i-é-teur), *n.*, dessinateur, peintre, *m.*
delinquency (dĕ-li'n'kwè'n'-), *n.*, délit, *m.*
delinquent (dĕ-li'n'kwè'n'te), *n.*, délinquant, *m.*, délinquante, *f.*
deliquate (dĕl-i-kwéte), *or* **deliquiate** (dĕ-lik-kwi-éte), *v.a.* and *n.*, liquéfier ; se liquéfier.
deliquation (dĕl-i-kwé-), *n.*, (ant.) déliquescence, *f.*
deliquesce (dĕl-i-kwèce), *v.n.*, tomber en déliquescence.
deliquescence, *n.*, déliquescence, *f.*
deliquescent, *adj.*, déliquescent.
deliquium (dĕ-lik'wi-eume), *n.*, (chem., deliquium, *m.* ; (med.) syncope, *f.*
delirious (dĕ-), *adj.*, en délire ; dans le délire.
deliriousness, *n.*, délire, *m.*
delirium (dĕ-lir-i-eume), *n.*, délire, *m.* — tremens ; *delirium tremens.*
deliver (dĕ-), *v.a.*, délivrer ; (letters—*les lettres*) distribuer ; (a letter, a parcel—*une lettre, un paquet*) remettre ; (goods. a place—*des marchandises, une place forte*) livrer ; (a speech—*un discours*) prononcer ; (a woman—*une femme*) délivrer, accoucher. To — from ; *délivrer de, sauver de.* To — in ; *délivrer ; donner.* To — up ; *livrer ; remettre ; rendre.* To — one's self up to ; *se livrer à.* To — a message to ; *remettre un message à.*
deliverance, *n.*, délivrance, *f.* ; acquitte-

ment par un jury ; (of a woman—*d'une femme*) accouchement, *m.*, délivrance, *f.*

deliverer, *n.*, libérateur, *m.*, libératrice, *f.* ; sauveur, *m.*

delivery, *n.*, délivrance, remise, *f.* ; (of speech—*d'un discours*) débit, *m.*, diction ; (com.) livraison ; (of letters—*des lettres*) distribution, *f.* ; (of a woman—*d'une femme*) accouchement, *m.*, délivrance, *f.*

dell, *n.*, creux ; vallon, *m.*

delphine, *adj.*, du Dauphin de France.

deludable (dè-lioud'a-b'l), *adj.*, qu'on peut tromper.

delude (dè-lioude), *v.a.*, tromper.

deluder, *n.*, trompeur, séducteur, *m.*

deluge (dèl'lioudje), *n.*, déluge, *m.*

deluge, *v.a.*, inonder.

delusion (dè-liou-jeune), *n.*, illusion, *f.*

delusive (dè-liou-cive), or **delusory** (-ço-), *adj.*, illusoire, trompeur.

delusiveness, *n.*, caractère illusoire, *m.*

delve (dèlve), *v.a.*, creuser ; fouir.

demagogue, *n.*, démagogue, *m.*

demain (di-méne), or **demesne** (di-mine), *n.*, domaine, *m.* ; propriété, *f.* ; bien-fonds, *m.*

demand (dè-mâ'n'de), *n.*, demande, *f.*

demand, *v.a.*, demander ; réclamer ; exiger.

demandable (-'a-b'l), *adj.*, exigible.

demandant, *n.*, (jur.) demandeur, *m.*, demanderesse, *f.*

demander, *n.*, personne qui demande, *f.*

demarcation (dì-mar-ké-), *n.*, démarcation, *f.*

demean (dè-mîne), *v.a.*, abaisser, avilir (l.u.); se conduire ; porter ; conduire ; traiter. To — one's self ; *se comporter.*

demeanour (dè-mî'n'eur), *n.*, conduite, *f.* ; maintien, *m.*

demency (di-), *n.*, démence, *f.*

demerit, *n.*, démérite, *m.* ; absence de mérite, *f.*

demerit, *v.a.*, (ant.) démériter.

demi (dèm'l), *adj.*, demi, à demi.

demi-deify (-di-i-fa'ye), *v.a.*, déifier à demi.

demi-devil (-dèv'l), *n.*, demi-démon, *m.*

demi-ditone (-daï-tône), *n.*, (mus.) tierce mineure ; petite tierce, *f.*

demi-god, *n.*, demi-dieu, *m.*

demi-john (-djone), *n.*, dame-jeanne, *f.*

demi-lance, *n.*, demi-pique, *f.*

demi-lune (-lioune), *n.*, (fort.) demi-lune, *f.*

demi-quaver (-kwé-), *n.*, (mus.) demi-croche, *f.*

demi-rep (-rèpe), *n.*, demi-vertu, *f.*

demisable (dè-maïz'a-b'l), *adj.*, (jur.) qui peut être affermé.

demise (di-maïze), *n.*, décès, *m.* ; mort; (jur.) translation de propriété, *f.*

demise, *v.a.*, donner à ferme ; léguer ; (jur.) faire transport de.

demission (dè-mish'eune), *n.*, relâchement, *m.* ; dégradation, *f.*

demi-tone (-tône), *n.*, demi-ton, *m.*

demi-wolf (-woulfe), *n.*, chien métis (from a wolf and a bitch—*de loup et de chienne*), *m.*

democracy, *n.*, démocratie, *f.*

democrat, or **democratist**, *n.*, démocrate, *m.*

democratic, or **democratical**, *adj.*, démocratique.

democratically, *adv.*, démocratiquement.

demolish (dè-), *v.a.*, démolir.

demolisher, *n.*, démolisseur, *f.*

demolition (-lish'eune), *n.*, démolition, *f.*

demon (dî-), *n.*, démon, diable, *m.*

demoniac, *n.*, démoniaque, *m.*, *f.*

demoniac (-mô-), or **demoniacal** (dèm'o-naï'a-), *adj.*, démoniaque.

demonian (-mô-), *adj.*, démoniaque.

demonology (-dji), *n.*, démonologie, *f.*

demonstrable (dè-mo'n'stra-b'l), *adj.*, démontrable.

demonstrably, *adv.*, par la démonstration.

demonstrate, *v.a.*, démontrer.

demonstration (-stré-), *n.*, démonstration, *f.*

demonstrative (-stra-), *adj.*, démonstratif ; qui montre clairement.

demonstratively, *adv.*, démonstrativement.

demonstrator (-stra-teur, ou -stré-), *n.*, démonstrateur, *m.*

demonstratory, *adj.*, qui tend à démontrer.

demoralization (dè-mor-al-i-zé-), *n.*, démoralisation, *f.*

demoralize (-aïze), *v.a.*, démoraliser.

demulcent (dè-meul-), *adj.*, adoucissant, émollient.

demur (dè-meur), *n.*, hésitation, objection ; difficulté, *f.*

demur, *v.n.*, hésiter ; balancer; temporiser ; (jur.) opposer une exception péremptoire. To — at ; *objecter, faire objection.*

demure (dè-mioure), *adj.*, réservé ; (b.s.) d'une modestie affectée.

demurely, *adv.*, gravement ; (b.s.) avec une modestie affectée.

demureness, *n.*, gravité ; (b.s.) modestie affectée, *f.*

demurrage (dè-meur'rèdge), *n.*, (com., nav.) indemnité pour surestarie, *f.*

demurrer (dè-meur'-), *n.*, personne qui hésite, qui balance ; (jur.) exception péremptoire, *f.*

demy (dè-ma'ye), *n.*, (of paper—*papier*) coquille, *f.*

den (dène), *n.*, antre, repaire, *m.* ; tanière, *f.*

denary (dè'n'-), *adj.*, qui contient le nombre dix; décimal.

denationalize (dè-nash'eu'n'al-aïze), *v.a.*, dénationaliser.

dendroid (dè'n'droïde), or **dendroidal** (-'al'-), *adj.*, (bot.) dendroïde.

deniable (dè-naï-a-b'l), *adj.*, niable.

denial (dè-naï-al), *n.*, refus, déni, *m.* ; dénégation, *f.* ; (of St. Peter—*de saint Pierre*) reniement, reniment, *m.*

denier (dè-naï'eur), *n.*, personne qui nie, *f.*

denigrate (dè'n'i-), *v.a.*, noircir; calomnier; dénigrer.

denigration (-gré-), *n.*, dénigrement, *m.* ; calomnie, médisance, *f.*

denization (dè'n'i-zé-), *n.*, dénization, *f.* ; droit de cité, *m.*

denizen (dè'n'i-z'n), or **denison** (dè'n'i-z'n), *n.*, (English plant) étranger qui a obtenu les petites lettres de naturalisation en Angleterre; citoyen, *m.*

denizen, *v.a.*, donner droit de cité à.

denominate (dè-), *v.a.*, nommer, appeler, désigner sous le nom de.

denomination (-né-), *n.*, dénomination, *f.* ; nom, *m.*

denominative, *adj.*, dénominatif.

denominator (-né-teur), *n.*, dénominateur, *n.*

denotation (dè'n'o-té-), *n.*, dénotation, *f.*

denote (dè-nôte), *v.a.*, dénoter, marquer, montrer.

denounce (dè-naou'n'ce), *v.a.*, dénoncer; déclarer.

denouncement, *n.*, dénonciation, déclaration, *f.*

denouncer, *n.*, dénonciateur, *m.*

dense (dè'n'se), *adj.*, dense ; épais.

density, *n.*, densité ; épaisseur, *f.*

dent (dè'n'te), *n.*, creux, *m.*, coche, *f.*

dent, *v.a.*, denteler, bossuer ; faire une coche, des coches.

dental (dèn'-), *adj.*, dentaire, des dents ; (gram.) dental.

dental, *n.*, (gram.) dentale, *f.* ; (conch.) dentale ; (arch.) modillon, *m.*

dentate (dè'n'-), *or* **dentated** (-'ède), *adj.*, (bot.) denté, dentelé.

denticle (dè'n'-ti-k'l), *n.*, (arch.) denticules, *m.pl.*

denticulate (dè'n'tik'iou-), *or* **denticulated** (-ède), *adj.*, (arch.) dentelé ; (bot.) denticulé.

denticulation, *n.*, dentelure, *f.*

dentifrice, *n.*, dentifrice, *m.*

dentil (dè'n'-), *or* **dental** (dè'n'-), *n.*, (arch.) modillon, *m.*

dentist, *n.*, dentiste, *m.*

dentition, *n.*, dentition, *f.*

denudate (dè-niou-), *or* **denude** (dè-nioude), *v.a.*, dénuder, dénuer, dépouiller.

denudation (-dé-), *n.*, dénudation, *f.*

denunciation (dè-neu'n'shi-), *n.*, dénonciation, déclaration, *f.*

denunciator (-é-teur), *n.*, dénonciateur, *m.*, dénonciatrice, *f.*

deny (dè-na'ye), *v.a.*, nier, démentir, dénier ; renier ; refuser. — *one's self*; *renoncer à soi-même ; faire dire qu'on n'est pas chez soi ; se refuser quelque chose.* To — anything to any one ; *refuser quelque chose à quelqu'un.*

deobstruct (di-ob-streucte), *v.a.*, désobstruer.

deobstruent (dè-ob-strou'-), *n.*, désobstruant, désobstructif, *m.*

deodand (di-), *n.*, amende, *f.*

deoppilate (dè-), *v.a.*, désopiler.

deoppilation (-lé-), *n.*, (ant.) désopilation, *f.*

deoppilative, *adj.*, (ant.) désopilatif.

deoppilative, *n.*, désopilant, désopilatif, *m.*

deoxidate (dè-), *v.a.*, désoxyder.

deoxidization (-'aïzé-), *n.*, désoxydation, *f.*

deoxidize (-daïze), *v.a.*, désoxyder.

deoxygenate (dè-oks'i-djè'n'-), *v.a.*, désoxygéner.

deoxygenation, *n.*, désoxygénation, *f.*

depart (dè-pârte), *n.*, départ, *m.*

depart, *v.n.*, partir ; sortir ; s'éloigner. To — from ; *s'écarter de.*

depart, *v.a.*, faire partir ; se départir ; dévier ; se désister. To — this life ; *mourir.*

department, *n.*, département, *m.* ; partie, *f.*

departure (-ioure), *n.*, départ ; éloignement, *m.* ; mort, *f.*

depasture (dè-pâst'ioure), *v.a.*, épuiser un pâturage ; nourrir.

depasture, *v.n.*, pâturer, brouter.

depauperate (dè-pô-peur'-), *v.a.*, appauvrir.

depend (dè-), *v.n.*, pendre ; dépendre ; demeurer dans la dépendance. To — on ; *dépendre de ; se fier à ; compter sur.*

dependable (-'a-b'l), *adj.*, sur lequel on peut compter.

dependance, *n.* *V.* **dependence**.

dependant, *or* **dependent**, *adj.*, dépendant ; pendant.

dependant, *or* **dependent**, *n.*, personne dépendante, *f.* ; subordonné, *m.*

dependantly, *or* **dependently**, *adv.*, dépendamment (l.u.).

dependence, *or* **dependency**, *n.*, dépendance ; confiance, *f.*

depender, *n.*, personne dépendante, *f.*

deperdition (dèp'èr-), *n.*, (ant.) déperdition, *f.*

dephlegm (dè-flème), *v.a.*, (ant.) déflegmer.

dephlegmation (dè-flè'm'é-), *n.*, déflegmation, *f.*

depict (dè-), *v.a.*, peindre, dépeindre.

depilate (dèp'-), *v.a.*, épiler.

depilation (-lé-), *n.*, épilation, *f.*

depilatory (-teuri), *adj.*, dépilatif ; dépilatoire, épilatoire.

depilatory, *n.*, dépilatoire, *m.*

deplorable (dè-plô-ra-b'l), *adj.*, déplorable.

deplorableness, *n.*, état déplorable, *m.*

deplorably, *adv.*, déplorablement ; pitoyablement.

deplore (dè-plôre), *v.a.*, déplorer.

deplorer, *n.*, personne qui déplore, *f.*

deploy (dè-plo'ye), *v.a.*, (milit.) déployer.

deploy, *v.n.*, (milit.) se déployer.

deplumation (dè-plou-me-), *n.*, action de plumer, *f.*

deplume (dè-ploume), *v.a.*, plumer.

deponent (dè-pô-), *n.*, déposant ; (gram.) déponent, *m.*

depopulate (dè-pop'iou-), *v.a.*, dépeupler.

depopulate, *v.n.*, se dépeupler.

depopulation (-lé-), *n.*, dépeuplement, *m.* ; dépopulation, *f.*

depopulator (-teur), *n.*, dépopulateur, destructeur, *m.*

deport (dè-pôrte), *n.*, port, *m.* ; conduite, *f.*

deport, *v.a.*, déporter. To — one's self; *se comporter.*

deportation (dè-por-té-), *n.*, déportation, *f.*

deportment (dè-pôrt'-), *n.*, maintien, *m.* ; tenue ; conduite, *f.*

deposal (dè-pô-zal), *n.*, (deprivation of a dignity—*privation d'une dignité*) déposition, *f.*

depose (dè-pôze), *v.a.* and *n.*, déposer.

deposer, *n.*, personne qui dépose, qui prive d'une dignité, *f.*

deposit (dè-poz'ite), *n.*, dépôt, *m.* ; arrhes, *f.pl.* To leave a —; *déposer des arrhes.*

deposit, *v.a.*, déposer.

depositary (dè-poz'-), *n.*, dépositaire, *f.*

deposition (dèp'o-zish'eune), *n.*, déposition, *f.*

depositor (-'eur), *n.*, (at a bank—*à une banque*) déposant, *m.* déposante, *f.* ; (com.) dépositeur, *m.*, dépositrice, *f.*

depository (-teuri), *n.*, dépôt, lieu où se garde la chose déposée, *f.*

depot (dé-pô), *n.*, dépôt, *m.*

depravation (dèp-ré-vé-), *n.*, dépravation, *f.*

deprave (dè-), *v.a.*, dépraver, gâter.

depraved (dè-prév'de), *adj.*, dépravé.

depravedly (-'èd'-), *adv.*, par dépravation.

depravedness (-'èd'-), *n.*, corruption, dépravation, *f.*

depravement, *n.*, dépravation, *f.*

depraver, *n.*, dépravateur, *m.*, dépravatrice, *f.*

depravity (dè-prav'-), *n.*, dépravation, *f.*

deprecate (dèp'ri-kéte), *v.a.*, détourner par la prière ; conjurer.

deprecation, *n.*, déprécation, supplication, *f.*

deprecative, *or* **deprecatory** (-teuri), *adj.*, de déprécation, de supplication.

depreciate (dè-pri-shi-), *v.a.*, déprécier.

depreciate, *v.n.*, se déprécier.

depreciation, *n.*, dépréciation, *f.*

depreciator (-teur), *n.*, dépréciateur, *m.*, dépréciatrice, *f.*

depredate (dèp'ri-), *v.a.*, piller, saccager, détruire.

depredate, *v.n.*, commettre des déprédations.

depredation (-dé-), *n.*, déprédation, *f.* ; ravage, *m.*

depredator (-teur), *n.*, pillard, déprédateur, *m.*

deprehend (dèp'ri-), *v.a.*, découvrir ; reconnaître.

deprehensible (-'i-b'l), *adj.*, qui peut être pris.

depress (dè-prèce), *v.a.*, baisser; abaisser; abattre; déprimer.

depression (-prèsh'eune), *n.*, abaissement; affaissement; (fig.) abattement, *m.*; (surg.) dépression, *f.*,

depressor (dè-prèss'eur), *n.*, oppresseur; (anat.) abaisseur, *m.*

deprivation (dèp'raïv'é-), *n.*, privation; perte, *f.*

deprive (dè-praïve), *v.a.*, priver; dépouiller.

depth (dèp'th), *n.*, profondeur; hauteur, *f.*; (of the seasons—*des saisons*) fort, cœur; (of the night—*de la nuit*) milieu; (print.)(of the letters —*des types*) corps, *m.*; (math.) hauteur, épaisseur, *f.* — of winter; *cœur de l'hiver*, *m.*

depulsion (dè-peul-sheune), *n.*, expulsion, *f.*

depurate (dèp'iou-), *v.a.*, dépurer.

depurate, *adj.*, dépuré.

depuration (-ré-), *n.*, dépuration, *f.*

depuratory (-teuri), *adj.*, dépuratoire.

deputation (dèp'iou-té-), *n.*, députation, *f.*

depute (dè-pioute), *v.a.*, député; déléguer.

deputy, *n.*, député, délégué, *m.* —governor; *lieutenant-gouverneur*, *m.* —chairman; *vice-président*, *m.* —mayor; *adjoint au maire*, *m.* —manager; *sous-directeur*, *m.*

deracinate, *v.a.*, déraciner.

derange (dè-ré'n'dje), *v.a.*, déranger; désorganiser.

derangement, *n.*, dérangement; trouble, *m.*; aliénation mentale, *f.*

derelict (dèr'i-), *adj.*, délaissé, abandonné.

derelict, *n.*, (jur.) objet abandonné, *m.*

dereliction, *n.*, abandon, *m.*

deride (dè-raïde), *v.a.*, tourner en dérision; railler.

derider, *n.*, moqueur, *m.*, moqueuse, *f.*; railleur, *m.*, railleuse, *f.*

deridingly, *adv.*, par dérision.

derision (dè-rij'eune), *n.*, dérision, *f.*; objet de dérision, *m.*

derisive (dè-raï-cive), *adj.*, dérisoire.

derisively, *adv.*, par dérision.

derisory (dè-raï-ceuri), *adj.*, dérisoire.

derivable (dè-raïv'a-b'l), *adj.*, dérivable; qui dérive, qui peut dériver.

derivation (dèr-i-vé-), *n.*, dérivation; origine, *f.*

derivative (dè-riv'-), *adj.*, dérivé; (med.) dérivatif.

derivative, *n.*, (gram.) dérivé; (mus.) accord dérivé; (med.) dérivatif, *m.*

derivatively, *adv.*, par dérivation.

derive (dè-raïve), *v.a.*, (water—*les eaux*) faire dériver; dériver; (gram.) faire dériver; (fig.) recueillir, retirer.

derive, *v.a.*, venir, provenir.

derm, **derma**, *or* **dermis** (deurm'), *n.*, (anat.) derme, *m.*

dernier (deur'ni-eur), *adj.*, (jur.) dernier.

derogate (dèr-o-ghéte), *v.a.*, déroger à; faire dérogation à.

derogate, *v.n.*, dégénérer; se dégrader. To — from; *déroger à; porter atteinte à*.

derogated (-ède), *part.*, diminué de valeur; dégradé, endommagé.

derogation (-ghé-), *n.*, dérogation, *f.*; détriment, *m.*; atteinte, *f.*

derogatorily, *adv.*, d'une manière qui porte atteinte.

derogatory, *adj.*, dérogatoire, qui porte atteinte.

dervis (deur-), *or* **dervise** (-vaïze), *n.*, dervis, derviche, *m.*

descant (dès'-), *n.*, chant; discours, *m.*; dissertation, *f.*

descant, *v.n.*, discourir. To — on; *commenter sur; s'appesantir sur*.

descend (dè-), *v.a.* and *n.*, descendre. To — upon; *tomber sur*.

descendant, *n.*, descendant, *m.*, descendante, *f.*

descendent, *adj.*, descendant; qui descend.

descension (dé-cè'n'sheune), *n.*, descente, *f.*

descent (dè'-), *n.*, descente; chute; descendance, postérité, *f.*

describe (dè-scraïbe), *v.a.*, décrire.

describer, *n.*, personne qui fait une description, *f.*; auteur d'une description, *m.*

descrier (dè-scraï'-), *n.*, personne qui découvre, *f.*

description (dè-scrip'-), *n.*, description, *f.*; (of a person —*d'une personne*) signalement, *m.*; qualité, sorte, *f.*

descry (dè-scra'ye), *n.*, découverte, *f.*

descry, *v.a.*, découvrir, apercevoir.

desecrate (dèss'i-), *v.a.*, profaner.

desecration (-cré-), *n.*, profanation, *f.*

desert (dèz'eurte), *n.*, mérite, *m.*; mérites, *m.pl.*; désert, *m.*; solitude, *f.*

desert (dèz'eurte), *adj.*, désert, solitaire.

desert (dè-zeurte), *v.a.*, abandonner; déserter.

desert (dè-zeurte), *v.n.*, déserter.

deserter (dè-zeurt'-), *n.*, déserteur; transfuge, *m.*

desertion (dè-zeur-), *n.*, désertion, *f.*, abandon, *m.*

desertless (dè-zeurt-), *adj.*, indigne, sans mérite.

deserve (dè-zeurve), *v.a.* and *n.*, mériter.

deservedly (-ède-), *adv.*, à bon droit, justement.

deserver, *n.*, personne méritante, *f.*

deserving, *adj.*, de mérite; méritant.

deshabille (dèss'a-bilé), *n.*, déshabillé, *m.*

desiccant (dè-cik'-), *adj.*, dessiccatif, siccatif.

desiccant, *n.*, dessiccatif, siccatif, *m.*

desiccate (dè-cik'-), *v.a.*, sécher, dessécher.

desiccate, *v.n.*, sécher, se dessécher.

desiccation (-'ké-), *n.*, dessiccation, *f.*

desiccative (dè-cik'-), *adj.*, dessiccatif, siccatif.

desiccative, *n.*, dessiccatif, siccatif, *m.*

desideratum (dè-cid'èr'é-teume), *n.* (*desiderata*), chose à désirer, *f.*

design (dè-çaïne), *n.*, dessein, projet; (drawing—*art*) dessin, *m.*

design, *v.a.*, dessiner; destiner; désigner; avoir le dessein.

designable (dè-çaï'n'ab'l), *adj.*, que l'on peut désigner.

designate (dèss'ig-néte), *v.a.*, désigner.

designation (dèss'ig-né-), *n.*, désignation, *f.*

designedly (dè-çaï'n'èd-), *adv.*, à dessein.

designer (dè-çaï'n'eur), *n.*, dessinateur; inventeur; (b.s.) machinateur, intrigant, *m.*

designing (dè-çaï'n'-), *adj.*, artificieux.

designless (dè-çaï'n'-), *adj.*, sans dessein.

designlessly, *adv.*, par inadvertance, sans dessein.

designment (dè-çaï'n'-), *n.*, (ant.) dessein, projet, *m.*

desirable (di-zaeur'a-b'l), *adj.*, désirable.

desire (di-zaeur), *n.*, désir, *m.*

desire (di-zaeur), *v.a.*, désirer; souhaiter; prier; ordonner.

desirer, *n.*, personne qui désire, *f.*

desirous (di-zaeur'-), *adj.*, qui désire; désireux, empressé.

desirously, *adv.*, avec désir.

desirousness, *n.*, désir, *m.*

desist (dè-ciste), *v.n.*, se désister; cesser.

desistance (dè-ci'st'-), *n.*, désistement, *m.*

desk (dèske), *n.*, pupitre, *m.*; (in a church-d'église) chaire, *f.*; (for music—à musique) lutrin, *m.*

desolate (dèss'o-), adj., désolé, isolé, solitaire.

desolate, v.a., désoler ; dévaster.

desolately, adv., d'une manière désolée.

desolation (-lé-), n., désolation, f.

despair (di-spére), n., désespoir, m.

despair, v.n., désespérer, se désespérer.

despairer, n., personne au désespoir, f.

despairingly, adv., d'une manière désespérée ; sans espoir.

despatch (dè-), or dispatch, n., dépêche ; promptitude, f.

despatch, or dispatch, v.a., dépêcher ; expédier.

despatchful, adj., expéditif, prompt.

desperado (dès-pi-ré-dô), n., énergumène ; homme dangereux, m.

desperate (dès-pé-), adj., désespéré, désespérant ; dont on désespère ; furieux ; qui désespère.

desperately, adv., en désespéré ; (l.u.) désespérément ; d'une manière désespérée ; terriblement, excessivement.

desperateness, n., fureur, furie, f.

desperation (-ré-), n., désespoir, m. ; fureur, exaspération, f.

despicable (dès-pi-ca-b'l), adj., méprisable.

despicableness, n., caractère méprisable, m.

despicably, adv., bassement, d'une manière méprisable.

despisable (dè-spaïz'a-b'l), adj., méprisable.

despise (dè-spaïze), v a., mépriser.

despisedness (dè-spaïz'èd-), n., avilissement, m.

despiser (dè spaïz'-), n., contempteur, m.

despising, n., mépris, m.

despisingly, adv., avec mépris.

despite (dè-spaïte), n., dépit, m. ; haine, f.

despite, v.a., dépiter.

despite, prep., en dépit de, malgré.

despiteful (-foule), adj., qui a du dépit.

despitefully, adv., avec dépit.

despitefulness, n., dépit, m.

despoil (dè-spoïl), v.a., dépouiller.

despoiler, n., spoliateur, m., spoliatrice, f.

despoliation (dè-spo-li-é-), n., spoliation, f.

despond (dè-spo'n'de), v.n., se décourager ; être abattu ; désespérer.

despondency, n., abattement, désespoir, m.

despondent, adj., découragé, abattu.

despondently, adv., dans l'abattement ; avec desespoir.

desponder, n., personne désespérée, f.

despot, n., despote, tyran, m.

despotic, or despotical (dès'-), adj., despotique.

despotically, adv., despotiquement ; en despote.

despotism (-'iz'm), n., despotisme, m.

desquamation (dès'kwa-mé-), n., desquamation, f.

dessert (dèz'zeurte), n., dessert. m.

destinate (dès-ti-), v.a., (ant.) destiner.

destination (-né-), n., destination, f.

destine (dès-tine), v.a., destiner.

destiny, n., destin, m. ; destinée, f.

destitute (dès-ti-tioute), adj., dépourvu, dénué ; dans le dénûment, dans la misère.

destitution (-ti-tiou-), n., dénuement, dénûment, m.

destroy (dè-stro'ye), v.a., détruire, exterminer.

destroyer, n., destructeur, m.

destructibility (dè-streuct'-), n., destructibilité, f.

destructible (dè-streuct'i-b'l), adj., destructible.

destruction, n., destruction, f. ; meurtre, carnage, m.

destructive, adj., destructeur, destructif.

destructively, adv., d'une manière destructive.

destructiveness, n., caractère destructeur, m.

desuetude (dèss'-wi-tioude), n., désuétude, f.

desultorily (dèss'-eul-teuri-), adv., par sauts et par bonds ; à bâtons rompus.

desultoriness, n., défaut de liaison. m.

desultory (dèss-eul-teuri), adj., par sauts et par bonds ; à bâtons rompus ; décousu ; sans suite ; changeant, irrégulier.

detach (dè-tatshe), v.a., détacher, séparer.

detachment, n., action de détacher, f. ; détachement, m.

detail (di-téle), n., détail, m.

detail, v.a., détailler.

detailer, n., narrateur de détails, m.

detain (di-téne), v.a., retenir ; tenir ; détenir.

detainer, n., personne qui retient ; détention, f. ; (jur.) mandat d'arrestation provisoire, m.

detect (di-tècte), v.a., découvrir ; surprendre.

detecter, n., personne qui découvre, f. ; dénonciateur, révélateur, m. ; chose qui découvre, f.

detection, n., découverte, f.

detective, n., agent, espion de la police criminelle, de la police secrète, m.

detent (di-), n., (horl.) détente, f.

detention (di-), n., action de retenir ; (jur.) détention, f.

deter (di-teur), v.a., détourner ; empêcher, retenir, arrêter ; effrayer.

deterge (di-teurdje), v.a., déterger.

detergent, adj., détergent, détersif.

detergent, n., détersif, m.

deteriorate (di-ti-), v.a., détériorer ; faire dégénérer.

deteriorate, v.n., (of things—des choses) se détériorer ; (pers.) dégénérer.

deterioration (-rio-ré-), n., (of things—des choses) détérioration ; (pers.) dégénération, f.

determinable (di-teur-mi-na-b'l), adj., déterminable.

determinate (di-teur-), adj., déterminé, établi, réglé ; définitif.

determinately, adv., déterminément.

determination (-né-), n., détermination ; (jur.) fin, expiration, f.

determinative, adj., déterminatif ; déterminant.

determine (di-teur-mine), v.a., déterminer.

determine, v.n., se déterminer ; se décider.

determined (-mi'n'de), adj., déterminé.

determinedly (-mi'n'dli), adv., déterminément.

detersion (di-teur-), n., détersion, f.

detersive (di-teur-), adj., détersif.

detersive, n., détersif, m.

detest (di-tèste), v.a., détester.

detestable, adj., détestable.

detestably, adv., détestablement.

detestation (-ès-té-), n., détestation, f.

detester, n., personne qui déteste, f.

dethrone (di-thrône), v.a., détrôner.

dethronement, n., détrônement, m.

dethroner, n., personne qui détrône, f.

detinue (dèt'i-niou), n., (jur.) instance pour détention illégale de biens meubles, f.

detonate (dèt'-o-), v.n., détoner.

detonate, v.a., faire détoner.

detonation (dèt'o-né-), n., détonation, f.

detort (di-teurte), v.a., détourner le sens de.

detour (dè-tour), n., détour, m.

detract (di-tracte), *v.n.*, enlever ; diminuer, rabattre. To — from ; (b.s.) *médire de*.

detracter, *n.*, détracteur, *m.*

detractingly, *adv.*, par détraction.

detraction (di-trac-), *n.*, action d'enlever ; détraction, *f.*; dénigrement, *m.*

detractive, *adj.*, détracteur.

detractory ('-eur-), *adj.*, dérogatoire ; détracteur.

detractress, *n.*, médisante, *f.*

detriment, *n.*, détriment ; préjudice ; dommage, *m.*

detrimental, *adj.*, préjudiciable, nuisible.

detrition (di-), *n.*, détrition, *f.*

detritus (di-traï-), *n.*, (geol.) détritus, débris, *m.*

detrude (dè-troude), *v.a.*, précipiter, repousser ; chasser, reléguer.

detruncate (di-treu'n'-), *v.a.*, tronquer.

detruncation, *n.*, coupe ; mutilation, *f.*

deuce (diouce), *n.*, deux, *m.*

deuce, *or* **deuse** (diouce), *n.*, (l. ex.) diable ; diantre, *m.* The —! *diantre! diable!* The — is in it ; *le diable s'en mêle*.

deuteronomy (diou-teur'-), *n.*, Deutéronome, *m.*

devastate (dèv'as-), *v.a.*, dévaster.

devastation, *n.*, dévastation, *f.*

develop (di-vèl'-), *v.a.*, développer.

development, *n.*, développement, dénouement, dénoûment, *m.* ; exposition, *f.*

devest (di-vèste), *v.a.*, (jur.) désinvestir de.

devexity (di-vèks'-), *n.*, courbure, *f.*

deviate (di-vi-), *v.n.*, dévier, se dévier ; s'égarer, s'écarter.

deviation, *n.*, déviation, *f.* ; égarement ; écart, *m.*

device (di-vaïce), *n.*, devise, *f.* ; dessein, projet ; artifice, moyen, *m.* ; invention, *f.*

devil (dèv'l), *n.*, diable, démon, *m.* She— ; *diablesse*, *f.* The —! *ah diable!* There is the — to pay ; *c'est le diable à confesser*.

devilet, *or* **deviling**, *n.* V. **devilkin**.

devilish (dèv'l-ishe), *adj.*, diabolique.

devilishly, *adv.*, diaboliquement, diablement.

devilishness, *n.*, caractère diabolique, *m.*

devilkin (dèv'l-), **devilet** (dèv'lète), *or* **deviling** (dèv'l-), *n.*, diablotin, *m.*

devious (di-vi-), *adj.*, détourné ; (fig.) errant, vagabond.

deviously, *adv.*, à tort.

devisable (dè-vaïz'-a-b'l), *adj.*, imaginable ; (jur.) (of property—*propriété*) disponible.

devise (dè-vaïze), *n.*, disposition testamentaire, *f.*

devise, *v.a.*, projeter ; imaginer, inventer ; tramer ; (jur.) disposer par testament de.

devise, *v.n.*, projeter.

devisee (dèv-i-zï), *n.*, (jur.) héritier institué. *m.*, héritière instituée, *f.*

deviser (dè-vaïz'-), *n.*, inventeur, *m.*

devisor (dè-vaï-zeur), *n.*, (jur.) testateur, *m.*, testatrice, *f.*

devoid (di-voïde), *adj.*, privé ; exempt ; dénué, dépourvu.

devoir (dèv'oir), *n.*, devoir, *m.*

devolution (dèv'o-liou-), *n.*, dévolution, *f.*

devolve (di-), *v.a.*, rouler.

devolve, *v.n.*, échoir, tomber ; confier ; être dévolu.

devote (di-vôte), *v.a.*, dévouer, vouer, consacrer.

devote, *adj.*, voué, dévoué.

devote, *n.*, dévot, *m* , dévote, *f.*

devotedness, *n.*, dévouement, dévoûment, *m.*

devotee (dèv'o-tï), *n.*, dévot, *m.*, dévote, *f.* ; (b.s.) faux dévot, *m.*, fausse dévote, *f.* ; bigot, *m.*, bigote, *f.*

devotion (di-vô-), *n.*, dévotion ; offrande ; prière, *f.*; empressement ; dévoûment, *m.*

devotional, *adj.*, (of things—*des choses*) de dévotion ; (pers.) porté à la dévotion.

devotionalist, *or* **devotionist**, *n.*, dévot, *m.*, dévote, *f.* ; (b.s.) faux dévot, *m.*, fausse dévote, *f.*

devour (di-va'-weur), *v.a.*, dévorer.

devourer, *n.*, monstre dévorant ; dévorateur, *m.*, dévoratrice, *f.*

devouringly, *adv.*, en dévorant.

devout (di-vaoute), *adj.*, dévot, pieux.

devoutless, *adj.*, indévot.

devoutlessness, *n.*, indévotion, *f.*

devoutly, *adv.*, dévotement.

devoutness, *n.*, dévotion, *f.*

dew (diou), *n.*, rosée, *f.*

dew, *v.a.*, couvrir de rosée ; mouiller, arroser, tremper.

dew-bent (-bè'n'te), *adj.*, qui plie sous la rosée ; chargé de rosée.

dew-bespangled (-bè-spa'n'g'l'de), *adj.*, parsemé de rosée.

dew-besprent, *adj.*, couvert de rosée.

dew-drop, *n.*, goutte de rosée, *f.*

dew-dropping, *adj.*, qui dégoutte de rosée.

dew-lap, *n.*, fanon, *m.*

dew-lapt, *adj.*, qui a un fanon ; à fanon.

dew-sprinkled (-spri'n'k'l'de), *adj.*, couvert de rosée.

dew-worm (-weurme), *n.*, (ent.) lombric terrestre ; ver de terre, *m.*

dewy (diou-i), *adj.*, de rosée ; couvert de rosée.

dexter (dèks'teur), *adj.*, droit; (her.) dextre.

dexterity (-tèr'-), *n.*, dextérité, adresse, *f.*

dexterous (-tèr'-), *adj.*, adroit ; habile.

dexterously, *adv.*, adroitement, habilement.

dexterousness, *n.*, dextérité, adresse, *f.*

dextral, *adj.*, droit.

dextrality, *n.*, situation à droite, *f.*

dextrine, *n.*, (chem.) dextrine, *f.*

dey, *n.*, dey, *m.*

diabetes (daï'a-bï-tize), *n. sing.* and *pl.*, (med.) diabète, *m.sing.*

diabetic, *or* **diabetical** (daï-a-bèt'-), *adj.*, diabétique.

diabolic, *or* **diabolical** (daï-a-), *adj.*, diabolique.

diabolically, *adv.*, diaboliquement.

diabolicalness, *n.*, caractère diabolique, *m.*

diachylum (daï-ak'i-leume), *or* **diachylon** (-lone), *n.*, diachylum, diachylon, *m.*

diacodium (daï-a-cô-di-eume), *n.*, diacode, *m.*

diaconal (daï-ac'o-), *adj.*, diaconal.

diacoustics (daï-a-caoustikse), *n.pl.*, diacoustique, *f.*

diadelphia (daï-a-), *n.*, diadelphie, *f.*

diadem (daï-a-), *n.*, diadème, *m.*

diademed (-dè'm'de), *adj.*, ceint d'un diadème.

diadrom (daï-a-), *n.*, vibration du pendule, *f.*

diaeresis (daï-ir-i-cîss), *n.*, (*diaereses*) tréma, *m.*; diérèse, *f.*

diagnostic (daï-ag-), *adj.*, diagnostique.

diagnostic, *n.*, diagnostique, *m.*

diagonal (daï-ag-), *adj.*, diagonal.

diagonal, *n.*, diagonale, *f.*

diagonally, *adv.*, diagonalement.

diagram (daï-a-), *n.*, diagramme, *m.*

dial (daï'al), *n.*, cadran, *m.* Sun-—; *cadran solaire*. *m.*

dialect (daï-a-), *n.*, dialecte ; langage, *m.*

dialectic, *or* **dialectical**, *adj.*, dialectique.

dialectically, *adv.*, dialectiquement.

dialectician (daï-a-lèc-tish'a'n), *n.*, dialecticien, *m.*

dialectics (daï-a-lèc-tikse), *n.pl.*, dialectique, *f.sing.*

dialling (daï-al'-), *n.*, gnomonique, *f.*

diallist (daï-al'-), *n.*, faiseur de cadrans, *m.*

dialogist (daï-al'o-djiste), *n.*, interlocuteur ; auteur de dialogues ; (l.u.) dialogiste, *m.*

dialogistic, or **dialogistical**, *adj.*, dialogique.

dialogistically, *adv.*, dialogiquement.

dialogue (daï-a-loghe), *n.*, dialogue ; entretien, *m.*

dialogue-writer (-raït'-), *n.*, auteur de dialogues, (l.u.) dialogiste, *m.*

dial-plate (daï-al-pléte), *n.*, cadran, *m.*

dial-work (-weurke), *n.*, (horl.) cadrature, *f.*

diameter (daï-am'i-), *n.*, diamètre, *m.*

diametral, diametric, or **diametrical** (daï-a-), *adj.*, diamétral.

diametrally, or **diametrically,** *adv.*, diamétralement.

diamond (daï'a-meu'n'de), *n.*, diamant ; (at cards—*cartes*) carreau ; (geom.) rhombe, *m.* Set of —s ; *garniture de diamants, f.* Cut —; *diamant taillé.* False —; *faux diamant ; diamant faux.* Polished —; *diamant poli.* Rough —; *diamant brut.* True —; *vrai diamant.* Wrought —; *diamant travaillé.* Glazier's —; *diamant de vitrier.* Rose —; *diamant en rose, m. ; rose, f.* — of the first water; *diamant de première eau.* To set a —; *monter un diamant.* —cutter; *diamantaire ; lapidaire, m.* —cutting ; *taille du diamant, f.*

diandria (daï-), *n.*, diandrie, *f.*

diapason (daï-a-pé-zone), *n.*, diapason, *m.*

diaper (daï-a-), *n.*, toile ouvrée, *f* ; (arch.) panneau à arabesques, *m.*

diaper, *v.a.*, varier de plusieurs couleurs, diaprer; ouvrer.

diaphaneity (daï'a-fa-ni-i-), *n.*, diaphanéité, *f.*

diaphanic, or **diaphanous,** *adj.*, diaphane.

diaphoresis (daï-a-fo-ri-cice), *n.*, diaphorèse, *f.*

diaphragm (daï-a-frame), *n.*, diaphragme, *m.*

diarist (daï-a-), *n.*, personne qui tient un journal, *f.*

diarrhœa (daï-a-ri-a), *n.*, diarrhée, *f.*

diarthrosis (daï-ar-thrô-cice), *n.*, diarthrose, *f.*

diary (daï-a-), *n.*, journal, *m.*

diastase (daï-as-téce), *n.*, (chem.) diastase, *f.*

. diastasis (daï-as-ta-cice), *n.*, (surg.) diastase, *f.*

diastole (daï-as-), *n.*, diastole, *f.*

diastyle (daï-a-staïle), *n.*, diastyle, *m.*

diathesis (daï-ath-i-cice), *n.*, diathèse, *f.*

diatonic (daï-a-), *adj.*, (mus.) diatonique.

diatribe (daï-a-traïbe), *n.*, diatribe, *f.*

dibber (dib'-), *n.*, (agri.) plantoir, *m.*

dibble (dib'b'l), *n.*, plantoir, *m.*

dibble, *v.a.*, (agri.) planter au plantoir.

dibstone (-stône), *n.*, palet, *m.*

dicacity (-ké-), *n.*, (ant.) caquet, babil, *m.*

dice (daïce), *n.pl. V.* **die** (noun).

dice-box (-bokse), *n.*, cornet à dés, *m.*

dicer, *n.*, joueur aux dés, *m.*

dichotomy (daï-cot'-), *n.*, dichotomie, *f.*

dickens! (dik'è'n'ze) *int.*, (l.ex.) diantre!

dicky, *n.*, siège de derrière, *m.* ; (shirt-front —*devant de chemise*) chemisette, *f.*

dicotyledon (daï-cot'i-li-), *n.*, (bot.) dicotylédone, *f.*

dicotyledonous, *adj.*, dicotylédone.

dictate, *n.*, précepte ; ordre, *m.*; inspiration, *f.*

dictate, *v.a.*, dicter.

dictation (dic-té-), *n.*, dictée, *f.*

dictator (-té-teur), *n.*, dictateur, *m.*

dictatorial (-tô-), *adj.*, dictatorial, de dictateur ; impérieux ; dogmatique ; arrogant.

dictatorship (-té-teur'-), *n.*, dictature, *f.*

dictatory (-té-teuri), *adj.*, arrogant ; dogmatique ; tranchant.

dicature (-té-tioure), *n.*, dictature, *f.*

diction (dik'sheune), *n.*, diction, *f.*

dictionary (dik'sheu'n'a-), *n.*, dictionnaire, *m.*

did, *v. V.* **do.**

didactic, or **didactical,** *adj.*, didactique.

didactically, *adv.*, didactiquement.

didapper (did'ap'eur), *n.*, (orni.) plongeon, *m.*

diddle (did'd'l), *v.n.*, chanceler en marchant ; vétiller ; perdre son temps.

diddle, *v.a.*, duper, (pop.) enfoncer, mettre dedans.

didelphys (daï-), *n.*, (mam.) didelphe, *m.*

didymous, *adj.*, (bot.) didyme.

didynamia (-né-), *n.*, (bot.) didynamie, *f.*

die (da'ye), *n.* (*dice*), dé à jouer, *m.* ; (fig.) chance, *f.*, hasard, *m.*

die (da'ye), *n.* (*dies*), (for stamping—*pour timbrer le papier, marquer les monnaies, &c.*) coin, *m.*

die (da'ye), *v.n.*, mourir ; s'éteindre. To — away ; *s'éteindre, se mourir.* To — off ; *s'éteindre.*

diesis (daï'i-cice), *n.*, (mus.) dièse, *m.* ; (print.) croix double (‡), *f.*

diet (daï'ète), *n.*, (assembly—*assemblée*) diète ; (food—*alimentation*) nourriture ; (med.) diète, *f.*, régime, *m.*

diet, *v.a.*, (med.) mettre à la diète, mettre au régime ; nourrir.

diet, *v.n.*, faire diète, être au régime ; se nourrir.

dietary, *n.*, diète, *f.*; régime alimentaire, *m.*

dietary, *adj.*, de diète.

dieter (daï-èt'-), *n.*, diététiste, *m.*

dietetic, or **dietetical** (daï'-), *adj.*, diététique.

dietetics (daï-), *n.pl.*, diététique, *f.*

dietine (daï'-è-), *n.*, diétine, *f.*

differ (dif'feur), *v.n.*, différer.

difference, *n.*, différence ; (quarrel—*querelle*) dispute, *f.*, différend, *m.*

difference, *v.a.*, différencier.

different, *adj.*, différent.

differential (-shal), *adj.*, différentiel.

differentiate, *v.a.*, (math.) différentier.

differently, *adv.*, différemment.

difficult (-keulte), *adj.*, difficile ; malaisé.

difficultly, *adv.*, difficilement.

difficulty (-keul-), *n.*, difficulté ; peine, *f.* ; embarras, *m.*

diffidence, *n.*, défiance, *f.* ; manque de confiance en soi-même, *m.* ; hésitation, *f.*

diffident, *adj.*, défiant ; timide ; hésitant.

diffidently, *adv.*, avec défiance ; avec hésitation ; timidement.

diffluent (dif'flou'-), *adj.*, (ant.) coulant, fluide.

difform, *adj.*, difforme, irrégulier.

difformity, *n.*, difformité, *f.*

diffraction, *n.*, diffraction, *f.*

diffuse (dif'fiouze), *adj.*, diffus, verbeux ; répandu.

diffuse, *v.a.*, répandre.

diffused (dif'fiouz'de), *past part.*, répandu ; irrégulier.

diffusedly (-fiouz'èd-), *adv.*, d'une manière étendue.

diffusely (-fiouz'-), *adv.*, diffusément.

diffusion (dif'fiou-jeune), *n.*, diffusion, dispersion ; propagation, *f.*

diffusive (-fiou-cive), *adj.*, qui se répand.

diffusively, *adv.*, au loin.

diffusiveness, *n.*, qualité de ce qui peut se répandre; abondance; extension, *f.*

dig, *v.a.* (*preterit and past part.*, Dug *or* Digged), creuser; bêcher; piocher; fouiller. To — out; *retirer*. To — up; *déterrer*.

dig, *v.n.*, bêcher, piocher; creuser la terre; faire des fouilles.

digest (daï-djèste), *n.*, digeste, *m.*

digest (di-djèste), *v.a.*, classer; (food—*nourriture*) digérer; (chem.) faire digérer.

digest, *v.n.*, digérer.

digester (di-), *n.*, (chem.) digesteur, *m.*

digestible (di-), *adj.*, digestible.

digestion (di-djèst'ieune), *n.*, digestion, *f.*; (fig.) examen approfondi, *m.*

digestive (di-), *adj.*, digestif.

digestive, *n.*, digestif, *m.*

digger (dig'gheur), *n.*, personne qui bêche, *f.*; terrassier; (for gold—*d'or*) chercheur d'or, mineur, *m.*

digging (-ghigne), *n.*, fouille, *f.*; déblai; terrassement, *m.*

dight (daïte), *v.a.*, (ant.) orner, parer.

digit (didj'ite), *n.*, mesure de 20 millimètres, *f.*; doigt; (arith.) chiffre, *m.*

digital (didj'i-), *adj.*, (anat.) digital.

digitate (didj'i-), *or* **digitated** (-ède), *adj.*, digité.

dignified (dig-ni-faïde), *adj.*, revêtu d'une dignité; plein de dignité, digne.

dignify (dig-ni-fa'ye), *v.a.*, élever à une dignité; donner de la dignité à; élever, illustrer; revêtir d'un titre.

dignitary (dig-ni-), *n.*, dignitaire, *m.*

dignity (dig-ni-), *n.*, dignité, *f.*

digraph (daï-), *n.*, digramme, *m.*

digress (di-), *v.n.*, faire une digression; s'écarter.

digression (di-grèsh'eune), *n.*, digression; faute, *f.*; écart, *m.*

digressional (-grèsh'eu'n'-), *adj.*, de digression, digressif.

digressive (di-), *adv.*, digressif.

digressively, *adv.*, digressivement.

dike (daïke), *n.*, digue, *f.*

dike, *v.a.*, diguer.

dilacerate (di-lass'eur'-), *v.a.*, dilacérer.

dilaceration (-'eur'é-), *n.*, dilacération, *f.*

dilaniation (di-lé-ni-é-), *n.*, (ant.) action de déchirer, action de mettre en pièces, *f.*

dilapidate, *v.a.*, délabrer, dilapider.

dilapidate, *v.n.*, se délabrer.

dilapidation (dil-ap-i-dé-), *n.*, délabrement, *m.*; dilapidation, *f.*

dilapidator (-dé-teur), *n.*, dilapidateur, *m.*; dilapidatrice, *f.*

dilatability (di-lét'-), *n.*, dilatabilité, *f.*

dilatable (di-lét'-a-b'l), *adj.*, dilatable.

dilatation (dil-a-té-), *n.*, dilatation, *f.*

dilate (daï-), *v.a.*, dilater, élargir, étendre.

dilate, *v.n.*, se dilater.

dilator (daï-lé-teur), *n.*, dilatateur, *m.*

dilatoriness (dil-a-teuri-), *n.*, lenteur, *f.*

dilatory (dil-a-teuri), *adj.*, négligent, lent, dilatoire.

dilemma (di-), *n.*, dilemme; embarras, *m.*

dilettante (dil-èt-ta'n'ti), *n.* (*dilettanti*), amateur des beaux arts; (mus.) dilettante, *m.*

diligence (dil-i-djè'n'ce), *n.*, diligence, assiduité; (coach—*voiture*) diligence, *f.*

diligent (dil-i-djè'n'te), *adj.*, diligent.

diligently, *adv.*, diligemment.

dill, *n.*, (bot.) anet, *m.*

dilucid (di-liou-), *adj.*, (ant.) clair, transparent.

dilucidate, *v.a.*, (ant.) éclaircir.

dilucidation (-ci-dé-), *n.*, (ant.) éclaircissement, *m.*

diluent (dil'iou-), *adj.*, délayant.

dilute (di-lioute), *v.a.*, détremper; délayer; (wine—*vin*) couper; (fig.) affaiblir.

diluter, *n.*, chose qui délaye, *f.*

dilution (di-liou-), *n.*, dilution, *f.*; délayement; (fig.) affaiblissement, *m.*

diluvial, *or* **diluvian** (di-liou-), *adj.*, diluvien.

dim, *adj.*, obscur, obscurci.

dim, *v.a.*, obscurcir; offusquer.

dimension, *n.*, dimension, proportion, étendue, *f.*

dimidiation (-mi-di-é-), *n.*, division en deux parties égales, *f.*

diminish, *v.a.*, diminuer, abaisser.

diminish, *v.n.*, diminuer.

diminishingly, *adv.*, désavantageusement.

diminution (-niou-), *n.*, diminution, *f.*

diminutive, *adj.*, petit, diminutif.

diminutive, *n.*, diminutif, *m.*

diminutively, *adv.*, dans de petites proportions; désavantageusement.

diminutiveness, *n.*, petitesse; exiguïté, *f.*

dimissory (-'is'seuri), *adj.*, dimissorial.

dimity, *n.*, basin, *m.*

dimly, *adv.*, obscurément.

dimmish, *adj.*, un peu obscurci; terne.

dimness, *n.*, état obscurci; obscurcissement, *m.*; obscurité, *f.*

dimple (di'm'p'l), *n.*, fossette, *f.*

dimple, *v.a.*, former en fossette.

dimple, *v.n.*, former des fossettes.

dimply, *adv.*, plein de fossettes.

din, *n.*, bruit étourdissant, *m.*

din, *v.a.*, étourdir.

dine (daïne), *v.n.*, dîner.

dine, *v.a.*, donner à dîner à; nourrir.

diner, *n.*, dîneur, *m.*

ding-dong (digu'dongne), *n.*, bruit des cloches, dine-dindon, *m.*

dinginess (di'n'-dji-), *n.*, couleur sombre, *f.*; air sombre, *m.*

dingle (di'n'-g'l), *n.*, vallon, *m.*

dingle-dangle (di'n'-g'l-da'n'-g'l), *adv.*, en pendillant.

dingy (di'n'-dji), *adj.*, sombre.

dining (daï'n'-), *n.*, action de dîner, *f.*; dîner, *m.*

dining-room (-roume), *n.*, salle à manger, *f.*

dining-rooms (-roum'ze), *n.pl.*, restaurant, *m.sing.*

dining-table (-té-b'l), *n.*, table à manger, *f.*

dinner (di'n'eur), *n.*, dîner, dîné, *m.* — time; heure de dîner, *f.*

dint (di'n'te), *n.*, coup, *m.*; coche, dent, marque d'un coup; force, puissance, *f.* By — of; à force de.

diat, *v.a.*, bossuer.

dinumeration (daï-niou-meur'é-), *n.*, énumération, *f.*; dénombrement, *m.*

diocesan (daï-o-ci-ça'n), *adj.*, diocésain.

diocesan, *n.*, évêque diocésain, *m.*

diocese (daï-ô-cice), *n.*, diocèse, *m.*

diœcia (daï-i-shi-a), *n.*, (bot.) diœcie, *f.*

dioptric, *or* **dioptrical** (daï-), *adj.*, dioptrique.

dioptrics (daï-op-trikse), *n.pl.*, dioptrique, *f. sing.*

diorama (daï-o-râ-), *n.*, diorama, *m.*

dip, *v.a.*, plonger; tremper; mouiller.

dip, *v.n.*, plonger; (of the needle—*de l'aiguille aimantée*) incliner; (mines) s'incliner. To — into; *s'engager dans*; *feuilleter*.

dip, *n.*, plongement, *m.*; (geol.; of the needle—*de l'aiguille aimantée*) inclinaison; (candle—*chandelle*) chandelle à la baguette, *f.*

diphthong (dip'thong), *n.*, diphtongue, *f.*

diploe (dip-lo-i), *n.*, (anat.) diploé, *m.*

diploma (di-plô-), *n.*, diplôme, *m.*

diplomacy (di-plô-), *n.*, diplomatie, *f.*

diplomatic, *adj.*, diplomatique.

diplomatics (-'ikse), *n.pl.*, diplomatique, . *sing.*

diplomatist (-plô-), *n.*, diplomate, *m.*

dipper, *n.*, plongeur, *m.*

dipping, *n.*, plongement, *m.*; (mines) inclinaison, *f.*

diptera (dip-tira), *or* **dipterans** (dip-ti-ra'n'ze), *n.pl.*, diptères, *m.pl.*

dipteral, *or* **dipterous** (-ti-), *adj.*, (ent.) diptère.

dire (daeur), *adj.*, terrible, affreux; cruel.

direct, *adj.*, direct, droit.

direct, *v.a.*, diriger; ordonner; enseigner, renseigner, donner des renseignements à. To — a letter; *adresser une lettre.*

direction, *n.*, direction, *f.*; ordre, *m.*, instruction, *f.*; sens, côté, *m.*; (of a letter—*d'une lettre*) adresse, *f.*; (of the wind—*du vent*) lit, *m.*

directive, *adj.*, rectif, qui dirige, qui guide.

directly, *adv.*, directement, immédiatement; (of time—*de temps*) tout de suite, immédiatement.

directness, *n.*, mouvement direct, *m.*; (fig.) droiture, *f.*

director (-teur), *n.*, directeur, guide, chef, *m.*

directory, *n.*, directoire; (for addresses—*d'adresses*) almanach des 25,000 adresses, *m.*

directress, *n.*, directrice, *f.*

direful (daeur'foule), *adj.*, terrible, affreux; cruel.

direfully, *adv.*, terriblement, affreusement, cruellement.

direfulness, *n.*, horreur, *f.*

direness (daeur'-), *n.*, horreur, *f.*

dirge (deurdje), *n.*, chant funèbre, *m.*

dirk (deurke), *n.*, dague, *f.*

dirt (deurte), *n.*, boue; saleté; fange; ordure; crotte, *f.*

dirt, *v.a.*, salir, souiller, crotter.

dirtily, *adv.*, salement; vilainement.

dirtiness, *n.*, saleté, malpropreté; (fig.) bassesse, *f.*

dirty, *adj.*, sale; crotté; malpropre; (fig.) vilain. — action; *action sale, f.*

dirty, *v.a.*, salir, crotter; souiller.

diruption (di-reup'-), *n.*, rupture, *f.*

disability (diss'-), *n.*, incapacité; impuissance; (jur.) inhabilité, *f.*

disable (diz'é-b'l), *v.a.*, rendre incapable; renverser; détruire; mettre hors de combat; (nav.) désemparer. —d soldier; *invalide, m.*

disabling, *adj.*, qui rend incapable; (jur.) qui frappe d'incapacité légale.

disabuse (diss'a-biouze), *v.a.*, désabuser.

disaccustom (diss'ac'keus'teume), *v.a.*, désaccoutumer, déshabituer.

disacquaintance (diss'ac'kwé'n't'-), *n.*, cessation de connaissance, *f.*

disadvantage (diss'ad-vâ'n'tédje), *n.*, désavantage, *m.*

disadvantage, *v.a.*, désavantager.

disadvantageous (-té-djeusse), *adj.*, désavantageux.

disadvantageously, *adv.*, désavantageusement.

disadvantageousness, *n.*, désavantage, *m.*

disaffect (diss'-), *v.a.*, aliéner les esprits; perdre l'amour, l'affection de.

disaffected (-ède), *adj.*, mal disposé.

disaffectedly, *adv.*, avec désaffection.

disaffectedness, *or* **disaffection**, *n.*, désaffection, *f.*

disaffirm (diss'af'feurme), *v.a.*, infirmer.

disaffirmance, *n.*, réfutation; (jur.) infirmation, *f.*

disafforest (diss'af'for'èste), *v.a.*, déclarer ne plus être forêt.

disaggregate (diss'ag'grï-), *v.a.*, désagréger.

disaggregation (diss'ag'grï-ghé-), *n.*, désagrégation, *f.*

disagree (diss'a-gri), *v.n.*, différer; ne pas s'accorder. To — with; *faire mal à; incommoder.* To — with any one; *ne pas s'accorder, être brouillé, avec quelqu'un.* To — to; *ne pas accéder à.*

disagreeable (diss'a-grï-a-b'l), *adj.*, désagréable; fâcheux.

disagreeableness, *n.*, désagrément, *m.*

disagreement (diss'a-grï-), *n.*, différence, *f.*; différend, désaccord, *m.*; brouillerie, *f.*

disallow (diss'al'laou), *v.a.*, désapprouver, rejeter, désavouer; ne pas admettre.

disallow, *v.n.*, ne pas permettre.

disallowable (-a-b'l), *adj.*, qui n'est pas permis.

disallowance, *n.*, défense, *f.*

disally (diss'al'la'ye), *v.a.*, (ant.) unir par mésalliance, mésallier.

disanchor (diz'angn'keur), *v.a.*, (ant.) faire chasser un vaisseau sur ses ancres.

disanimate (diz'-), *v.a.*, (ant.) cesser d'animer; décourager.

disanimation (diz'a'n'i-mé-), *n.*, mort, *f.*; découragement, *m.*

disappear (diss'ap'pire), *v.a.*, disparaître.

disappearance (diss'-), *n.*, disparition, *f.*

disappoint (diss'ap-pwaï'n'te), *v.a.*, contrarier; désappointer; frustrer; manquer de parole à; tromper.

disappointment (diss'ap-pwaï'n't'-), *n.*, contrariété, *f.*; désappointement, *m.*; espérance déçue, *f.*; contretemps, *m.*

disapprobation (diss'ap-pro-bé-), *n.*, désapprobation, *f.*

disapprobatory (diss'ap-pro-ba-teuri), *adj.*, désapprobateur.

disapprove (diss'ap-prouve), *v.a.*, désapprouver.

disarm (diz'ârme), *v.a.*, désarmer.

disarrangement (diss'ar-ré'n'dje-), *n.*, dérangement; désordre, *m.*

disarray (diss'ar-ré), *v.a.*, déshabiller; mettre en désarroi.

disarray, *n.*, désarroi, désordre, *m.*

disaster (diz'-), *n.*, désastre, *m.*

disaster, *v.a.*, frapper de désastres.

disastrous, *adj.*, désastreux.

disastrously, *adv.*, désastreusement.

disastrousness, *n.*, nature désastreuse, *f.*

disavow (diss'a-vaou), *v.a.*, désavouer.

disavowal, *n.*, désaveu, *m.*

disband, *v.a.*, licencier; congédier.

disband, *v.n.*, se séparer, se disperser; (milit.) être licencié.

disbanding, *n.*, licenciement, *m.*

disbark (-barke), *v.a.*, débarquer.

disbelief (-bi-life), *n.*, incrédulité, *f.*

disbelieve (-bi-live), *v.a.*, ne pas croire.

disbeliever, *n.*, incrédule, *m.*, *f.*

disbench (diz'bè'n'she), *v.a.*, chasser de son siège, chasser de son banc.

disbranch (diz'brâ'n'she), *v.a.*, ébrancher.

disbud (diz'beude), *v.a.*, ébourgeonner.

disburden (diz'beur-d'n), *v.a.*, décharger; (fig.) ouvrir.

disburse (diz'beurse), *v.a.*, débourser, dépenser.

disbursement, *n.*, déboursement, *m.*

disburser, *n.*, personne qui débourse, *f.*

disc (diske), *n.*, disque, *m.*

discard (dis'cârde), *v.a.*, congédier; écarter; exclure; renvoyer.

discase (dis'kéce), *v.a.*, déshabiller.

discern (diz'zeurne), *v.a.*, discerner, distinguer; juger.

discerner, *n.*, personne qui discerne ; personne qui juge, *f.*

discernible (diz'zeurn'i-b'l), *adj.*, perceptible, visible, discernable.

discernibleness, *n.*, visibilité, *f.*

discernibly, *adv.*, visiblement.

discerning. *adj.*, judicieux.

discerningly, *adv.*, avec discernement.

discernment, *n.*, discernement ; jugement, *m.*

discerp (dis'œurpe), *v.a.*, déchirer ; mettre en pièces.

discerpibility, *or* **discerptibility**, *n.*, qualité de ce qui peut être séparé, *f.*

discerptible (-ti-b'l), *adj.*, séparable.

discerption, *n.*, déchirement, *m.*

discharge (dis-tshârdje), *n.*, déchargement, *m.* ; émission, *f.* ; écoulement, *m.* ; (of fire-arms, arrows, water—*d'armes à feu, de flèches, d'eau*) décharge ; (from prison—*de prison*) libération, mise en liberté, *f.*, élargissement ; (of a duty —*d'un devoir*) accomplissement ; (of a servant— *de domestique*) congé ; (milit.) congé définitif, *m.*; (payment) quittance, *f.*

discharge (dis-tshârdje), *v.a.*, décharger ; (a servant— *domestiques*) congédier, renvoyer ; (from confinement—*de prison*) libérer, élargir ; (a debt— *une dette*) acquitter, payer ; (arrows— *des flèches*) décocher, lancer ; (fire-arms—*armes à feu*) décharger ; (a duty—*un devoir*) s'acquitter de, accomplir ; (milit., nav.) congédier.

discharger, *n.*, personne qui décharge, qui congédie, *f.*

disciple (dis'çaï'p'l), *n.*, disciple, *m.*

disciple, *v.a.*, enseigner, endoctriner.

discipleship, *n.*, état de disciple, *m.*

disciplinable (-a-b'l), *adj.*, disciplinable ; soumis à la discipline.

disciplinarian (-né-), *adj.*, disciplinaire.

disciplinarian. *n.*, personne rigide pour la discipline, *f.* ; (milit.) instructeur, *m.*

disciplinary, *adj.*, disciplinaire.

discipline, *n.*, discipline, *f.*

discipline, *v.a.*, discipliner.

disclaim (dis-cléme), *v.a.*, désavouer, renier.

disclaimer, *n.*, personne qui désavoue, qui renie, *f.* ; désaveu public, *m.*

disclose (-clôze), *v.a.*, découvrir, réveler ; mettre au jour.

discloser, *n.*, révélateur, *m.*, révélatrice, *f.*

disclosure (-clô'jeur), *n.*, déclaration, révélation ; découverte, *f.*

discoast, *v.n.*, (ant.) s'éloigner de la côte ; s'éloigner.

discolour (dis'keul'leur), *v.a.*, décolorer.

discolouration (dis'keul'leur-é-), *n.*, décoloration, *f.*

discomfit (dis-keu'm'fite), *n.*, défaite, déroute ; dispersion, *f.* ; renversement, *m.*

discomfit, *v.a.*, défaire ; mettre en déroute ; mettre en fuite ; disperser ; vaincre.

discomfiture (-'ioure), *n.*, défaite, déroute, ⊙ déconfiture, *f.*

discomfort (-keu'm'feurte), *n.*, désolation, *f.* ; désagrément, *m.*

discomfort, *v.a.*, affliger ; chagriner.

discomfortable (-a-b'l), *adj.*, (ant.) affligeant. désagréable.

discommend, *v.a.*, blâmer, censurer.

discommendable (-'a-b'l), *adj.*, blâmable, censurable.

discommendableness, *n.*, caractère blâmable, *m.*

discommendation, *n.*, blâme, *m.*

discommender, *n.*, désapprobateur, *m.*

discommode (-môde), *v.a.*, incommoder.

discommodious, *adj.*, (ant.) incommode.

discommon, *v.a.*, dépouiller du droit de vaine pâture.

discompose (-pôze), *v.a.*, déranger, troubler ; mettre hors de soi.

discomposure (-pô'jeur), *n.*, dérangement ; trouble, *m.*

disconcert (-ceurte), *v.a.*, déconcerter, troubler.

disconformity, *n.*, dissemblance, *f.*

discongruity (-grou-), *n.*, disconvenance, *f.*

disconnect. *v.a.*, désunir.

disconnection, *n.*, désunion, *f.*

disconsent, *v.n.*, différer ; ne pas s'accorder ; ne pas consentir.

disconsolate. *adj.*, inconsolable, désolé.

disconsolately, *adv.*, inconsolablement.

disconsolateness, *n.*, désolation, *f.*

disconsolation (-lé-), *n.*, (ant.) désolation, *f.*

discontent, *adj.*, mécontent.

discontent, *n.*, mécontentement, *m.*

discontent, *v.a.*, mécontenter.

discontented, *adj.*, mécontent.

discontentedly. *adv.*, avec mécontentement ; à contre-cœur.

discontentedness, *n.*, (ant.) mécontentement, *m.*

discontentment. *n.*, mécontentement, *m.*

discontinuance (-'iou-), *or* **discontinuation** (-'iou-é-), *n.*, cessation ; discontinuation, discontinuité, *f.*

discontinue (-ti'n'iou), *v.a. and n.*, discontinuer.

discontinuity (-niou-), *n.*, discontinuité, *f.*

discontinuous, *adj.*, (ant.) discontinu.

discord, **discordance**, *or* **discordancy**, *n.*, discorde ; (mus.) dissonance, *f.* ; discordance, *f.*

discordant, *adj.*, discordant.

discordantly, *adv.*, sans accord ; d'une manière discordante.

discount (dis-caou'n'te), *n.*, escompte, *m.* ; (abatement—*rabais*) remise ; (arith.) règle d'escompte, *f.* ; At a —; *sous escompte*. With a —; *sauf escompte*.

discount, *v.a.*, déduire, décompter ; (com.) escompter.

discount, *v.n.*, (com.) faire l'escompte.

discountable (-a-b'l), *adj.*, susceptible d'être escompté.

discountenance (-tè-), *n.*, défaveur, *f.* ; mauvais accueil, *m.*

discountenance, *v.a.*, décontenancer, désapprouver, décourager.

discountenancer, *n.*, personne qui décourage, *f.*

discounter, *n.*, (com.) escompteur, *m.*

discourage (-keur'édje), *v.a.*, décourager, rebuter.

discouragement, *n.*, découragement, *m.*

discourager, *n.*, personne qui décourage, *f.*

discourse (-côrse), *n.*, discours ; entretien, langage, *m.*

discourse, *v.n.*, discourir ; parler.

discourser, *n.*, discoureur. *m.*

discoursive, *adj.*, discursif ; dialogué.

discourteous (-kôrt'ieusse), *adj.*, impoli, incivil ; discourtois.

discourteously, *adv.*, discourtoisement, impoliment. incivilement.

discourtesy (-keur-té-ci), *n.*, impolitesse ; discourtoisie, *f.*

discover (-keuv'-), *v.a.*, découvrir ; montrer ; faire voir ; laisser percer.

discoverable (-a-b'l), *adj.*, qui peut être découvert ; facile à découvrir.

discoverer, *n.*, auteur d'une découverte ; révélateur, *m.*, révélatrice, *f.*

discovery, *n.*, découverte, *f.*

discredit (dis-crèd'ite), *n.*, discrédit ; déshonneur, *m.*

discredit, v.a., ne pas croire; décréditer; déshonorer; discréditer.

discreditable (-a-b'l), adj., qui décrédite; qui discrédite; déshonorant; honteux.

discreet (dis'crîte), adj., discret, prudent, sage.

discreetly, adv., discrètement, sagement, prudemment.

discreetness, n., discrétion, f.

discrepance, or **discrepancy** (-crèp'-),n., différence, contradiction, f.

discrepant, adj., différent; opposé.

discrete (dis'crîte), adj., séparé, discret; (arith.) simple.

discretion (-krèsh'eune), n., discrétion, prudence, sagesse, f.; jugement, m.

discretional, or **discretionary**(-krèsh'-), adj., discrétionnaire, à discrétion.

discretionally, or **discretionarily**, adv., à discrétion.

discretive (-cri'-), adj., disjonctif; séparé, discret, distinct.

discretively, adv., d'une manière disjonctive.

discriminable (-na-b'l), adj., qui peut être distingué.

discriminate, v.a. and n., distinguer.

discriminately, adv., distinctement.

discriminateness, n., distinction, f.

discriminating, adj., distinctif.

discrimination (-né-), n., distinction, f.; discernement, m. Without —; indistinctement.

discriminative (-né-), adj., distinctif, qui distingue.

discrown (-craoune), v.a., découronner; priver de la couronne.

disculpate (-keul-), v.a., disculper.

discumber (-keu'm'-), v.a., débarrasser, dégager.

discursive (-keur-), adj., errant; discursif; de raisonnement.

discursively, adv., d'une manière discursive.

discursory, adj., raisonnable, rationnel; d'argument.

discus (-keusse), n., disque, m.

discuss (-keusse), v.a., discuter.

discussion, n., discussion; analyse, f.

discutient (-kiou-shè'n'te), n., discussif, m.

disdain (diz'déne), n., dédain, m.

disdain, v.a., dédaigner.

disdainful (-foule), adj., dédaigneux.

disdainfully, adv., dédaigneusement.

disdainfulness, n., dédain, m.

disease (diz'ize), n., maladie, f.; mal, m.

disease, v.a., rendre malade.

diseased (diz'iz'de), adj., malade.

diseasedness (diz'iz'èd'-), n., état de maladie, m.

disedged (diz'édj'de), adj., émoussé.

disembark (diss'è'm'bàrke), v.a., désembarquer; débarquer.

disembark, v.n., débarquer.

disembarkation (-bàrk'-é-), or **disembarkment**, n., débarquement; désembarquement, m.

disembarrass (diss'-), v.a., débarrasser.

disembay (diss'-), v.a., dégager d'une baie.

disembitter (diss'-), v.a., adoucir.

disembodied (diss'è'm'bod'îde), adj., dépouillé de son corps; désincorporé.

disembody, v.a., dépouiller du corps; désincorporer.

disembogue (diss'è'm'bôghe), v.n., se décharger; déboucher; tomber dans (of rivers &c.—des fleuves, &c.); (nav.) déboucquer.

disembogue, v.a., jeter, décharger.

disemboguement (-boghe'-), n., débouchement; (nav.) débouquement, m.

disembosom (diss'è'm'bouz'eume), v.a., arracher au sein.

disembowel (diss'è'm'baouèl), v.a., retirer les entrailles.

disembroil (diss'è'm'broïl),v.a.,débrouiller.

disenable (diss'è'n'-é-b'l), v.a., rendre incapable.

disenamoured (diss'è'n'am'eurde), adj., qui n'est plus amoureux; désamourache.

disenchant (diss'è'n'tshâ'n'te), v.a., désenchanter.

disencumber (diss'è-n'keu'm'-), v.a., débarrasser, dégager.

disencumbrance, n., débarras, m.; délivrance, f.

disengage (diss'è'n'ghédje), v.a., dégager, débarrasser; délivrer; affranchir; libérer; détacher.

disengaged (-ghédj'de), adj., dégagé; libre; de loisir.

disengagement (-ghédj'-), n., dégagement, affranchissement, m.; libération, f.

disennoble (diss'è'n'nô-b'l), v.a., faire perdre la noblesse à; avilir.

disenroll (diss'è'n'rôl), v.a., effacer d'un registre.

disentangle (diss'è'n'ta'n'g'l), v.a.,démêler, débarrasser; débrouiller; dégager; (the feet—les pieds) dépêtrer.

disentanglement, n., démêlement; débrouillement; dégagement, m.

disenthral (diss'è'n'thrôl), v.a., affranchir; libérer.

disenthralment, n., affranchissement, m.

disenthrone (diss'è'n'thrône), v.a., détrôner.

disentitle (diss'è'n'taï't'l), v.a., dépouiller; priver du droit à.

disentrance (diss'è'n'-), v.a., réveiller d'un sommeil léthargique.

disentwine (diss'è'n'twaïne), v.a., désenlacer, séparer.

disespouse (diss'ès'paouze), v.a.,démarier; divorcer.

disesteem (diss'ès'tîme), n., déconsidération, mésestime, f.

disesteem, v.a., mésestimer.

disfavour (-fé-veur), n., défaveur, disgrâce, f.

disfavour, v.a., jeter la défaveur sur; voir avec défaveur.

disfiguration (-figh'iou-ré-), n., action de défigurer; difformité, f.

disfigure (-figh'ioure), v.a., défigurer; déformer.

disfigurement, n., état défiguré; enlaidissement; défaut, m.

disfranchise (-'shize), v.a., priver de ses privilèges; priver du droit électoral.

disfranchisement, n., privation de ses privilèges; privation du droit électoral, f.

disfurnish (-feur-), v.a., dépouiller, dégarnir; démeubler.

disgarnish (diz'gâr'-),v.a., dégarnir.

disglorify (diz'glô-ri-fa'ye), v.a., ne plus glorifier; humilier, dégrader.

disgorge (diz'gordje), v.a., vomir; rendre; se dégorger de; dégorger; rendre gorge.

disgorgement, n., vomissement, m.

disgrace (diz'-) ,n., disgrâce, honte, f.; déshonneur, m. To the — of; à la honte de. To be the — of; être la honte de; faire la honte de. To be in —; être en disgrâce.

disgrace, v.a., disgracier; déshonorer; avilir.

disgraceful (-foule), adj., infâme; honteux; déshonorant.

disgracefully, adv., honteusement; avec déshonneur; avec disgrâce.

disgracefulness, *n.*, infamie, honte, *f.*; déshonneur, *m.*

disgracer, *n.*, personne qui fait honte; personne qui déshonore, *f.*

disgracious (diz'gré-sheusse), *adj.*, disgracieux.

disguise (diz'gaïze), *n.*, déguisement; travestissement; (fig.) masque, voile, *m.*

disguise, *v.a.*, déguiser.

disguisement, *n.* *V.* **disguise**.

disguiser, *n.*, personne qui se déguise; personne qui déguise, *f.*

disguising, *n.*, déguisement, *m.*; mascarade, *f.*

disgust (diz'gheuste), *n.*, dégoût ennui, *m.*

disgust, *v.a.*, dégoûter; ennuyer.

disgustful (-foule), *adj.*, dégoûtant.

disgusting, *adj.*, dégoûtant.

disgustingly, *adv.*, dégoûtamment, d'une manière dégoûtante.

dish, *n.* (*dishes*), (utensil—*ustensile*) plat; (food—*nourriture*) mets, plat; (of a pair of scales—*de balances*) plat, plateau, *m.* —es; vaisselle, *f.* *sing.*·

dish, *v.a.*, mettre dans le plat; dresser, servir; apprêter. To — up; *mettre dans le plat*; *servir.*

dishabille (diss'a-bil), *n.*, déshabillé, *m.*

dishcloth (-cloth), *or* **dishclout** (-claoute), *n.*, torchon de cuisine, *m.*; lavette, *f.* *sing.*

dish-cover (-keuv'-), *n.*, couvercle, *m.*; cloche de plat, *f.*

dishearten (diss'hârt't'n), *v.a.*, décourager; désespérer, désoler.

disheir (diss'ère), *or* **disherit** (diss'hèr'-), *v.* (ant.). *V.* **disinherit**.

disherison (diss'hè-ri-z'n), *n.*, exhérédation, *f.*

dishevel (di-shè-vèl), *v.a.*, mettre en désordre; écheveler.

dishevelled (-vèlde), *adj.*, en désordre; échevelé.

dishonest (diz'o'n'èste), *adj.*, qui n'a pas de probité; qui n'est pas probe, déloyal; malhonnête; déshonnête; infidèle.

dishonestly, *adv.*, sans probité; déloyalement; malhonnêtement; déshonnêtement.

dishonesty, *n.*, improbité; déloyauté; malhonnêteté, *f.*

dishonour (diz'o'n'eur), *n.*, déshonneur, *m.*

dishonour, *v.a.*, déshonorer; avilir.

dishonourable (-a-b'l), *adj.*, (pers.) sans honneur; (of things—*des choses*) déshonorant.

dishonourer, *n.*, personne qui déshonore, *f.*; profanateur, *m.*

dishorn (diss'-), *v.a.*, arracher les cornes à.

dishumour (diss'-iou'meur), *n.*, mauvaise humeur, *f.*

dish-washer (-wôsh'-), *n.*, (orni.) lavandière, *f.*

dishwater (-wô-), *n.*, eau de vaisselle; lavure de vaisselle, *f.*

disimprovement (diss'i'm'prouve-), *n.*, progrès en arrière, *m.*

disinclination (diss'i'n'cli-né-), *n.*, éloignement, *m.*; aversion, indifférence, *f.*

disincline (-claïne), *v.a.*, indisposer, éloigner.

disincorporate (diss'i'n'-), *v.a.*, désincorporer.

disincorporation, *n.*, désincorporation, *f.*

disinfect (diss'i'n'-), *v.a.*, désinfecter.

disinfection, *n.*, désinfection, *f.*

disingenuity (diss'i'n'dji-niou-), *n.*, mauvaise foi, *f.*

disingenuous (-djè'n'iou-eusse), *adj.*, sans candeur, de mauvaise foi; dissimulé.

disingenuously, *adv.*, sans candeur; avec dissimulation; de mauvaise foi.

disingenuousness, *n.*, dissimulation; mauvaise foi, *f.*

disinherit (diss'i'n'hèr'-), *v.a.*, déshériter, exhéréder.

disinheritance, *n.*, exhérédation, *f.*

disinhume (diss'i'n'hioume), *v.a.*, exhumer.

disintegrable (diz'i'n'ti-gra-b'l), *adj.*, susceptible de se désagréger.

disintegrate (-grète), *v.a.*, désagréger.

disintegration (-gré-), *n.*, désagrégation, *f.*

disinter (diss'i'n'teur), *v.a.*, déterrer; exhumer.

disinterested (diz'i'n'tèr-èst'ède), *adj.*, désintéressé.

disinterestedly, *adv.*, avec désintéressement.

disinterestedness, *n.*, désintéressement, *m.*

disinterment (diss'i'n'teur-), *n.*, exhumation, *f.*

disinure (diss'i'n'ioure), *v.a.*, (ant.) désaccoutumer, déshabituer.

disinvite (diss'i'n'vaïte), *v.a.*, déprier.

disinvolve (diss'i'n'-), *v.a.*, (ant.) développer, dérouler; démêler.

disjoin (diz'djoï'ne), *v.a.*, déjoindre, disjoindre, désunir.

disjoint (diz'djoï'n'te), *v.a.*, démettre, désarticuler; disloquer; ·démonter; désunir, démembrer.

disjointed (-ède), *adj.*, désarticulé, disloqué, démis; démembré, démonté; décousu, sans suite.

disjointedly, *adv.*, séparément.

disjunct (diz'djeu'n'gn'k'te), *adj.*, disjoint.

disjunction (diz'-), *n.*, disjonction, séparation, *f.*

disjunctive (diz'djeu'n'gn'k'-), *adj.*, disjonctif, incapable d'union.

disjunctive, *n.*, (gram.) disjonctive, *f.*

disjunctively, *adv.*, séparément.

disk, *or* **disc**, *n.*, disque, *m.*

dislike (diz'laïke), *n.*, éloignement, *m.*; aversion, *f.*; dégoût, *m.* To take a — to any one; *prendre quelqu'un en aversion.* To have a — for; *avoir de l'éloignement pour.*

dislike, *v.a.*, ne pas aimer; avoir de l'éloignement pour; avoir du dégoût pour.

disliken (diz'laïk'n), *v.a.*, rendre dissemblable; défigurer.

dislikeness (-laïk'nèsse), *n.*, dissemblance, *f.*

disliker, *n.*, désapprobateur, *m.*

dislimb (diz'lime), *v.a.*, démembrer.

dislimn (dis-lime), *v.a.*, (ant.) effacer d'une peinture.

dislocate, *v.a.*, disloquer, démettre.

dislocation (-ké-), *n.*, dislocation; luxation, *f.*

dislodge (diz'-), *v.a.*, déloger; déplacer.

dislodge, *v.n.*, déloger.

disloyal (diz-lo'i'-), *adj.*, peu attaché au souverain; perfide, déloyal.

disloyally, *adv.*, avec peu d'attachement au souverain; perfidement; déloyalement.

disloyalty, *n.*, manque de fidélité au souverain, *m.*; défection, *f.*

dismal (diz'-), *adj.*, lugubre, sombre, horrible, triste.

dismally, *adv.*, lugubrement, horriblement, tristement, d'une manière sombre.

dismalness, *n.*, état lugubre, état sombre, *m.*; horreur; tristesse, *f.*

dismantle (diz'ma'n't'l), *v.a.*, dévêtir; dépouiller; (milit.) démanteler; (nav.) désarmer.

dismask (diz'mâske), *v.a.*, démasquer.

dismast (diz'mâste), *v.a.*, démâter.

dismasting, *n.*, démâtage, *m.*

dismay (diz'mè), *n.*, effroi, *m.*, terreur, épouvante, *f.*

dismay, *v.a.*, effrayer, terrifier, épouvanter.

dismember (diz'-), *v.a.*, démembrer.

dismembering, *n.*, démembrement, *m.*, mutilation, *f.*

dismemberment, *n.*, démembrement, *m.*, mutilation, *f.*

dismiss (diz'-), *v.a.*, renvoyer, congédier ; destituer.

dismissal, *n.*, renvoi, *m.* ; destitution, *f.*

dismission (diz'mish'eune), *n.*, renvoi, *m.* ; destitution, *f.*

dismortgage (diz'mor-ghédje), *v.a.*, dégrever un immeuble d'hypothèques.

dismount (diz'maou'n'te), *v.a.*, démonter, désarçonner ; faire descendre de cheval.

dismount, *v.n.*, descendre de cheval ; descendre.

disnaturalize (diz'nat'iou-ral-aïze), *v.a.*, dénaturaliser.

disnatured (diz'né-tiourde), *adj.*, dénaturé.

disobedience (diss'o-bi-), *n.*, désobéissance, *f.*

disobedient, *adj.*, désobéissant.

disobey (diss'o-bèy-), *v.a.*, désobéir ; désobéir à.

disobligation (diss'ob'li-ghé-), *n.*, acte désobligeant, *m.*

disoblige (diss'o-blaïdje), *v.a.*, désobliger.

disobliging, *adj.*, désobligeant.

disobligingly, *adv.*, désobligeamment.

disobligingness, *n.*, désobligeance, *f.*

disorbed (diz'orb'de), *adj.*, lancé hors de son orbite.

disorder (diz'-), *n.*, désordre, *m.* ; (illness—*mal*) indisposition, meladie, *f.*

disorder, *v.a.*, mettre en désordre ; déranger.

disordered (diz'or'deurde), *adj.*, en désordre ; dérangé ; déréglé, désordonné ; malade.

disorderly, *adj.*, en désordre, déréglé ; immoral ; vicieux.

disorderly, *adv.*, déréglément, en désordre.

disordinate (diz'-), *adj.*, (ant.) désordonné, déréglé.

disordinately, *adv.*, (ant.) désordonnément ; déréglément.

disorganization (diz'or-ga'n'i-zé-), *n.*, désorganisation, *f.*

disorganize (diz'or-ga'n'aïze), *v.a.*, désorganiser.

disown (diz'ône), *v.a.*, désavouer, nier.

disoxidate, **disoxidation** (diss'oks'idé-), **disoxygenate**, **disoxygenation** (diss-oks'i-djè'n'é-). *V.* deoxidate, &c.

dispair (dis'-), *v.a.*, dépareiller.

disparadised (-daïste), *adj.*, chassé du paradis.

disparage (dis'par'édje), *v.a.*, dépriser ; ravaler ; dénigrer ; (by marriage—*par mariage*) mésallier.

disparagement, *n.*, avilissement ; dénigrement ; déshonneur, *m.* ; (by marriage—*par mariage*) mésalliance, *f. Without* — to you ; *sans vouloir vous dénigrer ; sans déshonneur pour vous.*

disparager, *n.*, personne qui dénigre, qui déshonore, *f.*

disparagingly, *adv.*, avec dénigrement ; avec déshonneur.

disparate, *adj.*, disparate.

disparates (-rétse), *n. pl.*, disparates ; choses disparates, *f.pl.*

disparity, *n.*, disparité, inégalité, *f.*

dispark (dis'pârke), *v.a.*, déclore un parc; mettre en liberté.

dispart (dis'pârte), *v.a.*, diviser ; séparer; (artil.) marquer la mire sur un canon.

dispart, *v.n.*, être divisé, séparé ; se diviser ; se séparer.

dispassion (dis'pash'eune), *n.*, absence de passion, *f.* ; calme, *m.*

dispassionate, *adj.*, sans passion ; calme ; impartial.

dispassionately, *adv.*, sans passion ; avec calme ; avec impartialité.

dispauper, *v.a.*, rayer de la liste des indigents.

dispel, *v.a.*, dissiper, chasser.

dispensable (-sa-b'l), *adj.*, dont on peut se dispenser.

dispensary, *n.*, dispensaire, *m.*

dispensation (-sé-), *n.*, dispensation ; dispense, *f.*

dispensator (-sé-teur), *n.*, dispensateur, *m.*

dispensatory, *adj.*, qui a droit de donner dispense.

dispensatory, *n.*, codex ; dispensaire, *m.*

dispense, *v.a.*, distribuer, dispenser ; départir. To — with ; *se dispenser de; se passer de.*

dispenser, *n.*, dispensateur, *m.*, dispensatrice, *f.* ; distributeur, *m.*, distributrice, *f.*

dispeople (dis'pi-p'l), *v.a.*, dépeupler.

dispeopler (dis-pi-), *n.*, dépopulateur, dévastateur, *m.*

disperge (dis'peur'dje), *v.a.*, (ant.) répandre ; asperger.

disperse (dis'peurse), *v.a.*, disperser ; dissiper ; répandre.

disperse, *v.n.*, se disperser ; s'enfuir.

dispersedly (-'èdli), *adv.*, çà et là.

disperser, *n.*, personne qui disperse, qui dissipe, *f.* ; (b.s.) semeur, *m.*

dispersion (-zeune), *n.*, dispersion ; propagation, *f.*

dispirit, *v.a.*, décourager, abattre, démoraliser.

dispiritedness (-'èd'-), *n.*, abattement, découragement, *m.* ; démoralisation, *f.*

displace, *v.a.*, déplacer, déranger ; ôter.

displacement, *n.*, déplacement, *m.* ; révocation, destitution, *f.*

displacency (-plé-), *n.*, incivilité, *f.* ; déplaisir, *m.*

displant, *v.a.*, déplanter.

displantation (-té-), *n.*, déplantation, *f.*, déplantage, *m.*

display, *n.*, exposition, *f.* ; parade ; développement ; étalage ; faste ; (of troops—*de troupes*) déploiement, *m.*

display, *v.a.*, déployer ; étendre ; exposer ; développer ; étaler, faire parade de.

displeasant (-plèza'n'te), *adj.*, (ant.) désagréable.

displease (dis'plize), *v.a.*, déplaire ; déplaire à ; mécontenter ; contrarier.

displeasing, *adj.*, déplaisant, désagréable.

displeasure (dis'plèj'eur), *n.*, déplaisir ; courroux, *m.*

displode (-plôde), *v.n.*, faire explosion ; éclater.

displode, *v.a.*, faire faire explosion.

displosion (-jeune), *n.*, explosion, *f.*

displume (-ploume), *v.a.*, déplumer.

disport, (-pôrte), *n.*, divertissement, passetemps, *m.*, récréation, *f.*

disport, *v.n.*, se divertir, s'amuser.

disport, *v.a.*, divertir, amuser. To — one's self ; *s'amuser, se divertir.*

dispose (-pôz'-), *n.*, disposition, *f.* To have at one's — ; *avoir à sa disposition.*

dispose (-pôze), *n.*, (ant.) disposition, *f* ; caractère ; *m.*, manières, *f. pl.*

dispose, *v.a.*, disposer ; préparer ; arranger. To — of any one ; *se défaire de quelqu'un.* To — of one's time ; *employer son temps.* Evil —d ; *mal intentionné.* Well —d ; *bien intentionné.*

disposer, *n.*, personne qui dispose, *f.* ; distributeur, *m.*

disposition (-zish'-), *n.*, disposition, *f* (pers.) caractère, naturel, *m.*

dispossess (-poz'zèss), *v.a.*, déposséder, dépouiller ; priver.

dispossession (-poz'zèsh'eune), *n.*, dépossession, *f.*

dispossessor (-poz'zèss'-), *n.*, personne qui dépossède, *f.* ; spoliateur, *m.*, spoliatrice, *f.*

dispraise (-prèze), *n.*, blâme, reproche, *m.* ; défaveur, honte, *f.*

dispraise, *v.a.*, blâmer, censurer.

dispraiser, *n.*, censeur, critique, *m.*

dispraisingly, *adv.*, avec blâme ; avec reproche.

dispread (di-sprède), *v.n.* (preterit and past part., Dispread), s'étendre, se répandre.

dispread, *v.a.*, répandre,étendre.

disprize (-praize), *v.a.*, dépriser.

disproof (-proufe), *n.*, réfutation, *f.*

disproportion (-pôr-), *n.*, disproportion, *f.*

disproportion, *v.a.*, mal proportionner.

disproportionable (-a-b'l), *adj.*, inégal, disproportionné.

disproportionableness, *n.*, disproportion, *f.*

disproportionably, *adv.*, d'une manière disproportionnée ; inégalement.

disproportional, *adj.*, disproportionné.

disproportionally, *adv.*, d'une manière disproportionnée ; inégalement.

disproportionate, *adj.*, disproportionné.

disproportionately, *adv.*, d'une manière disproportionnée.

disproportionateness, *n.*, disproportion, *f.* ; caractère disproportionné, *m.*

disprove (-prouve), *v.a.*, réfuter.

disprover, *n.*, réfutateur, *m.*

dispunge (-peu'n'dje), *v.a.*, (ant.) effacer.

dispunishable (-peu'n'-ish-a-b'l), *adj.*, non punissable.

disputable (-piou-ta-b'l), *adj.*, disputable.

disputant, *n.*, disputant, *m.*

disputation (-té-), *n.*, dispute ; discussion,*f.*

disputatious (-piou-té-sheusse), *or* **disputative** (-piou-), *adj.*, disputeur.

dispute (-pioute), *n.*, dispute, *f.* ; débat, *m.* ; discussion, *f.*

dispute, *v.a.*, disputer ; discuter ; débattre.

dispute, *v.n.*, disputer ; discuter ; être en débat.

disputeless, *adj.*, incontestable, indisputable.

disputer, *n.*, disputeur, querelleur, *m.*

disqualification (dis-kwol-i-fi-ké-). *n.*, incapacité, *f.* ; (jur.) défaut de qualité, *m.* ; incapacité légale, *f.*

disqualify (-fa'ye), *v.a.*, rendre incapable ; frapper d'incapacité.

disquiet (-kwa-eute), *n.*, inquiétude,*f.*

disquiet, *v.a.*, inquiéter.

disquieter, *n.*, perturbateur, *m.*

disquietly, *adv.*, d'une manière inquiète, avec inquiétude.

disquietude (-tioude), *or* **disquietness**, *n.*, inquiétude, *f.*

disquisition (-kwi-zish'-), *n.*, disquisition ; recherche ; investigation,*f.*

disregard (-ri-gârde), *n.*, mépris, dédain, *m.* ; insouciance, *f.*

disregard, *v.a.*, ne pas considérer ; mépriser, négliger ; écarter ; éloigner ; regarder avec indifférence ; dédaigner ; ne faire aucun cas de.

disregardful (-foule), *adj.*, dédaigneux; insouciant.

disregardfully, *adv.*, négligemment ; dédaigneusement.

disrelish (diz'rèl'-), *n.*, dégoût, *m.* ; aversion, *f.*

disrelish, *v.a.*, avoir du dégoût pour ; avoir de l'aversion pour ; donner de l'aversion pour.

disreputable (-rèp'iou-ta-b'l), *adj.*, (pers.)

de mauvaise réputation. mal famé ; (of things —*des choses*) déshonorant.

disreputably, *adv.*, avec déshonneur ; honteusement.

disrepute (-rè-pioute), *n.*, discrédit, *m.*; mauvaise renommée ; mauvaise réputation,*f.*

disrespect (-ri-spèkte), *n.*, irrévérence, *f.*, manque d égards ; manque de respect, *m.*

disrespectful, *adj.*, irrespectueux.

disrespectfully, *adv.*, irrespectueusement ; avec irrévérence ; sans respect.

disrobe (diz'rôbe), *v.a.*, déshabiller ; dépouiller.

disrobe, *v.n.*, se déshabiller.

disroot (diz'route), *v.a.*, déraciner,arracher.

disruption (diz'reup'-), *n.*, rupture, *f.*

dissatisfaction, *n.*, mécontentement, *m.*

dissatisfactoriness, *n.*, impuissance de satisfaire, *f.*

dissatisfactory (-teuri), *adj.*, non satisfaisant.

dissatisfy (-fa'ye), *v.a.*, mécontenter.

dissect, *v.a.*, découper, disséquer.

dissection, *n.*, coupure, dissection, *f.*

dissector (-teur), *n.*, dissecteur, (iron.) disséqueur, *m.*

disseize (dis-size), *v.a.*, (jur.) déposséder illégalement.

disseizee (-zî), *n.*, (jur.) partie dépossédée illégalement, *f.*

disseizin (dis-si-zine), *n.*, (jur.) dépossession illégale, *f.*

disseizor. *n.*, (jur.) partie qui dépossède illégalement,*f.*

dissemble, *v.n.*, dissimuler ; faire l'hypocrite.

dissemble, *v.a.*, dissimuler, simuler.

dissembler, *n.*, dissimulé, *m.*,dissimulée,*f.*

dissemblingly, *adv.*, en dissimulant, avec dissimulation.

disseminate, *v.a.*, disséminer.

dissemination (-né-), *n.*, dissémination, *f.*

disseminator (-né-teur), *n.*, semeur, propagateur, *m.*

dissension, *n.*, dissension ; zizanie, *f.*

dissensious (-sheusse), *adj.* (of things —*des choses*) de dissension ; (pers.) porté à la dissension.

dissent, *n.*, dissentiment, *m.*

dissent, *v.n.*, différer, opposer ; différer de sentiment ; être d'une opinion contraire.

dissentaneous (-té-ni-), *adj.*, contraire, désagréable.

dissenter, *n.*, dissident, *m.*, dissidente, *f.*

dissentient (-shè'n'te), *adj.*, de dissentiment.

dissepiment (-sèp-), *n.*, (bot.) cloison, *f.*

dissert (dis'seurte), *v.n.*, (ant.) disserter ; discuter, disputer.

dissertation (-seur-té-), *n.*, dissertation, *f.*

dissertator (-té-teur), *n.*, auteur d'une dissertation ; dissertateur, *m.*

disserve (dis-seurve),*v.a.*,nuire à ; desservir.

disservice (-seur-), *n.*, mauvais service ; tort, *m.*

disserviceable, *adj.*, nuisible ; préjudiciable.

disserviceableness, *n.*, caractère préjudiciable, *m.*

disserviceably, *adv.*, d'une manière préjudiciable.

dissever (dis-sèv'-), *v.a.*, séparer ; enlever ; diviser ; désunir.

disseverance, *n.*, séparation ; division ; désunion, *f.*

dissidence, *n.*, dissidence,*f*

dissilition (-lish'-), *n.*, action d'éclater en plusieurs morceaux, *f.*

dissimilar. *adj.*, dissemblable ; dissimilaire.

dissimilarity, n., dissemblance, dissimilarité ; dissimilitude, f.

dissimulation (-'iou-lé-), n., dissimulation, f.

dissipable (-pa-b'l), adj., qui peut être dissipé.

dissipate, v.a., dissiper.

dissipation (-pé-), n., dissipation ; évaporation ; distraction, f.

dissociability (-sô-shi-), n., insociabilité, f.

dissociable, or **dissocial** (-sô-shi'-), adj., insociable.

dissociate (-sô-shi'-) v.a., désassocier ; séparer, désunir.

dissolubility, n., dissolubilité, f.

dissoluble (-sô-liou-b'l), adj., dissoluble ; soluble.

dissolute (-lioute), adj., dissolu.

dissolutely, adv., dissolument.

dissoluteness, n., dissolution, débauche, f.

dissolution (-liou-), n., dissolution ; mort, f.

dissolvable (diz'zolv'a-b'l), adj., soluble ; dissoluble.

dissolve (diz'zolve), v.a., dissoudre ; détruire.

dissolve, v.n., se dissoudre ; mourir. To — into tears ; fondre en larmes.

dissolvent, n., dissolvant, m.

dissolvent, adj., dissolvant.

dissolver, n., dissolvant, m.

dissonance, or **dissonancy**, n., dissonance ; discordance, f.

dissonant, adj., dissonant.

dissuade (-swéde), v.a., dissuader, détourner.

dissuader, n., personne qui dissuade, f.

dissuasion (-swé-jeune), n., dissuasion, f.

dissuasive (-swé-cive), adj., qui dissuade.

dissyllabic, adj., dissyllabe.

dissyllable (-sil'la-b'l), n., dissyllabe, m.

distaff (-tâfe), n., quenouille, f.

distain (-téne), v.a., tacher.

distance, n., distance, f. ; éloignement ; lointain, m. ; (fig.) réserve, f. ; (mus.) intervalle, m. In the —; au loin ; dans le lointain ; dans l'éloignement. Point of — ; (persp.) point de vue, m. To keep one's — ; se tenir à distance ; garder sa distance.

distance, v.a., éloigner ; dépasser, devancer ; distancer.

distant, adj., distant ; éloigné, lointain ; (fig.) réservé ; faible. A — likeness ; une faible ressemblance. He is very — ; il est très réservé.

distantly, adv., de loin ; à quelque distance ; d'une manière éloignée ; (fig.) avec réserve ; faiblement.

distaste (dis-téste), n., dégoût ; déplaisir, m.

distaste, v.a., dégoûter ; répugner.

distasteful (-foule), adj., dégoûtant, odieux ; désagréable ; offensant.

distastefulness, n., goût désagréable, m. ; aversion, f.

distemper, n., mal, dérangement, m. ; indisposition, maladie ; (vet.) épizootie ; (paint.) détrempe, f.

distemper, v.a., déranger, incommoder ; troubler ; (paint.) peindre en détrempe.

distemperate, adj., (ant.) immodéré ; maladif.

distemperature (-tioure), n., perturbation ; confusion, f. ; tumulte, m. ; indisposition, f.

distempered (-peurde), adj., incommodé, malade ; troublé ; immodéré.

distempering, n., art de peindre en détrempe, m.

distend, v.a., étendre ; dilater ; distendre.

distension, or **distention**, n., distension, f. ; écartement, m.

distensive (-'ive), adj., dilatable.

distich (-tike), n., distique, m.

distil, v.a., distiller ; faire tomber goutte à goutte.

distil, v.n., distiller ; tomber goutte à goutte ; égoutter, s'égoutter.

distillable (-la-b'l), adj., distillable.

distillation (-lé-), n., distillation, f.

distillatory (-la-teuri), adj., distillatoire.

distiller, n., distillateur, m.

distinct (-tign'kte), adj., distinct, distingué.

distinction, n., distinction, f.

distinctive, adj., distinctif.

distinctively, adv., distinctivement, d'une manière distinctive.

distinctiveness, n., caractère distinctif, m.

distinctly, adv., distinctement, clairement.

distinctness, n., caractère distinct, m. ; netteté, f.

distinguish (-tign'gwishe), v.a., distinguer.

distinguish, v.n., distinguer ; établir une distinction.

distinguishable, adj., que l'on peut distinguer ; qui mérite d'être distingué.

distinguished (-tign'gwish'te), adj., distingué.

distinguisher, n., observateur judicieux, m.

distinguishingly, adv., avec distinction ; d'une manière distinguée ; spécialement.

distinguishment, n., distinction, f.

distitle (-tait'l), v.a., priver du titre de ; priver du droit à.

distort, v.a., tordre, déformer ; contourner ; (one's features—les traits) décomposer ; (fig.) torturer.

distorted (-ède), adj., tordu ; contourné ; décomposé ; (fig.) torturé.

distortion, n., distorsion, f.

distract, v.a., diviser ; distraire ; jeter dans la confusion ; bouleverser ; mettre hors de soi.

distracted (-ède), adj., bouleversé, éperdu ; insensé, hors de soi.

distractedly, adv., follement ; confusément.

distractedness, n., folie, démence, f.

distracting, adj., cruel, atroce.

distraction, n., division, f. ; déchirement, trouble, m. ; confusion ; démence, f. To drive to — ; mettre hors de soi ; faire devenir fou.

distrain (-tréne), v.a. and n., saisir.

distrainable, adj., saisissable.

distrainer, n., saisissant, m., saisissante, f.

distraint, n., saisie, f.

distress, n., détresse, affliction, f., chagrin, m. ; (poverty—pauvreté) gêne, misère ; (jur.) saisie, f. ; (ant.) malheur, m., calamité, f.

distress, v.a., affliger ; désoler ; inquiéter ; (jur.) saisir.

distressful (-foule), adj., affligeant ; misérable ; de détresse ; malheureux.

distressfully, adv., cruellement.

distressing, adj., affligeant, désolant.

distribute (-'ioute), v.a., distribuer, répartir ; (justice) administrer.

distribution, n., distribution, répartition ; (justice) administration, f.

distributive, adj., distributif.

distributive, n., mot distributif, m.

distributively, adv., distributivement ; par distribution.

district (-trik'te), n., district, arrondissement, m. ; contrée, région, f.

distringas (dis-tri'n'gace), n., (jur.) ordre de saisir, m.

distrust (-treusté), n., méfiance, défiance, f.

distrust, v.a., se méfier de ; se défier de.

distrustful (-foule), adj., défiant ; méfiant ; réservé ; timide ; modeste.

distrustfully, adv., avec méfiance ; avec défiance.

distrustfulness, n., caractère méfiant, m.

disturb (-teurbe), v.a., troubler, déranger.

disturbance, *n.*, trouble; tumulte, *m.*; sonfusion; émeute, *f.*

disturber, *n.*, perturbateur, *m.*, perturbatrice, *f.*; (jur.) auteur de troubles, *m.*

disunion (diss'iou'n'ieune), *n.*, désunion, *f.*

disunite (diss'iou-naïte), *v.a.*, désunir, séparer.

disunite, *v.n.*, se désunir, se séparer.

disunity (diss'iou-ni-), *n.*, désunion, *f.*

disusage (diss'iou-zédge), *or* **disuse** (diss-iouce), *n.*, cessation d'usage; désuétude, *f.*

disuse (diss'iouze), *v.a.*, cesser de faire usage de; déshabituer.

disvouch (dis'vaoutshe), *v.a.*, contredire, infirmer.

ditch, *n.*, fossé, *m.*

ditch, *v.a.*, fossoyer.

ditch, *v.n.*, faire un fossé.

ditcher, *n.*, ouvrier qui creuse des fossés, *m.*

dithyramb, **dithyrambic**, *or* **dithyrambus** (dith-), *n.*, dithyrambe, *m.*

dithyrambic, *adj.*, dithyrambique.

ditone (daï-tône), *n.*, (mus.) diton, *m.*

dittander, *n.*, (bot.) cresson alénois, *m.*

dittany, *n.*, (bot.) dictame, *m.*; fraxinelle, *f.*

dittied (dit'tide), *adj.*, cadencé.

ditto (dit'tô), *adv.*, (com. fin.) idem, dito.

ditty, *n.*, chansonnette, chanson, *f.*

diuretic (daï-ou-rèt'-), *n.*, diurétique, *m.*

diuretic, *adj.*, diurétique.

diurnal (daï-eur'-), *n.*, journal; (c. rel.) diurnal, *m.*

diurnal, *adj.*, journalier, du jour; (med.) quotidien; (astron.) diurne.

diurnally, *adv.*, journellement.

divan (di-va'ne), *n.*, divan; conseil, *m.*

divaricate (daï-var'i-), *v.n.*, se séparer; se partager en deux; faire la fourche, fourcher.

divarication, *n.*, séparation, fourche, division en deux branches; intersection; croisement.

dive (daïve), *v. n.*, plonger; faire le plongeon. To —; *sonder, approfondir.*

divellent (di-vèl-), *adj.*, qui arrache, qui déchire.

diver (daïv'-), *n.*, plongeur; (orni.) plongeon, *m.*

diverge (di-veurdje), *v.n.*, diverger; (opt.) s'infléchir.

divergence, *or* **divergency** (-veur'djè'n-), *n.*, divergence, *f.*

divergent (-veur'djè'n'te), *adj.*, divergent.

divers (daï-vèrze), *adj.*, divers; plusieurs, quelques uns.

diverse (daï-vèrse), *adj.*, divers, différent.

diversely (-veurs'-), *adv.*, diversement.

diversification (di-veur-si-fi-ké-), *n.*, changement, *m.*; variation, *f.*

diversify (di-veur-si-fa'ye), *v.a.*, diversifier; varier.

diversion (-veur-), diversion, *f.*; divertissement, *m.*

diversity (-veur-), *n.*, diversite, variété, *f.*

divert (di-veurte), *v.a.*, divertir, réjouir, récréer; détourner, distraire; (milit.) faire diversion.

diverter, *n.*, personne qui distrait, qui divertit; chose qui distrait, *f.*

diverting, *adj.*, divertissant.

divertive, *adj.*, divertissant, amusant.

divest (di-vèste), *v.a.*, dépouiller; (jur.) dévêtir.

divestiture (-tioure), *n.*, action de se dépouiller, *f.*

divide (di-vaïde), *v.a.*, diviser; partager, distribuer; (in parliament—*parlement*), aller, mettre aux voix.

divide, *v.n.*, se diviser, se partager; (in parliament—*parlement*) aller aux voix.

dividend (di-vi-), *n.*, dividende, *m.*

divider (di-vaïd'-), *n.*, personne qui divise; chose qui divise, *f.*; distributeur; diviseur, *m.* divisé.

dividual, *or* **dividuous** (di-vi-diou-), *adj.*, divisé.

divination (di-vi-né-), *n.*, divination; prédiction, *f.*

divinatory (-teuri), *adj.*, divinatoire.

divine (di-vaïne), *adj.*, divin.

divine (di-vaïne), *n.*, ecclésiastique, prêtre; théologien, *m.*

divine (di-vaïne), *v.a.*, deviner; prédire.

divinely (di-vaï'n'-), *adv.*, divinement.

divineness (di-vaï'n'-), *n.*, divinité; nature divine, *f.*

diviner (di-vaï'n'-), *n.*, devin; devineur, *m.*; devineuse, *f.*

divineress, *n.*, devineresse, *f.*

diving (daïv'-), *n.*, plongeon, *m.*

diving-bell (daïv'-), *n.*, cloche à plongeur, cloche à plonger, *f.*

divinity (di-vi'n'-l-), *n.*, divinité; théologie, *f.*; (fig.) être céleste, *m.*

divisibility (-viz'-), *n.*, divisibilité, *f.*

divisible (-viz'i-b'l), *adj.*, divisible.

divisibleness, *n.*, divisibilité, *f.*

division (-vij'eune), *n.*, division, *f.*; partage, *m.*; scission, discorde; (mus.) roulade, *f.* Compound —; (arith.) *division composée; division complexe.*

divisionary (-vij'-), *adj.*, de division, divisionnaire.

divisor (-vaï'zeur), *n.*, diviseur, *m.*

divorce (-vôrce), *n.*, (jur.) divorce, *m.*; séparation, désunion, *f.* To sue for a —; *faire une demande en divorce.*

divorce, *v.a.*, (jur.) prononcer le divorce; séparer.

divorcement, *n.*, divorce, *m.*

divorcer, *n.*, personne qui divorce; cause de divorce, *f.*

divorcive, *adj.*, de divorce; qui entraîne le divorce.

divulge (di-veul'dje), *v.a.*, divulguer.

divulger, *n.*, divulgateur, *m.*; divulgatrice, *f.*

divulsion, *n.*, arrachement, *m.*; divulsion, *f.*

dizziness, *n.*, vertige, *m.*

dizzy, *adj.*, vertigineux, étourdissant; étourdi.

dizzy, *v.a.*, étourdir.

do (dou), *v.a.*, (preterit, Did; *past part.*, Done), faire; accomplir; (service, justice) rendre; (to finish—*terminer*) finir; (to cook—*cuisine*) cuire, faire cuire. To — good; *faire le bien.* To — evil; *faire le mal.* To — again, to — over again; *refaire.* To — up; *remettre en état; arranger; empaqueter* = *emballer.* To have nothing to — with; *n'avoir que faire de.* To — nothing; *ne faire rien; ne rien faire.* It is as good as done; *cela vaut fait.* To — up; *refaire.*

do, *v.n.*, se porter; se conduire; (to suit—*convenir*) aller, faire; (to finish—*terminer*) finir. How do you —? *comment vous portez-vous?* To — by; *agir envers; en agir avec.* To have to — with; *avoir affaire à; avoir affaire de; avoir à démêler avec.* To have done with; *en finir avec; avoir rompu avec.* To — without; *se passer de.* — ! *je l'en prie! je vous en prie!* Have done! *finissez! assez!* Will that —? *cela va-t-il? est-ce bien comme cela?* That will —; *c'est bien; cela suffit; cela va; c'est cela.* To — away with; *faire cesser; abolir; supprimer; se défaire de.*

docibility, *n.*, docilité, *f.*

docible (doss'i-b'l), *adj.*, docile.

docibleness, *n.*, docilité, *f.*

docile, *adj.*, docile.

docility, *n.*, docilité, *f.*

docimacy (-), *n.*, (metal.) docimasie, *f.*

dock, *v.a.*, (horses—*les chevaux*)courtauder; (dogs—*les chiens*) écourter; (fig.) rogner; (nav.)

mettre dans le bassin; (com., nav.) faire entrer aux docks.

dock, n., (stump of a horse's tail—*reste de la queue d'un cheval*) tronçon; (bot.) rumex, m.; patience, f.; (nav.)bassin; (com., nav.) dock, m. Dry —; *bassin d'échouage*, m. Floating —, wet —; *bassin à flot*, m.

dock-due (-diou). n., droit de bassin, droit de dock m.

docket (-'òte), n.. cote, étiquette; ouverture d'une faillite, f.; (jur.) extrait, m. To strike a —; *faire déclarer en faillite*.

docket, v.a., étiqueter; (jur.) faire un extrait de.

dock-gate (-ghéte), n., vanne de bassin, f.

dock-house (-haouce), n., hôtel de la compagnie des docks, m.

dock-master (-mâs-), n., gardien de dock, m.

dock-yard (-yârde), n., arsenal de port, arsenal de marine; chantier de construction, m.

doctor (-teur), n., docteur; médecin, m. — of divinity; *docteur en théologie*. — of laws; *docteur en droit*. — of physic; *docteur en médecine*. —'s Commons; *Collège des docteurs en droit*, m.

doctor (-teur), v.a., médeciner, médicamenter.

doctor (-teur), v.n., faire de la médecine.

doctoral (-teur-), adj., doctoral.

doctorally, adv., en docteur.

doctorate (-tor-), n., doctorat, m.

doctorate, v.a., faire docteur.

doctorly (-teur-), adv., (ant.) en docteur; doctoralement.

doctorship (-teur-), n., doctorat, m.

doctrinal, adj., de doctrine; dogmatique; doctrinal.

doctrine, n., doctrine, f.

document (dok'iou-), n., document, titre, m.; pièce, f.; précepte, m.

document, v.a., munir de documents; munir de titres.

documental, or **documentary**, adj., de documents; justificatif.

dodder, n..(bot.)cuscute, barbe-de-moine, f.

dodecagon (dô-dè-), n., (geom.) dodécagone, m.

dodecandria (dô-dè-), n., (bot.) dodécandrie, f.

dodge, v.n., changer de place; s'esquiver; biaiser.

dodge. v.a., esquiver.

dodger, n., biaiseur, m.. biaiseuse, f.

doe (dò), n., daine; chevrette, f.

doer (dou'eur), n., faiseur; auteur, m.

doff, v.a., ôter.

dog, n., chien; (andiron—*chenet*) chenet; (nav.) renard; (jest.) coquin, gaillard, m. Alpine —; *chien du grand Saint-Bernard*. Bull- —; *dogue*, m. House- —; *chien de garde, chien de basse-cour*. Lap- —; *chien de dame, bichon*, m. Watch- —; *chien de garde*. Sporting- —; *chien de chasse*. To go to the —s; *prendre le chemin de l'hôpital*. To set a — at any one; *haler un chien après quelqu'un*.

dog, v.a., suivre à la piste; espionner; harceler.

dogate. n., dogat. m.

dogbane. n. V. **dog's-bane**.

dogberry (-bèr'-), n., cornouille, f.

dogcheap (-tshipe), adj., à vil prix.

dogdays (-dèze), n.pl., jours caniculaires m.pl.; canicule, f.sing. To be in the —; *être dans la canicule*.

doge (dôdje), n., doge, m.

dog-faced (-féste), adj., à face de chien.

dog-fight (-faite), n., combat de chiens, m.

dogfish, n., (Ich.) roussette, f., chien de mer, squale, aiguillat, m.

dogged (-ghède), adj., bourru, hargneux; rébarbatif; acharné.

doggedly, adv., comme un chien; d'une manière hargueuse; opiniâtrément, avec acharnement.

doggedness, n., caractère hargneux, m.; opiniâtreté, f., acharnement, m.

dogger (-gheur), n.. (nav.) dogre, m.

doggerel (dog-gheur'-), adj., sans mesure; burlesque.

doggerel, n., vers sans mesure, vers burlesques, m.pl.

doggish (-ghishe), adj., de chien.

dog-hole (dog-hôl), n.. niche à chien, f.; (fig.) trou à chien, taudis, chenil, m.

dog-house (-haouce), n., niche à chien, f.

dog-keeper (-kîp'-), n., amateur de chiens, m.; personne qui possède des chiens, f.

dog-kennel (-kènel), n., chenil, m.

dog-leech (-lîtshe), n., médecin pour les chiens, m.

dog-legged (-lèg'de), adj., à patte de chien.

dogma, n., dogme, m.

dogmatic, or **dogmatical**, adj., dogmatique.

dogmatically, adv., dogmatiquement.

dogmaticalness, n., caractère dogmatique, m.

dogmatism, n., dogmatisme, m.

dogmatist, n., dogmatiste, m.

dogmatize (-taïze), v.n., dogmatiser.

dogmatizer (-taïz'-), n., dogmatiseur, m.

dog's-bane (dog'z'-), n., apocyn gobemouches; cynanque, m.

dog's-ear (dog'z'îre), n., corne, oreille, f., pli au coin d'une page de livre, m.

dog's-ear, v.a., faire des cornes aux pages d'un livre.

dog's-grass (dog'z'grâce), n., (bot.) chiendent, m.

dogsick, adj., qui a envie de vomir.

dog-star (-stâr), n., (astron.) Canicule, f.

dog-wood (-woude), n., (bot.) cornouille, f.; cornouiller, m.

doing (dou'-), n. (doings) faits, m.pl.; actions, f.pl.; fait, exploit, m.

dole (dôle), n., partage, m.; part; aumône, gratification, f.; coups, m.pl.

dole, v.a., distribuer avec parcimonie. To — out; *distribuer, répartir*.

doleful (-foule), adj., malheureux; plaintif; douloureux, triste, lugubre.

dolefully, adj., douloureusement, plaintivement, tristement.

dolefulness, n., tristesse, mélancolie, f.

dolesome (-seume), adj., triste, lugubre.

dolesomely, adv., tristement.

dolesomeness, n., tristesse, f.

doll, n., poupée, f.

dollar, n., dollar, m.

dolor (dò-leur), n.. douleur, f.; chagrin, m.

dolorous, adj., douloureux, triste.

dolorously, adv., douloureusement.

dolphin (-fine), n., dauphin, m.; (nav.) baderne, f.

dolt (dôlte), n., balourd, m., balourde, f.; benet; sot, m.

doltish, adj., sot; stupide.

doltishly, adv., avec balourdise; sottement.

domain, n., domaine, m., domaine, m.

dome (dôme), n., dôme, m.

domesday-book (dou'm'z'dè-bouke), n. V. **doomsday-book**.

domestic. n., domestique, m., f.

domestic, adj., domestique, de famille; du foyer domestique.

domestically, adv., dans son intérieur.

domesticate, v.a., rendre casanier; accoutumer à la vie domestique ; domestiquer, apprivoiser.

domestication (-ti-ké-), *n.*, retraite, *f.* ; (of animals—*des animaux*) apprivoisement, *m.*

domesticity, *n.*, domesticité, *f.*

domicile (-çail), *n.*, domicile, *m.*

domicile (-çail), *or* **domiciliate** (-cil'i-), *v.a.*, domicilier.

domiciliary (-cil'-), *adj.*, domiciliaire.

dominant, *adj.*, dominant.

dominant, *n.*, (mus.) dominante, *f.*

dominate, *v.n.*, dominer, prévaloir.

domination (-né-), *n.*, domination, *f.*

dominator (-né-teur), *n.*, dominateur, *m.*

domineer (-nîre), *v.n.*, dominer ; maîtriser ; tempêter ; commander en despote. To over ; *dominer sur ; maîtriser.*

dominical, *adj.*, dominical.

dominican, *adj.*, dominicain.

dominican, *n.*, dominicain, *m.*

dominion (-'ieunɔ), *n.*, domination, *f.* ; pouvoir, *m.* ; états, *m.pl.*

domino, *n.*, camail ; domino, *m.* In a —; *en domino.* To play at —es ; *jouer aux dominos.*

don, *n.*, don (title—*titre*); (jest.) grand seigneur, *m.*

don, *v.a.*, mettre; revêtir.

donation (-né-), *n.*, donation, *f.* ; don, *m.*

donative, *n.*, don, *m.* ; largesse, *f.*

done (deune). *V.* **do.**

donee (dô-nî), *n.*, donataire, *m.* ; *f.*

donkey, *n.*, âne, baudet, *m.*

donor (dô-), *n.*, donateur, *m.*, donatrice, *f.*

doodle (dou'd'l), *n.*, niais, *m.*

doom (doume), *v.a.*, condamner ; destiner.

doom, *n.*, arrêt ; sort, *m.*

doomsday (dou'm'z'dè), *n.*, jour du jugement dernier, *m.*

doomsday-book, *n.*, grand cadastre d'Angleterre, *m.*

door (dôr), *n.*, porte, *f.* ; (of a steam-engine—*de machine à vapeur*) registre, *m.* Folding —s ; *porte à deux battants.* House —; *porte de maison.* In —s ; *à la maison, chez soi.* Out of —s ; *hors de la maison, dehors.*

door-case (-kéce), *n.*, châssis de porte, *m.*

door-handle (-ha'n'd'l), *n.*, poignée de porte, *f.*

dooring, *n.*, châssis de porte, *m.*

door-jamb (-dja'm), *n.*, jambage de porte, *m.*

door-keeper (-kîp'-), *n.*, (of a house—*d'une maison*) concierge, portier ; (of public places—*d'un lieu public*) gardien, *m.*

door-knob (-nobe), *n.*, bouton de porte, *m.*

door-nail (-néle), *n.*, clou de marteau de porte, *m.*

door-porter, *n.*, (pers.) portier, concierge ; (thing—*chose*) arrête-porte, *m.*

door-post (-pôste), *n.*, dormant, montant de porte, *m.*

door-stead (-stède), *n.*, baie de porte, *f.*

door-way (-wè), *n.*, entrée de porte ; porte, *f.*

dor, *or* **dorr**, *n.*, (ent.) bourdon, *m.*

doradilla, *n.*, (bot.) doradille, *f.* ; cétérac officinal, *m.*

dorado (-ré-dô), *n.*, (ich.) dorade, *f.* ; (astron.) Dorade, *f.*, Xiphias, *m.*

doree (dô'rî), *n.*, (ich.) dorée, *f.*, zée, zée forgeron, *f.*

dorian, *adj.*, dorien.

doric, *adj.*, dorique.

dormancy, *n.*, repos, *m.*

dormant, *adj.*, endormi, assoupi ; (her.) dormant ; (capital) qui dort, mort ; (of partners—*d'associés*) commanditaire. To be —; *sommeiller ;* (capital) *dormir.*

dormer, *n.*, lucarne, *f.*

dormer-window (-wi'n'dô), *n.*, lucarne, *f.*

dormitive, *adj.*, dormitif.

dormitive, *n.*, dormitif, *m.*

dormitory (-teuri), *n.*, dortoir, *m.*

dormouse (-maouce), *n.*, (mam.) loir, *m.*

dornoc, *n.*, toile d'Écosse, *f.*

dorr, *or* **dorr-beetle** (-bî't'l), *n.* *V.* **dor**.

dorsal, *adj.*, dorsal.

dose (dôce), *n.*, dose, *f.*

dose, *v.a.*, médicamenter ; proportionner ; donner quelque chose d'un goût désagréable.

dossil, *n.*, bourdonnet, *m.*

dot, *n.*, point, *m.*

dot, *v.a.*, marquer de points; pointiller.

dotage (dô-tédje), *n.*, seconde enfance, *f.* ; radotage, *m.* ; tendresse extrême, *f.*

dotal (dô-), *adj.*, dotal.

dotard (dô-), *n.*, radoteur, *m.*

dotation (dô-té-), *n.*, dotation, *f.*

dote (dôte), *v.n.*, radoter, extravaguer. To —on ; *aimer éperdument; aimer à la folie ; raffoler de.*

doter (dôt'-), *n.*, radoteur, *m.*, radoteuse ; personne folle de, *f.*

dotingly (dôt'-), *adv.*, à la folie, avec extravagance.

dottard (dot'-), *n.*, arbre étêté, *m.*

double (deub'b'l), *n.*, double ; (print.) doublon, *m.* ; (mus.) variation, *f.*

double, *adv.*, double ; au double.

double, *v.a.*, doubler ; faire un pli à.

double, *v.n.*, doubler ; (fig.) biaiser.

double, *adj.*, double ; (pers.) voûté.

double-biting (-baït'-), *adj.*, à deux tranchants.

double-buttoned (-beut'n'de), *adj.*, à deux rangs de boutons.

double-dealer (-dîl'-), *n.*, trompeur, fourbe, *m.*

double-dealing, *n.*, dissimulation, hypocrisie, duplicité, fausseté, *f.*

double-dye (-da'ye), *v.a.*, teindre deux fois.

double-entendre (dou'b'l-à'n-tà'n'd'r), *n.*, mot à deux ententes, mot à double entente, *m.*

double-lock, *v.a.*, fermer à double tour.

double-minded (-maï'n'd'ède), *adj.*, faux, trompeur.

doubleness, *n.*, état double, *m.* ; duplicité, *f.*

doubler, *n.*, personne qui double, *f.* ; doubleur, *m.*, doubleuse, *f.*

doublet (deub'léte), *n.*, pourpoint ; doublet, *m.*

double-tongued (-teu'n'g'd), *adj.*, fourbe, dissimulé.

doubloon (doub'loune), *n.*, doublon, *m.*

doubly, *adv.*, doublement.

doubt, *n.*, doute, *m.*

doubt (daoute), *v.a.*, douter de.

doubt (daoute), *v.n.*, douter ; craindre.

doubter, *n.*, personne qui doute, *f.*

doubtful (-foule), *adj.*, douteux ; indécis.

doubtfully, *adv.*, d'une manière douteuse ; avec indécision.

doubtfulness, *n.*, doute, *m.* ; incertitude, *f.*

doubtingly, *adv.*, d'une manière douteuse.

doubtless, *or* **doubtlessly**, *adv.*, sans doute.

douceur (dou-ceur), *n.*, douceur, gratification, *f.*

doucine (dou-cîne), *n.*, (arch.) doucine, *f.*

dough (dô), *n.*, pâte, *f.*

doughnut (-neûte), *n.*, pet de nonne, beignet, *m.*

doughty (daou'ti), *adj.*, vaillant, brave.

doughy (dô-i), *adj.*, pâteux ; mou.

douse (daouce), *v.a.* and *n.*, plonger, jeter dans l'eau.

dove (deuve), *n.*, colombe, *f.* ; pigeon, *m.*

dove-colour (-keul'leur), *n.*, gorge-de-pigeon ; (of horses—*des chevaux*) isabelle, *m.*

dove-coloured (-keul'leur'de), *adj.*, gorge-de-pigeon ; (of horses—*des chevaux*) isabelle. —

dove-cot, *or* **dove-house** (-haouce), *n.*, colombier, *m.*

dovetail (-téle), *n.*, (carp.)queue d'aronde, *f.*

dovetail, *v.a.*, assembler à queue d'aronde.

dowager (daou'é-djeur), *n.*, douairière, *f.*

dowager, *adj.*, douairière.

dowcets (daou-cètse), *n.pl.*, (vet.) daintiers; rognons, *m.pl.*

dowdy (daou-di), *n.*, femme gauche et mal mise, *f.*

dowdy, *adj.*, gauche; mal mise; vulgaire.

dower, *or* **dowery** (daou'-), *n.*, douaire, *m.*; dot, *f.*; présent, don, *m.*

dowered (daou'eurde), *adj.*, doté.

dowerless, *adj.*, sans dot.

down (daoune), *n.*, duvet; (bot.) duvet, coton; (plain—*terrain plat*) plateau, bas, *m.*, plaine, *f.* The —s; *les dunes, f.pl.*

down, *prep.*, au bas de; en bas de; le long de; jusqu'en bas de.

down, *adv.*, en bas; à bas; bas; à terre; (of the wind—*du vent*) calme; (of the sun—*du soleil*) couché; (of the moon—*de la lune*) couchée; (of clocks, watches—*d'horloges, de montres*) arrêté; (fig.) sur le déclin, en défaveur. — with! *à bas!* Up and —; *çà et là.*

downcast (-câste), *adj.*, abattu.

downfall (-fôl), *n.*, chute; décadence, *f.*

downfallen (-fôl'n), *adj.*, tombé; déchu.

downhearted (-hârt'-ède), *adj.*, abattu.

downhill, *n.*, pente, *f.*

downhill, *adj.*, incliné; en pente.

downlook (-louke), *n.*, air morne, *m.*

downlooked (-louk'te), *adj.*, ayant l'air abattu.

downright (-raïte), *adj.*, direct; franc; vrai; (b.s.) fieffé.

downright, *adv.*, de haut en bas; tout à fait.

downsitting, *n.*, repos, *m.*

downward (-wôrde), *or* **downwards** (-wôrdze), *adj.*, penché; qui descend; descendant; incliné.

downward, *or* **downwards**, *adv.*, en bas; en descendant.

downy, *adj.*, de duvet; (fruit) duvèteux; (of birds—*des oiseaux*) duveté.

dowry, *n. V.* **dower**.

doxology (-dji), *n.*, doxologie, *f.*

doze (dôze), *v.n.*, être assoupi, sommeiller; avoir la tête lourde, vivre dans un état de stupeur; être à moitié endormi.

doze, *v.a.*, assoupir, appesantir, stupéfier. To —away; faire passer en dormant.

doze, *n.*, somme, *m.* To be in a —; *être assoupi.*

dozen (deuz'z'n), *n.*, douzaine, *f.*

doziness (dô-), *n.*, assoupissement, *m.*

dozy (dô-), *adj.*, assoupi, engourdi.

drab, *n.*, gris américain, *m.*; (woman—*femme*) coureuse, salope, *f.*

drab, *adj.*, gris américain.

drabble (drab'b'l), *v.n.*, pêcher des barbeaux à la ligne de fond.

drabble, *v.a.*, traîner dans la boue.

drabbling, *n.*, pêche de barbeaux à la ligne de fond, *f.*

drabbling, *adj.*, qui pêche des barbeaux à la ligne de fond.

drachm (drame), *n.*, drachme, *f.*

draco (dré-cô), *n.*, (astron.) Dragon; (zool.) dragon; feu follet, *m.*

draff (dráfe), *n.*, lavure, rinçure, lie, *f.*; balayures, *f.pl.*; rebut, *m.*

draft (dráfte), *n.*, tirage; trait; (sketch—*dessin*) dessin, plan, *m.*; (com.) traite, *f.*; (milit.) détachement, *m.* (depth of water—*profondeur d'eau*) tirant, *m.*

draft, *v.a.*, dessiner, rédiger; (milit.) détacher.

drag, *n.*, croc; harpon; train, radeau, *m.*; (nav.) drague, *f.*; (coach—*voiture*) diable; (of a coach—*de voiture*) sabot, *m.*, enrayure, *f.*; (of machinery—*de machines*) frein, sabot, *m.*

drag, *v.a.*, traîner; (nav.) draguer. To — away from; *arracher de.* To — in; *faire entrer de force.* To — out; *faire sortir de force; entraîner.* — for oysters; *pêcher des huîtres.*

drag, *v.n.*, se traîner; traîner; (nav.) (of the anchor—*de l'ancre*) chasser.

drag-chain (-tshéne), *n.*, chaîne de drague, *f.*

draggle (drag'g'l), *v.a.* and *n.*, traîner dans la crotte, traîner dans la boue; traîner par terre.

draggle-tailed (-tél'de), *adj.*, traîné dans la crotte; traîné dans la boue.

drag-hook (-houke), *n.*, croc, *m.*

drag-man (-ma'ne), *n.*, pêcheur à la seine; pêcheur à la drague, *m.*

drag-net (-nète), *n.*, seine, *f.*

dragoman (drag'o-ma'ne), *n.*, dragoman; drogman; truchemau; truchment, *m.*

dragon (dragh'eune), *n.*, dragon; (astron.) Dragon; (bot.) draconte, *m.*

dragon-beam (-bîme), *n.*, (carp.) contre-fiche, *f.*

dragonet (-eun'ète), *n.*, petit dragon, *m.*

dragonish, *adj.*, en forme de dragon; de dragon.

dragon-like (-laïke), *adj.*, en dragon; comme un dragon.

dragons-blood (-eu'n'z'bleude), *n.*, sang-de-dragon; sang-dragon, *m.*

dragons-head (-eu'n'z'hède), *n.*, (astron.) tête du dragon, *f.*; (bot.) dracocéphale, *m.*

dragon-tree (-trî), *n.*, (bot.) dragonnier, *m.*

dragoon (dra-goune), *n.*, (milit.) dragon, *m.*

dragoon, *v.a.*, livrer à la fureur du soldat; opprimer; harasser; persécuter; forcer par des mesures violentes; soumettre, assujettir, asservir par les armes.

dragoonade (-éde), *n.*, dragonnade, *f.*

drain (dréne), *v.a.*, tranchée, *f.*; égouttoir; fossé d'écoulement, *m.*

drain, *v.a.*, faire écouler; (a marsh, a river—*marais, rivière*) saigner, dessécher; (fig.) épuiser, saigner.

drainage (-édje), *n.*, écoulement, égouttage; desséchement; épuisement, *m.*

draining, *n.*, écoulement; égouttage, *m.*

drake, *n.*, canard, *m.* Ducks and —s; *ricochets, m.pl.*

dram, *n.*, drachme; (drink—*de liqueur*) goutte, *f.*

drama, *n.*, (dré-ma, *ou* dram'a), *n.*, drame, *m.*

dramatic, *or* **dramatical**, *adj.*, dramatique.

dramatist, *n.*, auteur dramatique; dramaturge, *m.*

dramatize (-taïze), *v.a.*, dramatiser.

draper (drép'-), *n.*, drapier; marchand de drap; marchand de nouveautés, *m.* Linen —; linger, *m.*, lingère, *f.*, marchand de linge, *m.*, marchande de linge, *f.*

drapery (-), *n.*, draperie, *f.*; nouveautés, *f.pl.*

drastic, *n.*, (med.) drastique, *m.*

drastic, *adj.*, drastique.

draught (dráfte), *n.*, tirage; trait; (of air—*d'air*) courant d'air; (of drink—*de liqueur*) coup d'air; (drawing—*dessin*) dessin, *m.*, esquisse, ébauche, *f.*; (of fish—*de pêche*) coup de filet, *m.*; quantité prise; (com.) traite, *f.*, mandat, *m.*; (depth of water—*profondeur d'eau*) tirant; (milit.) détachement, *m.*; (pharm.) potion, *f.*; *pl.* (game-jeu*) dames, *f.* Rough —; brouillon, *m.*

draught-board (-bôrde), *n.*, damier, *m.*

draught-compasses (-pass'ize), *n.*, compas à pointes changeantes, *m.*

draught-hole (-hôl), *n.*, (tech.) regard, *m.*

draughtsman, *n.*, dessinateur, *m.*

draw (drō), *v.a.* (*preterit*, Drew ; *past part.*, Drawn), tirer ; retirer ; traîner ; prendre, retirer ; (with a pencil—*avec un crayon*) dessiner ; (teeth—*les dents*) arracher ; (poultry—*la volaille*) vider ; (tech.) étirer. To — contracts ; *rédiger des contrats.* To — again ; *tirer de nouveau.* To — along ; *traîner.* To — aside ; *tirer à l'écart.* To — away ; *entraîner ; retirer, ôter.* To — back ; *tirer en arrière ; retirer.* To — down ; *tirer en bas ; faire descendre.* To — forth ; *tirer en avant ; faire avancer ; sortir.* To — in ; *tirer dedans ; faire entrer de force ; rentrer.* To — nearer ; *approcher.* To — off ; *tirer ; ôter.* To — on ; *mettre* (boots, gloves, &c.—*des gants, bottes, &c.*) ; *tirer* ; (fig.) *attirer ; amener.* To — out ; *tirer dehors ; faire avancer ; prolonger.* To — over ; *faire passer ; entraîner.* To — up ; *tirer en haut ; relever* ; (milit.) *ranger* ; (deeds, &c. —*titres, &c.*) *rédiger* ; (jur.) *dresser.*

draw, *v.n.*. tirer ; se resserrer ; se contracter ; (with a pencil—*avec un crayon*) dessiner. To — near ; *s'approcher.* To — together ; *se rassembler ; se réunir.* To — back ; *se retirer ; se reculer.*

drawback, *n.*, (com.) drawback ; (fig.) décompte, mécompte ; rabat-joie, *m.*

draw-bench (-bě'n'she), *n.*, (tech.) banc à tirer, *m.*

drawbridge, *n.*, pont-levis, *m.*

drawee (drō-i), *n.*, (com.) tiré, *m.*, tirée, *f.*

drawer (drō'eur), *n.*, tireur, *m.*, tireuse, *f.* ; puiseur ; arracheur ; (draughtsman—*de dessin*) dessinateur ; corps attirant ; (sliding box—*de meuble*) tiroir, *m.* ; (com.) tireur, *m.* Chest of —s ; *commode, f.*

drawers (drō'eurze), *n.pl.*, caleçon, *m. sing.* Pair of — ; *caleçon, m. sing.*

draw-gear (-ghīre), *n.*, attelage, *m.*

drawing, *n.*, tirage, *m.* ; action d'attirer, *f.* ; (sketch—*dessin*) dessin, *m.*

drawing-book (-bouke), *n.*, cahier à dessin, *m.*

drawing-frame (-frême), *n.*, (tech.) filière, *f.*

drawing-knife (-naïfe), *n.*, plane, *f.*

drawing-pen (-pène), *n.*, tire-ligne, *m.*

drawing-room (-roume), *n.*, salon, *m.* ; réception, *f.* To hold a — ; *recevoir.*

drawl (drōl), *v.a.*, passer en lambinant ; (one's words—*les mots*) traîner.

drawl, *v.n.*, traîner ses paroles.

drawl, *n.*, débit traînant ; son traînant, *m.*

drawling, *adj.*, traînant ; qui traîne ses paroles.

drawn (drō'ne), *adj.*, (combats) égal ; (of games—*jeux*) nul.

draw-stop, *n.*, (mus.) registre, *m.*

dray (drè), *n.*, camion, haquet, *m.*

dray-horse, *n.*, cheval de haquet, *m.*

dray-man, *n.*, camionneur ; haquetier, *m.*

drazel, *n.*, (ant.) saligaude, salope, *f.*

dread (drède), *n.*, crainte, *f.* ; effroi, *m.*

dread, *adj.*, redoutable, terrible.

dread, *v.a.*, craindre, redouter.

dread, *v.n.*, avoir peur.

dreadful (-foule), *adj.*, affreux, terrible.

dreadfully, *adv.*, terriblement, affreusement.

dreadfulness, *n.*, effroi, *m.* ; horreur, *f.*

dreadless, *adj.*, sans peur ; intrépide.

dreadlessness, *n.*, intrépidité, *f.*

dreadnaught (-nō'te), *n.*, audacieux, *m.* ; imperméable, vêtement imperméable, *m.*

dream (drī'me), *n.*, songe, rêve, *m.*

dream, *v.n.* (*preterit* and *past part.*, Dreamed *or* Dreamt), rêver, songer. To — of ; *rêver de.*

dream, *v.a.*, songer, rêver.

dreamer, *n.*, rêveur, *m.*, rêveuse, *f.*

dreamless, *adj.*, qui ne rêve pas ; qui n'a pas de songe ; sans rêve.

dreamlessly, *adv.*, sans rêver.

drearily (drèr'-), *adv.*, tristement, lugubrement.

dreariness, *n.*, tristesse, *f.*

dreary (drèr'i), *adj.*, triste, lugubre.

dredge (drèdje), *n.*, drèche ; (net—*filet*) drège ; drague, *f.*

dredge, *v.a.*, enfariner, saupoudrer ; draguer.

dredger, *n.*, pêcheur à la drague, *m.*

dregginess (drèg'ghi-), *n.*, qualité de ce qui a beaucoup de lie, *f.*

dreggy (drèg'ghi), *adj.*, féculent ; fangeux ; plein de lie.

dregs (drèg'ze), *n.*, lie, *f.* ; effondrilles, *f.pl.* ; restes, *m.pl.*

drench (drè'n'she), *n.*, breuvage, *m.*

drench, *v.a.*, tremper, submerger, mouiller ; (vet.) donner un breuvage à.

drencher, *n.*, personne qui trempe ; personne qui donne des breuvages à.

dress (drèce), *n.*, habillement, vêtement, *m.* ; mise ; toilette ; (of a woman—*de femme*) robe ; (milit.) tenue, *f.* Full — ; *grande toilette* ; (milit.) *grande tenue.*

dress, *v.a.*, habiller, vêtir ; parer, orner ; (a wound—*une blessure*) panser ; (agri.) donner une façon à ; (food—*aliments*) accommoder ; (cloth —*drap*) lustrer ; (manu.) apprêter ; (milit.) aligner. To — one's self ; *s'habiller ; faire sa toilette.*

dress, *v.n.*, s'habiller ; faire sa toilette ; (milit.) s'aligner.

dresser, *n.*, personne qui habille ; personne qui panse, *f.* ; (manu.) apprêteur, *m.*, apprêteuse ; (in a kitchen—*de cuisine*) table de cuisine, *f.* ; (med.) externe, *m.*

dressing, *n.*, toilette, *f.* ; (of a wound—*de blessure*) appareil, pansement ; (agri.) labour, *m.*, fumure, *f.* ; (manu.) apprêtage, *m.* ; (chastisement—*châtiment*) coups, *m.pl.*

dressing-case (-kéce), *n.*, nécessaire de toilette, *m.*

dressing-room (-roume), *n.*, cabinet de toilette, *m.*

dress-maker (-mék'-), *n.*, couturière, *f.*

dressy (drèss'i), *adj.*, qui aime la toilette ; habillé.

drib, *v.a.*, retrancher.

drib, *n.*, chiquet, *m.*

dribble (drib'b'l), *v.n.*, dégoutter ; baver.

dribblet, *n.*, chiquet, *m.*

drier (draï'-), *n.*, siccatif, dessiccatif, *m.*

drift, *v.a.*, chasser, pousser.

drift, *n.*, objet qui flotte au gré du vent, de l'eau ; tourbillon ; amas, *m.* ; (fig.) tendance, *f.*, but, *m.* ; (nav.) dérive, *f.*

drill, *n.*, (agri.) semoir ; (furrow— *le la terre*) sillon ; (manu.) coutil de fil ; (milit.) exercice ; (tech.) foret, *m.*

drill, *v.a.*, forer, percer ; (agri.) semer par sillons ; (milit.) exercer.

drill, *v.n.*, (agri.) semer par sillons ; (milit.) faire l'exercice.

drill-husbandry (-heuz'ba'n'd'-), *n.*, (agri.) semaille au semoir, *f.*

drilling, *n.*, (agri.) semis au semoir ; (milit.) exercice, *m.*

drill-machine (-ma-shīne), *n.*, (metal.) machine à forer, *f.*

drill-officer, *n.*, (milit.) officier instructeur, *m.*

drink (dri'n'ke), *n.*, boisson ; (fig.) ivresse, *f.*

drink, *v.n.* (*preterit*, Drank ; *past part.*, Drunk), boire. To — in ; *imbiber.* To — off ; *boire d'un coup.*

drink, *v.a.*, boire ; (fig.) s'abreuver de ; absorber.

drinkable (-'a-b'l), *adj.*, buvable, potable.
drinker, *n.*, buveur, *m.*, buveuse, *f.*
drinking, *adj.*, adonné à la boisson.
drinking, *n.*, action de boire; boisson, *f.*; boire, *m.*
drinking-house (-haouce), *n.*, cabaret, *m.*
drink-money (-meü'n'-nè), *n.*, pourboire, *m.*
drip, *n.*, goutte, *f.*; (arch.) larmier, *m.*
drip, *v.n.*, dégoutter.
drip, *v.a.*, faire dégoutter.
dripping, *n.*, graisse de rôti, *f.*; gouttes, *f.pl.*
dripping-pan (-pa'ne), *n.*, lèchefrite, *f.*
dripstone (-stône), *n.*, filtre; (arch.) larmier, *m.*
drive (draïve), *v.a.* (*preterit*, Drove; *past part.*, Driven), forcer, réduire; porter; (carriages, horses—*voitures, chevaux*) conduire, mener; chasser; pousser. To — away; *chasser*, renvoyer. To — back; *repousser*. To — in; *enfoncer*. To — off; *renvoyer, différer*. To — on; *pousser*. To — out; *faire sortir, chasser*.
drive, *v.n.*, mener, conduire; courir; se diriger; aller en voiture. To — by; *passer en voiture*. To — against; *pousser vers; s'élancer contre*. To — at; *tendre à; vouloir en venir à*.
drive, *n.*, promenade en voiture; (place—*lieu*) promenade pour les voitures, *f.*
drivel (driv'v'l), *n.*, bave, *f.*
drivel, *v.n.*, baver; radoter.
driveller (driv'l'-), *n.*, radoteur, *m.*, radoteuse, *f.*
driver (draïv'-), *n.*, personne qui pousse, qui chasse, *f.*; cocher, conducteur; (orni.) paille-en-cul, *m.*
drizzle (driz'z'l), *v.n.*, bruiner, brouillasser.
drizzle, *v.a.*, verser à petites gouttes.
drizzly, *adj.*, de bruine.
droll (drôl), *n.*, plaisant, farceur, *m.*
droll, *adj.*, plaisant, drôle.
droll, *v.n.*, faire le plaisant; faire le farceur.
drollery, *n.*, plaisanterie; drôlerie, farce, *f.*
dromedary (dreu'm'ë-), *n.*, dromadaire, *m.*
drone (drône), *n.*, bourdon; (pers.) fainéant, *m.*
drone, *v.n.*, bourdonner; (fig.) vivre dans la fainéantise; lambiner.
dronepipe (-païpe), *n.*, cornemuse, musette, *f.*
droning, *adj.*, fainéant; bourdonnant.
droning, *n.*, débit monotone, *m.*
dronish, *adj.*, fainéant.
droop (droupe), *v.n.*, tomber; faiblir, languir; se flétrir.
droop, *v.a.*, baisser, laisser tomber.
drooping, *adj.*, languissant.
droopingly, *adv.*, languissamment.
drop, *n.*, goutte; (of a gibbet—*de potence*) bascule, *f.*; (for the ear—*d'oreille*) pendant; (of a lock—*de serrure*) cache-entrée, *m.*; (nav.) chute, *f.*
drop, *v.a.*, laisser tomber; descendre de voiture en chemin; laisser échapper; (to desist —*cesser*) laisser là, quitter, abandonner. To — a letter into the post; *jeter une lettre à la poste*.
drop, *v.n.*, tomber en gouttes, dégoutter; tomber. To — away; *tomber l'un après l'autre*. To — down; *tomber*. To — into; *arriver inopinément*. To — off; *s'en aller, mourir*. To — out; *se dérober, s'esquiver*.
droplet (-lète), *n.*, gouttelette, *f.*
dropper, *n.*, (fishing—*pêche*) bout de ligne, *m.*
dropsical, *adj.*, hydropique.
dropsy, *n.*, hydropisie, *f.*
dropwort (-weurte), *n.*, (bot.) spirée, filipendule, *f.*
dross, *n.*, écume; (fig.) rouille; (metal.) scorie, *f.*
drossiness, *n.*, écume; (fig.) impureté, *f.*
drossy, *adj.*, écumeux, plein d'écume.

drought (draoûte), *n.*, sécheresse; soif, *f.*
droughtiness, *n.*, sécheresse, *f.*
droughty, *adj.*, sec; (pers.) altéré.
drove (drôve), *n.*, troupeau, *m.*
drover, *n.*, conducteur de bestiaux, *m.*
drown (draoune), *v.a.*, noyer; inonder, submerger. To be —ed; *être noyé*. To be —ing; *se noyer*.
drown, *v.n.*, se noyer.
drowse (draouze), *v.a.*, assoupir.
drowse, *v.n.*, s'assoupir.
drowsily, *adv.*, dans l'assoupissement; (fig.) nonchalamment.
drowsiness, *n.*, somnolence, *f.*; assoupissement, *m.*
drowsy, *adj.*, assoupi, endormi; léthargique; lourd, stupide.
drub (dreube), *v.a.*, rosser, étriller.
drub, *n.*, coup de bâton, *m.*; taloche, *f.*
drubbing, *n.*, roulée, *f.*
drudge (dreudje), *n.*, homme de peine; souffre-douleur, esclave, *m.*
drudge, *v.n.*, travailler sans relâche; s'échiner.
drudger, *n.*, homme de peine, *m.*
drudgery, *n.*, travail fatigant, travail pénible, *m.*; peine, corvée, *f.*
drudging, *n.*, travail pénible, *m.*
drudgingly, *adv.*, péniblement; laborieusement.
drug (dreughe), *n.*, drogue, *f.*
drug, *v.a.*, mettre des drogues dans; empoisonner; droguer.
drug, *v.n.*, ordonner des drogues, des médecines à.
drugget (dreug'ghète), *n.*, bure, *f.*
druggist (dreug'ghiste), *n.*, droguiste, *m.*
druid, *n.*, druide, *m.*
drum (dreume), *n.*, tambour, *m.*; caisse, *f.* — of the ear; *tympan, m.*
drum, *v.n.*, battre du tambour; tambouriner; faire le tambour; (fig.) tinter.
drum, *v.a.*, (milit.) chasser au son du tambour. To — out of; *chasser ignominieusement*.
drum-barrel, *n.*, (tech.) tambour, *m.*
drum-head (-hède), *n.*, dessus du tambour, *m.*
drum-hole (-hôle), *n.*, trou de la caisse du tambour, *m.*
drum-major (-mé-djeur), *n.*, tambour-major, *m.*
drum-maker (-mék'-), *n.*, faiseur de tambours, *m.*
drummer, *n.*, tambour, *m.*
drum-stick, *n.*, baguette de tambour, *f.*
drunk (dreu'n'ke), *adj.*, ivre, gris.
drunkard, *n.*, ivrogne, *m.*, ivrognesse, *f.*
drunken (dreug'n'k'n), *adj.*, ivre; ivrogne.
drunkenly, *adv.*, en ivrogne.
drunkenness, *n.*, ivrognerie; ivresse, *f.*
dry (dra'ye), *adj.*, sec; aride; altéré; (fig.) caustique, sévère. To be —; (pers.) *avoir soif; être altéré*; (of the weather—*du temps*) *faire sec*.
dry, *v.a.*, sécher; mettre a sec; dessécher. To — up; *sécher; dessécher*.
dry, *v.n.*, sécher. To — up; *tarir*.
dry-beat (-bîte), *v.a.*, battre légèrement.
dryer, *n.*, siccatif, dessiccatif, *m.*
dry-eyed (-a'ye'-dé), *adj.*, qui a l'œil sec; les yeux secs; sans larmes.
dry-foot (-foute), *adv.*, (hunt.) à la piste; à la trace.
drying, *adj.*, qui sèche, siccatif.
drying-house (-haouce), *n.*, essui, séchoir, *m.*; sécherie, *f.*
dryness, *n.*, sécheresse; aridité, *f.*
dry-rub (-reube), *v.a.*, frotter à sec, sans mouiller, pour nettoyer.
dry-salter (-sôlt'-), *n.*, marchand de salaisons, *m.*

dry-shod (-shode), *adj.*, à pied sec.
dry-stove (-stôve). *n.*, serre chaude, *f.*
dual (diou'-), *adj.*, duel.
dub (deube), *n.*, coup, *m.* -
dub. *v.a.*, créer, faire, armer chevalier; (b.s.) baptiser.
dubious (diou'-), *adj.*, douteux, incertain.
dubiously, *adv.*, douteusement.
dubiousness, *n.*, doute, *m.*; incertitude; Indécision, *f.*
ducal (diou-), *adj.*, ducal.
ducat (deuc'ate), *n.*, ducat, *m.*
duck (deuke), *n.*, (orni.) cane, *f.*, canard, *m.*; (nav.) toile à voile, *f.*; (plunging—*plonger*) plongeon; (term of endearment—*terme d'affection*) chou, chat, poulet, *m.*, poulette, *f.* Russian — ; *toile de Russie, f.*
duck. *v.a.*, plonger dans l'eau; plonger; (nav.) donner la cale à.
duck. *v.n.*, plonger; faire le plongeon.
duck-gun (-gheune), *n.*, canardière, *f.*
ducking, *n.*, action de plonger, *f.*; plongeon; (nav.) baptême des tropiques, *m.*
duck-legged (-lèg'de), *adj.*, à jambes de canard.
duckling. *n.*, caneton, *m.*; canette, *f.*
duck-meat (-mîte), *n.*, (bot.) lenticule, lentille d'eau, lentille de marais, lemne bossue, *f.*
ducks-foot (deukse'foute), *n.*, (bot.) serpentaire de Virginie, *f.*
duck-shooting (-shout'-), *n.*, chasse aux canards, *f.*
duck-stone (-stône), *n.*, (boy's game—*jeu de garçons*) sauvette, *f.*
ducky, *n.*, petit chat; petit chou, *m.*
duct (deucte), *n.*, conduit; canal; tube, *m.* Alimentary — ; *tube alimentaire, canal alimentaire.*
ductile (deuc'tile). *adj.*, ductile, souple.
ductileness, or ductility, *n.*, ductilité, flexibilité, *f.*
dudgeon (deud'jeune). *n.*, brouille; mauvaise part; (dagger—*poignard*) petite dague; colère intérieure, *f.* To take in — ; *prendre en mauvaise part.* In high — ; *fort en colère.*
due (diou), *adj.*, dû; convenable; juste.
due, *n.*, dû; droit, *m.*
due, *adv.*, droit, directement.
duel (diou'-), *n.*, duel; combat, *m.*
duel. *v.n.*, se battre en duel.
duel, *v.a.*, attaquer en duel.
duelling, *n.*, duel, *m.*
duellist, *n.*, duelliste, *m.*
duenna (diou'è'n'-), *n.*, duègne, *f.*
duet (deu'ète), *n.*, (mus.) duo, *m.*
duffel (deuf'-), *n.*, molleton de laine, *m.*
◀**dug** (deughe), *n.*, bout du sein, *m.*; (of animals that are milked—*de la vache, &c.*) trayon, *m.*
duke (diouke), *n.*, duc, *m.*
dukedom (-deume), *n.*, duché, *m.*; dignité de duc, *f.*
dulcet (deul'cète), *adj.*, doux, harmonieux.
dulcification (deul'-), *n.*, dulcification, *f.*
dulcify (deul-ci-fa'ye), *v.a.*, dulcifier.
dulcimer (deul'-), *n.*, tympanon, *m.*
dulcorate (deul'-), *v.a.*, édulcorer.
dulcoration (deul-co-ré-), *n.*, édulcoration, *f.*
dulia (diou-), *n.*, (theol.) dulie, *f.*
dull (deul), *adj.*, (of persons—*des personnes*) lourd, borné; (of the weather—*du temps*) lourd, triste; (of sound—*du son*) sourd; (melancholy —*mélancolique*) triste, sombre; (blunt—*d'un tranchant*) émoussé; (com.) plat, calme. — (of hearing; *qui entend dur; sourdaud; un peu sourd.* To be — (melancholy—*mélancolique*); *s'ennuyer.*
dull (deul), *v a.*, rendre lourd; lasser; émousser.

dull, *v.n.*, devenir lourd; s'hébéter.
dullard (deul'-), *n.*, lourdaud, *m.*
dull-brained (-bré'n'de), *adj.*, à l'esprit lourd; qui a l'esprit lourd.
dull-browed (-braou'de), *adj.*, au front sombre; qui a le front sombre.
dull-disposed (-pôz'de), *adj.*, disposé à la tristesse.
dull-eyed (-a'ye'-de), *adj.*, au regard sombre; mélancolique.
dull-head (-hède), *n.*, esprit lourd, *m.*
dull-sighted (-saït'ède), *adj.*, qui a la vue faible; à la vue faible.
dull-witted (-wit'tède), *adj.*, lourd d'esprit.
dully, *adv.*, durement; pesamment, tristement.
dulness, *n.*, stupidité; tristesse, *f.*; ennui; état émoussé, *m.*
duly (diou-li), *adv.*, dûment; justement.
dumb (deume), *adj.*; muet. — -waiter; *servante, f.*
dumbly (deu'm'li), *adv.*, sans rien dire, sans paroles.
dumbness (deu'm'nèce), *n.*, silence; mutisme, *m.*
dumfound, or dumfounder (deu'm'faou'n'd, -'eur), *v.a.*, confondre; abasourdir.
dummy (deu'm'-), *n.*, muet, *m.*, muette, *f.*; (whist) mort, *m.*
dump (deu'm'pe), *n.*, tristesse; mélancolie; rêverie, *f.* To be in the—s; *être triste comme un bonnet de nuit.*
dumpish, *adj.*, chagrin, mélancolique.
dumpishness, *n.*, tristesse, mélancolie, *f.*
dumpling (deu'm'p'-), *n.*, pommé, *m.*
dumpy, *adj.*, trapu; court et gros.
dun (deune), *adj.*, brun foncé; (of horses— *des chevaux*) bai brun, alezan foncé.
dun, *n.*, créancier importun, *m.*
dun, *v.a.*, importuner. To — any one with any thing; *corner quelque chose aux oreilles de quelqu'un.*
dunce (dou'n'ce), *n.*, ignorant, *m.*, ignorante, ganache, *f.*
duncery, *n.*, bêtise, *f.*
dun-coloured (-keul'leurde), *adj.*, brun foncé.
dung (deu'n'gne), *n.*, fiente, *f.*; (agri.) fumier, *m.*; (of mice, sheep, rabbits, &c.—*de souris, moutons, lapins, &c.*) crotte, *f.*; (of horses —*des chevaux*) crottin, *m.*; (of oxen, cows—*des bœufs, des vaches*) fiente, bouse, *f.*
dung, *v.a.*, fumer.
dung, *v.n.*, fienter.
dung-cart (-cärte), *n.*, tombereau à fumier, *m.*
dungeon (deu'n'djeu'ne), *n.*, cachot, *m.*
dung-fork (-forke), *n.*, fourche à fumier, *f.*
dunghill, *n.*, fumier; (fig.) taudis, *m.*, baraque, *f.*; (ant.) manant, *m.*
dunghill, *adj.*, de fumier; sale, ignoble.
dunging (deu'n'gn'-), *n.*, (agri.) fumure, *f.*; (manu.) bousage, *m.*
dungy (deu'n'gn'i), *adj.*, de fumier; vil.
dunnage (deu'n'nédje), *n.*, (nav.) fardage, *m.*
dunning (deu'n'-), *n.*, importunité; (curing codfish—*préparation de la morue*) salaison de la morue, *f.*
dunnish, *adj.*, qui tire sur le brun foncé.
duo (diou-ô), *n.*, duo, *m.*
duodecimal (diou-o-dèc'i-), *adj.*, duodécimal.
duodecimals (-malze), *n.*; (arith.) multiplication des nombres complexes, *f.*
duodecimo (diou-o-dèc'i-mô), *adj.*, in-douze.
duodecimo, *n.*, in-douze, *m.*
duodecuple (diou-o-dèk'iou-p'l), *adj.*, composé de douzièmes.
duodenum (diou-o-di-neume), *n.*, duodénum, *m.*

duoliteral (diou-o-lit-èr'-), *adj.*, composé de deux lettres.

dupe (dioupe), *n.*, dupe, *f.*

dupe, *v.a.*, duper.

dupion (diou-), *n.*, cocon double, *m.*

duple (diou-p'l), *adj.*, double.

duplicate (diou-pli-kéte), *adj.*, double.

duplicate, *n.*, double, duplicata, *m.* ; (of a pawnbroker—*de préteur sur gage*) reconnaissance, *f.*

duplicate, *v.a.*, plier en double.

duplication (diou-pli-ké-), *n.*, duplication, *f.*

duplicity (diou-), *n.*, double nature ; duplicité, *f.*

durability (diou-), *n.*, durabilité, *f.*

durable (diou-ra-b'l), *adj.*, durable.

durableness, *n.*, durabilité, *f.*

durably, *adv.*, durablement.

durance (diou-), *n.*, emprisonnement, *m.* ; (ant.) pouvoir d'endurer, *m.*, patience ; souffrance, *f.*

duration (diou-ré-), *n.*, durée, *f.*

duress (diou-), *n.*, emprisonnement, *m.* ; contrainte, *f.*

during (diour'-), *prep.*, pendant, durant.

dusk (deuske), *n.*, brune, *f.* ; crépuscule, *m.*

dusk, *adj.*, obscur, sombre.

duskily, *adv.*, obscurément.

duskish, *adj.*, sombre, foncé.

duskishly, *adv.*, obscurément.

dusky, *adj.*, obscur, sombre.

dust (deuste), *n.*, poussière ; poudre, *f.* ; (noise —*bruit*) train, tapage, *m.* Saw — ; *sciure, f.*

dust, *v.a.*, épousseter ; couvrir de poussière ; pulvériser.

dust-brush (-breushe), *n.*, plumeau, *m.*

duster, *n.*, torchon, *m.* ; vergette, *f.*, plumeau, *m.*, ⊙ époussette, *f.*,

dust-hole (-hôle), *n.*, trou aux ordures, *m.*

dustiness, *n.*, état poudreux, *m.*

dustman (-mane), *n.*, boueur, *m.*

dusty, *adj.*, poudreux, couvert de poussière; de poussière.

dutch (deutshe), *adj.*, hollandais.

dutch, *n.*, hollandais (language—*langue*), *m.*

dutchman, *n.*, Hollandais, *m.*

dutchwoman (-woum'ane), *n.*, Hollandaise. *f.*

duteous (diou-ti-), *adj.*, soumis, obéissant, respectueux.

dutiable (diou-ti-a-b'l), *adj.*, imposable, assujetti aux droits et impositions.

dutiful (diou-ti-foule), *adj.*, obéissant, soumis, respectueux, humble.

dutifully, *adv.*, avec soumission, respectueusement.

dutifulness, *n.*, soumission ; déférence, *f.*

duty (diou-ti), *n.*, devoir ; respect ; (at the customs—*douanes*) droit ; (milit.) service, *m.*

duumvir (diou-eu'm'veur), *n.*, duumvir, *m.*

duumvirate (-éte), *n.*, duumvirat, *m.*

dux (dioukse), *n.*, (in schools—*écoles, &c.*) sergent, premier, *m.*

dwale (dwéle), *n.*, (her.) couleur noire ; (bot.) belladone, *f.*

dwarf (dworfe), *n.*, nain, *m.*, naine, *f.*

dwarf, *adj.*, nain.

dwarf, *v.a.*, rapetisser.

dwarfish, *adj.*, de nain.

dwarfishly, *adv.*, en nain.

dwarfishness (dwarf'-), *n.*, taille de nain ; petitesse, *f.*

dwell (dwèle), *v.n.*, demeurer ; rester. To — on ; *s'étendre sur, appuyer sur ; s'arrêter à.*

dweller, *n.*, habitant, *m.*, habitante, *f.*

dwelling, *n.*, demeure, habitation, *f.*

dwelling-house (-haouce), *n.*, maison d'habitation, *f.* ; domicile, *m.*

dwindle (dwi'n'd'l), *v.n.*, diminuer ; dépérir ; dégénérer ; s'abréger.

dwindle, *v.a.*, diminuer, réduire ; briser ; disperser.

dye (da'ye), *v.a.*, teindre, colorer ; tacher.

dye, *n.*, teinture, teinte ; couleur ; empreinte, *f.*

dye-drug (-dreughe), *n.*, drogue de teinture ; drogue tinctoriale, *f.*

dye-house (-haouce), *n.*, teinturerie, *f.*

dyeing, *n.*, teinture, *f.*

dye-mill, *n.*, teinturerie, *f.*

dyer (da'y'eur), *n.*, teinturier, *m.*, teinturière, *f.*

dyer's-brown (-'z'braoune), *n.*, (bot.) herbe des teinturiers ; genestrolle, *f.*

dyer's-weed (-'z'wide), *n.*, (bot.) réséda des teinturiers, *m.* ; gaude, *f.*

dyer's-wood (-'z'woude), *n.*, (bot.) pastel des teinturiers, *m.* ; guède, *f.*

dyestuff (-steufe), *n.*, couleur pour teindre; matière tinctoriale, *f.*

dye-wood (-woude), *n.*, bois de teinture ; bois tinctorial, *m.*

dye-works (-weurkse), *n.pl.*, teinturerie, *f. sing.*

dying (daï'gne), *adj.*, mourant, moribond ; (of things—*des choses*) de la mort; suprême. — man ; *mourant, moribond, m.* — woman ; *mourante, moribonde, f.*

dyke (daike), *n.*, digue, *f.*; fossé ; (mines.) filon stérile, *m.*; (geol.) taille, *f.*

dynamic, or **dynamical** (di-), *adj.*, dynamique.

dynamics (di-na'm'ikse), *n.pl.*, dynamique, *f.sing.*

dynamometer (dyn'a-mo'm'i-), *n.*, dynamomètre, *m.*

dynastic, *adj.*, dynastique.

dynasty, *n.*, dynastie, famille, *f.*

dysenteric, or **dysenterical** (diss'è'n'-tèr'-), *adj.*, dysentérique.

dysentery (diss'è'n'tèr'i), *n.*, dysenterie, *f.*

dyspepsia, or **dyspepsy** (dis-pèp'-), *n.*, dyspepsie, *f.*

dyspnœa (disp'nî-a), *n.*, dyspnée, *f.*

dysury (diss'iou-ri), *n.*, dysurie, *f.*

E

e, cinquième lettre de l'alphabet, e, *m.* ; (mus.) mi, *m.*

each (itshe), *pron.* and *adj.*, chaque ; chacun, *m.*, chacune, *f.* — one ; *chacun, m., chacune, f.*

eager (i-gheur), *adj.*, vif, ardent, impatient, empressé ; (metal.) aigre.

eagerly, *adv.*, ardemment, impatiemment ; avec empressement.

eagerness, *n.*, ardeur, impatience, *f.* ; empressement, *m.*

eagle (i-g'l), *n.*, (orni., astron.) aigle, *m.* ; (her., Rom. hist.) aigle, *f.*

eagle-eyed (-a'ye'-dé), *adj.*, qui a des yeux d'aigle.

eagle-sighted (-saït'òde), *adj.*, à la vue d'aigle.

eagle-stone (-stóne), *n.*, (min.) aétite, pierre d'aigle, *f.*

eaglet (i-glète), *n.*, aiglon, *m.*

eagle-winged (-wign'de), *adj.*, à vol d'aigle.

eagre (i-gheur), *n.*, raz ; raz de marée, *m.*

ear (ir), *n.*, oreille, *f.* ; (of corn—*de blé*) épi, *m.* ; (of a porringer—*d'écuelle*) anse, *f.*

ear, *v.n.*, monter en épi.

earache (ir-éke), *n.*, mal d'oreille ; mal à l'oreille, *m.*

ear-bored (ir-bôrde), *adj.*, aux oreilles percées; qui a les oreilles percées.

ear-deafening (-dèf'ïn'-), *adj.*, étourdissant.

ear-drop, *n.*, pendant d'oreille, *m.*

ear-drum (-dreume), *n.*, (anat.) tympan; tambour de l'oreille, *m.*

eared (îr-de), *adj.*, qui a des oreilles; garni d'épis; (bot.) auriculé. Long- —; *aux longues oreilles.*

earl (eur'l), *n.*, comte, *m.*

ear-lap (ïr'lape), *n.*, lobe, bout inférieur de l'oreille, *m.*

earldom (eur'l'deume), *n.*, comté, *m.*

earless (ïr'lèce), *adj.*, sans oreilles.

earliness (eur'li'-), *n.*, heure peu avancée; précocité, *f.*

early (eur'li), *adv.*, de bonne heure; tôt; de bon matin; matinalement.

early, *adj.*, matinal, (pers.) matineux; prématuré, précoce; (hort.) hâtif.

earn (eurne), *v.a.*, gagner; acquérir.

earnest (eur'nèste), *adj.*, ardent, sérieux.

earnest, *n.*, sérieux, *m.*; (of money—*d'argent*) arrhes, *f.pl.* In —; *sérieux; au sérieux; de bonne foi.* In good —; *de bonne foi; pour tout de bon.* Are you in —? *parlez-vous sérieusement?*

earnestly, *adv.*, ardemment; sérieusement; instamment, avec empressement.

earnest-money (-meu'n'nè), *n.*, arrhes, *f.pl.*

earnestness, *n.*, ardeur, *f.*; empressement; sérieux, *m.*

earnings (eurn'ïgn'ze), *n.pl.*, gain; fruit du travail, *m.*

ear-pick (ïr-pike), *n.*, cure-oreille, *m.*

earpiercing (ïr-pîrs'-), *adj.*, qui perce l'oreille; au son perçant.

ear-ring (ïr-rigne), *n.*, boucle d'oreille, *f.*

ear-shaped (ïr-shép'te), *adj.*, en forme d'oreille; auriforme.

ear-shot (ïr-shote), *n.*, portée de l'oreille, *f.*

earth (eurth), *n.*, terre, *f.*

earth, *v.a.*, enterrer; enfouir. To — up; *déterrer;* (agri.) *butter.*

earth, *v.n.*, se terrer.

earthbag, *n.*, sac à terre, *m.*

earthbank, *n.*, jetée de terre, *f.*

earthboard (-bôrde), *n.*, (agri.) versoir, *m.*

earthborn, *adj.*, né de la terre.

earthbound (-baou'n'de), *adj.*, attaché à la terre.

earthbred (-brède), *adj.*, né de la terre.

earthen (eurth'n), *adj.*, de terre.

earthen-ware (-wére), *n.*, poterie; vaisselle de terre; faïence, *f.*

earthfed (-fède), *adj.*, nourri de substances terrestres.

earthflax, *n.*, amiante, *m.*

earthiness, or **earthliness**, *n.*, caractère terrestre, *m.*

earthling, *n.*, mortel, *m.*

earthly, *adj.*, terrestre.

earthly-minded (-maï'n'd'ède), *adj.*, mondain.

earthly-mindedness, *n.*, caractère mondain, *m.*

earth-nut (-neute), *n.*, (bot.) terre-noix, *f.*

earthquake (-kwéke), *n.*, tremblement de terre, *m.*

earthshaking (-shék'-), *adj.*, qui fait trembler la terre.

earthward (-worde), *adv.*, vers la terre.

earthwork (-weurke), *n.*, terrassement, *m.*, travaux de terrasse, *m.pl.*; (fort.) ouvrage en terre; parapet, *m.*

earthworm (-weurme), *n.*, ver de terre, *m.*

earthy, *adj.*, de terre; terrestre; terreux.

ear-trumpet (ïr-treu'm'pète), *n.*, cornet acoustique, *m.*

ear-wax (ïr-wakse), *n.*, cérumen, *m.*, cire, *f.*

earwig (ïr'wighe), *n.*, (ent.) forficule, *f.*; perce-oreille, *m.*

ease (îze), *n.*, aisance, aise, tranquillité, *f.*; repos, *m.* At —; *tranquille; à l'aise.* At one's —; *à l'aise; dans l'aisance.* To take one's —; *se mettre à l'aise.*

ease, *v.a.*, tranquilliser, calmer; soulager, alléger.

easeful (-foule), *adj.*, tranquille, paisible.

easel (î'z'l), *n.*, (paint.) chevalet, *m.*

easement, *n.*, soulagement, *m.*

easily, *adv.*, facilement, aisément.

easiness, *n.*, facilité; douceur, *f.*

east (îste), *n.*, est, orient, levant, *m.*

east, *adj.*, d'orient, oriental; d'est.

easter (îst'eur), *n.*, (Christian rel.—*des chrétiens*) Pâque, or Pâques, *m.* (*f.* in the plur.); (Jewish rel.—*des Juifs.*) Pâque, *f.*

easterly, *adj.*, d'orient; d'est.

easterly, *adv.*, vers l'orient, vers l'est.

eastern, *adj.*, oriental, d'orient, d'est.

eastward (îst'worde), *adv.*, vers l'orient; vers l'est.

easy (î-zé), *adj.*, aisé, facile; tranquille; doux, coulant; à l'aise; dans l'aisance. — of belief; *crédule.*

eat (île), *v.a.* (preterit, Eat, Ate; *past part.*, Eaten), manger; gruger; (to corrode—*corroder*) ronger. To — away; *consumer; ronger.* To — up; *manger entièrement; dévorer.*

eat, *v.n.*, manger. To — into; *ronger; faire des ravages dans.*

eatable (ît'a-b'l), *adj.*, mangeable, comestible, bon à manger.

eatable, *n.*, comestible.

eater, *n.*, mangeur, *m.*, mangeuse, *f.*

eating, *n.*, action de manger, *f.*; manger, *m.*

eating-house (-haouce), *n.*, restaurant, *m.* — keeper; *restaurateur; traiteur, m.*

eaves (îv'ze), *n.pl.*, bord des toits; (arch.) larmier, *m.*

eavesdrop, *v.n.*, écouter aux portes.

eavesdropper, *n.*, écouteur aux portes, *m.*

ebb (èbe), *v.n.*, refluer, baisser.

ebb, *n.*, reflux; (nav.) jusant, *m.*, èbe, ebbe, *f.*; (fig.) déclin, *m.* At a low —; *très bas.*

ebbing, *n.* V. **ebb.**

ebb-tide (-taïde), *n.*, reflux; (nav.) jusant, *m.*, èbe, ebbe, *f.*

eben (èb'è'ne), or **ebon** (èb'-), *n.*, ébène, *f.*

ebon, *adj.*, d'ébène.

ebonize (-'aïze), *v.a.*, ébéner.

ebony (èb'-), *n.*, ébène, *f.*; bois d'ébène, *m.*; (bot.) plaqueminier, ébénier, *m.*

ebony-tree (-trî), *n.*, (bot.) faux ébénier, *m.*, (bot.) plaqueminier, ébénier, *m.*

ebriety (è-brai-è-), *n.*, ébriété, ivresse, *f.*

ebrillade (i-bril'iade), *n.*, (man.) ⊙ébrillade, *f.*

ebriosity (î-bri-oss'-), *n.*, ivrognerie, *f.*

ebullience, or **ebulliency** (è-beull'-), *n.*, ébullition; effervescence, *f.*

ebullient, *adj.*, en ébullition, bouillonnant.

ebullition (èb'eul'-), *n.*, ébullition; effervescence, *f.*

ecce-homo (èk-sè-hô-mô), *n.*, ecce homo, *m.*

eccentric *adj.*, excentrique; original.

eccentric (èk'cè'n'-), *n.*, (geom.) cercle excentrique, *m.*

eccentricity *n.*, (geom.) excentricité; (fig.) originalité, *f.*

ecchymosis (èk'ki-mô-cice), *n.*, ecchymose, *f.*

ecclesiastes (èk-cli-zi-as-tize), *n.*, Ecclésiaste, *m.*

ecclesiastic (-cli-), *n.*, ecclésiastique, *m.*

ecclesiastic, or **ecclesiastical** (-cli-), *adj.*, ecclésiastique.

ecclesiastically (-cli-), *adv.*, ecclésiastiquement.

ecclesiasticus (-cli-), *n.*, Ecclésiastique, *m.*

echinus (i-ki-), *n.*, (conch.) oursin, *m.*; (arch.) échine, *f.*

echo (èk'ô), *n.*, écho, *m.*
echo, *v.a.*, répéter.
echo, *v.n.*, faire écho; retentir.
echoless, *adj.*, sans écho.
eclat (i-clâ), *n.*, éclat, *m.*
eclectic, *adj.*, éclectique.
eclectic, *n.*, éclectique, *m.*
eclecticism, *n.*, éclectisme, *m.*
eclipse, *n.*, éclipse, *f.*
eclipse, *v.a.*, éclipser.
eclipse, *v.n.*, s'éclipser.
ecliptic, *n.*, écliptique, *f.*
ecliptic, *adj.*, écliptique; de l'écliptique.
eclogue (èk'loghe), *n.* V. **æglogue.**
economic, or **economical**, *adj.*, (of things
—*des choses*) économique; (pers.) économe.
economically, *adv.*, économiquement.
economics, *n.pl.*, économique, *f.sing.*
economist, *n.*, économe; économiste, *m.*
Political —; *économiste.*
economize (-maïze), *v.a.*, économiser.
economize, *v.n.*, économiser; user d'économie.
economy, *n.*, économie, *f.*; système, *m.*
ecstasy (èk-sta-ci), *n.*, extase, *f.*; transport, *m.*
ecstatic, or **ecstatical**, *adj.*, extatique;
d'extase.
ectropium (èk-trô-), *n.*, ectropion, *m.*
edacious (è-dé-sheusse), *adj.*, vorace, gourmand.
edacity (è-dass'-), *n.*, voracité, gourmandise, *f.*
eddy (èd-), *n.*, (of water—*de l'eau*) contre-
courant, remous; (of wind—*du vent*) tourbillon, *m.*
eddy, *adj.*, tourbillonnant.
eddy, *v.n.*, tourbillonner.
eddy-water (-wô-), *n.*, remous, *m.*
eddy-wind (-wi'n'de), *n.*, revolin, *m.*
edematose (è-dè'm'a-tôss), or **edematous**,
adj., œdémateux.
eden (î-dène), *n.*, Éden, *m.*
edentalous, or **edentated** (è-dè'n'ta-, -té-
tède), *adj.*, édenté.
edge (èdje), *n.*, bord; (of sharp instruments
—*d'instruments tranchants*) fil, tranchant, *m.*;
(of a wood, forest—*d'un bois, d'une forêt*) lisière,
f.; (coin.) cordon, *m.*; (of a prism—*d'un prisme*)
arête saillante; (of a book—*d'un livre*) tranche,
f.; (fig.) glaive, *m.* To give an — to; *donner le
fil à.* To take off the —; *ôter le fil à.* To set
one's teeth on —; *agacer les dents.* To put to
the — of the sword; *passer au fil de l'épée.*
edge, *v.a.*, affiler; aiguiser; (to border—*border*) border; (carp.) abattre les angles; (fig.)
exaspérer, aiguillonner; inciter, pousser, exciter; provoquer. To — in; *faire entrer difficilement.* [Au figuré, on trouve quelquefois *egg*,
qui n'est qu'une orthographe erronée du mot
edge.]
edge, *v.n.*, s'avancer de côté.
edged (èdj'de), *adj.*, affilé, aigu. Two- —;
à deux tranchants.
edgeless, *adj.*, sans tranchant; émoussé.
edge-tool (-toule), *n.*, instrument tranchant, *m.*
edgewise (-waïze), *adv.*, de côté, sur le
bord.
edging, *n.*, bord, *m.*; bordure; garniture, *f.*
edible (èd'i-b'l), *adj.*, mangeable, comestible,
bon à manger.
edict (î-dicte), *n.*, édit, *m.*
edification (èd'i-fi-ké-), *n.*, édification, *f.*
edifice, *n.*, édifice, *m.*
edifier (èd'i-faï'-), *n.*, personne qui édifie, *f.*;
édificateur, *m.*
edify (èd'i-fa'ye), *v.a.*, édifier.
edifying, *adj.*, édifiant.
edifyingly, *adv.*, d'une manière édifiante.

edile (î-daïl), *n.*, édile, *m.*
edileship, *n.*, édilité, *f.*
edit (èd'ite), *v.a.*, publier; être éditeur de,
éditer; rédiger.
edition (è-dish'eune), *n.*, édition, *f.*
editor (èd'i-teur), *n.*, éditeur, *m.*; (of newspapers—*de journaux*) rédacteur, gérant, *m.*
editorship, *n.*, fonctions d'éditeur, *f.pl.*
educate (èd'iou-kéte), *v.a.*, élever, faire
l'éducation de, instruire.
education (èd-iou-ké-), *n.*, éducation, *f.*
educational, *adj.*, d'éducation.
educator (-két'eur), *n.*, instituteur, *m.*, institutrice, *f.*
educe (è-diouce), *v.a.*, tirer, faire sortir,
extraire.
eduction (è-deuk'-), *n.*, émission; décharge, *f.*
odulcorate (è-deul-co-réte), *v.a.*, édulcorer.
edulcoration, *n.*, édulcoration, *f.*
eel (îl), *n.*, anguille, *f.* — -spear; *trident, m.*
effable (èf'fa-b'l), *adj.*, (ant.) qui peut s'exprimer.
efface (-féce), *v.a.*, effacer.
effaceable (-féss'a-b'l), *adj.*, effaçable.
effect (èf'fècte), *n.*, effet, *m.*; action, *f.*; objet,
m. —s; (jur.) biens, *m.pl.* To take —; *faire effet,
porter coup.* To produce —; *faire de l'effet.*
effect, *v.a.*, effectuer, exécuter, accomplir.
effectible (-i-b'l), *adj.*, praticable.
effective, *adj.*, effectif, efficace.
effectively, *adv.*, effectivement; efficacement.
effectless, *adj.*, inefficace, sans effet; inutile.
effector (-teur), *n.*, auteur, producteur, *m.*
effectual (-'iou-), *adj.*, efficace.
effectually, *adv.*, efficacement.
effectuate (-'iou-éte), *v.a.*, effectuer.
effeminacy, *n.*, mollesse; délicatesse efféminée, *f.*
effeminate, *adj.*, efféminé, lâche, mou.
effeminate, *v.n.*, devenir efféminé; s'amollir.
effeminate, *v.a.*, efféminer.
effeminately, *adv.*, d'une manière efféminée; avec mollesse.
effeminateness, *n.*, mollesse; délicatesse
efféminée.
effervesce, *v.n.*, être en effervescence; faire
effervescence; (of beverages—*des breuvages*)
mousser.
effervescence, *n.*, effervescence, *f.*
effervescent, *adj.*, effervescent; mousseux
effete (èf'fîte), *adj.*, frappé de stérilité; usé;
émoussé; éventé.
efficacious (èf'fi-ké-sheusse), *adj.*, efficace.
efficaciously, *adv.*, efficacement; avec efficacité.
efficacy (èf'fi-ca-), *n.*, efficacité, *f.*
efficience, or **efficiency** (èf'fish'-), *n.*,
efficacité; action productrice, *f.*
efficient, *n.*, cause efficiente, *f.*; (math.)
facteur, *m.*
efficient, *adj.*, efficient; efficace.
efficiently, *adv.*, efficacement.
effigy (-dji), *n.*, effigie, *f.*; portrait, *m.*;
image, représentation, *f.*
efflation (èf'flé-), *n.*, souffle, *m.*
effloresce, *v.n.*, (chem.) effleurir, s'effleurir.
efflorescence, or **efflorescency**, *n.*, efflorescence; fleuraison, floraison, *f.*
efflorescent, *adj.*, efflorescent.
effluence, or **effluency** (èf'flou'-), *n.*,
effluence, émanation, *f.*
effluent, *adj.*, effluent; qui émane.
effluvium (èf'fliou-vi-eume), *n.* (*effluvia*),
exhalaison, *f.* effluve, *m.*
efflux (èf'fieukse), *n.*, écoulement, *m.*;
émanation, effusion, *f.*
effluxion (-fieuksh'-), *n.*, écoulement, *m.*
effort (ef'fòrte), *n.*, effort, *m.*

effrontery (èf'freu'n'ti-ri), *n.*, effronterie, *f.*

effulge (èf'feul'dje), *v.n.*, briller avec éclat, resplendir.

effulgence, *n.*, éclat, resplendissement, *m.*

effulgent, *adj.*, resplendissant, éclatant.

effuse (èf'fiouze), *v.a.*, épandre, verser.

effusion (èf-fiou-jeune), *n.*, effusioñ, *f.*; épanchement, *m.*

effusive (èf'fiou-cive), *adj.*, qui répand.

eft (èfte), *n.*,(zool.) salamandre,*f.*, mouron,*m.*

egad ! (è-gade), *int.*, ma foi !

egg (èghe), *n.*, œuf ; (arch.) ove, *m.* Addle —; œuf couvi. New-laid —; œuf frais.

egg, *v.a.* *V.* **edge**, *v.* (fig.).

egg-cup (-keupe), *n.*, coquetier, *m.*

egg-glass (-glâce), *n.*, sablier pour cuire les œufs à la coque, *m.*

egg-merchant (-meur-tsha'n'te), *n.*, coquetier, marchand d'œufs,*m.*

egg-nog (èghe-noghe), *n.*, lait de poule à l'eau-de-vie, au rhum, *m.*

egg-plant, *n.*, (bot.) morelle, mélongène; aubergine, *f.*

egg-shaped (-shép'te), *adj.*, en œuf ; (bot.) ovale.

egg-shell, *n.*, coque, coquille d'œuf, *f.*

egilops (i'dji-), *n.*, égilops, *m.*

eglantine (-taïne, ou -tine), *n.*, églantier,*m.*; (flower—*fleur*) églantine, *f.*

eglogue (èg-loghe), *n.* *V.* **æglogue.**

egoism (i-go-iz'me), *n.*, (philos.) égoïsme,*m.*

egoist (i-go-iste), *n.*, (philos.) égoïste, *m.*

egotism (èg-o tiz'me, ou ï-go-), *n.*, habitude de parler de soi, *f.* ; égoïsme; amour-propre, *m.* ; vanité, *f.*

egotist, *n.*, personne qui a l'habitude de parler de soi, *f.* ; égoïste, *m.*, *f.*

egotistic, *or* **egotistical**,*adj.*, qui a l'habitude de parler trop de soi ; égoïste.

egotize (i-go-taïze), *v.n.*, parler trop de soi; égoïser.

egregious (i-gri-djeusse), *adj.*, insigne, énorme ; fameux.

egregiously, *adv.*, d'une manière insigne; grandement ; énormément ; fameusement.

egregiousness, *n.*, caractère remarquable, *m.*

egress, *or* **egression** (i-gress, i-grèsh'-), *n.*, sortie, issue, *f.*

egret (i-grète), *n.*, aigrette, *f.*

egriot (i-gri-ote), *n.*, griotte, *f.*

egyptian (i-djip-'sha'ne), *adj.*, égyptien.

egyptian, *n.*, Egyptien, *m.*, Egyptienne, *f.*

eider (aï-), *or* **eider-duck** (-deuke), *n.*, (orni.) eider, *m.*

eider-down (-daoune), *n.*, édredon, *m.*

eight (è-te), *adj.*, huit.

eighteen (è-tine), *adj.*, dix-huit.

eighteenth (-ti'n'th), *adj.*, dix-huitième.

eightfold (-fôlde),*adj.*, octuple ; huit fois.

eighth (èt'th), *adj.*, huitième ; huit.

eighth,*n.*, (mus.) octave,*f.*

eighthly (èt'th'li), *adj.*, huitièmement.

eightieth (è-ti-èth), *adj.*, quatre-vingtième.

eightscore (-scôre), *adj.*, huit vingtaines, *f.pl.* ; cent soixante.

eighty (è-ti), *adj.*, quatre-vingts.

either (i-*theur*), *pron.*, l'un ou l'autre, *m.* *sing.* ; l'une ou l'autre, *f.sing.* ; les uns ou les autres, *m.pl.* ; les unes ou les autres, *f.pl.* ; chacun, *m.*, chacune, *f.* ; l'un d'eux, *m.*, l'une d'elles, *f.* ; (used negatively—*négativement*) aucun, *m.*, aucune, *f.*, ni l'un ni l'autre, *m.sing.*, ni les uns ni les autres, *m.pl.*, ni l'une ni l'autre, *f.sing.*, ni les unes ni les autres, *f.pl.*

either, *conj.*, ou, soit.

either, *adv.*, non plus.

ejaculate (è-djak'iou-léte), *v.a.*, lan~er ; prononcer avec ferveur ; éjaculer.

ejaculation, *n.*, action de lancer ; émission ; prière fervente ; éjaculation, *f.* ; élan, *m.*

ejaculatory, *adj.*, éjaculatoire ; (anat.) éjaculateur.

eject (è-djèate), *v.a.*, jeter, lancer ; chasser, expulser.

ejection, *n.*, expulsion,*f.* ; rejet, *m.* ; (med.) évacuation,*f.*

ejectment, *n.*, expulsion, *f.*

ejector, *n.*, auteur d'une expulsion, *m.*

eke (ike), *v.a.*, allonger, suppléer à. To — out ; suppléer à; prolonger.

elaborate (è-lab'o-réte), *adj.*, élaboré.

elaborate, *v.a.*, élaborer.

elaborately, *adv.*, d'une manière élaborée, laborieusement.

elaborateness, *n.*, élaboration, *f.* ; travail, *m.*

elaboration, *n.*, élaboration,*f.*

elapse (è-là'n'-), *v.a.* and *n.*, (ant.) lancer ; s'élancer.

elapse (è-), *v.n.*, s'écouler, passer, se passer.

elastic, *or* **elastical** (è-), *adj.*, élastique.

elastically, *adv.*, d'une manière élastique.

elasticity, *n.*, élasticité,*f.*

elate (i-léte), *adj.*, fier, enflé.

elate, *v.a.*, élever ; enfler ; exalter.

elatedly, *adv.*, orgueilleusement.

elation (i-lé-), *n.*, enflure (of mind—*de cœur*) ; vanité,*f.*, orgueil, *m.*

elbow (èl-bô), *n.*, coude ; (of an arm-chair—*de fauteuil*) bras, *m.* — -chair ; *fauteuil*, *m.* — -grease ; *huile de bras*, *f.* — -room ; *coudées franches,f.pl.* — -rest ; *accoudoir*, *m.*

elbow, *v.a.*, coudoyer ; presser.

elbow, *v.n.*, faire coude ; faire angle.

elder (èl-), *n.*, personne plus âgée qu'une autre ou que d'autres, *f.* ; doyen, ancien, *m.* ; (among the Jews, the Presbyterians—*parmi les Juifs et les Presbytériens*) ancien ; prêtre, *m.* ; (bot.) sureau, *m.*

elder, *adj.*, aîné, plus âgé.

elderly, *adj.*, qui tire sur l'âge.

eldership,*n.*,aînesse ; qualité d'ancien; *f.* ; (of the Presbyterians—*des Presbytériens*) conseil des anciens, *m.*

eldest (èl-dèste), *adj.*, le plus âgé, l'aîné.

elecampane (èl-i-ca'm'péne), *n.*, aunée, *f.*

elect (è-lèate), *adj.*, élu, choisi, nommé.

elect, *n.*, élu, *m.*

elect, *v.a.*, élire, nommer, choisir.

election, *n.*, élection,*f.* ; choix, *m.*

electioneer (-ire),*v.n.*, briguer les suffrages à une élection.

elective, *adj.*, électif, électoral.

electively, *adv.*, par choix ; par élection.

elector (-teur), *n.*, électeur, *m.*

electoral, *adj.*, électoral, d'électeur.

electorate, *n.*, électorat, *m.*

electric, *or* **electrical** (è-lèc-), *adj.*, électrique.

electric, *n.*, corps électrique non conducteur. *m.*

electrically,*adv.*, d'une manière électrique.

electrician (-trisha'ne), *n.*, électricien ; électrographe, *m.*

electricity, *n.*, électricité, *f.*

electrifiable (-faï-a-b'l), *adj.*, électrisable.

electrification (-fi-ké-), *n.*, électrisation, *f.*

electrify (-fa'ye), *v.a.*, électriser.

electrify, *v.n.*, s'électriser.

electrometer (-trom'i-), *n.*, électromètre, *m.*

electrophorus (i-lèc-), *n.*, électrophore, *m.*

electroscope (è-lèc-tro-scôpe), *n.*, électroscope, *m.*

electuary (è-lèct'iou-), *n.*, électuaire, *m.*

eleemosynary (èl-i-môz'-),*adj.*, de charité ; qui vit d'aumônes.

eleemosynary, *n.*, personne qui vit d'aumône ,*f.*

elegance.or **elegancy** (èl-i-), n.,élégance,f.
elegant, adj., élégant.
elegantly, adv., élégamment.
elegiac (è-li-dji-),or **elegiacal** (èl-i-djaï-a-), adj., élégiaque.
elegiac (èl-i-djaï-ake, ou è-li-dji-), n., vers élégiaque, m.
elegist, n., élégiaque; poète élégiaque, m.
elegit (è-lî-djite), n., (jur.) droit de saisir les bie·· s meubles et la moitié du revenu des terres, m.
elegy (èl'i-dji), n., élégie, f.
element (èl-i-), n., élément, m.
elemental, adj., élémentaire.
elementally, adv., littéralement.
elementarity, n., état élémentaire, m.
elementary, adj., élémentaire.
elephant (èl'i-), n., éléphant, m.
elephant-driver (-draïv'-), n., cornac, m.
elephantiasis (-taï-a-cice), n., éléphantiasis, f.
elephantine, adj., éléphantin.
elevate (èl-i-véte), v.a., élever, égayer, réjouir; exalter.
elevate, or **elevated**, adj., élevé.
elevation (èl-i-vé-), n., élévation, f.
elevator (-vé-teur), n., personne qui élève, f.; (anat.) élévateur, m.
elevatory (-vé-teuri), adj., élevant, qui élève.
elevatory, n., (surg.) élévatoire, m.
eleven (i-lèv'n), adj., onze.
eleventh (i-lèv'n'th), adj., onzième.
elf (èlfe), n. (elves), esprit follet, m.; fée, f.; lutin; nabot, m., nabote, f.
elf, v.a., entortiller les cheveux de telle manière qu'on ne puisse les démêler.
elfin, adj., des lutins.
elfin, n., nabot, m., nabote, f.; moutard, m.
elfish, adj., des lutins.
elf-lock, n., cheveux tordus en boucles comme par les lutins, m.pl.
elicit (è-), v.a., faire jaillir ; faire sortir; déduire.
elide, v.a., détruire, faire disparaître; (gram.) élider.
eligibility (èl-i-dji-), n., éligibilité ; préférence, f. ; avantage, m. ; convenance, f.
eligible (-dji-b'l), adj., éligible ; désirable, convenable.
eligibleness, n., avantage, m. ; préférence, f.
eligibly, adv., convenablement, avantageusement.
eliminate (è-li'm-), v.a., éliminer, chasser, expulser; élargir, affranchir.
elimination (-né-), n., élimination ; expulsion, f.
eliquate (èl-i-kwéte), v.a., (chem.)soumettre à la liquation, faire ressuer.
eliquation (-kwé-), n., liquation, f.; ressuage, m.
elision (i-lij'eune), n., élision ; division, f.
elisor (è-laï-çor), n., personne chargée de désigner le jury en cas de récusation contre le shérif, f.
elite (é-lite), n., élite, f.
elixate (è-liks-'), v.a., (ant.) faire cuire dans l'eau.
elixation (è-liks'é-), n., (ant.) élixation ; digestion, f.
elixir (i-liks-eur), n., élixir, m.; quintessence, f.
elk (èlke), n., (mam.) élan, m.
elke (èlke), n., (orni.) cygne sauvage, m.
ell, n., aune, f.
ellipsis, n. (ellipses), ellipse, f.
ellipsoid (-soïde), n., ellipsoïde, m.
elliptic, or **elliptical**, adj., elliptique.
elliptically, adv., elliptiquement.

ellipticity, n., ellipticité, f.
elm (èlme), n., (bot.) orme, m. Young —; ormeau, m.
elm-grove (-grôve), n., ormaie, f.
elocution (-kiou-), n., élocution ; parole, faculté de parler, f.
elogium, or **elogy** (èl'o-djieume, -dji), n. V. **eulogium**.
eloigne, or **eloin** (è-loi-ine), v.a., bannir; éloigner.
elongate, v.a., allonger; éloigner.
elongation (-ghé-), n., prolongement ; éloignement, m. ; (astron., med.) élongation, f.
elope (è-lôpe), v.n., quitter clandestinement la maison conjugale, la maison paternelle ; s'enfuir.
elopement, n., enlèvement consenti, m. ; fuite, f.
elops (i-lopse), n., espèce de poisson des mers équatoriales, f.
eloquence (èl-o-kwè'n'-), n., éloquence, f.
eloquent, adj., éloquent.
eloquently, adv., éloquemment.
else (èlse), adj., autre. Nothing — ; rien autre. What —? vous faut-il autre chose? quoi encore? quoi de plus?
else, adv., autrement; sans quoi.
elsewhere (èls'hwère), adv., ailleurs.
elucidate (è-liou-ci-), v.a., rendre lucide, éclaircir, élucider.
elucidation, n., éclaircissement, m. ; élucidation, f.
elucidator (è-liou-ci-dé-teur), n., commentateur, m.
elude (è-lioude), v.a., éluder, échapper à.
eludible (-'i-b'l), adj., qui peut être éludé.
elusive, adj., trompeur.
elute (è-lioute), v.a., laver, nettoyer.
elutriate (è-liou-), v.a., (chem.) décanter.
elysian (i-lij'i-a'ne), adj., élyséen. — **fields;** champs élysées, m.pl.
elysium (i-lij'i-eume), n., Élysée, m.
elytron (èl'i-), n. (elytra), élytre, m.
emaciate (i-mé-shi-éte), v.n., maigrir ; se décharner ; (bot.) s'étioler.
emaciate (i-mé-shi-éte), v.a., amaigrir ; devenir décharné ; (bot.) étioler.
emaciate, adj., maigre, décharné, émacié.
emaciation (-shi-é-), n., émaciation, maigreur, f. ; état décharné ; (bot.) étiolement, m.
emanate, v.n., émaner.
emanation (-né-), n., émanation, f.
emanative, adj., émané.
emancipate, v.a., émanciper, affranchir.
emancipate, or **emancipated** (-pét'ède), adj., émancipé.
emancipation (-pé-), n., émancipation, f. ; affranchissement, m.
emarginate (-mâr-dji-), v.a., ôter la marge.
emasculate (-kiou-), v.a., émasculer, châtrer; (fig.) affaiblir, énerver.
emasculate, adj., émasculé, châtré; efféminé.
emasculation (-kiou-lé-),n., émasculation ; mollesse, f.
embale, v.a., emballer.
embalm (è'm'bâ-me), v.a., embaumer; conserver.
embalmer, n., embaumeur, m.
embalming, n., embaumement, m.
embank, v.a., faire une digue, une levée; remblayer; encaisser.
embankment, n., levée, digue, f.; remblai; quai ; encaissement, m.
embargo (-bâr-), n., embargo, m.
embargo (-bâr-), v.a., mettre un embargo sur.
embark (-bârke), v.a., embarquer ; (fig.) engager.
embark, v.n., s'embarquer ; (fig.) s'engager.
embarkation (-ké-), n., embarquement, m.

embarrass, *v.a.*, embarrasser; gêner.

embarrassing, *adj.*, embarrassant.

embarrassment, *n.*, embarras; (in one's business—*des affaires*) dérangement, *m.*, gêne, *f.*

embassador (-deur), *n. V.* **ambassador**.

embassy, *n.*, ambassade, *f.*

embattle (-bat't'l), *v.a.*, ranger en ordre de bataille; (arch.) créneler.

embattle, *v.n.*, être rangé en ordre de bataille.

embattled (-bat't'l'de), *adj.*, crénelé.

embattlement, *n.*, crénelure, *f.*

embay (-bè), *v.a.*, renfermer dans une baie; baigner.

embed (-bède), *v.a.*, enfouir; emboîter.

embellish. *v.a.*, embellir.

embellishment. *n.*, embellissement, *m.*

ember-days (-dèze), *n.pl.*, Quatre-Temps, *m.pl.*

embers (-beurze), *n.pl.*, braise; cendre, *f.sing.*

ember-week (-wîke), *n.*, semaine des Quatre-Temps, *f.*

embezzle (-bèz'z'l), *v.a.*, détourner, dissiper.

embezzlement, *n.*, détournement, *m.*

embezzler, *n.*, auteur d'un détournement, *m.*

embitter, *v.a.*, rendre amer; (fig.) abreuver d'amertume, empoisonner.

emblaze, *or* **emblazon** (-blé-z'n), *v.a.*, blasonner; (fig.) embellir; publier, proclamer; exalter.

emblazoner, *n.*, écrivain héraldique; (fig.) écrivain pompeux, *m.*

emblazoury, *n.*, blason, *m.*; armes, armoiries, *f.pl.*

emblem, *n.*, emblème, *m.*

emblem, *v.a.*, être l'emblème de; représenter.

emblematic, *or* **emblematical**, *adj.*, emblématique.

emblematically, *adv.*, d'une manière emblématique.

emblematist, *n.*, auteur d'emblèmes, *m.*

emblematize (è'm-blè'm-a-taïze), *v.a.*, (ant.) figurer, représenter par emblèmes.

emblements, *n.pl.*, (agri.) fruits d'un terrain cultivé par le fermier, lesquels lui appartiennent quoique son bail expire avant la récolte, *m.pl.*

embody, *v.n.*, revêtir d'un corps; personnifier; incorporer.

embolden, *v.a.*, enhardir.

embolism, *n.*, embolisme; temps intercalé, *m.*

embosom (-bou-zeume), *v.a.*, placer au sein; ensevelir.

emboss, *v.a.*, relever en bosse; (gold.) bosseler; (linen—*le linge*) brocher; (cutlery—*coutellerie*) damasquiner; (sculpt.) travailler en bosse; graver en relief.

embossing, *n.*, relief; (arch.) bossage; (gold.) bosselage, *m.*; (of cutlery—*coutellerie*) damasquinerie, *f.*

embossment, *n.*, relief, *m.*; (sculpt.) bosse, *f.*

embottle (-bot't'l), *v.a.*, mettre en bouteilles.

embowel (-baou'èl), *v.a.*, arracher les entrailles; éventrer.

embrace, *n.*, embrassement, *m.*; étreinte, *f.*

embrace, *v.a.*, embrasser; saisir; accepter.

embracement, *n.*, embrassement, *m.*; étreinte, *f.*

embracer. *n.*, personne qui embrasse, *f.*; (of a jury—*d'un jury*) suborneur, *m.*

embrasure (-bréj'eur), *n.*, embrasure, *f.*

embrocate, *v.a.*, fomenter; bassiner.

embrocation (-ké-), *n.*, embrocation, *f.*

embroider (-broi-id'-), *v.a.*, broder.

embroiderer. *n.*, brodeur, *m.*; brodeuse, *f.*

embroidery, *n.*, broderie, *f.*

embroil (-broi-il), *v.a.*, brouiller, embrouiller; bouleverser.

embroilment, *n.*, embrouillement; désordre, *m.*; brouille, brouillerie, *f.*

embryo (è'm'-bri-ô), *or* **embryon** (-one), *n.*, embryon, *m.*

embryo, *or* **embryon**, *adj.*, d'embryon; à l'état d'embryon.

embryology (-dji), *n.*, embryologie, *f.*

emendable (-'a-b'l), *adj.*, corrigible.

emendation (-dé-), *n.*, correction, réforme, *f.*

emendator (-dé-teur), *a.*, correcteur, *m.*

emerald (èm-è-), *n.*, émeraude, *f.*

emerge (è-meurdge), *v.n.*, surgir; sortir.

emergence, *or* **emergency**, *n.*, action de surgir; circonstance imprévue; occurrence; conjoncture, *f.*

emergent (è-meur-djè'n'te), *adj.*, qui surgit; naissant; critique, difficile; (phys.) émergent. Upon — occasions; *dans les circonstances critiques.*

emeroids (èm'èr-oïdze), *n.pl.*, hémorroïdes, *f.pl.*

emersion (i-meur-sheune), *n.*, émersion; sortie, *f.*

emery (èm-èr-i), *n.*, émeri, *m.*

emetic (è-mèt'ike), *n.*, émétique, *m.*

emetic, *or* **emetical**, *adj.*, émétique.

emetically, *adv.*, comme un émétique.

emigrant (èm'i-), *n.*, émigrant, *m.*, émigrante, *f.*; (political—*politique*) émigré, *m.*, émigrée, *f.*

emigrant, *adj.*, émigrant.

emigrate, *v.n.*, émigrer.

emigration (-gré-), *n.*, émigration, *f.*

eminence, *or* **eminency** (èm-i-), *n.*, éminence, élévation; (fig.) grandeur, distinction, *f.* His — ; *son Éminence, f.*

eminent, *adj.*, éminent, élevé; distingué.

eminently, *adv.*, éminemment.

emir (i-mir), *n.*, émir.

emissary (èm'-), *n.*, émissaire, *m.*

emissary, *adj.*, d'émissaire; (anat.) excrétoire, excréteur.

emission (i-mish'eune), *n.*, émission, *f.*

emit (è-mite), *v.a.*, jeter, lancer, exhaler.

emmet (èm'mète), *n.*, fourmi, *f.*

emmew (èm'miou), *v.a.*, encager, enfermer.

emollescence (èm'-), *n.*, (metal.) amollissement, *m.*

emolliate (i-mol'yi-'éte), *v.a.*, amollir.

emollient (è-), *n.*, émollient, *m.*

emollient, *adj.*, émollient.

emollition, *n.*, amollissement, *m.*

emolument (è-mol'iou-), *n.*, émolument, avantage, *m.*

emotion (è-mô-), *n.*, émotion, *f.*

empale (è'm'pèle), *v.a.*, (to fortify—*fortifier*) palissader; (a man—*un homme*) empaler; (her.) partager; (fig.) environner.

empalement, *n.*, empalement, pal, *m.*

empanel (è'm'pa'n'èl), *v.a.*, (jur.) dresser la liste du jury; inscrire sur la liste du jury.

empassion (è'm'pash'-), *v.a.*, affecter, émouvoir, passionner.

emperor (è'm'peur'eur), *n.*, empereur, *m.*

emphasis (è'm'pha-cice), *n.* (*emphases*), force; énergie; emphase, *f.*; accent, *m.*

emphasize (-çaize), *v.a.*, appuyer sur un mot; enchérir, renchérir sur; prononcer avec force.

emphatic, *or* **emphatical**, *adj.*, énergique; expressif; accentué; emphatique.

emphatically, *adj.*, énergiquement, expressivement; avec force; d'une manière accentuée.

emphysema (è'm'fi-ci-), *n.*, emphysème, *m.*

emphyteusis (è'm'fi-tiou-cice), *n.*, emphytéose, *f.*

empire (è'm'paeur), n., empire, m.
empiric (è'm'-), n., empirique, m.
empiric, or **empirical**, adj., versé dans les expériences ; empirique.
empirically, adv., d'après des expériences ; empiriquement.
emplaster (è'm'plâs'-), v.a., (ant.) couvrir d'un emplâtre.
emplastic (è'm'plas'-), adj., (ant.) gluant, visqueux.
employ (è'm'plo'ye), n., emploi, m.
employ, v.a., employer, se servir de.
employable (-a-b'l), adj., qui peut servir ; que l'on peut employer ; employable.
employer, n., personne qui emploie, f. ; maître, m., maîtresse, f. ; patron, m., patronne, f. ; chef ; (com.) commettant, m.
employment, n., emploi, m. ; occupation, f.
empoison (è'm'pwaï-z'n), v.a., empoisonner.
empoisoner, n., empoisonneur, m., empoisonneuse, f.
empoisonment, n., empoisonnement, m.
emporium (è'm'pô-ri-), n., grand marché ; entrepôt, m.
empoverish (è'm'pov'èr'-), v.n., appauvrir.
empoverisher, n., chose, personne, qui appauvrit, f.
empoverishment, n., appauvrissement, m.
empower (è'm'pa'weur), v.a., autoriser, charger.
empress (è'm'-), n., impératrice, f.
emptier (è'm'ti-), n., videur, m., videuse, f.
emptiness (è'm'ti-), n., état de ce qui est vide ; vide, m. ; (fig.) vanité, inanité, f., néant, m.
empty (è'm'ti), v.a., vider.
empty, adj., vide ; à vide ; (fig.) vain, stérile.
empurple (è'm'peur'p'l), v.a., empourprer.
empyema (è'm'pi-î-), n., empyème, m.
empyreal, or **empyrean** (è'm'pir'i-), adj., empyrée.
empyrean, n., Empyrée, m.
empyreuma (è'm'pi-rou-), n., empyreume, m.
emulate (èm'iou-), v.a., s'efforcer d'égaler ; rivaliser avec.
emulation (-lé-), n., émulation ; rivalité, f.
emulative (-lé-), adj., émulatif.
emulator (-lé-teur), n., émule, m.,f. ; émulateur, m.
emulgent (è-meul-djè'n'te), adj., émulgent.
emulous, adj., émule, jaloux.
emulously, adv., avec émulation ; à l'envi.
emulsion (è-meul-), n., émulsion, f.
emulsive, adj., émulsif.
emunctory (è-meu'n'gn'k'to-), n., émonctoire, m.
enable (èn'é-b'l), v.a., rendre capable, mettre à même ; donner le moyen à ; mettre en état.
enact (èn'-), v.a., ordonner, arrêter ; (a law —une loi) passer, établir, faire, décréter ; (a part —un rôle) représenter, remplir, jouer, faire.
enactment, n., établissement d'une loi, m. ; ordonnance, f. ; décret ; acte législatif, m.
enactor (-'eur), n., auteur, m.
enallage (èn'al'ladje), n., (gram.) énallage, f.
enamel (èn'am'èle), n., émail, m.
enamel, v.a., émailler.
enameller, or **enamellist**, n., émailleur, m.
enamelling, n., émaillure, f.
enamel-work (-weurke), n., émaillure, f.
enamorado (èn'-), n., personne vivement éprise, f.
enamour (èn'am'eur), v.a., rendre amoureux ; rendre épris ; amouracher. To be —ed with ; être épris de, être amoureux de.
enarthrosis (èn'ar-thrô-cice), n., énarthrose, f.
enate (è-), adj., (ant.) qui naît de ; né de.

encage (è'n'kédje), v.a., encager ; enfermer dans une cage.
encamp (è'n'-), v.a. and n., camper.
encampment, n., campement, m.
encaustic (è'n'-), adj., (paint.) encaustique.
encaustic, n., peinture encaustique, f.
encave (è'n'-), v.a., encaver ; cacher.
enceinte (an'gn'sé'n'te), adj., enceinte.
enceinte, n., (fort.) enceinte, f.
encephalon (è'n'cèf'a-lone), n., (anat.) encéphale, m.
enchain (è'n'tshéne), v.a., enchaîner.
enchant (è'n'tshâ'n'te), v.a., enchanter.
enchanter, n., enchanteur, m.
enchanting, adj., enchanteur.
enchantingly, adv., par enchantement ; à ravir.
enchantment, n., enchantement, m.
enchantress, n., enchanteresse, f.
enchase (è'n'tshéce), v.a., enchâsser ; c'eseler ; enrichir de diamants, &c. ; peindre, représenter.
encircle (è'n'ceur'k'l), v.a., environner ; ceindre, entourer ; embrasser.
enclitic (è'n'-), n., (gram.) enclitique, f.
enclose (è'n'clôze), v.a., enclore, clore ; entourer, environner ; (parcels, letters—paquets, lettres) renfermer.
enclosed (-klôz'de), adj., entouré, environné ; (of parcels, letters—de paquets, de lettres) inclus, ci-inclus, sous ce pli.
encloser, n., personne qui renferme, f.
enclosure (-klôjeur), n., action de clore ; clôture, f. ; (space enclosed—espace) enclos, m., enceinte ; (thing enclosed—chose) chose incluse, f.
encloud (è'n'claoude), v.a., couvrir d'un nuage, de ténèbres ; envelopper.
encomiast (è'n'cô-), n., panégyriste, louangeur, m.
encomiastic, or **encomiastical**, adj., louangeur, laudatif.
encomiastically, adv., en panégyriste ; en forme de panégyrique.
encomium (è'n'cô-mi-), n., éloge, panégyrique, m.
encompass (è'n'keu'm'-), v.a., entourer ; enfermer.
encompassment, n., action d'entourer ; (fig.) circonlocution, f.
encore (an'gn'kôre), adv., bis.
encore, v.a., crier bis à.
encounter (è'n'caou'n'-), n., rencontre ; mêlée, f. ; incident, m.
encounter, v.a., rencontrer, affronter ; aborder ; aller au-devant de.
encounter, v.n., se rencontrer hostilement ; engager le combat ; s'affronter.
encounterer, n., personne qui aborde les autres, f. ; antagoniste, adversaire, m.
encourage (è'n'keur-édje), v.a., encourager.
encouragement, n., encouragement, m.
encourager, n., protecteur, m.
encouraging, adj., encourageant.
encouragingly, adv., d'une manière encourageante.
encroach (è'n'crôtshe), v.n., empiéter, abuser ; usurper.
encroacher, n., personne qui empiète, f. ; usurpateur, m., usurpatrice, f.
encroaching, adj., qui empiète toujours.
encroachingly, adv., par empiétement.
encroachment, n., empiétement, m. ; usurpation, f.
encumber (è'n'keu'm'-), v.a., encombrer, embarrasser.
encumbrance, n., encombrement, embarras, obstacle, m. ; charge, f.
encyclical (è'n'-), adj., encyclique.
encyclopedia, or **encyclopædia** (è'n'caï-clo-pî-), n., encyclopédie, f.
encyclopedian (è'n'ci-clô-pî-), **encyclo-**

pedic, *or* **encyclopedical** (è'n'çaï-clŏ-péd'-), *adj.,* encyclopédique.

encyclopedist (è'n'çaï-clo-pî-), *n.,* encyclopédiste, *m.*

encysted (è'n'cist'-ŏde), *adj.,* (med.) enkysté.

end (è'n'de), *n.,* bout, *m.* ; extrémité ; fin, *f.* ; but, objet, *m.,* fin, *f.,* intérêt ; (of time—*de temps*) bout, *m.* At the — of two months ; *au bout de deux mois.* Approaching —; *fin prochaine.* Odd — ; reste, *m.* By the — of ; *avant la fin de.* To no — ; *sans effet ; en vain.* To be at an — ; *être arrivé à sa fin.* To attain one's —s ; *parvenir à son but.* To come to a bad — ; *finir mal ; faire une mauvaise fin.* To make an — of ; *en finir avec.* To put an — to ; *mettre fin à ; mettre un terme à.*

end, *v.a.,* finir ; terminer ; achever.

end, *v.n.,* finir ; se terminer.

endamage (è'n'da'm'édje), *v.a.,* endommager, nuire à.

endamagement, *n.,* détriment, préjudice, *m.*

endanger (è'n'da'n'djeur), *v.a.,* exposer au danger, mettre en danger.

endangering, *n.,* tort, préjudice, détriment, *m.*

endear (è'n'dîre), *v.a.,* faire aimer, rendre cher.

endearment, *n.,* caresse, tendresse, *f.*

endeavour (è'n'dèv'eur), *n.,* effort, travail ; soin, *m.* ; tentative, *f.*

endeavour, *v.n.,* tâcher, s'efforcer, essayer, tenter.

endeavourer, *n.,* personne qui fait des efforts, qui s'efforce, *f.*

endemic (è'n'dè'm'-), *or* **endemial** (è'n'dî-), *adj.,* endémique.

ending (è'n'd'-), *n.,* fin, conclusion ; (gram.) terminaison, désinence, *f.*

endive (è'n'-), *n.,* chicorée, endive, escarole, *f.*

endless, *adj.,* infini, sans fin ; éternel.

endlessly, *adv.,* à l'infini ; éternellement.

endlessness, *n.,* perpétuité, *f.*

endorse (è'n'-), *v.n.,* (com.) endosser ; (fig.) sanctionner.

endorsee (è'n'dorsî), *n.,* (com.) porteur, *m.*

endorsement, *n.,* suscription *f.* ; (com.) endossement, endos, *m.* ; (fig.) sanction, *f.*

endorser, *n.,* (com.) endosseur, *m.*

endow (è'n'daou), *v.a.,* douer, doter.

endowment, *n.,* dotation, *f.* ; (fig.) don, *m.,* qualité, *f.*

end-piece (-pîce), *n.,* (tech.) bout, *m.*

endue (è'n'diou), *v.a.,* douer ; fournir ; revêtir ; investir.

endurable (è'n'diour'a-b'l), *adj.,* supportable.

endurance (è'n'diour'-), *n.,* patience, *f.* ; pouvoir d'endurer, *m.* ; souffrance, *f.*

endure (è'n'dioure), *v.n.,* durer ; endurer la souffrance.

endure, *v.a.,* endurer, souffrir, supporter.

endurer, *n.,* personne qui endure, *f.*

endways (è'n'd'wèze), *or* **endwise** (-waïze), *adv.,* bout à bout ; debout, perpendiculaire ; de champ.

eneid (è-ni-ide), *n.,* Enéide, *f.*

enemy (è-ni-mi), *n.,* ennemi, *m.,* ennemie, *f.*

energetic, *or* **energetical** (è-nèr-djèt'-), *adj.,* énergique.

energetically, *adv.,* énergiquement.

energize (è'n'èrdjaize), *v.a.,* donner de l'énergie à.

energumen (è'n'èr'ghiou-mène), *n.,* énergumène, démoniaque, *m.f.*

energy (è'n'èr-dji), *n.,* énergie, force, *f.*

enervate (è-neur-), *v.a.,* énerver.

enervation (-vé-), *n.,* état énervé, affaiblissement, *m.* ; (vet.) énervation, *f.*

enfeeble (èn'fi-b'l), *v.a.,* affaiblir.

enfeeblement, *n.,* affaiblissement, *m.*

enfeoff (è'n'fèfe), *v.a.,* inféoder.

enfeoffment, *n.,* inféodation, *f.*

enfilade (è'n'fi-léde), *n.,* enfilade, *f.*

enfilade, *v.a.,* enfiler.

enforce (è'n'fôr'-), *v.a.,* donner de la force à ; faire exécuter ; appliquer avec rigueur ; (fig.) fortifier.

enforceable (-'a-b'l), *adj.,* que l'on peut imposer ; qui peut être imposé.

enforcedly (-'èd'li), *adv.,* forcément ; de force.

enforcement, *n.,* acte de force, *m.* ; force ; action d'imposer de force ; exécution par la force, *f.*

enforcer, *n.,* personne qui emploie la force, *f.* ; agent, *m.*

enfranchise (è'n'fra'n'shize), *v.a.,* affranchir ; conférer droit de bourgeoisie à ; naturaliser.

enfranchisement, *n.,* affranchissement, *m.* ; admission au droit de bourgeoisie ; naturalisation, *f.*

enfranchiser, *n.,* personne qui affranchit, *f.*

engage (è'n'ghédje), *v.a.,* engager ; occuper ; (fig.) attaquer, combattre.

engage, *v.n.,* s'engager ; engager le combat ; livrer combat.

engagement, *n.,* engagement, *m.* ; occupation, *f.* ; (milit.) combat, *m.*

engaging, *adj.,* engageant, prévenant.

engagingly, *adv.,* d'une manière engageante.

engarrison (è'n'gar-ri-s'n), *v.a.,* mettre en garnison.

engender (è'n'djè'n'-), *v.a.,* engendrer, faire naître.

engender, *v.n.,* s'engendrer.

engine (è'n'djine), *n.,* machine, *f.* ; instrument ; (fig.) levier, moyen, agent, *m.* Fire- — ; *pompe à incendie, f.* Steam- — ; *machine à vapeur.* Single-acting — ; *machine à simple effet.* Double-acting — ; *machine à double effet.* Ten-horse power — ; *machine de la force de dix chevaux.* High-pressure — ; *machine à haute pression.*

engine-driver (-draiv'-), *n.,* conducteur de machines, *m.*

engineer (è'n'dji-nîre), *n.,* ingénieur ; (milit.) soldat du génie, officier du génie, *m.* Civil — ; *ingénieur civil.*

engineering, *n.,* art de l'ingénieur ; (milit.) génie, *m.*

engineering, *adj.,* de l'art de l'ingénieur ; du génie.

engine-house (-haouce), *n.,* bâtiment pour la machine ; dépôt de pompes à incendie, *m.*

engine-maker (-mék'-), *n.,* constructeur de machines ; mécanicien, *m.*

engine-making, *n.,* construction de machines, *f.*

engine-man, *n.,* machiniste ; (of steam-engines—*de machines à vapeur*) mécanicien ; ouvrier mécanicien, *m.*

engine-room (-roume), *n.,* chambre de la machine, *f.*

enginery (è'n'dji'n'ri), *n.,* génie, *m.* ; artillerie, *f.*

engine-shaft (-shâfte), *n.,* puits de machine, *m.*

engine-tender (-tè'n'd'-), *n.,* tender de machine, *m.*

engird (è'n'gheurde), *v.a.,* entourer, environner.

english (ign'glishe), *adj.,* anglais.

english, *n.,* Anglais ; (print.) saint-augustin, *m.*

english, *v.a.,* rendre en Anglais.

englishman, *n.,* Anglais, *m.*

englishwoman (-woum'-), *n.,* Anglaise, *f.*

23*

engorge (è'n'gordje), *v.a.*, gorger.

engorge, *v.n.*, se gorger de.

engrail (è'n'gréle), *v.a.*, engrêler.

engrain (è'n'gréne), *v.a.*, teindre en laine; teindre foncé.

engrave (è'n'-), *v.a.*, graver.

engraver ('-grév'-), *n.*, graveur, *m.*

engraving, *n.*, gravure, *f.* Dealer in —s; *marchand l'estampes, m.* Copper-plate —; *gravure en cuille-douce.* Stroke- —; *gravure au burin.* Wood- —; *gravure sur bois.* Steel- —; *gravure sur acier.*

engross (è'n'grôce), *v.a.*, (to copy—*copier*) grossoyer; (to forestall—*monopoliser*) accaparer; (to occupy—*occuper*) absorber.

engrosser, *n.*, personne qui grossoie, *f.*; (forestaller—*monopoleur*) accapareur, *m.*

engrossment, *n.*, action de grossoyer, *f.*; (forestalling—*accaparer*) accaparement, *m.*

enhance (è'n'hâ'n'ce), *v.a.*, enchérir, augmenter; rehausser.

enhancement, *n.*, enchérissement, *m.*; augmentation, *f.*

enigma (è-nig-), *n.*, énigme, *f.*

enigmatical, *adj.*, énigmatique; obscur.

enigmatically, *adv.*, énigmatiquement; obscurément.

enigmatist, *n.*, faiseur d'énigmes, *m.*

enjoin (è'n'djoï'ne), *v.a.*, enjoindre, prescrire.

enjoinment, *n.*, injonction, *f.*

enjoy (è'n'djo'é), *v.a.*, jouir, jouir de; posséder; goûter.

enjoyer, *n.*, personne qui jouit, *f.*

enjoyment, *n.*, jouissance, *f.*

enkindle (è'n'ki'n'd'l), *v.a.*, enflammer; exciter.

enlarge (è'n'lârdje), *v.a.*, agrandir, augmenter, étendre; (to set free—*mettre en liberté*) élargir.

enlarge, *v.n.*, grandir, s'agrandir, s'étendre.

enlargement, *n.*, agrandissement, accroissement, *m.*; augmentation, *f.*; (from prison—*d'emprisonnement*) élargissement, *m.*; (med.) dilatation, *f.*; (of the heart—*du cœur*) hypertrophie, *f.*; anévrisme, *m.*

enlight (è'n'laïte) (ant.), *or* **enlighten** (-laï-t'n), *v.a.*, illuminer; éclairer.

enlightener, *n.*, personne qui éclaire, *f.*

enlink (è'n'-), *v.a.*, enchaîner, lier.

enlist, *v.a.*, enrôler, inscrire; engager.

enlist, *v.n.*, s'enrôler.

enlistment, *n.*, enrôlement, engagement, *m.*

enliven (è'n'laïv'n), *v.a.*, vivifier; égayer, animer.

enlivener, *n.*, personne qui vivifie, qui égaie; chose qui vivifie, qui égaie, *f.*

enlivening, *adj.*, qui anime; qui égaie.

enmesh (è'n'mèshe), *v.a.*, (ant.) prendre au filet; embarrasser; attraper, prendre au piège.

enmity (è'n'-), *n.*, inimitié, *f.*

enneagon (è'n'ni-), *n.*, ennéagone, *m.*

enneandria (è'n'ni-), *n.*, (bot.) ennéandrie, *f.*

ennoble (è'n'nô-b'l), *v.a.*, anoblir; ennoblir; illustrer.

ennoblement, *n.*, anoblissement, *m.*

enormity (è-), *n.*, énormité; atrocité, *f.*; crime énorme, *m.*; irrégularité, *f.*

enormous, *adj.*, énorme; monstrueux; irrégulier.

enormously, *adv.*, énormément.

enormousness, *n.*, énormité, *f.*, excès de grandeur, *m.*

enough (i-neufe), *adj.*, assez. More than —; *plus qu'il n'en faut.* That is —; *c'en est assez; assez; en voilà assez.*

enrage (è'n'rédje), *v.a.*, faire enrager; irriter; exaspérer.

enrank (è'n'-), *v.a.*, mettre en rangs.

enrapt (è'n'-), *adj.*, (ant.) ravi.

enrapture (è'n'rapt'ioure), *v.a.*, transporter, ravir.

enravish (è'n'-), *v.a.*, ravir, transporter en extase.

enravishment, *n.*, ravissement, *m.*; extase, *f.*

enrich (è'n'ritshe), *v.a.*, enrichir.

enrichment, *n.*, enrichissement, *m.*

enridge (è'n'-), *v.a.*, mettre en sillons.

enring (è'n'-), *v.a.*, (ant.) entourer.

enrobe (è'n'rôbe), *v.a.*, vêtir, revêtir.

enroll (è'n'rôl), *v.a.*, enrôler, enregistrer.

enroller, *n.*, personne qui enregistre, qui enrôle, *f.*

enrolment, *n.*, enrôlement; enregistrement, *m.*

enroot (è'n'route), *v.a.*, enraciner; entrelacer.

enround (è'n'raou'n'de), *v.a.*, (ant.) environner, entourer.

ensanguine (è'n'sangn'gwine), *v.a.*, ensanglanter.

enschedule (è'n'skèd'ioul, *ou* -shèd'-), *v.a.*, inscrire; rapporter.

ensconce (è'n'-), *v.a.*, fortifier, mettre à couvert.

enseam (è'n'sîme), *v.a.*, coudre, ourler.

ensear (è'n'sîre), *v.a.*, cautériser; dessécher.

enshield (è'n'shîlde), *v.a.*, (ant.) couvrir; protéger.

enshrine (è'n'shraïne), *v.a.*, enchâsser; enfermer; placer au rang des saints.

enshroud (è'n'shraoude), *v.a.*, couvrir, abriter.

ensign (è'n'saïne), *n.*, enseigne, *f.*; signal; drapeau; (nav.) pavillon de poupe; (milit.) drapeau; (pers.) porte-drapeau, enseigne, *m.*

ensign-bearer (-bèr'-), *n.*, porte-drapeau, *m.*

ensigncy (è'n'si'n'ci), *n.*, grade de porte-drapeau, *m.*

enslave (è'n'-), *v.a.*, réduire à l'esclavage; asservir; rendre esclave, assujettir.

enslavement, *n.*, esclavage, asservissement, *m.*

enslaver, *n.*, personne, personne qui réduit à l'esclavage, *f.*; despote, tyran.

ensober (è'n'sô'-), *v.a.*, (ant.) rendre sobre; modérer.

ensue (è'n'siou), *v.n.*, s'ensuivre.

ensuing, *adj.*, suivant; prochain.

ensure (è'n'shioure), *v.a.* *V.* **insure.**

entablature (è'n'tab-la-tioure), *or* **entablement** (-té-b'l-), *n.*, (arch.) entablement, *m.*

entail (è'n'téle), *n.*, bien substitué, *m.*; substitution, *f.*

entail, *v.a.*, imposer; (fig.) léguer; (jur.) substituer.

entailment, *n.*, transmission; (jur.) substitution, *f.*

entame (è'n'téme), *v.a.*, dompter, subjuguer.

entangle (è'n'tangn'g'l), *v.a.*, emmêler; empêtrer; enchevêtrer; engager; (fig.) embrouiller, embarrasser.

entanglement, *n.*, état de ce qui est emmêlé, empêtré; (fig.) embrouillement, embarras, *m.*

entangler, *n.*, personne qui embrouille, *f.*; brouillon, *m.*, brouillonne, *f.*

entasis (è'n'ta-cice), *n.*, (arch.) galbe, renflement, *m.*

enter (è'n'-), *v.a.*, entrer dans; (to register—*enregistrer*) inscrire, enregistrer; (jur.) (an action—*un procès*) intenter; (book-keeping—*tenue des livres*) porter, inscrire.

enter, *v.n.*, entrer. To — into; *entrer dans, prendre part à.* To — upon; *commencer; entrer dans; entrer en possession de.*

entering, *n.*, entrée, *f.*

enterprise (è'n'teur-praïze), *n.*, entreprise, *f.*

enterprise, *v.a.,* entreprendre.

enterpriser, *n.,* personne entreprenante. *f.*

entertain (è'n'teur-téne), *v.a.,* (to receive—*recevoir*) accueillir, recevoir ; (to amuse—*amuser*) divertir ; (to feast—*féter*) régaler ; (an idea, &c. —*une idée, &c.*) entretenir : concevoir ; (with vain hopes—*d'un vain espoir*) amuser ; (a proposal—*proposition*) accepter.

entertainer, *n.,* personne qui accueille, qui divertit, qui conçoit, qui régale, *f.* ; amphitryon, *m.*

entertainment, *n.,* accueil, *m.* ; hospitalité, *f.* ; (feast—*fête*) repas, banquet ; (amusement) divertissement, amusement, *m.*

entertissued (è'n'teur-tish'ioude), *adj.,* entremêlé.

entheastic (è'n'thi-), *adj.,* doué de l'énergie divine.

enthral (è'n'thrôl), *v.a.,* asservir ; assujettir, tenir en servitude.

enthrone (è'n'thrône), *v.a.,* placer sur un trône ; (a bishop—*un évéque*) introniser.

enthronize (è'n'thrô-naize), *v.a.,* (ant.). *V.* **enthrone.**

enthusiasm (è'n'thiou'zi-az'me), *n.,* enthousiasme *m.*

enthusiast, *n.,* enthousiaste. *m.*

enthusiastic, *or* **enthusiastical,** *adj.,* enthousiaste.

enthusiastically, *adv.,* avec enthousiasme.

enthymeme (è'n'thi-nιeme),*n.,*(log.)enthymème, *m.*

entice(è'n'taïce),*v.a.,*attirer, inciter ; tenter, séduire.

enticement, *n.,* attrait, appas, *m.* ; tentation, séduction, *f.*

enticer, *n.,* séducteur, *m.,* séductrice, *f.* ; (thing—*chose*) appât, *m.*

enticing,*adj.,* séduisant, tentant, tentateur.

enticingly, *adv.,* d'une manière séduisante.

entire (è'n'taeur), *adj.,* entier.

entirely, *adv.,* entièrement.

entireness, *n.,* état entier, *m.* ; intégrité, *f.*

entitle (è'n'taï-t'l), *v.a.,* intituler, appeler ; donner droit.

entity (è'n'-), *n.,* être, *m.* ; entité, *f.*

entoil (è'n'toïl), *v.a.,* prendre dans des filets ; enlacer.

entomb (è'n'toume), *v.a.,* ensevelir.

entombment (è'n'toum'mè'n'te), *n.,* sépulture, *f.*

entomological (è'n'to-mol'o-dji-), *adj.,* entomologique.

entomologist, *n.,* entomologiste, *m.*

entomology (è'n'to-mol-o-dji), *n.,* entomologie, *f.*

entozoon (è'n'to-zô-), *n.* (*entozoa*), (ent.) entozoaire, *m.*

entrails (è'n'trél'ze), *n.pl.,* entrailles, *f.pl.*

entrance (è'n'trä'n'ce), *n.,* entrée, *f.* ; (beginning—*commencement*)commencement ; (nav.) avant, *m.*

entrance (è'n-trä'n'ce), *v.a.,* jeter dans un sommeil léthargique ; (fig.) extasier, ravir.

entrap, *v.a.,* prendre au piège ; attraper.

entreat (è'n'trìte), *v.a.,* supplier ; prier avec instance.

entreaty, *n.,* instance ; prière ; sollicitation, *f.*

entrepot (angn't'r'pô), *n.,* entrepôt, *m.*

entresol (angu't'r'-), *n.,* entresol,*m.*

entry (è'n'-), *n.,* entrée, *f.* ; (at the customs—*douanes*) droit d'inscription, *m.,* déclaration d'entrée, *f.* ; (of the mass—*de la messe*) introït, *m.* ; (registration—*enregistrement*) inscription, *f.* (book-keeping—*comptabilité*) By double — ; *en partie double* : by single — ; *en partie simple.*

entwine (è'n'twaïne), *v.a.,* enlacer, entrelacer : tresser.

entwine, *v.n.,* s'enlacer, s'entrelacer.

enucleate (è-niou-cli-), *v.a.,* (ant.) expliquer ; résoudre ; éclaircir.

enucleation (è-niou-cli-é-), *n.,* explication,*f.*

enumerate (è-niou-mèr'-), *v.a.,* énumérer.

enumeration (è-niou-mèr-é-), *n.,* énumération, *f.*

enunciate (i-neu'n'shi-), *v.a.,* énoncer.

enunciation (-shi-é-), *n.,* énonciation, *f.* ; (geom.) énoncé, *m.*

enunciative, *or* **enunciatory** (-teurl), *adj.,* énonciatif.

enunciatively, *adv.,.* d'une manière énonciative.

envelop (è'n'vèl'-), *v.a.,* envelopper, entourer.

envelop, *n.,* enveloppe,*f.*

envelopment, *n.,* enveloppement, *m.*

envenom (è'n'vè'n'eume), *v.a.,* envenimer ; rendre odieux.

enviable (è'n'vi-a-b'l), *adj.,* digne d'envie ; enviable.

envier, *n.,* envieux, *m.,* envieuse, *f.*

envious, *adj.,* envieux.

enviously, *adv.,* avec envie.

environ (è'n'vai-), *v.a.,* environner.

environs (è'n'vaï-ro'n'ze, *ou* -vi-), *n.pl.,* environs, *m.pl.*

envoy (è'n'vo'ye), *n.,* envoyé ; messager, *m.*

envy (è'n'-), *n.,* envie, *f.*

envy, *v.a.,* envier ; porter envie à.

enwheel (è'n'hwil), *v.a.,* entourer.

eolic (è-), *adj.,* éolique.

epact (i-), *n.,* épacte, *f.*

epaule (è-) *n.,* (fort.) épaule, *f.*

epaulet (è-), *n.,* épaulette, *f.*

epaulment, *n.,* (fort.) épaulement, *m.*

epenthesis (è-pè'n'thi-cice), *n.* (*epentheses*), épenthèse, *f.*

epergne (é-peurne), *n.,* surtout de table, *m.*

ephelis (èf'i-lice), *n.,* (med.) éphélide ; tache de rousseur,*f.*

ephemera (è-fèm'i-), *n.,* (ent.) éphémère, *m.* ; (med.) fièvre éphémère, *f.*

ephemeral, ephemeric, *or* **ephemerous** (-i-ral, -èr-ic, -èr'eusse), *adj.,* éphémère.

ephemeris (è-fèm'i-rice), *n.* (*ephemerides*), éphémérides, *f.pl.*

ephemerist, *n.,* auteur d'éphémérides, *m.*

ephesian (è-fi-zia'ne), *adj.,* éphésien.

ephesian, *n.,* Éphésien, *m.,* Éphésienne, *f.*

ephod (èf'-), *n.,* éphod, *m.*

epic (èp'-), *adj.,* épique.

epic, *n.,* poème épique, *m.*

epicene (èp'i-cêne), *adj.,* (gram.) épicène.

epicranium (èp'i-crē-ni-), *n.,* (anat.) épicrâne, *m.*

epicure (èp'i-kioure), *n.,* épicurien, *m.,* épicurienne, *f.* ; gastronome, gourmet, *m.*

epicurean (èp'i-kiou-ri-), *adj.,* d'Épicure ; épicurien ; de gastronome.

epicurean, *n.,* épicurien, sectateur d'Épicure, *m.*

epicureanism, *n.,* épicurisme (doctrine).*m.*

epicurism, *n.,* épicurisme, *m.* ; gastronomie, *f.*

epidemic, *or* **epidemical** (èp'i-dèm'-), *adj.,* épidémique.

epidemic, *or* **epidemy** (èp'i-dè'm'-), *n.,* épidémie, *f.*

epidermis (èp'i-deur'mice), *n.,* épiderme, *m.*

epigastrium (èp'i-), *n.,* (anat.) épigastre,*m.*

epiglottis (èp'-), *n.,* (anat.) épiglotte, *f.*

epigram (èp'-), *n.,* épigramme, *f.*

epigrammatic, *or* **epigrammatical,** *adj.,* (of things—*des choses*) épigrammatique ; (pers.) qui emploie l'épigramme.

epigrammatist, *n.,* épigrammatiste, *m.*

epigraph (èp-), *n.,* épigraphe,*f.*

epilepsy (èp'i-lèp-), *n.,* épilepsie, *f.*

epileptic, adj., épilept'que.
epilogistic (è-pil'o-djis-), adj., en forme
d'épilogue.
epilogize, or epiloguize (è-pil-o-ga.ze),
v.n., prononcer un épilogue.
epilogue (èp'i-), n., épilogue, m.
epiloguize (è-pil-o-gaize), v.a., ajouter en
forme d'épilogue.
epiphany (i-pif-), n., épiphanie, f.
epiploce (è-pip-lo-ci), n., (rhet.) gradation.f.
epiploon (è-pip-lo-one), n., (anat.) épiploon, m.
episcopacy (è-pis-cô-), n., épiscopat, m.
episcopal, adj., épiscopal.
episcopalian, adj., épiscopal.
episcopalian, n., épiscopal, m.
episcopally, adv., épiscopalement.
episcopate, n., épiscopat, m.
episcopate (è-pis-), v.n., faire les fonctions
d'évêque.
episode (èp'i-çôde), n., épisode, m.
episodic, or episodical, adj., épisodique.
episodically, adv., en forme d'épisode.
epispastic (èp-), adj., (med.) épispastique.
epispastic, n., épispastique, n.
epistle (è-pis's'l), n., épître, f.
epistler, n., (letter-writer—auteur de lettres)
épistolaire, m.
epistolary (è-), adj., épistolaire.
epistolic, or epistolical, adj., en forme
d'épître.
epistolize (-laïze), v.n., écrire des épîtres.
epistolizer, n., auteur d'épîtres, m.
epistolographic (è-), adj., qui a rapport à
l'art épistolaire.
epistolography, n., art épistolaire, m.
epistyle (èp'i-staile). n., (arch.) épistyle, f.
epitaph (èp'-), n., épitaphe, f.
epitasis (è-pit'a-cice), n., (rhet.) épitase. f.
epithalamium (èp'i-tha-lé-mi-), n., épithalame, m.
epithet (èp-i-thète), n., épithète, f.
epithetic, adj., d'épithète.
epitome (è-pit'o-mi), n., épitomé, m.
epitomist, n., auteur d'un épitomé, m.
epitomize (-maize), v.a., faire un épitomé
de; abréger, raccourcir.
epitomizer, n., auteur d'un épitomé; abréviateur, m.
epizootic (èp'-), adj., épizootique.
epizooty, n., épizootie, f.
epoch (èp-oke, ou i-poke), or epocha
(èp'o-ka), n., époque, f.
epode (èp'ôde), n., épode, f.
epopee (èp-o-pi), or epopœia (-pi-ia), n.,
épopée, f.
equability (i-kwa-), n., uniformité, égalité, f.
equable (i-kwa-b'l), adj., uniforme, égal.
equably, adv., avec égalité, avec uniformité.
equal (i-kwol), adj., égal, uniforme ; (fig.)
impartial, juste. — to ; de force à ; à la hauteur
de ; (of things—des choses) égal à. — with ; à
l'égal de.
equal, n., égal, m., égale, f.
equal, v.a., égaler.
equality, n., égalité, f.
equalization (-aizé-), n., état d'égalité, m.,
action d'égaliser; (jur.) égalisation, f.
equalize (-aize), v.a., égaliser, égaler.
equally, adv., également, pareillement.
equanimity (i-kwa-), n., égalité d'âme, f. ;
calme d'esprit, m. ; équanimité, f. (l.u.)
equanimous, adj., (ant.) doué d'égalité
d'âme ; doué de calme d'esprit ; équanime (l.u.).
equation (i-kwé-), n., équation, f.
equator (è-kwé-), n., équateur, m.
equatorial (è-kwa-tô-), adj., équatorial.
equerry (èk-wi-ri, ou i-kwèr-i), n., écuyer, m.
equestrian (è-kwès-), adj., équestre-

equestrian. n., cavalier, m.
equiangled (i-kwi-angn'g'l'de), or equiangular (-a'n'ghiou-), adj., équiangle.
equidistance (i-kwi-), n., equidistance, f.
equidistant, adj., équidistant.
equidistantly. adv., à égale distance.
equiformity (i-kwi-), n., égalité, uniformité, f.
equilateral (i-kwi-lat'èr-), adj., équilatéral;
équilatère.
equilateral, n., figure équilatérale. f.
equilibrate (i-kwi-laï-), v.a., équilibrer.
equilibration (-laï-bré-), n., équilibre, m.
equilibrious (i-kwi-li-), adj., en équilibre.
equilibriously, adj., en équilibre.
equilibrist (i-kwil'i-), n., bateleur, m.
equilibrity (i-kwi-), n., équilibre, m.
equilibrium (i-kwi-), n., équilibre. m. To
keep one's — ; garder l'équilibre. To remain in
— ; se tenir en équilibre.
equinal, or equine (è-kwaï-), adj., de
cheval
equinecessary (i-kwi-), adj., également
nécessaire.
equinoctial (i-kwi-nok-shal), adj., équinoxial, de l'équinoxe, des équinoxes.
equinoctial, n., ligne équinoxiale, f. ;
équateur céleste, m.
equinoctially, adv., dans la direction de la
ligne équinoxiale.
equinox (i-kwi-). n., équinoxe, m.
equinumerant (i-kwi-niou-mèr'-), adj., du
même nombre.
equip (i-kwipe), v.a., équiper.
equipage (èk'wi-pédje), n., équipage ; (nav.)
équipement, m. Tea — ; cabaret, m.
equipment (è-kwip'-), n., équipement, m.
equipoise (è-kwi-poïce), n., équilibre, m.;
pondération, f.
equipollence, or equipollency (i-kwi-),
n., équipollence ; force égale, f.
equipollent, adj., équipollent.
equipollently, adv., d'une manière équi-
pollente.
equiponderance, or equiponderancy
(i-kwi-po'n'dèr'-), n., équipondérance, f.
equiponderant, adj., équipondérant.
equitable (èk'wi-ta-b'l), adj., équitable,
juste.
equitableness, n., équité, f.
equitably, adv., équitablement.
equitation (èk'wi-té-), n., équitation. f.
equity (èk'wi-), n., équité, justice, f.
equivalence, or equivalency (è-kwiv'-),
n., équivalence, égalité de valeur; égalité de
force, f.
equivalent, adj., équivalent.
equivalent. n., équivalent, m.
equivalently, adv, d'une manière équiva-
lente.
equivocal (i-kwiv'-), adj., équivoque, ambigu.
equivocal, n., équivoque, f.
equivocally, adv., d'une manière équivoque.
equivocalness, n., équivoque, f., caractère
équivoque, m.
equivocate, v.a., user d'équivoque, équivoquer.
equivocation (-o-ké-), n., équivoque, f.
equivocator (-ké-teur), n., personne qui
use d'équivoque, f.
era (i-ra), n., ère ; époque, f.
eradiate (è-ré-di-), v.n., rayonner.
eradiation (-di-é), n., radiation, f.
eradicate (è-rad'i-), v.a., déraciner.
eradication (-'i-ké-), n., déracinement, m. ;
éradication, f.
eradicative (-'i-ké-), adj., éradicatif.
erase (è-réze), v.a., raturer, effacer.

erasement, *n.*, rature, *f.*
erasure (i-ré-jeur), *n.*, effaçure, rature, *f.*
ere (ère), *adv.* and *prep.*, avant que, plus tôt
que. — long ; *avant peu.*
erect (i-rèkte), *adj.*, droit ; haut ; élevé ;
levé ; dressé.
erect, *v.a.*, ériger, dresser, élever ; construire ; (fig.) établir, fonder.
erectable (i-rèk-ta-b'l), *or* **erectile** (i-rèk'-),
adj., que l'on peut dresser.
erection, *n.*, action de dresser ; érection,
construction, élévation ; (fig.) fondation, *f.*
erectly, *adv.*, droit.
erectness, *n.*, posture droite, *f.*
erector, *n.*, constructeur ; (fig.) fondateur ;
(anat.) muscle érecteur, *m.*
eremite (èr'i-maïte), *n.*, ermite, *m.*
ereption (è-rèp'-), *n.*, enlèvement, *m.* .
erethism (èr-i-thiz'me), *n.*, éréthisme, *m.*
ergo (eur-gô), *adv.*, ergo.
ergot (eur-gote), *n.*, ergot, *m.*
ergotine, *n.*, ergotine, *f.*
ermine (eur-), *n.*, hermine, *f.* ; roselet, *m.*
ermined (-mi'n'de), *adj.*, fourré d'hermine ;
revêtu d'hermine.
ern, *or* **erne** (eurne), *n.*, (orni.) orfraie, *f.*
erne, *or* **ærne** (eurne), *n.*, chaumière, *f.* ;
lieu de retraite, *m.*
erode (è-rôde), *v.a.*, corroder, ronger.
erodent (è-rôd'-), *n.*, (pharm.) caustique, *m.*
erosion (è-rô-jeune), *n.*, érosion, *f.*
erotic (è-), *n.*, composition erotique, *f.* ;
poème érotique, *m.*
erotic, *or* **erotical**, *adj.*, érotique.
erotomania (-mé-), *n.*, érotomanie, *f.*
erpetology (eur-pi-tol-o-dji), *n.*, erpétologie, *f.*
err (ère), *v.n.*, errer, s'égarer, s'écarter, se
tromper.
errable, *adj.*, sujet à errer.
errand (èr'-), *n.*, message, *m.* ; commission ;
course, *f.*
errand-boy (-boï), *n.*, garçon qui fait des
commissions, qui fait des courses; petit
messager, *m.*
errant (èr'-), *adj.*, errant, ambulant.
errantry, *n.*, vie errante, *f.* Knight —;
chevalerie errante, f.
erratic, *n.*, vagabond. *m.*
erratic, *or* **erratical**, *adj.*, errant ; (astron.,
med.) erratique.
erratically, *adv.*, sans règle, sans ordre.
erratum (èr-ré-), *n.* (*errata*), erratum,
errata, *m.*
erroneous (èr-rô-ni-), *adj.*, erroné, inexact.
erroneously, *adv.*, erronément.
erroneousness, *n.*, caractère erroné, *m.*;
fausseté, *f.*
error (èr-reur), *n.*, erreur, *f.* ; (theol.) péché,
m. —s excepted ; *sauf erreur.* In —; *dans
l'erreur.* To labour under — ; *être dans l'erreur.*
erst (eurste), *adv.*, autrefois, jadis.
erubescence, *or* **erubescency** (è-riou-),
n., érubescence ; rougeur, *f.*
erubescent, *adj.*, érubescent ; rougeâtre.
eructate (è-reuk'-), *v.a.*, avoir des éructa-
tions.
eructation (-té-), *n.*, éructation, *f.*
erudite (èr-iou-daïte, *ou* -dite), *adj.*, érudit.
erudition, *n.*, érudition, *f.*
eruginous (è-riou-dji-), *adj.*, érugineux.
eruption (è-reup'-), *n.*, éruption, *f.*
eruptive, *adj.*, éruptif.
erysipelas (èr-i-cip'i-lace), *n.*, érysipèle,
érésipèle, *m.*
erysipelatous (-cip'èl-), *adj.*, érésipélateux,
érysipélateux.
escalade (ès-ca-lé-de), *n.*, escalade, *f.*
escapade (ès-ca-péde), *n.*, escapade, *f.* ;
(man.) allure irrégulière, *f.*

escape (ès-), *n.*, évasion, fuite ; délivrance, *f.*
There is no — from it ; *il n'y a pas moyen d'y
échapper.* To make one's — ; *s'échapper.* To
have a narrow — ; *l'échapper belle.*
escape, *v.a.*, échapper à.
escape, *v.n.*, s'échapper, s'enfuir, se sauver;
(from prison—*d'une prison*) s'évader.
escapement, *n.*, échappement, *m.*
escarp (ès-càrpe), *v.a.*, (fort.) escarper.
escarpment, *n.*, (fort.) escarpement, *m.*
eschalot (èsh-a-), *n.*, échalote, ciboule, *f.*
eschar (ès-kar), *n.*, (surg.) escarre, *f.*
escheat (ès-tshite), *n.*, déshérence, *f.* ; bien
en déshérence ; (feudalism—*féodalité*) bien attribué au seigneur par suite de confiscation.
escheat, *v.n.*, tomber en déshérence :
(feudalism—*féodalité*) échoir au seigneur par
suite de confiscation.
eschew (ès-tshou), *v.a.*, éviter.
escort, *v.a.*, escorter.
escort, *n.*, escorte, *f.*
escritoire (ès-cri-twore), *n.*, écritoire, *f.*
esculent (ès-kiou-), *adj.*, esculent; comestible.
escutcheon (ès-keut'sheune), *n.*, écusson, *m.*
esoteric, *or* **esoterical** (ess'o-tèr'-), *adj.*,
ésotérique.
espalier (ès-pal'ieur), *n.*, espalier, *m.*
espalier, *v.a.*, mettre en espalier.
esparcet (ès-pâr-cète), *n.*, (bot.) esparcette, *f.*
esparto (ès-pâr-tô), *n.*, (bot.) sparte, *f.*
especial (ès-pèsh'al), *adj.*, spécial.
especially, *adv.*, spécialement, surtout,
particulièrement.
especialness, *n.*, spécialité, *f.*
esperance (ès-pè-), *n.*, espérance, *f.*
espial (ès-paï-), *n.*, espionnage, *m.*
espionage (ès-pi-o-nèdje, *ou* -naje), *n.*, espionnage, *m.*
esplanade (ès-pla-), *n.*, esplanade, *f.*
espousal (ès-paou-zal), *adj.*, nuptial, de mariage.
espousal, *n.*, adoption, *f.* —s ; *épousailles,
fiançailles, f.pl.*
espouse (è-spaouze), *v.a.*, épouser, fiancer;
(fig.) adopter, embrasser.
espouser, *n.*, protecteur, défenseur, *m.*
espy (è-spa'ye), *v.a.*, voir, découvrir, apercevoir.
esquire (ès-kwaer), *n.*, écuyer ; propriétaire, *m.*
essay (ès-sè), *n.*, essai, *m.* ; épreuve, *f.*
essay, *v.a.*, essayer, éprouver.
essence (ès'-), *n.*, essence, *f.* ; parfum, *m.*
essence, *v.a.*, parfumer.
essential (ès-sè'n'shal), *adj.*, essentiel.
essential, *n.*, essentiel, *m.*
essentiality, *n.*, caractère essentiel, *m.*
essentially, *adv.*, essentiellement.
essentialness, *n.*, extrême importance, *f.*
essoin (ès-swaine), *n.*, (jur.) excuse légitime, *f.*
essoin (ès'-), *v.a.*, (jur.) accorder un délai de
grâce à.
essoiner, *n.*, (jur.) avoué qui demande un
délai de grâce pour sa partie, *m.*
establish (ès-), *v.a.*, établir, affermir ; confirmer.
establisher, *n.*, personne qui établit, *f.*;
fondateur, *m.*
establishment, *n.*, établissement, *m.*, maison, *f.* ; état de maison, *m.* ; Église dominante, *f.*
estate (ès-), *n.*, (property—*propriété*) bien, *m.*,
propriété, terre, fortune, *f.* ; (condition) état,
rang, *m.* ; (jur.) propriété, masse des biens, *f.*,
(of a deceased person—*d'un décédé*) succession,
f.; (political body—*corps politique*) État, *m.* The
third —; *le tiers état, m.* Real —; (jur.) *masse
des biens immeubles, f.* Personal —; (jur.) *masse
des biens meubles, f.*

esteem (ès-tîme), *n.*, estime, *f.*

esteem, *v.a.*, estimer, considérer comme.

esteemer, *n.*, personne qui estime, *f.* ; appréciateur, *m.*

estimable (ès-ti-ma-b'l), *adj.*, dont on peut estimer la valeur ; estimable.

estimableness, *n.*, qualité estimable, *f.*

estimate (ès-), *n.*, estimation, appréciation, *f.* ; jugement ; (com.) devis, *m.* Rough —; *devis approximatif.*

estimate, *v.a.*, estimer, apprécier, évaluer ; juger ; calculer.

estimation (-mé-), *n.*, estimation, appréciation, opinion, *f.*

estimative, *adj.*, qui a la faculté d'apprécier ; d'opinion.

estimator (-méteur), *n.*, estimateur, *m.*

estival (ès-), *adj.*, d'été.

estivate, *v.n.*, (ant.) passer l'été.

estivation (-vé-), *n.*, séjour durant l'été, *m.* ; (bot.) estivation, *f.*

estop (è-), *v.a.*, (jur.) opposer une exception, opposer une fin de non-recevoir.

estoppel, *n.*, (jur.) exception, fin de non-recevoir, *f.*

estovers (ès-tô-veurze), *n.pl.*, (jur.) provision alimentaire, *f.sing.* ; aliments, *m.pl.*

estrange (ès-tré'n'dje), *v.a.*, aliéner, éloigner.

estrangement, *n.*, aliénation, *f.* ; éloignement, *m.*

estrapade (ès'tra-péde), *n.*, (man.) estrapade, *f.*

estray (ès-trè), *n.*, (jur.) épave, bête épave, *f.*

estreat (ès-trite), *n.*, (jur.) expédition, grosse, *f.* ; extrait authentique, *m.*

estreat, *v.n.*, faire une grosse, faire un extrait.

estrich (ès-trit'she), *n.*, duvet d'autruche, *m.*

estuary (èr-tiou-a-), *n.*, estuaire, *m.* ; (bathbain) étuve humide, *f.*

estuate (est'iou-éte), *v.n.*, se courroucer, s'emporter, bouillir ; s'agiter ; s'échauffer.

esurient (è-ziou-), *adj.*, affamé, vorace.

etc. (è't'ci-teura), (ab. of *et cætera*), &c., etc., et cætera.

etch (ètshe), *v.a.*, graver à l'eau-forte ; (fig.) tracer, dessiner.

etcher, *n.*, graveur à l'eau-forte, *m.*

etching, *n.*, gravure à l'eau-forte, *f.*

etching-needle (-nî'd'l), *n.*, pointe, *f.*

eteostic (ét'i-), *n.*, chronogramme, *m.*

eternal (i-teur-), *n.*, Éternel, *m.*

eternal, *adj.*, éternel.

eternalize (-'aïze), *v.a.*, éterniser.

eternally, *adv.*, éternellement.

eternity. *n.*, éternité, *f.* ;

eternize (-naïze), *v.a.*, éterniser.

ether (î-theur), *n.*, éther, *m.*

ethereal, *or* **ethereous** (î-theur-i-) *adj.*, éthéré ; céleste ; aérien.

ethic, *or* **ethical** (èth'-), *adj.*, éthique, moral.

ethically, *adv.*, suivant les principes de l'éthique.

ethics, *n.pl.*, morale, éthique, *f.sing.*

ethiop (î-thi-), *or* **ethiopian** (î-thi-ô-), *n.*, Éthiopien, *m.* ; Éthiopienne, *f.*

ethmoid (èth'moïde), *n.*, (anat.) ethmoïde, *os* ethmoïde, *m.*

ethmoid, *or* **ethmoidal**, *adj.*, ethmoïde, ethmoïdal.

ethnological (èth-nol-o-dj'ical), *adj.*, ethnologique.

ethnologist, *n.*, ethnologiste ; ethnographe, *m.*

ethnology (eth-nol-o-dji), *n.*, ethnologie ; ethnographie, *f.*

ethology (è-thol-o-dji), *n.*, éthologie, *f.*

etiolate (î-ti-). *v.n.*, s'étioler.

etiolate, *v.a.*, étioler.

etiolated, *adj.*, (bot.) étiolé.

etiolation (-lé-), *n.*, étiolement, *m.*

etiology (î-ti-ol-o-dji), *n.*, étiologie, *f.*

etiquette (èt'i-), *n.*, étiquette, *f.*, cérémonial de cour, *m.*

etruscan (è-treuss'-), *adj.*, étrusque.

etymological (èt'i-mo-lodj'i-), *adj.*, étymologique.

etymologist, *n.*, étymologiste, *m.*

etymology (èt'i-mol-o-dji), *n.*, étymologie, *f.*

eucharist (you-ka-), *n.*, eucharistie, *f.*

eucharistical, *adj.*, eucharistique.

euchology (you-kol'o-dji), *n.*, eucologe, *m.*

eucrasy (you-cra-ci), *n.*, (med.) eucraisie, *f.*

eudiometer (you-di-om'i-), *n.*, eudiomètre, *m.*

eudiometric, *or* **eudiometrical**, *adj.*, eudiométrique.

eudiometry, *n.*, eudiométrie, *f.*

eulogic, *or* **eulogical** (you-lodj'-), *adj.*, laudatif.

eulogically, *adv.*, avec éloge.

eulogist (you-), *n.*, panégyriste ; auteur d'éloges, *m.*

eulogium (you-lô-dji-), *or* **eulogy** (-lodji), *n.*, éloge, *m.*

eulogize (-lo-djaïze), *v.a.*, louer, faire l'éloge de.

eunomy (you-), *n.*, bonne législation, *f.*

eunuch (you-neuke), *n.*, eunuque, *m.*

eunuchate, *v.a.*, châtrer.

eupatory (you-pa-teuri), *n.*, (bot.) eupatoire, *f.*

euphemism (you-fèm'iz'me), *n.*, (rhet.) euphémisme, *m.*

euphonic, **euphonical** (you-fo'n'-), *or* **euphonious** (-fô-), *adj.*, euphonique.

euphony (-fo-), *n.*, euphonie, *f.*

european (you-ro-pî-), *adj.*, européen.

european, *n.*, Européen, *m.* ; Européenne, *f.*

eurythmy (you-rith'-), *n.*, (med.) régularité du pouls ; (arch.) eurythmie, *f.*

evacuant (è-vak'iou-), *n.*, évacuant, *m.*

evacuant, *adj.*, évacuant.

evacuate (è-vak'iou-), *v.a.*, évacuer, vider.

evacuation (è-vak'iou-é-), *n.*, évacuation ; sortie ; abolition, *f.*

evacuative, *adj.*, qui évacue.

evacuator (-ét'eur), *n.*, personne qui annule, *f.*

evade (è-véde), *v.n.*, s'échapper, s'esquiver.

evade, *v.a.*, échapper à.

evagation (èv'a-ghé-), *n.*, action d'errer ; excursion, *f.*

evanescence (èv'a-), *n.*, existence éphémère ; disparition, *f.*

evanescent, *adj.*, passager ; éphémère ; évanescent.

evangelic, *or* **evangelical** (è-va'n'dj'èl'-), *adj.*, évangélique.

evangelically, *adv.*, évangéliquement.

evangelism, *n.*, prédication de l'Évangile, *f.*

evangelist, *n.*, évangéliste, *m.*

evangelize (-'aïze), *v.a.*, évangéliser.

evanish (è-), *v.n.*, (ant.) disparaître, s'évanouir.

evanishment, *n.*, disparition, *f.*

evaporable (è-vap'o-ra-b'l), *adj.*, évaporable.

evaporate, *v.n.*, s'évaporer.

evaporate, *v.a.*, faire évaporer.

evaporation (-ré-), *n.*, évaporation, *f.*

evasion (i-vé-jeune), *n.*, moyen évasif ; subterfuge, *m.* ; défaite, *f.*

evasive (i-vé-cive), *adj.*, évasif.

evasively, *adv.*, évasivement.

evasiveness, *n.*, caractère évasif, *m.*

eve (îve), *n.*, soir, *m.* ; veille, *f.* ⚹ —: *le soir.* On the — of ; *à la veille de.*

even (î-v'n), *n.*, soir, *m.*

even, *adj.*, égal ; (smooth—*plat*) uni ; (level with—*à ras*) de niveau ; (of number—*des nombres*) pair. To be — with any one ; *rendre la pareille à quelqu'un* ; *être quitte avec quelqu'un.*

even, *adv.*, même ; aussi bien ; parfaitement. — as ; *comme.* — now ; *tout à l'heure.* — so ; *de même, ainsi.*

even, *v.a.*, égaler ; égaliser ; mettre de niveau.

even-handed (-ha'n'd'ède), *adj.*, impartial, équitable.

evening (ī-v'n'-), *n.*, soir, *m.* ; soirée, *f.* ; (fig.) déclin, *m.* In the— ; *le soir ; dans la soirée.* To-morrow — ; *demain soir ; demain au soir.*

evening, *adj.*, du soir. — party ; *soirée, f.*

evenly (ī-vè'n'-), *adv.*, également ; de niveau ; (fig.) impartialement.

evenness (ī-v'n'nèce), *n.*, égalité ; sérénité, *f.*

even-song (-so'n'g), *n.*, chant du soir, *m.* ; prière du soir, *f.* ; spir'-), *n.*, soirée, *f.*

event (è-vè'n'te), *n.*, événement, *m.* ; issue, *f.* ; (of a poem, a play, &c.—*d'un poème, d'une pièce, &c.*) dénouement, dénoûment, *m.* At all —s ; *à tout événement ; en tout cas ; à tout hasard.*

eventerate (è-vè'n'tèr'-), *v.a.*, éventrer.

eventful (-foule), *adj.*, plein d'événements.

eventide, *or* **evening-tide** (-taïde), *n.*, (ant.) déclin du jour ; soir, *m.*

eventilate (è-vè'n'-), *v.a.*, vanner.

eventual (è-vè'n'tiou-), *adj.*, éventuel ; final, définitif.

eventually, *adv.*, éventuellement ; définitivement.

ever (èv'eur), *adv.*, toujours ; jamais. For —; *pour toujours ; pour jamais ; à jamais ; à tout jamais.* For — and —; *pour toujours ; pour jamais ; à jamais ; (biblically—*biblique*) jusqu'à la fin des siècles.* Scarcely — ; hardly —; *presque jamais.* — and anon ; *de temps en temps ; de temps à autre.* Wine for — ! *vive le vin !* If I have — . . . . ; *si j'ai jamais* . . . .

ever-bubbling (-beub'-), *adj.*, toujours bouillonnant.

ever-burning (-beurn'-), *adj.*, inextinguible.

ever-during (-diour'-), *adj.*, éternel.

ever-green (-grīne), *adj.*, toujours vert.

evergreen, *n.*, plante toujours verte. *f.*

ever-honoured (-o'n'eurde), *adj.*, de glorieuse mémoire.

ever-lasting (-lâst'-), *adj.*, qui dure toujours ; éternel, perpétuel.

everlasting, *n.*, éternité, *f.* ; Éternel ; (bot.) gnaphale, *m.*, immortelle, *f.*

everlastingly, *adv.*, éternellement, à jamais.

everlastingness, *n.*, éternité ; durée perpétuelle. *f.*

ever-living (-liv'-), *adj.*, immortel.

evermore (-môre), *adv.*, toujours ; éternellement.

eversion (è-veur-), *n.*, (ant.) renversement, *m.*

every (èv'euri), *adj.*, chaque, tout, tous les. — body ; *tout le monde, chacun.* — day ; *tous les jours, chaque jour.* — other day ; *de deux jours l'un ; tous les deux jours.* —thing ; *tout.* — where ; *partout.*

evict (è-victe), *v.a.*, prouver ; (jur.) évincer.

eviction, *n.*, preuve ; (jur.) éviction, *f.*

evidence (èv'-), *n.*, évidence, déposition, preuve, *f.* ; témoignage ; (pers.) témoin, *m.* — for the prosecution ; *témoin à charge.* Prisoner's — ; *témoin à décharge.* King's —, Queen's — ; *témoin révélateur de ses complices.* Circumstantial — ; *preuves déduites des circonstances.* To give — ; *rendre témoignage ; déposer.*

evidence, *v.a.*, montrer avec évidence ; prouver, démontrer.

evident, *adj.*, évident.

evidential, *or* **evidentiary** (-shal, -shi-a-), *adj.*, d'évidence.

evidently, *adv.*, évidemment.

evil (ī-v'l), *adj.*, mauvais, malfaisant.

evil, *n.*, mal, *m.* ; crime ; maladie, *f.* King's — ; *écrouelles, f.pl.* Let — be to him that — thinks ; *honni soit qui mal y pense.*

evil, *adv.*, mal.

evil-affected (-af-fèkt'ède), *adj.*, mal disposé.

evil-doer (-dou'eur), *n.*, malfaiteur ; méchant, *m.*, méchante, *f.*

evil-favoured (-fé-veurde), *adj.*, laid, difforme.

evil-favouredness, *n.*, laideur, difformité, *f.*

evil-minded (-maï'n'd'-), *adj.*, mal intentionné.

evilness, *n.*, méchanceté, *f.*

evil-speaking (-spik'-), *n.*, médisance, *f.*

evil-worker (-weurk'-), *n.*, méchant, *m.*

evince (è-vi'n'-), *v.a.*, faire voir ; montrer, manifester.

evincible (-ci-b'l), *adj.*, qui peut être prouvé ; démontrable.

evincibly, *adv.*, incontestablement.

eviscerate (è-vis'cèr-), *v.a.*, éventrer, vider.

evocation (èv'o-ké-), *n.*, évocation, *f.*

evoke (è-vôke), *v.a.*, évoquer.

evolation (èv'o-lé-), *n.*, action de s'envoler ; volée, *f.*

evolute (èv'o-lioute), *n.*, (geom.) développée, *f.*

evolution (èv'o-liou-), *n.*, action de déployer ; (philos., milit.) évolution, *f.* ; (geom.) développement, *m.* ; (alg.) extraction des racines, *f.* ; (fig.) mouvement, *m.*

evolve (ī-volve), *v.a.*, dérouler ; développer ; (chem.) dégager.

evolve, *v.n.*, se dérouler ; se développer ; (chem.) se dégager.

evolvent, *n.*, (geom.) développante, *f.*

evomition (èv'-), *n.*, (ant.) vomissement, *m.*

evulgation (è-veul-ghé-), *n.*, (ant.) divulgation, *f.*

evulsion (ī-veul-), *n.*, évulsion, *f.*

ewe (you), *n.*, brebis, *f.*

ewer (you-eur), *n.*, aiguière, *f.*

ewry (you-ri), *n.*, office (in the Royal Household—*dans la maison du roi*), *m.*

exacerbate (ègz'ass'èr-), *v.a.*, irriter; (med.) rendre plus aigu ; empirer.

exacerbation, *or* **exacerbescence** (ègzass'èr-), *n.*, irritation ; aggravation ; (med.) exacerbation, *f.*

exact (ègz'-), *v.a.*, exiger.

exact, *v.a.*, commettre des exactions.

exact, *adj.*, exact, précis, strict.

exaction, *n.*, action d'exiger ; exaction, *f.*

exactly, *adv.*, exactement ; juste ; au juste.

exactness, *n.*, exactitude, justesse, *f.*

exacter, *or* **exactor** (-'eur), *n.*, exacteur, *m.* ; personne qui exige, *f.*

exaggerate (èg-cadj'è.'), *v.a.*, exagérer.

exaggeration (ègz'adj'èr'-é-), *n.*, exagération, *f.*

exaggeratory (-teuri), *adj.*, exagéré, exagératif.

exalt (ègz'ôlte), *v.a.*, exalter, élever.

exaltation (-ôl-té-), *n.*, exaltation, élévation, *f.*

examinant (ègz'-), *n.*, personne à examiner, *f.*

examinate, *n.*, personne qui est examinée, *f.*

examination (ègz'a'm'i-né-), *n.*, examen, *m.* ; vérification, *f.* ; (jur.) (of prisoners—*d'accusés*) interrogatoire, *m.* ; (of witnesses—*des témoins*) audition, *f.* Private —: (jur.) instruction, *f.* Post mortem —; *autopsie, f.*

examine (ègz'a'm'ine), *v.a.*, examiner ;

faire l'examen de ; visiter ; vérifier ; (jur.) interroger.

examiner,n., examinateur; interrogateur ; (jur.) juge d'instruction, m.

example (ègz'ä'm'p'l), n., exemple, m. To set an — ; donner l'exemple.

exanimate (ègz'a'n'·), adj., inanimé; abattu.

exanthema (èks'a'n'thèma), n. (exanthemata), exanthème, m.

exanthematous, adj., exanthémateux, exanthématique.

exasperate (ègz'as'pèr·), v.a., exaspérer; irriter.

exasperater (-'ét'eur), n., personne qui exaspère.f. ; provocateur, m.

exasperation (-pèr'é·), n., exaspération ; provocation.f.

excandescence, or **excandescency** (èks'ca'n'dès'·), n., incandescence ; (fig.) colère,f.

excandescent, adj., incandescent.

excarnate, or **excarnificate** (èks'cär·), v.a., décharner ; (anat.) excarner.

excarnification (-fi-ké·), n., excarnation,f.

excavate (èks'·), v.a., creuser ; excaver.

excavation (-vé·), n., excavation ; fouille; tranchée, f. ; déblai, m.

excavator (-vé-teur), n., terrassier, m.

exceed (èks'cìde), v.a., excéder, dépasser ; (fig.) surpasser.

exceeding, n., surcroît, excédent, m.

exceeding, adv., excessivement.

exceedingly, adv., excessivement, extrêmement.

excel (èks'cèl), v.a. and n., exceller, surpasser ; l'emporter sur. To — in ; exceller dans; surpasser dans.

excellence,or **excellency,** n., excellence, perfection, supériorité,f. His — ; son Excellence, f.

excellent, adj., excellent, parfait ; grand.

excellently, adv., excellemment ; parfaitement.

except (èks'cèpte), v.a., excepter.

except, v.n., (jur.) fournir ses exceptions. To — against, to — to ; s'opposer à ; récuser. - to a tribunal ; décliner la compétence d'un tribunal.

except, prep., excepté ; hors.

except, conj., à moins que, à moins de.

excepting, prep., excepté, hormis.

exception, n., exception ; objection, f. With this — ; à cette exception près. By way of - ; par exception. Without — ; sans exception. To take — at ; s'offenser de ; se formaliser de.

exceptionable (-a-b'l), adj., blâmable; répréhensible.

exceptioner, n., critique ; censeur, m.

exceptious (-sép'sheusse), adj., qui se formalise ; susceptible.

exceptiousness, n., susceptibilité, f.

exceptive, adj., exceptionnel.

exceptively, adv., exceptionnellement.

exceptless, adj., sans exception.

exceptor (-teur), n., critique, censeur, m.

excess. n., excès (arith.—of weight—de poids) excédent, m.

excessive, adj., excessif ; exagéré ; outré.

excessively, adv., excessivement, à l'excès.

exchange (èks-tshé'n'dje), n., échange ; (com.) change, m. ; (édifice) bourse, f. Average —; change commun. Current —; cours du change; cours, m. Foreign — ; change extérieur, change étranger. Nominal —; change nominal. Bill of —; lettre de change, f. Foreign bill of —; lettre de change sur l'étranger. First of —; première de change, f. Rate of —; taux du change, m. ; cote du change, f. In — for ; en échange de.

exchange, v.a., échanger ; changer.

exchange-office, n., bureau de change, m.

exchanger, n., changeur, m.

exchequer (èks-tshék'eur),n..trésor ; trésor royal; trésor de l'État, m. Court of —; cour de l'Échiquier.

exchequer, v.a., traduire devant la cour de l'échiquier.

exchequer-bill, n., bon du trésor, m.

excisable (-saïz'a'b'l), n., sujet à l'excise, à l'accise; (in France) sujet aux contributions indirectes.

excise (-saïze), n., (in England—en Angleterre) accise, excise,f. ; (in France—en France) contributions indirectes,f.pl., régie, f.

excise, v.a., soumettre à l'accise ; soumettre aux contributions indirectes.

exciseman (-ma'n), n., préposé de l'accise, employé de l'accise ; préposé des contributions indirectes, de la régie, employé des contributions indirectes, de la régie, m.

excision (-cijeune), n., destruction; (surg.) excision, f.

excitability (èx-saït'·), n., excitabilité, f.

excitable (èx-saït'é'b'l), adj., excitable.

excitation (èx-saït'é·), n., excitation, f.

excite (èx-saïte), v.a., exciter, animer.

excitement, n., excitation, f.; motif d'excitation, m.

exciter, n., excitateur, m. ; excitatrice, f. ; (fig.) mobile, m.

exclaim (-cléme), v.n., s'écrier ; se récrier. To — against ; se récrier contre.

exclaim, n., clameur, f.

exclaimer, n., personne qui s'écrie, qui se récrie, f. ; déclamateur, m.

exclamation (-mé·), n., exclamation, f. Note of — ; point d'exclamation, m.

exclamatory(-teuri), adj., de déclamateur; d'exclamation.

exclude (-cloude), v.a., exclure.

exclusion (-clou'jeune), n., exclusion, f.

exclusionist (-clou-jeun'iste), n., personne exclusive.

exclusive(-clou-cive), adj., exclusif ; d'exclusion. — of ; à l'exclusion de ; non compris.

exclusively, adv., exclusivement. — of ; à l'exclusion de.

excogitate (-codji'téte), v.a., inventer, créer, trouver à force de méditation.

excogitation (-codj'i-té·), n., méditation ; invention, f.

excommunicable (-miou·), adj., passible d'excommunication.

excommunicate (-miou-ni-kéte), v.a., excommunier.

excommunicate, n., excommunié, m., excommuniée, f.

excommunication (-ké·), n., excommunication, f.

excoriate (-cô-ri-éte), v.a.,écorcher ; (surg.) excorier.

excoriation, n., écorchure ; (surg.) excoriation, f.

excortication (-ké·), n., excortication, f.

excrement (-cri·), n., excrément, m.

excremental, or **excrementitious** (-ti-shi-eusse), adj., excrémenteux, excrémentiel, excrémentitiel.

excrescence, or **excrescency,** n., excroissance, f. ; (fig.) excès, rebut, m.

excrescent, adj., qui forme une excroissance ; surcroissant.

excrete (-crìte), v.a., excréter.

excretion (-cri·), n., excrétion, f.

excretive, or **excretory** (-cri-, -teuri), adj., excrétoire, excréteur.

excretory (-cri-teuri), n., vaisseau excrétoire, m.

excruciable (-crou-shi-a'b'l), adj., sujet à être tourmenté.

excruciate (-crou-shi-éte), *v.a.*, tourmenter affreusement.

excruciating, *adj.*, atroce, affreux.

excruciation, *n.*, tourment atroce, *m.*; affreuse torture, *f.*

exculpate (-keul'péte), *v.a.*, disculper.

exculpation, *n.*, excuse, justification, *f.*

exculpatory, *adj.*, qui disculpe, apologétique.

excursion (-keur-), *n.*, excursion, course, *f.*

excursive, *adj.*, qui erre; (fig.) décousu, vague, errant.

excursively, *adv.*, en errant.

excursiveness, *n.*, extravagance, *f.*

excusable (-kiouz'a'b'l), *adj.*, excusable.

excusableness, *n.*, caractère excusable, *m.*

excusatory (-teuri), *adj.*, d'excuse; apologétique.

excuse (-kiouze), *n.*, excuse, *f.* To offer an –; *présenter une excuse.*

excuse, *v.a.*, excuser. To – one's self for; *s'excuser de.* – me! *excusez!*

excuseless, *adj.*, sans excuse, inexcusable.

excuser, *n.*, personne qui excuse, *f.*; apologiste, *m.*, *f.*

exeat (èks'i'ate), *n.*, exeat (permission de s'absenter donnée à un étudiant des Universités anglaises).

execrable (èks'i-cra'b'l), *adj.*, exécrable.

execrably, *adv.*, exécrablement.

execrate (èks'i-créte), *v.a.*, exécrer.

execration, *n.*, exécration, *f.*

execratory (-cré-teuri), *n.*, formule d'exécration, *f.*

execute (èks'i-kioute), *v.a.*, exécuter; exercer.

execution, *n.*, exécution, *f.*; exercice; (slaughter—*tuerie*) massacre, carnage, *m.*; (jur.) saisie-exécution, *f.*

executioner, *n.*, exécuteur; bourreau; (jur.) exécuteur des hautes œuvres, *m.*

executive, *adj.*, exécutif.

executive, *n.*, pouvoir exécutif, gouvernement, *m.*

executor (-teur), *n.*, exécuteur; (jur.) exécuteur testamentaire, *m.*

executorial, *adj.*, d'exécuteur testamentaire.

executorship, *n.*, fonctions d'exécuteur testamentaire, *f.pl.*

executrix, *n.*, exécutrice testamentaire, *f.*

exegesis (èks'i'dji-cisse), *n.*, exégèse, *f.*

exegetical (-djét'-), *adj.*, exégétique.

exegetically, *adv.*, par exégèse; d'une manière exégétique.

exemplar (ègz'è'm'pleur), *n.*, modèle, *m.*

exemplarily, *adv.*, exemplairement.

exemplariness, *or* **exemplarity**, *n.*, qualité de ce qui est exemplaire, *f.*

exemplary (-plari), *adj.*, exemplaire; (her.) à armes parlantes.

exemplification (-ké-), *n.*, explication par des exemples; (jur.) ampliation, *f.*

exemplifier (-fa'eur), *n.*, personne qui donne l'exemple, *f.*

exemplify (-fa'ye), *v.a.*, démontrer par des exemples; donner un exemple de; (jur.) copier.

exempt (ègz'è'mt), *v.a.*, exempter.

exempt, *adj.*, exempt.

exemption, *n.*, exemption, *f.*

exenterate (ègz'è'n'tèr'éte), *v.a.*, ôter les entrailles à.

exenteration, *n.*, action d'ôter les entrailles, *f.*

exequatur (èks-i-koué-teur), *n.*, exequatur, *m.*

exequial (ègz'i-koui-), *adj.*, funéraire.

exequies (èks'i-kouize), *n.pl.*, obsèques, funérailles, *f.pl.*

exercisable (èks'èr-saïz'a'b'l), *adj.*, susceptible d'être exercé.

exercise (èks'èr-saïze), *n.*, exercice; (task—*devoir*) thème, *m.*; (milit.) manœuvre, *f.*, exercice. *m.*

exercise, *v.a.*, exercer; (animal) promener.

exerciser, *n.*, personne qui exerce; personne qui s'exerce, *f.*

exergue (ègz'eurghe), *n.*, exergue, *m.*

exert (ègz'eurte), *v.a.*, mettre en œuvre; montrer; accomplir; exercer avec effort, faire un effort. To – one's self; *faire des efforts;* *s'efforcer, tâcher.*

exertion, *n.*, effort; emploi, usage, *m.*

exestuation (ègz'ès-teu-é-), *n.*, effervescence, ébullition, *f.*

exeunt (èks'i-eu'nte), *v.n.*, (thea.) sortent.

exfoliate (èks'fô-li-éte), *v.n.*, s'exfolier.

exfoliation, *n.*, exfoliation, *f.*

exhalable (ègz'hé-la-b'l), *adj.*, qui peut s'évaporer; évaporable.

exhalation (-'ha-lé-), *n.*, exhalaison; exhalation, *f.*

exhale (ègz'héle), *v.a.*, exhaler, faire exhaler.

exhalement, *n.*, exhalaison, *f.*

exhaust (ègz'hôste), *v.a.*, épuiser; (phys.) aspirer.

exhausted, *adj.*, épuisé; (phys.) aspiré. I am quite – ; *je suis rendu.*

exhauster, *n.*, personne qui épuise; chose qui épuise. *f.*; (phys.) aspirateur, *m.*

exhaustible, *adj.*, épuisable.

exhausting, *adj.*, qui épuise; (phys.) d'aspiration. – pipe; *tuyau d'épuisement, m.*

exhaustion (ègz'hôst'ieune), *n.*, épuisement, *m.*; aspiration, *f.*

exhaustive, *adj.*, qui épuise; complet.

exhaustless, *adj.*, inépuisable.

exhibit (ègz'hibite), *v.a.*, exhiber, montrer, produire, exposer.

exhibiter, *n.*, personne qui montre, qui produit, *f.*; (at public exhibitions—*aux expositions publiques*) exposant, *m.*

exhibition (èks'hi-), *n.*, (action) exposition; (representation) représentation, *f.*, spectacle, *m.*; (in universities—*aux universités*) bourse fondée par un particulier; (jur.) exhibition, *f.* Industrial – ; *exposition de l'industrie.*

exhibitioner, *n.*, (in universities—*aux universités*) boursier, dont la bourse est fondée par un particulier, *m.*

exhibitive (ègz'-), *adj.*, représentatif.

exhibitively, *adv.*, d'une manière emblématique.

exhibitory, *adj.*, qui exhibe.

exhilarate (ègz'hil-a-réte), *v.a.*, réjouir, récréer; égayer.

exhilarating, *adj.*, qui égaie; réjouissant; exhilarant.

exhilaration, *n.*, réjouissance, *f.*

exhort (ègz'horte), *v.a.*, exhorter, solliciter.

exhort, *v.n.*, faire des exhortations.

exhortation (-té-), *n.*, exhortation, *f.*

exhortative, *adj.*, exhortatif.

exhortatory, *adj.*, exhortatoire.

exhorter, *n.*, personne qui exhorte, *f.*

exhumation (ègz'hiou-mé-), *n.*, exhumation, *f.*

exhume (ègz'hioume), *or* **exhumate** (-méte), *v.a.*, exhumer.

exigence, *or* **exigency** (èks'i'djè'nse, -ci), *n.*, exigence, *f.*; besoin, *m.*; situation critique, extrémité, *f.*

exigent, *adj.*, critique.

exigible (èks'i'dji-b'l), *adj.*, exigible.

exiguity (èks'i-ghiou-), *n.*, exiguïté, *f.*

exiguous (ègz'i-ghiou-eusse), *adj.*, exigu.

exile (ègz'aïle), *adj.*, mince, faible, peu considérable.

exile (èks'aïle), *n.*, exil, *m.*; (pers.) exilé, *m.*, exilée. *f.*

exile (èks'aïle, *ou* ègz'-), *v.a.*, exiler.

exilement, *n.*, exil, *m.*

exility (ègz'i-li-ti), *n.*, petitesse, faiblesse, *f*

exist, *v.n.*, exister.

existence, *n.*, existence, *f.*

existent, *adj.*, existant.

exit, *n.*, sortie, *f.*

exit (èks'ite), *n.*, (thea.) sort.

exitial (ègz'ish'al), *or* **exitious** (-sheusse), *adj.*, funeste ; mortel.

exodus (èks-ô-deusse), *n.*, Exode, *m.*; sortie, *f.*

exonerate (ègz-o'n'èréte), *v.a.*, décharger ; soulager ; exonérer.

exoneration, *n.*, décharge, *f.* ; soulagement, *m.*

exonerative, *adj.*, qui décharge ; qui soulage.

exophthalmia (èks'of-thal-), *n.*, exophtalmie, *f.*

exorable, *adj.*, exorable.

exorbitance, *or* **exorbitancy**, *n.*, excès, *m.*; extravagance, *f.*

exorbitant, *adj.*, exorbitant, excessif.

exorbitantly, *adv.*, exorbitamment ; excessivement.

exorcise (èks'or-saïze), *v.a.*, exorciser.

exorciser, *n.*, exorciste, *m.*

exorcism (-ciz'me), *n.*, exorcisme, *m.*

exorcist, *n.*, exorciste, *m.*

exordial (ègz'-), *adj.*, de l'exorde.

exordium (-dieume), *n.*, exorde, *m.*

exornation (èks'or-né-), *n.*, (ant.), embellissement, *m.*

exortive, *adj.*, de l'orient.

exossated (-sé-tède), *adj.*, (ant.) désossé.

exosseous (ègz-oeh-shi-eusse), *adj.*, sans os.

exostosis (-tô-cisse), *n.*, exostose, *f.*

exoteric, *adj.*, exotérique ; vulgaire.

exotery, *n.*, doctrine exotérique, *m.*

exotic, *adj.*, exotique.

exotic, *n.*, plante exotique, *f.*

expand, *v.a.*, faire épanouir, étendre, déployer ; dilater.

expand, *v.n.*, s'épanouir ; se répandre ; se dilater ; s'étendre ; se déployer.

expanse, *n.*, étendue, *f.*

expansibility, *n.*, expansibilité, *f*

expansible, *adj.*, expansible.

expansion, *n.*, expansion ; extension, *f.*; épanouissement, *m.*

expansive, *adj.*, expansif.

expansiveness, *n.*, expansibilité, *f*

ex parte, *adj.*, d'un seul côté ; d'une seule partie.

expatiate (èks-pé-shi-éte), *v.n.*, courir ; errer. To — on ; *s'étendre sur, discourir sur.*

expatiation (-pé-shi-é-), *n.*, extension ; irrégularité, *f.*

expatiator (-pé-shi-é-teur), *n.*, personne qui s'étend, qui discourt, *f.*

expatriate (-pé-tri-éte), *v.a.*, expatrier.

expect, *v.a.*, attendre ; espérer ; s'attendre à.

expectable, *adj.*, qui peut être attendu.

expectance, *or* **expectancy**, *n.*, attente, *f.*; espoir, *m.*; (jur.) expectative, *f.*

expectant, *adj.*, expectant.

expectant, *n.*, personne qui est dans l'attente ; personne qui est dans l'expectative, *f.*

expectation (-té-), *n.*, expectation, expectative, attente, espérance, *f.* He always lives in — ; *il vit toujours dans l'expectative.* In — of ; *dans l'attente de ; dans l'espérance de.* To answer one's —s ; *répondre à ses espérances.* Beyond one's —s ; *au delà de ses espérances.*

expecter, *n.*, personne qui attend, qui espère, *f.*

expectingly, *adv.*, dans l'attente.

expectorant, *adj.*, expectorant.

expectorant, *n.*, expectorant, *m.*

expectorate (-réte), *v.a.*, expectorer.

expectoration (-ré-), *n.*, expectoration, *f.*

expectorative (-ra-), *adj.*, expectorant.

expedience, *or* **expediency** (-pî-), *n.*, convenance, *f.* ; à-propos, *m.*

expedient, *n.*, expédient.

expediently, *adv.*, convenablement ; à propos.

expedite (-daïte), *adj.*, prompt, expéditif, vif, facile.

expedite, *v.a.*, expédier, hâter, dépêcher.

expeditely, *adv.*, promptement.

expedition, *n.*, expédition ; promptitude hâte, *f.*

expeditious (-pé-dish'eusse), *adj.*, expéditif, prompt.

expeditiously, *adv.*, rapidement ; promptement.

expeditive, *adj.*, expéditif.

expel, *v.a.*, expulser, chasser, faire sortir.

expellable, *adj.*, susceptible d'être chassé.

expeller, *n.*, personne qui chasse, qui expulse, *f.*

expend, *v.a.*, dépenser ; employer ; consacrer.

expenditure (-di-tioure), *n.*, dépense ; consommation, *f.* ; (fig.) emploi, sacrifice, *m.*

expense, *n.*, dépense, *f.* ; dépens, frais, *m.pl.* Free of — ; *sans frais ; franco.* At a great — ; *à grands frais.* To go to — ; *se mettre en dépense ; faire des frais.* At any — ; *à tout prix.*

expenseless, *adj.*, sans frais.

expensive, *adj.*, (pers.) dépensier ; (of things —des choses) dispendieux.

expensively, *adv.*, à grands frais ; dispendieusement.

expensiveness, *n.*, dépense ; prodigalité, *f.*

experience (-pî-ri-), *n.*, expérience, *f.* By —, from — ; *par expérience.*

experience, *v.a.*, éprouver ; faire l'expérience de.

experienced (èks'pî-ri-è'n'ste), *adj.*, qui a de l'expérience ; expérimenté.

experiencer, *n.*, personne qui fait des expériences, *f.*

experiment, *n.*, expérience, *f.*

experiment, *v.n. and n.*, expérimenter.

experimental, *adj.*, expérimental ; (pers.) qui procède par expérience, expérimenté.

experimentalist, *n.*, auteur d'expériences; expérimentateur, *m.*

experimentally, *adv.*, par expérience.

experimenter, *n.*, auteur d'expériences; expérimentateur, *m.*

expert (-peurte), *adj.*, expert, habile.

expertly, *adv.*, habilement.

expertness, *n.*, habileté, *f.*

expiable, *adj.*, que l'on peut expier.

expiate (-éte), *v.a.*, expier, réparer.

expiation (-pi-é-), *n.*, (ant.) expiation, *f.*

expiatory, *adj.*, expiatoire.

expilation (-lé-), *n.*, pillage, *m.*

expiration (-pi-ré-), *n.*, expiration ; cessation ; évaporation, *f.* ; (death—mort) dernier soupir, *m.*

expire (-paeur), *v.n.*, expirer ; mourir ; périr.

expire, *v.a.*, expirer ; exhaler,

expiring, *adj.*, expirant.

expiry (-piri), *n.*, expiration, *f.*

explain (-pléne), *v.a.*, expliquer, éclaircir.

explain, *v.n.*, s'expliquer.

explainable ('-a-b'l), *adj.*, explicable.

explainer, *n.*, explicateur ; commentateur, *m.*

explanation (-né-), *n.*, explication, *f.*; éclaircissement, *m.*

explanatory, *adj.*, explicatif.

expletive (-pli-), *adj.*, explétif.

expletive, *n.*, explétif, *m.*

explicable (-ca-b'l), *adj.*, explicable.

explicate (-kéte), *v.a.*, dérouler ; expliquer.

explication (-ké-), *n.*, déploiement, *m.* ; explication, *f.*

explicative, *adj.*, explicatif.

explicator (-ké-teur), *n.*, explicateur ; interprète, *m.*

explicatory, *adj.*, explicatif.

explicit, *adj.*, explicite ; clair.

explicitly, *adv.*, explicitement.

explicitness, *n.*, caractère explicite, *m.*

explode (-plóde), *v.a.*, rejeter ; repousser ; condamner.

explode, *v.n.*, faire explosion.

exploder, *n.*, personne qui repousse, qui condamne, *f.*

exploit (-ploate), *n.*, exploit ; haut fait ; fait d'armes, *m.*

exploration (-ré-), *n.*, exploration, *f.* ; examen, *m.* ; recherche, *f.*

explorator (-ré-teur), *n.*, explorateur, *m.*

exploratory, *adj.*, exploratoire ; explorateur.

explore (-plôre), *v a.*, explorer, examiner.

explorement, *n.*, recherche, exploration, *f.*

explorer, *n.*, explorateur, *m.*

explosion (-plô-jeune), *n.*, explosion, *f.*

explosive (-plô-cive), *adj.*, explosif.

exponent (-pô-), *n.*, (math.) exposant, *m.*

exponential (-shial), *adj.*, exponentiel.

export, *n.*, marchandise exportée ; qui peut être exportée, *f.*

export (-pôrte), *v.a.*, exporter.

exportation (-por-té-), *n.*, exportation, *f.* ; transport, *m.*

exporter, *n.*, exportateur, *m.*

expose, *v.a.*, exposer.

exposer, *n.*, personne qui expose, *f.*

exposition (-zi-), *n.*, exposition, *f.*

expositor (-teur), *n.*, interprète ; commentateur ; glossaire, *m.*

expostulate (-post'iou-léte), *v.n.*, se plaindre ; faire des reproches ; reprocher.

expostulation (-lé-), *n.*, reproche, *m* ; remontrance, *f.*

expostulator (-lé-teur), *n.*, personne qui fait des reproches, des remontrances, *f.*

expostulatory, *adj.*, de reproche ; de remontrance.

exposure (-pô-jeur), *n.*, exposition, *f.* ; danger ; scandale ; éclat, *m.*

expound (-pa-ou'n'de), *v.a.*, expliquer, exposer.

expounder, *n.*, interprète, *m.*

express, *n.*, exprès, *m.*

express, *adj.*, exprès ; formel ; d'une ressemblance exacte.

express. *v.a.*, exprimer ; représenter ; désigner.

expressible (-'si-b'l), *adj.*, exprimable.

expression, *n.*, expression ; énonciation, *f.*

expressive, *adj.*, expressif. To be — of ; *exprimer*.

expressively, *adv.*, avec expression.

expressiveness, *n.*, force d'expression, *f.*

expressly, *adv.*, expressément.

expressness, *n.*, (ant.) caractère formel, *m.*

expressure (-prè-shioure), *n.*, expression ; empreinte, *f.*

exprobrate (prô-bréte), *v.a.*, blâmer, reprocher.

exprobration (-bré-), *n.*, blâme, *m.*

exprobrative, *adj.*, de reproche.

expropriate (-prô-priéte), *v.a.*, abandonner.

expropriation (-prié-), *n.*, abandon, *m.* ; renonciation, *f.*

expugn (-pioune), *v.a.*, prendre d'assaut.

expugnable, *adj.*, expugnable.

expugnation (-peug-né-), *n.*, prise d'assaut ; conquête, *f.*

expulse (-peul'-), *v.a.*, expulser, chasser.

expulsion, *n.*, expulsion, *f.*

expulsive, *adj.*, expulsif.

expunction (-peu'n'k-), *n.*, effaçure, *f.*

expunge (-peu'n'dje), *v.a.*, effacer, rayer ; raturer.

expurgate (-peur-ghéte), *v.a.*, nettoyer ; (a book—*un livre*) purger.

expurgation, *n.*, nettoiement, *m.* ; purification, *f.*

expurgatory, *adj.*, expurgatoire.

exquisite (-kwi-zite), *adj.*, exquis ; (of pain—*douleur*) atroce, affreux.

exquisitely, *adv.*, d'une manière exquise ; exquisement.

exquisiteness, *n.*, goût exquis, *m.* ; perfection ; (of grief, pain—*du chagrin, de la douleur*) violence, *f.*

exsiccant, *adj.*, qui sèche, dessiccatif.

exsiccate (-kéte), *v.a.*, sécher, dessécher.

exsiccation, *n.*, sécheresse, *f.*, dessèchement, *m.*

exsiccative, *adj.*, dessiccatif, siccatif.

exspuition (-spiou-i-), *n.*, crachement, *m.*

exsuction (-ceuk-), *n.*, succion, *f.*

exsudation, *n. V.* **exudation**.

exsude. *V.* **exude**.

extant, *adj.*, qui existe, existant.

extemporal, *adj.*, (ant.) improvisé.

extemporally, *adv.*, (ant.) à l'improviste.

extemporaneous (èks-tè'm'po-ré-ni-eusse), *or* **extemporary** (-ra-), *adj.*, pour le moment ; improvisé.

extemporaneously, *adv.*, d'abondance.

extemporary. *V.* **extemporaneous**.

extempore (-pô-ri), *adv.*, sur-le-champ, sans préparation ; par improvisation.

extemporiness, *n.*, faculté d'improviser, *f.*

extemporize (-raïze), *v.n.*, improviser.

extemporizer, *n.*, improvisateur, *m.*, improvisatrice, *f.*

extend, *v.a.*, étendre, tendre ; continuer, prolonger.

extend, *v.n.*, s'étendre ; (of time—*du temps*) se prolonger.

extender, *n.*, personne qui étend ; chose qui étend, *f.*

extendible, *adj.*, extensible ; (jur.) saisissable.

extensible, *adj.*, extensible.

extensibleness, *or* **extensibility** (-tè'n'-), *n.*, extensibilité, *f.*

extension, *n.*, extension ; étendue, *f.*

extensive (-tè'n'-), *adj.*, étendu, vaste ; ample, grand.

extensively, *adv.*, d'une manière étendue ; avec étendue ; amplement.

extensor (-tè'n'-), *n.*, (anat.) extenseur, muscle extenseur, *m.*

extent (-tè'n'te), *n.*, étendue, *f.* ; (fig.) degré, point, *m.* ; (jur.) expertise pour estimer les biens d'un débiteur saisi, *f.*

extenuate (-tè'n'iouéte), *v.a.*, exténuer ; affaiblir, diminuer, atténuer.

extenuate, *adj.*, (ant.) petit ; maigre.

extenuation, *n.*, exténuation ; atténuation ; mitigation, *f.*

exterior (-ti-). *adj.*, extérieur, en dehors.

exterior, *n.*, (pers., things—*personnes, choses*) extérieur ; (pers.) physique, *m.*

exteriorly, *adv.*, extérieurement.

exterminate (-teur-mi-néte), *v.a.*, exterminer ; extirper ; (alg.) éliminer.

extermination, *n.*, extermination ; extirpation ; (alg.) élimination, *f.*

exterminator (-né-), *n.*, exterminateur, *m.*

exterminatory, *adj.*, d'extermination.

extermine (-teur), *v.a.*, (ant.) exterminer.

external (-teur-), *adj.*, extérieur, externe.

externally, *adv.*, extérieurement.

externals (-nalze), *n.pl.*, forme extérieure, *f.sing.* ; dehors, *m.sing.*

exterraneous (-teur'ra-ni-eusse), *adj.*, étranger.

extersion, *n.*, action d'essuyer, *f.*

extil, *v.n.*, (ant.) dégoutter.

extillation (-lé-), *n.*,(ant.)dégouttement, *m.*

extinct (-ti'n'k'te), *adj.*, éteint.

extinction, *n.*, extinction, *f.*

extinguish (-ti-n'gwishe), *v.a.*, éteindre; faire cesser; surpasser.

extinguishable (-'a-b'l), *adj.*, qu'on peut éteindre.

extinguisher, *n.*, (thing—*chose*) éteignoir, *m.*; personne qui éteint, *f.*

extinguishment, *n.*, extinction, *f.*

extirpable, *adj.*, que l'on peut extirper.

extirpate (-péte), *v.a.*, extirper.

extirpation, *n.*, action d'extirper; extirpation, *f.*

extirpator (-teur), *n.*, extirpateur, *m.*

extol, *v.a.*, exalter, élever, louer.

extoller, *n.*, panégyriste, *m.*

extolment, *n.*, panégyrique, *m.*; louange, *f.*

extorsive, *adj.*, qui extorque.

extorsively, *adv.*, par extorsion.

extort (-torte), *v.a.*, extorquer, arracher.

extorter, *n.*, personne qui extorque, *f.*; concussionnaire, *m.*

extortion, *n.*, extorsion; violence, *f.*

extortioner, *n.*, auteur d'extorsions; concussionnaire, *m.*

extra, *adj.*, d'extra; en sus; supplémentaire.

extra, *adv.*, en sus; de plus; au delà.

extract, *n.*, extrait, *m.*

extract, *v.a.*, extraire; tirer; (teeth—*les dents*) arracher.

extraction, *n.*, extraction, *f.*; (pharm.) extrait, *m.*

extractive, *adj.*, que l'on peut extraire; (chem.) extractif.

extractive, *n.*, (chem.) extractif, *n.*

extractor (-teur), *n.*, forceps, *m.*

extradition, *n.*, extradition, *f.*

extrados (-tré-dosse), *n.*,(arch.) extrados, *m.*

extrageneous (-tra-dji'ni-eusse),*adj.*, d'une autre espèce.

extra-judicial (-djiou-di'sh'al), *adj.*, extra-judiciaire.

extra-judicially, *adv.*, extrajudiciairement.

extra-limitary, *adj.*, au delà des limites.

extra-mission, *n.*, émission, *f.*

extra-mundane (-meu'n'dé-ne), *adj.*, au delà de ce monde.

extraneous (-tré-ni-eusse), *adj.*, étranger.

extraordinarily, *adv.*, extraordinairement.

extraordinariness, *n.*, caractère extraordinaire, *m.*; rareté, *f.*

extraordinary, *adj.*, extraordinaire.

extra-parochial (-rô-kial), *adj.*, qui n'est pas de la paroisse.

extra-provincial (-vi'n'-shal), *adj.*, qui n'est pas de la même province.

extra-regular (-rè-ghiou-leur), *adj.*, hors des règles.

extravagance, *or* **extravagancy** (-ga'n'ce,-'ci), *n.*, extravagance; bizarrerie, *f.*; prodigalité, *f.*, folles dépenses, *f.pl.*

extravagant, *adj.*, extravagant; bizarre; prodigue, dépensier; (of things—*des choses*) dispendieux.

extravagant (-ga'n'te), *n.*, extravagant, *m.*, extravagante, *f.*

extravagantly, *adv.*, d'une manière extravagante; prodigalement.

extravagantness, *n.*, extravagance, *f.*

extravasated (-cé-tède), *adj.*, extravasé.

extravasation, *n.*, extravasation, extravasion, *f.*

extreme (-trîme), *n.*, extrémité, *f.*; extrême, *m.* —s meet; *les extrêmes se touchent.* To an —; *jusqu'à l'extrême.* To carry to —s; *pousser à l'extrême.*

extreme, *adj.*, extrême.

extremely, *adv.*, extrêmement.

extremity (-tré-), *n.*, extrémité, *f.*; extrême, *m.*, calamité, *f.*; cas extrême, *m.*

extricable, *adj.*, qu'on peut dégager.

extricate (-kéte), *v.a.*, débarrasser, dégager; tirer d'affaire.

extrication, *n.*, action de débarrasser, de dégager, *f.*; dégagement, *m.*

extrinsic, *or* **extrinsical** (-tri'n'-), *adj.*, extrinsèque.

extrinsically, *adv.*, extrinsèquement, dehors.

extrude (-troude), *v.a.*, expulser; repousser.

extrusion (-trou-jeune), *n.*, expulsion, *f.*

extuberance, *or* **extuberancy** (-tiou-bèr'-), *n.*, protubérance, *f.*

extuberant, *adj.*, saillant.

exuberance, *or* **exuberancy** (ègz'lou-bèr'-), *n.*, exubérance, *f.*

exuberant, *adj.*, exubérant, surabondant.

exuberantly, *adv.*, avec exubérance.

exuberate (-bèr'éte), *v.n.*, surabonder.

exudation (èks'lou-dé-), *n.*, exsudation, *f.*

exude (èks'ioude), *v.n.*, exsuder.

exude, *v.a.*, faire exsuder.

exulcerate (ègz'eul-cè-réte), *v.a.*, exulcérer, ulcérer.

exulcerate, *v.n.*, s'ulcérer.

exulceration (-cèr'é-), *n.*, ulcération; (fig.) exaspération, *f.*

exult (ègz'eulte), *v.n.*, se réjouir; triompher de joie.

exultant, *adj.*, joyeux, triomphant.

exultation (-té-), *n.*, allégresse, *f.*; triomphe, *m.*

exustion (ègz'eust'-ieune), *n.*, combustion, *f.*

exuviæ (ègz'iou-vi-î), *n.pl.*, dépouilles, *f.pl.*

eyas (a'y'asse), *n.*, oiseau niais, *m.*

eye (a'ye), *n.*, œil, *m.*; (fig.) vue, *f.*; (persp.) point de vue; (of a needle—*d'une aiguille*) trou; (nav.) œillet; (bot., arch.,and in cheeses—*et du fromage*) œil, *m.*; (catch for a hook—*agrafe*) porte, *f.* —s; yeux. False —; œil postiche. Black —; œil noir, œil poché. Sore —s; *mal d'yeux*, *m.* Blind of one —; borgne. In the twinkling of an —; *en un clin d'œil.* Farther than the — can reach; *à perte de vue.* Before any one's —s; *sous les yeux de quelqu'un.* To be before any one's —; *avoir sous le nez.* To cry any one's — out; *s'épuiser en larmes.* With tears in one's —s; *les larmes aux yeux.* To have a black —; *avoir l'œil en compote, avoir un œil poché.* To have in one's —; *avoir dans l'œil; avoir en vue.* To tear out any one's —s; *arracher les yeux à quelqu'un.* To open any one's —s; *ouvrir les yeux à quelqu'un; dessiller les yeux de quelqu'un.* To shut one's —s to; *fermer les yeux sur.* To strike the —; *frapper les yeux.* To cast down one's —s; *baisser les yeux.*

eye, *v.a.*, regarder; contempler; suivre de, *j* yeux; (b.s.) lorgner.

eyeball (-bôl), *n.*, globe de l'œil, *m.*; prunelle, pupille, *f.*

eyebrow (-braou), *n.*, sourcil, *m.* To knit the —s; *froncer les sourcils.*

eyed (a'ye'-de), *adj.*, aux yeux. Blue —; *aux yeux bleus.*

eye-dazzling, *adj.*, éblouissant.

eye-drop (-drope), *n.*, larme, *f.*

eye-glance (-glâ'n'ce), *n.*, coup d'œil; regard, *m.*

eye-glass (-glâce), *n.*, lorgnon, *m.*; (opt.) oculaire verre oculaire, *m.* Single —; *monocle, m.*

Double —; *binocle; lorgnon à deux branches,* m. ; jumelle, *f.*

eye-hole (-hôle), n., (anat.) orbite, orbite de l'œil, *f.*

eyelash (-lashe), n., cil, m.

eyeless (-lèsse), adj., sans yeux ; aveugle.

eyelet, or **eyelet-hole** (-lète, -hôle), n., œillet (petit trou), m.

eyelid (-lide), n., paupière, *f.*

eyepiece (-pîce), n., (opt.) oculaire, m.

eye-salve (-sâve), n., (med.) onguent pour les yeux, m.

eyesight (-saïte), n., vue, *f.*

eyesore, n., chose qui blesse, qui offense l'œil, *f.*; objet d'aversion, m. ; bête noire, bête d'aversion, *f.*

eyestring (-strigne), n., fibre de l'œil, *f.*

eye-water (-wô-teur), n., collyre, m.

eyot (a'yote), n., îlot, m.

eyre (ére), n., (jur.) tournée (of judges—*de juges*), *f.*

eyry (ér'i), n., aire (of birds of prey—*des oiseaux de proie*), *f.*

F

f, sixième lettre de l'alphabet, f, m. *f.*; (mus.) fa, m.

fabaceous (fa-bé-sheusse), adj., de fève.

fabago, n., (bot.) fabago, m., fabagelle, *f.*, faux câprier, m.

fable (fé-b'l), n., fable, *f.*; apologue, m.

fable, v.a., feindre ; imaginer, inventer.

fabler, n., inventeur de fables, m.

fabric, n., édifice, ouvrage, m. ; fabrique, manufacture, fabrication ; étoffe, *f.*

fabric, v.a., fabriquer.

fabricate (-kéte), v.a., fabriquer, construire.

fabrication, n., construction, *f.*

fabricator, n., constructeur ; fabricateur, m., fabricatrice, *f.*

fabric-land (-la'n'de), n.pl., biens de fabrique, m.pl.

fabulist (-biou-), n., fabuliste, m.

fabulous (-biou-leusse), adj., fabuleux.

fabulously, adv., fabuleusement.

fabulousness, n., caractère fabuleux, m.

face (féce), n., visage, m. ; face, figure ; (fig.) apparence ; (impudence) audace ; (grimace) grimace ; (of a cannon—*d'un canon*) tranche ; (of a diamond—*d'un diamant*) facette, *f.*; (of a watch—*de montre*) cadran ; (of a wall—*de mur*) parement, m. ; (anat., arch., fort., geom.) face, *f.* To make —s at any one ; *faire des grimaces à quelqu'un.* To wash one's — ; *se laver la figure, se débarbouiller.* To put a good — on the matter ; *y faire bonne contenance.* To laugh in any one's — ; *rire au nez de quelqu'un.* To slap any one's — ; *donner un soufflet à quelqu'un.* Before any one's — ; *sous les yeux, à la barbe, au nez de quelqu'un.* — to — ; *face à face.* With a full — ; *de face.*

face, v.a., faire face à ; affronter ; (garments —*habits*) mettre un revers à, mettre un retroussis à ; (to cover—*couvrir*) revêtir.

face, v.n., prendre un faux dehors ; (milit.) faire front. To — about ; *faire volte-face.*

faced (féss'te), adj., à visage ; à figure. Double —; *à deux visages.* Full —; *qui a la figure pleine.* Fair —; *qui a beau visage.* Bold —; *effronté, impudent.*

faceless (-lèsse), adj., sans face.

face-painter (-pé'n't'eur), n., peintre de portraits, m.

face-painting, n., peinture de portraits, *f.*

facet (fass'ète), n., facette, *f.*

facetious (fa-ci-sheusse), adj., facétieux.

facetiously, adv., facétieusement.

facetiousness (-nèsse), n., facétie, *f.*

facies (fé-shi-ize), n., facies, m.

facile, adj., facile.

facileness (-nèsse), n., facilité, manque de fermeté, *f.*

facilitate (-téte), v.a., faciliter.

facilitation, n., action de faciliter ; facilité, *f.*

facility, n., facilité, *f.*

facing (fécigne), n., (of garments—*d'habits*) revers, retroussis ; (of structures—*de constructions*) parement, revêtement ; (milit.) front ; (fig.) extérieur, dehors, m.

fac-simile (-li), n., fac-similé, m.

fact, n., fait, m. Matter of —; *fait.* Matter-of-—man ; *homme positif,* m. In —; *en effet, au fait.* In point of —; *au fait.* To catch in the —; *prendre sur le fait.*

faction, n., faction ; discorde, *f.*

factionist, n., factieux, m.

factious (fak-shi-eusse), adj., factieux.

factiously, adv., factieusement.

factiousness (-nèsse), n., esprit factieux, m.

factitious (fak-tish'eusse), adj., factice.

factor (-teur), n., agent ; (com., math.) facteur, m.

factory, n., factorerie, manufacture, fabrique, *f.*

factotum (fak-tô-teume), n., factotum ; (print.) passe-partout, m.

factum (fak'teume), n., (math.) produit ; acte personnel, m.

facture (fak'tioure), n., (ant.) manière de faire, *f.*; art de faire, m.

faculty (fak'eul-), n., faculté, *f.*; pouvoir, talent, m. ; habileté, *f.*

facund, or **facundious** (fak'eu'n'de, -dieusse), adj., éloquent.

faddle, v.n., baliverner.

fade (féde), v.n., se faner, se flétrir ; s'évanouir.

fade, v.a., faner, flétrir.

fadge, v.n., s'accorder ; réussir.

fading, adj., qui se fane, qui se flétrit ; qui périt.

fadingly, adv., en se flétrissant.

fadingness (-nèsse), n., caractère périssable, m.

fady (fé-), adj., qui se fane, qui se flétrit.

fæces (fi-cèze), n.pl., matière fécale, *f.sing.*; (med.) fèces, *f.pl.*

fag, v.a., forcer à travailler, à piocher ; battre ; fatiguer.

fag, v.n., travailler, piocher.

fag, n., piocheur, travailleur ; souffre-douleur ; (knot in cloth—*nœud dans le drap*) nœud, m.

fag-end (-è'n'de), n., (of a tissue—*d'une étoffe*) lisière, *f.*; (com.) chef ; (nav.) (of a rope —*d'une corde*) bout ; (fig.) rebut, m.

fagot (fag'ote), n., fagot, m. ; (fort.) fascine, *f.*; (milit.) ⊙ passe-volant, m.

fagot, v.a., lier ensemble ; fagoter.

fail (féle), n., manque ; insuccès, m.

fail, v.a., manquer à ; faire défaut à.

fail, v.n., faillir, manquer ; échouer ; faiblir ; (com.) faire faillite.

failing, n., défaut, m. ; faute ; imperfection ; (com.) faillite, *f.*

failure (fél'ioure), n., manque, défaut ; affaiblissement, insuccès, m. ; affaire manquée, chute ; (com.) faillite, *f.*

fain (féne), adj., joyeux, heureux ; obligé.

fain, adv., bien volontiers.

faint (fé'n'te), adj., faible, abattu ; affaibli. — blue ; *bleu pâle.* — weather ; *temps mou.*

faint, v.n., s'évanouir, défaillir. To — away ; *s'évanouir.*

fainthearted (-hârt'ède), adj., poltron, sans cœur ; abattu.

faint-heartedly, *adv.*, lâchement ; dans l'abattement.

faint-heartedness (-nèsse), *n.*, manque de cœur, *m.* ; pusillanimité ; timidité, *f.*

fainting, *n.*, évanouissement, *m.* ; défaillance, *f.*

faintishness (fé'n't'ish'nèsse), *n.*, légère faiblesse, *f.*

faintly, *adv.*, faiblement, mollement ; dans l'abattement.

faintness (-nèsse), *n.*, faiblesse, *f.* ; abattement, *m.*

fainty, *adj.*, faible.

fair (fère), *adj.*, beau ; clair ; pur ; net ; (of the hair—*des cheveux*) blond ; (of the complexion —*du teint*) blanc ; (of the weather—*du temps*) beau ; (of the wind—*du vent*) bon, favorable ; (just—*raisonnable*) juste, équitable, probe, loyal ; (com.) courant ; (fig.) direct ; (fig.) bon, compétent ; (fig.) libéral. To be a — judge ; *être un bon juge.*

fair (fère), *adv.*, bien ; agréablement ; favorablement ; avec justice ; avec équité ; de bonne foi ; loyalement.

fair, *n.*, belle femme, belle ; (market—*marché*) foire, *f.* The — ; *le beau sexe, les belles.*

fair-haired (-hèr'de), *adj.*, aux cheveux blonds.

fair-hand (-ha'n'de), *adj.*, de belle apparence.

fairing, *n.*, cadeau de foire, *m.*

fairly, *adv.*, bien ; proprement ; complètement ; favorablement ; avec impartialité ; avec justice, honnêtement ; avec probité ; loyalement.

fairness (-nèsse), *n.*, beauté, clarté, pureté ; netteté ; (of the hair—*des cheveux*) couleur blonde ; (of the complexion—*du teint*) blancheur ; (justice) équité, probité ; justice ; loyauté, *f.*

fair-spoken (-spôk'è'n), *adj.*, à langue dorée.

fairy, *n.*, fée, *f.*

fairy, *adj.*, de fée ; féerique.

fairy-like (-laike), *adj.*, comme une fée.

faith (féth), *n.*, foi ; véracité, *f.* In —! *ma foi!* Breach of — ; (jur.) *violation de foi, f.*

faith! *int.*, ma foi ! en vérité !

faithful (-foule), *adj.*, fidèle.

faithfully, *adv.*, fidèlement.

faithfulness (-nèsse), *n.*, fidélité, *f.*

faithless (-lèsse), *adj.*, sans foi ; infidèle ; déloyal.

faithlessness (-lèss'nèsse), *n.*, infidélité ; déloyauté, *f.*

falcate. *or* **falcated** (-kéte, -két'ède), *adj.*, falciforme, courbe.

falchion (fàl'sheune), *n.*, glaive, *m.*

falcon (fô'k'n), *n.*, faucon, *m.*

falconer, *n.*, fauconnier, *m.*

falconet, *n.*, fauconneau, *m.*

faldstool (fàld'stoule), *n.*, prie-Dieu ; siège d'évêque ; siège pliant, *m.*

fall (fôl), *n.*, chute ; (of night—*de la nuit*) tombée ; (in price—*des prix*) baisse ; (of rain, of snow—*de pluie, de neige*) quantité tombée, *f.* ; chute des feuilles, *f.*, automne, *m.f.* There has been a — of snow ; *il est tombé de la neige.* To speculate on a — ; (com.) *jouer à la baisse.*

fall, *v.n.* (*preterit*, Fell ; *past part.*, Fallen), tomber ; retomber ; (in value—*de valeur*) baisser, diminuer ; (fig.) s'abaisser, descendre. To — away ; *maigrir, dépérir.* To — back ; *tomber en arrière, reculer.* To — down ; *tomber par terre.* To — from ; *abandonner, quitter.* To — in ; *tomber dedans ; s'écrouler ; s'ébouler* ; (milit.) *se ranger.* To —off ; *tomber.* To — on ; *tomber dessus ; attaquer.* To — out ; *tomber* ; (pers.) *se quereller, se brouiller* ; (of things—*des choses*) *arriver, advenir.* To — out with ; *se brouiller avec.* To — to ; *tomber en partage, échoir ; se mettre à ; se livrer à ; se rendre à ; se jeter sur ; tomber dessus.* To — into ; *se conformer à.*

fall, *v.a.*, laisser tomber ; diminuer ; (in America—*en Amérique*) abattre.

fallacious (fai-lé-sheusse), *adj.*, trompeur ; fallacieux, illusoire.

fallaciously, *adv.*, d'une manière trompeuse ; fallacieusement.

fallaciousness (-nèsse), *n.*, caractère trompeur, *m.* ; fausseté, *f.*

fallacy, *n.*, illusion, *f.* ; faux raisonnement ; sophisme, *m.*

fallibility, *n.*, faillibilité, *f.*

fallible (-li-b'l), *adj.*, faillible.

falling (fôl'-), *n.*, chute, *f.* — away ; *amaigrissement*, *m.* ; (fig.) *decadence*, *f.* — off ; *chute, défection ; apostasie, f.* — out ; *brouillerie. f.*

falling-sickness, *n.*, épilepsie, *f.* ; mal caduc ; haut mal, *m.*

tallow (fal'lô), *n.*, jachère, *f.*

fallow, *v.a.*, jachérer.

fallow, *adj.*, fauve ; (agri) en friche, en jachère ; (fig.) inculte.

fallow-finch (-fi'n'she), *n.*, (orni.) motteux, cul-blanc, *m.*

fallowness (-nèsse), *n.*, stérilité, *f.*

false (fôlse), *adj.*, faux ; (of imprisonment—*d'emprisonnement*) illégal.

falsefaced (-fés'-te), *adj.*, hypocrite.

false-hearted (-hâr't'ède), *adj.*, perfide, trompeur, au cœur faux.

false-heartedness (-nèsse), *n.*, perfidie, *f.*

falsehood (-houde), *n.*, fausseté, *f.* ; faux, *m.*

falsely, *adj.*, faussement.

falseness (-nèsse), *n.*, fausseté, *f.*

falsetto (fâl-), *n.*, (mus.) voix de tête, de fausset, *f.*, fausset, *m.*

falsifiable (fôls'i-faï'a'b'l), *adj.*, qui peut être falsifié.

falsification (-fi-ké-), *n.*, falsification, *f.*

falsifier (-faï'eur), *n.*, falsificateur ; faussaire, *m.*

falsify (-fa'ye), *v.a.*, falsifier ; altérer ; fausser.

falsity, *n.*, fausseté, *f.*

falter (fôl'-), *v.n.*, hésiter ; se troubler.

faltering, *n.*, hésitation, *f.* ; trouble, *m.*

falteringly, *adv.*, avec hésitation ; avec trouble.

fame (féme), *n.*, renommée, ⊙fâme, *f.*

famed (fén'de), *adj.*, renommé ; fameux

fameless (-lesse), *adj.*, sans renommée ; sans nom.

familiar, *n.*, ami intime ; démon ; esprit ; (Inquis.tion) familier, *m.*

familiar, *adj.*, de la famille ; familier. To be — with ; *être familier avec ; connaître familièrement.* To grow — ; *se familiariser.*

familiarity, *n.*, familiarité, *f.*

familiarize (-aïze), *v.a.*, familiariser.

familiarly, *adv.*, familièrement.

family, *n.*, famille, *f.* To be in the — way ; *être enceinte.*

famine, *n.*, famine, *f.*

famish, *v.a.*, affamer.

famish, *v.n.*, être affamé ; mourir de faim.

famishment, *n.*, faim extrême, *f.*

famous (fé'meusse), *adj.*, fameux.

famously, *adv.*, avec une grande renommée ; furieusement, prodigieusement, fameusement.

fan, *n.*, éventail, *m.* ; (of a windmill—*de moulin à vent*) aile, *f.* ; (agri.) van, *m.*

fan, *v.a.*, éventer ; (agri.) vanner ; (fig.) exciter.

fanatic, *or* **fanatical**, *adj.*, fanatique.

fanatic, *n.*, fanatique, *m.f.*

fanatically, *adv.*, d'une manière fanatique ; avec fanatisme.

fanaticism, *n.*, fanatisme, *m.*

fanaticize (-çaïze), *v.a.*, fanatiser.

fan-carrier, *n.*, porte-éventail, *m.*

fanciful (-foule), *adj.*, fantastique ; qui a des fantaisies ; fantasque.

fancifully, *adv.*, fantastiquement; capricieusement.

fancifulness, *n.*, caprice; caractère fantastique; caractère fantasque, *m.*

fancy, *n.*, imagination; fantaisie; idée, *f.*; goût, *m.* To take a — to any one; *prendre quelqu'un en affection.*

fancy, *adj.*, de fantaisie; (of a ball—*d'un bal*) costumé, travesti.

fancy, *v.a.*, s'imaginer; se figurer; avoir du goût pour.

fancy, *v.n.*, s'imaginer; se figurer.

fancy-framed (-fré'm'de), *adj.*, créé par l'imagination.

fancy-monger (-meu'n'gheur), *n.*, songe-ereux, *m.*

fancy-sick, *adj.*, qui a l'imagination malade.

fandango, *n.*, fandango, *m.*

fane (féne), *n.*, temple; fanum, *m.*

fanfaron (-rô'n), *n.*, fanfaron, *m.*

fanfaronade (-éde) *n.*, fanfaronnade, *f.*

fang (fan'gn), *n.*, griffe, serre; (of persons' teeth—*des dents humaines*) racine, *f.*; (of dogs—*de chien*) croc, *m.*; (of boars—*de sanglier*) défense, *f.*

fang, *v.a.*, saisir.

fanged (fan'gn'de), *adj.*, armé de dents; armé de griffes; armé de serres; armé de crocs; armé de défenses.

fangle (fan'gn'g'l), *n.*, (ant.) nouvelle mais stupide invention, *f.*

fangled (fan'gn'g'lde), *adj.*, (ant.) trop voyant; éclatant. New— ; *de nouvelle invention.*

fangless, *adj.*, sans dents, sans crocs; sans serres; sans griffes; sans défenses.

fanlight (-laïte), *n.*, fenêtre en éventail, *f.*, œil-de-bœuf, *m.*

fanlike (-laïke), *adj.*, en éventail.

fanmaker (-mék-), *n.*, éventailliste, *m.*

fannel, *or* **fanon**, *n.*, (c.rel.) fanon, *m.*

fanner, *n.*, personne qui évente, *f.*; vanneur, *m.*

fanshaped (-shépte), *adj.*, en éventail.

fan-stick, *n.*, lame d'éventail, *f.*

fantasied (-cide), *adj.*, travaillé par des fantaisies.

fantast, *or* **fantastic**, *n.*, personne fantasque, *f.*

fantastic, *or* **fantastical**, *adj.*, fantastique; (pers.) fantasque.

fantastically, *adv.*, fantastiquement; fantasquement.

fantasticalness, *n.*, fantaisie, *f.*; caractère fantasque, *m.*

fantasy (-ci), *n.*, fantaisie, *f.*

fantom. *V.* **phantom.**

faquir, *n.*, faquir, *m.*

far (fâre), *adv.*, loin; au loin; bien; de beaucoup; beaucoup. As — as; *aussi loin que;* *jusqu'à.* By —; *de beaucoup.* How — ? *jusqu'où ?* How — is it to . . . . ? *combien y a-t-il d'ici* . . . . ? So — as to; *jusqu'à.* In so — as; *en tant que.* Thus —; *jusque là; jusqu'ici.* — from; *loin de.* — from it; *bien loin de là; tant s'en faut.* The day was — spent; *la journée était en grande partie passée.* — inferior; *bien inférieur.*

far, *adj.*, lointain; éloigné; reculé.

farce (fârce), *v.a.*, farcir; enfler.

farce, *n.*, (thea.) farce, *f.*

farcical, *adj.*, de farce; burlesque.

farcically, *adv.*, burlesquement.

farcin, *or* **farcy** (fâr-), *n.*, (vet.) farcin, *m.*

fard (fârde), *v.a.*, farder.

fardel (fâr'-), *n.*, (ant.) fardeau; paquet, *m.*

fare (fére), *v.n.*, aller, se porter; se nourrir. To — ill; *être mal; faire mauvaise chère.* To — well; *faire bonne chère.*

fare, *n.*, course, *f.*; (price—*coût*) prix de la course, *m.*; (pers.) voyageur, *m.*; (food—*ali-*

mentation) chère, *f.*, plats, mets, *m.pl.* Bill of — ; *menu d'un repas*, *m.*; (at an eating-house — *au restaurant*) carte, *f.*

fare-well, *or* **farewell** (fèr'wèle), *n.*, adieu, *m.* To bid any one —; *dire adieu à quelqu'un.*

fare-well, *or* **farewell**, *adj.*, d'adieu.

fare-well, *or* **farewell**, *adv.*, porte-toi bien; portez-vous bien; adieu.

far-fetch (-fètshe), *n.*, (ant.) détour (ruse), *m.*

far-fetched (-fètsh'te), *adj.*, cherché au loin; amené, apporté de loin; recherché; tiré par les cheveux.

far-gone, *adj.*, avancé.

farina, *n.*, farine, *f.*; (bot.) pollen, *m.*; (chem.) fécule, *f.* Fossil —; *espèce de carbonate de chaux.*

farinaceous (-né'sheusse), *adj.*, farineux, farinacé.

farm (fârme), *v.a.*, affermer; exploiter; faire valoir. — out; *donner à ferme.*

farm (fârme), *n.*, ferme, *f.*

farmable (fârm'a'b'l), *adj.*, que l'on peut affermer.

farm-bailiff (-bé-life), *n.*, régisseur, de ferme, *m.*

farmer, *n.*, fermier, *m.*

farmery, *n.*, corps de ferme, *m.*

farm-house (-haouce), *n.*, ferme (habitation), *f.*

farming, *n.*, exploitation d'une ferme; agriculture, *f.*

farmost (fâr'môste), *adj.*, le dernier, le plus éloigné.

farm-yard (-yârde), *n.*, cour de ferme, *f.*

farness, *n.*, éloignement, *m.*; distance, *f.*

faro (fé'ro), *n.*, pharaon, *m.*

farraginous (far-radj'i-), *adj.*, composé de divers matériaux.

farrago (far-régô), *n.*, farrago, *m.*

farrier, *n.*, maréchal; maréchal ferrant; vétérinaire, artiste vétérinaire, médecin vétérinaire, *m.*

farrier, *v.n.*, exercer le métier de maréchal.

farrow (-rô), *n.*, cochonnée, *f.*

farrow, *adj.*, stérile.

farrow, *v.a.*, mettre bas.

far-sought (-sôte), *adj.*, cherche; recherché, tiré par les cheveux, forcé. — expressions; *expressions forcées, tirées par les cheveux, recherchées.* — learning; *savoir recherché.*

farthel (fârthèle), *v.a.*, (nav.) carguer, ferler.

farther (fârtheur), *adj.*, ultérieur, plus éloigné; autre, encore un.

farther, *adv.*, plus loin, de plus, ultérieurement; en outre.

farthermore. *adv.*, de plus.

farthest (fârthèste), *n.*, le plus loin.

farthing (fârthigne), *n.*, farthing (centime: 2.42); liard, *m.* Not to be worth a — ; *n'avoir pas un sou vaillant.*

farthing-gale (fârthing-ghéle), *n.*, cerceau; cerceau de jupon, *m.*

farthingsworth (fârthign'z'weurth), *n.*, quantité pour la valeur d'un farthing, *f.*

fasces (fas'size), *n.pl.*, faisceaux, *m.pl.*

fascia (fash'i'a), *n.*, (arch.) face, plate-bande; (astron.) bande; (anat.) aponévrose, *f.*, fascia; (surg.) bandage, *m.*

fascial (fas'sial), *adj.*, des faisceaux.

fasciated (fa-shi-ét'éde), *adj.*, à face.

fasciation (fa-shi-é-), *n.*, (bot.) fasciation, (surg.) bandage, *m.*

fascicle (fas'si-c'l), *n.*, (bot.) fascicule, *m.*

fascicular (fas-sik'iou-), *adj.*, (bot.) fasciculaire; fasciculé.

fasciculated (fas-si-kiou-lét'éde), *adj.*, (bot.) fasciculé.

fascinate (-néte), *v.a.*, fasciner; enchanter, charmer, *m.*

fascination (-né-), *n.*, fascination, charme, *m.*

fascine (-sine), *n.*, fascine, *f.*

fashion (fash'eune), *n.*, mode ; façon, forme, *f.* ; modèle, *m.* In — ; *à la mode.* It is the — ; *c'est la mode.* In the French — ; *à la française.* In the English — ; *à l'anglaise.* Out of — ; *passé de mode.* People of — ; *gens à la mode, m.pl.* Woman of — ; *femme à la mode, f.* Man of — ; *homme à la mode, m.*

fashion, *v.a.*, façonner, former.

fashionable (fash'eu'n'ab'l), *adj.*, à la mode ; élégant ; fashionable.

fashionableness, *n.*, élégance ; vogue, *f.*

fashionably, *adv.*, à la mode, élégamment.

fashionist, *n.*, façonnier, *m.*, façonnière, *f.*

fast (fâste), *n.*, jeûne, *m.*

fast, *v.n.*, jeûner.

fast, *adj.*, (firm—*adhérent*) ferme, fixé ; (quick —*prompt*) vite, rapide ; (faithful—*constant*) fidèle ; (of sleep—*du sommeil*) profond ; (of colours—*des couleurs*) bon teint ; (nav.) amarré ; (of a door, a window—*d'une porte, d'une fenêtre*) qui ne s'ouvre pas. To make — ; *attacher* ; (doors, windows—*portes, fenêtres*) *fermer* ; (nav.) *amarrer.*

fast, *adv.*, (firm—*avec force*) ferme ; fortement ; (quick—*avec célérité*) vite ; (of raining— *de la pluie*) fort, à verse ; (of one asleep—*du dormir*) profondément. To hold — ; *tenir ferme.*

fasten (fâs's'n), *v.a.*, fixer ; attacher, lier ; (windows, doors—*portes, fenêtres*) fermer.

fasten, *v.n.*, s'attacher.

fastener, *n.*, personne qui attache ; qui lie, *f.*

fastening, *n.*, attache ; fermeture, *f.*

faster (fâst'eur), *n.*, jeûneur, *m.*, jeûneuse, *f.*

faster, *adv.*, plus vite ; plus fort.

fastidiosity, *n.*, dédain ; goût difficile, *m.*

fastidious, *adj.*, dédaigneux ; difficile ; délicat.

fastidiously, *adv.*, dédaigneusement ; difficilement.

fastidiousness, *n.*, dédain ; goût difficile, *m.*

fastigiate, *or* **fastigiated** (fas-tidj'iéte, -tède), *adj.*, (bot.) fastigié.

fasting (fâst'-), *n.*, jeûne, *m.*

fasting-day, *n.*, jour de jeûne, jour maigre, *m.*

fastly (fâst'-), *adv.*, (ant.) ferme, fermement.

fastness (fâst'-), *n.*, fermeté, solidité ; (fig.) sécurité ; (stronghold—*forteresse*) place forte, *f.*

fastuous (fast'iou-), *adj.*, dédaigneux ; hautain ; fastueux.

fat (fate), *n.*, gras, *m.* ; graisse, *f.*

fat, *adj.*, gras ; gros.

fat, *v.a.*, engraisser.

fat, *v.n.*, engraisser ; être à l'engrais.

fatal, *adj.*, fatal, funeste, mortel.

fatalism, *n.*, fatalisme, *m.*

fatalist, *n.*, fataliste, *m.*

fatality, *n.*, fatalité, *f.*

fatally, *adv.*, fatalement, funestement, mortellement.

fatalness, *n.*, fatalité, *f.*

fate (féte), *n.*, destin, sort, *m.* The —s ; *les Parques, f.pl.*

fate, *v.a.*, destiner ; arrêter, décréter.

fated (fét'ède), *adj.*, destiné.

father (fâ-*theur*), *n.*, père, *m.* —s ; *pères* ; *ancêtres ; aïeux, m.pl.* Grand— ; *grand-père, m.* God— ; *parrain, m.* Step— ; -in-law ; *beau-père, m.* Almighty — ; *père éternel, m.* Holy — ; *saint père, m.*

father, *v.a.*, adopter. To — upon ; *attribuer à ; gratifier de.*

fatherhood (-houde), *n.*, paternité, *f.*

fatherland (-la'n'de), *n.*, pays natal, *m.*, patrie, *f.*

fatherless, *adj.*, orphelin, sans père.

fatherlessness, *n.*, état d'orphelin.

fatherliness, *adj.*, amour paternel, *m.*

fatherly, *adj.*, paternel ; de père.

fatherly, *adv.*, paternellement ; en père.

fathom (fath'eume), *n.*, toise ; (fig.) portée, *f.*

fathom (fath'eume), *v.a.*, sonder ; approfondir ; pénétrer.

fathomable (-'n-b'l), *adj.*, pénétrable.

fathomless, *adj.*, impénétrable ; insondable.

fatidic, *or* **fatidical,** *adj.*, fatidique.

fatiferous (-tif'èr'-), *adj.*, mortel.

fatigable (-ga-b'l), *adj.*, (ant.) qui se fatigue aisément.

fatigue (-tîghe), *n.*, fatigue, *f.* To stand — ; *supporter la fatigue.* To be worn out with — ; *n'en pouvoir plus de fatigue ; être rendu.*

fatigue, *v.a.*, fatiguer.

fatiguing, *adj.*, fatigant.

fatiscence, *n.*, fente, crevasse, *f.*

fatling, *n.*, bête grasse, *f.*

fatness, *n.*, graisse, *f.* ; (pers.) embonpoint, *m.* ; (fig.) fertilité, abondance, *f.*

fatten (fat't'n), *v.a.*, engraisser ; nourrir, alimenter.

fatten, *v.n.*, engraisser.

fattener, *n.*, personne qui engraisse, qui nourrit, *f.*

fattiness, *n.*, onctuosité, *f.*

fattish, *adj.*, un peu gras.

fatty, *adj.*, graisseux.

fatuity (fa-tiou-i-ti), *n.*, stupidité, imbécillité, sottise, *f.*

fatuous (fat'-iou-eusse), *adj.*, stupide, imbécile.

fatwitted, *adj.*, imbécile.

fauces (fô-cize), *n.pl.*, (anat.) isthme du gosier ; gosier, *m.*

faucet (fô-cète), *n.*, canule (in a cask—*d'un tonneau en perce*), cannelle, cannette, *f.*

faulchion (fôl-sheune), *n.* V. **falchion.**

fault (fôlte), *n.*, faute, *f.* ; défaut, *m.* To find — with ; *trouver à redire à.*

fault-finder (-fai'n'deur), *n.*, personne qui trouve toujours à redire, *f.* ; censeur, *m.*

faultily, *adv.*, d'une manière fautive.

faultiness, *n.*, défauts, *m.pl.* ; caractère fautif, *m.* ; imperfection, *f.*

faultless, *adj.*, sans défaut, sans faute ; parfait.

faultlessness, *n.*, perfection, *f.*

faulty, *adj.*, en faute, coupable ; fautif, erroné.

fauna (fô-), *n.*, faune, *f.*

fautor, *n.*, fauteur, *m.*

fautress, *n.*, fautrice, *f.*

favour (fé-veur), *n.*, faveur ; permission : grâce, *f.* ; (ribbons—*rubans*) couleurs, *f.pl.*, faveur, *f.* To wear a — ; *porter des couleurs.* To ask a — of ; *demander une faveur à.* To be in — with ; *être dans les bonnes grâces de.* By — ; *par la faveur.* By — of ; under — of ; *à la faveur de.*

favour, *v.a.*, favoriser ; gratifier ; ménager.

favourable, *adj.*, favorable.

favourableness, *n.*, caractère favorable, *m.* ; bienveillance, *f.*

favourably, *adv.*, favorablement.

favoured (fé-veurde), *adj.*, favorisé, Ill- — ; *de mauvaise mine.* Well- — ; *de bonne mine.*

favourer, *n.*, personne qui favorise, *f.* ; protecteur, partisan, *m.*

favourite (fé-veur'ite), *n.*, favori, *m.*, favorite, *f.*

favourite (fé-veur-ite), *adj.*, favori.

favourless, *adj.*, non favorisé.

fawn (fô'n), *n.*, (mam.) faon, *m.* ; (fig.) (pers.) caresse servile, basse flatterie ; (fig.) (of animals—*des animaux*) caresse, *f.*

fawn, *v.n.*, (of animals—*des animaux*) faonner. To — on ; (animal) *caresser* ; (pers.) *caresser servilement, flatter, flagorner.*

fawner, *n.*, flatteur servile ; flagorneur, *m.*

fawning, *n.*, (of animals—*des animaux*) caresse; (pers.) caresse servile; flatterie flagornerie, *f.*

fawningly, *adv.*, en caressant; d'une manière caressante; servilement.

fay (fé), *n.*, fée, *f.*

fay, *v.a.*, (carp.) joindre; affleurer.

fealty (fi-), *n.*, fidélité, *f.*

fear (fire), *n.*, crainte, peur, *f.* For — of; *de peur de, de crainte de.* From —; out of —; *par peur.* Bodily —; *crainte pour sa personne.*

fear, *v.a.*, craindre, avoir peur; redouter.

fear, *v.n.*, craindre; avoir peur, être craintif.

fearful (-foule), *adj.*, qui a peur; craintif; timide; terrible; (of things—*des choses*) effrayant.

fearfully, *adv.*, craintivement; avec crainte; avec effroi; terriblement; d'une manière effrayante.

fearfulness, *n.*, crainte, *f.*

fearless, *adj.*, sans peur; intrépide.

fearlessly, *adv.*, sans peur, sans crainte.

fearlessness, *n.*, intrépidité, *f.*

feasibility, *n.*, possibilité d'exécution, *f.*

feasible (fi-zi'b'l), *adj.*, faisable, exécutable.

feast (fiste), *n.*, festin, *m.*; fête, *f.*; régal, *m.*

feast, *v.a.*, donner un festin à; fêter, régaler, festoyer.

feast, *v.n.*, faire festin; se repaître.

feaster, *n.*, donneur de festins; amateur de bonne chère, *m.*

feastful (-foule), *adj.*, joyeux; de fête.

feasting, *n.*, festins; régals, *m.pl.*

feat, *n.*, action, *f.*; exploit; fait, haut fait, *m.*

feather (fèth'eur), *n.*, plume; (bot.) aigrette; (of a bird's wing and tail—*de la queue et des ailes d'oiseaux*) penne, *f.*; (milit.) plumet, *m.*

feather, *v.a.*, mettre des plumes à; orner d'une plume; (of birds—*des oiseaux*) côcher; (fig.) empenner, donner des ailes à; (to enrich —*enrichir*) emplumer.

feather-bed (-bède), *n.*, lit de plume, *m.*

feather-driver (-draïv'eur), *n.*, plumassier, *m.*

feathered (fèth'eurde), *adj.*, garni de plumes; emplumé; (of birds—*des oiseaux*) ailé, emplumé; (of arrows—*des flèches*) empenné; (fig.) enrichi.

feather-edged (-èdj'de), *adj.*, en biseau.

feather-grass (-grâce), *n.*, (bot.) stipe; stipe empennée, houque molle, *f.*

featherless, *adj.*, sans plumes.

feather-seller (-sèl'eur), *n.*, plumassier, *m.*

feather-trade (-tréde), *n.*, plumasserie, *f.*

feathery, *adj.*, garni de plumes, emplumé; (bot.) plumeux; (fig.) léger comme une plume; (of birds—*des oiseaux*) ailé, emplumé.

feature (fit'ioure), *n.*, trait, *m.*; figure, *f.*; trait caractéristique, *m.*; forme, *f.*

featured (fit'iourde), *adj.*, qui a des traits. Hard- —; *aux traits durs.*

featureless, *adj.*, sans traits.

febricitant, *adj.*, (med.) fébricitant, fiévreux.

febrifuge (fè-bri-fioud'je), *adj.*, fébrifuge.

febrifuge, *n.*, fébrifuge, *m.*

febrile (fi-braile, *ou* fè-), *adj.*, fébrile.

february (fèb'rou-), *n.*, février, *m.*

fecal (fi-), *adj.*, fécal, excrémentitiel.

feces (fi-cize), *n.* *V.* **fæces**.

fecial (fi-shi-al), *adj.*, fécial.

fecula (fèk'iou-), *n.*, (chim, *f.*; amidon, *m.*

feculence, *or* **feculency**, *n.*, féculence, *f.*

feculent, *adj.*, féculent.

fecund (fèc'un'n'd), *adj.*, fécond.

fecundate, *or* **fecundify** (-déte, -fa'ye), *v.a.*, féconder.

fecundation (-dé-), *n.*, fécondation, *f.*

fecundify, *v.a.* *V.* **fecundate**.

fecundity, *n.*, fécondité, *f.*

federal (fèd'èr-), *adj.*, fédéral.

federalism, *n.*, fédéralisme, *m.*

federalist, *n.*, fédéraliste, *m.*

federate (-éte), *adj.*, ligué, fédéré.

federation (-ré-), *n.*, fédération, alliance, *f.*

federative (-ré-), *adj.*, fédératif.

fee (fi), *n.*, (feudalism—*féodalité*) fief, *m.*; (jur.) propriété héréditaire, *f.*; (of doctors, &c.; —*de médecins, &c.*) honoraire, *m.*

fee, *v.a.*, payer; payer des honoraires à; graisser la patte à.

feeble (fi'b'l), *adj.*, faible.

feeble-minded (-maï'n'dède), *adj.*, faible d'esprit.

feebleness, *n.*, faiblesse, *f.*

feebly, *adv.*, faiblement.

feed (fide), *n.*, nourriture; (for cattle—*des bestiaux*) pâture, pâturage, *m.*

feed (fide), *v.a.*, nourrir; (cattle—*bestiaux*) paître, faire paître; (animal) donner à manger à.

feed, *v.n.*, se nourrir; (of animals—*des animaux*) paître, manger. To — upon; *se nourrir de; se repaître de.*

feeder, *n.*, personne qui nourrit, *f.*; mangeur, convive; (tech.) appareil d'alimentation, *m.*

feeding, *n.*, nourriture; (for cattle—*des bestiaux*) pâture, *f.*

feel (file), *n.*, toucher; attouchement; tact, *m.*

feel, *v.a.* (*preterit and past part.*, Felt), sentir; tâter; toucher; éprouver; ressentir; se ressentir de. To — any one's pulse; *tâter le pouls à quelqu'un.*

feel, *v.n.*, sentir; se sentir. To — for; *avoir de la sympathie pour.* To — cold; *avoir froid.* To — soft; *être doux au toucher.*

feeler, *n.*, personne qui sent, *f.*; (mol) tentacule, *f.*; (of a cat—*du chat*) moustache; (ent.) palpe, antenne, *f.*; (fig.) allusion détournée, *f.*

feeling, *n.*, attouchement, toucher, tact; sentiment, *m.*; sensibilité, *f.* To have no —; *n'avoir pas de sensibilité, n'avoir pas d'entrailles.*

feeling, *adj.*, touchant; sensible.

feelingly, *adv.*, d'une manière touchante; d'une manière sensible; sensiblement.

fee-simple (fi-si'm'p'l), *n.*, propriété libre, *f.*; (feudal—*féodalité*) fief simple, *m.*

feet (fite), *n.pl.* *V.* **foot**.

feetless, *adj.*, sans pieds.

feign (féne), *v.a.*, feindre, inventer, imaginer.

feign (féne), *v.n.*, feindre; dissimuler.

feigned (fé'n'de), *adj.*, feint, inventé; dissimulé; imaginé.

feignedly, *adv.*, avec feinte.

feigner, *n.*, personne qui feint, *f.*

feigning, *n.*, feinte; dissimulation, *f.*

feigningly, *adv.*, avec feinte.

feint (fé'n'te) *n.*, feinte, *f.*

feldspar, *or* **feldspath** (fèld'spâr, -spath), *n.*, (min.) feldspath, *m.*

feldspathic, *or* **feldspathose** (-spath'ik, -spath'oze), *adj.*, feldspathique.

felicitate (fi-li-ci-téte), *v.a.*, (ant.) féliciter; rendre heureux.

felicitation (fi-li-ci-té-), *n.*, félicitation, *f.*

felicitous (fi-), *adj.*, heureux.

felicitously, *adv.*, heureusement.

felicity (fi-), *n.*, félicité, *f.*; bonheur, *m.*

feline (fi-laïne), *adj.*, félin; de chat.

fell (fèle), *n.*, peau, fourrure, *f.*

fell, *adj.*, barbare, cruel.

fell, *v.a.*, abattre; assommer.

feller, *n.*, personne qui abat, *f.*

fellmonger (-meu'n'g'gheur), *n.*, marchand de peaux, *m.*

fellness, *n.*, cruauté, férocité, *f.*

felloe (fèl'lô), *n.* *V.* **felly**.

fellow (fèl'lô), *n.*, compagnon ; camarade ; garçon ; gaillard ; (b.s.) individu, drôle ; (of a university—*d'une université*) agrégé ; (of things —*des choses*) pendant, pareil, *m.* Bad —; *mauvais garnement, m.* Good —; *bon enfant, m.* Fine —; *beau garçon, m.* Poor —; *pauvre garçon, m.* Odd —; *drôle de corps, m.* Old —; *vieux bonhomme, m.* Bed—; *camarade de lit, m.* School- —; *camarade de classe, m.* These shoes are not —s ; *ces souliers ne sont pas pareils.* To be hail — well met; *se traiter de pair à compagnon.* Here is the — to this picture; *voici le pendant de ce tableau.*

fellow, *v.a.*, assortir ; associer.

fellow-creature (-krit-ioure), *n.*, semblable, *m., f.*

fellow-heir (-ère), *n.*, cohéritier, *m.*

fellow-helper (-hèlp'eur), *n.*, coadjuteur, *m.*, aide, *m.f.*

fellow-labourer (-lé-beur'eur), *n.*, collaborateur, *m.*

fellow-like (-laïke), *or* **fellowly**, *adj.*, sociable.

fellow-servant (-seur-), *n.*, compagnon de service, *m.*

fellowship, *n.*, société, confraternité, *f.*; (in universities—*des universités*) grade d'agrégé, *m.*; (arith.) règle de société, règle de compagnie, *f.*

fellow-soldier (-sôl'djeu'r), *n.*, frère d'armes, *m.*

fellow-student (-stiou'-), *n.*, condisciple, *m.*

felly (fèl'li), *adv.*, cruellement.

felly (fèl'li), *n.*, jante, *f.*

felo-de-se (fîlô-di-cî), *n.*, (jur.) suicide, *m.*

felon (fèl'o'n), *n.*, auteur d'un délit, d'un crime, d'un crime capital; criminel ; (med.) panaris, *m.*

felon, *adj.*, félon, traître ; inhumain.

felonious, *adj.*, félon, traître ; (jur.) criminel.

feloniously, *adv.*, en traître; (jur.)avec une intention criminelle.

felony, *n.*, (jur.) délit, crime, crime capital, *m.*

felt (fèlte), *n.*, feutre, chapeau de feutre, *m.*

felt, *or* **felter**, *v.a.*, feutrer.

felting, *n.*, feutrage, *m.*

felucca (fi-leuk'ka), *n.*, felouque, *f.*

female (fi-méle), *n.*, femme ; personne ; jeune personne ; (of animals only—*des animaux*) femelle, *f.*

female, *adj.*, féminin ; de femme ; (bot., and of animals—*des animaux*) femelle.

feme-covert, *or* **femme-covert** (fî'm'keuv'eurte), *n.*, (jur.) femme en puissance de mari, *f.*

feme-sole, *or* **femme-sole** (fî'm'sôle), *n.*, (jur.) fille, *f.*

feminacy, *or* **feminality** (fè'm'i-), *n.*, nature de femme, *f.*

feminine (fè'-m-i-), *adj.*, féminin ; efféminé. In the — gender; (gram.) *au féminin.*

femininely, *adv.*, comme une femme, en femme.

femoral (fè'm'o-), *adj.*, fémoral ; crural.

fen (fè'n), *n.*, marais, marécage, *m.*

fence (fè'n'ce), *n.*, clôture, enceinte, barrière, balustrade ; (art of fencing—*art de faire des armes*) escrime, *f.*

fence, *v.a.*, enclore ; mettre une clôture à ; mettre une enceinte à ; protéger, défendre. To — in ; *enclore.*

fence, *v.n.*, faire des clôtures ; (with foils—*avec des fleurets*) faire des armes, tirer des armes.

fenceless, *adj.*, ouvert ; sans clôture.

fencer, *n.*, tireur d'armes, *m.*

fencible (fè'n'ci'b'l), *adj.*, capable de défense.

fencibles, *n.pl.*, soldats pour la défense du territoire, lesquels ne peuvent être envoyés à l'étranger, *m.pl.*

fencing, *n.*, enceinte, clôture ; (with foils— *avec des fleurets*) escrime, *f.*

fencing-master (-mâs-teur), *n.*, maître d'armes. *m.*

fencing-school(-skoule),*n.*, salle d'armes,*f.*

fend·(fè'n'd), *v.a.*, se défendre de. — off; *parer ; écarter.*

fender, *n.*, garde-cendres, *m.* ; (nav.) défense, *f.*

fennel (fè'n'nèl), *n.*, fenouil ; aneth doux, *m.*

fennish, *or* **fenny** (fè'n'-), *adj.*, marécageux, des marais.

fenu-greek (fî-niou-grîke), *n.*, (bot.) fenugrec, senègre, senegré, senegrain, *m.*

feod (fioude), *n.*, fief, *m.*

feodal (fioud'-), *adj.*, féodal.

feodality (fioud'-), *n.*, féodalité, *f.*

feoff (fèfe), *v.a.*, investir d'un fief ; donner l'investiture à.

feoffee (fèf'fi), *n.*, personne investie d'un héritage foncier, *f.*

feoffer, *or* **feoffor** (fèf'eur), *n.*, personne qui investit d'un héritage foncier, *f.*

feoffment (fèf-), *n.*, inféodation, *f.* ; investissement d'un héritage foncier, *m.*

feracious (fi-ré-sheusse), *adj.*, fécond, fertile.

feracity (fî-ra-), *n.*, fertilité, *f.*

ferine (fi-raïne), *adj.*, sauvage, cruel.

ferineness (fî-raï'n'nèsse), *or* **ferity** (fî-), *n.*, férocité, *f.*

ferment (fèr-), *n.*, ferment, *m.* ; fermentation, *f.*

ferment, *v.n.*, fermenter.

ferment, *v.a.*, faire fermenter.

fermentable (-'a-b'l), *adj.*, fermentable.

fermentation (feur-mè'n-té-), *n.*, fermentation, *f.*

fermentative, *adj.*, fermentatif ; de fermentation.

fermentativeness, *n.*, qualité de ce qui est fermentatif, *f.*

fern (feurne), *n.*, fougère, *f.*

ferny, *adj.*, plein de fougère.

ferocious (fî-rô-sheusse), *adj.*, féroce.

ferociously, *adv.*, avec férocité.

ferociousness, *or* **ferocity** (fî-), *n.*, férocité, *f.*

ferreous (fèr-ri-), *adj.*, ferrugineux.

ferret (fèr'rète), *n.*, (mam.) furet, *m.* ; (tape —*ruban*) padou, *m.*

ferret, *v.a.*, fureter. To — out ; *traquer, dépister.*

ferreter, *n.*, fureteur, *m.*

ferriage (fèr'ri-édje), *n.*, pontonage, prix du passage dans un bac, *m.*

ferriferous (fèr'rif-èr'-), *adj.*, ferrifère.

ferruginated (fèr'riou'djinétède), *adj.*, rouilleux, rubigineux.

ferruginous, *or* **ferruginous** (fer'rioudji-n'-), *adj.*, ferrugineux.

ferrule (fèr-ril, *ou* fèr'reule), *n.*, virole, *f.*

ferry, *v.a.*, passer dans un bac. To — over, to — across ; *passer dans un bac.*

ferry, *v.n.*, passer l'eau.

ferry-boat (-bôte), *n.*, bac ; bateau de passeur, *m.*

ferry-man (-ma'n), *n.*, passeur ; (poet.) nocher, *m.*

fertile (feur'til), *adj.*, fertile, fécond.

fertilely, *adv.*, abondamment ; fertilement.

fertileness, *or* **fertility**, *n.*, fertilité, *f.*

fertilize (-aïze), *v.a.*, fertiliser.

ferula (fèr'iou-), *or* **ferule** (fèr'eule), *n.*, férule, *f.* ; (of the Eastern empire—*de l'empire d'Orient*) sceptre impérial, *m.*

ferule, *v.a.*, donner une férule à ; donner des férules à.

fervency (feur'vè'n-), *n.*, ardeur, ferveur, *f.*

fervent, *adj.*, ardent, fervent.
fervently, *adv.*, ardemment, avec ferveur.
fervid (feur-), *adj.*, ardent, chaud, vif.
fervidly *adv.*, avec chaleur ; ardemment.
fervidness, *n.*, chaleur, ardeur, *f.*
fervour (feur-veur), *n.*, chaleur ; ferveur, ardeur, *f.*
fescennine (-naïne), *adj.*, fescennin ; licencieux.
fescennine, *n. sing.*, vers fescennins, *m.pl.*
fescue (fès'kiou), *n.*, (ant.) touche. *f.*, pour montrer les lettres aux enfants qui apprennent à lire.
fesse, *n.*, (her.) fasce, *f.*
festal, *adj.*, de fête.
fester (fès'teur), *v.n.*, s'ulcérer ; se corrompre ; s'envenimer.
festival, *n.*, fête, *f.* ; festival, *m.*
festival, *adj.*, de fête.
festive, or **festivous**, *adj.*, de fête ; joyeux.
festivity, *n.*, fête ; gaîté, joie, *f.*
festoon (-toune), *n.*, feston, *m.*
festoon, *v.a.*, festonner.
festucine (-tiou-çaine), *adj.*, couleur de paille.
festucous, *adj.*, de paille.
fetch (fètshe), *n.*, ruse ; finesse, *f.* ; tour, *m.*
fetch, *v.a.*, chercher ; aller chercher ; amener ; apporter ; (of price—*prix*) rapporter ; (one's breath—*l'haleine*) prendre, reprendre ; (a pump —*pompe*) amorcer ; (a sigh—*soupir*) pousser ; (a blow—*un coup*) porter. To — away ; *emporter, emmener.* To — down ; *faire descendre, abaisser.* To — in ; *faire entrer.* To — off ; *ôter, enlever.* To — out ; *faire sortir, aller chercher.* To — up ; *monter, aller chercher.* These goods — a great deal ; *cette marchandise rapporte beaucoup.*
fetch, *v.n.*, se mouvoir.
fetcher, *n.*, chercheur, *m.*, chercheuse, *f.*
feticism, or **fetichism**, *n.*, fétichisme, *m.*
fetid, *adj.*, fétide.
fetidness, *n.*, fétidité, *f.*
fetlock (fèt'-), *n.*, fanon (of the horse—*du cheval*), *m.*
fetor (fi-teur), *n.*, fétidité, mauvaise odeur, *f.*
fetter (fèt'teur), *v.a.*, mettre dans les fers ; (fig.) entraver.
fetterless, *adj.*, sans fers ; sans entraves.
fetters (fèt'teurze), *n.*, fers, *m.pl.*; entraves, *f.pl.*
fettle (fèt't'l), *v.n.*, niaiser ; baliverner.
fetus (fi-), *n.*, fœtus, *m.*
feud (fioude), *n.*, fief, *m.* ; (quarrel—*querelle*) brouillerie, querelle, inimitié, dissension, *f.*
feudal, *adj.*, féodal.
feudalism, *n.*, féodalité, *f.*
feudality, *n.*, féodalité, *f.*
feudatory, *n.*, feudataire, *m.*
feudatory, *adj.*, feudataire, qui relève d'un seigneur.
feudist, *n.*, feudiste, *m.*
feuillemort (fwil'mor), *n.*, (colour—*couleur*) feuille-morte, *m.*
fever (fi-veur), *n.*, fièvre, *f.* Fit of — ; *accès de fièvre, m.* Burning — ; *fièvre ardente.* Intermittent — ; *fièvre intermittente.* Tertian —; *fièvre tierce.* Scarlet — ; *fièvre scarlatine.* Typhoid — ; *fièvre typhoïde.* Milk- — ; *fièvre de lait.* To be in a — ; *avoir la fièvre.*
fever, *v.a.*, donner la fièvre à.
feverfew (-fiou), *n.*, (bot.) pyrèthre, *m.* ; matricaire, *f.*
feverish, *adj.*, fiévreux ; fébrile ; brûlant.
feverishness, *n.*, indisposition fébrile ; (fig.) fièvre, *f.*
feverous, *adj.*, fiévreux ; fébrile ; inquiet.
fevery, *adj.*, qui a la fièvre.
few (fiou). *adj.*, peu de ; peu de gens. A — ; *peu de ; quelques ; quelques-uns, m., quelques-unes, f.* — people think thus ; *peu de gens pen-*

sent ainsi. Give me a — of these pears ; *donnez-moi quelques-unes de ces poires.*
fewness, *n.*, petit nombre, *m.* ; brièveté, *f.*
fib, *n.*, conte, mensonge, *m.* ; bourde, *f.*
fib, *v.n.*, mentir ; faire des contes.
fibber, *n.*, menteur, *m.*, menteus', *f.* ; faiseur de contes, *m.*, faiseuse de contes, *f.*
fibre (fai-beur), *n.*, fibre. *f.*
fibril (fai-bril), *n.*, (anat.) fibrille, *f.*
fibrilous, *adj.*, fibrilleux.
fibrous (fai-), *adj.*, fibreux.
fibula (fi-biou-), *n.*, (anat.) péroné, *m.* ; (surg.) suture, *f.*
fickle (fik'k'l), *adj.*, volage, inconstant.
fickleness, *n.*, inconstance, *f.*
fickly, *adv.*, avec inconstance.
fictile (fik'til), *adj.*, fait d'argile.
fiction (fik'sheune), *n.*, fiction, *f.*
fictitious (-tish'eusse), *adj.*, fictif ; factice.
fictitiously, *adv.*, fictivement.
fictitiousness, *n.*, caractère fictif, *m.*
fid, *n.*, (nav.) épissoir, *m.* ; (of a mast—*de mât*) clef, *f.*
fiddle, *n.*, violon, *m.*
fiddle, *v.n.*, jouer du violon ; (to trifle— *vétiller*) baguenauder.
fiddle, *v.a.*, jouer un air sur le violon.
fiddle-faddle, *n.*, (pop.) fadaise ; niaiserie ; sornette, *f.*
fiddle-faddle, *adj.*, (pop.) qui s'occupe de fadaises, de niaiseries, de sornettes.
fiddler, *n.*, joueur de violon ; ménétrier, *m.*
fiddle-stick, *n.*, archet de violon, *m.* ; (nonsense—*bêtise*) fadaise ; baliverne, *f.* — ! tarare !
fiddle-string (-strigne), *n.*, corde à violon, *f.*
fiddle-wood (-woude), *n.*, cytarexylon ; bois de guitare, *m.*
fiddling, *n.*, action de jouer du violon, *f.*
fidejussor (faï-di-djeuss'eur), *n.*, fidéjusseur, *m.*
fidelity, *n.*, fidélité, *f.*
fidget (fidjète), *v.n.*, se remuer ; se tourmenter ; frétiller, s'agiter.
fidget, *n.*, mouvement ; tourment, *m.* ; agitation, *f.* What a — you are ! *comme vous vous tourmentez !*
fidgety, *adj.*, remuant, inquiet ; tracassier.
fiducial (fi-diou-shal), *adj.*, confiant ; de fidéicommis
fiduciary (fi-diou-shi-), *adj.*, confiant ; fiduciaire.
fiduciary, *r.*, fiduciaire, *m.*
fie ! (fa'ye), *int.*, fi ! — for shame ! *fi l'horreur !* — on ... ! *fi de ... !*
fief (fife), *n.*, fief, *m.*
field (fîlde), *n.*, champ, *m.* ; campagne, *f.* — of battle ; *champ de bataille, m.* In the open —s ; *en pleins champs.* To take the — ; (milit.) *se mettre en campagne.*
field-bed (-bède), *n.*, lit de camp, *m.*
field-colours (-keul'leurze), *n.pl.*, (milit.) guidon, fanion, *m.sing.*
fieldfare (-fére), *n.*, (orni.) litorne, *f.*
field-marshal (-mâr-), *n.*, maréchal, *m.*
field-mouse (-maouce), *n.*, mulot, *m.*
field-officer, *n.*, officier supérieur, *m.*
field-piece (-pîce), *n.*, pièce de campagne, *f.*
field-staff (-stâfe), *n.*, (milit.) boutefeu, *m.*
fiend (fî'n'de), *n.*, esprit malin ; démon, *m.*
fiendish, *adj.*, diabolique, satanique. infernal.
fiendishness, *n.*, méchanceté infernale, *f.*
fierce (fîrce), *adj.*, féroce, farouche, furieux, violent.
fiercely, *adv.*, férocement ; furieusement.
fierceness, *n.*, férocité ; ardeur, *f.*
fieriness (faïeur'-), *n.*, fougue, *f.*
fiery, *adj.*, de feu ; ardent, fougueux.
fife (faïfe), *n.*, fifre, *m.*
fife, *v.n.*, jouer du fifre.
fifer, *n.*, fifre, joueur de fifre, *m.*

fifteen (fif'tïne), *adj.*, quinze.

fifteenth (fif'ti'n'th), *adj.*, quinzième.

fifteenth, *n.*, quinzième, *m.* ; (mus.) quin-zième, *f.*

fifth (fif'th), *adj.*, cinquième ; cinq. Charles the — ; *Charles Quint* (of Spain—*d'Espagne*). Pope Sixtus the — ; *le pape Sixte-Quint.*

fifth, *n.*, cinquième, *m.* ; (mus.) quinte, *f.*

fifthly, *adv.*, cinquièmement.

fiftieth (fif-ti-èth), *adj.*, cinquantième.

fifty, *adj.*, cinquante.

fig, *n.*, figue, *f.* ; (tree—*arbre*) figuier, *m.* A — for! *foin de! nargue de!* Not to care a — for ; *ne pas se soucier d'un fétu de.*

fig-eater (-ït'eur), *n.*, (orni.) figuier ; bec figue, *m.*

fig-garden (-gärd'n), *n.*, figuerie, *f.*

fig-house (-haouce), *n.*, serre à figuiers, *f.*

fight (faïte), *v.n.* (*preterit* and *past part.*, Fought), se battre ; combattre ; se combattre.

fight, *v.a.*, se battre avec ; combattre ; com-battre contre ; défendre ; (a battle—*une bataille*) livrer. To — hard ; *se battre avec acharnement.*

fight, *n.*, combat, *m.*

fighter, *n.*, combattant ; (b.s.) batailleur, bretteur, *m.*

fighting, *adj.*, qui combat ; (of things—*des choses*) de combat. — men ; *combattants, hommes de guerre, m.pl.*

fighting. *n.*, combat, *m.* ; combats, *m.pl.*

figmarigold (-gölde), *n.*, ficoïde, *f.*

figment (-mè'n'te), *n.*, fiction, *f.*

fig-orchard (-tsharde), *n.*, figuerie, *f.*

figpecker (-pèk'eur), *n.*, (orni.) becfigue, *m.*

fig-tree (-tri), *n.*, figuier, *m.*

figurability (figh'iou-), *n.*, figurabilité, *f.*

figurable, *adj.*, susceptible de recevoir une forme, une figure.

figural (figh'iou-), *adj.*, figuratif.

figurant (figh'iou-), *n.*, (thea) figurant, *m.*, figurante, *f.*

figurate (-réte), *adj.*, qui a une forme, une figure ; (math., mus.) figuré.

figurated (-rétède), *adj.*, formé ; figuré.

figuration (-ré-), *n.*, forme, formation ; (mus.) figure, *f.*

figurative (-ré-), *adj.*, figuratif ; figuré.

figuratively, *adv.*, figurément ; au figuré.

figurativeness, *n.*, caractère métamor-phique, *m.*

figure (figh'ioure), *n.*, figure ; forme, tour-nure, *f.* ; (arith.) chiffre, *m.* What a — you are ! *comme vous voilà fagoté, arrangé !* To cut a — ; *faire figure, faire une figure.* Academical — ; *académie, f.*

figure, *v.a.*, figurer, façonner ; former ; ima-giner. To — to one's self ; *se figurer, s'imaginer.*

figured (figh'iour'de), *adj.*, à dessin ; façonné, ouvragé.

figure-head (-hède), *n.*, (nav.) poulaine, *f.*

figurist (figh'iour'-), *n.*, figuriste, *m.*

figwort (-weurte),*n.*, (bot.) scrofulaire ; herbe aux écrouelles, *f.*

filaceous (-lé-sheusse), *adj.*, filamenteux.

filament, *n.*, filament ; (bot.) filet, *m.*

filamentous, *adj.*, filamenteux.

filbert (-beurte), *n.*, aveline, noisette, *f.*

filbert-orchard (-tsharde), *n.*, coudraie, *f.*

filbert-tree (-tri), *n.*, coudrier, avelinier, *m.*

filch (filshe), *v.a.*, escamoter, filouter, voler.

filcher, *n.*, filou, voleur. *m.*

file (faïle), *n.*, (tool—*outil*) lime, *f.* ; (of papers—*de papiers*) liasse, *f.*, dossier, *m.* ; (list) liste ; (of newspapers—*de journaux*) collection ; (milit.) file, *f.* Cunning — ; *fin matois*, *m.* Cun-ning old — ; *vieux renard, m.*

file, *v.a.*, limer ; enfiler ; (newspapers— *journaux*) faire une collection de ; (jur.) pro-duire ; (a schedule—*bilan*) déposer.

file, *v.n.*, (milit.) marcher sur un rang. To — off ; *défiler.*

file-cutter (-keut'-), *n.*, tailleur de limes, *m.*

file-cutting, *n.*, taille des limes, *f.*

file-leader (-lïd'-) *n.*, (milit;) chef de file,*m.*

filer, *n.*, limeur, *m.*

filial, *adj.*, filial.

filially, *adv.*, filialement.

filiation (fil-i-é-), *n.*, filiation, *f.*

filiform, *adj.*, filiforme.

filigrane (fail'i-grén e), *or* **filigree** (fil'i-gri), *n.*, filigrane, *m.*

filigraned (-gré'n'de), *or* **filigreed** (-gride), *adj.*, à filigrane.

filings (fail'ign'ze), *n.pl.*, limaille, *f. sing.*

fill, *n.*, suffisance, *f.* ; soûl, *m.*

fill, *v.a.*, emplir, remplir ; combler ; (to occupy —*tenir*) occuper, remplir. To — up ; *remplir, combler.*

fill, *v.n.*, se remplir.

filler, *n.*, personne qui remplit, *f.* ; remplis-sage, *m.*

fillet (-lète), *n.*, bandeau ; (bot.) filet ; (anat.) frein, filet, *m.* ; (arch.) astragale, *f.*, filet, *m.* — of veal ; *rouelle de veau, f.*

fillet, *v.a.*, nouer d'un bandeau ; (arch.) orner d'un filet.

filling, *n.*, action de remplir ; chose pour remplir, *f.* ; remplissage, *m.*

filling, *adj.*, qui remplit ; rassasiant.

fillip (fil'lipe), *n.*, chiquenaude, *f.*

fillip, *v.a.*, donner une chiquenaude à.

filly (fil'li), *n.*, pouliche ; (fig.) coquette, *f.*

film, *n.*, (bot.) pellicule ; (anat.) tunique, *f.* (med.) taie, *f.* ; (fig.) nuage, *m.*

film, *v.a.*, couvrir d'une tunique, d'une pelli-cule.

filmy, *adj.*, membraneux.

filter, *n.*, filtre, *m.*

filter, *v.a.*, filtrer.

filtering, *adj.*, filtrant.

filtering-machine, *n.*, filtre, *m.*

filth (filth), *n.*, ordure, saleté ; (fig.) corrup-tion, *f.*

filthily (-thi-), *adv.*, salement.

filthiness (-thi-), *n.*, saleté, *f.* ; ordures, *f.pl.* ; (fig.) corruption, *f.*

filthy (-thi-), *adj.*, sale ; (fig.) corrompu, ignoble, honteux.

filtrate (-tréte), *v.a.*, filtrer.

filtration (-tré-), *n.*, filtration, *f.*

fimbriate (-éte), *adj.*, (bot.) frangé.

fimbriated (-étède), *adj.*, (her.) bordé.

fin (fine), *n.*, (ich.) nageoire, *f.* ; (of flat fish— *de poissons plats*) *m.*, barbes, *f.pl.*

finable (faï'n'a'b'l), *adj.*, passible d'amende ; (of things—*des choses*) punissable d'une amende.

final (faï-), *adj.*, final, définitif, décisif.

finale (fi-nâ-lï), *n.*, (mus.) finale, *f.*

finally (faï-), *adv.*, enfin, finalement ; défini-tivement.

finance, *or* **finances**, *n.*, finance, *f.* ; finan ces. *f.pl.*

financial (-shial), *adj.*, financier.

financially, *adv.*, en matière de finances.

financier (-cïre), *n.*, financier.

finch (fi'n'she), *n.*, (orni.) pinçon, *m.*

find (faï'n'de), *v.a.* (*preterit* and *past part.*, Found), trouver ; (jur.) (guilty—*coupable*) déclarer ; (verdict) prononcer. To — in ; *pour-voir de.* — out ; *découvrir ; résoudre ; démasquer.*

finder, *n.*, trouveur, *m.*, trouveuse, *f.*

findfault (-fölte), *n.*, censeur, *m.*

finding, *n.*, découverte, *f.* ; (jur.) juge-ment, *m.*, déclaration, *f.*

fine (faïne), *adj.*, fin, délicat ; subtil ; (hand-some—*beau*) beau ; (fig.) bon. It is — ; (of the weather—*du temps*) *il fait beau.*

fine (faïne), *n.*, amende, *f.* ; pot-de-vin, *m.*

fine, *v.a.*, (to mulct—*mulcter*) mettre à

l'amende; condamner à une amende; (to refine —*raffiner*) affiner; (wine—*vin*) clarifier.

finedraw (-drô), *v.a.*, faire des reprises perdues à.

finedrawer, *n.*, ouvrier en reprises perdues, *m.*, ouvrière en reprises perdues, *f.*

finely, *adv.*, fin; délicatement; finement; subtilement; élégamment; (b.s.) joliment, de la belle manière.

fineness (faîne-), *n.*, finesse, délicatesse; pureté; subtilité; beauté, *f.*

finer (faîneur), *n.*, affineur, *m.*

finery (faî'n'ri), *n.*, parure, *f.*; ornement, *m.*; toilette, *f.*; beaux habits, *m. pl.*; (metal.) affinerie, *f.*, foyer d'affinerie, *m.*

fine-spoken (-spô'k'n) *adj.*, beau parleur.

fine-spun (-speune), *adj.*, filé fin; (fig.) subtil, délicat, délié.

finesse (finèce), *n.*, finesse, *f.*

finesse, *v.n.*, user de finesse, finasser.

fin-footed (fine-foutède), *adj.*, palmipède.

finger (fi'n'gheur), *n.*, doigt; (mus.) doigter, *m.*; (fig.) main, *f.* Fore—; *doigt indicateur; index, m.* Little —; *petit doigt.* Middle—; *doigt du milieu, médius.* Ring—; *annulaire, doigt annulaire.* To have anything at one's —s' ends; *savoir quelque chose sur le bout du doigt.* To point with one's —; *indiquer du doigt.*

finger, *v.a.*, toucher, manier; exécuter avec les doigts; (mus.) toucher.

finger, *v.n.*, (mus.) doigter.

finger-board (-bôrde), *n.*, (mus.) touche, *f.*; (of a violin—*de violon*) manche, *m.*

fingered (fi'n'gheurde),*adj.*,qui a des doigts; (bot.) digité; (main.) à doigts. Light—; *qui a la main légère; enclin à voler.*

finger-end (-è'n'de), *n.*, bout du doigt, *m.*

finger-fish, *n.*, (ich.) étoile de mer, *f.*; polynème, *m.*

finger-glass (-glàce), *n.*, bol pour se laver les doigts à table, *m.*

finger-grass (-gràce),*n.*,(bot.) digitale pourprée, *f.*

fingering, *n.*, touche, *f.*; maniement; ouvrage fait délicatement à la main; (mus.) doigter, *m.*

fingerling (fi'n'gheur-), *n.*, (ich.) saumoneau, *m.*

finger-parted (-pârtède), *adj.*, (bot.) digité.

finger-plate (-pléte) *n.*, plaque de propreté, *f.*

finger-stall (-stôl), *n.*, doigtier, *m.*

fingle-fangle (fi'n'g'l-fa'n'g'l), *n.*, (pop.) bagatelle, babiole, *f.*

finical, *adj.*, précieux, affété, prétentieux.

finically, *adv.*, précieusement, avec prétention.

finicalness, *n.*, afféterie, *f.*; ton précieux, *m.*

fining (faî'n-), (metal.) affinage, *m.*; (of wine —*du vin*) clarification, *f.*

finis (faî-nice), *n.*, fin, *f.*

finish, *v.a.*, finir, terminer; achever.

finish, *n.*, fini, *m.*

finished (fin'ishte), *adj.*, fini; parfait.

finisher, *n.*,exécuteur; cardeur en fin; (horl.) finisseur, *m.*

finishing, *adj.*, de perfectionnement.

finishing, *n.*, fini; achèvement, *m.*

finite (faï-naïte), *adj.*, fini.

finiteless, *adj.*,infini.

finitely (faï-naï't'li), *adv.*, d'une manière finie.

fin.teness, *n.*, caractère fini, *m.*; borne; limite, *f.*

finless, *adj.*, sans nageoires.

finlike (-laïke), *adj.*, en forme de nageoire.

finned (fi'n'de), *adj.*, qui a des nageoires; à nageoires.

finny, *adj.*, qui a des nageoires; à nageoires; (poet.) qui habite les eaux.

fintoed (fi'n'tôde), *adj.*, à doigts palmés, palmipède.

florin-grass (faï'o'ri'n'gràce), *n.*,(bot.) agrostide stolonifère, *f.*

fir(feur), *n.*, (bot.) sapin; bois de sapin, *m.*

fir-apple (-ap'p'l), *n.*, pomme de pin, *m.*

fire (faï'eur), *n.*, feu, incendie. *m.* Incendiary —; *incendie par malveillance.* —! *au feu!* To be on —; *être en feu.* To catch —; *prendre feu.* To make a —; *faire du feu.* To miss —; *rater.* To put out a —; *éteindre un feu, un incendie.* To set on —; to set — to; *mettre le feu à.* He will never set the Thames on —; *il n'a pas inventé la poudre.* To add fuel to the —; *jeter de l'huile sur le feu.* To put to — and sword; *mettre à feu et à sang.* To go through — and water for; *se mettre au feu pour.*

fire,*v.a.*, mettre le feu à; embraser; incendier; (fire-arms—*armes à feu*) tirer. To — with; *enflammer de.* To — off; *tirer.*

fire, *v.n.*, prendre feu; s'enflammer. To — at; *faire feu sur.* —! (milit.) *feu!*

fire-arms (-àrm'ze), *n.pl.*, armes à feu, *f.pl.*

fire-ball (-bôl), *n.*, (milit.) grenade, *f.*; (meteor) globe de feu, bolide, *m.*

fire-bar (-bàre), *n.*, barre de fourneau; barre de foyer, *f.*

fire-blast (-blàste), *n.*, (bot.) charbon, *m.*; rouille; nielle, *f.*

firebrand (-bra'n'de), *n.*, tison ardent, *m.*; (fig.) boutefeu, *m.*

fire-brick, *n.*, brique réfractaire, *f.*

fire-chest (-tshèste), *n.*, (nav.) coffre à feu, *m.*

fireclay, *n.*, (tech.) argile réfractaire, *f.*

fire-company (-keu'm'-), *n.*, compagnie de pompiers, *f.*

fire-damp (-da'm'pe),*n.*,feu grisou; grisou,*m.*

fire-dog, *n.*, chenet, *m.*

firedrake (-dréke), *n.*, dragon volant; feu follet, *m.*

fire-engine (-è'n'djine), *n.*, pompe à incendie, *f.*

fire-escape (-ès-képe), *n.*, appareil de sauvetage pour les incendies, *m.*

fire-fly (-fla'ye), *n.*, (ent.) lampyre; ver luisant, *m.*

fire-grate (-gréte), *n.*, grille de foyer, *f.*

fire-irons (-aï'eur'n'ze), *n.*, garniture de foyer, *f.*; (tech.) ringard; tisonnier, *m.* Set of —s; *garniture de foyer, f.*

firelock (-lòk), *n.*, arme à feu, *f.*; fusil, *m.*

fire-man (-ma'n), *n.*, pompier; (in factories —*industrie*) chauffeur, *m.*

fire-office, *n.*, bureau d'assurance contre l'incendie, *m.*

fire-pan (-pa'n), *n.*, bassinet, *m.*

fireplace (-pléce), *n.*, cheminée, *f.*; foyer de cheminée; âtre, *m.*

fire-proof (-proufe), *adj.*, à l'épreuve du feu.

firer, *n.*, incendiaire, *m.*

fire-screen (-scrine), *n.*, écran, *m.*

fire-ship (-shipe), *n.*, brûlot, *m.*

fireside (-saïde), *n.*, coin du feu, *m.*

fireside, *adj.*, du coin du feu.

firestone (-stône), *n.*, (min.) silex pyromaque, *m.*; pierre à feu, *f.*

fire-tile (-taïle), *n.*, (tech.) tuile réfractaire, *f.*

firewood (-woude), *n.*, bois à brûler, *m.*

firework (-weurke), *n.*, feu d'artifice. *m.* To let off —s; *tirer un feu d'artifice.* [*Firework* s'emploie généralement au pluriel.]

firing, *n.*, action d'incendier, *f.*; chauffage, *m.*; (milit.) feu, *m.*, fusillade; (vet.) cautérisation, *f.*

firing-iron (-aïeur'ne), *n.*, (vet.) fer à cautériser, *m.*

firkin (feur-ki'n), *n.*, quartaut, *m.*

firm (feurme), *adj.*, ferme, solide.

firm (feurme), *n.*, (com.) maison de commerce, raison sociale, *f.*

firm, *v.a.*, fixer, confirmer.

firmament (feur'-), *n.*, firmament, *m.*
firmamental, *adj.*, du firmament.
firman (feur-), *n.*, firman, *m.*
firmless, *adj.*, détaché de sa substance matérielle.
firmly. *adv.*, fermement ; solidement.
firmness, *n.*, fermeté ; solidité, *f.*
fir-plank (-pla'n'k), *n.*, planche de sapin ; sapine, *f.*
first (feurste), *adj.*, premier ; unième. Twenty — ; *vingt et unième.*
first, *adv.*, le premier ; premièrement, d'abord. — or last ; *tôt ou tard.* At — ; *d'abord.*
first-born, *adj.*, premier-né.
first-fruits (-froutse) *.*.*pl*, prémices, *f.pl.*
firstling, *n.*, premier-né, *m.*
firth (feurth), *n.*, estuaire, *m.*, embouchure, *f.* (of a river—*d'un fleuve*) ; détroit, *m.*
fir-tree (-trî), *n.*, (bot.) sapin, *m.*
fiscal (fiscal) *adj.*, fiscal.
fiscal, *n.*, fisc, *m.*
fish (fishe), *n.*, poisson, *m.* ; (at play—*au jeu*) fiche ; (nav.) jumelle, *f.* A fine kettle of — ; *une jolie affaire.*
fish,*v.n.*, pêcher. To go —ing : *aller à la pêche.*
fish, *v.a.*, pêcher ; fouiller dans ; (nav.) traverser, jumeler.
fish-bone (-bône), *n.*, arête de poisson, *f.*
fish-cart (-cârte), *n.*, voiture à poisson, *f.*
fish-curer (-kiour'-), *n.*, saleur, *m.*
fish-day, *n.*. jour maigre, *m.*
fisher, *n.*, pêcheur, *m.*
fisher-boat (-bôte), *n.*, bateau pêcheur, *m*
fisher-man (-ma'n), *n.*, pêcheur, *m.*
fishery, *n.*, pêche, pêcherie. *f.*
fish-fag, *n.*, poissarde, *f.*
fishful (-foule), *adj.*, poissonneux.
fish-hook (-houke), *n.*, hameçon, *m.*
fishify (-fa'ye), *v.a.*, convertir en poisson.
fishiness, *n.*, goût de poisson, *m.*
fishing, *n.*, pêche, *f.*
fishing-line (-laïne), *n.*, ligne, ligne à pêcher, *f.*
fishing-rod (-rode), *n.*, canne à pêcher, *f.*
fishing-tackle (-tak'k'l), *n.*, ustensiles de pêche, *m.pl.* ; attirail de pêche, *m.*
fish-kettle (-kèt't'l), *n.*, poissonnière (ustensile), *f.*
fishlike (-laïke), *adj.*, de poisson.
fish-market(-mâr-kète), *n.*, poissonnerie, *f.* ; marché au poisson, *m.*
fishmonger (-mun'n'g'gheur), *n.*, poissonnier ; marchand de poisson, *m.*
fish-pond, *or* **fish-pool** (-po'n'de, -poule), *n.*, étang ; vivier, *m.*
fish-slice (-slaïce), *n.*, truelle, *f.*
fish-spear (-spîre), *n.*, harpon, *m.*
fish-wife (-waïfe), *or* **fishwoman** (-woum'a'n), *n.*, poissonnière, marchande de poisson ; poissarde, *f.*
fishy, *adj.*, poissonneux ; qui sent le poisson.
fissiped (-pède), *adj.*, fissipède.
fissure (fish'ioure), *n.*, fissure, fente, *f.*
fissure, *v.a.*, fissurer ; faire des fentes à ; fendre.
fist, *n.*, poing, *m.*
fisticuffs (-keufse), *n.pl.*, coups de poing, *m.*
fistula (-tiou-), *n.*, fistule, *f*
fistular, *adj.*, fistuleux ; fistulaire.
fistuliform, *adj.*, fistulaire.
fistulous. *adj.*, fistuleux.
fit, *n.*, accès, paroxysme, *m.* ; attaque ; convulsion, *f.* By —s and starts ; *par accès ; à bâtons rompus, par sauts et par bonds.*
fit, *adj.*, propre ; juste ; à propos ; convenable ; capable.
fit, *v.a.*, convenir à ; arranger ; s'adapter à ; ajuster ; (tech.) encastrer ; (of clothes—*de vêtements*) aller à. To — to ; *accommoder à.* To — with ; *pourvoir de.* To — out ; *équiper, monter ;*

(a ship—*un vaisseau*) armer. To — in ; *encastrer.* To — up ; *arranger.* That coat —*e you* well ; *cet habit vous va bien.* To — any one for ; *préparer quelqu'un pour.*
fit, *v.n.*, convenir ; s'adapter à ; s'ajuster ; (of clothes—*de vêtements*) aller.
fitchet (-tshète), *or* **fitchew** (-tshiou), *n.*, (mam.) putois, *m.* ; belette, *f.*
fitly, *adv.*, à propos, convenablement, justement.
fitness, *n.*, convenance, propriété, *f.* ; à-propos, *m.*
fitter, *n.*, personne qui adapte, *f.* ; (tech.) ajusteur, *m.*
fitting, *adv.*, convenable ; à propos ; juste.
fitting, *n.*, adaptation, *f.* ; ajustement, *m.* — out ; (nav.) armement, *m.* ; (milit.) équipement, *m.*
fittingly, *adv.*, convenablement.
five (faïve), *n.* and *adj.*, cinq.
fivefold (-fôlde), *adv.*, cinq fois ; quintuple.
fives (faïv'ze), *n.*, (vet.) avives, *f.pl.*
fix, *v.a.*, fixer, attacher, arrêter. To — one's self ; *s'établir ; se fixer.*
fix, *v.n.*, se fixer. To — upon ; *se fixer sur, s'arrêter à.*
fixable (fiks'ab'l), *adj.*, qui peut être fixé.
fixation (fiks'é'-), *n.*, fixité ; place fixe ; fixation, *f.*
fixed (fiks'te, *ou* fiks'ède), *adj.*, fixe.
fixedly (fiks'èdli), *adv.*, fermement ; fixement.
fixedness (fiks'èd-), *n.*, fixité, *f.*
fixity, *n.*, fixité, *f.*
fixture (fiks'tioure), *n.*, stabilité, *f.* ; (in a house—*dans une maison*) meuble à demeure fixe ; immeuble, *m.*
flabbiness, *n.*, flaccidité ; nature flasque, *f.*
flabby, *adj.*, flasque ; mollasse.
flaccid (flak-side), *adj.*, flasque, faible.
flaccidity, *or* **flaccidness**, *n.*, flaccidité, *f.*
flag, *v.n.*, pendre, flotter ; (fig.) s'affaisser ; (fig.) se relâcher, faiblir.
flag, *v.a.*, laisser tomber ; (fig.) abattre.
flag, *n.*, (milit.) drapeau ; (nav.) pavillon, *m.* ; (bot.) algue. — of truce ; *drapeau blanc ; pavillon blanc.* Corn-— ; (bot.) *glaïeul, m.*
flagellate (fladj'el-léte), *v.a.*, flageller.
flagellation (fladj'èl-lé-), *n.*, flagellation, *f.*
flageolet (fladj'o-lète), *n.*, flageolet, *m.*
flagginess (flag'dji-), *n.*, état flasque, *m.*
flaggy (flag'dji), *adj.*, faible ; qui flotte ; insipide ; flasque.
flagitious (fla-djish'eusse), *adj.*, pervers ; infâme.
flagitiously, *adv.*, avec perversité ; d'une manière infâme.
flagitiousness, *y.*, perversité ; infamie, *f.*
flag-officer, *n.*, officier général de marine commandant une escadre, *m.*
flagon. *n.*, flacon ; pot, *m.*
flagrance, *or* **flagrancy** (flé-), *n.*, feu, *m.* ; chaleur ; notoriété ; énormité, *f.*
flagrant, *adj.*, flagrant.
flagrantly, *adv.*, d'une manière flagrante.
flag-ship, *n.*, vaisseau amiral, *m.*
flag-staff (-stâfe), *n.*, lance de drapeau, *f.* ; bâton de pavillon, *m.*
flag-stone (-stône), *n.*, dalle, *f.*
flail (fléle), *n.*, fléau (à battre le blé), *m.*
flake (fléke), *n.*, flocon, *m.* ; écaille, *f.*
flake, *v.a.*, former un flocon
flake,*v.n.*, s'écailler.
flaky, *adj.*, floconneux ; écailleux.
flam, *n.*, sornette, *f.* ; conte, *m.*
flam, *v.a.*, amuser par des sornettes.
flambeau, *n.*, flambeau, *m.*
flame (fléme), *n.*, flamme, *f.* ; feu, *m.*
flame, *v.n.*, flamber ; jeter de la flamme ; s'enflammer ; flamboyer.

flame-coloured (-keul'leurde), *adj.*, couleur de feu.

flameless, *adj.*, sans flamme.

flamen (flé-mène), *n.*, flamine, *m.*

flaming (flém'-), *adj.*, flamboyant; (fig.) merveilleux.

flamingly, *adv.*, avec éclat; merveilleusement.

flamingo (-mi'n'gô), *n.*, (orni.) phénicoptère, flamant, *m.*

flamy (flé-), *adj.*, de flamme; éclatant.

flanconade (-con'éde), *n.*, flanconade, *f.*

flange (fla'n'dje), *n.*, rebord; (railways) bandage, *m.*; saillie; bride; collerette, *f.*

flank, *n.*, flanc; côté, *m.*

flank, *v.a.*, flanquer; (milit.) prendre en flanc.

flanker, *n.*, (fort.) flanc; (milit.) flanqueur, *m.*

flanker, *v.a.*, (fort.) flanquer.

flannel, *n.*, flanelle, *f.*

flap, *n.*, tape, *f.*; léger coup; (of trousers—*de pantalon*) pont; (of a hat, a cap—*de chapeau, de casquette*) bord, *m.*; (of a pocket—*de poche*) patte, *f.*; (of a coat—*d'habit*) pan; (of a saddle—*de selle*) quartier; (of the ear—*de l'oreille*) bout, *m.*; (of a shoe—*de soulier*) oreille, *f.*

flap, *v.a.*, frapper légèrement; battre, agiter. To — its wings; *battre des ailes.*

flap, *v.n.*, battre légèrement; battre des ailes; pendre, retomber.

flap-eared (-îrde), *adj.*, qui a les oreilles pendantes.

flapper, *n.*, clapet; (orni.) halbran, *m.*

flare (flére), *v.n.*, étinceler; (of candles—*des chandelles*) filer.

flash, *n.*, éclat; (of water, of light—*de l'eau, de la lumière*) jet; éclair, *m.* — of lightning; éclair, *m.* — of wit; *trait d'esprit*, *m.*

flash (flashe), *v.a.*, luire; jaillir; étinceler. To — with; *briller de.*

flashily, *adv.*, superficiellement.

flashy, *adj.*, éclatant; brillant; insipide, fade.

flask, *n.*, bouteille, *f.*; flacon, *m.*; (artil.) flasque. *m.*

flasket (flâsk'ète), *n.*, corbeille, manne, *f.*

flat, *adj.*, plat; (of wine, beer, &c.—*de vin, bière, &c.*) éventé; (com.) calme; (mus.) bémol; (of sound—*du son*) grave; (fig.) net, clair, franc. — nosed; *camard; qui a le nez camus.* To get —; *s'aplatir*; (of wine, beer, &c.—*du vin, de la bière, &c.*) *s'éventer.*

flat, *n.*, surface unie, plaine, *f.*; terrain plat; (of a house—*d'une maison*) étage; (pers.) nigaud, niais; (mus.) bémol, *m.*

flat, *v.a.*, aplatir; (paint.) amortir; (fig.) affaiblir.

flat, *v.n.*, s'aplatir.

flatly, *adv.*, de niveau, à plat; (fig.) nettement, clairement.

flatness, *n.*, aplatissement, *m.*; égalité; (of wine, beer, &c.—*de vin, bière, &c.*) platitude, *f.*; goût éventé, *m.*; (of sound—*du son*) gravité; (fig.) insipidité, *f.*

flatten (flat't'n), *v.a.*, aplatir; aplanir; (fig.) affadir; (mus.) adoucir.

flatten, *v.n.*, s'aplatir; s'aplanir; (fig.) s'affadir.

flattening, *n.*, aplatissement; aplanissement, *m.*

flatter, *n.*, (pers.) aplatisseur; (thing—*chose*) aplatissoir, *m.*

flatter, *v.a.*, flatter.

flatterer, *n.*, flatteur, *m.*, flatteuse, *f.*

flattering, *adj.*, flatteur.

flatteringly. *adv.*, d'une manière flatteuse; avec flatterie, flatteusement.

flattery, *n.*, flatterie, *f.*

flattish (-tishe), *adj.*, un peu plat.

flatulence. *or* **flatulency** (-tiou-), *n.*, flatuosité; (med.) flatulence, *f.*; (fig.) vide, creux, *m.*

flatulent. *adj.*, flatueux; (med.) flatulent; (fig.) ampoulé, gonflé.

flatuosity, *n.*, (ant.) flatuosité, *f.*

flatuous, *adj.*, (ant.) flatueux.

flatwise, *adv.*, à plat.

flaunt (flô'n'te), *n.*, étalage, *m.*, vaine parure, *f.*, parade, *f.*; impertinence, *f.*

flaunt, *v.n.*, s'étendre; flotter; (fig.) se pavaner, briller.

flavour (flé-veur), *n.*, (of meat—*de la viande*) goût, fumet; (of tea, coffee, &c.—*du thé, du café, &c.*) arome; (of wine—*du vin*) fumet, bouquet, *m.*; (of flowers—*des fleurs*) senteur, *f.*, parfum, *m.*

flavour, *v.a.*, donner un arome à; donner un parfum à; donner un fumet à; donner du bouquet à.

flavoured (flé-veurde), *adj.*, qui a un arome un parfum; qui a un fumet, un bouquet, un goût savoureux.

flavourless, *adj.*, sans arome, sans senteur; sans parfum; sans goût; sans fumet; sans bouquet.

flavourous, *adj.*, odorant, savoureux; qui flatte le palais.

flavous (flé-), *adj.*, (ant.) jaune.

flaw (flô), *n.*, défaut, *m.*; (of a diamond—*du diamant*) glace; (in precious stones—*des pierres précieuses*) paille; brèche, fente; (nav.) risée de vent, *f.*; (jur.) nullité.

flaw, *v.a.*, fendre.

flawless, *adj.*, parfait, sans défaut.

flawy, *adj.*, qui a des défauts; défectueux.

flax, *n.*, lin, *m.*

flax-comb (-côme), *n.*, séran, *m.*

flax-dresser (-drès'-), *n.*, séranceur de lin, *m.*

flax-dressing, *n.*, peignage de lin; sérançage, *m.*

flaxen (flaks'n), *adj.*, de lin; blond.

flax-field (-fîlde), *n.*, linière, *f.*

flax-grower (-grô-), *n.*, cultivateur de lin, *m.*

flax-growing, *n.*, culture du lin, *f.*

flax-mill, *n.*, manufacture de lin, *f.*

flax-wench (-wè'n'she), *n.*, fileuse de lin, *f.*

flaxy, *adj.*, de lin; blond.

flay (flé), *v.a.*, écorcher.

flayer (flé-eur), *n.*, écorcheur.

flaying, *n.*, écorchement, *m.*

flea (flî), *n.*, puce, *f.*

flea-bite (-baïte), *n.*, piqûre de puce, *f.*

flea-bitten (-bit't'n), *adj.*, mordu des puces.

fleam (flîme), *n.*, (surg.) flammette; (vet.) flamme, *f.*

fleawort (-weurte), *n.*, herbe aux puces.

fledge (flèdje), *adj.*, garni de plumes.

fledge, *v.a.*, garnir de plumes.

flee (flî), *v.n.* (preterit *and past part.*, Fled), s'enfuir, fuir; prendre la fuite.

fleece (flîce), *n.*, toison, *f.*   Golden —; *toison d'or.*

fleece, *v.a.*, abattre la toison de; tondre; dépouiller; (fig.) écorcher.

fleeced (fliss'te), *adj.*, couvert d'une toison.

fleecer, *n.*, exacteur, spoliateur, écorcheur, *m.*

fleecy, *adj.*, laineux, floconneux.

fleer (flîre), *n.*, raillerie; grimace, *f.*

fleer, *v.a.* and *n.*, railler.

fleerer, *n.*, railleur, *m.*, railleuse, *f.*

fleet (flîte), *n.*, flotte, escadre, *f.*

fleet, *adj.*, vite, léger, rapide.

fleet, *v.n.*, passer rapidement, raser.

fleet, *v.n.*, fuir, passer; s'envoler.

fleeting, *adj.*, fugitif.

fleetly, *adv.*, vite, rapidement.

fleetness, *n.*, rapidité; légèreté à la course, vitesse, *f.*

flesh (flèshe), *n.*, chair, *f.*   Proud —; *bourgeons charnus, m.pl.*   Hard —; *durillon, m.*

flesh, v.a., repaître ; essayer, étrenner ; endurcir ; (hunt.) charner.

fleshbrush (-breushe), n., brosse à friction, f.

flesh-colour (-keul'leur), n., couleur de chair, f.

flesh-coloured (-keul'leurde), adj., couleur de chair ; incarnat.

flesh-day (-dè), n., jour gras, m.

fleshhook (-houke), n., croc, m.

fleshiness, n., état charnu, m.

fleshless, adj., maigre, décharné.

fleshliness, n., disposition charnelle, f.

fleshly, adj., de chair, de la chair ; charnel.

flesh-meat (-mîte), n., viande, f.

fleshment, n., excitation, f.

fleshpot (-pote), n., marmite pleine de viande, f. ; (of Egypt—d'Égypte) oignon, m.

flesh-red (-rède), adj., incarnat.

fleshy, adj., charnu ; de chair.

fleur-de-lis (fleur-dè-li), n., (her.) fleur de lis, f.

flew (fliou), n., babine, f.

flewed (flioude), adj., qui a des babines.

flexibility, n., flexibilité, f.

flexible, adj., qui peut se plier ; flexible.

flexion (flèk'sheune), n., courbure ; flexion, f.

flexor (flèk'seur), n., (anat.) fléchisseur ; muscle fléchisseur, m.

flexuose, or **flexuous** (flèk'shiou-eusse), adj., sinueux ; vacillant ; (bot.) flexueux.

flexure (flèk'sioure), n., flexion, génuflexion ; (geom.) courbure, f.

flicker, v.n., trémousser de l'aile ; voltiger ; ondoyer ; (of a light—d'une lumière) vaciller.

flickering, n., battement d'ailes, m. ; (fig.) vacillation, fluctuation, f.

flier (flaï'-), n., fugitif, fuyard ; (mec.) volant, m.

flight (flaïte), n., fuite, f. ; vol, m. ; (of birds, &c.—d'oiseaux, &c.) volée, f. ; (fig.) élan, essor, m. To betake one's self to — ; prendre la fuite.

flightiness, n., légèreté, étourderie, f

flighty, adj., fugitif ; étourdi, léger.

flimsiness (fli'm'zi-), n., légèreté ; pauvreté, f.

flimsy (fli'm'zi), adj., mince ; mollasse ; léger.

flinch (fli'n'she), v.n., reculer ; To — from ; se retirer de, fuir, manquer à.

flincher, n., personne qui recule, f. ; réfractaire, m.

fling (fligne), n., coup ; (fig.) trait, m.

fling, v.a. (preterit and past part., Flung), jeter, lancer. To — away ; jeter, prodiguer. To — down ; abattre, démolir. To — out ; jeter dehors. To — up ; jeter en haut ; abandonner.

fling, v.n., (man.) s'éparer ; (fig.) invectiver.

flinger, n., personne qui jette, f. ; railleur, m., railleuse, f.

flint (fli'n'te), n., caillou, m., pierre à fusil ; (fig.) roche ; dureté, f. —glass ; cristal d'Angleterre, m.

flinty, adj., de caillou ; caillouteux ; (fig.) dur, insensible.

flippancy (flip'p'a'n'-), n., ton léger ; verbiage, bavardage, m.

flippant (flip'pa'n'te), adj., inconsidéré, léger ; bavard. — tongue ; langue bien pendue.

flippantly, adv., légèrement ; inconsidérément ; avec mobilité.

flirt (fleurte), n., mouvement vif, m. ; (woman —d'une femme) coquette, f.

flirt, v.n., voltiger ; faire la coquette, coqueter.

flirt, v.a., jeter, lancer, agiter.

flirtation (fleur-té-), n., mouvement vif, m. ; coquetterie ; intrigue, f.

flit (flite), v.n., fuir ; voltiger.

flitch (flit'she), n., flèche de lard, f.

flitter (flit'teur), n., lambeau, m. ; guenille, f.

flitter-mouse (-maouce), n., chauve-souris, f.

float (flôte), n., chose qui flotte, f. ; radeau ;

(of wood—de bois) train ; flot, m. ; (of a fishing-line—de ligne à pêcher) flotte, f.

float, v.n., flotter ; faire la planche.

float, v.a., faire flotter.

float-board (-bôrde), n., aube, f.

floater, n., personne qui flotte ; personne qui fait la planche, f.

floating, adj., flottant.

float-stone (-stône), n., (min.) pierre flottante, f.

flocculent (flok'kiou-), adj., floconneux.

flock, n., troupeau, m. ; bande ; foule, troupe, f. ; (of a clergyman—d'un prêtre) ouailles, f.pl. ; (of wool, &c.—de la laine, &c.) flocon, m., bourre, f.

flock, v.n., s'attrouper ; se rassembler ; se porter en foule ; (of birds—des oiseaux) aller par bandes.

flock-surface (-seur-féce), n., velouté, m.

flog (flogbe), n., (ent.) taon, m.

flog, v.a., fouetter, fesser.

flogger (flogh'eur), n., fouetteur, m.

flogging (flogh'-), n., fouet, m., coups de fouet, m.pl.

flood (fleude), n., flux, déluge, m. ; inondation, f. — of tears ; torrent de larmes, m.

flood, v.a., inonder, submerger.

floodgate (-ghête), n., écluse, f.

flooding, n., (med.) hémorragie utérine ; perte, f.

flook, n. V. **fluke**.

flooking (flouk'-), n., (mines) interruption d'un filon métallique, f.

floor (flôrè), n., plancher ; (of a house—d'une maison) étage, m. ; (nav.) varangue, f. Inlaid — ; parquet, m.

floor, v.a., planchéier ; jeter par terre.

flooring, n., plancher ; parquet ; (nav.) fond, m.

florentine (-'è'n'-taïne), adj., florentin ; de Florence.

florentine, n., Florentin, m., Florentine, f.

florescence (-rès'cè'n'-), n., (bot.) floraison, fleuraison, f.

floret (flô'rète), n., fleurette, f.

florid, adj., fleuri ; florissant.

floridity, or **floridness**, n., teint fleuri ; style fleuri, m. ; fraîcheur, f.

floridly, adv., d'une manière fleurie.

florin (-ïne), n., florin, m.

florist, n., fleuriste, m. and f.

flosculous (-kiou-), adj., (bot.) flosculeux.

floss, n., (of silk—de soie) bourre, f. ; (metal.) chio, floss, m.

floss-silk, n., soie plate ; filoselle, bourre de soie, f. ; fleuret, m.

flotilla (-til'la), n., flottille, f.

flounce (flaou'n'ce), n., volant (de robe), m.

flounce, v.n., se débattre, s'agiter.

flounce, v.a., garnir de volants.

flounder (flaou'n'd'-), n., flet ; carrelet, m. ; plie franche, f.

flounder, v.n., se débattre.

flour (flaeur), n., farine, f.

flour, v.a., convertir en farine ; enfariner.

flourish (fleur'ishe), n., éclat, m. ; (with a sword —d'une épée) action de brandir, f. ; (rhet.) fleur, f. ; (with a pen—de la plume) trait, trait de plume, parafe ; (mus.) air rapide, m. ; (of a trumpet—de trompette) fanfare, f.

flourish, v.a., fleurir ; embellir ; (with a pen—avec une plume) parafer ; (a stick, a sword—une canne, une épée) brandir.

flourish, v.n., fleurir ; prospérer, être florissant ; (with a pen—avec une plume) faire des traits de plume ; (mus.) préluder ; (fig.) s'agiter ; (in speaking—du discours) parler d'une manière fleurie ; faire des phrases.

flourisher n., personne qui prospère, qui

brandit, qui fait des phrases, des traits de plume, *f.*

flourishing, *adj.*, florissant.

flourishingly,*adv.*,d'une manièreflorissante.

fiout (flaoute), *n.*, insulte, moquerie,*f.*

flout, *v.a.*, insulter; railler.

fiow (flô), *n.*, flux; épanchement, *m.*; effusion, *f.*

flow, *v.n.*, s'écouler. couler ; (of the sea—*de la mer*); fluer; (of the tide—*de la marée*) monter. To — in ; *affluer.*

flow, *v.a.*, inonder.

flower (flaou-eur), *n.*, fleur,*f.*

flower, *v.a.*, orner de fleurs artificielles, de figures de fleurs.

flower, *v.n.*, fleurir, être en fleur ; (of ale—*de la bière*) fermenter; (fig.) être en vogue.

flower-de-luce (dé-liouce), *n.*, fleur de lis, *f.*; (bot.) iris de Florence. *V.* **fleur de lis.**

flower-dust (-deuste), *n.*,(bot.) pollen, *m.* ; poussière fécondante,*f.*

flowered (flaoueurde), *adj.*, figuré ; à fleurs; fleuri.

floweret (-ète), *n.*, petite fleur ; fleurette,*f.*

flower-fence (-fè'n'ce), *n.*, (bot.) poinciane, poincillade,*f.*

flower-garden (-gârd'n),*n.*,jardin fleuriste; parterre,*m.*

flower-gentle (-djè'n't'l), *n.*, (bot.) amarante, *f.*

floweriness, *n.*, abondance de fleurs,*f.*

flower-leaf (-life), *n.*, (bot.) pétale, *m.*

flower-pot (-pote), *n.*, pot à fleurs ; vase à fleurs, *m.*

flower-show (-shô), *n.*, exposition de fleurs,*f.*

flower-stalk (-stôke), *n.*, (bot.) pédoncule, *m.*, hampe ; queue de fleur, *f.*

flower-stand (-sta'n'de), *n.*, jardinière (meuble),*f.*

flower-work (-weurke), *n.*, fleurs artificielles,*f.pl.*

flowery,*adj.*, orné de fleurs, plein de fleurs, fleuri ; (her.) fleuré.

flowing (flô-), *adj.*, coulant, qui déborde ; flottant ; (nav.) largue.

flowingly, *adv.*, coulamment ; avec abondance.

fluate (fliou-éte), *n.*, (chem.) fluate, *m.*

fiucan, *or* **fiuccan** (fliou-), *n. V.* **flooking.**

fluctuant (fleukt'-iou-), *adj.*, flottant ; incertain ; fluctueux.

fluctuate (fleukt'-iou-éte), *v.n.*, balancer, flotter ; être en agitation, fluctuer.

fluctuation (-'iou-é-), *n.*, balancement, doute, *m.* ; agitation, fluctuation,*f.*

fluder, *or* **fludder** (fleud'-), *n.*, (orni.) plongeon, *m.*

fiue (fliou), *n.*, duvet, poil, *m.* ; tuyau de cheminée, *m.*

fiuellen, *or* **fluellin** (fliou-èl-lène, -line), *n.*, (bot.) linaire élatinée ; véronique, *f.*

fluency (fliou-), *n.*, fluidité, facilité, volubilité,*f.*

fluent, *n.*, fil de l'eau, courant, *m.* ; (math.) intégrale,*f.*

fluent, *adj.*, coulant, aisé; abondant ; éloquent.

fluently, *adv.*, coulamment ; couramment.

flue-surface (-se'r-téce), *n.*, surface de chauffe,*f.*

fluid (fliou'-), *n.*, fluide, liquide, *m.* The blood is an animal — ; *le sang est un fluide animal.*

fluid, *adj.*, fluide, liquide. The water is — ; *l'eau est liquide.*

fluidity, *or* **fluidness**, *n.*, fluidité,*f.*

fluke (fliouke), *n.*, (ich.) plie franche, *f.*, Carrelet, *m.* ; patte d'ancre. *f.*

flummery (fleum'mèri), *n.*, gelée d'avoine, bouillie,*f.* ; (jest.) fadaises, sornettes,*f.pl.*

fluor (fliou-), *n.*, (min.) fluor, *m.* — spar; spath *fluor.*

flurry (fleur'-), *n.*, agitation, hâte, *f.*, désordre ; coup de vent, *m.*

flurry, *v.a.*, agiter, troubler; ahurir.

flush (fleushe), *n.*, rouge, *m.*; rougeur, *f.*; (at cards—*aux cartes*) flux ; (mus.) fredon ; (of joy —*de joie*) excès de joie, *m.*

flush, *v.a.*, colorer; faire rougir, rougir; (sewers, &c.—*des égoûts, &c.*) inonder (pour nettoyer) ; (hunt.) lever, faire lever, faire partir; animer, exciter, enfler.

flush, *v.n.*, rougir, (of the blood—*du sang*) monter au visage ; survenir; partir tout à coup; accourir ; briller, resplendir, rayonner.

flush, *adj.*, frais ; plein de vigueur; élevé ; animé.

flush-deck (-dèke), *n.*, (nav.) pont entier, *m.*

flusher, *n.*, (orni.) lanier, *m.*

flushing, *n.*, rougeur,*f.* ; rouge qui monte au visage, *m.* What can be more significant than this sudden — ? *quoi de plus expressif que cette rougeur subite?*

flushness, *n.*, fraîcheur, *f.* ; éclat, *m.* ; abondance, *f.*

fluster (fleus'teur), *v.a.*, déconcerter ; enivrer à moitié ; exciter ; échauffer.

fluster, *n.*, excitation ; confusion, *f.*; emportement, *m.*

flute (fiioute), *n.*, flûte ; (arch.) cannelure, *f.* Beaked — ; *flûte à bec.* German — ; *flûte allemande, flûte traversière.*

flute, *v.a.*, (arch.) canneler.

flute, *v.n.*, jouer de la flûte.

fluting (fliout'-), *n.*, (arch.) striure; cannelure, *f.*

flutist, *n.*, joueur de flûte, flûtiste, *m.*

flutter, *or* **fluttering** (fleut'-), *n.*, trémoussement; fracas, *m.*; agitation ; vibration ; ondulation,*f.*

flutter, *v.a.*, mettre en désordre; agiter; déranger.

flutter, *v.n.*, battre des ailes ; se trémousser ; voltiger.

flux (fleukse), *n.*, flux ; courant, *m.* ; dysenterie, *f.*

flux, *v.a.*, fondre; (med.) faire saliver, donner le flux de bouche à quelqu'un.

flux, *adj.*, inconstant, changeant.

flexibility, *n.*, fusibilité, *f.*

fluxing (fleuks'-), *n.*, salivation, *f.*, flux de bouche, *m.*

fluxion (fleuk'sheune), *n.*, fluxion,*f.*; écoulement, *m.*; (math.) fluxion différentielle, *f.*; infiniment petit, *m.*

fluxional, *adj.*, (math.) infinitésimal.

fluxionary, *adj.*, (math.) du calcul des fluxions.

fluxionist, *n.*, mathématicien versé dans le calcul des fluxions, dans le calcul différentiel, *m.*

fluxive, *adj.*, sans solidité; qui verse des larmes.

fly (fla'ye), *n.*, mouche ; voiture de place, de louage, *f.* Spanish — ; (ent.) *cantharide, f.* Gad — ; *taon, m.*

fly, *v.a.* (preterite, Flew; past part., Flown), fuir, éviter, quitter, abandonner. Sleep flies the wretched ; *le sommeil fuit les malheureux.* To — one's country ; *quitter, abandonner son pays.*

fly, *v.n.* (preterit, Flew ; past part., Flown), fuir; s'enfuir; voler, se sauver, prendre la fuite. To — on *or* at; *se jeter sur, s'élancer sur.* To — away ; *s'envoler, s'enfuir.* To — off; *reculer, biaiser.* To — back ; *faire un saut en arrière, reculer, se dédire.* To — back (of the horse—*du cheval*) ; *ruer.* To — open ; *s'ouvrir de soi-même.* To — up; *monter.* To — out; *s'élancer, se pré-*

24

cipiter dehors; *entrer en fureur.* To — into a passion; *s'emporter, se mettre en colère.* To — from justice; *se soustraire à la justice.* To — in a battle; *tourner le dos.* To — for refuge; *se réfugier.* To — the kingdom; *émigrer.* To — in pieces; *se rompre, éclater, se briser, voler en éclats.* To — abroad, about; *se répandre.*

fly-bane (-béne), *n.*, (bot.) silène, *f.*, attrape mouche, *m.*

fly-bitten ('-t'n), *adj.*, marqué de chiures de mouches.

fly-blow (-blō), *n.*, chiure de mouche, *f.*; œuf de mouche, *m.*

fly-blow, *v.a.*, gâter; corrompre.

fly-blown, *part.adj.*, gâté, corrompu; piqué des mouches.

fly-boat (-bôte), *n.*, (nav.) flûte, *f.*; flibot, *m.*

fly-catcher, *n.*, attrapeur de mouches; nigaud; gobe-mouches; *m.*; personne crédule, *f.*; (orni.) oiseau qui vit d'insectes ailés, *m.*

fly-fish, *v.n.*, pêcher à la ligne avec des mouches.

fly-flap, *n.*, chasse-mouches, émouchoir, *m.*

flying (fla'ylgne), *part.adj.*, volant. — camp; *camp volant.* — colours; *enseignes déployées.* — horse; *cheval ailé.* — report; *bruit qui court.*

fly-trap, *n.*, (bot.) attrape-mouche, *m.*

fly-wheel (-hwile), *n.*, (mec.) volant, *m.*

foal (fôle), *n.*, poulain, *m.*; pouliche, *f.*; petit d'une bête de somme, *m.* — of an ass; *ânon.*

foal, *v.n.*, pouliner.

foal-bit, *n.*, (bot.) chardon aux ânes.

foam (fôme), *n.*, écume, *f.*; bouillon, *m.*

foam, *v.n.*, écumer; jeter de l'écume; (nav.) moutonner; (fig.) être en colère.

foaming, *part.*, écumant; couvert d'écume.

foamy, *adj.*, écumeux.

fob, *n.*, gousset, ☉bourson, *m.*, petite poche; tromperi~, *f.*

fob, *v.a.*, duper, tromper, tricher, frauder.

focal (fô-), *adj.*, focal, du foyer; qui appartient au foyer.

focile (fô-çaïle), *n.*, (anat.) ☉focile, *m.* The greater —; *le grand focile (cubitus, tibia).* The lesser —; *le petit focile (radius, péroné).*

focus (fô-keusse), *n.*, (geom. and opt.) foyer, *m.* The — of a glass; *le foyer d'un verre.* The — of a parabole; *le foyer d'une parabole.*

fodder, *n.*, fourrage, *m.*; pâture, *f.*

fodder, *v.a.* and *n.*, affourrager, fourrager; (nav.). V. **fother.**

fodderer, *n.*, fourrageur, *m.*

foe (fô), *n.*, ennemi; adversaire; persécuteur, *m.*

fœtus (fî-), *n.*, fœtus, embryon, *m.*

fog, *n.*, brouillard; *m.*; brume; bruine, brouée, *f.*; (after grass—*luzerne*) regain, *m.*

fog, *v.n.*, s'exercer obscurément, en petit; traîner; se morfondre.

foggily (-'ghi), *adv.*, obscurément.

fogginess (-'ghi-), *n.*, (of the air—*de l'air*) état brumeux, obscur, *m.*; brouillard, *m.*, brume, *f.*

foggy (-'ghi), *adj.*, épais; brumeux; embrumé. It is —; *il fait du brouillard.*

foh! (feu), *int.*, fi! pouah!

foible (foi'b'l), *n.*, faible, *m.* Wise men know their own foible (weak side); *les gens d'esprit connaissent leur faible.*

foil (foïl), *n.*, défaite, *f.*; échec; (set off—*embellissement*) ornement; (fenc.) fleuret, *m.*; (for a stone—*de pierre précieuse*) feuille, *f.*; étain en feuilles, tain, *m*

foil, *v.a.*, vaincre; déjouer, faire échouer; désarmer; (set off—*embellir*) orner, parer.

foiler, *n.*, vainqueur; qui a gagné quelque avantage sur un autre.

foiling, *n.*, (hunt.) abattures, foulées, foulures, *f.pl.*, l'action d'orner; de défaire.

foin (foïne), *n.*, (fenc.) botte, *f.*; coup, *m.*

foin, *v.n.*, porter, ou allonger, une botte.

foist (foïste), *v.n.*, filou, *m.*; (nav.) fuste, *f.*

foist, *v.a.*, fourrer; interpoler; insérer; intercaler.

foistiness, *n.*, moisi, *m.*; moisissure; puanteur, *f.*

fold (fôlde), *n.*, (fig.) l'église; plissure, *f.*; pli, *m.*; enveloppe, *f.*; troupeau; parc, *m.* — of sheep; *bergerie.* Two-—; *double.* Three-—; *triple.* A hundred-—; *centuple.*

fold, *v.a.*, plisser; plier, ployer; envelopper. To — a letter; *plier une lettre.* To — sheep; *parquer des moutons.*

foldage (fôld'édje), *n.*, droit de parcage, *m.*

folder, *n.*, (pers.) plieur, *m.*, plieuse, *f.*; (tool —*outil*) plioir, *m.*

folding, *n.*, pliage; faudage, *m.*

folding, *part. adj.*, pliant; brisé. —-chair; *chaise pliante.* —-doors; *porte à deux battants.* —-screen; *paravent.* —-stick; *plioir.* —-bed; *lit pliant.*

foliaceous (fô-li-é-sheusse), *adj.*, (bot.) foliacé.

foliage (fô-li-édje), *n.*, feuillage; (paint.) feuille, *m.*

foliage, *v.a.*, orner de feuillage.

foliate (fô-), *v.a.*, réduire un métal en feuilles au marteau; étamer un miroir.

foliate, *or* **foliated**, *adj.*, (bot.) feuillé, muni de feuilles.

foliation (fô-lié-), *n.*, réduction d'un métal en feuilles, *f.*; étamage, *m.*; (bot.) feuillaison. *f.*

foliature (-tioure), *n.*, état de ce qui est en feuilles, *m.*

folier (fô-), *n.*, clinquant; oripeau, *m.*

folio (fô-liô), *n.*, in-folio, *m.*; page, *f.*; le chiffre qui désigne le numéro des pages d'un livre, folio, *m.*

folio, *v.a.*, (print.) paginer.

foliomort (fô-li-o-meurte), *adj.*, (colour—*couleur*) feuille-morte.

folk (fôke), *n.*, gens, personnes, *f.pl.*; monde, *m.* They are good kind of —; *ce sont de bonnes gens.*

folkmote (fôk'môte), *n.*, assemblée du peuple, *f.*

follicle (-'k'l), *n.*, (bot., anat.) follicule, *m.*

follow (-lô), *v.a.* and *n.*, suivre; poursuivre; succéder; imiter; s'ensuivre; s'appliquer; s'abandonner; continuer. To — the law; *étudier en droit.* As —s; *ainsi qu'il suit.* It does not — that; *il ne s'ensuit pas que.*

follower, *n.*, sectateur, *m.*; suite, *f.*; suivant; dépendant, partisan, *m.*

following, *part.adj.*, suivant. The year —; *l'année suivante.*

folly (fol'li), *n.*, folie, sottise, *f.*; vice; défaut, *m.*; ineptie, *f.*

foment, *v.a.*, échauffer; étuver; animer, fomenter.

fomentation (fô-mð'n'té-), *n.*, fomentation, *f.*

fomented, *part.adj.*, fomenté; étuvé.

fomenter, *n.*, fomentateur; fauteur, *m.*

fond, *adj.*, passionné; (foolish—*indiscret*) badin, folâtre; vain, fou; (kind—*tendre*) indulgent, bon. To be — of; *aimer.*

fondle (fo'n'd'l), *v.a.*, dorloter, caresser; raffoler. To — a child; *caresser un enfant.*

fondler, *n.*, celui qui dorlote; qui caresse.

fondling, *n.*, mignon, favori, enfant gâté, *m.*

fondly, *adv.*, tendrement; passionnément; à la folie.

fondness, *n.*, passion; douceur; tendresse, *f.*

font (fo'nte), *n.*, fonts baptismaux, *m.pl.*, source, fontaine; (print.) fonte, *f.*

fontanel (-nèle), *n.*, (surg.) cautère, *m.*; (anat.) fontanelle, *f.*

fontange (fo'n'ti'n'dje), *n.*, (head-dress knot —*nœud de rubans*) fontange, *f.*

fonticle (-'k'l), *n.*, (surg.) fonticule, exutoire, *m.*

food (foude), *n.*, nourriture, *f.* ; aliment, *m.*

foodful (-foule), *adj.*, nourrissant, nutritif ; abondant ; fertile.

fool (foule), *n.*, sot ; insensé, niais ; nigaud, *m.* To make a — of one ; *se jouer de quelqu'un.* To play the —; *badiner.*

fool, *v.a.* and *n.*, se moquer, badiner ; tromper. duper. To — one out of his money ; *plumer quelqu'un.*

fool-born. *adj.*, niais, idiot de naisssance.

foolery, *n.*, folie, sottise ; niaiserie ; badinerie, *f.*

fool-hardiness, *n.*, folle audace ; témérité, *f.*

fool-hardy,*adj.*,téméraire ; follement hardi.

foolish. *adj.*, simple, sot ; imbécile ; vain.

foolishly, *adv.*, follement, sottement ; folâtrement.

foolishness, *n.*, folie ; simplicité ; sottise, *f.*

fool's-cap, *n.*, papier écolier, *m.*

fool-trap, *n.*, attrape-nigaud, pont aux ânes, *m.*

foot (foute), *n.* (*feet*), pied, *m.* ; patte, *f.* — - soldiers ; *infanterie.* — of a pair of compasses ; *jambe.* — of a pillar ; *base, f.* — of a sail ; *fond.* — by —; *pied à pied.* Cat's- —; (bot.) *pied-dechat.* Dove's- — ; *pied-de-pigeon.* Hare—; *pied-de-lièvre, m.*

foot, *v.a.*, fouler aux pieds ; donner des coups de pied To — stockings; *ressemeler des bas.*

foot, *v.n.*, marcher, aller à pied ; danser.

football (-bôl), *n.*, ballon, *m.*

footboard (-bôrde), *n.*, marchepied, *m.* ; (of musical instruments—*d'instruments de musique*), pédale, *f.*

footboy (-boï), *n.*, petit laquais ; valet de pied, *m.*

footbridge, *n.*, passerelle, *f.*

footcloth (-cloth), *n.*, housse de pied, housse en souliers, *f.*

footed (-ède), *adj.*, qui a des pieds. Broad- —; *qui a le pied large.*

foot-guards (-gârdze), *n.pl.*, les gardes royaux à pied, *m.*

foothold (-hôlde), *n.*, espace couvert par le pied, *m.*

footing, *n.*, trace, piste ; situation, *f.* ; pied, établissement, *m.*

foot-lamps, or **foot-lights** (-laïtse), *n.pl.*, (thea.) rampe, *f. sing.*

footlicker, *n.*, esclave, vil flatteur, adulateur, *m.—*

footman (-ma'n), *n.*, laquais ; valet de pied ; fantassin, *m.*

footpace (-péce), *n.* ; (arch.) palier, *m.* ; estrade, *f.* ; pas à pas ; pas, *m.*

footpad, *n.*, voleur de grand chemin ; voleur à pied, *m.*

footpath (-pâth), *n.*, sentier ; trottoir, *m.*

foot-post, *n.*, messager à pied, *m.*

foot-race (-réce), *n.*, course à pied, *f.*

foot-rope (-rôpe), *n.*, (nav.) marchepied, *m.* ; ralingue de voile, *f.*

foot-rot (-rote), *n.*, (vet.) fourchet, *m.*

footstalk (-stôke), *n.*, (bot.) pétiole ; pédoncule, *m.*

footstall (-stôl), *n.*, étrier de femme, *m.*

footstep (-stèpe), *n.*, démarche ; trace, *f.* ; marchepied, *m.*

footstool (-stoule), *n.*, marchepied ; tabouret, *m.*

footway (-wè), *n.*, sentier ; trottoir, *m.*

fop, *n.*, petit-maître ; freluquet, damoiseau, *m.*

fopling, *n.*, petit fat ; dameret ; freluquet, *m.*

foppery, *n.*, niaiserie ; sottise ; afféterie, *f.*

foppish, *adj.*, recherché ; affecté ; vain.

foppishly, *adv.*, avec affectation ; avec vanité.

foppishness, *n.*, impertinence ; fatuité ; élégance affectée, *f.*

for, *prep.*, pour, par, de, à, pendant, malgré, nonobstant que. — your sake ; *pour l'amour de vous.* — pity ; *par pitié.* — the present ; *pour le présent.*

for, *conj.*, car ; afin que ; aussi bien.

forage (-'édje), *n.*, fourrage, *m.* ; provisions, *f. pl.*

forage, *v.n.*, fourager ; piller ; ravager ; désoler.

forager, *n.*, fourrageur, *m.*

foraging, *n.*, fourrage ; ravage, *m.* ; déprédation, *f.*

foraminous, *adj.*, troué, percé ; plein de trous ; criblé.

foray (fô'rè), *n.*, incursion, *f.*

forbear (-bère), *v.a.* and *v.*, cesser ; épargner ; supporter ; éviter ; se dispenser ; se retenir, s'abstenir ; s'arrêter ; traiter avec clémence ; ménager ; prendre patience.

forbearance, *n.*, abstinence ; clémence ; patience ; tolérance, *f.* ; ménagement, *m.*

forbid, *v.a.*, défendre, interdire ; prohiber.

forbiddance, *n.*, (l.u.) prohibition, défense, *f.*

forbiddenly, *adv.*, illicitement ; d'une manière illégitime.

forbidder, *n.*, personne qui défend, *f.*

forbidding, *n.*, défense, *f.* ; obstacle, *m.*

forbidding, *adj.*, rebutant ; repoussant, répulsif.

force (fôrce), *n.*, force ; violence ; contrainte ; nécessité, *f.*

force, *v.a.*, forcer, réduire, contraindre ; violer. To — back ; *repousser.* To — in ; *enfoncer*, cogner. To — out ; *chasser de force,* débusquer. To — a passage ; *forcer un passage.*

forced (fôrste), *past part. adj.*, forcé ; contraint ; obligé.

forcedly (fôrcèd'li), *adv.*, par force ; forcément ; par contrainte.

forceful (-foule), *adj.*, puissant, fort, vigoureux.

forcefully, *adv.*, par force, par violence ; fortement.

forceless, *adj.*, faible ; sans force.

forcemeat (-mîte), *n.*, godiveau, *m.* — balls ; *boulettes, f. pl.*

forceps (feur'cèpse), *n.pl.*, (surg.) pince, *f.* ; forceps, *m. sing.*

forcer (fôr-), *n.*, personne qui force, *f.* (mec.) piston foulant, *m.* —s ; *n.pl.*, (surg.) davier, *m.* (to draw teeth—*pour arracher des dents*).

forcible, *adj.*, puissant, efficace, emphatique, fort.

forcibleness, *n.*, force ; vigueur ; violence, *f.*

forcibly, *adv.*, puissamment ; par force ; fortement ; emphatiquement.

forcing, *part.*, contraignant ; (gard.) l'action de forcer, d'avancer, de hâter, de mûrir les fruits.

forcing-pump (-peu'm'pe), *n.*, pompe foulante, *f.*

ford (fôrde), *n.*, gué, *m.* ; (fig. and poet.) fleuve, *m.* ; onde, *f.*

ford, *v.a.*, passer à gué ; guéer.

fordable (fôrd'a'b'l), *adj.*, guéable ; qu'on peut passer à gué.

fore (fôre), *n.*, (nav.) avant, *m.* — and aft ; *de l'avant à l'arrière.*

fore, *adj.*, antérieur ; de devant. The — part ; *la partie antérieure ; le devant.*

fore, *adv.*, devant, auparavant, antérieurement.

fore-advise (-vaïze), *v.a.*, avertir, conseiller à l'avance.

fore-arm (-ârme), *n.*, avant-bras, *m.*

fore-arm, *v.a.*, armer, munir, fortifier par avance. Forewarned, forearmed ; ⊙*qui dit averti, dit muni ; un bon averti en vaut deux.*

fore-bode (bôde), *v.a.*, présager ; prédire ; pronostiquer.

fore-boder, *n.*, devin, *m.* ; personne qui prédit, *f.*

fore-boding, *n.*, présage, *m.*, prédiction, *f.*

fore-cast (-câste), *n.*, prévoyance, *f.* ; pressentiment ; projet, *m.*

fore-cast, *v.a.*, préméditer, prévoir ; projeter ; concerter.

fore-caster, *n.*, devin, *m.*, personne qui prémédite, ou prévoit.

forecastle (-câs's'l), *n.*, (nav.) château d'avant ; gaillard d'avant, *m.*

fore-choose (-tshouze), *v.a.*, élir d'avance ; choisir d'avance.

fore-chosen (-tshô'z'n), *part. adj.*, choisi d'avance ; élu d'avance.

fore-cited (-çaïl'ède), *adj.*, précité ; cité auparavant.

fore-close (-clôce), *v.a.*, exclure ; forclore ; prévenir.

fore-closure (-jioure), *n.*, empêchement, *m.* ; (jur.) forclusion, *f.*

fore-conceive (-cive), *v.a.*, préconcevoir.

fore-court (-côrte), *n.*, avant-cour, *f.*

fore-date, *v.a.*, antidater.

foredeck (-dèke), *n.*, (nav.) l'avant d'un navire ; gaillard d'avant, *m.*

fore-deem (fôr'dîme), *v.a.*, deviner ; conjecturer.

fore-design (-dè-çaïne), *v.a.*, préméditer, projeter ; prédestiner.

foreditch, *n.*, (fort.) avant-fossé, *m.*

fore-done (for'deune), *past part.*, détruit.

fore-doom (-doume), *v.a.*, prédestiner ; déterminer par avance.

foredoor (-dôre), *n.*, porte de devant, *f.*

fore-end (-è'n'de), *n.*, partie de devant ; partie antérieure, *f.*

forefather (-fâ-theur), *n.*, aïeul, ancêtre, *m.* —s ; *aïeux*.

forefinger (-fî'n'gheur), *n.*, index ; second doigt de la main, *m.*

forefoot (-foute), *n.*, pied de devant ; (nav.) brion, *m.*

forefront, *n.*, façade, face d'une maison, *f.*

fore-go (-gô), *v.a.*, céder, renoncer à, abandonner ; résigner ; se désister de ; précéder.

foregoer (-gô-eur), *n.*, aïeul ; précurseur ; prédécesseur, *m.*

fore-going (-gô'-), *part. adj.*, précédent. The — day ; *le jour précédent*.

foreground (-graou'n'de), *n.*, devant ; (paint.) premier plan, *m.*

foreguess (-ghèce), *v.a.*, deviner ; conjecturer ; pressentir.

forehand, *n.*, devant d'un cheval, *m.* ; partie principale, *f.*

forehand, *adj.*, fait trop tôt.

forehanded (-dède), *adj.*, fait à temps, de bonne heure, à propos ; formé en tête, en avant.

forehead (-hède), *n.*, front, *m.* ; (fig.) audace, assurance, effronterie, *f.* Low — ; *front bas*. High — ; *front haut*. — of a horse ; *chanfrein*. — cloth ; *bandeau, frontal*, *m.*

foreholding (-hôld'-), *n.*, présage, *m.* ; prédiction ; bonne aventure, *f.*

foreign (for'ine), *adj.*, étranger ; qui vient de dehors.

foreigner (for'in'eur), *n.*, étranger ; (jur.) aubain, (l.u.) *m.*

foreignness, *n.*, éloignement ; air étranger, *m.*

fore-imagine (-im'adj'ine), *v.a.*, présumer ; penser, concevoir d'avance.

forejudge (-djeu'dje), *v.a.*, préjuger ; juger par avance ; être prévenu.

forejudgment, *n.*, préjugé, *m.* ; prévention, *f.*

fore-know (-nô), *v.a.*, connaître, savoir d'avance ; prévoir.

fore-knowledge (nol'èdje), *n.*, prescience, prévision, *f.*

forel (for'èle), *n.*, parchemin (for the cover of books—*pour couverture de livre*), *m.*

foreland, *n.*, (geog.) promontoire, cap, *m.* ; pointe, *f.*

fore-lay, *v.a.*, surprendre dans une embuscade ; prévenir ; préétablir.

foreclock, *n.*, (nav.) goupille, *f.* ; toupet, *m.*, cheveux de devant, *m.pl.* To take time by the —; *saisir l'occasion aux cheveux*.

foreman, *n.*, chef ; premier ouvrier, contre-maître, *m.* ; (of a shop—*d'atelier*) chef d'atelier ; (of a jury—*d'un jury*) chef du jury ; (of a printing-office—*d'imprimerie*) prote, *m.*

foremast (-mâste), *n.*, (nav.) mât d'avant ; mât de misaine, *m.*

fore-mentioned (-mè'n'sho'n'de), *adj.*, dont on a fait mention auparavant, ci-dessus, mentionné ci-dessus ; (jur.) susmentionné.

foremost (-môste), *adj.*, premier ; le plus avancé de tous.

fore-named (-né'm'de), *adj.*, nommé auparavant ; susnommé.

forenoon (-noune), *n.*, avant midi ; matin, *m.*, matinée, *f.*

forenotice (-nô-), *n.*, avertissement, *m.* ; avis donné d'avance, *m.*

forensic, *or* **forensical** (fo-rè'n'-), *adj.*, (jur.) du barreau.

fore-ordain (fôr-or-déne), *v.a.*, préordonner ; prédestiner.

fore-part (-pârte), *n.*, devant, *m.* ; (nav.) proue ; tête, *f.*

forepast, *adj.*, passé.

fore-possessed (-poz'zèste), *adj.*, pris d'avance ; préoccupé.

forerank (-ra'n'ke), *n.*, premier rang ; front, *m.*

fore-reach (-ritshe), *v.a.*, (nav.) dépasser ; gagner sur.

foreroof (-roufe), *n.*, (arch.) avant-toit, *m.*

fore-run (fôr'reune), *v.a.*, précéder ; devancer ; présager ; prévenir ; arriver avant.

forerunner, *n.*, avant-coureur, précurseur ; prélude, *m.*

foresail (-séle), *n.*, (nav.) misaine.

foresay (-sè), *v.a.*, prédire, présager, prophétiser.

fore-see (-sî), *v.a.*, prévoir, pénétrer.

fore-shadow (-shad'ô), *v.a.*, figurer, représenter par un symbole, à l'avance.

foreshame (-shéme), *v.a.*, déshonorer, reprocher ; accuser.

foreship, *n.*, (nav.) avant d'un vaisseau.

fore-shorten (-shor't'n), *v.a.*, (paint.) raccourcir.

fore-show (-shô), *v.a.*, prédire ; pronostiquer ; faire voir par avance.

foresight (-saïte), *n.*, prévoyance ; (theol.) prescience ; (of fire-arms—*d'armes à jeu*) mire, *f.*

foresightful, *adj.*, prévoyant.

fore-signify (-sig'ni-fa'ye), *v.a.*, présager ; figurer, représenter par un symbole.

foreskin, *n.*, prépuce, *m.*

foreskirt (-skeurte), *n.*, basque, *f.* ; pan de devant ; devant, *m.*

foreslow (-slô), *v.a. and n.*, retarder, arrêter, empêcher, régliger ; tarder, s'amuser

forespeak (-spîke), *v.a. and n.*, prédire, défendre ; parler d'avance ; interdire.

forespeech (-spît'she), *n.*, prologue, exorde, avant-propos, *m.*

fore-spent (-spè'n'te), *adj.*, las, fatigué ; épuisé ; passé.

forespurrer (-speur'-), *n.*, avant-coureur, postillon, *m.*

forest (forèste), *n.*, forêt, *f.*

fore-stake (-stéke), *n.*, avant-pieu, *m.*

fore-stall (-stôl), *v.a.*, accaparer; anticiper; surprendre,

forestaller, *n.*, monopoleur, accapareur, *m.*

forest-born (forèste-), *adj.*, sauvage; né dans une forêt.

forested (-tède), *adj.*, couvert de forêts; garni d'arbres; boisé.

forester, *n.*, forestier, habitant d'une forêt, *m.*

fore-tackle (-tak'k'l), *n.*, (nav.) candelette, *f.*

fore-taste (-téste), *n.*, avant-goût, *m.*; anticipation, *f.*

fore-taste, *v.a.*, goûter par avance; avoir un avant-goût de.

foretell, *v.a.*, prédire, présager, prophétiser.

foreteller, *n.*, prophète, *m.*

forethink (för'thi'n'k), *v.a.* and *n.*, préméditer; prévoir; concevoir d'avance. projeter.

forethought (-thôte), *n.*, prévoyance; préméditation; prescience, *f.*

foretoken (-tô-k'n), *n.*, présage, pronostic; signe, *m.*

foretoken, *v.a.*, présager, pronostiquer.

foretooth (-touth), *n.*, dent de devant, *f.* The foreteeth; *les dents de devant; les incisives*, *f.pl.*

foretop, *n.*, sommet de devant; devant, *m.*, (head-dress—*coiffure*) fontange, *f.*; tour de cheveux. — gallant-mast; *perroquet.* — mast; *petit hunier*, *m.*

forevigil (-vid'jile), *n.*, avant-veille, *f.*

fore-vouched (-vaoutshe), *adj.*, déclaré d'avance; affirmé ci-devant.

foreward (fôr-wôrde), *n.*, (milit.) avant-garde, *f.*; premier rang; front, *m.*

fore-warn (-wôrne), *v.a.*, avertir par avance; précautionner.

forewheel (-hwile), *n.*, roue de devant, *f.*; train de devant, *m.*

forewind (-wi'n'de), *n.*, (nav.) vent en poupe, *m.*

forewish, *v.a.*, souhaiter, désirer par avance.

forewoman (-wouma'n), *n.*, première ouvrière, *f.*

fore-worn, *adj.*, (ant.) usé; gâté par le temps.

fore-wrist (-riste), *n.*, avant-poignet, *m.*

foreyard (-yârde), *n.*, (arch.) avant-cour; (nav.) vergue de misaine, *f.*

forfeit (-fîte), *n.*, amende; faute; forfaiture; confiscation, *f.*; gage; (in a bargain—*d'un marché*) dédit, *m.*

forfeit, *adj.*, confisqué; perdu.

forfeit, *v.a.* and *n.*, forfaire; manquer; confisquer; perdre. To — one's word: *manquer de parole.*

forfeitable, *adj.*, confiscable; sujet à confiscation.

forfeiture (-fit'ioure), *n.*, amende; confiscation; déchéance; forfaiture, *f.*

forfend (for-), *v.a.*, (ant.) défendre; prévenir; garder de; détourner. God — that; *Dieu me garde de.*

forfex (-fèkse), *n.*, pinces; tenettes, *f.pl.*; ciseaux, *m.pl.*

forge (fôrdje), *n.*, forge, *f.*

forge, *v.a.* and *n.*, forger, contrefaire; falsifier.

forger, *n.*, forgeur; inventeur; faussaire; faux monnayeur, *m.*

forgery, *n.*, falsification, *f.*; faux, *m.*

forget (-ghète), *v.a.*, oublier; perdre le souvenir de.

forgetful (-foule), *adj.*, oublieux; négligent.

forgetfulness, *n.*, oubli, *m.*; inattention; négligence, *f.*

forgetter *n.*, celui qui oublie.

forgive (-ghive), *v.a.*, pardonner; faire grâce de, faire remise de; remettre.

forgiveness, *n.*, pardon, *m.*; clémence; remise, grâce. *f.*

forgiver, *n.*, personne qui pardonne, *f.*

fork, *n.*, fourchette; fourche, *f.*

fork, *v.n.*, fourcher, se fourcher; finir en forme de fourche.

fork. *v.a.*, enlever avec la fourche; (agri.) fourcher.

forked (fork'te), *adj.*, fourchu; (bot.) bifurqué.

forkedly (fork'èd'li), *adv.*, en forme de fourche; en fourche.

forkedness (fork'èd'-), *n.*, fourchure, *f.*

fork-head (-hède), *n.*, pointe de flèche, *f.*

forlorn, *adj.*, abandonné; désespéré; délaissé; perdu. — hope; *enfants perdus.*

forlornness, *n.*, délaissement, abandon; état désespéré, *m.*; misère, *f.*

form, *n.*, forme, figure; formalité, *f.*; banc, *m.*; (of schools—*d'écoles*, &c.) classe, *f.*; (of horses —*des chevaux*) encolure, *f.*; (of a hare—*du lièvre*) gîte, *m.*; (print.) forme, *f.* To set a —; *composer une forme.* To take off a —; *lever une forme.* To wash the —; *laver la forme.*

form, *v.a.*, former; façonner; régler; concevoir.

formal, *adj.*, formel, précis; affecté; étudié; grave; cérémonieux.

formalist, *n.*, formaliste; façonnier; faux dévot, *m.*

formality, *n.*, formalité; cérémonie; affectation; bienséance, *f.*

formalize (-aïze), *v.a.*, (l.u.) modifier.

formalize, *v.n.*, (l.u.) être façonnier.

formally, *adv.*, avec formalité; en forme, formellement, expressément, par cérémonie.

formation (-mé-), *n.*, formation, *f.*

formative, *adj.*, formateur; plastique; qui a le pouvoir de former.

former, *n.*, formateur, *m.*; personne qui forme, qui fait, *f.*; forme, *f.*, moule, *m.*; (carp.) fermoir, *m.*

former, *adj.*, premier, précédent, celui-là; passé; ancien.

formerly, *adv.*, autrefois, jadis; anciennement.

formication (-ké-), *n.*, (med.) formication, *f.*; picotement, *m.*

formidable (-da'b'l), *adj.*, formidable, redoutable, terrible.

formidableness, *n.*, qualité, aspect formidable.

formidably, *adv.*, d'une manière formidable; terriblement.

formless, *adj.*, informe, irrégulier, confus.

formula (-miou-), *n.* (*formulæ*), (med. and math.) formule, *f.*

formulary, *n.*, formulaire, *m.*

fornicate (-k'éte), *v.n.*, commettre fornication; forniquer.

fornicate, *adj.*, (arch.) arqué, voûté.

fornication (-ké-), *n.*, fornication, *f.*; concubinage, *m.*; (theol.) idolâtrie, *f.*

fornicator (-ké-), *n.*, fornicateur; (l.ex.) putassier, *m.*

fornicatress (-ké-), *n.*, fornicatrice; concubine, *f.*

forsake (-séke), *v.a.*, délaisser, abandonner, renoncer à; se défaire de. To — a vice; *se corriger d'un vice.* — one's colours; *quitter les drapeaux, déserter.* — one's religion; *apostasier.*

forsaker, *n.*, personne qui abandonne, *f.*; déserteur, *m.*

forsaking, *n.*, abandon; abandonnement, *m.*; (rel.) apostasie, *f.*

forset, *n.*, coffret, petit coffre, *m.*

forsooth (-south), *adv.*, en vérité; ma foi; assurément.

forswear (-swére), *v.a.* and *n.*, abjurer; se parjurer; renoncer avec serment; renier. To — one's self; *se parjurer.*

forswearer, *n.*, parjure, *m.*

fort (fôrte), *n.*, fort, *m.*, forteresse, place forte, *f.*

fortalage (fôr-ta-lédje) (ant.), *or* **fortalice** (fôr-) *n.*, (fort.) donjon, *m.*, forteresse, *f.*

forth (fôrth), *adv.*, en avant; au dehors; au loin. And so —; *et ainsi de suite, et ainsi du reste.*

forth, *prep.*, hors de, de.

forthcoming (forth'keum'-), *adj.*, prêt à paraître, approchant, prochain.

forth-issuing (-ish'shiou-), *adj.*, sortant; s'avançant.

forthright (-raïte), *adv.*, tout droit; en avant.

forthwith (-with), *adv.*, incontinent, aussitôt, sur-le-champ; sans délai, tout de suite.

fortieth (-ti-èth), *adj.*, quarantième.

fortifiable (-fai'ab'l), *adj.*, qu'on peut fortifier.

fortification (-ké-), *n.*, fortification; place fortifiée, *f.*

fortifier (-faï'-), *n.*, ingénieur, *m.*, personne qui fortifie, *f.*

fortify (-fa'ye), *v.a.*, fortifier, munir.

fortin (fôrt'-), *n.*, fortin; petit fort, *m.*

fortitude (-tioude), *n.*, magnanimité; bravoure; force, force d'âme, *f.*, courage, *m.*

fortnight (-naïte), *n.*, quinze jours, *m.pl.*, quinzaine, *f.*

fortress, *n.*, forteresse, place forte, *f.* ; (fig.) appui, soutien, *m.*

fortuitous (-tiou-l-), *adj.*, fortuit, casuel accidentel.

fortuitously, *adv.*, fortuitement; par hasard; accidentellement.

fortuitousness, *n.*, hasard; accident, *m.*

fortunate (-tiou-), *adj.*, heureux, fortuné.

fortunately, *adv.*, heureusement; par bonheur.

fortunateness, *n.*, bonheur; succès, *m.*

fortune (fort'ioune), *n.*, fortune; destinée, *f.*; riche parti, *m.*, biens, *m.pl.*, richesses, *f.pl.* To have one's — told; *se faire dire la bonne aventure.*

fortune, *v.imp.*, arriver, advenir. It —d that; *il arriva que.* It —s that; *il arrive que.*

fortune-book (-bouke), *n.*, livre de bonne aventure, *m.*

fortuned (-tiou'n'de), *adj.*, riche; fortuné; favorisé de la fortune.

fortune-hunter (-heu'n't'-), *n.*, intrigant; aventurier; celui qui cherche à épouser une femme riche, *m.*

fortune-teller, *n.*, diseur de bonne aventure, *m.*

forty, *adj.*, quarante.

forum (fô-reume), *n.*, forum, *m.*, place publique, *f.*

forward (-wôrde), *adj.*, vif; entreprenant; hardi; avancé; empressé, prêt.

forward, *adv.*, en avant; (nav.) à l'avant.

forward, *v.a.* and *n.*, avan r, hâter; accélérer; envoyer, transmettre; faire pousser.

forwarder, *n.*, promoteur, *m.*; (of goods— *de marchandises*) envoyeur, consignateur, *m.*

forwardly, *adv.*, ardemment; avec empressement.

forwardness, *n.*, empressement; avancement; progrès, *m.*; ardeur; présomption, *f.*

fosse (foss), *n.*, fossé, *m.*; fosse, *f.*

fosset, *n.* V. **faucet.**

fosse-way (-wè). *n.*, grand chemin bâti par les Romains en Angleterre, *m.*

fossil, *n.* and *adj.*, fossile, *m.* — salt; *sel fossile.*

fossilize (-aïze), *v.a.*, pétrifier; convertir en fossile.

fossilize, *v.n.*, se fossiliser.

foster, *v.a.*, élever, nourrir; protéger.

fosterage (-édje), *n.*, fonction de nourrice; éducation, *f.*; salaire de nourrice, *m.*

foster-brother (-breuth'-), *n.*, frère de lait, *m.*

foster-child (-tshaïlde), *n.*, nourrisson, *m.*

fosterer, *n.*, nourrice, *f.*, nourricier, *m.*

foster-father (-fâ-theur), *n.*, père nourricier, *m.*

fostering, *n.*, nourriture, *f.*; tendres soins, *m.*

fostering, *part. adj.*, fécondant; tendre; maternel.

foster-mother (-meuth'-), *or* **foster-dam,** *n.*, nourrice, *f.*

foster-sister, *n.*, sœur de lait, *f.*

fother (foth'-), *v.a.*, (nav.) aveugler. To — a leak; *aveugler une voie d'eau.*

foul (faoul), *adj.*, sale, vilain, impur. A — stomach; *un estomac impur.* — wind; (nav.) *vent contraire.* — weather; *gros temps.* To run — of; *heurter, aborder par accident.* A — action; (fig.) *une action basse.* — dealing; *conduite déshonnête.*

foul, *v.a.*, salir, gâter, souiller, barbouiller, troubler; (of fire-arms—*d'armes à feu*) crasser.

foul-faced (-féss'te), *adj.*, laid, odieux, hideux.

foully, *adv.*, salement; bassement; vilainement; honteusement; d'une manière dégoûtante.

foul-mouthed (-maouth'de), *adj.*, grossier; qui tient des discours obscènes; insolent.

foulness, *n.*, saleté, impureté, laideur, turpitude, *f.*

found (faou'n'de), *v.a.*, fonder, poser les fondements de; établir; fondre, jeter en moule.

foundation (-dé-), *n.*, base, fondation, *f.*; fondement, commencement, *m.*; source, *f.*

founded (-dède), *part. adj.*, fondé, bâti, établi; (metal.) fondu, jeté en moule.

founder (-), *n.*, fondateur, auteur; (metal.) fondeur, *m.*; (vet.) courbature; fourbure, *f.*

founder, *v.a.* and *n.*, surmener un cheval, lui fouler les jambes; (nav.) couler à fond; (fig.) se méprendre; échouer.

foundered (-'eurde), *adj.*, (vet.) courbatu; fourbu.

foundery, *or* **foundry,** (faou'n'-), *n.*, fonderie, *f.*

foundling, *n.*, enfant trouvé; enfant abandonné, *m.*

foundress, *n.*, fondatrice, *f.*

fount, *or* **fountain** (faou'n'te, -téne), *n.*, fontaine, source, *f.*; jet d'eau, *m.*

fount, *n.*, (print.) V. **font.**

fountain-head (-hède), *n.*, source, origine, *f.*

fountainless, *adj.*, sans fontaine, sans eau.

fountful (-foulę), *adj.*, plein de sources.

four (fôre), *adj.*, quatre. — days; *quatre jours.*

fourfold (-fôlde), *adj.*, quatre fois autant, quadruple.

four-footed (-foutède), *adj.*, quadrupède, à quatre pieds.

fourscore, *adj.*, quatre-vingts.

foursquare (-skwére), *adj.*, carré; quadrangulaire.

fourteen (fôrténe), *adj.*, quatorze.

fourteenth (-ti'n'th), *adj.*, quatorzième.

fourth (-fôrth), *adj.*, quatrième. The — part; *la quatrième partie, le quart.*

fourthly (fôrthlï), *adv.*, quatrièmement.

four-wheeled (-hwílde), *adj.*, à quatre roues.

fowl (faoul), *n.*, oiseau, *m.*; volaille, *f.*; poulet, *m.*

fowl, *v.a.* and *n.*, tirer, chasser aux oiseaux. To go a —ing ; *aller à la chasse aux oiseaux.*

fowler, *n.*, oiseleur ; chasseur aux oiseaux, *m.*

fowling, *n.*, chasse aux oiseaux, *f.*

fowling-piece (-pice), *n.*, fusil de chasse, *m.*

fox (fokse), *n.* (*foxes*), renard ; rusé, *m.* Young — ; *renardeau, m.*

fox-chase (-tshéce), *n.*, chasse au renard.

fox-evil (-î-v'l), *n.*, (med.) alopécie, *f.*

foxglove, *n.*, (bot.) gantelée ; digitale, *f.*

fox-hound (-haou'n'de), *n.*, chien pour la chasse au renard, *m.*

fox-hunt *or* **fox-hunting**, *n.*, chasse au renard, *f.*

fox-hunter, *n.*, chasseur au renard, *m.*

foxish, *or* **foxlike** (-laïke), *adj.*, de renard ; rusé.

fox-kennel (-kè'n'nèle), *n.*, renardière, *f.*

foxship, *n.*, finesse, ruse, *f.*

foxtail (-téle), *n.*, (bot.) queue de renard, *f.*

fox-trap, *n.*, trappe, *f.*, piège à renard, *m.*

foxy, *adj.*, (ant.) de renard ; rusé ; roux.

fract, *v.a.*, (ant) fracasser, rompre, briser ; enfreindre.

fraction (frak'sheune), *n.*, fraction ; querelle ; brouillerie, *f.*

fractional, *or* **fractionary**, *adj.*, fractionnaire.

fractious (-sheusse), *adj.*, querelleur ; maussade hargneux, méchant, chicaneur.

fractiously, *adv.*, de mauvaise humeur.

fractiousness, *n.*, humeur querelleuse ; disposition à se fâcher, *f.*

fracture (frak'tioure), *n.*, fracture, rupture, *f.*

fracture, *v.a.* and *n.*, casser, rompre ; (surg.) se fracturer.

fragile (fradjî), *adj.*, fragile, frêle ; faible, délicat.

fragility, *n.*, fragilité ; instabilité ; faiblesse.

fragment, *n.*, fragment, reste, débris, *m.* Chosen —s of an author ; *analectes, m.pl.*

fragrance, *or* **fragrancy** (fré-), *n.*, odeur suave, *f.*, parfum, *m.*

fragrant, *adj.*, odoriférant ; qui sent bon.

fragrantly, *adv.*, avec un parfum agréable.

frail (fréle), *n.*, cabas, panier, *m.* A — of raisins ; *un cabas de raisins secs.*

frail (fréle), *adj.*, frêle, fragile, faible, périssable.

frailness, *or* **frailty**, *n.*, faiblesse, fragilité, infirmité, *f.*

frame (fréme), *n.*, forme ; charpente ; figure, *f.* ; châssis ; fût, *m.* ; (of picture—*de tableau*) cadre, *m.*, bordure, *f.* ; (of a ship—*de vaisseau*) couples, *m.pl.* ; (of artisans—*d'ouvriers*) métier, *m.* ; (of farriers—*de maréchaux ferrants*) travail, *m.* ; (of mind—*d'esprit*) disposition, *f.*

frame, *v.a.*, façonner, former, construire ; inventer ; exprimer ; régler ; former.

framed (fré'm'de), *part. adj.*, formé, fabriqué, fait.

framer, *n.*, ouvrier, auteur, artisan, *m.*

framework (-weurke), *n.*, ouvrage fait sur le métier ; (of a house—*de maison*) charpente, *f.*

franchise (fra'n'tshize), *n.*, franchise, immunité, *f.* ; privilège, *m.*

franchise, *v.a.*, affranchir ; exempter ; délivrer.

frangible (-dji'b'l), *adj.*, fragile, cassant, qui se brise aisément.

frank, *n.*, franc, *m.*, livre, *f.* ; enveloppe d'une lettre affranchie par privilège, *f.* ; chrétien, *m.*

frank, *adj.*, franc, libéral, généreux, sincère.

frank, *v.a.*, affranchir ; engraisser.

frankincense, *n.*, encens, *m.*

frankly, *adv.*, franchement ; sans contrainte.

frankness, *n.*, franchise, sincérité, bonté, *f.*

frantic, *adj.*, fou ; frénétique ; furieux. — with joy ; *ivre de joie.*

frantically, *adv.*, follement ; en frénétique; en furieux.

franticness, *n.*, folie, frénésie, fureur, *f.*

frap, *v.a.*, (nav.) ceintrer ; brider ; aiguilleter. To — a tackle ; *aiguilleter un palan.* To — a ship ; *ceintrer un vaisseau.*

frapping, *n.*, (nav.) aiguilletage.

fraternal (-teur-), *adj.*, fraternel.

fraternally, *adv.*, fraternellement, en frère.

fraternity, *n.*, fraternité, confrérie, société, *f.*

fratricide (-çaïde). *n.*, fratricide, *m.*

fraud, **fraudulence**, *or* **fraudulency** (fröd'iou-), *n.*, fraude, tromperie, superchcrie, circonvention, *f.*

fraudful, *or* **fraudulent** (-foule,-fröd'iou-), *adj.*, frauduleux, trompeur, de mauvaise foi.

fraudulently, *adv.*, frauduleusement ; en fraude.

fraught (fröte), *part. adj.*, rempli, chargé, plein.

fray (frè), *n.*, combat, *m.* ; querelle ; éraillure, *f.*

fray, *v.a.* and *n.*, érailler ; s'érailler ; effrayer, épouvanter.

freak (frike), *n.*, quinte, fantaisie ; boutade, *f.* ; caprice, *m.*

freak, *v.a.*, bigarrer ; tacheter ; varier.

freakish, *adj.*, quinteux, bizarre, fantasque.

freakishly, *adv.*, capricieusement, par fantaisie.

freakishness, *n.*, boutade ; bizarrerie, *f.*

freckle (frèk'k'l), *n.*, rousseur, tache de rousseur, *f.*

freckled, *or* **freckly** (frèk'k'lde), *adj.*, tacheté de rousseurs ; plein de rousseurs.

free (fri), *adj.*, libre, exempt ; sincère, franc, libéral ; aisé, dégagé ; (nav.) largue.

free, *v.a.*, affranchir, exempter ; délivrer. To — one's self ; *s'affranchir.*

freebooter (fri-bout'-), *n.*, bandit, voleur, pillard, picoreur, flibustier ; maraudeur, *m.*

freeborn, *adj.*, né libre.

freecost, *adv.*, sans frais, sans dépense ; gratis.

freedman (frid'ma'n'), *n.*, affranchi, homme libre, *m.*

freedom (fri-deume), *n.*, liberté ; immunité; maîtrise, aisance, *f.* ; (of a city—*de cité*) bourgeoisie, les franchises d'un bourgeois, *f.*

freehearted (-hârtède), *adj.*, libre, libéral, généreux.

freehold (-hôlde), *n.*, franc-fief, franc-alleu, *m.*

freeholder, *n.*, franc tenancier, *m.*

freely, *adv.*, librement, sans contrainte, gratuitement.

freeman (-ma'n), *n.*, bourgeois, citoyen, *m.*

freemason (-mé-s'n), *n.*, franc-maçon, *m.*

freemasonry (-mé-s'n-), *n.*, franc-maçonnerie, *f.*

freeminded (-maï'n'dède), *adj.*, sans souci ; libre de soins.

freeness, *n.*, sincérité, libéralité, candeur, *f.*

free-school (-skoul), *n.*, école gratuite ; école publique, *m.*

free-spoken (-spôk'n), *adj.*, qui dit librement sa pensée.

freestone (-stône), *n.*, pierre de taille, pierre sableuse. *f.*

freethinker (-thi'n'k'-), *n.*, esprit fort, libre penseur ; incrédule, *m.*

free-will, *n.*, libre arbitre, franc arbitre, *m.*

freeze (frize), *v.a.* and *n.*, geler, se geler, glacer, se glacer, congeler, se congeler.

freight (frète), *n.*, fret, nolis, nolissement, *m.*, cargaison, *f.*, chargement, *m.*

freight, *v.a.*, fréter, affréter, charger, noliser.

freighter, *n.*, fréteur, affréteur, *m.*
freighting, *n.*, affrétement. *m.*
french (frè'n'she), *adj.*, français. After the — fashion ; *à la française.*
french, *n.*, (language—*langue*) français, *m.*
french-horn, *n.*, cor de chasse, cornet à piston, *m.*
frenchify (-shifa'ye), *v.a.*, franciser ; donner les manières françaises.
frenchman, *n.*. Français, *m.*
frenchwoman (-wouma'n), *n.*, Française, *f.*
frenetic, *or* **frenetical** (-fri-nè't'-), *adj.*, frénétique, fou, furieux.
frenzy (frè'n'-), *n.*, frénésie, folie, *f.* ; égarement d'esprit, *m.*
frequence, *or* **frequency** (frt-kwè'n-), *n.*, fréquence ; multitude ; réitération, *f.*
frequent, *adj.*,fréquent ; ordinaire, commun.
frequent (fri-kwè'n'te), *v.a.*, fréquenter ; hanter.
frequentative, *n.*, (gram.) fréquentatif, *m.*
frequenter (fri-kwè'n't'-), *n.*, celui qui fréquente ; habitué, *m.*
frequenting (fri-), *n.*, fréquentation, ⊙hantise, *f.*
frequently (fri-), *adv.*, fréquemment, souvent.
fresco (frès-cô), *n.*, fresque ; (cool—*le frais*) fraîcheur, *f.*, frais, *m.* To paint in — ; *peindre à fresque.*
fresh, *or* **freshet** (frèshe, -'ète), *n.*, courant d'eau douce, *m.*, crue, *f.*
fresh (frèshe), *adj.*, frais ; récent ; vif ; nouveau ; vigoureux. — water ; *de l'eau douce.* — horses ; *chevaux de relais.* — complexion ; *un teint vif.* — in my memory ; *j'en ai la mémoire toute fraîche.*
freshen (frèsh'n), *v.a.* and *n.*, rafraîchir, devenir frais, fraîchir ; se rafraîchir, dessaler. The wind —s ; (nav.) *le vent fraîchit.*
freshly, *adv.*, fraîchement ; récemment, depuis peu.
freshman, *n.*, novice ; (acad.) étudiant de première année, *m.*
freshness, *n.*, fraîcheur ; nouveauté ; naïveté ; rapidité, *f.*
freshwater (-wô-teur). *adj.*, maladroit, inhabile, qui n'a point d'expérience, novice. — sailors ; *marins d'eau douce.*
fret (-frète), *n.*, (of liquor—*des liqueurs*) fermentation ; (mus.) touche ; (arch.) grecque ; (of silk—*de la soie*) éraillure ; (fig.) agitation de l'âme, *f.* ; (ant.) détroit, *m.*
fret, *v.a.*, chagriner ; fâcher ; corroder, ronger ; écorcher ; agiter ; courroucer ; découper ; relever en bosse.
fret, *v.n.*, se chagriner ; s'inquiéter ; se fâcher ; se vexer ; s'user, se couper. s'érailler ; se corroder ; s'agiter, se courroucer.
fretful (-foule), *adj.*, chagrin, acariâtre ; de mauvaise humeur.
fretfully, *adv.*, avec chagrin ; de mauvaise humeur ; avec irritation, avec dépit.
fretfulness, *n.*, humeur chagrine ; irritation, *f.* ; dépit, *m.*
fretting. *n.*, corrosif, *m.* ; (fig.) agitation ; commotion ; affliction ; (of the skin—*de la peau*) excoriation, *f.*
fretting, *adj.*, corrosif, corrodant ; (fig.) chagrinant, inquiétant.
fretty, *adj.*, relevé en bosse ; ciselé ; découpé ; (arch.) orné d'une grecque ; (her.) fretté. entrelacé.
fretwork (-weurke), *n.*, ouvrage relevé en bosse ; découpage, *m.* ; ciselure ; (arch.) grecque, *f.* ; (her.) entrelac, *m.*
friability, *or* **friableness** (frai-a-), *n.*, friabilité, *f.*
friable, *adj.*, friable ; facile à réduire en poussière, *m.*

friar (frai-), *n.*, religieux, moine, *m.*
friar-like (-laïke), *or* **friarly**, *adj.*, monacal, de moine.
friary, *n.*, confrérie, *f.* ; monastère, couvent de moines, *m.*
fribble, *v.n.*, s'amuser ; se jouer de ; chanceler.
fribble, *or* **fribbler**, *n.*. freluquet, *m.* ; personne frivole, *f.*, moqueur, *m.*
fricassee (-sî), *n.*, fricassée, *f.*
friction, *n.*, frottement, *m.*. friction, *f.*
friday (frai-), *n.*, vendredi, *m.* Good- — ; *vendredi saint.*
friend (frè'n'de), *n.*, ami, *m.*, amie, *f.* ; camarade, *m.*
friendless. *adj.*, sans amis ; délaissé, abandonné.
friendliness, *n.*, amitié ; bonté ; bienveillance, *f.*
friendly, *adj.*, serviable, d'ami, favorable, propice, utile.
friendship, *n.*, amitié, affection mutuelle, *f.*
frieze, *or* **frize** (frize), *n.*, frise, ratine, *f.* ; (arch.) gorgerin, *m.*, frise, *f.*
frigate (frigh'éte), *n.*, frégate, *f.*
frigefaction (fridj'i-), *n.*, refroidissement, *m.* ; l'action de refroidir, *f.*
fright (fraïte), *n.*, peur soudaine, *f.* ; épouvantail, *m.*, épouvante, frayeur, *f.*
fright, *or* **frighten** (fraït'n), *v.a.*, épouvanter, faire peur, effrayer.
frightful (fraït'foule), *adj.*, épouvantable, effroyable, affreux.
frightfully, *adv.*, effroyablement, affreusement.
frightfulness, *n.*, horreur, frayeur, *f.*
frigid (frid'jide), *adj.*, froid ; glacial ; privé de chaleur.
frigidity, *or* **frigidness**, *n.*, frigidité, froideur, *f.*
frigidly, *adv.*, froidement.
frigorific, *or* **frigorifical**, *adj.*, frigorifique, de froid.
frill, *v.n.*, (in falconry—*fauconnerie*) trembler de froid. The hawk —s ; *l'oiseau tremble de froid.*
frill, *n.*, jabot de chemise, *m.* ; fraise, *f.*
frill, *v.a.*, orner d'un jabot, de fronces.
fringe, *n.*, frange ; crépine, *f.* ; effilé ; bout, *m.*, extrémité, *f.*
fringe, *v.a.*, franger ; garnir de crépine.
fringemaker (-mék'-), *n.*, frangier, faiseur de franges, *m.*
fringy, *adj.*, à frange, à crépine.
frippery, *n.*, friperie, *f.*, vieux habits, haillons, *m.pl.*
frisk. *n.*, gambade, *f.* ; saut, frétillement, *m.*
frisk, *v.n.* and *a.*, sautiller, gambader, frétiller. se trémousser.
frisker, *n.*, homme folâtre, inconstant, *m.* ; personne qui sautille, frétille.
friskiness, *n.*, folâtrerie, gaîté, vivacité, *f.*
frisky, *or* **frisk**, *adj.*, fringant, gai, sémillant, vif, enjoué, frétillant. folâtre.
frit, *n.*, (glass manu.—*manuf. du verre*) fritte, *f.*
frith (frith). *n.*, détroit, *m.* ; estuaire, *m.*, embouchure, *f.* (of a river—*d'un fleuve*).
fritillary, *n.*, (bot.) fritillaire, *f.*
fritter, *n.*, beignet ; hachis frit ; ramequin, *m.*
fritter, *v.a.*, couper en morceaux ; dissiper, consumer. To — away ; *morceler*
frivolous, *adj.*, frivole, vain, léger, volage.
frivolously, *adv.*, d'une manière frivole ; superficiellement.
frivolousness, *n.*. frivolité, *f.*
frizz, *or* **frizzle** (-z'l), *v.a.*, friser ; frisoter, taper ; crêper.
frizzle (-z'l), *n.*, boucle de cheveux frisés, *f.* frisure.
frizzler, *n.*, friseur ; personne qui frise.
fro (frô), *adv.*, en arrière. To go to and — ; *aller çà et là ; aller et venir.*

frock. *n.,* froc; habit, *m.;* robe d'enfant; blouse, *f.;* (coat—*habit*) frac, *m.*

frockcoat (-côte), *n.,* redingote. *f.*

frog. *n.,* grenouille, *f.;* (of a horse's foot—*du pied du cheval*) fourchette, *f.*

frolic. *n.,* gaillardise, boutade, folie, *f.;* badinage, *m.*

frolic. *v.n.,* folâtrer, badiner, faire le fou; jouer; gambader.

frolicsome (-cœume), *adj.,* folâtre, gaillard, badin, espiègle, joyeux, fantasque.

frolicsomely, *adv.,* joyeusement; plaisamment, gaiement.

frolicsomeness, *n.,* gaillardise, boutade; folâtrerie, gaieté, espièglerie. *f.*

from, *prep.,* de; de devant; de par; de la part; depuis; dès, par; d'après; (above—*haut*) d'en haut; (afar—*loin*) de loin; (amidst—*milieu*) du milieu de; (among—*entre*) d'entre; (behind —*derrière*) de derrière; (beneath—*bas*) d'en bas; (beyond—*au delà*) d'au delà; (high—*haut*) de haut; (hence—*ici*) d'ici; (thence—*là*) de là; (under—*dessous*) de dessous; (within—*dedans*) de dedans; (without—*dehors*) de dehors.

frond, *n.,* (bot.) fronde, *f.;* feuillage, *m.*

frondation (-dé-), *n.,* (hort.) émondage, *m.*

frondescence (fro'n'd'ès'-), *n.,* (bot.) feuillage, *m.*

frondiferous, frondose, *or* **frondous.** *adj.,* frondifère, feuillu.

front (freu'n'te), *n.,* front, devant, portail, *m.;* face, façade, *f.;* (box—*loge*) première loge, loge de face, *f.;* (of a building) façade, *f.;* (room—*salle*) chambre sur le devant. *f.*

front (freu'n'te), *v.a.* and *n.,* rencontrer, faire face, faire tête; être vis-à-vis de.

frontage (freu'n't'-) *n.,* façade, *f.;* droit de façade, *m.*

frontal (-freu'n't'-), *n.,* fronteau, frontal; (arch.) fronton; bandeau, *m.*

fronted (freu'n't'ède), *adj.,* à façade; qui a un front.

frontier (fro'n'tîre), *n.* and *adj.,* frontière, limite, *f.;* (town—*ville*) ville frontière. *f.*

fronting (freu'n't'-) *adj.,* en face de; vis-à-vis; qui fait face.

frontispiece (freu'n'tis-pîce), *n.,* frontispice, *m.*

frontless (freu'n't'-), *a lj.,* effronté, déhonté, impudent.

frontlet (freu'n't'-), *n.,* fronteau, frontal, bandeau, *m.;* (artil.) mire, *f.*

frost. *n.,* gelée; glace, *f.* Hoar— —; *gelée blanche, f.* Glazed — ; *verglas, m.*

frost, *v.a.,* glacer; damasquiner.

frost-bitten (-bit'n), *adj.,* gelé.

frosted. *adj.,* glacé; damasquiné.

frostily, *adv.,* froidement; avec une froideur glaciale.

frostiness, *n.* froid glacial; grand froid, *m.*

frostnail (-néle), *n.,* clou à glace, *m.*

frost-work (-weurke), *n.,* glacé, *m.*

frosty, *adj.,* de gelée, glacé; (weather—*temps*) temps de gelée.

froth (froth). *n.,* écume, mousse, *f.;* bouillon, *m.;* crème fouettée, *f.;* (fig.) vain étalage de paroles. *m.*

froth. *v.n.,* écumer; mousser, jeter de l'écume.

frothily, *adv.,* avec de l'écume, légèrement; avec futilité; en bavardant.

frothy, *adj.,* écumeux; mousseux; plein de vent; (fig.) vain, frivole, verbeux.

frounce (fraou'n'ce), *v.a.,* friser; froncer.

frouzy (fraou-), *adj.,* sale, gras, moisi, vilain.

froward (frô-weurde), *adj.,* revêche, rude, chagrin, pervers, insolent, rude, opiniâtre, indocile.

frowardly, *adv.,* méchamment; insolemment; opiniâtrément; avec perversité.

frowardness. *n.,* humeur revêche; opiniâtreté; perversité, indocilité, insolence, *f.*

frown (fraou'ne), *n.,* froncement de sourcils, dédain; air refrogné; revers, *m.*

frown. *v.n.,* froncer les sourcils; être contraire; regarder de mauvais œil, se refrogner.

frowning. *adj.,* chagrin, rechigné.

frowningly, *adv.,* d'un air chagrin, de mauvais œil.

frozen (frôz'n), *part.adj.,* glacé, gelé, glacial.

fructiferous (freuk-tif eur'-), *adj.,* fertile, productif, fructifère.

fructification (-ké-), *n.,* fructification; fertilité; fécondation, *f.*

fructify (-fa'ye), *v.a.* and *n.,* fructifier, fertiliser, féconder, rapporter du fruit.

fructuous (freuk'tiou-), *adj.,* (ant.) utile, avantageux; fertile, fructueux, fécond.

frugal (friou-), *adj.,* frugal, économe, sobre, ménager.

frugality. *n.,* économie, frugalité; tempérance; sobriété, *f.*

frugally, *adv.,* frugalement; avec économie.

frugivorous (-djiv'-). *adj.,* frugivore.

fruit (froute), *n.,* fruit, *m.;* (fig.) avantage, profit, *m.* First— —s; *prémices, f.pl.*

fruit, *v.n.,* donner, produire du fruit.

fruitage (frout'édje), *n.,* fruitage, *m.*

fruit-basket (-baskète), *n.,* cuider, cueilloir, *m.*

fruit-bearer (-bèr'eur), *n.,* arbre fruitier; arbre qui porte du fruit, *m.*

fruiterer *n.,* fruitier, *m.,* fruitière, *f.*

fruitery. *n.,* fruiterie, *f.,* fruitier, *m.;* fruits, *m.pl.*

fruitful (-foule), *adj.,* fertile, abondant, fécond, chargé de fruit, utile.

fruitfully, *adv.,* fertilement, abondamment.

fruitfulness, *n.,* fertilité, abondance, fécondité, *f.*

fruit-grove (-grôve), *n.,* petit verger; jardin fruitier, *m.*

fruition (friou-ish'eune), *n.,* jouissance, possession, *f.*

fruitless (frout'-), *adj.,* stérile, infructueux, inutile, vain.

fruitlessly, *adv.,* inutilement, vainement, sans fruit.

fruit-market (-mâr-), *n.,* marché au fruit, *m.*

fruit-stalk (-stôke), *n.,* (bot.) pédoncule, *m.*

fruit-time (-taïme), *n.,* automne, *f.;* temps des fruits, *m.*

fruit-tree (-trî), *n.,* arbre fruitier, *m.* Wall —; *espalier.* Standard —; *arbre fruitier en plein vent.* Dwarf —; *arbre nain, m.*

fruit-wall (-wôl), *n.,* (hort.) espalier, *m.*

frumentaceous (friou-mè'n'té-sheusse), *adj.,* (bot.) frumentacé.

frumenty (friou-), *n.,* fromenté; bouillie de farine de froment, *f.*

frump (freu'm'pe), *v.a.* and *n.,* railler, plaisanter; se moquer de.

frush (freushe), *n.,* (vet.) fourchette du pied du cheval; excroissance cornée de la fourchette: suppuration fétide à la fourchette, *f.*

frush. *v.a.,* froisser; casser, briser, rompre.

frustraneous (freus-tré-ni-), *adj.,* (ant.) inutile, vain, sans profit.

frustrate (freus-), *adj.,* vain, inutile, nul, sans effet.

frustrate. *v.a.,* frustrer; dissiper; déconcerter; annuler.

frustration (-tré-), *n.,* privation, *f.;* insuccès; échec, *m.;* nullité, déception, *f.*

frustrative, *adj.,* (ant.) frustratoire: trompeur.

frustum (freus'teume), *n.* (*frusta*) fragment, tronc, *m.*

fry (fra'ye), *n.,* fretin, frai, *m.;* friture, *f.;* (fig.) foule, *f.,* amas, *m.*

24 *

fry, *v.a.*, frire ; fricasser.

frying-pan (-pane), *n.*, poêle à frire, *f.*

fub (feube), *n.*, (ant.) gros enfant, *m.*

fucate, *or* **fucated** (fiou-ké-), *adj.*, fardé, déguisé.

fucus (fiou-keusse), *n.*, fard ; rouge ; déguisement, *m.*

fuddle (feud'd'l), *v.a.* and *n.*, enivrer, soûler ; s'enivrer.

fuddler, *n.*, ivrogne, débauché, *m.*

fudge ! (feudje), *int.*, ah ! bah !

fudge, *n.*, (triv.) conte, *m.* ; baliverne, sottise, bêtise, absurdité, *f.*, galimatias, *m.*

fuel (fiou-), *n.*, chauffage ; combustible, *m.* To add — to the fire ; *verser de l'huile sur le feu.*

fuel, *v.n.*, alimenter en combustible ; entretenir le feu.

fugacious (fiou-ghé-sheusse), *adj.*, fugace, fugitif ; passager ; qui fuit.

fugaciousness, *or* **fugacity**, *n.*, fugacité, volatilité, instabilité, inconstance, *f.*

fugh ! (fou), *int.*, pouah !

fugitive (fiou dji-), *n.*, fugitif, transfuge, déserteur, réfugié, *m.*

fugitive, *adj.*, fugitif ; errant ; qui s'enfuit ; passager, inconstant.

fugitiveness, *n.*, fugacité, volatilité, inconstance, instabilité, *f.*

fugue (foughe), *n.*, (mus.) fugue, *f.* To maintain a — ; *faire une fugue.*

fulciment (feul-), *n.*, (ant.) (mec.) appui, point d'appui, *m.*

fulcrum (feul-creume), *n.*, (bot.) soutien, support ; (mec.) point d'appui ; palier, *m.*

fulfil (feul'file), *v.a.*, accomplir, remplir, achever, exécuter ; combler, satisfaire.

fulfiller, *n.*, personne qui accomplit, remplit, exécute, *f.*

fulfilling, *n.*, accomplissement, *m.*

fulfilment, *n.*, exécution, *f.*, accomplissement, *m.*

fulfraught, *adj.*, rempli, plein ; bien approvisionné.

fulgency (feul-djè'n'-), *n.*, vif éclat, resplendissement, *m.* ; splendeur ; clarté, *f.*

fulgent, *adj.*, reluisant, éclatant, brillant, resplendissant.

fulgid (feul'djid), *adj.*, (ant.) *V.* **fulgent.**

fulgidity, *or* **fulgor**, *n.*, éclat, *m.*, splendeur, *f.*

fulgurate (feul-ghiou-), *v.n.*, (ant.) émettre des éclairs.

fulguration (-ré-), *n.*, éclair, *m.* ; (chem.) fulguration, *f.*

fuliginosity, *n.*, (ant.) (chem.) fuliginosité, suie, *f.*

fuliginous (fiou-lidj'i-), *adj.*, fuligineux, plein de suie ; noir, sombre, triste.

full (foule), *n.*, plein ; comble, *m.* ; satiété ; mesure complète, *f.* ; soûl, *m.*

full, *adj.*, plein, rempli, ample, entier, complet ; rassasié ; (face) visage plein. — stop ; *point, m.* — moon ; *pleine lune, f.* — meal ; *un bon repas.* — eyes ; *de gros yeux, m.*

full, *v.a.*, fouler. To — cloth ; *fouler du drap.*

full, *adv.*, plein, en plein, pleinement, tout à fait. She is — twenty ; *elle a vingt ans accomplis.*

full-blown (-blône), *adj.*, tout à fait distendu, étendu, épanoui.

full-bodied (-bodide), *adj.*, gros ; replet.

full-bottomed (-bott'teu'm'de), *adj.*, à large fond.

full-butt (-beute), *adv.*, en se heurtant ; nez à nez.

full-dress, *n.*, grande tenue ; grande toilette, *f.*

full-drive (-draïve), *adv.*, au grand galop, ventre à terre, à bride abattue.

full-eared (-îr'de), *adj.*, rempli de grains ; mûr.

fuller (foul'-), *n.*, foulon, *m.*

fuller's-earth (foul'leurz'eurth), *n.*, terre à foulon, terre à dégraisser, *f.*

fullery, *n.*, foulerie, *f.* ; moulin à foulon, *m.*

full-eyed (-a'ye'de), *adj.*, ayant de gros yeux.

full-fed (-fède), *adj.*, gras ; bien nourri ; dodu.

full-grown (-grône), *adj.*, qui est parvenu à toute sa croissance. — girl ; *grande fille.*

full-growth (-grôth), *n.*, crue, *f.*, développement, accroissement, *m.*

fulling, *n.*, foulage, *m.*

fulling-mill, *n.*, moulin à foulon, *m.*

full-laden (-lèd'n), *adj.*, tout à fait chargé.

full-nigh (-na'ye), *adv.*, presque.

full-spread (-sprède), *adj.*, tout à fait étendu.

full-summed (-seu'm'de), *adj.*, entier ; complet dans toutes ses parties.

fully, *adv.*, pleinement, entièrement, amplement.

fulmar (feul'mar), *n.*, (orni.) pétrel, pinson de tempête, pinson de mer, *m.*

fulminant (feul'-), *adj.*, foudroyant ; (chem.) fulminant.

fulminate (feul'-), *v.a.* and *n.*, fulminer, tonner, faire un grand bruit.

fulmination (-né-), *n.*, fulmination, *f.*

fulminatory (-teuri), *adj.*, fulminant, fulminatoire.

fulness (foul-), *n.*, plénitude, abondance, *f.*

fulsome (feul'seume), *adj.*, dégoûtant ; honteux ; infâme ; nauséabond.

fulsomely, *adv.*, d'une manière dégoûtante ; d'une manière honteuse.

fulsomeness, *n.*, dégoût, *m.* ; infamie, honte, *f.*

fumage (fiou-médje), *n.*, fumage ; fouage, *m.*

fumatory (fiou-ma-teuri), *n.*, (bot.) fumeterre, *f.* ; fiel de terre, *m.*

fumble (feu'm'b'l), *v.a.* and *n.*, ranger maladroitement ; patiner, chiffonner ; fouiller ; tâtonner. — along ; *aller à tâtons.* — up ; *mal plier.*

fumbler, *n.*, maladroit, tâtonneur, patineur, *m.*

fumblingly, *adv.*, maladroitement.

fume (floume), *n.*, fumée, vapeur, exhalaison ; (fig.) colère, *f.*

fume, *v.a.* and *n.*, fumer, jeter de la fumée ; s'exhaler, s'évaporer ; s'échauffer, s'indigner, être en colère.

fumet (fiou-mète), *n.*, (hunt.) fumées (of the stag—*du cerf*) ; crottes (of the hare—*du lièvre*), *f. pl.*

fumette (fiou-), *n.*, (ant.) (cook.) fumet, *m.*

fumid (fiou-), *adj.*, enfumé ; fuligineux.

fumigate (fiou-), *v.a.* and *n.*, fumiger ; désinfecter.

fumigation, *n.*, fumigation, désinfection, *f.*

fumigator, *n.*, (surg.) fumigateur, *m.*

fumingly (fiou-), *adv.*, en colère.

fumitory (fiou-), *n.*, *V.* **fumatory.**

fumous, *or* **fumy** (fiou-), *adj.*, fumeux ; qui exhale des vapeurs.

fun (feune), *n.*, badinage, *m.*, plaisanterie ; gaieté, joie, gaillardise ; bourde, *f.* For — ; *pour badiner, pour rire.*

fun, *v.a.* and *n.*, cajoler ; se moquer de.

funambulist (fiou-), *n.*, funambule, voltigeur, danseur de corde, *m.*

function (feu'n'gk'sheune), *n.*, fonction ; faculté, occupation, *f.* ; métier, emploi, *m.*

functionary, *n.*, fonctionnaire, *m.*

fund (feunde), *n.*, fonds, capital, *m.* ; finance, *f.* The public —s ; *les fonds publics.* Sinking — ; *fonds d'amortissement.*

fund, *v.a.*, affecter des fonds ; placer, verser des fonds.

fundament (feu'n'-), *n.*, fondement ; siège, anus, *m.*

fundamental, adj., fondamental.

fundamentally, adv., fondamentalement, essentiellement.

funeral (fiou-nèr'-) n., enterrement, convoi funèbre, m.; funérailles, obsèques, f.pl.

funereal (fiou-ni-ri-), adj., triste, funèbre, lugubre, sépulcral.

fungosity (feu'n'goss'-), n., fongosité, f.

fungous (feu'n'-), adj., spongieux, fongueux, poreux.

fungus (feu'n'-), n., champignon, fongus, m.; excroissance de chair, f.

funicle (fiou-ni-k'l), n., petite corde, fibre, f.

funicular (fiou-nik'iou-), adj., (mec., math.) funiculaire; (bot.) fibreux, funiculé.

funk (feu'n'k), n., puanteur; étincelle, f.; amadou, m.

funnel (feu'n'-), n., entonnoir, tuyau, m.; (of a chimney—de cheminée) tuyau de cheminée, m.

funny (feu'n'-), adj., bouffon, facétieux, comique, drôle, risible, amusant.

fur (feur), n., fourrure, pelleterie, f.; poil, m.

fur, v.a., fourrer, garnir de fourrure; (a ship —vaisseau) doubler un vaisseau.

furacious (fiou-ré'-sheusse), adj., enclin à voler.

furbelow (feur-bi-lô), n., falbala, m.; pretin-taille, f.

furbelow, v.a., orner de falbalas, pretintailler.

furbish (feur-), v.a., fourbir, polir, brunir, éclaircir.

furbisher, n., fourbisseur, m.

furcation (feur-ké-), n., bifurcation; four-chure, f.

furchel, n., (of a coach—de voiture) armon, m.

furfur (feur-feur), n., dartre furfuracée, f.

furfuraceous (feur-feur-é-sheusse), adj., furfuracé; écailleux.

furious (fiou-), adj., furieux, frénétique, ou-tré, insensé.

furiously, adv., avec fureur; en insensé, en furieux, furieusement.

furiousness, n., furie, rage, frénésie, dé-mence, f.

furl (feurle), v.n., (nav.) ferler; ployer (the sails—les voiles).

furling-line, n., (nav.) raban de ferlage, m.; garcette à ferler, f.

furlong (feur-), n., la huitième partie d'un mille anglais; environ 200 mètres.

furlough (feur-lô), n., congé, semestre, m.; feuille de route, f.

furnace (feur-), n., fournaise, f.; four-neau, m.

furnish (feur-), v.a., fournir, pourvoir; (a house—une maison) garnir, meubler; (with linen —de linge), fournir du linge; (with arms—d'armes) armer.

furnisher, n., pourvoyeur, fournisseur, m.

furniture (feur-ni-tioure), n., appareil, équipage, m.; (print.) garniture, f.; (of a house —d'une maison) meubles, m.pl. A piece of —; un meuble.

furrier (feur-ri-eur), n., fourreur, pelletier, m.

furrow (feur-rô), n., ride, f.; sillon; rayon; conduit, m.

furrow, v.a., sillonner, rider.

furry (feur'ri), adj., fourré, couvert de fourrures.

further (feur'th eur), adj., ultérieur; autre; nouveau. — end; le fond, le bout. — obligation; surcroît d'obligation.

further (feur'theur), v.a. and n., avancer; aider; favoriser; pousser; appuyer.

further, adv., plus loin; de plus; ultérieure-ment; au delà; encore; outre cela.

furtherance, n., avancement, progrès, ap-pui, m.; aide, f.

furtherer, n., protecteur; promoteur, pa-tron; fauteur, m.

furthermore, adv., de plus; en outre; outre cela.

furthermore, conj., qui plus est, d'ailleurs.

furthermost (-môste), adj., le plus éloigné.

furthest (feur'thèste), adj., le plus éloigné; le plus reculé; ultérieur.

furthest, adv., à la distance la plus grande, le plus loin; à l'époque la plus reculée.

furtive (feur-), adj., furtif; dérobé; secret.

furtively, adv., furtivement, à la dérobée.

furuncle (fiou-reu'n'k'l), n., furoncle, clou, m.

fury (fiou-), n., furie, fureur, frénésie, rage, violence, fougue, f.

furze (feurze), n., (bot.) bruyère, brande, f.; genêt épineux, m.

furzy, adj., plein de bruyères.

fusarole (fiou-ça-rôl), n., (arch.) fusarolle, f.

fuscation (feus-ké-), n., action d'obscurcir, f., obscurcissement, m.

fuscous (feus'-), adj., terne, brun foncé, sombre.

fuse, n. V. **fusee**.

fuse (fiouze), v.a. and n., fondre, se fondre, liquéfier, fuser.

fusee (fiou-zî), n., (musket—arme à feu) fusil, m.; (hunt.) foulées; (of a watch or bomb —de montre, de bombe) fusée, f.

fusibility (fiouz'i-), n., fusibilité, f.

fusible (fiou-zi-), adj., fusible.

fusil (fiou-zile), n., (musket—arme à feu) fusil, m.; (her.) fusée, f.

fusileer, or **fusilier** (fiou-zi-lîre), n., (milit.) fusilier, m.

fusion (fiou-jeune), n., fusion; fonte des métaux, f.

fuss (feuce), n., fracas, bruit, embarras, m. To make a —; faire du bruit, de l'embarras.

fust (feuste), n., odeur de renfermé, f.; (arch.) fût, m.

fust, v.n., se moisir; sentir le renfermé.

fustian (feust'-), n., futaine, f.; (fig.) phébus, galimatias, m.

fustianist, n., écrivain boursouflé, m.

fustic (feus'-), n., ⊙fustel; fustet, m.

fustigate (feus'-), v.a., (ant.) fustiger; battre à coups de bâton.

fustiness (feus'-), n., moisissure; puan-teur, f.

fusty (feus'-), adj., chanci, puant; (air) renfermé.

futile (fiou-tile), adj., futile, vain; frivole.

futility, n., futilité, vanité, frivolité, f.; babil, caquet, bavardage, m.

futteril (feut'teur'ile), n., (min.) galerie d'extraction, f.

futtocks (feut'-), n.pl., (nav.) courbaton, genou, m.; allonge, f.

future (fiout'ioure), adj., futur, à venir.

future, or **futurity**, n., l'avenir, le futur, m.

futurely, adv., à l'avenir.

futurition (fiou-tiou-rish'-), n., futurition, f.

fuze (fiouze), n., (of a shell—de bomb') fusée, f.

fuzz (feuze), v.n., s'effiler, s'évaporer; voler en petits éclats.

fuzz, n., particules fines et légères, f.pl.; matière volatile, f. sing.

fuzzball (-bôl), n., (bot.) vesse de loup, f.

fy! or **fie!** (fa'ye), int., fi! fi donc! — for shame; fi! c'est une honte.

G

g, septième lettre de l'alphabet, g, m.; (mus.) sol, m.

gab, n., faconde, f.; bavardage, m.

gabardine (-dîne), n., souquenille; re-dingote, f., caban, balandras, m.

gabble (gab'b'l), n., babil, bourdonnement, bavardage, m.

gabble, v.n., bourdonner ; bavarder, babiller, causer, caqueter.

gabbler, n., babillard, causeur, bavard, m.

gabel, n., (ant.) impôt sur les denrées, m.

gabion (ghé-), n., (fort.) gabion, m.

gable (ghé-b'l), n., toit, pignon, m.

gable-end (-ě'n'de), m., bord d'un toit, m.

gad, n., coin d'acier, m. ; pointe, f. ; burin, poinçon, m.

gad, v.n., battre le pavé ; rôder ; courir çà et là. To — about : courir la pretantaine.

gadder, n., coureur, m., coureuse, f.

gaddingly (gad'-), adv., en rôdant ; en courant ça et là.

gadfly (-fla'ye), n., taon, m.

gaff, n., gaffe, f., harpon, m.

gaffer, n., (ant.) compère, m.

gaffle, n., éperon artificiel pour les coqs de combat, m.

gag, n., bâillon, m.

gag, v.a., bâillonner.

gage (ghédje), n., gage, m., assurance ; jauge, f., calibre, m. V. **gauge**.

gage, v.a., jauger ; gager.

gaggle, v.n., (ant.) crier comme une oie.

gag-tooth (-touth), n., surdent, f.

gaiety, or **gayety** (ghě-i-), n., gaieté, gaîté, f. ; enjouement, m. ; pompe, f. ; faste ; (pleasure —distraction) plaisir, m.

gaily, adv., gaiement, joyeusement.

gain (ghéne), n., gain, profit, avantage, lucre, m. ; (arch.) gaine, f.

gain, v.a. and n., gagner ; acquérir ; obtenir ; emporter ; (a victory—une victoire) remporter ; devenir riche. To — ground ; établir. To — over ; convertir. To — time ; prévenir, devancer. To — upon ; avoir l'avantage.

gainer, n., gagneur, m. ; personne qui gagne, f.

gainful (-foule), adj., profitable, lucratif, avantageux.

gainfully, adv., utilement ; avec profit.

gainfulness, n., avantage, profit, gain, m.

gaingiving (ghě'n'givigne), n., pressentiment ; soupçon, m. ; crainte, f.

gainless, adj., inutile ; qui n'est point profitable, sans profit.

gainlessness, n., inutilité, f.

gainly, adv., facilement ; avec dextérité ; adroitement.

gainsay (ghě'n'sě), v.a., contredire ; nier ; contrarier.

gainsayer (-sě-eur), n., contradicteur, adversaire, m.

gainsaying (-sě-igne), n., contradiction, opposition, f.

gainstand (ghě'n'sta'n'de), v.a., (ant.) résister à ; réprimer ; combattre.

gairish (ghér-), adj., fastueux, brillant ; folâtre.

gairishness, n., faste, brillant, luxe, m.

gait (ghéte), n., port, air, m. ; démarche ; (of a horse—du cheval) allure, f.

gaiter (ghét'-), n., guêtre, f.

gala (ghé-), n., gala, m. ; réjouissance, f.

galaxy, n., (astron.) voie lactée, galaxie ; réunion brillante, f.

gale, n., vent frais, m. ; (nav.) grain, coup de vent, m. ; brise, f.

gale, v.n., (nav.) voguer rapidement : courir devant le vent.

galea (ghé-li-), n., (bot.) coiffe, f. ; casque, m. ; (med.) céphalalgie générale, f.

galeas (-li-), n., (nav.) galéasse, f.

galeate, or **galeated** (ghé-li-), adj., casqué ; (bot.) ayant des fleurs en casque, f.pl.

galega (-li-), n., (bot.) rue de chèvre, f. ; galéga, m.

galena (-li-), n., mine de plomb ; galène, f.

galeopsis (gal-i-), n., (bot.) chanvre bâtard, galéopsis, m.

galiot, n., galiote ; petite galère, f.

galipot, n., encens blanc ; galipot, m.

gall (gôl), n., fiel ; amer, m., bile, f. ; (fig.) rancune, malice, f., chagrin, m. ; (bot.) noix de galle, f.

gall, v.a. and n., écorcher ; se couper ; se chagriner ; fâcher, irriter ; harasser.

gallant (gal'la'n'te), n., homme brave, vaillant, courageux ; galant homme.

gallant (gal-la'n'te), adj., gai ; bien mis : éclatant, voyant ; audacieux, brave, courageux, noble.

gallant (gal-lâ'nte), n., galant ; amant ; homme galant.

gallant (gal-lâ'nte), adj., galant, poli, courtois.

gallantly (gal'la'n'tli), adv., noblement ; généreusement ; bravement, courageusement.

gallantly (gal-lâ'ntli), adv., galamment ; poliment, courtoisement.

gallantry (gal'la'nt'-), n., galanterie, intrigue amoureuse ; générosité, valeur, bravoure, f.

galled (gôl'de), adj., écorché ; foulé ; blessé ; froissé ; piqué ; chagriné.

galleon (gal'li-eune), n., (nav.) galion, m.

gallery (gal'leu'ri), n., galerie, f. ; (chem.) galère, f.

galley (gal'li), n., galère, f. ; (boat—bateau) caïque, f. ; (print.) galée, f.

galley-slave, n., galérien, forçat, m.

galliard, n., (ant.) gaillard, m. ; (dance—danse) gaillarde, f.

galliardise, n., (ant.) gaillardise ; gaieté de jeunesse, f.

gallicism, n., gallicisme ; idiotisme français.

galligaskins (-ki'n'ze), n., chausses larges à l'antique ; braies, f.pl.

gallimaufry, n., galimafrée, f. ; galimatias, m. ; mélange ridicule ; salmigondis, m.

gallinaceous (-né-sheusse), adj., (orni.) gallinacé.

galling (gôll'-), n., inflammation, écorchure, f.

galling, adj., irritant, piquant, mordant, vexant ; incommode.

gallingale (gal'lin'ghéle), n., (bot.) souchet, m.

gallinule (gal'li-nioule), n., (orni.) poule d'eau, f.

gallipot (gal'li-), n., pot de faïence, m.

gall-nut (gôl'neute), n., noix de galle, f.

gallon (gal'lone), n., gallon, m. (quatre litres et demi).

galloon (gal'loune), n., galon, m. To bind with — ; galonner, border de galon.

gallop (gal'lope), n., galop, m. Full — ; grand galop. Easy — ; petit galop.

gallop, v.n., galoper, aller au galop.

galloper, n., cheval qui galope.

galloping, n., galop, m., galopade, f.

gallow (gal'lô), v.a., (ant.) effrayer, épouvanter, faire peur à.

galloway (gal'lo-wě), n., cheval de petite taille, bidet, m.

gallows (gal'leusse), n., potence, f., gibet, m. ; (print.) chevalet, m.

galoche (ga-lôshe), n., galoche, f.

galvanism (-'iz'me), n., galvanisme, m.

galvanize (-'aize), v.a., galvaniser.

gambade, n., guêtre, f. ; houseaux, m.pl., ☉ **gamache**, f.

gambit, n., (at chess—échecs) gambit, m.

gamble (ga'm'b'l), n., jouer gros jeu.

gambler, n., filou, joueur, escroc, brelandier, m.

gambling, n., jeu, m. ; maison de jeu, f.

gamboge (-bôdje), n., gomme-gutte, f.

gambol, n., gambade, f., saut de joie, bond, m.

gambol, *v.n.*, gambader, danser de joie, folâtrer.

gambrel, *n.*, jambe de derrière du cheval, *f.*

game, *n.*, jeu, *m.*, récréation; *f.*; gibier, *m.*; chasse, *f.*; (drawn game—*partie nulle*) refait, *m.*, partie nulle, *f.*

game, *v.a.* and *n.*, jouer; folâtrer, s'amuser, se divertir.

game-cock, *n.*, coq de combat, *m.*

gamekeeper (-kîp'-), *n.*, garde-chasse, *m.*

gamesome. *adj.*, folâtre, badin; ironique.

gamesomely, *adv.*, en badin; d'une manière folâtre.

gamesomeness, *n.*, badinage, *m.*; ironie, *f.*

gamester (ghé'm'steur), *n.*, joueur de profession, brelandier, *m.*

gaming-house (-haouce), *n.*, brelan, *m.*, maison de jeu, *f.*

gammer (ga'm'-), *n.*, commère, bonne femme, bonne mère, *f.*

gammon(ga'm'-), *n.*, jambon; toute-table, *m.*

gammon, *v.a.*, faire du jambon; embabouiner; (nav.) faire des liures; (at backgammon—*au trictrac*) battre.

gamut (ga'm'eute), *n.*, (mus.) gamme, *f.*

gander, *n.*, (orni.) jars, *m.*

gang, *n.*, bande, troupe; clique, cabale, séquelle, *f.*

gang, *v.n.*, aller, s'en aller, marcher.

ganglion (ga'n'gli-), *n.*, (anat.) ganglion, *m.*

gangrene (gan'gn'grîne), *n.*, gangrène, *f.*

gangrene, *v.a.* and *n.*, gangrener, se gangrener, être gangrené.

gangrenous, *adj.*, gangreneux.

gangway (ga'n'g'wè), *n.*, (nav.) passage étroit; passavant, *m.*; galerie du faux pont, *f.*

gannet (ga'n'nète), *n.*, (orni.) fou, *m.*; boubie, *f.*

ganny, *n.*, (orni.) coq d'Inde, dindon

gantlet, *or* **gantlope** (ga'n't'lète,-'lôpe), *n.*, gantelet, *m.*, baguettes, *f.pl.* To run the —; *passer par les baguettes*; (nav.) *courir la bouline.*

ganza, *n.*, oie sauvage, *f.*

gaol (djél), *n.*, prison, geôle, *f.*

gaol-book (-bouke), *n.*, livre d'écrou, *m.*

gaol-delivery (-dè-liv'èr'i). *n.*, élargissement, *m.*; action de vider les prisons, *f.*

gaoler (djél'eur), *n.*, geôlier, *m.*

gap, *n.*, brèche; ouverture, *f.*, vide, *m.*; (in a book—*dans un livre*) lacune, *f.* To stop a —; *boucher un trou; payer une dette.*

gape, *v.n.*, bâiller; s'ouvrir; bayer. To — after; *bayer après*, aspirer. To — at; *badauder.*

gape, *or* **gaping**, *n.*, bâillement, *m.*; fente, crevasse, ouverture, *f.*

gaper, *n.*, bâilleur, bayeur, *m.*

gaping. *part. adj.*, béant.

gap-toothed (-touth't), *adj.*, qui a les dents écartées.

garavances(-cèss), *n.*, (bot.) pois chiches, *m.*

garb, *n.*, façon, *f.*, costume; habit, habillement; manteau, dehors, *m.*

garbage (gâr'bèdje), *n.*, tripailles, *f.pl.*; curée, *f.*; restes, *m.pl.*

garble (gar'b'l), *v.a.*, trier, éplucher, cribler; (fig.) mutiler, tronquer (a quotation—*une citation*).

garbler, *n.*, personne qui trie; qui sépare le bon du mauvais; qui mutile, qui tronque (a quotation—*une citation*).

garboil(gar'boïl), *n.*, (ant.) désordre, trouble, *m.*, confusion, *f.*

gard. *V.* guard.

garden (gâr'd'n), *n.*, jardin, *m.*

garden, *v.a.*, jardiner.

gardener, *n.*, jardinier, *m.*

gardening, *n.*, jardinage, *m.*

garden-mould (-môlde). *n.*, terreau, *m*

garden-plot, *n.*, parterre, *m.*

gardon (gâr'done), *n.*, (ich.) gardon, *m.*

gare, *n.*, écouailles (coarse wool—*laine grossière*), *f.pl.*

garfish (gâr-), *n.*, (ich.) anguille de mer, orphie, *f.*

garganey (gâr-ga'n'i), *n.*, (orni.) sarcelle commune, *f.*

gargle (gâr-), *n.*, gargarisme, *m.*

gargle, *v.a.*, gargariser.

garish (gâr'-), *adj.*, trop voyant, extravagant, outré.

garishness, *n.*, excès d'éclat, *m.*, extravagance, *f.*

garland (gâr-), *n.*, couronne de fleurs, guirlande, *f.*

garlic (gâr-), *n.*, ail, *m.*, aulx, *pl.*

garlic-eater (-it'-), *n.*, mangeur d'ail; maraud, *m.*

garment (gâr-), *n.*, vêtement, habit, *m.*; parure, *f.*

garner (gâr-), *n.*, grenier à grain, *m.*

garner, *v.a.*, engranger; amasser, entasser.

garnet (gâr-), *n.*, grenat; (nav.) bredindin, *m.*

garnish (gâr-), *n.*, ornement, embellissement, *m.*, bienvenue; parure, garniture, *f.*

garnish, *v.a.* and *n.*, embellir, parer, garnir, orner.

garnishment, *or* **garniture**. *n.*, garniture, *f.*; ornement, embellissement, *m.*

garous (ghé-), *adj.*, de saumure de thon.

garran, *or* **garron** (gar'-), *n.*, bidet; mauvais cheval, criquet, *m.*, rosse, *f.*

garret (gar'rète), *n.*, galetas, grenier, *m.*

garreteer (-'ire), *n.*, habitant d'un galetas; (fig.) pauvre écrivain, *m.*

garrison (gar'is'n), *n.*, garnison, *f.*

garrison, *v.a.*, mettre garnison dans.

garron. *n.* *V.* **garran**

garrulity (gar-reu-), *n.*, loquacité, *f.*; babil, caquet, *m.*

garrulous, *adj.*, babillard, bavard.

garter (gar-), *n.*, jarretière, *f.*

garter, *v.a.*, attacher ses jarretières; lier avec une jarretière.

gas (gace), *n.* (*gases*), (chem.) gaz, *m.*

gas-burner (-beurn'-), *n.*, bec de gaz, *m.*

gasconade (-), *n.*, gasconnade, hâblerie, *f.*

gaseous (gaz'i-), *adj.*, gazeux.

gas-fitter (-fit'-), *n.*, gazier, ouvrier en gaz, *m.*

gash, *n.*, balafre, estafilade, *f.*

gash, *v.a.*, balafrer, taillader.

gashed (gash't), *adj.*, incisé, découpé.

gasify (gass'i-fa'ye), *v.a.*, (chem.) gazéifier.

gasket (gas'kète), *n.*, (nav.) garcette, *f.*, raban, *m.*

gaskins (gas'ki'n'ze), *n.pl.*, large culotte, *f.*

gas-light (-laïte), *n.*, éclairage au gaz, *m.*

gas-meter (-mî-), *n.*, compteur à gaz, *m.*

gasometer (gass'om'-), *n.*, gazomètre, *m.*

gasp (gâspe), *n.*, soupir; abois, *m.*; agonie, *f.*

gasp, *v.n.*, respirer avec peine. To — after; *soupirer après.* To — for life; *être près d'expirer.*

gast (gâste), *or* **gaster** (gâs-teur), *v.a.*, (ant.) effrayer, épouvanter, faire peur à.

gastralgia (-djia), *n.*, (med.) gastralgie, *f.*

gastric. *adj.*, (anat.) gastrique.

gastritis (-traï-), *n.*, (med.) gastrite, *f*

gastronome (-nôme), *or* **gastronomer** (-'o-meur), *n.*, épicurien, *m.*

gastronomic, *adj.*, gastronomique.

gastronomist. *n.*, gastronome, *m.*

gastronomy. *n.*, gastronomie, *f.*

gate, *n.*, porte, *f.*; portail, *m.*; barrière, *f.* Flood—; *vanne*; (in ponds—*d'étang*) bonde, *f.*

gateway (-wè), *n.*, porte cochère, porte d'entrée, *f.*

gather (gath'-), *n.*, pli, froncis, *m.*; fronçure, *f.*

gather, *v.a.*, cueillir; amasser, ramasser; assembler, rassembler, recueillir; froncer,

plisser. To — taxes; *percevoir les impôts.* To
— breath; *prendre haleine.* To — grapes;
vendanger. To — corn; *moissonner.* To —
strength; *se rétablir*; (fig.) *prospérer, s'affermir.*
To — wealth; *s'enrichir.* To — one's self up; *se
ramasser.*

gather (gath'-), *v.n.*, s'assembler, se rassembler; se condenser; s'épaissir. To — to a head;
commencer à mûrir; être prêt à suppurer.

gatherer, *n.*, collecteur, quêteur, cueilleur;
(of taxes) percepteur des impôts; (of grapes—*du
raisin*) vendangeur; (of corn—*du blé*) moissonneur, *m.*

gathering, *n.*, (agri.) récolte, cueillette;
(for charity—*de charité*) quête, collecte; (of
taxes—*des impôts*) perception; (assembly—
réunion) assemblée, foule; (tumor—*abcès*)
tumeur, *f.*, abcès, *m.*

gaud (gô'd), *n.*, parure, *f.*, ornement;
jouet, *m.*

gaudery, *n.*, parure fastueuse, *f.*, faste;
ornement, *m.*; bagatelle, babiole, *f.*

gaudily, *adv.*, fastueusement.

gaudiness, *n.*, faste, *m.*; ostentation, *f.*;
luxe, éclat, *m.*

gaudy, *n.*, (ant.) fête, réjouissance, *f.*;
festin, régal, *m.*

gaudy, *adj.*, fastueux; éclatant; trop voyant.
A — day; *un jour de régal, un gala.*

gauge (ghédje), *n.*, jauge; mesure, *f.*; (nav.)
tirant d'eau, *m.*; (mec.) manomètre, *m.*

gauge, *v.a.*, jauger; mesurer; étalonner.

gauger, *n.*, jaugeur, *m.*

gauging, *n.*, jaugeage, *m.* —rod; *jauge, f.*

gaul (gô'l), *n.*, Gaulois, *m.*; (country—*pays*)
Gaule. *f.*

gaulish, *adj.*, gaulois.

gaunt (gâ'nte), *adj.*, maigre, décharné,
élancé.

gauntlet (gâ'n't'-), *n.*, gantelet, *m.*

gauntly, *adv.*, maigrement.

gauze (gôze), *n.*, gaze, *f.*

gavel, *n.*, terrain, *m.*; terre; javelle, *f.*;
tribut, *m.*, corvée, *f.*

gavel-kind (-kaï'n'de), *n.*, partage égal des
terres.

gavot, *n.*, (dance—*danse*) gavotte, *f.*

gawk (gôke), *n.*, coucou; sot, niais; maladroit, *m.*

gawky, *n.*, grand maladroit, sot, niais, *m.*

gawky, *adj.*, gauche, stupide, maladroit.

gay, *adj.*, gai, réjoui, joyeux; pimpant;
leste.

gayety, *or* **gaiety**, *n.*, gaieté, *f.*; enjouement, éclat, plaisir, *m.*

gayly, *or* **gaily**, *adv.*, gaiement; avec éclat.

gaze (ghéze), *n.*, regard fixe, attentif, d'étonnement, *m.*; d'admiration, *f.*

gaze, *v.n.*, regarder fixement, contempler.

gazeful (-foule), *adj.*, (ant.) contemplatif.

gaze-hound (-haou'n'de), *n.*, lévrier, *m.*,
levrette, *f.*

gazelle, *n.*, gazelle, *f.*

gazer (ghéz'-), *n.*, contemplateur, spectateur, *m.*

gazette, *n.*, gazette. *f.*; journal, *m.*

gazetteer (-'tîre), *n.*, gazetier, nouvelliste;
dictionnaire géographique, *m.*

gazing-stock (ghéz'-), *n.*, spectacle; (fig.)
objet de mépris, *m.*

gazon (-zô'n), *n.*, (fort.) gazon, *m.*

gean (djîne), *n.*, (bot.) cerise sauvage, *f.*

gear (ghîre), *n.*, habit, habillement, *m.*;
marchandise, *f.*, attirail; colifichet, *m.*; (nav.)
apparaux, *m.pl.*, drisse, *f.*; (of a horse—*d'un
cheval*) harnais, *m.*

gearing (ghîr'-), *or* **gear**, *n.*, disposition
d'une machine, *f.*; appareil, *m.*

geck (ghèke), *n.*, (ant.) sot, *m.*; dupe, *f.*

geck, *v.a.*, duper tromper.

gee (dji), *v.n.*, hurhau! huhau! hue!

geese (ghîce), *n.*, (pl. of Goose) oies, *f.pl.*

geho (dji'hô), *v.n.* V. **gee.**

gelable (djèl'a'b'l), *adj.*, qui peut geler,
gelable.

gelatin (djèl'-), *n.*, gélatine, *f.*

gelatinate, *v.n.*, se prendre en gelée.

gelatinous, *adj.*, visqueux, gélatineux.

geld (ghèlde), *v.a.*, châtrer, couper, hongrer (horses—*les chevaux*).

gelder, *n.*, châtreur. *m.*

gelder-rose, *n.*, boule-de-neige, viorne, *f.*

gelding, *n.*, hongre, cheval coupé, *m.*

gelid, *adj.*, gelé, glacé.

gelidity, *or* **gelidness** (djèl'-), *n.*, gelée,
f., froid extrême, *m.*

golly (djèl'li), *n.*, gelée de fruits; viscosité,
f. V. **jelly.**

gelt (ghèlte), *n.*, animal châtré; clinquant, *m.*

gem (djème), *n.*, pierre précieuse, gemme,
f.; fleuron, bouton; bourgeon, *m.*

gem, *v.a.*, orner de pierres précieuses; bourgeonner; émailler.

geminate (djèm'-), *v.a.*, (ant.) doubler.

gemination (-né-), *n.*, (ant.) répétition, réduplication, *f.*

gemini (djèm'i'naï), *n.pl.*, (astron.) Gémeaux, *m.pl.*

geminous (djèm'-), *adj.*, (ant.) double, géminé, réitéré.

geminy (djèm'-), *n.*, (ant.) jumeaux, *m.pl.*;
paire, couple, *f.*

gemmary (djèm'-), *adj.*, de joyaux; de
pierres précieuses.

gemmeous (djèm'-), *adj.*, ressemblant aux
pierres précieuses.

gendarme (jà'n'dârm), *n.*, gendarme, *m.*

gender (djè'n'-), *n.*, genre, *m.*; espèce,
sorte, *f.*

gender, *v.a.* and *n.*, engendrer, produire;
s'accoupler.

genealogical (djèn'i-al'o-dji-), *adj.*, généalogique.

genealogist, *n.*, généalogiste, *m.*

genealogy (djèn'i-al-odji), *n.*, généalogie, *f.*

general (djèn'-), *n.*, général, chef, *m.*;
(milit.) générale, *f.*

general, *adj.*, général, commun, ordinaire.
Attorney- —; *procureur général.* Vicar- —;
vicaire général.

generalissimo, *n.*, généralissime, *m.*

generality, *n.*, généralité; la plupart;
diffusion générale; foule, *f.*

generalize (-aïze), *v.a.*, généraliser.

generally, *adv.*, en général, ordinairement,
généralement.

generalness, *n.*, généralité, grande étendue, *f.*

generalship, *n.*, généralat, talent de
général, *m.*; stratégie, *f.*

generant (djèn'èr'-), *n.*, générateur, *m.*;
puissance productrice, *f.*

generate, *v.a.* and *n.*, engendrer, produire;
s'accoupler.

generation (djèn'èr'é-), *n.*, génération,
race, famille; production, *f.*; siècle, *m.*

generative, *adj.*, génératif; producteur.

generator (-'eur), *n.*, générateur, *m.*

generic, *or* **generical** (djèn'èr'-), *adj.*,
générique, distinctif.

generosity, *or* **generousness** (djèn'èr'-),
n., générosité, magnanimité, libéralité, *f.*

generous, *adj.*, généreux; riche; abondant.

generously, *adv.*, généreusement; noblement, libéralement.

genesis (djèn'è-ciss), *n.*, Genèse, *f.*; (math.)
génération, *f.*

genet (djèn'ète), *n.*, genêt, *m.*; haquenée, *f.*

geneva (djè-ni-), *or* **gin** (dji'n), *n.*,
genièvre, *m*

genial (dji-), *adj.*, naturel; réjouissant; gai, enjoué.

genially, *adv.*, naturellement, gaîment.

geniculate (dji-nik'iou-), *or* **geniculated** (-le-tède), *adj.*, géniculé, en forme de genou; (bot.) qui a des nœuds.

geniculation, *n.*, union en forme de genou; nodosité, *f.*

genii (dji'-), *n.pl.*, génies, *m.pl.*

genio (dji-ni-ô), *n.*, (ant.) génie, esprit sublime, *m.*

genital (djè'n'-), *adj.*, génital, génératif.

genitals (djèn'i-talze), *n.pl.*, génitoires, *m.pl.*

genitive (djèn'-), *n.*, (gram.) génitif, *m.*

genius (djîn'-), *n.*, génie; talent, *m.*; disposition naturelle, *f.*

genteel (djèn-'til), *adj.*, de bon ton, comme il faut, distingué, de bon goût, joli, élégant, galant; poli, civil, noble.

genteelly, *adv.*, poliment, galamment, noblement, de bonne grâce, élégamment.

genteelness, *n.*, grâce, urbanité, élégance, *f.*, bon ton, *m.*

gentian (djè'n'sha'ne), *n.*, (bot.) gentiane, *f.*

gentile (djè'n'taïle), *n.*, païen, gentil, *m.*

gentilism (-taïl'iz'm), *n.*, paganisme, *m.*; idolâtrie, *f.*

gentility (-til'i-), *n.*, politesse, *f.*; agrément; bon ton, *m.*; naissance distinguée, *f.*

gentilize (-'aïze), *v.n.*, (ant.) vivre en gentil, en païen.

gentle (djè'n't'l)*, adj.*, doux, modéré; léger; gentil; bien né. — reader; *ami lecteur.*

gentle-folk (-fôke), *or* **gentle-folks** (-fôkse), *n.*, personnes de bon ton, distinguées, comme il faut, *f.pl.*; gens comme il faut, de condition, *m.pl.*

gentleman (-ma'n), *n.*, monsieur, homme de bon ton, comme il faut; (in the service of a sovereign—*au service d'un souverain*) gentilhomme, *m.*

gentleman-like (-laïke), *or* **gentleman-ly**, *adj.*, distingué, de bon ton, comme il faut, bien né.

gentlemanliness, *n.*, bon ton, urbanité, savoir-vivre, *m.*

gentleness, *n.*, douceur; bonté; bienveillance, *f.*

gentlewoman (-woum'a'n), *n.*, dame, femme de bon ton, de bonne famille, *f.*

gently, *adv.*, doucement, lentement, avec bonté.

gentry (djè'n'-), *n.*, petite noblesse; haute bourgeoisie, *f.*; (b.s., iron.) braves gens.

genuflection (dji-niou-flèk-sheune), *n.*, génuflexion, *f.*

genuine (djè'n'iou-ine), *adj.*, naturel, réel, pur, vrai.

genuinely, *adv.*, purement, réellement; naturellement.

genuineness, *n.*, réalité; authenticité; pureté, *f.*

genus (dji-), *n.* (*genera*), genre, caractère commun, *m.*; espèce, *f.*

geodesia (dji-o-di-cia), *or* **geodesy** (-ci) *n.*, (geom.) géodésie, *f.*; arpentage, *m.*

geognosy (dji-og'-no-ci), *n.*, science de la terre; géognosie, *f.*

geographer (dji-og'-ra-), *n.*, géographe, *m.*

geographical, *adj.*, géographique.

geography (dji-og'-ra-), *n.*, géographie, *f.*

geology (dji-ol-o-dji), *n.*, géologie, *f.*

geomancy (dji'-), *n.*, divination par la terre, géomance, géomancie, *f.*

geometer (dji-om'è-), *or* **geometrician** (dji-o-mi-trish'è'n), *n.*, géomètre, *m.*

geometric, *or* **geometrical**, *adj.*, géométrique, géométral.

geometrically, *adv.*, géométriquement, géométralement.

geometrician, *n.* *V.* **geometer.**

geometrize (-traïze), *v.n.*, procéder géométriquement.

geometry (dji-om'é-tri), *n.*, géométrie, *f.*

georama (dji-o-râ-ma), *n.*, géorama, *m.*

georgics (djor-djikse), *n.pl.*, géorgiques, *f.pl.*

georgium sidus (djor-dji-eume-saï-), *n.*, (astron.) Herschel, *m.*

geranium (dji-ré'-), *n.*, (bot.) bec-de-grue, *m.*

gerbua (gheur-biou-), *n.*, (mam.) gerboise, *f.*

gerent (dji-), *adj.*, portant.

gerfalcon (djeur-fô-k'n), *n.*, (orni.) gerfaut, *m.*

germ (djeurme), *n.*, germe, bourgeon, *m.*; pousse, *f.*; (bot.) embryon, *m.*

german (djeur-), *adj.*, germain; qui est parent, qui est proche; allemand. A cousin —; *un cousin germain.*

german (djeur-), *n.*, Allemand, *m.*, Allemande, *f.*; (language—*langue*) allemand, *m.*

germander (djeur-), *n.*, (bot.) germandrée, *f.*

germanic (djeur-), *adj.*, germanique.

germanism (djeur-), *n.*, germanisme, *m.*

germinate (djeur-), *v.n.*, germer, pousser, bourgeonner.

germination, *n.*, (bot.) germination, pousse, *f.*

gerund (djèr'eu'n'de), *n.*, (gram.) gérondif, *m.*

gest (djèste), *n.*, exploit, fait, *m.*; action, représentation, *f.*

gestation (djès-té-), *n.*, gestation, grossesse, *f.*

gesticulate (djès-tik-iou-), *v.n.*, gesticuler.

gesticulation, *n.*, gesticulation, *f.*

gesture (djèst'ioure), *n.*, geste; mouvement expressif, *m.*

gesture, *v.a.*, faire des gestes, gesticuler.

get (ghète), *v.a.* and *n.* (*preterit*, Got; *past part.*, Gotten *and* Got), gagner, acquérir, obtenir; remporter; avoir, tirer, faire, se faire, prendre; (to buy, to procure) acheter, procurer, se procurer; (to become) devenir, se faire; (to arrive, to reach) arriver, atteindre; (to fetch) aller chercher; (to find) trouver; (to go) aller; (to induce) engager, faire, obtenir de; (anything bad—*un malheur, &c.*) attraper, s'attirer. To — above; *surpasser.* To — abroad; *faire sortir, publier, devenir public.* To — away; *faire retirer, ôter; s'en aller; s'évader.* To — before; *prévenir, devancer.* To — by heart; *apprendre.* To — clear; *se tirer de.* To — down; *descendre; avaler.* To — forward; *avancer, profiter.* To — from; *tirer, arracher; se tirer, se débarrasser.* To — in; *entrer, faire entrer, engager; serrer; s'insinuer.* To — off; *tirer; débarrasser; vendre; échapper, se tirer, s'en tirer; ôter; s'ôter.* To — on; *mettre; avancer; réussir.* To — out; *sortir, tirer de, arracher, faire sortir.* To — through *or* over; *passer, surmonter, vaincre.* To — to; *arriver, aller, atteindre.* To — together; *amasser, assembler.* To — up; *lever, se lever; monter.* To — up again; *relever, ramasser; se relever.* To — upon; *monter sur.* To — well again; *se rétablir.* To — a fall; *tomber.* To — a footing; *s'établir.* To — friends; *se faire des amis.* To — ready; *préparer, apprêter, se préparer.* To — the better; *avoir l'avantage.* To — with child; (l.ex.) *engrosser.* To — old; *vieillir.* To — young again; *rajeunir.* To — married; *se marier.* To — rich; *s'enrichir.* To — made *or* done; *faire faire.* To — mended; *faire raccommoder.* To — to sleep; *s'endormir.* To — loose; *lâcher, relâcher, s'échapper.* To — drunk; *s'enivrer.*

getter (ghèt'-), *n.*, personne qui gagne.

getting (ghèt'-), *n.*, acquisition, *f.*; gain, profit, *m.*

gewgaw (ghiou-gô), *n.*, babiole, bagatelle *f.*; joujou, bijou, jouet, *m.*

gewgaw, *adj.*, éclatant, voyant, brillant mais sans valeur.

ghastful (gâst'foule), *adj.*, horrible, affreux.

ghastliness, *or* **ghastness**, ᵔ., pâleur; mine affreuse, *f.*; air terrible, *m.*

ghastly (gâst'-), *adj.*, de fantôme, pâle, triste, sombre.

gherkin (gheur-), *n.*, cornichon, *m.*

ghost (gôste), *n.*, esprit, *m.*; âme; ombre, *f.*; revenant, fantôme, *m.* The Holy —; *le Saint-Esprit.*

ghostlike (-laïke), *adj.*, de fantôme; flétri; pâle, triste, sombre.

ghostliness, *n.*, spiritualité, *f.*

ghostly, *adj.*, spirituel, divin; d'esprit, de revenant, d'apparitions.

giant (djaï'-), *n.*, géant, colosse, *m.*

giantess, *n.*, géante, *f.*

giant-like (-laïke), *adj.*, gigantesque; de géant.

giantship, *n.*, grandeur démesurée; forme gigantesque, *f.*

gibbe (ghibe), *n.*, vieux animal; un animal cassé de vieillesse, *m.*; (mec,)grue, *f.*

gibber (ghib'-), *v.n.*, barbouiller, bredouiller, baragouiner, parler sans articuler ses paroles.

gibberish (ghib'beur-), *n.*, baragouin, jargon, patois, *m.*

gibbet (djib'bète), *n.*, potence, *f.*; gibet *m.*; croix, *f.*

gibbet, *v.a.*, pendre à une potence; exposer sur un gibet.

gibbon (ghib'bône), *n.*, (mam.) gibbon, *m.*

gibbose (ghib'bôss), *or* **gibbous** (ghib'-), *adj.*, gibbeux, cornu, bossu.

gibbousness (ghib'-), *n.*, gibbosité, bosse, convexité, *f.*

gib-cat (ghib'-), *n.*, vieux chat décrépit; matou, *m.*

gibe (djaïbe), *n.*, lardon, sarcasme, *m.*; raillerie, moquerie, *f.*

gibe, *v.a. and n.*, gausser; railler; se moquer de, se rire de.

giber, *n.*, railleur. gausseur, *m.*

gibingly, *adv.*, d'un air railleur; ironiquement.

giblets (djib'lètse), *n.pl.*, abattis de volaille, &c., *m.pl.*, petite-oie, *f.*

giddily (ghid'-), *adv.*, étourdiment; capricieusement.

giddiness, *n.*, vertige, *m.*; étourderie, humeur folâtre, *f.*

giddy (ghid'dé'), *adj.*, étourdi, évaporé; volage, capricieux; (med.) vertigineux.

giddy-brained (-bré'n'dé), *or* **giddyheaded** (-hèd'ède), *adj.*, étourdi, écervelé, volage, léger.

giddy-paced (-pés'te), *adj.*, étourdi; qui erre de côté et d'autre.

gif (ghife), *conj.*, (ant.) si.

gift (ghif'te), *n.*, présent, don; talent, *m.*; grâce; donation, *f.* New year's — s; *présents du nouvel an, étrennes.*

gift, *v.a.*, douer, donner; inspirer.

gifted (-ède), *adj.*, doué; inspiré; illuminé.

gig (ghig), *n.*, (toy—*jouet*) toupie, *f.*, sabot; tilbury *m.*; (boat—*bateau*) chaloupe, *f.*

gigantic, **gigantical** (djaï-), *or* **gigantean** (djaï-ga'n-ti-), *adj.*, gigantesque; de géant.

giggle (ghig'g'l), *v.n.*, ricaner, rire sans raison.

giggle, *n.*, ricanement, *m.*

giggler, *n.*, ricaneur, rieur, *m.*

gigot (dji-gote), *n.*, gigot, *m.*

gild (ghilde), *v.a.*, dorer; embellir.

gilder, *n.*, doreur, *m.*; (Dutch coin—*monnaie hollandaise*) florin, *m.*

gilding, *n.*, dorure, *f.*, clinquant, oripeau, *f.*

gil-hooter (djil'hout'-), *n.*, (orni.) effraie, fresaie, chouette effraie, *f.*

gill (ghill), *n.*, (of the cock—*du coq*), barbe, *f.*;

(measure—*mesure*) roquille, *f.*, poisson, *m.*; (bot.) gléchome, lierre terrestre, *m.*; ruisseau, *m.*; clairière, *f.*; (of fish—*de poisson*)branchies, ouïes, *f. pl.*; (mam.) abajoue, *f.*; (bot.) feuillet, *m.*

gilly-flower, *n.*, girofiée, *f.*

gilt (ghilte), *n.*, (ant.) dorure, *f.*

giltedged (-èdj'de), *adj.*, doré sur tranche.

gilthead (-hède), *n.*, (ich.) daurade, *f.*

gim (djime), *adj.*, (ant.) net; pimpant; bien habillé.

gimcrack (djim'-), *n.*, joujou, *m.*, bagatelle, *f.*; mauvais mécanisme, *m.*, patraque, *f.*

gimlet (ghi'm'lète), *or* **gimblet**, *n.*, foret, *m.*, vrille, *f.*

gimmal, *or* **gimmer** (ghi'm-), *n.*, (ant.) mécanisme. mouvement, *m.*; machine, *f.*, ressort, *m.*; alliance, *f.*

gimp (ghi'm'pe), *n.*, guipure, *f.*; cordonnet, *m.*

gin (djine), *n.*, trébuchet, *m.*, trappe, *f.*; (liquor—*liqueur*) genièvre, *m.*, eau-de-vie de genièvre, *f.*; (mec.) grue à trois pieds, *f.*

gin, *v.a.*, prendre au trébuchet; égrener.

ginger (dji'n'djeur), *n.*, gingembre, *m.*

ginger-bread (-brède), *n.*, pain d'épice, *m.*

gingerly, *adv.*, (ant.) tout doucement; avec soin; adroitement.

gingerness, *n.*, (ant.) délicatesse, douceur; tendresse, *f.*

gingham (ghign'-), *n.*, guingan, *m.*

gingival (dji'n'dji-), *adj.*, des gencives.

gingle (dji'n'g'l), *n.*, tintement, tintin, *m.* V. **jingle.**

gingle, *v.a.*, tinter; faire sonner; (fig.) rimer. V. **jingle.**

gingling, *n.*, tintement, *n.*   The — of glasses; *le carillon des verres.*

ginnet (dji'n'nète), *n.*, bidet, mulet, *m.*

ginning, *n.*, égrenage, *m.*

ginseng (dji'n'sè'n'g), *n.*, (bot.) ginseng, *m.*

gipsy (djip'sé). *n.*, gipsy, bohémien, bohème, *m.*, gipsy, égyptienne, bohémienne; sorcière; fine matoise, *f.*

giraffe (dji-), *n.*, (zool.) girafe, *f.*, caméléopard, *m.*

gird (gheurde), *n.*, (l.u.) sarcasme, *m.*, raillerie, *f.*

gird, *v.a. and n.*, ceindre; pincer, railler.

girder, *n.*, (carp.) solive, traverse, *f.*

girdle (gheur'd'l), *n.*, ceinture, *f.*; ceinturon, *m.*

girdle, *v.a.*, ceindre; entourer, environner.

girdle-belt (-bèlte), *n.*, ceinturon, *m.*

girdler, *n.*, ceinturier, *m.*

girl (gheur'l), *n.*, fille; servante, domestique, *f.*

girlish, *adj.*, de fille; léger.

girlishly, *adv.*, en fille.

girt (gheurte), *or* **girth** (gheurth), *v.a.*, sangler, ceindre, entourer.

girth, *n.*, enceinte; ceinture, sangle, *f.*; contour, *m.*

gist (djiste), *n.*, fin, fin mot; point principal, *m.*

give (ghive). *v.a. and n.* (preterit, Gave; past part., Given), donner; rendre; (an answer, credit, one's compliments, one's love—*une réponse; crédit; compliments; amitiés*) faire; (one's respects—*respects*) présenter.   To — a call; *appeler; visiter, faire une visite.* To — a description; *décrire.* To — a fall; *faire tomber.* To — a guess; *deviner.* To — a look; *regarder.* To — a portion; *doter.* To — battle; *livrer bataille.* To — content; *contenter.* To — ear; *être attentif, écouter, prêter l'oreille.* To — fire; *tirer.* To — ground; *reculer; enfoncer.* To — heed; *prendre garde.* To — in charge; *charger; faire arrêter.* To — joy; *féliciter.* To — judg——; *rendre, prononcer jugement.* To — notice; *avertir.* To — one leave; *permettre.* To —

one's mind ; *s'adonner, s'attacher à.* To — place ;
céder, faire place. To — suck ; *allaiter.* To —
the slip ; *se dérober, faire faux bond, fausser
compagnie, s'échapper.* To — trouble ; *incommoder.* To — way ; *céder : enfoncer ; s'abandonner, se relâcher, s'affaisser, s'enfoncer.* To —
away ; *donner.* To — back again ; *rendre.* To
— forth ; *publier.* To — out ; *distribuer, rapporter, annoncer, se dire.* To — over ; *abandonner, céder : cesser, laisser, quitter.* To — up ;
*rendre, céder, se dessaisir, quitter, remettre, se
désister.* To — one's self up to ; *s'abandonner ;
s'adonner a.*

giver, n., donneur, donateur, m.

gizzard (ghiz'zeurde), n., gésier, m. ; (fig.)
esprit, m., imagination, f.

glacial (glé-shi'-), or **glacious** (glé-), adj.,
glacial, gelé.

glaciate (glé-shi-éte), v.a. and n., glacer,
geler ; se glacer, se congeler.

glaciation. n., (ant.) congélation, f.

glacier (gla-ci-eur), n., glacier, amas de
glace, m.

glacis (glé-ciss,ou glâ-), n., (fort.) glacis, m. ;
rampe, f.

glad. adj., content, charmé, bien aise, joyeux,
réjoui, heureux.

glad. v.n., se réjouir.

gladden (glad'd'n), v.a., réjouir, récréer,
rendr' heureux ; se réjouir, s'égayer.

glade (gléde), n., clairière ; percée ; avenue, f.

gladiator (glad'i-é-), n., gladiateur, m.

gladiole (-ôl), n., (bot.) glaïeul, m.

gladly. adv., volontiers, avec plaisir.

gladness, or **gladsomeness,** n., joie,
gaieté, allégresse, f. ; contentement, m.

gladsome, adj., enjoué, joyeux, réjouissant.

gladsomely, adv., joyeusement, volontiers.

gladwyn, n., (bot.) iris fétide, glaïeul
puant, m.

glair (glére), n., glaire ; hallebarde, f. ; blanc
d'œuf, m.

glair, v.a., (bookbind.) glairer.

glance glâ'n'-), n., regard, coup d'œil, m. ;
œillade, vue rapide, f.

glance, n., étinceler ; effleurer, raser ; jeter
un coup d'œil, des œillades ; insinuer. To —
over ; *parcourir.*

glancingly, adv., en passant ; légèrement.

gland (gla'n'de), n., (anat.) glande, f. ; (bot.)
gland, m.

glanders (gla'n'deurze),n.pl.,(vet.) morve, f.

glandiferous (-dif'eur'-), adj., qui porte des
glands.

glandular, or **glandulous** (-diou-), adj.,
(anat.) glandulaire, glanduleux.

glandule (-dioule), n., glandule, petite
glande, f.

glandulosity (-dioul'oss'-), n., glandes
conglobées, f.pl.

glare, n., vif éclat, éclat de lumière éblouissant, m. ; lueur, f. ; coup d'œil perçant, m.

glare, v.n., éblouir ; luire, briller ; regarder
d'un œil terrible.

glareous (glér'i-), adj., glaireux.

glaring (glér'-), adj., éblouissant, éclatant ;
choquant ; manifeste.

glass (glâce), n., verre, m. ; (window—*de
fenêtre*) vitre, f. Looking- — ; *miroir, m.. glace,
f.* Hour- — ; *sablier.* Weather- — ; *baromètre.*
Eye- — ; *lorgnon, m.* —es ; *lunettes, f.*

glass, adj., de verre.

glass, v.a., vitrer.

glass-beads (-bidze), n., rassade, verroterie, f.

glass-bottle (-bot't'l),n.,bouteille de verre, f.

glass-coach (-côtshe), n., voiture de remise,
de louage, f.

glass-furnace (-feur'-), n. fourneau de verrerie, m.

glass-gazing (-ghéz'-), adj., qui se mire
souvent.

glass-grinder (-graï'n'd'-), n., polisseur de
glaces, m.

glasshouse (-haouce), n., verrerie, f.

glass-maker (-mék'-), n., verrier, m.

glassman, n., marchand de verre, de verre
rie, m.

glass-metal (-mèt't'l), n., verre fondu, m.

glasswork (-weurke), n., manufacture du
verre, f.

glassworks (-weurkse), n., verrerie, manufacture de verre, f.

glassy, adj., vitré, vitreux ; fragile.

glaucoma (-cô-), n., (med.) opacité du cristallin, f. ; glaucome, m.

glaucous, adj., glauque ; verdâtre.

glave, n., (ant.) glaive, cimeterre, m.

glaze, v.a. and n., vitrer; vernir ; glacer.

glazier (glé-jeur), n., vitrier, m.

gleam (glime), n., rayon, m. ; lueur, vive
clarté, f.

gleam, v.n., rayonner, briller, luire.

gleamy, or **gleaming,** adj., étincelant,
brillant.

glean (gline), v.a. and n., glaner ; grappiller.

gleaner, n., glaneur, grappilleur, m.

gleaning, n., glanage, m. ; glanure, f.

glebe (glibe), n.., glèbe ; terre, f. ; sol, m.

glebous. or **gleby** (glib'-), adj., de gazon ;
plein de tourbe.

glede (glide), n., (orni.) milan, m.

glee (gli), n., gaillardise, joie ; (mus.)
chanson à reprise, f.

gleeful (-foule), adj., joyeux, gai.

gleek (glike), v.n., (ant.) ricaner ; se moquer.

gleet (glite), n., sanie ; blennorrhée, f. ;
pus, m.

gleet, v.n., produire de la sanie ; dégoutter.

gleety, adj., sanieux ; ichoreux.

glen (glène), n., vallon, m., vallée, f.

glene (gli-ni), n., (anat.) fosse, cavité
glénoïde, glénoidale, f. ; orbite, m.f. ; pupille de
l'œil, f.

glew (gliou), n. V. **glue.**

glib. adj., coulant ; glissant. A — tongue ;
langue bien pendue.

glib, v.a., châtrer ; rendre coulant.

glibly, adv., coulamment.

glibness, n., volubilité, f. ; cours, m.

glide (glaïde), v.n., couler doucement ;
glisser.

glimmer, or **glimmering,** n., lueur, f. ;
faible rayon, m.

glimmer, v.n., entreluire, luire faiblement ;
(of day-break—*du jour*) poindre.

glimpse (gli'm'pse), n., sillon de lumière, m.;
lueur, f. ; reflet ; rayon, m.

glimpse, v.n., paraître par lueurs.

glisten (glis's'n), or **glister** (glis'teur), v.n.,
étinceler, briller, reluire, éclater ; rayonner.

glistening, or **glistering,** n., lueur, f. ;
éclat, m.

glistening, or **glistering,** adj., luisant,
brillant.

glitter, n., éclat, lustre, m. ; splendeur, f.

glitter, v.n., éclater, briller, reluire, étinceler.

glittering, adj., brillant, luisant, étincelant.

glitteringly, adv., avec éclat.

gloar (glôre), v.n., loucher ; regarder de
travers.

gloat (glôte), v.n., jeter des œillades, couver
des yeux.

globard (glô-), n., (ent.) lampyre, ver
luisant, m.

globate, or **globated** (glô-bé-), adj.,
sphérique, en globe, globeux.

globe (glôbe), n., globe, m. ; sphère, boule, f.
The use of the —s (geog.) ; *la sphère.*

globe, *v.a.*, arrondir en forme de globe; mettre en boule.

globose (glo-bôss), **globous** (glô-). *or* **globular** (glob'iou). *adj.*, sphérique, globuleux, rond; (bot.) globeux.

globosity (glo-bôss'-), *n.*, rondeur, sphéricité, *f.*

globule (glob'ioule), *n.*, globule; petit corps sphérique, *m.*

glomerate (glom'eur'-), *v.a.*, assembler; arrondir; mettre en peloton.

glomerous, *adj.*, (ant.) pelotonné; (anat.) congloméré.

gloom, *or* **gloominess** (glou'm'-), *n.*, obscurité, *f.*; chagrin, *m.*; tristesse, *f.*

gloom, *v.n.*, être obscur; s'attrister.

gloomily, *adv.*, obscurément; d'un air triste.

gloomy, *adj.*, sombre, obscur; triste.

glorification (glô-ri-fi-ké-), *n.*, glorification; action de rendre gloire, *f.*

glorify (glô-ri-fa'ye), *v.a.*, glorifier; exalter; honorer.

glorious, *adj.*, glorieux; illustre; superbe.

gloriously, *adv.*, glorieusement, avec gloire.

glory (glô-), *n.*, gloire, honneur; (paint.) auréole, gloire, *f.*, nimbe, *m.*

glory, *v.n.*, se faire gloire, se glorifier.

gloss, *n.*, luisant, éclat, vernis, *m.*; glose, *f.*; (of stuffs—*des étoffes*) lustre, *m.*

gloss, *v.n.*, gloser; interpréter; lustrer; donner de l'éclat. To — over; *masquer, colorer.*

glossary, *n.*, glossaire; dictionnaire de mots obscurs, *m.*

glosser, *or* **glossarist**, *n.*, glossateur; commentateur; apprêteur, *m.*

glossiness, *n.*, poli, lustre, brillant, apprêt, *m.*

glossy, *adj.*, lustré, poli, éclatant, luisant.

glottis (glot'tiss), *n.*, (anat.) glotte, *f.*

glout (glaoute), *v.n.*, (l.u.) bouder, se refrogner; regarder de mauvais œil.

glove (gleuve), *n.*, gant, *m.*

glove, *v.a.*, ganter.

glover, *n.*, gantier, *m.*

glove-stick, *n.*, baguette à gants, *f.*; tourne-gants, *m.*

glow (glô), *n.*, chaleur; ardeur, *f.*; feu, éclat, *m.*

glow, *v.n.*, brûler, être embrasé; briller, luire.

glowing, *adj.*, éclatant; brûlant, embrasé; ardent, animé.

glowingly, *adv.*, vivement, chaleureusement, avec ardeur.

glowworm (-weurme), *n.*, ver luisant, *m.*

gloze (glôze), *v.a. and n.*, flatter; cajoler; caresser; gloser.

glozer, *n.*, flatteur, cajoleur, *m.*

glue (glou), *n.*, colle forte, *f.* Fish—; *colle de poisson, f.*

glue, *v.a.*, coller; attacher, unir.

glue-boiler (-boil'-), *n.*, fabricant de colle forte, *m.*

gluer, *n.*, colleur, *m.*

gluey, *or* **gluish**, *adj.*, gluant, collant, visqueux, glutineux.

glum (gleume), *adj.*, (l.ex.) chagrin, de mauvaise humeur.

glume (gloume), *n.*, (bot.) glume, balle, *f.*

glut (gleute), *n.*, surabondance, satiété, *f.*

glut, *v.a. and n.*, avaler, gorger, soûler; se rassasier; assouvir, s'assouvir; repaître, se repaître. To — one's self; *se gorger.*

gluteal (glou-ti-al), *adj.*, (anat.) fessier.

gluten (glou-tène), *n.*, gluten, *m.*

glutinous (glou-), *adj.*, glutineux, gluant, visqueux.

glutinousness, *n.*, viscosité, *f.*

glutton (gleut't'n), *n.*, gourmand, glouton, *m.*

gluttonize (gleut't'naïze), *v.n.*, être glouton.

gluttonous, *adj.*, glouton, gourmand, goulu, vorace.

gluttonously, *adv.*, en glouton, en gourmand, goulûment.

gluttony (gleut't'ni), *n.*, gourmandise, gloutonnerie, *f.*

glyn, *n.* *V.* glen.

glyptics, *n.*, art de graver en pierres précieuses, *m.*; glyptique, *f.*

gnar (nâr), *or* **gnarl** (nârl), *v.n.*, murmurer, gronder; être revêche, bourru rebours.

gnarled (nârl'de), *or* **gnarly** (nâr-), *adj.*, noueux; plein de nœuds.

gnash (nashe), *v.a.*, grincer les dents.

gnashing, *n.*, grincement de dents, *m.*

gnat (nate), *n.*, (ent.) cousin; moucheron, *m.*

gnatsnapper (nate'-), *n.*, (orni.) pivoine, gobe-mouche, *m.*

gnaw (nô), *v.a.*, ronger; corroder; mordre.

gnawer, *n.*, rongeur, *m.*

gnawing, *n.*, rongement, *m.*; corrosion, *f.*

gnawing, *adj.*, corrosif, rongeant.

gneis (nice), *n.*, (min.) gneiss, *m.*

gnome (nôme), *n.*, gnome, *m.*, gnomide, *f.*; esprit, *m.*

gnomon (nô-mone), *n.*, style de cadran solaire, *m.*

gnomonics (no-mo'n'ikse), *n.*, gnomonique, *f.*

gnostic (nos-tik), *n.*, gnostique, *m.*

go (gô), *v.n.* (preterit, Went; *past part.*, Gone), aller, s'en aller; passer; partir, marcher. To — about; *faire le tour, se détourner; entreprendre.* To — abroad; *sortir, partir, voyager.* To — against; *s'opposer, avoir de la répugnance.* To — along; *poursuivre son chemin, accompagner, passer.* To — ashore; *débarquer, aborder.* To — aside; *se mettre de côté.* To — astray; *s'égarer.* To — asunder; *aller séparément.* To — away; *s'en aller, se retirer, sortir.* To — back; *reculer, s'en retourner.* To — backwards; *reculer.* To — backwards and forwards; *aller et venir, se contredire.* To — beyond; *passer, surpasser.* To — by; *passer auprès, passer; se régler; souffrir; devancer, surpasser.* To — down; *descendre, se coucher, ⊙avaler; rétrograder.* To — for; *aller chercher, passer pour.* To — forth; *sortir.* To — forward; *avancer, pousser, profiter, poursuivre.* To — from; *quitter, partir de.* To — from the matter; *s'écarter.* To — halves; *être de moitié.* To — in; *entrer.* To — near; *approcher.* To — off; *quitter; tirer.* To — off (of goods—*de marchandises*); *se vendre, s'écouler.* To — on; *avancer, continuer.* To — out; *sortir; s'éteindre.* To — over; *passer, traverser.* To — through; *passer, passer au travers, enfiler, percer, fendre; subir, souffrir.* To — up; *monter.* To — up and down; *courir de côté et d'autre.* To — upon; *entreprendre, se fendre.* To — with; *accompagner.* To — without; *se passer de.*

goad (gôde), *n.*, aiguillon de bouvier, aiguillade, *f.*

goad (gôde), *v.a.*, aiguillonner, piquer; (fig.) exciter.

goal (gôle), *n.*, but, terme; point de départ, *m.*

goat (gôte), *n.*, chèvre, *f.* He——; *bouc, m.* She——; *chèvre, f.*

goatherd, *n.*, chevrier, *m.*

goatish, *adj.*, lascif, de bouc.

goat-sucker (-seuk'-), *n.*, (orni.) crapaud volant, tette-chèvre, engoulevent, *m.*

gobble (gob'b'l), *v.a.*, gober; fagoter; avaler.

gobbler, *n.*, glouton, goulu, avaleur, *m.*

gobetween (gô-bi-tvêne), *n.*, médiateur; courtier; entremetteur, *m.*

goblet (gob'lète), *n.*, gobelet, *m.*; coupe, *f.*

goblin (gob'line), *n.*, lutin, spectre, gobelin, fantôme, *m.*

go-by (gô-ba'ye), *n.*, mauvaise raison, défaite,

f., détour, artifice, m. ; action d'éluder ; de passer sans faire attention ; d'écarter ; de repousser ; de changer, f.

go-cart (gŏ-cârte), n., chariot pour apprendre aux petits enfants à marcher, m.; petite chaise à roulettes. f.

god, n., Dieu, m. Would to —; plût à Dieu!

godchild (-tshaïlde), n., filleul, m., filleule. f.

goddaughter, (-dŏ'-) n., filleule. f.

goddess (-'dèce), n., déesse, divinité, f.

godfather (-fâ-theur), n., parrain, m.

godhead (-hède), n., divinité, f.

godless, adj., athée, impie.

godlike (-laïke), adj., divin.

godliness, n., sainteté, piété. f.

godling, n., divinité inférieure, f.

godly, adj., pieux, dévot, saint.

godly, adv., religieusement, dévotement.

godly-head (-hède), n., (ant.) bonté, équité, f.

godmother (-meuth'eur), n., marraine, f.

godship, n., divinité, f.

godson (-seune), n., filleul, m.

godward (-wŏrde), adv., (ant.) vers, envers Dieu.

godwit (-wite), n., (orni.) francolin, m., barge, f.

goer (gŏ'-) n., marcheur.   Comers and —s; allants et venants.   Play- — ; amateur du théâtre, m.

goggle (gog'g'l), v.n., regarder de travers, loucher.

goggle-eyed (-a'ye'de), adj., louche ; aux grands yeux.

goggles (gog'g'lze), n.pl., lunettes, f.pl. ; (for horses—pour les chevaux) œillères, f.pl.

going (gŏ'-), n., marche, démarche, allure, f.

goitre (goï'teur), n., (med.) goitre, m.

gola (gŏ-), n., (arch.) cymaise, doucine. f.

gold (gŏlde), n., or, m.   A — -mine ; une mine d'or.   A — ring ; un anneau d'or.

goldbeater (-bit'-), n., batteur d'or, m.

goldbeater's-skin (-'teur'z'skine), n., baudruche, f.

goldbound (-baou'n'de), adj., couvert d'or, entouré d'or.

gold-digger (-dig'gheur), n., chercheur d'or, m.

gold-drawer (-drŏ'-), n., tireur d'or, m.

gold-dust (-deuste), n., poudre d'or, f.

golden, adj., d'or.

goldenly, adv., splendidement.

goldfinch (-fin'she), n., (orni.) chardonneret, m.

gold-finder (-faï'n'd'-), n., orpailleur ; (iron.) / vidangeur, m.

gold-finer (-faï'n'-), n., affineur d'or, m.

goldfish, n., (ich.) poisson rouge, m.

golding, n., pomme qui a la chair rougeâtre, f.

goldsmith (-smith), n., orfèvre, m.

gold-spink (-spi'n'k), n., (orni.) bruant commun, m.

gome (gôme), n., cambouis, m.

gomphosis (go'm'-phŏ-ciss), n., (anat.) gomphose, articulation immobile des os, f

gondola, n., gondole, f.

gondolier (-lire), n., gondolier, m.

gone (gone), past part. (of to go), allé, part. He is — ; il s'en est allé ; (dead—trépassé) il est mort.

gonfalon, or **gonfanon,** n., (her.) gonfalon, gonfanon ; (ant.) drapeau, étendard, m.

goriometry (gŏ-), n., goniométrie, f.

gonorrhœa (-or-rî'-), n., (med.) gonorrhée, f.

good (goûde), adj., bon, d'un bon naturel, honnête ; convenable ; solide.

good, n., bien ; avantage ; profit, m. , utilité, f.

good, adv., bien, bon.   Very — ; fort bien. As — ; aussi bien.

good! int., eh bien ! eh ! de grâce !

good-breeding (-brid'-), n., éducation, politesse, f.

good-conditioned (-dish'eu'n'de), adj., bien conditionné ; en bon état.

good-friday (-fraï-), n., vendredi saint, m.

good-humour (-hiou-meur), n., bonne humeur, f., enjouement, m.

good-humoured (-hiou-meur'de), adj., de bonne humeur, enjoué.

goodliness, n., beauté, grâce, f.

good-luck (-leuke), n., bonheur, m., prospérité, f.

goodly, adj., beau, bel, joli, m.

goodman (-ma'n) n., bon homme, compère, m.

good-nature (-nét'ioure), n., bonté, bonhomie, humanité, complaisance, f.

good-natured (-nét'iourde), adj., d'un bon naturel, bénin, bon.

goodness, n., bonté, m. ; probité, f.

good-now! (-nao) int., à la bonne heure !

goods (goûdze), n., meubles, effets, biens, m.pl. ; marchandises, f.pl.

good-will, n., bienveillance, bonne volonté, bonté, f.

good-woman (-woum'a'n), or **goody,** n., bonne femme, dame, f.

goose (gouce), n. (geese), oie, f. ; idiot, imbécile, m. ; (tailor's—de tailleur) carreau, m.   A green — ; un oison. A wild- — ; une oie sauvage.

gooseberry (-bèr'-), n., groseille à maquereau, groseille verte, f.

goose-grass (-grâce), n., (bot.) grateron, rièble, m. ; râpette, f.

gooseneck (-nèke), n., (nav.) crochet, m.

gorbelly, n., (ant.) gros ventre, m., grosse panse, f.

gorcock, n., (orni.) coq de bruyère, m.

gorcrow (-crŏ), n., (orni.) corneille, f.

gord (gŏrde), n., dé pipé, m.

gore (gŏre), n., sang figé, m. ; pièce de terre triangulaire ; longue pièce d'étoffe triangulaire, coupée en pointe, f.

gore, v.a., piquer, percer ; couper en pointe.

gorge (gordje), n., gosier, m., gorge, f.; jabot, m. ; (fort.) gorge, f.

gorge, v.a., gorger, remplir, avaler, rassasier.

gorge, v.n., se gorger ; avaler.

gorgeous (gor'djeusse), adj., superbe, magnifique, somptueux, éclatant.

gorgeously, adv., superbement, magnifiquement.

gorgeousness, n., magnificence, pompe, splendeur, f.

gorgerin (gor'djeur'ine), n., (arch.) gorgerin, colarin, m.

gorget (gor'djète), n., gorgerin, hausse-col, m. ; (surg.) gorgeret, m.

gorhen (-hène), n., poule de bruyère, f.

goring, n., piqûre, f., coup de corne, m.

gormand (gor-), or **gourmand** (gŏr-), n., gourmand ; goulu, glouton, m.

gormandize (-aïze), v.n., bâfrer, goinfrer, gourmand, m.

gormandizer (-aïz'-), n., glouton, goinfre, gourmand, m.

gormandizing (-aïz'-), n., gourmandise, gloutonnerie, f.

gorse, n., (bot.) bruyère, brande, f.; genêt, m.

gory (gŏ-), adj., sanglant, couvert de sang caillé.

goshawk (goss'hŏke), n., (orni.) autour, m.

gosling (goz'-), n., oison ; chaton, m.

gospel (gos'pèl), n., évangile, m.

gospel, v.a., évangéliser.

gospeller, n., évangéliste ; sectaire, m.

gossamer (gos'sa-), *n.*, filandres, *f.pl.* ; duvet de plantes, *m.*

gossip, *n.*, commère, causeuse ; babillarde, *f.* ; caquet, bavardage, *m.*

gossip, *v.n.*, jaser, caqueter, babiller, bavarder.

gossipping, *n.*, commérage, bavardage, *m.*

gothic (goth'-), *adj.*, gothique.

gothicize (goth-iss'aïze), *v.a.*, rendre gothique ; ramener à la barbarie.

go-to! (gô-tou),*int.*, allons ! çà ! sus ! courage !

gouge (gaoudje), *n.*, gouge, *f.*

gourd (gourde), *n.*, gourde ; calebasse, citrouille, *f.*

gourdiness, *n.*, (vet.) enflure à la jambe, *f.*

gourd-worm (-weurme), *n.*, douve, *f.*

gourdy, *adj.*, gros; (vet.) enflé aux jambes.

gourmand, *n.* V. **gormand**.

gout (gaoute), *n.*, (med.) goutte, *f.* ; (taste) goût, *m.*

gouty, *adj.*, goutteux.

govern (gheuv'eurne),*v.a.*, gouverner, régir, diriger, tenir en bride.

governable (-'a-b'l), *adj.*, qui peut être gouverné, docile, gouvernable.

governance, *n.*, gouvernement, *m.*, administration, *f.*

governess, *or* **governante**, *n.*, institutrice, gouvernante, *f.*

government, *n.*, gouvernement, *m.*, administration, direction, *f.* ; (gram.) régime, *m.*

governor (gheuv'eur-neur), *n.*, gouverneur ; instituteur.

gowan (gaw'a'n), *n.*, (bot.) pâquerette commune, marguerite, *f.*

gowl (gaoul), *v.n.*, (ant.) hurler.

gown (gaoune), *n.*, robe; toge, *f.* Night- — ; peignoir, *m.* Morning- —, dressing- — ; *robe de chambre, f.*

gowned (gaou'n'de), *adj.*, vêtu d'une robe, en robe.

gownman (-ma'n), *or* **gownsman** (gaou'n'z'-), *n.* (-men), homme de robe, *ou* de robe longue, *m.* ; (pl.) gens de robe.

grabble (grab'b'l), *v.a.* and *n.*, tâter, tâtonner ; aller à tâtons ; fouir ; déraciner ; s'étirer.

grace (gréce), *n.*, grâce, bonté, faveur, *f.* ; pardon, *m.* ; agrément, bon air, *m.* ; grandeur, *f.* ; (rel.) grâces. *f.pl.*

grace, *v.a.*, orner, embellir ; illustrer.

graced (gréss'te), *adj.*, orné, doué, bien fait; vertueux.

graceful (-foule), *adj.*, beau, gracieux, agréable, bien fait, enjoué.

gracefully, *adv.*, gracieusement, de bonne grâce.

gracefulness, *n.*,bonne grâce, *f.*, agrément, charme, *m.*, beauté, *f.*

graceless, *adj.*, sans grâces, désagréable ; abandonné, effronté, dépravé.

gracenote (-nôte), *n.*, (mus.) note d'agrément, *f.*

graces (grè-cize), *n.pl.*, (myth.) Grâces, *f.pl.*

gracile (grass'il), *or* **gracilent** (grass'-), *adj.*, (ant.) grêle, mince, menu, petit.

gracility, *n.*, (ant.) gracilité, ténuité, petitesse, *f.*

gracious (gré-sheuss), *adj.*, gracieux, bénin, bon, favorable, agréable, propice.

graciously, *adv.*, gracieusement, obligeamment, humainement.

graciousness, *n.*, bonté, bénignité ; bienfaisance, *f.*

gradation (gra-dé-), *n.*, gradation, *f.*; degré, *m.*

gradatory (-teuri), *n.*, escalier, perron, *m.*

grade, *n.*, grade; degré, *m.*

gradient, *adj.*, avançant ; ambulant

gradient, *n.*, (railways)pente, rampe, *f.*

gradual (grad'iou-), *n.*, montée, *f.* ; gradin ; (liturgy) graduel, *m.*

gradual, *adj.*, graduel, par degrés, gradué, réglé.

graduality, *n.*, gradation, progression régulière, *f.*

gradually, *adv.*, graduellement, par degrés, pas à pas, peu à peu.

graduate (grad'iou-), *n.*, gradué, *m.*

graduate, *v.a.*, graduer.

graduate, *v.n.*, prendre ses degrés à une université, se faire graduer.

graduation (-'iou-e-), *n.*, graduation ; gradation, *f.*

graff (grâfe), *n.*, fossé, *m.*, fosse, *f.*

graft (grâf'te) *v.*, greffe, ente, *f.*, empeau, *m.*

graft, *v.a.* and *n.*, greffer, enter.

grafter, *n.*, personne qui ente, greffeur.

grafting, *n.*, (hort.) greffe, *f.*

grafting-knife (-naïfe), *n.*, greffoir, ⊙entoir, *m.*

grain (gréne), *n.*, grain ; pépin, *m.* ; veine, *f.* ; fil, *m.* — of allowance; *indulgence.* — of wood; veine de bois. Against the — ; *à contre-cœur, malgré soi.*

grain, *v.a.*, grener, greneler ; peindre en décors.

grained (gré'n'de), *adj.*, grenu ; dur.

grainer, *n.*, peintre décorateur, *m.*

grains (gré'n'ze), *n.*, drèche, *f.*, marc, *m.*

grainy, *adj.*, plein de grains, grenelé.

grallic, *adj.*, (orni.) échassier.

graminous (-mi'n'i-eusse), *adj.*, (bot.) graminée, herbeux, herbacé.

graminivorous, *adj.*, herbivore.

grammar, *n.*, grammaire, *f.*

grammarian (-mé-), *n.*, grammairien, *m.*

grammar-school (-scoule), *n.*, école où l'on enseigne le latin et le grec, *f.*

grammatic, *or* **grammatical**,*adj.*, grammatical ; de grammaire.

grammatically, *adv.*, grammaticalement.

grammaticize (-çaïze), *v.a.*, rendre une expression grammaticale ; faire le grammatiste ; écrire grammaticalement.

grampus, *n.*, (ich.) épaulard, orque, *m.*

granadilla, *n.*, (bot.) grenadille, fleur de la passion, *f.*

granary, *n.*, grenier, *m.* ; grange, *f.*

grand (gra'n'de), *adj.*, grand, superbe, noble, illustre, sublime, grandiose.

grandam, *n.*, grand'mère ; vieille femme, *f.*

grand-child (-tshaïlde), *n.*, petit-fils, *m.*, petite-fille, *f.*

grand-daughter (-dô-teur), *n.*, petite-fille, *f.* A great — ; *une arrière-petite-fille.*

grandee (gra'n'dī), *n.*, personne de marque, *f.*, grand, *m.*

grandeur (-'ieur),*n.*, grandeur, *f.*, éclat, *m.*, pompe, splendeur, *f.*

grand-father (-fâ-theur), *or* **grand-sire** (-saeur), *n.*, grand-père, aïeul, *m.* A great — ; *un bisaïeul.*

grandiloquence (-kwè'n'se), *n.*, langage pompeux, *m.* ; emphase, *f.*

grandiloquent (-kwè'n'te), *or* **grandiloquous** (-kweusse), *adj.*, (of speeches—*discours*) sublime, pompeux ; enflé.

grandinous, *adj.*, (ant.) plein de grêle.

grandly, *adv.*, grandement ; fastueusement.

grand-mother (-meuth'eur),*n.*, grand'mère, aïeule, *f.* A great — ; *une bisaïeule.*

grand-son (-seune), *n.*, petit-fils, *m.* A great —; *un arrière-petit-fils.*

grange (gré'n'dje), *n.*, ferme, métairie, grange, *f.*

granite, *n.*, (min.) granit, *m.*

granitel, *n.*, (min.) marbre granitelle; granit à petits grains, *m.*

granivorous, *adj.*, granivore.

grant (gra'n'te), *n.*, octroi, *m.*, concession, *f.*, don, privilège, *m.*

grant, *v.a.*, donner, accorder, céder ; avouer ; entériner ; octroyer. To — a pardon ; *pardonner* ; accorder une grâce.

grantable (-'a-b'l), *adj.*, qui peut être accordé.

granted (-ède), *part. adj.*, accordé, octroyé ; avoué ; reconnu ; d'accord.

grantee (-tî), *n.*, donataire, concessionnaire. *m.*, *f.*

granter, *or* **grantor** (-tor), *n.*, donateur ; cédant. *m.*

granular, *or* **granulary** (-'iou-), *adj.*, en grains ; grenelé, grenu, granulé, granulaire.

granulate (-'iou), *v.a.*, greneler, grener, granuler.

granulation (-lé), *n.*, granulation. *f.*

granule (-'ioule), *n.*, petit grain, granule, *m.*

granulous, *adj.*, grenu, granuleux.

grape (grépe), *n.*, raisin, *m.* ; vigne, *f.* A bunch of —s ; *une grappe de raisin.*

grape-shot (grépe-shote), *n.*, (milit.) mitraille, *f.*

grapestone (grépe-stône), *n.*, pépin de raisin, *m.*

grape-vine (-vaïne), *n.*, vigne, *f.*

graphic, *or* **graphical**, *adj.*, graphique, bien tracé, exact, parfait.

graphically, *adv.*, graphiquement, exactement.

graphite (-'aïte), *n.*, graphite, plombagine, *m.*

graphometer (-fo'mi'-), *n.*, (math.) graphomètre, *m.*

grapnel, *n.*, grappin, *m.*, petite ancre, *f.*

grapple (grap'p'l), *n.*, grappin, croc, harpon, *m.* ; lutte, *f.*, combat de lutteurs, *m.*

grapple, *v.a.*, accrocher ; grappiner, harponner, arrêter ; happer. To — a ship ; *accrocher un navire.*

grapple, *v.n.*, en venir aux mains, se saisir de ; lutter ; (nav.) en venir à l'abordage ; (fig.) combattre. To — with ; *combattre, en venir aux prises, en venir aux mains.*

grapy (grépi), *adj.*, de raisin.

grasp (grâsp), *n.*, poignée ; prise ; étreinte ; possession, *f.* ; pouvoir, *m.*

grasp, *v.a.*, empoigner, saisir, prendre avec la main, gripper.

grasp, *v.n.*, s'emparer ; tâcher d'attraper, de saisir.

grasper, *n.*, personne qui empoigne ; homme avide, ambitieux.

grasping, *adj.*, avide, cupide, ambitieux.

grass (grâce), *n.*, herbe, verdure, *f.* ; foin, gazon, *m.*

grasshopper (-hop'-), *n.*, sauterelle, cigale, *f.*

grassiness, *n.*, herbage, *m.* ; qualité d'être herbeux, *f.*

grass-plot (-plote), *n.*, boulingrin, *m.*, pelouse, *f.* ; tapis vert, *m.*

grassy, *adj.*, herbu, herbeux.

grate (grète), *n.*, grille, *f.* ; grillage, *m.* ; jalousie, *f.* ; gril ; treillis, *m.*

grate, *v.a.* and *n.*, râper, égruger ; griller ; frotter. To — the teeth ; *grincer les dents.* To — up ; *fermer d'un treillis.*

grateful (grèt'-foule), *adj.*, reconnaissant ; agréable ; délicieux.

gratefully, *adv.*, avec gratitude ; avec reconnaissance ; agréablement.

gratefulness, *n.*, gratitude, reconnaissance, *f.* ; agrément, *m.*

grater, *n.*, râpe, *f.* ; égrugeoir, *m.* ; racloir, *m.*

gratification (-fi-ké-), *n.*, gratification ; récompense ; volupté ; satisfaction, *f.*

gratify (-fa'ye), *v.a.*, gratifier, satisfaire, récompenser.

gratifying (-ti-fa-igne), *adj.*, satisfaisant, agréable, flatteur.

grating (grèt'-), *n.*, grille, *f.*, grillage ; (nav.) égrruttoir, *m.*

grating, *adj.*, rude, dur, discordant ; qui choque l'oreille.

gratingly, *adv.*, rudement.

gratis (gré-tiss), *adv.*, gratuitement, gratis, pour rien.

gratitude (-tioude), *n.*, gratitude, reconnaissance, *f.*

gratuitous (-tiou-i-), *adj.*, gratuit ; volontaire ; bénévole.

gratuitously, *adv.*, gratuitement ; bénévolement.

gratuity (-tiou-i-) *n.*, don, présent, *m.*, gratuité, largesse, *f.* ; pourboire, *m.*

gratulate (grat'iou-), *v.a.*, féliciter, congratuler.

gratulation (-lé-), *n.*, félicitation, congratulation, *f.*

gratulatory. *adj.*, congratulateur, congratulatoire, congratulant.

grave (gréve), *n.*, sépulcre, *m.*, tombe, fosse, *f.*

grave, *adj.*, grave, sérieux, réservé, retenu, modeste ; (gram.) grave.

grave, *v.a.* and *n.*, graver, tailler, ciseler. To — a ship ; *espalmer et suiver.*

grave-clothes (-clôze), *n.*, linceul, drap mortuaire, suaire, *m.*

grave-digger (-dig'gheur), *n.*, fossoyeur, *m.*

gravel (grav'èl), *n.*, gravier, *m.* ; (med.) gravelle, *f.* A — -pit ; *une sablonnière, f.*

gravel, *v.a.*, sabler, couvrir de gravier ; embarrasser, inquiéter.

graveless (grév'-), *adj.*, sans sépulture.

gravelly (grav'èl-li), *adj.*, graveleux, sablonneux.

gravely (grév'li), *adv.*, gravement, sérieusement, modestement.

graven (grév'n), *past. part.* (of to grave), gravé, taillé, ciselé. A — image ; *une image taillée.*

graveness (grév'-), *n.*, gravité, contenance grave, *f.*

graveolent (gré-vi-), *n.*, (ant.) à odeur forte.

graver (grév'-), *n.*, graveur ; burin, *m.*

graves (grév'z), *n.pl.* V. **greaves.**

gravestone (-stône), *n.*, tombeau, *m.*, tombe, *f.*

gravidation (-dé-), *or* **gravidity**, *n.*, (ant.) grossesse, *f.*

graving (grév'-), *n.*, gravure, *f.* ; (nav.) action d'espalmer. — -tool ; *burin, m.*

gravitate, *v.n.*, graviter ; peser.

gravitation (-té-), *n.*, gravitation, pesanteur, *f.* ; poids, *m.*

gravity, *n.*, air sérieux *m.*, gravité ; pesanteur, *f.*, grave, *m.*

gravy (gré-vé), *n.*, jus, suc de viande, coulis, *m.*

gray, *or* **gray-brook**, *n.*, (zool.) blaireau, taisson, *m.*

gray, *or* **grey** (gré), *adj.*, gris ; (fig.) vieux.

graybeard (-bírde), *n.*, barbe grise, *f.* ; vieillard, grison, barbon, *m.*

gray-eyed (-a'ye-de), *adj.*, qui a les yeux gris.

gray-haired (-hèr'de), *adj.*, qui a les cheveux gris, grison, chenu.

gray-headed (-hèd'ède), *adj.*, qui a la tête grise.

grayhound, *n.* V. **greyhound.**

grayish, *adj.*, grisâtre.

grayling, *n.*, (ich.) ombre-chevalier, umble, *m.*

grayness, *n.*, couleur grise, *f.*

graywacke (-wac'ki), *n.*, (min.) grès des houillères, psammite. *m.*

graze, *v.a.*, effleurer, raser, friser.

graze, *v.n.*, paître, faire paître, brouter.

grazier (gré-jeur), *n.*, engraisseur de bétail, éleveur, *m.*

grease (grîce), *n.*, graisse, *f.*, oing, *m.*

grease (grîze), v.a., graisser; frotter de graisse.

greasiness (griz'-), n., crasse, graisse, saleté, f.

greasy (griz'i), adj., graisseux, taché de graisse ; crasseux, sale.

great (grète), n., (ant.) le gros, le tout, m.

great, adj., grand, gros ; noble, illustre, important. — with child; enceinte. The — ; les grands, m.pl.

greatbellied (-bel'ide), adj., ventru.

great-granddaughter (-dô'-), n., arrière-petite-fille, f.

great-grandfather (-fâ-theur), n., bisaïeul, m.

great-grandmother (-meuth-eur), n., bisaïeule, f.

great-grandson (-seune), n., arrière-petit-fils, m.

great-hearted (-hârt'ède), adj., courageux, généreux.

greatly, adv., grandement, fort, beaucoup.

greatness, n., grandeur, dignité ; grosseur ; sublimité ; énormité, f.

greave (grîve), n., grève, jambière, armure pour les jambes, f.

greaves (griv'ze), or **graves**, n.pl., cretons, m.pl.

grecian (gri'sha'n), n. Grec ; (antiq.) Helléniste ; (one versed in the Greek language — érudit versé dans la langue grecque) helléniste, m.

grecian, adj., grec.

grecism (gri'ciz'm), n., hellénisme, idiotisme grec, (l.u.) grécisme, m.

grecize (gri-çaîze), v.a., gréciser; traduire en grec.

greed (gri'de), n., cupidité, avidité ; gourmandise, gloutonnerie, f.; (fig.) passion, f., désir ardent, m.

greedily (grid'-), adv., goulûment ; avidement, avec avidité.

greediness, n., cupidité, avidité ; gourmandise, gloutonnerie, f.; (fig.) désir ardent, m., passion, f.

greedy (grid'-), adj., cupide, avide ; gourmand, goulu, vorace ; passionné. — of honour; ambitieux. — of money ; avare, cupide.

greedy-gut (-gheute), n., (triv.) glouton, gourmand, m.

greek (grîke), n., Grec, m., Grecque, f.; (language—langue) grec, m.

greek, adj., grec.

green (grîne), adj., vert ; frais ; novice.

green, n., vert, m., verdure, f. ; gazon, m.

green, v.a., verdir, faire verdir.

greenbroom (-broume), n., (bot.) genêt épineux, m.

greencloth (-clôth), n., tapis vert, m. The board of — ; la cour du tapis vert, de la maison royale.

green-eyed (-a'ye'-de), adj., aux yeux verdâtres.

greenfinch (-fi'n'she), n., (orni.) verdier, bréant, m.

greengage (-ghédje), n., prune de reine-Claude, f.

greengrocer (-grô-ceur), n., fruitier, m., fruitière, f.

greenhouse (-haouce), n., serre, f.

greenish, adj., verdâtre.

greenly, adv., vertement ; nouvellement, prématurément ; sans expérience.

greenness, n., verdure, f.; fraîcheur, verdeur, f.

greenroom (-roume), n., foyer de théâtre, m.

greens (gri'n'ze), n.pl., (gard.) légumes, m.pl. ; herbes potagères, f.pl.

greensickness, n., (med.) chlorose, f., pâles couleurs, f.pl.

greensward (-swôrde), n., pelouse, f.; gazon m.

greenwood (-woude), n., bois vert, m.

greet (grî'te), v.a., saluer, congratuler.

greeting, n., salutation, f., salut, m.

gregal (gri'-) adj., (ant.) de troupeau.

gregarious (gri-ghé-), adj., qui va en troupe, par bandes.

gregorian (gri-gô-), adj., grégorien.

grenade (gri-), n., (artil.) grenade, f.

grenadier (grè'n'a-dire), n., grenadier, m.

grey, adj. V. **gray**.

greyhound, or **grayhound** (grè-haou'n'de), n., lévrier, m., levrette, f.

grice (graîce), n., jeune cochon ; marcassin, m.

gride (graîde), v.a., couper, trancher, fendre.

gridelin (grid'è-), n., gris de lin, m.

gridiron (grid'ai'eur'ne), n., gril, m.

grief (grîfe), n., douleur, tristesse, f.; chagrin, déplaisir, m.

grievance (griv'-), n., grief; tort, abus, m.; peine, f.

grieve (grîve), v.a., chagriner, attrister ; fouler, opprimer.

grieve, v.n., se chagriner, s'attrister.

grievingly, adv., avec douleur, avec chagrin.

grievous (griv'-), adj., grief, douloureux, affligeant ; cruel, énorme, atroce, fâcheux.

grievously, adv., grièvement ; gravement, cruellement.

grievousness, n., grièveté, énormité ; affliction, calamité, f.; chagrin, m.

griffin, or **griffon**, n., (orni.) griffon, gypaète, m.

grig, n., petite anguille, f. ; gaillard, m.

grill (grile), v.a., griller, mettre sur le gril.

grillade (gril-léde), n., grillade, viande grillée, f.

grim, adj., refrogné, chagrin ; horrible.

grimace (gri-mece), n., grimace, f.; faux semblant, m.

grimalkin, n., vieux chat, m.

grime (graîme), n., saleté, noirceur, f., barbouillage, m.

grime, v.a., salir, barbouiller, tacher, noircir.

grimly (gri'm'-), adv., d'un air refrogné, horriblement, hideusement.

grimness (gri'm'-), n., air refrogné, visage sévère, m.

grin (grine), n., grimace, contortion de la bouche, f.; piège, m.

grin, v.a., ricaner, grimacer ; tordre la bouche.

grind (graï'n'de), v.a. (pret. and past part., Ground), moudre ; mâcher ; broyer ; grincer ; (knives, &c.—couteaux, &c.) aiguiser, émoudre ; opprimer, fouler.

grinder, n., émouleur ; broyeur ; meunier, m.

grinding, n., broiement, m., mouture, f.

grindstone (-stône), n., meule ; pierre à aiguiser, à repasser, f.

grinner (gri'n'-), n., ricaneur ; grimacier, m.

grinningly, adv., en ricanant, en grimaçant.

grip, n., petit fossé, m.

gripe (graîpe), n., poignée ; prise, étreinte, f.; serrement, m. ; (nav.) bas du taille-mer, m. ; (fig.) oppression, vexation, f.

gripe, v.a., empoigner, saisir, gripper, serrer.

gripe, v.n., causer des tranchées, donner la colique ; gripper, agripper, escroquer ; (nav.) serrer le vent de trop près.

gripes (graîpse), n.pl., colique, f., tranchées ; (nav.) risses de chaloupe, f.pl.

gripingly, adv., avec des tranchées.

gris-amber (griss'a'm'-), n., ambre gris, m.

grise (graîze), n., cochon ; pas, m.; marche d'escalier, f.

griskin (griss'-), n., côtelette de porc, f.

grisly (griz'-), adj., hideux, affreux, horrible.

grisly-bear (-bère), *n.*, ours gris d'Amérique, *m.*

grist (griste), *n.*, mouture, farine, *f.* ; (fig.) gain, profit, *m.*

gristle (gris's'l), *n.*, cartilage, *m.*

gristly (gris's'li),*adj.*, cartilagineux.

grit (grite), *n.*, sable, gravier, *m.* ; limaille,*f.*

grit, *v.n.*, craquer, frotter violemment.

grits, *n.pl.* *V.* **groats**.

grit-stone (-stône), *n.*, (min.) grès dur, *m.*

grittiness, *n.*, qualité graveleuse,*f.*

gritty, *adj.*, graveleux, plein de sable.

grizelin, *n.* *V.* **gridelin**.

grizzle (griz'z'l), *n.*, grisaille, *f.* ; grison, gris, *m.*

grizzled (gríz'z'l'de), *adj.*, grison.

grizzly, *adj.*, grisâtre.

groan (grône), *or* **groaning** (grô'n'-), *n.*, gémissement, soupir, *m.* ; plainte, *f.* ; grognement, *m.*

groan, *v.n.*, gémir, soupirer ; grogner.

groat -(grôte), *n.*, quatre pence, monnaie anglaise ; environ 40 centimes, monnaie française. He is not worth a — ; *il n'a pas le sou.*

groats (grôtse), *n.pl.*, gruau d'avoine, *m.*, farine grossière,*f.*

grocer (grô-œur), *n.*, épicier, *m.*

grocery (grô-œuri), *n.*, épicerie,*f.*

grog, *n.*, grog, *m.*

grogram,*n.*, étoffe à gros grains, filoselle,*f.*

groin (gro-i-ne), *n.*, aine,*f.*

groined (gro-i'n'de), *adj.*, (arch.) à arête, d'arête.

gromwell, *or* **gromil**, *n.*,(bot.) lithosperme, grémil, *m.*

groom (groume), *n.*, palefrenier, valet d'écurie, garçon, valet, groom, *m.*

groove (grouve), *n.*, rainure, coulisse,*f.*

groove, *v.a.*, évider ; creuser en gorge.

grope (grôpe), *v.n.*, tâter, tâtonner ; patiner. To —, to — along ; *aller à tâtons.*

gross, *n.*, gros, *m.*, grosse ; masse,*f.*

gross, *adj.*, gros, épais ; grossier, rude.

grossly, *adv.*, grossièrement ; lourdement.

grossness, *n.*, grossièreté,*f.*

grot, *or* **grotto**,*n.*, grotte,*f.*

grotesque, *adj.*, grotesque.

ground (graou'n'de), *n.*, terre,*f.*, terrain, *m.* ; bien-fonds, *m.* ; sol ; fondement, sujet, motif, *m.*, raison,*f.* ; (of pictures, of flowered cloths— *de peintures, d'étoffes à fleurs*) fond, *m.* The —s of a gentleman's seat ; *le parc, les jardins, d'une maison de campagne.*

ground, *v.a.*, fonder, établir, enseigner ; appuyer, motiver ; mettre à sec ; faire le fond. To — a ship ; *échouer un vaisseau.*

ground (*past part.* of to grind), broyé, moulu ; (fig.) opprimé, foulé ; (sharpened—*émoulu*) aiguisé.

groundage (-'édje), *n.*, droit d'ancrage, droit de port, *m.*

grounded (-'ède), *part. adj.*, fondé, établi, enseigné ; mis à terre.

groundedly (-'èdli), *adv.*, sur de bons principes, solidement ; avec raison.

ground-floor (-flôre),*n.*, rez-de-chaussée, *m.*

groundivy (-aïvi), *n.*, lierre terrestre, *m.*

groundless. *adj.*, mal fondé, sans raison.

groundlessly, *adv.*, sans fondement, sans raison.

groundlessness, *n.*, mánque de fondement, *m.* ; futilité,*f.*

groundling, *n.*, homme de bas étage, *m.* ; (ich.) loche,*f.*

ground-plate, *n.*, (carp.) sablière, sole,*f.*

ground-plot, *n.*, sol, plan ; fondement, *m.* ; base,*f.*

ground-rent, *n.*, rente foncière; *f.*

grounds (graou'n'dze), *n.pl.*, sédiment, *m.*, lie,*f.* ; marc de café : principes, *m.pl.*

groundsel, *n.*, (bot.) seneçon, *m.*

groundsill, *or* **groundsel**, *n.*, seuil, *m.*

groundwork (-weurke), *n.*, fond, plan, *m.* ; base, fondation, *f.*

group (groupe),*n.*, groupe;(hort.) massif, *m.*

group, *v.a.*, grouper, agrouper.

grouse(graouze), *n.*,(orni.) coq de bruyère,*m.*

grout (graoute), *n.*, sédiment ; son, *m.* ; pomme,*f.* ; mortier, *m.*

grove (grôve), *n.*, bocage, bosquet, *m.*

grovel (grov'v'l), *v.n.*, ramper, se traîner.

groveller, *n.*, homme rampant, *m.*

grow (grô), *v.n.* (*pret.*, Grew, *past part.*, Grown), croître ; devenir ; se faire. To — again ; *recroître ; reprendre racine; redevenir.* To — into fashion ; *venir à la mode.* To — out of fashion; *passer de mode.* To — into ; *venir, passer.* To — into favour; *s'insinuer dans les bonnes grâces.* To — out of esteem ; *perdre son crédit.* To — out of favour; *perdre les bonnes grâces.* To — out of kind; *dégénérer.* To — out of use ; *passer, vieillir.* To — towards an end ; *s'achever, tendre à la fin.* To — up; *croître, lever.* To — up again ; *revenir.* To— old ; *vieillir.* To — dear; *enchérir.* To — less; *diminuer.* To — near or on ; *approcher.* To — tame; *s'apprivoiser.* To — weary; *se lasser, s'ennuyer.* To — young again ; *rajeunir.* To — better; *s'améliorer, se remettre.* To — big; *grossir.* To — cold; *se refroidir.* To — fat; *engraisser.* To — handsome; *embellir.* To — hot; *s'échauffer.* To — rich ; *s'enrichir.* To — sleepy ; *s'assoupir.* To — strong; *se fortifier.* To — lean ; *maigrir.* To — ugly ; *enlaidir.* To — worse ; *empirer ; être plus mal.*

grow, *v.a.*, cultiver, semer.

grower, *n.*, cultivateur, planteur, *m.*

growing, *adj.*, naissant ; croissant.

growl (graoul), *n.*, grognement, grondement, *m.*

growl, *v.n.*, grogner, gronder, murmurer.

grown (grône), (*part.* of to grow), crû ; fait ; devenu. —, full— girl; *grande fille.* —people ; *les grandes personnes, f., les adultes, m.*

growth (grôth), *n.*, croissance,*f.*, accroissement; (produce—*produit*) crû; progrès, *m.* ; augmentation,*f.*

grub (greube), *n.*, ver ; (fig.) nain, *m.* ; (l.ex.) nourriture, *f.*, aliments, *m.pl.*

grub, *v.a.*, défricher, essarter, déraciner.

grudge (greudje), *n.*, rancune, animosité, mauvais vouloir, *m.*

grudge, *v.a.* and *n.*, regretter ; reprocher ; envier ; plaindre, pleurer.

grudgingly, *adv.*, à contre cœur, avec peine, à regret.

gruel (grou'ěl), *n.*, gruau, *m.*

gruff (greufe), *adj.*, bourru, rechigné ; rude.

gruffily, *adv.*, d'un air rechigné ; rudement.

gruffness, *n.*, mauvais naturel, *m.* ; rudesse,*f.*

grum (greume), *adj.*, arrogant, sévère ; refrogné.

grumble (greu'm'b'l),*v.n.*, grommeler, murmurer, se plaindre, grogner.

grumbler, *n.*, grondeur, grogneur, grognon, *m.*

grumbling, *n.*, murmure, *m.* ; plainte. *f.*

grumblingly, *adv.*, d'un air chagrin, en grognant.

grume (groume), *n.*, grumeau, *m.*

grumly, *adv.*, d'un air mécontent ; de travers ; opiniâtrement.

grumose (-môze), *or* **grumous** (-meusse). *adj.*, grumeleux ; épais.

grunt (greu'n'te), *n.*, grognement (des pourceaux), *m.*

grunt, *v.n.*, grogner, grommeler.

grunter, *n.*, grognard ; cochon, *m.*

grunting, *n.*, grognement, *m.* ; plainte. *f.*

gruntling, *n.*, petit cochon, goret. *m.*

guaiacum (gwa-ya-keume), *n.*, gaïac. *m.*

guano (goua-nô), *n.*, guano, *m.*

guarantee, *or* **guaranty** (gar'a'n'ti), *n.*, garant, *m.* caution. *f.*

guarantee, *v.a.*, garantir,être garant.

guard (gârde), *n.*, garde, défense, *f.* ; (man —homme)garde, *m.* —house; *corps de garde, m.* Extraordinary night— ; *bivouac, m.*

guard, *v.a.*, garder. défendre, protéger.

guard, *v.n.*, se garder, se tenir en garde.

guarder, *n.*, gardien, *m.*

guardian (gâr-di-a'n), *n.*, gardien ; (of minors—de mineurs) tuteur ; curateur, *m.*

guardian. *adj.*, gardien, tutélaire.

guardianship, *n.*, curatelle, tutelle ; protection, défense, *f.*

guard-irons (-aïeur'n'ze), *n.*, chasse-pierres, *m.*

guardless, *adj.*, sans défense ; exposé ; délaissé.

guardship, *n.*, (nav.) vaisseau de garde ; garde-côte, *m.*

gubernation (ghiou-beur-né-), *n.*, gouvernement, *m.*, direction, *f.*

gudgeon (gheud'jeune), *n.*, (ich.) goujon, *m.* ; (fig.) dupe, *f.*

guerdon (gheur'-), *n.*, récompense, *f.*

guerilla, *n.*, guérilla, *f.*

guess (ghèce), *n.*, conjecture, *f.*

guess, *v.a.* and *n.*, deviner, conjecturer.

guesser, *n.*, conjectureur, devineur, *m.*

guesswork (-weurke), *n.*, supposition, *f.*

guest (ghèste), *n.*, convié, hôte, *m.*, convive, *m.,f.*

guest-chamber (-tshé'm'beur), *n.*, salle à manger, *f.*, réfectoire, *m.*

guggle (gheug'g'l), *v.n.* V. **gurgle**.

guggling, *n.*, glouglou, *m.*

guidage (gaïd'édje), *n.*, salaire du guide, *m.*

guidance (gaïd'-), *n.*, conduite, *f.* ; auspices, *m.pl.*

guide (gaïde), *n.*, guide, conducteur ; directeur, *m.*

guide, *v.a.*, conduire, guider ; diriger.

guideless, *adj.*, sans guide.

guild (ghilde), *n.*, corps de métier, *m.* ; corporation, *f.* ; tribut, *m.*

guilder (ghild'-) *n.*, (Dutch coin—monnaie hollandaise) florin, *m.*

guildhall (-hôl), *n.*, hôtel de ville, *m.*, maison de ville, maison commune, mairie, *f.*

guile (gaïl), *n.*, fraude, fourberie ; astuce, *f.*

guileful (-foule), *adj.*, fourbe, trompeur ; astucieux.

guilefully, *adv.*, astucieusement ; frauduleusement ; en traître.

guilefulness, *n.*, fourberie, *f.* ; artifice, *m.*

guileless, *adj.*, franc, sincère.

guiler, *n.*, trompeur, traître, *m.*

guillotine (ghil'lo-tine), *n.*, guillotine, *f.*

guilt (ghiltè), *n.*, crime, forfait, *m.*

guiltily, *adv.*, criminellement.

guiltiness, *n.*, crime, *m.*, méchanceté, culpabilité, *f.*

guiltless, *adj.*, innocent ; pur.

guiltlessly, *adv.*, innocemment, sans crime.

guiltlessness, *n.*, innocence ; pureté, *f.*

guilty, *adj.*, coupable.

guinea (ghi'n'é), *n.*, guinée, *f.*

guinea-dropper (-drop'-), *n.*,fripon,filou,*m.*

guinea-hen (-hène), *n.*, pintade, *f.*

guinea-pepper (-pèr'-),*n.*,poivre d'Inde,*m.*

guinea-pig, *n.*, cochon d'Inde, *m.*

guise (gaïze), *n.*, guise, manière, façon, *f.*, masque, *m.*

guitar (ghi-târ), *n.*, guitare, *f.*

gules (ghioulze), *n..* (her.) gueules. *m.*

gulf (gheulfe),*n.*, golfe, *m.*, baie, *f.* ; gouffre, abîme, *m.*

gulfy, *adj.*, plein de golfes.

gull (gheule), *n..* (orni.) mouette ; (fig.) dupe ; fraude, fourberie, tromperie,*f.*

gull, *v.a..* tromper, duper, attraper.

gull-catcher (-catsh'-), *or* **guller**, *n* , fourbe, imposteur, trompeur, *m.*

gullery, *n.*, fraude, imposture, *f.*

gullet (gheul'lète), gosier, *m.*, gorge, *f.* ; (of a bottle—de bouteille) goulot, *m.*

gullibility, *n..* crédulité, *f.*

gullible (gheul'lib'l), *adj..* crédule, facile à duper.

gully (gheul'-), *n.*, ravin, *m.*

gully, *v.n.*, couler avec bruit.

gully-hole (-hôle), *n.*, égout, *m.*

gulosity (ghiou-loss'-), *n.*, gourmandise, voracité, *f.*

gulp (gheulpe), *n.*, goulée, gorgée, *f.* ; trait, *m.*

gulp, *v.a.*, avaler, gober.

gum (gheume), *n.*, gomme ; (of the teeth— des dents) gencive, *f.*

gum, *v.a.*, gommer.

gumminess,*or* **gummosity** (ant.), *n.*, viscosité, *f.*

gumming, *n.*, gommage, *m.*

gummous, *or* **gummy** *adj.*, gommeux, gluant.

gums (gheum'ze), *n.pl.*, gencives, *f.pl.*

gun (gheune), *n.*, fusil, mousquet, *m.*, arme à feu, *f.* Great — ; *canon, m.*

gun-boat (-bôte), *n.*, (nav.) chaloupe canonnière, *f.*

gun-carriage (-car'ridje), *n.*, affût de canon, *m.*

gun-deck (-dèke), *n.*, (nav.) batterie, *f.*

gunnel, *or* **gunwale**, *n.*, (nav.) plat-bord, *m.*

gunner, *n.*, canonnier, *m.*

gunnery, *n.*, art du canonnier, *m.*

gunport (-pôrte), *n.*, (nav.) sabord, *m.*

gunpowder (-paou-deur), *n.*, poudre à canon, *f.* The — plot ; *la conspiration des poudres.*

gun-rack, *n.*, (milit.) ratelier, *m.*

gunroom (-roume), *n.*, (nav.) sainte-barbe, *f.*

gunshot (-shote). *n.*, (range—portée) portée de fusil ; portée de canon, *m.*

gunsmith (-smith), *n.*, armurier, arquebusier, *m.*

gunstick, *n.*, baguette, *f.* ; (artil.) refouloir, ⊙chargeoir, *m.*

gunstock, *n.*, monture, *f.*, fût, bois de fusil, *m.*

gunter's-chain (gheu'n'teurz'tshéne), *n.*, chaîne d'arpentage, *f.*

gurge (gheurdje), *n.*,goufre, abîme, *m.*

gurgle (gheur'g'l), *v.n.*, faire glouglou.

gurnard,*or* **gurnet** (gheur-), *n.*,(ich.) rouget, rouget grondin, grondin rouge,*m.*, trigle. *f.*

gush, *or* **gushing** (gheush'-), *n.*, saillie ; *f.* jaillissement, *m.*

gush (gheushe), *v.n.*, saillir, jaillir, ruisseler. To — out in tears ; *fondre en larmes.*

gusset (gheus'sète), *n.*, gousset, *m.*

gust (gheuste), *n.*, goût ; désir,*m.* ; jouissance, *f.* ; bouffée, *f.*, coup ; transport, accès, *m.* — of wind ; *bouffée de vent, coup de vent, revolin.* — of passion ; *accès de colère, m.*

gustable (gheust'a-b'l), *adj.*, qui peut être goûté.

gustful (-foule), *adj.*, savoureux, de bon goût.

gusty (gheusti), *adj.*, orageux, venteux.

gut (gheute), *n.*, boyau, intestin, *m.* ; *pl.*, canal alimentaire, estomac et intestins, *m.*

gut (gheute), *v.a.*, éventrer, vider ; (fig) voler, piller.

gut-spinner, *n.*, boyaudier, *m.*

guttated (gheut'té-tède), *adj.*, aspergé, en gouttes.

gutter (gheut'-), *n.*, gouttière, *f.* ; ruisseau.

m ; cannelure, *f.* — of lead ; *chéneau, m.* — of a cross-bow ; *coulisse, f.*

gutter, *v.a.*, canneler ; sillonner.

gutter, *v.n.*, dégoutter ; s'égoutter ; couler. The candle —s ; *la chandelle coule.*

gutter-spout (-spaoute), *n.*, gargouille, *f.*

gutter-tile (-taïle), *n.*, faitière, tuile creuse,*f.*

guttle(gheut't'l), *v.a.* and *n.*, bâfrer, goinfrer.

guttler, *n.*, bâfreur, goinfre, *m.*

guttling, *n.*, bâfre, *f.*

guttulous (gheut'tiou-),*adj.*, en gouttelette.

guttural (gheut'teur-), *adj.*, guttural.

gutturally, *adv.*, gutturalement.

guzzle (guz'z'l), *v.a.* and *n.*, boire avidement, lamper, ingurgiter.

guzzler, *n.*, buveur, ivrogne, *m.*

gybe (djaïbe), *n.* V. **gibe.**

gymnasium (dji'm'né-ji-eume), *n.*, gymnase, *m.*

gymnastic, *adj.*, gymnastique.

gymnastics, *n.pl.*, gymnastique, *f.*

gymnic, or **gymnical** (dji'm'-), *adj.*, (antiq.) gymnique.

gymnospermous (dji'm'no-speurm'-),*adj.* (bot.) gymnosperme.

gynarchy (dji'n'ar-ki),*n.*, gouvernement des femmes, *m.*

gypse, or **gypsum** (djipse, -seume), *n.*, (min.) gypse, *m.*

gypseous (djip'si-), *adj.*,gypseux.

gyration (djaï'r'é-), *n.*, mouvement giratoire, *m.*

gyre (djaïre), *n.*, cercle, *m.*; giration, *f.*, mouvement giratoire, *m.*

gyromancy (djaï-), *n.*, gyromancie, *f.*

gyve (djaïve), *v.a.*, mettre les fers aux pieds, enchaîner.

gyve (djaïve), *n.*, fers qu'on met aux pieds des prisonniers, *m.pl.*

H

h, huitième lettre de l'alphabet, h, *m.*, *f.*

ha! (hâ)! *int.*, ha! ha!

habeas corpus (hé-bi-ass'cor-peusse), *n.*, habeas corpus, *m.*

haberdasher, *n.*, mercier, marchand de nouveautés. A —'s shop; *magasin de nouveautés, m.*

haberdashery, *n.*, mercerie, *f.*

haberdine (-dîne), *n.*, morue sèche, merluche salée, *f.*

habergeon (-bèr-dji-), *n.*,haubergeon, corselet, *m.*

habiliment, *n.*, habillement, apprêt; équipage, *m.*

habilitate, *v.a.*, (ant.) rendre capable de, habiliter. qualifier.

habilitation (-té-), *n.*, (ant.), habilitation, qualification, *f.*

hability, *n.*, (ant.) habileté, faculté; (jur.) habilité, *f.*

habit, *n.*, habitude, coutume, *f.*; (dress-*costume*) habit, habillement, *m.* Riding- —; *habit de cheval, m., amazone, f.* — of the body; *complexion, f., tempérament, m.*

habit, *v.a.*, habiller, vêtir.

habitable (-a-b'l), *adj.*, habitable.

habitant, *n.*, (ant.) habitant, *m.*

habitation (hab'i-té-), *n.*, habitation, *f.*, domicile, *m.*; demeure, *f.*, séjour, *m.*

habitual (-bit'iou-), *adj.*, habituel.

habitually, *adv.*, habituellement, d'habitude.

habituate (-bit'iou-), *v.a.*, habituer, accoutumer.

habitude (-tioude), *n.*, habitude, coutume, routine, *f.*

habnab, *adv.*, (ant.) au hasard; téméraire-ment.

hack, *v.a.*, hacher, couper, écharper; tuer.

hack, *v.n.*, devenir commun; se louer.

hackle (hac'k'l), *n.*, mouche artificielle pour pêcher; filoselle; filasse; soie écrue, *f.*, séran, séran çoir, *m.*

hackle, *v.a.*, sérancer; déchirer.

hackney (hak'ni), or **hack**, *n.*, cheval de louage, *m.*

hackney (hak'ni), *v.a.*, avilir par l'usage; exercer, pratiquer.

hackney-coach (-côtshe), *n.*, fiacre, carrosse de louage, *m.*

hackneyed (-nîde), *adj.*, avili par l'usage; commun.

haddock, *n.*, cabillaud, *m.*, petite morue, *f.*

hæmaturia (hi-mat'iou-), *n.*, (med.) hématurie, *f.*

hæmoptysis (hi-mop-ti-cice), *n.*, (med.) hémoptysie, *f.*

haft (hâfte), *n.*, manche, *m.*, poignée, *f.*

haft, *v.a.*, emmancher.

hag, *n.*, sorcière, vieille salope, furie, *f.*

hag, *v.a.*, tourmenter; effrayer.

haggard, *adj.*, hagard, farouche; laid.

haggardly, *adv.*, d'une manière hideuse, d'un air hagard.

haggish (hag'ghish), *adj.*, laid, difforme.

haggle (hag'g'l), *v.n.*, marchander; barguigner; chipoter.

haggler, *n.*, barguigneur, chipotier, marchandeur, *m.*

hagiographer (hé-dji-o-), *n.*, hagiographe, auteur qui a écrit sur les saints, *m.*

hagiology (hé-dji-), *n.*, traité des choses saintes, *m.*

hag-ridden (-rid'd'n), *adj.*, qui a le cauchemar.

hail (héle), *n.*, grêle, *f.*; salut, *m.*, santé, *f.*

hail, *int.*, salut! salut à vous!

hail, *v.a.*, saluer; (nav.) héler.

hail, *v.n.*, grêler.

hail-fellow (-fèl-lô), *n.*, ami, compagnon intime, *m.*

hailshot(-shote), *n*, mitraille, chevrotine,*f.*

hailstone (-stône), *n.*, grêlon, grain de grêle, *m.*

haily, *adj.*, de grêle.

hair (hère), *n.*, cheveu; poil, *m.*; chevelure. *f.*; (of a beast—*d'un animal*) poil, crin, *m.*; (of a boar—*du sanglier*), soies, *f.pl.* Head of —; *cheveux, m.pl., chevelure, f.sing.* Against the —; *à contre-poil, à contresens.* To a—; *exactement.*

hairbreadth (-brèd'th), *n.*, épaisseur d'un cheveu, *f.* He had a — escape; *il l'a échappé belle.*

hairbrush (-breushe), *n.*, brosse à cheveux,*f.*

haircloth (-c'oth), *n.*, haire, *f.*, cilice, *m.*

hairdresser (-drèss'-), *n.*, coiffeur, *m.*

haired (hèr'de), *adj.*, aux cheveux. Red— ; *qui a les cheveux rouges, aux cheveux rouges.*

hairiness, *n.*, (ich.) quantité de cheveux, *f.*

hairless, *adj.*, chauve, sans cheveux.

hair-sieve (-sive), *n.*, tamis de crin, *m.*

hair-worker (-weurk'-), *n.*, crinier, *m.*

hairy, *adj.*, velu, chevelu, poilu.

hake (héke), *n.*, (ich.) merlus,*m.*, merluche,*f.*

halberd (hôl'beurde), *n.*, hallebarde, *f.*

halberdier (-dire), *n.*, hallebardier, *m.*

halcyon (hal-ci-o'ne), *n.*, (orni.) alcyon, *m.*, *adj.*, tranquille, serein. — days; *des jours heureux.*

hale (héle), *adj.*, robuste, sain, vigoureux.

hale, *v.a.*, haler, tirer, traîner avec violence.

haler, *n* . personne qui tire, *f.*

half (hâfe), *n.* (*halves*), moitié, *f.*, demi, *m.*, demie, *f.* One hour and a — ; *une heure et demie.* To divide in halves ; *partager par moitié.*

half, *adj.*, demi.
half, *adv.*, à demi, à moitié.
half-blooded (-bleud'ède), *adj.*, dégénéré ; de sang croisé, de race croisée.
half-bred (-brède), *adj.*, métis ; bas.
half-brother (-breu'*th*'-), *n.*, frère consanguin *ou* utérin, *m.*
half-moon (-moune), *n.*, demi-lune, *f.*
half-pay (-pè), *n.*, demi-solde, *f.*
half-penny (-pèn'ni), *n.*, un sou ; cinq centimes, *m.*
half-pint (-paï'n'te), *n.*, demi-pinte, *f.*
half-sister, *n.*, sœur consanguine *ou* utérine, *f.*
half-sphere (-sfire), *n.*, hémisphère, *m.*
half-sword (-sorde), *n.*, combat chaud, combat corps à corps, *m.*
half-way (-wè), *adv.*, à mi-chemin.
half-wit (-wite), *n.*, niais, esprit faible, idiot, *m.*, idiote, *f.*
half-witted (-'tède), *adj.*, niais, sot, timbré, idiot.
balituous (ha-lît'iou-), *adj.*, (ant.) fumeux, vaporeux.
hall (hôl), *n.*, salle, *f.* ; palais ; barreau ; vestibule, manoir, *m.*
halleluiah, *or* **hallelujah** (hal-li-liou-ya), *n.*, alléluia, *m.*
halliard, *n.*, (nav.) drisse, *f.*
halloo (-'lou), *n.*, huée, *f.*, holà, *m.*
halloo, *v.a.*, héler ; huer ; exciter par des cris.
halloo! *int.*, holà ! holà ho !
hallow (hal'lô), *v.a.*, sanctifier ; consacrer, dédier.
hallowmas (-mâss), *n.*, la Toussaint, *f.*
hallucination (hal'liou-ci-né-), *n.*, hallucination ; méprise, bévue, *f.*
halm (hô'm), *n.*, paille, *f.* ; chaume, *m.*
halo (hé-lô), *n.*, halo, cercle lumineux, *m.* ; auréole, *f.*
halser (hô'ceur), *n.*, (nav.) haussière, *f.*
halt (hôlte), *n.*, halte, *f.* ; boitement, *m.*
halt, *adj.*, boiteux ; estropié.
halt, *v.n.*, boiter ; s'arrêter, faire halte.
halter, *n.*, licou, *m.*, corde, *f.* ; boiteux, *m.*
halter, *v.a.*, enchevêtrer, mettre un licou.
halve (hâve), *v.a.*, partager en deux.
ham, *n.*, jambon, jarret, *m.*
hamate (hé-), *or* **hamated** (-ède), *adj.*, crochu ; garni de crochets.
hamlet, *n.*, hameau, petit village, *m.*
hammer, *n.*, marteau, *m.* ; enchère, *f.*
hammer, *v.a.*, marteler, forger.
hammer, *v.n.*, avoir de la peine ; hésiter ; bégayer.
hammer-cloth (-cloth), *n.*, housse de siège, *f.*
hammer-dressed (-drès'te), *adj.*, dégrossi au marteau ; (of stone—*de pierre*) équarri.
hammering, *n.*, bruit des marteaux, *m.*
hammock, *n.*, hamac, branle, *m.*
hamper, *n.*, mannequin, *m.* ; hotte, *f.*, panier, *m.*
hamper, *v.a.*, embarrasser, empêtrer.
ham-string (-strigne), *n.*, tendon du jarret, *m.*
ham-string, *v.a.* (preterit and past part., Ham-strung), couper les jarrets à.
hanaper, *n.*, trésorerie, *f.*, échiquier, *m.*
hand, *n.*, main, *f.* ; (measure—*mesure*) palme, *m.* ; signature, *f.* ; (at cards—*aux cartes*) jeu, *m.* ; (of a watch—*d'une montre*) aiguille, *f.* A horse fifteen —s high ; *cheval qui a quinze palmes.* — to —; *corps à corps.*
hand, *v.a.*, donner avec la main ; transmettre, conduire, mener ; passer ; (nav.) ferler les voiles.
hand-barrow (-bar'rô), *n.*, civière, *f.*, brancard, *m.*
hand-basket, *n.*, panier à anse, *m.*, bourriche, *f.*

hand-bell, *n.*, clochette, sonnette, *f.*
hand-bill, *n.*, prospectus, *m.* ; affiche, *f.* ; serpe, *f.*
hand-book (-bouke), *n.*, manuel, *m.*
hand-breadth (-brèd'th), *n.*, paume, *f.* ; empan, *m.*
handcuff (-keufe), *n.*, menotte, *f.*
handcuff, *v.a.*, mettre les menottes à, emmenotter.
handful (-foule), *n.*, poignée ; brassée, *f.* ; (fig.) petit nombre, peu, *m.*
handgallop, *n.*, petit galop, *m.*
hand-grenade (-gri-), *n.*, grenade, *f.*
handgun (-gheune), *n.*, fusil, *m.*
handicraft, *n.*, métier, *m.* ; main-d'œuvre, *f.*
handicraftsman, *n.*, artisan ; manœuvre, *m.*
handily, *adv.*, adroitement ; avec dextérité.
handiness, *n.*, adresse, dextérité, *f.*
handi-work (-weurke), *n.*, ouvrage manuel, *m.*, main-d'œuvre, *f.* ; œuvre, *f.*
handkerchief (-tshife), *n.*, mouchoir, *m.*
handle (ha'n'd'l), *n.*, anse, *f.*, manche, *m.* ; (of a sword—*d'une épée*) poignée ; (of a pump—*de pompe*) brimbale ; (of a frying pan—*de poêle*) queue ; (of a printing-press—*de presse*) manivelle, *f.* ; (of a wheelbarrow—*de brouette*) bras, *m.*
handle (ha-), *v.a.*, manier, toucher ; traiter
hand-leather (lèth'-), *n.*, manique, *f.*
handling, *n.*, maniement, *m.*
handmaid (-méde), *n.*, servante, *f.*
handmill, *n.*, moulin à bras, *m.*
handrail (-réle), *n.*, garde-fou, *m.* ; rampe, *f.*
handsaw (-sô), *n.*, petite scie, scie à main, *f.*
handsel, *n.*, étrenne (première vente), *f.*
handsel, *v.a.*, étrenner.
hands off! *int.*, à bas les mains ! ôtez vos mains ! ôtez-vous !
handsome, *adj.*, beau, bel ; élégant ; gracieux ; bien fait.
handsomely, *adv.*, joliment ; galamment ; convenablement ; avec grâce.
handsomeness, *n.*, beauté ; élégance ; grâce ; générosité, *f.*
handspike (-spaïke), *n.*, levier ; (nav.) anspect, *m.*
handvice (-vaïce), *n.*, étau à main, *m.*
hand-writing (-raït'-), *n.*, écriture, *f.*
handy, *adj.*, adroit, habile ; commode.
handy-blow (-blô), *or* **handy-cuff** (-keufe), *n.*, coup donné avec la main, *m.*
handy-dandy, *n.*, jeu de main, *m.*
hang (hain'gn), *v.a.* (preterit and past part., Hanged *or* Hung), pendre, suspendre ; tendre ; pencher ; (nav.) monter, mettre en place. [En général, *hanged* s'emploie en parlant du supplice.]
hang, *v.n.*, pendre, être pendu ; être retardé, pencher. To — a room ; *tapisser une chambre.* To — about ; *s'attacher.* To — back ; *reculer.* To — by ; *appendre.* To — down ; *baisser.* To — loose ; *pendiller.* To — out ; *arborer.* To — over ; *pencher ; menacer.* To — together ; *s'accorder.* To — the rudder ; *monter le gouvernail.*
hanger, *n.*, coutelas, couteau de chasse, *m.*
hanger-on, *n.*, écornifleur ; parasite, *m.*
hanging, *n.*, pendaison ; tenture, *f.*
hangings, *n.pl.*, tapisserie, tenture, *f.*
hangman, *n.*, bourreau, *m.*
hank, *n.*, peloton ; écheveau ; (nav.) anneau de bois, *m.*
hanker, *v.n.*, désirer ardemment ; soupirer après ; avoir bien envie ; convoiter.
hankering, *n.*, penchant, *m.*, inclination ; grande envie, *f.*, vif désir, *m.*
hap, *v.n.*, advenir, arriver par hasard.
hap, *or* **hap-hazard**, *n.*, hasard, sort ; accident, *m.* ; fortune, *f.*
hapless, *adj.*, misérable ; infortuné.
haply, *adv.*, par hasard ; peut-être.

happen, *v.n.*, arriver, avenir ; se passer; tomber.

happily, *adv.*, heureusement, par bonheur.

happiness, *n.*, félicité, *f.*, bonheur, *m.*

happy, *adj.*, heureux, fortuné.

harangue, *n.*, harangue, *f.*, discours oratoire, *m.*

harangue, *v.a.*, haranguer, faire un discours.

haranguer (ha-ra'n'gh'eur), *n.*, harangueur, orateur, *m.*

harass, *n.*, désordre ; ravage, dégât, *m.*

harass, *v.a.*, harasser, lasser, fatiguer.

harbinger (hâr-bi'n'djeur), *n.*, avant-coureur, précurseur; fourrier, *m.*

harbour (hâr-beur), *n.*, havre, port ; refuge; gîte, *m.*

harbour, *v.a.* and *n.*, loger ; recéler ; héberger; (fig.) entretenir, avoir. How can you — such a thought ? *comment pouvez-vous entretenir, avoir, une pareille idée?*

harbourage (-édje), *n.*, abri, asile, *m.*; retraite, *f.*

harbourer, *n.*, receleur, *m.*

harbourless, *adj.*, sans port, sans abri, sans asile.

hard (hârde), *adj.*, dur, ferme, solide ; difficile, rude, cruel, rigoureux. — cherries ; *guignes, f.pl.* — -drinking ; *débauche.* — frost ; *forte gelée, f.* — of belief; *incrédule.* — of hearing; *dur d'oreille.* — to deal with; *intraitable.* — words; *dureté, f.pl.*

hard, *adv.*, fort, fort et ferme, rudement ; difficilement ; beaucoup.

hardbound (-baou'n'de), *adj.*, constipé.

hard-by (-ba'ye), *adv.*, tout près, auprès.

harden, *v.a.*, endurcir, durcir, rendre dur.

harden, *v.n.*, durcir, s'endurcir, devenir dur.

hardfavoured (-fé-veurde), *adj.*, laid ; disgracié de la nature.

hardfought (-fôte), *adj.*, fortement contesté ; acharné, opiniâtre.

hardhanded (-ède), *adj.*, dont les mains sont endurcies au travail.

hard-hearted (-hârt'ède), *adj.*, dur, insensible, cruel.

hard-heartedness, *n.*, dureté de cœur, insensibilité, inhumanité, *f.*

hardihood (-houde), *n.*, hardiesse, audace, intrépidité, *f.*

hardily, *adv.*, hardiment ; sévèrement ; sans mollesse.

hardiness, *n.*, hardiesse, *f.*; tempérament robuste, *m.*

hard-laboured (-lé-beurde), *adj.*, travaillé avec soin, élaboré.

hardly, *adv.*, à peine ; rudement.

hardmouthed (-maouth'de), *adj.*, insensible au frein ; grossier, dur en paroles.

hardness, *n.*, dureté, fermeté, solidité; rigueur, difficulté ; avarice, *f.*

hards (hardze), *n.pl.*, chènevottes, *f.pl*; étoupe, *f.*

hardship, *n.*, dureté ; fatigue, misère, privation, *f.*; travail, *m.*

hardware (-wére), *n.*, quincaille, quincaillerie, *f.*

hardwareman, *n.*, quincaillier, *m.*

hardy, *adj.*, hardi, courageux ; fort, robuste.

hare (hére), *n.*, lièvre, *m.* A young — ; *levraut, m.*

harebell, *n.*, (bot.) scille penchée, jacinthe des prés, *f.*

harebrained (-bré'n'de), *adj.*, écervelé ; volage, léger.

harefoot (-foute), *n.*, (bot.) pied-de-lièvre, *m.*

harelip, *n.*, bec-de-lièvre, *m.*

harem (hé-), *n.*, harem, *m.*

hare's-ear (-z'îre), *n.*, (bot.) buplèvre, *m.*, oreille-de-lièvre, *f.*

haricot (-cô), *n.*, (cook.) haricot. *m.*

hark (-hârke), *or* **hearken** (hârk'-), *v.n.*, écouter, prêter l'oreille, entendre.

hark! *int.*, écoutez !

harl (hârle), *n.*, filaments du chanvre, *m.pl.* ; filasse, *f.*

harlequin (hâr-li-kine), *n.*, arlequin, *m.*

harlot (hâr-lote), *n.*, (l.ex.) putain, prostituée, *f.*

harlotry, *n.*, prostitution, *f.*, libertinage, *m.*

harm (hârme), *n.*, tort, dommage, préjudice, mal, malheur, *m.*

harm, *v.a.*, nuire, faire du mal.

harmful (-foule), *adj.*, nuisible, malfaisant ; dangereux.

harmfully, *adv.*, dangereusement ; avec préjudice ; d'une manière nuisible.

harmfulness, *n.*, préjudice, dommage, *m.*

harmless, *adj.*, innocent, inoffensif.

harmlessly, *adv.*, innocemment.

harmlessness, *n.*, innocence, *f.*

harmonic, *or* **harmonical**, *adj.*, harmonique, musical.

harmonious (-mô-), *adj.*, harmonieux ; mélodieux.

harmoniously, *adv.*, harmonieusement, mélodieusement.

harmoniousness (-mô-), *or* **harmony**, *n.*, harmonie ; mélodie ; concorde, *f.*; accord, *m.*

harmonize (-mô-naize), *v.a.*, rendre harmonieux ; cadencer ; accorder ; ajuster.

harmonize, *v.n.*, s'accorder ; correspondre.

harmonizer, *n.*, conciliateur ; (mus.) harmoniste, *m.*

harness, *n.*, harnais, *m.*

harness, *v.a.*, harnacher, enharnacher.

harness-maker (-mék'-), *n.*, fabricant de harnais, sellier ; bourrelier, *m.*

harness-making (-mek'-), *n.*, fabrication de harnais ; bourrellerie, *f.*

harp (hârpe), *n.*, harpe, *f.*

harp, *v.n.*, pincer, *ou* jouer de la harpe ; répéter ; répétailler.

harper, *n.*, joueur de harpe, harpiste, *m.*

harping-iron (-aï'eurne), *or* **harpoon** (-poune), *n.*, harpon, *m.*

harpooner, *n.*, harponneur, *m.*

harpsichord (hârp'si-corde), *n.*, clavecin, *m.*

harpy, *n.*, harpie, *f.*

harridan, *n.*, haridelle, rosse, *f.*

harrier, *n.*, lévrier, *m.*; (orni.) soubuse, *f.*, busard, *m.*

harrow (har'rô), *n.*, herse, *f.*

harrow, *v.a.*, herser, déchirer ; agiter; torturer.

harrower, *n.*, herseur, *m.*

harry, *v.a.*, (ant.) harceler, harasser, tourmenter; piller.

harsh (hârshe), *adj.*, rude, âpre; dur ; sévère.

harshly, *adv.*, rudement ; sévèrement ; âprement.

harshness, *n.*, rudesse, âpreté ; sévérité, *f.*

harslet (hârs'-), *or* **haslet** (hâs'-), *n.*, fressure de cochon, *f.*

hart (hârte), *n.*, cerf, *m.*

harts-horn, *n.*, corne de cerf ; (med.) essence de corne de cerf, *f.*

hartstongue (-teu'n'ghe), *n.*, (bot.) scolopendre, langue-de-cerf, *f.*

hart-wort (-weurte), *n.*, (bot.) séséli de Marseille, *m.*

harum-scarum (hér'eume-skér'eume), *adj.*, écervelé, braque, étourdi ; en l'air.

harvest (hârvèste), *n.*, moisson ; récolte, *f.*

harvest, *v.a.*, moissonner ; récolter.

harvester, *or* **harvestman** (-ma'n), *n.*, moissonneur, *m.*

harvest-home (-hôme), *n.*, chanson du moissonneur ; fête des moissonneurs quand la moisson est finie, *f.*

harvest-time (-taïme), *n.*, temps de la moisson, *m.*

hash, *n.*, hachis, *m.*, galimafrée, capilotade, *f.*

hash, *v.a.*, hacher, couper en petits morceaux.

haslet, *n. V.* **harslet.**

hasp (hâspe), *n.*, fermoir, crochet ; anneau, *m.*

hasp, *v.a.*, fermer avec des crochets, accrocher, verrouiller.

hassock, *n.*, paillasson, agenouilloir, *m.*

haste (héste), *n.*, hâte, vitesse ; diligence ; colère, *f.*

haste, *or* **hasten** (hé's'n), *v.a.*, hâter, dépêcher, presser.

haste, *or* **hasten**, *v.n.*, se hâter, se dépêcher, se presser.

hastener, *n.*, personne qui se hâte, *f.*

hastily (hés'-), *adv.*, à la hâte ; brusquement ; en colère.

hastiness, *n.*, promptitude, hâte, *f.* ; emportement, *m.*

hastings, *n.pl.*, primeur, *f.*, fruits, légumes précoces, hâtifs, *m.pl.* Green —; *pois hâtifs, m.pl.*

hasty (hés'ti), *adj.*, prompt, diligent ; pétulant, violent, emporté.

hasty-pudding (-poud'digne), *n.*, bouillie, *f.*

hat, *n.*, chapeau, *m.* —s off ! *chapeaux bas !*

hatband, *n.*, cordon de chapeau, bourdalou, *m.*

hatbox, *or* **hatcase** (-kéce), *n.*, boîte à chapeau, *f.*

hatch, *n.*, couvée ; éclosion ; découverte ; porte coupée ; (nav.) écoutille, *f.*

hatch, *v.a.*, faire éclore ; produire ; tramer ; hacher, faire des hachures.

hatch, *v.n.*, couver, être prêt à éclore.

hatchel, *n.*, séran, peigne à chanvre, échanvroir, sérançoir, *m.*

hatchel, *v.a.*, sérancer, passer par le séran ; échanvrer ; vexer.

hatcheller, *n.*, séranceur, *m.*

hatcher, *n.*, inventeur, auteur, *m.*

hatches (hatsh'ize), *n.pl.* (nav.) panneaux des écoutilles, *m.pl.*

hatchet (hatsh'ète), *n.*, cognée, hachette, *f.*

hatchment, *n.*, (her.) écusson, *m.*, armoiries, *f.pl.*

hatchway (-wè), *n.*, (nav.), écoutille, *f.*

hate (héte), *n.*, haine, aversion, inimitié, *f.*

hate, *v.a.*, haïr, détester, abhorrer.

hateful (-foule), *adj.*, haïssable, odieux, détestable.

hatefully, *adv.*, odieusement.

hatefulness, *n.*, qualité odieuse, abomination, noirceur, *f.*

hater (hét'eur), *n.*, ennemi, *m.*, personne qui hait, *f.*

hatred (hé'trède), *n.*, haine, aversion, inimitié, *f.*

hatter (hat'teur), *n.*, chapelier, *m.*

hattock, *n.*, tas de gerbes de blé, *m.*

hauberk (-beurke), *n.*, haubert, *m.* ; cotte de mailles, cuirasse, *f.*

haughtily (hô-ti), *adv.*, hautainement, fièrement.

haughtiness, *n*, hauteur, fierté, arrogance, *f.*

haughty (hô-ti), *adj.*, altier, fier, hautain, arrogant.

haul (hôl), *n.*, action de tirer, de traîner, *f.* ; tiraillement ; coup de filet, *m.*

haul, *v.a.*, tirer ; tirailler ; haler ; traîner.

haum (hôme), *n.*, chaume, *m.* ; paille, *f.*

haunch (hân'she), *n.*, hanche, *f.* ; (of venison—*de renaison*) cuisse, *f.*

haunt (hâ'n'te), *n.*, repaire ; lieu que l'on fréquente, *m.* ; habitude, *f.*

haunt, *v.a.*, hanter, fréquenter, visiter souvent.

haunter, *n.*, personne qui hante, *f.* ; visiteur habituel, *m.*

haunting, *n.*, fréquentation, hantise, *f.*

hautboy (hô-boï), *n.*, hautbois, *m.*

have (hève), *v.a.* (*preterit* and *past part.*, Had), avoir, tenir.

haven (hé'v'n), *n.*, havre, port ; asile, *m.*

having (hav'igne), *n.*, avoir, *m.* ; possession, fortune, *f.* ; biens, *m.pl.*

havoc, *n.*, dégât, ravage, *m.*

havoc, *v.a.*, ravager, dévaster.

haw (hô), *n.*, fruit de l'aubépine, *m.* ; (vct.) caroncule, *f.*

haw, *v.n.*, hésiter en parlant ; ânonner.

hawk (hôke), *n.*, épervier, faucon, *m.*

hawk, *v.a.* and *n.*, chasser à l'oiseau ; colporter.

hawk-bell, *n.*, grelot ; (her.) grillet, *m.*

hawked (hôk'te), *adj.*, aquilin ; crié dans les rues.

hawker, *n.*, colporteur, *m.*

hawse-hole (hôce-hôl), *n.*, (nav.) écubier, *m.*

hawser (hôss'-), *or* **halser** (hôss'-), *n.*, (nav.) haussière, *f.*, grelin, câblot, *m.*

hawthorn (hô-thorne), *n.*, aubépine, *f.*

hay, *n.*, foin, *m.*

haybird (-beurde), *n.*, (orni.) grand pouillot, *m.*

haycock, *n.*, (agri.) veillotte, *f.*

hayharvest (-vèste), *n.*, fenaison ; récolte des foins, *f.*

hayloft, *n*, grenier à foin, fenil, *m.*

haymaker (-mék'-), *n.*, faneur ; faucheur, *m.*

haymaking (-mék'-), *n.*, fenaison, *f.*

hay-market (-mâr-kète), *n.*, marché au foin, *m.*

hayrick, *or* **haystack**, *n.*, meule de foin, *f.*

hazard, *n.*, hasard, *m.* ; (at cards—*aux cartes*) chance, *f.*

hazard, *v.a.*, risquer, hasarder.

hazard, *v.n.*, se hasarder ; s'aventurer.

hazarder, *n.*, personne qui hasarde, *f.*

hazardous, *adj.*, hasardeux ; dangereux.

hazardously, *adv.*, hasardeusement, dangereusement.

haze, *n.*, brouillard, *m.* ; brume, *f.*

hazel (hé-z'l), *or* **hazel-tree** (-tri), *n.*, noisetier, coudrier, *m.*

hazel, *adj.*, de coudrier ; couleur de noisette.

hazel-nut (-neute), *n.*, noisette, *f.*

hazy (héz'i), *adj.*, brumeux.

he (hi), *pron.*, il, celui, lui. [*He* s'emploie souvent comme préfixe pour désigner les animaux mâles. Ex.: *he-elephant*, éléphant mâle ; *he-goat*, bouc.]

head (hède), *n.*, tête, *f.* ; chef ; (nav.) avant, éperon, *m.* ; (of hair—*cheveux*) chevelure, *f.*, cheveux, *m.pl.* ; (of a book—*de livre*) titre, *m.* ; (of a river—*de rivière*) source ; (of an arrow—*de flèche*) pointe ; (of a cane—*de canne*) pomme ; (of a wild boar—*de sanglier*) hure, *f.* ; (of a college—*de collège*) principal, *m.*

head, *v.a.*, conduire, commander en chef ; se mettre à la tête de ; diriger ; (pins—*épingles*) entêter ; (nails—*clous*) façonner la tête de.

head, *adj.*, principal, en chef.

headache (-éke), *n.*, mal de tête, *m.* ; migraine, *f.*

headband, *n.*, bandeau, *m.*, bande, *f.*

header, *n.*, chef ; (of nails—*de clous*) ouvrier qui façonne les têtes ; (of pins—*d'épingles*) entêteur, *m.*

headdress, *n.*, coiffe ; coiffure, *f.*

headiness, *n.*, emportement, *m.* ; impétuosité ; étourderie ; (of drink—*des boissons*) qualité capiteuse, *f.*

heading, *n.*, (print.) lettrine, *f.* ; (of casks—*de tonneaux*) fond, *m.*

headland, *n.*, cap, *m.* ; pointe, *f.*

headless, *adj.*, sans tête ; sans chef.

headlong, *adv.*, la tête en avant, la tête la première ; (fig.) à corps perdu, en étourdi, de gaieté de cœur.

headlong, *adj.*, escarpé ; (fig.) irréfléchi, inconsidéré.

headman (-ma'ne), *n.*, chef, *m.*

headmost, (-môste), *adj.*, de tête, en tête, à la tête, le premier.

headpiece (-pîce), *n.*, armet, casque, *m.* ; (fig.) tête, caboche, *f.*

head-quarters (-kwor-teurze), *n.pl.*, quartier général, *m.sing.*

headship, *n.*, autorité suprême, *f.*

headsman (hèdz'ma'ne), *n.*, bourreau, *m.*

headstall (-stôl), *n.*, têtière, *f.*

head-stick, *n.*, (nav.), corne, *f.* ; bois de foc, *m.*

headstone (-stône), *n.*, pierre angulaire ; pierre tumulaire, tombe, *f.*

headstrong, *adj.*, opiniâtre, têtu, obstiné.

headway, *n.*, (nav.) marche, *f.*

heady, *adv.*, violent ; emporté ; impétueux ; (of drink—*des boissons*) capiteux.

heal (hîl), *v.a.*, guérir ; cicatriser ; (fig.) apaiser.

heal, *v.n.*, guérir ; se guérir ; se cicatriser.

healer, *n.*, guérisseur, *m.*, guérisseuse, *f.*

healing, *adj.*, propre à guérir ; salutaire. The — art ; *l'art de guérir.*

healing, *n.*, guérison, *f.*

health (hèlth), *n.*, santé, *f.* ; toast, *m.* ; (jur.) salubrité, *f.* To drink any one's — ; *boire à la santé de quelqu'un.*

healthful (-foule), *adj.*, bien portant ; en bonne santé ; sain, salubre ; salutaire.

healthfully, *adv.*, en bonne santé ; salutairement.

healthfulness, *n.*, santé ; salubrité, *f.*

healthily, *adv.*, en santé ; sainement.

healthiness, *n.*, santé ; salubrité ; nature salutaire, *f.*

healthless, *adj.*, malade, infirme, faible, valétudinaire.

healthy, *adj.*, bien portant ; en bonne santé ; sain ; salutaire.

heam (hîme), *n.*, (of animals—*des animaux*) arrière-faix, délivre, *m.*

heap (hîpe), *n.*, tas, monceau, amas, *m.*

heap, *v.a.*, entasser, amonceler. To — up ; *entasser ; amonceler.*

heaper, *n.*, personne qui entasse, *f.*

heapy, *adj.*, entassé, amoncelé.

hear (hîre), *v.a.*, (*preterit and past part.*, Heard), entendre, entendre dire ; écouter ; (fig.) apprendre ; (fig.) exaucer. To — say ; *entendre dire ; ouïr dire.*

hear, *v.n.*, entendre ; écouter. To — of ; *entendre parler de.* To — from any one ; *recevoir des nouvelles de quelqu'un.* To — of any one ; *avoir des nouvelles de quelqu'un.* Let us — from you ; *donnez-nous de vos nouvelles.*

heard (heurde), *past part.* V. **hear.**

hearer, *n.*, personne qui écoute, qui entend, *f.* ; auditeur, assistant, *m.*

hearing, *n.*, (the sense—*sens*) ouïe ; (of witnesses—*de témoins*) audition ; (jur.) audience, *f.* To be hard of — ; *avoir l'oreille dure.* He said it in my — ; *il l'a dit devant moi.*

hearken (hàrk'ène), *v.n.*, écouter.

hearkener, *n.*, écouteur, *m.*, écouteuse, *f.*

hearsay (hîr'sè), *n.*, oui-dire, *m.*

hearse (heurse), *n.*, corbillard, char funèbre, *m.*

hearse, *v.a.*, mettre dans le cercueil ; (fig.) ensevelir.

heart (hàrte), *n.*, cœur ; (centre) centre, *m.* ; (nav.) moque, *f.* By — ; *par cœur.* To take to — ; *prendre à cœur.*

heart-ache (-éke), *n.*, douleur de cœur, *f.* ; chagrin, *m.* ; affliction, *f.*

heart-bond, *n.*, (mas.) parpaing, *m.*

heart-break (-brèke), *n.*, crève-cœur, *m.*

heart-breaking, *n.*, déchirement de cœur, *m.*

heart-breaking, *adj.*, qui fend le cœur ; navrant.

heart-broken (-brôk'n), *adj.*, qui a le cœur navré, brisé.

heartburn (-beurne), *n.*, ardeur d'estomac, (med.) gastralgie, cardialgie, *f.*

heart-burning, *n.*, ardeur d'estomac ; (fig.) aigreur, animosité, *f.*

heart-dear (-dire), *adj.*, chéri.

heart-ease (-ize), *n.*, paix du cœur, *f.*

hearted (hàrtède), *adj.*, doué d'un cœur. Broken- — ; *qui a le cœur navré, brisé.* Good- — ; *qui a bon cœur.* Hard- — ; *au cœur dur.* Light- — ; *au cœur gai.* Open- — ; *au cœur sincère.* franc. Tender- — ; *tendre.* Stout- — ; *courageux.*

heartedness, *n.*, cœur, *m.*, de cœur, du cœur. Cold- — ; *froideur de cœur, insensibilité, f.* Hard- — ; *dureté de cœur, f.*

hearten (hàr't'n), *v.n.*, encourager ; animer.

hearth (hàrth), *n.*, âtre ; foyer, *m.*

hearth-rug (-reughe), *n.*, tapis de foyer, *m.*

hearthstone (-stône), *n.*, pierre de cheminée, *f.*

heartily (hàrt'ili), *adv.*, cordialement ; de bon cœur ; vigoureusement ; (of eating—*manger*) de bon appétit.

heartiness (hàrt'-), *n.*, sincérité ; cordialité ; (of the appetite—*de l'appétit*) force, *f.*

heartless (hàrt'-), *adj.*, sans cœur ; lâche.

heartlessly, *adv.*, sans cœur ; lâchement.

heartlessness, *n.*, manque de courage, *m.* ; insensibilité, *f.*

heart's-blood, or **heart-blood** (-bleude), *n.*, le plus pur de son sang, *m.* ; (fig.) essence, *f.*

heart's-ease (hàrt's'ize), *n.*, (bot.) pensée sauvage, *f.*

heart-sick, *adj.*, qui a la mort dans l'âme ; qui a le cœur mort.

heart-sore, *n.*, plaie du cœur, *f.*

heart-string (-strigne), *n.pl.*, fibre, *f.*, nerf, tendon, *m.*, du cœur.

heart-struck (-streuke), *adj.*, touché au cœur ; consterné ; terrifié ; atterré.

heart-wounded (-wou'n'dède), *adj.*, blessé au cœur.

hearty (hàrti), *adj.*, du cœur ; sincère ; cordial ; robuste ; (of meals—*repas*) abondant ; (of eaters—*mangeur*) fort.

heat (hîte), *n.*, chaleur, ardeur ; (fig.) colère, animosité, *f.*

heat, *v.a.*, chauffer, échauffer.

heat, *v.n.*, chauffer ; s'échauffer.

heated (hit'ède), *adj.*, chauffé ; échauffé.

heater (hît'-), *n.*, personne qui chauffe ; chose qui chauffe, *f.* ; moine (pour chauffer), *m.*

heath (hîth), *n.*, lande, bruyère, *f.*

heath-cock, *n.*, coq de bruyère, *m.*

heathen (hi-th'n), *n.* (heathen ou heathens), païen, *m.*, païenne, *f.*

heathen, *adj.*, païen.

heathenish, *adj.*, de païen.

heathenishly, *adv.*, en païen.

heathenism, *n.*, paganisme, *m.* ; (fig.) barbarie, *f.*

heathy (hîth'i), *adj.*, plein de bruyères.

heave (hîve), *n.*, secousse, *f.* ; soulèvement, *m.* ; élévation ; agitation, *f.*

heave, *v.a.* (*preterit*, Heaved, Hove ; *past part.*, Heaved, Hoven), lever ; élever ; soulever ; jeter, lancer : (a sigh—*un soupir*) pousser ; (nav.) haler, virer.

heave, *v.n.*, haleter, soulever ; (of the heart—*du cœur*) palpiter, battre ; (nav.) haler, virer. To — to ; (nav.) *mettre en panne.* To — in sight ; (nav.) *paraître ; être en vue.*

heaven (hèv'n), *n.*, ciel, *m.* ; cieux, *m.pl.*

heaven-born, *adj.*, divin, céleste.

heaven-bred (-brède), *adj.*, céleste.

heaven-built (-bilte), *adj.*, céleste.

heavenly, adj., céleste.
heavenly, adv., d'une manière céleste ; divinement.
hoaver (hïv'-), n., chargeur, porteur, m.
heaves (hïv'ze), n.pl., (vet.) pousse, f.sung.
heavily (hèv'-), adv., pesamment ; lourdement.
heaviness (hèv'-), n., pesanteur ; lourdeur. f. ; poids, m. ; (fig.) tristesse, f.
heaving (hïv'-), adj., qui se soulève ; soulevé.
heaving (hïv'-), n., agitation ; (of the sea—de la mer) soulèvement, m.
heavy (hèv'-), adj., lourd, pesant ; (of the sea —de la mer) gros ; (of the roads—des routes) gras ; (fig.) triste.
hebdomadal, or **hebdomadary**, adj., hebdomadaire.
hebdomadary, n., membre d'un chapitre, chanoine, m.
hebetate (hèb'i-), v.a., hébéter.
hebetation, n., état hébété, m.
hebraism (hï-bra-iz'm), n., hébraïsme, m.
hebrew (hï-brou), n., Hébreu ; Israélite, m., f. ; (language—langue) hébreu, m.
hebrew, adj., hébraïque ; hébreu ; israélite.
hecatomb (hèk'a-toume), n., hécatombe, f.
heckle (hèk'k'l), v.a., sérancer.
heckle, n., séran, sérançoir, m.
heckler, n., séranceur, m.
hectare (hèk'târ), n., hectare, m.
hectic, or **hectical**, adj., hectique ; étique.
hectogram, or **hectogramme**, n., hectogramme, m.
hectolitre, n., hectolitre, m.
hectometre (-mé'tr), n., hectomètre, m.
hector (-teur), n., fendant, fier-à-bras ; matamore, m.
hector, v.n., faire le fendant.
hector, v.a., malmener.
hedge (hèdje), n., haie, f.
hedge, v.a., entourer d'une haie ; border.
hedge, v.n., se cacher ; bouder ; parier pour et contre.
hedgebill, or **hedging-bill**, n., serpe, f. ; croissant, m.
hedge-born,adj.,né dans la boue ; vil,obscur.
hedge-hog (-hoghe), n., hérisson, f.
hedge-note (-nôte), n., poésie de carrefour, de la halle, f.
hedge-pig, n., jeune hérisson, m.
hedger, n., faiseur de haies, m.
hedgesparrow(-rô), n., fauvette d'hiver, f.
heed (hïde), n., attention, f. ; soin, m. To give—; faire attention. To take—; prendre garde.
hoed, v.a., observer,écouter ; faire attention à.
heedful (-foule), adj., attentif, vigilant.
heedfully. adv., attentivement ; avec soin.
heedfulness, n., attention, vigilance, f. ; soin, m.
heedless, adj., étourdi, inattentif.
heedlessly, adv., sans soin, négligemment ; par mégarde.
heedlessness, n., inattention, négligence, étourderie, f.
heel (hïl), n., talon ; éperon, m.
heel, v.n., danser ; (nav.) avoir un faux côté. To — over (nav.) ; donner la bande, être à la bande.
heel, v.a., mettre un talon à ; (a cock—un coq de combat) armer.
heel-piece (-pïce), n., bout ; talon, m.
heft (hèfte), n., poids, m.
hegira (hi-dji-ra, ou hèdj'i-ra), n., hégire, f.
heifer (hèf'-), n., génisse, f.
heighho ! (hï'hô), int., ho ! ah !
height (haïte), n., élévation, hauteur, f. ; (fig.) plus haut point, comble ; (centre) fort, cœur, m.

heighten (haï't'n), v.a., relever, rehausser, embellir, orner ; accroître.
heinous (hè-), adj., odieux, affreux, atroce.
heinously, adv., odieusement,affreusement, atrocement, avec atrocité.
heinousness, n., atrocité, énormité, f.
heir (ère), n., héritier ; successeur, m.
heiress. n., héritière, f.
heirless, adj., sans héritier.
heirloom (-loume), n., meuble de famille, m,
heirship, n., hérédité, f.
heliac (hi-li-), or **heliacal** (hi-laï-), adj. héliaque.
heliocentric, or **heliocentrical** (hi-), adj., héliocentrique.
helioscope (hi-li-o-scôpe), n., hélioscope, m.
heliotrope (hi-li-o-trôpe), n., (bot., min.) héliotrope, m.
helix (hi-likse), n. (helices), hélice ; (anat.) hélix, limaçon, m.
hell, n., enfer, m.
hell-cat, n., furie, harpie, f.
hellebore (-li-bôre), n., (bot.) ellébore, m.
hellenic (hèl-lè'n'-), adj., hellénique.
hellenism, n., hellénisme, m.
hellenist, n., helléniste, m.
hell-hound (-haou'n'de), n., chien de l'enfer ; (fig.) tison d'enfer, m.
hellish, adj., infernal, d'enfer.
hellishly, adv., infernalement.
hellishness, n., caractère infernal, m.
helm, n., timon, gouvernail, m.
helm, v.a., guider ; conduire.
helmet (-mète), n., casque, m.
helminthic (-thike), n., (med.) anthelminthique ; vermifuge, m.
helminthology (-thol-o-dji), n., helminthologie, f.
helmsman (hèlm'z'ma'n), n., timonier, m.
help (hèlpe), n., aide, f. ; secours ; remède, m. ; ressource, f. — ! au secours !
help (hèlpe), v.a.,aider, secourir, assister, empêcher ; (at table—à table) servir. I cannot — it ; je n'y puis rien. How can it be —ed ? qu'y faire ? que voulez-vous ? How can I — it ? que voulez-vous que j'y fasse ?
help, v.n., aider ; se défendre, s'empêcher. I cannot — saying ; je ne puis m'empêcher de dire.
helper, n., aide ; auxiliaire, m.
helpful (-foule), adj., secourable ; utile.
helpless, adj., sans secours, faible, impuissant ; sans ressource.
helplessly, adv., sans secours ; faiblement ; sans ressource.
helplessness, n., faiblesse, impuissance, destitution, f.
helpmate, n., aide, compagnon, m., compagne, f.
helter-skelter, adv., pêle-mêle, sens dessus dessous.
helve, n., manche de hache, m.
helve, v.a., emmancher une hache.
helvetic, adj., helvétique.
hem (hème), n., ourlet ; bord, m.
hem, v.a., ourler ; border. To — in ; enfermer ; entourer.
hem, int., hem !
hem, v.n., faire hem.
hematite (hè'm'a-taïte),n.,(min.) hématite,f.
hematocele (hi-ma-to-cïle), n., hématocèle, f.
hematosis (hi-ma-to-ciss), n., hématose, f.
hemerocallis (hèm'i-) n.,hémérocalle, f.
hemi (hè-mi), prefixe grec ἡμί, demi, semi.
hemicycle (-caï'k'l), n., hémicycle, m.
hemiplegy (-plèdj'i), hémiplégie, f.
hemiptera (hi-mip-tira), n.pl., (ent.) hémiptères, m.pl.
hemisphere (hèm'i-sfire), n., hémisphère, m.

hemispheric. *or* **hemispherical,** *adj.*, hémisphérique.

hemistich (hèm'is'tike), *n.*, hémistiche, *m.*

hemlock (hèm'-), *n.*, ciguë, *f.*

hemoptysis (hi-mop-ti-ciss), *n.* *V.* **hæmoptysis.**

hemorrhage (hèm'or-'radje), *n.*, hémorragie, *f.*

hemorrhoidal (-roïd'-), *adj.*, hémorroïdal.

hemorrhoids (-roïd'ze), *n.pl.*, hémorroïdes, *f.pl.*

hemp (hè'm'pe), *n.*, chanvre, *m.*; étoupe, *f.*

hemp-comb (-côme), *n.*, séran, sérançoir, *m.*

hemp-dresser (-dress'-), *n.*, séranceur, chanvrier, *m.*

hempen (hèm'p'n), *adj.*, de chanvre.

hemp-field (-filde), *n.*, chènevière, *f.*

hemp-seed (-side), *n.*, chènevis, *m.*

hen (hène), *n.*, poule ; femelle, *f.*

henbane (hè'n'-), *n.*, jusquiame, *f.*

hence (hè'n'-), *adv.*, d'ici ; de là ; loin d'ici.

henceforth (-forth), *adv.*, désormais ; dorénavant.

henceforward (-worde), *adv.*, dorénavant, désormais.

hen-coop (-coupe), *n.*, cage à poule, mue, *f.*

hendecagon (hè'n'dèk-'), *n.*, (geom.) endécagone, hendécagone, *m.*

hendecasyllabic (hè'n'dèk'-), *adj.*, hendécasyllabe.

hendecasyllable, *n.*, hendécasyllabe, *m.*

hen-hearted (-hârt'ède), *adj.*, lâche, poltron.

hen-house (-haouce), *n.*, poulailler, *m.*

hen-pecked (-pèk'te), *adj.*, gouverné par sa femme.

hen-roost (-rouste), *n.*, juchoir, *m.*

hepatic, *or* **hepatical** (hè-),*adj.*, hépatique.

hepatite (hèp'a-taïte), *n.*, (min.) hépatite, *f.*

hepatitis (-taï-tice),*n.*, (med.) hépatite, *f.*

heptagon (hèp'ta-gone), *n.*, (geom.) heptagone, *m.*

heptandria (hèp'-), *n.*, (bot.) heptandrie, *f.*

heptarchy (hèp'tàr-ki), *n.*, heptarchie, *f.*

her (heure), *pron.*, (person.) elle, la, lui; (possess.) son, sa, ses.

herald (hèr'-), *n.*, héraut ; messager, *m.*

herald, *v.a.*, proclamer. To — into ; *introduire dans.*

heraldic, *adj.*, héraldique.

heraldry, *n.*, science héraldique, *f.* ; blason, *m.*

herb (eurbe), *n.*, herbe, *f.*

herbaceous (-bé-sheusse), *adj.*, herbacé.

herbage (-bédje), *n.*, herbage, pâturage, *m.*

herbal (heurbal), *n.*, herbier, *m.*

herbal, *adj.*, des herbes.

herbalist, *n.*, herboriste, *m.*

herbarium (hèr-bé-rieume), *n.* (*herbariums*), (bot.) herbier, *m.*

herbary (heur-), *n.*, jardin botanique, *m.*

herbescent (hèr'-), *adj.*, herbeux.

herbivorous, *adj.*, herbivore.

herborist, *n.*, herboriste, *m.*

herborization (heur-bo-ri-zé-), *n.*, herborisation, *f.*

herborize (hèr-bo-raïze), *or* **herbarize** (heur-ba-raïze), *v n.*, herboriser.

herbous (ant.), *or* **herby** (heurb'-), *adj.*, herbu, herbeux.

herb-shop (-shope), *n.*, herboristerie, *f.*

herbwoman (heurbwoum'a'n), *n.*, herbière, *f.*

herculean (hèr-kiou-li-) *adj.*, herculéen.

herd (heurde), *n.*, troupeau, *m.* ; troupe, *f.*

herd, *v.n.*, vivre en sociétés ; vivre en troupes.

herdsman (heurdz'-), *n.*, pâtre, *m.*

here (hîre), *adv.*, ici ; par ici.

hereabout (-abaoute), *or* **hereabouts** (-a-baoutse), *adv.*, par ici ; près d'ici.

hereafter. *adv.*, désormais, dorénavant ; dans la vie future.

hereat. *adv.*, à ceci, à cela.

hereby (-ba'ye), *adv.*, par ce moyen, par là ; par ceci.

hereditament (hèr'i-), *n.*, (jur.) bien, *m.*

hereditarily (hi-rèd'-), *adv.*, héréditairement.

hereditary (hi-rèd'-), *adj.*, héréditaire.

herein (hir -), *adv.*, en ceci ; ici.

hereof (hîr'ove), *adv.*, de ceci, de cela.

hereon (hîr'-), *adv.*, là-dessus ; sur ceci, sur cela.

heresiarch (hè ri-zi-ârke),*n.*,hérésiarque,*m.*

heresiarchy (-ki), *n.*, principale hérésie, *f.*

heresy (hèr'i-ci), *n.*, hérésie, *f.*

heretic (hèr'i-), *n.*, hérétique, *m.*,*f.*

heretical, *adj.*, hérétique.

heretically, *adv.*, en hérétique ; avec hérésie.

hereto (hîr-tou), *or* **hereunto** (hîr-eu'n'tou), *adv.*, à ceci, à cela.

heretofore (hîr-tou-fôre), *adv.*, jusqu'à présent ; jadis.

hereupon (hîr-eup'-), *adv.*,là-dessus, sur ces entrefaites.

herewith (hîr-with), *adv.*, là-dessus ; avec ceci.

heritable (hèr-it-a-b'l), *adj.*, qui peut hériter.

heritage (-tédje), *n.*, héritage, *m.*

hermaphrodite (-daïte), *n.*, hermaphrodite, *m.*

hermeneutics (heur-mi-niou-tikse), *n.pl.*, herméneutique, *f.sing.*

hermetic, *or* **hermetical** (hèr-mèt'-), *adj.*, hermétique.

hermit (heur-), *n.*, ermite, hermite, *m.*

hermitage (-'édje), *n.*, ermitage, hermitage, *m.*

hermitical (hèr'-), *adj.*, d'ermite.

hernia (heur'-), *n.*, (med.) hernie, *f.*

hero (hî-rô), *n.* (*heroes*), héros, *m.*

heroic (hi-rô-ike), *adj.*, héroïque.

heroical (hi-rô-i-), *adj.*, héroïque.

heroically, *adv.*, héroïquement.

heroi-comic, *or* **heroi-comical** (hi-rô-i-), *adj.*, héroï-comique.

heroine (hèr-o-ine, *ou* hî-), *n.*, héroïne,*f.*

heroism (hèr-o-iz'me, *ou* hi-ro-), *n.*, héroïsme, *m.*

heron (hèr-), *n.*, (orni.) héron, *m.*

herpes (heur-pize), *n.*, (med.) herpès, *m.* ; dartre, *f.*

herpetic (heur-pi-), *adj.*, (med.) herpétique, dartreux.

herpetology (heur-pi-tol'o'dji), *n.*, erpétologie, *f.*

herring (hèr-), *n.*, hareng, *m.* Red —; *hareng saur.* — **woman** ; *harengère,f.*

hers (heurze), *pron.*, (person.) d'elle, à elle ; (possess.) le sien, la sienne, les siens, les siennes.

herse (heurse), *n.*, (fort.) herse, *f.*

herself (heur-), *pron.*, elle-même, se, soi.

hesitancy (hèz'-), *n.*, incertitude, *f.*

hesitate (hèz'-), *v.n.*, hésiter, balancer.

hesitating (-tét'-), *adj.*, hésitant, qui hésite.

hesitatingly, *adv.*, avec hésitation.

hesitation (hèz'it-té-), *n.*, hésitation, *f.*

heteroclite (hèt-i-ro-claïte), *n.*, mot hétéroclite, *m.* ; chose hétéroclite, *f.*

heteroclitic, *or* **heteroclitical** (-clit'-), *adj.*, hétéroclite.

heterodox (hèt-èr-), *adj.*, hétérodoxe.

heterodoxy, *n.*, hétérodoxie, *f.*

heterogeneity (hèt-i-rô-dji'n'i-), *n.*, hétérogénéité, *f.*

heterogeneous, heterogene, *or* **heterogeneal,** *adj.*, hétérogène.

heteroscian (hèt-i-rosh'a'n), *n.*, (geog.) hétérosciens, *m.pl.*

hew (hiou), *v.a.* (*preterit*, Hewed ; *past part.*, Hewn), tailler, couper.

hewer. *n.*, (of stone—*de pierre*) tailleur ; (of wood—*de bois*) charpentier, *m.*

hexagon (hèks'-), *n.*, hexagone, *m.*

hexagonal, *adj.*. hexagone.

hexahedron (hèks'a-hî-), *n.*, hexaèdre, *m.*

hexameter (héks'am'i-), *n.*, hexamètre, *m.*

hexametrical, *adj.*, hexamètre.

hexandria (hèks'-), *n.*, hexandrie, *f.*

hey ! (hè) *int.*, hé ! hein !

heyday, *n.*, beaux jours, *m.pl.* ; force, *f.*

heyday ! *int.*, ouais ! hé !

hiatus (haï-é-), *n.*, brèche, lacune, *f.* ; hiatus, *m.*

hibernate (haï-), *v.n.*, hiverner.

hibernian (haï-beur-), *n.*, Hibernien, *m.*, Hibernienne, *f.*

hibernian, *adj.*, hibernien.

hiccough (hik-kofe), *or* **hiccup** (hik-keupe), *n.*. hoquet, *m.*

hiccough, *or* **hiccup**, *v.n.*, avoir le hoquet.

hidden (hid'd'n), *adj.*, caché, secret.

hide (haïde), *n.*, peau, *f.* ; cuir, *m.*

hide (haïde), *v.n.* (*preterit*, Hid ; *past part.*, Hid, Hidden), se cacher.

hide, *v.a.*, cacher ; dérober à la vue.

hidebound (haïde-baou'n'de), *adj.*, (vet.) dont la peau adhère aux muscles.

hideous (hid'i-), *adj.*, hideux, horrible, affreux.

hideously, *adv.*, hideusement.

hideousness. *n.*, caractère hideux, *m.* ; laideur hideuse ; difformité, *f.*

hider (haïd'-), *n.*, personne qui cache, *f.*

hiding (haïd'-), *n.*, coups, *m.pl.*, roulée, *f.* To give any one a — ; (triv.) *tanner la peau à quelqu'un.*

hie (ha'ye), *v.n.*, se hâter ; courir.

hierarch (haï-i-rār-ke), *n.*, hiérarque. *m.*

hierarchal, *or* **hierarchical**, *adj.*, hiérarchique.

hierarchy (haï-i-rār-ki), *n.*, hiérarchie, *f.*

hieroglyphic (haï-i-ro-), *n.*, hiéroglyphe ; symbole, *m.*

hieroglyphic, *or* **hieroglyphical**, *adj.*, hiéroglyphique.

hieroglyphically, *adv.*, par hiéroglyphes.

hierophant (haï-èr-), *n.*, hiérophante, *m.*

higgle (hig'g'l),*v.n.*,vendre des denrées dans les rues ; barguigner.

higgledy-piggledy (hig-glè-di-pig-glè-di), *adv.*, (pop.) pêle-mêle, sens dessus dessous.

higgler, *n.*, marchand des rues, regrattier, *m.*

high (ha'ye), *adj.*, haut, élevé, grand ; sublime ; fier, altier ; important. — price ; *prix* élevé. To speak of any one in — terms ; *parler de quelqu'un en termes flatteurs.*

high, *n.*, haut ; ciel, *m.*

high, *adv.*, haut, hautement; grandement; solennellement.

high-blown (-blône), *adj.*, enflé.

high-born. *adj.*. de haute naissance.

high-flier (-flaï'-), *n.*, enthousiaste, *m.*

high-flown (-flône), *adj.*, fier ; enflé, outré.

high-flying (-flaï'gne), *adj.*, extravagant.

highland (-la'n'd), *n.*, pays montagneux, *m.*

highlander. *n.*, montagnard. *m.*

high-low (-lô), *n.*, soulier à recouvrement, *m.*

highly (ha'ye'li), *adv.*, hautement : d'une manière élevée ; grandement, fortement.

highmettled (-mèt't'l'de), *adj.*, audacieux.

high-minded (-maï'n'd'ède),*adj.*,ambitieux, fier

highmost (-môste), *adj.*, le plus haut.

highness (ha'ye'nèce), *n.*, hauteur, élévation ; chèrté ; (title—*titre*) Altesse : (title of the Sultan—*titre du Sultan*) Hautesse, *f.*

high-spirited (-'ède), *adj.*, fier, audacieux.

hight (haïte), *adj.*, nommé, appelé.

high-water (-wô-teur), *n.*, haute marée, *f.*

high-way (-wè), *n.*, grand chemin, *m.*

highway-man (-ma'n), *n.*, voleur de grand chemin, *m.*

hilarity (haï-), *n.*, hilarité, *f.*

hill, *n.*, montagne, colline, *f.* ; coteau, *m.*

hill, *v.a.*, (agri.) chausser.

hilliness, *n.*, nature montueuse, *f.*

hillock, *n.*, monticule, *m.* ; hauteur, colline, *f.*

hilly, *adj.*, montagneux, accidenté.

hilt, *n.*, poignée, *f.*

hilum (haï-leume), *n.*, (bot.) hile, *m.*

him. *pron.*, (pers.) lui, le ; (demonstr.) celui.

himself, *pron.*, lui-même ; se, soi. He thinks — : *il se croit.*

hind (haï'n'de), *n.*, biche, *f.* ; domestique, *m. f.* : valet de ferme ; paysan ; rustre, *m.*

hind (haï'n'de), *adj.*, de derrière.

hinder (haï'n'd'-), *adj.*, derrière, postérieur.

hinder (hi'n'-), *v.a.*, empêcher, détourner ; gêner ; retarder.

hinderance, *or* **hindrance** (hi'n'-), *n.*, obstacle. *m.* ; entrave, *f.*

hinderer (hi'n'-), *n.*, personne qui empêche; chose qui empêche, *f.*

hindermost (hai'n'd'eur-môste), *or* **hindmost** (haï'n'd'-môste), *adj.*, dernier.

hinge (hi'n'dje), *n.*, gond, *m.* ; charnière, *f.* ; (fig.) ressort, pivot, *m.*

hinge, *v.a.*, garnir de gonds; (fig.) plier, courber.

hinge, *v.n.*, tourner sur, rouler sur.

hint (hi'n'te), *n.*, allusion indirecte, *f.* ; avis ; demi-mot, *m.* ; insinuation, *f.*

hint, *v.a.*, donner à entendre, suggérer.

hint, *v.n.*, faire allusion, *f.*

hip, *n.*, hanche, *f.*

hip (hipe), *v.a.*, rendre déhanché, disloquer.

hip-bone (-bône), *n.*, (anat.) ischion, *m.*

hipgout (-gaoute), *n.*, sciatique, *f.*

hip-joint (-djoï'n'te), *n.*, (anat.) articulation coxo-fémorale, *f.*

hippocentaur (hip-po-cè'n'-), *n.*, hippocentaure, *m.*

hippocras (-crace), *n.*, hypocras, *m.*

hippodrome (-drôme), *n.*, hippodrome, *m.*

hippogriff, *n.*, hippogriffe, *m.*

hippolith (-lith), *n.*, (vet.) hippolithe, *f.*

hippomane (-méne), *n.*, hippomane, *m.*

hippopotamus (-meusse),*n.*, hippopotami, hippopotame, *m.*

hip-roof (-roufe), *n.*, (arch.) croupe, *f.*

hipshot, *adj.*, déhanché.

hip-stone (-stône), *n.*, (min.) pierre néphrétique, *f.* ; jade, *m.*

hire (haeur), *n.*, louage, prix de louage; loyer, *m.*

hire, *v.a.*, louer ; prendre à louage. To — one's self out ; *se louer.*

hireling (haeur'-), *n.*, personne salariée, *f.* ; mercenaire, *m.*

hireling, *adj.*, salarié ; mercenaire.

hirer. *n.*, personne qui loue, *f.*

hiring, *n.*, louage, *m.*

hirsute (hir-sioute), *adj.*, hérissé ; velu.

his (hize), *pron.*, (person.) de lui, à lui ; (possess.) son, sa, ses ; le sien, la sienne ; les siens, les siennes.

hispid (haï-), *adj.*, velu ; (bot.) hispide.

hiss, *n.*; sifflement ; sifflet, *m.*

hiss. *v.a.* and *n.*, siffler.

hissing, *n.*, sifflement; sifflet, *m.*

hissing, *adj.*, sifflant.

hist ! *int.*, chut !

historian (-tô-), *n.*, historien, *m.*

historic, *or* **historical**, *adj.*, historique.

historically, *adv.*, historiquement.

historiographer (-to-), *n.*, historiographe, *m.*

history, *n.*, histoire, *f.*: historique, *m.*

history-piece (-pîce) *n.*, tableau d'histoire, *m.*

histrion, *n.*, (ant.) comédien; histrion, *m.*

histrionic. (ant.), *or* **histrionical**. *adj.*, du comédien; de la scène; de la comédie; d'histrion.

histrionism. *n.*, représentation scénique, *f.*, théâtre, *m.*

hit, *n.*, coup, *m.*; chance,*f.* Lucky —; coup heureux, *m.*

hit, *v.a.* and *n.* (preterit and past part., Hit), donner un coup à; frapper, heurter; rencontrer; (fig.) atteindre le but; arriver; s'accorder; réussir. To — against: donner contre. To — home; porter coup. To — upon; trouver, rencontrer, se ressouvenir de, tomber sur.

hitch, *v.n.*, se trémousser; se nouer; (man.) s'entrecouper.

hitch, *v.a.*, accrocher; (nav.) amarrer.

hitch, *n.*, empêchement, *m.*; entrave, *f.*; (nav.) nœud, *m.*, clef, *f.*

hither (hith'-), *adv.*, ici, par ici; y.

hither, *adj.*, de ce côté-ci; en deçà; le plus rapproché: citérieur.

hithermost (-môste), *adj.*, le plus proche.

hitherto (-tou), *adv.*, jusqu'ici, jusqu'à présent.

hitherward (-wõrd), *or* **hitherwards** (-wõrdze), *adv.*, de ce côté-ci.

hive (haïve), *n.*, ruche, *f.*; essaim, *m.*

hive, *v.a.*, mettre dans une ruche.

hive, *v.n.*, vivre dans la même ruche; vivre ensemble.

hiver (haïv'eur), *n.*, apiculteur, *m.*

hives (haïv'ze), *n.*, (med.) croup, *m.*; varicelle pustuleuse, *f.*

ho, *or* **hoa**!*int.*, hé! ho!

hoar (hôre), *adj.*, blanc, blanchi, chenu.

hoard (hôrde), *n.*, monceau, amas; magot, *m.*

hoard, *v.a.* and *n.*, amasser.

hoarder, *n.*, thésauriseur, accapareur, *m.*

hoar-frost (hôr'froste), *n.*, gelée blanche, *f.*

hoariness, *n.*, blancheur, *f.*

hoarse (hôrse), *adj.*, enroué, rauque.

hoarsely, *adv.*, d'une voix enrouée, rauque.

hoarseness, *n.*, enrouement, *m.*; raucité, *f.*

hoary (hôr'i), *adj.*, blanc; blanchi; aux cheveux gris; chenu.

hoax (hôkse), *v.a.*, mystifier.

hoax, *n.*, mystification, *f.*; canard, *m.*

hob, *n.*, (of a fire-grate—de grille de foyer) plaque, *f.*; (of a wheel—de roue) moyeu, *m.*; (peasant—campagnard) paysan, rustre, manant; lutin, *m.*

hob, *v.n.*, boire avec quelqu'un.

hobbingly, *adv.*, en clochant.

hobble (hob'b'l), *n.*, clochement, *m.*; (fig.) difficulté, nasse, *f.*, embarras, *m.*

hobble. *v.n.*, clocher, clopiner; marcher avec des béquilles: marcher gauchement.

hobble, *v.a.*, mettre dans l'embarras.

hobby, *n.*, cheval de bois; dada, *m.*, marotte, *f.*

hobby-horse, *n.*, cheval de bois, dada, *m.*; marotte, *f.*

hob-goblin (-gob'line), *n.*, lutin, spectre, fantôme, *m.*

hoblike (-laïke), *adj.*, en paysan, en rustre.

hobnail (-néle), *n.*, clou à fer à cheval; (fig.) paysan, rustre, manant, *m.*

hobnailed (-nél'de), *adj.*, garni de clous à grosses têtes; (fig.) grossier.

hobnob, *v.n.*, boire avec quelqu'un; trinquer.

hobnob, *adv.*, au hasard; pêle-mêle; à prendre ou à laisser.

hock, *n.*, (of a horse—du cheval) jarret; (wine —rin) hock, vin du Rhin, *m.*

hockle (hoc'k'l), *v.a.*, couper le jarret à.

hocus pocus (hô'keusse po'keusse), *n.*, tour de passe-passe, *m.*; jonglerie, *f.*

hocus, *v.a.*, (l.ex.) escamoter.

hod, *n.*, (mas.) oiseau, *m.*

hodge-podge, *n.*, salmigondis. hochepot,*m.*

hodiernal (hô-di-eur-), *adj.*, d'aujourd'hui.

hoe (hô), *n.*, houe, *f.*

hoe, *v.a.* and *n.*, houer.

hog, *n.*, pourceau, cochon, porc, *m.*

hoggish. *adj.*, de cochon; (fig.) grossier.

hoggishly, *adv.*, en cochon.

hoggishness,*n.*,cochonnerie; gloutonnerie; (fig.) grossièreté, *f.*

hogherd (hog'heurde), *n.*, porcher, *m.*

hogmane (-méne), *n.*, crinière en brosse, *f.*

hogshead (hog'z'hède), *n.*, demi-pièce (de litres238.4509),*f.*

hogsty (hog'sta'ye), *n.*, étable à cochons, *f.*

hogwash (-wõshe), *n.*, lavure; lavure de vaisselle, *f.*

hoi, *v.n.*, dia!

hoiden (hoï'd'n), *n.*, garçonnière, *f.*

hoiden, *v.n.*, garçonner.

hoiden, *or* **hoidenish**, *adj.*, garçonnier.

hoist (hoïste), *v.a.*, guinder; lever, hausser, hisser.

hoist, *n.*, effort; (nav.) guindant, *m.*

hoity-toity ! (hoï-ti-toï-ti), *int.*, bah!

hoity-toity, *adj.*,étourdi, irréfléchi, léger.

hold (hôlde), *n.*, action de tenir; prise, *f.* (support) soutien, *m.*; serre; griffe; (fortress) place forte; (nav.) cale, *f.*; (mus.) point d'orgue, *m.* To get, to take — of; prendre; saisir; empoigner; se saisir de. To let go one's —; lâcher prise.

hold,*v.a.* (preterit and past part., Held), tenir; retenir; arrêter; soutenir; contenir; garder; conserver; considérer comme; regarder comme; avoir; occuper; célébrer. To — fast; tenir ferme. To — together; tenir ensemble. To — one's self; se retenir; se regarder. To — back; retenir. To — forth; tendre; avancer; mettre en avant. To — in; retenir. To — off; tenir éloigné; tenir à distance. To — on; continuer de tenir; persévérer dans. To — out; tendre; présenter; offrir; supporter; endurer. To — up; lever; soulever; soutenir; maintenir; présenter; exposer. To — any one to his promise; astreindre quelqu'un à tenir sa promesse. To — one's tongue; se taire.

hold, *v.n.*, tenir; se soutenir; se maintenir; rester; durer; être vrai; supporter; endurer. To — fast; tenir ferme, avec force. To — good; être vrai; ne pas se démentir. To — together; tenir ensemble. To — back; se tenir en arrière. To — forth; haranguer; pérorer. To — in; se contenir; se retenir. To — on; tenir toujours; tenir bon; aller toujours. To — out; tenir bon. To — up; se soutenir; (of the rain—de la pluie) cesser.

holdback, *n.*, empêchement, obstacle, *m.*; entrave, *f.*

holder, *n.*, personne qui tient; (thing—objet) chose pour tenir, poignée, anse, *f.*, manche; (possessor—possesseur) détenteur; (com.) porteur, *m.*

holdfast (-fâste), *n.*, crampon; croc; (tech.) valet. *m.*

holding, *n.*, possession; prise; influence. *f.*

hole (hôle), *n.*, trou; antre, *m.*; caverne; ouverture, *f.*

hole, *v.n.*, trouer; (at billiards—au billard) blouser.

holidam (hol'i-dame), *n.*, (ant.) la sainte Vierge, *f.*

holiday (-lè), *n.*, jour de fête, *m.*; fête, *f.*; congé, campos, *m.* —s; vacances, *f.pl.* Bank—: fête légale.

holiday, *adj.*, de jour de fête, de fête; de jour de congé, de congé; de vacances.

holily, *adv.*, saintement.

holiness, *n.*, sainteté, *f.*

25

holland, *n.*, toile de Hollande, *f.*
hollands,*n.pl.*,genièvre de Hollande, *m.sing.*
hollo (hol'lô), *n.*, huée, *f.* ; holà, *m.*
hollo (hol'lô), *v.n.*, huer, crier.
holloa!*or* **hollo**! (hol'lôa,-lô), *int.*, holà ! hé !
hollow (-lô), *n.*, creux; antre, *m.* ; caverne, cavité, *f.*
hollow, *adj.*, creux, vide ; (of sound—*du son*) sourd.
hollow, *v.a.*, creuser.
hollowness, *n.*, creux, vide, *m.* ; (fig.) fausseté, *f.*
holly, *n.*, (bot.) houx, *m.*
holly-grove (-grôve), *n.*, houssaie, *f.*
holly-hock, *n.*, aloée ; rose trémière ; passerose, *f.*
holm (hôlme), *n.*, îlot ; terrain d'alluvion ; chêne vert, *m.* ; yeuse, *f.*
holocaust, *n.*, holocauste, *m.*
holograph, *n.*, (jur.) olographe, *m.*
holothuria (-lô-thiou-), *n.*, (zool.) holothurie, *f.*
holster (hôl-), *n.*, fonte de pistolet, *f.*
holy (hô-), *adj.*, saint, sacré ; bénit. —-Ghost ; *le Saint-Esprit.* — land ; *terre sainte.* — -water ; *eau bénite.* —-week ; *la semaine sainte.*
homage (-édje), *n.*, hommage, *m.*
homager (-édj'-), *n.*, hommager, *m.*
home (hôme), *n.*, chez soi ; logis ; foyer domestique ; intérieur, *m.* ; demeure, maison, *f.* ; pays, *m.* At —; *chez soi ; à la maison.*
home, *adj.*, de la maison, domestique ; qui porte coup, bon.
home, *adv.*, chez soi, au logis ; à la maison ; dans son pays ; (fig.) directement, vigoureusement.
homebred (-brède), *adj.*, naturel ; domestique.
homefelt (-fèlte), *adj.*, intime, du cœur, intérieur.
home-keeping (-kîp'-), *adj.*, sédentaire, casanier.
homeliness, *n.*, caractère domestique, *m.* ; simplicité, grossièreté ; (of the face—*du visage*) sans beauté, *f.*
homely, *adj.*, de la maison ; de ménage ; simple ; ordinaire ; commun.
homemade (-méde), *adj.*, de ménage ; fait à la maison ; de fabrication indigène.
homesick, *adj.*, qui a le mal du pays.
home-sickness, *n.*, mal du pays, *m.* ; nostalgie, *f.*
home-speaking (-spîk'-), *n.*, discours énergique, *m.*
homespun (-speune), *adj.*, fait à la maison, de ménage, grossier ; sans façon.
homestall (-stôl), *or* **homestead** (-stède), *n.*, château et dépendances ; lieu de naissance ; domicile originaire, *m.*
homeward (-wôrde), *or* **homewards** (-wôrdze), *or* **homeward-bound** (-baou'n'de), *adv.*, vers la maison ; vers son pays ; (nav.) de retour.
homicidal (-çaï'-), *adj.*, homicide ; meurtrier.
homicide (-çaïde), *n.*, homicide, *m.*
homily, *n.*, homélie, *f.*, sermon, *m.*
homocentric (hô-), *adj.*, (astron.) homocentrique ; (math.) concentrique.
homœopathic, *or* **homœopathical** (hô-mi-op-a-thi-), *adj.*, homéopathique.
homœopathist, *n.*, homéopathe, *m.*
homœopathy, *n.*, homéopathie, *f.*
homogeneal, *or* **homogeneous** (-dji-ni-), *adj.*, homogène, semblable.
homogenealness, homogeneity, *or* **homogeneousness** (-dji-ni-), *n.*, homogénéité, *f.*
homologous, *adj.*, (geom.) homologue.
homonym, *n.*, homonyme, *m.*

homonymous, *adj.*, homonyme.
homonymy, *n.*, homonymie ; ambiguïté, *f.*
homophony, *n.*, homophonie, *f.*
hone (hône), *n.*, pierre à rasoir, pierre à l'huile, *f.*
hone, *v.a.*, affiler sur la pierre.
honest (on'èste), *adj.*, honnête ; loyal ; probe, intègre, de bonne foi. — man ; *homme de bien.*
honestly, *adv.*, honnêtement ; avec probité ; de bonne foi ; sincèrement.
honesty, *n.*, honnêteté, probité, bonne foi, loyauté, intégrité, franchise, *f.*
honey (heu'n'i), *n.*, miel, *m.*
honey, *v.a.*, mettre du miel dans, sucrer avec du miel.
honey, *v.n.*, parler tendrement.
honey-bag, *n.*, premier estomac de l'abeille, *m.*
honey-comb (-côme), *n.*, rayon de miel, gâteau de miel, *m.*
honey-cup (-keupe), *n.*, (bot.) nectaire, *m.*
honey-dew (-diou), *n.*, miellat, *m.*
honeyed (heu'n'ède), *adj.*, emmiellé ; doux ; miellé ; mielleux.
honey-flower (-fla'weur), *n.*, (bot.) grand mélianthe, *m.* ; fleur miellée, *f.*
honey-guide (-gaïde), *n.*, (orni.) indicateur, *m.*
honey-moon (-moune), *n.*, lune de miel, *f.*
honey-suckle (-seuc'k'l), *n.*, chèvrefeuille, *m.*
honey-wort (-weurte), *n.*, (bot.) mélinet ; sison, *m.*
honorary, *adj.*, honoraire.
honour (o'n'or), *n.*, honneur, *m.* ; dignité, estime, *f.* ; (at cards—*aux cartes*) figure, *f.*
honour, *v.a.*, honorer, faire honneur à ; glorifier.
honourable, *adj.*, honorable.
honourableness, *n.*, caractère honorable ; honneur, *m.*
honourably, *adv.*, honorablement.
honourer, *n.*, personne qui honore, *f.*
hood (houde), *n.*, coiffe de femme, *f.* ; capuchon, chaperon, *m.*
hood, *v.a.*, encapuchonner ; couvrir ; (a hawk —*un faucon*) chaperonner.
hoodwink (-wi'n'ke), *v.a.*, bander les yeux à ; (fig.) en imposer.
hoof (houfe), *n.*, sabot ; ongle, *m.*
hoof, *v.n.*, marcher.
hoof-bound (-baou'n'de), *adj.*, (vet.) encastelé.
hook (houke), *n.*, crochet, croc ; (for fishing —*de pêche*) hameçon, *m.* ; (sickle—*faucille*) faucille, *f.* — and eye ; *agrafe et porte*, *f.*
hook, *v.a.*, accrocher ; agrafer ; prendre à l'hameçon.
hooked (houk'te), *adj.*, crochu, recourbé.
hookedness (houk'èd'-), *n.*, forme crochue ; courbure, *f.*
hook-nose (-nôze), *n.*, nez aquilin, *m.*
hook-nosed (-nôz'de), *adj.*, qui a un nez aquilin.
hoop (houpe), *n.*, cerceau ; cercle, *m.* ; (of a wheel—*de roue*) jante, *f.* ; (cry—*cri*) cri, *m.*
hoop, *v.a.*, cercler ; entourer ; garnir de jantes.
hoop, *v.n.*, crier ; pousser des cris.
hooper, *n.*, cerclier, *m.*
hooping, *n.*, action de crier ; vocifération, *f.*
hooping-cough (-kô'fe), *n.*, coqueluche, *f.*
hoot (houte), *v.a.*, huer.
hoot, *v.n.*, huer.
hoot, *or* **hooting**, *n.*, huée, *f.*
hop (hope), *n.*, sautillement ; (bot.) houblon, *m.*
hop, *v.a.*, houblonner.
hop, *v.n.*, sautiller ; folâtrer.
hope (hôpe), *n.*, espérance ; attente, *f.* ; espoir, *m.*
hope, *v.a.*, espérer ; s'attendre à.

hope, *v.n.*, espérer.
hopeful (hôp'foule), *adj.*, de grande espérance ; qui promet beaucoup.
hopefully, *adv.*, de manière à faire espérer beaucoup ; avec espoir.
hopefulness, *n.*, bon espoir, *m.*
hopeless, *adj.*, sans espoir.
hoper, *n.*, personne qui espère, *f.*
hopingly, *adv.*, avec espoir.
hopper (hop'peur), *n.*, personne qui sautille ; (of a mill—*de moulin*) trémie, *f* ; (agri.) semoir, *m.*
hopping, *n.*, clochement, *m.*
hop-pole (-pôle), *n.*, perche à houblon, *f.*
hopscotch (hop'scotshe), *n.*, marelle, *f.*
horal, or **horary** (hô-), *adj.*, horaire.
horde (hôrde), *n.*, horde, *f.*
horehound (hôr'haou'n'de), *n.*, (bot.) marrube, *m.*
horizon (ho-raï'-), *n.*, horizon, *m.*
horizontal (hor-i-), *adj.*, horizontal.
horizontally, *adv.*, horizontalement
horn, *n.*, corne, *f.*; (of stags—*du cerf*) bois, *m.* ; (ent.) antenne, *f.* ; (mus.) cor, cornet, *m.*
hornbeam (-bîme), *n.*, (bot.) charme, *m.* ; charmille, *f.*
hornblende, *n.*, hornblende, *f.*
hornbook (-bouke), *n.*, abécédaire, *m.*
horned (horn'de), *adj.*, cornu, à cornes.
horned-owl (horn'd'aoul), *n.*, (orni.) duc, *m.*
hornet (hor-nète), *n.*, (ent.) frelon, *m.*
hornfish, *n.*, (ich.) aiguille de mer ; orphie, *f.*
hornpipe (-païpe), *n.*, danse des matelots, *f.*
hornwork (-weurke), *n.*, (fort.) ouvrage à corne, *m.*
hornwort (-weurte), *n.*, (bot.) cornifle, *m.* ; mille-feuille cornue, *f.*
horny, *adj.*, calleux ; de corne.
horological (hor-o-lodj'-), *adj.*, d'horloge; d'horlogerie.
horology (-dji), *n.*, horlogerie, *f.*
horoscope (-scôpe), *n.*, horoscope, *m.*
horrent (hor'rè'n'te), *adj.*, hérissé.
horrible (hor'ri-b'l), *adj.*, horrible, affreux.
horribleness, *n.*, caractère affreux, *m.*; horreur, *f.*
horribly, *adv.*, horriblement ; affreusement.
horrid (hor'ride), *adj.*, affreux, horrible.
horridness, *n.*, horreur, *f.*; caractère horrible, *m.*
horrific, *adj.*, horrible ; affreux.
horripilation (hor-ri-pi-lé-), *n.*, (med.) horripilation, *f.*
horrisonous (hor-riss'o-), *adj.*, qui a un son horrible.
horror, *n.*, horreur, *f.*
horror-stricken (-strick'n), or **horror-struck** (-streuke), *adj.*, frappé d'horreur.
horse, *n.*, cheval, *m.* ; (milit.) cavalerie, *f.* ; (tech.) chevalet, *m.*
horse, *v.a.*, monter un cheval ; porter ; (of horses—*du cheval*) saillir, couvrir.
horseback, *n.*, dos de cheval, *m.* Oir—; à cheval.
horsebean (-bîne), *n.*, petite fève, féverole, *f.*
horseblock, *n.*, montoir, *m.*
horseboy (-boï), *n.*, valet d'écurie, palefrenier, *m.*
horsebreaker (-brèk'-), *n.*, personne qui dresse les chevaux, *f.* ; piquer, *m.*
horsechestnut (-tshès'neute), *n.*, marron d'Inde; (tree—*arbre*) marronnier d'Inde, *m.*
horsecloth (-clôth), *n.*, housse, *f.*
horsefly (-fla'ye), *n.*, taon, *m.*
horse-gin (-djine), *n.*, manège, *m.*
horseguard (-gârde), *n.*, garde à cheval, *m.*
horseguards (-gârd'ze), *n.pl.*, gardes à cheval, *m.pl.*

horsehair (-hère), *n.*, crin de cheval, *m.*
horselaugh (-lâfe), *n.*, rire outré, **rire** grossier, *m.*
horseleech (-lîtshe), *n.*, sangsue, *f.*
horselitter (-lit'teur), *n.*, litière, *f.*
horseload (-lôde), *n.*, charge d'un cheval, *f.*
horseman, *n.*, cavalier, écuyer, *m.* To be a good — ; *être bon écuyer, bien monter à cheval.*
horsemanship, *n.*, manège, *m.* : équitation, *f.*
horsepath (-pâth), *n.*, chemin de halage, *m.*
horsepicker (-pick'-), *n.*, cure-pied, *m.*
horseplay, *n.*, jeu de main, *m.* ; raillerie grossière, *f.*
horsepond (-po'n'de), *n.*, étang pour les chevaux, abreuvoir, *m.*
horse-race, *n.*, course de chevaux, *f.*
horse-radish, *n.*, raifort, *m.*; rave sauvage, *f.*
horseshoe (-shou), *n.*, fer de cheval; fer à cheval, *m.*
horsestealer (-stîl'-), *n.*, voleur de chevaux, *m.*
horse-trappings (-trap'pign'ze), *n.*, harnais, *m.*
horse-twitchers, *n.pl.*, (vet.) morilles, *f.pl.*
horsewhip (-hwipe), *n.*, fouet, *m.*; cravache, *f.*
horsewhip, *v.a.*, fouetter ; donner des coups de cravache à.
horsewoman (-woum'a'n), *n.*, cavalière, écuyère, *f.*
hortation (-té-), *n.*, exhortation, *f.*
hortative (-ta-), *n.*, incitation, *f.*
hortatory, *adj.*, exhortatoire, d'exhortation.
horticultural (-keult'iour'-), *adj.*, d'horticulture ; horticultural.
horticulture (-keult'ioure), *n.*, horticulture, *f.*
horticulturist (-keult'iour'-), *n.*, horticulteur, *m.*
hortulan (hort'iou-), *adj.*, du jardinier.
hosanna (ho-za'n'-), *n.*, hosanna, *m.*
hose (hôze), *n.*, bas, *m.pl.* ; chaussure, *f.* ; (pipe—*conduit*) tuyau élastique, *m.*, (nav.) manche, *f.*
hosier (hô-jeur), *n.*, marchand de bas, chaussetier, bonnetier, *m.*
hosiery (hô-jeur'i), *n.*, bonneterie, *f.*
hospitable (-ta-b'l), *adj.*, hospitalier.
hospitably, *adv.*, avec hospitalité ; charitablement.
hospital, *n.*, hôpital ; hospice, *m.*
hospitality, *n.*, hospitalité, *f.*
host (hôste), *n.*, hôte ; hôtelier, aubergiste, *m.* ; armée, foule, multitude ; (c.rel.) hostie, *f.*
host, *v.a.* and *n.*, loger.
hostage (host'édje), *n.*, otage ; (fig.) gage, *m.*
hostel (hô-tèle), *n.* (ant.) *V.* hotel.
hostelry (hôs'tèl-), *n.*, (l.u.) hôtel, *m.* ; auberge, hôtellerie, *f.*
hostess (hôst'-), *n.*, hôtesse, *f.*
hostile, *adj.*, hostile, ennemi.
hostilely, *adv.*, hostilement, d'une manière hostile.
hostility, *n.*, hostilité, *f.*
hostler (os'leur), *n.*, valet d'écurie, garçon d'écurie, *m.*
hot, *adj.*, chaud, ardent, brûlant : (fig.) violent, échauffé. To be —; *avoir chaud.* To grow —; *s'échauffer.* To make —; *chauffer.* To be burning —; *brûler, être brûlant.* — baths ; *bains chauds, thermes, m.pl.*
hotbed (-bède), *n.*, couche ; serre chaude, *f.*
hotbrained (-bré'n'de), or **hotheaded** (-hèd'ède), *adj.*, violent, fougueux, emporté.
hotchpotch, *n.*, hochepot, salmigondis, *m.*
hot-cockles (-kok'k'l'ze), *n.*, (game—*jeu*) main-chaude, *f.*
hotel (hô-tèl), *n.*, hôtel, *m.* ; hôtellerie, **au**berge, *f.*

hothouse (-haouce), *n.*, serre chaude, *f.*

hotly, *adv.*, avec chaleur, chaudement; vivement.

hot-mouthed (-maouth'de), *adj.*, entêté, obstiné, opiniâtre.

hotness, *n.*, chaleur; passion, violence, fureur, *f.*

hotpress (-prèce), *v.a.*, presser à chaud; (cloth—*le drap*) catir; (paper—*le papier*) satiner.

hotspur (-speur), *n.*, homme violent, fougueux, *m.*

hough (hoke), *n.*, jarret (of animals—*d'animaux*), *m.*

hough (hoke), *v.a.*, couper les jarrets à.

hound (haou'n'de), *n.*, chien de chasse, chien courant, *m.*

hound, *v.a.*, chasser au chien courant; (fig.) exciter, presser.

houndfish, *n.*, aiguillat, squale, chien de mer, *m.*

hour (aou'eur), *n.*, heure, *f.* An — and a half; *une heure et demie.* Half an —; *une demi-heure.* An — ago, an — since; *il y a une heure.* Within an —, an — hence; *dans une heure.* In a lucky —; *dans un moment heureux.* To keep good —s; *rentrer, se coucher de bonne heure.* To keep bad —s; *rentrer, se coucher tard, à des heures indues.*

hour-glass (-glàce), *n.*, sablier, *m.*

hour-hand (-ha'n'de), *n.*, aiguille des heures, petite aiguille, *f.*

hourly (aou'eur'li), *adj.*, fréquent, continuel.

hourly, *adv.*, à toute heure, à tout moment.

hour-plate, *n.*, cadran, *m.*

house (haouce), *n.*, maison, *f.*; bâtiment, *m.*; demeure, habitation; (family—*famille*) race, famille; (thea.) salle, *f.* A religious —; *une maison religieuse, un couvent, un monastère.* A nobleman's —; *un hôtel.* The — of lords; *la chambre des pairs.* The — of commons; *la chambre des communes.* The two —s of parliament; *les deux chambres du parlement.* A town- —; *une maison de ville.* A country- —; *une maison de campagne.* To keep a good —; *tenir bonne table.* To keep open —; *tenir table ouverte.*

house, *v.a.*, loger, recevoir chez soi, donner le couvert à, héberger; (things—*chose*), serrer. To — cattle; *établer le bétail.* To — corn; *serrer le blé, mettre le blé en grange.*

house, *v.n.*, loger, demeurer, se mettre à couvert.

housebreaker (-brèk'-), *n.*, voleur avec effraction, brigand, *m.*

housebreaking, *n.*, vol avec effraction, *m.*

house-dog, *n.*, chien de garde, *m.*

houseful, *n.*, chambrée, *f.*

household (-hôlde), *n.*, maisonnée (pop.), maison, famille, *f.*; domestique; ménage, *m.*

household, *adj.*, domestique; de ménage. — goods; *meubles, m.pl.* —utensils; *ustensiles de ménage, m.pl.*

householder, *n.*, chef de famille, maître de maison, *m.*

household-stuff (-steufe), *n.*, meubles, *m* pl.; mobilier, ameublement, *m.*

housekeeper (-kîp'-), *n.*, chef de famille, *m.*; femme de charge, *f.*

housekeeping, *n.*, ménage, *m.*; économie domestique, *f.*

houseleek (-lîke), *n.*, (bot.) joubarbe, *f.*

houseless, *adj.*, qui n'a point de maison, de demeure, d'habitation; sans asile.

house-maid (-méde), *n.*, servante, *f.*

house-rent, *n.*, loyer d'une maison, *m.*

house-room (-roume), *n.*, place, *f.*; espace, abri, logement, *m.*

house-top, *n.*, faîte, toit, *m.*

house-warming (-wôr'm'-), *n.*, pendre la crémaillère, *f.*

housewife (-waïfe), *n.*, ménagère, maîtresse

de maison, *f.*; (case for needles &c.—*boîte d ouvrage*), nécessaire de femme, *m.*

housewifely, *adj.*, de ménagère; de ménage.

housewifely, *adv.*, économiquement, en bonne ménagère.

housewifery, *n.*, ménage, *m.*; économie domestique, *f.*

housing, *n.*, logement, *m.*; (of horses—*de chevaux*) housse, *f.*

hovel, *n.*, chaumière, cabane; baraque, hutte, cahute, *f.*

hover (heuv'-), *v.n.*, voltiger, planer, se balancer, voler par dessus, prendre l'essor.

how (haou), *adv.*, comment, de quelle manière, combien, que, quel. — do you do? *comment vous portez-vous?* He related to us — it happened; *il nous raconta de quelle manière la chose s'était passée.* You see — I love you; *vous voyez combien je vous aime.* — amiable virtue is; *que la vertu est aimable.* — old are you? *quel âge avez-vous?* — long have you been here? *combien y a-t-il que vous êtes arrivé? Depuis quand êtes-vous ici?*

howbeit (haou-bî-ite), *adv.*, (ant.). V. **however**.

however (haou-èv-) or **howsoever** (haou-çɔ-èv'-), *adv.*, cependant, quoi qu'il en soit, néanmoins, pourtant; (before an adj.— *devant quelque adj.*) quelque . . . que. — rich he may be; *quelque riche qu'il soit.*

howitz (haou'itz), or **howitzer** (haou-it-zeur), *n.*, obusier, *m.*

howl (haoul), *n.*, hurlement, cri, *m.*

howl, *v.n.*, hurler.

howlet (haou-lète), *n.*, (orni.) hulotte, *f.*

howling (haoul'-), *n.*, hurlement; cri, *m.*

howling, *adj.*, qui hurle; qui pousse des hurlements.

hoy (hoï), *n.*, (nav.) vaisseau côtier, ⊙ heu, *m.*

hoy! *int.*, hé! holà!

hubbub (heub'beube), *n.*, tumulte, grabuge, charivari, vacarme, tintamarre, *m.*

huckaback (heuk'a-), *n.*, toile ouvrée, *f.*

huckle (heuck l), *n.*, (ant.) hanche; bosse, *f.*

huckle-backed (-bak'te), *adj.*, bossu, voûté.

huckle-bone (-bône), *n.*, (ant.) os de la hanche, *m.*

huckster (heuck'-), *n.*, revendeur, regrattier, *m.*

huckster, *v.n.*, revendre en détail, vendre du regrat.

hucksteress (heuck'steur'-), *n.*, regrattière, *f.*

huddle (heud'd'l), *n.*, désordre, *m.*; confusion; foule, *f.* All in a —; *pêle-mêle, en désordre, confusément.*

huddle, *v.a.*, brouiller, confondre ensemble, mêler, jeter pêle-mêle.

huddle, *v.n.*, se fouler, se mêler, se coudoyer, se presser en désordre.

hue (hiou), *n.*, teint, *m.*; couleur, *f.*; (cry—*cri*) huée, *f.*, cri, *m.* Flowers of all —s; *fleurs de toutes les couleurs.* — and cry; *cri de haro, m.*; (journal) *gazette de poursuites judiciaires, f.* To raise a — and cry after one; *crier haro sur quelqu'un.*

huff (heufe), *n.*, emportement, accès de colère, mouvement d'arrogance, *m.*

huff, *v.a.*, gonfler; enfler; maltraiter, brusquer; (at draughts—*aux dames*) souffler.

huff, *v.n.*, gonfler; s'enfler. To — at; *pester contre.*

huffer, *n.*, vantard, fanfaron, *m.*

huffish, *adj.*, fanfaron; arrogant; fier.

huffishly, *adv.*, avec fanfaronnerie; avec arrogance; fièrement.

huffishness, *n.*, pétulance; vanterie; arrogance, *f.*

hug (heughe), *n.*, embrassade, accolade, *f.*

hug, *v.a.*, embrasser, serrer entre les bras;

chérir. To — the wind ; (nav.) *pincer le vent.* To — the land ; (nav.) *serrer la terre, côtoyer.*

huge (hioudje), *adj.*, vaste, grand, immense, énorme.

hugely, *adv.*, énormément, immensément, extrêmement, grandement.

hugeness, *n.*, grandeur énorme, *f.*

hugger-mugger (heug'gheur-meug-gheur), *n.*, secret, *m.* ; saleté, négligence. *f.* In — ; *en secret.* In — fashion ; *salement : négligemment.*

hulk (heulke), *n.*, carcasse, *f.* —s ; *pontons, m.pl.*

hull (heul), *n.*, (of a ship—*de vaisseau*) coque ; (of walnuts, &c.—*de noix, &c.*) cosse, écale, *f.*

hull, *v.a.*, (a ship—*un vaisseau*) percer le bordage d'un vaisseau d'un coup de canon ; (walnuts, &c.—*noix, &c.*) écosser, écaler.

hull, *v.n.*, flotter au gré du vent. To — to ; *mettre à sec.*

hully, *adj.*, à écales.

hum (heume), *n.*, bourdonnement ; murmure, *m.*

hum, *v.a.* and *n.*, fredonner ; bourdonner ; murmurer.

human (hiou-ma'n), *adj.*, humain.

humane (hiou-méne), *adj.*, bon, bénin ; humain, qui a de l'humanité ; bienfaisant.

humanely (hiou-mé'n'li), *adv.*, humainement ; avec humanité.

humanist (hiou-), *n.*, personne qui connaît la nature humaine, *f.* ; humaniste, *m.*

humanity (hiou-), *n.*, humanité, *f.*

humanize (hiou-ma'n'aïze), *v.a.*, humaniser ; adoucir.

human-kind (-kaï'n'de), *n.*, genre humain, *m.*

humanly, *adv.*, humainement.

humble (heu'm'b'l, *ou* eu'm'-), *adj.*, humble.

humble, *v.a.*, humilier.

humble-bee (-bi), *n.*, bourdon, *m.* ; abeille sauvage, *f.*

humbleness, *n.*, humilité, *f.*

humble-plant, *n.*, (bot.) sensitive, *f.*

humbler, *n.*, personne qui humilie ; chose qui humilie, *f.*

humbles (eu'm'b'l'ze), *n.pl.*, nombles, *f.pl.*

humbly, *adv.*, humblement.

humbug (heu'm'beughe), *n.*, hâblerie, blague, *f.* ; (pers.) hâbleur, blagueur, charlatan, *m.*

humbug, *v.a.*, friponner, tromper ; faire le charlatan ; conter des sornettes à.

humdrum (heu'm'dreu'me), *n.*, personne lente et paresseuse, *f.* ; lendore (pop.), fainéant, *m.*

humdrum, *adj.*, monotone ; (pers.) assommant, lourd, hébété.

humect, *or* **humectate** (hiou-mèk't), *v.a.*, humecter.

humectation (-mèk'té'-), *n.*, humectation, *f.* ; arrosement, *m.*

humeral, *adj.*, huméral.

humerus(hiou-mèr'-), *n.*,(anat.)humérus, *m.*

humid (hiou-), *adj.*, humide.

humidity, *n.*, humidité, *f.*

humiliating (hiou-mil'iét'-), *adj.*,humiliant.

humiliation (hiou-mil'ié-), *n.*, humiliation,*f.*

humility (hiou-mil-), *n.*, humilité, *f.*

hummer (heum'-), *n.*, personne qui fredonne, qui bourdonne ; chose qui bourdonne, *f.*

humming, *n.*, bourdonnement ; fredonnement, *m.*

humming-bird (-beurde), *n.*, oiseau-mouche ; colibri, *m.*

humoral (you-mor'-), *adj.*, humoral.

humorist (you-mor'-), *n.*, personne spirituelle. *f.* ; plaisant, *m.* ; personne qui n'obéit qu'à ses propres inclinations. *f.*

humorless (hiou-), *adj.*, sans esprit, sans caractère.

humorous (hiou-), *adj.*, spirituel ; plaisant ; fantasque ; bizarre ; capricieux.

humorously, *adv.*, spirituellement ; bizarrement ; capricieusement.

humorousness, *n.*, caractère spirituel ; esprit ; caractère fantasque, bizarre, capricieux, *m.*

humorsome (hiou-mor-seume), *adj.*, de mauvaise humeur ; pétulant ; spirituel ; plaisant.

humorsomely, *adv.*. de mauvaise humeur ; avec méchanceté ; spirituellement.

humour (hiou-meur), *n.*, humeur : disposition, *f.* ; caractère ; goût, caprice ; esprit, *m.* ; gaîté, *f.* To be in a good, a bad — ; *être de bonne, de mauvaise humeur.* To put any one in a good — ; *mettre quelqu'un en bonne humeur.* To put out of — ; *mettre de mauvaise humeur.* In a — for ; *en veine de ; en train de ; disposé à ; d'humeur à.* The —s of the human body ; *les humeurs du corps humain.*

humour, *v.a.*, complaire à ; laisser faire à ; flatter ; chercher à plaire à.

humoured (hiou-meur'de), *part.*, satisfait, contenté ; qu'on écoute trop, pour qui l'on a trop d'indulgence. Ill- — ; *de mauvaise humeur.* Good- — ; *de bonne humeur.*

hump (heu'm'pe), *n.*, bosse, *f.*

humpbacked (-'bak'te), *adj.*, bossu.

hunch (heu'n'she), *v.a.*, faire une bosse à ; coudoyer.

hunch (heu'n'she), *n.*, bosse (on the back—*au dos*), *f.* ; gros morceau, *m.* ; bribe *f.*

hunchback (-bake), *n.*, bossu, *m.*, bossue, *f.*

hunchbacked (-bak'te), *adj.*, voûté, bossu.

hundred (heu'n'drède), *adj.*, cent.

hundred, *n.*, cent, *m.* ; centaine ; (territorial division), centurie. *f.*. canton, *m.*

hundred-fold (-fôlde), *adj.*, centuple.

hundredth (-drèd'th), *adj.*, centième.

hundredth, *n.*, centième, *m.*

hundredweight (-wè-te),*n.*, quintal, cent,*m.*

hungarian (heu'n'ghé-), *adj.*, hongrois.

hungarian. *n.*, Hongrois, *m.*, Hongroise, *f.* ; (language—*langue*) hongrois, *m.*

hunger (heu'n'gheur), *n.*, faim ; (fig.) soif, *f.*

hunger, *v.n.*, avoir faim, être affamé. To — after ; *languir après* ; *être affamé de ; avoir soif de.*

hunger-bit, *or* **hunger-bitten** (-bit't'n), *adj.*, affamé ; pressé par la faim.

hungered (-gheurde), *adj.*, qui a faim, affamé.

hungerly (-gheur-), *or* **hungrily,** *adv.*, avec un appétit dévorant, avidement.

hunger-starved (-stàrv'de), *adj.*, affamé ; dévoré par la faim.

hungry, *adj.*, affamé ; qui a faim ; famélique. To be — ; *avoir faim.*

hunks (heu'n'kse), *n.*, ladre, harpagon. *m.*

hunt (heu'n'te), *n.*, chasse à courre ; (pack of hounds—*des chiens*) meute, *f.*

hunt (heu'n'te), *v.a.*, chasser, courre, courir ; poursuivre. To — out ; *découvrir, dépister.* To — down ; *harceler, persécuter, mettre aux abois.*

hunt. *v.a.*, chasser ; aller à la chasse.

hunter, *n.*, chasseur ; (horse—*cheval*) cheval de chasse ; (dog—*chien*) chien de chasse, *m.*

hunting, *n.*, chasse ; (fig.) recherche, *f.*

huntress, *n.*, chasseresse. *f.*

huntsman, *n.*, chasseur, piqueur, veneur, *m.*

huntsmanship, *n.*, chasse, *f.* ; qualités d'un chasseur, *f.pl.*

hurd (heurde), *n.*, (nav.) toron, *m.*

hurdle (heur'd'l), *n.*, claie ; (milit.) fascine, *f.*

hurds (heurdze), *n.pl.*, étoupe, *f.sing.*

hurdy-gurdy (heur'di-gheur'di), *n.*, vielle,*f.*

hurgil (heur'ghil), *n.*, (orni.) cigogne à sac, *f.* : marabout, *m.*

hurl (heurle), *n.*, action de précipiter, de lancer, *f.*

hurl, *v.a.*, précipiter, lancer, jeter.

hurler, *n.*, personne qui lance, *f.*

hurly-burly (heur'li-beur-li), *n.*, brouhaha ; tintamare, *m.*

hurrah, (hour'râ), *n.*, hourra, *m.*

hurricane (heur-ri-), *n.*, ouragan, *m.* ; tempête, *f.*

hurried (heur-ride), *adj.*, précipité, pressé.

hurrier (heur-ri-), *n.*, personne qui se hâte, qui hâte, qui presse, *f.*

hurry (heur-ri-), *n.*, hâte, *f.*; (fig.) tumulte, *m.*, confusion, *f.* To be in a—; *être pressé.* Done in a—; *fait à la hâte ; fait avec précipitation.*

hurry, *v.a.,* presser; précipiter; faire dépêcher. To —away ; *emmener précipitamment.*

hurry, *v.n.,* se dépêcher; se presser; se hâter.

hurt (heurte), *n.*, mal, *m.* ; blessure, *f.* ; (fig.) tort, préjudice, *m.*

hurt, *v.a.,* blesser ; faire mal à; faire du mal à ; (fig.) nuire à, offenser, blesser, choquer.

hurt, *v.n.,* faire du mal ; faire mal.

hurter, *n.*, personne qui blesse, *f.*; auteur d'un mal, d'une blessure, d'un tort, *m.*

hurtful (-foule), *adj.*, nuisible, pernicieux.

hurtfully, *adv.,* d'une manière nuisible ; pernicieusement.

hurtfulness, *n.*, qualité nuisible, *f.* ; tort, préjudice, *m.*

hurtless, *adj.*, qui ne fait point de mal ; innocent ; intact.

hurtlessly, *adv.,* innocemment.

hurtlessness, *n.*, qualité de ce qui n'est pas nuisible, *f.*

husband (heuz'ba'n'd), *n.*, mari, époux, *m.*

husband, *v.a.,* ménager, économiser

husbandless, *adj.*, sans mari.

husbandly, *adj.*, ménager.

husbandman, *n.*, laboureur, cultivateur, *m.*

husbandry, *n.*, labourage, *m.*; industrie agricole; frugalité, économie domestique, *f.*

hush (heushe), *adj.*, silencieux, paisible.

hush ! *int.*, chut !

hush, *v.n.,* se taire; faire silence.

hush, *v.a.,* taire ; faire taire, imposer silence à ; (fig.) calmer. To— up ; *étouffer, taire.*

hush-money (-meu'n'nè), *n.*, argent qu'on donne pour faire taire quelqu'un, *m.*; prime du silence, *f.*, (fam.) chantage, *m.*

husk (heuske), *n.*, (of grain—*de grain*) balle ; (bot.) cosse, glume, gousse, *f.*

husk, *v.a.,* (fruit and vegetables—*fruits et légumes*) écosser ; (grain.) vanner.

husked (heusk'te), *adj.*, (of fruit and vegetables—*de fruits et légumes*) écossé ; à cosse ; (grain) vanné.

huskiness, *n.*, sécheresse, rugosité, *f.*; (of the voice—*de la voix*) raucité, *f.*

husky (heus'-), *adj.*, cossu ; rude, âpre ; (of the voice—*de la voix*) rauque.

hussar (heuz'zàr), *n.*, hussard, *m.*

hussy (heuz'zi), *n.*, coquine ; gueuse, *f.*

hustings (heus'tign'ze), *n.*, estrade (pour haranguer les assemblées en plein air), *f.* ; lieu où se tenaient les élections, *m.*

hustle (heus's'l), *v.n.,* se pousser, se presser, se bousculer.

hustle, *v.a.,* bousculer, presser.

huswife (hewz'zif), **huswifery** (heuz'-), *v. housewife, &c.*

hut (heute), *n.*, hutte ; (milit.) baraque, *f.*

hut, *v.n.,* (milit.) se hutter, se baraquer.

hut, *v.a.,* loger dans des baraques.

hutch (heutshe), *n.*, huche, *f.* ; (for rabbits —*pour lapins*) clapier, *m.*

huzza ! (heuz'zâ), *int.*, hourra !

hyacinth (haï-a-ci'n'th), *n.*, hyacinthe, jacinthe, *f.*

hyades (haï'a-dize), *n.pl.*, hyades, *f.pl.*

hybrid (haï-bride), *n.*, hybride, *m.*

hybrid, *adj.*, hybride.

hydra (haï-dra), *n.*, hydre, *f.*

hydragogue (haï-), *n.*, (med.) hydragogue, *m.*

hydrangea (haï-dra'n'dji-a), *n.*, (bot.) hortensia, *m.*

hydraulic, *or* **hydraulical** (haï-), *adj.*, hydraulique.

hydraulics, *n.pl.*, hydraulique, *f.sing.*

hydrocele (haï-dro-cèle), *n.*, (med.) hydrocèle, *f.*

hydrocephalus (haï-dro-cèf'a-), *n.*, hydrocéphale. *f.*

hydrochlorate (haï-dro-klo-), *n.*, (chem.) hydrochlorate, *m.*

hydrochloric (haï-dro-klô-), *adj.*, hydrochlorique, chlorhydrique.

hydrocotyle (haï-drô-co-ti-li), *n.*, (bot.) hydrocotyle, *f.*

hydrodynamic (haï-dro-daï), *adj.*, hydrodynamique.

hydrodynamics, *n.pl.*, hydrodynamique, *f. sing.*

hydrogen (haï-dro-djène), *n.*, (chem.) hydrogène, *m.*

hydrogenize (-'aïze), *v.a.,* (chem.) hydrogéner.

hydrographer (haï-), *n.*, hydrographe, *m.*

hydrographical, *adj.*, hydrographique.

hydrography, *n.*, hydrographie, *f.*

hydrology (haï-drol'o-dji), *n.*, hydrologie, *f.*

hydromel, *n.*, (pharm.) hydromel, *m.*

hydrometer (haï-dro'm'i-), *n.*, hydromètre ; pèse-liqueur, *m.*

hydrometric, *or* **hydrometrical,** *adj.*, hydrométrique.

hydrometry, *n.*, hydrométrie, *f.*

hydrophobia, *or* **hydrophoby** (haï-dro-fô-), *n.*, hydrophobie ; rage, *f.*

hydrophobic, *adj.*, hydrophobe.

hydrophyte (haï-dro-faïte), *n.*, (bot.) hydrophyte, algue, *f.*

hydropic, *or* **hydropical** (haï-), *adj.*, hydropique.

hydropneumatic (haï-dro-niou-mat'ike), *adj.*, hydropneumatique.

hydrostatic, *or* **hydrostatical** (haï-), *adj.*, hydrostatique.

hydrostatically, *adv.,* suivant l'hydrostatique.

hydrostatics, *n.pl.*, hydrostatique, *f. sing.*

hydrotic (haï-), *n.*, (med.) hydragogue, *m.*

hydrotic, *adj.*, (med.) hydragogue, ☉ hydrotique.

hydruret (haï-drou-rète), *n.*, (chem.) hydrure, *m.*

hyemation (haï-i-m'é-), *n.*, hiémation, *f.*

hyena (haï-i-), *n.*, hyène, *f.*

hygeine (haï-dji-aïne), *or* **hygiene** (haï-dji-îne), *n.*, hygiène, *f.*

hygieual, *or* **hygienic** (haï-dji-è'n'-), *adj.*, hygiénique.

hygrometer (haï-gro'm'i-), *n.*, hygromètre, *m.*

hygrometric. *or* **hygrometrical** (-gro'm'-), *adj.*, hygrométrique.

hygrometry (haï-gro'm'i-), *n.*, hygrométrie, *f.*

hymen (haï-mène), *n.*, hymen, hyménée, *m*

hymeneal, *or* **hymenean** (haï-mi-ni-), *adj.*, de l'hymen ; de l'hyménée ; nuptial.

hymeneal, *or* **hymenean,** *n.*, chant d'hyménée, *m.*

hymenoptera, *or* **hymenopters** (haï-mè'n'op'tèr-, -teurze), *n.pl.*, (ent.) hyménoptères, *m.pl.*

hymenopteral, *adj.*, hyménoptère.

hymn (hime), *n.*, (ode) hymne, *m.* ; (rel.) hymne, *f.*

hymn, *v.a.,* célébrer par des hymnes.

hymn, *v.n.,* chanter des hymnes.

hymn-book (-bouke), *n.*, livre d'hymnes, *m.*

hyosciamus (haï-os-saï-a-), *n.*, (bot.) jusquiame, *f.*

hyp (hipe), *v.a.*, rendre hypocondriaque.

hyp, *n.*, hypocondrie, *f.*

hypallage (haï-pal-la-dji), *n.*, (rhet.) hypallage, *m.*

hyperbaton (haï-peur-), *n.*, (rhet.) hyperbate, *f.*

hyperbola (haï-peur-), *n.*, (geom.) hyperbole, *f.*

hyperbole (haï-peur-bo-li), *n.*, (rhet.) hyperbole, *f.*

hyperbolic, or **hyperbolical,** *adj.*, hyperbolique.

hyperbolically, *adv.*, hyperboliquement.

hyperbolist, *n.*, faiseur d'hyperboles, *m.*

hyperbolize (-laïze), *v.a.*, qualifier hyperboliquement.

hyperbolize, *v.n.*, user de l'hyperbole, parler par hyperbole.

hyperborean (haï-pèr-bo-ri-), *adj.*, hyperboréen, hyperborée.

hypercritic (haï-pèr-), *n.*, hypercritique, *m.*

hypercritical, *adj.*, hypercritique.

hypercriticism, *n.*, critique exagérée, *f.*

hyphen (haï-fène), *n.*, tiret; trait d'union, *m.*

hypnotic, *adj.*, hypnotique, narcotique, soporifique.

hypnotic, *n.*, (med., pharm.) narcotique, soporifique, hypnotique, *m.*

hypochondriac (hip-o-co'n'-), *n.*, hypocondriaque, hypocondre, *m.*

hypochondriacal, *adj.*, hypocondriaque, hypocondre.

hypocrisy (hi-pok'ri-ci), *n.*, hypocrisie, *f.*

hypocrite, *n.* hypocrite, *m.*, *f.*

hypocritic, or **hypocritical,** *adj.*, hypocrite.

hypocritically, *adv.*, hypocritement, en hypocrite, par hypocrisie.

hypogastrium (hip-), *n.*, hypogastre, *m.*

hypoglossal (hip-), *n.*, hypoglosse, *f.*

hypopium (haï-pô-), *n.*, (surg.) hypopyon, *m.*

hypostasis (haï-pos-ta-cice), *n.*, hypostase, *f.*

hypostatic, or **hypostatical** (haï-), *adj.*, hypostatique.

hypostatically, *adv.*, hypostatiquement.

hypotenuse (haï-poth'i-niouze), *n.*, hypoténuse, *f.*

hypothesis (haï-poth'i-cice), *n.*, hypothèse, *f.*

hypothetic, or **hypothetical,** *adj.*, hypothétique.

hypothetically, *adv.*, hypothétiquement.

hyson (haï-çone), *n.*, thé hyson, *m.*

hyssop, *n.*, hysope, *f.*

hysteric, or **hysterical** (his'tèr-), *adj.*, hystérique.

hysterics, *n.pl.*, attaque de nerfs; hystérie, *f. sing.*

hysterocele (his'tèr'o-cile), *n.*, (med.) hystérocèle, *f.*

hysterotomy, *n.*, hystérotomie, *f.*

I

i, neuvième lettre de l'alphabet, i, *m.*

i, *pron.,* je, moi. — speak; *je parle.* Who speaks? *qui est-ce qui parle?* —; moi. It is —; *c'est moi.* It is — who speak; *c'est moi qui parle.*

iambic (aï-), *adj.*, iambique; iambe.

iambic, or **iambus,** *n.*, iambe, *m.*

ibex (aï-bèkse), *n.*, (mam.) bouquetin, *m.*

ibis (aï-bice), *n.*, (orni.) ibis, *m.*

ice (aïce), *n.*, glace, *f.*

ice, *v.a.*, glacer; frapper.

iceberg (aïce-beurghe), *n.*, montagne de glace; banquise, *f.*, banc de glace, *m.*

ice-boat (-bôte), *n.*, bateau-traîneau, *m.*

ice-bound (-baou'n'de), *adj.*, fermé par les glaces; entouré de glace.

ice-breaker (-brèk'-), *n.*, brise-glace, *m.*

ice-cream (-crime), *n.*, crème glacée, glace, *f.*

iced (aïste), *adj.*, glacé; à la glace; (of wine, &c.—*du vin, &c.*) frappé.

ice-house (-haouce), *n.*, glacière, *f.*

icelander, *n.*, Islandais, *m.*, Islandaise, *f.*

icelandic, *adj.*, islandais; d'Islande.

ice-plant, *n.*, ficoïde cristalline; glaciale, glacée, plante glacée, *f.*

ichneumon (ik'niou-), *n.*, ichneumon, *m.*

ichnographic, or **ichnographical** (ik'nog'-), *adj.*, ichnographique.

ichnography (ik'nog'-), *n.*, ichnographie, *f.*

ichor (aï-kor), *n.*, (med.), ichor, pus, *m.*

ichorous, *adj.*, ichoreux.

ichthyolite (ik-thi-o-laïte), *n.*, ichtyolithe, *m.*

ichthyological (ik'thi-ol-o-djik'-), *adj.*, ichtyologique.

ichthyology (ik'thi-ol-o-dji), *n.*, ichtyologie, *f.*

icicle (aï-cik'k'l), *n.*, petit glaçon, *m.*

iciness (aï-), *n.*, froid glacial, *m.*

iconoclast (aï-), *n.*, iconoclaste, *m.*

iconography (aï-), *n.*, iconographie, *f.*

iconolater (aï-co-nol'é-), *n.*, iconolâtre, *m.*

iconology (aï-co-nol-o-dji), *n.*, iconologie, *f.*

icosahedron (aï-cô-ça-hi-), *n.*, (geom.) icosaèdre, *m.*

icterical (ik'tèr'-), *adj.*, ictérique.

icterus (ik'tèr-), *n.*, (med.) ictère, *m.*, jaunisse, *f.*

icy (aï-cy), *adj.*, de glace; glacé, glacial.

idea (ci-dî-eu), *n.*, idée, *f.* To have an — of; *avoir, se faire une idée de.*

ideal, *adj.*, idéal; (philos.) mental.

ideal, *n.*, idéal, *m.*

idealism (-'iz'me), *n.*, idéalisme; spiritualisme, *m.*

idealist, *n.*, idéaliste; spiritualiste, *m.*

idealize (-aïze), *v.n.*, former des idées; idéaliser.

ideally, *adv.*, en idée, mentalement.

identical (aï-), *adj.*, identique.

identically, *adv.*, identiquement.

identification (-fi-ké-), *n.*, identification, *f.*

identify (aï-dè'n'ti-fa-ye), *v.a.*, identifier, constater l'identité de; reconnaître.

identify, *v.n.*, s'identifier.

identity (aï-dè'n'ti-ti), *n.*, identité, *f.*

ideological (aï-di-ol-o-dj'-), *adj.*, idéologique.

ideologist, *n.*, idéologue, idéologiste, *m.*

ideology (aï-di-ol-o-dji), *n.*, idéologie, *f.*

ides (aïd'ze), *n.pl.*, ides, *f.pl.*

idiocy, *n.*, imbécilité, *f.*; idiotisme, *m.*

idiom, *n.*, idiome, idiotisme; génie d'une langue, *m.* The —s of our language; *les idiotismes de notre langue.*

idiomatic, or **idiomatical,** *adj.*, qui tient de l'idiome; qui renferme un idiotisme; idiotique, idiomatique.

idiomatically, *adv.*, conformément à l'idiome; d'une manière idiomatique.

idiopathic (-thike), *adj.*, idiopathique.

idiopathically, *adv.*, par idiopathie.

idiopathy (id-i-op-a-thi), *n.*, (med.) idiopathie, *f.*

idiosyncrasy (id-i-o-ci'n'-cra-ci), *n.*, idiosyncrasie, *f.*

idiot (id-i-ote), *n.*, idiot, *m.*, idiote, *f.* imbécile, *m.*, *f.*

idiotcy (-ot'ci), *n.*, imbécillité, *f.*; idiotisme, *m.*

idiotic, or **idiotical,** *adj.*, idiot, idiotique; d'imbécile; imbécile.

idiotish, *adj.*, idiot, idiotique; imbécile.

idiotism (-iz'me), *n.*, (idiom—*expression*)

idiotisme, *m.*; (idiocy—*idiotic*) imbécillité, *f.*; idiotisme, *m.*

idle (aï'd'l), *adj.*, fainéant, oisif, paresseux, désœuvré; inutile, indolent. — fellow; *fainéant: paresseux.* — hours; *heures de loisir, f. pl.*

idle, *v.n.*, faire le paresseux, fainéanter; passer dans la paresse. To — away one's time; *perdre son temps.*

idle-headed (-hèd'ède), *adj.*, étourdi.

idleness, *n.*, paresse, fainéantise; oisiveté, inutilité, *f.*; désœuvrement, *m.*

idler, *n.*, fainéant, *m.*, fainéante, *f.*; désœuvré, *m.*, désœuvrée, *f.*; paresseux, *m.*, paresseuse, *f.*; oisif, *m.*

idly, *adv.*, dans la paresse; oisivement; en paresseux; avec indolence; oiseusement; nonchalamment; inutilement.

idol (aï-), *n.*, idole, *f.*

idolater, or **idolist**, *n.*, idolâtre; adorateur, *m.*

idolatress, *n.*, femme idolâtre, *f.*

idolatrize (-traïze), *v.n.*, idolâtrer.

idolatrize, *v.a.*, adorer; idolâtrer.

idolatrous, *adj.*, idolâtre.

idolatrously, *adv.*, avec idolâtrie; à l'idolâtrie.

idolatry, *n.*, idolâtrie, *f.*

idolish, *adj.*, idolâtre.

idolist, *n.* *V.* **idolater**.

idolize (-aïze), *v.a.*, idolâtrer; adorer; aimer jusqu'à l'idolâtrie; faire une idole de.

idyl (aï-), *n.*, idylle, *f.*

if, *conj.*, si. — not; *sinon; si ce n'est.*

igneous (ig-ni-), *adj.*, igné, de feu.

igniferous (ig-nif'èr'-), *adj.*, ignifère.

ignipotent (ig-nip-), *adj.*, qui préside au feu.

ignis-fatuus (ig-niss-fat'iou-), *n.* (*ignes-fatui*), feu follet, *m.*

ignite (ig-naïte), *v.a.*, enflammer; mettre en ignition.

ignite, *v.n.*, s'enflammer; entrer en ignition.

ignitible (ig-naït'i-b'l), *adj.*, inflammable.

ignition (ig-nish'-), *n.*, ignition, *f.*

ignivomous (ig-niv'-), *adj.*, ignivome.

ignoble (ig-nô-b'l), *adj.*, ignoble, roturier.

ignobleness, *n.*, ignobilité; roture, *f.*

ignobly, *adv.*, ignoblement; dans la roture; d'une manière ignoble, basse.

ignominious (ig-no-mi'n'-), *adj.*, ignominieux, indigne; (jur.) infamant.

ignominiously, *adv.*, ignominieusement; indignement; (jur.) d'une manière infamante.

ignominy (ig-no-), *n.*, ignominie; (jur.) infamie, *f.*

ignoramus (ig-no-ré-), *n.*, ignare, *m.*, *f.*; ignorant, *m.*; ignorante, *f.*

ignorance (ig-no-), *n.*, ignorance, *f.*

ignorant, *adj.*, ignorant; étranger; inconnu. To be — of; *ignorer; ne pas savoir; ne pas connaître.*

ignorantly, *adv.*, ignoramment; par ignorance.

ignore, *v.a.*, (jur.) déclarer qu'il n'y a pas lieu à poursuivre; ignorer; écarter; mépriser; dédaigner; ne pas vouloir reconnaître (une personne).

ileum (il-î-), *n.*, (anat.) iléon, *m.*

ileus (il-i-), *n.*, (med.) iléus, *m.*; colique de miséréré, *f.*

ilex (aï-lèkse), *n.*, houx, *m.*

ilia, *n.pl.*, flancs, *m.pl.*; région lombaire, *f.sing.*

iliac, *adj.*, iliaque. — passion; *passion iliaque, f.*

iliad, *n.*, iliade, *f.*

ill (il), *n.*, mal. *m.*

ill, *adj.*, mauvais, méchant; (of the health—*de la santé*) malade.

ill, *adv.*, mal; peu. —able to; *peu capable de.*

illapse, *n.*, introduction; attaque, *f.*; accès, *m.*

illation (il-lé-), *n.*, conséquence; déduction; conclusion, *f.*

illative, *adj.*, que l'on peut conclure.

illative, *n.*, terme conclusif, *m.*

illaudable (-a-b'l), *adj.*, peu louable.

illaudably, *adv.*, d'une manière peu louable.

ill-designing (-dè-çaï'n'-), *adj.*, malintentionné.

ill-doing (-dou'-), *n.*, mal, *m.*; mauvaise action, *f.*

illegal (il-lî-), *adj.*, illégal, illicite.

illegality, *n.*, illégalité, *f.*

illegalize (-aïze), *v.a.*, rendre illégal.

illegally, *adv.*, illégalement.

illegibility (il-lèdj'i-), *n.*, état illisible, *m.*

illegible (-lèdj'i-b'l), *adj.*, illisible, ⊙ inlisible.

illegibly, *adv.*, illisiblement; d'une manière illisible.

illegitimacy (il-li-djit'i-), *n.*, illégitimité, *f.*

illegitimate, *adj.*, illégitime; non autorisé.

illegitimately, *adv.*, illégitimement.

illegitimation (-'i-mé-), *n.*, illégitimité, *f.*

illeviable (il-lèv'-i-a-b'l), *adj.*, qui ne peut être levé.

ill-fated (-fét'ède), *adj.*, infortuné, malheureux.

ill-favoured (-fé-veurde), *adj.*, disgracieux; vilain; laid.

ill-favouredly, *adv.*, disgracieusement; mal.

ill-favouredness, *n.*, figure disgraciée; laideur, *f.*

illiberal (il-lib'èr-), *adj.*, illibéral; peu généreux; mesquin; borné; inélégant.

illiberality, *n.*, illibéralité; mesquinerie, *f.*; manque de générosité; manque de lumière, *m.*; petitesse; inélégance, *f.*

illiberally, *adv.*, sans libéralité; sans générosité; mesquinement; d'une manière bornée; sans élégance.

illicit, *adj.*, illicite.

illicitly, *adv.*, illicitement.

illicitness, *n.*, nature illicite, *f.*

illimitable (-a-b'l), *adj.*, illimitable.

illimitably, *adv.*, d'une manière illimitable.

illimited (-ède), *adj.*, illimité.

illimitedness, *n.*, nature illimitée; infinité, *f.*

illiterate (-'èr'éte), *adj.*, illettré.

illiterately, *adv.*, en homme illettré.

ill-meaning (-mîn'-), *adj.*, malintentionné.

ill-minded (-maï'n'd'-), *adj.*, mal disposé; enclin au mal.

ill-nature (-nét'ieure), *n.*, mauvais naturel, *m.*

ill-natured (-nét'ieurde), *adj.*, de mauvais naturel; méchant.

ill-naturedly, *adv.*, méchamment.

ill-naturedness, *n.*, mauvais naturel, *m.*

illness, *n.*, maladie, *f.*; mal, *m.*; indisposition, *f.*

illogical (il-lodj'i-cal), *adj.*, peu logique; illogique.

illogically, *adv.*, peu logiquement; illogiquement.

illogicalness, *n.*, absence de logique; illogicité, *f.*

ill-omened (-ô-mè'n'de), *adj.*, de mauvais présage.

ill-seeming (-sîm'-), *adj.*, d'un aspect peu agréable.

ill-sounding (-saou'n'd'-), *adj.*, sans harmonie; malsonnant.

ill-spirited (-spirit'ède), *adj.*, mal disposé.

ill-starred (-stär'de), *adj.*, né sous une mauvaise étoile ; fait sous une mauvaise étoile.

ill-suiting (-siout'-), *adj.*, malséant.

ill-timed (-taï'm'de), *adj.*, hors de saison ; déplacé ; importun.

illude (il-lioude), *v.a.*, décevoir, tromper.

illume (il-lioume), *v.a.*, illuminer.

illuminate (il-liou-), *v.a.*, éclairer ; illuminer ; éclaircir ; (to decorate—*colorier*) enluminer.

illuminate, *n.*, illuminé, *m.*, illuminée, *f.*

illuminating, *adj.*, qui éclaire.

illuminating, *n.*, enluminure, *f.*

illumination (-mi-né-), *n.*, illumination, *f.* ; (fig.) éclat, *m.*. splendeur, *f.*

illuminative, *adj.*, illuminatif.

illuminator (-né-), *or* **illuminer**, *n.*, personne qui éclaire, chose qui éclaire, *f.* ; illuminateur ; (paint.)enlumineur,*m.*, enlumineuse,*f.*

illumine, *v.a.*, éclairer.

illuminee (il-liou-mi'n'i), *n.* (*illuminati*), illuminé, *m.*, illuminée,*f.*

illuminism, *n.*, illuminisme, *m.*

illusion (il-liou-jeune), *n.*, illusion,*f.*

illusive (il-liou-cive), *adj.*, illusoire.

illusively, *adv.*, illusoirement.

illusiveness, *n.*, caractère illusoire, *m.*

illusory (il-liou-çô-),*adj.*, illusoire.

illustrate (il-leus'-), *v.a.*, illustrer ; expliquer ; démontrer ; faire voir ; prouver ; orner.

illustration (il-leus-tré-), *n.*, illustration ; explication,*f.* ; éclaircissement, *m.*

illustrative, *or* **illustratory** (-tré-) *adj.*, qui éclaircit ; explicatif ; qui rend illustre.

illustratively, *adv.*, pour servir d'explication.

illustrious, *adj.*, illustre ; glorieux ; beau.

illustriously, *adv.*, d'une manière illustre ; avec éclat ; glorieusement.

illustriousness,*n.*,illustration,*f.*;éclat,*m.*

ill-visaged (-viz'adj'de), *adj.*, laid.

i'm (aï'm), *ab de* I am ; *je suis.*

image (i'm'adje), *n.*, image,*f.*

image, *v.a.*, représenter, figurer, peindre.

image-breaker (-brèk'eur), *n.*, briseur d'images ; iconoclaste, *m.*

imagery, *n.*, images. *f.pl.* ; forme ; apparence,*f.* ; chimères ; visions,*f.pl.*

image-vendor (-vè'n'deur), *n.*, marchand d'images, *m.*

image-worship (-weur-), *n.*, idolâtrie, *f.* ; culte des images, *m.*

imaginable (i'm'adj'-i'n'-a-b'l), *adj.*, imaginable.

imaginary (i'm'adj'i'n'), *adj.*, imaginaire, de l'imagination.

imagination (i'm'adj'i-né-), *n.*, imagination, conception,*f.*

imaginative. *adj.*, imaginatif.

imagine (i'n'adj'ine), *v.a.*, imaginer ; s'imaginer ; (jur.) préméditer.

imagine, *v.n.*, s'imaginer ; se figurer.

imaginer, *n.*, personne qui imagine, *f.*

imagining, *n.*, création, conception, *f.*

imbathe (i'n'bé'the),*v.a.*, baigner ; plonger, pénétrer.

imbecile (i'm'bi-cile), *adj.*, imbécile ; faible.

imbecility, *n.*, imbécillité ; impuissance, *f.*

imbed (i'm'bède), *v.a.*, fixer ; empâter ; sceller ; encastrer.

imbibe (i'n'baïbe), *v.a.*, imbiber, absorber ; puiser, prendre ; être imbu de.

imbiber,*n.*,chose qui imbibe,*f.*;absorbant,*m.*

imbibition (i'm'bi-bish'-), *n.*, imbibition,*f.*

imbitter (i'm'bit'-). *V.* **embitter.**

imbody. *V.* **embody.**

imbolden. *V.* **embolden.**

imbosk.*v.a.*,cacher,dérober à la vue (comme par un buisson).

imbosk. *v.n.*, (ant.) être caché, se cacher.

imbosom (-bouz'eume). *V.* **embosom.**

imbow (i'm'bô), *v.a.*, voûter.

imbrangle (i'm'bra'n'g'l), *v.a.*, empêtrer ; entortiller, embarrasser.

imbricated (-két'-ède), *adj.*, en tuile faitière ; en forme de tuile creuse ; imbriqué.

imbrication (-bri-ké'-), *n.*, imbrication,*f.*

imbroglio (i'm' brôl'yi-ô), *n.*, imbroglio, *m.*

imbrown (-braoune), *v.a.*, rembrunir ; assombrir.

imbrue (-brou), *v.a.*, tremper ; souiller.

imbrute (-broute), *v.a.*, abrutir.

imbrute,*v.n.*, s'abrutir.

imbue (-biou), *v.a.*, imbiber ; pénétrer ; inspirer ; teindre.

imitability, *n.*, qualité de ce qui est imitable, *f.*

imitable (-a-b'l), *adj.*, imitable.

imitate, *v.a.*, imiter ; contrefaire.

imitation (-i-té-), *n.*, imitation ; contrefaçon, *f.* ; (paint.) pastiche, *m.*

imitative (-i-té-), *adj.*, qui imite, imitatif ; imitateur.

imitator (-i-té-), *n.*, imitateur, *m.*, imitatrice, *f.* ; contrefacteur, *m.*

immaculate (-'mak'iou-), *adj.*, sans tache, immaculé.

immaculately,*adv.*,sans tache; purement.

immaculateness, *n.*, pureté sans tache,*f.*

immane. *adj.*, vaste; énorme; atroce.

immanely, *adv.*, énormément ; atrocement.

immanency, *n.*, qualité inhérente, *f.*

immanent, *adj.*, inhérent, intrinsèque ; immanent.

immanity, *n.*, barbarie, atrocité,*f.*

immartial (-mâr-shal), *adj.*, peu martial ; peu guerrier.

immask (-mâske), *v.a.*, masquer.

immaterial (-ma-ti-), *adj.*, immatériel ; indifférent, égal. It is — ; *peu importe, c'est égal.*

immaterialism (-iz'me), *n.*, immatérialisme, *m.*

immaterialist, *n.*, immatérialiste, *m.*

immateriality, *n.*, immatérialité,*f.*

immaterialize (-aize), *v.a.*, rendre immatériel.

immaterially, *adv.*, immatériellement ; sans importance.

immature (-tioure), *adj.*, pas mûr ; pas mûri ; sans être mûr ; prématuré.

immaturely, *adv.*, prématurément ; avant la maturité.

immatureness, *or* **immaturity**, *n.*, immaturité ; prématurité, *f.*

immeasurable (-mèj'iou-ra-b'l), *adj.*, incommensurable.

immeasurably, *adv.*, outre mesure ; sans mesure.

immediacy (-mi-di-). *n.*. indépendance,*f.*

immediate (-mi-), *adj.*, immédiat ; instantané.

immediately, *adv.*, immédiatement ; tout de suite ; sur-le-champ ; incessamment.

immediateness. *n.*, caractère immédiat, *m.* ; grande promptitude, *f.*

immedicable (-mèd'i-ca-b'l), *adj.*, irrémédiable ; incurable.

immelodious (-mèl-ô-), *adj.*, peu mélodieux.

immemorable (-mè'm'o-ra-b'l), *adj.*, immémorable.

immemorial (-mi-mô-), *adj.*, immémorial , de temps immémorial.

immemorially, *adv.*, immémorialement ; de temps immémorial.

immense. *adj.*. immense.

immensely, *adv.*, immensément.

immensity, *n.*, immensité,*f.*

immensurability (-mè'n'siou-), *n.*, incommensurabilité, *f.*

25*

immensurable (-ra-b'l), *adj.*, incommen-surable.

immensurate, *adj.*, immense.

immerge (-meurdje), .*v.a.*, plonger; im-merger.

immerse (-meurse), *v.a.*, plonger, enfoncer; immerger.

immersion, *n.*, immersion, *f.*

immesh (-mèshe),*v.a.*, prendre dans un filet; envelopper, enlacer.

immethodical (-mè-thod'-), *adj.*, peu mé-thodique; sans méthode.

immethodically, *adv.*, sans méthode.

immethodicalness (-thod'-), *n.*, absence de méthode, *f.*

immigrant, *n.*, immigrant, *m.*

immigrate, *v.a.*, immigrer.

immigration (-gré-), *n.*, immigration, *f.*

imminence, *n.*, imminence, *f.*; (l.n.) péril, *m.*

imminent, *adj.*, imminent.

immingle (-mi'n'g'l), *v.a.*, mêler.

imminution (-mi-niou-), *n.*, diminution. *f.*

inamiscibility, *n.*, inmiscibilité, *f.*

immission, *n.*, immission, *f.*

immit, *v.a.*, introduire.

immix, *v.a.*, mêler.

immixable (-miks'a-b'l), *adj.*, qui ne peut être mêlé.

immobility, *n.*, immobilité, *f.*

immoderate (-mod'èr'-), *adj.*, immodéré.

immoderately, *adv.*, immodérément.

immoderation (-'èrè-), *n.*, excès; défaut de modération, *m.*; immodération, *f.*

immodest, *adj.*, immodeste; peu modeste; impudique.

immodestly, *adv.*, immodestement; sans modestie; impudiquement.

immodesty, *n.*, immodestie; impudeur, impudicité, *f.*

immolate (-mô-), *v.a.*, immoler.

immolation (-lé-), *n.*, immolation, *f.*; sa-crifice, *m.*

immolator (-lé-), *n.*, immolateur, *m.*

immoral, *adj.*, déréglé, immoral.

immorality, *n.*, immoralité, *f.*

immorally, *adv.*, immoralement.

immortal, *adj.*, immortel; perpétuel.

immortality, *n.*, immortalité; (jur.) per-pétuité, *f.*

immortalization (-tal'aïzé-), *n.*, immortali-sation, *f.*

immortalize (-aïze); *v.a.*, rendre immortel; immortaliser, perpétuer.

immortally, *adv.*, immortellement; éter-nellement.

immortification (-fi-ké-), *n.*, immortifica-tion, *f.*

immovability (-mouv'-), *n.*, immobilité, *f.*

immovable (-mouv'-a-b'l), *adj.*, immobile; inébranlable; (fig.) insensible; (jur.) immeuble.

immovableness, *n.*, immobilité, *f.*; carac-tère inébranlable, *m.*; (fig.) insensibilité, *f.*

immovably, *adv.*, d'une manière immobile; inébranlablement; (fig.) insensiblement.

immundicity (-meu'n'd'-), *n.*,(ant.)immon-dicité, *f.*

immunity (-miou-), *n.*, immunité, exemp-tion, *f.*

immure (-mioure), *v.a.*, entourer de murs; enfermer; claquemurer, tenir captif.

immusical (-miou-zi-), *adj.*, peu harmo-nieux; sans harmonie.

immutability (-miou-ta-), *n.*, immuabilité, immutabilité, *f.*

immutable (-miou-ta-b'l), *adj.*, invariable; immuable; irrévocable.

immutableness, *n.*, immuabilité, immuta-bilité, *f.*

immutably, *adv.*, immuablement; irrévo-cablement.

immutation (-miou-té-). *n.*, changement, *m.*

immute (-mioute), *v.a.*, changer.

imp (i'm'pe), *n.*, rejeton; diablotin, démon; (urchin—*gamin*) petit drole; (of the devil—*du diable*) suppôt, *m.*; (bot.) greffe, *f.*

imp, *v.a.*, (ant.) enter; greffer; allonger, agrandir; insérer.

impact, *v.a.*, presser; serrer.

impact, *n.*, contact; choc, *m.*; empreinte, *f.*; (phys.) inpact, *m.*

impair, *v.a.*, détériorer; (fig.) nuire à, affai-blir, altérer, délabrer.

impair, *adj.*, indigne.

impairer, *n.*, personne qui détériore, qui affaiblit, chose qui détériore, qui affaiblit, *f.*

impairment, *n.*, détérioration, diminution, altération, *f.*; délabrement, *m.*

impale. *V.* empale.

impalpability, *n.*, impalpabilité, *f.*

impalpable (-pa-b'l), *adj.*, impalpable; (fig.) subtil.

impanation (-né-), *n.*, impanation, *f.*

impanel, *v.a.*, dresser une liste du jury; in-scrire sur la liste du jury.

imparadise (-daïce), *v.a.*, placer dans un paradis; combler de bonheur.

imparasyllabic, *adj.*, imparisyllabique.

impardonable (-a-b'l), *adj.*, impardon-nable.

imparity, *n.*, disparité, imparité, dispropor-tion; inégalité, *f.*

impark (-pârke), *v.a.*, parquer.

imparl (-pârle), *v.n.*, (jur.) obtenir une remise pour proposer un arrangement.

impart (-pârte), *v.a.*, accorder, donner; con-férer; communiquer; faire savoir, instruire; faire part à.

impartial (-pâr-shal), *adj.*, impartial.

impartiality, *n.*, impartialité, *f.*

impartially, *adv.*, impartialement.

impartibility (-pârt'-), *n.*, communicabi-lité; indivisibilité; impartibilité, *f.*

impartible (-pârt'i-b'l),*adj.*, communicable; indivisible; impartable.

impartment, *n.*, communication, *f.*

impassable (-pâss'a-b'l), *adj.*, impraticable; infranchissable.

impassableness, *n.*, état impraticable; état infranchissable, *m.*

impassibility (-pas'si-), *n.*, impassibilité, *f.*

impassible (-pas'si-b'l), *adj.*, impassible.

impassibleness, *n.*, impassibilité, *f.*

impassion (-pash'-), *v.a.*, passionner.

impassioned (-pash'eu'n'de), *adj.*, pas-sionné.

impassive (-pas'sive), *adj.*, impassible, in-sensible.

impassively, *adv.*, impassiblement; avec insensibilité.

impassiveness, *n.*, impassibilité, *f.*

impastation (-pés-té-), *n.*, impastation, *f.*

impaste (-péste), *v.a.*, pétrir; réduire en pâte; (paint.) empâter.

impatience (-pé-shè'n'se), *n.*, impatience, *f.*

impatient(-pé-shè'n'te),*adj.*, impatient. To get —; *s'impatienter*; *devenir impatient.* — of, at, for, under, to; impatient de.

impatiently, *adv.*, impatiemment.

impawn (-pône), *v.a.*, engager; garantir.

impeach (-pitshe), *v.a.*, mettre en accusa-tion; accuser; attaquer; dénoncer.

impeachable (-pitsh'a-b'l), *adj.*, sujet à être mis en accusation; accusable.

impeacher, *n.*, personne chargée de soute-nir une accusation, *f.*; accusateur, *m.*

impeachment, *n.*, mise en accusation; accusation; atteinte, *f.*; blâme, *m.*

impearl (-peurle), v.a., former en perles, orner de perles.

impecoability (-pèk'ka-), n., impeccabilité, f.

impeccable (-pèk'ka-b'l), adj., impeccable.

impede (-pîde), v.a., empêcher; mettre obstacle à; retarder.

impediment (-pèd'i-), n., empêchement; obstacle, m.; entrave, difficulté, f.

impel (-pèl), v.a., pousser; mettre en mouvement; forcer; exciter.

impeller, n., force impulsive, f.; moteur, m.

impend (-pè'n'de), v.n., être suspendu; être imminent, menacer.

impendence, or **impendency**, n., imminence, f.

impendent, adj., imminent.

impenetrability (-pè'n'i-tra-), n., impénétrabilité, f.

impenetrable (-pè'n'i-tra-b'l), adj., impénétrable; inaccessible; insensible.

impenetrableness. V. **impenetrability.**

impenetrably, adv., impénétrablement.

impenitence. or **impenitency** (-pè'n'i-), n., impénitence, f.

impenitent. adj., impénitent.

impenitently, adv., dans l'impénitence.

impennate, or **impennous** (-pè'n'-), adj., sans plumes; sans ailes, aptère.

imperative (-pèr'a-), adj., impératif.

imperative, n., impératif, m. In the —; à l'impératif.

imperatively, adv., impérativement.

imperceptible (-pèr'cèp'ti-b'l), adj., imperceptible.

imperceptibleness, n., imperceptibilité, f.

imperceptibly, adv., imperceptiblement.

imperfect (-peur-fèctè), adj., imparfait; incomplet.

imperfection (-pèr-fèk'-),n., imperfection, f.

imperfectly (-peur-), adv., imparfaitement.

imperfectness (-peur-),n., état imparfait, m.

imperforable (-peur-fo-ra-b'l), adj., qui ne peut être percé, qui ne peut être perforé.

imperforate (-peur-), or **imperforated** (-rét'ède), adj., imperforé.

imperforation (-ré-), n., imperforation, f.

imperial (-pî-), adj., impéri l; royal, souverain; (of paper—papier) grand jésus.

imperial (-pî-), n., (beard—barbe) impériale, royale; (of a diligence—de diligence) impériale, f.; (arch.) dôme, m., coupole moresque, f.

imperialist, n., impérialiste, m. — s; impériaux (soldiers of the German Emperor—soldats de l'empereur d'Allemagne).

imperiality, n., pouvoir impérial, m.

imperially, adv., impérialement; en empereur; en roi.

imperious (-pî-), adj., impérieux; dominant; (l.u.) puissant.

imperiously, adv., impérieusement.

imperiousness, n., caractère impérieux, m.; arrogance; hauteur impérieuse, f.

imperishable (-pèr'ish'a-b'l), adj., impérissable.

imperishableness, n., impérissabilité, f.

imperishably, adv., impérissablement.

impermanence (-peur-), n., défaut de permanence, m.

impermanent, adj., peu permanent.

impermeability (-peur-mi-), n., imperméabilité, f.

impermeable (-peur-mi-a-b'l), adj., imperméable.

impersonal (-peur-), adj., impersonnel; unipersonnel.

impersonality, n.,défaut d'individualité, m.

impersonally, adv., impersonnellement; unipersonnellement.

impersonate (-peur-), v.a., personnifier.

impersonated (-ét'ède), adj., personnifié.

impersonation (-so'n'é-), n., personnification, f.

imperspicuity (-pèr-spik'iou-), n., défaut de clarté, m.

imperspicuous, adj., qui n'est pas clair; obscur.

impersuasible (-per-sioué-ci-b'l), adj., qu'on ne peut pas persuader.

impertinence. or **impertinency**(-peur-). n., chose étrangère; (rudeness—impolitesse) impertinence; (trifle—bagatelle) futilité, f.

impertinent, adj., étranger, déplacé; (rude —impoli) impertinent; (trifling—insignifiant) futile.

impertinent, n., impertinent, m., impertinente, f.

impertinently, adv., d'une manière étrangère; (rudely—impoliment) impertinemment.

imperturbable (-pèr-teur-ba-b'l), adj., imperturbable.

impervious (-peur-), adj., impraticable; impénétrable; imperméable.

imperviously, adv., d'une manière impénétrable.

imperviousness, n., impénétrabilité; imperméabilité, f.

impetrate (-pi-), v.a., obtenir par la prière; impétrer.

impetration (-pi-tré-), n., impétration, f.

impetuosity (-pèt'iou-o-ci-), n., impétuosité, f.

impetuous (-pèt' iou-), adj., impétueux.

impetuously, adv., impétueusement.

impetuousness, n., impétuosité, f.

impetus (-pi-), n., impulsion; force impulsive; impétuosité, f.

impierceable (-pirs'a-b'l), adj., qu'on ne peut percer.

impiety (-paï-è-), n., impiété, f.

impinge (-pi'n'dje), v.n., heurter; frapper.

impious (-pi-), adj., impie.

impiously, adv., d'une manière impie; en impie.

implacability (-plé-ka-), n., implacabilité; haine implacable, f.

implacable (-plé-ka-b'l), adj., implacable, acharné.

implacableness, n., implacabilité, f.

implacably, adv., implacablement.

implant, v.a., planter; implanter; graver.

implantation (-pla'n'té-), n., implantation, f.

implausibility (-plô-zi-), n., manque de plausibilité, m.; invraisemblance, f.

implausible (-plô-zi-b'l),adj., peu plausible; invraisemblable.

implausibly, adv., d'une manière peu plausible; invraisemblablement.

implead (-plîde), v.a., poursuivre en justice, accuser.

impleader, n., personne qui poursuit en justice, f.; accusateur, m., accusatrice, f.

implement (-pli-), n., outil; instrument; ustensile, m.

implex (-plèkse), adj., implexe.

implicate. v.a., impliquer; compromettre.

implication (-ké-), n., implication; induction, f.

implicit. adj., implicite; aveugle.

implicitly, adv., implicitement.

implicitness, n., caractère implicite. m.; foi implicite, f.

implied (-plaîde), adj., implicite, tacite.

impliedly.adv., implicitement; tacitement.

implore (-plôre), v.a. and n., implorer.

implorer, n., personne qui implore, f.

implumed(l'm'plou'm'de), or **implumous** (-plou'm'-), adj., sans plumes, privé de plumes.

imply (-pla'ye), v.a., impliquer ; signifier ; vouloir dire.

impoison (-pwaï-z'n). V. **empoison**.

impolicy, n., nature impolitique ; mauvaise politique ; inconvenance ; maladresse, f.

impolite (-laïte), adj., impoli, malhonnête.

impolitely, adv., impoliment ; malhonnête- ment.

impoliteness, n., impolitesse ; malhonnê- teté, f.

impolitic, adj., peu politique, maladroit ; of things—des choses) impolitique.

impoliticly, adv., impolitiquement.

imponderability (-dèr'-), n., impondéra- bilité, f.

imponderable (-dèr-a-b'l), or **impon- derous** (-dèr'-), adj., impondérable.

imporosity (-pô-ro-ci-), n., imporosité, f.

imporous (-pô-), adj., imporeux.

import (-pôrte), n., portée, f.; sens, m. ; importance ; (of words—des mots) valeur ; (com.) Importation, f.

import, v.a., importer ; introduire ; signifier indiquer.

importance, n., importance, f.

important, adj., important.

importantly, adv., avec importance ; d'une manière importante.

importation (-té-), n., importation, f.

importer (-pôrt'-), n., importateur, m.

importless (-pôrt'-), adj., (ant.) sans im- portance.

importunate (-port'iou-), adj., importun ; pressant.

importunately, adv., importunément, avec importunité.

importunateness, n., importunité, f.

importune (-tioune), v.a., importuner.

importunity, n., importunité, f.

imposable (-pôz'a-b'l), adj., qui peut être imposé; qu'on peut imposer.

impose (-pôze), v.a., imposer. To—upon (to deceive—tromper) any one ; en imposer à, trom- per, quelqu'un.

imposer, n., personne qui impose, f.

imposing, adj., imposant.

imposing, n., (print.) imposition, f.

imposing-stone (-stône), n., (print.) marbre, m.

imposition (-po-zish'-), n., imposition, f. ; (tax—contribution) impôt, m. ; (deceit—trom- perie) imposture, f. ; (at school—d'école, &c.) pensum, m.

impossibility, n., impossibilité, f. ; im- possible, m. There is no doing —s ; à l'impossible nul n'est tenu.

impossible (-pos'si-b'l), adj., impossible.

impost (-pôste), n., impôt ; droit d'entrée, m. ; (arch.) imposte, f.

imposthumate (-post'iou-), v.n., abcéder ; ⊙apostumer.

imposthumation, n., formation d'un apostème, f. ; apostume ; apostème, abcès, m.

imposthume (-post'ioume), n., apostème, apostume, abcès, m.

impostor (-pos'teur), n., imposteur, m.

imposture (-post'loure), n., imposture, f.

impotence, or **impotency**, n., impuis- sance ; faiblesse, f.

impotent, adj., impuissant ; faible ; (med.) impotent, perclus.

impotently, adv., avec impuissance ; faible- ment.

impound (-paou'n'de), v.a., mettre en fourrière ; enfermer.

impracticability. V. **impracticable- ness**.

impracticable (-ca-b'l), adj., impraticable, inexécutable ; insociable, intraitable.

impracticableness, n., impraticabilité, impossibilité, insociabilité, f.

impracticably, adv., d'une manière im- praticable.

imprecate (-pri-), v.a., faire des impréca- tions contre ; maudire.

imprecation (-pri-ké-), n., imprécation, f.

imprecatory (-pri-ké-), adj., imprécatoire ; d'imprécation.

impregn(-prī'ne), v.a., imprégner; féconder.

impregnable (-prèg-na-b'l), adj., impre- nable ; inexpugnable ; inébranlable.

impregnably, adv., de manière à être im- prenable.

impregnate (-prèg-), v.a., imprégner ; féconder.

impregnated (-prèg-nét'ède), adj., im- prégné ; fecondé.

impregnation (-prèg'-né-), n., imprégna- tion ; fécondation, f.

impreparation (-prèp'a-ré-), n., (ant.) man- que de preparation, m.

imprescriptibility (-pri-scrip-),n., impres- criptibilité, f.

imprescriptible (-pri-scrip-ti-b'l), adj., im- prescriptible.

impress (-prèce), n., impression, empreinte ; (of sailors—de matelots) presse, f.

impress, v.a., imprimer ; empreindre ; (fig.) graver ; (fig.) pénétrer ; impressionner ; (sailors —matelots) presser.

impressibility, n., qualité de ce qui peut recevoir une empreinte ; sensibilité, f.

impressible (-près'si-b'l), adj., qui peut recevoir une empreinte ; impressionnable ; sen- sible.

impression (-prèsh'-), n., impression ; empreinte ; idée, f.

impressive (-près'-), adj., qui fait une pro- fonde impression ; frappant, touchant ; impres- sionnable.

impressively, adv., de manière à faire impression ; d'une manière touchante, d'une manière pénétrante.

impressiveness, n., force, puissance, na- ture touchante, nature pénétrante, f.

impressment, n., réquisition ; (of sailors— de matelots) presse, f.

impressure (-prèsh'-), n., empreinte, im- pression, f.

imprest (-prèste), n., prêt, m ; arrhes, f.pl.

imprimatur (-mé-teur), n., permis d'im- primer, m.

imprint (-pri'n'te), v.a., imprimer ; em- preindre ; graver.

imprint, n., nom de l'éditeur sur le frontis- pice, m.

imprison (-priz'z'n), v.a., emprisonner, enfermer.

imprisonment (-priz'-), n., emprisonne- ment, m. ; prison ; détention, f. False —; détention illégale.

improbability, n., improbabilité ; invrai- semblance, f.

improbable (-'a-b'l), adj., improbable ; in- vraisemblable.

improbably, adv., improbablement ; invrai- semblablement.

improbity, n., improbité, f.

improficience, or **improficiency** (-fish'è'n'-), n., défaut de progrès, m.

impromptu (-tiou), adj., impromptu, im- provisé.

impromptu, adv., par improvisation, d'a- bondance.

impromptu, n., impromptu, m.

improper, adj., (pers.) qui convient peu ; (of things—des choses) peu convenable, peu propre, inconvenant.; (of language—*du langage*) impropre. — character; *personne de mauvaise réputation, f.* He is an — person for that employment; *il convient peu à cet emploi ; il est peu fait pour cet emploi.*

improperly, *adv.,* d'une manière peu convenable; d'une manière inconvenante; avec inconvenance; à tort; improprement; mal à propos.

impropriate (-prô-), *v.a.,* approprier; (canon law—*droit canon*) séculariser.

impropriate, *adj.,* sécularisé.

impropriation (-prô-pri-é-), *n.,* sécularisation, *f.*; bénéfice sécularisé, *m.*

impropriator (-prô-pri-é-teur), *n.,* possesseur d'un bénéfice sécularisé, *m.*

impropriety (-praï-é-), *n.,* inconvenance; (of language—*du langage*) impropriété, *f.*

improsperity (-pèr'-), *n.,* (ant.) défaut de prospérité, *m.*

improsperous, *adj.,* (ant.) peu prospère; malheureux.

improsperously, *adv.,* (ant.) sans prospérité; malheureusement.

improvability (-prouv'-),*n.,*perfectibilité,*f.*

improvable (-prouv'a-b'l), *adj.,* susceptible d'amélioration, de perfectionnement; qu'on peut perfectionner.

improvably, *adv.,* de manière à pouvoir être amélioré.

improve (-prouve), *v.a.,* améliorer, perfectionner; utiliser; profiter de; faire faire des progrès à; faire avancer; (money—*de l'argent*) faire valoir; (land—*de la terre*) bonifier; (to embellish—*orner* embellir; (to cultivate—*exploiter*) faire valoir, exploiter. To be —d; *avoir fait des progrès* ; (in beauty—*en beauté*) *être embelli.*

improve, *v.n.,* s'améliorer; se perfectionner; se bonifier; faire des progrès; avancer; (to embellish—*devenir plus beau*)embellir, s'embellir; (com.) hausser, augmenter de prix. To — on anything; *perfectionner quelque chose.*

improvement, *n.,* amélioration, *f.*; perfectionnement; (in learning—*du savoir*) progrès, avancement, *m.*; instruction, *f.*; (use—*usage*) emploi, *m.*; application pratique,*f.*; (embellishment—*ornementation*) embellissement, *m.*

improver, *n.,* personne qui améliore, qui perfectionne, qui utilise, *f.*; réformateur, *m.*; réformatrice; cause d'amélioration, *f.*

improvidence (-prov'-),*n.,* imprévoyance,*f.*

improvident, *adj.,* imprévoyant.

improvidently, *adv.,* avec imprévoyance; sans prévoyance.

improvisation(-vi-cé-), *n.,* improvisation,*f.*

improvisatore (-ça-tô-ri), *n.* (*improvisatori*), improvisateur, *m.*

improvisatrice (-ça-trè-tsha), *n.,* improvisatrice,*f.*

imprudence (-prou-), *n.,* imprudence, *f.*

imprudent, *adj.,* imprudent. An — act; *une imprudence.*

imprudently, *adv.,* imprudemment.

impuberty (i'm-piou-bèr-ti), *n.,* impuberté, *f.*

impudence, or **impudency** (-piou-), *n.,* impudence, effronterie,*f.*

impudent, *adj.,* impudent, effronté.

impudently, *adv.,* impudemment, effrontément.

impugn (-peu'ne), *v.a.,* attaquer, combattre.

impugner, *n.,* adversaire; antagoniste, *m.*

impulse (-peulse), or **impulsion** (-peulsh'-), *n.,* impulsion, *f.*; mouvement; motif, *m.*

impulsive, *adj.,* impulsif.

impulsively, *adv.,* par impulsion; par un mouvement involontaire.

impunctuality (-peu'n'gn'k't'iou-), *n.* *V.* **unpunctuality.**

impunity (-piou-), *n.,* impunité,*f.* With —; *impunément.*

impure (-pioure), *adj.,* impur; impudique; immonde.

impurely, *adv.,* impurement; impudiquement; d'une manière immonde.

impurity (-piou-ri-), *n.,* impureté; impudicité; immondice, *f.*

impurple (-peur'p'l), *v.a.,* empourprer.

imputable (-piou-ta-b'l), *adj.,* imputable.

imputation (-piou-té-), *n.,* imputation; prévention; accusation, *f.*

imputative (-piou-), *adj.,* imputable; imputatif.

imputatively, *adv.,* par imputation.

impute (-pioute), *v.a.,* imputer, attribuer.

imputer, *n.,* personne qui attribue, qui impute,*f.*

imputrescible (-piou-très-ci-b'l), *adj.,* non sujet à la putréfaction; imputrescible.

in, *prep.,* en, dans; à; par; pour; sur; (among—*parmi*) chez. — his country; *dans son pays.* — the country (out of town—*hors de la ville*); *à la campagne.* — an hour; *dans, en une heure.* They came — bands; *ils sont venus par bandes.* — self-defence; *pour sa propre défense.* One — ten; *un sur dix.* You must expect that — children; *il faut s'attendre à cela chez les enfants.* He will start — one hour; *il partira dans une heure.* It will take him one hour to do that; *il fera cela en une heure.*

in, *adv.,* (at home—*pas dehors*) chez soi, à la maison, y; (in power—*gouvernant*) au pouvoir; là dedans, en dedans, dedans. Is my brother —? *mon frère est-il à la maison, est-il chez lui, y est-il?* No, he is not —; *non, il n'y est pas, il n'est pas chez lui, il n'est pas à la maison.* The Whigs are — now; *les Whigs sont au pouvoir à présent.* To be — for it; *être dedans ; s'être mis dedans.* To have — (pers.)*faire entrer;* (things —*choses*) *faire provision de ; acheter, se procurer.* I have had my coals —; *j'ai fait ma provision de charbon de terre.* My hand is — ; *je suis en train, en veine.* —! (nav.) *amène!* Put it —; *mettez-le dedans.*

inability, *n.,* état de ne pas pouvoir; manque de moyens, *m.*; impuissance; incapacité; inhabileté,*f.*

inabstinence, *n.,* intempérance, *f.*

inaccessibility, *n.,* inadmissibilité,*f.*; inaccessibilité, *f.*

inaccessible (-cès'-si-b'l), *adj.,* inaccessible, inabordable, impénétrable.

inaccuracy (-kiou-), *n.,* inexactitude,*f.*

inaccurate (-'kiou-), *adj.,* inexact.

inaccurately, *adv.,* inexactement.

inaction, *n.,* inaction, *f.*

inactive, *adj.,* inactif; (of things—*des choses*) sans action, d'inaction, inerte.

inactively, *adv.,* inactivement; dans l'inactivité.

inactivity, *n.,* inactivité,*f.*; manque d'action, *m.*; inertie,*f.*

inadequacy (-i-kwa-), *n.,* insuffisance; disproportion,*f.*; état incomplet; (philos.) état inadéquat, *m.*

inadequate (-i-kwate), *adj.,* insuffisant; disproportionné; incomplet; (philos.)inadéquat.

inadequately, *adv.,* insuffisamment; imparfaitement; incomplètement; d'une manière disproportionnée; d'une manière inadéquate.

inadequateness. *V.* **inadequacy.**

inadmissibility, *n.,* inadmissibilité,*f.*

inadmissible (-si-b'l), *adj.,* inadmissible.

inadvertence, or **inadvertency** (-veur-), *n.,* inadvertance,*f.*

inadvertent, *adj.,* négligent.

inadvertently (-veur-), *adv.,* par mégarde, par inadvertance.

inaffability, *n.,* défaut d'affabilité, *m.*

inaffable (-fa-b'l), *adj.*, peu affable.

inalienable (-'el-iè'n'a-b'l), *adj.*, inaliénable ; inséparable.

inalienableness, *n.*, inaliénabilité, *f.*

inalienably, *adv.*, d'une manière inaliénable.

inalimental, *adj.*, (ant.) qui n'est pas nourrissant.

inalterability (-tèr'a-), *n.*, inaltérabilité, *f.*

inalterable (-tèr'a-b'l), *adj.*, (ant.) inaltérable.

inane, *adj.*, vide.

inanimate, *adj.*, inanimé.

inanition (-nish'-), *n.*, inanition, *f.*

inanity, *n.*, vide, *m.* ; inanité, *f.*

inappetence, *or* **inappetency** (-ap-pi-), *n.*, inappétence, *f.*

inapplicability (-ap-pli-ca-), *n.*, inapplicabilité, *f.*

inapplicable (-pli-ca-b'l), *adj.*, inapplicable.

inapplication (-pli-ké-),*n.*, inapplication,*f.*

inapposite (-po-cite), *adj.*, peu approprié ; inapplicable ; peu conforme, peu juste.

inappreciable(-pri-shi-a-b'l),*adj.*, inappréciable.

inapprehensible (-pri-hè'n'-si-b'l), *adj.*, incompréhensible.

inapprehensive (-cive), *adj.*, inattentif.

inapproachable (-prôtsh-a-b'l), *adj.*, inabordable, inaccessible.

inappropriate (-prô-pri-éte), *adj.*, peu approprié.

inaptitude (-ti-tioude), *n.*, inaptitude, *f.*

inarable (-a-b'l), *adj.*, qui ne peut être labouré.

inarch (-ârtshe), *v.a.*, (hort.) enter par approche.

inarticulate (-tik'iou-léte), *adj.*, inarticulé.

inarticulately, *adv.*, d'une manière inarticulée ; confusément, indistinctement.

inarticulateness, *or* **inarticulation**, *n.*, défaut d'articulation, *m.*

inartificial (-fish'al), *adj.*, peu artificiel ; naturel, sans art.

inartificially, *adv.*,inartificiellement ; naturellement ; sans art.

inattention, *n.*, inattention ; distraction, *f.*

inattentive, *adj.*, inattentif ; distrait ; inappliqué.

inattentively, *adv.*, peu attentivement ; avec distraction ; sans attention.

inaudible (-di-b'l), *adj.*, inaudible.

inaudibly, *adv.*, à ne pouvoir être entendu.

inaugural (-ghiou-), *adj.*, inaugural.

inaugurate, *v.a.*, inaugurer, dédier.

inauguration (-ré'-), *n.*, inauguration, *f.*

inauguratory, *adj.*, d'inauguration.

inauration (-ré-), *n.*, dorure, *f.*

inauspicious (-spish'-), *adj.*, funeste, peu propice.

inauspiciously, *adv.*, sous de mauvais auspices ; d'une manière funeste.

inauspiciousness, *n.*, mauvais auspices, *m.pl.*

inbeing (-bi'-), *n.*, inhérence, *f.*

inboard (-bôrde), *adv.*, dans la cale d'un vaisseau.

inborn, *adj.*, inné.

inbreathed (-brith'de), *adj.*, communiqué par la respiration ; inspiré.

inbred (-brède), *adj.*, inné, né en soi.

inbreed (-bride), *v.a.* (*preterit* and *past part.*, Inbred), faire naître ; créer ; produire.

inca, *n.*, Inca, *m.*

incage (-kédje), *v.* *V.* encage.

incalculable(-kiou-la-b'l),*adj.*, incalculable.

incalculably,*adv.*, incalculablement ; d'une manière incalculable.

incalescence, *or* **incalescency** (-lès'-), *n.*, chaleur naissante, *f.*

incameration (-mèr-é-),*n.*, incamération,*f.*

incandescent (-dès'-), *adj.*, incandescent.

incantation (-té), *n.*, incantation, *f.* ; enchantement, *m.*

incantatory (-ta-to-), *or* **incanting**, *adj.*, par incantation.

incanton, *v.a.*, réunir en cantons.

incapability, *or* **incapableness**(-ké-pa-), *n.*, incapacité, *f.*

incapable (-ké-pa-b'l), *adj.*, incapable ; non susceptible.

incapacious (-pé-shi-), *adj.*, de peu de capacité ; (fig.) étroit, borné.

incapaciousness, *n.*, défaut d'espace, *m.* ; (fig.) étroitesse, *f.*

incapacitate (-pass'i-), *v.a.*, rendre incapable ; (jur.) frapper d'incapacité, rendre inhabile.

incapacitation (-ci-té-), *n.*, défaut de capacité, *m.* ; privation de capacité légale, *f.*

incapacity, *n.*, incapacité ; (jur.) inhabilité, *f.*

incarcerate (-câr-cèr'-), *v.a.*, incarcérer.

incarcerate, *adj.*, incarcéré.

incarceration (-cèr'é-), *n.*, incarcération, *f.* ; (surg.) étranglement, *m.*

incarn (-cârne), *v.a.*, couvrir de chair.

incarn, *v.n.*, se couvrir de chair.

incarnate (-câr-), *adj.*, incarné.

incarnate, *v.a.*, revêtir de chair ; vivifier.

incarnation (-né-), *n.*, incarnation, *f.*

incarnative (-câr-na-), *adj.*, incarnatif.

incarnative, *n.*, incarnatif, *m.*

incase (-kéce), *v.a.*, encaisser ; couvrir, enfermer, enchâsser.

incastellated (-tèl-lét'éde), *adj.*, enfermé dans un château.

incatenation (-cat'i-né-), *n.*, enchaînement, *m.*

incautious (-cô-shi-), *adj.*, inconsidéré, imprudent.

incautiously, *adv.*, imprudemment, inconsidérément.

incautiousness, *n.*, imprudence, *f.*

incavated (-vét'éde), *adj.*, creusé.

incavation (-vé-), *n.*, excavation, *f.*

incendiary, *n.*, incendiaire ; (fig.) boutefeu, *m.*

incendiary, *adj.*, incendiaire.

incense (i'n'cè'n's), *n.*, encens, *m.*

incense (i'n'cè'n's), *v.a.*, encenser.

incense (i'n'cè'n's), *v.a.*, courroucer ; irriter ; exaspérer ; provoquer.

incensement, *n.*, courroux, *m.* ; irritation, exaspération, *f.*

incension (-cè'n'sh'-), *n.*, embrasement, *m.*

incensive (-cive), *adj.*, qui irrite ; exaspérant ; qui courrouce.

incensor, *n.*, provocateur, *m.*

incensory, *n.*, encensoir, *m.*

incentive (-tive), *n.*, aiguillon ; motif, *m.*

incentive, *adj.*, qui excite ; qui encourage.

inception (-cèp'-), *n.*, commencement, *m.*

inceptive, *adj.*, qui commence ; qui marque le commencement ; (gram.) inchoatif.

inceptor, *n.*, commençant, *m.*

inceration (-ci-ré-), *n.*, action de couvrir de cire, *f.*

incertitude (-ceur-ti-tioude), *n.*, incertitude, *f.*

incessancy (-cès'-), *n.*, durée non interrompue, *f.*

incessant, *adj.*, incessant ; continuel.

incessantly, *adv.*, sans cesse, continuellement.

incest, *n.*, inceste, *m.*

incestuous (-cèst'iou-), *adj.*, incestueux.

incestuously, *adv.*, incestueusement.

incestuousness, *n.*, état incestueux, *m.*

inch (i'n'sh), *n.*, pouce (centimètres 2·530954).

m̃. Within an — of; *à deux doigts de.* By —es; *peu à peu, à coups d'épingle; à petit feu.*

inch, *v.a.,* pousser peu à peu ; faire avancer peu à peu.

inch, *v.n.,* avancer peu à peu ; reculer peu à peu.

inchmeal (-mîl), *n.,* pièce d'un pouce de long, *f.* By — ; *pouce par pouce; à coups d'épingle ; à petit feu.*

inchoate (ign'co'éte), *adj.,* commencé.

inchoate. *v.a.,* commencer.

inchoately, *adv.,* au premier degré.

inchoation, *n.,* commencement, *m.*

inchoative (-cô-a-tive), *adj.,* qui commence; inchoatif.

incidence, *or* **incidency,** *n.,* accident, *m.* ; (geom.) incidence, *f.*

incident, *n.,* incident, *m.*

incident. *adj.,* accidentel ; qui arrive ; qui appartient ; (gram., opt.) incident.

incidental, *adj.,* accidentel, fortuit ; (gram.) incident.

incidentally, *adv.,* incidemment ; fortuitement.

incinerate (-ci'n'èr'éte), *v.a.,* incinérer.

incineration, *n.,* incinération, *f.*

incipiency, *n.,* commencement, *m.*

incipient, *adj.,* qui commence, premier, naissant.

incise (-çaïze), *v.a.,* couper, tailler; inciser.

incised (-çaïz'de), *adj.,* incisé.

incision (-cij'eune), *n.,* incision, coupure, *f.*

incisive (-çaï-cive), *adj.,* incisif.

incisor (-çaï-çor), *n.,* dent incisive ; incisive, *f.*

incisory, *adj.,* incisif ; tranchant.

incisure (-cij'eur), *n.,* incision, *f.*

incitation (-ci-té-), *n.,* incitation, *f.*

incite (-çaïte), *v.a.,* inciter, exciter, animer, stimuler, encourager.

incitement (-çaïť-), *n.,* encouragement, aiguillon, motif, stimulant, *m.*

incivil, *adj.,* incivil, impoli.

incivility, *n.,* incivilité, malhonnêteté, *f.*

incivism (-'iz'me), *n.,* incivisme, *m.*

inclemency (-clè'm'-), *n.,* inclémence; (of the weather—*du temps*)inclémence, intempérie ; (pers.) inflexibilité, dureté, *f.*

inclement (-clè'm'-), *adj.,* inclément ; (pers.) inflexible, dur.

inclinable (-claï'n'a-b'l), *adj.,* enclin, porté.

inclination (-cli-né-), *n.,* inclinaison, pente; (of the head or body—*de la tête, du corps*) inclination, *f.* ; (liking—*disposition*) penchant, goût, *m.,* inclination, *f.* From — ; *par inclination, par goût.*

inclinatorily (-claï'n'-a-), *adv.,* par inclinaison.

inclinatory (-claï'n'a-), *adj.,* qui incline ; incliné.

incline (-claïne), *v.a.,* incliner, pencher, porter.

incline, *v.n.,* incliner, baisser, pencher ; être enclin, être disposé ; (math.) s'incliner.

inclined (-claï'n'de), *adj.,* incliné ; enclin, disposé.

incliner, *n.,* cadran solaire incliné, *m.*

inclining, *adj.,* incliné ; penché.

inclip, *v.a.,* étreindre ; entourer ; embrasser.

incloister (-cloïs'-), *v.a.,* cloîtrer.

inclose (-clôze), *v. V.* **enclose.**

incloud (-claoude), *v.a.,* envelopper d'un nuage ; obscurcir.

include (-cloude), *v.a.,* comprendre, renfermer. Including; *comprenant, compris, y compris.* Including the ladies ; *y compris les dames ; les dames y comprises.*

included (-cloud'ède), *adj.,* renfermé ; compris ; y compris,

inclusion (-clou-jeune), *n.,* action de renfermer, de comprendre, *f.*

inclusive (-clou-cive), *adj.,* inclusif, qui renferme, qui comprend. — of ; *y compris.*

inclusively, *adv.,* inclusivement.

incoagulable (-agh'iou-la-b'l), *adj.,* qui ne peut se coaguler.

incoercible (-co-eur-ci-b'l), *adj.,* incoercible.

incog., *adv.,* incognito.

incogitance, *or* **incogitancy** (-codj'i-), *n.,* irréflexion, *f.*

incogitant. *adj.,* irréfléchi.

incogitantly, *adv.,* sans réflexion.

incogitative (-codji-ta-tive), *adj.,* incapable de penser.

incognito (-cog-ni-tô), *adv.,* incognito.

incoherence, *or* **incoherency** (-hi-), *n.,* incohérence, *f.*

incoherent (-hi-), *adj.,* incohérent.

incoherently, *adv.,* sans cohérence; d'une manière incohérente.

incombustibility, *or* **incombustible- ness** (-beus'-), *n.,* incombustibilité, *f.*

incombustible (-beus'ti-b'l), *adj.,* incombustible.

income (-keume), *n.,* rente, *f.* ; revenu, *m.* ; rentes, *f.pl.* ; revenus, *m.pl.*

incommensurability (-'mè'n's'iou-ra-), *n.,* incommensurabilité, *f.*

incommensurable(-mè'n's'iou-ra-b'l),*adj.,* incommensurable.

incommensurably, *adv.,* incommensurablement.

incommensurate, *adj.,* disproportionné ; incommensurable.

incommensurately, *adv.,* d'une manière disproportionnée.

incommodate (-mo-déte), *or* **incommode** (-môde), *v.a.,* incommoder, gêner, déranger.

incommodious (-mô-di-), *adj.,* incommode.

incommodiously, *adv.,* incommodément.

incommodiousness, *or* **incommodity,** *n.,* incommodité, *f.*

incommunicability, *or* **incommuni- cableness** (-miou-ni-ca-), *n.,* incommunicabilité, *f.*

incommunicable (-miou-ni-ca-b'l), *adj.,* incommunicable.

incommunicably, *adv.,* d'une manière incommunicable.

incommunicated (-két'ède), *adj.,* (ant.) qui n'a pas été communiqué.

incommunicating (-két'-), *adj.,* sans communication.

incommunicative (-két'-), *adj.,* peu communicatif.

incommutability, *or* **incommutable- ness** (-miout'a-), *n.,* non-commuabilité, *f.*

incommutable (-miout-a-b'l), *adj.,* incommuable.

incompact, *or* **incompacted** (-pact'ède), *adj.,* non compact ; qui n'est pas serré.

incomparable (-pa-ra-b'l), *adj.,* incomparable.

incomparableness, *n.,* qualité de ce qui est incomparable, *f.*

incomparably, *adv.,* incomparablement.

incompassionate (-pash'eu'n'éte), *adj.,* peu compatissant ; sans compassion.

incompassionately, *adv.,* sans compassion.

incompassionateness, *n.,* défaut de compassion, *m.*

incompatibility (-pat-i-), *n.,* incompatibilité, *f.*

incompatible (-pat'i-b'l),*adj.,* incompatible.

incompatibly, *adv.,* incompatiblement.

incompetence, *or* **incompetency** (-pi-), *n.,* insuffisance ; impuissance ; (jur.) incapacité, incompétence, *f.*

incompetent, *adj.*, impuissant, insuffisant; incompétent; (jur.) incompétent, incapable.

incompetently, *adv.*, insuffisamment; (jur.) incompétemment.

incomplete (-plîte), *adj.*, imparfait; inachevé, incomplet.

incompletely, *adv.*, incomplètement; imparfaitement.

incompleteness, *n.*, état incomplet, inachevé, imparfait, *m.*

incomplex (-plèkse), *adj.*, incomplexe.

incompliance (-plaï'a'n'ce), *n.*, manque de complaisance, *m.*; raideur, *f.*

incompliant, *adj.*, peu complaisant.

incomposed (-pôz'de), *adj.*, dérangé, troublé.

incomposite (-poz'ite), *adj.*, incomposé; (arith.) premier.

incomprehensibility, *or* **incomprehensibleness** (-pri-hè'n'-), *n.*, incompréhensibilité, *f.*

incomprehensible (-si-b'l), *adj.*, incompréhensible.

incomprehensibly, *adv.*, incompréhensiblement.

incomprehensive (-pri-hè'n'cive), *adj.*, peu étendu; borné.

incompressibility (-près'si-), *n.*, incompressibilité, *f.*

incompressible (-près'si-b'l), *adj.*, incompressible.

inconcealable (-cîl'a-b'l), *adj.*, qu'on ne peut cacher; qui ne peut se cacher.

inconceivable (-civ'a-b'l), *adj.*, inconcevable.

inconceivableness, *adj.*, nature inconcevable, *f.*

inconceivably, *adv.*, inconcevablement.

inconclusive (-clou-cive), *adj.*, peu concluant.

inconclusively, *adv.*, d'une manière peu concluante.

inconclusiveness, *n.*, nature peu concluante, *f.*

inconcoct, *or* **inconcocted** (-coct'ède), *adj.*, (ant.) indigeste; peu mûr.

inconcoction, *n.*, immaturité, *f.*

incondensability (-sa-), *n.*, non-condensabilité, *f.*

incondensable (-sa-b'l), *adj.*, non-condensable.

incondite (-daïte, *ou* -dîte), *adj.*, irrégulier.

inconformity, *n.*, (ant.) *V.* **non-conformity.**

incongruity (-grou-), *n.*, incongruité; inconvenance, *f.*

incongruous (-grou-), *adj.*, incongru, inconvenant.

incongruously, *adv.*, incongrûment; peu convenablement.

inconsequence (-si-kwè'n'-), *n.*, fausse conséquence; fausse déduction, *f.*

inconsequent, *or* **inconsequential** (-si-kwè'n'te,-shal), *adj.*, mal déduit; peu important.

inconsequentially, *adv.*, illogiquement.

inconsiderable (-èr'a-b'l), *adj.*, peu important; de peu de considération; sans importance; peu considérable; peu sensible; petit.

inconsiderableness, *n.*, manque d'importance, *m.*; petitesse, *f.*

inconsiderate (-sid'èr'-), *adj.*, inconsidéré, irréfléchi.

inconsiderately, *adv.*, inconsidérément; sans réflexion.

inconsiderateness, *or* **inconsideration**, *n.*, irréflexion; inconsidération, *f.*

inconsistence, *or* **inconsistency** (-sist'è'n'-), *n.*, inconséquence; contradiction; incompatibilité; versatilité, *f.*

inconsistent, *adj.*, inconséquent; incompatible.

inconsistently, *adv.*, contradictoirement; incompatiblement; inconséquemment.

inconsolable (-sôl'a-b'l), *adj.*, inconsolable.

inconsolably, *adv.*, inconsolablement.

inconsonance, *or* **inconsonancy**, *n.*, discordance, *f.*; manque de conformité, *m.*

inconsonant, *adj.*, discordant; peu conforme.

inconspicuous (-spik'iou-), *adj.*, qui n'est pas en vue; peu marquant; peu remarquable.

inconstancy, *n.*, inconstance; diversité, *f.*

inconstant, *adj.*, inconstant, volage.

inconstantly, *adv.*, inconstamment; avec inconstance.

inconsumable (-sioum'a-b'l), *adj.*, qui ne peut être consumé; qui ne peut être consommé.

inconsummate (-seum'méte), *adj.*, non consommé, non accompli.

inconsummateness (-seum'mét'-), *n.*, état de ce qui n'est pas consommé, de ce qui n'est pas accompli, *m.*

incontestable (-tès'ta-b'l), *adj.*, incontestable.

incontestably, *adv.*, incontestablement.

incontinence, *or* **incontinency** (-ti-nè'n'-), *n.*, incontinence, *f.*

incontinent, *adj.*, incontinent.

incontinently, *adv.*, avec incontinence; immédiatement.

incontrovertible (-tro-veurt'i-b'l), *adj.*, incontroversable; incontestable.

incontrovertibly, *adv.*, incontestablement.

inconvenience, *or* **inconveniency** (-vi'n'iè'n'-), *n.*, incommodité, gêne; disconvenance, *f.*; inconvénient, *m.*

inconvenience (-vi-ni-è'n'ce), *v.a.*, déranger; incommoder; gêner.

inconvenient (-vi'n'-), *adj.*, incommode; gênant.

inconveniently, *adv.*, incommodément.

inconvertible (-veurt'i-b'l), *adj.*, non convertible.

inconvincible (-ci-b'l), *adj.*, incapable de conviction; qui n'est pas à convaincre.

inconvincibly, *adv.*, sans possibilité de conviction.

incorporal, *adj.*, incorporel; immatériel.

incorporality, *n.*, incorporalité, immatérialité, *f.*

incorporally, *adv.*, d'une manière incorporelle; immatériellement.

incorporate, *v.a.*, incorporer; constituer en corps; former en corporation; (com.) constituer en compagnie, constituer en société.

incorporate, *v.n.*, s'incorporer.

incorporation (-ré-), *n.*, incorporation, *f.*

incorporeal (-pô-ri-), *adj.*, incorporel.

incorporeally, *adv.*, d'une manière incorporelle; immatériellement.

incorporeity (-pô-rî-i-), *n.*, incorporéité, *f.*

incorrect (i'n-cor-rècte), *adj.*, incorrect, inexact.

incorrectly, *adv.*, incorrectement; inexactement.

incorrectness, *n.*, incorrection; inexactitude, *f.*

incorrigibility, *or* **incorrigibleness** (-cor-ri-iji-), *n.*, incorrigibilité, *f.*

incorrigible (-dji-b'l), *adj.*, incorrigible.

incorrigibly, *adv.*, incorrigiblement.

incorrupt, *or* **incorrupted** (-cor-reupt, -'ède), *adj.*, non corrompu: pur.

incorruptible, *or* **incorruptibleness** (-cor-reup-ti-), *n.*, incorruptibilité, *f.*

incorruptible (-ti-b'l), *adj.*, incorruptible.

incorruption (-reup'-), *n.*, incorruptibilité; incorruption, *f.*

incorruptive, *adj.*, incorruptible.

incorruptness, *n.*, incorruptibilité; pureté, *f.*

incrassate (-cras'séte), *v.a.* and *n.*, épaissir; engraisser; s'épaissir; s'engraisser.

incrassate, *or* **incrassated** (-cras'séte, -'ède), *adj.*, épaissi; engraissé.

incrassation (-sé-), *n.*, épaississement, *m.*

incrassative (-sat'ive), *adj.*, incrassant.

increase (-crìce), *n.*, crue, augmentation, *f.*; accroissement, surcroît: (fig.) produit, rejeton; (of the moon—*de la lune*) croissant, *m.*

increase, *v.a.*, augmenter, faire croître, grossir; accroître. To — to; *porter à.*

increase, *v.n.*, croître; accroître; s'accroître; grossir; augmenter; s'augmenter; prendre de l'accroissement.

increaseful (-foule), *adj.*, (ant.) abondant.

increaser, *n.*, personne, chose qui accroît, qui augmente, *f.*

increasing, *adj.*, croissant.

increate, *or* **increated**(-cri-éte,-'ède), *adj.*, incréé.

incredibility,*or* **incredibleness**(-crèd'-), *n.*, caractère incroyable, *m.*; incrédibilité, *f.*

incredible (-crèd'i-b'l), *adj.*, incroyable.

incredibly, *adv.*, incroyablement.

incredulity(-cri-diou-), *n.*, incrédulité, *f.*

incredulous (-crèd'iou-), *adj.*, incrédule.

incredulousness, *n.*, incrédulité, *f.*

increment (-cri-), accroissement, *m.*; (math.) différentielle, quantité différentielle, *f.*

increpation (-cri-pé-), *n.*, réprimande, *f.*

increscent (-crès'-),*adj.*, croissant.

incriminate (-cri'm'-i-), *v.a.*, incriminer.

incrust, *or* **incrustate** (-creust,-téte), *v.a.*, incruster.

incrustation (-té-), *or* **incrustment**, *n.*, incrustation; croûte,*f.*

incubate (-kiou-), *v.a.*, couver.

incubation (-bé-), *n.*, incubation, *f.*

incubus (-kiou-beusse), *n.*, cauchemar; incube, *m.*

inculcate (-keul-), *v.a.*, inculquer.

inculcation (-ké-), *n.*, inculcation, *f.*

inculpable (-keul-pa-b'l), *adj.*, irrépréhensible.

inculpate (-keul-), *v.a.*, blâmer; censurer; inculper.

inculpation (-pé-), *n.*, blâme, *m.*; censure, inculpation,*f.*

inculpatory (-pa-teuri), *adj.*, qui blâme.

incult, *or* **incultivated** (-keulte, -vét'ède), *adj.*, (ant.) inculte.

incultivation (-keul-ti-vé-), *or* **inculture** (-tioure), *n.*, (ant.) inculture,*f.*

incumbency (-keu'm'-), *n.*, état d'un objet couché sur un autre; devoir, *m.*; charge, *f.*; (ecc.) possession d'un bénéfice, *f.*

incumbent, *n.*, titulaire; bénéficier, *m.*

incumbent,*adj.*, couché; appuyé; obligatoire; (bot.) incombant.

incumber (-keu'm'-), *v. V.* **encumber**.

incur (-keur), *v.a.*, encourir. s'attirer.

incur, *v.n.*, (ant.) se présenter; s'offrir.

incurability, *or* **incurableness** (-kiou-ra-), *n.*, incurabilité,*f.*

incurable (-kiou-ra-b'l), *adj.*, incurable.

incurable, *n.*, incurable, *m.*,*f.*

incurably, *adv.*, incurablement, sans.remède.

incurious (-kiou-), *adj.*, peu curieux; sans curiosité.

incuriously, *adv.*, sans curiosité; avec incuriosité

incuriousness, *or* **incuriosity** (-rioss'i-), *n.*, incuriosité, *f.*

incursion (-keur-), *n.*, incursion,*f.*

incurvate (-keur-), *v.a.*, courber.

incurvate, *adj.*, courbé.

incurvation (-vé-), *n.*, incurvation, courbure,*f.*

incurve (-keurve), *v.a.*, courber.

incurvity, *n.*, incurvation; courbure,*f.*

incus, *n.*, (anat.) enclume (ossicle of the ear —*osselet de l'oreille*),*f.*

indagate (-da-ghéte), *v.a.*, rechercher.

indagation (-ghé-), *n.*, recherche,*f.*

indagator, *n.*, scrutateur, *m.*

indart (-dárte), *v.a.*, darder.

indebted(-dèt'ède),*adj.*, endetté; redevable.

indebtedness, *n.*, état de dette, *m.*

indecency (-di-), *n.*, indécence,*f.*

indecent (-di-), *adj.*, indécent; déshonnête.

indecently, *adv.*, indécemment.

indeciduous (-di-cid'iou-), *adj.*, persistant.

indecision (-di-sij'-), *n.*, indécision,*f.*

indecisive (-di-çaï-cive), *adj.*, peu décisif; indécis.

indecisively, *adv.*, d'une manière indécise.

indecisiveness, *n.*, état indécis, *m.*

indeclinable (-di-claï'n'a-b'l), *adj.*, indéclinable.

indecomposable (-dî-co'm'póz'a-b'l), *adj.*, indécomposable.

indecomposableness, *n.*, nature indécomposable,*f.*

indecorous (-dèk'o-, *ou* -di-cô-), *adj.*, contraire au décorum; qui blesse le décorum; indécent; inconvenant.

indecorously, *adv.*, avec inconvenance; incongrûment.

indecorousness, *n.*, manque de décorum, *m.*; messéance; inconvenance,*f.*

indecorum (-di-cô-), *n.*, manque de décorum, *m.*; messéance; inconvenance,*f.*

indeed (-dîde), *adv.*, en effet, en vérité; vraiment; il est vrai; à dire vrai; à la vérité. —! *vraiment! allons donc! comment!* (iron.) *par exemple!*

indefatigable (-di-fat'-i-ga-b'l), *adj.*, infatigable.

indefatigableness, *n.*, caractère infatigable, *m.*

indefatigably, *adv*, infatigablement; sans relâche.

indefeasibility (-di-fi-zi-), *n.*, inaliénabilité; imprescriptibilité; indestructibilité,*f.*

indefeasible (-di-fi-zi-b'l), *adj.*, inaliénable; imprescriptible.

indefeasibly, *adv.*, avec inaliénabilité; avec imprescriptibilité; d'une manière indestructible.

indefectibility (-di-fèct'i-), *n.*, indéfectibilité,*f.*

indefectible (-di-fèct-i-b'l), *adj.*, indéfectible.

indefective (-di-fèk'tive), *adj.*, non défectueux.

indefensible (-di-fè'n'si-b'l), *adj.*, qui n'est pas défendable; insoutenable; inexcusable.

indefensibly, *adv.*, inexcusablement.

indefensive (-di-fè'n'sive), *adj.*, sans défense.

indeficiency (-di-fish'-), *n.*, perfection,*f.*

indeficient (-di-fish-), *adj.*, parfait; sans défaut.

indefinable (-di-faï'n'a-b'l), *adj.*, indéfinissable.

indefinite (-dèf'i-), *adj.*, indéfini.

indefinitely, *adv.*, indéfiniment.

indefiniteness, *n.*, nature indéfinie,*f.*

indeliberate (-di-lib'èr'-), *adj.*, indélibéré.

indeliberately, *adv.*, d'une manière indélibérée; sans délibération.

indelibility, *or* **indelibleness** (-dèl'i-), *n.*, indélébilité,*f.*

indelible (-dèl-i-b'l), *adj.*, indélébile, ineffaçable.

indelibly, *adv.*, d'une manière indélébile; ineffaçablement.

indelicacy (-dèl'i-), *n.*, indélicatesse,*f.*
indelicate (-dèl'i-kéte), *adj.*, indélicat.
indelicately, *adv.*, avec indélicatesse ; d'une manière indélicate.
indemnification (-dè'm'ni'-fi-ké-), *n.*, indemnisation ; indemnité,*f.*
indemnify (-dè'm'ni-fa'ye), *v.a.*, dédommager, indemniser.
indemnity (-dè'm'ni-ti), *n.*, dédommagement, *m.*; indemnité,*f.* Act of — ; *amnistie, f.*
indemonstrable (-di-mo'n'stra-b'l), *adj.*, indémontrable.
indent (-dè'n'te), *n.*, dentelure ; échancrure, coupure, (stamp—*impression*) empreinte,*f.*
indent, *v.a.*, denteler ; ébrécher ; échancrer ; (to bind out by indentures—*engager par contrat d'apprentissage*)mettre en apprentissage;(print.) rentrer.
indent, *v.n.*, denteler le bord de papier, de parchemin ; (to contract—*contracter*) passer contrat.
indentation (-té-), *n.*, dentelure ; échancrure,*f.*
indented (-'ède), *adj.*, dentelé ; bossué, (bound out by indentures—*mis en apprentissage par contrat*) obligé par un contrat d'apprentissage.
indenture (-'ioure), *n.*, (jur.) titre, *m.* —s ; *contrat d'apprentissage, m.sing.*
indenture, *v.a.*, mettre en apprentissage.
independence, *or* **independency** (-di-), *n.*, indépendance,*f.*
independent (-di-), *adj.*, indépendant.
independent, *n.*, indépendant, *m.*
independently, *adv.*, indépendamment ; dans l'indépendance ; avec indépendance.
indescribable (-di-scraib'a-b'l), *adj.*, indescriptible.
indesert (-di-ceurte),*n.*,défaut de mérite,*m.*
indestructibility (-di-streuk'ti-), *adj.*, indestructibilité,*f.*
indestructible (-di-streuk'ti-b'l), *adj.*, indestructible.
indeterminable (-di-teur-mi-na-b'l), *adj.*, indéterminable ; interminable.
indeterminably, *adv.*, d'une manière indéterminable.
indeterminate (-di-teur-mi-), *adj.*, indéterminé, indécis.
indeterminately, *adv.*, indéterminément.
indeterminateness, *n.*, nature indéterminée,*f.* ; manque de précision, *m.*
indetermination (-né-), *n.*, indétermination,*f.*
indevote (-di-vôte), *or* **indevoted** (-'ède), *adj.*, (ant.) peu dévoué.
indevotion, *n.*, indévotion,*f.*
indevout (-di-vaoute), *adj.*, indévot.
indevoutly, *adv.*, indévotement, *m.*
index, *n.*, indice, indicateur, *m.* ; (of books —*de livre*) table des matières,*f.* ; (of Latin books—*de livres latins*) index ; (anat.) index, doigt indicateur, *m.* ; (of a logarithm—*de logarithme*) caractéristique, *f.* ; (of a globe—*d'un globe*) index ; (alg., arith.) exposant, *m.* — expurgatory ; *index expurgatoire; index, m.*
indexical (-dèks'i-), *adj.*, qui a la forme d'une table des matières ; qui appartient à une table des matières.
indexically, *adv.*, en forme de table des matières.
index-plate, *n.*, plaque à index,*f.* ; indicateur, *m.*
indexterity (-tèr'-), *n.*, indextérité, *f.*; manque de dextérité,*m.* ; maladresse,*f.*
indian, *adj.*, Indien ; des Indiens.
indian, *n.*, Indien, *m.*, Indienne,*f.*
indian-like (-laike), *adj.*, comme l'Indien ; en Indien.
indicant, *adj.*, (med.) indicatif.

indicate, *v.a.*, indiquer ; annoncer ; marquer.
indication (-di-ké-), *n.*,indication,*f.* ; signe ; indice, *m.*
indicative, *adj.*, indicatif. — mood ; *mode indicatif.*
indicative, *n.*, indicatif, *m.* In the — ; *à l'indicatif.*
indicator (-ké-teur), *n.*, indicateur, indice, *m.*
indicatory (-ké-to-ri), *adj.*,qui indique, qui montre.
indict (i'n'dite), *v.a.*, (jur.) poursuivre, attaquer, traduire en justice.
indictable (-dait'a-b'l), *adj.*, (jur.) passible d'être poursuivi ; (of things—*des choses*) qualifié crime, qualifié délit.
indiction (-dik'-), *n.*, indiction ; proclamation,*f.*
indictment (-daït'-), *n.*, accusation,*f.* Bill of — ; *acte d'accusation, m.* To find an — ; *prononcer une mise en accusation.*
indifference, *or* **indifferency** (-dif-fèr'-), *n.*, indifférence,*f.*
indifferent (-dif'fèr-), *adj.*, indifférent, passable ; médiocre.
indifferently, *adv.*, indifféremment ; passablement ; médiocrement.
indigence, *or* **indigency** (-di-djè'n'-), *n.*, indigence,*f.*
indigenous (-didj'i-), *adj.*, du pays, indigène.
indigent (-di-djè'n'te), *adj.*, nécessiteux, indigent.
indigest, *or* **indigested** (-di-djèst,-'ède), *adj.*, indigeste, non digéré ; informe.
indigestible (-djèst'i-b'l), *adj.*, indigeste, difficile à digérer.
indigestion (-di-djèst'ieune),*n.*;indigestion, *f.* ; mal d'estomac, *m.*
indignant (-dig-na'n'te), *adj.*, indigné, irrité.
indignantly, *adv.*, avec indignation.
indignation (-dig-né-), *n.*, indignation,*f.* To give vent to one's — ; *faire éclater son indignation.*
indignity (-dig-ni-ti), *n.*, indignité, *f.*; outrage, *m.*
indigo (-di-gô), *n.*, (bot.) indigo, *m.*
indigo-tree (-trî), *n.*, indigotier, *m.*
indirect (-di-rècte), *adj.*, indirect, oblique, détourné.
indirection, *or* **indirectness** (-di-rèk'-,-rèct'-), *n.*, voie détournée ; obliquité ; mauvaise foi,*f.*
indirectly, *adv.*, indirectement.
indiscernible (-diz-ceur-ni-b'l),*adj.*, imperceptible ; indiscernable.
indisciplinable (-pli'n'a-b'l), *adj.*, indisciplinable.
indiscipline (-pline), *n.*, indiscipline,*f.*
indiscoverable (-dis-keuv'èr-a-b'l), *adj.*, qu'on ne peut découvrir.
indiscreet (-dis-crîe), *adj.*, indiscret, irréfléchi.
indiscreetly, *adv.*, indiscrètement.
indiscretion (-dis-krish'-), *n.*, indiscrétion, imprudence,*f.*
indiscriminate (-dis-cri'm'i-), *adj.*, confus ; indistinct ; sans distinction.
indiscriminately, *adv.*, sans distinction, confusément.
indiscriminating (-nét'-), *adj.*, qui ne fait pas de distinction, aveugle.
indispensable (-dis-pè'n'sa-b'l), *adj.*, indispensable.
indispensableness, *n.*, nécessité, indispensabilité,*f.*
indispensably, *adv.*, indispensablement.

indispo¦e (-dis-póze), *v.a.*, indisposer, déranger, incommoder ; détourner, éloigner.

indisposed (-póz'de), *adj.*, indisposé, dérangé.

indisposedness (-pozèd'-), *n.*, répugnance, *f.* ; dérangement, *m.*

indisposition (-dis-po-zish'-), *n.*, indisposition, répugnance, *f.* ; éloignement, *m.*

indisputable (-dis-piou-ta-b'l), *adj.*, incontestable, indisputable.

indisputableness, *or* **indisputability**, *n.*, évidence, *f.* ; caractère incontestable, *m.*

indisputably, *adv.*, incontestablement, sans contredit.

indisputed (-'ède), *adj.*, incontesté, reconnu.

indissolubility (-dis'so-liou-bi-), *n.*, indissolubilité, *f.*

indissoluble (-liou'b'l), *adj.*, indissoluble.

indissolubleness, *n.*, indissolubilité, *f.*

indissolubly, *adv.*, indissolublement.

indistinct (-dis-ti'n'cte), *adj.*, indistinct, confus.

indistinction *or* **indistinctness**, *n.*, confusion, *f.* ; défaut de distinction, *m.*

indistinctly, *adv.*, indistinctement, sans ordre.

indistinguishable (-dis-ti'n'gwish'a-b'l), *adj.*, indistinct.

indisturbance (-dis-teurb'-), *n.*, calme, *m.*

indite (-daïte), *v.a.*, rédiger ; dicter.

inditement, *n.*, rédaction ; dictée, *f.*

individable (-di-vaïd'a-b'l), *adj.*, indivisible.

individual (-di-vid'iou-), *n.*, individu ; particulier, *m.*

individual, *adj.*, individuel, seul, unique.

individuality, *n.*, individualité, *f.*

individualize (-aïze), *v.a.*, individualiser.

individually, *adv.*, individuellement, isolément.

individuate (-di-vid'iou-), *v.a.*, individualiser.

individuation (-'iou-é-), *n.*, individualisation, *f.*

indivisibility, *or* **indivisibleness** (-di-viz'i-), *n.*, indivisibilité, *f.*

indivisible (-viz'i-b'l), *adj.*, indivisible.

indivisibly, *adv.*, indivisiblement.

indocible (-doss'i-b'l), *or* **indocile** (-doss'il), *adj.*, indocile.

indocility, *n.*, indocilité, *f.*

indoctrinate (-doc-tri'n'-), *v.a.*, endoctriner, instruire.

indoctrination (-tri'n'é-), *n.*, instruction, *f.*

indolence, *or* **indolency**, *n.*, indolence, *f.*

indolent, *adj.*, indolent.

indolently, *adv.*, nonchalamment, indolemment.

indomitable (-ta-b'l), *adj.*, indomptable.

indorsable (-'a-b'l), *adj.*, (com.) transférable par endossement.

indorse, *v.a.*, charger (on the back—*sur le dos*) ; (com.) endosser.

indorsee (-sî), *n.*, (com.) porteur, *m.*

indorsement, *n.*, endossement, endos, *m.*

indorser, *or* **indorsor** (-'eur), *n.*, (com.) endosseur, *m.*

indrench (-drè'n'she), *v.a.*, plonger, submerger.

indubious (-diou-bi-), *adj.*, certain, non douteux.

indubitable (-diou-bi-ta-b'l), *adj.*, indubitable.

indubitably, *adv.*, indubitablement.

induce (-diouce), *v.a.*, porter à, engager, amener, décider, déterminer ; induire, entraîner ; (a thing—*une chose*) causer, produire.

inducement, *n.*, incitation, raison, *f.* ; motif, mobile, stimulant, *m.*

inducer, *n.*, instigateur, *m.* ; chose qui porte, qui engage, qui détermine ; personne qui porte, qui engage, qui détermine, *f.*

inducible (-diou-ci-b'l), *adj.*, qui peut être induit, inféré, causé, produit.

induct (-deuk'te), *v.a.*, mettre en possession, installer, établir.

inductile (-til), *adj.*, inductile.

inductility, *n.*, inductilité, *f.*

induction (-deuk'-), *n.*, installation, induction ; prise de possession, *f.*

inductive (-deuk'tive), *adj.*, qui amène, qui décide ; par induction.

indue (-diou). *V.* **endue**.

indulge (-deuldje), *v.a.*, tolérer, favoriser, permettre, accorder ; se permettre, satisfaire, écouter, se laisser aller, se livrer, (pers.) avoir trop d'indulgence pour. To — any one with a thing ; *accorder, permettre quelque chose à quelqu'un.* To — one's self ; *s'écouter, se soigner.*

indulge, *v.n.*, se laisser aller à, se livrer à, s'abandonner à, s'adonner à.

indulgence, *or* **indulgency** (-deul-djè'n'-), *n.*, plaisir, *m.* ; faveur, *f.* ; abandon, *m.* ; indulgence ; clémence ; (c.rel.) indulgence, *f.*

indulgent, *or* **indulgential** (-deul-djè'n'te, -shal), *adj.*, indulgent, facile ; qui se laisse aller, qui se livre.

indulgently, *adv.*, avec douceur, avec indulgence.

indurate (-diou-), *v.a.*, endurcir, durcir ; (med.) indurer.

indurate, *v.n.*, s'endurcir, durcir ; (med.) s'indurer.

induration (-diou-ré-), *n.*, durcissement, endurcissement, *m.* ; (med.) induration, *f.*

industrial (-deus'-), *adj.*, industriel ; industrieux.

industrious (-deus'-), *adj.*, laborieux ; diligent ; qui aime le travail.

industriously, *adv.*, laborieusement, assidûment, diligemment.

industry (-deus'tri), *n.*, travail ; amour du travail, *m.* ; assiduité, *f.* ; (fig.) empressement, *m.*, ardeur, *f.*

indweller (-dwèl'-), *n.*, habitant, *m.*, habitante, *f.*

indwelling, *adj.*, intérieur ; du cœur.

inebriant (-i-bri-), *or* **inebriating** (-i-briét'-), *adj.*, enivrant.

inebriate (-i-bri-), *v.a.*, enivrer ; infatuer.

inebriate, *v.n.*, s'enivrer.

inebriation (-i-bri-é-), *or* **inebriety** (-i-braï-i-ti), *n.*, ivresse, ébriété, *f.*

inedited (-èd'it'ède), *adj.*, inédit.

ineffability, *or* **ineffableness** (-èf'-fa-), *n.*, ineffabilité, *f.*

ineffable (-èf'fa-b'l), *adj.*, ineffable.

ineffably, *adv.*, ineffablement.

ineffective (-èf'fèk'tive), *adj.*, inefficace, sans effet, ineffectif.

ineffectual (-èf'fèk'tiou-), *adj.*, inefficace, inutile, vain.

ineffectually, *adv.*, inutilement, sans efficacité.

ineffectualness, *n.*, inefficacité, *f.*

ineffervescence (-èf'fèr'vès'-), *n.*, défaut d'effervescence, *m.*

ineffervescent, *adj.*, non effervescent, non mousseux.

ineffervescibility, *n.*, qualité de ce qui n'est pas effervescent, *f.*

ineffervescible ('-ci-b'l), *adj.*, incapable d'effervescence.

inefficacious (i'n-èf-fi-ké-sheusse), *adj.*, inefficace.

inefficaciously, *adv.*, inefficacement.

inefficacy (-èf'i-ca-ci), *n.*, inefficacité, *f.*

inefficiency (-èf-fi-shè'n'ci), *n.*, inefficacité, *f.*

inefficient (-èf-fi-shè'n'te), *adj.*, inefficace ; insuffisant.

inefficiently, adj., inefficacement, sans efficacité.

inelastic (-i-las-), adj., non élastique.

inelasticity (-i-las-ti-ci-ti), n., non-élasticité, f.

inelegance, or **inelegancy** (-èl-i-, -ci), inélégance, f.

inelegant (-èl-i-), adj., sans élégance ; sans goût, inélégant.

inelegantly, adv., sans élégance.

ineligibility (-èl'i-dji-), n., inconvenance ; (pol.) inéligibilité, f.

ineligible (-èl-i-dji'-b'l), adj.; peu convenable ; (pol.) inéligible.

ineloquent (-èl'o-kwè'n'te), adj., sans éloquence, inéloquent.

ineloquently, adv., sans éloquence.

inept (-èpte), adj., inepte, faible ; sot.

ineptitude (-ti-tioude), or **ineptness** (-èpt'-), n., inaptitude, f.

ineptly, adv., sottement, ineptement.

inequal (-i-kwol), adj., inégal.

inequality (-i-kwol'i-ti), n., inégalité ; insuffisance, f.

inequitable (-èk'wi-ta-b'l), adj., peu équitable.

inerrability, or **inerrableness** (-eur-ra-), n., (ant.) infaillibilité, f.

inerrable (-eur-ra-b'l), adj., (ant.) infaillible.

inerrably, adv., infailliblement.

inert (-eurte), adj., inerte.

inertia (-eur-shi-a), n., inertie, force d'inertie, f.

inertly (-eurt'-), adv., lourdement, d'une manière inerte.

inertness (-eurt'-), n., inertie, f.

in esse (-ès'si), adj., positif, réel.

inestimable (-ès-ti-ma-ù'l), adj., inestimable ; incalculable.

inestimably, adv., incalculablement.

inevident (-èv'i-), adj., caché, inévident.

inevitability, or **inevitableness** (-èv'i-), n., impossibilité d'être évité, inévitabilité, f.

inevitable (-èv'i-ta-b'l), adj., inévitable, inéluctable.

inevitably, adv., inévitablement.

inexact (-ègz'-), adj., inexact.

inexactness, n., inexactitude, f.

inexcusable (-kiou-za-b'l), adj., inexcusable.

inexcusableness, n., tort inexcusable ; caractère inexcusable, m.

inexcusably, adv., inexcusablement.

inexecution (-èks'i-kiou-), n., inexécution, f.

inexhalable (-ègz'hè-la-b'i), adj., qui ne s'évapore pas.

inexhausted (-ègz'haust'ède), adj., inépuisé.

inexhaustible (-ti-b'l), adj., inépuisable.

inexhaustibleness, n., nature inépuisable, f.

inexhaustibly, adv., inépuisablement.

inexhaustive, or **inexhaustless** (ant.), adj., inépuisable.

inexistence (i'n-ègz'-), n., non-existence, inexistence, f.

inexistent, adj., non existant, inexistant.

inexorability, or **inexorableness** (-èks'o-), n., caractère inexorable, m. ; inflexibilité, f.

inexorable (-èks'o-ra-b'l), adj., inexorable, inflexible.

inexorably, adv., inexorablement.

inexpedience, or **inexpediency** (-èks'pi-), n., inopportunité, inconvenance, f.

inexpedient, adj., inopportun, mal à propos, inconvenable. To deem it — to ; ne pas juger convenable de.

inexperience (-èks'pi-), n., inexpérience, f.

inexperienced (-è'n'ste), adj., inexpérimenté.

inexpert (-èks'peurte), adj., inexpérimenté, maladroit, inhabile.

inexpiable (-èks'pi-a-b'l), adj., inexpiable.

inexpiably, adv., d'une manière inexpiable.

inexplicable (-èks'pli-ca-b'l), adj., inexplicable.

inexplicably, adv., inexplicablement.

inexplicit (-èks'pli-ci'te), adj., inexplicite, obscur.

inexpressible (-si-b'l), adj., inexprimable ; inouï.

inexpressibly, adv., d'une manière inexprimable.

inexpressive, adj., inexpressif, dénué d'expression.

inexpugnable (-peug-na-b'l), adj., imprenable ; inexpugnable.

inextinct (-èks'ti'n'k'te), adj., non éteint.

inextinguishable (-èks'ti'n'gwish'a-'b'l), adj., inextinguible.

inextricable (-ca-b'l), adj., inextricable ; qu'on ne peut pas débrouiller.

inextricableness, n., nature inextricable, f.

inextricably, adv., inextricablement.

ineye (i'n'a'-ye), v.a., greffer en écusson.

infallibility, or **infallibleness**, n., infaillibilité, f.

infallible (-fal'li-b'l), adj., infaillible, immanquable.

infallibly, adv., infailliblement, immanquablement.

infame, v.a., (ant.) diffamer.

infamous (-fé-), adj., infâme, indigne.

infamously, adv., d'une manière infâme ; indignement, affreusement.

infamousness, or **infamy** (-fé-), n., infamie, f.

infancy, n., enfance, f. ; bas âge, m ; (jur.) minorité, f.

infant, n., enfant en bas âge, petit enfant ; (jur.) mineur, m., mineure, f. — school ; salle d'asile, f.

infant, adj., en bas âge, dans l'enfance ; (fig.) naissant, à sa naissance, qui commence. — colony ; colonie naissante, f.

infanta, n., infante, f.

infante, n., infant (of Spain, Portugal— d'Espagne, de Portugal), m.

infanticide (-caïde), n., infanticide, m.

infantile, or **infantine** (-taïl,-taïne), adj., enfantin, d'enfant.

infant-like (-laïke), adj., enfantin.

infantry, n., infanterie, f.

infatuate (-fat'iou-), v.a., infatuer, entêter, engouer, enivrer, enorgueilli ; troubler l'esprit de.

infatuation (-fat'iou-é-), n., entêtement ; enivrement ; vertige, m. ; infatuation, f.

infeasibility, or **infeasibleness** (-fi-zi-), n., nature impraticable, f.

infeasible (-fï-zi-b'l), adj., impraticable, infaisable.

infect (-fèk'te), v.a., infecter, empester.

infecter, n., personne qui infecte, qui empeste ; chose qui infecte, qui empeste, f.

infection (-fèk'-), n., infection, corruption ; contagion, f.

infectious (-fèk-sheusse), adj., contagieux, infect, pestilentiel.

infectiously, adv., par infection, par contagion.

infectiousness, n., nature contagieuse ; nature infecte ; contagion, infection, f.

infective (-fèk-tive), adj., contagieux.

infecund (-fék'eu'n'de), adj., stérile, infécond.

infecundity, n., stérilité, infécondité, f.

infelicitous (-fi-lici'i-), adj., malheureux.

infelicity, n., infortune, f. ; malheur, m.

infer (-feur), v.a., inférer, conclure ; déduire.

inferable, or **inferrible** (-'a-b'l,-fèr-ri-b'l), adj., qui peut être inféré, à inférer.

inference (-fèr'-), n., conséquence, conclusion, déduction, f.

inferior (-fi-rior), adj., inférieur.

inferior, n., inférieur, m.

inferiority, n., infériorité, f.

infernal (-feur-), adj., infernal, d'enfer.

infernal, n., habitant de l'enfer, m.

infernally, adv., infernalement.

infertile (-feur-taïl), adj:, stérile, infertile.

infertility(-feur-til'-), n., infertilité, f.

infest (-fèste), v.a., infester ; attaquer.

infestation (-té-), n., infestation, f. ; ravage, m.

infeudation (-fiou-dé-), n., inféodation, f.

infidel (-dèle), adj., infidèle, incrédule, impie;

infidel, n., infidèle ; incrédule, impie, m.,f.

infidelity (-dèl'-),n.,infidélité ; incrédulité,f.

infiltrate, v.n., s'infiltrer.

infiltration (-tré-), n., infiltration, f.

infinite(-fi-nite), adj., infini ; perpétuel.

infinitely, adv., infiniment; fort, à l'infini.

infiniteness, n., infinité ; immensité,f.

infinitesimal (-fi'n'i-tèss'i-), adj., infinitésimal, infiniment petit.

infinitive, n., infinitif, m.

infinitive, adj., infinitif.

infinitude (-tioude), n., infinité,f.

infinity, n., infinité ; immensité, f.

infirm (-feurme), adj., infirme, faible ; maladif.

infirmary(-feurm'-), n., infirmerie,f.

infirmity, or **infirmness** (-feurm'-), n., infirmité; faiblesse, f.

infirmly (-feurm'-), adv., déblement, faiblement.

infix (-fikse), v.a., fixer, inculquer; enfoncer.

inflame (-fléme), v.a., enflammer, embraser; exciter, irriter.

inflame. v.n., s'enflammer.

inflammability, or **inflammableness** (-fla'm'-), n., inflammabilité, f.

inflammable (-fla'm'ma-b'l), adj., inflammable; (of coal—de la houille) flambant.

inflammation (-fiam'mé-), n., inflammation; fluxion, f. — of the lungs; inflammation du poumon. — of the chest; fluxion de poitrine.

inflammatory (-flam-ma-), adj., inflammatoire ; incendiaire.

inflate (-fléte), v.a., enfler, gonfler, bouffir.

inflated, part., enflé, gonflé; (style) boursouflé.

inflation(-flé-), n., enflure,f.; gonflement, m

inflect (-flèk'te), v.a., fléchir; varier; détourner ; (the voice—la voix) moduler ; (opt.) infléchir.

inflection, n., inflexion; variation, f.

inflective. adj., flexible.

inflexibility, or **inflexibleness** (-flèks'-), n., inflexibilité, f.

inflexible(-flèks-i-b'l),adj., inflexible.

inflexibly. adv., inflexiblement.

inflict (-flik'te), v.a., infliger; (pain—peine) faire.

inflicter, n., personne qui inflige, f. ; auteur d'un mal. m.

infliction (-flik'-), n., infliction, f.; châtiment, m.

inflictive. adj., inflictif.

inflorescence (-rès'-). n., (bot.) disposition des fleurs, inflorescence, f.

influence (-fiou-), n., influence, f.

influence. v.a., influer sur; influencer.

influential (-fiou-è'n'shal), adj., influent, qui a de l'influence.

influentially. adv., avec influence.

influenza (-fiou'è'n'-), n., grippe, f.

influx (-fleukse), or **influxion** (l'n-fleuk'sheune), n., affluence; abondance, f.

infold (-fôlde), v.a., envelopper.

infoliate (-fô-li-), v.a., couvrir de feuilles.

inform. v.a., instruire, informer, avertir; faire savoir. To — one's self; s'instruire, s'éclairer; (of a fact—d'un fait) s'informer.

inform, v.n., dire, montrer ; (against—contre) faire une dénonciation contre, dénoncer.

inform. adj., informe.

informal, adj., non en forme; irrégulier, fautif.

informality, n., défaut de formalité, vice de forme, m.

informant. n., accusateur, m.; personne qui fait savoir, qui informe,f.

information (-mé-), n., nouvelle, information,f. ; avis ; renseignement, m ; instruction,f.; connaissances, f.pl.; savoir, m. ; (jur.) dénonciation, révélation, délation ; enquête, f. To get — on ; se procurer des renseignements sur. To lay an — against; dénoncer.

informer, n., délateur, dénonciateur, révélateur, m.

informidable (-da-b'l), adj., qui n'est pas à craindre, peu formidable.

informous, adj., (ant.) difforme, informe.

infraction (-frak'-), n., infraction; contravention, f.

infractor (-'eur), n., infracteur ; violateur, m.

infrangible (-dji-b'l), adj., qui ne peut être brisé ; qui ne peut enfreindre.

infrequency, or **infrequence** (-fri-), n., rareté, f.

infrequent (-frl-), adj., rare.

infrigidate (-fridj-), v.a., refroidir.

infringe (-fri'n'dje), v.a., enfreindre.

infringement (-n., infraction, violation,f.; violement, m.

infringer, n., infracteur, violateur, m., violatrice, f.

infuriate (-fiou-), adj., furieux, enragé.

infuriate, v.a., rendre furieux, mettre en fureur.

infuriated, adj., furieux, en fureur, furibond.

infuse (-fiouze), v.a., infuser ; faire infuser; verser, introduire; (fig.) communiquer, inspirer, pénétrer. To be infused ; s'infuser.

infusibility (-fiou-zi-), n., infusibilité,f.

infusible (-fiou-zi-b'l), adj., infusible.

infusion (-fiou-jeune), n., infusion; suggestion ; inspiration,f.

infusive (-fiou-zive), adj., absorbant.

infusoria (-fiou-çô-), n.pl., animalcules infusoires; infusoires, m.pl.

infusory (-fiou-çô-), n. (infusories, infusoria), animalcule infusoire, m.

infusory (-fiou-ço-), adj., infusoire.

ingathering (i'n'gath'eur-), n., récolte, f.

ingeminate (-djè'm'-), v.a., redoubler; répéter.

ingemination (-djè'm'i-né-), n., redoublement, m. ; répétition, f.

ingenerate (-djè'n'èr'-), adj., incréé.

ingenious (-dji'n'-), adj., ingénieux; qui a du savoir ; qui a du talent ; de mérite ; de talent ; spirituel ; savant.

ingeniously, adv., ingénieusement; spirituellement.

ingeniousness, n., caractère ingénieux; génie ; art ; mérite ; talent, m. ; habileté,f.

ingenite (-djè'n'-), adj., inné.

ingenuity (-dji-niou-i-). n., caractère ingénieux; génie; art; mérite; talent, m.; habileté, f.

ingenuous (-djè'n'iou-), adj., ingénu, naïf; noble ; généreux ; (birth—naissance) honorable.

ingenuously, adv., ingénument; naïvement.

ingenuousness, n., ingénuité, naïveté,f.

ingestion (-djèst'ieune), *n.*, ingestion, action d'avaler, *f.*

inglorious (-glô-), *adj.*, sans gloire; déshonorant, honteux ; inglorieux.

ingloriously, *adj.*, sans gloire; honteusement ; avec déshonneur.

ingot (i'n'gote), *n.*, lingot, *m.*

ingot-mould (-môlde), *n.*, lingotière, *f.*

ingraft (-gráfte), *v.a.*, greffer, enter; (fig.) graver.

ingraftment, *n.*, greffe ; ente, *f.*

ingrain (-gréne), *v.a.*, teindre en laine.

ingrate, *n* , ingrat, *m.*, ingrate, *f.*

ingrateful (-foule), *adj.*, ingrat.

ingratiate (-gré-shi-), *v.a.*, insinuer dans les bonnes grâces; concilier la faveur. To — one's self with; *s'insinuer dans les bonnes grâces de ; se concilier la faveur de.*

ingratitude (-tioude), *n.*, ingratitude, *f.*

ingredient (-gri-), *n.*, ingrédient ; élément, *m.*

ingress, *n.*, entrée, *f.*

ingression (-grèsh'-), *n.*, action d'entrer; entrée, *f.*

inguinal (-ign'gwi-), *adj.*, (anat.) inguinal.

ingulf (-gheulfe), *v.a.*, engouffrer; engloutir.

ingurgitate (-gheur'dji-), *v.a.*, avaler avidement; ingurgiter.

ingurgitate, *v.n.*, boire avec excès, ingurgiter.

inhabit, *v.a.* and *n.*, habiter; habiter dans ; vivre, demeurer.

inhabitable (-ta-b'l), *adj.*, habitable.

inhabitance, or **inhabitancy**, *n.*, habitation, *f.*

inhabitant, *n.*, habitant, *m.*, habitante ; (jur.) personne domiciliée, *f.*

inhabitation (-bi-té-), *n.*, habitation, *f.*

inhabited, *adj.*, habité.

inhabiter, *n.*, habitant, *m.*, habitante, *f.*

inhalation (-hél'é-), *n.*, inhalation, absorption des gaz; inspiration, *f.*

inhale, *v.a.*, aspirer ; respirer ; humer.

inhaler (-hél'-), *n.*, personne qui aspire, qui respire, *f.*

inharmonic, or **inharmonical**, *adj.*, peu harmonieux ; inharmonieux.

inharmonious (-mô-), *adj.*, peu harmonieux ; inharmonieux.

inharmoniously, *adv.*, sans harmonie ; inharmonieusement.

inhere (hire), *v.n.*, être inhérent, s'attacher.

inherence (-hi-), *n.*, inhérence, *f.*

inherent, *adj.*, inhérent ; inséparable.

inherently, *adv.*, par inhérence.

inherit (-hèr'-), *v.a.*, hériter; recueillir.

inherit, *v.a.*, hériter.

inheritable (-hèr'i-ta-b'l), *adj.*, héréditaire; transmissible par héritage.

inheritably, *adv.*, en héritage.

inheritance, *n.*, héritage, *m.* ; succession ; hérédité, *f.*

inheritor, *n.*, héritier, *m.*

inheritress, or **inheritrix**. *n.*, héritière, *f.*

inherse (-heurse), *v.a.*, mettre, enterrer dans un tombeau.

inhesion (-hi-jeune), *n.*, inhérence, *f.*

inhibit, *v.a.*, arrêter, prohiber, empêcher, interdire; défendre.

inhibition, *n.*, interdiction ; défense ; prohibition, *f.*

inhoop (-houpe), *v.a.*, enfermer.

inhospitable (-ta'b'l), *adj.*, inhospitalier.

inhospitableness, or **inhospitality**, *n.*, inhospitalité, *f.*

inhospitably, *adv.*, inhospitalièrement.

inhuman (-hiou-), *adj.*, inhumain.

inhumanity, *n.*, inhumanité, *f.*

inhumanly (-ma'n'-), *adv.*, inhumainement, avec inhumanité.

inhumate (-hiou-), or **inhume** (-hiou'-), *v.a.*, inhumer.

inhumation (-mé-), *n.*, inhumation, *f.*

inimical. *adj.*, ennemi, hostile, contraire.

inimically. *adv.*, hostilement ; en ennemi.

inimitability, *n.*, qualité de ce qu'on ne peut imiter, *f.*

inimitable (-ta-b'l), *adj.*, inimitable.

inimitably, *adv.*, inimitablement.

iniquitous (-ik'wi-), *adj.*, inique.

iniquity (-ik'wi-), *n.*, iniquité, *f.*

initial (-ish'-), *adj.*, initial ; premier.

initial. *n.*, initiale, *f.*

initially, *adv.*, au premier degré ; au commencement.

initiate (-ish'i-éte), *v.a.*, initier ; commencer.

initiate, *v.n.*, faire le premier acte.

initiate, *adj.*, initié ; du commencement.

initiate, *n.*, initié, *m.*, initiée, *f.*

initiation, *n.*, initiation, *f.*

initiative, *adj.*, initiateur.

initiative, *n.*, initiative, *f.*

initiatory, *adj.*, initiateur.

inition, *n.*, (ant.) commencement, *m.*

inject (-djèk'te), *v.a.*, injecter; jeter.

injection (-djèk'-), *n.*, injection ; (med.) injection, *f.*, lavement, *m.*

injudicial (-djiou-dish'-), *adj.*, qui n'est pas dans les formes judiciaires ; extrajudiciaire.

injudicious (-djiou-dish'-), *adj.*, peu judicieux ; injudicieux.

injudiciously, |*adv.*, peu judicieusement ; injudicieusement.

injudiciousness, *n.*, manque de jugement, *m.*

injunction (-djeu'n'g'n'k'-),*n.*, injonction,*f.* ; commandement, *m.*

injure (-djeur), *v.a.*, nuire à, faire tort à ; faire mal à ; blesser ; porter atteinte à ; outrager ; (a thing—*chose*) faire du mal à, gâter ; (med.) léser, faire une lésion à ; (surg.) intéresser.

injurer, *n.*, personne qui nuit à, qui fait tort à, qui fait mal à, qui blesse, qui porte atteinte à, qui outrage, *f.* ; auteur d'un tort, d'un outrage, *m.*

injurious (-djiou-ri-), *adj.*, qui nuit à, qui fait tort à, qui fait mal à, qui blesse, qui porte atteinte à, qui outrage ; nuisible ; injurieux, outrageant, injuste.

injuriously, *adv.*, injustement ; à tort ; injurieusement ; outrageusement.

injury (-djiouri), injure, *f.* ; tort, mal, préjudice, *m.* ; injustice, *f.* ; (to goods—*de marchandises*) dégât, dommage ; détriment, *m.* ; (med.) lésion, *f.* To the — of ; *au détriment de.*

injustice (-djeus'-), *n.*, injustice, *f.*

ink. *n.*, encre, *f.* Indian- — ; *encre de Chine, de la Chine.* Marking- — ; *encre à marquer.* Printing- — ; *encre d'impression.* Blot of — ; *pâté, m.*

ink, *v.a.*, barbouiller d'encre ; (print.) encrer.

inkbag, *n.*, (mol.) poche à encre, *f.*

ink-box, *n.*, encrier, *m.*

ink-case (-kéce), *n.*, écritoire, *f.* ; encrier, *m.*

inkfish, *n.*, (mol.) seiche, sèche, *f.*

inkhorn, *n.*, écritoire, *f.*

inkiness, *n.*. état de ce qui est taché d'encre, *m.* ; noirceur, *f.*

inking-roller (-rôl-), *n.*, (print.) rouleau, *m.*

inking-table (-té-b'l), *n.*, (print.) table d'encrier, *f.*

inkle (ign'k'l), *n.*, ruban de fil, *m.*

inkling, *n.*. avis ; désir, *m.* ; envie, *f.*

ink-manufacturer (-fak'tiour'-), *n.*, fabricant d'encre, *m.*

inkstand (-sta'n'de), *n.*, encrier, *m.* ; écritoire, *f.*

ink-trough (-trofe), *n.*,(print.) encrier, *m.*

inky, *adj.*, d'encre ; taché d'encre.

inlaid (-léde), *adj.*, marqueté, incrusté.

inland (-'a'n'de), *adj.*, intérieur ; de l'intérieur ; (of letters of exchange—*de lettres de change*) sur l'intérieur ; (geog.) méditerrané.

inland, *n.*, intérieur (d'un pays), *m.*

inlander, *n.*, habitant de l'intérieur d'un pays, *m.*

inlapidate, *v.a.*, (ant.) pétrifier.

inlaw (-lô), *v.a.*, purger de la mise hors la loi.

inlay (-lè), *n.*, marqueterie, *f.*

inlay, *v.a.*, marqueter ; incruster.

inlayer (-lè-eur), *n.*, marqueteur, *m.*

inlaying (-lè-igne), *n.*, art de la marqueterie, *m.*

inlet (-lète), *n.*, entrée, *f.* ; passage, *m.* ; voie, *f.* ; (geog.) petit bras de mer, *m.*

inly (i'n'li), *adj.*, intérieur ; secret ; interne.

inly, *adv.*, intérieurement ; dedans ; dans le cœur ; secrètement.

inmate (i'n'méte), *n.*, habitant, *m.*, habitante, *f.* ; (lodger—*locataire*) pensionnaire, locataire, *m.*, *f.*

inmate, *adj.*, interne ; intérieur ; admis comme habitant.

inmost (-môste), *adj.*, le plus intérieur ; intime ; dernier.

inn, *n.*, auberge, *f.* ; hôtel, *m.* ; taverne, *f.* — of court : *école de droit*, *f.* To put up at an — ; *descendre à une auberge*.

inn, *v.n.*, loger.

inn, *v.a.*, loger ; (agri.) rentrer, engranger.

innate (i'n'néte), *adj.*, inné.

innately; *adv.*, d'une manière innée.

innateness, *n.*, qualité de ce qui est inné,*f.*

innavigable (-nav'i-ga-b'l), *adj.*, innavigable.

inner (i'n'neur), *adj.*, intérieur, de l'intérieur.

. **innermost** (-môste), *adj.*, le plus intérieur ; intime ; dernier.

inning, *n.*, (agri.) rentrée, *f.* —s; (at cricket—*à la crosse*) jeu, *m.* ; (lands abandoned by the sea—*terrains abandonnés par la mer*) relais de la mer, *m.pl.*

innkeeper (-kip'-), *n.*, aubergiste, hôtelier, hôte, *m.*

innocence, *or* **innocency**,*n.*, innocence, *f.*

innocent, *adj.*, innocent ; permis, légitime.

innocent, *n.*, innocent, *m.* ; (l.u.) idiot, *m.*, idiote, *f.*

innocently, *adv.*, innocemment.

innocuous (-nok'kiou-), *adj.*, non nuisible ; innocent.

innocuously, *adv.*, innocemment, sans nuire.

innocuousness, *n.*, innocuité, *f.*

innovate, *v.a.*, innover.

innovate, *v.n.*, innover ; faire des innovations.

innovating, *adj.*, novateur.

innovation (-vé-), *n.*, innovation. *f.*

innovator (-vét'eur), *n.*, novateur, innovateur, *m.*

innoxious (-no'k'sheusse), *adj.*, non nuisible ; innocent.

innoxiously,*adv.*, innocemment, sans nuire.

innoxiousness, *n.*, innocuité, *f.*

innuendo (-niou-è'n'dô), *n.*, insinuation, *f.*

innumerable (-niou-mèr'a-b'l), *adj.*, innombrable, infini.

innumerably, *adv.*, sans nombre ; innombrablement.

innumerous (-niou-mèr'-), *adj.*, innombrable.

inobservable (-zeurv'a-b'l), *adj.*, inobservable.

inobservance (-zeur-), *or* **inobservation** (-zeur-vé-), *n.*, inobservation, *f.*

inoculate (-ok'iou-), *v.a.*, inoculer ; (hort.) écussonner.

inoculation (-ok'iou-lé-), *n.*, inoculation ; (hort.) action d'écussonner, *f.*

inoculator (i'n-ok'iou-lét'eur), *n.*, inoculateur, *m.*, inoculatrice ; (hort.) personne qui écussonne, *f.*

inodorous (i'n'ô-), *adj.*, inodore.

inoffensive. *adj.*, inoffensif, inoffensant.

inoffensively, *adv.*, inoffensivement.

inoffensiveness, *n.*, caractère inoffensif,*m.*

inofficial (-fish'al), *adj.*, inofficiel.

inofficially, *adv.*, inofficiellement.

inofficious (-fish'eusse), *adj.*, inofficieux.

inoperative (-'op'èr'-), *adj.*, qui n'opère pas.

inopportune (-tioune), *adj.*, inopportun.

inopportunely, *adv.*, inopportunément.

inordinacy, *n.*, nature désordonnée ; fureur,*f.* ; dérèglement, *m.*

inordinate, *adj.*, déréglé, désordonné, démesuré.

inordinately, *adv.*, d'une manière désordonnée ; démesurément ; déréglément.

inordinateness. *V.* **inordinacy**.

inordination (-né-), *n.*, dérèglement, *m.*

inorganic, *or* **inorganical**, *adj.*, inorganique.

inorganically, *adv.*, d'une manière inorganique.

inorganized (-'aïz'de), *adv.*, inorganique.

inosculate (-os'kiou-), *v.a.*, unir.

inosculate. *v.n.*, s'anastomoser.

inosculation (-os'kiou-lé-), *n.*, inosculation, anastomose, *f.*

inquest (i'n'kwèste), *n.*, enquête ; recherche, *f.*

inquietude (i'n'kwa-eu-tioude), *n.*, inquiétude, *f.*

inquinate (-kwi-), *v.a.*, corrompre, souiller.

inquination (-kwi-né-), *n.*, souillure, *f.*

inquirable (-kwa'eur'a-b'l), *adj.*, qu'on peut examiner ; sujet à enquête.

inquire (-kwa'eur), *v.a.*, s'enquérir de, s'informer de ; demander ; s'adresser. To — into ; *s'informer de ; faire une enquête sur*. To — after ; *demander des nouvelles de*. — within ; *s'adresser ici*. I will —, I will — about it ; *je m'en informerai*. He —d after your health ; *il a demandé des nouvelles de votre santé*. — at the baker's, of the baker ; *adressez-vous chez le boulanger, au boulanger*.

inquire, *v.n.*, s'informer de ; demander.

inquirer, *n.*, personne qui s'enquiert, qui s'informe, *f.* ; investigateur,*m.*, investigatrice,*f.*

inquiring, *adj.*, investigateur.

inquiry, *n.*, demande ; investigation ; enquête, recherche, *f.* Inquiries ; *informations, f.pl.*, renseignements, *m.pl.* On — ; *en allant aux informations, aux renseignements*. To make inquiries ; *aller aux informations, aux renseignements*. To make inquiries after ; *prendre des informations, des renseignements sur ; s'informer de*. Without — ; *sans demander, sans prendre des renseignements*.

inquisition (i'n'kwi-zish'-), *n.*, inquisition ; recherche, investigation ; (jur.) enquête, *f.*

inquisitional, *or* **inquisitionary** (-kwi-zish'-), *adj.*, assidu dans ses recherches ; inquisitorial.

inquisitive (-kwiz'-), *adj.*, curieux ; (b.s.) indiscret.

inquisitively, *adv.*, avec curiosité ; (b.s.) indiscrètement.

inquisitiveness, *n.*, curiosité ; (b.s.) indiscrétion, *f.*

inquisitor (-kwiz'i-teur), *n.*, inquisiteur, *m.*

inquisitorial (-kwiz'i-to-), *adj.*, inquisitorial ; d'enquête.

inquisitorious (-kwiz'i-to-), *adj.*, (ant.) inquisitorial.

inrail (-réle), v.a., environner de balustres, griller.

inroad (-rôde), n., incursion, irruption, f., empiètement, m.

insalubrious (-liou-bri-), or **insalutary** (-sal'iou-). adj., insalubre.

insalubrity (-liou-), n., insalubrité, f.

insane, adj.,fou, insensé, aliéné.

insanely, adv., en aliéné ; en insensé ; follement.

insaneness. V. **insanity**.

insanity (i'n'sa'n'-), n., aliénation d'esprit, folie, démence, f.

insatiable (-sé-shi-a-b'l), adj., insatiable.

insatiableness, n., insatiabilité, f.

insatiably, adv., insatiablement.

insatiate (-sé-shi-éte), adj., insatiable.

insatiately, adv., insatiablement.

insaturable (-sat'iou-ra-b'l), adj., insaturable.

inscribe (-scraïbe), v.a., inscrire ; dédier ; graver, empreindre.

inscriber, n., personne qui inscrit, f. ; auteur d'une inscription, d'une dédicace, m.

inscription (-skrip'-), n., inscription, f. ; (title—titre) titre, m. ; (dedication—dédicace) dédicace, f.

inscriptive. adj., qui porte une inscription.

inscrutability, or **inscrutableness** (-skreu-), n., inscrutabilité ; impénétrabilité, f.

inscrutable (-skreu-ta-b'l),adj., inscrutable, impénétrable.

inscrutably, adv., impénétrablement.

insculp (-skeulpe), v.a., (l.u.) sculpter ; graver.

insculpture (-skeulpt'ioure), n., (l.u.) inscription sculptée, gravée, f.

inseam (-sîme), v.a., empreindre, marquer, coudre.

insecable (-sî-ca-b'l), adj., insécable, indivisible.

insect (-sèk'te), n., insecte, m.

insect, adj., vil, méprisable.

insectator (-sèk'tèt'eur), n., (l.u.) persécuteur, m.

insectile. adj., de la nature de l'insecte.

insectivorous, adj., insectivore.

insecure (-sî-kioure), adj., sans sécurité ; exposé au danger ; en danger, chanceux.

insecurely, adv., sans sécurité; sans sûreté.

insecurity, n., manque de sécurité ; danger, m.; incertitude, f.

insensate, adj., insensé.

insensibility, n., insensibilité, f. ; défaut de sens, m.

insensible (-sî-b'l), adj., insensible ; vide de sens.

insensibleness, n., insensibilité, f.

insensibly, adv., insensiblement, peu à peu.

insentient (-sè'n'shè'n'te), adj., insensible, privé de sentiment.

inseparable (-sèp'a-ra-b'l), adj., inséparable.

inseparableness, n., état de ce qui est inséparable, m. ; inséparabilité, f.

inseparably, adv., inséparablement.

insert (-seurte), v.a., insérer.

insertion, n., insertion, f.

inservient (-seur-vi-), adj., utile.

inshell, v.a., (ant.) renfermer dans la coquille.

inshrine (-shraïne), v. V. **enshrine**.

inside (-saïde), n., dedans, intérieur, m.

inside, adj., intérieur, d'intérieur, de l'intérieur.

inside, adv., à l'intérieur ; en dedans.

insidiate, v.n., s'embusquer.

insidiator (-sid'i-ét'eur), n., personne qui s'embusque, f.

insidious, adj., perfide, traître ; insidieux,

insidiously, adv., perfidement ; insidieusement.

insidiousness, n., perfidie, trahison ; (of things—des choses) nature insidieuse, f.

insight (i'n'saïte), n., connaissance, f. ; éclaircissement, renseignement, m.

insignia (i'n'sig-ni-a), n.pl.,insignes, m.pl. ; marques distinctives, f.pl.

insignificance, or **insignificancy** (-signif'i-), n., insignifiance, f.

insignificant (-sig-nif'i-), adj., insignifiant.

insignificantly, adv., d'une manière insignifiante ; avec insignifiance.

insincere (-cîre), adj., peu sincère ; dissimulé, faux.

insincerely, adv., peu sincèrement ; sans sincérité ; faussement.

insincerity (-cèr'i-ti), n., manque de sincérité, m. ; dissimulation, fausseté, f.

insinew (i'n'si'n'niou), v.a., (ant.) donner des nerfs à ; donner des forces à.

insinuant (-si'n'iou),v.a., adj., (ant.) insinuant, persuasif.

insinuate (-si'n'iou-),v.a., insinuer ; glisser.

insinuate, v.n., s'insinuer ; se glisser.

insinuating, adj., insinuant.

insinuation (-si'n'iou-é-), n., insinuation, f.

insinuative, adj., insinuant.

insipid, adj., insipide, fade.

insipidness, or **insipidness**, n., insipidité, fadeur, f.

insipidly, adv., insipidement ; fadement.

insipience. n., folie, extravagance, f.

insist, v.n., insister.

insistent, adj., appuyé.

insitiency (i'n'sish'i-è'n'ci), n., absence de soif, f.

insition (-sish'-), n., insertion, greffe, f.

insnare, v.a., faire tomber dans un piège ; prendre au piège ; enlacer, surprendre.

insnarer, n., personne qui tend des pièges, f.

insobriety. (-braï-è-ti), n., manque de sobriété, m. ; intempérance, f.

insociable (-shi-a-b'l),adj., (ant.) insociable.

insociably, adv., insociablement.

insolate, v.a., exposer au soleil.

insolation (-lé-), n., exposition au soleil, f.

insolence, or **insolency**, n., insolence, f.

insolent, adj., insolent.

insolently, adv., insolemment.

insolidity, n., insolidité, f.

insolubility,or **insolubleness** (-sol'iou-), n., insolubilité, f.

insoluble (-sol'iou-b'l), adj., insoluble.

insolvable (-va-b'l), adj., insoluble, indissoluble : qui ne peut être payé.

insolvency, n., insolvabilité, faillite ; (of things—des choses) insuffisance, f. Act of —; loi autorisant la cession de biens, f.

insolvent, adj., insolvable ; (of things—des choses) insuffisant. — Act ; loi autorisant la cession de biens, f. Benefit of the — Act ; bénéfice de cession. To take the — Act ; être admis au bénéfice de cession.

insolvent, n., débiteur, m., débitrice, f., insolvable.

insomnia, n., insomnie, f.

insomnious, adj., qui a des insomnies.

insomuch (-sô-meutshe), adv., au point ; à un tel point ; si bien ; en tant que.

inspect (-spèk'te), v.a., inspecter, examiner, visiter ; surveiller ; vérifier.

inspection (-spèk'-), n., inspection, f. ; examen, m. ; visite ; vérification ; surveillance, f.

inspector (-spèk'-), n., examinateur, surveillant, vérificateur, inspecteur, m.

inspectorship, n., place d'inspecteur; surveillance, f.

insphere (-sfìre), *v.a.*, mettre dans une sphère.

inspirable (-spa'eur'a-b'l), *adj.*, respirable.

inspiration (-spi-ré-), *n.*, (inhaling air—*inhalation de l'air*) aspiration; (respiration) respiration; (infusion of ideas into the mind—*suggestion de pensées*) inspiration, *f.*

inspiratory (-spa'eur'a-), *adj.*, inspirateur, respiratoire.

inspire (-spaeur), *v.a.*, (to breathe into—*pousser de l'air par la bouche*) souffler dans; souffler; (to draw into the lungs—*attirer dans les poumons*) aspirer; (to infuse into the mind—*suggérer*) inspirer.

inspire, *v.n.*, aspirer.

inspired (-spaeurde) *adj.*, inspiré.

inspirer, *n.*, être qui inspire, *m.*

inspiring, *adj.*, inspirateur; inspirant.

inspirit (-spir'ite), *v.a.*, animer, encourager.

inspissate, *v.a.*, épaissir.

inspissation (-'sé-), *n.*, épaississement, *m.*

instableness, *or* **instability**, *n.*, instabilité, *f.*

instable (-sté-b'l), *adj.*, peu stable; inconstant.

install (-stòl), *v.a.*, installer.

installation (-stòl'lé-), *n.*, installation, *f.*

instalment (-stòl'-), *n.*, installation *f.*; (l.u.) siège; (of money—*d'argent*) paiement partiel, acompte, *m.*

instance, *n.*, demande, instance, *f.*; exemple, *m.*; occasion, *f.*; cas, *m.* For —; *par exemple.* In the first —; *dans le principe*; *pour la première fois.*

instance, *v.a.*, citer pour exemple.

instance, *v.n.*, citer des exemples.

instant, *adj.*, instant, urgent, pressant; immédiat; (of the month—*du mois*) courant.

instant, *n.*, instant, moment, *m.*

instantaneous (-té-ni-), *adj.*, instantané.

instantaneously, *adv.*, instantanément.

instantaneousness, *n.*, instantanéité, *f.*

instanter, *adv.*, immédiatement, sans délai.

instantly, *adv.*, à l'instant; tout de suite; sur-le-champ; (urgently—*d'une manière pressante*) instamment, avec instance.

instate, *v.a.*, établir, mettre, placer.

instauration (-ré-), *n.*, restauration, réparation, *f.*

instead (-stède), *adv.*, à sa place, à la place, en place. — of; *au lieu de, en place de, à la place de.* To be — of; *tenir lieu ds.*

insteep (-stîpe), *v.a.*, tremper, baigner, mouiller.

instep (-stèpe), *n.*, cou-de-pied; (anat.) tarse; (of a horse—*du cheval*) canon, *m.*

instigate, *v.a.*, exciter, inciter, entraîner, instiguer.

instigation (-ghé-), *n.*, instigation, *f.*

instigator (-ghét'eur), *n.*, instigateur, *m.*, instigatrice, *f.*

instil, *v.a.*, instiller; (fig.) graver, inculquer dans l'esprit.

instillation (-stil'lé-), *n.*, instillation; (fig.) action de graver, d'inculquer dans l'esprit, *f.*

instiller (-stil'leur), *n.*, personne qui instille; (fig.) personne qui grave, qui inculque dans l'esprit, *f.*

instinct, *n.*, instinct, *m.*

instincted, *adj.*, animé.

instinctive, *adj.*, instinctif.

instinctively, *adv.*, instinctivement; par instinct.

institute (-sti-tioute), *n.*, institution, *f.*; principe, *m.*, maxime, *f.*; learned society—*société savante*) institut, *m.* —s; (jur.) *institutes*, *f.pl.*; (l.u.) *instituts*, *m pl.*

institute, *v.a.*, instituer, établir; commencer; (a lawsuit—*un procès*) intenter; (an ecclesiastic—*un ecclésiastique*) investir.

institution (-sti-tiou-), *n.*, institution; (of an ecclesiastic—*d'un ecclésiastique*) investiture, *f.*

institutionary, *adj.*, élémentaire.

institutist (-tiou-tiste), *n.*, auteur d'ouvrages élémentaires, *m.*

institutor (-tiout'eur), *n.*, fondateur, *m.*, fondatrice, *f.*; instituteur, *m.*, institutrice, *f.*

instruct (-streuk'te), *v.a.*, instruire, enseigner; donner des instructions à.

instruction (-streuk'-), *n.*, instruction; leçon, *f.*

instructive (-streuk'-), *adj.*, instructif.

instructively, *adv.*, d'une manière instructive.

instructor (-streuk'teur), *n.*, instituteur; professeur, *m.*

instructress, *n.*, institutrice, *f.*

instrument (-strou-), *n.*, instrument; (jur.) acte, titre, *m.*

instrumental, *adj.*, instrumental; d'instrument; cause.

instrumentality, *n.*, concours, moyen, *m.*; action, *f.*

instrumentally, *adv.*, comme moyen; (mus.) par des instruments de musique.

instrumentalness. *V.* **instrumentality**.

insubjection (-seub'djèk'-), *n.*, révolte, *f.*

insubmission (-seub'-), *n.*, manque de soumission, *m.*

insubordinate (-seub'-), *adj.*, insubordonné.

insubordination (-seub'or-di-né-), *n.*, insubordination, *f.*

insufferable (-seuf'feur'a-b'l), *adj.*, insupportable, intolérable; détestable.

insufferably, *adv.*, insupportablement; intolérablement; détestablement.

insufficience, *or* **insufficiency** (-seuf-fish'-), *n.*, insuffisance, *f.*

insufficient, *adj.*, insuffisant.

insufficiently, *adv.*, insuffisamment.

insufflation (-seuf-flé-), *n.*, insufflation, *f.*

insular, *or* **insulary** (-siou-), *adj.*, insulaire.

insular, *n.*, insulaire, *m.f.*

insulate (-siou-), *v.a.*, isoler.

insulated, *adj.*, isolé.

insulation (-siou-lé-), *n.*, action d'isoler, *f.*; isolement, *m.*

insulator (-siou-lét'eur), *n.*, (phys.) isoloir, *m.*

insult (-seulte), *n.*, insulte, injure, *f.* To offer an — to any one; *faire insulte, faire une insulte à quelqu'un.*

insult, *v.a.*, faire insulte à, insulter, outrager, injurier.

insult, *v.n.*, triompher insolemment, se comporter insolemment, insulter à.

insulter, *n.*, insulteur, auteur d'une insulte, *m.*

insulting, *adj.*, insultant, outrageant, outrageux, injurieux.

insultingly, *adv.*, insolemment, outrageusement, injurieusement, d'une manière insultante.

insuperable (-siou-pèr'a-b'l), *adj.*, insurmontable.

insuperableness, *or* **insuperability** (-siou-pèr'-), *n.*, qualité insurmontable, *f.*

insuperably (-siou-pèr'-), *adv.*, insurmontablement, d'une manière insurmontable.

insupportable (-seup-pòrt'a-b'l), *adj.*, insupportable, intolérable.

insupportableness, *n.*, nature insupportable, *f.*

insupportably, *adv.*, insupportablemen intolérablement.

insuppressible (-seup'près'i-b'l), *adj.*, qu'on ne peut supprimer; (of laughter—*du rire*) inextinguible, irrésistible.

insuppressive, *adj.*, (ant.) qui ne se supprime pas.

insurable (-shour'a-b'l), *adj.*, susceptible d'être assuré.

insurance (-shour'-) *n.*, assurance. *f.* Life-—; *assurance sur la vie.* Fire-—; *assurance contre l'incendie.* —broker ; *courtier d'assurances, m.* —company ; *compagnie d'assurances, f.* — office ; *bureau d'assurances, m.* Marine — company ; *chambre des assurances, f.*

insure, (-shoure), *v.a.* and *n.*, assurer, garantir.

insured (-shour'de), *n.*, assuré, *m.*, assurée, *f.*

insurer (-shour'-), *n.*, assureur, *m.*

insurgent (-seur-djè'n'te), *n.*, insurgé, *m.*

insurgent, *adj.*, insurgé.

insurmountable (-seur-maou'n't'a-b'l), *adj.*, insurmontable ; infranchissable.

insurmountably, *adv.*, insurmontablement.

insurrection (-seur-rèk'-), *n.*, insurrection, *f.* ; soulèvement, *m.*

insurrectionary (-seur-rek'shʼ-), *adj.*, insurrectionnel.

insusceptibility (-seus'cèp-), *n.*, manque de susceptibilité, *m.*

insusceptible (-seus-cèp'ti-b'l), *adj.*, insusceptible.

intactible (-'ib'l), *adj.*, (ant.) intactile ; intangible.

intagliated (i'n'tal'yé-tède), *adj.*, en intaille.

intaglio (i'n'tal'yō), *n.*, (arts.) intaille, *f.*

intangibility, *or* **intangibleness** (-dji-), *n.*, intangibilité, *f.*

intangible (-dji-b'l), *adj.*, intangible, intactile.

intangibly, *adv.*, d'une manière intangible.

integer (i'n'ti-djeur), *n.*, entier, nombre entier, *m.*

integral (-ti-), *n.*, entier ; intégral ; (chem.) intégrant ; (alg.) intégral.

integral, *n.*, intégrité, totalité, *f.* ; tout, *m.* ; (math.) intégrale, *f.*

integrant (-ti-), *adj.*, intégrant.

integrate (-ti-), *v.a.*, rendre entier ; (math.) intégrer.

integration (-ti-grè-), *n.*, action de rendre entier ; (math.) intégration, *f.*

integrity (-tèg'-), *n.*, intégrité ; probité, pureté, *f.*

integument (-tègh'iou-), *n.*, tégument, *m.*

intellect (-tèl'lèk'te), *n.*, intelligence, faculté intellectuelle, *f.* ; esprit ; intellect, *m.*

intellection (-lèk'sheune), *n.*, intellection, *f.*

intellective, *adj.*, intelligent ; intellectuel ; (philos.) intellectif.

intellectual (-lèk't'iou-), *adj.*, intellectuel, idéal.

intellectualist, *n.*, personne qui exagère les facultés de l'intelligence, *f.*

intellectually, *adv.*, intellectuellement.

intelligence (-li-djè'n'ce), *n.*, intelligence, *f.* ; esprit, *m.* ; (information) nouvelle, *f.*, nouvelles, *f.pl.* renseignements, *m.pl.*, avis ; (concord —concorde) accord, *m.*, intelligence, *f.*

intelligence, *v.a.*, transmettre des nouvelles à ; informer.

intelligence-office, *n.*, bureau de renseignements, *m.*

intelligencer, *n.*, personne qui fournit des renseignements, *f.* ; donneur de nouvelles, *m.*, donneuse de nouvelles, *f.* ; messager, *m.* ; (newspaper—*journal*) gazette; *f.*, moniteur, *m.*

intelligency, *n.*, (ant.) *V.* **intelligence**.

intelligent (-'li-djè'n'te), *adj.*, intelligent.

intelligential (-shal), *adj.*, intellectuel, spirituel.

intelligibility, *or* **intelligibleness** (-dji-), *n.*, intelligibilité, *f.*

intelligible (-dji-b'l), *adj.*, intelligible.

intelligibly, *adv.*, intelligiblement.

intemperament (-tè'm'pèr a-), *n.*, mauvais état, mauvais tempérament, *m.*

intemperance (-tè'm'per'-), *n.*, intempérance, *f.*

intemperancy, *n.*, (ant.). *V.* **intemperance.**

intemperate (-tè'm'pèr-), *adj.*, déréglé, intempérant ; désordonné ; démesuré ; (of the weather—*du temps*) non tempéré.

intemperately (-tè'm'pèr-ét'li), *adv.*, ⊙intempéramment, avec intempérance, démesurément, immodérément.

intemperateness, *n.*, dérèglement, *m.* ; (of the weather—*du temps*) intempérie, *f.*

intend, *v.a.*, se proposer, avoir dessein, avoir l'intention, compter, vouloir ; (to reserve—*réserver*) destiner.

intendant, *n.*, intendant, *m.*

intended, *adj.*, projeté ; intentionnel.

intended, *n.*, (pop.) prétendu, futur époux, *m.*, prétendue, future épouse, *f.* ; futur, *m.*, future, *f.*

intendedly, *adv.*, à dessein.

intender, *n.*, auteur d'une intention, *m.*

intendment, *n.*, intention, *f.*

intenerate (-tè'n'èr'-), *v.a.*, attendrir, adoucir, amollir.

inteneration (-tè'n'èr'é-), *n.*, amollissement, *m.*

intense, *adj.*, (strained—*extrême*) tendu ; (vehement) véhément, chaleureux, ardent ; (application) opiniâtre, acharné ; (of heat, cold—*du chaud, du froid*) intense ; (of suffering, pain—*souffrance, douleur*) vif, fort.

intensely, *adv.*, intensivement, avec intensité ; avec opiniâtreté ; chaleureusement ; avec acharnement ; vivement ; fortement.

intenseness, *n.*, tension, intensité ; force, violence ; ardeur ; opiniâtreté, *f.*, acharnement, *m.* ; (of thought—*d'esprit*) contention, *f.*

intension, *n.*, (l.u.) tension, *f.*

intensity. *V.* **intenseness**.

intensive, *adj.*, intensif.

intent, *n.*, dessein, but, objet ; sens, *m.*, portée, signification, *f.* To all —s ; *dans tous les sens.*

intent, *adj.*, fort attentif, fort attaché, fort appliqué.

intention, *n.*, intention, *f.* ; dessein, but, *m.*

intentional, *adj.*, intentionnel ; d'intention.

intentionally, *adv.*, avec intention, à dessein.

intentioned (-tè'n'sheu'n'de), *adj.*, intentionné.

intentive, *adj.*, (ant.) fort appliqué, fort attentif.

intentively, *adv.*, (ant.) fort attentivement.

intently, *adv.*, fort attentivement ; avec une grande force d'application.

intentness, *n.*, forte attention, forte application, *f.*

inter (-teur), *v.a.*, enterrer, inhumer, ensevelir.

interact (-tèr'-), *n.*, intermède, *m.*

intercalar, *or* **intercalary** (-teur) *adj.*, intercalaire.

intercalate (-teur-), *v.a.*, intercaler.

intercalation (-lé-), *n.*, intercalation, *f.*

intercede (-tèr'cîde), *v.n.*, intercéder.

interceder, *n.*, intercesseur, *m.*

intercept (-tèr-cèpte), *v.a.*, intercepter ; arrêter, surprendre.

intercepter, *n.*, personne qui intercepte, qui arrête, qui surprend, *f.*

interception, *n.*, interception ; interruption, *f.*

intercession (-tèr-cèsh'-), *n.*, intercession, *f.*

intercessor (-tèr-cès'-), *n.*, intercesseur, *m.*

interchain (-tèr-tshéne), *v.a.*, enchaîner.

interchange (-tèr-tshè'n'dje), *n.*, échange, *m.* ; (fig.) variété, *f.*

interchange, *v.a.,* changer mutuellement, échanger.

interchangeable (-tèr-tshé'n'dj'a-b'l), *adj.,* échangeable ; qui se succède alternativement.

interchangeableness, *n.,* nature échangeable ; succession alternative, *f.*

interchangeably, *adv.,* alternativement, réciproquement.

intercipient (-tèr'-), *n.,* personne qui intercepte, qui arrête ; chose qui intercepte, qui arrête, *f.*

intercipient, *adj.,* qui intercepte, qui arrête.

interclude (-tèr-cloude), *v.a.,* intercepter, interrompre.

interclusion (-tèr-clou-jeune), *n.,* obstacle, *m.*

intercolumniation (-tèr-co-leu'm'-ni-é-), *n.,* entre-colonne, entre-colonnement, *m.*

intercommon, *v.a.,* manger à la même table; user en commun du droit de pâturage sur les biens communaux.

intercommunicate (-tèr-co'm'miou-), *v.a.,* communiquer ensemble.

intercommunication (-tèr-co'm'-miou-niké'-), *n.,* communication réciproque, *f.*

intercommunity, *n.,* communication réciproque, *f.*

intercostal, *adj.,* intercostal.

intercourse (-tèr-côrse), *n.,* correspondance, *f.* ; commerce, *m.* ; relations, *f.pl.*

intercurrent (-tèr-keur'-), *adj.,* (med.) intercurrent.

interdict (-tèr'dik'te'), *v.a.,* interdire, interdire à, défendre à, défendre.

interdict (tèr-dik'te). *or* **interdiction** (-dik'-), *n.,* interdiction, défense, prohibition, *f.*; (canon law—*droit canon*) interdit, *n.*

interdictory. *adj.,* d'interdiction.

interest (-tèr'èste), *v.a.,* intéresser. To — one self in ; *s'intéresser à.*

interest (i'n'tèr'èste), *n.,* intérêt, *m.* ; intérêts, *m.pl.* ; (influence) pouvoir, crédit, *m.,* protection, *f.* Compound — ; *intérêt composé ; intérêt des intérêts.* At —, upon — ; *à intérêt.* To one's — ; *dans son intérêt.* To promote any one's — ; *favoriser les intérêts de quelqu'un.* To have — with ; *avoir du crédit auprès de.* To give one's — to any one ; *accorder sa protection à quelqu'un.* To make — with any one ; *mettre quelqu'un dans ses intérêts.* To bear — ; *porter intérêt.* To pay the — ; (fin.) *servir les intérêts.* To put out to — ; *placer à intérêt.* To pay with — ; *payer avec usure.*

interested, *adj.,* intéressé.

interesting, *adj.,* intéressant.

interfere (-tèr-fîre), *v.n.,* intervenir, se mêler, s'entre-mettre ; s'ingérer, s'immiscer; (to clash—*s'opposer*) être en conflit, s'entre-choquer; (to hinder—*empêcher*) mettre obstacle à, déranger ; (man) s'entre-tailler, se couper.

interference (-tèr-fîr'-), *n.,* intervention, *f.*; (collision) choc, *m.,* collision ; (man.) atteinte, *f.*

interfluent, *or* **interfluous** (-teur-flou-), *adj.,* qui coule entre deux.

interfulgent (-tèr-feul-djè'n'te), *adj.,* reluisant entre.

interfused (-tèr-fiou'z'de), *adj.,* répandu entre.

interim (-tèr-), *n.,* intérim, intervalle, *m.,* entrefaites, *f.pl.* In the — ; *en attendant; sur ces entrefaites, dans l'intérim.* Ad — ; *par intérim.*

interior (-ti-), *adj.,* intérieur.

interior, *n.,* intérieur, *m.*

interiorly, *adv.,* intérieurement.

interjacent (-ter-djé-), *adj.,* situé entre, intermédiaire.

interject (-tèr'djèk'te), *v.a.,* interjeter ; jeter entre ; interposer ; insérer.

interjection (-tèr'djèk'-), *n.,* interjection, *f.*

interjectional, *adj.,* interjeté.

interjoin (-tèr'djoï'ne), *v.a.,* unir, marier réciproquement.

interjoist (-tér'djwaïste), *n.,* entrevous, *m.*

interknowledge (-tèr'nol'èdje), *n.,* connaissance mutuelle, *f.*

interlace (-tèr'-), *v.a.,* entremêler ; entrelacer.

interlapse (-tèr'lapse), *n.,* entre-temps, intervalle, *m.*

interlard (-tèr-lârde), *v.a.,* entrelarder.

interleaf (-tèr'life), *n.,* feuillet intercalé, feuillet blanc, *m.*

interleave (-tèr-lîve), *v.a.,* interfolier.

interline (-tèr-laïne), *v.a.,* écrire entre les lignes, (l.u.) interlinéer, interligner.

interlineal, interlinear, *or* **interlineary** (-tèr-li'n'i-), *adj.,* interlinéaire.

interlineary, *n.,* livre interfolié, *m.*

interlineation (-tèr-li'n'i-é-), *n.,* interlinéation ; intercalation, *f.*

interlining (-tèr'laï'n'-), *n.,* action d'interligner, *f.*; entrelignes, interlignes, *f.pl.*

interlink (-tèr-), *v.a.,* joindre les chaînons ; enchaîner ; lier.

interlocution (-tèr-lo-kiou-), *n.,* interlocution, *f.* ; dialogue, *m.*

interlocutor (-tèr-lok'iou-), *n.,* interlocuteur, *m.*

interlocutory, *adj.,* (jur.) interlocutoire ; de dialogue.

interlope (-tèr'lôpe), *v.n.,* être intrus ; (com.) faire le commerce interlope.

interloper, *n.,* intrus, *m.,* intruse, *f.*; (com.) courtier marron, *m.*

interlucent (-tèr-liou-), *adj.,* reluisant entre.

interlude (-tèr-lioude), *n.,* intermède, entr'acte, *m.*

interluder, *n.,* acteur dans un intermède, *m.*

interlunar, *or* **interlunary** (-tèr-liou-), *adj.,* interlunaire.

intermarriage (-tèr-mar'rédje), *n.,* double mariage entre deux familles, *m.*

intermarry (-tèr'-), *v.n.,* faire un double mariage entre deux familles ; se marier les uns avec les autres.

intermeddle (-tèr-mèd'd'l), *v.n.,* se mêler, s'entremêler.

intermeddler, *n.,* personne qui se mêle des affaires d'autrui, *f.* ; médiateur officieux, *m.*, médiatrice officieuse, *f.*

intermeddling, *n.,* intervention officieuse, *f.*

intermediacy (-tèr-mi-), *n.,* intervention, *f.*

intermedial (-tèr-mi-), *adj.,* intermédiaire.

intermediary (-tèr-mi-), *n.,* (l.u.) intervention, *f.* ; intermédiaire, *m.*

intermediate (-tèr'mi-), *adj.,* intermédiaire.

intermediately, *adv.,* intermédiairement.

interment (-teur-), *n.,* enterrement, *m.*; sépulture, *f.*

intermigration (-tèr-mi-gré-), *n.,* émigration réciproque, *f.*

interminable (-teur-mi-na-b'l), *adj.,* interminable, éternel.

interminably, *adv.,* d'une manière interminable.

interminate (-teur-mi-), *adj.,* illimité ; sans bornes.

intermingle (-tèr-mi'n'g'l), *v.a.,* mêler ; entremêler.

intermingle, *v.n.,* se mêler ; s'entremêler.

intermission (-tèr'mish'-), *n.,* intermission, *f.* ; relâche, *m.* ; cessation, *f.*

intermissive (-tèr'-), *adj.,* intermittent.

intermit (-tèr'-), *v.a.,* interrompre, discontinuer, cesser, arrêter.

intermit, *v.n.,* discontinuer, cesser, s'arrêter.

intermittent (-tèr-), *adj.,* intermittent.

intermittent, *n.,* fièvre intermittente, *f.*

intermittingly (-tèr-), *adv.,* avec intermission ; par intervalle.

intermix (-tèr-), *v.a.*, entremêler, mélanger, mêler.

intermix, *v.n.*, s'entremêler ; se mélanger ; se mêler.

intermixture (-tèr-mixt'ieur), *n.*, mélange; assaisonnement, *m.*

intermodillion (-tèr-), *n.*, entre-modillon, *m.*

intermundane (-tèr'meu'n'-), *adj.*, entre les mondes.

intermuscular (-tèr'meus'kiou-), *adj.*, intermusculaire.

intermutation (i'n-tèr-miou-té-sheune), *n.*, échange, *m.*

internal (-teur-). *adj.*, interne, intérieur.

internally, *adv.*, intérieurement.

international (-tèr'nash'-), *adj.*, international.

interneciary (-tèr-ni-shi-), **internecinal** (-tèr-nè-ci-), **internecine**, or **internecive** (-tèr-ni-), *adj.*, meurtrier ; mortel.

internecion(-tèr'ni-sheune), *n.*, massacre,*m.*

internode. *n.*, entre-nœud, *m.*

internuncio (-tèr-neu'n'ci-ô), *n.*, entremetteur ; (of the pope) internonce, *m.*

interpellation (-tèr-pèl'lé-), *n.*, appel, *m.* ; interruption; interpellation, *f.*

interpledge (-tèr-plèdje),*v.a.*, échanger des gages.

interpoint (-tèr-pwaï'n'te), *v.a.*, marquer par des points; entrecouper.

interpolate (-teur-), *v.a.*, interpoler; intercaler.

interpolation (-lé-), *n.*, interpolation ; intercalation,*f.*

interpolator (-lét'eur), *n.*, interpolateur, *m.*

interposal (-tèr-pôz'-). *n.*, intervention, *f.*

interpose (-tèr-pôze). *v.a.*, interposer, placer entre ; faire intervenir , offrir.

interpose, *v.n.*, s'interposer ; intervenir ; interrompre.

interposer, *n.*, médiateur, *m.*, médiatrice ; personne qui s'interpose, *f.*

interposition, *n.*, interposition ; intervention, *f.*

interpret (-teur-prète), *v.a.*, interpréter, expliquer, définir.

interpretable (-'a-b'l), *adj.*, que l'on peut interpréter.

interpretation (-té-), *n.*, interprétation, *f.*

interpretative (-teur-pri-ta-), *adj.*, interprétatif.

interpretatively, *adv.*, par interprétation.

interpreter(-teur-prèt'eur),*n.*,interprète,*m.*

interregnum (-tèr-règ'-), or **interreign** (-tèr-réne), *n.*, interrègne, *m.*

interrer(-teur'reur),*n.*,personne qui enterre, qui ensevelit,*f.*

interrogate (-tèr-ro-), *v.a.* and *n.*, interroger, questionner.

interrogation (-tèr-ro-ghé-), *n.*, interrogation, question,*f.* Note of — ; *point d'interrogation, m.*

interrogative (-tèr-rogh'a-), *adj.*, interrogatif.

interrogative, *n.*, terme interrogatif, *m.*

interrogatively, *adv.*, par forme d'interrogation ; (gram.) interrogativement.

interrogatory (-tèr'ro-ghé-), *n.*, interrogatoire, *m.* ; interrogations, *f.pl.*

interrogatory, *adj.*, interrogatif.

interrupt (-tèr'reupte),*v.a.*, interrompre.

interrupt, *adj.*, séparé, entr'ouvert.

interrupted. *part.*, interrompu, séparé.

interruptedly, *adv.*, avec interruption.

interrupter, *n.*, interrupteur, *m.*, interruptrice,*f.*

interruption, *n.*, interruption ; intervention,*f.*; obstacle, *m.*

interscapular (-tèr'scap'iou-), *adj.*, interscapulaire.

interscind (-tèr'çi'n'de), *v.a.*, (ant.) entrecouper.

interscribe (-tèr'scraïbe),*v.a.*, interligner.

intersect (-tèr'sèk'te), *v.a.*, entrecouper; (geom.) couper.

intersect, *v.n.*, (geom.) se couper.

intersection (-tèr'sèk'-), *n.*, action d'entrecouper ; (geom.) intersection,*f.*

intersert (-tèr'ceurte), *v.a.*, insérer, intercaler.

intersertion(-teur-ceur-), *n.*, insertion,*f.*

interspace (-tèr-), *n.*, intervalle ; espacement, *m.*

intersperse (-tèr-speurse),*v.a.*, entremêler ; parsemer ; disperser.

interstellar (-tèr-stèl'-), *adj.*, interstellaire.

interstice (-tèr-, *ou* -teur-), *n.*, interstice ; intervalle, *m.*

interstitial (-tèr-stish'-), *adj.*, qui contient des interstices ; intermédiaire.

intertexture (-tèr-tèxt'ieur), *n.*, entrelacement, *m.*

intertie (-tèr-ta'ye),*n.*, (carp.) entretoise; (of a roof—*detoit*) sablière, *f.*

intertropical(-tèr-), *adj.*, intertropical.

intertwine (-tèr-twaïne), or **intertwist** (-tèr'-).*v.a.*, entrelacer.

interval (-tèr'-), *n.*, intervalle ; espacement, *m.*

intervene (-tèr-vîne), *v.n.*, (of space, places —*espace, lieux*) être, se trouver entre ; (pers.) intervenir ; (of circumstances—*circonstances*) arriver, survenir, avoir lieu ; (of time—*du temps*) s'écouler, arriver.

intervening, *adj.*, (pers.) intervenant ; (of space, places, time—*espace, temps, lieux*) intermédiaire. — *party ; intervenant, m.,intervenante;* (jur.) *partie intervenante, f.* — *peace; paix durant l'intervalle, f.*

intervention (-tèr-vè'n'-), *n.*, intervention ; (of things—*des choses*) interposition, action,*f.*

intervert (-tèr-veurte), *v.a.*, intervertir.

interview (-tèr-viou),*n.*, entrevue,*f.*

intervolve (-tèr-), *v.a.*, envelopper l'un dans l'autre.

interweave (-tèr-wîve), *v.a.*, entrelacer, tresser, tisser ensemble, entremêler.

interweaving, *n.*, tissu ; entrelacement, *m.*

interworking (-weurk'-), *n.*, action réciproque,*f.*

interwreathed (-tèr-rîth'de), *adj.*, tissu en guirlande.

intestable (-tès-ta-b'l), *adj.*, intestable, incapable de tester.

intestacy (-tès-taci). *n.*, mort intestat, *f.*

intestate (-tès-), *adj.*, (of the deceased—*du décédé*) intestat; (of the heir—*de l'héritier*) ab intestat.

intestate. *n.*, intestat, *m.*

intestinal (-tès-), *adj.*, intestinal.

intestine (-tès-), *adj.*, intestin.

intestine, *n.*, intestin, *m.*

inthral (-thrôl),*v.a.* V. **enthral**.

inthralment, *n.*, asservissement, esclavage, *m.* ; servitude,*f.*

inthrone (-thrône), *v.* V. **enthrone**.

intimacy, *n.*, intimité, liaison intime,*f.*

intimate, *adj.*, intime ; intimement lié.

intimate, *n.*, intime, *m.,f.*

intimate, *v.a.*, faire entendre ; donner à entendre ; signifier ; faire comprendre.

intimately (-mét'li), *adv.*, intimement.

intimation (-mé-). *n.*, avis indirect, *m.*

intimidate, *v.a.*, intimider.

intimidation (-dé-), *n.*, intimidation, *f.*

into (i'n'tou), *prep.*, dans, en ; (math.) par, multiplié par.

intolerable (-tol'èr'a-b'l), adj., intolérable, insupportable.
intolerableness, n., nature insupportable, f.
intolerably, adv., intolérablement, insupportablement.
intolerance (-tol'èr'-), n., intolérance, f.
intolerant, adj., intolérant. — of; *incapable de supporter*.
intolerant, n., intolérant, m., intolérante, f.
intolerated (-tol'èr'é-), adj., qui n'est pas toléré.
intoleration (-tol'èr'é-), n., intolérance, f.
intomb (-toume), v.a., descendre dans la tombe; enterrer.
intonate, v.n., retentir; tonner; (mus.) solfier.
intonation (-tô'n'é-), n., intonation, f.
intone (-tône), v.a., chanter.
intorsion, or **intortion** (-torsh'eune), n., intorsion, f.; entortillement m.
intort, v.a., entortiller, entrelacer.
intoxicate, v.a., enivrer.
intoxicated (-toks'i-két'-), adj., ivre; (fig.) transporté, enivré.
intoxicating, adj., enivrant.
intoxication (-toks'i-ké-), n., ivresse, f.; enivrement, m.
intractability, or **intractableness**, n., humeur intraitable, indocilité, f.
intractable (-ta-b'l), adj., intraitable; indocile.
intractably. adv., d'une manière intraitable.
intrados (-tré-doss), n., intrados, m., douelle intérieure, f.
intransitive, adj., (gram.) intransitif.
intransitively, adv., dans un sens intransitif.
intransmutability (-miou-), n., non-transmutabilité, f.
intransmutable (-miou-ta-b'l), adj., intransmuable.
intrant, adj., entrant, pénétrant.
intreasure (-trèj'eur), v.a., (ant.) garder comme un trésor.
intreatful (-trit'foule), adj., suppliant.
intrench (-trè'n'she), v.a., (milit.) retrancher, se retrancher.
intrench, v.n., envahir; empiéter; creuser, fouiller, faire des tranchées.
intrenchment, n., retranchement, m.
intrepid (-trèp'-), adj., intrépide.
intrepidity, n., intrépidité, f.
intrepidly, adv., intrépidement.
intricacy, n., embrouillement, embarras, m.; complication, difficulté, f.
intricate, adj., embrouillé; embarrassé; compliqué.
intricately, adv., d'une manière embrouillée, embarrassée, compliquée.
intricateness. V. **intricacy**.
intrigue (-trighe), n., intrigue, f.
intrigue, v.n., intriguer.
intriguer, n., intrigant, m., intrigante, f.
intriguing (-trigh'igne), adj., intrigant.
intriguingly. adv., par intrigue.
intrinsic, or **intrinsical**, adj., intrinsèque.
intrinsically, adv intrinsèquement.
introduce (-diouce), v.a., introduire; faire entrer; (persons to one another—*une personne à une autre*) présenter, faire connaître. — him; *faites-le entrer*. — your friend to me; *présentez-moi votre ami; faites-moi connaître votre ami*. To — a fashion; *introduire une mode*.
introducer. n., introducteur, m.
introduction (-deuk'-), n., introduction; présentation, f.
introductive (-deuk'-), adj., qui sert d'introduction.
introductory (-deuk'-), adj., d'introduction; qui sert d'introduction.

introit (-trô-), n., introït, m.
intromission (-mish'-), n., introduction. admission; (phys.) intromission, f.
intromit, v.a., admettre.
introspect (-trô-spèk'tè), v.a., examiner l'intérieur de.
introspection (-trô-spèk'-), n., introspection, f.
introsusception (-trô-ceus'sèp'-), n. V. **intussusception**.
introvert (-veurte), v.a., tourner en dedans; diriger intérieurement.
intrude (-troude), v.n., se présenter sans être invité; se présenter; s'introduire; se faufiler; être intrus; être importun. To — on any one; *importuner quelqu'un*.
intrude, v.a., introduire (par importunité). To — one's self; *se présenter sans être invité; se présenter; s'introduire; se faufiler; être intrus*. To — one's self on any one; *importuner quelqu'un*.
intruder, n., importun, m., importune, f.; intrus, m., intruse, f.
intrusion (-trou-jeune), n.. intrusion, importunité; usurpation, f.; empiètement, m.
intrusive (-trou-cive), adj., importun.
intrust (-treuste), v.a., confier. To — any one with anything; *confier quelque chose à quelqu'un*.
intuition (-tiou-ïsh'), n., intuition, f.
intuitive (-tiou-i-), adj., intuitif d'intuition.
intuitively, adv., par intuition; intuitivement.
intumesce (-tiou-mèce), v.n., s'enfler.
intumescence, n., intumescence, f.
inturgescence (-teur-djès'-), n.. (ant.) gonflement, m.; enflure, f.
intussusception (-teus'seus'cèp'-), n., invagination, intussusception, f.
intwine (-twaï'ne), v.a. V. **entwine**.
inuendo. n. V. **innuendo**.
inula (-iou-), n., (bot.) aunée, f.
inumbrate (-eu'm-), v.a., ombrager.
inunction (-'eu'n'k'-), n., (ant.) onction, f.
inunctuosity (-'eu'n'k't'iou-oss'-), n., défaut d'onctuosité, m.
inundant (-'eu'n-), adj., qui inonde.
inundate (-'eu'n'-), v.a., inonder.
inundation (-eu'n'dé-), n., inondation, f.
inurbaneness (-'eur-bé'n'-), or **inurbanity** (-'eur-ba'n'-), n., défaut d'urbanité, m.
inure (-'youre), v.a., accoutumer, habituer, endurcir, aguerrir, rompre.
inurement, n., habitude, f.
inurn (-eurne), v.a., mettre dans une urne; enterrer.
inustion (-eust'i'eune), n., ustion, f.
inutility (-iou-), n., inutilité, f.
invade (-véde), v.a., envahir; attaquer; saisir.
invader, n., envahisseur, m.
invading, adj., envahissant.
invaletudinary (-i-tiou-), adj., valétudinaire.
invalid, adj., infirme, faible; (jur.) invalide.
invalid (-lide), n., malade, m., f.; personne malade, f.; (worn out soldier, sailor—*marins, soldats infirmes*) invalide, m.
invalidate, v.a., invalider, infirmer.
invalidity, n., faiblesse; (jur.) invalidité, f.
invalidness, n., faiblesse, f.
invaluable (-'iou-a-b'l), adj., inestimable.
invaluably, adv., d'une manière inestimable.
invariability, or **invariableness** (-vé-ri-), n., invariabilité, f.
invariable (-vé-ri-a-b'l), adj., invariable.
invariably, adv., invariablement.
invasion (-vé-jeune), n., invasion, f.; envahissement, m.
invasive (-vé-cive), adj., envahissant.

invective, *n.*, invective, *f.*
invective, *adj.*, satirique; injurieux.
invectively, *adv.*, avec invective; injurieusement.
inveigh (-vê), *v.n.*, se déchaîner, invectiver.
inveigher (-vê-eur), *n.*, personne qui invective, qui se répand en invectives, *f.*
inveigle (-vï'g'l), *v.a.*, séduire, attirer, capter, enjôler.
inveiglement, *n.*, séduction, captation, *f.*
inveigler, *n.*, enjôleur, *m.*, enjôleuse, *f.*; séducteur, *m.*; séductrice, *f.*
invent, *v.a.*, inventer; (to contrive falsely—*des mensonges*) controuver, inventer.
invention, *n.*, invention; (fiction) invention; (forgery—*mensonge*) chose controuvée, *f.*
inventive, *adj.*, inventif.
inventor, *n.*, inventeur, *m.*
inventorially, *adv.*, en forme d'inventaire.
inventory, *n.*, inventaire, *m.*
inventory, *v.a.*, inventorier.
inventress, *n.*, inventrice, *f.*
inverse (-veurse), *adj.*, inverse.
inversely, *adv.*, en sens inverse; en raison inverse; inversement.
inversion (-veur-), *n.*, inversion, *f.*; (fig.) (log., mus.) renversement, *m.*
invert (-veurte), *v.a.*, tourner sens dessus dessous, renverser; intervertir.
invertebral (-veur-ti-), *adj.*, invertébré.
invertebrate (-veur-ti-), *n.*, (zool.) invertébré, *m.*
invertebrate, *or* **invertebrated** (-veurti-bréte, -'ède), *adj.*, invertébré.
inverted (-veurt'-), *adj.*, renversé; inverse.
invertedly, *adv.*, dans un ordre renversé; en sens inverse.
invest (-vèste), *v.a.*, vêtir, revêtir; (milit.) investir; (money—*de l'argent*) placer.
investigable (-vès'ti-ga-b'l), *adj.*, susceptible d'investigation.
investigate (-vès'ti-), *v.a.*, rechercher; faire une enquête sur; faire des investigations sur.
investigation (-vès'ti-ghé-), *n.*, investigation, recherche, *f.*
investigative (-vès'ti-ghé-), *adj.*, investigateur.
investigator (-vès'ti-ghé-teur), *n.*, investigateur, *m.*, investigatrice, *f.*
investiture, *or* **investure** (-vès'ti-tioure, -vès'tioure), *n.*, investiture, *f.*
investive (-vès'-), *adj.*, qui revêt; qui investit.
investment (-vèst'-), *n.*, action de vêtir, de revêtir, *f.*; vêtement; (of money—*d'argent*) placement; (milit.) investissement, *m.*
inveteracy (-vèt'èr-a-), *n.*, caractère invétéré; acharnement, *m.*
inveterate (-vèt'èr'-), *adj.*, invétéré; acharné. To grow —; *s'invétérer.*
inveterate, *v.a.*, invétérer.
inveterately, *adv.*, d'une manière invétérée; avec acharnement.
inveterateness (-vèt'èr'èt'-), *n.*, état invétéré; acharnement, *m.*
inveteration (-vèt-èr'é-), *n.*, action de laisser invétérer, *f.*
invidious, *adj.*, odieux, envieux; irritant.
invidiously, *adv.*, odieusement.
invidiousness, *n.*, odieux, *m.*; envie, *f.*
invigorate, *v.a.*, renforcer, fortifier; donner de la vigueur à.
invigorating, *adj.*, fortifiant.
invigoration (-o-ré-), *n.*, action de fortifier, de donner de la vigueur, *f.*; état de vigueur, *m.*
invincible (-ci-b'l), *adj.*, invincible.
invincibleness, *n.*, nature invincible, *f.*
invincibly, *adv.*, invinciblement.
inviolability, *or* **inviolableness** (-vaï-o-), *n.*, inviolabilité, *f.*
inviolable (-vaï-o-la-b'l), *adj.*, inviolable.

inviolably, *adv.*, inviolablement.
inviolate (-vaï-o-), *adj.*, inviolable; entier, intact.
invious, *adj.*, impraticable.
inviscate, *v.a.*, engluer.
invisibility, *or* **invisibleness** (-viz'i-), *n.*, invisibilité, *f.*
invisible (-viz'i-b'l), *adj.*, invisible.
invisibly, *adv.*, invisiblement.
invitation (-vi-té-), *n.*, invitation. *f.*
invitatory (-vaï-ta-), *adj.*, invitatif, qui renferme une invitation.
invitatory, *n.*, (c.rel.) invitatoire, *m.*
invite (-vaïte), *v.a.*, inviter, engager.
inviter (-vaït'-), *n.*, personne qui invite, *f.*; hôte, *m.*
inviting (-vaït'-), *adj.*, engageant, attrayant.
invitingly, *adv.*, d'une manière engageante.
invitingness (-vaït'ign'-nèce), *n.*, nature engageante, *f.*
invitrifiable, *adj.*, non vitrifiable.
invocate, *v.a.*, invoquer.
invocation (-vo-ké-), *n.*, invocation, *f.*
invoice (-voïce), *n.*, facture, *f.*
invoice, *v.a.*, facturer.
invoke (-vôke), *v.a.*, invoquer.
involucral (-liou-), *adj.*, involucral.
involucre (-vo-liou-keur), *or* **involucrum** (-liou-creu-me), *n.*, involucre, *m.*
involuntarily (-vol'eu'n'-), *adv.*, involontairement.
involuntariness (-vol'eu'n'-), *n.*; caractère involontaire, *m.*
involuntary (-vol'eu'n'-), *adj.*, involontaire.
involute (-li'oute), *n.*, (geom.) développante, *f.*
involution (-li'ou-), *n.*, action d'envelopper; complication; (gram.) incise; (arith., alg.) élévation aux puissances, *f.*
involve, *v.a.*, (to envelop—*couvrir*) envelopper; (to comprise—*inclure*) comprendre; impliquer; (to cause—*causer*) entraîner; (to plunge—*jeter dans*) plonger; (to entangle—*embarrasser*) entortiller; (alg.) élever à une puissance. To — one's self; *s'endetter.* To be — d; *être endetté.* To — in difficulties; *plonger dans des difficultés.* She has greatly —d him; *elle l'a obéré de dettes.* That —s expense; *cela entraîne de la dépense.*
involved, *adj.*, (of persons—*personnes*) accablé de dettes; (of things—*choses*) grevé de dettes; dans la gêne. To be in — circumstances; *être dans un état de gêne.*
involvement, *n.*, embarras pécuniaire, *m.*; difficulté, gêne, *f.*
invulnerability, *or* **invulnerableness** (-veul-nèr'-), *n.*, invulnérabilité, *f.*
invulnerable (-veul-nèr'a-b'l), *adj.*, invulnérable.
inwall (-wôl), *v.a.*, entourer de murs.
inward (-worde), *adj.*, intérieur, interne.
inward, *or* **inwards**, *adv.*, en dedans; intérieurement.
inwardly, *adv.*, intérieurement.
inwardness, *n.*, intimité, *f.*
inwards, *n.*, entrailles d'animal, *f.pl.*; viscères, *m.pl.*
inweave (-wive), *v.a.* (*preterite*, Inwove; *past part.*, Inwoven), enlacer.
inwrap (-rape), *v.a.*, envelopper; (fig.) ravir.
inwreathe (-rithe), *v.a.*, couronner d'une guirlande; ceindre, couronner.
inwrought (-rôte), *adj.*, tissu.
iodine (aï-o-), *n.*, (chem.) iode, *m.*
ioduret (aï-o-diou-rète), *n.*, (chem.) iodure, *m.*
ionic (aï-o'n'-), *adj.*, ionique; ionien.
iota (aï-o-), *n.*, iota; rien, zest, *m.*
ipecacuanha (ip-i-kak'iou-), *n.*, (bot.) ipécacuana, *m.*
irascibility, *n.*, irascibilité, *f.*
irascible (-ci-b'l), *adj.*, irascible.

ire (aéur,, *s.*, colère, ⊙ire, *f.*; courroux, *m.*

ireful (-foule), *adj.*, furieux, courroucé.

irefully, *adv.*, avec courroux, avec colère.

iridium (i-rid'ieume), *n.*, iridium, *m.*

iris (aï-rice), *n.* (*irides*), iris, *m.*

irisated (aï-riss'ét'-), *or* irised (aï-riste), *adj.*, irisé.

irish (aïr'-), *adj.*, irlandais.

irish, *n.*, (language—*langue*) irlandais, *m.*

irishism, *n.*, locution irlandaise, *f.*

irishman, *n.*, Irlandais, *m.*

irishwoman (-woum'-), *n.*, Irlandaise, *f.*

iris-root (-route), *n.*, racine d'iris, *f.*

irk (eurke), *v.a. imp.*, répugner ; fatiguer, ennuyer.

irksome (-seume), *adj.*, pénible, ennuyeux ; fatigant.

irksomely, *adv.*, d'une manière fatigante, ennuyeusement.

irksomeness, *n.*, ennui, *m.* ; fatigue, *f.*

iron (aï'eurne), *n.*, fer ; (tech.) ferrement, *m.* Flat- —; *fer à repasser, m.* Wrought —; *fer forgé, m.* Cast- —; *fonte, f.* Old —; *ferraille, f.* Sheet- —; *tôle, f.*

iron, *adj.*, de fer.

iron, *v.a.*, ferrer ; (linen—*le linge*) repasser; (to shackle—*enchaîner*) mettre les fers à.

iron-bound (-baou'n'de), *adj.*, cerclé de fer ; garni de fer ; (shackled—*enchaîné*) chargé de fers.

iron-brake, *n.*, brimbale, *f.*

iron-clad, *adj.*, cuirassé.

iron-filings (-faïl'ign'ze), *n.pl.*, limaille de fer, *f.sing.*

iron-founder (-faou'n'd'-), *n.*, fondeur en fer, *m.*

iron-foundry, *n.*, fonderie de fer, *f.*

iron-glance, *n.*, fer spéculaire, fer oligiste, *m.*

iron-gray, *adj.*, gris de fer,

iron-hearted (-hârt'-), *adj.*, au cœur de fer.

ironic, *or* ironical (aï-ro'n'-), *adj.*, ironique.

ironically, *adv.*, ironiquement.

ironist (aï-reu'n'-), *n.*, personne qui emploie l'ironie, *f.*

iron-manufactory (-'iou-fak'-), *n.*, usine de fer, *f.*

iron-manufacture (-iou-fakt'ioure), *n*, fabrication du fer, *f.*

iron-master (-mâs'-), *n.*, maître de forges, *m.*

iron-monger (-meun'gn'gheur), *n.*, quincaillier, *m.*

iron-mongery (-meun'gn'gheuri), *n.*, quincaillerie, *f.*

iron-mould (-môlde), *n.*, (stain—*tache*) tache de rouille; (vessel—*vase*) lingotière, *f.*

iron-ore (-ôre), *n.*, minerai de fer, *m.*

iron-stone (-stône), *n.*, minerai de fer, *m.*

iron-wire (-waeur), *n.*, fil de fer, *m.*

iron-wood (-woude), *n.*, bois de fer, *m.*

iron-work (-weurke), *n.*, ferrure, *f.* ; ouvrage en fer, *m.*

iron-works (-weurkse), *n.pl.*, usine de fer, *f.sing.*

iron-wort (-weurte), *n.*, sidéritis, *m.* ; crapaudine, *f.*

irony (aï-ro'n'i), *n.*, ironie, *f.*

irony (aï-eur'n'i), *adj.*, de fer.

irradiance, *or* irradiancy (-'ré-di-), *n.*, rayonnement; rayon, *m.*

irradiate (-'ré-di-), *v.a.*, rayonner sur ; éclairer.

irradiate, *v.n.*, rayonner ; resplendir.

irradiate, *adj.*, rayonnant.

irradiation (-'ré-di-é-), *n.*, irradiation, splendeur, *f.*

irrational (ir-rash'eu'n'-), *adj.*, irraisonnable ; déraisonnable ; (geom.) irrationnel.

irrationality, *n.*, déraison, *f.* ; nature irraisonnable, *f.*

irrationally, *adv.*, sans raison, déraisonnablement.

irreclaimable (ir-ri-clé'm-a-b'l), *adj.*, incorrigible; indomptable.

irreclaimably, *adv.*, incorrigiblement.

irreconcilable (ir-rèk'o'n'çaïl'a-b'l), *adj.*, irréconciliable ; inconciliable.

irreconcilableness, *n.*, nature irréconciliable ; incompatibilité, *f.*

irreconcilably, *adv.*, irréconciliablement.

irreconciled, *adj.*, non réconcilié ; non expié.

irreconcilement, *n.*, non-réconciliation ; incompatibilité, *f.*

irreconciliation, *n.*, non-réconciliation, *f.*

irrecoverable (ir-ri-keuv'èr-a-b'l), *adj.*, irréparable; perdu sans ressource ; (fin.) irrécouvrable.

irrecoverableness, *n.*, nature irréparable; perte sans ressource, *f.*

irrecoverably, *adv.*, irréparablement; sans ressource; sans remède.

irredeemable (ir-ri-dî'm'-a-b'l), *adj.*, irrémédiable ; (fin.) irrachetable, non rachetable.

irredeemableness, *n.*, nature irrémédiable ; (fin.) nature non rachetable, *f.*

irreducible (ir-ri-diou-ci-b'l), *adj.*, irréductible.

irreducibleness, *n.*, irréductibilité, *f.*

irrefragability, *or* irrefragableness (ir-rèf'ra-ga-), *n.*, nature irréfragable, *f.*

irrefragable (ir-rèf-ra-ga-b'l), *adj.*, irréfragable, irréfutable.

irrefragably, *adv.*, irréfragablement.

irrefutable (ir-ri-fiout'a-b'l, *ou* -rèf-), *adj.*, irréfutable.

irrefutably, *adv.*, d'une manière irréfutable.

irregular (ir-règh'iou-), *adj.*, irrégulier, déréglé, désordonné.

irregular, *n.*, soldat de corps franc, *m.*

irregularity, *n.*, irrégularité ; conduite déréglée, *f.*

irregularly, *adv.*, irrégulièrement.

irrelative (ir-rèl'a-), *adv.*, sans liaison ; sans rapport.

irrelevancy (ir-rèl-i-), *n.*, nature étrangère, *f.*

irrelevant (ir-rèl-i-), *adj.*, inapplicable, étranger.

irreligion (ir-ri-lidj'-), *n.*, irréligion, *f.*

irreligious (ir-ri-lidj'-), *adj.*, irréligieux.

irreligiously, *adv.*, irréligieusement.

irreligiousness, *n.*, irréligion, *f.*

irremeable (ir-ri-mi-a-b'l), *adj.*, dont on ne peut revenir ; sans retour.

irremediable (ir-ri-mî-di-a-b'l), *adj.*, irrémédiable.

irremediableness, *n.*, nature irrémédiable, *f.*

irremediably, *adv.*, irrémédiablement.

irremissible (ir-ri-mis'si-b'l), *adj.*, irrémissible.

irremissibleness, *n.*, qualité irrémissible, *f.*

irremovability (ir-ri-mouv'-), *n.*, fermeté inébranlable; inamovibilité, *f.*

irremovable (ir-ri-mouv'a-b'l), *adj.*, immuable ; inamovible.

irremovably, *adv.*, d'une manière immuable.

irremunerable (ir-ri-miou-nèr-a-b'l), *adj.*, qu'on ne peut récompenser.

irreparability (ir-rèp'a-ra-), *n.*, nature irréparable, irréparabilité, *f.*

irreparable (ir-rèp'a-ra-b'l), *adj.*, irréparable.

irreparably, *adv.*, irréparablement.

irrepealability (ir-ri-pîl'-), *n.*, irrévocabilité, *f.*

irrepealable (ir-ri-pīl'a-b'l), adj., irrévocable.

irrepealably, adv., irrévocablement.

irrepleviable (ir-ri-plèv'i-a-b'l), or **irreplevisable** (-sa-b'l), adj.,(jur.)dont on ne peut obtenir la mainlevée.

irreprehensible (ir-rèp'ri-hè'n'si-b'l), adj., irrépréhensible.

irreprehensibleness, n., nature irrépréhensible, f.

irreprehensibly, adv., d'une manière irrépréhensible; irrépréhensiblement.

irrepressible (ir-ri-prèss'-i-b'l), adj., irrépressible; (of laughter—du rire) inextinguible.

irreproachable (ir-ri-prôtsh'a-b'l), adj., irréprochable.

irreproachableness, n., irréprochabilité, f.

irreproachably, adv., irréprochablement.

irreprovable (ir-ri-prouv'a-b'l), adj., irrépréhensible, irréprochable.

irreprovably, adv., irrépréhensiblement, irréprochablement.

irresistance (ir-ri-zist'-), n., non-résistance, f.

irresistibility, or **irresistibleness** (ir-ri-zist'-), n., irrésistibilité, f.

irresistible (ir-ri-zist'i-b'l), adj., irrésistible.

irresistibly, adv., irrésistiblement.

irresoluble (ir-rèz'o-liou-b'l), adj., insoluble.

irresolubleness, n., insolubilité, f.

irresolute (ir-rèz'o-lioute), adj., irrésolu.

irresolutely, adv., irrésolument.

irresoluteness, or **irresolution**, n., irrésolution, f.

irresolvability, or **irresolvableness** (irri-zol-), n., insolubilité, f.

irresolvable (ir-ri-zol-va-b'l), adj., insoluble.

irrespective (ir-ri-spèk'-), adj., indépendant.

irrespectively, adv., indépendamment.

irrespirable (ir-rès'-pi-ra-b'l), adj., irrespirable.

irresponsibility (ir-ri-spo'n'si-), n., irresponsabilité, f.

irresponsible(ir-ri-spo'n'si-b'l), adj., irresponsable.

irretrievable (ir-ri-trīv'a-b'l), adj., irréparable, irrémédiable.

irretrievably, adv., irréparablement.

irreverence (ir-rèv'èr'-), n., irrévérence, f.

irreverent, adj, irrévérent, irrévérencieux.

irreverently, adv., irrévéremment, avec irrévérence.

irreversible (ir-rl-veur-si-b'l), adj., irrévocable.

irreversibly, adv., irrévocablement.

irrevocability, or **irrevocableness** (irrèv'-), n., irrévocabilité, f.

irrevocable (ir-rèv'o-ca-b'l), adj., irrévocable.

irrevocably, adv., irrévocablement.

irrhetorical (ir-rhi-), adj., qui n'est pas bien tourné, sans éloquence.

irrigate, v.a., arroser, irriguer.

irrigation (-ghé-), n., arrosement, m.; irrigation, f.

irriguous (-righ'iou-), adj., arrosé, humide.

irritability, n., irritabilité, f.

irritable (-ta-b'l), adj., irritable.

irritant, adj., irritant.

irritant, n., irritant, m.

irritate, v.a., irriter; provoquer.

irritating (-tét'igne), adj., irritant.

irritation (-ri-té-), n., irritation, f.

irroration (ir-ro-ré-), n., (ant.) irroration, f.

irruption (ir-reup'-), n., irruption, f.

irruptive (-reup'-), adj., qui fait irruption.

isabel (iz'-), n., isabelle, m.

isabel-coloured (-keul'leurde), adj., isabelle.

ischium (is-ki-), n., ischion, m.

ischuretic (is-kiou-rèt'-), adj., (ant.) ischurétique.

ischury (is-kiou-), n., ischurie, f.

isinglass (aï'zign'-glàce), n., colle de poisson, f.

isinglass-stone (-stône), n., talc, m.

islam, or **islamism** (iz-,-iz'me), n., islamisme, m.

island (aï-la'n'de), n., île, f.

islander (aï-la'n'd'-), n., insulaire, m., f.

isle (aïl), n., île, f.

islet (aï-lète), n., îlot, m. ; petite île, f.

isochronal, or **isochronous** (aï-çok'-), adj., isochrone.

isolate (aïz'-), v.a., isoler.

isolated (aïz'o-lét'-), adj., isolé.

isolation (aïz'o-lé-), n., isolement, m.

isosceles (aï-ços'ci-lize), adj., isocèle.

israelite (iz'ra-èl'aïte), n., Israélite, m., f.

israelitic, or **israelitish**, adj., israélite.

issuable (ish'shiou-a-b'l), adj., qu'on peut émettre, qu'on peut rendre; (jur.) des sessions.

issue (ish'shiou), n., issue; (egress—sortie) sortie, f., écoulement, m.; (sending out—émission) distribution, expédition, f.; (ultimate result —conséquence finale) résultat, m., conclusion, issue, f.; (progeny—progéniture) enfants, m.pl., postérité, f.; (surg.) exutoire, (l.u.) fonticule, m.; (fin.) émission; (jur.) question, f. To die without —; mourir sans enfants, sans postérité.

issue, v.a., publier; expédier; (fin.)émettre; (jur.) donner, lancer.

issue, v.n., sortir, jaillir, découler; (to end—finir) se terminer, être l'issue; (to accrue—arriver) provenir de; (milit.) faire une sortie; (jur.) dépendre de la solution d'une question.

issueless, adj., sans enfants, sans postérité.

issue-peas (-pīze), n.pl., pois à cautère, m.pl.

issuer, n., personne qui émet, f.

isthmus (ist'meusse), n., isthme, m.

it (ite), pron., il, m., elle, f.; le, m., la, f.; lui, m., f.; ce; cela. — must be; il le faut. — is over ; c'est fini. — is I who said —; c'est moi qui l'ai dit. — is they who said —; ce sont eux qui l'ont dit. — rains; il pleut. Of —; en. At —, in —, to —; y.

italian (i-tal'ya'ne), adj., italien.

italian, n., Italien, m., Italienne, f.; (language—langue) italien, m.

italic, n., italique, m.

italic, adj., italique.

italicize (-çaïze), v.a., imprimer en italique.

itch (itshe), n., démangeaison ; (disease—maladie) gale, f.

itch, v.n., avoir des démangeaisons ; démanger à.

itching, n., démangeaison, f.

itchy, adj., galeux.

item (aï-tème), adv , item.

item, n., article, item, m.

iterant (it'èr-), adj., qui répète.

iterate (it'èr-). v.a., réitérer, répéter.

iteration (it'èr'é-), n., réitération, répétition, f.

iterative (it'èr'é-), adj., répété, itératif.

itinerant (i-ti'n'èr-), adj., ambulant.

itinerant, n., personne ambulante, f.; prédicateur ambulant, m.

itinerary (i-ti'n'èr'-), n., itinéraire, m.

itinerary, adj., ambulant.

its (pron., son, m.s.a.; ses, m., f.pl.; sa, sien, m., la sienne, f.; les siens, m.pl., les siennes, f.pl.

itself, pron., lui-même, m., elle-même, f.; soi-même, m.; même, m.f. Virtue —; la vertu même.

ives (aï'vize), n., (vet.) avives, f.pl.

ivory (aï-vo-), *n.*, ivoire, *m.*
ivory, *adj.*, d'ivoire.
ivory-black, *n.*, noir d'ivoire, *m.*
ivory-turner (-teurn'-), *n.*, tourneur en ivoire, *m.*
ivory-worker (-weurk'-), *n.*, ivoirier, *m.*
ivy (aï-vi), *n.*, lierre, *m.*
ivy-berry (-bèr-ri), *n.*, grain de lierre, *m.*
ivyed, *or* **ivied** (aï-vide), *adj.*, couvert de lierre.
ivy-mantled (-ma'n't'l'de), *adj.*, couvert de lierre.

J

J, dixième lettre de l'alphabet, j, *m.*
jabber, *v.n.*, jaboter, jacasser; bredouiller.
jabber, *n.*, bredouillement; baragouinage, *m.*
jabberer, *n.*, bredouilleur, *m.*, bredouilleuse, *f.*; baragouineur, *m.*, baragouineuse, *f.*
jabbering, *n.*, bredouillement, baragouinage, *m.*
jacent (djé-), *adj.*, étendu au long; couché.
jack (djake), *n.*, (spit—*broche*) tourne-broche; (ich.) brocheton; (frame for sawing wood on—*pour scier le bois*) chevalet, *m.*; (pitcher—*vase*) outre, *f.*; (lifting jack—*machine à crémaillère*) cric; (at bowls—*aux boules*) cochonnet; (flag—*drapeau*) pavillon, *m.* — -with-a-lantern; *feu follet*, *m.* — of all trades; *factotum*, *m.*
jackal, *n.*, chacal, *m.*
jackalent (-a-lè'n'te), *n.*, benêt, nigaud, *m.*
jackanapes (-épse), *n.*, singe; fat, *m.*
jackass, *n.*, âne, baudet, bourriquet, *m.*, (fig.) âne, bête, imbécile, *m.*
jack-boot (-boute), *n.*, botte à genouillère, *f.*
jackdaw (-dô), *n.*, (orni.) choucas, *m.*
jacket, *n.*, veste, jaquette, *f.*; (for women—*de femme*) corsage, canezou, *m.*; (tech.) chemise, *f.*
jack-ketch (-kètshe), *n.*, bourreau, *m.*
jackpudding (-poud'-), *n.*, pierrot, bouffon, paillasse, *m.*
jacksauce (-sôss), *n.*, impertinent; drôle, *m.*
jack-sprat (-sprate), *n.*, jeune étourdi, écervelé, *m.*
jack-tar (-târ), *n.*, loup de mer, marin, matelot, *m.*
jacobin, *n.*, Jacobin, *m.*
jacobin, *adj.*, jacobin; de jacobin.
jacobin, *n.*, jacobin (monk—*moine*), *m.*
jacobinie, *or* **jacobinical,** *adj.*, jacobin; de jacobin.
jacobinism (-iz'me), *n.*, jacobinisme, *m.*
jacobinize (aïze), *v.a.*, entacher de jacobinisme.
jacobite (-baïte), *n.*, jacobite, *m.*
jacobite, *adj.*, jacobite.
jacobitism (-baït'iz'me), *n.*, principes des jacobites, *m.pl.*
jacob's-staff (djé-cob'z'stâfe), *n.*, bâton de pèlerin, bourdon de pèlerin, *m.*; canne à poignard, *f.*; bâton de Jacob; (astron.) astrolabe, *m.*
jacobus (djé-cô-), *n.*, jacobus, *m.*
jaconet, *n.*, jaconas, *m.*
jaculate (djak'iou-), *v.a.*, lancer.
jaculation (djak'iou-lé-), *n.*, action de lancer, *f.*
jaculator (djak'iou-lé-teur), *n.*, personne qui lance, *f.*
jaculatory, *adj.*, jaculatour; jaculatoire.
jade, *n.*, haridelle, rosse; (woman—*femme*) coquine, friponne, *f.*
jade, *v.a.*, surmener, harasser; fatiguer.
jade, *v.n.*, se fatiguer; se décourager.
jaded, *adj.*, surmené, harassé; excédé de fatigue; usé.
jadish, *adj.*, de rosse, de haridelle; (fig.) coquin, fripon.

jag, *or* **jagg,** *n.*, dent de scie; (bot.) laciniure; (fig.) brèche, *f.*
jag, *or* **jagg,** *v.a.*, ébrécher.
jaggedness (djag'ghèd'-), *n.*, dentelure, *f.*
jaggy (djag'ghi), *adj.*, dentelé, ébréché; (bot.) lacinié.
jaguar (djagh'iou'âr), *n.*, jaguar, *m.*
jah (djâ), *n.*, Jéhovah, *m.*
jail (djéle), *n.*, prison, geôle, *f.*
jail-bird (-beurde), *n.*, gibier de potence, *m.*
jailer, *or* **jail-keeper** (-kîp'-), *n.*, geôlier, *m.*
jakes (djékse), *n.*, latrines, *f.pl.*
jalap, *n.*, jalap, *m.*
jam, *n.*, conserve; confiture, *f.*
jam, *v.a.*, serrer, presser, fouler.
jamb (djame), *n.*, jambage; (of a chimney—*de cheminée*) chambranle, *m.* — post; *montant*, *m.*
jane, *n.*, coutil satiné, *m.*
jangle (djan'gn'g'l), *v.a.*, faire discorder.
jangle, *v.n.*, se quereller; se chamailler.
jangler, *n.*, querelleur, *m.*
jangling, *n.*, son discordant, *m.*; querelle, *f.*, chamaillis, *m.*
janitor (-teur), *n.*, portier, concierge, *m.*
janizarian, *adj.*, des janissaires.
janizary, *n.*, janissaire, *m.*
jansenism (dja'n'sè'n'iz'me), *n.*, jansénisme, *m.*
jansenist, *n.*, janséniste, *m.*
january (dja'n'iou-), *n.*, janvier, *m.*
japan, *n.*, laque, *m.*
japan, *v.a.*, vernisser de laque; vernir.
japanese (-ize), *adj.*, japonais.
japanese, *n.*, Japonais, *m.*, Japonaise, *f.*; (language—*langue*) japonais, *m.*
japanner, *n.*, vernisseur, *m.*
jar (djâr), *v.n.*, (of sound—*du son*) être discordant; (to quarrel—*disputer*) se disputer, se quereller; (to vibrate—*vibrer*) vibrer; (to clash —*s'opposer*) être contraire, heurter, choquer, jurer.
jar (djâr), *v.a.*, secouer; faire trembler; faire vibrer; choquer, heurter.
jar (djâr), *n.*, (vessel—*vase*) jarre, cruche, *f.*; bocal, *m.*; (harsh sound—*son désagréable*) son discordant, *m.*; (vibration) vibration; (dispute) contestation, *f.*, conflit, *m.* On a —, on the —; *entr'ouvert, entre-bâillé.*
jardes (djardze), *n.pl.*, (vet.) jardons, *m.pl.*
jargon (djâr-), *n.*, jargon, *m.*
jarring (djâr'-), *n.*, (dispute) querelle, contestation, *f.*; (harsh sound—*son désagréable*) bruit discordant, *m.*
jarring, *adj.*, en contestation; discordant.
jasmine (djaz'-, *ou* djas'-), *n.*, jasmin, *m.*
jasper, *n.*, jaspe, *m.*
jasperated (-peur'ét'ède), *adj.*, jaspé.
jaundice (djâ'n'dice), *n.*, ictère, *m.*; jaunisse, *f.*
jaundiced (-diste), *adj.*, qui a la jaunisse.
jaunt (dja'n'te), *n.*, tournée, promenade, course, *f.*
jaunt, *v.n.*, courir çà et là; faire des promenades, faire des courses.
jauntiness, *n.*, gaieté; légèreté, *f.*; (showiness—*parade*) étalage, *m.*
jaunty, *adj.*, léger; (showy—*éclatant*) voyant.
javelin (djav'-), *n.*, javeline, *f.*; javelot, *m.*
jaw (djô), *n.*, mâchoire; (of a horse—*d'un cheval*) ganache; (pop.) (abuse—*injurieux*) gueule, *f.* —s; *gueule*; (fig.) porte, serre, *f.sing.* *étreintes*, *f.pl.* The —s of death; *les étreintes de la mort.* Lock—; *trismus*, *m.*
jaw, *v.a.*, (pop.) criailler après; dire des sottises à.
jaw, *v.n.*, (pop.) gueuler.
jawbone (djô-bône), *n.*, mâchoire, *f.*; os maxillaire, *m.*
jawfallen (-fôl'n), *adj.*, abattu, attristé.

26

jaw-set (-sète), *adj.*, (med.) qui a le trismus.

jay, *n.*, (orni.) geai, *m.*

jealous (djèl'-), *adj.*, jaloux.

jealously, *adv.*, jalousement.

jealousness, *n.*, jalousie, *f.*

jealousy (djèl'euss'i), *n.*, jalousie, *f.*

jears (djirze), *n.pl.*, (nav.) drisse, *f. sing.*

jeer (djire), *n.*, raillerie, moquerie, *f.*

jeer, *v.a.*, railler, se moquer de.

jeer, *v.n.*, railler, se railler, se moquer.

jeerer, *n.*, railleur, *m.*, railleuse. *f.*; moqueur, *m.*, moqueuse, *f.*

jeering, *adj.*, railleur, moqueur.

jeering, *n.*, raillerie, moquerie, *f.*

jeeringly, *adv.*, en raillant.

jehovah (dji-hô-), *n.*, Jéhovah, *m.*

jejune (dji-djioune), *adj.*, vide; aride, pauvre, maigre.

jejuneness, *n.*, vide, *m.*; aridité, pauvreté, *f.*

jelly (djèl'-), *n.*, gelée, *f.*; coulis, *m.*

jennet (djè'n'nète), *n.*, genêt, *m.*

jenny (djè'n'ni), *n.*, mule-Jenny, jenny, *f.*, métier à filer le coton, *m.*

jeofail (djè'fal), *n.*, (jur.) erreur, omission, *f.*

jeopard, *or* **jeopardize** (djèp'ard, -'aïze), *v.a.*, hasarder, risquer.

jeoparder, *n.*, personne qui hasarde, qui risque, *f.*

jeopardous, *adj.*, hasardeux, chanceux; périlleux, dangereux.

jeopardously, *adv.*, d'une manière hasardeuse, périlleuse, chanceuse; dangereusement.

jeopardy (djèp'ard'i), *n.*, péril, danger, *m.*

jerboa (djeur'-), *n.*, (mam.) gerboise, *f.*

jeremiade (djè-ri-maï-), *n.*, jérémiade, *f.*

jerfalcon (djeur-fôl-), *n.*, gerfaut, *m.*

jerk (djeurke), *n.*, saccade; secousse, *f.*

jerk, *v.a.*, donner une saccade à; pousser, lancer; (mam.) saccader.

jerkin (djeur-), *n.*, pourpoint; (orni.) gerfaut mâle, *m.*

jess, *n.*, (hawking—*fauconnerie*) laisse, *f.*; ruban, *m.*

jessamine (djès'sa-), *n.*, jasmin, *m.*

jest (djèste), *n.*, plaisanterie, facétie, *f.*; bon mot; mot pour rire, *m.*; (laughing-stock—*plastron*) risée, *f.* In — ; *par plaisanterie, pour badiner.* To be in — ; *badiner.*

jest, *v.n.*, plaisanter, badiner. To — at; *rire de, railler sur.*

jest-book (-bouke), *n.*, recueil de bons mots, *m.*

jester, *n.*, plaisant, farceur, diseur de bons mots, railleur, *m.*, railleuse, *f.*; (buffoon—*bouffon*) bouffon, *m.*

jesting, *adv.*, de plaisanterie; pour rire; badin.

jesting, *n.*, plaisanterie, *f.*; badinage, *m.*

jesuit (djèz'iou-ite), *n.*, jésuite, *m.*

jesuitic, *or* **jesuitical**, *adj.*, jésuitique.

jesuitically, *adv.*, jésuitiquement; en jésuite.

jesuitism, *n.*, jésuitisme, *m.*

jet (djète), *n.*, (min.) jais, jaiet; (of water—*d'eau*) jet d'eau, jet, *m.*

jet, *v.n.*, s'élancer; (to strut—*marcher fièrement*) se pavaner, se carrer.

jet d'eau (jé-dô), *n.*, jet d'eau, *m.*

jetsam, **jetsom**, **jetson**, *or* **jetteson**, *n.*, (jur.) jet, jet de marchandises à la mer, *m.*

jetteau (djèt'tô), *n.*, jet d'eau, *m.*

jettee (djèt'tî), *n.*, saillie, *f.*

jetty (djèt'ti), *adj.*, couleur de jais.

jetty (djèt'-), *n.*, jetée, *f.* — -head; (nav.) môle, *m.*, jetée, *f.*

jetty, *v.n.*, être en saillie, faire saillie, saillir, déborder.

jew (djiou), *n.*, Juif, Israélite, *m.*

jewel (djiou'èl), *n.*, jovau, bijou, *m.*; pierre précieuse, *f.*; (horl.) diamant. *m.* — -case; *écrin, m.*

jewel, *v.a.*, orner de bijoux; parer de pierreries; (horl.) placer des rubis dans un mouvement de montre.

jewel-house (-haouce), *or* **jewel-office**, *n.*, conservatoire des joyaux de la couronne, *m.*

jeweller, *n.*, joaillier, bijoutier, *m.*

jewellery, *or* **jewelry**, *n.*, joaillerie, bijouterie, *f.*

jewess (djiou-èce), *n.*, Juive, *f.*

jewish, *adj.*, juif, des Juifs; judaïque.

jewishly, *adv.*, en juif; en juive.

jew's-harp (djiouz'hàrpe), *n.*, guimbarde, *f.*

jezebel (djèz'i-bèl), *n.*, mégère, *f.*

jib (djibe), *n.*, (nav.) foc, *m.*

jig (djighe), *n.*, gigue (dance—*danse*), *f.*

jig, *v.n.*, danser une gigue.

jigger (djig'gheur), *n.*, (print.) visorium, *m.*

jilt, *n.*, coquette, *f.*

jilt, *v.a.*, faire la coquette à l'égard de; planter là; duper, tromper.

jilt, *v.n.*, faire la coquette; coqueter.

jingle (djign'-g'l), *n.*, (of bells—*de cloches*) tintement; (of glasses, metals—*de verres, de métaux*) cliquetis; (little bell—*sonnette*) grelot, *m.*; (correspondence of sound in rhyme—*consonance*) concordance, *f.*

jingle, *v.n.*, (of bells—*des cloches*) tinter; (of glasses—*des verres*) s'entre-choquer; (of chains—*de chaînes*) retentir.

jingle, *v.a.*, (bells—*cloches*) faire tinter; (glasses—*verres*) choquer; (chains—*chaînes*) faire retentir.

job, *n.*, affaire, chose à faire, *f.*; travail: ouvrage, *m.*; (among workmen—*d'ouvriers*) tâche, *f.*; (print.) ouvrage de ville; (b.s.) tripotage, *m.* By the — ; *à forfait;* (among workmen—*d'ouvriers*) *à la tâche; aux pièces.*

job, *v.n.*, frapper avec un instrument aigu, enfoncer un instrument aigu dans quelque chose; (to hire—*prendre à louage*) louer; (to let—*donner à louage*) louer; (b.s.) tripoter.

job, *v.n.*, travailler à la tâche; (in the public stocks—*dans les fonds publics*) agioter, spéculer; louer des chevaux, des voitures.

jobber, *n.*, ouvrier à la tâche; (in the public stocks—*sur les fonds publics*) agioteur, spéculateur; (b.s.) tripotier, *m.*

jobbernowl (djob'beur'nôl), *n.*, benêt, butor, *m.*

jobbing, *n.*, ouvrage à la tâche; (in the public stocks—*dans les fonds publics*) agiotage; (print.) ouvrage de ville; (b.s.) tripotage, *m.*

jockey, *n.*, jockey; (cheat—*escroc*) maquignon, fripon, *m.*

jockey, *v.a.*, duper, tromper.

jockeyship, *n.*, équitation, *f.*

jocose (-côce), *adj.*, plaisant, badin.

jocosely, *adv.*, en plaisantant, en badinant.

jocoseness, *n.*, enjouement, badinage, *m.*

jocular (djok'iou-), *adj.*, plaisant, gai, badin.

jocularly, *adv.*, en plaisantant, gaîment.

jocund, *adj.*, joyeux, enjoué, gai.

jocundly, *adv.*, joyeusement, gaîment.

jocundness, *n.*, joie, gaîté, *f.*; enjouement, *m.*

jog, *n.*, secousse légère, *f.*; attonchement pour éveiller l'attention; obstacle, *m.*

jog, *v.n.*, remuer; se mouvoir, voyager, marcher, paresseusement, lentement, lourdement. To — on; *aller doucement; aller son petit bonhomme de chemin.*

jog, *v.a.*, toucher, pousser, du coude, de la main pour éveiller l'attention; éveiller l'attention en touchant, en poussant légèrement.

jogger (djog'gheur), *n.*, personne qui marche lourdement, personne qui donne une secousse, *f.*

jogging (djog'ghigne), *n.*, secousse légère; motion saccadée, *f.*

joggle (djog'g'l), *v.a.*, secouer, remuer, pousser, tout à coup, mais légèrement.

jogtrot (djog'trote), *n.*, petit trot, *m.*

join (djwaine), *v.a.*, joindre; (to overtake—*rattraper*) rejoindre; réunir; se joindre à.

join, *v.n.*, se joindre; se toucher.

joinder (djwaï'n'-), *n.*, (jur.) réponse à une exception, *f.*

joined (djwaï'n'de), *adj.*, (bot.) conné, coadné, conjoint.

joiner (djwaï'n'-), *n.*, menuisier, *m.*

joinery, *n.*, menuiserie, *f.*

joining, *n.*, action de joindre; jonction, *f.*

joint (djwaï'n'te), *n.*, jointure, *f.*; joint, *m.*; (anat.) articulation, *f.*; (bot.) nœud, *m.*, articulation, *f.* — of meat; *pièce de viande*, *f.*; *rôti, m.* Out of —; *disloqué, démis, luxé*; (fig.) *dérangé.* To put one's arm out of —; *se disloquer, se démettre le bras.*

joint, *v.a.*, couper dans la jointure, dans l'articulation; former de jointures, d'articulations.

joint, *adj.*, réuni; commun.

jointed, *adj.*, articulé; jointé; joint.

jointer, or **jointing-plane**, *n.*, varlope, *f.*

joint-guardian (-gâr-di-ane), *n.*, cotuteur, *m.*

joint-heir (-ère), *n.*, cohéritier, *m.*

jointly, *adv.*, conjointement; d'accord, de concert.

joint-oil (-oïl), *n.*, synovie, *f.*

joint-pin, *n.*, goupille, *f.*

joint-racking (-rak'-), *adj.*, convulsif.

jointress, *n.*, douairière, *f.*

joint-stock, *n.*, fonds commun, *m.* — company; *société anonyme*, *f.*

jointure (djwaï'n't'ioure), *n.*, douaire, *m.*

jointure, *v.a.*, assigner un douaire à.

joist (djwaïste), *n.*, solive, *f.*; madrier, *m.*

joist, *v.a.*, poser des solives à, des madriers à.

joke (djô'ke), *n.*, bon mot; mot pour rire, *m.*; plaisanterie, *f.* In —; *par plaisanterie; pour rire.* To crack one's —; *avoir le mot pour rire.* To crack a —; *dire un bon mot.* To be in —; *plaisanter.* To be no —; *passer la plaisanterie.*

joke, *v.a.*, plaisanter, railler.

joke, *v.n.*, plaisanter; badiner; rire; faire le farceur.

joker, *n.*, diseur de bons mots, plaisant, farceur, *m.*

joking, *n.*, plaisanterie, farce, *f.*

jokingly, *adv.*, en plaisantant; pour rire.

jole (djôle), *n.*, joue; (of a fish *de poisson*) hure, *f.* Cheek by —; *tête à tête.*

jolily (djol'-), *adv.*, joyeusement; gaillardement.

joliness, or **jollity**, *n.*, joie, gaieté, allégresse, gaillardise, *f.*

jolly, *adj.*, gai, joyeux, gaillard.

jolly-boat (-bôte), *n.*, petit canot, *m.*

jolt (djôlte), *n.*, cahot, *m.*

jolt, *v.a.* and *n.*, cahoter.

jolter, *n.*, personne qui cahote, chose qui cahote, *f.*

jolthead (djôlt'hède), *n.*, balourd, butor, *m.*

jolting, *n.*, cahotage, *m.*

jonquil (djo'n'kwil), *n.*, (bot.) jonquille, *f.*

jorden, *n.*, pot de chambre, vase de nuit, *m.*

jostle (djos's'l), or **justle** (djeus's'l), *v.a.*, coudoyer, pousser, bousculer.

jostling, *n.*, action de coudoyer, *f.*

jot (djote), *n.*, iota, brin, *m.*

jot, *v.a.*, noter; prendre note de.

journal (djeur-), *n.*, journal, *m.*; feuille publique, *f.*; (com.) journal, livre-journal, *m.*

journalism, *n.*, journalisme, *m.*

journalist, *n.*, journaliste, *m.*

journalize (-'aïze), *v.a.*, insérer dans un

journal; (book-keeping—*comptabilité*) porter au journal.

journey (djeur-nè), *n.*, voyage (by land—*par terre*), *m.* To take a —; *faire un voyage.* A pleasant — to you! *bon voyage!* By slow journeys; *à petites journées.*

journey, *v.n.*, voyager.

journeying, *n.*, voyage, *m.*

journey-man, *n.*, garçon; ouvrier, *m.* — tailor; garçon tailleur, *m.*

journey-work (-weurke), *n.*, ouvrage à la journée, *m.*

joust (djousta), *n.*, joute, *f.*

joust, *v.a.*, jouter.

jovial (djô-), *adj.*, jovial, joyeux.

joviality, *n.*, humeur joviale; jovialité, joie, *f.*

jovially, *adv.*, jovialement, joyeusement.

jovialness, *n.*, humeur joviale; joie, *f.*

jowl (djôle), *n.* V. **jole**.

jowler, *n.*, chien de chasse, *m.*

joy (djoè), *n.*, joie, *f.* To wish any one —; *faire des compliments de félicitation à quelqu'un.*

joy, *v.n.*, se réjouir.

joy, *v.a.*, (ant.) réjouir; féliciter.

joyful (-foule), *adj.*, joyeux.

joyfully, *adv.*, joyeusement.

joyfulness, *n.*, allégresse, joie, *f.*

joyless, *adj.*, sans joie.

joylessly, *adv.*, sans joie.

joylessness, *n.*, absence de joie, *f.*

joyous (djoè-yeusse), *adj.*, joyeux.

joyously, *adv.*, joyeusement.

joyousness, *n.*, joie, *f.*

jubilant (djiou-), *adj.*, qui pousse des cris de joie.

jubilation (djiou-bi-lé-), *n.*, réjouissances de triomphe, *f.pl.*; jubilation, *f.*

jubilee (djiou-bi-lî), *n.*, (of the Jews—*des Juifs*; c. rel.) jubilé, *m.*; réjouissance, jubilation, allégresse, *f.*

jucundity (djeu-keu'n'-), *n.*, agrément, *m.*

judaic, or **judaical** (djiou-dé-), *adj.*, judaïque.

judaically, *adv.*, judaïquement.

judaism (djiou-dé-iz'ne), *n.*, judaïsme, *m.*

judaize (djiou-dé-aïze), *v.n.*, judaïser.

judas-tree (djiou-dass-tri), *n.*, (bot.) gainier commun; arbre de Judée, *m.*

judcock (djeud'-), *n.*, (orni.) petite bécassine, *f.*

judge (djeudje), *n.*, juge; connaisseur, *m.* Assistant —; *assesseur, m.* To be a — of; *se connaître à, se connaître en.* To be a —; *être juge; s'y connaître.*

judge, *v.a.* and *n.*, juger.

judgeship, *n.*, fonctions de juge; *f.pl.*; dignité de juge; judicature, *f.*

judgment, *n.*, jugement; (of Heaven—*du Ciel*) châtiment, *m.*, punition, *f.*; (jur.) jugement, arrêt, *m.* In my —; *à mon avis.* To have a correct —; *avoir l'esprit juste.*

judgment-day (-dè), *n.*, jour du jugement; jugement dernier, *m.*

judgment-hall (-hôl), *n.*, salle de justice, *f.*

judgment-seat (-sîte), *n.*, tribunal, *m.*

judicable (djiou-di-ca-b'l), *adj.*, qui peut être jugé.

judicative (-ca-), *adj.*, qui a la faculté de juger.

judicatory, *adj.*, de justice; qui rend la justice.

judicatory, *n.*, cour de justice; justice, *f.*

judicature (djiou-di-ca-teur), *n.*, judicature, justice; cour de justice, *f.*

judicial (djeu-dish'al), *n.*, judiciaire, juridique.

judicially, *adv.*, judiciairement; juridiquement.

judiciary (djiou-dish'i-a-ri), *adj.*, judiciaire

judicious (djiou-dish'-), *adv.*, judicieux; sage.

judiciously, *adv.*, judicieusement.

judiciousness, *n.*, jugement, *m.*: sagesse, *f.*

jug (djeughe), *n.*, pot, *m.*

juggle. *n.*, jonglerie, *f.*; tour de gobelets: tour de passe-passe. *m.*

juggle (djeug'g'l), *v.n.*, faire des tours de passe-passe; escamoter: tromper; jongler.

juggle. *v.a.*, jouer, duper, escamoter.

juggler, *n.*, jongleur, bateleur, joueur de gobelets. escamoteur, *m.*

jugglery, *n.*, tour de jongleur, d'escamoteur, *m.*; jonglerie, *f.*

juggling, *n.*, jonglerie, *f.*; batelage, escamotage, *m.*

juggling. *adj.*, qui fait des tours de passe-passe; qui escamote; trompeur.

jugglingly, *adv.*, par jonglerie, en fourbe.

jugular (djiou-ghiou-), *adj.*, jugulaire.

jugular, *n.*, jugulaire, *f.*

juice (djiouce), *n*, jus: suc, *m.*

juice. *v.a.*, humecter de jus. de suc.

juiceless, *adj.*, sans jus; sans suc.

juiciness, *n.*, abondance de jus, *f.*

juicy, *adj.*, juteux; plein de jus.

jujube (djiou-djioube), *n.*, jujube; (tree—*arbre*) jujubier, *m.*

julep (djiou-lèpe), *n.*, julep, *m.*

julian (djioul'ya'ne), *adj.*, julien.

julus (djiou-), *n.*, (bot.), chaton, *m.*

july (djiou-laï), *n.*, juillet, *m.*

jumart (djiou-marte), *n.*, jumart, *m.*

jumble (djeu'm'b'l), *v.a.*, jeter pêle-mêle, confondre, mêler, brouiller.

jumble, *v.n.*, se mêler confusément; se brouiller.

jumble, *n.*, pêle-mêle, brouillamini, *m.*; confusion, *f.*

jump (djeu'm'pe), *n.*, saut, *m.*

jump, *v.n.*, sauter; cahoter; (pop.)(to agree —*concorder*) s'accorder. To — over; *sauter par dessus.* To — up; *monter en sautant; se lever précipitamment.* To — out of; *sauter hors de.* To — out of bed; *sauter à bas du lit.*

jump, *v n.*, sauter.

jumper. *n.*, sauteur, *m.*, sauteuse, *f.*

junction (djeu'n'k'-), *n.*, jonction, *f.*, (of *roads—des routes*) croisement, carrefour, *m.*

juncture (djeu'n'gn'k't'ioure), *n.*, joint, *m.*; jointure; (critical time—*moment critique*) conjoncture, *f.*, moment critique, *m.*

june (djioune), *n.*, juin, *m.*

jungle (djeu'n'g'l), *n.*, jungle, *f.*; fourré, *m.*

junior (djiou'n'ieur), *adj.*, jeune, cadet.

junior, *n.*, cadet; inférieur en âge, *m.*

juniper (djiou-ni-), *n.*, (bot.) genièvre, *m.*

juniper-berry (-bèr-ri), *n.*, graine de genièvre, *f.*; genièvre, *m.*

juniper-tree (-tri), *n.*, genévrier, *m.*

junk (djeu'n'ke), *n.*, (ship—*vaisseau*) jonque, *f.*; (old cordage—*vieux cordage*) bout de câble, de corde, *m.*

junket (djeu'n'kète), *n.*, régal en cachette, *m.*

junket. *v.n.*, se régaler en cachette; faire bonne chère.

junta, *or* **junto** (djeu'n'ta. -tô), *n.*, junte; faction, cabale, *f.*

juratory (djiou-), *adj.*, juratoire.

juridical (djiou-), *adj.*, juridique.

juridically, *adv.*, juridiquement.

jurisconsult (djiou-ris'co'n'seulte), *n.*, jurisconsulte, *m.*

jurisdiction (djiou-ris-dik'-), *n.*, juridiction *f.*

jurisdictional, *adj.*, juridictionnel.

jurisdictive. *adj.*, qui a juridiction.

jurisprudence (djiou-ris'prou'-), *n.*, jurisprudence, *f.*

jurist (djiou-), *n.*, juriste, jurisconsulte, *m.*

juror (djiou-), *n.*, jure, *m.* Petty — : *juré de jugement.* Grand —: *juré d'accusation.* Foreman of the —; *chef du jury, m.*

jury (djiou-ri), *n.*, jury, juri, *m.* Petty —; *jury de jugement.* Grand —: *jury d'accusation.*

jury-box, *n.*, banc du jury. *m.*

juryman. *n.*, juré, *m.*

jury-mast, *n.*, (nav.) mut de rechange, de fortune, *m.*

just (djeuste). *adj.*, juste, exact: fidèle.

just, *adv.*, juste, justement: au juste; un peu; tout. To have —; *venir de.* He has — gone out; *il vient de sortir.* — let us see; *voyons un peu.* — by; *tout près.* — as; *de même que.* — now; *tout à l'heure.* This child is — like his father; *cet enfant est tout le portrait de son père.*

justice (djeus-tice), *n.*, justice; justesse, *f.* — of the peace; *juge de paix, m.* Chief- —; (in England—*d'Angleterre) premier juge;* (in France —*en France) conseiller de cour, m.*

justiceship, *n.*, dignité de juge, *f.*

justiciable (djeus'tish'i-a-b'l), *adj.*, justiciable.

justiciary (djeus'tish'i-), *n.*, justicier; (jur.) (in England—*en Angleterre) premier juge;* (in France—*en France) président de cour, m.*

justifiable (djeus-ti-fi-a-b'l), *adj.*, justifiable; légitime, permis.

justifiableness. *n.*, caractère justifiable, *m.*

justifiably, *adv.*, d'une manière justifiable; légitimement.

justification (djeus-ti-fi-ké-), *n.*, justification, *f.*; (jur.) moyens de défense, *m.pl.*

justificative (djeus-ti-fi-ka-), *adj.*, justificatif.

justificatory (djeus-ti-fi-ké-teuri), *adj.*, justificatif.

justifier (djeus-ti-faï-eur), *n.*, personne qui justifie, *f.*; justificateur, *m.*

justify (djeus-ti-fa-ye), *v.a.*, justifier; (print.) justifier, parangonner.

justify, *v.n.*, cadrer ensemble; (print.) (pers.) justifier; (of plates—*de planches*) être de la même justification.

justifying, *n.*, (print.) justification, *f.*, parangonnage, *m.*

justle, *v.a.* V. **jostle.**

justle (djeus's'l), *v.n.*, se heurter; s'entrechoquer.

justle, *n.*, heurt; choc; coup, *m.*

justly (djeust'li), *adv.*, exactement, justement; à bon droit, à bon titre.

justness (djeust'-), *n.*, justesse, *f.*, (equity—*équité*) justice; (accuracy—*exactitude*) justesse, *f.*

jut (djeute), *v.n.*, avancer, déborder, faire saillie. To — out; *bomber.*

jut, *n.*, saillie, *f.*

jute, *n.*, jute, chanvre de l'Inde, *m.*

jutty (djeut'ti), *v.a.*, avancer, déborder, dépasser.

jutty, *n.*, saillie; jetée, *f.*

juvenile (djiou-vi-naïl), *adj.*, (of things—*des choses*) juvénile, de jeunesse, de la jeunesse; (pers.) jeune.

juvenileness (djiou-vi-naïl'-), *or* **juvenility** (djiou-vi-nil'i-ti), *n.*, jeunesse, *f.*

juxtaposited (djeux-ta-poz'-), *adj.*, juxtaposé.

juxtaposition (djeux'ta-po-zish'-), *n.*, juxtaposition, *f.* In —; *juxtaposé; à côté l'un de l'autre.*

K

k, onzième lettre de l'alphabet, k, *m.*

kale, *or* **kail** (kéle), *n.*, chou, *m.*

kaleidoscope (ka-laï-do-scôpe), *n.*, kaléidoscope, *m.*

kalendar, *n. V.* **calendar**

kali (ké-li), *n.*, kali, *m.*

kalif, *n. V.* **calif.**

kangaroo (-ga-rou), *n.*, kanguroo, *m.*

kaoline (ké-o-), *n.*, kaolin, *m.*

kaw (cô), *n.*, croassement, *m.*

kaw, *v.n. V.* **caw.**

keckle (kèc'k'l), *v.a.*, (nav.)congréer,fourrer le câble.

kedge (kèdje), *n.*, (nav.) ancre à touer, *f.*

kedge, *v.a.*, (nav.) touer.

keel (kil), *n.*, quille; carène, *f.*

keel, *v.a.*, (to navigate—*voguer*) naviguer, fendre les eaux; (to turn up the keel—*tourner la quille en l'air*) montrer le dessous.

keelage (kil'édje), *n.*, droit d'ancrage, *m.*

keelhaul, *v.a.*, (nav.) donner la cale à.

keeling, *n.*, morue franche, *f.*; cabillaud, *m.*

keelson, *n.*, contre-quille, *f.*

keen (kine), *adj.*, (sharp—*tranchant*) affilé, acéré, aiguisé; (eager—*empressé*) vif, ardent, âpre; (bitter—*amer*) sanglant, poignant, amer, mordant; (piercing—*perçant*) pénétrant, perçant, piquant.

keenly, *adv.*, avec un fil acéré; vivement, ardemment, âprement; d'une manière sanglante, poignante, mordante; amèrement; d'une manière pénétrante, piquante.

keenness, *n.*, (of edge—*de tranchant*) finesse; (eagerness—*empressement*) ardeur, âpreté; (rigour—*rigueur*) nature pénétrante, perçante, piquante, *f.*; (asperity—*âpreté*) mordant, *m.*, amertume, nature mordante, sanglante, *f.*; (acuteness—*acuité*) nature pénétrante, *f.*

keep (ki-pe), *v.a.* (*preterit and past part.*, Kept), tenir, retenir, garder, avoir; (to solemnize—*solenniser*) observer, célébrer; (to preserve —*conserver*) entretenir, conserver; (to obey—*obéir*) observer; (to fulfil—*remplir*) tenir, remplir; (to continue—*persévérer*) continuer; (to board—*nourrir*)nourrir, entretenir; (to have in one's pay—*payer*) avoir; (to restrain—*modérer*) retenir; (a school, an inn, &c.—*une école, une auberge, &c.*)tenir; (lodgers—*locataires*)prendre; (sheep, fowls, &c.—*moutons, volailles, &c.*) élever. To — away; *tenir éloigné.* To — back; *retenir; tenir en réserve.* To — down; *tenir en bas;* (fig.) *retenir, comprimer, contenir,* (com.) *maintenir à bas prix.* To — from danger; *préserver du danger.* To — any one from any thing; *détourner quelqu'un de quelque chose.* To — any one from doing any thing; *empêcher quelqu'un de faire quelque chose.* To — in; (to provide with—*pourvoir de*) *fournir de, entretenir de;* (to shut in—*confiner*) *tenir enfermé,* (to repress—*réprimer*) *retenir;* (at school—*à l'école*) *mettre en retenue, consigner, priver de récréation.* To — off; *tenir éloigné.* To — on (one's clothes—*ses habits*); *garder,* (to feed on—*alimenter*) *nourrir de.* To — out; *faire rester dehors;* (fig.) *écarter, éloigner.* To — to; *tenir fermé.* To — any one to it, to his work; *faire travailler, faire marcher quelqu'un.* To — under; *tenir dessous;* (fig.) *contenir, retenir, assujettir.* To — up; *tenir en haut; tenir en l'air; tenir levé; soutenir;* (to prolong—*augmenter la durée*) *prolonger, continuer;* (to maintain—*maintenir*) *entretenir;* (to prevent from going to bed—*empêcher de se coucher*) *faire veiller;* (com.) *maintenir un prix.* To — one's bed, one's room; *garder le lit, la chambre.* To — house; *avoir une maison.* To — a secret; *garder un secret.* To — one's word; *garder sa parole.* To — silent; *garder le silence; se taire.* To — a promise; *remplir une promesse.* To — a servant; *avoir un domestique.* To — company with; *tenir compagnie à;* (to court—*chercher à plaire*) *courtiser, faire la cour à.* To — a great deal of company; *recevoir beaucoup de monde.* To — any one at home; *faire rester quelqu'un à la maison.* To father —s her at home; *son père la garde auprès de lui, la garde à la maison.*

keep, *v.n.*, se tenir; rester; (to last—*durer*) se garder, se conserver; (to dwell—*habiter*) demeurer. To — away; *se tenir éloigné; s'absenter.* To — back; *se tenir en arrière;* (fig.) *se tenir à l'écart.* To — down; *rester en bas;* (fig.) *se contenir, se comprimer.* To — in; *rest.) dedans;* (at home—*chez soi*) *rester à la maison;* (fig.) *se contenir, se retenir, se cacher.* To — off; *se tenir éloigné, s'éloigner;* (nav., milit.) *tenir le large.* To — on; *aller en avant; continuer, aller toujours, aller son train.* To — out; *rester dehors; s'éloigner.* To — out of the way; *s'absenter; se tenir caché.* To — to; *rester fidèle à, tenir ferme à;* (to keep shut—*rester fermé*) *se tenir fermé.* To — to one's word, one's promise; *tenir sa parole, remplir sa promesse.* To — to the laws; *observer les lois.* To — under; *se tenir dessous;* (fig.) *se contenir.* To — up; *se tenir en haut, se tenir levé;* (fig.) *se soutenir, se maintenir;* (to continue —*durer*) *se continuer, se prolonger;* (not to go to bed—*passer la nuit éveillé*) *veiller, ne pas se coucher.* — there ! *restez là !* To — it up; *aller toujours; s'en donner.* These apples — well; *ces pommes se gardent, sont de bonne garde.* Meat does not — well; *la viande ne se garde pas, n'est pas de bonne garde.*

keep, *n.*, (stronghold—*forteresse*) donjon (of a castle—*de château*); (support—*appense, soin*) entretien; (condition) état, *m.*, condition, *f.*; cachot, *m.*; (l.u.) tutelle, contrainte,*f.* The — of a horse; *l'entretien d'un cheval.*

keeper, *n.*, garde; gardien; surveillant, *m.*

keeping, *n.*, garde; surveillance; conservation; (fodder—*aliments*) nourriture; (congruity —*congruité*) harmonie,*f.*, unisson, *m.*; (paint.) harmonie, *f.* In —; *en harmonie; à l'unisson.*

keepsake (ki'p'séke), *n.*, souvenir d'amitié; souvenir, keepsake, *m.*

keg (kèghe), *n.*, caque, *f.*; petit baril, *m.*

kelp (kèlpe), *n.*, soude brute, *f.*; caillotis, *m.*

kelson (kèl-), *n. V.* **keelson.**

ken (kène), *n.*, vue; portée de la vue, *f.*

ken, *v.a.*, voir de loin; apercevoir; savoir; comprendre.

kennel (kèn'nèl), *n.*, (of a dog—*de chien*) chenil; (of a fox—*du renard*) terrier; (of wild beasts—*d'animaux sauvages*)trou; (gutter—*cours d'eau*) ruisseau, *m.*; (pack of hounds—*chiens de chasse*) meute, *f.*

kennel, *v.n.*, (of the dog—*du chien*) se coucher, se loger; (of the fox—*du renard*) se terrer.

kennel, *v.a.*, mettre dans un chenil.

kennel-stone (-stône), *n.*, (arch.) caniveau, *m.*; (mas.) culière, *f.*

kentledge (kèn't'lèdje), *n.*, (nav.) gueuse *f.*; saumon, *m.*

kept (kèpte). *V.* **keep.**

kerchief (keur'tshif), *n.*, fichu, ⊙couvre-chef, *m.*

kerchiefed, or **kerchieft** (keur'tshif'te), *adj.*. habillé; coiffé.

kerf (keurfe), *n.*, trait de scie; trait, *m.*

kermes (keur-mize), *n.*, kermès, *m.*

kern (keurne), *v.n.*, durcir; se former en grain.

kern (keurne), *n.*, fantassin irlandais, *m.*

kernel (keur-nèl), *n.*, amande; (of fruit—*de fruit*) graine, *f.*; (of pulpy fruit—*des fruits pulpeux*) pépin; (of corn—*du blé, &c.*) grain, *m.*; (med.) glande, *f.*

kernel, *v.n.*, se former en grain.

kernelly, *adj.*, de grains, de pépins.

kersey (keur-zè), *n.*, gros drap, *m.*

kerseymere (keur-zè-mire), *n.*, casimir. *m.*

kestrel (kès-trèl), *n.*, (orni.) crécerelle, crecerelle, *f.*; émouchet, *m.*

ketch (kèt'she), *n.*, (nav.) quaiche, *f.*

ketchup (kètsh'eupe), *n.* *V.* **catsup**.
kettle (kèt't'l), *n.*, bouilloire, *f.* Tea— ;
bouilloire, *f.*
kettle-drum (-dreume), *n.*, timbale, *f.*
key (ky), *n.*, clef, *f.* ; (book—*livre*) corrigé ;
(bot.) chaton, *m.* ; (mus.) clef, tonique, *f.* ; ton,
m. ; (in an organ, a harpsichord—*d'instruments
de musique*) touche, *f.* ; (on the side of rivers, &c.)
—*sur le bord de rivières &c.*), quai, *m.*
keyage (ky'-adje), *n.*, quaiage, quayage, *m.*
key-board (-bôrde), *n.*, (mus.) clavier, *m.*
keyed (ky'-de), *adj.*, (mus.) à touches ;
adapté à une clef, à un ton.
key-groove (-grouve), *n.*, cannelure, *f.*
keyhole (-hôl), *n.*, trou de serrure, *m.*
key-note (-nôte), *n.*, (mus.) tonique, *f.*
keystone (-stône), *n.*, clef de voûte, *f.*
khan (kâ'ne), *n.*, kan, *m.*
kibe (kaibe), *n.*, engelure, gerçure, *f.*
kibed (kaïb'de), *adj.*, qui a des engelures ;
gercé.
kick, *n.*, coup de pied, *m.* ; (of animals—*des
animaux*) ruade, *f.*
kick, *v.a.*, donner un coup de pied à ; donner
des coups de pied à ; frapper du pied. To—
down ; *renverser d'un coup de pied*. To — out ;
chasser à coups de pied.
kick, *v.n.*, donner des coups de pied ; (of animals—*des animaux*) ruer, regimber.
kicker, *n.*, personne qui donne des coups de
pied, *f.* ; (man.) rueur, *m.*, rueuse, *f.*
kicking, *n.*, coups de pied ; coups, *m.pl.* ; (of
animals—*des animaux*) ruades, *f.pl.*
kicking-strap, *n.*, plate-longe, *f.*
kickshaw (-shô), *n.*, colifichet, *m.*
kick-up (-eupe), *n.*, (pop.) esclandre, tapage, *m.*
kid, *n.*, chevreau, cabri, *m.* ; petit baquet,
m. ; (nav.) gamelle, *f.* ; fagot ; fagot de bruyère,
de genêt, *m.*
kid, *adj.*, de chevreau. — gloves ; *gants de
chevreau.*
kid, *v.n.*, (of the goat—*de la chèvre*) chevroter,
mettre bas ; faire un baquet.
kidder, *n.*, regrattier, *m.*
kiddow (kid'dô), *n.*, (orni.) guillemot, *m.*
kidnap, *v.a.*, enlever un homme, une femme,
un enfant.
kidnapper, *n.*, auteur d'un enlèvement
d'homme, de femme, d'enfant, *m.*
kidney (-'né), *n.*, rein ; (of animals—*des animaux*) rognon, *m.* ; (sort—*espèce*) trempe, sorte, *f.*
kidney-bean (-bîne), *n.*, haricot, *m.*
kidney-shaped (-shépte), *adj.*, en forme
de rein, de rognon.
kidney-vetch (-vèt'she), *n.*, (bot.) vulnéraire, *f.*
kilderkin (-dèr'-), *n.*, demi-baril, *m.*
kill, *v.a.*, tuer ; faire mourir.
killer, *n.*, tueur, *m.*
kiln, *n.*, four, *m.* Brick— ; *four à briques.*
Lime— ; *four à chaux.*
kiln-dry (-dra'ye), *v.a.* (*preterite and past
part.*, Kiln-dried), sécher au four.
kilogram, *n.*, kilogramme, *m.*
kilolitre (-li'teur), *n.*, kilolitre, *m.*
kilometre (-mê-teur), *n.*, kilomètre, *m.*
kilt, *or* **kelt** (kèlte), *n.*, jupon de montagnard
écossais, *m.*
kimbo (ki'm'bô), *adj.*, crochu, courbé, plié.
kin, *n.*, parenté, *f.* ; parent, *m.*, parente, *f.* ;
allié, *m.*, alliée, *f.* Next of — ; *le plus proche
parent, m., la plus proche parente, f.*
kin, *adj.*, parent, allié.
kind (kaï'n'de), *adj.*, (pers.) bon ; plein de
bonté, bienveillant, bienfaisant ; (obliging—
obligeant) complaisant ; (of things—*des choses*)
bon. bienfaisant.
kind (kaï'n'de)- *n.*, genre, *m.* ; sorte : race,
espèce, *f.*

kindle (ki'n'd'l), *v.a.*, allumer ; (fig.) éveiller,
réveiller.
kindle, *v.n.*, s'allumer ; (fig.) s'embraser,
s'éveiller, se réveiller.
kindler, *n.*, personne qui allume, qui enflamme ; chose qui allume, qui enflamme, *f.*
kindliness (kaï'n'd'-), *n.*, bienveillance,
bonté, *f.*
kindly (kaï'n'd'li), *adj.*, bienfaisant, bon.
kindly (kaï'n'd'li), *adv.*, avec bienveillance ;
avec bonté ; complaisamment.
kindness (kaï'n'd'-), *n.*, bienveillance, bonté ;
complaisance ; amitié, *f.* ; service ; acte de bienveillance, *m.* Act of — ; *acte de bienveillance,
m. ; amitié, f.*
kindred (kï'n'-), *n.*, parenté ; affinité, *f.* ;
parents, *m.pl.* ; (fig.) rapport, *m.*
kine (kaine), *n.* (*pl.* of cow), vaches, *f.pl.*
king (kigne), *n.*, roi, *m.* ; (at draughts—*aux
dames*) dame damée ; dame, *f.*
king, *v.a.*, élever à la royauté ; (at draughts
—*aux dames*) damer.
kingcraft (-crâfte), *n.*, art de régner, *m.* ;
politique de roi, politique astucieuse, *f.*
kingcup (-keupe), *n.*, (bot.) bouton d'or, *m.*
kingdom (kign'deume), *n.*, royaume ; (fig.)
empire, *m.*, région, *f.* ; (natur. hist.) règne, *m.*
United — ; *Royaume-Uni.*
kingfisher, *n.*, (orni.) martin-pêcheur, *m.*
kinghood (kign'houde), *n.*, royauté, dignité
de roi, *f.*
kingless (kign'-), *adj.*, sans roi ; qui n'a pas
de roi.
kinglet (kign'lète) *n.*, roitelet, *m.*
kinglike (kign'laïke), *adj.*, en roi ; comme
un roi.
kingling (kign'-), *n.*, roitelet, *m.*
kingly (kign'-), *adj.*, royal, de roi.
kingly, *adv.*, royalement ; en roi.
king's-bench (kign'z'bè'n'she), *n.*, cour du
banc du roi, *f.*
king's-evil (kign'z'i-v'l), *n.sing.*, écrouelles, *f.pl.*
kingship (kign'-), *n.*, royauté, *f.*
king-spear (kign'z'spire), *n.*, (bot.) asphodèle rameux, *m.*
kino (kaï-nô), *n.*, kino, *m.* ; résine kino ;
gomme de Gambie, *f.*
kinsfolk (ki'n'z'fôke), *n.*, parents, *m.pl.*
kinsman (ki'n'z'-), *n.*, parent, allié, *m.*
kinswoman (ki'n'z'woum'-), *n.*, parente,
alliée, *f.*
kiosk, *n.*, kiosque, *m.*
kirb (keurbe), *n.* *V.* **curb.**
kirb-stone (keurb'stône), *n.* *V.* **curb-
stone.**
kirk (keurke), *n.*, église de l'Ecosse, *f.*
kirschwasser (keursh'wôs'seur), *n.*, kirsch-
wasser ; kirsch, *m.*
kirtle (keur't'l), *n.*, manteau ; jupon, *m.*
kirt-roof (keurt'roufe), *n.*, toit pyramidal, *m.*
kiss, *n.*, baiser, *m.*
kiss, *v.a.*, baiser, embrasser
kisser, *n.*, baiseur, *m.*, baiseuse, *f.*
kissing, *n.*, action de baiser, *f.* ; baisement,
m. ; baisers, embrassements, *m.pl.*
kissing-crust (-creuste), *n.*, baisure, *f.*
kit, *n.*, (mus.) violon de poche, *m.*, pochette ;
(tech.) tinette, *f.* ; (milit.) équipement ; attirail ;
baquet à poisson ; jeune chat, petit chat, chaton,
m., jeune chatte, petite chatte, *f.*
kitchen (kit'shine), *n.*, cuisine, *f.* — garden ; *jardin potager, m.* — stuff ; *graisses de
cuisine, f.pl.*
kitchen-maid (-méde), *n.*, fille de cuisine, *f.*
kitchen-range (-rè'n'dje), *n.*, cuisine anglaise, *f.*
kitchen-wench (-wè'n'she), *n.*, laveuse de
vaisselle, *f.*
kitchen-work (-weurke), *n.*, cuisine, *f.*

kite (kaïte), n., (orni.) milan ; (toy—_jouet_), cerf-volant ; (rapacious person—_personne avide_) vautour, m.

kitten (kit't'n), n., chaton, petit chat, m. petite chatte, f.

kitten, v.n., chatter.

klick, n., cliquet, m. ; claque, f.

klick, v.n., faire un petit bruit aigu.

knab (nabe), or knabble (nab'b'l), (ant.) v.a., croquer.

knack (nake), n., (toy—_jouet_) colifichet, m., babiole ; (adroitness—_dextérité_) adresse, f., chic, tic, m.

knacker (nak'-), n., équarrisseur ; (maker of toys—_fabricant de joujoux_) bimbelotier, m.

knackish (nakishe), adj., artificieux, trompeur.

knackishness (nakish'-), n., artifice, m.

knag (naghe), n., nœud, m. ; cheville, f.

knaggy (nag'ghi), adj., noueux ; (fig.) hargneux.

knap (nape), n. V. knob.

knapple (nap'p'l), v.n., (ant.) se briser en craquant.

knapsack (nap'-), n., (milit.) sac, havresac, m.

knapweed (nap'wïde), n., jacée, f.

knar (nâr), adj., nœud, m.

knarled (nârl'de), adj., noueux ; plein de nœuds.

knave (néve), n., fripon, fourbe, coquin ; (at cards—_aux cartes_) valet, m.

knavery (név'ri), n., friponnerie ; fourberie, coquinerie ; (waggishness—_espièglerie_) malice, f.

knavish (név'-), adj., fripon, de fripon ; de coquin ; de fourbe ; (waggish—_espiègle_) malin, malicieux.

knavishly (név'-), adv., en fripon ; en fourbe ; (waggishly—_par espièglerie_) malicieusement, avec malice.

knavishness (név'-), n., coquinerie ; fourberie, f.

knead (nîde), v.a., pétrir.

kneading (nïd'-), n., pétrissage, m.

kneading-trough (nïd'ign'trofe), n., pétrin, m. ; huche, f.

knee (nï), n., genou, m. ; (nav.) courbe, f. ; (mec.) coude, m. On one's —s ; _à genoux_.

knee-cap (nï-cape), n., genouillère ; (anat.) rotule, f.

knee-crooking (nï-crouk'igne), adj., obséquieux.

kneed (nï-de), adj., qui a des genoux ; (bot.) géniculé ; (tech.) coudé.

knee-deep (nï-dïpe), adj., à la hauteur du genou ; jusqu'aux genoux.

knee-high (nï-ha'ye), adj. V. knee-deep.

kneel (nïl), v.n., s'agenouiller. To — down ; se mettre à genoux.

kneeler (nïl'-), n., personne qui s'agenouille ; personne agenouillée, f.

kneeling (nïl'-), n., action de s'agenouiller ; génuflexion, f.

kneepan (nï-pa'ne), n., rotule, f.

knee-tribute (nï-trib'ioute), n., hommage de la génuflexion, f.

knell (nèl), n., glas, m.

knick-knack (nik'nake), n., brimborion, m. ; babiole, f. ; colifichet, m.

knife (naïfe), n. (knives), couteau ; (tech.) coupoir, m. ; épée, f., poignard, m. Carving— ; _couteau à découper_. Table— ; _couteau de table_. Dessert— ; _couteau à dessert_. Clasp— ; _couteau pliant_. Pruning— ; _serpette_, f.

knife-blade (naïfe-bléde), n., lame de couteau, f.

knife-board (naïfe-bórde), n., planche à couteaux, f.

knife-grinder (naïfe-graï'n'd'-), n., rémouleur, repasseur de couteaux ; gagne-petit, m.

knife-rest (naïfe-rèste), n., porte-couteau, m.

knife-tray (naïfe-trè), n., boîte à couteaux, f.

knight (naïte), n., chevalier ; (at chess—_aux échecs_) cavalier, m.

knight (naïte), v.a.; créer chevalier ; armer chevalier.

knight-errant (naïte-èr'-), n., chevalier errant, m.

knight-errantry (naïte-èr'-), n., chevalerie errante, f.

knighthood (naït'houde), n., chevalerie, f.

knightliness (naït'-), n.sing., devoirs de chevalier, m.pl.

knightly (naït'-), adj., de chevalerie.

knit (nïte), v.a., tricoter ; (the brows—_les sourcils_) froncer ; (fig.) joindre, attacher.

knittable (nït'ta-b'l), adj., qui peut être tricoté.

knitter (nït'-), n., tricoteur, m., tricoteuse, f.

knitting (nït'-), n., tricotage, m. ; (fig.) union, f.

knitting-needle (nït'tign'nïd'd'l), n., aiguille à tricoter, f.

knittle (nït't'l), n., (nav.) raban, m.

knob (nobe), n., protubérance, f. ; (of a door—_de porte_) bouton fixe, bouton ; (in wood—_dans le bois_) nœud, m.

knobbed (nob'b'de), adj., qui a des protubérances ; qui a des nœuds ; noueux.

knobbiness (nob'-), n., nature noueuse, f.

knobby (nob'-), adj., plein de protubérances ; plein de nœuds ; noueux.

knock (noke), v.a., frapper, heurter, cogner. To — about ; _frapper de tout côté_ ; (fig.) _ballotter_. To — down ; _faire tomber (par un coup)_ ; _renverser_; _terrasser_. To — in ; _enfoncer, cogner_. To — off ; _faire sauter_ ; (to get through—_accomplir_) _faire_, _achever_. To —s off a good deal of work ; _il fait bien de la besogne_. To — out ; _faire sortir (à force de coups)_ ; _faire sauter_. To — up ; (to awake—_réveiller_) ; _réveiller (en frappant à la porte)_ ; (to fatigue—_fatiguer_) _éreinter_.

knock (noke), v.n., frapper, heurter, cogner. To — at the door ; _entendre frapper à la porte_.

knocker (nok'-), n., personne qui frappe, f. ; (of r.door—_de porte_) marteau, m.

knocking (nok'-), n.sing., coups ; coups de marteau, m.pl.

knoll (nôl), n., monticule, tertre, m.

knoll (nôl), v.a., sonner, tinter.

knoll (nôle), v.n., tinter.

knot (note), n., nœud ; (group of persons—_assemblage de personnes_) groupe, cercle ; (group of things—_assemblage de choses_) groupe, m. ; (difficulty—_difficulté_) difficulté ; (epaulet—_nœud d'épaule_) aiguillette, f. ; (association) lien ; (nav.) bot.) nœud, m.

knot (note), v.a., faire des nœuds ; se nouer.

knot (note), v.a., nouer ; lier ; (fig.) embrouiller.

knotgrass (note'grâce), n., (bot.) renouée, centinode, trainasse, f.

knotless (not'-), adj., sans nœuds.

knotted (not'-), adj., noueux.

knottiness (not'-), n., abondance de nœuds, f. ; (fig.) embrouillement, m.

knotty (not-), adj., noueux ; (hard—_résistant_) dur ; (intricate—_compliqué_) embarrassant, embrouillé.

knout (naoute), n., knout, m.

know (nô), v.a. and n. (preterit, Knew ; past part., Known), (by the mind—_par l'esprit_) savoir, posséder ; (by the senses—_par les sens_) connaître ; (to recognize—_se remettre dans l'esprit_) reconnaître. To — by heart ; _savoir par cœur_. To — by sight ; _connaître de vue_. To — any thing ; _savoir quelque chose_. To — any one ; _connaître quelqu'un_. To — one's lesson ; _savoir sa leçon_.

To — two languages ; *posséder deux langues*. **To** let any one — any thing ; *faire savoir, faire con- naître, faire part de, quelque chose à quelqu'un.* **To** —*again* ; *remettre, reconnaître.* Not to — one from the other ; *ne pouvoir distinguer l'un de l'autre.* **To** — of ; *connaître ; avoir connaissance de.* **To** — how to read and write ; *savoir lire et écrire.* **He** —s ; *il le sait.*

knowable (nô-a-b'l), *adj.*, qu'on peut savoir.
knower (nô'-), *n.*, connaisseur, *m.*
knowing (no'-), *adj.*, savant, intelligent ; in- struit ; (cunning—*sagace*) fin, rusé.
knowing (nô'-), *n.*, savoir, *m.*
knowingly (nô'-), *adv.*, sciemment ; (cun- ningly—*avec sagacité*) avec ruse, avec finesse.
knowledge (nô-lèdje), *n.*, savoir, *m.* ; con- naissances, *f.pl.*, science, *f.* To one's — ; *à sa connaissance.*
knuckle (neuk'k'l), *n.*, articulation, jointure, *f.* ; (of meat—*viande*) jarret, *m.* ; (of a hinge—*de charnière*) jointure, *f.*
knuckle (neuk'k'l), *v.n.*, se rendre ; mettre les pouces. **To** — to, under ; *se rendre ; mettre les pouces.*
knuckled (neuk'k'lde), *adj.*, articulé.
koran (kô-), *n.*, Coran, Koran, *m.*
kreutzer (kreut'zeur), *n.*, kreutzer, *m.*

L

L., douzième lettre de l'alphabet, l, *m.*, *f.*
la ! (lô), *int.*, là ! vois donc ! voyez donc ! tiens ! tenez !
la, *n.*, (mus.) la, *m.*
labarum, *n.*, labarum, *m.*
labefaction (lab'i-fak'-), *n.*, affaiblissement, déclin, *m.*
label (lé'b'l), *n.*, étiquette, *f.* ; écriteau, *m.* ; (jur.) codicille, *m.* ; (of a deed—*d'un titre*) queue, *f.* ; (her.) lambel, *m.*
label, *v.a.*, étiqueter.
labent (lé-) *adj.*, tombant, glissant.
labial (lé-), *adj.*, labial.
labial, *n.*, labiale, *f.*
labiate, *or* **labiated** (lé-bi-éte, -'ède), *adj.*, labié.
labiodental (lé-bi-o-) *adj.*, labial et dental.
laboratory, *n.*, laboratoire, *m.*
laborious (la-bô-), *adj.*, laborieux ; (of things —*des choses*) pénible, laborieux.
laboriously, *adv.*, laborieusement, pénible- ment.
laboriousness, *n.*, nature laborieuse, *f.* ; la- beur, *m.*
labour (lé-beur), *n.*, travail, labeur, ouvrage, *m.* ; peine, *f.* ; travail d'enfant, *m.* The —s of Hercules ; *les travaux d'Hercule.* To lose one's — ; *perdre sa peine.* To be in — ; *être en travail d'enfant.* Hard — ; *travail pénible;* (prison) *travail dans l'intérieur de la prison.*
labour, *v.a.*, travailler ; (to till—*cultiver*) labourer ; (to urge—*presser*) pousser, poursuivre ; (to beat—*frapper*) (l.u.) battre ; (fig.) élaborer, travailler.
labour, *v.n.*, travailler ; (to be in distress— *souffrir*) souffrir ; (to be in travail—*être en travail*) être en travail d'enfant ; (to strive—*s'efforcer*) chercher, s'efforcer, s'évertuer. **To** — under a disease ; *être travaillé par une maladie, être at- taqué d'une maladie.* **To** — under an error ; *être dans l'erreur.*
labourer, *n.*, homme de peine, ouvrier, *m.* Bricklayer's — ; *manœuvre, m.* Day- — ; *jour- nalier, m.*
laboursome (-seume), *adj.*, (ant.) pénible, difficile.
laburnum (leu-beur-), *n.*, aubours, faux ébénier, *m.*
labyrinth (-ri'nth), *n.*, labyrinthe, dédale, *m.*

lac, *n.*, laque (résine), *f.* — of rupees ; *lac de roupies* (environ 250,000 *francs*).
lace (léce), *n.*, dentelle, *f.* ; passement, galon ; (a snare—*piège*) collet, filet ; (a string—*cordon*) ruban, lacet, cordon, *m.* Brussels — ; *dentelle de Bruxelles, f.*, *point de Bruxelles, m.* Gold, silver— ; *galon d'or, d'argent, m.* Boot- — ; *lacet de bottine.* Stay- — ; *lacet de corset.*
lace, *v.a.*, (to fasten—*attacher*) lacer ; (to beat —*battre*) rosser, battre ; (to adorn with lace— *orner*) garnir de dentelle, galonner ; (fig.) orner.
laced (léss-te), *adj.*, lacé ; garni de dentelle ; galonné ; (of coffee—*de café*) à l'eau-de-vie.
lace-embroiderer (-è'm'broïd'-), *n.*, bro- deur en dentelle, *m.*, brodeuse en dentelle, *f.*
lace-frame, *n.*, métier à dentelle, *m.*
lacemaker (-mék'-), *or* **lace-manufac- turer** (-ma'n'iou-fakt'iour'-), *n.*, fabricant de dentelles, passementier, *m.*
laceman, *n.*, marchand de dentelles, passe- mentier, *m.*
lace-manufacture (-ma'n'iou-fakt'ioure), *n.*, fabrication de dentelles, passementerie, *f.*
lace-merchant (-meur'tsh'a'n'te), *n.*, né- gociant en dentelles, *m.*
lacerable (lass'èr-a-b'l), *adj.*, lacérable.
lacerate (lass'èr'-), *v.a.*, déchirer, lacérer.
lacerate, *or* **lacerated** (lass'èr'éte,-'ède), *adj.*, déchiré ; (bot.) lacéré.
laceration (lass'èr'é-), *n.*, déchirure, *f.* ; déchirement, *m.* ; lacération, *f.*
lacerative, *adj.*, qui déchire.
lace-runner (-reun'-), *n.*, brodeur en dentel- le, *m.*, brodeuse en dentelle, *f.*
lace-trade, *n.*, commerce des dentelles, *m.* ; passementerie, *f.*
lacewoman (-woum'-), *n.*, marchande de dentelles ; passementière, *f.*
lace-work (-weurke), *n.*, dentelle ; passe- menterie, *f.*
lachrymal (lak'ri-), *adj.*, lacrymal.
lachrymary, *adj.*, lacrymatoire.
lachrymation (lak'ri-mé-), *n.*, action de pleurer, *f.* ; pleurs. *m.pl.*
lachrymatory, *n.*, lacrymatoire, *m.*
laciniate, *or* **laciniated**, *adj.*, orné de frange ; (bot.) lacinié.
lack, *or* **lac**, *n.*, lac, *m.* — of rupees ; *lac de roupies* (about £10,000).
lack, *n.*, besoin, manque, *m.* ; privation, *f.*
lack, *v.a.*, manquer ; manquer de, être dénué de.
lack, *v.n.*, manquer ; être dans le besoin.
lackadaisical (-dé-zi-), *adj.*, minaudier.
lackadaisy ! (-dé-zi). *V.* **lack-a-day.**
lack-a-day ! (-dè), *int.*, hélas ! ah !
lackbrain (-bréne), *n.*, homme sans tête, imbécile, *m.*
lacker, *or* **lacquer**, *n.*, laque, vernis, *m.*
lacker, *or* **lacquer**, *v.a.*, vernisser de laque ; laquer.
lackey, *n.*, laquais, *m.*
lackey, *v.a.*, servir en laquais ; faire le la- quais auprès de ; flatter.
lackey, *v.n.*, faire le laquais.
lacklustre (-leusteur), *adj.*, sans éclat ; sans brillant.
laconic, *or* **laconical**, *adj.*, laconique.
laconically, *adv.*, laconiquement.
laconism (-niz'me), *n.*, laconisme, *m.*
lactage (-tédje), *n.*, (ant.) laitage, *m.*
lactary, *n.*, laiterie, *f.*
lactary, *adj.*, laiteux ; lacté ; lactaire.
lactation (-té-), *n.*, lactation, *f.*
lacteal (-ti-). *adj.*, lacté.
lactean, *or* **lacteous** (-ti-), *adj.*, de lait, laiteux.
lactescence (-tès'-), *n.*, lactescence, *f.*
lactometer (-to'm'i-), *n.*, lactomètre, galac- tomètre, *m.*

lad, n., garçon, jeune homme ; gaillard, m. Well, my — ; eh bien, mon garçon, mon ami, mon brave!

ladder, n., échelle, f. ; escalier, m. Scaling- — ; échelle de siège. Rope- — ; échelle de corde.

ladder-rope (-rôpe), n., (nav.) tire-veille, f.

lade (léde), v.a., charger ; (water—eau)puiser, tirer ; mettre.

lade, v.n., (ant.) tirer, puiser de l'eau.

laden (léd'è'ne), adj., (nav.) chargé ; (fig.) accablé, oppressé.

lading (léd'-), n., chargement, m. Bill-of—; connaissement, m.

ladle (léd'l), n., cuiller à pot, cuiller à potage ; (of a water-mill—de moulin à eau)aube, palette, f.

lady (lé-di), n. (ladies), dame, femme, f. Young— ; demoiselle ; jeune dame, f. Yes, my — ; (to a countess—à une comtesse) oui, madame la comtesse ; (a viscountess—à une vicomtesse) oui, madame la vicomtesse, &c. Ladies! mesdames! mesdemoiselles!

lady-bird (-beurde), **lady-bug** (-beughe), **lady-cow** (-cao), or **lady-fly** (fla'ye), n., bête à bon Dieu, bête de la Vierge ; coccinelle, f.

lady-day (-dè), n., le vingt-cinq mars, m. ; fête de l'Annonciation, f.

lady-like (-laïke), adj., de bon ton ; comme il faut ; qui a l'air distingué ; (delicate) délicat. She is very — ; elle a très bon ton, l'air très comme il faut, un air très distingué.

lady-love (-leuve), n., dame de ses pensées, f.

lady's-comb (-di'z'côme), n., (bot.) aiguille de berger, f. ; peigne de Vénus, m.

ladyship, n., madame, f. Her —, your—; (of a countess—d'une comtesse) madame la comtesse ; (of a viscountess—d'une vicomtesse) ; madame la vicomtesse, &c.

lady's-mantle (-di'z'ma'n't'l), n., (bot.) alchimille, f. ; pied-de-lion, m.

lady's-seal (-sil), n., (bot.) sceau-de-Notre-Dame, m.

lady's-slipper (-slip'-), n., (bot.) sabot de Vénus, sabot des vierges, soulier de Notre-Dame, m.

lady's-smock (-di'z'-), n., (bot.) cardamine, f. ; cresson, m.

lag, adj., (ant.) dernier, tardif ; en retard.

lag, n., dernier, traînard, m. ; (of things—des choses) dernière classe, lie, f.

lag, v.n., rester en arrière, se traîner, lambiner ; (of things—des choses) traîner

lag, v.a., ralentir.

lagger (lag'gheur), n., traîneur, traînard, lambin, m.

laggings (lag'ghi'n'ze), n.pl., couchis, m.

lagoon (lé-goune), or **lagune** (lé-ghioune), n., lagune, f.

lagophthalmia, n., lagophtalmie, f.

laic (lé-ike), n., laïque, m.

laic, or **laical**, adj., laïque.

laid, past part. (of to lay), posé ; (nav.) désemparé ; (of paper—du papier) vergé. New- — eggs ; œufs frais, m.pl.

lair (lére), n., repaire, m. ; reposée, f. ; (of a wolf—du loup) liteau, m. ; (of a boar—du sanglier) bauge, f.'

laird (lérde), n., seigneur, m.

laity (lé-), n. sing., laïques, m.pl.

lake (léke), n , lac, m. ; (colour—couleur) laque, f.

lakelike (-laïke), adj., en forme de lac.

lake-weed (-wide), n., (bot.) renouée, persicaire, f.

lama (lé-), n., (of the Tartars—des Tartares) lama ; (mam.) lama, llama, m.

lamantin, n., lamantin, m.

lamb (lame), n., agneau, m. God tempers the wind to the shorn — ; à brebis tondue, Dieu mesure le vent.

lamb, v.a., agneler.

lambative, or **lambitive**, adj., (med.) à lécher.

lambent, adj., qui effleure ; léger ; folâtre.

lambkin (la'm'kine), n., agnelet, petit agneau, m.

lamb-like (la'm'laïke), adj., d'agneau.

lamb's-lettuce (la'm'z'lèt'teuce), n., doucette, valérianelle, f.

lamb's-skin (la'm's'skine), n., peau d'agneau, f.

lamb's-wool (la'm'z'woul). n., laine d'agneau, laine agneline ; (beer—bière) bière mêlée avec de la pulpe de pommes cuites, f.

lame (léme), adj., boiteux, estropié ; (of language—du langage) boiteux, qui cloche ; (fig.) imparfait. To walk — ; boiter.

lame, v.a., estropier.

lamella, n., lamelle, f.

lamellar, adj., lamelleux, feuillé.

lamellarly, adv., par lamelles.

lamellate, or **lamellated**, adj., lamellé.

lamely (lé'm'li), adv., en boitant ; en clochant ; (fig.) imparfaitement, mal.

lameness (lé'm'-), n., état d'une personne estropiée, boiteuse ; boitement, m. ; (of a horse—du cheval) boiterie ; (fig.) imperfection, f.

lament (la'-), v.n., se lamenter. To—for ; pleurer. To—over ; pleurer ; se lamenter sur ; gémir de, s'affliger de.

lament, v.a., se lamenter sur ; pleurer ; s'affliger de ; gémir sur ; se désoler de.

lament, n., lamentation, f.

lamentable (la-mè'n't'a-b'l), adj., lamentable ; pitoyable ; déplorable.

lamentably, adv., lamentablement ; déplorablement ; pitoyablement.

lamentation (-mè'n'té-), n., lamentation, f.

lamented, adj., regrettable ; regretté.

lamenter, n., personne qui se lamente, qui fait des lamentations, f.

lamenting, n., lamentation, f.

lamia (lé-mi-a), n., lamie, f.

lamina (la'mi'na), n. (laminæ), lame, f. ; (bot.) limbe, m.

laminar, adj., composé de lames.

laminated (-né-tède), adj., lamelleux, lamellé.

lammas, n., le premier jour d'août, m. ; fête de saint Pierre-aux-Liens, m.

lamp, n., lampe ; (fig.) lumière, f. Argand —; lampe d'Argant, f. ; quinquet, m. Solar —; lampe solaire, f. Illumination- —; lampion, m. Safety- —; lampe de sûreté. Foot- —s ; (thea.) rampe, f. sing.

lampass, n., (vet.) lampas, m.

lampblack, n., noir de fumée, m.

lamp-lighter (-laït'-), n., allumeur, m.

lamp-maker (-mék'-), n., lampiste, m.

lampoon (-poune), n., satire personnelle, chanson satirique, f. ; libelle, m.

lampoon, v.a., écrire un libelle, une satire contre.

lampooner, n., auteur d'une satire personnelle ; libelliste, m.

lampoonry, n., satire personnelle, f.

lamp-post (-pôste), n., lampadaire, m. ; colonne lampadaire, f. To hang up at the — ; mettre à la lanterne.

lamprey, or **lampron**, n., lamproie, f.

lamp-stand (la'm'p-sta'n'd), n., dessous de lampe, m.

lanate, or **lanated** (lé-néte, -'ède) adj., laineux.

lance (là'n'-), n., lance, f.

lance, v.a., percer d'un coup de lance ; (surg.) donner un coup de lancette à ; ouvrir avec une lancette, percer avec une lancette ; percer, ouvrir.

lanceolate, or **lanceolated** (-ci-o-léte, -'ède), adj., lancéolé.

K
L

26 *

lancer, *n.*, lancier, *m.*
lancet (-ète), *n.*, lancette; (arch.) ogive, *f.*
lanch (là'n'she). *V.* **launch.**
lanching, *n. V.* **launching.**
lancinate, *v.a.*, déchirer.
lancination (-né-), *n.*, déchirement, *m.*
land, *n.*, terre, *f.*; pays; (jur.) bien-fonds, *m.* Arable —; *terre labourable*, *f.*, *terroir, m.* Promised —; *terre promise, terre de promission.* Holy —; *Terre Sainte.* To make —; (nav.) *atterrer.* To lose sight of —; (nav.) *perdre terre.*
land, *v.a. and n.*, débarquer; mettre à terre.
landau, *n.*, landau (*pl.* landaus), *m.*
land-chain (-tehéne), *n.*, (surveying—*lever des plans*) chaîne d'arpentage, *f.*
landed, *adj.*, foncier; territorial; de biens-fonds. —*property*; *propriété foncière, territoriale, f.*
landfall (-fôl), *n.*, succession inattendue de biens-fonds, *f.*; (nav.) atterrissement, *m.*
land-flood (-fleude), *n.*, inondation, *f.*
land-force (-fôrce), *n.*, troupes de terre, *f.pl.*
landgrave (-gréve), *n.*, landgrave, *m.*
landgraviate (-grév-i-éte), *n.*, landgraviat, *m.*
landholder (-hôld-), *n.*, propriétaire foncier, *m.*
landing, *n.*, débarquement; (at the top of a staircase—*d'escalier*) palier, *m.* — -place; (at which to disembark—*pour débarquer*) débarcadère; (arch.) perron, *m.*
landjobber, *n.*, spéculateur sur les biens fonciers. *m.*
landlady (-lé-di), *n.*, (of houses—*d'une maison*) propriétaire; (of a lodging house—*de maison garnie*) maîtresse; (of an inn, an hotel—*d'auberge, d'hôtel*) maîtresse d'auberge, d'hôtel, aubergiste, hôtesse; (of a manor—*de manoir*) dame de manoir, châtelaine, dame châtelaine, *f.*
landless, *adj.*, sans terre.
landlocked (-lok'te), *adj.*, enfermé entre des terres.
landloper (la'n'd-lôp'-), *or* **landlouper** (-la'oup'-), *n.*, vagabond, *m.*
landlord (-lorde), *n.*, propiétaire; (of an inn—*d'auberge*) hôte; maître d'un hôtel, *m.*
landlubber (-leub'-), *n.*, (nav.) marin d'eau douce, veau de rivière, *m.*
landman (la'n'd'z'ma'ne), *n.*, homme de terre; soldat de l'armée de terre, *m.*
landmark (-mârke), *n.*, borne, limite, *f.*; signal, *m.*
land-measurer (-mèj'eur'-), *n.*, arpenteur, *m.*
land-owner (-ô'n'-), *n.*, propriétaire foncier, *m.*
landscape, *n.*, paysage; point de vue, coup d'œil, *m.* — -painter; *paysagiste, m.*
landslide (-slaïde), *or* **landslip** (-slipe), *n.*, éboulement de terre de dimensions considérables, *m.*
landsman (la'n'd'z'ma'ne), *n.*, homme de terre; matelot sans expérience, *m.*
land-tax, *n.*, impôt foncier, *m.*; contribution foncière, *f.*
land-ties (-taï'ze), *n.pl.*, (carp.) palée, *f.sing.*
land-turn (-teurne), *n.*, (nav.) brise de terre, *f.*
land-waiter (-wét'-), *n.*, douanier de côte, vérificateur, *m.*
landward (-worde *adv.*, du côté de la terre.
lane. *n.*, petite rue, ruelle, *f.*; (out of town—*hors de la ville*) sentier, chemin, *m.*
langrage (-grédje), *or* **langrel-shot**, *n.*, (nav., artil.) mitraille, *f.*
language (langn'gwadje), *n.*, langue, *f.*; (way of speaking—*manière de parler*) langage, *m.* Bad —; *mauvais style, m.*; (offensive language—*langage offensant*) grossièretés, *f.pl.* Good —; *bon style, m.*; *belles paroles, f.pl.*

languid (langn'gwide), *adj.*, languissant, faible.
languidly, *adv.*, languissamment.
languidness, *n.*, langueur, faiblesse, *f.*
languish (langn'gwishe), *v.n.*, languir.
languishing, *adj.*, languissant, langoureux.
languishingly, *adv.*, d'une manière languissante, languissamment, langourcusement.
languishment, *or* **languor**, *n.*, langueur, *f.*
laniard (-ârde), *n. V.* **lanyard.**
laniferous, *or* **lanigerous** (-èr-, -nidj'èr-), *adj.*, lanifère.
lank, *adj.*, grêle, mince, maigre, décharné, fluet; languissant; flasque, mou, lâche. — hair; *cheveux plats, m.pl.* To make —; *amaigrir, décharner.* To grow —; *s'amaigrir, maigrir.*
lankly, *adv.*, mollement; maigrement.
lankness, *n.*, maigreur; mollesse, *f.*
lanky, *adj.*, fluet. — fellow; *grand flandrin.*
lanner, *n.*, (orni.) lanier, *m.*
lanneret, *n.*, (orni.) laneret, *m.*
lansquenet (-ki-nète), *n.*, lansquenet, *m.*
lantern, *n.*, lanterne, *f.*; (on a building—*sur un édifice*) belvédère; (nav.) fanal, *m.* Dark —; *lanterne sourde.* Magic —; *lanterne magique.*
lantern-jaws (-djôze), *n.*, joues creuses, *f.pl.*; visage maigre, *m.*
lanuginous (-nïou-dji-), *adj.*, lanugineux.
lanyard, *n.*, (nav.) garant, *m.*, corde, aiguillette, ride, *f.*
lap, *n.*, giron, *m.*; genoux, *m.pl.*; (fig.) sein; (of a coat—*d'habit*) pan; (of the ear—*de l'oreille*) bout, *m.* In the — of; *au sein de.* In my —; *sur mes genoux.*
lap, *v.a.*, (animals—*des animaux*) laper; (to wrap—*couvrir*) envelopper, plier, rouler.
lap, *v.n.*, laper; avancer, s'étendre sur. To — over; *retomber, recouvrir.*
lapdog, *n.*, bichon, *m.*
lapel. *n.*, revers d'habit, de redingote, *m.*
lapidary, *n.*, lapidaire; joaillier, *m.*
lapidary, *adj.*, lapidaire. — style; *style lapidaire.*
lapidate, *v.a.*, (ant.) lapider.
lapidation (-dé-), *n.*, (ant.) lapidation, *f.*
lapideous (-pid'i-), *adj.*, pierreux.
lapidescence, *n.*, pétrification, *f.*
lapidific, *or* **lapidifical**, *adj.*, lapidifique.
lapidify (-fa'ye), *v.a.*, lapidifier.
lapidify, *v.n.*, se lapidifier.
lapis-lazuli (-la-ziou-la'ye), *n.*, lapis-lazuli, *m.*
laplander, *n.*, Lapon, *m.*, Laponne, *f.*
lappet, *n.*, pan, *m.*
lapse (lapse), *n.*, (fault—*faute*) faute, erreur, *f.*; manquement; (deviation) écart, manque; (of time—*de temps*) laps, cours, *m.*, marche; (fall—*chute*) chute, *f.*
lapse, *v.n.*, s'écouler, passer; tomber; faillir.
lapwing, *n.*, (orni.) vanneau, *m.*
lapwork (-weurke), *n.*, enveloppe, *f.*; recouvrement, *m.*
larboard (lâr-bôrde), *n.*, (nav.) bâbord, *m.*
larceny (lâr-ci-), *n.*, larcin, vol, *m.*
larch (lârtshe), *n.*, (bot.) mélèze, *m.*
lard (lârde), *n.*, saindoux, *m.*
lard, *v.a.*, larder; piquer; assaisonner.
larder (lâr-), *n.*, offices, *f.pl.*; dépense, *f.*; garde-manger, *m.*
larding-pin, *or* **larding-needle** (-nî-d'l), *n.*, lardoire, *f.*
lares (lé-rize), *n.pl.*, lares, dieux lares, *m.pl.*
large (lâr-dje), *adj.*, grand, gros; étendu, considérable, fort; (nav.) largue. — sum; *forte somme.* As — as life; *de grandeur naturelle.* At —; *en liberté; libre; en général; au long; au large.*
largely. *adv.*, amplement, largement, grandement; libéralement; au long.

largeness, n., grandeur; grosseur,étendue, f.
largess (lâr-djèce), n., largesse, libéralité, f.
largition (-djish'-), n., action de donner, f.
lark (lârke), n., alouette; mauviette; (trick —tour) escapade, f.
lark's-heel, or **larkspur** (-hîl, -speur), n., (bot.) pied-d'alouette, m.
larum, n., alarme, f.
larva (lâr-), n. (larvæ), (ent.) larve, f.
larvated (lâr-vét'-), adj., masqué.
larynx, n., larynx, m.
lascar (-'câr), n., lascar, matelot indien, m.
lascivious, adj., impudique, voluptueux, lascif.
lasciviously, adv., lascivement.
lasciviousness, n., impudicité, lasciveté, f.
lash, n., coup de verge, coup de fouet, m.; (ant.) (for dogs—de chien) laisse, f.; (fig.) coup, trait. Eye —es; cils, m.
lash, v.a., sangler, cingler, fouetter; (nav.) amarrer; (to tie—lier) attacher; (fig.) crosser, censurer, parler fortement contre, flageller; châtier, battre.
lash, v.n., faire claquer un fouet; éclater; s'emporter.
lasher, n., fouetteur, m.; (nav.) corde d'amarrage, f.
lashing,n.,coups de fouet, m.pl.; châtiment, m.; (nav.) ligne d'amarrage, f.
lass (lâce), n., fillette, jeune fille, f.
lassitude (-tioude),n., ennui,m.; lassitude,f.
last (lâste), n., dernier, dernier moment, m.; fin; dernière parole; (for shoes—de souliers, &c.) forme,f.; (weight—poids) last, laste, m. At —; à la fin, enfin. Till the —, to the —; jusqu'à la fin, jusqu'au dernier moment. To breathe one's —; rendre le dernier soupir.
last, adj., dernier, passé. — but one; avant-dernier.
last, v.n., durer; se garder.
last, adv., dernièrement; enfin; pour la dernière fois, la dernière fois.
lasting, adj., durable, permanent; (of colours—des couleurs) bon teint.
lastingly, adv., d'une manière durable.
lastingness (lâst'ign'nèce), n., durée, f.
lastly, adv., en dernier, en dernier lieu; enfin.
latch (lat'she), n., loquet, m.; cadole, f.
latch, v.a., fermer au loquet.
latchet (-ôte), n., boucle, f., cordon de soulier, m.
latchkey (-ky), n., passe-partout, m.
late, adj., tardif; (of time—de l'heure) avancé; (former—prédécesseur;\ précédemment) ancien, dernier, ci-devant, ex; (dead—mort) feu; (recent—nouveau) récent, dernier. Of — years; ces dernières années. The —st posterity; la postérité la plus reculée.
late, adv., tard; sur la fin; (of persons—des personnes) en retard. At —st; au plus tard. It is getting —; il se fait tard. Of —; dernièrement, récemment.
lated, adj., (ant.) surpris par la nuit, attardé.
lateen-sail (lé-tîne-sél), n., (nav.) voile latine, f.
lately, adv., dernièrement, récemment, depuis peu.
latency (lé-), n., état de ce qui est caché, m.
lateness, n., arrivée tardive, f.; retard, m.; (of the hour—de l'heure) heure avancée, f., temps avancé, m.; (hort.) tardiveté, f.
latent (lé-), adj., caché, secret, latent.
later (lét'-), adj., postérieur, ultérieur.
later, adv., plus tard.
lateral (lat'èr'-), adj., de côté, latéral.
laterally, adv., latéralement, de côté.
lath (lâth), n., latte, f.
lath, v.a., latter.
lathe (léthe), n., tour (à tourner le bois, &c.),m.
lather (lâth'-), n., mousse, écume, f.

lather (lâth'-), v.a., savonner, couvrir de savon.
lather (lâth'-), v.n., mousser.
lathy (lâth'i), adj., de latte; flasque, faible.
latin (lat'ine), adj. and n., latin.
latinism (-'iz'me), n., latinisme, m.
latinist (-'iz'me), n., latiniste, m.
latinity, n., latinité, f.
latinize (-'aize), v.a., latiniser.
latish (lét'-), adj., un peu tard; un peu en retard.
latish (lét'-), adv., un peu tard.
latitude (-tioude), n., latitude; étendue, f.; (nav.) parage, m.
latitudinarian (-tiou-di-né-), adj. and n., tolérant, latitudinaire.
latria (lé-), n., latrie, f.
latten, n., fer-blanc; étain en feuille; cuivre jaune fin, m.
latten-brass (-brâce), n., cuivre laminé, m.
latter (lat'-), adj., dernier; moderne, récent. The —; ce dernier, ces derniers, celui-ci, ceux-ci, m.; cette dernière, ces dernières, celle-ci, celles-ci, f.
latterly, adv., depuis peu, dernièrement.
lattermath (-mâth), n., regain, m.
lattice, or **lattice-work** (lat'ice,-weurke), n., treillis, treillage, m.
lattice, v.a., treillisser; former en treillis.
laud, n., louange, f.; (c.rel.) laudes, f.pl.
laud, v.a., louer, célébrer.
laudable (-'a-b'l), adj., louable, digne de louanges.
laudableness, n., qualité louable, f.; mérite, m.
laudably, adv., louablement.
laudanum (lô-da-), n., laudanum, opium, m.
laudatory, or **laudative**, n., éloge, panégyrique, m.
laudatory, adj., laudatif, louangeur.
lauder, n., louangeur, panégyriste, m.
laugh (lâfe), n., rire, ris, m. Loud —; gros rire, éclat de rire. To burst into a loud —; partir d'un grand éclat de rire. To have a good — at; se bien moquer de; rire beaucoup de.
laugh (lâfe), v.n., rire. To — at; se moquer de; rire de, railler; se jouer de. To burst out —ing; rire aux éclats, éclater de rire. To — out; partir d'un éclat de rire. To — in any one's face; rire au nez à quelqu'un. To — immoderately; rire à gorge déployée.
laughable (lâf'a-b'l), adj., risible.
laugher (lâf'-), n., rieur, m., rieuse, f.
laughing (lâf'-), adj., rieur, qui aime à rire.
laughing (lâf'-), n., rire, m.; action de rire, f.
laughingly (lâf'-), adv., en riant, gaîment.
laughing-stock (lâf'-), n., risée, f.; jouet, plastron, m.
laughter (lâf'teur), n., rire, ris, m.; (b.s.) risée, moquerie, f. Burst of —; éclat de rire, m. To break out into —; éclater de rire.
launch (lân'she), v.n., se lancer. To — out into; se jeter dans; se lancer dans; s'étendre sur.
launch, v.a., lancer; (a ship—un vaisseau) lancer; lancer à l'eau; mettre à l'eau, à la mer.
launch, n., lançage, m.; mise à l'eau; (boat —bateau) chaloupe, f.
launching, n., lançage, m.; mise à l'eau, f.
launder (lân'-), n., blanchisseuse, f.; (mines) auge, f.
launderer, n., blanchisseur, m.
laundress, n., blanchisseuse, f.
laundry, n., buanderie, f.
laureate (-ri-), adj., couronné de lauriers, lauréat.
laureate, v.a., couronner.
laureation (-ri-é-), n., action de couronner un lauréat, f.; couronnement, m.
laurel, n., laurier. m. — -wreath; couronne de laurier, f.

laurelled (lor'èlde), *adj.*, couronné de lau-rier.

laurustine (-reus'-), *n.*, (bot.) viorne-tin, *f.*; laurier-tin, *m.*

lava (lé-va. *ou* là-va), *n.*, lave, *f.*

lavatory, *n.*, lavoir, *m.* ; (pharm.) lotion, *f.*

lave (léve), *v.a.*, laver, arroser, baigner.

lave, *v.n.*, se laver, se baigner.

laveer (la-vîr), *v.n.*, louvoyer.

lavender, *n.*, (bot.) lavande, *f.*

lavender-cotton (-cot't'n), *n.*, (bot.) santo-line, garde-robe, citronnelle, *f.*

lavender-water (-wô-), *n.*, eau de lavande, *f.*

laver (lé-), *n.*, lavoir, bassin, *m.*

lavish (lav'-), *adj.*, prodigue ; excessif.

lavish, *v.a.*, prodiguer.

lavisher, *n.*, prodigue, *m.* To be a — of ; *être prodigue de.*

lavishly, *adv.*, prodigalement.

lavishment, *or* **lavishness**, *n.*, prodiga-lité, *f.*

law (lô), *n.*, lot, *f.* ; droit, *m.* ; jurisprudence, *f.* Civil — ; *droit civil ; droit romain.* Criminal — ; *droit criminel.* To go to ; *recourir à la justice.* To study — ; *étudier le droit.* To be at — ; *être en procès.* To lay down the — ; *expliquer la loi.*

law-book (-bouke), *n.*, livre de jurispru-dence, *m.*

law-breaker (-brèk'-), *n.*, transgresseur de la loi, *m.*

law-day (-dè), *n.*, jour d'audience, *m.*

law-expenses (-èks'pè'n'size), *n.*, frais de procédure, *m.pl.*

lawful (-foule), *adj.*, légal ; légitime ; licite ; permis.

lawfully, *adv.*, légalement ; légitimement.

lawfulness, *n.*, légalité ; légitimité, *f.*

lawgiver (-ghiv'-), *n.*, législateur, *m.*

lawgiving (-ghiv'-), *adj.*, législatif.

lawless, *adj.*, sans loi ; arbitraire ; illégal ; (fig.) sans frein.

lawlessly, *adv.*, sans loi ; illégalement.

lawlessness, *n.*, illégalité ; licence, *f.*

lawmaker (-mék'-), *n.*, législateur, *m.*

lawn, *n.*, (linen—*linge*) linon, *m.* ; (open space —*terrain*) pelouse, *f.*, tapis vert, *m.* The bi-shop's — ; (fig.) *la chape d'évêque.*

lawn, *adj.*, de linon.

lawny, *adj.*, uni comme une pelouse ; fait de linon.

lawsuit (-sioute), *n.*, procès, *m.*

law-term (-teurme), *n.*, terme de loi, terme de palais, *m.*

lawyer, *n.*, légiste ; homme de loi ; juriscon-sulte ; avoué, *m.*

lawyer-like (-laïke), *or* **lawyerly**, *adj.*, en homme de loi.

lax, *n.*, diarrhée, *f.*

lax, *adj.*, relâché, lâche, mou ; dissolu, licen-cieux ; vague, obscur.

laxation (laks'é-), *n.*, action de relâcher, *f.* ; relâchement, *m.*

laxative (laks'a-), *adj.*, laxatif.

laxative, *n.*, laxatif, *m.*

laxativeness, *n.*, qualité laxative, *f.*

laxity, *or* **laxness**, *n.*, relâchement, état lâche ; (med.) relâchement, dévoiement, *m.* ; flaccidité, *f.* ; (want of exactness—*défaut de pré-cision*), manque d'exactitude, obscurité, *f.* — of moral ; *relâchement de mœurs.*

laxly, *adv.*, mollement, avec nonchalance, sans vigueur ; sans exactitude.

laxness, *n.* V. **laxity**.

lay, *v.* V. **lie**, *v.*

lay, *v.a.* (*preterit* and *past part.*, Laid), placer, mettre, poser, déposer, coucher ; (to beat down —*renverser*) abattre ; (to calm—*calmer*) calmer, apaiser ; (a bet—*un pari*) faire ; (eggs—*des œufs*) pondre ; (a snare—*un piège*) tendre, dresser ; (the

cloth—*la nappe*) mettre ; (the dust —*la poussière*) abattre ; (an indictment—*des poursuites*) inten-ter ; (a tax—*un impôt*) imposer ; (nav.) (cable) commettre. To — aside ; *mettre de côté, ôter, quit-ter.* To — before ; *soumettre à ; mettre sous les yeux de.* To — by ; *mettre de côté, garder, réserver.* To — down arms; *mettre bas, poser, déposer les armes;* (a principle, a foundation—*un principe, une base*) poser ; (to give up—*abandonner*) quitter, renoncer à. To — down one's life for ; *donner sa vie pour.* To — one's self down ; *se coucher.* To — in ; *faire une provision de, se procurer.* To — hold of ; *s'emparer de, saisir.* To — on ; *appli-quer ;* (blows—*des coups*) porter ; (colour—*couleur*) étendre. To — a fault on ; *imputer une faute à.* To — open ; *mettre à nu ;* (fig.) *exposer.* To — out ; *arranger ;* (a garden, a road—*un jardin, une route*) tracer ; (money—*de l'argent*) dépenser, dé-bourser ; (a corpse—*un cadavre*) ensevelir. To — over ; *étendre, couvrir, incruster.* To — up ; *mettre de côté, garder, amasser ;* (to make ill—*rendre malade*) rendre malade, faire garder le lit, la chambre ; *tenir enfermé.* To — it on ; (to beat—*battre*) étriller ; (to lie—*mentir*) broder, exagérer ; (in price—*de prix*) surfaire.

lay, *v.n.*, pondre. To — about ; *frapper de tout côté.* To — on ; *frapper fort ;* en découdre ; (of expenses—*de dépenses*) y aller grand train.

lay, *n.*, (row—*rang*) rangée ; (layer—*couche*) couche, *f.* ; (wager—*gageure*) pari, *m.*, mise, *f.* ; (meadow—*prairie*) pré, *m.*, prairie, *f.* ; (song—*chanson*) chant, *m.*

lay, *adj.*, lai, laïc, laïque.

lay-clerk (-clârke, *ou* -cleurke), *n.*, chantre, *m.*

layer (lè'eur), *n.*, personne qui pose, *f.* ; (tech.) poseur ; (founder—*fondateur*) fondateur, *m.*, fondatrice ; (a stratum—*couche*) couche, *f.*, lit, *m.* ; (geol.) couche, assise, *f.*, étage, *m.* ; (hort.) marcotte, *f.* ; (shoot of a plant—*pousse de plante*) rejeton, *m.* ; (hen—*poule*) pondeuse, *f.*

lay-figure, *n.*, (paint.) mannequin, *m.*

laying (lè-igne), *n.*, mise, pose, *f.* ; posage, *m.* ; (of eggs—*d'œufs*) ponte, *f.*

layman, *n.*, laïque ; (paint.) mannequin ; (in a cathedral—*de cathédrale*) chantre, *m.*

lazar, *n.*, lazare, *m.*

lazaretto, *or* **lazar-house** (-haouce), *n.*, lazaret, *m.*

lazar-like (-laïke), *or* **lazarly**, *adj.*, lé-preux.

laze, *v.n.*, (ant.) paresser, fainéanter.

laze, *v.a.*, (ant.) perdre dans la paresse.

lazily (lé-), *adv.*, lentement, en paresseux, dans la paresse, dans la fainéantise.

laziness (lé-), *n.*, fainéantise, paresse, *f.*

lazing (léz'-), *adj.*, paresseux, fainéant.

lazulite (laz'iou-laïte), *n.*, (min.) lazulite, lapis, lapis-lazuli, *m.*

lazy (lé-), *adj.*, fainéant, paresseux ; (of a horse—*cheval*) mou, lent ; (of life—*vie*) indolent. de paresse.

lea (li), *or* **ley** (li), *n.*, pré, clos, *m.* ; prairie, plaine, *f.*

leach (litshe), *n.*, cendre de lessive, *f.*

leach, *v.a.*, lessiver.

leachtub (-teube), *n.*, cuve à lessive, *f.* ; cuvier, *m.*

lead (lède), *n.*, (metal) plomb. *m.* ; (print.) interligne, *f.* ; (nav.) plomb de sonde, *m.*, sonde, *f.* ; (for pencils—*pour crayons*) mine de plomb, *f.* —s; (of a house—*de maison*) plombs (des toits) ; toit de plomb. — —wire ; *fil de plomb, m.* White— ; *céruse, f. ; blanc de céruse, m.* Sheet— ; *plomb en feuille.* — -work ; *plombage, m.* — -works, —manufactory ; *plomberie, f. sing.*

lead (lède), *v.a.*, plomber, couvrir de plomb ; (print.) interligner.

lead (lîde), *n.*, conduite, direction. *f.* ; com-mandement, *m.* ; influence ; présidence, *f.* ; pas ; (at billiards—*au billard*) acquit ; (at cards—*aux* cartes) devant, m., main, f.; (at play—au jeu) début, m., ouverture, f. To take the —; marcher en avant; dominer, primer, présider.

lead (lède), v.a., (preterit and past part., Led), mener, guider, conduire; (to command—commander) conduire, commander, diriger; (to induce—engager) porter, faire, induire; (a life—une vie) mener. To — about; mener de tous côtés, partout. To — astray; égarer, détourner de la bonne voie. To — back; ramener, reconduire. To — in; introduire. To — into; entraîner dans. To — off; détourner; emmener. To — out; faire sortir, conduire dehors. To — out of the way; égarer.

lead (lède), v.n., conduire; mener; dominer; (at play—au jeu) jouer le premier, avoir la main, débuter.

leaded (lèd'ède), adj., (print.) interligné.

leaden (lèd'd'n), adj., de plomb; (fig.) lourd.

leader (lid'-), n., conducteur, guide, chef, meneur, premier, commandant, m.; (of a news-paper—de journal) article principal, premier Paris, premier Londres, &c.; (man.) cheval de volée; (mus.) chef d'orchestre, de musique; (in parliament—au parlement) orateur principal, orateur qui dirige la discussion, m.

leading (lid'-), adj., premier, principal. — card; première carte, f. — hand; premier en carte, m. — man; chef, m. — strings; lisières, f.pl. — word; premier mot, m. — note (mus.); note sensible, f.

leading (lid'-), n., conduite, direction, f.

leadsman (lèd'z'-), n., (nav.) sondeur, m.

leady (lèd'i), adj., couleur de plomb, m.

leaf (life), n. (leaves), feuille, f.; (of a book—de livre) feuillet, m.; (of a door—de porte) battant, m.; (of a table—de table) rallonge, f. To turn over the leaves; feuilleter. To turn over a new — (fig.); changer de propos et de conduite.

leaf, v.n., porter des feuilles.

leafage (lif'édje), n., feuillage épais, m.

leaf-gold (-gôlde), n., or en feuille, m.

leafless, adj., sans feuilles, effeuillé.

leaflet, n., petite feuille; (bot.) foliole, f.

leafstalk (-stôke), n., (bot.) pétiole, m.

leafy, adj., feuillé, feuillu, couvert de feuilles.

league (lighe), n., ligue; (measure—mesure) lieue, f.

league, v.n., se liguer.

leagued (lig'de), adj., ligué.

leaguer (ligh'eur), n., confédéré, ligueur, m.

leak (like), n., voie d'eau; perte d'eau; fuite, f. To spring a —; faire eau, faire une voie d'eau.

leak, v.n., couler, faire eau, fuir.

leakage (lik'édje), n., coulage, m.; fuite, f.; voies d'eau, f.pl.

leaky, adj., qui coule, qui fuit; (nav.) qui a des voies d'eau, qui fait eau de partout; (fig.) bavard, indiscret.

lean (line), n., maigre, m.

lean, adj., maigre; stérile; chétif. To grow, to get —; maigrir. To make —; amaigrir.

lean, v.a., pencher; s'appuyer, s'incliner; (to rest—reposer) reposer. To — over; avancer. To — to; tendre à; incliner à; pencher vers.

lean, v.a., faire pencher, incliner; appuyer, reposer.

leaning, n., penchant; penchement, m.

leanly, adv., maigrement, stérilement.

leanness, n., maigreur, f.; amaigrisse-ment, m.

leap (lipe), n., saut; accouplement, m. — frog; cheval fondu, m. — -year; année bissextile, f. To take a —; faire un saut.

leap, v.a., sauter, franchir; (of animals—des animaux) saillir, couvrir.

leap, v.n., sauter, s'élancer, se précipiter. To — for joy; sauter de joie.

leaper, n., sauteur, m., sauteuse, f.

leaping, adj., qui saute, qui fait des sauts.

leapingly, adv., en sautant; par sauts.

learn (leurne), v.a., apprendre.

learn (leurne), v.n., apprendre, s'instruire. To — to read; apprendre à lire.

learned (leurn'ède), adj., savant, docte. — man; savant, m.

learnedly (leurn'èd'li), adv., savamment.

learner (leurn'-), n., écolier; apprenti; élève, m.

learning (leurn'-), n., étude; littérature, science, instruction, f.; savoir, m. Polite —; belles-lettres, f.pl. Man of —; savant; homme instruit, m.

lease (li'ce), n., bail, m. Long —; bail à longues années, à long terme. — of ground; bail à ferme. Building- —; bail emphytéotique. On a —; à bail.

lease (li'ce), v.a., louer, donner à bail; (land—terres) affermer.

lease (lize), v.n., glaner.

leasehold (-hôlde), n., tenure par bail, par bail emphytéotique, f.

leaseholder, n., locataire par bail; pro-priétaire par bail emphytéotique, m.f.

leaser (liz'eur), n., glaneur, glaneuse, f.

leash (lishe), n., laisse, attache, f.

leash, v.a., mener en laisse, attacher.

leasing-making (liz'ign'mék'-), n., offen-se au souverain par des discours outrageants, f.

least (liste), adj., moindre, plus petit.

least, adv., moins. At —; au moins. At the —; pour le moins, tout au moins. Not in the —; point du tout, nullement, pas le moins du monde.

leather (lèth' eur), n., cuir, m., peau, f. — dresser; peaussier, m. — seller; mégissier; pelletier; marchand de cuir, m.

leather (lèth' eur), v.a., garnir de cuir; (to beat—battre) (pop.) étriller, rosser, épousseter, avec une courroie.

leathern (lèth'-), adj., de cuir, de peau.

leathery (lèth'-), adj., semblable à du cuir, coriace.

leave (live), n., permission, f.; congé, m. On —; en congé. To take — of; prendre congé de, dire adieu à. With your —; avec votre per-mission. To give —; donner la permission, per-mettre. To take French —; prendre la permis-sion sous son bonnet. By any one's —; par permission de quelqu'un.

leave (live), v.n., partir; cesser. To — off; cesser, s'arrêter, en rester, finir.

leave (live), v.a. (preterit and past part., Left), laisser; (to quit a person—personne) quitter; (a place—lieu) quitter, partir de; (to discontinue—discontinuer) cesser. I — that to you; je m'en rapporte à vous. To — about; laisser traîner. To — alone; laisser seul, laisser tranquille; laisser. To — off; laisser, laisser de côté, quitter; cesser, discontinuer. To — out; supprimer, omettre, oublier. To be left; rester. There is some wine left; il reste du vin. To be left till called for; poste restante; (of parcels—paquets) bureau restant. To have left; avoir de reste, avoir encore. I have nothing left; il ne me reste rien.

leaved (liv'de), adj., feuillé, à feuilles.

leaven (lèv'v'n), n., levain, m.; levure, f.

leaven (lèv'v'n), v.a., fermenter, faire lever, gâter.

leavenous (lèv'-), adj., qui contient du levain; corrompu, gâté.

leavings (liv'ign'z), n., restes, m. pl.; bribes, f.pl.

lecher (lètsh'-), n., libertin, débauché, m.

lecherous, adj., lascif, débauché, libertin.

lecherously, adv., lascivement, lubrique-ment, en libertin.

lecherousness, or **lechery**, n., lasciveté, f.; libertinage, m.

lectern (lĕk'teurne), *n.* *V.* **lettern.**

lection (lĕk'-), *n.*, leçon, *f.* ; texte d'auteur. *m.*

lecture (lĕkt'ieur), *n.*, discours; sermon, *m.*; leçon ; (fig.) mercuriale, semonce, *f.* Course of —s; *cours, m.*

lecture (lĕkt'ieur), *v.a.*, donner des leçons à, faire un cours à ; (fig.) sermonner, réprimander, faire un sermon à.

lecture (lĕkt'ieur), *v.n.*, faire un cours, donner des leçons, professer ; (fig.) sermonner, faire des sermons.

lecturer, *n.*, lecteur ; professeur ; (rel.) prédicateur, *m.*

lectureship, *n.*, professorat, *m.*

lecturing, *n.*, cours publics, *m.pl.* ; leçons publiques, *f.pl.*

led (lĕde), *past part.* *V.* **lead.** — horse; *cheval de main, m.*

ledge (lĕdje), *n.*, rebord, bord, *m.* ; (nav.) chaîne de rochers, *f.*, récif, *m.* ; (layer—*strate*) couche, *f.*

ledger (lĕdj'eur), *n.*, grand livre, *m.*

lee (lî), *n.*, (nav.) côté de dessous le vent, *m.*

lee, *adj.*, (nav.) sous le vent.

lee-board (-bôrde), *n.*, (nav.) semelle, dérive, *f.*

leech (lîtshe), *n.*, sangsue, *f.* ; (doctor—*docteur*) médecin, *m*: — rope ; (nav.) *ralingue de chute, f.* — -lines; *cargues-boulines, f.pl.*

leech, *v.a.*, médicamenter, médeciner.

lee-gage (-ghédje), *n.*, (nav.) dessous du vent, *m.*

leek (lîke), *n.*, (bot.) poireau, porreau, *m.*

leer (lîre), *n.*, œillade, *f.* ; regard affecté, *m.*

leer, *v.n.*, lorgner, regarder de côté, du coin de l'œil.

leeringly, *adv.*, par une œillade.

lees (lîze), *n.*, lie, *f.* ; sédiment, *m.*

leeward (lî-wörde), *adv.*, (nav.) sous le vent.

leeward, *adj.*, (nav.) sous le vent; (of the tide—*de la marée*) qui porte sous le vent.

leeway (lî-wè), *n.*, (nav.) dérive, *f.*

left (lĕfte), *past part.* *V.* **leave**, *v.*

left (lĕfte), *adj.*, gauche. On the — ; *à gauche.*

left-handed, *adj.*, gaucher ; (fig.) gauche. — marriage; *mariage de la main gauche, m.*

left-handedness (-ha'n'dĕd'-), *n.*, usage habituel de la main gauche, *m.*

left-handiness, *n.*, gaucherie, *f.*

leg (lĕghe), *n.*, jambe ; (of birds, insects—*des oiseaux, des insectes*) patte ; (of boots—*de bottes*) tige; (of poultry—*de volaille*) cuisse, *f.* ; (of furniture—*de meubles*) pied; (of mutton—*de mouton*) gigot, *m.* To be on one's —s ; *être sur pied, être debout.* To have sea—s; *avoir le pied marin.*

legacy (lĕg'-), *n.*, legs, *m.*

legal (lî-), *adj.*, légal, judiciaire, juridique, licite.

legality (lè-), *n.*, légalité, *f.*

legalize (lî-gal'aize), *v.a.*, légaliser, autoriser.

legally (lî-), *adv.*, selon les lois, juridiquement, légitimement, légalement.

legatary (lĕg'-), *n.*, légataire, *m.*

legate (lĕg'-), *n.*, légat ; délégué, *m.*

legatee (lĕg'a-tî), *n.*, légataire, *m.*

legation (li-ghé-), *n.*, légation, *f.*

legator (li-), *n.*, légateur, testateur, *m.*, légatrice, testatrice, *f.*

legend (lî-djè'n'de, *ou* lĕdj'-), *n.*, légende ; chronique, *f.*

legendary (lĕdj'-), *adj.*, légendaire.

legendary, *n.*, légende, *f.* ; légendaire, *m.*

legerdemain (lĕdj'èr'di-méne), *n.*, tour d'escamoteur, de passe-passe, d'adresse, *m.*

legged (lĕg'de), *adj.*, qui a des jambes.

legging (lĕg'ghigne), *n.*, grande guêtre, *f.*

legibility, *or* **legibleness** (lĕdj'-), *n.*, lisibilité, netteté d'écriture, caractère lisible.

legible (lĕdj'l-b'l), *adj.*, lisible, qu'on peut lire.

legibly, *adv.*, lisiblement.

legion (lî'djeune), *n.*, légion, *f.*

legionary, *adj.*, légionnaire; de légion.

legionary, *n.*, légionnaire ; soldat légionnaire, *m.*

legislate (lĕdj'-), *v.n.*, faire des lois.

legislation (lĕdj'is-lé-), *n.*, législation, *f.*

legislative (-lé-), *adj.*, législatif.

legislator (-lé-teur), *n.*, législateur, *m.*

legislature (lĕdj'is-lét'ieur), *n.*, législation, législature, *f.*

legitimacy (li-djit'-), *n.*, légitimité, *f.*

legitimate, *adj.*, légitime.

legitimate, *v.a.*, légitimer.

legitimately, *adv.*, légitinement.

legitimation (-'i-mé-), *n.*, légitimation, *f.*

legitimatist, *or* **legitimist**, *n.*, légitimiste, *m.*, *f.*

legitimize (-maïze), *v.a.*, légitimer.

legume (lègh'ioume), *or* **legumen** (li-ghiou-mène), *n.*, légume, *m.*

leguminous (lègh'iou-), *adj.*, légumineux.

leisurable (li-jeur'a-b'l), *adj.*, fait à loisir.

leisurably, *or* **leisurely**, *adv.*, à loisir, peu à peu.

leisure (li-jeur), *n.*, loisir, *m.* ; commodité, *f.*

lemma (lĕm'-), *n.*, (math.) lemme, *m.*

lemon (lĕm'-), *n.*, citron, limon, *m.*

lemonade (lè'm'o'n'éde), *n.*, limonade, *f.*

lemon-grass (-grâce), *n.*, (bot.) schénanthe, jonc odorant, *m.*

lemon-peel (-pîl), *n.*, écorce de citron, *f.*

lemon-plant, *n.*, (bot.) verveine, *f.*

lemon-tree (-tri), *n.*, citronnier, *m.*

lemur (lìmeur), *n.*, (mam.) lémurien, maki, *m.*

lemures (lèm-iou-rize), *n.pl.*, lémures, *f.pl.*, mânes, *m.pl.*

lend (lè'n'de), *v.a*, prêter; (on hire—*en location*) louer.

lender, *n.*, prêteur, *m.*, prêteuse, *f.*

lending, *n.*, prêt, *m.*

length (lè'n'gn'th), *n.*, longueur; étendue, *f.*; (degree—*degré*) degré, point, *m.* ; (of time—*du temps*) durée, *f.*, espace, *m.* Full — ; *en pied, de grandeur naturelle.* At full — (not (abridged—*non abrégé*); *tout au long.* At great — ; *fort au long, longuement.* Two feet in — ; *deux pieds de longueur.* To go to great —s ; *aller bien loin.* To go the — of thinking ; *aller jusqu'au point de (jusqu'à) penser.* At — ; *enfin, à la fin;* (lengthily—*longuement*) *au long.* To fall full — ; *tomber tout de son long.*

lengthen (lè'n'gn'th'n), *v.a.*, allonger, étendre ; rallonger ; (time—*temps*) prolonger. To — out; *étendre, prolonger.*

lengthen, *v.n.*, s'allonger, devenir plus long, s'étendre ; (of time—*du temps*) se prolonger ; (of days—*des jours*) grandir, croître.

lengthening, *n.*, prolongement, *m.* ; (of time—*du temps*) prolongation, *f.*

lengthily (lè'n'gn'th'-), *adv.*, longuement.

lengthiness, *n.*, longueur, *f.*

lengthways, *or* **lengthwise**, *adv.*, en longueur, de long, en long.

lengthy, *adj.*, un peu long, un peu trop long.

lenience, *or* **leniency** (lì-), *n.*, douceur, indulgence, *f.*

lenient (lì-), *adj.*, doux, adoucissant ; (med.) lénitif.

lenify (lè'n'i-fa'ye), *v.a.*, adoucir, lénifier, mitiger.

lenitive, **lenient**, *or* **leniment** (lè'n'-), *n.*, (med.) lénitif, calmant, émollient, *m.*

lenitive (lè'n'-), *adj.*, lénitif, calmant, émollient.

lenity (lè'n'-), *n.*, douceur ; indulgence, *f.* To show — to ; *avoir de l'indulgence pour.*

lens (lè'n'se), *n.* (*lenses*), (opt.) lentille, loupe, *f.*

lens-shaped (-shép'te), *adj.*, lenticulaire, lenticulé.

lent (lè'n'te), *n.*, carême, *m.* Mid- —; *la mi-carême, f.*

lenten, *adj.*, de carême.

lenticular (-tik'iou-), *adj.*, en forme de lentille, lenticulaire.

lentiform, *adj.*, lenticulaire, lenticulé.

lentil (lè'n'tile), *n.*, (bot.) lentille, *f.*

leo (li-ô), *n.*, (astron.) Lion, *m.*

leonine (li-o-naïne), *adj.*, de lion, léonin.

leoninely, *adv.*, en lion, comme un lion.

leopard (lèp'arde), *n.*, léopard, *m.*

leper (lèp'eur), *n.*, lépreux, *m.*

lepidopteral, *adj.*, (ent.) lépidoptère.

lepidopters (lèp'i-dop-teurze), *or* **lepidoptera** (-ti-ra), *n.*, (ent.) lépidoptères, *m.pl.*

leporine (lèp-o-raïne), *adj.*, de lièvre.

leprosity (li-pross'-), *n.*, (ant.) *V.* **leprosy.**

leprosy (lèp'ro-ci), *n.*, lèpre, *f.*

leprous (lèp'reusse), *adj.*, lépreux, ladre.

lesion (li-jeune), *n.*, lésion, contusion, *f.*

less (lèce), *adj.*, moindre, plus petit, inférieur.

less, *adv.*, moins. The — .... the more ....; *moins* .... *plus* .... —and —; *de moins en moins.* So much the —; *d'autant moins.* A man —; *un homme de moins.*

less, *n.*, moins; moindre, inférieur. *m.*

lessee (lès'sî), *n.*, locataire à bail, *m., f.*; (jur.) preneur, *m.*

lessen, *v.a.*, apetisser, rapetisser; diminuer, amoindrir; (to lower—*abaisser*) rabaisser.

lessen, *v.n.*, diminuer, s'amoindrir, se rapetisser ; s'abaisser.

lessening, *n.*, amoindrissement, *m.*; diminution, *f.*

lesser, *adj.*, moindre, plus petit ; (geog.) mineur, petit.

lesson (lès's'n), *n.*, leçon ; répétition, *f.*

lesson, *v.a.*, instruire, enseigner.

lessor (lès'sor, *ou* -'seur), *n.*, bailleur, *m.*

lest (lèste), *conj.*, de peur que, de crainte que ; (after to fear—*après to fear*) que.

let (lète), *v.a.*, (*preterit* and *past part.*, Let), (to permit—*permettre*) laisser, permettre, souffrir ; (to cause, make—*causer*) faire ; (a house—*maison*) louer. To — alone (pers.); *laisser tranquille, laisser seul*; (a thing—*chose*) *laisser, laisser là.* To — it alone ; *n'en rien faire, ne pas s'en mêler.* To — blood; *saigner.* To — fly; *tirer, faire partir.* To — know ; *faire savoir.* To — loose; *lâcher, déchaîner.* To — see; *faire voir; montrer.* To — be, to be —; *maison à louer.* — him come; *qu'il vienne.* — us go; *allons.* To — in; *faire, laisser entrer; ouvrir la porte à.* To — into; *faire, laisser entrer; initier; communiquer.* To — off; *laisser partir, laisser échapper*; (of fire-arms—*d'armes à feu*) *tirer, faire partir, décharger.* To — down; *faire descendre; laisser, abattre.* To — out; *laisser sortir;* (a house—*maison*) *louer*; (fire—*le feu*) *laisser éteindre.* To — up, up-stairs; *faire, laisser monter.*

let, *n.*, empêchement; obstacle, *m.*

lethal (li-thal), *adj.*, mortel, fatal.

lethargic, *or* **lethargical** (lè-thâr-djike, -dji-cal), *adj.*, léthargique.

lethargy (lèth'ar-dji), *n.*, léthargie, *f.*

lethargy, *v.a.*, frapper de léthargie, faire tomber en léthargie.

lethe (li-thè), *n.*, (myth.) Léthé ; oubli, *m.*

lethean (lè-thi'a'n), *adj.*, du Léthé, de l'oubli.

letheferous (lè-thif'èr-), *adj.*, (ant.) léthifère, mortel.

letter (lèt'teur), *n.*, lettre, *f.* — of attorney; *procuration, f.* — of mark; *lettre de marque, f.*

— of exchange; *lettre de change, f.* — -box; *boîte aux lettres, f.* — -case; *porte-lettres, m.*; (print.) *casse, f.*

letter, v.a., (a book—*un livre*) mettre le titre au dos.

letter, *n.*, personne qui laisse, qui permet; personne qui empêche, qui entrave, *f.*

letter-carrier (-car'ri-eur), *n.*, facteur, *m.*

lettered (let'teur'de), *adj.*, lettré, savant; littéraire ; (bookbind.) avec le titre marqué au dos.

lettering, *n.*, titre, *m.*

lettern (lèt'tèrne), *n.*, lutrin, *m.*

letter-press, *n.*, impression typographique, *f.*

letter-proud (-praoude), *adj.*, fier de son savoir.

letter-writer (-raït'-), *n.*, personne qui aime à écrire des lettres, *f.*; auteur épistolaire; (book —*livre*) recueil de lettres, *m.*

letting (lèt'-), *n.*, louage, m., location, *f.* ; (of land—*de terres*) affermage, *m.*

lettuce (lèt'tice), *n.*, laitue, *f.* Cabbage- —; *laitue pommée.* Cos- —; *laitue romaine.*

leucorrhœa (liou-cor-rhi-a), *n.*, leucorrhée, *f.*; fleurs blanches, *f.pl.*

levant (li-, *ou* lè-), *n.*, Levant, Orient, *m.*

levant, *adj.*, oriental, du Levant, de l'Orient.

levantine (li-va'n'tine, *ou* lèv'a'n'taïne), *n.*, levantine (stuff—*étoffe*), *f.*

levee (lèv'è), *n.*, lever, *m.*; réception, *f.* To hold a —; *recevoir.* A — will be held; *il y aura réception.*

level (lèv'èl), *n.*, niveau, *m.* ; surface unie ; visée, *f.*; pays plat, *m.* On a —; *de niveau.* Dead —; *niveau parfaitement uni.*

level, *adj.*, uni, de niveau, égal. — with; *au niveau de, de niveau avec.*

level, *v.a.*, aplanir, niveler, mettre de niveau; (fire-arms—*armes à feu*) pointer, ajuster, viser; (a blow—*coup*) porter, assener, lancer ; (to throw down—*abattre*) renverser. To — to the ground; *raser, détruire, renverser.* To — at; *viser à; porter un coup à.*

level, *v.n.*, viser, mettre en joue, pointer, ajuster; s'aplanir, se niveler.

leveller, *n.*, aplanisseur; niveleur, *m.*

levelling, *n.*, nivellement ; aplanissement ; pointage, *m.*

levelling-staff (-stâfe), *n.*, mire de nivellement, *f.*, jalon, *m.*

levelness, *n.*, niveau, *m.*; égalité, *f.*

leven (lèv'è'n), *n.*, levain, *m.* *V.* **leaven.**

lever (li-veur), *n.*, levier, *m.*; bascule, *f.*

leveret (lèv'eur'ète), *n.*, levraut, *m.*

leviable (lèv'i-a-b'l), *adj.*, qui peut être levé.

leviathan (lè-vaï-a-tha'n), *n.*, léviathan, *m.*; baleine, *f.*

levigate (lèv'-), *v.a.*, (pharm.) broyer, pulvériser; aplanir; polir.

levigation (lèv'i-ghé-), *n.*, lévigation, pulvérisation, *f.*

levitation (lèv'i-té-), *n.*, action de rendre léger; légèreté, *f.*

levite (li-vaïte), *n.*, lévite, prêtre, *m.*

levitical (lè-vit'i-), *adj.*, lévitique, des lévites.

leviticus (lè-vit'i-keusse), *n.*, Lévitique, *m.*

levity (lèv'-), *n.*, légèreté, inconstance, *f.*

levy (lèv'i), *n.*, levée, conscription militaire, *f.*

levy, *v.a.*, lever; (a fine—*amende*) imposer.

lewd (lioude), *adj.*, dissolu, impudique, débauché, déréglé, licencieux, dépravé, luxurieux.

lewdly, *adv.*, licencieusement, impudiquement, dans la débauche, dans le débordement.

lewdness, *n.*, impudicité, luxure, débauche, dépravation, *f.*; libertinage, débordement, *m.*

lewdster, *n.*, libertin, débauché, *m.*; impudique, *m.*

lexicographer (lèks'-), *n.*, lexicographe, *m.*

lexicographic, adj., lexicographique.
lexicography, n., lexicographie, f.
lexicology (lěks'ĭ-co -o-djĭ), n., lexicologie, f.
lexicon (lěks'ĭ-), n., lexique, dictionnaire, m.
ley (lĭ), n., champ, m., pâturage, m.
leyden-jar (lī-dē'n-djär), or **leyden-phial** (-faī'al), n., (phys.) bouteille de Leyde, f.
liability (laī'a-), n., responsabilité; condition de ce qui est sujet, exposé, f. Liabilities; (com.) engagements, m.pl., passif, m.s. Their — to accidents; comme ils sont exposés, sujets à des accidents.
liable (laī'a-b'l), adj., sujet, exposé, passible, responsable.
liableness, n. V. **liability**.
liar (laī'ar), n., menteur, m., menteuse, f.
lias (laī'ace), n., lias, m.
libation (laī-bé-), n., libation, f.
libbard (lib'ärde), n., (ant.) léopard, m.
libel (laī-běl), n., libelle, m.; publication diffamatoire, diffamation, f.
libel, v.a., diffamer; (jur.) libeller.
libel, v.n., (ant.) répandre des libelles, des calomnies.
libeller, n., diffamateur, libelliste, m.
libelling, n., diffamation, f.
libellous, adj., diffamatoire.
liber (laī-běre), n., (bot.) liber, m.
liberal (lib'ěr'-), adj., libéral, généreux.
liberal, n., libéral, m.
liberalism (-'ĭz'me), n., libéralisme, m.
liberality, n., libéralité, f.
liberalize (-'aīze), v.a., rendre libéral, libéraliser.
liberally, adv., libéralement.
liberate, v.a., rendre libre, affranchir, libérer, mettre en liberté; délivrer.
liberation (lib'ěr-é-), n., mise en liberté, f., élargissement; affranchissement, m.; libération, délivrance, f.
liberator (-'ěr'éteur), n., libérateur, m.; libératrice, f.
libertine, adj., libertin.
libertine (lib'eur-tine, ou -taïne), n., libertin, m., libertine, f.
libertinism (-tǐ'n'ĭz'me), n., libertinage, m.
liberty (lib'eur'tĭ), n., liberté, f. To be at —; être en liberté; être libre. To set at —; mettre en liberté, donner la liberté à. To take the — of; prendre la liberté de. Liberties; privilèges, m.pl.; franchises, f.pl. To take liberties; prendre des libertés, prendre des licences.
libidinous, adj., libertin, libidineux.
libidinously, adv., avec luxure.
libidinousness, n., luxure, f.
librarian (laī-bré-), n., bibliothécaire, m.
library (laī-), n., bibliothèque, f.
librate (laī-), v.n., balancer.
librate, v.n., balancer; se tenir en équilibre.
libration (laī-bré-), n., balancement, équilibre, m.; (astron.) libration, f.
libratory, adj., de libration; en équilibre.
lice (laīce), n. V. **louse**.
license (laī-), n., licence, liberté, f., dérèglement; (thea.) privilège, m.; (of a preacher—de prédicateur) autorisation; (of tobacconists, vendors of excisable articles—de marchands de tabac, liqueurs, &c.) licence, f.; (of a bookseller, a printer—de libraire, d'imprimeur, &c.) brevet, m.; (com.) patente, f. Marriage—; dispense de bans, f. Gun —; port d'arme; permis de chasse, m. Government—; licence accordée par le gouvernement.
license, v.a., autoriser, accorder une autorisation à; (a printer, a bookseller—imprimeur, libraire) breveter; (theatre) accorder un privilège à; (of tobacconists and vendors of excisable articles—marchands de tabac, de vin, &c.) accorder une licence à; (com.) patenter.
licensed (laī-cě'n'ste), adj., autorisé;

(printers, booksellers—imprimeurs, libraires) breveté; (theatres) privilégié; (com.) patenté.
licenser (laī-), n., agent qui accorde les autorisations; censeur, m.
licentiate (laī-cè'n'shi-éte), n., licencié, m.
licentiate, v.a., permettre, autoriser.
licentious (laī-cè'n'shi-eusse), adj., licentieux, libertin, déréglé.
licentiously, adv., licencieusement.
licentiousness, n., licence, f.; dérèglement, libertinage, m.
lichen (laī-kè'n, ou litsh'ě'n), n., (bot.) lichen, m.
licit, adj., licite, légal.
licitly, adv., licitement.
licitness, n., légalité, f.
lick n., (pop.) coup, m.; action de lécher; la chose léchée, f. — on the head; taloche, f. — in the face; giffla, f.
lick, v.a., lécher; laper; (to beat — battre) (pop.) flanquer des coups à, rosser
lickerish, adj., friand; avide.
lickerishly, adv., avec friandise.
lickerishness, n., friandise, f.
licking, n., coups, m.pl.; roulée, rossée, f.
licorice, or **liquorice**, n., réglisse, f.
lictor, n., licteur, m.
lid, n., couvercle, m.; (of the eye—de l'œil) paupière, f.
lie (la'ye), n., mensonge; démenti, m. To give the — to; donner un démenti à.
lie (la'ye), v.n. (preterit, Lay; past part., Lain), être couché; coucher; se coucher; reposer; être; être situé; se trouver; s'appuyer; rester; demeurer; consister; (nav.) être mouillé, être à l'ancre. To — about; traîner. To — by; (pers.) se reposer, se tenir en réserve; (of things—choses) être tenu en réserve. To — down; coucher, être couché, se coucher. To — in; être en couches; faire ses couches. The town —s between two valleys; la ville est située, se trouve entre deux vallées. It —s against the wall; il s'appuie contre le mur. The whole —s in this; le tout repose sur ceci. The difference —s in this; la différence consiste en ceci. Here —s; ci-git. To let any thing —; laisser là quelque chose. To — under a mistake; se tromper; être dans l'erreur. It —s in my power to; il dépend de moi de. To — heavy on; peser sur; tourmenter. My honour —s at stake; il y va de mon honneur. To — alongside; être bord à bord.
lie (la'ye), v.n., mentir.
lief (lîfe), adj., (ant.) bien-aimé; cher.
lief (lîfe), adv., volontiers. I had as —; j'aime autant.
liege (lî'dje), n., vassal lige; souverain; suzerain, m.
liege, adj., lige, fidèle.
liege-man, n., homme lige, m.
lien (lî-è'n, ou laī'è'n), n., (jur.) gage, nantissement, m.
lier (laī'eur), n., personne qui est couchée, f.
lieu (liou), n., lieu, remplacement, m. In — of; au lieu de; en place de; à la place de; en remplacement de. [Ne s'emploie qu'avec in.]
lieutenancy (lèf'tě'n'-, ou liou-), n., lieutenance, f.
lieutenant (lèf'tě'n'- ou liou-), n., lieutenant, m.
lieutenantship, n., lieutenance, f.
life (laïfe), n. (lives), vie, f.; vivant, m.; (fig.) vie, âme, vivacité, f.; mouvement; (paint., sculpt.) naturel, m., nature, f. Prime of — ; fleur de l'âge, f. Fashionable—; beau monde, m. Single —; célibat, m. At that time of —; à cet âge. During his, her —; de son vivant. For —; à vie; pour toute la vie, sa vie. Never in one's —; jamais de sa vie. From —; d'après nature. I cannot for the — of me; je ne le peux pour tout au monde. To the —; exactement. The streets

are full of —; *les rues sont pleines de mouvement.*
To depart this —; *mourir ; quitter cette vie.* To
fly for one's —; *chercher son salut dans la fuite.*
To give — to; *animer ; donner de la vie à, de
l'âme à.*

life-blood (-bleude), *n.*, le plus pur de son
sang; (fig.) sang, *m.*, vie, âme, *f.*

life-boat (-bôte), *n.*, canot de sauvetage, *m.*

life-buoy (-bou'é), *n.*, bouée de sauvetage, *f.*

life-consuming (-siou'm'-), *adj.*, qui fait
dépérir.

lifegiving (-ghiv'-), *adj.*, qui donne la vie;
fortifiant.

lifeguard (-gârde), *n.*, garde du corps, *m.*

lifeguards, *n.pl.*, garde du corps, *f.sing.*;
gardes du corps, *m.pl.*

lifeguardsman (-gârd'z'ma'n), *n.*, garde du
corps, *m.*

lifeless, *adj.*, sans vie; inanimé, mort; (fig.)
sans âme, sans vigueur, sans mouvement.

lifelessly, *adv.*, sans vie; sans âme, sans
vigueur, sans mouvement.

lifelessness, *n.*, absence de vie; absence
d'âme, absence de mouvement, *f.*

lifelike (-laïke), *adj.*, comme un être vivant.

life-line (-laïne), *n.*, (nav.) garde-corps,
garde-fou, *m.*

lifepreserver (-pri-ceur'-), *n.*, appareil de
sauvetage; (truncheon—*gourdin*) assommoir, *m.*

liferent, *n.*, rente viagère, *f.*

life-string (-strigne), *n.*, nerf vital, *m.*

lifetime (-taïme), *n.*, vie, *f.*; vivant, *m.*

life-weary (-wî-ri), *adj.*, las de la vie.

lift, *n.*, action de lever, de soulever, *f.*, effort;
coup de main, *m.*; charge, *f.* To give a — to;
donner un coup d'épaule à, un coup de main à.

lift, *v.a.*, lever, élever, enlever, soulever,
hausser; relever.

lifter, *n.*, personne qui lève, qui élève, qui
enlève, qui soulève, qui hausse, *f.*

lifting, *n.*, action de lever, *f.*

ligament, *n.*, ligament; lien, *m.*

ligamental, *or* **ligamentous**, *adj.*, liga-
menteux.

ligation (li-ghé-), *n.*, action de lier, *f.*;
lien, *m.*

ligature (lig'a-tioure), *n.*, action de lier;
(mus.) liaison; (print., surg.) ligature, *f.*

light (laïte), *n.*, lumière, clarté, *f.*; jour, *m.*;
lueur, *f.*; (paint.) jour, *m.*, lumière, *f.*; (arch.)
jour, *m.* Day—; *jour, m.* Moon—; *clair de
lune, m.* By the — of; *à la lumière de, à la
clarté de.* It is —; *il fait jour ; il fait clair.* To
give —; *éclairer.* By —; *à la lumière.*

light, *adj.*, léger; (fig.) agile; facile; (of
light and colour—*de lumière, de couleur*) clair.

light, *v.a.* (*preterit and past part.*, Lighted,
Lit), allumer; (to give light to) éclairer. To — a
candle; *allumer une chandelle.* To — the streets;
éclairer les rues.

light, *v.n.*, s'abattre. To — upon; *tomber
sur ; retomber.*

light-bearer (-bèr'-), *n.*, porte-flambeau, *m.*

light-borne, *adj.*, (man.) léger à la main.

lighten, *v.a.*, alléger; (to alleviate—*adoucir*)
soulager; (to cheer — *animer*) égayer ; (to dissipate darkness—*dissiper l'obscurité*) éclairer.

lighten, *v.n. imp.*, faire des éclairs, éclairer.

lighter, *n.*, allumeur, *m.*, allumeuse; (nav.)
allège, gabare, *f.*

lighterage (laït'eur'édje), *n.*, frais d'allège, *m.pl.*

lighter-man, *n.*, gabarier, *m.*

light-fingered (-fi'n'gheurde), *adj.*, qui a les
doigts crochus, fripon.

light-foot (-foute), *or* **light-footed** (-'ède),
adj., au pied léger; agile.

light-headed (-hèd'-), *adj.*, qui a la tête
légère; étourdi; en délire.

light-headedness, *n.*, étourderie, *f.*; délire, *m.*

light-hearted (-hârt'-), *adj.*, enjoué, gai,
réjoui.

light-house (-haouce), *n.*, phare, fanal, *m.*

lighting, *n.*, éclairage, *m.*

lightless, *adj.*, sans lumière; sans clarté.

lightly, *adv.*, légèrement ; avec légèreté ; à
la légère; lestement; facilement; gaîment.

lightness, *n.*, légèreté; agilité, *f.*

lightning, *n.*, éclair, *m.*, foudre, *f.*; (alleviation—*adoucissement*) soulagement, *m.* — -rod;
paratonnerre, m. Flash of —; *éclair, m.*

lightning-glance (-glâ'n'ce), *n.*, éclair, *m.*

lights (laïtse), *n.*, poumons (of animals—
des animaux), *m.pl.*; (of calves, &c.—*de veau, &c.*)
mou, *m.*

lightsome (-seume), *adj.*, clair; éclairé;
égayant.

lightsomeness, *n.*, clarté; gaîté; légèreté, *f.*

ligneous (lig-ni-), *adj.*, ligneux.

lignify (lig-ni-fa'ye), *v.a.*, (bot.) convertir en
bois.

lignify, *v.n.*, se lignifier.

lignum-vitæ (lig-neume-vaï-ti), *n.*, gaïac,
bois de gaïac; bois de gaïac râpé, *m.*

like (laïke), *n.*, chose pareille, *f.*; pareil, *m.*,
pareille, *f.*; même chose, *f.* To do the — ; *en
faire autant.*

like, *adj.*, semblable, tel, même, pareil, égal,
ressemblant ; vraisemblable. That is something
— ! *à la bonne heure !* To look — ; *avoir l'air de ;
ressembler.* Does this portrait look — me? *est-
ce que ce portrait me ressemble?*

like, *adv.*, comme; en; tel que, telle que;
probablement. That is just — you ; *c'est bien
vous.*

like, *v.a.*, aimer; trouver à son goût; trouver
bien ; prendre goût à; trouver convenable;
aimer; convenir; vouloir, vouloir bien; être
curieux. I begin to — it; *je commence à y
prendre goût.* As you — ; *comme vous jugerez
convenable ; comme vous voudrez.* I should — to
go there; *je voudrais bien y aller.* If you — ; *si
vous voulez.*

likelihood (-houde), *or* **likeliness**, *n.*,
vraisemblance, apparence, probabilité, *f.*

likely, *adj.*, vraisemblable; probable. — to;
fait pour ; propre à ; de nature à.

likely, *adv.*, probablement ; vraisemblablement. He is — to come ; *il viendra probablement, il est probable qu'il viendra.*

liken (laïk'n), *v.a.*, comparer; faire ressembler à.

likeness, *n.*, ressemblance; apparence, *f.*;
portrait, *m.*

likewise (-waïze), *adv.*, pareillement, de
même, aussi.

liking, *n.*, gré; goût, *m.*; inclination ; amitié,
affection, *f.*

lilac (laï-lake), *n.*, lilas, *m.*

liliaceous (lil'i-é-sheusse), *adj.*, (bot.) liliacé.

lilied (lil'ide), *adj.*, orné de lis.

lily, *n.*, lis, *m.* — of the valley ; *muguet, m.*

limail (laï-méle), *or* **limature** (laï-ma-
tioure), *n.*, limaille, *f.*

limb (lime), *n.*, (of the body—*du corps*) membre ; (edge—*bord*) bord, *m.*; (of a tree—*d'arbre*)
grosse branche, *f.*; (astron., bot.) limbe, *m.*

limb, *v.a.*, (to dismember—*arracher les
membres*) démembrer; (to supply with limbs —
fournir des membres) donner des membres à.

limbed (li'm'de), *adj.*, membré. Large — ;
membru.

limber (li'm'beur), *adj.*, souple, flexible;
(fig.) faible; agile.

limberness, *n.*, souplesse; (fig.) faiblesse,
fragilité, *f.*

limbers (li'm'beurze), *n.pl.*, (artil.) caisson, *m.*

limbless (li'm'-), *adj.*, sans membres.

limb-meal (li'm'mîl), *adv.*, morceau par morceau.

limbo (li'm'bô), *or* **limbus**, *n.*, limbes, *m.pl.*, prison, *f.*

lime (laï'me), *n.*, chaux ; (for catching birds —*pour attraper les oiseaux*) glu, *f.* ; (tree—*arbre*) limonier ; (linden) tilleul ; (fruit) citron, *m.*

lime, *v.a.*, gluer ; prendre au gluau ; (fig.) prendre dans un piège.

lime-burner (-beurn'-), *n.*, chaufournier, *m.*

lime-hound (-haoun'de), *n.*, limier, *m.*

lime-juice (-djiouce), *n.*, jus de citron, *m.*

lime-kiln, *n.*, chaufour, four à chaux, *m.*

lime-pit. *n.*, fosse à chaux, *f.*

limestone (-stône), *n.*, pierre calcaire ; pierre à chaux, *f.*

lime-tree (-trî), *n.*, limonier ; tilleul, *m.*

lime-twig, *n.*, gluau, *m.*

limit, *n.*, limite, *f.*, bornes, *f.pl.*

limit, *v.a.*, limiter, borner.·

limitable (-'a-b'l), *adj.*, qu'on peut limiter.

limitarian (-mit'é-), *adj.*, limitatif.

limitary, *adj.*, limitrophe.

limitation, *n.*. limitation, restriction ; réserve, (jur.) prescription, *f.*

limited, *adj.*, limité, borné ; (math.) déterminé.

limitedly, *adv.*, avec des limites, avec des bornes.

limitedness, *n.*, état limité, état borné, *m.*

limiter, *n.*, personne qui limite, chose qui limite, *f.*

limn (lime), *v.a.*, enluminer ; peindre à l'aquarelle ; (fig.) peindre.

limner (li'm'neur), *n.*, enlumineur, *m.*, en- lumineuse, *f.* ; (fig.) peintre, *m.*

limning (li'm'igne), *n.*, enluminure ; peinture à l'aquarelle, aquarelle ; (fig.) peinture, *f.*

limous (laï-meusse), *adj.*, limoneux.

limp (li'm'pe), *adj.*, mou, flasque.

limp, *v.n.*, clocher, boiter, clopiner.

limper, *n.*, personne qui cloche, *f.* ; boiteux, *m.*, boiteuse, *f.*

limpet (li'm'pète), *n.*, lépas, *m.* ; patelle, *f.*

limpid. *adj.*, limpide.

limpidness, *n.*, limpidité, *f.*

limpingly (li'm'pign'li), *adv.*, en boiteux, en clochant.

limy (laï'm'l), *adj.*, calcaire ; (viscous—*vis- queux*) gluant.

lin, *n.*, (ant.) mare, flaque d'eau ; chute d'eau, cataracte, *f.*

linchpin (li'n'sh'pi'n), *n.*, esse ; clavette d'essieu, *f.*

linden, *or* **linden-tree** (-trî), *n.*, tilleul, *m.*

line (laïne), *n.*, ligne ; (railways) voie, *f.* ; (of business—*profession*) genre d'affaires, *m.*, spécia- lité, partie ; *f.* ; (poet.) vers ; (short letter—*petite lettre*) mot, *m.* ; (limit) limite ; (fort., geog., geom., milit., tech.) ligne, *f.* Ship of the —; *vaisseau de ligne, m.* Troops of the —; *troupes de ligne, f.pl.* Send me a—; *écrivez-moi un mot.*

line, *v.a.*, garnir ; (garments—*vêtements*) doubler, garnir ; (fort.) fortifier ; (to trace) tracer ; (to border) border ; (mas.) revêtir.

lineage (li'n'i-édje), *n.*, lignée, race, fa- mille, *f.*

lineal (li'n'l'-), *adj.*, linéaire ; (genealogy— *généalogie*) direct, en ligne directe ; (jur.) linéal.

lineally, *adv.*, en ligne droite.

lineament (li'n'i-a-), *n.*, trait, linéament, *m.*

linear (li'n'i-), *adj.*, linéaire.

lineation (li'n'i-é-), *n.*, délinéation, *f.*

linen, *n.*, toile, toile de lin, *f.* ; lin ; (clothes —*vêtements*) linge, *m.* Clean — ; *linge blanc, m.* Dirty — ; *linge sale, m.*

linen, *adj.*, de toile, de lin ; de linge.

linen-cloth (-clôth), *n.*, toile de lin, *f.*

linen-draper (-dré-), *n.*, marchand de toiles ; linger, *m.*, lingère, *f.*

linenpress, *n.*, armoire à linge, *f.*

linenyarn, *n.*, fil de lin, *m.*

linger (li'n'gheur), *v.n.*, traîner, languir ; tarder.

linger, *v.a.*, (ant.) faire traîner ; retarder.

lingerer, *n.*, traînard, lambin, *m.*

lingering, *n.*, retardement, délai, *m.* ; len- teur, *f.*

lingering, *adj.*, qui tarde ; qui lambine ; qui traîne, lent ; languissant. —illness ; *maladie de langueur, f.*

lingeringly, *adv.*, en traînant ; lentement ; avec langueur.

lingo (li'n'gô), *n.*, langage ; jargon, *m.*

linguacious (li'n'goué-sheusse), *adj.*, (ant.) babillard.

lingual (li'n'gwal), *adj.*, lingual.

linguist (li'n'gwiste), *n.*, linguiste, *m.*

lingwort (lign'weurte), *n.*, angélique, *f.*

liniment, *n.*, liniment, *m.*

lining (laï'nigne), *n.*, (of garments—*de vêtements*) doublure ; garniture, *f.* ; (mas.) re- vêtement, *m.*

link (li'n'ke), *n.*, chaînon, anneau, *m.* ; (torch) torche, *f.*, flambeau, *m.*

link, *v.a.*, lier ; joindre ; enchaîner.

linkboy (-boï), *or* **linkman**, *n.*, porte flambeau, *m.*

linnet (li'n'nète), *n.*, linotte, *f.*

linseed (-sîde), *n.*, graine de lin, *f.*

linseed-meal (-mîle), *n.*, farine de graine de lin, *f.*

linseed-oil (-oïl), *n.*, huile de lin, *f.*

linsey, *or* **linsey-woolsey** (li'n'sé-woul'sè), *adj.*, de tiretaine ; (fig.) grossier, bas, vil.

linsey-woolsey, *n.*, tiretaine, *f.*

linstock (li'n'stoke), *n.*, (artil.) boutefeu, *m.*

lint (li'n'te), *n.*, filasse ; (surg.) charpie, *f.*

lintel (li'n'-), *n.*, linteau, *m.*

lion (laï'o'n), *n.*, lion, *m.*

lioness (laï'o'n'-), *n.*, lionne, *f.*

lion-hearted (-hârt'-), *adj.*, de lion ; cœur de lion.

lion's-foot (-'z'foute), *n.*, (bot.) pied-de- lion, *m.*

lion's-tail · (-'z'téle), *n.*, (bot.) queue-de- lion, *f.*

lip, *n.*, lèvre, *f.* ; (of things—*des choses*) bord, *m.* ; (of some beasts—*de quelques animaux*) babine, *f.*

lip, *v.a.*, baiser ; embrasser.

lipless, *adj.*, sans lèvres.

lipogram, *n.*, lipogramme, *m.*

lipogrammatic, *or* **lipogrammatical**, *adj.*, lipogrammatique.

lipogrammatist, *n.*, lipogrammatiste, *m.*

lipothymy (-poth'-), *n.*, lipothymie, *f.*

lipped (lip'te), *adj.*, qui a des lèvres ; (bot.) labié. Blubber—; *lippu.*

lippitude (-tioude), *n.*, lippitude, chassie, *f.*

lip-salve (-salve), *n.*, pommade pour les lèvres, *f.*

lip-strap, *n.*, fausse gourmette, *f.*

liquable (li-kwa-b'l), *adj.*, liquéfiable.

liquate (laï-kwéte), *v.a.*, (ant.) fondre, liqué- fier.

liquation (li-kwé-), *n.*, liquation, *f.*

liquefaction (lik'wè-fak'-), *n.*, liquéfaction.

liquefiable (lik'wè-faï-a-b'l), *adj.*, liquéfiable.

liquefier (-faï'eur), *n.*, chose qui liquéfie, *f.*

liquefy (lik'wè-fa'yé), *v.a.*, liquéfier, fondre.

liquefy, *v.n.*, se liquéfier.

liquescency (li-kwès'-), *n.*, fusibilité, *f.*

liquescent, *adj.*, fusible.

liquid (lik'wide), *n.*, (substance) liquide, *m.* ; (gram.) liquide, *f.*

liquid, *adj.*, liquide, doux, coulant ; (of the letter L—*de la lettre L*) mouillé.

liquidate (lĭk'wĭ-déte), *v.a.*, tirer au clair ; adoucir ; (com.) liquider, solder.

liquidation ('-wĭ-dé-), *n.*, liquidation ; action de solder, *f.*

liquidity, *or* **liquidness**, *n.*, liquidité, *f.*

liquor (lĭk'eur), *n.*, liqueur, *f.*

liquor, *v.a.*, mouiller ; arroser.

liquorice, *n. V.* **licorice.**

lisp, *n.*, action de parler du bout des dents, *f.* ; grasseyement, *m.*

lisp, *v.a.* and *n.*, prononcer, parler du bout des dents ; grasseyer, bégayer, balbutier.

lisper, *n.*, personne qui parle du bout des dents, *f.* ; grasseyeur, *m.*, grasseyeuse, *f.*

lisping, *adj.*, qui parle du bout des dents ; qui balbutie, qui grasseye.

lispingly, *adv.*, en parlant du bout des dents ; en balbutiant, en grasseyant.

list, *n.*, liste ; (arena—*champ*) lice, arène, *f.* ; (nav.) faux côté, *m.* ; (selvage of cloth—*bord d'étoffe*) lisière, *f.* ; (arch.) listel, *m.* ; (limit) limite, barrière, *f.*. Civil —; *liste civile.*

list, *v.a.*, garnir de lisière ; (to enrol—*mettre sur le rôle*) enrôler, enregistrer ; écouter ; faire attention ; enclore un terrain pour un tournoi, un combat, &c.

list, *v.n.*, s'engager ; s'enrôler ; (to choose—*choisir*) vouloir, désirer.

listed (list'éde), *adj.*, rayé, à raies.

listel, *n.*, (arch.) listel, *m.*

listen (lis's'n), *v.a.* and *n.*, écouter.

listener (lis's'neur), *n.*, auditeur ; écouteur, *m.*

listless (list'less), *adj.*, nonchalant ; insouciant ; inattentif.

listlessly (list'-), *adv.*, nonchalamment ; avec insouciance ; inattentivement.

listlessness (list'-), *n.*, nonchalance, insouciance ; inattention, *f.*

list-shoe (-shou), *n.*, chausson, *m.*

litany, *n.*, litanie, *f.*

literal (lĭt'èr'-), *adj.*, littéral ; par des lettres.

literality, *n.*, sens littéral, *m.*

literally, *adv.*, littéralement.

literalness. *n.*, littéralité, *f.*

literary (lĭt'èr'-), *adj.*, littéraire, lettré.

literati (lĭt'èr'é-ta'ye), *n.pl.*, hommes de lettres, littérateurs ; savants, *m.pl.*

literature (lĭt'èr'a'-tioure), *n.*, littérature, *f.*

litharge (lĭth'adje), *n.*, litharge, *f.*

lithe (laïthe), *adj.*, pliant, flexible, souple.

litheness (laïth'-), *n.*, flexibilité, souplesse, *f.*

lithiasis (li-thaï'a-cice), *n.*, (med.) lithiase, lithiasie, *f.*

lithocolla (lĭth'-), *n.*, lithocolle, *f.*

lithograph (lĭth'-), *v.a.*, lithographier.

lithograph, *n.*, lithographie, *f.*

lithographer, *n.*, lithographe, *m.*

lithographic, *or* **lithographical**, *adj.*, lithographique.

lithographically, *adv.*, par la lithographie.

lithography, *n.*, lithographie, *f.*

lithologic (li-thol'o-djike), *or* **lithological** (-dji-cal), *adj.*, lithologique.

lithologist (li-thol'o-djiste), *n.*, lithologue, *m.*

lithology (li-thol'o-dji), *n.*, lithologie, *f.*

lithontriptic (lĭth'-), *n.*, lithontriptique, *m.*

lithophagous (li-thoph'-), *adj.*, lithophage.

lithophyte (lĭth'o-phaïte), *n.*, lithophyte, *m.*

lithotome (lĭth'-), *n.*, lithotome, *m.*

lithotomic. *adj.*, de, par, la lithotomie.

lithotomist, *n.*, lithotomiste, *m.*

lithotomy, *n.*, lithotomie, *f.*

lithotrity (li-thot-, *ou* lith'o-traï-), *n.*, lithotritie, *f.*

litigant, *n.*, plaideur, *m.*, plaideuse, *f.*

litigant, *adj.*, en litige, litigant.

litigate, *v.a.*, plaider, disputer.

litigate, *v.n.*, plaider être en procès.

litigation (-ti-ghé-), *n.*, litige, procès, *m.*

litigious (-tĭdj'eusse), *adj.*, litigieux, contentieux ; (pers.) processif.

litigiously, *adv.*, en chicaneur, (l.u.) contentieusement.

litigiousness, *n.*, chicane ; humeur processive, *f.* ; esprit litigieux, *m.*

litorn, *n.*, (orni.) grosse grive, litorne, *f.*

litotes (laï-to-tize), *n.*, (rhet.)litote, exténuation, *f.*

litre (lĭ-teur), *n.*, litre, *m.*

litter, *n.*, (vehicle—*véhicule*) brancard, *m.*, civière, litière ; (of a stable—*d'écurie, &c.*) litière, *f.* ; (b.s.) fumier, fouillis, *m.* ; (of animals—*des animaux*) portée, ventrée, *f.*

litter, *v.a.*, (a stable—*une écurie, &c.*) pourvoir de litière, faire la litière à ; (fig.) mettre en désordre, en fouillis, salir ; (of animals—*des animaux*) mettre bas.

little (lĭt't'l), *n.*, peu, *m.*

little (lĭt't'l), *adj.*, petit, faible, minime, exigu. — one ; *enfant, petit enfant, m.*

little (lĭt't'l), *adv.*, peu, un peu, pas beaucoup, peu de chose, peu de, guère de. But— ; *guère* (with *ne* before a verb). A— : *un peu.* Not a — ; *pas mal, pas peu.* By — and — ; *petit à petit, peu à peu.* As — as possible ; *le moins possible.* Ever so — : *tant soit peu.*

littleness, *n.*, petitesse, *f.*

littoral, *adj.*, maritime, littoral, riverain.

liturgic (lit'eur'djike), *or* **liturgical** (-djik'-), *adj.*, liturgique.

liturgy (lit'eur'dji), *n.*, liturgie.

live (laïve), *adj.*, en vie ; vivant ; vif ; (of coals —*de charbons*) ardent.

live (live), *v.n.*, vivre ; (reside—*résider*) demeurer, habiter. To— away ; *avoir un grand train de maison ; faire bonne chère, faire joyeuse vie.* To — out of the house one is usually occupied in ; *ne pas demeurer à la maison.* To — by ; *vivre de.* To — from hand to mouth ; *vivre au jour le jour, au jour la journée.* To — in London ; *demeurer à Londres, habiter Londres.* To — on, upon ; *vivre de, se nourrir de, subsister de.* To — up to ; *vivre selon.* Enough to — on ; *de quoi vivre.* Long — the Queen ! *vive la Reine !*

live (live), *v.a.*, mener (une vie).

lived (liv'de), *adj.*, de vie. Long — ; *qui vit longtemps, de longue vie.* Short — ; *qui vit peu de temps, d'une courte vie ;* (of things—*des choses*) *passager, qui dure peu de temps.* High— ; *ae haut ton, qui vit grandement.*

livelihood (laïv'li-houde), *n.*, vie, nourriture, subsistance, *f.* ; gagne-pain, *m.*

liveliness (laïv'-), *n.*, vivacité ; gaieté, *f.*

livelong (laïv'-), *adj.*, durable, permanent, long, éternel. The — day ; *tout le long du jour.*

lively (laïv'-), *adj.*, vif, gai, enjoué, animé ; (of place—*lieu*) vivant, gai.

lively (laïv'-), *adv.*, vivement ; gaiement.

liver (liv'eur), *n.*, (anat.) foie ; (pers.) vivant. High — ; *viveur, m., personne qui vit bien, qui fait bonne chère, f.*

liver-coloured (-keul'leurde), *adj.*, rouge foncé.

livery (liv'èr'i), *n.*, livrée ; (of horses—*de chevaux*) pension, *f.* ; (of the city of London—*de la cité de Londres*) notables, électeurs municipaux, *m.pl.* ; (jur.) mise en possession ; (of minors —*des mineurs*) émancipation, *f.* Full — ; *grande livrée.* Undress — ; *petite livrée* (of horses—*des chevaux*). To put out at — ; *mettre en pension.* Out of — ; *sans livrée.*

livery (liv'èr'i), *v.a.*, mettre, habiller en livrée ; galonner.

livery-man (-ma'n), *n.*, homme qui porte la livrée, *f.* ; (of the city of London—*de la cité de Londres*) notable, électeur municipal, *m.*

livery-servant (-seur'-), *n.* domestique en livrée, *m.*

livery-stable (-sté-b'l), *n.*, écurie de chevaux à louer; pension pour les chevaux, *f.*
livery-stable-keeper (-kip'-), *n.*, loueur de chevaux, loueur de voitures, *m.*
livid, *adj.*, livide, pâle.
lividity, *or* **lividness**, *n.*, lividité, *f.*
living (liv'-), *n.*, (ecc.) bénéfice, *m.*, cure, *f*; (livelihood—*vie*) vie, subsistance, existence, *f.* For a —; *pour vivre; pour gagner sa vie.*
living (liv'-), *adj.*, vivant; vif; vivifiant. While —; *de son vivant.* The —(*n.pl.*); *les vivants, m.pl.*
livre (lî-veur), *n.*, ⊙livre, *f.*; franc, *m.*
lixivial, *or* **lixivious**, *adj.*, de lessive, ⊙lixiviel.
lixiviate, *v.a.*, (chem.) lessiver.
lixivium, *n.*, lessive, *f.*
lizard, *n.*, lézard, *m.*
lo! (lô). *int.*, voici, voilà, voyez.
loach (lôtshe), *n.*, (ich.) loche, dormille, *f.*
load (lôde), *n.*, charge, *f.*; fardeau, *m.*; (cartful—*charge de charrette*) charretée; quantité, *f.*
load (lôde), *v.a.*, charger, combler.
loader, *n.*, chargeur.
loading, *n.*, charge, *f.*; (com.) chargement, *m.*
loadsman (lôd'z'-), *n.*, (ant.) pilote côtier, *m.*
loadstone (-stône), *n.*, aimant, *m.*
loaf (lôfe), *n.*, pain, *m.* — of bread; *pain.* —-sugar; *sucre en pain, m.* — of sugar; *pain de sucre.*
loam (lôme), *n.*, marne, *f*; mélange de terre glaise et de sable, *m.*
loam (lôme), *v.a.*, marner.
loamy, *adj.*, argileux, glaiseux, marneux.
loan (lône), *n.*, prêt; emprunt, *m.*
loan (lône), *v.a.*, prêter.
loan-bank, *n.*, mont-de-piété, *m.*
loan-fund, *n.*, caisse d'emprunt, *f.*
loath (lôth), *adj.*, fâché, peiné. To be —; *avoir de la répugnance, être fâché;* (imp.) *répugner.*
loathe (lôthe), *v.a.*, hair; avoir du dégoût pour, de l'aversion pour. I — meat; *la viande me répugne.*
loather (lôth'-), *n.*, personne qui hait, qui a en horreur, qui a du dégoût pour, *f.*
loathful (lôth'foule), *adj.*, dégoûtant.
loathing (lôth'-), *adv.*, dégoût, *m.*; aversion, répugnance, horreur, *f.*
loathingly (lôth'-), *adv.*, à contre-cœur, avec répugnance, avec dégoût, à regret.
loathly (lôth'-), *adj.*, odieux, affreux, dégoûtant.
loathly (lôth'-), *adv.*, à regret, à contre-cœur, avec répugnance.
loathness (lôth'-), *n.*, répugnance, *f.*; dégoût, *m.*
loathsome (lôth'seume), *adj.*, dégoûtant; horrible, odieux.
loathsomeness (lôth'-), *n.*, qualité dégoûtante, *f.*; dégoût, *m.*
lob, *n.*, rustre, lourdaud, butor, *m.*
lob, *v.a.*, laisser tomber.
lobate (lô-), **lobated** (lô-bét'-), *or* **lobed** (lôb'de), *adj.*, lobé.
lobby, *n.*, antichambre, *f.*; couloir; (thea.) foyer, *m.*
lobe (lôbe), *n.*, lobe, *m.*
lobed. *adj.* V. **lobate**.
loblolly-boy (-boi), *n.*, (nav.) infirmier, *m.*
lobsided (-caïd'-), *adj.*, qui a un côté plus lourd que l'autre.
lobster, *n.*, écrevisse de mer, *f.*; homard, *m.*
lobule (lob'ioule), *n.*, (anat.) lobule, *m.*
local (lô-), *adj.*, local.
locality, *n.*, localité, situation, *f.*, endroit, *m.*; existence, *f.*
localization (-'aïzé-), *n.*, localisation, *f.*
localize (lôcal'aïze), *v.a.*, localiser.
locally, *adv.*, localement.

locate (lô-), *v a.*, placer, établir, fixer.
location (lo-ké-), *n.*, situation, *f.*; emplacement, placement, établissement, *m.*
loch (loke), *n.*, (geog.) lac, *m.*
loch (loke), *or* **lohoch** (lô-hoke), *n.*, (pharm.) looch, lok, *m.*
lochia (lo-ki-a), *n.*, lochies, *f.pl.*
lock, *n.*, serrure, *f.*; (of a canal—*de canal*) écluse; (of a fire-arm—*d'arme à feu*) platine; (of a pond—*d'étang*) bonde; (of hair—*des cheveux*) touffe, mèche, boucle, *f.*; (of wool—*de laine*) flocon, *m.* Under — and key; *sous clef.* —s; *cheveux, m.pl.; boucles de cheveux, f.pl.* Double —; *serrure à double tour, f.*
lock, *v.a.*, fermer à clef; (print.) serrer; (to clasp—*étreindre*) serrer, presser; (a canal—*un canal*) écluser. To—in; *enfermer, renfermer.* To — one out; *fermer la porte à quelqu'un.* To — up; *serrer, enfermer, tenir sous clef;* (pers.) *mettre au violon, mettre en prison, coffrer;* (print.) *serrer.* To double —; *fermer à double tour.*
lock, *v.n.*, fermer à clef; s'enfermer; (tech.) s'adapter.
lockage (lok'édje), *n.*, écluses, *f.pl.*; péage d'écluse, *m.*
lock-chamber (-tshé'm'-), *n.*, sas d'écluse, *m.*
locked-jaw (lok'te-djô), *or* **lockjaw** (-djô), *n.*, tétanos, trismus, *m.*
locker, *n.*, (nav.) parquet; boulin, *m.*
locket, *n.*, (jewel—*bijou*) médaillon; fermoir, *m.*; agrafe; agrafe de fourreau d'épée, *f.*
lock-gate, *n.*, porte d'écluse, *f.*
lock-keeper (-kip'-), *n.*, éclusier, *m.*
lockram, *n.*, toile grossière, *f.*; locrenan, *m.*
locksmith (-smith), *n.*, serrurier, *m.*
locomotion (lô-co-mô-), *n.*, locomotion, *f.*
locomotive (lô-co-mô-), *adj.*, mobile, locomotif.
locomotive (lô-co-mô-), *n.*, locomotive, *f.*
locust (lô-keuste), *n.*, sauterelle, cigale, locuste, *f.*; (bot.) caroubier, *m.*
locust-tree (-trî), *n.*, faux acacia, robinier, *m.*
lode (lôde), *n.*, filon, *m.*
lodge, *n.*, maisonnette; loge; (of a stag—*du cerf*) reposée; (of wild beasts—*d'animaux sauvages*) tanière; (of freemasons—*de francs-maçons*) loge, *f.*
lodge, *v.a.*, loger; abriter; (to deposit—*faire un dépôt*) déposer; (to throw in—*jeter*) planter; (a complaint—*une plainte*) déposer, porter; (money—*de l'argent*) déposer.
lodge, *v.n.*, loger, se loger. The ball—d in a hillock; *la balle se logea dans un tertre.*
lodger, *n.*, locataire, *m.*, *f.*
lodging, *n.*, logis, logement, *m.*; chambre, *f.*; appartement, *m.* Furnished —s; *chambres garnies, f.pl.; appartement meublé, m. sing.*
lodging-house (-haouce), *n.*, hôtel garni; logis, *m.*
lodgment (lodj'-), *n.*, logement; dépôt, *m.*
loft, *n.*, étage; grenier, *m.*
loftily, *adv.*, haut; (fig.) pompeusement, fièrement, d'une manière sublime.
loftiness, *n.*, hauteur, *f.*; ordre élevé, *m.*; fierté; pompe, sublimité, *f.*
lofty, *adj.*, haut, élevé, sublime; pompeux, fier, altier.
log (loghe), *n.*, souche, bûche, *f.*; (nav.) loch, *m.*
logarithm (-rithme), *n.*, logarithme, *m.*
logarithmetic, **logarithmetical**, **logarithmic**, *or* **logarithmical** (-rith-), *adj*, logarithmique.
log-board (-bôrde), *n.*, (nav.) table de loch, *f.*
logbook (-bouke), *n.*, (nav.) livre de loch; journal de navigation, *m.*
logged (log'de), *adj.*, (nav.). V. **water-logged**.
logger-head (-hède), *n.*, sot, lourdaud, *m.*; bûche, *f.* To fall to —s; *en venir aux mains.*

loggerheaded (-hèd'-), *adj.*, sot, lourd, stupide.

logic (lod'jike), *n.*, logique, *f.*

logical, *adj.*, logique; de la logique.

logically, *adv.*, logiquement.

logician (lod'jish'-), *n.*, logicien, *m.*

logman (log'-), *n.*, porteur de bois; (in America—*en Amérique*) bûcheron, *m.*

logomachy (-go'm'a-ki), *n.*, logomachie, *f.*

logwood (-woude), *n.*, campêche, bois de campêche, *m.*

lohoch, *n.*   *V.* **loch.**

loin (loïne), *n.*, (of meat—*de viande*) longe, *f.* —s; (anat.) lombes, reins, *m.pl.*

loiter (loï-teur), *v.n.*, tarder, traîner, muser; (on the way—*en chemin*) s'amuser en chemin.

loiter, *v.a.*, perdre.

loiterer, *n.*, traînard, musard, flâneur, *m.*

loitering, *n.*, négligence, flânerie, paresse, *f.*

loitering, *adj.*, négligent, fainéant, paresseux, traîneur, lambin.

loiteringly, *adv.*, en paresseux, en fainéant.

loll, *v.n.*, s'étaler; se pencher, s'appuyer; (of the tongue—*de la langue*) pendre.

loll, *v.a.*, laisser pendre; tirer.

lollipop, *n.*, sucre d'orge, *m.*

lone (lône), *adj.*, isolé, solitaire; délaissé.

loneliness, *n.*, solitude, *f.*; isolement, *m.*

lonely, *adj.*, solitaire; isolé.

loneness, *n.*, solitude, *f.*

lonesome (-seume), *adj.*, solitaire.

lonesomeness, *n.*, solitude, *f.*

long (lon'gn), *v.n.*, avoir bien envie; tarder. I — to go there; *j'ai bien envie, il me tarde d'y aller.* To — for; *soupirer après; avoir un grand désir de.*

long, *adj.*, long; étendu. To be three feet —; *avoir trois pieds de long, être long de trois pieds.* In the — run; *à la longue.* A — time; *longtemps, depuis longtemps, pendant longtemps.*

long, *adv.*, fort; (of time—*de temps*) longtemps, longuement; depuis longtemps; pendant longtemps; le long de; durant. A — extended line; *une ligne fort étendue.* How — have you been here? *combien de temps y a-t-il que vous êtes ici?* Have you been here — ? *y a-t-il longtemps que vous êtes ici?* All night —; *tout le long de la nuit.* Ere — ; *bientôt, avant peu.* — ago; *il y a longtemps, depuis longtemps.* Not — ago; *il n'y a pas longtemps.* All one's life —; *toute sa vie durant.* Not — before; *peu de temps avant.* Not — after; *peu de temps après.* Before —; *avant peu, sous peu, bientôt.*

longanimity, *n.*, longanimité, *f.*

longboat (-bôte), *n.*, chaloupe, *f.*

longe (leu'n'dje), *n.*, (man.) longe; (fenc.) botte, *f.*

longe (leu'n'dje), *v.n.*, (man.) mettre à la longe; (fenc.) pousser une botte.

longer (lon'gh'eur), *n.*, personne qui a un grand désir, *f.*

long-established (-ès-tab'lish'te), *adj.*, établi depuis longtemps.

longeval, *or* **longevous** (-dji-), *adj.*, qui vit longtemps.

longevity (-djè'v'-), *n.*, longévité, *f.*

longe-whip (leu'n'dj'houipe), *n.*, (man.) chambrière, *f.*

long-forgotten, *adj.*, oublié depuis longtemps.

longimetry (-djim'è-), *n.*, (geom.) longimétrie, *f.*

longing (lon'gh'-), *n.*, désir ardent, *m.*; envie, passion, *f.*

longingly (lon'gh'-), *adv.*, avec ardeur, passionnément.

longish (lon'gh'-), *adj.*, passablement long.

longitude (-dji-tioude), *n.*, longitude, *f.* — in; (nav.) *longitude arrivée.* — by account; *longitude estimée.* — by time-keeper; *longitude*

par le chronomètre. — by lunar observations; *longitude observée.* Board of —; *bureau des longitudes, m.*

longitudinal (-dji-tiou-), *adj.*, longitudinal.

longitudinally, *adv.*, longitudinalement.

long-legged (-lèg'de), *adj.*, à longues jambes.

long-lived (-liv'de), *adj.*, qui vit longtemps; qui dure longtemps, de longue durée.

long-lost, *adj.*, perdu depuis longtemps.

longness (lon'g'nèce), *n.*, (ant.) longueur, *f.*

long-sighted (-saït'-), *adj.*, à longue vue; qui a une longue vue; (med.) presbyte.   I am —; *j'ai la vue longue.*

long-sightedness, *n.*, longue vue; presbytie, *f.*

long-sufferance (-seuf'-), *n.*, patience, clémence, *f.*

long-suffering, *n.*, longanimité, patience, *f.*

long-suffering, *adj.*, plein de longanimité; endurant, patient.

longways (-wèze), *or* **longwise** (-waïze), *adv.*, en long.

long-winded, *adj.*, de longue haleine.

loo (lou), *n.*, (card game—*jeu de cartes*) mouche, *f.*

loobily (lou-), *adj.*, niais, nigaud.

looby (lou-), *n.*, nigaud, niais, sot, *m.*

loof (leufe), *n.*, (nav.) lof, *m.*

loof (leufe), *v.n.*, (nav.) venir au lof.

look (louke), *n.*, regard, air, *m.*; apparence, *f.*; coup d'œil, *m.* To give a — in; *faire une petite visite; entrer en passant.* Good —s; *bonne mine, f. sing.*

look, *v.a.*, regarder. To — down; *contenir par des regards; dompter par des regards.* To — out; *chercher.* To — over; *jeter un coup d'œil sur; parcourir des yeux;* (a lesson—*une leçon*) *repasser;* (any one's shoulder—*par dessus les épaules*) *regarder par dessus les épaules.* To — any one in the face; *regarder quelqu'un en face.*

look, *v.n.*, regarder. To — about; *regarder autour de soi; avoir l'œil ouvert.* To — after; *regarder à; chercher; soigner; veiller à.* To — at; *regarder.* To — away; *détourner ses regards.* To — back; *regarder en arrière;* (fig.) *jeter un regard rétrospectif.* To — down; *regarder en bas; baisser les yeux.* To — for; *chercher;* (to expect —*espérer*) *s'attendre à.* To — forward; *regarder devant soi;* (fig.) *attendre avec impatience.* To — forward to; *s'attendre à.* To — in; *faire une petite visite, entrer en passant.* To — into; *regarder dans;* (fig.) *examiner.* To — on; *regarder; considérer; donner sur; être spectateur.* To — over; *regarder par dessus;* (fig.) *fermer les yeux sur.* To — to; *veiller à; avoir soin de; prendre garde à; s'adresser à.* To — through; *regarder à travers; parcourir.* To — up; *regarder en haut; lever les yeux; relever la tête;* (com.) *être en voie de hausse.* To — any one up; *aller voir quelqu'un.* To — anything up; *chercher quelque chose.* To — up to; *regarder; mettre son espoir en; compter sur; se reposer sur.* To — down upon any one; *regarder quelqu'un du haut de sa grandeur.* To — ill; *avoir mauvaise mine; avoir l'air malade.* That —s ill; *cela a mauvaise apparence.* To — well; *avoir bonne mine; avoir l'air bien portant;* (of things—*des choses*) *avoir une belle apparence.* To — like; *avoir l'air de; ressembler; être ressemblant.* Our house —s on the river; *notre maison donne sur la rivière.* — sharp; *dépêchez-vous.* To — out; *être sur ses gardes; avoir l'œil au guet;* (milit.) *être en observation;* (nav.) *être en vigie.* To — out of; *regarder par.* To — upon; *regarder; considérer.*

looker, *n.*, regardant, *m.* — on; *spectateur, assistant, m.*

looking, *n.*, action de regarder, *f.*; regard, *m.*

looking-glass (-glâce), *n.*, miroir, *m.*; glace, *f.*

look-out (-aoute), *n.*, vue. *f.*; guet, *m.*; (nav.) découverte, vigie, *f.* To keep a —; avoir l'œil au guet.

loom (loume), *n.*, métier de tisserand; (of an oar—*de rame*) manche, *m.*

loom, *v.n.*, paraître; (nav.) être en mirement.

loom-gale (-ghéle), *n.*, (nav.) petit vent frais, *m.*

looming, *n.*, mirage, *m.*

loon (loune), *n.*, coquin, drôle, chenapan; (orni.) plongeon imbrim, grand plongeon, *m.*

loop (loupe), *n.*, bride, *f.*; (tech.) tenon; nœud coulant, *m.*

loophole (-hôl), *n.*, trou, *m*; ouverture; (in a ship, in a wall—*dans un vaisseau, un mur*) meurtrière; (fig.) échappatoire, défaite, *f.*

loopholed (-hôld), *adj.*, troué; à meurtrières.

loose (louce), *n.*, liberté, *f.*

loose (louce), *adj.*, délié, détaché, défait; ample; peu serré; qui n'est pas ferme; (fig.) relâché, lâche, vague, peu rigide; décousu, sans liaison; (b.s.) licencieux, libre.

loose (louce), *v.a.*, détacher; délier; relâcher; délivrer, lâcher.

loosely *adv.*, librement; lâchement; négligemment; vaguement; (b.s.) licencieusement.

loosen (lous's'n), *v.a.*, détendre, lâcher, relâcher, délier; détacher; défaire; desserrer.

looseness, *n.*, état desserré; état détendu; relâchement; caractère vague; caractère lâche, *m.*; (b.s.) licence, *f.*; (med.) dévoiement, cours de ventre, *m.*

loosestrife (-straïfe), *n.*, (bot.) lysimaque, lysimachie, *f.*

lop (lope), *n.*, élagage, ébranchement, *m.*

lop, *v.a.*, élaguer, émonder, ébrancher.

lopper, *n.*, élagueur, *m.*

loquacious (lo-kwé-), *adj.*, loquace.

loquacity (-kwass'-), *n.*, loquacité, *f.*

lord (lorde), *n.*, seigneur; maître, *m.* Our —; notre Seigneur, *m.*

lord, *v.n.*, dominer, faire le maître. To — it over any one; *tyranniser quelqu'un.*

lordlike (-laïke), *adj.*, de seigneur; noble.

lordliness, *n.*, dignité; hauteur, *f.*; orgueil, *m.*

lordling, *n.*, petit seigneur, gentillâtre, *m.*

lordly, *adj.*, de seigneur; noble; arrogant, altier, fier.

lordly, *adv.*, en seigneur; avec arrogance.

lordship, *n.*, pouvoir, *m.*; seigneurie, *f.*

lore (lôre), *n.*, savoir, *m.*; science, doctrine, *f.*

loricate, *v.a.*, enduire.

lorication, *n.*, action d'enduire, *f.*

lorimer, *n.*, (ant.) sellier, harnacheur, *m.*

loriot, *n.*, (orni.) loriot, *m.*

losable (louz'a-b'l), *adj.*, perdable.

lose (louze), *v.a.* and *n.* (preterit and past part, Lost), perdre. To — any one anything; faire perdre quelque chose à quelqu'un. To — by; perdre à; (in value—*valeur*) perdre de sa valeur.

loser (louz'eur), *n.*, personne qui perd, *f.*; (at play—*au jeu*) perdant, *m.*

loss, *n.*, perte, *f.*; (hunt.) défaut, *m.* At a —; dans l'embarras; embarrassé; (hunt.) en défaut.

lot, *n.*, sort, destin, *m.*, destinée; (quantity—*quantité*) quantité, grande quantité, *f.*; (of persons—*de personnes*) tas; (at a sale—*à une vente*) lot, *m.*; (com.) partie, *f.* To draw —s; tirer au sort. By —; par le sort; au sort.

lot, *v.a.*, assigner; lotir.

lote (lôte), *n.*, (bot.) jujubier; lotus, lotos, *m.*; (ich.) lotte, *f.*

lotion (lô-), *n.*, lotion, *f.*

lottery, *n.*, loterie, *f.*

lotting, *n.*, (com.) lotissement, *m.*

loud (laoude), *adj.*, haut; élevé, éclatant; fort, grand; bruyant. In a — voice; à haute voix.

loudly, *adv.*, haut; fort; hautement, à haute voix; avec grand bruit; d'une manière éclatante.

loudness, *n.*, force, *f.*; bruit; retentissement, *m.*

lounge (laou'n'dje), *v.n.*, badauder, flâner; vivre dans la paresse; être couché, être étendu. To — away; passer en flânant.

lounge, *n.*, (stroll—*flânerie*) promenade; (gait—*allure*) démarche nonchalante, *f.* (place —*lieu*) rendez-vous, *m.*

lounger, *n.*, badaud, flâneur, *m.*

lounging-chair (-tshére), *n.*, bergère, *f.*

louse (laouce), *n.* (lice), pou, *m.*

louse (laouze), *v.a.*, épouiller.

lousewort (laouss'weurte), *n.*, pédiculaire; herbe aux poux, *f.*

lousily (laouz'-), *adv.*, en pouilleux.

lousiness (laouz'-), *n.*, état pouilleux, *m.*

lousy (laouz'-), *adj.*, pouilleux.

lout (laoute), *n.*, rustre, benêt, butor, *m.*

loutish, *adj.*, benêt, rustre.

loutishly, *adv.*, en benêt, en rustre.

lovable (leuv'a-b'l), *adj.*, digne d'être aimé; aimable.

lovage (leuv'adje), *n.*, (bot.) angélique à feuilles d'ache, *f.*

love (leuve), *v.a.*, aimer, chérir, affectionner.

love (leuve), *n.*, amour, *m.*; amitié, *f.*; (term of endearment—*terme d'affection*) amour, ami, *m.*, amie, *f.* For —; par amour. To play for —; jouer pour rien, pour le plaisir. To be in —; être amoureux. To be in — with; être amoureux de, être épris de. To make — to; faire la cour à. To fall in — with; devenir amoureux de, devenir épris de. Give her my —; faites-lui mes amitiés.

love-apple (-ap'p'l), *n.*, tomate; pomme d'amour, *f.*

love-knot (-note), *n.*, lac d'amour, nœud, *m.*

loveless, *adj.*, sans amour; insensible.

love-letter (-let'teur), *n.*, billet doux, poulet, *m.*

love-lies-a-bleeding (leuv'laïz'é-blid'-), *n.*, (bot.) amarante, *f.*

lovelily, *adv.*, avec amabilité.

loveliness, *n.*, amabilité; beauté, nature ravissante, *f.*

lovelorn, *adj.*, abandonnée de son amant; abandonné de son amante; délaissé.

lovely, *adj.*, aimable, charmant, séduisant, gracieux, joli, beau; digne d'amour.

love-making (-mék'-), *n.*, cour, *f.*; assiduités, *f.pl.*

love-potion (-pô-), *n.*, philtre, *m.*

lover, *n.*, amant, *m.*, amante, *f.*; ami, *m.*, amie, *f.*; amoureux; amateur, *m.*

love-secret (-sè-krète), *n.*, secret d'amour, *m.*

lovesick, *adj.*, malade d'amour.

lovesong, *n.*, chanson d'amour, *f.*; romance, *f.*

lovesuit (-sioute), *n.*, cour, *f.*; assiduités, *f.pl.*

love-tale (-téle), *n.*, histoire galante, *f.*; roman, *m.*

love-thought (-thôte), *n.*, pensée d'amour; pensée amoureuse, *f.*

love-token, *n.*, gage d'amour, *m.*

lovetrick, *n.*, amourette, *f.*

loving, *adj.*, aimant, affectueux, qui aime; (of things—*des choses*) d'amour; affectueux.

loving-kindness (-kaï'n'd'-), *n.*, bonté, miséricorde, *f.*

lovingly, *adv.*, avec amour; tendrement; affectueusement.

low (lô), *adj.*, bas; peu élevé; profond; petit; faible; commun; vulgaire; (of fever—*de fièvres*) lent; (in spirits—*du moral*) abattu. In a — voice; d'une voix faible; à voix basse. To bring —; affaiblir.

low, *adv.*, bas; profondément; à voix basse; à bas prix.

low, v.n., beugler, mugir.

low-born, adj., de basse naissance.

low-bred (-brède), adj., mal élevé ; vulgaire.

lower (lô-eur), n., (l.u.) état nébuleux ; air sombre, m.

lower (lô-eur), adj., plus bas ; inférieur ; (geog.) bas.

lower (laou-eur), v.n., (to frown—se refrogner) froncer les sourcils, se refrogner ; (of the weather—du temps) s'assombrir, s'obscurcir, se couvrir ; (fig.) menacer. The sky —s ; le temps se couvre.

lower (lô-eur), v.a., baisser, abaisser ; descendre ; (to humiliate—humilier) rabaisser, humilier, ravaler ; (to diminish—amoindrir) diminuer, affaiblir ; (com.) baisser.

lowering (lô-eur'-), n., abaissement, m. ; diminution, f.

lowering (laou-eur'-), adj., couvert, sombre ; menaçant, refrogné, rechigné. — look ; air refrogné, m. — weather ; temps couvert, m.

loweringly (laou-eur'-), adv., d'un air refrogné, tristement ; d'une manière sombre, menaçante.

lowermost (lô-eur-môste), or **lowest** (lô-èste), adj., le plus bas.

lowery (laou-euri), adj., nébuleux, triste ; sombre.

lowing (lô'igne), n., mugissement, beuglement, m.

lowland (lô-), n., pays bas ; terrain bas, bas-fond, m. ; plaine, f.

lowliness (lô-), n., humilité ; bassesse, petitesse, f.

lowly (lô-), adj., humble ; bas, vil.

lowly (lô-), adv., humblement, bassement.

lown (laou'ne), n., vaurien, drôle, m.

lowness (lô-nèce), n., situation basse ; petitesse ; profondeur ; (mus.) gravité ; (weakness—défaut de force) faiblesse, f. ; (of spirits—du moral) abattement, m. ; (humility—humilité) humilité ; (vulgarity—vulgarité) vulgarité, bassesse, f. The — of the price ; le bas prix.

low-priced (-praïs'te), adj., à bas prix.

low-spirited, adj., abattu, triste.

low-spiritedness, n., tristesse, mélancolie, f.

low-water (-wô-), n., marée basse, f.

loxodromic, adj., loxodromique.

loxodromics, n.pl., loxodromie, f.

loyal (lo'yal), adj., attaché au gouvernement, au souverain, fidèle.

loyalist, n., personne attachée au gouvernement, au souverain, f.

loyally, adv., fidèlement.

loyalty, n., attachement au gouvernement, au souverain, m. ; fidélité, f.

lozenge (loz'è'n'dje), n., pastille ; (pharm.) tablette, pastille ; (geom., her.) losange, m.

lozenged (-'è'n'dj'de), adj., en losange.

lubber (leub'-), n., lourdaud, rustre, manant, paltoquet ; (nav.) marin d'eau douce, m.

lubberly, adj., grossier, maladroit, gauche.

lubberly, adv., en lourdaud ; grossièrement.

lubric, or **lubrical** (liou-), adj., (slippery—coulant) glissant ; (unsteady—volage) inconstant ; (lewd—lascif) lubrique.

lubricant (liou-), n., chose qui lubrifie, f.

lubricate (liou-), v.a., adoucir.

lubricator (liou-bri-két'eur), n., chose qui lubrifie, qui adoucit, f.

lubricity (liou-), n., nature glissante ; inconstance ; lubricité, f.

lubrifaction (liou-bri-fak-), or **lubrification** (-fi-ké-), n., lubrification, f.

luce (-liouce), n., lis ; (ich.) brochet, m.

lucent (liou-), adj., (ant.) luisant, brillant.

lucern (liou-), n., (bot.) luzerne, f.

lucid (liou-), adj., lucide ; lumineux ; limpide, transparent.

lucidly, adv., lucidement, clairement.

lucidness, or **lucidity**, n., transparence, limpidité, lucidité, clarté, f. ; éclat, m.

lucifer (liou-), n., (astron.) lucifer, m ; (match—allumette) allumette chimique, f.

luciferian, adj., de Lucifer.

luciferous, adj., qui éclaire.

luck (leuke), n., hasard ; bonheur, m. ; fortune, chance, f. Good- — ; bonne fortune, f. ; bonheur, m. Ill- — ; mauvaise fortune, f. ; malheur, m. By good- — ; par bonheur. By ill- — ; par malheur. Pot- — ; la fortune du pot, f.

luckily, adv., heureusement, par bonheur.

luckiness, n., bonheur, m.

luckless, adj., malheureux.

lucky, adj., heureux ; (of things—des choses) heureux, propice, favorable.

lucrative (liou-), adj., lucratif.

lucratively, adv., lucrativement.

lucre (liou-keur), n., lucre, m.

lucubrate (liou-kiou-), v.n., travailler de nuit, veiller.

lucubration, n., élucubration, f.

lucubratory, adj., d'élucubration ; nocturne.

luculent (liou-kiou-), adj., limpide, clair ; évident.

ludicrous (liou-), adj., plaisant, risible.

ludicrously, adv., plaisamment, risiblement.

ludicrousness, n., plaisant, m. ; plaisanterie, f.

luff (leufe), v.n., (nav.) venir au lof, lofer.

luff, n., (nav.) lof, m. ; aulofée, f.

lug (leughe), n., (pop.) chose lourde à tirer, f. ; fardeau, m.

lug, v.a., traîner ; tirer ; tirailler. To — out ; tirer, tirer dehors ; faire sortir ; (a sword—une épée) dégainer, mettre flamberge au vent.

lug, v.n., traîner ; se traîner.

luggage (leug'ghédje), n., bagage ; attirail, m.

lugger (leug'gheur), n., (nav.) lougre, chasse-marée, m.

lugubrious (liou-ghiou-), adj., lugubre.

lukewarm (liouk'wôrme), adj., tiède.

lukewarmly, adv., tièdement.

lukewarmness, n., tiédeur, f.

lull (leule), v.a., endormir ; bercer ; assoupir ; calmer. To — to sleep ; endormir.

lull, v.n., se calmer.

lull, n., chose qui endort, f. ; calmant, m.

lullaby (leul'la-ba'ye), n., chanson pour endormir les enfants, f.

luller (leul'-), n., personne qui endort par des chants, f. ; endormeur, m.

lulling (leul'-), adj., endormant, calmant.

lumachel (liou-ma-kèle), n., lumachelle, f.

lumbago (leu'm'bé-go) n., lumbago, m. ; courbature, f.

lumbar (leu'm'-), adj., lombaire.

lumber (leu'm'-), n., gros meubles, m. ; vieilleries, f.pl. ; rebut, fatras, m.

lumber, v.a., entasser sans ordre ; remplir de fatras.

lumber, v.n., se traîner lourdement.

lumber-house (-haouce), **lumber-room** (-roume), n., décharge, f. ; grenier, m.

lumbering, n., action d'entasser sans ordre, de remplir de fatras, de vieilleries, f.

lumbrical (leu'm'-), adj., lombrical.

luminary (liou-), n., corps lumineux ; luminaire ; flambeau, m.

luminous (liou-), adj., lumineux.

luminously, adv., d'une manière lumineuse.

luminousness, n., propriété lumineuse ; clarté ; lucidité, f.

lump (leu'm'pe), n., masse, f. ; morceau ; bloc ; monceau, m. — -sugar ; sucre en pain, m. — of sugar ; morceau de sucre. In the — ; en gros, en bloc.

lump, v.a., mettre en bloc ; mettre en masse.
lumper, n., ouvrier déchargeur du port, m.
lumping, adj., gros ; pesant.
lumpish, adj., gros, épais, lourd, grossier.
lumpishly, adv., lourdement; grossièrement.
lumpishness, n., lourdeur ; grossièreté, f.
lumpy, adj., grumeleux, plein de grumeaux.
lunacy (liou-), n., folie, démence ; aliénation mentale, f. Commission de — ; *conseil de famille, m. ; jury d'examen pour cas d'aliénation mentale*, f.
lunar (liou-), adj., lunaire ; en forme de lune.
lunarian (liou-), n., habitant de la lune.
lunary (liou-), n., (bot.) lunaire, f.
lunate, or **lunated** (liou-), adj., en demilune.
lunatic (liou-), adj., de fou, d'aliéné.
lunatic (liou-), n., aliéné, m., aliénée, f. ; fou, m., folle, f.
lunation (liou-né-), n., lunaison, f.
lunch(leu'n'sh),or **luncheon**(leu'n'sh'eune), n., second déjeuner. goûter, m.
lunch, v.n., faire son second déjeuner ; goûter.
lune (lioune), n., croissant, m., (geom.) lunule ; (leash—*attache*) laisse, f.
lunette (liou-), n., lunette, f.
lung (leun'gn), n., poumon, m. ; (of the calf, &c.—*du veau*, &c.) mou. m.
lunge, n., (fenc.) botte, f.
lunge (leu'n'dje), v.n., (fenc.) porter une botte.
lunged (leun'gn'de),adj.,nourvu de poumons.
lung-grown (-grône), adj., (med.) qui a les poumons adhérents à la plèvre.
lungwort (-weurte), n., (bot.) pulmonaire ; épervière des murailles, f.
luniform (liou-), adj., en lune ; luniforme.
lunisolar (liou-ni-çô-), adj., luni-solaire.
lunt (leu'n'te), n., (artil.) mèche, f.
lupine (liou-païne), n., (bot.) lupin, m.
lurch (leurtshe), n., (nav.) embardée, f.; coup de gouvernail, m. ; (at tricktrack—*au trictrac*) bredouille, partie double, f. To leave in the — ; *faire faux bond à ; planter là ; laisser dans l'embarras*.
lurch (leurtshe), v.n., jouer de ruse ; (nav.) faire des embardées, s'embarder.
lurcher, n., personne aux aguets, f. ; (dog—*chien*) chien qui guette et saisit le gibier ; glouton, gourmand, m.
lure (lioure), n., leurre, appât, m. ; amorce, f.
lure (lioure), v.a., leurrer, amorcer, attirer ; (hawking—*fauconnerie*) appeler.
lurid (liou-), adj., sombre ; lugubre.
lurk (leurke), v.n., être aux aguets ; être en embuscade, se tenir caché.
lurker, n., personne aux aguets, personne en embuscade, personne qui se cache, f.
lurking, adj., d'embuscade ; aux aguets.
lurking (leurk'-), n., aguets, m.pl. ; embuscade, f.
lurking-place, n., embuscade ; cachette, f.
luscious (leush'eusse), adj., mielleux, très sucré ; très succulent ; délicieux.
lusciously, adv., avec douceur ; délicieusement.
lusciousness, n., nature très succulente ; excessive douceur, f.
lusorious (liou-co-), or **lusory** (liou-co-), adj., amusant.
lust (leuste), n., désir, m., convoitise, impudicité, luxure, f.
lust (leuste), v.n., convoiter ; désirer immodérément.
lustful (-foule), adj., convoiteux, impudique, luxurieux.
lustfully, adv., avec convoitise; impudiquement ; avec luxure.
lustfulness, n., convoitise. impudicité, luxure, f.

lustily (leust'-), adv., vigoureusement.
lustiness, n., vigueur, f. ; embonpoint, m.
lusting (leust'-), (ant.). V. **lust**.
lustless (leust'-), adj., sans vigueur, sans force.
lustral, or **lustrical** (leus-), adj., lustral.
lustrate (leus'-), v.a., (ant.) purifier.
lustration (leus-tré-), n., lustration, f.
lustre (leus'teur), n., (gloss—*éclat*) lustre, brillant ; (chandelier) lustre, candélabre ; (space of time—*espace de temps*) lustre ; (fig.) éclat, m., splendeur, f.
lustring (leus'-), n., taffetas, m.
lustrous (leus'-), adj., brillant, lustré.
lusty (leust'i), adj., vigoureux, robuste, fort ; copieux.
lutanist (liout'-), n., joueur de luth, m.
lute (lioute), n., (mus.) luth ; (chem.) lut, m.
lute (lioute), v.a., (chem.) luter.
lute-maker (-mék'-), n., luthier, m.
lutheran (liou-theur-), adj., luthérien.
lutheran (liou-theur-), n., luthérien, m., luthérienne, f.
lutheranism (liou-theur'a'n'iz'me), n., luthéranisme, m.
luthern (liou-theurne), n., (arch.) lucarne, f.
luting (liout'-), n., (chem.). V. **lute**.
lutist (liout'-), n., joueur de luth, m.
lux, or **luxate** (leux'-), v.a., luxer.
luxation (leuks'é-), n., luxation, f.
luxuriance, or **luxuriancy** (leux'ziou-), n., exubérance, surabondance, luxuriance, f.
luxuriant (leux'ziou-), adj., exubérant, surabondant, fort riche, luxuriant.
luxuriantly (leux'ziou-), adv., avec exubérance ; avec grande abondance.
luxuriate (leux'ziou-), v.n., croître avec abondance ; être en pleine fertilité. To — in ; *se livrer avec abandon à*.
luxurious (leuks'iou-), adj., de luxe, somptueux ; adonné au luxe ; voluptueux, luxurieux.
luxuriously (leuks'iou-), adv., avec luxe ; somptueusement; voluptueusement ; luxurieusement.
luxuriousness (leuks'iou-), n., luxe, m. ; luxure, volupté, f.
luxurist (leuks'iou-), n., personne qui aime le luxe, f.
luxury (leuks'iou-ri), n., luxe, m. ; somptuosité ; volupté, luxure, f.
lycanthropy (laï-ca'n'thro-), n., lycanthropie, f.
lyceum (laï-ci-), n., lycée, m.
lychnis (lik'-), n., lychnis, m.; croix de Jérusalem, f.
lycopodium (laï-co-pô-), n., (bot.) lycopode, m.
lydian, adj., lydien.
lye (la'ye), n., lessive, f.
lye-trough (-trofe), n., baquet à lessive, m.
lying (la'yigne), n., mensonge, m.
lying, adj., menteur ; (of things—*des choses*) mensonger.
lying-in, n. sing., couches, f.pl. — hospital ; *hospice pour les femmes en couches; hospice de la maternité*, m.
lyingly, adv., mensongèrement.
lying to (la'yign'tou), part., (nav.) en panne.
lymph (li'm'fe), n., lymphe, f.
lymphate, or **lymphated** (-féte, -'ède), adj., (ant.) fou de peur ; fou, furieux.
lymphatic (-fat'-), adj., lymphatique.
lymphatic, n., vaisseau lymphatique, m.
lymphe-duct (-deuk'te), n., vaisseau lymphatique, m.
lynx (li'n'kse), n., lynx, m.
lynx-eyed (-a'ye'-de), adj., aux yeux de lynx.
lyre (laeur), n., lyre, f.
lyric, or **lyrical** (liz'-), adj., lyrique.

lyric, *n.*, lyrique, poème lyrique, *m.*
lyricism (-ciz'-me), *n.*, ouvrage lyrique, *m.*
lyrist (laeur'-), *n.*, joueur de lyre, *m.*

M

m, treizième lettre de l'alphabet, *m.*, *f.*
mab, *n.*, Mab, reine des fées ; saligaude, *f.*
mab, *v.n.*, s'habiller négligemment.
macadamize (-'aïze), *v.a.*, macadamiser.
macaroni (-rô-), *n.*, macaroni ; (fop—*fat*) fat, petit-maître, *m.*
macaronic, *adj.*, macaronique.
macaronic, *n.*, macaronée, *f.*
macaroon (-roune), *n.*, macaron, *m.*
macaw-tree (-cô-tri), *n.*, cocotier du Brésil, *m.*
mace (méce), *n.*, masse, *f.* ; macis, *m.*
mace-bearer (-bèr'-), *n.*, massier, bedeau, *m.*
macerate, *v.a.*, amaigrir ; macérer.
maceration (-'eur'é-), *n.*, amaigrissement, *m.* ; macération, *f.*
machiavelian (mak'-), *adj.*, machiavélique.
machiavelism, *n.*, machiavélisme, *m.*
machicolation (matsh'i-co-lé-), *n.*, (fort.) mâchicoulis, *m.*
machinal (mak'-, *ou* ma-shi-), *adj.*, machinal.
machinate, *v.a.*, machiner.
machination (mak'i-né-), *n.*, machination, *f.*
machinator (mak'i-né-), *n.*, machinateur, *m.*
machine (ma-shine), *n.*, machine ; mécanique, *f.* ; instrument ; (poet.) merveilleux, *m.*
machine-factory, *n.*, atelier de construction de machines, *m.*
machine-made, *adj.*, fait à la mécanique ; à la mécanique.
machine-minder (-maï'n'd'-), *n.*, surveillant de machine, *m.*
machinery (ma-shï'n'euri), *n.*, mécanique, *f* ; mécanisme, *m.* ; machines, *f.pl.* ; (poet.) merveilleux, *m.*
machinist (ma-shï'n'-), *n.*, machiniste, *m.*
mackerel (mak'eur'èl), *n.*, maquereau, *m.*
mackle (mak'l), *n.*, (print.) maculature, *f.*
macle (mé'k'l), *n.*, (min.) macle, macre, *f.*
mactation (mak'té-), *n.*, immolation, *f.*
macula (mak'iou-), *or* **macule** (mak'ioul), *n.* (*maculæ*), tache ; (astron.) macule, *f.*
maculate (mak'iou-), *v.a.*, tacher, gâter, maculer.
maculation (mak'iou-lé-), *n.*, action de tacher ; maculation, *f.*
mad, *v.n.*, être fou.
mad, *adj.*, fou, aliéné, en démence, insensé ; (of animals—*des animaux*) enragé, furieux ; — with any one ; *furieux contre quelqu'un.* — with pain ; *fou de douleur.* — for, after ; *fou de.* To drive —; *faire devenir fou ; faire perdre la tête à.* To go —; *devenir fou ; (of animals—des animaux) devenir enragé.* Raving —; *fou à lier, fou furieux.*
madam, *n.*, madame, *f.*
mad-apple (-ap'p'l), *n.*, (bot.) morelle comestible, mélongène, *f.*
mad-brain (-brène), *or* **mad-brained** (-brè'n'de), *adj.*, écervelé, timbré, fou.
madcap, *n.*, fou, *m.*, folle, *f.* ; écervelé, *m.*, écervelée, *f.*
madcap, *adj.*, étourdi, écervelé ; fou.
madden, *v.a.*, rendre fou ; faire devenir fou ; faire enrager.
madden (mad'd'n), *v.n.*, devenir fou ; tomber en démence.
maddening, *adj.*, à rendre fou ; qui rend fou.
madder (mad'deur), *n.*, garance, *f.*

madder, *v.a.*, garancer.
madder-coloured (-keul'leurde), *adj.*, garancé.
madder-dyeing (-da'yigne), *n.*, garançage, *m.*
madder-dyer (-da'yeur), *n.*, garanceur, *m.*
maddering, *n.*, garançage, *m.*
madder-root (-route), *n.*, alizari, *m.* ; garance, *f.*
madefaction (ma-di-fak-), *n.*, madéfaction, *f.*
madefy (mad'i-fa'ye), *v.a.*, madéfier.
madeira (ma-di-ra, *ou* -dé-), *n.*, vin de Madère, *m.*
mad-headed (-hèd'-), *adj.*, écervelé ; à tête folle.
madhouse (-haouce), *n.*, maison de fous ; maison d'aliénés, *f.* ; petites-maisons, *f.pl.* Private—; *maison particulière de fous, d'aliénés, f.*
madly, *adv.*, follement, furieusement ; en fou.
madman, *n.*, aliéné, insensé, fou, *m.*
madness, *n.*, aliénation mentale, démence, fureur, folie ; (of animals—*des animaux*) rage, *f.*
madonna, *n.*, madone, *f.*
madrepore (mad'ri-pôre), *n.*, madrépore, *m.*
madrier (mad'rire), *n.*, (fort.) madrier, *m.*
madrigal, *n.*, madrigal, *m.*
madwort (-weurte), *n.*, (bot.) globulaire, alysse, *f.*
magazine (-zine), *n.*, (milit.) magasin, *m.* ; (periodical—*écrit périodique*) revue ; (nav.) soute aux poudres, *f.*
maggot, *n.*, larve, *f.* ; asticot ; (whim—*fantaisie*) caprice, *m.*, lubie, quinte, *f.*
maggoty, *adj.*, véreux ; plein de mites, de vers ; (whimsical—*fantasque*) quinteux, capricieux.
magi (mé'dja-ye), *n.pl.*, mages, *m.pl.*
magian (mé-dji-), *n.*, mage, *m.*
magian, *adj.*, des mages.
magianism, *n.*, magisme, *m.*
magic (madj'-), *n.*, magie, *f.*
magic, *or* **magical** (madj'-), *adj.*, magique.
magically, *adv.*, par magie.
magician (ma-djish'-), *n.*, magicien, *m.*, magicienne, *f.*
magisterial (madj'is-ti-), *adj.*, magistral ; de maître ; de magistrat.
magisterially, *adv.*, en maître ; magistralement.
magisterialness, *n.*, ton de maître, ton magistral, *m.*
magistracy (madj'-), *n.*, magistrature, *f.*
magistral (madj'-), *adj.*, (ant.) magistral.
magistrate (madj'-), *n.*, magistrat, juge de paix, *m.*
magistrate, *adj.*, de magistrat.
magna-charta (mag-na-kär-) *n.*, la grande charte ; loi fondamentale, *f.*
magnanimity (mag-na-), *n.*, magnanimité, *f.*
magnanimous (mag-na'n'-), *adj.*, magnanime.
magnanimously, *adv.*, magnanimement.
magnate (mag-néte), *n.*, magnat ; grand, *m.*
magnesia (mag-nî-zi-a), *n.*, magnésie, *f.*
magnesian (mag-nî-zi-), *adj.*, magnésien. — limestone ; *magnésium, m.*
magnet (mag-nète), *n.*, aimant, *m.* ; pierre d'aimant, *f.*
magnetic, *or* **magnetical** (mag-), *adj.*, magnétique ; aimanté ; attractif.
magnetic (mag-), *n.*, aimant, *m.*
magnetically (mag-), *adv.*, par le magnétisme.
magneticalness (mag-), *n.*, propriété magnétique, *f.*
magnetics (mag-), *n.pl.*, science du magnétisme, *f.*
magnetism (mag-nèt'iz'me), *n.*, magné-

tisme, *m.* ; puissance attractive, *f.* Animal —; magnétisme animal, *m.*

magnetize (mag-nèt'aïze), *v.a.*, aimanter ; magnétiser.

magnetize (mag-nèt'aïze), *v.n.*, s'aimanter.

magnific, *or* **magnifical** (mag-), *adj.*, magnifique.

magnifically (mag-), *adv.*, magnifiquement.

magnificence (mag-), *n.*, magnificence, *f.*

magnificent (mag-), *adj.*, magnifique, superbe.

magnificently (mag-), *adv.*, magnifiquement.

magnifico (mag-), *n.*, grand seigneur, *m.*

magnifier (mag-ni-faï'-), *n.*, verre grossissant, *m.* ; personne qui exalte, *f.* ; panégyriste, *m.*

magnify (mag-ni-fa'ye), *v.a.*, magnifier ; grossir ; exalter ; exagérer.

magnifying (mag-ni-fa'yigne), *adj.*, qui grossit ; exagératif. — -glass ; *verre grossissant, m.* ; *loupe, f.*

magniloquence (mag-), *n.*, emphase, *f.* ; style pompeux, *m.*

magniloquent (mag-), *adj.*, emphatique ; pompeux.

magnitude (mag-ni-tioude), *n.*, grandeur ; importance, *f.*

magnolia (mag-nô-), *n.*, (bot.) magnolia, magnolier, *m.*

magpie (-pa'ye), *n.*, pie, *f.*

mahogany, *n.*, acajou ; bois d'acajou ; mahogon, *m.*

mahomedan, *or* **mahometan** (-ho'm'è-), *adj.*, mahométan.

mahomedan, *or* **mahometan** (-ho'm'è-), *n.*, mahométan, *m.*, mahométane, *f.*

mahometanism (-iz'me), *n.*, mahométisme, *m.*

maid (méde), *n.*, vierge ; fille, jeune fille ; (servant—domestique) bonne, servante, domestique, fille, (of an upper class—de classe supérieure)demoiselle, *f.* ; (ich.) ange de mer, *m.* — of all work ; *bonne à tout faire.* Nursery— , nurse— ; *bonne d'enfant, f.* Lady's— ; *femme de chambre, f.* Chamber— ; *fille de chambre, f.* Kitchen— ; *fille de cuisine, f.* House— ; *servante, f.*

maiden (méd'n), *n.*, fille, jeune fille, demoiselle, *f.*

maiden (méd'n), *adj.*, de fille, de jeune fille ; virginal ; de vierge ; (fig.) pur, neuf, vierge ; (of a speech—d'un discours) de début. — name ; *nom de demoiselle, m.* —lady ; demoiselle, *f.*

maiden-hair, *n.*, capillaire, *m.*

maidenhead (méd'n'hède), *or* **maidenhood** (-houde). *n.*, virginité, pureté, *f.*

maiden-like (-laïke), *adj.*, en jeune fille ; pudique.

maidenliness, *n.*, tenue de jeune fille ; pudeur de jeune fille, *f.*

maidenly, *adj.*, virginal ; de jeune fille ; modeste, chaste.

maidenly, *adv.*, en jeune fille ; modestement, avec pudeur ; pudiquement.

maidhood, *n.*, virginité, *f.*

maid-servant (-seurv'-), *n.*, servante, *f.*

mail (méle), *n.*, maille ; (coach—voiture) malle, malle-poste, *f.* ; courrier, *m.* ; (at the post-office—des postes) dépêche, *f.* Coat of — ; *cotte de maille, f.*

mail (méle), *v.a.*, expédier ; mettre une cotte de maille.

mail-bag, *n.*, valise, *f.*

mail-coach (-kôtshe), *n.*, malle-poste, *f.* ; courrier, *m.*

mail-guard (-gârde), *n.*, courrier de la malle, *m.*

mail-packet (-pak'ète), *n.*, paquebot de poste, *m.*

maim (méme), *v.a.*, estropier, mutiler ; (fig.) mutiler, tronquer ; paralyser.

maim, *n.*, perte de l'usage d'un membre ; perte ; mutilation, *f.*

main (méne), *adj.*, principal, premier ; vaste, grand ; important, essentiel. — land ; *continent, m.* — -mast ; grand mât, *m.* — - sail ; *grande voile, f.* — sea ; *haute mer, f.* — - topmast ; *grand mât de hune, m.* — -yard ; *grande vergue, f.*

main (méne), *n.*, (gross—masse) gros, principal ; (ocean) océan ; (continent) continent, *m.* ; (strength—force) force, *f.* ; (duct) grand conduit ; (cock-fight) combat de coqs, *m.* In the — ; *pour la plupart* ; *en général.* With might and — ; *de toutes ses forces.*

mainly, *adv.*, principalement ; puissamment.

mainpernable (mé'n'peur-na-b'l), *adj.*, (jur.) recevable à fournir caution.

mainpernor (-neur), *n.*, (jur.) caution, *f.*

mainprise (mé'n'praïze), *n.*, mise en liberté sous caution, *f.*

mainprise, *v.a.*, mettre en liberté sous caution.

mainswear (mé'n'swère), *v.n.*, se parjurer.

maintain (mé'n'té'n), *v.a.*, maintenir, entretenir ; soutenir ; conserver ; (to keep in food, &c.—soutenir) entretenir.

maintain, *v.n.*, maintenir ; soutenir.

maintainable (-'a-b'l), *adj.*, qui peut être maintenu ; soutenable ; tenable.

maintainer, *n.*, personne qui maintient, qui conserve, qui soutient, qui nourrit, qui entretient, *f.*

maintenance (mé'n'tè'n'-), *n.*, maintien, entretien, soutien, *m.* ; conservation, *f.* ; moyen d'existence, *m.* ; (jur.) pension alimentaire, *f.*

maize (méze), *n.*, maïs, blé de Turquie, *m.*

majestic, *or* **majestical** (ma-djès'-), *adj.*, majestueux.

majestically (ma-djès'-), *adv.*, majestueusement.

majesticalness (ma-djès'-), *n.*, air majestueux, *m.*

majesty (mad'jesté), *n.*, majesté, *f.* His, her — ; *sa majesté, f.*

major (mé-djeur), *adj.*, plus grand ; majeur.

major (mé-djeur), *n.*, (log.) majeure ; (jur.) personne majeure, *f.* ; (of infantry—d'infanterie) chef de bataillon ; (of cavalry—de cavalerie) chef d'escadron, *m.* — -general ; *général de division, lieutenant général, m.* Drum— ; *tambour-major, m.*

majoration (madj'or'é-), *n.*, (ant.) augmentation, *f.*

major-domo (mé-djeur-dô'mô), *n.*, majordome, *m.*

majority (ma-djor'-), *n.*, majorité, *f.* ; (milit.) grade de chef de bataillon, d'escadron, *m.*

make (méke), *n.*, façon, forme, construction, structure ; fabrique ; tournure, *f.* ; complément, *m.*

make (méke), *v.a.* (preterit and past part., Made), faire ; façonner ; (to render) rendre ; (to force—obliger) faire, forcer, contraindre ; (money—de l'argent) faire, amasser, gagner ; (a pen—une plume) tailler ; (to reach—arriver à) gagner, atteindre ; (nav.) découvrir ; (to represent) représenter ; (to fabricate—fabriquer) inventer. To — free with ; (pers.) *traiter sans façon* ; (things—choses) *ne pas se gêner pour se servir de, pour prendre.* To — too free with ; (pers.) *prendre des libertés avec* ; (drink—boisson) *prendre trop de.* To — account of. much of ; *faire grand cas de.* To — a great deal of ; *profiter beaucoup de* ; *tirer beaucoup de profit de.* To — nothing by ; *ne tirer aucun parti de, aucun profit de.* To — out ; (to understand—saisir) *venir à bout de comprendre;* (to discover the meaning of—*découvrir la signification*) *déchiffrer, découvrir;* (to furnish—*pourvoir*) *fournir, produire;* (to prove—*prouver*) *établir;* (to draw up—*dresser*) *rédiger ;* (a bill—*un mémoire*) *dresser.* To — over to; *céder à; transférer à.* To — up; *compléter;* (clothes—*vétements*) *façonner ;* (a quarrel—*une querelle*) *accommoder, arranger ;* (accounts—*des comptes*) *faire régler, établir ;* (to supply—*fournir*) *suppléer à, tenir compte de;* (to compensate—*compenser*) *dédommager de;* (print.) *mettre en pages.* To — it up; *se raccommoder.* To — nothing of; *ne rien comprendre à ;* (not to be scrupulous—*étre sans scrupule*) *ne pas se faire un scrupule de ;* (to find no difficulty in—*ne pas trouver difficile*) *n'avoir aucune difficulté à.* He is not such a fool as you — him; *il n'est pas aussi bête que vous le représentez.* To — ill; *rendre malade.* To — sick; *faire vomir.* To — well; *faire bien ;* (to restore to health—*rendre la santé*) *guérir.* He —s clothes well; *il fait bien les habits; il travaille bien.* To — the bed; *faire le lit.* To — up a lip; *faire la moue.* To — a fool of; *se jouer de.* To — a mistake; *se tromper.* To — land; *découvrir la terre.* To — one's escape; *se sauver.* To — angry; *fâcher.* To — good; *soutenir, prouver, défendre.* To — haste; *se dépécher, se hâter.* To — less; *apetisser, amoindrir.* To—ready; *préparer.* To—again; *refaire.*

make (méke), *v.n.*, (of the tide—*de la marée*) monter. To — at; *s'avancer sur; courir sur; s'élancer sur.* To — away with; *se défaire de; détruire.* To — away with one's self; *se donner la mort, se suicider, se détruire.* To — to; *s'avancer à; se rendre à; se diriger vers.* To — for; *tendre à; favoriser;* (to go to—*se diriger vers*) *aller à, se rendre à;* (to sail to—*se diriger vers*) *faire voile pour.* To — toward; *se diriger vers.* To — as if ; *faire semblant de, avoir l'air de.* To — up to; *s'approcher de; s'avancer vers;* (fig.) *faire des avances à, faire la cour à.* To — up for ; *tenir lieu de ; suppléer à, dédommager, compenser.* To — against; *nuire à.* To — nothing in ; *ne contribuer en rien à ; ne prouver rien en.* This argument — nothing *in* his favour; *cet argument ne prouve rien en sa faveur.* This argument —s against his cause; *cet argument nuit à sa cause.*

makebate, *n.*, brouillon, boutefeu, *m.*
makepeace (-pîce), *n.*, pacificateur, *m.*
maker, *n.*, créateur, faiseur, fabricant, *m.*
maker-up (-eupe), *n.*, (print.) metteur en pages, *m.*
makeshift, *n.*, pis aller; expédient, *m.*
makeweight (-wête), *n.*, complément de poids ; (fig.) remplissage, *m.*
making (mék'-), *n.*, création ; façon ; fabrication ; forme, *f.*
making-up (mék'ign'eupe), *n.*, (print.) mise en pages, *f.*
malachite (-kaïte), *n.*, malachite, *f.*
malacology ('-o-djî), *n.*, malacologie, *f.*
maladministration (-tré-), *n.*, mauvaise administration, maladministration, *f.*
malady (-dî), *n.*, maladie, *f.*
malaga, *n.*, vin de Malaga, *m.*
malanders (-deurze), *n.pl.*, (vet.) malandres. *f. pl.*
malapert (-peurte), *adj.*, malappris, impertinent.
malapertly, *adv.*, en malappris ; impertinemment ; avec insolence.
malapertness, *n.*, impertinence, insolence, *f.*
malapropos, *adv.*, mal à propos.
malaria, *n.*, air malfaisant, *m.* ; exhalaison malsaine, *f.*
malconformation (-form'é-), *n.*, mauvaise conformation, *f.*

malcontent, *n.*, mécontent, *m.*
malcontent, *or* **malcontented**, *adj.*, mécontent.
malcontentedly, *adv.*, avec mécontentement.
malcontentedness, *n.*, mécontentement, *m.*
male, *adj.*, mâle; masculin.
male, *n.*, mâle, *m.*
malediction (mal'i-), *n.*, malédiction, *f.*
malefaction (mal-i-fak'-), *n.*, méfait, crime, *m.*
malefactor (mal'i-fac-), *n.*, malfaiteur, criminel, *m.*
malefic (-lèf'-), *adj.*, (ant.) maléfique.
malefice (mal'i-), *n.*, (ant.) maléfice, *m.*
maleficence (-lèf'-), *n.*, malfaisance, *f.*
maleficent (-lèf'-), *adj.*, malfaisant.
male-practice, *n.* *V.* **mal-practice**.
malevolence (-lèv'-), *n.*, malveillance, *f.*
malevolent (-lèv'-), *adj.*, malveillant ; (astrol.) maléfique.
malevolently (-lèv'-), *adv.*, avec malveillance.
malfeasance (-fî-za'n'ce), *n.*, (jur.) malfaisance, *f.* ; méfait, *m.*
malice, *n.*, malice; malveillance ; méchanceté ; (jur.) intention criminelle, *f.* To bear any one —; *vouloir du mal à quelqu'un; en vouloir à quelqu'un.* With — prepense; *avec préméditation.*
malicious (ma-lish'eusse), *adj.*, malveillant; méchant; (jur.) criminel.
maliciously, *adv.*, avec malveillance; méchamment; (jur.) criminellement.
maliciousness, *n.*, malignité, malice, malveillance, *f.*
malign (ma-laïne), *adj.*, malin.
malign (ma-laïne), *v.a.*, diffamer; maltraiter; nuire à.
malign (ma-laïne), *v.n.*, avoir de la rancune.
malignancy (ma-lig-), *n.*, malignité, *f.*
malignant (ma-lig-), *adj.*, malin, méchant; malfaisant ; (med.) malin.
malignantly (ma-lig-), *adv.*, malignement ; avec malignité ; avec méchanceté.
maligner (ma-laï'n'eur), *n.*, personne maligne, *f.* ; diffamateur, détracteur, *m.*
malignity (ma-lig-). *V.* **malignancy**.
malignly (ma-laï'n'-). *V.* **malignantly**.
malkin (mô'-), *n.*, balai à laver, écouvillon, (nav.) faubert, *m.* ; (pers.) salope, gaupe, *f.*
mall (môl), *n.*, gros maillet, *m.*
mall (môl), *v.a.*, frapper d'un maillet ; battre; (fig.) tracasser.
mall (mèl, *ou* mal), *n.*, mail (place—*lieu*), *m.*
malleability, *or* **malleableness** (mal'li-), *n.*, malléabilité, *f.*
malleable (mal'li-a-b'l), *adj.*, malléable.
malleate (mal'li-), *v.a.*, marteler.
malleation (mal'li-), *n.*, action d'étendre à coups de marteau, *f.*
mallet (mal'li-), *n.*, maillet, *m.*
mallow, *or* **mallows** (-lô, lôze), *n.*, mauve, *f.* Marsh— ; *guimauve*, *f.*
malmsey (mà'm'zê), *n.*, malvoisie, *f.*
mal-practice, *n.*, action illicite ; menée; malversation, *f.*
malt (môlte), *n.*, drèche, *f.* ; malt, *m.*
malt-distillery, *n.*, brasserie, *f.*
malt-floor (-flôre), *n.*, aire de germoir, *m.*
malt-horse, *n.*, cheval pour broyer la drèche ; (fig.) lourdaud, *m.*
malt-house (-haouce), *n.*, germoir, *m.*
malting (môlt'-), *n.*, maltage, *m.*
malt-kiln (-kilne), *n.*, touraille, *f.* ; four à drèche, *m.*
malt-liquor (-lik'eur), *n.*, boisson d'orge brassée ; bière, *f.*
maltman (môlt'ma'n), *n.*, malteur; marchand de drèche, *m.*

maltreat (mal-trìte), *v.a.*, maltraiter, malmener.

maltreatment (mal-trìte-), *n.*, mauvais traitement, *m.*

maltster (mõlt'-), *n.* *V.* **maltman**.

malt-worm (mõlt-weùrme), *n.*, buveur de bière; ivrogne, *m.*

malvaceous (mal-vé-sheusse),*adj.*,malvacé.

malversation (-vèr-sé-), *n.*, malversation,*f.*

mamaluke (-liouke), *or* **mameluke** (-'i-liouke), *n.*, mameluk, mamelouk, *m.*

mamma. *n.*, maman, mère,*f.*

mammalia (-'mé-li-a), *n.pl.*, mammifères, *m.pl.*

mammalogist (-'o-djiste), *n.*, mammalogiste, mammologiste, *m.*

mammalogy (-'o-dji), *n.*, mammalogie, mammologie,*f.*

mammary, *adj.*, mammaire.

mammet (-mète), *n.*, poupée, *f.*

mammifer (-fère), *n.*, mammifère, *m.*

mammiferous, *adj.*, mammifère.

mammiform, *adj.*, mammiforme.

mammillary, *adj.*, mamillaire.

mammon. *n.*, Mammon, *m.*

mammonist, *n.*,adorateur de Mammon, *m.*

mammoth (-moth), *n.*, mammouth, *m.*

man (ma'n), *n.* (men), homme, *m.* ; (at chess —aux échecs) pièce; (at draughts—aux dames) dame,*f.*; pion; (servant—serviteur) domestique, valet; (workman—ouvrier)ouvrier, *m.* Well, my —! eh bien,mon brave! — -servant; domestique, *m.* — cook; cuisinier, *m.* Head—; chef, *m.* —and wife; mari et femme. —-of-war; vaisseau de guerre, *m.* —'s estate; âge virii, *m.; virilité,f.*

man, *v.a.*, garnir d'hommes; (a ship—un vaisseau) garnir de monde, fournir de monde, de marins; équiper; (a pump—une pompe) armer; (a prize—une prise) amariner; (a hawk—un faucon) apprivoiser; (fig.) fortifier.

manacle (-'a-k'l), *v.a.*, mettre les menottes à; emmenotter; garotter.

manacles (-a-k'l'ze), *n.pl.*, menottes,*f.pl.*

manage (-'édje), *v.a.*, conduire, gouverner, régir, diriger; (to spare—épargner) ménager; (com,) gérer; (a horse—un cheval) traiter, dompter.

manage, *v.n.*, s'arranger.

manageable (-'édj'a-b'l), *adj.*, qui peut être conduit, dirigé, régi; docile; traitable; maniable.

manageableness (-'édj'a-), *n.*, qualité de ce qui peut être conduit, dirigé, régi; douceur, docilité,*f.*

management (-'édj'-), *n.*, conduite, direction, régie, administration, *f.*; gouvernement. *m.*; (com.) gestion,*f.*; (contrivance—invention) artifice; savoir-faire, *m.*

manager (-'édj'-), *n.*, directeur; gérant; régisseur; chef; (thea.) directeur, *m.* Stage-—; régisseur, *m.*

managing (-'édj'-), *n.*, gestion, direction,*f.*

managing (-'édj'-), *adj.*, qui conduit, qui dirige; directeur; gérant. — -man; gérant; chef, *m.*

manchineel (ma'n'sh-i-nìl), *n.*, mancenillier, *m.*

manciple (-ci-p'l), *n.*, pourvoyeur, *m.*

mandamus (-dé-), *n.*, mandement, *m.*

mandarin (-rine), *n.*, mandarin, *m.*

mandatary, *or* **mandatory**, *n.*, mandataire, *m.*

mandate,*n.*, mandement; mandat; ordre,*m.*

mandatory, *adj.*, qui ordonne.

mandible (-di-b'l), *n.*, mandibule,*f.*

mandibular (-di-biou-), *adj.*, de la mandibule

mandolin, *n.*, mandoline,*f.*

mandore (-dòre), *n.*, mandore,*f*

mandrake (-dréke), *or* **mandragora**, *n.*, (bot.) mandragore,*f.*

mandrel, *n.*, mandrin, *m.*

mandrill. *n.*, (mam.) mandrill, *m.*

manducate (-diou-), *v.a.*, mâcher.

manducation (-diou-ké-), *n.*, mastication; manducation,*f.*

mane (méne), *n.*, crinière. *f.*

maneater (ma'n'ìt'eur), *n.*, cannibale, anthropophage, *m.*

maned (mé'n'de), *adj.*, qui porte une crinière.

manege (ma-nèje), *n.*. manège, *m.*

manes (mé-nize), *n.pl.*, mânes, *m.pl.*

manful (ma'n'foule),*adj.*,mâle, viril; brave, hardi; digne.

manfully, *adv.*, en homme; virilement, hardiment, vaillamment; noblement, dignement.

manfulness, *n.*, bravoure,*f.*

manganese (-nize), *n.*, manganèse, *m.*

mange (ma'n'dje), *n.*, gale de chien,*f.*

mangel-wurzel (man'gn'g'l-weurz'l), *n.*, betterave,*f.*

manger (mé'n'djeur), *n.*,crèche,mangeoire,*f.*

manginess (ma'n'dji-), *n.*, état galeux, *m.*

mangle (ma'n'g'l), *v.a.*, déchirer, déchiqueter; mutiler, estropier; (linen—du linge) calandrer, cylindrer.

mangle. *n.*, cylindre au linge, *m.*, calandre, *f.*; (bot.) mangle, *m.*

mangler, *n.*, personne qui mutile,*f.*; (of linen—de linge) cylindreur, calandreur, *m.*

mangling, *n.*, cylindrage, calandrage, *m.*

mango (ma'n'gô), *n.*, mangue,*f.*

mangostan, *n.*, mangouste,*f.*

mango-tree (-tri), *n.*, manguier, *m.*

mangrove (man'gu'grâve), *n.*,(bot.) mangle, manglier, palétuvier, *m.*

mangy (ma'n'dji), *adj.*, galeux.

man-hater (ma'n'hét'eur), *n.*, misanthrope, *m.*

manhood (-houde), *n.*, virilité, *f.*; âge viril, *m.* — suffrage; suffrage universel.

mania (mé-), *n.*, folie; rage; manie, *f.*

maniac, *or* **maniacal** (iné-), *adj.*, furieux; fou; enragé.

maniac (mé-), *n.*, fou furieux, *m.*, folle furieuse, *f.*; fou, *m.*, folle,*f.*

manichean (-ki-a'n), *adj.*, des manichéens.

manichean, *or* **manichee** (-ki), *n.*, manichéen, *m.*, manichéenne,*f.*

manicheism (-ki-iz'me), *n.*,manichéisme,*m.*

manichord, *or* **manichordon** (-kord'-), *n.*, manichordion, *m.*

manifest (-fèste), *v.a.*, manifester, témoigner, laisser voir; montrer.

manifest, *adj.*, manifeste, évident.

manifest, *n.*, (nav.) manifeste. *m.*

manifestation (-fèst'é-), *n.*, manifestation,*f.*

manifestible (-fèst'i-b'l), *adj.*, facile à rendre maniteste.

manifestly. *adv.*, manifestement.

manifestness, *n.*, évidence,*f.*

manifesto (-fès'tô), *n.*, manifeste, *m.*

manifold (-fôlde), *adj.*, nombreux, en grand nombre; divers; multiple.

manifoldly, *adv.*, de diverses manières; diversement.

manifoldness, *n.*, multiplicité,*f.*

manikin, *n.*, bout d'homme; nabot; mannequin. *m.*

manioc (mé-), *n.*, manioc, *m.*

maniple (-i-p'l), *n.*, manipule, *m.*

manipular (-nip'iou-), *adj.*, manipulaire.

manipulate, *v.a.*, manipuler.

manipulation (-nip'iou-lé-), *n.*, manipulation, *f.*

manipulator (-lét'eur), *n.*, manipulateur,*m.*

man-killer. *n.*, meurtrier, assassin, *m.*

mankind (-kaï'n'de), *n.*, genre humain, *m.*; espèce humaine, *f.*

man-like (-laïke), *adj.*, d'homme; viril; mâle, vigoureux.

manliness. *n.*, air d'homme; air mâle, *m.*; bravoure; vigueur; dignité, *f.*

manly, *adj.*, d'homme; viril; mâle; vigoureux.

manly, *adv.*, en homme de cœur; noblement, courageusement; comme un homme.

man-midwife (-waïfe), *n.*, accoucheur, *m.*

manna, *n.*, manne, *f.*

manner. *n.*, manière, *f.*; genre, *m*; sorte, façon; espèce; coutume; habitude, *f.* —s; mœurs, *f.pl.*; politesse, *f.* After the — of; à la manière de; à la façon de. The —in which; la manière dont. In a —; en quelque sorte. To have no —s; ne savoir pas vivre. All —s of things; toutes espèces, toutes sortes de choses. Good —s; bonnes manières, *f.pl.*; bon ton, *m.sing.* Ill —s; mauvaises manières, *f.pl.*; mauvais ton, *m.sing.*

manner, *v.a.*, former aux belles manières, former au bon ton.

mannerism (-'iz'me), *n.*, uniformité de manières, *f.*; air maniéré, *m.*

mannerist, *n.*, personne maniérée, *f.*; maniériste. *m.*, *f.*

mannerliness, *n.*, civilité, *f.*

mannerly, *adj.*, poli, civil.

mannerly, *adv.*, poliment.

manners (man'neurze), *n.*, manières polies; mœurs, *f.pl.* *V.* **manner.**

mannish, *adj.*, d'homme, mâle; hommasse.

manœuvre (ma-niou-veur), *n.*, manœuvre, *f.*

manœuvre (ma-niou-veur), *v.n.*, manœuvrer.

manœuvre, *v.a.*, faire manœuvrer.

manœuvrer, *n.*, conducteur de manœuvres; tacticien, manœuvrier, *m.*

manœuvring, *n.*, manœuvres, *m.pl.*

manometer (-'èt'-), *n.*, manomètre, *m.*

manometrical, *adj.*, manométrique.

manor, *n.*, manoir, *m.*; seigneurie, *f.*

manor-house (-haouce), *or* **manor-seat** (-sìte), *n.*, manoir, *m.*

manorial, *adj.*, seigneurial.

man-rope (-rôpe), *n.*, (nav.) tire-veille, *f.*

manse, *n.*, ferme, *f.*; presbytère, *m.*

mansion (-sheune), *n.*, maison seigneuriale, *f.*; hôtel, *m.*; grande maison, *f.*; (fig.) habitation, *f.*; séjour, *m.*

mansion-house (-haouce), *n.*, hôtel, *m.*, grande maison, *f.*; hôtel du Lord-maire de Londres, *m.*

manslaughter (ma'n'slô-teur), *n.*, homicide sans préméditation, par imprudence, *m.*

manslayer (ma'n'slè-eur), *n.*, meurtrier, homicide, *m.*

mansuetude (ma'n'swit'ioude), *n.*, (ant.) mansuétude, *f.*

mantel (ma'n'tl), *n.*, partie horizontale de chambranle de cheminée, *f.*

mantelet, *or* **mantlet**, *n.*, mantelet, *m.*

mantelpiece, **mantel-piece** (-pìce), *or* **mantel-shelf**, *n.*, chambranle de cheminée. *m.*

mantilla, *n.*, mantille, *f.*

mantle, *n.*, mante, *f.*; manteau; (arch.) manteau; (her.) lambrequin; (fig.) voile, *m.*

mantle, *v.a.*, couvrir; voiler.

mantle, *v.n.*, s'étendre; se répandre; (to revel —se divertir) se réjouir; (to rush to the face—se porter au visage) monter à la figure. To—to the view; s'offrir à la vue. The mantling bowl; le bol qui se couvre d'écume.

mantling, *n.*, (her.) manteau, *m.*

mantua (-tiou-a), *n.*, robe de femme, *f.*

mantua-maker (-mék'-), *n.*, couturière, *f.*

manual (-'iou-), *adj.*, manuel, de la main.

manual, *n.*, manuel, *m.*

manually, *adv.*, manuellement.

manufactory (ma'n'iou-fak'-), *n.*, manufacture, fabrique; usine, *f.*

manufactural (-'iou-fakt'iou-), *adj.*, de manufacture; de fabrique; d'usine; manufacturier.

manufacture (-'iou-fakt'ieur), *n.*, manufacture, fabrique, industrie; industrie manufacturière; fabrication, *f.* —s; industrie manufacturière, *f.*; produits des manufactures, *m.pl.*

manufacture, *v.a.*, manufacturer, fabriquer.

manufacture, *v.n.*, se livrer à la manufacture, à l'industrie.

manufacturer, *n.*, manufacturier, fabricant; (workman—ouvrier) industriel, *m.*

manufacturing, *adj.*, manufacturier; de manufacture; de fabrique; industriel.

manumission (-'iou-mish'-), *n.*, manumission, *f.*; affranchissement *m.*

manumit (-'iou-mite), *v.a.*, affranchir.

manurable (-'iour'a-b'l), *adj.*, labourable; qui peut être engraissé, fumé.

manure (-nioure), *n.*, engrais, *m.*

manure (-nioure), *v.a.*, engraisser, amender, fumer.

manurer, *n.*, agriculteur qui engraisse les terrains, *m.*

manuscript (-'iou-scripte), *n.*, manuscrit, *m.*

manuscript. *adj.*, manuscrit.

many (mè'n'i), *n.*, multitude, foule, *f.*; grand nombre; *m.* A great —; beaucoup; un grand nombre. A very great —; un très grand nombre. — think thus; beaucoup de personnes pensent ainsi.

many (mè'n'i), *adj.*, nombreux; beaucoup de; bien; du, de la, des; plusieurs, maint; plus d'un. — persons; beaucoup de personnes; bien des personnes. — nations; de nombreuses nations. —a man; maint homme. —a time; mainte fois. Full —a; maint; plus d'un; bien des. As —as; autant que. How—? combien? Too—; trop; trop de. So —; tant, tant de.

many-cleft (-clèfte), *adj.*, qui a de nombreuses fissures; multifide.

many-coloured (-keul'leurde), *adj.*, de diverses couleurs; diversement coloré.

many-cornered (-cor'neur'de), *adj.*, qui a plusieurs coins; qui a plusieurs angles; (geom.) polygone.

many-flowered (-flaour'de), *a* *lj.* qui a plusieurs fleurs; multiflore.

many-headed (-hèd'-), *adj.*, qui a plusieurs têtes; à plusieurs têtes.

many-languaged (-lan'gn'gwédj'de), *adj.*, de diverses langues, de divers idiomes.

many-leaved (-liv'de), *adj.*, à beaucoup de feuilles; (bot.) polyphylle.

many-mastered (-mâs'teur'de), *adj.*, soumis à beaucoup de maîtres.

many-nationed (-né-sheu'n'de), *adj.*, de nations diverses.

many-parted (-pârt'-), *adj.*, multipartite.

many-peopled (-pi'p'l'de), *adj.*, fort populeux.

many-petaled (-pèt'alde), *adj.*, (bot.) polypétale.

many-sided (-saïd'-), *adj*, qui a plusieurs côtés; polygone.

many-toned (-tô'n'de), *adj.*, de divers sons; de sons variés.

many-twinkling, *adj.*, étincelant, scintillant.

many-valved (-valv'de), *adj.*, qui a de nombreuses soupapes; (conch.) multivalve.

map, *n.*, carte; carte géographique; carte

de géographie, *f*. — of the world ; *mappe-monde*, *f*.

map, *v.a.*, dessiner une carte ; tracer une carte.

maple. *or* **maple-tree** (mé-p'l-trî), *n.*, érable. *m*.

mappery, *or* **mapping**, *n.*, cartographie, *f*.

mar (mâr), *v.a.*, gâter, abimer ; (fig.) troubler.

marabout (-boute), *n.*, marabout, *m*.

marasmus (-raz'-), *n.*, (med.) marasme, *m*.

maraud, *v.n.*, marauder.

marauder. *n.*, maraudeur, *m*.

marauding, *n.*, maraude ; picorée, *f*.

maravedi, *n.*, maravédis (Spanish coin—*monnaie d'Espagne*). *m*.

marble (mâr'b'l), *adj.*, de marbre ; marbré.

marble (mâr'b'l), *n.*, marbre, *m*. ; (toy—*jouet*) bille, (l.u.) chique, *f*.

marble, *v.a.*, marbrer.

marble-cutter (-keut'-), *n.*, marbrier, *m*.

marbled (mâr'b'l'de), *adj.*, marbré.

marble-hearted (-hârt-), *or* **marble-breasted** (-brèst'-), *adj.*, inexorable ; cruel ; insensible ; à cœur de marbre.

marble-quarry (-kwôr'-), *n.*, carrière de marbre ; marbrière, *f*.

marble-works (-weurkse), *n.pl.*, marbrerie, *f. sing*.

marbling, *n.*, marbrure, *f*.

marcasite (mâr-ca-caït'e-), *n.*, (min.) marcassite, *f*.

marcasitic (mâr-ca-cit'-), *adj.*, de marcasite.

march (mârtshe), *n.*, marche ; course, *f*. ; progrès ; (month—*mois*) mars, *m*. Dead—; *marche funèbre*, *m*.

march (mârtshe), *v.n.*, marcher, se mettre en marche. To — off ; *se mettre en marche ; plier bagage, s'en aller*. To — in ; *entrer*. To — out ; *sortir*. To — on ; *marcher, avancer*. To — back ; *retourner ; revenir ; reculer*. To — down ; *descendre*.

march (mârtshe), *v.a.*, faire marcher ; mettre en marche ; conduire, diriger. To — off ; *mettre en marche ; faire décamper*. To — out ; *faire sortir*. To — up ; *faire avancer ; faire monter*. To — down ; *faire descendre*. To — in ; *faire entrer*. To — into ; *conduire à*.

marcher, *n.*, commandant de marche (frontier—*frontière*), *n*.

marches (mârtsh'èze), *n.pl.*, marche (frontiers—*frontière*), *f.sing*.

marching, *n.*, marche, *f*.

marchioness (mâr'sheu'n'èce), *n.*, marquise, *f*.

marcid (mâr-), *adj.*, maigre, décharné ; flétri.

mare (mére), *n.*, cavale, jument, *f*.

mareschal (mâr'shal), *n.*, maréchal, *m*.

margarite (mâr'ga-raïte), *n.*, perle, *f*., (min.) mica nacré, *m*.

margay (mâr-), *n.*, (mam.) margay, chat-tigre, *m*.

margin (mâr'djine), *n.*, (of paper, &c.—*de papier, &c.*) marge, *f*. ; (of a river, a lake, &c. —*de rivière, lac, &c.*) bord, *m*.

margin, *v.a.*, border ; marginer ; marger.

marginal, *adj.*, de marge ; marginal ; de bord.

marginated (-dji'n'ét'-), *adj.*, qui a une marge ; marginé.

margrave (mâr'gréve), *n.*, margrave, *m*.

margraviate, *n.*, margraviat, *m*.

marigold (-gôlde), *n.*, (bot.) souci, *m*.

marinate, *v.a.*, mariner.

marine, *n.*, marine, *f*. ; (milit., nav.) soldat de marine, *m*.

marine (-rîne), *adj.*, marin, de mer ; naval.

mariner, *n.*, marin, matelot, *m*.

marish (mér'-), *n.*, marais, *m*.

marital, *adj.*, marital.

maritally, *adv.*, maritalement.

maritime (-time), *or* **maritimal**, *adj.*, maritime.

marjoram (mâr'djor'-), *n.*, marjolaine, *f*.

mark (mârke), *n.*, marque, *f*. ; (at school— *à l'école*) point ; (on the skin—*sur la peau*) signe ; (to aim at—*pour viser*) but, blanc. *m*., cible, *f*. ; (notice) avis, avertissement, *m*. ; (reprisal—*de corsaire*) marque, lettre de marque, *f*. ; (coin) marc ; (weight—*poids*) marc, *m*. ; (signature) marque, *f*. . Near the —; *près de la réalité, de la vérité*. Over the —; *au-dessus de la réalité, de la vérité ; exagéré*. Under the —; *au-dessous de la réalité, de la vérité*.

mark (mârke), *v.a.* and *n.*, marquer, remarquer ; faire attention à.

marker, *n.*, marqueur, *m* ; personne qui remarque, qui fait attention, *f*.

market (mâr'kète), *n.*, marché, *m*. ; halle, *f*. ; (com.) débouché, marché, *m*., place, *f*. ; (sale—*vente*) débit, *m*., vente ; (pers.) masse des acheteurs, *f*. ; (price—*prix*) cours, prix, *m*. In our —; (com.) *sur notre place*. To find a — for ; *trouver un débouché pour*.

market, *v.a.*, acheter au marché ; vendre au marché.

marketable ('-a-b'l), *adj.*, propre à la vente, de bonne vente ; (com.) marchand ; (of price— *de prix*) courant.

market-garden (-gâr'd'n), *n.*, marais, jardin maraîcher, *m*.

market-gardener (-gâr'd'n'eur), *n.*, maraîcher, *m*.

market-house (-haouce), *n.*, marché, *m* ; halle, *f*.

marketing, *n.*, marché, *m*.

market-place, *n.*, place du marché, *f*.

market-price (-praïce), *or* **market-rate** (-réte), *n.*, cours du marché, prix courant, *m*.

market-town (-taoune), *n.*, ville à marché, *f*. ; bourg, *m*.

market-woman (-woum'-), *n.*, femme de la halle, *f*.

marking, *n.*, action de marquer, *f*.

marksman (mârks'-), *n.*, tireur ; bon tireur, *m*.

marl (mârle), *n.*, marne, *f*.

marl (mârle), *v.a.*, marner.

marline (mâr-laïne), *n.*, (nav.) merlin, *m*.

marline-spike (-spaïke), *n.*, (nav.) épissoir, *m*.

marling (mârl'-), *n.*, marnage, *m*.

marl-pit, *n.*, marnière, *f*.

marlstone (-stône), *n.*, marne dure, *f*.

marly, *adj.*, marneux.

marmalade (mâr-), *n.*, marmelade, *f*.

marmorean (mâr-mor-î-), *adj.*, de marbre.

marmot. *n.*, marmotte, *f*.

maroon (-roune), *n.*, nègre libre, *m*.

maroon (-roune), *v.a.*, abandonner sur une île déserte.

marplot (mâr'plote), *n.*, brouillon, *m*., brouillonne, *f*.

marque (mârke), *n.*, marque ; lettre de marque, *f*. Letter of —; *lettre de marque, f*.

marquee (mâr-ki), *n.*, marquise (tente), *f*.

marquetry (mâr'kèt'ri), *n.*, marqueterie, *f*.

marquis (mâr'kwice), *or* **marquess** (mâr'kwè'ce), *n.*, marquis, *m*.

marquisate (-kwiss'éte), *n.*, marquisat, *m*.

marrer (mâr-), *n.*, personne qui gâte, qui abîme ; personne qui trouble, qui dépare, qui détruit, *f*.

marriage (mar'ridge), *n.*, mariage, *m*. ; noce, *f*. ; noces, *f.pl.*

marriageable (-ridj'a-b'l), *adj.*, mariable, nubile.

marriage-articles (-âr'ti'k'l'ze), *n.pl.*, contrat de mariage, *m*.

marriage-contract, *or* **marriage-treaty** (-tri'té), *n.*, contrat de mariage, *m.*
marriage-license (-laï-), *n.*, dispense de bans, *f.*
marriage-portion (-pŏr-), *n.*, dot, *f.*
marriage-settlement (-sèt't'l-mè'n't), *n.*, douaire, *m.*
married (ma-ride), *past part.*, marié ; (of things—*des choses*) conjugal.
marrow (mar-rō),*n.*,moelle ; (fig.) essence,*f.*
marrow, *v.a.*, remplir de moelle.
marrow-bone (-bône), *n.*, os à moelle, *m.* Upon one's —s (fam) ; *à genoux.*
marrow-fat, *n.*, pois carré, *m.*
marrowless, *n.*, sans moelle,
marrowy (mar-rō-i), *adj.*, moelleux ; médullaire.
marry, *v.a.*, marier ; se marier à ; épouser ; (fig.) unir intimement, marier.
marry, *v.n.*, se marier. To — again ; se *remarier.* To be married ; *se marier.*
marsh (marshe), *n.*, marais, *m.*
marshal (mâr-), *p.* , maréchal ; (nav.) prévôt, *m.* Field- — ; *maréchal, m.* ; (in France) *maréchal de France, m.*
marshal, *v.a.*, ranger, régler, ordonner ; placer en ordre.
marshaller,*n.*, ordonnateur, régulateur,*m.*
marshalsea (-sï), *n.*, ancien nom de la prison de Southwark, à Londres.
marshalship, *n.*, dignité de maréchal,*f.*
marsh-mallow (-mal'lo), *n.*, guimauve, *f.*
marshy (marsh'i), *adj.*, marécageux ; de marais.
mart (mârte), *n.*, marché, entrepôt, *m.*
martello-tower (-taou'eur), *n.*, tour bâtie sur le bord de la mer en Angleterre pour opposer l'invasion du pays,*f.*
marten (mâr-tène), *n.*, (mam.) martre, maite,*f.*
martial (mâr-shal), *adj.*,martial ; de guerre, de bataille ; militaire ; guerrier, belliqueux. — l iw ; *code martial, m.* — nation ; *nation guerrière, belliqueuse,f.*
martially, *adv.*, martialement.
martin (mâr'tine), *n.*, (orni.) martinet, *m.*
martinet, *n.*, personne rigide pour la discipline,*f.* ; (orni.) martinet, *m.* —s ; (nav.) *martinets, m.pl.*
martingal (mâr-), *or* **martingale** (-ghéle), *n.*, martingale, *f.*
martinmas (mâr-), *n.*, la St.-Martin,*f.*
martlet (mârt'-), *n.*, (orni.). *V.* **martinet** (orni.).
martyr (mâr-teur), *n.*, martyr,*m.*,martyre,*f.*
martyr (mâr-teur), *v.a.*, martyriser.
martyrdom (-deume), *n.*, martyre, *m.*
martyrology (mâr-teur-ol'o-dji), *n.*, martyrologe, *m.*
marvel (mâr-),*n.*, merveille, chose merveilleuse,*f.*
marvel (mâr-),*v.n.*, s'émerveiller, s'étonner. To — at ; *s'émerveiller de ; s'étonner de.*
marvellous, *adj.*, merveilleux.
marvellously, *adv.*, merveilleusement ; à merveille.
marvellousness, *n.*, caractère merveilleux ; merveilleux, *m.*
masculine (mas-klou-), *adj.*, mâle ; (gram.) masculin ; (b.s.) hommasse.
masculine, *n.*, masculin. In the — ; *au masculin.*
masculinely, *adv.*, virilement, en homme.
masculineness, *n.*, caractère mâle, *m.*
mash, *n.*, mélange, *m.* ; tripotage ; (in breweries—*de brasserie*) mélange, fardeau, *m.*
mash, *v.a.*, écraser, broyer, mêler, mélanger ; (in breweries—*de brasserie*) brasser.
mashing, *n.*, mélange, fardeau, *m.*
mash-tub (-teube), *n.*, cuve, *f.* ; brassin, *m.*

mashy, *adj.*, mêlé ; mélangé ; écrasé ; broyé.
mask (mâske), *n.*, masque, *m.* ; mascarade, *f.* ; (arch.) mascaron, *m.*
mask, *v.a.*, masquer ; déguiser.
mask, *v.n.*, se masquer.
masker *n.*, masque (pers.), *m.*
mason (mé-s'n), *n.*, maçon, *m.* Free-— ; *franc-maçon, m.* Stone-— ; *maçon.* Master —; *maître maçon, m.* Journeyman—; *compagnon, m.*
masonic (mé-ço'n'-), *adj.*, maçonnique.
masonry (mé-co'n'-), *n.*, maçonnage, *m.*; maçonnerie, *f.* Free-— ; *franc-maçonnerie, f.*
masquerade (mas-kèr'éde), *n.*, mascarade, *f.* ; masque, *m.*
masquerade (mas-kèr'éde), *v.n.*, se masquer ; faire une mascarade.
masquerader, *n.*, masque (pers.), *m.*
mass (mâsse), *n.*, masse,*f.* ; amas, gros, *m.*; (crowd—*foule*) multitude, foule ; (c. rel.) messe, *f.* A — of things ; *une foule de choses.* High— ; (c. rel.) *messe haute, grande messe, grand' messe.* Low—; (c. rel.) *messe basse, petite messe.* — book ; *livre de messe, missel, m.* —priest ; *prêtre officiant. m.*
massacre (mass'a-keur), *n.*, massacre, *m.*
massacre, *v.a.*, massacrer.
massacrer, *n.*, massacreur, *m.*
massicot, *n.*, (chem.) massicot, *m.*
massiness, *or* **massiveness** (mâs'-), *n.*, nature massive ; solidité,*f.*
massive, *or* **massy** (mâs'-), *adj.*, massif, solide.
massively, *adv.*, en masse, massivement.
mast (mâste), *n.*, (nav.) mât, *m.* —s; *mâts, m.pl.* ; *mâture, f. sing.* Fore—; *mât de misaine.* Main—; *grand mât.* Spare —; *mât de rechange.* Mizzen-—; *mât d'artimon.* Jury-—; *mât de fortune.* Before the—; *sur le gaillard d'avant.* Half—high; *à mi-mât.*
mast, *v.a.*, (nav.) mâter.
mast, *n.*, (fruit) (of the chestnut—*du châtaignier*) châtaigne, *f.*; (du marronnier) marron, *m.*; (of the oak—*du chêne*) gland, *m.* ; (of the hazel—*du noisetier*) noisette ; (of the beech—*du hêtre*) faîne, *f.*
masted, *adj.*, mâté.
master (mâs'teur), *n.*, maître ; (nav.) maître d'équipage ; (of clerks—*d'employés*) chef, patron ; (of workmen—*d'ouvriers*) maître, patron, bourgeois ; (of a school—*d'école*) maître, maître de pension, chef d'institution, maître d'école ; (of a college—*de collège*) régent ; (of ceremonies) maître des cérémonies ; (of fêtes) ordonnateur ; (appellation given to children — *appliqué aux enfants*) monsieur ; (possessor) possesseur ; ⊙messire, *m.* ; (of a merchantman—*de vaisseau marchand*) capitaine, *m.* — of arts ; *maître-ès-arts.* —passion ; *passion dominante, f.* To be — of ; *posséder ; être maître de.* To be thoroughly — of ; *posséder à fond ; savoir à fond ; être parfaitement maître de.* Head—; *principal, proviseur, m.*
master, *v.a.*, maîtriser ; se rendre maître de ; vaincre ; l'emporter sur ; venir à bout de ; surmonter ; dominer ; apprendre, posséder.
master-builder (-bild'-), *n.*, entrepreneur ; architecte, *m.*
masterdom (-deume), *n.*, domination, *f.*
masterful (-foule), *adj.*, de maître ; impérieux ; habile.
master-hand, *n.*, main de maître, *f.* He is a — at it ; *il y est passé maître.*
master-key (-kï), *n.*, passe-partout, *m.*
masterless, *adj.*, sans maître.
masterliness, *n.*, talent de maître, *m.* ; grande habileté,*f.*
masterly, *adj.*, de maître ; de main de maître ; parfait ; (imperious—*altier*) impérieux.

masterly, *adv.*, en maître.

master-piece (-pîce), *n.*, chef-d'œuvre, *m.*

mastership, *n.*, pouvoir de maître, *m.*; autorité; habileté; supériorité, *f.*; (office) fonctions de maître, *f.pl.*

master-string (-strigne), *n.*, corde principale, *f.*

master-stroke (-strôke), *n.*, coup de maître, *m.*

master-touch (-teutshe), *n.*, coup de maître, *m.*, touche de maître, *f.*

master-work (-weurke), *n.*, chef d'œuvre, *m.*

master-wort (-weurte), *n.*, (bot.) impératoire, *f.*

mastery, *n.*, supériorité, puissance; prééminence; domination, *f.*, empire, *m.*; (knowledge —*savoir*) connaissance parfaite, perfection *f.*

masthead (-hède), *n.*. tête de mât, *f.*

mastic, *n.* V. **mastich**.

masticate, *v.a.*, mâcher.

mastication (-ti-ké-), *n.*, mastication, *f.*

masticatory, *n.* and *adj.*, masticatoire, *m.*

mastic, *or* **mastich** (-tike), *n.*, (resin—*résine*) mastic, *m.* — -tree; *lentisque, m.*

masticot, *n.* V. **massicot**.

mastiff, *n.*, dogue; mâtin, *m.*

mastless, *adj.*, sans mât.

mastlin (maz'line), *n.*, méteil, *m.*

mast-maker (-mék'-), *n.*, mâteur, *m.*

mastodon, *n.*, mastodonte, *m.*

mastoid (-toïde), *adj.*, (anat.) mastoïde, mastoïdien.

mat, *n.*, (of rush—*en roseaux*) natte, *f.*; (of straw—*en paille*) paillasson, *m.* Door- —; *paillasson, m.*

mat, *v.a.*, couvrir de nattes; couvrir de paillassons; natter, tresser.

matadore (-dôre), *n.*, matadore, *m.*

match (matshe), *n.*, (contest—*joute*) lutte; partie, *f.*; concours, *m.*; (in running), sailing, rowing, driving—*de coureurs; de bateaux, &c.*) course, joute, *f.*; (in fighting—*lutte*) combat, *m.*, lutte, *f.*

match, *n.*, (an equal—*égal*) pareil, égal; (marriage—*mariage*) mariage, *m.*, alliance, *f.*; (person to be married—*personne à marier*) parti, *m.* To be a bad — ; (of things—*des choses*) aller mal ensemble. To be a good — ; (of things—*dès choses*) aller bien ensemble; être assorti. To make a good —; *faire un bon mariage; épouser un bon parti.* To make a bad —; *faire un mauvais mariage; épouser un mauvais parti.* To be a — for; *être de taille à; pouvoir se disputer à.* You are not a — for him; *vous n'êtes pas de taille à entrer en lice avec lui, à concourir avec lui.* Love- —; *mariage d'inclination, m.* Prudent —; *mariage de raison, de convenance, m.*

match, *n.*, (combustible substance) allumette; (artil.) mèche. Lucifer- —; *allumette chimique, f.*

match, *v.a.*, (to equal—*être égal*) égaler; (to oppose as equal — *opposer comme égal*) tenir tête à, se mesurer avec; (to proportion—*ajuster*) proportionner; (to marry—*allier*) marier, allier, donner en mariage; (colours, stuffs—*couleurs, étoffes*) assortir; (pairs of things—*objets en paires*) apparier; (horses, pictures, &c.—*chevaux, tableaux, &c.*) appareiller.

match, *v.n.*, (to be united in marriage—*contracter mariage*) s'allier, se marier, s'unir; (to correspond—*correspondre*) assortir, s'assortir; (of pairs of things—*d'objets en paires*) être pareil; être le pendant de.

matchable (-'a-b'l), *adj.*, comparable; égal.

matchbox, *n.*, porte-allumettes, *m.*; boîte à allumettes, *f.*

matchless, *adj.*, incomparable, sans pareil.

matchlessly, *adv.*, incomparablement.

---

matchlessness, *n.*, état de ce qui est incomparable, *m.*; grande supériorité, *f.*

matchlock, *n.*, platine à mèche, *f.*; fusil à mèche, *m.*

match-maker (-mék'-), *n.*, marieur, *m.*; marieuse, *f.*; faiseur de mariages, *m.*. faiseuse de mariages, *f.*; courtier de mariages, *m.*, courtière de mariages, *f.*; fabricant d'allumettes, *m*

match-making (-mék'-), *n.*, action de faire des mariages; de faire des allumettes, *f.*

match-tub (-teube), *n.*, (artil.) baril à mèches, *m.*

mate (méte), *n.*, camarade, *m.*, *f.*; compagnon, *m.*, compagne, *f.*; (nav.) second, aide, contre-maître; (at chess—*aux échecs*) mat, *m.*

mate, *v.a.*, (to marry—*donner en mariage*) marier; (to equal—*être égal*) égaler, assortir, apparier; (to oppose—*opposer*) résister à, s'opposer à, tenir tête à; (to subdue — *réduire*) subjuguer, humilier; (to crush—*anéantir*) écraser; (at chess—*aux échecs*) mater.

mateless, *adj.*, sans compagnon, sans compagne.

mater (mé-teur), *n.*, (anat.) mère, *f.* Dura —; (anat.) *dure-mère, f.* Pia —; *pie-mère, f.*

material (-tî-), *adj.*, matériel; essentiel, important, sensible, considérable.

material (-tî-), *n.*, matière; étoffe, *f.* —s; *matériaux, m.pl.* Raw —; *matière première, f.*

materialism (-tî-ri-al-iz'me), *n.*, matérialisme, *m.*

materialist (-tî-), *n.*, matérialiste, *m.*

materiality (-tî-), *n.*, matérialité; importance, *f.*

materialize (-tî-ri-al-aïze), *v.a.*, matérialiser.

materially (-tî-), *adv.*, matériellement; essentiellement.

materialness (-tî-), *n.*, matérialité; (fig.) importance, *f.*

materia medica (ma-tî-ri-a-mèd'i-ca), *n.*, matière médicale, *f.*

maternal (-teur-), *adj.*, maternel.

maternally (-teur'), *adv.*, maternellement.

maternity (-teur-), *n.*, maternité, *f.*

mat-grass (-grâce), *n.*, nard; roseau des tables, *m.*

math (math), *n.*, récolte, *f.*

mathematic, *or* **mathematical** (-mathè-), *adj.*, mathématique, de mathématique.

mathematically (math-), *adv.*, mathématiquement.

mathematician (math-), *n.*, mathématicien, *m.*

mathematics (math-), *n.pl.*, mathématiques, *f.pl.*

matin, *adj.*, matinal; du matin.

matin (ma-tine), *n.*, matin, *m.*

matins (-tî'n'ze), *n.pl.*, matines, *f.pl.*

mat-maker (-mék'-), *n.*, nattier, faiseur de paillassons, *m.*

matrass, *n.*, (chem.) matras, *m.*

matricaria (-ké-ri-a), *n.*, (bot.) matricaire, *f.*

matrice (mé-trice), *n.*, matrice, *f.*; (anat.) utérus, *m.*, matrice; (dy.) couleur matrice, *f.*

matricidal (-çaïd'-), *adj.*, matricide.

matricide (-çaïde), *n.*, matricide, *m.*

matriculate (-trik'iou-), *v.a.*, immatriculer.

matriculate, *adj.*, immatriculé.

matriculate, *n.*, (bot.) matriculaire, *m.*

matriculation (-trik'iou-lé-), *n.*, immatriculation, matricule, *f.*

matriculation-book (-bouke), *n.*, registre matricule, *m.*

matrimonial (-mô-), *adj.*, conjugal; matrimonial, de mariage.

matrimonially (-mô-), *adv.*, conjugalement.

matrimony, *n.*, mariage, *m.*

matrix (mé-), *n.* *V.* **matrice.**

matron (mé-), *n.*, dame, femme; dame respectable, femme respectable; mère; mère de famille; (jur.) ⊙matrone, *f.*

matronage (mat'ron'édje), *n.*, dames, femmes; mères de famille, *f.pl.*

matronal, *or* **matron-like** (-laïke), *adj.*, respectable; sévère; maternel; de mère; de matrone.

matronly (mé-), *adj.*, qui tire sur l'âge; d'un certain âge.

matross, *n.*, (nav.) canonnier servant; (milit.) soldat du train, *m.*

matte, *n.*, (metal.) matte, *f.*

matter (mat'teur), *n.*, matière; chose; affaire, *f.*; fond; sujet; (med.) pus, *m.*, matière, *f.*; (jur.) moyen; (space of time—*laps de temps*) espace de temps, *m.*; (distance) distance; (suit —*procès*) cause, *f.*, sujet de plainte, *m.*; (import —*portée*) importance, *f.* The — I speak of; *le sujet dont je parle.* It is a very easy —; *c'est une chose bien facile.* In —; *dans le fond.* What is the —? *qu'y a-t-il? de quoi s'agit-il?* Nothing; *il n'y a rien.* What is the — with you? *qu'avez-vous?* Nothir.g; *je n'ai rien.* What is the — in hand? *de quoi s'agit-il?* What —? *qu'importe?* No —! *n'importe!* It is no great —; *ce n'est pas grand'chose.* For that —, for the — of that; *quant à cela.* In — of; *en fait de.*

matter, *v.n.imp.*, importer. What —s? *qu'importe?* It —s; *il importe.* It —s not, it —s little; *n'importe; il n'importe; peu importe.*

matterless, *adj.*, sans matière.

mattery, *adj.*, (med.) purulent.

matting, *n.*, (of straw—*en paille*) paillasson, *m.*; (of rush—*en roseau*) natte, *f.*

mattock, *n.*, pioche, *f.*

mattress (mat'trèce), *n.*, matelas, *m.*

mattress-maker (-mék'-), *n.*, matelassier, *m.*, matelassière, *f.*

maturant (mat'lou-), *n.*, (med.) maturatif, *m.*

maturate (mat'lou-), *v.n.*, mûrir; (med.) suppurer.

maturate, *v.a.*, mûrir; (med.) faire suppurer.

maturation (-ré-), *n.*, maturité; (med.) suppuration, *f.*

maturative, *adj.*, qui mûrit; qui fait mûrir; (med.) maturatif.

mature (-tioure), *adj.*, mûr.

mature, *v.a.*, mûrir, faire mûrir.

mature, *v.n.*, mûrir; (com.) échoir.

maturely, *adv.*, mûrement.

matureness, *or* **maturity,** *n.*, maturité; (of bills—*de lettres de change*, *f.*) échéance, *f.* To come to —; (of bills—*lettres de change*, *&c.*) échoir.

mat-weed (-wide), *n.*, stipe tenace, sparte, *f.*

maudlin, *n.*, (bot.) aigremoine, *f.*

maudlin, *adj.*, à moitié ivre; (fig.) insipide.

maugre (mô-gheur), *adv.*, (jest.) malgré, en dépit de.

maul, *v.a.*, rosser; rouer de coups.

maul, *n.* *V.* **mall.**

maul-stick, *n.*, appui-main, *m.*

maunday-thursday (mâ'n'dè-theur'z'dè), *n.*, jeudi saint, jeudi absolu, jeudi de l'absoute, *m.*

mausolean, *adj.*, de mausolée.

mausoleum, *n.*, mausolée, *m.*

maw (mô), *n.*, (of birds—*des oiseaux*) jabot, *m.*; (of animals—*des animaux*) panse, *f.*

mawkish (môk'-), *adj.*, fade, dégoûtant, insipide.

mawkishness, *n.*, fadeur, insipidité, *f.*

mawmish (mô-), *adj.*, nauséabond.

maw-worm (mô-weurme), *n.*, ver intestinai; (fig.) tartufe, *m.*

maxillar, *or* **maxillary,** *adj.*, maxillaire.

maxim, *n.*, maxime, *f.*

maxim-monger (-meun'gn'gheur), *n.*, débitaut de maximes, *m.*

maximum, *n.*, maximum, *m.*

may, *v.auxil.*, pouvoir. — be; *peut-être.* That — be; *cela se peut.* He — go; *il peut sortir.* — I! *puisse-je!*

may (mè), *n.*, (month—*mois*) mai, *m.* —bloom: aubépine, *f.*; (fig.) *printemps de la vie, m.*

may, *v.a.*, cueillir des fleurs le matin du premier mai.

may-bug (-beughe), *n.*, hanneton, *m.*

may-bush (-boushe), *n.*, aubépine *f.*

may-day (mè-dè), *n.*, premier mai, *m.*

may-flower (-flaoueur), *n.*, fleur d'aubépine, *f.*

may-game, *n.*, jeu de mai, jeu de la Saint-Philippe, *m.*

mayhem (mè-hème), *n.*, (jur.) mutilation, *f.*

may-lady (-lédi), *n.*, reine de la Saint-Philippe, *f.*

may-lord (-lorde), *n.*, roi de la Saint-Phi. lippe, *m.*

may-morn, *n.*, (fig.) fraîcheur, vigueur, *f.*

mayor (mé-eur), *n.*, maire, *m.*

mayoralty (mé-eur'-), *n.*, mairie, *f.*

mayoress (mé-eur'-), *n.*, femme du maire, *f.*

may-pole (-pôl), *n.*, mai, arbre du premier mai, *m.*

maze (méze), *n.*, labyrinthe; dédale; (fig.) embarras, *m.*, perplexité, *f.*

maze, *v.a.*, jeter dans l'embarras; embarrasser; troubler.

mazourka, *n.*, mazourka, masurka, masourque, *f.*

mazy (méz'i), *adj.*, de labyrinthe; (fig.) confus; embrouillé.

me (mi), *pron.*, me, moi. Of —, from —; *de moi.* To —; *moi; à moi; me.*

mead (mide), *n.*, hydromel; (meadow—*champ*) pré, *m.*, prairie, *f.*

meadow (mèd'ô), *n.*, prairie, *f.*, pré, *m.*

meadow-saffron, *n.*, colchique, *f.*

meadow-sweet (-swite), *n.*, spirée; herbe aux abeilles, reine des prés, *f.*

meadowy (mèd'ô-i), *adj.*, de pré, de prairie.

meagre (mi-gheur), *adj.*, maigre; pauvre.

meagrely, *adv.*, maigrement; pauvrement.

meagreness, *n.*, maigreur; pauvreté, *f.*

meal (mil), *n.*, farine, *f.*; (repast) repas, *m.*

mealiness (mil'-), *n.*, propriété farineuse; (fruit) nature cotonneuse, *f.*

mealman, *n.*, (mealmen) farinier; marchand de farine, *m.*

meal-time (-taïme), *n.*, heure du repas, *f.*

meal-tub (-teube), *n.*, farinière, huche, *f.*

mealy (mil'i), *adj.*, farineux; poudreux, (fruit) cotonneux.

mealy-mouthed (-maouth'de), *adj.*, qui a la bouche doucereuse; qui a la langue dorée.

mealy-mouthedness (-maouthd'-), *n.*, bouche doucereuse; langue dorée, *f.*

mealy-tree (-tri), *n.*, (bot.) viorne commune, bourdaine blanche, *f.*

mean (mîne), *adj.*, (wanting dignity—*défaut d'honneur*) bas; (despicable—*vil*) bas, méprisable, vil, abject; (of little value—*de peu de valeur*) médiocre; (low-minded—*bas*) mesquin, commun; (humble) pauvre, petit, chétif; (avaricious—*avare*) sordide, avare, regardant; (middle—*au milieu*) moyen.

mean (mîne), *n.*, milieu, terme moyen; (log.) moyen, terme moyen, *m.*; (math.) moyenne proportionelle, moyenne; (mediocrity) médiocrité. —s (*sing.*) moyen, *m.*; voie, *f.*; —s (*pl.*); moyens; revenus, *m.pl.*; fortune, *f.sing.* By —s of; *au moyen de.* By this —s present; by some —s or other; *de manière ou d'autre.* By all —s; *par tous les moyens; absolument; à toute force; certainement.* By no —s; *par aucun moyen; en aucune manière; aucunement; nulle*

ment. To live on one's —s; *vivre de ses revenus, de sa fortune.*

mean, *v.a.* (preterit and past part., Meant),(to signify—*signifier*) signifier, vouloir dire; (to intend—*se proposer*) se proposer, avoir en vue, vouloir. To — for; *destiner à.* What does that word — ? *que veut dire ce mot?* What do you — ? *que voulez-vous dire?* I meant that for you; *je vous destinais cela.*

mean, *v.n.,* avoir l'intention de; se proposer; avoir en vue, vouloir; entendre. To — well to; *vouloir le bien de.*

meander (mi-a'n'-), *n.,* méandre; dédale, labyrinthe, *m.*; sinuosité, *f.*

meander, *v.n.,* serpenter; aller en serpentant; former des sinuosités.

meander. *v.a.,* faire serpenter.

meandering, meandrian, meandrous, òr meandry, *adj.,* qui serpente; qui va en serpentant; onduleux, sinueux.

meaning (mi'n'-), *adj.,* significatif; (pers.) à intentions. Ill—; *à mauvaises intentions.* Well—; *à bonnes intentions, bien intentionné.*

meaning (mi'n'-), *n.,* (signification) signification, *f.,* sens, *m.*; (intention) intention, *f.,* dessein, *m.*; (thought—*idée*) pensée, *f.* What is the — of that? *que veut dire cela? que signifie cela?* That is not my —; *ce n'est pas là ce que je veux dire, ce n'est pas là ma pensée.* Double —; *double sens.* To know the — of anything; *savoir ce que quelque chose signifie, veut dire.*

meanly (mi'n'-),*adv.,* bassement; méprisablement, vilement, abjectement ; médiocrement, mesquinement, pauvrement; chétivement; sordidement.

meanness (mi'n'-), *n.,* bassesse, *f.* ; caractère méprisable, caractère vil. caractère abject, *m.* ; médiocrité ; pauvreté; mesquinerie, lésinerie,*f.*

mean-spirited, *adj.,* sans cœur; lâche.

meantime, *or* **meanwhile** (-taîme,-whaîle), *adv.,* dans l'intervalle; en attendant. In the —; *sur ces entrefaites.*

mease (mîce), *n.,* quantité de cinq cents, *f.*

measled (mi'z'l'de),*adj.,* atteint de rougeole; couvert de taches de rougeole.

measles (mi'z'l'ze), *n.pl.,* rougeole, *f.sing.*; (of swine—*du porc*) ladrerie, *f.*

measurable (mèj'eur'a-b'l), *adj.,* mesurable ; (moderate—*limité*) modéré.

measurableness (mèj'eur'-), *n.,* qualité de ce qui est mesurable ; mensurabilité, *f.*

measurably (mèj'eur'-), *adv.,* avec mesure; modérément.

measure (mèj'eur), *n.,* mesure ; (of a number —*d'un nombre*) division, partie aliquote ; (mus., poet.,dancing) mesure; (fig.) capacité, *f.* The — of my days; *le nombre de mes jours.* To take —s; *prendre des mesures.* To take legal —s ; *avoir recours aux voies légales.* To take any one's — for à coat; *prendre la mesure d'un habit à quelqu'un.* In—; *avec mesure.* In a great —; *en grande partie.* In some —; *en quelque sorte.* Beyond all —, without —; *outre mesure, sans mesure, sans bornes.* To —; *sur mesure.*

measure (mèj'eur), *v.a.,* mesurer; (land—*la terre*) arpenter; (solids—*les solides*) métrer.

measure (mèj'eur), *v.n.,* avoir. This —s ten feet; *ceci a dix pieds de longueur.*

measured (mèj'eur'de), *adj.,* mesuré; égal, uniforme.

measureless (mèj'eur'-), *adj.,* qui ne peut être mesuré; immense, infini, illimité.

measurement (mèj'eur'-), *n.,* mesurage, *m.*; mesure,*f.* ; (of land—*de terrain*) arpentage, *m.*

measurer (mèj'eur'-), *n.,* mesureur ; (of land —*de terrain*)arpenteur; (of buildings—*de bâtiments*) toiseur, *m.*

measuring (mèj'eur'-), *n.,* mesurage, *m*

meat (mîte), *n.,* viande; (food—*aliment*) nourriture, *f.,* aliment, *m.* Roast —; *rôti, m.*

Boiled —; *bouilli, m.* Broken —; *graillon, m.* Brown —; *viande noire.* White —; *viande blanche.* Butcher's—; *viande de boucherie;* grosse viande. (Green —; (for animals—*pour les animaux*) vert, *m.* That is my — and drink ; *c'est ce qui me fait vivre.* Force — ball ; *andouillette, f.*

meath (mîth),*n.,* breuvage, *m.*

meatus (mi-é-), *n.,* (anat.) méat, conduit. *m.*

mechanic (mi-ka'n'ike), *n.,* mécanicien ; artisan, ouvrier, *m.*

mechanic, *or* **mechanical**(mi-ka'n'-), *adj.,* mécanique; d'ouvrier; d'artisan; de la classe ouvrière ; (acting without intelligence—*agissant sans intelligence*) machinal.

mechanically (mi-ka'n'-), *adv.,* mécaniquement ; (without intelligence—*sans intelligence*) machinalement.

mechanicalness (mi-ka'n'-), *n.,* nature mécanique; nature machinale.*f.*

mechanician (mèk-a-nish'a'n), *n.,* mécanicien, *m.*

mechanics (mi-ka'n'-ikse), *n.pl.,* mécanique, *f.sing.*

mechanism (mèk'a'n'iz'me), *n.,* mécanisme, *m.*; mécanique,*f.*

mechanist (mèk'a'n'-), *n.,* mécanicien ; constructeur de machines, *m.*

mechlin (mèk'line),*n.,* malines (dentelle),*f.*

meconium (mi-cô-), *n.,* méconium, *m.*

medal (mèd'-), *n.,* médaille, *f.*

medallic (mi-), *adj.,* de médaille.

medallion (mi-dal'ieune), *n.,* médaillon, *m.*

medallist (mèd'-), *n.,* médailliste, *m.*

meddle (mèd'd'l), *v.n.,* se mêler des affaires d'autrui. To — with; *toucher à ; se mêler de ; s'occuper de; intervenir dans; s'immiscer dans.*

meddler, *n.,* personne qui se mêle des affaires d'autrui,*f.* ; fâcheux; intrigant; fureteur, *m.*

meddlesome (-seume), *or* **meddling,** *adj.,* qui se mêle des affaires d'autrui ; intrigant.

meddlesomeness, *n.,* disposition à se mêler des affaires d'autrui ; intrigue, *f.*

mediæval (mèd'i-i-), *adj.,* du moyen âge.

medial (mi-), *adj.,* moyen ; (gram.) médial.

median (mi-), *adj.,* (anat.) médian.

mediant (mi-), *n.,* (mus.) médiante, *f.*

mediastinum (mèd'i-as-taï-), *n.,* (anat.) médiastin, *m.*

mediate (mî-), *v.n.,* être médiateur.

mediate, *v.a.,* obtenir par la médiation.

mediate,*adj.,* médiat. interposé.

mediately, *adv.,* médiatement.

mediation (mî-di-é-), *n.,* médiation ; entremise; intercession,*f.* ; intermédiaire, *m.*

mediatization (mî-di-a-taïzé-), *n.,* médiatisation, *f.*

mediatize (mî-di-a-taïze), *v.a.,* médiatiser.

mediator (mî-di-é-teur), *n.,* médiateur, *m.*

mediatorial, *or* **mediatory,** *adj.,* de médiateur.

mediatorship, *n.,* office de médiateur, *m.*

mediatrix (mî-di-é-), *n.,* médiatrice, *f.*

medic (mèd'-). *n.,* (bot.) luzerne, *f.*

medicable (mèd'i-ca-b'l), *adj.,* guérissable, curable.

medical (mèd'-), *adj.,* médical; de médecin, de médecine. — man; *médecin, m.*

medically, *adv.,* en médecine; sous le rapport médical.

medicament (mèd'-), *n.,* médicament, *m.*

medicamental. *adj.,* médicamenteux.

medicamentally,*adv.,* en forme de médicament.

medicaster (mèd'-), *n.,* médicastre, charlatan, *m.*

medicate (mèd'-), *v.a.,* donner des propriétés médicales à ; (to treat with medicine—*donner des médicaments*) médicamenter.

medication (mèd'i-ké-), *n.*, action de donner des propriétés médicales ; action de médicamenter, *f.*

medicinal (mè-diss'i-), *adj.*, médicinal.

medicinally, *adv.*, médicinalement.

medicine (mèd'i-cine), *n.*, médecine, *f.* ; remède ; médicament, *m.*

medicine-chest (-tshèste), *n.*, droguier, *m.* ; pharmacie, *f.*

mediety (mè-daï-ô-), *n.*, état mitoyen, *m.*

mediocre (mi-di-ô-keur), *adj.*, médiocre.

mediocrist (mi-di-ô-), *n.*, personne de talents médiocres, personne médiocre, *f.*

mediocrity (mi-di-ok'-), *n.*, médiocrité, *f.*

meditate (mèd'-), *v.a.*, méditer.

meditate, *v.n.*, méditer. To — on ; *méditer sur ; méditer.*

meditated, *adj.*, médité, projeté.

meditation (mèd'i-té-), *n.*, méditation, *f*

meditative, *adj.*, méditatif ; de méditation.

mediterranean, *or* **mediterraneous** (mèd'i-tèr-rè-ni-), *adj.*, méditerrané. — sea ; *mer méditerranée, f.*

mediterranean, *n.*, Méditerranée, *f.*

medium (mi-), *n.* (*media*), milieu, terme moyen ; médium ; (log.) moyen terme, moyen, *m.* ; (math.) moyenne proportionnelle, moyenne, *f.* ; (agent) agent intermédiaire ; (means—*instrument*) moyen, intermédiaire, *m.* ; voie, entremise, *f.* Circulating — ; *agent monétaire, agent de circulation, m.* Through the — of ; *par l'intermédiaire de, par l'entremise de.*

medlar (mèd'-), *n.*, (fruit) nèfle, *f.* ; (tree—*arbre*) néflier, *m.*

medley (mèd'li), *adj.*, mêlé, mixte.

medley, *n.*, mélange, *m.* ; bigarrure, *f.* ; (mus.) pot pourri, *m.*

medulla (mi-deul'la), *n.*, moelle, *f.*

medullar (mi-), *or* **medullary** (mèd'-), *adj.*, de moelle, médullaire.

meed (mîde), *n.*, récompense, *f.* ; prix, *m.*

meek (mîke), *adj.*, doux, humble, soumis.

meeken (mi'k'n), *v.a.*, adoucir.

meek-eyed (-a'ye'-dé), *adj.*, au regard doux.

meekly, *adv.*, avec douceur ; humblement.

meekness, *n.*, douceur ; humilité, *f.*

meer (mîre), *n.* and *adj.* V. **mere**.

meered (mîr'de), *adj.*, (ant.). V. **mered**.

meerschaum (mîr-), *n.*, écume de mer, *f.*

meet (mîte), *v.a.* (*preterit* and *past part.*, Met) rencontrer ; faire la rencontre de ; (to find—*contrer*) trouver, recevoir ; (to join—*approcher*) joindre, rejoindre ; (to face—*affronter*) faire face à, affronter ; (to appear before—*paraître devant*) se présenter devant ; (in society—*en société*) voir ; (a bill—*une lettre de change, &c.*) faire honneur à. To — one's engagements ; *faire face à ses engagements.* Persons met together ; *des personnes réunies ensemble.* Persons met from all parts ; *des personnes réunies, rassemblées de toutes parts.*

meet, *v.n.*, se rencontrer ; se voir ; (to assemble—*s'assembler*) se réunir, s'assembler ; (to join —*se joindre*) se joindre, se rejoindre. To — with (a person—*une personne*) ; *rencontrer, se trouver avec* ; (thing—*chose*) *rencontrer, découvrir* ; (misfortune—*malheur*) *éprouver, subir, essuyer* ; (good fortune—*bonheur*) *éprouver* ; (kindness, a reception—*bonté, accueil*) *recevoir.*

meet (mîte), *adj.*, propre, convenable, à propos.

meeter (mît'-), *n.*, personne qui en rencontre une autre, *f.*

meeting (mît'-), *n.*, rencontre ; (interview—*rendez-vous*) entrevue ; (assembly—*réunion*) assemblée, réunion, *f.* ; (of rivers—*de rivières*) confluent, *m.*, jonction ; (of roads—*de routes*) jonction, *f.* ; (of dissenters—*de dissidents*) office, service, *m.*

meeting-house (-haouce), *n.*, maison de réunion, *f.* ; (of dissenters—*de dissidents*) temple, *m.*

meetly, *adv.*, convenablement, à propos ; comme il faut.

meetness, *n.*, propriété, convenance, *f.*

megrim (mi-grime), *n.*, migraine, *f.* ; vertige, *m.*

melancholic (mèl'a'n'kol'-), *adj.*, mélancolique, triste.

melancholic (mèl'a'n'kol'-), *n.*, (pers.) mélancolique, hypocondriaque, hypocondre, *m.*, *f.* ; (state—*état*) mélancolie, *f.*

melancholily, *adv.*, mélancoliquement.

melancholiness, *n.*, mélancolie, *f.*

melancholy, *n.*, hypocondrie, mélancolie, tristesse, *f.*

melancholy, *adj.*, hypocondriaque, mélancolique, triste (of things—*des choses*) triste, cruel, lugubre, affligeant.

melilot, *n.*, (bot.) mélilot, *m.*

meliorate (mil'yo-réte), *v.a.*, améliorer.

meliorate, *v.n.*, s'améliorer.

melioration (mil'yo-r-é), *n.*, amélioration, *f.*

melliferous (mèl'lif'èr-), *or* **mellific** (mèl'lif'-), *adj.*, mellifère.

mellification (-ik'é-), *n.*, mellification, *f.*

mellifluence (-lif'liou-), *n.*, douceur constante, *f.*

mellifluent, *or* **mellifluous**, *adj.*, qui abonde en miel ; doux, plein de douceur ; suave.

mellow (mèl'lô), *adj.*, mou ; mol ; (fruit) blet ; (paint.) moelleux ; (in liquor—*à moitié ivre*) entre deux vins, en train, gai ; (of land—*d'une terre*) meuble ; (fig.) doux, moelleux, mélodieux.

mellow, *v.a.*, mûrir ; faire mûrir ; (fruit) rendre blet ; (paint.) donner du moelleux à ; (land—*terrain*) ameublir ; (fig.) rendre mélodieux, rendre doux ; adoucir, amollir. To—into; *amener à.*

mellow, *v.n.*, mollir, mûrir ; (fruit) devenir blet ; (paint.) prendre du moelleux ; (of land—*terrain*) devenir meuble ; (fig.) devenir mélodieux, s'adoucir, s'amollir.

mellowly, *adv.*, d'une manière douce, moelleuse, mélodieuse.

mellowness, *n.*, maturité, *f.* ; état d'un fruit blet ; (paint.) moelleux ; état d'un terrain meuble, *m.* ; (fig.) mollesse, douceur, *f.*, moelleux, *m.*

melodious (mè-lô-di-), *adj.*, mélodieux.

melodiously, *adv.*, mélodieusement.

melodiousness, *n.*, mélodie, *f.*

melodize (mèl'o-daïze), *v.a.*, rendre mélodieux.

melodrama, *or* **melodrame** (mèl-o-drā-ma, -drâme), *n.*, mélodrame, *m.*

melody (mèl'-), *n.*, mélodie, *f.*

melon (mèl'-), *n.*, melon, *m.*

melon-bed (-bède), *n.*, melonnière, *f.*

melt (mèlte), *v.a.*, fondre, faire fondre ; résoudre ; (fig.) attendrir, fléchir ; faire faiblir.

melt, *v.n.*, fondre, se fondre ; se résoudre ; (fig.) fléchir, faiblir, s'attendrir. To — into tears ; *fondre en larmes.*

melter, *n.*, fondeur, *m.*

melting, *adj.*, qui fond ; (fruit) fondant ; (of the weather—*du temps*) étouffant ; (fig.) attendrissant, touchant.

melting, *n.*, fusion, *f.* ; attendrissement, *m.*

melting-house (-haouce), *n.*, fonderie, *f.*

meltingly, *adv.*, en se fondant ; (fig.) d'une manière attendrissante.

meltingness, *n.*, pouvoir de fondre, d'attendrir.

melwel (mèl-wèl), *n.*, (ich.) merlus, *m.* ;

merluche (mèr-), *n.*, (ich.) merlus, *m.* ;

member (mè'm'beur), *n.*, membre, *m.*

membered (mè'm'beurde), *adj.*, membré ; qui a des membres.

membership, *n.*, qualité de membre ; société, *f.*

membranaceous,membraneous,mem-branous, or **membraniferous** (mè'm'brè-né-shi-eusse, -bré-ni-, -bré-, -ifèr-), *adj.*, membraneux.

membrane (mè'm'bréne), *n.*, membrane; (min.) couche superficielle, *f.*

. **memento** (mi-mè'n'tô), *n.*, souvenir, mémento, *m.*

memoir (mt-), *n.*, mémoire, *m.*

memorable (mè'm'o-ra-b'l), *adj.*, mémorable.

memorably, *adv.*, mémorablement.

memorandum (mè'm'o-ra'n'deume), *n.*, (*memoranda*, *-dums*). note, *f.*; (com.) bordereau, *m.*

memorandum-book (-bouke), *n.*, agenda; com.) carnet, *m.*

memorial (mi-mô-), *n.*, souvenir, *m.*; commémoration; (note) note, *f.*, mémoire, *m.*; (petition) requête, pétition, demande, *f.*; mémorial, *m.*

memorial, *adj.*, propre à conserver le souvenir; commémoratif; de la mémoire.

memorialist (mi-mô-), *n.*, auteur d'une requête, d'une demande, auteur de mémoire, pétitionnaire, *m.*

memorialize (mi-mô-ri-al'aïze), *v.a.*, présenter une demande à, une requête à; adresser un mémoire à.

memorize (mè'm'o-raïze), *v.a.*, conserver la mémoire de; faire ressouvenir de.

memory (mè'm'-), *n.*, mémoire, *f.*, souvenir, *m.* In — ; *en souvenir de.* To the best of my — ; *autant qu'il m'en souvient.* From — ; *de mémoire.* Within the — of man; *de mémoire d'homme.* Good, bad — ; *bonne, mauvaise mémoire.*

memphian (mè'm'fi-a'n), *adj.*, de Memphis; ténébreux.

men (mène), *n.pl.* *V.* **man.**

menace (mè'n-), *n.*, menace, *f.*

menace, *v.a.*, menacer.

menacer, *n.*, personne qui menace, *f.*

menacing, *adj.*, menaçant.

menage (mè-nâje), or **menagery** (mi-nâji-ri), *n.*, ménagerie, *f.*

mend (mè'n'de), *v.a.*, raccommoder; réparer; (a pen, pencil—*plume, crayon*) tailler; (one's pace—*l'allure*) hâter; (fig.) corriger, avancer, réformer, rétablir, améliorer.

mend, *v.n.*, se corriger, s'améliorer, se réformer, se rétablir. My health is —ing; *ma santé se rétablit.*

mendable (-a-b'l), *adj.*, susceptible de raccommodage; susceptible de réparation; réparable; (fig.) corrigible.

mendacity (mè'n-), *n.*, mensonge, *m.*; fausseté, *f.*

mender (mé'n'd'-), *n.*, réparateur, raccommodeur, *m.*, raccommodeuse; (fig.) personne qui corrige, qui améliore, qui réforme, *f.*, correcteur, *m.*

mendicancy (mè'n-), *n.*, mendicité, *f.*

mendicant (mè'n-), *adj.*, mendiant; de mendicité. — friar; *frère mendiant, moine mendiant, m.*

mendicant, *n.*, mendiant, *m.*, mendiante, *f.*

mendicity (mè'n-), *n.*, mendicité, *f.*

menial (mî-), *n.*, domestique, *m., f.*

menial, *adj.*, domestique, de domestique; (fig.) bas, avilissant.

meninges (mè-ni'n'djïze), *n.pl.*, (anat.) méninges, *f.pl.*

meniscus (mi-nis'-), *n.*, (opt.) ménisque, *m.*

meniver (mè'n-), or **miniver** (mi'n'-), *n.*, petit-gris, *m.*

menology (mi-nol'o-dji), *n.*, ménologe, *m.*

mensal (mè'n'-), *adj.*, de table.

menses (mè'n'sïze), *n.pl.*, (med.) menstrues, *f.pl.*

menstrual (mè'n'strou-), *adj.*, mensuel; (med.) menstruel.

menstruum (mè'n'strou-), *n.*, dissolvant, ⊙menstrue, *m.*

mensurability (mè'n's'iou-), *n.*, mensurabilité, *f.*

mensurable (mè'n's'iou-ra-b'l), *adj.*, mesurable.

mensuration (mè'n's'iou-ré-), *n.*, mesurage, *m.*; mensuration, *f.*

mental (mè'n'-), *adj.*, mental, intellectuel, moral.

mentally, *adv.*, mentalement, intellectuellement, moralement.

mention (mè'n'-), *n.*, mention, *f.*

mention, *v.a.*, mentionner, faire mention de; parler de. Do not — it! *n'y faites pas attention!* I am much obliged to you; *je vous suis très obligé.* Do not — it; *il n'y a pas de quoi.*

mentor (mè'n'-), *n.*, mentor, *m.*

mentorial, *adj.*, qui renferme des conseils.

mephitic, or **mephitical** (mi-faï'-), *adj.*, méphitique.

mephitis (mi-faï'-), or **mephitism** (mèf'i-tiz'me), *n.*, méphitisme, *m.*

meracious (mi-ré-shi-eusse), *adj.*, (ant.) pur, fort.

mercantile (meur-ca'n'taïl), *adj.*, mercantile, de commerce. — establishment; *maison de commerce, f.*

mercenarily (meur-ci-), *adv.*, mercenairement.

mercenariness, *n.*, vénalité, *f.*; caractère mercenaire, *m.*

mercenary (meur-ci-), *adj.*, mercenaire, vénal.

mercenary, *n.*, mercenaire, *m., f.*

mercer (meur-ceur), *n.*, mercier, *m.*, mercière, *f.*

mercery, *n.*, mercerie, *f.*

merchandise (meur'tsha'n'daïze), *n.*, marchandise, *f.*

merchandise, *v.n.*, (l.u.) négocier, trafiquer.

merchant (meur'tsha'n'te), *n.*, négociant, commerçant, marchand, *m.*, marchande, *f.* Coal— ; *marchand de charbon.*

merchant, *adj.*, commercial; marchand.

merchantable (-a-b'l), *adj.*, marchand. In a — state; *marchand; en état d'être livré au commerce.*

merchant-like (-laïke), *adj.*, en négociant, en marchand, en commerçant.

merchant-man, or **merchant-ship**, *n.*, vaisseau marchand, *m.*

merchant-service (-seur), *n.*, marine marchande, *f.*

merciful (meur-ci-foule), *adj.*, miséricordieux, clément; indulgent.

mercifully, *adv.*, miséricordieusement; avec clémence.

mercifulness, *n.*, miséricorde, clémence, *f.*

merciless, *adj.*, sans miséricorde; sans clémence, cruel, implacable, impitoyable.

mercilessly, *adv.*, sans miséricorde; impitoyablement, sans pitié.

mercurial (meur-kiou-), *adj.*, de Mercure; de mercure; ardent, vif; mercuriel.

mercurial, *n.*, (preparation) préparation mercurielle; (fig.) personne vive, *f.*

mercurification (-fi-ké-), *n.*, mercurification, *f.*

mercury (meur-kiou-), *n.*, (astron., myth.) Mercure; (metal.) mercure, *m.*; (bot.) mercuriale; (fig.) ardeur, vivacité, *f.*

mercury, *v.a.*, enduire d'une préparation mercurielle.

mercy (meur-ci), *n.*, merci, miséricorde, *f.*; (compassion) compassion; (clemency) clémence; (pardon) grâce, *f.*, pardon, *m.* — ! *grâce!* For —'s sake; *par grâce.* At the — of; *à la merci*

de. To be at the — of: *être à la discrétion de.*
To cry — : *demander grâce.*
mercy-seat (-site), *n.. propitiatoire. m.*
mere (mire), *n., lac, m.* : (boundary—*limite*) *borne, f.*
mere (mire), *adj.. pur, simple* : (b.s.) *fieffé. franc.*
mered (mir'de), *adj.. de borne. de limite.*
merely (mir'-), *adv.. simplement. seulement. purement : uniquement.*
mere-stone (-stone), *n., borne, limite. f.*
meretricious (mèr'i-trish'euss), *adj., de courtisane* ; (fig.) *d'emprunt. faux.*
meretriciously. *adv., en courtisane.*
meretriciousness. *n.. conduite de courtisane, f.*
merganser (meur-), *n.. (orni.) harle huppé, harle, m.*
merge (meurdje), *v.a.. laisser fondre ; éteindre.*
merge, *v.n.. s'éteindre : se perdre.* To — into ; *se fondre dans : se confondre avec.*
meridian (mi-), *n., méridien ; midi ;* (fig.) *apogée, m.*
meridian, *adj., méridien ; de midi : dans son apogée.*
meridional (mi-), *adj., méridional ; du méridien.*
meridionality, *n.. exposition au midi. f.*
meridionally, *adv.. dans la direction du midi ; au midi.*
merit (mè-), *n., mérite, m.*
merit, *v.a., mériter.*
meritorious (mèr'i-to-), *adj., méritoire.*
meritoriously, *adv., méritoirement.*
meritoriousness, *n., mérite, m.*
merlin (meur-), *n., (orni.) émerillon, m.*
merlon (meur-), *n., (fort.) merlon, m.*
mermaid (meur-méde), *n., sirène, f.*
merrily (mèr-), *adv.. joyeusement, gaiment, avec allégresse.*
merriment (mèr'-),*n., gaîté, joie, allégresse, réjouissance. f.*
merriness (mèr'-), *n., gaîté, joie, allégresse; réjouissance, f.*
merry (mèr'-), *adj., joyeux, allègre, gai ;* (b.s.) *plaisant.* To make — : *se divertir ; être gai.* To make — with ; *se réjouir de ; se divertir de ;* (b.s.) *plaisanter sur.*
merry. *n.. (bot.) guigne, f.*
merry-andrew (-a'n'drou. *n., paillasse, m.*
merry-andrew. *adj., de paillasse.*
merry-make (-méke), *v.n., se réjouir. se divertir.*
merry-making (-mék'-), *n.. réjouissance ; fête ; gaicté, f.*
merry-thought (-thôthe), *n . lunette de volaille. f.*
mersion (meur'-). *n., immersion. f.*
meseems. *v.imp., il me semble.*
mesenteric (mèz'è'n'tèr'-), *adj.. mésentérique.*
mesentery (mèz'è'n'tèr'i), *n., (anat.) mésentère. m.*
mesh (mèshe), *n.. maille. f.:* (of brewers — *de brasseurs*) *marc, m.*
mesh. *v.a.. prendre au filet.*
meshy. *adj.. de mailles. en réseau.*
mesial (mi-ci-). *adj.. (anat.) médian : interne.*
meslin (mèz'-), *n.. méteil. m.*
mesmeric (mèz'mèr'-). *adj., mesmérique.*
mesmerism (mèz'mèr'iz'me). *n., mesmérisme, m.*
mesmerize (-aïze). *v.a.. magnétiser.*
mesmerizer (-aïz'-. *n.. magnétiseur. m.*
mess (mèce, *n.. (dish—mets) nets, plat. m.:* (milit.) (of officers—*des officiers*) *pension. messe, f.:* (of non-commissioned officers—*des sous-officiers*) *pension. f.;* (of privates—*des soldats*) *ordinaire, m.;* (nav.) (of officers—*des officiers*) *table.*

f.; (of seamen—*des matelots*) *plat, m.* : (medley—*masse confuse*) *gâchis. m.;* (dirt—*ordure*) *saleté;* (of animals—*des animaux*) *ration. f.* To be in a — : *être dans le gâchis : être sale.* To be in a fine — ; *être dans de beaux draps : être dans un bel état.* What a —! *quel gâchis! quelle saleté!*
mess. *v.n.. manger ensemble :* (to dirt—*salir*) *faire du gâchis.* To — together : *être à la même pension; être du même ordinaire : manger à la même gamelle : faire plat ensemble.*
mess. *v.a., donner à manger à ;* (to dirt—*salir*) *salir.*
message (mès-sédje), *n.. message, m.*
messenger (mès-sè'n'djeur), *n.. messager ; avant-coureur. m. ; (nav.) tournevire, f.*
messiah (mès-saï'a), *n , Messie. m.*
messieurs (mèsh'eurze),*n.pl.,messieurs,m.p'.*
messmate, *n., camarade de pension, d'ordinaire, de gamelle, de table. de plat, m.*
messuage (mès'wadje), *n., maison et dépendances. f.pl.*
metacarpal (mèt'-), *adj.. métacarpien.*
metacarpus (mèt'-), *n., (anat.) métacarpe, m.*
metage (mi-tédje), *n.. mesurage de la houille ; prix de ce mesurage. m.*
metal (mèt'-), *n.. métal ;* (for roads—*pour les routes*) *cailloutis, empierrement ;* (fig.) *courage, cœur, m.*
metal-bed (-bède), *n.. encaissement de route, m.*
metalepsis (mèt'a-lèp-), *n., (rhet.) métalepse, f.*
metaleptic. *adj. de métalepse.*
metaleptically, *adv., par métalepse.*
metalled (mèt'al'de), *adj., (of roads—de routes), empierré, en empierrement ; ferré, caillouté.*
metallic, or metallical (mèt'-), *adj., métallique.*
metalliferous (-'if'èr'-), *adj., métallifère.*
metallist, *n., ouvrier en métaux ; métallurgiste. m.*
metallization (-laïzé), *n., métallisation, f.*
metallize (-laize), *v.a., métalliser.*
metallography, *n.. métallographie, f.*
metallurgic (-leur'djike), *or* **metallurgical** (-djik'-), *adj., métallurgique.*
metallurgist (-leur'djiste), *n., métallurgiste. m.*
metallurgy (-leur'dji), *n., métallurgie, f.*
metal-man, *n.. ouvrier en métaux, m.*
metal-stone (-stône),*n., argile schisteuse. f.*
metamorphose (mèt'a-mor-fôce), *v.a.. metamorphoser.*
metamorphosis (mèt'a-mor-fo-cice), *n., métamorphose,f.*
metaphor (mèt'-). *n., métaphore, f.*
metaphoric, or metaphorical. *adj.. métaphorique.*
metaphorically, *adv., métaphoriquement.*
metaphorist, *n., personne qui emploie la métaphore, f.*
metaphrase (mèt'a-frèze), *or* **metaphrasis** (mi taf'ra-cice), *n.. métaphrase, f.*
metaphysic. or metaphysical (mèt'a-f'z'-), *adj.. métaphysique.*
metaphysically. *adv..métaphysiquement.*
metaphysics (-fiz'ikse), *n.pl., métaphysique. f.sing.*
metaplasm (mèt'a-plaz'me), *n.,(gram.) métaplasme, m.*
metastasis (mi-tas-ta-cice), *n., (med.) métastase. f.*
metatarsal (mèt'a-târ-), *adj., métatarsien.*
metatarsus (mèt'a-târ-), *n., (anat.) métatarse, m.*
metathesis (mi-tath'i-cice), *n.. (gram.) métathèse, f.*
meto (mite), *v.a., mesurer.*

mete, *n.*, mesure, *f.*

metempsychose (mi-tè'm'si-kôze), *v.a.*, faire subir la métempsycose à.

metempsychosis (-kô-cice), *n.*, métempsycose. *f.*

meteor (mi-ti-), *n.*, météore, *m.*

meteoric, *adj.*, météorique.

meteorite (-aïte), *or* **meteorolite** (-laïte), *n.*. (l.u.) météorolithe, aérolithe, *m.*

meteorologic (-djike), *o* **meteorological** (-djik'-), *adj.*, météorologique.

meteorology (mi-ti-or-ol-o-dji), *n.*, météorologie, *f.*

meteorous, *adj.*, de météore.

meter (mit'-), *n.*, mesureur, *m.*

mete-stick (mit'-), *n.*, (nav.) niveau, *m.*

metheglin (mi-thèg'linc), *n.*, hydromel, *m.*

methinks (mi-thi'n'kse),*v.imp.*, il me semble.

method (meth'-), *n.*, méthode; manière; voie, *f.*; moyen; ordre, *m.*

methodic, *or* **methodical**, *a-lj.*, méthodique.

methodically, *adv.*, méthodiquement.

methodism, *n.*, méthodisme, *m.*

methodist, *n.*, méthodiste, *m.*

methodistic, *a-lj.*, méthodiste.

methodize (-aïze), *v.a.*, donner de la méthode à ; ranger, régler.

methought (mi-thôte), *v.imp.*, il me semblait.

metonymic, *or* **metonymical** (mi-to'n'-), *adj.*, employé par métonymie.

metonymically, *adv.*, par métonymie.

metonymy (mi-to'n'-), *n.*, métonymie, *f.*

metope (mèt'o-pi), *n.*, (arch.) métope, *f.*

metoposcopical (mèt'-), *adj.*, métoposcopique.

metoposcopy (mèt'-), *n.*, métoposcopie, *f.*

metre (mi-teur), *n.*, (measure—*mesure*,) mètre (poet.), vers, *m.*. mesure, *f.*

metrical (mèt'-), *adj.*, métrique; en vers, de mesure.

metrically, *adv.*, d'après le système métrique; d'une manière métrique, en vers.

metrology (mi-trol'o-dji), *n.*, métrologie, *f.*

metronome (mèt'ro-nôme), *n.*, métronome, *m.*

metropolis (mi-), *n.*, capitale, métropole, *f.*

metropolitan, *adj.*, de la capitale; métropolitain.

metropolitan, *n.*, métropolitain, *m.*

mettle (mèt't'l), *n.*, fougue, ardeur, *f.*; (fig.) courage, cœur, *m.*

mettled (mèt't'l'de), *adj.*, vif, ardent; fougueux; courageux.

mettlesome (-seume), *adj.*, fougueux, ardent; vif.

mettlesomely, *adv.*, avec ardeur, avec fougue.

mettlesomeness, *n.*, fougue, ardeur, *f.*

mew (miou), *n.*, (orni.)mouette; (cage) mue, sage; prison, *f.* —s; écuries, *f.pl.*

mew (miou), *v.a.*, (to shut up—*confiner*) enfermer ; (to change—*changer*) renouveler, changer.

mew (miou), *v.n.*, (of cats—*des chats*) miauler; (to moult—*muer*) muer; (to change—*changer*) changer.

mewing, *n.*, mue, *f.*; (of a cat—*du chat*) miaulement, *m.*

mewl (mioule), *v.n.*, vagir, pousser des vagissements.

mewler, *n.*,personne qui pousse des vagissements, *f.*

mewling, *n.*, vagissement, *m.*

mezereon (mi-zi-ri-), *n.*, (bot.) mézéréon, bois gentil, *m.*

mezzanine (-nîne), *n.*, (arch.) mezzanine, *f.*

mezzo-relievo (-ri-li-vô). *n.*, demi-relief, *m.*

mezzo-tint, *or* **mezzo-tinto** (-ti'n'te,-tô), *bois. m.*

n., mezzo-tinto, *m.*; gravure à la manière noire, *f.*

miasm (maï'az'me), *or* **miasma** (mi-az'-), *n.* (*miasmata*), miasme, *m.*

mica (maï-), *n.*,(min.) mica, *m.*

micaceous (maï-ké-shi-eusse), *adj.*, (min.) micacé.

mice (maïce), *n.pl.* V. **mouse.**

michaelmas (maïk'èl'-), *n.*, la Saint-Michel, *f.* — day ; *la Saint-Michel.*

miche (mish), *v.n.*, (ant.) dérober, voler; se cacher.

mickle (mik'k'l), *a-lj.*, beaucoup.

microcosm (maï-cro-coz'me), *n.*, microcosme, *m.*

micrometer (maï-cro'm'-i-teur), *n.*, micromètre, *m.*

microscope (maï-cro-scôpe), *n.*, microscope, *m.*

microscopic, *or* **microscopical**, *adj.*, microscopique.

microscopically, *adv.*, au microscope.

mid, *adj.*, du milieu ; moyen ; intérieur.

mid-age (-édje), *n.*, âge moyen, *m.*

mid-course (-côrse), *n.*, milieu du chemin; milieu, *m.*

mid-day (-dè), *n.*, midi, *m.*

mid-day, *a-lj.*, de midi.

middle (mid'd'l), *n.*, milieu, centre, *m.*

middle, *adj.*, du milieu, du centre; central; (middling—*médiocre*) médiocre; moyen. — — aged; d'âge moyen; entre deux âges. — ages; moyen-âge, *m.sing.* — -sized; de taille médiocre.

middleman, *n.*, principal locataire; intermédiaire, *m.*

middlemost (-môste), *adj.*, le plus au milieu ; central.

middling, *adj.*, médiocre, moyen ; passable ; (com.) bon, ordinaire.

middlingly, *adv.*, passablement ; médiocrement ; moyennement.

mid-heaven (-hèv'v'n), *n.*, milieu du ciel, *m.*

mid-land, *adj.*, méditerrané, intérieur.

mid-leg (-lèghe), *n.*, mi-jambe, *f.*

mid-lent, *n.*, mi-carême, *f.*

midmost (-môste), *adj.*, au milieu, au centre; central.

midnight (-naïte), *n.*, minuit, *m.*

midrib, *n.*, (bot.) nervure médiane, *f.*

midriff, *n.*, (anat.) diaphragme, *m.*

mid-sea (-si), *n.*, pleine mer, *f.*; milieu de la mer, *m.*

midship, *n.*, (nav.) milieu du vaisseau, *m.* — -frame ; (nav.) *maître couple*, *m.* — -beam; *maître bau, m.*

midshipman, *n.*, aspirant de marine, élève de marine ; enseigne de marine, *m.*

midships, *adv.*, (nav.) par le travers.

midst, *n.*, milieu ; fort, *m.*

midst, *adv.*, au milieu, parmi.

mid-stream (-strîme), *n.*, milieu du courant; milieu du fleuve, *m.*

midsummer (-seum'-), *n.*, milieu de l'été, *m.* ; la Saint-Jean, *f.* —day; *la Saint-Jean.*

mid-watch (-wôtshe), *n.*, milieu de la veillée, *m.*

midway (-wè), *n.*, milieu du chemin; milieu, *m.*

midway, *adj.*, à mi-chemin.

midway, *adv.*, à mi-chemin ; à moitié chemin.

midwife (-wife, *ou* -waïfe), *n.*, sage-femme, accoucheuse, *f.*

midwife,*v.n.*, remplir l'office d'accoucheuse.

midwifery (mid'wif'ri), *n.*, art des accouchements, *m.* ; assistance d'accoucheuse ; obstétrique, *f.*

mid-winter (-wi'n'teur),*n.*,cœur de l'hiver,*m.*

mid-wood (-woude), *n.*, milieu du bois, des bois. *m.*

mien (mîne), *n.*, mine, *f.* ; air, *m.*

miff, *n.*, bouderie, fâcherie, brouillerie, brouille, *f.*

miffed (mifte), *adj.*, fâché, brouillé.

might (maïte), *n.*, puissance, force, *f.* With — and main ; *à corps perdu ; de toutes ses forces.*

mightily, *adv.*, fortement, vigoureusement, grandement, puissamment.

mightiness, *n.*, grandeur, puissance, *f.*

mighty, *adj.*, fort, puissant, vigoureux ; vaste ; grand, important.

mighty, *adv.*, fort, très, bien.

mignonette (mi'n'ieu'nète), *n.*, (bot.) réséda, *m.*

migrate (maï-), *v.n.*, faire une migration ; émigrer.

migration (maï-gré-), *n.*, migration, *f.*

migratory (maï-gré-), *adj.*, émigrant ; nomade ; migratoire. — birds ; *oiseaux voyageurs.*

milch (milshe), *adj.*, à lait, laitière. — cow ; *vache laitière. vache à 'ait, f.*

mild (maïlde), *adj.*, doux ; (of drink—*de boisson*) léger.

mildew (mil'diou), *n.*, tache d'humidité, *f.* ; (on plants—*sur les plantes*) blanc, *m.*, rouille, *f.*

mildew (mil'diou). *v.a.*, frapper de blanc, de rouille ; gâter par l'humidité ; souiller.

mildewed (mil'dioude), *adj.*, gâté par la rouille, par l'humidité.

mildly (maïld'-), *adv.*, doucement ; modérément.

mildness (maïld'-), *n.*, douceur, *f.*

mile (maïle), *n.*, mille, *m.*

mileage (maïl'édje), *n.*, prix par mille ; péage par mille, *m.*

mile-post (-pôste), *or* **mile-stone** (-stône), *n.*, borne milliaire, *f.*

milfoil (-foïl), *n.*, achillée ; mille-feuille, *f.*

miliary, *adj.*, (med.) miliaire.

militant. *adj.*, militant ; qui combat.

militarily, *adv.*, militairement.

military, *adj.*, militaire.

military, *n.*, militaires, *m.pl.* ; militaire, *m.sing.* ; troupe, armée, *f.*

militate, *v.n.*, militer.

militia (mi-lish'ya), *n.*, milice, *f.*

milk, *n.*, lait, *m.*

milk, *v.a.*, traire.

milk-diet (-daï'ète), *n.*, régime de laitage, *m.*

milken, *adj.*, laiteux.

milker, *n.*, personne qui trait, *f.*

milkiness, *n.*, nature laiteuse ; (fig.) douceur, *f.*

milklivered (-liv'eurde), *adj.*, qui a du lait dans les veines ; lâche, poltron.

milkmaid (-méde), *n.*, laitière, fille de laiterie, *f.*

milkman (-ma'n), *n.*, laitier, *m.*

milkpail (-péle), *n.*, seau à lait, *m.*

milkpan (-pa'n), *n.*, jatte à lait, *f.*

milk-porridge, *or* **milk-pottage** (-'tédje), *n.*, soupe au lait, *f.*

milk-pot, *n.*, pot à lait, *m.*

milksop, *n.*, poule mouillée (pers.), *f.*

milk-tooth (-toutb), *n.*, dent de lait, *f.*

milk-van, *n.*, wagon à lait, *m.*

milk-white (-hwaïte), *adj.*, blanc comme le lait.

milk-woman (-woum'-), *n.*, laitière, *f.*

milkwort (-weurte), *n.*, (bot.) euphorbe, *f.*

milky, *adj.*, laiteux, doux.

milky-way (-wè), *n.*, voie lactée, *f.*

mill, *n.*, moulin, *m.* ; (factory—*manufacture*) filature, manufacture, fabrique, usine, *f.* ; (coin.) moulinet, *m.* ; (of cloth—*du drap*) croisure, *f.* Wind- ; *moulin à vent.* Water- —; *moulin à eau*, *m.* ; *roue hydraulique, f.* Cotton, silk- —; *filature de coton, de soie.* Flax- —; *manufacture de toile.* To bring grist to the — ; *faire venir l'eau au moulin.*

mill, *v.a.*, moudre ; (to full—*fouler*) fouler ; (coin.) fabriquer au moulinet ; (chocolate—*chocolat*) faire mousser ; (pop.) donner une volée de coups de poing.

mill-bar (-bàr), *n.*, barre laminée, *f.*

mill-board (-bôrde), *n.*, carton, *m.*

millboard-maker, *n.*, cartonnier, *m.*

mill-course, *n.*, coursier, bief, *m.*

mill-dam, *n.*, barrage de moulin, *m.*

mill-dust (-deuste), *n.*, folle farine, *f.*

milled (milde), *adj.*, foulé. Double- ; *cuir de laine ; croisé.*

millenarian (mil'lè'n'-), *n.*, millénaire, *m.*

millenarian, *adj.*, de mille ans ; du millénaire.

millenary (mil'lè'n'-), *adj.*, millénaire, du millénaire.

millenial (mil'lè'n'-), *adj.*, millénaire, du millénaire.

millenium (mil'lè'n'-), *n.*, millénaire, *m.* (les mille ans avant le jugement dernier).

millepede (mil'li-pède), *n.*, mille-pieds ; myriapode, *m.*

millepore (mil-li-pôre), *n.*, millépore, *m.*

miller (mil'leur), *n.*, meunier, *m.* —'s wife; *meunière, f.*

miller's-thumb (mil'leur'z'theume), *n.*, (ich) meunier, chabot, *m.*

millesimal (mil'lèss'i-), *adj.*, (arith.) de millième.

millet (-'lète), *or* **millet-grass** (-grâce), *n.*, (bot.) millet, mil, *m.*

mill-handle (-ha'n'd'l), *n.*, queue de moulin à bras, *f.*

mill-hopper, *n.*, trémie, *f.*

mill-horse, *n.*, cheval de moulin, *m.*

mill-house (-haouce), *n.*, maison du moulin, *f.* ; atelier des meules, *m.*

milliard (mil-li-àrde), *n.*, milliard, billion, *m.*

milliary, *adj.*, milliaire.

milligram, *n.*, milligramme, *m.*

millilitre (-li-teur), *n.*, millilitre, *m.*

millimeter (-mî-teur), *n.*, millimètre, *m.*

milliner, *n.*, marchande de modes ; modiste, *f.* Man- — ; *marchand de modes ; modiste, m.*

millinery, *n.sing.*, modes (parures de femmes), *f.pl.*

million, *n.*, million, *m.*

millionary, *adj.*, de millions, par millions.

millionnaire (mil'ieun'ére), *n.*, millionnaire, *m.*

millionth (mil'ieu'n'tb), *adj.*, millionième.

millionth, *n.*, millionième, *m.*

mill-moth (-moth), *n.*, (ent.) blatte, *f.*

mill-owner (-ô'n'eur), *n.*, propriétaire de moulin ; chef de fabrique, manufacturier, *m.*

mill-race. *V.* **mill-course**.

mill-stone (-stône), *n.*, meule de moulin, *f.* ; (fig.) poids, *m.*, charge ; (min.) pierre meulière, *f.* To have a — about one's neck ; *avoir un poids sur les épaules ; avoir la corde au cou.*

mill-tooth (-toutb), *n.*, dent molaire, *f.*

millwright (-raïte), *n.*, constructeur de moulins, *m.*

milt, *n.*, rate ; (of fishes—*des poissons*) laite, laitance, *f.*

milt, *v.n.*, (ich.) féconder.

milter, *n.*, poisson laité, *m.*

mimetic, *or* **mimetical** (mi-mi-), *adj.*, d'imitation.

mimic, *or* **mimical**. *adj.*, imitateur ; (of things—*des choses*) imitatif, mimique.

mimic, *n.*, mime, imitateur, *m.*

mimic, *v.a.*, contrefaire, imiter ; mimer.

mimicking, *or* **mimicry** (-cra'ye), *n.*, mimique, imitation, *f.*

minacious (mi-né-shieusse), *adj.*, menaçant ; comminatoire.

minaret (-rète), *n.*, minaret, *m.*

minatory, *adj.*, menaçant, comminatoire.
mince (mi'n'ce), *v.a.*, hacher menu ; (meat —*la viande*) émincer ; (fig.) atténuer, adoucir. Not to — the matter ; *ne pas mâcher ce qu'on pense* ; *ne pas le mâcher.* To — one's words ; *manger ses mots.*
mince, *v.n.*, (in walking—*de la marche*) marcher à petits pas affectés ; (in speaking—*du parler*) parler avec une délicatesse affectée ; minauder.
minced-meat, *or* **mince-meat** (mi'n's'te-mîte), *n.*, hachis, *m.*
minced-pie, *or* **mince-pie** (-pa'-ye), *n.*, pâté de fruits et de viande hachés, *m.*
mincing, *adj.*, affecté, minaudier.
mincing-knife (-naïfe), *n.*, hachoir, *m.*
mincingly, *adv.*, en petits morceaux ; (fig.) avec minauderie.
mind (maï'n'de), *n.*, (understanding—*entendement*) esprit, *m.*, intelligence ; (intention) intention ; (inclination) envie, *f.*, désir, *m.* ; (opinion) opinion, pensée, idée, *f.*, avis, sentiment ; (memory—*mémoire*) souvenir, *m.*, mémoire ; (heart, soul—*cœur*, *âme*, *f.*, moral ; (taste—*goût*) goût, *m.* Nobleness of —; *noblesse d'âme, f.* To be of the same —; *être du même avis.* To alter one's —; *changer d'avis, d'idée.* To have a — to ; *avoir envie de.* To find a thing to one's —; *trouver une chose à son goût.* To speak one's —; *dire sa pensée.* To make up one's — ; *se décider.* To call to — ; *se rappeler à l'esprit.* To put any one in — of any thing ; *rappeler quelque chose au souvenir de quelqu'un ; faire souvenir quelqu'un de quelque chose ; faire penser quelqu'un à quelque chose.* To go out of one's —; *perdre la tête ; perdre la raison.* To be out of one's —; *avoir perdu la tête, la raison ; être hors de son bon sens.* That went out of my —; *cela m'est sorti de la tête.* To know one's —; *savoir ce qu'on veut.* To be easy, uneasy in one's —; *avoir, n'avoir pas l'esprit tranquille.* In my —; *dans mon esprit ;* (opinion) *à mon avis.* Of sound —; *sain d'esprit.* Of unsound —; *qui n'est pas sain d'esprit.* A noble —; *une belle âme.* A grovelling —; *une âme de boue.*
mind, *v.a.*, (to attend to—*s'occuper*) s'occuper de, songer à, faire attention à ; (to obey—*obéir*) obéir à, écouter ; (to nurse—*soigner*) soigner, garder ; (to watch—*surveiller*) surveiller ; (to care about—*s'intéresser*) s'inquiéter de, regarder à. Do not — it ; *ne faites pas attention à cela.* I do not — it ; *je n'y fais pas attention ; cela m'est égal.* Never — him ; *ne faites pas attention à lui ; ne l'écoutez pas.* I do not — what they say ; *je ne m'inquiète pas de ce qu'on dit.* I do not — the money ; *je ne regarde pas à l'argent.*
mind, *v.n.*, avoir envie. Never — ; *n'importe ; peu importe ; c'est égal ; ça ne fait rien.*
minded, *adj.*, disposé ; porté. High—; *qui a l'esprit élevé ; noble, magnanime.* Low—; *qui a l'esprit bas ; vil, commun.* Feeble—; *qui a l'esprit faible.* Sober—; *d'un esprit sobre ; sage, raisonnable.* Double—; *irrésolu.*
mindedness, *n.*, disposition, *f.*
mindful (-foule), *adj.*, attentif ; soigneux.
mindfully, *adv.*, attentivement ; soigneusement.
mindfulness, *n.*, attention, *f.* ; soin, *m.*
mindless, *adj.*, inattentif, insouciant ; (without mind—*sans esprit*) sans facultés intellectuelles ; (stupid) stupide, sot. — of ; *oublieux de ; sans égard pour.*
mine (maïne), *pron.*, le mien, *m.*, la mienne, *f.* ; les miens, *m.pl.*, les miennes, *f.pl.* ; à moi.
mine, *n.*, mine, *f.* ; minerai, *m.*
mine (maïne), *v.a.*, miner ; (fig.) saper.
mine, *v.n.*, creuser une mine ; (to work a mine—*faire valoir une mine*) exploiter une mine ; (fig.) employer de sourdes menées pour nuire à quelqu'un.

mine-burner (maï-ne-beurn'-), *n.*, grilleur de minerai, *m.*
mine-dial (-daï'al), *n.*, demi-cercle suspendu, *m.*
mine-digger (-dig'gheur), *n.*, mineur, *m.*
miner (maï'n'-), *n.*, mineur, *m.*
mineral (mi'n'èr'-), *adj.*, minéral.
mineral, *n.*, minéral, *m.*
mineralist, *n.*, minéralogiste, *m.*
mineralization (mi'n'èr'al-aïzé-), *n.*, minéralisation, *f.*
mineralize (-aïze), *v.a.*, (chem.) minéraliser.
mineralizer (-aïz'-), *n.*, minéralisateur, *m.*
mineralizing, *adj.*, minéralisateur.
mineralogical (-'o-djik'-), *adj.*, minéralogique.
mineralogically (-'o-djik'-), *adv.*, en minéralogie.
mineralogist (-'o-djiste), *n.*, minéralogiste, *m.*
mineralogy (-'o-dji), *n.*, minéralogie, *f.*
minever (mi'n'i-veur), *n.*, petit-gris (fur—*fourrure*), *m.*
mingle (mîgn'g'l), *n.*, mélange, *m.*
mingle, *v.a.*, mélanger, mêler. To — with ; *mêler, entremêler : confondre avec.*
mingle, *v.n.*, se mêler, se mélanger ; s'entremêler ; se confondre.
mingler, *n.*, personne qui mêle, *f.*
mingling, *n.*, action de mélanger, *f.* ; mélange, *m.*
miniate (mi'n'i-), *v.a.*, vermillonner.
miniature (-a-tioure), *n.*, miniature, *f.*
miniature-painter (-pé'n't'-), *n.*, miniaturiste ; peintre en miniature, *m.*
minikin, *n.*, (pin—*épingle*) camion ; (minion—*favori*) mignon, *m.*, mignonne, *f.*
minikin, *adj.*, petit, chétif, mignon.
minim, *n.*, (dwarf—*très petite personne*) nain. *m.*, naine ; (mus.) blanche, *f.* ; (ich.) véron ; (Franciscan—*moine*) minime, *m.*
minimum, *n.*, minimum, *m.*
minimus, *n.*, le plus petit des êtres.
mining (maï'n'-), *adj.*, de mines ; de mineur.
mining, *n.*, exploitation des mines, *f.* ; travail dans les mines, *m.*
minion (mi'n'ieune), *n.*, mignon, *m.*, mignonne, *f.* ; favori, *m.* ; (print.) mignonne, *f.*
minionly, *adv.*, avec mignardise.
minionship, *n.*, état de mignon, de favori, *m.*
minious, *adj.*, rouge.
minister, *n.*, ministre ; (ecc.) ministre, pasteur, *m.* — of State ; *ministre d'État.* Prime —; *premier ministre.*
minister, *v.a.*, fournir ; donner.
minister, *v.n.*, servir ; (ecc.) officier. To — to ; (to relieve—*soulager*) assister, venir au secours de ; (to contribute to—*aider*) contribuer à ; (to humour—*complaire*) se prêter à ; (to provide for—*fournir*) pourvoir à ; (to give medicine to—*administrer médecine*) donner un remède à.
ministerial (-is-ti-), *adj.*, de ministère ; du pouvoir exécutif ; ministériel ; d'ecclésiastique, ecclésiastique.
ministerially, *adv.*, ministériellement.
ministrant, *adj.*, qui sert ; subordonné.
ministration (-tré-), *n.*, service ; ministère, *m.*
minium, *n.*, minium, *m.*
miniver, *n.*, *V.* **meniver**.
minnow (-nô), *n.*, (ich.) véron, *m.*
minor (maï-), *n.*, mineur, *m.*, mineure, *f.* ; (friar—*moine*) mineur, *m.* ; (log.) mineure, *f.*
minor (maï-), *adj.*, moindre ; petit ; mince ; de second ordre ; (mus., geog.) mineur.
minorite (maï-nor-aïte), *n.*, (ecc.) mineur, frère mineur, *m.*

minority, *n.*, minorité, *f.*

minotaur, *n.*, Minotaure, *m.*

minster. *n.*, cathédrale, *f.*

minstrel, *n.*, ménestrel, chanteur, musicien. *m.*

minstrelsy, *n.*, chant des ménestrels, art du ménestrel, *m.* ; musique, *f.* ; chant, *m.*

mint (mi'n'te), *n.*, (bot.) menthe, *f.* Pepper—; menthe poivrée, *f.*

mint (mi'n'te), *n.*, monnaie, *f.* ; hôtel de la monnaie, *m.*, (fig.) mine, *f.*, trésor, *m.* ; (b.s.) fabrique, forge, *f.* Master of the—; directeur de la monnaie, *m.*

mint, *v.a.*, monnayer ; frapper ; (fig.) forger, fabriquer, inventer. controuver.

mintage (mi'n'tédje), *n.*, objet monnayé ; (duty—impôt) droit de monnayage, *m.*

minter, *n.*, monnayeur ; (fig.) forgeur ; inventeur, *m.*

mintman. *n.*, monnayeur, *m.*

mintmaster (-mâs-), *n.*, directeur de la monnaie, *m.* ; (b.s.) forgeur ; inventeur, *m.*

minuend (mi'n'ou-è'n'de), *n.*, (arith.) nombre dont il faut soustraire, *m.*

minuet (mi'n'iou-ète), *n.*, menuet, *m.*

minus, *n.*, (alg., print.) moins, *m.*.

minus, (maï-neusse), *adv.*, moins.

minute (mi-nioute), *adj.*, menu, très petit ; minutieux ; mince.

minute (mi'n'eute, ou mi'n'ite), *n.*, minute ; (astron., geom., arch.) minute ; (note) note, *f.*

minute, *v.a.*, minuter, prendre note de.

minute-book (-bouke), *n.*, carnet, agenda ; journal ; (jur.) plumitif, *m.*

minute-glass (-glàce), *n.*, sablier à minutes, *m.*

minute-hand (-ha'n'de), *n.*, aiguille des minutes ; grande aiguille, *f.*

minutely, *adj.*, qui arrive à chaque minute ; de toutes les minutes.

minutely (min'eutly), *adv.*, à chaque minute.

minutely (mi-niout'li), *adv.*, minutieusement ; exactement ; en détail.

minuteness (mi-niout'-), *n.*, petitesse, exiguïté, *f.* ; détails minutieux, *m.pl.*

minute-watch (-wôtshe), *n.*, montre à minutes, *f.*

minute-wheel (-hwîle), *n.*, (horl.) roue des minutes, *f.*

minutiæ (mi-niou-shi-î), *n.pl.*, minuties, *f.pl.*

minx (mign'kse), *n.*, coquine, friponne, *f.*

miny (maï-ni), *adj.*, riche en mines ; souterrain.

miracle (mir'a'k'l), *n.*, miracle, *m.* By a—; par miracle.

miracle-monger (-moeun'gheur),*n.*, faiseur de miracles, *m.*

miraculous (-rak'iou-), *adj.*, miraculeux.

miraculously, *adv.*, miraculeusement, par miracle.

miraculousness, *n.*, caractère miraculeux, *m.*

mirage (mî-raje), *n.*. mirage, *m.*

mire (maï'eur), *n.*, boue, bourbe, fange, *f.* ; (place—lieu) bourbier, *m.* ; (ant.) fourmi, *f.*

mire (maï'eur), *v.a.* and *n.*, embourber ; enfoncer dans la bourbe, dans un bourbier ; s'embourber, s'enfoncer dans la bourbe, dans un bourbier.

miriness (maï'eur'-), *n.*, état de ce qui est couvert de boue, de bourbe ; état boueux, *m.* ; saleté, *f.*

mirkiness (meurk'-), *n.*, obscurité, *f.* ; ténèbres. *f.pl.*

mirky (meurk'-), *adj.* V. murky.

mirror (-reur), *n.*. miroir, *m.*

mirth (meurth). *n.*, gaîté, réjouissance, joie, *f.*

mirthful (-foule), *adj.*, gai, joyeux, allègre.

mirthfully, *adv.*, gaiment ; joyeusement ; avec allégresse.

miry (ma'ïeuri), *adj.*, fangeux, bourbeux.

misacceptation (miss'ac-cèp-té-), *n.*, interprétation erronée, *f.*

misadventure (miss'ad-vè'n'tïoure), *n.*, mésaventure, *f.*

misadventured (-tiourde), *adj.*, malheureux.

misadvised (miss'ad-vaïz'de), *adj.*, mal avisé.

misalliance (miss'al'laï'-), *n.*, mésalliance,*f.*

misallied (-laïde), *adj.*, mésallié.

misanthrope (miz'a'n'thrôpe), *or* **misanthropist** (-thro-), *n.*, misanthrope, *m.*

misanthropic, *or* **misanthropical** (miss'-), *adj.*, (pers.) misanthrope ; (of things—choses) misanthropique.

misanthropy (miss'-), *n.*, misanthropie, *f.*

misapplication (miss'ap-pli-ké-), *n.*, fausse application, *f.*

misapply (miss'ap'pla'ye), *v.a.*, faire une mauvaise application de ; appliquer mal à propos.

misapprehend (miz'ap-pri-hè'n'de), *v.a.*, mal entendre, comprendre mal.

misapprehension (miss'ap-pri-hè'n'-), *n.*, malentendu, *m.* ; méprise,*f.*

misarrange (miss'ar'rè'n'dje),*v.a.*, arranger mal.

misascribe (miss'as'craïbe), *v.a.*, attribuer à tort.

misassign (miss'as'saïne), *v.a.*, assigner à tort.

misattend (miss'-), *v.a.*, méconnaître ; ne pas écouter.

misbecome (miss'bi-keume), *v.a.*, messeoir à ; convenir mal à.

misbecoming, *adj.*, inconvenant, messéant.

misbecomingly, *adv.*, d'une manière inconvenante.

misbecomingness, *n.*, inconvenance,*f.*

misbegot, *or* **misbegotten** (miss'bi'-), *adj.*, illégitime, bâtard.

misbehave (miss'bi-hève), *v.n.*, se comporter mal, se conduire mal. To — one's self; se conduire mal, se comporter mal.

misbehaviour (miss'bi-hév'ïeur), *n.*, mauvaise conduite, inconduite,*f.*

misbelief (miss'bi-lîfe), *n.*, fausse croyance, incrédulité,*f.*

misbeliever (miss'bi-liv'-), *n.*, mécréant, infidèle, incrédule, *m.*

misbelieving, *adj.*, infidèle, incrédule.

misbestow (miss'bi-stô), *v.a.*, donner à tort.

miscalculate (miss'cal-klou-), *v.a.*, mal calculer, supputer mal, compter mal.

miscalculation (-kiou-lé-),*n.*,calcul erroné, *m.* ; supputation erronée, *f.* ; mécompte, *m.*

miscarriage (miss'car'ridge), *n.*, (failure—défaut de succès) insuccès ; coup manqué, *m.* ; affaire manquée ;(ill conduct—mauvaise conduite) erreur, faute ; (of women—des femmes) fausse couche, *f.*

miscarry, *v.n.*, (to fail—échouer) ne pas réussir, manquer, éc'jouer, avorter ; (not to arrive —se perdre) ne pas arriver à sa destination, s'égarer ; (of women—des femmes)faire une fausse couche.

miscast (miss'câste), *v.a.* (preterit, past part.. Miscast), compter mal.

miscellanarian (-la-né-), *adj.*, de miscellanées ; de mélanges.

miscellaneous (-lé-ni-), *adj.*, mêlé, varié ; général ; de mélanges. — works ; mélanges, *m.pl.*

miscellanist, *n.*, auteur de miscellanées ; auteur de mélanges, *m.*

miscellany, *n.* (miscellanea), mélange, *m.* ; miscellanées, miscellanea, *m.pl.*

mischance (mis'tshâ'n'ce), *n.*, mauvaise chance, *f.* ; malheur, accident fâcheux, revers, *m.*; infortune, *f.*

27 *

mischaracterize (mis-ca-rac-tèr'aïze), v.a., défigurer.

mischarge (mis'tshärdje), v.a., porter à tort sur un compte.

mischarge, n., somme portée à tort sur un compte.

mischief (mis'tshife), n., mal ; dommage ; tort, m. To do — ; faire du mal. To be in — ; faire quelque mal. To make — ; semer la discorde, brouiller les gens.

mischief-maker (-mék'-), n., personne qui aime à brouiller les gens, f. ; semeur de discorde ; brouillon, m.

mischief-making, adj., qui sème la discorde ; qui brouille les gens.

mischievous (mis'tshè-veusse), adj., (pers.) méchant, porté au mal, malfaisant ; (of things— des choses) malfaisant, mauvais, nuisible, pernicieux, funeste, méchant ; (of children—des enfants) méchant, enclin au mal.

mischievously, adv., méchamment, mal, d'une manière malfaisante ; malicieusement ; par méchanceté ; pernicieusement, nuisiblement, funestement.

mischievousness, n., caractère malfaisant, m. ; nature malfaisante ; disposition au mal ; (of children—des enfants) malice, méchanceté, f.

mischoose (mis'tshouze), v.a. (preterit, Mischose ; past part., Mischosen), choisir mal.

miscible (mis-ci'b'l), adj., miscible.

miscitation (mis-saï-té-)n.,fausse citation,f.

miscite (mis-saïte), v.a., citer à faux.

misclaim (mis-cléme), n., fausse prétention, f.

miscomputation (-co'm'piou-té-), n., erreur de calcul, f. ; mécompte, m.

miscompute (-piout), v.a., calculer mal.

misconceive (-cive), v.a. and n., concevoir mal ; juger mal.

misconceived (-civ'de), adj., mal conçu.

misconception (-cèp-), n.,fausse conception, f. ; malentendu, m.

misconduct (-deuk'te), n., mauvaise conduite ; incondite ; (management—direction) mauvaise gestion, f.

misconduct, v.a., conduire mal ; (to manage —diriger) mal gérer. To — one's self ; se conduire mal.

misconduct, v.n., se conduire mal.

misconjecture (-djèk'tioure), n., fausse conjecture, f.

misconjecture, v.a. and n., conjecturer à faux ; faire de fausses conjectures.

misconstruction (-streuk'-), n., interprétation fausse, f. ; contresens, m.

misconstrue (-strou), v.a., interpréter mal ; dénaturer.

misconstruer, n., personne qui interprète mal, f.

miscorrect, v.a., corriger à tort, à faux.

miscount (-caou'n'te), v.a.,compter mal.

miscount, v.n., se mécompter.

miscreant (-kri-),n.,mécréant ; misérable,m.

misdate, v.a., dater mal ; mettre une date fausse.

misdate, n., date erronée ; fausse date, f.

misdeed (-dîde), n., méfait, crime, m.

misdeem (-dîme),v.a., juger mal.

misdemean (-di-mîne), v.a., conduire mal. To — one's self ; se conduire mal.

misdemeanour (-di-mî'n'eur),n., mauvaise conduite, f. ; (jur.) délit ; crime, m.

misdirect, v.a., (letters, &c.—lettres, &c.) adresser mal ; (pers.) enseigner mal ; diriger mal.

misdo (-dou), v.a. (preterit, Misdid ; past part., Misdone),malfaire ; commettre des fautes.

misdoer (-dou'-), n., auteur d'une faute ; malfaiteur, m.

misdoing (-dou'-), n., faute, f. ; méfait, m.

misdoubt (mis-daoute), n., soupçon ; doute, m.

misdoubt, v.a. and n., douter, soupçonner.

misemploy (miss'è'm'plo'ye), v.a.,employer mal ; faire un mauvais emploi de.

misemployment, n., mauvais emploi, m.

misentry (miss'è'n'-), n., inscription fausse, inscription erronée, f.

miser (maï-zeur), n., avare, m.

miserable (miz'eur'a-b'l), adj., misérable, malheureux, triste.

miserableness, n., état malheureux, état misérable, m.

miserably, adv., misérablement, malheureusement, tristement.

miserere (mi-zi-ri-rî), n., (c. rel.) miséréré, m.

miserly (maïz'eur'-), adj., d'avare, avare.

misery (miz'èr'i), n., misère, f.

misestimate (miss'ès-), v.a., estimer à tort.

misfashion, v.a., former mal.

misfeasance (mis-fi-za'n'ce), n., (jur.) dommage, m.

misform, v.a., former mal.

misfortune (-fort'ioune), n., malheur, m. ; infortune, f.

misgive (-ghive), v.a. (preterit, Misgave ; past part., Misgiven), faire craindre à ; inspirer des craintes à.

misgiving (-ghiv'-), n., crainte, f. ; pressentiment de mal ; soupçon, m.

misgotten (-got't'n), adj., mal acquis.

misgovern (-gheuv'eurne), v.a., gouverner mal, régir mal.

misgoverned (-gheuv'eurn'de), adj., mal gouverné ; rude ; grossier.

misgovernment, n., mauvais gouvernement, m. ; mauvaise administration, f. ; (disorder) dérèglement, m.

misguidance (-gaïd'-), n.,fausse direction,f.

misguide (-gaïde), v.a., mal guider, égarer.

misguided, adj., mal guidé ; (fig.) aveugle.

mishap (miss'hape), n., contretemps ; malheur, m.

mishmash, n., mélange ; micmac, fatras,m.

misimprove (miss'i'm'prouve), v.a., employer mal, abuser de.

misimprovement, n., mauvais emploi, m.

misinfer (miss'i'n'feur), v.a., conclure à tort.

misinform (miss'-), v.a., informer mal ; enseigner mal.

misinformation (-for-mé-), n., faux avis, faux renseignement, m. ; fausse information, fausse nouvelle, f.

misinformer, n., personne qui donne de faux renseignements, de fausses nouvelles,f.

misinstruct (miss'i'n'streuk'te), v.a., instruire mal.

misinstruction (-treuk'-), n.,fausse instruction, f.

misinterpret (miss'i'n'teur-prète), v.a., interpréter mal ; dénaturer.

misinterpretation (-prè-té-), n., fausse interprétation, f. ; contresens, m.

misinterpreted, adj., mal interprété.

misinterpreter, n., personne qui interprète mal, f. ; faux interprète, m.

misjoin (miss'djoïne), v.a., joindre mal.

misjudge (-djeudje), v.a., juger mal.

misjudge, v.n., se tromper dans son jugement.

misjudgment (-djeudj'-) n., jugement erroné, m.

mislay (-lè), v.a. (preterit and past part., Mislaid), égarer.

mislayer (miss-lè-eur), n., personne qui place mal ; personne qui égare, f.

misle, or **mistle** (miz'z'l), v.n., bruiner, brouillasser.

mislead (-lîde), v.a. (preterit and past part.,

Misled), induire en erreur, égarer; fourvoyer; tromper.

misleader, *n.,* personne qui induit en erreur, *f.* ; trompeur, corrupteur, *m.*

mislen (miz'lène), *n.,* méteil, *m.*

misly (miz'li), *adj.,* de bruine, de brouillard.

mismanage (-édje), *v.a.,* gérer mal; conduire mal; diriger mal.

mismanage, *v.n.,* se conduire mal; s'arranger mal.

mismanagement, *n.,* mauvaise gestion; mauvaise conduite, *f.* ; mauvais arrangement, *m.*

misname, *v.a.,* nommer mal.

misnomer (-nô-), *n.,* erreur de nom, *f.* ; faux nom, *m.*

misobserve (miss'ob'zeurve), *v.a.,* observer mal.

misogamist (mi-ço-), *n.,* misogame, *m.*

misogyny (mi-çodj'-), *n.,* misogynie, *f.*

mispersuade (-peur-swède), *v.a.,* persuader à tort.

mispersuasion (-swé-jeune), *n.,* fausse persuasion, fausse opinion, *f.*

misplace, *v.a.,* placer mal; déplacer.

misplaced (-plés'te), *adj.,* mal placé; déplacé.

misplead (-plîde), *v.a.,* (jur.) faire erreur dans la production des moyens de droit.

misprint (-pri'n'te), *n.,* faute d'impression, *f.*

misprint, *v.a.,* imprimer incorrectement.

misprision (-prij'eune), *n.,* (jur.) négligence, *f.,* oubli, *m.* ; crime d'un degré au dessous du crime capital, *m.* ; (ant.) mépris, *m.* — of treason ; *simple connaissance du crime de trahison, et action de le cacher f.* — of felony ; *action de cacher un crime ou un délit, f.*

misprize (-praïze), *v.a.,* (ant.) se méprendre; mépriser.

misproceeding (-cîd'-), *n.,* procédé irrégulier, *m.* ; irrégularité, *f.*

mispronounce (-naou'n'ce), *v.a.* and *n.,* prononcer incorrectement.

mispronunciation (-neu'n'cié-), *n.,* fausse prononciation ; prononciation incorrecte, *f.*

misproportion (-pôr-), *v.a.,* proportionner mal.

misquotation (-kwôt'é-), *n.,* fausse citation, *f.*

misquote (-kwôte), *v.a.,* citer à faux.

misrate, *v.a.,* évaluer à faux.

misrecital (-ri-çaï-), *n.,* récit inexact, *m.*

misrecite (mis-ri-çaïte), *v.a.,* réciter mal, inexactement.

misreckon (-rèk'k'n), *v.a.,* calculer mal.

misrelate (-ri-léte), *v.a.,* rapporter inexactement.

misrelation (-ri-lé-) *n.,* rapport erroné, *m.*

misremember (-ri-mè'm'-), *v.a.,* se rappeler inexactement.

misreport (-ri-pôrte), *v.a.,* rapporter inexactement.

misreport (-ri-pôrte), *n.,* faux rapport; rapport inexact, *m.*

misrepresent (-rèp'ri-zè'n'te), *v.a.,* représenter sous de fausses couleurs; dénaturer.

misrepresentation (-zè'n'té-), *n.,* faux rapport, *m.*

misrepresenter, *n.,* personne qui représente sous de fausses couleurs, qui dénature, *f.*

misreputed (-ri-piout'-), *adj.,* mal apprécié.

misrule (-roule), *n.,* confusion, *f.* ; désordre; gouvernement tyrannique, *m.*

miss, *n.,* mademoiselle, demoiselle, *f.* — A. ; *mademoiselle A.*

miss, *n.,* (loss—*privation*) perte, *f.,* manque, *m.* ; (mistake—*erreur*) erreur, méprise, *f.*

miss, *v.n.,* manquer ; ne pas porter; (ab billiards—*au billard*) manquer à toucher. To be —ing; (pers.) *être absent;* (of things—*des choses*) *manquer.*

miss, *v.a.,* manquer; (to omit—*manquer*) omettre, sauter; (at billiards—*au billard*) manquer à toucher; (to perceive the want of—*remarquer l'absence de*) s'apercevoir de l'absence de, du manque de; regretter vivement. To—one's mark; *manquer son coup.*

missal, *n.,* missel, *m.*

missay (mis'sè), *v.a.,* dire mal ; médire de.

missaying (-sè'igne), *n.,* expression incorrecte, *f.*

missend, *v.a.* (*preterit* and *past part.,* Missent), mal diriger, adresser mal.

misserve (mis'seurve), *v.a.,* servir mal, desservir.

misshape (mis'shépe), *v.a.,* former mal; défigurer.

misshaped (mis'shép'te), *or* **misshapen** (-shé-p'n), *adj.,* difforme.

missile (mis'sil), *adj.,* de jet, de trait; lancé.

missile (mis'sil), *n.,* projectile, *m.* ; arme de trait, arme de jet, *f.*

mission (mish'eune), *n.,* mission, *f.*

missionary, *n.,* missionnaire, *m.*

missive (mis'sive), *adj.,* missive; (of weapons—*armes*) de jet, de trait.

missive (mis'sive), *n.,* missive; lettre missive, *f.*

misspeak (mis'spîke), *v.a.* (*preterit,* Misspoke; *past part.,* Misspoken), articuler mal.

misspell, *v.a.,* épeler mal; orthographier mal.

misspelling, *n.,* orthographe vicieuse, *f.*

misspend, *v.a.,* dépenser mal à propos; gaspiller.

misstate (mis'stéte), *v.a.,* exposer inexactement ; rapporter inexactement.

misstatement, *n.,* rapport inexact, rapport erroné, *m.*

mist, *n.,* brouillard, *m.* ; brume, *f.*

mist, *v.a.,* couvrir d'une vapeur ; obscurcir.

mistakable (-ték'a-b'l), *adj.,* susceptible de méprise : qui prête à méprise.

mistake, *n.,* erreur, méprise, *f.* To make a —; *faire une méprise; se tromper.*

mistake, *v.a.* (*preterit,* Mistook; *past part.,* Mistaken), se tromper de; se tromper sur; se méprendre à; prendre pour. He mistook me for you ; *il me prenait pour vous.*

mistake, *v.n.,* se tromper, se méprendre, s'abuser. To be —n; *se tromper, se méprendre, s'abuser.*

mistaken *f.*-ték'n), *adj.,* (pers.) qui se trompe; (of things—*des choses*) faux, mal entendu, erroné.

mistakenly (-té-kè'n'll), *adv.,* par méprise.

mistaker, *n.,* personne qui se trompe, *f.* ; auteur de méprise, *m.*

mistaking (-ték'-), *n.,* méprise, erreur, *f.*

mistakingly, *adv.,* par méprise.

misteach (-tîtshe), *v.a.* (*preterit* and *past part.,* Mistaught), enseigner mal.

mistell, *v.a.* (*preterit* and *past part.,* Mistold), raconter inexactement.

mistemper (-tè'm'-), *v.a.,* tempérer mal; troubler.

misterm (-teurme), *v.a.,* qualifier mal.

mistful (-foule), *adj.,* brumeux ; couvert de brouillards.

mistime (-taïme), *v.a.,* régler mal ; prendre mal son temps.

mistiness, *n.,* état brumeux, *m.* ; obscurité, *f.*

mistle (miz'l), *v.n.* V. **misle.**

mistletoe (miz z'l'tô), *n.,* (bot.) gui, *m.*

mist-like (-laïke), *adj.,* comme un brouillard; brumeux.

mistrain (-tréne), *v.a.,* mal élever; (animal) mal dresser.

mistranslate, *v.a.,* traduire incorrectement.

mistranslation (-lé-), *n.,* traduction incorrecte, *f.* ; contresens, *m.*

mistreat (-trîte), v.a., maltraiter.

mistreatment, n., mauvais traitement, m.

mistress (-trèce, ou mis'sice), n., maîtresse ; madame ; (intended—future) prétendue ; (of a school—d'école) maitresse institutrice, f.

mistrust (-treuste), n., méfiance, défiance,f.

mistrust, v.a., se méfier de; soupçonner.

mistrustful (-foule), adj., méfiant, défiant.

mistrustfully, adv., avec méfiance.

mistrustfulness, n., défiance, méfiance, f.

mistrustless (-treust'-), adj., qui ne se méfie pas ; confiant.

mistune (-tioune), v.a., accorder mal; désaccorder.

mistutor (-tiou-), v.a., instruire mal ; diriger mal.

misty, adj., couvert de brouillards ; brumeux.

misunderstand (miss'eu'n'deur-), v.a. (preterit and past part., Misunderstood), comprendre mal ; se méprendre sur le sens des paroles de.

misunderstanding, n., conception erronée, f. ; (mistake—erreur) malentendu, m. ; (quarrel —querelle) mésintelligence, f.

misusage (miss'iou-zadje), n., mauvais traitements, m.pl. ; abus, mauvais usage, mauvais emploi, m.

misuse (miss'iouce , n., abus ; mauvais usage, mauvais emploi, m.; application erronée, f. ; mauvais traitements, m.pl.

misuse, v.a., abuser de; (to treat ill—rudoyer) maltraiter.

misvouch (-vaoutshe), v.a., attester faussement.

miswear (miss'wére), v.n. (preterit and past part., Misworn), être d'un mauvais user.

miswrite (miss'raïte), v.a. (preterit, Miswrote; past part., Miswritten), écrire incorrectement.

miswrought (miss'rôte), adj., mal travaillé ; mal fait.

misyoke (miss'yôke), v.n., s'unir mal.

miszealous (mis-zêl'eusse), adj., (ant.) animé d'un faux zèle.

mite (maïte), n., (ent.) mite, f. ; (money—argent) denier ; (fig.) rien, m. —s ; (ent.) mites, f.pl. ; acares, m.pl.

mithridate (mith'ri-déte), n., (pharm.) mithridate, m.

mitigable (-ga-b'l), adj., susceptible de mitigation, susceptible d'adoucissement.

mitigant, adj., qui mitige ; qui tempère ; adoucissant.

mitigate, v.a., mitiger, adoucir; calmer, modérer, apaiser.

mitigation (-ghé-), n., mitigation, f. ; adoucissement, m.

mitigator (-ghé-), n., personne qui mitige, qui adoucit ; chose qui mitige, qui adoucit, f.

mitre (maï-teur), n., mitre, f. ; (arch.) onglet, m.

mitre, v.a., orner d'une mitre ; (arch.) assembler en onglet.

mitred (maï-teurde), adj., orné d'une mitre ; mitré ; (arch.) en onglet.

mitriform, adj., mitriforme.

mitten, n., mitaine, f.

mittimus, n., mandat de dépôt; ordre de renvoi de pièces, m.

mity (maï-ti), adj., qui a des mites ; rempli de mites.

mix, v.a., mêler ; se mélanger ; (pharm.) mixtionner.

mix, v n., se mélanger ; se mêler.

mixed (mix'te), adj., mélangé, mêlé ; (math.) fractionnaire.

mixedly (m'ksèd'li), adv., avec mélange d'une manière mixte.

mixer, n., personne qui mêle, qui mélange, f.

mixtilineal, or **mixtilinear**, adj., (geom.) mixtiligne.

mixtion (mixt'ieune), n., mixtion, f. ; mélange, m.

mixtly, adv., avec mélange ; d'une manière mixte.

mixture (mixt'ieur), n., mélange, m. ; (pharm.) mixtion, potion,f.

mizmaze, n., (pop.) labyrinthe, dédale, m.

mizzen (miz'z'n), n., artimon, m.

mizzen-mast (-mâste),n., mât d'artimon,m.

mizzle (miz'z'l), v.a., bruiner, brouillasser.

mizzy, n., fondrière, f.

mnemonic, or **mnemonical** (ni-mo'n'-), adj., mnémonique.

mnemonics (ni-mb'n'-), n.pl., mnémonique, mnémotechnie, f.sing.

moan (mône), n.,gémissement, m. ;lamentation, f.

moan, v.n., gémir, se lamenter.

moan, v.a., gémir sur; se lamenter sur ; lamenter.

moanful (-foule), adj., lugubre, triste, plaintif.

moanfully, adv., d'un ton plaintif, tristement.

moat (môte), n., (fort.) fossé, m.

moat, v.a., (fort.) entourer d'un fossé.

mob (mobe), v.a., houspiller ; (to wrap up—envelopper) coiffer, affubler.

mob, n., foule ; populace ; cohue ; canaille ; (head-dress—coiffure) cornette, f. Riotous — ; attroupement, rassemblement, m.

mobbish, adj., tumultueux ; de la populace, de la foule.

mobcap, n., cornette (coiffure de femme), f.

mobile (mo-bile), adj., (ant.) mobile.

mobility, n., mobilité ; (activity—activité) activité ; (inconstance—inconstance) légèreté ; canaille, racaille, populace, f.

moble (mob'l), v.a., (ant.) envelopper d'un capuchon ; affubler.

mock, v.a., se moquer de ; se rire de, se jouer de ; railler; tromper.

mock, v.n., se moquer. To — at ; se moquer de, se rire de ; se jouer de ; railler.

mock, adj., dérisoire ; de moquerie ; burlesque ; (false—imité) faux. — poem ; poème burlesque. — prophet ; faux prophète. — style ; style comique.

mock, n., moquerie, raillerie ; (sport—amusement) risée, f., jouet, m.

mockable (-a-b'l), adj., exposé à la moquerie.

mocker, n., moqueur, m.; moqueuse, f. ; railleur, m., railleuse, f. ; (impostor—fourbe) imposteur, trompeur, m.

mockery, n., moquerie, raillerie, dérision ; (sport—jouet) risée ; (illusion) illusion, f. ; (imitation) semblant, m.

mocking, n., moquerie ; dérision, f.

mocking-bird (-beurde), n., oiseau moqueur, m.

mockingly, adv., en se moquant ; d'un ton moqueur.

mocking-stock, n., risée, f.

modal (mô-), adj., modale.

modality (mo-), n., modalité, f.

mode (môde), n., mode, façon, manière, f. ; (gram., music, philos.) mode, m.

model, n., modèle, m. ; (representation) présentation, f. ; (mould—matrice) moule, m.

model, v.a., modeler ; faire, former d'après un modèle.

modeller (mod'èl'eur), n., inventeur ; homme à projets, m.

moderate (mod'ér-),adj., modéré ; modique, ordinaire ; passable ; raisonnable ; médiocre.

moderate, v.a., modérer, adoucir, tempérer.

moderately, adv., modérément ; modiquement ; passablement ; raisonnablement ; médiocrement.

moderateness, n., modération; modicité, f.; état moyen, m.

moderation (-'ér'é-), n., modération; retenue, mesure, f. With —; *moderément*.

moderator (-'ér'é-teur), n., modérateur, m., modératrice, f.; président, m.

moderatorship, n., fonctions de modérateur, f.pl.; présidence, f.

modern (mod'eurne), adj., moderne, nouveau, récent.

modern, n. (*moderns*), moderne, m.

modernism (-'iz'me), n., forme moderne, f.

modernist, n., partisan des modernes, m.

modernize (-'aize), v.a., moderniser; rendre moderne.

modernizer, n., personne qui modernise, f.

modernness, n., nouveauté, f.

modest (mod'èste), adj., modeste; pudique.

modestly, adv., modestement.

modesty, n., modestie; pudeur, f.

modicum, n., petite portion; pitance, f.

modifiable (-faï-a-b'l), adj., qui peut être modifié.

modification (-fi-ké-), n., modification, f.

modifier (-faï'eur), n., personne qui modifie; chose qui modifie, f.

modify (-fa'ye), v.a., modifier, limiter.

modify, v.a., faire des modifications.

modillion (mo-dil'ieune), n., (arch.) modillon, m.

modish (mô-), adj., à la mode.

modishly, adv., à la mode.

modishness, n., fureur pour la mode; affectation de suivre la mode, f.

modulate (mod'iou-), v.a., moduler.

modulation (mod'iou-lé-), n., modulation; mélodie, f.

modulator, n., personne qui module; chose qui module, f.

module (mod'ioule), n., (arch.) module, m.

modus (mô-deusse), n., mode, m., manière, f.; (jur.), compensation pour la dîme, f.

modwall (-wôl), n., (orni.) pivert, m.

mogul (-gheule), n., Mogol, m.

mohair (mô-hére), n., poil de chèvre de Turquie, m.

mohammedan, n., Mahométan, m., Mahométane, f.

mohammedanism, n., mahométisme, m.

mohawk, or **mohock** (mô-), n., scélérat, brigand, m.

moidore (môï-dôre), n., (Portuguese coin—*monnaie portugaise*) moidore, m.

moiety (mwa-é-), n., moitié, f.

moil (moïl), v.a., mouiller, barbouiller; fatiguer.

moil, v.n., fatiguer; se fatiguer; travailler fort; s'échiner. To toil and —; *suer sang et eau*.

moire (moïré), n., moire, f.

moist (moïste), adj., moite, humide.

moisten (moïs't'n), v.a., rendre humide; humecter, rendre moite.

moistener, n., personne qui rend humide; chose qui rend humide, f.

moistness (moïs't'-), or **moisture** (moïst'ïoure), n., moiteur, humidité, f.

molar (mô-), adj., molaire.

molasses (-cize), n.pl., mélasse, f.sing.

mole (môle), n., (mam.) taupe, f.; (on the skin—*sur la peau*) marque de naissance, f., signe, grain de beauté, m.; (med.) môle, f.; (mound—*remblai*) pile, digue; (of a port—*de port de mer*) jetée, f., môle, m.

molecast (-câste), n., taupinière, f.

mole-catcher, n., taupier, m.

mole-cricket (-ète), n., taupe-grillon, m., courtilière, f.

molecular (-lèk'iou-), adj., moléculaire.

molecule (-'è-kioule), n., molécule, f.

mole-eyed (-a'ye'-de), adj., qui a de très petits yeux; aveugle.

molehill, n., taupinière, f.

molest (-lèste), v.a., molester; vexer.

molestation (-lès-té-), n., action de molester, molestation, f.; encombre, m.; vexation, contrariété, f.

molester, n., personne qui moleste, qui vexe, f.; importun, m., importune, f.; fâcheux, m.

molestful (-foule), adj., contrariant, importun.

mole-track, n., trainée de taupe, f.

mole-trap, n., taupière, f.

molinism (-'iz'me), n., molinisme, m.

molinist, n., moliniste, m., f.

mollient. *V.* **emollient**.

mollifiable (-faï-a-b'l), adj., qui peut être amolli.

mollification (-fi-ké-), n., mollification, f.; amollissement, adoucissement, m.

mollifier (-faï'-), n., personne qui amollit, qui apaise; chose qui amollit, qui apaise, f.; émollient, m.

mollify (-fa'ye), v.a., amollir, mollifier, calmer, adoucir; apaiser.

mollusc (-leuske), **molluscan** (-leus'-), or **mollusk** (-leuske), n. (*mollusca*), mollusques, m.pl.

molluscan, or **molluscous**, adj., des mollusques.

molten (môl't'n), adj., fondu, de métal fondu, de fonte.

molybdenum (-di-), n., (min.) molybdène, m.

moment (mô-), n., moment, m.; importance, f. In a —; *dans un moment*. He stops every —; *il s'arrête à tout moment, à tous moments*.

momentarily, adv., momentanément.

momentary, adj., momentané, passager.

momentous (mo-mè'n't'-), adj., important.

momentum (mo-mè'n'-), n., (mec.) moment, m., quantité de mouvement, vitesse acquise, f.

monachal (-kal), adj., monacal.

monachism (-kiz'me), n., monachisme, m.

monad (-'ade), n., monade, f.

monadelphia (-dèl-), n., (bot.) monadelphie, f.

monadic, or **monadical**, adj., des monades.

monandria, n., (bot.) monandrie, f.

monarch (mo'n'arke), n., monarque; roi, m., reine, f.

monarch, adj., suprême.

monarchal (-'ark'-), adj., de monarque; souverain.

monarchic, or **monarchical** (-'ark'-), adj., monarchique.

monarchically (-'ark'-), adj., monarchiquement.

monarchist, n., monarchiste, m.

monarchize (-'ark'aïze), v.n., faire le roi.

monarchy (-'ark'i), n., monarchie, f.

monastery (-tèr'i), n., monastère, m.

monastic, or **monastical**, adj., monastique.

monastic, n., moine, m.

monastically, adv., en moine.

monasticism (-ciz'me), n., vie monastique, f.

monday (meu'n'dè), n., lundi, m.

mone (môn), n., (man.) guenon, f.

monetary (-'è-ta-), adj., monétaire.

money (meu'n'nè), n., argent, m.; monnaie, f. Bad, base, counterfeit, — ; *fausse monnaie*. Odd — ; *appoint; compte borgne*, m.; *passe*, f. Ready — ; *argent comptant*. Pocket- — ; *menus plaisirs*, m.pl. Public — ; *deniers publics*, m.pl. — dormant (lying dead—*mort*); *argent mort*. Bank — ; *monnaie de banque; monnaie banco*. Copper — ; *monnaie de cuivre*, f.; *billon*, m. Paper- — ; *papier-monnaie*, m. Silver —

monnaie d'argent, argent blanc. Bag of —; *sac d'argent : group, m.* For —; *au comptant.* To coin —; *battre monnaie.* To earn —; *gagner de l'argent.* To get in —; *faire rentrer des fonds.* To make —; *gagner, faire de l'argent.* To put — out to interest ; *placer de l'argent.* To receive —; *recevoir, toucher de l'argent.* To fetch —; *rapporter de l'argent.* To be worth —; *avoir de l'argent, avoir du bien ;* (of things—*des choses*) *avoir de la valeur, avoir du prix.* To have — with one's self, about one's self ; *avoir de l'argent sur soi.* A man of —; *un homme opulent.*

money-agent (-é-djé'u'te), *n.,* banquier, *m.*

money-box, *n.,* tirelire, *f.*

money-broker (-brô-), *n.,* courtier de change, *m.*

money-change (-tshé'n'dje), *n.,* change de monnaie ; *change, m.*

money-changer (-tshé'n'djeur), *n.,* changeur, *m.*

moneyed (meu'n'ède), *adj.,* riche, opulent, qui a de l'argent; (of things—*des choses*) consistant en argent. — man ; *capitaliste, homme opulent, m.*

money-getting (-ghèt'-), *adj.,* cupide; intéressé.

money-jobber (-djob'-), *n.,* agioteur, *m.*

money-lender, *n.,* prêteur d'argent ; bailleur de fonds, *m.*

moneyless, *adj.,* sans, argent, sans le sou, pauvre.

money-matter, *n.,* affaire pécuniaire, affaire d'argent, *f.*

money-scrivener (-scriv'è'n'-), *n.,* courtier de change, *m.*

money's-worth (-'è'z'weurth), *n.,* valeur de l'argent, *f.*; objet de valeur, *m.* To have one's —; *en avoir pour son argent.*

money-wort (-weurte), *n.,* (bot.) lysimaque nummulaire ; herbe aux écus, *f.*

monger (meu'n'gu'gheur), *n.,* marchand, débitant, *m.*

mongrel (meu'n'-), *adj.,* métis ; mélangé. — dog ; *chien métis, m.*

morgrel, *n.,* métis, *m.,* métisse, *f.*

monition, *n.,* admonition, *f.* ; avertissement, avis, *m.* ; indication, *f.*

monitive, *adj.,* d'admonition, d'avis.

monitor (-teur), *n.,* moniteur, *m.*

monitorial, *adj.,* d'admonition ; d'avertissement ; monitorial ; (of instruction—*d'enseignement*) par des moniteurs ; (of schools—*d'école*) qui a des moniteurs.

monitory, *adj.,* d'admonition ; d'avertissement ; monitoire.

monitory, *n.,* admonition, *f.* ; avertissement, avis ; (ecc.) monitoire, *m.*

monitress, *n.,* monitrice, *f.*

monk (meu'n'ke), *n.,* moine, religieux, *m.*

monkery, *n.,* moinerie, *f.*

monkey (meun'gn'ké),*n.,* singe, *m.* ; guenon, *f.* ; (of piledrivers—*de sonnette*) mouton ; (pers.) babouin, *m.,* babouine, guenon, *f.*

monk-fish, *n.,*(ich.) angelot ; ange de mer,*m.*

monkhood (-houde), *n.,* moinerie, *f.*

monkish, *adj.,* de moine. monacal.

monochord (-korde), *n.,* (mus.) monocorde, *m.*

monochromatic (-krôm'-), *adj.,* monochrome.

monocotyle. *V.* **monocotyledonous.**

monocotyledon (li-),*n.,* (bot.) monocotylédone, *f.*

monocotyledonous, *adj.,* monocotylédone.

monocular, or **monoculous** (-ok'iou-), *adj.,* borgne.

monodist, *n.,* auteur d'une monodie, *m.*

monody, *n.,* monodie, *f.* ; monologue, *m.*

monoecia (-i-shia), *n.,*(bot.) monœcie,*f.*

monogamist, *n.,* monogame, *m.*

monogamous, *adj.,* monogame.

monogamy, *n.,* monogamie, *f.*

monogram, *n.,* monogramme, *m.*

monography, *n.,* monographie, *f.*

monologue (-loghe), *n.,* monologue, *m.*

monomane, or **monomaniac,** *n.,* monomane, *m.,f.*

monomania (-mé-nia), *n.,* monomanie, *f.*

monomaniac, *adj.,* monomane.

monome (-ôme), *n.,* (alg.) monôme, *m.*

monopetalous, *adj.,* (bot.) monopétale.

monophyllus, *adj.,* (bot.) monophylle.

monopolist, *n.,* monopoleur, accapareur,*m.*

monopolize (-laïze), *v.a.,* faire le monopole de ; monopoliser ; accaparer.

monopolizer (-laïz'-), *n.,* monopoleur ; accapareur, *m.*

monopoly, *n.,* monopole ; accaparement, *m.*

monopteral (-tè-), *adj.,* (arch.) monoptère.

monosepalous (-cèp'-), *adj.,* (bot.) monosépale, monophylle.

monospermous (-speur-), *adj.,* (bot.) monosperme.

monostich (-stik), *n.,* monostique, *m.*

monosyllabic, *adj.,* monosyllable, monosyllabique.

monosyllable, *n.,* monosyllabe, *m.*

monotone (-tône), *n.,* monotonie, *f.*

monotonous (-ot'o-), *adj.,* monotone.

monotonously, *adv.,* avec monotonie ; d'une manière monotone.

monotony (-ot'o-), *n.,* monotonie, *f.*

monsoon (-soune), *n.,* mousson, *f.*

monster, *v.a.,* rendre monstrueux.

monster, *n.,* monstre, *m.*

monster, *adj.,* monstre.

monstrance, *n.,* ostensoir, *m.*

monstrosity, *n.,* monstruosité, *f.*

monstrous, *adj.,* monstrueux ; horrible ; prodigieux.

monstrously, *adv.,* monstrueusement ; horriblement ; prodigieusement, furieusement.

monstrousness, *n.,* monstruosité, *f.*

montanic, *adj.,* montueux.

month (meu'n'th), *n.,* mois, *m.* Calendar —; *mois solaire.* Lunar —; *mois lunaire.* By the —; *au mois.*

monthly (meu'n'th'-), *adj.,* mensuel ; tous les mois.

monthly, *adv.,* mensuellement, tous les mois.

monument (-'iou-), *n.,* monument ; (tomb—*tombe*) tombeau, monument, *m.,* tombe, *f.*

monumental, *adj.,* de monument ; monumental ; de la tombe, du tombeau.

monumentally, *adv.,* en monument.

mood (moude), *n.,* humeur, disposition, *f.* ; (gram., log., mus.) mode, *m.* To be in the — for ; *être d'humeur à ; être disposé à ; être en train de.*

moodiness, *n.,* humeur ; mauvaise humeur ; tristesse, *f.*

moody, *adj.,* de mauvaise humeur ; triste, morne, chagrin.

moon (nioune), *n.,* lune, *f.* Full —; *pleine lune.* New —; *nouvelle lune.*

moon-beam (-bîme), *n.,* rayon de la lune ; rayon lunaire, *m.*

moon-blindness (-blaï'n'd'-), *n.,* (vet.) ophtalmie périodique, *f.*

moon-calf (-k .fe), *n.,* monstre ; (dolt—*sot*) imbécile ; idiot, *m.* ; conception fausse ; (med.) môle, *f.*

mooned (mou'n'de), *adj.,* en forme de croissant. — horns ; *cornes en forme de croissant.*

moonet (-ète), *n.,* petite lune, *f.*

moon-eye (-'a'ye), *n.,* œil affecté d'ophtalmie périodique, *m.*

moon-eyed (-a'ye'-de), *adj.*, myope ; qui voit peu ; aveugle ; (vet.) lunatique.

moonish, *adj.*, lunatique.

moonless. *adj.*, sans lune ; sans clair de lune.

moonlight (-laite), *n.*, clair de lune, *m.* By — ; *au clair de lune.*

moonlight (-laite), *adj.*, au clair de lune ; éclairé par la lune.

moon-loved (-leuv'de), *adj.*, aimé au clair de lune.

moon-seed (-side), *n.*, (bot.) ménisperme, *m.*

moon-shaped (-shēp'te), *adj.*, en forme de lune, en forme de croissant ; (bot.) lunulé.

moonshine (-shaine), *n.*, clair de lune. *m.*; (jest.) lune, *f.*, mois, *m.* ; (rubbish—*sornette*) vétille, *f.*

moonshine, or **moonshiny,** *adj.*, de clair de lune. éclairé par la lune.

moon-struck (-streuke), *adj.*, lunatique.

moonwort (-weurte), *n.*, (bot.) lunaire, *f.*

moony, *adj.*, de la lune ; en forme de lune.

moor (moure), *n.*, More, Maure, *m.*, *f.* ; lande, bruyère. *f.* ; marais, *m.*

moor, *v.a.*, amarrer.

moor, *v.n.*, s'amarrer.

moor-berry (-bèr'-), *n.*, (bot.) canneberge, *f.*

moor-cock, or **moor-fowl** (-faoul), *n.*, coq de bruyère. *m.*

moor-hen, *n.*, (orni.) poule d'eau, *f.*

mooring, *n.*, (nav.) amarrage, *m.* — s : corps *mors, m.pl.*

mooring-post (-pôste), *n.*, poteau d'amarre, *m.*

mooring-shaft (-shâfte), *n.*, puits d'amarre, *m.*

moorish, or **moory,** *adj.*, marécageux.

moorish, *adj.*, (of the Moors—*moresque*) des Maures ; mauresque, moresque, more, maure.

moor-land, *n.*, marais ; pays marécageux, *m.*

moose (mouce), *n.*, élan d'Amérique, *m.*

moot (moute), *n.*, question à débattre, question à discuter ; thèse, *f.*

moot, *v.a.*, discuter, débattre ; soulever.

moot, *v.n.*, débattre un point de droit.

moot, *adj.*, discutable. — case, — point ; *question discutable, question à décider.*

mooted, *adj.*, débattu.

mooter. *n.*, soutenant. *m.*

mooting, *n.*, conférence, discussion, *f.* ; débat, *m.*

mop, *n.*, balai à laver ; écouvillon ; (nav.) faubert, *m.*

mop, *v.a.*, laver avec un balai ; essuyer avec un balai ; (nav.) fauberter ; (a gun, an oven—*un canon, un four*) écouvillonner.

mope (mōpe), *v.a.*, hébéter ; attrister

mope, *v.n.*, être triste ; être mélancolique ; languir, s'ennuyer ; être hébété.

mope, *n.*, personne triste ; personne qui s'ennuie toujours ; personne hébétée, *f.*

mope-eyed (-a'ye'de), *adj.*, myope.

mopish (môp'-), *adj.*, triste ; abattu ; qui s'ennuie, hébété.

mopishly, *adv.*, tristement ; dans l'abattement.

mopishness, *n.*, tristesse ; stup'dité, *f.*; abattement ; ennui. *m.*

moppet, or **mopsey,** *n.*, poupée ; marionnette ; (fondling name—*terme d'affection*) poponne, *f.*

mopsical, *adj.*, myope.

mopus (mō-), *n.*, personne hébétée. *f.*

moral, *adj.*, moral.

moral *n.*, morale, moralité, *f.*

moralist, *n.*, moraliste, *m.* ; personne morale, *f.*

morality. *n.*, morale ; moralité, *f.*

moralization (-aizé-), *n.*, morale, moralité, *f.*

moralize (-aize), *v.a.*, (to explain in a moral sense—*expliquer*) donner un sens moral à : (to render moral—*moraliser*) rendre moral, corriger les mœurs de, moraliser.

moralize. *v.n*, moraliser, faire de la morale.

To — on ; *moraliser sur. faire de la morale sur.*

moralizer, *n.*, personne qui moralise, qui fait de la morale, *f.* ; moraliseur, *m.*

morally, *adv*, moralement ; au moral, dans un sens moral.

morals (-alze), *n.pl.*, mœurs, *f pl.* ; moralité, *f.*

morass, *n.*, marais. marécage, *m.*

morassy, *adj.*. marécageux.

morbid, *adj.*, maladif, malsain, morbide.

morbidness, *n.*, état maladif, état morbifique. *m.*

morbific, or **morbifical,** *adj.*, morbifique.

morbose (-bôce), *adj.*, malsain.

morbosity, *n.*, (ant.) état maladif. *m.*

mordacious (-dé-sheusse), *adj.*, mordant, piquant.

mordaciously, *adv.*, d'une manière mordante, piquante.

mordacity (-dass'-), *n.*, mordacité, *f.*

mordant. *n.*, mordant, *m.*

mordicant (-ant,) *adj.*) mordant.

mordication (-di-ké), *n.*, mordication ; corrosion. *f.*

more (môre), *adj.*, plus ; plus de ; encore ; plus nombreux ; davantage. —money ; *plus d'argent.* Some — ; *encore un peu ; encore quelques-uns ; davantage.* No — of that! *assez de cela !* Give me some — ; *donnez-m'en encore.* Give me some — apples ; *donnez-moi encore des pommes.* It is — ; *c'est davantage.* They are — than we, there are — of them than of us ; *ils sont plus nombreux que nous.* One — ; *encore un ; un de plus.* — than ; *plus que ;* (followed by a number—*devant un nombre*) plus de.

more (môre), *adv.*, plus ; davantage, encore. Once — ; *encore une fois.* Much — ; *beaucoup plus, bien plus, bien davantage.* — and — ; *de plus en plus.* No — ; *pas davantage.* No — ! *assez !* The — ; *d'autant plus ; davantage.* So much the — ; *d'autant plus ; d'autant mieux ; à plus forte raison.* The — you speak the less you will learn ; *plus vous parlerez, moins vous apprendrez.* Nothing — than ; *pas plus que.*

moreen (-rine), *n.*, damas de laine, *m.*

morel, *n.*, (bot.) morille, *f.*

moreover (mōr'ô-veur), *adv.*, de plus, outre cela, d'ailleurs.

moresque, *adj.*, moresque, mauresque.

moresque. *n.*, (paint.) moresque, mauresque, peinture moresque, *f.*

morfoundering (-faou'n'd'-), *n.*, (vet.) morfondure *f*

morganatic, *adj.*, morganatique, de la main gauche.

moribund (-beu'n'de), *adj.*, (ant.) moribond.

morigeration (-ridj'èr'é-), *n.*, (ant.) obséquiosité, *f.*

morigerous, *adj.*, (ant.) obéissant.

moriliform, *adj.*, en forme de morille.

morinel, *n.*, (orni.) guignard, *m.*

morion (mô-), *n.*, morion, *m.*

morn, *n.*, matin, *m.* ; aurore, *f.*

morning, *n.*, matin, *m.* ; matinée, *f.* Every — ; *tous les matins.* All the — ; *toute la matinée.* In the — ; *le matin ; dans la matinée.* In the course of the — ; *dans la matinée.*

morning, *adj.*, du matin ; matinier. — gown ; *robe de chambre, f.* — -star ; *étoile du matin, f.*

morocco (-'cô), *n.*, maroquin, *m.*

morocco-leather (-lèth'eur), *n.*, maroquin, *m.* ; peau de maroquin, *f.*

morocco-paper (-pé'-), *n.*, papier maroquin, *m.*

morose (-rôce), *adj.*. morose.

morosely, *adv.*, d'une manière morose.
moroseness. *or* **morosity**, *n.*, morosité, *f.*
morphew (-fiou), *n.*, (med.) morphée, *f.*
morphia, *or* **morphine**, *n.*, morphine, *f.*
morris, *or* **morris-dance**, *n.*, moresque, danse moresque, *f.*
morris-dancer, *n.*, danseur de la moresque, *m.*, danseuse de la moresque, *f.*
morrow (mor'rô), *n.*, demain; lendemain. Good-—; *bonjour.* To-—; *demain.* The day after to-—; *après demain.*
morse, *n.*, morse, *m.*; vache marine, *f.*; cheval marin, *m.*
morsel, *n.*, morceau, *m.*; pièce, *f.*
morsure (-sheur), *n.*, (ant.) morsure, *f.*
mort (morte), *n.*, saumon de trois ans, *m.*; (hunt.) mort, *f.*
mortal, *adj.*. (deadly—*mortel*) mortel, fatal, meurtrier, funeste; (human—*humain*) des mortels, humain.
mortal, *n.*, mortel, *m.*, mortelle, *f.*
mortality, *n.*, mortalité; nature humaine; humanité; mort, *f.* Bills of —; *états de mortalité, m pl.; tables de mortalité, f.pl.*
mortalize (-aïze), *v.a.*, rendre mortel.
mortally, *adv.*, mortellement.
mortar, *n.*, (tech., artil., mas.) mortier, *m.*
mortar-mill, *n.*, manège à mortier, *m.*
mortgage (mor-ghédje), *n.*, hypothèque, *f.* To pay off a —; *purger une hypothèque.*
mortgage, *v.a.*, hypothéquer.
mortgagee (-ghédji), *n.*, créancier hypothécaire. *m.*
mortgageor *or* **mortgager** (-ghédj'or, -'eur), *n.*, débiteur sur hypothèque, *m.*
mortiferous (-èr'-), *adj.*, mortel, funeste; mortifère.
mortification (-fi-ké-), *n.*, mortification; gangrène, *f.*
mortified (-faïde), *adj.*, mortifié; affligé; (med.) gangrené.
mortifiedness, *n.*, état de mortification, *m.*
mortifier, *n.*, personne qui mortifie; chose qui mortifie, qui fait gangrener, *f.*
mortify (-ti-fa'ye), *v.a.*, mortifier; (med.) déterminer la gangrène dans, faire gangrener.
mortify, *v.n.*, se mortifier; (med.) se gangrener.
mortise (-tice), *n.*, mortaise, *f.*
mortise, *v.a.*, emmortaiser; assembler à mortaise.
mortmain (mort'méne), *n.*, mainmorte, *f.*
mortuary (mort'iou-a-ri), *n.*, droit mortuaire, *m.*
mortuary, *adj.*, mortuaire.
mosaic (-zé-), *adj.*, en mosaïque; (pertaining to Moses—*de Moïse*) mosaïque. — work; *ouvrage en mosaïque, m.; mosaïque, f.*
mosk, *or* **mosque**, *n.*, mosquée, *f.*
mosquito (-ki-), *n.*, mosquito, *m.*
moss, *v.a.*, couvrir de mousse.
moss, *n.*, mousse, *f.*; (bog—*marécage*) marais, *m.*
moss-clad, *or* **moss-grown** (-grône), *adj.*, couvert de mousse; moussu.
mossiness. *n.*, état moussu, *m.*
moss-land, *n.*, dépôt tourbeux, *m.*
moss-trooper (-troup-'), *n.*, maraudeur, bandit, *m.*
mossy, *adj.*, moussu.
most (môste), *adj.*, le plus; la plupart. The — part ; *la plus grande partie.* — men; *la plupart des hommes.*
most, *adv.*, le plus; très, fort. The — modest man in the world; *l'homme du monde le plus modeste.* The animals that man has admired are . . .; *les animaux que l'homme a le plus admirés sont . . . .* — vile; *très, fort; bien, excessivement, vil.*
most, n., la plupart, *f.*; le plus grand nom-

bre, *m.* At —; *au plus; tout au plus.* To make the — of; *tirer le meilleur parti de.*
mostic, *n.*, appui-main, *m.*
mostly (môst'-), *adv.*, pour la plupart; le plus souvent; ordinairement.
mote (môte), *n.*, atome; (in the eye—*dans l'œil*) fétu, *m.*
motet (-tète), *n.*, (mus.) motet, *m.*
moth (moth), *n.* (*moths*), phalène; teigne, gerce, *f.*; (fig.) ver rongeur, *m.*
moth-eaten (-it'-), *adj.*, rongé des vers.
mother (meuth'eur), *n.*, mère; (familiar term of address—*apostrophe familière*) bonne mère, bonne vieille, bonne femme, *f.*; (slimy substance in liquors—*moisissure de liqueurs*) moisi, *m.*, moisissure, *f.* Grand-—; *grand'mère.* Step-—; *belle-mère.* To be a — to; *être une mère pour.*
mother, *adj.*, mère; maternel; national; (of churches—*église*) métropolitain. — -country; *mère patrie, f.* — -tongue; *langue maternelle, f.*
mother, *v.a.*, servir de mère à; adopter.
mother, *v.n.*, (of liquors—*des liqueurs*) se moisir.
motherhood (-houde), *n.*, maternité, *f.*
mother-in-law (-lô), *n.*, belle-mère, *f.*
mother-land, *n.*, mère patrie, *f.*
motherless, *adj.*, sans mère; orphelin de mère.
motherly, *adj.*, maternel, de mère; (in look —*en apparence*) qui a l'air d'une mère de famille.
motherly, *adv.*, maternellement; en mère.
mother-of-pearl (-ov'peurle), *n.*, nacre de perle, *f.*
mother-water (-wô-teur), *n.*, eau mère, *f.*
mother-wit, *n.*, esprit naturel, *m.*
mothery, *adj.*, (of liquids—*des liquides*) moisi.
moth-worm (-weurme), *n.*, teigne des habits; teigne, *f.*
mothwort (moth'weurte), *n.*, (bot.) agripaume, *f.*
mothy (moth'i), *adj.*, plein de teignes, de gerces.
motion (mô-), *v.n.*, faire une proposition, faire une motion. To — to; *faire signe à.*
motion, *v.a.*, proposer.
motion, *n.*, mouvement, *m.*; motion, *f.*; (astron.) mouvement, *m.*; (proposal—*proposition*) motion, proposition; (med.) selle, *f.*; (signal) signe, *m.* The laws of —; *les lois du mouvement, f.pl.* Perpetual —; *mouvement perpétuel, m.* Diurnal —; *mouvement diurne, m.* To make a —; *faire une motion, une proposition.* To carry a —; *faire adopter une motion.* To put in —; *mettre en mouvement; imprimer le mouvement à.*
motionless, *adj.*, immobile.
motion-rod, *n.*, bielle de parallélogramme, *f.*
motive (mô-), *adj.*, moteur, qui fait agir. — power; — force; *force motrice, f.; moteur, m.*
motive, *n.*, motif, mobile, *m.* To allege, to state a — for, the — of; *motiver; exposer le motif de.*
motled (mott'l'd), *or* **motley** (-lè), *adj.*, bigarré, mêlé, varié, mélangé.
motor (mô-teur), *n.*, moteur, *m.*; force motrice, *f.*; mobile, *m.*
motory (mô-), *adj.*, qui donne le mouvement, moteur.
mottle (mott'l), *v.a.*, madrer, moirer; (soap —*savon*) marbrer.
mottled (mott'l'de), *adj*, pommelé, saumoné, tacheté; (of wood—*du bois*) madré, moiré; (of soap—*du savon*) marbré.
motto (-tô), *n.* (*mottoes*), devise, *f.*
mould (môlde), *n.*, (earth—*terre*) terreau, *m.*, terre végétale, terre, *f.*; (mouldy part—*moisissure*) moisi, *m.*, moisissure, *f.*; (cast—*matrice*) moule, *m.*, forme, *f.*; (fig.) modèle;

(arch.) panneau, *m.*, moulure, *f.*; (nav.) gabari,
gabarit. *m.*

mould, *v.a.*, mouler, modeler, faire, former;
(to make mouldy—*rendre moisi*) moisir.

mould, *v n.*, (to become mouldy—*devenir
moisi*) se moisir.

mouldable (môld'a-b'l), *adj.*, susceptible
d'être moulé.

moulder, *n.*, mouleur; (fig.) formateur, *m.*

moulder, *v.n.*, dépérir, fondre; se réduire
en poudre, en poussière; se réduire. To —
away; *tomber en poussière; dépérir, se dissiper.*

moulder, *v.n.*, réduire en poussière.

mouldering, *adj.*, qui se réduit en poussière, qui dépérit, qui tombe en ruines.

mouldiness (môld'-), *n.*, moisissure, *f.*,
moisi; rebut, *m.*

moulding, *n.*, moulure, *f.*; panneau, *m.*

moulding-plane, *n.*, (carp.) doucine, *f.*

mouldwarp (-wôrpe), *n.*, taupe, *f.*

mouldy (môld'i), *adj.*, moisi, ⊙chanci. To
become (get) — ; *se moisir*, ⊙*se chancir*.

moult (môlte), *v.n.*, muer.

moulting, *or* **moult**, *n.*, mue, *f.*

mound (maou'n'de), *n.*, levée, digue, *f.*;
rempart; (arch.) remblai, *m.*

mound, *v.a.*, fortifier par un rempart, faire
une digue à.

mount (maou'n'te), *n.*, mont, monticule, *m.*,
montagne, *f.*

mount, *v.a.*, monter; monter sur. To —
the throne; *monter sur le trône.*

mount, *v.n.*, monter, s'élever; monter à
cheval.

mountain, *n.*, montagne, *f.*; (fig.) monceau,
m. Waves — high; *des vagues hautes comme des
montagnes.*

mountain, *adj.*, de la montagne, des montagnes; agreste; vaste, énorme; montagnard.

mountaineer (-tén'ire), *n.*, montagnard, *m.*,
montagnarde, *f.*

mountain-girl (-gheurle), *or* **mountain-
maid** (-méde), *n.*, jeune montagnarde, *f.*

mountainous, *adj.*, montagneux, de montagnes, montueux; (fig.) énorme.

mountainousness, *n.*, situation élevée,
nature montagneuse, *f.*

mountain-stream (-strime), *n.*, ravin,
torrent, *m.*

mountant, *adj.*, montant.

mountebank (maou'n'tè-), *n.*, charlatan,
saltimbanque, *m.*

mountebank, *v.a. and n.*, tromper, duper,
charlataner.

mountebankery, *n.*, charlatanisme, *m.*;
charlatanerie, *f.*; tours de charlatan, *m.pl.*

mounted, *adj.*, monté; à cheval; (*pl.*) pour-
vus de chevaux.

mounter, *n.*, personne qui monte, *f.*;
(tech.) monteur, *m.*

mounting, *n.*, montée, *f.*; (tech.) montage;
(equipment) équipement, *m.*

mountingly, *adv.*, en montant.

mourn (môrne), *v.a.*, pleurer, déplorer.

mourn, *v.n.*, pleurer, se lamenter; porter le
deuil.

mourner, *n.*, (hired—*loué*) pleureur, *m.*,
pleureuse, *f.*; (in funerals—*aux enterrements*)
personne qui est du convoi, qui suit le convoi;
personne qui pleure, personne affligée, *f.* Chief
— ; *personne qui mène le deuil, f.* To be a —, one
of the —s; *suivre le deuil, être du convoi.* To be
chief — ; *mener le deuil.*

mournful (-foule), *adj.*, triste, lugubre,
fatal; lamentable, déplorable.

mournfully, *adv.*, d'un air lugubre, d'une
manière lugubre; tristement, lamentablement,
déplorablement.

mournfulness, *n.*, deuil, *m.*; affliction,
tristesse, douleur, *f.*

mourning, *n.*, deuil, *m.*; affliction, *f.* Deep
— ; *grand deuil.* To be in — for; *être en deuil
de, porter le deuil de.* To go into — ; *prendre le
deuil, se mettre en deuil.* To wear — ; *être en
deuil.*

mourning, *adj.*, affligé; triste.

mourningly, *adv.*, d'une manière lugubre,
tristement, lugubrement.

mouse (maouce), *n.*, souris, *f.*; (nav.)
bouton, *m.*, pomme, *f.* Field- — ; *mulot, m.* —
coloured; *poil de souris.*

mouse, *v.a.*, prendre des souris.

mouse, *v.a.*, (nav.) aiguilleter.

mouse-hole (-hôle), *n.*, trou de souris, *m.*

mouser, *n.*, preneur de souris. *m.*

mouse-trap (-trape), *n.*, souricière, *f.*

mouth (maouth), *n.* (*mouths*), bouche: (of
things—*des choses*) ouverture, entrée, *f.*, orifice,
m. ;(of ravenous beasts—*des carnassiers*) gueule;
(of rivers, instruments—*des fleuves, des instruments de musique*) embouchure; (of cannon—*de
canons*) bouche; (wry face—*moue*) grimace, *f.*
To make any one's — water; *faire venir l'eau à
la bouche à quelqu'un.*

mouth (maouth), *v.a.*, crier; déclamer; insulter; (to take in the mouth—*mettre dans la
bouche*) avaler, dévorer, gober; saisir avec la
bouche; mettre dans la bouche.

mouth (maouth), *v.n.*, crier, brailler; déclamer, pérorer, vociférer.

mouthed (maouth'de).*adj.*, qui a une bouche.
Foul- — ; *mal embouché.* Hard- — ; (man.) *qui a
la bouche dure, qui n'a point de bouche.* Mealy — ;
doucereux. Wide- — ; *qui a la bouche large.*

mouther (maouth'eur), *n.*, braillard, criailleur; péroreur, *m.*

mouth-friend (-frè'n'de), *n.*, faux ami, *m.*

mouthful (-foule), *n.* (*mouthfuls*), bouchée, *f.*
At a — ; *d'une seule bouchée.*

mouth-honour (-o'n'or), *n.*, égards feints,
m.pl.: déférence feinte, *f.*

mouthing (maouth'-), *n.*, criaillerie, déclamation, *f.*

mouthless (maouth-), *adj.*, sans bouche.

mouthmade (-méde), *adj.*,-faux, sans sin
cérité.

mouth-piece (-pîce), *n.*, embouchure, *f.*;
bocal; (pers.) organe, orateur, interprète, *m.*

movable (mouv'a-b'l), *adj.*, mobile; meuble.

movableness, *n.*, mobilité, *f.*

movables (mouv'a-b'lze), *n.*, biens meubles;
meubles, *m.pl.*

movably, *adv.*, d'une manière mobile.

move (mouve), *v.a.*, (to shake, stir—*bouger*)
remuer; (to give motion to—*imprimer un mouvement*) mouvoir, faire mouvoir, mettre en mouvement, faire marcher, faire aller; (to take, carry
away—*emporter*) transporter, porter; (to excite,
induce—*engager*) exciter, pousser, porter, engager; (to affect—*affecter*) toucher, émouvoir;
(to produce—*causer*) produire, faire naître, soulever; (to propose—*proposer*) faire la motion de,
proposer, demander; (at chess—*aux échecs*)
jouer. To — to pity; *toucher, émouvoir.* To be
—d by; *se laisser émouvoir, toucher par.* To —
away; *éloigner, enlever, ôter.* To — back; *remettre à sa place, rapporter.* To — backward; *reculer* To — down; *baisser, descendre.* To —
forward; *avancer.* To — off; *ôter, enlever.* To
— out; *sortir.* To — round; *tourner.* To — up;
monter, hausser.

move, *v.n.*, bouger, se remuer, se mouvoir;
(to go, advance—*aller, avancer*) se mettre en
mouvement, aller, partir, marcher, s'avancer, se
transporter; (of an army—*d'une armée*) s'ébranler; (to stir—*bouger*) s'agiter, se remuer; (to
change residence—*changer de demeure*) déménager; (to turn—*tourner*) tourner; (to propose—
proposer) faire une motion, proposer, demander;
(at chess—*aux échecs*) jouer. To — away; *s'éloi-*

guer, s'en aller. To — back; *reculer, se reculer.*
Tu ~. down; *descendre.* To — forward, to — on;
avancer, s'avancer, marcher. To — off: *s'éloigner,*
filer. To — out; *sortir.* To — round; *se retour-*
ner, se tourner, tourner. To — up; *monter, avan-*
cer. To — in; *emménager; entrer, rentrer.*

move, *n.*, mouvement; (at chess—*aux échecs*)
trait, coup, *m.* To have the —. to play the first
—; *jouer le premier, avoir le trait.* Masterly —;
coup de maître, coup de partie. Lucky —; *coup de*
bonheur. To recall a —; *rejouer.* Whose — is it?
à qui est-ce à jouer? It is my —; *c'est à moi à*
jouer.

moveless (mouv -), *adj.*, immobile.

movement (mouv'-), *n.*, mouvement, *m.*;
agitation, *f.*

mover (mouv'), *n.*, moteur; mobile, *m.*;
force motrice, *f.*; (proposer—*celui qui propose*)
auteur d'une motion, d'une proposition, *m.*
First —; *principe moteur, force motrice.*

moving (mouv'-), *adj.*, (having motion—*en*
mouvement) mouvant, mobile; (giving motion—
qui met en mouvement) moteur; (affecting—*atten-*
drissant) touchant, émouvant, attendrissant,
pathétique, qui émeut. — power; *force motrice,*
f.; moteur, m.

moving, *n.*, mouvement. *m.*; impulsion, *f.*

movingly, *adv.*, d'une manière touchante,
attendrissante, pathétiquement.

movingness, *n.*, air touchant, *m.*; nature
touchante, *f.*; pathétique, *m.*

mow (maou), *n.*, monceau, tas de foin, de
gerbes, *m.*

mow (mô) *v.a.* and *n.*, faucher; (to heap up
—*amonceler*) mettre en tas, en meule; (fig.)
moissonner. To — down; *moissonner, abattre,*
faire tomber.

mower (mô-), *n.*, faucheur, *m.*

mowing (mô-), *n.*, fauchage, *m.*; fauche, *f.*
— time; *fauchaison, f.; temps de faucher, m.*

moxa, *n.*, moxa, *m.*

moyle (mo-ile), *n.*, (ant.) mule, *f.*, mulet, *m.*

mr. (ab. of Mister), Monsieur; M.

mrs. (ab. of Mistress), Madame; Mme.

much (meutshe), *adv.*, beaucoup de; beaucoup, bien, fort, très; (nearly—*presque*) à peu
près. Read —; *lisez beaucoup.* — more; *bien*
plus. So —; *tant; tant de.* So — as; *taut que,*
autant que; assez pour. In so — as; *d'autant*
plus que. Too —; *trop, de trop; trop de.* As —;
autant de. How —; *combien, combien de.* As —
as; *autant que; le plus.* To make — of; *faire*
grand cas de, tirer grand parti de, faire valoir,
estimer beaucoup. So — for; *voilà pour.*

mucid (miou-), *adj.*, moisi; qui a un goût de
relent.

mucidness, *n.*, moisissure, *f.*; relent, *m.*

mucilage (miou-cil'édje), *n.*, mucilage, *m.*

mucilaginous, *adj.*, mucilagineux.

muck (meuke), *n.*, fumier, *m.*; fiente, *f.*;
objet méprisable, *m.*

muck, *v.a.*, fumer; (to dirty—*salir*) salir.

muckhill, *n.*, tas de fumier, *m.*

muckiness, *n.*, saleté, ordure, *f.*

muckle (meuk'k'l), *adj.*, (ant.) beaucoup.

mucksweat (-swète), *n.*, sueur abondante, *f.*

muck-worm (-weurme), *n.*, ver de fumier, *m.*;
(miser—*avare*) ladre, *m.*

mucky, *adj.*, sale, malpropre.

mucous (miou-), *adj.*, glaireux, muqueux.

muculent (miou-kiou-), *adj.*, muqueux.

mucus (miou-), *n.*, mucosité, *f.*; mucus, *m.*

mud (meude), *n.*, boue, bourbe, vase, fange,
f. To stick in the —; *s'embourber.* — building; *bousillage, m.* —-wall; *mur de terre, mur*
de bousillage, m.

mud, *v.a.*, embourber, salir, couvrir de boue,
crotter; (a liquid—*un liquide*) troubler.

muddily, *adv.*, salement; d'un air sombre.

muddiness,*n.*,état boueux, état bourbeux,*m.*

muddle (meud'd'l), *v.a.*, hébéter; troubler,
étourdir.

muddle, *v.n.*, barboter, se salir; être troublé.

muddle, *n.*, fange, *f.*; état troublé, *m.*

muddled (meud'd'l'de), *adj.*, trouble, troublé; hébété, lourd; confus.

muddy, *adj.*, boueux, bourbeux, fangeux;
limoneux, vaseux; crotté, couvert de boue;
(stupid—*stupide*) lourd, borné, hébété; (dark—
marâtre) couleur de boue; (of precious stones—
des pierres précieuses) nuageux.

muddy, *v.a.*, troubler; salir, crotter.

muddy-headed (-hèd'ède),*adj.*, lourd, borné, sot, hébété.

mud-fish, *n.*, (ich.) limande, *f.*

mud-sill, *n.*, (of a bridge—*de pont*) grillage,
m.; plateforme, *f.*

mudwort (-weurte), *n.*, (bot.) petit plantain
d'eau, *m.*

mue (miou), *v.n.*, muer.

muff (neufe), *n.*, manchon; (pers.) maladroit, *m.*

muffin (meuf'-), *n.*, espèce de galette, *f.*

muffle (meuf'f'l), *v.a.*, emmitoufler; envelopper; affubler; (a bell—*une cloche*) assourdir;
(a drum—*un tambour*) voiler; (the eyes—*les yeux*)
bander; (fig.) couvrir, cacher. To — up; *affu-*
bler, envelopper.

muffle, *v.n.*, parler sourdement, marmotter.

muffle, *n.*, (chem.) moufle, *m.*

muffle-furnace (-feur-nace), *n.*, (chem.)
fourneau à moufle, *m.*

muffler, *n.*, cache-nez, *m.*

mufflon (meuf'-), *n.*, (mam.) mouflon, *m.*

mufti (meuf'-), *n.*, mufti, muphti, *m.*

mug (meughe), *n.*, gobelet, *m.*

muggy (meug'ghi), *or* **muggish** (-ghishe),
adj., couvert, humide, lourd.

mughouse (-haouce), *n.*, cabaret borgne, *m.*

mugil (miou-djil), *n.*, (ich.) muge, mulet, *m.*

mugwort (meug'weurte), *n.*, (bot.) armoise,
herbe de St.-Jean, *f.*

mulatto (miou-lat'tô), *n.*, mulâtre, *m.*, *f.*,
mulâtresse, *f.*

mulberry (meul'bèr'-), *n.*, mûre, *f.*; (tree—
arbre) mûrier, *m.*

mulct (meulkte), *v.a.*, amende, *f.*

mulct, *v.a.*, mettre à l'amende, mulcter.

mule (mioule), *n.*, mulet, *m.*, mule, *f.*; (orni.)
mulet, *m.*; (for spinning—*à filer*) mule-jenny, *f.*,
métier à filer en fin. *m.*

mule-driver (-draïv'-),*or* **muleteer** (miou-
lèt'ire), *n.*, muletier.

mule-jenny (mioul'djè'n'-), *n.*, mule-jenny,
f.; métier à filer en fin, *m.*

mule-spinning, *n.*, filage à la mule-jenny,*m.*

muleteer, *n.* *V.* **mule-driver**.

mule-twist, *n.*, fil de la mule-jenny, *m.*

mulewort (-weurte), *n.*, herbeaux mulets, *f.*

muliebrity (miou-li-éb'-), *n.*, nubilité, *f.*;
état de femme, *m.*; nature efféminée; mollesse, *f.*

mulish (mioul'-), *adj.*, de mulet.

mull (meul), *v.a.*, faire chauffer et épicer;
adoucir; énerver.

mulled (meul'de), *adj.*, (of wine—*de vin*)
chaud et épicé.

mullen (meul'line), *or* **mullein** (meu'line),
n., (bot.) molène, *f.*; bouillon-blanc, *m.*

muller (meul'-), *n.*, molette (à broyer), *f.*

mullet (meul'-), *n.*, (ich.) mulet, surmulet, *m.*

mulligrubs (meul'li-greubze), *n.*, mauvaise
humeur; colique, *f.*; tranchées, *f.pl.*

mullion (meul'ieune), *n.*, (arch.) meneau, *m.*

multangular (meult'an'gn'ghiou-), *adj.*,
multangulaire, multangulé.

multicapsular (meul-ti-cap'siou-), *adj.*,
(bot.) multicapsulaire.

multifarious (meul-ti-fé-), *adj.*, varié,
différent, multiplié.

multifariously, *adv.*, diversement; avec une grande diversité.

multifariousness, *n.*, diversité; multiplicité, *f.*

mul+ifid, *or* **multifidous** (meul-ti-), *adj.*, multifide.

multiflorus (meul-ti-flô-), *adj.*, multiflore.

multifold (-fôlde), *adj.*, nombreux, varié.

multiform, *or* **multiformous** (meul-), *adj.*, qui a plusieurs formes, varié, multiforme.

multiformity, *n.*, diversité de formes, *f.*

multilateral (meul-), *adj.*, à plusieurs côtés; multilatère.

multiloquence (meul-), *n.*, bavardage, *m.*; loquacité, *f.*

multiloquous, *adj.*, bavard, loquace.

multinodate, *or* **multinodous** (meul-ti-nô-), *adj.*, qui a beaucoup de nœuds.

multiparous (meul-), *adj.*, multipare.

multiped (meul-ti-pède), *n.*, (ent.) multipède, cloporte, *m.*

multiple (meul'ti-p'l), *adj.* and *n.*, multiple, *m.*

multipliable (meul-ti-plaï-a-b'l), *adj.*, multipliable.

multiplicand (meul'-), *n.*, multiplicande, *m.*

multiplicate (meul-), *adj.*, multiplié.

multiplication (meul-ti-pli-ké-), *n.*, multiplication, *f.*

multiplicator (meul-ti-pli-ké-), *n.*, multiplicateur, *m.*

multiplicity (meul-), *n.*, multiplicité, *f.*

multiplied (meul-ti-plaïde), *adj.*, multiplié; réitéré, nombreux.

multiplier (meul-ti-plaï'-), *n.*, (arith.) multiplicateur, multiplieur, *m.*

multiply (meul-ti-pla'ye), *v.a.*, multiplier.

multiply, *v.n.*, multiplier, se multiplier.

multiplying, *adj.*, multipliant. — -glass; *multipliant; verre multipliant, m.*

multipotent (meul-), *adj.*, très-puissant, d'une puissance variée.

multisiliquous (meul-), *adj.*, multisiliqueux.

multitude (meul-ti-tioude), *n.*, multitude, *f.*

multitudinous, *or* **multitudinary** (meul-ti-tiou-), *adj.*, très-nombreux, diversifié, vaste, immense.

multivagant, *or* **multivagous** (meul-ti-va-), *adj.*, (ant.) vagabond, errant de tous côtés, qui voit beaucoup de pays.

multivalve (meul-), *or* **multivalvular** (-valv'iou-), *adj.*, (conch., bot.) multivalve.

multivalve, *n.*, (conch.) multivalve, *f.*

multivious (multi-), *adj.*, (ant.) à plusieurs voies, qui a plusieurs chemins.

multocular (meult'ok'iou-), *adj.*, ayant plus de deux yeux.

mum (meume), *adj.*, silencieux, muet. To be —; avoir la bouche close, la bouche cousue.

mum! *int.*, bouche close! chut! motus!

mumble (meu'm'b'l), *v.n.*, marmotter; mâchonner.

mumble-news (-niouze), *n.*, conteur de nouvelles, forgeur de contes, *m.*

mumbler, *n.*, grogneur; marmotteur, *m.*; grogneuse, marmotteuse, *f.*

mumblingly, *adv.*, en marmottant; en mâchonnant.

mum-budget! (meu'm'beudj'ète), *int.*, (ant.) silence! motus!

mumm (meume), *v.n.*, se masquer.

mummer, *n.*, masque, *m.*

mummery, *n.*, mascarade; momerie, *f.*

mummification (-mi-fi-ké-), *n.*, momification, *f.*

mummiform, *adj.*, en forme de momie.

mummify (meum'mi-fa'ye), *v. a.*, momifier.

mumming, *n.*, mascarade, *f.*

mummy, *n.*, momie, *f.* To beat to a —; rouer de coups.

mump (meu'm'pe), *v.a.*, marmotter; (to cheat—tromper) attraper, duper; (to nibble—ronger) grignoter, machonner; (to beg—mendier) mendier.

mump, *v.a.*, marmotter; mâchonner; gueuser.

mumper, *n.*, gueux, *m.*, gueuse, *f.*

mumping, *n.*, ruse de gueux; grimace, *f.*

mumpish, *adj.*, de mauvaise humeur, rechigné, chagrin.

mumps (meu'm'pse), *n.*, (med.) oreillons, *m. pl.*; mauvaise humeur, *f.*

munch (meu'n'she), *v.a.* and *n.*, mâcher de grosses bouchées.

mundane (meu'n'-), *adj.*, mondain, du monde.

mundanity (meu'n'-), *n.*, (ant.) mondanité, *f.*

mundation (meu'n'dé-), *n.*, (ant.) nettoyage, *m.*; (med.) mondification, *f.*

mundatory, *adj.*, mondificatif; détersif.

mundification (meu'n'di-fi-ké-), *n.*, mondification, *f.*

mundificative, *adj.*, mondificatif, détersif.

mundify (meu'n'di-fa'ye), *v.a.*, (ant.) (med.) mondifier, nettoyer, déterger.

mundivagant (meu'n'-), *adj.*, qui court le monde.

munerary (miou-nèr'-), *adj.*, donné en présent.

mungrel, *n.* and *adj.* *V.* mongrel.

municipal (miou-), *adj.*, municipal.

municipality, *n.*, municipalité, *f.*

munificence (miou-), *n.*, munificence, *f.*

munificent, *adj.*, libéral, généreux.

munificently, *adv.*, libéralement, avec munificence.

muniment (miou-), *n.*, fortification, place forte, *f.*; fort, *m.*; défense, *f.*; (jur.) document, titre, *m.* — -room; archives, *f.pl.*

munition (miou-), *n.*, munition; fortification, *f.*

munition-ship, *n.*, transport, vaisseau de transport, *m.*

mural, *adj.*, mural, de mur.

murder (meur-), *n.*, meurtre, assassinat, homicide, *m.*; (fig.) meurtre, grand dommage, *m.* — ! à l'assassin!

murder, *v.a.*, assassiner, tuer; (to do badly —faire mal) massacrer, estropier; (a language— une langue) écorcher. To — a name; estropier un nom.

murderer, *n.*, meurtrier, assassin, *m.*

murderess, *n.*, femme homicide, femme qui a commis un assassinat, (l.u.) meurtrière, *f.*

murdering, *adj.*, assassin, meurtrier.

murderous, *adj.*, homicide, meurtrier, assassin, sanguinaire.

murderously, *adv.*, par le meurtre, par l'assassinat, en assassin, d'une manière meurtrière.

mure (mioure), *n.*, (ant.) mur, *m.*

mure, *v.a.*, murer.

murex (miou-rèkse), *n.*, murex, *m.*

muriate (miou-ri-éte), *n.*, (chem.) muriate, *m.*

muriatic, *adj.*, muriatique.

murine (miou-raïne), *adj.*, de souris, des souris.

murk (meurke), *n.*, obscurité, *f.*; ténèbres, *f.pl.*

murkiness (meurk'-), *n.*, obscurité, *f.*; ténèbres, *f.pl.*

murky, *adj.*, sombre, obscur, ténébreux, noir.

murmur (meur-meur), *n.*, murmure, *m.*

murmur, *v.n.*, murmurer.

murmurer, *n.*, murmurateur, *m.*, personne qui murmure, *f.*

murmuring, *adj.*, murmurant, murmurateur.

murmuring, *n.*, murmure, *m.*; murmures, *pl.*

murmuringly, *adv.*, en murmurant, par des murmures.

murmurous, *adj.*, qui excite des murmures.

murrain (meur-rine), *n.*, épizootie, *f.*

murre (meurre), *n.*, (orni.) pingouin commun, *m.*

murrey (meur-rè), *adj.*, rouge foncé.

muscadel, muscadine, *or* **muscatel** (meus-), *n.*, muscat, vin muscat, raisin muscat, *m.*; (pear—*poire*) muscadelle, *f.*

muscadel, *or* **muscatel** (meus-), *adj.*, muscat.

muscat (meus-), *n.*, vin muscat; raisin muscat, *m.*

muscle (meus's'l), *n.*, (anat.) muscle, *m.*; (mol.) moule, *f.*

muscosity (meus'coss'-), *n.*, état moussu, *m.*

muscovado (meus-co-vé-), *n.*, moscouade, *f.*; sucre brut, *m.*

muscular, *or* **musculous** (meus-kiou-), *adj.*, musculaire; musculeux.

muscularity, *n.*, constitution musculaire, constitution musculeuse, *f.*

muscularly, *adv.*, par l'action musculaire; vigoureusement.

musculite (meus-kiou-laïte), *n.*, moule pétrifiée, *f.*

musculous, *adj.* V. **muscular**.

muse (miouze), *n.*, muse; rêverie, méditation, *f.* In a —; *rêveur, pensif.*

muse (miouze), *v.n.*, méditer, rêver; être distrait, rêveur, pensif. To —on; *rêver à, songer à, réfléchir à, sur.*

muse, *v.a.*, penser à, réfléchir à, méditer.

museful (-foule), *adj.*, taciturne, rêveur, pensif.

musefully, *adv.*, pensivement, d'une manière rêveuse.

muser, *n.*, rêveur; penseur; distrait, *m.*

museum (miou-zi-), *n.*, musée, muséum, *m.*

mushroom (meush'roume), *n.*, champignon, (upstart—*parvenu*) parvenu, *m.*

mushroom-bed (-bède), *n.*, couche de champignons, champignonnière, *f.*

mushroom-house (-haouce), *n.*, serre à champignons, *f.*

music (miou-zic), *n.*, musique; harmonie, *f.* To set to —; *mettre en musique.*

musical (miou-zi-), *adj.*, musical, harmonieux, mélodieux. — instrument; *instrument de musique, m.* —box; *boîte à musique, f.*

musically, *adv.*, en musique, musicalement, harmonieusement, avec harmonie.

musicalness, *n.*, harmonie; mélodie, *f.*

music-book (-bouke), *n.*, cahier de musique, *m.*

musician (miou-zish'-), *n.*, musicien, *m.*, musicienne, *f.* —s; *musiciens, m.pl.*; *musique, f.sing.*

music-mad, *adj.*, mélomane.

music-pen, *n.*, griffe à graver la musique, *f.*

music-publisher (-peub'-), *n.*, éditeur de musique, *m.*

music-room (-roume), *n.*, salle de musique, de concert, *f.*

music-seller, *n.*, marchand de musique, *m.*

music-stand, *n.*, pupitre à musique; lutrin, *m.*

music-stool (-stoul), *n.*, tabouret de piano, *m.*

musing (miouz'-), *n.*, méditation, contemplation; rêverie, *f.*

musk (meuske), *n.*, musc; (mam.) chevrotain, porte-musc, *m.*

musk, *v.a.*, musquer.

musk-cat, *n.*, musc, *m.*; chèvre à musc, *f.*

musket (meus'kète), *n.*, fusil, mousquet, *m.*

musketeer (-'ire), *n.*, mousquetaire; fusilier, *m.*

musketoon (-'oune), *n.*, mousqueton, *m.*

musketry, *n.*, mousqueterie, *f.*; fusils. Discharge of —; *fusillade, f.*

muskiness (meusk'-), *n.*, odeur de musc, *f.*

musk-melon (meusk'mèl'-), *n.*, melon muscat, *m.*

musk-pear (-'père), *n.*, poire musquée, *f.*

musk-rose (-rôze), *n.*, rose musquée, *f.*

musk-seed (-sïde), *n.*, (bot.) graine d'ambrette, *f.*

musky (meusk'-), *adj.*, musqué, de musc.

muslin (meuz'-), *adj.*, de mousseline.

muslin, *n.*, mousseline, *f.*

muslin-sewer (-sô'eur), *n.*, brodeur en mousseline, *m.*, brodeuse en mousseline, *f.*

musrole (meuz'rôle), *n.*, muserolle, *f.*

mussel (meus's'l), *n.*, moule, *f.*

mussulman (meus'seul'-), *n.*, Musulman, *m.*, Musulmane, *f.*

mussulman, *adj.*, à la manière des Musulmans; en Musulman; musulman.

mussulmanish, *adj.*, musulman.

must (meuste), *v.n.*, falloir; devoir. I —; *il le faut.* I —dine; *il me faut dîner; il faut que je dîne.* I —do it; *il faut que je le fasse.* You —return to Paris; *il faut que vous retourniez à Paris.*

must (meuste), *v.a.*, moisir.

must, *v.n.*, (to grow mouldy—*rendre moisi*) moisir; se moisir.

must (meuste), *n.*, moût, *m.*

mustache (meus'tàshe), *or* **mustachio** (-tà-shiô), *n.*, (*mustaches*) moustache, *f.*

mustachioed (-ôde), *adj.*, qui porte des moustaches; à moustaches.

mustard (meus-tarde), *n.*, moutarde, *f.*; sénevé, *m.*

mustard-pot (-pote), *n.*, moutardier, *m.*

mustard-seed (-sïde), *n.*, graine de moutarde, *f.*

mustee (meus-tï), *n.*, métis, *m.*, métisse, *f.*

musteline (meus-tï-laïne), *adj.*, de belette.

muster (meus-), *n.*, appel, *m.*; réunion; revue, *f.*; rassemblement, *m.*; contrôles, *m.pl.* To pass —; *passer à la revue*; (fig.) *passer.*

muster, *v.a.*, faire l'appel de; réunir; rassembler.

muster, *v.n.*, s'assembler; se réunir; (milit.) faire l'appel, répondre à l'appel.

muster-book (-bouke), *n.*, rôle; contrôle; (nav.) rôle d'équipage, *m.*; (milit.) matricule, *f.*, registre matricule d'un régiment, *m.*

muster-master (meus-teur-mâs-teur), *n.*, (milit.) major, *m.*

mustily (meus-), *adv.*, avec un goût moisi; avec un goût de renfermé.

mustiness (meus'ti-), *n.*, moisi; (closeness —*renfermé*) relent, renfermé, *m.*

musty, *adj.*, moisi; (close—*renfermé*) qui sent le relent, qui sent le renfermé; (old—*vieux*) suranné; (pers.) engourdi, lourd.

mutability (miou-), *or* **mutableness** (miou-ta-b'l-), *n.*, mutabilité; instabilité; inconstance, *f.*

mutable (miou-ta-b'l), *adj.*, changeant, inconstant, peu stable.

mutation (miou-té-), *n.*, mutation, *f.*; changement, *m.*

mute (mioute), *adj.*, muet; silencieux.

mute, *n.*, muet, *m.*, muette, *f.*; (mus.) sourdine; (gram.) lettre muette; (at a funeral—*d'enterrement*) personne placée à la porte d'une maison mortuaire, *f.*; (jur.) accusé qui refuse de répondre, *m.*; (of birds—*d'oiseaux*) fiente, *f.*

mute, *v.n.*, (of birds—*des oiseaux*) fienter.

mutely, *adv.*, en muet; silencieusement.

muteness, *n.*, mutisme, silence, *m.*

mutilate (miou-), *v.a.*, mutiler, tronquer.

mutilate, *or* **mutilated**, *adj.*, mutilé; (bot.) incomplet.

mutilation (miou-ti-lé-), *n.*, mutilation, *f.*

mutilator (-ti-lé-teur), *n.*, mutilateur, *m.*, mutilatrice, *f.*

mutineer (miou-ti-nîre), *n.*, mutin; révolté, *m.*

mutinous (miou-), *adj.*, mutin, mutiné (of soldiers, sailors—*de soldats, de marins*).

mutinously, *adv.*, en mutin (in the army, navy—*dans l'armée, la marine*).

mutinousness, *n.*, mutinerie, résistance (of soldiers, sailors—*dans l'armée, la marine*), *m.*

mutiny, *n.*, mutinerie; révolte, *f.* (in the army, navy—*dans l'armée, la marine*).

mutiny, *v.n.*, se mutiner; se révolter (in the army, navy—*dans l'armée, la marine*).

mutter (meut'teur), *n.*, murmure, *m.*

mutter, *v.a.*, marmotter, marmonner; murmurer.

mutter, *v.n.*, marmotter, marmonner; gronder.

mutterer, *n.*, personne qui marmotte, qui marmonne, *f.*; marmotteur; mécontent, *m.*

mutteringly, *adv.*, en marmottant, en marmonnant.

mutton (meut't'n), *n.*, mouton, *m.* Leg of —; *gigot*, *m.*

mutton-chop (-tshope), *n.*, côtelette de mouton, *f.*

mutton-fist, *n.*, main grossière, *f.*

mutual (miout'iou-), *adj.*, mutuel, réciproque.

mutuality, *n.*, réciprocité, *f.*

mutually, *adv.*, mutuellement.

mutule (miout-ioule), *n.*, (arch.) mutule, *f.*

muzzle (meuz'z'l), *n.*, (of animals—*des animaux*) museau, *m.*; (of fire-arms—*d'armes à feu*) bouche, *f.*; (of bellows—*d'un soufflet*) canon, bec, tuyau, *m.*; (fastening for the mouth—*pour la gueule*) muselière, *f.*

muzzle, *v.n.*, approcher le museau.

muzzle, *v.a.*, museler.

muzzle-nag, *n.*, (artil.) ceinture de la bouche, *f.*

my (ma'ye), *pron.*, mon, *m.*, ma, *f.*; mes, *pl.m.,f.*

myography (maï-og'-), *n.*, myographie, *f.*

myological (maï-ol-o-dj'-), *adj.*, myologique.

myology (maï-ol-o-dji), *n.*, myologie, *f.*

myopy (maï-o-pi), *n.*, myopie, *f.*

myosotis (maï-ô-çô-), *n.*, (bot.) myosotis, *m.*

myotomy (maï-ot'-), *n.*, myotomie, *f.*

myriad, *n.*, myriade, *f.*

myriameter (-mî-teur), *n.*, myriamètre, *m.*

myrmidon (meur-mi-), *n.*, mirmidon, *m.*

myrobalan (mi-) *n.*, (bot.) myrobolan, *m.*

myrrh (meur), *n.*, myrrhe, *f.*

myrtiform (mir-), *adj.*, (anat.) myrtiforme.

myrtle (mir't'l), *n.*, myrte, *m.*

myrtle-berry (-bèr'-), *n.*, baie de myrte, *f.*

myself (ma'ye-cèlfe), *pron.*, moi-mênie; me.

mystagogue (-goghe), *n.*, mystagogue, *m.*

mysterious (mis-ti-), *adj.*, mystérieux.

mysteriously, *adv.*, mystérieusement.

mysteriousness, *n.*, mystère, *m.*; nature mystérieuse, *f.*

mysterize (-tè-raïze), *v.a.*, faire un mystère de.

mystery (-tè-ri), *n.*, mystère, secret, *m.*

mystic, *n.*, mystique, *m.*

mystic, *or* **mystical**, *adj.*, mystique; emblématique.

mystically, *adv.*, mystiquement.

mysticalness, *n.*, mysticisme, *m.*; mysticité, *f.*

mysticism (-ciz'me), *n.*, mysticisme, *m.*, mysticité, *f.*

mystification (-fi-ké-), *n.*, mystification, *f.*

mystify (-fa'ye), *v.a.*, envelopper de mystère.

myth (mith), *n.*, mythe, *m.*

mythic, *or* **mythical** (mith'-), *adj.*, de mythe; fabuleux.

mythologic, *or* **mythological** (-thol'-o-dji'-), *adj.*, mythologique.

mythologically, *adv.*, mythologiquement.

mythologist, *n.*, mythologue, mythologiste, *m.*

mythologize (-djaïze), *v.a.*, interpréter par la mythologie.

mythology (-o-dji), *n.*, mythologie, *f.*

N

n, quatorzième lettre de l'alphabet, n, *f.*

nab, *v.a.*, gripper, happer; gober.

nabob (né-), *n.*, nabab, *m.*

nacarat, *adj.*, nacarat.

nacarat, *n.*, nacarat, *m.*

nacre (né-keur), *n.*, nacre, *f.*

nacreous (né-kri-), *adj.*, nacré.

nadir (né-), *n.*, nadir, *m.*

nag, *n.*, bidet, jeune cheval, *m.*

naiad (né-), *n.*, (myth.) naïade, *f.*

nail (nèle), *n.*, clou, *m.*; (of claws, fingers, toes—*des pattes, des doigts, des orteils*) ongle; (measure—*mesure*) un seizième de yard (centimèt. 5.50), *m.* To cut one's —ʒ; se couper, se tailler les ongles. To bite one's —ʒ; se ronger les ongles. To drive in a —; enfoncer, ficher un clou. To pay down on the —; payer écus sonnants, payer rubis sur l'ongle.

nail, *v.a.*, clouer; clouter; (a cannon—*un canon*) enclouer. To — any one; prendre quelqu'un au mot; y prendre quelqu'un. To — up; clouer; fermer avec des clous; (a window, a door, &c.—*une fenêtre, une porte, &c.*) condamner.

nail-brush (-breushe), *n.*, brosse à ongles, *f.*

nailer, *n.*, cloutier, *m.*

nailery, *n.*, clouterie, *f.*

nail-head (-hède), *n.*, tête de clou, *f.*

nail-headed (-hèd'ède), *adj.*, à tête de clou.

nail-maker (-mék'-), *n.*, cloutier, *m.*

nail-making (-mék'-), *n.*, fabrication des clous, *f.*

nail-manufactory (-ma'n'iou-fac-), *n.*, clouterie, *f.*

nail-shank (-), *n.*, tige de clou, *f.*

nail-trade, *n.*, clouterie, *f.*

nail-works (-weurkse), *n.pl.*, clouterie, *f.sing.*

naive (né-ïve), *adj.*, naïf.

naively, *adv.*, naïvement.

naivete (né-èv'té), *n.*, naïveté, *f.*

naked (né'kède), *adj.*, (not covered—*découvert*) nu, à nu; (open to view—*visible*) à découvert, ouvert, dégarni; (defenceless—*sans défense*) sans défense, exposé sans défense; (evident) évident, manifeste; (simple) simple, pur; (print.) dégarni; (bot.) dépouillé. With the eye; à l'œil nu. Stark —; tout nu; nu comme la main.

naked, *n.*, (of a column—*de colonne*) fût, (of a wall—*de mur*) nu, *m.*

nakedly, *adv.*, à nu; sans défense; simplement, purement; manifestement, ouvertement; nûment.

nakedness, *n.*, nudité, *f.*; état sans défense, *m.*, (plainness—*clarté*) évidence, clarté, *f.*; (fig.) dénûment, *m.*

namby-pamby, *adj.*, prétentieux, musqué.

name, *n.*, nom; (fame—*renommée*) renom, *m.*, renommée, *f.* Christian —; prénom, nom de baptême. What is your —? comment vous appelez-vous? By —; de nom. To go by the —

of; *être nommé* : *être connu sous le nom de.* In the
— of; *au nom de; sous le nom de; de la part de.*
The house is in the — of; *la maison est sous le
nom de.* He came in-my —; *il est venu de ma
part.*

name, *v.a.*, nommer, appeler; intituler. To
be —d; *s'appeler, se nommer*; (of things—*des
choses*) *être appelé, nommé, intitulé; s'appeler,
se nommer.* What are you —d? *comment-vous
appelez-vous?* Do not — it; *n'y faites pas attention; n'en parlez pas*; (in answering thanks
—*réponse à des remercîments*) *il n'y a pas de quoi.*

named (né'm'de), *adj.*, qui a un nom;
nommé, désigné, mentionné. Above —; *ci-
dessus nommé.*

nameless, *adj.*, sans nom, anonyme; inconnu.

namely, *adv.*, savoir, nommément.

namer, *n.*, personne qui appelle, qui nomme, *f.*

namesake (né'm'céke), *n.*, homonyme, *m.*

nankeen (-kîne), *n.*, nankin, *m.*

nap, *n.*, (of cloth, hats—*du drap, des chapeaux*) poil; (of plants—*des plantes*) duvet;
(sleep—*sommeil*) somme; (top of a hill—*sommet
de colline*) haut, *m.*; (protuberance) éminence,
touffe, *f.*, bouton, *m.* Afternoon —; *sieste, f.*

nap, *v.n.*, faire un somme; sommeiller; (fig.)
s'endormir, manquer de vigilance.

nape (népe), *n.*, nuque, *f.*; chignon, *m.*

naphtha (nap'tha), *n.*, naphte, *m.*

napkin, *n.*, serviette, *f.*

napless, *adj.*, sans poil; râpé.

nappiness, *n.*, (of cloth—*du drap*) abondance de poils; (sleepiness—*somnolence*) envie de
faire un léger somme, *f.*

nappy, *adj.*, écumeux; poilu.

nap-taking (-ték'-), *n.*, faire souvent la
sieste.

narcissus, *n.*, (bot.) narcisse, *m.*

narcotic, or **narcotical**, *adj.*, narcotique.

narcotic, *n.*, narcotique, *m.*

narcoticness, *n.*, qualité narcotique, *f.*

narcotine (nâr-co-taïne), *n.*, (chem.) narcotine, *f.*

nard (nârde), *n.*, nard, *m.*

nardine (nàr'd'aine), *adj.*, de nard.

nares (né-rize), *n.pl.*, narines, *f.pl.*

narrable (-ra-b'l), *adj.*, (ant.) qui peut être
raconté.

narrate, *v.a.*, raconter, narrer.

narration (nar-ré-), *n.*, narration, *f.*; récit, *m.*

narrative (-ré-), *n.*, récit, narré, *m.*

narrative, *adj.*, narratif; qui aime à conter.

narratively, *adv.*, en forme de narration.

narrator (-rét'eur), *n.*, narrateur, conteur, *m.*

narrow (-rô), *adj.*, étroit; (contracted, of
confined views—*rétréci, à vues étroites*) rétréci,
borné, étroit; (accurate—*correct*) exact, soigneux, scrupuleux, attentif; (near—*proche*) de
près; (not liberal—*chiche*) mesquin. To be in
— circumstances; *être à l'étroit.* To have a —
escape; *l'échapper belle.* — mind; *esprit borné.*
— -minded; *à l'esprit borné.*

narrow, *v.a.*, rendre étroit, rétrécir, étrécir.

narrow, *v.n.*, devenir étroit; se rétrécir.

narrower (-rô-eur), *n.*, personne qui rétrécit; chose qui rétrécit, *f.*

narrowing (-rô-igne), *n.*, rétrécissement, *m.*

narrowly, *adv.*, étroitement; à l'étroit;
d'une manière rétrécie, bornée; exactement,
soigneusement, scrupuleusement, attentivement; de près; mesquinement.

narrowness, *n.*, étroitesse, *f.*; rétrécissement, *m.*; petitesse, mesquinerie, *f.*

narrows (-rôze), *n.pl.*, détroit; défilé, *m.sing.*

narwal, or **narwhal** (nâr-), *n.*, (mam.)
narval, *m.*; licorne de mer, *f.*

nasal (né-zal), *a.dj.*, nasal, du nez.

nasal, *n.*, (gram.) nasale, *f.*; (med.) errhin,
médicament errhin; (of a helmet—*de casque*)
nasal, *m.*

nasality, *n.*, nasalité, *f.*

nasally, *adv.*, nasalement.

nascent, *adj.*, naissant.

nastily, *adv.*, salement, malproprement;
(fig.) grossièrement; vilainement.

nastiness, *n.*, saleté, malpropreté, grossièreté, *f.*

nasturtium (nas-teur-shi-eume), *n.*, (bot.)
capucine; graine de capucine, *f.*

nasty, *adj.*, sale, malpropre; (fig.) sale, vilain.
— boy; *vilain enfant*; *vilain, vilain sale, m.*

natal (né-), **natalitial** (-lish'al), or
natalitious (-lish'eusse), *adj.*, natal; de la
naissance; du jour natal.

natant (né-), *adj.*, (bot.) flottant.

natation (na-té-), *n.*, natation, *f.*

natatorial (né-ta-tô-), or **natatory** (-to-),
adj., natatoire.

nation (né-), *n.*, nation, *f.*; peuple, *m.*

national (nash'-), *adj.*, national.

nationality, *n.*, nationalité, *f.*

nationalize (-aïze), *v.a.*, rendre national,
nationaliser.

nationally, *adv.*, nationalement.

nationalness, *n.*, caractère national, *m.*

native (né-), *adj.*, naturel, natif; natal; du
pays, de son pays; de naissance; paternel,
maternel; indigène; primitif; (min.) natif. —
genius; *le génie naturel, m.* — soil; *sol natal,
m.* — place; *pays, lieu de naissance, m.* —
tongue; *langue maternelle, f.* — productions;
productions indigènes, f.pl.

native, *n.*, natif; naturel, indigène, *m.*

natively, *adj.*, de naissance; naturellement;
originairement.

nativeness, *n.*, état naturel, *m.*

nativity, *n.*, nativité; naissance, *f.*; lieu de
naissance, *m.* The — of our Saviour; *la nativité
de Notre-Seigneur.*

natron (né-), *n.*, (min.) natron, natrum, *m.*

natural (nat'iou-), *n.*, idiot, imbécile; (mus.)
bécarre, *m.*

natural, *adj.*, naturel; réel; naïf; (mus.)
bécarre.

naturalism (-'iz'me), *n.*, naturalisme, *m.*

naturalist, *n.*, naturaliste, *m.*

naturalization (-'aïzé-), *n.*, naturalisation, *f.*

naturalize (-aïze), *v.a.*, naturaliser.

naturally, *adv.*, naturellement.

naturalness, *n.*, naturel; caractère naturel,
m.; naïveté, *f.*

nature (nét'-), *n.*, nature, *f.*; naturel, *m.*
Good- —; *bon naturel, m.*; bonté, bonhomie, *f.*
Ill- —; *mauvais naturel, m.*; méchanceté, *f.*

natured (nét'ieur'de), *adj.*, de nature; de
naturel. Good- —; *d'un bon naturel; bon.* Ill-
—; *de mauvais naturel; méchant*; (of things—
des choses) *mauvais; ingrat.*

naturedly, *adv.* Good- —; *avec bonté; avec
bonhomie.* Ill- —; *méchamment; avec méchanceté
braver; défier.*

naught (nôte), *n.*, rien; (arith.) zéro, *m.*
To set at —; *ne faire aucun cas de; mépriser;*

naught, *adv.*, nullement; aucunement.

naught, *adj.*, méchant, mauvais.

naughtily, *adv.*, par méchanceté.

naughtiness, *n.*, méchanceté, *f.*

naughty, *adj.*, méchant. — trick; *méchanceté, f.*

naumachy (-ki), *n.*, naumachie, *f.*

nausea (nô-shi-a), *n.*, nausée, *f.*; soulèvement de cœur, *m.*

nauseate (nô-shi-éte), *v.n.*, avoir des nausées; (fig.) être dégoûté.

nauseate, *v.a.*, donner des nausées; avoir des
nausées de; dégoûter; (med.) faire vomir.

nauseating. *adj.*, nauséabond ; dégoûtant.

nauseous (nô-sheusse), *adj.*, nauséabond ; dégoûtant.

nauseously, *adv.*, d'une manière nauséabonde ; d'une manière dégoûtante.

nauseousness, *n.*, nature nauséabonde, *f.* ; dégoût, *m.*

nautic, *or* **nautical**, *adj.*, nautique, de marin.

nautilus, *n.*, nautile, argonaute, *m.*

naval (né-), *adj.*, naval, maritime ; de la marine.

nave, *n.*, (of a church—*d'église*) nef, *f.* ; (of a wheel—*de roue*) moyeu, *m.*

navel (né-v'l), *n.*, nombril ; (fig.) centre, cœur, *m.*

navel-string (-strigne), *n.*, cordon ombilical, *m.*

navel-wort (-weurte), *n.*, (bot.) cotylédon, cotylet, *m.*

navigable (-ga-b'l), *adj.*, navigable.

navigableness, *n.*, navigabilité, *f.*

navigate, *v.a.* and *n.*, naviguer, naviguer sur ; gouverner.

navigation (-ghé-), *n.*, navigation, *f.*

navigation-laws (-lôze), *n.pl.*, code maritime, *m.* ; législation maritime, *f.*

navigator (-ghé-teur), *n.*, navigateur, *m.*

navy (né-), *n.*, marine, *f.* Mercantile — ; *marine marchande*, *f.*

navy-agency (-é-djè'n'-), *n.*, agence pour la marine, *f.*

navy-agent (-é-djè'n'te), *n.*, agent pour la marine, *m.*

navy-bills (-bil'ze), *n.pl.*, lois et ordonnances maritimes, *f.pl.*

navy-board (-bôrde), *n.*, conseil de la marine, *m.*

navy-office, *n.*, bureaux de la marine, *m.pl.*

navy-yard, *n.*, arsenal maritime, *m.*

nay, *adv.*, non, nenni ; même ; qui plus est.

nazarene (-rine). *n.*, Nazaréen, *m.*, Nazaréenne, *f.*

nazarite (-raïte), *n.*, Nazaréen, *m.*

neal (nîl), *v.* *V.* **anneal**.

neapolitan, *adj.*, napolitain ; de Naples.

neapolitan (ni-a-), *n.*, Napolitain, *m.*, Napolitaine, *f.*

neap-tide (-taïde), *n.*, morte-eau ; morte marée, *f.*

near (nîr), *adj.*, proche ; près ; près de ; rapproché ; (parsimonious—*parcimonieux*) serré, parcimonieux, très regardant ; (stingy—*ménager*) chiche ; (intimate—*intime*) précieux, chéri, cher ; (faithful—*fidèle*) exact, fidèle. — relation ; *proche parent*, *m.*, *proche parente*, *f.*

near, *adv.*, près ; près de ; de près ; presque. To draw — ; *s'approcher*. To draw — to ; *s'approcher de*. Nothing — ; *à beaucoup près*.

near, *prep.*, près de, auprès de.

near, *v.a.* and *n.*, s'approcher de, s'approcher.

nearly, *adv.*, de près ; à peu près ; environ ; presque ; (parsimoniously—*parcimonieusement*) chichement, mesquinement.

nearness, *n.*, proximité ; (close union—*union intime*) union étroite ; (parsimony—*parcimonie*) parcimonie, mesquinerie, *f.*

near-sighted (-saït'-), *adj.*, qui a la vue basse, myope.

neat (nîte), *n.*, gros bétail ; *m.*, vache, *f.*

neat (nîte), *adj.*, (clean—*propre*) net, propre, soigné, rangé ; (pure—*pur*) pur, chaste ; (unadulterated—*non frelaté*) pur ; (unadorned—*sans ornement*) propre, simple ; de bon goût.

neatherd (-heurde), *n.*, bouvier, vacher, *m.*

neatly, *adv.*, proprement ; nettement ; d'une manière soignée, purement, chastement ; simplement ; (dexterously—*avec dextérité*) adroitement ; avec bon goût.

neatness, *n.*, propreté, netteté ; pureté ; simplicité, *f.*

nebula (nèb'lou-), *n.*, nuage, *m.* ; (astron.) nébuleuse, étoile nébuleuse, *f.*

nebulose, *or* **nebulous**, *adj.*, nébuleux, obscur.

nebulosity, *n.*, état nébuleux, *m.* ; nébulosité, *f.*

necessaries (nèss'ès-sa-rize), *n.*, nécessaire, *m.* : nécessités. *f.pl.*

necessarily, *adv.*, nécessairement, de nécessité.

necessariness, *n.*, nécessité, *f.*

necessary (nèss'ès-sa-ri) *adj.*, nécessaire ; (unavoidable—*inévitable*) obligé, forcé, péremptoire. If — ; *s'il le faut ; au besoin. It is — ; il faut.*

necessary, *n.*, garde-robe, *f.*, commodités, *f.pl.*, lieux, lieux d'aisances, *m.pl.*, cabinet d'aisances, *m.*

necessitate (niss'ès-si-), *v.a.*, nécessiter, obliger, contraindre.

necessitation (-si-té-), *n.*, obligation, contrainte, *f.*

necessitous (ni-cès-si-teuse), *adj.*, nécessiteux, dans le besoin ; (of things—*des choses*) de nécessité, de besoin.

necessitousness, *n.*, nécessité, *f.* ; besoin, *m.*

necessity (ni-cès-sï'-), *n.*, nécessité ; (indigence) nécessité, *f.*, besoin, *m.* From — ; *par nécessité ; par besoin.* To make a virtue of — ; *faire de nécessité vertu.* To be under the — of ; *se trouver dans la nécessité de.*

neck (nèke), *n.*, cou ; (of bottles, &c.—*de bouteilles*, &c.) cou, goulot ; (of musical instruments—*d'instruments de musique*) manche ; (of meat—*de viande*) collet ; (of a mountain—*de montagne*) col, *m.* ; (of land—*de terre*) langue, *f.* Stiff-—; torticolis, *m.* — and shoulders (of animals—*des animaux*) ; encolure, *f.* To break any one's — ; *casser le cou à quelqu'un.*

neckcloth (-clôth), *n.*, cravate, *f.*

necked (nèk'te), *adj.*, qui a un cou. Stiff-—; *au cou raide* ; (fig.) altier, arrogant. Long-—; *au long cou.* Short-—; *qui a le cou court*, *au cou court.*

neckerchief (nèk'èr tshif), *n.*, fichu, *m.*

necklace, *n.*, collier, *m.*

necklaced (-léss'te), *adj.*, marqué comme d'un collier.

neckland, *n.*, langue de terre, *f.*

neckweed (-wide), *n.*, chanvre, *m.*

neorological (nèk'rol'o-dj'-), *adj.*, nécrologique.

necrologist (nèk'rol-o-djiste), *n.*, nécrologue, *m.*

necrology (nek'rol-o-dji), *n.*, nécrologie, *f.*

necromancer (nèk'-), *n.*, nécromancien, *m.*, nécromancienne, *f.* ; nécromant, *m.*

necromancy (nèk'-), *n.*, nécromancie, œnécromance, *f.*

necromantic, *adj.*, de nécromancie.

necromantic. *n.*, tour de nécromancie, *m.*

necromantically, *adv.*, par nécromancie.

necrosis (ni-crô-cice), *n.*, nécrose, *f.*

nectar, *n.*, nectar, *m.*

nectareal, *or* **nectarean** (-ri-), *adj.*, de nectar ; nectaréen ; nectaré.

nectared (nèk-tarde), *adj.*, de nectar.

nectareous (-ri-), *adj.* *V.* **nectareal**.

nectarine. *V.* **nectareal**.

nectarine, *n.*, brugnon, *m.*

nectarize (-aïze), *v.a.*, sucrer.

nectarous. *V.* **nectareal**.

nectary, *n.*, (bot.) nectaire, *m.*

need (nide), *n.*, besoin. *m.* ; nécessité. *f.* ; (indigence) besoin, *m.*, nécessité, misère, *f.* In case of — ; *au besoin ; en cas de nécessité.* What — is there of that ? *quel besoin y a-t-il de ...? quelle* *nécessité y a-t-il pour cela?* There is no — of that; *il n'y a pas besoin de cela.* To be in —; *être dans le besoin, dans la misère.*

need (nide), *v.n.*, avoir besoin; devoir; avoir; (imp.) falloir, être nécessaire.

need, *v.a.*, avoir besoin de.

needer, *n.*, personne qui a besoin, *f.*

noodful (-foule), *adj.*, nécessaire.

needfully, *adv.*, nécessairement.

needfulness, *n.*, besoin, *m.*; nécessité, *f.*

needily, *adv.*, dans le besoin; par besoin.

neediness, *n.*, indigence, nécessité, *f.*; besoin, *m.*

needle (nî-d'l), *n.*, aiguille, *f.* To thread a —; *enfiler une aiguille.* Netting- —; *navette, f.* Sewing- —; *aiguille à coudre, f.* Darning- —; *aiguille à repriser, f.* Eye of a —; *trou d'aiguille, m.*

needle, *v.n.*, se cristalliser en aiguilles.

needle, *v.a.*, cristalliser en aiguilles.

needle-case (-kéce), *n.*, étui, *m.*

needle-fish, *n.*, (ich.) aiguille, *f.*

needleful (-foule). *n.*, aiguillée, *f.*

needler, *or* **needle-maker** (-mék'-), *n.*, aiguillier, *m.*

needless, *adj.*, inutile.

needlessly, *adv.*, inutilement.

needlessness, *n.*, inutilité, *f.*

needle-work (-weurke), *n.*, ouvrage à l'aiguille, *m.*

needs (nîdze), *adv.*, nécessairement, absolument. I must —; *je dois nécessairement . . . .*; *il faut absolument que je . . . .* He must —; *il doit nécessairement . . . .*; *il faut absolument qu'il . . . .*

needy (nîd'-), *adj.*, indigent, nécessiteux, pauvre.

nefand (nî-), *or* **nefandous** (nî-), *adj.*, (ant.) détestable, abominable.

nefarious (ni-fé-), *adj.*, exécrable, atroce, abominable, infâme.

nefariously, *adv.*, exécrablement, atrocement, abominablement; avec infamie.

negation (ni-ghé'-), *n.*, négation, négative, *f.*

negative (nèg'-a-), *n.*, négative, négation, *f.*

negative, *adj.*, négatif.

negative, *v.a.*, décider négativement; (in parliament—*parlement*) rejeter.

negatively, *adv.*, négativement, avec négation.

negativeness, *n.*, qualité négative, *f.*

neglect (nèg'-), *n.*, négligence, *f.*; oubli, *m.*

neglect, *v.a.*, négliger.

neglecter, *n.*, négligent, *m.*, négligente, *f.*

neglectful (-foule), *adj.*, négligent; nonchalant.

neglectfully, *adv.*, négligemment; nonchalamment.

negligee (nèg-li-jé), *n.*, négligé, *m.*

negligence (nèg-li-djè'n'ce), *n.*, négligence; nonchalance, *f.*; oubli, *m.*

negligent (nèg-li-djè'n'te), *adj.*, négligent.

negligently, *adv.*, négligemment; par négligence.

negotiability (ni-gô-shi-), *n.*, négociabilité, *f.*

negotiable (ni-gô-shi-a-b'l), *adj.*, négociable.

negotiate (ni-gô-shi-), *v.a.*, négocier.

negotiate, *v.n.*, négocier, être en négociation.

negotiation (ni-gô-shi-é-), *n.*, négociation, *f.*

negotiator (ni-gô-shi-ét'eur), *n.*, négociateur, *m.*

negress (nî-grèce), *n.*, négresse, *f.*

negro (nî-), *n.*, nègre, *m.* — boy; *jeune nègre: négrillon, m.* — girl; *jeune négresee; négrillonne, f.*

negus (nî-), *n.*, vin chaud, vin cuit, négus, *m.*

neigh (né), *v.n.*, hennir.

neigh (né), *n.*, hennissement, *m.*

neighbour (né-beur), *n.*, voisin, *m.*, voisine, *f.*; (biblically—*biblique*) prochain, *m.* Next-door —; *plus proche voisin.* To be next-door —s; *demeurer porte à porte.*

neighbour, *adj.*, voisin.

neighbour, *v.n.*, avoisiner.

neighbourhood (né-beur'houde), *n.*, voisinage, *m.*; alentours, environs, *m.pl.*

neighbouring, *adj.*, voisin; du voisinage; des alentours; approximatif.

neighbourly, *adj.*, de voisin. — act; *trait de bon voisin, m.*

neighbourly, *adv.*, en voisin; en bon voisin.

neighing (né-igne), *n.*, hennissement, *m.*

neither (nî-*theur*), *pron.*, ni l'un ni l'autre, *m.*, ni l'une ni l'autre, *f.*; ni les uns ni les autres, *m.pl.*, ni les unes ni les autres, *f.pl.*

neither, *conj.*, ni; non plus.

nem. con. (nème-) (*ab.* of Nemine contradicente), sans voix dissidente.

nemean (ni-mî-), *adj.*, néméen; de Némée.

nemoral, *or* **nemorous** (nèm'-), *adj.*, des bois.

nenuphar (nə'n'îou-fâr), *n.*, (bot.) nénuphar, *m.*

neologic, *or* **neological** (ni-ô-lodj'-), *adj.*, néologique.

neologism (ni-ol'o-djiz'me), *n.*, néologisme, *m.*

neologist (ni-ol-o-djiste), *n.*, néologue; néologiste, *m.*

neology (ni-ol-o-dji), *n.*, néologie, *f.*

neophyte (nî-o-faïte), *n.*, néophyte; novice, *m., f.*

neoteric (nî-o-tèr'-), *adj.*, moderne.

neoteric, *n.*, moderne, *m.*

nepenthe (ni-pè'n'thi), *n.*, panacée, *f.*, népenthès, *m.*

nepenthes (ni-pè'n'thize) *n.*, (bot.) népenthès, *m.*

nephew (nèv'viou), *n.*, neveu, *m.* Grand-—; *petit-neveu, m.*

nephritic, *or* **nephritical** (nè-), *adj.*, néphrétique.

nephritic, *n.*, néphrétique, *m.*

nephritis (nè-fraï-), *n.*, néphrite, *f.*

nepotism (nèp'o-tizme), *n.*, népotisme, *m.*

nereid (nî-ri-ide), *n.*, néréide, *f.*

nerite (nî-raïte), *n.*, nérite, *f.*

neroli (nèr-), *n.*, néroli, *m.*

nerve (neurve), *n.*, nerf, *m.*; (arch., bot.) nervure, *f.*

nerve, *v.a.*, donner du nerf à, de la force à.

nerved (neurv'de), *adj.*, fortifié, vigoureux; (bot.) nervé.

nerveless, *adj.*, sans nerf; sans vigueur, sans force.

nervine (neur-), *adj.*, nervin.

nervine, *n.*, nervin, *m.*

nervose (neur-vôce), *adj.*, (bot.) nervé.

nervous (neur-), *adj.*, nerveux, vigoureux; (med.) nerveux; (bot.) nervé.

nervously, *adv.*, nerveusement; avec vigueur.

nervousness, *n.*, nerf, *m.*; vigueur, *f.*; (med.) état nerveux, *m.*

nervy (neur-), *adj.*, (ant.) nerveux; vigoureux.

nescience (nèsh'i-è'n'ce), *n.*, ignorance, *f.*

nest (nèste), *n.*, nid, *m.*; (brood of birds—*couvée*) nichée; (fig.) nichée, *f.*, repaire, *m.*; (of boxes, cases, &c.—*de boîtes, de caisses, &c.*) caisse à tiroirs, *f.*, casier, *m.* To have found a mare's one's —; *faire son nid; faire ses orges.* A — of thieves; *un repaire de voleurs.* — egg; *nichet, m.*

nest, *v.n.*, nicher, faire un nid.

nestle (nès's'l), *v.n.*, nicher; se nicher, se fixer.

nestle, *v.n.*, nicher, loger; chérir.

nestling (nès's'l'-), *adj.*, nouvellement éclos; encore au nid.

nestling (nès'ligne), *n.*, petit oiseau nouvellement éclos, encore au nid, *m.*

net (nète), *n.*, filet, rets; réseau; (textile fabric —*tissu*) tulle, *m.*

net, *v.a.*, (com., fin.) donner net, produire un bénéfice net.

net, *v.n.*, faire du filet.

net, *adj.*, net; pur.

nether (nèth'eur), *adj.*, inférieur, bas.

nethermost (-môste), *adj.*, le plus bas.

netting, *n.*, réseau, rets; filet, *m.*

nettle (nèt't'l), *n.*, ortie, *f.*

nettle, *v.a.*, piquer; aigrir.

nettler, *n.*, personne qui pique, qui aigrit; chose qui pique, qui aigrit, *f.*

nettle-rash, *n.*, (med.) urticaire, *f.*

net-work (-weurke). *n*, réseau, lacis, *m.*

neuralgia (niou-ral-djia), *n.*, (med.) névralgie, *f.*

neurological (niou-rol-o-dj'-), *adj.*, névrologique.

neurologist (niou-rol'o-djiste), *n.*, névrolographe, *m.*

neurology (niou-rol-o-dji), *n.*, névrologie, *f.*

neuropter (niou-), *n.*, névroptère, *m.*

neuropteral, *or* **neuropterous**, *adj.*, névroptère.

neurotic (niou-), *adj.*, névritique; nervin.

neurotic, *n.*, (disease—*maladie*) névrite, *f.*; (remedy—*remède*) nervin, *m.*

neurotomy, *n.*, névrotomie, *f.*

neuter (niou-), *adj.*, neutre.

neuter, *n.*, neutre, *m.*; personne neutre, *f.*; (gram., ent.), neutre, *m.*

neutral (niou-), *adj.*, neutre; indifférent.

neutrality, *n.*, neutralité; indifférence, *f.*

neutralization (-aïzé-), *n.*, neutralisation, *f.*

neutralize (-aïze), *v.a.*, neutraliser.

neutrally, *adv.*, neutralement.

neuvaines (niou-vé'n'ze), *n. pl.*, neuvaine, *f.*

never (nèv'-), *adv.*, jamais; ne ... jamais; pas; ne ... aucunement; ne ... nullement; quelque ... que ce soit. — I *jamais!* I have — seen it; *je ne l'ai jamais vu.* — a word; *pas un mot.* Be — so idle; *ne soyez jamais si paresseux.*

nevertheless (-*th*i-), *adj.*, néanmoins, toutefois, cependant, pourtant.

new (niou), *adj.*, neuf, nouveau, nouvel; (of bread—*pain*) tendre, frais; (unaccustomed—*inaccoutumé*) neuf, novice; frais, récent; (recently commenced, recently appeared—*commencé, paru récemment*) nouveau, nouvel. Bran-—, brand-—; *battant neuf.* Speck and span—; *tout battant neuf.* — from; *frais de.* A — hat; *un chapeau neuf.* — wine; *du vin nouveau.* The — moon; *la nouvelle lune.* ◄ — work; *un nouvel ouvrage.* A — book; (not used—*tout neuf*) *un livre neuf;* (newly out—*récemment publié*) *un livre nouveau;* (a different one—*différent*) *un nouveau livre.* A — word; *un mot nouveau.* — comer; *nouveau venu, m.* —laid eggs; *œufs frais, m.pl.* — year; *nouvel an, m.* —year's-day; *le jour de l'an, m.* — year's-gifts; *étrennes, f.pl.*

nowel (niou-èl), *n.*, noyau d'escalier, *m.*

new-fangled (niou-fan'gn'g'l'de), *adj.*, nouvellement inventé.

newing (niou'igne), *n.*, levure, *f.*

nowish (niou'ishe), *adj.*, assez neuf; assez nouveau; assez récent, assez frais; (of bread—*pain*) assez tendre, assez frais.

newly (niou-). *adv.*, nouvellement, fraîchement, récemment.

newness niou-), *n.*, nouveauté; (want of practice—*défaut de pratique*) inexpérience; (innovation) innovation, *f.*

news (niouze). *n.*, nouvelle, *f.*; nouvelles,

f.pl. What is the —s? *quelles sont les nouvelles? qu'y a-t-il de nouveau?*

news-boy (-boï), *n.*, marchand, porteur de journaux, *m.*

newsman, *n.*, commissionnaire pour les journaux; marchand de journaux, *m.*

news-monger (-meu'n'gheur), *n.*, débitant de nouvelles, *m.*

newspaper (-pé-), *n.*, journal, *m.*; feuille, gazette, *f.*

newsvendor, *n.*, commissionnaire pour les journaux; marchand de journaux, *m.*

newt (nioute), *n.*, petit lézard, *m.*

newtonian (niou-tô-), *adj.*, newtonien.

newtonian, *n.*, newtonien, *m.*

new-year's-day (niou-yeur'z'dè), *n.*, le jour de l'an *m.*

new-year's-gift (-ghifte), *n.*, étrennes, *f.pl.*

next (nèkste), *adj.*, (in degree—*en degré*) le plus proche, voisin; (in place—*de lieu*) le plus près; (in succession—*successivement*) suivant, premier; (of past time—*du passé*) suivant; (of future time—*du futur*) prochain; (fig.) voisin, rapproché, suivant, prochain; futur. The — interview; *la prochaine entrevue.* The — world; *l'autre monde; la vie future; la vie à venir.* He will come — month; *il viendra le mois prochain.* He came — day; *il est venu le jour suivant, le lendemain.*

next (nèkste), *adv.*, à côté de; après; immédiatement après; ensuite; le premier, *m.*, la première, *f.*; les premiers, *m.pl.*, les premières, *f.pl.* — to; *à côté de;* (nearly—*presque*) *à peu près, presque.* — to nothing; *presque rien.* — to impossible; *à peu près, presque impossible.* He sat — to me; *il était assis à côté de moi.* He came —; *il vint immédiatement après.* What — ? *après? et après? ensuite?*

nias (naï'ace), *n.* (ant.) *V.* **eyas.**

nib, *n.*, (of a bird, a pen—*d'oiseau, de plume*) bec, *m.*; (point—*pointe, extrémité*) pointe, *f.*, bout, *m.*

nibbed (nib'de), *adj.*, qui a un bec, une pointe; à bec; à pointe. Hard-—; *qui a le bec dur.* Soft—; *qui a le bec flexible.*

nibble (nib'b'l), *n.*, coup de dent, de bec, *m.*

nibble, *v.a.*, mordiller; grignoter; (of fish—*de poisson*) mordre à l'hameçon; (of birds—*des oiseaux*) becqueter; (the grass, &c.—*l'herbe, &c.*) brouter.

nibble, *v.n.*, mordiller; grignoter; brouter; mordre. To — at; *mordiller, grignoter, brouter; mordre;* (to carp at—*médire*) *gloser sur, faire la critique de.*

nibbler, *n.*, personne qui mordille, qui grignote, *f.*; animal qui mordille, qui grignote, qui broute; poisson qui mord à l'hameçon; (carper —*médisant*) gloseur, *m.*, gloseuse, *f.*; critique, *m.*

nice (naïce), *adj.*, (to the taste—*au goût*) bon, agréable, friand; (delightful—*charmant*) joli; (delicate—*délicat*) délicat, fin; (exact—*correct*) exact, juste; (scrupulous—*scrupuleux*) scrupuleux; (fastidious—*difficile*) difficile, sévère, rigide, prude; (refined—*raffiné*) recherché, subtil; (acute—*délié*) subtil, pénétrant; (well-behaved—*de bonne conduite*) (of children—*des enfants*) sage, gentil; (amiable—*aimable*) gentil, aimable, charmant, bon; (jest.) joli. A — dinner; *un bon dîner.* —tints; *des nuances délicates.* You are very —! *vous êtes bien difficile!* A — child; *un enfant gentil, sage.* A very — girl; *une demoiselle bien aimable, bien gentille; une petite fille très sage.* A — little wife; *une bonne petite femme.* A — man; *un homme aimable.* You are a — fellow! a — man! *vous êtes un joli garçon!*

nicely, *adv.*, bien; agréablement; avec friandise; délicatement; finement; exactement; justement; scrupuleusement; difficilement;

sévèrement, rigidement, avec pruderie ; avec recherche ; subtilement ; avec pénétration ; gentiment ; avec amabilité, aimablement ; joliment ; (jest.) joliment.

niceness, n., goût agréable, m. ; délicatesse, finesse ; exactitude, justesse, f. ; soin scrupuleux m. ; sévérité, rigidité, pruderie ; recherche, f. ; raffinement, m. ; subtilité ; pénétration ; gentillesse ; amabilité, f.

nicety, n., délicatesse, finesse, f. ; (delicate management—*attention*) soin scrupuleux, m. ; (precision) exactitude, justesse, f. Niceties (*friandises, délicatesses, douceurs, f.pl.* To a — ; à *point ; très bien.* The niceties of a language ; *les délicatesses d'une langue.*

nicho (nishe), n., niche, f.

nick, n., moment précis ; moment critique ; (northern myth.—*mythol. du nord*) esprit malfaisant, m. ; (notch—*coche*) entaille, f. ; (print.) cran, m. Old— ; *le diable*, m. In the — of time ; *juste à point : à propos ; à point nommé.*

nick, v.a., (to hit—*tomber juste*) rencontrer juste ; (to notch—*faire une coche*) faire une entaille dans : (a horse—*un cheval*) anglaiser.

nickel (-'èl), n., (min.) nickel, m.

nicker (-'eur), n., filou m.

nickname, n., sobriquet, m.

nickname. v.a., donner un sobriquet à.

nicotian (ni-kô-sha'n), n., (bot.) nicotiane, f.

nictate, or **nictitate**, v.n., clignoter.

nictation (nik'té-), or **nictitation** (nik'ti-té-), n., clignotement, m. ; (med.) nictation, nictitation, f.

nidification (-fi-ké-), n., nidification, f.

nidor (naï-), n., odeur, senteur, f.

nidorosity (naï-dor-o-ci-), n., (ant.) (med.) éructation nidoreuse, f.

nidorous. adj., nidoreux.

nidulation (nid'iou-lé-), n., couvaison, f.

nidus (naï-), n., nid, m.

niece (nîce), n., nièce, f. Grand— ; petite-nièce.

niggard, adj., chiche, avare, vilain, ladre.

niggard, n., avare, ladre, vilain, lésineur, m.

niggard. v.a., donner mesquinement.

niggardish, adj., assez avare, assez chiche.

niggardliness, n., mesquinerie, ladrerie, avarice sordide, lésinerie, f.

niggardly, adv., avec ladrerie, avec avarice, en avare, en ladre.

niggardly, adj., mesquin, ladre, chiche, lésineur. — doings ; *vilenies, lésineries, f.pl.*

nigger (nig'gheur), n., (pop.) nègre, m., négresse, f.

nigh (na'-ye), adv., presque, de près ; près de. To draw — ; *approcher ; s'approcher.*

nigh. adj., proche, rapproché ; près ; près de.

nighly, adv., presque, à peu près.

nighness, n., proximité, f.

night (naïte), n., nuit, f. ; soir, m. ; (thea.) représentation, f. It is — ; *il fait nuit.* At — ; *la nuit, de nuit.* Good — ! *bonsoir* ! A good —'s rest to you ! *bonne nuit* ! All — ; *toute la nuit.* Every — ; *toutes les nuits ; tous les soirs.* Twelfth— ; *le jour des Rois*, m., *l'Épiphanie*, f.

night-born, adj., né des ténèbres.

night-brawler (-brôl'-), n., tapageur de nuit, m.

night-cart (-cârte), n., voiture de vidange, f.

nighted, adj., obscur, sombre.

night-fall (-fôl), n., tombée de la nuit, chute du jour, f.

night-fire (-faï'eur), n., feu de nuit ; feu follet, m.

night-foundered (-faou'n'deurde), adj., égaré la nuit ; (of ships—*des vaisseaux*) sombré au milieu de la nuit.

night-hag, n., sorcière de nuit, f.

night-hawk (-hôke), n., hulotte, huette, f.

nightingale (naït'i'n'ghéle), n., rossignol, m.

nightly, adj., nocturne, de nuit.

nightly, adv., de nuit ; chaque nuit, toutes les nuits ; (till midnight—*jusqu'à minuit*) tous les soirs.

nightman, n., vidangeur, m.

nightmare, n., cauchemar, m.

night-piece (-pîce), n., (paint.) tableau de nuit, m.

nightshade (-shéde), n., (bot.) solanum, m. ; morelle. f. Deadly — ; *belladone*, f.

night-soil (-soïle), n.sing., vidanges, f.pl.

night-time (-taïme), n., nuit (temps), f. In the — ; *pendant la nuit.*

night-walk (-wôke), n., promenade nocturne, f.

night-walker, n., rôdeur nocturne, m. ; somnambule, m., f.

night-walking, adj., qui rôde la nuit ; somnambule.

night-walking, n., action de rôder la nuit, f. ; courses de nuit, f.pl. ; somnambulisme, m.

night-watch (-wôtshe), n., garde de nuit, f.

night-work (-weurke), n., veille, f., travail de nuit. m. ; vidange (de fosses), f.

nigrescent (naï-grès'-), adj., noirâtre.

nihilism (naï-hil'iz'me), or **nihility**, n., néant, m.

nill, n., étincelle, f.

nill, v.a., refuser, ne pas vouloir. — I, will I ; *bon gré, mal gré.*

nilometer (naï-lom'i-), n., nilomètre, m.

nimble (ni'm'b'l), adj., agile, actif, ingambe, léger, leste, vif, dispos.

nimble-footed (-fout'-), adj., au pied léger ; leste.

nimbleness, n., légèreté ; agilité ; vivacité, f.

nimble-witted, adj., à l'esprit vif.

nimbly, adv., agilement ; lestement.

nimbus (-beusse), n., (paint., sculpt.) nimbe, (meteorol.) nimbus, m.

nincompoop (ni'n'keu'm'poupe), n., niais, sot, nicodème, m.

nine (naëne), n. and adj., neuf.

ninefold (-fôlde), adj., neuf fois autant.

nineholes (-hôl'ze), n., balle au pot, f.

ninepins (-pi'n'ze), n.pl., quilles, f.pl.

ninescore (-scôre), n. and adj., cent quatre-vingts.

nineteen (-tîne), adj., dix-neuf.

nineteenth (-ti'n'th), adj., dix-neuvième.

ninetieth (naë'n'ti-èth), adj., quatre-vingt-dixième.

ninety, adj., quatre-vingt-dix.

ninny, n., nigaud, m., nigaude, f. ; benêt, m.

ninth (na'é'nth), adj., neuvième.

ninthly, adv., neuvièmement.

nip, n., action de saisir, f. ; (with the nails, the teeth—*avec les ongles, les dents*)coup d'ongle, coup de dent, m. ; (cut—*coupure*)coupure, f. ; (of plants —*des plantes*)brûlure (par le froid), f. ; (sarcasm) sarcasme, trait piquant, lardon, ⊙biscard ; (sip —*du boire*) petit coup, m.

nip, v.a., pincer ; pincer le bout de ; couper le bout de ; mordre ; (plants—*des plantes*) brûler (par le froid) ; (to blast—*faner*) flétrir ; (fig.) piquer ; (nav.) amarrer ; saisir. To — off ; *couper : couper le bout de ; pincer ; pincer le bout de.*

nipper, n., pince, f. —s ; *pincettes, pinces, f.pl.* ; (nav.) *garcette de tournevire, f.*

nipping, adj., mordant, piquant ; (of cold— *du froid*) perçant.

nippingly, adv., d'une manière piquante.

nipple (nip'p'l), n., mamelon, tetin, m. ; (of fire-arms—*d'armes à feu*) cheminée, f.

nipple-wort (-weurte), n., lampsane, f.

nit. n., (ent.) lente, f.

nitrate (naï-), n., nitrate, m.

nitre (naï-teur), n., nitre, m.

nitre-works (-weurkse), n.pl., salpêtrière, f.

nitriary (naï-), n., (min.) nitrière, f.

nitric (naï-), *adj.*, nitrique.
nitrify (naï-trï-fa'-ye), *v.a.*, nitrifier.
nitrogen (naï-tro-ájène), *n.*, nitrogène, azote, *m.*
nitrogenous (naï-tro-djè'n-),*adj.*,nitrogéné.
nitrous, *or* **nitry** (naï-), *adj.*. nitreux.
nitty, *adj.*, couvert de lentes.
niveous (niv'ï-), *adj.*, de neige ; neigeux.
no (nô), *adj.*, nul, aucun ; pas, point ; pas de ; ue . . . . pas de ; ne . . . . point de. —where ; *nulle part.* There is — means to ; *il n'y a pas moyen de.*
no, *adv.*, non, ne, pas. — matter ; *n'importe.* — more ; *pas davantage.*
nob, *n.*, caboche, boule, *f.*
nobiliary, *n.*, nobiliaire, *m.*
nobilitate, *v.a.*, (ant.) anoblir.
nobilitation (-li-té-), *n.*, anoblissement, *m.*
nobility, *n.*, noblesse, *f.*
noble (nô-b'l), *n.*, gentilhomme, noble, *m.*
noble, *adj.*, noble, illustre, grand ; généreux.
nobleman, *n.*, noble, gentilhomme, *m.*
nobleness, *n.*, noblesse, grandeur, *f.*
nobles (nô-b'l'ze), *n.*, noblesse, *f.* ; corps des nobles, *m.*
noblewoman (-woum'a'n), *n.*, femme noble, *f.*
nobly, *adv.*, noblement ; de noble rang ; de noble condition.
nobody (nô-), *n.*, personne, *f.* ; rien, *m.* — knows it ; *personne ne le sait.* — I know — ; *je ne connais personne.* Who is there ? *qui est-là !* — ; *personne.* To be — ; *n'être rien du tout.*
nocent (nô-), *adj.*, nuisible.
noctambulation (-biou-lé-), *n.*, noctambulisme, *m.*
noctambulist, *n.*, noctambule, *m.*, *f.*
noctivagant, *or* **noctivagous**, *adj.*, qui court pendant la nuit.
noctivagation (-va-ghé-), *n.*, course nocturne, *f.*
noctuary (-tiou-), *n.*, rapport de ce qui se passe la nuit, *m.*
nocturn (-teurne), *n.*, nocturne, *m.*
nocturnal (-teur-), *n.*, télescope de nuit, *m.*
nocturnal, *adj.*, nocturne, de nuit.
nod, *n.*, signe de tête, salut, *m.* ; inclination de tête, *f.* ; balancement, *m.*
nod. *v.n.*, faire un signe de tête ; incliner la tête ; s'incliner ; (to be drowsy—*avoir sommeil*) s'assoupir ; (to tremble—*trembler*) trembler, s'agiter ; se plier, se balancer. To — to ; *faire un signe de tête à ; saluer.*
nod, *v.n.*, exprimer par une inclination de tête, montrer par une inclination de tête.
nodated (nô-dét'-), *adj.*, noueux.
nodder, *n.*,personne qui fait une inclination de tête; personne assoupie, *f.*
noddle (nod'd'l), *n.*, caboche, tête, *f.*
noddy, *n.*, sot, benêt, *m.*
node (nôde), *n.*, nœud ; (med.) nodus, *m.*
nodose (no-dôce), *adj.*, noueux.
nodosity (no-dô-ci-ti), *n.*, nœud, *m.* ; nodosité, *f.*
nodular (nod'iou-), *adj.*, en forme de nodule.
nodule (nod'ioule), *n.*, nodule, *m.*
noduled (nod'ioulde), *adj.*, en nodule.
nog, *n.*, petit pot, *m.* ; (beer—*bière*) bière, *f.* ; (tree-nail—*cheville*) cheville de bois employée dans la construction des vaisseaux, *f.*; pavé en bois, *m.*
noggin (-ghine), *n.*, petit pot de bois, *m.*
nogging (-ghigne), *n.*, (mas.) cloison de briques, *f.*
noise (noïze), *n.*, bruit ; tapage ; fracas ; (in the ears—*dans les oreilles*) tintement, bourdonnement ; (fig.) éclat, retentissement, *m.* To make a —; *faire du bruit.* What a — ! *quel fracas ! quel tapage !*

noise, *v.a.*, publier, répandre, ébruiter. To — abroad ; *répandre au loin ; faire circuler.*
noise, *v.n.*, faire du bruit ; retentir.
noiseless, *adj.*, sans bruit ; silencieux ; tranquille, calme.
noiselessly, *adv.*, sans bruit ; silencieusement.
noiselessness, *n.*, tranquillité, *f.*
noise-maker (-mék'-), *n.*, tapageur, *m.*
noisily, *adv.*, bruyamment.
noisiness, *n.*, grand bruit ; tumulte, *m.*
noisome (noï-ceume), *adj.*, dégoûtant; malsain ; infect ; nuisible.
noisomely, *adv.*, d'une manière infecte.
noisomeness, dégoût, *m.* ; infection, *f.*
noisy (noï-zi), *adj.*, bruyant, turbulent, tumultueux ; tapageur.
nolens-volens (nô-lè'n'ze vô-lè'n'ze), *adv.*, de gré ou de force ; bon gré, mal gré.
noli me tangere, *n.*, noli me tangere, *m.*
nomad, *or* **nomadic**, *adj.*, nomade.
nomad, *or* **nomade** (-made), *n.*, nomade, *m.*
nomadize (-daïze), *v.n.*, mener une vie nomade.
nombles (neu'm'b'lze), *n.pl.*, entrailles de cerf, *f.pl.*
nomenclator (nô-mè'n'clé-teur), *n.*, nomenclateur, *m.*
nomenclatress, *n.*, nomenclateur (femme), *f.*
nomenclature (-klét'ieur), *n.*, nomenclature, *f.*
nominal, *adj.*, nominal ; de nom.
nominal, *or* **nominalist**, *n.*, nominaliste, (*pl. nominaux*), *m.*
nominally, *adv.*, de nom ; nommément ; nominalement.
nominate, *v.a.*, nommer; désigner; (a candidate to the electors—*un candidat aux électeurs*) présenter, proposer.
nominately, *adv.*, nommément.
nomination (-né-), *n.*, nomination ; présentation, *f.*
nominative, *adj.*, au nominatif ; du nominatif.
nominative, *n.*, (gram.), nominatif, *m.*
nominator (-né-teur), *n.*, personne qui nomme (to an office, &c.—*à un emploi, &c.*), *f.* ; nominateur, *m.*
nominee (-nî), *n.*, personne nommée, présentée, *f.*
nomothetic, *or* **nomothetical** (-thèt'-), *adj.*, législatif.
non, *adv.*, non ; défaut, manque, *m.* ; absence, *f.*
non-ability, *n.*, inhabilité, *f.*
non-acquaintance (-ak'kwè'n't'-), *n.*, défaut de connaissance, *m.* ; ignorance, *f.*
nonage (no'n'édje), *n.*, minorité, *f.*
non-appearance (-pîr'-), *n.*, absence, *f.* ; défaut de comparution, *m.*
non-attendance, *n.*,manque de présence, *m.*
nonce, *n.*, (ant.) dessein, effet, but, *m.* For the — ; *cet effet ; pour cette fois-ci.*
non-claim (-cléme), *n.*, défaut de réclamation, *m.*
non-compliance (-plaï'-), *n.*, non-acquiescement, refus d'acquiescer, *m.*
non-complying (-pla'yigne), *adj.*, qui refuse d'acquiescer.
non-conducting (-deuk't'-), *adj.*, non-conducteur.
non-conductor (-deuk't'eur), *n.*, non-conducteur, *m.*
non-conformist, *n.*, non-conformiste, *m.*
non-conformity, *n.*, défaut de conformité, *m.*; non-conformité, *f.*
non-contagious (-té'djeusse), *adj.*, non-contagieux.

non-contag'ousness, *n.*, caractère non contagieux, *m.*

nondescript, *adj.*, qui n'a pas encore été décrit ; indéfinissable.

nondescript, *n.*, chose qui n'a pas encore été décrite ; chose indéfinissable, *f.*

none, *adj.*, nul, *m.*, nulle, *f.* ; aucun, *m.*, aucune, *f.* ; pas un, *m.*, pas une, *f.* ; personne, *m.* ; aucun ; pas ; point.

non-electric, *adj.*, non électrique.

non-electric, *n.*, substance non électrique, *f.*

non-emphatic, *or* **non-emphatical**, *adj.*, peu énergique.

non-entity, *n.*, non-existence ; chose qui n'existe pas, *f.*

non-episcopal, *adj.*, non épiscopal.

non-episcopalian, *n.*, Presbytérien, *m.*

non-essential (-shal), *n.*, chose non essentielle, *f.*

nonesuch (neu'n'seutshe), *n.*, sans pareil, *m.*

non-execution (-ègz'è-kiou-), *n.*, inexecution, *f.*

non-existence, *n.*, non-existence ; chose qui n'existe pas, *f.*

non-exportation (-por-té-), *n.*, non-exportation, *f.*

nonius (nô-ni-), *n.*, nonius, vernier, *m.*

non-juring (-djiour'-), *adj.*, qui refuse de prêter serment de fidélité.

non-juror (-djiou-), *n.*, personne qui refuse de prêter serment d• fidélité, *f.*

non-malignant (-lig-), *adj.*, qui n'a pas de qualité maligne ; innocent.

non-metallic, *adj.*, non métallique.

non-natural (-nat'iou-), *n.*, cause qui n'est pas naturelle, *f.*

non-observance (-zeurv'-), *n.*, inobservation, *f.*

nonpareil (-rèl), *n.*, supériorité hors ligne ; (bot., print.) nonpareille, *f.*

nonpareil, *adj.*, nonpareil ; sans égal.

non-payment, *n.*, non-payement ; défaut de payement, *m.*

non-performance, *n.*, inexécution, *f.*

nonplus (-pleusse), *n.*, embarras, quia, bout, *m.*

nonplus, *v.a.*, mettre au pied du mur; mettre à quia ; embarrasser.

non-ponderosity (-dèr'o-ci-), *n.*, défaut de poids, *m.*

non-ponderous (-dèr-), *adj.*, non pesant.

non-pressure (-prèsh'eur), *n.*, absence de pression, *f.*

non-production (-deuk'-), *n.*, non-production, *f.*

non-proficiency (-fish'è'n'-), *n.*, défaut de force, manque de savoir, *m.* ; faiblesse, *f.*

non-proficient (-fish'è'n'te), *adj.*, peu fort, peu savant ; faible.

non-resemblance (-ri-zè'm'-), *n.*, dissemblance, *f.*

non-residence (-rèz'-), *n.*, non-résidence, *f.*

non-resident, *adj.*, non résident.

non-resident, *n.*, non résident, *m.*

non-resistance (-ri-zist'-), *n.*, non-résistance, *f.*

nonsense, *n.*, nonsens, *m.* ; bêtise, sottise, *f.* ; galimatias, *m.* ; absurdité, baliverne, *f.* — ! *allons donc ! laissez donc ! quelle sottise !*

nonsensical, *adj.*, vide de sens ; bête, sot, absurde.

nonsensically, *adv.*, contre le bon sens, contre le sens commun ; bêtement, sottement, absurdement.

nonsensicalness, *n.*, absurdité, bêtise, sottise, *f.*

non-sensitive, *adj.*, sans perception.

non-solution (-liou-), *n.*, non-solution, *f.*

non-solvency, *n.*, insolvabilité, *f.*

non-solvent, *adj.*, insolvable.

non-sparing (-spèr'-), *adj.*, qui n'épargne personne.

nonsuit (-sioute), *n.*, (jur.) désistement, *m.*

nonsuit, *v.a.*, mettre hors de cour.

non-usance (-you-za'n'ce), *n.*, non-usage, *m.*

non-user (-youz'-), *n.*, non-exercice de fonctions ; non-usage, *m.*

noodle (noud'l), *n.*, nigaud, benêt, sot, *m.*

nook (nouke), *n.*, coin, recoin ; enfoncement, *m.*

noon (noune), *n.*, midi ; (fig.) milieu, *m.*

noonday, *adj.*, méridional, de midi.

noonday, *n.*, plein jour ; midi, *m.*

nooning, *n.*, (sleep—*somme*) méridienne, *f.* ; (repast—*repas*) goûter, repas de midi, *m.*

noonstead (-stède), *n.*, position du soleil à midi, *f.*

noontide (-taïde), *n.*, heure de midi, *f.* ; midi, *m.*

noose (nouce, *ou* nouze), *n.*, nœud coulant, *m.*

noose, *v.a.*, attacher par un nœud coulant; (fig.), prendre dans un piège.

nopal (nô-), *n.*, nopal, *m.*

nope, *n.*, bouvreuil, *m.*

nor, *conj.*, ni ; ni . . . . ne ; pas . . . non plus.

normal, *adj.*, normal ; (geom.) perpendiculaire.

normal, *n.*, (geom.) normale, *f.*

norman, *adj.*, normand.

norman, *n.*, Normand, *m.*, Normande, *f.*

north (north), *n.*, nord, septentrion, *m.*

north, *adj.*, du nord, de nord, septentrional.

north-east (-iste), *n.*, nord-est, *m.*

northerly, *or* **northern** (north'-), *adj.*, septentrional, du nord.

northerly (north'-), *adv.*, au nord ; vers le nord.

north-star (north-), *n.*, étoile polaire, *f.*

northward (north'wôrde), *adj.*, vers le nord ; au nord.

northward, *or* **northwards** (-wôrd'ze), *adv.*, vers le nord, au nord.

north-west (north'wèste), *n.*, nord-ouest, *m.*

north-wind (north'wi'n'de), *n.*, vent du nord, *m.*

norwegian (-wi dji-), *adj.*, norwégien, norvégien.

norwegian, *n.*, Norwégien, *m.*, Norvégienne, *f.*

nose (nôze), *n.*, nez ; (of animals—*des animaux*) museau ; (of bellows—*du soufflet*) tuyau, *m.* To blow one's — ; *se moucher.* To put any one's — out of joint ; *supplanter quelqu'un* ; *couper l'herbe sous le pied à quelqu'un.* To speak through one's — ; *parler du nez.* Pug—, snub—, turned-up — ; *nez épaté, camus, retroussé.*

nose, *v.a.*, sentir ; (to oppose—*résister*) tenir tête à.

nosed (nôz'de), *adj.*, au nez ; qui a le nez fin. Pug—, snub—; *qui a le nez épaté.* Flat-— ; *camus, camard.*

nosegay (-ghè), *n.*, bouquet, *m.*

noseless, *adj.*, sans nez.

nosocomial (nô-ço-kô-), *adj.*, (med.) nosocomial.

nosological (-çol'o-dj'-), *adj.*, nosologique.

nosologist (-çol'o-djiste), *n.*, nosologiste, *m.*

nosology (-çol-o-dji), *n.*, nosologie, *f.*

nostalgia (-djia), *n.*, nostalgie, *f.*

nostoc, *n.*, (bot.) nostoc, crachat de lune, *m.*

nostril, *n.*, narine, *f.* ; (of a horse—*du cheval*) naseau, *m.*

nostrum, *n.*, élixir merveilleux, *m.* ; panacée, *f.*

not, *adv.*, ne . . . . pas ; ne . . . . point ; non ; pas ; non pas. — at all ; *point du tout.* — but that; non *que; non pas que ; ce n'est pas que.* I do — see ; *je ne vois pas.* Good or — ; *bon ou non.* — here; *pas ici.*

notable (nôt'a-b'l), *adj.*, notable ; insigne.

notable, *n.*, notable, *m.*

notableness, *n.*, nature remarquable, *f.*

notably, *adv.*, notablement ; remarquablement. — well ; *parfaitement bien.*

notarial (-té-), *adj.*, de notaire ; notarial, notarié.

notary (nô-), *or* **notary-public** (-peub'-), *n.*, notaire, *m.*

notation (no-té-), *n.*, notation ; numération écrite, *f.*

notch, *n.*, coche, entaille ; dent, *f.* ; (tech.) cran, *m.*

notch, *v.a.*, entailler ; tailler inégalement ; ébrécher ; faire une coche à, une entaille à.

notchboard (-bôrde), *n.*, (arch.) limon d'escalier, *m.*

notchwheel (-hwîl), *n.*, (horl.) roue de compte, *f.*

note (nôte), *n.*, note, marque, *f.* ; signe, *m.* ; (letter—*missive*) billet, *m.*, lettre ; (reputation) marque, distinction, *f.* ; (com.) billet, *m.* ; (mus.) note, *f.*, ton ; (gram.) point, *m.* Bank— ; *billet de banque*, *m.* — of exclamation ; *point d'admiration, point d'exclamation, m.* To take a — of ; *prendre note de.* Leading— ; (mus.) *note sensible.*

note, *v.a.*, noter ; prendre note de, marquer, remarquer.

note-book (-bouke), *n.*, cahier de notes ; carnet, *m.*

noted, *adj.*, distingué, remarquable, fameux, célèbre ; (b.s.) noté, insigne, bien connu.

notedly, *adv.*, avec attention.

notedness, *n.*, célébrité, *f.*

noteless, *adj.*, peu distingué ; peu remarquable ; obscur.

noter, *n.*, personne qui remarque, *f.* ; annotateur, *m.*

nothing (neuth'-), *n.*, rien, néant ; zéro, *m.* Good for — ; *bon à rien.* — at all ; *rien du tout.* To make — of ; *ne rien comprendre à* ; (not to be scrupulous—*sans scrupule*) *ne pas se faire scrupule de* ; (to find no difficulty in—*ne pas trouver difficile*) *n'avoir aucune difficulté à.* A good-for— ; *un vaurien*, *m.*

nothing, *adv.*, en rien ; nullement, aucunement.

nothingness, *n.*, néant, rien, *m.*

notice (nô-tice), *n.*, connaissance ; attention ; notice, *f.* ; (warning—*avertissement*) avis ; (to quit—*de déménager*) congé, *m.* ; (jur.) notification, *f.* Biographical — ; *notice biographique.* Take — ; *avis.* To take — of ; *prendre connaissance de* ; *faire attention à.* To rise to — ; *se faire connaître.* To attract — ; *attirer l'attention.* At short — ; *à court délai.*

notice, *v.a.*, prendre connaissance de, remarquer, noter ; faire connaître ; faire attention à.

noticeable (-a-b'l), *adj.*, que l'on remarque ; perceptible ; remarquable.

notification (-fi-ké-), *n.*, notification, *f.* ; avertissement, *m.*

notify (nô-ti-fa'ye), *v.a.*, faire connaître, faire savoir ; notifier.

notion (nô-), *n.*, notion, idée, pensée, opinion, *f.* ; sentiment, *m.*

notional, *adj.*, idéal, chimérique ; (pers.) qui se repaît de chimères.

notionally, *adv.*, idéalement.

notoriety (nô-to-raï-è-), *n.*, notoriété, *f.*

notorious (no-tô-), *adj.*, notoire, évident, manifeste ; (b.s.) fieffé, insigne.

notoriously, *adv.*, notoirement.

notoriousness, *n.*, notoriété, *f.*

notus (nô-teusse), *n.*, vent du sud, *m.*

notwithstanding (-with'-), *conj.*, nonobstant, malgré, en dépit de.

nought (nôte), *n.* V. **naught**.

noun (naou'ne), *n.*, (gram.) nom, substantif, *m.*

nourish (neur'-), *v.a.*, nourrir ; entretenir.

nourishable (-a-b'l), *adj.*, qui peut être nourri.

nourisher, *n.*, personne qui nourrit ; chose qui nourrit, *f.* ; nourricier, *m.*

nourishing, *adj.*, nourrissant, nutritif.

nourishment, *n.*, nourriture, *f.*

novel, *adj.*, neuf, nouveau, nouvel.

novel, *n.*, roman, *m.* ; nouvelle, *f.*

novelist, *n.*, novateur ; (writer—*écrivain*) romancier, nouvelliste, *m.*

novelty, *n.*, nouveauté, *f.*

novel-writer (-raït'-), *n.*, romancier, *m.*

november, *n.*, novembre, *m.*

novenary, *n.*, neuvaine, *f.*

novenary, *adj.*, de neuf.

novennial, *adj.*, de neuf en neuf ans.

novercal (-veur-), *adj.*, de marâtre.

novice, *n.*, novice, *m.*, *f.*

noviciate, *n.*, noviciat, *m.*

now (nao), *adv.*, maintenant, à présent, actuellement ; (of the past—*du passé*) alors, pour lors. Till — ; *jusqu'ici* ; *jusqu'alors.* Just — ; *tout à l'heure* ; *à l'instant.* — and then ; *de temps en temps.*

now, *conj.*, or...

now, *n.*, présent ; présent moment, *m.*

nowadays (nao-a-dèze), *adv.*, aujourd'hui, de nos jours.

nowhere (nô-wère), *adv.*, nulle part.

nowise (nô-waïze), *adv.*, en aucune manière ; nullement.

noxious (nok-sheusse), *adj.*, nuisible, pernicieux.

noxiously, *adv.*, d'une manière nuisible ; pernicieusement.

noxiousness, *n.*, qualité nuisible, *f.*

nozle, *or* **nozzle** (noz'z'l), *n.*, nez ; museau ; groin ; bec, tuyau, bout, *m.*

nucleus (nîou-kli-), *n.*, noyau ; nucleus, *m.*

nude (nioude), *adj.*, nu ; (jur.) nul.

nudity (nion-), *n.*, nudité, *f.*

nugacity (nîou-gass'-), *n.*, futilité, frivolité, *f.*

nugation (nîou-ghé-), *n.*, futilité, frivolité, *f.*

nugatory (nîou-ga-), *adj.*, futile, frivole ; inefficace.

nuisance (nîou-ça'n'ce), *n.*, dommage aux propriétés, *m.* ; peste, plaie, *f.* ; ennui, *m.* What a —! *quel ennui ! comme c'est ennuyeux !* He is a — to every one ; *c'est une peste pour tout le monde.* Commit no — ; *il est défendu de déposer ou de faire aucune ordure.*

nul (neul), *adj.*, (jur.) aucun.

null (neul), *adj.*, nul. — and void ; (jur.) *nul et de nul effet.*

null, *v.a.*, annuler.

nullify (neul'li-fa'ye), *v.a.*, rendre nul ; annuler, casser.

nullity (neul'li-ti), *n.*, nullité, *f.*

numb (neume), *adj.*, engourdi, transi.

numb, *v.a.*, engourdir, transir.

number (neu'm'beur), *n.*, nombre, *m.* ; quantité, *f.* ; (of things in succession, as houses, &c. —*de choses placées en ordre, telles que les maisons dans les rues, &c.*) numéro, *m.* ; (of publications —*d'écrits périodiques*) livraison, *f.* ; (gram., math., rhet.) nombre, *m.* ; (harmony) harmonie, *f.* ; (poet.) vers, *m.* Cardinal, ordinal, odd, even — ; *nombre, cardinal, ordinal, impair, pair.*

number, *v.a.*, nombrer, compter, supputer ; (things in succession, as houses, &c.—*choses dans un certain ordre*) numéroter.

numberer, *n.*, personne qui nombre, qui suppute, qui compte, qui numérote, *f.*

numbering, *n.*, action de compter, de supputer, *f.* ; numérotage, *m.*

numberless, *adj.*, sans nombre ; innombrable.

numbness (neu'm'nèce), *n.*, engourdissement, *m.* ; torpeur, *f.*

numerable (niou-mèr'a-b'l), *adj.*, qui peut être compté.

numeral (niou-mèr'-),*n.*, lettre numérale, *f.*; chiffre, *m.*

numeral, *adj.*, numéral, numérique.

numerally, *adv.*, numériquement.

numerary (niou-mèr'-), *adj.*, numéral.

numeration (niou-mèr'é-),*n.*, numération.*f.*

numerator (niou-mèr'é-),*n..* numérateur, *m.*

numeric, *or* **numerical**, *adj.*, numérique.

numerically, *adv.*, numériquement.

numerist (niou-mèr'-), *n.*, (ant.) calculateur, *m.*

numerous (niou-mèr'-), *adj.*, nombreux.

numerously, *adv.*, en grand nombre.

numerousness, *n.*, nombre, grand nombre, *m.*; (mus., poet.) cadence, harmonie, mélodie, *f.*

numismatic, *or* **numismatical** (niou-miz'-), *adj.*, numismatique.

numismatic, *adj.*, numismatique.

numismatics, *n.pl.*, numismatique, *f.*

numismatist, *or* **numismatologist** ('-o-djiste), *n.*, numismate, numismatiste, *m.*

numismatology (-o-dji), *n.*, numismatique, *f.*

numismatography, *n.*, numismatographie, *f.*

nummary, nummular, *or* **nummulary** (neu'n'miou-), *adj.*, monétaire.

nummulite (neu'm'miou-laïte), *n.*, nummulaire, nummulite, *f.*

numskull (neu'm'skeul),*n.*, benêt, lourdaud, nigaud, balourd, *m.*

numskulled (neu'm'skeul'de), *adj.*, imbécile, nigaud, balourd.

nun (neune), *n.*, religieuse; nonne, (jest.) nonnain, nonnette, *f.*

nunciature (neu'n'shi-a-tiour), *n.*, (ant.) nonciature, *f.*

nuncio (neu'n'shi-ô), *n.*, nonce, *m.*

nuncupative (neu'n'kiou-), *or* **nuncupatory** (ant.), *adj.*, nominal; de nom; qui déclare solennellement; (of wills—*des testaments*) nuncupatif.

nundinal, *or* **nundinary** (neu'n'-), *adj.*, de foire, de jour de marché; (antiq.) nundinal.

nundinal, *n.*, lettre nundinale, *f.*

nunnery (neu'n'-), *n.*, couvent de religieuses, *m.*

nuptial (neup'shal), *adj.*, nuptial, de noces.

nuptials (-shalze), *n.pl.*, noces, *f.pl.*

nurse (neurse), *n.*, (for infants—*de petits enfants*) nourrice; (for children—*d'enfants*) bonne d'enfant; (for the sick—*de malades*) garde-malade, garde, *f.*; (in hospitals—*dans les hôpitaux*) infirmier,*m.*,infirmière; (fig.)mère,*f.* —-maid; *bonne d'enfant.* —-child; *nourrisson, m.* To put out to —; *mettre en nourrice.*

nurse, *v.a.*, nourrir, allaiter, garder; (the sick—*les malades*) soigner, garder; (fig.) alimenter, soigner, entretenir, ménager.

nurser, *n.*, personne qui alimente, *f.*

nursery (neurs'-), *n.*, chambre des enfants; (gard., fig.) pépinière; (of silk-worms—*de vers à soie*) magnanerie, *f.*

nursery-garden (-gâr'd'n), *n.*, pépinière, *f.*

nursery-maid (-méde), *n.*, bonne d'enfant,*f.*

nursery-man, *n.*, pépiniériste, *m.*

nursling (neurs'-), *n.*, nourrisson; (fig.) mignon, *m.*, mignonne, *f.*

nurture (neurt'ieur), *n.*, nourriture; instruction, éducation, *f.*

nurture, *v.a.*, nourrir, alimenter; élever.

nut (neute), *n.*, noisette, *f.*; (of a screw—*d'une vis*) écrou, *m.*; (of a fiddle-bow—*d'archet*) hausse,*f.*; (of stringed instruments—*d'instruments à cordes*) sillet, *m.* —-shell; *coquille de noisette, f.* —-tree; *noisetier, m.*

nut, *v.n.*, cueillir des noisettes. To go nutting; *aller cueillir la noisette.*

nutation (niou-té-), *n.*, nutation, *f.*

nutbrown (-braoune), *adj.*, châtain.

nutcracker, *n.*, casse-noisette, casse-noix, *m.*

nutgall (-gôl), *n.*, noix de galle, *f.*

nuthook (-houke), *n.*, croc, crochet aux noix; (ant.) filou.

nutmeg, *n.*, muscade, *f.* —-tree; *muscadier, m.*

nutrient (neu-), *n.*, nourriture, *f.*; aliment, *m.*

nutrient, *adj.*, nourrissant, nutritif.

nutriment (neu-), *n.*, nourriture, *f.*; aliment, *m.*

nutrimental, *adj.*, nourrissant, nutritif.

nutritious (niou-tri-sheusse), *or* **nutritive** (niou-tri-tive), *adj.*, nutritif, nourrissant, alimenteux, nourricier.

nux-vomica (neuks'vo-), *n.*, noix vomique, *f.*

nuzzle (neuz'z'l), *v.a.*, (to nurse—*soigner*) nourrir, entretenir; (to nestle—*nicher*) nicher, loger; (to hide—*cacher*) cacher; (to insnare—*attraper*) prendre au piège; (to root up—*arracher*) déraciner; (a hog—*un porc*) mettre un anneau au nez.

nuzzle, *v.n.*, fouiller avec le groin; se fourrer la tête dans.

nye (na'ye), *n.*, (of pheasants—*des faisans*) troupe, *f.*

nymph (ni'm'fe), *n.*, nymphe, *f.*

nymphean (-phî-), *or* **nymphish**, *adj.*, de nymphe.

nymph-like (-laïke), *or* **nymphly** (-phli), *adj.*, comme une nymphe.

nymphomania, *or* **nymphomany**, *n.*, nymphomanie, érotomanie, *f.*

O

o, quinzième lettre de l'alphabet, o, *m.*

oaf (ôfe), *n.*, enfant de fée; (dolt—*imbécile*) benêt, idiot, *m.*

oafish, *adj.*, stupide, idiot.

oafishness, *n.*, stupidité, *f.*

oak (ôke), *n.*, chêne; chêne rouvre; (woodbois) chêne, bois de chêne, *m.* —-tree; *chêne.* Holm-—; *yeuse, f.; chêne vert. m.*

oak-apple (-ap'p'l), *n.*, noix de galle; pomme de chêne, *f.*

oaken, *adj.*, de chêne.

oak-grove (-grôve), *n.*, chênaie, *f.*

oakling, *n.*, jeune chêne, *m.*

oakum (ôk'eume), *n.*, étoupe, *f.* —-boy; (nav.) mousse de calfat, calfatin, *m.*

oaky, *adj.*, de chêne; dur comme le chêne.

oar (ôre), *n.*, rame, *f.*; aviron, *m.*

oar, *v.n.*, ramer.

oar, *v.a.*, diriger à la rame.

oared (ôr'de), *adj.*, à rames, à avirons. Eight--boat; *bateau à huit rames, m.*

oar-maker (-mék'-), *n.*, avironnier, *m.*

oarsman (ôrz'-), *n.*, rameur, *m.*

oary, *adj.*, en forme de rame.

oasis (ô-é-cice), *n.*, oasis, *f.*

oast (ôste), *n.*, four à houblon, *m.*

oat. *V.* oats.

oatcake (ôt'kéke), *n.*, gâteau d'avoine, *m.*

oaten (ôt'ène), *adj.*, d'avoine.

oat-grass (ôt'grâce), *n.*, avoine, *f.*

oath (ôth), *n.*, serment; (b.s.) juron, jurement, serment, *m.* On —, on one's —; *sous serment; sous la foi du serment.* To put any one on his —; *faire prêter serment à quelqu'un.* To take —, an —; *prêter serment.* To break one's —; *manquer à; fausser son serment.* Tremendous —; *gros juron.* Volley of —s; *bordée de jurements.* To rap out an —; *lâcher un jurement.*

oath-breaking (-brèk'-), *n.*, violation de serment, *f.*; parjure, *m.*

oat-malt (-mölt), *n.*, dièche d'avoine, *f.*

oat-meal(-mil),*n.*, gruau d'avoine,*m.* ; farine d'avoine, *f.*

oats (ôtse), *n.pl.*, avoine, *f.sing.* To sow one's wild — ; *jeter ses premiers feux, faire ses farces.*

obduracy (-diou-), *n.*, endurcissement, *m.* ; impénitence, *f.*

obdurate(-diou-),*adj.*, endurci, impénitent ; inflexible.

obdurately, *adv.*, opiniâtrément, avec endurcissement, avec impénitence.

obdurateness, or **obduration**. *V.* **obduracy.**

obdured (-diour'de), *adj.*, (ant.) endurci, inflexible.

obedience(-bi-), *n.*, obéissance ; soumission, *f.* In — to ; *par obéissance à.*

obedient, *adj.*, obéissant, soumis.

obediential,*adj.*, respectueux, de soumission ; obédientiel.

obediently, *adv.*, avec obéissance ; avec soumission.

obeisance, or **obeisancy** (o-bé-, *ou* o-bi-), *n.*, révérence, *f.* ; salut, *m.*

obeliscal,*adj.*, en forme d'obélisque.

obelisk (ob-è-), *n.*, obélisque, *m.* ; (print.) croix,*f.*

obeseness, or **obesity** (o-bi-), *n.*, obésité,*f.*

obey (o-bè), *v.a.*, obéir, obéir à ; écouter ; (jur.) obtempérer.

obeyer, *n.*, personne qui obéit,*f.*

obfuscate (-feus'-),*v.a.*, offusquer, obscurcir.

obfuscation(-feus'-),*n.*, obscurcissement,*m.*

obit (ô-), *n.*, obit, *m.*

obitual (o-bit'iou-), *adj.*, de l'obit.

obituary, *adj.*, obituaire ; nécrologique.

obituary, *n.*, obituaire, *m.* ; nécrologie,*f.*

object, *n.*, objet ; but ; (gram.) complément, régime ; (milit.) objectif, *m.* ; (pop.) personne ridicule, effroyable, *f.* ; objet effrayant, *m.*, horreur,*f.* That is an — of consequence ; *c'est important.*

object, *v.a.*, objecter ; opposer.

object, *v.n.*, objecter ; s'opposer. Do you — to having the door shut? *vous opposez-vous à ce que la porte soit fermée?*

object-glass (-glâce), *n.*, verre objectif, objectif, *m.*

objection (-jèk'-), *n.*, objection, difficulté,*f.* Have you any — ? *vous opposez-vous à ce que* . . . ?

objectionable (-a-b'l), *adj.*, reprochable, répréhensible ; inadmissible.

objective, *adj.*, objectif ; (gram.) du complément, du régime.

objective, *n.*, (gram.) complément, régime, *m.*

objectively, *adv.*, objectivement ; (gram.) comme un régime.

objectiveness, or **objectivity**, *n.*, état d'un objet, *m.*

objectless,*adj.*, sans but, sans objet.

objector, *n.*, personne qui fait une objection,*f.*

objurgation (-jeur-ghé-), *n.*, vive réprimande ; objurgation,*f.*

objurgatory (-jeur-ga-), *adj.*, objurgatoire, de réprimande, de reproche.

oblate, *adj.*, aplati vers les pôles.

oblateness, *n.*, aplatissement, *m.*

oblation (ob-lé-), *n.*, oblation, offrande, *f.*

oblectation (-lèk'té-), *n.*, joie, *f.* ; délices, *f.pl.*

obligate, *v.a.*, obliger, astreindre.

obligation (-ghé-), *n.*, obligation, *f.* ; engagement, *m.* Under an — to; *dans l'obligation de.* To be under an — to any one ; *avoir une obligation à quelqu'un.*

obligatory,*adj.*, obligatoire.

oblige (-blaïdje), *v.a.*, obliger, faire plaisir à ; (to force—*forcer*) obliger, astreindre.

obligee (-bli-dji), *n.*, créancier, *m.*, créancière. *f.*

obligement(-blaïdj'-) *n.*,(ant.) obligation,*f.*

obliger, *n.*, personne qui oblige, *f.*

obliging, *adj.*, obligeant, officieux.

obligingly, *adv.*, obligeamment ; officieusement.

obligingness (-blaïdj'ign-nèce), *n.*, obligeance. *f.*

obligor (ob-li-), *n.*,(jur.) obligé, *m.*, obligée, *f.* ; débiteur, *m.*, débitrice,*f.*

obliquation (-likwé-), *n.*,(ant.) obliquité,*f.*

oblique,*adj.*, oblique ; indirect, détourné. — dealings ; *procédés détournés, m.pl.*

obliquely, *adv.*, obliquement ; indirectement, d'une manière détournée.

obliqueness (-blîk'-), *or* **obliquity** (-likwi-), *n.*, obliquité ; (fig.) irrégularité,*f.*

obliterate (-èr-), *v.a.*, effacer ; faire oublier ; oblitérer.

obliteration,*n.*, action d'effacer ; effaçure,*f.*

oblivion. *n.*, oubli, *m.* Act of — ; *amnistie,f.*

oblivious, *adj.*, d'oubli, oublieux.

oblong, *adj.*, oblong.

oblong, *n.*, figure oblongue,*f.*

oblongly, *adv.*, d'une forme oblongue,*f.*

oblongness, *n.*, forme oblongue.

obloquy (-kwi), *n.*, reproche ; blâme, *m.* ; censure,*f.*

obmutescence (-miou-tès'-), *n.*, perte de la parole, *f.* ; silence, *m.*

obnoxious (-nok'sheusse), *adj.*, (hurtful—*dommageable*) nuisible ; (odious—*odieux*) odieux, offensant ; (reprehensible) répréhensible, blâmable ; (liable—*sujet à*) sujet, exposé, soumis.

obnoxiously, *adv.*, d'une manière offensante, d'une manière répréhensible ; odieusement ; dans un état de sujétion.

obnoxiousness, *n.*, odieux, *m.* ; sujétion,*f.*

obnubilate (-niou-), *v.a.*, (ant.) obscurcir.

obnubilation (-niou-bi-lé-), *n.*, obscurcissement, *m.*

obolus, or **obole** (-ôle), *n.*, obole,*f.*

obreption (-rèp-), *n.*, surprise ; obreption,*f.*

obreptitious (-rèp-ti-sheusse), *adj.*, fait par surprise ; obreptice.

obscene (-sine), *adj.*, obscène, sale ; grossier.

obscenely, *adv.*, d'une manière obscène ; avec obscénité.

obsceneness,or **obscenity**,*n.*, obscénité,*f.*

obscuration (-skiou-ré-), *n.*, obscurcissement, *m.*

obscure (-skioure), *adj.*, obscur ; de la nuit ; des ténèbres ; caché.

obscure, *v.a.*, obscurcir ; offusquer ; cacher ; éclipser.

obscurely, *adv.*, obscurément ; dans l'obscurité.

obscureness, or **obscurity**,*n.*,obscurité,*f.*

obsecrate (-si-), *v.a.*, (ant.) supplier, conjurer, implorer.

obsecration (-si-cré-), *n.*, obsécration,*f.*

obsequies (-si-kwize), *n.pl.*, obsèques, *f.pl.*

obsequious (-sî-kwi-eusse), *adj.*, soumis ; obéissant ; obséquieux.

obsequiously, *adv.*, avec soumission ; avec obéissance ; obséquieusement.

obsequiousness,*n.*,soumission,obéissance ; soumission obséquieuse,*f.*

observable (-zeurv'a-b'l), *adj.*,remarquable ; digne de remarque ; appréciable ; observable.

observably, *adv.*, remarquablement ; d'une manière appréciable ; d'une manière observable.

observance (-zeurv'-), *or* **observancy** (ant.), *n.*, observance ; pratique, *f.* ; accomplissement ; (respect) respect, *m.*

observanda (-zeurv'-), *n.pl.*, choses à observer, *f.pl.*

observant (-zeur-), *adj.*, observateur, atten-

tif. — of ; *attentif à ; attentif à observer, à pratiquer.*

observation (-zeur-vé-), *n.*, observation ; attention, *f.*

observator (-zeur-vé-), *n.*, observateur, *m.*, observatrice, *f.*

observatory (-zeùrv'a-), *n.*, observatoire, *m.*

observe (-zeurve), *v.a.*, observer, remarquer ; faire observer, faire remarquer.

observer, *n.*, observateur, *m.*

observing, *adj.*, observateur ; attentif.

observingly, *adv.*, attentivement.

obsidian, *n.*, obsidiane, obsidienne, *f.*

obsidional, *adj.*, obsidional.

obsignation (-sig-né-), *n.*, (ant.) ratification, confirmation, *f.*

obsignatory (-sig na-), *adj.*, confirmatif.

obsolescence, *n.*, état de ce qui vieillit, *m.*

obsolescent, *adj.*, qui vieillit.

obsolete (-lite), *adj.*, vieilli, suranné, vieux ; tombé en désuétude.

obsoleteness, *n.*, état de désuétude, *m.* ; désuétude, *f.*

obstacle (-sta-k'l), *n.*, obstacle, empêchement, *m.*

obstetric, *or* **obstetrical** (-stèt'-), *adj.*, d'accouchement ; obstétrique.

obstetrication (-tri-ké-), *n.*, accouchement, *m.*

obstetrician (-trish'-), *n.*, accoucheur, *m.*

obstetrics (-stèt'rikse), *n.pl.*, obstétrique, *f.sing.*

obstinacy, *n.*, obstination, opiniâtreté, *f.* ; acharnement, *m.* ; (med.) résistance, *f.*

obstinate, *adj.*, opiniâtre, obstiné ; entier ; acharné ; têtu, entêté ; (med.) rebelle.

obstinately, *adv.*, obstinément ; opiniâtrément ; avec entêtement.

obstinateness. *V.* **obstinacy**.

obstipation (-pé-), *n.*, action de boucher ; (med.) constipation, *f.*

obstreperous (-strèp'èr'-), *adj.*, turbulent ; tapageur ; très bruyant ; étourdissant.

obstreperously, *adv.*, avec turbulence ; d'une manière étourdissante ; à grand bruit.

obstreperousness, *n.*, grand bruit, *m.* ; turbulence, *f.*

obstriction, *n.*, obligation, *f.*

obstruct (-streuk't), *v.a.*, empêcher, obstruer, boucher ; barrer ; mettre obstacle à.

obstructer, *n.*, personne qui obstrue, qui bouche, qui barre, qui met obstacle à, *f.*

obstruction (-streuk'-), *n.*, empêchement ; embarras ; obstacle, *m.* ; (med.) obstruction, *f.*

obstructive (-streuk-), *or* **obstruent** (-strou-), *adj.*, qui empêche, qui obstrue, qui bouche, qui barre, qui met obstacle à ; embarrassant ; (med.) obstructif, opilatif.

obtain (-téne), *v.a.*, obtenir ; procurer ; se procurer ; recevoir ; posséder, tenir.

obtain, *v.n.*, exister, régner ; s'établir.

obtainable (-'a-b'l), *adj.*, qu'on peut se procurer ; à obtenir.

obtainer, *n.*, personne qui obtient, *f.*

obtainment, *n.*, action d'obtenir ; obtention, *f.*

obtest (-tèste), *v.a.*, supplier, conjurer, invoquer.

obtestation (-tès-té-), *n.*, supplication, prière, *f.*

obtrude (-troude), *v.a.*, imposer, présenter ; présenter de force.

obtrude, *v.n.*, s'imposer ; s'introduire de force ; être importun.

obtruder, *n.*, importun, *m.*

obtrusion (-trou-jeune), *n.*, introduction forcée ; importunité, *f.*

obtrusive (-trou-cive), *adj.*, importun.

obtrusively, *adv.*, d'une manière importune ; avec importunité.

obtund (-teu'n'de), *v.a.*, émousser ; (fig.) adoucir, amortir, assoupir.

obturating (-tiou-ré-), *adj.*, obturateur.

obturation (-tiou-ré-), *n.*, (ant.) obturation, obstruction, *f.*

obturator (-tiou-ré-teur), *n.*, obturateur, *m.*

obtuse (-tiouce), *adj.*, obtus ; émoussé ; (of sound—*du son*) sourd.

obtuse-angled (-tiouce-an'g'l'de),*or* **obtus-angular** (-an'gn'ghiou-), *adj.*, obtusangle.

obtusely, *adv.*, d'une manière obtuse ; (stupidly—*avec stupidité*) stupidement ; (dully—*du son*) sourdement.

obtuseness, *n.*, état émoussé, *m.* ; stupidité, *f.*

obtusion (-tiou-jeune), *n.*, action d'émousser, *f.* ; résultat de cette action, *m.*

obumbration (-eu'm'bré-), *n.*, obscurcissement, *m.*

obverse (-veurse), *adj.*, (bot.) obcordé.

obverse. *n.*, (of medals, coins—*de médailles, de monnaies*) obverse ; (print.) recto, *m.*

obvert (-veurte), *v.a.*, tourner vers.

obviate, *v.a.*, obvier à ; prévenir.

obvious, *adj.*,·évident, sensible, clair ; qui saute aux yeux ; visible.

obviously, *adv.*, évidemment, clairement, sensiblement.

obviousness, *n.*, évidence, clarté, *f.*

occasion (-ké-jeune), *n.*, occasion, rencontre ; (cause) cause, occasion, *f.* ; sujet ; (need—*besoin*) besoin, *m.*, nécessité, *f.* There is no — for ; *il n'y a pas besoin de ; il n'est pas besoin de.* To profit by the — ; *profiter de l'occasion.* On — ; *au besoin.* On the first — ; *à la première occasion.* On all —s ; *en toute occasion ; en toute rencontre.*

occasion, *v.a.*, occasionner, donner lieu à, causer, produire.

occasional, *adj.*, occasionnel, d'occasion ; accidentel, casuel.

occasionality, *n.*, adaptation à l'occasion, *f.*

occasionally, *adv.*, occasionnellement ; par occasion, parfois ; de temps en temps.

occasioner, *n.*, cause, *f.* ; auteur, *m.*

occasive (-ké-cive), *adj.*, (astron.) occase. /

occident, *n.*, occident, *m.*

occidental, *or* **occiduous** ('-lou-), *adj.*, (ant.) occidental.

occipital, *adj.*, (anat.) occipital.

occiput (-peute), *n.*, occiput, *m.*

occlude (-cloude), *v.a.*, fermer.

occlusion (-clou-jeune), *n.*, action d'enfermer ; (med.) occlusion, *f.*

occult (-keulte), *adj.*, occulte.

occultation (-té-), *n.*, occultation, *f.*

occultness (-keult'-), *n.*, secret, *m.*

occupancy (ok'kiou-), *n.*, occupation, *f.*

occupant, *n.*, personne qui occupe un lieu, *f.* ; possesseur, occupant, *m.*

occupation (ok'kiou-pé-), *n.*, occupation, *f.* ; emploi, *m.* ; (possession) occupation, possession, *f.*

occupier, *n.*, possesseur ; (of houses—*de maisons*) habitant, *m.*, habitante, *f.*

occupy (ok'kiou-pa-ye), *v.a.*, occuper ; employer. To be occupied in, with ; *s'occuper de.*

occur (ok'keur), *v.n.*, se présenter, se rencontrer, s'offrir ; venir ; survenir, arriver. A thought —ed to me ; *une pensée me vint.* An accident has —ed to me ; *il m'est arrivé un accident.*

occurrence (-keur'-), *n.*, occurrence, rencontre, *f.* ; événement, incident, *m.*

occursion (ok'keur'-), *n.*, choc, heurt, *m.*

ocean (ô-sha'n), *n.*, océan, *m.* ; (fig.) immensité, *f.*

ocean, *adj.*, de l'océan.

oceanic (-shi-), *adj.*, océanique.

ocellated (-cèl-), *adj.*, qui ressemble à un œil ; ocellé.

ochre (ô-keur), *n.*, ocre, *f.*

ochreous (ô-keur'-), *or* **ochrey** (-kré), *adj.*, d'ocre; ocreux.

ocrea (oc'-ri-), *n.*, (bot.) gaine, *f.*

octagon, *n.*, octogone. *m.*

octagonal, *or* **octaugular**, *adj.*, octogone.

octahedron (-hi-), *n.*, (geom.) octaèdre, *m.*

octandria, *n.*, (bot.) octandrie, *f.*

octandrian, *adj.*, (bot.) octandre.

octant, *n.*, octant, *m.*

octave (-téve), *n.*, octave, *f.*

octavo (-té-vô), *n.*, in-octavo, *m.*

octennial, *adj.*, de huit ans.

octile (-taïl), *n.*, octil, aspect octil, *m.*

october (-tô-beur), *n.*, octobre, *m.*

octogenarian (-djè-né-), *or* **octogenary** (-djè-), *n.*, octogénaire, *m.f.*

octogenary, *adj.*, d'octogénaire.

octosyllable (-cil'la-b'l), *n.*, mot de huit syllabe, *m.*

octuple (-tiou'p'l), *adj.*, octuple.

ocular (ok'iou-), *adj.*, oculaire.

ocularly, *adv.*, de ses propres yeux.

oculate (ok'iou-), *or* **oculated** (-lét'-), *adj.*, qui a des yeux; que l'on sait par les yeux.

oculist (ok'iou-), *n.*, oculiste, *m.*

odd, *adj.*, impair; (surplus) de surplus, de reste, quelques; (of money—*argent*) d'appoint; de reste; (singular—*peu ordinaire*) étrange, singulier; (droll—*drôle*) bizarre, drôle, original, baroque; (leisure—*de loisir*) perdu; (not fellows —*de choses en paires*) déparié; (of books, &c.—*de livres, &c.*) dépareillé.

oddity, *n.*, singularité; bizarrerie, *f.*; (pers.) original, *m.*, originale, *f.*; travers, *m.*

oddly, *adv.*, étrangement, singulièrement; bizarrement.

oddness, *n.*, singularité; étrangeté; bizarrerie, *f.*

odds (odze), *n.*, (inequality—*défaut d'égalité*) inégalité, disparité, *f.*; (advantage—*avantage*) avantage, *m.*, supériorité; (quarrel—*querelle*) dispute, querelle, *f.*, différend, *m.* At —; *on querelle.* To set at —; *brouiller.* To have the — against one's self; *avoir affaire à plus fort que soi.* — and ends; *petits bouts, fragments, m.pl.*

ode (ôde), *n.*, ode, *f.*

odeon (ô-di-), *or* **odeum** (-di-), *n.*, odéon, ⊙ odéum, *m.*

odious (ô-di-), *adj.*, odieux, détestable.

odiously, *adv.*, odieusement.

odiousness, *n.*, nature odieuse, *f.*; odieux, *m.*

odium (ô-), *n.*, odieux, *m.*

odometer (-'i-teur), *n.*, odomètre, compte-pas, *m.*

odontalgia, *or* **odontalgy** (ô-do'n-tal'dji-a, -dji), *n.*, odontalgie, *f.*

odontalgic, *n.*, odontalgique, *m.*

odontoid (-toïde), *adj.*, odontoïde.

odontology (-tol'o-dji), *n.*, odontologie, *f.*

odorant, odorate, odorating, *or* **odoriferous**, *adj.*, odorant, odoriférant.

odoriferously, *adv.*, avec un parfum.

odoriferousness, *n.*, parfum, *m.*

odorous, *adj.*, odorant.

odour (ô-deur), *n.*, odeur, senteur, *f.*; parfum, *m.*

odourless, *adj.*, inodore; sans odeur.

oeconomy. *V.* economy.

oecumenical (ik'iou-mè'n-), *adj.*, écuménique, œcuménique.

oecumenically (-'ik-), *adv.*, œcuméniquement, œcuméniquement.

oedema (i-di-), *n.*, œdème, *m.*

oeiliad (i-il'-), *n.*, œillade, *f.*

oesophagus (i-çof'-), *n.*, œsophage, *m.*

of (ove), *prep.*, de. — late; *dernièrement.* — old; *autrefois.* The best — men; *le meilleur des hommes.*

off (ôf), *adv.*, loin; de distance; (paint.) avec relief; (broken off—*brisé, interrompu*) rompu,

manqué, cessé; (separated—*séparé*) de dessus, séparé, enlevé; (nav.) au large. The house is a mile —; *la maison est à un mille de distance.* — and on; *avec interruption.* — with that; *ôtez, enlevez cela.* — with him; *emmenez-le.* I am —; *je m'en vais, je file.* Hats — ! *chapeaux bas!* To be well, badly —; *être bien, mal dans ses affaires, heureux, malheureux.*

off, *adj.*, le plus éloigné; (man.) hors main.

off. *prep.*, (nav.) à la hauteur de, devant.

offal, *n.*, abattis, *m.*; issue, *f.*; reste de viande, *m.*; chair grossière, *f.*; (refuse—*restes*) rebut, *m.*

offcut (-keute), *n.*, (print.) petit carton de feuilles, *m.*

offence, *n.*, offense, *f.*; outrage, *m.*; injure, *f.*; (jur.) atteinte, contravention, violation de la loi et du droit, *f.*, délit, crime; (scandal) scandale, *m.*; (attack) attaque, agression, *f.* Capital —; *crime capital.* To commit an — against ; *faire outrage à* ; (jur.) *porter atteinte à.* To take —; *se formaliser; s'offenser.* To give —; *choquer, offenser.*

offend, *v.a.*, offenser, choquer; outrager, blesser; scandaliser.

offend, *v.n.*, déplaire; commettre une offense; commettre un péché; se scandaliser. To — against; *nuire à;* (the law—*la loi*) *violer, transgresser.*

offender, *n.*, offenseur, coupable; pécheur; (jur.) contrevenant, délinquant, criminel, *m.* An old —; *coutumier du fait; repris de justice, m.*

offendress, *n.*, coupable; pécheresse, *f.*

offenseful (-foule), *adj.*, offensant.

offenseless, *adj.*, inoffensif; innocent.

offensive, *adj.*, offensant; injurieux; choquant, blessant; (assailant—*attaque*) offensif.

offensive, *n.*, offensive, *f.*

offensively, *adv.*, d'une manière offensante, injurieuse, blessante; offensivement.

offensiveness, *n.*, nature offensante, blessante, choquante, injurieuse, *f.*

offer, *v.a.*, offrir. To — violence; *faire violence.* To — one's self, itself; *s'offrir, se présenter.*

offer, *v.n.*, s'offrir; se présenter; faire l'offre de; (to attempt—*tenter*) essayer. To — to; *faire l'offre de.*

offer, *n.*, offre; (attempt—*essai*) tentative, *f.*; essai, *m.*

offerable (of'feur-a-b'l), *adj.*, que l'on peut offrir.

offerer, *n.*, personne qui offre, *f.*; sacrificateur, *m.*

offering, *n.*, offrande, *f.*; sacrifice, *m.*

offertory (-fèr-), *n.*, offertoire, *m.*; offerte, *f.*

off-hand, *adv.*, d'abord; au premier abord, sans réflexion, sur-le-champ, sans préparation.

off-hand, *adj.*, tranchant, cru, brusque.

office, *n.*, (service) office, service; (duty—*obligation*) devoir; (employment—*emploi*) emploi, *m.*, charge, *f.*, fonctions, *f.pl.*; (power—*charge*) pouvoir, *m.*, place, *f.*; (apartment—*lieu*) bureau, (private—*particulier*) cabinet, *m.*; (of lawyers—*d'hommes de loi*) étude, *f.*; (rel.) office, *m.* —s; (of a house—*d'une maison*) offices, *f.pl.*; (out-houses—*dépendances*) communs, *m.pl.*

office-keeper (-kîp'-), *n.*, buraliste, *m.*

office-lead (-lède), *n.*, serre-papiers, *m.*

officer, *n.*, officier; (of state—*d'état*) dignitaire; (of the government—*du gouvernement*) fonctionnaire; (of justice—*de justice*) agent; (of a court—*d'un tribunal*) huissier, *m.*

officer, *v.a.*, fournir des officiers à.

officered (of'fi-ceurde), *adj.*, commandé; pourvu d'officiers.

official (-fish'al), *n.*, fonctionnaire; (eec.) official, *m.*

official, *adj.*, officiel, public.

officially, *adv.*, officiellement.

28

officialty, n., officialité, f.
officiate (of-fish'i-),v.n., exercer ses fonctions; exercer.
officiate, v.n., donner, conférer.
officiating,adj.,qui fait ses fonctions ; (ecc.) officiant, desservant.
officinal, adj., (pharm.) officinal.
officious (-sheusse), adj., officieux ; (kind—complaisant) bienveillant.
officiously (-sheus'-), adv., officieusement; (kindly—complaisamment) avec bienveillance ; complaisamment.
officiousness,n.,empressement officieux,m.
offing, n., (nav.) large, m.
offscouring (-skaeur'-), n., rebut, m.
offset, n., (hort.) rejeton, m.; (com.) compensation ; (arch.) retraite,f.
off-side (-saïde), n., (man.) hors de la main, hors-main ; côté droit, m.
offspring, n., enfant, m. ; enfants, m.pl.; descendant, m. ; descendants, m.pl. ; race, postérité,f. ; (fig.) fruit, produit, m.
off-take (-téke), n., (mines) galerie d'écoulement, f.
offward (-wôrde), adv., vers le large, vers la mer.
oft, often (of'f'n), oftentimes (-taï'm'ze), or ofttimes, adv., souvent.
ogee (o-djï), n., (arch.) cymaise, f.
ogive (o-djive), n., ogive, f.
ogive, adj., en ogive.
ogle (ô-g'l), n., œillade, f.
ogle, v.a., lorgner ; lancer des œillades à.
ogler, n., lorgneur, m., lorgneuse,f.
ogling, n., lorgnerie, f.
ogre (ô-gheur), n., ogre, m.
ogress, n., ogresse,f.
oh! int., oh !
oil (oïl), n., huile,f.
oil, v.a., huiler.
oilbag, n., (orni.) glande oléifère,f.
oilcake, n., (agri.) tourteau, m.
oil-case (-kéce), n., toile cirée (pour vêtement), f.
oil-cloth (-cloth), n., toile cirée (pour meuble), f.
oil-colour (-kenl'eur),n., couleur à l'huile,f.
oiliness, n., onctuosité ; nature huileuse,f.
oilman, n., marchand d'huile, m.
oil-mill, n., huilerie, f.
oilnut (-neute), n., (bot.) noix de ben,f.
oilnut-tree (-trî), n., ricin, palmachristi, m.
oil-plant, n., plante oléagineuse,f.
oil-press, n., pressoir à l'huile, m.
oil-shop, n., magasin d'huile, m.
oil-skin, n.,toilecirée; (of a hat—de chapeau) coiffe en toile,f.
oily, adj., huileux, onctueux, oléagineux.
ointment (oaï'n't'-), n., onguent, m.
old (ôlde), adj., vieux, vieil ; âgé ; ancien, antique. How — are you? quel âge avez-vous ? I am ten years — ; j'ai dix ans. At ten years — ; à l'âge de dix ans. Ten years — ; âgé de dix ans. The — world ; l'ancien monde. An — man ; un vieillard, un vieux, un vieil homme,; un homme vieux. An — shoe ; un vieux soulier. To grow — ; vieillir. The —est ; le plus âgé ; le doyen d'âge. Of — ; anciennement.
olden (ôld'ène). adj., (ant.) vieux, ancien.
old-fashioned. adj., suranné ; à l'ancienne mode ; (pers.) de vieille roche.
oldish, adj., un peu vieux.
oldness, n., vieillesse, f. ; âge avancé, m., ancienneté ; vétusté,f.
oleaginous (ô-li-adj'-), adj., oléagineux.
oleaginousness, n., nature oléagineuse, f.
oleander (ô-li-), n., (bot.) laurier-rose, laurose, oléandre, m.
oleraceous (o-li-ré-sheusse), adj., (bot.) oléracé, potager.

olfact, v.a., (ant.) flairer, sentir.
olfactory, adj., olfactif.
olibanum, n., oliban, m.
oligarchal, oligarchic, or oligarchical (-gàrk'-), adj., oligarchique.
oligarchy (-gàrki), n., oligarchie,f.
oligist, or oligistic (-djist'-), adj., (min.) oligiste.
olio (ô-li-ô), n.,(cook.)olla podrida,f. ; (mus.) recueil d'airs, m.
olitory, adj., potager.
olivary, adj., olivaire.
olivaster, adj., olivâtre.
olive, n., olive, f. —-tree; olivier, m., yard ; jardin des olives, m.
olympiad, n., olympiade,f.
olympian, adj., Olympien ; Olympique.
olympic, adj., olympique.
olympics, n.pl., jeux olympiques, m.
olympus, n., Olympe, m.
ombre (ô'm'beur), n., hombre, m.
omega (ô-mè-), n., oméga, m.
omelet (o'm'lète), n., omelette, f.
omen (ô-mè'ne), n., augure, présage, m.
omened (ô-mè'n'de), adj., d'augure. Ill-—; de mauvais augure.
omentum (o'mèn'n'-), n., (anat.) épiploon, m.
ominous (o'm'-), adj., de mauvais présage; nistre.
ominously, adv., de mauvais augure.
ominousness, n., mauvais augure, m.
omissible (-si-b'l), adj., qui peut être omis.
omission (-mish'-), n., omission,f.
omissive, adj., qui commet des omissions.
omit, v.a., omettre ; manquer ; négliger.
omittance, n., (ant.) omission, f.
omnibus (-beusse), n. (omnibuses), omnibus, m.
omnifarious (-fé-), adj., de toutes sortes; varié.
omniferous (-nif'èr'-),adj., produisant tout.
omniform, adj., omniforme.
omnipotence, or omnipotency, n., omnipotence, toute-puissance,f.
omnipotent, adj., tout-puissant.
omnipotent. n., Tout-Puissant, m.
omnipotently, adv., avec omnipotence, avec toute-puissance.
omnipresence (-prèz'-), n., omniprésence,f.
omnipresent (-prèz'-), adj., omniprésent.
omnipresentness (-prèz'è'n'shal), adj., qui implique l'omniprésence.
omniscience, or omnisciency (-nish'-), n., omniscience,f.
omniscient, adj., omniscient; qui sait tout.
omnium, n., omnium, m.
omnivorous, adj., omnivore.
omoplate, n., (anat.) omoplate, f.
on, prep., sur ; à ; de ; en ; lors de. — foot; à pied. — high; en haut. — horseback ; à cheval. — purpose ; à dessein, exprès. — that day; ce jour-là. — the left; à gauche. — the right; à droite. — the table; sur la table. — my honour; sur mon honneur. Loss — loss ; perte sur perte. — credit; à crédit. A ring — the finger; une bague au doigt. — one; sur soi. To play — the piano (&c.); jouer du piano. — Monday; lundi.
on,adv., dessus; (forward—en avant) en avant, avant, avancé; (continuation) toujours; (succession) de suite. Read —; lisez toujours. — ! en avant! And so —; et ainsi de suite. Play —; continuez de jouer.
onager (o'n'a-djeur), n., (mam.) onagre, m.
onanism (ô-), n., (med.) onanisme, m.
once (weu'n'ce), adv., une fois ; autrefois ; jadis — upon a time ; une fois. — for all ; une fois pour toutes. All at —; tout d'un coup, tout à coup. — I knew how to sing; autrefois je savais chanter.
one (weu'ne). adj., un, m.,une,f. ; un seul, m., une seule, f. ; unique ; seul, un certain. — man ;

un homme. He has but — child ; *il n'a qu'un seul enfant.* There is — Charles ; *il y a un certain Charles.* — by — ; *un à un.* It is all — ; *c'est la même chose; celu revient au même; c'est tout un ; c'est égal.* — and all; *tous jusqu'au dernier.*

one, *pron.,* on, l'on; celui, *m.,* celle. *f.*; quelqu'un ; un homme, *m.,* une femme, *f.*; — sees that every day ; *on voit cela, cela se voit tous les jours.* He is — who ; *c'est un homme qui.* He is the — who; *c'est celui qui.* A good thing and a 'bad —; *une bonne chose et une mauvaise.* Any —; *quelqu'un ; le premier venu, tout le monde ; qui -que ce soit; personne.* Some —; *quelqu'un.* No —; *personne.* Every —; *chacun ; tout le monde.* — another ; *l'un l'autre, l'une l'autre ; les uns les autres, les unes les autres.*

one-eyed (weu'n'a-ye'-de), *adj.,* borgne.

oneirocritic. *or* **oneirocritical** (o-naï-), *adj.,* de l'onirocritique; d'un interprétateur de songes.

oneirocritic, *n.,*.interprétateur de songes, *m.*

oneirocritics, *n.pl.,* onirocritie, onirocritique,*f.*

oneiromancy (-naï-), *n.,* oniromancie, *f.*

oneness (weu'n'-), *n.,* unité, *f.*

onerate (o'n'é-), *v.a.,* (ant.) charger.

oneration (-ré-), *n.,* charge, *f.*

onerose (-i-rôce), *or* **onerous** (-'èr'-), *adj.,* onéreux.

one's self (weu'n'-), *pron.,* soi-même; se.

onion, *n.,* ognon, oignon, *m.*

only (ô'n'-), *adj.,* seul ; unique.

only, *adv.,* seulement ; uniquement ; ne .... que.

onomatopoeia (-pî-ya), *n.,* (gram.) onomatopée,*f.*

onset, *n.,* commencement ; abord ; premier choc ; (attack—*attaque*) assaut, *m.,* attaque,*f.*

onslaught(-slôte), *n.,*.attaque,*f.*; assaut, *m.*

ontologic, *or* **ontological** (-o-dj'-), *adj.,* ontologique.

ontologist (-djiste), *n.,* ontologiste, *m.*

ontology (-dji), *n.,* ontologie,*f.*

onus (ô-), *n.* (*onera*), fardeau, poids, *m.*

onward (-wôrde), *adv.,* en avant; plus loin ; progressivement.

onward,*adj.,* qui conduit en avant ; avancé ; progressif.

onyx (ô-nikse), *n.,* (min.) onyx, *m.*

oolite (ô-o-laïte), *n.,* (geol.) oolithe, *m.*

oolitic (ô-o-lit'-), *adj.,* oolithique.

ooze (ouze), *n.,* vase, *f.*; limon; suintement, *m.*

ooze,*v.n.,* suinter, s'écouler, filtrer.

oozing, *n.,* suintement, *m.*

oozy,*adj.,* vaseux, limoneux.

opacity, *n.,* opacité ; (fig.) obscurité,*f.*

opacous (-pé-), *adj.,* opaque ; (fig.) obscur.

opal (ô-),*n.,* (min.) opale,*f.*

opaline, *adj.,* d'opale.

opaque (-pèke), *adj.,* opaque ; (fig.) obscur.

opaqueness, *n.,* opacité, *f.*

open (ô-p'n). *v.a..* ouvrir ; (a bottle—*une bouteille*) déboucher ; (to explain—*expliquer*) expliquer ; (to reveal—*révéler*) révéler, exposer ; (a letter—*une lettre*) ouvrir, décacheter.

open, *v.n.,* s'ouvrir ; (to begin to appear—*commencer à paraître*) se découvrir.

open, *adj.,* ouvert ; à découvert ; nu, à nu ; (of the weather—*du temps*) doux; (print.) blanc ; (frank) franc, sincère, ouvert ; (fig.) exposé, en butte ;(mus.) vide. —handed ; *libéral.* —hearted. *franc.* —heartedly ;*franchement.* —heartedness ; *franchise, f.* —weather ; temps doux. —eyed ; *rigilant.* — to an engagement ; *libre pour un engagement.* Wide —; *grand ouvert.* In the — air ; *en plein air.* In the —sea ; *en pleine mer.*

opener. *n.,* personne qui ouvre, *f.* ; ouvreur, *m.,* ouvreuse,*f.*: interprète ; (med.) apéritif, *m.*

opening, *adj,,* apéritif.

opening, *n.,* ouverture,*f.*; commencement ; début. *m.* ; chance de réussite, *f.* ; (at play—*au jeu*) début ; (com.) débouché, *m.*

openly, *adv.,* ouvertement ; sincèrement, franchement.

openness, *n.,* situation ouverte ; (of the weather—*du temps*) douceur ; (frankness—*franchise*) franchise, sincérité,*f.*

opera (op'ra), *n.,* opéra, *m.* — -glass; *lorgnette, f.* — -hat; *claque, m.* — -house; *opéra, m.,* salle d'opéra, *f.*

operant (op'èr'-), *adj.,* actif.

operate (op'èr'-), *v.a.,* opérer, agir ; avoir son effet.

operatic, *or* **operatical,** *adj.,* d'opéra; lyrique.

operation (op'èr'é-), *n.,* opération ; action, *f.* ; effet, *m.*

operative (op-èr'a-), *adj.,* manuel ; ouvrier ; des ouvriers ; (efficacious—*efficace*) actif, efficace.

operative, *n.,* artisan, ouvrier, travailleur, *m.*

operator (op'èr-é-teur), *n.,* personne qui opère ; chose qui opère,*f.* ; agent; (surg.) opérateur, *m.*

opercular (o-peur-kiou-), *adj.,* (bot.) operculé.

operculate, *or* **operculated,** *adj.,*operculé; operculaire.

operculum (-peur-kiou-), *n.,* opercule, *m.*

operose (op'èr-ôce), *or* **operous,** *adj.,* laborieux ; pénible ; fatigant.

operoseness, *n.,* nature fatigante, laborieuse,*f.*

ophite (ô-faïte),.*n.,* ophite, marbre ophite, *m.*

ophiuchus (o-faï-eu-keusse), *n.,* (astron.) Serpentaire, *m.*

ophthalmia, *or* **ophthalmy** (-thal-), *n.,* ophtalmie,*f.*

ophthalmic (-thal-), *adj.,* ophtalmique.

ophthalmology (-thal-mol-o-dji), *n.,* ophtalmologie,*f.*

opiane (ô-pi-ène), *n.,* narcotine,*f.*

opiate (ô-),*n.,* opiat, électuaire, *m.* ; ⊙opiate,*f.*

opiate (ô-), *adj.,* (med.) narcotique ; (fig.)'qui endort.

opine (-païne),*v.n.,* opiner ; être d'avis ; penser.

opiniated (-ni-ét'-), *adj.,* opiniâtre ; entêté.

opiniative (-ni-é-), *adj.,* obstiné, opiniâtre, entêté.

opiniativeness, *n.,* opiniâtreté,*f.* ; entêtement, *m.* : obstination,*f.*

opinion(-pi'n'yeune),*n.,*opinion,*f.*.avis, sentiment; jugement. *m.* ; idée, pensée,*f.* That's a matter of —; *c'est une affaire d'opinion.* To give one's — ; *donner son opinion, son avis.* To have a high — of ; *avoir une haute opinion de.* To be of — that ; *être d'avis que.* To be of the.— of ; *être de l'avis de.* To be entirely of the — of ; *être entièrement de l'avis de : abonder dans le sens de.* To state one's —; *dire son avis, son sentiment, sa pensée.* In the — of ; *selon l'opinion de.* In my —; *à mon avis.*

opinionate, *or* **opinionated,** *adj.,* opiniâtre, entêté, obstiné ; suffisant.

opinionately, *adv.,*opiniâtrément ; obstinément : avec suffisance.

opinionative, *adj.,* opiniâtre, entêté ; suffisant.

opinionatively, *adv.,* opiniâtrément, obstinément ; avec suffisance.

opinionativeness, *n.,* opiniâtreté,*f.* ; entêtement, *m.* : suffisance,*f.*

opinioned (-pi'n'yeu'n'de), *adj.,* attaché à son opinion ; plein de soi-même.

opinionist, *n.,* personne obstinément attachée à son opinion ; personne suffisante,*f.*

opium (ô-), *n.,* opium, *m.*

opobalsam (-bôl-), *n.,* opobalsamum, *m.*

opodeldoc. *n.* opodeldoch, opodeltoch, *m.*

opossum, *n.,* (mam.) opossum, sarigue, *m.*

oppilate, *v.a.,* (ant.) opiler.

oppilation (-lé-), *n.,* opilation, *f.*

opponency (-pô-), *n.,* thèse académioue, *f.*

opponent (-pô-), *n.,* antagoniste, adversaire, *m.*

opponent, *adj.,* opposé, en face ; contraire.

opportune (-tioune), *adj.,* opportun ; à propos.

opportunely, *adv.,* à propos; en temps opportun.

opportuneness, *n.,* opportunité, *f.*

opportunity, *n.,* occasion, opportunité, *f.*

oppose (op-pôze), *v a.,* opposer, s'opposer à ; résister à ; combattre.

oppose, *v.n.,* s'opposer ; faire des objections.

opposeless, *adj.,* qui ne souffre pas d'opposition ; irresistible.

opposer, *n.,* personne qui s'oppose à, *f.;* antagoniste, adversaire, concurrent, rival, *m.*

opposite (op-po-zite),*adj.,*opposé ; vis-à-vis ; en face ; (contrary—*contraire*) opposé, contraire. The — sex ; *l'autre sexe.*

opposite. *n.,* opposé ; (adversary—*antagoniste*) adversaire, *m.*

oppositely, *adv.,* en face ; à l'opposite ; (adversely—*contre*) en sens opposé.

oppositeness, *n.,* situation opposée, *f.;* état opposé, *m.*

opposition (-zish'eune), *n.,* situation opposée ; opposition ; (competition —*concurrence*) concurrence, *f.* ; (obstacle) obstacle, empêchement. *m.* ; (resistance) résistance ; (repugnance) répugnance, *f.* In — to ; *par opposition a.* To be in the — ; *être de l'opposition.*

oppositive (-poz'-), *adj.,* qui peut être opposé.

oppress, *v.a.,* opprimer ; oppresser ; écraser.

oppression (-prèsh'-), *n.,* oppression, *f.* ; accablement, abattement, *m.* — of the heart ; *serrement de cœur, m.*

oppressive, *adj.,* accablant, oppressif.

oppressively, *adv.,* d'une manière oppressive ; avec accablement.

oppressiveness, *n.,* caractère oppressif, *m.* ; nature accablante, *f.*

oppressor, *n.,* oppresseur, *m.*

opprobrious (-prô-), *adj.,* infamant ; injurieux ; d'opprobre.

opprobriously, *adv.,* avec opprobre.

opprobriousness, *n.,*nature infamante, *f.;* opprobre. *m.*

opprobrium (-prô-), *n.,* opprobre. *m.*

oppugn (-pioune), *v.a.,* combattre, attaquer.

oppugnancy (-peug-na'n'-), *or* **oppugnation** (-peug-né-), *n.,* opposition, resistance, *f.*

oppugner (-piou'n'-), *n.,* personne qui attaque, qui combat, *f.* ; adversaire, antagoniste, *m.*

optative (op-té-), *adj.,* optatif.

optic, *n.,* œil. *m.*

optic. *or* **optical,** *adj.,* optique.

optically. *adv.,* par l'optique.

optician (-tish'-), *n.,* opticien, *m.*

optics. *n.pl.,* optique, *f.sing.*

optimacy, *n.,* noblesse, *f.* ; corps des nobles, *m.*

optime (-mi), *n.,* élève de deuxième, de troisième série en mathématiques, *m.*

optimism. *n.,* optimisme, *m.*

optimist, *n.,* optimiste, *m.,f.*

optimity, *n.,* état de ce qui est le meilleur, *m.* ; excellence, *f.*

option (op'sheune), *n.,* option, *f.* ; choix, *m.* ; faculté, *f.*

optional, *adj.,* laissé au choix ; facultatif ; optatif.

opulence, *or* **opulency** (op'iou-), *n.,* opulence, *f.* ; richesses, *f.pl.*

opulent, *adj.,* opulent, riche.

opulently. *adv.,* opulemment.

opuscle (ô-peus's'l), *or* **opuscule** (-kioule), *n.,* opuscule, *m.*

or, *conj.,* ou ; (negatively—*négation*) ni. — else ; *ou, ou bien, autrement.* Either you — he ; *ou vous ou lui.*

or, *n.,* (her.) or, *m.*

orach, orache, *or* **orrach** (or'atshe), *n.,* (bot.) arroche, *f.*

oracle (or'a-k'l). *n.,* oracle, *m.*

oracular, *or* **oraculous** (ô-rak'iou-), *adj.,* qui rend des oracles ; d'un ton d'oracle ; d'oracle.

oraculousness. *n.,* ton d'oracle, *m.*

oral (ô-), *adj.,* oral.

orally, *a lv.,* oralement.

orange (or'a'n'dje), *n.,* orange, *f.* — -tree **:** *oranger, m.* — chips ; *orangeat, m.* — -house ; *orangerie, f.* — -peel ; *écorce d'orange, f.*

orangeade, *n.,* orangeade, *f.*

orange-coloured (-keul'ieurde), *adj.,* orangé; couleur d'orange, orangé.

orange-flower (-fla'weur), *n.,* fleur d'orange, *f.*

orange-musk (-meuske), *n.,* poire-orange musquée, *f.*

orangery (-djer'i), *n.,* orangerie, *f.*

orange-woman (-woum'a'n), *n.,* marchande d'oranges, *f.*

orang-outang (ô-ran'gn-ou-tan'gn), *n.,* (mam.) orang-outang, *m.*

oration (ô-ré-), *n.,* discours, *m.* ; harangue, oraison. *f.*

orator (-teur), *n.,* orateur, *m.*

oratorial (-tô-), *or* **oratorious** (ant.), *adj.,* oratoire.

oratorian, *n.,* oratorien, *m.*

oratorically, *adv.,* oratoirement.

oratorio (-tô-), *n.,* oratoire ; (mus.) oratorio, concert spirituel, *m.*

oratory (-teuri), *n.,* art oratoire, *m.* ; éloquence, *f.* ; (chapel—*chambre de prière*) oratoire, *m.*

orb, *n.,* globe ; corps sphérique ; orbe, *m.* ; orbite: sphère, *f.* ; cercle, *m.* ; (of time—*du temps*) révolution, période, *f.*

orb, *v.a.,* arrondir, former en cercle ; couvrir.

orbed (orb'de), *adj.,* rond, circulaire, sphérique.

orbic, *adj.,* sphérique.

orbicular (-bik'iou-), *adj.,* circulaire, sphérique ; orbiculaire.

orbicularly, *adv.,* orbiculairement, sphériquement : en rond.

orbicularness, *n.,* sphéricité, forme orbiculaire, *f.*

orbiculate, *or* **orbiculated.** *V.* **orbicular.**

orbiculation (-iou-lé-), *n.,* forme orbiculaire, *f.*

orbit, *n.,* orbite, *f.* ; orbe, *m.*

orbital, *or* **orbitual,** *adj.,* (anat.) orbitaire.

orc. *n.,* (ich.) épaular i, *m.* ; orque,*f.*

orchal (-kal), *or* **orchel** (-kèl), *n.,* (bot.) roccelle ; oreille des teinturiers, *f.*

orchanet (-ka-), *n.,* orcanète, *f.*

orchard (-tsharde), *n.,* verger, *m.* ; pommeraie, *f.*

orcharding,*n.,*culture des arbres fruitiers,*f.*

orchardist, *n.,* jardinier qui cultive les arbres fruitiers, *m.*

orchestra (-kès-). *n.,* orchestre, *m.*

orchestral, *adj.,* d'orchestre ; de l'orchestre.

orchis (-kiss), *n.,* (bot.) orchis, *m.*

ordain (-déne), *v.a.,* ordonner, décréter, prescrire ; établir ; (ecc.) ordonner ; (biblically—*biblique*) élire, choisir.

ordainable (-'a-b'l), *adj.,* que l'on peut ordonner.

ordainer, *n.,* ordonnateur, instituteur **:** (ecc.) ordinant, *m.*

ordaining, *adj.*, ordonnateur; (ecc.) ordinant.

ordeal (-di-), *n.*, (antiq.) ordalie; épreuve, *f.*, jugement de Dieu, *m.*

order, *n.*, ordre; règlement, *m.*; règle. *f.*; arrêté; (arch., her., milit.) ordre, *m.*; (fin.) ordonnance, *f.*; (thea., &c.) billet de faveur, *m.*; (class—*classe*) classe, *f.*; (for goods—*à un marchand*) commande, demande, *f.*; (draft—*traite*) mandat, *m.* —s ;(eco.)ordres, *m.pl.* —! à l'ordre! In — to; *pour, afin de; dans le but de; dans le dessein de; dans l'intention de.* In — that: *afin que; pour que.* To —; (of bills—*de traites, &c.*) à ordre; (of clothes, &c.—*de vêtements, &c.*) de commande. Made to —; *sur commande.* By —; *par ordre;* (com.) *d'ordre.* In —; *en règle; en bonne forme.* Till further —s ; *jusqu'à nouvel ordre.* Out of —; *dérangé: détraqué.* In alphabetical —; *par ordre alphabétique.* In —s; (ecc.) *dans les ordres.* — of the day; *ordre du jour.* To call to —; *rappeler à l'ordre.* To keep in —; *tenir dans l'ordre; tenir dans le devoir.* To keep —; *maintenir l'ordre.* To put out of —; *déranger; mettre en désordre; détraquer.* To set in —; *mettre en ordre: mettre de l'ordre dans.* Higher —s; *classes élevées; hautes classes, f.* Lower —s ; *basses classes ; classes inférieures.*

order, *v.a.*, ordonner, ordonner à, donner l'ordre à; (to regulate—*ordonner*) régler, arranger, disposer; (to conduct—*conduire*) diriger, conduire, guider; (things, as clothes, &c.— *choses telles que vêtements, &c.*) commander, demander.

orderer, *n.*, ordonnateur, régulateur, *m.*; personne qui commande, *f.*

ordering, *n.*, ordonnance, disposition, *f.*

orderless. *adj.*, sans ordre; désordonné.

orderliness, *n.*, ordre, *m.*; méthode; régularité, *f.*

orderly, *n.*, officier d'ordonnance, *m.*

orderly, *adj.*, réglé, régulier; en bon ordre; méthodique; tranquille. — officer; *officier d'ordonnance, f.*

orderly, *adv.*, dans l'ordre, avec ordre.

ordinal, *n.*, nombre ordinal; rituel, *m.*

ordinal, *adj.*, ordinal.

ordinance, *n.*, ordonnance; loi, *f.*; ordre, *m.*

ordinarily, *adv.*, ordinairement; d'ordinaire.

ordinary, *n.*, ordinaire, *m.*; chose ordinaire; table d'hôte, *f.*; (of a prison—*de prison*) aumônier, *m.*

ordinary, *adj.*, ordinaire.

ordinate, *adj.*, régulier.

ordinate, *n.*, (geom.) ordonnée, *f.*

ordinately. *adv.*. régulièrement.

ordination (-né-), *n.*, tendance; (ecc.) ordination, *f.*

ordnance, *n.*, artillerie, *f.*

ordonnance, *n.*. (paint.) ordonnance, *f.*

ordure (ord'yeur), *n.*, ordure, *f.*

ore (ôre), *n.*. minerai, *m.*; mine, *f.*; métal, *m.*

ore-hearth (-hârth), *n.*, (metal.) fourneau de fusion, *m.*

orfrays (-fréze), *n.*, (ant.) orfroi, *m.*

orgal. *n.*, tartre brut, *m.*

organ, *n.*, organe; (mus.) orgue. *m.sing.*; orgues, *f.pl.*

organ-blower (-blô'eur), *n.*, souffleur d'orgue, *m.*

organ-builder (-bild'-), *n.*, facteur d'orgues. *m.*

organ-case (-kéce), *n.*. buffet d'orgue, *m.*

organic, *or* **organical**, *adj.*, organique; des organes.

organically, *adv.*, organiquement.

organicalness, *n.*. état organique, *m.*

organism (-'iz'me), *n.*, organisme, *m.*

organist, *n.*, organiste, *m.*

organization (-aïzé-), *n.*, organisation, *f.*

organize (-aïze),*v.a.*, organiser, constituer.

organ-loft, *n.*, tribune d'orgue, *f.*

organography, *n.*, organographie, *f.*

organ-pipe (-païpe), *n.*, tuyau d'orgue, *m.*

organ-stop, *n.*, jeu d'orgue, *m.*

organzine. *n.*, organsin. *m.*

organzine, *v.a.*, organsiner.

orgeat (-jate), *n.*, orgeat. *m.*

orgies (-djize), *n.pl.*, orgies, *f.pl.*

orient (ô-), *n.*, orient, est, *m.*

orient, *adj.*, levant; naissant; d'orient; oriental; (fig.) brillant, éclatant.

oriental, *adj.*, oriental; d'Orient.

oriental, *n.*, natif de l'Orient, *m.*

orientalist, *n.*, orientaliste, *m.*

orifice, *n.*, orifice, trou, *m.*; ouverture, *f.*

origan, *or* **origanum**, *n.*, (bot.) origan, *m.*

origin, *n.*, origine, source, *f.*

original (o-ridj'-), *n.*, original, *m.*

original, *adj.*, original, originel, primitif.

originality, *n.*, originalité, *f.*

originally, *adv.*, originairement; dans l'origine; d'une manière originale.

originalness, *n.*, originalité, *f.*

originate (o-ridj'-), *v.n.*, provenir; dériver; tirer son origine.

origination (o-ridj'i-né-), *n.*, génération, origine, *f.*

originator (-teur), *n.*, cause première, *f.*; mobile; auteur, *m.*

orillon, *n.*, (fort.) orillon, *m.*

oriole (ô-ri-ôl), *n.*, (orni.) loriot, *m.*

orion (o-raï-), *n.*, (astron.) Orion, *m.*

orison (or'i-zeune), *n.*, oraison, *f.*

orle, *n.*, (her.) orle, *m.*

orle, **orlet**, *or* **orlo**, *n.*, (arch.) orle, *m.*

orlop, *n.*, (nav.) faux pont, *m.*

ornament, *n.*, ornement, *m.*

ornament, *v.a.*, orner, décorer; ornementer.

ornamental, *adj.*, ornemental.

ornamentally, *adv.*, pour servir d'ornement.

ornate, *adj.*, orné, beau, élégant.

ornateness, *n.*, état de ce qui est orné, *m.*; élégance, *f.*

ornithologic (-thol'o-djik), *adj.*, ornithologique.

ornithologist (-thol'o-djist), *n.*, ornithologiste, ornithologue, *m.*

ornithology (-thol'o-dji), *n.*, ornithologie, *f.*

ornithomancy (-tho'm'-), *n.*, ornithomancie, *f.*

orologist (-djist), *n.*, personne versée dans l'orologie, *f.*

orology (-dji), *n.*, orologie, *f.*

orphan, *n.*, orphelin, *m.*, orpheline, *f.*

orphan, *adj.*, orphelin.

orphan, *v.a.*, rendre orphelin.

orphanage (-'édje), *n.*, état d'orphelin; orphelinat, *m.*

orphanism (-iz'me), *n.*, état d'orphelin, *m.*

orpiment, *n.*, orpiment, *m.*

orpin, *n.*, (paint.) orpin, orpiment, *m.*

orpine (-païne), *n.*, (bot.) orphin, *m.*, sarcelle d'été, reprise, grassette, *f.*

orrery (or-ré-), *n.*, planétaire. *m.*

orris, *n.*, passement, *m.*; (bot.) iris, *m.*

ort, *n.*, fragment. débris. rebut. *m.*

orthodox (-tho-). *adj.*, orthodoxe.

orthodoxly (-tho-), *adv.*, d'une manière orthodoxe.

orthodoxy (-tho-), *n.*, orthodoxie, *f.*

orthoepist (-tho-è-), *n.*, personne qui prononce bien, *f.*

orthoepy (-tho-è-), *n.*, prononciation correcte, *f.*

orthogon (-tho-), *n.*, (geom.) figure orthogonale, *f.*

orthogonal (-tho-), *adj.*, (geom.) orthogonal.

orthographer, *or* **orthographist** (-tho-), *n.*, orthographiste, *m.*

orthographic, *or* **orthographical** (-tho-), *adj.*, d'orthographe ; bien orthographié ; orthographique.

orthographically (-tho-), *adv.*, orthographiquement, selon les règles de l'orthographe, de l'orthographie.

orthography (-tho-), *n.*, orthographe, orthographie; (arch., fort., geom., persp.) orthographie, *f.*

orthopedic (-thop'i-), *adj.*, orthopédique.

orthopedist (-thop'i-), *n.*, orthopédiste, *m.*

orthopedy (-thop'i-), *n.*, orthopédie, *f.*

orthopnœa (-thop-ni-), *n.*, orthopnée, *f.*

ortive, *adj.*, ortive.

ortolan, *n.*, ortolan, *m.*

orts, *n.pl.*, restes, *m.pl.* ; épluchures, *f.pl.*

orval, *n.*, orvale, *f.*

oryctography, *n.*, oryctographie, *f.*

oryctology (-o-dji), *n.*, oryctologie, *f.*

oscillate, *v.n.*, osciller; balancer, hésiter.

oscillation (-cil-lé-), *n.*, oscillation, *f.*

oscillatory, *adj.*, oscillatoire.

oscitancy, *or* **oscitation**, *n.*, bâillement, *m.*; nonchalance, *f.*

oscitant, *adj.*, qui bâille ; nonchalant.

osculation (-kiou-lé-), *n.*, (geom.) osculation, *f.*

osculatory (-kiou-lé-), *adj.*, (geom.) osculateur.

osculatory, *n.*, (ecc.) paix, patène, *f.*

osier (ô-jère), *n.*, osier, *m.*

osier-ground (-graou'n'de), *n.*, oseraie, *f.*

osmazome (oz'ma-zo'm), *n.*, osmazôme, *f.*

osmund (oz'meu'n'de), *n.*; (bot.) osmonde, *f.*

osprey, *n.*, (orni.) orfraie, *f.*; aigle de mer, *m.*

osselet (os'lè-), *n.*, (vet.) osselet, *m.*

osseous (osh'i-), *adj.*, osseux.

ossicle (os'si-k'l), *n.*, osselet, *m.*

ossification (-fi-ké-), *n.*, ossification, *f.*

ossify (-fa-ye), *v.a.*, ossifier.

ossify, *v.n.*, s'ossifier.

ossuary (os-shiou-), *n.*, charnier; ossuaire, *m.*

ostensibility, *n.*, caractère ostensible, *m.*

ostensible, *adj.*, ostensible.

ostensibly, *adv.*, ostensiblement.

ostensive, *adj.*, évident.

ostent, *n.*, apparence, *f.*; signe, *m.*

ostentation (-tè'n'-té-), *n.*, ostentation, *f.*; faste, étalage, *m.*

ostentatious (-té-sheusse), *adj.*, plein d'ostentation ; fastueux; de parade.

ostentatiously, *adv.*, fastueusement, avec ostentation, avec étalage.

osteocolla (os-ti-), *n.*, ostéocolle, *f.*

osteogeny (-ti-odj'è-), *n.*, ostéogénie, *f.*

osteography (-ti-), *n.*; (anat.) ostéographie, *f.*

osteolite (os-ti-o-laïte), *n.*, ostéolithe, *m.*

osteologer, *or* **osteologist** (-odj'-), *n.*, auteur d'un traité d'ostéologie, *m.*

osteologic, *or* **osteological** (-o-dj'-), *adj.*, ostéologique.

osteologically, *adv.*, selon l'ostéologie.

osteology (-o-dji), *n.*, ostéologie, *f.*

osteotomy (-ti-o-to-), *n.*, (anat.) ostéotomie, *f.*

ostiary, *n.*, embouchure de fleuve, *f.*

ostler (os'leur), *n.*, valet d'écurie, *m.*

ostracism (-ciz'me), *n.*, ostracisme, *m.*

ostracite (-çaïte), *n.*, ostracite, *f.*

ostracize (-çaïze), *v.a.*, frapper d'ostracisme.

ostrich (-tritshe), *n.*, (orni.) autruche, *f.*

otalgia, *or* **otalgy** (-dj'-), *n.*, otalgie, *f.*

other (euth'-), *pron.*, autre; autrui. Every — ; *tous les deux; de deux* . . . *l'un*.

otherwhere, *adv.*, ailleurs.

otherwhile (-hwaïle), *or* **otherwhiles** (-hwaïlze), *adv.*, dans un autre temps.

otherwise (-waïze), *adv.*, autrement.

ottar, *or* **otto** (-tô), *n.*, essence de roses; huile essentielle, *f.*

otter, *n.*, loutre, *f.*

ottoman, *adj.*, ottoman.

ottoman, *n.*, ottomane, *f.*, divan, sofa; (Turk—*Turc*) Ottoman, *m.*

ought (ôte), *n. V.* **aught.**

ought (ôte), *v. defective*, devoir. You — to do it; *vous devriez le faire.*

ounce (aou'n'ce), *n.*, (weight—*poids*) once, *f.* ; (mam.) once, *f.*

our (aou'eur), *adj.*, notre, *sing.* ; nos, *pl.* — self ; *nous-même.*

ouranography (aou-), *n.*, uranographie, *f.*

ours (aoueurze), *pron.*, le nôtre, *m.*, la nôtre, *f.* ; les nôtres, *pl.m.*, *f.* ; à nous.

ourselves (aeur-cèlv'ze), *pron.*, nous-mêmes ; nous.

ousel (o-z'l), *n.*, merle aquatique, *m.*

oust (aouste), *v.a.*, débusquer ; (jur.) évincer, déposséder.

ouster (aoust'-), *n.*, (jur.) éviction, dépossession, *f.*

out (aoute), *v.a.*, expulser.

out (aoute), *n.*, (print.) bourdon, *m.*

out (aoute), *adv.*, (on the outside—*hors de*) dehors ; (abroad—*hors de la maison*) sorti ; (milit.) sur pied ; (disclosed—*révélé*) découvert, connu; (extinct—*éteint*) éteint ; (at an end—*au bout*) épuisé, usé, fini ; (without—*sans*) sans ; (*to the end—jusqu'à la fin*) jusqu'au bout, jusqu'à la fin ; (loudly, without restraint—*hautement*) haut, hautement, ouvertement, à haute voix ; (not in the hands of the owner—*hors des mains du propriétaire*) loué, prêté ; (puzzled—*interdit*) embarrassé, dans l'embarras ; (in error—*dans l'erreur*) dans l'erreur ; (of clothes, shoes, &c.—*de vêtements, souliers, &c.*) percé, troué ; (not in power—*non au pouvoir*) non au pouvoir, ne . . . plus au pouvoir, non en fonctions, ne . . . plus en fonctions. —! *dehors!* — with him ! *à la porte!* — with it ! *dites ce que c'est ! finissez!* *achevez! voyons!* — of ; *hors de ; sans ; dans ; par.* To be — of ; *être sans ; manquer de.* To be — of pocket ; *perdre.* I was fifty pounds — of pocket by it ; *j'y ai perdu cinquante livres.* — of friendship; *par amitié.* To read — of a book; *lire dans un livre.* — of money; *sans argent.* — and — ; *à ne plus en revenir ; d'importance.* — of hatred ; *par haine.* — of hand ; *tout de suite.* — of measure; *outre mesure.* — of hope; *sans espérance.* — of favour; *disgracié.* — of place; *hors de place.* — of sight; *à perte de vue; hors de vue.* — of humour ; *de mauvaise humeur.* Where are you going ? *où allez-vous ?* —; *je vais sortir.*

outact, *v.a.*, dépasser ; faire plus que.

outbalance, *v.a.*, l'emporter sur, surpasser.

outbar, *v.a.*, fermer par des barres.

outbid, *v.a.* (*preterit*, Outbid, Outbade; *past part.*, Outbidden. Outbid), enchérir, surenchérir ; enchérir sur ; renchérir sur.

outbidder, *n.*, enchérisseur, *m.*

outblown (-blône), *adj.*, enflé, gonflé.

outbound (-baou'n'de), *adj.*, en destination pour l'étranger.

outbrave, *v.a.*, surpasser en bravoure ; braver, défier.

outbrazen (-bré-z'n), *v.a.*, vaincre d'effronterie ; traiter effrontément.

outbreak (-brèk-), *n.*, explosion ; émeute, *f.*

outbreathe (-brîthe), *v.a.*, avoir l'haleine plus longue qu'un autre ; (*v.n.*) (to expire—*mourir*) expirer.

outbuild (-bilde), *v.a.*, (*preterit and past part.*, Outbuilt), surpasser en construction ; surpasser en solidité.

outbuilding, *n.*, bâtiment extérieur, *m.*

outburn (-beurne), *v.a.*, brûler plus qu'un autre.

outcast (-câste), *n.*, proscrit, exilé, *m.*

outcast, *adj.*, expulsé, proscrit, exilé, abandonné.

outcrop, *n.*, (geol.) affleurement, *m.*

outcry (-cra-ye), *n.*, grand cri, *m.* ; hauts cris, *m.pl.* ; clameur, *f.*, clameurs, *f.pl.* ; (sale—*vente*) criée, *f.*

outdare, *v.a.*, surpasser en audace; défier ; affronter.

outdo (-dou), *v.a.* (*preterit*, Outdid ; *past part.*, Outdone), surpasser ; exceller sur.

outdwell, *v.n.*, (*preterit* and *past part.*, Outdwelt), rester trop longtemps, demeurer au delà de.

outer. *adj.*, extérieur, du dehors ; externe.

outerly, *adv.*, extérieurement ; au dehors ; à l'extérieur.

outermost (-môste), *adj.*, le plus en dehors ; le plus extérieur ; le plus externe.

out-face (-féce), *v.a.*, faire baisser les yeux à ; affronter, défier.

outfall (-fôl), *n.*, embouchure, *f.*

outfawn (-fône), *v.a.*, surpasser en flatterie.

outfit, *n.*, armement, équipement ; trousseau, *m.*

outflank, *v.a.*, (milit.) déborder, tourner.

outflow (-flô), *v.a.*, découler, provenir, venir.

outflow, *n.*, émigration, *f.*

outfly (-fla-ye), *v.a.* (*preterit*, Outflew ; *past part.*, Outflown), surpasser dans son vol; dépasser.

outfool (-foule), *v.a.*, dépasser en folie.

outfrown (-fraoune), *v.a.*, froncer les sourcils plus qu'un autre ; mater, abattre.

outgeneral, *v.a.*, surpasser comme général; l'emporter sur.

outgive (-ghive), *v.a.* (*preterit*, Outgave ; *past part.*, Outgiven), surpasser en libéralité.

outgo, *v.a.* (*preterit*, Outwent ; *past part.*, Outgone), devancer, surpasser, dépasser ; circonvenir, tromper, abuser.

outgoing, *n.*, sortie, *f.* ; extrême limite, *f.*

outgrow (-grô), *v.a.* (*preterit*, Outgrew ; *past part.*, Outgrown), grandir plus que ; surpasser en croissance ; dépasser, surpasser.

out-guard (-gârde), *n.*, garde avancée. *f.*

out-herod (-hèr'-), *v.a.*, dépasser en cruauté. That —s Herod ; *cela dépasse tout.*

outhouse (-haouce), *n.*, pavillon, *m.* ; dépendance, *f.* —s ; *communs*, *m.pl.*

outjest, *v.a.*, accabler de plaisanteries; réduire au silence, interdire à force de plaisanteries.

outjuggle (-djeug'g'l), *v.a.*, surpasser en ruse; duper.

outknave (-néve), *v.a.*, surpasser en fourberie.

outlandish. *adj.*, étranger ; grossier, rude.

outlast, *v.a.*, surpasser en durée ; survivre à.

outlaw (-lô), *n.*, personne mise hors la loi, *f.* ; proscrit, *m.*

outlaw (-lô), *v.a.*, mettre hors la loi ; proscrire, bannir.

outlawry, *n.*, mise hors la loi, proscription, *f.*

outlay, *n.*, dépense, *f.* ; déboursés, *m.pl.*

outleap (-lîpe), *n.*, sortie, fuite, *f.*

outlet, *n.*, issue ; sortie, *f.* ; passage ; débouché, *m.* ; voie d'écoulement, *f.* ; (of a roof snoot—*de gouttière*) gargouille, *f.*

outlie (-la'ye), *v.a.*, surpasser en mensonge.

outlier (-la'yeur), *n.*, non-résident (geol.) lambeau détaché, *m.*

outline (-laï'ne), *n.*, contour, *m.* ; esquisse, *f.* ; premier jet, aperçu, *m.*

outline, *v.a.*, dessiner le contour de ; esquisser.

outlive, *v.a.*, survivre à.

outliver, *n.*, survivant, *m.*, survivante, *f.*

outlook (-louke), *v.a.*, faire baisser les yeux à ; affronter ; braver ; mater ; observer, veiller.

out-look, *n.*, vigilance, *f.*

outlustre (-leus'teur), *v.a.*, surpasser en lustre, éclipser.

outlying (-la'yigne), *adj.*, éloigné.

outmarch (-mârtshe), *v.a.*, devancer.

outmost (-môste), *adj.*, le plus en dehors; extrême, le plus éloigné.

outpace (-péce), *v.a.*, devancer, dépasser.

out-parish, *n.*, paroisse extérieure, *f.*

out-part (-pârte), *n.*, partie extérieure, *f.*

outpass, *v.a.*, dépasser ; devancer.

outpoise (-poîze), *v.a.*, peser plus que; surpasser en poids.

out-porch (-pôrtshe), *n.*, portique extérieur; parvis, *m.*

outpost (-pôste), *n.*, (milit.) avant-poste, *m.*, garde avancée, *f.*

outpour (-pôre), *v.a.*, verser à grands flots.

outpouring, *n.*, effusion, *f.* ; épanchement, *m.*

outpray, *v.a.*, prier plus que ; prier avec plus de ferveur que.

outpreach (-prîtshe), *v.a.*, prêcher mieux que; surpasser par la prédication.

outprize (-praîze), *v.a.*, surpasser en valeur.

outrage (-rédje), *n.*, outrage, affront, *m.* ; (jur.) atteinte, *f.*

outrage, *v.a.*, outrager.

outrageous (-ré'djeusse), *adj.*, outrageux, outrageant ; furieux, violent ; (tumultuous— *bruyant*) tumultueux, turbulent ; (excessive— *excessif*) outré, exagéré ; (enormous— *immense*) énorme.

outrageously, *adv.*, outrageusement ; violemment, furieusement ; avec turbulence; d'une manière outrée ; énormément.

outrageousness. *n.*, nature outrageuse, nature outrageante ; violence, fureur, turbulence, énormité, *f.*

outreach (-rîtshe), *v.a.*, dépasser ; outrepasser.

outreason (-rî-z'n), *v.a.*, surpasser en raisonnement.

outreckon (-rèk'k'n), *v.a.*, dépasser dans ses calculs.

outride (-raîde), *v.a.* (*preterit*, Outrode ; *past part.*, Outridden), devancer à cheval.

outrider (-raîd'-), *n.*, piqueur, chasseur, *m.*

outright (-raîte), *adv.*, sur-le-champ; tout de suite ; (completely—*complètement*) entièrement ; (without constraint—*sans retenue*) sans gêne, sans contrainte.

outrival (-raï-), *v.a.*, l'emporter sur.

outroar (-rôr), *v.a.*, crier plus fort que.

outroot (-route), *v.a.*, déraciner.

outrun (-reune), *v.a.* (*preterit*, Outran ; *past part.*, Outrun), devancer à la course ; devancer.

outsail (-séle), *v.a.*, dépasser à la voile; dépasser.

outsell, *v.a.*, (*preterit* and *past part.*, Outsold), vendre plus que, plus vite que ; obtenir de plus hauts prix que.

outset, *n.*, début, commencement ; principe, *m.*

outshine (-shaîne), *v.a.* (*preterit* and *past part.*, Outshined, or Outshone), surpasser en éclat; surpasser ; éclipser.

outshoot (-shoute), *v.a.*, (*preterit* and *past part.*, Outshot), tirer plus loin que.

outside (-saîde), *n.*, dehors, extérieur, *m.* ; (of a diligence—*de diligence*) impériale, banquette, *f.* At the —; *tout au plus.*

outside, *adj.*, extérieur, externe.

outside, *adv.*, en dehors; (of a diligence— *de diligence*) sur l'impériale, sur la banquette.

outsit. *v.a.* (*preterit* and *past part.*, Outsat), être assis plus longtemps que.

outskirt (-skeurte), *n.*, extrémité, *f.*; bord; (of a town—*d'une ville*) faubourg, *m.*; (of a wood —*d'un bois*) lisière, *f.*

outsleep (-slîpe), *v.a.* (*preterit* and *past part.*, Outslept), dormir plus longtemps que, dormir au-delà de.

outspeak (-spîke), *v.a.* (*preterit*, Outspoke; *past part.*, Outspoken), parler plus que; dépasser.

outsport (-sporte), *v.a.*, surpasser en badinage, pousser trop loin le badinage.

outspread (-sprède), *v.a.* (*preterit* and *past part.*, Outspread), étendre, déployer; répandre.

outstand. *v.a.* (*preterit* and *past part.*, Outstood), rester au-delà de; durer plus que.

outstanding, *adj.*, en saillie; (of bills—*de factures, &c.*) non payé, encore dû; (com.) en suspens, courant.

outstare, *v.a.*, faire baisser les yeux à; décontenancer.

outstep (-stèpe), *v.a.*, devancer; dépasser.

outstorm. *v.a.*, gronder plus fort que; braver; défier.

out-street (-strîte), *n.*, rue écartée; rue à l'extrémité d'une ville; rue de faubourg, *f.*

outstretch (-strètshe), *v.a.*, étendre.

outstretched (-strètsh'te), *adj.*, étendu; ouvert.

outstride (-straïde), *v.a.*(*preterit*,Outstrode; *past part.*, Outstridden), enjamber mieux que; devancer.

outstrip, *v.a.*, gagner de vitesse; devancer; surpasser.

outswear (-swére), *v.a.* (*preterit*, Outswore; *past part.*, Outsworn), jurer mieux que; l'emporter en serments sur.

outsweeten (-'swît'-). *v.a.*, surpasser en douceur; l'emporter en douceur sur.

outtalk (-tôke), *v.a.*, parler plus que; causer plus que; réduire au silence.

outthrow (-thrô), *n.*,(geol.) faille,*f.*; rejet. *m.*

outtongue (-teu'n'ghe), *v.a.*, parler plus haut que; réduire au silence.

outvalue (-val'you),*v.a.*, surpasser en valeur.

outvenom (-vè'n'eume), *v.a.*, surpasser en venin.

outvie (-va'ye), *v.a.*, l'emporter sur; surpasser.

outvillain (-vil'li'n), *v.a.*, surpasser en scélératesse.

outvote (-vôte), *v.a.*, l'emporter à la pluralité des voix sur.

outwalk (-wôke), *v.a.*, marcher mieux que; devancer.

out-wall (-wôl), *n.*, mur extérieur, *m.*

outward (-worde),*adj.*,extérieur; superficiel.

outward, *n.*, extérieur, dehors, *m.*

outward, *or* **outwards** (-wordze) *adv.*, à l'extérieur; au dehors, extérieurement; (of ships —*de vaisseaux*), pour l'étranger.

outwardly, *adv.*, extérieurement, à l'extérieur; au dehors.

outwatch (-wotsch), *v.a.*, veiller plus que.

outweigh (-wè), *v.a.*, peser plus que; l'emporter sur.

outwit, *v.a.*, surpasser en finesse; duper; attraper, (pop.) mettre dedans.

outwork (-weurke), *n.*, (fort.) ouvrage extérieur, *m.*

outworth (-weurth), *v.a.*, (ant.) surpasser en prix.

outwrite (-raïte), *v.a.* (*preterit*, Outwrote; *past part.*, Outwritten), écrire plus que.

oval (ô-), *adj.*, ovale.

oval, *n.*, ovale, *m.* — in a wall; *œil-de-bœuf, m*

ovarious (ô-vé-), *adj.*, d'œufs.

ovary (ô-), *n.*, ovaire, *m.*

ovate, *or* **ovated** (ô-vét'-), *adj.*, (bot.) ovale.

ovation, *n.*, ovation, *f.*

oven (euv'v'n), *n.*, four, *m.* — fork; *fourgon, râble, m.* — full; *fournée, f.* Dutch —; *rôtissoire, cuisinière, f.*

over (ô-veur). *prep.*, (above—*au dessus*) au-dessus de; par-dessus; sur; (during—*pendant*) durant, pendant; (upon—*sur*) sur, sur la surface de; (across—*au travers*) à travers, au travers de; (on the other side—*au delà*) de l'autre côté, au delà de; (about—*dans*) dans, par. — the water; *de l'autre côté de l'eau.* — hill and dale; *par monts et par vaux.* To walk — the field; *marcher dans, à travers le champ.* — the table; *sur la table.* — winter; *pendant l'hiver.* The water is — one's shoes; *l'eau est au-dessus des souliers.* To be placed — any one; *être placé au-dessus de,* surveiller quelqu'un.

over, *adv.*, (from side to side—*d'un côté à l'autre*) d'un côté à l'autre; (on the opposite side—*au delà*) de l'autre côté; (on the surface), above the top—*sur le dessus*) par-dessus, au-dessus; (throughout—*complètement*) partout, tout, entièrement; (ended—*terminé*) fini, passé; (more than the quantity assigned—*de plus que la quantité voulue*) de reste. A table ten feet —; *une table de dix pieds de large.* He is —; *il est de l'autre côté.* To walk —; *marcher par-dessus.* You are splashed all —; *vous êtes éclaboussé partout.* To have something —; *avoir de reste.* —and—; *mille fois, sans cesse, incessamment.* To be all —; *être fini.* To be all — with; *en être fait de.* I am glad it is —; *je suis content que ce soit fini.*

overabound (-abaou'n'de), *v.n.*, surabonder.

overact, *v.a.* and *n.*, outrer, exagérer, charger.

overall (-ôl), *n.*, surtout, pardessus. —s; *pantalon de voyage, m.sing.*

overarch (-ârtshe), *v.a.*, voûter; couvrir d'une voûte.

overawe (ô-veur-ô), *v.a.*, imposer le respect à; intimider.

overbalance, *n.*, excédent, *m.*; prépondérance, *f.*

overbalance. *v.a.*, peser plus que, surpasser; l'emporter sur.

overbalancing, *n.*, prépondérance, *f.*

overbear (-bère), *v.a.* (*preterit*, Overbore; *past part.*, Overborne), subjuguer, dompter; accabler, vaincre; surmonter.

overbearing, *adj.*, dominateur; impérieux; arrogant.

overbend, *v.a.* (*preterit* and *past part.*, Overbent), plier trop, courber trop.

overbid, *v.a.* (*preterit*, Overbade; *past part.*, Overbidden), offrir trop pour; enchérir sur.

overblow (-blô), *v.n.* (*preterit*, Overblew; *past part.*, Overblown), surventer.

overblow,*v.a.*, dissiper par le vent.

overboard (-bôrde), *adv.*, hors le bord; à la mer.

overbuilt (-bilte), *adj.*, chargé de bâtiments; chargé.

overburden (-beur-d'n), *v.a.*, surcharger.

overbusy (-biz'zé), *adj.*, trop affairé; qui s'ingère dans les affaires des autres.

overbuy (-ba'ye), *v.a.*(*preterit* and *past part.*, Overbought), acheter trop cher.

overcanopy, *v.a.*, couvrir d'un pavillon; couvrir.

overcare (-kére), *n.*, excès de soucis, *m.*

overcareful, *adj.*, (over-attentive—*trop attentif*) soigneux à l'excès; (over-solicitous—*trop soucieux*) soucieux à l'excès.

overcarry, *v.a.*, entraîner; emporter.

overcast (-câste), *adj.*, couvert, nuageux; obscur.

overcast (-câste), *v.a.* (*preterit* and *past part.*, Overcast), obscurcir; (to compute—*supputer*) porter trop haut; (needlework—*ouvrage à l'aiguille*) surjeter.

overcautious (-cŏ-sheusse), *adj.*, par trop prudent.

overcharge (-tshârdje), *v.a.*, surcharger ; (in price—*de prix*) survendre, faire payer trop cher, surfaire ; (fire-arms—*armes à feu*) mettre une charge trop forte dans.

overcharge, *n.*. charge excessive, *f.* ; (in price—*prix*) prix trop élevé, *m.*

overcloud (-claoude), *v.a.*, couvrir de nuages ; obscurcir.

overcloy (-clo'ye), *v.a.*, rassasier.

overcolour (-keul'leur), *v.a.*, charger de couleur; colorer trop ; charger ; exagérer; outrer.

overcome (-keume), *v.a.* (*preterit*, Overcame ; *past part.*, Overcome), subjuguer; dompter ; triompher de ; vaincre ; surmonter.

overcome, *v.n.*, vaincre ; être victorieux; l'emporter. I am quite —; *je n'en puis plus.*

overcomer, *n.*, vainqueur, *m.*

overcomingly, *adv.*, en vainqueur.

overconfidence.*n.*.tropgrande confiance,*f.*

overcount (-caou'n'te), *v.a.*, évaluer trop; priser trop.

overcover (-keuv'-), *v.a.*, couvrir entièrement.

overcredulous (-crèd'iou-leusse), *adj.*, trop crédule.

overdate, *v.a.*, postdater.

overdo (-dou), *v.a.* (*preterit*, Overdid : *past part.*, Overdone), faire trop; exagérer ;outrer; (eatables—*comestibles*) faire trop cuire ; (to fatigue—*fatiguer*) harasser, fatiguer.

overdo (-dou), *v.n.*, faire trop ; trop travailler.

overdone, *adj.*, trop cuit.

overdose (-dôce), *n.*, dose trop forte, *f.*

overdraw (-drô), *v.a.* (*preterit*, Overdrew; *past part.*, Overdrawn), excéder, dépasser le montant de son crédit ; tirer trop.

overdrawing (-drô-igne), *n.*, (com.) action de dépasser, d'excéder son crédit, *f.*

overdress, *v.a.*, habiller trop; trop charger de parure.

overdrink, *v.n.* (*preterit*, Overdrank; *past part.*. Overdrunk), boire à l'excès.

overdrive (-draïve), *v.a.* (*preterit*, Overdrove; *past part.*, Overdriven), faire marcher trop vite; pousser trop loin; (of animals—*des animaux*) surmener.

overdry (-dra'ye), *v.a.*, sécher trop.

overdue (-diou), *adj.*, échu, non payé, en souffrance. ; en retard.

overeager (-ĭ-gheur), *adj.*, trop empressé.

overeagerly (-ĭ-gheur-), *adv.*, avec trop d'empressement.

overeagerness (-ĭ-gheur-), *n.*, excès d'empressement, *m.*

overestimate, *v.a.*, surestimer ; estimer trop ; évaluer trop haut.

overeye (-a-ye), *v.a.*, (l.u.), surveiller; observer, remarquer.

overfall (-fôl), *n.*, (nav.) bas fond, *m.*

overflow (-flô), *v.n.*, déborder ; se déborder ; (fig.) regorger.

overflow, *v.a.*, faire déborder ; inonder.

overflow, *n.*. inondation, *f.* ; débordement, *m.* ; (fig.) surabondance, *f.*, excès, *m.*

overflowing (-flô-igne), *adj.*, qui déborde; (fig.) surabondant; qui regorge.

overflowing, *n.*, débordement; épanchement, *m.*

overflowingly, *adv.*, à l'excès; surabondamment.

overfly (-fla'ye), *v.a.*, passer au vol; voler au-delà de.

overforward (-worde), *adj.*, trop empressé; trop hardi.

overforwardness, *n.*, empressement excessif, *m.* ; hardiesse excessive, *f.*

overfraught (-frôte), *adj.*, surchargé.

overfreight (-frête), *v.a.*, surcharger.

overfruitful (-frout'foule), *adj.*, trop fertile, trop fécond.

overglance, *v.a.*, parcourir des yeux, voir à la hâte.

overgo (-gô), *v.a.* (*preterit*, Overwent ; *past part.*, Overgone), dépasser.

overgrow (-grô), *v.a.* (*preterit*, Overgrew; *past part.*, Overgrown), (of plants—*de plantes*) couvrir, croître au-dessus de ; s'élever au-dessus de ; (pers., animal) grandir au-dessus de.

overgrow, *v.n.*, croître trop ; (pers.) grandir trop ; (animal) grossir trop.

overgrown (-grône), *adj.*, (with plants—*de plantes*) couvert, plein; trop grand; trop puissant ; énorme.

overgrowth (-grôth), *n.*, accroissement excessif. *m.*

overhandle (-ha'n'd'l), *v.a.*, manier trop ; toucher trop souvent.

overhang, *v.n.* (*preterit* and *past part.*, Overhung), pencher, surplomber.

overhang (-han'gn'g), *v.a.*, pencher sur ; être suspendu sur ; (fig.) menacer.

overhanging (-ghigne), *adj.*, en surplomb.

overharden, *v.a.*, endurcir trop.

overhaste (-héste), *n.*, précipitation : trop grande hâte, *f.*

overhastily (-hést'-), *adv.*, avec précipitation ; trop à la hâte.

overhastiness (-hést'-), *n.*, précipitation ; trop grande hâte, *f.*

overhasty (-hést'-), *adj.*, précipité ; trop emporté.

overhaul, *v.a.*, examiner de nouveau ; visiter, inspecter ; (nav.) gagner.

overhead (-hède), *adv.*, au-dessus de la tête ; en haut.

overhear (-hir), *v.a.* (*preterit* and *past part.*, Overheard), entendre par hasard ; surprendre.

overheat (-hîte), *v.a.*, échauffer trop.

overjoy (-jo-é), *v.a.*, transporter de joie; ravir.

overjoy, *n.*, transport de joie; transport ; ravissement, *m.*

overlabour (-lé-beur), *v.a.*, faire travailler à l'excès ; travailler trop, élaborer trop.

overlade, *v.a.* (*preterit*, Overladed; *past part.*, Overladen), surcharger.

overland, *adj.*, par voie de terre.

overlap, *v.a.*, recouvrir.

overlap, *n.*, recouvrement, *m.*

overlarge (-lârdje), *adj.*, trop gros; trop grand.

overlargeness, *n.*, grosseur excessive; grandeur excessive ; largeur excessive, *f.*

overlay, *v.a.* (*preterit* and *past part.*, Overlaid), couvrir ; étouffer ; (fig.) obscurcir. To—a child ; *étouffer un enfant.*

overleap (-lîpe), *v.n.*, sauter par-dessus; sauter.

overleather (-lèth'-), *n.*, empeigne, *f.*

overliberal, *adj.*, trop libéral ; trop généreux.

overlight (-laïte), *n.*, lumière trop forte, *f.*

overload (-lôde), *v.a.*, surcharger.

overlong (-lon'gn'g), *adj.*, trop long.

overlook (-louke), *v.a.*, (to view from on high, applied to persons—*voir de haut ; des personnes*) avoir vue sur, planer sur ; (applied to things —*des choses*) dominer, commander ; (to see from behind—*regarder par derrière*) regarder, regarder pardessus l'épaule de ; (to view fully—*examiner complètement*) parcourir en entier, voir en entier ; (to superintend—*veiller à*) surveiller ; (to review —*reviser*) revoir, retoucher ; (to excuse—*excuser*) fermer les yeux sur, avoir de l'indulgence pour, ne vouloir pas voir ; (to pass by, to neglect— *négliger*) laisser échapper, ne pas remarquer.

overlooker, n., inspecteur, surveillant, m.
overlooking, f., surveillance, f.
overlove (-leuve), v.a., aimer trop.
overmasted (-mâst'-), adj., trop haut mâté.
overmaster (-mâs-), v.a., maîtriser, surmonter.
overmatch, n., force supérieure, f.; vainqueur, m.
overmatch (-matshe), v.a., opposer une force supérieure à; surmonter, être trop fort pour, accabler.
overmeasure(-mèj'eur), v.a., évaluer trop; priser trop.
overmeasure. n., trop bonne mesure, f.
overmerit (-mèr'-), n., mérite excessif, m.
overmerry (-mèr'-), adj., trop gai.
overmix, v.a., mêler trop.
overmodest, adj., trop modeste.
overmuch (-meutshe), n., trop; excès, m.
overmuch, adj., excessif; trop grand, trop de; à l'excès.
overmuch, adv., trop, excessivement.
overofficious (-fish'eusse), adj., trop officieux.
overpaid, adj., trop payé; payé trop cher.
overpaint (-pé'n'te), v.a., surcharger de couleur.
overpass (-pâce), v.a., passer sur; passer, franchir; omettre; ne pas remarquer.
overpay, v.a., surpayer; payer trop; payer libéralement; payer trop cher.
overpeople(-pî'p'l), v.a., peupler trop; surcharger de population.
overpersuade (-pèr-swéde), v.a., persuader par importunité.
overpicture (-tieur), v.a., surpasser la représentation de.
overplus (-pleusse), n., surplus; excédent; trop-plein, m.
overpoise, v.a., peser plus que; (fig.) l'emporter sur, surpasser.
overpoise (-poize), n., poids plus fort, m.; (fig.) prépondérance, f.
overpolish, v.a., polir trop.
overponderous (-dèr'-), adj., trop pesant.
overpost (-pôste), v.a., passer rapidement sur.
overpower (-paou'eur), v.a., être trop fort pour; vaincre; subjuguer; accabler.
overpowering, adj., accablant; écrasant.
overpoweringly, adv., excessivement.
overpress, v.a., presser vivement; vaincre à force (d'instances); accabler; opprimer.
overprize (-praize), v.a., évaluer trop, estimer trop.
overprompt, adj., trop prompt; trop vif.
overpromptness, n., promptitude excessive; précipitation, f.
overproportion (-pôr-), v.a., diviser en parties trop grandes.
overrank (-ran'gn'k), adj., trop gras; surabondant.
overrate (-réte), v.a., évaluer trop, priser trop.
overreach (-ritshe), n., (man.) action de forger; (vet.) nerf-férure, f.
overreach, v.a., aller au-delà de; dépasser; (to deceive—abuser) tromper; jouer; duper.
overreach, v.n., (man.) forger.
overreacher, n., trompeur, m., trompeuse, f.
overreaching, n., action de dépasser; duperie, f.
override (-raïde), v.a. (preterit, Overrode; past part., Overridden), surmener; excéder de fatigue.
overripe (-raïpe), adj., trop mûr.
overripen (-raï-p'n), v.a., mûrir trop.
overroast (-rôste), v.a., rôtir trop.
overrule (-roule), v.a., dominer; gouverner; régir; maîtriser; (jur.) rejeter.

overruler, n., gouverneur; régisseur; directeur, m.
overruling, adj., qui gouverne; qui régit; dominant.
overrun (-reune), v.a. (preterit, Overran; past part., Overrun), couvrir; (to infest—infester) envahir, faire une irruption dans; infester; ravager; (to outrun—dépasser) devancer, passer; (print.) remanier; (to overflow—inonder) déborder.
overrunner, n., envahisseur, ravageur, m.
overrunning, n., envahissement; (print.) remaniement, m.
oversea (-sî), adj., d'outre-mer.
oversee (-sî), v.a. (preterit, Oversaw; past part., Overseen), surveiller.
overseer (-sî-eur), n., surveillant; (of the poor—des pauvres) percepteur et administrateur de la taxe des pauvres; (print.) prote; (of a factory, &c.—de manufacture, &c.) contremaître, m.
overset, v.a. (preterit and past part., Overset), renverser; (a vehicle—une voiture) verser; (a boat—un bateau) faire chavirer; (fig.) renverser, bouleverser.
overset, v.n., se renverser; (of vehicles—des voitures) verser; (of boats—des bateaux) chavirer, faire capot.
overshade (-shéde), v.a., ombrager; (fig.) jeter dans l'ombre, obscurcir.
overshadow (-shad'ô), v.a., ombrager; protéger; jeter dans l'ombre; éclipser.
overshadower, n., personne qui jette de l'ombre sur, qui éclipse; chose qui jette de l'ombre sur, qui éclipse, f.
overshoes (-shouze), n.pl., galoches, f.pl.
overshoot (-shoute), v.a. (preterit and past part., Overshot), porter trop loin, aller trop avant; dépasser le but.
overshot (-shote), adj., en dessus; dépassé.
oversight (-saïte), n., méprise, inadvertance, f.; oubli, m.; (superintendence—surveillance) surveillance, f.
oversize (-saïze), v.n., enduire.
overskip, v.a., sauter par-dessus; sauter.
oversleep (-slîpe), v.a. (preterit and past part., Overslept), dormir au-delà de son heure. To—one's self; dormir trop; rester endormi.
overslip, v.a., glisser sur; passer, négliger.
oversnow (-snô), v.a., couvrir de neige.
oversoon (-soune), adv., trop tôt.
overspent, adj., harassé, épuisé.
overspread (-sprède), v.a. (preterit and past part., Overspread), couvrir; se répandre sur.
overstand (-sta'n'd), v.a. (preterit and past part., Overstood), insister trop sur; tenir trop à.
overstate (-stéte), v.a., exagérer.
overstep (-stèpe), v.a., passer; dépasser; surpasser.
overstock, n., surabondance, f.
overstock, v.a., remplir trop; surcharger.
overstore, v.a., approvisionner à l'excès.
overstrain (-stréne), v.n., faire de trop grands efforts.
overstrain, v.a., forcer trop; pousser trop loin.
overstrew (-strou, ou -strô), v.a., répandre sur; joncher.
oversway (-swè), v.a., dominer; gouverner; dissuader.
overswell, v.a., faire déborder; inonder.
overt (ô-veurte), adj., ouvert, évident, manifeste.
overtake (-téke), v.a. (preterit, Overtook; past part., Overtaken), atteindre, rattraper. rejoindre.
overtask (-tâske), v.a., surcharger de travail; mettre à l'épreuve.
overtax, v.a., surtaxer.
overthrow (-thrô), v.a. (preterit, Over-

threw ; *past part.*, Overthrown), renverser ; bouleverser ; défaire, détruire.

overthrow, *n.*, renversement ; bouleversement, *m.* ; défaite ; ruine, *f.*

overthrower, *n.*, personne qui renverse, qui détruit, qui défait, *f.*

overthwart (-thw'arte), *adj.*, opposé ; d'en face ; (cross—*brusque*) contraire, bourru.

overthwartness (-thwart'-), *n.*, opposition, *f.* ; mauvais caractère, *m.*

overtire (-taeur), *v.a.*, fatiguer trop ; harasser.

overtly (ô-veurt'-), *adv.*, ouvertement ; manifestement.

overtop, *v.a.*, dépasser le sommet de ; être plus grand que ; surpasser.

overtrip, *v.a.*, passer légèrement.

overtrust (-treuste), *v.a.*, se fier trop à.

overture (ô-veur-tioure), *n.*, ouverture, *f.* ; (mus.) prélude, *m.*, ouverture, *f.*

overturn (-teurne), *v.a.*, renverser ; bouleverser ; (a vehicle—*une voiture*) verser ; (a boat—*un bateau*) faire chavirer.

overturn, *n.*, renversement, *m.*

overturner, *n.*, personne qui renverse, qui bouleverse, *f.* ; destructeur, *m.*

overturning, *n.*, renversement ; bouleversement, *m.*

overvaluation (-val'iou-é-), *n.*, surévaluation ; estimation trop élevée, *f.*

overvalue (-val'iou), *v.a.*, surévaluer ; évaluer trop ; priser trop.

overveil (-vél),*v.a.*, couvrir d'un voile ; couvrir.

overweak (-wike), *adj.*, trop faible.

overweary (-wi-ré), *v.a.*, excéder de fatigue.

overween (-wine), *v.n.*, être présomptueux ; se flatter, se faire illusion.

overweening, *adj.*, présomptueux.

overweeningly, *adv.*, présomptueusement.

overweigh (-wè), *v.a.*, peser plus que ; (fig.) l'emporter sur.

overweight (-wète), *n.*, surplus de poids, *m.*

overwhelm (ô-veur-hwèlme), *v.a.*, accabler, écraser.

overwhelming, *adj.*, accablant, écrasant.

overwhelmingly, *adv.*, d'une manière accablante.

overwing (-wigne), *v.a.*, (milit.) (ant.) déborder.

overwise (-waïze), *adj.*, par trop sage.

overwork (-weurke), *v.a.*, (*preterit* and *past part.*, Overworked, Overwrought), faire travailler au-delà de ses forces ; accabler de travail ; fatiguer ; (a horse—*un cheval*) surmener ; travailler trop.

overworn, *adj.*, accablé de fatigue, usé.

overwrought (ô-veur-rôte), *adj.*, trop travaillé.

overzealous (-zèl'leusse), *adj.*, trop zélé.

ovicular (ô-vik'iou-), *adj.*, propre à l'œuf ; de l'œuf.

ovine (ô-vine), *adj.*, ovine, de la brebis.

oviparous, *adj.*, ovipare.

ovoid (ô-voïde), *adj.*, ovoïde, en forme d'œuf.

ovolo (ô-vo-lô), *n.*, (arch.) ove, *m.*

owe (ô), *v.n.*, devoir, être redevable de.

owing (ô-igne), *adj.*, dû. — to ; *à cause de* ; *grâce à.*

owl (aoul), *n.*, hibou, *m.*

owler, *n.*, contrebandier, *m.*

owlet, *n.*, hulotte, *f.*

owlish, *adj.*, de hibou.

owl-light (-laïte), *n.*, tombée de la nuit, *f.*

own (ô'ne), *adj.*, propre (à soi). Of my — ; *à moi.* My — ; *à moi* ; *le mien.* At his — house ; *chez lui.*

own, *v.a.*, avouer, confesser, convenir ; (to possess—*posséder*) être propriétaire de, avoir, jouir de, posséder.

owner, *n.*, propriétaire, possesseur, *m.*

ownership, *n.*, propriété, *f.*

ox, *n.* (*oxen*), bœuf, *m.*

oxalic, *adj.*, oxalique.

ox-driver (-draiv'-), *n.*, bouvier, *m.*

oxeye (a-ye), *n.*, (bot.) buphthalme, œil de bœuf, *m.* ; (orni.) mésange charbonnière, *f.*

ox-eyed (-a-ye'de), *adj.*, aux yeux de bœuf.

oxfly (-fla-ye), *n.*, taon, *m.*

oxidable (-'a-b'l), *adj.*, oxydable.

oxidate, *v.a.*, oxyder.

oxidation, *n.*, oxydation, *f.*

oxide (oks'ide), *n.*, oxyde, *m.*

oxidize (-'aïze), *v.a.*, oxyder.

oxidizement (-aïz'-), *n.*, oxydation, *f.*

oxonian (-'ô-ni-), *n.*, étudiant de l'université d'Oxford.

ox-stall (-stôl), *n.*, étable à bœufs, *f.*

ox-tongue (-teu'n'ghe), *n.*, (bot.) buglosse,*f.*

oxygen (-djène), *n.*, oxygène, *m.*

oxygenate (-djè'n'-), *v.a.*, oxygéner.

oxygenation (-djè'n'é-), *n.*, oxygénation, *f.*

oxygenize (-djè'n'aïze), *v.a.*, oxygéner.

oxygenizement (-djè'n'aïz'-), *n.*, oxygénation, *f.*

oxygenous (-djè'n'-), *adj.*, d'oxygène.

oxygon, *n.*, (geom.) triangle oxygone, *m.*

oxygonal, *adj.*, oxygone.

oxymel, *n.*, oxymel, *m.*

oxytone (-tône), *n.*, son aigu, *m.*

oxytone (-tône), *adj.*, qui a un son aigu.

oyer (ô-yeur), *n.*, (jur.) audition, *f.* — and terminer ; *audition et jugement.*

oyez! (ô-yèss), *int.*, oyez ! écoutez ! faites silence !

oyster (oïs-teur), *n.*, huître, *f.* — -shell ; *écaille d'huître, f.*

oyster-bed (-bède), *n.*, banc d'huîtres, *m.*

oyster-brood (-broude), *n.*, frai d'huîtres,*m.*

oyster-fishery, *n.*, pêche des huîtres, *f.*

oyster-wench, or **oyster-woman** (-woum a'n), *n.*, marchande d'huîtres ; écaillère, *f.*

P

p, seizième lettre de l'alphabet, p, *m.*

pabular, or **pabulous** (pab'iou-), *adj.*, alimentaire.

pabulum (pab'iou-). *n.*, aliment, *m.*

pace, *n.*, pas ; (man.) pas, *m.* At a great — ; *à grands pas.* To mend, to hurry one's — ; *hâter, presser le pas.*

pace, *v.n.*, aller au pas ; aller ; marcher.

pace, *v.a.*, mesurer ; arpenter ; toiser ; faire marcher ; faire aller au pas

paced (pèste), *adj.*, qui a le pas . . . ; à pas. Slow- — ; *qui a le pas lent.* Thorough- — ; *consommé.*

pacer, *n.*, personne qui marche, *f.* ; cheval qui va bien au pas, *m.*

pacha (pa-shô), *n.*, pacha, *m.*

pachalic, *n.*, pachalik, *m.*

pachyderm (pak'i-deurme), *n.*, pachyderme, *m.*

pachydermatous (pak'i-deur-),*adj.*,pachyderme.

pacific, *adj.*, pacifique ; calme, paisible ; (geog.) pacifique ; équinoxial.

pacification (-fi-ké-), *n.*, pacification, *f.*

pacificator (-ké'-teur), *n.*, pacificateur, *m.*

pacificatory, *adj.*, pacifique.

pacifier (-faï'eur), *n.*, pacificateur, *m.*

pacify (-fa'ye), *v.a.*, pacifier, apaiser, calmer.

pack, *n.*, paquet ; ballot ; fardeau, *m.* ; (band —*troupe*) bande ; (of hounds—*de chiens*) meute, *f.* ; (of cards—*de cartes*) jeu, *m.*

pack, *v.a.*, emballer ; encaisser ; (fish, meat

—*poisson, viande*) mettre en baril ; (herrings—*harengs*) encaquer ; (cards—*cartes*) préparer ; (jury, &c.) trier subrepticement

pack, *v.n.*, s'emballer ; s'encaisser ; faire sa malle. To — off ; *décamper* ; plier *bagage*. To send —ing ; *envoyer paître, envoyer promener*.

package (-'édje), *n.*, emballage, encaissement ; (packet—*paquet*) colis, ballot ; paquet, *m.*

packer, *n.*, emballeur, *m.*

packet, *n.*, paquet, *m.*

packet. or **packet-boat.** *n.*, paquebot, *m.*

packhorse, *n.*, cheval de bât, *m.*

packing, *n.*, emballage, encaissement, *m.* ; (tech.) garniture, *f.*

packing-plate, *n.*, plateau de garniture, *m.*

packing-press, *n.*, presse à empiler, *f.*

packsaddle (-sad'd'l), *n.*, bât, *m.*

packthread (-thrède), *n.*, fil d'emballage, *m.* ; ficelle, *f.*

pact, *n.*, pacte, *m.*

pad, *n.*, coussinet, bourrelet ; tampon, *m.* ; (of a saddle—*de selle*) sellette, *f.* ; (man.) cheval dressé au pas ; (thief—*voleur*) voleur de grand chemin, *m.*

pad, *v.n.*, voler sur le grand chemin ; (to travel—*voyager*) aller lentement.

pad, *v.a.*, ouater ; garnir, rembourrer.

padder, *n.*, (ant.) voleur de grands chemins, *m.*

padding, *n.*, ouate ; garniture, *f.*

paddle (pad'd'l), *n.*, rame courte ; pagaie ; (of a wheel—*de roue*) palette, aube ; (tech.) rame ; (of a lock-gate—*de biez*) pale, ventelle, *f.*

paddle, *v.n.*, ramer ; aller à la pagaie ; patrouiller ; patauger.

paddle, *v.n.*, faire aller à la pagaie ; pagayer.

paddle-beam (-bîme), *n.*, grand bau de roue à aubes, *m.*

paddle-box. *n.*, tambour de roue, *m.*

paddle-door (-dôre), *n.*, vanne, *f.*

paddle-hole (-hôle), *n.*, acqueduc à siphon, *m.*

paddler, *n.*, personne qui patrouille, qui patauge, *f.* ; rameur, *m.*

paddle-shaft (-shâfte), *n.*, arbre de pale, arbre de roue, *m.*

paddle-wheel (-hwîl), *n.*, roue à pales, roue à aubes. *f.*

paddock. *n.*, pré ; (l.u.) gros crapaud, *m.*

padlock, *n.*, cadenas, *m.*

padlock, *v.a.*, cadenasser.

pæony (pî-), *n.*, (bot.) pivoine, *f.*

pagan (pa'te), *adj.*, païen.

pagan, *n.*, païen, *m.*, païenne, *f.*

paganish *adj.*, païen.

paganism (pé-ga'n'iz'm-), *n.*, paganisme, *m.*

paganize (-aize), *v.a.*, rendre païen.

paganize, *v.n.*, se conduire en païen.

page (pédje), *n.*, (pers.) page, *m.* ; (of a book —*de livre*) page, *f.*

page, *v.a.*, (print.) paginer ; faire le service de page.

pageant (pédj'è'n'te), *n.*, spectacle, *m.* ; parade, pompe, *f.*

pageant, *adj.*, de spectacle ; de parade ; pompeux.

pageant, *v.a.*, faire parade de ; donner en spectacle.

pageantry, *n.*, parade, *f.* ; spectacle, *m.* ; pompe, *f.* ; faste, *m.*

page-paper, *n.*, (print.) porte-page, *m.*

paginal (padj'-), *adj.*, composé de pages, des pages.

paging (pédj'-), *n.*, (print.) pagination, *f.*

pagod (pé-), or **pagoda** (-gô-), *n.*, pagode, *f.*

paid, *adj.*, acquitté ; pour acquit ; payé.

pail, *n.*, seau, *m.*, (nav.) baille, *f.*

pailful (pél-foule), *n.*, seau, *m.*, quantité contenue dans un seau, *f.*

pain, *n.*, douleur, peine, *f.*, mal, *m.* —s ; (care—*souci*) peine, *f.* To give any. one — ;

(mental—*au moral*) *faire de la peine à quelqu'un* ; (physical—*au physique*) *faire mal à, causer des douleurs à quelqu'un.* To suffer — ; *souffrir.* To take —s ; *se donner de la peine.* To take —s with ; *soigner.*

pain (pé'n), *v.a.*, faire mal à ; causer de la douleur à ; faire de la peine à ; attrister, tourmenter ; peiner, affliger.

painful (-foule), *adj.*, douloureux, pénible, laborieux.

painfully, *adv.*, douloureusement ; péniblement.

painfulness, *n.*, douleur, nature douloureuse, peine, fatigue, *f.*

painless, *adj.*, sans douleur, sans peine.

painstaker (pé'n'z'ték'-) *n.*, personne qui se donne de la peine, personne laborieuse, *f.*

painstaking, *adj.*, qui se donne de la peine ; laborieux.

paint (pé'n'te), *n.*, couleur ; peinture, *f.* ; (for the face—*pour le visage*) fard, rouge, *m.*

paint, *v.a.*, peindre ; (fig.) peindre, dépeindre ; (the face—*le visage*) farder.

paint, *v.n.*, peindre ; (fig.) peindre, dépeindre ; se farder.

painter, *n.*, peintre ; (nav.) câbleau, *m.* House— ; *peintre en bâtiments, m.*

painting, *n.*, peinture, *f.* ; tableau, *m.*

painture (pé'n't'ieur), *n.*, (l.u.) peinture, *f.*

pair, *n.*, paire, couple, *f.*

pair, *v.a.*, accoupler ; (pers.) unir ; (birds—*oiseaux*) accoupler ; (colours—*couleurs*) marier ; fig.) assortir.

pair, *v.n.*, (of birds—*des oiseaux*) s'accoupler, s'apparier ; (fig.) s'assortir. To — off ; (in parliament—*parlement*) *s'abstenir par compensation de votes contraires.*

pairing, *n.*, accouplement ; appariment, *m.* ; (of partridges—*des perdrix*) pariade. —, — off ; (in parliament—*parlement*) *absence convenue d'un membre ministériel et d'un membre de l'opposition, f.*

palace (pal'éce), *n.*, palais, *m.*

paladin (-kine), *n.*, paladin, *m.*

palanquin (-'a-b'l), *n.*, palanquin, *m.*

palatable (-'a-b'l), *adj.*, agréable au goût ; bon ; de bon goût.

palatableness, *n.*, goût agréable, *m.* ; saveur agréable, *f.*

palatal (pé-), *adj.*, (gram.) palatale.

palatal, *n.*, palatale, *f.*

palate (pal'ate), *n.*, palais (de la bouche), *m.* ; (taste—*sens*) goût, *m.*

palatial (pa-lé-shal), *adj.*, du palais.

palatinate, *n.*, palatinat, *m.*

palatine, *adj.*, palatin.

palatine, *n.*, palatin, *m.*

palaver (-lâ-), *n.*, flagornerie (pop.); conférence, délibération, *f.*

palaver, *v.a.* and *n.*, flagorner (pop.); conférer, délibérer.

palaverer, *n.*, flagorneur, *m.*, flagorneuse, *f.*

pale, *adj.*, pâle, blême ; (fig.) faible.

pale, *v.a.*, pâlir, faire pâlir.

pale, *v.n.*, pâlir.

pale, *n.*, pieu ; palis ; (punishment—*supplice*) pal, *m.* ; (inclosure—*enclos*) enceinte, *f.* ; (fig.) giron, sein, *m.*

pale, *v.a.*, entourer de palis ; palissader ; renfermer. To — up ; *paliser.*

pale-eyed (-a-ye'de), *adj.*, aux yeux ternes.

pale-faced (-féste), *adj.*, au teint pâle.

palely, *adv.*, avec pâleur.

paleness, *n.*, pâleur, *f.*

paleography (pé-li-), *n.*, paléographie, *f.*

paleous (pé li-), *adj.*, pailleux.

paletot, *n.*, paletot, *m.*

palfrey (pâl'-), *n.*, palefroi ; cheval de parade, *m.*

palification (-fi-ké-), *n.*, (arch.) palification, *f.*; pilotage, pilotis, *m.*

paling (pǒl'-), *n.*, palissade, *f.*

palinode (-'ôde), *or* **palinody**, *n.*, palinodie, *f.*

palisade (-céde), *or* **palisado** (-cé-dô), *n.*, palissade, *f.*

palisade, *v.a.*, palissader.

palish (pél'-), *adj.*, un peu pâle; blafard; pâlot.

pall (pôl), *n.*, poêle, drap mortuaire; (of an archbishop—*d'archevêque*) pallium; (mantle—*vêtement*) manteau, *m.*   — -bearer; *personne qui porte un coin du drap mortuaire, f.*

pall, *v.n.*, (of liquors—*des liqueurs*) s'éventer; (to become insipid—*devenir insipide*) devenir fade, insipide; (fig.) s'affaiblir, perdre sa force.

pall, *v.a.*, (to cloak—*envelopper*) couvrir d'un manteau de parade; revêtir; (to make vapid—*rendre insipide*) éventer; (to weaken—*affaiblir*) affaiblir; (to cloy—*rassasier*) rassasier, blaser; (to dispirit—*abattre*) décourager.

palladium (pal-lé-), *n.*, palladium, *m.*

pallet, *n.*, lit de veille; grabat, *m.*; (paint., surg.) palette, *f.*; (hort.) palette, levée, *f.*   — -knife; *spatule, f.*

palliate, *v.a.*, pallier.

palliation (-li-é-), *n.*, palliation, *f.*

palliative, *adj.*, qui pallie; palliatif.

palliative, *n.*, palliatif, *m.*

pallid, *adj.*, pâle, pâlot.

pallidity, *or* **pallidness**, *n.*, pâleur, *f.*

pallidly, *adv.*, avec pâleur.

pallium, *n.*, pallium, *m.*

pall-mall (pèl-mèl), *n.*, mail, *m.*

palm (pâme), *n.*, (of the hand—*de la main*) paume, *f.*; (bot.) palmier, *m.*; (branch—*branche*) palme; (nav.) patte, *f.*; (measure—*mesure*) palme, *m.*   — -Sunday; *dimanche des Rameaux, m.*   — -tree; *palmier, m.*

palm, *v.a.*, cacher dans la paume de la main; escamoter; (to impose—*tromper*) imposer; (to handle—*toucher*) manier. To — a thing upon any one for; *faire passer à quelqu'un une chose pour.*

palma-christi (-kris'-), *n.*, palma-christi, ricin, *m.*

palmate, *or* **palmated** (-mét'-), *adj.*, palmé.

palmer (pâ-meur), *n.*, pèlerin; croisé, *m.*

palmiferous, *adj.*, palmifère.

palmiped, *adj.*, (orni.) palmipède.

palmister, *n.*, chiromancien, *m.*

palmistry, *n.*, chiromancie, *f.*; escamotage, *m.*

palmy (pâ'm'é), *adj.*, chargé de palmiers; (fig.) beau, glorieux, victorieux.

palp, *n.*, (ent.) palpe, *f.*

palpability, *or* **palpableness**, *n.*, nature palpable, *f.*

palpable (-pa-b'l), *adj.*, palpable.

palpably, *adv.*, palpablement.

palpation (-pé-), *n.*, attouchement, *m.*

palpebral (pal-pè-). *adj.*, (anat.) palpébral.

palpitate, *v.n.*, palpiter.

palpitation (-pi-té-), *n.*, palpitation, *f.*

palsical (pôl-zi-), *adj.*, paralytique; paralysé.

palsied (pôl-zîde), *adj.*, frappé de paralysie; paralysé.

palsy (pôl-zi), *n.*, paralysie, *f.*

palsy (pôl-zi), *v.a.*, paralyser.

palter (pôl-), *v.a.*, tergiverser; biaiser.

palterer (pôl-), *n.*, tergiversateur, *m.*

paltriness (pôl-), *n.*, mesquinerie; nature chétive, *f.*

paltry (pôl-), *adj.*, chétif; méchant, mesquin; qui fait pitié; pitoyable; pauvre.

paly (pé-), *adj.*, pâle; (her.) divisé par pals.

pamper, *v.a.*, nourrir à l'excès; choyer; bien traiter, flatter, dorloter.

pampered (-peur'de), *adj.*, trop nourri; riche; abondant.

pamphlet, *n.*, brochure, *f.*; (b.s.) pamphlet, *m.*

pamphlet, *v.a.*, écrire des brochures; des pamphlets.

pamphleteer (-flèt'îre), *n.*, auteur de brochures; pamphlétaire, *m.*

pan, *n.*, terrine; casserole; poêle, *f.*; (of a gun—*de fusil à pierre*) bassinet, *m.*

panacea (-cî-a), *n.*, panacée, *f.*

panado (-né-dô), *n.*, panade, *f.*

pancake (-kéke), *n.*, crêpe, *f.*

pancratic, *or* **pancratical**, *adj.*, (antiq.) du pancratiaste.

pancratist, *n.*, (antiq.) pancratiaste, *m.*

pancreas (pan'gn'krî-ace), *n.*, (anat.) pancréas, *m.*

pandect, *n.*, traité complet, *m.*   —s; *pandectes, f.pl.*

pandemonium (-di-mô-), *n.*, pandémonium, *m.*

pander, *n.*, complaisant; ministre complaisant des amours, des galanteries, *m.*

pander, *v.a.*, faire le complaisant (en amours, en galanteries).

pander, *v.n.*, être le complaisant de, être le ministre complaisant de (en amours, en galanteries).

panderism, *n.*, métier de complaisant (en amours, en intrigues); métier d'entremetteur, *m.*

pane, *n.*, carreau, *m.*; vitre, *f.*   — of glass; *carreau.*

panegyric, *or* **panegyrical** (pa'n-i-djir'-), *adj.*, de panégyrique.

panegyric, *n.*, panégyrique, *m.*

panegyrist (-i-djir'-), *n.*, panégyriste, *m.*

panegyrize (pa'n-i-djir'aize), *v.a.*, faire le panégyrique de.

panegyrize, *v.n.*, faire un panégyrique.

panel, *n.*, (arch.) panneau, *m.*; (jur.) tableau, *m.*, liste, *f.*

panel, *v.a.*, faire des panneaux à.

paneless (pé'n-), *adj.*, sans carreau, sans vitre.

pang (pan'gn), *v.a.*, faire souffrir des angoisses à, tourmenter, faire souffrir.

pang, *n.*, angoisse; douleur, *f.*; saisissement, *m.*

panic, *n.*, panique; terreur panique, *f.*   — struck; *saisi d'une terreur panique.*

panic, *adj.*, panique.

panic-grass (-grace), *n.*, (bot.) panic, panis, *m.*

panicle (pa'n'i-k'l), *n.*, (bot.) panicule, *f.*

paniculate (-'ik-iou-), *or* **paniculated** (-lét'-), *adj.*, (bot.) paniculé, en panicule.

panification (-fi-ké-), *n.*, panification, *f.*

pannade, *n.*, (man.) courbette, *f.*

pannage (-nédje), *n.*, glandée, *f.*; panage, *m.*

pannel, *n.*, (saddle—*selle*) bât; (of a hawk—*de faucon*) gésier, *m.*

paunier (pa'n-ieur), *n.*, panier, *m.*

panoply, *n.*, panoplie, armure complète, *f.*

panorama (-râ-), *n.*, panorama, *m.*

panoramic, *or* **panoramical** (-râ-), *adj.*, panoramique, panoramique.

pansy (-zé), *n.*, (bot.) pensée, *f.*

pant, *n.*, palpitation, *f.*; battement, *m.*

pant, *v.n.*, battre, haleter, palpiter. To — after; *soupirer après.*

pantaloons (-lou'n'ze), *n.*, pantalon à plods; (pl.) pantalon; (thea.) pantalon, *m.*

panter, *n.*, personne dont le cœur palpite, *f.*

pantess, *n.*, pantoiement, *m.*

pantheism (-thi-iz'me), *n.*, panthéisme, *m.*

pantheist, *n.*, panthéiste, *m.*

pantheistic, *or* **pantheistical** (-thi-), *adj.*, panthéiste.

pantheon (-thi-), *n.*, panthéon, *m.*

panther (-theur), *n.*, panthère. *f.*

pantile (-tail), *n.*, tuile faitière ; faitière, *f*

panting, *n.*, battement de cœur, *m.* ; palpitation, *f.* ; (fig.) désir ardent, *m.*

pantingly, *adv.*, en palpitant.

pantler, *n.*, panetier, *m.*

pantofle (-tou-f'l), *n.*, pantoufle ; (of the pope—*du pape*) mule, *f.*

pantometer, *n.*, (geom.) pantomètre. *m.*

pantomime (-tô-maime), *n.*, pantomime, *f.* ; (pers.) pantomime, *m.*

pantomimic, *or* **pantomimical**, *adj.*, de pantomime ; pantomime.

pantomimist, *n.*, pantomime, *m.*

panton-shoe (-shou), *n.*, (of horses—*pour chevaux*) fer à pantoufle, *m.*, pantoufle, *f.*

pantry, *n.*, garde-manger, *m.* ; office, dépense, *f.*

pap, *n.*, tetin, teton, *m.* ; mamelle. *f.* ; mamelon, *m.* ; (food—*nourriture*) bouillie ; (of fruit —*des fruits*) pulpe, *f.*

pap, *v.a.*, nourrir de bouillie.

papa (-pà), *n.*, papa, père, *m.*

papacy (pé-pa-), *n.*, papauté, *f.*

papal (pé-), *adj.*, papal, du pape.

papaverous (-pé-veur'-), *adj.*, de pavot.

papaw (-pô), *n.*, (bot.) papaye, *f.* —*tree* ; *papayer*, *m.*

paper (pé-peur), *n.*, papier, *m.* ; feuille de papier ; (newspaper—*journal*) feuille, *f.*, journal, papier public ; (article) morceau, article ; (fin.) papier-monnaie, *m.* ; (com.) papier, *m.*, valeurs, *f.pl.*. Brown —; *papier gris.* Foreign —; *papier pelure ; papier pelure d'oignon.* Gilt-edged —; *papier doré sur tranche.* Imperial —; *papier jésus.* Stained —; *papier peint.* Stamped —; *papier timbré.* Waste —; *papier de rebut, m. ;* (print.) *maculature, f.* Whity brown —; *papier bulle.* Blotting—; *papier brouillard.* Foolscap, foolscap—; *papier écolier.* Letter-—, note—; *papier à lettres.* Petition—; *papier ministre.* Printing—; *papier à imprimer ; papier d'impression.* Tissue-—; *papier de soie ; papier joseph ; papier serpente.* — holder, —-weight ; *serre-papiers, m.* —s; *papiers, titres, mémoires, manuscrits, m.pl.*

paper, *adj.*, de papier ; (fig.) faible.

paper, *v.a.*, (a room—*une chambre*) décorer de papier ; tapisser de papier ; (to wrap—*envelopper*) mettre dans-du papier.

paper-credit (-crèd'-), *n.*, crédit sur effets ; papier-monnaie, *m.*

papered (-peur'de), *adj.*, décoré de papier ; tapissé de papier.

paper-faced (-fés'te), *adj.*, à figure de papier mâché.

paper-hanger (-han'gn'eur), *n.*, colleur de papier, *m.*

paper-hangings, *n.pl.*, papier-tenture, papier peint, *m.*

paper-knife (-naïfe), *n.*, couteau à papier ; plioir, *m.*

paper-maker (-mék'-), *n.*, fabricant de papier, papetier, *m.*

paper-making (-mék'-), *n.*, fabrication du papier, *f.*

paper-manufactory (-'iou-fak-), *n.*, papeterie ; fabrique de papier, *f.*

paper-manufacturer (-'iou-fak-tiour'-), *n.*, fabricant de papier, papetier, *m.*

paper-mill, *n.*, moulin à papier, *m.* ; papeterie, *f.*

paper-money (-meu'n-nè), *n.*, papier-monnaie, *m.*

paper-rush (-reushe), *n.*, papyrus, papyrier, *m.*

paper-stainer (-sté'n'-), *n.*, fabricant de papier peint ; dominotier, *m.*

paper-staining (-sté'n'-), *n.*, fabrication du papier peint ; dominoterie, *f.*

paper-trade (-tréde), *n.*, papeterie. *f.*

paper-war (-wor), *n.*, guerre de plume. *f.*

papescent (-pèz'-), *adj.*, pulpeux.

papess, *n.*, papesse, *f.*

papier-mâché (pap'l-è-mâ-shè), *n.*, papier mâché, *m.*

papilio (pa-pil'yô), *n.*, papillon, *m.*

papilionaceous (-né-sheusse), *adj.*, (bot.) papilionacé, papillonacé.

papilla (pa-pil-la), *n.*, (anat.) papille, *f.*

papillary, **papilloes**, *or* **papillous**, *adj.*, papillaire.

papillate, *v.n.*, (anat.) se former en papille.

papism (pé-piz'm), *n.*, papisme, *m.*

papist (pé-), *n.*, papiste, *m.*

papistic, *or* **papistical** (pé-), *adj.*, papistique.

papistry (pé-), *n.*, papisme, *m.*

pappose, *or* **pappous**, *adj.*, (bot.) duveteux.

pappus, *n.*, (bot.) aigrette, *f.*

pappy, *adj.*, comme de la bouillie ; mou ; succulent.

papyrus (pa-paï-), *n.* (*papyri*) papyrus, *m.*

par (pàr), *n.*, égalité, *f.* ; (com.) pair, *m.* At —; *au pair.*

parable (par'a-b'l), *n.*, parabole, *f.*

parable, *v.a.*, représenter par une parabole.

parabola, *n.*, (math.) parabole, *f.*

parabole (-bô-li), *n.*, (rhet.) similitude ; comparaison, *f.*

parabolic, *or* **parabolical**, *adj.*, par parabole ; parabolique ; allégorique.

parabolically, *adv.*, paraboliquement.

paraboloid (-loïde), *n.*, (solid) paraboloïde, *m.* ; (parabola) ⊙ paraboloïde, *f.*

parachute (-shioute), *n.*, parachute, *m.*

paraclete (-clìte), *n.*, paraclet, *m.*

parade (pa-réde), *n.*, parade, *f.* ; étalage, faste, *m.* ; (fenc., milit.) parade, *f.*

parade, *v.a.*, faire parade de ; (milit.) faire faire la parade à.

parade, *v.n.*, se donner en spectacle ; marcher ; (milit.) faire la parade.

paradigm (-dime), *n.*, paradigme, *m.*

paradise (-daïce), *n.*, paradis, *m.*

paradisiacal (-di-saï-), *adj.*, du paradis.

paradox, *n.*, paradoxe, *m.*

paradoxical, *adj.*, paradoxal.

paradoxically, *adv.*, d'une manière paradoxale.

paradoxicalness (-doks'-), *n.*, caractère paradoxal, *m.*

paragoge (-gô-dji), *n.*, paragoge, *f.*

paragogic, *or* **paragogical** (-godj'-), *adj.*, paragogique.

paragon, *n.*, parangon, modèle ; modèle parfait, chef-d'œuvre ; (print.) parangon, *m.*

paragram, *n.*, jeu de mots, calembour, *m.*

paragrammatist, *n.*, faiseur de jeux de mots, faiseur de calembours, *m.*

paragraph, *n.*, paragraphe ; alinéa, *m.* ; (poet.) strophe, *f.* ; (in newspapers—*de journal*), article, *m.*

paragraphic, *or* **paragraphical**, *adj.*, composé de paragraphes.

paragraphically, *adv.*, par paragraphes.

paralipsis (-lèp-), *n.*, paralipse, *f.*

paralipomena (-po'm'i-), *n.pl.*, Paralipomènes, *m.pl.*

parallactic, *or* **parallactical**, *adj.*, parallactique.

parallax, *n.*, (astron.) parallaxe, *f.*

parallel, *adj.*, parallèle ; (fig.) semblable, pareil. To run —with ; *être parallèle à ; aller parallèlement à ;* (fig.) *se conformer à.*

parallel, *n.*, ligne parallèle ; direction parallèle ; (fort.. geom.) parallèle, *f.* ; (geog.) parallèle, *m.* ; (fig.) comparaison, conformité, *f.*, parallèle, *m.* To draw a — between ; *établir un parallèle entre.*

parallel, *v.a.*, mettre dans une ligne parallèle à ; placer parallèlement ; (fig.) correspondre à, ressembler à, mettre en parallèle.

parallelism (-'iz'm), *n.*, parallélisme, *m.* ; (fig.) ressemblance, comparaison, *f.*

parallelly, *adv.*, parallèlement.

parallelogram, *n.*, parallélogramme, *m.*

parallelogramic, *or* **parallelogramical**, *adj.*, parallélogrammatique.

parallelopiped ('-o-païe-), *or* **parallelopipedon** (-pip'i-), *n.*, (geom.) parallélipipède, parallélépipède, *m.*

paralogism (-djz'm), *or* **paralogy** (-dji), *n.*, paralogisme, *m.*

paralogize (-djaïze), *v.n.*, faire de mauvais raisonnements.

paralysis (-cice), *n.*, paralysie, *f.*

paralytic, *or* **paralytical**, *adj.*, paralytique.

paralytic, *n.*, paralytique, *m.*, *f.*

paralyze (-laïze), *v.a.*, paralyser.

parameter ('-i-teur), *n.*, (geom.) paramètre, *m.*

paramount (-maou'n'te), *adj.*, souverain, dominant ; en chef ; suprême. — to ; *supérieur à.*

paramount, *n.*, souverain, chef, *m.*

paramour, *n.*, amant, *m.*

paranymph (-ni'm'fe), *n.*, paranymphe ; (support) soutien, *m.*

parapet, *n.*, parapet, *m.*

paraphernal, *adj.*, paraphernal.

paraphernalia (-feur-né-), *n.pl.*, (jur.) paraphernaux, *m.pl.* paraphernal ; attirail, *m.sing.* ; ornements, *m.pl.*

paraphimosis (-mô-cice), *n.*, paraphimosis, *m.*

paraphrase (-fréze), *n.*, paraphrase, *f.*

paraphrase, *v.a.*, paraphraser.

paraphrast, *n.*, paraphraste, *m.*

paraphrastic, *or* **paraphrastical**, *adj.*, en forme de paraphrase.

paraphrastically, *adv.*, en forme de paraphrase.

paraplegy (-pledj'i), *n.*, paraplégie, *f.*

paraselene (-sè-li-ni), *n.*, (astron.) parasélène, *f.*

parasite (-ça-ïte), *n.*, parasite, *m.* ; (bot.) plante parasite, *f.*

parasitic, *or* **parasitical** (-cit'-), *adj.*, de parasite ; (bot., ent.) parasite.

parasitically, *adv.*, en parasite.

parasitism (-cit'-iz'm), *n.*, conduite de parasite, *f.*

parasol (-çol), *n.*, ombrelle, *f.* ; parasol, *m.*

parboil (pâr-boïl), *v.a.*, faire bouillir à demi ; faire cuire à demi ; bouillir à demi ; cuire à demi.

parcœ (pâr-ci), *n.*, (myth.) Parques, *f.pl.*

parcel, *n.*, (bundle—*paquet*) paquet, *m.* ; (a part—*portion*) parcelle, portion, partie, *f.* ; (a number, in contempt—*un certain nombre, par mépris*) tas, *m.* ; (com.) partie, *f.* ; envoi, *m.* Bill of —s ; *facture, f.*

parcel, *or* **parcel out**, *v.a.*, morceler ; partager ; distribuer par parcelles.

parcenary (pâr-cè-), *n.*, (jur.) indivis (par succession), *m.*

parcener (pâr-cè'n-), *n.*, (jur.) propriétaire indivis (par succession), *m.*

parch (pârtshe), *v.a.*, brûler, rôtir ; dessécher (par la chaleur).

parch, *v.n.*, se brûler ; se rôtir ; se dessécher (par la chaleur).

parchedness (pârtsh'èd-), *n.*, état brûlé, état rôti, état desséché, *m.* ; aridité, *f.*

parching (pârtsh'-), *adj.*, brûlant, dévorant.

parchment (pârtsh'-), *n.*, parchemin, *m.* —maker ; *parcheminier, m.* —works ; *parcheminerie, f.sing.*

pard (pârde), *n.*, léopard, *m.*

pardon (pâr'd'n), *n.*, pardon, *m.* ; grâce, *f.* To ask any one —; *demander pardon à quelqu'un.*

pardon, *v.a.*, pardonner, pardonner à ; faire grâce de ; gracier.

pardonable (pâr-do'n'-a-b'l), *adj.*, graciable, pardonnable ; (of persons—*des personnes*) digne de pardon.

pardonableness, *n.*, nature pardonnable, *f.*

pardonably, *adv.*, d'une manière pardonnable.

pardoner (pâr'dn'-), *n.*, personne qui pardonne, *f.*

pardoning (pâr'd'n'-), *adj.*, qui pardonne ; clément ; miséricordieux.

pare, *v.a.*, rogner ; ébarber ; (fruit) peler ; (man.) rogner. To — one's nails ; *se rogner, se couper les ongles.*

paregoric (par-i-), *adj.*, parégorique, anodin.

paregoric, *n.*, parégorique, anodin, *m.*

parenchyma (-rè'n'ki-), *n.*, parenchyme, *m.*

parent (pér'-), *n.*, père, *m.*, mère, *f.* —s ; *père et mère, parents.*

parentage (pér'è'nt'édje), *n.*, naissance, extraction, *f.*

parental, *adj.*, de père, de mère ; paternel, maternel.

parenthesis (-rè'n'thi-cice), *n.* (*parentheses*), parenthèse, *f.* In a —; *entre parenthèses.*

parenthetic, *or* **parenthetical** (-thèt'-), *adj.*, par parenthèse ; (pers.) qui emploie souvent des parenthèses.

parenthetically (-thèt'-), *adv.*, par parenthèse.

parenticide (-caïde) *n.*, parricide, *m.*

parentless (pér'-), *adj.*, sans père ni mère.

parer (pér'-), *n.*, personne qui rogne, qui ébarbe, qui pèle, *f.* ; (thing—*chose*) ébarboir, *m.*

parget (pâr-djète), *n.*, pierre à plâtre, *f.* ; gypse ; (mas.) crépi, *m.*

parget, *v.a.*, (mas.) crépir.

pargeter (pâr-), *n.*, (mas.) ouvrier qui crépit ; plâtrier, *m.*

pargeting, *n.*, crépi, *m.*

parhelion, *or* **parhelium** (-hî'-), *n.* (*parhelia*), parélie, parhélie, *m.*

pariah (pâ-ri-à), *n.*, paria, *m.*

parial (pér'al-), *or* **pair royal** (pér'-), *n.*, trois cartes de la même sorte, *f.pl.* ; brelan, *m.*

parian (pé-), *adj.*, de Paros.

parietal (pa-raï-èt'-), *adj.*, de mur ; (anat.) pariétal.

parietary (-raï-è-ta-), *n.*, (bot.) pariétaire, *f.*

paring (pér'igne), *n.*, pelure ; rognure, épluchure, *f.*

paring-knife (-naïfe), *n.*, tranchet, *m.*

parish, *adj.*, de la commune ; communal ; (ecc.) de la paroisse, paroissial.

parish, *n.*, commune ; (ecc.) paroisse, *f.*

parishioner, *n.*, habitant de la commune ; (ecc.) paroissien.

parisian (-rish'i-), *adj.*, de Paris, parisien.

parisian, *n.*, Parisien, *m.*, Parisienne, *f.*

parisyllabic, *or* **parisyllabical**, *adj.*, parisyllabique.

paritor, *n.*, appariteur, huissier, *m.*

parity, *n.*, parité, *f.*

park (pârke), *n.*, parc ; (artil.) parc, *m.*

park, *v.a.*, enfermer dans un parc ; parquer.

parlance (pâr-), *n.*, conversation, *f.* ; langage, *m.*

parley (pâr-), *n.*, pourparler, *m.* ; conférence, *f.* To beat a —; *battre la chamade.*

parley, *v.n.*, être en pourparler ; parlementer.

parliament (pâr-lè-), *n.*, parlement, *m.* ; chambre, *f.* ; chambres, *f.pl.* House of —; *palais du parlement, m.* ; *chambre, f.* Act of —; *loi, f.*

parliamentarian (-té-), *or* **parliamen-**

teer (-tire), n., (English hist.—hist. d'Angleterre) parlementaire, m.

parliamentary, adj., parlementaire; du
parlement.

parlour (pâr-leur), n., petit salon; parloir, m.

parlous (pâr-), adj., (ant.) périlleux; fin,
rusé.

parmesan (pâr-mè-za'n), adj., de Parme.
— cheese; parmesan, m.

parochial (-rô-ki-), adj., de la commune;
communal; (ecc.) de la paroisse. paroissial.

parochially, adv., par commune; par paroisse.

parodic, or **parodical**, adj., parodié, travesti.

parody, n., parodie. f.; adage, proverbe, m.

parody, v.a., parodier, travestir.

parol, or **parole** (-rôle), n., (jur.) parole, déclaration de vive voix, f.; plaidoyer, m.

parol, or **parole** (-rôle), adj., oral; verbal;
de vive voix.

parole, n., parole; (milit.) parole, f.; (watchword) mot d'ordre, m.

paronomasia (-mé-zi-), n., paronomase, f.

paronomastic, or **paronomastical**,
adj., par forme de paronomase.

paronymous, adj., paronyme.

paroquet (-kète), n., perruche, f.

parotid (-rô-), adj., parotidien.

parotis (-rô-), n., parotide, f.

paroxysm (-iz'm), n., paroxysme, accès, m.

parrel, n., (nav.) racage, m.

parricidal (-çaïd'-), adj., parricide.

parricide (-çaïde), n., parricide, m.

parrot, n., perroquet, m.; perruche, f.

parry, v.a., parer; éluder.

parse (pârse), v.a., (gram.) analyser.

parsimonious (pâr-si-mô-), adj., parcimonieux.

parsimoniously, adv., avec parcimonie.

parsimoniousness, or **parsimony**, n.,
parcimonie, f.

parsing (pârs'-), n., (gram.) analyse, f.

parsley (pârs-), n., persil, m.

parsnip (pârs-), n., panais, m.

parson (pâr-s'n), n., curé, pasteur, m.

parsonage (pâr-s'n-édje), n., presbytère,
m.; cure, f. — house; presbytère, m.

part (pârte), n., partie; (portion) portion,
part, f.; (thea.) rôle; (side, defence—parti)
parti, m.; défense; (of a book—de livre) livraison, f.; (quarter—quartier) quartier, m.; (mus.)
partie, f. —s; (talent) talent, m., moyens, m.pl.;
(country—contrée) pays, m., pays, m.pl.; contrées,
f.pl. In —; en partie. In —s; par livraisons.
In a great —; en grande partie. For my —;
pour ma part, pour moi. To take any one's —;
prendre le parti, la défense de quelqu'un. On any
one's —; de la part de quelqu'un. In good —;
en bonne part.

part, v.a., partager; séparer; diviser; (nav.)
casser; (chem.) faire le départ de.

part, v.n., se séparer; se quitter; (nav.) aller
en dérive. To — with; se défaire de; abandonner, céder: se dessaisir de.

partake, v.n. (preterit, Partook; past part.,
Partaken), participer à; prendre part à. To —
of; prendre part à; participer à; (to have something of—avoir quelque chose de) participer de.

partaker (-têk'-), n., personne qui prend
part, f.; participant, m.

parter (pârt'-), n., personne qui sépare, f.

parterre (pâr-tère), n., (hort.) parterre, m.

partial (pâr-shal), adj., (biassed—prévenu)
partial; (not total—en partie) partiel; particulier. To be — to (to like—aimer); aimer.

partiality (pâr-shi-), n., partialité; prédilection, f.; goût, m.

partialize (pâr-shal' aïze) v.a., (ant.) rendre
partial

partially (pâr-shal-), adv., partialement;
partiellement.

partibility, n., divisibilité, f.

partible (pârt'i-b'l), adj., divisible.

participable (-pa-b'l), adj., à quoi l'on peut
participer.

participant, adj., participant, qui partage.

participant, n., participant, m.

participate, v.a., participer à, partager.

participate, v.n., avoir une part. To — in;
prendre part à; participer à; s'associer à. To
— of; participer de.

participation (pâr-ti-ci-pé-), n., participation; part, f.

participative (-pét'-), adj., capable de participer.

participial. adj., de la nature du participe.

participially, adv., comme participe.

participle (pâr-ti-cip'l), n., (gram.) participe, m.

particle (pâr-ti-k'l), n., particule; molécule,
f.; grain, m.; la plus petite partie, f.

particular (pâr-tik'iou-leur), adj., particulier; spécial; précis, exact, minutieux; (scrupulous—scrupuleux) scrupuleux; (over nice—trop
délicat) difficile, exigeant; (singular—singulier)
remarquable, étrange. — in one's dress; recherché dans sa toilette. To be — in choosing
things; bien choisir, faire un bon choix.

particular, n., particularité, f.; détail;
point circonstancié. m.; circonstance, f. In
—; particulièrement; en particulier.

particularity, n., particularité, f.; détail,
m.; point circonstancié, m.

particularize (-'aïze), v.a., particulariser,
spécifier.

particularize (-'aïze), v.n., entrer dans des
particularités.

particularly (-leur'li), adv., particulièrement; individuellement.

parting (pârt'-), adj., de séparation; d'adieu.

parting, n., séparation, f.; départ; adieu, m.

partisan (pâr-ti-za'n), n., partisan; (staff—
bâton) bâton de commandement, m.; (halbert—
hallebarde) pertuisane, f.

partition (par-tish'-), n., (division) partage,
m., répartition; division; séparation; (bot..
carp.) cloison, paroi, f.; (separated part—portion
séparée) endroit à part, m.

partition, v.a., partager; (carp.) séparer
par une cloison.

partitive (pâr-), adj., (gram.) partitif.

partitively, adv., comme partitif.

partly (pârt'-), adv., en partie.

partner (pârt'-), n., personne qui partage,
f.; (com.) associé, m., associée, f.; (mate—camarade) compagnon, m., compagne, f.; sociétaire,
m., f.; (in dancing—danse) danseur, m., danseuse, f., cavalier, partenaire, m., dame, f.; (at
cards—aux cartes) partenaire, m. Sleeping —;
associé commanditaire; commanditaire, m.

partner, v.a., associer à; se joindre à.

partnership, n., association, société, f.

partridge (pâr-), n., perdrix, f.

parturient (-tiou-), adj., prête à enfanter;
(of animals—des animaux) prête à mettre bas.

parturition (pâr-tiou-rish'-), n., enfantement, m., parturition, f.

party (pâr-), n., parti, m., partie, f.; (milit.)
parti, m.; (pers.) partie, personne, f., individu,
m.; (of pleasure—de plaisir) partie; (company
—compagnie) réunion, société, f., monde, m.;
(one concerned—intéressé) partie intéressée, f.,
intéressé, complice, m. Evening —; soirée, f.
Leader of a —; chef de parti, m. To go to a —;
aller en soirée. To go to a dinner —; aller dîner
en ville. To be of the —; être de la partie. To
be a — to; prendre part à; être complice de.
Will you join our —? voulez-vous être des nôtres?

party-coloured (-keul'leurde), adj.. bigarré.

party-man, *n.*, factieux ; homme de parti,*m.*
party-wall (-wôl), *n.*, mur mitoyen, *m.*
parvenu (pär-vi-niou), *n.*, parvenu, *m.*
paschal (pas-kal), *adj.*, pascal.
pasch-flower, *or* **pasque-flower** (pask-fla-oueur),*n.*,(bot.) pulsatille, coquelourde, herbe du vent, *f.*
pasquil (-kwil), *or* **pasquin** (-kwine), *n.*, pasquin, *m.*
pasquil, *or* **pasquin**, *v.a.*, faire des pasquinades sur.
pasquilant (-kwi-),*or* **pasquiller** (-kwil'-), *n.*, faiseur de pasquinades, *m.*
pasquin. *V.* **pasquil**.
pasquin, *or* **pasquinade** (-kwi'n'-), *v.a.*, faire des pasquinades sur.
pasquinade (-kwi'n'-), *n.*, pasquinade, *f.*
pass, *v.n.*, passer ; se passer ; (to occur—*arriver*) se passer ; (to die—*décéder*) mourir ; (of time—*du temps*) passer, se passer, s'écouler ; (to give judgment—*rendre un arrêt*) prononcer un jugement. To — away, off ; *passer, se passer.* To — by; *passer à côté.* To — on ; *passer son chemin.* To — for ; *passer pour.* To — out ; *sortir.* To — over; *franchir ; passer ; s'écouler.*
pass, *v.a.*, passer ; passer par; (to transfer—*transporter*) transférer, faire passer ; (to pronounce—*rendre*) prononcer ; (a law—*une loi*) faire rendre ; (compliment) faire; (one's word—*sa parole*) engager ; (accounts—*des comptes*) approuver ; (fig.) passer, surpasser. To — a trick on ; *jouer un tour à.* To — away ; *passer, employer.* To — by ; (near—*près*) passer à côté de ; (beyond—*au delà*) passer au delà de ; (to omit—*négliger*) omettre, sauter ; ne pas faire attention à ; (to forgive—*pardonner*) pardonner. To — for ; *faire passer pour.* To — over ; *franchir, passer, traverser*; (to pardon—*passer sur*) pardonner ; (to omit—*omettre*) passer ; sauter, omettre; *ne pas voir.* To bring to — ; *amener ; faire arriver.* To be brought to — ; *arriver.*
pass, *n.*, (entrance—*entrée*) passage, défilé ; (permission) permis ; (passport) passeport ; (for vagrants and impotent persons—*vagabonds et impotents*) ordre de transporter des vagabonds et des infirmes à leur demeure respective ; (state —*état*) état, *m.*, extrémité, *f.* ; (nav.) congé, *m.*, lettres de mer, *f.pl.* ; (fenc.) passe, *f.*
passable (-a-b'l),*adj.*, praticable; pénétrable; (of water—*rivières, &c.*) navigable ; (tolerable) passable, tolérable.
passably, *adv.*, passablement ; tolérablement.
passade (-çâde), **passado** (-çâ-dô), *or* **pass**, *n.*, (fenc.) botte, passe, *f.*
passade (-çâde), *n.*, (man.) passade, *f.*
passage (-cédje), *n.*, (passing over—*action de passer*) passage, *m.*, traversée, *f.* ; (road—*route*) chemin, accès, *m.* ; (entrance—*entrée*) entrée, *f.* ; (arch.) couloir, corridor ; (man., mus., and of a book—*et de livre*) passage, *m.*
passage (-cédje), *v.a.* and *n.*, (man.) passager.
passenger (-djeur), *n.*, (on boats—*sur un vaisseau*) passager, *m.*, passagère, *f.* ; (in the street—*dans la rue*) passant, *m.* ; (in vehicles—*en voiture*) voyageur, *m.*, voyageuse, *f.*
passer, *or* **passer-by** (pâss'eur,-ba'ye), *n.*, passant, *m.*
passerine (pass'eur'ine), *adj.*, (orni.) de passereau.
passibility, *or* **passibleness**, *n.*, passibilité, *f.*
passible (-si-b'l), *adj.*, passible.
passing, *adj.*, (exceeding—*extrême*) extrême, éminent ; (ephemeral—*éphémère*) passager, éphémère.
passing, *adv.*, extrêmement, éminemment, étonnamment.
passing, *n.*, passage ; cours, *m.*

passing-bell, *n.*, glas, *m.*
passing-place, *n.*, (railways) gare d'évitement ; voie supplémentaire, *f.*
passion (pash'-), *n.*, passion ; (anger—*courroux*) colère, *f.*, courroux, emportement ; (zeal—*zèle*) zèle, *m.*, ardeur, *f.* In a — ; *en colère.* To fly into, to put one's self into a — ; *se mettre en colère; s'emporter.*
passionary (pash'-), *n.*, légendes des martyrs,*f.pl.*
passionate (pash'-), *adj.*, colère, colérique, irascible, vif, emporté ; (of things—*des choses*) passionné, ardent.
passionately (pash'-), *adv.*, de passion ; passionnément ; avec emportement, avec colère ; ardemment.
passionateness (pash'-), *n.*, caractère passionné ; caractère irascible, colérique, *m.*
passion-flower (-fla-weur), *n.*, (bot.) passiflore, grenadille, *f.*
passion-week (-wike), *n.*, semaine sainte, *f.*
passive, *adj.*, passif.
passively, *adv.*, passivement.
passiveness, *n.*, nature passive ; passibilité, *f.*
passless (pâss'-), *adj.*, sans passage.
passover (pâss'ô-), *n.*, Pâque, *f.*
passport (pâss'-), *n.*, passeport, *m.*
past (pâst), *adj.*, passé. — a child ; *qui a passé l'enfance.* — cure; *incurable.* — dispute ; *incontestable.* These — days; *ces jours derniers.*
past, *prep.*, au delà de ; au-dessus de ; hors de ; (of age—*de l'âge*) plus de ; (of the hour—*de l'heure*) passé, sonné, et. He is — ten ; *il a plus de dix ans.* It is — ten ; *il est dix heures passées, sonnées.* It is — twelve ; *il est midi sonné, passé.* Half— twelve; *midi et demi.*
past, *n.*, passé, *m.*
paste (péste),*n.*,(dough—*pâte de farine*) pâte ; (cement—*colle de pâte*) colle ; (paint.) maroufle, *f.* ; (imitation gem—*pierre fausse*) stras, *m.*
paste, *v.a.*, coller. To — up; poser, afficher.
pasteboard (-bôrde), *n.*, carton, *m.* —maker ; cartonnier, *m.*
pasteboard, *adj.*, de carton.
pastel (-), *n.*, pastel, *m.*
pastern (pâs-teurne), *n.*, pâturon, *m.*
pasticcio (pas-tit'shi-ô), *n.*,mélange ; (mus.) pastiche, *m.*
pastil (pâs-), *n.*, pastel, crayon de pastel, *m.* ; (pharm.) pastille, *f.*
pastime (pâs'taïme), *n.*, passe-temps, *m.* ; récréation, *f.*
pastor (pâs-teur), *n.*, pasteur ; pâtre ; (milit.) pâtureur, *m.*
pastoral (pâs-), *adj.*, pastoral.
pastoral, *n.*, pastorale, églogue, *f.*
pastorally, *adv.*, pastoralement.
pastorless, *adj.*, sans pasteur.
pastorlike (-laïke), *or* **pastorly**, *adj.*, pastoral ; de pasteur.
pastorship, *n.*, fonctions pastorales, *f. pl.*
pastry (pés'-), *n.*, pâtisserie, *f.*
pastry-cook (-couke), *n.*, pâtissier, *m.*
pasturable (pâst'ieur'a-b'l), *adj.*, propre au pâturage ; de pâturage.
pasturage (-édje), *n.*, pâturage, *m.*
pasture (pâst'ieur), *n.*, pâture, *f.* ; (hunt.) viandis, *m.*
pasture, *v.n.*, paître.
pasture, *v.a.*, faire paître.
pasture-land, *n.*, pâturage, *m.*
pasty (pés'ti), *n.*, pâté, *m.*
pasty, *adj.*, pâteux.
pat, *adj.*, à propos, tout juste.
pat, *n.*, tape, *f.*
pat, *v.a.*, donner une tape à.
patache (-tâshe), *n.*, patache, *f.*
patch, *n.*, pièce, *f.* ; morceau, *m.* ; (for the

pat 882 pay

face—*pour le visage*) mouche, *f.* —work;
rapiécetage, *m.*

patch, *v.a.*, mettre des pièces à; rapiécer, raccommoder; (the face—*le visage*) mettre des mouches à. To — up; *plâtrer.*

patcher, *n.*, ravaudeur, *m.*, ravaudeuse, *f.*

patchery, *n.*, ravaudage, *m.*

patching, *n.*, rapiécetage, *m.*

pate, *n.*, caboche; (of a calf—*du veau*) peau de tête de veau, *f.*; (fort.) pâté, *m.*

pated (pét'-), *adj.*, à caboche. Shallow— —; *à caboche vide.*

patefaction (-ti-fak-), *n.*, manifestation, *f.*

paten, or patin, *n.*, patène, *f.*

patent (pat'- *ou* pét'-), *adj.*, patent; breveté.

patent, *n.*, lettres patentes, *f.pl.*; privilège; brevet, brevet d'invention, *m.* To take out a —; *prendre un brevet.*

patent, *v.a.*, accorder par lettres patentes; breveter.

patentable (-a-b'l), *adj.*, susceptible d'être breveté.

patentee (-tî), *n.*, personne munie de lettres patentes, *f.*; concessionnaire; breveté, *m.*, brevetée, *f.*

paternal (-teur-), *adj.*, paternel.

paternally, *adv.*, paternellement.

paternity (-teur-), *n.*, paternité, *f.*

paternoster, *n.*, Pater, *m.*; patenôtre. *f.*

path (pâth), *n.*, chemin, sentier, *m.*; (astron.) route, *f.*; cours, *m.*; (fig.) voie, *f.* Beaten —; *sentier battu.* By— —; *sentier détourné.* Foot— —; *trottoir, m.*

pathetic, or pathetical (-thèt'-), *adj.*, pathétique.

pathetic (-thèt'-), *n.*, pathétique, *m.*

pathetically (-thèt'-), *adv.*, pathétiquement.

- patheticalness (-thèt'-), *n.*, pathétique, *m.*

pathless (pâth'-), *adj.*, sans sentier; (fig.) inconnu, désert.

pathologic, *or* pathological (-thol'o-dj'-), *adj.*, pathologique.

pathologically (-thol'-), *adv.*, pathologiquement.

pathologist (-thol'-), *n.*, pathologiste, *m.*

pathology (-thol'o-dji), *n.*, pathologie, *f.*

pathos (pé-thoss), *n.*, pathétique *m.* (rhet.) pathos, *m.*

pathway (pâth'wè), *n.*, sentier; chemin, *m.*

patibulary (-tib'iou-), *adj.*, patibulaire.

patience (pé-shè'n'ce), *n.*, patience; (bot.) patience, parelle, *f.* To lose — ; *perdre patience; être à bout de patience.* To put out of —: *impatienter; faire perdre patience à.* To get out of — ; *s'impatienter.*

patient (pé-shè'n'te), *n.*, malade, *m.*, *f.*

patient, *adj.*, patient.

patiently, *adv.*, patiemment.

patin, *n.* V. paten.

patly, *adv.*, juste, à propos.

patness, *n.*, justesse, *f.*; à-propos, *m.*

patriarch (pé-tri-ârke), *n.*, patriarche, *m.*

patriarchal, *or* patriarchic, *adj.*, patriarcal.

patriarchate, *or* patriarchship, *n.*, patriarcat, *m.*

patrician (-trish'-), *adj.*, patricien.

patrician, *n.*, patricien, *m.*, patricienne, *f.*; patrice, *m.*

patrimonial (-mô-), *adj.*, patrimonial, de patrimoine.

patrimonially, *adv.*, comme patrimoine; par héritage.

patrimony, *n.*, patrimoine, *m.*

patriot (pé-), *n.*, patriote, *m.*, *f.*

patriotic, *or* patriotic, *adj.*, patriotique.

patriotically, *adv.*, patriotiquement; en patriote.

patriotism (-'iz'm), *n.*, patriotisme, *m.*

patrol, *n.*, patrouille, *f.*

patrol (-trôl), *v.n.*, faire la patrouille; patrouiller.

patron (pé-), *n.*, patron; protecteur, *m.*

patronage (-'édje), *n.*, patronage, appui, *m.*; protection, *f.*

patronal, *adj.*, patronal.

patroness (pé-), *n.*, patronne, protectrice, *f.*

patronize (-'aïze), *v.a.*, favoriser, protéger, patroniser.

patronizer (-'aïzeur), *n.*, protecteur, *m.*, protectrice, *f.*

patronless, *adj.*, sans protecteur.

patronymic, *adj.*, patronymique.

patten, *n.*, socque à l'anglaise; (arch.) soubassement, *m.*

patter, *v.n.*, frapper avec bruit (comme la grêle, la pluie); fouetter.

pattern, *n.*, patron, modèle; (specimen, sample—*spécimen, échantillon*) échantillon, *m.*

pattern, *v.a.*, imiter; servir de modèle à.

patty, *n.*, petit pâté, *m.*

patty-pan, *n.*, moule à pâté; (pers.) gâtesauce, *m.*

patulous (pat'iou-), *adj.*, (bot.) étalé.

paucity, *n.*, petit nombre, *m.*; paucité, *f.*

paunch (pâ'n'sh, *ou* pô'n'sh), *n.*, panse; (nav.) baderne, *f.*

paunch, *v.a.*, éventrer.

pauper, *n.*, pauvre, indigent, *m.*

pauperism, *n.*, paupérisme, *m.*

pause (pôze), *n.*, pause, *f.*; intervalle; (poet.) repos; (mus.) point d'orgue, *m.*

pause, *v.n.*, faire une pause, s'arrêter; délibérer; réfléchir. To — upon; *bien considérer.*

pauser, *n.*, personne qui fait une pause, qui délibère, *f.*

pausingly, *adv.*, après une pause.

pave, *v.a.*, paver. To — a way for; *frayer un chemin à.*

pavement, *n.*, pavé; trottoir; pavement, *m.*

paver, pavier, *or* pavior (pé-), *n.*, paveur, *m.*

pavilion, *n.*, pavillon, *m.*; tente, *f.*

pavilion, *v.a.*, munir de pavillons, de tentes; abriter sous un pavillon, une tente.

paving (pév'-), *n.*, pavement, pavage, *m.*

paving-beetle (-bit't'l), *n.*, hie, demoiselle, *f.*

paving-stone (-stône), *n.*, pavé, *m.*

pavior. V. paver.

pavonine (-naïne), *adj.*, ressemblant à une queue de paon; irisé, gorge-de-pigeon.

pavonine (-naïne), *n.*, (min.) queue-de-paon, *f.*, sulfure de cuivre irisé, *m.*

pavy, *n.*, (bot.) pavie, *m.*

paw (pô), *n.*, patte, *f.*

paw (pô), *v.a.*, frapper du pied; (to handle—*toucher*) manier, manier rudement.

paw (pô), *v.n.*, trépigner; (of horses—*des chevaux*) piaffer.

pawn (pô'n), *n.*, gage; nantissement; (at chess—*aux échecs*) pion, *m.* In —; *en gage; engagé.*

pawn, *v.a.*, engager; mettre en gage; mettre au mont-de-piété.

pawnbroker (-brôk'-), *n.*, prêteur sur gage, commissionnaire du mont-de-piété, *m.*

pawnee (pô'n'î), *n.*, prêteur sur gage, *m.*

pawner, *n.*, emprunteur sur gage, *m.*

pawnshop, *n.*, mont-de-piété, *m.*; (in England—*en Angleterre*) boutique de prêteur sur gage, *f.*

pax, *n.*, (ecc.), paix, *f.*

pay, *n.*, paye, solde, *f.*; salaire, *m.* Full —; *solde entière.* Half —; *demi-solde.*

pay, *v.a.*, payer, acquitter; s'acquitter de; (fin.) verser; (bring in—*produire*) rapporter; (compliments, attention) faire; (attentions) avoir; (honour—*honneur*) rendre; (visits—*visites*) rendre, faire. To — lack ; *rendre, rembourser, restituer.* To — down ; *payer argent comptant.* To — off ; *payer ; liquider ;* (nav.) *espalmer, goudronner, suiver, suiffer.* To — away ; *payer ;* (nav.) *filer.* To — out ; *lâcher ; ralentir ; étendre ; laisser courir ;* (fig.) *donner son fait à, rendre la pareille à.* To — in ; *verser.*

payable (pé-a-b'l), *adj.*, payable.
pay-bill, *n.*, (milit.) feuille de prêt, *f.*
pay-day, *n.*, jour de payement, *m.*
payee (pé-î), *n.*, (com.) porteur, *m.*
payer (pé-eur), *n.*, payeur, *m.*
paymaster (-mâs-), *n.*, payeur ; (milit.) trésorier, *m.*
payment, *n.*, payement, paiement, *m.*
pea (pî), *n.*, pois, *m.* ; (nav.) patte, *f.* Green —s ; *petits pois ; pois verts, m.pl.*
peace (pîce), *n.*, paix ; tranquillité, *f.* ; (jur.) ordre public, *m.* — -officer ; *officier de police, m.*
peaceable (-'a-b'l), *adj.*, paisible, tranquille.
peaceableness, *n.*, caractère paisible, *m.* ; tranquillité, *f.*
peaceably, *adv.*, paisiblement, tranquillement.
peaceful (-foule), *adj.*, paisible ; tranquille.
peacefully, *adv.*, paisiblement, tranquillement.
peacefulness, *n.*, tranquillité, *f.*
peaceless, *adj.*, sans paix ; sans tranquillité.
peace-maker (-mék'-), *n.*, pacificateur, *m.*
peach (pît-she), *n.*, pêche, *f.* ; (tree—*arbre*) pêcher, *m.* — -colour ; *couleur de fleur de pêcher, f.* — -coloured ; *de couleur de fleur de pêcher.*
pea-chick (-tshike), *n.*, paonneau, *m.*
peacock, *n.*, paon, *m.*
peahen (pî-hène), *n.*, paonne, *f.*
peak (pike), *n.*, pointe, *f.* ; sommet ; (geog.) pic, *m.* ; (of a mountain—*de montagne*) cime, *f.*
peal (pîle), *n.*, bruit ; retentissement ; (of thunder—*du tonnerre*) éclat, coup ; (of bells—*de cloches*) carillon, *m.* — of ordnance ; *décharge d'artillerie, f.*
peal, *v.n.*, retentir, résonner ; gronder.
peal, *v.a.*, faire retentir, faire résonner.
pea-pod, *n.*, pois en cosse, *m.pl.*
pear (pére), *n.*, poire, *f.*
pearl (peurle), *n.*, perle ; (print.) parisienne, sédanoise ; (med.) taie perlée de la cornée, *f.* ; (her.) argent, *m.*
pearl-ashes, *n.pl.*, perlasse ; potasse d'Amérique, *f.*
pearled (peurlde), *adj.*, orné de perles ; (her.) perlé.
pearl-eyed (-a'ye-de), *adj.*, qui a une taie sur l'œil.
pearl-fishery *n.*, pêche de perles, *f.*
pearl-grass (-grâce), *n.*, (bot.) sagine, herbe aux perles, *f.*
pearl-powder (-paou-), *or* **pearl-white** (-hwaîte), *n.*, blanc de perle, *m.*
pearl-shell, *n.*, huître perlière ; nacre, *f.*
pearl-white, *n.* V. **pearl-powder.**
pearly, *adj.*, de perle.
pearmain (pèr-méne), *n.*, (hort.) pomme-poire, *f.*
pear-tree (-trî), *n.*, poirier, *m.*
peasant (pèz'-), *n.*, paysan, *m.*, paysanne, *f.*
peasant, peasant-like (-laike), *or* **peasantly**, *adj.*, de paysan ; rustique.
peasantry (-), *n.*, paysans, gens de la campagne, *m.pl.*
pease (pîze), *n.pl.* V. **pea.**
pea-shell, *n.*, cosse de pois, *m.*
pea-shooter (-shout'-), *n.*, sarbacane, *f.*
peat (pîte), *n.*, tourbe, *f.* ; (mines) dépôt tourbeux, *m.*
peat-moss, *n.*, tourbe, *f.* ; (mines) dépôt tourbeux, *m.*
pebble (pèb'b'l), *n.*, caillou, *m.*

pebble-w .-weurke), *n.*, liocage, cailloutage, *m.*
pebbly, *adj.*, plein de caillou ; caillouteux.
peccability (pèk'ka-), *n.*, disposition au péché, *f.*
peccable (pèk'ka-b'l), *adj.*, peccable.
peccadillo (pèk'ka-dil-lô), *n.*, peccadille, *f.*
peccancy (pèk'-), *n.*, mauvaise qualité, *f.* ; vice, *m.*
peccant (pèk'-), *adj.*, qui pèche, pécheur ; peccant, coupable.
peck (pèke), *n.*, picotin, *m.* ; (quantity) quantité, *f.*
peck, *v.a.*, becqueter, percer à coups de bec.
pecker, *n.*, oiseau qui becquète ; pivert, *m.*
pectinal (pèk'-), *adj.*, de peigne ; pectiné.
pectination (pèk'ti-né-), *n.*, action de peigner, *f.*
pectoral (pèk'-), *n.*, pectoral, *m.*
pectoral, *adj.*, pectoral.
peculate (pèk'iou-), *v.n.*, être coupable de péculat.
peculation (pèk'iou-lé-), *n.*, péculat, *m.*
peculator (-lé-teur), *n.*, auteur d'un péculat, *m.*
peculiar (pi-kiou-li-eur), *adj.*, particulier, spécial ; singulier.
peculiar, *n.*, propriété particulière ; (canon law—*droit canon*) chapelle privilégiée, *f.*
peculiarity, *n.*, propriété particulière ; chose particulière ; singularité, particularité, *f.*
peculiarize (-aize), *v.a.*, approprier.
peculiarly, *adv.*, particulièrement ; singulièrement.
pecuniary (pi-kiou-), *adj.*, pécuniaire.
pedagogic, *or* **pedagogical** (-godj'-), *adj.*, pédagogique.
pedagogism (-djîz'm), *n.*, (ant.) pédagogie, *f.*
pedagogue (pèd'a-goghe), *n.*, pédagogue, *m.*
pedagogue, *v.a.*, enseigner en pédagogue.
pedagogy (-godj'î), *n.*, pédagogie, *f.*
podal (pèd'-), *n.*, pédale, *f.*
pedal (pî-), *adj.*, du pied.
pedant (pèd'-), *n.*, pédant, *m.*
pedantic, *or* **pedantical** (pèd'-), *adj.*, pédant, pédantesque.
pedantically, *adv.*, pédantesquement.
pedantize (-aize), *v.n.*, (ant.) faire le pédant, pédanter, pédantiser.
pedantry (pèd'-), *n.*, pédanterie, *f.*
peddle, *v.a.*, colporter.
peddle, *v.n.*, s'occuper de bagatelles ; baguenauder, niaiser ; faire le colportage.
peddler, *n.*, colporteur, *m.*
peddlery, *n.*, marchandise de colporteur, *f.* ; colportage, *m.*
peddling, *adj.*, futile, mesquin.
pedestal (pèd'-), *n.*, piédestal, *m.*
pedestrian (pi-dès-), *adj.*, à pied ; pédestre.
pedestrian, *n.*, piéton ; marcheur, *m.*
pedestrious (pi-dès'-), *adj.*, pédestre.
pedicel (pèd'i-cèl), *or* **pedicle** (pèd'i-k'l), *n.*, pédicelle, pédoncule, *m.*
pedicular (pi-dik'iou-), *adj.*, pédiculaire.
pedigree (pèd'i-grî), *n.*, généalogie, *f.*
pediluvy (pèd'i-leu-), *n.*, pédiluve, *m.*
pediment (pèd'-), *n.*, fronton, *m.*
pedlar, *or* **pedler** (pèd'-). V. **peddler.**
pedometer (pi-deum'i-), *n.*, pédomètre, odomètre, compte-pas, *m.*
pedometrical, *adj.*, de pédomètre.
peduncle (pi-deun'k'l), *n.*, (bot.) pédoncule, *m.*
peduncular (pi-deun'k'iou-), *adj.*, (bot.) pédonculaire.
pedunculate (pi-deun'k'iou-), *adj.*, (bot.) pédonculé.
peel (pîl), *n.*, peau ; (of oranges, lemons—

d'*oranges, de citrons*) écorce, *f.* ; (print.) étendoir, *m.* ; (shovel—*pelle*) pelle de four, *f.*

peel, *v.a.*, peler; ôter l'écorce de; (fig.) dépouiller, piller ; (barley—*orge*) monder.

peel, *v.n.*, se peler; s'écailler.

peeler, *n.*, personne qui pèle,*f.* ; (plunderer —*pillard*) pillard, *m.*

peep (pîpe), *n.*, (of day—*du jour*) point, *m.*, pointe, aube, *f.*; (look—*regard*) coup d'œil, regard, *m.* — -hole; *judas, m.*

peep, *v.n.*, (to look—*regarder*) regarder ; (to appear—*paraître*) paraître, poindre, percer.

peeper, *n.*, spectateur caché, *m.* ; personne qui regarde à la dérobée, *f.*; (chicken—*petit poulet*) poussin, *m.*

peer (pîr), *n.*, pair ; égal, pareil ; compagnon, *m.*

peer, *v.n.*, paraître; poindre; (to look—*regarder*) regarder.

peerage (pîr'édje), *n.*, pairie, *f.*

peeress, *n.*, pairesse, *f.*

peerless, *adj.*, incomparable ; sans égal.

peerlessly, *adv.*, sans pareil ; sans égal.

peerlessness, *n.*, supériorité incomparable, *f.*

peevish (pî-), *adj.*, chagrin, bourru, maussade, hargneux.

peevishly, *adv.*, maussadement.

peevishness, *n.*, maussaderie ; humeur chagrine, humeur bourrue, *f.*

peewit (pî-), *n.*, (orni.) vanneau, *m.*

peg (pèghe), *n.*, cheville, patère, *f.*; point, *m.* To come down a — ; *baisser d'un cran.*

peg, *v.a.*, cheviller.

pegasus (pèg'a-ceusse), *n.*, Pégase, *m.*

pelamis (pèl'a-), (ich.) pélamide, *f.*

pelf (pèlf), *n.*, argent, *m.*; richesses mal acquises, *f.pl.*

pelican (pèl'-), *n.*, pélican, *m.*

pelisse (pè-lîce), *n.*, pelisse, *f.*

pellet (pèl'-), *n.*, balle, boule, *f.*

pellicle (pèl-li-k'l), *n.*, pellicule, *f.*

pellitory (pèl'li-teuri), *n.*, (bot.) pariétaire,*f.*

pell-mell, *adv.*, pêle-mêle.

pellucid (pèl-liou-), *adj.*, transparent; clair; pellucide.

pellucidity, *or* **pellucidness**, *n.*, transparence; clarté, *f.*

pelt (pèlte), *n.*, peau, *f.* — -monger; *peaussier, m.*

pelt (pèlte), *v.a.*, assaillir, jeter, lancer, lapider. To — any one with any thing; *lancer quelque chose à quelqu'un.*

pelting, *adj.*, furieux ; (of rain—*de la pluie*) battant.

pelting, *n.*, attaque, *f.*; assaut, *m.*

peltry, *n.*, pelleterie, *f.*

pelvic, *adj.*, (anat.) pelvien.

pelvis, *n.*, (anat.) bassin, *m.*

pen (pèn), *n.*, plume, *f.*; (for poultry—*pour la volaille*) poulailler ; (for cattle—*pour les bestiaux*) parc, enclos, *m.*

pen, *v.a.*, écrire; rédiger; coucher par écrit; (cattle—*les bestiaux*) parquer. To — up; *enfermer, parquer.*

penal (pî-), *adj.*, passible d'une amende ; punissable ; pénal.

penalty (pèn'-), *n.*, peine. amende, *f.*

penance (pèn'-), *n.*, pénitence, *f.*

pen-blade (-blède), *n.*, lame à tailler les plumes, *f.*

pencase (-kéce), *n.*, étui à plumes, *m.*

pence (pèn'ce), *n.pl.* *V.* **penny.**

pencil (pèn'-), *n.*, pinceau; crayon; (opt.) faisceau, *m.* Drawing —; *crayon à dessin.* — - case ; *portecrayon, m.*

pencil, *v.a.*, peindre; dessiner.

pencil-shaped (-shép'te), *adj.*, en forme de pinceau ; pénicillé.

pencraft (-crâfte), *n.*, art d'écrire, *m.*, calligraphie, *f.*

pen-cutter (-keut'-), *n.*, taille-plume, *m.*

pendant (pèn'-), *n.*, pendant, *m.*; (nav.) flamme, *f.* Broad —; *guidon, m.*

pendence, *n.*, penchant, *m.* ; pente, inclinaison,*f.*

pendency, *n.*, (jur.) litispendance, *f.*, suspens, *m.*

pendent, *adj.*, pendant; saillant.

pendentive, *n.*, (arch.) pendentif, *m.*

pending, *adj.*, pendant, non décidé.

pending, *prep.*, pendant.

pendule (-dioule), *n.* *V.* **pendulum.**

pendulosity (-diou-loss'-), *or* **pendulousness** (-diou-leus'-), *n.*, état de ce qui est pendant, suspendu, *m.*

pendulous (-diou-), *adj.*, pendant ; oscillant.

pendulum (-diou-leume), *n.*, pendule, balancier, *m.* — -clock ; *pendule, f.* — -bob ; *lentille de pendule, f.* — -rod ; *verge de pendule,f.*

penetrability (pè'n'i-), *n.*, pénétrabilité, *f.*

penetrable (pè'n'i-tra-b'l), *adj.*, pénétrable; sensible.

penetrancy, *n.*, pénétration, *f.*

penetrant, *adj.*, pénétrant.

penetrate (pè'n'i-), *v.a.* and *n.*, pénétrer.

penetrating, *adj.*, pénétrant.

penetration (pè'n'i-tré'-), *n.*, pénétration, *f.*

penetrative, *adj.*, pénétrant.

penful (-foule), *n.*, plumée, *f.*

penguin (pè'n'gwine), *n.*, (orni.) pingouin, *m.*

pen-holder (-hôld'-), *n.*, porte-plume, *m.*

penicil (pè'n'i-), *n.*, (med.) plumasseau, *m.* ; tente de charpie, *f.*

peninsula (pè'n'i'n-siou-), *n.*, péninsule; presqu'île,*f.*

peninsular, *adj.*, en forme de péninsule; péninsulaire.

peninsulate, *v.a.*, faire une péninsule de.

peninsulated (-lét'-), *adj.*, en forme de péninsule.

penitence, *or* **penitency**, *n.*, pénitence, *f.*; repentir, *m.*

penitent, *adj.*, pénitent, repentant.

penitent, *n.*, pénitent, *m.*, pénitente, *f.*

penitential (-tè'n'shal), *adj.*, de pénitence ; pénitentiaux, *m.pl.*, pénitentielles, *f.pl.*

penitential, *n.*, pénitentiel, *m.*

penitentiary (-tè'n'sha-), *adj.*, pénitentiaire.

penitentiary, *n.*, pénitencier ; pénitent, *m.*, pénitente, *f.* ; maison pénitentiaire,*f.*

penitently, *adv.*, avec pénitence.

penknife (pè'n'naïfe), *n.*, canif, *m.*

penman (pè'n'ma'n), *n.*, calligraphe ; auteur, écrivain, *m.*

penmanship, *n.*, écriture, *f.*

pennant (pè'n'-), *n.*, pennon, *m.*

pennate, *or* **pennated** (pè'n'nét'-), *adj.*, ailé ; (bot.) penné.

penner, *n.*, écrivain, rédacteur, *m.*

penniless, *adj.*, sans le sou ; pauvre.

penning, *n.*, écriture ; rédaction, *f.*; (of cattle—*des bestiaux*) parcage, *m.*

pennon, *n.*, pennon, *m.*

penny (pè'n'-), *n.* (*pence*, ou *pennies*), deux sous, décime ; penny, *m.* — -royal ; (bot.) pouliot, *m.* — -weight ; *penny-weight* (gramme 1·5545.), *m.* — -worth ; *pour deux sous ; pour son argent.* — -wort ; *hydrocotyle, m.*

penny-wise (-waïze), *adj.*, ménager de bouts de chandelle.

pensile (pè'n'sil), *adj.*, suspendu ; pendant.

pensileness, *n.*, état de ce qui est suspendu, *m.*

pension (pè'n'sheune), *n.*, pension, rente; retraite, *f.* Retiring —; *pension de retraite.*

pension, *v.a.*, pensionner.

pensionary, *n.*, pensionnaire, *m.*

pensionary, *adj.*, pensionné ; (of things—*des choses*) par pension.

pensioner, *n.*, pensionnaire ; (Cambridge) étudiant ordinaire ; (milit., nav.) invalide, *m.*

pensive, *adj.*, pensif, triste.

pensively, *adv.*, d'une manière pensive ; tristement.

pensiveness, *n.*, air pensif, *m.* ; tristesse, *f.*

penstock, *n.*, vanne, *f.*

pentagon, *n.*, pentagone, *m.*

pentagonal, *adj.*, pentagone.

pentameter (pè'n'ta'm'i-), *adj.*, pentamètre.

pentameter, *n.*, pentamètre, *m.*

pentandria, *n.*, (bot.) pentandrie, *f.*

pentarchy (-tàr-ki), *n.*, pentarchie, *f.*

pentateuch (-teuke), *n.*, Pentateuque, *m.*

pentecost (-tì-côste), *n.*, Pentecôte, *f.*

pentecostal, *adj.*, de la Pentecôte.

pentecostals (-taize), *n.pl.*, offrandes de la Pentecôte, *f.pl.*

penthouse (-haouce), *n.*, appentis, *m.*

pentile (-taïle), *n.*, tuile faitière ; faîtière, *f.*

penult (pî-neulte), **penultima** (pi-neul-), *n.*, pénultième, pénultième syllabe, *f.*

penultimate, *adj.*, pénultième.

penumbra (pi-neu'm-), *n.*, (astron.) pénombre, *f.*

penurious (pi-niou-), *adj.*, avare ; sordide ; (of things—*des choses*) pauvre.

penuriously, *adv.*, avec pénurie.

penuriousness, *n.*, pénurie, *f.*

penury (pè'n'-), *n.*, pénurie, *f.*

pen-wiper (-waïp'-), *n.*, essuie-plume, *m.*

peony (pî-), *n.*, (bot.) pivoine, *f.*

people (pî-p'l), *n.*, peuple ; (the vulgar—*le vulgaire*) peuple, vulgaire ; (persons in general—*tout le monde*) on, monde *m.*, personnes, *f.pl.* ; gens, *m.pl.* — say ; on dit.

people, *v.a.*, peupler.

pepper (pèp'-), *n.*, poivre, *m.* — -tree ; *poivrier*, *m.* —wort ; *passerage*, *m.*

pepper, *v.a.*, poivrer ; (to beat—*battre*) cribler de coups.

pepper-box, or **pepper-castor** (-càst'-), *n.*, poivrier, *m.* ; poivrière, *f.*

pepper-corn, *n.*, grain de poivre, *m.* ; (fig.) bagatelle, *f.*

peppermint (-mi'n'te), *n.*, menthe poivrée, *f.*

pepper-vine (-vaïne), *n.*, vigne vierge, *f.*

per (peur), *prep.*, par ; (com.) le, *m.*, la, *f.*, les, *pl.* A shilling — hundred ; *un schelling le cent.*

peradventure (pèr'ad-vè'n'tieur), *adv.*, par hasard, d'aventure, peut-être.

perambulate (-biou-), *v.a.*, parcourir à pied.

perambulation (-biou-lé-), *n.*, action de parcourir à pied ; tournée, *f.*

perambulator (-biou-lé-teur), *n.*, odomètre, pédomètre, compte-pas, *m.* ; voiture d'enfant, *f.*

perceivable (pèr-cîv'a-b'l), *adj.*, apercevable, perceptible.

perceivably, *adv.*, perceptiblement ; d'une manière apercevable ; sensiblement.

perceive (pèr-cîve), *v.a.*, apercevoir ; s'apercevoir de ; remarquer ; sentir ; percevoir.

perceiver, *n.*, personne qui s'aperçoit, qui remarque, *f.*

percentage (pèr-cè'n't'édje), *n.*, droit de . . . pour cent ; salaire, *m.* A — ; *tant pour cent.*

perceptibility (pèr-), *n.*, perceptibilité, perception, *f.*

perceptible (pèr'cèp-ti-b'l), *adj.*, perceptible ; apercevable.

perceptibly, *adv.*, perceptiblement ; d'une manière apercevable.

perception (pèr-cèp'-), *n.*, action de s'apercevoir ; perception ; observation, *f.*

perceptive (pèr-cèp-), *adj.*, perceptif.

perceptivity, *n.*, faculté de perception, *f.*

perch (peurtshe), *n.*, perche, *f.* ; (of birds—

des oiseaux) perchoir, *m.* ; (ich.) perche ; (measure—*mesure*) perche (mètre 5·0291), *f.*

perch (peurtshe), *v.a.* and *n.*, percher ; se percher.

perchance (pèr'tshä'n'ce), *adv.*, par hasard ; peut-être ; par aventure.

perching (peurtsh'-), *adj.*, qui perche ; percheur.

percipient, (pèr-) *adj.*, doué de perception.

percipient, *n.*, être doué de perception, *m.*

percolate (peur-), *v.a.*, filtrer, passer.

percolate, *v.n.*, filtrer.

percolation (peur-co-lé-), *n.*, filtration, *f.*

percussion (pèr-keush'-), *n.*, percussion, *f.* — -cap ; *capsule*, *f.*

percussive (pèr'keus'-). or **percutient** (pèr-keush'-), *adj.*, qui frappe.

perdition (pèr-dish'-), *n.*, perdition, ruine, *f.* ; enfant perdu, *m.*

perdu, *adj.*, (milit.) perdu ; perdu, abandonné ; accoutumé aux entreprises désespérées.

perdu, or **perdue**, *adv.*, caché ; en embuscade.

peregrinate (pèr'i-), *v.n.*, visiter l'étranger, voyager.

peregrination (pèr'i-gri-né-), *n.*, pérégrination, *f.* ; voyage ; séjour à l'étranger, *m.*

peregrine (pèr'i-grine), *n.*, (orni.) pèlerin, faucon pèlerin, *m.*

peremption (pèr-). *n.*, (ant.) péremption, *f.*

peremptorily (pèr-), *adv.*, péremptoirement.

peremptoriness (pèr'-), *n.*, caractère péremptoire ; ton tranchant, *m.*

peremptory (pèr'-), *adj.*, péremptoire, tranchant, absolu.

perennial (pèr'è'n'-), *adj.*, qui dure l'année ; perpétuel ; (bot.) vivace.

perennial, *n.*, plante vivace, *f.*

perennially, *adv.*, continuellement ; perpétuellement.

perennity (pèr'è'n'-), *n.*, (ant.) perpétuité, *f.*

perfect (peur-fèkte), *adj.*, parfait ; achevé ; complet, accompli.

perfect, *v.a.*, rendre parfait ; achever ; perfectionner ; accomplir, compléter.

perfecter, *n.*, personne qui rend parfait, qui complète, qui perfectionne ; chose qui complète, qui perfectionne, *f.*

perfectibility, *n.*, perfectibilité, *f.*

perfectible (pèr-fèk-ti-b'l), *adj.*, perfectible.

perfection (pèr-fèk'-), *n.*, perfection, *f.* To — ; *en perfection.*

perfectionist (pèr-fèk'-), *n.*, personne qui prétend à la perfection, *f.*

perfective, *adj.*, qui rend parfait.

perfectively, *adv.*, de manière à rendre parfait.

perfectly, *adv.*, parfaitement, à fond.

perfectness, *n.*, perfection, *f.*

perfidious (pèr-), *adj.*, perfide.

perfidiously, *adv.*, perfidement.

perfidiousness, or **perfidy**, *n.*, perfidie, *f.*

perflate (pèr-), *v.a.*, (ant.) souffler à travers.

perflation (pèr-flé-), *n.*, action de souffler à travers, *f.*

perfoliate (pèr-fô-), *adj.*, (bot.) perfolié.

perforate (peur-), *v.a.*, percer d'outre en outre ; perforer.

perforation (peur-of-ré-), *n.*, trou d'outre en outre, percement, *m.* ; ouverture, perforation, *f.*

perforative, *adj.*, perforatif.

perforator, *n.*, (surg.) perforatif, *m.*

perforce (pèr'-), *adv.*, forcément, par force ; de force.

perform (pèr-), *v.a.*, exécuter, accomplir ; faire ; (thea.) donner, jouer, représenter ; (to fulfil—*remplir*) remplir, s'acquitter de.

perform, v.a., (of actors—*d'acteurs*) jouer; tof musiciens—*de musiciens*) exécuter, jouer.

performable (-'ab'l), adj., faisable, exécutable, praticable.

performance, n., exécution, f. ; acte, accomplissement ; exercice ; (thing done—*chose faite*) ouvrage, m., œuvre ; (thea.) représentation, f.

performer, n., auteur, m. ; personne qui exécute, qui accomplit, f. ; (thea.) artiste, m., f., acteur, m., actrice, f., comédien, m., comédienne, f. ; (mus.) artiste, m., f., exécutant, m.

perfume (pèr-fioume, ou peur-), n., parfum, m.

perfume, v.a., parfumer. embaumer.

perfumer, n., parfumeur, m., parfumeuse, f.

perfumery, n., parfumerie, f.

perfunctorily (pèr-feu'n'k-, ou peur-), adv., négligemment ; légèrement.

perfunctoriness (pèr'feu'n'k-, ou peur-), n.. négligence, f.

perfunctory, adj., négligent, léger ; fait par manière d'acquit.

perfuse (pèr-fiouze), v.a., répandre partout.

perhaps (pèr-), adv., peut-être.

peri (pi-), n., péri, m., f.

perianth (pèr-i-an'th), or **perianthium** (-thi-), n., (bot.) périanthe, m.

peribolus (pi-), n., (arch.) péribole, m.

pericardium (pèr-i-câr-), n., (anat.) péricarde, m.

pericarp, or **pericarpium** (pèr-i-câr-), n., (bot.) péricarpe, m.

pericranium (pèr-i-cré-), n., péricrâne, m.

periculous (pi-rik'iou-), adj., (ant.) périlleux, dangereux.

peridot (pèr-), n., péridot, m.

perigee (pèr-i-djî), or **perigeum** (-djî-), n., (astron.) périgée, m.

perigord-stone (pèr-i-gord'stône),n.,(min.) périgueux, m.

perihelion, or **perihelium** (pèr-i-hî-), n., (astron.) périhélie, m.

peril (pèr'-), n., péril, danger, m. At one's —; *à ses risques et périls*.

peril, v.a., mettre en péril.

peril, v.a., être en péril.

perilous, adj., périlleux.

perilously, adv., périlleusement.

perilousness, n., nature périlleuse, f.; danger, m.

perimeter (pi-ri'm'i-), n., périmètre, m.

perinæum (pèr'i-nî-), n., (anat.) périnée, m.

period (pi-), n., période, f. ; temps, espace, m. ; (portion of time—*portion de temps*) durée, f. ; temps, m.; (epoch—*époque*) époque ; (end—*fin*) fin, limite, f., terme, m.; (astron., chron., gram.) période, f. ; (in punctuating—*ponctuation*) point, m. To put a — to ; *mettre fin à*. To form a —; *faire époque*.

periodic, or **periodical** (pi-), adj., périodique.

periodical, n., ouvrage périodique, m.

periodically, adv., périodiquement.

periodicity, n., périodicité, f.

periœci (pèr-i-î-ça'ye), or **periecians** (pèr-i-î-sha'n'ze), n.pl., (geog.) périœciens, m.pl.

periosteum (pèr-i-os-ti-), n., (anat.) périoste, m.

periostitis (pèr-i-os-taï-tice), n., (med.) périostose, f.

peripatetic (pèr'i-pa-tèt-), adj., péripatéticien.

peripatetic, n., péripatéticien, m.

peripateticism, n., péripatétisme, m.

periphery (pi-rif'i-), n., périphérie, circonférence, f.

periphrase (pèr-i-frèze), v.a., exprimer par une périphrase.

periphrasis (pi-rif'ra-cice), n. (*periphrases*), périphrase, f.

periphrastic, or **periphrastical** (pèr'-), adj., de périphrase ; périphrastique.

periphrastically, adv., par périphrase.

periplus (pèr-), n., périple, m.

peripptery (pi-rip-ti-), n., (arch.) périptère, m.

periscii (pè-rish'i-a'ye), n., périsciens, m.pl.

perish (pèr'-), v.n., périr ; dépérir.

perishable (-a-b'l), adj., périssable.

perishableness, n., nature périssable, f.

peristaltic (pèr'-),adj., (med.) péristaltique.

peristerion (pèr-is-tî-), n. V. **vervain**.

peristyle (pèr-i-staïl), or **peristylium** (pèr-i stil'-), n., (arch.) péristyle, m.

peritoneum (pèr'it'oni-), n., péritoine, f.

periwig (pèr-), n., perruque, f. — -maker; perruquier, m.

periwig, v.a., coiffer d'une perruque.

periwinkle (pèr'i-wign'k'l), n., (bot.) pervenche, f. ; (mol.) bigorneau, m.

perjure (peur-djioure), v.a., parjurer. To — one's self ; *se parjurer*.

perjurer, n., parjure ; faux témoin, m.

perjurious, adj., parjure.

perjury (peur-djiouri), n., parjure ; faux témoignage, faux serment, m. Wilful — ; *parjure prémédité*.

perk (peurke), adj., vif, éveillé.

perk, v.n., lever la tête avec affectation.

perk, v.a., parer, orner.

perkin (peur-), n., petit cidre, m.

permanence, or **permanency** (peur-), n., permanence, f.

permanent, adj., permanent ; en permanence.

permanently, adv., en permanence.

permeability (peur-mi-), n., perméabilité, f.

permeable (-mi-a-b'l), adj., pénétrable, perméable.

permeate (peur-mi-), v.a., pénétrer.

permeation (peur-mi-é-), n., pénétration, f.

permissible (pèr-mis'si-b'l), adj., qui peut être permis.

permission (pèr-mish'-), n., permission, f.; permis, m.

permissive (pèr-), adj., qui permet, tolérant ; permis.

permissively, adv., avec permission ; sans empêchement.

permistion (pèr-mist'ieune), or **permixtion** (per-mikst'ieune), n., mixtion, f.

permit (pèr-), v.a., permettre ; permettre à.

permit, n., permission, f., permis ; congé, m.

permutable (pèr-miou-ta-b'l), adj., permutable.

permutation (peur-miou-té-), n., permutation, f. ; (com.) échange, m.

pernicious (pèr-nish'-), adj., pernicieux.

perniciously, adv., pernicieusement.

perniciousness, n., nature pernicieuse, f.

pernoctation (peur-noc-té-), n., veille, f.

peroration (pèr-o-ré-), n., péroraison, f.

peroxide (pè,'-), n., péroxyde, m.

perpendicular (peur-pè'n-dik'iou-), adj., perpendiculaire.

perpendicular, n., ligne perpendiculaire ; perpendiculaire, f.

perpendicularity, n., perpendicularité, f.

perpendicularly, adv., perpendiculairement.

perpend-stone (-stône), n., parpaing, m.; pierre faisant parpaing, pierre parpaigne, f.

perpetrate (peur-pi-), v.a., perpétrer, commettre.

perpetration (-pi-tré-), n., perpétration, f.

perpetrator, n., auteur d'un crime ; coupable, m.

perpetual (peur-pèt'iou-), adj., perpétuel, continuel ; constant.

perpetually, adv., perpétuellement, continuellement.

perpetuate (pèr-pèt'iou-), v.a., perpétuer.

perpetuation (pèr-pèt'iou-é-), n., perpétuation, f.

perpetuity (peur-pi-tiou-), n., perpétuité, f.

perplex (pèr-), v.a., embarrasser, embrouiller, brouiller; rendre perplexe, jeter dans la perplexité.

perplexedly, adv., d'une manière embrouillée; avec embarras.

perplexedness, or **perplexity**, n., embrouillement; embarras, m.: perplexité, f.

perquisite (peur-kwi-zite), n., revenant-bon, émolument, m. —s; revenants-bons; profits éventuels; émoluments, m.pl.; casuel, revenu casuel, m.

perquisition (peur-kwi-zish'-), n., perquisition, f.

perron (pèr-reune), n., perron, m.

perroquet (pè-ro-kète), n., perruche, f.

perry (pèr-), n., poiré, m.

persecute (peur-si-kioute), v.a., persécuter.

persecuting, adj., persécuteur.

persecution, n., persécution, f.

persecutor, n., persécuteur, m., persécutrice, f.

perseverance (peur-si-vir-), n., persévérance, f.

persevere (peur-si-vîre), v.n., persévérer.

persevering, adj., persévérant.

perseveringly, adv., avec persévérance.

persian (peur-shi-), or **persic** (peur-), adj., de Perse; persan.

persian, n., Persan, m., Persane, f.; (antiq.) Perse; (language—langue) perse, m.; (stuff—étoffe) marceline, f.

persicaria (pèr-), n., (bot.) renouée d'Orient, grande persicaire, herbe vierge, f.

persist (pèr-), v.n., persister.

persistence, or **persistency**, n., persistance; opiniâtreté, f.

persistent, or **persisting**, adj., (bot.) persistant.

persistive, adj., persévérant.

person (peur-), n., personne, f.; personnage, caractère, m.; (gram.) personne, f. —s; personnes. f.pl.; gens, pl.m., f.; monde, m. A —; une personne; quelqu'un, quelqu'une. —s say so; on le dit. Young —s; les jeunes gens. In —; en personne. No —; personne, m.

personable (peur-ceu'n'a-b'l), adj., de bonne mine; beau de sa personne.

personage (peur-ceu'n'édje), n., personnage, m., personne, f.

personal, adj., personnel.

personality, n., personnalité, f.

personally, adv., personnellement.

personate, v.a., passer pour, se faire passer pour un autre; représenter; feindre; jouer; jouer le rôle de; ressembler.

personate, v.a., passer pour un autre.

personation (peur-ceu'n'é-), n., action de se faire passer pour un autre, f.

personator, n., personne qui passe pour une autre, f.; acteur, m.

personification (-fi-ké-), n., personnification, f.

personify (-i-fa-ye), v.a., personnifier.

personnel (pèr-so-nèl), n., personnel, m.

perspective (pèr-spèk'-), adj., perspectif, m.

perspective, n., perspective, f.; aspect, m. — -glass; lunette d'approche, f.

perspectively, adv., par une lunette; selon les règles de la perspective.

perspicacious (peur-spi-ké-sheusse), adj., pénétrant, clairvoyant, perspicace; (of the sight—de la vue) perçant.

perspicaciousness (peur-spi-ké-sheus'-), n., vue perçante, f.

perspicacity (peur-), or **perspicacy** (ant.), n., vue pénétrante, perspicacité; sagacité; clarté, f.

perspicuity, or **perspicuousness** (peur-spi-kiou-), n., clarté, perspicuité, f.

perspicuous, adj., clair, net.

perspicuously, adv., nettement, avec clarté.

perspirability (per-spaeur'-), n., nature transpirable, f.

perspirable (-a-b'l), adj., transpirable.

perspiration (peur-spi-ré-), n., transpiration, sueur, f.

perspirative, or **perspiratory** (peur-spaeur'et-), adj., sudorifère, sudorifique.

perspire (pèr-spaeur), v.n., transpirer.

persuade (pèr-swéde), v.a., persuader; persuader à; déterminer, décider. To — from; dissuader.

persuader, n., personne qui persuade, f.

persuasibility, or **persuasibleness** (-ci-), n., caractère d'être facile à persuader, m.

persuasible (-ci-b'l), adj., que l'on peut persuader; à qui l'on peut persuader; ⊙persuasible.

persuasion (-swé-jeune), n., persuasion; croyance; opinion; (creed—foi) croyance, opinion religieuse, f.

persuasive (-swé-cive), adj., persuasif, persuadant.

persuasively, adv., d'une manière persuasive.

persuasiveness, n., force persuasive, f.

persuasory (-swé-ço-), adj., persuasif.

pert (peurte), adj., éveillé; (saucy—impudent) impertinent, insolent; (ant.) vif.

pert, n., impertinent, m., impertinente, f.; insolent, m., insolente, f.

pertain (pèr-téne), v.n., appartenir; concerner, se rapporter.

pertinacious (peur-ti-né-sheusse), adj., persévérant; opiniâtre; obstiné.

pertinaciously, adv., avec persévérance; obstinément; opiniâtrément.

pertinaciousness, or **pertinacity**, n., persévérance; obstination, opiniâtreté, f.

pertinence, or **pertinency** (peur-), n., convenance; justesse, f.

pertinent (peur-), adj., pertinent, convenable, à propos.

pertinently, adv., pertinemment, convenablement; à propos.

pertly (peurt'-), adv., avec vivacité; (saucily—impudemment) impertinemment, insolemment.

pertness (peurt'-), n., vivacité; (sauciness—impudence) impertinence, insolence, f.

perturbation (pèr-teur-bé-), n., bouleversement, trouble, m.; agitation; perturbation, f.

perturbator, or **perturber**, n., perturbateur, m.

perturbed (pèr-teurb'de), adj., troublé, inquiet, agité.

pertuse (pèr-tiouze), or **pertused** (-tiouz'de) (ant.), adj., percé, foré.

pertusion (pèr-tiou-jeune), n., percement; trou, m.

peruke (pèr-ouke), n., perruque, f.

peruke, v.a., coiffer d'une perruque.

peruke-maker (-mék'-), n., perruquier, m.

perusal (pi-riou-zal), n., lecture, f. Worthy of —; digne d'être lu.

peruse (pi-riouze), v.a., lire attentivement; lire, parcourir.

peruser, n., lecteur, examinateur, m.

peruvian (pi-riou-), adj., péruvien.

pervade (pèr-), v.a., pénétrer; pénétrer dans; régner dans; se répandre dans.

pervasion (pèr-vé-jeune), n., pénétration, f.

perverse (pèr-veurse), adj., pervers, méchant; mauvais.

perversely, *adv.*, avec perversité ; mechamment.

perverseness, *or* **perversity**, *n.*, perversité ; méchanceté. *f.*

perversion, *n.*, perversion, *f.*

pervert (pèr-veurte), *v.a.*, pervertir.

perverter, *n.*, corrupteur. *m.*, corruptrice,*f.*

pervertible, *adj.*, qui peut être perverti.

pervicacious (peur-vi-ké-sheusse), *adj.*, obstiné.

pervicaciously, *adv.*, avec opiniâtreté.

pervious (peur-), *adj.*, pénétrable ; abordable ; perméable.

perviousness, *n.*, pénétrabilité ; perméabilité, *f.*

pesade (pi-zâde),·*n.*, (man.) pesade, *f.*

pessary (pès-), *n.*, (med.) pessaire, *m.*

pessimist (pès-), *n.*, pessimiste, *m.*

pest (pèste), *n.*, peste. *f.*

pester (pès'-), *r.a.*, tourmenter, ennuyer, assommer.

pesterer,*n.*,ennuyeux,importun,fâcheux.*m.*

pest-house (-haouce), *n.*, maison de pestiférés, *m*

pestiferous (pès-tif'èr'-), *adj.*, pestifère, pestilentiel ; pestiféré ; malfaisant, funeste.

pestilence (pès-),·*n.*, peste, pestilence, *f.*

pestilent(pès-),*adj.*,pestilentiel, contagieux; (troublesome—*fatigant*) méchant ; malfaisant ; funeste; malicieux.

pestilential (-lè'n'shal), *adj.*, pestilentiel ; malfaisant, funeste.

pestilently,*adv.*, fatalement, mortellement.

pestle (pès-t'l), *n.*, pilon, *m.*

pet (pè't), *n.*, boutade, *f.*; dépit ; accès d'humeur ; (lamb—*agneau*) agneau élevé à la cuiller ; (fondling—*chéri*) favori, *m.*, favorite, *f.* To be in a —; *être piqué, être dépité ; se dépiter*.

pet, *r.a.*, choyer, dorloter, gâter.

petal (pèt'-*or* pi-), *n.*, (bot.) pétale. *m.*

petaled (pèt'alde), *or* **petalous**, *adj.*, à pétale ; pétalé.

petard (pi-târde), *n.*, (milit.) pétard, *m.*

petasus (pèt-a-ceusse), *n.*, pétase, *m.*

pet-cock, *n.*, robinet d'essai, *m.*

petersham (pî-teur-), *n.*, ratine, *f.*

petiole (pèt'i-ôle), *n.*, (bot.) pétiole, *m.*

petition (pi-tish'-), *n.*, requête, pétition, demande, *f.*; placet, *m.*; supplication, supplique, prière, *f.* Right of —; *droit de pétition, m.*

petition, *r.a.*, supplier ; présenter une pétition à ; pétitionner.

petitionarily, *adv.*, par voie de pétition ; par supplication.

petitionary, *adj.*, suppliant ; de supplication.

petitionee, *n.*, personne contre laquelle on a présenté une pétition,*f.*

petitioner, *n.*, pétitionnaire, *m.*, *f.*; suppliant, *m.*, suppliante, *f.*

petitioning, *n.*, pétition, *f.*

petrean (pi-tri-), *adj.*, de rocher, pierreux.

petrel (pèt-rèl), *n.*, pétrel, *m.*

petrescence (pi-très'-), *n.*, pétrification, *f.*

petrescent, *adj.*, qui se pétrifie.

petrifaction (pèt-ri-fak-), *or* **petrification** (-fi-ké-), *n.*, pétrification, *f.*

petrifactive (pèt-), *or* **petrific** (pi-), *adj.*, pétrifiant.

petrify (pèt-ri-fa-ye), *v.a.* and *n.*, pétrifier; se pétrifier.

petrol (pi-), *or* **petroleum** (pi-trô-li-), *n.*, huile de pétrole, *f.*

petronel (pèt'-), *n.*, pistolet d'arçon, *m.*

petro-silex (pè-tro-caï-lèkse), *n.*, pétrosilex,*m.*

petrous (pî-), *adj.*, pierreux.

petticoat (pèt'ti-côte), *n.*, jupe,*f.* ; jupon,

m.; (of little boys—*de petits garçons*) jaquette,*f.* —-government ; *régime du cotillon, m.*

pettifog (pèt'-), *c.n.*, avocasser.

pettifogger (-gheur), *n.*, homme de loi, avoué, avocat ; chicaneur, *m.*

pettifoggery (-gheri), *n.*, chicane,*f.*

pettifogging (-ghigne), *adj.*, chicaneur; chicanier.

pettiness (pèt'-), *n.*, petitesse. *f.*

pettish (pèt'-), *adj.*, qui a des boutades ; bourru.

pettishly,*adv.*, par boutade; d'une manière bourrue; de dépit, par dépit.

pettishness,*n.*, aigreur ; humeur bourrue,*f.*

pettitoes (pèt'ti-tôze), *n.*, pieds de cochon, *m.pl.* ; (jest.) pattes, *f.pl.*

in **petto**, *adv.*, in petto.

petty (pèt'-), *adj.*, petit ; mesquin, chétif ; (jur.) inférieur.

petulance, *or* **petulancy** (pèt'-iou-), *n.*, pétulance ; impertinence,*f.*

petulant, *adj.*, pétulant ; impertinent, insolent.

petulantly, *adv.*, pétulamment ; avec pétulance ; insolemment, impertinemment.

petuntze (pi-teu'n'se), *n.*, pétunsé, pétunzé, *m.*

pew (piou), *n.*, banc d'église ; banc, *m.* Churchwarden's —; *banc de l'œuvre, banc d'œuvre, m.*

pewet (pî-wète), *or* **pewit** (pi-wîte), *n.*, (orni.) huppe, *f.* ; pouillot, *m.*

pewter (piou-), *n.*, étain, *m.*; potée d'étain,*f.*

pewterer, *n.*, potier d'étain, *m.*

phaeton (fé-î-), *n.*, phaéton ; (orni.) paille-en-queue, *m.*

phalanx, *n.* (*phalanges*). phalange, *f.*

phantasm (-taz'm), *or* **phantasma** (-taz'-), *n.*, vision, illusion, *f.*

phantasmagoria (-taz ma-gô-), *or* **phantasmagory** (-taz'-), *n.*, fantasmagorie,*f.*

phantom, *n.*, fantôme. *m.*

pharaon (fé-), *n.* *V.* **faro**.

pharisaic, *or* **pharisaical** (-cé-ik, -cé-i-cal). *adj.*, pharisaïque.

pharisaicalness, *n.*, pharisaïsme, *m* .

pharisean, *adj.*, pharisaïque.

pharisee (-cî), *n.*, pharisien, *m.*, pharisienne,*f.*

pharmaceutic,*or* **pharmaceutical**(fàrma-ciou-), *adj.*, pharmaceutique.

pharmaceutically, *adv.*, suivant la pharmaceutique.

pharmaceutics, *n.pl.*, pharmaceutique, *f.* *sing.*

pharmacologist (-djiste), *n.*, auteur qui traite de la pharmacologie, *m.*

pharmacology (-dji), *n.*, pharmacologie, *f.*

pharmacopoeia (-pî-ia),*n.*,pharmacopée,*f.*

pharmacopolist, *n.*, pharmacien, apothicaire, (jest.) pharmacopole, *m.*

pharmacy, *n.*, pharmacie, *f.*

pharos (fé-), *n.*, phare. *m.*

pharynx, *n.*, (anat.) pharynx, *m.*

phase (féze), *or* **phasis** (fé-cice) *n.* (*phases*). phase, *f.*

pheasant (fèz'-), *n.*, faisan, *m.* Hen— ; *faisande, faisane, poule faisane, f.*

pheasantry (fèz'-), *n.*, faisanderie, *f.*

pheese (fize), *r.a.*, peigner, étriller ; rabattre.

phenomenon (n-no'm'i-), *n.* (*phenomena*), phénomène. *m.*

phial (faï-), *n.*, fiole, *f.*

philanthropic, *or* **philanthropical**, *adj.*, philanthropique.

philanthropist (n-), *n.*, philanthrope, *m.*,*f.*

philanthropy, *n.*, philanthropie,*f.*

philharmonic, *adj.*, philharmonique.

philhellenist (-hèl'lè'n'-),*n.*, philhellène, *m*

philippic, *n.*, philippique,*f.*

philippize (-païze), *v.n.*, faire des philippiques, invectiver.

philologer (-djeur), *or* **philologist** (-djiste), *n.*, philologue, linguiste, *m.*

philologic, *or* **philological** (-o-dj'-), *adj.*, philologique.

philology (-dji-), *n.*, philologie, linguistique, *f.*

philomel, *or* **philomela** (-mi-la), *n.*, philomèle, *f.*, rossignol, *m.*

philomot, *adj.*, feuille-morte.

philosopher (-loss'-),*n.*,philosophe; savant; moraliste; physicien, *m.* —'s stone; *pierre philosophale.* Natural —; *physicien, m.*

philosophic, *or* **philosophical** (-çof'-), *adj.*, philosophique; de morale; de physique.

philosophically,*adv.*,philosophiquement; par la morale, par la physique.

philosophism (-fiz'me),*n.*,philosophisme,*m.*

philosophist, *n.*, philosophiste, faux philosophe, *m.*

philosophistic, *or* **philosophistical**, *adj.*, de philosophiste.

philosophize (-faïze), *v.n.*, philosopher.

philosophy, *n.*, philosophie; morale; physique. *f.* Natural —; *physique,f.*

philter, *n.*, philtre, *m.*

philter, *v.a.*, donner un philtre à.

phimosis (-mô-cice), *n.*, (med.) phimosis, *m.*

phiz, *n.*, visage, *m.*; trogne. *f.*

phlebotomist (fli-), *n.*, phlébotomiste, *m.*

phlebotomize (fli-bot'o-maïze), *v.a.*, saigner.

phlebotomy (fli-bot'-), *n.*, phlébotomie, saignée,*f.*

phlegm (flème), *n.*, flegme, phlegme, *m.*; pituite,*f.*

phlegmatic, *or* **phlegmatical** (flèg-), *adj.*,flegmatique, phlegmatique; pituiteux.

phlegmatically, *adv.*, flegmatiquement.

phlegmon(flèg-), *n.*,(med.)phlegmon, flegmon, *m.*

phlegmonous (flèg-), *adj.*, (med.) phlegmoneux, flegmoneux.

phlogistic (-djis'-),*adj.*, phlogistique.

phlogiston (-djis-), *n.*, phlogistique, *m.*

phoca (fô-), *n.*, (mam.) phoque, *m.*

phœbus (fi-),*n.*, Apollon; Phébus; soleil, *m.*

phœnix (fi-), *n.*, phénix, *m.* —like; *comme le phénix.*

pholas, *n.*, pholade,*f.*

phonic, *adj.*, phonique, phonétique.

phonics, *n.pl.*, phonique, phonétique,*f.sing.*

phonography, *n.*, phonographie, *f.*

phonology (-dji), *n.*, phonologie,*f.*

phosphate, *n.*, phosphate, *m.*

phosphor, *n.*, phosphore; (astron.) Lucifer, *m.*

phosphoresce (-rès'ce), *v.n.*, être phosphorescent.

phosphorescence (-rès'-), *n.*, phosphorescence,*f.*

phosphorescent(-rès'-),*adj.*,(chem.)phosphorescent.

phosphoric, *adj.*, phosphorique.

phosphorus, *or* **phosphor**, *n.*, (chem.) phosphore, *m.*; (astron.)étoile du matin,*f.* — box; *briquet phosphorique, m.*

phosphuret (-fiou-), *n.*, (chem.) phosphure, *m.*

phosphuretted (-fiou-),*adj.*, (chem.) phosphuré.

photogenic (-todj'-), *adj.*, photogénique.

photographer, *or* **photographist**, *n.*, photographe, *m.*

photographic, *adj.*, photographique.

photography (-toj'-), *n.*, photographie, *f.*

photometer (-to'm'i-), *n.*, photomètre, *m.*

photometric, *or* **photometrical**, *adj.*, photométrique.

photometry (-to'm'i-), *n.*, photométrie, *f.*

phrase (-frèze), *n.*, phrase; locution,*f.*

phrase, *v.a.*, exprimer; appeler, nommer.

phraseologic, *or* **phraseological**(fré-zi-ol-o-dj'-), *adj.*, phraséologique.

phraseologist, *n.*, phraseur, *G.*phrasier,*m.*

phraseology (fré-zi-ol-o-dji), *n.*, phraséologie,*f.*

phrenetic (fri-nèt'-), *adj.*, fou, frénétique.

phrenic (frè'n'-), *adj.*, (anat.) phrénique.

phrenitis (fri-naï-). *n.*, frénésie. *f.*

phrenologic, *or* **phrenological** (fri-nol-odj'-), *adj.*. phrénologique.

phrenologist, *n.*, phrénologiste, phrénologue, *m.*

phrenology(fri-nol-o-dji),*n.*,phrénologie,*f.*

phrensy (frè'n'zi),*or* **frenzy**,*n.*, frénésie,*f.*

phthisical (fthiz-ik'-),*adj.*, phtisique.

phthisis (fthiz'-), *n.*, phtisie,*f.*

phylacter, *or* **phylactery**, *n.*, phylactère, *m.*

phyllite (fil'laïte), *n.*, phyllithe, *m.*

physic (fiz'-), *n.*, médecine,*f.*; remède, *m.*, —s; *physique,f.sing.*

physic,*v.a.*, médicamenter; médeciner; droguer; (to cure—*guérir*) guérir.

physical, *adj.*, physique; (med.) médical; médicinal, de médecine.

physically, *adv.*, physiquement.

physician (fi'zish'-), *n.*, médecin, *m.*

physics (fiz'-), *n.pl.*, physique,*f.sing.*

physiognomer,*or* **physiognomist** (fiz'i-og-no-), *n.*, physionomiste, *m.*

physiognomic, *or* **physiognomical** (fiz'iog-no-, *ou* fiz'i-o'n'o-), *adj.*, de la physionomie; physiognomonique.

physiognomy (fiz'i-og-no-,*ou* -o'n'o-mi), *n.*, physionomie; physiognomonie,*f.*

physiographical (fiz'-), *adj.*, physiographique.

physiography (fiz'-), *n.*, physiographie,*f.*

physiologer, *or* **physiologist** (fiz'i-ol-odj'-), *n.*, physiologiste, *m.*

physiological (fiz'i-ol-odj'-), *adj.*, physiologique.

physiologically, *adv.*, de, par la physiologie.

physiology (fiz'i-ol'o-dji), *n.,* physiologie,*f.*

phytography, *n.*, phytographie, *f.*

phytolite (fit'o-laïte), *n.*, phytolithe, *f.*

phytology (fi-tol'o-dji), *n.*, phytologie,*f.*

pia mater (paï-a-mé-teur), *n.*, (anat.) pie-mère,*f.*

pianet, *n.*, (orni.) petit pivert, *m.*

pianino, *n.*, (mus.) pianino, *m.*

pianist, *n.*, pianiste, *m.,f.*

piano, *or* **piano-forte** (pi-â-no-fôr-té), *n.*, piano, *m.* Grand—; *piano à queue.* Cabinet—; *grand piano droit.* Square, upright —; *piano carré, droit.* —-maker; *facteur de pianos, m.*

piaster, *n.*, piastre,*f.*

piazza, *n.*, arcade, galerie; place,*f.*; passage, *m.*

pibroch (paï-broke), *n.*, pibroch, *m.*, cornemuse écossaise; musique de cornemuse.*f.*

pica (paï-), *n.*, (print.) cicéro, *m.*; (orni.) pie,*f.*; (med.) pica, *m.*

picaroon (-roune), *n.*, pilleur, pirate, forban, *m.*

pick, *n.*, (a tool—*outil*) pic, *m.*; (print.) ordure, *f.*; (choice—*le meilleur*) choix, *m.*

pick, *v.a.*, (to pull off—*retirer*) enlever, ôter; (to gather—*cueillir*) cueillir; (to choose—*choisir*) prendre, choisir, trier; (a bone—*un os*) ronger; (a quarrel—*querelle*) chercher; (a fowl, &c.—*volaille, &c.*) plumer; (a pocket—*les poches*) voler à la tire; (a lock—*serrure*) crocheter; éplucher. To — one's nose; *se nettoyer le nez*; tourmenter, son nez. To — one's teeth, one's nails; *se curer les dents, les ongles.* To — off, to — out; *enlever,*

ôter; (to choose—*choisir*) tr*i*er, choisir. To — up; *ramasser, rel·ver; raccrocher.*

pick, v.n., faire avec délicatesse et soin ; (to eat—*manger*) pignocher. To — up again ; *reprendre ses forces; se refaire.*

pickaback. *adv.,* sur le dos.

pickaxe (pik'akse), *n.,* pioche, *f.,* pic, *m.*

picked (pikte), *adj.,* épluché ; (pointed— *pointu*) pointu ; (choice—*choisi*) d'élite, choisi.

pickedness (pik'ẽd'-), *n.,* état pointu, *m.*

pickeer (pick'īre), *v.a.,* (ant.) picorer; escarmoucher.

picker, *n.,* cueilleur, *m.,* cueilleuse, *f.* ; éplucheur, *m.,* éplucheuse, *f.* ; (tool — *outil*) pioche, *f.*

pickerel, *n.,* (ich.) brocheton, *m.*

picket, *n.,* pieu, piquet ; (cards—*cartes*, milit.) piquet, *m.*

picket. *v.a.,* enfermer de piquets ; (milit.) former en piquet.

picking, *n.,* action de cueillir, d'ôter, d'enlever, de choisir, *f.* ; épluchement, cueillage; glanage ; triage, *m.* —*s;* *épluchures* ; (fig.) *choses à recueillir, f.pl.*

pickle (pick'l), *n.,* saumure, *f.* —*s ; conserves au vinaigre, f.pl. ; marinade, f.* To be in a fine—; *être dans un bel état, dans de beaux draps, dans la sauce.*

pickle, *v.a.,* mariner, saler; confire au vinaigre.

pickled (pick'lde), *adj.,* salé ; mariné ; confit au vinaigre.

picklock, *n.,* crochet à serrure; (pers.) crocheteur de serrures, *m.*

pickpocket, *or* **pickpurse** (-peurse), *n.,* filou, voleur à la tire; coupeur de bourses, *m.*

pickthank (-tha'n'k), *n.,* flagorneur, *m.*

picnic, *n.,* pique-nique, *m.*

pictorial (-tô-). *adj.,* de peintre ; illustré.

pictorially, *adv.,* par des peintures.

picture (pikt'ieur), *n.,* peinture, *f.;* tableau, portrait, *m.*

picture (pikt'ieur), *v.a.,* peindre, dépeindre, décrire.

picturesque (pikt'iou-rèske), *adj.,* pittoresque.

picturesque, *or* **picturesqueness,** *n.,* pittoresque, *m.*

picturesquely, *adv.,* d'une manière pittoresque.

piddle (pid'd'l), *v.n.,* s'occuper de bagatelles, pignocher, niaiser; uriner.

piddler, *n.,* personne qui pignoche, qui s'occupe de bagatelles, *f.*

piddling, *adj.,* futile, frivole.

pie (pâ'-ye), *n.,* (of meat—*de viande*) pâté, *m.,* (fruit) tourte ; (orni.) pie, *f.;* (print.) pâté, *m.,* pâte, *f.*

piebald (pâ'-ye-bôld), *adj.,* (of horses—*des chevaux*) pie.

piece (pîce), *n.,* (of large dimensions—*de grandes dimensions*) pièce, *f.* ; (a portion, a bit, a hunch—*petite portion*) morceau ; (fragment) fragment, bout ; (action) acte, exemple, *m.* ; (of money, of poetry, &c.—*d'argent, de poésie, &c.*) pièce ; (artil.) pièce ; (paint.) scène, *f.;* tableau, *m.;* (for mending—*pour raccommoder*) pièce ; (of wine— *de vin*) pièce, *f.* A — of water; *une pièce d'eau.* The —s of a machine; *les pièces d'une machine.* A — of soap, of bread; *un morceau de savon, de pain.* A theatrical —; *une pièce de théâtre.* To break to — s; *mettre en morceaux, en pièces; tomber en morceaux, en pièces.* To fall to —s; *se démonter ; tomber en pièces.* To take to —s; *démonter ; se démonter.* To fly to —s; *voler en éclats.* All of a —; *d'une seule pièce ; d'un seul morceau; tout d'une pièce.* A—; *chacun ; par tête ; la pièce.* What a — of a man! *quel bout d'homme !*

piece, *v.a.,* rapiécer, rapetasser, mettre une

---

pièce à : allonger. To — out ; *allonger.* To —up; plâtrer.

piece, *v.n.,* se joindre ; s'unir.

piece-hand, *n.,* (print.) paquetier, *m.*

pieceless, *adj.,* entier.

piecemeal (piss'mîl), *adv.,* en pièces, par pièces, pièce à pièce; par morceaux; peu à peu.

piecer, *n.,* ravaudeur, *m.,* ravaudeuse, *f.*

piecework (-weurke), *n.,* ouvrage fait à la pièce, *m.*

pied (pâ'-ye'de), *adj.,* bigarré ; (of horses— *des chevaux*) pie.

piedness (pâ'-ye'-d'-), *n.,* bigarrure, *f.*

pier (pi'eur), *n.,* jetée, *f.* ; embarcadère, *m.;* (of a bridge) pile, *f.;* (arch.) contrefort, trumeau, *m.*

pierage (pi-eur'édje), *n.,* droit de jetée, *m.*

pierce (pîr-ce, *ou* pieur-ce), *v.a.,* percer, pénétrer ; pénétrer dans.

piercer, *n.,* perçoir, *m.;* (mines) épinglette ; (pers.) perceur, celui qui perce, *m.*

piercing, *adj.,* perçant; pénétrant ; (of sound —*du son*) perçant, aigu.

piercingly, *adv.,* d'une manière perçante, d'une manière pénétrante.

piercingness, *n.,* pénétration, *f.;* son aigu, *m.*

pier-glass (-glâce), *n.,* glace en trumeau, *f.*

pier-shaft (-shâfte), *n.,* fût vertical de pile, *m.*

pier-table (-té-b'l), *n.,* console, *f.*

pietist (paï-èt-), *n.,* piétiste, *m., f.*

piety (paï-è-), *n.,* piété, *f.*

pig, *n.,* cochon, *m.,* cochonne, *f.* ; porc, pourceau ; (metal.) lingot, saumon, *m.* Sucking-—; *cochon de lait, m.*

pig, *v.a.* and *n.,* cochonner; vivre en pourceau ; mettre bas.

pig-driver (-draïv'-), *n.,* porcher, *m.*

pigeon (pidj'n), *n.,* pigeon, *m.* ; (pers.) dupe, *f.*

pigeon-dung (-dea'n'gn), *n.,* colombine, *f.*

pigeon-hearted (-hârt'-), *adj.,* timide, craintif.

pigeon-hole (-hôl), *n.,* boulin, *m.;* (for papers, &c.—*pour papiers, &c.*) case, *f.*

pigeon-house (-haouce), *n.,* pigeonnier, colombier, *m.*

pigeon-livered (-liv'eur'de), *adj.,* sans fiel, doux.

pigeon-toed (-tôde), *adj.,* qui marche avec les pieds en dedans.

piggery (pig'gheur'i), *n.,* toit à cochons, *m.*

pig-headed (-hèd'ède), *adj.,* à grosse tête ; stupide.

pigmean (-mî-), *adj.,* de pigmée.

pigment, *n.,* couleur, *f.;* pigment, *m.*

pigmy, *n.,* pigmée, *m.*

pigmy, *adj.,* de pigmée ; très petit.

pig-nut (-neute), *n.,* (bot.) terre-noix, *f.*

pig-sty (-sta'ye), *n.,* toit à cochons, *m.*

pig-tail (-téle), *n.,* queue (de cheveux, *f.;* (tobacco—*tabac*) tabac en corde, *m.*

pike (païke), *n.,* pique, *f.;* (ich.) brochet, *m.*

piked (païk'te), *adj.,* pointu.

pikeman (païk'-), *n.,* piquier, *m.*

pikestaff (païk'stâf), *n.,* bois de pique ; bâton pointu, *m.*

pilaff, *n.,* pilau, *m.*

pilaster, *n.,* pilastre, *m.;* colonne plaquée, *f.*

pilchard (piltsh'-), *n.,* (ich.) sardine, *f.*

pile (païl), *n.,* pile, *f.;* tas, monceau ; (of firearms—*d'armes à feu*) faisceau, *m.;* (building— *bâtiment*) construction, *f.,* édifice, bâtiment, *m* ; (of shot—*de boulets*) pile, *f.* ; (arch.) pieu, pilotis, *m.* ; (phys.) pile, *f.* Funeral —; *bûcher, m.*

pile (païl), *v.a.,* entasser, empiler, amonceler ; (milit.) mettre en faisceau.

pile, *v.a.,* piloter; enfoncer des pieux.

pileate, *or* **pileated** (pil-i-), *adj.,* en forme de chapeau.

pile-driver (-draïv'-), n., (mec.) sonnette, f.; (nav.) bâtiment canard, m.

pile-engine (-è'n'dji'n), n. V. **pile-driver** (mec.).

pile-planking, n., plancher sur pilotis, m.; plate-forme sur pilotis, f.

pile-planks, n., palplanches, f.pl.

piler (païl'-), n., personne qui empile, qui entasse, f.; empileur, m.

piles (païl'ze), n., (med.) hémorroïdes, f.pl.

pileus (païl'i-), n., (bot.) chapeau, m.

pile-work (-weurke), n., pilotage, m.; pilotis, m.

pilfer, v.a., dérober, voler.

pilfer, v.n., voler, dérober; commettre un larcin, un petit vol.

pilferer, n., auteur d'un petit vol, d'un larcin; petit voleur; larron, m.

pilfering, n., petit vol; larcin, m.

pilferingly, adv., par vol, par larcin.

pil-garlick (-gâr'-), n., personne chauve par suite de maladie, f.; pauvre diable, m.

pilgrim, n., pèlerin, m., pèlerine, f.

pilgrimage ('-édje), n., pèlerinage, m.

piling (païl'-), n., empilement; amoncellement; (arch.) ouvrage en pilotis, pilotage, m.

pill, n., pilule, f.

pill, v.a., administrer des pilules à; (to rob—voler) piller, voler.

pill, v.n., piller, voler.

pillage (pil-lédje), n., pillage, sac, saccagement, m.

pillage, v.a., saccager, piller.

pillager, n., pillard, m.

pillar (pil'-), n., pilier, m.; colonne, f.; (support) support, m., fondation, f.; (monument) monument, m.

pillared (pil-larde), adj., soutenu par des colonnes; à colonnes.

pillar-plate, n., (horl.) platine, f.

pillion (pil'ieune), n., coussinet, m.; selle de femme, f.

pillory, n., pilori, m.

pillory, v.a., pilorier, mettre au pilori.

pillow (pil'lô), n., oreiller; (nav.) coussin du mât de beaupré; (of a plough—de charrue) (tech.) coussinet, m. — -case; taie d'oreiller, f.

pillow, v.a., poser, coucher (comme sur un oreiller); servir d'oreiller à, soutenir.

pilose (pi-lôce), or **pilous** (pi-), adj., poilu; (bot.) capillaire.

pilosity (pi-loss'-), n., abondance de poils, f.

pilot (paï-), n., pilote; (coat—vêtement) paletot-pilote, m. — -boat; bateau-pilote, m.

pilot, v.a., piloter; servir de pilote à; conduire, diriger.

pilotage (paï-lot'édje), n., droit de pilotage, m.

piloting (paï-lot'-), n., pilotage, m.

pimenta, or **pimento** (-tô), n., (bot.) piment, m.

pimp, n., entremetteur; maquereau, m.

pimp, v.n., faire l'entremetteur; faire le maquereau.

pimpernel, or **pimpinella**, n., (bot.) pimprenelle, f.

pimple (pi'm'p'l), n., pustule, f.; bourgeon, bouton. m

pimpled (pi'm'p'l'de), adj., bourgeonné, pustuleux.

pin, n., épingle; (peg—cheville) cheville; (linchpin—esse) esse, clavette; (of a hinge—de charnière) fiche, f.; (of a pulley—de poulie) essieu, m.; (bolt, tree-nail—boulon) cheville, f.; (centre) centre; (valueless thing—bagatelle) fétu, rien, m., valeur d'une épingle, f. Rolling- —; rouleau, m. Not to care a — for; se moquer pas mal de; se soucier comme de l'an quarante de. To be upon — s and needles; être sur des charbons.

pin, v.a., attacher avec une épingle; attacher

avec une cheville; attacher; clouer; arrêter; cheviller. To — down; attacher avec une épingle; (tech.) cheviller. To — any one down to; clouer, lier quelqu'un à. To — up; attacher avec une épingle, trousser avec une épingle.

pinafore, n., blouse; blouse d'enfant, f.; tablier, m.

pinaster, n., (bot.) pinastre, m.

pincase (-kéce), n., étui à épingles, m.

pincers (pi'n'ceurze), n.pl., pince, f.sing.; tenailles, f.pl.

pinch (pi'n'sh), n., (of salt, &c —de sel, &c.) pincée; (of snuff—de tabac) prise; (straits—pénurie) gêne, extrémité, nécessité, f., besoin; (gripe—pincement) pinçon, m., meurtrissure faite en pinçant; (distress—détresse) angoisse, f.

pinch, v.a., pincer; (of clothes—des vêtements) serrer, gêner; (of cold—du froid) pincer; (to deprive—priver) priver, refuser à; (to press hard—presser) serrer de près; (to distress—faire souffrir) faire pâtir; (to straiten—gêner) gêner, mettre dans la gêne, mettre à l'étroit. To — one's self; se priver du nécessaire. To — off; arracher, emporter.

pinch, v.a., pincer; (to be straitened—être dans la gêne) se gêner, être dans la gêne.

pinchbeck, n., similor, m.

pincher, n., personne qui pince; chose qui pince, f.

pinchfist, or **pinchpenny**, n., pince-maille; ladre, m.

pincushion (-keush'ieune), n., pelote à épingles, f.

pindaric, adj., pindarique.

pindaric, n., ode pindarique, f.

pindust ('-deuste), n., limaille d'épingles, f.

pine (païne), n., (tree—arbre) pin; (fruit) ananas (wood—bois) bois de pin, m.

pine, v.n., languir, dépérir. To — after; languir après, soupirer après. To — away; languir, dépérir.

pineal (pai'n'i-), adj., (anat.) pinéal.

pine-apple (-ap'p'l), n., ananas, m.

pine-nut (-neute), n., pomme de pin, f.

pinery (paï'n'ri), n., serre d'ananas, f.

pin-feather (pi'n'fèth'-), n., petite plume, f.; duvet, m.

pinfeathered (-fèth'eur'de), adj., dont les plumes commencent à naître.

pinfold, n., bergerie, f.; parc, m.

pinion (pi'n'ieune), n., aileron, m.; (feather —plume) plume, f.; (quill—plume) bout d'aile; (tech.) pignon, m.; (fetters—attache) liens, pour les bras, m.pl.

pinion, v.a., lier les ailes à; couper le bout de l'aile à; lier les bras à; lier, attacher; garrotter, enchaîner.

pinioned (pi'n'ieu'n'de), adj., ailé; les bras liés, attachés.

pink, n., (bot.) œillet; (ich.) véron, m.; (nav.) pinque, f.; (model) modèle; (colour—couleur) rose, m.

pink, adj., couleur de rose; rose.

pink, v.a., travailler à jour; percer.

pin-maker (-mék'-), n., épinglier, m.

pin-money, n., épingles (don, gratification), f.pl.

pinna, n., (conch.) pinne marine, f.

pinnace (pi'n'néce), n., barque; pinasse, f.; grand canot du capitaine, m.

pinnacle (-na-k'l), n., tour, tourelle, f.; pinacle; faîte, m.; of glory; faîte de la gloire, m.

pinnacle, v.a., pourvoir de tours; (fig.) élever.

pinnate, pinnated (-nét'-), or **pinnulate** (-niou-léte), adj., (bot.) penné, pinné.

pinner, n., cornette, f.; bonnet, m.

pinnock, n., (orni.) mésange, f.

pint (païn'te), n., pinte (litre 0.5679), f.

pintle (pin't'l), *n.*, petite épingle ; (artil.) cheville ouvrière, *f.*

pioneer (pai-o-nîeur), *n.*, pionnier, *m.*

piony (paï-o-), *n.*, (bot.) pivoine, *f.*

pious (paï-), *adj.*, pieux, dévot, pie.

piously, *adv.*, pieusement.

pip, *n.*, pépie, *f.* ; (on cards—*aux cartes*) point ; (fruit) pépin, *m.*

pip, *v.n.*, crier.

pipe (païpe), *n.*, (mus.) pipeau, chalumeau ; (long tube, tech.) tuyau, conduit, *m.* ; (to smoke out of—*à tabac*) pipe, *f.* ; (key of the voice—*de la voix*) son, *m.* ; (measure—*mesure*) pipe (477 litres), *f.* ; (mines) amas horizontal ; (nav.) sifflet, *m.* Main — ; *tuyau principal.*

pipe (païpe), *v.a.*, jouer du chalumeau ; jouer d'un instrument à vent ; (of birds—*des oiseaux*) siffler ; (nav.) appeler à coups de sifflet.

pipe, *v.n.*, jouer d'un instruments à vent.

pipe-clay, *n.*, terre à pipe, *f.*

piped (païp'te), *adj.*, à tuyau ; tubulé ; (of keys—*de clefs*) foré.

piper (païp'-), *n.*, joueur de flûte ; joueur d'instrument à vent, *m.*

piperine, *n.*, piperin, *m.*, piperine, *f.*

piping (païp'-), *adj.*, faible, languissant. — hot (pop.) ; *tout bouillant, tout chaud.*

piping (païp'-), *n.*, liséré, *m.*

pipkin, *n.*, pot de terre, *m.*

pippin, *n.*, (bot.) reinette, pomme de reinette, *f.*

piquancy (pi-ka'n'-), *n.*, goût piquant ; piquant, *m.*

piquant (pi-ka'n'te), *adj.*, piquant.

piquantly, *adv.*, d'une manière piquante.

pique (pîke), *n.*, pique, brouille, brouillerie, *f.* ; (punctilio—*point*) point, *m.*

pique (pîke), *v.a.*, piquer, offenser. To — one's self on ; *se piquer de ; se glorifier de.*

piquet (pi-kète), *n.*, (cards—*cartes*, milit.) piquet, *m.*

piracy (paï-), *n.*, piraterie ; (lit.) contrefaçon, *f.*

pirate (paï-), *n.*, pirate, forban, écumeur de mer ; (lit.) contrefacteur, plagiaire, *m.*

pirate, *v.a.*, voler en pirate ; (lit.) contrefaire.

pirate, *v.n.*, pirater ; exercer la piraterie ; (lit.) faire la contrefaçon ; commettre un plagiat.

pirated, *adj.*, de contrefaçon ; de plagiat.

piratical, *adj.*, de pirate ; (lit.) de contrefaçon.

piratically, *adv.*, en pirate ; en contrefaçon.

pirating, *adj.*, de piraterie, de contrefaçon.

pirogue (pi-rôghe), *n.*, pirogue, *f.*

pirouette, *n.*, pirouette, *f.*

pirouette, *v.n.*, pirouetter.

piscary, *n.*, (jur.) droit de pêche, *m.*

piscatory, *or* **piscatorial** (-tô-), *adj.*, de la pêche ; de pêcheur.

Pisces (pi-cize), *n.pl.*, (astron.) les Poissons, *m.pl.*

piscina (-ci-), *n.*, piscine, *f.*

piscine, *adj.*, de poisson.

piscivorous, *adj.*, piscivore.

pish! *int.*, bah !

pish, *v.n.*, dire bah.

pismire (-maire), *n.*, (ent.) fourmi, *f.*

piss, *n.*, urine, *f.* ; pissat, *m.*

piss, *v.n.*, pisser, uriner.

piss, *v.a.*, pisser.

pissabed, *n.*, (bot.) pissenlit, *m.*

pissasphalt, *n.*, (min.) pissasphalte, *m.*

piss-burnt (-beurn'te), *adj.*, taché d'urine.

pissing, *n.*, pissement, *m.*

pissing-evil (-i-v'l), *n.*, (vet.) diabète ; relâchement de la vessie, *m.*

pissing-place, *n.*, pissoir, *m.*

pistachio (-tâ-klô), *n.*, pistache, *f.*

piste (piste), *n.*, piste, trace, *f.*

pistil, *n.*, (bot.) pistil, *m.*

pistol, *n.*, pistolet, *m.* — -case ; *boîte à pistolets*, *f.* — -shot ; *coup de pistolet.* Within -- shot ; *à portée de pistolet.*

pistol, *v.a.*, tuer d'un coup de pistolet.

pistole (-tôle), *n.*, pistole, *f.*

pistol-gallery, *n.*, tir au pistolet, *m.*

piston, *n.*, piston, *m.*

pit, *n.*, fosse ; cavité, *f.* ; creux ; (thea.) parterre ; (mines) puits ; (of the stomach—*de l'estomac*) creux, *m.* ; (of the arm—*du bras*) aisselle ; (for cock-fighting—*pour combat de coqs*) arène ; (mark—*marque*) marque, empreinte ; (of the small-pox—*de petite vérole*) marque, trace ; (grave—*tombe*) fosse ; (biblically—*biblique*) citerne, *f.* ; abîme, *m.*

pit, *v.a.*, creuser ; marquer de petits creux. To — with ; *marquer de.* To — against ; *opposer à.*

pitapat, *n.*, palpitation, *f.* ; battement de cœur, *m.*

pitapat, *adv.*, en palpitant, en battant. To go — ; *palpiter, battre.*

pitch, *n.*, (degree—*point*) point, degré ; (highest rise—*au plus haut*) plus haut point, plus haut degré, comble, *m.* ; (slope—*inclinaison*) pente, *f.*, penchant, versant, *m.* ; (stature) taille, stature ; (elevation) élévation, hauteur ; (arch., tech.) portée, *f.* ; (mus.) ton, diapason, *m.* ; (of a roof—*de toit*) pente ; (of the belt of a wheel—*de roue*) épaisseur ; (substance) poix, *f.*

pitch, *v.a.*, lancer, jeter ; précipiter ; (with a fork—*avec une fourche*) jeter avec la fourche ; (to fix—*établir*) asseoir, fixer ; (a tent—*tente*) dresser ; (camp) asseoir ; (mus.) donner le ton à ; (to smear with pitch—*poisser*) enduire de poix, poisser.

pitch, *v.n.*, (of vehicles—*de voitures*) plonger ; (of ships—*de vaisseaux*) plonger, tanguer ; (of birds—*des oiseaux*) s'abattre ; (a camp—*un camp*) camper ; (to fall—*tomber*) tomber. To — into ; *se jeter dans, se précipiter dans, plonger dans* ; (to fall foul of—*tomber dessus*) tomber dessus. To — upon ; *choisir ; faire choix de ; s'arrêter à.*

pitch-board (-bôrde), *n.*, planche de support, équerre, *f.*

pitch-coal (-côle), *n.*, jais, jaïet, *m.*

pitched (pitsh'te), *adj.*, rangé.

pitcher, *n.*, cruche, *f.*

pitch-farthing (-fàr-*thigne*), *n.*, fossette, *f.*

pitchfork, *n.*, fourche, *f.*

pitching, *n.*, (of vehicles—*de voitures*) plongement ; (of ships—*de vaisseaux*) plongement, tangage, *m.*

pitching, *adj.*, incliné ; en pente.

pitchy, *adj.*, poissé ; de poix ; enduit de poix ; (fig.) sombre.

pit-coal (-côle), *n.*, charbon de terre, *m.* ; houille, *f.*

piteous (pit'i-), *adj.*, digne de pitié ; piteux ; (compassionate—*compatissant*) compatissant ; (pitiful—*pitoyable*) pitoyable.

piteously, *adv.*, de manière à exciter la pitié ; avec compassion ; pitoyablement ; piteusement.

piteousness, *n.*, tristesse ; pitié, compassion, *f.*

pitfall (-fôl), *n.*, trappe, *f.* ; piège, *m.*

pitfall, *v.a.*, faire tomber dans une trappe, dans un piège.

pith (pith), *n.*, sève, moelle ; (force) force, énergie ; (quintessence) quintessence ; (importance) importance, *f.*, poids, *m.*

pith (pith), *v.a.*, ôter la moelle épinière à.

pithily (pith'-), *adv.*, fortement, avec force, énergiquement, avec énergie.

pithiness (pith'-), *n.*, force, vigueur, énergie, *f.*

pithless(pith'-), *adj.*, sans sève, sans moelle ; (fig.) sans énergie, sans force.

pithy (pith'-), *adj.*, plein de sève ; moelleux ; (fig.) fort, énergique, vigoureux.

pitiable (pit'i-a-b'l), *adj.*, digne de pitié ; pitoyable.

pitiableness, *n.*, état pitoyable, *m.*

pitiful (-foule), *adj.*, pitoyable ; (compassionate—*compatissant*) compatissant.

pitifully, *adv.*, pitoyablement ; avec compassion.

pitifulness. *n.*, caractère pitoyable, *m.* ; (pity—*pitié*) pitié, *f.*

pitiless, *adj.*, impitoyable, sans pitié, sans compassion.

pitilessly, *adv.*, impitoyablement ; sans pitié.

pitilessness, *n.*, caractère impitoyable, *m.* ; cruauté, *f.*

pitman, *n.*, scieur de long qui est au-dessous ; (mines) mineur, *m.*

pittance, *n.*, pitance ; légère portion ; légère dose, *f.*

pituite (pit'iou-aïte), *n.*, pituite, *f.*

pituitous (pit'iou-it'-). *adj.*, pituiteux.

pity, *n.*, pitié, *f.* ; dommage, *m.* For —'s sake ; *par pitié.* It is a — ; *c'est dommage.*

pity, *v.a.*, avoir pitié de, prendre en pitié ; plaindre. He is to be pitied ; *il est à plaindre.*

pivot, *n.*, pivot, *m.*

pix, *n.*, (coin.) boîte des monnaies d'or et d'argent à essayer, *f.* ; (c.rel.) ciboire, saint ciboire, *m.*

pize ! (païze), *int.*, peste ! malepeste !

pizzle (niz-z'l), *n.*, (of an ox—*de bœuf*) nerf, *m.*

placable (plé-ca-b'l), *adj.*, que l'on peut apaiser ; plicable.

placableness, *n.*, disposition facile à apaiser, *f.*

placard (-cârde), *n.*, placard, *m.*, affiche, *f.*

place, *n.*, place, *f.* ; endroit, lieu, *m.* ; (employment—*occupation*) place, *f.*, emploi ; (rank —*rang*) rang, *m.*, condition, *f.* ; (priority—*priorité*) pas, *m.*, préséance ; (milit.) place, place de guerre ; (space—*espace*) place, *f.*, espace ; (for a house, &c.—*de maison, &c.*) emplacement, *m.* Come to my — ; *venez chez moi.* In — of ; *à la place de ; au lieu de.* In one's, in its— ; *à sa place.* In the first — ; *en premier lieu ; d'abord.* To take — ; *avoir lieu.* Out of — ; *déplacé.*

place, *v.a.*, placer, mettre.

placeman, *n.*, fonctionnaire public, *m.*

placenta, *n.*, (anat., bot.) placenta, *m.*

placer, *n.*, personne qui place, *f.* ; (gold-digging—*recherche de l'or*) placer, *m.*

placid, *adj.*, placide, doux, tranquille, calme, serein, paisible.

placidly, *adv.*, placidement. doucement, tranquillement, avec calme, paisiblement.

placidness. *n.*, placidité, *f.*, calme, *m.* ; douceur, sérénité, tranquillité, *f.*

plagal (plé-), *adj.*, (mus.) plagal.

plagiarism (plé-ghi-a-riz'm). *n.*, plagiat, *m.*

plagiarist, *or* **plagiary** (plé-ghi-), *n.*, plagiaire, *m.*

plagiarize (plé-ghi-a-raïze), *v.a.*, s'approprier par plagiat.

plagiary, *adj.*, plagiaire.

plague (pléghe), *n.*, peste ; (fig.) plaie, *f.*, fléau, tourment, *m.*

plague (pléghe) *v.a.*, infecter de la peste ; (fig.) être une peste pour, une plaie pour, un fléau pour, un tourment pour ; tourmenter, ennuyer ; (pop.) embêter.

plaguily (plé-ghi-), *adv.*, furieusement, terriblement.

plaguy (plé-ghi), *adj.*, maudit ; méchant.

plaice (pléce), *n.*, (ich.) plie, *f.* ; carrelet, *m.*

plaid (plade), *n.*, étoffe écossaise, *f.* ; (garment—*vêtement*) manteau écossais, *m.*

plain (pléne), *n.*, plaine, *f.*

plain, *adj.*, (level—*de niveau*) uni, plat, plain ; (simple) (pers.) simple, sans façon ; (of things —*des choses*) simple ; (frank—*ouvert*) franc, sincère ; (evident) évident, clair ; (undisguised— *sans déguisement*) pur, franc ; (ordinary—*ordinaire*) commun, ordinaire ; (ugly—*laid*) laid ; (of stuffs—*des étoffes*) uni ; (of language—*du langage*) bon. — truth ; *pure vérité, franche vérité, f.*

plain. *adv.*, (frankly—*ouvertement*) franchement, sincèrement ; (evidently—*manifestement*) évidemment, clairement ; (distinctly—*nettement*) distinctement, intelligiblement.

plain, *v.a.*, aplanir.

plain-chant, *or* **plain-song**, *n.*, plain-chant, *m.*

plain-dealing (-dil'-), *n.*, droiture, probité, *f.*

plain-dealing, *adj.*, probe.

plainly, *adv.*, franchement, sincèrement, ouvertement, bonnement ; évidemment, clairement ; simplement ; distinctement ; (with a level surface—*à surface plate*) de niveau.

plainness, *n.*, (levelness—*de niveau*) surface plane, unie ; égalité ; (fig.) franchise, sincérité ; évidence, clarté ; nature ordinaire ; laideur, *f.*

plain-spoken, *adj.*, qui parle à cœur ouvert.

plaint (plé'n'te), *n.*, plainte ; lamentation ; (jur.) plainte, *f.*

plaintful (-foule), *adv.*, (ant.) plaintif.

plaintiff, *n.*, demandeur ; plaignant, *m.*

plaintive, *adj.*, plaintif.

plaintively, *adv.*, plaintivement.

plaintiveness, *n.*, nature plaintive, tristesse, *f.*

plaintless, *adj.*, (ant.) qui ne se plaint pas ; sans plainte.

plain-work (-weurke), *n.*, ouvrage à l'aiguille uni, *m.*

plait (pléte), *n.*, pli, *m.* ; (of hair—*de cheveux*) tresse, *f.*

plait, *v.a.*, plisser ; (hair—*les cheveux*) tresser ; (fig.) entortiller.

plaiter, *n.*, personne qui plisse, qui tresse, *f.* ; tresseur, *m.*, tresseuse, *f.*

plaiting, *n.*, action de plisser ; plissure, *f.* ; plissement, *m.*

plan, *n.*, plan ; (project) plan, dessein, projet, *m.* Raised — ; *élévation, f.* To raise, to take a — ; *lever un plan.*

plan, *v.a.*, tracer un plan ; (fig.) projeter.

plane (pléne), *n.*, (geom.) plan, *m.*, surface plane, *f.* ; (persp.) plan ; (carp.) rabot ; (print.) taquoir, *m.*

plane, *v.a.*, raboter ; (print.) taquer.

plane, *or* **plane-tree** (-tri), *n.*, platane. *m.*

planer, *n.*, raboteur ; (print.) taquoir, *m.*

planet, *n.*, planète, *f.*

planetarium (-ët'é-), *n.*, (astron.) planétaire, *m.*

planetary, *adj.*, planétaire.

planet-struck (-streuke), *adj.*, sous l'influence des planètes ; flétri, brûlé.

planimetric, *or* **planimetrical** (-mèt'-), *adj.*, planimétrique.

planimetry (-ni'm'è-), *n.*, (geom.) planimétrie, *f.*

planing (plé'n'-), *n.*, rabotage, *m.* — *machine*, *machine à raboter*, *f.*

planish (pla'n'-), *v.a.*, planer.

planisher, *n.*, planeur, *m.*

planisphere (-sfire), *n.*, planisphère, *f.*

plank, *n.*, planche, *f.* ; ais ; (nav.) bordage, *m.*

plank, *v.a.*, planchéier ; (a ship—*un vaisseau*) border.

planking, *n.*, planchéiage ; (of a ship—*d'un vaisseau*) bordage, *m.*

planner, *n.*, auteur d'un plan, d'un projet ; projeteur, *m.*

plant, *v. n.*, planter.

plant, *n.*, (bot.) plante, *f.*, plant ; (tech.) matériel, *m.*

plant,*v.a.*,planter; (to found—*fonder*) fonder, établir ; (to place—*placer*) poser, placer ; (cannon —*canon*) pointer, braquer.

plantain (-tine), *n.*, (bot.) plantain, *m.*

plantain, *or* **plantain-tree** (-trî), *n.*, bananier, *m.*

plantation (-té-), *n.*, plantation ; (colony—*colonie*) colonie, *f.* ; (in America—*en Amérique*) plantage ; (establishment—*établissement*) établissement, *m.*, fondation,*f.*

planter, *n.*, planteur, colon ; (fig.) propagateur, *m.*

planticle (-ti-k'l), *n.*, jeune plant, *m.*

planting, *n.*, plantation ; (arch.) pose,*f.*

plantlet, *n.*, (bot.) plantule, *f.*

plash,*n.*,flaque d'eau; (hort.) branche coupée en partie,*f.*

plash, *v.n.*, patauger, barboter.

plash, *v.a.*, éclabousser ; jeter de l'eau sur ; entrelacer.

plashy, *adj.*, gâcheux, boueux.

plaster (plâs-), *n.*, plâtre ; (pharm.) emplâtre, *m.* — of Paris ; *plâtre de Paris.* — -work ; *plâtrage, m.* Old —; *plâtras, m.*

plaster, *v.a.*, plâtrer ; (med.) mettre un emplâtre à.

plasterer, *n.*, plâtrier; mouleur, *m.*

plastering, *n.*, plâtrage, *m.*

plastic. *or* **plastical.** *adj.*, plastique.

plasticity, *n.*, nature plastique, plasticité, *f.*

plastron, *n.*, plastron, *m.*

plat, *n.*, petite pièce de terre,*f.*

plat. *or* **platting**, *n.*, tresse,*f.*

plat. *v.a.*, tresser, tisser.

platane. *n.*, (bot.) platane, *m.*

platband, *n.*, plate-bande, *f.*

plate, *n.*, assiette ; (metal) plaque ; (gold and silver articles—*articles d'or et d'argent*) vaisselle plate, *f.* ; (prize—*prix*) prix en vaisselle plate, *m.* ; (of a lock—*de serrure*, tech.) platine,*f.* ; (print.) cliché, *m.* ; (engr.) planche ; (armour—*armure*) armure de plaques de fer, *f.* Dinner—; *assiette plate.* Soup—; *assiette à soupe.* Piece of —; *pièce d'argenterie, f.* Silver— ; *vaisselle d'argent, argenterie.* Gold— ; *vaisselle d'or,f.*

plate, *v.a.*, plaquer ; (to beat into thin pieces —*former en plaques*) réduire en plaques. en lames ; (to arm—*cuirasser*) revêtir d'une armure de plaques ; (to adorn with plate—*orner*) orner de plaques ; (mirrors—*miroirs*) étamer; (to cover with gold or silver—*couvrir d'or ou d'argent*) plaquer, dorer, argenter.

plateau (pla-tô), *n.*, plateau, *m.*

plate-cover (-keuv'-), *n.*, cloche d'assiette, *f.*

plated (plét-), *adj.*, plaqué.

plateful (-foule), *n.*, assiettée, *f.*

plate-layer (-lé-eur), *n.*, (railways) poseur de rails, *m.*

platen, *n.*, (print.) platine, *f.*

plate-stand, *n.*, porte-assiette, *m.*

platform, *n.*, plate-forme ; estrade ; (railways) gare, *f.* ; (plan) plan, modèle, *m.* ; ichnographie, *f.* ; (of a bridge—*de pont*) tablier, *m.* ; (arch.) plate-forme,*f.*

platina, *or* **platinum,** *n.*, platine, *f.*

plating (plét'-), *n.*, opération de plaquer, *f.* ; art de plaquer, *m.*

platonic. *or* **platonical** (plé-), *adj.*, platonicien ; platonique.

platonically, *adv.*, d'une manière platonique.

platonism (plé-to-niz'm), *n.*, platonisme, *m.*

platonist (plé-to-), *n.*, platonicien, *m.*

platoon (pla-toune), *n.*, (milit.) peloton, *m.* Firing by —; *feu de peloton, m.*

platter, *n.*, grand plat ; (pers.) tresseur, *m.*, tresseuse,*f.*

---

plaudit, *n.*, applaudissement, *m.*

plausibility, *or* **plausibleness** (plô-zi-), *n.*, plausibilité, *f.*

plausible (-zi-b'l),*adj.*, plausible ; (pers.) qui emploie des arguments plausibles ; à langue dorée.

plausibly (-zi-), *adv.*, plausiblement, d'une manière plausible.

plausive (-cive), *adj.*, d'applaudissement; plausible.

play, *v.a.*, (to put in motion—*mettre en mouvement*) faire jouer ; (to act—*jouer*) jouer, représenter, faire, feindre ; (sportive—*de jeu*) déployer gaîment ; (a game—*un jeu*) jouer, faire ; (a trick—*un tour*) jouer, faire ; (mus.) jouer de; (the piano, the organ—*piano, orgue*) jouer de; toucher ; (the harp, the guitar—*harpe, guitare*) pincer de. To — the fool ; *badiner; folâtrer;* faire la bête. To — off ; *déployer, faire voir;* (tricks—*tours*) *faire, jouer.*

play, *v.n.*, jouer ; (to move—*remuer*) se mouvoir; (to frolic—*jouer*) folâtrer, s'amuser, badiner ; tech.) travailler ; (mus.) jouer, exécuter ; (of precious stones—*pierres précieuses*) briller. To — against; *jouer, jouer contre.* To — at; *jouer à.* To — on, upon ; (mus.) *jouer de;* (the piano, organ—*piano, orgue*) *jouer de; toucher;* (the harp, the guitar—*harpe, guitare*) *pincer de;* (to mock —*se moquer*) *se jouer de.* To — with; *jouer avec;* (to trifle with, to mock—*se moquer*) *se jouer de.* To — fair; *jouer bon jeu.* To — false ; *jouer faux; tromper.* To — high, low ; *jouer gros jeu, jouer petit jeu.* To — for love; *jouer pour l'honneur, pour le plaisir.*

play, *n.*; jeu ; badinage, *m.*; (recreation) récréation, *f.* ; (scope—*étendue*) essor, *m.*, carrière ; (mus.) exécution, *f.* ; (tech.) jeu ; (playhouse—*théâtre*) spectacle, théâtre, *m.* ; (book—*livre*) comédie, pièce de théâtre ; (representation) représentation, *f.*, spectacle, *m.* In —; *pour badiner, pour rire.* At —; *en jouant, en récréation;* (gambling—*jeu pour de l'argent*) *au jeu.* To be in full —; *avoir libre essor, pleine carrière.* To give — to; *donner essor à, carrière à.* To give full — to; *donner beau jeu à ; bien traiter.* Full of —; *badin.* By—; *jeu de scène, jeu muet.* Fair —; *franc jeu; bon jeu, jeu de bonne guerre.* Foul —; *mauvais jeu; mauvais tour, m.; perfidie, f.; trait de perfidie, m.*

playbill, *n.*, affiche de spectacle,*f.* ; programme de spectacle, *m.*

playbook (-bouke), *n.*, recueil de pièces de théâtre, livre de comédies, *m.* ; pièce de théâtre,*f.*

playday, *n.*, jour de récréation ; jour de congé, *m.*

playdebt (-dète), *n.*, dette de jeu,*f.*

player,*n.*, joueur, *m.*, joueuse, *f.* ; (thea.) acteur, *m.*, actrice,*f.*, comédien, *m.*, comédienne, *f.*, artiste, *m.,f.* ; (mus.) exécutant, *m.*, artiste, *m.,f.*, (b.s.) joueur, *m.*, joueuse,*f.* ; (idler—*oisif*) fainéant, *m.*, fainéante,*f.*

playfellow (-lô). *n.*, compagnon, *m.*, compagne,*f.*, camarade de jeu, *m.,f.*

playful (-foule). *or* **playsome** (-ceume), *adj.*, qui aime à jouer ; folâtre, badin.

playfully,*adv.*, d'une manière badine; en badinant ; avec enjouement.

playfulness, *or* **playsomeness**, *n.*, badinage, enjouement, *m.* ; gaîté, *f.*

playgame. *n.*, jeu d'enfants, *m.*

play-goer (-gô-eur), *n.*, habitué de spectacle, *m.*, habituée de spectacle,*f.* ; coureur de spectacles, *m.*, coureuse de spectacles,*f.*

playgoing,*adj.*, qui va souvent au spectacle; qui court les spectacles.

play-ground (-graou'n'de), *n.*, cour de récréation, *f.*

play-hour (-haoueur), *n.*, heure de récréation,*f.* —s; *récréation, f.sing.*

playhouse (-haouce), *n.*, salle de spectacle, *f.*; théâtre, *m.*; comédie, *f.*

playmate. *V.* **play-fellow.**

play-room (-roume), *n.*, salle de récréation, *f.*

plaything (-thigne), *n.*, jouet, joujou, *m.*

play-time (-taïme), *n.*, heures de récréation, *f.pl.*; récréation, *f. sing.*

playwright, *or* **playwriter** (-raït'-), *n.*, faiseur de pièces de théâtre, *m.*

plea (plî), *n.*, (jur.) moyen, plaid, *m.*, exception, *f.*; (lawsuit—*instance*) procès, *m.*, cause; (justification) justification, défense; (urgent prayer—*prière instante*) supplication, *f.* Court of Common —s; *cour des plaids communs, f.*

plead (plîde), *v.n.*, plaider; se défendre; (jur.) se déclarer; (to allege—*alléguer*) déclarer, alléguer, faire valoir. To — for; *parler en faveur de.* To — with; *intervenir auprès de.* To — guilty; *se déclarer coupable.*

plead (plîde), *v.a.*, plaider, défendre; (to maintain—*soutenir*) soutenir; (to allege—*alléguer*) déclarer, alléguer, faire valoir; (to offer in excuse—*s'excuser*) s'excuser sur. To — against; *opposer à.*

pleadable (-a-b'l), *adj.*, qui peut être plaidé, qui peut être allégué; (jur.) plaidable.

pleader (plîd'-), *n.*, avocat; défenseur, *m.*

pleading (plîd'-), *n.*, plaidoirie, *f.* —s; *débats, m.pl.*

pleasant (plèz'-), *adj.*, agréable, charmant; aimable; gracieux; gai.

pleasantly, *adv.*, agréablement; d'une manière charmante, aimable; gaîment; (ludicrously—*risiblement*) plaisamment.

pleasantness, *n.*, agrément, charme, *m.*; gaîté, *f.*

pleasantry, *n.*, plaisanterie, *f.*

please (plîze), *v.a.*, plaire à; faire plaisir à; charmer; contenter. To be —d; *être content;* (with—*de*) *être content de;* (to—*à*) *se plaire à, se plaire un plaisir de, daigner, vouloir bien.* You are —d to say so; *cela vous plaît à dire.* To — one's self ; *se contenter ; faire son choix;* (in—*à*) *se plaire à.*

please, *v.n.*, plaire. To — to; *plaire à; vouloir bien; vouloir; daigner.* If you —; *s'il vous plaît.* As you —; *comme il vous plaira; comme bon vous semblera, comme vous voudrez.* If I —; *si cela me plaît.* — God; *s'il plaît à Dieu.* — to lift up your hand; *veuillez lever la main.*

pleaseman (plîz'-), *n.*, (ant.) flagorneur, *m.*

pleaser (plîz'-), *n.*, complaisant, *m.*, complaisante, *f.*; courtisan, *m.*

pleasing (plîz'-), *adj.*, agréable, charmant, aimable, gracieux; (of things—*des choses*) riant, agréable.

pleasing, *n.*, action de plaire, *f.*; agrément, *m.*

pleasingly, *adv.*, agréablement, avec amabilité; gracieusement; d'une manière riante.

pleasingness, *n.*, agrément, charme, *m.*; amabilité, nature gracieuse; nature riante, *f.*

pleasurable (plèj'eur'-a-b'l), *adj.*, agréable, charmant.

pleasurableness, *n.*, agrément, charme, *m.*

pleasurably, *adv.*, agréablement.

pleasure (plèj'eur), *n.*, plaisir; agrément, charme; (will—*vouloir*) gré, *m.*, volonté, *f.* At —; *à volonté.* At my —; *à mon gré.* What is your —? *qu'y a-t-il pour votre service?* To afford — to; *faire plaisir à.* To take — in; *prendre plaisir à.* To make a — of; *mettre son plaisir à.* To esteem it a — to; to make a — of; *se faire un plaisir de.*

pleasure, *v.a.*, plaire à, contenter.

pleasure-ground (-graou'n'de), *n.*, parc d'agrément, *m.*

pleasure-house (-haouce), *n.*, maison de plaisance, *f.*

plebeian (plè-bî-ya'n), *n.*, plébéien. *m.*, plébéienne, *f.*

plebeian, *adj.*, plébéien, vulgaire.

pledge, *n.*, gage, garant, *m.*; garantie, *f.*; nantissement: (toast) toast; (milit.) otage. *m.*; (jur.) caution, *f.* To put in —; *mettre en gage; engager.*

pledge, *v.a.*, engager; mettre en gage; (to vouch for—*répondre de*) garantir; (toast) faire raison à.

pledgee (plèd'jî), *n.*, créancier gagiste, *m.*

pledger, *n.*, personne qui met en gage, *f.*; débiteur sur gage; garant, *m.*

pledget, *n.*, (surg.) plumasseau, *m.*

pleiads (plî-yadze), *or* **pleiades** (plî-yédize), *n.*, Pléiades, *f.pl.*

plenarily (plî-), *adv.*, pleinement, complètement.

plenariness (plî-), *n.*, plénitude, *f.*

plenary (plî-), *adj.*, plein, complet, entier; (indulgence) plénière.

plenilunar, *or* **plenilunary** (plè'n'î-liou-), *adj.*, de pleine lune.

plenipotence, *or* **plenipotency** (plè-), *n.*, plein pouvoir, *m.*

plenipotent, *adj.*, qui a plein pouvoir.

plenipotentiary (-tè'n'shia-), *adj.*, plénipotentiaire; (of things—*des choses*) plein et entier.

plenipotentiary, *n.*, plénipotentiaire, *m.*

plenist (plî'-), *n.*, partisan du plénisme, *m.*

plenitude (plè'n'î-tioude), *n.*, plénitude, *f.*; état complet, *m.*

plenteous (plè'n'tî-), *adj.*, abondant.

plenteously, *adv.*, abondamment.

plenteousness, *n.*, abondance, *f.*

plentiful (plè'n'tî-foule), *adj.*, abondant, en abondance.

plentifully, *adv.*, abondamment.

plentifulness, *n.*, abondance, *f.*

plenty (plè'n'ti), *n.*, abondance, *f.* Horn of —; *corne d'abondance, f.*

plenty, *adj.*, abondant; en abondance.

pleonasm (plî-o-naz'm), *n.*, pléonasme, *m.*

pleonastical, *adj.*, pléonastique.

pleonastically, *adv.*, par pléonasme; d'une manière pléonastique.

plethora, *or* **plethory** (plèth'-), *n.*, pléthore, *f.*

plethoric, plethorical, *or* **plethoretic**. *adj.*, pléthorique.

pleura (plioura), *n.*, (anat.) plèvre, *f.*

pleurisy (pliou-ri-ci), *n.*, (med.) pleurésie, *f.*

pleuritic, *or* **pleuritical**, *adj.*, pleurétique.

plexus, *n.*, (anat.) plexus, *m.*

pliability (plaï-), *n.* *V.* **pliableness.**

pliable (plaï-a-b'l), *adj.*, pliable; pliant, souple, flexible.

pliableness, *n.*, souplesse, flexibilité, *f.*

pliancy (plaï-), *n.*, flexibilité, *f.*

pliant (plaï-), *adj.*, pliant, souple, flexible.

pliantness, *n.*, souplesse, flexibilité, *f.*

plicate (plaï-), *or* **plicated** (-két'-), *adj.*, (bot.) plié, plissé.

plicature (plic'a-tioure), *or* **plication** (plik'é-), *n.*, (ant.) action de ployer, *f.*; pli, double; pliage, *m.*

plier (plaï'-), *n.*, (nav.) boulinier, *m.*

pliers (plaï-eurze), *n.pl.*, pinces, *f.pl.*

pliform (plaï-), *adj.*, en forme de pli.

plight (plaïte), *n.*, état, *m.*; condition, *f.*; (pledge—*nantissement*) gage, *m.*

plight, *v.a.*, engager.

plighter, *n.*, personne qui engage, chose qui engage, *f.*

plinth (pli'n'th), *n.*, (arch.) plinthe, *f.*; (of a wall—*de mur*) bandeau, *m.*

plod, *v.n.*, marcher laborieusement; s'appliquer à, piocher.

plodder, *n.*, piocheur, *m.* A mere —; *un bon boueux.*

plodding, adj., laborieux, d'un travail soutenu.

plodding, n., travail laborieux, travail soutenu, pénible, m.

plot, n., (stratagem,conspiracy—conspiration) complot, m., trame; (of a dramatic piece—d'une comédie, &c.) intrigue, f.; (of ground—de terrain) petite pièce de terre, f., petit terrain, petit champ; (in surveying—lever des plans) plan de terrain, m. To lay a —; ourdir, tramer un complot, ourdir une trame.

plot, v.n., comploter; (of things—des choses) se tramer.

plot, v.a., comploter, tramer; former le plan de; (in surveying—arpentage) rapporter.

plotter, n., personne qui forme des plans, des projets; conspirateur, m.

plotting, n., stratagèmes, m.pl.; complot, m.; (in surveying—arpentage) action de rapporter, f.

plotting-scale, n., échelle à rapporter, f.

plough (plaô), n., charrue; (fig.) culture, agriculture, f.; (bookbind.) rognoir; (carp.) bonnet de deux pièces, m.

plough (plaô), v.a., labourer; passer la charrue sur; (bookbind.) rogner; (carp.) creuser; (fig.) sillonner, fendre.

plough, v.n., labourer.

ploughable (-a-b'l), adj., labourable, arable.

plough-boy (-boï), n , valet de charrue; jeune laboureur, m.

plougher (plaô'eur), n., laboureur, cultivateur, m.

ploughing (plaô-igne), n., labourage, labour, m.

plough-land (-la'n'de), n., terre de labour, f.

ploughman, n., valet de charrue; laboureur; paysan, m.

ploughshare, n., soc de charrue, m.

plough-tail (-téle), n., manche de charrue, m.

plover (pleuv'-), n., (orni.) pluvier, m.

pluck (pleuke), v.a., tirer; (flowers, fruit—fleurs, fruit) cueillir; (poultry—volaille) plumer; (at examinations—aux examens) faire fruit sec. To — away, off; arracher, enlever. To — up; arracher, déraciner; (courage) reprendre. To be —ed; (at examinations—aux examens) être fruit sec.

pluck, n., action de tirer; (of animals—des animaux) fressure, f.; (courage) cœur, courage, m.

plucker, n., personne qui arrache, qui plume, f.; cueilleur, m., cueilleuse, f.

plug (pleughe), n., tampon; (of a water-cock —de robinet) piston, m.

plug, v.a., tamponner.

plum (pleume), n., prune, f.; (raisin) raisin sec; (£100,000) cent mille livres sterling; (pers.) millionnaire, m. —cake; baba, m. —pudding; plum-pudding; pouding au raisin de Corinthe, m. —tree; prunier, m.

plum (pleume), v.a., (mines) niveler au demi-cercle (avec fil à plomb).

plumage (pliou-médje), n., plumage, m. (of hawks—des faucons) pennage, m.

plumb (pleume), **plumb-line** (-laïne), n. **plumb-rule** (-roule), n., plomb, fil à plomb, m.

plumb (pleume), adv., à plomb, droit.

plumb (pleume), v.a., mettre à plomb.

plumbaginous (-hadj'-), adj., de plombagine.

plumbago (-bá-gô), n., (min.) plombagine, f.

plumbean, or **plumbeous** (-bi-), adj., de plomb.

plumber (pleum'eur), n., plombier, m.

plumbery (pleum'eur'i), n., plomberie, f.

plumbiferous (pleum'b if'èv'-), adj., plombifère.

plumbing (pleum'm'igne), n., plomberie, f.

plumb-line (-laïne), n. fil à plomb, m.

plume (ploume), n., plume, f.; panache, plumet; (pride—vanité) orgueil, m.; (token of honour—signe d'honneur) palme, f.; honneur, m.

plume (ploume), v.a., plumer; orner d'un plumet, d'un panache, d'une plume; (of birds—des oiseaux) nettoyer. To — itself; (of birds—des oiseaux) nettoyer ses plumes. To — one's self upon; se piquer de, se glorifier de.

plumeless (ploum'-), adj., sans plumes; sans plumet, sans panache, sans plume.

plumelet (ploum'-), n., (bot.) plumule, f.

plumigerous (pleu-midj-èr'-), adj., qui porte des plumes.

plummet (pleum'-), n., (for sounding—à sonder) sonde, f.; plomb; (tech.) plomb, fil à plomb; (weight—poids) contrepoids, m.

plumming (pleum'-), n., (mines) nivellement au demi-cercle, m.

plumose (pleu-môce), or **plumous** (pliou-), adj., de plumes; plumeux.

plumosity (pleu-môss'-), n., (ant.) état de ce qui a des plumes, m.

plump (pleum'p), adj., dodu, potelé; replet; (blunt—bourru) brusque; (downright—franc) net.

plump, adv., tout d'un coup; lourdement.

plump, v.a., rendre dodu, rendre potelé; engraisser; donner de l'embonpoint à; enfler.

plump, v.n., tomber comme une masse; tomber tout-à-coup; (to enlarge—grossir) s'enfler; s'engraisser.

plumper, n., chose qui enfle; (lie—mensonge) bourde, f.; (vote) double vote, m.

plumpish, adj., grasset, grassouillet.

plumply, adv., nettement; rondement.

plumpness, n., état potelé; embonpoint, m.

plum-porridge, n., soupe au raisin, f.

plumule (pliou-mioule), n. V. **plumelet.**

plumy (pliou-), adj., couvert de plumes; orné d'un plumet, d'un panache, d'une plume.

plunder (pleun'-), n., pillage; saccagement; butin, m.

plunder, v.a., piller, saccager.

plunderer, n., pillard, pilleur, rapineur, m.

plunge (pleun'dje), n., action de plonger, f.; plongeon; (difficulty—difficulté) embarras, m.

plunge, v.a., plonger, précipiter.

plunge, v.n., se plonger, se précipiter, se jeter.

plungeon (pleu'n'djeune), n., (orni.) plongeon, m.

plunger (pleu'n'dj'-), n., plongeur; (hydr.) piston plongeur, plongeur, m.

pluperfect (plou-peur-fek't), adj., (gram.) plus-que-parfait.

plural (plou-), adj., de plus d'un; (gram.) pluriel. —, n., pluriel, m.

pluralist (plou-), n., ecclésiastique qui jouit de plus d'un bénéfice, m.

plurality (pleu-), n., pluralité, f.

plurally (plou-), adv., dans un sens de pluralité; (gram.) au pluriel.

plus (pleuss), adv., (alg.) plus.

plush (pleushe), n., peluche; futaine, f.

pluvial (plou-), or **pluvious** (-vieusse), adj., pluvieux; pluvial.

pluvial, n., (c.rel.) pluvial, m.

pluviameter (plou-vi-am'i-), n., udomètre, m.

ply (pla'ye), n., pli, m.

ply (pla'ye), v.a., s'appliquer à, s'attacher à; manier; (to practice—pratiquer) exercer, employer, appliquer; (to urge—presser) presser, solliciter.

ply (pla-ye), v.n., plier, céder; (to work steadily—travailler avec constance) travailler ferme; (to go in haste—aller à la hâte) se rendre à la hâte; (to busy one's self—s'occuper de) s'occuper; (nav.) aller à la bouline, bouliner; (of vehicles—de voitures, &c.) faire le service.se tenir.

plyer (pla'-yeur), *n.*, personne qui travaille, those qui travaille, *f.* —s; (fort.) bascule, *f.sing.*

pneumatic, *or* **pneumatical** (niou-mat'-), *adj.*, pneumatique.

pneumatics, *n.pl.*, pneumatique, *f.sing.*

pneumatocele (niou-mat'o-cile), *n.*, (med.) pneumatocèle, *f.*

pneumatological (niou-ma-tol'o-dj'-),*adj.*, pneumatologique.

pneumatology (niou-ma-tol'o-dji),*n.*,pneumatologie, *f.*

pneumonia (niou-mô-), *or* **pneumony** (niou-mo-), *n.*, pneumonie, *f.*

pneumonic (niou-), *adj.*, pneumonique.

pneumonic, *n.*, (med.) pneumonique, *m.*

poach (pôtshe), *v.a.*, faire bouillir légèrement; (to begin—*commencer*) commencer, entamer; (to steal—*dérober*) voler, piller; (to spear —*darder*) harponner; (eggs—*œufs*) pocher.

poach, *v.n.*, braconner; (of the earth—*de la terre*) être humide et plein de creux.

poachard (pôtsh'-), *n.*, (orni.) millouin, *m.*

poacher (pôtsh'-), *n.*, braconnier, *m.*

poachiness (pôtsh'-), *n.*, humidité, *f.*

poaching (pôtsh'-), *n.*, braconnage, *m.*

poachy (pôtsh'-), *adj.*, humide, mou.

pock, *n.*, grain de petite vérole, *m.*

pocket, *n.*, poche, *f.*; (fob—*de gilet*) gousset, *m.*; (of a billiard-table—*de billard*) blouse, *f.* To spare any one's —; *ménager la bourse de quelqu'un.* To be out of — by ; *perdre à.*

pocket, *v.a.*, empocher; mettre dans la poche; soustraire, dérober; (affront) avaler.

pocket-book (-bouke), *n.*, portefeuille, *m.*

pocket-glass (-glâce),*n.*,miroir de poche,*m.*

pocket-hole (-hôle), *n.*, ouverture de la poche, *f.*

pocket-money (-meu'n'nè),*n.*, argent pour les menus plaisirs, *m.*; menus plaisirs, *m.pl.*; (of children—*des enfants*) semaine, *f.*

pock-hole (-hôl), *or* **pock-mark** (-màrke), *n.*, marque de petite vérole, *f.*

pockiness, *n.*, état d'une personne attaquée de la petite vérole, *m.*

pock-marked (-màrk'te), *or* **pock-pitted**, *adj.*, marqué de la petite vérole, grêlé.

pocky, *adj.*, attaqué de la petite vérole; couvert de grains de petite vérole.

pod, *n.*, cosse; gousse, *f.*

pod, *v.a.*, écosser.

pod, *v.n.*, produire des cosses, des gousses.

podagrical, *adj.*, podagre; (of things—*des choses*) de la goutte.

podded, *adj.*, muni de cosse, de gousse; à cosse, à gousse.

podder, *n.*, personne qui ramasse des cosses, des gousses, *f.*

poem (pô-ème), *n.*, poème, *m.*; poésie, *f.*; vers, *m.pl.*

pœony (pi-), *n.* V. **pæony.**

poesy (pô-è-ci), *n.*, poésie, *f.*

poet (pô-ète), *n.*, poète, *m.*

poetaster (pô-èt'-), *n.*, poètereau, rimailleur, *m.*

poetess (pô-èt'-), *n.*, poétesse, femme poète,*f.*

poetic, *or* **poetical**, *adj.*, poétique.

poetically, *adv.*, poétiquement.

poetics, *n.pl.*, poétique, *f.sing.*

poetize (pô-èt'aïze), *v.n.*, écrire en poète, poétiser.

poetry (pô-è-), *n.*, poésie, *f.*

poh ! *int.*, bah !

poignancy (pwa-na'n'-), *n.*, piquant, *m.*; pointe; nature poignante, *f.*

poignant (pwa'na'n'te), *adj.*, piquant, mordant; poignant, cuisant.

poignantly, *adv.*, d'une manière piquante, cuisante, poignante.

point (pwaï'n'te), *n.*, point, *m.*; (sharp end— *bout aigu*) pointe; (aiglet—*aiguillette*) aiguil-

lette; (of an epigram—*d'une épigramme*) pointe; (engr.) pointe, pointe sèche,*f.*; (astron.,geom., gram., mus.) point, *m.*; (geog.) pointe,*f.*; (at cards—*aux cartes*) point, *m.*; (print.) pointure; (railways) aiguille,*f.*, rail mobile; (of the compass—*de la boussole*) quart de vent, *m.*, aire de vent, *f.*; (of a sail—*de voile*) garcette de ris; (of a cable—*de câble*) queue de rat,*f.*; (in falconry —*fauconnerie*) point, *m.*; (quality—*qualité*) qualité, *f.*; (aim, purpose—*but*) but, *m.*, fins, *f.pl.* Brussels —; *point de Bruxelles.* Self-acting —; (railways) aiguille à contre-poids. At the — of; *au point de.* At the — of death; *à l'article de la mort.* On the — of; *sur le point de.* In — of; *sous le rapport de; en fait de.* In all —s; *en tout point; de tous points.* To be to the —; *aller au fait.* To come to the —; *venir au fait, arriver au fait.* To make a — of; *se faire un devoir de, une loi de.* To gain one's —; *arriver à ses fins.* — -blank; *de but en blanc; directement.*

point (pwaï'n'te),*v.a.*, (to sharpen—*émoudre*) aiguiser, affiler; (to make pointed—*rendre pointu*) tailler, faire une pointe à; (to direct— *diriger*) diriger; (fire-arms—*armes à feu*) pointer, braquer, mettre en joue; (to punctuate—*ponctuer*) ponctuer, pointer; (to mark with vowel points—*marquer*) marquer de points-voyelles; (a sail—*une voile*) garnir de garcettes de ris; (cable) garnir de queues de rat; (mas.) jointoyer. To — out; montrer au doigt; signaler; faire remarquer. To — the finger at any one; *montrer quelqu'un au doigt.* To be, to get — ed at; *se faire montrer au doigt.*

point (pwaï'n'te), *v.n.*, pointer; (mas.) jointoyer; (of dogs—*de chiens*) faire un arrêt, tomber, se mettre en arrêt; (nav.) garnir de garcettes de ris, garnir de queues de rat. To — at; *montrer du doigt;* (b.s.) *montrer au doigt.* To — to; *indiquer, montrer;* (of things—*des choses*) *indiquer; se tourner vers.*

pointed, *adj.*,(sharp—*aigu*)à pointe, pointu; (epigrammatic—*sarcastique*) épigrammatique, piquant; (personal—*personnel*) personnel. — style; (arch.) *style Gothique, m.*

pointedly, *adv.*, d'une manière piquante; positivement, expressément; directement.

pointedness, *n.*, forme pointue, *f.*; aspérité; pointe; tournure épigrammatique, *f.*

pointer, *n.*, index, *m.*; aiguille, *f.*; (dog— *chien*) chien d'arrêt, *m.*; (railways) aiguille, *f.*, rail mobile, *m.*

pointing, *n.*, (artil.) pointement, pointage; (mas.) jointoiement, *m.*; (gram.) ponctuation,*f.*

pointing-stock, *n.*, objet de mépris, *m.*; risée, *f.*

pointless, *adj.*, sans pointe; fade.

pointsman, *n.*, (railways) aiguilleur, *m.*

poise (pwaïze), *n.*, poids, *m.*; pondération, importance, *f.*; équilibre, *m.*

poise, *v.a.*, peser; donner du poids à; balancer; équilibrer, tenir en équilibre; pondérer.

poison (pwaï-z'n), *n.*, poison, *m.*

poison, *v.a.*, empoisonner.

poisoner, *n.*, empoisonneur,'*m.*, empoisonneuse, *f.*

poison-nut (-neute), *n.*, (bot.) noix vomique,*f.*

poisonous, *adj.*, empoisonné, vénéneux, venimeux.

poisonously, *adv.*, avec venin.

poisonousness, *n.*, nature vénéneuse, *f.*; poison, *m.*

poison-tree (-tri), *n.*, (bot.)upas de Java, *m.*

poke (pôke), *n.*, sachet, *m.*; poche, *f.* To buy a pig in a —; *acheter chat en poche.*

poke, *v.a.* and *n.*, fourrer; (to push—*pousser*) pousser; (the fire—*le feu*) attiser, remuer, fourgonner; (of cattle—*des bestiaux*) donner des cornes contre. To — about; *pousser ;* (the fire—

le fsu) remuer; fouiller, farfouiller. To — after, for ; *chercher ; chercher à tâtons.* To — fun at; *se rire de, se moquer de.*

poker, *n.*, tisonnier ; fourgon, *m.*

poke-weed (-wîde), *n.*, (bot.) morelle à grappes. *f.*

poking, *adj.*, servile; obscur ; sale. — -hole; *taudis, m.*

poking, *n.*, action de pousser, *f.* ; (of the fire —*du feu*) remuage, *m.*

polacca, or **polacre,** *n.*, (nav.) polacre, polaque, *f.*

polar (pô-), *adj.*, polaire.

polarity, *n.*, polarité, *f.*

polarization (pô-lar-aïzé-),*n.*,polarisation,*f.*

polarize (pô-lar'aïze), *v.a.*, polariser.

pole (pôle), *n.*, perche, *f.*; (staff—*bâton*) bâton ; (of a carriage—*de voiture*) timon ; (of a dancer—*de danseur*) balancier, *m.* ; (of a stable—*d'écurie*) barre, *f.* ; (nav.) pible, *m.* ; (of a mast—*de mât*) flèche ; (measure—*mesure*) perche (mètres 5·02911), *f.*; (astron.. geog.) pôle, *m.* Under bare —s; (nav.) *à sec.* Greasy —; *mât de cocagne, f.*

pole (pôle), *v.a.*, mettre des perches à; (to bear—*porter*) porter sur une perche; (to impel—*pousser*) faire avancer au moyen d'une perche.

pole (pôle), *n.*, Polonais, *m.*, Polonaise, *f.*

pole-axe (pôl'akse), *n.*, hache d'armes, *f.*

polecat (pôl'cate), *n.*, putois, *m.*

polemic, or **polemical** (-lè'm'-),*adj.*, polémique.

polemic (-lè'm'-), *n.*, écrivain polémique, *m.*

polemics (po-lè'm'-), *n.pl.*, polémique, *f.sing.*

pole-star, *n*, étoile polaire, *f.*

polianthes (po-li-a'n'thize), *n.*, (bot.) tubéreuse, *f.*

police (-lîce), *n.*, police, *f.* — -court ; *tribunal de simple police, m.* — -officer ; *agent de police, m.* — -spy; *espion de police ; mouchard,m.*

policed (po-lîste), or **policied** (-cide), *adj.*, policé.

policeman, *n.*, agent de police, sergent de ville, ❀archer, *m.*

policy, *n.*, politique ; (com.) police, *f.* — of insurance; *police d'assurance.* Life— ; *police d'assurance sur la vie.* Fire— ; *police d'assurance contre l'incendie.*

poling (pôl'-), *n.*, bordage; blindage, *m.*

polish (pô-), *adj.*, polonais.

polish (pol'-), *n.*, poli, *m.* ; (fig.) élégance, *f.*

polish (pol'-), *v.a.*, polir ; (fig.) policer. To — up ; *polir, dérouiller ;* (pers.) *façonner, dégourdir.*

polish, *v.n.*, se polir ; (fig.) se façonner, se dégourdir.

polishable (pol'ish-a-b'l), *adj.*, susceptible de poli.

polished (po-lish'te), *adj.*, poli ; (pers.) de manières élégantes ; policé.

polisher, *n.*, polisseur ; (thing—*outil*) polissoir, *m.*

polishing, *n.*, polissure, *f.* ; poli ; polissage, *m.*

polite (-laïte), *adj.*, poli.

politely. *adv.*, poliment.

politeness (-laït'-), *n* , politesse, *f.*

politic (pol'i-tike), *adj.*, politique, fin.

political. *adj.*, politique.

politically. *adv.*, politiquement.

politician (pol'i-tish'-), *n.*, politique, *m.*

politicly, *adv.*, politiquement ; d'une manière fine.

politics, *n.pl.*, politique, *f.sing.*

polity, *n.*, constitution politique, *f.* ; gouvernement, *m.*

poll (pôl), *n.*, (head—*tête*) tête ; (register of persons—*registre*) liste de personnes ; (register of electors—*registre d'électeurs*) liste électorale, liste

d'électeurs,*f.* ; collège électoral, *m.* ; élection,*f.*; (parrot—*perroquet*) jacquot ; jacot, *m.*

poll, *v.a.*, (to clip—*couper*) tondre ; (trees—*arbres*) étêter ; (electors—*électeurs*) inscrire ; se faire inscrire; (to vote—*voter*) donner son vote, voter.

pollard, *n.*, (hort.) têtard ; (meal—*farine*) mélange de son et de farine, *m.*

pollard, *v.a.*, (hort.) étêter.

polled (pôl'd), *adj.*, sans cornes ; étêté.

pollen (pol'lène), *n.*, (agri.) recoupe,*f.* ; (bot.) pollen. *m.*

poller (pôll'-), *n.*, personne qui enregistre les votes, *f.* ; (voter—*électeur*) votant, *m.* ; (hort.) personne qui étête les arbres, *f.*

pollevil (pol'i-v'l). *n.*, (vet.) taupe, *f.*

pollicitation (-ci-té-), *n.*, promesse ; (jur.) pollicitation, *f.*

poll-tax, *n.*, capitation, *f.*

pollute (pol-lioute), *v.a.*, polluer, souiller, profaner ; flétrir, corrompre, pervertir ; rendre impur.

pollute *adj.*, souillé.

pollutedness (-liout'ed'-), *n.*, impureté ; pollution; souillure, *f.*

polluter (-liout'-), *n.*, personne qui pollue, qui profane, qui souille, *f.* ; corrupteur, *m.*, corruptrice, *f.*

pollution (-liou-), *n.*, pollution ; profanation ; souillure, *f.*

polonese (-nîze), *n.*, (garment—*vêtement*) polonaise, *f.*

poltroon (-troune), *n.*, poltron, *m.*, poltronne, *f.*

poltroonery, *n.*, poltronnerie, *f.*

polyadelphia *n.*, (bot.) polyadelphie, *f.*

polyandria, *n.*, (bot.) polyandrie, *f.*

polyanthus (-theusse), *n.*, primevère, *f.*

polygamia, *n.*, (bot.) polygamie, *f.*

polygamian, *n.*, (bot.) plante polygame,*f.*

polygamist, *n.*, polygame, *m.f.*

polygamous, *adj.*, polygame.

polygamy, *n.*, polygamie, *f.*

polyglot, *adj.*, polyglotte.

polyglot, *n.*, polyglotte, *f.*

polygon, *n.*, polygone, *m.*

polygonal, or **polygonous,** *adj.*, polygone.

polyhedral (-hî-), **polyhedrical** (-hî-), or **polyhedrous** (-hi-), *adj.*, à plusieurs faces, à plusieurs côtés ; polyédrique.

polyhedron (-hî-), *n.*, (geom.) polyèdre, *m.*

polymathic (-math'ike),*adj.*,polymathique.

polymathy (-thi). *n.*, polymathie, *f.*

polynome (-nôme), *n.*, (alg.) polynôme, *m.*

polypetalous (-pèt'a-), *adj.*, (bot.) polypétale, *f.*

polypier (-pié), *n.*, polypier, *m.*

polypode (-pôde), *n.*, (ent.) mille-pieds, *m.*

polypody (-pode), *n.*, (bot.) polypode, *m.*

polypus. *n.*, polype, *m.*

polysyllabic, *adj.*, polysyllabique, polysyllabe, *f.*

polysyllable, *n.*, polysyllabe, *m.*

polytechnic (-tèk'-), *adj.*, polytechnique.

polytheism (-thi-iz'me),*n.*,polythéisme, *m.*

polytheist (-thi-), *n.*, polythéiste, *m.*

polytheistic, or **polytheistical** (-thi-), *adj.*, polythéiste.

pomace (peu'm'éce), *n.*,marc de pommes,*m.*

pomaceous (peu'm'é-sheusse), *adj.*, de pommes ; de marc de pommes.

pomade. *n.*, pommade, *f.*

pomatum (-mé-), *n.*, pommade, *f.*

pomatum. *v.a.*, pommader.

pome-citron (peu'm'-), *n.*, (bot.) cédrat, *m.*

pomegranate (peu'm'gra'n'éte),*n.*,grenade, *f.*; (tree—*arbre*) grenadier, *m.*

pommel (peu'm'mèl), *n.*, pommette, *f.* ; (of

a saddle, a sword—*de selle, d'épée*) pommeau, *m.*
pommel, *v.a.*, rosser, frotter.
pomp, *n.*, pompe, *f.*; éclat, faste, *m.*
pompion (peu'm'pi'eune), *n.*, citrouille, courge *f.* ; potiron, *m.*
pomposity (-poss'-), *n.*, pompe ; emphase, *f.* ; pathos, *m.*
pompous, *adj.*, pompeux, fastueux, emphatique.
pompously, *adv.*, pompeusement; fastueusement ; emphatiquement.
pompousness, *n.*, pompe, emphase, *f.* ; pathos ; éclat, *m.*
pond, *n.*, étang, vivier, *m.* ; mare, *f.*
pond, *v.a.*, établir un étang.
ponder, *v.a.*, peser, considérer, méditer ; réfléchir à.
ponder, *v.n.*, méditer, réfléchir.
ponderability (-dèr'-), *n.*, pondérabilité, *f.*
ponderable (-dèr'a-b'l), *adj.*, pondérable.
ponderation (-dèr'é-), *n.*, (ant.) pondération, *f.*
ponderer, *n.*, personne qui pèse, qui considère, qui médite, *f.*
ponderingly, *adv.*, avec méditation ; avec réflexion.
ponderosity (-dèr'oss'-), *n.*, pesanteur, gravité, *f.*
ponderous, *adj.*, pesant ; important ; fort.
ponderously, *adv.*, avec grand poids ; pesamment.
ponderousness, *n.*, poids, *m.* ; pesanteur, gravité, *f.*
pond-weed (-wîde), *n.*, (bot.) potamot, potamogéton flottant, épi d'eau, *m.*
pongo (pon'gn'gô), *n.*, (mam.) pongo, *m.*
poniard, *n.*, poignard, *m.*
poniard, *v.a.*, poignarder.
pontage (-tédje), *n.*, pontonage, *m.*
pontiff, *n.*, pontife, *m.*
pontific, or **pontifical,** *adj.*, pontifical ; (magnificent—*superbe*) magnifique; des prêtres.
pontifical, *n.*, pontifical, *m.* —s ; *habits pontificaux.*
pontifically, *adv.*, pontificalement, en pontife.
pontificate, *n.*, pontificat, *m.*
pontine, *adj.*, pontin.
pontlevis (po'nt-li-vice), *n.*, pont-levis, *m.*
pontoon (-toune), *n.*, ponton, *m.* —bridge ; *pontons, m.pl.* —train ; *équipage de pont, m.*
pony (pô-), *n.*, poney, ponet, petit cheval, *m.*
poodle (pou-d'l), *n.*, caniche, chien caniche, *m.*
pool (poul), *n.*, étang, *m.* ; mare ; (at cards—*aux cartes*) poule, *f.*
poop (poupe), *n.*, dunette, poupe, *f.*; arrière, *m.*
poor (pour), *adj.*, pauvre ; indigent ; (unhappy —*infortuné*) malheureux ; (trifling, paltry—*mesquin*) méchant, triste ; (bad—*misérable*) mauvais. The — (*pl.*); *les indigents.* A — man ; *un homme pauvre.* — little fellow ; *pauvre petit.* The — fellow ; *le malheureux.* To have a — opinion of ; *avoir une triste opinion de.* The patient has passed a — night ; *le malade a passé une mauvaise nuit.* A — excuse ; *une mauvaise excuse.* — fare ; *mauvaise chère.* As — as a church mouse ; *gueux comme un rat d'église.*
poor-box, *n.*, tronc des pauvres, *m.*
poor-law (-lô), *n.*, loi sur les pauvres, *f.*
poorly, *adj.*, indisposé, souffrant.
poorly, *adv.*, pauvrement ; mal, tristement.
poorness, *n.*, pauvreté ; indigence ; (mediocrity—*incapacité*) médiocrité; (meanness—*vileté*) bassesse; (barrenness—*stérilité*) stérilité ; (bad quality—*qualité*) mauvaise qualité, *f.*
poor-rate, *n.*, taxe des pauvres, *f.*
poor-spirited, *adj.*, lâche ; sans cœur.
poor-spiritedness, *n.*, lâcheté, *f.* ; manque de cœur, *m.*

pop, *n.*, son vif, aigu, sec, *m.*
pop, *v.n.*, entrer, sortir, subitement, précipitamment. To — in ; *entrer subitement, précipitamment.* To — off ; *s'en aller subitement, précipitamment.* To — out ; *sortir subitement, précipitamment.* To — up ; *se lever subitement, précipitamment.*
pop, *v.a.*, pousser subitement, précipitamment. To — off ; *renvoyer subitement.* To — up ; *faire monter subitement.* To — the question ; *demander en mariage subitement ; lâcher le grand mot tout à coup.*
pop, *adv.*, soudain, tout à coup ; crac !
pope (pôpe), *n.*, pape ; (of the Greek church —*de l'église grecque*) pope, *m.*
popedom (pôp'deume), *n.*, papauté, *f.*
pope-joan (pôp'djône), *n.*, (game—*jeu*) nain jaune, *m.*
popeling (pôp'-), *n.*, papiste, *m.*
popery (pôp'-), *n.*, papisme, *m.*
popgun (-gheune), *n.*, (toy—*jouet*) canonnière, *f.*
popinjay (-djé), *n.*, perroquet ; (fop—*petit maître*) freluquet, fat, damoiseau, *m.*
popish, *adj.*, papiste ; (of things—*des choses*) de papiste.
popishly, *adv.*, en papiste.
poplar, *n.*, (bot.) peuplier, *m.*
poplin, *n.*, popeline, *f.*
popliteal (-plit'i-), or **poplitic,** *adj.*, poplité.
poppy, *n.*, pavot, *m.* ; œillette, *f.*
poppy-head (-hède), *n.*, tête de pavot ; (arch.) poupée, *f.*
populace (pop'iou-), *n.*, populace, *f.*
popular (pop'iou-), *adj.*, populaire.
popularity, *n.*, popularité, *f.*
popularize (-aize), *v.a.*, populariser.
popularly, *adv.*, populairement.
populate, *v.a.*, peupler.
populate, *v.n.*, se peupler
population (pop'iou-lé-), *n.*, population, *f.*
populous, *adj.*, populeux.
populously, *adv.*, d'une manière populeuse.
populousness, *n.*, abondance d'habitants, *f.*
porcelain (-ci-léne), *n.*, porcelaine, *f.* ; (bot.) pourpier, *m.*
porch (pôrtshe), *n.*, porche, portique, *m.* ; (antiq.) portique, *m.*, doctrine du portique, *f.*
porcine (-çaïne), *adj.*, de porc, du porc.
porcupine (-kiou-païne), *n.*, porc-épic, *m.*
pore (pôre), *n.*, pore, *m.*
pore (pôre), *v.n.*, regarder avec grande attention. To — on, over ; *fixer les yeux sur ; avoir les yeux fixés sur, collés sur ; pâlir sur.*
poriform (pôr'-), *adj.*, poriforme.
poriness (pôr'-), *n.*, porosité, *f.*
porism (pô-riz'me), *n.*, porisme, *m.*
poristic, or **poristical** (pô-), *adj.*, poristique.
pork (pôrke), *n.*, porc, *m.*
pork-bone (-bône), *n.*, savouret de porc, *m.*
pork-butcher (-bout'sheur), *n.*, charcutier, *m.*
pork-chop (-tshope), *n.*, côtelette de porc, *f.*
porker, *n.*, porc ; cochon, *m.*
porket, or **porkling** (pôrk'-), *n.*, jeune porc, jeune cochon, *m.*
porosity (pô-ross'-), or **porousness** (pô-), *n.*, porosité, *f.*
porous (pô-), *adj.*, poreux.
porphyre. *V.* **porphyry.**
porphyritic, or **porphyritical,** *adj.*, porphyrique, porphyritique.
porphyrize (-raize), *v.a.*, faire ressembler au porphyre.
porphyry, *n.*, porphyre, *m.*
porpoise (por-peusse), *n.*, marsouin, pourceau de mer, *m.*
porraceous (por-ré-sheusse), *adj.*, porracé

porret, n., (bot.) échalotte, f.

porridge, n., potage, m. ; soupe, f. ⌐ -pot ; pot, m. ; marmite, f.

porringer (-djeur), n., écuelle, f.

port (pôrte), n., (harbour—port de mer) port; (carriage—démarche) port, maintien. air, m. tenue, f. ; (nav.) sabord ; (side—côté) bâbord ; (wine—vin) Porto, m.

port, v.a., porter ; (nav.) mettre la barre à bâbord.

portable (-'a-b'l), adj., portatif.

portableness, n.. nature, forme portative, f.

portage (pôrt'édje), n., portage, port, m.

portal (pôr-), n., portail ; (of a door—de porte) tambour, m. ; (fig.) porte, f.

portamento, portamento-voice, n., (mus.) port de voix, m.

port-charges (-tshârdjize), n.pl., frais de port, m.pl.

port-crayon (pôrte-kré-eune), n., porte-crayon, m.

portcullis (pôrt'keul-lice),n., (fort.) herse, f. **portcullis**, v.a., défendre par une herse ; fermer, barrer, obstruer.

porte (pôrte), n., Porte, f. Sublime — ; Sublime Porte.

portend, v.a., présager ; augurer.

portent, n., présage sinistre, mauvais augure, m.

portentous, adj., de mauvais augure ; de sinistre présage ; monstrueux, prodigieux.

porter (pôr-), n., porteur, commissionnaire ; crocheteur, portefaix ; (door-keeper—portier) portier, concierge, m.

porter, n., (liquor—boisson) porter, m.

porterage (-'édje), n., port ; portage ; (business of a door-keeper—garde d'une porte) état de portier, de concierge, m.

portfolio (pôrt'fô-liô), n., portefeuille, m.

porthole (-hôl), n., sabord, m.

portico (-cô), n., portique, m.

portion (pôr-), n., portion, part ; (dowry—dot) dot, f.

portion, v.a., partager, distribuer ; doter.

portioner, n., personne qui fait les portions, qui fait une répartition, f. ; répartiteur, m.

portlast (pôrt'lâste), or **portoise** (pôr-toîze), n., plat-bord, m.

port-lid, n., mantelet de sabord, m.

portliness (pôrt-), n., port majestueux, m.

portly (pôrt'-), adj., de noble port ; (corpulent) corpulent.

portman (pôrt'-), n., habitant d'un port, m.

portmanteau (pôrt'ma'n'tô), n., valise, f. ; portemanteau, m.

portrait (pôr-tréte), n., portrait, m. Full-length — ; portrait en pied. Half-length — ; portrait en buste. To have one's — taken ; se faire peindre ; faire faire son portrait.

portrait-painter (-pé'n't'eur), n., peintre de portraits, m.

portraiture (-tioure), n., portraiture, f. ; portrait, tableau, m.

portray (pôr), v.a., peindre ; dépeindre.

portrayer (pôr-tré-eur), n., peintre, m.

portress (pôr-), n., portière, concierge, f.

portuguese (pôr-tiou-ghize), adj., portugais.

portuguese, n., Portugais, m.. Portugaise, f. ; (language—langue) portugais, m

pory (pô-), adj., poreux.

pose (pôze), v.a., embarrasser, confondre ; poser des questions difficiles à.

poser (pôz'-), n., personne qui embarrasse, qui confond ; (caing—chose) question embarrassante, chose qui ferme la bouche, qui met à quia, f.

position (-zish'-), n., (situation) position ; (state—état) position, condition, f., état ; (principle laid down—principe) principe avancé, principle, m. ; (advancement of a principle—pose

d'un principe) position ; (gram., milit.) position ; (arith.) fausse position, règle de fausse position, f. In a — to ; en position de ; en état de.

positive (poz'-), adj., positif ; absolu ; précis, exact ; (confident—confiant) sûr, certain ; (decisive—décidé) décisif, tranchant.

positive, n., positif ; (gram.) positif, m.

positively, adv.,positivement ; absolument ; précisément, exactement ; décisivement, d'une manière tranchante.

positiveness, n., réalité ; nature positive ; nature absolue, f. ; caractère positif ; caractère absolu, m. ; précision, exactitude, f. ; ton décisif, ton tranchant, m.

posse (pos'sé), n.,force publique d'un comté. (crowd—assemblage) cohue, foule, f.

possess (poz'zèss), v.a., posséder ; être possesseur de ; être en possession de ; (to occupy—occuper) occuper ; (to obtain possession of—prendre possession) s'emparer de, se rendre maître de. To — one's self of ; se rendre maître de ; s'emparer de. To be —ed of ; être possesseur de. —ed with the devil ; possédé du démon.

possession(poz'zèsh'-), n., possession;(thing possessed—chose possédée) possession, f., bien, m.; (jur.) possession, f., (of real property—bien immobilier) possessoire, m. To enter in — ; entrer en possession. To take — of ; prendre possession de ; entrer en jouissance de ; (to seize—saisir) s'emparer de ; (jur.) se saisir de.

possessive (poz-zès'-), n., possessif, m.

possessive, adj., qui possède ; (gram.) possessif.

possessor (poz'zès'-), n., possesseur ; (of a bill—d'une lettre de change, &c.) porteur, m.

possessory, adj., qui possède ; possessoire.

posset, n., lait caillé au vin, &c., m.

posset, v.a., faire cailler.

possibility, n., possibilité, f.

possible (-si-b'l), adj., possible ; absolument.

possibly, adv., peut-être.

post (pôste), n., poteau ; (of a door) montant ; (milit.) poste ; (employment—occupation) poste, m., place ; (post-office—poste aux lettres) poste, f.; (paper—papier) écu, m. By the — ; par la poste, par le courrier. By return of — ; par le retour du courrier. To travel — ; voyager en poste.

post, v.a., coller sur un poteau, &c. ; afficher ; (letters—lettres) jeter à la poste, mettre à la poste, déposer à la poste ; (milit.) poster ; (in book-keeping—tenue des livres) porter au grand livre. To — up ; poser, afficher.

post, v.n., voyager en poste, aller en poste ; courir la poste ; marcher rapidement ; voler. To — off ; s'en aller en poste ; s'en aller à la hâte.

postage (pôstédje), n., port de lettre, port, m. To pay the — of ; payer le port de ; affranchir.

postage-stamp (-sta'm'p), n., timbre-poste, m.

postboy (-boï), n., postillon, m.

postchaise (tshéze), or **post-coach** (-côtsh), n., chaise de poste, f.

postdate, n., postdate, f.

postdate, v.a., postdater.

postday, n., jour de courrier, m.

postdiluvial, or **postdiluvian** (pôst'diliou-), adj., postdiluvien.

postdiluvian (pôst'dill-ou-),n.,personne qui a vécu postérieurement au déluge, f.

poster (nôst'-), n., courrier, m ; (bill—affiche) affiche, f.

posterior (-ti-rieur), adj., postérieur.

posteriority, n., postériorité, f.

posteriors (-ti-ri-eurze), n.pl., parties postérieures, f.pl. ; postérieur, m.sing.

posterity (-tèr'-), n., postérité, f.

postern (pôs-), n., porte de derrière ; porte dérobée ; (fort.) poterne, f.

postern. *adj.*, de derrière ; dérobé.

post-existence (pôst'-), *n.*, existence postérieure, *f.*

postfix (pôst'-), *n.*, (gram.) terminaison ; particule finale, *f.*, suffixe, *m.*

postfix. *v.a.*, (gram.) ajouter une terminaison, une particule finale.

post-hackney, *n.*, cheval de poste, *m.*

post-haste (-héste), *adj.*, très prompt.

post-haste, *adv.*, train de poste, en grande diligence.

post-horse, *n.*, cheval de poste, *m.*

post-house (-haouce), *n.*, poste aux chevaux, *f.* ; bureau de poste, *m.*

posthumous (post'hiou-), *adj.*, posthume.

posthumously, *adv.*, après la mort.

postil, *n.*, (ant.) note marginale ; apostille, *f.*

postil, *v.a.*, (ant.) commenter ; apostiller.

postil, *v.n.*, (ant.) faire des notes marginales, des apostilles.

postiller, *n.*, (ant.) commentateur, *m.*

postillion (-lieune), *n.*, postillon, *m.*

posting (pôst'-), *n.*, voyage en poste ; louage de chevaux de poste, *m.*

postliminiar, *or* **postliminious** (pôst-), *adj.*, subséquent.

postman (pôst'-), *n.* (postmen), facteur de la poste, facteur, *m.*

postmark (-mârke), *n.*, marque de la poste, *f.* ; timbre de la poste, *m.*

postmaster (-mâst'-), *n.*, directeur de poste, *m.* — -general ; *directeur général des postes*, *m.*

post-meridian (-mi-), *adj.*, de l'après-midi.

post mortem, *n.*, autopsie, *f.* — examination ; *autopsie*, *f.*

post-note (-nôte), *n.*, (com.) mandat de banque, *m.*

post-obit (-ôbite), *n.*, (jur.) contrat exécutoire après décès, *m.*

post-office, *n.*, bureau de poste, *m.* ; poste ; poste aux lettres ; boîte aux lettres ; administration des postes, *f.* To be left at the — ; till called for ; *poste restante*.

post-paid (-péde), *adj.*, affranchi, franc de port ; port payé.

postpone (pôst'pône), *v.a.*, ajourner ; différer ; remettre ; (to esteem less—*faire moins cas de*) estimer moins.

postponement, *n.*, ajournement, *m.* ; remise, *f.*

postponer, *n.*, personne qui ajourne, qui remet, qui diffère, *f.*

postscenium (pôst-cî-), *n.*, postscénium, *m.*

postscript, *n.*, postscriptum, *m.* ; apostille, *f.*

post-stage (-stédje), *n.*, relais de poste, *m.*

post-town (-taoune), *n.*, ville où il y a un bureau de poste ; ville où il y a une poste aux chevaux.

postulant (-tiou-), *n.*, postulant, *m.*, postulante, *f.*

postulate (post'iou-), *v.a.*, postuler, solliciter ; s'arroger.

postulate, *n.*, postulat, *m.*

postulation (post'iou-lé-), *n.*, supplication ; supposition ; cause, demande, *f.*

postulatory (post'iou-lé-), *adj.*, supposé, sans preuve.

postulatum (-tiou-lé-), *n.*, postulat, *m.*

posture (post'ieur), *n.*, posture, position, pose, *f.* ; état, *m.* ; (paint.) attitude, pose, *f.*

posture, *v.a.*, placer dans une certaine posture.

posy (pô-zi), *n.*, devise, *f.*

pot, *n.*, pot, *m.* ; marmite, *f.* (pop.) To go to —; *s'en aller au diable*.

pot, *v.a.*, empoter, mettre en pot.

potable (pô-ta-b'l), *adj.*, potable.

potable, *n.*, chose potable, *f.*

potableness, *n.*, qualité d'être potable, *f.*

potash, *or* **potassa**, *n.*, potasse, *f.*

potassium, *n.*, potassium, *m.*

potation (po-té-), *n.*, débauche ; libation, *f.*

potato (-té-tô), *n.* (potatoes), pomme de terre, *f.*

potbellied (-bèl'li'de), *adj.*, pansu, ventru.

potbelly, *n.*, grosse panse, *f.* ; gros ventre, *m.*

pot-boy (-boï), *n.*, garçon de cabaret, *m.*

pot-companion (-pa'n'ieune), *n.*, camarade de bouteille ; compagnon de débauche, *m.*

potency (pô-), *n.*, puissance, autorité, *f.* ; pouvoir, *m.*

potent (pô-), *adj.*, puissant, fort.

potentate (pô-), *adj.*, potentat, *m.*

potential (pô-tè'n'shal), *adj.*, virtuel, efficace ; (gram., med.) potentiel.

potential, *n.*, chose virtuelle, *f.*

potentiality, *n.*, virtualité, *f.*

potentially, *adv.*, virtuellement.

potently, *adv.*, puissamment.

pother (poth'-), *n.*, confusion, *f.* ; tumulte ; tintamarre, *m.*

pother, *v.a.*, tourmenter, ennuyer, tarabuster.

pother, *v.n.*, se trémousser.

potherb (-eurbe), *n.*, herbe potagère, *f.*

pothook (-houke), *n.*, (pot.) crémaillère, *f.* ; (in writing—*écriture*) jambage ; (scrawl—*mauvaise écriture*) griffonnage, *m.*

pothouse (-haouce), *n.*, cabaret, *m.*

potion (pô-), *n.*, potion, *f.* ; breuvage, *m.*

pot-lid, *n.*, couvercle, *m.*

potluck (-leuke), *n.*, fortune du pot, *f.*

potman, *n.*, garçon de cabaret, *m.*

potstone (-stône), *n.*, (min.) pierre ollaire, *f.*

pottage (pot'tédje), *n.*, potage, *m.*

potter, *n.*, potier, *m.*

pottery, *n.*, poterie, *f.*

potting, *n.*, mise en pot ; (tippling—*boire*) boisson, *f.*

pottle (pot't'l), *n.*, quatre pintes, *f.pl.* ; (for fruit—*de fruit*) petit panier, pot, *m.*

pot-valiant, *adj.*, brave le verre en main.

pouch (paoutshe), *n.*, poche, *f.* ; sachet, *m.* ; (belly—*ventre*) grosse panse, bedaine ; (of animals—*des animaux*) bourse ; (of monkeys—*des singes*) abajoue, *f.*

pouch, *v.a.*, empocher ; (of birds—*des oiseaux*) avaler.

pouched (paoutshte), *adj.*, à bourse, marsupial ; (orni.) à poche.

poulterer (pôl-teur'-), *n.*, poulailler ; marchand de volaille, *m.*

poultice, *n.*, cataplasme, *m.*

poultice (pôl-tice), *v.a.*, appliquer un cataplasme à.

poultry (pôl-tri), *n.*, volaille, *f.* — -house ; *poulailler*, *m.* — -yard ; *basse-cour*, *f.*

pounce (paou'n'ce), *n.*, sandaraque ; poudre de sandaraque ; ponce ; (of birds—*des oiseaux*) griffe, serre, *f.*

pounce, *v.n.*, fondre sur.

pounce, *v.a.*, poudrer (de sandaraque) ; poncer ; saisir ; percer, perforer ; (of birds—*des oiseaux*) saisir avec les serres.

pound (paou'n'de), *n.*, (weight—*poids*) livre ; (coin—*monnaie*) livre sterling (fr. 25) ; livre ; (inclosure—*enceinte*) fourrière, *f.* — , apothecaries' weight ; *livre* (grammes 373·239). — avoirdupois weight ; *livre* (grammes 450·541). By the —; *à la livre*. So much in the —; *tant pour cent*.

pound, *v.a.*, piler, broyer ; battre ; (animal) mettre en fourrière ; (metal.) bocarder.

poundage (-édje), *n.*, pondage, *m.* ; commission de tant par livre, *f.*

poundbreach (-brîtshe), *n.*, infraction de fourrière, *f.*

pounder, *n.*, pilon, *m.* A twenty-four—; (artil.) *un canon de vingt-quatre livres de balle*, *m.*, *une pièce de vingt-quatre*, *f.* ; (ball—*boulet*) *boulet de vingt-quatre*, *m.*

pounding, *n.*, broiement; pillage; (metal.) bocardage. *m.*

pound-keeper (-kip'-), *n.*, gardien de fourrière, *m.*

pour (pore), *v.a.*, verser; répandre. To — forth; *verser; répandre.* To — in; *verser dans; lancer.* To — out; *verser; répandre; décharger; lâcher.*

pour, *v.n.*, couler; se précipiter; (of the rain —*de la pluie*) pleuvoir à verse.

pourer, *n.*, personne qui verse, *f.*

pout (paoute), *n.*, bouderie, moue; (ich.) lamproie, *f.*; (orni.) francolin, *m.*

pout, *v.n.*, bouder; faire la mine, faire la moue; déborder, saillir. To — at; *bouder.* To — one's lip; *faire la moue.*

pouting, *adj.*, qui fait la mine, qui fait la moue; saillant.

pouting, *n.*, bouderie, moue, mine, *f.*

poverty, *n.*, pauvreté, misère, *f.* To come to —; *tomber dans la misère.*

powder (paoudeur), *n.*, poudre, *f.* Tooth- —; *poudre dentifrice.* To waste — and shot; *tirer sa poudre aux moineaux.*

powder, *v.a.*, réduire en poudre; piler; pulvériser; (the hair—*les cheveux*) poudrer; (to sprinkle with salt—*saler*) saupoudrer de sel.

powder-box, *n.*, poudrier, *m.*

powder-cart (-cârte), *n.*, caisson, *m.*

powder-chest (-tshèste), *n.*, caisson à poudre, *m.*

powder-flask, or **powder-horn**, *n.*, poire à poudre, flasque, *f.*

powdering, *n.*, pulvérisation; action de poudrer les cheveux; salaison, *f.*

powdering-tub (-teube), *n.*, saloir, *m.*

powder-magazine (-zîne), *n.*, poudrière; (nav.) soute aux poudres, *f.*

powder-mill, *n.*, poudrière, *f.*; moulin à poudre, *m.*

powder-puff (-peufe), *n.*, houppe à poudrer, *f.*

powder-room (-roume), *n.*, (nav.) soute aux poudres, *f.*

powdery, *adj.*, poudreux; friable.

power (paou'eur), *n.*, pouvoir, *m.*; force, puissance, *f.*; (ability—*capacité*) talent, *m.*; moyens, *m.pl.*, forces, *f.pl.*; (faculty—*faculté*) faculté; (military force—*force militaire*) armée, puissance militaire, *f.*, forces, *f.pl.*; (mec.) effet, travail, *m.*, puissance; force; (math.) puissance, *f.* To the utmost of one's —; *de tout son pouvoir; autant que possible; autant que faire se peut.* To have it in one's —; *être en pouvoir de; avoir en son pouvoir de; être à même de.* A machine of eight-horse —; *une machine de la force de huit chevaux.*

powerful (-foule), *adj.*, puissant; fort; efficace.

powerfully, *adv.*, puissamment, fortement, efficacement.

powerfulness, *n.*, puissance, force, énergie, efficacité, *f.*

powerless, *adj.*, impuissant, faible; inefficace.

power-loom (-loume), *n.*, métier à tisser, métier mécanique, *m.*

power-owner (-ô'n'eur), *n.*, propriétaire de métier mécanique, *m.*

pox, *n.*, (l.ex.) vérole, *f.* Chicken- —; *vérole volante.* Small- —; *petite vérole.* Cow- —; *vaccine, f.*

poy (pwaï), *n.*, balancier, *m.*

pozzuolana, or **pozzolana** (-lâ-), *n.*, pouzzolane, *f.*

practicability, or **practicableness**, *n.*, nature praticable; possibilité. *f.*

practicable (-ca-b'l), *adj.*, praticable, faisable.

practical, *adj.*, pratique; praticien.

practically, *adv.*, pratiquement; en pratique, dans la pratique.

practicalness, *n.*, nature, qualité pratique, *f.*

practice, *n.*, pratique, (custom—*coutume*) habitude, coutume, *f.*, usage; (exercise) exercice, *m.*; (of doctors, barristers—*de médecins, d'avocats*) clientèle, *f.*; (artifice) artifice, stratagème, *m.*; (arith.) méthode des parties aliquotes; (jur.) pratique, *f.*

practise (-tice), *v.a.*, pratiquer, mettre en pratique; (to commit—*commettre*) commettre, exercer; (profession) exercer, pratiquer; (mus.) étudier.

practise, *v.a.*, pratiquer; exercer; (to try artifices—*user de stratagème*) employer des pratiques, employer des menées; (mus.) étudier, s'exercer.

practiser, *n.*, personne qui pratique, qui met en pratique, *f.*; praticien, *m.*

practising, *adj.*, praticien; en exercice.

practitioner (-tish'eu'n'eur), *n.*, praticien; médecin praticien, *m.*

præcognita (pri-cog-), *n.pl.*, choses connues, *f.pl.*

præmunire, or **premunire** (pri-miou-niri). *n.*, (jur.) atteinte portée aux droits du souverain ou des chambres, *f.*

prætexta (pri-), *n.*, (antiq.) prétexte, robe prétexte, *f.*

prætorium (pri-), *n.*, (antiq.) prétoire, *m.*

pragmatic, *adj.*, pragmatique. — sanction; *pragmatique sanction; pragmatique, f.*

pragmatic, or **pragmatical**, *adj.*, prêt à se mêler des affaires d'autrui; importun.

pragmatically, *adv.*, en se mêlant des affaires d'autrui; avec importunité.

pragmaticalness, *n.*, disposition à se mêler des affaires d'autrui; importunité, *f.*

pragmatist, *n.*, (ant.) personne qui se mêle des affaires d'autrui, *f.*; importun, *m.*

prairy, or **prairie**, *n.*, prairie, *f.*

praise (prèze), *n.*, louange, *f.*; éloge, *m.* To bestow — on; *donner des louanges à, des éloges à.*

praise, *v.a.*, louer, faire l'éloge de; (biblically —*biblique*) louer, célébrer, glorifier.

praiseless, *adj.*, sans louange; sans éloge.

praiser, *n.*, distributeur d'éloges; approbateur; louangeur, *m.*

praiseworthily (préz'weur-thi-), *adv.*, d'une manière louable.

praiseworthiness (-weur-thi-), *n.*, mérite, *m.*

praiseworthy (préz'weur-thi), *adj.*, louable; digne d'éloge.

pram, or **prame**, *n.*, (nav.) prame, *f.*

prance, *v.n.*, se cabrer; (pers.) se carrer.

prancer, *n.*, cheval qui se cabre, *m.*

prancing, *n.*, action de se cabrer, *f.*

prank, *n.*, escapade; fredaine; farce; niche, *f.*; tour, *m.* To play a — on; *faire une farce à, une niche à, un tour à.* To play one's —s; *faire des siennes.*

prank, *adj.*, badin; espiègle; malin.

prank, *v.a.*, attifer, orner, parer.

prankish, *adj.*, badin; espiègle; malin.

prate, *v.n.*, jaser, babiller, bavarder.

prate, *v.a.*, débiter; dire sottement.

prate, *n.*, babil, caquet, caquetage, bavardage, *m.*

prater (prét'-), *n.*, jaseur, jaseuse, *f.*; caqueteur, *m.*, caqueteuse, *f.*; bavard, *m.*, bavarde, *f.*; babillard, *m.*, babillarde, *f.*

pratingly (prét'-), *adv.*, en bavard, en babillard.

pratique (prat'ike), *n.*, pratique, *f.*

prattle (prat't'l), *n.*, caquet, babil, bavardage, parlage, *m.*, jaserie, *f.*

prattle, *v.n.*, babiller, jaser, caqueter, bavarder.

prattler, *n.*, bavard, *m.*, bavarde, *f.*; babillard, *m.*, babillarde, *f.*; caqueteur, *m.*, caqueteuse, *f.*; jaseur, *m.*, jaseuse, *f.*

pravity, *n.*, dépravation, *f.*

prawn (pro'n), *n.*, crevette, salicoque, *f.*

praxis, *n.*, pratique, *f.*; exercice; exemple, *m.*

pray (prè), *v.a.*, prier, supplier; (jur.) demander, requérir. **I — you**; *je vous prie, je vous en prie; de grâce.*

pray, *v.n.*, prier.

prayer (pré-ère, *ou* prére), *n.*, prière; supplication; (jur.) demande, *f.* **—book**; *livre de prières, rituel, m.*

prayerful (-foule), *adj.*, porté à la prière; qui prie beaucoup.

prayerfully, *adv.*, par beaucoup de prières.

preach (pritshe), *v.n.*, prêcher.

preach, *v.a.*, prêcher. **To — up**; *prêcher; prôner.*

preacher, *n.*, prédicateur; (b.s.) prêcheur, prédicant. *m.*

preaching, *n.*, prédication, *f.*

preachment, *n.*, sermon, *m.*

pre-acquaintance (pri-ac-kwé'n't'-), *n.*, connaissance préalable, *f.*

pre-acquainted (pri-ac-kwé'n'tède), *adj.* familier auparavant.

pre-adamic, *or* **pre-adamitic** (-'It'ike), *adj.*, préadamite.

pre-adamite (pri-ad'a'm'aïte), *n.*, préadamite, *n., f.*

pre-administration (pri-ad-mi'n'is-tré-), *n.*, administration antérieure, *f.*

pre-admonish (pri-), *v.a.*, avertir au préalable; prévenir préalablement.

pre-admonition (pri-), *n.*, avertissement préalable, avertissement antérieur, *m.*

preamble (pri-a'm'b'l), *n.*, préambule, avant-propos; exposé des motifs, *m.*

preamble, *v.a.*, faire un préambule à; faire précéder.

preambulate (pri-a'm'biou-), *v.a.*, marcher devant.

preambulatory, *adj.*, (ant.) antécédent.

pre-appoint (pri-ap-poï'n'te), *v.a.*, nommer auparavant.

pre-apprehension (pri-ap-pri-hè'n'-), *n.*, opinion formée d'avance; prévention, *f.*

pre-audience (pri-), *n.*, (jur.) préséance d'avocats aux audiences, *f.*

prebend (prèb'-), *n.*, prébende, *f.*

prebendal, *adj.*, de prébende.

prebendary, *n.*, chanoine prébendé; prébendier, *m.*

precarious (pri-ké-), *adj.*, précaire; (of the weather—*du temps*) incertain.

precariously, *adv.*, précairement.

precariousness, *n.*, nature précaire, incertitude, *f.*

precative (prèk'-), *or* **precatory** (-teuri), *adj.*, suppliant, de supplication.

precaution (pri-co-), *n.*, précaution, *f.* By way of **—**; *par précaution.*

precaution, *v.a.*, précautionner, avertir, prémunir.

precautional, *or* **precautionary**, *adj.*, de précaution.

precede (pri-cîde), *v.a.*, précéder; avoir le pas sur.

precedence, *or* **precedency** (pri-cî-), *n.*, priorité; (superiority) supériorité; (in rank—*rang*) préséance, *f.*, pas, *m.* To have **— of**; *avoir le pas sur.*

precedent (pri-cî-), *adj.*, précédent, antécédent.

precedent, *n.*, précédent, *m.*; (jur.) décision de la cour, *f.*

precedented, *adj.*, autorisé par un précédent.

precedently, *adv.*, précédemment.

preceding (pri-cî-), *adj.*, précédent.

precentor (pri-cè'n'teur), *n.*, chantre; grand chantre, *m.*

precept (pri-cèpte), *n.*, précepte, *m.*

preceptive (pri-cèp'-), *adj.*, de préceptes; didactique, instructif.

preceptor (pri-cèp-teur), *n.*, précepteur, instituteur, *m.*

preceptorial (pri-cèp-tô-), *adj.*, de précepteur, d'instituteur.

preceptory (prè-cèp-teuri), *adj.*, de préceptes.

preceptory, *n.*, maison religieuse d'éducation, *f.*

preceptress (pri-cèp-), *n.*, institutrice, *f.*

precession (pri-cèsh'-). *n.*, action de précéder; (astron.) précession, *f.*

precinct (pri-), *n.*, limite, borne; juridiction, *f.*; ressort, *m.*

precious (prèsh'eusse), *adj.*, précieux; de prix; (b.s.) fameux, fier.

preciously, *adv.*, précieusement; (b.s.) fameusement, fièrement, furieusement.

preciousness, *n.*, nature précieuse, *f.*; haut prix, *m.*; grande valeur, *f.*

precipe (pri-ci-pi), *n.*, (jur.) sommation, *f.*

precipice (près'i-), *n.*, précipice, *m.*

precipitability (pri-), *n.*, propriété de se précipiter, *f.*

precipitable (pri-cip'i-ta'-b'l), *adj.*, précipitable.

precipitance, *or* **precipitancy** (pri-), *n.*, précipitation, *f.*; empressement excessif, *m.*

precipitant, *adj.*, qui se précipite; précipité.

precipitant (pri-), *n.*, (chem.) précipitant, *m.*

precipitantly, *adv.*, précipitamment.

precipitate (pri-), *adj.*, précipité; qui se précipite.

precipitate. *n.*, précipité, *m.*

precipitate, *v.a.*, précipiter. To be **—d**; (chem.) *se précipiter.*

precipitate, *v.n.*, se précipiter; se précipiter.

precipitately, *adv.*, précipitamment.

precipitation (pri-cip-i-té-), *n.*, précipitation, *f.*

precipitator (pri-cip-i-té-teur), *n.*, personne qui précipite, *f.*

precipitous (pri-), *adj.*, escarpé; de précipice; (fig.) précipité.

precipitously, *adv.*, en précipice; (fig.) précipitamment.

precipitousness, *n.*, escarpement, *m.*; nature escarpée; précipitation, *f.*

precise (pri-çaïce), *adj.*, précis, exact scrupuleux; formel.

precisely, *adv.*, précisément; exactement; scrupuleusement.

preciseness, *n.*, précision, exactitude, *f.*; scrupule, *m.*; formalité, *f.*

precision (pri-cij'-), *n.*, précision, *f.*

precisive (pri-çaï-cive), *adj.*, (ant.) précis.

preclude (pri-cloude), *v.a.*, exclure; empêcher; écarter.

preclusion (pri-clou-jeune), *n.*, exclusion, *f.*

preclusive (pri-clou-cive), *adj.*, qui exclut; qui empêche, qui écarte.

preclusively, *adv.*, avec exclusion.

precocious (pri-cô-sheuse), *adj.*, précoce.

precociousness, *or* **precocity**, *n.*, précocité, *f.*

precognition (pri-cog-), *n.*, connaissance antérieure, *f.*

precompose (pri-co'm-pôze), *v.a.*, composer d'avance.

preconceit (pri-co'n'cîte), *n.*, opinion conçue d'avance, *f.*; préjugé, *m.*; prévention, *f.*

preconceive (pri-co'n'cive), *v.a.*, concevoir d'avance ; juger d'avance ; (philos.) préconcevoir.
preconceived (-civ'de), *adj.*, formé d'avance ; (philos.) préconçu.
preconception (pri-), *n.*, opinion formée d'avance ; prévention, *f.* ; préjugé, *m.*
preconcert (pri-co'n'certe), *v.a.*, concerter d'avance.
preconsign (pri-co'n'çaine), *v.a.*, transférer d'avance.
preconstitute (pri-co'n'sti-tioute), *v.a.*, constituer préalablement.
precontract (pri-), *n.*, contrat préalable, *m.*
precontract, *v.a.* and *n.*, contracter préalablement.
precordial (pri-), *adj.*, (anat.) précordial.
precursor (pri-keur-seur), *n.*, précurseur, avant-coureur, *m.*
precursory, *adj.*, précurseur.
predaceous (pri-dé-sheusse), *adj.*, qui vit de proie.
predatory (prèd'-), *adj.*, de pillards ; de pillage ; de rapine ; de vol ; pillard.
predecease (pri-di-cice), *v.n.*, prédécéder.
predecessor (prèd'i-cès'seur), *n.*, prédécesseur, devancier, *m.* —s ; *ancêtres*, *m.pl.*
predesign (pri-dè-çaine), *v.a.*, projeter d'avance.
predestinarian (pri-dès-ti-né-), *n.*, prédestinatien. *m.*
predestinate (pri-dès-), *adj.*, prédestiné.
predestinate, *or* **predestine** (pri-dès-), *v.a.*, prédestiner.
predestination (pri-dès-ti-né-), *n.*, prédestination, *f.*
predestinator (pri-dès-ti-né-teur), *n.*, prédestinatien, *m.*
predestine, *v.a. V.* **predestinate**.
predetermination (pri-di-teur-mi-né-), *n.*, prédétermination, *f.*
predetermine (pri-di-teur-), *v.a.*, arrêter d'avance ; prédéterminer.
predial (pri-), *adj.*, qui consiste en terres ; attaché à la terre ; qui provient de la terre.
predicable (prèd'i-ca-b'l), *adj.*, ⊙prédicable.
predicable, *n.*, (log.) universel, (*pl.*) universaux, *m.*
predicament (pri-dik'-) *n.*, catégorie, *f.* ; ordre ; (state—*état*) état, *m.*, passe, position, *f.* ; (log.) prédicament, *m.*
predicant (prèd'-), *n.*, (ant.) personne qui affirme, *f.*
predicate (prèd'-), *n.*, (log.) prédicat, attribut, *m.*
predicate (prèd'-), *v.a.*, (log.) affirmer ; donner pour attribut.
predicate, *v.n.*, (log.) affirmer.
predication (prèd'-), *n.*, affirmation, *f.*
predicatory (prèd'-), *adj.*, affirmatif.
predict (pri-), *v.a.*, prédire.
prediction (pri-), *n.*, prédiction, *f.*
predictive (pri-), *adj.*, qui prédit ; prophétique.
predictor (pri-dic-teur), *n.*, personne qui prédit, *f.* ; prophète, *m.*
predigestion (pri-di-djès'tieune), *n.*, digestion précipitée, *f.*
predilection (pri-di-lèk'-), *n.*, prédilection, *f.*
predispose (pri-dis-pôze), *v.a.*, disposer d'avance ; prédisposer.
predisposition, *n.*, disposition antérieure ; prédisposition, *f.*
predominance, *or* **predominancy** (pri-), *n.*, prédominance, *f.* ; ascendant, pouvoir, *m.* ; prépondérance ; (med.) prédominance, *f.*
predominant (pri-), *adj.*, prédominant.
predominantly, *adv.*, d'une manière prédominante.
predominate (pri-), *v.n.*, dominer.
predominate, *v.n.*, prédominer.

predomination (pri-do'm'i né-), *n.*, influence supérieure, *f.*
predoomed (pri-dou'm'de), *adj.*, condamné d'avance.
pre-elect (pri-i-lèk'tè), *v.a.*, élire auparavant.
pre-election (pri-i-lèk'-), *n.*, élection antérieure ; élection faite d'avance, *f.*
pre-eminence (pri-è'm'r), *n.*, prééminence, supériorité, *f.*
pre-eminent (pri-è'm'-), *adj.*, prééminent, supérieur.
pre-eminently (pri-), *adv.*, d'une manière prééminente ; supérieurement.
pre-emption (pri-è'm'-), *n.*, préemption, *f.*
preen (pri'n), *v.a.*, (of birds—*des oiseaux*) nettoyer les plumes.
pre-engage (pri-è'n'ghédje), *v.a.*, engager d'avance.
pre-engagement (pri-è'n'ghédj'-), *n.*, engagement antérieur, *m.*
pre-establish (pri-ès'-), *v.a.*, préétablir.
pre-examination (pri-ègz'a'm'i-né-), *n.*, examen préalable, *m.*
pre-examine (pri-ègz'a'm'-), *v.a.*, examiner préalablement.
pre-exist (pri-ègz'-), *v.n.*, préexister.
pre-existence (pri-ègz'ist'-), *n.*, préexistence, *f.*
pre-existent, *adj.*, préexistant.
preface (prèf'-), *n.*, préface, *f.* ; avant-propos, *m.*
preface, *v.a.*, faire une préface à ; faire précéder.
preface, *v.a.*, dire comme préface ; dire en forme de préface.
prefatory (prèf'-), *or* **prefatorial** (·tô-), *adj.*, qui sert de préface ; préliminaire.
prefect (pri-fèkte), *n.*, préfet, *m.*
prefecture (prèf'èk-tioure), *or* **prefectship**, *n.*, préfecture, *f.*
prefer (pri-feur), *v.a.*, préférer ; aimer mieux ; (to advance—*promouvoir*) avancer, élever ; (to offer—*offrir*) présenter, offrir ; (to make—*faire*) présenter, former. To — a complaint, an accusation ; *former une plainte, une accusation.*
preferable (-'a-b'l), *adj.*, préférable.
preferableness, *n.*, nature préférable, *f.*
preferably, *adv.*, préférablement, de préférence.
preference (prèf'èr'-), *n.*, préférence, *f.*
preferment (pri-feur-), *n.*, avancement, *m.* ; promotion ; (superior place—*emploi supérieur*) place supérieure, *f.*
preferrer (pri-feur-), *n.*, personne qui préfère, *f.*
prefiguration (pri-figh'iou-ré-), *n.*, représentation antérieure, *f.* ; symbole, *m.*
prefigurative (pri-figh'iou-ré-), *adj.*, symbolique, typique.
prefigure (pri-figh'ieure), *v.a.*, figurer d'avance.
prefix (pri-), *v.a.*, mettre devant ; arrêter d'avance.
prefix (pri-), *n.*, (gram.) préfixe, *m.*
preform (pri-), *v.a.*, (ant.) former d'avance.
prefulgency (pri-feul-djè'n'-), *n.*, éclat resplendissant, *m.*
pregnancy, *n.*, grossesse ; (fig.) fécondité, *f.*
pregnant (prèg-), *adj.*, enceinte, grosse ; (fig.) gros, plein, fertile, fécond, inventif.
pregnantly (prèg-), *adv.*, avec fertilité.
prehensile, *or* **prehensory** (pri-hè'n'-), *adj.*, préhensile.
prejudge (pri-djeudje), *v.a.*, condamner d'avance, préjuger.
prejudgment (pri-djeudj'-), *n.*, jugement par avance, *m.*
prejudicate (pri-djou-di-), *v.a.* and *n.*, condamner d'avance ; préjuger.

prejudicated (-két'éde), *part.*, préjugé ; prévenu.

prejudication (-di-ké-), *n.*, action de préjuger, *f.*

prejudicative (-két'-), *adj.*, qui préjuge.

prejudice (prèd'jiou-dice), *v.a.*, (to bias—*prévenir*) prévenir, donner des préventions à, des préjugés à ; (to injure—*nuire*) préjudicier à, faire tort à, nuire à, porter préjudice à, porter dommage à.

prejudice (prèd'jiou-dice). *n.*, (bias—*prévention*) prévention, *f.*, préjugé ; (injury—*tort*) préjudice, tort, dommage, *m.* To my —; *à mon préjudice.* To do any one a — ; *faire tort, faire un préjudice à quelqu'un.*

prejudiced (-diste), *adj.*, prévenu ; à préjugés ; à préventions ; qui a des préjugés.

prejudicial (prèd'jiou-dish'-), *adj.*, préjudiciable, nuisible.

prejudicialness, *n.*, nature préjudiciable, *f.*

pre-knowledge (prî-nol'èdje), *n.*, connaissance antérieure, *f.*

prelacy (prèl'-), *n.*, prélature, *f.* ; épiscopat, *m.*

prelate (prèl'-), *n.*, prélat, *m.*

prelateship (prèl'èt'shipe), *n.*, prélature, *f.*

prelatic, *or* **prelatical** (pri-lat'-), *adj.*, de prélat.

prelatically, *adv.*, en prélat.

prelatism (prèl'at-'iz'm), *n.*, (ant.) épiscopat, *m.*

prelature (prèl'at'ioure), *n.*, prélature, *f.*

prelect (pri-lèk'te), *v.n.*, lire un discours en public.

prelection (pri-lèk'-), *n.*, discours lu en public, ou devant un auditoire privé, *m.*

prelector (pri-lèkt'eur), *n.*, professeur, lecteur, *m.*

pre-libation (pri-laï-bé-), *n.*, avant-goût, *m.*

preliminarily *adv.*, préliminairement.

preliminary (pri-), *adj.*, préliminaire ; préalable.

preliminary, *n.*, préliminaire, préalable, *m.*

prelude (prèl'ioude), *n.*, prélude, *m.*

prelude (pri-lioude), *v.a.* and *n.*, préluder, préluder à.

preluder, *n.*, personne qui prélude, *f.*

preludious (pri-lioud'-), *adj.*, (ant.) qui sert de prélude, préparatoire.

prelusive (pri-liou-cive), *or* **prelusory** (-ço-), *adj.*, préliminaire, préparatoire.

premature (pri-ma-tioure), *adj.*, prématuré.

prematurely, *adv.*, prématurément.

prematureness, *or* **prematurity,** *n.*, prématurité, *f.*

premeditate (pri-mèd'-), *v.a.*, préméditer ; méditer d'avance.

premeditate, *v.n.*, méditer d'avance.

premeditated (-tèt'ède), *adj.*, prémédité.

premeditately (-tèt'-), *adv.*, avec préméditation.

premeditation (-té-sheune), *n.*, préméditation, *f.*

premier (pri-mi-eur), *adj.*, premier (de rang).

premier (pri-mi-eur), *n.*, premier ministre ; (France) président du conseil des ministres, *m.*

premiership, *n.*, dignité de premier ministre ; présidence du conseil des ministres, *f.*

premise (pri-maize), *v.a.*, exposer d'avance ; (log.) poser les prémisses de.

premise, *v.n.*, poser des prémisses.

premises (prè'm'iss'ize), *n.pl.*, lieux, *m.pl.* ; lieu, établissement, local, *m.sing.* ; (jur.) intitulé, *m.sing.* ; (log) prémisses, *f.pl.* On the — ; *dans l'établissement : sur les lieux.*

premium (pri-), *n.*, prix ; prix d'encouragement, *m.* ; récompense ; (com., fin.) prime, *f.* At a — ; *à prime.*

premonish (pri-), *v.a.*, prévenir.

premonishment, *or* **premonition** (pri-), *n.*, avis préliminaire, *m.*

premonitory (pri-mo'n'i-teuri), *adj.*, qui avertit d'avance.

premonstrants (pri-), *n.pl.*, Prémontrés, *m.pl.*

premorse (pri-), *adj.*, (bot.) mordu.

premotion (pri-mô-),*n.*,(theol.) prémotion,*f.*

premunire. *V.* **præmunire.**

prenomen (pri-nô-mène), *n.*, prénom, *m.*

prenominate (pri-), *v.a.*, nommer d'avance.

prenominate, *adj.*, déjà nommé, susnommé.

prenomination (-mi-né-), *n.*, privilège d'être nommé le premier, *m.*

prenotion (pri-nô-), *n.*, prénotion, *f.*

preobtain (pri-ob-téne), *v.a.*, obtenir d'avance.

preoccupancy (pri-). *n.*, possession antérieure, *f.* ; droit d'occupation, *m.*

preoccupation (pri-oc-keu-pé-), *n.*, occupation antérieure ; (anticipation) préoccupation, anticipation, *f.*

preoccupy (pri-oc-keu-pa'ye), *v.a.*, occuper avant un autre ; occuper le premier ; (fig.) préoccuper, prévenir, donner des préjugés à.

preominate (pri-), *v.a.*, (ant.) pronostiquer ; présager.

preopinion (pri-o-pi'n'ieune), *n.*, opinion formée d'avance, *f.* ; préjugé, *m.*

preordain (pri-or-déne), *v.a.*, ordonner d'avance ; prédéterminer.

preordinance (pri-), *n.*, ordonnance antérieure, *f.*

preordination (pri-or-di-né-), *n.*, détermination antérieure ; (theol.) prédétermination, *f.*

prepaid (pri-), *adj.*, affranchi.

preparation (prèp'a-ré-), *n.*, préparation, *f.* ; préparatif, apprêt ; (state—*état*) état, *m.*, condition ; (anat., mus , pharm.) préparation, *f.* To make —s for ; *faire des préparatifs, des apprêts pour.*

preparative (pri-par-ô-), *adj.*, préparatoire ; qui prépare.

preparative, *n.*, préparatif ; apprêt, préparatoire, *m.*

preparatively, *adv.*, d'une manière préparatoire.

preparatory (pri-), *adj.*, préparatoire ; qui prépare.

prepare (pri-), *v.a.*, préparer ; (to set—*placer*) disposer ; apprêter ; (to provide—*pourvoir*) se pourvoir de, fournir ; (food—*aliments*) apprêter.

prepare, *v.n.*, se préparer ; se disposer ; s'apprêter.

preparedly, *adv.*, par des mesures préparatoires.

preparedness, *n.*, état de préparation, *m.*

preparer, *n.*, personne qui prépare, qui dispose, qui apprête ; chose qui prépare, qui apprête, *f.*

prepay (pri-), *v.a.*, payer d'avance ; (letters —*lettres*) affranchir.

prepayment (pri-pé-), *n.*, payement d'avance ; (of letters—*de lettres*) affranchissement, *m.*

prepense (pri-pè'n'sé), *adj.*, (jur.) prémédité.

prepollence, *or* **prepollency** (pri-), *n.*, prépondérance, supériorité, *f.*

prepollent, *adj.*, supérieur.

preponderance, *or* **preponderancy** (pri-po'n'-dèr-), *n.*, supériorité de poids ; prépondérance, *f.*

preponderant, *adj.*, qui surpasse en poids ; prépondérant.

preponderate, *v.a.*, surpasser en poids ; (fig.) l'emporter sur.

preponderate, *v.n.*, peser le plus ; (fig.) avoir la prépondérance, l'emporter.

preponderation (pri-po'n'dĕr'ĕ-), n., supériorité de poids; prépondérance, f.

preposition (prèp'o-zish'-), n., préposition, f.

prepositional, adj., prépositif.

prepositive (pri-poz'-), adj., prépositif.

prepositive, n., mot prépositif, m.; particule prépositive, f.

prepositor (pri-poz'i-teur), n., moniteur, m.

prepossess (pri-poz'zèss), v.a., occuper antérieurement; (fig.) préoccuper, prévenir; (the mind, the heart—l'esprit, le cœur) gagner.

prepossessing, adj., prévenant; qui prévient en sa faveur; avenant, agréable.

prepossession, n., possession antérieure; (fig.) prévention, f., préjugé, m.

preposterous (pri-pos-tèr'-), adj., dont l'ordre est renversé; absurde, déraisonnable.

preposterously, adv., dans un ordre renversé; à rebours; absurdement, déraisonnablement.

preposterousness, n., ordre renversé, m.; absurdité, déraison, f.

prepuce (pri-piouce), n., prépuce, m.

prerequire (pri-ri-kwaeur), v.a., demander préalablement.

prerequisite, adj., nécessaire auparavant.

prerequisite (pri-rèk'wi-zite), n., chose nécessaire au préalable, f.

preresolve (pri-ri-zolve), v.a., résoudre d'avance.

prerogative (pri-), n., prérogative, f. — court; cour de la prérogative, f. —office; greffe de la cour de la prérogative, m.

presage (prèss'adje), n., présage, m.

presage (pri-cédje), v.a. and n., présager.

presageful (-foule), adj., qui renferme des présages, qui abonde en présages.

presagement, n., présage, m.

presbyter (prèz'-), n., ancien; prêtre; (presbyterian) presbytérien, m., presbytérienne, f.

presbyterial, or **presbyterian** (prèz-bi-ti-), adj., de presbytère; presbytérien.

presbyterian (prèz-bi-ti-), n., presbytérien, m., presbytérienne, f.

presbyterianism, n., presbytérianisme; presbytéranisme, m.

presbytery, n., presbytère; (religion) presbytéranisme, m.

prescience (pri-shi-), n., prescience, f.

prescient (pri-shi-), adj., doué de prescience.

prescious (pri-shi-), adj., qui sait d'avance.

prescribe (pri-scraïbe), v.a., prescrire, ordonner.

prescribe, v.n., faire la loi; (med.) faire une ordonnance.

prescript (prt-), adj., prescrit.

prescript, n., (l.u.) chose prescrite, f.; précepte, m., (med.) ordonnance, f.

prescriptible (pri-script'i-b'l), adj., (jur.) prescriptible.

prescription (pri-), n., action de prescrire; ordonnance, f.; précepte, m.; prescription, f.; (med.) ordonnance; (jur.) prescription, f.

prescriptive (pri-), adj., établi par prescription.

presence (prèz'-), n., présence, f.; (mienmine) port, air, m., mine; (persons assembled—assemblée) réunion, société; (apartment—salle) salle d'audience, f.; (pers.) personnage supérieur, m. — of mind, présence d'esprit.

presence-chamber (-tshé'm'beur), or **presence-room** ('-roume), n., salle de réception, f.

presension (pri-cè'n'-), n., pressentiment, m.

present (prèz'-), adj., présent; actuel; (of the month—du mois) courant; (attentive) attentif. In the — tense; au présent. At the — moment; à présent; actuellement, présentement.

present, n., (time—temps, gram.) présent; (gift—don) présent; cadeau, don, m., —s; (jur.)

présentes, f. pl. At —; à présent; actuellement; présentement. In the —; (gram.) au présent. Know all men by these —s; à tous ceux qui ces présentes verront. To make a —; faire un cadeau. To make any one a — of any thing; faire don, faire cadeau de quelque chose à quelqu'un.

present (pri-zè'n'te), v.a., présenter; offrir; (to a benefice) présenter; (jur.) déférer au tribunal compétent. To — somebody with something; faire présent de, faire don de, faire cadeau de quelque chose à quelqu'un.

presentable (-a-b'l), adj., présentable.

presentaneous (prèz'è'n'té-), adj., présent; immédiat; qui opère sur-le-champ.

presentation (prèz'è'n'té-), n., présentation; (representation) représentation; (eec.) présentation, f. On —; à présentation.

presentative, adj., (eec.) dont le patron a le droit de présentation.

presentee (prèz'è'n'ti), n., (eec.) personne présentée à un bénéfice, f.

presenter (pri-zè'n't'-), n., personne qui présente, f.

presentiment (pri-cè'n't'-), n., pressentiment, m.

presently (prèz'-), adv., tout à l'heure; bientôt; tantôt.

presentment (pri-zè'n't-), n., présentation, apparence; (jur.) dénonciation spontanée, f.

preservable (pri-zeurv'a-b'l), adj., qui peut être préservé, qui peut être conservé.

preservation (prèz'èr-vé-), n., conservation; préservation, f.

preservative, or **preservatory** (pri-zeur-), n., préservatif, m.

preservative, or **preservatory**, adj., préservateur; préservatif; conservateur.

preserve (pri-zeurve), n., confiture, f.; (inclosure—enclos) réserve, f., parc pour la conservation du gibier, m.

preserve, v.a., préserver; conserver, garder; (fruit) confire.

preserver, n., personne qui préserve, qui conserve; chose qui préserve, qui conserve, f.; conservateur, m., conservatrice, f.; préservatif, sauveur, m.; personne qui fait des confitures, f. Eye —s; conserves (lunettes), f. pl.

preside (pri-zaïde), v.n., présider.

presidency (prèz'-), n., présidence, f.

president (prèz'-), n., président, m. Vice- —; vice-président, m.

presidential (prèz'i-dè'n'shal), adj., présidentiel; présidentiel; de président; qui préside.

presidentship, n., présidence, f.

presidial, or **presidiary** (pri-cid'-), adj., de garnison; à garnison.

presignification (pri-cig-), n., action de montrer d'avance, de signifier d'avance, f.

presignify (pri-cig-ni-fa-ye), v.a., montrer d'avance; signifier d'avance.

press (prèce), v.a., presser; serrer; (to urge —presser) presser, pousser; (to embrace—embrasser) serrer, presser, étreindre; (sailors—matelots) exercer la presse contre, presser; (paper—papier) glacer, satiner; (fruit) presser; (manu.) mettre en presse. To — upon; appuyer sur; insister sur; faire sentir à. To — a thing on any one; imposer une chose à quelqu'un. To — down; presser; appuyer fortement sur. To — out; exprimer; pressurer. To — hard; presser fort; (to be hard with—suivre) serrer de près. To cold- —; to hot —; satiner à froid, à chaud. To be —ed for time; être pressé.

press, v.n., presser; pousser; (to encroach —empiéter) empiéter; (to approach—approcher) approcher, s'approcher; avancer; (to crowd—affluer) se presser, affluer. To — upon; presser.

press, n., pressoir, m.; presse; (print.) presse; (crowd—foule) presse, foule; (closet—

armoire) armoire ; (urgency—*urgence*) urgence, presse ; (levy of men for service—*levée de recrues*) presse, *f.* — of sail ; (nav.) *force de voiles, f.* Printing— ; *presse d'imprimerie.* — -error ; *faute d'impression, f.* In the —; *sous presse.* To go to —; *mettre sous presse.*

press-bed (-bède), n., lit en armoire, m.

pressed (près-te), adj., satiné.

presser, n., personne qui appuie, qui insiste, f. ; presseur ; pressureur, m.

press-gang, n., presse, f.

pressing, adj., pressé ; urgent ; pressant.

pressing, n., action de presser, f. ; (tech.) pressage ; (fruit) pressurage, m.

pressingly, adv., d'une manière urgente ; d'une manière pressante ; instamment.

pressman, n. (*pressmen*), pressureur ; presseur ; (print.) pressier, imprimeur, m.

press-money (-meu'n'nè), n., gratification à un homme enrôlé par la presse, f.

press-point (-pwai'n'te), n., tulle, m.

pressure (prèsh'eur), n., action de presser ; (phys.) pression ; (impulse—*mouvement*) impulsion, force ; (urgency—*presse*) urgence ; presse ; (calamity—*malheur*) calamité ; oppression, f. ; (weight—*poids*) poids, m. ; (impression) impression, f. ; (fruit) pressurage, m. High, low, mean —; *haute, basse, moyenne pression.*

pressure-engine (-è'n'djine), n., machine à presser, f.

pressure-gauge (-ghédje), n., manomètre, m.

press-warrant (-wor'-), n., autorisation de presser, d'exercer la presse, f.

presswork (-weurke), n., ouvrage fait à la presse ; (print.) tirage, m.

prestation (près-té-), n., prestation, redevance, f.

prestation-money (-meu'n'nè), n., prestation payée aux évêques, f.

presto (près-tô), adv., preste, prestement ; (mus.) presto.

presumable (pri-ziou'm'a-b'l), adj., présumable.

presumably, adv., probablement.

presume (pri-zioume), v.a., présumer.

presume, v.n., présumer trop ; se permettre, oser, prendre la liberté. To — upon ; *présumer trop de ; se flatter de.*

presumer, n., personne qui présume, f. ; arrogant, m.

presuming, adj., présomptueux.

presumption (-zeu'm'-), n., présomption, f.

presumptive (pri-zeu'm'-), adj., présumé ; (presumptuous—*arrogant*) présomptueux ; (jur.) présomptif.

presumptively, adv., par présomption.

presumptuous (pri-zeu'm'pt'iou-), adj., présomptueux.

presumptuously, adv., présomptueusement.

presumptuousness, n., présomption, f.

presupposal (pri-ceup'poz'-), n., présupposition, f.

presuppose (pri-ceup'poze), v.a., présupposer.

presupposition, n., présupposition, f.

presurmise (pri-ceur-maïze), n., idée formée antérieurement, f., soupçon, m.

pretence (pri-), n., prétexte ; faux semblant, m.; défaite, feinte ; (claim—*réclamation*) prétention, f. To make — to ; *faire semblant de.* Under — of ; *sous prétexte de ; sous couleur de.*

pretend (pri-), v.a., prétexter ; affecter ; feindre ; faire semblant de.

pretend (pri-), v.n., prétendre ; avoir des prétentions ; feindre. To — to be dead ; *feindre d'être mort ; faire le mort.*

pretended, adj., prétendu, faux, feint.

pretender (pri-), n., personne qui prétexte, qui feint, qui fait semblant de, f.; prétendant, m., prétendante, f. ; (hist.) prétendant, m.

pretendingly, adv., avec suffisance, présomptueusement.

pretension (pri-), n., prétention, f. To have —s to ; *avoir des prétentions à.* To have —s to beauty (of women—*des femmes*) ; *avoir des prétentions.* Of great —s ; à *prétentions.* Of no —s ; *sans prétentions.*

preterimperfect (pri-teur-i'm'peur-fèkte), n., imparfait, m.

preterit (prèt'èr'-), n., (gram.) prétérit, m.

preterition (prèt'èr'ish'-), or **preteriteness**, n., état d'une chose passée, m. ; (rhet.) prétérition, f.

pretermission (pri-teur-mish'-), n., omission ; (rhet.) prétermission, prétérition, f.

pretermit (pri-teur-), v.a., omettre ; passer sous silence.

preternatural (pri-teur-nat'iou-), adj., surnaturel ; contre nature.

preternaturally, adv., surnaturellement.

preternaturalness, n., état surnaturel ; état contre nature, m.

preterperfect (pri-teur-peur-fèkte), n., plus-que-parfait, m.

preterpluperfect (-plou-), n., prétérit antérieur, m.

pretext (pri-), n., prétexte ; faux semblant, m.; couleur ; feinte, défaite, f. Under — of; *sous prétexte de ; sous couleur de.*

pretor (pri-teur), n., préteur ; magistrat, m.

pretorial, adj., de préteur ; des préteurs.

pretorian, adj., prétorien.

pretorship, n., préture, f.

prettily (prèt'-), adv., joliment ; gentiment.

prettiness (prèt'-), n., gentillesse, élégance, beauté, f.

pretty (prèt'-), adj., joli ; gentil ; (b.s., jest.) joli, beau. — little fellow; *joli petit garçon.* — fellow; (b.s.) *joli garçon.*

pretty, adv., assez ; passablement. — well ; *assez bien.*

pretty-spoken (-spôk'ène), adj., gentil ; qui parle joliment.

pretypify (pri-tip'i-fa-ye), v.a., figurer d'avance.

prevail (pri-vél), v.n., prévaloir ; régner ; avoir du pouvoir ; avoir de l'influence ; (to succeed—*avoir du succès*) réussir. To — on ; *obtenir de ; décider, persuader, entraîner.* To — over ; *prévaloir sur, l'emporter sur.* To — with ; *avoir de l'empire sur, avoir de l'influence sur ; prévaloir auprès de ; prédominer auprès de.* To be —ed on ; *se laisser persuader ; se laisser entraîner.*

prevailing, adj., dominant, régnant ; (efficacious—*effectif*) efficace.

prevailment, n., ascendant, pouvoir, empire, m.

prevalence, or **prevalency** (prèv'a-), n., ascendant, empire, pouvoir, m. ; influence ; efficacité, f.

prevalent, adj., régnant, dominant, général ; (victorious—*vainqueur*) victorieux ; (efficacious—*effectif*) efficace.

prevalently, adv., efficacement, puissamment.

prevaricate (pri-var'i-), v.n., prévariquer ; tergiverser ; user de collusion.

prevarication (pri-var'i-ké-), n., prévarication ; tergiversation, f.

prevaricator (pri-var'i-ké-teur), n., prévaricateur ; auteur d'une collusion, m.

prevenient (pri-vi-), adj., prévenant.

prevent (pri-), v.a., empêcher, prévenir, détourner.

preventer, n., personne qui prévient, qui empêche ; chose qui prévient, qui empêche ; (nav.) fausse manœuvre, f.

preventible (-'l-b'l), *adj.*, qui peut être prévenu, qui peut être empêché.

preventingly, *adv.*, pour empêcher, pour prévenir.

prevention (pri-), *n.*, empêchement, obstacle, *m.*

preventive (pri-), *n.*, chose qui prévient, qui empêche, *f.* ; préservatif, *m.*

preventive, *adj.*, préventif ; propre à empêcher, propre à prévenir.

preventively, *adv.*, pour prévenir, pour empêcher.

previous (pri-), *adj.*, précédent, antérieur, préalable.

previously, *adv.*, précédemment ; antérieurement ; préalablement ; auparavant.

previousness, *n.*, antériorité, priorité, *f.*

prevision (pri-vij'eune), *n.* (ant.) prévision, *f.*

prewarn (pri-wörne), *v.a.*, avertir.

prey (prē), *n.*, proie, *f.* To be a — to ; *être en proie à.*

prey (prē), *v.n.*, butiner, piller ; faire sa proie de ; (fig.) miner, ronger.

preyer (prē-eur), *n.*, spoliateur, *m.*, spoliatrice (*thing—chose*) chose qui mine, qui ronge, *f.*

price (praïce), *n.*, prix, *m.* ; récompense, *f.* Market- —; *cours ; prix du marché, prix courant, m.* Cost- —; *prix coûtant.* Low —; *bas prix.* The lowest — ; *le dernier prix; le plus juste prix.* Under —; *à vil prix.* Half- —; *à moitié prix.* High —; *prix élevé.* At any —; *coûte que coûte; à tout prix.*

price-current (-keur'-), *n.*, prix courant, *m.*

priceless, *adj.*, (invaluable—*inestimable*) sans prix, inappréciable; (without value—*sans valeur*) sans prix, sans valeur.

prick, *n.*, pointe, *f.* ; piquant ; (goad— *aiguillon*) aiguillon, *m.* ; (puncture—*piqûre*) piqûre ; (remorse—*remords*) douleur cuisante, *f.*, remords ; (mark—*but*) but, blanc, *m.* ; (fixe ; place—*place fixée*) place marquée, *f.*, point, *m.* ; (of a hare—*du lièvre*) trace, *f.*

prick, *v.a.*, piquer ; (the ears—*les oreilles*) dresser ; (to fix—*fixer*) enfoncer par la pointe ; (to designate by a puncture—*piquer*) désigner, marquer, piquer ; (to spur—*éperonner*) piquer ; (to goad—*aiguillonner*) aiguillonner ; (to incite— *porter*) pousser, exciter ; (to sting with remorse— *déchirer de remords*) tourmenter de remords ; (to affect with pain—*peiner*) faire éprouver une douleur poignante à ; (liquors—*liqueurs*) rendre piquant ; (mus.) noter ; (nav.) pointer. To — off ; *marquer, désigner.* To — up the ears; *dresser les oreilles.*

prick, *v.n.*, piquer ; piquer des deux ; (to dress one's self out—*se parer*) se parer ; (to become acid—*devenir acide*) devenir piquant.

pricker, *n.*, personne qui pique, *f.* ; piqueur, *m.* ; (thing—*chose*) pointe, *f.* ; piquant, *m.* ; (tech.) épinglette, *f.*

pricking, *n.*, action de piquer, *f.* ; picotement, *m.*

pricking, *adj.*, qui pique ; piquant.

prickle (prik'k'l), *n.*, aiguillon, piquant, *m.* ; épine, *f.*

prickle-back, *n.*, (ich.) épinoche, *f.*

prickliness, *n.*, abondance de piquants, *f.*

prickly, *adj.*, plein de piquants ; (bot.) armé d'aiguillons, armé d'épines.

pricksong (-son'gn), *n.*, air noté, air modulé, *m.*

prickwood (-woude), *n.*, (bot.) fusain, *m.*

pride (praïde), *n.*, orgueil, *m.* ; fierté, *f.* ; (ostentation) faste ; (ornament) ornement, *f.* Honest — ; *noble orgueil.* Puffed up with — ; *bouffi d'orgueil.* To humble any one's — ; *rabattre, rabaisser l'orgueil, la fierté de quelqu'un.*

pride, *v.n.*, rendre orgueilleux. To — one's self on ; *être fier de ; se faire une gloire de.*

prier (praï'eur), *n.*, personne qui examine, qui scrute, *f.*

priest (pris'te), *n.*, prêtre, *m.* High- — ; *grand prêtre.*

priestcraft, *n.*, intrigues de prêtre, *f. pl.*

priestess, *n.*, prêtresse, *f.*

priesthood (-houde), *n.*, prêtrise, *f.*, sacerdoce, *m.* ; (b.s.) prêtraille, *f.*

priestlike (-laïke), *adj.*, de prêtre.

priestliness, *n.*, manières de prêtre, *f. pl.*

priestly, *adj.*, de prêtre, sacerdotal.

priestridden (-rid'd'n), *adj.*, gouverné par les prêtres.

prig, *v.a.*, escamoter ; chiper.

prig, *n.*, freluquet, faquin, fat, *m.*

prill, *n.*, (ich.) turbot, *m.*

prim, *adj.*, affecté, précieux, tiré à quatre épingles.

prim, *v.a.*, parer avec affectation.

prima, *n.*, (print.) réclame, *f.*

primacy (praï-), *n.*, primatie; primauté, *f.*

primage (praï-médje), *n.*, (nav.) allocation au capitaine et à l'équipage d'un navire pour le chargement des marchandises embarquées, *f.*

primarily (praï-), *adv.*, primitivement ; originairement.

primariness (praï-), *n.*, qualité de ce qui est primitif, *f.*

primary (praï-), *adj.*, primitif ; premier ; principal ; primaire, élémentaire.

primate (praï-), *n.*, primat, *m.*

primateship, *n.*, primatie, *f.*

primatial (praï-ma-shal), *or* **primatical** (praï-), *adj.*, primatial.

prime (praïme), *adj.*, principal ; premier ; de premier rang, de premier ordre ; (first in quality —*qualité*) de première qualité, excellent ; (early —*précoce*) précoce ; (arith.) premier.

prime (praïme), *n.*, (dawn—*aube*) aurore, aube, *f.*, point du jour ; (beginning—*commencement*) commencement, *m.*, premiers temps, *m. pl.*, origine, *f.* ; (spring—*saison*) printemps, *m.* ; (best part—*le meilleur*) meilleure partie, fleur, élite, *f.*, meilleur, *m.* ; (perfection) comble de perfection, *m.* ; (fenc.) prime, *f.* ; (chem.) rapport le plus simple, *m.* ; (c.rel.) prime ; (fig.) beauté, force, fraîcheur, fleur, *f.*, printemps, *m.* — of life ; *fleur de l'âge.* To be in one's — ; *être à la fleur de l'âge.* To be in its, their — ; *être dans toute sa beauté, dans toute sa fleur ;* (of fruit, flowers—*fruits, fleurs*) être en pleine saison.

prime (praïme), *v.a.*, (of fire-arms—*armes à feu*) amorcer ; (paint.) imprimer.

primely (praï'm'-), *adv.*, (originally—*originairement*) en premier lieu, primitivement ; (most excellently—*excellemment*) parfaitement, on ne saurait mieux.

primeness (praï'm'-), *n.*, excellence, *f.*

primer (pri'm'-), *n.*, (spelling-book—*abécédaire*) premier livre de lecture ; (c.rel.) livre d'heures, *m.*, heures canoniales, *f. pl.* ; (print.) romain, *m.* ; (milit.) épinglette, *f.*

primero (pri-mi-), *n.*, (gram—*jeu*) prime, *f.*

primeval, *or* **primevous** (praï-mi-), *adj.*, primitif, premier.

primigenial, *or* **primigenous** (praï-mi-dji-), *adj.*, (ant.) premier-né.

priming (praï'm'-), *n.*, amorce, *f.* ; (paint.) impression, *f.*

priming-horn, *n.*, corne d'amorce, *f.* ; pulvérin, *m.*

priming-pan, *n.*, (of fire-arms—*d'armes à feu*) bassinet, *m.*

priming-powder (-paou-), *n.*, pulvérin, *m.*

priming-wire (-waeur), *n.*, (artil.) épinglette, *f.* ; dégorgeoir, *m.*

primitial (praï-mish'-), *adj.*, qui concerne les prémices.

primitive (pri'm'-), *adj.*, primitif.

primitively, *adv.*, primitivement.

primitiveness, *n.*, nature primitive, *f.*,

primness (pri'm'-), n., affectation, afféterie, f.

primogenial (praï-mo-dji-), adj., premier-né ; primordial ; primitif.

primogenitor (praï-mo-djè'n'i-teur), n., premier père, m.

primogeniture (praï-mo-djè'n'i-tioure), n., primogéniture, f.

primogenitureship, n., droit de primogéniture ; droit d'aînesse, m.

primordial, or **primordiate** (praï-), adj., primordial.

primordial, n., origine, f. ; premier principe, m.

primrose (-rôze), n., (bot.) primevère, f. — bed ; planche de primevères, f.

prince, n., prince, m.

prince. r.n., faire le prince.

princelike (-laïke), adj., digne d'un prince ; de prince.

princeliness, n., caractère de prince, m. ; munificence de prince, f.

princely, adj., qui a un air de prince, de princesse ; qui a un rang de prince, de princesse ; de prince, de princesse ; princier ; digne d'un prince, d'une princesse ; royal, auguste ; magnifique, riche.

princely, adv., en prince, en princesse.

princess, n., princesse, f. — -feather ; amaranthe, f.

principal, adj., principal, premier ; (mus.) fondamental.

principal, n., (chief—chef) partie principale, f., chef ; (leader—chef) chef ; (master—maître) patron ; (of a college—d'un collège) proviseur ; (of a school—d'une école) chef, maître ; (com.) associé principal ; commettant ; (jur.) auteur principal ; (capital) capital, m., capitaux, m.pl., principal, m. — and agent ; commettant et agent.

principality, n., principauté, f.

principally, adv., principalement.

principalness, n., rang principal, m.

principle (-ci-p'l), n., principe, m. To be a man of — ; avoir des principes. Of no — ; sans principes.

principle, v.a., donner des principes à ; graver fortement dans l'esprit ; persuader fortement.

principled (-ci-p'l'de), adj., qui a des principes. Ill- — ; qui a de mauvais principes. Well- — ; qui a de bons principes.

print, v.a., imprimer ; (to mark—marquer) faire une empreinte sur, laisser une trace sur. —ed by ; imprimé par ; (on books—des livres) imprimerie de. —ed for ; imprimé pour ; (on books—des livres) librairie de, chez.

print, v.n., imprimer ; se faire imprimer.

print, n., (mark—marque) empreinte, trace, marque ; (of books—des livres) impression, f. ; (printed book—livre imprimé) imprimé, m. ; (engraving—gravure) estampe, gravure, f. ; (newspaper—journal) journal, m., feuille, f. ; (print.) caractère ; (mould—matrice) moule, m. ; (stuff—étoffe) indienne, toile peinte, f. This book is out of — ; l'édition de ce livre est épuisée.

print-dress, n., robe d'indienne, de toile peinte, f.

printed, adj., imprimé.

printer, n., imprimeur, m. Letter-press — ; typographe, m. Lithographic — ; imprimeur lithographe.

printing, n., impression ; imprimerie, f.

printing-machine (-ma-shîne), n., presse mécanique, f.

printing-office, n., imprimerie, f.

printless, adj., qui ne laisse point de trace.

print-seller, n., marchand d'estampes, m.

print-shop, n., magasin d'estampes, m.

prior (praï-), n., prieur, m.

prior (praï-), adj., antérieur. — to ; avant de.

prioress (praï'-), n., prieure, f.

priority (pri-), n., priorité, f.

priorship (praï-), n., priorat, m.

priory (praï-), n., prieuré, m.

prism (priz'-), n., prisme, m.

prismatic, or **prismatical** (priz'-), adj., prismatique.

prismatically (priz'-), adv., en forme de prisme.

prismoid (priz'moïde), n., corps prismatique, m.

prison (priz'z'n), n., prison, f. To be in — ; être en prison. To break out of — ; forcer sa prison ; s'évader. To take out of — ; retirer de prison. Out of — ; hors de prison.

prison, v.a., emprisonner ; captiver.

prison-bars (-bârze), or **prison-base** (-bêce), n., (game—jeu) barres, f.pl.

prisoner, n., prisonnier, m., prisonnière, f. ; prévenu, m., prévenue, f. ; accusé, m., accusée, f. To take — ; faire prisonnier.

prison-house (-haouce), n., prison, f.

prisonment, n., emprisonnement, m. ; captivité, f.

pristine, adj., primitif ; ancien.

prithee ! (prith'i), int., de grâce ! je vous en prie !

privacy (praï-), n., retraite, solitude, f. ; secret, m. In — ; dans son intérieur, en son particulier.

private (praï-), adj., privé ; (retired—retiré) retiré ; (secret) secret ; (personal—personnel) particulier ; (of dress—vêtements) bourgeois, de ville ; (jur.) à huis clos. — individual ; simple particulier.

private, n., message secret, m. ; affaire privée, f. ; (soldier—soldat) simple soldat, m. In — ; en particulier ; en son particulier ; dans son intérieur ; (jur.) à huis clos.

privateer (praï-vé-tîre), n., corsaire, m.

privateer, v.n., (nav.) faire la course.

privateering, n., (nav.) course, f.

privately (praï-vét'-), adv., en particulier ; en secret.

privation (pri-vé-), n., privation ; perte, absence, f.

privative (praï-va-), adj., qui cause privation ; privatif ; négatif.

privative (praï-va-), n., négation, f. ; (gram.) privatif, m.

privatively (praï-va-), adv., négativement.

privet, n., (bot.) troène, m.

privilege (-lèdje), n., privilège, m.

privilege (-lèdje), v.a., accorder un privilège, des privilèges, (l.u.) privilégier.

privileged (-lèdj'de), past part., privilégié.

privily (priv'-), adv., secrètement.

privity (priv'-), n., connaissance secrète, f.

privy (priv'-), adj., privé, secret, caché ; dérobé. — to ; instruit de, qui a connaissance de. —-council ; conseil privé, m. —-councillor ; conseiller privé, m. —-purse ; cassette, f. — seal ; petit sceau, m.

privy (priv'-), n., lieux, lieux d'aisance, m.p'., garde-robe, f., privé, m., latrines, commodités, f.pl. ; (jur.) ayant droit, ayant cause, m.

prize (praize), n., (things taken—choses prises) prise, f. ; (reward—récompense) prix ; (in a lottery—de loterie) lot, m. ; bonne fortune, aubaine, f. ; (nav.) bâtiment pris, m., prise, f.

prize, v.a., priser, évaluer, estimer.

prize-fighter (-faït'-), or **prizer** (praïz'-), n., boxeur qui se bat pour des prix, boxeur de profession, m.

prize-man, n., lauréat, m.

prize-money (-meu'n'nè), n., part de prise, f.

prizer (praïz'-), n., personne qui évalue, qui estime, f.

prize-taker (-ték'-), *n.*, remporteur de prix, *m.*

probability, *n.*, probabilité, *f.*

probable (-'a-b'l), *adj.*, probable.

probably, *adv.*, probablement.

probang (prô-ban'gn), *n.*, sonde œsophagienne, *f.*

probate (prô-), *n..* (jur.) acte probatif de la sincérité et de la validité d'un testament, *m.*

probation (pro-bé-), *n.*, épreuve ; probation, *f.*

probational, *or* **probationary** (pro-bé-), *adj.*, qui sert d'épreuve ; de probation.

probationer (pro-bé-), *n.*, personne admise à l'examen, *f.*, candidat ; (novice) novice, *m.*

probationership, *n.*, candidature, *f.* ; noviciat, *m.*

probative (prô-), *adj.*, d'épreuve, qui sert d'épreuve.

probatory (prô-), *adj.*, d'épreuve ; qui sert d'épreuve, probatoire ; probatif.

probe (prôbe), *n.*, (surg.) stylet, *m.* ; sonde, *f.*

probe (prôbe), *v.a.*, (surg.) sonder ; (fig.) sonder, approfondir.

probe-scissors (-ciz'zeurze), *n.pl.*, ciseaux boutonnés, *m.pl.*

probity (prôb'-), *n.*, probité, *f.* Of — ; *de probité ; probe.*

problem, *n.*, problème, *m.*

problematical, *adj.*, problématique.

problematically, *adv.*, problématiquement.

proboscis, *n.* (*proboscides*), trompe, *f.*

procedure (-cid'ieur), *n.*, procédé, *m.* ; manière de procéder, *f.*

proceed (-cîde), *v.n.*, poursuivre ; continuer ; (to act—*agir*) agir, procéder, s'y prendre ; (to make progress—*avancer*) avancer, marcher ; faire des progrès ; passer outre. To — against ; (jur.) procéder contre, diriger des poursuites contre. To — from ; procéder de, passer de, tirer son origine de, provenir de, naître de. To — on ; (to continue—*continuer*) poursuivre, continuer ; procéder d'après, agir d'après. To — to ; se mettre à ; passer à ; commencer ; (to go to—*aller*) se rendre à, aller à. To — with ; continuer, poursuivre ; (to act towards—*se comporter*) en agir avec.

proceeder (-cîd'-), *n.*, personne qui avance, qui fait des progrès, *f.*

proceeding (-cîd'-), *n.*, procédé, *m.* —s ; mesures, *f.pl.* ; actes, *m.pl.* ; (jur.) procédure, *f.*, poursuites, *f.pl.* Book of —s ; procès-verbal ; registre des procès-verbaux, *m.*

proceeds (-cîd'ze), *n.pl.*, produit, rapport, *m.*

procerity (-cèr'-), *n.*, haute stature, haute taille, *f.*

process, *n.*, (progress—*progrès*) progrès ; (course—*tendance*) cours, *m.*, marche, (of time—*du temps*) suite ; (operation) opération, *f.*, procédé, *m.* ; (anat.) apophyse, *f.* ; (jur.) procès, *m.* ; sommation de comparaître, *f.*

procession (-cèsh'-), *n.*, cortège, *m.* ; procession, *f.*

processional (-cèsh'-), *adj.*, de cortège ; processionnel.

processional, *n.*, processionnal, *m.*

processionary (-cèsh'-), *adj.*, de cortège ; processionnel.

prochronism (prô-kron'-iz'm), *n.*, prochronisme, *m.*

proclaim (-cléme), *v.a.*, proclamer, déclarer, publier ; (to outlaw—*proscrire*) mettre hors la loi.

proclaimer (-clé'm'-), *n.*, personne qui proclame, qui déclare, qui publie, *f.* ; proclamateur, *m.*

proclamation (-cla-mé-), *n.*, proclamation, publication ; ordonnance, *f.* ; édit, *m.*

proclive, *or* **proclivous** (-claï'-), *adj.*, incliné.

proclivity, *n.*, inclination, *f.* ; penchant, *m.* ; (facility of learning—*facilité à apprendre*) disposition pour l'étude, *f.*

proconsul (-seul), *n.*, proconsul, *m.*

proconsular (-seul'-), *adj.*, proconsulaire.

proconsulship, *n.*, proconsulat, *m.*

procrastinate, *v.a.*, remettre de jour en jour ; différer de jour en jour, retarder.

procrastinate, *v.n.*, temporiser.

procrastination (-ti-né-), *n.*, retardement, *m.* ; remise, *f.*

procrastinator (-ti-né-), *n.*, personne qui use de délais, qui diffère de jour en jour, *f.* ; temporisateur, temporiseur, *m.*

procreant (prô-cri-), *adj.*, (ant.) fécond ; qui procrée.

procreate (prô-cri-), *v.a.*, procréer ; produire.

procreation (prô-cri-é-), *n.*, procréation ; production, *f.*

procreative, *adj.*, de procréation ; de production.

procreativeness, *n.*, faculté de procréer, *f.*

procreator (prô-cri-é-teur), *n.*, personne qui procrée, *f.* ; animal qui procrée ; père, *m.*

proctor (-teur), *n.*, homme d'affaires ; agent in universities—*des universités*) censeur ; (in ecclesiastical courts—*des cours ecclésiastiques*) procureur, *m.*

proctor (-teur), *v.n.*, diriger, conduire.

proctorage (-teur'édje), *n.*, métier d'agent d'affaires, *m.*

proctorial, *adj.*, de censeur.

proctorship, *n.*, fonctions de censeur, *f.pl.*

procumbent (-keu'm'-), *adj.*, couché ; (bot.) procombant.

procurable (-kiour'a-b'l), *adj.*, facile à se procurer, à trouver ; qu'on peut se procurer.

procuration (prok'iou-ré-), *n.*, procuration ; gestion des affaires d'autrui, *f.*

procurator (prok'iou-ré-teur), *n.*, agent d'affaires ; (jur.) procureur, *m.*

procure (-kioure), *v.a.*, procurer ; faire avoir ; obtenir, se procurer ; (to cause—*causer*) causer, amener, occasionner.

procurement, *n.*, action de procurer ; entremise, *f.*

procurer (-kiour'-), *n.*, personne qui procure, qui obtient, qui fait avoir ; chose qui procure, qui obtient, qui fait avoir, *f.* ; (b.s.) entremetteur, *m.*

procuress (-kiour'-), *n.*, entremetteuse, *f.*

prodigal, *adj.*, prodigue. The — son ; *l'enfant prodigue.*

prodigal, *n.*, prodigue, *m.*

prodigality, *n.*, prodigalité, *f.*

prodigally, *adv.*, prodigalement ; avec prodigalité.

prodigious (-didj'euss) *adj:*, prodigieux.

prodigiously (-didj'-), *adv.*, prodigieusement.

prodigiousness (-dîdj'-), *n.*, nature prodigieuse ; énormité, *f.*

prodigy (prod'i-dji), *n.*, prodige, *m.*

prodition (-dish'-), *n.*, (ant.) trahison, *f.*

produce, *v.a.*, produire ; (geom.) prolonger.

producer, *n.*, personne qui produit ; chose qui produit, *f.* ; producteur, *m.*

producible (-diou-ci-b'l), *adj.*, qui peut être produit ; productible.

producibleness, *n.*, productibilité, *f.*

product (prod'eukte), *n.*, produit ; (effect—*résultat*) effet ; (arith., geom.) produit, *m.*

productile (-deuk'-), *adj.*, qui peut être allongé, ductile.

production (-deuk'-), *n.*, production, *f.* ; (chem.) produit, *m.*

productive (-deuk'-). *adj.*, productif ; d'un bon rapport. To be — of ; *produire.*

productiveness, *n.*, nature productive, *f.* ; bon rapport, *m.*

proem (prô-è'm), *n.*, préface, *f.* ; proème, *m.*

proemial, *adj.*, de proème ; de préface.

profanation (-né-), *or* **profanity**, *n.*, profanation, *f.*

profane, *adj.*, profane.

profane, *v.a.*, profaner.

profanely (-fé'n'-), *adv.*, avec profanation.

profaneness (-fé'n'-), *n.*, conduite profane, impiété, *f.* ; langage profane, *m.*

profaner (-fé'n'-), *n.*, profanateur, *m.*

profanity. *V.* **profanation**.

profess, *v.a.*, professer ; faire profession de ; déclarer, dire.

profess, *v.n.*, se déclarer ; se dire.

professed (pro-fèste), *adj.*, déclaré, avoué ; (ecc.) profès.

professedly (-fèss'èd'-), *adv.*, ouvertement ; de profession ; par son propre aveu.

profession (-fèsh'-), *n.*, profession ; déclaration ; (calling—*profession*) profession, *f.*, état, métier, *m.*

professional (-fèsh'-), *adj.*, de sa profession ; qui a rapport à une profession ; professionnel. — **man** ; *homme de profession libérale, m.*

professionally (-fèsh'-), *adv.*, de profession ; (by calling—*par profession*) par profession, par état.

professor, *n.*, personne qui professe, qui fait profession de foi publique, *f.* ; (teacher—*professeur*) professeur, *m.*

professorial, *adj.*, de professeur.

professorship, *n.*, professorat, *m.* ; chaire de professeur, place de professeur, *f.*

professory, *adj.*, de professeur.

profest. *V.* **professed**.

proffer, *n.*, offre ; proposition ; (essay—*essai*) tentative, épreuve, *f.*, essai, *m.*

proffer, *v.a.*, offrir, proposer ; (to essay—*essayer*) essayer, tenter.

profferer, *n.*, personne qui offre, *f.*

proficience, *or* **proficiency** (-fish'-), *n.*, progrès, *m.* ; force, *f.* To have attained great —; *avoir fait de grands progrès.*

proficient (-fish'-), *n.*, personne qui a fait de grands progrès ; personne versée dans un art, une science, *f.* ; maître, *m.*, maîtresse, *f.*

profile (prô-faïle), *n.*, profil, *m.* In — ; en, de profil.

profile (prô-faïle), *v.a.*, profiler.

profit, *n.*, profit ; (advantage—*avantage*) avantage, *m.*, utilité, *f.* ; (com.) bénéfice, profit, *m.* Gross — ; *bénéfice brut.* Net — ; *bénéfice net.* To make a — by ; *faire son profit de* ; (com.) *bénéficier sur.*

profit, *v.a.*, profiter à ; faire du bien à ; (to improve—*améliorer*) améliorer, perfectionner. To be —ed by ; *gagner à* ; *profiter de.* To — one's self by ; *profiter de.*

profit, *v.n.*, (to improve—*progresser*) faire des progrès ; (to be of use—*être utile*) être utile. To — by ; *profiter de* ; *profiter à* ; *profiter sur* ; *tirer du profit de.* Things that — not ; *des choses qui ne servent à rien.*

profitable (-a-b'l), *adj.*, profitable, utile ; (lucrative—*de gain*) lucratif.

profitableness, *n.*, avantage ; profit, *m.* ; utilité ; nature profitable ; nature lucrative, *f.*

profitably, *adj.*, avantageusement, utilement ; avec profit.

profiting, *n.*, profit ; avantage, *m.*

profitless, *adj.*, sans profit ; sans avantage.

profligacy, *n.*, dérèglement, abandonnement, *m.* ; dissolution ; atrocité, scélératesse, *f.*

profligate, *adj.*, abandonné au vice ; sans mœurs ; scélérat ; déréglé, dissolu ; atroce, vicieux.

profligate, *n.*, scélérat, abandonné, *m.*, abandonnée, *f.* ; mauvais sujet, *m.*

profligately (-ghét'-), *adv.*, sans mœurs ; dissolument.

profligateness (-ghét'-), *n.*, dérèglement, abandonnement, *m.* ; dissolution ; atrocité, scélératesse, *f.*

profluent (-flou-), *adj.*, qui coule en avant.

pro forma, pour la forme ; (com.) simulé.

profound (-faou'n'de), *adj.*, profond.

profound, *n.*, abîme, gouffre ; (fig.) l'Océan, *m.*

profoundly, *adv.*, profondément.

profoundness, *or* **profundity** (-feu'n'-), *n.*, profondeur, *f.*

profuse (-fiouce), *adj.*, prodigue ; (of things —*des choses*) extravagant, abondant, excessif.

profusely (-fious'-), *adv.*, profusément ; avec profusion ; avec prodigalité.

profuseness (-fious'-), *n.*, profusion ; prodigalité, *f.*

profusion (-fiou-jeune), *n.*, profusion ; prodigalité, *f.*

prog, *v.n.*, rôder çà et là à la recherche de vivres ; gueuser, voler, piller.

prog, *n.*, vivres mendiés ; vivres, *m.pl.* ; (pers.) mendiant, *m.*, mendiante, *f.*

progenitor (-djè'n'i-teur), *n.*, aïeul, ancêtre, premier père ; (jur.) ascendant, *m.*

progeny (prodj'i-), *n.*, race, lignée, postérité, famille, *f.* ; descendants, *m.pl.*

prognosis (prog-nô-cice), *n.*, (med.) prognostic, pronostic, *m.*

prognostic (prog-nos-), *adj.*, (med.) prognostique.

prognostic, *n.*, pronostic ; (med.) prognostic, pronostic, *m.*

prognosticable (-ca-b'l), *adj.*, que l'on peut pronostiquer.

prognosticate (prog-), *v.a.*, pronostiquer ; prédire.

prognostication (-ti-ké-), *n.*, présage ; pronostic, *m.*

prognosticator (-ti-ké-teur), *n.*, pronostiqueur, *m.*

program, programma, *or* **programme** (prô-), *n.*, programme ; avant-propos, *m.* ; préface, *f.*

progress, *n.*, progrès ; cours, *m.* ; course, marche, *f.* ; (state journey—*voyage de prince*) voyage, *m.* ; (of a judge—*de juge*) tournée, *f.* ; (advance in knowledge—*en savoir*) progrès, *m.pl.* To report — ; (in parliament—*parlement*) *faire un rapport à la chambre du travail du comité.* To make — ; (in knowledge—*en savoir*) *faire des progrès.*

progress, *v.n.*, s'avancer ; continuer son cours ; s'étendre progressivement ; progresser ; (in knowledge—*en savoir*) faire des progrès, avancer.

progression (-grèsh'-), *n.*, progression, *f.* ; progrès, *m.* ; (course) course, *f.*, voyage, *m.* ; (math.) progression, *f.*

progressional (-grèsh'-), *adj.*, qui est en progrès ; progressif.

progressive, *adj.*, progressif.

progressively, *adv.*, progressivement.

progressiveness, *n.*, marche progressive, *f.*

prohibit, *v.a.*, défendre à ; interdire à ; défendre ; prohiber.

prohibiter, *n.*, personne qui défend à, qui interdit à, *f.*

prohibition (-bish'-), *n.*, prohibition ; défense, interdiction ; (jur.) défense de statuer, *f.* Writ of — ; *défense de statuer.*

prohibitive, *or* **prohibitory**, *adj.*, prohibitif.

project (-djèk'te), *n.*, projet, *m.*

project (-djèk'te), *v.a.*, projeter.

project, *v.n.*, se projeter ; saillir ; être en saillie ; (arch.) ressauter.

projectile (-djèk'-), *adj.*, (mec.) projectile.

projectile, *n.*, projectile, *m.*

projecting, *adj.*, en saillie.
projection (-djèk'-), *n.*, projection; saillie, *f.*; (arch.) ressaut, *m.*
projector (-djèkt'eur), *n.*, projeteur; homme à projets, *m.*
projecture (-djèkt'leur), *n.*, (arch.) projecture, *f.*
prolapse (-lapse), *or* **prolapsus**, *n.*, (surg.) prolapsus; renversement, *m.*; (med.) chute, hernie, *f.*
prolate, *adj.*, (geom.) allongé.
prolegomena, *n.pl.*, prolégomènes, *m.pl.*
prolepsis (-lèp-), *n.*, (rhet.) prolepse, *f.*; (chron.) anachronisme, *m.*
proleptic, *or* **proleptical** (-lèp'-), *adj.*, précédent; (med.) proleptique; (rhet.) de prolepse.
proleptically, *adv.*, proleptiquement.
proliferous (-lif'èr-), *adj.*, prolifère, proligère.
prolific, *or* **prolifical**, *adj.*, fécond; fécondant; prolifique.
prolificacy, *n.*, fécondité, fertilité, *f.*
prolifically, *adv.*, avec fécondité, avec fertilité.
prolification (-fi-ké-), *n.*, fertilisation, fécondation, fécondance, *f.*
prolificness, *n.*, fécondité, fertilité, *f.*
prolix (prô-), *or* **prolixious**, *adj.*, prolixe.
prolixity, *or* **prolixness**, *n.*, prolixité, *f.*
prolixly, *adv.*, avec prolixité; prolixement.
prolocutor (-lok'iou-teur), *n.*, président d'une assemblée du clergé, *m.*
prolocutorship, *n.*, présidence d'une assemblée du clergé, *f.*
prologue (prol'oghe), *n.*, prologue, *m.*
prologue, *v.a.*, introduire par un prologue.
prelong (-lon'gn). *v.a.*, prolonger; retarder. To be — ed ; *se prolonger ; être prolongé.*
prolongation (prô-lo'n'ghé-), *n.*, prolongement, *m.*; prolongation, *f.*
prolonger (-gheur), *n.*, personne qui prolonge, chose qui prolonge, *f.*
promenade (-nâde, *ou* -néde), *n.*, promenade; (place—*lieu*) promenade, *f.*
promenade, *v.n.*, se promener.
promenader, *n.*, promeneur, *m.*
promethean (-mi-thi-), *adj.*, de Prométhée.
prominence, *or* **prominency**, *n.*, proéminence; saillie; (fig.) distinction, *f.*
prominent, *adj.*, proéminent, qui fait saillie; (large) prononcé; (eminent) éminent, marquant, distingué; (principal) principal; (conspicuous—*apparent*) marquant, remarquable; (paint.) prononcé.
prominently, *adv.*, d'une manière proéminente; en saillie; d'une manière distinguée; d'une manière marquée; d'une manière prononcée.
promiscuous (-kiou-), *adj.*, mêlé; en commun; général; confus, sans ordre; (min.) croisé.
promiscuously, *adv.*, généralement, en général; en commun; confusément, pêle-mêle.
promiscuousness, *n.*, mélange; caractère général, *m.*; promiscuité, confusion, *f.*
promise (-ice), *n.*, promesse, *f.*; (hope—*espoir*) espérances, *f.*; (biblically—*biblique*) promission, *f.*, espérances, *f.pl.* To make a —; *faire une promesse. Of great —; de grandes espérances, qui donne de grandes espérances.* The Land of — ; *la Terre de promission.*
promise, *v.a.* and *n.*, promettre. I — you ! *je vous le promets!*
promise-breach (-brîtshe), *n.*, violation d'une promesse, *f.*
promise-breaker (-brèk'-), *n.*, personne qui viole sa promesse, *f.*
promised (-miste), *adj.*, promis; (biblically —*biblique*) promis, de promission.
promisee (-miss'î). *n.*, personne à qui l'on a fait une promesse, *f.*; (jur.) stipulant, *m.*

promiser. *n.*, personne qui fait une promesse, *f.*; auteur d'une promesse; prometteur, *m.*, prometteuse, *f.*
promising (-miss'-), *adj.*, qui promet; qui donne des espérances.
promisor (-miss'eur. *ou* -or), *n.*, (jur.) promettant, *m.*
promissorily, *adv.*, par manière de promesse.
promissory, *adj.*, qui contient une promesse. — *note; billet à ordre, m.*
promontory, *n.*, promontoire, *m.*
promote (-môte), *v.a.*, favoriser, encourager, protéger; inspirer; donner de l'avancement à; élever; promouvoir.
promoter (-môt'-), *n.*, personne qui favorise, qui encourage, *f.*; protecteur, *m.*, protectrice, *f.*; promoteur, *m.*, promotrice. *f.*; patron. *m.*
promotion (-mô-), *n.*, promotion, *f.*; avancement, *m.*; protection; élévation, *f.*
promotive (-môt'-), *adj.*, qui favorise, qui protège, qui encourage.
prompt (pro'm'te), *v.a.*, exciter, pousser; dicter, inspirer; suggérer; (thea.) souffler.
prompt (pro'm'te), *adj.*, prompt, empressé; (com.) comptant.
prompt-book (-bouke), *n.*, (thea.) livre du souffleur, *m.*
prompter, *n.*, (thea.) souffleur, *m.*
promptitude (pro'm'ti-tioude), *n.*, promptitude, *f.*
promptly (pro'm't'-), *adv.*, promptement.
promptness (pro'm't'-), *n.*, promptitude, *f.*; empressement, *m.*
promptuary (pro'm't'iou-), *n.*, magasin, dépôt, *m.*
promulgate (pro-meul-), *v.a.*, promulguer; publier; divulguer.
promulgation (-ghé-), *n.*, promulgation; publication; divulgation, *f.*
promulgator (-ghét'eur), *n.*, personne qui promulgue, qui publie, qui divulgue, *f.*
pronation (pro-né-), *n.*, (anat.) pronation, *f.*
pronator (-nét'eur), *n.*, (anat.) pronateur, *m.*
prone (prône), *adj.*, (not erect—*penché*) courbé, penché, incliné; (declivous—*déclive*) incliné, penché, en pente; (precipitous—*précipité*) qui se précipite; (disposed—*enclin*) disposé, enclin, porté; (lying with the face downward—*couché à plat ventre*) couché le visage tourné vers la terre.
proneness, *n.*, position courbée, penchée, inclinée; (declivity—*déclivité*) inclinaison, pente; (disposition—*caractère*) disposition, inclination, *f.*, penchant, *m.*; (lying with the face downward—*être couché à plat ventre*) position d'une personne couchée le visage tourné vers la terre, *f.*
prong (pro'n'gn), *n.*, (fork—*fourche*) fourche, *f.*; (of a fork—*de fourche*) fourchon; (of a dinnerfork—*de fourchette*) fourchon, *m.*, dent, *f.*
pronged (pro'n'gn'de), *adj.*, à fourchons.
pronominal, *adj.*, pronominal.
pronominally, *adv.*, pronominalement.
pronoun (prô-naou'n), *n.*, pronom, *m.*
pronounce (-naou'n'ce), *v.a.*, prononcer; déclarer.
pronounce, *v.n.*, prononcer; se prononcer.
pronounceable (-'a-b'l), *adj.*, qui peut se prononcer.
pronouncer, *n.*, personne qui prononce, *f.*
pronunciation (-neu'n'shi-é-), *n.*, prononciation, *f.*; (rhet.) débit, *m.*
pronunciative (-shi-é-), *adj.*, dogmatique.
proof (proufe), *n.*, (proof—*essai*) épreuve; (alg., arith.) preuve; (of spirit—*de l'alcool*) preuve, *f.*; (print.) épreuve, *f.* — against ; *à l'épreuve de.* In — of; *pour preuve de.* To come to the — ; *en venir à la preuve.*
proofless, *adj.*, sans preuve
proof-puller (-poul'-). *n.*, (print.) faiseur d'épreuves, *m.*

proof-sample (proof-sa'm'p'l), *n.*, (com.) preuve. *f.*

proof-stick. *n.*, sonde, *f.*

prop, *n.*, appui, soutien, étai, support ; (carp) étai, étançon ; (hort.) tuteur, échalas ; (fig.) appui, soutien, *m.*

prop, *v.a.*, appuyer, soutenir, étayer ; (carp.) étayer, étançonner ; (hort.) échalasser.

propagable (-ga-b'l), *adj.*, susceptible de propagation.

propaganda. *n.*, doctrines à propager, *f.pl.* ; propagande ; propagande, *f.*

propagandism (-diz'me), *n.*, esprit de propagande ; propagandisme, *m.*

propagandist, *n.*, membre de la propagande, propagandiste, *m.*

propagate, *v.a.*, propager ; accroitre : (to spread—*répandre*) étendre, répandre, porter au loin ; (to produce—*produire*) produire, créer, enfanter.

propagate. *v.n.*, se propager.

propagation (-pa-ghé-), *n.*, propagation, *f.*

propagator (-ghét'eur), *n.*, personne qui propage, *f.* ; propagateur, *m.*

propel. *v.a.*, mouvoir ; faire marcher ; faire avancer ; mettre en mouvement ; lancer.

propeller, *n.*, propulseur, moteur, *m.*

propelling. *adj.*, moteur.

propense (-pè'n'sé), *adj.*, enclin, porté, disposé.

propensity, *or* **propension.** *n.*, penchant, *m.* ; propension, tendance, inclination, *f.* ; goût, *m.*

proper, *adj.*, (peculiar—*particulier*) propre, particulier ; (natural—*naturel*) propre, naturel ; (one's own—*de propriété*) propre, à soi ; (fit—*convenable*) propre, convenable, à propos ; (correct) propre, exact ; (not figurative—*d'expressions*) propre ; (handsome—*beau*) beau. — name ; *nom propre.* To deem it — to ; *juger convenable de ; juger à propos de.* It is — to ; *il est bien de ; il convient de.*

properly, *adv.*, proprement ; particulièrement, justement ; naturellement ; exactement ; convenablement ; bien — speaking ; *à proprement parler : proprement parlant.* He acted — ; *il a bien agi.*

property. *n.*, (ownership—*possession*) propriété ; (thing owned—*chose possédée*) propriété, *f.*, bien, *m.*, biens, *m pl.* ; (quality—*vertu*) propriété, qualité, *f.* ; (characteristic—*caractéristique*) propre ; (disposition) caractère ; (thea.) accessoire, *m.* Funded — ; *biens en rentes.* Landed — ; *biens fonciers ; bien-fonds.* Real — ; *biens immeubles.* Personal — ; *biens mobiliers, biens meubles.* Literary — ; *propriété littéraire.* Man of — ; *homme qui a du bien, qui a de la fortune.*

property-man. *n.*, fournisseur de théâtre, *m*

property-tax, *n.*, impôt sur les propriétés, *m.*

prophecy (prof'i-cî), *n.*, prophétie. *f.*

prophesier (-i-caï-eur), *n.*, prophète, *m.*

prophesy (prof'i-ça-ye), *v.a.*, prophétiser.

prophesy, *v.n.*, prononcer des prophéties.

prophesying (-i-ça-vigne), *n.*, prophétie, *f.*

prophet, *n.*, prophète, *m.*

prophetess, *n.*, prophétesse, *f.*

prophetic, *or* **prophetical,** *adj.*, prophétique.

propinquity (-pi'n'gn'kwi-), *n.*, proximité ; parenté, *f.*

propitiable (-pish'i-a-b'l), *adj.*, que l'on peut rendre propice.

propitiate (pro-pish'i-), *v.a.*, rendre propice, rendre favorable ; apaiser.

propitiation (-pish'i-é-), *n.*, action de rendre propice. d'apaiser ; propitiation, *f.*

propitiator (-pish'i-é-teur), *n.*, personne qui rend propice, *f.*

propitiatory, *adj.*, propitiatoire.

propitiatory, *n.*, propitiatoire, *m.*

propitious (-pish'eusse), *adj.*, propice, favorable.

propitiously, *adv.*, favorablement, d'une manière propice.

propitiousness. *n.*, bonté, disposition favorable ; (of things—*des choses*) nature favorable, nature propice, *f.*

proplasm (prô-plaz'me), *n.*, moule, *m.* ; matrice, *f.*

propolis. *n.*, propolis, *f.*

proponent (pro-pô-), *n.*, auteur d'une proposition, *m.*

proportion. *n.*, proportion, *f.* ; rapport, *m.* ; (arith, math.) proportion ; (geom) raison, *f.* In — to ; *en proportion de.* In — as ; *à mesure que, en proportion ; à proportion que.*

proportion (-pôr-), *v.a.*, proportionner.

proportionable (-a-b'l), *adj.*, qui peut être proportionné ; à proportion ; proportionné.

proportionably, *adv.*, proportionnément, à proportion.

proportional, *adj.*, en proportion ; proportionnel.

proportional. *n.*, (geom.) proportionnelle, *f.*

proportionality. *n.*, proportionnalité, *f.*

proportionally. *adv.*, proportionnellement.

proportionate, *r.a.*, proportionner.

proportionate, *adj.*, proportionné.

proportionately, *adv.*, en proportion ; proportionnellement.

proportionateness, *n.*, proportion ; (math.) proportionnalité, *f.*

proportionless, *adj.*, sans proportion.

proposal (-pô-zal), *n.*, proposition, offre, *f*

propose (-pôze), *v.a.*, proposer ; offrir, présenter.

propose, *v.n.*, se proposer.

proposer, *n.*, personne qui propose, *f.* ; auteur d'une proposition, *m.*

proposition (-pô-zish'-), *n.*, proposition, *f.*

propositional, *adj.*, de proposition.

propound (-paou'n'de), *v.a.*, proposer, exposer ; mettre en avant.

propounder. *n.*, personne qui propose, qui expose, qui met en avant, *f.*

propping. *n.*, appui, soutien ; (carp.) étayement ; (hort.) échalassement, *m.*

proprætor (pri-teur), *n.*, propréteur, *m.*

proprietary (-praï-è-), *n.*, propriétaire, *m.*

proprietary, *adj.*, de propriété ; de propriétaire.

proprietor (-praï-è-teur). *n.*, propriétaire, *m.*

proprietress, *n.*, propriétaire, *f.*

propriety (-praï-è-), *n.*, convenance, *f.*, convenances, *f.pl.* ; bienséance, *f.* ; bienséances, *f.pl.* ; propriété, *f.* To keep within the bounds of — ; *garder les convenances, les bienséances.*

propulsion (-peul-), *n.*, propulsion, *f.*

propulsive (-peul-). *adj.*, propulsif.

prop-wood (-woude), *n.*, étai vertical, *m.*

prorata, à proportion : au prorata.

prorogation (prô-ro-ghé-). *n.*, prorogation, *f.*

prorogue (-rôghe), *v.a.*, proroger.

proruption (-reup-), *n.*, éruption, explosion, *f.*

prosaic (-zaïke), *adj.*, prosaïque.

prosaicism (-zaï-ciz'm), *or* **prosaism** (-zaï'z'm), *n.*, prosaïsme, *m.*

prosaist (-zaïste). *n.*, prosateur, *m.*

prosal (prô-zal), *adj.*, (ant.). *V.* **prosaic.**

proscenium (-ci-), *n.*, proscenium, *m.*, avant-scène, *f.*

proscribe (-scraïbe). *v.a.*, proscrire.

proscriber, *n.*, proscripteur, *m.*

proscription. *n.*, proscription, *f.*

proscriptive, *adj.*, de proscription.

prose (prôze), *n.*, prose, *f.* — -writer ; *prosateur, m.*

prose (prôze), *v.a.*, écrire en prose ; raconter ennuyeusement.

prosecute (pross'i-kioute), *v.a.*, poursuivre, continuer ; persévérer dans ; (jur.) poursuivre, diriger des poursuites contre, poursuivre en justice.

prosecution (-kiou-), *n.*, poursuite ; continuation ; (jur.) poursuite, *f.*, poursuites, *f.pl.* ; accusation, *f.*

prosecutor (-kiout'eur), *n.*, personne qui poursuit, qui continue, *f.* ; (jur.) plaignant, *m.*, plaignante, *f.*

proselyte (pross'i-laïte), *n.*, prosélyte, *m.*, *f.*

proselyte, *v.a.*, faire un prosélyte ; convertir.

proselytism (pross'i-li-tiz'm), *n.*, prosélytisme, *m.*

proser (prôz'-), *n.*, prosateur ; (b.s.) conteur ennuyeux, conteur fastidieux, *m.*

prosodial (-çô-), *or* **prosodical** (-çod'-), *adj.*, prosodique.

prosodian, *or* **prosodist** (pross'o-), *n.*, personne versée dans la prosodie, *f.*

prosody (pross'-o-), *n.*, prosodie, *f.*

prosopopœia (pross'o-po-pî-ya), *n.*, prosopopée, *f.*

prospect, *n.*, vue, perspective, *f.* ; point de vue, coup d'œil, *m.* ; (expectation) espoir, *m.*, espérance, perspective, *f.*, avenir, *m.* To have fine — s before one's self ; *avoir devant soi un bel avenir.*

prospective (-spèk-), *adj.*, en perspective ; (provident—*prévoyant*) prévoyant ; (of extensive prospect—*d'étendue*) d'une vue étendue ; (viewing at a distance—*de vue*) de longue vue. — glass ; *lunette d'approche, f.*

prospectively, *adv.*, en perspective ; pour l'avenir.

prospectus (-spèk-). *n.*, prospectus, *m.*

prosper, *v.a.*, faire prospérer ; faire réussir ; favoriser.

prosper, *v.n.*, prospérer, réussir.

prosperity (-pèr'-), *n.*, prospérité, *f.*

prosperous (-pèr'-), *adj.*, prospère ; (of things—*des choses*) florissant, heureux.

prosperously, *adv.*, avec prospérité ; heureusement ; avec bonheur.

prosperousness, *n.*, prospérité, *f.*

prostate, *adj.*, prostatique. — gland ; *prostate, f.*

prosthesis (-thi-cice), *n.*, (gram.) prosthèse, (surg.) prothèse, *f.*

prosthetic (-thèt'-), *adj.*, de prosthèse ; (surg.) prothétique.

prostitute (-tioute), *n.*, prostituée, *f.* ; (mercenary—*mercenaire*) vil mercenaire, *m.*

prostitute, *v.a.*, prostituer.

prostitute, *adj.*, prostitué.

prostitution (-ti-tiou-), *n.*, prostitution, *f.*

prostitutor (-tiou-teur), *n.*, personne qui prostitue, qui se prostitue, *f.*

prostrate, *v.a.*, (to lay flat—*mettre à plat*) coucher ; (to throw down—*jeter à bas*) abattre, renverser ; (to overthrow—*renverser*) détruire, ruiner, perdre ; (to reduce—*anéantir*) réduire entièrement, jeter dans l'abattement, dans l'anéantissement, anéantir. To — one's self ; *se prosterner.*

prostrate, *adj.*, prosterné, couché ; (fig.) abattu. To be utterly — ; *être dans l'anéantissement ; être abattu ; être épuisé de fatigue.*

prostration (-tré-), *n.*, (throwing down—*renversement*) renversement, *m.* ; (bowing—*prosternement*) prosternation, *f.* ; (dejection) abattement, anéantissement, *m.* ; (med.) prostration, *f.*

prostyle (prô-staïle), *n.*, prostyle, *m.*

prosy (prô-zi), *adj.*, lourd, ennuyeux, assommant.

protasis (-cice), *n.*, protase, *f.*

protatic, *adj.*, protatique.

protean (prô-ti-), *adj.*, de Protée ; protéen.

protect (-tèkte), *v.a.*, protéger ; défendre, garantir.

protection (-tèk-), *n.*, protection ; défense ; (safeguard—*écrit*) sauvegarde, *f.*, passeport, sauf-conduit, *m.* ; (exemption) privilège d'être exempt d'arrestation, *m.*

protective, *adj.*, protecteur.

protector (-teur), *n.*, protecteur, *m.*, protectrice, *f.* ; (jur.) tuteur, curateur d'un bien substitué, *m.*

protectorate, *or* **protectorship**, *n.*, protectorat, *m.*

protectress, *n.*, protectrice, *f.*

protend, *v.a.*, étendre, allonger.

protest (prô-), *n.*, protestation, *f.* ; (com.) protêt ; (of a skipper—*de capitaine de navire*) rapport énonçant les avaries, *m.* Under — ; (com.) *protesté.*

protest (pro-), *v.a.*, protester, attester ; (com.) protester, faire protester.

protest, *v.n.*, protester.

protestant, *adj.*, protestant.

protestant, *n.*, protestant, *m.*, protestante, *f.*

protestantism, *n.*, protestantisme. *m.*

protestation (prot'ès-té-), *n.*, protestation, *f.*

protester, *n.*, personne qui proteste, *f.* ; (com.) créancier qui fait faire un protêt, *m.*

prothonotary (pro-tho'n'-), *n.*, protonotaire ; (jur.) greffier, *m.*

protocol (prô-), *n.*, protocole, *m.*

protomartyr (prô-to-mâr-teur), *n.*, protomartyr ; premier martyr, *m.*

prototype (prô-to-taïpe), *n.*, prototype, *m.*

protoxide, *n.*, protoxyde, *m.*

protract, *v.a.*, prolonger ; faire durer ; (to defer—*remettre*) ajourner, différer.

protractor, *or* **protractor** (-teur), *n.*, personne qui prolonge, *f.*

protraction, *n.*, prolongation, *f.*

protractive, *adj.*, qui prolonge, qui diffère.

protractor, *n.*, (instrument) rapporteur, *m.* ; personne qui prolonge, *f.*

protrude, *v.a.*, pousser en avant, pousser dehors.

protrude (-trioude), *v.n.*, s'avancer, sortir, faire saillie.

protrusion (-triou-jeune), *n.*, action de pousser en avant ; saillie, *f.*

protrusive (-triou-cive), *adj.*, qui pousse en avant.

protuberance (-tiou-bèr-), *n.*, saillie, éminence, proéminence, avance ; protubérance ; (knoll —*colline*) éminence, hauteur ; (anat.) protubérance, *f.*

protuberant, *adj.*, en saillie, proéminent.

protuberate, *v.n.*, s'enfler ; être en saillie.

proud (pra-oude), *adj.*, fier ; (arrogant) hautain, orgueilleux, superbe, arrogant ; (magnificent—*magnifique*) beau, magnifique, superbe ; (grand) noble, beau, grand ; (animal) en chaleur. To be — of ; *être fier de, s'enorgueillir de.* — flesh ; *bourgeons charnus, m.pl., chair baveuse, f.*

proudly, *adv.*, fièrement, orgueilleusement.

provable (prouv'a-b'l), *adj.*, qui peut se prouver, prouvable.

prove (prouve), *v.a.*, (to try, to experience—*essayer*) éprouver, faire l'épreuve de ; (to establish, to confirm—*établir, confirmer*) prouver ; (arith.) faire la preuve de ; (a debt—*créance*) produire des titres de ; (a will—*testament*) vérifier. To — one's self, itself ; *se montrer.*

prove, *v.n.*, éprouver ; (to be found to be—*être*) se montrer, se trouver, se trouver être ; (of things—*des choses*) se trouver, se trouver être ; (to be—*être*) être.

proveditor (-vèd'i-teur), *or* **provedore** (prô-vi-dôr), *n.*, pourvoyeur ; (milit.) commissaire des vivres, *m.*

proveditore (-vèd'it'or), *n.*, (in Italy—*en Italie*) provéditeur, *m.*

proven (prouv'è'n), *adj.*, prouvé.
provencial (prô-vè'n'shial), *adj.*, provençal ; de Provence.
provender, *n.*, fourrage, *m.* ; nourriture (for animals—*pour les animaux*), *f.* ; (provisions) provisions, *f.pl.*, vivres, *m.pl.*
prover (prouv'-), *n.*, personne qui éprouve, qui prouve ; chose qui éprouve, qui prouve, *f.*
proverb (prov'eurbe), *n.*, proverbe, *m.*
proverb. *v.n.*, parler par proverbes.
proverbial (-veur-), *adj.*, proverbial, qui fait proverbe.
proverbialist, *n.*, personne qui parle par proverbes, *f.*
proverbially, *adj.*, proverbialement.
provide (-vaïde), *v.a.*, pourvoir, fournir ; préparer. To — one's self with ; *se pourvoir de.* To be —d for ; *être pourvu ; avoir son avenir assuré.*
provide, *v.n.*, pourvoir. To — against ; *se pourvoir contre.* To — for ; *pourvoir à.*
provided, *conj.*, pourvu que. —that; *pourvu que.*
providence, *n.*, prévoyance ; (theol.) providence; (foresight—*prévoyance*) prévoyance ; prudence, *f.*
provident, *adj.*, prévoyant ; prudent.
providential (-shial), *adj.*, providentiel.
providentially, *adv.*, d'une manière providentielle ; par la providence.
providently, *adv.*, prudemment, avec prévoyance.
provider (-vaïd'-), *n.*, personne qui pourvoit, *f.* ; pourvoyeur, *m.*
province, *n.*, province, *f.* ; (business—*affaire*) département, ressort, *m.* ; occupation, affaire, *f.* ; fonctions, attributions, *f.pl.*
provincial (-shal), *adj.*, provincial ; de province.
provincial, *n.*, provincial, *m.*, provinciale, *f.*
provincialism (-shal'iz'm), *n.*, provincialisme, *m.*
provinciality (-shal'-), *n.*, caractère provincial, *m.*
provincialship, *n.*, provincialat, *m.*
provine (-vaïne), *v.n.*, (agri.) provigner.
provining, *n.*, (agri.) provignement, *m.*
provision (-vij'eune), *n.*, action de pourvoir ; (stipulation) précaution, mesure de prévoyance ; (stock—*approvisionnement*) provision ; (jur.) disposition, *f.* —s ; vivres, comestibles, *m.pl.*, munitions de bouche, *f.pl.* To lay in a — of ; *faire provision de.* To make — against, for ; *prendre des précautions contre.* To make a — for any one ; *pourvoir aux besoins de quelqu'un ; assurer l'avenir de quelqu'un.*
provision, *v.a.*, approvisionner de vivres.
provisional, *or* **provisionary** (-vij'-), *adj.*, provisoire ; provisionnel.
provisionally, *adv.*, provisoirement, par provision ; provisionnellement.
provisionary, *adj.* V. **provisional**.
provision-merchant (-meur-tsha'n't), *n.*, négociant en comestibles, *m.*
provision-warehouse (-wér'haouce), *n.*, magasin de comestibles, *m.*
proviso (-vaï-zô), *n.*, condition, clause, *f.* With that —, with the — that ; *pourvu que ; à condition que.*
provisor (-vaï-zeur), *n.*, ecclésiastique nommé par le pape à un bénéfice avant la mort du bénéficier, *m.*
provisory (-vaï-ço-), *adj.*, provisoire ; conditionnel.
provocation (-ké-), *n.*, provocation, *f.*
provocative, *n.*, provocation, *f.* ; aiguillon, stimulant, *m.*
provocative (-vô-ka-), *adj.*, qui provoque ; provocatif.
provoke (-vôke). *v.a.*, provoquer ; exciter ;

inciter ; (to enrage—*mettre en colère*) fâcher, irriter, contrarier ; (to challenge—*défier*) défier. To — laughter ; *faire rire.* To — a smile ; *faire sourire.*
provoker. *n.*, personne qui provoque, *f.* ; provocateur, *m.*, provocatrice, *f.* ; chose qui provoque, *f.*
provoking, *adj.*, provoquant ; irritant, contrariant.
provokingly, *adv.*, d'une manière provoquante, irritante, contrariante.
provost (prov'oste), *n.*, prévôt ; (of a college —*de collège*) proviseur ; (in Scotland—*en Écosse*) maire, *m.*
provost (-vô), *n.*, (milit.) prévôt. — -marshal ; *grand- prévôt* ; (nav.) *commissaire-rapporteur*, *m.*
provostship (-vô-shipe), *n.*, prévôté, *f.* ; provisorat, *m.* ; mairie, *f.*
prow (praou), *n.*, proue, *f.*
prowess (praou-èss), *n.*, bravoure, valeur ; prouesse, *f.*
prowl (praoul), *v.n.*, rôder. To — about ; *rôder çà et là ; rôder par; rôder dans.*
prowler, *n.*, rôdeur, *m.*
proximate, *adj.*, prochain.
proximately. *adv.*, immédiatement.
proximity, *n.*, proximité, *f.*
proxy, *n.*, (pers.) fondé de pouvoir, mandataire, délégué, *m.* ; (thing—*chose*) procuration délégation, *f.*
proxyship, *n.*, fonctions d'un fondé de pouvoir, *f.pl.*
prude (proude), *n.*, prude, *f.*
prudence (prou-), *n.*, prudence, sagesse, *f.*
prudent. *adj.*, prudent, sage.
prudential (-shal), *adj.*, de prudence ; dicté par la prudence.
prudentially, *or* **prudently**, *adv.*, prudemment.
prudentials (-shalze), *n.pl.*, maximes de sagesse, *f.*
prudery (prou-), *n.*, pruderie, *f.*
prudish (prou-), *adj.*, prude ; de prude.
prudishly, *adv.*, en prude ; avec pruderie.
prune (proune), *n.*, pruneau, *m.* ; prune sèche, *f.*
prune, *v.a.*, (hort.) élaguer, tailler, émonder ; rogner ; (to trim—*ajuster*) arranger, ajuster.
prune, *v.n.*, (jest.) s'ajuster, s'attifer.
prunello (prou-nè'-lô), *n.*, (stuff—*étoffe*, fruit) prunelle, *f.*
pruner (prou'n'-), *n.*, personne qui élague, qui émonde, *f.* ; élagueur, *m.*
pruniferous, *adj.*, qui porte des prunes.
pruning (prou'n'-), *n.*, (hort.) action d'émonder, d'élaguer ; taille, *f.*
pruning-hook (-houke), *or* **pruning-knife** (-naïfe). *n.*, serpette, *f.*
pruning-shears (-shirze), *n.pl.*, sécateur, *m. sing.*
prurience. *or* **pruriency** (prou-), *n.*, démangeaison, *f.* ; prurit ; (fig.) désir immodéré, *m.*
prurient (prou-), *adj.*, qui démange ; (fig) qui brûle de désir.
pruriginous (-ridj'-), *adj.*, prurigineux.
prussian (preush'a'n), *adj.*, prussien ; de Prusse.
prussian, *n.*, Prussien, *m.*, Prussienne, *f.*
prussic (preus'-), *adj.*, prussique.
pry (pra'ye), *v.n.*, scruter. To — into ; *scruter ; fouiller dans ; fourrer le nez dans ; se mêler de ; épier.* To — about ; *fourrer le nez partout.*
pry, *n.*, regard scrutateur ; regard indiscret, *m.* Paul —; brouillon ; homme qui se mêle de tout, *m.*
prying (pra-yigne), *adj.*, scrutateur, curieux ; indiscret.

prying, *n.*, curiosité; exacte recherche; indiscrétion, *f.*

pryingly, *adv.*, curieusement; indiscrètement.

psalm (sâme), *n.*, psaume, *m.* — -book; *livre de psaumes; psautier, m.*

psalmist (sal'-, *ou* sä'm'iste), *n.*, psalmiste; (c.rel.) chantre, *m.*

psalmody (sal-), *n.*, psalmodie, *f.*

psalter (sôl'-), *n.*, psautier, *m.*

psaltery (sôl-), *n.*, psaltérion, *m.*

pseudo (siou-dô), *adj.*, pseudo, faux.

pseudonymous (siou-), *adj.*, pseudonyme.

pshaw! (shô), *int.*, bah! baste!

psychologic, *or* **psychological** (saï-kol-odj'-), *adj.*, psychologique.

psychologist (saï-kol'odj'iste), *n.*, psychologiste, psychologue, *m.*

psychology (saï-kol'o-dji), *n.*, psychologie, *f.*

ptisan (tiz'-), *n.*, tisane, *f.*

puberty (piou-bèr-), *n.*, puberté, *f.*

pubes (piou-bize), *n.*, (bot.) pubescence, *f.*

pubescence (piou-bès'-), *n.*, puberté; (bot.) pubescence, *f.*

pubescent (piou-bès-), *adj.*, qui entre dans l'âge de puberté; pubère; (bot.) pubescent.

public (peub'-), *adj.*, public.

public, *n.*, public, *m.* — -house; *cabaret, m; auberge, f.*

publican (peub'-), *n.*, publicain; (innkeeper—*aubergiste*) cabaretier, aubergiste, *m.*

publication (peub'li-ké-), *n.*, publication, *f.*

publicist (peub'-), *n.*, publiciste, *m.*

publicity (peub'-), *n.*, publicité, *f.*

publicly (peub'-), *adv.*, publiquement.

publicness (peub'-), *n.*, publicité, *f.*

public-spirited, *adj.*, qui s'occupe du bien général.

publish (peub'-), *v.a.*, publier.

publisher, *n.*, personne qui publie, *f.*; éditeur; publicateur, *m.*

puce (piouce), *or* **puce-coloured** (-keulleurde), *adj.*, puce.

puceron (piou-ci-), *n.*, (ent.) puceron, *m.*

puck (peuke), *n.*, esprit follet; lutin, *m.*

pucker (peuk'-), *v.a.*, rider; (needlework—*ouvrage à l'aiguille*) faire goder; (clothes—*vêtements*) faire grimacer.

pucker, *v.n.*, grimacer.

pucker (peuk'-), *n.*, ride; (in needlework—*ouvrage à l'aiguille*) poche, *f.*

pudder (peud'-), *n.*, fracas, tumulte, tapage, *m.*

pudder, *v.n.*, faire du tapage, faire du tumulte.

pudder, *v.a.*, embarrasser, confondre.

pudding (poud'-), *n.*, pouding, *m.* Black—; *boudin; boudin noir, m.*

pudding-pie (-pa'ye), *n.*, pâté, *m.*

pudding-sleeve (-slive), *n.*, grande manche, *f.*

pudding-stone (-stône), *n.*, (min.) poudingue, *m.*

pudding-time (-taïme), *n.*, heure du dîner, *f.*; à point nommé, *m.*

puddle (peud'd'l), *n.*, flaque d'eau; mare, *f.*; gâchis; (mas.) corroi, *m.*

puddle, *v.a.*, troubler; rendre bourbeux; embourber, crotter; (metal.) puddler; (mortar—*mortier*) corroyer; (a wall—*un mur*) remblayer.

puddling, *n.*, (mas.) corroi; (metal.) puddlage, *m.*

puddly, *adj.*, bourbeux, trouble, boueux.

pudency (piou-), *n.*, modestie; pudeur, *f.*

pudenda (piou-), *n.pl.*, parties honteuses, *f.pl.*

pudicity (piou-), *n.*, pudicité, *f.*

puerile (piou-eur'aïl), *adj.*, puéril.

puerilely, *adv.*, puérilement.

puerility (piou-eur'il'-), *n.*, puérilité, *f.*

puerperal (piou-eur-peur'-), *adj.*, (med.) puerpéral.

puerperous (piou-eur-peur'-), *adj.*, en couche puerpérale.

puff (peuf), *n.*, (breath—*souffle*) souffle, *m.*; (of wind—*de vent*) bouffée, *f.*; (pastry—*pâtisserie*) feuilletage, *m.*; (for powdering the hair —*à poudrer*) houppe à poudre, *f.*; (on dresses—*de robe*) bouillon, *m.*; (advertisement—*annonce*) pouf, *m.*, annonce emphatique, *f.*

puff, *or* **puff-ball** (-bôl), *n.*, (bot.) vesse-de-loup; vesse-loup, *f.*

puff, *v.a.*, souffler; (to swell—*gonfler*) bouffir, enfler; (to praise—*louer*) faire mousser, louer emphatiquement. To — away; *dissiper; chasser;* To — up; *enfler; bouffir.*

puff, *v.n.*, souffler; (to swell—*gonfler*) bouffir; (to swell the cheeks—*enfler les joues*) bouffer; (to breathe with vehemence—*de la respiration*) haleter; (fig.) faire des poufs, faire des annonces emphatiques.

puffer, *n.*, personne qui souffle, *f.*; faiseur de poufs, faiseur d'annonces emphatiques, *m.*

puffin (peuf'-), *n.*, plongeon de mer, *m.*

puffiness (peuf'-), *n.*, enflure, *f.*; (surg.) empâtement, *m.*

puffingly (peuf'-), *adv.*, en haletant; avec enflure; par des poufs.

puffy (peuf'-), *adj.*, bouffi, enflé; (style) boursouflé.

pug (peughe), *n.*, bichon; (monkey—*singe*) petit singe, *m.*

pug (peughe), *v.a.*, (mas.) hourder; (tech.) pilonner.

pug, *or* **pug-dog**, *n.*, roquet, *m.*

pugging (peug-ghigne), *n.*, (mas.) hourdage, hourdis; pilonnage, *m.*; aire de plancher, *f.*

pugging-mortar, *n.*, bauge, *f.*

pugh! (pou), *int.*, nargue! fi donc!

pugilism (piou-djil'iz'm), *n.*, pugilat, *m.*

pugilist, *n.*, pugiliste, boxeur, *m.*

pugilistic, *adj.*, de pugilat.

pug-mill, *n.*, (brick-making—*briqueterie*) pétrin, *m.*

pugnacious (peug-né-sheusse), *adj.*, enclin à se battre; querelleur.

puisne (piou-ni), *adj.*, inférieur.

puissance (piou-is'sa'), *n.*, puissance, *f.*

puissant, *adj.*, puissant.

puissantly, *adv.*, puissamment.

puke (piouke), *n.*, vomitif, émétique; vomissement, *m.*

puke, *v.n.*, vomir.

puker, *n.*, vomitif, émétique, *m.*; (pers.) personne qui vomit, *f.*

pulchritude (peul-kri-tioude), *n.*, beauté, *f.*

pule (pioule), *v.n.*, piauler; (to whine—*murmurer*) pleurnicher.

puling, *n.*, cri de petit poulet; cri de pleurnicheur, *m.*

pulingly, *adv.*, en piaulant; en pleurnichant.

pull (poule), *n.*, action de tirer, *f.*; coup de main; (rowing—*ramer*) coup de rame, *m.*, coups de rame, *m.pl.*; (effort) effort, *m.*, tâche, *f.*; (violence) secousse, *f.*; (advantage—*arantage*) avantage; (draught—*du boire*) coup, trait, *m.*; contest—*lutte*) lutte, *f.* A — on the -water; *une promenade sur l'eau.* Hard —; *rude effort; rude tâche.*

pull (poule), *v.a.*, tirer; (to gather—*cueillir*) cueillir; (to tear—*déchirer*) déchirer; (print.) tirer. To — asunder, apart; *déchirer en deux.* To — away; *arracher.* To — back; *faire reculer;* tirer en arrière. To — down; *faire descendre;* (to demolish—*démolir*) démolir, abattre; (to abase —*abaisser*) abaisser, rabattre. To — off; *arracher,* enlever; ôter; (one's clothes—*vêtements*) ôter; (one's boots—*bottes*) tirer, ôter. To — in; *tirer dedans; rentrer.* To — in pieces; *mettre en pièces.* To — ou (as boots, &c.—*bottes, &c.*); *mettre.* To — out; *tirer dehors; tirer; arracher;*

faire sortir : sortir ; (hair, teeth—*cheveux, dents*) arracher. To — up; *tirer en haut ; arracher ; déraciner ; extirper.*

pull, *v.n.,* tirer ; (to row—*ramer*) ramer ; (of horses, carriages, &c.—*des chevaux, voitures, &c.*) to — up ; *arrêter ; s'arrêter ; descendre.*

puller, *n.,* tireur ; arracheur. *m.*

pullet (poul'-), *n.,* poulette, *f.* Fat —; *poularde, f.*

pulley (poul'-), *n.,* poulie, *f.*

pulling (poul'-), *n.,* tirage ; (agri.) arrachage, *m.*

pullulate (peu'liou-), *v.n.,* germer.

pullulation (peul-liou-lé-), *n.,* action de germer. *f.*

pulmonary (peul-), *adj.,* pulmonaire.

pulmonic (peul-), *adj.,* pulmonaire ; (pers.) phtisique, pulmonique.

pulmonic, *n.,* médicament pectoral, *m.* ; (pers.) pulmonique, phtisique, *m.,f.*

pulp (peulpe), *n.,* substance molle ; (of fruit —*des fruits*) chair, pulpe ; (marrow—*moelle*) moelle ; (bot.) pulpe, *f.,* parenchyme, *m.* ; (for making paper—*pour faire du papier*) pâte, bouillie, *f.*

pulp (peulpe), *v.a.,* enlever la chair de, enlever l'enveloppe de ; décortiquer.

pulpiness (peulp'-), *n.,* nature molle ; nature pulpeuse, *f.*

pulpit (poul-), *n.,* (ecc.)chaire ; (pol.) tribune, *f.* ; (for auctioneers—*de commissaires-priseurs*) bureau, *m.* — cloth ; *tapis de chaire, m.*

pulpous, *or* **pulpy** (peul-), *adj.,* pulpeux.

pulsate (peul-), *v.n.,* avoir des pulsations.

pulsatile (peul-), *adj.,* de percussion.

pulsation (peul-sé-), *n.,* pulsation, *f.*

pulsatory (peul-sé-), *adj.,* (med.) pulsatif.

pulse (peulse), *n.,* pouls, *m.* ; (phys.) pulsation ; (bot.) plante légumineuse, *f.,* légume, *m.* High, low —; *pouls élevé, faible.* Irregular, regular —; *pouls déréglé,réglé.* Strong, weak —; *pouls élevé, faible.* Quick —; *pouls fréquent.* Wiry —; *pouls sec.* To feel any one's —; *tâter le pouls à quelqu'un ;* (fig.) *pressentir quelqu'un sur quelque chose.*

pulsion (peul-), *n.,* action de pousser en dehors, *f.*

pulverable (peul-vèr-a-b'l), *adj.,* pulvérisable.

pulverization (-vèr'aïzé-), *n.,* pulvérisation. *f.*

pulverize (peul-vèr'aïze), *v.a.,* pulvériser; réduire en poudre.

pulverous (peul-vèr'-). *adj.,* poudreux.

pulverulence (peul-vir'iou-), *n.,* pulvérulence. *f.*

pulverulent, *adj.,* pulvérulent.

pumice (piou-mice), *or* **pumice-stone** (-stône). *n.,* ponce, pierre ponce, *f.*

pumice, *v.a.,* poncer.

pumiceous (piou-mish'eusse), *adj.,* ponceux.

pummel. *V.* **pommel.**

pump, *n.,* pompe, *f.* ; (shoe—*chaussure*) escarpin, *m.* Fire— ; *pompe à incendie.* Stomach-— ; *pompe stomacale.* Sucking— ; *pompe aspirante.* Forcing— ; *pompe foulante.* Air- — ; *pompe pneumatique.* To fetch the — ; *amorcer la pompe.*

pump, *v.a.,* pomper ; (fig.) sonder, tirer les vers du nez à. To — anything out of any one ; *tirer quelque chose de quelqu'un.*

pump, *v.n.,* pomper.

pump-bore, *n.,* âme de pompe. *f.*

pump-brake, *n.,* brimbale de pompe, *f.*

pumper, *n.,* personne qui pompe ; chose qui fait aller la pompe, *f.*

pump-gauge (-ghédje), *n.,* sonde de pompe. *f.*

pump-gear (-ghîre), *f.,* garniture de pompe, *f.*

pumpion (peu'm'p'ieune), *or* **pumpkin,** *n.,* citrouille, courge,*f.* ; potiron, *m.*

pump-lift, *n.,* reprise de pompe, *f.*

pump-spear (-spîre), *n.,* tige de pompe, *f.*

pun (peune), *n.,* calembour, *m.*

pun, *v.n.,* faire des calembours.

pun, *v.n.,* persuader par des calembours.

punch (peu'n'she), *n.,* (instrument) emporte-pièce ; (buffoon—*bouffon*) polichinelle ; (beverage —*boisson*) punch, ☉ ponche ; (blow—*coup*) coup de poing ; (short man—*homme de petite taille*) courtaud ; (horse) cheval ramassé ; *m.*

punch, *v.a.,* percer ; (to hit—*frapper*) donner un coup de poing à. To — out ; *enlever à l'emporte-pièce.*

punch-bowl (-bôl), *n.,* bol à punch, *m.*

puncheon (peu'n'sh'eune), *n.,* poinçon ; (carp.) montant, *m.* ; (of beer—*de bière*) pièce (litres 332·6876); (of wine—*de vin*) pièce (litres 318), *f.*

puncher, *n.,* personne qui enlève à l'emporte-pièce, *f.* ; (thing—*chose*) emporte-pièce, *m.*

punchinello (peu'n'shi-nèl'lô), *n.,* polichinelle, *m.*

punchy, *adj.,* ramassé, trapu, courtaud.

punctated (peu'n'k-tét'-), *adj.,* en pointe.

punctiform (peu'n'k-), *adj.,* en forme de pointe.

punctilio (peu'n'k-til'iô). *n.,* exactitude scrupuleuse ; pointillerie, formalité. *f.*

punctilious (peu'n'k-), *adj.,* d'une exactitude scrupuleuse ; pointilleux.

punctiliously, *adv.,* avec une exactitude scrupuleuse ; d'une manière pointilleuse.

punctiliousness, *n.,* exactitude scrupuleuse ; nature pointilleuse ; pointillerie, *f.*

puncto (peu'n'k-tô), *n.,* forme ; (fenc.) pointe, *f.*

punctual (peun'gu.'kt'iou-), *adj.,* ponctuel, exact.

punctualist, *n.,* personne pointilleuse pour les formes, sur le cérémonial, *f.*

punctuality, *n.,* ponctualité, exactitude, *f.*

punctually, *adv.,* ponctuellement, exactement.

punctualness, *n.,* ponctualité, exactitude, *f.*

punctuate (peu'n'kt'iou-), *v.a.,* ponctuer.

punctuation (peu'n'k-tiou-é-), *n.,* ponctuation, *f.*

puncture (peun'gn'kt'ieur), *n.,* piqûre, *f.*

puncture. *v.a.,* piquer ; faire une piqûre à.

pungency (peu'n'djè'n'-), *n.,* nature piquante ; acrimonie ; âcreté ; aigreur, *f.* ; piquant, *m.*

pungent (peu'n'djè'n'te). *adj.,* piquant ; acrimonieux ; âcre ; cuisant ; poignant.

punic (piou-), *adj.,* punique.

puniceous (piou-nish'eusse), *adj.,* de pourpre ; pourpré.

puniness (piou-), *n.,* petitesse ; nature chétive, *f.*

punish (peu'n'-), *v.a.,* punir, châtier.

punishable (peu'n'ish-a-b'l), *adj.,* punissable.

punishableness, *n.,* caractère punissable, *m.*

punisher, *n.,* personne qui punit, *f.*

punishment, *n.,* punition ; peine, *f.* ; châtiment, *m.*

punitive (peu'n'-), *adj.,* pénal.

punitory, *adj.,* (ant.) qui tend à punir, qui punit.

punster (peu'n'-), *n.,* calembouriste, *m.*

punt (peu'n'te), *v.a.,* (boat—*bateau*) conduire à la gaffe.

punt, *v.n.,* (at play—*au jeu*) ponter.

punt, *n.,* ras de carène, *m.*

punter, *n.,* ponte, *m.*

puny (piou-), *adj.,* petit ; faible ; mesquin.

puny, *n.*, novice, *m.*, *f.* ; personne sans expérience, *f.*

pup (peupe). *v.n.*, chienner ; mettre bas.

pup, *n.*, petit chien, petit, *m.* ; petite chienne, *f.*

pupa (piou-), *or* **pupe** (pioupe), *n.* (*pupæ*), (ent.) pupe, chrysalide, nymphe, *f.*

pupil (piou-), *n.*, élève, *m.f.* ; écolier, *m.*, écolière, *f.* ; pupille, *m.f.* ; (of the eye—*de l'œil*) pupille, prunelle, *f.*

pupilage (-édje), *n.*, état d'élève, *m.* ; minorité, *f.*

pupilary (piou-), *adj.*, pupillaire.

puppet (peup'-), *n.*, marionnette ; poupée, *f.*, poupard, *m.* ; bamboche, *f.*

puppet-man, *n.*, maître d'un spectacle de marionnettes, *m.*

puppet-show (-shô), *n.*, spectacle de marionnettes, *m.* ; marionnettes, *f.pl.*

puppy (peup'-), *n.*, petit chien, *m.*, petite chienne, *f.* ; petit, *m.*, (pers.) fat, faquin, drôle, *m.*

puppy. *v.n.*, chienner, mettre bas.

puppyism, *n.*, fatuité, *f.*

pur, *or* **purr** (peur), *v.n.*, (of the cat—*du chat*) filer ; faire le rouet.

pur, *or* **purr**, *n.*, murmure du chat, *m.*

purblind (peur-blai'n'de), *adj.*, qui a la vue courte ; myope ; (animal) qui voit peu, aveugle.

purblindness, *n.*, vue courte ; myopie, *f.*

purchasable (peur'tshéss'a-b'l), *adj.*, qu'on peut acheter ; à acheter.

purchase (peur-tchéce), *n.*, achat, *m.* ; acquisition, emplette ; (mec.) puissance, prise ; (jur.) obtention, *f.* ; (nav.) appareil, *m.* — money ; *prix d'achat*, *m.*

purchase (peur-tchéce), *v.a.*, acheter, acquérir ; faire l'achat de ; (to obtain—*obtenir*) obtenir, gagner.

purchaser (peur-tchéss'-), *n.*, acquéreur ; acheteur, *m.*

pure (pioure), *adj.*, pur ; (b.s.) vrai, franc. — from ; *exempt de.*

purely. *adv.*, purement.

pureness, *n.*, pureté, *f.*

purgation (peur-ghé-). *n.*, purgation, *f.*

purgative, *n.*, purgatif, *m.*

purgative, *adj.*, purgatif.

purgatorial (peur-ghé-tô-), *adj.*, du purgatoire.

purgatorian (peur-ghé-tô-), *adj.*, (ant.). *V.* **purgatorial**.

purgatory (peur-), *n.*, purgatoire, *m.*

purgatory, *adj.*, qui purifie ; expiatoire.

purge (peurdje), *n.*, purgation, *f.* ; purgatif, *m.*

purge, *v.a.*, purger ; nettoyer, purifier ; clarifier ; épurer.

purger, *n.*, personne qui purge, qui épure, qui nettoie, qui purifie ; chose qui purge, qui épure, qui nettoie, qui purifie, *f.*

purging, *n.*, diarrhée ; (fig.) épuration, *f.*

purification (piou-ri-fi-ké-), *n.*, purification ; épuration, *f.*

purificative. *or* **purificatory** (piou-ri-fi-ké-), *adj.*, qui purifie.

purifier (piou-ri-faï-), *n.*, personne qui purifie, qui épure ; chose qui purifie, qui épure, *f.* ; purificateur, *m.*

puriform (piou-), *adj.*, (med.) puriforme.

purify (piou-ri-fa'ye), *v.a.*, purifier ; épurer.

purify, *v.n.*, se purifier ; s'épurer.

purism (piou-riz'm), *n.*, purisme, *m.*

purist, *n.*, puriste, *m.*

puritan (piou-), *adj.*, puritain.

puritan, *n.*, puritain, *m.*, puritaine, *f.*

puritanic, *or* **puritanical**, *adj.*, de puritain, puritain.

puritanism (-'iz'm), *n.*, puritanisme, *m.*

purity (piou-), *n.*, pureté, *f.*

purl (peurle), *n.*, bordure en broderie ; (of

lace—*de dentelle*) engrêlure ; (beverage—*boisson*) bière à l'absinthe, *f.* ; (of brooks—*des ruisseaux*) doux murmure, gazouillement, *m.*

purl, *v.a.*, orner de broderie.

purl, *v.n.*, murmurer, gazouiller.

purlieu (peur-liou), *n.*, alentour, confin, *m.* ; limite, *f.* —s ; *environs, confins, m.pl.* ; *voisinage*, *m.sing.*

purlin (peur-), *n.*, (carp.) ventrière, *f.*

purling (peurl'-), *adj.*, murmurant.

purling (peurl'-), *n.*, murmure, gazouillement, *m.*

purloin (peur-lwaïne), *v.a.*, soustraire, dérober, voler, détourner.

purloiner, *n.*, voleur, *m.*, voleuse ; personne qui soustrait, qui dérobe, *f.*

purloining, *n.*, soustraction, *f.* ; vol, détournement, *m.*

purple (peur-p'l), *adj.*, de pourpre, pourpré.

purple (peur-p'l), *n.*, pourpre, *m.* ; (dye, fig.) pourpre, *f.*

purple. *v.a.*, teindre en pourpre ; empourprer ; rougir.

purples (peur-p'l'ze), *n.*, fièvre pourprée, *f.*

purplish, *adj.*, tirant sur le pourpre ; purpurin.

purport (peur-), *n.*, but, objet ; (sense—*signification*) sens, *m.* ; (import—*force*) portée, *f.*

purport, *v.a.*, tendre à montrer ; signifier.

purpose (peur-poss), *n.*, but, effet, *m.*, fin, *f.* ; dessein, projet, *m.*, intention, *f.* ; besoin ; usage ; but d'intérêt, *m.* On —; *exprès ; à dessein.* To no —; *sans effet ; inutilement ; en vain ; en pure perte.* To little —; *à peu d'effet ; en vain.* To the —; *à propos.* Foreign to the —; *étranger au but.* To what —? *à quoi bon ! à quel effet ?* For one — only ; (man.) *à une main ; pour un seul usage.* To answer, to take one's —; *faire son affaire ; arranger quelqu'un.* To answer a —; *remplir un but.* To answer no —; *être inutile ; ne servir de rien.* To come to the —; *venir au fait.* To gain one's —; *en venir à ses fins.* To answer the — of ; *faire l'office de.* That is nothing to the —; *cela ne fait rien à l'affaire ; cela ne veut rien dire.*

purpose (peur-poss), *v.a.*, se proposer, avoir le dessein ; avoir l'intention ; avoir le projet.

purposely, *adv.*, à dessein, exprès.

purpura (peur-piou-), *n.*, (med.) purpura, *m.*

purpure (peur-piour), *n.*, (her.) pourpre, *m.*

purpuric (peur-piou-), *adj.*, purpurique.

purr. *v.n.* *V.* **pur**.

purring, *n.* *V.* **pur**, *n.*

purring (peur'-), *adj.*, (of the cat—*du chat*) qui file, qui fait le rouet ; (med.) frémissement cataire.

purse (peurse), *n.*, bourse, *f.* ; (prize) prix, *m.* Privy —; *cassette*, *f.*

purse, *v.a.*, embourser ; mettre en bourse ; (fig.) plisser.

purse-net, *n.*, filet en bourse, *m.*

purse-proud (-praoude), *adj.*, fier de son argent.

purser, *n.*, agent comptable, *m.* —'s steward ; *distributeur des vivres*, *m.*

pursiness (peur-), *n.*, boursouflure. enflure ; (of breath—*de l'haleine*) courte haleine, *f.*

purslain (peurs'line), *n.*, (bot.) pourpier, *m.*

pursuable (peur-siou-a-b'l), *adj.*, qu'on peut poursuivre.

pursuance (peur-siou-), *n.*, poursuite ; suite, conséquence, *f.* In — of ; *en conséquence de ; en vertu de.*

pursuant (peur-siou-), *adj.*, en conséquence, par suite ; conforme. — to ; *conformément à.*

pursue (peur-siou), *v.a.*, poursuivre ; suivre ; chercher.

pursuer, *n.*, personne qui poursuit, *f.* ; poursuivant. *m.*

pursuit (peur-sioute), *n.*, poursuite ; recherche ; occupation, profession, *f.* ; —s ; travaux, *m.pl.* ; occupations, *f.pl.* ; carrière, *f.*, études, *f.pl.* In — of ; *à la poursuite de, à la recherche de.*

pursuivant (peur-swi-), *n.,* poursuivant d'armes, *m.* — at arms ; *poursuivant d'armes.*

pursy (peur-), *adj.,* bouffi ; poussif.

purulence, *or* **purulency** (piou-riou-), *n.,* purulence, *f.*

purulent (piou-riou-), *adj.,* purulent.

purvey (peur-), *v.a.,* faire provision de; pourvoir; fournir; procurer.

purvey, *v.n.,* faire ses provisions; se pourvoir.

purveyance (peur-vé-), *n.,* provisions, *f.pl.* ; approvisionnement, *m.*

purveyor (peur-vé-eur), *n.,* pourvoyeur, *m.*

pus (peuss), *n.,* pus, *m.*

push (poush), *n.,* coup, *m.*; impulsion; poussée, poussade, *f.* ; (attack—*attaque*) assaut, *m.,* attaque, *f.* ; (critical moment—*conjoncture*) moment critique, *m.,* conjoncture, extrémité, *f.* At a —, on a —; *dans un moment critique, à l'extrémité; comme un pis aller.*

push (poush), *v.n.,* pousser ; faire un effort; se pousser; attaquer. To — at; *pousser; attaquer.* To — away; *pousser toujours.* To — off ; (nav.) *pousser au large.* To — on, forward; *pousser en avant; s'avancer; se pousser dans le monde.* To — on to; *pousser jusqu'à; donner un coup de pied jusqu'à.*

push, *v.a.,* pousser; (to urge—*presser*) presser, importuner. To — away ; *repousser,* éloigner. To — back ; *repousser ; faire reculer.* To — down ; *faire tomber.* To — any one down the stairs ; *faire dégringoler l'escalier à quelqu'un.* To — forward; *avancer, faire avancer.* To — in; *faire entrer.* To — off; *repousser ; lancer; pousser au large.* To — on ; *pousser ; faire avancer.* To — out; *pousser dehors; faire sortir.* To — up; *faire monter.* To be —ed for money; *être à court d'argent.* To be —ed for an answer; *être embarrassé pour répondre.*

pusher, *n.,* personne qui pousse, *f.*; pousseur, *m.*

pushing, *adj.,* qui se pousse ; qui pousse ; (enterprising—*hardi*) entreprenant.

pushpin, *n.,* poussette, *f.*

pusillanimity (piou-cil'-), *n.,* pusillanimité, *f.*

pusillanimous, *adj.,* pusillanime.

pusillanimously, *adv.,* pusillanimement.

pusillanimousness (piou-cil'-), *n.,* pusillanimité, *f.*

puss (pouss), *n.,* (cat—*chat*) minon, minet, *m.,* minette, *f.* ; (hare—*lièvre*) lièvre, *m.*

pustular, pustulate, *or* **pustulous** (peust'iou-), *adj.,* couvert de pustules ; pustuleux.

pustulate (peust'iou-), *v.a.,* former en pustules.

pustule (peust'ioule), *n.,* pustule, *f.*

put (poute), *v.a.* (*preterit* and *past part.,* Put), mettre ; poser ; placer ; (to suppose—*conjecturer*) supposer, poser ; (to offer—*offrir*) offrir, proposer. To — about ; *faire passer ; faire circuler.* To — away ; *serrer, cacher ;* (to take away) *ôter ;* (a wife—*une épouse*) *répudier.* To — back; *reculer ; faire reculer.* To — replace—*replacer*) *replacer, remettre.* To — by; *mettre de côté, serrer.* To — down; *déposer, poser ; mettre par terre;* (to suppress—*supprimer*) *supprimer ;* (to confound—*confondre*) *réduire au silence, confondre.* To — forth; *mettre en avant ; étendre, tendre, avancer;* (to display—*déployer*) *déployer;* (leaves, flowers—*des feuilles, des fleurs*) *pousser.* To — in; *mettre dedans ; mettre, passer ;* (to insert—*insérer*) *insérer.* To — off; *ôter ;* (to defer—*différer*) *remettre, retarder, différer.* To — on; (to advance—*avancer*) *avancer;* (to assume

—*assumer*) *prendre ;* (to attribute to—*attribuer*) *mettre sur le compte de, attribuer à, imputer à ;* (clothes—*vêtements*) *mettre.* To — out; *mettre dehors; mettre à la porte ;* (to extinguish—*éteindre*) *éteindre ;* (to confuse—*confondre*) *embarrasser, déranger, troubler ;* (money—*argent*) *placer ;* (flowers, leaves—*fleurs, feuilles*) *pousser ;* (to display—*déployer*) *déployer.* To — over; *mettre dessus ; mettre au-dessus de.* To — to ; *mettre à;* (to refer to—*référer*) *s'en référer à ;* (to harness—*harnacher*) *atteler.* To — up; *mettre en haut ; réduire à; contraindre; mettre à; engager à ;* (to replace—*replacer*) *remettre ;* (to pack—*emballer*) *empaqueter, emballer ;* (a prayer —*une prière*) *faire, offrir.* To — any one up to any thing; *donner le mot à quelqu'un; mettre quelqu'un au courant de quelque chose.* To — to the sword ; *passer au fil de l'épée.* To be — to it ; *être embarrassé ; avoir du fil à retordre; avoir fort à faire.* To — together; *mettre ensemble; rapprocher ; réunir ;* (a piece of mechanism—*assembler les pièces d'un ouvrage, d'un mécanisme*) *monter.* To — any one on his trial; *mettre quelqu'un en jugement, en cause.* To — an affront on any one ; *faire affront à quelqu'un.*

put (poute), *v.n.,* (to germinate—*germer*) germer, pousser; (nav.) se mettre. To — forth; *annoncer, déclarer, publier ;* (to bud—*germer*) *germer, pousser.* To — in; (nav.) *entrer au port, relâcher ;* (at play—*au jeu*) *mettre au jeu.* To — in for ; *se mettre sur les rangs pour.* To — off; *pousser au large.* To — on ; *aller vite.* To — to sea; *mettre à la voile.* To — up ; *loger.* To — up at ; *descendre à.* To — up for; *se mettre sur les rangs pour.* To — up with; *souffrir, endurer, supporter, avaler, digérer ;* (to make shift with— *se contenter de*) *s'accommoder de, s'arranger de.*

put (poute), *n.,* nécessité, extrémité, *f.*

putative (piou-té-), *adj.,* supposé, réputé; (of fathers—*d'un père*) putatif.

putid (piou-), *adj.,* (l.u.), bas, vil, indigne.

putidness, *n.,* (l.u.) bassesse, indignité, *f.*

putlog (peut'-), *n.,* boulin, *m.*

put-off, *n.,* défaite, excuse, échappatoire, *f.,* faux-fuyant, *m.*

putrefaction (piou-tri-fak'-), *n.,* putréfaction, *f.*

putrefactive (piou-tri-fak-), *adj.,* de putréfaction ; putréfactif.

putrefy (piou-tri-fa'ye), *v.a.,* putréfier; corrompre.

putrefy, *v.n.,* se putréfier, pourrir.

putrescence (piou-très'-), *n.,* état de putréfaction, *m.*

putrescent (piou-très'-), *adj.,* en état de putréfaction; putride ; putréfié.

putrid (piou-), *adj.,* putride.

putridness, *or* **putridity** (piou-), *n.,* pourriture, putridité, *f.*

putter (pout'-), *n.,* personne qui met, qui pose, qui place, *f.* ; faiseur, *m.,* faiseuse, *f.*

putter-on, *n.,* instigateur, *m.*

putting (pout'-), *n.,* action de mettre, de placer ; mise, *f.*

putty (peut'-), *n.,* potée d'étain, *f.*; (for glaziers—*de vitrier*) mastic ; ciment, *m.*

puzzle (peuz'z'l), *n.,* embarras, *m.,* difficulté, *f.* ; (toy—*jouet*) jeu de patience, casse-tête, *m.*

puzzle (peuz'z'l), *v.a.,* intriguer, embarrasser, démonter ; (one's brains—*l'esprit*) s'alambiquer l'esprit, la cervelle.

puzzle (peuz'z'l), *v.n.,* être embarrassé.

puzzle-headed (-hèd'ède), *adj.,* qui a la tête pleine d'idées creuses.

puzzler, *n.,* personne qui embarrasse ; chose qui embarrasse, *f.*

puzzuolana (peuz-ziou-ô-là-), *n.* V. **pozzuolana.**

pygmean (-mî-), *adj.,* de pygmée.

pygmy, *n.,* pygmée, *m.*

pyloric (-lô-), *adj.*, (anat.) pylorique.
pylorus (-lô-), *n.*, (anat.) pylore, *m.*
pyracanth (-ca'n'th), *n.*, (bot.) pyracanthe, *f.* ; buisson ardent, *m.*
pyramid. *n.*, pyramide, *f.*
pyramidal, pyramidic, *or* **pyramidical**, *adj.*, pyramidal.
pyramidically, *adv.*, en pyramide.
pyre (paeur), *n.*, bûcher, *m.*
pyriform, *adj.*, pyriforme, piriforme.
pyrites (-raï-tize), *n. sing.* and *pl.*, pyrite, *f.*
pyritous, *adj.*, (min.) pyriteux.
pyroligneous (-lig-ni-), **pyrolignic,** *or* **pyrolignous** (-lig-), *adj.*, pyroligneux.
pyrometer (-ro'm'i-), *n.*, pyromètre, *m.*
pyrophorus, *n.*, pyrophore, *m.*
pyrotechnic, *or* **pyrotechnical** (-tèk'-), *adj.*, pyrotechnique.
pyrotechnics (-tèk'-), *n.pl.*, pyrotechnie, *f.sing.*
pyrotechnist (-tèk'-), *n.*, personne versée dans la pyrotechnie, *f.*
pyrotechny (-tèk'-), *n.*, pyrotechnie, *f.*
pyroxene(pir'oks'ïne),*n.*,(min.) pyroxène,*m.*
pyrrhic, *n.*, pyrrhique ; danse pyrrhique,*f.* ! (poet.) pyrrhique, *m.*
pyrrhonic, *adj.*, pyrrhonien.
pyrrhonism (-niz'm), *n.*, pyrrhonisme, *m.*
pyrrhonist, *n.*, pyrrhonien, *m.*
pythagorean (-thag-o-rî-), *n.*, pythagoricien, *m.*, pythagoricienne, *f.*
pythagoric, *or* **pythagorical** (-thag-), *adj.*, pythagoricien.
pythagorism (-thag-o-riz'm), *n.*, pythagorisme, *m.*
pythian (pith'-), *adj.*, pythien ; pythique, de la pythie.
pythoness (pith'-), *n.*, pythonisse, *f.*
pythonic (pith'-), *adj.*, de devin.
pythonist (pith'-), *n.*, devin, *m.*
pyx, *n. V.* **pix.**

Q

q. dix-septième lettre de l'alphabet, q, *m.*
quack (kwake), *n.*, charlatan ; empirique ; marchand d'orviétan, *m.*
quack, *v.n.*, faire le charlatan ; faire le gascon ; hâbler ; (of ducks—*des canards*) nasiller.
quack, *adj.*, de charlatan ; d'empirique.
quackery (kwak'ri), *n.*, charlatanisme, empirisme. *m.* ; charlatanerie,*f.*
quackish, *adj.*, de charlatan ; d'empirique ; charlatanesque.
quackism (-'iz'm), *n.*, charlatanisme, *m.*
quacksalver, *n.*, marchand d'orviétan, *m.*
quadragesima (kwôd-ra-djèss-), *n.*, Quadragésime,*f.* — Sunday ; *dimanche de la Quadragésime, m.*
quadragesimal. *adj.*, quadragésimal.
quadragesimals (-molze), *n.*, offrandes de la mi-carême,*f.pl.*
quadrangle (kwôd-ra'n'g'l), *n.*, quadrangle. *m.*
quadrangular (-ghiou-), *adj.*, quadrangulaire.
quadrant (kwôd'-), *n.*, quart ; quart de cercle ; octant, *m.* — of altitude ; *quart de cercle mural. m.*
quadrantal. *adj.*, de quart de cercle.
quadrat (kwôd'-), *n.*, (print.) quadrat, cadrat, *m.*
quadrate (kwôd'-), *adj.*, carré.
quadrate, *n.*. carré ; (astrol.) quadrat aspect. *m.*
quadrate. *v.n.*, cadrer.
quadratic (kwad'-), *adj.*, carré ; (alg.) quadratique.

quadratrix (kwad'-), *n.*, carré, *m.* ; figure carrée ; (geom.) quadratrice,*f.*
quadrature (kwôd'-ra-tioure), *n.*, quadrature,*f.* ; carré, *m.*
quadrennial (kwôd'-), *adj.*, de quatre ans ; quadriennal, quatriennal.
quadrennially, *adv.*, tous les quatre ans.
quadrible (kwôd-ri-b'l), *adj.*, qui peut être carré.
quadrifid (kwôd'-), *adj.*, (bot.) quadrifide.
quadriga (kwôd-raï-), *n.*, quadrige, *m.*
quadrilateral (kwôd'ri-lat'èr'-), *adj.*, quadrilatéral.
quadrilateral, *n.*. quadrilatère, *m.*
quadrille (ka-drile), *n.*, (cards—*jeu de cartes*) quadrille ; (mus., danc.) quadrille, *m.*, contredanse,*f.*
quadrillion (kwôd'-), *n.*. septillion, *m.*
quadrinomial (kwôd-ri-nô-), *n.*, quadrinôme, *m.*
quadripartite (kwa-drip-ar-ta'ite), *adj.*, quadriparti, quadripartite.
quadrisyllable (kwôd-ri-cil-la-b'l), *n.*, quadrisyllabe, *m.*
quadroon (kwôd-roune), *n.*, quarteron, *m.*, quarteronne,*f.*
quadrumane (kwôd-rou-), *n.*, quadrumane, *m.*
quadrumanous, *adj.*, quadrumane.
quadruped (kwôd-rou-), *n.*, quadrupède, *m.*
quadrupedal, *adj.*, quadrupède.
quadruple (kwôd-rou-p'l),*n.*, quadruple, *m.*
quadruple, *adj.*, quadruple.
quadruple, *v.a.*, quadrupler.
quadruplicate (kwôd-rou-), *v.a.*, quadrupler.
quadruplicate, *adj.*, quadruplé.
quadruplication (-pli-ké-), *n.*, action de quadrupler,*f.*
quadruply, *adv.*, au quadruple.
quaff (kwaf), *v.n.*, boire copieusement ; vider (en buvant) ; (fig.) savourer, humer ; (b.s.) s'abreuver de.
quaff, *v.a.*, boire copieusement ; boire.
quaffer, *n.*, buveur, *m.*
quaggy (kwag-ghi), *adj.*, marécageux.
quagmire (kwag-maeur), *or* **quag,** *n.*, fondrière,*f.*
quail (kwéle), *n.*, caille,*f.*
quail, *v.n.*, perdre courage, faiblir ; reculer, se troubler ; se cailler, se coaguler.
quail (kwéle), *v.a.*, (ant.) écraser, vaincre, abattre, dompter.
quail-pipe (-païpe), *n.*, courcaillet, appeau, *m.*
quaint (kwén-te), *adj.*, (odd—*original*) singulier, bizarre, original ; (unusual—*singulier*) extraordinaire, étrange ; (affected—*affecté*) affecté, prétentieux ; (fine spun—*recherché*) recherché, apprêté ; (pretty—*joli*) gentil, joli.
quaintly.*adv.*, singulièrement, bizarrement, originalement ; extraordinairement, étrangement ; d'une manière affectée, d'une manière prétentieuse ; d'une manière recherchée, d'une manière apprêtée ; gentiment.
quaintness. *n.*, singularité, bizarrerie, originalité ; nature extraordinaire, nature étrange ; gentillesse,*f.*
quake (kwéke), *v.n.*, trembler ; tremblo'er.
quake, *n.*, tremblement, *m.*
quaker, *n.*, quaker, quacre, trembleur, *m.*
quakeress, *n.*, quakeresse,*f.*
quakerism (-iz'm), *n.*, quakerisme, *m.*
quakerly, *adv.*. de quaker.
quaking (kwék'-), *n.*, tremblement, *m.*; terreur,*f.*
quaking, *adj.*, tremblant ; tremblotant.
quakingly. *adv.*, en tremblant.
qualification (kwôl'i-fi-ké-), *n.*. qualité, qualité requise ; capacité ; (diminution) diminu-

tion. *f.*, affaiblissement, *m.* ; (modification) modification, restriction ; (denomination) dénomination, désignation, *f.*

qualified (kwŏl'i-faide), *adj.*, qui a les qualités requises ; apte, capable, propre ; autorisé : modifié ; tempéré.

qualify (kwŏl'i-fa'ye), *v.a.*, donner les qualités requises à ; rendre apte, rendre capable, rendre propre, préparer ; autoriser, donner le droit de ; qualifier ; (to modify—*changer*) modifier ; (to soften—*tempérer*) adoucir, modérer ; (to regulate—*régler*) déterminer, fixer.

qualifying (kwŏl'i-fa-yigne), *adj.*, (gram.) qualificatif.

quality (kwŏl'-), *n.*, qualité, *f.* ; (acquirement—*acquis*) talent, *m.*

qualm (kwâme), *n.*, mal au cœur, *m.* ; nausée ; envie de vomir, *f.* ; (scruple—*de conscience*) scrupule, *m.*

qualmish (kwâm'-), *adj.*, qui a mal au cœur ; qui a des nausées ; qui a envie de vomir.

qualmishness, *n.*, envie de vomir ; nausée, *f.*

quandary (kwo'n'dé-), *n.*, embarras, *m.* ; incertitude ; difficulté, *f.*

quantitative, *or* **quantitive** (kwŏ'n'-); *adj.*, (ant.) appréciable sous les rapports de la quantité.

quantity (kwo'n-), *n.*, quantité, *f.*

quantum (kwo'n-), *n.*, montant, total, *m.* ; quantité, *f.*

quarantine (kwor'a'n-tine), *n.*, quarantaine, *f.* To perform — ; *faire quarantaine.*

quarantine, *v.a.*, faire faire quarantaine à.

quarrel (kwor'rèl), *n.*, querelle, dispute, *f.* ; démêlé, *m.* ; (cause of dispute) sujet de querelle, *m.*, cause de querelle, *f.* To fasten a — on any one ; *chercher querelle, chercher noise à quelqu'un.*

quarrel, *v.n.*, quereller ; se quereller ; se disputer. To — with ; *se quereller avec.* To want to — with ; *chercher querelle à.* To have —led with ; *être en querelle avec ; être brouillé avec.*

quarreller, *n.*, querelleur, *m.*, querelleuse, *f.*

quarrelling, *n.*, querelle ; dispute, *f.*

quarrellous, *or* **quarrelsome**, *adj.*, querelleur. — man ; *querelleur, m.* — woman ; *querelleuse, f.*

quarrelsomely, *adv.*, en querellant.

quarrelsomeness, *n.*, caractère querelleur, *m.* ; humeur querelleuse, *f.*

quarry (kwor'-), *n.*, carrière de pierre ; (hunt.) curée ; (prey—*proie*) proie, *f.*

quarry, *v.a.*, tirer d'une carrière.

quarrying, *n.*, extraction de la carrière, *f.*

quarryman, *n.*, carrier, *m.*

quart (kwŏrte), *n.*, quart (litre 1·135860), *m.*

quartan (kwor-), *n.*, fièvre quarte, *f.* ; (of a measure—*de mesure*) quart, *m.*

quartan, *adj.*, (med.) quart.

quartation (kwor-té-), *n.*, (metal.) quartation, inquartation, *f.*, inquart, *m.*

quarter (kwor-), *v.a.*, partager en quarts ; diviser en parties, diviser en parties distinctes ; (her.) écarteler ; (to lodge—*loger*) loger ; (troops —*des troupes*) faire le logement de. To draw and — ; *écarteler.*

quarter, *v.a.*, loger ; (milit.) être en quartier.

quarter, *n.*, (fourth part—*quatrième partie*) quart ; (of a hundred-weight—*d'un cent*) quart de quintal (kilo. 12·899) ; (astron., her., milit., vet.) quartier ; (of a city, of a shoe, of lamb—*de ville, de soulier, d'agneau*) quartier ; (region) endroit, parage, *m.*, contrée, *f.* ; (particular part —*partie*) endroit, côté ; (of the year, of schooling —*de l'année, d'école*) trimestre ; (of rent—*de loyer*) terme ; (mercy—*merci*) quartier ; (of a ship—*de vaisseau*) arrière, *m.*, hanche, *f.* Head—s ; *quartier général, m.sing.* False —; (vet.) *faux quartier.* There is nothing to hope from that —; *il n'y a rien à espérer de ce côté-là.* From all

—s ; *de tous côtés ; de toutes parts ; de tous les points.*

quarterage (-'édje), *n.*, pension trimestrielle, *f.*

quarter-bill, *n.*, (nav.) rôle d'équipage, *m.*

quarter-day, *n.*, terme, *m.*

quarter-deck, *n.*, gaillard d'arrière, *m.*

quarterer, *n.*, celui qui écartèle, bourreau, *m.*

quartering, *n.*, division par quarts, *f.* ; (milit.) logement militaire ; (punishment—*supplice*; her.) écartèlement, *m.*

quarterly, *adj.*, trimestriel ; de quart.

quarterly, *adv.*, par trimestre.

quarter-master (-mâs-), *n.*, (milit.) ☉ quartier-maître, officier de casernement ; (nav.) contremaître, *m.*

quartern (kwor-teurne), *n.*, quart de pinte (litre 0·142), *m.* A — loaf ; *un pain de quatre livres.*

quarter-pace, *n.*, (arch.) quartier tournant, repos, *m.*

quarter-sessions (-sèsh'eu'n'ze), *n.*, session trimestrielle, *f.*

quarter-staff (-stâf), *n.*, bâton ; bâton de garde forestier, *m.*

quartet (kwor-tète), *or* **quartetto** (-tèt'tô), *n.*, (mus.) quatuor, *m.*

quartile (kwor-), *n.*, aspect quartile, *m.* ; quadrature, *f.*

quarto (kwŏr-tô), *adj.*, in-quarto.

quarto, *n.*, in-quarto, *m.*

quartz (kwŏrtz), *n.*, quartz, *m.*

quartzy, *adj.*, quartzeux.

quash (kwôshe), *v.a.*, briser ; écraser ; réprimer ; (jur.) annuler, casser.

quash, *v.n.*, s'agiter avec bruit.

quasi (kwé-ça'ye), *adv.*, quasi.

quasi contract, *n.*, quasi-contrat, *m.*

quasimodo (kwa-ci-mô-dô), *n.*, Quasimodo, *f.*

quassation (kwŏ-cé-), *n.*, ébranlement, *m.* ; secousse, *f.*

quassia (kwosh'l-a), *n.*, quassia ; (tree—*arbre*), quassier, *m.*

quater-cousins (ké-tèr-keuz'z'n'z), *n.pl.*, cousins jusqu'au quatrième degré, *m.pl.*

quaternary (kwa-teur-), *n.*, quatre, *m.*

quaternary, *adj.*, quaternaire.

quaternion (kwa-teur-), *n.*, nombre quatre, *m.* ; compagnie de quatre, *f.*

quaternity (kwa-teur-), *n.*, nombre quatre, *m.*

quatrain (kwŏt'ra'n), *n.*, quatrain, *m.*

quaver (kwé-), *n.*, tremblement de la voix ; (mus.) croche, *f.*, trille, *m.*

quaver, *v.n.*, faire trembler sa voix ; trembler ; (mus.) triller, cadencer.

quaverer, *n.*, personne qui fait trembler sa voix, *f.*

quavering, *n.*, trille, *m.* ; cadence, *f.*

quaver-rest (-'rèste), *n.*, (mus.) demi-soupir, *m.*

quay (kî), *n.*, quai, *m.*

quay, *v.a.*, garnir de quais.

quean (kwi'n), *n.*, femme de mauvaise vie, coquine, guenipe, *f.*

queen (kwi'n), *n.*, reine ; (at cards, at draughts —*aux cartes, aux dames*) dame ; (at chess—*aux échecs*) dame, reine, *f.*

queen, *v.a.*, faire la reine ; jouer le rôle de la reine ; (at chess—*aux échecs*) aller à dame.

queenlike (-lïke), *or* **queenly**, *adv.*, de reine ; comme une reine ; semblable à une reine.

queer (kwir), *adj.*, bizarre, étrange, singulier ; original ; drôle de. A — fellow ; *un drôle de corps, un original.*

queer, *v.a.*, mettre à quia.

queerly, *adv.*, étrangement ; bizarrement ; originalement, singulièrement.

queerness, n., étrangeté, bizarrerie, originalité, singularité, f.

quell (kwèl), v.a., réprimer, étouffer, dompter, apaiser.

quell, v.n., s'éteindre.

queller, n., personne qui réprime, qui étouffe, f.; dompteur, m.

quench (kwĕ'n'she), v.a., éteindre; (to check —contenir) amortir; (to repress—réprimer) étouffer; (to still —calmer) apaiser; (one's thirst —la soif) étancher, éteindre.

quench, v.n., se refroidir.

quenchable (-'a-b'l), adj., qu'on peut éteindre, qu'on peut étancher.

quencher, n., personne qui éteint; chose qui éteint, f.

quenchless, adj., inextinguible.

quercitron (kwèr-), n., (bot.) quercitron, m.

querimonious (kwèr'i-mô-), adj., qui fait des plaintes.

querimoniously, adv., avec plainte.

querimoniousness, n., habitude de se plaindre, f.

querist (kwī-), n., personne qui fait une question, f.; questionneur, m.; questionneuse, f.

querulous (kweur-lou-), adj., plaintif.

querulousness, n., habitude de se plaindre, f.

query (kwī-), n., question, f.

query, v.a., faire une question, des questions.

query (kwī), v.n., s'informer de; questionner, interroger.

quest (kwèste), n., enquête, recherche; (request—demande) demande, sollicitation, f.

question (kwèst'-), n., question, interrogation, demande; (discussion) discussion; (subject of debate—sujet de discussion) question, proposition, f., sujet, m.; (in parliament—parlement) interpellation; (math.) question, f., problème, m.; (torture) question, torture, f. A pretty —! belle question; la belle demande! An unfair —; une question indiscrète; une indiscrétion, f. To ask a —; faire une question. To call in —; mettre en question; révoquer en doute. That is out of the —; cela est hors de question. Without a —; sans aucun doute. Beyond all —; hors de doute.

question, v.a., questionner, interroger; (to doubt—douter) mettre en question, mettre en doute, révoquer en doute, douter de.

question, v.n., interroger; questionner; faire des questions. I — whether it would not be better to; je ne sais pas s'il ne vaudrait pas mieux.

questionable (-'a-b'l), adj., contestable, douteux, incertain.

questionableness, n., caractère douteux, caractère incertain, m.

questionary, adj., en forme de question; qui contient des questions.

questioner, n., questionneur, m., questionneuse, f.; interrogateur, m., interrogatrice, f.

questionist, n., questionneur, m., questionneuse, f.

questionless, adj., sans doute.

questor (kwès-teur), n., questeur, m.

questorship, n., questure, f.

questuary (kwèst'iou-), adj., intéressé; avide de gain.

questuary, n., collecteur, m.

quib (kwibe), n., (ant.) sarcasme; mot piquant, m.

quibble (kwib'b'l), n., argutie, chicane, f., quolibet. m.

quibble, v.n., faire des arguties; faire des quolibets; ergoter; chicaner; turlupiner.

quibbler, n., faiseur de quolibets. m., faiseuse de quolibets, f.; ergoteur, m., ergoteuse, f.; chicaneur, m., chicaneuse, f.

quibbling. n., chicane, f.

quick (kwike), n., vif, m.; chair vive, f. The —; (pl.) les vivants.

quick, adj., (living—en vie) vif, vivant; (of flesh—de la chair) vif; (rapid) rapide, prompt; (brisk—actif) vif, ardent; (intelligent) intelligent; (of the pulse, the breath—du pouls, de l'haleine) fréquent. — ear; oreille fine. —sale; prompt débit. Be —! dépêchez-vous!

quick, adv., vite, promptement, rapidement.

quick, v.a., étamer, mettre le tain à.

quickbeam (-bîme), n., (bot.) sorbier, m.

quicken (kwik'k'n), v.a., animer, vivifier; accélérer, hâter.

quicken, v.n., prendre vie, s'animer.

quickener, n., être qui vivifie; principe vivifiant, m.; chose qui accélère, f.

quickening, adj., vivifiant, excitant; qui vivifie; qui ranime.

quicklime (-laïme), n., chaux vive, f.

quickly (kwik'-), adv., vite, rapidement, promptement; bientôt.

quickness, n., vitesse; promptitude; vivacité; (perception) facilité; (of the pulse, the breath—du pouls, de l'haleine) fréquence, f.

quicksand (-ça'n'de), n., sable mouvant, m.

quickset, n., plante vive, f. — hedge; haie vive, f.

quickset. v.a., entourer d'une haie vive.

quicksighted (-saït'-), adj., qui a la vue bonne; clairvoyant, pénétrant.

quick-sightedness, n., vue perçante; (fig.) sagacité, f.

quicksilver, n., vif-argent, mercure, m.

quicksilvered (-veurde), adj., étamé.

quicksilvering, n., étamage, m.

quickwitted, adj., qui a l'esprit vif.

quid (kwide), n., chique, f.

quiddany (kwid'-), n., marmelade de coings, f.

quiddative (kwid'-), adj., qui constitue l'essence d'une chose.

quiddity (kwid'-), n., quiddité, essence, f.

quiddle (kwid'd'l), v.a., niaiser, lambiner.

quiddler, n., lambin, m., lambine, f.

quiddling, n., niaiserie. f.

quidnunc (kwid-'neu'n'ke), n., curieux insatiable, m.

quid pro quo, n., (jur.) équivalent.

quiesce (kwaï-), v.n., (hebr. gram.) être quiescent.

quiescence, or **quiescency**, n., quiétude, f., repos, m.; (hebr. gram.) être quiescent (of letters —des lettres).

quiescent (kwaï-ès'-), adj., paisible, en repos, calme, tranquille; (hebr. gram.) quiescent.

quiescent, n., (hebr. gram.) lettre quiescente, f.

quiet (kwa-eute), n., tranquillité, f.; repos; calme, m.; paix; quiétude, f.

quiet, adj., tranquille, en repos, calme, paisible. To keep —; tenir tranquille; se tenir tranquille. To be —; être tranquille; rester tranquille; se taire.

quiet, v.a., tranquilliser, apaiser, calmer; adoucir; faire taire.

quieter, n., personne qui tranquillise, qui calme, qui apaise; chose qui tranquillise, f.; pacificateur, m.

quieting, n., action d'apaiser, f.

quieting, adj., calmant; tranquillisant.

quietism, n., (kwa-èt'-), n., quiétisme, m.

quietist, n., quiétiste, m.

quietly (kwa-eut'-), adv., tranquillement, paisiblement.

quietness (kwa-eut'-), n., tranquillité; paix, f.; calme; repos, m.

quietsome (-ceume), adj., calme, paisible, tranquille.

quietude (kwa-eut'ioude), n., quiétude, tranquillité, f.

qui 923 rab

quietus (kwa-i-), *n.*, repos, *m.*; tranquillité; (discharge—*quitus*) libération, *f.*
quill (kwile), *n.*, plume, *f.*; (of a porcupine—*de porc-épic*) piquant, *m.*
quill, *v.a.*, plisser; (mus.) emplumer; (needlework—*ouvrage à l'aiguille*) rucher.
quill-driver (-draïv'-), *n.*, gratte-papier, fesse-cahier, *m.*
quilling (kwil'-), *n.*, plissement, *m.*; (needlework—*ouvrage à l'aiguille*) ruche, *f.*
quilt (kwilte), *n.*, couvre-pied piqué, couvre-pied, *m.*
quilt, *v.a.*, piquer; (nav.) garnir.
quilting, *n.*, piqué, *m.*; (nav.) garniture, *f.*
quilt-maker (-mék'-), *n.*, faiseur de couvre-pieds piqués, *m.*
quinary, *or* **quinate** (kwaï-), *adj.*, quinaire.
quince (kwi'n'ce), *n.*, coing, *m.* —*tree*; *cognassier, m.*
quincuncial (kwi'n'keu'n'shal), *adj.*, en quinconce.
quincunx (kwi'n'keun'gn'kse), . *n.*, quinconce, *m.*
quindecagon (kwi'n'dèk'-), *n.*, quindécagone, *m.*
quindecemvir (kwi'n'dï-cè'm'veur), *n.*, quindécemvir, *m.*
quindecemvirate, *n.*, quindécemvirat, *m.*
quinia (kwi-), *or* **quinine** (kwi-nîne, *ou* -naïne), *n.*, quinine, *f.*
quinquagesima (kwi'n'kwa-djèss'-), *n.*, quinquagésime, *f.*
quinquangular (kwi'n'kwan'gn'gh'iou-), *adj.*, quinquangulaire.
quinquennial (kwi'n'kwè'n'-), *adj.*, quinquennal.
quinquereme (kwi'n'kwi-rîme), *n.*, quinquerème, *f.*
quinquina (kwi'n'kwaï-), *n.*, quinquina, *m.*
quinsy (kwi'n'zi), *n.*, esquinancie, *f.*
quint (kwi'n'te), *n.*, quinte, *f.*
quintain (kwi'n'téne), *n.*, quintaine, *f.*
quintal (kwi'n'-), *n.*, quintal, *m.*
quintessence (kwi'n'tèss'-), *n.*, quintessence, *f.*
quintetto (kwi'n'tèt'-), *n.*, (mus.) quintette, quintetto, *m.*
quintile (kwi'n'tile), *adj.*, (astron.) quintil.
quintillion (kwi'n'-), *n.*, nonillion, *m.*
quintuple (kwi'n'tiou-p'l), *adj.*, quintuple.
quintuple, *v.a.*, quintupler.
quip (kwipe), *n.*, mot piquant, lardon, *m.*
quip, *v.a.*, railler amèrement.
quire (kwaeur), *n.*, chœur, *m.*; (of paper—*de papier*) main, *f.*
quire, *v.n.*, chanter en chœur; faire chorus.
quirister (kwaeur'-), *n.*, (l.u.) choriste, *m.*
quirk (kweurke), *n.*, sarcasme; mot piquant, *m.*; (quibble—*détour*) argutie, *f.*, détour, subterfuge, *m.*; air irrégulier; (arch.) contour, *m.*
quirkish (kweurk'-), *adj.*, de détour; de subterfuge, d'argutie.
quit (kwite), *v.a.*, quitter; sortir de; abandonner; (to pay—*acquitter*) payer. Notice to —; *congé, m.* To — cost; *payer les frais.* To — scores; *être quitte à quitte.*
quit, *adj.*, quitte.
quitch-grass (kwitsh'grâce), *n.*, chiendent, *m.*
quitclaim (kwit'cléme), *v.a.*, (jur.) renoncer à ses droits à.
quite (kwaïte), *adv.*, tout à fait, entièrement, complètement.
quit-rent, *n.*, cens, *m.*
quits (kwitse), *adv.*, quitte. To be —; *être quitte; être quitte à quitte.*
quittance (kwit'-) *n.*, quittance; (reward—*récompense*) récompense, *f.*
quitter (kwit'-), *n.*, personne qui quitte , *f.*

quitter-bone (-bône), *n.*, (vet.) bleime, solbature, sole battue, *f.*
quiver (kwiv'-), *n.*, carquois, *m.*
quiver (kwiv'-), *v.n.*, trembler; frissonner; (of flesh—*de la chair*) palpiter.
quivered (kwiv'eurde), *adj.*, armé d'un carquois.
quivering, *n.*, tremblement, frissonnement, *m.*
quixotic (kwiks'-), *adj.*, de don Quichotte; extravagant.
quixotism (kwiks'ot'iz'm), *or* **quixotry**, *n.*, don quichotisme, *m.*; extravagance, *f.*
quiz (kwize), *n.*, énigme; question obscure, *f.*; (pers.) persifleur, railleur, *m.*, railleuse, *f.*
quiz, *v.a.*, railler, persifler; (to look at—*regarder*) lorgner.
quizzical, *adj.*, railleur, qui aime le persiflage; de persiflage.
quizzing, *n.*, raillerie, *f.*, persiflage, *m.*; lorgnerie, *f.*
quizzing-glass (-glâce), *n.*, lorgnon, *m.*
quodlibet (kwod-li-), *n.*, subtilité, raison subtile, *f.*
quoif (kwaïfe), *n.*, coiffe, *f.*
quoif, *v.a.*, coiffer.
quoiffure (kwaïf'floure), *n.*, coiffure, *f.*
quoin (kwaïne), *n.*, coin, *m.*; encoignure, encognure; (arch.) arête, *f*; (print.) coin, *m.*
quoin-post (-pôste), *n.*, poteau cornier, *m.*
quoit (kwaïte), *n.*, palet; (antiq.) disque, *m.*
quoit, *v.n.*, jouer au palet;
quondam (kwo'n-), *adj.*, ci-devant, d'autrefois, de jadis.
quorum (kwô-), *n.*, nombre suffisant, nombre compétent, *m.*; (of justices—*de juges*) commission de juges de paix, *f.*
quota (kwô-), *n.*, quote-part; quotité, *f.*; contingent, *m.*
quotation (kwo-té-), *n.*, citation; (com.) cote, *f.*; (print.) cadrat creux, *m.*
quote (kwôte), *v.a.*, citer, alléguer; (com.) coter.
quoter (kwôt'-), *n.*, citateur, *m.*
quoth (kwôth), *v.n.*, dire.
quotidian (kwô-), *n.*, fièvre quotidienne; (daily thing—*de tous les jours*) chose journalière, *f.*
quotidian (kwô-), *adj.*, quotidien.
quotient (kwô-shè'n'te), *n.*, quotient, *m.*

R

r, dix-huitième lettre de l'alphabet, r, *m.*, *f.*
rabate, *v.n.*, (a hawk—*faucon*) (ant.) ramener.
rabbet, *n.*, (arch.) saillie; rainure, *f.*; chanfrein, *m.*
rabbet, *v.a.*, (arch.) faire une saillie dans; faire une rainure à; chanfreiner.
rabbet-plane, *n.*, guillaume, *m.*
rabbi (rab-bi, *ou* -ba'ye), *or* **rabbin** (-bine), *n.*, rabbin, *m.*
rabbinic, *n.*, dialecte rabbinique, *m.*
rabbinical, *adj.*, rabbinique.
rabbinism (-'iz'm), *n.*, rabbinisme, *m.*
rabbinist, *n.*, rabbiniste, *m.*
rabbit, *n.*, lapin, *m.* Young — ; *lapereau, m.* —'s nest; *rabouillère, f.* Welsh — ; *rôtie au fromage, f.*
rabble (rab'b'l), *n.*, populace, canaille; foule tumultueuse, *f.*
rabdology (-o-djl), *n.*, rabdologie, *f.*
rabdomancy, *n.*, rabdomancie, *f.*
rabid, *adj.*, (pers.) forcené, furieux; (of the appetite—*de l'appétit*) canin, dévorant; (of

animals—*des animaux*) enragé, qui a la rage, hydrophobe.

rabidness, *n.*, rage ; fureur, *f.*

rabies (rab'i-èss), *n.*, (med.) rage, hydrophobie, *f.*

.**race**, *n.*, (breed—*génération*) race ; (root—*racine*) racine, *f.* ; (of wine—*du vin*) goût de terroir, goût âpre *m.* ; (running contest—*course*) course ; (course) course, carrière, *f.* ; (tide—*marée*) ras, raz, *m.* Horse-—; *course de chevaux.*

race, *v.n.*, courir, courir de toute sa force, à toutes jambes, à bride abattue.

race-course (-côrse), *n.*, terrain de course, hippodrome, *m.* ; arène, *f.*

race-horse, *n.*, cheval de course, *m.*

racemation (rass'i-mé-), *n.*, grappe ; culture du raisin, *f.*

raceme (-cîme), *n.*, (bot.) grappe, *f.*

racer (ré-), *n.*, coureur ; cheval de course, *m.*

races (ré-cize), *n.pl.*, courses de chevaux, *f.pl.*

raciness (ré-), *n.*, caractère distinctif ; (of wine—*du vin*) goût de terroir, fumet, bouquet, *m.*

racing (ré-), *adj.*, qui court ; de course.

rack, *n.*, (of a stable—*d'étable*) râtelier ; (instrument for stretching—*pour étendre*) chevalet, *m.* ; (instrument of torture) roue, *f.* ; (horl.) rochet ; (print.) rayon, *m.* ; (tech.) crémaillère ; (torture) torture, *f.* ; (for plates, bottles, &c.—*d'assiettes, de bouteilles, &c.*) dressoir, râtelier ; (of mutton, veal—*de mouton, de veau*) bout saigneux ; (liquor—*liqueur*) rack, arack, *m.* To put to the — ; *mettre à sa torture, à la question.*

rack, *v.a.*, mettre à la roue ; (to torment—*tourmenter*) mettre à la torture, torturer, tourmenter ; (to harass by exaction—*pressurer*) commettre des exactions sur, pressurer ; (nav.) aiguilleter ; (liquor—*liqueur*) soutirer. To — off ; *soutirer.* To — one's brains ; *se creuser la cervelle.*

rack, *v.n.*, commettre des exactions.

racker, *n.*, personne qui torture, *f.*

racket, *n.*, fracas, tapage, tintamarre, *m.*, crierie, *f.* ; caquet, *m.* ; (at tennis—*à la paume*) raquette, *f.*, battoir, *m.* ; (game—*jeu*) paume, *f.*

racket, *v.a.*, relancer à coups de raquette.

racket, *v.n.*, faire un tintamarre ; faire du tapage.—*ing* noise ; *tapage, m.*

rackety (rak'èt'), *adj.*, de tapage, de tintamarre.

racking, *adj.*, de torture ; (flying—*de fuite*) qui fuit.

racking, *n.*, torture, *f.* ; (tech.) étendage ; (of liquors—*des liqueurs*) soutirage, *m.*

racking-pace, *n.*, (man.) traquenard, *m.*

rack-rent, *n.*, loyer excessif. égal au produit annuel de l'immeuble, *m.*

rack-rented, *adj.*, qui paye un loyer excessif, égal au produit annuel de l'immeuble.

rack-renter, *n.*, personne qui paye un loyer excessif, égal au produit annuel de l'immeuble *f.*

racy (ré-), *adj.*, (of wine—*du vin*) qui a un goût de terroir, qui a du bouquet ; (fig.) vif, attrayant, piquant, original (of the style, of the language—*du style, du langage*).

.**raddle** (rad'd'l), *v.a.*, tresser.

radial (ré-), *adj.*, radial.

radiance or **radiancy** (ré-), *n.*, rayonnement ; éclat, *m.*

radiant (ré-), *adj.*, rayonnant ; radieux ; éclatant ; (bot.) radiant, radié ; (her.) radié.

radiant (ré-), *n.*, point lumineux ; point rayonnant, *m.*

radiantly, *adv.*, en rayonnant ; d'une manière radieuse.

radiary (ré-), *n.*, (zool.) radié, *m.*

radiate (ré-), *v.n.*, rayonner.

radiate, *adj.*, (bot.) radié.

radiating (ré-diét'-), *adj.*, rayonnant ; radieux.

radiation (ré-di-é-), *n.*, rayonnement, *m.*

radical, *adj.*, radical ; fondamental.

radical, *n.*, radical ; primitif, *m.*

radicalism (-iz'm), *n.*, radicalisme, *m.*

radically, *adv.*, radicalement ; essentiellement.

radicant, *adj.*, radicant.

radicate, *v.a.*, enraciner.

radication (rad'i-ké-), *n.*, radication, *f.*

radicle (rad'i-k'l), *or* **radicule** (-kioule), *n.*, (bot.) radicule, *f.*

radish, *n.*, radis, *m.* ; rave, *f.* Turnip-—; *petite rave.* Horse-— ; *raifort, m.*

radius (ré-), *n.*, rayon ; rais ; (anat.) radius, *m.*

radix (ré-), *n.* (radices), racine ; (logarithms) base, *f.*

raff, *n.*, (mob—*canaille*) populace, *f.* ; (jumble —*pêle-mêle*) fatras, *m.*

raffle (raf'f'l), *n.*, loterie, *f.*

raffle, *v.n.*, mettre en loterie.

raffle, *v.n.*, faire une loterie.

raffler, *n.*, personne qui met à la loterie, *f.*

raft (râfte), *n.*, radeau, *m.*

rafter, *n.*, poutre, *f.* ; chevron, *m.*

raftered (râf-teurde), *adj.*, à poutres ; à chevrons.

rafting (râft'-), *n.*, flottage en train, *m.*

raftsman (râfts'-), *n.*, flotteur, *m.*

rag, *n.*, (piece of cloth torn off—*morceau déchiré d'une étoffe*) chiffon ; (tatter—*guenille*) haillon, lambeau, *m.*, guenille, loque, *f.* In —s ; *en haillons, en loques, en guenilles, déguenillé.*

ragamuffin (-menf'fine), *n.*, gueux, maroufle, *m.*

rag-bolt (-bôlte), *n.*, cheville à fiche, *f.*

rage (rédje), *n.*, (anger—*colère*) fureur, rage, *f.*, emportement, *m.* ; (violent desire) passion, furie, rage, manie ; (of things—*des choses*) fureur, force, violence, *f.* To fly, to get into a — ; *se mettre en colère, entrer en colère ; s'emporter.* To put into a — ; *mettre en colère.* To be all the — ; *faire fureur.*

rage, *v.n.*, (pers.) être furieux, être en fureur, se courroucer, être courroucé, s'emporter ; (of things—*des choses*) se courroucer, être en fureur ; (to ravage—*ravager*) faire des ravages, sévir.

rageful (-foule), *adj.*, furieux, violent.

rag-gatherer (-gath'-), *n.*, chiffonnier, *m.*

ragged (rag-ghède), *adj.*, (pers.) en haillons, en guenilles, déguenillé ; (of things—*des choses*) en lambeaux, en loques, déchiré.

raggedly (-ghèd'-), *adv.*, en lambeaux, en guenilles.

raggedness (-ghèd'-), *n.*, état de ce qui est en haillons, *m.* ; guenilles, *f.pl.*, lambeaux, *m.pl.* ; (roughness—*inégalité*) inégalité, rudesse, *f.*

raging (ré'dji'-), *adj.*, courroucé, furieux. — fever ; *fièvre ardente, f.*

raging, *n.*, fureur ; violence, *f.*

ragingly, *adv.*, avec fureur ; furieusement.

ragman, *n.*, marchand de chiffons ; chiffonnier, *m.*

ragout (râ-gou), *n.*, ragoût, *m.*

ragstone (-stône), *n.*, tuf, *m.*

rag-wheel (-hwile), *n.*, (tech.) hérisson, *m.*

ragwort (-weurte), *n.*, (bot.) jacobée, herbe de Saint-Jacques, *f.*

rail (réle), *n.*, (bar of wood, of metal—*barre de bois, de métal*) barre, *f.*, barreau, *m.* ; (of a staircase—*d'escalier*) rampe ; (carp.) traverse, *f.* ; (balustrade) garde-fou, garde-corps, *m.*, grille, barrière ; (nav.) lisse, *f.* ; (railways) rail, *m.* Hand-—; *lisse, f.* —s ; *garde-fou, garde-corps, m., grille, f.* To run off the —s ; *dérailler ; sortir de la voie.*

rail (réle), *v.a.* garnir d'un garde-fou ; garnir d'une grille, griller. To — in ; *fermer avec une grille ; griller.* To — round ; *entourer d'une grille ; entourer d'un garde-fou.*

rail (réle), *v.n.*, dire des injures; injurier, outrager.

railed (rél'de), *adj.*, à voie. Double---; *à double voie.*

railer (rél'-), *n.*, personne qui injurie, qui outrage. *f.*; frondeur, *m.*

railing (rél'-), *n.*, injures, *f.pl.*; outrage, *m.*

railing, *adj.*, injurieux; outrageant.

railing, *n.*, grille; *f.*, garde-fou, garde-corps. *m.*

railingly, *adv.*, injurieusement, outrageusement.

raillery (rél'lèr'i), *n.*, raillerie, *f.*

railroad (rél-rôde), *or* **railway** (rél'wè), *n.*, chemin de fer, *m.*; voie de fer, voie ferrée, *f.*

raiment (ré-), *n.*, vêtement, *m.*; vêtements, *m.pl.*

rain (ré'ne), *n.*, pluie, *f.* Pelting —; *pluie battante.* To pour with —; *pleuvoir à verse.*

rain (ré'ne), *v.n.*, pleuvoir; tomber de l'eau; (fig.) tomber en pluie, *f.* It —s; *il pleut; il tombe de l'eau.*

rain. *v.a.*, faire pleuvoir; faire tomber.

rainbow (-bô), *n.*, arc-en-ciel, *m.*

rain-gauge (-ghédje), *n.*, udomètre, *m.*

raininess, *n.*, temps pluvieux, *m.*

rain-water (-wŏ-), *n.*, eau de pluie, eau pluviale, *f.*

rainy (ré-), *adj.*, pluvieux, de pluie. It looks —; *le temps est à la pluie.*

raise (réza). *v.a.*, lever; élever; hausser; soulever; (to build—*bâtir*) élever, bâtir, fonder; (to produce—*produire*) produire, faire naître; (to enlarge—*agrandir*) grandir, augmenter, accroître; (to excite—*exciter*) soulever, exciter; (a cry—*un cri*) pousser; (to propagate—*propager*) semer, faire courir; (the dead—*les morts*) ressusciter; (troops, taxes, a siege—*troupes, impôts, siège*) lever; (dough—*pâte*) faire lever; (evil spirits—*esprits malins*) évoquer; (courage) faire reprendre à, relever; (prices—*prix*) hausser; (money—*argent*) trouver; (live stock—*bétail*) élever; (hopes—*espérances*) donner, redonner. To— up; *lever; élever; soulever; hausser.*

raiser (réz'-), *n.*, personne qui lève, qui élève, qui soulève, qui hausse, *f.*; auteur; fondateur, *m.*, fondatrice, *f.*; (agri.) cultivateur; (of live stock—*de bétail*) éleveur, *m.*; chose qui lève, qui élève, qui soulève, qui hausse, *f.*

raisin (ré-z'n), *n.*, raisin sec; raisin, *m.*

raising (réz'-), *n.*, action de lever, d'élever, de hausser, de soulever; (foundation) fondation; production, *f.*; agrandissement, *m.*, augmentation, *f.*, accroissement, *m.*; excitation; (of taxes, of troops—*d'impôts, de troupes*) levée; (of spirits —*d'esprits*) évocation, *f.*; (of live stock—*de bétail*) élevage, *m.*, élève, *f.*; (of plants, &c.—*de plantes, &c.*) culture, *f.*

raising-piece (-pice), *n.*, (carp.) sablière, *f.*

raja, *or* **rajah** (râ-dja, *ou* ré-djâ), *n.*, raja, rajah, *m.*

rake, *n.*, râteau, *m.*; (nav.) quête, *f.*; (libertine) libertin, abandonné, *m.*

rake, *v.a.*, (to gather with a rake—*assembler avec un râteau*) râteler; (to scrape—*gratter*) ratisser, racler;(to collect—*ramasser*) rassembler, ramasser; (to search—*chercher*) fouiller dans; (milit.) enfiler. To— off; *enlever au râteau.* To — out; *dégager;*(the fire—*le feu*) *éteindre.* To— together; *ramasser.* To— up; *ramasser; ramasser au râteau.* To— up the fire; *couvrir le feu de cendre.*

rake, *v.a.*, (to scrape—*racler*) gratter; (to search—*chercher*) fouiller; (to lead a dissolute life—*se livrer au libertinage*) libertiner.

rakehell, *n.*, débauché, libertin, *m.*

raker, *n.*, râteleur, *m.*

rakeshame, *n.*, impudent, éhonté, *m.*

raking (rék'-), *n.*, ratissage; râtelage, *m.*;

(quantity raked—*quantité*) râtelée, *f.*; (ground raked—*terrain*) terrain râtelé, *m.*

raking, *adj.*, (milit.) d'enfilade.

rakish (rék'-), *adj.*, dissolu, débauché, libertin.

rakishly, *adv.*, en libertin.

rakishness, *n.*, débauche, *f.*; libertinage, *m.*

rally, *v.a.*, rallier, assembler; (to banter—*railler*) railler (pers.).

rally. *v.n.*, se rallier, se rassembler; (to banter—*railler*) railler, railler de, se railler.

rally, *n.*, (milit.) ralliement, *m.*; (bantering —*raillerie*) raillerie, *f.*

rallying, *n.*, ralliement, *m.*; (bantering—*raillerie*) raillerie, *f.*

ram, *n.*, (mam., astron.) bélier, *m.* Battering —; *bélier, m.*

ram, *v.a.*, enfoncer; battre à la hie, damer, tasser; (to stuff—*farcir*) fourrer; (artil.)bourrer

ramadan, *n.*, ramadan, ramazan, *m.*

ramage (-'adje), *n.*, (ant.) ramage, *m.*

ramble (ra'm'b'l), *n.*, course, excursion, *f.*

ramble, *v.n.*, courir çà et là; errer; rôder; (fig.) divaguer. To — about; *errer par, errer partout, courir de tous côtés.*

rambler, *n.*, personne qui court çà et là, qui erre, *f.*; rôdeur; promeneur, *m.*, promeneuse, *f.*

rambling, *n.*, courses, excursions, promenades, *f.pl.*; (fig.) divagations, *f.pl.*

rambling, *adj.*, qui erre çà et là; errant, vagabond; plein de divagations; vague.

ramification (-fi-ké-), *n.*, ramification, *f.*

ramify (-fa'ye), *v.n.*, se ramifier.

ramify, *v.a.*, diviser en ramifications.

rammer, *n.*, personne qui enfonce, qui bat à la hie, *f.*; (artil.) refouloir; (pile-driver—*de sonnette*) mouton, *m.*; (of a gun—*de fusil*)baguette; (for driving stones, &c.—*pour enfoncer les pavés, &c.*) hie, demoiselle, *f.*

rammish, *adj.*, rance.

rammishness, *n.*, rancidité, *f.*

ramous, *adj.*, rameux, branchu.

ramp, *v.n.*, grimper; (to leap—*sauter*) sauter, folâtrer.

ramp, *n.*, saut, bond, élan, *m.*; (slope—*déclivité*) rampe, *f.*

rampancy, *n.*, exubérance; influence, *f.*; pouvoir, empire, *m.*

rampant, *adj.*, dominant, régnant; prédominant; exubérant; (her.) rampant.

rampart, *n.*, rempart, *m.*

rampion, *n.*, (bot.) raiponce, *f.*

ramrod, *n.*, baguette, *f.*; (of a cannon—*de canon*) refouloir, *m.*

rance. *v.a.*, étayer, soutenir.

rancescent (-cès-), *adj.*, qui devient rance.

rancid, *adj.*, rance.

rancidity, *or* **rancidness**, *n.*, rancissure, rancidité, *f.*

rancorous (ran'gn'-), *adj.*, rancunier.

rancorously, *adv.*, avec rancune, par rancune.

rancour (ran'gn'keur), *n.*, rancune; (corruption) corruption, *f.*

random (-deume), *n.*, aventure, *f.*, hasard, *m.* At —; *au hasard; à l'aventure.* To speak at —; *parler à tort et à travers.*

random (-deume), *adj.*, au hasard; fait au hasard; (artil.) à toute volée, tiré à toute volée, perdu.

random-shot, *n.*, coup perdu; coup à toute volée, *m.*

range (ré'n'dje), *n.*, (row—*rang*) rangée, *f.*, rang, *m.*; (class) classe, *f.*, ordre, *m.*; (excursion) excursion, course; (extent—*étendue*) étendue, portée, *f.*; essor, *f.*; (space) espace, *m.*; (reach—*portée*) portée, *f.*; (of a ladder—*d'échelon*) échelon, *m.*; (kitchen grate—*fourneaux de cuisine*) grille de cuisine, *f.*, fourneaux, *m.pl.*; (sieve—*bluteau*) sas à farine, bluteau, m. ; (of mountains—*de montagnes*) chaîne, *f.*

range (ré'n'dje), *v.a.*, (arch., print.) aligner; (nav.) ranger ; (to rove over—*errer parmi*) parcourir ; (to pass over—*passer*) franchir ; (to arrange—*arranger*) arranger, ranger.

range, *v.n.*, errer; (to lie—*se trouver*) être situé ; (nav.) ranger la côte ; (to vary—*varier*) varier.

ranger (ré'n'dj'-), *n.*, officier forestier ; (dog —*chien*) chien courant, *m.*

rangership, *n.*, fonctions d'officier forestier, *f.pl.*

ranging (ré'n'dj'-), *n.*, action de ranger ; action de franchir, *f.* ; arrangement; (arch., print.) alignement, *m.*

rank, *n.*, (row, class, dignity—*rang, classe, dignité,* milit.) rang, *m.*   To rise from the —s ; *s'élever, sortir des grades inférieurs* ; *être nommé officier après avoir été simple soldat.* To close the —s; *serrer les rangs.*

rank, *adj.*, (rank—*âcre*) rance ; (strong—*fort*) fort; (gross—*grossier*) grossier, rude ; (excessive) excessif, extrême ; (fertile) fertile, fécond ; (of vigorous growth—*de végétation vigoureuse*) vigoureux, fort.

rank, *v.a.*, ranger.

rank, *v.n.*, se ranger, être rangé ; prendre rang, occuper un rang.

rankish, *adj.*, un peu rance.

rankle (ran'gu'k'l), *v.n.*, s'envenimer, s'enflammer.

rankly, *adv.*, avec rancidité ; fortement ; grossièrement, rudement ; excessivement, extrêmement ; fertilement, avec fécondité ; vigoureusement.

rankness, *n.*, rancissure, rancidité, *f.* ; goût fort, *m.* ; abondance, *f.* ; excès, *m.*

ransack, *v.a.*, saccager ; piller ; fouiller.

ransacking, *n.*, saccagement, pillage, *m.*

ransom (-ceume), *n.*, rançon, *f.* ; rachat, *m.*

ransom (-ceume), *v.a.*, rançonner ; racheter.

ransomer, *n.*, personne qui rachète, qui délivre, *f.*

ransomless, *adj.*, sans rançon.

rant, *n.*, déclamation extravagante, *f.* ; paroles ampoulées, *f.pl.* ; phébus, galimatias, *m.*

rant, *v.n.*, déclamer avec extravagance ; extravaguer ; tempêter.

ranter, *n.*, déclamateur extravagant, *m.*

ranting, *adj.*, d'une déclamation extravagante.

ranula (ra'n'iou-), *n.*, (med.) ranule, grenouillette, *f.*

ranunculus (ra-neu'n'klou-), *n.*, (bot.) renoncule, *f.*

rap, *n.*, tape, *f.* ; coup sec, *m.*

rap, *v.n.*, frapper. To — out; *lâcher.*

rap, *v.a.*, transporter ; charmer ; (to snatch away—*enlever*) enlever, arracher.

rapacious (ra-pé-sheuse), *adj.*, rapace.

rapaciously, *adv.*, avec rapacité.

rapaciousness, or **rapacity,** *n.*, rapacité, *f.*

rape, *n.*, rapt, enlèvement ; (jur.) viol; *m.* ; (bot.) navette, *f.* ; colza, *m.*

rape-cake, *n.*, tourteau de colza, *m.*

rape-oil, *n.*, huile de colza, *f.*

rapid, *n.* (rapids) rapide, *m.*

rapid, *adj.*, rapide.

rapidity, *n.*, rapidité, *f.*

rapidly, *adv.*, rapidement.

rapidness, *n.*, rapidité, *f.*

rapier (ré-pi-ère), *n.*, rapière, *f.*

rapine, *n.*, rapine, *f.*

rappee (-pi), *n.*, tabac râpé ; râpé, *m.*

rapper, *n.*, personne qui frappe, *f.* ; (thing —*chose*) marteau, *m.*

rapt, *past part.*, ravi, transporté, extasié.

rapter, or **raptor,** *n.*, ravisseur, *m.*

raptorial, or **raptorious,** *adj.*, de proie.

rapture (rapt'ieur), *n.*, ravissement, transport ; enthousiasme, *m.* ; extase, *f.*

raptured (rapt'ieurde), *adj.*, ravi, transporté, extasié.

rapturous (rapt'ieur'-), *adj.*, ravissant.

rapturously, *adv.*, avec transport ; avec enthousiasme.

rare, *adj.*, rare ; (thinly scattered—*pas serré*) clairsemé ; (excellent) beau ; (phys.) rare, raréfié ; (nearly raw—*pas très cuit*) peu cuit, saignant.

raree-show (ré-ri-shô), or **rare-show,** *n.*, spectacle ambulant, *m.* ; curiosité, *f.*

rarefaction (rar'i-fak-), *n.*, raréfaction, *f.*

rarefiable (rar-i-faï-a-b'l), *adj.*, qui peut se raréfier.

rarefy (rar'i-fa'ye), *v.a.*, raréfier.

rarefy, *v.n.*, se raréfier.

rarefying, *adj.*, raréfiant, raréfactif.

rarely (rér'-), *adv.*, rarement.

rareness, or **rarity** (rér'-), *n.*, rareté ; (phys.) raréfaction, *f.*

rascal (râs'-), *n.*, coquin, fripon, polisson, *m.* ; (lean—*maigre*) maigre ; (mean —*bas*) misérable.

rascality, *n.*, friponnerie ; (populace) canaille, *f.*

rascallion (-cal'ieune), *n.*, malotru, drôle, faquin, polisson, *m.* ; canaille, *f.*

rascally (râs-), *adj.*, de coquin, de fripon ; (worthless—*vil*) misérable.

rase (réze, *ou* réce), *v.a.*, (to graze—*effleurer*) raser, friser, effleurer ; (to erase—*effacer*) rayer, effacer ; (to overthrow—*renverser*) raser.

rash, *n.*, (med.) éruption, *f.*

rash, *adj.*, téméraire ; irréfléchi, inconsidéré.

rash, *v.a.*, tailler en pièces ; couper en morceaux, en tranches.

rasher, *n.*, tranche, barde, *f.* — of bacon ; *tranche de lard, f.*

rashly, *adv.*, témérairement ; inconsidérément.

rashness, *n.*, témérité ; précipitation ; nature irréfléchie, *f.*

rasp (râspe), *n.*, (tool—*outil*) râpe ; (surg.) rugine, *f.*

rasp, *v.a.*, râper ; (bread—*pain*) chapeler ; (surg.) ruginer.

raspatory, *n.*, rugine, ⊙raspatoire, *f.*

raspberry, *n.*, framboise, *f.*

raspberry-bush (-boushe), *n.*, framboisier, *m.*

rasping, *n.*, râpage, *m.* —s ; *râpure, f.sing.* ; (of bread—*de pain*) chapelure, *f.sing.*

rasure, *n.*, effaçure, rature, *f.*

rat, *n.*, rat ; (pers.) transfuge, *m.*   To smell a — ; *se douter de quelque chose.*

rat, *v.n.*, tourner casaque.

ratable (ré-ta-b'l), *adj.*, qui peut être évalué ; (liable to taxation—*sujet à l'impôt*) imposable.

ratably (ré-ta-), *adv.*, à proportion.

ratafia, *n.*, ratafia, *m.*

ratan, *n.*, rotin, rotang, *m.*

rat-catcher, *n.*, preneur de rats, *m.*

ratch, *n.*, (horl.) rochet, *m.*

ratchet, *n.*, (horl.) guide-chaîne, *m.* ; (tech.) dent d'engrenage, *f.* ; (of a lock—*de serrure*) rochet, *m.*

ratchet-engine (è'n'djine), *n.*, machine à tailler les dents d'engrenage, *f.*

ratchet-wheel (-hwîle), *n.*, roue d'engrenage, roue à dents ; (horl.) roue d'échappement, roue à rochet, *f.*

rate, *n.*, (standard—*taux*) prix, taux ; (degree of value—*degré de valeur*) taux, cours ; (price—*prix*) prix ; (degree—*degré*) degré, rang ordre, *m.* ; (allowance—*allocation*) quantité ; (degree of speed—*degré de vitesse*) vitesse, *f.* ;

(pace—vitesse) train, m., vitesse, f.; (nav.) rang, m.; (tax—impôt) contribution, f., impôt, m. First— ; de première force ; (of rank—de rang) de premier ordre ; (of quality—de qualité) de première qualité. At any — ; coûte que coûte ; à quelque prix que ce soit ; à tout événement. At the — of ; à... eux de ; à raison de ; (of speed—de vitesse) a la vitesse de. At the — you are going at, you will soon be ruined ; au train dont vous allez, vous vous ruinerez bientôt.

rate, v.a., évaluer ; tarifer ; estimer ; apprécier ; (to place in a class, as a ship—classer) classer, donner un rang à, donner un ordre à ; (to assess—asseoir) imposer, taxer ; (to chide—réprimander) gronder vertement, réprimander, faire une mercuriale à.

rate, v.n., faire une estimation. To — as ; être classé comme ; être estimé à ; avoir le rang de.

rate-book (-bouke),n.,registre pour l'assiette et la perception d'un impôt, m.

rate-payer (-pé-eur), n., contribuable, m.

rater, n., estimateur, m.

rath (râth), adj., (ant.) hâtif, précoce.

rather (râth-), adv., plutôt ; mieux ; un peu ; quelque peu ; assez. I would — ; j'aimerais mieux, je voudrais plutôt. — ill ; un peu malade. Or — ; ou plutôt : ou pour mieux dire. Anything — than ; rien moins que. — pretty ; assez joli.

ratification (-fi-ké-), n., ratification, f.

ratifier (-faï'-), n., personne qui ratifie ; chose qui ratifie, f.

ratify (-fa'ye), v.a., ratifier.

rating (rét'-), n., estimation ; (chiding—réprimande) gronderie, f.

ratio (ré-shi-ô), n., proportion, raison, f.; rapport, m. In the — of ; dans le rapport de, à raison de.

ratiocination (rash'i-oss'i-né-), n., raisonnement, m.

ration (ré-), n., ration, f.

rational (rash'eu'n'-), adj., (endowed with reason—raisonnable) doué de raison, raisonnable ; (agreeable to reason, judicious—judicieux) raisonnable ; (arith., astron.) rationnel.

rational (rash'eu'n'-), n., être raisonnable, être doué de raison, m.

rationale (rash'i-o-né-li), n., analyse raisonnée, f.

rationalism (rash'eu'n-al-iz'm), n., rationalisme, m.

rationalist, n., rationaliste, m.

rationality, n., faculté de raisonner, f.; raisonnement, m. ; raison, justesse ; (philos.) rationalité, f.

rationally, adv., raisonnablement ; (philos.) rationnellement.

rationalness, n., raison, justesse, f.

rat's-bane, n., mort aux rats, f.

rat-tail, or **rat's-tail** (-téle), n., (vet.) queue-de-rat, f.

rattan, n., rotin, rotang, m.

ratteen (rat'tîne), n., ratine, f.

rattery, n., ratière, f.

rattinet, n., petite ratine, f.

rattle (rat't'l), v.a., faire résonner, faire retentir ; (to stun with noise—étourdir) remplir de bruit, étourdir ; (to scold—réprimander) gronder vertement.

rattle, v.n., faire du bruit ; résonner, retentir ; (to speak—parler) bavarder. To — on ; aller toujours. To — over ; résonner sur.

rattle (rat't'l), n.. (noise—son) bruit : (talk—parler) bavardage ; (med.) râle, m. ; (toy—jouet) hochet, m. ; (for a policeman—d'agent de police) crécelle, f. Death— : râle de la mort. m.

rattle-brained (-bré'n'de), or **rattle-headed** (-hèd'ède), adj., étourdi.

rattles (rat't'l'ze), v.pl., (med.)croup, m.sing.

rattle-snake, n., serpent à sonnettes ; crotale, m.

rattle-traps, n., effets, m.pl. ; affaires, choses, f.pl.

rattling, adj., d'un bruit vif et rapide.

rattling, n., bruit, bruissement, m.

rat-trap, n., ratière, f.

raucity, n., son rauque, m. ; (of the voice—de la voix) raucité, rudesse, âpreté, f.

ravage (rav'adje), n., ravage, m.

ravage, v.a., ravager.

ravager, n., ravageur ; dévastateur, m.

rave, v.n., délirer, avoir le délire, être en délire ; extravaguer.

ravel, v.a., entortiller ; (fig.) embrouiller. To — out ; effiler, démêler, débrouiller.

ravel (rav-v'l), v.n., s'embrouiller ; s'entortiller ; s'effiler.

ravelin (rav'line), n., (fort.) ravelin, m., demi-lune, f.

ravellings (rav'èl'lign'z),n.pl., effilures, f.pl.

raven (ré-v'n), n., (orni.) corbeau, m. ; (prey—proie) proie ; (plunder—rapine) rapine, f.

raven (rév-v'n), v.a., manger avec voracité, dévorer ; obtenir par violence.

raven, v.n., être avide de proie ; voler, piller.

ravener, n., dévorateur, vorace ; (orni.) oiseau de proie, m.

ravening, adj., vorace.

ravening, n., voracité, f.

ravenous (rav'v'n'-), adj., vorace, dévorant ; carnassier.

ravenously, adv., avec voracité.

ravenousness, n., voracité, rapacité, f.

raver (rév'-), n., énergumène, m.

ravin (rav'v'n), n., proie ; rapacité, f.

ravine (ra-vîne), n., ravin, m. ; ravine, f.

raving (rév'-), adj., furieux, frénétique ; fou. — mad ; fou enragé ; fou à lier ; fou furieux.

raving, n., délire, m. ; frénésie, f.

ravingly, adv., furieusement ; avec frénésie ; en frénétique.

ravish (rav'-), v.a., ravir ; enlever ; (to delight—enchanter) ravir, transporter ; (to violate—commettre un viol) violer.

ravisher, n., ravisseur, m. ; personne qui ravit, qui transporte, f.

ravishing, adj., ravissant.

ravishing, n., ravissement, m.

ravishingly, adv., à ravir ; d'une manière ravissante.

ravishment, n., ravissement ; enlèvement ; viol, m.

raw (rô), adj., (not cooked—non cuit) cru ; (bare—écorché) vif, ulcéré ; (unripe—non mûr) peu mûr ; (inexperienced—novice) sans expérience, inexpérimenté, novice, neuf ; (untried—non essayé) nouveau, non essayé ; (of liquors—des boissons) pur, sans eau ; (of the weather—du temps) froid et humide ; (of silk—soie) grège ; (of hides—des peaux) brut ; (of sugar, of materials—de sucre, &c.) brut.

rawbone (-bône), or **rawboned** (-bô'n'de), adj., qui n'a que la peau et les os ; maigre.

rawhead (-hède), n., loup-garou, m.

rawly, adv., sans expérience.

rawness, n., crudité, f. ; (of the weather—du temps) froid et humidité ; (soreness—ulcération) état ulcéré, m. ; (inexperience) inexpérience, ignorance, f.

ray (rè), n., rayon ; (fig.) éclat, rayon, m. ; (ich.) raie, f.

ray, v.a., rayer.

rayless, adj., sans rayon ; sans lumière.

raze (réze), v.a., raser, abattre ; déraciner.

razee (ra-zî), n., (nav.) vaisseau rasé, m.

razor (ré-zor), n., rasoir, m. ; (of a boar—du sanglier) défense, f.

razor-bill (ré-), n., (orni.) pingouin commun, m.

razor-fish (ré-), *n.*, (Ich.) rasoir, rason, *m.*
reabsorb (ri-), *v.a.*, réabsorber, absorber de nouveau.
reabsorption (ri-), *n.*, réabsorption, absorption nouvelle, *f.*
reaccess (ri-), *n.*, nouvel accès, *m.*; visite renouvelée, *f.*
reach (ritshe), *n.*, (extent—*étendue*) étendue; (power of extending to—*puissance d'étendre*) portée, *f.*; (power—*pouvoir*) pouvoir, *m.*: (intellectual power (*des facultés intellectuelles*) portée, capacité, étendue; (artifice) ruse, *f.*; (effort to vomit—*effort pour vomir*) effort pour vomir, *m.* Out of any one's —; *hors de la portée de quelqu'un*. Within any one's —; *à la portée de quelqu'un*.
reach, *v.a.*, atteindre; (to hand—*passer*) passer, donner; (to touch—*toucher*) toucher; (to attain—*parvenir*) arriver à, parvenir à, atteindre; (to extend—*étendre*) étendre. To — down; descendre. The letter will — you to-morrow; *la lettre vous parviendra demain.* — me that book; *passez-moi ce livre.*
reach, *v.n.*, s'étendre; (to penetrate—*pénétrer*) pénétrer; (of fire-arms—*des armes à feu*) porter; (to make efforts to vomit—*s'efforcer de vomir*) faire des efforts pour vomir. To — after; *s'efforcer d'atteindre.*
reacher, *n.*, personne qui atteint; personne qui passe quelque chose à quelqu'un, *f.*
reaching, *n.*, efforts pour vomir, *m.pl.*
react (ri-), *v.a.*, jouer de nouveau; représenter de nouveau; rejouer.
react, *v.n.*, réagir; résister.
reacting, *adj.*, réactif.
reaction (ri-), *n.*, réaction; résistance, *f.*
read (rède), *past part.*, qui a de la lecture. To be well —; *avoir beaucoup de lecture; avoir lu beaucoup.*
read (ride), *v.a.* (*preterit* and *past part.*, Read), lire; faire la lecture de. To — again; *relire.* — on; *continuer à lire.* To — out; *lire tout haut.* To — over; *parcourir.* To — over and over again; *lire et relire.*
readable (rid'a-b'l), *adj.*, lisible, qui peut se lire avec plaisir.
reader (rid'-), *n.*, lecteur, *m.*, lectrice, *f.*; (print.) correcteur, *m.*; (person fond of reading—*qui aime la lecture*) personne qui aime la lecture, *f.*, liseur, *m.*, liseuse, *f.*
readership, *n.*, fonctions d'ecclésiastique qui lit les prières, *m.*
readily (rèd'-), *adv.*, tout de suite, promptement, aisément; (willingly—*volontiers*) volontiers, avec bonne volonté, avec empressement, sans hésiter.
readiness (rèd'-), *n.*, état de ce qui est prêt, *m.*, (promptitude) promptitude; (facility) facilité; (willingness—*bonne volonté*) bonne volonté, *f.*, empressement, *m.* — of mind; *présence d'esprit, f.*
reading (rid'-), *n.*, lecture; (in criticism—*critique*) teneur; (lecture—*discours public*) leçon; interprétation, explication, *f.*
reading-book (-bouke), *n.*, livre de lecture, *m.*
reading-boy (-boï), *n.*, (print.) apprenti qui lit la copie, *m.*
reading-closet (-clôz'-), *n.*, (print.) cabinet de correcteur, *m.*
reading-desk, *n.*, pupitre; lutrin, *m.*
reading-room (-roume), *n.*, cabinet de lecture, *m.*
readjourn (ri-ad-jorne), *v.n.*, ajourner de nouveau.
readjust (ri-ad-jeuste), *v.a.*, rajuster.
readjustment (ri-ad-jeust'-), *n.*, rajustement, *m.*
readmission, *or* **readmittance** (ri-), *n.*, réadmission, *f.*
readmit (ri-), *v.a.*, réadmettre.

readopt (ri-), *v.a.*, adopter de nouveau.
readorn (ri-), *v.a.*, orner de nouveau.
ready (rèd'-), *adj.*, (quick—*vif*) prompt; (dexterous—*adroit*) qui a de la facilité; (quick of apprehension—*prompt à comprendre*) vif; (of money—*argent*) comptant; (prepared—*préparé*) prêt; (willing—*de bonne volonté*) empressé; (inclined—*enclin*) porté; (near at hand—*proche*) le premier venu, sous la main; (easy, short—*facile, court*) facile, court. To make —; *préparer.*
ready (rèd'-), *adv.*, tout.
ready-made (-méde), *adj.*, tout fait; confectionné.
ready-witted, *adj.*, spirituel.
reaffirm (ri-af'feurme), *v.a.*, affirmer de nouveau.
reaffirmance (ri-af'feurm'-), *n.*, nouvelle affirmation, *f.*
reagent (ri-é-djè'n'te), *n.*, réactif, *m.*
reaggravation (ri-ag-gra-vé-), *n.*, (canon-law—*droit canon*) réaggrave, *f.*
real (ri-), *adj.*, réel; vrai; véritable; (jur.) réel, immeuble.
real (ri-), *n.*, réal (Spanish coin—*monnaie d'Espagne*), *m.*
realgar (ri-), *n.*, (min.) réalgar, *m.*
realist (ri-), *n.*, réaliste, *m.*
reality (ri-), *n.*, réalité, *f.*; réel; (philos.) réalisme, *m.*
realization (ri-al'i-zé-), *n.*, réalisation; (of money—*d'argent*) conversion en bien-fonds, *f.*
realize (ri-al-aïze), *v.a.*, réaliser; (to believe as real—*croire*) regarder comme réel, croire à la réalité de; se rendre compte de; (to feel in all its force—*comprendre*) sentir dans toute sa force; (money, property—*argent, propriété*) convertir en bien-fonds. To be —d; *se réaliser.*
reallege (ri-al'lèdje), *v.a.*, alléguer de nouveau.
really (ri-), *adv.*, réellement, en réalité, en effet, vraiment.
realm (rèl'm), *n.*, royaume, pays, *m.*
realty (ri-), *n.*, (jur.) caractère immobilier, *m.*
ream (rîme), *n.*, rame, *f.*
reanimate (ri-), *v.a.*, ranimer.
reanimation (ri-a'n'i-mé-), *n.*, action de ranimer, *f.*
reannex (ri-), *v.a.*, annexer de nouveau.
reannexation (ri-a'n'nèks'é-), *n.*, action d'annexer de nouveau, *f.*
reap (rîpe), *v.a.*, moissonner; récolter; (to obtain—*obtenir*) retirer, recueillir.
reap, *v.n.*, moissonner; faire la moisson.
reaper, *n.*, moissonneur, *m.*; moissonneuse, *f.*
reaping, *n.*, moisson, *f.*
reaping-hook (-houke), *x.*, faucille, *f.*
reaping-time (-taime), *n.*, moisson, *f.*
reapparel (ri-), *v.n.*, rhabiller.
reappear (ri-ap-pîr), *v.n.*, reparaître.
reappearance (ri-ap-pî'r'-), *n.*, réapparition, *f.*
reapplication (ri-ap-pli-ké-), *n.*, nouvelle application, *f.*; nouvel emploi, *m.*; nouvelle demande, nouvelle sollicitation, *f.*
reapply (ri-ap-pla'ye), *v.a.*, appliquer de nouveau; adresser de nouveau.
reapply, *v.n.*, s'appliquer de nouveau; s'adresser de nouveau.
reappoint (ri-ap-pwaï'n'te), *v.a.*, arrêter de nouveau; instituer de nouveau; rétablir; désigner de nouveau; indiquer, fixer de nouveau; renommer à des fonctions.
reappointment, *n.*, nouveau rendez-vous, *m.*; nouvelle nomination, *f.*
reapportion (ri-ap-), *v.a.*, répartir de nouveau.
reapportionment (ri-), *n.*, nouveau partage, *m.*; nouvelle répartition, *f.*
rear (rîre), *n.*, dernier rang, *m.*; queue, *f.*; (milit.) arrière-garde, *f.*; (of buildings, &c.—*de*

bâtiments, &c.) derrière, *m.* To attack in the —; *attaquer par derrière, m.* To attack in the —; *attaquer par derrière; en queue.*

rear (rîre), *v.a.*, élever ; relever.

rear, *v.n.*, se cabrer.

rear, *adj.*, peu cuit ; saignant.

rear-admiral, *n.*, contre-amiral, *m.*

rearmouse (-maouce), *n.*, chauve-souris, *f.*

rear-rank, *n.*, dernier rang, *m.*

rearward (-wôrde), *n.*, arrière-garde, queue, *f.*

reascend (rî-), *v.a.* and *n.*, remonter.

reason (rî-z'n), *n.*, raison, *f.* By — of ; *en raison de ; pour cause de.* For —s best known to myself ; *pour des raisons à moi connues.* To speak — ; *parler raison.*

reason (rî-z'n), *v.n.*, raisonner ; arguer.

reason, *v.a.*, raisonner. To — into ; *entraîner à.* To — out of ; *détourner de.*

reasonable (rî-z'n'a-b'l), *adj.*, raisonnable.

reasonableness, *n.*, caractère raisonnable, *m.* ; raison. modération, *f.*

reasonably, *adv.*, raisonnablement.

reasoner (rî-z'n'-), *n.*, raisonneur, *m.*, raisonneuse, *f.* ; logicien, *m.*

reasoning (rî-z'n'-), *n.*, raisonnement, *m.*

reasonless, *adj.*, sans raison.

reassemblage (rî-as'sè'm'bladje), *n.*, assemblage nouveau, *m.*

reassemble (rî-as'sè'm'b'l), *v.a.*, assembler de nouveau.

reassemble, *v.n.*, s'assembler de nouveau.

reassert (rî-as'seurte), *v.a.*, soutenir de nouveau ; déclarer de nouveau ; avancer de nouveau ; affirmer de nouveau ; (rights—*droits*) revendiquer de nouveau.

reassign (rî-as'saïne), *v.a.*, assigner de nouveau ; fixer de nouveau ; appliquer de nouveau.

reassimilate (rî-), *v.a.*, assimiler de nouveau.

reassimilation (rî-as-sim'î-lé-), *n.*, nouvelle assimilation, *f.*

reassume (rî-as-sloume), *v.a.*, prendre de nouveau ; reprendre.

reassurance (rî-a-shiour'-), *n.*, réassurance, *f.*

reassure (rî-a-shioure), *v.a.*, rassurer ; (com.) réassurer.

reassurer, *n.*, réassureur, *m.*

reattach (rî at'tatshe), *v.a.*, rattacher.

reattachment, *n.*, nouvel attachement, *m.*

reattempt (rî-), *v.a.*, essayer de nouveau, tenter de nouveau ; faire une nouvelle tentative.

reavow (rî-a-vaou), *v.a.*, avouer de nouveau.

rebaptism (rî-bap-tiz'm), *n.*, nouveau baptême, *m.*

rebaptization (rî-bap-taïzé-), *n.*, nouveau baptême, *m.*

rebaptize (rî-bap-taïze), *v.a.*, rebaptiser.

rebate (rî-), *n.*, diminution ; réfaction ; (arith.) règle d'escompte ; (carp.) feuillure, *f.*

rebate, *v.a.*, émousser ; diminuer ; (carp.) faire une feuillure à.

rebatement, *n.*, diminution, *f.* ; (com.) rabais, *m.*

rebec (rî-bèke), *n.*, rebec, *m.*

rebel (rèb'èl), *n.*, rebelle, révolté, *m.*

rebel, *v.n.*, se révolter, se soulever, se rebeller.

rebeller, *n.*, (ant.) rebelle, *m.*

rebellion (rî-bel'ieune), *n.*, rébellion, *f.*

rebellious (rî-bèl'-), *adj.*, rebelle, révolté.

rebelliously, *adv.*, en rebelle.

rebelliousness, *n.*, rébellion, *f.*

rebellow (rî-bèl-lô), *n.*, mugir de nouveau.

reblossom (rî-blos'seume), *v.n.*, refleurir.

rebound (rî-baou'n'de), *n.*, rebondissement, contre-coup. *m.*

rebound, *v.n.*, rebondir, retentir.

rebound (rî-ba-ou'n'de), *v.a.*, faire rebondir ; répéter ; faire retentir.

rebrace (rî-), *v.a.*, attacher de nouveau ; lier de nouveau ; serrer de nouveau ; (the nerves) —*les nerfs*) tendre, fortifier de nouveau.

rebreathe (rî-brithe), *v.n.*, respirer de nouveau.

rebuff (rî-beuf), *n.*, rebuffade, *f.* ; échec ; refus, *m.*

rebuff, *v.a.*, rebuter, repousser.

rebuild (rî-bilde), *v.a.* (preterit and past part., Rebuilt), rebâtir, reconstruire.

rebukable (rî-biouk'a-b'l), *adj.*, répréhensible, blâmable.

rebuke (rî-biouke), *n.*, réprimande, *f.* ; reproche, blâme, *m.* ; rebuffade, *f.* ; (in Scripture — *Écriture sainte*) châtiment, *m.*, punition, *f.*

rebuke, *v.a.*, réprimander, blâmer, reprendre, censurer ; faire des reproches à ; (in Scripture—*Écriture sainte*) châtier, réprimander.

rebuker, *n.*, personne qui réprimande, qui censure, qui fait des reproches, *f.* ; censeur, *m.*

rebukingly, *adv.*, avec une réprimande.

rebus (rî-), *n.*, rébus, *m.*

rebut (rî-beute), *v.a.*, rebuter, repousser.

rebut, *v.n.*, riposter ; (jur.) dupliquer.

rebutter (rî-beut'-), *n.*, (jur.) duplique, *f.*

recall (rî-côl), *n.*, rappel, *m.* ; révocation ; rétractation, *f.*

recall, *v.a.*, rappeler ; rétracter ; révoquer.

recallable (rî-côl'a-b'l), *adj.*, révocable.

recant (rî-), *v.n.*, se rétracter, se dédire.

recant, *v.a.*, rétracter, se dédire de.

recantation (rî-ca'n'té-), *n.*, rétractation, palinodie, *f.*

recanter, *n.*, personne qui se rétracte, qui se dédit, qui abjure, *f.*

recapacitate (rî-), *v.a.*, remettre en état de.

recapitulate (rî-ca-pit'iou-), *v.a.*, récapituler, résumer.

recapitulation (rî-ca-pit'iou-lé-), *n.*, récapitulation, *f.* ; résumé, *m.*

recapitulatory, *adj.*, récapitulatif.

recaption (rî-), *n.*, (jur.) reprise, *f.*

recaptor, *n.*, personne qui reprend une prise, *f.*

recapture (rî-capt'ieur), *n.*, reprise ; (l. u.) recousse, rescousse, *f.*

recapture (rî-capt'ieur), *v.a.*, reprendre.

recarry (rî-), *v.a.*, (pers.) remener ; (things —*choses*) reporter, rapporter, ramener.

recast (rî-câste), *v.a.* (preterit and past part., Recast), mouler de nouveau, refondre ; (metal.) couler de nouveau ; (arith.) additionner de nouveau.

recede (rî-cîde), *v.n.*, reculer ; s'éloigner ; se retirer ; (to desist—*renoncer*) se désister.

receipt (rî-cîte), *n.*, (act of receiving—*action de recevoir*) réception ; (place—*lieu*) recette, *f.* ; bureau de recette, *m.* ; (recipe—*formule*) recette, *f.* ; (com.) reçu, *m.*, quittance, *f.*, acquit, *m.* —s (money received) ; *recette, f. sing., recettes, f.pl.* Acknowledgment of — ; *accusé de réception, m.* To acknowledge the — of ; *accuser réception de.* To put a — to ; *acquitter ; mettre un acquit à.* — in full of all demands ; *quittance pour solde de tout compte.*

receipt, *v.a.*, donner un reçu pour, donner une quittance pour, acquitter, mettre un acquit à.

receipt-book (-bouke), *n.*, livre de recettes, *m.*

receivable (rî-cîv'a-b'l), *adj.*, recevable, admissible ; (com.) à recevoir.

receive (rî-cîve), *v.a.*, recevoir ; accueillir ; (money—*argent*) recevoir, toucher ; (stolen goods—*choses volées*) recéler. —d ; *reçu ; pour acquit.*

30

receivedness (ri-cĭv'ĕd'-), *n.*, adoption générale, *f.*

receiver (ri-cĭv'-), *n.*, personne qui reçoit, *f.*; percepteur, receveur, *m.*, receveuse, *f.*; (of stolen objects—*d'objets volés*) receleur, *m.*, receleuse, *f.*; (chem.) récipient, *m.*

receiving (ri-cĭv'-), *n.*, réception, *f.*; (jur.) recèlement, *m.*

receiving-house (-haouce), *n.*, petite poste, boîte aux lettres; (of the Royal Humane Society —*de la société royale de secours aux noyés*) maison de secours pour les noyés, *f.*; (of parcels delivery companies—*de petites messageries*) dépôt de paquets pour les petites messageries, *m.*

receiving-ship, *n.*, vaisseau Cayenne, *m.*

recelebrate (ri-cĕl'i-), *v.a.*, célébrer de nouveau.

recelebration (rĭ cĕl'i-bré'-), *n.*, nouvelle célébration, *f.*

recency (rĭ-cĕn'se), *n.*, nouveauté; date récente, *f.*

recense (ri-cĕn'se), *v.a.*, reviser, recenser.

recension (ri-), *n.*, énumération; revue, *f.*; examen, *m.*

recent (rĭ-), *adj.*, récent, frais, nouveau.

recently, *adv.*, récemment, fraîchement, nouvellement.

recentness, *n.*, nouveauté; date récente, *f.*

receptacle (ri-cĕp'ta-k'l), *n.*, asile, refuge; réceptacle; (anat.) réservoir; (bot., hydraul.) réceptacle, *m.*

reception (ri-cĕp-), *n.*, action de recevoir; réception, *f.*; accueil, *m.*; (readmission) rentrée; (opinion generally admitted—*opinion générale*) opinion reçue, *f.* For the — of; *pour recevoir.*

receptive (ri-cĕp-tĭve), *adj.*, susceptible de recevoir, qui reçoit.

recess (ri-), *n.*, retraite; (suspension) suspension, *f.*; (holidays—*vacances*) vacances, *f.pl.*; (secret) secret; (of the heart—*du cœur*) repli; (arch.) enfoncement, *m.*, embrasure, *f.*

recession (ri-cĕsh'-), *n.*, retraite, *f.*; désistement, *m.*; (of the equinoxes—*des équinoxes*) précession, *f.*

rechange (ri-tshé'n'dje), *v.a.*, rechanger.

recharge (ri-tshârdje), *v.a.*, renvoyer l'accusation à; (milit.) recharger.

recheat (ri-tshîte), *n.*, (hunt.) rappel, *m.*

recheat, *v.n.*, sonner le rappel.

rechoose (ri-tshouze), *v.a.*(*preterit*, Rechose; *past part.*, Rechosen), choisir de nouveau.

recipe (rĕss'-'-pĭ), *n.*, récipé, *m.*; recette; ordonnance de médecin, *f.*

recipient (ri-), *n.*, personne qui reçoit; chose qui reçoit, *f.*; (chem.) récipient, *m.*

reciprocal (ri-), *adj.*, réciproque, mutuel; (of contracts—*des contrats*) synallagmatique, bilatéral.

reciprocal, *n.*, (math.) réciproque, *f.*

reciprocally, *adv.*, réciproquement, mutuellement.

reciprocalness, *n.*, réciprocité, *f.*

reciprocate, *v.a.*, échanger réciproquement; échanger,-⊙réciproquer.

reciprocate, *v.n.*, agir réciproquement.

reciprocating (ri-cip-ro-két'-), *adj.*, alternatif; de va-et-vient.

reciprocation (ri-cip-ro-ké-), *n.*, réciprocité, réciproquation; (mec.) révolution, *f.*

reciprocity (rĕss'-), *n.*, réciprocité, *f.*

recision (ri-cij'eune), *n.*, rescision, *f.*

recital (ri-çaï-), *n.*, récit, narré, exposé, *m.*; répétition; narration, relation; (enumeration) énumération, *f.*

recitation (rĕss'i-té-), *n.*, récit; narré, exposé, *m.*; répétition; narration, relation; (in schools—*aux écoles*) récitation, *f.*

recitative (rĕss'i-ta-tĭve), *adj.*, (mus.) en récitatif.

recitativo (rĕss'i-ta-tĭve), *or* **recitativo** (-tĭ-vó), *n.*, récitatif; récit, *m.*

recitatively, *adv.*, (mus.) en récitatif.

recite (ri-çaïte), *v.a.*, réciter, faire le récit de; raconter; rapporter; répéter; (to enumerate—*énumérer*) énumérer.

recite, *v.n.*, réciter les leçons.

reciter, *n.*, personne qui récite, qui fait le récit de, qui raconte, *f.*; récitateur; narrateur, *m.*, narratrice, *f.*; énumérateur, *m.*, énumératrice, *f.*

reck (rèke), *v.a.*, (ant.) se soucier de, faire cas de.

reck, *v.n.*, (ant.) se soucier de; importer. What —s it? *qu'importe?*

reckless (rĕk'-), *adj.*, insouciant; téméraire.

recklessly, *adv.*, témérairement; avec insouciance.

recklessness, *n.*, insouciance, témérité, *f.*

reckon (rĕk'k'n), *v.a.*, calculer, compter; considérer comme; estimer. To — up; *additionner.*

reckon, *v.n.*, compter. To — on; *compter sur*; faire fond sur.

reckoner, *n.*, calculateur, chiffreur, *m.* Ready —; *prompt calculateur*; (book—*livre*) barème, *m.*

reckoning, *n.*, calcul; compte, *m.*; (nav.) estime, *f.* Short —s make long friends; *les bons comptes font les bons amis.*

reckoning-book (-bouke), *n.*, livre de comptes, *m.*

reclaim (ri-cléme), *v.a.*, réclamer, redemander; revendiquer; (to restrain—*retenir*) retenir, arrêter; (to tame—*apprivoiser*) apprivoiser; (to reform—*corriger*) amender, corriger, ramener au bien; (a hawk—*faucon*) apprivoiser, dresser. To — from; *faire revenir de.*

reclaim, *v.n.*, réclamer.

reclaimable (-'a-b'l), *adj.*, qui peut être réclamé; qui peut être corrigé; qui peut être amendé; qui peut être ramené au bien.

reclaimant, *n.*, réclamateur, opposant, *m.*

reclaimless, *adj.*, incorrigible.

reclamation (rĕk-la-mé-), *n.*, réclamation, demande, *f.*; recouvrement, *m.*

reclination (rĕk-li-né-), *n.*, position inclinée, *f.*

recline (ri-claïne), *adj.*, penché, incliné.

recline (ri-claïne), *v.a.*, incliner, pencher, appuyer.

recline, *v.n.*, s'incliner, se pencher, s'appuyer, se reposer.

reclining (ri-claï'n'-), *adj.*, incliné, penché.

reclose (ri-clôce), *v.a.*, refermer.

recluse (ri-cliouce), *adj.*, reclus; (of things —*des choses*) de reclus, séparé.

recluse (ri-cliouce), *n.*, reclus, *m.*, recluse, *f.*

reclusely, *adv.*, en reclus.

recluseness, *n.*, retraite, *f.*

reclusion (ri-cliou-jeune), *n.*, réclusion, réclusion, retraite, *f.*

reclusive (ri-cliou-cive), *adj.*, de reclus.

recoagulation (ri-co-agh'iou-lé-), *n.*, seconde coagulation, *f.*

recognition (rĕk'og-ni-), *n.*, reconnaissance, action de reconnaître, *f.*

recognitor (ri-cog-ni-teur), *n.*, membre d'un jury d'assises, juré, *m.*

recognizable (ri-cog-ni-za-b'l), *adj.*, reconnaissable.

recognizance (ri-cog-ni-za'n'ce), *n.*, reconnaissance, action de reconnaître, *f.*; (jur.) obligation authentique de faire quelque acte particulier, *f.*; verdict d'un jury, *m.*

recognize (rĕk'og-naïze), *v.a.*, reconnaître.

recognize, *v.n.*, (jur.) souscrire une obligation authentique de faire quelque acte particulier.

recognizee (ri-cog-ni-zï), *n.*, personne au

profit de laquelle on souscrit une obligation authentique, *f.*

recognizor (ri-cog-ni-), *n.*, personne qui souscrit une obligation authentique, *f.*

recoil (ri-coïl), *n.*, recul, *m.* ; (fig.) répugnance, révolte. *f.*

recoil, *v.n.*, reculer ; retomber.

recoiling, *n.*, recul, *m.* ; (fig.) répugnance, révolte, *f.*

recoin (ri-coïne), *v.a.*, refondre.

recoinage ('-édje), *n.*, refonte; monnaie de refonte, *f.*

recollect (rèk'-), *v.a.*, se souvenir de ; se rappeler ; se ressouvenir de ; se remettre. — it ; *souvenez-vous-en.*

recollect (ri-), *v.a.*, recueillir, rassembler, réunir.

recollection (rèk'-), *n.*, souvenir, ressouvenir, *m.* ; mémoire, *f.* To have no — of ; *ne pas se rappeler ; n'avoir pas le souvenir de.* To have some — of ; *avoir un souvenir de.* To the best of my — ; *autant que je puis m'en souvenir.*

recollet (ri-), *n.*, récollet, *m.*

recolonization (ri-col-o-ni-zé-), *n.*, nouvelle colonisation, *f.*

recolonize (ri-col-o-naïze), *v.a.*, coloniser de nouveau.

recombination (ri-co'm'bi-né-), *n.*, combinaison nouvelle, *f.*

recombine (ri-co'm'baïne), *v.a.*, combiner de nouveau.

recomfort (ri-keu'm'feurte), *v.a.*, reconforter ; consoler de nouveau, ranimer.

recommence (ri-), *v.a.*, recommencer.

recommend (rèk'-), *v.a.*, recommander.

recommendable ('-a-b'l), *adj.*, recommandable.

recommendation (rèk'om'mè'n'dé-), *n.*, recommandation ; (on a petition—*sur une pétition*) apostille, *f.*

recommendatory, *adj.*, de recommandation ; d'éloge.

recommender, *n.*, personne qui recommande, *f.*

recommission (ri-), *v.a.*, renommer à une charge ; charger de nouveau d'une commission.

recommit (ri-), *v.a.*, renvoyer en prison, devant une commission.

recommitment, *or* **recommittal** (ri-), *n.*, nouvelle incarcération, *f.*

recommunicate (ri-co'm'miou-), *v.a.*, communiquer de nouveau.

recompense (rèk'-), *n.*, récompense ; réparation, compensation, *f.* ; dédommagement ; retour, *m.*

recompense (rèk'-), *v.a.*, récompenser ; donner en retour ; dédommager ; compenser ; réparer.

recompilement (ri-co'm'païl'-), *n.*, nouvelle compilation, *f.*

recompose (ri-co'm'pôze), *v.a.*, recomposer ; calmer de nouveau ; tranquilliser, remettre ; (print.) recomposer.

reconcilable (rèk'o'n'çaïl-a-b'l), *adj.*, réconciliable ; (of things—*des choses*) qui peut s'arranger, conciliable.

reconcilableness (-çaïl'-), *n.*, possibilité de réconciliation, de conciliation, d'arrangement ; compatibilité, *f.*

reconcile (rèk'o'n'çaïle), *v.a.*, réconcilier ; mettre d'accord, raccommoder, concilier ; apaiser, accorder : (biblically—*biblique*) faire rentrer en grâce. To be — d with ; *être réconcilié avec.* To — one's self to a thing ; *se faire à une chose.*

reconcilement (-çaïl'-), *n.*, réconciliation, *f.* ; raccommodement, *m.*

reconciler (-çaïl'-), *n.*, réconciliateur, *m.*, réconciliatrice, *f.* ; conciliateur, *m.*, conciliatrice, *f.*

reconciliation (rèk'o'n'-èll-i-é-), *n.*, réconciliation, *f.* ; raccommodement, *m.* ; (of things —*des choses*) conciliation ; (biblically—*biblique*) expiation, *f.*

reconciliatory (-éil'-), *adj.*, de réconciliation, conciliateur.

recondensation (ri-co'n'dè'n'sé-), *n.*, nouvelle condensation, *f.*

recondense (ri-), *v.a.*, condenser de nouveau.

recondite (rèk'o'n'daïte), *adj.*, secret, profond, caché; abstrus, abstrait.

reconduct (rèk'o'n'deuk'te), *v.a.*, reconduire.

reconfirm (ri-co'n'feurme), *v.a.*, confirmer de nouveau.

reconjoin (ri-co'n'djwaïne), *v.a.*, rejoindre.

reconnoissance (ri-co'n'nois'-), *n.*, (milit.) reconnaissance, *f.*

reconnoitre (rèk'o'n'noï-teur), *v.a.*, (milit.) reconnaître, faire la reconnaissance de.

reconnoitre, *v.n.*, reconnaître, faire une reconnaissance.

reconnoitring, *adj.*, (milit.) de reconnaissance.

reconquer (ri-ko'n'keur), *v.a.*, reconquérir.

reconsecrate (ri-co'n'si-), *v.a.*, consacrer de nouveau.

reconsecration (ri-co'n'si-), *n.*, consécration nouvelle, *f.*

reconsider (ri-), *v.a.*, considérer de nouveau ; revenir sur.

reconsideration (ri-), *n.*, considération nouvelle, nouvelle réflexion, *f.* ; nouvel examen, *m.*

reconvene (ri-co'n'vîne), *v.a*, réunir de nouveau ; assembler de nouveau.

reconversion (ri-co'n'veur-), *n.*, nouvelle conversion, *f.*

reconvert (ri-co'n'veurte), *v.a.*, convertir de nouveau.

reconvey (ri-co'n'vê), *v.a.*, transporter de nouveau ; reporter, ramener ; (jur.) rétrocéder.

reconveyance (ri-co'n'vê-), *n.*, nouveau transport, *m.* ; (jur.) rétrocession, *f.*

record (ri-), *n.*, registre, *m.* ; marque, *f.* ; souvenir, signe, monument, *m.* —s ; *archives ; annales ; notes, f.pl.* Public —s ; *archives, f.pl.* On — ; *dans les annales de l'histoire ; inscrit, enregistré.* To make a — of ; *tenir registre de.* Keeper of the —s; *archiviste, greffier, m.* — office ; *archives, f.pl. ; greffe, m.*

record, *v.a.*, enregistrer; inscrire ; (to imprint—*imprimer*) graver, imprimer ; (to celebrate—*célébrer*) célébrer ; (in history—*dans l'histoire*) rapporter.

recorder, *n.*, receveur de l'enregistrement; archiviste; (jur.) premier officier judiciaire d'une ville, *m.*

recouch (ri-caoutshe), *v.n.*, rentrer dans son antre.

recount (ri-caou'n'te), *v.a.*, raconter, réciter.

recountment, *n.*, récit, rapport, *m.*

recourse (ri-côrse), *n.*, recours, *m.* To have — to ; *recourir à ; avoir recours à.*

recover (ri-keuv'-), *v.a.*, recouvrer, retrouver, ravoir, reprendre; reconquérir; (to reach—*atteindre*) parvenir à, atteindre ; (a loss—*une perte*) réparer ; (health—*la santé*) recouvrer ; rétablir ; (jur.) obtenir ; (com.) recouvrer, récupérer. To — one's self ; *se remettre ; revenir à soi.*

recover, *v.n.*, se rétablir, guérir, se guérir ; se relever, se remettre, se refaire ; (jur.) gagner son procès, gagner sa cause.

recoverable ('-a-b'l), *adj.*, qui peut être recouvré ; recouvrable ; réparable ; (of invalids— *des malades*) guérissable.

recovery (ri-keuv'-), *n.*, recouvrement, *m.* ; reprise, *f.* ; (of one's health—*de la santé*) recouvrement, *m.*, guérison, *f.*, rétablissement

æ.; (jur.) adjudication. *f.* Past —; *incurable*: (of things—*des choses*) *sans remède.*

recreant (rèk'ri-), *n.*, lâche, poltron, *m.*

recreant, *adj.*, lâche, poltron; faux, traître.

recreate (rèk'ri-), *v.a.*, récréer, réjouir, divertir, distraire.

recreate (rèk'ri-), *v.n.*, se récréer, se distraire, se divertir.

recreate (rî-cri-), *v.a.*, recréer.

recreation (rèk'ri-é-), *n.*, récréation; distraction, *f.*; divertissement, *m.*

recreative (rèk'ri-), *adj.*, récréatif, divertissant.

recreatively, *adv.*, d'une manière récréative.

recreativeness; n., qualité récréative, *f.*

recrement (rèk'ri-), *n.*, (metal.) scorie, *f.*; (med.) récrément, *m.*

recremental (rèk'ri-), **recrementitial** (-tish'-), *or* **recrementitious** (-tish'-), *adj.*, (metal.) plein de scories; (med.) récrémenteux, récrémentitiel.

recriminate (ri-), *v.a.*, récriminer contre.

recriminate, *v.n.*, récriminer.

recrimination (ri-cri'm'i-né-), *n.*, récrimination, *f.*

recriminator (ri-cri'm'i-né-teur), *n.*, personne qui récrimine, *f.*

recriminatory, *adj.*, récriminatoire.

recross (ri-), *v.a.*, traverser de nouveau; repasser.

recrudescence, *or* **recrudescency** (ri-crou-dès'-), *n.*, (ant.) recrudescence, *f.*

recrudescent (ri-crou-dès'-), *adj.*, (ant.) recrudescent.

recruit (ri-croute), *n.*, recrue, *f.*; (fig.) renfort, *m.*

recruit, *v.a.*, recruter; (to strengthen—*renforcer*) renforcer, réparer. To — one's self; *se remettre, se refaire.*

recruit, *v.n.*, se recruter; se refaire, se remettre, reprendre.

recruiting, *or* **recruitment** (ri-crout'-), *n.*, recrutement, *m.*

recrystallization (ri-cris-tal-li-zé-), *n.*, nouvelle cristallisation, *f.*

recrystallize (ri-cris-tal-laïze), *v.a.*, se cristalliser de nouveau.

rectangle (rèk'ta'n'g'l), *n.*, rectangle, *m.*

rectangled (rèk'ta'n'g'l'de), *adj.*, rectangle.

rectangular (-ghiou-), *adj.*, rectangulaire, rectangle, angle droit.

rectangularly, *adv.*, avec des angles droits.

rectifiable (-faï-a-b'l), *adj.*, susceptible de rectification; qui peut se rectifier.

rectification (-fi-ké-), *n.*, rectification, *f.*

rectifier (-faï-eur), *n.*, rectificateur.

rectify (rèk-ti-fa'ye), *v.a.*, rectifier; redresser.

rectilinear, rectilineal, *or* **rectilineous** (-li'n'i-), *adj.*, rectiligne.

rectitude (rèk'ti-tioude), *n.*, rectitude, *f.*

rector (rèk'teur), *n.*, curé; (of a university—*d'université*) recteur; (of religious orders—*d'ordre religieux*) directeur, supérieur, *m.*

rectorial, *adj.*, rectoral; de curé.

rectorship, *n.*, cure, *f.*; (of a university—*d'université*) rectorat, *m.*

rectory, *n.*, cure, *f.*; presbytère; (of universities—*d'université*) rectorat, *m.*

rectum, *n.*, (anat.) rectum, *m.*

recumbence, *or* **recumbency**(ri-keu'm'-), *n.*, état d'une personne couchée, *m.*

recumbent (ri-keu'm'-), *adj.*, couché, étendu; (idle—*oisif*) en repos, oisif.

recuperation (ri-kiou-pèr'é-), *n.*, récupération, *f.*

recuperative, *or* **recuperatory** (ri-kiou-pèr'-), *adj.*, qui tend à recouvrer.

recur (ri-keur), *v.n.*, revenir; se représenter; (to have recourse—*s'adresser à*) avoir recours.

recurrence, *or* **recurrency** (ri-keur'-), *n.*, retour; recours, *m.* Of frequent —; *qui revient souvent, qui arrive souvent.*

recurrent (ri-keur'-), *adj.*, qui revient de temps en temps.

recourse (ri-keur-), *or* **recurve** (-keurve), *v.a.*, recourber.

recurvate, *or* **recurved** (ri-keurv'de), *adj.*, recourbé.

recurvation (-keurv'é-), *or* **recurvity** (-keurv'i-), *n.*, courbure, *f.*

recurvous, *adj.*, recourbé.

recusancy (rèk'iou-za'n'-), *n.*, non-conformité, *f.*

recusant (rèk'iou-za'n'te), *n.*, non-conformiste, *m.*

recusant, *adj.*, qui refuse de se conformer.

recusation (rèk'iou-zé-), *n.*, récusation, *f.*

recuse (ri-kiouze), *v.a.*, récuser.

red (rède), *n.*, rouge, *m.*

red, *adj.*, rouge. — -hot; *tout rouge, tout chaud.* — -coat; *soldat, m.* — -deer; *cerf, m.* — face; *visage enluminé, m.* — herring; *hareng saur, m.* — -lead; *vermillon, m.*

redan (ri-), *n.*, (fort.) redan, *m.*

redbreast (-brèste),*n.*,(orni.) rouge-gorge,*m.*

redden (rèd'd'n), *v.a.* and *n.*, rougir.

reddendum, *n.*, (jur.) stipulation de loyer,*f.*

reddish (rèd'-), *adj.*, rougeâtre.

reddishness, *n.*, couleur rougeâtre, *f.*

reddition (rèd'dish'-), *n.*, reddition; restitution; (explanation—*explication*) explication, *f.*

reddle (rèd'd'l), *n.*, rubrique (craie rouge), sanguine; (min.) ocre rouge,*f.*

redeem (ri-dîme), *v.a.*, racheter; (fin.) racheter, rembourser; (things pawned—*objets engagés*) dégager, retirer; (fig.) dégager, délivrer, compenser.

redeemable (-'a-b'l), *adj.*, rachetable; remboursable.

redeemableness, *n.*, nature remboursable; qualité de ce qui est rachetable, *f.*

redeemer (ri-dî'm'-), *n.*, Rédempteur, *m.*; personne qui rachète, *f.*; libérateur, *m.*, libératrice, *f.*

redeeming, *adj.*, qui rachète, qui compense; réparateur; compensatoire.

redeliberate (ri-dé-lib'èr'-), *v.n.*, délibérer de nouveau.

redeliver (ri-dè-), *v.a.*, restituer; (to deliver again—*libérer de nouveau*) délivrer de nouveau.

redelivery (ri-di-), *n.*, restitution; nouvelle délivrance,*f.*

redemand (ri-di-), *v.a.*, redemander.

redemand, *n.*, demande en restitution, *f.*

redemandable (-'a-b'l), *adj.*, qui peut être redemandé.

redemise (ri-di-mize),*v.a.*,(jur.) rétrocéder.

redemise, *n.*, (jur.) rétrocession, *f.*

redemption (ri-dè'm'sheune), *n.*, rédemption,*f.*; rachat, *m.*; délivrance, *f.*; (jur.) rachat, réméré, *m.*

redemptive, *or* **redemptory** (ri-dè'm'-). *adj.*, payé pour la rançon.

redented (ri-), *adj.*, (bot.) denté en scie.

redescend (ri-), *v.n.*, redescendre.

redintegrate (ri-di'n'ti-), *adj.*, réintégré, rétabli, renouvelé.

redintegrate (ri-di'n'ti-), *v.a.*, réintégrer, rétablir; renouveler.

redintegration (-ti-gré-), *n.*, réintégration, *f.*; renouvellement; rétablissement, *m.*

rediscount (ri-dis-caou'n'te),*v.a.*, réescompter.

redispose (ri-dis-pôze), *v.a.*, disposer de nouveau.

redisseizin (ri-dis-sî-zîne), *n.*, (jur.) nouvelle

saisine contre celui qui s'est dessaisi après avoir recouvré, *f.*

redisseizor (ri-dis-sî-), *n.*, (jur.) personne qui après avoir recouvré une chose, s'en dessaisit, *f.*

redissolve (ri-diz-zolve), *v.a.*, dissoudre de nouveau.

redistil (ri-), *v.a.*, distiller de nouveau.

redistillation(ri-),*n.*,nouvelle distillation,*f.*

redistribute (ri-dis-trib'ioute), *v.a.*, distribuer de nouveau.

redistribution, *n.*, nouvelle distribution,*f.*

redness, *n.*, rougeur, *f.*

redolence, *or* **redolency** (rèd'-), *n.*, parfum, *m.* ; odeur agréable, senteur, *f.*

redolent, *adj.*, qui a un parfum de, odoriférant, parfumé.

redouble (ri-deub'b'l), *v.a.* and *n.*, redoubler.

redoubt (ri-daoute), *n.*, (fort.) redoute, *f.*

redoubtable (-'a-b'l), *adj.*, redoutable.

redoubted, *adj.*, redouté.

redound (ri-daou'n'de), *v.n.*, rejaillir, revenir ; (to contribute—*aider*) contribuer ; (to result—*s'ensuivre*) résulter.

redpole, *or* **redpoll** (-pôle), *n.*, (orni.) linotte, *f.*

redraft (ri-drâfte), *v.a.*, dessiner de nouveau ; rédiger de nouveau.

redraft, *n.*, nouveau dessein; nouveau brouillon, *m.*; (com.) retraite,*f.*

redraw (ri-drô), *v.a.*, retirer ; faire un nouveau brouillon ; (com.) faire retraite.

redress (ri-), *v.a.*, redresser ; faire justice à ; secourir, soulager ; réparer.

redress, *n.*, redressement, *m.* ; justice ; réparation ; réformation, *f.*, soulagement, *m.*

redresser, *n.*, redresseur, réparateur, *m.*

redressible (-'i-b'l), *adj.*, réparable.

redressive, *adj.*, qui apporte du secours.

redressless,*adj.*, irréparable ; sans remède.

red-shanks, *n.*, (bot.) renouée persicaire, herbe vierge, persicaire, *f.*

red-tail (-tèle), *n.*, (orni.) rouge-queue, *m.*

reduce (ri-diouce), *v.a.*, réduire, diminuer, rabaisser.

reducer, *n.*, personne qui réduit, *f.*

reducible (-'i-b'l), *adj.*, réductible.

reducibleness, *n.*, qualité de ce qui est réductible, *f.*

reduct (ri-deukte), *n.*, réduit, *m.*

reduction (ri-deuk-), *n.*, réduction, diminution, *f.*

reductive, *adj.*, réductif.

reductive, *n.*, agent réductif, *m.*

reductively, *adv.*, par réduction, *f.*

redundance, *or* **redundancy** (ri-deu'n'-), *n.*, redondance, surabondance, *f.*

redundant (ri-deu'n'-), *adj.*, redondant ; surabondant.

redundantly, *adv.*, avec superfluité, d'une manière redondante.

reduplicate (ri-diou-), *v.a.*, redoubler.

reduplicate, *adj.*, double.

reduplication (ri-diou-pli-ké-), *n.*, réduplication,*f.* : redoublement, *m.*

reduplicative (ri-diou-pli-ké-), *adj.*, réduplicatif ; double.

re-echo (ri-èk'o'), *v.a.*, répéter ; renvoyer.

re-echo, *v.n.*, résonner, retentir ; répondre.

re-echo, *n.*, écho répété ; retentissement, *m.*

reed (ride), *n.*, roseau; (musical pipe—*pipeau*) chalumeau, *m.* ; (of wind instruments—*d'instruments à vent*) anche,*f.*

reeded (rid'-), *adj.*, couvert de roseaux.

reeden (rid'-), *adj.*, de roseau.

reed-grass (-grâce), *n.*, roseau, *m.*

re-edification (ri-èd'i-fi-ké-), *n.*, réédification.*f.*

re-edify (ri-èd'i-fa'ye), *v.a.*, réédifier, rebâtir.

reedless, *adj.*, sans roseaux.

reedy, *adj.*, plein de roseaux.

reef (rife), *n.*, recoif ; (of a sail—*d'une voile*) ris, *m.*

reef, *v.a.*, (nav.) prendre un ris, des ris.

reef-line (-laïne), *n.*, (nav.) garcette de ris,*f.*

reefy, *adj.*, plein de rescifs, plein de rocs.

reek (rike), *n.*, fumée, vapeur, exhalaison,*f.*

reek, *v.n.*, fumer ; s'exhaler.

reeky, *adj.*, enfumé, noirci.

reel (rile), *n.*, dévidoir ; touret, *m.* ; bobine, *f.* ; (dance—*danse*) branle, *m.* Scotch —; *écussaise*,*f.*

reel, *v.a.*, dévider.

reel, *v.n.*, chanceler ; vaciller ; tourner.

re-elect (ri-i-), *v.a.*, réélire.

re-election (ri-i-lèk-), *n.*, réélection,*f.*

re-eligibility (ri-èl'i-dji-), *n.*, rééligibilité,*f.*

re-eligible (ri-èl'i-dji-b'l), *adj.*, rééligible.

re-embark (ri-è'm'bârke), *v.a.*,rembarquer.

re-embark, *v.n.*, se rembarquer.

re-embarkation (ri-è'm'bâr-ké-), *n.*, rembarquement, *m.*

re-embattle (ri-è'm'bat't'l), *v.a.*, remettre en bataille.

re-embody (ri-), *v.a.*, réincorporer.

re-emerge (ri-i-meur-dje), *v.n.*, ressortir.

re-enact (ri-è'n'-), *v.a.*, ordonner, décréter, de nouveau.

re-enactment, *n.*, remise en vigueur, *f.* ; rétablissement, *m.*

re-enforce (ri-è'n'fôrce). *V.* **reinforce**

re-engage (ri-è'n'ghédje),*v.a.*, rengager.

re-engage, *v.n.*, se rengager.

re-enjoy (ri-è'n'djo'ye), *v.a.*, jouir de nouveau.

re-enkindle (ri-è'n'-), *v.a.*, rallumer.

re-enlist (ri-è'n'-), *v.a.*, enrôler de nouveau.

re-enlist, *v.n.*, se rengager.

re-enter (ri-è'n'-), *v.a.* and *n.*, rentrer.

re-entering, *adj.*, rentrant.

re-enthrone (ri-è'n'thrône), *v.a.*, remettre sur le trône.

re-entrance (ri-è'n'-), *n.*, rentrée, *f.*

re-establish (ri-ès-), *v.a.*, rétablir ; réintégrer.

re-establisher, *n.*, restaurateur, *m.*

re-establishment, *n.*, rétablissement, *m.* ; réintégration,*f.*

reeve (rive), *v.a.*,(nav.)passer une manœuvre dans.

re-examination (ri-ègz'a'm'i-né-), *n.*, nouvel examen, *m.*

re-examine (ri-ègz'-), *v.a.*, examiner de nouveau ; revoir.

re-exchange (ri-èks'tsché'n'dje), *n.*, nouvel échange ; rechange, *m.*

re-export (ri-èks'-), *v.a.*, réexporter.

re-export, *n.*, marchandise réexportée,*f.*

re-exportation (ri-èks-pôr-té-),*n.*, réexportation,*f.*

refection (ri-fèk'-), *n.*, réfection, *f.*; repas; rafraîchissement, *m.*

refective (ri-fèk-), *adj.*, restaurant.

refectory (ri-), *n.*, réfectoire, *m.*

refer (ri-feur), *v.a.*, référer ; renvoyer ; rapporter ; adresser ; adresser pour des renseignements.

refer, *v.n.*, (of things—*des choses*) se référer, référer, se rapporter, avoir trait, avoir rapport ; faire allusion ; (pers.) s'en rapporter, se référer, s'adresser.

referable (ri-feur'a-b'l). *V.* **referrible**.

referee (rè'fèr'i), *n.*, arbitre, *m.*

reference (rèf'èr'-), *n.*, renvoi; (respect) regard, rapport, *m.* ; (allusion)allusion; (recommendation) recommandation,*f.* ; (for character —*sur la moralité*) renseignement,*m.* ; (pers.) personne chez laquelle on peut prendre des renseignements, *f.* ; (print.) renvoi, *m.*, lettrine,*f.* ;

(jur.) renvoi, *m.* In — to; *à l'égard de; par rapport à.* To have — to; *se rapporter à; faire allusion à.* To give a — to any one; *donner une référence, indiquer quelqu'un pour fournir des renseignements.* To go for a —; *aller aux renseignements.* To have good —s; *avoir de bonnes recommandations, de bonnes références.*

referendary (rèf'-), *n.*, référendaire, *m.*

re-ferment (ri-fèr-), *v.a.*, faire fermenter de nouveau.

referrible (ri-feur-ri-b'l), *adj.*, qui peut être référé, qui peut être rapporté.

refine (ri-faïne), *v.a.*, épurer; purifier; polir; (metal.) affiner; (liquids—*liquides*) épurer; (sugar, saltpetre—*sucre, salpêtre*) raffiner.

refine, *v.n.*, s'épurer, se purifier; s'affiner, se raffiner; (of liquids—*des liquides*) s'épurer.

refined (ri-faï'n'de), *adj.*, épuré; pur; affiné; poli; raffiné.

refinedly (-èd'-), *adv.*, avec raffinement.

refinedness (-èd'-), *n.*, état d'affinage; état d'épuration; état de raffinage; raffinement; poli, *m.*; pureté; politesse, *f.*

refinement (ri-faï'n'-), *n.*, raffinement; poli, *m.*; pureté; politesse, *f.*; (of sugar, saltpetre—*de sucre, de salpêtre*) raffinage; (metal.) affinage, *m.*; (of liquids—*des liquides*) épuration, *f.*

refiner (-faï'n'-), *n.*, personne qui épure, qui purifie, *f.*; (of sugar, saltpetre—*de sucre, de salpêtre*) raffineur; (metal.) affineur, *m.*

refinery (ri-faï'n'-), *n.*, (metal.) affinerie; (of sugar—*de sucre*) raffinerie, *f.*

refining (ri-faï'n'-), *n.*, raffinage, affinage, *m.*; (of liquids—*des liquides*) épuration, *f.*

refit (ri-), *v.a.*, réparer; (nav.) radouber.

reflect (ri-), *v.a.*, réfléchir; faire rejaillir; reféter. To be —ed; *être réfléchi; se réfléchir.*

reflect, *v.n.*, réfléchir; faire réflexion; faire ses réflexions. To — on; (to bring reproach to —*amener des reproches à*) retomber sur, rejaillir sur; (to censure—*censurer*) censurer, fronder, critiquer, jeter le blâme sur. To be —ed on; *être blâmé, être censuré, être un sujet de blâme, être un sujet de censure.*

reflected, *adj.*, réfléchi; reflété.

reflectent, *adj.*, qui se réfléchit.

reflecting (-flèkt'-), *adj.*, réfléchi; réflecteur.

reflectingly, *adv.*, avec réflexion; (censure) avec blâme.

reflection (ri-flèk'-), *n.*, réflexion, *f.*; reflet, *m.*; (of the mind—*de l'esprit*) réflexion; (censure) censure, critique, *f.*, reproche, blâme, *m.* To cast —s on; *censurer, critiquer, blâmer.* On —; *en y réfléchissant.*

reflective, *adj.*, qui réfléchit; réfléchissant; réflecteur.

reflector, *n.*, personne qui réfléchit, *f.*; (phys.) réflecteur, *m.*

reflex (ri-flèkse), *adj.*, réfléchi; (paint.) reflété.

reflex, *n.*, (paint.) reflet, *m.*

reflexibility, *n.*, réflexibilité, *f.*

reflexible (-'i-b'l), *adj.*, réflexible.

reflexion. *V.* reflection.

reflexity, *n.*, réflexibilité, *f.*

reflexive, *adj.*, qui a rapport au passé.

reflexively, *adv.*, en arrière.

reflorescence (ri-), *n.*, nouvelle floraison, *f.*

reflourish (ri-fleur'-), *v.n.*, refleurir.

reflow (ri-flô), *v.n.*, refluer.

refluctuation (ri-fleuk'tiou-é-), *n.*, nouvelle fluctuation, *f.*; reflux, *m.*

refluence, *or* **refluency** (rèf'liou-), *n.*, reflux, *m.*

refluent, *adj.*, qui reflue.

reflux (ri-fleukse), *n.*, reflux, *m.*

reform (ri-), *n.*, réforme, *f.*

reform (ri-), *v.a.*, réformer.

reform (ri-), *v.n.*, se réformer

re-form (ri-), *v.a.*, reformer

reformation (rèf'or-mé-), *n.*, réformation, réforme, *f.*

re-formation (ri-form'-é-), *n.*, formation nouvelle, *f.*

reformer, *or* **reformist** (ri-), *n.*, réformateur, *m.*

reforming (ri-), *adj.*, qui réforme, qui conduit à la réformation.

reformist. *n.* *V.* **reformer.**

refortification (ri-for-ti-fi-ké-), *n.*, nouvelle fortification, *f.*

refortify (ri-for-ti-fa'ye), *v.a.*, refortifier.

re-found (ri-faou'n'de), *v.a.*, refondre; fonder de nouveau.

refract (ri-), *v.a.*, réfracter.

refracting (ri-), *adj.*, réfringent; à réfraction.

refraction (ri-), *n.*, réfraction, *f.*

refractivo (ri-), *adj.*, réfractif.

refractoriness (ri-), *n.*, résistance, opiniâtreté; obstination, mutinerie, *f.*

refractory (ri-), *adj.*, mutin, revêche, indocile, insoumis, intraitable, rebelle; réfractaire; (chem.) réfractaire.

refractory (ri-), *n.*, personne insoumise, personne indocile, personne intraitable, *f.*

refragable (rèf-ra-ga-b'l), *adj.*, que l'on peut réfuter.

refrain (ri-fréne), *v.a.*, retenir; contenir, réprimer.

refrain, *v.n.*, se retenir, se contenir; s'abstenir; se garder; s'empêcher.

refrain (ri-fréne), *n.*, refrain, *m.*

refrangibility (ri-fra'n'dji-), *n.*, réfrangibilité, *f.*

refrangible (ri-fra'n'dji-b'l), *adj.*, réfrangible.

refresh (ri-frèshe), *v.a.*, rafraîchir; soulager; délasser; refaire; récréer. To — one's self; *se rafraîchir; se délasser, se remettre, se refaire.*

refresher, *n.*, personne qui rafraîchit qui délasse; chose qui rafraîchit, qui délasse, *f.*; (extra fee—*augmentation d'honoraires*) honoraires extra (à un homme de loi), *m. pl.*

refreshing, *adj.*, rafraîchissant; qui délasse; récréatif, délassant.

refreshment (ri-frèsh'-), *n.*, rafraîchissement; délassement, *n.*; récréation, *f.*

refrigerant (ri-), *n.*, réfrigérant, *m.*

refrigerant (ri-fridj'èr'-), *adj.*, réfrigérant.

refrigerate (ri-fridj'èr-), *v.a.*, rafraîchir; réfrigérer.

refrigeration (ri-fridj'èr'é-), *n.*, réfrigération, *f.*

refrigerative, *or* **refrigeratory** (ri-fridj'èr'-), *n.*, réfrigératif, rafraîchissant; (chem.) réfrigérant, *m.*

refrigerative, *or* **refrigeratory** (ri-fridj'èr'-), *adj.*, (med.) rafraîchissant, réfrigératif; (chem.) réfrigérant.

refuge (rèf-fioudje), *n.*, refuge, *m.* To take —; *se réfugier.*

refuge, *v.a.*, donner un refuge à.

refugee (rèf'iou-dji), *n.*, réfugié, *m.*, réfugiée, *f.*

refulgence, *or* **refulgency** (ri-feul-dj'-), *n.*, éclat, *m.*; splendeur, *f.*

refulgent (ri-feul-djè'n'te), *adj.*, éclatant, resplendissant.

refund (ri-feu'n'de), *v.a.*, rembourser; (jur.) refonder.

refusable (ri-fiou-za-b'l), *adj.*, refusable.

refusal (ri-fiou-zal), *n.*, refus; choix de refuser ou d'accepter, *m.* To meet with a —; *éprouver un refus.* To have the — of; *avoir le choix de refuser ou d'accepter.* On his —; *sur son refus.*

refuse (rèf'iouze), *n.*, rebut, *m.*

refuse, *adj.*, de rebut.

refuse (ri-fiouze), *v.a.*, refuser. That is not to be —d; *cela n'est pas de refus.*

refuse, *v.n.*, refuser.
refuser, *n.*, personne qui refuse, *f.*; refuseur, *m.*, refuseuse, *f.*
refutable (ri-fiout'a-b'l), *adj.*, qui peut être réfuté; réfutable.
refutation (rèf'iou-té·), *n.*, réfutation, *f.*
refute (ri-fioute), *v.a.*, réfuter.
refuter, *n.*, réfutateur, *m.*
regain (ri-ghéne), *v.a.*, regagner, reprendre, ressaisir, reconquérir.
regal (rî-), *adj.*, royal; régalien.
regal (rî-), *n.*, (mus.) (ant.) régale, *m.*
regale (ri-ghéle), *n.*, régale, *f.*; droit régalien, *m.*; (feast) festin, *m.*, fête, *f.* (donnée à des ambassadeurs ou autres personnes de distinction).
regale (ri-ghéle), *v.a.*, régaler; réjouir.
regale (ri-ghéle), *v.n.*, se régaler.
regalement (ri-ghél'-), *n.*, rafraîchissement, *m.*
regalia (ri-ghé-), *n.*, insignes de la royauté; droits régaliens, *m.pl.*
regality (ri-), *n.*, royauté, *f.*
regally (rî-), *adv.*, royalement.
regard (ri-gârde), *n.*, égard, *m.*; (esteem—*estime*) considération, *f.*, respect; (reference) égard, rapport, *m.*; (in the forest laws—*eaux et forêts*) inspection, *f.*; (ant.) regard, *m.*; (eminence) distinction, *f.* —s; *amitiés, f.pl.*; *compliments, m.pl.* Give my —s to your brother; *dites mille choses de ma part à monsieur votre frère; faites mes amitiés à monsieur votre frère.* With — to; *par rapport à; relativement à; à l'égard de; quant à.* Out of — for; *par égard pour.* To pay — to; *avoir égard à; faire attention à; écouter.*
regard (ri-gârde), *v.a.*, regarder, considérer; (to mind—*faire attention*) avoir égard à, prendre garde à, regarder à.
regardable (-'a-b'l), *adj.*, (ant.) regardable.
regarder, *n.*, regardant; (of forests—*de forêts*) inspecteur, *m.*
regardful (-foule), *adj.*, soigneux; attentif.
regardfully, *adv.*, attentivement; avec égard.
regarding (ri-gârd'-), *prep.*, touchant, concernant, à l'égard de, quant à.
regardless, *adj.*, peu soigneux; inattentif. — of; *sans se soucier de; sans avoir aucun égard à; sans regarder à; sans faire aucun cas de.*
regardlessly, *adv.*, avec indifférence.
regardlessness, *n.*, insouciance, indifférence, *f.*
regatta (ri-), *n.*, régate, *f.*
regency (ri-djè'n'-), *n.*, régence, *f.*·
regeneracy (ri-djè'n'èr'-), *n.*, état régénéré, *m.*
regenerate (ri-djè'n'èr'-), *adj.*, régénéré.
regenerate (ri-djè'n'èr'-), *v.a.*, régénérer.
regenerateness, *n.*, état régénéré, *m.*
regenerating, *adj.*, régénérateur.
regeneration (ri-djè'n'èr'é-), *n.*, régénération, *f.*
regenerator, *n.*, régénérateur, *m.*, régénératrice, *f.*
regeneratory, *adj.*, régénérateur.
regent (ri-djè'n'te), *n.*, régent, *m.*
regent, *adj.*, régent; dominant, régnant.
regentess (rî-djè'n'-), *n.*, régente, *f.*
regentship, *n.*, régence, *f.*
regerminate (ri-djeur-), *v.n.*, regermer.
regicide (rèdj'i-çaïde), *n.*, régicide, *m.*
regimen (rèdj'i-mène), *n.*, régime; (med.) régime, *m.*, diète, *f.*; (gram.) régime, *m.*
regiment (rèdj'-), *n.*, régiment, *m.*
regiment, *v.a.*, enrégimenter.
regimental, *adj.*, du régiment.
regimentals (-talze), *n.pl.*, uniforme, *m.*
regiminal, *adj.*, (med.) diététique.

region (ri-djeune), *n.*, région; contrée, *f.*
register (rèdj'-), *n.*, registre; (jur.) greffier; (print., of organs—*d'orgues*) registre; (of stoves —*de poêles, &c.*) registre, *m.*, trappe, *f.*
register, *v.a.*, enregistrer; enrôler; porter sur les rôles; (print.) pointer.
registership, *n.*, fonctions d'archiviste, fonctions de greffier, *f.pl.*
registrar, *or* **registrary** (rèdj'-), *n.*, gardien, teneur des registres; (jur.) greffier; archiviste, *m.*
registration (rèdj'is-tré-), *n.*, enregistrement, *m.*; inscription, *f.*
registry (rèdj'-), *n.*, enregistrement, *m.*; inscription, *f.*
registry-book (-bouke), *n.*, livre d'enregistrement, livre d'inscription, *m.*; matricule, *f.*
reglet (règ'-), *n.*, réglette, *f.*
regnancy (règ'-), *n.*, règne, *m.*
regnant (règ'-), *adj.*, régnant.
regorge (ri-gordje), *v.a.*, vomir; (to swallow again—*avaler de nouveau*) ravaler.
regraft (rî-), *v.a.*, regreffer.
regrant (rî-), *v.a.*, accorder de nouveau; rendre.
regrant (rî-), *n.*, concession nouvelle, *f.*
regrate (ri-), *v.a.*, (to offend—*offenser*) offenser, choquer; (to sell—*revendre*) revendre; (mas.) regratter.
regrator (ri-grét'-), *n.*, revendeur, *m.*, revendeuse, *f.*
regrating (ri-grét'-), *n.*, revente, *f.*; (mas.) regrattage, *m.*
regreet (ri-grîte), *v.a.*, resaluer; rendre le salut à.
regreet, *n.*, échange de saluts, *m.*
regress (ri-grèss), *n.*, retour; regrès, *m.*
regression (ri-grèsh'-), *n.*, retour, *m.*; (rhet.) régression, *f.*
regressive, *adj.*, régressif, qui retourne.
regressively, *adv.*, régressivement, en retour·ant.
regret (ri-), *n.*, regret, *m.* To feel —; *éprouver, avoir du regret.*
regret (ri-), *v.a.*, regretter, avoir regret.
regretful (-foule), *adj.*, plein de regrets; regrettable.
regretfully, *adv.*, avec regret, à regret.
regular (règh'iou-), *adj.*, régulier; réglé; en règle; (geom., gram., milit.) régulier; (real—*réel*) vrai, véritable; (downright—*parfait*) franc, fieffé, parfait.
regular (règh'-), *n.*, régulier, *m.*
regularity (règh'iou-), *n.*, régularité, *f.*
regularly, *adv.*, régulièrement; réglément; véritablement; vraiment, franchement.
regulate (règh'iou-), *v.a.*, régler; ordonner; mettre en ordre; (horl.) régler.
regulation (règh'-iou-lé-), *n.*, règlement, *m.*
regulator (règh'iou-lé-teur), *n.*, régulateur, *m.*
regurgitate (ri-gheur-dji-), *v.a.*, vomir, revomir, rejeter.
regurgitate, *v.n.*, regorger.
regurgitation (ri-gheur-dji-té-), *n.*, rejet; regorgement, *m.*
re-habilitate (rî-), *v.a.*, réhabiliter.
re-habilitation (rî-ha-bil'î-té-), *n.*, réhabilitation, *f.*
re-hear (rî-hîr), *v.a.*, entendre de nouveau.
re-hearing (rî-hîr'-), *n.*, nouvelle audition, *f.*
rehearsal (ri-heurs'-), *n.*, récit, *m.*; récitation; (thea.) répétition, *f.*
rehearse (ri-heurse), *v.a.*, réciter; répéter; (to narrate—*narrer*) raconter, rapporter; (thea.) répéter.
rehearser, *n.*, personne qui récite; (thea.) personne qui répète, *f.*
re-heat (rî-hîte), *v.a.*, réchauffer; (tech.) recuire.

re-heating (ri-hit'-), n., recuite, f.
reign (rêne), n., règne ; royaume, m. ; souveraineté, f. In the — of ; sous le règne de.
reign (rêne), v.n., régner.
reigning, adj., régnant ; dominant.
re-imbursable (ri-i'm'beurs'a-b'l), adj., remboursable.
re-imburse (ri-i'm'beurse), v.a., rembourser.
re-imbursement, n., remboursement, m.
re-imburser, n., personne qui rembourse, f.
re-implant (ri-i'm'-), v.a., replanter.
re-import (ri-), v.a., réimporter.
re-importation (ri-i'm'por-té-), n., réimportation, f.
re-importune (ri-i'm'-por-tioune), v.a., importuner de nouveau.
re-impregnate (ri-i'm'prèg-), v.a., imprégner de nouveau.
re-impress (ri-), v.a., imprimer de nouveau.
re-impression (ri-i'm'prèsh'-), n., réimpression, f.
re-imprison (ri-i'm'priz'eune), v.a., remettre en prison.
re-imprisonment, n., nouvel emprisonnement, m.
rein (rêne), n., rêne, bride, f. To keep a tight — over any one ; tenir la bride courte, tenir la bride serrée à quelqu'un. To give the — to ; rendre la bride à : lâcher la bride à.
rein, v.a., conduire à la bride, conduire, gouverner ; brider ; (to restrain—retenir) brider, contenir. To — in ; retenir.
reindeer (rê'n'dir), n., renne, m.
reinforce (ri-i'n'fôrce), v.a., (milit.) renforcer ; (fig.) fortifier.
reinforcement, n., secours, appui ; (milit.) renforcement, renfort, m.
re-ingratiate (ri-i'n'gré-shi-), v.a., faire rentrer en grâce ; remettre en grâce.
re-inhabit (ri-), v.a., habiter de nouveau.
reinless (rê'n'-), adj., sans rênes ; sans frein.
re-insert (ri-i'n'seurte), v.a., insérer de nouveau.
re-insertion (ri-i'n'seur'-), n., insertion nouvelle, f.
· re-inspect (ri-), v.a., inspecter de nouveau.
re-inspection, n., nouvelle inspection, f.
re-inspire (ri-i'n'spaeur), v.a., inspirer de nouveau ; ranimer.
re-install (ri-i'n'stôl), v.a., réinstaller ; rétablir.
re-instalment (ri-), n., réinstallation, f. ; rétablissement, m.
re-instate (ri-), v.a., rétablir ; réintégrer.
re-instatement, n., rétablissement, m. ; réintégration, f.
re-integrate (ri-i'n'ti-), v.a., réintégrer.
re-interrogate (ri-i'n'tèr-), v.a., interroger de nouveau.
re-introduce (ri-i'n'tro-diouce), v.a., introduire de nouveau.
re-invest (ri-i'n'vèste), v.a., revêtir ; investir de nouveau ; (money—argent) replacer.
re-investment (ri-), n., nouvel investissement ; replacement, m.
re-invigorate (ri-), v.a., rendre de la vigueur à.
re-issue (ri-ish'iou), n., nouvelle émission, f.
re-issue (ri-ish'iou), v.a., émettre de nouveau.
re-iterate (ri-i'teur-), v.a., réitérer.
re-iteration (ri-it'eur'é-), n., réitération, f.
reject (ri-djèk'te), v.a., rejeter.
rejectable ('a-b'l), adj., rejetable, à rejeter.
rejecter, n., personne qui rejette, f.
rejection, n., rejet, m.
rejective, adj., qui rejette.
rejoice (ri-djwaice), v.a., réjouir.
rejoice, v.n., se réjouir.

rejoicer, n., personne qui se réjouit, f.
re-join (ri-djwaine), v.a., rejoindre.
rejoin, v.n., répliquer, répondre.
rejoinder, n., repartie, réponse ; réplique, f.
rejoint (rè-djwaï'n'te), v.a., rejoindre ; (mas.) rejointoyer.
rejointing, n., action de rejoindre, f. ; (mas.) rejointoiement, m.
re-judge (ri-djeudje), v.a., rejuger.
rejuvenate (ri-djiou-vi-), or rejuvenize (-vè'n'aïze), v.a., rajeunir.
rejuvenescence, or rejuvenescency (ri-djiou-vè-nès'-), n., rajeunissement. m.
re-kindle (ri-ki'n'd'l), v.a., enflammer de nouveau ; rallumer.
re-land (ri-), v.a. and n., débarquer.
relapse (ri-), n., rechute, f.
relapse, v.n., retomber.·
relate (ri-), v.a., raconter ; rapporter ; réciter; conter.
relate, v.n., se rapporter ; avoir rapport; être relatif.
related (ri-lét'), adj., qui a relation, qui a rapport; relatif ; (by blood—par le sang) allié, parent.
relater (ri-lét'-), n., raconteur, conteur, narrateur, m.
relating (ri-lét'-), adj., relatif, qui a rapport, qui a trait ; qui se rapporte.
relation (ri-lé-), n., (recital—récit) relation, f., récit, rapport ; (analogy—analogie) rapport, m., relation ; (alliance) parenté, f. ; (pers.) parent, m., parente, f. —s ; (intercourse— commerce d'amitié, &c.) relations, f.pl ; rapports, m.pl.
relational (ri-lé-), adj., de la même famille.
relationship (ri-lé-), n., parenté ; relation, f.
relative (rèl'-), n., parent, m., parente, f. ; (gram.) relatif ; (log.) terme relatif, m.
relative (rèl'-), adj., relatif.
relatively, adv., relativement.
relativeness (rèl'-), n., relation, f. ; rapport, m. ; (log.) relativité, f.
relax (ri-), v.a., relâcher, détendre, débander; lâcher ; se relâcher de ; (fig.) relâcher, délasser, distraire. To — one's mind ; se distraire, se délasser.
relaxable ('-a-b'l), adj., qui peut être relâché.
relaxation (rèl'aks'é-), n., relâchement, relâche ; (med.) relâchement, m., relaxation, f. ; (fig.) relâchement, délassement, m., distraction, f.
relaxing, adj., qui relâche ; (med.) relâchant, laxatif.
relay (ri-lè), n., relais, m.
release (ri-lîce), n., élargissement, m. ; délivrance ; libération f. ; (jur.), abandon, m. ; (from an obligation—d'une obligation) décharge, f.
release (ri-lîce), v.a., relâcher, élargir ; dégager, délivrer, relever, abandonner ; (from an obligation—d'une obligation) décharger.
releasee (ri-liss'î), n., (jur.) abandonnataire, m.f.
releaser (ri-liss'-), n., personne qui délivre, qui décharge, qui dégage, f. ; libérateur, m., libératrice, f.
releasor, n., (jur.) personne qui abandonne, f.
relegate (rèl'i-), v.a., (ant.) reléguer. .
relegation (rèl'i-ghé-), n., (ant.) relégation, f.
relent (ri-), v.n., s'amollir ; se ramollir ; (pers.) se radoucir, fléchir, céder, s'adoucir, s'attendrir.
relenting (ri-), n., ramollissement ; (pers.) radoucissement, attendrissement, m.
relentless (ri-), adj., inflexible, sans pitié, impitoyable, inexorable, implacable.

relentlessly, *adv.*, impitoyablement.

relentlessness. *n.*, rigueur, dureté, *f.*

relessee (ri-lès'si), *n.*, abandonnataire, *m.,f.*

relessor (ri-lès'seur), *n.*, personne qui donne une décharge, *f.*

relevance, *or* **relevancy** (rèl'i-), *n.*, dépendance, convenance, relation, *f.*

relevant (rèl'i-), *adj.*, relatif ; applicable ; pertinent.

reliable (ri-laï'a-b'l), *adj.*, à qui l'on peut se fier, sur lequel on peut compter ; digne de confiance.

reliableness, *or* **reliability** (ri-laï-), *n.*, qualité d'être digne de confiance, *f.*

reliance (ri-laï'-), *n.*, confiance, *f.* To place — on ; *avoir confiance dans ; se fier à ; compter sur ; mettre sa confiance dans, en.*

relic (rèl'-), *n.*, reste, *m.* ; (saint, martyr) relique, *f.* —s ; *restes, m.pl.* ; *dépouille mortelle, f.* ; *cendre, f.* ; *cendres, f.pl.*

relict (rèl'-), *n.*, veuve, *f.*

relief (ri-life), *n.*, (from pain, &c.—*de douleur, &c.*) soulagement, adoucissement, allégement ; (assistance) secours, *m.*, aide ; (milit.) action de relever une sentinelle, *f.* ; (milit.) soldat qui relève une sentinelle, *m.* ; (redress—*réparation*) redressement, *m.*, réparation, *f.* ; (feudalism—*féodalité*, paint., sculpt.) relief, *m.* Demi—; (paint., sculpt.) *demi-relief.* To afford, to give —; *donner du soulagement* ; (assistance) *donner des secours.* Parish —; *secours du bureau de bienfaisance.*

relier (ri-laï'-), *n.*, personne qui met sa confiance, personne qui a confiance, *f.* To be a — on ; *avoir confiance dans ; mettre sa confiance dans, en ; compter sur.*

relieve (ri-live). *v.a.*, (from pain, &c., to give ease to—*de douleur, &c.*) soulager ; (to alleviate—*alléger*) adoucir, alléger ; (to deliver—*délivrer*) délivrer ; (to assist—*assister*) secourir, aider, subvenir aux besoins de ; (milit.) relever ; (to right—*réformer*) redresser ; (to abate—*mitiger*) adoucir, tempérer ; (to set off—*faire ressortir*) relever, donner du relief à.

reliever (ri-liv'-). *n.*, personne qui soulage, qui adoucit, qui secourt, qui aide ; chose qui soulage, qui adoucit, qui secourt, qui aide, *f.*

relieving (ri-liv'-), *n.*, soulagement, allégement, adoucissement ; secours, *m.* ; aide, *f.*

relieving-officer (ri-liv'-), *n.*, employé chargé de distribuer les secours, *m.*

relievo (ri-li-vô), *n.*, relief, *m.*

re-light (ri-laïte), *v.a.*, rallumer ; éclairer de nouveau.

religion (ri-lid'jeune), *n.*, religion, *f.*

religionist, *n.*, bigot, fanatique, *m.*

religious (ri-lid'jeusse), *adj.*, religieux ; de religion ; de piété.

religious, *n.*, religieux, *m.*, religieuse, *f.*

religiously, *adv.*, religieusement ; avec piété.

religiousness, *n.*, piété, *f.*

relinquish (ri-lin'gn'kwish), *v.a.*, abandonner ; quitter ; renoncer à.

relinquisher. *n.*, personne qui abandonne ; personne qui renonce, *f.*

relinquishment, *n.*, renonciation, *f.* ; abandon, désistement, *m.*

reliquary (rèl'i-kwa-), *n.*, reliquaire, *m.*

re-liquated (ri-li-kwét'-), *adj.*, (metal.) de liquation.

relish (rèl'-). *n.*, goût, *m.*, saveur, *f.* ; (fig.) parfum ; (charm) charme, *f.* ; (titbit—*friandise*) morceau friand, *m.*, friandise, *f.* To give a — to ; *relever le goût de.*

relish (rèl'-), *v.a.*, (to give a taste to—*donner du goût*) donner du goût à, relever le goût de ; (to like—*aimer*) trouver goût à, goûter, savourer, aimer.

relish, *v.n.*, avoir bon goût, être d'un goût

agréable ; (to give pleasure—*faire plaisir*) faire plaisir, être agréable ; (to have a flavour—*avoir du parfum*) avoir un parfum, une saveur, de.

relishable, *adj.*, qui a bon goût.

re-live (ri-liv'), *v.n.*, revivre.

relucent (ri-liou-), *adj.*, clair, transparent.

reluctance, *or* **reluctancy** (ri-leuk-), *n.*, répugnance, *f.*

reluctant (ri-leuk'-), *adj.*, qui a de la répugnance ; qui balance ; qui agit à contre-cœur ; (of things—*des choses*) qui résiste, forcé. I am — to ; *j'ai de la répugnance à ; je répugne à ; il me répugne de.*

reluctantly (ri-leuk'-), *adv.*, avec répugnance, à contre-cœur.

reluctate (ri-leuk'-). *v.n.*, (ant.) résister.

reluctation (ri-leuk-té-), *n.*, (ant.) résistance, répugnance, *f.*

relume (ri-lioume), *v.a.*, rallumer.

relumine (ri-liou-), *v.a.*, (ant.) V. **relume**.

rely (ri-la'-ye), *v.n.*, compter sur, se reposer sur, se fier à, faire fond sur, avoir confiance dans, en.

remain (ri-mé'n), *v.n.*, rester, demeurer. There — ; there —s ; *il reste.* To have —ing ; *avoir de reste.* It —s for me to ; *il me reste à.* To — till called for ; (of letters—*des lettres*) *poste restante.*

remainder (ri-mé'n'-), *n.*, reste, restant, *m.* ; (jur.) réversibilité à terme fixe, *f.*

remainder, *adj.*, de reste.

remaining, *adj.*, de reste ; restant.

remains (ri-mé'n'ze), *n.pl.*, restes ; débris, *m.pl.* ; cendres, *f.pl.*, cendre, dépouille mortelle, *f.* Mortal — ; *restes mortels ; cendres ; cendre ; dépouille mortelle.*

re-make (ri-), *v.a.* (preterit and *past part.*, Remade), refaire.

re-man (ri-), *v.a.*, remettre du monde dans ; armer de nouveau.

remand (ri-mâ'n'd), *v.a.*, rappeler ; contremander ; (jur.) renvoyer à une autre audience.

remand, *n.*, renvoi à une autre audience, *m.*

remark (ri-mârke), *n.*, remarque, *f.*

remark (ri-mârke), *v.a.*, remarquer, observer ; faire remarquer, faire observer.

remarkable ('-a-b'l), *adj.*, remarquable.

remarkableness, *n.*, caractère remarquable, *m.*

remarkably, *adv.*, remarquablement.

remarker, *n.*, observateur, *m.*, observatrice, *f.*

re-marry (ri-), *v.a.*, remarier.

re-marry, *v.n.*, se remarier.

remasticate (ri-). *v.a.*, remâcher.

remediable (ri-mi-di-a-b'l), *adj.*, à quoi l'on peut remédier, réparable, remédiable.

remedial (ri-mî-), *adj.*, destiné à remédier, réparateur.

remediless (ri-mèd'-), *adj.*, incurable ; irréparable ; sans remède.

remedilessness, *n.*, incurabilité, *f.*

remedy (rè'm'i-), *n.*, remède, *m.* Past — ; *sans remède.*

remedy, *v.a.*, remédier à, porter remède à.

remember (ri-mè'm-), *v.a.*, se souvenir de, se ressouvenir de ; se rappeler ; rappeler au souvenir. If I — rightly ; *s'il m'en souvient bien.* — me to him ; *rappelez-moi à son souvenir ; diteslui mille choses de ma part.*

rememberer, *n.*, personne qui se souvient, qui se ressouvient, qui se rappelle, *f.*

remembrance, *n.*, souvenir, ressouvenir ; (token—*témoignage*) souvenir ; (memorandum) mémorandum, *m.*, note, *f.* In —of ; *en souvenir de ; en mémoire de.* To bring a thing to any one's — ; *rappeler une chose au souvenir de quelqu'un.* Give him my —s ; *rappelez-moi à son souvenir ; dites-lui mille choses de ma part.*

remembrancer, *n.*, personne qui fait sou-

30 *

venir, *f.* ; (thing—*chose*) souvenir ; (of the ex-chequer—*du Trésor*) secrétaire, *m.*

remigrate (rè'm'-), *v.n.*, émigrer de nou-veau ; retourner.

remigration (rè'm'i-gré-), *n.*, nouvelle émi-gration, *f.*

remind (ri-maï'n'de), *v.a.*, rappeler ; rap-peler au souvenir ; remettre dans l'esprit, faire souvenir, faire ressouvenir. — him of that ; *rappelez-lui cela, faites-le souvenir de cela.*

reminiscence, *or* **reminiscency** (rè'm'-), **x.**, réminiscence, *f.*

reminiscential (-shal), *adj.*, de réminis-cence.

remise (ri-maïze), *v.a.*, (jur.) quitter, céder, abandonner.

remiss (ri-), *adj.*, nonchalant ; négligent, lent, inexact ; sans soins ; mou.

remissible (-'si-b'l), *adj.*, rémissible ; gracia-ble.

remission (ri-), *n.*, rémission, *f.*, relâche-ment, radoucissement, adoucissement, *m.* ; (pardon) remise, grâce, *f.*, pardon, *m.* — of sins ; *rémission des péchés.*

remissly (ri-), *adv.*, négligemment, noncha-lamment, lentement, sans soin.

remissness (ri-), *n.*, nonchalance, lenteur, négligence, inexactitude, *f.*

remit (ri-), *v.a.*, (to relax—*relâcher*) se re-lâcher de, calmer, diminuer, affaiblir ; (to for-give—*pardonner*) faire grâce de, faire remise de, pardonner, remettre ; (to give up—*livrer*) li-vrer, remettre ; (to refer—*référer*) renvoyer ; (to restore—*rendre*) remettre dans, rendre à ; (to send back—*renvoyer*) renvoyer ; (money—*argent*) remettre, faire une remise de.

remit, *v.n.*, se relâcher ; se calmer ; dimi-nuer ; s'affaiblir.

remittal, *or* **remitment** (ri-), *n.*, renvoi en prison ; (forgiveness) pardon, *m.* ; remise, *f.*

remittance (ri-), *n.*, (com.) remise, *f.*

remitter (ri-), *n.*, personne qui pardonne, qui fait remise, qui fait grâce ; (of money—*d'argent*) personne qui fait une remise de fonds, *f.*

remnant (rè'm'-), *n.*, reste, *m.* ; (of stuff—*d'étoffe*) coupon, *m.*

remodel (ri-mod'l), *v.a.*, refondre.

remodelling, *n.*, refonte, *f.*

re-molten (ri-môl't'n), *adj.*, refondu.

remonstrance (ri-), *n.*, remontrance, *f.* ; (c. rel.) ostensoir, *m.*

remonstrant (ri-), *adj.*, de remontrance ; qui remontre.

remonstrant (ri-), *n.*, personne qui fait des remontrances, *f.* ; (hist.) remontrant, *m.*

remonstrate (ri-), *n.*, remontrer, repré-senter. To — with : *faire des remontrances à.*

remonstrator (ri-mo'n'stré-teur), *n.*, per-sonne qui fait des remontrances, *f.*

remora (rè'm'-), *n.*, (ich.) rémora, *m.*

remorse (ri-), *n.*, remords, *m.*

remorseful (-foule), *adj.*, rempli de re-mords ; déchiré de remords.

remorseless (ri-), *adj.*, sans remords ; sans pitié.

remorselessly. *adv.*, sans remords.

remorselessness, *n.*, cruauté, inhumanité, barbarie, *f.*

remote (ri-môte), *adj.*, éloigné, lointain ; reculé, écarté, retiré.

remotely, *adv.*, au loin, de loin ; d'une manière éloignée ; légèrement.

remoteness, *n.*, éloignement, *m.* ; nature éloignée, *f.* ; degré éloigné, *m.* ; faiblesse, *f.*

re-mould (ri-môlde), *v.a.*, mouler de nou-veau.

re-mount (ri-maou'n'te), *v.a.* and *n.*, re-monter.

re-mounting, *n.*, (milit.) remonte, *f.*

removability (ri-mouv'-), *n.*, amovibilité, *f.*

removable (ri-mouv'a-b'l), *adj.*, amovible ; transportable.

removal (ri-mouv'-), *n.*, (of residence—*de résidence*) changement de domicile, déménage-ment ; (from office—*d'emploi*) déplacement, renvoi, *m.*, destitution, *f.* ; (of a grievance—*grief*) redressement, *m.* ; (of a disease—*de maladie*) guérison ; (of bandages—*de bandages*) levée, *f.* ; (change of place—*changement de lieu*) change-ment de place ; déplacement ; enlèvement, *m.*

remove (ri-mouve), *n.*, (change of place—*changement de lieu*) changement de place, *m.* ; (translation) translation, *f.*, transport ; (re-moval—*de maison*) déménagement ; (departure—*départ*) départ ; (at chess, draughts—*aux échecs, aux dames*) coup ; (step—*un pas*) degré, *m.* ; (dis-tance) distance ; (dish—*plat*) entrée, *f.*

remove (ri-mouve), *v.a.*, (to place at a dis-tance—*écarter*) éloigner ; (to put from its place —*changer de place*) déplacer ; (to set aside—mettre à l'écart) ôter, enlever, écarter ; (to take away—*enlever*) ôter, enlever ; (to transport—*transférer*) transporter ; (from office—*d'emploi*) déplacer, démettre, destituer ; (furniture—*mobilier*) déménager ; (bandages) lever ; (ob-stacle) lever ; (a disease—*maladie*) chasser ; (jur.) porter à une autre cour ; (by death—*par la mort*) enlever ; (from school—*d'une école*) re-tirer.

remove (ri-mouve), *v.n.*, s'éloigner ; s'ôter, s'écarter ; se déplacer ; se transporter ; (to change residence—*de demeure*) changer de domi-cile, déménager.

remover, *n.*, personne qui ôte, qui éloigne, qui déplace, *f.*

remunerability (ri-miou-nèr'-), *n.*, qualité de ce qui peut être rémunéré, *f.*

remunerable (ri-miou-nèr'a-b'l), *adj.*, qui mérite récompense.

remunerate (ri-miou-nèr'-), *v.a.*, rémuné-rer ; rétribuer ; salarier, payer.

remunerated (ri-miou-nèr'ét'-), *adj.*, ré-muneré ; rétribué ; salarié, payé.

remunerating (ri-miou-nèr'ét'-), *adj.*, qui rétribue ; de rémunération, lucratif.

remuneration (ri-miou-nèr'é-), *n.*, rémuné-ration ; rétribution, *f.*

remunerative (-nèr'é-), *or* **remuneratory** (-nèr'a-teuri), *adj.*, qui rétribue ; rémunérateur, rémunératif, rémunératoire.

re-murmur (ri-meur-meur), *v.a.* and *n.*, répéter en murmurant ; répondre en murmu-rant.

renal (ri-), *adj.*, (anat.) rénal.

renard (rè'n'-), *n.*, renard, maître renard, *m.*

renascency (ri-nas'-), *n.*, renaissance, *f.*

renascent (ri-nas'-), *adj.*, renaissant.

renascible (-ci-b'l), *adj.*, (ant.) qui peut renaître ; qui renaît.

re-navigate (ri-), *v.a.*, naviguer de nouveau sur.

re-navigate, *v.n.*, naviguer de nouveau.

rencounter (rè'n'caou'n'-), *n.*, rencontre, *f.* ; choc, *m.* ; (combat) rencontre, *f.*, combat, *m.*

rencounter (rè'n'caou'n'-), *v.a.*, rencontrer hostilement.

rencounter, *v.n.*, se rencontrer, se heurter ; se choquer ; (to fight—*combattre*) se rencontrer hostilement, se battre.

rend, *v.a.* (preterit and past part., Rent), dé-chirer : fendre. To — the heart ; *fendre le cœur.* To — asunder ; *déchirer en deux, fendre en deux.*

render, *v.a.*, rendre ; (mas.) appliquer.

render, *n.*, reddition ; (payment of rent—*payement de loyer*) redevance, *f.* ; (account given —*rapport*) compte rendu, *m.*, explication, *f.* ; (pers.) fendeur, *m.*, fendeuse ; personne qui dé-chire, *f.*

renderable (-a-b'l), *adj.*, qui peut être rendu.

rendez-vous (rŏ'n'dĭ-vou),*n.*,rendez-vous,*m.*
rendez-vous, *v.n.*, se donner rendez-vous ;
se réunir.
rendezvous, *v.a.*, donner rendez-vous à;
réunir.
rendition (rĕ'n'dĭsh'-), *n.*, reddition, *f.*
renegade (rĕ'n'ĭ-), *or* **renegado** (-ghé-dô),
n.. renégat, transfuge : (vagabond) vagabond, *m.*
re-nerve (rĭ-neurve), *v.a.*, redonner du nerf
à ; redonner de la vigueur à.
renew (ri-niou), *v.a.*, renouveler ; renouer.
renewable (-a'b'l), *adj.*, renouvelable.
renewal, *n.*, renouvellement, *m.*
renewedness (ri-nioud'-), *n.*, renouvellement, *m.* ; rénovation, *f.*
renewer, *n.*, rénovateur, *m.*, rénovatrice, *f.*
renewing, *adj.*, rénovateur.
renewing, *n.*, renouvellement, *m.*
reniform (rĕ'n'-), *adj.*, réniforme.
renitence, *or* **renitency** (ri-naï-), *n.*, rénitence ; résistance, *f.*
renitent (ri-naï-), *adj.*, rénitent ; résistant.
rennet, *n.*, présure ; caillette, *f.*
rennet, *or* **rennetting**, *n.*,reinette, pomme
de reinette, *f.*
renounce (ri-naou'n'-ce), *v.a.* and *n.*, renoncer ; renoncer à ; renier.
renouncement, *n.*, renoncement, *m.* ; renonciation, *f.*
renouncer, *n.*, personne qui renonce, *f.*
renovate (rĕ'n'-), *v.a.*, renouveler, faire renaître.
renovating (rĕ'n'o-vét'-), *adj.*, rénovateur.
renovation (rĕ'n'o-vé-), *n.*, rénovation, *f.*, renouvellement, *m.*
renown (ri-naou'n), *n.*, renommée, *f.*; renom, *m.*
renowned (ri-naou'n'de), *adj.*, renommé.
renownedly, *adv.*, avec renom; avec une
grande renommée ; glorieusement.
rent, *n.*, (fissure)déchirement, *m.*, déchirure,
fente, *f.* ; (in garments—*des vêtements*) accroc,
m., déchirure, *f.* ; (schism) schisme, *m.* ; (min.)
fente, fissure, *f.* ; rente, redevance, *f.* ; (of farms
—*de ferme*) fermage ; (of houses, rooms—*de
maisons, chambres, &c.*) loyer, *m.* Heavy —;
gros loyer. High, low —; *loyer élevé, faible.*
rent, *v.a.*, (to let out—*donner en location*)
louer, donner à louage, donner à ferme, donner
à loyer ; (to ·take—*prendre en location*) louer,
prendre à louage, prendre à ferme, prendre à
loyer ; arrenter.
rent, *v.n.*, se louer.
rentable (-'a-b'l), *adj.*, qui peut être loué.
rental, *n.*, état de rentes ; livre censier, *m.*
renter, *n.*, bailleur, propriétaire qui donne à
loyer, à ferme ; (lessee—*preneur*) locataire ; (of
a farm—*de ferme*) fermier, *m.*
renter, *v.a.*, faire des reprises perdues à.
renterer, *n.*, ouvrier en reprises perdues,
m., ouvrière en reprises perdues, *f.*
rent-roll, *n.*, état de revenus, livre censier,*m.*
renunciation (ri-neu'n'shi-é-), *n.*, renonciation, *f.* ; renoncement, *m.*
renverse (rĕ'n'veurse), *adj.*, (her.) renversé.
re-obtain (rĭ-), *v.n.*, obtenir de nouveau.
re-open (rĭ-ô-), *v.a.*, rouvrir, ouvrir de nouveau.
re-oppose (rĭ-op-pôze),*v.a.*, opposer de nouveau.
re-ordain (rĭ-or-dé'n), *v.a.*, réordonner.
re-ordination (rĭ-or-di-né-), *n.*, réordination, *f.*
re-organization (rĭ-or-ga'n'aïzé-), *n.*, réorganisation, *f.*
re-organize (rĭ-or-ga'n'aïze), *v.a.*, réorganiser.
re-pacify (rĭ-pa-ci-fa'-ye), *v.a.*, pacifier de
nouveau.
repair (ri-pére),*v.a.*,réparer; raccommoder ;

rétablir; (nav.) radouber ; (an injury—*un dommage*) réparer, indemniser.
repair (ri-pére), *n.*, réparation,*f.*; rétablissement, entretien ; (nav.) radoub; séjour, *m.*, 'demeure ; action de se rendre d'un lieu à un autre,*f.*
To be out of —; *être en mauvais état ; avoir besoin de réparation ; avoir besoin d'être raccom-
modé.* To be in good —; *être en bon état ; être bien
entretenu.* To keep in —; *entretenir en bon état.*
repair (ri-pére), *v.n.*, aller; se rendre ; se
transporter.
repairer, *n.*, réparateur, *m.*, réparatrice, *f.* ;
(tech.) répareur, *m.*
repand, *or* **repandous** (ri-), *adj.*, (bot.)
godronné.
reparable (rèp'a-ra-b'l), *adj.*, réparable.
reparably, *adv.*, d'une manière réparable.
reparation (rèp'a-ré-), *n.*, action de réparer ;
réparation, *f.* ; rétablissement, *m.*
reparative (ri-par-a-), *adj.*, qui répare ; réparateur.
repartee (rèp'ar-tî), *n.*, repartie, *f.*
repartee (rèp'ar-tî), *v.n.*, repartir, riposter.
repass (rî-pàss),*v.a.* and *n.*, repasser.
repast (ri-pàste), *n.*, repas, *m.*
repast (ri-pàste), *v.a.*, repaître.
repay (ri-pè), *v.a.* (*pretcrit* and *past part.,*
Repaid), rembourser; payer, rendre ; récompenser; payer de retour ; revaloir.
repayable (ri-pè-a-b'l), *adj.*, payable, remboursable.
re-payment (rî-pè-), *n.*, payement, remboursement, *m.*
repeal (ri-pîl), *v.a.*, révoquer, abolir,abroger.
repeal (ri-pîl), *n.*, révocation, abrogation,
abolition, *f.*
repealable (-'a-b'l), *adj.*, révocable.
repealer, *n.*, personne qui révoque, qui
abroge, *f.* ; partisan de la révocation, *m.*
repeat (ri-pîte), *v.a.*, répéter, redire ; réciter.
repeat (ri-pîte), *n.*, répétition ; (mus.) reprise, *f.*
repeatedly (ri-pît'èd'-), *adv.*, à plusieurs
reprises ; souvent.
repeater, *n.*, rediseur, *m.*, rediseuse, *f.* ;
(nav.) répétiteur, *m.* ; (horl.) montre à répétition, *f.*
repeating, *adj.*, qui répète ; (horl.) à répétition.
repel (ri-pèl), *v.a.*, repousser ; (med.) répercuter.
repellency (ri-pèl'-), *n.*, force répulsive,*f.*
repellent (ri-pèl'-), *n.*, répercussif, révulsif, *m.*
repellent, *adj.*, répulsif.
repeller, *n.*, personne qui repousse, chose
qui repousse, *f.* ; (thing—*chose*) repoussoir, *m.*
repent (ri-), *v.a.* and *n.*, se repentir de ; se
repentir.
repent (rî-), *adj.*, rampant.
repentance (ri-), *n.*, repentir, *m.* ; repentance, *f.*
repentant (ri-), *adj.*; repentant.
repentant (ri-), *n.*, personne repentante,
f. ; pénitent, *m.*, pénitente, *f.*
repenter, *n.*, personne repentante,*f.*
repenting, *n.*, repentir, *m.*
repentingly, *adv.*, avec repentir.
re-people (ri-pi-p'l), *v.a.*, repeupler.
re-peopling (ri-pî-), *n.*, repeuplement, *m.*
repercuss (ri-peur-keuss), *v.a.*, (ant.) répercuter.
re-percussion (ri-peur-keush'-), *n.*, répercussion, *f.*
re-percussive (ri-peur-keuss'-), *adj.*, répercussif ; répercutant.
repertory (rèp'èr-), *n.*, répertoire, recueil, *m.*
repetend (rèp'i-), *n.*, (arith.) période, *f.*
repetition (rèp'i-tish'-),*n.*,répétition ; (mus.)

reprise, répétition ; (recital—*de mémoire*) récitation, *f.*

repine (ri-païne), *v.n.*, se plaindre ; murmurer ; s'affliger ; gémir.

repiner, *n.*, personne qui se plaint, qui murmure, qui s'afflige, qui gémit, *f.* ; mécontent, *m.*, mécontente, *f.*

repining, *adj.*, disposé à s'affliger, à gémir ; disposé à se plaindre, à murmurer.

repiningly, *adv.*, avec affliction ; avec des plaintes ; en murmurant.

replace (ri-), *v.a.*, replacer ; remettre en place ; (to make good—*indemniser*) remplacer.

replacement (ri-plés'-), *n.*, remise en place ; remplacement, *m.* ; (surg.) réduction, *f.*

re-plait (ri-pléte), *v.a.*, replisser ; replier.

re-plant (ri-), *v.a.*, replanter.

replantation (ri-pla'n'té-), *n.*, replantation, *f.*

replead (ri-plide), *v.a.*, replaider.

repleader, *n.*, nouveaux débats, *m.pl.*

replenish (ri-plè'n-), *v.a.* and *n.*, remplir ; se remplir.

replete (ri-plite), *adj.*, plein, rempli.

repletion (ri-plī-), *n.*, plénitude ; (med.) réplétion, *f.*

repleviable (ri-plèv'-a-b'l), *or* **replevizable** (-za-b'l), *adj.*, (of things—*des choses*) dont on peut obtenir la mainlevée ; (pers.) dans le cas d'être admis à fournir caution.

replevin (ri-plèv'-), *n.*, mainlevée sur caution, *f.*

replevy (ri-plèv'-), *v.a.*, (jur.) (pers.) obtenir la mainlevée sur caution, admettre à fournir caution ; (of things—*des choses*) donner mainlevée de, cautionner.

replication (rèp'li-ké-), *n.*, réponse, réplique, *f.*

replier (ri-plaï-), *n.*, personne qui réplique, qui répond, *f.*

reply (ri-pla'ye), *n.*, réplique, réponse, *f.*

reply (ri-pla'ye), *v.a.* and *n.*, répliquer, répondre.

re-polish (ri-), *v.a.*, repolir.

report (ri-pôrte), *v.a.*, rapporter ; raconter, dire, réciter ; faire le rapport de. It is —ed ; *on rapporte que ; on dit que ; le bruit court que.*

report, *v.n.*, faire un rapport.

report (ri-pôrte), *n.*, (account—*relation*) rapport, compte rendu ; (rumour—*rumeur*) rapport, bruit, ouï-dire ; compte rendu ; (story—*narration*)récit, *m.* ; (repute—*réputation*)réputation ; (of fire-arms—*d'armes à feu*) détonation, *f.* ; (jur.) procès-verbal, rapport, *m.*

reporter, *n.*, rapporteur ; auteur d'un récit, auteur d'un compte rendu ; (short-hand writer—*sténographe*) sténographe ; (correspondent) correspondant, *m.*

reporting, *n.*, comptes rendus, *m.* ; sténographie ; correspondance, *f.*

reportingly, *adv.*, par ouï-dire.

reposal (ri-pô-zal), *n.*, action de mettre confiance, *f.*

repose (ri-pôze), *v.n.*, se reposer ; reposer. To — on ; *se reposer sur ; se fier à ; se confier à.*

repose, *v.a.*, reposer ; (to confide—*confier*) mettre sa confiance, confier.

repose (ri-pôze), *n.*, repos, *m.*

reposedness (ri-pôz'èd'-), *n.*, état de repos,*m.*

reposit (ri-poz'-), *v.a.*, déposer.

reposition (ri-poz'ish'-), *n.*, (ant.) remise en place ; (surg.) réduction, *f.*

repository (ri-poz'i-teuri), *n.*, dépôt ; (min.) dépôt, gisement, bassin, *m.*

re-possess (ri-poz'zèss), *v.a.*, rentrer en possession de, reposséder.

re-possession (ri-poz-zèsh'-), *n.*, rentrée en possession, *f.*

reprehend (rèp'ri-), *v.a.*, reprendre ; réprimander ; censurer, blâmer.

reprehender, *n.*, personne qui reprend, qui réprimande, *f.* ; censeur, critique, *m.*

reprehensible (rèp-ri-hè'n'si-b'l), *adj.*, répréhensible.

reprehensibleness, *n.*, nature répréhensible, *f.*

reprehensibly, *adv.*, d'une manière répréhensible.

reprehension (rèp'ri-), *n.*, répréhension,*f.*

reprehensive (rèp'ri-); *or* **reprehensory** (-seuri), *adj.*, de reproche.

represent (rèp'ri-zè'n'te), *v.a.*, représenter.

representant (rèp'ri-zè'n'-), *n.*, représentant. *m.*

representation (rèp'-ri-zè'n'té'-), *n.*, représentation,*f.*

representative (rèp'ri-zè'n'ta-), *adj.*, représentatif ; qui représente.

representative, *n.*, représentant, *m.* ; (of things—*des choses*) représentation, *f.*

representatively, *adv.*, d'une manière représentative ; par représentation.

representativeness, *n.*, (philos.) représentation, *f.*

representer, *n.*, personne qui représente, chose qui représente, *f.* ; représentant, *m.*

repress (ri-prèss), *v.a.*, réprimer.

represser, *n.*, personne qui réprime, *f.*

repression (ri-prèsh'-), *n.*, répression, *f.*

repressive (ri-près'-), *adj.*, répressif.

repressively, *adv.*, d'une manière répressive.

reprieve (ri-prive), *n.*, sursis, répit, *m.*

reprieve, *v.a.*, accorder un sursis ; surseoir à l'exécution de ; accorder un répit à.

reprimand (rèp'-), *n.*, réprimande, *f.*

reprimand, *v.a.*, réprimander ; blâmer

re-print (ri-), *n.*, réimpression, *f.*

re-print, *v.a.*, réimprimer.

reprisal (ri-praï-zal), *n.*, représaille ; (jur.) reprise, *f.*

reproach (ri-prôtshe), *n.*, reproche, *m.* ; (shame—*honte*) honte, *f.*, opprobre, *m.*

reproach, *v.a.*, reprocher ; faire un reproche à ; blâmer, accuser. To be —ed with ; *recevoir des reproches de.*

reproachable (-a-b'l), *adj.*, reprochable, digne de reproche.

reproachful (-foule), *adj.*, plein de reproches ; digne de reproche ; injurieux ; honteux, d'opprobre.

reproachfully, *adv.*, avec reproche ; injurieusement, avec insulte ; avec honte.

reprobate (rèp'-), *n.*, vaurien, mauvais garnement ; (theol.) réprouvé, *m.*

reprobate (rèp'-), *adj.*, (pers.) en état de réprobation ; frappé de réprobation ; (of things—*des choses*) de réprobation, de réprouvé.

reprobate, *v.a.*, réprouver ; frapper de réprobation.

reprobateness (rèp'ro-bét'-), *n.*, état de réprobation, *m.*

reprobater (-bét'-), *n.*, personne qui réprouve, *f.*

reprobation (-bé-), *n.*, réprobation, *f.*

reproduce (ri-pro-diouce), *v.a.*, reproduire.

reproducer, *n.*, personne qui reproduit ; chose qui reproduit, *f.* ; (animal) reproducteur,*m.*

reproduction (ri-pro-deuk-), *n.*, reproduction, *f.*

reproductive (-deuk'-), *or* **reproductory** (-teuri), *adj.*, reproducteur ; de la reproduction.

reproof (ri-proufe), *n.*, répréhension, réprimande, *f.* ; reproche, *m.*

reprovable (ri-prouv'a-b'l), *adj.*, répréhensible.

reprove (ri-prouve), *v.a.*, censurer ; blâmer, reprendre, réprimander.

reprover, *n.*, personne qui blâme, qui censure, qui reprend, *f.* ; censeur, *m.*

reproving, *adj.*, réprobateur ; de réprobation.

re-prune (ri-proune), *v.a.*, élaguer de nouveau.

reptile (rèp'-), *n.*, reptile, *m.*

reptile, *adj.*, reptile ; rampant.

republic (ri-peub'-), *n.*, république ; chose publique, *f.*

republican (ri-peub'-), *adj.*, républicain.

republican, *n.*, républicain, *m.*

republicanism (-ca'n'iz'm), *n.*, républicanisme, *m.*

re-publication (ri-peub'li-ké-), *n.*, republication, *f.* ; (of a will—*de testament*) renouvellement, *m.*

re-publish (ri-peub'-), *v.a.*, republier ; publier une nouvelle édition de ; (a will—*testament*) renouveler.

repudiable (ri-piou-di-a-b'l), *adj.*, qui peut être répudié.

repudiate (ri-piou-), *v.a.*, répudier.

repudiation (ri-piou-), *n.*, répudiation, *f.*

repugnance, *or* **repugnancy** (ri-peug-), *n.*, répugnance ; résistance ; (contrariety) contrariété, *f.*

repugnant (ri-peug-), *adj.*, répugnant ; qui répugne ; contraire. It is — to me to ; *il me répugne de.*

repugnantly, *adv.*, avec répugnance.

re-pullulate (ri-peul-liou-), *v.n.*, repulluler.

re-pullulation (ri-peul-liou-lé-), *n.*, action de repulluler, *f.*

repulse (ri-peulse), *v.a.*, repousser ; rebuter.

repulse, *n.*, échec, refus, *m.* ; rebuffade, *f.*

repulser, *n.*, personne qui repousse, *f.*

repulsion (ri-peul-), *n.*, répulsion ; action de rebuter, *f.*

repulsive (ri-peul-), *or* **repulsory** (-seuri), *adj.*, rebutant ; (forbidding—*repoussant*) repoussant ; (phys.) répulsif.

repulsiveness, *n.*, caractère repoussant, caractère rebutant, *m.*

repulsory, *adj. V.* **repulsive**.

re-purchase (ri-peur-tshéce), *v.a.*, racheter.

re-purchase, *n.*, rachat, *m.*

reputable (rèp'iou-ta-b'l), *adj.*, (pers.) honorable, en bonne réputation ; (things—*choses*) honorable, compatible avec la bonne réputation.

reputably, *adv.*, avec honneur ; honorablement.

reputation (rèp'iou-té-), *n.*, réputation, renommée, *f.* To get a — ; *se faire une réputation.*

repute (ri-pioute), *v.a.*, réputer.

repute (ri-pioute), *n.*, réputation, renommée, *f.* ; renom, *m.* Of — ; *de renom ; renommé.*

reputed (ri-piout'-). *adj.*, réputé, censé ; (of fathers—*d'un père*) putatif.

reputedly, *adv.*, suivant l'opinion commune.

reputeless, *adj.*, (ant.) déshonorant.

request (ri-kwèste), *n.*, requête, demande, prière, *f.* In — ; *en crédit, en vogue* ; (com.) demandé, recherché. At the — of ; *à la demande de : sur la demande de ; à la prière de ; à la requête de.*

request (ri-kwèste), *v.a.*, demander ; prier.

requester, *n.*, personne qui fait une demande, qui fait une prière, qui fait une requête, *f.* ; demandeur, *m.*, demandeuse, *f.* ; solliciteur, *m.*, solliciteuse, *f.*

re-quicken (ri-kwik'k'n), *v.a.*, raviver, ranimer.

requiem (ri-kwi-è'm), *n.*, requiem, *m.*

requirable (ri-kwaeur'a-b'l), *adj.*, que l'on peut exiger.

require (ri-kwaeur), *v.a.*, exiger, requérir, demander, réclamer ; (to want—*falloir*) avoir besoin de, falloir. To be —d ; *falloir.* It is ; *il faut.* It is —d. of me ; *il faut que je ; on demande, on exige que je.* Two are —d ; *il en faut deux.*

requirement, *n.*, exigence ; condition requise ; nécessité, *f.* ; besoin, *m.*

requirer, *n.*, personne qui requiert, qui demande, qui exige, *f.*

requisite (rèk'wi-zite), *adj.*, requis, exigé, voulu ; nécessaire. It is —to ; *il faut.*

requisite (rèk'wi-zite), *n.*, qualité requise, condition requise ; chose requise ; chose nécessaire, *f.*

requisitely, *adv.*, nécessairement.

requisiteness, *n.*, nécessité absolue, *f.*

requisition (rèk'wi-zish'-), *n.*, réquisition ; demande, requête, *f.*

requital (ri-kwaeu-), *n.*, récompense, *f.* ; retour, *m.* In — of ; *en récompense de ; en retour de.*

requite (ri-kwaite), *v.a.*, récompenser, payer ; reconnaître ; rendre ; payer de retour.

requiter, *n.*, personne qui récompense, qui rend, *f.*

rere-ward, *n.*, arrière-garde, *f.*

re-sail (ri-céle), *v.n.*, retourner à la voile ; remettre à la voile.

re-sale (ri-céle), *n.*, revente, *f.*

re-salute (ri-ça-lioute), *v.a.*, saluer de nouveau ; rendre le salut à.

rescind (ri-ci'n'de), *v.a.*, rescinder ; abolir ; annuler ; révoquer.

rescission (ri-cij'eune), *n.*, rescision ; annulation, révocation, abrogation, *f.*

rescissory (ri-), *adj.*, rescisoire.

rescript (ri-), *n.*, rescrit, *m.*

rescriptively, *adv.*, par rescrit.

rescue (rès'kiou), *n.*, délivrance, *f.* ; secours, *m.* ; délivrance par force ; (jur.) violation de saisie, *f.* To the — ; *au secours!*

rescue (rès'kiou), *v.a.*, sauver ; délivrer ; reprendre ; secourir, délivrer par force ; (jur.) ressaisir.

rescuer, *n.*, personne qui délivre par force, *f.* ; sauveur ; libérateur, *m.*, libératrice, *f.*

research (ri-ceurtshe), *n.*, recherche ; examen.

research, *v.a.*, rechercher ; examiner ; chercher de nouveau.

researcher, *n.*, auteur de recherches, *m.*

re-seat (ri-cite), *v.a.*, rasseoir, replacer.

re-seize (ri-cize), *v.a.*, ressaisir ; (jur.) séquestrer.

re-seizer, *n.*, personne qui saisit de nouveau, *f.*

re-seizure (ri-ci-jeur), *n.*, seconde saisie, *f.*

re-sell (ri-), *v.a.* (*preterit* and *past part.*, Re-sold), revendre.

resemblance (ri-zè'm'-), *n.*, ressemblance ; image, *f.*

resemble (ri-zè'm-b'l), *v.a.*, ressembler à.

resent (ri-zè'n'te), *v.a.*, ressentir ; sentir vivement ; se ressentir de ; se venger de.

resenter, *n.*, personne animée de ressentiment ; personne qui se venge, *f.*

resentful (-foule), *adj.*, plein de ressentiment ; haineux, vindicatif. — of ; *qui se ressent de ; qui se ressent vivement de : qui se venge de.*

resentfully, *or* **resentingly**, *adv.*, avec ressentiment.

resentive (ri-cè'n'-), *adj.*, (ant.) plein de ressentiment ; vindicatif.

resentment (ri-zè'n't'-), *n.*, ressentiment, *m.*

reservation (rèz'èr-vé-), *n.*, réserve ; restriction, arrière-pensée ; (jur.) réserve, réservation, *f.* ; (in America—*en Amérique*) terrain réservé, *m.*

reservatory (ri-zeurv'a-teuri), *n.*, réservoir, *m.*

reserve (ri-zeurve), *n.*, réserve ; (modesty, caution—*retenue*) réserve, retenue ; (exception) restriction ; (thought withheld—*restriction mentale*) arrière-pensée ; (jur.) réserve, réservation, *f.* Body of — ; (milit.) *corps de réserve, m.*

reserve (ri-zeurve), *v.a.*, réserver, se réserver ; conserver, garder.

reserved (ri-zeurv'de), *adj.*, réservé ; qui a de la retenue.

reservedly (ri'zeurv'èd'-), *adv.*, avec retenue, avec réserve.

reservedness (ri-zeurv'èd'-), *n.*, réserve, retenue, *f.*

reserver, *n.*, personne qui réserve, *f.*

reservoir (rèz'èr-voir), *n.*, réservoir ; puisard, *m.*

re-set, *v.a.* (rĭ-cète), (*preterit* and *past part.*, Re-set), (print.) recomposer, composer de nouveau.

re-set (ri-cète), *n.*, (print.) recomposition, *f.*

re-settle (ri'cèt't'l), *v.a.*, rétablir, arranger de nouveau, installer de nouveau.

re-settle (rĭ-cèt't'l), *v.n.*, s'installer de nouveau ; s'établir de nouveau ; (of lees—*lie*, *sédiment*) se rasseoir, se reposer.

re-settlement (ri-), *n.*, rétablissement, *m.* ; réinstallation ; (of lees—*lie*, *sédiment*) nouvelle formation, *f.*

re-ship (ri-), *v.a.*, rembarquer.

re-shipment (ri-), *n.*, rembarquement, *m.*

reside (ri-zaïde), *v.n.*, résider, demeurer.

residence, *or* **residency** (rèz'-), *n.*, résidence, demeure, *f.* ; séjour ; domicile, *m.*

resident (rèz'-), *n.*, habitant, *m.*, habitante, *f.* ; résident, *m.*

resident, *adj.*, résidant.

residentiary (rèz'i-dè'n'shi-), *adj.*, de résident ; qui a une résidence.

residentiary (rèz'i-dè'n'shi-), *n.*, ecclésiastique obligé à résidence, *m.*

residual (rèz'i-diou-), *adj.*, pour le reste ; du reste.

residuary (rèz'i-diou-), *adj.*, pour le reste ; du reste ; (of legatees—*de légataires*) universel.

residue (rèz'i-diou), *n.*, reste, (of debts—*de créances*) reliquat, *m.*

residuum (ri-zid'lou-eume), *n.*, (chem.) résidu ; (jur.) résidu, reste, *m.*

resign (ri-zaïne), *v.a.*, résigner ; (to submit—*soumettre*) soumettre ; (to yield—*céder*) renoncer à ; (functions—*emploi, &c.*) se démettre de, donner sa démission de ; abandonner, céder. To be —ed ; *se résigner ; être résigné.*

re-sign (rĭ-çaïne), *v.a.*, signer de nouveau.

resignation (rèz'ig-né-), *n.*, résignation ; soumission ; cession, *f.* ; abandon, *m.* ; (of functions—*d'emploi, &c.*) démission, *f.* To send in one's —; *donner sa démission.*

resigned (ri-zaï'n'de), *adj.*, résigné.

resignedly (ri-zaï'n'èd'-), *adv.*, avec résignation.

resigner, *n.*, démissionnaire ; résignant, *m.*

resilience, *or* **resiliency** (ri-cil'-), *n.*, rebondissement, *m.*

resilient (ri-cil'-), *adj.*, rebondissant.

resilition (ri-cil'-), *n.* *V.* **resilience**.

resin (rèz'i'n), *n.*, résine ; colophane, *f.*

resinous (rèz'-), *adj.*, résineux.

resinousness (rèz'-), *n.*, qualité résineuse ; propriété résineuse, *f.*

resipiscence (rèss'-), *n.*, (ant.) résipiscence, *f.*

resist (ri-ziste), *v.a.*, résister à ; se raidir contre ; se refuser à.

resist (ri-ziste), *v.n.*, résister.

resistance (ri-zist'-), *n.*, résistance ; (jur.) rébellion, *f.*

resistant (ri-zist'-), *n.*, personne qui résiste, chose qui résiste, *f.*

resister, *n.*, personne qui résiste, *f.*

resistibility (ri-zist'-), *n.*, qualité de ce qui est résistible ; résistance, *f.*

resistible (ri-zist'i-b'l), *adj.*, résistible, à quoi l'on peut résister.

resisting (ri-zist'-), *adj.*, résistant.

resistless (ri-zist'-), *adj.*, irrésistible ; sans défense.

resoluble (rèz'o-llou-b'l), *adj.*, dissoluble, réductible.

resolute (rèz'o-lioute), *adj.*, déterminé, résolu.

resolutely, *adv.*, résolument.

resoluteness, *n.*, résolution, fermeté, *f.*

resolution (rèz'o-liou-), *n.*, résolution ; (of deliberative bodies—*de corps délibérants*) décision ; (math.) résolution, solution, *f.*

resolutive (rèz'o-liou-), *adj.*, résolutif, résolvant.

resolvable (ri-zolv'a-b'l), *adj.*, qu'on peut résoudre ; résoluble.

resolve (ri-zolvé), *n.*, résolution ; décision, *f.*

resolve (ri-zolve), *v.a.*, résoudre ; (to melt—*fondre*) dissoudre, fondre ; (to inform—*informer*) informer, instruire ; (med., math.) résoudre ; (of deliberative bodies—*de corps délibérants*) arrêter, décider.

resolve, *v.n.*, (to determine—*décider*) résoudre, décider, se résoudre, se décider ; (to melt—*fondre*) se résoudre, se dissoudre, se fondre, fondre.

resolvedly (ri-zolv'èd'-), *adv.*, résolument.

resolvedness (ri-zolv'èd'-), *n.*, résolution, fermeté, *f.*

resolvent (ri-zolv'-), *n.*, dissolvant ; (med.) résolvant, résolutif, *m.*

resolver, *n.*, personne qui prend une résolution, *f.*

resolving, *n.*, résolution, *f.*

resonance (rèz'o-), *n.*, résonance, *f.*

resonant (rèz'-), *adj.*, résonnant.

resorb (ri-çorbe), *v.a.*, résorber.

resorbent (ri-çorb'-), *adj.*, absorbant ; dévorant ; qui engloutit.

resort (ri-zorte), *n.*, (application—*recours*) recours, *m.* ; (visiting—*fréquentation*) fréquentation, *f.* ; (concourse) concours, *m.*, affluence ; (assembly—*réunion*) assemblée, *f.* ; (place—*lieu*) rendez-vous ; (jur.) ressort, *m.* In the last — ; *en dernier ressort.*

resort (ri-zorte), *v.n.*, (to apply—*avoir recours*) recourir à, avoir recours ; (to go—*aller*) se rendre, aller, fréquenter.

resorter, *n.*, personne qui fréquente, *f.*

resound (ri-zaou'n'de), *v.n.*, retentir ; résonner ; avoir du retentissement.

resound, *v.a.*, renvoyer le son de ; faire résonner ; faire retentir ; célébrer ; sonner de nouveau.

resound. *v.a.* and *n.*, sonner de nouveau.

resounding, *n.*, retentissement ; résonnement, *m.*

resounding, *adj.*, retentissant.

resource (ri-çorce), *n.*, ressource, *f.*

resourceless, *adv.*, sans ressource.

re-sow (ri-çô), *v.a.* (preterit, Re-sowed ; past part., Re-sown), ressemer.

respect (ri-spèkte), *n.*, respect, *m.* ; considération, *f.* ; égards, *m.pl.* ; (reference—*rapport*) égard, rapport, *m.* —s ; *respects, hommages, m.pl.* In — to ; *par rapport à ; à l'égard de.* In every — ; *sous tous les rapports ; à tous égards.* In some —s ; *sous quelques rapports.* In some —; *en quelque sorte.* Out of — to ; *par égard pour, par respect pour.* To pay — to ; *avoir des égards pour, avoir du respect pour.* To pay one's — to ; *rendre ses respects à ; offrir ses hommages à.*

respect (ri-spèkte), *v.a.*, respecter, considérer ; avoir de la considération pour ; honorer ; (of things—*des choses*) se rapporter à, regarder, concerner. To — the person ; *faire acception de personne.*

respectability, *n.*, position honorable, *f.* ; caractère honorable ; caractère respectable, crédit, *m.*, considération ; (com.) notabilité ; (of external appearance, of dress, &c.—*de l'extérieur, des vêtements, &c.*) décence, *f.*, extérieur décent,

m. Of —; *dans une position honorable; de considération dans le monde; comme il faut.* Of no —; *sans considération dans le monde.*

respectable (-'a-b'l), *adj.*, respectable, honorable, notable, dans une position honorable. de considération dans le monde, comme il faut; (*of things—des choses*) respectable, passable, qui n'est pas mal.

respectableness, *n.*, caractère respectable, *m.*

respectably, *adv.*, respectablement; honorablement; comme il faut; passablement, pas mal.

respecter, *n.*, personne qui respecte, *f.*

respectful (-foule), *adj.*, respectueux.

respectfully, *adv.*, respectueusement, avec respect.

respectfulness, *n.*, respect, caractère respectueux, *m.*

respecting, *prep.*, par rapport à, à l'égard de, quant à.

respective, *adj.*, respectif; relatif.

respectively, *adv.*, respectivement, relativement.

respirable (ré-spaeur'a-b'l), *adj.*, respirable.

respiration (rès-pi-ré-), *n.*, respiration, *f.*; (*repose—repos*) repos, *m.*

respirator (-ré-teur), *n.*, respirateur, *m.*

respiratory, *adj.*, (anat.) respiratoire.

respire (ri-spaeur), *v.n.*, respirer; (*to rest—se reposer*) se reposer, respirer.

respire, *v.a.*, respirer.

respite (rès-pite), *v.a.*, donner du répit à; suspendre, différer; (jur.) surseoir, surseoir à.

respite (rès-pite), *n.*, répit, relâche; (jur.) sursis, *m.*

resplendence, *or* **resplendency** (ri-splè'n'-), *n.*, resplendissement; éclat, *m.*; splendeur, *f.*

resplendent (ri-splè'n'-), *adj.*, resplendissant.

resplendently, *adv.*, d'une manière resplendissante.

respond (ri-spo'n'de), *v.a.*, répondre; s'accorder.

respondent (ri-spo'n'-), *n.*, répondant; (jur.) défendeur, *m.*, défenderesse, *f.*

respondent (ri-spo'n'-), *adj.*, qui répond, correspondant.

respondentia (ri-spo'n'dè'n'shia), *n.*, (com.) prêt à la grosse, *m.*

response (ri-spo'n'se), *n.*, réponse, *f.*

responsibility (ri-spo'n'-), *n.*, responsabilité; (jur.) solidarité, *f.*

responsible (ri-spo'n'si-b'l), *adj.*, responsable; solidaire.

responsibleness, *n.*, responsabilité, *f.*

responsive, *adj.*, qui répond, qui correspond; responsif.

responsively, *adv.*, d'une manière correspondante.

responsiveness, *n.*, accord, *m.*; correspondance, *f.*

responsory, *adj.*, responsif.

responsory, *n.*, répons, *m.*

ressault (rès'sôlte), *n.*, (arch.) ressaut, *m.*

rest (rèste), *n.*, (remainder—*restant*) reste, restant, *m.*; (the others—*d'autres*) les autres, *m.pl.*

rest (rèste), *n.*, (repose) repos; (support) appui; (poet.) repos, *m.*; (mus.) pause, *f.*; (of a lance—*de lance*) arrêt; (tech.) support, *m.* To —; *en repos.* To set at —; *mettre en repos.* Crotchet- —; *soupir, m.* Quaver- —; *demisoupir, m.* Demi-quaver-—; *quart de soupir, m.* Minim —; *demi-pause, f.*

rest, *v.n.*, se reposer, reposer; dormir; (to lean—*s'appuyer*) reposer, se reposer, s'appuyer, s'arrêter; (to rely—*se fier*) se reposer, se fier, se confier, s'en remettre; (to be satisfied—*être satisfait*) s'en tenir, s'arrêter; (to be—*être*) de-

meurer, se tenir pour; (to remain—*rester*) demeurer, rester.

rest, *v.a.*, reposer; faire reposer; appuyer.

re-stem (ri-stème), *v.a.*, rebrousser.

restful (-foule), *adj.*, en repos, paisible.

restfully, *adv.*, en repos, paisiblement.

resting, *n.*, repos, *m.* — -place; *lieu de repos, m.*

resting-stick, *n.*, appui-main, *m.*

restitution (rès-ti-tiou-), *n.*, restitution, *f.*

restive (rès-), *adj.*, rétif; (obstinate—*obstiné*) opiniâtre.

restiveness, *n.*, naturel rétif *m.*; opiniâtreté, obstination, *f.*

restless, *adj.*, sans repos; inquiet; agité; turbulent.

restlessly (rèst'-), *adv.*, sans repos; avec inquiétude; avec turbulence.

restlessness, *n.*, absence de repos; inquiétude; agitation; turbulence, *f.*

restorable (ri-stôr'a-b'l), *adj.*, qui peut être rendu; qui peut être rétabli; qui peut être restauré.

restoration (rès-tô-ré-), *n.*, (re-establishment—*rétablissement*) rétablissement, *m.*; restitution, restauration, *f.*; (of health—*de la santé*) rétablissement, *m.*

restorative (ri-stô-ra-), *n.*, restaurant, *m.*

restorative, *adj.*, restaurant; restauratif; fortifiant.

restore (ri-stôre), *v.a.*, (to return—*rendre*) restituer, rendre; (to bring back—*ramener*) ramener; (to cure—*guérir*) rétablir, restaurer; (to make restitution—*rendre*) restituer; (to replace—*replacer*) remettre, ramener; (to recover—*rétablir*) restituer, rétablir; (to rebuild—*restaurer*) restaurer, rétablir; (paint., sculpt.) restaurer.

restorer, *n.*, restituteur, restaurateur, *m.*, restauratrice, *f.*

restrain (ri-strène), *v.a.*, retenir; contenir; réprimer, gêner. To — from; *éloigner de; détourner de; empêcher de; interdire à.* To — to; *restreindre à.*

restrainable (ri-strè'n'a-b'l), *adj.*, qui peut être retenu, contenu, réprimé.

restrainedly (-'èd'-), *adv.*, d'une manière restreinte.

restrainer, *n.*, personne qui retient, qui contient, qui réprime; chose qui retient, qui contient, qui réprime, *f.*

restraining, *adj.*, qui restreint, restrictif.

restraint (ri-strè'n'te), *n.*, contrainte, gêne; entrave; restriction, *f.*; frein, *m.*

restrict (ri-strikte), *v.a.*, restreindre.

restriction (ri-strik'-), *n.*, restriction, *f.*

restrictive, *adj.*, restrictif.

restrictively, *adv.*, avec restriction.

restringency (ri-stri'n'dj'-), *n.*, astringence, *f.*

restringent (ri-stri'n'dj'-), *adj.*, restringent, astringent.

restringent, *n.*, restringent, astringent, *m.*

re-subjection (ri-ceub-djèk'-), *n.*, nouvel assujettissement, *m.*

re-sublimation (ri-ceub-li-mé-), *n.*, sublimation nouvelle, *f.*

result (rè-zeulte), *n.*, (consequence) résultat; (resilience—*rebondissement*) rebondissement, *m.*

result (rè-zeulte), *v.n.*, résulter; (to rebound—*rebondir*) rebondir.

resultant (rè-zeul-), *n.*, (mec.) résultante, *f.*

resumable (ri-ziou'm'a-b'l), *adj.*, qui peut être repris, que l'on peut reprendre.

resume (ri-zioume), *v.a.*, reprendre; renouer; continuer.

resume, *n.*, résumé, *m.*

re-summon (ri-ceu'm'meune), *v.a.*, sommer de nouveau; citer de nouveau.

resumption (ri-zeu'm'p-), *n.*, reprise, *f.*

resumptive (ri-zeu'm'p-), *adj.*, qui reprend.

resurrection (rèz'eur-rèk'-), *n.*, résurrection, *f.*

resurrectionist, *n.*, résurrectionniste, *m.*

resurrection-man, *n.*, résurrectionniste, voleur de cadavres, *m.*

re-survey (ri-ceur-vè), *v.a.*, revoir; arpenter de nouveau.

resurvey, *n.*, revision, *f.*; nouvel examen; réarpentage, *m.*

resuscitate (ri-ceus-ci-). *v.a.*, ressusciter, faire revivre, rappeler à la vie; ranimer.

resuscitate, *v.n.*, revivre, renaître; ressusciter.

resuscitation (ri-ceus-ci-té-), *n.*, résurrection, *f.*; retour à la vie, *m.*; (of the arts, &c. —*des arts, &c.*) renaissance, *f.*; (chem.) renouvellement, *m.*

resuscitator (-té-teur), *n.*, résurrecteur, *m.*

retail (ri-tél), *n.*, détail, *m.*; vente en détail, *f.* — -dealer; *marchand en détail; détaillant, m.*

retail (ri-téle), *v.a.*, vendre en détail, détailler; (fig) débiter, redire.

retailer, *n.*, détaillant, *m.*, détaillante, *f.*; débitant, *m.*, débitante, *f.*; (fig.) débiteur, *m.*, débiteuse, *f.*

retain (ri-téne), *v.a.*, retenir, garder; conserver; (by a fee—*par des arrhes*) engager; (to hire—*louer*) prendre à son service.

retainable (-'a-b'l),*adj.*, qui peut être retenu.

retainer, *n.*, personne qui retient, qui garde, qui conserve, *f.*; (attendant—*suivant*) suivant, *m* , suivante, *f.*; (adherent) adhérent, partisan; (fee—*honoraires*) honoraires donnés d'avance, *m.pl.* —s; *suite, f. sing.*

retaining, *adj.*, qui retient, qui garde, qui conserve, qui engage. — -wall; *mur de soutènement.* — -fee; *honoraires donnés d'avance, m.pl.*

re-take (ri-), *v.a.* (preterit, Re-took; *past part.*, Re-taken), reprendre.

re-taking, *n.*, reprise, *f.*

retaliate (ri-), *v.a.*, rendre; rendre la pareille de; prendre sa revanche; user de représailles pour.

retaliate (ri-), *v.n.*, rendre la pareille; prendre sa revanche; user de représailles.

retaliation (ri-tal-i-é-), *n.*, pareille, représaille, *f.*; représailles, *f.pl.*; revanche, peine du talion, *f.*

retaliatory, *adj.*, de représaille, en représaille.

retard (ri-tárde), *v.a.*, retarder; ralentir; différer.

retardation (-dé-), *n.*, retardement, *m.*; (mec.) retardation, *f.*

retarder, *n.*, personne qui retarde; cause de retard, *f.*

retardment, *n.*, retardement, retard, *m.*

retch (ritshe, *ou* rètshe), *v.n.*, faire des efforts pour vomir.

retching, *n.*, efforts pour vomir, *m.pl.*

re-tell (ri-), *v.a.* (preterit and *past part.*, Re-told), redire, répéter.

retention (ri-), *n.*, action de retenir, *f.*; souvenir, *m.*; (med. philos.) rétention, *f.*

retentive (ri-), *adj.*, qui retient; rétentif; (of the memory—*de la mémoire*) tenace, fidèle.

retentiveness, *n.*, faculté de retenir, *f.*; pouvoir rétentif, *m.*; (of the memory—*de la mémoire*) fidélité, ténacité, *f.*

reteration (ri-tè-ré-), *n.*, (print.) retiration, *f.*

reticence, *or* **reticency** (rèt'-), *n.*, réticence, *f.*

reticle (rèt'i-k'l), *n.*, petit filet, *m.*

reticular (ri-tik'iou-), *adj.*, réticulaire.

reticulate ri-tik'iou-), *or* **reticulated** (-lét'-), *adj.*, réticulé.

reticulation (ri-tik'iou-lé-), *n.*, disposition rétiforme, *f.*

reticule (rèt'-kioule), *n.*, sac à ouvrage, ridicule, *m.*

retiform ,rèt'-), *adj.*, rétiforme.

retina (rèt'-), *n.*, rétine, *f.*

retinue (rèt'i-niou), *n.*, suite, *f.*; cortège, *m.*

retire (ri-taeur), *v.n.*, se retirer.

retired (ri-taeur'de), *adj.*, retiré, secret, caché; (of places—*d'endroits*) écarté, retiré. On the — list; *en retraite.*

retiredly, *adv.*, d'une manière retirée; dans la retraite.

retiredness, *n.*, retraite, solitude, *f.*; isolement, *m.*

retirement (ri-taeur'-), *n.*, retraite, solitude, *f.*; isolement, *m.*

retiring, *adj.*, qui se retire, qui fuit le monde; réservé, timide. — -pension; *pension de retraite, f.*

re-told (ri-tôlde), *adj.*, répété; redit.

retort (ri-torte), *n.*, riposte, réplique; (chem.) cornue, *f.*

retort (ri-), *v.n.*, riposter, répliquer.

retort, *v.a.*, renvoyer; rétorquer.

retorter, *n.*, personne qui rétorque, qui riposte, qui renvoie, *f.*

retorting, *n.*, renvoi, *m.*; rétorsion, *f.*

retortion, *n.*, rétorsion, *f.*

ro-toss (ri-), *v.a.*, rejeter, relancer.

re-touch (ri-teutshe), *v.a.*, retoucher.

re-trace (ri-), *v.a.*, retracer; reprendre; revenir sur; rechercher; examiner; (one's steps—*ses pas*) revenir sur, retourner sur; (one's way—*son chemin*) reprendre.

retract (ri-), *v.a.*, rétracter; retirer.

retract, *v.n.*, se rétracter, se dédire.

retractable (-'a-b'l), *adj.*, qui peut être rétracté.

retractation (-trak-té-), *n.*, rétractation, *f.*

retractile (ri-trakt'il), *adj.*, rétractile.

retraction (ri-trak'-), *n.*, rétraction, *f.*; rétractation, *f.*

retraxit (ri-traks'-),*n.*, jur.)désistement, *m.*

retreat (ri-trite), *n.*, retraite, *f.*

retreat (ri-trite), *v.n.*, se retirer ; (milit.) se retirer, faire retraite, battre en retraite.

retrench(ri-),*v.a.*,retrancher; retrancher de.

retrenchment (ri-), *n.*, retranchement, *m.*; réduction des dépenses, économie, *f.*; (milit.) retranchement, *m.*

retribute (ri-trib'ioute), *v.a.*, récompenser, rétribuer.

retributer, *n.*, personne qui rémunère, qui rétribue, *f.*

retribution (rèt'ri-biou-), *n.*, récompense, rémunération, rétribution, *f.*; (b.s.) châtiment, *m.*, vengeance, *f.*

retributive, *or* **retributory** (ri-trib'iou-), *adj.*, qui récompense; distributif.

retrievable (ri-triv'a-b'l), *adj.*, qui peut être réparé.

retrieve (ri-trive), *v.a.*, (to restore—*restaurer*) restaurer, rétablir; (to repair—*réparer*) réparer; (to regain—*regagner*) regagner, recouvrer, retrouver, récupérer, se récupérer de; (to recall—*ramener*) retirer.

retroaction (ri-), *n.*, rétroaction, *f.*

retroactive (ri-), *adj.*, rétroactif.

retroactively, *adv.*, rétroactivement.

retrocede (ri-tro-cide), *v.a.*, rétrocéder.

retrocession (ri-tro-cèsh'-), *n.*, rétrocession, *f.*

retroduction (ri-tro-deuk'-), *n.*, action de ramener, *f.*

retrogradation (rèt'ro-gra-dé-), *n.*, rétrogradation, *f.*

retrograde (rèt'ro-gréde), *v.n.*, rétrograder.

retrograde, *adj.*, rétrograde, en arrière.

retrogression (rè'tro-grès'-), *n.*, mouvement rétrograde, *m.*, rétrogradation, *f.* ; (geom.) rebroussement, *m.*

retrospect (rèt'-), *n.*, regard en arrière; examen, *m.*

retrospection (rèt'-), *n.*, action de regarder en arrière; faculté de regarder en arrière, *f.*; regard en arrière; examen, *m.*

retrospective (rèt'-), *adj.*, rétrospectif; qui regarde en arrière; rétroactif.

retrospectively, *adv.*, rétrospectivement, rétroactivement.

retroversion (rèt'ro-veur-), *n.*, rétroversion, *f.*; renversement, *m.*

retrovert (rèt'ro-veurte), *v.a.*, renverser.

retting (rèt'-), *n.*, rouissage, *m.*

retting-pit, *n.*, routoir; rutoir, *m.*

retund (ri-teu'n'de), *v.a.*, (ant.) émousser.

return (ri-teurne), *v.n.*, (to come back—*revenir*) revenir, rentrer; (to go back—*retourner*) retourner; rentrer; (to answer—*répondre*) répondre.

return (ri-teurne), *v.a.*, (to give back—*rendre*) rendre; (to send back—*renvoyer*) renvoyer; (to repay—*restituer*) rendre, restituer; (to give in recompense—*récompenser*) rendre ;•(an answer —*réponse*) rendre, faire; (to render an account—*rendre compte*) faire un rapport de, rapporter, rendre compte de; (to report officially—*fournir un état officiel*) faire l'état de; (verdict) rendre; (candidates—*candidats*) élire, nommer. The money —s interest; *l'argent rapporte intérêt.*

return (ri-teurne), *n.*, (coming back, going back—*revenir*, *retourner*) retour, *m.*; (coming back—*rentrer*) rentrée, *f.*; (sending back—*renvoyer*)renvoi, *m.*; putting back—*replacer*) remise en place, *f.*; (revolution, periodical renewal—*révolution*, *retour périodique*) retour; (profit) profit, gain, produit, *m.*; (restitution) restitution, *f.*; (retribution) retour; (reimbursement—*remboursement*) remboursement; (milit.) état, *m.*; (election) élection, *f.*; (jur.) renvoi; (arch.) retour; (report—*rapport*) rapport, compte rendu, relevé, état, *m.*; (of funds—*de fonds*) rentrée, *f.*; (of health—*de la santé*) retour; (com.) montant des opérations, montant des remises, *m.* —s; *produit. m. sing.* On —; (com.) en dépôt; en commission. In — for; *en retour de.* Small profits and quick —s; *petits profits, promptes ventes.*

returnable (-'a-b'l), *adj.*, restituable; qui doit être rendu; qui doit être renvoyé; (com.) en commission.

return-day, *n.*, (jur.) jour du renvoi du mandat et de la comparution, *m.*

returner, *n.*, personne qui rend, qui rembourse, qui renvoie, qui fait des remises d'argent, *f.*

returning-officer, *n.*, rapporteur du procès-verbal des élections; fonctionnaire chargé de renvoyer les actes officiels, *m.*

return-side (-saïde), *n.*, (arch.) côté en retour, *m.*

reunion (ri-yeu'n'yeune), *n.*, réunion, *f.*

reunite (ri-you-naïte), *v.a.*, réunir.

reveal (ri-vîl), *v.a.*, révéler.

reveal (ri-vîl), *n.*, (arch.) jouée, *f.*

revealer, *n.*, révélateur, *m.*, révélatrice, *f.*

reveille (ri-vèl'ié), *n.*, (milit.) réveil, *m.*; diane, *f.*

revel (rèv'èl), *n.*, divertissement, *m.*; réjouissances. *f.pl.*, ébats, *m.pl.*; fête bruyante, orgie, *f.*

revel (rèv'èl), *v.n.*, se réjouir; se divertir; s'ébattre; faire une orgie; (pop.) riboter. To— in; *se livrer à; s'abandonner à.*

revelation (rèv'i-lé-), *n.*, révélation; Apocalypse, *f.*

reveller (rèv'èl'-), *n.*, personne qui se réjouit, qui se divertit, qui fait une orgie, *f.*; convive, joyeux convive, viveur, riboteur, *m.*

revelling, *or* **revelry** (rèv'èl'-), *n.*, fêtes,

réjouissances, *f.pl.*; divertissements, ébats, *m.pl.*; orgie, *f.*

revenge (ri-vè'n'dje), *n.*, vengeance; (at play—*au jeu*) revanche, *f.*

revenge (ri-vè'n'dje), *v.a.*, venger; se venger de; revancher; se revancher de. To be —d; *se venger de.* To be —d on, to — one's self on; *se venger de.*

revengeful (-foule), *adj.*, qui respire la vengeance; vindicatif; vengeur.

revengefully, *adv.*, par vengeance; vindicativement.

revengefulness, *n.*, caractère vindicatif; esprit de vengeance, *m.*

revengeless, *adj.*, sans vengeance.

revenger, *n.*, vengeur, *m.*, vengeresse, *f.*

revengingly, *adv.*, par vengeance.

revenue (rèv'i-niou), *n.*, revenu; (of the state—*de l'état*), revenu, fisc, trésor, *m.* Public —; *revenus publics, revenus de l'état, m.pl.*

revenue-board (-bôrde), *n.*, administration des revenus publics, *f.*

reverberant (ri-veur-bèr'-),*adj.*, qui renvoie; réverbérant.

reverberate (ri-veur-bèr'-), *v.a.*, réverbérer; répercuter; renvoyer.

reverberate (ri-veur-bèr'-), *v.n.*, réverbérer; se répercuter.

reverberate (ri-veur-bèr'-), *adj.*, qui réverbère, qui répercute, qui réfléchit, qui renvoie.

reverberation (ri-veur-bèr'é-), *n.*, réverbération; répercussion, *f.*

reverberatory, *adj.*, à réverbère.

reverberatory (ri-veur-bèr'a-teuri), *n.*, four à réverbère, fourneau à réverbère, foyer à réverbère, *m.*

revere (ri-vîre), *v.a.*, révérer, respecter.

reverence (rèv'èr'-), *n.*, révérence, *f.*; respect, *m* ; (title, bow—*titre, salutation*) révérence, *f.*

reverence (rèv'èr'-), *v.a.*, révérer, respecter.

reverencer, *n.*, personne qui révère, qui respecte, *f.*

reverend (rèv'èr'-), *adj.*, vénérable, respectable, (of the clergy—*du clergé*) révérend. Most —; *révérendissime.*

reverent (rèv'èr'-), *adj.*, révérencieux.

reverential, *adj.*, de révérence, de respect; (of fear—*de crainte*) révérencielle.

reverentially, *or* **reverently**, *adv.*, avec révérence, avec respect; révérencieusement, respectueusement.

reverer (ri-vîr'-), *n.*, personne qui révère, qui respecte, *f.*

reversal (ri-veur-), *n.*, annulation; cassation, *f.*

reverse (ri-veurse), *n.*, (change—*changement*) vicissitude, *f.*; (misfortune—*infortune*) revers; (contrary—*contraire*) opposé, contraire; (of a page—*d'une page*) revers, verso; (of a medal—*de médaille*) revers, *m.*

reverse (ri-veurse), *adj.*, contraire.

reverse (ri-veurse), *v.a.*, renverser; mettre en sens inverse; (jur.) infirmer, réformer.

reversed (ri-veurs'te), *adj.*, renversé; (jur.) cassé, infirmé.

reversedly (ri-veurs'èd'-), *adv.*, en sens inverse.

reverseless, *adj.*, qui ne peut être renversé.

reversely, *adv.*, en sens inverse, inversement.

reversible (ri-veurs'i-b'l), *adj.*, réformable, annulable.

reversion (ri-veur-), *n.*, réversion, *f.*; retour; bien qui fait retour, *m.*; (of offices—*de charges*) survivance; (succession) succession, *f.*

reversionary, *adj.*, réversible; (of offices—*de charges*) de survivance.

reversioner, *n.*, personne investie d'un droit

de réversion, d'un droit de retour, *f.*; (of offices —de charges) survivancier, *m.*

revert (ri-veurte), *v.n.*, revenir; retourner; faire retour.

revert, *v.a.*, faire retourner.

revert (ri-veurte),*n.*,(mus.) renversement,*m.*

revertible (ri-veurt'i-b'l), *adj.*, réversible.

revertive, *adj.*, qui retourne; qui change.

revery, *or* **reverie** (rèv'i-ri), *n.*, rêverie, *f.*

revest (ri-vèste), *v.a.*, revêtir; investir de nouveau.

revest, *v.n.*, (jur.) retourner, faire retour.

revestiary (ri-vèst'-), *n.*, vestiaire, *m.*

revetement (ri-vit'-), *n.*, (fort.) revêtement, *m.*

re-vibrate (ri-vaï-), *v.n.*, vibrer en retour.

re-vibration (ri-vaï-bré-), *n.*, vibration en retour, *f.*

re-victual (rî-vit't'l), *v.a.*, ravitailler.

re-victualling (rî-vit't'l-), *n.*, ravitaillement, *m.*

review (ri-viou), *n.*, revue; (revision) revision; (periodical—écrit périodique) revue; (of a book—d'un livre) analyse, critique, *f.*, compte rendu, *m.*; (milit.) revue; (jur.) revision, *f.*

review (ri-viou), *v.a.*, (to see again—voir de nouveau) revoir; (to examine—examiner) revoir, repasser, passer en revue, faire la revue de; (a book—un livre) analyser, rendre compte de; (milit.) passer en revue, faire la revue de.

reviewer, *n.*, personne qui passe en revue,*f.*; auteur d'une analyse, d'une critique; rédacteur de revue; critique, *m.*

revile (ri-vaïle), *v.a.*, injurier, insulter, outrager.

revilement, *n.*, injure, insulte, *f.*

reviler,*n.*,personne qui injurie,qui insulte,*f.*

reviling (ri-vaïl'-), *n.*, insulte, injure, *f.*

reviling, *adj.*, diffamatoire, outrageant.

revilingly, *adv.*, injurieusement, outrageusement.

revindicate (rî-), *v.a.*, revendiquer.

revisal (ri-vaï-zal), *n.*, revision, *f.*

revise (ri-vaïze),*n.*,(print.) deuxième épreuve d'auteur,*f.*

revise (ri-vaïze), *v.a.*, revoir, reviser, faire la revision de.

reviser (ri-vaïz'-), *n.*, personne qui revoit,*f.*; reviseur, *m.*

revision(ri-vij'eune), *n.*, revision, *f.*

revisional, *or* **revisionary** (ri-vij'-), *adj.*, de revision.

re-visit (rî-viz'-), *v.a.*, revisiter; revoir, retourner à.

revival (ri-vaï-), *n.*, retour à la vie, renouvellement, *m.*; renaissance; remise en vigueur,*f.*

revive (ri-vaïve), *v.a.*, faire revivre; rappeler à la vie; ressusciter; renouveler; rauimer; raviver; remettre en vigueur; (chem.) vivifier.

revive, *v.n.*, revivre, ressusciter; se ranimer; se raviver; renaître; (chem.) se revivifier.

reviver, *n.*, personne qui fait revivre, qui ranime, qui ravive, qui ressuscite; chose qui fait revivre, qui ranime, qui ravive, qui ressuscite, *f.*, restaurateur, *m.*, restauratrice, *f.*

revivification (rî-viv'i-â-ké-), *n.*, revivification,*f.*

revivify (rî-viv'i-fa'ye), *v.a.*, revivifier.

reviviscence, *or* **reviviscency** (rèv'i-vis'-), *n.*, retour à la vie, *m.*; résurrection; renaissance,*f.*

revivor (ri-vaï-veur), *n.*, (jur.) reprise de procès,*f.*

revocable (rèv'o-ca-b'l), *adj.*, révocable

revocableness, *n.*, qualité d'être révocable; révocabilité,*f.*

revocably, *adv.*, révocablement.

revocation (rèv'o-ké-), *n.*, révocation; abjuration, *f.*; rappel, *m.*

revoke (ri-vôke), *v.a.*, révoquer.

revoke, *v.n.*, (at cards—aux cartes) renoncer.

revoke (ri-vôke), *n.*, renonce,*f.*

revolt (ri-), *n.*, révolte,*f.*

revolt, *v.n.*, se révolter, se soulever.

revolt, *v.a.*, révolter, soulever.

revolted, *adj.*, révolte; en révolte; soulevé;

revolter, *n.*, révolté, rebelle, *m.*

revolting, *adj.*, révoltant.

revolution (rèv'o-liou-), *n.*, révolution. *f.*; (of a wheel—de roue) tour, *m.*, révolution,*f.*

revolutionary, *adj.*, révolutionnaire.

revolutionist, *n.*, révolutionnaire, *m.*

revolutionize (rèv'o-liou-sheu'n'aïze), *v.a.*, révolutionner, mettre en révolution.

revolve (ri-), *v.a.*, tourner; (in the mind—dans l'esprit) retourner, repasser, rouler, penser à.

revolve, *v.n.*, tourner; retourner; (astron.) tourner, faire sa révolution.

revolvency, *n.*, mouvement de révolution, *m.*

revolving, *adj.*, tournant; qui retourne; (astron.) qui fait sa révolution, qui tourne.

revulsion (ri-veul-), *n.*, révulsion, répercussion,*f.*

revulsive (ri-veul-), *adj.*, (med.) révulsif.

reward (ri-wôrde), *n.*, récompense, *f.*; prix, *m.*

reward (ri-wôrde), *v.a.*, récompenser.

rewardable (-'a-b'l), *adj.*, digne de récompense.

rewardableness, *n.*, qualité de ce qui est digne de récompense,*f.*

rewarder, *n.*, rémunérateur, *m.*, rémunératrice, *f.*

re-warehouse (rî-wér'haouce), *v.a.*, (com.) remettre en magasin.

re-write (rî-raïte), *v.a.*, récrire.

rhabarbarate (ra-bâr-ba-), *adj.*, imprégné de rhubarbe.

rhabdology (-'o-dji), *n.*, rabdologie,*f.*

rhabdomancy,*n.*, rabdomancie,*f.*

rhapsodical, *adj.*, de rapsodie.

rhapsodist, *n.*, rapsodiste; (antiq.) rapsode, *m.*

rhapsody, *n.*, rapsodie,*f.*

rhenish (rè'n'-), *adj.*, du Rhin; (geog.) rhénan.

rhetian (rî-shî-), *adj.*, rhétien.

rhetor (rî-), *n.*, rhéteur, *m.*

rhetoric (rèt'-), *n.*,rhétorique; éloquence,*f.*

rhetorical, *adj.*, de la rhétorique.

rhetorically, *adv.*, suivant les règles de la rhétorique; en rhétoricien.

rhetorician (rèt'o-rish'a'n), *n.*, rhétoricien; rhéteur, *m.*

rhetorize (rèt'o-raïze), *v.n.*, faire de la rhétorique.

rhetorize, *v.a.*, représenter par une figure de rhétorique.

rheum (roume), *n.*, rhume; catarrhe, *m.*; pituite; (bot.) rhubarbe, *f.*

rheumatic (rou-), *adj.*, rhumatismal, rhumatique.

rheumatism (rou-ma-tiz'm), *n.*, rhumatisme, *m.*

rheumy (roumi),*adj.*,rhumatismal; rhumatisant; humide.

rhino (raï-nô), *n.*, (pop.) écus, jaunes, *m.pl.*

rhinocerial (raï-no-ci-), *adj.*, de rhinocéros.

rhinoceros (raï-noss'i-), *n.*, rhinocéros, *m.*

rhodian (rô-), *adj.*, de Rhodes.

rhodium (rô-), *n.*, (chem.) rhodium, *m.*

rhododendron (rô-), *n.*, (bot.) rhododendron, *m.*

rhomb, *or* **rhombus**, *n.*, rhombe, *m.*

rhombo, *n.*, (ich.) rhombe, *m.*

rhomboid (-boïde), *n.*, rhomboïde, *m.*

rhomboidal (-boïd'-), *adj.*, rhomboïdal.

rhonchus (ron'gn'keusse),*n.*,(med.) râle, *m.*

rhubarb (rou-bârbe), *n.*, rhubarbe, *f.*

rhumb (reu'm'be), *n.*, (nav.) rumb, *m.*

rhumb-line (-laine), *n.*, (nav.) rumb de vent, *m.*

rhyme (raïme), *n.*, rime, *f.* ; vers, *m.*

rhyme, *v.a.* and *n.*, rimer ; (b. s.) rimailler.

rhymeless. *adj.*, sans rime.

rhymer. **rhymester**, *or* **rhymist** (raï'm'-) *n.*, rimeur ; rimailleur, *m.*

rhymic, *adj.*, de rime.

rhymist, *n.*   *V.* **rhymer**.

rhythm (rith'm), *or* **rhythmus** (rith-), *n.*, rythme, *m.*

rhythmical, *adj.*, rythmique.

rib, *n.*, côte; (bot.) nervure, côte; (carp.) entretoise, *f.*, tirant, étançon, *m.*; (of a roof—*de toit*) ferme; (arch.) nervure, *f.*; (nav.) membre, *m.*, côte; (in cloth—*du drap*) côte; (pop.) (wife—*épouse*) moitié, *f.*

rib, *v.a.*, pourvoir de côtes; (cloth, &c.—*drap*, *&c.*) faire des côtes à.

ribald, *n.*, débauché ; libertin, *m.*

ribald, *adj.*, licencieux ; vil, bas.

ribaldish, *adj.*, (ant.) licencieux, déshonnête.

ribaldry, *n.*, langage licencieux, *m.*

riband, *n.*   *V.* **ribbon**.

ribbed (rib'de), *adj.*, muni de côtes ; (of cloth, &c.—*drap*, *&c.*) à côtes.

ribbon, *n.*, ruban ; ruban de soie ; (shred—*lambeau*) lambeau, *m.* — -trade ; *rubanerie, f.* — -weaver ; *rubanier, m.*

rib-wall (-wôl), *n.*, (mines) compartiment, *m.*

rice (raïce), *n.*, riz, *m.* — -plantation ; *rizière, f.*

rich (ritsh), *adj.*, riche ; (opulent) riche, opulent ; (fertile) fertile, fécond ; (succulent) succulent ; (highly seasoned—*épicé*) de haut goût ; (costly, valuable—*coûteux, précieux*) précieux ; (splendid) magnifique, superbe, beau ; (fig.) délicieux, exquis.

riches (ritsh'éze), *n.pl.*, richesses, *f.pl.*, richesse, *f.sing.*

richly, *adv.*, richement ; (truly—*réellement*) grandement, amplement, bien.

richness, *n.*, richesse ; opulence ; fécondité ; fertilité ; nature succulente, *f.* ; haut goût, *m.* ; qualité précieuse ; magnificence, *f.* ; goût délicieux, goût exquis ; prix, *m.*

ricinus, *n.*, (bot.) ricin, *m.*

rick, *n.*, meule, *f.* ; monceau, *m.*

rickets, *n.pl.*, rachitis, rachitisme, *m.*

rickety (-èt'i), *adj.*, (med.) noué, rachitique ; (fig.) détraqué, dérangé, en mauvais état.

ricochet (rik'o-shè), *n.*, (artil.) ricochet, *m.*

rid. *v.a.* (*preterit*, Rid ; *past part.*, Rid, Ridden), défaire, délivrer, débarrasser. To — one's self of ; *se défaire de*. To get — of ; *se débarrasser de ; se défaire de*. To have got — of ; *être débarrassé de*.

riddance, *n.*, délivrance, *f.*, débarras, *m.* A good —! *bon débarras!*

riddle (rid'd'l), *n.*, énigme, *f.* ; (sieve—*tamis*) crible, *m.*

riddle, *v.n.*, parler énigmatiquement.

riddle, *v.a.*, (to perforate—*perforer*) cribler ; (wheat—*le blé*) cribler ; (to solve—*expliquer*) résoudre, expliquer.

riddler, *n.*, personne qui parle par énigmes, *f.*

riddling, *n.*, (metal.) lavage au crible, *m.*

riddlingly, *adv.*, par énigmes.

ride (raïde), *v.n.* (*preterit*, Rode ; *past part.*, Ridden), (on horseback—*à cheval*) aller à cheval, être à cheval, se promener à cheval, monter à cheval ; (in a vehicle—*en voiture*) aller en voiture, être en voiture, se promener en voiture ; (print.) chevaucher ; (man.) monter ; (to be borne on a fluid—*sur un fluide*) être porté, flotter, voguer. To — on ; *monter sur ; être monté sur*. To — at anchor ; *être à l'ancre*. To — easy ; *ne*

pas fatiguer à cheval; (nav.) *ne pas fatiguer à l'ancre*. To — hard ; (nav.) *fatiguer à l'ancre*. The vessel —s on the sea ; *le vaisseau vogue sur la mer*. The flag —s in the air ; *le drapeau flotte dans l'air*. To — over ; *venir à cheval, aller à cheval ; parcourir ;* pers.) *passer sur, renverser*. To — out a gale ; *tenir bon sur ses ancres dans un coup de vent*.

ride, *v.a.*, monter ; (to take to, to lead—*conduire*) mener.

ride (raïde), *n.*, (on horseback—*à cheval*) promenade à cheval ; (in a vehicle—*en voiture*) promenade en voiture ; (in an omnibus, a cab—*en omnibus, en fiacre*) course ; (place—*lieu*) promenade, *f.*

rider, *n.*, personne à cheval, personne en voiture, *f.* ; cavalier ; écuyer, *m.*, écuyère ; (document) annexe ; (com.) allonge ; (fly-sheet—*feuille détachée*) feuille volante ; (of an ore—*de minerai*) matrice, *f.* Gentleman —; *écuyer amateur*. Rough —; *casse-cou, m.*

ridge, *n.*, (top—*faîte*) sommet, *m.* ; cime ; (elevation) élévation, hauteur ; (of mountains—*de montagnes*) chaîne ; (of a mountain—*d'une montagne*) crête, *f.*; (of a roof—*d'un toit*) faîte ; (agri.) sillon, *m.*

ridge. *v.a.*, sillonner ; surmonter ; (agri.) faire des sillons dans.

ridgel, *or* **ridgeling**. *n.*, animal à demi châtré, *m.*

ridge-piece (-pîce), *or* **ridge-plate**, *s.*, (carp.) faîtage, faîte, *m.*

ridgy, *adj.*, sillonné.

ridicule (-kioule), *n.*, ridicule, objet de risée, *m.*

ridicule, *v.a.*, tourner en ridicule, ridiculiser.

ridiculer, *n.*, personne qui tourne en ridicule, *f.*

ridiculous (-dik'iou-), *adj.*, ridicule ; (laughable) risible. — thing ; *chose ridicule, f. ; ridicule, m.*

ridiculously, *adv.*, ridiculement.

ridiculousness, *n.*, ridicule, *m.*

riding (raïd'-), *n.*, action de monter à cheval, *f.* ; art de monter à cheval, *m.*, équitation ; promenade en voiture, à cheval ; (place—*lieu*) promenade, *f.* ; (print.) chevauchage ; (of Yorkshire—*dans le Yorkshire*) arrondissement, *m.*

riding-coat (-côte), *n.*, habit de cheval, *m.*, redingote de voyage, *f.*

riding-habit (raïd'-), *n.*, habit d'amazone, *m.* ; amazone, *f.*

riding-hood (-houde), *n.*, chaperon de voyage, *m.* Little red — ; *petit chaperon rouge.*

riding-master (-mâs-), *n.*, maître d'équitation, *m.*

riding-school (-skoul), *n.*, école d'équitation, *f.* ; manège, *m.*

ridotto (-tô), *n.*, redoute, assemblée pour danser, &c., *f.*

rife (raïfe), *adj.*, qui règne, qui domine ; régnant.

rifely, *adv.*, communément, abondamment.

rifeness, *n.*, abondance, grande quantité, fréquence, *f.*

riffraff, *n.*, (of things—*des choses*) rebut, *m.*, racaille, *f.* ; (pers.) gens de rien, *m.pl.*, lie du peuple, racaille, canaille, *f.*

rifle (raï-f'l), *v.a.*, piller ; dévaliser ; (of firearms—*d'armes à feu*) carabiner, rayer.

rifle, *n.*, fusil à balle forcée, *m.* ; carabine, *f.* —s ; (men—*hommes*) (milit.) *carabiniers, m.*

rifleman, *n.* (*riflemen*), carabinier, *m.*

rifler (raï-), *n.*, pillard, *m.*

rig, *n.*, (dress—*habillement*) accoutrement, *m.* ; (woman—*femme*) libertine ; (trick—*tour*) farce, *f.* ; (nav.) grément, gréement, *m.*

rig, *v.a.*, équiper, accoutrer ; (nav.) garnir, gréer.

rigadoon (-doune), *n.*, rigodon, *m.*

rigation (ri-ghé-), *n.*, (ant.) irrigation, *f.*
rigger (-gheur), *n.*, personne qui s'accoutre, *f.* ; (nav.) gréeur, *m.*
rigging (-ghigne), *n.*, équipement, accoutrement, *m.* ; (nav.) agrès, *m.pl.*, gréement, grément, *m.*, manœuvres,manœuvres de gréement, *f.pl.* Standing, running —; manœuvres dormantes, courantes.
rigging-loft, *n.*, (nav.) atelier de garniture. *m.*
riggle (rig-g'l), *v.n.*, frétiller ; se tortiller ; s'agiter.
right (raïte), *adj.*, (straight—*droit*) droit ; (direct) direct, en ligne droite ; (becoming—*sortable*) convenable ; (lawful—*licite*) légitime ; (true—*réel*) vrai,véritable, bon ; (equitable) droit, juste, bon ; (side—*côté*) droit ; (com.) régulier ; (that which is meant—*ce qu'on veut*) qu'il faut. To be —; avoir raison ; (of things—*des choses*) convenir ; (of an account—*d'un compte*) être juste; être bien le compte. That is —; c'est bien ; c'est cela. The — road ; la route directe ; (fig.) le bon chemin. All —; en route! allez! c'est bon! c'est bien! Bon! Bien! All's —; tout va bien. That served you —; c'est bien fait. To go the — way to work ; s'y prendre bien. That is not the — thing ; ce n'est pas là ce qu'il faut. To set —; mettre en bon ordre, mettre en règle ; (to rectify—*corriger*) rectifier ; (a watch—*une montre*) régler ; (pers.) éclairer, mettre sur la bonne voie.
right, *adv.*, (straight—*droit*) droit, tout droit ; (justly—*justement*) juste, justement, droit, droitement ; (properly—*convenablement*) comme il faut, bien ; (before titles—*devant un titre*) très ; (very—*très*) très, furieusement.
right, *n.*, droit, *m.* ; (justice) justice, raison, *f.*, droit ; (property—*propriété*) bien ; (interest—*intérêt*) intérêt ; (right side—*côté*) côté droit, *m.*. droite, *f.* — of way ; droit de passage. Bill of —s ; déclaration des droits et privilèges politiques d'un peuple, *f.* In — of ; par le droit de. Of —; de droit, de plein droit. In one's own —; en propre. On the —; à droite. On one's —; à sa droite. To set to —s ; mettre en bon ordre, mettre en règle ; (pers.) mettre à la raison, faire voir à. To know the —s of ; savoir le fin mot de.
right, *v.a.*, (pers.) faire droit à. rendre justice à ; (things—*choses*) redresser ; (a ship—*vaisseau*) redresser ; (the helm—*gouvernail*) dresser.
right, *v.n.*, se redresser, se relever.
righteous (raït'i'eusse), *adj.*, juste, droit.
righteously, *adv.*, justement.
righteousness, *n.*, droiture, justice, *f.*
righter, *n.*, redresseur, *m.*
rightful (-foul), *adj.*, légitime.
rightfully, *adv.*, légitimement.
rightfulness,*n.*, justice ; rectitude, équité, *f.*
right-handed, *adj.*, droitier.
right-hearted (-hârt'-), *adj.*, qui a le cœur bien placé.
rightly, *adv.*, droitement, bien, justement ; (properly—*proprement*) convenablement, comme il faut ; (not erroneously—*sans erreur*) juste ; (exactly—*exactement*) bien.
right-minded (-maï'n'd'-), *adj.*, qui a l'esprit juste, droit.
right-mindedness, *n.*, justesse d'esprit, droiture, *f.*
rightness, *n.*, rectitude ; droiture ; justesse ; (straightness—*ligne droite*) direction droite. *f.*
rigid (ridj'-), *adj.*, rigide, raide.
rigidity, *n.*, rigidité ; raideur, *f.*
rigidly, *adv.*, rigidement ; avec raideur.
rigidness, *n.*, rigidité ; raideur, *f.*
riglet, *n.*, (print.) réglet, *m.*, réglette, *f.*
rigmarole (-rôle), *n.*, amphigouri, rabâchage ; conte à dormir debout, galimatias, *n.*
rigol, *n.*, (ant.) cercle, diadème. *m.*
rigor. *n.*, (med.) froid. *m.*, fièvre en froid, *f.*

rigorous, *adj.*, rigoureux ; sévère ; de rigueur.
rigorously, *adv.*, rigoureusement ; à la rigueur.
rigorousness, *n.*, rigueur, *f.*
rigour (righ'eur), *n.*, rigueur, sévérité, *f.*
rill, *n.*, petit ruisseau, *m.*
rill, *v.n.*, couler en petit ruisseau.
rillet, *n.*, petit ruisseau, *m.*
rim,*n.*,bord, *m.* ; (of wheels—*de roue*) jante,*f.*
rim, *v.a.*, mettre un bord à.
rime (raïme), *n.*, givre, *m.* ; gelée blanche, *f.*
rime (raïme), *v.n.*, geler blanc.
rimose (ri-môce), *or* **rimous** (raï-), *adj.*, (bot.) crevassé.
rimple, *n.*, ride, *f.* ; pli. *m.*
rimple (ri'm'p'l), *v.a.*, rider ; plier.
rimpling, *n.*, ride,*f.*
rimy (raï-), *adj.*, couvert de givre, couvert de gelée blanche.
rind (raï'n'de), *n.*, écorce, peau, pelure, *f.*
ring (rigne), *n.*, (circle—*cercle*) cercle, rond ; (of metal, &c.—*de métal, &c.*) anneau, *m.* ; (for the fingers—*pour les doigts*) bague, *f.*, anneau ; (round a wound—*autour d'une plaie*) ⊙ceine ; (bot.) cerne ; (nav.) anneau, organeau, *m.*. boucle ; (of a wheel—*de roue*) jante, *f.* ; (astron.) anneau, *m.* In a —; en rond. Wedding —; alliance ; alliance de mariage, *f.* ; anneau nuptial, *m.* Split —; anneau brisé.
ring, *v.a.*, mettre un anneau à.
ring, *n.*,(sound—*bruit*) son, tintement, retentissement ; (on a bell—*de sonnette*) coup de sonnette, *m.* ; (chime—*de cloches*) sonnerie, *f.* Give a —; sonnez.
ring, *v.a.* (preterit, Rang ; past part., Rung), sonner, tinter. To — with ; résonner de; retentir de.
ring, *v.n.*, sonner, tinter ; (of the ears—*des oreilles*) tinter.
ring-bone (-bône), *n.* (vet.) forme, *f.*
ringer, *n.*, sonneur, *m.*
ringing (rign'igne), *n.*, action de sonner, *f.* ; tintement ; retentissement ; (of bells—*des cloches*) son. *m.* — in the ears ; tintement d'oreilles.
ringleader (rign'lid'-), *n.*, chef d'émeute, meneur, *m.*
ringlet (rign'lète), *n.*, petit anneau, *m.* ; (of hair—*de cheveux*) boucle de cheveux, *f.*
ring-shaped (-shép'te), *adj.*, annulaire.
ring-streaked (-strik'te), *adj.*, annelé.
ring-tail (-tél), *n.*, (orni.) paille-en-queue ; (nav.) tapecu, *m.*
ring-worm (-weurme), *n.*, impétigo, *m.* ; dartre à la tête, *f.*
rinse, *v.a.*, rincer.
rinser, *n.*, personne qui rince, *f.*
rinsing, *n.*, action de rincer, *f.* ; rinçage, *m.*
riot (raï'ote), *n.*, émeute, *f.* ; rassemblement tumultueux ; attroupement ; (uproar—*tapage*) vacarme, tumulte, *m.* ; (feasting—*orgies*) festins, *m.pl.*, orgies, *f.pl.*, dissipation ; intempérance, *f.* ; excès, *m.*
riot (raï'ote), *v.n.*, faire une émeute ; faire du vacarme, faire du tumulte ; se réjouir, se divertir ; faire des orgies, faire des excès ; riboter.
riot-act, *n.*, loi contre les émeutes, *f.* To read the — ; faire les trois sommations.
rioter, *n.*, séditieux, mutin ; émeutier ; débauché, *m.*
riotous (raï'ot'-), *adj.*,séditieux,tumultueux ; (luxurious—*débauché*) déréglé, dissipé, intempérant, débauché.
riotously, *adv.*, tumultueusement ; séditieusement ; avec excès, avec intempérance ; dans les plaisirs, dans les orgies.
riotousness, *n.*, caractère tumultueux, caractère séditieux ; dérèglement, *m.* ; intempérance, dissipation, débauche, *f.*
rip,*v.a.*,ouvrir, fendre, déchirer. To — from ;

arracher de. To — off ; *arracher, enlever.* To — open ; *ouvrir* ; (in needlework—*ouvrage à l'aiguille*) *découdre.* To — out of; *arracher de.* To — up; *ouvrir, fendre, déchirer. labourer* ; (to search—*chercher*) *pénétrer, exhumer.*

rip, *n.,* ouverture en long; déchirure, fente ; (blackguard—*vaurien*) canaille, *f.*

ripe (raïpe), *alj.,* mûr; (consummate—*consommé*) parfait.

ripely, *adv.,* mûrement; à temps, à propos.

ripen (raï'p'n), *v.a.,* mûrir, faire mûrir.

ripen, *v.n.,* mûrir; venir à maturité.

ripeness (raïp'-), *n.,* maturité; (fitness — *convenance*) à-propos, *m.,* opportunité, *f.*

ripening (raïp'-), *n.,* maturation ; action de mûrir, *f.* ; progrès vers la maturité, *m.*

ripper, *n.,* personne qui ouvre, qui fend, qui déchire, qui laboure, qui découd, *f.* ; (nav.) déchireur, *m.*

ripping, *n.,* action de fendre, de déchirer, de labourer, d'arracher; ouverture en long, *f.*

ripple (rip'p'l), *v.n.,* se rider; bouillonner.

ripple, *v.a.,* rider; faire bouillonner.

ripple, *n.,* (of water—*de l'eau*) ride, *f.,* bouillon, *m.*

rippler, *n.,* (nav.) chasse-marée, *m.*

rippling, *n.,* action de se rider, de rider, *f.* ; bouillonnement ; (nav.) remous de courant, *m.*

rise (raïze) *v.n.* (*preterit,* Rose ; *past part.,* Risen), se lever; (after a fall, a misfortune, &c. —*après une chute, un malheur, &c.*) se relever ; (to swell—*enfler*) s'élever, monter ; (to augment— *s'accroître*) s'augmenter, s'agrandir, s'accroître ; (of waters—*des eaux*) s'accroître, s'élever, monter, hausser; (of price—*des prix*) hausser, monter, s'élever, augmenter; (of bread, &c.—*du pain, &c.*) renchérir; (to rebel—*se révolter*) se lever, se soulever; (of courts—*des tribunaux*) se lever ; (of assemblies—*d'assemblées*) se séparer; (to sound—*duson*) s'élever, monter; (of the dead —*des morts*) ressusciter; (to gain elevation, rank —*obtenir de l'élévation, un rang*) s'élever; (to grow —*croître*) s'élever, hausser; (to ascend—*monter*) s'élever, monter ; (to have its source in, to spring —*avoir sa source*) naître, venir, s'élever. To — again; *se relever.* To — out of; *sortir de; naître de ; provenir de.* To — to view; *s'offrir à la vue, se présenter à la vue.* To — up; *se lever; se soulever.* I — when the sun —s ; *je me lève avec le soleil.*

rise (raïze), *n.,* lever, *m.* ; (elevation) élévation ; (ascent—*ascension*) ascension ; (of a hill. &c.—*d'une colline, &c.*) montée ; (of waters—*des eaux*) crue; (in price—*des prix*) hausse, augmentation, *f.,* renchérissement, *m.* ; (source) source, naissance, origine ; (increase—*accroissement*) augmentation. *f.* ; (promotion) avancement, *m.* To give — to ; *donner naissance à ; faire naître.* To take its — ; *prendre naissance ; avoir sa source.* On the — ; (com.) en hausse.

riser (raïz'-), *n.,* personne qui se lève, *f.* ; (of a stair—*d'escalier*) degré, *m.,* marche, *f.* Early — ; *personne matineuse, f.* To be an early — ; *être matineux.*

risibility (riz'-), *n.,* risibilité, *f.*

risible (riz'i-b'l), *adj.,* risible.

rising (raïz'-), *adj.,* levant; qui s'élève ; naissant.

rising (raïz'-), *n.,* action de se lever, de se relever, *f.* ; (from bed—*du lit;* of the sun—*du soleil*) lever, *m.* ; (act of ascending—*ascension*) ascension ; (of a hill—*de colline*) montée ; (elevation) élévation ; (of waters—*des eaux*) crue ; (of assemblies, a court—*d'assemblées, de tribunaux*) clôture ; (resurrection) résurrection ; (med.) tumeur. *f.* ; (insurrection) soulèvement, *m.*

risk, *n.,* risque, péril, *m.* At one's — ; *à ses risques et périls.*

risk, *v.a.,* risquer, hasarder.

risker, *n.,* personne qui risque, *f.*

rite (raïte), *n.,* rite, rit, *m.*

ritornello (ri-tor-nèl-lô), *n.,* (mus.) ritournelle, *f.*

ritual (rit'iou-), *n.,* rituel, *m.*

ritual. *a lj.;* rituel, du rit.

ritualist, *n.,* ritualiste, *m.*

ritually, *ado.,* selon le rit.

rival (raï-), *n.,* rival, *m.,* rivale, *f.* ; émule, *m., f.*

rival, *adj.,* rival.

rival (raï-), *v.a.* and *n.,* rivaliser avec, rivaliser.

rivalry, *or* **rivalship** (raï-), *n.,* rivalité, *f.*

rive (raïve), *v.a.* and *n.,* fendre; se fendre.

rivel (riv'v'l), *v.a.,* rider; dessécher; recroqueviller.

river (raï'ver), *n.,* fendeur, *m.*

river (riv'er), *n.,* rivière, *f.* ; fleuve, *m.* Down the — ; *en descendant le fleuve ; en aval.* Up the — ; *en remontant le fleuve ; en amont.*

river-dragon. *n.,* crocodile, *m.* ; (fig.) the King of Egypt (Milton).

river-god. *n.,* dieu de rivière ; fleuve, *m.*

river-horse. *n,* hippopotame, *m.*

rivet, *n.,* rivet, *m.* ; rivure ; (for china—*pour porcelaine, &c.*) attache, *f.*

rivet, *v.a.,* river ; (fig.) fixer, clouer, consolider.

rivulet (riv'lou-), *n.,* ruisseau, *m.*

rix-dollar, *n.,* rixdale, risdale, *f.*

roach (rôtsh), *n.,* (ich.) gardon, *m.*

road (rôde), *n.,* route, *f.* : chemin, *m.* : chaussée, voie, *f.* ; (nav.) rade ; (fig.) voie, route, *f.,* chemin, *m.* Carriage- — ; *voie charretière.* High — ; *grand chemin, grand'route.* Rail- — ; *chemin de fer.* Turnpike- —; *chemin à barrière.* By- — ; *chemin détourné.* Beaten — : *chemin battu.* Heavy — ; *chemin rompu.* Cross- — ; *chemin de traverse.*

road-embankment, *n.* remblai de route, *m.*

road-engineer (-è'n'dji-nîre), *n.,* ingénieur des routes, *m.*

roader. *n.,* vaisseau en rade, *m.*

road-fence. *n.,* clôture de route, *f.*

road-labourer (-léb'eur'-), *n.,* cantonnier, *m.*

road-maker (-mék'-), *n.,* constructeur de routes, *m.*

road-making, *n.,* construction de routes, *f.*

road-scraper (-scrép'-), *n.,* racloir ; rabot ; (pers.) boueur, *m.*

road-side (-saïde), *n.,* bord de la route, *m.*

roadstead (-stède), *n.,* (nav.) rade, *f.*

roadster. *n.,* bidet ; (nav.) navire en rade, *m.*

roadway, *n.,* chaussée; (of a bridge—*de pont*) voie, *f.*

roam (rône), *v.a.* and *n.,* errer, rôder ; rôder dans, parmi.

roamer, *n.,* personne qui erre, *f.* ; promeneur, *m.,* promeneuse, *f.*

roaming (rô'm'-), *n.,* course vagabonde, *f.*

roan (rône), *adj.,* rouan.

roan-tree (-trî), *n.,* (bot.) sorbier des oiseaux, *m.*

roar (rôre), *n.,* (of the lion—*du lion*) rugissement ; (of the bull, &c.—*du taureau, &c.*) mugissement ; cri ; bruit, fracas ; (of laughter—*de rire*) éclat, grand éclat ; (of horses—*des chevaux*) cornage, *m.*

roar, *v.n.,* (of the lion—*du lion*) rugir ; (of the bull, &c.—*du taureau, &c.*) mugir ; (of thunder, cannon—*du tonnerre, du canon*) gronder ; (to cry aloud—*crier fort*) crier : pousser des cris ; tempêter ; (of horses—*des chevaux*) corner.

roarer, *n.,* animal qui rugit ; animal qui mugit : (of horses—*des chevaux*) corneur, *m.* ; (pers.) crieur, criard, *m.,* crieuse, criarde, *f.*

roaring. *n.* V. roar.

roaring (rôr'-), *adj.,* mugissant, rugissant.

roaringly, *adv.,* en rugissant.

roast (rôste), *v.a.,* rôtir ; faire rôtir ; cuire ;

griller, faire cuire ; (metal.) griller ; (to banter—*railler*) railler, plaisanter vivement.

roast, *adj.*, rôti. — meat ; *rôti*, *m*.

roast, *n.*, rôti, *m*. ; (fig.) haute main, *f*. To rule the —; *avoir la haute main*.

roaster, *n.*, personne qui fait rôtir, *f*. ; rôtisseur, *m*. ; (pig—*porc*) cochon de lait pour rôtir, *m*. ; (thing—*chose*) rôtissoire, cuisinière, *f*.

roasting (rôst'-), *n.*, action de rôtir, de faire rôtir, de griller, de brûler ; cuisson, *f*. ; (metal.) grillage, *m*. ; (bantering—*raillerie*) raillerie mordante, *f*.

rob, *n.*, (pharm.) rob, *m*.

rob, *v.a.*, voler ; voler à main armée ; piller ; dépouiller ; dérober ; frustrer ; priver.

robber, *n.*, voleur, *m*. ; voleuse, *f*. ; voleur à main armée ; brigand, *m*. High-way —; *voleur de grand chemin*.

robbery, *n.*, vol ; vol à main armée ; brigandage ; larcin, *m*. ; soustraction, *f*.

robe (rôbe), *n.*, robe, *f*.

robe (rôbe), *v.a.*, vêtir d'une robe.

robe (rôbe), *v.n.*, se revêtir de sa robe.

robin, *or* **robin-redbreast** (-rèd'brèste), *n.*, (orni.) rouge-gorge, *m*.

robinia, *n.*, (bot.) robinier, *m*.

roborant, *adj.*, fortifiant ; (med.) corroborant, roboratif.

robust (ro-beuste), *adj.*, robuste, vigoureux.

robustly, *adv.*, robustement, vigoureusement.

robustness, *n.*, vigueur, force, *f*.

roc, **rock**, *or* **rukh** (reuke), *n.*, rouc, rock, (fabulous bird of Eastern tales—*oiseau fabuleux des contes orientaux*).

rocambole (-bôl), *n.*, rocambole, *f*. ; ail d'Espagne, *m*.

roche-alum (rotsh'al'eume), *or* **rock-alum**, *n.*, alun de roche, *m*.

rochet (rotsh'-), *n.*, rochet (surplis), *m*.

rock, *n.*, roche, *f*. ; rocher, roc ; (sugar—*sucre*) sucre d'orge, sucre de pomme ; (geol.) terrain, *m.*, roche, *f*. ; (at sea—*en mer*) écueil, *m*. —s ; (shoals—*à fleur d'eau*) récif, rescif, *m.sing.* ; (flax around a distaff—*filasse qui garnit la quenouille*) poupée, quenouillée, *f*. ; (fabulous bird—*oiseau fabuleux*) V. **roc**. — -crystal ; *cristal de roche*, *m*.

rock, *v.a.*, bercer, remuer ; balancer.

rock, *v.n.*, se balancer.

rock-basin (-bé's'n), *n.*, bassin de roche, *m*.

rocker, *n.*, personne qui berce ; berceuse ; (thing—*chose*) bascule, *f*.

rocket, *n.*, fusée volante ; (bot.) roquette, *f*.

rock-head (-hède), *n.*, (geol.) crête de roche, *f*.

rockiness, *n.*, abondance de roches, *f*.

rocking, *n.*, action de bercer, *f*. ; balancement, *m*.

rocking-chair (-tshére), *n.*, chaise à bascule, *f*.

rocking-horse, *n.*, cheval à bascule, *m*.

rockless, *adj.*, sans rochers.

rock-rose (-rôze), *n.*, (bot.) ciste, *m*.

rock-work (-weurke), *n.*, rocaille, *f*. ; mur de roche, *m*.

rocky, *adj.*, plein de rochers ; de rocher ; rocheux ; rocailleux.

rocou. V. **arnotto**.

rod, *n.*, verge ; baguette ; tringle ; (of a pump —*de pompe*) tige ; (for fishing—*à pécher*) canne à pêche ; (tech.) verge ; (measure—*mesure*) perche (mètres 5·0291) ; (birch—*de bouleau*) verge, *f*. ; verges, *f.pl.* ; (of a shepherd—*de berger*) houlette, *f*. To have a — in pickle for any one ; *en garder bonne à quelqu'un*.

rodents (rô-), *n.pl.*, (mam.) rongeurs, *m.pl.*

rodomont, *n.*, rodomont, *m*.

rodomont, *adj.*, de rodomont.

rodomontade, *n.*, rodomontade, *f*.

rodomontade, *v.n.*, faire le rodomont.

roe (rô), *n.*, chevrette, biche, *f*. ; (of fish—*de poisson*) œufs de poisson, *m.pl.* Hard —; *œufs de poisson*, *m.pl.* ; *frai*, *m*.' Soft —; *laite*, *laitance*, *f*.

roebuck (rô-beuke), *n.*, chevreuil, *m*.

roed (rôde), *adj.*, à frai ; à laite.

rogation (ro-ghé-), *n.*, rogation, *f*.

rogue (rôghe), *n.*, coquin, fripon, fourbe ; (jest.) malin, espiègle, farceur ; (jur.) vagabond, *m*.

roguery (rôgh'-), *n.*, coquinerie, friponnerie, fourberie ; malice, espièglerie, *f*. ; (jur.) vagabondage, *m*.

rogueship (rôgh'-), *n.*, coquinerie, *f*.

roguish (rôgh'ishe), *adj.*, coquin, fripon, fourbe ; (jest.) malin, espiègle.

roguishly (rôgh'ish'-), *adv.*, en coquin ; en fripon, en fourbe ; (jest.) malicieusement, avec espièglerie.

roguishness (rôgh'-), *n.*, coquinerie, friponnerie, fourberie ; malice, espièglerie, *f*.

roister, *or* **roisterer** (roïs'-), *n.*, (ant.) tapageur, fanfaron, *m*.

roister, *or* **roist** (roïst), *v.n.*, (ant.) faire du tapage ; faire le fanfaron.

roll (rôl), *n.*, (act of rolling—*acte de rouler*) roulement, *m.*, roulade, *f*. ; (round mass—*corps rond*) rouleau ; (of a ship—*d'un vaisseau*) roulis ; (of a drum—*de tambour*) roulement ; (loaf—*pain*) petit pain ; (of tobacco—*de tabac*) rouleau, *m.*, carotte, *f*. ; (metal.) laminoir ; (list—*liste*) rôle ; tableau, contrôle, *m*. —s ; *rôle*, *m.*, *rôles*, *m.pl.*, *contrôle*, *m.*, *contrôles*, *m.pl.* ; (annals—*annales*) *annales*, *f.pl.*

roll, *v.a.*, rouler ; (metal.) laminer. To —down ; *rouler en bas*. To — up ; *rouler en haut* ; (to inwrap—*enrouler*) rouler ; enrouler. To — one's self up ; *s'enrouler, se pelotonner*.

roll, *v.n.*, rouler, se rouler ; (to revolve—*tourner*) faire sa révolution ; (milit.) faire un roulement. To — away ; *s'éloigner en roulant* ; (of time—*du temps*) *s'écouler*. To — off ; *tomber de*. To — up ; *se rouler, s'enrouler*. To — by ; *passer en roulant*.

roller, *n.*, rouleau ; cylindre, *m*. ; (caster—*de meuble*) roulette, *f*. ; (print.) rouleau ; (tech.) tambour ; (metal.) cylindre, laminoir ; (bandage) rouleau, *m.*, bande roulée, *f*. ; (of a lock—*de serrure*) galet ; (orni.) rollier, *m*. Garden-—; *cylindre de jardin*.

rolling, *n.*, roulement ; roulage ; (of a ship—*d'un vaisseau*) roulis ; (metal.) laminage, *m*.

rolling-mill, *n.*, laminoir, *m*. ; machine à cingler le fer, *f*.

rolling-pin, *n.*, rouleau, *m*.

roll-muster (-meus'-), *n.*, contrôle, *m*.

rolls-court (rôlz'côrte), *n.*, cour des rôles, *f*.

rolly-polly, *n.*, (game—*jeu*) balle au pot, *f*.

roman (rô-), *n.*, Romain, *m*. ; Romaine, *f*. ; (print.) romain, *m*.

roman, *adj.*, des Romains, romain ; (print) romain ; (of the nose—*du nez*) aquilin.

romance, *n.*, roman ; (mus.) romance, *f*.

romance, *v.n.*, faire des romans.

romancer, *n.*, romancier, conteur, *m*.

romance-writer (-raït'-), *n.*, romancier, *m*.

romancing, *adj.*, de roman (fiction).

romanesque, *adj.*, (arch., linguist.) roman (paint.) romanesque.

romanish, *n.*, langue romane, *f*. ; roman, *m*.

romanism (-'iz'm), *n.*, religion catholique romaine, *f*.

romanist, *n.*, catholique romain, *m.*, catholique romaine, *f*.

romanize (-'aïze), *v.a.*, latiniser ; convertir au catholicisme romain.

roman-like (-laïke), *adj.*, à la romaine.

romantic, *adj.*, romanesque ; romantique,

romantically, adv., romanesquement ; d'une manière romantique.

romanticist, n., romantique, m.

romanticness, n., caractère romanesque, m., nature romantique, f.

romescot, or **romepenny** (rô'm'-), n., denier de Saint-Pierre, m.

romish, adj., romain.

romp, n., fille joyeuse, gamine, folâtre, f. ; (play—jeu) jeu rude, m.

romp, v.n., jouer rudement ; folâtrer ; gambader, batifoler.

romping, n., jeu rude, m.

rompish, adj., rude ; folâtre.

rompishness, n., folâtrerie, f. ; batifolage, m.

rondeau, or **rondo,** n. (rondeaux, rondoes), rondeau, m.

rood (roude), n., le quart d'une acre, m. ; (rel.) crucifix, m.

rood-loft, n., galerie du crucifix, f.

roof (rouf), n., toit ; (of the mouth—de la bouche) palais, m. ; (of a coach—de voiture) impériale ; (fig.) voûte, f. — -tile ; faîtière, tuile faîtière, f. — -work ; toiture, f.

roof, v.a., couvrir d'un toit ; couvrir ; (to shelter—mettre à l'abri) abriter.

roofing, n., toiture, f.

roofless, adj., sans toit ; (unsheltered—sans abri) sans abri.

roofy, adj., couvert d'un toit.

rook (rouke), n., (orni.) grolle, freux ; (cheat —filou) tricheur, capon, filou, m. ; (at chess—aux échecs) tour, f.

rook, v.a. and n., friponner ; tricher.

rookery, n., lieu habité par des freux ; (bad place—lieu de débauche) mauvais lieu, m.

rooky, adj., rempli de freux.

room (roume), n., (apartment—chambre) chambre, salle ; (of a suite of apartments—dans un appartement) pièce, f. ; (space—étendue) espace, m., place ; (place—endroit) place ; (stead—lieu) place, f., lieu ; (fig.) lieu, motif, m., matière, f. ; (workshop—atelier) atelier, m. Powder— ; (nav.) soute aux poudres, f. Bed— ; chambre à coucher. Dining— ; salle à manger. There is no — ; il n'y a pas de place. To make — ; faire de la place ; faire place.

room, v.n., loger.

roomer, n., (nav.) vaisseau spacieux, m.

roomful (-foule), n., chambre pleine ; chambrée, f.

roominess, n., nature vaste, nature spacieuse, grandeur, f.

roomy, adj., spacieux, vaste.

roost (rouste), n., juchoir, perchoir, m.

roost, v.n., jucher, se percher.

root (route), n., racine ; (first ancestor—premier ancêtre) souché ; (original cause—cause première) source ; (mus.) base ; (lower part—bas) fondation, f., fondement, m. ; (aig., arith., bot., gram.) racine, f. To take— ; prendre racine.

root, v.a., enraciner ; fixer en terre ; laisser enraciner ; (to turn up the earth—la terre) fouiller la terre avec le groin. To — out ; to — up ; déraciner, extirper.

root, v.n., s'enraciner ; prendre racine ; fouiller avec le groin.

root-bound (-baou'n'de), adj., attaché par la racine.

rooted, adj., enraciné. — out ; déraciné, extirpé.

rootedly, adv., profondément.

rooter, n., personne qui laisse enraciner ; personne qui déracine, f. ; exterminateur, m., exterminatrice, f.

rootlet, n., (bot.) radicule, f.

root-stock, n.,(bot.) rhizome, m. ; souche, f.

rooty, adj., plein de racines.

ropalic, adj., en forme de massue.

rop (rôpe), n., corde, f., cordage, m. ; (nav.) manœuvre, f., cordage ; (of birds—des oiseaux) intestin, m. ; (of onions—d'oignons) glane, f. Tight— ; corde tendue ; corde raide.

rope, v.n., filer.

rope-barrel (-'rèl), n., tambour, m.

rope-dancer, n., danseur de corde, m., danseuse de corde, f. ; funambule, m., f.

rope-ladder, n., échelle de corde, f.

rope-maker (-mék'-), n., cordier, m.

rope-making (-mék'-), n., corderie, fabrication de cordes, f.

roper, n., cordier, m.

rope-roll (-rôl), n., tambour, m.

ropery, n., corderie, f. ; (trick—tour) tour pendable, m.

rope-trick, n., tour pendable, f.

rope-walk (-wôke), n., corderie, f.

rope-yarn, n., fil de caret, m.

ropiness (rô-), n., viscosité, nature filamenteuse, f.

ropish, or **ropy** (rô-), adj., qui file ; visqueux ; filamenteux.

roriferous (-rif'èr'-), adj., qui amène la rosée.

rosaceous (-zé-sheusse), adj., (bot.) rosacé.

rosary (rô-za-ri), n., roseraie, f. ; (c.rel.) rosaire, m.

rose (rôze), n., rose ; (of a watering-pot—d'arrosoir) pomme ; (of ribbon—de ruban) rosette, f. There is no — without a thorn ; il n'y a pas de rose sans épines. Under the — ; sous la cheminée, sous le manteau.

roseate (rô-ji-), adj., de rose ; rosé ; orné de roses.

rose-bay, n., laurier-rose ; laurose, rhododendron, rosage, m. Dwarf — ; rhododendron, m.

rosebud (-beude), n., bouton de rose, m.

rose-bush (-boushe), n., rosier, m.

rose-campion, n., lychnide coronaire, coquelourde ; coquelourde des jardiniers, f.

rose-cheeked (-tshîk'te), adj., aux joues de rose.

rose-colour (-keul'leur), n., rose, m.

rose-coloured (-keul'leurde), adj., couleur de rose ; rose ; vermeil.

rosegall (-gôl), n., (bot.) bédegar, bédeguar, m.

rose-like (-laïke), adj., en rose.

rose-lipped (rôz'lip'te), adj., aux lèvres rosées.

rose-mallow (-lô), (bot.) rose trémière ; passe-rose, f.

rosemary, n., (bot.) romarin, m.

rosequartz (-kwörtze), n., quartz rosé, m.

rose-tribe (-traïbe), n.sing., rosacées, f.pl.

rose-water (-wô-), n., eau de rose ; eau rose, f.

rose-window (-dô), n., rosace, f.

rosewood (-woude), n., (bot.) bois de rose, bois de Chypre, palissandre, m.

rose-work (-weurke), n.sing., rosaces, f.pl.

rosicrucian (rôz'i-crou-shi-), n., rose-croix, m.

rosicrucian, adj., des rose-croix.

rosin (roz'-), n. V. **resin.**

rosin, v.a., frotter de résine ; frotter de colophane.

rosiness (rô-zi-), n., rose, vermillon, m. ; couleur rose, f.

rosiny (roz'-), adj., résineux.

rosland, n., bruyère (place—lieu), f. ; terrain marécageux, m.

rosset, n., (mam.) roussette, rougette, f.

roster, n., (milit.) règlement, m. ; cadres, m.pl.

rostral, adj., rostral.

rostrate, or **rostrated** (-trét'-), adj., armé d'un bec ; (natur. hist.) rostré.

rostrum, n., (of a ship—de vaisseau) bec, éperon, m. ; (pulpit—tribune) rostres, m.pl., tri-

bune aux harangues, *f.* ; (of an alembic—*d'alam-bic*) bec : (natur. hist.) rostre, *m.*

rosy (rō-zi), *adj.*, rose, rosé, de rose ; vermeil.

rosy-bosomed (-bou-zeu'm'de), *adj.*, au sein de rose.

rosy-coloured (-keul'leurde), *adj.*, aux couleurs de rose.

rosy-crowned (-craou'n'de), *adj.*, couronné de roses.

rosy-fingered (-fi'n'gheurde), *adj.*, aux doigts de rose.

rosy-tinted, *adj.*, rosé.

rot, *n.*, pourriture ; (vet.) clavelée, *f.*, claveau, *m.*

rot, *v.a.*, pourrir ; faire pourrir ; carier.

rot, *v.n.*, pourrir, se pourrir ; se carier.

rotaug (ro-tan'gn), *n.*, rotang, rotin, *m.*

rotary (rō-), *adj.*, rotatoire.

rotation (ro-té-), *n.*, rotation ; succession, *f.* ; roulement, *m.*

rotator (ro-té-teur), *n.*, muscle rotateur, *m.*

rotatory (rō-ta-teuri), *adj.*, de rotation ; alternatif : (anat.) rotateur ; (mec.) rotatoire.

rote (rōte), *n.*, routine, *f.* By — ; *par cœur.*

rote, *v.a.*, apprendre par cœur.

rote, *v.n.*, rouler, alterner.

rotten (rot't'n), *adj.*, pourri, carié ; (of teeth —*des dents*) gâté. To smell — ; *sentir le pourri.*

rottenness, *n.*, pourriture ; carie, *f.* ; pourri, *m.*

rotten-stone (-stône). *n.*, terre pourrie, *f.*

rotund (-teu'n'de), *adj.*, rond.

rotunda, *or* **rotundo**, *n.*, rotonde, *f.*

rotundity, *n.*, rondeur ; rotondité, *f.*

rouble, *n. V.* **ruble.**

roucou, *n.*, (bot.) roucouyer ; roucou, *m.*

rouge (rouje), *n.*, rouge, fard, *m.*

rouge, *v.n.*, mettre du rouge.

rouge, *v.a.*, mettre du rouge à ; farder.

rough, *adj.*, rude ; (harsh to the taste—*âcre au goût*) âpre ; (rugged—*rugueux*) rude, raboteux ; (shaggy—*hérissé*) hérissé ; (of features—*des traits*) rude ; (of roads—*des routes*) raboteux : (of the sea—*de la mer*) agité, gros ; (of the weather—*du temps*) rigoureux, gros ; (of precious stones—*des pierres précieuses*) brut : (violent) violent ; (coarse in manners—*de manières grossières*) brusque, grossier. — copy ; *brouillon.*

rough, *v.a.*, rendre rude ; ébaucher, dégrossir.

roughcast (-câste), *v.a.*, ébaucher ; (mas.) crépir.

roughcast, *n.*, ébauche, *f.* ; (mas.) crépi, *m.*

roughcasting, *n.*, crépi, ravalement, *m.*

rough-coat (-côte), *v.a.*, (mas.) crépir, ravaler.

rough-coating, *n.*, crépi, ravalement, *m.*

roughdraught (-drâfte), *n.*, ébauche, *f.* ; brouillon, *m.*

roughdraw (-drō), *v.a.*, ébaucher.

roughen (reuff'n), *v.n.*, devenir rude.

roughening, *n.*, action de rendre rude, *f.*

rough-footed (-fout'-), *adj.*, pattu.

rough-hew (-hiou), *v.a.*, ébaucher ; dégrossir.

rough-hewn, *adj.*, ébauché ; dégrossi.

roughing (reuf'-), *n.*, ébauchage, *m.*

roughly (reuf'-), *adv.*, rudement ; grossièrement : âprement.

roughness (reuf'-), *n.*, aspérité ; rudesse ; (austereness to the taste—*âcreté de goût*) âpreté ; (of the sea—*de la mer*) agitation : (of the wind—*du vent*) violence ; (of the weather—*du temps*) rigueur ; (of features—*des traits*) rudesse ; (coarseness of manners—*grossièreté de manières*) grossièreté, rudesse, *f.*, manières impolies, manières grossières, *f.pl.*, brusquerie, *f.* ; (of roads—*des rout s*) état raboteux, *m.*

rough-shod, *adj.*, ferré à glace.

roughwork (-weurke), *v.a.*, travailler grossièrement.

roughwrought (-rôte), *adj.*, travaillé grossièrement. fait grossièrement.

rouleau, *n.* (*rouleaux*), rouleau, *m.*

roulette, *n.*, roulette, *f.*

rounce (raou'n'ce), *n.*, (print.) manche de barreau, *m.*

round (raou'n'de), *n.*, (circle—*cercle*) rond, cercle, *m.* ; (tech.) rondelle, *f.* ; (of a ladder—*d'échelle*) échelon, *m.* ; (of beef—*de bœuf*) rouelle ; (of applause—*d'applaudissements*) salve : (milit.) décharge, *f.* ; (fenc.) assaut, *m.* ; (milit.) ronde, *f.* ; (revolution) tour ; (walk round—*tour*) tour, *m.*, tournée, *f.* In a — ; *en rond.* To go the —s ; *faire la tournée, la ronde.*

round (raou'n'de), *v.a.*, arrondir ; (to encircle ? —*entourer*) environner, entourer ; (to walk round —*faire le tour*) faire le tour de ; (nav.) haler ; (a cape—*un cap*) doubler.

round, *v.n.*, s'arrondir ; (to go round—*aller en rond*) faire la ronde.

round, *adj.*, rond ; en rond ; (large—*considé-rable*) rond, grand, joli, bon ; (full—*plein*) rond, arrondi ; (candid—*franc*) rond, facile, coulant ; (positive—*positif*) absolu.

round, *adv.*, (circularly—*circulairement*) en rond ; (on all sides—*de tous côtés*) autour, tout autour, à l'entour, à la ronde. All — ; *tout autour.* To hand — ; *passer à la ronde.* To go — ; *faire le tour* ; *faire un détour.* To get — ; *tourner* : (of the health—*de la santé*) *se rétablir, se refaire.*

round, *prep.*, autour de. To go — the garden ; *faire le tour du jardin.* To get — any one ; *entortiller quelqu'un.*

roundabout (-'abaoute), *adj.*, détourné ; (ample) vaste, ample.

roundabout, *n.*, jeu de bagues, *m.* ; (garment—*vêtement*) veste, *f.*

roundelay (raou'n'di-), *n.*, rondeau, *m.*

rounders, *n.pl.*, balle au camp, *f.sing.*

roundhead, *n.*, (hist.) tête ronde, *f.*

roundhouse (-haouce), *n.*, violon, *m.* ; (in a ship of war—*sur un vaisseau de guerre*) bouteilles des sous-officiers, *f.pl.* ; (in a merchant-ship—*sur un navire marchand*) chambre du conseil, *f.*

rounding (raou'n'd'-), *n.*, (nav.) fourrure de câble, *f.* — of the side ; (nav.) rentrée des œuvres mortes, *f.*

roundish (raou'n'd'-), *adj.*, arrondi, presque rond ; (pers.) rondelet.

roundishness, *n.*, forme arrondie, forme presque ronde, *f.*

roundlet, *n.*, petit rond, petit cercle, *m.*

roundly, *adv.*, (circularly—*circu'airement*) en rond ; (plainly—*simplement*) rondement, franchement : (completely—*complètement*) rondement, complètement ; (briskly—*vite*) rondement, bon train.

round-man, *n.*, homme de tournée, *m.*

roundness, *n.*, rondeur ; (plainness—*fran-chise*) rondeur, franchise, *f.* ; (positiveness—*caractère positif*) caractère absolu, *m.*

round-robin, *n.*, pièce revêtue de signatures en rond, *f.*

rouse (raouze), *v.a.*, réveiller, éveiller : exciter ; soulever ; (nav.) haler ; (animal) faire lever.

rouse, *v.n.*, se réveiller ; s'éveiller ; s'exciter, se soulever.

rouser, *n.*, personne qui réveille, qui éveille, qui soulève, qui excite ; chose qui réveille, qui éveille, qui soulève, qui excite, *f.*

rousing (raouz'-), *adj.*, qui réveille, qui éveille ; (of fire—*du feu*) grand, bon.

rout (raoute), *n.*, (party—*partie*) réunion nombreuse, *f.*, rout, *m.* ; (multitude) foule, multitude ; (milit.) déroute, *f.* ; (jur.) association de trois personnes ou plus pour commettre un acte de violence, *f.*

rout (raoute), *v.a.*, mettre en déroute.
route (route), *n.*, route, *f.*
routine (rou-tine), *n.*, routine ; manière routinière, *f.*
rove (rôve), *v.n.*, rôder ; courir ; (fig.) divaguer.
rove, *v.a.*, errer dans ; parcourir, courir ; (in spinning—*filage*) passer dans une maille, boudiner.
rover, *n.*, coureur, *m.* ; (fickle person—*personne changeante*) inconstant, *m.*, inconstante, *f.* ; (pirate) écumeur de mer, pirate, corsaire ; (in spinning—*filage*) boudineur, *m.*
roving (rôv'-), *adj.*, errant, qui court ; vagabond.
roving, *n.*, boudinage; *m.*
roving-frame, *n.*, boudinoir, *m.* ; lanterne, *f.*
rovingly, *adv.*, en rôdant ; en divaguant.
row (raou), *n.*, (tumult—*tumulte*) tapage vacarme, *m.* ; querelle, *f.* ; chamaillis, *m.*, batterie, rixe, *f.*
row (rô), *n.*, (rank—*rang*) rang, *m.*, rangée ; (of figures—*de chiffres*) colonne ; (on the water—*sur l'eau*) promenade sur l'eau, promenade en bateau. *f.* All of a —; *en rang d'oignons.*
row (rô), *v.a.*, conduire à la rame; (nav.) nager.
row (rô), *v.n.*, ramer ; (nav.) nager.
rowel (raou-èl), *n.*, (of a spur—*d'éperon*) molette ; (of a bit—*de mors*) bossette, *f.* ; (vet.) séton, *m.*
rowel (raou-èl), *v.a.*, (vet.) appliquer un séton a.
rower (rô-eur), *n.*, rameur ; (nav.) nageur, canotier, *m.*
rowing (rô-), *adj.*, (nav.) qui va à la nage; à rames.
rowlock (rô-), *n.*, toletière. *f.*
row-port (rô-), *n.*, sabord d'aviron, *m.*
royal (roi-ial), *adj.*, royal, de roi ; (of paper—*papier*) grand raisin. —. assent; *consentement du roi, m.*
royal, *n.*, (nav.) perroquet volant; (paper—*papier*) grand raisin, *m.* ; (of a stag—*de cerf*) branche, *f.* ; (artil.) petit mortier; (milit.) soldat du premier régiment d'infanterie, *m.*
royalism ('-iz'm), *n.*, royalisme, *m.*
royalist, *n.*, royaliste, *m.*
royalize (-'aïze), *v.a.*, rendre royal.
royally, *adv.*, royalement, en roi.
royalty, *n.*, royauté ; prérogative royale, *f.*
rub (reube), *v.a.*, frotter; (med.) frictionner ; (to tease—*taquiner*) contrarier. To — away ; *enlever par le frottement.* To — down ; *frotter ;* (a horse—*un cheval*) bouchonner. To — off; *enlever par le frottement : faire disparaître.* To — out; *enlever, effacer.* To — up; *frotter, dérouiller ;* (to polish—*polir*) polir ; (to excite—*exciter*) exciter. To — through; *se frayer un chemin à travers.* To — on; *aller son petit bonhomme de chemin.*
rub (reube), *n.*, frottement ; frottage, *m.* ; (difficulty—*embarras*) difficulté, *f.*, point difficile, obstacle, embarras : (sarcasm—*raillerie*) lardon, coup de patte, *m.* At the —; *au fait et au prendre.*
rubber (reub'-), *n.*, (pers.) frotteur ; (thing—*chose*) frottoir ; (whist) robre rob; (file—*lime*) carreau, *m.* ; (whetstone—*pierre à aiguiser*) pierre à aiguiser ; (at cards—*aux cartes*) partie liée, *f.* India—— ; *caoutchouc, m., gomme élastique. f.*
rubbing (reub'-), *n.*, frottement ; frottage *m.* (hunt.) frayoir, *m.* ; (med.) friction, *f.*
rubbish (reub'-), *n.*, décombres ; débris, déblais ; gravois, gravats, *m.pl.* ; ordures. *f.pl.* ; (anything worthless—*chose sans valeur*) drogue, *f.*, fumier, rebut, *m.* ; (mingled mass—*masse*) masse informe, *f.*
rubbish-cart (-cârte), *n.*, tombereau, *m.*
rubbishing (reub'-), *adj.*, de rebut ; de rien.

rubbish-pan, *n.*, panier aux ordures, *m.*
rubble-stone (reub'b'l-stône), *n.*, pierre brute ; blocaille, *f.* ; moellon brut, blocage, *m.*
rubble-work (-weurke), *n.*, maçonnerie brute de moellons, maçonnerie de blocaille, *f.*
rubefacient (rou-bi-fé-shè'n'te), *adj.*, (med.) rubéfiant.
rubescent (riou-bès-), *adj.*, rubescent.
rubican (rou-), *adj.*, rubican.
rubicund (rou-bi-keu'n'de), *adj.*, rubicond.
rubied (rou-bid), *adj.*, rouge, de rubis.
rubification (rou-bi-fi-ké-), *n.*, (med.) rubéfaction, *f.*
rubify (rou-bi-fa'ye), *v.a.*, rubéfier.
ruble (rou-b'l), *n.*, rouble, *m.*
rubric (rou-), *n.*, rubrique. *f.*
rubric (rou-), *v.a.*, orner de rouge.
rubric, or **rubrical**, *adj.*, rouge.
rubrical, *adj.*, renfermé dans les rubriques.
rubricate (rou-), *v.a.*, tacher de rouge.
rubricate, *adj.*, taché de rouge.
rub-stone (reub'stône), *n.*, pierre à aiguiser. *f.*
ruby (rou-), *adj.*, vermeil, de rubis, couleur de rubis.
ruby (rou-), *n.*, (min.) rubis, *m.* ; (chem.) rubine, *f.* ; (colour—*couleur*) teinte rouge, *f.*, incarnat, *m.*, couleur rouge, *f.* ; (blain—*pustule*) rubis, *m.*
ruby (rou-), *v.a.*, rendre rouge.
ructation (reuk-té-), *n.*, action de roter, éructation, *f.*
rudder (reud'-), *n.*, gouvernail, *m.*
rudder-case (-kéce), *n.*, boîte de gouvernail, *f.*
ruddiness (reud'-), *n.*, rougeur, *f.* ; teint rouge, fraîcheur de teint, *f.* ; incarnat, *m.*
ruddle (reud'd'l), *n.*, rubrique, sanguine, craie rouge, *f.*
ruddle-man, *n.*, ouvrier qui extrait la rubrique, *m.*
ruddy (reud'-), *adj.*, rouge, vermeil ; (pers.) au teint vermeil.
rude (roude), *adj.*, (uneven—*inégal*) rude, grossier ; (impolite—*impoli*) impoli, malhonnête ; (violent, impetuous—*impétueux*) rude, violent, sévère, dur ; (harsh, inclement—*dur*) rude, rigoureux ; (barbarous—*barbare*) barbare, grossier, rustique.
rudely, *adv.*, rudement ; grossièrement ; impoliment, malhonnêtement ; violemment ; sévèrement, durement ; rigoureusement.
rudeness (roud'-), *n.*, rudesse ; grossièreté ; violence ; sévérité, dureté ; rigueur, *f.*
rudenture (rou-dè'n'tioure), *n.*, (arch.) rudenture, *f.*
ruderary (rou-dèr'-), *adj.*, (bot.) rudéral.
rudiment (rou-), *n.*, rudiment, *m.*
rudimental, *r.a.*, enseigner les rudiments à.
rudimental, or **rudimentary**, *adj.*, rudimentaire; élémentaire.
rue (rou), *v.a.*, se repentir de ; regretter, déplorer.
rue (rou), *n.*, (bot.) rue. *f.*
rueful (rou-foule), *adj.*, triste, lamentable. Knight of the — countenance ; *chevalier de la triste figure, m.*
ruefully, *adv.*, tristement, déplorablement.
ruefulness, *n.*, tristesse, *f.*
ruff (reuf). *n.*, fraise, *f.* ; tour de gorge, *m.* ; (milit.) rappel, roulement de tambour, *m.*
ruff (reufe), *v.a.*, donner un coup de baguette à.
ruffian (reuf'ya'n), *n.*, brigand, bandit, (brute) brutal, *m.*
ruffian (reuf'ya'n), *adj.*, de brigand, de bandit ; brutal.
ruffian, *v.n.*, faire le brigand, faire le bandit ; être brutal.
ruffianism ('-iz'm). *n.*, brigandage, *m.* ; extrême grossièreté, brutalité, *f.*

ruffianly, *adj.*, de brigand, de bandit ; brutal.

ruffle (reuf'l), *n.*, manchette, *f.* ; (agitation) trouble, *m.*, agitation, *f.* ; (milit.) rappel, roulement de tambour, *m.*

ruffle (reuf'fl), *v.a.*, (to wrinkle—*froisser*) froncer, froisser, chiffonner ; (to agitate—*agiter*) troubler, agiter ; (to throw into disorder—*mettre en désordre*) mettre en désordre, déranger ; (milit.) rappeler, battre le rappel.

ruffle, *v.n.*, se troubler, s'agiter ; s'ébouriffer ; (to flutter—*voltiger*) battre des ailes, voleter ; jouer négligemment.

rug (reughe), *n.*, (for beds—*de lit*) couverture de bure, *f.* ; (for rooms—*de chambre*) tapis de pied, tapis de foyer, *m.*

rugged (reug'ghède), *adj.*, (rough—*rude*) tempétueux, rude ; (uneven—*rugueux*) raboteux ; (harsh—*âpre*) âpre ; (surly—*hargneux*) renfrogné ; refrogné.

ruggedly (reug'ghèd'-), *adj.*, rudement ; âprement.

ruggedness (reug'ghèd'-), *n.*, aspérité ; nature raboteuse ; âpreté ; rudesse, *f.*

rugine (rou-djine), *n.*, rugine, *f.*

rugose (rou-gôce), *or* **rugous** (rou-), *adj.*, ridé ; rugueux.

rugosity (rou-gôss'i-), *n.*, rugosité, *f.*

ruin (rou-), *n.*, ruine ; perte, *f.* To go to — ; s'en aller, tomber en ruine ; (pers.) courir à sa perte.

ruin (rou-), *v.a.*, ruiner ; perdre.

ruin, *v.n.*, tomber en ruine.

ruination (rou-i'né-), *n.*, (ant.) ruine, *f.*

ruiner, *n.*, destructeur, *m.*, destructrice, *f.*

ruiniform, *adj.*, ruiniforme.

ruinous, *adj.*, (decayed—*en ruine*) ruineux, en ruine ; destructif, ruineux.

ruinously, *adv.*, ruineusement.

ruinousness, *n.*, caractère ruineux, *m.*

rule (roule), *n.*, règle, *f.* ; (government—*gouvernement*) gouvernement, pouvoir, empire, *m.*, autorité, *f.* ; (instrument) règle ; (print.) filet, réglet, *m.*, réglette, *f.* ; (jur.) ordonnance, *f.* To make it a — to ; se faire une règle de. There is no — without exception ; il n'y a point de règle sans exception. To lay out by — and line ; tirer au cordeau.

rule (roule), *v.a.*, (to govern—*gouverner*) gouverner, régir ; (to determine—*déterminer*) régler, déterminer ; (to conduct—*conduire*) régler, diriger ; (paper, &c.—*papier, &c.*) régler.

rule, *v.n.*, gouverner. To — over ; régner sur.

ruler, *n.*, gouverneur ; gouvernant, souverain, *m.* ; (instrument) règle, *f.* ; (workman—*ouvrier*) régleur, *m.*

ruling (roul'-), *adj.*, dominant.

rum (reu'm), *adj.*, drôle ; drôle de ; original. A — fellow ; un drôle de corps.

rum, *n.*, rhum, rum, *m.*

rumble (reu'm'b'l), *v.n.*, gronder, bruire ; (of vehicles—*des voitures*) résonner, retentir.

rumble (reu'm'b'l), *n.*, siège de derrière, *m.*

rumbler, *n.*, chose qui bruit, qui gronde, *f.*

rumbling, *n.*, bruit sourd, grondement ; (of vehicles—*des voitures*) retentissement, bruit, *m.*

rumbling, *adj.*, qui bruit, qui gronde ; (of vehicles—*des voitures*) retentissant ; (of sound—*du son*) sourd.

ruminant (rou-), *adj.*, ruminant.

ruminant, *n.*, ruminant, *m.*

ruminate (rou-), *v.a.* and *n.*, (of animals—*des animaux*) ruminer. To — on (fig.); méditer sur, réfléchir à, ruminer.

rumination (rou-mi-né-), *n.*, rumination ; méditation, réflexion, *f.*

rummage (reum'médje), *v.a.*, chercher en fouillant, fouiller, remuer ; farfouiller.

rummage, *v.n.*, faire un remue-ménage ; farfouiller.

rummage (reum'médje), *n.*, remuement, remue-ménage, *m.*

rummer (reu'm'-), *n.*, (ant.) grand verre. *m.*

rumour (rou-meur), *n.*, rumeur, *f.* ; bruit, *m.* ; renommée, *f.*

rumour, *v.a.*, faire courir le bruit de.

rumourer, *n.*, auteur d'un bruit, d'une rumeur, *m.*

rump (reu'm'pe), *n.*, croupe ; (of meat—*de viande*) culotte, *f.* ; (pers., birds—*des oiseaux*) croupion ; (hist.) croupion, *m.* — -steak ; bifteck, *m.*

rumple (reu'm'p'l), *n.*, pli, *m.* ; froissure. *f.*

rumple (reu'm'p'l), *v.a.*, chiffonner, froisser.

rumpus (reu'm'-), *n.*, grand bruit ; grave différend, *m.*

rumwort (-weurte), *n.*, moût de rhum, *m.*

run (reune), *v.n.* (preterit, Ran ; past part., Run), courir ; marcher ; (to hasten up to—*courir à*) accourir ; (to flee—*fuir*) se sauver ; (to extend—*s'étendre*) courir, s'étendre ; (to leak—*être fendu*) fuir ; (to flow—*couler*) couler ; (to melt—*fondre*) fondre ; (to turn—*tourner*) tourner ; (to be—*être*) être ; (to be circulated—*circuler*) courir, circuler ; (to slide—*glisser*) glisser ; (to be wheeled—*rouler*) rouler ; (of public coaches, boats—*de voitures, de bateaux publics*) aller, faire le service ; (of the eyes—*des yeux*) couler, pleurer ; (of time—*du temps*) s'écouler, écouler, passer ; (of writings—*des écrits*) être conçu ; (of paper—*du papier*) boire ; (of prices—*des prix*) aller ; (of bills—*de billets*) courir ; (of ships—*de vaisseaux*) filer ; (of ulcers—*d'ulcères*) couler, suppurer ; (of candles—*de chandelles*) couler ; (of meteors—*de météores*) filer. To — about ; courir çà et là. To — after ; chercher ; rechercher ; poursuivre. To — against ; courir contre ; se précipiter sur, se jeter sur. To — aground ; échouer. To — at ; courir sur, attaquer. To — away ; s'enfuir ; fuir ; se sauver ; (of horses—*des chevaux*) s'emporter, prendre le mors aux dents ; (of time, liquids—*du temps, des liquides*) s'écouler. To — away with ; se sauver avec ; emporter ; enlever. To — away with the idea ; se mettre dans la tête, s'imaginer. To — back ; retourner en courant ; retourner vite. To — down ; courir en bas ; descendre. To — for ; courir chercher. To — from ; fuir de ; s'enfuir de ; s'échapper de. To — in ; entrer ; entrer précipitamment. To — into ; entrer dans ; (danger) se jeter dans ; (dissipation) se livrer à ; (of colours—*des couleurs*) se fondre. To — off ; s'enfuir ; fuir ; se sauver, s'échapper. To — on ; continuer ; aller toujours ; (to talk—*bavarder*) parler sans cesse, parler toujours ; (to refer to—*référer*) rouler sur ; porter sur ; s'attacher à. To — out ; courir dehors ; sortir ; (to expire—*expirer*) expirer, finir ; tirer à sa fin. To — over ; passer dessus ; passer sur ; parcourir ; (pers.) passer sur, écraser ; (a book—*un livre*) parcourir ; (a street, &c.—*une rue, &c.*) passer, traverser ; (of glasses, &c.—*des verres, &c.*) déborder. To — through ; parcourir, traverser ; (to dissipate—*dissiper*) manger, dissiper, gaspiller. To — up ; courir en haut ; monter. To — up to ; courir à ; (to amount to—*monter à*) s'élever à, monter à. To — upon ; rouler sur ; porter sur ; s'attacher à. The sea — s high ; la mer est haute. To — to seed ; monter en graine. To — into debt ; s'endetter. To — out only for an instant ; ne faire que sortir et rentrer.

run (reune), *v.a.*, (to incur—*encourir*) courir, encourir ; (to melt, to cast—*fondre, jeter en moule*) fondre, couler ; (to smuggle—*introduire en contrebande*) faire entrer par contrebande ; (to pursue—*poursuivre*) parcourir, suivre, poursuivre ; (to drive, to thrust—*enfoncer*) pousser, enfoncer, fourrer ; (to mark, as a line—*tracer*) tirer ; (to cause to fly—*faire marcher*) faire marcher ; (to cause to pass—*faire passer*) passer, faire courir ; (to wheel—*rouler*) rouler. To — down ; lasser à *la course* ; (a ship—*un vaisseau*) *couler, couler bas, couler à fond* ; (pers.) *réduire au silence, fermer la bouche à* ; (to decry—*décrier*) *ravaler* ; (hunt.) *forcer*. To — hard ; *presser* ; *serrer de près*. To — in ; *enfoncer*. To — a thorn into one's foot ; *s'enfoncer une épine dans le pied*. To — into difficulties ; *jeter. précipiter dans des difficultés*. To — into debt ; *endetter*. To — out ; *faire sortir* ; (to exhaust—*épuiser*) *épuiser* ; (to waste—*prodiguer*) *dissiper* ; (to extend—*étendre*) *étendre* ; (print.) *composer en alinéa*. To — over ; *passer rapidement sur* ; *examiner rapidement* ; *parcourir*. To — through ; *percer de part en part* ; *percer d'outre en outre* ; *transpercer* ; (to peruse—*parcourir un écrit*) *parcourir*. To — a sword through any one ; *passer une épée à travers le corps de quelqu'un*. To — up ; *monter en courant* ; (to build—*bâtir*) *élever, bâtir* : (an account—*un compte*) *faire monter*. To — the risk ; *courir le risque*.

run (reune), *n.*, (act of running—*acte de courir*) *course, f.* ; (series—*série*) *cours, m.*, suite, *f.* ; (process—*procédé*) *cours, m.*, marche, *f.* ; (course) *courant* ; (success—*succès*) *succès* ; (censure) cri, *m.*, clameur, opposition ; (on a bank, &c.—*sur une banque, &c.*) descente, irruption, invasion, *f.* ; (voyage) *voyage* ; (generality—*généralité*) *commun, m.* ; (of millstones—*de meules de moulin*) paire ; (at play—*au jeu*) veine, *f.* In the long —; *à la longue, à la fin.*

runagate (reu'n'a-ghéte), *n.*, fugitif ; apostat, renégat ; vagabond ; déserteur, *m.*

runaway (reu'n'a-wè), *n.*, fuyard, *m.*, fuyarde, *f.* ; fugitif, *m.*, fugitive, *f.* ; déserteur, *m.*

rundle (reu'n'd'l), *n.*, cylindre ; (of a ladder —*d'échelle*) échelon, *m.*

rundlet (reu'n'-), *n.*, baril, *m.*

rune (roune), *n.*, caractère runique, *m.*

runer (rou'n'-), *n.*, barde runique, *m.*

rung (reun'gn), *n.*, (nav.) alle : extrémité de la cale ; varangue, *f.* ; façons, *f.pl.*

runic (rou-), *adj.*, runique.

runner (reu'n'-), *n.*, coureur ; messager, courrier ; (racer—*coureur*) coureur ; (of an umbrella—*de parapluie*) coulant ; (bot.) rejeton ; (of a strawberry plant—*de fraisier*) filet, *m.* ; (nav.) itague, *f.* ; (tech.) anneau mobile, *m.* ; (of a mill—*de moulin*) meule supérieure, *f.*

runnet (reu'n'-), *n.*, présure, caillette, *f.*

running (reu'n'-), *n.*, course, *f.* ; écoulement, *m.* ; (of wounds—*de plaies*) suppuration, *f.* ; (of the nose—*du nez*) écoulement, *m.*

running (reu'n'-), *adj.*, courant ; (consecutive—*consécutif*) consécutif, de suite ; (print., nav.) courant ; (of water—*d'eau*) courant, vif ; (of accounts—*de comptes*) courant ; (of bills—*de billets*) à échoir ; (of wounds—*de blessures*) en suppuration. — -horse ; *cheval de course*. — knot ; *nœud coulant*.

runt (reu'n'te), *n.*, animal rabougri, *m.*

rupee (rou-pî), *n.*, roupie, *f.*

rupture (reupt'ieur), *n.*, rupture ; (med.) rupture, hernie, descente, *f.*

rupture (reupt'ieur), *v.a.*, rompre.

rupture, *v.n.*, se rompre.

rupture-wort (-weurte), *n.*, (bot.) herniaire, herniole, turquette, *f.*

rural (rou-), *adj.*, champêtre, rural.

ruralist (rou-), *n.*, habitant de la campagne, *m.*, habitante de la campagne, *f.*

rurally, *adv.*, d'une manière rurale, ruralement.

rush (reushe), *n.*, jonc ; (thing of trivial value—*chose sans valeur*) fétu, rien, *m.*

rush (reushe), *v.n.*, se lancer, s'élancer ; se jeter ; se précipiter, courir à. To — forward ; *s'élancer en avant* ; se précipiter en avant. To — in ; se précipiter dans, s'élancer dans. To — upon ; se précipiter sur. To — out ;

s'élancer dehors ; se précipiter dehors ; sortir brusquement. To — through ; s'élancer à travers.

rush (reushe), *n.*, (violent motion—*mouvement impétueux*) mouvement précipité ; flot ; choc ; effort, *m.* There was a — to ; *on se précipita pour.*

rush-broom (-broume), *n.*, genêt jonciforme, genêt d'Espagne, *m.*

rushiness (reush'-), *n.*, abondance de joncs, *f.*

rushlight (-laïte), *n.*, chandelle de veille, *f.*

rush-like (-laïke), *adj.*, comme un jonc ; faible comme un jonc.

rush-nut (-neute), *n.*, (bot.) souchet comestible, *m.*

rushy (reush'-), *adj.*, plein de joncs ; fait de jonc ; de jonc.

rusk (reuske), *n.*, biscotin. *m.* ; biscotte, *f.*

russet (reus'-), *n.*, roussâtre ; d'un brun rouge ; (rustic—*rustique*) grossier, rustique.

russet (reus'-), *n.*, brun rouge ; roux ; (dress —*vêtement*) habit de paysan, *m.*

russet, *or* **russeting** (reus'-), *n.*, reinette grise, *f.*

russian (reush'a'n), *adj.*, russe, de Russie.

russian, *n.*, Russe, *m.*, *f.* ; (language—*langue*) russe, *m.*

rust (reuste), *n.*, rouille ; rouillure ; moisissure ; (in grain—*des grains*) rouille, *f.* Black —; *nielle, f.* ; *charbon, m.* Brown —; *carie, f., noir, m.*

rust (reuste), *v.n.*, se rouiller.

rust, *v.a.*, rouiller.

rustic (reus-), *adj.*, rustre ; rustique ; rude.

rustic (reus-), *n.*, rustaud, rustre, paysan, *m.*

rustically, *adv.*, rustiquement.

rusticalness, *n.*, rusticité, *f.*

rusticate, *v.n.*, demeurer à la campagne :

rusticate, *v.a.*, reléguer à la campagne ; (at universities—*aux universités*) expulser temporairement.

rusticated (reus-ti-két'-), *adj.*, relégué à la campagne.

rustication (reus-ti-ké-), *n.*, vie de campagne ; (at universities—*aux universités*) expulsion temporaire, *f.*

rusticity (reus-tiss'-), *n.*, simplicité rustique ; rusticité, *f.*

rustily (reust'-), *adv.*, dans un état de rouille.

rustiness (reust'-), *n.*, état de rouille, *m.*

rustle (reus's'l), *v.n.*, bruire ; frôler ; faire frou-frou.

rustle, *or* **rustling** (reus's'l), *n.*, frôlement ; bruissement, *m.*

rustling (reus's'l'-), *adj.*, qui bruit, qui frôle, qui fait frou-frou ; frémissant.

rusty (reust'-), *adj.*, rouillé ; (angry—*en colère*) fâché.

rut (reute), *n.*, (in a road—*de route*) ornière, *f.* ; (of deer, &c.—*des fauves*) rut, *m.*

rut (reute), *v.n.*, être en rut.

rut, *v.a.*, remplir d'ornières ; creuser des ornières dans.

ruthful (routh'foule), *adj.*, (ant.) compatissant.

ruthfully, *adv.*, avec compassion.

ruthless (routh'-), *adj.*, impitoyable ; sans pitié ; insensible.

ruthlessly, *adv.*, sans pitié.

ruthlessness, *n.*, dureté de cœur, cruauté, *f.* ; caractère sans pitié, *m.*

rutilant (rou-), *adj.*, (ant.) brillant, éclatant.

rutted (reut'-), *adj.*, coupé d'ornières.

rutting (reut'-), *n.*, rut, *m.*

ruttish (reut'-), *adj.*, lascif.

ryder (raïd'-), *n.*, *V.* **rider** (com.).

rye (ra'ye), *n.*, seigle, *m.*

rye-grass (-grâce), *n.*, fromental, faux froment, *m.*

s. dix-neuvième lettre de l'alphabet, s, *m.*, *f.*

sabbatarian (-té-), *n.*, sabbataire, *m.*, *f.*; sabbatéen, *m.*, sabbatéenne, *f.*

sabbatarian, *adj.*, sabbataire, sabbatéen.

sabbath (-bath), *n.*, sabbat; (fig.) repos, *m.*

sabbath, *adj.*, saint; religieux.

sabbath-breaker (-brèk'-), *n.*, violateur du sabbat. *m.*

sabbath-breaking, *n.*, violation du sabbat, *f.*

sabbathless, *adj.*, sans sabbat; sans repos.

sabbatic, or **sabbatical**, *adj.*, sabbatique; du sabbat.

sabian, or **sabæan** (-bi-), *n.*, Sabéen, *m.*, Sabéenne, *f.*

sabian, *adj.*, sabéen; (geog.) de Saba (modern Mareb), sabéen.

sabianism (-'iz'm), *n.*, sabéisme, sabisme, sabaïsme, *m.*

sabine (-'ine), *n.*, (bot.) sabine. *f.*

sable (sé-b'l), *n.*, (mam.) martre zibeline; zibeline, *f.*; (her.) sable; (garment—*habillement*) vêtement de deuil, *m.*

sable (sé-b'l), *adj.*, de zibeline; de martre zibeline; (her.) de sable; (fig.) noir, sombre, de deuil.

sabliere (sâ-bli-ère), *n.*, (carp.) sablière, *f.*

sabre (sé-beur), *n.*, sabre, glaive, *m.*

sabre, *v.n.*, sabrer.

sabulosity (sab'iou-loss'-), *n.*, nature sablonneuse, *f.*

sabulous (sab'iou-), *adj.*, sablonneux.

sac, *n.*, sac, *m.*; (anat.) bourse, *f.*

saccade (sak'kéde), *n.*, (man.) saccade, *f.*

sacchariferous (sak'ka-rif'èr'-), *adj.*, saccharifère.

saccharify (sak'kâr-i-fa'ye), *v.a.*, saccharifier.

saccharine (-rine), *adj.*, saccharin.

sacerdotal (sass'èr-dô-), *adj.*, sacerdotal.

sachel (satsh'-), *n.*   V. **satchel.**

sack, *n.*, sac, *m.*; (measure—*mesure*) sac (hectolitre 1·09043), *m.*; (of an abscess—*d'abcès*) poche, *f.*; (wine—*vin*) vin de Xérès; vin d'Espagne; (of a town—*d'une ville*) sac, saccagement, *m.*   To give the —; to; renvoyer, remercier.   To get the —; *être renvoyé.*

sack, *v.a.*, (to pillage—*piller*) saccager, piller; (to put in a sack—*mettre en sac*) ensacher; (to discharge—*renvoyer un domestique, &c.*) renvoyer, remercier.

sackage (sak'édje), *n.*, saccagement, saccage, sac, *m.*

sackcloth (-cloth), *n.*, toile à sac, *f.*; (biblically—*biblique*) sac, *m.*

sacker, *n.*, saccageur, *m.*

sackful (-foule), *n.*, sachée, *f.*

sacking, *n.*, (of a town—*d'une ville*) sac, saccagement *m.*; (cloth—*toile*) toile à sac; (of a bed—*de lit*) sangle, *f.*

sacral (sé-), *adj.*, (anat.) sacré.

sacrament, *n.*, sacrement, *m.*   To receive the —; *communier.*   To administer the last — to: *administrer les derniers sacrements à.*

sacramental, *adj.*, sacramental; sacramentel.

sacramentally, *adv.*, sacramentalement; sacramentellement.

sacramentarian, or **sacramentary**, *n.*, sacramentaire. *m.*

sacramentarian, or **sacramentary**, *adj.*, de sacrement, du sacrement.

sacred (sé-crède), *adj.*, sacré; saint. — to; *consacré à.*

sacredly, *adv.*, saintement; religieusement.

sacredness, *n.*, sainteté, *f.*; caractère saoré, *m.*

sacrific, or **sacrifical**, *adj.*, sacrificatoire.

sacrifice (-faïce), *v.a.* and *n.*, sacrifier.

sacrifice (-faïce), *n.*, sacrifice, *m.*; victime, *f.*   To fall a — to; *être victime de.*

sacrificer (-faïss'-), *n.*, sacrificateur, *m.*

sacrificial (-fish'ial), or **sacrificatory**, *adj.*, sacrificatoire, des sacrifices.

sacrilege (-lèdje), *n.*, sacrilège, *m.*

sacrilegious (-lidj'-), *adj.*, sacrilège.

sacrilegiously, *adv.*, sacrilègement; avec sacrilège.

sacrilegiousness, *n.*, caractère sacrilège, *m.*

sacrilegist (-lèdj'-), *n.*, sacrilège, *m.*, *f.*

sacrist (sé-), *n.*, sacristain; copiste de musique à l'usage du chœur des églises, *m.*

sacristan, *n.*, sacristain, *m.*

sacristy, *n.*, sacristie, *f.*

sad, *adj.*, triste.   To make —; *rendre triste; attrister.*

sadden, *v.a.* and *n.*, attrister; s'attrister.

saddle (sad'd'l), *n.*, selle, *f.*; (of a bowsprit —*de beaupré*) taquet; (of a yard—*de vergue*) croissant, *m.*   Side— —; *selle de dame.*

saddle, *v.a.*, seller.   To — with; *charger de.*   To be — d with; *avoir sur le dos.*

saddle-backed (-bak'te), *adj.*, en selle; (arch.) en dos d'âne.

saddle-bags (-bag'ze), *n.pl.*, sacoche, bourse, *f.*

saddle-bow (-bô), *n.*, arçon, *m.*

saddle-cloth (-cloth), *n.*, housse de cheval, *f.*

saddle-maker (-mék'-), *n.*, sellier; bourrelier, *m.*

saddler, *n.*, sellier, *m.*

saddlery, *n.*, sellerie, *f.*

saddle-tree (-trî), *n.*, bois de selle; pontet, *m.*

sadducean (sad-diou-ci-), *adj.*, saducéen.

saducee (sad-diou-ci), *n.*, saducéen, *m.*, saducéenne, *f.*

sadducism (-ciz'm), or **sadduceeism** (-ci-iz'm), *n.*, saducéisme, *m.*

sadly, *adv.*, tristement. — hurt; *grièvement blessé.*   To be — d with; *avoir grand besoin de.*

sadness, *n.*, tristesse, *f.*

safe, *adj.*, sauf; sain et sauf; (trustworthy—*digne de confiance*) sûr; (secure—*sans danger*) sûr. — from; *à l'abri de: en sûreté contre.*

safe, *n.*, garde-manger; coffre-fort, *m.*

safe-conduct (-co'n'deuk'te), *n.*, sauf-conduit, *m.*; escorte, *f.*

safe-guard (-gârde), *n.*, sauvegarde; protection, *f.*

safe-keeping (-kip'-), *n.*, bonne garde; sûreté, *f.*

safely, *adv.*, sain et sauf; sûrement; en sûreté; sous bonne garde.

safeness, *n.*, sûreté, *f.*

safety, *n.*, sûreté, *f.*; salut, *m.*   To seek — in flight; *chercher son salut dans la fuite.*

safety-lamp, *n.*, lampe de sûreté, *f.*

safflower (saf'fla-weur), *n.*, (bot.) carthame; (dy.) safranum, *m.*

saffron (saf'reune), *n.*, safran, *m.*

saffron, *adj.*, safrané; couleur de safran; de safran.

saffron, *v.a.*, safraner.

saffron-plantation (-pla'n'té-), *n.*, safranière, *f.*

saffron-seed (-sîde), *n.*, graine de perroquet, *f.*

saffrony, *adj.*, safrané.

sag, *v.a.*, (ant.) courber, faire plier sous un fardeau.

sag, *v.n.*, plier, fléchir, être courbé.

sagacious (sa-ghé-shieusse), *adj.*, sagace; pénétrant.

sagaciously, *adv.*, avec pénétration, avec sagacité.

sagaciousness, or **sagacity**, *n.*, sagacité; pénétration, *f.*

sage (sédje), *n.*, sage, philosophe, *m.*
sage, *adj.*, sage ; prudent.
sage, *n.*, (bot.) sauge, *f.*
sagely, *adv.*, sagement ; prudemment.
sagging (sag-ghigne), *or* **sag**, *n.*, courbure, *f.*
sagittal (sadj'-), *adj.*, sagittale.
sagittarius (sadj-it'té-), *n.*, (astron.) le Sagittaire, *m.*
sagittary (sadj'it-), *n.*, sagittaire, *m.*
sagittary, *adj.*, sagittale.
sagittate (sadj'-), *adj.*, (bot.) sagitté.
sago (sé-gô), *n.*, sagou, *m.*
sagoin (sa-goïne), *n.*, (mam.) sagouin, *m.*
sago-tree (-trî), *n.*, sagouier ; sagoutier, *m.*
sagy (-sé-dji), *adj.*, plein de sauge ; qui a un goût de sauge.
sail (séle), *n.*, voile ; (of a windmill—*de moulin*) aile ; (ship—*vaisseau*) voile ; (on the water—*sur l'eau*) course à la voile, *f.* Fore- — : *misaine : voile de misaine, f.* Main— ; *grande voile.* Top- — : *hunier, m.* Gallant- — ; *voile de perroquet.* To set — ; *mettre à la voile ; faire voile.* To carry a press of — ; *faire force de voiles.*
sail, *v.n.*, faire voile ; cingler, naviguer ; mettre à la voile ; appareiller ; aller ; voguer. To — along the coast ; *côtoyer.*
sail, *v.n.*, naviguer sur, voguer sur.
sailable (sél'a-b'l), *adj.*, navigable.
sail-cloth (-cloth), *n.*, toile à voile. *f.*
sailer (-r), voilier, *m.* Fast, heavy — ; *bon, mauvais voilier.*
sailing, *n.*, navigation ; marche, *f.* ; (setting sail—*appareiller*) appareillage ; (flight—*vol d'oiseaux, &c.*) vol, *m.*, course, *f.*
sailing, *adj.*, à voiles. — -ship : *bâtiment à voiles, m.* Fast- — ship : *bâtiment d'une marche rapide ; fin voilier, m.*
sail-loft, *n.*, voilerie, *f.* ; magasin à voiles, *m.*
sail-maker (-mék'-), *n.*, voilier, *m.*
sail-making (-mék'-), *n.*, voilerie, *f.*
sailor, *n.*, marin ; matelot, *m.* Fresh-water — ; *marin d'eau douce.*
sail-yard (-yàrde), *n.*, vergue, *f.*
sainfoin (sé'n'foïne), *or* **saintfoin** (sé'n't'-), *n.*, (bot.) sainfoin, *m.*
saint (sé'n't), *n.*, saint, *m.*, sainte, *f.* One's —'s day ; *sa fête, f.* All —s' day ; *jour de la Toussaint, m. ; la Toussaint, f.*
saint, *v.a.*, mettre au rang des saints ; canoniser.
saint, *v.n.*, faire le saint.
sainted, *adj.*, saint ; sacré ; canonisé.
saintlike (-laïke), *or* **saintly**, *adj.*, saint ; semblable à un saint.
saintly, *adv.*, saintement, en saint.
saintship, *n.*, sainteté, *f.*
sake, *n.*, égard ; but, *m.* ; cause, *f.* For your —; *par égard pour vous ; à cause de vous : pour vous.* For the — of annoying me ; *pour le plaisir de me vexer.* For pity's —; *par pitié.* For God's —; *pour l'amour de Dieu : je vous en supplie.* For the — of appearances ; *pour sauver les apparences.* For the — of going there ; *dans le but, pour le plaisir d'y aller.* For the — of health ; *pour cause de santé.* For the — of money ; *pour l'amour de l'argent.*
saker (sé-keur), *n.*, (orni.) sacre, *m.*
sakeret (sak'èr'-), *n.*, (orni.) sacret, *m.*
salable (sél'a-b'l), *adj.*, vendable ; de bonne vente.
salableness, *n.*, facilité de vente. *f.*
salably, *adv.*, d'une manière vendable.
salacious (sa-lé-shieusse), *adj.*, lubrique ; lascif.
salaciously, *adv.*, lubriquement ; lascivement.
salacity (-lass'-), *n.*, lubricité ; lasciveté, *f.*
salad, *n.*, salade, *f.*
salad-bowl (-bôl), *n.*, saladier, *m.*

salading, *n.*, salade, *f.*
salamander, *n.*, salamandre, *f.*
salamandrine (-drine), *adj.*, de salamandre ; qui tient de la salamandre.
salaried (-ride), *adj.*, salarié.
salary, *n.*, appointements, *m.pl.* ; (of high functionaries—*de hauts fonctionnaires*) traitement ; (fig.) salaire, *m.*
sale, *n.*, vente, *f.* ; débit, *m.* Deed of — ; *contrat de vente, m.* Bill of — ; *lettre de vente, f.* — by auction ; *vente aux enchères.* Private — ; *vente à l'amiable.* To put up for — ; *mettre en vente.* Dull — ; *vente difficile.* Quick — ; *vente facile.*
saleable (sél'a-b'l), *adj.* V. **salable.**
saleableness, *n.* V. **salableness.**
saleably, *adv.* V. **salably.**
salep (sa-lèp), *n.* V. **salop.**
salesman (sélz'-), *n.*, commis ; (of clothes—*d'habits*) marchand d'habits ; (of cattle—*de bestiaux*) marchand de bestiaux, *m.*
salework (-weurke), *n.*, ouvrage de pacotille, *m.* ; camelote, pacotille, *f.*
salic, *adj.*, salique.
salient (sé-), *adj.*, saillant ; qui saute ; qui bondit.
saliferous (-lif'èr-), *adj.*, salifère.
salifiable (-faï-a-b'l), *adj.*, (chem.) salifiable.
salification (-fi-ké-), *n.*, (chem.) salification, *f.*
salify (sal'i-fa'ye), *v.a.*, (chem.) salifier.
salination (-né-), *n.*, salaison, *f.* ; salage, *m.*
saline (-laïne), *adj.*, salin.
saline (-laïne), *n.*, source salée, *f.*
salinous (-laï-), *adj.*, salin.
saliva (-laï-), *n.*, salive, *f.*
salival, *or* **salivary** (-laï-), *adj.*, salivaire.
salivate (sal'i-), *v.a.*, faire saliver.
salivation (sal'i-vé-), *n.*, salivation, *f.*
salivous (-laï-), *adj.*, de salive.
sallow (sal'lô), *adj.*, blême.
sallowness, *n.*, couleur blême, *f.* ; teint blême, *m.*
sally, *n.*, excursion ; (arch., of wit—*d'esprit*) saillie, *f.* ; (of youth—*de jeunesse*) écart, *m.* ; (milit.) sortie, *f.*
sally, *v.n.*, (milit.) sortir ; faire une sortie.
sally-port, *n.*, (milit.) poterne, *f.* ; (nav.) sabord de fuite (in a fire-ship—*d'un brûlot*), *m.*
salmagundi (-gheu'n'-), *n.*, salmigondis, *m.*
salmon (sa'm'eune), *n.*, saumon, *m.*
salmon-fishery, *n.*, pêche du saumon, *f.*
salmon-trout (-traoute), *n.*, truite saumonée, *f.*
saloon (sa-loune), *n.*, salle de réception, *f.* ; salon, *m.*
salop (sé-), *or* **saloop** (sa-loupe), *n.*, salop, *m.*
salsify (-fi), *n.*, (bot.) salsifis cultivé des jardins ; salsifis, *m.*
salt (sôlt), *n.*, sel, *m.* ; —s ; (pharm.) sel, *m. sing.* Epsom —s ; *sel Anglais, sel d'Epsom.* Attic —; *sel Attique.* Not to be worth one's —; *ne pas valoir le pain qu'on mange.*
salt, *adj.*, salé ; d'un goût salin ; (abounding with salt—*abondant en sel*) qui abonde en sel ; (lecherous—*lascif*) lubrique.
salt, *v.a.*, saler ; saupoudrer de sel. To — down; *saler.*
saltation (sal-té-), *n.*, action de sauter ; (palpitation) palpitation, *f.*
salt-box, *n.*, salière de cuisine, *f.* ; saloir, *m.*
salt-cat, *n.*, salignon, *m.*
salt-cellar, *n.*, salière, *f.*
salter (sôlt'-), *n.*, saunier ; (drysalter—*saleur*) saleur, marchand de salaisons, *m.*
saltern (sôlt'-), *n.*, saunerie ; saline, *f.*
salt-fish, *n.*, poisson salé, *m.* ; saline, salaison, *f.*
saltier, *or* **saltire** (sal-tîre), *n.*, (her.) sautoir, *m.* — -wise ; *en sautoir.*
salting (sôlt'-), *n.*, salaison, *f.* ; salage, *m.*

salting-tub (-teube), *n.*, saloir, *m.*

saltish (sōlt'-), *adj.*, un peu salé; saumâtre.

saltishness, *n.*, goût salin, *m.*

salt-lake. *n.*, lac salé, *m.*

saltless (sōlt'-). *adj.*, sans sel; fade.

saltly (sōlt'-), *adv.*, avec un goût de sel.

salt-maker (-mék'-), *n.*, saunier, *m.*

salt-marsh, *n.*, marais salant, *m.*

salt-meat (-mîte), *n.*, viande salée; salaison, *f.*; salé, *m.*

salt-mine (-maîne), *or* **salt-pit**, *n.*, saline; mine de sel, *f.*

saltness (sōlt'-), *n.*, salure, *f.*

saltpetre (sōlt'pî-teur), *n.*, salpêtre, *m.*

saltpetre-maker (-mék'-), *n.*, salpêtrier, *m.*

saltpetre-pit, *n.*, nitrière, *f.*

saltpetre-works (-weurkse), *n.pl.*, salpêtrière, *f.* *sing.*

saltpetrous (-pît'-). *adj.*, salpêtreux.

salt-springs (-sprign'ze), *n.pl.*, sources salées, *f.pl.*

saltwater (-wō-), *n.*, eau de mer; eau salée, *f.*

saltwork (-weurke), *n.*, saline, saunerie, *f.*

saltwort (-weurte), *n.*, soude; herbe au verre: salicote; salicorne, *f.*

salty (sōlt'-), *adj.*, salé; qui a un goût de sel.

salubrious (-liou-), *adj.*, salubre.

salubriously, *adv.*, d'une manière salubre.

salubrity (-liou-), *n.*, salubrité, *f.*

salutariness (sal'iou-), *n.*, caractère salutaire, *m.*

salutary (sal'iou-), *adj.*, salutaire.

salutation (sal'iou-té-), *n.*, salut, *m.*; salutation, *f.*

salute (sa-lioute), *n.*, salut; (kiss—*baiser*) baiser; (milit., nav.) salut, *m.*; (of guns—*de canons*) salve, *f.*

salute, *v.a.*, saluer; (to kiss—*baiser*) baiser; (milit., nav.) saluer.

saluter, *n.*, personne qui salue, *f.*

salutiferous (sal'iou-tif'èr-), *adj.*, salutaire.

salvage (-vèdje), *n.*, sauvetage, *m.* — money; *prix du sauvetage*, *m.*

salvation (sal-vé-), *n.*, salut, *m.*

salve (sâve), *n.*, onguent; (remedy—*remède*) remède, baume, *m.* Lip—; *pommade pour les lèvres, f.*

salve, *v.a.*, guérir avec des onguents; (to remedy—*remédier*) secourir, remédier à. To — over: *cajoler.*

salver (sal-veur), *n.*, plateau, *m.*; soucoupe, *f.*

salvo (sal-vō), *n.*, réserve; restriction; (of artillery—*d'artillerie*) salve, *f.*

salvor (sal-veur), *n.*, sauveteur, *m.*

samaritan, *n.*, Samaritain, *m.*, Samaritaine, *f.*

samaritan, *adj.*, samaritain.

same, *adj.*, même. It is all the —; *c'est égal; c'est tout un; c'est tout de même; c'est la même chose.* It is all the — to me: *cela m'est égal; cela m'est parfaitement égal.* Much about the —; *à peu près de même.* To do the —; *faire de même; en faire autant.* The very —; *le même.*

sameness, *n.*, identité; similitude; (uniformity—*uniformité*) uniformité, monotonie, *f.*

samlet, *n.*, saumoneau, *m.*

samphire (-faï'eur), *n.*, bacile, fenouil marin, *m.*; crête-marine, passe-pierre, perce-pierre, christe marine, *f.*

sample (sa'm'p'l), *n.*, échantillon, *m.*; montre, *f.*, exemple, *m.*

sample, *v.a.*, échantillonner.

sample-bottle (-bot't'l), *n.*, bouteille à échantillon, *f.*

sampler, *n.*, modèle; (for needle-work—*ouvrage à l'aiguille*) canevas, *m.*

sampling, *n.*, échantillonnage, *m.*

sanability, *or* **sanableness**, *n.*, curabilité, *f.*

sanable (-'a-b'l), *adj.*, curable; guérissable.

sanative (-tîve), *or* **sanatory**, *adj.*, curatif.

sanativeness, *n.*, vertu curative, *f.*

sanatory, *adj.* *V.* **sanative.**

san-benito (sa'n'bè'n'î-tō), *n.*, san-benito, *m.*

sanctification (-fi-ké-), *n.*, sanctification. *f.*

sanctified (-faïde), *adj.*, sanctifié; (b.s.) béat.

sanctifier (-faï'-), *n.*, sanctificateur, *m.*

sanctify (-fa'ye), *v.a.*, sanctifier.

sanctifying (-fa'yigne), *adj.*, sanctifiant; béat.

sanctimonious (-mô-), *adj.*, dévot; (b.s.) béat.

sanctimoniously, *adv.*, avec un air de sainteté.

sanctimoniousness, *n.*, dévotion affectée, *f.*

sanctimony (-mo-), *n.*, sainteté; dévotion, *f.*

sanction, *n.*, sanction, *f.*

sanction. *v.a.*, sanctionner.

sanctitude (-tioude), *n.*, sainteté, *f.*

sanctity (san'gn'k-ti-ti), *n.*, sainteté, *f.*

sanctuarize (-'iou-a-raïze), *v.a.*, (ant.) servir de sanctuaire à.

sanctuary (san'gn'kt'iou-), *n.*, sanctuaire; asile; refuge, *m.* To take —; *se réfugier dans un sanctuaire.*

sand, *n.*, sable; grain de sable, *m.* To be bedded in the —; (nav.) *être engravé; être ensablé.*

sand, *v.a.*, sabler.

sandal, *n.*, sandale, *f.*

sandal, *or* **sandal-wood** (-woude), *n.*, sandal, santal, bois de santal, de sandal, *m.*

sandarac, *or* **sandarach** (-rake), *n.*, sandaraque, *f.*

sand-bag. *n.*, (milit.) sac à terre, *m.*

sand-bank, *n.*, banc de sable, *m.*

sand-blind (-blaï'n'de), *adj.*, qui a la vue trouble.

sand-box, *n.*, poudrière, *f.*; (bot.) sablier, *m.*

sand-coloured (-keul'leurde), *adj.*, couleur de sable.

sand-crack, *n.*, (vet.) bleime, *f.*

sanded, *adj.*, sablé; sablonneux.

sand-flood (-fleude), *n.*, mer de sable, *f.*

sandiness, *n.*, nature sablonneuse, *f.*; (colour—*couleur*) blond ardent, *m.*; couleur vive, *f.*

sandish, *adj.*, sablonneux.

sand-paper (-pé-), *n.*, papier sablé; papier de verre, *m.*

sand-piper (-païp'-), *n.*, (orni.) bécasseau, *m.*

sand-pit, *n.*, sablière; sablonnière, *f.*

sandstone (-stône), *n.*, grès, *m.*

sandwich (-'widje), *n.*, sandwich, *f.*

sandy, *adj.*, sablonneux; de sable; (of colour —*de couleur*) d'un blond ardent, roux.

sane, *adj.*, sain d'esprit.

sang-froid (san'gn-froi), *n.*, sang-froid, *m.*

sanguiferous (sa'n'gwif'èr-), *adj.*, qui renferme du sang.

sanguification (-gwi-fi-ké-), *n.*, (med.) sanguification, hématose, *f.*

sanguify (sa'n'gn'gwi-fa'ye), *v.n.*, se sanguifier.

sanguinary (-gwi'n'-), *adj.*, sanguinaire.

sanguine (sa'n'gn'gwine), *adj.*, sanguin; (ardent) ardent, vif; (confident—*confiant*) plein de confiance, confiant. — hopes; *de vives espérances.* Beyond my most — hopes; *au-delà de toutes mes espérances.*

sanguinely, *adv.*, ardemment; avec confiance.

sanguineness, *n.*, nature sanguine; (ardour —*ardeur*) ardeur; (confidence—*confiance*) confiance, *f.*

sanguineous (-gwi'n'i-), *adj.*, sanguin.

sanhedrim (-hi-), *n.*, sanhédrin, *m.*

sanicle (-'i-k'l), *n.*, (bot.) sanicle, *f.*

sanies (sé-ni-îze), *n.*, (med.) sanie, *f.*

sanious (sé-ni-), *adj.*, sanieux.

sanitary, *adj.*, sanitaire.

sani y, *n.*, état d'un esprit sain *m.*

sanscrit, *n.*, sanscrit, *m.*

santaline (-line), *n.*, (chem.) santaline, *f.*

sap, *n.*, (bot.) : sève ; (milit.) sape, *f.*

sap, *v.a.*, saper.

sap, *v.n.*, saper ; aller à la sape.

sapajo, *or* **sapajou** (-djô), *n.*, (mam.) sapajou, *m.*

sapan, *or* **sapan-wood** (-woude), *n.*, sapan, bois de sapan. *m.*

sapan-tree (-trî), *n.*, (bot.) sapan, *m.*

sap-colour (-keul'leur), *n.*, couleur végétale, *f.*

sapgreen (-grîne), *n.*, (paint.) vert de vessie, *m.*

sapid, *adj.*, sapide.

sapidity, *or* **sapidness**, *n.*, sapidité, *f.*

sapience (sé-), *n.*, sagesse, *f.*

sapient (sé-), *adj.*, sage ; doué de sagesse.

sapiential (sé-piè'n-shal), *adj.*, (rel.) sapientiaux, *adj.m.pl.*

sapless, *adj.*, sans sève; sec ; desséché.

sapling, *n.*, plant ; plantard ; plançon, *m.*

sapodilla, *or* **zapotilla**, *n.*, sapote, sapotille, *f.* —-tree; *sapotillier, sapotier, m.*

saponaceous (-né-sheusse), *adj.*, saponacé.

saponification (-fi-ké-), *n.*, saponification, *f.*

saponify (-fa'ye), *v.a.* and *n.*, saponifier ; se saponifier.

sapor (sé-), *n.*, saveur, *f.*

saporific (sap'-), *adj.*, saporifique.

saporous, *adj.*, sapide, qui a du goût, qui a de la saveur.

sapota, *n.*, (bot.) sapotier, sapotillier, *m.* ; (fruit) sapote, sapotille, *f.*

sapper, *n.*, (milit.) sapeur, *m.*

sapphic, *n.*, saphique, *m.*

sapphire (saf'ir), *n.*, saphir, *m.*

sapphirine (-ine), *adj.*, de saphire, ressemblant au saphir.

sappiness, *n.*, abondance de sève, *f.*

sappy, *adj.*, plein de sève ; de sève ; séveux ; polish—*sot*) sot.

saraband, *n.*, sarabande, *f.*

saracen, *n.*, Sarrasin, *m.*

saracen, *adj.*, sarrasin.

saracenic, *adj.*, sarracénique; (arch.) sarrasin.

sarcasm (sâr-caz'm), *n.*, sarcasme, *m.*

sarcastic, *or* **sarcastical**, *adj.*, sarcastique.

sarcastically, *adv.*, avec sarcasme ; d'une manière sarcastique.

sarcenet (sârs'nète), *n.*, florence, *m.*

sarcocele (sâr-co-cîle), *n.*, (med.) sarcocèle, *m.*

sarcological (-'ô-djik'-), *adj.*, de la sarcologie.

sarcology (-'o-dji), *n.*, sarcologie, *f.*

sarcoma (-cô-), *n.*, (med.) sarcome, *m.*

sarcomatous, *adj.*, (med.) sarcomateux.

sarcophagous (-gheusse), *adj.*, carnivore.

sarcophagus (-gheusse), *n.*, sarcophage, *m.*

sarcotic, *adj.*, sarcotique.

sarcotic, *n.*, sarcotique, *m.*

sard (sârde), *or* **sardoin** (-doïne), *n.*, (min.) sardoine, *f.*

sardine (sâr-dîne), *n.*, (ich.) sardine, *f.*

sardinian, *n.*, Sarde, *m.,f.*

sardinian, *adj.*, sarde.

sardonian, *or* **sardonic**, *adj.*, sardonique; sardonien.

sardonyx (sâr-), *n.*, sardonyx, sardoine, *f.*

sarmentose (sâr-mè'n-tôce), *or* **sarmentous** (-teusse), *adj.*, (bot.) sarmenteux.

sarplier (sâr-plîre), *n.*, serpillière, *f.*

sarrasine (-cîne), *n.*, (fort.) sarrasine, *f.*

sarsaparilla (sâr-), *n.*, salsepareille, *f.*

sarsenet *n.* *V.* **sarcenet.**

sash, *n.*, ceinture, *f.* ; (of a window—*de fenêtre*) châssis. *m.* French — ; croisée, *f.*

sash, *v.a.*, parer d'une ceinture ; (carp.) munir d'un châssis.

sash-frame, *n.*, (carp.) châssis dormant, *m.*

sash-window (-dô), *n.*, fenêtre à châssis, fenêtre à guillotine. *f.*

sassafras, *n.*, (bot.) sassafras, *m.*

satan (sé-), *n.*, Satan, *m.*

satanic, *or* **satanical** (sé-), *adj.*, satanique.

satanically (sé-), *adv.*, d'une manière satanique

satanism (sé-ta'n-iz'm), *n.*, esprit satanique, *m.*

satchel, *n.*, sachet, petit sac, *m.* ; gibecière, *f.* ; (of lawyers—*d'hommes de loi*) sac de procès, sac, *m.*

sate, *v.a.*, rassasier.

sateless, *adj.*, insatiable.

satellite (-tèl'laïte), *n.*, satellite, *m.*

satellitous (-lish'eusse), *adj.*, de satellite.

satiate (sé-shi-éte), *v.a.*, rassasier.

satiate, *adj.*, rassasié.

satiety (sa-taï-è-), *n.*, satiété, *f.*

satin, *n.*, satin, *m.*

satin, *adj.*, de satin ; satiné. —-ribbon ; ruban de satin, *m.*

satinet, *n.*, satinade, *f.*

satining, *n.*, satinage, *m.*

satire (sat'a'eur, *ou* sat'eur), *n.*, satire, *f.*

satiric, *or* **satirical** (-tir'-), *adj.*, satirique.

satirically, *adv.*, satiriquement.

satirist (sat'ir'-), *n.*, satiriste, *m.*

satirize (sat'ir'aïze), *v.a.*, satiriser.

satisfaction, *n.*, satisfaction, *f.* ; (discharge —*payement*) acquittement, *m.* ; (amends—*réparation*) réparation ; (concession, apology—*excuse*) satisfaction, raison, réparation, *f.* To give — ; (to please, to suit—*plaire, convenir*) donner de la satisfaction; (to apologize—*faire des excuses*) donner satisfaction ; (to fight—*se battre en duel*) rendre raison.

satisfactorily, *adv.*, d'une manière satisfaisante.

satisfactoriness, *n.*, pouvoir de satisfaire ; caractère satisfaisant, *m.*

satisfactory, *adj.*, satisfaisant satisfactoire.

satisfier (-faï'-), *n.*, personne qui satisfait, *f.*

satisfy (-fa'ye), *v.a.*, satisfaire ; satisfaire à ; contenter; (to convince—*convaincre*) convaincre; (a debt—*une dette*) acquitter ; (the appetite—*l'appétit*) rassasier. To — one's vengeance ; assouvir sa vengeance. To — one's appetite ; se rassasier. To be satisfied cf ; *être convaincu de.* To be satisfied with ; *être satisfait de ; être content de.* To be rather more than satisfied ; *en avoir plus qu'assez.*

satisfy, *v.n.*, satisfaire à.

satrap (sé-), *n.*, satrape, *m.*

satrapal (sé-), *adj.*, de satrape.

satrapy (sé-tra-pi), *n.*, satrapie, *f.*

saturable (sat'iou-ra-b'l), *adj.*, saturable.

saturant, *adj.*, saturant.

saturate (sat'iou-), *v.a.*, saturer.

saturation (sat'iou-ré-), *n.*, saturation, *f.*

saturday (sat'eurne), *n.*, samedi, *m.*

saturn (sat'eurne), *n.*, Saturne, *m.*

saturnalia (-'eur-né-), *n.pl.*, saturnales, *f.pl.*

saturnalian, *adj.*, des saturnales.

saturnian, *adj.*, de Saturne.

saturnine (sat'eur-naïne), *adj.*, sombre ; taciturne.

satyr (sé-teur, *ou* sat'ir), *n.*, satyre, *m.*

satyriasis (sat'i-raï-a-cice), *n.*, (med.) satyriasis, *m.*

satyrium, *n.*, (bot.) satyrion, *m.*

sauce (sôss), *n.*, sauce; (insolence) insolence, impertinence, (l. as.) gueule, *f.* Butter-— ; *sauce blanche.* Sweet — ; *sauce douce.*

sauce, *v.a.*, assaisonner ; (the palate—*le pa*

lais) flatter; (to be impudent to—*être insolent envers*) dire des insolences à, dire des sottises à.

sauce-boat (-bôte), *n.*, saucière, *f.*

saucebox, *n.*, insolent, *m.*, insolente, *f.*; impertinent, *m.*, impertinente, *f.*

saucepan, *n.*, casserole, *f.*

saucer, *n.*, soucoupe, *f.*

saucily (sô-), *adv.*, insolemment; impertinemment.

sauciness (sô-), *n.*, insolence; impertinence, *f.*

saucisse, or **saucisson** (sôs'-), *n.*, (milit.) saucisson, *m.*

saucy (sô-), *adj.*, insolent; impertinent.

sauer-kraut (saor-kraoute), *n.*, choucroute, *f.*

saunter (sô'n'-), *v.n.*, flâner; badauder; se promener sans objet. To — away the time; *perdre son temps à flâner.*

saunterer, *n.*, flâneur, *m.*, flâneuse, *f.*; badaud, *m.*, badaude, *f.*

sauntering, *n.*, flânerie; badauderie, *f.*

sauntering, *adj.*, de flâneur, de badaud.

sauria, or **saurians** (sô-), *n.pl.*, sauriens. *m.pl.*

saurian, *adj.*, saurien.

sausage (sô-cédje), *n.*, saucisse, *f.*; saucisson, *m.*

savage (sav'édje), *adj.*, sauvage; féroce; barbare; farouche, furieux.

savage (sav'édje), *n.*, sauvage, *m.*, *f.*

savagely, *adv.*, sauvagement, d'une manière sauvage; en sauvage; (brutally—*avec brutalité*) brutalement.

savageness, *n.*, état sauvage, *m.*; nature sauvage, nature barbare, nature farouche, *f.*

savagery, *n.*, férocité; barbarie; (of plants —*des plantes*) végétation sauvage, *f.*

savagism (sav'a-djiz'm), *n.*, sauvagerie, *f.*

savanna, or **savannah**, *n.*, savane, *f.*

save, *v.a.*, sauver; (to spare—*sauver*) épargner, éviter, sauver; (to put by—*mettre de côté*) réserver; (to economize—*économiser*) économiser, ménager, épargner; (not to lose—*ne pas manquer*) ne pas manquer, ne pas perdre, arriver à temps pour. In order to — the post; *pour ne pas manquer la poste.* God — the Queen! *Dieu sauve la reine! Vive la reine!*

save, *v.n.*, économiser.

save, *prep.*, hormis; excepté; sinon; si ce n'est; sauf.

save-all (-ôl), *n.*, brûle-tout, *m.*

saver (sév'-), *n.*, (liberator—*libérateur*) sauveur, libérateur, *m.*, libératrice, *f.*; (economiser —*ménager*) économe, ménager, *m.*, ménagère, *f.*

savin (sav'-), or **sabine** (sab'ine), *n.*, (bot.) sabine, *f.*

saving (sév'-), *n.*, épargne; économie; (reservation) réservation, *f.*

saving (sév'-), *adj.*, (pers.) économe, ménager; (of things—*des choses*) économique. — grace; *grâce qui sauve.*

saving (sév'-), *prep.*, sauf; excepté.

savingly (sév'-), *adv.*, pour le salut; (frugally —*frugalement*) avec économie; économiquement.

savingness (sév'-), *n.*, épargne; économie. *f.*; (biblically—*biblique*) salut, *m.*

savings-bank (sév'igu'z'-), *n.*, caisse d'épargne, *f.*

saviour (sév'ior), *n.*, Sauveur, *m.*

savonet (sav'-), *n.*, savonette, *f.*

savory (sé-), *n.*, (bot.) sarriette, *f.*

savour (sé-vor), *n.*, saveur, *f.*; goût, *m.*; odeur, *f.*

savour (sé-vor), *v.a.*, goûter avec plaisir; savourer.

savour, *v.n.*, avoir le goût de; sentir.

savourily (sé-vor'-), *adv.*, savoureusement; avec goût.

savouriness, *n.*, goût agréable, *m.*; bonne saveur, *f.*

savourless, *adj.*, qui est sans goût, sans saveur; fade.

savourly, *adj.*, savoureux.

savourly, *adv.*, savoureusement; avec goût.

savoury (sé-vori), *adj.*, savoureux; qui a de la saveur.

saw (sô), *n.*, scie, *f.*

saw (sô), *n.*, (saying—*dicton*) proverbe; adage; dicton, *m.* An old —; *un vieux dicton.*

saw (sô), *v.a.* and *n.*, scier; se scier.

saw-bones (-bô'n'ze), *n.*, (medical student— *étudiant en médecine*) carabin, *m.*

saw-dust (-deuste), *n.*, sciure, *f.*

saw-fish, *n.*, (ich.) scie de mer, *f.*

saw-mill, *n.*, scierie, *f.*

saw-pit, *n.*, fosse de scieurs de long, *f.*

saw-yard (-yârde), *n.*, scierie, *f.*

sawyer (sô-yeur), *n.*, scieur; scieur de long, *m.* —'s block; *chantier, m.*

saxatile (saks'a-), *adj.*, saxatile; de rocher.

saxifrage (sak'ci-frédje), *n.*, (bot.) saxifrage, *f.*

saxifragous (sak'si-fra-), *adj.*, saxifrage.

saxon, *adj.*, saxon, de Saxe.

saxon, *n.*, Saxon, *m.*, Saxonne, *f.*; (language —*langue*) Saxon, *m.*

say, *v.a.* (preterit and *past part.*, Said), dire, parler; marquer; réciter. I —! *dites donc! dis donc!* Let us — no more about it; *n'en parlons plus.* They —; *on dit.* My watch —s one o'clock; *ma montre marque une heure.*

say, *n.*, dire; mot; mot à dire; ce qu'on a à dire, *m.*

saying (sé-igne), *n.*, mot, proverbe, dicton, *m.*; sentence, maxime, expression, *f.* As the — is; *comme on dit.*

scab, *n.*, croûte; gale, rogne, *f.*

scabbard, *n.*, fourreau, *m.*; gaine, *f.* — maker; *gainier, m.*

scabbed (scab'de), *adj.*, couvert de plaies; galeux; (vile—*vil*) vil.

scabbedness (scab'bèd'-), *n.*, état galeux, *m.*

scabby, *adj.*, couvert de plaies; galeux.

scabellum, *n.*, (arch.) scabellon, *m.*

scabious (ské-), *adj.*, scabieux.

scabious (ské-), *n.*, (bot.) scabieuse, *f.*

scabrous (ské-), *adj.*, scabreux; raboteux.

scabrousness, *n.*, nature scabreuse, *f.*

scaffold, *n.*, échafaud; *m.* To ascend the —; *monter sur l'échafaud.*

scaffold, *v.a.*, échafauder; mettre un échafaud à; (fig.) soutenir, supporter.

scaffoldage (-'édje), *n.*, échafaudage, *m.*; estrade, *f.*

scaffolding, *n.*, échafaudage, *m.*; estrade, (fig.) charpente, *f.* — -pole; *perche d'échafaudage, f.*

scagliola (scal'yi-ô-), *n.*, scagliola (kind of stucco—*espèce de stuc*) *m.*

scalable (ské-la-b'l), *adj.*, que l'on peut escalader.

scalade (sca-lâde), *n.*, escalade, *f.*

scald (scôlde), *n.*, brûlure; (med.) teigne, *f.* — head; *teigne.*

scald (scôlde), *v.a.*, échauder; brûler; faire bouillir. To — one's self; *s'échauder; se brûler.* To — one's hand; *s'échauder la main.*

scalding (scôld'-), *n.*, action d'échauder; brûlure, *f.* — -house, — -tub; *échaudoir, m.* — in the urine; (l ex.) *ardeur d'urine, chaude-pisse, f.*

scalding (scôld'-), *adj.*, bouillant. — -hot; *tout bouillant.*

scale, *n.*, échelle, *f.*; (balance) bassin, plateau, *m.*; (gradation,mus.,math., geog.) échelle; (of a fish—*de poisson*) écaille; (milit.) escalade; (bot.) écaille, *f.* —s, pair of —s; *balance, f. sing.* Sliding —; *échelle mobile.* On a large —; *sur une grande échelle.*

scale, *v.a.*, (to climb—*grimper*) escalader ; (to pick off —*enlever*) écailler ; (a cannon—*un canon*) souffler.

scale, *v.n.*, s'écailler.

scaled (skélde), *adj.*, écaillé, écailleux.

scaleless (skél'-), *adj.*, sans écailles.

scale-maker (mék'-), *n.*, balancier, fabricant de balances, *m.*

scalene (sca-lîne), *adj.*, (geom.) scalène ; (cone) oblique.

scalene (sca-lîne), *n.*, (geom.) triangle scalène, *m.*

scaliness (skél'-), *n.*, nature écailleuse, *f.*

scaling (skél'-), *n.*, (climbing—*escalade*) escalade, *f.* ; (peeling off—*écaillage*) écaillage, *m.* — -ladder ; *échelle de siège, f.*

scall (scôl), *n.*, teigné, *f.*

scalled (scôlde), *adj.*, teigneux.

scallion (scal'lieune), *n.*, ciboule, *f.*

scallop (skol'leupe), *n.*, pétoncle ; coquille ; (notching—*dent*) dentelure, *f.* ; (in needlework —*ouvrage à l'aiguille*) feston, *m.*

scallop (skol'leupe), *v.a.*, denteler ; (in needlework—*ouvrage à l'aiguille*) festonner.

scalp, *n.*, cuir chevelu ; crâne ; os frontal ; (fig.) front, *m.*

scalp, *v.a.*, scalper.

scalpel, *n.*, (surg.) scalpel, *m.*

scalper, *n.*, (surg.) rugine, *f.*

scalping, *n.*, action de scalper, *f.*

scalping-knife (-naïfe), *n.*, couteau à scalper, *m.*

scaly (skél'î), *adj.*, écailleux ; à écailles ; (stingy—*ladre*) chiche.

scammony, *n.*, (bot.) scammonée, *f.*

scamp, *n.*, chenapan, mauvais sujet, *m.* ; canaille, *f.* Young — ; *petit polisson, m.*

scamper, *v.n.*, courir. To — off, to — away ; *détaler ; décamper lestement ; s'en aller bien vite.*

scan, *v.a.*, examiner minutieusement ; scruter ; mesurer des yeux ; (verses—*vers*) scander.

scandal, *n.*, scandale, *m.* ; honte ; médisance, *f.* To raise — ; *faire du scandale.* To be a — to ; *être une honte pour.*

scandalize (-aïze), *v.a.*, scandaliser ; (to defame—*diffamer*) médire de, diffamer.

scandalizing (-aïz'-), *adj.*, scandaleux.

scandal-monger (-meu'n'gheur), *n.*, médisant ; colporteur de médisances, *m.*

scandalous, *adj.*, scandaleux ; honteux ; diffamatoire, médisant.

scandalously, *adv.*, scandaleusement; honteusement ; avec médisance.

scandalousness, *n.*, caractère scandaleux, scandale. *m.*

scandent, *adj.*, (bot.) grimpant.

scanning, *n.*, examen minutieux, *m.* (in poetry—*poésie*) action de scander, prosodie, *f.*

scansion (-sheune), *n.*, action de scander, *f.*

scant, *v.a.*, restreindre, rétrécir, resserrer.

scant, *v.n.*, (nav.) (of the wind—*du vent*) refuser ; diminuer, faiblir.

scant. *V.* **scanty**.

scantily, *adv.*, (narrowly—*étroitement*) étroitement, d'une manière rétrécie ; (insufficiently—*insuffisamment*) faiblement, d'une manière insuffisante, peu abondamment, chétivement, mesquinement.

scantiness, *n.*, (narrowness—*étroitesse*) étroitesse, *f.*, état rétréci, *m.*, limites étroites, *f.pl.* ; (insufficiency—*insuffisance*) faiblesse, insuffisance, mesquinerie, *f.*

scantle (sca'n't'l), *v.a.*, couper en morceaux.

scantling (-), *n.*, faible quantité, *f.* ; fragment, *m.* ; (nav.) échantillon, *m.* ; (carp.) volige, *f.*

scanty, *adv.*, (narrow—*étroit*) étroit, rétréci, étriqué ; (poor, insufficient—*pauvre*, *insuffisant*) faible, insuffisant, chétif, mesquin ; (of

the hair—*des cheveux*) clairsemé. — of ; *sobre de ; avare de.*

scape, *n.*, (bot.) hampe ; (arch.) apophyge ; (ant.) mauvaise raison, défaite, mauvaise excuse, *f.*, prétexte, *m.*

scape-goat (-gôte), *n.*, bouc émissaire, *m.*

scape-grace, *n.*, vaurien, mauvais garnement, *m.*

scapement, *n.*, (horl.) échappement, *m.*

scapula, *n.*, omoplate, *f.*

scapular, *adj.*, scapulaire.

scapulary, *n.*, scapulaire, *m.*

scar (scâr), *n.*, cicatrice ; balafre, *f.*

scar (scâr), *v.a.*, faire une cicatrice à ; cicatriser ; balafrer.

scar, *or* **scarus**, *n.*, (ich.) scare, *m.*

scarab, *or* **scarabee** (-bî), *n.*, (ent.) scarabée, *m.*

scaramouch (-maoutshe), *n.*, scaramouche, *m.*

scarce (skérce), *adj.*, rare.

scarcely, *adv.*, à peine ; presque pas ; difficilement. — ever ; *presque jamais.*

scarceness, *or* **scarcity** (skér'-), *n.*, rareté ; disette, *f.*

scare (skére), *v.a.*, effrayer, épouvanter, effaroucher.

scarecrow (skér'crô), *n.*, épouvantail, *m.* ; (orni.) guifette noire, *f.*

scarf (scârfe), *n.* (*scarfs*), écharpe, *f.* ; (carp.) assemblage, *m.*

scarf, *v.a.*, nouer en écharpe ; (carp.) assembler.

scarfed (scârf'te), *adj.*, paré d'une écharpe ; (carp.) assemblé.

scarfing, *n.*, (carp.) assemblage, *m.*

scarfskin, *n.*, épiderme, *m.*

scarification (-fi-ké-), *n.*, scarification, *f.*

scarificator (-fi-ké-teur), *n.*, scarificateur, *m.*

scarifier (-faï'-), *n.*, (thing—*chose*) scarificateur ; (pers.) chirurgien qui scarifie, *m.*

scarify (-fa'ye), *v.a.*, scarifier.

scarlatina (scâr-la-tî-), *n.*, fièvre scarlatine; scarlatine, *f.*

scarlatinous, *adj.*, écarlate ; (med.) de scarlatine.

scarlet (scâr-), *n.*, écarlate, *f.*

scarlet, *adj.*, écarlate ; vermeil ; (med.) scarlatine.

scarlet-fever (-fî-), *n.*, fièvre scarlatine, *f.*

scarlet-runner (-reun'-), *n.*, haricot rouge, *m.*

scarp (scârpe), *n.*, (fort.) escarpe ; (her.) écharpe, *f.*

scarus, *n. V.* **scar**.

scatch, *n.*, (ant.) escache, *f.*

scate, *n. V.* **skate**.

scate, *v.a. V.* **skate**.

scater, *n. V.* **skater**.

scath (scath), *n.*, dommage ; mal, *m.*

scath (scath), *v.a.*, endommager ; nuire à.

scathless (scath'-), *adj.*, sans dommage ; sans perte.

scatter, *v.a.*, disperser ; répandre ; dissiper ; éparpiller.

scatter, *v.n.*, se disperser ; se répandre.

scattered (scat'teurde), *adj.*, dispersé ; répandu ; dissipé ; éparpillé.

scattering, *adj.*, épars ; éparpillé.

scatteringly, *adv.*, éparsement, d'une manière éparse ; de loin en loin, de loin à loin ; çà et là.

scavenger (sca-vè'n'djeur), *n.*, boueur ; balayeur, *m.*

scene (cîne), *n.*, scène, *f.* ; (place—*lieu*) théâtre, *m.* ; (thea.) scène, décoration, *f.* —s ; (thea.) décors, *m.pl.*

scenery (cî'n'ri), *n.*, scène ; vue ; perspective, *f.* ; paysage, *m.* ; (thea.) scène, *f.*, décorations, *f.pl.*, décors, *m.pl.*

scenic (cï'n'-), or **scenical** (cè'n'-). adj., scénique.

scenographic, or **scenographical** (ci-nog'-), adj., scénographique.

scenographically (ci-nog'-), adv., scénographiquement.

scenography (ci-nog'-), n., scénographie, f.

scent (sè'n'te), n., odeur; senteur, f.; parfum, m.; (track—du boar) piste; (of the boar—du sanglier) trace, f.; (of the dog—du chien) nez, m.; (of the stag—du cerf) voie, f. Upon the right —; sur la voie. On the wrong —; en défaut.

scent (sè'n'te), v.a., parfumer; (of animals—des animaux) sentir, flairer.

scent-bottle (-bot't'l), n., flacon à odeur, m.

scent-box, n., cassolette; boîte à parfums, f.

scentless, adj., inodore; sans odeur, sans parfum.

sceptic (skèp'-), n., sceptique, m., f.

sceptic, or **sceptical** (skèp'-), adj., sceptique.

sceptically (skèp'-), adv., sceptiquement; avec scepticisme.

scepticism (skèp'ti-ciz'm), n., scepticisme, m.

sceptre, n., sceptre, m.

sceptre (sèp'teur), v.a., revêtir d'un sceptre.

sceptred (sèp'teurde), adj., portant le sceptre.

schedule (shèd'youle), n., rouleau, m.; liste, f.; inventaire; (com.) bilan, m. To file a —; déposer son bilan.

scheme (skïme), n., plan; projet, m.

scheme (skïme), v.a. and n., projeter; faire des projets.

schemer (skï'm'-), n., faiseur de projets; homme à projets, (b.s.) intrigant, m.

scheming (skï'm'-), adj., à projets; qui fait des projets.

schism (ciz'm), n., schisme, m.

schismatic (ciz'mat'ik), n., schismatique, m., f.

schismatic, or **schismatical** (ciz'-), adj., schismatique.

schismatically (ciz'-), adv., en schismatique.

schismaticalness (ciz'-), n., disposition schismatique, f.

schismatize (ciz'ma-taïze), v.n., faire schisme.

schismless (ciz'-), adj., sans schisme.

scholar (skol'-), n., écolier, m., écolière, f.; disciple, m.; élève, m., f.; (learned person—savant) érudit, m., érudite, f., homme instruit, savant, m.; savante, f.; (at public schools—des collèges) boursier, m. Day- —; externe, m. Good Latin —; bon latiniste, m.

scholar-like (-laïke), adj., d'écolier; d'érudit, de savant; savant.

scholar-like (-laïke), adv., en écolier; en érudit, en savant.

scholarship, n., érudition, f.; savoir, m.; (at public schools—aux collèges) bourse, f.

scholastic, or **scholastical**, adj., scolastique.

scholastic, n., scolastique, m.

scholastically, adv., scolastiquement.

scholasticism (-ciz'm), n., scolastique, f.

scholiast (skô-), n., scoliaste, m.

scholium (skô-), n., (scholia, ou scholiums), scolie, f.; (math.) scolie, m.

school (skoule), n., école; pension; institution, f.; pensionnat, m.; classe, salle, f. Boarding- —; pension; pensionnat. Fencing —; salle d'armes. Day- —; externat, m. —-room; classe, f. Infant- —; salle d'asile. National —; école communale. At —; en pension; à l'école.

school, v.a., enseigner, instruire; (to reprimand—gronder) réprimander, faire la leçon à.

school-boy (-boï), n., écolier, m. Still a —; encore sur les bancs, encore au collège.

school-day, n., jour de classe, m. —-s; temps des études, m. sing.; études, f. pl.

school-fellow (-fèl'lô), n., camarade de pension, de classe, d'école, m., f.; condisciple, m.

school-girl (-gheurle), n., écolière, f.

schooling (skoul'-), n., instruction; (reprimand—réprimande) réprimande, f.

schoolman (skoul'-), n., savant; philosophe, scolastique, m.

school-master (skoul-mâs-), n., maître d'école, maître de pension; chef d'institution, m.

school-mistress (skoul-mis-trèce), n., maîtresse d'école, maîtresse de pension, f.

school-time (skoul-taïme), n., classe, f.; temps de la classe, m.

schooner (skou'n'-), n., (nav.) goëlette, f.

sciagraphic, or **sciagraphical** (saï-ag'-), adj., de la sciagraphie.

sciagraphy (saï-ag'-), n., sciagraphie, sciographie, f.

sciatic (saï-), adj., sciatique.

sciatica (saï-), n., sciatique, f.

science (saï-è'n'ce), n., science, f.

sciential (saï-è'n'shial), adj., qui produit la science.

scientific, or **scientifical** (saï-), adj., (pers.) de science, savant; (of things—des choses) scientifique.

scientifically (saï-), adv., scientifiquement.

scilla n., (bot.) scille, f.

scillitic, adj., (bot.) scillitique.

scimitar, n., cimeterre, m.

scintillant, adj., scintillant.

scintillate, v.n., scintiller.

scintillation (ci'n'til'lé-), n., scintillation, f.

sciolism (saï-o-liz'm), n., connaissance superficielle, f.

sciolist (saï-), n., demi-savant, m.

scion (saï-), n., (bot.) scion, m.

scioptic, adj., scioptique.

scioptic, or **scioptric** (saï-), adj., scioptique.

scioptics (saï-), n., science scioptique, f.

sciroc, or **scirocco**, n., V. sirocco.

scirrhosity (skaïr'-ross'-), n., squirrosité, f.; endurcissement squirreux, m.

scirrhous (skaïr'-), adj., squirreux.

scirrhus, or **scirrhus** (skaïr'-), n., squirre, m.

scissible (-ci'b'l), or **scissile** (-cile), adj., scissile; sécable.

scission (sij'eune), n., scission; séparation, f.

scissors (ciz'zeurze), n., pl., ciseaux, m., pl. Pair of —; paire de ciseaux, f. —-sheath; étui à ciseaux, m.

sclavonian, or **sclavonic**, adj., sclave.

sclerophthalmia (sclèr'oph-thal-), n., (med.) sclerophthalmie, f.

sclerotic, adj., (anat.) sclérotical.

sclerotic, n., sclérotique, f.

scobiform, adj., scobiforme.

scobs, n., pl., râpure, scorie, f. sing.

scoff, n., raillerie; moquerie, f.

scoff, v.a., railler; se moquer de; se rire de. — at me? pourquoi vous moquez-vous de moi?

scoffer, n., railleur, m., railleuse, f.; moqueur, m., moqueuse, f.

scoffing, n., raillerie, f.

scoffing, adj., railleur.

scoffingly, adv., avec raillerie, avec moquerie.

scold (scôlde), v.n., gronder; crier.

scold, v.a., gronder; crier après; criailler après.

scold (scôlde), n., grondeuse, criailleuse; (scolding—gronderie) gronderie, f.

scolding (scôld'-), n., gronderie, criaillerie, f.

scolding (scôld'-), *adj.*, grondeur; criailleur.

scoldingly (scôld'-), *adv.*, en grondant; en criaillant.

scollop, *n. V.* **scallop**.

scolopendra, *n.*, (ent.) scolopendre, *f.*

scolopendrium, *n.*, (bot.) scolopendre vraie, doradille, *f.*

sconce, *n.*, chandelier à bras, candélabre, *m.*; (head—*tête*) caboche, *f.*

scoop (scoupe), *n.*, grande cuiller ; (nav.) écope, escope ; (for cheese—*à fromage*) sonde *f.* ; (for coal—*à charbon*) seau à charbon ; (of brewers—*de brasseurs*) fourquet ; (stroke—*coup* coup, *m.*

scoop (scoupe), *v.a.*, vider ; ôter, évider. T— out*; *enlever, ôter (en creusant, en puisant) creuser ; évider.*

scooper (scoup'-), *n.*, personne qui évide, qui vide, qui creuse, *f.*

scope (scôpe), *n.*, (aim—*fin*) but, *m.*, visée, *f.* ; dessein, *m.*, vue, *f.* ; (space—*étendue*) espace, *m.*, place, *f.* ; (liberty—*liberté*) liberté, carrière, *f.*, essor, *m.* To have — enough ; *avoir assez de place, d'espace.* To have full — ; *avoir libre carrière ; liberté entière.*

scorbutic, or **scorbutical** (-biou-), *adj.*, scorbutique.

scorbutically (-biou-), *adv.*, par le scorbut.

scorch (scortshe), *v.a.* and *n.*, roussir, brûler, rôtir.

scorching (scortsh-), *adj.*, brûlant, ardent, très chaud. — -hot ; *tout brûlant.*

score (scôre), *n.*, (notch—*coche*) entaille, coche ; (mus.) partition ; (line—*ligne*) ligne, *f.*, trait ; (motive—*motif*) motif, *m.*, raison, *f.* ; chapitre ; compte ; (bill—*écot*) compte, écot ; (twenty—*vingt*) vingt, *m.*, vingtaine, *f.* On that — ; *sur ce chapitre, à cet égard.* On the — of ; *sur l'article de ; à titre de ; en raison de.* Upon what —? *à quel titre? en vertu de quoi?* Three— ; *soixante.* Four—; *quatre-vingts.*

score (scôre), *v.a.*, faire une coche à, entailler ; marquer ; (as a debt—*comme créance*) porter sur un compte ; (mus.) orchestrer.

scorer (scôr'-), *n.*, marqueur, *m.*

scoria (scô-), *n.* (*scoriæ*), scorie, *f.*

scoriaceous (scô-ri-a-shieusse), *adj.*, scoriacé.

scorification (scô-ri-fi-ké-), *n.*, scorification, *f.*

scorify (scô-ri-fa'ye), *v.a.*, scorifier.

scoring (scôr'-), *n.*, (mus.) orchestration, *f.*

scorn, *v.a.*, dédaigner ; mépriser.

scorn, *v.n.*, dédaigner, mépriser. To — at ; *montrer du mépris pour ; traiter avec mépris ; railler.* To — to fly ; *dédaigner de fuir.* To — to tell a lie ; *mépriser le mensonge.*

scorn, *n.*, mépris, dédain ; (subject of contempt—*sujet de mépris*) objet de dédain, *m.* To laugh to — ; *couvrir de honte et de mépris.*

scorner, *n.*, personne qui méprise, *f.*; railleur, railleuse, *f.*

scornful (-foule), *adj.*, méprisant; dédaigneux.

scornfully, *adv.*, dédaigneusement ; avec mépris ; avec dédain.

scornfulness, *n.*, caractère méprisant, caractère dédaigneux, *m.*

scorning, *n.*, mépris; dédain, *m.*

scorpion, *n.*, (ent.) scorpion, *m.*

scorpion-grass (-grâce), *n.*, (bot.) myosotis, *m.* ; grémillet, *m.*

scorpion-wort (-weurte), *n.*, (bot.) herbe au scorpion, *f.*

scortatory (-ta-teuri), *adj.*, de libertinage ; de débauche.

scorzonera (-zo-ni-), *n.*, (bot.) scorsonère, *f.*

scot, *n.*, écot, *m.*; contribution, *f.* To pay — and lot; *payer les contributions communales.*

scot, *v.a.*, enrayer.

scot, *n.*, Écossais, *m.*, Écossaise, *f.*

scotch (scotshe), *adj.*, écossais. —man ; *Écossais, m.* —woman ; *Écossaise, f.*

scotch (scotshe), *v.a.*, (tech.) arrêter ; (a wheel—*une roue*) enrayer ; (to cut—*couper*) entamer, taillarder.

scotch, *n.*, (of a wheel—*de roue*) enrayure, *f.* ; (tech.) arrêt, *m.* ; (cut—*coupure*) taillade, *f.*

scotch-hopper, *n.*, (game—*jeu*) marelle, *f.*

scoter, *n.*, (orni.) macreuse, *f.*

scot-free (-fri), *adj.*, exempt de payement; exempt de contribution ; sans frais ; (unhurt—*sans mal*) sain et sauf.

scotia (scô-shi-a), *n.*, (arch.) scotie, *f.*

scotticisme (-ciz'm), *n.*, idiotisme écossais, *m.*

scottish, *adj.*, écossais.

scoundrel (scaou'n'-), *n.*, misérable; scélérat; drôle; gueux, *m.* ; canaille, *f.*

scoundrel, *adj.*, scélérat; misérable; de drôle.

scoundrelism (-'iz'm), *n.*, scélératesse, *f.*

scour (scaeur), *v.a.*, écurer; nettoyer; décrasser; (articles of dress—*vêtements*) dégraisser ; (to purge—*purger*) purger ; (to roam—*parcourir*) parcourir ; (to pass quickly over—*effleurer rapidement*) raser ; (a room—*une chambre*) nettoyer ; (coppers—*batterie de cuisine*) écurer.

scour, *v.n.*, écurer; nettoyer ; (to rove—*errer*) courir ; (to be purged—*être relâché*) avoir le dévoiement.

scourer, *n.*, écureur, *m.*, écureuse, *f* ; nettoyeur, *m.*, nettoyeuse, *f.* ; (of articles of dress—*de vêtements*) dégraisseur, *m.*, dégraisseuse, *f.*; coureur ; (purgation) violent purgatif, *m.*

scourge (skeurdje), *n.*, fouet; fléau, *m.*

scourge (skeurdje), *v.a.*, fouetter ; flageller; châtier ; affliger.

scourger, *n.*, flagellateur, fléau, *m.*; personne qui afflige ; chose qui afflige, *f.*

scourging, *n.*, flagellation, *f.*

scouring (scaeur'-), *n.*, écurage ; nettoyage; (of articles of dress—*de vêtements*) dégraissage, *m.* ; (purging—*dévoiement*) diarrhée, *f.*

scout (scaoute), *n.*, éclaireur, *m.* ; vedette, *f.* à la découverte.

scout (scaoute), *v.n.*, aller en éclaireur ; aller à la découverte.

scout, *v.a.*, rejeter ; repousser avec indignation.

scovel (skeuv'l), *n.*, écouvillon, *m.*

scowl (scaoul), *v.n.*, se refrogner ; froncer le sourcil.

scowl (scaoul), *n.*, refrognement ; froncement de sourcil ; air refrogné ; sombre regard; aspect menaçant, *m.*

scowling, *adj.*, refrogné, renfrogné.

scowlingly, *adv.*, d'un air refrogné ; avec un aspect menaçant.

scrabble (scrab'b'l), *v.n.* and *a.*, gribouiller.

scrag, *n.*, corps décharné ; (of meat—*de viande*) bout saigneux, *m.*

scragged (-ghède), or **scraggy** (-ghi), *adj.*, décharné ; inégal ; rude ; raboteux.

scraggily (-ghi-), *adv.*, avec maigreur ; avec rudesse.

scragginess (-ghi-), *n.*, état décharné, état raboteux, *m.* ; inégalité ; rudesse, *f.*

scramble (scra'm'b'l), *v.n.*, avancer à l'aide des pieds et des mains ; (of children—*des enfants*) jouer à la gribouillette. To — for; *chercher à attraper, à saisir, tâcher d'empoigner, se battre pour avoir.* To — up ; *grimper.*

scramble, *n.*, action de grimper ; dispute pour avoir ; (among children—*parmi les enfants*) gribouillette, *f.*

scrambler, *n.*, personne qui grimpe, *f.*; chercheur, *m.* ; personne qui cherche à empoigner, qui se bat pour avoir, *f.*

scrambling. *V.* **scramble.**

scranch (scra'n'she), *v.a.*, broyer avec les dents; croquer.

scrap, *n.*, morceau; fragment; (of paper —*de papier*) chiffon, bout, *m.* —s; (remains—*restes*) restes, *m.pl.*: bribes, *f.pl.*

scrap-book (-bouke), *n.*, album. *m.*

scrape (scrépe), *v.a.*, gratter; décrotter; racler; ratisser; (chem.) décaper; (engr.) ébarber; (the fiddle—*violon*) racler. To —one's shoes; *décrotter ses souliers.* To — up, together; *ramasser.* To — off; *gratter.*

scrape, *v.n.*, gratter; (to play the fiddle—*jouer du violon*) racler. To bow and —; *faire des salamalecs.*

scrape (scrépe), *n.*, coup de grattoir; grattage; frottement, *m.*; (difficulty—*difficulté*) affaire, *f.*, embarras, guêpier, bourbier, *m.*; (bow—*salutation*) révérence, *f.* To get into a —; *s'attirer une affaire; se mettre dans l'embarras; se mettre dedans.*

scrape-penny, *n.*, grippe-sou, *m.*

scraper (scrép'-), *n.*, grattoir; racloir, *m.*; ratissoire; (tech.) curette, *f.*; (engr.) ébarboir; (for shoes—*pour la chaussure*) décrottoir; (on a fiddle—*de violon*) racleur, *m.*

scraping (scrép'-), *n.*, ratissure, *f.*; grattage; frottement; raclage, *m.*; raclure, *f.*

scratch (scratshe), *n.*, égratignure, *f.*; coup d'ongle, *m.*; (wig—*perruque*) tignasse, *f.* Old —; *le diable, m.* To come to the —; *en venir au fait et à prendre.*

scratch, *v.a.*, gratter; égratigner. She —ed out his eyes; *elle lui arracha les yeux avec ses ongles.* To— out; *raturer; rayer; barrer, effacer.*

scratch, *v.n.*, gratter; égratigner.

scratcher, *n.*, personne qui égratigne, qui gratte; chose qui gratte, *f.*; (instrument) grattoir, *m.*

scrawl (scröl) *n.*, griffonnage; barbouillage, *m.*

scrawl (scröl), *v.a.* and *n.*, griffonner; barbouiller.

scrawler, *n.*, griffonneur, *m.*, griffonneuse, *f.*; barbouilleur, *m.*, barbouilleuse, *f.*

scray, *n.*, (orni.) hirondelle de mer, *f.*

screak (skrike), *v.n.*, crier.

screak (skrike), *n.*, cri; cri aigu, *m.*

scream (scrime), *n.*, cri; cri perçant, *m.* To give a —; *jeter un cri.*

scream (scrime), *v.n.*, crier; pousser un cri. To — out; *pousser un cri, des cris; jeter les hauts cris.*

screaming (scri'm'-), *adj.*, aigu; (pers.) qui crie.

screaming, *n.*, cris, *m.pl.*

screech (scritshe), *n.*, cri; cri aigu, *m.*

screech (scritshe), *v.n.*, crier; jeter un cri; pousser un cri; (to sing badly—*mal chanter*) glapir.

screech-owl (-aoul), *n.*, (orni.) chat-huant, *m.*, chouette, *f.*

screen (scrine), *n.*, paravent; écran, *m.*; (sieve—*claie*) claie, *f.*; (of an altar—*d'autel*) arrière-dos, *m.*; (arch.) boiserie, grille; (fig.) défense, *f.* Folding—; *paravent à feuilles, m.* Fire——.—hand-—; *écran.*

screen (scrine), *v.a.*, mettre à couvert; abriter; mettre à l'abri; (to sift—*passer*) passer à la claie.

screw (scrou), *n.*, vis, *f.*; (pers.) pince-maille, *m.*; (nav.) hélice; vis d'Archimède, *f.*

screw, *v.a.*, visser; (to press—*serrer*) presser, serrer; (to oppress—*opprimer*) opprimer, pressurer; (to distort—*déformer*) déformer. To— down; *visser; fermer à vis;* (to oppress—*pressurer*) opprimer, pressurer. To — in; *faire entrer en vissant.* To — one's self in; *se glisser dedans.* To — up; *fermer à vis; visser.*

screw-arbor, *n.*, axe de vis, *m.*

screw-bolt (-bôlte), *n.*, boulon à vis, *m.*

screw-cap, *n.*, bouchon à vis, *m.*

screwdriver (-draiv'-), *n.*, tournevis, *m.*

screwed (scrou'de), *adj.*, à vis.

screwer (scrou'-), *n.*, personne qui visse; chose qui visse, *f.*

screw-jack (-djack), *n.*, (tech.) cric, *m.*

screw-making (-mck'-), *n.*, fabrication de vis, *f.*

screw-nail (-néle), *n.*, clou à vis, *m.*

screw-nut (-neute), *n.*, écrou de vis, *m.*

screw-plate, *n.*, filière, *f.*

screw-plug (-pleughe), *n.*, cheville vissée, *f.*; tampon à vis, *m.*

screw-ship (scrou-), *n.*, bâtiment, vaisseau à hélice, *m.*

screw-wheel (-hwîle), *n.*, roue-vis, *f.*

screw-worm (-wcurme), *n.*, filet de vis, *m.*

scribble (scrib'b'l), *or* **scribbling**, *n.*, griffonnage; barbouillage, *m.*

scribble (scrib'b'l), *v.a.* and *n.*, griffonner; barbouiller.

scribbler, *n.*, griffonneur, *m.*, griffonneuse, *f.*; barbouilleur, *m.*, barbouilleuse, *f.*; écrivassier, *m.*

scribe (scraïbe), *n.*, scribe; écrivain, *m.*

scribe (scraïbe), *v.a.*, (carp.) étriquer.

scrip, *n.*, (fin.) action provisoire; inscription, *f.*; (of paper—*de papier*) chiffon; (wallet—*besace*) petit sac, *m.*

script, *n.*, (print.) anglaise, *f.*

scriptory (scrip-teuri), *adj.*, écrit; par écrit.

scriptural (script'ieu-ral), *adj.*, de l'Écriture Sainte; scriptural.

scripture (script'ieur), *n.*, Écriture Sainte; Écriture, *f.*

scripturist, *or* **scripturalist** (script'ieur'-), *n.*, personne versée dans l'Écriture Sainte, *f.*

scrivener (scriv'neur), *n.*, notaire; courtier, *m.*

scrofula (scrof'ou-), *n.*, scrofules; écrouelles, *f.pl.*

scrofulous (scrof'iou-), *adj.*, scrofuleux.

scroll (scrôle), *n.*, rouleau; (arch.) enroulement, *m.*

scrotum (scrô-), *n.*, (anat.) scrotum, *m.*

scrub (screube), *n.*, homme de rien; pauvre diable, *m.*; chose de rien, *f.*

scrub (screube), *v.a.*, frotter fort; laver, écurer.

scrub, *v.n.*, travailler fort; s'éreinter. To — hard for a living; *gagner sa vie péniblement.*

scrubbing-brush (-breushe), *n.*, brosse à écurer, *f.*

scrubby (screub'-), *adj.*, mauvais; méchant; misérable.

scruple (scrou-p'l), *n.*, scrupule; (weight—*poids*) scrupule, *m.* Without a —; *sans scrupule.*

scruple (scrou-p'l), *v.n.*, se faire scrupule; se faire un scrupule; balancer; hésiter.

scrupler, *n.*, scrupuleux, *m.*, scrupuleuse, *f.*

scrupulosity (scrou-piou-loss'-), *n.*, scrupule, *m.*

scrupulous (scrou-piou-), *adj.*, scrupuleux. Over —; *trop scrupuleux; méticuleux.*

scrupulously. *adv.*, scrupuleusement.

scrupulousness, *n.*, scrupule, *m.*

scrutable (scrou-ta-b'l), *adj.*, qu'on peut scruter.

scrutator (scrou-té-teur), *n.*, scrutateur, *m.*

scrutinize (scrou-ti-naïze), *v.a.*, scruter; examiner à fond; rechercher.

scrutinizer, *n.*, scrutateur, *m.*

scrutinizing, *adj.*, scrutateur.

scrutiny, *n.*, examen sévère, *m.*; recherche minutieuse, *f.*; scrutin, *m.*

scrutoire (scrou-toire), *n.*, pupitre pour écrire, *m.*

scud (skeude), n., (thin cloud—*léger nuage*) léger nuage chassé par le vent, m. ; (flight—*course*) course rapide, f.

scud (skeude),v.n.,s'enfuir ; se sauver ; (nav.) faire vent arrière, courir devant le vent. To — under bare poles ; *courir à sec, courir à mâts et à cordes.*

scuffle (skeuf-f'l), n., lutte, bagarre, rixe, f.

scuffle (skeuf'f'l), v.n., lutter, se battre, se houspiller.

scuffler, n., lutteur, m.

scuffling, n., lutte, f.

sculk (skeulk),v.n., se cacher ; se tenir caché. To — after ; *suivre à la dérobée.*

sculker, n., personne qui se cache, f. ; (fig.) lâche, cagnard, m.

sculking, adj., qui se cache. — -place ; *cachette, f.* — -fellow ; *lâche, cagnard, m.*

scull (skeule), n., aviron à couple, m. ; godille, f. ; (brainpan.) V. skull.

scull (skeule), v.a., godiller.

scull-cap. V. skull-cap.

sculler, n., godilleur ; (boat—*bateau*) batelet, canot, m.

scullery, n., lavoir de cuisine, m. — -maid ; *fille de cuisine ; souillon, f.*

scullion, n., marmiton ; laveur de vaisselle, m., laveuse de vaisselle, f.

scullionly, adj., de marmiton ; vil ; bas.

sculptile (skeulp'tile), adj., (ant.) ciselé ; sculpté.

sculptor (skeulp'teur), n., sculpteur, m.

sculpture (skeulpt'ieur), n., sculpture ; ciselure, f.

sculpture (skeulpt'ieur), v.a., sculpter ; ciseler.

sculptured (skeulpt'ieurde), adj., sculpté ; ciselé.

scum (skeume), n., écume ; (metal.) scorie, crasse, f. ; (refuse—*rebut*) rebut, m. ; lie, f. The — of the people ; *la lie du peuple, f.*

scum, v.a., écumer.

scumber (skeu'm'beur), n., crotte du renard, f.

scummer (skeu'm'-), n., écumoire, f.

scumming (skeu'm'-), n., action d'écumer, f. ; écumage, m. —s ; *écume, f.sing.*

scupper (skeup'-),*or* scupper-hole (-hôle), n., (nav.) dalot, m.

scupper-hose (-hôze), n., cuir des dalots, m.

scurf (skeurfe), n., croûte ; (med.) desquamation farineuse, f.

scurfiness (skeurf'-), n., état dartreux, m.

scurfy (skeurf'-), adj., dartreux.

scurrility (skeur'-). n., sourrilité, grossièreté ; incivilité ; malhonnêteté ; indécence ; raillerie grossière, f.

scurrilous (skeur'-), adj., grossier ; incivil ; malhonnête ; indécent.

scurrilously, adv., grossièrement ; malhonnêtement ; indécemment.

scurrilousness. V. scurrility.

scurvily (skeur'-), adv., bassement, indignement, vilement ; (stingily—*mesquinement*) avec ladrerie.

scurviness (skeur'-), n., état scorbutique ; (fig.) caractère vil, m. ; (stinginess—*mesquinerie*) ladrerie, f.

scurvy (skeur'-), n., scorbut, m.

scurvy (skeur'-), adj., atteint du scorbut ; scorbutique ; (vile, mean—*bas, misérable*) vil, méprisable ; (stingy—*mesquin*) ladre.

scurvy-grass (-grâce), n.,(bot.) cochléaria, cranson, m.

scut (skeute), n., queue, f.

scutage (skiou-tédje), n., écuage, m.

scutcheon (skeutsh'eune), n. V. escutcheon.

scutiform (skiou-), adj., scutiforme.

scuttle (skeut't'l), n., panier, seau ; (quick

pace—*marche rapide*) pas précipité, m. ; (nav.) écoutille, f. Coal- — ; *seau, panier à charbon.*

scuttle (skeut't'l), v.a., (nav.) couler bas ; couler à fond.

scuttle, v.n., aller à pas précipités.

scythe (saïthe), n., faux, f.

scythian (ci-thi-), adj., des Scythes.

scythian (ci-thi-), n., Scythe, m., f.

sea (sî), n., mer, f. ; (wave—*vague*) coup de mer, m., lame ; (large quantity—*grande quantité*) multitude, f., déluge, m., mer, f. Beyond the —s ; *outre mer ; au delà des mers.* Half- —s over ; *à demi ivre ; dans les vignes du seigneur ; entre deux vins.* To ship a — ; *recevoir un coup de mer.* Rough — ; *grosse mer ; mer houleuse.* On the high- —s ; *sur la haute mer.* On the open — ; *en pleine mer.*

sea-adder, n., (ich.) couleuvre de mer, f.

sea-anemone (-a-nè'm'o-ni), n., (zool.) anémone de mer, f.

sea-ape (-épe), n., singe de mer, m.

sea-bank, n., rivage de la mer ; môle, brise-lames, m.

sea-bat, n., poisson volant, m.

sea-bear (-bère), n., ours blanc, ours polaire, ours marin, m.

sea-beard (-birde), n., barbe de mer, f.

sea-boat (-bôte), n., navire qui se comporte bien à la mer, m.

sea-born, adj., né de la mer ; né sur mer.

sea-bound (-baou'n'de), adj., borné par la mer.

sea-boy (-boï), n., novice ; mousse, m.

sea-breach (-britshe), n., irruption de la mer, f.

sea-breeze (-brîze), n., brise de mer, f.

sea-built (-bilte), adj., bâti pour la mer.

sea-calf (-kâfe), n., veau marin, m.

sea-card (-cârde), n., rose des vents, f.

sea-chart (-tshârte), n., carte marine, f.

sea-chest (-tshèste), n., coffre de bord, m.

sea-coast (-côste), n., côte de la mer, f.

sea-cormorant, n., corbeau de mer ; cormoran, m.

sea-devil (-dèv'v'l), n., (ich.) baudroie, f.

sea-dog, n., (mam.) phoque, veau marin, m.

sea-encircled (-cir-k'l'de),adj.,entouré par la mer.

seafarer (-fér'-), n., homme de mer, m.

seafaring (-fér'-), adj., marin ; de marin. — man ; *marin, m.*

sea-fennel (-fè'n'-), n.,(bot.) fenouil marin, m.

sea-fight (-faïte), n., combat naval, m.

sea-fish, n., poisson de mer, m.

sea-fowl (-faoule), n., oiseau de mer, m.

sea-fox, n., (ich.) renard marin, m.

sea-gauge (-ghédje), n., tirant d'eau, m.

sea-girt (-gheurte), adj., entouré de la mer.

sea-grass (-grâce), n., herbe marine, f.

sea-green (-grîne), n., vert de mer, m. ; (bot.) saxifrage, f.

sea-green, adj., vert de mer, vert d'eau.

sea-gull (-gheule), n., mouette, f.

sea-hedge-hog (-hèdj'-), n., poursille, m.

sea-holm (-hôlme), n., petite île inhabitée, f.

sea-horse, n., (ich.) hippocampe, cheval marin ; (mam.) hippopotame ; morse, m.

sea-king (-kigne), n., roi des pirates, m.

seal (sîl), n., cachet, sceau ; (jur.) scellé ; (mam.) veau marin, phoque, m. The —s of state ; *les sceaux de l'État.* Privy- — ; *petit sceau.* Great- — ; *grand sceau.* To affix the —s ; *apposer les scellés.* Under one's — ; *sous seing privé.* His writings bear the — of genius ; *ses écrits sont marqués du sceau du génie.*

seal, v.a., sceller ; (letters, parcels, &c.—*lettres, paquets, &c.*) cacheter ; (to shut—*clore*) fermer, clore ; (arch.) sceller. To — up ; *mettre le sceau à ; sceller ; (letters. &c.—lettres, &c.) cacheter.*

seal, v.n., mettre un sceau.

sea-legs (-lèg'ze), n.pl., pied marin, m. sing.

sealer, n., scelleur, m. ; personne qui cachette, f.

sealing, n., action de sceller, de cacheter, f. ; (arch.) scellement, m.

sealing-wax, n., cire à cacheter. f.

sea-lion (-laï-o'n), n., lion marin, m.

seal-ring, n.. bague gravée en cachet, f.

seam (sime), n.. couture, f. ; (of a mast—de mât) joint, m. ; (mines) couche; (geol.) veine ; (scar—cicatrice) cicatrice, f. ; (measure—mesure) huit boisseaux, m.

seam, v.a., joindre; faire une couture à; cicatriser, couturer. —ed with the small-pox; couturé de la petite vérole.

sea-maid (-méde), n., nymphe océanique; sirène, f., lamantin, m.

seaman, n., marin, matelot, m.

seamanship, n., navigation, f.; matelotage, art nautique, m.

sea-mark (-mârke), n., (nav.) reconnaissance, f.

sea-mew (-miou), n., mouette, f.

seamless, adj., sans couture.

seam-rent, n., décousure, f.

seamster, n., couturier, m.

seamstress, n., couturière; lingère; ouvrière en linge, f.

seamy, adj., à couture ; plein de coutures.

sea-nettle (-nèt't'l), n., méduse, ortie de mer, f.

sea-nymph, n., nymphe de l'océan, f.

sea-owl (-aoul), n., (ich.) cycloptère, m.

sea-pad, n., (ich.) astérie, étoile de mer, f.

sea-piece (-pîce), n., (paint.) marine, f.

sea-plant, n., plante marine, f.

seaport (-pôrte), n., port de mer, m. — town; port de mer, m. ; ville maritime, f.

sear (sîre), adj., sec ; séché. — leaf ; feuille morte, f.

sear (cîre), v.a., brûler; cautériser; dessécher; (vet.) mettre le feu à, appliquer un cautère à.

search (seurtshe), n., recherche; (jur.) perquisition ; (at the customs) visite, f. To go in — of ; aller à la recherche de. A vain — ; une vaine recherche. To be in — of ; être à la recherche de.

search (seurtshe), v.a., faire une recherche dans ; (to probe—sonder) sonder ; (to examine—examiner) examiner, fouiller; (pers.) visiter, fouiller; (jur.) faire une perquisition dans, visiter; (at the customs—à la douane) visiter, fouiller dans.

search, v.n., chercher; fouiller. To — after ; rechercher. To — for ; chercher. To — into ; faire des recherches sur ; approfondir.

searchable (-'a-b'l), adj., qu'on peut chercher, qu'on peut fouiller.

searcher, n., personne qui cherche, qui recherche, qui fouille, f. ; (inquirer—investigateur) investigateur, m., investigatrice, f. ; (b.s.) chercheur, m., chercheuse, f. ; (trier—examinateur) sondeur, scrutateur ; (at the customs—à la douane) visiteur, m., visiteuse, f.

searching (seurtsh'igne) n., examen, m.; recherche, f.

searching. adj., scrutateur ; pénétrant.

searchingly (seurtsh'ign'-), adv., avec pénétration ; d'un regard scrutateur.

searchingness (seurtsh'ign'nèce), n., subtilité, f. ; examen profond, m.

searchless, adj.. impénétrable; inscrutable.

search-warrant (-wôr'-), n., (jur.) mandat de perquisition, m.

sear-cloth (-cloth), n., emplâtre, m.

searedness (sîr'èd-), n., sécheresse; (fig.) insensibilité, f.

sea-risk, n., périls de la mer, risque de mer, m.

sea-robber, n., pirate; corsaire, m.

sea-room (-roume), n., eau à courir, f. ; large, m.

sea-rover (-rov'-), n., écumeur de mer, m.

sea-serpent (-seur-), n., serpent de mer, m.

sea-service (-seur-vice), n., service de la marine, m.

sea-shell, n., coquillage, m.; coquille de mer, f.

sea-shore, n., rivage de la mer, rivage, m.

sea-sick. adj., qui a le mal de mer.

sea-sickness. n.. mal de mer, m.

sea-side (-saïde), n., bord de la mer, m.

season (si-z'n), n., saison, f. ; (fig.) temps, moment opportun, m. In — ; de saison ; (in time—à temps) à temps, en temps opportun. Out of — ; hors de saison. For a — ; pendant une saison ; pour un temps. In due — ; en temps et saison.

season (si-z'n), v.a., (cook.) assaisonner ; (to give a zest to—relever) relever le goût de ; (to temper—modérer) tempérer, modérer ; (to imbue —imprégner) imprégner ; (to fit—habituer) accoutumer ; (to make—faire) faire; (to prepare for a climate—acclimater) acclimater ; (wood—les bois) préparer, sécher.

season, v.n., s'acclimater ; (of wood—du bois) se préparer, se sécher.

seasonable (-'a-b'l), adj., de saison ; à propos ; convenable.

seasonableness, n., opportunité, f. ; à-propos, m.

seasonably, adv., de saison ; à propos.

seasoner, n., (pers.) assaisonneur ; (thing —chose) assaisonnement, m.

seasoning, n., assaisonnement, m. ; (of wood —du bois) préparation, f., séchage, m.

seat (sîte), n., siège ; (bench, form—banc) banc ; (abode—résidence) séjour, m., demeure, f. ; (mansion—château) château ; (place where any thing is established—lieu d'installation) siège ; (site—lieu) emplacement, m., situation, f. ; (tribunal) tribunal, m. ; (place—endroit) place ; (man.) assiette, f. ; (of trousers—de pantalon) fond, m. ; (of a water-closet—de commodités) lunette, f., siège, m. To have a — in parliament ; siéger au parlement. To vacate one's — in parliament ; donner sa démission. To put a — to a pair of trousers ; mettre un fond à un pantalon. To take a — ; s'asseoir. To keep one's — ; rester assis ; (on horseback—à cheval) rester en selle.

seat (sîte), v.a., asseoir ; faire asseoir ; (to fix—établir) fixer, établir ; (to place—placer) placer ; (to fit up with seats—pourvoir de sièges) garnir de sièges ; (trousers—pantalon) mettre un fond à. To — one's self ; s'asseoir. Pray be —ed ; donnez-vous la peine de vous asseoir ; veuillez vous asseoir.

seating, n., (of trousers—de pantalon) fond, m.

sea-tossed (-tos'te), adj., ballotté par la mer.

sea-urchin (-eur-tshine), n., (ich.) oursin, m.

sea-walled (-wôl'de), adj., entouré de la mer.

seaward (-wôrde), adj., tourné vers la mer.

seaward, adv., vers la mer, du côté de la mer.

sea-water (-wô'-), n., eau salée ; eau de mer, f.

sea-weed (-wîde), n., aigue ; plante marine, f.

sea-worthiness (-weur-thi-) n., navigabilité, f.

sea-worthy (-weur-thi), adj., qui peut tenir la mer ; en bon état de navigation.

sebaceous (si-bé-sheusse), adj., sébacé.

sebate (si-), n., (chem.) sébate, m.

secant (si-), n.. (geom.) sécante, f.

secant (si-), adj., sécant.

secede (si-cîde), *v.n.*, se séparer ; faire scission.

seceder, *n.*, scissionnaire, *m.,f.*

seceding, *adj.*, scissionnaire.

secern (si-ceurne), *v.a.*, sécréter.

secernent (si-ceurn'-), *n.*, médicament qui excite les sécrétions, *f.*

secernment (si-ceurn'-), *n.*, sécrétion, *f.*

secession (si-cèsh'-),*n.*,séparation,scission,*f.*

seclude (si-clioude), *v.a.*, séparer ; écarter, éloigner ; retirer; exclure. To — one's self; *se retirer ; se renfermer.*

secluded, *adj.*, retiré.

seclusion (si-cliou-jeune), *n.*, retraite,*f.*

seclusive (si-cliou-cive), *adj.*,qui tient dans la retraite.

second (sèk'eu'n'de),*adj.*,second; deuxième; (inferior—*inférieur*) inférieur. Every — day; *tous les deux jours.* A — Nero ; *un autre Néron.* — -cousin; *cousin issu de germain.* — -lieutenant; *lieutenant en second; sous-lieutenant.* To be — to none; *n'être inférieur à personne ; ne le céder à personne.*

second, *n.*, (in a duel—*dans un duel*) témoin ; (supporter—*soutien*) second, *m.*; (of time—*de temps*) seconde ; (mus.) seconde, *f.*

second, *v.a.*, seconder, aider; appuyer. To — a motion; *appuyer une motion.*

secondarily, *adv.*, secondairement.

secondariness, *n.*,caractère secondaire,*m.*

secondary, *adj.*, secondaire; accessoire; (subaltern—*inférieur*) subalterne.

secondary, *n.*, député; délégué, *m.*

seconder, *n.*, personne qui seconde, qui appuie,*f.*

second-hand, *adj.*, d'occasion ; de hasard.

secondly, *adv.*, secondement.

second-rate, *adj.*, de second ordre.

second-sight (-saïte), *n.*, seconde vue,*f.*

second-sighted, *adj.*, qui a le don de seconde vue.

secrecy (sî-cri-ci), *n.*, secret, *m.* ; (solitude) solitude ; (closeness—*discrétion*) discrétion,*f.* I rely upon your — ; *je compte sur votre discrétion.*

secret (sè-crète), *adj.*, secret; (secluded—*écarté*) retiré. To keep — ; *tenir secret.*

secret (sè-crète), *n.*, secret, *m.* In — ; *en secret; secrètement, à la dérobée.* To keep a — ; *garder un secret.* To tell a — to; *confier un secret à.*

secretary (sèk'ri-), *n.*, secrétaire, *m.* — 's office ; *secrétariat, m.* : *secrétairerie,f.*

secretaryship (sèk'ri-), *n.*, secrétariat, *m.*

secrete (si-crîte), *v.a.*, cacher ; tenir secret ; celer ; (physiolog.) (to secern—*sécréter*)sécréter.

secretion (si-cri-), *n.*, sécrétion,*f.*

secretitious (sèk-ri-tish'eusse), *adj.*, provenant de la sécrétion.

secretiveness (si-crî-tiv'-),*n.*,sécrétivité,*f.*

secretly (si-crèt'-), *adv.*, secrètement, en secret ; (inwardly—*à l'intérieur*) intérieurement.

secretness (si-crèt'-), *n.*, fidélité à garder un secret,*f.* ; caractère secret, *m.*

secretory (si-crî-teuri), *adj.*, sécrétoire.

sect, *n.*, secte,*f.*

sectarian (sèc-té-), *adj.*, de sectaire.

sectarian, *n.*, sectaire, sectateur, *m.*

sectarianism (-'iz'm),*n.*,esprit de secte,*m.*

sectarist, *or* **sectary**, *n.*, sectaire, *m.*

sectator (sèc-té-), *n.*, sectateur, *m.*

sectile, *adj.*, (min.) sectile.

section, *n.*, section ; coupe, *f.* Cross — ; *coupe transversale.*

sectional, *adj.*, de section.

sector, *n.*, (geom.) secteur ; (instrument) compas de proportion, *m.*

secular (sèk'iou-), *adj.*, séculier, temporel ; (mus.) profane ; (coming once in a hundred years—*d'un siècle*) séculaire.

secular, *n.*, séculier, laïque ; (in churches—*d'église*) chantre, *m.*

secularity, *n.*, sécularité, mondanité, *f.*

secularization (-'i-zé-), *n.*, sécularisation,*f.*

secularize (-'aize), *v.a.*, séculariser; rendre séculier.

secularly, *adv.*, séculièrement.

secularness, *n.*, sécularité, mondanité, *f.*

secund (sî-keu'n'de), *adj.*, unilatéral.

secundines (sèk'eu'n-daï'n'ze), *n.pl.*, (med.) secondines, *f.pl.*

secure (si-kioure), *adj.*, (pers.) dans la sécurité, en sûreté; (of things—*des choses*) sûr, assuré. — against, — from ; *en sûreté contre; à couvert de ; à l'abri de.* — of ; *sûr de.*

secure (si-kioure), *v.a.*, (to make safe—*protéger*) mettre en sûreté, défendre ; (make certain —*assurer*) assurer, s'assurer ; (to insure—*garantir*) assurer, garantir; (to make fast—*consolider*) assurer, affermir; (to seize and confine—*s'emparer*) s'assurer de, s'emparer de; (a place in a coach, &c.—*une place dans une voiture, &c.*) retenir.

securely, *adv.*, en sûreté; sûrement ; avec sécurité ; sans danger.

secureness, *n.*, (ant.) sécurité,*f.*

securer, *n.*, défenseur, *m.* ; (thing—*chose*) défense,*f.*

securiform, *adj.*, (bot.) sécuriforme.

security (si-kiou-), *n.*, sécurité ; sûreté, *f.* ; (pledge—*nantissement*) nantissement, *m.*, garantie ; (jur.) caution, *f.* To give — ; *fournir un cautionnement; donner des garanties;* (jur.) *fournir caution.*

sedan-chair (si-da'n'tshère), *n.*, chaise à porteurs,*f.*

sedate (si-), *adj.*, posé ; calme ; tranquille.

sedately, *adv.*, posément ; tranquillement.

sedateness, *n.*, manières posées, *f.pl.* ; calme, *m.* ; tranquillité,*f.*

sedative (sèd'-), *adj.*, sédatif.

sedative, *n.*, sédatif, *m.*

sedentarily (sèd'-), *adv.*, sédentairement.

sedentariness (sèd'-), *n.*, vie sédentaire,*f.*

sedentary (sèd'-),*adj.*, sédentaire; (inactive —*inerte*) inactif, inerte.

sedge (sèdje), *n.*, laîche,*f.*, carex, *m.*

sedged (sèdj'de), *adj.*, de laîche, de carex.

sedgy, *adj.*, plein de laîche.

sediment (sèd'-), *n.*, sédiment; dépôt, *m.* ; lie,*f.*

sedition (si-dish'-), *n.*, sédition,*f.*

seditionary (si-), *n.*, séditieux, *m.*

seditious (si-di-sheusse), *adj.*, séditieux.

seditiously, *adv.*, séditieusement.

seditiousness,*n.*, esprit séditieux ; caractère séditieux, *m.* ; excitation à la sédition,*f.*

seduce (si-diouce), *v.a.*, séduire.

seducement, *n.*, séduction,*f.*

seducer, *n.*, séducteur, *m.*, séductrice,*f.*

seducible (-'i-b'l), *adj.*, quel'on peut séduire.

seducing, *adj.*, séduisant.

seduction (si-deuk'-), *n.*, séduction,*f.*

seductive (si-deuk'-),*adj.*, séducteur ; séduisant.

sedulity (si-diou-). *V.* **sedulousness.**

sedulous (sèd'iou-), *adj.*, assidu ; diligent; appliqué.

sedulously, *adv.*, assidûment; diligemment : avec application.

sedulousness, *n.*, assiduité, diligence : application,*f.*

see (sî), *n.*, siège, *m.* Holy — ; *saint-siège.*

see (sî), *v.a.* (preterit, Saw ; *past part.*, Seen), voir. He — s nobody ; *il ne voit personne.* To be seen ; *être vu ; se voir.* To — any one off; *voir partir quelqu'un.* To — any one out; *reconduire quelqu'un.* To — any one home, to the door ; *conduire quelqu'un jusque chez lui, jusqu'à la porte.* To — a thing out ; *voir finir une chose.* I saw him through his difficulties ; *je l'ai tiré de son embarras.*. Fit to be seen ; *présentable.*

see (sî), *v.n.*, voir. To — about ; *penser à.* To — to; *avoir soin de; veiller à; prendre garde à.* To — that; *avoir soin que; veiller à ce que.* I shall — that all be ready ; *j'aurai soin que tout soit prêt.* — to it; *veillez-y; prenez-y garde.* Let us —; *voyons.* You —; *voyez-vous.* —! *voyez!*

seed (sîde), *n.*, semence ; (of vegetables—*des végétaux*) graine ; (fig.) semence, race, *f.* To run to —; *monter en graine.*

seed, *v.n.*, grener; produire de la graine; monter en graine.

seed, *v.a.*, semer.

seed-bud (-beude), *n.*, germe, *m.*

seed-cake, *n.*, gâteau anisé, *m.*

seed-coat (-côte), *n.*, épisperme, arille, *m.*

seed-leaf (-lîfe), *n.*, feuille séminale, *f.*

seedling, *n.*, plante semée, *f.*

seed-lip, *or* **seed-lop**, *n.*, semoir, *m.*

seed-pearl (-peurle), *n.*, semence de perle, *f.*

seed-plot, *n.*, semis, *m.*

seedsman (sîdz-), *n.*, grainier, grènetier; (sower—*semeur*) semeur, *m.*

seed-time (-taïme), *n.*, semailles, *f.pl.*

seed-vessel, *n.*, péricarpe, *m.*; enveloppe de la graine, *f.*

seedy (sîd'-), *adj.*, grenu; (of brandy—*eau-de-vie*) aromatise ; (worn out—*usé*) râpé; (pers.) abattu, éreinté, fatigué.

seeing (sî-), *n.*, vue; vision, *f.*

seeing, *conj.*, vu que ; puisque. — that; *vu que; puisque.*

seek (sîke), *v.a.* (*preterit* and *past part.*, Sought), chercher; demander; (one's life, property—*la vie, les biens de*) en vouloir à. To — out; *chercher; rechercher; quêter.*

seek, *v.n.*, chercher. To — for; after; *chercher; rechercher.* To — to; *faire tout son possible pour; chercher à;* (to apply to—*s'adresser*) *s'adresser à.*

seeker, *n.*, chercheur, *m.*, chercheuse, *f.*

seeking, *n.*, recherche, *f.*

seem (sî'm), *v.n.*, sembler; paraître. To — to; *faire semblant de; feindre de.* It —s to me; *ce me semble; il me semble.* Without —ing to; *sans faire semblant de.*

seemer, *n.*, personne qui fait semblant, *f.*; hypocrite, *m.,f.*

seeming, *n.*, semblant; extérieur, *m.*; apparence, *f.*; dehors, *m.*; (opinion) opinion, *f.*

seeming, *adj.*, (pers.) qui paraît, qui semble, qui fait semblant; (of things—*des choses*) spécieux.

seemingly, *adv.*, en apparence; apparemment.

seemingness, *n.*, apparence spécieuse, *f.*

seemliness, *n.*, bienséance; bonne grâce; convenance, *f.*

seemly, *adj.*, bienséant; convenable. That is not — in a girl; *cela n'est pas bienséant pour une demoiselle.*

seemly, *adv.*, avec bienséance; convenablement.

seer (sî-eur), *n.*, personne qui voit, *f.*; spectateur, *m.*, spectatrice, *f.*; (prophet) prophète, voyant, *m.* Sight- —; *amateur de spectacles, m.*

seesaw (sî-çô), *n.*, bascule, balançoire, *f.*; (mec.) va-et-vient, *m.*

seesaw, *v.n.*, faire la bascule.

seethe (sîthe), *v.a.* and *n.*, faire bouillir; cuire; bouillir.

seether (sîth'-), *n.*, marmite, *f.*

segar, *or* **cigar** (ci-gâr), *n.*, cigare, *m.*

segar-case, *n.*, porte-cigare, *m.*

segment (sèg'-), *n.*, segment, *m.*; portion, *f.*; morceau, *m.*

segregate (sèg'ri-), *v.a.*, séparer.

segregation (sèg-ri-ghé-), *n.*, séparation, *f.*; isolement, *m.*

seigneurial (sî-nîou-ri-), *adj.*, seigneurial.

seignior (sîn'ieur), *n.*, seigneur, *m.* The Grand- —; *le Grand Seigneur, le sultan.*

seigniorage (-édje), *n.*, seigneuriage, *m.*

seignory (sîn'ieur'i), *n.*, seigneurie; suzeraineté, *f.*

seine (sîne), *n.*, (net—*filet*) seine, *f.*

seizable (sîz'a-b'l), *adj.*, saisissable.

seize (sîze), *v.a.*, saisir; se saisir de; s'emparer de; (nav.) aiguilleter; (jur.) saisir. To — again ; *ressaisir.* To — upon; *se saisir de; s'emparer de.*

seizer, *n.*, personne qui saisit; *f.*; (jur.) saisissant, *m.*

seizin (sîz'-), *n.*, (jur.) saisine, *f.*

seizing, *n.*, action de saisir, *f.*; (nav.) aiguilletage, *m.*

seizure (sîj'eur), *n.*, saisie; (gripe, thing seized—*serrement; chose saisie*) prise; (taking possession—*prendre possession*) prise de possession ; (jur.) saisie, saisie-arrêt, *f.*

seldom (sèl-deume), *adv.*, rarement; peu souvent.

seldomness, *n.*, rareté, *f.*

select (si-lèkte), *adj.*, choisi; d'élite; distingué.

select, *v.a.*, choisir.

selected, *adj.*, choisi.

selectedly, *adv.*, avec choix.

selection (si-lèk'-), *n.*, choix; recueil, *m.*

selectness, *n.*, bon choix, choix distingué, *m.*

selector, *n.*, personne qui choisit, qui fait un recueil, *f.*

selenite (sèl'i-naïte), *n.*, (chem.) sélénite, *f.*; (min.) gypse, *m.*

selenitic, *or* **selenitical** (sèl'i-nit'-), *adj.*, séléniteux.

selenium (si-lî-), *n.*, (chem.) sélénium, *m.*

selenographic, *or* **selenographical** (sèl'i-nog-), *adj.*, sélénographique.

selenography (sèl'i-nog-), *n.*, sélénographie, *f.*

self (sèlfe), *pron.* (*selves*), soi; soi-même; même. My—, thy—, him—, her—, it—; *moi-même, toi-même, lui-même, elle-même, se.* Our-selves, yourselves, themselves; *nous-mêmes, vous-mêmes, eux-mêmes, elles-mêmes, se.* One's —; *se.* *soi-même.* I shave my—; *je me rase moi-même.* He knows how to enrich him—; *il sait s'enrichir.* By one's —; *seul; tout seul; de soi-même.* I dine by my—; *je dîne seul.* Her gracious —; *sa gracieuse personne.*

self-abased (-a-bés'te), *adj.*, humilié par le sentiment de sa honte.

self-abasing (-a-bés'-), *n.*, humiliation, *f.*

self-abasing (-a-béss'-), *adj.*, qui fait honte à soi-même.

self-abuse (-a-biouss), *n.*, abus de soi-même, *m.*

self-accusing (-ak'kiouz'-), *adj.*, qui s'accuse soi-même.

self-acting, *adj.*, automoteur ; qui agit de soi-même.

self-admiration (-mi-ré-), *n.*, admiration de soi-même, *f.*

self-admiring (-ad-maeur'-), *adj.*, qui s'admire soi-même.

self-adoring, *adj.*, qui s'adore soi-même.

self-affairs (-af'fair'ze), *n.pl.*, affaires personnelles, *f.pl.*

self-affrighted (-af'fraït'-), *adj.*, effrayé de soi-même.

self-aggrandizement (-daïz'-), *n.*, agrandissement de soi-même, *m.*

self-applause (-plôze), *n.*, applaudissement de soi-même, *m.*

self-approving (-prouv'-), *adj.*, qui s'approuve soi-même.

self-assumed (-as'sioum'de), *adj.*, de sa propre autorité.

self-banished (-ban-ish'te), *adj.*, qui s'exile volontairement.

self-begotten (-bi-got't'n), *adj.*, créé par soi-même ; produit par soi-même.

self-born, *adj.*, né de soi-même.

self-centred (-cè'n'teur'de), *adj.*, fixé sur son propre centre.

self-charity (-tshar'-), *n.*, amour de soi, *m.*

self-command, *n.*, empire sur soi-même, *m.* ; retenue, *f.*

self-conceit (-co'n'site), *n.*, suffisance ; vanité, *f.* ; amour-propre, *m.*

self-conceited, *adj.*, suffisant ; vain, rempli l'amour-propre.

self-conceitedness. *V.* **self-conceit.**

self-condemnation (-dè'm'né-), *n.*, condamnation de soi-même, *f.*

self-confidence, *n.*, confiance en soi-même, *f.*

self-confident, *adj.*, confiant en soi-même.

self-conscious (-co'n'sheusse), *adj.*, qui a la connaissance de soi-même.

self-consciousness (-sheus'-), *n.*, connaissance de soi-même, *f.*

self-consuming (-sioum'-), *adj.*, qui se consume soi-même ; qui s'épuise ; qui se détruit.

self-contradiction, *n.*, contradiction avec soi-même, *f.*

self-contradictory, *adj.*, qui se contredit.

self-control, *n.*, empire sur soi-même, *m.*

self-convicted, *adj.*, convaincu par soi-même.

self-conviction (-vik'-), *n.*, conviction par soi-même, *f.*

self-created (-cri-ét'-), *adj.*, créé par soi-même.

self-deceit (-dè-cite), *n.*, illusion, *f.*

self-deceived (-dè-cîv'de), *adj.*, qui se trompe soi-même.

self-deception (-dè-cèp'-), *n.*, illusion, *f.*

self-defence (-dè-), *n.*, défense personnelle ; propre défense, *f.* In — ; *dans sa propre défense.*

self-delusion (-dè-llou-jeune), *n.*, illusion, *f.*

self-denial (-dè-naï-). *n.*, abnégation de soi-même, *f.* ; renoncement à soi-même, *m.*

self-denying (-dè-na-yigne), *adj.*, qui fait abnégation de soi-même ; qui s'oublie soi-même.

self-dependent (-dè-), *adj.*, qui dépend de soi-même ; indépendant.

self-destroyer (-dè-stro-yeur), *n.*, suicide, *m.*

self-destruction (-dè-streuk'-), *n.*, suicide, *m.*

self-destructive (-dè-streuk'-), *adj.*, qui tend à se détruire.

self-determination (-dè-teur-mi-né-), *n.*, détermination par soi-même, *f.*

self-determining (-dè-teur-mi'n'-), *adj.*, qui se détermine de soi-même.

self-devoted (-dè-vot'-), *adj.*, dévoué volontairement ; dévoué par soi-même.

self-devouring (-dè-vaeur'-), *adj.*, qui se dévore soi-même.

self-educated (-èd'iou-két'-). *adj.*, instruit par soi-même ; qui a fait sa propre éducation.

self-education (-èd'iou-ké-), *n.*, instruction due à soi-même, *f.*

self-elected (-è-lèkt'-), *adj.*, élu par soi-même.

self-elective (-è-lèkt'-),' *adj.*, qui a le droit de s'élire soi-même, d'élire ses membres.

self-endeared (-è'n-dir'dè), *adj.*, épris de soi-même.

self-enjoyment (-è'n'djo-ye-), *n.*, satisfaction intérieure, *f.*

self-esteem (-ès-tîme), *n.*, estime de soi-même, *f.*

self-evidence (-èv'-), *n.*, évidence en soi, *f.*

self-evident, *adj.*, évident en soi ; évident.

self-evidently, *adv.*, d'une manière évidente en soi.

self-exaltation (-ègz-al-té-),*n.*, élévation de soi-même, *f.*

self-exalting (-ègz-ôlt'-), *adj.*, qui s'élève en soi-même.

self-examination (-ègz'a'm'-i-né-), *n.*, examen de soi-même, *m.*

self-excusing (-èks'kiouz'-), *adj.*, qui s'excuse soi-même.

self-existence (-ègz'ist'-), *n.*, existence par soi-même, *f.*

self-existent, *adj.*, qui existe par soi-même.

self-flattering, *adj.*, qui se flatte soi-même.

self-flattery, *n.*, flatterie de soi-même, *f.*

self-glorious, *adj.*, vain ; glorieux.

self-governed (-gheuv'èrn'de), *adj.*, gouverné par soi-même, indépendant.

self-government (-gheuv'èrn'-), *n.*, empire sur soi-même, *m.* ; indépendance, *f.*

self-heal (-hîl), *n.*, (bot.) brunelle, prunelle, brunelle commune, *f.*

self-healing, *adj.*, qui se guérit soi-même.

self-imposture (-post'ieur), *n.*, illusion, *f.*

self-interest (-tèr'èste), *n.*, intérêt personnel, *m.*

self-interested, *adj.*, intéressé.

self-invited (-vait'-), *adj.*, invité par soi-même.

selfish (sèlf'-), *adj.*, égoïste.

selfishly, *adv.*, égoïstement, avec égoïsme, d'une manière égoïste.

selfishness, *n.*, égoïsme, *m.*

self-judging (-djeudj'-), *adj.*, qui se juge soi-même.

self-knowing (-nô-igne), *adj.*, instruit par soi-même.

self-knowledge (-no-lèdje), *n.*, connaissance de soi-même, *f.*

self-love (-leuve), *n.*, amour de soi ; égoïsme ; amour-propre, *m.*

self-loving. *adj.*, égoïste ; personnel.

self-motion (-mô-), *n.*, mouvement propre ; mouvement spontané, *m.*

self-moved (-mouv'de), *adj.*, mû spontanément.

self-moving (-mouv'-), *adj.*, qui se meut de soi-même ; automoteur.

self-murder (-meur-), *n.*, suicide, *m.*

self-murderer, *n.*, suicide, *m.*

self-neglecting (-nèg-lèkt'-), *n.*, oubli de soi-même, *m.*

self-opinioned (-o-pi'n'ieu'n'de), *adj.*, prévenu en faveur de son opinion.

self-pleasing (-pliz'-), *adj.*, qui se plaît à soi-même.

self-possession (-poz'zèsh'-), *n.*, empire sur soi-même ; calme ; sang-froid, *m.*

self-praise (-préze),*n.*, éloge de soi-même,*m.*

self-preservation (-pré-zeur-vé-), *n.*, conservation de soi-même, *f.*

self-preserving (-pri-zeurv'-), *adj.*, qui se conserve soi-même ; (of things—*des choses*) qui se conserve de soi-même.

self-regulating (-règh'iou-lét'-), *adj.*, automoteur, agissant de soi-même.

self-repelling (-ri-pèl'-), *adj.*, d'une répulsion spontanée.

self-reproach (-ri-prôtshe), *n.*, reproche de soi-même, *m.*

self-reproached (-ri-prôtsh'te), *adj.*, qui se fait des reproches à soi-même.

self-reproved (-ri-prouv'de), *adj.*, réprouvé par soi-même.

self-reproving (-ri-prouv'-), *adj.*, qui se réprouve soi-même.

self-reproving, *n.*, réprobation de soi-même, *f.*

self-restrained (-ri-stré'n'de), *adj.*, contenu par soi-même.

31▲

self-restraining (-ri-strế'n'-), adj., qui se contient soi-même.

self-restraint (-ri-strế'n'te), n., contrainte qu'on s'impose à soi-même, f.

self-same, adj., exactement le même; même.

self-seeker, n., égoïste, m., f.; personne qui ne pense qu'à soi, f.

self-seeking (-sĭk'-), adj., personnel; intéressé; égoïste.

self-slaughter (-slŏ-), n., suicide, m.

self-styled (-stail'de), adj., soi-disant.

self-subdued (-seub'dioude), adj., dompté par soi-même.

self-sufficiency (-seuf'fish'ĕ'n'ci), n., suffisance, f.

self-sufficient (-seuf'fish'ĕ'n'te), adj., suffisant.

self-taught (-tŏte), adj., instruit par soi-même.

self-tormenting, adj., qui se tourmente.

self-upbraiding (-eup'brĕd'-), adj., qui se fait des reproches à soi-même.

self-violence (-vaï-), n., violence contre soi-même, f.

3elf-will, n., obstination, f.

self-willed (-wil'de), adj., obstiné, volontaire.

self-worship (-weur-), n., adoration de soi-même, f.

self-wrong (-ron'gn), n., tort à soi-même, m.

sell, v.a. (preterit and past part., Sold), vendre. To be sold; à vendre. To — wine for five shillings a bottle; vendre du vin cinq schellings la bouteille. To — out; vendre; vendre tout. To — off; liquider.

sell, v.n., se vendre. To — off; se liquider. To — out; vendre; (of the army—dans l'armée anglaise) vendre son grade.

sellander, or **sellender**, n., (vet.) solandre, f.

seller, n., vendeur, m., vendeuse, f.; marchand, m., marchande, f.

selling-out (-aoute), n., vente totale; (of the army—dans l'armée anglaise) vente de son grade, f.

selvage (sĕl-védje), or **selvedge** (-vèdje), n., lisière, f.

selvaged (-védj'de), adj., à lisière.

semaphore (sè'm'a-fŏre), n., sémaphore, m.

semaphorically, adv., par le télégraphe marin.

semblance, n., ressemblance; image, f.; (show—apparences) semblant, m., apparence, f.

semen (sĭ-mè'n), n., semence, f.

semi (sè'm'ĭ), adj., semi, demi, à demi.

semi-annular (-a'n'niou-), adj., semi-annulaire.

semi-barbarian (-bar-bé-), adj., semi-barbare.

semi-breve (-brĭve), n., (mus.) ronde, f.

semi-circle (-cir-k'l), n., demi-cercle, m.

semi-colon (-cŏ-), n., point et virgule, m.

semi-cylindrical, adj., semi-cylindrique.

semi-diaphanous (-daï-), adj., semi-transparent; à moitié diaphane.

semi-floret, n., demi-fleuron, m.

semi-flosculous (-flos'kiou-), adj., semi-flosculeux.

semi-lunar (-liou-), adj., en demi-lune; semi-lunaire.

semi-metal, n., demi-métal, m.

semi-metallic, adj., demi-métallique.

seminal (sè'm'-), adj., séminal.

seminality, n., nature séminale, f.

seminarist (sè'm'-), n., séminariste, m.

seminary, n., pépinière, f.; (ecc.) séminaire, m.; (school—école) institution, f., pensionnat, m., école, f.; (seminary priest—prêtre) séminariste, prêtre instruit dans un séminaire, m.

seminary (sè'm'-), adj., séminal.

semination (sè'm'i'né-), n., sémination, propagation, f.

seminiferous (-nif'èr'-), adj., séminifère.

seminific, adj., qui forme de la semence.

seminification (-nif'i-ké-), n., propagation de semence, de graine, f.

semi-opaque, adj., demi-opaque.

semi-orbicular (-bik'iou-), adj., demi orbiculaire.

semi-ovate (-ŏ-), adj., semi-ové.

semi-oxygenated (-djè'n'ét'-), adj., à demi oxygéné.

semiped (-pède), n., demi-pied; m.

semipedal (-pĭ-), adj., long d'un demi-pied.

semi-pellucid (-pèl-liou-), adj., demi-transparent.

semi-proof (-proufe), n., semi-preuve, f.

semi-quadrate (-kwŏd'-), adj., semi-quartile.

semi-quaver (-kwé-), n., (mus.) double croche, f.

semi-quaver, v.a., chanter par doubles croches.

semi-quintile, adj., semi-quintil.

semi-sextile, adj., semi-sextil.

semi-spherical (-sfèr'-), adj., demi-sphérique.

semi-spheroidal (-sfĭ-roïd'-), adj., demi-sphéroïdal.

semi-tertian (-teur-sha'n), n., (med.) fièvre double-tierce.

semi-tone (-tŏne), n., (mus.) demi-ton, m.

semi-tonic (-tŏ'n'-), adj., de demi-ton.

semi-transparency, n., demi-transparence, f.

semi-transparent, adj., demi-transparent.

semi-vitreous (-vit'ri-), adj., demi-vitreux.

semi-vitrified (-vit'ri-faide), adj., demi-vitrifié.

semi-vocal adj., de demi-voyelle.

semi-vowel (-vaou-èl), n., demi-voyelle, f.

sempervirent (sè'm'pèr-vaï-), adj., toujours vert.

sempiternal (-teur-), adj., éternel, sempiternel.

sempiternity (-teur-), n., éternité, f.

sempster (sè'm'steur), n., couturier; linger, m.

sempstress (sè'm'strèss), n., couturière; lingère, f.

senary (sè'n'-), adj., composé de six.

senate (sè'n'-), n., sénat, m.

senate-house (-haouce), n., sénat, m.

senator (sè'n'-), n., sénateur; (biblically—biblique) ancien, m.

senatorial, or **senatorian**, adj., sénatorial; sénatorien; du sénat.

senatorially, adv., comme sénateur; en sénateur; par le sénat.

senatorship, n., sénatorerie, f.

senatus consultum (sĭ-né-teus'co'n'seul-), n., sénatus-consulte, m.

send (sè'n'de), v.a. (preterit and past part., Sent), envoyer; faire partir; expédier; (to bestow—accorder) accorder, donner; (to inflict —infliger) infliger; (to diffuse—répandre) répandre. To — away; renvoyer; congédier. To — back; renvoyer. To — down; faire descendre. To — forth; produire; lancer; (a groan—un gémissement) pousser; (of trees, &c.—des arbres, &c.) pousser; (to emit—émettre) émettre, répandre, exhaler. To — in; faire entrer; (to deliver—remettre) livrer. To — off; faire partir, renvoyer, expédier. To — out; envoyer dehors; faire sortir; (to send on an errand—donner une commission) envoyer en course. To — to health to; envoyer la santé à. To — pestilence among; envoyer la peste chez. To — word to; envoyer dire à; faire dire à.

send, v.n., envoyer; (nav.) tanguer. To —

for any one, anything; *envoyer chercher quel-qu'un, quelque chose ; faire venir quelqu'un, quelque chose.* They have sent for you ; *on vous a envoyé chercher.*

sender, *n.,* personne qui envoie, *f.* ; (com.) expéditeur, *m.*

sending, *n.,* envoi, *m.* ; expédition, *f.*

senega, *or* **seneka** (sè'n'ï-), *n.,* (bot.) poly-gale, polygala, *m.*

senescence (si-nès'-), *n.,* déclin, *m.*

seneschal (sè'n'ès-shal), *n.,* sénéchal, *m.*

sengreen (sè'n'gri'n), *n.,* (bot.) joubarbe, *f.*

senile (si-naïle), *adj.,* de vieillard ; sénile.

senility (si-nil'-). *n.,* vieillesse, sénilité, *f.*

senior (si'n'ieur), *adj.,* aîné ; (in office—*en office*) plus ancien, *m.* Mr. A. — ; *M. A.* aîné ; *M. A. père.*

senior, *n.,* aîné, *m.,* aînée, *f.* ; (in office—*en office*) ancien, *m.,* ancienne, *f.* ; (in a firm—*d'une maison de commerce*) associé principal ; (old man—*vieux*) vieillard, *m.*

seniority, *n.,* supériorité d'âge ; ancienneté, *f.*

senna (sè'n'-), *n.,* séné, *m.*

se'nnight (sè'n'naïte), *n.,* huit jours, *n.pl.* ; huitaine, *f.* To this day — ; *à huitaine.* Next Tuesday — ; *de mardi en huit.*

sennit (sè'n'nite). *n.,* (nav.) garcette, *f.*

senocular (sè'n'ok'iou-), *adj.,* qui a six yeux.

sensation (sè'n'sé-), *n.,* sensation, *f.* ; sentiment, *m.* To make a — ; *faire sensation.*

sense (sè'n'se), *n.,* (perception) sens ; (understanding—*entendement*) sens, esprit, *m.,* raison ; (sensation) sensation ; (sensibility—*sensibilité*) sensibilité, *f.* ; (opinion) sens, sentiment ; avis, *m.,* opinion, *f.* ; (consciousness—*sens*) sentiment ; (signification) sens, *m.,* signification ; (reason—*raison*) raison, *f.* Common- —; *sens commun.* Good —; *bon sens.* A man of — ; *un homme de bon sens.* In a good, a bad — ; *en bonne, en mauvaise part.* To speak — ; *parler raison.* To be in one's right —s ; *être dans son bon sens.* To be out of one's —s ; *être hors de son bon sens.* To drive any one out of his —s ; *faire perdre la tête à quelqu'un.* To come to one's —s ; *reprendre ses sens ; reprendre connaissance ;* (fig.) *revenir à la raison.* To take the — of an assembly ; *prendre l'avis d'une assemblée.* Against all —; *contre le sens commun.*

senseless. *adj.,* sans connaissance ; (insensible) insensé, privé de sentiment ; (unreasonable —*déraisonnable*) insensé, déraisonnable.

senselessly, *adv.,* d'une manière insensée ; déraisonnablement.

senselessness, *n.,* déraison, *f.* ; manque de bon sens, *m.* ; sottise ; absurdité, *f.*

sensibility, *n.,* sensibilité, *f.* ; sentiment, *m.* False — ; *sensiblerie, f.*

sensible (sè'n'si-b'l), *adj.,* (perceptible by the senses, having moral perception, intelligence—*perceptible aux sens ; doué de perception intellectuelle et morale*) sensible ; (sensitive—*sensitif*) sensible ; (intelligent) sensé, raisonnable ; (conscious—*conscient*) avec toute sa connaissance, conscient. To be — of ; *être sensible à ; avoir le sentiment de.* A — man ; *un homme sensé.* — to cold ; *sensible au froid.* — of injury ; *sensible aux injures.* He was not — ; *il était sans connaissance.* — balance ; *balance sensible.* — thermometer ; *thermomètre sensible.* That is a — deed ; *voilà une action sensée.*

sensibleness, *n.,* (sensibility—*sensibilité*) sensibilité ; (possibility of being perceived by the senses—*perception par les sens*) perceptibilité, perception ; (intelligence) intelligence, *f.,* sens, bon sens, esprit, *m.,* raison, *f.*

sensibly. *adv.,* sensiblement ; (intelligently —*intelligemment*) sensément, sagement, raisonnablement.

sensitive (sè'n'si-tive), *adj.,* sensible ; sensitif.

sensitively, *adv.,* d'une manière sensible.

sensitiveness, *n.,* sensibilité, *f.*

sensitive-plant, *n.,* (bot.) sensitive, *f.*

sensorial (sè'n'sô-), *adj.,* du sentiment ; des sens.

sensorium, *or* **sensory** (sè'n'sô-), *n.,* sensorium ; organe des sens, *m.*

sensual (sè'n'shiou-), *adj.,* sensuel ; des sens.

sensualism (sè'n'shiou-al'iz'm), *n.,* sensualisme, *m.*

sensualist, *n.,* sensualiste, *m.,f.*

sensuality, *n.,* sensualité, *f.*

sensualize (-'aïze), *v.a.,* rendre sensuel.

sensually, *adv.,* sensuellement ; d'une manière voluptueuse.

sensuous (sè'n'shiou-eusse), *adj.,* qui affecte les sens.

sentence (sè'n'tè'n'ce), *n.,* (gram.) phrase, période ; (maxim—*maxime*) maxime, sentence ; (opinion) opinion, *f.,* avis, *m.* ; (judgment—*jugement*) sentence, *f.,* jugement, arrêt, *m.* To pass — of death on ; *condamner à mort ; prononcer une sentence de mort contre.*

sentence, *v.a.,* prononcer une sentence, un jugement, un arrêt contre ; condamner.

sentential (sè'n'tè'n'shal), *adj.,* de phrases, de périodes.

sententious (sè'n'tè'n'sheusse), *adj.,* sententieux ; laconique.

sententiously, *adv.,* sentencieusement ; laconiquement.

sententiousness, *n.,* caractère sententieux, *m.*

sentient (sè'n'shi-è'n'te), *adj.,* sensitif.

sentient, *n.,* être sensitif, *m.*

sentiment, *n.,* sentiment ; avis, *m.* ; pensée, *f.* ; (toast) toast ; (sensibility—*sensibilité*) sentiment, *m.*

sentimental, *adj.,* sensible ; plein de sentiment ; sentimental.

sentimentalism (-'iz'm), *n.,* sentimentalisme, *m.*

sentimentalist, *n.,* personne sentimentale, *f.*

sentimentality, *n.,* sensiblerie ; vive sensibilité, *f.*

sentinel, *or* **sentry,** *n.,* sentinelle, *f.* ; factionnaire, *m.* To stand — ; *faire sentinelle, être en faction.*

sentry-box, *n.,* guérite ; (on a rampart—*sur un rempart*) vedette, *f.*

separability, *or* **separableness** (sèp'a-ra-), *n.,* caractère séparable, *m.* ; divisibilité, *f.*

separable (-ra-b'l), *adj.,* séparable, divisible.

separate (sèp'a-). *adj.,* séparé ; disjoint ; (distinct) distinct ; (disunited—*séparé*) désuni.

separate, *v.a.,* séparer ; disjoindre ; désunir.

separate, *v.n.,* se séparer ; se disjoindre.

separated (sèp'a-rét'-), *adj.,* séparé ; divisé ; à part.

separately (-rét'li), *adv.,* séparément ; à part.

separateness (-rét'-), *n.,* séparation, *f.* ; état de ce qui est séparé, *m.*

separation (sèp'a-ré-), *n.,* action de séparer ; séparation ; dissolution ; désunion, *f.*

separatist (sèp'a-ra-), *n.,* séparatiste, *m.*

separator (-ré-teur), *n.,* personne qui sépare, *f.*

separatory, *adj.,* séparateur, qui sépare.

sepia (si-), *n.,* sépia, *f.*

sepoy (si-pwaï), *n.,* cipaye, *m.*

seps (sèpse), *n.,* seps, *m.*

sept (sèpte), *n.,* clan, *m.,* race, famille, *f.*

septangular (-tan'gn'ghiou-), *adj.,* (geom.) à sept angles.

september, *n.,* septembre, *m.*

septenary (sèp-tè'n'-), *adj.,* septénaire.

septennial (sèp-tè'n'-), *adj.,* septennal

septennially, *adv*., tous les sept ans.
septentrion (sèp-tè'n'-), *n*., septentrion, *m*.
septentrional, *adj*., septentrional.
septfoil (sèpt'fwaïl), *n*., (bot.) tormentille, *f*.
septic, *adj*., (med.) septique.
septic, *n*., (med.) poison septique, *m*.
septifolious, *adj*., (bot.) qui a sept feuilles.
septilateral, *adj*., qui a sept côtés.
septinsular (-siou-), *adj*., aux sept îles.
septuagenarian, *or* **septuagenary** (sèp-tiou-a-dji-né-,-adj'i-na), *n*., septuagénaire, *m*..*f*.
septuagenary, *adj*., de soixante-dix ans; septuagénaire, *f*.
septuagesima (sèp-tiou-a-djèss'-), *n*., septuagésime, *f*.
septuagint (sèp-tiou-a-dji'n'te), *n*., version des Septante, *f*.
septuple (sèp-tiou-p'l), *adj*., septuple.
sepulchral (si-peul-kral), *adj*., sépulcral.
sepulchre (sèp'eul-keur), *n*., sépulcre, *m*.
sepulchre, *v.a*., servir de sépulcre à; ensevelir.
sepulture (sèp'eul-tioure), *n*., sépulture, *f*.
sequaciousness (si-kwa-sheus-), *n*., disposition à suivre, *f*.
sequel (si-kwèl), *n*., suite; conséquence, *f*. In the —; *par la suite; dans la suite*.
sequence (si-kwè'n'ce), *n*., suite; série, *f*.; ordre de succession, *m*.; (c. rel.); at cards—*aux cartes*) séquence, *f*.
sequentially (si-kwè'n'shal'-), *adv*., en succession.
sequester (si-kwès'teur), *v.a*., séquestrer. To — one's self; *se séquestrer; se retirer*.
sequester, *v.n*., se séquestrer; (of widows—*des veuves*) renoncer à la succession de son mari.
sequestered (-teurde), *adj*., retiré; (jur.) en séquestre.
sequestrable (-'ra-b'l), *adj*., qui peut être séquestré.
sequestrate. *V*. **sequester**.
sequestration (-tré-), *n*., prise de possession, *f*.; séquestre, *m*.; (retirement) retraite, *f*., isolement, *m*.
sequestrator (-tré-teur), *n*., (jur.) séquestre, *m*.
sequin (si-kwî'n), *n*., sequin, *m*.
seraglio (si-ral'ió), *n*., sérail, *m*.
seraph (sèr'-), *n*. (*seraphim*), séraphin, *m*.
seraphic, *or* **seraphical**, *adj*., séraphique.
serass (sè-rass), *n*., (orni.) sérasse, *f*.
sere (sire), *adj*. *V*. **sear**.
serenade (sèr'i-), *n*., sérénade, *f*.
serenade, *v.a*., donner une sérénade à.
serenade, *v.n*., sérénader, donner des sérénades.
serene (si-rîne), *adj*., serein; calme; (bright—*brillant*) brillant; (title—*titre*) sérénissime.
serene, *v.a*., rendre serein; rasséréner.
serenely, *adv*., avec sérénité.
sereneness (si-rî'n'-), *or* **serenity** (si-rè'n'-), *n*., sérénité, *f*.
serf (seurfe), *n*., serf, *m*.
serge (seurdje), *n*., serge, *f*. — -maker; *serger, sergier, m*. — manufactory, — trade; *sergerie, f*.
sergeant (sâr-djè'n'te), *n*., huissier; (of infantry—*d'infanterie*) sergent; (of cavalry—*de cavalerie*) maréchal des logis; (jur.) avocat de premier rang, *m*. — -major; (of infantry—*d'infanterie*) sergent-major; (of cavalry—*de cavalerie*) maréchal des logis chef, *m*.
sergeantship, *n*., fonctions d'huissier, *f.pl*.; grade de sergent, grade de maréchal des logis; (jur.) rang d'avocat de première classe, *m*.
sericeous (si-rish'eusse), *adj*., (bot.) soyeux.
series (si-rize), *n*., suite; succession; série, *f*.
serious (si-), *adj*., sérieux. To take for —; *prendre au sérieux. Is he — ? parle-t-il sérieusement?*

seriously, *adv*., sérieusement.
seriousness, *n*., sérieux, *m*.
serjeant. *V*. **sergeant**.
sermon (seur-),*n*.,sermon: prône; prêche, *m*.
sermon, *v.a*., (ant.) sermonner.
sermonize (-aïze), *v.n*., prêcher; sermonner : faire des sermons.
sermonizer (-'aïz'-), *n*., sermonneur, *m*.. sermonneuse. *f*.
serosity (si-ross'-), *n*., sérosité. *f*.
serous (si-), *or* **scrose** (si-rôce), *adj*., séreux.
serpent (seur-), *n*., (reptile, astron., mus., fig.) serpent; (firework—*pièce d'artifice*) serpenteau, *m*.
serpentaria (seur-pè'n'té-), *n*., (bot.) serpentaire, *f*.
serpentarius, *n*., (astron.) Serpentaire, *m*
serpent-eater (-ît'-), *n*., (orni.) messager, *m*.
serpent-fish, *n*., (ich.) serpent de mer, *m*.
serpentine (seur-pè'n'taïne), *adj*., de serpent; qui serpente; qui va en serpentant; sinueux; tortueux; (of verse—*de vers*) qui commence et qui finit par le même mot. —-worm; *serpentin, m*.
serpentine,*or* **serpentine-stone** (-stône), *n*., (min.) serpentine, *f*.
serpentize (-'aïze), *v.n*., serpenter.
serpent-like (-laïke), *adj*., de serpent.
serpent's-tongue, *n*., (bot.) langue-de-serpent,*f*.
serrate, *or* **serrated** (sèr-), *adj*., en scie, à engrenage, dentelé; serré; denticulé.
serration (ant.), *or* **serrature** (-'loure), *n*., denteture, *f*.
serrulation (sèr-riou-lé-), *n*., dentelure, *f*.
serum (si-), *n*., sérum, *m*.
servant (seur-), *n*., serviteur, *m*., servante, *f*.; (domestic) domestique, *m*., *f*., servante, bonne, *f*.; (bondman—*esclave*) esclave; (of God —*de Dieu*) serviteur, *m*., servante, *f*. Your — ! *votre serviteur! votre servante!* — of all work; *bonne à tout faire*. Man—; *domestique, m*. Woman—; *domestique, servante, bonne, f*. Maid—; *servante, bonne*. — -boy; *petit domestique*.
serve (seurve), *v.a*., servir; (to treat—*traiter*) traiter, en user avec, agir avec; (to fulfil—*remplir*) servir à, remplir; (to satisfy—*contenter*) satisfaire, contenter; (to comply with—*se conformer*)s'accommoder à; (to obey—*obéir*)obéir à; (to be a slave to—*être assujetti*) être esclave de; (an apprenticeship—*apprentissage*) faire; (a gun —*un canon*) servir; (a trick—*un tour*) jouer; (a church—*une église*) desservir; (a rope—*un cordage*) fourrer, garnir; (a writ—*une sommation*, &c.) signifier. To — out; (to distribute—*distribuer*) distribuer; (to be revenged on—*se venger*) rendre la monnaie de sa pièce à, payer; (time—*son temps*) servir. To — up; servir. It —ed you, him, &c., right; *c'est bien fait*.
serve, *v.n*., servir; (in the army, &c.—*dans l'armée,* &c.) servir, être au service; (to be convenient—*être propre à*) être convenable, être favorable; (to be in subjection—*être assujetti*) être esclave. To — as; *servir de*. To — for nothing; *ne servir de rien; ne servir à rien*.
service (seur-vice), *n*., service; (favour—*faveur*) service, office, *m*., faveur, *f*.; (use—*usage*) avantage, *m*., utilité, *f*.; (worship—*culte*) service, office; (duty—*obligation*) devoir; (nav., milit.) service, *m*.; (of a rope—*d'un cordage*) fourrure, *f*.; (milit.) exploit; (homage—*hommage*) hommage, *m*.; (of a writ—*une citation*, &c.) signification, *f*.; (of china, of plate, &c.— *de porcelaine, d'argenterie*, &c.) service, *m*. Divine —; *office divin*. Tea- —; *cabaret à thé; service à thé, m*. Secret — money; *fonds secrets, m.pl*. In —, out at —; (of servants—*des dome-*

tiques) en service, en condition. Out of —; (of servants—*des domestiques) sans place.* Of —; *utile.* On —; *de service.* To do — to ; *être utile à ; faire du bien à.* To do any one a —; *rendre un service à quelqu'un.*

serviceable (-a-b'l), *adj.*, (pers.) utile, serviable ; (of things—*des choses*) avantageux, utile, qui peut servir.

serviceableness, *n.*. (pers.) disposition serviable, disposition à rendre service, *f.* ; (of things—*des choses*) avantage, *m.*, utilité, *f.*

serviceably, *adv.*, utilement, d'une manière utile.

service-book (-bouke), *n.*, rituel, *m.*

servile (seur-vaïl), *adj.*, servile ; (in subjection—*asservi*) asservi.

servilely, *adv.*, servilement.

servileness, or **servility**, *n.*, (slavery—*esclavage*) servitude ; (baseness—*bassesse*) servilité, bassesse, *f.*

serving (seurv'-), *n* , (nav.) fourrage, *m.*

serving, *adj.*, servant ; qui sert.

serving-maid (-méde), *n.*, servante, *f.*

serving-man, *n.*, serviteur, *m.*

servitor (seur-vi-teur), *n.*, serviteur, *m.* ; (at Oxford University—*à l'université d'Oxford*) étudiant servant, *m.*

servitorship, *n.*, condition d'un serviteur, *f. V.* **servitor**.

servitude (seur-vi-tioude), *n.*, servitude, *f.* ; asservissement, *m.*

sesame (sèss'a-mi), *n.*, (bot.) sésame, *m.*

sesamoid, or **sesamoidal** (sèss'a-mwaïd-), *adj.*, (anat.) sésamoïde.

seseli (sèss-i-), *n.*, (bot.) séséli, *m.*

sesquialter, sesquialteral, or **sesquialterate** (sès-kwi-), *adj.*, sesquialtère.

sesquipedal (sès-kwip'i-), or **sesquipedalian** (-pi-dé-), *adj.*, qui contient un pied et demi.

sesquiplicate (sès'kwi-), **sesquitertian** (-teur-sha'n), or **sesquitertional** (-teursho'n'-), *adj.*, sesquitierce.

sesquitone (-tône), *n.*, (mus.) tierce mineure, *f.*

sessile (sès'sile), *adj.*, sessile.

session (sèsh'-), *n.*, session ; séance, *f.* —s ; *assises, f.pl.* Quarter—s ; *assises trimestrielles ; audiences trimestrielles, f.pl.*

sess-pool, *n. V.* **cess-pool**.

sesterce (sès-teurce), *n.*, sesterce, *m.*

set, *v.a.*, (preterit and past part.—Set), poser ; (to put—*mettre*) mettre; (to place—*placer*) placer ; (to fix—*fixer*) fixer; (to plant—*planter*) planter ; (to appoint—*indiquer*) indiquer; (to regulate—*régulariser*) régler, déterminer ; (to sharpen—*aiguiser*) repasser, affiler, (tools—*outils*) affûter; (to begin to sing—*commencer à chanter*) entonner ; (to spread—*déployer*) déployer ; (to oppose—*résister*) opposer ; (an example—*un exemple*) donner ; (a bone—*un os*) remettre, remboîter; (precious stones—*les pierres précieuses*) monter, enchâsser; (a hen—*une poule*) faire couver ; (a clock, &c.—*une pendule, &c.*) mettre à l'heure, régler ; (the land—*la terre*) (nav.) relever; (a task—*une tâche*) donner, imposer ; (milk—*du lait*) laisser reposer ; (a trap—*un piège*) dresser, tendre; (of dogs—*des chiens*) arrêter, tomber en arrêt sur. To — against; *opposer à.* To — a-going; *faire aller ; mettre en mouvement.* To — apart; *mettre à part ; mettre de côté.* To — aside; *mettre de côté; écarter;* (to annul—*annuler*) casser, infirmer ; (to reject—*rejeter*) rejeter. To — at; *exciter, agacer contre, exciter après.* To — a dog at; *haler un chien après, contre.* To — by; *mettre de côté ;* (to reject—*rejeter*) rejeter. To — by the ears; *brouiller.* To — down ; *poser ; mettre à terre, mettre par terre ;* (to establish—*établir*) établir, *arrêter :* (to register—*inscrire*) coucher par écrit, mettre par écrit, inscrire ; (to relate—*mentionner*)

rapporter ; (from a vehicle—*d'une voiture*) descendre ; (fig.) *mettre à sa place.* To — down as; *considérer comme.* To — forth; *manifester, montrer ; faire paraître ;* (to publish—*publier*) publier, *énoncer ;* (to display—*déployer*) déployer. To — forward; *avancer ;* (to promote—*favoriser*) favoriser. To — off ; (to adorn—*orner*) *orner, parer, embellir ;* (to eulogize—*louer*) *rehausser ;* (to place against as an equivalent—*donner un equivalent*) *compenser.* His clothes — off his form; *ses vêtements dessinaient son corps.* To — on; *exciter, pousser ;* (to employ—*employer*) *employer.* To — on edge; *agacer.* To — on fire; *mettre le feu à, incendier ;* (fig.) *enflammer, mettre en feu.* To — out; (to assign—*allouer*) *assigner, allouer ;* (to mark—*tracer*) *marquer, tracer ;* (to adorn—*embellir*) *orner, embellir ;* (to set off—*orner*) *rehausser.* To — over ; *établir sur ; préposer à.* To — up ; (to erect—*bâtir*) *ériger, élever, dresser ;* (to establish—*établir*) *établir ;* (to found—*fonder*) *fonder, établir ;* (to exalt—*exalter*) *élever, exalter ;* (to place in view—*montrer*) *mettre en évidence ;* (to utter loudly—*crier*) *pousser, jeter ;* (to advance —*avancer*) *mettre en avant, avancer ;* (print.) *composer ;* (a carriage—*une voiture*) *se donner.* To — up a laugh ; *se mettre à rire.* To be hard —; *être bien embarrassé.* To — at ease; *mettre à l'aise ; rendre tranquille.* To — to music; *mettre en musique.* To — sail ; *mettre à la voile, appareiller.* To — the sails ; *hisser, déferler les voiles.* To — one's self about ; *se mettre à.* To — free ; *mettre en liberté.* All sails —; *toutes voiles dehors.* To — in order ; *arranger.*

set, *v.n.*, (of the sun. &c.—*du soleil, &c.*) se coucher ; (to be fixed—*s'établir*) se fixer ; (to congeal—*se coaguler*) se coaguler, se figer, se prendre ; (to plant—*planter*) planter ; (of the tide—*de la marée*) se diriger ; (of plants—*des plantes*) prendre racine, prendre ; (arch., mas.) prendre, prendre du corps ; (hunt.) chasser au chien d'arrêt; (of dogs—*des chiens*) arrêter, tomber en arrêt. The sun is —ting ; *le soleil se couche.* To — about; *se mettre à.* To — forward; *se mettre en marche; se mettre en chemin.* To — in ; *commencer ;* (of the weather—*du temps*) *se mettre à.* Winter has — in ; *l'hiver a commencé.* It — in wet; *le temps se mit à la pluie.* To — off ; *se mettre en route, se mettre en chemin, partir.* To — on ; (to begin—*commencer*) *commencer ;* (to assault—*assaillir*) *attaquer.* To — out; *partir ;* (to begin—*débuter*) *commencer, débuter.* To — to ; *se mettre à.* To — up; *s'établir.* To — up for ; *se donner pour ; avoir des prétentions à.*

set, *adj.*, (regular—*régulier*) régulier ; (fixed —*fixe*) fixe, immobile ; (firm—*ferme*) ferme, résolu ; (prescribed—*prescrit*) prescrit, établi ; (of battles—*de batailles*) rangé; (of speech—*de discours*) d'apparat, préparé ; (of phrases—*d'expressions*) d'usage, toût fait, fixe. — square ; *équerre, f.*

set, *n.*, (collection) collection, réunion, *f.* ; (of china or other ware—*de porcelaine, &c.*) service, *m.* ; (of ornaments, ribbons, &c.—*d'ornements, de rubans, &c.*) garniture ; (of precious stones—*de pierres précieuses*) parure, *f.* ; (of chairs, tables, &c.—*de tables, de chaises*) assortiment ; (of trees, &c.—*d'arbres, &c.*) rang, *m.*, rangée, *f.* ; (opinions —*d'opinions*) système, *m.*; (of studs—*de boutons*) garniture; (pers.) réunion, *f.*, assemblage, corps, *m.*, (b.s.) clique, bande, troupe, *f.*; (young plant —*jeune plante*) plant, *m.* ; (game—*jeu*) partie, *f.*; (bet at dice—*pari aux dés*) pari ; (of the sun, &c. —*du soleil, &c.*) coucher, *m.* To be at a dead —; *être à quia ; rester court.* To make a dead — upon ; *mettre au pied du mur ; attaquer vivement.*

setaceous (si-té-sheusse), *adj.*, sétacé.

set-down (-daoune), *n.*, semonce, *f.*; savon, *m.*

setiferous (si-tif'èr-), *adj.*, sétifère.

setiform (si-ti-), *adj.*, sétiforme.

set-off, *n.*, (counterbalance—*compensation*)

compensation, *f.* ; (decoration) embellissement. *m.* ; (in a wall—*d'un mur*) retraite, *f.* As a — against ; *par contre* ; *en compensation de.*

seton (sī-t'n), *n.*, séton, *m.*

setous (sī-), *or* **setose** (si-tôce), *adj.*, à poil ude. hérissé.

set-out (-aoute), *n.*, attirail ; étalage. *m.*

settee (sèt'tî), *n.*, canapé, *m.*

setter (sèt'teur), *n.*, (dog—*chien*) chien d'arrêt ; (mus.) compositeur ; (fig.) embaucheur, *m.*

setter-on, *n.*, instigateur, *m.*, instigatrice, *f.*

setting, *n.*, action de poser, de placer, de mettre, *f.* ; (of the sun, &c.—*du soleil, &c.*) coucher, *m.* ; (of mus.) mise en musique, *f.* ; (of a bone—*d'un os*) emboîtement, remboîtement ; (of precious stones—*de pierres précieuses*) montage, *m.*, enchâssure, *f.* ; (of the compass—*de la boussole*)relèvement, *m.* —*dog* ; *chien d'arrêt*, *m.* — in ; *commencement*, *m.* — off ; *départ*, *m.* — on ; *instigation*, *f.* — out ; *départ* ; (commencement) *début*, *m.* — rule ; *filet à composer*, *m.* — stick ; *composteur*, *m.* — up ; *établissement*, *m.* ; (print.) *composition*, *f.*

settle (sèt't'l), *n.*, banc, *m.*

settle (sèt't'l), *v.a.*, (to fix—*fixer*) fixer, établir ; (to establish, to marry—*marier*) établir ; (to determine—*décider*) déterminer, décider, arrêter ; (to colonize—*coloniser*) coloniser ; (to tranquillize—*calmer*) tranquilliser, calmer ; (to adjust —*arranger*) accommoder, arranger ; (questions, &c.) résoudre ; (a minister—*un ministre*) installer ; (to pay—*acquitter*) payer ; (a quarrel— *une querelle*) arranger, ajuster ; (lees—*lie*) faire déposer ; (accounts—*comptes*) régler, arrêter ; (to make close—*rendre compact*, arch., mas.) tasser, faire tasser. To — a pension on ; *assigner une pension à ; constituer une pension à.* To — the land ; (nav.) *noyer la terre.*

settle, *v.n.*, (to sink to the bottom—*précipiter*) se rasseoir ; reposer ; déposer ; (to fix one's residence—*se fixer*) s'établir, se fixer ; (to marry— *se marier*) s'établir ; (to become fixed after change, as of the wind—*se fixer après un changement*, *comme le vent*) se fixer ; (to repose—*reposer*) reposer ; (to become calm—*se calmer*) se calmer, se tranquilliser ; (to determine—*se décider*) se déterminer. se décider ; (to become compact—*devenir compact*, arch., mas.) tasser, se tasser ; (to come to an agreement—*s'arranger*) prendre des arrangements, s'arranger. To — down ; *se fixer*, *s'établir*. To — dc vn to ; *s'appliquer à ; se faire à.* To let — ; *laisser reposer.*

settlement, *n.*, (act of settling—*acte de s'établir*) établissement ; (subsidence—*précipité*) dépôt, *m.*, action de tomber au fond ; (act of giving possession—*acte de donner possession*) mise en possession ; (jur.) institution, *f.* ; (jointure— *douaire*) douaire, *m.* ; (of an annuity—*d'unerente*) constitution, *f.* ; (marriage and housekeeping —*mariage et ménage*) établissement, *m.* ; (a becoming stationary—*devenir stationnaire*) fixation ; (colonization—*colonisation*) colonisation ; (colony—*colonie*) colonie, *f.*, établissement ; (of disputes, &c.—*de disputes, &c.*) ajustement, arrangement, accommodement ; (of accounts—*de comptes*) règlement, *m.* ; (of a question, &c.— *d'une question, &c.*) solution ; (of a minister—*d'un ministre*) installation, *f.* ; (legal residence—*domicile légal*) domicile légal, *m.* ; (liquidation) liquidation, *f.*, (arch., mas.) tassement, *m.* Act of —; *loi de la succession au trône, f.* Deed of —; *acte de constitution*, *m.* Marriage- — ; *douaire*, *m.*

settler, *n.*, colon, *m.*

settling, *n.*, (act of settling—*action de s'établir*) établissement, *m.* ; (subsidence—*tomber au fond*) précipitation, *f.* ; (marriage and housekeeping—*se marier et tenir maison*) établissement, *m.* ; (of an annuity—*d'une rente*) constitution ; (a becoming stationary—*devenir stationnaire*) fixation ; (colonization—*colonisation*) colo-

nisation, *f.* ; (of disputes, &c.—*de disputes, &c.*) ajustement, arrangement, accommodement, *m.* ; (of questions—*de questions*) solution, *f.* ; (of accounts—*de comptes*) règlement ; (arch., mas.) tassement, *m.* —s ; *sédiment, dépôt, m., lie, f.*

set-to (-tou), *n.*, dispute, *f.* ; chamaillis, *m.* ; batterie, *f.*

seven (sèv'n), *adj.*, sept.

sevenfold (-fôlde), *adj.* and *adv.*, septuple, de sept fois ; sept fois.

seven-hilled (-hilde), *adj.*, aux sept collines.

sevennight (sè'n'naïte), *n.* *V.* se'nnight.

sevenscore (-scôre), *adj.*, cent quarante.

seventeen (-tîne), *adj.*, dix-sept.

seventeenth (-tî'n'th), *adj.*, dix-septième.

seventh (sèv'n'th), *adj.*, septième.

.**seventh**, *n.*, septième, *m.* ; (mus.) septième, *f.*

seventhly, *adv.*, septièmement.

seventieth (-tièth), *adj.*, soixante-dixième.

seventy (-tî), *adj.*, soixante-dix. The —, the Septuagint ; *les Septante, m.pl.*

sever (sèv'-), *v.a.*, séparer ; disjoindre.

sever, *v.n.*, faire une séparation ; se séparer.

several (sèv'rol), *adj.*, plusieurs ; (divers) divers ; (different) différent ; (distinct) distinct, séparé ; (particular—*particulier*) particulier.

severally, *adv.*, séparément ; en particulier.

severance (sèv'-), *n.*, disjonction, *f.*

severe (si-vîre), *adj.*, sévère ; (cruel) cruel ; rigorous—*rigoureux*) rigoureux, rude ; (violent) violent, grand ; (acute—*aigu*) aigu, vif. A — winter ; *un hiver rigoureux.* A — cold ; *un gros rhume.*

severely (si-vîr'-), *adv.*, sévèrement ; cruellement ; rigoureusement.

severity (si-vèr'-), *n.*, sévérité ; (rigour— *rigueur*) rigueur, *f.*

sow (sô), *v.a.* and *n.*, coudre.

sewer (sô'eur), *n.*, personne qui coud ; couturière, couseuse, *f.*

sewer (siou-eur), *n.*, (subterranean channel —*canal souterrain*) égout ; cloaque ; conduit pour les eaux souterraines, *m.*

sewerage (siou-eur-édje), *n.*, égout ; système d'égouts, *m.* ; égouts, *m.pl*

sewing (sô-igne), *n.*, action de coudre ; couture, *f.*

sewing-silk (sô-ign'-), *n.*, soie à coudre, *f.*

sex, *n.*, sexe, *m.* The fair — ; *le sexe, le beau sexe, m.*

sexagenarian (sèks-a-dji-né-), *n.*, sexagénaire, *m., f.*

sexagenary (sèks-adj'i-), *adj.*, sexagénaire.

sexagesima (sèks-a-djèss'-), *n.*, Sexagésime, *f.*

sexagesimal, *adj.*, sexagésimal.

sexangle (sèks-an'gn'g'l), *n.*, hexagone, *m.*

sexangled (-g'l'de), *or* **sexangular** (-ghiou-), *adj.*, hexagone.

sexangularly, *adv.*, en hexagone.

sexennial (sèks'è'n-), *adj.*, sexennal.

sexennially, *adv.*, tous les six ans.

sexlocular (sèks'lok'iou-), *adj.*, (bot.) sexloculaire.

sextain (sèks'tine), *n.*, sixain, sizain, *m.*

sextant, *n.*, sextant, *m.*

sextile, *n.*, (astron.) aspect sextil, *m.*

sexton (sèks'teu'ne), *n.*, fossoyeur ; sacristain, *m.*

sextonship, *n.*, charge de fossoyeur, de sacristain, *f.*

sextuple (sèks-tiou-p'l), *adj.*, sextuple, *n.*

sexual (sèk'shiou-), *adj.*, sexuel.

sexualist, *n.*, partisan de la doctrine des sexes parmi les plantes, *m.*

sexuality, *n.*, distinction des sexes, *f.*

shabbily, *adv.*, (of dress—*des vêtements*) avec des habits râpés ; (meanly—*mesquinement*) d'une manière méprisable, mesquinement.

shabbiness, *n.*, (of dress—*des vêtements*),

état râpé. *m.* ; (meanness—*bassesse*) petitesse, bassesse, mesquinerie, *f.*

shabby, *adj.*, (of clothes) usé, râpé ; (clothed shabbily—*mal vétu*) vêtu d'habits râpés, mal vêtu ; (mean—*bas*) mesquin, bas. petit, vilain. That is very — of you ; *c'est bien mal à vous ; c'est bien petit de votre part.* — fellow ; *homme mesquin.* What ! you won't give me a pair of gloves? oh ! what a — fellow you are ! *quoi ! vous ne voulez pas me donner une paire de gants ? oh ! que vous êtes vilain !*

shackle (shak'k'l), *v.a.*, enchaîner ; garrotter ; (fig.) entraver.

shackles (shak'k'l'ze), *n.pl.*, fers, *m.* ; chaînes ; (fig.) entraves, *f.pl.*

shad. *n.*, (ich.) alose, *f.*

shaddock, *n.*, (bot.) pamplemousse, *f.*

shade, *n.*, ombre, *f.* ; ombrage ; (of a lamp, &c.—*de lampe*) abat-jour, *m.* ; (of colour—*de couleur*) nuance ; (spirit—*esprit*) ombre ; (paint.) ombre, *f.* The —s of night ; *les ombres de la nuit.*

shade, *v.a.*, ombrager ; couvrir d'ombre ; (to obscure—*assombrir*) obscurcir ; (to protect—*protéger*) protéger ; (paint.) ombrer ; (to mark with gradations of colour—*nuancer*) nuancer.

shaded (shéd'-), *adj.*, à l'ombre ; (paint.) ombré ; (of places—*d'endroits*) ombragé.

shader (shéd'-), *n.*, personne qui met à l'ombre ; chose qui met à l'ombre, qui fait ombre, *f.*

shadiness (shéd'-), *n.*, ombrage ; état ombreux, *m.* ; ombre, *f.*

shading (shéd'-), *n.*, ombrage, *m.* ; action d'ombrer, *f.*

shadow (shad'ô), *n.*, ombre ; (type) figure, *f.*, type, signe, *m.* ; (protection) ombre, *f.*, abri, *m.* Under the — of an angel's wing ; *à l'ombre de l'aile d'un ange.* The great —s of a picture ; *les grandes ombres d'une peinture.* To pass like a — ; *passer comme une ombre.*

shadow, *v.a.*, ombrager ; couvrir de son ombre ; (colours—*couleurs*) nuancer ; (to protect —*abriter*) protéger, abriter ; (to represent faintly —*ébaucher*) esquisser ; ébaucher ; (to represent typically—*représenter par un type*) représenter ; (to hide—*couvrir*) cacher, couvrir ; (paint.) ombrer.

shadowing (shad'ô-igne), *n.*, action d'ombrer, de nuancer, *f.*

shadowless. *adj.*, sans ombre.

shadow-works (-weurkse), *n.pl.*, ombres chinoises, *f.pl.*

shadowy (shad'ô-ï), *adj.*, couvert d'ombre ; ombragé ; (gloomy—*sombre*) sombre, ténébreux ; (typical—*typique*) typique, figuré ; (unreal—*illusoire*) chimérique ; (obscure) obscur.

shady (shéd'i), *adj.*, couvert d'ombre ; ombragé ; ombreux ; (sheltered—*abrité*) à l'ombre.

shaft (shâf'te), *n.*, (arrow—*trait*) flèche, *f.*, dard, trait ; (mines) puits ; (of a carriage—*de voiture*) timon ; (of a cart—*de charrette*) brancard ; (of a quill—*de plume*) tuyau ; (of a lance—*de lance*) bois ; (of a column—*de colonne*) fût ; (of a weapon—*d'arme*) manche ; (mec.) arbre, *m.* To sink a — ; *percer un puits.* Main — ; (mec.) *arbre moteur.*

shafted, *adj.*, à manche ; (her.) à tête de lance.

shag, *n.*, (cloth—*étoffe*) peluche, *f.* ; (hairpoil) poil rude ; (tobacco—*tabac*) caporal, *m.*

shag, *adj.*, poilu ; velu.

shag, *v.a.*, rendre poilu ; rendre hérissé ; rendre raboteux.

shagged (-ghède), or **shaggy** (-ghi), *adj.*, poilu ; velu ; hérissé ; raboteux ; inégal. A — dog ; *un barbet. m.*

shaggedness (-ghèd'-), or **shagginess** (-ghi-), *n.*, état poilu ; état hérissé, *m.*

shagreen (-grîne), *n.*, chagrin, *m.*, peau de chagrin. *f.*

shagreen, *adj.*, de peau de chagrin.

shah, *n.*, Schah, *m.*

shake, *n.*, secousse ; (agitation) agitation, *f.*, tremblement, *m.* ; (in wood—*dans du bois*) fente, *f.* ; (mus.) tremblement, *m.* — of the hand ; poignée de main, *f.* A — -down ; *un lit fait à la hâte ; le coucher, m.*

shake, *v.a.* (*preterit,* Shook ; *past part.*, Shaken),secouer ; ébranler ; branler, remuer ; agiter ; (to weaken, to move—*affaiblir, toucher*) ébranler ; (mus.) cadencer. To — hands with ; *serrer la main à ; donner une poignée de main à.* To — one's head ; *secouer la tête.* To — to pieces ; *faire tomber en pièces.* To — off ; secouer ; *faire tomber ;* (to get rid of—*se débarrasser de*) *se débarrasser de ; se défaire de.* To — up ; remuer. To — the table ; *remuer la table.*

shake, *v.n.*, s'ébranler ; trembler ; trembloter. To — with cold ; *trembler de froid.* His hand —s ; *la main lui tremble.*

shaken (shék'n), *adj.*, (of wood—*du bois*) fendillé.

shaker (shék'-), *n.*, personne qui tremble, qui fait trembler, qui ébranle, qui secoue ; chose qui fait trembler, qui ébranle, qui secoue, *f.* —s ; (sect—*secte*) trembleurs, *m.pl.*

shaking (shék'-), *n.*, secousse, *f.* ; ébranlement ; tremblement, *m.* Hand— — ; *serrement de main, m.*

shako (shék'ô), *n.*, shako, schako, *m.*

shaky (shék'i), *adj.*, infirme ; débile ; faible ; (of things—*des choses*) peu solide ; (of wood—*du bois*) éclaté.

shale, *n.*, coque ; (min.) argile schisteuse, *f.*

shale-stone (-stône), *n.* V. shale (min.).

shall, *v.* auxil. (*preterit,* Should), devoir ; vouloir. I — go ; *j'irai.* — I go? *irai-je !* dois-je aller ? You — do it ; *je veux que vous le fassiez.*

shalloon (-loune), *n.*, serge fine, *f.*

shallop (-lô), *n.*, chaloupe, *f.*

shallot, *n.* V. eschalot.

shallow (-lô), *adj.*, peu profond ; superficiel ; (slight—*léger*) léger ; (silly—*superficiel*) borné ; (of water—*de l'eau*) bas.

shallow (-lô), *n.*, haut-fond, bas-fond, *m.*

shallow-brained (-lô-bré'n'de), *adj.*, à cervelle creuse ; borné.

shallowly, *adv.*, de peu de profondeur ; superficiellement.

shallowness, *n.*, manque de profondeur, *m.* ; nature superficielle, *f.* ; esprit superficiel, *m.*

shalm (shâme), *n.*, (ant.) V. shawm.

shalot, *n.* V. eschalot.

sham, *n.*, feinte, *f.*

sham, *adj.*, feint ; faux ; simulé ; prétendu ; postiche. — fight ; *petite guerre.*

sham, *v.a.*, feindre, simuler ; tromper. To — upon ; *faire accroire à.* To — lameness, illness ; *feindre d'être boiteux, malade.* To — Abraham ; *jouer l'innocence patriarcale ; feindre d'être malade.*

sham, *v.n.*, user de feintes.

shamble (-b'l), *v.n.*, marcher lourdement.

shambles (-b'l'ze), *n.pl.*, boucherie ; (mines) niche, retraite, *f.*

shambling, *adj.*, à démarche lourde.

shambling, *n.*, démarche lourde, *f.* ; pas lourd, *m.*

shame, *n.*, honte ; pudeur ; (dishonour—*déshonneur*) honte, *f.*, opprobre, *m.* From —, for —, out of — ; *de honte.* For — ! *fi donc !* — ! *quelle honte ! c'est honteux ! honte !* To cry — at ; *crier à l'infamie contre.* To be the — of ; *être, faire la honte de.* To be lost to all — ; *avoir perdu toute honte.*

shame, *v.a.*, faire honte à ; (to mock at—*se moquer*) se moquer de ; (to disgrace—*déshonorer*) déshonorer.

shamefaced (-féste), *adj.*, honteux ; timide.

shamefacedly (-fést'li), *adv.*, avec mauvaise honte ; timidement.
shamefacedness (-fést'nèce), *n.*, mauvaise honte ; timidité, *f.*
shameful (-foule), *adj.*, honteux ; (indecent) indécent, déshonnête.
shamefully, *adv.*, honteusement ; indécemment.
shamefulness, *n.*, opprobre, *m.*
shameless, *adj.*, éhonté, effronté ; impudent.
shamelessly, *adv.*, sans honte ; effrontément ; impudemment.
shamelessness, *n.*, effronterie ; impudence, *f.*
shamer (shém'-), *n.*, personne qui fait honte ; chose qui fait honte, *f.*
shammed (sha'm'de), *adj.*, faux ; prétendu, feint, simulé.
shammer (sha'm'-), *n.*, personne qui feint, *f.* ; trompeur, *m.*, trompeuse, *f.* ; imposteur, *m.*
shamois, shamoy, *or* **shammy,** *n.*, chamois, *m.*
shampoo (-pou), *v.a.*, masser.
shampooing (-pou-igne), *n.*, massage, *m.*
shamrock, *n.*, trèfle, *m.*
shank, *n.*, jambe, *f.* ; (tibia) tibia, os de la jambe ; (of a horse—*du cheval*) canon, *m.* ; (of instruments—*d'instruments*) tige,*f.* ; (of a pipe —*de pipe*) tuyau, *m.* ; (of a button—*de bouton*) queue ; (of an anchor—*d'ancre*) tige, verge ; (of a key—*de clef*) tige,*f.* ; (of a column—*de colonne*) fût, *m.*
shanked (shan'gn'k'te), *adj.*, à jambe ; à tige ; à queue.
shape, *n.*, forme ; figure ; (pers.) tournure, taille ; (idea—*idée*) idée ; (of a bonnet—*de chapeau*) forme, carcasse, *f.* In the — of ; *en forme de.*
shape, *v.a.*, former ; (to regulate—*régulariser*) régler, modeler ; (to direct—*diriger*) diriger.
shape, *v.n.*, cadrer ; convenir.
shapeless, *adj.*, informe, sans forme.
shapelessness. *n.*, état informe, *m.*
shapely, *adj.*, bien fait ; bien formé.
shard (shârde), *n.*, têt ; tesson, *m.* ; (bot.) carde, *f.* ; (of an insect—*d'insecte*) étui, *m.* ; (of a snail—*de colimaçon*) coquille, *f.*
share, *n.*, (portion) part, portion, *f.* ; (part allotted—*portion allouée*) part,*f.* ; (interest—*intérêt*) intérêt, *m.* ; (in a railway, a mine, &c.— *dans un chemin de fer, une mine, &c.*) action, *f.* ; (of a plough—*de charrue*) soc, *m.* To have a — in ; *avoir part à ; avoir un intérêt dans.* To fall to any one's — ; *échoir à quelqu'un en partage.* To go —s ; *partager.* In half —s ; *de compte à demi.*
share, *v.a.*, partager.
share, *v.n.*, partager ; avoir part à. To — in ; *avoir part à ; participer à.*
shareholder (-hôld'-), *n.*, actionnaire, *m.*,*f.*
sharer, *n.*, personne qui partage, qui participe, *f.* ; (jur.) partageant, *m.* Joint— ; *copartageant, m.*
sharing (shér'-), *n.*, partage, *m.*
shark (shârke), *n.*, (ich.) requin ; (sharper— *escroc*) chevalier d'industrie, escroc, filou, *m.*
shark, *v.a.*, écornifler.
shark, *v.n.*, filouter ; vivre d'écornifleries ;
sharker, *n.*, chevalier d'industrie ; escroc ; écornifleur, *m.*
sharking, *n.*, escroquerie, écorniflerie, *f.*
sharp (shârpe), *adj.*, tranchant, affilé ; (pointed—*aigu*) pointu, aigu, à pointe acérée ; (acute of mind—*d'un esprit délié*) vif, intelligent, pénétrant, fin ; (of children—*des enfants*) éveillé, dégourdi ; (piercing—*perçant*) perçant, pénétrant ; (acid—*aigre*) acide, piquant ; (biting— *mordant*) mordant, piquant, vif, amer, acerbe, aigre ; (rigid—*sévère*) rigide, sévère ; (subtle—

délié) subtil, fin ; (ardent) vif, ardent ; (violent) violent, fort ; (fierce—*furieux*) vif, vigoureux, rude ; (keen—*aigu*) aigu, vif ; (of sound—*du son*) aigre, perçant ; (mus.) dièse. A — edge ; *un fil tranchant.* A — appetite ; *un grand appétit.* — pain ; *douleur vive.* A — contest ; *une contestation vive, violente.* To look — ; *se dépêcher.* As — as a needle ; (pers.) (pop.) *fin comme tout.*
sharp, *n.*, (mus.) dièse, *m.*
sharp, *v.a.*, aiguiser ; affiler ; (mus.) diéser.
sharp-edged (-èdj'de), *adj.*, bien affilé ; (carp.) à vive arête.
sharpen (shârp'n), *v.a.*, aiguiser, affiler ; (to point—*faire une pointe à*) rendre pointu, rendre aigu ; (to make active—*rendre vif*) rendre vif ; (to make acid—*aigrir*) aigrir, rendre acide, rendre piquant ; (to make biting—*rendre mordant*) rendre amer, rendre acerbe, rendre aigu ; (the intellect, the sight—*l'intelligence, la vue*) rendre vif, rendre pénétrant, aiguiser ; (the appetite—*l'appétit*) aiguiser. ouvrir ; (pain— *une douleur*) rendre vif, rendre aigu ; (desire— *un désir*) exciter ; (mus.) diéser.
sharpen, *v.n.*, s'aiguiser.
sharper, *n.*, aigrefin ; escroc ; chevalier d'industrie, *m.*
sharply, *adv.*, avec un fil tranchant ; avec une pointe aiguë ; (rigorously—*durement*) rigoureusement ; (vigorously—*vivement*) vigoureusement, rudement, vivement, âprement, avec âpreté ; (roughly—*vertement*) vivement, vertement, avec aigreur ; (violently—*fortement*) violemment, fortement ; (acutely—*vigoureusement*) d'une manière pénétrante, d'une manière perçante. To answer — ; *répondre avec aigreur, vivement.*
sharpness, *n.*, (keenness of an edge—*finesse de tranchant*) qualité de ce qui est tranchant ; (keenness of a point—*acuité*) qualité de ce qui est pointu ; (acidity—*acidité*) acidité ; (of pain, grief—*de la douleur, du chagrin*) force, violence ; (of language—*de langage*) aigreur, amertume,*f.*, piquant, *m.* ; (acuteness of intellect—*d'esprit*) intelligence, *f.*, (of children—*des enfants*) esprit éveillé, *m.* ; (quickness of perception—*rapidité de perception*) pénétration ; (of the weather— *du temps*) rigueur, *f.* ; (of sound—*du son*) son aigu, *m.*
sharp-set, *adj.*, affamé ; vorace ; avide.
sharp-shooter (-shout'-) *n.*, bon tireur ; tirailleur, *m.*
sharp-sighted (-saït'-), *adj.*, qui a la vue perçante.
sharp-witted, *adj.*, qui a l'esprit pénétrant.
shatter, *v.a.*, briser, fracasser ; mettre en pièces ; (to rend—*déchirer*) déchirer ; (to derange —*déranger*) déranger ; (to impair—*détruire*) altérer ; abîmer.
shatter, *v.n.*, se briser, se fracasser.
shatter-brained (shat'teur-bré'n'de), *or* **shatter-pated** (-pét'-), *adj.*, timbré ; (heedless —*étourdi*) étourdi.
shatters (shat'teur'ze), *n.pl.*, pièces, *f.pl.* ; morceaux ; éclats, *m.pl.* To break into — ; *faire voler en éclats.*
shattery, *adj.*, cassant ; fragile.
shave, *v.a.*, raser ; faire la barbe à ; (animal) tondre ; (just to touch—*effleurer*) raser ; (to fleece —*voler*) plumer, écorcher ; (tech.) planer ; (carp.) raboter ; (paper—*papier*) rogner. To — one's self ; *se raser, se faire la barbe.* To get —d ; *se faire raser, se faire faire la barbe.*
shave, *v.n.*, raser ; (to shave one's self—*se raser*) se raser, se faire la barbe.
shave, *n.*, plane, *f.*
shave-grass (-grâce), *n.*, (bot.) prêle,*f.*
shaveling (shév'-), *n.*, tonsuré, *m.*
shaver (shév'-), *n.*, barbier ; (plunderer— *fripon*) écorcheur, fripon ; (sharp man *to deal*

with—*malin*) fin matois; (youngster—*adolescent*) blanc-bec, moutard, *m.*

shaving (shév'-), *n.*, action de raser, *f.*; (of wood, &c.—*de bois, &c.*) copeau, *m.*

shaving-box. *n.*, boîte à savonnette, *f.*

shaving-brush (-breushe), *n.*, blaireau, *m.*

shaving-cloth (-cloth), *n.*, linge à barbe, *m.*

shawl (shôl), *n.*, châle, *m.*

shawm (shô'm), *n.*, (ant.) hautbois; cornet à bouquin, chalumeau, *m.*

she (shi), *pron.*, elle, *f.* [*She* s'emploie souvent comme préfixe pour désigner les animaux femelles. Ex.: — -goat, *chèvre*; — -cat, *chatte*; — -bear, *ourse*.]

sheaf (shif), *n.*, gerbe; javelle, *f.*; (of arrows —*de flèches*) faisceau, *m.*

sheaf, *v.a.*, engerber; mettre en gerbe, javeler.

shear (shîr), *v.a.* (*preterit*, Sheared; *past part.*, Sheared, Shorn), tondre; couper.

shear, *v.n.*, se séparer.

shear-bill, *n.*, (orni.) coupeur d'eau, *m.*

shearer. *n.*, tondeur, *m.*, tondeuse, *f.*

shearing (shîr-), *n.*, tonture; tonte, *f.*

shearing-machine (-ma-shîne), *n.*, tondeuse mécanique, *f.*

shearling (shîr), *n.*, brebis qui n'a été tondue qu'une fois, *f.*

shearman (shîr-), *n.*, tondeur de drap, *m.*

shears (shîrze), *n.pl.*, grands ciseaux, *m.pl.*; cisailles, *f.pl.*

sheath (shîth), *n.* (*sheaths*), fourreau; étui, *m.*; gaine, *f.*; (ent.) étui, élytre, *m.*; (anat., bot.) gaine, *f.* — -maker; *gaînier, m.*

sheathe (shîthe), *v.a.*, mettre dans un étui; (a sword, &c.—*une épée, &c.*) rengainer; (to cover—*couvrir*) couvrir, revêtir; (to fit with a sheath—*pourvoir d'un fourreau*) munir d'un fourreau; (fig.) plonger; (a ship—*un vaisseau*) doubler.

sheathing (shîth'-), *n.*, bordage; (nav.) doublage, *m.*

sheath-winged (shîth-wign'de), *adj.*, (ent.) à étui; à élytre.

• sheathy (shîth'i), *adj.*, qui forme un fourreau, un étui, une gaine.

sheave (shive), *n.*, (nav.) rouet, réa, ria, *m.*

shed (shède), *n.*, hangar; appentis; atelier, *m.*; (hovel—*baraque*) bicoque, *f.* Cow— —; *étable à vaches,*

shed, *v.a.* (*preterit* and *past part.*, Shed), répandre, faire couler; (of trees—*des arbres*) laisser tomber; (of animals—*des animaux*) jeter, changer; (to emit—*émettre*) répandre, exhaler; (to keep off—*éloigner*) garantir de; (tears—*des larmes*) verser. To —over; *répandre sur; verser sur.*

shed, *v.n.*, éloigner; empêcher d'entrer.

shedder. *n.*, personne qui répand, qui verse, qui fait couler, *f.*

shedding, *n.*, action de répandre; effusion, *f.*

sheen (shîne), *n.*, splendeur, *f.*; éclat, *m.*

sheen, *or* **sheeny,** *adj.*, éclatant; brillant.

sheep (shipe), *n.*, brebis, *f.*; mouton; (silly fellow—*imbécile*) sot, *m.*; (fig.) brebis, *f.*; (skin —*peau*) mouton, *m.*, basane, *f.*

sheep-cot, *n.*, parc à moutons, *m.*

sheepfold (-fôlde), *n.*, bercail, *m.*; bergerie, *f.*

sheephook (-houke), *n.*, houlette, *f.*

sheepish. *adj.*, penaud; bête, timide.

sheepishly, *adv.*, en penaud; d'un air bête, timidement.

sheepishness, *n.*, timidité, *f.*

sheep-master (-mâs-), *n.*, éleveur de moutons, *m.*

sheep's-eye (-'a-ye) *n.*, œillade, *f.*; yeux doux, *m.pl.* To cast —; *faire les yeux doux à.*

sheep-shank, *n.*, (nav.) jambe de chien, *f.*

sheep-shearer (-shîr'-), *n.*, tondeur de moutons, *m.*

sheep-shearing (-shîr'-), *n.*, tonte, *f.*

sheep-skin, *n.*, mouton, *m.*; peau de mouton, *f.*

sheep-stealer (-stîl'-), *n.*, voleur de moutons. *m.*

sheep-stealing, *n.*, vol de moutons, *m.*

sheepwalk (-woke), parc à moutons; pâturage à moutons, *m.*

sheer (shîr), *adj.*, pur. —nonsense; *pure sottise.*

sheer (shîr), *n.*, (nav.) tonture; courbure longitudinale des ponts et du bordage extérieur d'un bâtiment, *f.* —s; *machine à mâter, f. sing.*

sheer, *v.n.*, (nav.) faire des embardées. To — off; *fuir.*

sheer-hooks (-houkse), *n.*, grappin, *m.*

sheer-hulk (-heulke), *n.*, machine à mâter flottante, *f.*

sheers (shîrze), *n.pl.*, bigue, *f.*; bigues. *f.pl.*

sheet (shî'te), *n.*, drap, *m.*; (of paper, of metals—*de papier, de métaux*) feuille; (of water, &c.—*d'eau, &c.*) nappe, pièce; (nav.) écoute, *f.* Winding-—; *linceul, m.*

sheet (shî'te), *v.a.*, couvrir; envelopper.

sheet, *v.n.*, (nav.) border une écoute.

sheet-anchor (-an'gn'k'eur), *n.*, ancre de miséricorde, maîtresse ancre; (fig.) planche de salut, *f.*

sheet-copper, *n.*, cuivre en planches, *m.*

sheeting, *n.*, toile pour draps de lits, *f.*; (lining—*doublage*) blindage, *m.*

sheet-iron (-aï-eur'n), *n.*, tôle, *f.*

sheet-lead (-lède), *n.*, plomb en feuille. *m.*

sheet-piles, *or* **sheeting-piles** (-pailze), *n.pl.*, madriers, *m.pl.*; palplanches, *f.pl.*

sheets, *n.pl.*, (nav.) écoutes, *f.pl.*

shelf (shèlfe), *n.*, tablette, planche, *f.*; rayon; (nav.) banc de sable, écueil, récif, *m.*; (min.) couche, *f.*

shelfy, *adj.*, plein d'écueils.

shell, *n.*, (of eggs, of fruit—*d'œufs, de fruits*) coque, coquille, écale; (of peas—*de pois*) cosse; (of oysters—*d'huîtres*) écaille; (mol.) coquille; (coffin—*cercueil*), bière, *f.*; cercueil de sapin; (artil.) obus, *m.*, bombe, *f.*; (outer part—*extérieur*) extérieur, *m.*, écorce; (of a house—*de maison*) carcasse; (mus.) lyre, *f.*

shell, *v.a.*, ôter la coque de, la coquille de; (peas—*pois*) écosser.

shell, *v.n.*, s'écaler.

shell-fish, *n.*, coquillage; mollusque. *m.*

shell-work (shèl'weurke), *n.*, coquillage, *m.*

shelly, *adj.*, couvert de coquillages.

shelter (shèl-), *n.*, abri; couvert; (protection) abri, refuge, *m.*, protection, *f.* To take —; *s'abriter; se mettre à l'abri.* Under — from; à *l'abri de, à couvert de.*

shelter, *v.a.*, abriter; mettre à l'abri; protéger, garantir.

shelter, *v.n.*, s'abriter.

shelterless, *adj.*, sans abri; sans asile.

shelve (shèlve), *v.a.*, mettre sur des tablettes; (fig.) mettre de côté; se débarrasser de.

shelve, *v.n.*, aller en pente; incliner.

shelving, *adj.*, en pente; en talus; incliné.

shelvy. *V.* **shelfy.**

shepherd (shèp'eurde), *n.*, berger; pâtre; (fig.) pasteur. *m.*

shepherdess, *n.*, bergère, *f.*

shepherdish, *adj.*, de berger; pastoral.

shepherdly. *adj.*, pastoral.

shepherd's-purse (-peurse), *n.* (bot.) capselle, *f.*

sherbet (shèr-), *n.*, sorbet, *m.*

sheriff (shèr'-), *n.*, shérif, *m.*

sheriffalty. *V.* **shrievalty.**

sherry, *n.*, vin de Xérès, *m.*

shew-bread (shô-), *n.* *V.* **show-bread.**

shewer. *n.* *V.* **shower.**

shibboleth (-lèth), *n.*, marque distinctive d'un parti, *f.*

shield (shïlde), *n.*, bouclier, *m.* ; (of Minerva —*de Pallas*) égide, *f.* ; (fig.) bouclier, *m.*, égide, *f.* ; (hort.) écusson ; (her.) écu, écusson, *m.*

shield, *v.a.*, couvrir d'un bouclier. To — from ; *couvrir de; mettre à l'abri de ; défendre de, protéger de : garantir de.*

shield-bearer (-bèr'-), *n.*, écuyer, *m.*

shift, *n.*, (change—*changement*) changement ; (expedient) expédient, *m.*, ressource, *f.* ; (mean refuge—*petit moyen*) biais, détour ; (trick to escape detection—*défaite*) faux-fuyant, *m.*, défaite, *f.* ; (mus.) démanché, *m.* ; (chemise) chemise de femme, *f.* To use —s ; *user de biais.* To make — to ; *s'arranger pour ;* (to do with difficulty—*faire avec peine*) avoir de la peine à. Not to know what — to make ; *ne savoir à quel saint se vouer.* My last — ; *ma dernière ressource.*

shift, *v.a.*, changer ; transporter. To — off ; *secouer ; éviter ; se délivrer de.*

shift, *v.n.*, (to change place—*changer de place*) changer de place ; (to vary—*varier*) changer ; (to resort to expedients—*avoir recours à des expédients*) trouver des expédients, s'arranger ; (to change dress—*changer d'habits*) changer de vêtements ; (to practise indirect methods—*biaiser*) user de faux-fuyants, biaiser. To — for one's self ; *s'arranger.*

shifter, *n.*, personne qui change, *f.* ; (person who uses artifice—*personne qui use de subterfuges*) biaiseur, *m.*, biaiseuse, *f.* ; (nav.) aide-coq, *m.* Scene— ; *machiniste, m.*

shifting, *n.*, changement, *m.* ; (evasion—*détour*) défaite, *f.*, subterfuge, détour, *m.*

shifting, *adj.*, changeant ; (deceitful—*trompeur*) qui use de détours.

shiftingly, *adv.*, en changeant ; (deceitfully —*trompeusement*) par des détours.

shiftless, *adj.*, sans ressource ; sans expédient.

shilling, *n.*, schelling. *m.*

shilly-shally, *n.*, hésitation ; irrésolution, *f.*

shilly-shally, *v.n.*, hésiter, être irrésolu.

shin, or **shin-bone** (-bône), *n.*, tibia, os de la jambe, *m.*

shindy, *n.*, tapage, *m.*

shine (shaïne), *n.*, splendeur, *f.*, éclat ; (of the weather—*du temps*) beau temps, *m.*

shine (shaïne), *v.n.* (preterit and past part., Shone), luire ; reluire ; briller. The sun —s ; *il fait du soleil.* The moon —s ; *il fait clair de lune.*

shingle (shïng'l), *n.*, galet ; caillou ; (carp.) bardeau. *m.*

shingle, *v.a.*, couvrir de bardeaux.

shingles (shïng'l'ze), *n.pl.*, (med.) zona, zoster, *m.sing.*

shining (shaï'n'-), *adj.*, luisant ; reluisant ; brillant.

shining, *n.*, brillant : éclat, *m.*

shiny (shaï'n'-), *adj.*, luisant ; reluisant ; brillant.

ship, *n.*, navire ; vaisseau ; bâtiment, *m.* Merchant— ; *navire, vaisseau marchand.* — of war ; *vaisseau de guerre.* Store— ; *vaisseau de transport.* First-class — ; *vaisseau de premier rang.* — of the line ; *vaisseau de ligne.* Her Majesty's — ; *vaisseau de la marine royale.* To take — ; *s'embarquer.*

ship, *v.a.*, embarquer ; charger ; mettre à bord ; (a sea—*une vague*) recevoir, embarquer ; (the rudder—*le gouvernail*) monter ; (oars—*les avirons*) armer.

ship, *v.n.*, s'engager dans la marine ; s'embarquer.

ship-board (-bôrde), *n.*, planche de vaisseau, *f.*

ship-boy (-boï), *n.*, mousse, *m.*

ship-broker (-brôk'-), *n.*, courtier maritime, *m.*

ship-builder (-bïld'-), *n.*, constructeur de vaisseaux, *m.*

ship-building, *n.*, construction de vaisseaux ; architecture navale, *f.*

ship-chandler (-tshä'n'd'-), *n.*, fournisseur de navires, *m.*

ship-holder (-hôld'-), *n.*, propriétaire de vaisseaux, *m.*

shipless, *adj.*, sans vaisseau.

ship-load (-lôde), *n.*, chargement, *m.* ; cargaison, *f.*

ship-master (-mâs-), *n.*, patron de navire, *m.*

shipmate, *n.*, camarade de vaisseau, *m.*

shipment, *n.*, chargement ; embarquement, *m.*

ship-money (-meu'n'nè), *n.*, impôt pour la construction des vaisseaux, *m.*

ship-owner (-ô'n'-), *n.*, armateur, *m.*

shipper, *n.*, négociant qui fait le commerce maritime, *m.*

shipping, *n.*, vaisseaux ; navires, *m.pl.* ; forces navales, *f.pl.* ; (loading—*chargement*) chargement, *m.* To take — ; *s'embarquer.*

shipping. *adj.*, maritime ; naval.

ship-scraper (-scrép'-), *n.*, gratte-navire, *m.*

ship-shape, *adv.*, bien ; proprement.

shipwreck (-rèke), *n.*, naufrage, *m.*

shipwreck, *v.a.*, faire faire naufrage à. To be —ed ; *faire naufrage; être naufragé.*

shipwrecked (-rèk'te), *adj.*, naufragé.

shipwright (-raïte), *n.*, constructeur de vaisseaux, *m.*

shire (shïre, ou shaeur), *n.*, comté, *m.*

shirt (sheurte), *n.*, chemise d'homme ; chemise, *f.* Night— ; *chemise de nuit.* To sell the — off one's back ; *vendre jusqu'à sa chemise.*

shirt, *v.a.*, couvrir d'une chemise.

shirting, *n.*, toile, *f.*, calicot, *m.*, pour chemises.

shirtless, *adj.*, sans chemise.

shist, or **shistus**, *n.*, (min.) schiste, *m.*

shistic, or **shistous**, *adj.*, (min.) schisteux.

shittah, or **shittim**, *n.*, (Script.—*Bible*) bois de sétim, *m.*

shittle-cock (shït't'l-), *n.* V. **shuttlecock.**

shive (shaïve), *n.*, morceau, fragment, *m.*

shiver (shiv'-), *n.*, (min.) schiste ; (nav.) rouet ; (fragment) fragment, morceau, éclat ; (trembling—*tremblement*) frissonnement, *m.* To break to —s ; *faire voler en éclats.* To have the —s ; *avoir le frisson.*

shiver (shiv'-), *v.a.*, briser en morceaux ; fracasser ; faire voler en éclats ; (a sail—*une voile*) faire fasier ; (a mast—*un mât*) casser.

shiver, *v.n.*, se briser en morceaux ; voler en éclats ; (of sails—*de voiles*) fasier ; (to tremble —*trembler*) trembler, tressaillir ; (with cold—*de froid*) grelotter ; (with cold, fear—*de froid, de crainte*) frissonner.

shivering, *adj.*, tremblant ; tremblotant ; frissonnant.

shivering, *n.*, action de briser en morceaux, *f.* ; (trembling) frissonnement, frisson, tremblement, *m.*

shiveringly, *adv.*, en tremblant ; en grelottant.

shivery, *adj.*, qui vole en éclats ; cassant.

shoal (shôle), *n.*, (multitude) multitude, foule, *f.* ; (shallow) bas-fond, haut-fond ; (of fish—*de poissons*) banc, *m.* ; (of a river—*de rivière*) barre, *f.*

shoal (shôle), *v.n.*, affluer ; s'attrouper ; (of fish—*des poissons*) se réunir en banc ; (of water—*de l'eau*) diminuer en profondeur.

shoal. *adj.*, bas ; peu profond.

shoaliness, *n.*, manque de profondeur ; grand nombre de hauts-fonds, *m.*

shoaly, *adj.*, plein de hauts-fonds.

shock, *n.*, choc ; (impression) dégoût, coup, saisissement, *m.* ; (in electricity—*de l'élec-*

tricité) secousse, *f.* ; (of corn) tas, *m.* — -dog ;
barbet, m.

shock, *v.a.,* choquer, heurter ; (to strike
with horror, disgust—*inspirer de l'horreur, du
dégoût*) frapper d'horreur, dégoûter ; (to offend
—*offenser*) choquer, offenser, blesser ; (corn,
sheaves—*blé, gerbes*) mettre en tas.

shock, *v.n.,* choquer, offenser, blesser.

shock-headed (-hèd'-), *adj.,* à épaisse chevelure.

shocking, *adj.,* (meeting—*heurt*) qui se
choque ; (frightful—*hideux*) affreux, horrible ;
(offensive—*offensant*) blessant, offensant, choquant ; (disgusting—*dégoûtant*) repoussant, dégoûtant.

shockingly (-'ign-li), *adv.,* affreusement,
horriblement.

shockingness (-'ign-nèce), *n.,* horreur ;
nature affreuse, *f.*

shod, *past part.,* ferré.

shoe (shou), *n.* (*shoes*), soulier ; (of animals—
pour animaux) fer, *m.* ; (of a sleigh—*de traîneau*)
semelle, *f.,* sabot ; (of a carriage—*de voiture*)
sabot, *m.* ; (of an anchor—*d'ancre*) semelle, *f.* ;
(tech.) coussinet, *m.* List— -s ; *chaussons, m.pl.*
Over— -s ; *claques, galoches, f.pl.* Snow— -s ;
raquettes, f.pl. Wooden— -s ; *sabots, m.pl.* To
stand in any one's —s ; *être à la place de
quelqu'un.* To be waiting for any one's old —s ;
attendre après la défroque de quelqu'un. To take
off one's —s and stockings ; *se déchausser.* To
buy one's — of ; *acheter ses souliers à ; se faire
chausser par, chez.* To make —s for any one ;
*faire des souliers pour quelqu'un ; chausser quel-
qu'un.*

shoe (shou), *v.a.* (preterit and past part.,
Shod), chausser ; (animal) ferrer ; (an anchor—
une ancre) garnir les pattes de ; (tech.) saboter.

shoe-black, *n.,* décrotteur, *m.*

shoe-boy (-boï), *n.,* petit décrotteur, *m.*

shoe-buckle (-beuk'l), *n.,* boucle de soulier, *f.*

shoe-horn, or **shoeing-horn,** *n.,* chausse-
pied, *m.,* corne, *f.*

shoeing (shou-igne), *n.,* action de ferrer, *f.*

shoeing-hammer, *n.,* brochoir, *m.*

shoe-latchet, *n.,* cordon de soulier, *m.*

shoe-leather (-lèth'-), *n.,* cuir de soulier, *m.*
To save — ; *pour épargner ses souliers.*

shoeless, *adj.,* sans souliers.

shoemaker (-mék'-), *n.,* cordonnier, *m.*

shoemaking (-mék'-), *n.,* cordonnerie, *f.*

shoer (shou-eur), *n.,* personne qui chausse,
f. ; (farrier—*maréchal ferrant*) maréchal ferrant, *m.*

shoe-string, *n.,* cordon de soulier, *m.*

shoot (shoute), *v.a.* (preterit and past part.,
Shot), (with fire-arms—*des armes à feu*) tirer, décharger, faire partir ; (an arrow—*une flèche*) tirer,
décocher, lancer ; (to dart—*darder*) lancer, jeter,
darder ; (to strike—*frapper*) frapper, atteindre ;
(to push forth—*pousser*) pousser ; (to push out
—*faire sortir*) faire sortir ; (to traverse rapidly
—*passer rapidement*) traverser rapidement ;
(carp.) ajuster ; (to kill—*tuer*) tuer ; (to kill with
a gun—*tuer avec un fusil*) fusiller ; (a bolt—*un
verrou*) tirer, mettre, pousser ; (the contents of
anything—*le contenu de quelque chose*) décharger.
To—at any one with a gun, to—a gun at any one ;
tirer un coup de fusil à quelqu'un, sur quelqu'un.
To—any one with a gun ; *tuer quelqu'un d'un
coup de fusil.* To — dead ; *tuer raide.* Ney was
shot ; *Ney a été fusillé.* He has shot me ; *il m'a
atteint.* I shot him in the leg ; *je l'ai atteint
d'un coup de fusil à la jambe, je lui ai logé une
balle dans la jambe.* Trees — branches ; *les arbres
poussent des branches.* To — forth ; *pousser* ; (to
dart—*darder*) lancer, darder. To — off ; *tirer,
décharger* ; (to carry away—*enlever*) emporter.
The ball shot his leg off ; *le boulet lui emporta*

la jambe. To — out ; *lancer.* To — through ;
traverser, transpercer, percer d'outre en outre. The
ball shot him through the heart ; *la balle lui
traversa le cœur ; la balle le tua en lui traversant
le cœur.*

shoot, *v.n.,* (to bud—*pousser*) pousser,
croître ; (to run along—*s'élancer*) s'élancer,
courir, s'avancer ; (to feel a quick darting pain
—*avoir des élancements*) éprouver des élancements à ; (of stars—*des étoiles*) filer. To —
ahead ; *courir en avant ; se précipiter en avant.*
To — ahead of ; *devancer, dépasser.* To — at ;
tirer sur. To — forth ; *s'avancer, s'élancer.* To
— forward ; *s'élancer en avant.* To — into ; *se
former en, se développer en, se projeter en ; se précipiter dans.* To — out ; *s'élancer dehors* ; (to
project—*avancer*) se projeter, s'avancer. To —
through ; *traverser, pénétrer.* To — up a man,
to a man ; *devenir homme.* My temples — ;
j'éprouve des élancements aux tempes. To go
out —ing ; *aller à la chasse.*

shoot (shoute), *n.,* coup ; (branch—*branche*)
jet, rejeton ; (young pig—*jeune cochon*) goret, *m.* ;
(of an arch—*d'arche*) poussée, *f.*

shooter, *n.,* tireur ; chasseur ; archer, *m.*

shooting, *m.,* tir.*m.* ; décharge, *f.* ; décoch-
ment, *m.* ; (hunt.) chasse au tir, *f.* ; (of pain—
d'une douleur) élancement, *m.* ; (of plants—*des
plantes*) pousse, *f.*

shooting, *adj.,* (of pain—*d'une douleur*) qui
élance ; (of a star—*d'une étoile*) filante.

shooting-gallery, *n.,* tir, *m.*

shooting-pocket, *n.,* gibecière, *f.*

shooting-stick, *n.,* (print.) décognoir, *m.*

shop, *n.,* magasin, *m.* ; boutique, *f.* ; (workshop—*atelier*) atelier, *m.* To keep a — ; *tenir un
magasin, une boutique.* To keep — ; *garder le
magasin, la boutique.*

shop-board (-bôrde), *n.,* établi, *m.*

shop-book (-bouke), *n.,* livre de comptes, *m.*

shop-boy (-boï), *n.,* garçon de magasin, *m.*

shop-girl (-gheurle), *n.,* fille de boutique ;
demoiselle de magasin, *f.*

shopkeeper (-kip'-), *n.,* marchand, *m.,* marchande, *f.* ; boutiquier, *m.,* boutiquière, *f.*

shop-lifter (-lif'-), *n.,* voleur (m.), voleuse (*f.*), qui
vole dans les boutiques.

shop-lifting, *n.,* vol dans une boutique, *m.*

shopman, *n.,* commis de magasin, de boutique ; commis, *m.*

shopwoman (-woum'-), *n.* V. **shop-girl.**

shorage (shôr'édje), *n.,* droit de rivage, *m.*

shore (shôre), *n.,* (of the sea—*de la mer*)
rivage, *m.,* côte, *f.* ; (of a river—*de rivière*) rive, *f.* ;
(carp.) étai, étançon ; (nav.) accotoir, accore, *m.*
To go on — ; *aller à terre.* Along the — ; *près
de la terre.*

shore, *v.a.,* (carp.) étayer ; étançonner ;
(nav.) accorer.

shoreless, *adj.,* sans côte ; sans rivage.

shoreling, or **shorling,** *n.,* peau de mouton
vivant qui vient d'être tondu, *f.* ; mouton qui
vient d'être tondu, *m.*

shorl, *n.,* (min.) schorl, *m.*

shorn, *past part.* V. **shear.**

short, *adj.,* court ; (insufficient—*insuffisant*)
insuffisant ; (abrupt—*brusque*) brusque ; (brief—
bref) bref ; (stature) petit ; (of earth, marl—*de
terre, de marne*) friable ; (gram., mus.) bref ;
(limited—*limité*) borné. Nothing — of murder ;
rien au-dessous du meurtre. To be — of ; *être
court de ; être à court de* ; (of things—*de choses*)
être au-dessous de. To fall — ; *être à court ; manquer ; être insuffisant.* To fall — of ; *être au-dessous de.* To fall — of my expectations ; *ne pas
répondre à mon attente.* To fall — in ; *manquer à.*
To cut — ; *couper court à ; couper la parole à* ;
abréger. To stop — ; *s'arrêter tout court.* In — ;
bref, en un mot, enfin.

short, *n.*, court, *m.* To know the long and the — of; *savoir le long et le court de.*

short, *adb.*, court; peu; tout court.

short-breathed (-brth'de), *adj.*, qui a l'haleine courte.

shortcoming (-keun'-), *n.*, insuffisance, faute. *f.*; déficit, *m.*

short-dated (-dét'-), *adj.*, à courte date; à courte échéance.

shorten (short'n), *v.a.*, raccourcir; accourcir; (to abridge—*abréger*) abréger; (to diminish—*diminuer*) diminuer; (to deprive—*priver*) priver; (to contract—*resserrer*) resserrer.

shorten. *v.n.*, se raccourcir; s'accourcir; s'abréger; diminuer; se resserrer.

shortening, *n.*, raccourcissement; accourcissement; resserrement, *m.*; diminution, *f.*

shorthand, *n.*, sténographie, *f.* — writer; *sténographe, m.*

shortjointed (-djwai'n't'-), *adj.*, court-jointé.

short-lived (-liv'de), *adj.*, d'une courte vie; qui vit peu; de courte durée; passager.

shortly, *adv.*, bientôt; sous peu; dans peu de temps; (briefly—*brièvement*) brièvement.

shortner, *n.*, personne qui abrège, qui raccourcit, qui diminue; chose qui abrège, qui diminue, qui raccourcit, *f.*

shortness, *n.*, court; (of space—*d'espace*)peu d'étendue, *m.*; (stature) petitesse; (brevity—*brièveté*) brièveté; (imperfection) faiblesse, imperfection; (mus., gram.) brièveté, *f.* — of breath; *courte haleine, f..* — of waist; *courte taille, f.* — of memory; *faiblesse de la mémoire, f.*

short-rib, *n.*, fausse côte, *f.*

shorts (shortze), *n.pl.*, son, *m.sing.*

shortsight (-saïte), *n.*, vue courte, myopie, *f.*

short-sighted (-saït'-), *adj.*, qui a la vue courte, myope.

short-sightedness, *n.*, vue courte, myopie, *f.*; (fig.) manque de clairvoyance, *m.*

short-waisted, *adj.*, à courte taille.

short-winded, *adj.*, à courte haleine.

short-witted, *adj.*, qui a peu d'esprit.

shot, *n.*, (of a fire-arm—*d'une arme à feu*) coup; (from a bow—*d'un arc*) trait, *m.*; (for a rifle—*de fusil*) balle, *f.*; (for cannon—*de canon*) boulet; (for a fowling-piece—*de fusil de chasse*) plomb, *m.*; (reach—*portée*) portée, *f.*; (reckoning —part) écot, *m.* Small —; *menu plomb, m.*; dragée, *f.* Grape-—; *mitraille, f.* Canister-—; case-—; *boîte à mitraille, f.* Bar-—; *boulet ramé.* Chain-—; *boulets enchaînés.* Random-—; *coup perdu.* Spent —; *balle morte.* To waste powder and —; *tirer sa poudre aux moineaux.* To be a good —; *être bon tireur.* To fire a —; *tirer un coup.* Without firing a —; *sans coup férir.* Within —; *à portée de.* Within ear-—; *à la portée de l'oreille.* Within cannon —; *à portée de canon.* At a —; *d'un seul coup.*

shot, *v.a.*, charger à boulet

shot-belt, *n.*, ceinture de chasse, *f.*

shot-casting (-cast'-), *n.*, fonte de plomb de chasse, *f.*

shot-free (-fri), *adj.* V. **scot-free**.

shot-hole (-hôle), *n.*, trou de balle, *m.*

shot-locker, *n.*, parc à boulets, *m.*

shotten (shot't'n), *adj.*, en saillie; (of a bone —*d'un os*) disloqué; (of fish—*d'un poisson*) qui a déchargé son frai.

shot-tower, *n.*, tour à plomb de chasse, *f.*

should (shoude), *v.* V. **shall**.

shoulder (shôl'deur), *n.*, épaule; (tech.) languette, *f.* To shrug up one's —s; *hausser les épaules.* Round —s; *dos rond, m.sing.* To put one's — to the wheel; *mettre la main à la pâte.* To show any one the cold —; *battre froid à quelqu'un.*

shoulder (shôl-), *v.a.*, charger sur les épaules; (to push—*pousser*) pousser avec violence; (arms) porter

shoulder-belt, *n.*, baudrier, *m.*; bandoulière. *f.*

shoulder-blade, *n.*, omoplate, *f.*

shouldered (shôl-deurde), *adj.*, à épaules. Broad- —; *qui a les épaules larges; aux larges épaules.* Round- —; *qui a le dos rond.*

shoulder-knot (-note), *n.*, nœud d'épaule, *m.*

shoulder-shotten (-shot't'n), *adj.*, épaulé.

shoulder-slip, *n.*, dislocation de l'épaule, *f.*

shoulder-strap, *n.*, bretelle, *f.*

shoulder-wrench (-rè'n'she), *n.*, effort d'épaule, *m.*

shout (shaoute), *v.n.*, crier; pousser un cri; faire des acclamations; crier.

shout, *n.*, cri; cri de joie, *m.*; acclamation, *f.*

shouter, *n.*, personne qui fait des acclamations, *f.*

shouting, *n.*, acclamation, *f.*; cris, *m.pl.*

shove (sheuve), *v.a.*, pousser. To — away; *repousser, éloigner.* To — from; *repousser de, éloigner de.* To — back; *faire reculer; repousser.* To — down; *pousser en bas; faire tomber.* To — off; *repousser; (a boat—un bateau) pousser à l'eau.* To — out; *pousser dehors; faire sortir.*

shove, *v.n.*, pousser. To — away; *pousser toujours; (to push off—s'éloigner) s'éloigner.* To — by; *bousculer.* To — off; *s'éloigner; pousser au large.*

shove (sheuve), *n.*, poussée, *f.* To give a — to; *pousser, donner une poussée à.*

shovel (sheuv'v'l), *n.*, pelle, *f.* Fire- —; *pelle à feu.*

shovel. *v.a.*, ramasser avec la pelle; jeter avec la pelle; amasser. To — in; *ramasser avec la pelle; jeter avec la pelle.*

shovelful (-foule), *n.*, pelletée, *f.*

shoveller (-leur), *n.*, (orni.) souchet, *m.*

show (shô), *v.a.*, (preterit, Showed; past part., Showed, Shown), montrer; faire voir; exposer à la vue; (to prove—*prouver*) démontrer; (to manifest—*témoigner*) manifester, témoigner, montrer; (to make known—*faire connaître*)faire connaître; (to explain—*expliquer*) expliquer; (attention, kindness, &c.—*attention, bonté, &c.*) témoigner, avoir. To — any one in; *introduire quelqu'un; faire entrer quelqu'un.* To — any one out; *reconduire quelqu'un.* To — any one up; *faire monter quelqu'un; (to unmask—démasquer) démasquer quelqu'un; montrer quelqu'un dans ses vraies couleurs.* To—off; *étaler; faire parade de.*

show, *v.n.*, se montrer. To — off; *poser; se donner des airs.*

show (shô), *n.*, (superficial appearance—*extérieur*) apparence, *f.*; (spectacle) spectacle; (ostentatious parade—*ostentation*) étalage, *m.*, ostentation, montre, parade; (pomp—*pompe*) pompe, *f.*, apparat, *m.*; (semblance) semblance, apparence, figure; (exhibition) exposition, *f.*; (external appearance—*extérieur*) extérieur; (phantom—*fantôme*) fantôme, *m.* Cattle-—; *exposition de bétail, f.* Dumb-—; *jeu muet, m.*; pantomime, *f.* To make a — of; *faire parade de; faire étalage de; étaler;* (to pretend—*feindre*) faire semblant de. For —; *pour les apparences; pour faire parade.*

show-bottle (-bot't'l), *n.*, (of chemists—*de pharmaciens*) flacon de montre, *m.*

show-bread (-brède), *n.*, pain de proposition, *m.*

show-case (-kéce), *n.*, montre, *f.*

shower, *or* **shewer** (shô-eur), *n.*, personne qui montre, qui fait voir, *f.*

shower (shaou-eur), *n.*, averse, ondée; (copious supply—*abondance*) pluie; (of blows, stones, &c.—*de coups, de pierres, &c.*) pluie, grêle, *f.* April —; *giboulée de Mars, f.*

shower (shaou-eur), *v.a.*, inonder de pluie; arroser; (to bestow liberally—*accorder libéralement*) verser, faire pleuvoir.

shower-bath (shaou-eur-bâth), *n.*, douche, *f.*

showerless (shaou-eur-), *adj.*, sans pluie; sans ondée.

showery (shaou-euri), *adj.*, pluvieux.

show-glass (-glâce), *n.*, montre, *f.*

showily (shô-ili), *adv.*, avec éclat; d'une manière voyante; pompeusement; fastueusement.

showiness (shô-i-), *n.*, éclat excessif, *m.*; pompe, *f.*; faste, étalage, *m.*

showman (shô-), *n.*, directeur de spectacle forain, *m.*

show-window (-dô), *n.*, montre, *f.*; étalage, *m.*

showy (shô-i), *adj.*, éclatant; voyant; fastueux.

shred (shrède), *n.*, bande, *f.*; lambeau; fragment, bout; (hort.) lien pour palisser, *m.*

shred. *v.a.*, couper en lambeaux.

shredless, *adj.*, sans lambeau.

shrew (shrou), *n.*, mégère; grondeuse; pie-grièche, *f.* — -mouse; *musaraigne*, *f.* Taming the —; *la mégère mise à la raison*.

shrewd (shroude), *adj.*, sagace; clairvoyant, pénétrant, malin, fin, rusé; (of things—*des choses*) fin, adroit, subtil, malin.

shrewdly, *adv.*, avec sagacité; avec clairvoyance; avec pénétration, avec malice, avec finesse; adroitement; subtilement; avec adresse.

shrewdness. *n.*, sagacité; clairvoyance, pénétration, malice, finesse, ruse, subtilité, adresse, *f.*

shrewish (shrou-ish), *adj.*, grondeur; acariâtre.

shrewishly (shrou-ish'-), *adv.*, en mégère; en grondeuse; en pie-grièche.

shrewishness (shrou-ish'-), *n.*, humeur acariâtre, humeur de mégère, *f.*

shriek (shrike), *n.*, cri; cri perçant, *m.*

shriek (shrike), *v.n.*, crier; jeter un cri perçant; jeter des cris. To — out; *crier, jeter les hauts cris*.

shrieking, *n.*, cris perçants, *m.pl.*

shrievalty (shriv'-), *n.*, fonctions de shérif, *f.pl.*; juridiction de shérif, *f.*

shrike (shraïke), *n.*, (orni.) lanier, laneret, *m.*; pie-grièche, *f.*

shrill, *adj.*, aigu; perçant; aigre, grêle; glapissant: (mus.) aigu.

shrill, *v.n.*, produire un son aigu; glapir. To — forth; *exprimer d'une voix aiguë; chanter d'une voix aiguë*.

shrillness, *n.*, son aigu, ton aigu; son perçant, ton perçant, *m.*

shrilly, *adv.*, d'un ton aigu, d'un ton perçant.

shrimp, *n.*, crevette, chevrette, *f.*; (pers.) bout d'homme, nain, *m.*, naine, *f.*

shrine, *n.*, châsse, *f.*; reliquaire; (fig.) autel, *m.*

shrink, *v.n.* (preterit and past part., Shrunk), rétrécir, se rétrécir, s'étrécir; reculer, se retirer; (to shrivel—*se rider*) se rider; (to diminish—*diminuer*) diminuer, baisser; (of wood—*du bois*) se contracter, se resserrer. To — back; *reculer*. To — from; *reculer devant; trembler devant; avoir horreur de*. To—up; *rétrécir; se rétrécir; s'étrécir; se recoquiller*.

shrink, *v.a.*, rétrécir; rider. To — to; *diminuer; se réduire à*.

shrink, *n.*, rétrécissement, étrécissement, *m.*: (contraction) contraction, *f.*

shrinkage (shri'nk'édge), *n.*, rétrécissement, étrécissement, *m.*

shrinker, *n.*, personne qui recule, *f.*

shrinking, *n.*, rétrécissement, *m.*; contraction; (act of running back—*se retirer*) action de reculer, de se retirer; (of timber—*des bois*) contraction, *f.*

shrive (shraïve), *v.a.* (preterit, Shrove; past part., Shriven), confesser.

shrivel (shriv'v'l), *v.n.*, se rider; se ratatiner; se recroqueviller.

shrivel, *v.a.*, faire ratatiner, faire recroqueviller; rider, grésiller.

shroud (shraoude), *n.*, (winding-sheet—*suaire*) linceul, suaire; (shelter—*abri*) abri, couvert, *m.* —s; (nav.) haubans, *m.pl.*

shroud (shraoude), *v.a.*, (to shelter—*couvrir*) mettre à l'abri, mettre à couvert, abriter, couvrir; (to dress for the grave—*ensevelir*) ensevelir, mettre dans un linceul, dans un suaire; (to conceal—*cacher*) cacher, couvrir, dérober à la vue.

shroud, *v.n.*, s'abriter.

shroudless, *n.*, sans linceul.

shroudy (shraoud'-), *adj.*, qui abrite; qui sert d'abri.

shrove-tide (shrov'taïde), *n.*, les jours gras, *m.pl.*

shrove-tuesday (-tiouz'dè), *n.*, mardi gras, *m.*

shrub (shreube), *n.*, (bot.) arbrisseau; arbuste; (drink) grog, *m.*

shrub (shreube), *v.a.*, purger d'arbrisseaux; purger d'arbustes.

shrubbery, *n.*, plantation d'arbrisseaux, *f.*; arbrisseaux, *m.pl.*

shrubby, *adj.*, plein d'arbrisseaux, *f.*; (resembling a shrub—*ressemblant à un arbuste*) qui ressemble à un arbuste; (consisting of shrubs—*consistant en arbrisseaux*) d'arbrisseaux.

shrug (shreughe), *n.*, haussement d'épaules, *m.*

shrug (shreughe), *v.a.*, hausser. To —, to — up one's shoulders; *hausser les épaules*.

shrug, *v.n.*, hausser les épaules.

shudder (sheud-), *v.n.*, frissonner; frémir.

shudder (sheud-), *n.*, frissonnement; frémissement, *m.*

shuffle (sheuf'f'l), *v.a.*, mettre en confusion; brouiller; mêler; (cards—*les cartes*) mêler, battre; (to cheat—*tromper*) duper, tromper. To — off; *éluder; se débarrasser de; éconduire*. To — into; *glisser adroitement dans; introduire adroitement dans*. To — any one out of anything; *escamoter quelque chose à quelqu'un*. To — up; *faire à la hâte; bâcler*.

shuffle, *v.n.*, (at cards—*aux cartes*) battre les cartes; (to change position—*changer de position*) changer de position; (to prevaricate—*biaiser*) tergiverser, chicaner, biaiser; (to shift—*s'arranger*) se tirer d'affaire, s'arranger; (to show the feet—*agiter les pieds*) battre des pieds; (to move with an irregular gait—*se mouvoir irrégulièrement*) traîner les jambes. To — along; *traîner les jambes*. To — off; *reculer honteusement*.

shuffle (sheuf'f'l), *n.*, (pushing—*poussée*) poussée, action de pousser, ☉poussade; (confusion) confusion, *f.*; (artifice) artifice, tour, *m.*; (evasion—*détour*) défaite, *f.*, faux-fuyant, *m.*

shuffler, *n.*, biaiseur, chicaneur, *m.*, chicaneuse, *f.*; (of cards—*aux cartes*) personne qui bat les cartes, *f.*

shuffling, *adj.*, (pers.) chicaneur, biaiseur; (of things—*des choses*) évasif.

shuffling, *n.*, action de mettre en confusion, *f.*; (irregular gait—*démarche traînante*) marche traînante, *f.*; (of cards—*des cartes*) battement des cartes, *m.*; (artifice) ruses, *f.pl.*, détours, artifices, *m.pl.*, chicane, *f.*

shufflingly, *adv.*, d'une manière évasive; par chicane, par artifice; (with an irregular gait—*avec une démarche traînante*) en traînant les pieds.

shun (sheune), *v.a.*, éviter; fuir.

shunless, *adj.*, inévitable.

shunt (sheu'n'te), *n.*, (railways) ligne, gare d'évitement, *f.*

shut (sheute), *v.a.*, fermer. To — again; *refermer*. To — close; *fermer bien*. To — from; *exclure de*. To — in; *enfermer*. To — off;

intercepter. To — out ; *exclure ;* (to intercept — *arrêter*) *intercepter ;* (to shut the door against— *fermer la porte au nez de*) *fermer la porte à.* -To be — out all night ; *trouver la porte fermée et être obligé de coucher dehors.* To — out from ; *exclure de.* To — up ; *fermer ;* (to confine— *enfermer*) *enfermer, mettre sous les verrous ;* (a door, a window—*une porte, une fenêtre*) *con- damner ;* (to end—*finir*) *terminer, finir.*

shut, *v.n.*, fermer ; se fermer.

shut, *n.*, action de fermer, clôture, *f.*

shutter, *n.*, personne qui ferme, *f.* ; (of a window—*de fenêtre*) volet, *m.*, persienne, *f.* ; (door—*de porte*) guichet, *m.*

shuttle (sheut't'l), *n.*, navette, *f.*

shuttle-cock. *n.*, volant, *m.* Battledore and — ; *volant, m.*

shy (sha'ye), *adj.*, timide ; sauvage, farouche ; (reserved—*réservé*) réservé ; (suspicious—*soup- çonneux*) soupçonneux, ombrageux ; (cautious— *prudent*) circonspect, prudent ; (of horses—*des chevaux*) ombrageux. To be — of using ; *crain- dre d'employer.*

shy (sha'ye), *v.n.*, faire un écart ; être om- brageux ; être sur l'œil.

shyly, *adv.*, timidement ; avec réserve ; avec prudence, avec circonspection.

shyness (sha'ye-nèce), *n.*, timidité ; sau- vagerie ; retenue ; réserve ; (of horses—*des chevaux*) nature ombrageuse, *f.*

sialagogue (saï-al-a-goghe), *n.*, (med.) sia- lagogue, *m.*

siberian (si-bi-), *adj.*, sibérien ; de la Sibérie.

siberite (sib'i-raïte), *n.*, sibérite, *f.*

sibilant, *adj.*, sifflant, sibilant.

sibilant, *n.*, (gram.) lettre sifflante, *f.*

sibilation (-lé-), *n.*, sibilation, *f.*

sibyl. *n.*, sibylle, *f.*

sibylline (-laïne), *adj.*, sibyllin.

sicamore, *n.* V. **sycamore**.

siccative, *adj.*, siccatif.

siccative, *n.*, siccatif, *m.*

siccity (sik-ci-), *n.*, siccité, *f.*

sice (saïze), *n.*, (at dice—*aux dés*) six, *m.*

sick, *adj.*, (ill—*malade*) malade ; (affected with nausea—*atteint de nausées*) qui a des nausées, qui a mal au cœur. — of ; *dégoûté de ; las de.* — of a fever ; *malade de la fièvre.* To feel :—*avoir mal au cœur ; avoir des nausées.* To be — at stomach ; *avoir mal au cœur.* To be — at heart ; *avoir la mort dans le cœur, dans l'âme.* To turn —; *commencer à éprouver des maux de cœur.* To make — ; *donner mal au cœur à.* — unto death ; *malade à la mort.*

sick. *n.pl.*, malades, *pl. m., f.*

sick-berth (-beurth), *n.*, (nav.) poste des malades, *m.*

sick-brained (sik-bré'n'de), *adj.*, malade d'esprit.

sicken (sik'k'n), *v.a.*, rendre malade ; (to dis- gust—*dégoûter*) lasser, ennuyer, dégoûter ; (to make squeamish—*donner mal au cœur*) faire soulever le cœur à.

sicken, *v.n.*, tomber malade ; (to be satiated —*se rassasier*) se rassasier ; (to languish—*languir*) languir. To— of ; *se dégoûter de.* To — at ; *éprouver des maux de cœur à.* I —ed at the sight of that thing ; *la vue de cette chose me fit éprouver des maux de cœur, me souleva le cœur.* To — into ; *dégénérer en.*

sickener (sik'k'n-), *n.*, ennui, *m.* ; chose ennuyeuse, *f.* To give any one a — ; *embêter, ennuyer quelqu'un.*

sickish, *adj.*, maladif ; (nauseating—*qui cause des nausées*) nauséabond. To feel — ; *avoir un léger mal de cœur.*

sickishness, *n.*, disposition au mal de cœur, qualité de ce qui est nauséabond, *f.*

sickle (sik'k'l), *n.*, faucille, *f.*

sickled (sik'k'l'de), *adj.*, à faucille.

sickliness, *n.*, défaut de santé, *m.* ; mau- vaise santé ; (of places, climates—*de lieux, de climats*) insalubrité, *f.*

sick-list, *n.*, (milit., nav.) rôle des malades, *m.*

sickly, *adj.*, (pers.) maladif, d'une mauvaise santé ; (of things—*des choses*) maladif ; (producing disease—*producteur de maladie*) insalubre, mal- sain ; (languid—*en langueur*) languissant. To grow — ; *devenir maladif ; languir.*

sickly, *adv.*, d'une manière maladive.

sickness, *n.*, maladie, *f.* ; (nausea—*nausée*) mal de cœur, *m.* Sea— ; *mal de mer, m.*

side (saïde), *n.*, côté ; flanc ; (edge, border— *bord*) bord ; (of a mountain—*de montagne*) versant ; (party—*parti*) parti, *m.* Along— ; *bord à bord.* Blind— ; *côté faible.* Off— ; (man.) *hors montoir, m.* Near— ; (man.) *mon- toir, m.* Wrong— ; *mauvais côté ;* (of stuffs—*des étoffes*) envers, *m.* — by — ; *côte à côte.* On all —s ; *de tous côtés ; de toute part.* On the other — ; *de l'autre côté.* On whose — are you? *de quel parti êtes-vous?* To change —s ; *changer de parti.* To choose —s ; (for games—*au jeu*) *choisir les partenaires.* To hold one's —s for laughter ; *se tenir les côtés de rire.*

side, *adj.*, de côté ; latéral ; (indirect) in- direct, oblique.

side (saïde), *v.n.*, (to lean on one side—*pen- cher*) pencher d'un côté ; (pers.) s'engager dans un parti. To — with ; *se mettre du même côté que ;* (to agree with—*s'entendre avec*) *se mettre de l'opinion de.*

side-board (-bôrde), *n.*, buffet, *m.* ; (nav.) planche de roulis, *f.*

side-box, *n.*, loge de côté, *f.*

side-face, *n.*, figure de côté, de profil, *f.*

sidelong (saïd'lon'gn), *adj.*, de côté ; obli- que.

sidelong. *adv.*, de côté ; latéralement.

sideral (sid'èr-), *or* **sidereal** (saï-di-ri-), *adj.*, des astres ; sidéral.

siderated (sid'èr'ét'-), *adj.*, sous l'influence des planètes.

siderocalcite (sid'i-ro-cal-çaïte), *n.*, (min) sidérocalcite, *m.*

sideroclepte (sid'i-ro-klèp'-ti), *n.*, (min.) sidéroclepte, *m.*

siderographical (sid-i-), *adj.*, sidérogra- phique.

siderographist (sid'i-), *n.*, sidérographe, *m.*

siderography (sid'i-), *n.*, sidérographie, *f.*

side-saddle (-sad'd'l), *n.*, selle de femme, *f.*

sidesman (saïd'z'-), *n.*, marguillier adjoint ; (party-man—*homme de parti*) homme de par- ti, *m.*

side-stick, *n.*, (print.) biseau de côté, *m.*

side-table (-té-b'l), *n.*, table à placer contre le mur ; (for children—*pour les enfants*) petite table, *f.*

sideways (saïd'wèze), *or* **sidewise** (-waïze), *adv.*, de côté ; latéralement.

siding (saïd'-), *n.*, engagement dans un parti, *m.*

siding, *or* **siding-place**, *n.*, (railways) gare d'évitement ; voie de chargement et de déchar- gement, *f.*

sidle (saïd'l), *v.n.*, marcher de côté ; (to be on the side—*être couché sur le côté*) être sur le côté.

siege (sidje), *n.*, siège, *m.* To lay — to ; *mettre le siège devant, faire le siège de, assiéger.* To raise the — ; *lever le siège.*

sienite (saï-i-naïte), *n.* V. **syenite**.

siesta. *n.*, sieste, *f.*

sieve (sive), *n.*, crible ; sas ; tamis, *m.*

sieve-box, *n.*, caisse à crible, *f.*

sift, *v.a.*, cribler ; tamiser ; passer au crible, au sas, au tamis ; (fig.) sonder. To — out ; *venir à bout de découvrir ;* (to scrutinize— *approfondir*) *examiner scrupuleusement, appro- fondir.*

sifter, *n.*, cribleur, *m.*, cribleuse, *f.* ; (sieve —*tamis*) tamis, sas, crible, *m.*

sifting, *n.*, tamisage ; sassement ; (fig.) examen, approfondissement, *m.* —s ; *criblure, f.sing.*

sigh (sa-ye), *n.*, soupir, *m.* To fetch a —; *jeter, pousser un soupir.*

sigh (sa-ye), *v.n.*, soupirer. To — over; *gémir sur.* To — after; *soupirer après.*

sigh, *v.a.*, se lamenter sur; pleurer; (to express by sighs—*exprimer par des soupirs*) exprimer par des soupirs.

sigher (sa'y'eur), *n.*, personne qui soupire, *f.*; soupirant, *m.*

sighing (sa'yigne), *n.*, soupirs, *m.pl.*

sight (saïte), *n.*, (faculty of vision—*faculté de voir*) vue ; (act of seeing—*action de voir*) vue, -vision ; (view—*vue*) vue ; (eye—*œil*) vue, *f.*; regards, yeux, *m.pl.* ; (of a quadrant—*d'un quart de cercle*) lumière ; (of fire-arms—*d'armes à feu*) mire, *f.* ; (spectacle) spectacle, *m.*, vue, *f.* A fine — ; *un beau spectacle.* At — ; *à première vue; à livre ouvert ;* (com.) *à vue.* Three days after — ; *à trois jours de vue.* At first — ; *à première vue; de prime abord.* By — ; *de vue.* In — ; *en vue; à la portée de la vue.* Out of — ; *hors de vue.* Out of — out of mind ; *loin des yeux, loin du cœur.* In — of ; *à la vue de ; devant.* With in — ; *à portée de la vue.* Within — of ; *en vue de.* To come in — ; *commencer à paraître.* To lose — of ; *perdre de vue.* Not to lose — of, not to let out of one's — ; *ne pas perdre de vue.* To take — ; *viser ; prendre son point de mire.* To take a — of ; *jeter un coup d'œil sur.* To know by —; *connaître de vue.* I hate the —of him, her, &c. ; *sa présence m'est odieuse ; je l'ai en horreur ; c'est ma bête noire.* To lose, to recover one's — ; *perdre; recouvrer la vue.* To vanish out of — ; *disparaître.* ¦To take a —at any one; *faire un pied de nez à quelqu'un.*

sightless, *adj.*, privé de la vue ; aveugle ; (offensive—*désagréable à l'œil*) laid, vilain, qui blesse la vue.

sightlessly, *adv.*, aveuglément ; d'une manière qui blesse la vue.

sightlessness, *n.*, cécité, *f.* ; aveuglement, *m.*

sightliness, *n.*, beauté, *f.* ; charme, *m.*

sightly, *adj.*, beau ; beau à voir ; charmant ; (open to the view—*visible*) en vue, visible.

sightsman (saït'z'-), *n.*, personne qui lit la musique à première vue, *f.*

sigil (sidj'-), *n.*, sceau, *m.*

sigillative (sidj'-), *adj.*, bon pour cacheter ; de cire.

sigmoid, *or* **sigmoidal** (-moïd'-), *adj.*, sigmoïde.

sign (saïne). *n.*, signe, *m.* ; (sign-board—*enseigne*) enseigne, *f.* ; (alg., med., astron.) signe, *m.* To give —s of ; *donner signe de.* — -manual ; *seing, m.*

sign (saïne), *v.a.*, signer.

signal (sig-nal), *n.*, signal, *m.*

signal (sig-nal), *adj.*, signalé.

signal-chest (-tshèste), *n.*, coffre aux signaux, *m.*

signal-gun (-gheune), *n.*, coup de canon de signal, *m.*

signalize (-'aïze), *v.a.*, signaler.

signal-light (-laïte), *n.*, fanal, *m.*

signally, *adv.*, d'une manière signalée.

signal-word (-weurde), *n.*, signal, mot d'ordre, *m.*

signatory (sig-na-teuri), *adj.*, de sceau.

signature (sig-na-tioure), *n.*, signature, *f.*; (stamp—*marque*) cachet, *m.*, marque, empreinte ; (mus.) armure, *f.* Joint — ; *signature collective.*

sign-board (-bôrde), *n.*, enseigne, *f.*

signer (saï'n'eur), *n.*, signataire, *m.*, *f.*

signet (sig-nète), *n.*, sceau ; cachet privé

du souverain, *m*, — -ring ; *bague à cachet, f.* Writer to the — (in Scotland) ; *avoué (en Écosse), m.*

significance, *or* **significancy** (sig-nif'-). *n.*, (meaning—*sens*) signification, *f.*, sens, *m.* ; (force) force, énergie, *f.* ; (importance) poids, *m.*, importance, *f.*

significant (sig-nif'-), *adj.*, significatif ; signifiant.

significantly, *adv.*, d'une manière significative.

signification (sig-ni-fi-ké-), *n.*, signification, *f.*

significative (sig-nif'i-ca-), *adj.*, significatif ; signifiant.

significatively, *adv.*, significativement, d'une manière significative.

significator (sig-nif'i-ké-teur), *n.*, signe, *m.*.

significatory, *adj.*, significatif.

signify (sig-ni-fa'ye),*v.a.*,(to mean—*signifier*) vouloir dire, signifier ; (to make known—*informer*) faire connaître ; (to import—*être important*) importer. To — to ; *signifier à, déclarer à, notifier à, annoncer à.* What does it — ? *qu'importe ?* It does not —; *cela ne signifie rien, cela ne veut rien dire; cela importe peu · n'importe.*

signior (sî'n'ieur), *n.*, seigneur, *m.*

signiory (sî'n'ieuri), *n.*, seigneurie, *f.*

sign-post (-pôste), *n.*, poteau d'enseigne, *m.*

silence (saï-), *n.*, silence, *m.* ; (taciturnity—*taciturnité*) taciturnité, *f.* To keep — ; *faire silence ; faire faire silence.* To reduce to — *réduire au silence.* —! *silence!*

silence (saï-), *v.a.*, réduire au silence ; imposer silence à ; interdire la parole à ; (to stop—*arrêter*) mettre un terme à, arrêter, faire cesser, étouffer. To — complaints ; *étouffer les plaintes.*

silent (saï-),*adj.*, silencieux ; muet ; (taciturn —*taciturne*) taciturne ; (calm—*calme*) calme, tranquille ; (of letters—*lettres*) muet. To be —; *faire silence, garder le silence ; se taire.* Keep those children — ; *faites garder le silence à ces enfants ; faites taire ces enfants.* To remain —; *garder le silence.* Real grief is —; *le vrai chagrin est muet.* — system ; *système du silence, m.*

silentiary (si-lè'n'shi-a-ri), *n.*, personne qui prête serment de garder le silence, *f.* ; (of a court—*d'un tribunal*) huissier audiencier, *m.*

silently (saï-), *adv.*, silencieusement ; en silence ; sans bruit.

silentness (saï-), *n.*, silence, *m.*

silesian (si-li-shi-), *adj.*, de Silésie.

silex (saï-lèkse), *or* **silica**,*n.*, (min.) silice,*f.*

silicious, *adj.*, siliceux.

silicium (si-lish'i-), *or* **silicon**, *n.*, (min.) silicium, *m.*

silicule (-kioule), **silicula** (-lik'iou-), *or* **silicle** (-'i-k'l), *n.*, (bot.) silicule, *f.*

siliculous (-kioul'-), *or* **siliculose** (-lôce), *adj.*, (bot.) siliculeux.

silique (si-lîke), *n.*, (bot.) silique, *f.*

siliquose (-kwôce), *or* **siliquous** (-kweuzs), *adj.*, (bot.) siliqueux.

silk, *n.*, soie, *f.* ; (for sewing—*à coudre*) fil de soie, *m.*, soie à coudre, *f.* Floss— ; *soie plate ; filoselle, f.* Raw — ; *soie crue ; soie grège.* Twisted — ; *soie torse, f.* Unbleached — ; *soie écrue.* Bleached — ; *soie blanchie.*

silk, *adj.*, de soie.

silk-district, *n.*, pays séricole, *m.*

silken (silk'n), *adj.*, de soie ; soyeux ; (soft—*doux*) soyeux, doux, moelleux.

silken (silk'n), *v.a.*, rendre doux, rendre moelleux.

silk-engine (-è'n'djine),*n.*, moulin à organsiner, *m.*

silk-goods (-goudze), *n.pl.*, soierie, *f.*; soieries, *f.pl.*

silk-handkerchief (-keur-tshife), *n.*, foulard, *m.*

silkiness, *n.*, nature soyeuse, *f.*; donœur, *f.*

silk-mercer (-meur-ceur), *n.*, marchand de soieries, *m.*, marchande de soieries, *f.*

silk-mill, *n.*, fabrique de soierie, *f.*

silk-spinner, *n.*, filateur de soie, *m.*

silk-spinning, *n.*, filature de soie, *f.*

silk-thread (-thrède), *n.*, fil de soie, *m.*

silk-thrower (-thrô-), *or* **silk-throwster** (-thrôst'-), *n.*, moulineur ; moulinier, *m.*

silk-throwing (-thrô-igne), *n.*, moulinage de la soie, *m.*

silk-trade, *n.*, commerce de la soierie, *m.*

silk-wares (-wér'ze), *n.*, soieries, *f.pl.*

silk-weaver (-wiv'-),*n.*,tisserand de soie, *m.*

silk-worm (-weurme), *n.*, ver à soie, *m.*

silky, *adj.*, de soie ; soyeux ; (soft—*doux*) soyeux, moelleux, doux.

sill, *n.*, seuil, racinal ; (of a door—*de porte*) seuil, *m.*; (of a window—*de fenêtre*) allège, *f.* Ground —; *semelle, f.*

sillabub (-beube), *n.* *V.* **syllabub.**

sillily, *adv.*, sottement ; bêtement ; niaisement.

silliness, *n.*, sottise, nigauderie ; niaiserie ; bêtise, *f.*

sillometer (-mît'-), *n.*, (nav.) sillomètre, *m.*

silly, *adj.*, sot, nigaud ; niais ; bête. He is — (idiotic—*idiot*); *c'est un idiot.* — thing ; *chose sotte, sottise, nigauderie ;* (pers.) *bête, f., nigaud, m., nigaude, f., sot, m., sotte, f.*

silurus (-liou-), *n.*, (ich.) silure, *m.*

silvan, *adj.*, des bois ; des forêts.

silvanite (-'nîte), *n.*, tellure, *m.*

silver, *n.*, (metal.) argent ; (money—*monnaie*) argent ; argent blanc, *m.*; (plate—*vaisselle, couverts, &c.*) argenterie, *f.*

silver, *adj.*, d'argent ; (of colour—*couleur*) argenté, argentin ; (of sound—*du son*) argentin.

silver, *v.a.*, argenter ; (a mirror—*un miroir*) étamer.

silver-beater (-bît'-), *n.*, batteur d'argent, *m.*

silver-bust (-beuste), *n.*, (bot.) barbe-de-Jupiter. *f.*

silverer, *n.*, argenteur, *m.*

silver-eyed (-a'ye-de), *adj.*, (of needles—*aiguilles*) à tête d'argent ; (of horses—*des chevaux*) vairon.

silver-fish, *n.*, (ich.) cyprin doré, poisson rouge, *m.*

silver-gilt (-ghilte), *n.*, vermeil, *m.*

silver-glance, *n.*, (min.) argent rouge, *m.*

silver-headed (-hèd'-), *adj.*, qui a la tête blanchie ; (of things—*des choses*) à pomme d'argent.

silvering, *n.*, argenture, *f.*

silver-leaf (-lîfe), *n.*, argent battu, *m.sing.*; feuilles d'argent, *f.pl.*

silverly, *adv.*, comme l'argent ; de couleur d'argent.

silver-mounted (-maou'n't-), *adj.*, monté en argent.

silver-plate, *n.*, argenterie ; vaisselle d'argent, *f.*

silver-shafted (-shâft'-), *adj.*, au carquois d'argent.

silversmith (-smith), *n.*, orfèvre, *m.*

silver-weed (-wîde), *n.*, (bot.) potentille ansérine ; argentine, *f.*

silver-winged (-wign'de), *adj.*, aux ailes argentines.

silvery, *adj.*, d'argent ; (of colour—*couleur*) argenté, argentin ; (of sound—*du son*) argentin.

simar (-mâr), *or* **simare** (-mére), *n.*, simarre, *f., m.sing.*

simaruba (-riou-), *n.*, (bot.) simarouba, *m.*

similar, *adj.*, semblable ; pareil ; similaire.

similarity, *n.*, ressemblance, similitude ; similarité, *f.*

similarly, *adv.*, de la même manière ; d'une manière semblable.

simile (-lî), *n.*, comparaison ; similitude, *f.*

similitude (-tioude), *n.*, similitude ; comparaison, *f.*

simitar, *n.* *V.* **scimitar.**

simmer, *v.n.*, bouillir lentement ; mitonner.

simoniac (-mô-), *or* **simonist**, *n.*, simoniaque, *m.*

simoniacal, *or* **simonious**, *adj.*, simoniaque.

simoniacally, *adv.*, avec simonie.

simony, *n.*, simonie, *f.*

simoom (-moume), *n.*, simoun, *m.*

simous (saï-), *adj.*, camus ; concave.

simpor, *n.*, sourire niais, *m.*

simper, *v.n.*, sourire niaisement.

simperer, *n.*, personne qui sourit niaisement, *f.*

simpering, *n.*, sourire niais, *m.*

simperingly, *adv.*, avec un sourire niais.

simple (si'm'p'l), *adj.*, simple.

simple, *n.*, simple, *m.*

simple, *v.n.*, recueillir des simples.

simple-hearted (-hârt'-), *adj.*, ingénu, candide.

simple-minded (-maï'n'd'-), *adj.*, simple, ingénu.

simple-mindedness (-maï'n'd'-), *n.*, ingénuité. candeur, simplicité, *f.*

simpleness, *n.*, simplicité, *f.*

simpler, *n.*, personne qui recueille des simples, *f.*

simpleton, *n.*, niais, nigaud, *m.*

simplicity, *n.*, simplicité, *f.*

simplification (-fi-ké-), *n.*, simplification, *f.*

simplify (-fa'ye), *v.a.*, simplifier.

simplist, *n.*, personne qui connaît les simples, *f.*

simply, *adv.*, simplement ; bonnement ; (merely—*simplement*) simplement, bonnement ; (foolishly—*sottement*) avec simplicité ; (of itself —*de soi*) de soi-même.

simulate (si'm'iou-), *v.a.*, feindre ; contrefaire, simuler.

simulation (si'm'iou-lé-), *n.*, simulation ; feinte, *f.*; déguisement, *m.*

simultaneous (-meul-té-ni-), *adj.*, simultané.

simultaneously, *adv.*, simultanément.

simultaneousness (-meul-té-ni-), *or* **simultaneity** (-meul-ta-ni-i-), *n.*, simultanéité, *f.*

sin, *n.*, péché, *m.* Original —; *péché originel*

sin, *v.n.*, pécher.

sinapism (-piz'm), *n.*, sinapisme, *m.*

since, *conj.*, puisque. — you like it ; *puisque vous l'aimez.*

since, *prep.*, depuis ; depuis que. — then ; *depuis ce temps. depuis lors.* — I saw him ; *depuis que je ne l'ai vu.*

since, *adv.*, depuis. Long —; *il y a longtemps.* Two years —; *il y a deux ans.* It happened —; *cela est arrivé depuis.*

sincere (-cîre), *adj.*, sincère ; de bonne foi.

sincerely, *adv.*, sincèrement.

sincereness, *or* **sincerity**, *n.*, sincérité ; bonne foi, *f.*

sinciput (-peute), *n.*, (anat.) sinciput, *m.*

sine (saïne), *n.*, (geom.) sinus, *m.*

sinecure (saï-ni-kioure, *ou* si'n'i-kioure), *n.*, sinécure, *f.*

sinecurist (saï-ni-kiour'-), *n.*, sinécuriste, *m.*

sine die (saï-nî-da'y'î), *adv.*, indéfiniment.

sinew (si'n'iou), *n.*, nerf ; tendon, *m.* —s ; (fig.) nerf, *m.sing.*

sinew, *v.n.*, attacher comme avec des tendons.

sinewed (si'n'iou'de), *adj.*, nerveux ; vigoureux.

sinewless, *adj.*, sans nerf ; sans vigueur ; énervé.

sinew-shrunk (-shreu'n'ke), *adj.*, (vet.) efflanqué.

sinewy (si'n'iou-i), *adj.*, nerveux.

sinful (-foule), *adj.*, pécheur ; criminel ; coupable de péché ; (of things—*des choses*) criminel, coupable.

sinfully. *adv.*, criminellement ; en pécheur.

sinfulness, *n.*, méchanceté ; criminalité, *f.*

sing (signe), *v.a.* (*preterit*, Sang ; *past part.*, Sung), chanter.

sing, *v.n.*, chanter ; (to make a shrill sound —*produire un son aigu*) siffler.

singe (si'n'dje), *v.a.*, flamber ; roussir.

singe (si'n'dje), *n.*, action de flamber, de roussir ; (slight burn—*brûlure*) légère brûlure, *f.*

singer (sign'eur), *n.*, chanteur, *m.*, chanteuse. *f.* ; (in a church—*d'église*) chantre ; (bird—*oiseau*) oiseau chanteur, *m.*

singing (sign'igne), *adj.*, qui chante ; (of birds —*des oiseaux*) chanteur.

singing (sign'igne), *n.*, chant ; (of the wind —*du vent*) sifflement.

singing-bird (-beurde), *n.*, oiseau chanteur, *m.*

singing-book (-bouke), *n.*, livre de chant, *m.*

singing-boy (-boï), *n.*, enfant de chœur, *m.*

singingly, *adv.*, en chantant.

singing-man, *n.*, chantre, *m.*

singing-master (-mâs-), *n.*, maître de chant, *m.*

singing-mistress, *n.*, maîtresse de chant, *f.*

singing-school (-skoule), *n.*, école de chant, *f.*

single (si'n'g'l), *adj.*, (one—*unique*) seul, simple, unique ; (individual—*personnel à*) individuel, particulier ; (uncompounded, not double —*simple, non composé*) simple ; (unmarried—*célibataire*) non marié, célibataire, dans le célibat ; (bot.) simple ; (in Scripture—*biblique*) simple, sincère. — combat ; combat singulier. — man ; homme non marié ; célibataire : homme dans le célibat ; garçon. — woman ; femme non mariée ; femme dans le célibat. — life ; célibat, *m.*

single (si'n'g'l), *v.a.*, choisir ; (to separate— *séparer*) séparer. To — out ; choisir ; distinguer de la foule, du nombre.

single-handed. *adj.*, seul ; tout seul.

single-hearted (-hârt'-), *adj.*, sincère ; honnête, franc.

single-heartedness (-hârt'èd'-), *n.*, sincérité, *f.*

singleness, *n.*, unité ; (sincerity—*franchise*) sincérité, *f.*

single stick, *n.*, bâton, gourdin ; jeu du bâton, *m.*

singly, *adv.*, (individually—*individuellement*) individuellement, un à un ; (sincerely—*franchement*) sincèrement ; (by one's self—*tout seul*) seul, à part.

singsong (sign'son'gn), *n.*, chant monotone, *m.*

singular (sign'ghiou-), *n.*, singulier, *m.*

singular (sign'ghiou-), *adj.*, singulier ; (remarkable—*remarquable*) singulier ; (not compound—*non composé*) simple ; (gram.) singulier, au singulier.

singularity, *n.*, singularité, *f.*

singularly, *adv.*, singulièrement ; (gram.) au singulier

sinical, *adj.*, (geom.) de sinus.

sinister, *adj.*, sinistre ; méchant ; (her.) gauche.

sinisterly, *adv.*, sinistrement ; d'une manière sinistre.

sinistrous, *adj.*, sinistre ; méchant ; (side— *côté*) gauche.

sinistrously, *adv.*, sinistrement ; d'une manière sinistre : avec méchanceté ; (of left-handed persons—*des gauchers*) en gaucher.

sink, *n.*, évier ; cloaque, *m.* ; (sewer—*égout*) égout, *m.*, (l.u.) cloaque, *f.* ; (print.) tremperie, *f.*

sink, *v.n.* (*preterit*, Sank, Sunk ; *past part.*, Sunk), aller au fond ; tomber au fond ; s'enfoncer ; (to decrease—*décroître*) diminuer, baisser, s'abaisser ; (to decline—*décliner*) décliner, s'affaiblir ; (to decay—*dépérir*) périr ; (to be overwhelmed—*être accablé*) succomber ; (to fall —*tomber*) se laisser tomber ; (of vessels—*des vaisseaux*) couler à fond ; (of price—*des prix*) baisser ; (of courage, of the spirits—*du moral*) être abattu ; (of patients—*des malades*) décliner, s'affaiblir ; (of the sun—*du soleil*) descendre ; (of buildings, &c.—*de bâtiments*) tasser, se tasser. To — down ; aller au fond, s'enfoncer ; (to fall prostrate—*tomber*) s'affaisser, tomber ; (of the sun—*du soleil*) descendre, se coucher. To — down on ; se laisser tomber sur. To — down to ; s'habituer à, se faire à ; (to decrease to—*décroître*) baisser jusqu'à, diminuer jusqu'à. To — into ; s'enfoncer dans ; (to penetrate—*pénétrer*) pénétrer dans, entrer dans ; (to fall into—*tomber*) tomber dans ; (to degenerate into—*dégénérer*) dégénérer en.

sink, *v.a.*, faire tomber au fond ; enfoncer ; (to degrade—*dégrader*) abaisser ; (to diminish— *décroître*) diminuer, faire baisser ; (to depress— *décourager*) abattre ; (to plunge into destruction —*ruiner*) perdre ; (to cause to decline—*faire décliner*) affaiblir ; (to waste—*prodiguer*) dissiper ; (fin.) amortir ; (of a ship—*un vaisseau*) couler à fond, couler bas ; (a well, a shaft—*un puits*) percer, creuser ; (money—*argent*) placer à fonds perdus : débourser. —ing the others ; non compris les autres.

sinker, *n.*, poids, (on a fish-line—*de ligne à pêcher*) plomb, *m.*

sinkhole (-hôle), *n.*, trou d'évier ; puisard, *m.*

sinking, *n.*, (of money—*d'argent*) placement à fonds perdus ; déb-oursés ; (fin.) amortissement : (of wells, shafts—*de puits*) percement, creusage ; (of buildings—*de bâtiments*) tassement, *m.*

sinking-fund (-feu'n'de), *n.*, fonds d'amortissement, *m.* ; caisse d'amortissement, *f.*

sinkstone (-stône), *n.*, pierre d'évier, *f.*

sinless, *adj.*, sans péché ; innocent ; impeccable.

sinlessness, *n.*, innocence ; impeccabilité, *f.*

sinner, *n.*, pécheur, *m.*, pécheresse, *f.*

sinnet, *n.*, (nav.) garcette, *f.*

sin-offering, *n.*, sacrifice expiatoire, *m.*

sinoper, *n.*, (min.) sinople, *m.*

sinople, *n.*, (her., min.) sinople, *m.*

sinter, *n.*, (min.) dépôt calcaire, *m.*

sinuate (si'n'iou-), *v.n.*, contourner ; faire aller en serpentant.

sinuate (si'n'iou-), *adj.*, (bot.) sinué.

sinuosity (si'n'iou-oss'-) ; *n.*, sinuosité, *f.*

sinuous. or **sinuose** (si'n'iou-), *adj.*, sinueux ; tortueux.

sinus (saï-), *n.*, ouverture ; cavité ; (geog.) baie. *f.* ; (anat.) sinus, *m.*

sip, *n.*, petit coup (of drinking—*en buvant*), *m.*

sip, *v.a.*, buvotter ; (to extract—*extraire*) extraire, sucer.

sip, *v.n.*, buvotter, siroter.

siphilis, siphilitic. V. **syphilis**, &c.

siphon (saï-), *n.*, siphon, *m.*

sipper, *n.*, personne qui buvotte, qui sirote, *f.*

sir (seur), *n.*, monsieur ; (before the name of a baronet or knight—*titre donné aux baronets et aux chevaliers*) sir, *m.* — count : seigneur comte.

sire (saeur), *n.*, père ; (in addressing the king —*du roi*) Sire, *m.* —s ; pères, aïeux, *m.pl.* Grand- ; grand-père, *m.*

siren (saï-), *n.*, sirène, *f.*

siren (saï-), *adj.*, de sirène.

sirius. *n.*, (astron.) Sirius, *m.*

sirloin (seur-loï'n), *n.*, aloyau, *m.* ; surlonge, *f.*

sirname. *V.* **surname.**

sirocco, *n.,* siroco, ☉ siroc, *m.*

sirrah, *n.,* coquin; fripon, *m.*

sirup (sir'eupe), *n.,* sirop, *m.*

siruped (sir'eup'te), *adj.,* au sirop.

sirupy, *adj.,* sirupeux.

siskin, *n.,* (orni.) tarin, *m.*

sister, *n.,* sœur, *f.* The fatal —s; *les Parques, f.pl.*

sisterhood (-houde), *n.,* société de sœurs, *f.*

sister-in-law (-lô), *n.,* belle-sœur, *f.*

sisterly, *adj.,* de sœur.

sit, *v.n.* (*preterit* and *past part.,* Sat), s'asseoir; être assis; (to stay—*rester*) rester, demeurer; (of assemblies, courts, judges, &c.—*d'assemblées, de tribunaux, de juges, &c.*) siéger, tenir séance, se réunir; (of clothes—*de vêtements*) aller; (of birds—*d'oiseaux*) couver; (for one's portrait— *pour un portrait*) poser. To be —ting; *être assis.* To — down; *s'asseoir.* To — down to table; *se mettre à table.* To — down before the town; (milit.) *mettre le siège devant la ville.* To be — -ting down; *être assis.* To — in judgment on; *juger.* To — in parliament; *siéger au parlement.* To — on; (to be imprinted on—*être empreint*) *être empreint sur, s'imprimer sur, se peindre sur;* (to become—*convenir*) *seoir à, convenir à.* To — heavy on; *peser sur.* To — up; *se tenir droit;* (to rise from a recumbent position—*se lever*) *se mettre sur son séant;* (not to go to bed—*ne pas se coucher*) *passer la nuit, veiller.* To—up with; *veiller.* To — close; *se serrer.* To — loose, tight; (of clothes—*des vêtements*) *être large;* être *étroit, être serré.*

sit, *v.a.,* asseoir; (a horse—*à cheval*) se tenir sur, monter. To — out; *rester jusqu'à la fin de.* To — one's self down; *s'asseoir.*

site (saïte), *n.,* situation, *f.;* emplacement; (of a landscape—*d'un paysage*) site, *m.*

sitfast (-fâste), *n.,* (vet.) cor; durillon, *m.*

sitter, *n.,* personne sédentaire; (paint.) personne qui pose, *n.,* modèle, *m.;* (hen—*poule*) couveuse, *f.*

sitting, *n.,* séance; (of a court—*d'un tribunal*) audience; (incubation) incubation; (in a church—*à l'église*) place; (paint.) séance, *f.*

sitting, *adj.,* assis; (of birds—*des oiseaux*) qui couve; (bot.) sessile.

situate, *or* **situated** (sit'iou-é), *adj.,* situé; (jur.) sis; (pers.) placé. This is how I am —; *voici comme je suis placé; voici ma position.*

situation (sit'iou-é-), *n.,* situation; (place— *emploi*) place, *f.,* emploi, *m.;* (condition) place, position, *f.* To have a good —; *avoir une bonne place, un emploi lucratif.* In a —; *en place.* Out of a —; *sans place.*

six (sikse), *adj.,* six.

six, *n.,* six, *m.* To be at —es and sevens; *être sens dessus dessous.*

sixfold (-fôlde), *adj.,* sextuple.

sixpence, *n.,* six pence; pièce de six pence (60 centimes), *f.*

sixpenny, *adj.,* de six pence.

sixscore (-scôre), *adj.,* cent vingt.

sixteen (-tîne), *adj.,* seize.

sixteenth (-tî'n'th), *adj.,* seizième.

sixth (siks'th), *adj.,* sixième.

sixth, *n.,* sixième, *m.;* (mus.) sixte, *f.*

sixthly (siks'th'-), *adv.,* sixièmement.

sixtieth (siks-ti-èth), *adj.,* soixantième.

sixty, *adj.,* soixante.

sizar (saï-), *n.,* étudiant servant (of the Cambridge university—*à l'université de Cambridge*), *m.*

size (saïze), *n.,* grandeur; taille; (bulk— *masse*) grosseur, *f.,* volume, *m.,* dimension, *f.;* (calibre) calibre, *m.;* (portion) portion, *f.;* (com.) numéro, *m.;* (glue—*colle*) colle; colle forte, *f.;* (tech.) encollage; (of shoemakers—*de cordonnier*) compas, *m.* A man of his —; *un homme de sa*

taille. What is your —? (for gloves, &c.—*de gants, &c.*) *quel est votre numéro?*

size (saïze), *v.a.,* ajuster; calibrer; (to cover with size—*enduire de colle*) coller; encoller.

sizeable (saïz'a-b'l), *adj.,* d'une bonne grosseur; de volume considérable.

sized (saïz'de), *adj.,* de grosseur; de taille; de volume; de grandeur. Middle— —; *de moyenne taille, de grandeur moyenne.*

sizer. *V.* **sizar.**

sizestick (saïz'-), *n.,* (of shoemakers—*de cordonnier*) compas, *m.*

siziness (saïz'-), *n.,* viscosité, *f.*

sizy (saïz'-), *adj.,* glutineux, visqueux; gluant.

skain. *V.* **skein.**

skate, *n.,* (ich.) raie, raie blanche, *f.;* (for sliding—*pour patiner*) patin, *m.*

skate, *v.n.,* patiner.

skater, *n.,* patineur, *m.*

skeet, *n.,* (nav.) écope, escope, *f.*

skeg, *n.,* (bot.) prune sauvage, *f.*

skegger (skèg'gheur), *n.,* saumoneau, *m.*

skein (ské'n'), *n.,* écheveau, *m.*

skeleton (skèl'é-), *n.,* (anat.) squelette, *m.;* (fig.) charpente; carcasse; (tech.) carcasse, monture, (of an umbrella—*de parapluie*) carcasse, *f.* — -key; crochet, *m.* — regiment; cadres *d'un régiment, m.*

skeptic. *V.* **sceptic.**

sketch (skètahe), *n.,* esquisse, *f.;* croquis, *m.;* ébauche, *f.*

sketch, *v.a.,* esquisser; ébaucher; croquer. To — out; esquisser; *faire le croquis de.*

sketch-book (-bouke), *n.,* cahier de croquis; album, *m.*

skew (skiou), *adv.,* obliquement; en biais.

skew, *adj.,* oblique; de biais.

skew-back, *n.,* (arch.) redan, *m.*

skew-bridge, *n.,* pont oblique, pont de biais, *m.*

skewer (skiou-eur), *n.,* brochette, *f.* Small —; *hâtelet, m.*

skewer, *v.a.,* attacher avec des brochettes.

skid, *n.,* chaîne à earrayer; enrayure; (nav.) défense, *f.*

skid, *v.a.,* enrayer.

skiff, *n.,* esquif, *m.*

skiff, *v.a.,* traverser dans un esquif.

skilful (-foul), *adj.,* adroit; habile; industrieux.

skilfully, *adv.,* adroitement; habilement.

skilfulness, *n.,* adresse; habileté, *f.;* talent, *m.*

skill, *n.,* habileté; dextérité; adresse, industrie, *f.;* savoir-faire, talent, *m.*

skilled (skilde), *adj.,* habile; adroit. —in; *versé dans.*

skilless, *adj.,* sans habileté; sans adresse; maladroit; sans talent.

skillet, *n.,* casserole; marmite, *f.*

skim, *v.a.,* écumer; écrémer; (fig.) écumer; raser, effleurer.

skim, *v.n.,* passer légèrement; glisser. To — over; *effleurer, raser.*

skim, *n.,* écume; (of milk—*du lait*) crème, *f.*

skimmer, *n.,* écumoire, *f.;* (orni.) bec-enciseaux, *m.*

skim-milk, *or* **skimmed-milk** (ski'm'de-), *n.,* lait écrémé, *m.*

skimming, *n.,* écrémage, *m.* —s; écume, *f.sing.*

skin, *v.a.,* écorcher; (to cover with skin— *couvrir de peau*) couvrir de peau; (to cover superficially—*couvrir légèrement*) couvrir superficiellement. To — a flint; *tondre sur un œuf.* To — over; *couvrir superficiellement.*

skin, *v.n.,* se couvrir de peau.

skin, *n.,* peau, *f.;* (of certain animals—*de quelques animaux*) cuir, *m.* To be nothing but —

and bone; *n'avoir que la peau et les os.* Next to one's —; *sur la peau.*

skin-deep (-dipe), *adj.*, de l'épaisseur de la peau; (fig.) superficiel, léger.

skinflint, *n.*, pince-maille, fesse-mathieu, ladre, *m.*

skink (skignʹk), *n.*, (zool.) scinque, *m.*

skinless, *adj.*, sans peau; qui a la peau fort mince.

skinner, *n.*, écorcheur; (dealer in skins—*marchand de peaux*) peaussier, *m.*

skinniness, *n.*, maigreur, *f.*; état décharné, *m.*

skinny, *adj.*, de peau; maigre; décharné.

skip, *n.*, saut; bond, *m.*

skip, *v.n.*, sauter, sautiller, bondir.

skip, *v.a.*, sauter; omettre, passer.

skip-jack (-djake), *n.*, parvenu, *m.*

skip-kennel (-kèʹn'-), *n.*, saute-ruisseau; galopin, *m.*

skipper, *n.*, (of a merchant vessel—*d'un navire marchand*) patron; (dancer—*danseur*) danseur, *m.*, danseuse, *f.*, sauteur, *m.*, sauteuse, *f.*; (thoughtless person—*étourdi*) étourdi; (ent.) ver de fromage, *m.*

skipping, *n.*, action de sauter, de danser, *f.*

skippingly, *adv.*, par sauts; par bonds.

skipping-rope (-rôpe), *n.*, corde; corde pour sauter, *f.*

skirmish (skeur-), *n.*, escarmouche; lutte, contestation, querelle, *f.*

skirmish (skeur), *v.n.*, escarmoucher.

skirmisher, *n.*, tirailleur, ☉escarmoucheur, *m.*

skirmishing, *n.*, escarmouche, *f.*

skirret, *n.*, (bot.) berle, *f.*, chervis, *m.*

skirt (skeurte), *n.*, (of a coat—*d'un habit*) pan, *m.*, basque; (of a gown—*de robe*) jupe, *f.*; (of animals—*d'animaux*) diaphragme, *m.*; (of a town, a forest, &c.—*de ville, de forêt, &c.*) lisière, extrémité, *f.*, bord, *m.*

skirt (skeurte), *v.a.*, border, longer.

skirt, *v.n.*, vivre au bord de; être sur les bords.

† **skirting**, *or* **skirting-board** (-bôrde), *n.*, plinthe, *f.*

skit, *n.*, raillerie, *f.*

skittish, *adj.*, (shy—*timide*) timide, sauvage; (fickle—*volage*) capricieux, volage, inconstant; (of horses—*des chevaux*) ombrageux.

skittishly, *adv.*, (shyly—*timidement*) timidement; (changeably—*avec inconstance*) avec inconstance.

skittishness, *n.*, timidité; (fickleness—*inconstance*) inconstance; (of horses—*des chevaux*) nature ombrageuse, *f.*

skittle, *n.*, quille (jouet), *f.*

skittle-ground (-graouʹn'de), *n.*, quillier, *m.*

skolezite (skolʹèzʹaïte), *n.*, (min.) scolésite, *f.*

skonce. *V.* **sconce**.

skreen. *V.* **screen**.

skulk (skeulke), *v.n.*, se cacher, se tenir caché. To — in; *entrer furtivement, à la dérobée.* To — out; *sortir furtivement, à la dérobée.*

skull (skeul), *n.*, crâne, *m.*

skullcap, *n.*, bonnet; (milit.) casque, *m.*

sky (skaʹye), *n.*, ciel, *m.*

sky-colour (-keulʹleur), *n.*, azur, bleu de ciel, *m.*

sky-coloured (-keulʹleurde), *adj.*, azuré, bleu de ciel.

sky-dyed (-daï-de), *adj.*, teint en azur, en bleu de ciel.

skyey, *adj.*, du ciel; éthéré.

skyish, *adj.*, qui ressemble au ciel.

sky-lark (-lârke), *n.*, alouette des champs, *f.*

sky-larking, *n.*, polissonneries; mauvaises plaisanteries; (toying—*badinage*) folâtreries, *f.pl.*

skylight (-laïte), *n.*, lucarne, *f.*; vasistas, *m.*; (nav.) claire-voie, *f.*

skyrocket, *n.*, fusée volante, *f.*

slab, *n.*, (metal.) plaque; (of stone—*pierre*) plaque, table, pierre plate, *f.*; (print.) marbre, *m.*; (carp.) planche; (for an epitaph—*de tombe*) pierre sépulcrale, (tablet—*tablette*) tablette, *f.*

slabber, *v.n.*, baver.

slabber, *v.a.*, baver sur.

slabberer, *n.*, personne qui bave, *f.*

slabbering, *adj.*, baveux.

slack, *n.*, (small coal—*de la houille*) petit charbon; (of ropes—*de cordages*) mou, *m.*

slack, *adj.*, lâche; (slow—*lent*) lent; (remiss—*négligent*) négligent, nonchalant; (weak—*faible*) faible, mou; (com.) faible.

slack, *adv.*, à demi; en partie.

slack, *or* **slacken**, *v.a.*, relâcher, détendre; (to relax—*relâcher*) relâcher de, se relâcher; (to mitigate—*mitiger*) affaiblir, adoucir; (to make slower—*ralentir*) ralentir; (to repress—*réprimer*) retenir, arrêter; (fire—*le feu*) amortir; (lime—*chaux*) éteindre. To — out; (nav.) *mollir.*

slack, *or* **slacken** (slakʹk'n), *v.n.*, se relâcher, se détendre; (to be remiss—*se relâcher*) se relâcher; (to become more slow—*devenir plus lent*) se ralentir; (to lose cohesion—*perdre sa cohésion*) mollir; (to abate—*diminuer*) diminuer, baisser; (to become less violent—*devenir moins violent*) diminuer d'intensité; (to flag—*pendre*) pendre; se relâcher; (of lime—*de la chaux*) s'éteindre.

slacked (slakʹte), *adj.*, éteint.

slacken (slakʹk'n), *n.*, scorie, *f.*

slacking, *n.*, (of lime—*de la chaux*) extinction, *f.*

slackly, *adv.*, d'une manière lâche, lâchement; (negligently—*négligemment*) négligemment, nonchalamment.

slackness, *n.*, relâchement, *m.*; (remissness—*négligence*) négligence, nonchalance, *f.*, relâchement, *m.*; (slowness—*lenteur*) lenteur; (weakness—*faiblesse*) faiblesse, mollesse, *f.*

slag, *n.*, scorie, *f.*

slake (sléke), *v.a.*, éteindre; (thirst—*la soif*) éteindre, étancher; (lime—*la chaux*) éteindre.

slam, *n.*, action de fermer bruyamment une porte; (at cards—*aux cartes*) vole, *f.*

slam, *v.a.*, fermer une porte bruyamment, avec violence; (at cards—*aux cartes*) faire la vole.

slander, *n.*, médisance; calomnie; (disgrace—*déshonneur*) honte, *f.*, opprobre; (ill name—*mauvaise réputation*) mauvais renom, *m.*, mauvaise renommée; (jur.) diffamation, *f.*

slander, *v.a.*, médire de; calomnier.

slanderer, *n.*, médisant, *m.*, médisante, *f.*; calomniateur, *m.*, calomniatrice, *f.*; (jur.) diffamateur, *m.*, diffamatrice, *f.*

landering, *adj.*, médisant.

slanderous, *adj.*, (of things—*des choses*) de médisance, calomnieux; diffamatoire, diffamant; (pers.) médisant.

slanderously, *adv.*, avec médisance; calomnieusement.

slanderousness, *n.*, caractère diffamatoire, *m.*

slang, *n.*, argot, *m.*

slank, *n.*, algue, *f.*

slant, *v.a.*, rendre oblique, faire biaiser.

slant, *v.n.*, être oblique; être en pente; biaiser.

slant, *or* **slanting**, *adj.*, oblique; de biais. Cut —; *coupé en biais, en talus.*

slant, *or* **slanting**, *n.*, direction oblique, *f.*; biaisement, talus, *m.*

slantingly, **slantly**, *or* **slantwise** (-waize), *adv.*, obliquement; en biais, en talus.

slap, *n.*, tape, claque, *f.*; coup, *m.* — on the face; *soufflet, m.*

slap, *adv.*, voilà que; pan!

slap, *v.a.*, taper; claquer; frapper; (any one's

face—*au visage*) souffleter. He —ped my face ;
il m'a donné un soufflet, il m'a souffleté.

slapdash, *adv.*, tout d'un coup ; pan !

slapper, *n.*, personne qui soufflette, *f.* That's
a — ! *en voilà un fameux ! en voilà une bonne !*

slapping. *n.*, action de frapper, *f.* ; coups ;
(on the face—*au visage*) soufflets, *m.,pl.*

slash, *n.*. taillade, coupure ; (on the face—*au
visage*) balafre, *f.*

slash,.*v.a.*,taillader ; (the face—*le visage*) balafrer ; (a whip—*un fouet*) faire claquer ; (to lash—
fouetter) fouetter. To— right and left ; *tailler
à droite et à gauche.*

slasher. *n.*, personne qui taillade, qui balafre, qui fouette, *m.*

slate. *n.*, ardoise, *f.* ; (min.) schiste, *m.*

slate. *v.a.*, couvrir en ardoise.

slate-axe (-akse), *n.*, hache à ardoise, *f.*

slate-clay, *n.*, argile schisteuse. *f.*

slate-coloured (-keul'leurde), *adj.*, ardoisé.

slate-knife (-naïfe),*n.*.couperet à ardoise,*m.*

slate-pencil, *n.*. crayon d'ardoise, *m.*

slate-quarry (-kwŏr-), *n.*, carrière d'ardoise,
ardoisière, *f.*

slater (-slét'-), *n.*, couvreur en ardoise, *m.*

slating (-slét'-), *n.*, toiture en ardoise, *f.*

slatter (slat'-),*v.n.*,s'habiller négligemment,
malproprement.

slattern, *n.*, femme négligente, femme malpropre, *f.*

slatternly, *adj.*, négligent, malpropre.

slatternly, *adv.*, négligemment ; malproprement.

slaty (slé-ti), *adj.*, d'ardoise ; (of colour—
couleur) ardoisé.

slaughter (slŏ-), *n.*, tuerie ; boucherie, *f.*
(massacre) massacre, *m.*

slaughter, *v.a.*, tuer, égorger ; massacrer
(animal) tuer, abattre.

slaughter-house (-haouce), *n.*, tuerie, *f.* ;
abattoir, *m.*

slaughterman, *n.*, abatteur, tueur, *m.*

slaughterous, *adj.*. meurtrier.

slave, *n.*, esclave, *m.*,*f.* A — to ; *esclave de.*

slave. *v.n.*, travailler comme un esclave ;
s'échiner.

slave-born. *adj.*, né dans l'esclavage.

slave-driver (-draïv'-), *n.*, commandeur
d'esclaves, *m.*

slave-grown (-grŏ'n), *adj.*, produit par le
travail des esclaves.

slave-like (-laïke), *adj.*, d'esclave ; comme
un esclave.

slave-owner (-ŏ'n'-), *n.*. propriétaire d'esclaves, *m.*

slaver (slév'-),*n.*. négrier ; bâtiment négrier ;
bâtiment de traite, *m.*

slaver (slav'-), *n.*, bave. *f.*

slaver (slav'-), *v.n.*, baver.

slaver (slav'-), *v.a.*, couvrir de bave.

slaverer (slav'-), *n.*, personne qui bave, *f.*

slavery (slév'-), *n.*, esclavage, *m.*

slave-ship, *n.*, négrier ; bâtiment négrier ;
bâtiment de traite, *m.*

slave-trade. *n.*, traite des noirs, traite des
nègres ; traite, *f.*

slavish (slév'-), *adj.*, d'esclave ; servile, assujettissant.

slavishly (slév'-), *adv.*, en esclave ; servilement.

slavishness (slév'-), *n.*, servilité, *f.*

slavonic (sla-), *adj.*, slave ; slavon, esclavon.

slavonic, *n.*, slavon. esclavon, *m.*

slay, *v.a.* (*preterit*, Slew ; *past part.*, Slain),
tuer, égorger ; massacrer.

slayer (slè-eur), *n.*, tueur, meurtrier, *m.*

sleaziness (slî-), *n.*, nature flasque, nature
molle, *f.*

sleazy (slî-). *adj.*, clair ; flasque, mou ; mince.

sled, *n.*, traineau, *m.*

sled, *v.a.*, transporter sur un traineau.

sledding, *n.*, transport en traineau, *m.*

sledge, *n.*, traineau ; (hammer—*marteau*)
marteau à deux mains, *m.*

sledge-driver (-draïv'-), *n.*, conducteur de
traineau, *m.*

sledge-hammer, *n.*, marteau à deux
mains, *m.*

sleek (slike), *adj.*, lisse ; luisant ; (of horses—
des chevaux) d'un beau poil ; (fig.) doux.

sleek. *v.a.*, lisser.

sleekly, *adv.*, doucement ; gentiment.

sleekness, *n.*, surface lisse ; (fig.) douceur *f.*

sleek-stone (-stône), *n.*, lissoir, *m.*

sleeky, *adj.*, lisse.

sleep (slipe), *n.*, sommeil, *m.* Want of — ;
d faut de sommeil, m.: insomnie, f. Sound.
deep — : *profond sommeil.* Restless — : *sommeil
agité.* To go to — ; *s'endormir.* He did not get
a wink of — all night ; *il n'a pu fermer l'œil de
toute la nuit.* To wake out of one's — ; *s'éveiller.*
To wake up out of one's —, to start up out of
one's — ; *se réveiller en sursaut.* To be dying
with — ; *n'en pouvoir plus de sommeil.* Overcome with — ; *accablé de sommeil.*

sleep (slipe), *v.n.* (*preterit* and *past part.*,
Slept), dormir : (to stay for the night, as at an
inn—*rester pendant la nuit à une auberge, &c.*)
coucher. He slept at my house last night ; *il a
couché chez moi cette nuit.* To — like a top ;
dormir comme une marmotte, comme un sabot. To
— in peace ; *reposer en paix.* To — till late in
the day ; *dormir fort avant dans la journée ; faire
la grasse matinée.* To — at night, in the day ;
dormir la nuit, le jour. To — out ; *découcher.* To
— soundly ; *dormir profondément.* To — off the
effects of wine, to — one's self sober ; *cuver son
vin.* To — a dream out ; *finir un rêve ; dormir
jusqu'à ce qu'on ait fini un rêve.*

sleeper, *n.*, dormeur, *m.*, dormeuse, *f.* :
(arch.) lambourde, traversine, semelle de bois ;
(in ships—*de vaisseau*) guirlande de genou ;
(railways) traverse, *f.* ; (animal) animal hiber-
nant, *m.*

sleepily, *adv.*, en dormant ; (heavily—*lourdement*) lourdement ; (stupidly—*stupidement*) bêtement.

sleepiness, *n.*, assoupissement, *m.* : envie
de dormir, *f.*

sleeping, *n.*, sommeil ; repos, *m.*

sleeping, *adj.*, endormi, dormant ; (of partners—*d'associés*) commanditaire. — partner ;
commanditaire, m.

sleepless. *adj.*, sans sommeil ; sans repos.
— nights ; *nuits sans sommeil ; insomnies, f.pl.*

sleeplessness, *n.*, insomnie, *f.*

sleepy. *adj.*, qui a sommeil : qui a envie de
dormir ; (asleep—*dormant*) endormi ; (somniferous—*soporifique*) somnifère, soporifique ;
(lazy—*paresseux*) inactif : (heavy—*lourd*) lourd ;
(of pears—*poire*) blette. To be, to feel — ; *avoir
sommeil : avoir envie de dormir.*

sleepy-head (-hède), *n.*, personne endormie. *f.* : paresseux, *m.*, paresseuse, *f.* ; (fam.)
endormi, *m.*. endormie, *f.*

sleepy-looking (-louk'-), *adj.*, qui a l'air
endormi, qui a l'air d'avoir sommeil.

sleet (slite), *n.*, grésil, *m.*

sleet, *v.n.*, grésiller.

sleety, *adj.*, de grésil.

sleeve (slive), *n.*, manche, *f.* To laugh in
one's — ; *rire dans sa barbe : rire sous cape.*

sleeve. *v.a.*, mettre des manches à.

sleeve-board (-bŏrde), *n.*, passe-carreau,
m.

sleeve-button (-beut't'n), *n.*, bouton de
manche, *m.*

sleeved (sliv'de), *adj.*, à manches.

sleeveless, *adj.*, sans manches.

sleigh (slè), *n.*, traineau, *m.*

sleighing (slè-igne), *n.*, transport par traineau, *m.*

sleight (slaïte), *n.*, ruse, *f.* ; tour d'adresse, escamotage, *m.* — *of hand* ; *passe-passe* ; *tour de passe-passe*, *m.*

sleightful (-foule), *or* **sleighty**, *adj.*, adroit ; rusé.

sleightily (slaït'-), *adv.*, adroitement, avec adresse.

slender (slè'n'-), *adj.*, mince ; svelte, délié, élancé ; (slight, weak—*léger*, *faible*) faible, léger ; (abstemious—*sobre*) sobre ; (not amply supplied —*peu fourni*) pauvre, chétif, exigu ; (small—*petit*) petit. — waist ; *taille svelte, taille élancée, f.* — blade ; *lame mince, f.* — stalk ; *tige déliée, f.* — repast ; *léger repas, m.* — hopes ; *faibles espérances, f. pl.*

slenderly, *adv.*, d'une manière élancée, d'une forme svelte ; légèrement, sobrement, pauvrement, chétivement ; faiblement.

slenderness, *n.*, finesse, *f.* ; état mince, *m.*, forme svelte, déliée, élancée ; (weakness—*faiblesse*) faiblesse, légèreté ; (spareness—*pauvreté*) sobriété, pauvreté, *f.* ; (want of plenty—*exiguité*) état chétif, *m.*, exiguïté, petitesse, *f.*

sley (slè), *n.*, peigne de tisserand, *m.*

slice (slaïce), *n.*, tranche ; (of poultry—*de volaille*) aiguillette ; (of a melon—*de melon*) côte ; (round slice—*tranche ronde*) rouelle ; (spatula—*spatule*) spatule, *f.* Fish—; *truelle, f.* — of bread and butter ; *tartine de beurre, beurrée, f.*

slice (slaïce), *v.a.*, couper par tranches, couper par aiguillettes.

slick, *adv.*, tout de suite ; d'emblée.

slide (slaïde), *n.*, glissade ; glissoire, *f.* ; (of umbrellas, parasols—*de parapluies, d'ombrelles*) coulant, *m.* ; (tech.) coulisse, *f.*, chariot ; (of a steam-engine—*de machine à vapeur*) tiroir, *m.* ; (inclined plane—*déclivité*) descente, *f.* ; (mines) filon argileux, *m.*

slide, *v.n.* (preterit, Slid, *past part.*, Slidden), glisser ; couler ; (mec.) mouvoir en coulisse. To — away ; *glisser toujours* ; (to pass—*s'écouler*) glisser, s'écouler. To — down ; *glisser en bas* ; *descendre en glissant.* To — in ; *se glisser dans, se faufiler dans.* To — into ; *tomber dans, passer insensiblement dans.*

slide, *v.a.*, glisser. To — in ; *glisser dans.*

slider (slaïd'-), *n.*, glisseur, *m.* ; (mec.) coulisse, *f.*

slide-rest, *n.*, support à coulisse, à chariot, *m.*

slide-valve, *n.*, soupape à tiroir, *f.*

sliding (slaïd'-), *n.*, glissade ; action de glisser, *f.*

sliding, *adj.*, glissant, à coulisse.

sliding-rule (-roule), *n.*, règle à calcul, règle logarithmique, règle à coulisse, *f.*

sliding-scale, *n.*, échelle mobile ; règle à calcul, *f.*

slight (slaïte), *adj.*, mince ; léger ; faible. A — wound ; *une légère blessure, f.*

slight, *n.*, manque d'égard, manque de respect, *m.*

slight (slaïte), *v.a.*, manquer d'attention à ; manquer à ; traiter sans égard ; négliger ; mépriser ; faire peu de cas de ; dédaigner.

slighter, *n.*, personne qui dédaigne, qui fait peu de cas de, qui méprise, qui néglige, *f.*

slighting, *n.*, mépris ; manque d'égard, *m.*

slightingly, *adv.*, avec peu d'égard ; avec mépris.

slightly, *adv.*, légèrement, négligemment ; à la légère ; faiblement.

slightness, *n.*, légèreté ; faiblesse, *f.*

slighty, *n.*, *adj.*, superficiel ; léger.

slily (slaï-), *adv.*, en sournois ; avec malice, avec ruse ; sournoisement.

slim, *adj.*, svelte, mince ; délié, élancé ; (slight—*léger*) léger, faible.

slime (slaïme), *n.*, vase *f.* ; limon, *m.*

slime-pit, *n.*, bassin de dépôt, *m.*

sliminess (slaï'm'-), *n.*, viscosité ; nature limoneuse, *f.*

slimness (sli'm'-), *n.*, forme svelte ; légèreté, faiblesse, *f.*

slimy (slaï'm'-), *adj.*, vaseux ; limoneux, visqueux.

sliness (slaï-), *n.*, fronde ; (for a broken limb—*pour un bras cassé*) écharpe ; (nav.) élingue, *f.* ; (blow—*coup*) coup de fronde ; coup, *m.* To carry one's arm in a — ; *porter, avoir le bras en écharpe.*

sling, *v.a.* (preterit and past part., Slung), lancer avec une fronde ; (to suspend—*suspendre*) suspendre ; (nav.) élinguer. To — the hammocks ; *tendre les hamacs.* To — any thing over one's shoulder ; *mettre quelque chose en bandoulière.*

slinger (slign'eur), *n.*, frondeur, *m.*

slink, *v.a.* (preterit and past part., Slunk), s'échapper ; se dérober. To — away ; *s'échapper à la dérobée, se dérober, s'esquiver, se retirer.* To — out ; *sortir à la dérobée ; s'esquiver.*

slip, *v.n.*, glisser, couler ; faire un faux pas. To — away ; *s'échapper, s'esquiver ; se dérober, s'en aller furtivement.* To — down ; *tomber.* To — in ; *glisser dedans ; entrer furtivement.* To — into ; *se glisser dans.* To — off ; *s'échapper, s'esquiver, se dérober, s'en aller furtivement.* To — off from ; *glisser de.* To — over ; *glisser sur, sauter.* To — out ; *glisser dehors ; s'échapper, s'esquiver, sortir furtivement.* To — out of ; *sortir de . . . . à la dérobée ; s'échapper de* ; (to throw off—*rejeter*) *se dégager de.* My foot —ped ; *mon pied glissa, le pied me glissa.*

slip, *v.a.*, glisser ; couler ; (to lose—*perdre*) perdre, laisser échapper ; (to escape from—*s'échapper*) quitter à la dérobée ; (to let loose—*lâcher*) lâcher ; (to throw off—*se débarrasser*) se dégager de ; (to tear off—*enlever*) arracher, enlever ; (cable) filer. To — in ; *introduire ; glisser dans ; couler dans.* To — into ; *glisser dans.* To — off ; *enlever, ôter.* To — on ; *passer, mettre.*

slip, *n.*, (sliding—*glissade*) action de glisser, glissade ; (fault—*erreur*) erreur, méprise, *f.* ; faux pas, *m.*, faute ; (long piece—*bande*) bande ; (leash —*attache*) laisse, *f.* ; (twig—*petite branche*) brin, plant, *m.*, bouture, *f.* ; (print.) placard, *m.* ; (thea.) coulisse ; (of a river, a harbour—*de rivière, de port*) cale, *f.* ; (writing-copy—*modèle d'écriture*) exemple ; (petticoat—*jupon*) jupon ; (geol.) déplacement de strates, *m.* — of land ; *bande de terre, f.* Land—; *éboulement de terre, m.* There's many a — between the cup and the lip ; *de la main à la bouche, se perd souvent la soupe.* To give any one the — ; *faire faux bond à quelqu'un ; fausser compagnie à quelqu'un ; planter quelqu'un là.* It is a — of the tongue ; *c'est un mot échappé.* He made a — of the tongue ; *la langue lui a fourché.* — of the pen ; *faute de plume, f.*

slip-board (-bôrde), *n.*, coulisse, *f.*

slip-knot (-note), *n.*, nœud coulant, *m.*

slipper, *n.*, pantoufle ; (of the pope—*du pape*) mule, *f.* ; (bot.) soulier de Notre-Dame, *f.*

slippered (slip'peurde), *adj.*, en pantoufles.

slipperily, *adv.*, d'une manière glissante.

slipperiness, *n.*, nature glissante ; (uncertainty—*incertitude*) incertitude ; (of the tongue —*de la langue*) volubilité, *f.*

slippery, *adj.*, glissant ; (not easily held—*difficile à tenir*) difficile à tenir ; (uncertain—*incertain*) incertain, peu sûr ; (unstable—*changeant*) peu stable, variable, inconstant ; (lubricious—*lascif*) lubrique. It is very — out of doors ; *il fait très glissant ; le pavé est très glissant, très gras.* — promises ; *des promesses peu sûres.*

slipshod, *adj.*, chaussé en savates. To go about — ; *traîner la savate.* — style ; *style décousu.*

slipslop, *n.*, ripopée, *f.*

slit, *v.a.* (preterit and past part., Slit), fendre.

slit, *v.n.*, se fendre.
slit, *n.*, fente, *f.*
slitter, *n.*, fendeur, *m.*, fendeuse, *f.*
slitting, *n.*, fenderie, *f.*
slitting-mill, *n.*, fenderie, *f.*
sliver (slaï-), *v.a.*, couper par tranches.
sliver (slaï-), *n.*, tranche, *f.*
slobber, *v.n.*, baver.
slobber, *v.a.*, baver sur.
slobber, *n.*, bave, *f.*
slobbery, *adj.*, baveux.
sloe (slô), *n.*, (bot.) prunelle, *f.*
sloe-tree (-trî-), *n.*, prunier épineux ; prunellier, *m.*
sloop (sloupe), *n.*, (nav.) sloop, sloupe, *m.*
slop, *v.a.*, boire salement ; répandre ; tacher, salir, avec un liquide.
slop, *n.*, gâchis, *m.* —s ; rinçure, *f.* ; (mean liquor—*mauvaise boisson, mélange*) ripopée, *f.* V. **slops**.
slop-basin (-béss'n), *or* **slop-bowl** (-bôl), *n.*, bol à rinçure, *m.*
slope (slôpe), *n.*, pente, *f.* ; talus ; penchant, *m.* ; (in a garment—*de vêtements*) échancrure, *f.*, biais, *m.*
slope (slôpe), *v.a.*, incliner ; couper en biais ; taluter ; échancrer.
slope, *v.n.*, pencher ; aller en pente, aller en talus ; biaiser, aller en biais.
slopewise (slôp'waïze), *or* **slopingly** (slôp'-), *adv.*, obliquement ; en biais ; avec échancrure ; en talus.
sloping (slôp'-), *adj.*, de biais ; échancré ; (of land—*de terrain*) en talus, en pente.
sloping (slôp'-), *n.*, pente, *f.* ; biais ; (of land—*de terrain*) talus, *m.*, rampe, pente, obliquité, *f.*
slop-pail (-pèle), *n.*, seau aux eaux sales, *m.*
sloppiness (slop'-), *n.*, état bourbeux, état boueux, *m.*
sloppy, *adj.*, gâcheux ; humide, bourbeux.
slops, *n.pl.*, habits de pacotille, de camelote ; pantalons ; caleçons, *m.pl.* ; literie, *f.* ; eaux sales, *f.pl.* ; mauvaise nourriture liquide, telle que soupe, &c., *f.*
slop-seller (slop'sèl'eur), *n.*, confectionneur d'habits de pacotille, *m.*
slop-shop, *n.*, boutique d'habits de pacotille, *f.*
slot, *n.*, barre de bois, *f.* ; (ant.) foulées, *f. pl.*, voie, *f.*, (of a deer—*du chevreuil*).
sloth (slôth), *n.*, (idleness—*paresse*) paresse, fainéantise ; (slowness—*lenteur*) lenteur, *f.* ; (mam.) paresseux, *m.*
slothful (slôth'foule), *adj.*, paresseux ; fainéant ; indolent.
slothfully, *adv.*, d'une manière paresseuse, avec fainéantise, en fainéant ; avec paresse ; en paresseux.
slothfulness, *n.*, paresse ; fainéantise ; indolence, *f.*
slot-hole (-hôle), *n.*, rainure, *f.*
slouch (slaoutshe), *n.*, inclination ; (gait—*allure*) démarche lourde, *f.* ; (pers.) gros manant, *m.*
slouch (slaoutshe), *v.n.*, marcher en inclinant le corps ; avoir une démarche de paysan, lourde.
slouch, *v.a.*, rabattre ; rabaisser.
slouched (slaoutsh'te), *adj.*, rabattu. — hat : *chapeau rabattu*.
slouching, *adj.*, incliné ; rabattu ; rabaissé.
slough (sleufe), *n.*, peau ; dépouille ; (med.) exfoliation gangreneuse, *f.*
slough (sleufe), *v.n.*, (med.) s'exfolier.
slough (slaou), *n.*, fondrière, *f.* ; bourbier, *m.*
sloughy (slaou-î), *adj.*, bourbeux.
sloughy (sleuf'î), *adj.*, gangreneux.
sloven (sleuv'e'n), *n.*, homme malpropre ; saligaud, *m.*, saligaude ; femme malpropre, *f.*

slovenliness (sleuv'è'n'-), *n.*, malpropreté ; saleté ; négligence, *f.*
slovenly, *adj.*, négligent ; malpropre, sale.
slovenly, *adv.*, malproprement ; négligemment.
slow (slô), *adj.*, lent ; (late—*en retard*) tardif ; (dull—*stupide*) lourd ; (inactive—*inactif*) indolent, paresseux ; (of clocks, watches—*des pendules, des montres, &c.*) en retard. That clock is ten minutes too — ; *cette horloge est en retard de, retarde de dix minutes.* To be — of speech ; *parler lentement.*
slow, *v.a.* and *n.*, ralentir ; se ralentir.
slowly, *adv.*, lentement ; avec lenteur ; tardivement.
slowness, *n.*, lenteur ; (dullness—*stupidité*) lourdeur, *f.* ; (dilatoriness — *manque d'activité*) naturel lent, *m.* ; (of clocks, watches—*de pendules, de montres, &c.*) retard, *m.*
slow-paced (-pés'te), *adj.*, qui a le pas lent.
slow-worm (-weurme), *n.*, orvet, *m.*
slub (sleube), *n.*, boudinage, *m.*
slub (sleube), *v.a.*, boudiner.
slubber, *n.*, boudineur, *m.*, boudineuse, *f.*
slubber, *v.a.*, bousiller ; salir.
slubberdegullion (sleub'beur-dî-gheul-lieune), *n.*, (triv.) vaurien ; va-nu-pieds, *m.*
slubbing (sleub'-), *n.*, boudinage, *m.*
slubbing-machine (-ma-shîne), *n.*, boudinoir, *m.*
slue (sliou), *v.a.*, (nav.) faire pivoter.
slug (sleughe), *n.*, (mol.) limace, *f.* ; limaçon ; (lazy fellow—*fainéant*) fainéant, paresseux ; (hindrance—*difficulté*) obstacle ; (for a gun—*de fusil*) lingot, *m.*, chevrotine, *f.*
sluggard (sleug-garde), *n.*, fainéant, *m.*, fainéante, *f.* ; paresseux, *m.*, paresseuse, *f.* ; dormeur, *m.*, dormeuse, *f.*
sluggard, *adj.*, paresseux ; fainéant ; apathique ; inerte.
sluggishly (sleug-ghish'-), *adv.*, avec paresse ; avec fainéantise ; avec apathie ; avec indolence ; avec inertie.
sluggishness (sleug-ghish'-), *n.*, paresse ; fainéantise ; inertie, *f.*
sluggy (sleug-ghî), *adj.*, (ant.) V. **sluggish**.
sluice (sliouce), *n.*, écluse ; vanne, *f.*, clapet, *m.* ; (opening—*ouverture*) issue ; (source) source, *f.* Falling — ; *barrage mobile, m.*
sluice (sliouce), *v.a.*, lâcher par une écluse ; lâcher par une vanne ; lâcher les chasses ; (to pour over—*verser*) verser à flots sur ; répandre à flots sur.
sluicy (sliouss'i), *adj.*, à flots ; par torrents.
slumber (sleu'm'-), *n.*, sommeil ; assoupissement ; repos, *m.*
slumber, *v.n.*, sommeiller ; dormir ; faire un somme.
slumberer, *n.*, personne qui sommeille, qui dort, *f.* ; dormeur, *m.*, dormeuse, *f.*
slumbering (sleu'm'-), *n.*, sommeil, assoupissement, *m.*
slumbering, *adj.*, qui sommeille.
slumberingly, *adv.*, en dormant, en sommeillant.
slumberous, *adj.*, qui invite au sommeil ; assoupissant ; (sleepy—*dormant*) endormi.
slur (sleur), *n.*, tache, *f.* ; (print.) barbouillage ; (mus.) coulé, *m.*, liaison, *f.*
slur (sleur), *v.a.*, (to soil—*salir*) tacher, salir ; souiller ; (to pass lightly—*toucher légèrement sur*) glisser sur, passer légèrement sur ; (to conceal —*cacher*) cacher, voiler ; (mus.) lier ; (print.) barbouiller. To — over ; *passer légèrement sur.*
slurring (sleur'-), *n.*, (mus.) liaison, *f.*
slut (sleute), *n.*, saligaude ; salaude ; souillon ; friponne, *f.*
sluttish, *adj.*, salaude ; de souillon ; de salaude, de saligaude ; sale, malpropre.

sluttishly, *adv.*, en salaude, en saligaude, en souillon, malproprement, salement.

sluttishness, *n.*, malpropreté ; saleté, *f.*

sly(sla'ye), *adj.*, sournois ; rusé ; fin ; (arch — *malicieux*) malin. On the —; *à la sourdine.*

sly-boots (-boutse), *n.*, sournois ; (arch — *child—espiègle*) petit malin, *m.*, petite maligne, *f.*, espiègle, *m.*, *f.*

slyly (sla'ye-li), *adv.*, finement, avec ruse, en sournois ; (archly—*maliciousement*) avec malice ; sournoisement, malicieusement.

smack, *n.*, (boat—*bateau*) bateau de pêche ; (kiss—*baiser*) gros baiser ; (taste—*saveur*) goût, *m.*, saveur ; (smattering—*connaissance imparfaite*) connaissance superficielle, teinture, *f.* ; (of a whip—*d'un fouet*) claquement, *m.* ; (slap—*claque*) tape, claque ; (small quantity—*petite quantité*) légère quantité, *f.*, soupçon, *m.*

smack, *v.n.*, (to kiss—*baiser*) baiser ; (of whips, of the lips—*d'un fouet, des lèvres*)claquer. To — of ; *avoir un goût de ; sentir le ; se ressentir de.*

smack, *v.n.*, (to kiss—*baiser*) baiser ; (to slap—*taper*) donner une claque à ; (a whip, the lips—*un fouet, les lèvres*) faire claquer.

smacking, *adj.*, qui claque ; (of kisses—*de baisers*) retentissant.

small (smŏl), *adj.*, petit ; (slender—*délié*) délié ; (fine—*menu*) fin, menu ; (minute—*exigu*) minime, exigu ; (weak—*faible*) faible, léger ; (not considerable—*sans importance*) peu considérable, peu important. — improvement ; *légers progrès, m.pl.* — beer ; *de la petite bière.*

small (smŏl), *n.*, partie mince ; (of an anchor—*d'ancre*) tige, *f.* ; (of the leg—*de la jambe*) bas, *m.* — of the back ; *chute des reins, f.*

smallage (-'édje), *n.*, (bot.) ache, *f.*

small-clothes (-clôze), *n.pl.*, culotte, *f.sing.*

smallness, *n.*, petitesse ; (fineness—*ténuité*) finesse, ténuité, *f.* ; (inconsiderableness—*manque d'importance*) peu d'importance, *m.*, faiblesse, exiguïté, *f.*

small-pox, *n.*, petite vérole, *f.*

smally, *adv.*, petitement ; en petite quantité.

smalt (smŏlte), *n.*, smalt ; bleu d'azur ; (blue glass—*verre bleu*) smalt, verre bleu, *m.*

smart (smârte), *adj.*, (pricking—*aigu*) cuisant, douloureux, vif, aigu ; (severe—*piquant*) mordant, poignant, piquant ; (vigorous— *vigoureux*) vigoureux, vif, rude ; (brisk—*fort*) bon, fort ; (pertinent—*à propos*) bon, vif, subtil, fin, à propos ; (spruce—*coquet*) beau, élégant, pimpant, coquet.

smart (smârte), *n.*, cuisson ; (anguish— *angoisse*) douleur poignante, *f.*

smart, *v.n.*, cuire ; (to feel pain of mind—*de douleur morale*) éprouver une vive douleur, souffrir. To — for ; *supporter la peine de.* To make any one — for any thing ; *faire payer cher quelque chose à quelqu'un.* My hand —s ; *la main me cuit.*

smarten (smârt'è'n), *v.a.*, faire beau. To — one's self up ; *se faire beau.*

smarting, *n.*, cuisson ; douleur vive, *f.*

smarting, *adj.*, cuisant ; douloureux.

smartly, *adv.*, (with pain—*avec douleur*) d'une manière cuisante, douloureusement ; (sharply—*vivement*) d'une manière mordante, d'une manière piquante, vivement ; (vigorously —*rudement*) vigoureusement, rudement ; (showily—*élégamment*) coquettement, avec recherche, élégamment.

smart-money (-meu'n'nè), *n.*, indemnité, *f.* ; dédit. *m.* ; gratification pour blessure, *f.*

smartness, *n.*, (poignancy—*douleur*) poignante, nature cuisante ; (vigour—*vigueur*) vigueur, rudesse ; (vivacity—*vivacité*) vivacité ; (of dress—*des vêtements*) coquetterie, élégance, *f.*

smart-ticket, *n.*, certificat de blessure, *m.*

smart-weed (-wîde), *n.*, (bot.) renouée versicaire, *f.*

smash, *r.a.*, écraser ; briser. To — to pieces ; *briser en morceaux.*

smatter. *V.* **smattering.**

smatter, *v.n.*, parler en ignorant. To — of ; *parler en ignorant de ; n'avoir qu'une connaissance superficielle de.*

smatterer, *n.*, demi-savant, bavard ignorant. homme superficiel, *m.*

smattering, *n.*, connaissance superficielle, teinture, teinte, *f.*

smear (smîre), *v.a.*, enduire ; couvrir ; barbouiller.

smell, *n.*, (faculty—*sens*) odorat ; (of a dog— *du chien*) flair, *m.* ; (odour—*odeur*) odeur, senteur, *f.*, parfum, *m.* To be offensive to the —; *blesser l'odorat.*

smell, *v.a.* (preterit and past part., Smelt, Smelled), sentir ; flairer. To — out ; *flairer, découvrir.* To — a rat ; *se défier de quelque chose, soupçonner quelque chose.*

smell, *v.n.*, sentir ; (to emit a bad odour— *émettre une mauvaise odeur*) sentir, sentir mauvais ; (of animals—*des animaux*) sentir, flairer. To —, — bad, nasty ; *sentir mauvais.* To — good, nice ; *sentir bon.* To — of smoke ; *sentir la fumée.* To — at ; *sentir, flairer.* Nasty —ing ; *qui sent mauvais.* Sweet —ing ; *qui sent bon ; odoriférant.*

smeller, *n.*, personne qui sent, *f.* ; flaireur ; (the nose—*le nez*) nez ; (blow—*coup*) coup de poing sur le nez, *m.*

smelling, *n.*, odorat, *m.*

smelling-bottle (-bot't'l), *n.*, flacon d'essence, de senteur, *m.*

smelt, *n.*, éperlan, *m.*

smelt, *v.a.*, fondre.

smelter, *n.*, (metal.) fondeur, *m.*

smeltery, *n.*, (metal.) fonderie, *f.*

smelting, *n.*, (metal.) fonte, *f.*

smerk (smeurke), *v.n.* *V.* **smirk.**

smew (smiou), *n.*, (orni.) plongeon, *m.*

smicker, *v.n.*, regarder amoureusement, lascivement.

smile (smaïle), *n.*, souris ; sourire, *m.*

smile (smaïle), *v.n.*, sourire. To — on ; *sourire à.* To — into ; *sourire jusqu'à ce que:* To — any one into a good humour ; *sourire à quelqu'un jusqu'à ce qu'il soit de bonne humeur.*

smiler, *n.*, personne qui sourit, *f.*

smiling, *adj.*, souriant ; (of things—*des choses*) riant.

smilingly, *adv.*, en souriant.

smilingness, *n.*, air souriant, *m.*

smirch (smeurtshe), *v.a.*, salir, barbouiller.

smirk (smeurke), *v.n.*, sourire avec affectation ; affecter un air de bonté, de douceur.

smirk (smeurke), *n.*, sourire affecté, *m.*

smite (smaïte), *v.a.* (preterit, Smote ; past part., Smitten), frapper ; (to destroy—*détruire*) détruire ; (to punish—*punir*) châtier, frapper ; (to affect with passion—*rendre amoureux*) passionner, embraser, charmer. To be smitten with a woman ; *être épris, être passionné, être amoureux d'une femme.* To be desperately smitten with ; *être extrêmement épris de, éperdument amoureux de.*

smite (smaïte), *v.n.*, se heurter ; se choquer.

smiter (smaït'-), *n.*, personne qui frappe, *f.*

smith (smith), *n.*, forgeron ; (fig.) ouvrier ; auteur, *m.*

smithery (smith'euri), *n.*, forge, *f.* ; (work— *travail*) ouvrage de forge, de forgeron, *m.*

smithy (smithi), *n.*, forge, *f.*

smiting-line (smaït'igne-laïne), *n.*, (nav.) cordage pour baisser l'artimon, *m.*

smitten (smit't'n), *past part.* *V.* **smite.**

smock, *n.*, chemise de femme, *f.*

smock-faced (-fés'te), adj., pâlot ; d'un visage efféminé.

smockfrock, n., sarrau, m.

smockless, adj., sans chemise.

smoke (smôke), v.n., fumer ; (to raise dust—faire de la poussière) faire lever la poussière ; (to suffer—souffrir) souffrir. Do you —? fumez-vous !

smoke (smôke), v.a., fumer ; enfumer ; (to smell out—dépister) flairer, découvrir ; (to banter—railler) se moquer de, berner ; (tobacco—tabac) fumer. To — out ; enfumer ; chasser par la fumée.

smoke (smôke), n., fumée ; (vapour—vapeur) vapeur, f. To end in — ; s'en aller en eau de boudin.

smokebox, n., boîte à fumée, f.

smokeconsuming (-co'n'sioum'-), adj., fumivore.

smoke-dried (-draïde), adj., fumé.

smoke-dry (-dr'ye), v.a., fumer.

smoke-jack (-djake), n., tournebroche à courant d'air, m.

smokeless, adj., sans fumée.

smoker (smôk'-), n., fumeur, m.

smokiness, n., état enfumé, m.

smoking, adj., fumant. — -hot ; tout chaud. — -room. — -divan ; estaminet, m.

smoking, n., habitude de fumer ; action de fumer, f. To be fond of — ; aimer la pipe ; aimer à fumer.

smoky, adj., qui fume ; plein de fumée ; (black—noir) enfumé, noir. — chimney ; cheminée qui fume.

smooth (smouth), adj., uni, (even—égal) égal ; (not rough—uni) doux ; (glossy—lisse) lisse ; (gently flowing ; bland—s'écoulant avec tranquillité ; doux) doux ; (bot.) glabre.

smooth (smouth), v.a., aplanir ; lisser ; polir ; (to flatter—flatter) flatter ; (to calm—calmer) calmer, adoucir ; (to make even—aplanir) aplanir, unir, adoucir ; (to make easy, to free—favoriser) faciliter. To — down ; unir, adoucir ; (to cajole—cajoler) cajoler.

smoothen (smouth'n), v.a., unir ; aplanir.

smoother (smouth'-), n., personne qui aplanit, qui unit, f.

smooth-faced (smouth'fés'te), adj., imberbe ; (fig.) qui a l'air doux ; (b.s.) papelard. — villain ; tartufe, m.

smoothing (smouth'-), n., action d'unir, f. ; adoucissement ; aplanissement, m.

smoothing-iron (smouth'igne-aï-eur'n), n., fer à repasser, m.

smoothly (smouth'-), adv., uniment, doucement ; (with even flow—d'un cours égal) doucement ; (easily—facilement) aisément, facilement ; (blandly—avec douceur) doucement, avec douceur.

smoothness (smouth'-), n., égalité ; douceur, f.

smother (smeuth'eur), v.a., suffoquer ; asphyxier ; étouffer ; (to suppress—réprimer) étouffer, éteindre.

smother, v.n., suffoquer, étouffer.

smother (smeuth'-), n., grande fumée ; grande poussière, f.

smothering (smeuth'-), n., suffocation, f. ; étouffement, m.

smothering (smeuth'-), adj., étouffant, suffocant.

smoulder (smôld'-), v.n., couver.

smouldering (smôld'-), adj., qui couve.

smuggle (smeug'g'l), v.n., faire la contrebande.

smuggle, v.a., passer en contrebande ; faire passer par contrebande. To — in ; faire entrer par contrebande.

smuggled (smeug'g'l'de), adj., de contrebande.

smuggler, n., contrebandier ; (ship—navire) bâtiment chargé de contrebande, m.

smuggling, n., contrebande, fraude, f.

smut (smeute), n., noir ; (in corn—dans les blés) charbon, m., nielle, f. ; (obscenity—obscénité) gravelure, f.

smut (smeute), v.a., noircir ; tacher ; (corn—le blé) nieller, carier.

smut, v.n., se noircir ; (of corn—du blé) se carier.

smut-balls (-bôlze), n., (bot.) noir, m.

smutch (smeutshe), v.a., noircir ; barbouiller.

smuttily (smeut'-), adv., en noircissant ; (obscenely—avec obscénité) d'une manière graveleuse, salement.

smuttiness, n., noirceur, f. ; (obscenity—obscénité) nature graveleuse, obscénité, f.

smutty, adj., noir ; enfumé ; (of corn—du blé) carié, niellé ; (obscene) graveleux, grivois, obscène.

snack, n., portion ; part, f. ; (hasty repast—petit repas fait à la hâte) morceau, morceau sur le pouce, m. To go —s ; partager le gâteau. To take a — ; manger un morceau.

snaffle (snaf'f'l), n., bridon ; filet, m.

snaffle, v.a., mettre un bridon à.

snag, n., nœud, m. : (branch—branche) branche, f., jet, m.

snagged, or **snaggy**, adj., noueux.

snail (snél), n., limaçon ; colimaçon ; (pers.) lambin, m., lambine, f.

snail-clover (-klô-), or **snail-trefoil** (-trī-foil), n., (bot.) luzerne, f.

snail-like (-laïke), adj., de limaçon, comme un limaçon.

snail-like, adv., en limaçon ; (slowly—lentement) comme une tortue.

snake, n., serpent, m. A — in the grass ; quelque anguille sous roche. Rattle— ; serpent à sonnettes, m.

snake, v.a., (nav.) congréer.

snake-root (-route), n., (bot.) serpentaire ; bistorte, f.

snake's-head (-'hède), n., (bot.) fritillaire, f.

snake-weed (-wíde), n., (bot.) renouée, bistorte, f.

snake-wood (-woude), n., bois de couleuvre, m.

snakish (snék'-), adj., de serpent.

snaky (snék'-), adj., de serpent ; (having serpents—qui a des serpents) hérissé de serpents ; (sly—rusé) de serpent, rusé ; (winding—serpentant) tortueux, sinueux, qui va en serpentant.

snap, v.n., se casser, se rompre. To — at ; tâcher de mordre, de happer ; (fig.) gourmander, brusquer. To — in two ; se casser en deux.

snap, v.a., casser, rompre ; (a whip, one's fingers—un fouet, les doigts) faire claquer ; (to seize suddenly—saisir tout à coup) happer, empoigner. To — in two ; casser en deux. To — off ; casser. To — up ; happer ; (to reprimand—gourmander) brusquer, gourmander ; relever vivement.

snap, n., cassure, f. ; (bite—morsure) coup de dent ; (of a whip, the fingers—d'un fouet, des doigts) claquement ; (greedy fellow—glouton) glouton, m. ; (theft—vol) prise, f. ; (catch—crochet) crochet d'arrêt, m.

snapdragon, n., (bot.) muflier, m.

snapper, n., personne qui happe, f. ; bourru, m., bourrue ; personne hargneuse, acariâtre, f.

snappish, adj., disposé à happer ; hargneux ; (peevish—acariâtre) bourru, hargneux, acariâtre.

snappishly, adv., d'une manière bourrue ; d'une manière hargneuse.

snappishness, n., humeur bourrue ; humeur hargneuse, acariâtre, f.

snare (snére), n., piège, m.

snarl, v.n., grogner ; gronder.

snarler, n., grognard, m., grognarde. f. s,

grogneur, *m.*, grogneuse, *f.* ; homme hargneux, *m.*, femme hargneuse, *f.*

snarling, *adj.*, grognard, grogneur, bourru ; hargneux.

snary (snér'-), *adj.*, qui embrouille ; insidieux.

snatch, *n.*, action de saisir avidement ; prise, *f.* ; (fragment) petit morceau, fragment ; (short fit of vigour—*accès d'activité*) éclair, accès passager, *m.*, échappée, *f.* By —es ; *par accès ; par échappées.*

snatch, *v.a.*, saisir avidement ; se saisir de ; gripper. To — from ; *arracher à.* To — up ; *ramasser, empoigner.* To—at ; *chercher à saisir.*

snatch-block, *n.*, (nav.) poulie coupée, *f.*

snatcher, *n.*, personne qui saisit avidement, *f.* Body— ; *résurrectionniste ; voleur de cadavres, m.*

snatchingly, *adv.*, avidement ; brusquement.

sneak (snīke), *v.n.*, (to truckle—*s'humilier*) ramper : (to steal away—*s'esquiver*) s'en aller furtivement. To — away ; *s'en aller à la dérobée, s'en aller furtivement ; s'esquiver ; s'en aller la tête baissée.*

sneak, *n.*, homme rampant ; pied plat, *m.*

sneaking, *adj.*, rampant ; bas ; servile ; (niggardly—*mesquin*) ladre, chiche.

sneakingly, *adv.*, furtivement ; servilement.

sneakingness, *n.*, caractère rampant, *m.* ; servilité, *f.*

sneer (snīre), *n.*, rire moqueur, ris moqueur, *m.* ; ricanerie, *f.*

sneer (snīre), *v.n.*, ricaner. To — at ; *se moquer de.*

sneerer, *n.*, ricaneur, *m.*, ricaneuse, *f.*

sneering, *n.*, ricanement, *m.*

sneering, *adj.*, ricaneur.

sneeringly, *adv.*, en ricanant.

sneeze (snīze), *n.*, éternuement, *m.*

sneeze (snīze), *v.n.*, éternuer.

sneezing, *n.*, éternuement, *m.*

snicker, *or* **snigger** (snig'gheur), *v.n.*, rire sous cape.

sniff, *n.*, reniflement, *m.*

sniff, *v.a.*, aspirer.

sniff, *v.n.*, renifler.

sniffer, *n.*, renifleur, *m.*, renifleuse, *f.*

sniffing, *n.*, reniflement, *m.*

snigger. *V.* **snicker**.

sniggle (snig'g'l), *v.a.*, prendre au piège.

snip, *n.*, coup de ciseaux ; (shred—*lambeau*) morceau coupé, *m.* ; (share—*part*) portion, *f.*

snip, *v.a.*, couper.

snipe (snaïpe), *n.*, (orni.) bécassine, *f.*

snipper, *n.*, coupeur, *m.*, coupeuse, *f.*

snipsnap, *n.*, dialogue piquant, *m.*

snivel (sniv'v'l), *n.*, roupie, *f.*

snivel (sniv'v'l), *v.n.*, avoir la roupie ; (to cry —*pleurnicher*) pleurnicher.

sniveller (sniv'èl'-), *n.*, pleurnicheur, *m.*, pleurnicheuse, *f.*

snivelling (sniv'èl'-), *adj.*, pleurnicheur.

snivelling (sniv'èl'-), *n.*, pleurnicherie, *f.*

snively (sniv'èl'-), *adj.*, roupieux ; (whining —*pleurard*) pleurnichant.

snob, *n.*, personne de mauvais ton, *f.* ; goujat ; malotru, *m.*, malotrue, *f.*

snobbish. *adj.*, de mauvais ton, de malotru.

snore (snōre), *v.n.*, ronfler.

snore, *n.*, ronflement, *m.*

snorer, *n.*, ronfleur, *m.*, ronfleuse, *f.*

snoring, *n.*, ronflement, *m.*

snort, *v.n.*, ronfler.

snorting, *n.*, ronflement, *m.*

snot, *n.*, morve, *f.*

snotter, *n.*, (nav.) collier, *m.*

snotty, *adj.*, morveux ; couvert de morve.

snotty-nosed (-nōz'de), *adj.*, morveux.

snout (snaoute), *n.*, museau, *m.* ; (of a pig—*du*

---

cochon) groin : (of a wild boar—*du sanglier*) boutoir ; (of things—*des choses*) bout, bec ; (of a pipe, of a pair of bellows—*de pipe, de soufflet*) tuyau, *m.*

snouted (snaout'-), *adj.*, à museau, à groin, à bout, à bec, à tuyau.

snouty, *adj.*, qui ressemble à un museau.

snow (snō), *n.*, neige, *f.* There has been a fall of — ; *il est tombé de la neige.*

snow, *v.n.*, neiger ; tomber de la neige.

snow-ball (-bōl), *n.*, boule de neige, pelote de neige, *f.* —, —-tree ; (bot.) *boule de neige, viorne, f.*

snow-drift, *n.*, monceau de neige, *m.*

snow-drop, *n.*, (bot.) perce-neige, *f.*

snow-flake, *n.*, flocon de neige, *m* ; (bot.) nivéole printanière, *f.*

snow-flood (-fleude), *n.*, inondation produite par la fonte des neiges, *f.*

snow-like (-laïke), *adj.*, de neige ; comme la neige.

snow-shoe (-shou), *n.*, raquette, *f.*

snow-slip (-joli), *n.*, avalanche, *f.*

snow-water (-wō-), *n.*, eau de neige, *f.* ; la neige.

snow-white (-hwaïte), *adj.*, blanc comme la neige.

snowy (snō-i), *adj.*, de neige ; neigeux ; (white like snow—*blanc*) blanc comme la neige ; (pure—*sans tache*) pur, sans tache. — weather ; *un temps de neige.*

snub (sneube), *n.*, nœud (in wood—*dans le bois*), *m.*

snub (sneube), *v.a.*, (to nip—*couper*) couper le bout de ; (to rebuke—*gourmander*) réprimander, gourmander, brusquer.

snub-nose (-nōze), *n.*, nez, camus, *m.*

snub-nosed (-nōz'de). *adj.*, camus.

snuff (sneufe), *n.*, (of a wick—*de mèche*) lumignon ; (candle-end—*bout de chandelle*) bout de chandelle, *m.* ; of a candle—*de chandelle*) mouchure, *f.* ; (tobacco—*tabac*) tabac à priser, tabac, *m.* To take — ; *priser, prendre du tabac.* To be up to — ; *ne pas se moucher du pied.* To put up to — ; *dégourdir.*

snuff, *v.a.*, aspirer ; humer ; (to scent—*sentir*) flairer ; (a candle—*une chandelle*) moucher.

snuff, *v.n.*, renifler.

snuffbox, *n.*, tabatière, *f.* Musical — ; *tabatière à carillon, à musique, f.*

snuffer, *n.*, moucheur, *m.*

snuffers (sneuf'feurze), *n.pl.*, mouchettes, *f.pl.*

snuffers-stand (-feurze-), *n.*, porte-mouchettes, *m.*

snuffle (sneuf'f'l), *v.n.*, parler du nez ; nasiller, nasillonner.

snuffler, *n.*, (pers.) nasilleur, *m.*, nasilleuse ; (thing—*chose*) nasillard, *m.*, nasillarde, *f.*

snuffles (sneuf'f'lze), *n.pl.*, enchifrènement, *m.sing.*

snuffling, *n.*, nasillement, *m.*

snuff-taker (-ték'-), *n.*, priseur, *m.*, priseuse, *f.*

snuffy, *adj.*, barbouillé de tabac.

snug (sneughe), *v.n.*, se serrer ; se presser.

snug, *adj.*, (convenient—*agréable*) commode et petit ; (neat—*joli*) gentil ; (lying close—*resserré*) serré. He has a — place ; *il a une bonne petite place.* We are very — here ; *nous sommes on ne peut mieux ici.* A — house ; *une petite maison bien commode.*

snuggery (sneug'gheurl), *n.*, endroit petit et commode, *m.*

snuggle (sneug'g'l), *v.n.*, se serrer ; se presser, se tenir serré.

snugly, *adv.*, petitement et commodément ; en se serrant l'un contre l'autre, les uns contre les autres. To live — ; *vivre agréablement.*

snugness (sneug-), *n.*, commodité, petitesse et commodité, agréable petitesse, *f.*

32

so (sô), *adv.*, (thus—*ainsi*) ainsi; (in such a degree—*à un tel point*) si, tellement, tant; (in this manner—*de cette manière*) ainsi, de cette manière, comme cela, comme ça; (in the same manner—*de la même manière*) de même; (be it so—*soit*) soit. —, you are here at last! *eh bien! vous voici, enfin!* I think —; *je le pense.* —, he went; *ainsi, il est parti.* He is — obstinate; *il est si entêté; il est tellement entêté.* — many; — much; *tant.* —much the better; *tant mieux.* Make it —; *faites-le ainsi, faites-le de cette manière.* As blight destroys flowers, — does dissipation destroy the mind; *de même que la brousissure détruit les fleurs, ainsi la débauche détruit l'esprit.* — —; *ni trop mal ni trop bien; passablement; comme ça.* — that; *de sorte que; si bien que.* If —; *if it is —; s'il en est ainsi.* Not —; *il n'en est rien; il n'en est pas ainsi; non pas.* And — on; *et ainsi de suite; et ainsi du reste.* — it is; *c'est ainsi.* Mr. — and —; *Monsieur un tel.* — long as; *aussi longtemps que; tant que.* — far; *jusqu'ici; jusque là.* Why —? *pourquoi cela?*

so, *conj.*, pourvu que. — that; *de sorte que; si bien que;* (provided that—*à condition que*) *pourvu que.*

soak (sôke), *v.a.*, tremper; abreuver, baigner. To — in; *absorber, boire.*

soak, *v.n.*, tremper; s'imbiber; (to drink intemperately—*boire avec excès*) pomper. To — into; *s'infiltrer dans; pénétrer dans.*

soak (sôke), *n.*, trempage, m. To put in —; *mettre tremper.*

soakage (sôk'édje), *n.*, action de tremper, *f.*; trempage, m.

soaker, *n.*, personne qui trempe, *f.*; (hard drinker—*ivrogne*) biberon, ivrogne, m.

soaking, *adj.*, qui trompe; qui s'infiltre; qui pénètre. A — rain; *une pluie battante, f.*

soap (sôpe), *n.*, savon, m. Mottled —; *savon marbré; savon madré.* Soft —; *savon noir;* (cajolery—*cajolerie*) flagornerie, cajolerie, *f.* Shaving— —; *savon pour la barbe.* Scented —; *savon de toilette; savon parfumé.*

soap, *v.a.*, savonner.

soapball (-bôl), *n.*, savonnette, *f.*

soapberry-tree (-bèr'ri-tri), *n.*, (bot.) savonnier, m.

soapboiler (-boïl'-), *n.*, savonnier, m.

soapdish, *n.*, boîte à savon, *f.*

soap-house (-haouce), *n.*, savonnerie, *f.*

soapstone (-stône), *n.*, pierre de lard, stéatite, pagodite, *f.*

soapsuds (-seudze), *n.pl.*, eau de savon, *f.*

soapwort (-weurte), *n.*, (bot.) saponaire, *f.*

soapy, *adj.*, savonneux.

soar (sôre), *n.*, essor; élan, m.

Soar (sôre), *v.n.*, prendre l'essor, son essor, s'élever. To — over; *planer sur.*

soaring, *n.*, essor, élan, m.

soaring, *adj.*, ardent; qui plane, qui s'élève.

sob, *v.n.*, sangloter; pousser des sanglots.

sob, *n.*, sanglot, m.

sobbing, *n.sing.*, sanglots, *m.pl.*

sober (sô-beur), *adj.*, sobre, tempérant; (not intoxicated—*non ivre*) pas ivre; (not mad—*pas fou*) sensé, raisonnable; (not visionary—*non visionnaire*) sobre, modéré; (grave) grave, sérieux; (calm—*posé*) calme, rassis. To be —; *être sobre;* (not to be drunk—*ne pas être gris*) *n'être pas ivre, n'avoir pas bu; être à jeun.*

sober (sô-), *v.a.*, dégriser; désenivrer; (fig.) rendre raisonnable.

soberly, *adv.*, sobrement, avec tempérance; sensément; raisonnablement; modérément, gravement, sérieusement.

sober-minded (-maï'n'd'-), *adj.*, modéré; sage, raisonnable.

sober-mindedness, *n.*, modération; sagesse, *f.*

soberness (sô-), *or* **sobriety** (so-braï-i-), *n.*,

sobriété, tempérance; (moderation) sagesse, modération, *f.*; (calmness—*calme*) calme, sang froid; (seriousness—*gravité*) sérieux, m.

sociability (sô-shi-), *n.*, sociabilité, *f.*

sociable (sô-shi-a-b'l), *adj.*, sociable; qui aime la société.

sociable. *n.*, calèche à bateau, *f.*

sociableness, *n.*, sociabilité, *f.*

sociably (sô-shi-), *adv.*, sociablement, d'une manière sociable.

social (sô-shal), *adj.*, social; sociable.

socialism (sô-shal'iz'm), *n.*, socialisme, m.

socialist (sô-shal'-), *n.*, socialiste, m., *f.*

sociality (sô-shal'-) sociabilité, *f.*

socially (sô-shal'-), *adv.*, socialement; d'une manière sociale; d'une manière sociable.

socialness (sô-shal'-), *n.* V. **sociality**.

society (sô-çaï-i-), *n.*, société, *f.*; monde, m.; réunion, *f.* Fashionable —; *beau monde.* To go into —; *aller dans le monde.* Charitable —; *société de bienfaisance.* Learned —; *société littéraire.*

socinian, *n.*, socinien, m., socinienne, *f.*

socinian. *adj.*, socinien.

socinianism (-'iz'm), *n.*, socinianisme, m.

sock, *n.*, chaussette, *f.*; (of a plough—*de charrue*) soc; (shoe—*chaussure*) socque; (comedy —comédie) socque, brodequin, m., comédie, *f.*

socket, *n.*, emboîture, *f.*; (of a tooth—*de dent*) alvéole, m.; (of the eye—*de l'œil*) orbite; (of tools—*d'outils*) douille, *f.*; (of a lamp—*de lampe*) bec, m.; (of a candlestick, &c.—*de chandelier, &c.*) bobèche, *f.*

sockless, *adj.*, sans chaussettes.

socle (sok'l), *n.*, (arch.) socle, m.

socratic, *or* **socratical** (-al), *adj.*, socratique.

socratically, *adv.*, d'après la méthode de Socrate.

socratism (-'iz'm), *n.*, philosophie de Socrate, *f.*

socratist, *n.*, disciple de Socrate, m.

sod, *n.*, gazon, m.; motte, *f.*

sod, *adj.*, de gazon, de mottes.

sod, *v.a.*, gazonner.

soda (sô-), *n.*, (min.) soude, *f.*

sodality, *n.*, société; confrérie, *f.*

soda-water (-wô-), *n.*, eau de Seltz, *f.*

sodden. V. **seethe**.

soddy, *adj.*, revêtu de gazon; plein de mottes.

sodium (sô-), *n.*, sodium, m.

sodomite (-aïte), *n.*, sodomite, m.

sodomy, *n.*, sodomie, *f.*

soever (so-èv'-), *adj.*, . . . que ce soit; . . . qui soit . . . How—; *quelque . . . que.* What things —; *quelques choses que ce soient.*

sofa (sô-), *n.*, canapé, sofa, sopha, m.

sofett (sô-), *n.*, petit canapé, m.

soffit, *n.*, (arch.) soffite; plafond de cor niche, m.

soft, *adj.*, mou, mol. mollet; (to the touch—*au toucher*) doux; (delicate—*délicat*) délicat; (yielding—*facile*) doux, facile, coulant; (tender —tendre) tendre; (mild—*doux*) doux; (effeminate—*efféminé*) mou, efféminé; (still—*calme*) calme, paisible, doux; (weak—*faible*) faible; (foolish—*sot*) sot, niais; (gram.) doux.

soft, *adv.*, mollement; doucement; paisiblement.

soft! *int.*, doucement!

soften (sof'f'n), *v.a.*, amollir, ramollir; (to make less harsh, to palliate—*pallier*) adoucir; (to make easy—*faciliter*) rendre facile; (to calm —apaiser) calmer, adoucir, apaiser, radoucir; (to make less glaring—*adoucir*) adoucir; (to enervate—*énerver*) efféminer, amollir, affaiblir; (to move—*toucher*) attendrir, adoucir, fléchir; (paint.) adoucir.

soften (sof'f'n), *v.n.*, s'amollir, se ramollir; s'adoucir; devenir facile; se calmer, s'adoucir;

s'apaiser, se radoucir, devenir efféminé. s'affaiblir, s'attendrir, fléchir.

softening (sof'f'n'-),*n.*, amollissement; adoucissement; affaiblissement; attendrissement; (paint.) adoucissement, *m.*

soft-headed (-hèd'-), *adj.*, niais; sot.

soft-hearted (-hårt'-). *adj.*, tendre, compatissant.

softly (soft'-), *adv.*, mollement; (of sound— *du son*) bas, doucement; (placidly—*paisiblement*) avec calme, paisiblement, doucement; (tenderly—*tendrement*) tendrement, doucement, avec tendresse; (gently—*délicatement*) doucement.

softner (sof'n'eur), *n.*, personne qui amollit, qui ramollit, qui adoucit, qui pallie; chose qui amollit, qui ramollit, qui adoucit, qui pallie; (paint.) brosse à adoucir, *m.*

softness (soft'-), *n.*, mollesse; (to the touch —*au toucher*) douceur; (mildness—*douceur*) douceur; (effeminacy—*mollesse*) délicatesse efféminée, mollesse; (weakness—*faiblesse*) faiblesse; (silliness—*bétise*) niaiserie; (gentleness—*douceur*) douceur, facilité; (timorousness—*timidité*) timidité, *f.*

soho! (so-hô), *int.*, holà!

soil (soïl), *n.*, (stain—*tache*) tache, souillure; (dirt—*ordure*) ordure, saleté, *f.*; (manure—*fumier*) engrais, fumier; (land—*terre*) sol, terroir, *m.*, glèbe, terre, *f.*

soil (soïl), *v.a.*, salir; souiller; (to defile— *souiller*) profaner, souiller; (to manure—*fumer un champ*) engraisser, fumer; (cattle—*bestiaux*) nourrir de vert.

soil-bound (-baou'n'de), *adj.*, attaché à la glèbe, au sol.

soiling, *n.*, nourrissage au vert, *m.*

soilless (soïl-lèce), *adj.*, sans terre.

soirée(swâ-ré), *n.*, soirée, *f.*

sojourn (sô-djeurne), *n.*, séjour, *m.*

sojourn (sô-djeurne), *v.n.*, séjourner.

sojourner, *n.*, habitant temporaire, *m.*

sojourning, *n.*, séjour, *m.*

sojournment, *n.*, séjour, *m.*

sol. *n.*, (myth.) soleil; (mus.) sol; G., *m.*

solace (sol'-), *n.*, consolation, *f.*; soulagement, *m.*

solace, *v.a.*, consoler; égayer; (to allay—*soulager*) soulager. To — one's self with; *se consoler par.*

solander, *n.*, solandre, *f.*

solar, *or* **solary** (sô-), *adj.*, solaire; du soleil; (anat., bot.) solaire.

solder, *n.*, soudure, *f.*

solder, *v.a.*, souder; joindre.

solderer, *n.*, personne qui soude, *f.*

soldering, *n.*, soudure, *f.* —*-iron*; *soudoir; fer à souder, m.*

soldier (sôl-djeur), *n.*, soldat; militaire, *m.* Foot—; *fantassin,m.* Private—; *simple soldat.*

soldier-like (-laïke), *or* **soldierly,** *adj.*, de soldat, de militaire; militaire, martial.

soldiership, *n.*, qualités militaires, *f.pl.*; état militaire, *m.*; bravoure, *f.*

soldiery, *n.*, troupes, *f.pl.*; soldats, militaires, *m.pl.*; (b.s.) soldatesque, *f.*

sole (sôle), *adj.*, seul; unique; (jur.) non marié.

sole (sôle), *n.*, (of the foot—*du pied*) plante; (of a shoe—*d'une chaussure*) semelle; (of a hoof —*du sabot d'un cheval, &c.*) sole; (ich.) sole, *f.*; (of a rudder—*de gouvernail*) talon, *m.*

sole (sôle), *v.a.*, mettre des semelles à; ressemeler.

solecism ('-ciz'm), *n.*, solécisme, *m.*

solecist (sol'i-), *n.*, personne qui fait des solécismes. *f.*

solecistic, or solecistical (sol'i-), *adj.*, qui tient du solécisme; incorrect.

solecistically, *adv.*, avec des solécismes; incorrectement.

solecize (sol'i-çaïze), *v.n.*, faire des solécismes.

solely (sôl'-), *adv.*, seulement; uniquement.

solemn (sol'è'm), *adj.*, solennel; (grave) grave.

solemness, *or* **solemnity** (sol'è'm'-), *n.*, solennité; (gravity—*sérieux*) gravité, *f.*

solemnization (sol'è'm'naïzé-), *n.*, solennisation; célébration solennelle, *f.*

solemnize (sol'è'm'naïze), *v.a.*, solenniser; célébrer solennellement.

solemnly (sol'è'm'-), *adv.*, solennellement.

soleness (sôl'-), *n.*, caractère unique, *m.*; nature unique, *f.*

solenite (sô-lè'n'aïte), *n.*, solénite, *f.*, solen pétrifié, *m.*

sol-fa (-fâ), *v.n.*, solfier.

sol-faing (sol-fâ-igne), *n.*, solfiation, action de solfier, *f.*

solfeggio (sol-fè-dji-ô), *n.*, solfège, *m.*

solicit, *v.a.*, solliciter; briguer; demander; postuler; (to invite—*inviter*) inviter, attirer.

solicitation ('-i-té-), *n.*, sollicitation; (excitement) excitation, *f.*

solicitor (-teur), *n.*, solliciteur; (jur.) avoué, *m.* —*-general*; *procureur général.*

solicitous, *adj.*, désireux. — about; *qui a de la sollicitude pour; soigneux de; attentif à.* — for; *inquiet de.* — of, — to; *désireux de; qui tient à.*

solicitously, *adv.*, avec sollicitude.

solicitress, *n.*, solliciteuse, *f.*

solicitude (-tioude), *n.*, sollicitude, *f.*

solid, *adj.*, solide; massif; (firm—*ferme*) ferme; (grave) grave, posé; (cubic—*cube*) cube. To become —; *se solidifier.*

solid, *n.*, solide, *m.*

solidification (-fi-ké-), *n.*, solidification, *f.*

solidify (-fa'ye), *v.a.*, solidifier.

solidify (-fa'ye), *v.n.*, se solidifier.

solidity, *n.*, solidité, *f.*; état massif; (pers.) caractère posé, *m.*, gravité, *f.*

solidly, *adv.*, solidement.

solidness. *V.* **solidity.**

solidungulous (-deun'ghiou-), *adj.*, solidongulé; solipède.

soliloquize (-kwaïze), *v.n.*, faire un soliloque.

soliloquy (-kwi), *n.*, soliloque, monologue, *m.*

soliped (-pède), *adj.*, solipède.

soliped, *n.*, solipède, *m.*

solitaire (-tére), *n.*, solitaire, *m.*

solitarian (-té-), *n.*, solitaire, *m.*

solitarily, *adv.*, solitairement.

solitariness, *n.*, solitude; retraite, *f.*; isolement, *m.*

solitary, *n.*, solitaire, *m.*

solitary, *adj.*, solitaire; (gloomy— *sombre*) triste, sombre; (single—*unique*) seul, unique. — confinement; *emprisonnement cellulaire; secret, m.*

solitude (-tioude), *n.*, solitude, *f.*

solivagant, *or* **solivagous**, *adj.*, errant seul.

solmization (-mi-zé-), *n.*, solfiation, action de solfier, *f.*

solo (sô-lô), *n.*, solo, *m.*

solomon's-seal (-mo'n'z'sile), *n.*, (bot.) sceau-de-Salomon, *m.*

solstice, *n.*, solstice, *m.*

solstitial (-tish'-), *adj.*, solsticial.

solubility (sol'iou-), *n.*, solubilité, *f.*

soluble (-'iou-b'l), *adj.*, soluble.

solubleness, *n.* *V.* **solubility.**

solution (-liou-), *n.*, solution; dissolution, *f.*

solutive, *adj.*, dissolvant.

solvability, *n.*, solvabilité, *f.*

solvable, or solvible (-'b'l), *adj.*, soluble,

résoluble; (that can be paid—*qui peut être payé*) qui peut être payé.

solve, *v.a.*, résoudre ; (to remove—*dissiper*) dissiper, éclaircir.

solvency, *n.*, solvabilité, *f.*

solvent, *n.*, dissolvant, *m.*

solvent, *adj.*, dissolvant ; (able to pay—*solvable*) solvable ; (sufficient to pay—*suffisant pour payer*) suffisant pour payer.

somatic, *or* **somatical**, *adj.*, (ant.) corporel ; qui a rapport au corps.

somatology (sô-ma-tol'o-dji), *n.*, somatologie, *f.*

sombre (sô'm'beùr), *or* **sombrous** (so'm'-), *adj.*, sombre.

some (seume), *adj.*, du, *m.* ; de la, *f.* ; de l', *m. f.* ; des, *pl.m.*, *f.* ; quelque ; un peu de ; certain ; à peu près, environ. — six or seven persons; *quelque six ou sept personnes, environ six ou sept personnes.* — persons say ; *quelques personnes disent.* — persons who were there said ; *des personnes qui y étaient ont dit.* — bread; *du pain.* He has — wit; *il a quelque peu d'esprit.* — one; *quelqu'un*, *m.*, *quelqu'une*, *f.*

some, *pron.*, en ; quelques-uns, *m.pl.*, quelques-unes, *f.pl.* ; les uns, *m.pl.*, les unes, *f.pl.* ; une partie, *f.* — went one way and — another ; *les uns allèrent d'un côté, et les autres d'un autre.* Have you received all your books ? No, but I have received — of them ; *avez-vous reçu tous vos livres? Non, mais j'en ai reçu une partie, quelques-uns.* Give me —; *donnez m'en.* Give him —; *donnez-lui-en.*

somebody, *n.*, quelqu'un, *m.*, quelqu'une, *f.* — else; *quelque autre* To be —; *être quelque chose.*

somehow (-haou), *adv.*, d'une façon ou d'une autre ; de manière ou d'autre.

somersault (seum'eur-sôlte), *or* **somerset** (seum'eur-), *n.*, saut périlleux, *m.* ; culbute, *f.*

something (-thigne), *n.*, quelque chose; (before an *adj.* -*devant* un adj.) quelque chose de, *m.* ; (at a small distance—*près*) à peu de distance; (adverbially—*adverbialement*) un peu, quelque peu, tant soit peu. He has a — about him which pleases every one ; *il a un je ne sais quoi qui plaît à tout le monde.* — good ; *quelque chose de bon.*

sometime (-taïme), *adv.*, un de ces jours ; (formerly—*autrefois*) autrefois. — or other ; *un de ces jours, un beau jour ; une fois ou une autre.*

sometimes (-taï'm'ze), *adv.*, quelquefois ; parfois ; tantôt. — rich, — poor ; *tantôt riche, tantôt pauvre.*

somewhat, *n.*, quelque chose,*f.* ; quelque peu ; tant soit peu ; un peu, *m.*

somewhat, *adj.*, un peu ; quelque peu ; tant soit peu.

somewhere, *adv.*, quelque part. — else ; *ailleurs, autre part.*

somewhile (-hwaïle), *adv.*, pendant un temps ; pendant quelque temps.

sommite (so'm'aïte), *n.*, (min.) sommite, *f.*

somnambulism (-biou-liz'm), *n.*, somnambulisme, *m.*

somnambulist (-biou-liste), *n.*, somnambule, *m.*, *f.*

somniferous (-if'èr'-), *or* **somnific**, *adj.*, somnifère.

somnolence, *or* **somnolency**, *n.*, envie de dormir ; somnolence, *f.*

somnolent, *adj.*, accablé de sommeil ; somnolent.

son (seune), *n.*, fils, *m.* —-in-law ; *beau-fils*, gendre. Grand— ; *petit-fils.* God— ; *filleul, m.*

sonata (-nâ-ta), *n.*, sonate, *f.*

song (son'gn), *n.*, romance, *f.* ; chant ; (hymn—*hymne*) chant, cantique ; (poet.) poème, *m.*, poésie, *f.*, vers, *m.pl.* ; (lay—*lai*) chanson, *f.*,

couplet, *m.* ; (trifle—*bagatelle*) rien, *m.*, bagatelle, *f.* Old — ; (trifle—*bagatelle*) rien, *m.*, bagatelle, *f.* Drinking— ; *chanson à boire.*

song-book (-bouke), *n.*, chansonnier, *m.*

songless, *adj.*, qui ne chante pas.

songster, *n.*, chanteur ; (bird—*oiseau*) chantre ; (book—*livre*) chansonnier, *m.*

songstress, *n.*, chanteuse, *f.* ; (bird—*oiseau*) chantre, *m.*

song-writer (-raït'-), *n.*, chansonnier, *m.*

soniferous (-if'èr'-), *adj.*, résonnant.

sonnet, *n.*, sonnet, *m.*

sonneteer (-nèt'ire), *n.*, auteur de sonnets ; (b.s.) poétereau, *m.*

sonnetize (-aïze), *v.n.*, faire des sonnets.

sonometer (-'i-teur), *n.*, sonomètre, *m.*

sonorific, *adj.*, sonnant.

sonorous (so-nô-), *adj.*, sonore.

sonorously, *adv.*, d'une manière sonore.

sonorousness, *n.*, sonorité, *f.* ; son éclatant, *m.*

sonship (seun'n'-), *n.*, qualité de fils ; filiation, *f.*

soochong, *or* **souchong** (sou-shon'gn), *n.*, souchong, *m.*

soon (soune), *adv.*, bientôt ; (early—*tôt*) tôt, de bonne heure ; (willingly—*volontiers*) volontiers. Too — ; *trop tôt.* As — as ; *aussitôt que, dès que ; le plus tôt que.* I would as — remain as go ; *j'aimerais autant rester que de m'en aller.* —er ; *plus tôt* ; (rather—*plutôt*) plutôt. —er than ; *plus tôt que ;* (rather than) *plutôt que.*

soot (soute), *n.*, suie, *f.*

soot, *v.a.*, couvrir de suie.

soot-bag, *n.*, sac à suie, *m.*

sooth (south), *n.*, (ant.) vérité ; réalité, *f.* In — ; *en vérité.*

soothe (south*e*), *v.a.*, (to flatter—*flatter*) flatter, caresser ; (to assuage—*calmer*) adoucir, calmer ; (to please—*plaire*) charmer.

soother (south'-), *n.*, personne qui calme, qui adoucit ; chose qui calme, qui adoucit, *f.* ; calmant, adoucissant, *m.* ; (flatterer—*flatteur*) flatteur, flatteuse, *f.*

soothing (south'-), *adj.*, (assuaging—*calmant*) adoucissant ; (flattering—*flatteur*) flatteur.

soothsay (south'sè), *v.n.*, prophétiser ; prédire.

soothsayer (south'sè-eur), *n.*, devin, *m.*, devineresse, *f.* ; prophète ; augure, *m.* ; diseur, *m.*, diseuse, *f.*, de bonne aventure.

sootiness (sout'-), *n.*, état d'être couvert de suie, *m.*

sootish (sout'-), *adj.*, de suie.

sooty (sout'-), *adj.*, (producing soot—*produisant de la suie*) qui produit de la suie ; (consisting of soot—*consistant en suie*) de suie, fuligineux ; (foul with soot—*souillé de suie*) noir de suie ; (black—*noir*) noir ; (dusky—*sombre*) sombre, obscur.

sop, *n.*, soupe, *f.* ; morceau trempé ; (present) présent, *m.*, douceur, *f.*

sop, *v.a.*, tremper.

soph, *n.*, étudiant de seconde, de troisième année, *m.*

sophi (sô-fî), *n.*, Sophi, *m.*

sophism (sof'iz'm), *n.*, sophisme, *m.*

sophist, *n.*, sophiste, *m.*

sophistic, *or* **sophistical**, *adj.*, sophistique.

sophistically, *adv.*, d'une manière trompeuse.

sophisticate, *or* **sophisticated**, *adj.*, falsifié ; frelaté ; sophistiqué.

sophisticate, *v.a.*, sophistiquer ; falsifier ; frelater.

sophistication (-ti-ké-), *n.*, sophistication ; falsification ; frelaterie, *f.* ; frelatage, *m.*

sophisticator (-ti-ké-tor), *n.*, sophistiqueur, frelateur, *m.*

sophistry, n., sophismes, m.pl. ; sophistiquerie, f.

soporiferous (-rif'èr'-), adj., soporifère.

soporiferousness (-rif'èr'-), n., soporifique, m. ; propriété soporifère, f.

soporific, adj.,soporifique ; soporatif, soporifère.

soporific, n., soporifique ; soporatif, soporifère, m.

soporous, or **soporose** (-rôce), adj., (med.) soporeux.

sopper, n., personne qui trempe, f.

sopranist (-prä-), n., sopraniste, m.,f.

soprano (-prä-nô), n., soprano, m.

sorb, n., (bot.) sorbier ; cormier, m.

sorbate, n., (chem.) malate, m.

sorbic, adj., (chem.) sorbique, malique.

sorbonist, n., sorboniste, m,

sorcerer, n., sorcier ; magicien, m.

sorceress, n., sorcière ; magicienne, f.

sorcerous, adj., de sorcellerie, de sortilège.

sorcery, n., sorcellerie, f. ; sortilège ; enchantement, m. ; magie, f.

sordawalite (-val'aïte), n., (min.) sordawalite, f.

sordes (-dize), n.pl., (med.) saburre, f.sing.

sordet, or **sordine** (-dîne), n., (mus.) sourdine, f.

sordid, adj., sale ; sordide ; vil ; bas.

sordidly, adv., sordidement ; d'une manière vile.

sordidness, n., (dirtiness—saleté) saleté ; (meanness—bassesse) bassesse ; (niggardliness—avarice) avarice sordide, f.

sore (sôre), n., plaie, f. ; (in Scripture—biblique) ulcère ; (mam.) chevreuil de quatrième année, m.

sore (sôre), adj., (tender—douloureux) sensible ; (susceptible) susceptible, sensible ; (affected with inflammation—enflammé) malade ; (afflictive—cruel) douloureux, cruel ; (violent) violent, grand, rude. To have — eyes, ears ; avoir mal aux yeux, un mal d'yeux, mal aux oreilles, un mal d'oreille. To have a — foot ; avoir mal au pied. To make — ; rendre sensible, rendre malade ; (to irritate—irriter) irriter.

sore, adv., douloureusement, grièvement ; (greatly—considérablement) grandement, fortement, gravement, profondément.

sorel, n., chevreuil de troisième année, m.

sorely (sôr-), adv., douloureusement, grièvement, vivement, fortement, cruellement, rudement, sévèrement.

soreness (sôr-), n., sensibilité ; douleur, f. ; mal, m. ; (susceptibility—sensibilité) susceptibilité, sensibilité, f.

sorites (so-raï-tize), n., (log.) sorite, m.

sorrel, n., (bot.) oseille ; (colour—couleur) couleur alezan, saure, f.

sorrel, adj., alezan, saure.

sorrily, adv., tristement, pauvrement, chétivement ; pitoyablement.

sorriness, n., triste état, m. ; nature pitoyable, f.

sorrow (sor-rô), n., chagrin, m. ; douleur ; affliction, peine, tristesse, f. To one's — ; à son grand chagrin ; à sa grande douleur.

sorrow (sor-rô), v.n., être affligé ; avoir du chagrin ; s'affliger.

sorrowful (-foule), adj., triste ; affligé ; chagrin ; mélancolique ; (of things—des choses) affligeant, attristant, funeste, pénible, douloureux.

sorrowfully, adv., avec chagrin ; avec douleur ; tristement.

sorrowfulness, n., chagrin, m. ; tristesse, douleur, f.

sorrowing (sor-rô-igne), n., chagrin, m.

sorrowless, adj., sans chagrin ; sans douleur ; exempt de chagrin ; exempt de douleur.

sorry, adj., fâché, contrarié, affligé, peiné ; (melancholy—triste) mélancolique, triste ; (poor, worthless—misérable, sans valeur) triste, méchant, pitoyable. To be — for any one ; être fâché pour quelqu'un. To be — for any thing ; être fâché de quelque chose. I am — for it ; j'en suis fâché, peiné.

sort (sorte), n., (species—espèce) .sorte, f., genre, m., espèce ; (manner—manière) manière, sorte, façon ; (class—classe) classe, condition ; (pair—paire) paire f. To be out of —s ; n'être pas dans son assiette. To put out of —s ; déranger, bouleverser. In some — ; en quelque sorte, en quelque manière, en quelque façon. A woman of the right — ; une bonne pâte de femme.

sort (sorte), v.a., classer, distribuer ; séparer; assortir ; réunir ; (letters—lettres) trier; (cards—cartes) appareiller. To — out ; assortir, trier, séparer. To — from ; séparer de. To — with ; (to be joined with—joindre) se joindre à, s'unir à, se lier avec ; (to suit—convenir) s'accorder avec, convenir à.

sortable (-a-b'l), adj., qui peut être classé, distribué, trié ; (ant.) (fitting—convenable) convenable, sortable.

sortably, adv., (ant.) convenablement, d'une manière sortable.

sorted, adj., assorti, trié, arrangé, séparé

sorter, n., trieur, m., trieuse, f.

sortie (-tî), n., (milit.) sortie, f.

sortilege (-lèdje), n., tirage au sort, m.

sortilegious (-lèdj'eusse), adj., de tirage au sort.

sorting, n., triage, arrangement, m.

sortition, n., (ant.) tirage au sort, m.

sot (sote), n., sot, m., sotte, bête, f. ; (drunkard —ivrogne) ivrogne, m., ivrognesse, f.

sot, v.a. V. besot.

sot, v.n., ivrogner.

sottish, adj., (stupid—sot) sot, stupide, hébété ; (drunken—abruti) abruti par l'ivrognerie.

sottishly, adv., (stupidly—sottement) sottement ; stupidement ; (drunkenly—d'ivrogne) en ivrogne.

sottishness, n., sottise ; bêtise ; stupidité, f. ; (drunkenness—abrutissement) abrutissement par l'ivrognerie, m.

sou, n., sou, m.

souchong, n. V. soochong.

soul (sôle), n., âme ; (creature) âme, f., être, m., créature, f. With all my — ; de toute mon âme. Poor — ; pauvre chère âme. Simple — ; bonhomme, m., bonne femme, f. Good — ; bonne créature ; bonne pâte d'homme, bonne pâte de femme. All —s' day ; fête des morts, f.

soul-destroying (-dè-stro-yigne), adj., qui perd l'âme.

soul-felt, adj., senti dans l'âme, au fond de l'âme.

soulless, adj., sans âme ; apathique.

soul-saving (-sév'-), adj., qui sauve l'âme.

soul-searching (-seurtsh'-), adj., qui remue l'âme.

soul-selling, adj., trafiquant en créatures humaines.

soul-sick, adj., malade d'esprit.

soul-stirring (-steur'-), adj., qui remue l'âme.

soul-vexed (-vèks'te), adj., tourmenté jusqu'au fond de l'âme.

sound (saou'n'de), n., (strait—détroit) détroit, m. ; (surg.) sonde, f. ; (noise—bruit) son, m.

sound (saou'n'de), adj., sain ; en bon état ; (of the mind—de l'esprit) sain ; (of the health—de la santé) bon, solide ; (of sleep—du sommeil) profond ; (of blows—de coups) bon, fort, vigoureux ; (valid—valide) valide ; (correct) légitime ;

(well founded—*juste*) bien fondé. — thrashing; *bonne raclée, f.*

sound, *adv.*, profondément; d'importance.

sound, *v.n.*, sonner; rendre un son; retentir; résonner; (to search the depth of water—*profondeur d'eau*) sonder, jeter la sonde.

sound, *v.a.*, sonner de; faire sonner; faire résonner; (proclaim—*publier*)proclamer,publier, faire retentir; (to try the depth of, to examine—*profondeur d'eau; examiner*) sonder.

soundable (-'a-b'l), *adj.*, qu'on peut sonder.

sound-board (-bôrde). V. **sounding-board.**

sound-headed (-hèd'-), *adj.*, qui a la tête saine; qui a une bonne tête.

sound-hearted (-hârt'-), *adj.*, affectionné, sincère.

sounding, *adj.*, à son; résonnant; retentissant.

sounding, *n.*, action de sonner, *f.*; retentissement, résonnement, *m.*, résonance, *f.*; (of wounds, water, &c.—*de blessures, d'eau, &c.*) action de sonder, *f.*, sondage, *m.*

sounding-board, *n.*, (mus.) table d'harmonie, *f.*; (of a pulpit—*d'une chaire*) abat-voix, *m.*

sounding-lead (-lède), *n.*, sonde, *f.*

sounding-line (-laïne), *n.*, ligne de sonde; sonde, *f.*

sounding-post (-pôste), *n.*, (mus.) âme,*f.*

soundings (-'ign'ze), *n.pl.*, sondes, *f.pl.*

soundless, *adj.*, (unfathomable—*sans fond*) insondable, que l'on ne peut sonder; (having no sound—*dépourvu de son*) sans son; sans bruit.

soundly, *adv.*, (healthily—*sainement*) avec santé; (lustily—*fortement*) vigoureusement, rudement, d'importance, ferme; (without fallacy—*sans fausseté*) sainement; (firmly—*fermement*) solidement, profondément; (of sleeping—*du dormir*) profondément, d'un profond sommeil. — beaten; *bien, joliment battu; rossé d'importance.*

soundness, *n.*, état sain; bon état, *m.*; solidité; (strength—*force*) force, vigueur; (rectitude) rectitude, justesse, pureté; (of the body—*du corps*) santé,*f.*

soup, *n.*, potage, *m.*; soupe, *f.* Gravy—; *consommé, m.* Vegetable—; *potage à la julienne.* Turtle—; *potage à la tortue.* Mock-turtle—; *potage à la tête de veau; tête de veau en tortue, soupe, potage à la financière.*

sour (sa-eur), *adj.*, aigre; sûr; acide; (fig.) aigre, âpre, morose. To make —; *aigrir.* To turn —; *s'aigrir.*

sour (sa-eur), *v.a.*, aigrir; (chem.) acidifier; (fig.) aigrir, empoisonner.

sour, *v.n.*, s'aigrir. To —into; *tourner en; dégénérer en.*

source (sôrce), *n.*, source,*f.*

sourish (sa-eur'-), *adj.*, aigret; suret; aigrelet.

sourly (sa-eur-), *adv.*, avec aigreur; (fig.) aigrement, âprement, avec aigreur.

sourness(sa-eur-), *n.*, aigreur, acidité; (fig.) âpreté, aigreur,*f.*

souse (saouce), *n.*, marinade,*f.*

souse (saouce), *v.a.*, mariner; plonger dans l'eau; (to strike—*frapper*) frapper avec violence.

souse, *v.n.*, fondre sur; se jeter, se précipiter sur.

souse (saouce), *adv.*, tout à coup.

south (saouth). *n.*, sud, midi, *m.*

south, *adj.*, sud, du sud; méridional.

south, *adv.*, vers le midi; vers le sud, au sud.

south-east (-1ste). *n.*, sud-est, *m.*

south-east, *adj.*, sud-est, du sud-est.

south-eastern (-1st'eur'n), *adj.*, du sud-est.

southerly (soth' eur-), *adv.*, vers le sud.

southern (soth'eur'n), *adj.*, du sud; du midi: méridional.

southernly (soth-eur'n'-), *adj.*, sud, du sud; méridional.

southernmost (-môste), *adj.*, le plus au sud.

southern-wood (-woude), *n.*, (bot.) aurone des jardins; citronnelle,*f.*

southing (saouth'-), *n.*, mouvement vers le sud; (astron.) passage au méridien, *m.*; (of a ship—*d'un vaisseau*) route au sud, *f.*

southing (saou th'-), *adj.*, qui se dirige vers le sud.

southmost (saouth'môste), *adj.*, le plus au sud.

southward, *adv.*, vers le sud; au sud.

southward (saouth'wôrde), *n.*, pays méridionaux, *m.pl.*; midi, *m.*

south-west (-wèste), *n.*, sud-ouest, *m.*

south-west, *adj.*, sud-ouest; du sud-ouest.

south-westerly (-wòst'eur-), *adj.*, de sud-ouest; du sud-ouest; sud-ouest.

south-western (-wèsteur'n), *adj.*, de sud-ouest; du sud-ouest; sud-ouest.

souvenir (souv'nîr), *n.*, souvenir, *m.*

sovereign (sov'eur'ine), *n.*, souverain, *m.* souveraine, *f.*; (gold coin—*monnaie d'or*) souverain (20 shil.=25 f.), *m.*

sovereign, *adj.*, souverain.

sovereignly, *adv.*, souverainement.

sovereignty, *n.*, souveraineté,*f.*

sow (saou), *n.*, truie; (metal.) gueuse, *f.*; (of lead—*de plomb*) saumon, *m.*

sow (sô), *v.a.* (preterit, Sowed; *past part.,* Sown), semer, ensemencer. To — one's wild oats;*jeter ses premiers feux; faire ses farces.*

sow (sô), *v.n.*, semer; faire les semailles.

sow-thistle (saou-this's'l), *n.*, (bot.) laiteron, *m.*

sower (sô-eur), *n.*, semeur, *m.*

sowing (sô-igne), *n.*, semailles, *f.pl.*; (fig.) propagation, *f.* —-time; *temps de semer;* (agri.) *temps des semailles, m.*

soy (swaï), *n.*, soy, soui, *m.*

spa (spâ), *n.*, source d'eau minérale, *f.*

space, *n.*, espace, *m.*; étendue, *f.*; (quantity of time—*laps de temps*) espace de temps; (short time—*temps court*) court espace de temps; (mus.) espace, interligne, *m.*

space, *v.a.*, (print.) espacer.

space-line (-laïne), *n.*, interligne, *f.*

spacious (spé-sheusse),*adj.*, spacieux; d'une grande étendue; vaste.

spaciously, *adv.*, amplement, spacieusement.

spaciousness, *n.*, nature spacieuse; immensité; vaste étendue, *f.*

spaddle (spad'd'l), *n.*, petite bêche, *f.*

spade, *n.*, bêche, *f.*; (in cards—*aux cartes*) pique; (hunt.) daim de trois ans, *m.*

spade, *v. a.*, bêcher.

spadebone (-bône), *n.*, omoplate, *f.*

spadeful (-foule), *n.*, pelletée, *f.*

spadille (spa-dil), *or* **spadilio** (-dil-iô), *n.*, spadille, as de pique, *m.*

spadix (spé-), *n.*, (bot.) spadice, *m.*

spahi, *or* **spahee** (spâ-hî), *n.*, spahi, *m.*

spalt (spôlte), *n.*, (min.) spalt, *m.*

span, *n.*, empan, *m.*; main, *f.*; (short space of time—*court espace de temps*) moment, instant, *m.*; (arch.) ouverture; (of an arch—*d'arche*) corde; (of horses, oxen—*de chevaux, de bœufs*) paire,*f.*

span, *v.a.*, mesurer par empan; mesurer de la main; (nav.) saisir, brider.

spandrel, *n.*, (of an arch—*d'arche*) naissance, *f.*; (of a bridge—*de pont*) tympan, *m.*

spanfarthing (-fâr-thigne), *n.*, (game—*jeu*) fossette,*f.*

spangle (span'gn'g'l), *n.*, paillette,*f.*

spangle (span'gn'g'l), *v.a.*, pailleter; parsemer de paillettes.

spaniard, *n.*, Espagnol, *m.*, Espagnole, *f.*

spaniel, *n.*, épagneul ; (fig.) flatteur, *m.*

spaniel, *v.n.*, faire le chien couchant.

spaniel, *adj.*, de chien couchant ; rampant.

spanish, *adj.*, espagnol ; d'Espagne.

spanish-broom (-broume), *n.*, genêt d'Espagne, *m.*

spanish-fly (-fla'ye), *n.*, cantharide, *f.*

spank, *v.a.*, (pop.) donner une claque.

spank, *v.n.*, se mouvoir rapidement.

spanker, *n.*, gros gaillard, *m.*; personne qui marche à grands pas, *f.*; (nav.) basse voile d'artimon, *f.*

spanking, *adj.*, fort ; gros ; qui marche à grands pas.

span-long (-lon'gn), *adj.*, de la longueur d'un empan.

spanner, *n.*, personne qui mesure par empan, *f.* ; (of a carbine—*de fusil*) platine, *f.* ; (mec.) clef à boulon, clef à levier, *f.*

span-new (-niou), *adj.*, tout neuf.

spar (spâr), *n.*, (nav.) espar ; (min.) spath, *m.*

spar (spâr), *v.n.*, se quereller ; se disputer ; se battre.

sparable (-ra-b'l), *n.*, clou à soulier, *m.*

sparadrap, *n.*, (med.) (ant.) sparadrap, *m.*

spare, *v.a.*, épargner ; ménager ; (to economize—*économiser*) économiser ; (to do without—*se passer de*) se passer de ; (to omit—*omettre*) s'épargner, s'éviter ; (to let have—*donner*) donner, céder ; (to forbear to punish, destroy, &c.—*ménager*) épargner. To — any one a pain; *épargner une peine à quelqu'un.* To have to —; *avoir de reste, avoir de trop.*

spare, *v.n.*, économiser ; épargner ; vivre frugalement ; faire des économies ; (to forbear —*s'abstenir*) s'abstenir ; (to use mercy—*user de miséricorde*) être clément.

spare, *adj.*, (scanty—*modique*) modique, faible, pauvre ; (superfluous—*superflu*) de reste, de trop ; (lean—*maigre*) maigre, chétif, sec; (of time—*de temps*) de loisir, libre; (nav.) de rechange. — of ; *sobre de ; économe de ; ménager de.* — bed ; *lit de reste ; lit au service des amis, m.*

spareness (spér'-), *n.*, maigreur, *f.*

sparer (spér'-), *n.*, personne économe; personne qui épargne, *f.*

sparing (spér'-), *adj.*, (little—*peu*) peu de ; (scanty—*modique*) modique, faible, pauvre, peu abondant ; (saving—*ménager*) économe, ménager, éparghant ; (parsimonious—*mesquin*) parcimonieux. — of ; *sobre de, économe de.*

sparingly (spér'-), *adv.*, sobrement ; frugalement, avec parcimonie ; modérément ; économiquement ; (seldom—*rarement*) peu souvent.

sparingness (spér'ign'nèce), *n.*, économie, épargne, modération ; parcimonie, *f.*

spark (spârke), *n.*, étincelle ; lueur, *f.* ; éclat, *m.* ; (gay man—*dandy*) galant, petit-maître, mirliflore, *m.*

sparkish (spârk'l), *adj.*, vif ; brillant ; élégant.

sparkle (spârk'l), *n.*, étincelle, *f.*

sparkle (spârk'l), *v.n.*, étinceler ; pétiller ; briller ; (of beverages—*des boissons*) mousser.

sparkler, *n.*, personne qui brille ; chose qui étincelle, *f.*

sparklet, *n.*, petite étincelle, *f.*

sparkling, *n.*, pétillant ; étincelant ; (of beverages—*des boissons*) mousseux.

sparklingly, *adv.*, d'une manière étincelante ; avec éclat ; en pétillant.

sparklingness (-lign'nèce), *n.*, étincellement, pétillement ; éclat, brillant, *m.*

sparling (spâr-), *n.*, (ich.) éperlan, *m.*

sparring (spâr'-), *n.*, querelle ; dispute, *f.* ; (in boxing—*boxe*) prélude de combat, *m.*

sparrow (-rô), *n.*, (orni.) moineau ; passereau, *m.* Hedge- —; *fauvette d'hiver, f.*

sparrow-hawk (-hôke), *n.*, (orni.) épervier, *m.*

sparrow-wort (-weurte), *n.*, (bot.) passerine, *f.*

sparry (spâr-), *adj.*, (min.) spathique ; de spath.

sparse (spârse), *adj.*, épars.

sparsedly (spârs'èd'-), *adv.*, d'une manière éparse.

spartan (spâr-), *n.*, Spartiate, *m.*, *f.*

spartan, *adj.*, spartiate.

spasm (spaz'm), *n.*, spasme, *m.*

spasmodic, *or* **spasmodical** (spaz'-), *adj.*, spasmodique.

spasmodic, *n.*, (med.) antispasmodique, *m.*

spasmology (spaz'mol'o-djï), *n.*, spasmologie, *f.*

spat, *n.*, frai des mollusques ; jeune mollusque ; coup, *m.*

spathaceous (spa-thé-sheusse), *adj.*, (bot.) spathacé ; spathé.

spathe (spêthe), *n.*, (bot.) spathe, *f.*

spathic (spath-), *adj.*, (min.) spathique.

spathiform (spath'-), *adj.*, (min.) spathiforme.

spathose (-thôce), *or* **spathous** (spé-theuss), *adj.*, (bot.) spathé.

spatter, *v.a.*, éclabousser ; crotter ; (to defame—*diffamer*) diffamer, noircir ; ternir ; (liquids—*liquides*) répandre, verser.

spatter, *v.n.*, cracher.

spatterdashes (-dash'ize), *n.pl.*, houseaux, *m.pl.*

spatula (-'iou-), *n.*, spatule, *f.*

spavin, *n.*, (vet.) éparvin ; épervin, *m.*

spavined (spav'i'nde), *adj.*, (vet.) qui a des éparvins.

spawl (spôl), *n.*, (ant.) crachat, *m.*

spawl (spôl), *v.n.*, cracher en parlant.

spawn (spô'n), *n.*, frai ; (fig.) produit, *m.*, engeance, race, *f.*

spawn (spô'n), *v.n.*, frayer ; naître.

spawn, *v.a.*, engendrer par du frai ; engendrer.

spawner, *n.*, poisson femelle, *m.*

spawning, *n.*, frai, *m.* ; action de frayer, *f.* - -time ; *temps où les poissons fraient, temps du frai, m.*

spay (spè), *v.a.*, châtrer, couper.

speak (spike), *v.n.*, (preterit, Spoke; *past part.*, Spoken), parler ; dire. To — with ; *s'entretenir avec, causer avec, parler avec.* So to — ; *pour ainsi dire.* To — ill of ; *dire du mal de.* To — well of ; *dire du bien de ; parler avantageusement de.* To — up ; *parler plus haut ; parler hardiment.* To — out ; *parler tout haut.*

speak, *v.a.*, parler ; dire ; (to proclaim—*proclamer*) proclamer, publier ; (to celebrate—*célébrer*) célébrer ; (to express—*exprimer*) montrer, manifester, exprimer, dire ; (to accost—*accoster*) accoster ; (to communicate) communiquer, porter ; (nav.) héler. To — the truth; *dire la vérité.* To — one's mind ; *dire sa pensée.* To — a language; *parler une langue.* To — English ; *parler anglais.* To his shame be it spoken ; *soit dit à sa honte.* Ships spoken with ; *vaisseaux hélés.* I beg leave to — ; *je demande la parole.* French spoken here ; *ici on parle français.*

speakable (-'a-b'l), *adj.*, exprimable; que l'on peut dire.

speaker, *n.*, personne qui parle, *f.*, orateur ; parleur ; (of the House of Commons—*de la Chambre des Communes*) président, *m.* Eternal —; *parleur sempiternel.*

speaking, *n.*, action de parler ; parole, *f.* ; langage ; discours, parler, *m.* ; (in college—*au collège*) déclamation, *f.*

speaking-pipe (-païpe), *n.*, cordon acoustique, *m.*

speaking-trumpet (-treu'm'-), *n.*, portevoix ; cornet acoustique, *m.*

spear (spïre), *n.*, lance, *f.* ; harpon, *m.* ; épieu, *m.*

spear (spïre), *v.a.*, percer d'un coup de lance, d'un coup d'épieu ; harponner.

spear-foot (-foute), *n.*, pied de derrière, *m.*

spear-grass (-grâce), *n.*, chiendent, *m.*

spear-hand, *n.*, main droite, *f.*

spearman, *n.*, lancier, *m.*

spearmint, *n.*, menthe verte, *f.*

spearwort (-weurte), *n.*, renoncule, *f.*

special (spèsh'al), *adj.*, qui désigne une espèce ; spécial ; (peculiar—*particulier*) particulier ; (extraordinary—*extraordinaire*) extraordinaire, remarquable ; (uncommon—*rare*) peu commun ; (chief—*chef*) premier. — constable ; *constable spécial, temporaire, m.* — department ; *spécialité, f.*

speciality. *V.* **specialty.**

specialize (spèsh'al'aïze), *v.a.*, spécifier ; particulariser.

specially, *adv.*, particulièrement ; spécialement ; principalement ; surtout.

specialty, *n.*, spécialité, *f.* ; (jur.) contrat sous seing privé, *m.*

specie (spï-shi), *n.*, numéraire, *m.* ; espèces, *f.pl.*

species (spï-shize), *n.*, espèce, *f.* ; genre, *m.* ; sorte ; (money—*monnaie*) espèce, *f.*, espèces, *f.pl.*, numéraire, *m.* ; (representation) image ; (appearance—*apparence*) apparence, *f.* ; (show—*exhibition*) (ant.) spectacle, *m.*

specific (spi-), *n.*, spécifique, *m.*

specific, *or* **specifical** (spi-), *adj.*, spécifique.

specifically, *adv.*, spécifiquement.

specificate (spi-), *v.a.*, (ant.) spécifier.

specification (spi-ci-fi-ké-), *n.*, spécification ; (thing specified—*chose spécifiée*) chose spécifiée, *f.* ; (estimate—*devis*) devis, *m.*

specify (spèss'i-fa'ye), *v.a.*, spécifier ; particulariser.

specimen (spèss'i-mè'n), *n.*, spécimen ; modèle ; échantillon, *m.*

specious (spi-sheuss), *adj.*, spécieux ; agréable à la vue.

speciously, *adv.*, spécieusement.

speciousness, *n.*, nature spécieuse ; apparence spécieuse, *f.*

speck (spèk), *n.*, tache ; marque, *f.* ; point, *m.* ; (med.) taie, *f.*

speck, *v.a.*, tacher ; marquer.

speckle (spèk'k'l), *n.*, petite tache ; (on animals—*des animaux*) moucheture, *f.*

speckle, *v.a.*, tacheter ; marqueter ; moucheter.

speckled (spèk'k'l'de), *adj.*, tacheté ; marqueté ; moucheté ; truité.

speckledness, *n.*, couleur tachetée ; couleur marquetée : couleur truitée ; moucheture, *f.*

spectacle (spèk'ta-k'l), *n.*, spectacle, *m.*

spectacled (-tak'l'de), *adj.*, qui porte des lunettes.

spectacle-glasses (-glâcize), *n.pl.*, verres de lunettes, *m.pl.*

spectacle-maker (-mék'-), *n.*, opticien, *m.*

spectacles (-tak'l'ze), *n.pl.*, lunettes ; besicles, *f.pl.*

spectacular (-tak'iou-), *adj.*, de spectacle.

spectator (-té-teur), *n.*, spectateur, *m.*, spectatrice, *f.* ; assistant, *m.*

spectatorial, *adj.*, de spectateur.

spectatorship, *n.*, action de regarder ; position de spectateur ; vue ; vision, *f.*

spectatress, *or* **spectatrix** (spèk-té-), *n.*, spectatrice, *f.*

spectral, *adj.*, de spectre.

spectre (spèk-teur), *n.*, spectre ; fantôme, *m.*

spectrum (spèk-treume), *n.* (*spectra*), (opt.) spectre solaire, *m.*

specular (spèk'iou-), *adj.*, favorable à la vue ; (min.) spéculaire.

speculate (spèk'iou-), *v.n.*, spéculer ; méditer ; contempler avec attention ; (com.) spéculer. To — on ; *jouer sur ; jouer à.* To — in ; *spéculer sur.*

speculation (spèk'iou-lé-), *n.*, spéculation ; méditation ; contemplation ; (com.) spéculation, *f.*

speculative (spèk'iou-), *adj.*, spéculatif ; (com.) spéculateur, qui spécule, (of things—*choses*) de spéculation.

speculatively, *adv.*, en théorie ; dans la spéculation.

speculativeness, *n.*, caractère spéculatif, *m.*

speculator (-lé-teur), *n.*, personne qui se livre à la spéculation, *f.* ; (com.) spéculateur, *m.*

speculatory, *adj.*, qui se livre à la spéculation.

speculum (spèk'iou-), *n.* (*specula*), miroir ; (surg.) speculum, *m.*

speech (spîtshe), *n.*, parole, *f.* ; (oration—*oraison*) discours, *m.*, harangue, *f.* ; (language—*langue*) langage ; (talk—*paroles*) discours, langage, *m.*, paroles, *f.pl.*, entretien ; (gram.) discours, *m.*, oraison, *f.* The parts of — ; *les parties du discours, f.pl.* Maiden— ; *discours de début.* To be slow of — ; *parler lentement.*

speechifier (-faï-eur), *n.*, péroreur, *m.*

speechify (spîtsh'i-fa-ye), *v.n.*, pérorer.

speechless, *adj.*, privé de la parole ; muet, interdit. To be — ; *avoir perdu la parole.* To be taken — ; *perdre la parole.*

speechlessness, *n.*, privation de la parole, *f.* ; mutisme, *m.*

speech-maker (-mék'-), *n.*, faiseur de discours, *m.*

speed (spîde), *n.*, vitesse ; rapidité ; hâte ; diligence, *f.* ; (success—*succès*) succès, *m.*, réussite, *f.* At full — ; (of horses—*des chevaux*) à franc étrier ; à bride abattue ; à toute bride ; ventre à terre ; (of vehicles—*de voitures*) à grande vitesse ; (pers.) à toutes jambes. God— ; Good— to you ! *bon succès ! bonne chance !* With all possible — ; *en toute hâte.* At the height of its — ; *de toute sa vitesse.*

speed, *v.a.*, faire partir à la hâte, dépêcher, expédier ; (to hurry—*hâter*) hâter, accélérer ; (to prosper—*faire réussir*) favoriser, faire prospérer, faire réussir ; (to furnish in haste—*fournir à la hâte*) fournir à la hâte ; (to kill—*tuer*) tuer, expédier, dépêcher.

speed, *v.n.*, (to make haste—*se hâter*) se hâter, se dépêcher ; (to succeed—*réussir*) réussir, avoir du succès, prospérer ; (to fare—*être*) être, se trouver.

speed-gauge (-ghédje), *n.*, sillomètre, *m.*

speedily, *adv.*, vite ; rapidement, promptement ; en toute hâte.

speediness, *n.*, rapidité ; vitesse ; célérité, promptitude ; hâte, *f.*

speedwell, *n.*, (bot.) véronique, *f.*

speedy, *adj.*, rapide ; vite ; prompt.

spell, *n.*, charme ; (turn of work—*tour de travail*) tour ; coup de main ; (nav.) temps, *m.*

spell, *v.a.*, (to name the letters—*nommer les lettres*) épeler ; (to write with the proper letters —*orthographier*) orthographier, écrire ; (to charm—*charmer*) charmer, mettre sous le charme ; (nav.) relever. To — out—*d'chiffrer*, découvrir, lire.

spell, *v.n.*, épeler ; orthographier correctement, écrire correctement ; (to read unskilfully —*lire*) lire mal, ânonner.

spell-bound (-baou'n'de), *adj.*, sous le charme.

speller, *n.*, personne qui épèle, *f.* ; ortho-graphiste, *m.*, *f.* To be a bad — ; *ne pas savoir son orthographe.*

spelling, *n.*. épellation ; orthographe, *f.*

spelling-book (-bouke), *n.*, syllabaire, *m.*

spelt. *n.*, (bot.) épeautre ; (min.) spalt, *m.*

spelter, *n.*, zinc, *m.*

spencer, *n.*, spencer, *m.*

spend, *v.at.* (*preterit* and *past part.*, Spent), dépenser ; (to waste—*gaspiller*) prodiguer, gas-piller, perdre, dissiper, manger ; (to consume, to exhaust—*consumer*) épuiser ; (time—*le temps*) passer ; (a mast—*un mât*) casser. The ball had spent its force ; *la balle avait perdu sa force.* To — money on ; *dépenser son argent à.*

spend, *v.n.*, dépenser ; faire de la dépense ; (to be lost—*se perdre*)se perdre; (to be consumed —*s'épuiser*) se consumer, s'épuiser.

spender, *n.*, dépensier, *m.*, dépensière, *f.* ; dissipateur, *m.*, dissipatrice, *f.*

spending, *n.*, action de dépenser; dépense, *f.*

spendthrift (-thrif'te), *n.*, dépensier, *m.*, dépensière, *f.* ; prodigue ; mange-tout ; bourreau d'argent, *m.*

spent, *adj.*, (of balls—*balle*) morte ; (of masts —*mât*) cassé.

spergula (speur-ghiou-), *n.*, (bot.) sper-gule, *f.*

sperm (speurme), *n.*, sperme ; (of fish, frogs — *des poissons, des grenouilles*) frai, *m.*

spermaceti (speur-ma-cî-), *n.*, sperma ceti, sperme, blanc de baleine, *n.*

spermatic, or **spermatical** (speur-), *adj.*, de sperme ; spermatique.

spermatocele (spèr'mat'o-cîle), *n.*, (med.) spermatocèle, *f.*

spermatology(speur-ma-tol-o-dji),*n.*,sper-matologie, *f.*

spew (spiou), *v.a.*, vomir. To — up ; *vomir.*

spew, *v.n.*, vomir.

spewer (spiou-eur), *n.*, personne qui vomit, *f.*

spewing (spiou-igne), *n.*. vomissement, *m.*

sphacel. *V.* **sphacelus.**

sphacelate (sfass'i-), *v.n.*, (med.) se sphacé-ler, être frappé de sphacèle.

sphacelate, *v.a.*, sphacéler, frapper de sphacèle.

sphacelus (sfass'i-),*n.*, sphacèle, *m.*

sphene (sfîne), *n.*, (min.) sphène, *m.*

sphenoid. or **sphenoidal** (sfî-noïde, -noïd'-), *adj.*, sphénoïde ; sphénoïdal.

sphere (sfîre), *n.*, sphère, *f.*

sphere (sfîre), *v.a.*, former en sphère ; arron-dir ; (to place in a sphere—*mettre dans une sphère*) placer dans une sphère.

spheric, or **spherical** (sfèr'-), *adj.*, sphé-rique.

spherically, *adv.*, sphériquement.

sphericalness, or **sphericity,** *n.*, sphéri-cité, *f.*

spherics, *n.pl.*, théorie de la sphère, *f.* *sing.*

spheroid (sfî-roïde), *n.*, sphéroïde, *m.*

spheroidal, spheroidic, or **spheroi-dical** (sfî-, *adj.*, sphéroïdal.

spheroidity (sfî-roï'd'-), *n.*, forme de sphéroïde, *f.*

spherometer (sfî-ro'm'i-),*n.*,sphéromètre,*m.*

spherule. *n.*. petit corps sphérique, *m.*

spherulite (sfèr'iou-laïte), *n.*, sphérulite, *f.*

sphery (sfîr'i), *adj.*, sphérique.

sphincter (sfi'n'k'teur), *n.*, sphincter, *m.*

sphinx, *n.*, sphinx ; (ent.) sphinx. *m.*

spica-bandage (-ba'nd'édje), *n.*, (surg.) spica, *m.*

spice (spaïce), *n.*, épice, *f.* ; épices, *f.pl.* ; (small quantity—*très petite quantité*) teinte, nuance, *f.*

spice (spaïce), *v.a.*, épicer ; assaisonner avec des épices.

spicer (spaïss'eur), *n.*, personne qui épice, *f.*

spicery (spaï-ceuri), *n.*, épices, *f.pl.* ; épi-cerie, *f.*, magasin d'épices, *m.*

spiciness (spai-), *n.*, goût épicé, goût aro-matisé, *m.*

spick-and-span, *adj.*, brillant. — new ; *tout battant neuf.*

spiculate (spik'iou-), *v.a.*, armer d'une pointe ; tailler en pointe.

spicy (spaï-), *adj.*, fertile en épices ; épicé ; (fragrant—*odoriférant*) aromatique, parfumé ; (showy—*pimpant*) pimpant, flambant.

spider (spaï-), *n.*, araignée, *f.* —'s web ; *toile d'araignée, f.*

spider-like (-laïke), *adj.*, d'araignée ; comme une araignée.

spider-work (-weurke),*n.*,toile d'araignée,*f.*

spigot, *n.*, fausset, *m.*

spike (spaïke), *n.*, pointe; (of wood—*de bois*) cheville, *f.* ; (of corn—*de blé*)épi,*m.* Marling- — ; (nav.) *épissoir, m.*

spike (spaïke), *v.a.*, clouer ; (a cannon--*un canon*) enclouer.

spikelet (spaïk'-), *n.*, (bot.) épillet, *m.*

spikenail (-néle), *n.*, clou barbelé, *m.* ; che-ville barbelée, *f.*

spikenard (spaïk'-), *n.*, nard indien, *m.*

spiky (spaïk'-), *adj.*, à pointe aiguë ; pointu.

spill, *n.*, cheville; goupille, *f.* ; fausset ; pieu, *m.*

spill, *v.a.* (*preterit* and *past part.*, Spilt, Spilled), répandre ; verser ; renverser ; (nav.) carguer.

spill, *v.n.*, se verser, se répandre.

spiller, *n.*, personne qui répand, qui renverse, qui verse, *f.*

spin, *v.a.* (*preterit* and *past part,* Spun), filer ; (a top—*une toupie*) faire tourner ; (hay—*du foin*) tordre. To — out ; *allonger ; prolonger ; étendre ; faire durer, tirer en longueur.*

spinage (spi'n'édje), or **spinach** (-'atshe), *n.*, (bot.) épinard, *m.* ; (cook.) épinards. *m.pl.*

spinal (spaï-), *adj.*, spinal ; (of the spinal cord—*de la moelle épinière*) épinière ; (of the back-bone—*du rachis*) rachidien.

spindle (spi'n'd'l), *n.*, fuseau ; (rod on which a thing turns—*pivot*) pivot, *m.* ; (horl.) fusée ; (of a compass—*de la boussole*) aiguille, *f.* ; (mec.) essieu ; (of a vane—*de girouette*) fer ; (tech.) axe, *m.* ; (in spinning-mills—*de filatures*) broche, *f.* ; (nav.) pivot du cabestan, *m.*

spindle-legs(-lèg'ze),or**spindle-shanks,** *n.pl..* jambes de fuseau, *f.pl.*

spindle-shanked (-sha'n'k'te), *adj.*, qui a des jambes de fuseau

spindle-shaped (-shép'te), *adj.*, fusiforme.

spindle-tree (-trî), *n.*, fusain, *m.*

spine (spaïne), *n.*, épine du dos, *f.* ; (bot.) épine, *f.*

spinel, or **spinelle** (spaï-) *n.*, (min.) spi-nelle, *m.*

spinet, *n.*, (mus.) épinette, *f.*

spiniferous (spaï-nif'èr-), or **spinigerous** (-nidj'èr-), *adj.*, spinifère.

spinner, *n.*, fileur, *m.*, fileuse, *f.* ; filateur, *m.* ; (spider—*araignée*) araignée, *f.*

spinning, *n.*, filature, *f.* ; filage, *m.*

spinning-factory, *n.*, filature, *f.*

spinning-frame, *n.*, métier à filer, *m.*

spinning-jenny (-djè'n'-), *n.*, métier à filer en gros, *m.* ; mule-jenny, *f.*

spinning-machine(-ma-shîne),*n.*,machine à filer, *f.*

spinning-mill. *n.*, filature, *f.*

spinning-wheel (-hwîle), *n.*, rouet à filer.*m.*

spinosity (spaï-noss'-), *n.*, présence d'épines ; (fig.) difficulté épineuse, *f.*

spinous (spaï-), *adj.*, épineux.

spinozism (-ziz'm), *n.*, spinosisme, *m.*

spinozist, *n.*, spinosiste, *m.*

32 *

spinster, *n.*, fileuse; (jur.) femme non mariée, *f.*

spinstry, *n.*, filage, *m.*

spinthere (-thîre), *n.*, (min.) sphène vert, *m.*

spiny (spaï-), *adj.*, plein d'épines; (perplexed —*épineux*) difficile, épineux.

spiracle (spaï-ra-k'l), *n.*, trou, *m.*; ouverture, *f.*; pore; (bot.) stomate; (ent.) stigmate, *m.*

spiral (spaï-), *adj.*, spiral.

spiral (spaï-), *n.*, spirale, *f.*

spirally, *adv.*, en spirale.

spiration (spaï-ré-), *n.*,(ant.) respiration, *f.*

spire (spaeur), *n.*, spirale; (of a steeple—*de clocher*) aiguille, flèche, *f.*; (top—*sommet*) point le plus élevé, sommet; (of grass—*d'herbe*) brin,*m.*

spire (spaeur), *v.n.*, s'élever en flèche; (of grain—*de graines*) germer.

spired (spaeur'de), *adj.*, à flèche.

spirit, *n.*, (breath—*haleine*) souffle; (soul of man—*âme humaine*) esprit, *m.*, âme; (ardour, fire—*ardeur, cœur*) ardeur, force, vigueur, verve, *f.*, feu, entraînement; (courage) courage, caractère, cœur; (genius—*génie*) génie; (vigour of intellect—*vigueur d'esprit*) esprit, *m.*, intelligence, *f.*; (temper—*caractère*) caractère, *m.*, nature, disposition, *f.*, esprit; (immaterial substance— *substance incorporelle*) esprit; (immaterial being —*être incorporel*) esprit, *m.*; (turn of mind—*tour d'esprit*) disposition, *f.*, esprit, sentiment, *m.*; (perception) perception, *f.*, sentiment, *m.*; (eager·desire—*désir ardent*) esprit, *m.*, ardeur, rage,*f.*; (person of activity—*personne active*) esprit entreprenant, *m.*; (essence) essence, *f.*; (of troops—*de troupes*) moral; (apparition) esprit, fantôme, spectre; (liquor—*liqueur*) spiritueux, *m.*, liqueur spiritueuse, *f.*; (chem com.) esprit, *m.* —**s**; *gaîté, bonne humeur, f.sing.*; *entrain, m.sing.* In —**s**; *gai; en train; de bonne humeur.* To put in —**s**; *égayer; mettre de bonne humeur.* Party-—; *esprit de parti.* Ardent—; *esprit ardent; caractère ardent.* Ardent —**s**; *liqueurs fortes, f.pl.*; *spiritueux, m.pl.* Depressed —**s**, low —**s**; *abattement; accablement, m.sing.* Good —**s**, high —**s**; *gaîté, f.sing.*; *entrain, m.sing.*; *bonne humeur, f.sing.* Evil-—; *mauvais génie, m.* Raw —**s**; *liqueurs pures, sans eau, f.pl.* To labour under depression of —**s**; *être abattu; être dans l'abattement.* To raise any one's —**s**; *égayer quelqu'un, remonter le courage à quelqu'un; mettre quelqu'un de bonne humeur.* To raise a —; *évoquer un esprit.* Proof-—; *esprit de preuve.* A man of —; *un homme de cœur, de caractère.*

spirit, *v.a.*, animer; encourager; exciter.

spirited, *adj.*, animé, plein de cœur, plein de courage, plein de caractère; plein d'ardeur; ardent; chaleureux; entraînant; plein de force, plein de vigueur; vigoureux; fort; vif; plein de verve; (of horses—*des chevaux*) fougueux, vif, ardent. Bold-—; *hardi.* High-—; *de caractère; plein de cœur.* Low-—; *abattu; dans l'abattement.* Mean-—; *sans cœur, sans caractère.* Poor-—; *sans cœur, sans caractère, lâche.*

spiritedly, *adj.*, avec cœur, avec caractère, avec courage; courageusement; avec ardeur; ardemment; chaleureusement; avec force, avec vigueur; vivement; fortement; vigoureusement.

spiritedness,*n.*,cœur; courage; caractère; feu, *m.*; ardeur; chaleur, *f.*; entraînement, *m.*; verve; force; vigueur, *f.*; (of horses— *des chevaux*) fougue, ardeur, *f.* Bold-—; *hardiesse, f.* High-—; *caractère, cœur.* Low- —; *abattement, m.* Mean-—; *manque de cœur, m.*; *lâcheté, f.*

spiritless, *adj.*, inanimé, sans âme; (destitute of vigour—*dépourvu de vigueur*) languissant, sans caractère,—sans ardeur, sans force; (without courage—*sans courage*) sans cœur, sans courage; (dejected—*accablé*) abattu, accablé, dans l'abattement, dans l'accablement.

spiritlessly, *adj.*, sans cœur, sans courage.

spiritlessness, *n.*, manque de caractère; manque de cœur; manque d'ardeur; manque de force, *m.*

spirit-level (-lèv'-), *n.*, niveau à bulle d'air, *m.*

spiritous, *adj.*,'spirituel; ardent; (of alcohol —*d'alcool*) rectifié; épuré.

spirit-room (-roume), *n.*, (nav.) cale au vin, *f.*

spirit-stirring (-steur'-), *adj.*, qui réveille l'âme; qui excite le cœur.

spirit-trade, *n.*,commerce des spiritueux,*m.*

spiritual (-'iou-), *adj.*, spirituel.

spiritualism (-'iou-al'iz'm), *n.*, spiritualisme, *m.*

spiritualist, *n.*, spiritualiste, *m./f.*

spirituality, *n.*, spiritualité,*f.*; spirituel,*m.*

spiritualization (-'aï-zé-), *n.*, spiritualisation, *f.*

spiritualize (-'iou-al'aïze),*v.a.*,spiritualiser.

spiritually, *adv.*, spirituellement.

spirituous (-'iou-), *adj.*, spiritueux.

spirituousness, *n.*, propriété spiritueuse,*f.*

spirt (speurte), *n.*, jaillissement; rejaillissement; (sudden effort—*effort soudain*) accès, *m.*, boutade, saillie, *f.*

spirt (speurte), *v.a.*, faire jaillir; faire rejaillir.

spirt, *v.n.*, saillir; jaillir; rejaillir; s'élancer.

spiry (spaeur'-), *adj.*, spiral; en spirale; en flèche.

spissated (-sé-), *adj.*, épaissi.

spissitude (-tioude), *n.*, nature épaissie, *f.*

spit, *n.*, broche; (depth of earth pierced by the spade—*profondeur d'un coup de bêche*) terre bêchée; pelletée, *f.*; (saliva—*salive*) crachat, *m.*, salive, *f.* He is the very —of his father; *c'est son père tout craché.*

spit, *v.a.* (preterit and past part., Spit), embrocher; mettre à la broche; (to eject from the mouth—*cracher*) cracher, rejeter.

spit, *v.n.*, cracher; saliver. To — in any one's face; *cracher au visage à quelqu'un.*

spite (spaïte), *n.*, dépit, *m.*; haine; rancune, *f.* In — of; *en dépit de, malgré.* Out of —; *par dépit.* To have a — against any one; *garder rancune à quelqu'un; en vouloir à quelqu'un.*

spite (spaïte), *v.a.*, dépiter; avoir du dépit contre.

spiteful (-foule), *adj.*, plein de dépit; rancunier, méchant.

spitefully, *adv.*, par dépit; par haine; par rancune, par méchanceté.

spitefulness, *n.*, dépit, *m.*; rancune; méchanceté; haine,*f.*

spitter, *n.*, personne qui embroche, *f.*; (deer—*cerf*) daguet; (pers.) cracheur, *m.*, cracheuse,*f.*

spitting, *n.*, crachement, *m.*

spitting-box, *n.*, crachoir, *m.*

spittle (spit't'l), *n.*, salive, *f.*; crachat, *m.*

spittoon (-toune), *n.*, crachoir, *m.*

splanchnic (spla'nk'-),*adj.*, (anat.) splanchnique.

splanchnology (splan'gn'k-nol'o-dji), *n.*, (anat.) splanchnologie, *f.*

splash, *v.a.*, éclabousser.

splash, *v.n.*, patauger.

splash, *n.*, éclaboussure, *f.*

splash-board (-bôrde), *n.*, garde-crotte, *m.*

splasher, *n.*, personne qui éclabousse, *f.*

splashy, *adj.*, gâcheux; bourbeux.

splay, *v.a.*, épauler (a horse—*un cheval*); (arch.) ébraser; évaser.

splay, *n.*, écartement, évasement; (arch.) ébrasement, *m.*

splay-foot, *or* **splay-footed** (-fout'-), *adj.*, qui a les pieds larges, *ou* tournés en dehors.

splay-mouth (-maouth),*n.*,grande bouche,*f.*

spleen (splîne), *n.*, rate ; (anger—*fiel*) haine, *f.*, fiel, *m.*, animosité, bile, *f.* ; (melancholy—*mélancolie*) spleen, *m.*, mélancolie, humeur noire, *f.* To have the — ; *avoir le spleen, broyer du noir ; avoir l'humeur noire.*

spleened (splî'n'de), *adj.*, dératé.

spleenful (-foule),**spleeny,** or **spleenish**, *adj.*, irrité,chagrin ; (melancholy—*mélancolique*) mélancolique, splénétique.

splendent, *adj.*, resplendissant ; éclatant.

splendid, *adj.*, (shining—*luisant*) resplendissant, éclatant ; (brilliant—*éclatant*) brillant, éclatant ; (sumptuous—*somptueux*) somptueux, splendide ; (magnificent—*magnifique*) magnifique.

splendidly, *adv.*, d'une manière resplendissante ; avec éclat ; brillamment ; somptueusement, splendidement ; magnifiquement.

splendour (splè'n'deur), *n.*, splendeur, *f.* ; éclat, *m.*

splenetic, *adj.*, atrabilaire ; splénétique ; chagrin.

splenetic, *n.*, hypocondriaque, *m.*, *f.*

splenic, or **splenical,** *adj.*,(anat.)splénique.

splenitive, *adj.*, (ant.) emporté ; colère ; irascible.

splent, *n.*, (vet.) suros, *m.*

splice (splaïce), *n.*, (nav.) épissure, *f.*

splice (splaïce), *v.a.*, (nav.) épisser ; (carp.) joindre à onglet.

splicing-fid (splaïss'-), *n.*, épissoir, *m.*

splint, or **splinter,** *n.*, éclat, éclat de bois, *m.* ; (of a bone—*d'os*) esquille ; (surg.) attelle, éclisse, *f.* ; (vet.) suros, *m.* ; (small—*petit*) écharde, épine, *f.* To fly into —s ; *voler en éclats.*

splint, or **splinter,** *v.a.*, faire éclater, briser en éclats ; (surg.) éclisser, mettre une attelle à.

splint-bone (-bône), *n.*, péroné, *m.*

splinter, *v.n.*, se briser en éclats.

splinter-bar, *n.*, barre d'appui des ressorts, *f.*

splintery, *adj.*, (min.) écailleux, à écailles.

split, *v.a.* (preterit and past part., Split), fendre ; briser ; (a sail—*une voile*) crever. To — one's sides with laughing ; *crever de rire.* To — asunder ; *fendre en deux.* To — into ; *diviser en.*

split, *v.n.*, se fendre. To — into ; *se fendre en.* To — with laughter ; *crever de rire.*

splitter, *n.*, fendeur, *m.*, fendeuse, *f.*

splutter (spleut'-), *n.*, tracas ; tapage, *m.*

splutter (spleut'-), *v.n.*, bredouiller.

spoil (spoïl), *n.*, dépouille, *f.* ; butin, *m.* ; (of animals—*des animaux*) dépouille, *f.*

spoil, or **spoil-bank,** *n.*, déblai ; lieu de dépôt de déblai, *m.*

spoil (spoïl), *v.a.*, (to corrupt—*gâter*) corrompre ; (to destroy—*détruire*) détruire, ruiner ; (to injure—*abîmer*) gâter, abîmer ; (to seize by violence—*prendre de force*) se saisir de, s'emparer de. To — a child ; *gâter un enfant.* To — of ; *spolier de ; dépouiller de.* To — sport ; *troubler la fête.*

spoil, *v.n.*, se corrompre ; se gâter ; (to practise plunder—*extorquer*) exercer des spoliations.

spoiled (spoïl'de), *adj.*, gâté ; abîmé.

spoiler, *n.*, personne qui gâte, qui abîme, *f.* ; (plunderer—*pillard*) spoliateur, *m.*, spoliatrice, *f.*

spoiling, *n.*, spoliation ; action de gâter, *f.*

spoil-sport, *n.*, trouble-fête, *m.*

spoke (spôke), *n.*, rais, rayon, *m.*

spoken (spôk'n), *past part.* V. **speak.**

spoke-shave, *n.*, (carp.) plane, *f.*

spokesman (spôks'-), *n.*, orateur, *m.* ; personne qui porte la parole, *f.*

spoliate (spô-), *v.a.*, dépouiller ; spolier ; piller.

spoliate, *v.n.*, exercer des spoliations.

spoliation (spô-li-é-), *n.*, spoliation, *f.*

spondaic, or **spondaical** (-daï-), *adj.*, spondaïque.

spondee (-dî), *n.*, spondée, *m.*

spondyle (-dil), *n.*, (anat.) spondyle, *m.* ; vertèbre, *f.*

sponge (speu'n'dje), *n.*, éponge, *f.* ; (artil.) écouvillon, *m.*

sponge, *v.a.*, éponger; (artil.) écouvillonner.

sponge (speu'n'dje), *v.n.*, boire : (to gain things by mean acts—*obtenir par des bassesses*) piquer l'assiette. To — on ; *écornifler.*

sponger, *n.*, personne qui éponge. *f.* ; (fig.) pique-assiette, écornifleur, *m.*, écornifleuse, *f.*

sponginess, *n.*, nature spongieuse, *f.*

sponging, *n.*, action d'éponger ; (fig.) écorniflerie, *f.*

sponging-house (-haouce), *n.*, maison d'huissier, *f.*

spongious, *adj.*, spongieux.

sponk, *n.*, amadou, *m.*

sponsal, *adj.*, conjugal.

sponsion, *n.*, garantie, *f.*

sponsor (-seur), *n.*, parrain, *m.*, marraine, *f.* ; (surety—*caution*) garant, *m.*

spontaneity (-nî-i-), *n.*, spontanéité, *f.*

spontaneous (-té-ni-), *adj.*, spontané.

spontaneously, *adv.*, spontanément.

spontaneousness, *n.*, spontanéité, *f.*

spontoon (-toune), *n.*,esponton ; sponton, *m.*

spool (spoul), *n.*, bobine, *f.*

spool (spoul), *v.a.*, bobiner.

spoom (spoume), *v.n.*, (nav.) courir vent arrière.

spoon (spoune), *n.*, cuiller, cuillère, *f.* ; (simpleton—*sot*) niais, sot, *m.* Table- — ; *cuiller à soupe.* Dessert- — ; *cuiller à dessert.* Tea- — ; *cuiller à thé.* Gravy- — ; *cuiller à ragoût.*

spoonbill, *n.*, (orni.) palette, *f.*

spoondrift, *n.*, (nav.) embrun, *m.* ; éclaboussure ; poussière d'eau de mer, *f.*

spoonful (-foule), *n.*, cuillerée, *f.*

spoonmaker (-mék'-), *n.*, cuilleriste, *m.*

spoonmeat (-mîte), *n.*, aliment liquide, *m.*

spoonwort (-weurte), *n.*, (bot.) cochléaria, *m.* ; herbe aux cuillers, *f.*

spoony, *adj.*, niais, sot. — on ; *amoureux de.*

sporadic, or **sporadical,** *adj.*, (med.) sporadique.

sport (spôrte), *n.*, sport, jeu, divertissement, amusement, *m.* ; récréation ; (mockery—*raillerie*) moquerie, raillerie, *f.* ; (plaything—*joujou*) jouet ; (of words—*de mots*) jeu, *m.* ; (hunt., shooting—*chasse*) chasse, *f.* ; (fishing—*pêche*) pêche, *f.* To be the — of ; *être le jouet de.* To make a — of ; *se jouer de ; se rire de.* To spoil — ; *troubler la fête.*

sport (spôrte), *v.a.*, (to divert—*amuser*) divertir ; (to represent—*représenter*) représenter ; (to exhibit—*exhiber*) étaler, faire parade de.

sport, *v.n.*, se divertir, s'amuser ; se récréer ; folâtrer, badiner. To — with (to trifle with—*bafouer*) ; *se jouer de ; se faire un jeu de.*

sporter, *n.*, personne qui se divertit, qui s'amuse, qui se récrée, *f.*

sportful (-foul), *adj.*, joyeux ; enjoué ; folâtre, badin.

sportfully, *adv.*, avec enjouement ; en riant ; en plaisantant, pour badiner, pour rire.

sportfulness, *n.*, enjouement, *m.* ; gaieté humeur joyeuse ; plaisanterie, folâtrerie, *f.* ; badinage, *m.*

sporting, *n.*, divertissement, *m.* ; (hunt., shooting—*chasse*) chasse; (fishing—*pêche*) pêche, *f.*

sportive, *adj.*, enjoué ; gai ; badin, folâtre.

sportiveness, *n.*, enjouement, *m.* ; gaieté, folâtrerie, humeur badine, *f.*

sportsman, *n.*, chasseur ; amateur de la chasse, amateur de la pêche, *m.*

spot, *n.*, tache ; (stain on character, &c.—*atteinte à la réputation, &c.*) tache, souillure, *f.* ; (place—*lieu*) endroit, lieu, *m.*, place ; (astron.)

tache, *f.* A — of ground; *morceau de terre. m.*
On the —; *sur le lieu; sur la place;* (immediately) *sur-le-champ.*

spot, *v.a.*, tacher; tacheter; moucheter; (to blemish—*flétrir*) tacher, souiller.

spotless. *adj.*, sans tache; pur.

spotlessness, *n.*, pureté, *f.*

spotted. *adj.*, tacheté; moucheté; (of tigers —*du tigre*) tigré.

spottedness, *n.*, tachetures; mouchetures, *f.pl.*

spotter. *n.*, personne qui fait des taches, *f.*

spotty, *adj.*, couvert de taches; moucheté; taché, tacheté.

spousal (spaou-zal), *adj.*, nuptial; matrimonial; conjugal,

spousals (-zalze), *n.pl.*, épousailles; noces, *f.pl.*

spouse (spaouze), *n.*, époux, *m.*, épouse, *f.*; mari, *m.*, femme, *f.*

spouseless, *adj.*, sans époux; sans épouse.

spout (spaoute), *n.*, tuyau; tuyau de décharge; canal; (of a pitcher, &c.—*d'une écuelle, &c.*) bec, goulot, *m.*; (of a house—*de maison*) gouttière; (mines) ouverture, *f.*; (at sea—*en mer*) siphon, *m.*, trombe, *f.* Up the —; (in pawn—*èn gage*) *en gage;* (pop.) *chez ma tante.*

spout (spaoute), *v.n.*, jaillir, rejaillir, s'élancer; (to declaim—*déclamer*) déclamer.

spout, *v.a.*, verser, lancer, jeter; (to declaim —*déclamer*) déclamer; (to pawn—*engager*) mettre en gage.

spouter, *n.*, déclamateur, *m,*

spouting, *n.*, jaillissement; rejaillissement, *m.*; (declamation) déclamation, *f.*.

sprain (spré'n), *n.*, entorse; foulure, *f.*

sprain (spré'n), *v.a.*, donner une entorse à; fouler; se fouler; se donner une entorse à. I have —ed my wrist; *je me suis foulé le poignet.* He has — ed his ankle; *il s'est donné une entorse à la cheville.*

sprat, *n.*, (ich.) sprat, *m.* To catch a herring; *donner un œuf pour avoir un bœuf.*

sprawl (spröl), *v.n.*, s'étendre; s'étaler; (to move when lying down—*s'agiter, étant par terre*) s'agiter, se débattre.

spray, *n.*, (branch—*branche*) brin, *m.*; brindille, ramille, *f.*; (of the sea—*de la mer*) embrun de la mer, embrun, *m.*

spread (sprède), *v.a.* (*preterit and past part.,* Spread), étendre; déployer; (to cover—*couvrir*) couvrir, s'étendre sur; (to propagate—*propager*) répandre, propager; (to emit—*émettre*) répandre, exhaler; (to scatter—*répandre*) répandre; (a sail —*une voile*) déferler, déployer; (a net—*un filet*) tendre; (*une tente*) dresser; (a disease—*une maladie*) répandre, propager. To — the table; *mettre le couvert; dresser la table.* To — abroad; *répandre au loin.* To — over; *répandre sur; épandre sur.* To — out; *étendre.* To — the report of; *répandre, faire courir, propager le bruit de.* A paleness — her face; *une pâleur s'étendait sur son visage.*

spread, *v.n.*, s'étendre; se déployer; se répandre; se propager; s'exhaler; s'épandre.

spread (sprède), *n.*, étendue; (expansion) expansion; (propagation) propagation, *f.*; (feast—*festin*) régal, *m.*

spreader, *n.*, propagateur, *m.* He was the — of that report; *c'est lui qui a propagé ce bruit.* She was the — of that calumny; *c'est elle qui a répandu cette calomnie.*

spreading, *n.*, action de s'étendre, de se répandre; propagation, *f.*

spree (spri), *n.*, fredaine, *f.*

sprig. *n.*, brin, *m.*; brindille, *f.*; rejeton, surgeon. scion. *m.*; (in embroidery—*de broderie*) branche, *f.* — of nobility; *hobereau, m.*

sprig, *v.a.*, orner de branches; broder des branches sur.

spriggy (sprig-ghi), *adj.*, chargé de brindilles; chargé de rejetons.

spright (spraïte), *n.*, spectre; esprit; fantôme, *m.*; apparition, *f.*

sprightful (-foul), *adj.*, vif; animé; enjoué.

sprightfully, *adv.*, vivement; avec ardeur.

sprightfulness, *n.*, ardeur; vivacité, *f.*

sprightless (spraït'-), *adj.*, sans ardeur; froid; inanimé.

sprightliness, *n.*, vivacité; gaieté, *f.*; enjouement, feu, *m.*

sprightly (spraït'-), *adj.*, enjoué, vif, animé, gai, sémillant.

spring, *v.n.* (*preterit*, Sprung, Sprang; *past part.*, Sprung), (to begin to grow—*commencer à croître*) pousser, croître; (to spurt out—*jaillir*) jaillir, rejaillir; (to begin to appear—*commencer à paraître*) surgir, commencer, paraître, poindre; (to blaze into sight—*naître*) venir au jour, naître; (to be descended—*descendre*) descendre; (to thrive—*prospérer*) prospérer, s'élever; (to leap, to shoot—*s'élancer*) se lancer, s'élancer; (to rise from a covert—*sauter hors du couvert*) se lever. To — at; *tâcher de saisir.* To — back; *s'élancer en arrière; reculer;* (of things—*des choses*) *faire ressort.* To — forth; *pousser, croître;* (to spurt out—*jaillir*) jaillir, rejaillir. To — forward; *s'élancer en avant.* To — from; (to issue from—*provenir de*) sortir de, naître de, provenir de, découler de, dériver de. To — in; *se précipiter dans, sauter dans.* To — on; *se précipiter sur; s'élancer sur, sauter sur.* To — out; *s'élancer dehors;* (to spurt out—*jaillir*) jaillir, rejaillir. To — over; *sauter, franchir.* To — up; (to rise up—*se lever vite*) se lever précipitamment; (to grow—*croître*) pousser, croître, lever; (of young persons—*de personnes jeunes*) grandir.

spring, *v.a.*, (to rouse—*faire lever*) faire lever, faire partir; (to produce quickly—*produire rapidement*) produire; (to cause to explode—*faire sauter*) faire sauter; (nav.: a leak—*une voie d'eau*) faire; (a mast, a yard—*un mât, une vergue*) faire consentir; (a trap—*un piège*) faire jouer; (a rattle—*une crécelle*) sonner.

spring, *n.*, (leap—*saut*) saut, élan; (resilience—*ressort*) ressort; (elastic power—*force élastique*) ressort, *m.*, élasticité, *f.*; (elastic plate, wire, &c.—*ressort métallique*). ressort; (active power—*force*) ressort, *m.*; (fountain, source—*fontaine*) source; (cause) cause, origine, *f.*; (season—*saison*) printemps, *m.*; (nav.) fente, *f.* Main- —; *grand ressort.* To take a —; *prendre son élan.* In the —; *au printemps.*

spring-box, or **springbuck** (-beuke), *n.*, gazelle africaine, *f.*

spring-box, *n.*, (horl.) barillet, *m.*

spring-carriage (-kar-ridje), *n.*, voiture suspendue, *f.*

springe (spri'n'dje), *n.*, lacet, *m.*; lacs, *m.pl.*

springe (sprin'dje), *v.a.*, prendre au lacet, prendre aux lacs.

springer (sprin'djeur), *n.*, (hunt.) traqueur, rabatteur, *m.*; (arch.) imposte, *f.*

springgun (-gheune), *n.*, fusil à ressort, *m.*

spring-head (-hède), *n.*, grande source, *f.*

springiness (sprign'i-), *n.*, élasticité (abundance of springs—*abondance de sources*) abondance de sources; (wetness—*humidité*) humidité, *f.*

springing (sprign'-), *n.*, action de s'élancer, de lancer, *f.*; élan, saut, *m.*; (increase—*crue*) croissance, crue; (arch.) naissance, *f.*

springing-level (sprign'igne-lèv'-), *n.*, (arch.) niveau des naissances, *m.*

springing-line (sprign'igne-laïne), *n.*, (arch.) ligne de naissance, *f.*; montant, *m.*

spring-tide (-taïde), *n.*, (nav.) grande marée, maline, *f.*

spring-time (-taïme), *n.*, printemps, *m.*

spring-water (-wô-), *n.*, eau de source, *f.*

spring-wheat (-hwîte), n., blé de mars, m.

springy (sprign'i), adj., élastique; (abounding in springs—abondant en sources) plein de sources.

sprinkle (spri'n'k'l), n., petite quantité répandue, f.

sprinkle, v.imp., pleuvoir un peu.

sprinkle (spri'n'k'l), v.a., répandre; parsemer; saupoudrer; (with water—d'eau) arroser; (with holy-water—d'eau bénite) asperger. To — with salt; saupoudrer de sel. —d with gold; parsemé d'or.

sprinkler, n., personne qui asperge, qui arrose; chose qui asperge, f. Holy-water- —; aspersoir, goupillon, m.

sprinkling, n., action de répandre, de saupoudrer; aspersion, f.; arrosement, m.'; (small quantity—petite quantité) petite quantité, f. A — of rain; quelques gouttes de pluie.

sprit, n., (sprout—jet) jet, rejeton, m.; (nav.) livarde, f.

sprit, v.n., (ant.) pousser; germer.

sprite (spraïte), n., spectre; esprit; fantôme, m.

sprit-sail (-séle), n., voile à livarde; civadière, f.

sprocket-wheel (-hwîle), n., (mec.) hérisson, m.

sprout (spraoute), n., jet; chou vert, m. Brussels- —s; choux de Bruxelles.

sprout (spraoute), v.n., pousser; germer.

spruce (sprouce), adj., paré; orné; requinqué; pimpant.

spruce (sprouce), v.n., se parer; se requinquer.

spruce (sprouce), n., sapin, m.; épinette, f.

sprucely, adv., d'une manière pimpante, avec recherche.

spruceness, n., recherche, f.; air pimpant, air requinqué, m.

spud (speude), n., petit couteau, m.; (agri.) béquille, f.

spud (speude), v.a., béquiller.

spume (spioume), n., écume, f.

spume (spioume), v.n., écumer.

spumescence (spiou-), n., état spumeux, m.

spumid, spumous, or **spumy** (spiou-), adj., écumeux; plein d'écume; spumeux.

spunge. V. sponge.

spunging-house. V. sponging-house.

spunk (speu'n'ke), n., amadou; (pop.) (spirit —courage) cœur, m.

spun-yarn (speun'yârne), n., (nav.) bitord, m. — -winch; moulinet, m.

spur (speur), n., éperon; (of cocks—des coqs) ergot; (in grain—des grains) ergot; (carp.) arcboutant; (bot., fort.) éperon; (incitement—excitant) aiguillon stimulant, m. On the — of the moment; sous l'impulsion du moment.

spur (speur), v.a., éperonner; piquer des deux; (to incite-exciter) stimuler, aiguillonner, exciter, pousser, presser, encourager; (to put spurs on—mettre des éperons à) armer d'éperons, mettre des éperons à. To — on; presser, aiguillonner.

spur, v.n., jouer des éperons; avancer; (ant.) voyager rapidement.

spurgall (-gôl), n., blessure d'éperon, f.

spurgall (-gôl), v.a., blesser avec l'éperon.

spurge (speurdje), n., (bot.) euphorbe, m. Caper- — ; épurge, f.

spurious (spiou-), adj., faux; (adulterated —frelaté) falsifié, sophistiqué; (of writings—d'écrits) apocryphe; (med., bot.) faux; (jur.) illégitime. — edition; édition de contrefaçon.

spuriously, adv., faussement; (of books—de livres) par contrefaçon.

spuriousness, n., falsification; sophistication; fausseté; nature apocryphe; (jur.) illégitimité, f.

spur-maker (-m^r'k'-), n., éperonnier. m.

spurn (speurne), n., mépris, dédain, m.

spurn (speurne), v.a., pousser du pied; (to reject with disdain—rejeter avec mépris) rejeter avec mépris, rejeter dédaigneusement, repousser dédaigneusement; (to treat with disdain—traiter avec mépris) traiter avec mépris, mépriser.

spurn, v.n., gigoter. To — at; repousser dédaigneusement; rejeter dédaigneusement; dédaigner, mépriser.

spurner, n., personne qui méprise, qui dédaigne, f.; contempteur, f.

spurred (speurde), adj., éperonné; (of rye, of cocks—du seigle, des coqs) ergoté.

spurrier (speur'-), n., cavalier qui use de l'éperon, m.

spurrier (speur'-), n., éperonnier, m.

spurt (speurte), v.a. V. spirt.

spur-wheel (-hwîle), n., (tech.) hérisson, m.

sputter (speut'-), n., salive, f.; (noise—bruit) vacarme; (stammering—bredouillement) bredouillement, m.

sputter (speut'-), v.n., cracher.

sputter, v.a., cracher en parlant; (to utter indistinctly—bredouiller) bredouiller; (of pens—des plumes) cracher; (of things burning—de choses qui brûlent) siffler.

sputterer, n., personne qui crache en parlant, f.; bredouilleur, m., bredouilleuse, f.

spy (spa'ye), n., espion, m., espionne, f.

spy (spa'ye), v.a., voir; apercevoir; découvrir; épier. To — out; trouver, découvrir.

spy, v.a., scruter, épier.

spy-boat (-bôte), n., petite corvette, f.

spy-glass (-glâce), n., longue-vue, lunette d'approche, f.

squab (skwôbe), n., coussin; sofa; (young pigeon—jeune pigeon) pigeonneau, m.

squab (skwôbe), adj., dodu; potelé; (of birds —des oiseaux) sans plumes.

squab, adv., lourdement; avec violence; rudement.

squabble (skwab'b'l), n., dispute; bagarre; querelle, f.; (print.) soleil, m.

squabble (skwab'b'l), v.n., se quereller; se chamailler.

squabbler, n., querelleur, m., querelleuse, f.

squabbling, n., querelle, f.; chamaillis, m.

squab-pie (-pa'ye), n., pâté de pigeonneaux, m.

squad (skwôde), n., escouade; clique, f.

squadron (skwôd'reune), n., (of cavalry—de cavalerie) escadron; (of infantry—d'infanterie) bataillon. m.; (nav.) escadre, division, f.

squadroned (skwôd'reu'n'de), adj., formé en carré; rangé en escadron.

squalid (skwôl'-), adj., crasseux; sale.

squalidly, adv., salement, malproprement.

squalidness, n., malpropreté; crasse; saleté, f.

squall (skwôl), n., cri; (of wind—de vent) coup de vent, grain, m., rafale, f.

squall (skwôl), v.n., crier; brailler; piailler; criailler.

squaller, n., crieur, m., crieuse, f.; brailleur, m., brailleuse, f.; criard, m., criarde, f.; criailleur, m., criailleuse, f., braillard, m., braillarde, f.

squalling, n., criaillerie, f.; cris, m.pl.

squally, adj., exposé à des coups de vent; tempétueux.

squalor (skwé-), n., saleté; crasse, f.

squamiform (skwé-), adj., squamiforme.

squamigerous (skwa-midj'èr-), adj., squameux.

squamose (skwa-môce), or **squamous** (skwé-), adj., squameux; écailleux.

squander (skwo'n'-), v.a., dissiper; gaspiller; dépenser follement.

squanderer (skwo'n'-), n., dissipateur, m., dissipatrice, f.; gaspilleur, m., gaspilleuse, f.; prodigue, m., f.

squandering, *n.*, dissipation, *f.*; gaspillage, *m.*

square (skwére), *n.*, carré; (on stuffs—*sur les étoffes*) carreau; (equality—*égalité*) niveau, pied d'égalité, *m.*, égalité; (rule—*règle*) règle, *f.*; (carp.) équarrissage, *m.*; (arith.) carré, *m.*; (on a chessboard—*d'échiquier*) case, *f.* Set —; *équerre, f.*

square (skwére), *v.a.*, carrer; (to regulate—*régler*) régler; (to fit—*adapter*) proportionner; (carp.) équarrir; (arith.) carrer; (accounts—*comptes*) balancer, solder; (a yard—*une vergue*) brasser carré.

square, *v.n.*, cadrer; s'accorder; (to quarrel —*se disputer*) se quereller. To — up to any one; *s'avancer vers quelqu'un en posture de combat à coups de poing.*

square, *adj.*, carré; (leaving no balance—*soldé*) balancé, soldé; (true—*vrai*) vrai; (fair—*juste*) équitable, juste; (honest—*honnête*) honnête; (carp.) d'équarrissage; (math., nav.) carré. To make an account — ; *balancer un compte.*

square-built (-bilte), *adj.*, bâti en carré; taillé carrément.

squarely, *adv.*, carrément; (fairly—*équitablement*) honnêtement, justement, équitablement.

squareness (skwér'-), *n.*, forme carrée, *f.*

square-rigged (-rig'de), *adj.*, mâté à carré.

square-sail (-séle), *n.*, voile carrée, *f.*

squarish (skwér'-), *adj.*, à peu près carré.

squarrose (skwar'rôse), *or* **squarrous** (skwar'-), *adj.*, (bot.) squarreux.

squash (skwosh), *v.a.*, écraser; (jur.) casser.

squash (skwosh), *n.*, chose molle; (fall—*chute*) chute lourde, *f.*; écrasement, *m.*; (bot.) gourde, courge, *f.*

squat (skwote), *adj.*, accroupi; blotti; (short and thick—*trapu*) trapu, ramassé.

squat (skwote), *v.n.*, se tapir; s'accroupir; se blottir.

squat (skwote), *n.*, accroupissement, *m.*

squatter, *n.*, personne accroupie, blottie, *f.*; animal accroupi, blotti, *m.*

squatting, *n.*, action de s'accroupir, de se blottir, *f.*; accroupissement, *m.*

squaw (skwô), *n.*, femme; épouse (among the savages of Northern America—*chez les sauvages de l'Amérique du Nord*), *f.*

squeak (skwîke), *n.*, cri; cri aigre, *m.*

squeak (skwîke), *v.n.*, crier; (of musical instruments—*d'instruments de musique*) jurer.

squeaker, *n.*, personne qui crie, *f.*; criard, *m.*; criarde, *f.*; animal qui crie, *m.*

squeaking, *adj.*, qui crie; criard; (of musical instruments—*d'instruments de musique*) qui jure.

squeal (skwîle), *v.n.*, crier.

squeamish (skwi-), *adj.*, (of the stomach—*de l'estomac*) qui se soulève; (fastidious—*difficile*) trop délicat, trop difficile; délicat, difficile. To be —; *faire le difficile.*

squeamishly, *adv.*, trop délicatement.

squeamishness, *n.*, (of the stomach—*de l'estomac*) disposition à se soulever; (fastidiousness—*délicatesse outrée*) délicatesse exagérée, *f.*

squeeze (skwîze), *n.*, action de serrer, de presser; compression, *f.*; (of the hand—*de la main*) serrement, *m.*

squeeze (skwîze), *v.a.*, serrer; presser. To — out; *exprimer.* To — through; *forcer à travers.*

squeeze, *v.n.*, serrer, presser. To — through; *se forcer à travers.* To — out of; *sortir de . . . en pressant, en poussant.*

squeezing, *n.*, action de presser, de serrer; pression, *f.*; (that which is squeezed out—*substance exprimée*) pressurage, *m.*

squib (skwibe), *n.*, pétard, *m.*; (lampoon—*satire*) satire personnelle, *f.*

squib (skwibe), *v.n.*, lancer des pétards; lancer des satires personnelles.

squill (skwil), *n.*, (bot.) scille; (ich.) squille, *f.*

squinancy (skwi'n'-), *n.*, (bot.) aspérule, *f.*

squint (skwi'n'te), *adj.*, louche; (fig.) d'un regard méfiant.

squint (skwi'n'te), *n.*, regard louche, *m.*

squint (skwi'n'te), *v.n.*, loucher; (fig.) s'écarter de la droite ligne.

squint-eyed (-a-ye'de), *adj.*, louche, oblique; indirect; méchant; qui regarde de côté.

squinting, *n.*, action de loucher, *f.*; strabisme, *m.*

squintingly, *adv.*, en louchant.

squire (skwa'eur), *n.*, écuyer; (of a lady—*d'une dame*) cavalier; chevalier; squire, *m.* [title donné en Angleterre au propriétaire le plus influent, mais non noble, d'un village.]

squire (skwa-eur), *v.a.*, servir d'écuyer; servir de cavalier à; escorter.

squirely, *adj.*, d'écuyer, de cavalier.

squireship, *n.*, qualité d'écuyer, de cavalier, *f.*

squirrel (skwir'rèl), *n.*, écureuil, *m.*

squirt, *n.*, seringue, *f.*; (small quick stream —*petit jet d'eau*) jet d'eau, *m.*

squirt (skweurte), *v.a.*, seringuer.

squirter, *n.*, personne qui seringue, *f.*

stab, *n.*, coup; coup mortel; coup de poignard, coup d'épée, coup de couteau, *m.*

stab, *v.a. and n.*, poignarder; percer; frapper; porter un coup de poignard à, un coup d'épée à, un coup mortel à; donner un coup de couteau à; faire une blessure mortelle.

stabber, *n.*, personne qui donne un coup de poignard; personne qui frappe, *f.*

stabbing, *n.*, coup d'épée, coup de poignard, *m.*

stabiliment, *n.*, appui; soutien, *m.*

stabilitate, *v.a.*, (ant.) consolider; rendre stable.

stability, *or* **stableness** (sté-b'l'nèce), *n.*, stabilité; fixité; (pers.) constance, fermeté, *f.*

stable (sté-b'l), *adj.*, stable; fixe; (pers.) constant, ferme.

stable (sté-b'l), *v.a.*, (cattle—*bestiaux*) établer; (horses—*chevaux*) loger.

stable (sté-b'l), *n.*, (for horses—*pour les chevaux*) écurie; (for cattle—*pour les bestiaux*) étable, *f.*

stable-boy (-boï), *or* **stable-man**, *n.*, valet d'écurie, *m.*

stableness. *V.* **stability.**

stable-yard (-yârde), *n.*, cour d'écurie, *f.*

stabling (sté-), *n.*, action d'établer, *f.*; (for horses—*pour chevaux*) écuries, (for cattle—*pour les bestiaux*) étables, *f.pl.*

stably (sté-), *adv.*, d'une manière stable.

stack, *n.*, (of chimneys—*de cheminées*) souche; (of hay, &c.—*de foin, &c.*) meule; (of wood—*de bois*) pile, *f.*

stack, *v.a.*, (wood—*du bois*) empiler; (hay, &c. —*du foin, &c.*) amenlonner, mettre en meule.

stack-yard (-yârde), *n.*, cour de ferme, *f.*

stacte (stac-ti), *n.*, myrrhe, *f.*

staddle (stad'd'l), *n.*, (young tree—*jeune arbre*) baliveau; (support) appui; (of hay—*de foin*) support, *m.*

staddle (stad'd'l), *v.a.*, laisser des baliveaux; (hay—*foin*) faire un support à une meule.

staddle-roof (-roufe), *n.*, toit d'une meule de foin, *m.*

stadium (sté-), *n.*, stade, *m.*

stadtholder (-hôld'-), *n.*, stathouder, *m.*

stadtholderate, *n.*, stathoudérat, *m.*

staff (stâf), *n.*, bâton; bourdon; gourdin; (milit.) état-major, *m.*; (poet.) stance, strophe; (mus.) portée, *f.*; (nav.) bâton, mâtereau; (support) soutien, appui, bâton; (badge of office—*insigne*) bâton de commandement, *m.* Flag— ; *bâton de pavillon.* Field-marshal's —; *bâton de*

maréchal, *m.* Medical —; (milit.) *service de santé*, *m.* Bread is the — of life; *le pain est le soutien de la vie.*

stag, *n.*, cerf, *m.*

stage (stédje), *n.*, (platform—*plate-forme*) estrade; (thea.) scène, *f.*; théâtre; (degree of advance—*phase*) degré, *m.*, période, phase, *f.*; (relay—*relais*) relais; (of a press—*de presse*) établi, *m.*; (for a mountebank—*de saltimbanque*) tréteaux, *m.pl.*;(nav.) échafaud,plancher; (arch.) échafaud, *m.* To come on, to go on the —; *entrer en scène.* To go on the —(to turn actor—*devenir acteur*); *se faire acteur.* To quit the —(the profession—*la profession*); *quitter le théâtre.* To go off the —; *quitter la scène.*

stage, or **stage-coach** (-côtshe), *n.*, diligence; voiture publique, *f.*

stage-dancer, *n.*, baladin, *m.*

stage-directions (-di-rèk'-), *n.pl.*, indications scéniques,*f.pl.*

stage-play, *n.*, pièce de théâtre, *f.*

stage-player (-plé-eur), *n.*, acteur, *m.*, actrice,*f.*

stager (stédj'-), *n.*, routier, *m.* Old —; *vieux routier.*

stagevil (stagh'i-v'l), *n.*, (vet.) tétanos, *m.*

staggard, *n.*, cerf de quatre ans, *m.*

stagger (stag-gheur), *v.a.*, faire chanceler; faire vaciller; (to cause to waver—*faire hésiter*) faire chanceler, faire fléchir, faire hésiter; (to shock—*émouvoir*) saisir, émouvoir.

stagger (stag-gheur), *v.n.*, chanceler, vaciller; (to fail—*faiblir*) chanceler, faiblir, fléchir; (to hesitate—*hésiter*) hésiter, balancer.

staggering (-gheur'-), *n.*, action de chanceler, de fléchir, de faiblir,*f.*; chancellement, *m.*; hésitation,*f.*

staggering (-gheur'-), *adj.*, chancelant; vacillant; qui ébranle; saisissant.

staggeringly (-gheur'-), *adv.*, en chancelant; (with hesitation—*avec hésitation*) avec hésitation.

staggers (-gheurze), *n.*, (vet.) vertige, vertigo, *m.*

stag-horn-tree (-trî), *n.*, (bot.) sumac de Virginie, *m.*

stagnancy (stag'-), *n.*, stagnation, *f.*

stagnant (stag'-), *adj.*, stagnant; dans un état de stagnation; (fig.) inactif.

stagnate (stag'-), *v.n.*, être stagnant; être dans un état de stagnation.

stagnation (stag-né-), *n.*, stagnation, *f.*

stag-worm (-weurme), *n.*, œstre des cerfs,*m.*

staid (stéde), *adj.*, rassis; sérieux; grave, posé.

staidness (stéd'-), *n.*, gravité, *f.*; sérieux; caractère rassis, caractère posé, *m.*

stain (sté'n), *n.*, tache, (coloured spot—*endroit coloré*) tache; (disgrace—*déshonneur*) tache, flétrissure, souillure; (shame—*honte*) honte, *f.*, opprobre, *m.*

stain (sté'n), *v.a.*, tacher; (fig.) tacher, souiller, flétrir, ternir, entacher; (paint.) colorier, mettre en couleur; (dy.) teindre.

stained (sté'n'de), *adj.*, taché; (fig.) souillé, terni, entaché; (paint.) mis en couleur; (dy.) teint; (of glass—*verre*) de couleur.

stainer (sté'n'-), *n.*, personne qui tache,*f.*; (dy.) teinturier, *m.*

stainless, *adj.*, sans tache.

stair, *n.*, degré, *m.*; marche,*f.* —s; *escalier*, *m.sing.* Back- —s; *escalier de service.* To be up —s; *être en haut.* To be down —s; *être en bas.*

stair-case (-kéce), *n.*, cage d'escalier, *f.*; escalier, *m.* Back- —; *escalier de service.* Private —; *escalier dérobé.* Winding —; *escalier en limaçon.*

stair-head (-hède), *n.*, haut de l'escalier, *m.*

stair-rod, *n.*, tringle de marche d'escalier,*f.*

stake, *v.a.*, (to wager—*gager*) parier, gager;

(to risk—*risquer*) exposer, risquer; (at play—*au jeu*) mettre au jeu; (to defend with stakes—*garnir de pieux*) garnir de pieux; (to pierce with a stake—*percer d'un pieu*) percer avec un pieu; (to sharpen—*aiguiser*) faire une pointe à un pieu. To — out; *jalonner.*

stake. *n.*, pieu; poteau; jalon; (at cards—*aux cartes*) enjeu; (funeral pile—*amas de bois*) bûcher, *m.* To be at —; *y aller de.* My life is at —; *il y va de ma vie.* To perish at the —; *mourir sur le bûcher.*

stalactical, *adj.*, stalactitique.

stalactite (-taïte), *n.*, stalactite,*f.*

stalagmite (-maïte), *n.*, stalagmite, *f.*

stale, *adj.*, vieux, vieil, vieille; (worn out—*usé*) suranné; vieilli, passé, usé; (of bread—*du pain*) rassis; (of liquors—*des liqueurs*) plat, éventé. — mate (chess—*échecs*); pat, *n.m.* To give a — mate (chess—*échecs*); *faire pat.*

stale, *n.*, urine, *f.*; (handle—*manche*) long manche; (at chess—*aux échecs*) pat, *m.*

stale, *v.n.*, (of animals—*des animaux*) uriner.

stale, *v.a.*, user, détruire.

staleness (stél'-), *n.*, vieillesse, *f.*; état suranné; (of liquor—*des liqueurs*) évent; (of bread—*du pain*) état rassis, *m.*, dureté, *f.*

staling (stél'-), *n.*, (of animals—*des animaux*) action d'uriner,*f.*

stalk (stôke), *n.*, tige; (of a plant—*de plante*) tige, *f.*; (of a flower—*de fleur*) queue, *f.*, pédoncule; (of a leaf—*de feuille*) pétiole; (of a quill—*de plume*) tuyau, *m.*; (walk—*allure*) démarche hautaine,*f.*

stalk (stôke), *v.n.*, marcher fièrement; (to go behind a cover—*avancer en cachette*) aller à la dérobée. To — over; *arpenter, parcourir.*

stalked (stôk'te), *adj.*, à tige; qui a une tige.

stalker (stôk'-), *n.*, personne à la démarche fière,*f.*

stalking (stôk'-), *n.*, (hunt.) traque,*f.*

stalking-horse (stôk'igne-), *n.*, cheval factice; (fig.) prétexte, masque, *m.*

stalky (stôk'-), *adj.*, comme une tige; dur.

stall (stôl), *n.*, stalle; (for cattle—*pour les bestiaux*) étable; (for horses—*pour les chevaux*) écurie, *f.*; (in a stable—*dans une écurie, une étable*) compartiment, *m.*, case,*f.*; (shed—*hangar*) échoppe, *f.*; (of a butcher—*de boucher*) étal; (for the sale of things in the open air—*pour vendre en plein air*) étalage; (in Scripture—*biblique*) cheval, *m.*

stall (stôl),*v.a.*, établer; mettre à l'étable.

stallage (stôl'édje), *n.*, autorisation de vendre en plein air, dans un marché,*f.*; droit payé pour cette autorisation, *m.*

stall-feed (-fîde), *v.a.*, nourrir à l'étable, au fourrage.

stall-feeding (-fîd'-), *n.*, nourrissage au fourrage, *m.*

stall-food (-foude), *n.*, nourriture au fourrage,*f.*

stallion (stal'ieune), *n.*, étalon, *m.*

stall-keeper (-kip'-), *n.*, étalagiste, *m.*

stalwart(stôl'-),*or* **stalworth**(stôl'weurth), *adj.*, vaillant; fort; vigoureux.

stamen (sté-),*n.* (*stamina*),base; force vitale; texture; chaîne (of linen—*du linge*),*f.*

stamen (sté-), *n.*, (*stamens*), (bot.) étamine,*f.*

stamened (sté-mè'n'de), *adj.*, (bot.) staminé.

stamin (sté-), *n.*, (stuff—*étoffe*) étamine,*f.*

stamina, *n.pl.* V. **stamen.**

staminal, *adj.*, staminal.

staminate, *v.a.*, douer de la force vitale; donner une base solide à.

stamineous (-mi'n'i-), *adj.*, stamineux.

staminiferous (-nif'èr'-), *adj.*, staminifère.

stamin-maker (-mék'-), *n.*, étaminier, *m.*

stammer, *v.a.* and *n.*, bégayer, balbutier. To — through; *balbutier.*

stammerer, *n.*, bègue, *m.*,*f.*

stammering, *n.*, bégaiement; balbutiement, *m.*

stammering, *adj.*, qui bégaie; qui balbutie; bègue.

stammeringly, *adv.*, en bégayant; en balbutiant.

stamp, *v.a.*, frapper du pied; (to impress—*marquer*) empreindre, marquer, imprimer; (to imprint—*empreindre*) empreindre, imprimer; graver; (coin.) monnayer, frapper; (gold, silver —*or, argent*) contrôler; (coin.) estamper; (paper, parchment—*papier, parchemin*) timbrer; (metal.) bocarder; (goods—*marchandises*) estampiller. To — one's reputation; *mettre le sceau à sa réputation.* He has had his plate —ed; *il a fait contrôler sa vaisselle.*

stamp, *n.*, (instrument) estampe, *f.*, coin, poinçon, *m.*; (impression) empreinte, marque, *f.*; (on gold, on silver—*sur l'or, l'argent*) contrôle; (on paper parchment—*sur le papier, le parchemin*) timbre; (metal.) bocard; (coin.) coin, poinçon, *m.*; (on goods—*sur des marchandises*) estampille, *f.*; (character—*trempe*) caractère, genre, *m.*, trempe; (character of reputation —*marque*) marque, empreinte, *f.*, coin, sceau; (of the foot—*du pied*) coup frappé sur la terre, le plancher, &c., avec le pied; (postage-stamp —*de la poste*) timbre-poste, *m.* Post-office- —; *timbre de la poste.* Postage—; *timbre-poste.* To be of the right —; *être marqué au bon coin.*

stamp-act, *n.*, loi sur le timbre, *f.*

stamp-duty (-diou-ti), *n.*, droit de timbre, *m.*

stamper, *n.*, pilon; (metal.) bocard; (pers.) timbreur, *m.*

stamping, *n.*, action d'empreindre, d'imprimer, *f.*; (of gold, of silver—*d'or, d'argent*) contrôlage; (of paper, parchment—*de papier, de parchemin*) timbrage; (coin.) monnayage; (metal.) bocardage, *m.*; (with the feet—*du pied*) action de taper du pied, *f.*

stamping-mill, *n.*, bocard, *m.*

stamp-laws (-lôze), *n.pl.*, lois sur le timbre, *f.pl.*

stamp-mill, *n.*, moulin à estamper, *m.*

stamp-office, *n.*, bureau de timbre; bureau de papier timbré, *m.*

stanch. or **staunch** (stä'n'she), *adj.*, (strong —*fort*) solide, fort; (firm—*ferme*) ferme; (zealous—*zélé*) zélé; (hunt.) sûr.

stanch (stä'n'she), *v.a.*, étancher; arrêter.

stanch, *v.n.*, s'arrêter.

stancher, *n.*, personne qui étanche; chose qui étanche, *f.*

stanching, *n.*, étanchement, *m.*

stanchion (stä'n'sheune), *n.*, étançon, *m.*; (nav.) épontille, *f.*

stanchless, *adj.*, qui ne peut pas être étanché.

stanchness, *n.*, solidité; (fig.) fermeté, *f.*

stand, *v.n.* (preterit and past part., Stood), être debout; se tenir debout; rester debout; (to keep on one's legs—*être debout*) se soutenir; (to be still on its foundation—*exister encore*) être debout, se trouver, être; (to be, to remain —*rester*) se tenir, rester, demeurer, être; (to be placed or situated—*être situé*) se trouver, être; (to become erect, as the hair—*se dresser*) se dresser; (to stop—*s'arrêter*) s'arrêter, arrêter, rester, demeurer, faire halte; (to be stationary—*ne pas se mouvoir*) rester stationnaire; (to continue—*durer*) durer; (to maintain a posture of defence—*se maintenir en défense*) se défendre; (to be placed with regard to order or rank—*occuper un certain rang*) se trouver, être; (to consist—*consister*) consister; (to maintain one's ground—*se maintenir en sa place*) se maintenir; (to continue living—*conserver la vie*) vivre; (to offer one's self as a candidate—*se porter candidat*) se présenter comme candidat; (to place one's self—*se placer*) se mettre, se tenir;

(to stagnate—*être en stagnation*) être stagnant; (to remain, to make delay—*différer*) rester; (to persevere—*persister*) persévérer, persister; (to adhere—*adhérer*) s'attacher; (nav.) porter; (milit.) faire halte; (of cabs—*de fiacres*) stationner; (of colour—*des couleurs*) être bon teint. ne pas passer. To — against; *résister à; tenir contre.* To — back; *se reculer; se tenir en arrière;* se tenir à l'écart. To — by; *se trouver à côté de;* assister à; *être auprès;* (to support—*soutenir*) soutenir, défendre; (to rest on for confirmation— *reposer sur*) reposer sur; (nav.) *se tenir près.* To — by one's self; *être tout seul.* To — for; (to support—*supporter*) soutenir; (to be in lieu of— *remplacer*) tenir lieu de, être à la place de; (to signify—*vouloir dire*) signifier, représenter; (nav.) faire route pour. To — for nothing; *ne compter pour rien;* (to stop at nothing—*ne reculer devant rien*) ne s'arrêter à rien, ne s'effrayer de rien. To — fast; *tenir ferme; tenir bon.* To — forth; *se mettre en avant; s'avancer.* To — from; *venir de.* To — good; *être valide.* To — in; *rentrer;* (to cost—*coûter*) revenir à, coûter; (nav.) *donner dedans.* To — in for; *se diriger vers.* To — in fear of; *craindre; avoir peur de.* To — in any one's light; *se tenir au jour de quelqu'un.* To — in the way; *barrer le passage; faire obstacle.* To — off; *se tenir éloigné, se tenir à l'écart;* (nav.) *porter au large;* (nav.) *être à la hauteur de.* — off! *au large!* To — on; *se tenir sur;* (to rely on—*compter sur*) s'appuyer sur, compter sur. To — on ceremony; *faire des façons.* To — out; *être en saillie, être en relief;* (to resist—*résister*) résister, tenir ferme; (nav.) porter au large. To — out from; *se distinguer parmi.* To — out against; *tenir tête à, résister à, s'opposer à.* To — out of the way; *s'ôter du chemin, se garer.* — out of my light; *ôtez-vous de mon jour.* To — with; *s'accorder avec.* To — still; *se tenir tranquille.* To — to; *persister dans; s'appliquer à; persévérer dans;* (to abide by—*adhérer à*) *s'en tenir à, adhérer à, rester fidèle à.* To — to sea; *porter au large.* To — together; *se tenir ensemble, s'accorder.* To — up; *se lever, se tenir debout.* To — up against; *opposer; s'attaquer à.* To — up for; *se lever pour; défendre;* soutenir. To — upon; (to concern—*concerner*) concerner, regarder; (to value—*faire cas de*) estimer; (to insist upon—*insister*) insister sur. How does the price of wheat — ? *quel est le prix du blé?* How do these things — ? *où en sont ces affaires?* How do you — with him? *quelle est votre position vis-à-vis de lui?* comment vous trouvez-vous placé à son égard? As matters — ; *au point où en sont les choses; sur le pied où sont les choses.* It —s to reason; *la raison le veut ainsi.* How do we — ? *où en sommes-nous?* (at school— *aux écoles*) quelles sont nos places?

stand, *v.a.*, (to endure—*endurer*) endurer, souffrir, supporter, soutenir; (to abide by— *subir*) subir; (to treat to—*régaler*) payer. To — fire; *soutenir le feu.* To — the enemy's fire; *essuyer le feu de l'ennemi.* To — cold; *supporter le froid.* To — fatigue; *soutenir la fatigue.* To — one's ground; *défendre son terrain; se maintenir sur son terrain.* To — it; *le souffrir.* What are you going to — ? *qu'allez-vous nous payer?* I will — some drink; *je vous paierai à boire.* To — the risk; *courir le risque.* To — a joke; *entendre raillerie.* To — the test; *subir l'épreuve.*

stand, *n.*, (halt—*halte*) arrêt, *m.*, halte, stagnation; (place) place, *f.*; (stall—*boutique en plein vent*) étalage, *m.*; (act of opposing—*résistance*) résistance, *f.*; (highest point—*sommet*) point culminant; (young tree—*jeune arbre*) jeune arbre, *m.*; (platform—*plate-forme*) estrade, *f.*; (rest for anything—*support*) dessous, pied, porte- . . .; (tech.) support, *m*; (of cabs—*de fiacres*) place, station, *f.*; (for umbrellas—*à* *parapluies*) porte-parapluie ; (for a lamp—*de lampes*) dessous, pied, *m.* — -still ; *arrêt.* To come to a — -still ; *arrêter.* At a — -still : *arrêté, suspendu.* To come to a — ; *s'arrêter.* To put to a — ; *embarrasser : mettre au pied du mur.* To make a — ; *s'arrêter, faire halte.* To make a — against ; *se soulever contre ; résister à ; faire une levée contre.*

standard, *n.*, étendard, drapeau ; (nav.) pavillon ; (of weights, measures—*de poids et mesures*) étalon, type ; (coin.) titre légal ; (bot.) étendard ; (tree—*arbre*) arbre en plein vent ; (regulator—*régulateur*) régulateur ; (fig.) type, modèle, régulateur, *m.*

standard, *adj.*, qui sert de modèle ; (coin.) au titre ; (of books—*de livres*) classique ; (of weights, measures—*de poids et mesures*) qui sert d'étalon ; (of trees—*d'arbres*) en plein vent ; (of price—*de prix*) régulateur ; (fig.) régulateur.

standard-bearer (-bèr'-), *n.*, porte-étendard ; porte-drapeau, *m.*

stander, *n.*, personne qui se tient debout, *f.*

standing, *adj.*, (established—*fixe*) établi ; (lasting—*solide*) durable, solide ; (permanent) permanent ; (stagnant) stagnant, dormant ; (fixed—*établi*) fixé, à demeure ; (not cut down—*debout*) sur pied ; (of rigging—*d'agrès*) dormant ; (fig.) constant, fixe, invariable. — rules ; *règles fixes, f.pl.* — account ; *compte courant.* Long-— account ; *compte d'ancienne date, m.*

standing, *n.*, action de se tenir debout ; (continuance—*continuation*). durée, date ; (station—*rang*) place, *f.* ; (power to stand—*force*) pouvoir de se tenir debout, *m.* ; (rank—*rang*) position, *f.*, rang ; (stall—*boutique en plein vent*) étalage, *m.*, boutique, *f.* Of long —; *d'ancienne date ; ancien.* An officer of twenty years —; *un officier de vingt années de service.*

standish, *n.*, écritoire, *f.*

stand-point (-pwaï'n'te), *n.*, point d'arrêt, *m.* ; base. *f.* ; point de vue, *m.*

stand-up (-eupe), *adj.*, montant. — collar ; *col droit, m.*

stannary, *adj.*, d'étain.

stannic, *adj.*, (chem.) stannique.

stanniferous (-nif'ër'-), *adj.*, (metal.) stannifère.

stanza, *n.*, stance ; strophe, *f.*

staphyloma (-lô-), *n.*, staphylôme, *m.*

staple (sté-p'l), *n.*, (emporium—*entrepôt*) marché, entrepôt ; (of wool, flax, &c.—*de laine, de lin,&c.*) brin,*m.*; (of cotton) soie ; (of land—*de terre*) qualité, *f.* ; (loop of iron—*crampon*) crampon de fer, *m.* ; (of a lock—*de serrure*) gâche ; (nav.) boucle, *f.* ; (fig.) objet principal, *m.*

staple (sté-p'l), *adj.*, (established—*établi*) établi, fixe ; (principal) principal ; (fit to be sold—*de vente*) marchand, de commerce.

star (stâr), *n.*, étoile, *f.* ; astre ; (print.) astérisque, *m.* ; étoile, *f.* ; (decoration) crachat, *m.*, décoration, *f.* North-—, Pole-— ; *étoile du nord, étoile polaire.* —-of-Bethlehem ; (bot.) ornithogale, *m.* ; *dame d'onze heures, f.*

star (stâr), *v.a.*, étoiler ; parsemer d'étoiles ; parsemer.

starboard (stâr'bōrde), *n.*, tribord, *m.*

starboard, *adj.*, de tribord.

starboard, *adv.*, tribord.

starch (stârtshe), *n.*, amidon ; empois, *m.* ; (fig.) raideur, *f.*

starch (stârtshe), *v.a.*, empeser.

star-chamber (-tshé'm-), *n.*, chambre étoilée. *f.*

starched (stârtsh'te), *adj.*, empesé ; (fig.) empesé, raide, guindé.

starchedness (stârtsh'ëd'-), *n.*, tenue empesée ; raideur, *f.*

starchly, *adv.*, d'une manière empesée ; avec raideur.

starch-maker (-mék'-), *n.*, amidonnier, *m.*

starch-works (-weurkse), *n.pl.*, amidonnerie, *f.sing.*

starchy, *adj.*, empesé ; (fig.) empesé, guindé.

stare, *n.*, regard fixe ; regard ébahi, *m.* ; (orni.) étourneau, *m.*

stare, *v.a.* and *n.*, regarder fixement. To — at ; *regarder fixement ; contempler ; considérer ; fixer ses regards sur ; ouvrir de grands yeux à.* To — any one in the face ; *regarder quelqu'un en face ;* (of things—*des choses*) *sauter aux yeux à quelqu'un.* To — any one out ; *faire baisser les yeux à quelqu'un.*

starer, *n.*, personne qui regarde fixement, *f.*

starfish, *n.*, (ich.) astérie, étoile de mer. *f.*

starflower (-fla'weur), *or* **star-of-bethlehem** (-ov'bèth'li-), *n.*, (bot.) ornithogale, *m.*

star-gazer (-ghéz'-), *n.*, astrologue, *m.*

star-gazing (-ghéz'-), *n.*, astrologie, *f.*

staring (stér'-), *n.*, action de regarder fixement, *f.*

staring (stér'-), *adj.*, (of colours—*des couleurs*) voyant, éclatant.

staringly, *adv.*, fixement ; entre les deux yeux.

stark (stârke), *adv.*, tout, tout à fait ; entièrement. — naked ; *tout nu.*

stark (stârke), *adj.*, vrai, pur, franc ; (strong—*fort*) fort ; (stiff—*raide*) raide. — nonsense ; *pure bêtise, f.*

starless (stâr-), *adj.*, sans étoiles.

starlight (-laïte), *n.*, lumière des étoiles, lumière stellaire, *f.*

starlight (-laïte), *or* **starlit** (-lite), *adj.*, étoilé.

starlike (-laïke), *adj.*, qui ressemble à une étoile ; étoilé ; brillant.

starling (stâr-), *n.*, (orni.) étourneau, sansonnet ; (of a bridge—*de pont*) avant-bec, brise-glace, *m.*

star-paved (-pév'de), *adj.*, parsemé d'étoiles ; étoilé.

starproof (-proufe), *adj.*, impénétrable à la lumière des étoiles.

starred (stâr'de), *adj.*, étoilé ; parsemé d'étoiles. Ill-— ; *né sous une mauvaise étoile ; voué au malheur.*

starry (stâr'-), *adj.*, étoilé ; (fig.) étincelant, brillant.

starstone (-stône), *n.*, (min.) saphir astérite, *m.*

start (stârte), *v.n.*, tressaillir ; (to set out—*partir*) partir, se mettre en route ; (of persons, horses, &c.—*racing—terme de courses de chevaux, &c.*) partir. To — aside ; *se jeter de côté.* To — back ; *se jeter en arrière ; reculer.* To — from ; *sortir de ;* (to get up from—*se lever*) *se lever précipitamment de.* To — off ; *partir.* To — out ; *se jeter dehors ; sortir précipitamment.* To — out of ; *sortir de.* To — out of one's sleep ; *se réveiller en sursaut.* To — up ; *se lever précipitamment ;* (fig.) *naître, surgir.*

start, *v.a.*, (to alarm—*effrayer*) alarmer ; (to rouse—*lever*) lever, faire lever, débucher ; (to send off—*faire partir*) faire partir ; (to invent—*inventer*) inventer, découvrir ; (to establish—*établir*) établir ; (to bring into notice—*soulever*) faire naître ; soulever, mettre en avant ; (question) soulever ; (a bone—*un os*) déboîter.

start (stârte), *n.*, tressaillement ; (spring—*saut*) saut ; (sally, sudden fit—*accès soudain*) élan ; (first motion—*premier pas*) premier pas, premier mouvement, *m.* By —s ; *par sauts ; par élans ;* (fig.) *par boutades, à bâtons rompus.* By fits and —s ; *à bâtons rompus, par sauts et par bonds.* To get the — ; *prendre les devants.* To get the — of ; *prendre les devants sur ; devancer.*

starter, *n.*, personne qui tressaille ; (of a question, &c.—*d'une question, &c.*) personne qui soulève, qui met en avant, *f.* ; (founder—*auteur*)

fondateur, auteur; (dog—*chien*) chien qui lève le gibier, *m.*

startful (-foule), *adj.*, sujet à tressaillir ; (of horses—*des chevaux*) ombrageux.

startfulness, *n.*, disposition à tressaillir ; (of horses—*des horses*) nature ombrageuse, *f.*

starting, *n.*, tressaillement ; mouvement subit ; (departure—*départ*) départ, *m.*

startingly, *adv.*, par élans ; (fig.) par boutades, à bâtons rompus.

starting-note (-nôte), *n.*, échappatoire, *f.*

starting-post (-pôste), *n.*, poteau de départ, *m.* ; barrière, *f.*

startist, *adj.*, sujet à tressaillir ; (of horses—*des chevaux*) ombrageux.

startle (stâr-t'l), *n.*, alarme, *f.* ; tressaillement ; saisissement, *m.*

startle (stâr-t'l). *v.n.*, tressaillir ; frémir.

startle, *v.a.*, faire tressaillir ; effrayer ; faire frémir ; faire peur.

startling, *adj.*, effrayant ; atterrant ; très étonnant.

starve (stârve), *v.a.*, faire mourir de faim ; affamer ; réduire par la faim. To — with cold ; *faire mourir de froid.* To — out ; *réduire, vaincre par la faim.*

starve, *v.n.*, mourir de faim. To — with cold ; *mourir de froid ;* (fig.) *languir.*

starveling, *n.*, animal affamé, *m.* ; (plant—*plante*) plante affamée, *f.* ; (pers.) affamé, meurt de faim, famélique, *m.*

starveling (stârv-'), *adj.*, affamé ; famélique.

starwort (-weurte), *n.*, (bot.) aster, *m.*

state, *n.*, (condition) état, *m.*, condition, *f.* ; (political body, government—*organisation politique*) État ; (body of men united by profession—*membres d'une profession*) ordre ; (rank—*rang*) rang, *m.* ; (pomp—*pompe*) pompe, grande cérémonie, *f.*, apparat, *m.* ; (grandeur) grandeur, dignité, *f.* ;(canopy—*dais*) dais, *m.* —s-general ; *états généraux, m.pl.* Married — ; *vie conjugale.* In — ; *en grande cérémonie.* Lying in — ; *exposition sur un lit de parade.* To lie in — ; *être exposé sur un lit de parade.*

state, *v.a.*, (to set—*fixer*) régler, fixer, arrêter ; (to express—*exprimer*) exposer, énoncer, dire ; (math.) poser ; (an account—*un compte*) établir, dresser.

statecraft (-crâfte), *n.*, politique, *f.*, ruses de la politique, *f.pl.*

stated (stét'-), *adj.*, réglé ; fixé.

statedly, *adv.*, régulièrement.

state-house (-haouce), *n.*, salle des États, *f.*

stateless, *adj.*, sans apparat, sans pompe.

stateliness, *n.*, majesté, noblesse, grandeur, *f.* ; caractère imposant, air imposant, *m.* ; (dignity—*dignité*) dignité, *f.* ; (b.s.) faste, *m.*, ostentation, *f.*, grands airs, *m.pl.*

stately, *adj.*, plein de grandeur ; imposant ; grand ; majestueux ; (magnificent—*superbe*) magnifique, superbe ; (elevated in sentiment—*de sentiments élevés*) plein de dignité, noble, élevé ; (b.s.) fastueux.

statement, *n.*, exposé ; énoncé ; compte rendu, récit, dire, rapport, *m.*, assertion, *f.* ; (of an account—*de compte*) relevé, *m.* ; (act of stating—*exposé*) exposition, *f.* Verbal — ; *rapport verbal.*

state-monger (-meu'n'gheur), *n.*, personne qui se mêle de politique, *f.*

state-prison (-priz'z'n), *n.*, prison d'État, *f.*

state-prisoner (-priz'z'neur), *n.*, prisonnier d'État, *m.*

stater (stét'-), *n.*, personne qui énonce, qui rapporte, *f.*

state-room, *n.*, salle de réception, *f.*

statesman (stéts'-), *n.*, homme d'état, *m.*

statesmanlike (-laïke), *adj.*, d'homme d'état.

statesmanship, *n.*, fonctions de l'homme d'état ; connaissances de l'homme d'état, *f.pl.*

stateswoman (stéts'woum'-), *n.*, femme politique, *f.*

state-trial (-traï-), *n.*, procès politique, *m.*

static, *or* **statical**, *adj.*, de la statique ; pour peser.

statice (sté-taï-ci), *n.*, (bot.) statice, *f.*

statics, *n.pl.*, statique, *f.sing.*

station (sté-), *n.*, station ; place, *f.* ; (office) poste ; (character—*caractère*) caractère, *m.* ; (rank—*rang*) position, condition ; (railways) station, *f.*, (chief one—*principale*) embarcadère, débarcadère, *m.*, gare, *f.* — in life ; *position sociale.*

station, *v.a.*, placer ; poser ; poster.

stational (sté-), *adj.*, de station ; (c. rel.) stationnale.

stationary (sté-), *adj.*, stationnaire ; fixé.

stationer (sté-), *n.*, papetier ; petit libraire, *m.* —s' hall ; *dépôt de la librairie, m.* Entered at —s' hall ; *déposé à la librairie centrale.*

stationery (sté-). *n.*, papeterie, *f.*

station-house (-haouce), *n.*, corps de garde de police, *m.*

station-master (-mâs-), *n.*, chef de station, *m.*

station-staff (-stâfe), *n.*, jalon, *m.*, perche d'arpenteur, *f.*

statistical, *or* **statistic**, *adj.*, statistique.

statistician (-tish'a'n), *n.*, statisticien, *m.*

statistics, *n.pl.*, statistique, *f.sing.*

statuary (stat'iou-), *n.*, statuaire, *f.* ; (pers.) statuaire, *m.*

statue (stat'iou), *n.*, statue, *f.*

statue (stat'iou), *v.a.*, placer comme une statue ; (to form a statue of—*faire une statue*) former en statue.

stature (stat'ieur), *n.*, stature ; taille, *f.*

statutable (stat'iou-ta-b'l),*adj.*,statué ; (jur.) prévu par la loi.

statutably, *adv.*, conformément aux statuts ; conformément aux lois.

statute (stat'ioute), *n.*, statut, *m.* ; loi, *f.* — of bankruptcy ; *déclaration de faillite, f.*

statutory (stat'iou-), *adj.*, établi par des statuts ; établi par la loi.

stave (stéve), *n.*, (of a cask—*de tonneau*) douve ; (mus.) portée, *f.* ; (of a song—*de chanson*) couplet ; (of a psalm—*de psaume*) verset, *m.*

stave, *v.a.*, (preterit and past part., Stove, Staved), briser ; crever ; (a cask—*un tonneau*) défoncer. To — in ; *crever, briser.* To — off ; *chasser avec un bâton ;* (fig.) *repousser, tenir éloigné.*

stavesacre (stév'z'é-keur), *n.*, (bot.) staphisaigre, herbe aux poux, *f.*, pied-d'alouette, *m.*

stay, *v.n.* (preterit and past part., Staid), rester, demeurer ; séjourner ; (to continue—*continuer*) continuer, rester. To — at ; *rester à, demeurer à.* To — at any one's ; *rester, être, demeurer chez quelqu'un.* To — away ; *s'éloigner, s'absenter.* To — for ; *attendre.* To — in ; *rester chez soi, à la maison.* To — up ; *veiller.* To — up for ; *attendre.* — there ; *restez là.*

stay, *v.a.*, (to stop—*arrêter*) arrêter, retenir ; (to restrain—*réprimer*) réprimer, retenir, contenir ; (to support—*soutenir*) soutenir, fortifier ; (to prop up—*étayer*) étayer ; (nav.) donner vent devant. To — the stomach ; *soutenir l'estomac.*

stay, *n.*, (abode—*séjour*) séjour, *m.* ; (stability—*stabilité*) stabilité, *f.* ; (support) soutien, appui ; (arch., nav.) étai ; (tech.) arrêt, *m.* ; (carp.) entretoise, *f.* ; (obstacle) obstacle ; (mec.) support, *m.* —s ; *corset, m.* Main— ; (nav.) *grand étai.*

stayer (stè-eur), *n.*, soutien ; appui, *m.*

staylace, *n.*, lacet, *m.*

stay-maker (-mék'-), *n.*, fabricant de corsets ; faiseur de corsets, *m.*, faiseuse de corsets, *f.*

stays (stéze), *n.pl.*, corset, *m.sing.*

stay-sail (-sél), n., (nav.) voile d'étai, f. ; foc, m.

'**stay-supporter**(-seup-pôrt'-),n.,étançon,m.

stead (stède), n., lieu, m. ; place, f. In any one's — ; au lieu de; à la place de quelqu'un. To stand in — ; être utile.

stead (stède), v.a., servir ; rendre service ; être utile ; aider.

steadfast (-fâste), adj., ferme ; solide ; (re-solute—résolu) ferme ; (constant) constant, fixe.

steadfastly, adv., fermement ; avec constance.

steadfastness, n.,stabilité ; fermeté ; (fig.) constance, f.

steadily (stèd'-),adv.,fermement ; (without irregularity—régulièrement) d'une manière rangée ; (without inconstance—constamment) avec constance, avec fermeté ; (resolutely—résolument) avec assurance, fermement, avec fermeté.

steadiness, n., fermeté ; (of conduct—de conduite) conduite rangée ; (constancy—constance) constance ; (resolution) assurance, fermeté, f.

steady, adj., ferme ; assuré ; (in conduct—conduite) rangé, posé ; (assiduous—constant) assidu ; (regular—régulier) régulier ; (constant) constant, ferme ; (of the wind—du vent) fait. — ! restez tranquille ! (nav.) comme ça.

steady. v.a., affermir ; assurer.

steak (stéke), n., tranche ; (of pork—de porc) côtelette, f. ; (beefsteak—de bœuf) bifteck, m.

steal (stîle), v.a. (preterit, Stole; past part., Stolen), voler, dérober, soustraire ; (to gain, to win—gagner) gagner, séduire. To — a march on ; gagner une marche sur. To — all hearts ; gagner tous les cœurs. To — a glance ; dérober un regard.

steal, v.n., voler. To — away ; s'en aller à la dérobée, furtivement ; s'esquiver ; se dérober. To — down ; descendre à la dérobée, furtivement. To — from ; se dérober à. To — in ; entrer à la dérobée, furtivement. To — into ; se glisser furtivement dans. To — out ; sortir à la dérobée, furtivement.

stealer, n., voleur, m., voleuse, f.

stealing, n., vol, m.

stealth (stèlth). n., vol, m. By — ; à la dérobée ; furtivement, en cachette.

stealthful (-foule), adj., voleur.

stealthfully, adv., comme un voleur.

stealthfulness, n., disposition au vol, à voler, f.

stealthily, adv., à la dérobée ; en cachette.

stealthy (stèlth'-), adj., fait à la dérobée ; dérobé ; furtif.

steam (stîme), n., vapeur ; (of a little liquid—d'une petite quantité de liquide) fumée, f. With its — on ; en vapeur. With all its — on ; en pleine vapeur. To put the — on ; mettre en vapeur. The — is on ; la machine est en vapeur. The — is up ; la machine est en pleine vapeur. To get up the — ; chauffer la vapeur, chauffer. To shut off the — ; stopper ; arrêter la machine.

steam (stîme), v.n., émettre de la vapeur ; fumer. To — away ; s'évaporer.

steam, v.a., passer à la vapeur ; (cook.) cuire à la vapeur.

steam-boat (-bôte). n., bateau à vapeur, m.

steam-boiler (-boïl'-), n., chaudière à vapeur, f.

steam-carriage (-car-ridje), n., voiture à vapeur, f.

steam-casing (-késs'-), n., chemise, f.

steam-engine (-è'n'djine), n., machine à vapeur, f. Double-acting, single-acting — ; machine à vapeur à double effet, à simple effet.

steamer. n., bateau à vapeur ; bâtiment à vapeur ; navire à vapeur ; vapeur ; steamer, m. ; (cook.) marmite à vapeur, f.

steam-gauge(-ghédje), n., manomètre, m. ; éprouvette, f.

steam-navigation (-vi-ghé'-), n., navigation à vapeur, f.

steam-packet, n., paquebot à vapeur, m.

steam-pipe (-païpe), n., tuyau à vapeur, tuyau d'apport, tuyau de prise de vapeur. m. Waste- — ; tuyau de dégagement de la vapeur.

steam-piston, n., piston de machine à vapeur, m.

steam-ship, n., bâtiment à vapeur, m.

steam-tight (-taïte), adj., imperméable à la vapeur.

steam-tug (-teug), n., remorqueur à vapeur, m.

steam-vessel (-vès's'l), n., bâtiment à vapeur, m.

steam-whistle (-hwis's'l), n., sifflet de machine à vapeur ; sifflet à vapeur, m.

stearine (stî-), n., (chem.) stéarine, f.

steatite (sti-a-taïte), n., (min.) stéatite, f.

steed (stîde), n., coursier, m.

steel (stîle), n., acier ; (to sharpen knives on —à aiguiser) fusil ; (to strike a light on—pour obtenir du feu) briquet ; (weapon—arme) fer, m., épée, f. ; (hardness—dureté) fer, m. Heart of — ; cœur de fer, m.

steel, adj., d'acier, de fer. —-pen ; plume d'acier, de fer ; plume métallique, f.

steel (stîl), v.a., acérer ; garnir d'acier ; (to make obdurate—endurcir) endurcir ; (to arm—armer) armer, fortifier. To — one's heart against ; s'endurcir le cœur contre.

steel-clad, adj., revêtu d'acier.

steeliness, n., dureté d'acier ; (fig.) dureté de fer, insensibilité, f.

steel-wire (-waeur), n., fil d'acier, m.

steel-works (-weurkse), n.pl., aciérie,f.sing.

steely, adj., d'acier ; (fig.) dur, de fer.

steelyard (-'yârde), n., romaine, f. ; (small one—petite) peson, m.

steep (stîpe), adj., escarpé ; raide ; à pic.

steep (stîpe), n., pente rapide, f. ; précipice, m.

steep (stîpe), v.a., tremper ; (plants, drugs —plantes, drogues) infuser ; (fig.) plonger.

steeping, n., action de tremper, f. ; trempage, m.

steeping-place, n., routoir, m.

steeping-vat, n., trempoire, f.

steeple (stip'l), n., clocher, m.

steeple-chase (-tshéce), n., course au clocher, f.

steepled (stîp'l'de), adj., à clocher ; qui a un clocher.

steeply, adv., en pente rapide.

steepness, n., raideur ; descente escarpée, pente rapide, f.

steepy, adj., escarpé, raide.

steer, n., bouvillon, m.

steer (stîre), v.a., (nav.) gouverner, diriger ; (fig.) conduire, guider.

steer (stîre), v.n., (nav.) gouverner ; (fig.) se conduire, se diriger.

steerage (stîr'édje), n., timonerie, f. ; (in merchant-ships—dans les navires marchands) logement des matelots ; (of the helm—du gouvernail) effort du gouvernail ; (fig.) gouvernement, m., conduite, f. —-passenger ; passager de bord, m.

steerage-way, n., (nav.) vitesse, f., sillage, m.

steerer, n., timonier ; pilote, m.

steering, n., action de gouverner, f. ; gouvernement, m.

steering-wheel (-hwile), n., roue du gouvernail, f.

steersman (stirz'-), n., (nav.) pilote ; timonier, m.

steganographic, *or* **steganographical** (stèg'-), *adj.*, stéganographique.

steganographist, *n.*, personne versée dans l'art d'écrire en chiffres. *f.*

steganography (stèg'-), *n.*, stéganographie, *f.*

stellar, *or* **stellary** (stèl'-), *adj.*, stellaire ; étoilé.

stellate (stèl'-). *or* **stellated** (-'lét'-), *adj.*, en étoile : (bot.) radié, rayonné.

stelliferous (stèl-lif-èr'-), *adj.*, stellifère.

stelliform, *adj.*, stelliforme.

stellion (stèll'ieune), *n.*, (ent.) stellion, *m.*

stem (stème), *n.*, tige ; (of a flower—*de fleur*) queue,*f.* ; (stock of a family—*tronc d'une famille*) tronc. *m.*, souche ; (branch of a family—*branche d'une famille*) branche, *f.*, rejeton, *m.* ; (mus.) queue,*f.* ; (of a pen—*de plume*) tuyau, *m.* ; (nav.) étrave, *f.*, avant, *m.* From — to stern; *de l'avant à l'arrière.*

stem (stème), *v.a.*, arrêter; refouler; (to resist—*s'opposer*) résister à, s'opposer à. To — the tide; *aller contre la marée, refouler la marée.*

stem-leaf (-life). *n.*,(bot.)feuille caulinaire,*f.*

stemless, *adj.*, sans tige.

stemple (stè'm'p'l), *n.*, (mines) traverse,*f.* ; poteau ; étai, *m.*

stench (stè'n'she), *n.*, mauvaise odeur; puanteur,*f.*

stench, *v.a.*, empuantir; infecter.

stencil, *v.a.*, peindre au patron.

stencil (stè'n'-), *n.*, patron, *m.*

stenographer (sti-), *n.*,sténographe. *m.*

stenographic, *or* **stenographical** (sti-), *adj.*, sténographique.

stenography (sti-), *n.*, sténographie, *f.*

stentorian (stè'n'-), *adj.*, de stentor.

stentorophonic,*adj.*, à voix de stentor.

step (stèpe), *v.n.*, faire un pas ; marcher pas à pas; passer. To — aside; *faire un pas à l'écart.* To — back; *faire un pas en arrière, reculer.* To — down; *descendre; venir.* Just — down to my house; *venez chez moi pour un instant.* To — forward; *faire un pas en avant; s'avancer.* To — in; *entrer; entrer pour un instant; faire une petite visite.* To — into; *entrer dans; entrer dans . . . . pour un instant.* To — into an estate, a good place; *entrer en possession d'une terre; entrer dans une bonne place.* To — on; *marcher sur.* To — out; *sortir; sortir pour un instant.* (to quicken one's pace—*marcher plus vite*) *allonger le pas.* To — up; *monter.* To — up to; *s'avancer vers; s'approcher de.* To — over; *traverser, franchir.*

step, *v.a.*, poser le pied; (nav.) presser.

step (stèpe), *n.*, pas; (of stairs—*d'escalier*) degré, *m.*, marche, *f.*; (progression) progrès, *f.*; acheminement, *m.*; (gait—*allure*) marche, démarche; (measure—*mesure*) démarche, *f.*, pas, *m.*; (of a capstan, a mast—*de cabestan, de mât*) carlingue,*f.*; (of a door—*de porte*) pas, seuil; (of a ladder—*d'échelle*) échelon; (of a carriage—*de voiture*) marchepied; (of a shaft, a wheel—*de colonne, de roue*) piédestal, *m.* —s ; (ladder—*échelle*) *marchepied.* To take a —; *faire un pas;* (fig.) *faire une démarche.* Within a —of ; *à deux pas de.* A few —s off; *à deux pas d'ici.* To retrace one's —s : *revenir sur ses pas; rebrousser chemin.*

step-brother (-breuth'-), *n.*, beau-frère, *m.*

step-child (-tshaïlde), *n.*, beau-fils, *m.*, belle-fille, *f.*

step-daughter (-dô-teur), *n.*, belle-fille, *f.*

step-father (-fâ-*theur*), *n.*, beau-père, *m.*

step-mother (-meuth'-), *n.*, belle-mère; (b.s.) marâtre,*f.*

steppe (stèpe), *n.*, steppe,*f.*

stepper (stèp'-), *n.*, (man.) cheval qui a de l'action, *m.*

stepping, *n.*, marche: action de marcher pas à pas. *f.*

stepping-stone (-stóne). *n.*. marchepied, *m.*

step-son (-seune). *n.*, beau-fils, *m.*

step-stone (-stóne), *n.*, pas, seuil. *m.*

stercoraceous (steur-co-ré-sheusse), *or* **stercoral** (steur-), *adj.*, stercoraire.

stercoration (steur-co-ré-), *n.*, stercoration ; action de fumer une terre. *f.*

stere (stire), *n.*. stère, *m.*

stereographic. *or* **stereographical** (stèr'i-). *adj.*, stéréographique.

stereographically, *adv.*,stéréographique-ment.

stereography (stèr'i-). *n.*. stéréographie. *f.*

stereometrical (stèr'i-), *adj.*, stéréométrique.

stereometry (stèr'i-). *n.*, stéréométrie. *f.*

stereotomical (stèr'i-),*adj.*, stéréotomique.

stereotomy (stèr'i-), *n.*, stéréotomie. *f.*

stereotype (stèr'i-o-taïpe), *n.*, cliché ; clichage. *m.*

stereotype, *adj.*, stéréotype ; cliché. — printing, — printing-office; *stéréotypie, f.*

stereotype, *v.a.*, clicher; stéréotyper.

stereotype-plate, *n.*, cliché, *m.*

stereotyper, *n.*, clicheur, stéréotypeur. *m.*

stereotyping,*n.*, clichage; stéréotypage,*m.*

stereotypographer (-ti-pog'-), *n.*, stéréotypeur, *m.*

stereotypography (-ti-pog'-), *n.*, stéréotypie,*f.*

sterile (stèr'ile), *adj.*, stérile ; (bot.) stérile, mâle, à étamines.

sterility, *n.*, stérilité,*f.*

sterlet (steur-lète). *n.*, (ich.) sterlet, *m.*

sterling (steur-), *or* **starling** (stâr-), *n.*, (of a bridge—*de pont*) avant-bec, brise-glace. *m.*

sterling (steur-), *adj.*, sterling; (fig.) pur, vrai, de bon aloi.

stern (steurne), *adj.*, sévère; austère; (harsh —*dur*) dur, rigide; (afflictive—*cruel*) rigoureux.

stern (steurne), *n.*, poupe, *f.* ; arrière, *m.*

stern-chase (-tshéce), *or* **stern-chaser** (-tshéss'-), *n.*, canon de retraite, *m.*

sterned (steurn'de), *adj.*, à poupe. Round-— ship ; *vaisseau à poupe ronde, m.*

stern-frame, *n.*, (nav.) arcasse,*f.*

sternly, *adv.*, sévèrement; austèrement ; rigidement; durement ; rigoureusement.

sternness, *n.*, sévérité; austérité ; rigidité ; dureté ; rigueur,*f.*

sternpost (-póste), *n.*, étambot, *m.*

sternum (steur-), *n.*, sternum, *m.*

sternutation (steur-niou-té-), *n.*, éternuement, *m.*

sternutative *or* **sternutatory**,*adj.*, ster-nutatoire ; sternutatif.

stern-way, *n.*, culée,*f.*

stet (stète), *v.n.*, (print.) bon.

stethoscope (stèth'o-scôpe), *n.*, stétho-scope, *m.*

stew (stiou), *n.*, (hot-house—*serre*) étuve; serre ; (of meat—*de viande*) étuvée, *f.*, ragoût, *m.* ; (fruit, pigeons) compote, *f.* ; (brothel—*mauvais lieu*) maison de prostitution,*f.* To be in a —; *être sur le gril.*

stew (stiou), *v.a.*, étuver ; faire un ragoût de ; (fruit, pigeons) mettre en compote.

stew, *v.n.*, cuire à l'étuvée ; cuire en ragoût ; (fruit, pigeons) cuire en compote ; (pers.) cuire dans sa peau.

steward (stiou-), *n.*, maître d'hôtel ; régisseur ; intendant ; (of a college—*de collège*) économe ; (of a ball—*d'un bal*) commissaire ; (nav.) commis des vivres ; (in Scripture—*biblique*) dispensateur, *m.* —'s room ; *soute du commis des vivres,f.*

stewardship,*n.*, intendance, *f.* ; office de maître d'hôtel; office de régisseur ; (in a college —*de collège*) économat,*m.*

stewpan, *n.*, casserole. *f.*

stibial, *adj.,* antimonial.

stibiated (stib'i-ét'-), *adj.,* stiblé.

stibium, *n.,* antimoine, *m.*

stich (stike), *n.,* vers; (ant.) (of the Bible) verset, *m.*

stichwort (stitsh'weurte), *or* **stitchwort** (-weurte), *n.,* (bot.) camomille; stellaire, *f.*

stick, *n.,* bâton, *m.*; canne, *f.*; (of a tree—*d'arbre*) tronc, *m.,* tige, *f.*; (thrust with a pointed instrument—*coup porté avec un instrument pointu*) coup; (of sealing-wax, chocolate, &c.—*de cire à cacheter, de chocolat, &c.*) bâton; (of a fiddle—*de violon*) archet, *m.*; (small stick—*petit bâton, de baguette, f.* Blow with a —; *coup de bâton, de canne.*

stick, *v.a.* (preterit and past part., Stuck), (to pierce—*percer*) percer; (with paste, &c.—*avec de la colle, &c.*) coller, attacher; (to fix in—*fixer*) fixer; (a sheep—*un mouton*) saigner. To — into; *piquer dans; enfoncer dans; ficher dans.* To — on; *fixer;* (with paste, &c.—*avec de la colle, &c.*) coller, attacher; afficher. To — out; *faire saillir; faire ressortir.* To — up; *dresser; mettre droit; mettre;* (to paste up—*afficher*) coller, afficher. To — round with; *garnir tout autour de.* Stuck-up people; *parvenus, m.pl., parvenues, f.pl.*

stick, *v.n.,* (to adhere—*adhérer*) se coller, coller, s'attacher, adhérer; (to remain—*rester*) rester, demeurer; (to get embedded—*être pris dans*) être engagé, pris, demeurer engagé, pris; (to get embarrassed—*s'embarrasser*) s'embarrasser; (to stop short—*s'arrêter*) s'arrêter, rester court. To — at; *s'arrêter devant; reculer devant; hésiter devant.* To — by; *rester fidèle à; soutenir; s'en tenir à.* To — close, fast; *s'attacher fortement; adhérer fortement; s'arrêter court, s'embarrasser; rester pris; rester engagé dans la boue, &c.* To — close to work; *travailler d'arrache-pied.* To — on; *s'attacher; se coller.* To — out; *faire saillie; ressortir; bomber;* (not to give in—*ne pas céder*) tenir bon, *ferme, tenir toujours bon, ferme;* persister. To — to; *s'attacher à;* (to persevere in—*persister*) persévérer dans; (to abide by—*s'en tenir*) s'en tenir à; (to be constant to—*demeurer fidèle*) s'attacher à, rester fidèle à. To — up; *se dresser; se redresser.*

stickiness, *n.,* nature gluante; viscosité; ténacité, *f.*

sticking-plaster (-plâs-), *n.,* taffetas d'Angleterre, *m.*

stickle (stik'l), *v.n.,* prendre part; (to contend—*disputer*) se débattre; se disputer; (to pass from one side to the other—*changer de parti*) flotter. To — for; *insister pour avoir.*

stickle-back (stik'l-), *n.,* (ich.) épinoche, *f.*

stickler, *n.,* (in a duel—*dans un duel*) second, témoin; (contender—*champion*) disputeur obstiné, champion, *m.* He is a great — for; *il tient beaucoup à.*

sticky, *adj.,* gluant, collant; glutineux; visqueux, poisseux; poissé.

stiddy, *n.,* enclume, *f.*

stiff, *adj.,* raide, rigide; (not liquid—*solide*) dur, ferme; (constrained—*contraint*) raide, gêné, contraint; (stubborn—*entêté*) opiniâtre, dur; (strong—*fort*) fort. As — as a poker; *raide comme une barre de fer.* To grow —; *devenir raide; se raidir.* — gale; *vent carabiné.*

stiffen, *v.a.,* raidir; endurcir; (to make torpid—*engourdir*) engourdir; (paste—*pâte*) durcir, rendre ferme.

stiffen, *v.n.,* se raidir; raidir; s'endurcir; s'engourdir; (of paste—*de la pâte*) durcir, devenir ferme.

stiffener (stif'neur), *n.,* (of boots—*de bottes*) sous-contrefort; (of shoes—*de souliers*) cambrillon; (of a cravat—*de cravate*) col, *m.*

stiffening (stif'nigne), *n.,* soutien, *m.*

stiff-hearted (-hârt'-), *adj.,* opiniâtre, obstiné.

stiffly, *adv.,* avec raideur; avec opiniâtreté.

stiff-necked (-nòk'te), *adj.,* raide; obstiné; opiniâtre.

stiffness, *n.,* raideur; (of paste, liquids—*de pâte, de liquides*) consistance; (constraint—*contrainte*) raideur, gêne, contrainte; (harshness—*dureté*) dureté; (obstinacy—*entêtement*) opiniâtreté, raideur, *f.*

stiff-starched (-stârt'sh'te), *adj.,* empesé.

stifle (staï-f'l), *v.a.,* étouffer; suffoquer. To — a report; *étouffer un bruit.* We are —ing here; *nous étouffons ici.*

stifle (staï-f'l), *n.,* rotule, *f.*; (vet.) grasset; (disease—*maladie*) vessigon du grasset, *m.*

stifle-joint (staï-f'l-djwaï'n'te), *n.,* (vet.) grasset, *m.*

stifling (staï-), *adj.,* étouffant; suffocant.

stigma, *n.* (stigmata), stigmate, *m.*; marque; flétrissure, *f.*; (bot.) stigmate, *m.*

stigmatic, *or* **stigmatical,** *adj.,* stigmatique.

stigmatically, *adv.,* avec un stigmate; avec une flétrissure.

stigmatize (-taïze), *v.a.,* stigmatiser; marquer; flétrir.

stilar (staï-), *adj.,* de style de cadran solaire.

stile (staïl), *n.,* barrière, *f.*; (of a dial—*de cadran solaire*) style, *m.,* aiguille, *f.* Turn—; *tourniquet, m.*

stiletto (sti-lèt'tô), *n.,* stylet; (for needle-work—*pour ouvrage à l'aiguille*) poinçon, *m.*

still, *n.,* alambic; (calm—*silence*) calme, *m.*

still, *adj.,* tranquille; calme; paisible; (silent—*silencieux*) silencieux, taciturne. Be —; *restez tranquille.*

still, *adv.,* encore; toujours; (nevertheless—*cependant*) cependant; néanmoins, toutefois.

still, *v.a.,* arrêter; calmer.

stillatitious (-tish'euse), *adj.,* stillatoire.

stillborn, *adj.,* mort-né.

stillburn (-beurne), *v.a.,* brûler en distillant.

stiller, *n.,* personne qui apaise, qui calme, *f.*

stillhouse (-haouce), *n.,* distillerie, *f.*

stillicidious, *adj.,* stillatoire.

stilling, *n.,* action de calmer, d'apaiser, *f.*; (stand for casks—*pour tonneaux*) chantier, *m.*

still-life (-laïfe), *n.,* (paint.) nature morte, *f.*

stillness, *n.,* tranquillité, *f.*; calme; silence, repos, *m.*; (taciturnity) taciturnité, *f.*

still-room (-roume), *n.,* distillerie, *f.*

stilly, *adv.,* silencieusement; (calmly—*tranquillement*) avec calme, paisiblement, tranquillement.

stilt, *n.,* échasse, *f.*; (of a bridge—*de pont*) pilotis, pieu, *m.* To be on —s; *être monté sur des échasses.*

stilt, *v.a.,* élever sur des échasses.

stilt-bird (-beurde), *n.,* (orni.) échasse, *f.*

stimulant (stim'iou-), *n.,* stimulant, *m.*

stimulant (stim'iou-), *adj.,* stimulant.

stimulate (stim'iou-), *v.a.,* stimuler; aiguillonner; exciter.

stimulating (stim'iou-lét'-), *adj.,* stimulant; excitant.

stimulation (-'iou-lé-), *n.,* stimulation, *f.*

stimulative (-'iou-lé-), *adj.,* stimulant, stimulateur.

stimulative, *n.,* stimulant, *m.*

stimulator (-'iou-lé-teur), *n.,* personne qui stimule, qui excite, *f.*; stimulant, *m.*

stimulus (-'iou-), *n.,* stimulant; aiguillon; (med.) stimulus; (bot.) dard, aiguillon, *m.*

sting (stigne), *n.,* aiguillon; dard, *m.*; (thrust of a sting into the flesh—*piqûre d'aiguillon*) piqûre, *f.*; (fig.) aiguillon, *m.,* morsure, *f.*; (of an epigram—*d'une épigramme*) pointe, *f.* The —s of remorse; *les aiguillons du remords.*

sting (stigne), *v.a.* (*preterit and past part.*, Stung), piquer; (fig.) piquer, fâcher, irriter. Stung with remorse; *bourrelé, tourmenté, de remords.*

stinger (stign'eur), *n.*, chose qui pique, qui blesse, qui irrite, *f.* He gave him a blow, a regular —; *il lui appliqua un coup, mais un fameux.*

stingily (sti'n'dji-), *adv.*, chichement; avec avarice; sordidement.

stinginess (sti'n'dji-), `n.`, mesquinerie; ladrerie; avarice, lésinerie, *f.*

stingless (stign'-), *adj.*, sans aiguillon; sans dard.

stingo (stign'gô), *n.*, vieille bière, *f.*

stingy (sti'n'dji), *adj.*, avare; mesquin; ladre; chiche.

stink (stign'ke), *n.*, puanteur; mauvaise odeur, *f.* What a — there is here! *comme il sent mauvais ici!*

stink (stign'ke), *v.n.* (*preterit and past part.*, Stunk), puer; sentir mauvais.

stinkard (stign'kàrde), *n.*, (mam.) puant (fig.) goujat, *m.*

stinker (stign'k'-), *n.*, chose puante, *f.*

stinking (stign'k'-), *adj.*, puant.

stinkingly (stign'k'-), *adv.*, avec une mauvaise odeur; en puant.

stinkpot, *n.*, composition puante, *f.*; (artil.) pot à feu, *m.*

stinkstone (-stône), *n.*, pierre puante, *f.*

stint (stign-, (limit—*borne*) borne, limite, restriction; (portion) part, portion, *f.*

stint, *v.a.*, limiter; borner; restreindre; rogner. To — one's self; *se refuser le nécessaire.* To — one's self of; *se priver de.*

stinter, *n.*, personne qui limite, qui restreint; chose qui limite, qui restreint, *f.*

stipe (staïpe), *n.*, (bot.) stipe; pédicule, *m.*

stipel (staïp'-), *n.*, (bot.) stipelle, *f.*

stipend (staï-), *n.*, appointements, *m.pl.*; salaire, *m.*

stipend (staï-), *v.a.*, stipendier; soudoyer; salarier; solder.

stipendiary (staï-), *adj.*, salarié, (l.u.) stipendiaire.

stipendiary (staï-), *n.*, salarié; stipendié, *m.*

stipple (stip'p'l), *v.a.*, pointer; pointiller.

stippling, *n.*, pointillage, *m.*; points, *m.pl.*

stiptic. *V. styptic.*

stipula (stip'iou-), *n.*, (bot.) stipule, *f.*

stipulate (stip'iou-), *v.n.*, stipuler; convenir.

stipulation (stip'iou-lé-), *n.*, contrat, *m.*; convention; (bot., jur.) stipulation, *f.*

stipulator (stip'iou-lét'-), *n.*, partie contractante; partie stipulante, *f.*

stir (steur), *n.*, remuement; mouvement, *m.*; agitation, *f.*; bruit, *m.*; (disturbance—*trouble*) tumulte, trouble, mouvement séditieux, *m.*

stir (steur), *v.a.*, remuer; (to agitate—*agiter*) agiter; (to incite—*exciter*) exciter, pousser; (to excite—*irriter*) exciter, irriter. To — round; *tourner, remuer.* To — up; *remuer;* (to incite—*pousser*) exciter, pousser; (to excite—*irriter*) exciter, irriter; (to enliven—*animer*) animer, réveiller.

stir, *v.n.*, remuer, se remuer; se mouvoir; bouger. Do not —; *ne bougez pas.* To — abroad, out; *bouger de chez soi, sortir de chez soi.* To be —ring; *être debout, être levé.* He is not —ring yet; *il n'est pas encore levé; il ne fait pas encore jour chez lui.*

stirless (steur-), *adj.*, immobile.

stirrer (steur'-), *n.*, personne qui remue; personne en mouvement, *f.*; (instigator—*instigateur*) instigateur, *m.*, instigatrice, *f.* Early —; *personne matineuse.* Late —; *personne qui se lève tard.*

stirring (steur'-), *adj.*, remuant; actif.

stirrup (stir-reupe), *or* **stirrup-iron** (-aï eur'n), *n.*, étrier, *m.*

stirrup-leather (-lèth'-), *n.*, étrivière, *f.*

stirrup-oil (-oïl), *n.*, huile de cotret, *f.*

stitch, *n.*, point, *m.*; (in knitting—*de tricot*) maille, *f.* — in the side; *point de côté, m.* To put a — to; *faire un point à.* Back-—; *arrière-point.* Cross-—; *point croisé.* Open-work —; *point à la turque, point à jour.*

stitch, *v.a.*, piquer; coudre; (books—*les livres*) brocher. To — up; *coudre; faire un point à.*

stitch, *v.n.*, piquer; coudre.

stitched (stitsh'te), *adj.*, piqué; (of books—*de livres*) broché.

stitcher, *n.*, couseuse, *f.*; piqueur, *m.*, piqueuse, *f.*; (of books—*de livres*) brocheur, *m.*, brocheuse, *f.*

stitchery, *n.*, arrière-point, *m.*; (of books—*de livres*) brochure, *f.*

stiver (staï-), *n.*, (Dutch coin—*monnaie hollandaise*) stiver; (fig.) liard, sou, *m.* Not to have a —; *n'avoir pas le sou, m.*

stoat (stôte), *n.*, (mam.) hermine, *f.*

stoccado (stok'ké-dô), *n.*, estocade, *f.*

stock, *n.*, (race) souche, *f.*, tronc, *m.*, race, famille, *f.*; (store—*provision*) fonds, *m.*, provision, *f.*; (of wood, stone—*de bois, de pierre*) bloc; (cravat—*cravate*) col; (at cards—*aux cartes*) talon, *m.*; (bot.) girofiée; (print.) fonte; (of fire-arms—*d'armes à feu*) monture, *f.*, bois, *m.*; (handle—*manche*) manche; (of an anchor—*d'ancre*) jas; (of a tree—*d'arbre*) tronc, *m.*; (stupid person—*imbécile*) bûche, *f.*; (hort.) sujet, *m.*, ente, *f.*; (on a farm—*de ferme*) bétail, *m.*, bestiaux, *m.pl.*; (log—*bois*) bûche, *f.*; (capital) capital, fonds, *m.*, capitaux, *m.pl.*; (goods on hand—*com.*) marchandises en magasin, *f.pl.*; (manu.) matériel, *m.*, monture, *f.*; (centre-bit—*mèche de vilbrequin*) cintre, *m.*, mèche anglaise, *f.*; (tech.) fût, *m.*, souche, *f.*; (in book-keeping —*comptabilité*) capital, *m.* —s; (fin.) fonds, fonds publics, *m.pl.*, rentes, *f.pl.*, effets, effets publics, *m.pl.*; (for ship building—*cale de construction de vaisseau*) chantier, *m. sing.*, cale de construction, *f.sing.*; (punishment—*châtiment*) bloc, *m.sing.* Dead —; *mobilier mort, m.* Live —; *mobilier vif, bétail, m.*, bestiaux, *m.pl.* Working —; *matériel, m.* To take —; *faire l'inventaire.* To take in —; *recevoir des marchandises.* To lay in a —of; *faire une provision de.* On the —s; *sur le chantier.* In the —s; (punishment—*châtiment*) *au bloc.* — in trade; *marchandises disponibles, f.pl.; fonds de commerce, m.* — on hand; *marchandises en magasin, f.pl.; approvisionnement, m.* India —; *fonds de la compagnie des Indes.*

stock, *v.a.*, fournir; pourvoir; monter; approvisionner; (a farm—*une ferme*) pourvoir de bétail; (a country—*un pays*) peupler; (a warren —*une garenne*) peupler; (a fish-pond—*un étang*) empoissonner; (cards—*cartes*) rassembler.

stockade, *n.*, (fort.) palissade, *f.*

stockade, *v.a.*, (fort.) palissader.

stock-book (-bouke), *n.*, livre de magasin, *m.*

stockbroker (-brô-), *n.*, agent de change, *m.*

stockdove (-deuve), *n.*, pigeon ramier, *m.*

stock-exchange (-èks'tshé'n'dje), *n.*, bourse pour les fonds publics; compagnie des agents de change, *f.*

stockfish, *n.*, stockfisch, *m.*; morue séchée à l'air, *f.*

stockholder (-hôld'-), *n.*, rentier, *m.*, rentière, *f.*; actionnaire, *m.*, *f.*; détenteur de fonds publics, *m.*

stocking, *n.*, bas, *m.* Silk —; *bas de soie.*

stocking-frame, *n.*, métier à bas, *m.*

stocking-stitch, *n.*, tricot au crochet, *m.*

stocking-trade, *n.*, bonneterie, *f.*

stockjob (-djobe), v.a. and n., agioter ; jouer dans les fonds.

stockjobber (-djob'-), n., spéculateur dans les fonds publics; agioteur, m.

stockjobbing (-djob'-), n., jeu sur les fonds publics ; agiotage, m.

stock-loom (-loume), n., métier à bas, m.

stocks, n.pl. V. **stock**.

stock-still, adj., immobile.

stocky, adj., trapu.

stoic (stoïke), n., stoïcien, m., stoïcienne, f.

stoic, or **stoical** (stoïk'-), adj., stoïcien ; (of things—des choses) stoïque.

stoically, adv., stoïquement.

stoicalness, n., stoïcisme, m.

stoicism (stoï-ciz'm), n., stoïcisme, m.

stoker (stô-), n., ouvrier chauffeur ; chauffeur, m.·

stole (stôle), n., étole ; (antiq.) stole, f. Groom of the ~; premier gentilhomme de la chambre, m.

stolid (stol'), adj., lourd ; stupide.

stolidity, or **stolidness** (stol'-), n., pesanteur, stupidité, f.

stomach (steum'ake), n., estomac ; (appetite —appétit) appétit, m., faim, f. To turn one's —; soulever le cœur. It goes against his —; il n'a pas de goût pour cela ; le cœur ne lui en dit pas. To stay any one's —; apaiser la faim à quelqu'un.

stomach (steum'ake), v.a., se fâcher de ; s'estomaquer de ; (to brook—avaler) endurer, digérer, souffrir. I cannot — that ; je ne peux pas digérer cela.

stomach-ache (-ôke), n., mal à l'estomac, m. ; douleur d'estomac, f.

stomached (steum'ak'te), adj., fâché ; en colère ; estomaqué.

stomacher (steum'a-keur), n., corsage lacé, m.

stomachful (-foule), adj., opiniâtre ; têtu.

stomachfulness, n., obstination ; opiniâtreté, f.

stomachic (sto-mak'ike), n.,stomachique,m.

stomachic, or **stomachical**, adj., stomacal ; stomachique.

stomachless, adj., sans appétit.

stomach-pump (-peu'm'pe), n., (surg.) pompe stomacale, f.

stone (stône), n., pierre, f.; (of fruit—des fruits) noyau ; (of grapes—du raisin) pépin ; (anat.) testicule ; (med.) calcul, m., pierre ; (of a mill—de moulin) meule ; (gem—gemme) pierre précieuse, pierre, f.; (min.) grès ; (weight—poids) stone (kilog. 6·3190), m. ; (fig.) pierre, f., rocher, m. Precious —s ; pierres précieuses, pierreries, f.pl. Philosopher's —; pierre philosophale. To leave no — unturned ; remuer ciel et terre. Not to leave a —standing ; ne pas laisser pierre sur pierre. A heart of —; un cœur de rocher.

stone (stône), adj., de pierre ; de grès. — bottle; bouteille de grès.

stone (stône), v.a., lapider ; (mas.) garnir de pierres, maçonner ; (to harden—endurcir) endurcir ; (fruit) vider.

stone-blind (-blaï'n'de), adj., complètement aveugle.

stone-borer (-bôr'-), n., (ent.)lithophage, m.

stone-bow (-bô), n., arbalète à jalet, f.

stone-chatter (-tshat'-), n., (orni.) traquet, m.

stone-crop, n., (bot.) orpin, m.

stone-cutter (-keut'-), n., tailleur de pierre, m.

stone-cutting (-keut'-), n., taille de la pierre, f.

stone-fruit (-froute), n., fruit à noyau, m.

stone-hearted (-hârt'-), adj., qui a un cœur de rocher.

stone-horse, n., cheval entier, m.

stone-mason (-mé-s'n), n., maçon, m.

stone-pit, n., carrière de pierre, f.

stone's-throw (-thrô), n., jet de pierre, m. Within a —; à la portée d'une pierre; à deux pas.

stone-ware, n., grès, m. ; poterie de terre,f.

stone-work (-weurke), n.,ouvrage de maçonnerie, m. ; maçonnerie, f.

stone-yard (-yârde), n., chantier de pierre, m.

stoniness, n., nature pierreuse ; (fig.) dureté, f.

stoning, n., lapidation ; (of roads, &c.—des routes, &c.) partie empierrée ; (of fruit—des fruits) action de vider, f.

stony (stô'n'i), adj., de pierre ; (abounding in stone—abondant en pierres) pierreux ; (fig.) de rocher, dur, cruel, insensible ; (petrifying— pétrifiant) pétrifiant.

stool (stoule), n., tabouret ; escabeau, m. ; sellette ; (med.) selle ; (hort.) plante mère, f. Foot— ; tabouret. Camp— ; pliant, m. Close— ; chaise percée, f. — of repentance; sellette, f.

stoop (stoupe), v.n., se pencher ; se baisser ; se courber ; (of birds—des oiseaux) se poser ; (of birds of prey—des oiseaux de proie) s'abattre, fondre ; (fig.) s'abaisser ; s'incliner ; descendre ; se soumettre ; s'humilier ; s'avilir ; (to acknowledge inferiority—se soumettre) céder. To —down ; se baisser. Carthage —ed to Rome; Carthage se soumit à Rome.

stoop, v.a., pencher, incliner, baisser.

stoop (stoupe), n., inclination ; (of birds of prey—des oiseaux de proie)action de s'abattre, de fondre ; (vessel—vase) cruche, f. ; (fig.) abaissement, m. He has a slight —; il a le dos légèrement voûté.

stooping (stoup'-), adj., qui se penche, qui se soumet ; penché, courbé. In a — posture ; dans une posture courbée.

stoopingly (stoup'-), adv., en se baissant; en se courbant.

stop, n., action de s'arrêter ; (halt—halte) halte ; pause ; (interruption) interruption, f. ; retardement ; (hindrance—obstacle) obstacle, empêchement, m. ; (prohibition of sale—défense de vendre) vente prohibée, f. ; (of an organ— d'orgue) jeu ; (of a flute—de flûte) trou ; (gram.) signe de ponctuation ; (nav., tech.) arrêt, m. To put a —to ; arrêter, suspendre ; mettre fin à. Full — ; point, m.

stop, v.a., arrêter ; suspendre ; (to hinder— entraver) empêcher, entraver, gêner ; (mus.) presser ; (gram.) ponctuer ; (a hole—un trou) boucher ; (the breath—l'haleine) couper. To — payment; suspendre, cesser ses payements. To — any one's salary; faire une retenue sur les appointements de quelqu'un. To —any one from ; empêcher quelqu'un de. To — up ; boucher, fermer ; (to obstruct—faire obstacle) obstruer ; (a street— une rue) encombrer, barrer. — thief ! au voleur !

stop, v.n., s'arrêter ; arrêter ; (nav.) parer ; (com.) cesser ses payements. — there (leave off—cesser) ; restez-en là. To — for any body; attendre quelqu'un.

stop-cock, n., robinet d'arrêt, m.

stop-gap, n., bouche-trou, m.

stoppage (-pédje), n., interruption ; fermeture ; obstruction ; action d'arrêter, de boucher, d'interrompre ; (of salary—de salaire) retenue, f. ; (of payment—de payement) suspension, f. ; (in the streets—dans les rues) embarras, encombrement, m.

stopper, n., personne qui arrête, qui ferme, qui bouche ; chose qui arrête, qui ferme, qui bouche, f. ; (of a bottle—d'une bouteille) bouchon, m. ; (nav.) bosse, f.

stopper, v.a., boucher ; mettre un bouchon à ; (nav.) bosser.

stop-plank, n., (carp.) poutrelle, f.

stopple (stop'p'l), n., bouchon, m.

stop-watch (-wôtshe), n., montre à arrêt, f.

storage (stŏr'édje), *n.*, magasinage, *m.*

storax, *n.*, (pharm.) storax, styrax, *m.* — tree ; *styrax, aliboufier, m.*

store (stōre), *n.*, provision ; quantité ; abondance, *f.* ; (warehouse—*magasin*)magasin,dépôt ; arsenal ; (fig.) fonds, trésor, *m.* —s ; *matériel, m.sing.* ; (milit., nav.) *vivres, m.pl.* ; *munitions, f.pl.* ; *matériel de guerre, m.* In — ; *en réserve.* To lay in a — of ; *faire une provision de.*

store, *v.a.*, pourvoir; munir; approvisionner ; (fig.) enrichir, orner. To — up ; *amasser.*

store-house (-haouce), *n.*, magasin; dépôt ; grenier public, *m.*

store-keeper (-kip'-), *n.*, garde-magasin ; marchand; (nav.) commissaire garde-magasin, *m.*

storer, *n.*, personne qui amasse, *f.*

storeship, *n.*, gabare, *f.* ; transport, bâtiment de transport, *m.*

storied (stŏ-ride), *adj.*, historié ; rapporté par l'histoire.

stork, *n.*, (orni.) cigogne, *f.*

stork's-bill, *n.*, (bot.) bec-de-grue, *m.*

storm, *n.*, orage, *m.* ; tempête, *f.* ; (milit.) assaut; (fig.) orage, *m.* To take by — ; *prendre d'assaut.*

storm, *v.a.*, donner l'assaut à.

storm, *v.n.*, faire de l'orage ; (pers.) tempêter.

storm-beaten (-bit'n), *adj.*, battu par la tempête.

storm-bell, *n.*, tocsin, *m.*

storminess, *n.*, état orageux, *m.*

storming, *n.*, (milit.) assaut, *m.*

storm-jib (-djibe), *n.*, (nav.) trinquette, *f.* ; tourmentin, *m.*

stormy, *adj.*, orageux ; à l'orage.

story (stŏ-), *n.*, histoire, *f.* ; conte, *m.* ; historiette, *f.* ; (falsehood—*fausseté*) conte, mensonge ; (of a house—*de maison*) étage, *m.* As the — goes ; *à ce que dit l'histoire.* The best of the — ; *le plus beau de l'histoire.* Always the old — ; *toujours la même chanson.* That is quite another — ; *c'est une autre paire de manches.* To tell stories (falsehoods—*faussetés*) ; *dire des mensonges.* On the first, second, third — ; *au premier, au second, au troisième ; au premier étage, &c.*

story-book (-bouke), *n.*, livre de contes, *m.*

story-rod, *n.*, (carp.) perche d'étage, *f.*

story-teller, *n.*, (narrator—*narrateur*) conteur, *m.*, conteuse, *f.* ; (liar—*menteur*) menteur, *m.* ; menteuse, *f.*

stout (staoute), *n.*, bière forte, *f.*

stout, *adj.*, (strong—*fort*) vigoureux, fort ; (brave) brave, courageux, vaillant ; (resolute—*résolu*) ferme, décidé, résolu ; (large —*gros*) gros, fort; corpulent, qui a de l'embonpoint ; (of things—*des choses*) vigoureux, fort, ferme, solide. To have a — heart; *avoir du cœur.* To grow —; *engraisser ; prendre de l'embonpoint.*

stoutly, *adv.*, vigoureusement ; courageusement, vaillamment; fortement ; bravement, fermement ; résolument.

stoutness, *n.*, (strength—*force*) vigueur ; (bulk—*grosseur*) corpulence, *f.*, embonpoint, *m.* ; (boldness—*hardiesse*) intrépidité, bravoure ; (obstinacy—*entêtement*) obstination, *f.*

stove (stōve), *n.*, poêle ; (for washing, cookery—*de blanchissage, de cuisine*) fourneau, *m.* ; (for the feet—*pour les pieds*) chaufferette ; (drying-room—*étuve*) étuve ; (hort.) serre, serre chaude, *f.*

stover (stŏ-), *n.*, fourrage, *m.*

stove-room (-roume), *n.*, étuve, *f.*

stow (stō), *v.a.*, arranger ; placer ; déposer ; mettre ; mettre en place ; (nav.) arrimer.

stowage (stŏ-édje), *n.*, mise en place, *f.* ; arrangement, magasinage ; (nav.) arrimage, *m.*

strabism (-biz'm), or **strabismus** (-bis'-). *n.*, strabisme, *m.*

straddle (strad'd'l), *v.a.*, enfourcher ; être à califourchon sur.

straddle, *v.n.*, écarter les jambes ; marcher les jambes écartées.

straggle (strag'g'l), *v.n.*, s'écarter ; se détacher ; errer ; rôder ; être écarté, être éloigné ; (milit.) traîner.

straggler, *n.*, personne qui s'éloigne, qui se sépare, qui erre, *f.* ; rôdeur, *m.*, rôdeuse, *f.* ; (milit.) traîneur, traînard, *m.*

straggling, *adj.*, écarté ; séparé ; éloigné ; égaré ; épars ; (bot.) divariqué. — house ; *maison isolée.*

straight (strête), *adj.*, droit; (narrow—*étroit*) étroit ; (upright—*droit*) droit, équitable, juste. To make — ; *dresser, rendre droit.* To make things — ; *arranger les choses.*

straight, *adv.*, droit ; (immediately—*sans délai*) sur-le-champ, aussitôt, tout de suite, incontinent. — on ; *tout droit.*

straighten (strê-t'n), *v.a.*, rendre droit ; redresser ; (to make narrow—*rétrécir*) étrécir, rétrécir, resserrer ; (to reduce to difficulties—*embarrasser*) gêner, embarrasser.

straightener, *n.*, redresseur, *m.* ; chose qui redresse, *f.*

straightforward (-fôr-worde), *adj.*, droit, franc.

straightforwardly, *adv.*, avec droiture, avec franchise.

straightforwardness, *n.*, droiture, franchise, *f.*

straightly, *adv.*, droit ; (tightly—*étroitement*) étroitement.

straightness, *n.*, qualité de ce qui est droit ; (rectitude droiture; (narrowness—*étroitesse*) étroitesse, *f.*, étrécissement, rétrécissement, *m.* ; (tightness—*tension*) tension, *f.*

straightway, *adv.*, sur-le-champ ; à l'instant; immédiatement.

strain (strê'n), *v.a.*, tendre trop ; forcer ; (to constrain—*forcer*) contraindre, forcer ; (to sprain —*fouler*) se fouler ; (to make tighter—*serrer*) serrer, resserrer ; (animal) forcer, outrer ; (liquids—*liquides*) filtrer, passer, (fig.) forcer, outrer, faire violence à. To — one's self; *se donner un effort.* To — every nerve to ; *faire tous les efforts possibles pour.* To — out; *exprimer.* To — after ; *faire de grands efforts pour produire.*

strain, *v.n.*, s'efforcer ;(of liquids—*des liquides*) se filtrer.

strain (strê'n), *n.*, (stretching—*extension*) extension, *f.* ; (sprain—*foulure*) effort, *m.*, entorse, foulure, *f.* ; (style) style, caractère, *m.*, manière, *f.* ; (song—*chant*) chant, *m.*, (note) accords, accents, *m.pl.* ; (disposition) disposition naturelle, *f.* ; (manner of speech—*du parler*)ton ; (nav.) effort ; (fig.) élan, essor, *m.*

strainer, *n.*, passoire, *f.* ; filtre, *m.*

straining, *n.*, action de forcer, d'outrer, de fouler; tension excessive, *f.* ; (filtration) filtrage, *m.* — after ; *grands efforts pour produire, m.pl.*

straining-piece, *n.*, (carp.) contrevent, *m.*

strait (strête), *adj.*, étroit ; (strict) strict, rigide, rigoureux ; (intimate—*intime*) étroit, intime; (difficult—*gêné*) difficile, embarrassé, gêné ; (stingy—*serré*) avare, serré ; (straight—*droit*) droit.

strait, *n.*, (geog.) détroit, *m.* ; (distress—*gêne*) gêne, difficulté, *f.*

straiten, *v.a.*, étrécir ; rétrécir ; resserrer ; (fig.) embarrasser, gêner. In —ed circumstances ; *gêné dans ses affaires ; gêné.*

straitlaced (-lés'te), *adj.*, lacé étroitement, (constrained—*raide*) raide, contraint ; (strict) rigide, sévère.

straitly, *adv.*, étroitement ; (strictly—

strictement) strictement ; (intimately—*intime-ment*) étroitement, intimement.

straitness, *n.*, étroitesse, *f.* ; (difficulty—*gêne*) embarras, *m.*, gêne ; (strictness—*rigueur*) rigueur, *f.* ; (scarcity—*rareté*) manque, *m.*

straits, *n.pl.*, (geog.) détroit, *m.sing.*

strait-waistcoat (-wést'côte), *or* **strait-jacket** (-djak'kète), *n.*, camisole de force, *f.*

stramineous (-mi'n'i-), *adj.*, de paille.

stramony, *n.*, (bot.) stramonium, *m.*

strand, *n.*, rivage, *m.* ; grève, *f.* ; (of a rope —*d'une corde*) toron, cordon, *m.*

strand, *v.a.*, jeter à la côte ; échouer.

strand, *v.n.*, échouer.

stranding, *n.*, échouement, échouage, *m.*

strange (strė'n'dje),*adj.*,étrange ; singulier ; (unknown, foreign—*inconnu, étranger*) étranger.
— to say ; *chose étrange.*

strangely, *adv.*, étrangement ; singulièrement.

strangeness. *n.*, (foreignness—*de ce qui est étranger*) caractère de ce qui est étranger, *m.* ; (singularity—*bizarrerie*) singularité, étrangeté, bizarrerie, *f.*

stranger (stré'n'djeur), *n.*, étranger, *m.*, étrangère, *f.* I am a — to that ; *je suis étranger à cela.* He is a — to me ; *il m'est étranger ; il m'est inconnu.* To become quite a — ; *devenir rare comme les beaux jours ; devenir bien rare.*

strangle (stran'gn'gl), *v.a.*, étrangler.

strangler, *n.*, étrangleur, *m.*

strangles (stra'n'g'lze), *n.pl.*, (vet.) étran-guillon, *m.sing.*

strangle-weed (-wide), *n.*, (bot.) oroban-che, *f.*

strangling, *n.*, étranglement, *m.* ; strangulation,*f.*

strangulated (stra'n'ghiou-), *adj.*, (surg.) étranglé.

strangulation (-ghiou-lé-), *n.*, strangulation, *f.* ; (surg.) étranglement, *m.*

strangury (stra'n'ghiou-) *n.*, (surg.) stran-gurie, *f.*

strap, *n.*, courroie, *f.* ; (of iron—*de fer*) lien ; (for trousers—*de pantalons*) sous-pied, *m.* Razor- — ; *cuir à rasoir, m.*

strap, *v.a.*, attacher avec une courroie ; (a razor—*un rasoir*) repasser ; (to beat—*battre*) donner les étrivières à.

strappado (-pé-dô), *n.*, estrapade, *f.*

strappado (-pé-dô), *v.a.*, estrapader ; tor-turer.

strapper, *n.*, gaillard bien découplé, *m.*, gaillarde bien découplée,*f.*

strapping. *adj.*, bien découplé.

strap-shaped (-shép'te), *adj.*, (bot.) ligulé.

strata (stré-), *n.pl. V.* **stratum**.

stratagem (-'a-dje'm), *n.*, stratagème, *m.*

strategy (-'è-dji), *n.*, stratégie, *f.*

stratification (-ti-fi-ké-), *n.*,stratification,*f.*

stratify (-'i-fa'ye), *v.a.*, stratifier.

stratocracy. *n.*, stratocratie, *f.*

stratography, *n.*, stratographie, *f.*

stratum (stré-), *n.* (*strata*), couche ; strate, *f.* ; étage, *m.*

straw (strô), *n.*, paille, *f.* ; (fig.) fétu, *m.* Not to be worth a — ; *ne pas valoir un fétu.* Not to care a — for ; *se soucier comme d'un fétu de. comme de l'an quarante de.* To pick —s ; *enfiler des perles.* Man of — ; *homme de paille.*

strawberry, *n.*, (fruit) fraise, *f.* ; (plant—*plante*) fraisier, *m.*

strawberry-tree (-tri), *n.*, arbousier, *m.*

straw-built (-bilte). *adj.*, fait de paille.

straw-colour (-keul'leur), *n.*, couleur paille,*f.*

straw-coloured (-keul'leurde),*adj.*, paille, couleur paille.

straw-cutter (-keut'-), *n.*, hache-paille, *m.*

straw-hat, *n.*, chapeau de paille, *m.*

straw-platter, *n.*, nattier, *m.*

straw-stuffed (-steuf'te), *adj.*, rembourré de paille.

strawy (strô-i), *adj.*, de paille ; comme la paille.

stray, *v.n.*, errer ; vaguer ; s'éloigner ; s'écarter ; s'égarer.

stray, *adj.*, égaré ; (jur.) épave.

stray, *n.*, bête épave, *f.*

strayer (stré-eur), *n.*, personne qui erre ; qui vague ; personne errante, égarée, *f.*

straying (stré-igne), *n.*, égarement, *m.*

streak (strike), *n.*, raie ; (nav.) virure, *f.*, bordage, *m.*

streak (strike),*v.a.*, rayer, barioler,bigarrer.

streaky, *adj.*, rayé.

stream (strime), *n.*, courant ; (of a river—*d'une rivière*) fil, courant ; (river—*cours d'eau*) fleuve, cours d'eau, ruisseau, *m.*, rivière, *f.* ; (fig.) cours, jet, flot, torrent, flux, *m.* Moun-tain- — ; *torrent, m.* Against the — ; *contre le courant.*

stream (strîme), *v.n.*, couler ; (to issue in streaks—*sortir en jets*) jaillir ; (of a flag, &c.—*d'un drapeau*) flotter. To — with ; *ruisseler de.*

stream, *v.a.*, rayer ; orner de raies.

streamer, *n.*, drapeau ; étendard, *m.* ; en-seigne ; (nav.) banderole ; (astron.) aurore boréale, *f.*

streaming, *adj.*, sillonné de ruisseaux ; ruisselant.

streamlet, *n.*, petit ruisseau ; filet d'eau, *m.*

stream-works (-weurkse), *n.pl.*, (metal.) mines d'étain de lavage, *f.pl.*

street (strite), *n.*, rue, *f.* By- — ; *rue écartée.* In the open — ; *en pleine rue.*

street-door (-dôre), *n.*, porte sur la rue, porte d'entrée, *f.*

street-walker (-wôk'eur), *n.*, coureuse, prostituée. *f.*

strength (strègn'th), *n.*, force, *f.* ; (pers.) forces, *f.pl.* ; (of materials—*de la matière*) résis-tance, force, *f.* With all my — ; *de toutes mes forces.* Upon the — of ; *sous l'influence de.*

strengthen (strègn'th'n), *v.a.*, fortifier ; affermir ; raffermir.

strengthen. *v.n.*, se fortifier ; s'affermir ; se raffermir, se renforcer.

strengthener, *n.*, contrefort, *m.* ; chose qui fortifie, *f.* ; (med.) fortifiant. *m.*

strengthless (strègn'th'-), *adj.*, sans force ; faible.

strenuous (strè'n'iou-eusse), *adj.*, zélé ; ferme ; ardent ; (bold—*hardi*) intrépide, cou-rageux, vaillant, ardent ; (of things—*des choses*) ardent, vigoureux.

strenuously, *adv.*, avec zèle ; ardemment ; intrépidement, courageusement, vaillamment.

strenuousness, *n.*, zèle, *m.* ; ardeur ; activité, *f.*

stress, *n.*, importance ; force. *f.* ; poids ; (gram.) accent prosodique ; accent tonique, accent, *m.* ; (of the weather—*du temps*) violence, *f.* ; (mec.) effort, *m.* To lay a — upon ; *s'appuyer sur ; mettre l'accent prosodique sur.*

stretch, *v.a.*, (to extend in a line—*tendre*) tendre, bander ; (to extend in breadth—*étendre*) étendre, étirer ; (to spread as wings—*ouvrir, comme des ailes*) étendre, déployer ; (to strain—*forcer*) forcer ; (to enlarge, as gloves—*agrandir, comme des gants*) élargir ; (fig.) forcer, outrer. To — one's self out full length ; *s'étendre tout de son long.* To — forth the hand ; *tendre la main.*

stretch.*v.n.*,s'étendre ; s'étirer ; se déployer ; (to become larger—*devenir plus large*) s'élargir, prêter ; (nav.) s'étendre ; (to exaggerate—*exa-gérer*) s'étendre, gasconner. To — from ; *s'éten-dre de.* To — over ; *s'étendre sur.*

stretch, *n.*, tension ; (force of body—*force corporelle*) force, *f.* ; (strain—*effort*) effort, *m.* ;

(min.) direction ; (nav.) bordée ; (fig.) étenduc, portée, f.

stretcher, n., personne qui étend ; chose qui étend, f. ; (arch.) carreau ; (of a boat—*de bateau*) traversin, m. ; (to carry a person on—*pour transporter quelqu'un*) civière, f.

stretching, n.,tension, f. ; élargissement,m.

strew (strou), v.a., répandre ; semer. To — with ; *parsemer de ; couvrir de ; joncher de*.

strewing (strou'-), n., action de répandre ; jonchée, f.

striæ (straï-i), n.pl., stries, striures, f.pl. ; (arch.) cannelure, f.

striate (straï-), or **striated** (straï-ét'-), adj., strié.

striation (straï-é-), n., stries, f.pl. ; nature striée, f.

striature (straï-a-tioure), n., disposition des stries, f.

strickle (strik'k'l), or **strickler**, n., racloire, radoire, f.

strict, adj., (exact) exact, strict ; (rigorous—*sévère*) rigoureux, sévère, strict ; (tight—*étroit*) étroit, tendu, serré.

strictly, adv., (exactly—*exactement*) exactement, strictement ; (rigorously—*rigoureusement*) rigoureusement, sévèrement, strictement ; (tightly—*étroitement*) étroitement, d'une manière tendue.

strictness, n., (exactness—*exactitude*) exactitude rigoureuse ; (rigour—*sévérité*) rigueur, sévérité ; (tightness—*tension*) tension, f.

stricture (strikt'ieur), n., (stroke—*trait*) trait, m. ; (censure) critique, observation critique, f. ; (med.) rétrécissement ; étranglement,m.

stride (straïde), n., pas ; grand pas, m. ; enjambée, f. To make rapid —s ; *avancer à grands pas*.

stride (straïde), v.n. (*preterit*, Strode ; *past part.*, Stridden), marcher à grands pas ; (to straddle—*enjamber*) se mettre à califourchon. To — over ; *enjamber*.

stride, v.a., enjamber.

stridulous (strid'iou-), adj., strident ; perçant.

strife (straïfe), n., lutte ; querelle, contestation ; dispute, f. ; (opposition) contraste, m. To be at — ; *être en contestation, en querelle*.

strifeful (-foule), adj., querelleur ; chicaneur.

strigose (straï-gôce), or **strigous** (straï-), adj., (bot.) hispide.

strike (straïke), v.a. (*preterit* and *past part.*, Struck), frapper ; (to dash—*jeter*) jeter ; (coin.) frapper ; (to affect—*affecter*) frapper, saisir ; (to produce—*produire*) produire ; (metal.) battre ; (a bargain—*un marché*) faire ; (a mast—*un mât*) abaisser ; (a flag—*pavillon*) amener ; (ground—*la terre*) toucher ; (a light—*le briquet*) battre ; (a measure—*une mesure*) rader ; (a blow—*un coup*) porter ; (root—*racine*) prendre ; (balance)établir ; (a musical instrument—*instrument de musique*) jouer de, toucher ; (a tent—*tente*) lever ; (of clocks, &c.—*de pendules*, &c.) sonner. To — down ; *abattre*. To — in ; *enfoncer*. To — off ; *enlever ; retrancher* ; (to erase—*biffer*) *effacer, rayer, biffer* ; (print.) *tirer*. To — out ; *faire jaillir* ; (to erase—*biffer*) *effacer, rayer, biffer* ; (to devise—*inventer*) *former, imaginer, inventer, créer*. To — up ; *entonner ; commencer à jouer*. To — any one in the face ; *frapper quelqu'un à la figure*. To — with astonishment ; *frapper d'étonnement*. To — dead ; *frapper de mort*. The clock is striking nine ; *la pendule sonne neuf heures*. It strikes me ; *il me semble*.

strike, v.n.,frapper ; (to be stranded—*échouer*) toucher ; (to lower a ship's flag—*amener le pavillon d'un vaisseau*) baisser pavillon, amener ; (of clocks, &c.—*de pendules*, &c.) sonner ; (hort.) prendre racine, pousser des racines ; (of workmen

—*d'ouvriers*) faire grève, se mettre en grève. To — against ; *frapper contre, donner contre, heurter contre*. To — at ; *tâcher de frapper, vouloir frapper* ; (fig.) *s'attaquer à, attenter à*. To — in ; *arriver tout à coup*. To — in with ; *se conformer à* ; (to join with—*joindre*) *se joindre à*. To — out ; *se lancer*. To — out into ; *se lancer dans* ; *se jeter dans*. To — up ; *commencer à jouer*.

strike (straïke), n., radoire, racloire ; (geol.) inclinaison de strate ; (of workmen—*d'ouvriers*) grève, f.

striker (straïk'-), n., personne qui frappe, f. ; (in Scripture—*biblique*) homme en colère, m.

striking (straïk'-), adj., frappant ; remarquable ; (of colour—*couleur*) marquant, tranchant.

striking, n., action de frapper ; (of clocks. &c.—*des horloges*, &c.) action de sonner, f. ; (metal.) battage, m.

striking-floor (-flôr), n., aire de battage, f.

strikingly, adv., d'une manière frappante, remarquablement.

strikingness (straïk'ign'nèce), n., caractère frappant, m. ; nature remarquable, f.

string, n., ficelle ; corde, f. ; (of a purse, of shoes—*de bourse, de souliers*) cordon ; (of beads—*de perles*, &c.) fil, m. ; (of a bonnet—*de chapeau*) bride ; (mus.) corde ; (of a bow—*d'arc*) corde, f. ; (of the tongue—*de la langue*) filet ; (of plants —*des plantes*) filet, fil, m. ; fibre, f. ; (of meat, of leguminous plants—*de viande, de légumineuses*) filandres, f.pl. ; (list—*liste*) kyrielle, enfilade, f. ; (fig.) fil, m. To have two—s to one's bow ; *avoir deux cordes à son arc*.

string, v.a. (*preterit* and *past part.*, Strung), garnir de ficelle ; munir de cordes ; (to strengthen —*fortifier*) fortifier ; (mus.) accorder ; (beads—*perles*, &c.) enfiler ; (leguminous plants—*légumineuses*) effiler.

string-board (-bôrde), n., (of a staircase—*d'escalier*) limon intérieur, m.

string-course (-côrse), n., (arch.) cordon, m.

stringed (strign'de), adj., à cordes.

stringent (stri'n'djè'n'te), adj., qui serre ; (fig.) rigoureux, strict.

stringhalt (-hôlte), n., (vet.) éparvin sec, m.

stringless (strign'-), adj., sans cordes.

stringy (strign'i), adj., filamenteux ; fibreux ; filandreux.

strip, n., bande, f.

strip, v.a., (to undress—*déshabiller*) déshabiller ; (a tree—*un arbre*) écorcer ; (nav.) dégréer ; (to rob—*voler*) dévaliser. To — of ; *dépouiller de*. To — from ; *enlever à ; ôter à*. To — off ; *enlever, ôter, arracher*.

strip, v.n., se déshabiller.

stripe (straïpe), n., raie ; barre ; (long piece —*longue pièce d'étoffe*, &c.) bande, f. ; (with a whip—*avec un fouet*) coup, m. ; (wale—*meurtrissure d'un coup de fouet*) marque, empreinte, f. ; (milit.) galon ; chevron ; (punishment—*punition*) châtiment, m.

stripe (straïpe), v.a., rayer, barrer.

striped (straïp'te), adj., rayé ; à raies.

stripling (strip'-), n., tout jeune homme ; adolescent, m.

stripper, n., personnne qui enlève, qui dépouille, qui écorce, f.

strive (straïve), v.n. (*preterit*, Strove ; *past part.*, Striven), s'efforcer, tâcher ; faire des efforts. To — against, with ; *lutter contre, lutter avec ; se disputer avec, rivaliser avec*.

striver (straïv'-), n., personne qui fait des efforts, qui lutte, qui rivalise, f.

striving (straïv'-), n., lutte, f. ; efforts, m.pl.

strobile (strô-baïle), n., (bot.) strobile, m.

stroke (strôke), n., coup ; (dash—*trait*) trait ; (of a brush—*de pinceau*) coup de pinceau ; (of a pen—*de plume*) trait de plume ; (of an oar —*de rame*) coup d'aviron ; (of a piston—*de pis-

ton) coup, mouvement; (effort) effort, *m*.; (touch—*trait*) touche,*f*., trait, coup, *m*. Great — of business; *grande affaire, f.* Back- —; *coup de revers.* Down- —; (in writing—*d'écriture*) plein, *m.* Up- —; (in writing—*d'écriture*) délié, *m.* Straight — ;(in writing—*d'écriture*) bâton,*m.*

stroke(strôke), *v.a.*, passer la main sur; caresser; flatter avec la main; frotter douce-ment.

stroker (strôk'-), *n.*, personne qui caresse, qui flatte avec la main, qui frotte doucement,*f.*

strokesman (strôk's'-), *n.*, (nav.) brigadier de rameurs, *m.*

stroking (strôk'-), *n.*, caresses, *f.pl.*; action de caresser,*f.*

stroll (strôle), *n.*, promenade; flânerie, *f.*

stroll (strôle), *v.n.*, errer; flâner; se pro-mener à l'aventure.

stroller (strôl'-), *n.*, coureur; flâneur, *m.*, flaneuse, *f.*; (vagabond) vagabond; (actor— *acteur*) comédien ambulant, *m.*, comédienne ambulante,*f.*

strolling (strôl'-), *adj.*, qui erre; de flâneur; ambulant. — actor; *comédien ambulant.*

strong(stron'gn), *adj.*, fort; (robust—*robuste*) vigoureux; (firm—*ferme*) ferme; (ardent) ardent, chaud; (of the memory—*de la mémoire*) tenace; (vehement) véhément, violent. To smell — of; *avoir une forte odeur de.* An army a hundred thousand —; *une armée forte de cent mille hommes.*

strong-backed (-bak'te), *adj.*, fort des reins.

strong-coloured (-keul'leurde), *adj.*, forte-ment coloré.

stronger (stron'gn'-gheur), *adj.*, plus fort.

strongest (stron'gn'ghèste), *adj.*, le plus fort.

strong-fisted, *adj.*, qui a un poignet vigou-reux.

strong-handed, *adj.*, qui a les mains fortes; (employing many hands—*ayant beaucoup d'ouvriers*) qui a beaucoup d'ouvriers.

stronghold (-hôlde), *n.*, place forte, *f.*

strongly (stron'gn'gli), *adv.*, fortement; (firmly—*fermement*) fermement; (vehemently— *violemment*) véhémentement.

strong-minded (-maï-), *adj.*, à esprit fort.

strong-set, *adj.*, fortement bâti.

strontia (-shi-a), **strontian** (-shi-a'n), or **strontites** (-taï-tize), *n.*, (chem.) strontiane,*f.*

strop, *n.*, cuir à repasser; cuir à rasoir, *m.*; (nav.) élingue,*f.* Razor- —; *cuir à rasoir.*

strop, *v.a.*, repasser sur le cuir.

strophe (strô-fi), *n.*, stance, strophe,*f.*

structural (streuk'tiou-), *adj.*, de structure.

structure (streuk't'ieur), *n.*, construction, structure,*f.*; (building—*bâtiment*)édifice, monu-ment, *m.*, construction, *f.*; (anat.) tissu, *m.*

struggle (streug-g'l), *n.*, lutte,*f.*; violent effort,*m.*

struggle (streug-g'l), *v.n.*, lutter; faire de violents efforts; se débattre; se démener.

struggler, *n.*, personne qui lutte, qui fait de violents efforts, qui se débat,*f.*

struggling, *n.*, lutte,*f.*; effort, *m.*

strum *v.a.*, taper sur; (mus.) massacrer.

struma(strou-), *n.*, (bot.) renflement, *m.*; (med.) strume, scrofule,*f.*

strumose (strou-môce), or **strumous** (strou-), *adj.*, strumeux.

strumpet (streu'm'-), *n.*, prostituée,*f.*

strumpet, *adj.*, prostituée.

strumpet (streu'm'-), *v.a.*, débaucher.

strut (streute), *n.*, démarche fière, *f.*; (carp.) étai, *m.*

strut (streute), *v.n.*, se pavaner; se carrer.

strutter, *n.*, personne qui se pavane, qui se carre,*f.*

struttingly, *adv.*, en se carrant; en se pava-nant.

strutting-piece (-pîce), *n.*, (carp.) contre-vent, *m.*

strychnia, or **strychnine** (strik'-), *n.*, strychnine,*f.*

stub (steube), *n.*, souche,*f.*; chicot, *m.*

stub (steube), *v.a.*, déraciner, arracher.

stubbed (steub'de), *adj.*, tronqué; épais; trapu; obtus; (blunt—*mousse*) émoussé; (not delicate—*non délicat*) grossier.

stubbedness (steub'èd'-), *n.*, état de souche, état de chicot; (bluntness—*état mousse*) état émoussé, *m.*

stubble (steub'b'l), *n.*, chaume, *m.*; éteule, esteuble,*f.*

stubborn (steub'-), *adj.*, obstiné; opiniâtre; têtu; entêté; (inflexible) inflexible; (stiff—*raide*) raide, inflexible; (of metals—*des métaux*) réfrac-taire; (constant) opiniâtre. — ass; *âne entêté, têtu.*

stubbornly, *adv.*, obstinément; opiniâtré-ment.

stubbornness (steub'-), *n.*, opiniâtreté,*f.*; entêtement, *m.*; obstination; (inflexibility— *inflexibilité*) inflexibilité; (stiffness—*raideur*) raideur, inflexibilité; (of metals—*des métaux*) nature réfractaire,*f.*

stubby (steub'-), *adj.*, plein de chaume; plein d'éteule; (short and thick—*court et gros*) petit et gros; (pers.) trapu.

stucco (steuk'kô), *n.*, stuc; ouvrage de stuc, *m.*

stucco (steuk'kô), *v.a.*, revêtir de stuc.

stud (steude), *n.*, clou, *m.*; (on harness—*de harnais*) bossette, *f.*; (of a shirt—*de chemise*) bouton; (carp.) montant; (ornamental knob— *d'ornement*) bouton, clou; (of horses—*de chevaux*) haras,*m.*

stud (steude), *v.a.*, garnir de clous; (fig.) semer, parsemer.

stud-book (-bouke), *n.*, registre des chevaux de pur sang, *m.*

studding-sail (steud'dign'séle), *n.*, (nav.) bonnette, *f.*

student (stiou-), *n.*, étudiant, *m.*; personne studieuse,*f.* Law- —; *étudiant en droit.* Medi-cal —; *étudiant en médecine.*

stud-groom (-grou'm), *n.*, piqueur, *m.*

stud-horse, *n.*, étalon de haras, *m.*

studied (steud'ide), *adj.*, (learned—*savant*) instruit; érudit; (of things—*des choses*) étudié; (premeditated—*prémédité*) prémédité.

studier (steud'-), *n.*, étudiant, *m.*; personne qui étudie,*f.*

studio (stou-diô), *n.*, atelier (of painter, &c. —*de peintre, &c.*), *m.*

studious (stiou-), *adj.*, studieux; adonné à l'étude; (diligent) diligent; (careful—*soigneux*) soigneux; (deliberate—*étudié*) délibéré; (con-templative—*pensant*) contemplatif; (favourable to study—*propre à l'étude*) favorable à l'étude. — of; *adonné à l'étude de;* (attentive to—*atten-tif*) attentif à, soigneux de. To be — to; *s'étudier à, chercher à; travailler à; être empressé de.* He is very — to please; *il cherche, il s'étudie beau-coup à plaire.*

studiously, *adv.*, studieusement; (carefully —*soigneusement*) soigneusement; attentivement.

studiousness, *n.*, attachement à l'étude, *m.*; étude,*f.*

study (steud'i), *n.*, étude; (attention) atten-tion, *f.*, soin, *m.*, application, *f.*; (apartment— *chambre*) cabinet d'étude; cabinet, *m.*; (paint.) étude; (reverie) rêverie,*f.* To make it one's — to; *s'étudier à, chercher à; s'appliquer à.*

study (steud'i), *v.a.*, étudier.

study, *v.n.*, étudier; travailler; (to endeav-our—*s'efforcer*) s'étudier, chercher, s'appliquer; (to muse—*songer*) méditer.

stuff (steufe), *n.*, (matter indefinitely—*ma-tière*) matière, *f.*; (fabric—*tissu*) étoffe, *f.*; (manu.)

stoff, m.; (materials—*matériaux* : *tissus*) matériaux, m.pl., étoffe, f.; (nav.) suif. doublage. m.; (essence) essence. f.; (mas.) mortier, m.; (rubbish—*chose sans valeur*) drogue, f., fatras, m. —! *bah! sottises!* What —! *quelles sottises!* Wretched —; *méchante drogue; misérable chose.* Nasty —; *mauvaise chose; de la cochonnerie.* Silly —; *des sottises; des sornettes.* That is all — and nonsense; *c'est tout de la bétise : bah! ce sont des bétises.*

stuff (steufe), v.a., remplir; bourrer; farcir; boucher; (cook.) farcir; (dead animals—*des animaux morts*) empailler; (furniture—*des meubles*) rembourrer. To — in; *bourrer.* To — up; *bourrer;* (a hole—*un trou*) boucher; (the nose—*le nez*) enchifrener. —ed up with nonsense; *plein d'affectation.*

stuff, v.n., se remplir; se bourrer.

stuffing, n., bourre; (cook.) farce, f.

stuffing-box, n., boîte à étoupe, f.; serreétoupe, m.

stultify (steul-ti-fa'ye), v.a., hébéter; abrutir; (jur.) alléguer la faiblesse d'esprit de. To — one's self; *se rendre ridicule.*

stultiloquence (steul-til'o-kwè'n'ce), or **stultiloquy** (-kwi), n., sottise, f.; babillage, m.

stum (steume), n., moût; râpé, m.

stum (steume), v.a., passer par le râpé.

stumble (steu'm'b'l), n., faux pas, m.; (blunder—*bévue*) bévue, f.

stumble (steu'm'b'l), v.n., trébucher; broncher; faire un faux pas; (to err—*errer*) faillir; (of animals—*des animaux*) broncher. To — upon; *rencontrer par hasard, tomber sur.*

stumble, v.a., faire trébucher, faire broncher, faire faire un faux pas à; (to puzzle—*embarrasser*) embarrasser.

stumbler, n., personne qui trébuche, qui bronche, qui fait un faux pas, qui fait des bévues, f.

stumbling, n., trébuchement, m.

stumbling, adj., qui fait des faux pas, qui bronche; qui fait des bévues; (puzzling—*embarrassant*) embarrassant.

stumbling-block, or **stumbling-stone**, n., pierre d'achoppement, f.

stump (steu'm'pe), n., tronçon; (of a limb—*d'un membre*) moignon; (of a tooth—*d'une dent*) chicot; (of a cabbage—*de chou*) trognon; (of a pen—*de plume*) bout; (of a tree—*d'arbre*) tronçon, chicot, m.; (in drawing—*dessin*) estompe, f. —s; (at cricket—*à la crosse*) guichet, m. Stir your —s; *alerte! remuez-vous.*

stump (steu'm'pe), v.a., (to lop—*couper*) ne laisser qu'un tronçon de; (in drawing—*de dessin*) estomper; (to take all from—*enlever tout à*) mettre à sec. To — out; *mettre à sec.*

stump-orator (-or'a-teur), n., orateur de carrefour, m.

stumpy, adj., plein de tronçons; (pers.) trapu.

stun (steune), v.a., étourdir; (fig.) étourdir abasourdir.

stunning (steu'n'-), adj., étourdissant; (big grand—*gros; grandiose*) fameux.

stunt (steu'n'te), v.a., empêcher de croître; rendre rabougri.

stunted, adj., rabougri. To become —; *se rabougrir.*

stuntedness, n., état rabougri, m.

stupe (stioupe), n., (med.) lotion; fomentation; (pers.) imbécile. m., f., bête, f.

stupe (stioupe), v.a., bassiner. fomenter.

stupefaction (stiou-pi-fak-), n., stupéfaction, f.; étonnement, m.

stupefactive (stiou-pi-fak-), adj., stupéfactif; stupéfiant.

stupefier (stiou-pi-faï-), n., chose qui hébète, qui assoupit, qui stupéfie, f.

---

stupefy (stiou-pi-fa'ye), v.a., hébéter; abrutir; stupéfier.

stupendous (stiou-), adj., étonnant; prodigieux.

stupendously, adv., prodigieusement; étonnamment.

stupendousness, n., grandeur prodigieuse, f.

stupid (stiou-), adj., stupide: sot; bête. To become —; *devenir stupide, s'abétir, abétir.* — thing; *stupidité, f.;* (pers.) *bêta, m., bête, f.*

stupidity, n., stupidité; bêtise; sottise, f.

stupidly, adv., stupidement; sottement; bêtement.

stupidness. V. **stupidity**.

stupor (stiou-peur), n., stupeur, f.

stuprate (stiou-), v.a., violer; déshonorer; ravir.

stupration (stiou-pré-), n., rapt; viol, m.

sturdily (steur-), adv., hardiment, fortement, vigoureusement.

sturdiness, n., hardiesse; vigueur; force, f.

sturdy (steur-), adj., hardi; vigoureux; fort.

sturdy (steur-), n., (vet.) tournis; tournoiement, m.

sturgeon (steur-djeune), n., (ich.) esturgeon, m.

stutter (steut'-), v.a. and n., bégayer; balbutier.

stutterer, n., bègue, m., f.

stuttering, n., bégaiement, m.

stutteringly, adv., en bégayant; en balbutiant.

sty (sta'ye), n., étable à cochons, f., toit à cochons, m.; (on the eye—*de l'œil*) orgelet, compère-loriot, m.

sty, v.a., mettre dans une étable, dans un toit à cochons.

stygian (stidj'i-), adj., stygien; du styx.

style (staïle), n., style; genre, m.; manière, f.; ton; (probe—*sonde*) stylet; (bot.: of a dial; and in chronology; graver—*de cadran solaire; de chronologie;* burin) style, m. In good —; *dans le bon genre; d'un bon goût.* In grand —; *dans le grand genre.* In bad —; *dans le mauvais genre, d'un mauvais goût.* To live in —; *avoir un train de maison.* To live in first-rate —; *avoir un grand train de maison.* To go on in fine —; *aller grand train.* He gave it me in fine —; *il m'en a dit d'une belle manière; il m'a arrangé d'une belle façon; il m'a fait une verte semonce.* She has no — about her; *elle n'a pas de ton.* His — is bad; *son style est mauvais.*

style (staïle), v.a., appeler; donner le titre de . . . . à. . . . To — one's self; *s'appeler; se faire appeler; se donner le titre de.*

stylet (staï-), n., stylet, m.

styliform (staï-), adj., (bot.) styliforme.

stylish (staï-), adj., élégant; de bon ton; de haut ton; dans le bon genre.

stylite (staï-laïte), adj., stylite.

stylobate (staï-), n., (arch.) stylobate, m.

styloid (staï-loïde), adj., (anat.) styloïde.

styptic (stip-), n., styptique, m.

styptic, or **styptical**, adj., (med.) styptique.

stypticity, n., stypticité, f.

stythe (staïthe), n., grisou; gaz inflammable, m.

suability (siou-), n., sujétion à une action civile, f.

suable (siou-a-b'l), adj., (jur.) capable d'être poursuivi.

suasible (soua-ci-b'l), adj., (ant.) facile à persuader.

suasive (soué-cive, or **suasory** (soué-çori), adj., persuasif.

suasively, adv., d'une manière persuasive.

suavity (souèv'-), n., suavité, f.

subacid (seub-), adj., acidule.

subacrid (seub'-), adj., un peu âcre.

subact (seub'-), *v.a.*, subjuguer ; réduire.
sub-action (seub'-), *n.*, réduction, *f.*
sub-agent(seub'é-djè'n'te), *n.*, sous-agent, *m.*
sub-almoner (seub'al-meu'n'-), *n.*, second aumônier, *m.*
subaltern (seub'al-teurne), *adj.*, subalterne.
subaltern, *n.*, subalterne ; officier au-dessous de chef de bataillon, officier subalterne, *m.*
subalternate, *adj.*, successif, alternatif.
subalternation (seub'al-teur-né-), *n.*, alternation, *f.*
subaquatic(seub'a-kwat'-),*or* **subaqueous** (seub'é-kwi-), *adj.*, sous l'eau.
subastral (seub'-), *adj.*, terrestre.
sub-basement (seub-béss'-), *n.*, (arch.) soubassement, *m.*
sub-brigadier (seub-brig'a-dîre), *n.*,(milit.) enseigne, cornette, *m.*
subcelestial (seub-ci-lèst'-), *adj.*, terrestre.
sub-chanter (-tshâ'n'-), *n.*, sous-chantre, *m.*
sub-commissioner (seub-com'mish'-), *n.*, sous-commissaire, *m.*
sub-committee (seub-), *n.*, sous-comité, *m.*
sub-constellation (seub-co'n'stèl-lé-), *n.*, constellation de second ordre, *f.*
sub-contractor (seub-co'n'trac-teur), *n.*, sous-entrepreneur, *m.*
subcostal (seub-), *adj.*, sous-costal.
subcutaneous (seub-kiou-té-ni-), *n.*, sous-cutané.
sub-deacon (seub-dî-k'n), *n.*,sous-diacre, *m.*
sub-deaconry, *or* **subdeaconship**, *n.*, sous-diaconat, *m.*
sub-dean (seub-dîne), *n.*, sous-doyen, *m.*
sub-deanery, *n.*, sous-doyenné, *m.*
subdivide (seub-di-vaïde), *v.a.*, subdiviser.
subdivide, *v.n.*, se subdiviser.
subdivision (seub-di-vij'eune), *n.*, subdivision, *f.*
sub-dominant (seub-), *n.*, (mus.) sous-dominante, *f.*
subduable (seub-diou-a-b'l), *adj.*, domptable
subdual (seub-diou-), *n.*, réduction, *f.* ; assujettissement, *m.*
subduce (seub-diouce), *or* **subduct** (seub-deuk'te), *v.a.*, soustraire ; retirer.
subduction (seub-deuk'-), *n.*, soustraction, *f.* ; enlèvement, *m.*
subdue (seub-diou), *v.a.*, subjuguer ; soumettre ; réduire ; dompter ; assujettir ; vaincre ; maîtriser.
subduer, *n.*, vainqueur, *m.* ; chose qui subjugue, qui maitrise, *f.*
subduple (seub-diou-p'l), *adj.*, (math.) sous-double.
subduplicate (seub-diou-), *adj.*, sous-doublé.
suberic (siou-bèr'-), *adj.*, (chem.) subérique.
subinfeudation (seub'i'n'fiou-dé-), *n.*, sous-inféodation, *f.*
subjacent (seub-djé-), *adj.*, sujet à ; situé au dessous ; inférieur ; sous-jacent.
subject (seub-djèk'te), *adj.*, assujetti ; soumis ; sujet.
subject (seub-djèkte), *n.*, sujet, *m.* ; personne, *f.* ; (gram.) sujet ; (mus.) motif, *m.*
subject (seub-djèkte), *v.a.*, assujettir ; soumettre ; (to make liable—*exposer*) rendre sujet, exposer. To — one's self to ; *s'exposer à*. — of a fugue ; (mus.) *demande*, *f.*
subjection (seub-djèk'-), *n.*, sujétion ; soumission, *f.* ; assujettissement, *m.* To bring under —; *assujettir ; soumettre.*
subjective (seub-djek'-), *adj.*, subjectif.
subjectively, *adv.*, subjectivement.
subject-matter (seub-), *n.*, sujet, *m.*, matière, *f.*
subjoin (seub-djwaïne), *v.a.*, ajouter ; joindre. —ed ; *ci-joint.*
subjugate (seub-djiou-), *v.a.*, subjuguer ; assujettir ; soumettre.

subjunction (seub-djeu'n'k'-), *n.*, jonction, *f.* In — to ; *joint à.*
subjunctive (seub-djeu'n'k'-), *n.*, (gram.) subjonctif, *m.* In the — ; *au subjonctif.*
subjunctive.*adj.*, joint, ajouté. — mood ; (gram.) *subjonctif*, *m.*
sub-king (seub-), *n.*, roi tributaire, *m.*
sublapsarian (seub-lap-sé-), *adj.*, sublapsairien.
sublapsarian, *n.*, sublapsaire, *m.*,*f.*
sublapsarianism ('iz'm), *n.*, sublapsarianisme, *m.*
sublation (seub'lé-), *n.*, enlèvement, *m.*
sublet (seub-), *v.a.* (*preterit* and *past part.*, Sublet), sous-louer.
sub-librarian (seub-laï-bré-), *n.*, sous-bibliothécaire, *m.*
sub-lieutenant (seub-lèf'tè'n'-), *n.*, (artil.) sous-lieutenant, *m.*
sublimable (seub'laï-ma-b'l), *adj.*, (chem.) sublimable.
sublimableness, *n.*, (chem.) qualité de ce qui peut être sublimé, *f.*
sublimate (seub'li-), *v.a.*, élever ; (chem.) sublimer.
sublimate, *n.*, (chem.) sublimé, *m.*
sublimate, *adj.*, (chem.) sublimé.
sublimation (seub'li-mé-), *n.*, (chem.) sublimation, *f.*
sublime (seub'laïme), *adj.*, élevé ; haut ; (fig.) sublime, imposant, majestueux, élevé.
sublime, *n.*, sublime, *m.*
sublime (seub'laïme), *v.a.*, élever ; exalter ; (chem.) sublimer.
sublime, *v.n.*, se sublimer.
sublimely, *adv.*, d'une manière sublime ; sublimement.
sublimeness, *n.*, sublimité, *f.* ; sublime, *m.*
subliming-pot (seub'laïm'-), *n.*, (chem.) sublimatoire, *m.*
sublimity (seub'li'm'-), *n.*, élévation, hauteur ; (fig.) sublimité, *f.*, sublime, *m.*, grandeur, élévation, *f.*
sublingual (seub'lign'gwal), *adj.*, (anat.) sublingual.
sublunar, *or* **sublunary** (seub'liou-), *adj.*, sublunaire.
submarine (seub'ma-rîne), *adj.*, sous-marin.
submerge (seub-meurdje), *v.a.*, submerger.
submerge, *v.a.*, plonger dans l'eau.
submerse (seub-meurse), *v.a.*, submerger.
submersion (seub-meur-), *n.*, submersion, *f.*
submission (seub-mish'-), *n.*, soumission ; résignation, *f.*
submissive (seub-), *adj.*, soumis ; humble ; résigné.
submissively, *adv.*, humblement ; avec soumission.
submissiveness, *n.*, soumission, *f.*
submit (seub-), *v.a.*, soumettre ; déférer.
submit, *v.n.*, se soumettre ; se résigner.
submitter, *n.*, personne qui se soumet, *f.*
submultiple (seub-meul-ti-p'l), *n.*, arith.) sous-multiple, *m.*
subnormal (seub-), *n.*, (geom.) sous-normale, *f.*
subnude (seub-nioude), *adj.*, (bot.) presque nu.
subordinate (seub-), *adj.*, inférieur ; subordonné.
subordinate, *n.*, subordonné, *m.*
subordinate, *v.a.*, subordonner ; (to make subject—*soumettre*) assujettir.
subordinately, *adv.*, subordonnément ; en sous-ordre ; (in descending—*en descendant*) en descendant, par gradation.
subordination (seub-or-di-né-), *n.*, subordination ; soumission, *f.* ; rang inférieur, *m.*
suborn (seub-), *v.a.*, suborner ; corrompre ; séduire ; acheter.

subornation (seub-or-né-), *n.*, subornation; corruption ; séduction, *f.*

suborner, *n.*, suborneur, *m.*, suborneuse, *f.*

sub-pavement (seub-pév'-), *n.*, sous-fondation, *f.*

subperpendicular (seub-peur-pè'n'dik-lou-), *n.*, (geom. sous-perpendiculaire, sous-normale, *f.*

subpœna (seub-pî-), *n,,* (jur.) citation ; assignation, *f.*

subpœna, *v.a.*, (jur.) citer ; assigner.

sub-prior (seub-prai-), *n.*, sous-prieur, *m.*

sub-purchaser (seub-peur-tshé-ceur), *n.*, acheteur en seconde main, *m.*

sub-rector (seub-rèk'teur), *n.*, sous-recteur, *m.*

subreption (seub-rèp-), *n.*, subreption, *f.*

subreptitious (seub-rèp-tish'-), *adj.*, subreptice.

subreptitiously, *adv.*, subrepticement.

subrogation (seub-ro-ghé-), *n.*, (jur.) subrogation, *f.*

subrotund (seub-ro-teu'n'de), *adj.*, (bot.) presque rond.

subsalt (seub-sōlte), *n.*, (chem.) sous-sel, *m.*

subscapular (seub-scap'lou-), *adj.*, sous-scapulaire.

subscribe (seub-scraïbe), *v.a.*, souscrire ; signer. To — five francs to; *souscrire pour la somme de cinq francs à.*

subscribe, *v,n.*, souscrire. To — to a newspaper, &c.; *s'abonner, prendre un abonnement, à un journal; être abonné à un journal.*

subscriber, *n.*, souscripteur ; signataire ; (to a newspaper, &c.—*à un journal, &c.*) abonné, *m.*, abonnée, *f.*

subscription (seub-scrip'-), *n.*, souscription; signature, *f.*; (to a newspaper, &c.—*à un journal*) abonnement, *m.*

sub-section (seub'sèk'-), *n.*, subdivision, *f.*

subsequence, or **subsequency** (seub-sikwè'n'-), *n.*, postériorité, *f.*

subsequent, *adj.*, subséquent ; postérieur.

subsequently, *adv.*, ensuite ; par la suite ; subséquemment.

subserve (seub-seurve), *v.a.*, servir subordonnément ; être dépendant de ; servir d'instrument à.

subservience, or **subserviency** (seub-seur-), *n.*, concours, *m.* ; utilité, *f.*

subservient, *adj.*, utile ; (subordinate—*subordonné*) subordonné. To make — to; *faire servir à.*

subserviently, *adv.*, en sous-ordre, utilement.

subside (seub-saïde), *v.a.*, tomber au fond ; (to become tranquil—*s'apaiser*) se calmer, s'apaiser ; (to sink—*s'affaisser*) s'affaisser ; (of buildings —*de bâtiments*) tasser ; (to abate—*diminuer*) baisser, s'abaisser.

subsidence, or **subsidency** (seub-saï-), *n.*, affaissement, *m.* ; (of liquids—*des liquides*) action de tomber au fond, *f.*, dépôt ; (of buildings—*de bâtiments*) tassement, *m.*

subsidiary (seub-si-), *adj.*, subsidiaire ; auxiliaire.

subsidiary, *n.*, auxiliaire, *m.*

subsidize (seub-si-daïze), *v.a.*, subventionner ; donner des subsides à.

subsidy (seub-si-), *n.*, subside, *m.* ; subvention, *f.*

subsist (seub-), *v.n.*, exister ; subsister. To - on ; *subsister de ; vivre de.*

subsist, *v.a.*, faire subsister.

subsistence, or **subsistency,** *n.*, (being —*exister*) existence ; (means of support—*moyens d'existence*) subsistance, *f.*, entretien, moyens d'existence, *m.* ; (inherence) inhérence, *f.*

subsistent, *adj.*, existant, qui existe ; (inherent) inhérent.

subsoil (seub-soïle), *n.*, (agri.) sous-sol, *m.*

sub-species (seub-spî-shîze), *n.*, sous-espèce, *f.*

substance (seub-), *n.*, substance, *f.* ; (means of living—*moyens*) moyens d'existence ; (goods —*propriété*) biens, *m.pl.*

substantial (seub-sta'n'shal), *adj.*, (belonging to substance—*existant*) de substance, qui existe, substantiel ; (real—*réel*) réel, vrai ; (solid, stout—*fort*) solide, fort, substantiel ; (material—*matériel*) matériel, corporel ; (well off—*riche*) aisé, à l'aise. — proof; *preuve matérielle.* — meal; *repas solide.* — speech; *discours substantiel.* — food; *nourriture substantielle.* — man; *homme à son aise.*

substantiality, *n.*, existence réelle, *f.*

substantially, *adv.*, (solidly—*fortement*) solidement, fortement ; (really—*réellement*) réellement, vraiment ; (in substance—*matériellement*) en substance; (at one's ease—*dans l'aisance*) à l'aise, dans l'aisance ; (theol.) substantiellement.

substantialness, *n.*, solidité ; force, *f.*

substantials (-shalze), *n.pl.*, parties essentielles, *f.pl.* ; (succulent food—*d'aliments*) aliments substantiels, *m.pl.*

substantiate (seub-sta'n'shi-), *v.a.*, faire exister ; (to establish by proof—*constater*) prouver, établir.

substantive (seub-), *adj.*, indépendant ; (gram. ; of colours—*des couleurs*) substantif.

substantive, *n.*, (gram.) substantif, *m.*

substantively, *adv.*, en substance ; (gram.) substantivement.

substile, *n. V.* **substyle.**

substitute (seub-sti-tioute), *v.a.*, substituer.

substitute (seub-sti-tioute), *n.*, substitut ; remplaçant ; représentant, mandataire ; (milit.) remplaçant, *m.* ; (thing—*chose*) chose qui remplace, *f.* That is a — for; *cela remplace ; cela sert pour remplacer.*

substitution (seub-sti-tiou-), *n.*, substitution ; (gram.) syllepse, *f.*

substract (seub-), *v.a. V.* **subtract.**

substratum (seub-strê-), *n.* (*substrata*), (min.) couche inférieure, *f.* ; (philos.) substratum ; (agri.) sous-sol, *m.*

substruction (seub-streuk-), or **substructure** (-streukt'leur), *n.*, fondation, substruction, *f.*

substylar (seub-staïl'-), *adj.*, de soustylaire.

substyle (seub-staïle), *n.*, soustylaire, *f.*

subsultive, or **subsultory** (seub-seul-), *adj.*, à soubresauts.

subsultorily, *adv.*, par soubrésauts.

subsultus (seub-seul-), *n.*, (med.) soubresaut, *m.*

subtangent (seub-ta'n'djè'n'te), *m.*, (geom.) sous-tangente, *f.*

subtartarean (seub'tar-tar'i-), *adj.*, sous le Tartare ; infernal.

subtend (seub-), *v.a.*, sous-tendre.

subtense (seub-), *n.*, (geom.) sous-tendante ; corde, *f.*

subterfuge (seub-tèr-floudje), *n.*, subterfuge ; détour, faux-fuyant, *m.*

subterrane (seub-tèr-), *n.*, souterrain, *m.*

subterranean, or **subterraneous** (seub-tèr-ré-nî-), *adj.*, souterrain.

subtile (seub-tile), *adj.*, subtil ; fin ; (acute —*perçant*) aigu, perçant ; (cunning—*fin*) subtil, fin, adroit ; (deceitful—*trompeur*) trompeur.

subtileness, subtility, or **subtilty** (seub-), *n.*, subtilité, *f.*

subtility, *n. V.* **subtileness.**

subtilization (seub-til'aïzé-), *n.*, subtilisation, *f.*

subtilize (seub-til'aïze), *v,n.*, subtiliser.

subtilize, *v.a.*, rendre subtil.

subtle (seut't'l), *adj.*, subtil ; rusé ; (cunning —*fin*) subtil, fin.

subtleness (seut't'l'-), _n._, finesse, _f._; artifice, _m._

subtly (seut't'li),_adv._,finement,avec finesse; artificieusement, avec artifice.

subtract (seub-), _v.a._, soustraire; retrancher; ôter; déduire.

subtracter, _n._, personne qui soustrait, qui retranche, _f._

subtraction, _n._, retranchement, _m._; (arith.) soustraction, _f._

subtractive, _adj._, qui tend à soustraire, à retrancher.

subtrahend, _n._, (arith.) nombre à retrancher, _m._

sub-tutor (seub-tiou-teur), _n._, sous-précepteur, _m._

subulate (siou-biou-), _adj._, (bot.) subulé.

suburb (seub'eurbe), _n._, faubourg, _m._ —s; alentours, environs, _m.pl._

suburban, suburbial, _or_ **suburbian** (seub-eur-), _adj._, suburbain.

suburbicarian (seub'eurb'i-ké-), _adj._, suburbicaire.

subvention (seub-), _n._, subvention,_f._

subversion (seub-veur-), _n._, subversion,_f._; renversement, _m._

subversive, _or_ **subversionary** (seub-veur-), _adj._, subversif.

subvert (seub-veurte), _v.a._, subvertir, renverser, bouleverser.

subverter, _n._, destructeur, _m._, destructrice,_f._

subworker (seub-weurk'-), _n._, auxiliaire; aide, _m._

succedaneous (seuk-ci-dé-ni-), _adj._, qui remplace, _f._; succédané.

succedaneum (seuk-ci-dé-ni-), _n._, chose qui remplace, _f._; succédané, _m._

succeed (seuk-cide), _v.n._, succéder; (to prosper—_prospérer_) réussir, succéder. He —s in every thing; _il réussit en tout; tout lui réussit, lui succède._

succeed (seuk'cide), _v.a._, succéder à; suivre; (to prosper—_favoriser_) faire réussir, faire succéder. To — each other; _se succéder._

succeeding, _adj._, (of the past—_du passé_) suivant; (of the future—_du futur_) à venir, futur; (successive) successif.

success (seuk'cèss), _n._, succès, _m._; réussite, _f._ To have —; _avoir du succès; réussir._

successful (-foule), _adj._, qui réussit; heureux. To be —; _avoir du succès; réussir._

successfully, _adv._, heureusement; avec succès.

successfulness, _n._, réussite, _f._; succès, _m._

succession (seuk'cèsh'-), _n._, succession; suite, _f._; (to the throne—_au trône_) avènement, _m._; (lineage—_lignée_) postérité, _f._; (right to inherit—_habilité à hériter_) droit de succession, _m._; (mus.) succession; (agri.) rotation, _f._ In —; _successivement._

successive (seuk'-), _adj._, successif.

successively, _adv._, successivement.

successiveness, _n._, nature successive, _f._

successless, _adj._, sans succès; malheureux, infortuné.

successor (seuk'cèss'eur), _n._, successeur, _m._

succinct (seuk'cignk'te), _adj._, succinct.

succinctly, _adv._, succinctement.

succinctness, _n._, concision; brièveté, _f._

succory (seuk'-), _n._, (bot.) chicorée, _f._

succour (seuk'keur), _v.a._, secourir; aider; (a mast—_un mât_) renforcer; (cable) fortifier.

succour (seuk'keur), _n._, secours, _m._; aide; assistance, _f._

succourer, _n._, personne qui donne du secours, qui apporte du secours, _f._

succourless, _adj._, sans secours.

succulence, _or_ **succulency** (seuk'kiou-), _n._, abondance de suc,_f._; suc, _m._

succulent, _or_ **succulous** (seuk'kiou-),_adj._, succulent; plein de jus, plein de suc.

succumb (seuk'keu'm), _v.n._, succomber, céder.

succussation (seuk'keus'sé-), _or_ **succussion** (-keush'-), _n._,action de secouer; secousse,_f._

such (seutshe), _adj._, tel; certain. — an one; _un tel, m.,une telle, f._ — an one as; _tel que._ — as you; _tel que vous._ — as do not like; _ceux qui n'aiment pas; tels qui n'aiment pas._ — as it is; _tel quel, m., telle quelle, f._ — and —; _tel et tel._ These verses are of — a poet; _ces vers sont de tel poète._ Mr. — an one; _Monsieur un tel._ We have walked — a way that; _nous avons tellement marché que._ He remained — a time that; _il est resté si longtemps que._ It is — a way; _c'est si loin._ He is — a bore; _il est si ennuyeux, si assommant._ Continue —; _continuez ainsi, tel._ At — a time; _à un tel moment._ You are — a man ! _vous êtes si galant, si brave, si farceur, &c._ It is no —thing; _il n'en est rien._

suck (seuke),_v.a._, sucer; (the teat—_le sein_) teter, téter; (to inhale) aspirer, pomper; (to absorb—_absorber_) absorber, boire. To — in; _sucer ;_ (to absorb—_engloutir_) absorber ; (to inhale —_aspirer_) aspirer; (to believe—_croire_) gober. To — in with one's milk; _sucer avec le lait._ To — out; _sucer; tirer, vider (en suçant)._ To — up; _aspirer ;_ (to absorb—_engloutir_) absorber. To — out of; _puiser dans, tirer de._

suck, _v.n._, sucer; (of young things—_des jeunes êtres_) teter, téter; (to draw in—_absorber_) aspirer.

suck (seuke), _n._, sucement, _m._; aspiration,_f._; (milk—_lait_) lait; (sugar-stick—_sucre d'orge_) sucre d'orge, _m._ To give — to; _donner le sein à, donner à téter à, allaiter._

sucker, _n._, suceur; (of a pump—_de pompe_) piston; (ent.) suçoir; (bot.) drageon, _m._

sucket (seuk'-), _n._, sucrerie, _f._

sucking, _n._, sucement, _m._; succion; (of liquids—_de liquides_) aspiration, _f._

sucking, _adj._, qui suce; qui tette; qui absorbe; qui aspire. —child; _enfant à la mamelle._ —pig; _cochon de lait._

sucking-bottle (-bot't'l), _n._, biberon, _m._

sucking-fish, _n._, rémora, _n._; rémore, _f._; sucet, _m._

sucking-pump (-peu'm'p), _n._, pompe aspirante, _f._

suckle (seuk'k'l), _v.a._, allaiter; nourrir.

suckling (seuk'-), _n._, enfant à la mamelle nourrisson; (animal) animal qui tette encore, _m._

suction (seuk'-), _n._, succion; aspiration; absorption,_f._; sucement, _m._

suctorial, _or_ **suctorious** (seuk'tô-), _adj._, suceur.

sudation (siou-dé-), _n._, sudation, _f._

sudatory (siou-), _adj._, sudatoire.

sudden (seud'-),_adj._,subit; soudain ;inopiné; imprévu. — death; _mort subite, f._

sudden, _n._, événement soudain, _m._ All of a —; _tout à coup._

suddenly, _adv._, subitement; soudainement; tout à coup, soudain.

suddenness, _n._, soudaineté; promptitude,_f._

sudoriferous (siou-do-rif'èr'-), _adj._, (anat.) sudoripare.

sudorific (siou-), _n._, sudorifique, _m._

sudorific, _adj._, sudorifique; sudorifère.

suds (seudze), _n.pl._, eau de savon; lessive, _f. sing._

sue (siou), _v.a._, poursuivre; poursuivre en justice; (of a hawk—_du faucon_) s'essuyer. To — out; _obtenir par pétition._ To — for; _poursuivre en._ To — for damages; _poursuivre en dommages-intérêts._

sue, _v.n._, poursuivre en justice. To — for; _solliciter, demander._ To — to; _s'adresser à._

suet (siou-ète), _n._, graisse,_f._

suety (siou-èt'-), *adj.*, de graisse; gras; ressemblant à la graisse.

suffer (seuf'-), *v.a.*, souffrir; supporter; endurer; (to undergo—*subir*) subir; (to permit—*permettre*) souffrir, laisser, permettre; (to sustain—*éprouver*) éprouver, essuyer. To — losses; *éprouver des pertes.* To — punishment; *subir, souffrir une peine.* — me to tell you; *permettez moi de vous dire, souffrez que je vous dise.* To — one's self to be deceived; *se laisser tromper.*

suffer, *v.n.*, souffrir. To — for; *souffrir de; pâtir de, porter la peine de.*

sufferable (seuf'feur'-a-b'l), *adj.*, supportable; tolérable; permis.

sufferably, *adv.*, d'une manière supportable.

sufferance (seuf'feur'-), *n.*, (toleration—*permission*) tolérance, permission; (endurance—*souffrance*) souffrance; (patience) patience, modération, *f.* Bill of —; *lettre d'exemption des droits de la douane, f.* You are here only on —; *vous n'êtes ici que par tolérance.* At —; (jur.) *par tolérance.*

sufferer, *n.*, personne qui souffre; victime, *f.*; patient, *m.*; (one who permits—*celui qui permet*) personne qui permet, *f.* Fellow- —; *compagnon d'infortune.* To be a — by; *être victime de.* Yes, but I am the —; *oui, mais c'est moi qui en souffre, qui en pâtis.*

suffering, *n.*, souffrance, douleur, *f.*

sufferingly, *adv.*, avec douleur, en souffrant.

suffice (seuf'faïze), *v.a.*, suffire à; satisfaire.

suffice, *v.n.*, suffire. — it to say; *qu'il suffise de dire.*

sufficience, *or* **sufficiency** (seuf'fish'è'n'-), *n.*, suffisance; (ability—*moyens*) capacité; (competence—*fortune*) fortune suffisante, aisance; (vanity—*vanité*) suffisance, *f.* A — of; *suffisamment de, assez de.*

sufficient (seuf'fish'è'n'te), *adj.*, suffisant; assez; (fit—*apte*) capable. — for; *suffisant pour, qui suffit à.* — unto the day is the evil thereof; *à chaque jour suffit sa peine.*

sufficiently, *adv.*, suffisamment, assez.

suffix (seuf'-), *n.*, (gram.) terminaison, *f.*; suffixe, *m.*

suffocate (seuf'-), *v.a.*, suffoquer; étouffer; asphyxier.

suffocating (seuf'fo-két'-), *adj.*, suffocant; asphyxiant.

suffocatingly, *adv.*, d'une manière suffocante.

suffocation (seuf'fo-ké-), *n.*, suffocation, *f.*; étouffement, *m.*

suffocative (-fo-ké-), *adj.*, suffocant; étouffant.

suffragan (seuf'-), *n.*, suffragant, *m.*

suffragan, *adj.*, suffragant. — bishop; *évêque suffragant, m.*

suffrage (seuf'frédje), *n.*, suffrage, *m.* Manhood- —; *suffrage universel.* —s; (in the liturgy—*liturgie*) suffrages, *m.pl.*

suffrutex (seuf-frou-tèkse), *n.*, (bot.) sous-arbrisseau, *m.*

suffumigate (seuf'fiou-), *v.a.*, (med.) fumiger.

suffumigation (seuf'fiou-mi-ghé-), *n.*, suffumigation, *f.*

suffuse (seuf'fiouze), *v.a.*, couvrir; se répandre sur, s'épancher sur. Her face was —ed with blushes; *une rougeur s'était répandue sur son visage.*

suffusion (seuf'fiou-jeune), *n.*, action de couvrir, *f.*; épanchement; (med.) épanchement, *m.*, suffusion, *f.*; (surg.) cataracte, *f.*

sugar (shoug'-), *n.*, sucre, *m.* Brown —; *sucre brun.* Moist —; *cassonade, f.* Raw —; *sucre brut.* Barley- —; *sucre d'orge.* Loaf of —; *pain de sucre, m.* Lump of —; *morceau de sucre, m.* Lump- —; *sucre en pain.* — and water; *eau sucrée, f.*

sugar, *v.a.*, sucrer; (fig.) adoucir.

sugar-baker (-bék'-), *n.*, raffineur de sucre, *m.*

sugar-basin (-bé-s'n), *n.*, sucrier, *m.*

sugar-candy, *n.*, sucre candi, *m.*

sugar-cane, *n.*, canne à sucre, *f.*

sugared (shough'eurde), *adj.*, sucré; doux; mielleux.

sugar-house (-haouce), *n.*, sucrerie, *f.*

sugar-loaf (-lôfe), *adj.*, en pain de sucre.

sugar-loaf, *n.*, pain de sucre, *m.*

sugar-maple, *n.*, (bot.) érable à sucre, *m.*

sugar-mill, *n.*, moulin à sucre, *m.*

sugar-mite (-maïte), *n.*, (ent.) lépisme du sucre, *m.*

sugar-mould (-môlde), *n.*, forme à sucre, *f.*

sugar-nippers, *n.pl.*, pinces à sucre, *f.pl.*

sugar-plantation (-pla'n'té-), *n.*, plantation de cannes à sucre, *f.*

sugar-planter, *n.*, planteur de cannes à sucre, *m.*

sugar-plum (-pleu'm), *n.*, dragée, *f.*

sugar-refiner (-ri-faï'n'-), *n.*, raffineur de sucre, *m.*

sugar-refinery (-ri-faï'n'-), *n.*, raffinerie de sucre, *f.*

sugar-refining, *n.*, raffinage du sucre, *m.*

sugar-tongs (-to'n'gze), *n.pl.*, pinces, pinces à sucre, *f.pl.*

sugar-trade, *n.*, commerce des sucres, *m.*

sugar-work (-weurke), *n.*, sucrerie, *f.*

sugary (shoug'-), *adj.*, sucré; sucrin; (fond of sugar—*aimant le sucre*) qui aime le sucre.

sugescent (siou-djèss'-), *adj.*, qui sert à l'allaitement.

suggest (seud'jèste), *v.a.*, suggérer; inspirer. To be —ed; *se suggérer.*

suggester (seud'jèst'-), *n.*, personne qui suggère, *f.*

suggestion (seud'jèst'ieu'n), *n.*, suggestion, inspiration; impulsion; (b.s.) instigation; (jur.) déposition sans serment, *f.* On my —; *à ma suggestion.*

suggestive (seud'jèst'-), *adj.*, qui inspire; qui suggère.

suicidal (siou-i-çaï'-), *adj.*, de suicide.

suicide (siou-i-çaïde), *n.*, suicide, *m.* To commit —; *se suicider.*

suit (sioute), *n.*, collection, *f.*; nombre complet; assortiment, *m.*; (at cards—*aux cartes*) couleur, *f.*; (solicitation) sollicitation, demande; (petition) pétition, requête; (courtship—*cour*) recherche en mariage, cour; (pursuit—*poursuite*) poursuite; (jur.) action, poursuite, *f.*; procès, *m.* To bring a —; (jur.) *intenter une action, une poursuite.* — of armour ; *armure complète, f.* — of clothes ; *habillement complet, m.* To follow —; (at cards—*aux cartes*) servir, donner de la couleur jouée.

suit (sioute), *v.a.*, (to adapt—*adapter*) adapter, approprier; (to become—*convenir*) convenir à, aller à, arranger; (to please—*plaire*) plaire à; (to clothe—*habiller*) revêtir. That just —s me; *cela me convient, me va, m'arrange, fait mon affaire.* To — the action to the word; *mettre ses actions d'accord avec ses paroles, faire répondre ses actions à ses discours.* If that — you; *si cela vous convient, vous plaît.*

suit, *v.n.*, s'accorder; convenir.

suitable (siout-a-b'l), *adj.*, convenable. — to; *adapté à.*

suitableness, *n.*, convenance, *f.*; accord, *m.*; conformité, *f.*

suitably, *adv.*, convenablement; conformément.

suite (souîte), *n.*, suite, *f.*; cortège, *m.*; (series—*série*) suite; (of rooms—*de chambres*) enfilade, *f.* — of apartments; *appartement, m.*

suitor (siout'eur), *n.*, pétitionnaire, *m.*, *f.*; solliciteur, *m.*, solliciteuse, *f.*; suppliant, *m.*,

suppliante, *f.* ; (lover—*amoureux*) amant, soupirant ; (jur.) plaideur, *m.*, plaideuse, *f.*

suitress (siou-), *n.*, suppliante, *f.*

sulcate (seul-), or **sulcated** (-két'-), *adj.*, (bot.) sillonné.

sulk (seulke), *v.n.*, bouder ; faire la mine. To — with ; *bouder.*

sulkily, *adv.*, en boudant ; en faisant la mine.

sulkiness, *n.*, bouderie ; humeur boudeuse, *f.*

sulking, *n.*, bouderie, *f.*

sulky (seulk'-), *adj.*, boudeur ; qui fait la mine. To be — ; *être boudeur ; bouder.*

sulky (seulki), *n.*, (carriage—*voiture*) désobligeante, *f.*

sullen (seul'-), *adj.*, maussade de mauvaise humeur ; morose, bourru ; (malignant—*malfaisant*) malfaisant ; (intractable—*intraitable*) obstiné, revêche, intraitable ; (gloomy—*triste*) sombre, triste ; (sorrowful—*funeste*) affligeant, funeste.

sullenly, *adv.*, maussadement, de mauvaise humeur ; (malignantly—*avec malignité*) malignement ; (intractably—*avec rudesse*) d'une manière intraitable ; (gloomily—*tristement*) tristement.

sullenness (seul'-), *n.*, maussaderie ; mauvaise humeur ; morosité ; (malignity—*méchanceté*) malignité ; (intractableness—*caractère difficile*) humeur intraitable ; (gloominess—*humeur sombre*) humeur sombre, tristesse, *f.*

sully (seul'-), *v.a.*, souiller ; ternir.

sully, *v.n.*, se ternir.

sulphate (seul-), *n.*, sulfate, *m.*

sulphatic, *adj.*, sulfaté.

sulphite (seul-faïte), *n.*, sulfite, *m.*

sulphur (seul-feur), *n.*, soufre, *m.*

sulphurate, *adj.*, sulfuré.

sulphurate, *v.a.*, convertir en sulfure.

sulphuration (seul-feu-ré-), *n.*, sulfuration, *f.*

sulphureous, sulphurous, or **sulphury**, *adj.*, (chem.) sulfureux.

sulphureousness, *n.*, état sulfureux, *m.*

sulphureously, *adv.*, au moyen du soufre.

sulphuret, *n.*, sulfure, *m.*

sulphuretted, *adj.*, sulfuré.

sulphuric, *adj.*, sulfurique.

sulphurous, or **sulphury**, *adj.* V. **sulphureous**.

sulphur-wort (-weurte), *n.*, (bot.) peucédan ; fenouil de porc, *m.*

sultan (seul-, *ou* soul-), *n.*, sultan ; (of Egypt —*d'Égypte*) soudan, *m.*

sultana (seul-tâ-nâ, *ou* -té-), or **sultaness** (-ta'n'-), *n.*, sultane, *f.*

sultanry, *n.*, sultanie, *f.*

sultanship, *n.*, sultanat, *m.* His — ; *Sa Hautesse, f.*

sultriness (seul-), *n.*, chaleur étouffante, *f.*

sultry (seul-), *adj.*, d'une chaleur étouffante ; étouffant, suffocant. It is very — ; *il fait une chaleur étouffante.*

sum (seu'm), *n.*, somme, *f.* ; (compendium—*sommaire*) résumé ; (height—*comble*) comble, *m.* ; (arith.) règle, *f.* ; (in Scripture—*biblique*) dénombrement, *m.* To set any one a — ; (arith.) *poser une règle à quelqu'un.* — total ; *somme totale, f.* ; *total, m.*

sum, *v.a.*, additionner ; (to condense—*resserrer*) résumer. To — up ; (arith.) additionner, *faire l'addition de, le total de, la somme de, prendre la somme de, le total de ; résumer.* — ming up ; addition ; (jur.) résumé, *m.*

sumac, or **sumach** (sou-make), *n.*, sumac, *m*

sumless, *adj.*, incalculable.

summarily (seu'm'-), *adv.*, sommairement.

summary (seu'm'-), *n.*, sommaire, précis, résumé, *m.*

summary, *adj.*, sommaire.

summer (seu'm'-), *n.*, été, *m.*

summer, *v.a.*, tenir chaudement.

summer, *v.n.*, passer l'été.

summer, *n.*, (arch.) sommier, coussinet ; (carp.) poitrail, *m.*

summer-freckle (-frèk'k'l), *n.*, tache de rousseur, *f.*

summer-house (-haouce), *n.*, pavillon, *m.* : (residence) habitation d'été, *f.*

summer-sault, or **summer-set**, *n.* V. **somersault**.

summer-tree (-trî), *n.*, (carp.) lambourde. *f.*

summit (seu'm'-), *n.*, sommet, *m.* ; cime, *f.* ; (fig.) comble, faîte, *m.*

summit-level (-lèv'v'l), *n.*, point de partage, *m.*

summon (seu'm'meu'n), *v.a.*, convoquer ; sommer ; (jur.) citer, assigner ; (to call—*appeler*) appeler, demander, réclamer, inviter. To — away ; *appeler, réclamer.* To — up ; (to excite—*exciter*) exciter ; (to call up—*rassembler*) rassembler. To — a meeting ; *convoquer une assemblée.* To — the rioters to disperse ; *sommer les émeutiers de se disperser.*

summoner, *n.*, personne qui convoque, qui cite, qui somme, *f.* ; (jur.) huissier commis, *m.*

summons (seu'm'meu'n'ze), *n.*, sommation ; convocation ; invitation, *f.* ; appel, *m.* ; (jur.) assignation, citation, *f.*, mandat de comparution, *m.* To take out a — against ; *envoyer une assignation à.*

sump (seu'm'pe), *n.*, réservoir de marais salant ; (mines) puisard, *m.*

sumpter-horse (seu'm'teur-), *n.*, cheval de somme, *m.*

sumptuary (seu'm'p-tiou-), *adj.*, ' somptuaire.

sumptuous (seu'm't'iou-eusse), *adj.*, somptueux.

sumptuously, *adv.*, somptueusement.

sumptuousness, *n.*, somptuosité, *f.*

sun (seu'n), *n.*, soleil ; (fig.) éclat, *m.* The — is down, up ; *le soleil est couché, levé.* The — is high up ; *il fait grand soleil.* The — shines ; *il fait du soleil.* To worship the rising — ; *adorer le soleil levant.*

sun, *v.a.*, chauffer au soleil. To — one's self ; *se chauffer au soleil.*

sunbeam (-bî'm), *n.*, rayon de soleil, *m.*

sunbeat (-bite), *adj.*, exposé au soleil.

sun-bright (-braïte), *adj.*, qui a l'éclat du soleil, *m.*

sunburning (-beurn'-), *n.*, hâle, *m.*

sunburnt, *adj.*, brûlé par le soleil ; hâlé, basané.

sunclad, *adj.*, revêtu de l'éclat du soleil ; radieux.

sunday, *n.*, dimanche, *m.*

sunder, *v.a.*, séparer ; couper ; rompre.

sunder, *n.*, séparation en deux parties, *f.* In — ; *en deux.*

sundew (-diou), *n.*, (bot.) rosée-du-soleil, *f.*, rossolis, *m.*

sundial (-daï-al), *n.*, cadran solaire, *m.*

sun-dried (-draïde), *adj.*, séché au soleil.

sundries (-drize), *n.*, diverses choses, *f. pl.* ; faux frais ; (com.) divers, *m. pl.*

sundry, *adj.*, divers.

sunfish, *n.*, (ich.) molle, lune de mer, *f.*

sunflower (-fla-weur), *n.*, hélianthe ; soleil, tournesol, *m.*

sunless, *adj.*, sans soleil.

sunlight (-laïte), *n.*, lumière du soleil, *f.*

sunlike (-laïke), *adj.*, semblable au soleil.

sunny, *adj.*, de soleil ; (bright—*luisant*) brillant comme le soleil ; (exposed to the sun—*exposé au soleil*) exposé au soleil ; (coloured by the sun—*coloré par le soleil*) coloré du soleil ; (fig.) riant, heureux. — side of a hill ; *côté d'une colline exposé au soleil.* — side of nature ; *le beau côté de la nature.* It is — ; *il fait du soleil.*

33

sunproof (-proufe), *adj.*, impénétrable aux rayons du soleil.

sunrise (-raïze), *or* **sunrising** (-raïz'-), *n.*, lever du soleil ; soleil levant, *m.*

sun-rose, *n.*, (bot.) hélianthème, *m.* ; fleur du soleil, *f.*

sunset, *or* **sunsetting**, *n.*, coucher du soleil ; soleil couchant, *m.*

sunshine (-shaîne), *n.*, clarté du soleil, *f.* ; soleil ; (fig.) bonheur, éclat, *m.* In the —; *au soleil.*

sunshine, *or* **sunshiny**, *adj.*, de soleil, brillant comme le soleil.

sunstroke (-strôke), *n.*, coup de soleil, *m.* ; insolation, *f.*

sup (seupe); *n.*, petit coup, *m.* ; goutte légère, gorgée, *f.*

sup (seupe), *v.a.*, (to sip—*siroter*) boire à petits coups, humer, siroter ; (to give supper to —*donner un souper à*) donner à souper à. To up ; *boire.*

sup, *v.n.*, souper.

superable (siou-pèr'a-b'l), *adj.*, surmontable.

superableness, *n.*, qualité de ce qui est surmontable, possibilité de surmonter, *f.*

superably, *adv.*, de manière à être surmonté.

superabound (siou-pèr'a-baou'n'de), *v.n.*, surabonder.

superabundance (siou-pèr'a-beu'n'-), *n.*, surabondance, *f.*

superabundant, *adj.*, surabondant.

superabundantly, *adv.*, surabondamment.

superacidulated (siou-pèr'a-cid'iou-lét'-), *adj.*, trop acidulé.

superadd (siou-pèr'-), *v.a.*, surajouter.

superaddition, *n.*, surcroît, *m.* ; chose surajoutée, *f.*

superannuate (siou-pèr'a'n-niou-), *v.a.*, rendre suranné ; affaiblir par l'âge ; (to pension off—*mettre à la retraite*) mettre à la retraite.

superannuated, *adj.*, suranné ; (pensioned off —*retraité*) mis à la retraite, retraité, en retraite.

superannuation (siou-pèr'a'n'niou-é-), *n.*, incapacité produite par l'âge ; (pensioning off—*mise en retraite*) mise à la retraite ; pension de retraite, *f.*

superb (siou-peurbe), *adj.*, superbe.

superbly, *adv.*, superbement.

supercargo (siou-pèr'câr-gô), *n.*, subrécargue, *m.*

supercelestial (siou-pèr-ci-lès-), *adj.*, plus que céleste.

superciliary (siou-pèr'-), *adj.*, (anat.) sourcilier.

supercilious, *adj.*, hautain, arrogant, impérieux, fier.

superciliously, *adv.*, avec hauteur ; arrogamment, fièrement.

superciliousness, *n.*, hauteur, arrogance, *f.*

supereminence, *or* **supereminency** (siou-pèr'è'm'-), *n.*, prééminence, supériorité, *f.*

supereminent (siou-pèr'è'm'-), *adj.*, suréminent, prééminent, très supérieur.

supereminently, *adv.*, très éminemment.

supererogate (siou-pèr'èr'-), *v.n.*, faire plus que l'on n'est obligé.

supererogation (-'èr'o-ghé-), *n.*; surérogation, *f.*

supererogatory, *adj.*, surérogatoire.

superexalt (siou-pèr-ègz'ôlte), *v.a.*, élever très haut.

super-exaltation (-ègz'ôl-té-), *n.*, élévation au suprême degré, *f.*

super-excellence (siou-pèr'-), *n.*, excellence supérieure, *f.*

superexcellent, *adj.*, très excellent.

super-excrescence (siou-pèr'èks-krès'-), *n.*, excroissance, *f.*

super-fecundity (siou-pèr-fi-keu'n'-), *n.*, fécondité excessive, *f.*

superfetate (siou-pèr-fi-), *or* **superfete** (-fîte), *v.n.*, concevoir par superfétation, *f.*

superficial (siou-pèr-fish'al), *adj.*, de superficie ; superficiel ; (fig.) superficiel, léger.

superficiality, *n.*, superficialité, *f.*

superficially, *adv.*, superficiellement.

superficialness, *n.*, nature superficielle, *f.* ; manque de profondeur, *m.*

superficies (siou-pèr-fish'ize), *n.*, superficie, *f.*

superfine (siou-pèr-faïne), *adj.*, superfin, très fin.

superfluity (siou-pèr-flou-), *n.*, superfluité, *f.* ; superflu, *m.*

superfluous (siou-peur-flou-eussè), *adj.*, superflu.

superfluously, *adv.*, avec superfluité.

superfluousness, *n.*, superfluité, *f.* ; superflu, *m.*

superflux (siou-pèr-fleukse), *n.*, (ant.) superflu, *m.*

superhuman (siou-pèr-hiou-), *adj.*, surhumain.

superimpose (siou-pèr'i'm'pôze), *v.a.*, superposer.

superimposition, *n.*, superposition, *f.*

superincumbent (siou-pèr-i'n'keu'm-), *adj.*, placé au-dessus, superposé.

superinduce (siou-pèr'i'n'diouce), *v.a.*, ajouter, donner en plus.

superinduction (-i'n'deuk'-), *n.*, introduction ; action d'ajouter en plus, *f.*

superintellectual (siou-pèr'i'n'tèl-lôkt'iou-), *adj.*, au-dessus de l'intelligence.

superintend (siou-pèr'-), *v.a.*, surveiller.

superintendence, *or* **superintendency**, *n.*, surintendance ; surveillance ; direction, *f.*

superintendent, *n.*, chef ; surintendant, *m.*, surintendante, *f.* ; surveillant, *m.*, surveillante, *f.* ; (in reformed churches—*des églises réformées*) supérieur, *m.*

superior (siou-pi-), *adj.*, supérieur.

superior, *n.*, supérieur, *m.*, supérieure, *f.*

superiority, *n.*, supériorité, *f.*

superlative (siou-peur-), *adj.*, au suprême degré ; suprême ; le plus haut ; (gram.) superlatif.

superlative, *n.*, (gram.) superlatif, *m.*

superlatively, *adv.*, au superlatif, au suprême degré, superlativement.

superlativeness, *n.*, suprême degré, *m.*

superlunar, *or* **superlunary** (siou-pèr-liou-), *adj.*, au delà de la lune.

supermundane (siou-pèr-meu'n'-), *adj.*, au-dessus du monde.

supernal (siou-peur-), *adj.*, supérieur ; céleste.

supernatant (siou-pèr-né-), *adj.*, qui surnage.

supernatation (siou-pèr-né-té-), *n.*, action de surnager, *f.*

supernatural (siou-pèr-nat'iou-), *adj.*, surnaturel.

supernaturalism, *n.*, surnaturalité, *f.*

supernaturally, *adv.*, surnaturellement.

supernaturalness, *n.*, caractère surnaturel, *m.*

supernumerary (siou-pèr-niou-mi-), *adj.*, surnuméraire ; (of things—*des choses*) supplémentaire.

supernumerary, *n.*, surnuméraire ; (thea.) figurant, comparse, *m.*

superplus (siou-pèr-pleusse), *n.*, surplus, excédent, *m.*

superpose (siou-pèr-pôze), *v.a.*, superposer.

superposition, *n.*, superposition, *f.*

superroyal (siou-pèr-), *adj.*, (paper—*papier*) jésus.

supersalt (siou-pèr-sôlte), *n.*, (chem.) sursel, *m*

supersaturate (siou-pèr-sat'iou-), *v.a.*, sursaturer.

supersaturation (-sat-iou-ré-), *n.*, sursaturation, *f.*

superscribe (siou-pèr-scraïbe), *v.a.*, mettre une suscription, une adresse, une inscription à.

superscript, *or* **superscription** (sioupèr-), *n.*, action de mettre une suscription; adresse, suscription; (coin.) légende, *f.*

supersecular (siou-pèr-sèk'iou-), *adj.*, au-dessus des choses mondaines.

supersede (siou-pèr-cide), *v.a.*, (to set aside —*écarter*) faire abandonner; (to suspend—*arrêter*) suspendre; (to come in the room of—*remplacer*) se substituer à, remplacer; (to be put in the room of—*remplacer*) remplacer.

supersedeas (siou-pèr-ci-di-), *n.*, (jur.) sursis, *m.*

superstition (siou-pèr-), *n.*, superstition, *f.*

superstitionist, *n.*, homme superstitieux, femme superstitieuse.

superstitious (siou-pèr-stish'eusse), *adj.*, superstitieux.

superstitiously, *adv.*, superstitieusement.

superstitiousness, *n.*, caractère superstitieux, *m.*

superstratum (siou-pèr-stré-), *n.*, couche superposée, *f.*

superstruct (siou-pèr-streukte), *v.a.*, bâtir sur, surélever un bâtiment.

superstruction. *V.* **superstructure.**

superstructive, *adj.*, bâti sur une autre bâtisse.

superstructure (-streukt'ieur), *n.*, édifice, *m.*; construction; superstructure, *f.*

supersubstantial (siou-pèr-seub-sta'n-shal), *adj.*, plus que substantiel.

supersubtle (siou-pèr-seut't'l), *adj.*, trop rusé.

supersulphuretted (siou-pèr-seul-feur'-), *adj.*, sursulfuré.

supertare (siou-pèr-), *n.*, (com.) surtare, *f.*

superterrene (siou-pèr-tèr-rîne), *adj.*, au-dessus du sol.

superterrestrial (siou-pèr-tèr-rès'-), *adj.*, au-dessus des choses terrestres.

supertonic (siou-pèr-), *n.*, (mus.) surtonique, *f.*

supervene (siou-pèr-vîne), *v.n.*, survenir.

supervenient, *adj.*, qui survient; survenant.

supervention, *n.*, arrivée inopinée; (jur.) survenance, *f.*

supervise (siou-pèr-vaïze), *v.a.*, surveiller, veiller à.

supervision, *n.*, surveillance, inspection, *f.*

supervisor (-vaï-zeur), *n.*, inspecteur, surveillant; reviseur, *m.*

supination (siou-pi-né-), *n.*, supination, *f.*

supinator (-teur), *n.*, supinateur, *m.*

supine (siou-païne), *adj.*, couché sur le dos; renversé; incliné; (fig.) nonchalant, oisif, indolent.

supine (siou-païne), *n.*, supin, *m.*

supinely, *adv.*, couché sur le dos; (fig.) nonchalamment, avec négligence.

supineness, *n.*, supination; (fig.) indolence, nonchalance, *f.*

supper (sup-peur), *n.*, souper, soupé, *m.* Lord's —; Cène; sainte Cène, *f.*

supperless, *adj.*, sans souper.

supper-time (-taïme), *n.*, temps de souper, *m.*

supplant (seup'-), *v.a.*, supplanter; (to trip up the heels of—*donner un croc-en-jambe*) renverser par un croc-en-jambe.

supplantation (-pla'n't'é-), *n.*, supplantation, *f.*

supplanter, *n.*, supplantateur, *m.*

supple (seup'p'l), *adj.*, souple, flexible; (flattering—*flatteur*) flatteur, caressant.

supple (seup'p'l), *v.a.*, assouplir.

supple, *v.n.*, s'assouplir.

supplement (seup-pli-), *n.*, supplément, *m.*

supplemental, *or* **supplementary**, *adj.*, supplémentaire.

suppleness (seup'p'l'-), *n.*, souplesse, flexibilité, *f.*

suppletory (seup-pli-teuri), *adj.*, supplétif.

suppliant (seup-), *adj.*, suppliant.

suppliant (seup-), *n.*, suppliant, *m.*, suppliante, *f.*; (jur.) requérant, *m.*, requérante, *f.*

suppliantly, *adv.*, en suppliant.

supplicant (seup-), *n.*, suppliant, *m.*, suppliante, *f.*

supplicate (seup-), *v.a.*, supplier; implorer.

supplication (-pli-ké-), *n.*, supplication; supplique; prière, *f.*

supplicatory (-ké-teurl), *adj.*, suppliant, de supplication.

supplier (seup-plaï-), *n.*, personne qui fournit, *f.*; fournisseur, *m.*

supply (seup-pla'ye), *n.*, provision, fourniture, *f.*; approvisionnement, *m.* Supplies (of parliament—*parlement*); subsides, *m.pl.*, budget des dépenses, *m.sing.* To vote the supplies; voter les subsides, le budget, les dépenses. To cut off the supplies of; couper les vivres à. To take in a — of; faire une provision de. Bill of —; projet de loi de finance. Committee of —; comité de subsides et dépenses, *m.*

supply (seup-pla'ye), *v.a.*, (to furnish—*fournir*) fournir; offrir; (to serve instead of—*remplacer*) suppléer à, remplacer; (a vacancy—*vacance*) remplir; (wants—*besoins*) pourvoir à, subvenir à; (com.) être fournisseur de. To — with; fournir à; pourvoir de; approvisionner de; alimenter de. To — what is wanting; suppléer à ce qui manque. To — the poor with food; fournir de la nourriture, de quoi manger aux pauvres. I — him with goods; je lui fournis des marchandises. I — him; je suis son fournisseur.

supplying (seup-pla-yigne), *n.*, fourniture, *f.*; approvisionnement, *m.*

support (seup-porte), *n.*, action de supporter, de soutenir, *f.*; (prop—*soutien*) soutien, support, appui; (upholding—*appui*) maintien; (subsistence—*subsistance*) entretien, soutien, *m.*, nourriture, subsistance, *f.*; (fig.) soutien, appui, *m.*, protection, *f.* In — of; à l'appui de. For my —; pour mon entretien. With the favour of your —; à la faveur de votre appui, de votre protection.

support (seup-porte), *v.a.*, soutenir; supporter; porter; (to endure—*endurer*) supporter, endurer, souffrir; (to sustain, to uphold—*supporter*) soutenir; (to second—*seconder*) appuyer; (to keep up—*maintenir*) soutenir, entretenir; (to provide with the necessaries of life—*nourrir*) entretenir, nourrir, soutenir, pourvoir à. To — one's self; se soutenir; (to keep one's self—*se suffire*) s'entretenir; se suffire à soi-même.

supportable (-'a-b'l), *adj.*, supportable; (that can be maintained—*soutenable*) soutenable.

supportableness, *n.*, état supportable, état tolérable, *m.*

supporter, *n.*, personne qui supporte, qui soutient, *f.*; (prop—*soutien*) support, soutien; (her.) support; (adherent) adhérent, partisan; (sustainer—*appui*) appui, soutien; (defender—*protecteur*) défenseur, *m.*

supportless, *adj.*, sans soutien; sans appui.

supposable (seup-pôz'a-b'l), *adj.*, supposable.

supposal (seup-pôz'-), *n.*, supposition, *f.*

suppose (seup-pôze), v.a., supposer. That
being —d; cela supposé. —d to be; supposé être;
censé être.

supposer, n., personne qui suppose, f.

supposition (seup-po-zish'-),n.,supposition;
hypothèse, f.

suppositional, adj., hypothétique.

supposititious (seup-poz'i-tish-), adj., supposé; faux; contrefait.

supposititiously, adv., par une supposition, hypothétiquement.

supposititiousness, n., nature fausse, f.

suppositive (seup-poz'i-tive), adj., supposé.

suppositive, n., mot qui implique supposition, m.

suppositively, adv., par supposition, par
hypothèse.

suppository (seup-poz'i-teuri), n., suppositoire, m.

suppress (seup'près), v.a., (to overpower—
réprimer) réprimer; (to withhold from publicity
—taire) taire, supprimer; (to stifle—étouffer)
étouffer; (to stop—arrêter) arrêter.

suppression (seup-prèsh'-), n., suppression;
répression, f.

suppressive, adj., qui réprime, qui supprime, qui étouffe; répressif.

suppressor, n., personne qui réprime, qui
supprime, qui étouffe, f.

suppurate (seup-piou-), v.n., suppurer.

suppuration (-piou-ré-), n., suppuration, f.

suppurative, n., suppuratif, m.

suppurative, adj., suppuratif.

supputation (seup-piou-té-), n., supputation, f.

suppute (seup pioute), v.a., (ant.) supputer,
calculer.

supraciliary (siou-), adj., sourcilier.

supramundane (siou-pra-meu'n'-), adj.,
supramondain.

supranaturalism (siou-pra-nat'iou-ral-
iz'm), n., surnaturalité, f.

suprarenal (siou-pra-ri-), adj., surrénal.

supravulgar (siou-pra-veul-), adj., au-dessus du vulgaire.

supremacy (siou-prè'm'-), n., suprématie, f.

supreme (siou-pri'me), adj., suprême.

supremely, adv., au suprême degré; (of
authority—d'autorité) avec une autorité suprême.

sural (siou-), adj., sural.

surbase (seur-béss), n., (arch.) corniche de
lambris d'appui, f.

surbased (seur-bés'te), adj., surbaissé; à
corniche.

surbate (seur-), v.a., meurtrir les pieds en
marchant; (vet.) rendre solbatu; (to harass—
fatiguer) harasser.

surcharge (seur-tshârdje), n., surcharge, f.

surcharge, v.a., surcharger.

surcharger, n., personne qui surcharge, f.

surcingle (seur-cign'g'l), n., ceinture, f.;
surfaix, m.

surcingled (-cign'g'lde), adj., lié avec un
surfaix.

surcle (ceur-k'l), n., petit rejeton, m.

surd (seurde), adj., (math.) incommensurable, ⊙ sourd; (linguist.) fort.

surd (seurde), n., (math.) quantité incommensurable, quantité irrationnelle; (linguist.)
forte, consonne forte, f.

sure (shoure), adj., sûr, certain; (not liable
to failure—assuré) sûr, assuré; (permanent) permanent; (secure, steady—sûr) sûr; (stable)
stable. To be — of; être sûr de, certain de. His
income is —; son revenu est sûr, assuré. A —
man; un homme sûr. To have a — eye; avoir le
coup d'œil sûr. Be —, to be —; sûrement, assurément, certainement, à coup sûr. As — as a gun;
sûr comme père et mère. To be — to; ne pas

manquer de. Be — of; soyez sûr de. To be —
not to; se garder de; être sûr de ne pas. To
make — of; (to secure—s'emparer) s'assurer de,
s'emparer de; (to think one is sure to—se croire
sûr) se croire sûr de; (to rely on—compter sur)
compter sur.

sure (shoure), adv., sûrement, à coup sûr.

surely, adv., sûrement, assurément; certainement, à coup sûr; en sûreté.

sureness, n., certitude, f.

surety (shour-), n., (certainty—certitude) certitude; (safety—sécurité) sûreté, sécurité, f.;
(support)soutien,appui; (evidence)témoignage,
m., confirmation, f.; (jur.) garant, m., caution, f.

suretyship (shour-), n., cautionnement, m.

surf (seurfe), n., (nav.) ressac, m.

surface (seur-), n., surface, f.

surfeit (seur-fite), n., excès de table; rassasiement, m.

surfeit (seur-fite), v.a., rassasier; (fig.)
dégoûter, fatiguer.

surfeit, v.n., être rassasié.

surfeiter, n., glouton, m., gloutonne, f.

surfeiting, n., gloutonnerie, f.

surge (seurdje), n., lame, vague, houle, f.

surge (seurdje), v.n., s'enfler, s'élever.

surge, v.a., (nav.) larguer; choquer.

surgeon (seur-djeune), n., chirurgien; médecin, m. Assistant- —; (milit., nav.) aide-
chirurgien.

surgery (seur-dje-ri), n., chirurgie, f.;
(apartment—chambre) laboratoire, m.

surgical (seur-djic'-), adj., chirurgical; de
chirurgie.

surgy (seur-dji), adj., houleux.

surlily (seur-), adv., avec morosité; d'une
manière hargneuse.

surliness, n., morosité, f.; caractère hargneux, m.

surloin (seur-loï'n). V. **sirloin**.

surly (seur-), adj., morose; hargneux,
bourru.

surmise (seur-maïze), n., soupçon, m.; conjecture, f.

surmise (seur-maïze), v.a., se douter de;
s'imaginer, soupçonner.

surmiser, n., personne qui se doute de, qui
s'imagine, qui soupçonne, f.

surmising, n., soupçon, m.; conjecture, f.

surmount (seur-maou'n't), v.a., surmonter;
(to conquer—vaincre) surmonter, vaincre; (to
surpass—surpasser) excéder, surpasser.

surmountable (-'a-b'l), adj., surmontable.

surmounter, n., personne qui surmonte,
qui vainc, f.

surmullet (seur-meul'-), n., (ich.) surmulet, m.

surmulot (seur-miou-), n., (mam.) surmulot, m.

surname (seur-), n., nom de famille; (name
added to the original name—surnom) surnom,m.

surname (seur-), v.a., surnommer.

surpass (seur-pàss), v.a., surpasser, exceller
sur, l'emporter sur.

surpassable (-'a-b'l), adj., qui peut être
surpassé.

surpassing, adj., éminent, supérieur,
éclatant.

surpassingly, adv., éminemment, supérieurement, avec éclat.

surplice (seur-plice), n., surplis, m.

surpliced (seur-plis'te), adj., à surplis.

surplice-fees (-fize), n.pl., casuel, m.s.

surplus (seur-pleuss), n., surplus, excédent;
(jur.) actif net, m.

surplusage (-'édje), n., surplus, m.; (jur.)
superfluité, f.

surprisal (seur-praï-zal), n., surprise, f.

surprise (seur-praïze), n., surprise, f.;
étonnement, m.; (unexpected event—événement

inattenlu) surprise, *f.*, coup de main, *m.* To be taken by —; *être surpris; être pris par surprise; être pris au dépourvu.* To recover from one's —: *revenir de sa surprise.*

surprise (seur-praïze), *v.a.*, surprendre, prendre par surprise; prendre au dépourvu; étonner. Surprising to say; *chose surprenante.* To be —d at. with: *être surpris de.* I am —d that you should go there; *je m'étonne de ce que vous y alliez.*

surprising, *adj.*, surprenant, étonnant.

surprisingly, *adv.*, d'une manière surprenante; étonnamment.

surrebut (seur-ri-beute), *v.n.*, (jur.) faire une triplique, tripliquer.

surrebutter, *n.*, (jur.) triplique, *f.*

surrejoinder (seur-ri-djwaï'n deur), *v.n.*, (jur.) faire une duplique, dupliquer.

surrejoinder (seur-ri-djwaï'n'deur), *n.*.(jur.) duplique, *f.*

surrender (seur-rè'n'-),*n.*,(milit.) reddition; (of a claim—*d'un droit*) renonciation, *f.*, abandon, *m.*; (com.) cession; (of an estate for life or years—*d'un domaine à vie,* ou *temporairement*) reddition; (of a bankrupt—*d'un failli*) action de se mettre à la disposition de ses syndics, *f.*

surrender (seur-). *v.a.*, rendre, livrer; (to resign—*se démettre*) abandonner, renoncer à; (jur.) rendre. To — one's self; *se rendre; se livrer;* (jur.) *se constituer prisonnier ;* (of a bankrupt—*d'un failli*) *se mettre à la disposition de ses syndics.*

surrender, *v.n.*, se rendre; (of a bankrupt —*d'un failli*) se mettre à la disposition de ses syndics. To — to take one's trial; *se constituer prisonnier au jour du jugement.*

surrenderee, *n.*, (jur.) personne à qui une reddition est faite, *f.*

surrenderor, *n.*, (jur.) personne qui fait une reddition, *f.*

surreptitious (seur-rèp-tish'eusse), *adj.*, subreptice.

surreptitiously, *adv.*, subrepticement.

surrogate (seur-), *n.*, délégué, *m.*

surrogate (seur-), *v.a.*, (jur.) substituer; subroger.

surround (seur-raou'n'de), *v.a.*, environner, entourer; cerner; ceindre.

surrounding, *adj.*, environnant.

surtout (seur-toute), *n.*, surtout, *m.*; redingote, *f.*

survene (seur-vîne), *v.a.*, (ant.) survenir.

survey (seur-vè), *n.*, vue, *f.*; coup d'œil; (examination—*examen*) examen, *m.*; inspection, *f.*; (math.) levé, lever des plans: arpentage, *m.* Trigonometrical —; *triangulation, f.*

survey (seur-vè), *v.a.*, promener sa vue sur, contempler; (to examine—*inspecter*) examiner, inspecter; (math.) lever le plan de: arpenter.

surveying, *n.*, arpentage; levé, lever des plans, *m.*

surveying-wheel (-hwîl), *n.*, pédomètre, compte-pas, *m.*

surveyor (seur-vè-eur). *n.*, (of land—*de terres*) arpenteur, arpenteur-géomètre; (of buildings, &c.—*de bâtiments, &c.*) inspecteur; ♭commissaire voyer; (examiner—*examinateur*) examinateur: (overseer—*surveillant*) inspecteur, surveillant. *m.*

surveyorship, *n.*, inspection: place d'inspecteur, &c., *f.*

survival (seur-vaï-), *n.*, survie, *f.*

survivance (seur-vaï-), *n.*, survivance, *f.*

survive (seur-vaïve), *v.a.* and *n.*, survivre à; survivre.

surviving, *adj.*, survivant.

survivor (seur-vaïv'-), *n.*, survivant. *m.*, survivante, *f.*

survivorship, *n.*, survivance, *f.*

susceptibility (seus'cèp'-), *n.*, faculté de recevoir, d'admettre; susceptibilité; sensibilité, *f.*

susceptible -(seus'cèp-ti-b'l), *adj.*, susceptible; (fig.) sensible.

susceptibly, *adv.*, d'une manière susceptible.

susceptive (seus-cèp'-), *adj.*, capable de recevoir, susceptible.

suscipiency (seus-ci-pi-ò'n-), *n.*, réception, admission, *f.*

suscipient (seus-ci-pi-è'n'te), *adj.*, qui prend, qui admet, qui reçoit.

suscipient (seus-ci-pi-è'n'te), *n.*, personne qui admet, qui reçoit, *f.*

suscitate (seus'-), *v.a.*, (ant.) susciter.

suscitation (seus-ci-té-), *n.*, (ant.) ⊙suscitation, *f.*

suspect (seus-pèk'te), *v.a.*, soupçonner; (to doubt—*douter*) douter de, se défier de, soupçonner; (to imagine to be guilty—*suspecter*) soupçonner, suspecter; (to conjecture—*se douter de*) se douter de, soupçonner, conjecturer. We ought not to — those we employ; *il ne faut pas soupçonner ceux que l'on emploie.*

suspect, *v.n.*, soupçonner. I — he has . . . ; *je le soupçonne d'avoir . . . ; je soupçonne qu'il a . . .*

suspectedly (-pèkt'èd-), *adv.*, de manière à exciter les soupçons.

suspectedness (-pèkt'èd'-), *n.*, caractère suspect, *m.*

suspecter, *n.*, personne qui soupçonne, *f.*

suspectful (-foule), *adj.*, soupçonneux.

suspectless, *adj.*, sans soupçon; (not suspected—*non soupçonné*) qui n'est pas soupçonné.

suspend (seus-), *v.a.*, suspendre.

suspender, *n.*, personne qui suspend, *f.*; (bandage) suspensoire, suspensoir, *m.*

suspense (seus-), *n.*, suspens, *m.*; incertitude, indécision, *f.*; (jur.) suspension, *f.* In —; *en suspens.*

suspensibility, *n.*, propriété de pouvoir être suspendu, *f.*

suspensible (seus-pè'n'si-b'l), *adj.*, qui peut être suspendu.

suspension (seus-pè'n'sheune), *n.*, suspension, *f.*

suspension-bridge, *n.*, pont suspendu, *m.*

suspensor (seus'-), *n.*, suspensoir, suspensoire, *m.*

suspensory, *adj.*, suspenseur.

suspicion (seus-pish'eune), *n.*, soupçon, *m.*; suspicion, *f.*

suspicious (seus-pish'eusse), *adj.*, soupçonneux; (liable to suspicion—*suspect*) suspect. That looks — to me; *cela me paraît suspect.*

suspiciously, *adv.*, avec soupçon; d'une manière suspecte.

suspiciousness, *n.*, caractère soupçonneux, *m.*; défiance; (liability to be suspected—*nature suspecte*) nature suspecte, *f.*

suspiration (seus-paï-ré-), *n.*, soupir, *m.*

sustain (seus-té'n),*v.a.*, soutenir, supporter; (to feed—*nourrir*) entretenir, nourrir, soutenir; (to endure—*souffrir*) endurer, souffrir, soutenir; (to assist—*assister*) soutenir, appuyer; (to maintain) soutenir; (to hold—*tenir*) tenir, retenir; (mus.) soutenir; (a loss—*une perte*) éprouver, essuyer, faire.

sustainable(seus-té'n'a-b'l),*adj.*,soutenable.

sustainer, *n.*, personne qui supporte; chose qui supporte. *f.*; appui, soutien, *m.*

sustenance (seus-té'n'-), *n.*, alimentation, subsistance; (food—*nourriture*) subsistance, nourriture, *f.*; provisions, *f.pl.*, vivres, *m.pl.*

sustentation (seus-tè'n'té-), *n.*, soutien, *m.*; (maintenance—*subsistance*) subsistance, *f.*

susurration (siou-ceur-ré-), *n.*, (ant.) susurration, *f.* ; murmure, *m.*

sutile (siou-til), *adj.*, cousu ; fait au moyen de la couture.

sutler (seut'-), *n.*, vivandier, *m.*, vivandière, *f.* ; cantinier, *m.*, cantinière, *f.*

suttee (seut'ti), *n.*, suttee, suttie, *f.*

suttle (seut't'l), *adj.*, (of weight—*de poids*) net.

suturated (siout'iou-rét'-), *adj.*, réuni par une suture.

suture (siout'ieur), *n.*, suture, *f.*

suzerain (siou-zi-ré'n), *n.*, suzerain, *m.*, suzeraine, *f.*

suzerainty, *n.*, suzeraineté. *f.*

swab (swôbe), *n.*, (nav.) faubert, *m.*

swab (swôbe), *v.a.*, fauberter.

swabber, *n.*, fauberteur, *m.*

swaddle (swod'd'l), *v.a.*, emmailloter.

swaddle (swod'd'l), *n.*, maillot, *m.* ; langes, *m.pl.*

swaddling, *n.*, emmaillotement, *m.*

swaddling-clothes (-clôze), *n.*, maillot, *m.sing.* ; langes, *m.pl.*

swag (swag), *v.n.*, s'affaisser.

swag-bellied (-bèl'lide), *adj.*, à gros ventre ; pansu.

swagger (swag-gheur), *v.n.*, faire le rodomont, faire le fanfaron, faire le crâne ; (to boast —*se vanter*) se vanter, gasconner. To — along ; marcher d'un air fanfaron.

swaggerer, *n.*, rodomont, fanfaron, bravache, crâne ; (boaster—*vantard*) vanteur, vantard, gascon, *m.*

swaggering, *n.*, rodomontade, fanfaronnade, crânerie ; (boasting—*vanterie*) vanterie, gasconnade, *f.*

swaggering, *adj.*, fanfaron, de fanfaron, de crâne ; (boasting—*de gascon*) vantard, de gascon.

swaggy (swag-ghi), *adj.*, pendant.

swain (swé'n), *n.*, berger ; pastoureau ; amant, *m.*

swallow (swol'lô), *n.*, gosier, *m.* ; arrière-bouche ; (what is swallowed at once—*quantité avalée en une fois*) gorgée ; (voracity—*voracité*) voracité ; (orni.) hirondelle, *f.* What a — ! (jest.) *quelle avaloire !*

swallow (swol'lô), *v.a.*, avaler ; (to ingulf—*engloutir*) engloutir ; (to absorb, to occupy—*occuper*) absorber ; (to consume—*consumer*) consumer ; (to believe—*croire*) avaler, gober. To — down ; *avaler* ; (fig.) *avaler, gober.* To — up ; *avaler* ; (to inguli—*engloutir*) engloutir ; (to absorb—*consumer*) absorber, consumer. To be —ed 'up by the waves ; *être englouti par les vagues.*

swallow-fish, *n.*, (ich.) trigle ; hirondelle de 'mer, *f.*

swallowing, *n.*, action d'avaler, de consumer ; absorption, *f.* ; engloutissement, *m.*

swallow's-tail (swol'lô'z'téle), *n.*, (carp.) queue d'aronde, *f.*

swallow-stone (-stône), *n* , pierre d'hirondelle, *f.*

swallow-wort (-weurte), *n.*, (bot.) asclépiade, *f.*, asclépias, dompte-venin, *m.*

swamp, *n.*, marais, marécage, *m.*

swamp, *v.a.*, enfoncer dans ; (a boat—*un bateau*) faire chavirer ; (fig.) plonger dans de graves difficultés. To be —ed ; (of boats—*des bateaux*) chavirer.

swampy, *adj.*, marécageux.

swan, *n.*, cygne, *m.*

swan's-down (swa'n'z'daou'n), *n.*, duvet de cygne ; (cloth—*drap*) drap de vigogne, *m.*

swan-skin (-ski'n), *n.*, molleton, *m.*

sward (sworde), *n.*, gazon, *m.* ; pelouse, *f.*

sward (sworde), *v.a.*, produire du gazon ; (to cover with sward—*gazonner*) couvrir de gazon, gazonner.

swardy, *adj.*, couvert de gazon ; gazonneux.

swarm (swôrme), *n.*, essaim, *m.* — of ants ; fourmilière, *f.*

swarm (swôrme), *v.n.*, essaimer ; (fig.) s'attrouper, accourir en foule. To — with ; fourmiller de.

swarth (swôrth), *adj.* V. **swarthy**.

swarth (swôrth), *n.*, coup de faux. *m.*

swarthily (swôrth'-), *adv.*, d'un teint basané, hâlé.

swarthiness, *or* **swarthness**, (swôrth'-), *n.*, teint basané, *m.*

swarthish (swôrth'-), *adj.*, un peu basané, un peu hâlé.

swarthy (swôrthi), *adj.*, basané, hâlé.

swarthy (swôrthi), *v.a.*, rendre basané ; hâler.

swash (swôsh), *n.*, grand rejaillissement d'eau, *m.* ; (ant.) (blustering—*rodomontade*) fanfaronnade, *f.*

swath (swôth), *n.*, (agri.) andain, *m.*

swathe (swéthe), *v.a.*, emmailloter.

swathe (swéthe), *n.*, maillot, lange, *m.*

sway, *n.*, (swing of a weapon—*d'une arme*) course ; (any thing moving with bulk and power —*masse*) masse ; (preponderation—*supériorité*) prépondérance, *f.* ; (power—*puissance*) pouvoir, empire, sceptre, *m.*, puissance ; (influence) influence, *f.*

sway, *v.a.*, manier, porter ; (to bias—*influencer*) influencer, influer sur ; (to rule—*régir*) gouverner, régir. To — from ; *détourner de.*

sway, *v.n.*, pencher, incliner ; (to govern—*régir*) gouverner. To — with ; *influer sur ; avoir de l'influence sur.* To — up ; *guinder ; hisser.*

swaying (swé-igne), *n.*, (vét.) effort, *m.*

swear (swére), *v.a.* (*preterit*, Swore ; *past part.*, Sworn), (witnesses, a jury—*des témoins, un jury*) faire prêter serment à, déférer le serment à ; (an oath—*serment*) prêter. To — in ; assermenter. To — treason against ; *déclarer coupable de trahison sous la foi du serment.*

swear (swére), *v.n.*, jurer ; prêter serment ; faire serment ; (to blaspheme—*blasphémer*) jurer. To — to ; *jurer de.* To — like a trooper ; *jurer comme un charretier.*

swearer, *n.*, personne qui prête serment, *f.* ; (blasphemer—*blasphémateur*) jureur, *m.* What a — she is ! *comme elle jure !*

swearing, *n.*, action de jurer, *f.* ; serments ; (blaspheming—*blasphèmes*) jurements, *m.pl.* — in ; *action d'assermenter, f.*

sweat (swète), *n.*, sueur ; (fig.) sueur, *f.*, sueurs, *f.pl.* By the — of one's brow ; *à la sueur de son front.*

sweat (swète), *v.n.*, suer ; (tech.) faire ressuer. To — out ; *faire passer par la sueur.*

sweater, *n.*, personne qui fait suer, *f.*

sweatily, *adv.*, en suant, avec sueur.

sweatiness, *n.*, sueur, *f.* ; état de sueur, *m.*

sweating, *n.*, sueur, action de suer, *f.*

sweating-house (-haouce), *n.*, étuve, *f.*

sweating-iron (-aïeur'n), *n.*, couteau de chaleur, *m.*

sweating-room (-roume), *n.*, (med.) étuve, *f.* ; (agri.) séchoir, *m.*

sweating-sickness, *n.*, fièvre miliaire, *f.*

sweaty (swèt'-), *adj.*, en sueur ; (consisting of sweat—*de sueur*) de sueur ; (laborious—*laborieux*) qui fait suer, pénible.

swede (swîde), *n.*, Suédois, *m.*, Suédoise, *f.*

swedish (swîd'-), *adj.*, suédois.

sweep (swîpe), *v.a.* (*preterit* and *past part.*, Swept), balayer ; (a chimney—*une cheminée*) ramoner ; (the lyre—*la lyre*) frapper ; (a river—*une rivière*) draguer. To — away, off ; *balayer ;* enlever. To — up ; *balayer.* To — from ; *balayer une chambre.* Her dress —s the ground ; *sa robe balaie la terre.*

sweep, *v.n.*, passer rapidement ; (to pass with pomp—*passer pompeusement*) passer avec

pompe, marcher pompeusement. To — along, over; *passer rapidement sur*; *brûler*.

sweep (swipe), *n.*, balayage; (stroke with a broom—*coup de balai*) coup de balai; (metal.) fourneau de coupelle; (oar—*rame*) aviron de galère; (chimney-sweep—*ramoneur*) ramoneur, *m.*; (the compass of any turning body—*courbe décrite par un corps en tournant*) courbe décrite, *f.*; (the compass of any thing flowing—*étendue. course d'un fluide qui s'écoule*) cours, *m.*, course, *f.*; (the compass of a stroke—*étendue linéaire, course*) coup, *m.*, ligne; (tech.) cambrure, courbe, *f.*

sweeper, *n.*, balayeur, *m.*, balayeuse, *f.*; (of chimneys—*de cheminées*) ramoneur, *m.*

sweeping, *n.*, balayage; (of chimneys—*de cheminées*) ramonage, *m.* —s; *balayures ordures, f.pl.*

sweep-net, *n.*, épervier, *m.*

sweepstake, or **sweepstakes**, *n.*, joueur qui gagne une poule, *m.*

sweepstakes, *n.pl.*, (horse-racing—*course de chevaux*) poule, *f.*; joueur qui gagne la poule, *m.*; (gaming—*jeu*) poule, *f.*

sweepy (swip-), *adj.*, qui passe rapidement; (wavy—*ondulé*) onduleux, ondoyant, ondulé.

sweet (swite), *n.*, (sweet substance—*sucrerie*) chose douce, chose sucrée, sucrerie, *f.*; (perfume—*odeur*) parfum; (word of endearment—*terme d'affection*) chéri, *m.*, chérie, *f.*, doux ami, *m.*, douce amie; (something pleasing—*chose agréable*) douceur, *f.*

sweet (swite), *adj.*, (to the taste—*au goût*) doux, sucré; (fragrant—*odoriférant*) doux, odoriférant; (melodious—*mélodieux*) doux, suave, mélodieux; (to the eye—*à l'œil*) qui flatte les yeux; (beautiful—*beau*) beau; (fresh—*frais*) doux, frais; (mild—*doux*) doux; (not stale—*non gâté*) bon, frais; (jest.) joli. You're a — youth! (jest.) *vous êtes joli garçon!*

sweet-bread (-brède), *n.*, ris de veau, *m.*

sweet-brier (-braï-), *n.*, églantier odorant, *m.*

sweeten (swit't'n), *v.a.*, sucrer; (to make mild, to soften—*adoucir*) adoucir; (to make pleasing—*rendre agréable*) adoucir, rendre agréable; (a room, the air—*une chambre, l'air*) purifier, désinfecter; (the soil—*le sol*) fertiliser; (water, butter, &c.—*eau, beurre, &c.*) rafraîchir; (medicine—*une médecine*) édulcorer; (paint.) adoucir.

sweetener, *n.*, chose qui sucre; (fig.) chose qui adoucit; personne qui adoucit, *f.*

sweetening, *n.*, action de sucrer, de rendre doux, de rafraîchir; purification, désinfection; (of the soil—*du sol*) fertilisation; ((f medicine—*d'une médecine*) édulcoration, *f.*; (of pain—*d'une douleur*) adoucissement, *m.*

sweetheart (-hârte), *n.*, amant, *m.*, amante, *f.*; bon ami, *m.*, bonne amie, *f.*

sweeting, *n.*, pomme douce, *f.*

sweetish, *adj.*, douceâtre.

sweetishness, *n.*, goût douceâtre, *m.*

sweetly, *adv.*, doucement; agréablement, mélodieusement; avec douceur.

sweet-marjoram (-mâr-djo-), *n.*, marjolaine commune, *f.*

sweetmeat (-mîte), *n.*, sucrerie, *f.*; bonbon, *m.*; confiture, *f.*

sweetness, *n.*, douceur; saveur sucrée, *f.*; (melody—*mélodie*) douceur, mélodie; (fragrance—*parfum*) douceur, *f.*, parfum, *m.*; (mildness—*douceur*) douceur; (freshness—*fraîcheur*) fraîcheur; (of eatables—*de comestibles*) bonté; (fig.) douceur, *f.*, charme. *m.*

sweet-pea (-pi), *n.*, pois de senteur, *m.*

sweet-scented, or **sweet-smelling**, *adj.*, odoriférant, odorant.

sweet-tempered (-tè'm'peurde), *adj.*, d'un caractère doux.

sweet-toned (-tô'n'de), *adj.*, d'un son doux, au son doux.

sweet-weed (-wide), *n.*, (bot.) capraire théiforme, *f.*

sweet-william, *n.*, œillet barbu, œillet de poète, bouquet parfait, *m.*

swell (swèl), *v.n.* (preterit, Swelled; past part., Swelled, Swollen), enfler, s'enfler; se gonfler; (to increase by any addition—*s'accroître*) grossir; (to bulge out—*bomber*) faire le ventre, bomber; (to become larger—*croître*) grandir; (to strut—*se carrer*) se carrer, s'enfler; (of sound—*du son*) augmenter. To — along; *se carrer en marchant*. To — into; s'élever en; grandir en; se convertir en, *devenir*; (h.s.) dégénérer en. To — to; s'élever à. To — out; bomber; faire le ventre. To — with pride; bouffir d'orgueil. To — with rage; bouffer, bouffir de colère.

swell, *v.a.*, enfler, gonfler; (to aggravate—*aggraver*) aggraver; (to raise to arrogance—*rendre orgueilleux*) bouffir, faire bouffer; (to enlarge—*agrandir*) grandir, grossir, élever; (mus.) enfler. To be —ed with pride; *être bouffi d'orgueil*.

swell (swèl), *n.*, bombement, *m.*; (elevation) élévation, montée; (of sound—*du son*) augmentation, *f.*; (of the sea—*de la mer*) vagues, *f.pl*; houle; (mus.) pédale d'expression, *f.*; (of an organ—*d'orgue*) récit, *m.*; (pers.) fashionable de mauvais goût, fashionable, freluquet. *m.* What a — she is! *quelle toilette elle a!* To be dressed a —; *être pimpant*.

swelling, *n.*, (tumour—*tumeur*) enflure; (morbid enlargement—*gonflement morbide*) bouffissure, *f.*; (protuberance) gonflement, bombement, *m.*, bosse, grosseur, *f.*; (of anger, grief, pride—*de colère, chagrin, orgueil*) mouvement, transport, *m.*

swelling, *adj.*, qui enfle; qui s'enfle, qui se gonfle; qui bouffe; qui grossit; (turgid—*ampoulé*) enflé, ampoulé; (growing larger—*croissant*) grandissant; (of sound—*du son*) augmentant.

swell-mob, *n.*, corps des filous de Londres, *m.*

swelter (swèlt-), *v.n.*, étouffer de chaleur, être accablé de chaleur.

sweltry (swèl-), *adj.*, étouffant.

swerve (sweurve), *v.n.*, errer; (to incline—*incliner*) incliner; (to climb—*grimper*) grimper. To — from; *s'écarter de, s'éloigner de, dévier de.*

swerving (sweurv-), *n.*, action d'errer, de s'écarter, de s'éloigner; déviation, *f.*

swift, *adj.*, rapide; (prompt) prompt, vif; (in running—*à la course*) vite, vite à la course; léger, léger à la course.

swift, *n.*, bobine, *f.*; (orni.) martinet; (erpetolog.) lézard gris, *m.*

swifter, *n.*, (nav.) ceinture, *f.*; (of the capstan—*du cabestan*) garde-corps, *m.*

swifter, *v.a.*, (nav.) mettre une ceinture à; (the capstan—*le cabestan*) placer le garde-corps.

swiftly, *adv.*, vite, vitement, rapidement, promptement, vivement, agilement.

swiftness, *n.*, rapidité; promptitude, vitesse, *f.*

swift-sailing (-sél'-), *adj.*, fin voilier, de marche rapide.

swift-winged (-wign'de), *adj.*, à l'aile rapide.

swig, *v.a.* and *n.*, boire à longs traits. To — at; *humer*.

swig, *n.*, long trait en buvant; (of liquor—*de boisson*) grand coup, coup sur coup, *m.*

swill, *n.*, lavure de vaisselle, lavure, *f.*; (of liquor—*de boisson*) grand coup, coup sur coup, *m.*

swill, *v.a.*, boire avidement; (to inebriate—*enivrer*) enivrer, griser.

swill, *v.n.*, s'enivrer; pomper.

swiller, *n.*, ivrogne, *m.*

swillings (swill'ign'ze), *n.pl.*, lavure de vaisselle, *f. sing.*

swill-tub (teube), *n.*, baquet à cochon, *m.*

swim, *v.n.* (*preterit*, Swam; *past*, *part.*, Swum),nager; (to float—*flotter*) flotter,nager, surnager; (to glide along—*glisser*) glisser, filer; (to be dizzy—*avoir le vertige*) avoir des vertiges; (of the head—*de la tête*) tourner; (to be overflowed —*être inondé*) être inondé. To — across; *traverser à la nage*. To — out of one's depth; *perdre pied*. To — over; *passer à la nage*. To — with; *suivre; se laisser aller à*.

swim, *v.n.*, passer à la nage; (wheat—*du blé*) faire flotter.

swim, *n.*, (ich.) vessie natatoire, *f.*

swimmer, *n.*, nageur, *m.*, nageuse,*f.*; (orni.) palmipède, *m.*

swimming, *n.*, natation, *f.*; (dizziness— *étourdissement*) vertige, *m.*

swimmingly, *adv.*, aisément ; d'emblée.

swimming-school (-skoule), *n.*, école de natation,*f.*

swimming-tub (-teube), *n.*, baquet, *m.*

swindle (swi'n'd'l), *v.a.*, escroquer. To — out of ; *escroquer à*.

swindle (swi'n'd'l), *n.*, escroquerie,*f.*

swindler,*n.*, escroc; chevalier d'industrie,*m.*

swindling, *n.*, escroquerie,*f.*

swine (swaï'n), *n. sing.* and *pl.*, cochon, pourceau, *m.*

swine-herd (-heurde), *n.*, porcher, *m.*

swine-pipe (-païpe), *n.*, (orni.) mauvis, *m.*

swine-pox, *n.*, varicelle ; varicelle verruqueuse,*f.*

swine-stone (-stône), *n.*, pierre puante ; pierre sonnante,*f.*

swine-sty (-sta'ye), *n.*, toit à cochons, *m.*

swing (swigne), *n.*, (oscillation) oscillation, vibration,*f.* ; (motion from one side to the other —*mouvement oscillatoire*) mouvement d'un côté à l'autre, balancement, *m.*; (apparatus to swing in—*pour se balancer*) balançoire; (free course— *libre essor*) libre carrière, *f.*, libre essor, élan, *m.* ; (sweep of a moving body—*course d'un corps en mouvement*) courbe décrite, ligne parcourue,*f.*

swing (swigne), *v.a.*, faire vibrer ; balancer; (to wave—*agiter*) agiter ; (to brandish—*brandir*) brandir, brandiller.

swing, *v.n.*, vibrer ; se balancer ; (of a ship— *d'un vaisseau*) éviter ; (to be hanging—*être pendant*) pendiller.

swing-bar, *n. V.* **swing-tree**.

swing-bridge, *n.*, pont tournant, *m.*

swinge (swi'n'dje), *v.a.*, rosser, étriller, battre.

swinger (swign'-), *n.*, personne qui se balance,*f.* ; frondeur, *m.*

swing-gate, *n.*, porte à bascule,*f.*

swinging (swign'-), *n.*, vibration,*f.* ; balancement, *m.*

swinging (swign'-),*adj.*, énorme.

swingingly (swign'-), *adv.*, énormément.

swingle (swign'g'l),*v.a.*, battre.

swing-tree (-tri), *n.*, volée,*f.*

swinish (swaï'n'-), *adj.*, de cochon ; grossier, sale.

swinishly (swaï'n'-), *adv.*, salement, comme un cochon.

swipe (swaïpe), *n.*, coup fort, *m.*

swipes (swaïp'se), *n.pl.*, mauvaise petite b'ère, *f.sing.*

swiss, *n.*, Suisse, *m.*, Suissesse, *f.*

swiss, *adj.*, suisse.

switch (switshe), *n.*, badine, houssine, gaule; (railways) aiguille,*f.*, rail mobile, *m.*

switch, *v.a.*, donner des coups de badine à, des coups de houssine à, houssiner.

switchman, *n.*, (railways) aiguilleur, *m.*

switch-tail (-téle), *n.*, queue à tous crins,*f.*

swivel, *n.*, tourniquet; porte-mousqueton ; (artil.) pierrier, *m.*

swoon (swoune), *v.n.*, s'évanouir, se trouver mal; tomber en défaillance.

swoon (swoune), *n.*, évanouissement, *m.* ; syncope, défaillance,*f.*

swooning, *n.*, évanouissement, *m.* ; défaillance, *f.*

swoop (swoupe), *v.a.*, fondre sur; (to seize —*s'emparer*) s'emparer de, enlever.

swoop (swoupe), *n.*, (of birds of prey—*des oiseaux de proie*) action de fondre sur la proie, *f.*; coup, *m.* At one fell —; *d'un seul coup*.

swop, *v.a.*, troquer, changer.

sword (sôrde), *n.*, épée, *f.* ; sabre ; (fig.) fer, glaive, *m.* — in hand; *l'épée à la main.* To put to the —; *passer au fil de l'épée.* To put to fire and —; *mettre à feu et à sang.* — of justice ; *glaive de la justice.*

sword-bearer (-bèr'-), *n.*, porte-épée, *m.*

sword-belt, *n.*, ceinturon, porte-épée, *m.* ¡

sword-blade, *n.*, lame d'épée. *f.*

sword-cane, *n. V.* **sword-stick**.

sword-cutler (-keut'-), *n.*, fourbisseur, *m.*

sword-fight (-faïte), *n.*, combat à l'épée, *m.*

sword-fish, *n.*, espadon, *m.*

sword-grass (-grâce),*n.*,(bot.) morgeline,*f.*

sword-hilt, *n.*, poignée d'épée,*f.*

sword-knot (-note), *n.*, nœud d'épée, *m.*

sword-player (-plè-eur),*n.*,tireur d'épée, *m.*

sword-shaped (-shép'te), *adj.*, ensiforme, gladié.

swordsman (sôrd'z'-), *n.*, tireur d'armes, *m.* ; lame, *f.*

sword-stick, *n.*, canne à épée,*f.*

sworn (swôrne), *adj.*, juré ; assermenté; (of enemies—*d'ennemis*) juré ; (of friends—*d'amis*) intime.

sybarite (-raïte), *n.*, sybarite, *m.*

sybaritic, *or* **sybaritical** (-rit'-), *adj.*, sybaritique.

sycamore (-môre), *n.*, sycomore, érable blanc, *m.*

sycophancy, *or* **sycophantcy** (ant.), *n.*, adulation, flagornerie, *f.*

sycophant (-fa'n'te), *n.*, flagorneur, *m.*, flagorneuse, *f.*; adulateur, *m.*, adulatrice,*f.*

sycophant, *v.n.*, flagorner.

sycophantic, *adj.*, de flagorneur, de parasite.

sycophantize (-'aïze),*v.n.*(ant.). *V.* **sycophant**, *v.*

sycophantry, *n.*, adulation, flagornerie,*f.*

syenite (saï-è'n'aïte), *n.*, (min.) syénite, *f.*

syllabic, *or* **syllabical**, *adj.*, syllabique.

syllabically, *adv.*, syllabiquement, par syllabes.

syllabication (-bi-ké-), *n.*, syllabation, syllabisation,*f.*

syllable (sil'la-b'l), *n.*, syllabe,*f.*

syllabub (-beube), *n.*, caillé de lait au vin, au cidre. *m.*

syllabus, *n.*, extrait, résumé; (c.rel.) syllabus, *m.*

syllepsis, *n.*, syllepse, *f.*

syllogism (-lo-djiz'm), *n.*, syllogisme, *m.*

syllogistic, *or* **syllogistical** (-lo-djist'-), *adj.*, syllogistique.

syllogistically (-lo-djist'-), *adv.*, par un syllogisme.

syllogization (-lo-djazé-), *n.*, raisonnement par syllogismes, *m.*

syllogize (-lo-djaïze), *v.n.*, raisonner par syllogismes.

syllogizer (-lo-djaïz'-). *n.*, personne qui raisonne par syllogismes,*f.*

sylph, *n.*, sylphe, *m.* ; sylphide, *f.*

sylphid, *n.*, sylphide, *f.*

sylvan, *adj.*, champêtre, des bois, des forêts.

sylvan,*n.*, (myth.) sylvain; (rustic—*paysan*) paysan, *m.*

sylvanite (-va'n'aïte), *n.*, (min.) tellure, *m.*

symbol, *n.,* symbole ; signe symbolique ; (alg.) symbole, signe, *m.*

symbolic, or **symbolical,** *adj.,* symbolique.

symbolically, *adv.,* d'une manière symbolique, par symbole.

symbolization (-bol'aïzé-), *n.,* symbolisation, *f.*

symbolize ('-aïze), *v.n.,* symboliser, avoir du rapport.

symbolize, *v.a.,* faire accorder.

symbology ('-o'dji), *n.,* art d'exprimer par des symboles, *m.*

symmetral (-mèt'-), *adj.,* mesurable.

symmetrical (-mèt'-), *adj.,* symétrique.

symmetrically, *adv.,* symétriquement.

symmetrist (-mèt'-), *n.,* grand observateur de la symétrie, *m.*

symmetrize (-mèt'raïze), *v.a.,* faire symétriser, rendre symétrique.

symmetry (-mè-), *n.,* symétrie, *f.*

sympathetic, or **sympathetical** (-thèt'-), *adj.,* sympathique.

sympathetically (-thèt'-), *adv.,* sympathiquement ; par sympathie.

sympathize (-thaïze), *v. n.,* sympathiser, compatir.

sympathy (-thi), *n.,* sympathie, *f.*

symphonious (-phô-), or **symphonic,** *adj.,* harmonieux.

symphonist, *n.,* symphoniste, *m.*

symphony, *n.,* (harmony—*harmonie*) harmonie ; (instrument, composition) symphonie, *f.*

symphysis (-fi-cice), *n.,* (anat.) symphyse ; (surg.) fermeture d'une ouverture naturelle ; première indication de cicatrisation d'une blessure, sans suppuration, *f.*

symposium (-pô-zi-), *n.,* banquet, *m.*

symptom (sī'm-to'm), *n.,* symptôme, indice, *m.*

symptomatic, or **symptomatical** (sī'm-to'm'-), *adj.,* symptomatique.

symptomatically, *adv.,* par des symptômes.

symptomatology (-o'dji), *n.,* symptomatologie, *f.*

syneresis (-'ir'i-cice), *n.,* synérèse ; crase, *f.*

synagogical (-go-djic'-), *adj.,* de la synagogue.

synagogue (-goghe), *n.,* synagogue, *f.*

synalepha (-li-), *n.,* synalèphe, *f.*

synarthrosis (-thrô-cice), *n.,* (anat.) synarthrose, *f.*

synchondrosis (-ko'n'drô-cice), *n.,* (anat.) synchondrose, *f.*

synchronal (sign'kro), *n.,* événement contemporain, *m.*

synchronal, or **synchronical** (sign-kro-), *adj.,* synchronique, contemporain.

synchronically (sign'kro-), *adv.,* d'une manière synchronique.

synchronism (sign'kro-niz'm), *n.,* synchronisme, *m.*

synchronize (sign'kro-naïze), *v.n.,* être contemporain.

synchronous (-kro-), *adj.,* synchrone, synchronique.

synchysis (-ki-cice), *n.,* synchyse, *f.*

syncopate, *v.a.,* (gram.) élider ; (mus.) syncoper.

syncopation (-pé-), *n.,* élision ; (mus.) syncope, *f.* ; contre-temps, *m.*

syncope (sign'ko-pi), *n.,* syncope, *f.*

syncretism (-cri-tiz'm), *n.,* syncrétisme, *m.*

syndic, *n.,* syndic, *m.*

syndicate, or **syndicship,** *n.,* syndicat, *m.*

syndicate, *v.a.,* contrôler, censurer.

synecdoche (-nèk'do-ki), *n.,* synecdoche, synecdoque, *f.*

synneurosis (si'n'niou-rô-ciee), *n.,* synévrose, *f.*

synocha (-ka), or **synochus** (-keusse), *n.,* synoque, *f.*

synod, *n.,* synode, *m.* ; (astron.) conjonction, *f.*

synodal, *adj.,* synodal.

synodic, or **synodical,** *adj.,* synodique.

synodically, *adv.,* synodalement.

synonyme, *n.,* synonyme, *m.*

synonymize (-maïze), *v.a.,* exprimer par des synonymes.

synonymous, *adj.,* synonyme.

synonymously, *adv.,* comme synonyme.

synonymy, *n.,* synonymie, *f.*

synopsis, *n.* (*synopses*), synopsis, *m.*

synoptical, *adj.,* synoptique.

synoptically, *adv.,* d'une manière synoptique.

synovia (-nô-), *n.,* synovie, *f.*

synovial (-nô-), *adj.,* synovial.

syntactical, *adj.,* syntaxique, conforme aux règles de la syntaxe.

syntax, *n.,* syntaxe, *f.*

synthesis (-thi-cice), *n.* (*syntheses*), synthèse, *f.*

synthetic, or **synthetical** (-thèt'-), *adj.,* synthétique.

synthetically (-thèt'-), *adv.,* synthétiquement.

syphilis, *n.,* syphilis, *f.*

syphilitic, *adj.,* syphilitique. ?

syriac, *n.,* syriaque, *m.*

syriac, *adj.,* syriaque.

syrian, *adj.,* syrien.

syrian, *n.,* Syrien, *m.,* Syrienne, *f.*

syrianism (-'iz'm), *n.,* idiotisme syriaque, *m.*

syringa, *n.,* (bot.) seringa, *m.*

syringe (sir'i'n'dje), *n.,* seringue, *f.*

syringe (sir'i'n'dje), *v.a.,* seringuer ; injecter.

syringotomy, *n.,* syringotomie, *f.*

syrup (sir'eupe), *n.*   *V.* **sirup.**

system, *n.,* système, *m.*

systematic, or **systematical,** *adj.,* systématique.

systematically, *adv.,* systématiquement.

systematist, or **systematizer** (-taïz'-), *n.,* auteur de système, *m.*

systematization (-taïzé-), *n.,* réduction en système, *f.*

systematize (-taïze), *v.a.,* systématiser, réduire en système.

systole, *n.,* systole, *f.*

systyle (-'taïle), *n.,* systyle, *m.*

syzygy (-i-dji), *n.,* syzygie, *f.*

T

t, vingtième lettre de l'alphabet, t, *m.*

tabard (-bàrde), or **taberd** (-beurde), *n.,* tabar, *m.*

tabaret, *n.,* satin rayé pour rideaux, *m.*

tabby, *n.,* tabis ; (cat—*chat*) chat tigré, *m.*

tabby, *adj.,* tacheté, moucheté, tavelé, tigré.

tabby, *v.a.,* tabiser.

tabefaction (-i-fak'-), *n.,* dépérissement, marasme, *m.*

tabefy (-i-fa-ye), *v.n.,* amaigrir, dépérir.

tabellion, *n.,* tabellion, *m.*

tabernacle (-èr-na-k'l), *n.,* tabernacle ; sanctuaire, *m.*

tabernacle, *v.n.,* habiter, séjourner.

tabernacular (-nak'iou-), *adj.,* treillissé.

tabid, *adj.,* tabide ; attaqué de marasme.

tabidness, *n.,* dépérissement, marasme, *m.*

tablature (-tioure), *n.,* (mus.) ⊙tablature ; (paint.) peinture, *f.*

33 *

tab 1034 **tak**

table (té-b'l), *n.*, table ; (tablet—*tablette*) tablette, table, *f.* ; (paint.) tableau, *m.* ; (arch.) tablette, *f.* ; (persp.) plan perspectif, *m.* ; (anat.) table ; (catalogue) table, *f.*, catalogue, *m.* ; (synopsis) table synoptique ; (of the hand—*de la main*) paume ; (among jewellers—*jouillerie*) table ; (index) table des matières. *f.* —s ; (draughts—*jeu*) dames, *f.pl.* The Lord's — ; *la sainte table ; la table du Seigneur.* Astronomical, chronological —s ; *tables astronomiques, chronologiques.* Office- — ; *bureau, m.* Folding- — ; *table brisée.* Dining-, tea-, work-, card-, writing- — ; *table à manger, à thé, à ouvrage, à jouer, à écrire.* Kitchen- — ; *table de cuisine.* Night- — ; *table de nuit.* Raised — ; (sculpt.) *abaque, m.* To keep open — ; *tenir table ouverte.* Good, poor — ; *bonne, pauvre table.* Frugal — ; *table frugale.* Side- — ; (for children—*d'enfants*) *petite table.* To keep a good — ; *avoir, tenir bonne table.* To sit down to — ; *se mettre à table.* To remain long at — ; *rester longtemps à table.* To be left under the — ; (of persons intoxicated—*de personnes ivres*) *rester sous la table.* To rise from — ; *se lever, sortir de table.* To turn the —s upon ; *tourner les chances contre.* The —s are turned ; *les choses ont changé de face.* To lay, to be upon the — ; (in Parliament—*au Parlement*) déposer, être déposé sur le bureau. The pleasures of the — ; *les plaisirs de la table.* All the — ; *toute la table.*

table, *v.a.*, (to form catalogues—*dresser des catalogues*) cataloguer ; (to board—*nourrir*) donner la table à, nourrir ; (carp.) assembler.

table, *v.n.*, être en pension ; manger.

tableau (tab'lô), *n.*, tableau, *m.*

table-beer (-bïr), *n.*, petite bière, *f.*

table-bell, *n.*, sonnette de table, *f.*

table-book (-bouke), *n.*, tablettes, *f.pl.*

table-cloth (-cloth), *n.*, nappe, *f.*

table-cover (-keuv'-), *n.*, tapis de table, *m.*

table-d'hôte (tâ-b'l-dôte), *n.*, table d'hôte, *f.*

table-land, *n.*, (geog.) plateau, *m.*

table-linen, *n.*, linge de table, *m.*

tabler (té-), *n.*, commensal, *m.*

table-shore, *n.*, rivage plat, *m.*

table-spoon (-spoune), *n.*, cuiller à soupe, *f.*

table-spoonful (-foule), *n.*, grande cuillerée, *f.*

tablet, *n.*, plaque ; tablette, *f.*

table-talk (-tôke), *n.*, propos de table. *m.pl.*

tabling (té-), *n.*, formation d'un tableau ; classification, *f.* ; (carp.) assemblage, *m.*

tabour (té-bor), *n.*, tambourin, *m.*

tabour (té-bor), *v.n.*, tambouriner.

tabourer, *n.*, tambourin, tambourineur, *m.*

tabouret (tab'eur'-), *n.*, petit tambourin, *m.*

tabouret (tab'ou-rè), *n.*, tabouret, *m.*

tabourine, (téb'eur'ine), *n.*, tambourin, *m.*

tabular (tab'iou-), *adj.*, en forme de table ; (having the form of plates—*de forme plate*) en forme de plaque ; (set in squares—*à carreaux*) disposé en carrés ; (set down in tables—*tabulaire*) disposé en tables, tabulaire.

tabulate (tab'iou-), *v.a.*, disposer en forme de tables ; (to shape with a flat surface—*aplanir*) aplanir.

tabulated (tab'iou-), *adj.*, en table.

tace (té-ci), *or* **tacet** (ta-cète), *n.*, (mus.) tacet, *m.*

tacit, *adj.*, tacite, implicite.

tacitly, *adv.*, tacitement, implicitement.

taciturn (-teurne), *adj.*, taciturne.

taciturnity (-teur-ni-), *n.*, taciturnité, *f.*

tack, *n.*, (nail—*clou*) broquette, pointe, *f.* ; petit clou, *m.* ; (nav.) bord, *m.*, bordée ; (of a sail—*de voile*) amure, *f.*, point du vent ; (of a flag—*d'un drapeau*) œillet, *m.*

tack, *v.a.*, attacher ; (to fasten slightly—*clouer*) clouer légèrement, mettre une pointe à ;

(to sew slightly—*coudre*) coudre légèrement ; bâtir.

tack, *v.n.*, (nav.) virer vent devant. To - about ; *virer de bord ; louvoyer, bordailler, bor deyer.*

tacker. *n.*, personne qui attache, *f.*

tackle (tak'k'l), *n.*, poulie ; moufle, *f.* ; (for fishing, &c.—*à pêche, &c.*) attirail ; (nav.) palan, *m.* ; (weapons—*armement*) armes, *f.pl.*

tackle, *v.a.*, (to supply with tackle—*fournir, pourvoir*) pourvoir de poulies, de palans ; (to seize—*empoigner*) empoigner, s'emparer de.

tackle-block, *n.*, moufle ; (nav.) poulie de palan, *f.*

tackling, *n.*, attirail ; (nav.) palan, *m.*

tact, *n.*, tact, toucher ; (skill—*talent*) tact, *m.*

tactic, *or* **tactical**, *adj.*, tactique.

tactician (tish'ia'n), *n.*, tacticien, *m.*

tactics, *n.pl.*, tactique, *f.sing.*

tactile, *adj.*, tactile.

tactility, *n.*, tact, toucher, *m.*

taction, *n.*, taction ; (geom.) tangence, *f.*

tadpole (-pôle), *n.*, têtard, *m.*

tænia (tî-), *n.*, ténia, ver solitaire, *m.*

taffeta, *or* **taffety** (-fi-), *n.*, taffetas, *m.*

taffrail, *or* **tafferel**, *n.*, couronnement de la poupe, *m.*

taffy, *n* .*V.* toffy.

taffyman, *n.*, marchand de sucre d'orge, *m.*

tafia (tâ-), *n.*, tafia, *m.*

tag, *n.*, fer, ferret, *m.* —-rag people ; *racaille, canaille, f.* —-rag and bobtail ; *quatre tondus et un pelé.*

tag, *v.a.*, (a lace—*un lacet*) ferrer ; (to join) joindre, lier, attacher, coudre. To — with ; *joindre à, faire suivre de.*

tag-sore, *n.*, (vet.) clavelée, *f.*, claveau, *m.*

tail (téle), *n.*, queue ; (extremity—*bout*) extrémité, *f.* ; bout ; (of a cart—*d'une charrette*) derrière ; (of a plough—*d'une charrue*) manche ; (nav.) fouet, *m.* ; (mus.) queue ; (of a comet, a pacha, a letter—*de comète, de pacha, de lettre*) queue ; (of a storm—*d'un orage*) fin, *f.* To turn — ; *s'enfuir ; tourner le dos.*

tail (téle), *v.a.*, tirer par la queue.

tailboard (-bôrde), *n.*, derrière de charrette, *m.*

tailed (tél'de), *adj.* à queue ; caudé.

tailing, *n.*, (arch.) corbeau, *m.* ; queue, *f.*

tailor (té-), *n.*, tailleur, *m.*

tailor (té-), *v.n.*, exercer l'état de tailleur.

tailoress, *n.*, ouvrière qui fait des vêtements d'homme ; culottière, tailleuse, *f.*

tailoring, *n.*, état de tailleur ; ouvrage de tailleur, *m.*

tailpiece (-pîce), *n.*, queue, *f.* ; cul-de-lampe, *m.* ; (mus.) touche, *f.*

tail-pointed (-pwaï'n't'-), *adj.*, (bot.) caudé.

tail-rope (-rôpe), *n.*, corde de remorque, *f.*

taint (té'n'te), *v.a.*, corrompre, altérer ; (to infect—*infecter*) infecter ; (to sully—*souiller*) ternir, souiller ; (meat—*viande*) gâter.

taint, *v.n.*, se corrompre ; (of meat—*de la viande*) se gâter.

taint (té'n'te), *n.*, corruption ; infection ; souillure ; (blemish—*défaut*) tache, *f.* Free from — ; *sans tache* ; (of meat—*de la viande*) bon, qui n'est pas gâté.

taintless, *adj.*, sans infection, sans tache.

tainture (té'n'tieur), *n.*, souillure, tache, *f.*

take, *v.a.* (preterit, Took ; past part., Taken), prendre ; (to understand—*comprendre*) comprendre ; (to arrest—*arrêter*) arrêter ; (to convey—*conduire*) conduire, mener ; (to lead away—*emmener*) emmener ; (to adopt—*adopter*) adopter ; (to suppose—*conjecturer*) supposer, s'imaginer ; (to fascinate—*séduire*) fasciner, séduire ; (to choose—*choisir*) choisir ; (to admit—*admettre*) admettre ; (to require—*exiger*) falloir, prendre ; (to endure—*souffrir*) endurer, souffrir ; (to copy—*copier*) copier, saisir ; (portrait) faire ; (impres=ion) recevoir : (revenge, satisfaction—*vengeance*) avoir, tirer ; (affront) recevoir. essuyer, subir. To — about ; *conduire partout.* To — again ; *reprendre.* To — away ; *emmener* ; (things—*choses*) emporter ; (to deprive of—*ôter*) *priver de.* ôter ; (to remove—*d'placer*) ôter ; (dinner-things, &c.—*le couvert*) desservir. To — away from ; *prendre à. ôter à.* To — back ; *reprendre* ; (to carry back—*remmener*) remmener, (things—*choses*) remporter. To — down ; *descendre* ; (to humble—*abaisser*) humilier, *abaisser, rabattre* ; (to swallow—*avaler*) prendre, avaler ; (to pull down—*démolir*) abattre, *démolir* ; (to write down—*écrire*) prendre note de, *coucher par écrit* ; (at school—*d'école*) prendre la place de. To — for ; *prendre pour* ; *regarder comme.* To — from ; *prendre de, accepter de* ; (to deprive of—*ôter*) prendre à, enlever à, ôter à, dérober à ; (to subtract—*soustraire*) soustraire à. retrancher de ; (to detract—*retirer*) enlever à, diminuer de. To — in ; rentrer ; (to enclose—*entourer*) enclore ; (to comprise—*renfermer*) comprendre, renfermer, embrasser ; (to contract—*resserrer*) resserrer, rétrécir, rentrer ; (to receive—*recevoir*) recevoir, prendre ; (to receive in one's house—*admettre chez soi*) recevoir chez soi ; (to hold—*contenir*) contenir ; (to cheat—*tromper*) tromper, mettre dedans ; (garments—*vêtements*) rendoubler, remplier ; (sails—*voiles*) carguer, ferler, serrer ; (a periodical—*écrit périodique*), recevoir ; .(lodgers—*locataires*) prendre, recevoir ; (washing, needlework, &c.—*blanchissage, ouvrage à l'aiguille, &c.*) s'occuper de ; (provisions, a stock, &c.—*des provisions, un assortiment, &c.*) faire sa provision de ; (shop goods—*marchandises*) recevoir. To — in hand ; *prendre en main ; se mettre après.* To — in one's hand ; *prendre dans la main.* To — into ; admettre dans, à. To — off ; enlever, ôter ; (to cut off—*couper*) couper, trancher ; (to destroy—*enlever*) détruire ; enlever ; (to invalidate—*affaiblir*) affaiblir ; (to swallow—*avaler*) avaler ; (to purchase—*acheter*) prendre, acheter ; (to copy—*copier*) copier ; (to mimic—*imiter*) contrefaire ; (to lead away—*emmener*) emmener ; (a mask—*un masque*) lever ; (clothes—*vêtements*) ôter ; (to withdraw—*retirer*) retirer. To — off the stage ; retirer du théâtre. To — off from ; détourner de ; (to lessen—*diminuer*) diminuer. To — off the mind from ; détourner l'esprit de. To — one's self off ; s'en aller. Death has —n him off ; la mort nous l'a enlevé. To — out ; faire sortir ; (things—*choses*) sortir ; (teeth—*dents*) arracher ; (stains—*taches*) ôter, enlever ; (for a walk—*promenade*) promener. To — out of ; sortir de ; tirer de. To — up ; porter en haut ; (to raise—*lever*) soulever ; (to pick up—*ramasser*) relever, ramasser ; (to buy—*acheter*) acheter ; (to borrow—*emprunter*) emprunter ; (to begin—*commencer*) commencer, entamer ; (to engross, to occupy—*occuper*) prendre, occuper ; (to arrest—*arrêter*) prendre, arrêter, empoigner ; (to reprimand—*réprimander*) réprimander, relever, reprendre ; (to begin where another leaves off—*commencer au point où un autre cesse*) continuer ; (to extend over—*comprendre*) embrasser ; (to adopt—*adopter*) adopter ; (to espouse—*épouser*) épouser ; (to take in hand—*se charger de*) prendre en main, se charger de ; (to collect—*lever*) lever, prélever ; (to carry up—*monter*) monter ; (to lead up—*faire monter*) faire monter ; (a bill—*une facture, &c.*) payer, acquitter, faire honneur à ; (a surg.) attacher avec une ligature, lier. To — up into ; faire monter dans. To — prisoner ; faire prisonnier. To — refuge in ; se réfugier dans. To — it into one's head to, that ; se mettre dans la tête de, que. It —s . . . . to : il faut . . . . To — any one to be ; prendre quelqu'un pour. To be —n with ; être enchanté de ; être épris de. To be —n ill ; se trouver mal ; tomber malade. To be —n with

illness ; tomber malade. To be —n with cholera ; être attaqué du choléra. To be —n giddy ; être pris de vertiges. To be —n with pains in the stomach : éprouver des tiraillements d'estomac. How old do you — me for ? quel âge me donnez-vous ? I — you to be thirty ; je vous donne trente ans.

take. v.n., (to please—*plaire*) plaire ; (to succeed—*réussir*) avoir du succès. réussir. prendre ; (to catch—*prendre*) prendre, opérer. To — after ; imiter ; (to resemble—*ressembler*) ressembler, tenir de. To — on ; se lamenter. s'affliger. To — to ; (to go towards—*aller vers*) se diriger vers ; (to take refuge in—*se réfugier*) se réfugier dans ; (to resort to—*recourir à*) avoir recours à ; (to apply to—*s'appliquer*) s'appliquer à. se livrer à, se mettre à ; (to be fond of persons—*prendre en amitié*) s'attacher à, prendre en amitié ; (to be fond of things—*des choses*) prendre du goût à, mordre à.

take-in. n., volerie, f. ; (trick—*tour*) tour ; (pers.) voleur, charlatan, fripon, m.

taker (tèk'-), n., preneur, m., preneuse, f.

taking (tèk'-), n., action de prendre ; prise : arrestation, f. ; (distress of mind—*angoiss.*) trouble, m.

taking (tèk'-), adj., attrayant ; (infectious—*contagieux*) contagieux.

takingly, adv., d'une manière attrayante.

takingness (tèk'-), n., attrait, m.

talaria (té-lé-), n.pl., (myth.) talonnières, f.pl.

talbot, n., lévrier, m.

talc, n., talc, m.

talcky, talcose (-côce), or **talcous,** adj., talcique, de talc ; (containing talc—*renfermant du talc*) contenant du talc.

talc-slate, n., talc feuilleté, m.

tale, n., conte, récit, m. ; histoire ; historiette, f. ; (reckoning—*compte*) compte, m. To tell —s ; faire des rapports.

talebearer (-bèr'-), n., rapporteur, m., rapporteuse, f.

tale-bearing (-bèr'-), n., action de rapporter ce qu'on a vu ou entendu, f. ; bavardage, m.

tale-bearing (-bèr'-), adj., qui rapporte ce qui a été vu ou entendu.

taled (té-lède), n., taled, m.

taleful (tél'foule), adj., riche de contes ; riche en récits.

talent (tal'-), n., talent ; (coin—*monnaie*) talent, m.

talented, adj., de talent.

tales (té-lize), n., juré spécial supplémentaire, m.

taleteller, n., conteur, m., conteuse, f.

talisman (tal'iz'-), n., talisman, m.

talismanic, or **talismanical** (tal'iz'-),adj., talismanique.

talk (tôke), v.n. and a., parler ; converser ; causer ; (to prate—*jaser*) bavarder, jaser ; dire. To — of ; parler de, causer de ; parler, causer. To — to ; (to advise—*conseiller*) faire des reproches à ; reprendre doucement ; faire la morale à. To — to one's self ; parler en soi-même, parler à son bonnet, se parler à soi-même. To — of politics, to — politics ; parler politique. To — nonsense ; dire des sottises, dire des bêtises. To — away the time ; passer le temps à causer. To — any one into ; persuader quelqu'un de. To — any one out ; l'emporter par la parole sur quelqu'un. To — any one out of ; dissuader quelqu'un de. To — over ; parler de ; causer de : (to cajole—*cajoler*) cajoler.

talk (tôke), n., conversation, f. ; entretien, m. ; causerie ; (prattling—*babillage*) jaserie, f. ; bavardage ; (report—*rumeur*) bruit ; (conversation) entretien, sujet de conversation, m. ; propos, m.pl.

talkative (tôk'é-), adj., causeur ; bavard.

talkativeness (tŏk'é-), *n.*, loquacité, *f.* ; caquet, bavardage, *m.*

talker (tŏk'-), *n.*, causeur, *m.*, causeuse, *f.* ; parleur, *m.*, parleuse, *f.* ; (b.s.) bavard, *m.*, bavarde, *f.* ; (boaster—*vantard*) vantard, *m.*, vantarde, *f.*

talking (tŏk'-), *n.*, conversation ; causerie, *f.* ; (b.s.) bavardage, *m.*

talking (tŏk'-), *adj.*, causeur ; bavard.

tall (tŏl), *adj.*, (pers.) grand ; haut (things—*choses*), grand.

tallage (-lédje), *n* , (ant.) taille, *f.* ; impôt, *m.*

tallage (-lédje), *v.a.*, (ant.) imposer, taxer.

tallness (tŏl'-), *n.*, (pers.) haute taille, grandeur ; (of things—*des choses*) grandeur, hauteur, *f.*

tallow (-lô), *n.*, suif, *m.*

tallow, *v.a.*, suiver, suiffer.

tallow-chandler (-tsha'n'd'-), *n.*, fabricant de chandelles, chandelier, *m.*

tallow-faced (-fés'te), *adj.*, à figure maladive; pâle.

tallow-grease (-grîce), *n.*, suif, *m.*

tallowish (-lô-ishe), *adj.*, de la nature du suif.

tallow-tree (-trî), *n.*, (bot.) arbre à suif, *m.*

tallowy (-lô-i), *adj.*, de suif ; graisseux.

tally, *v.a.*, faire des coches sur une taille ; (to fit—*adapter*) ajuster, adapter ; (nav.) border.

tally, *v.n.*, s'accorder. To — with; *s'accorder avec ; s'ajuster à ; cadrer avec ; s'adapter.*

tally, *n.*, taille (petit bâton), *f.* ; (com.) tempérament ; (fellow—*pareil*) pendant, *m.*

tally-ho! (-hô), *exc.*, (hunt.) taïaut.

tally-man, *n.*, personne qui marque la taille, *f.* ; (com.) marchand qui vend à tempérament, *m.*

tally-shop, *n.*, boutique où l'on paie à tempérament, *f.*

tally-trade, *n.*,commerceà tempérament,*m.*

talmud (-meude), *n.*, talmud, *m.*

talmudic, talmudical, *or* **talmudistic,** *adj.*, talmudique.

talmudist, *n.*, talmudiste, *m.*

talon, *n.*, serre, *f.* ; (arch.) talon, *m.*

talus (té-), *n.*, (anat.) astragale, *f.* ; (arch.) talus, *m.*

tamable (té'm'a-b'l), *adj.*, qui peut être apprivoisé; domptable.

tamableness, *n.*, nature qui peut être apprivoisée, nature domptable ; facilité d'apprivoiser, *f.*

tamarind, *n.*, (fruit) tamarin, *m.*

tamarind, *or* **tamarind-tree**, *n.*, tamarin, tamarinier, *m.*

tamarisk, *n.*, tamaris, tamarise, tamarix, *m.*

tambour (ta'm'bour), *n.*, tambour de basque; (arts, arch.) tambour, *m.*

tambour (ta'm'bour), *v.a.*, broder au tambour.

tambourine (-bo-rîne), *n.*, tambour de basque, *m.*

tame, *v.a.*, apprivoiser, dompter, priver ; rendre domestique; (fig.) subjuguer, dompter, réprimer.

tame, *adj.*, apprivoisé ; privé, domestique; (spiritless—*faible*) traitable ; fade, pâle, sans couleur ; (subdued—*subjugué*) soumis.

tamely, *adv.*, avec soumission ; sans résistance; servilement ; (without force—*sans force*) sans force, sans couleur.

tameness, *n.*, état apprivoisé, *m.* ; domesticité, *f.*; (want of force—*manque de force*) manque de force, manque de couleur, *m.*; (submission—*obéissance*) soumission, servilité, *f.*

tamer (té'm'-), *n.*, personne qui apprivoise, *f.* ; (of wild beasts—*d'animaux sauvages*) dompteur, *m.*

taminy, *n.*, étamine, *f.*

tamkin, *n.* *V.* **tampion.**

tamper, *v.a.*, (to practise secretly—*agir en secret*) machiner, agir dans l'ombre. To — with (of things—*des choses*) ; *faire de petites expériences* ; (to meddle with—*s'ingérer*) se mêler de ; (a witness—*un témoin*) pratiquer, suborner. *tâcher de gagner* ; (objects—*objets*) toucher à, déranger, abîmer.

tampering, *n.*, action de toucher à, de déranger, d'abîmer ; de se mêler de; de suborner ; menée secrète, *f.*

tamping-bar (-bâr), *n.*, bourroir, *m.*

tampion, *n.*, tampon de canon, *m.*

tamtam, *n.*, tam-tam, *m.*

tan, *n.*, tan, *m.* Waste —; tannée, *f.*

tan, *v.a.*, tanner ; (to sun-burn—*hâler*) basaner, hâler.

tanager (-'a-djeur), *n.*, (ornl.) tangara, *m.*

tan-bed (-bède), *n.*, (hort.) couche de tan, *f.*

tan-colour (-keul'leur), *n.*, tanné, *m.*

tandem, *n.*, tandem ; cabriolet découvert à deux chevaux en flèche, *m.*

tang (tan'gu), *n.*, arrière-goût; mauvais goût, *m.*

tangency (ta'n'djè'n'ci), *n.*, tangence, *f.*

tangent (-djè'n'te), *n.*, tangente, *f.* To go off at a — ; *s'emporter tout de suite.*

tangential (-djè'n'shial), *adj.*, (geom.) tangent.

tangibility (-dji-), *n.*, tangibilité, *f.*

tangible (-dji-b'l), *adj.*, tangible; tactile.

tangle (tan'gn'g'l), *n.*, état emmêlé, état embrouillé, *m.* It is in a — ; *c'est tout embrouillé.*

tangle (tan'gn'g'l), *v.a.* *V.* **entangle.**

tau-house (-haouce), *n.*, tannerie, *f.*

tank, *n.*, réservoir, *m.* ; cuve ; (of a pump—*de pompe*) bâche, *f.*

tankard, *n.*, pot à couvercle, *m.*

tanling, *n.*, (ant.) personne hâlée, *f.*

tanner, *n.*, tanneur, *m.*

tannery, *n.*, tannerie, *f.*

tannic, *adj.*, tannique.

tannin, *n.*, tanin, *m.*

tanning, *n.*, tannage, *m.*

tanning-liquor (-lik'eur), *n.*, jus de tannée, *m.*

tan-pit, *n.*, fosse à tan, *f.*

tan-stove (-stôve), *n.*, (hort.) serre à tannée, *f.*

tansy (-zi), *n.*, tanaisie, herbe aux vers, *f.*

tantalism (-liz'm), *n.*, supplice de Tantale, *m.* ; torture, *f.*

tantalization (laïzé-), *n.*, action de torturer; tentation, *f.*

tantalize (-laïze), *v.a.*, se jouer de, torturer ; tenter.

tantalizer (-laïz'-), *n.*, personne qui torture, *f.*

tantalizing (-laïz'-), *adj.*, tentant.

tantamount (maou'n'te), *adj.*, équivalent.

tantivy, *adv.*, à fond de train ; à bride abattue.

tantling, *n.*, (ant.) personne tentée, *f.*

tantrums (-treu'm'ze), *n.pl.*, mauvaise humeur ; grande mauvaise humeur, *f. sing.*

tan-vat, *n.*, fosse à tan, *f.*

tan-waste (-wéste), *n.*, tannée, *f.*

tan-yard (-yârde), *n.*, tannerie, *f.*

tap, *n.*, (blow—*coup léger*) tape, *f.*, coup ; (of an inn, &c.—*d'auberge, &c.*) comptoir, *m.* ; (of a cask—*de tonneau*) cannelle, cannette. *f.* ; (tech.) taraud, *m.*

tap, *v.a.*, (to strike—*taper*) taper ; (surg.) percer ; faire la ponction ; (wine, &c.—*rin, &c.*) tirer ; (a cask—*un tonneau*) mettre en perce ; (a tree—*un arbre*) inciser ; (tech.) tarauder; (metal.) faire la coulée à.

tap, *v.n.*, taper ; frapper.

tap-borer (-bôr'-), *n.*, taraud. *m.*

tape, *n.*, ruban de fil, ruban de coton, *m.*

taper (té-), *n.*, petite bougie, *f.* ; cierge, *m.*

taper (té-), *v.a.*, tailler en pointe.

taper. *v.n.*, se terminer en pointe.

taper, *or* **tapering** (té-), *adj.*, terminé en pointe; effilé; (conical—*conique*) en forme de cône, conique.

taperingly. *adv.*, en pointe.

taperness (té-), *n.*, qualité de ce qui se termine en pointe, *f.*

tapestried (tap'ès-tride), *adj.*, tapissé.

tapestry (tap'ès-), *n.*, tapisserie, *f.*

tapestry-maker (-mék'-), *n.*, tapissier, *m.*

tape-worm (-weurm), *n.*, ténia; ver solitaire, *m.*

tap-hole (-hôle), *n.*, (metal.) trou de coulée, *m.*

tapioca. *n.*, tapioca, *m.*

tapir (té-), *n.*, (mam.) tapir, *m.*

tapis (tap-pi), *n.*, tapis, *m.*

taplash, *n.*, lie du tonneau, *f.*

tapping, *n.*, ponction; (metal.) coulée, *f.*

taproom (-roume), *n.*, salle; salle des buveurs, *f.*

taproot (-route), *n.*, (bot.) pivot, *m.*; racine pivotante, *f.*

tap-rooted, *adj.*, à racine pivotante.

tapster, *n.*, garçon de cabaret. *m.*

tar (târ), *n.*, goudron; (sailor—*marin*) matelot, loup de mer, *m.*

tar (târ), *v.a.*, goudronner.

tarantismus (-tiz'-), *n.*, (med.) tarentisme, *m.*

tarantula (-tiou-), *n.*, (ent.) tarentule, *f.*

tardigradous (târ-di-gré-), *adj.*, (ant.) tardigrade.

tardily (târ-), *adv.*, lentement; tardivement.

tardiness (târ-), *n.*, lenteur; (reluctance—*aversion*) répugnance, *f.*; (lateness—*délai*) retard, *m.*

tardy (târ-), *adj.*, lent; (late—*tardif*) en retard, tardif; (unwilling—*qui répugne*) qui a de la répugnance, mal disposé.

tardy-gaited (târ-), *adj.*, à la marche traînante.

tare, *n.*, ivraie; (com.) tare, *f.*

tare, *v.n.*, (com.) tarer; prendre la tare de.

target (târ-ghète), *n.*, cible, *f.*; but, blanc, *m.*; (shield—*bouclier*) targe, *f.*

targeteer (târ-ghèt'ire), *n.*, homme armé d'une targe; (antiq.) peltaste, *m.*

tariff, *n.*, tarif, *m.*

tariff, *v.a.*, tarifer.

tarin, *n.*, (orni.) tarin, *m.*

tar-lake, *n.*, lac d'asphalte, *m.*

tarnish. *v.a.*, ternir; (fig.) souiller, flétrir.

tarnish. *v.n.*, se ternir.

tarpaulin, *or* **tarpawling** (-pô-), *n.*, prélart, *m.*

tarpeian, *adj.*, Tarpéien.

tar-pit, *n.*, puits à goudron, *m.*

tarrace, **tarrass**, *or* **trass**, *n.*, trass, *m.*

tarragon, *n.*, (bot.) estragon, *m.*

tarrier, *n.*, personne qui tarde, *f.*; (dog—*chien*) terrier, *m.*

tarry, *v.n.*, (to stay—*rester*) rester, s'arrêter; (to delay—*différer*) tarder, différer.

tarry (târ-), *adj.*, de goudron.

tarrying, *n.*, retard, *m.*

tarsal (târ-), *adj.*, tarsien, du tarse.

tarsel (târ-), *n.*, tiercelet. *m.*

tarsus (târ-), *n.*, tarse; cartilage tarse. *m.*

tart (târte), *n.*, tarte. tourte. *f.* — -dish: tourtière, *f.*

tart (târte). *adj.*, aigre. âcre; acide; (fig.) aigre, mordant, piquant, âcre.

tartan (târ-), *n.*, tartan. *m.*; (vessel—*navire*) tartane, *f.*

tartar (târ-), *n.*, (chem., of the teeth—*des dents*) tartre, *m.*

tartar (târ-), *n.*, Tartare. *m.*, *f.*; (fig.) bourru, *m.* To catch a —; s'attaquer à plus fort que soi.

tartarean, *or* **tartareous** (târ-té-), *adj.*, du Tartare.

tartareous (târ-), *adj.*, (chem.) tartareux.

tartaric (târ-), *adj.*, tartrique, tartarique.

tartarine (târ-), *n.*, potasse, *f.*

tartarous (târ-), *adj.*, tartareux.

tartish (târ-), *adj.*, aigrelet.

tartly (târt-), *adv.*, avec âcreté; avec aigreur; (fig.) vertement, avec aigreur, sévèrement.

tartness (târt-), *n.*, acidité, aigreur, âcreté; (fig.) aigreur, sévérité, *f.*

tartrate (târ-), *n.*, tartrate, *m.*

tartuffe (târ-teufe), *n.*, tartufe, hypocrite, cafard, *m.*

tartuffish (târ-teuf'-), *adj.*, de tartufe; cafard.

task (tâske), *n.*, tâche, *f.*; travail, ouvrage, *m.*; besogne; charge, *f.*; (lesson—*leçon*) devoir; (punishment—*punition*) pensum, *m.* To take to —; *réprimander; blâmer.*

task, *v.a.*, donner une tâche à; charger de travail.

tasker, *n.*, personne qui donne une tâche, *f.*

taskmaster (-mâs-), *n.*, personne qui impose des tâches, *f.*; (b.s.) maître. oppresseur, *m.*

taskwork (-weurke), *n.*, tâche, *f.*

tassel, *n.*, gland, *m.*; (large one—*de grande dimension*) houppe, *f.*; (arch.) tasseau; (hawk—*faucon*) tiercelet d'autour, *m.*

tasselled, *adj.*, à glands; orné de glands.

tasses (tass'ize), *or* **tassets** (tass'ètse), *n.pl.*, tassette, *f.sing.*

tastable (tést'-a-b'l), *adj.*, qui peut être goûté; savoureux.

taste. *v.a.*, goûter; (liquids—*boissons*) déguster; (fig.) goûter, goûter de, sentir, savourer.

taste. *v.n.*, goûter. To — of; goûter de. *goûter;* (to have a smack of—*avoir un goût de*) avoir un goût de, sentir le; (just to taste—*goûter*) effleurer; (to experience—*éprouver*) sentir, *éprouver, goûter, subir :* (to be tinctured with—*avoir une odeur de*) sentir. To — good, bad ; avoir un bon, un mauvais goût.

taste, *n.*, goût, *m.*; (small quantity—*petite quantité*) idée, *f.*, soupçon; (specimen) échantillon. spécimen, *m.*; (of beverages—*des boissons*) dégustation, *f.* My mouth is out of —; *ma bouche n'est pas disposée à goûter.* There is no disputing about —s ; *il ne faut pas disputer des goûts.* Every one to his — ; *chacun à son goût.* To one's — ; *à son goût.* To dress with — ; *s'habiller avec goût.* That is good. bad — ; *c'est de bon, de mauvais goût.* From, out of — ; *par goût.*

tasteful (tést'foule), *adj.*, savoureux; (having good taste—*de bon goût*) de bon goût.

tastefully (-foul'-), *adv.*, avec goût.

tasteless, *adj.*, fade, insipide.

tastelessly, *adv.*, insipidement.

tastelessness, *n.*, insipidité, fadeur, *f.*

taster (tést'-), *n.*, personne qui goûte, *f.*; (of beverages—*de boissons*) dégustateur; (dram cup—*verre à liqueur*) petit verre; (of cheese—*de fromage*) petit morceau, *m.*

tasting (tést'-), *n.*, goût, *m.*; gustation; (of beverages—*des boissons*) dégustation, *f.*

tasty (tést'-), *adj.*, de goût, de bon goût.

tatter, *n.*, haillon, lambeau, *m.*; guenille, *f.*

tatter. *v.a.*, déchirer.

tatterdemalion (-di-), *n.*, homme déguenillé. va-nu-pieds. gueux, *m.*

tattered (tat'teurde), *adj.*, (pers.) déguenillé; (of garments—*des vêtements*) en lambeaux, en guenilles, en haillons.

tattle (tat't'l). *n.*, babil, caquet, bavardage, *m.*; cancans, *m.pl.*

tattle (tat't'l), *v.n.*, babiller, jaser, caqueter, bavarder; cancaner.

tattler. *n.*, bavard. *m.*, bavarde, *f.*; babillard, *m.*, babillarde, *f.*; cancanier. *m.*, cancanière, *f.*

tattling, *adj.*, babillard, bavard; cancanier, *m.*

tattoo (tat'tou), *v.a.*, tatouer.

tattoo (tat'tou), *n.*, tatouage, *m.* ; (milit.) retraite, *f.*

tattooing (tat'tou-), *n..* tatouage, *m.*

taught (tôte), *adj.*, raide, tendu ; (of sails—*des voiles*) enflé, plein.

taunt (tà'n'te, *ou* tô'n'te), *n.*, injure en paroles, *f.* ; (bitter reproach—*reproche*) reproche sanglant, reproche amer, *m.* ; (invective) invective, raillerie, *f.* ; sarcasme, *m.*

taunt (tà'n'te, *ou* tô'n'te), *v.a.*, reprocher vivement à ; outrager ; injurier ; dire des injures à, railler, censurer.

taunt, *adj.*, (nav.) haut.

taunter, *n.*, personne qui fait des reproches sanglants, qui injurie, qui outrage, *f.* ; railleur, *m.*, railleuse, *f.*

tauntingly, *adv.*, injurieusement, avec raillerie ; d'une manière insultante.

taurus, *n.*, (astron.) le Taureau, *m.*

tautochrone (-krône), *n.*, courbe tautochrone, *f.*

tautochronous (-krô'n'-), *adj.*, tautochrone.

tautologic, *or* **tautological** (-lodj'-), *adj.*, tautologique.

tautologize (-djaïze), *v.n.*, se répéter.

tautology (-dji), *n.*, tautologie, *f.*

tavern (tav'eurne), *n.*, taverne ; auberge, *f.* ; cabaret. *m.*

tavern-hunter (-heu'n't'-), *n.*, pilier de cabaret. *m.*

tavern-keeper (-kip'-), *n.*, aubergiste, cabaretier, *m.*

taw (tô), *n..* bille à jouer, *f.*

taw (tô), *v.a.*, passer en mégie, mégisser.

tawdrily (tô-), *adv.*, avec un faux éclat; d'une manière voyante.

tawdriness (tô-), *n.*, faux éclat ; mauvais goût, *m.*

tawdry (tô-), *adj.*, éclatant ; voyant ; de faux éclat.

tawer (tô-), *n.*, mégissier, *m.*

tawing (tô-), *n.*, mégisserie, mégie, *f.*

tawny (tô-ni), *adj.*, basané, tanné, hâlé, (animal) fauve.

tax, *n.*, impôt, *m.* ; contribution, imposition, taxe, *f.* ; (fig.) taxe, *f.*, impôt, fardeau, *m.* ; (censure) censure,*f.* Assessed —es : *contributions directes.* Income— — ; *impôt sur le revenu, m.* ; *taxe du revenu. f.*

tax, *v.a.*, imposer ; frapper d'un impôt ; taxer ; (to accuse—*accuser*) taxer, accuser ; (to censure—*blâmer*) censurer ; (fig.) taxer, mettre à contribution ; (jur.) taxer.

taxable (taks'a-b'l), *adj.*, imposable ; qui peut être taxé.

taxation (taks'é-), *n.*, taxation ; (jur.) taxation, taxe. *f.*

taxer (taks'-), *n.*, personne qui impose une taxe, *f.* ; (jur.) taxateur, *m.*

tax-free (-fri), *adj.*, exempt d'impôts.

tax-gatherer (-gath'eur'-), *n.*, percepteur des contributions, *m.*

taxidermy (taks'i-deur-), *n..* taxidermie, *f.*

tax-payer (-pè-eur), *n.*, contribuable, *m.*

tazetta, *n.*, (bot.) narcisse, *m.*

tea (ti), *n.*, thé ; (broth—*bouillon*) bouillon,*m.* ; (infusion) eau, tisane, infusion, *f.* Beef- — ; *bouillon, consommé, m.*

tea-board (-bôrde), *n..* cabaret, plateau, *m.*

tea-caddy, *or* **tea-canister**, *n.*, boîte à thé. *f.*

teach (titshe), *v.a.* (preterit and *past part.*, Taught), (pers.) enseigner, instruire ; (things—*choses*) enseigner, apprendre ; (any manual labour—*travail manuel*) montrer ; (to lecture on —*professer*) professer ; (to accustom—*habituer*) apprendre, habituer ; (to suggest to the mind—*suggérer*) communiquer ; (to signify—*signifier*)

indiquer. To — any one French ; *enseigner, apprendre le français à quelqu'un.*

teach, *v.n.*, enseigner, professer.

teachable (titsh'a-b'l), *adj.*, disposé à apprendre ; (docile) docile.

teachableness, *n.*, disposition à apprendre ; (docility—*docilité*) docilité, *f.*

teacher. *n.*, maître, *m.*, maîtresse, *f.* ; instituteur, *m.*, institutrice, *f.* ; professeur (preacher—*prédicateur*) prédicateur ; prédicateur laïque, *m.*

teaching, *n.*, enseignement, *m.* ; instruction, *f.*

tea-dealer (-dîl'-), *n.*, marchand de thé. *m.*

tea-dust (-deuste), *n..* poudre de thé, *f.*

tea-equipage (-èk'wi-pédje), *n.*, cabaret à thé, *m.*

tea-grower (-grô-), *n.*, cultivateur de thé,*m.*

teak (tike), *n.*, (bot.) teck, tek, *m.*

tea-kettle (-kèt't'l), *n.*, bouilloire, *f.*

teal (tîle), *n.*, (orni.) sarcelle, *f.*

team (time), *n.*, attelage, *m.* ; ligne, file, *f.*

team (time), *v.a.*, transporter du déblai au remblai.

tea-merchant, *n.*, marchand de thé, *m.*

teaming, *n.*, transport du déblai au remblai, *m.*

teaming-road (-rôde), *n.*, chemin provisoire de transport, *m.*

teamster, *n.*, conducteur d'un attelage, *m.*

tea-party, *n.*, thé, *m.*

tea-pot, *n.*, théière, *f.*

tear (ti-eur), *n.*, larme, *f.* ; pleur, *m.* To shed — s ; *verser des larmes.* To shed bitter —s ; *pleurer à chaudes larmes.* To burst into —s ; *fondre en larmes.* To be drowned in —s ; *avoir les yeux noyés de larmes.* To affect to —s ; *toucher jusqu'aux larmes.* With —s in one's eyes ; *les larmes aux yeux.* All in —s ; *tout en pleurs ; tout éploré.*

tear (tère), *v.a.* (preterit, Tore; *past part.*, Torn), déchirer; (the hair—*les cheveux*) arracher ; (fig.) arracher. To — asunder ; *déchirer en deux.* To — away, down, off, out; *arracher.* To — from; *arracher à.* To — up ; *arracher ;* (to tear to pieces—*mettre en pièces*) *mettre en morceaux.*

tear (tère), *v.n.*, s'agiter ; se démener. To — along ; *aller ventre à terre.*

tear (tère), *n.*, déchirure ; (injury done to things in use—*dommage*) détérioration, *f.*

tearer (tèr'-), *n.*, personne qui déchire ; (one that rages—*personne en colère*) personne qui se démène, *f.*

tear-falling (ti-eur-fôl'-), *adj.*, qui répand des larmes, funeste.

tearful (ti-eur-foule), *adj.*, tout en larmes ; rempli de larmes.

tearing (tèr'-), *n.*, déchirement ; arrachement, *m.*

tear-shaped (ti-eur-shép'te), *adj.*, (tech.) larmeux.

tease (tîze), *v.a.*, tracasser, tourmenter ; contrarier ; asticoter, taquiner ; chicaner ; (to card—*carder*) carder ; (cloth—*drap*) lainer.

teasel (ti-zèl), *n.*, (bot.) cardère. *f.* ; chardon à foulon, à bonnetier, *m.* ; cardère à foulon, a bonnetier, *f.*

teaseler (ti-zèl'-), *n.*, laineur, *m.*, laineuse,*f.*

teaser (tiz'-), *n.*, tracassier, *m.*, tracassière, *f.* ; taquin, *m.*, taquine, *f.* ; chicaneur, *m.*, chicaneuse, *f.*

tea-service (-seur-vice), *n.*, cabaret, service à thé, *m.*

teasling (tîz'-), *n.*, lainage ; ratinage, *m.*

tea-spoon (-spoune), *n.*, cuiller à thé, *f.*

teat (tîte), *n.*, mamelon, tetin ; (of animals—*des animaux*) mamelon. *m.*, tette, *f.*

tea-table (-té-b'l), *n.*, table à thé, *f.*

tea-things (-thign'ze), *n.pl.*, service à thé, *m.sing.*

tea-tray, *n.*, plateau, *m.*

tea-tree (-trî), *n.*, thé; arbre à thé, *m.*

tea-urn (-eurne), *n.*, fontaine à thé, *f.*

techily (tètsh'-), *adv.*, maussadement; d'une manière hargneuse.

tochiness (tètsh'-), *n.*, maussaderie; humeur hargneuse, *f.*

technical (tèk-), *adj.*, technique; de l'art.

technicality, *or* **technicalness** (tèk-), *n.*, caractère technique, *m.*

technically (tèk-), *adv.*, techniquement; suivant l'art.

technics (tèk-), *n.pl.*, technique, *f.sing.*

technological (tèk-nol-o-dj'-), *adj.*, technologique; des arts.

technology (tèk-nol'o-dji), *n.*, technologie; terminologie, *f.*

techy (tètshi), *adj.*, maussade; hargneux, bourru.

ted, *v.a.*, (agri.) répandre.

tedder, *v.a.*, lier par une attache; attacher.

te deum (ti-di-), *n.*, Te Deum, *m.*

tedious (tîd'-), *adj.*, ennuyeux, fastidieux, fatigant; (slow—*lent*) lent, trop long.

tediously (tîd'-), *adv.*, ennuyeusement; fastidieusement.

tediousness (tîd'-), *n.*, ennui, *m.*; fatigue; nature fastidieuse; (slowness—*lenteur*) lenteur fatigante; (prolixity—*prolixité*) prolixité, longueur, *f.*

tedium (tî-), *n.*, ennui, *m.*; fatigue, *f.*

teem (tî'me), *v.n.*, enfanter; être fécond. To — with; *être plein de; abonder en; regorger de.*

teem, *v.a.*, enfanter; produire.

teemer, *n.*, personne qui enfante, *f.*

teemful (-foul), *adj.*, (ant.) fécond, fertile; (brimful—*plein*) plein jusqu'au bord.

teemless, *adj.*, stérile.

teens (tî'n'ze), *n.pl.*, l'âge de treize à dix-neuf ans, *m.sing.*

teeth (tîth),*n.pl.* V. **tooth.**

teeth (tîthe), *v.n.*, faire ses dents.

teething (tîth'-), *n.*, dentition, *f.*

teeth-range (tîth-rè'n'dje), *n.*, denture, *f.*

teetotal (tî-tô-), *adj.*, de tempérance.

teetotaler (tî-tô-),*n.*, personne qui s'abstient entièrement de bière et de boissons spiritueuses, *f.*, abstème. *m f.*

teetotalism (tî-tô-tal'iz'm), *n.*, abstinence entière de bière et de boissons spiritueuses, *f.*

teetotum (tî-tô-), *n.*, toton, *m.*

tegular (tègh'iou-), *adj.*. de tuile.

tegularly, *adv.*, en tuile.

tegument (tègh'iou-), *n.*, tégument, *m.*

tegumentary, *adj.*, tégumentaire.

teil-tree (tîle-), *n.*, tilleul, *m.*

telamones (tèl'a-mô-nîze), *n.pl.*, (arch.) télamons, *m.pl.*

telegraph (tèl'i-), *n.*, télégraphe, *m.* Electric —; *télégraphe électrique.*

telegraph, *v.a.*, télégraphier.

telegraphic, *adj.*, télégraphique.

telescope (tèl'i-scôpe), *n.*, télescope, *m.*; lunette d'approche, *f.*

telescope-shell, *n.*, (conch.) turbo, *m.*

telescopic, *adj.*, télescopique.

tell, *v.a.* (*preterit* and *past part.*, Told), dire; faire part de; (to narrate—*narrer*) raconter; conter; (to teach—*enseigner*) apprendre, dire; (to disclose—*révéler*) révéler, dévoiler, rapporter; (to count—*compter*) compter, énumérer; (to confess—*confesser*) avouer; (to publish—*publier*) publier, proclamer; (to discover—*découvrir*) découvrir, trouver; (to explain—*expliquer*) expliquer, dire. To — by; *juger à.* To — off; *énumérer.* Don't — me! *laissez donc!* — that to others; *à d'autres.* I have been told; *on m'a dit; j'ai entendu dire.* It is told of; *on le dit de.* To — any one any thing; *dire quelque chose à quelqu'un; faire part de quelque chose à quelqu'un.*

tell, *v.n.*, dire; raconter; (to take effect— *agir*) faire son effet; porter; porter coup. To — of; (pers.) dénoncer; (things—*choses*) dire. To — up; *monter.*

teller, *n.*, diseur, *m.*, diseuse, *f.*; raconteur, *m.*, raconteuse, *f.*; (in parliament—*du parlement*) scrutateur; (of the exchequer—*du trésor*) agent comptable; (thing—*chose*) compteur, *m.*

tell-tale, *n.*, rapporteur, *m.*, rapporteuse, *f.*; (mec.) compteur; (nav.) axiomètre, *m.*

tell-tale, *adj.*, bavard; qui fait des rapports.

tellurium (tèl-liou-), *n.*, (chem.) tellure, *m.*

temerarious (tè'm'èr'é-), *adj.*, téméraire.

temerity (ti-mèr'-), *n.*. témérité, *f.*

temper, *n.*, caractère; naturel, *m.*; (humour —*humeur*) humeur, *f.*, caractère, *m.*; (anger) colère, *f.*; (calmness of mind—*calme*) sang-froid, calme, *m.*; (of steel, &c.—*de l'acier, &c.*) trempe; (mixture—*mélange*) combinaison, *f.*, mélange, *m.*; in (sugar-works—*raffinage du sucre*) matière à défécation, *f.* Out of —; *de mauvaise humeur.* In a good—; *de bonne humeur.* To lose one's —, to get out of —; *sortir de son caractère; se mettre en colère; s'emporter; perdre son sang-froid.* To put out of —; *mettre de mauvaise humeur.* To keep one's —; *garder son sang-froid; ne pas sortir de son caractère.* A man of a violent —; *un homme d'un caractère emporté.* He has a bad — but a good heart; *il a un mauvais caractère, mais un bon cœur.*

temper, *v.a.*, (to mix—*mêler*) mélanger, combiner; (to adjust—*ajuster*) ajuster, proportionner; (to modify—*modifier*) tempérer; (to soften—*mitiger*) adoucir; (mus.) tempérer; (steel, &c.—*l'acier, &c.*) tremper. Ill—ed; *qui a un mauvais caractère, qui a le caractère mal fait.* Good—ed; *qui a un bon caractère, qui a le caractère bien fait.*

temperament (-peur'-), *n.*, constitution, *f.*; tempérament; (medium—*milieu*) milieu, équilibre; (mus.) tempérament, *m.*

temperamental, *adj.*, de tempérament; constitutionnel.

temperance (-peur-), *n.*, tempérance; sobriété, modération, *f.* — society; *société de tempérance.*

temperate (-peur'-), *adj.*, tempéré; modéré; (pers.) tempérant, sobre; (calm—*calme*) calme; (in speech—*en paroles*) réservé; (geog.) tempéré.

temperately, *adv.*, avec sobriété, avec tempérance; modérément; avec calme; avec réserve.

temperateness, *n.*, modération, douceur, *f.*; (calmness—*calme*) calme, *m.*

temperative, *adj.*, qui tempère, qui modère.

temperature (-tioure), *n.*, température; (constitution) constitution, *f.*, tempérament, *m.*; modération, *f.*

tempest (-pèste), *n.*, tempête, *f.*; orage, *m.* — -beaten; *battu par la tempête.* — -tossed; *ballotté par la tempête.*

tempestuous (-pèst'iou-), *adj.*, orageux; tempétueux.

tempestuously, *adv.*, d'une manière orageuse.

tempestuousness, *n.*, état orageux. *m.*

templar, *n.*, templier; (law-student—*étudiant en droit*) étudiant en droit, *m.*

temple (tè'm'p'l), *n.*, temple, *m.*; (anat.) tempe, *f.*

temple-bone (-bône), *n.*, (anat.) os temporal. *m.*

templet, *n.*, (mas.) panneau, patron, *m.*

temporal, *adj.*, temporel; (anat.) temporal.

temporality, *n.* (*temporalities, temporals*), bien temporel, revenu temporel, *m.*

temporally, *adv.*, temporellement.

temporaneous (-ré-ni-), *adj.*, (ant.) temporaire.

temporarily, *adv.*, temporairement.

temporariness, *n.*, état temporaire, *m.*
temporary. *adj.*. temporaire.
temporization (-raïzé-),*n*..temporisation,*f.*
temporize (-raize), *v.a.*, temporiser; s'accommoder.
temporizer (-raïz'-), *n.*, temporisateur, temporiseur, *m.*
temporizing (-raïz'-), *adj.*, temporisateur. qui temporise; accommodant.
tempt, *v.a.*, tenter,; (to incite—*pousser*) *excite* r, pousser: (to draw—*entraîner*) entraîner; *t* to try—*essayer*) tenter, essayer; (in Scripture—*biblique*) tenter, éprouver.
temptable (-'a-b'l), *adj.*, sujet à la tentation.
temptation (tè'm'té-), *n.*, tentation, *f.*; entraînement, *m.*
tempter (tè'm't'-), *n.*, tentateur, *m.*, tentatrice, *f.*
tempting (tè'm't'-), *adj.*, tentant. entraînant, tentatif.
temptingly, *adv.*. d'une manière tentative, d'une manière tentante; d'une manière entraînante.
temptress (tè'm't'-), *n.*, tentatrice,*f.*
ten. *adj.*, dix. About —, some ten; *une dizaine: une dizaine de.*
ten, *n.*, dix, *m.*; dizaine, *f.*
tenable (tè'n'a-b'l), *adj.*, soutenable; tenable.
tenacious (tè-né-sheusse), *adj.*, tenace. — of ; *qui tient à ; fortement attaché à.*
tenaciously, *adv.*, d'une manière tenace.
tenacity (ti-nass'-), *n.*, ténacité,*f.*
tenacy (tè'n'-), *n.* (ant.). *V. tenacity.*
tenaille (ti-nél), *n.*, (fort.) tenaille,*f.*
tenaillon (tè-nél-li-eune), *n.*, (fort.) tenaillon, *m.*
tenancy (tè'n'-), *n.*, location,*f.*
tenant, *v.a.*, tenir à loyer; être locataire de.
tenant, *n.*, locataire, *m.,f.*; habitant, *m.*, habitante. *f.*; (of a farm—*d'une ferme*) fermier,*m.*
tenantable (-'a-b'l), *adj.*, logeable; locatif.
tenantableness, *n.*, état locatif, *m.*
tenantless, *adj.*, sans locataire; sans habitant; vide.
tench, *n.*, (ich.) tanche,*f.*
tend, *v.a.*, garder; soigner; avoir soin de; veiller sur.
tend, *v.n.*, (nav.) éviter. To — upon ; *servir.* To — to; *se diriger vers ;* (to aim at—*viser à*) *tendre à ;* (to contribute to—*contribuer*) *tendre à, contribuer à.*
tendency, *n.*, tendance,*f.*
tender, *n.*, (nurse—*garde-malade*) garde,*f.* ; (nav.) aviso; transport, bâtiment de transport; bâtiment de servitude; (railways) tender, *m.*; (offer—*offre*) offre; (for contracts—*de contrats*) soumission; (of an oath—*d'un serment*) action de déférer. *f.* Legal —; *monnaie légale, f.* ; *cours légal, m.*
tender. *v.a.*, offrir, présenter; (an oath—*un serment*) déférer; (contracts—*contrats*) soumissionner.
tender. *adj.*, tendre; (easily pained—*sensible*) tendre, sensible; (effeminate—*efféminé*) délicat, mou; (young—*jeune*) tendre; (mild—*doux*) doux; (compassionate—*compatissant*) tendre, compatissant; (dear—*cher*) cher, tendre; (of flowers—*des fleurs*) délicat, de serre; (ticklish—*scabreux*) délicat. scabreux. — of ; *soucieux de ; jaloux de.*
tender-hearted (-hârt'-), *adj.*, compatissant, sensible, au cœur tendre.
tender-heartedly, *adv.*, avec sensibilité.
tender-heartedness, *n.*, sensibilité,*f.*
tenderling, *n.*, enfant chéri; (of a deer—*des fauves*) premier bois, *m.*
tenderly, *adv.*, tendrement; doucement; délicatement; (with pity—*avec pitié*) avec compassion.
tenderness, *n.*, tendresse; (screness, sensi-

bility—*sensibilité*)sensibilité; (softness—*mollesse*)? mollesse, délicatesse; (kind attention—*soins*) sollicitude,*f.*. égards, *m.pl.* ; (scrupulousness—*scrupule*) scrupule; (care—*soin*) soin, *m.*; (expression) douceur. *f.*
tending, *n.*,.(nav.) évitage, *m.*
tendinous, *adj.*, tendineux; plein de tendons.
tendon. *n.*, tendon, *m.*
tendril, *n.*, vrille,*f.*; cirre. *m*
tendril. *adj.*, (bot.) grimpant.
tenebrous (tè'n'i-), *adj.*, ténébreux.
tenebrousness, *or* **tenebrosity**, *n.*, ténèbres, *f.pl.* ; obscurité, *f.*
tenement (tè'n'i-), *n.*, habitation, maison. *f.* ; appartement, *m.*
tenemental, *adj.*. en location; susceptible de location.
tenesmus (ti-nèz'-), *n.*. ténesme, *m.*
tenet (tè'n'-), *n.*, dogme, *m.*; doctrine, *f.*
tenfold (-fôlde), *adj.*, décuple.
tennis, *n.*, paume, *f.*
tennis-court (-côrte), *n.*, jeu de paume, *m.*
tenon (tè'n'-), *n.*, tenon, *m.*
tenor (tè'n'-), *n.*, (strain—*cours*) style, ton. *m.* : teneur,*f.* ; (character—*caractère*) caractère; (sense—*sens*) sens, esprit; (mus.) ténor; (instrument) alto, *m.*, viole,*f.*
tense (tè'n'-), *n.*, (gram.) temps, *m.*
tense, *adj.*, tendu, raide.
tenseness, *n.*, tension, raideur,*f.*
tensible (tè'n'si-b'l), *or* **tensile** (-sile), *adj.*, extensible.
tension, *n.*, tension; extension,*f.*
tensive, *adj.*, qui tend, qui raidit.
tensor (tè'n'seur), *n.*, (anat.) extenseur, *m.*
tent, *n.*, tente; (surg.) tente,*f.*
tent, *v.n.*, camper.
tent, *v.a.*, (surg.) sonder.
tentacle (tè'n'ta-k'l), *n.*, (ent.) tentacule, *m.*
tentative (tè'n'ta-), *adj.*, d'essai, expérimental.
tentative (tè'n'ta-), *n.*, tentative,*f.*; essai,*m.*
tented, *adj.*, couvert de tentes; (pers.) campé, habitant sous des tentes.
tenter, *n.*, crochet à étendre les draps, *m.* To be on the —s ; *être dans des transes.*
tenter, *v.a.*, (of cloth—*des draps*) ramer.
tenter, *v.n.*, s'étendre.
tenter-frame, *n.*, (to stretch cloth—*pour étendre les draps*) rame,*f.*
tenter-hook (-houke), *n.*, clou à crochet, *m.*
tentering, *n.*, ramage, *m.*
tenth (tè'n'th), *adj.*, dixième.
tenth (tè'n'th), *n.*, dixième, *m.*; (tithe—*dîme*) dîme; (mus.) dixième,*f.*
tenthly (tè'n'th-), *adv.*, dixièmement.
tenuity (ti-niou-i-), *n.*, ténuité; minceur; (of the air—*de l'air*) raréfaction,*f.*
tenuous (ti-niou-), *adj.*, mince, ténu; (of the air—*de l'air*) rare, raréfié.
tenure (tè'n'ieur), *n.*. mouvance, tenure. *f.*
tepefaction (tèp'i-fak'-), *n.*, action de tiédir, *f.*
tepefy (tèp'i-fa'ye), *v.a.*, rendre tiède; attiédir.
tepefy, *v.n.*, tiédir.
tepid (tèp'-), *adj.*, tiède.
tepidity, *or* **tepidness** (tèp'-), *n.*, tiédeur; tépidité, *f.*
tepor (tî-), *n.*, douce chaleur. *f.*
terce (teurce), *n.*, (cask—*tonneau*) tiers d'une pipe, *m.*
tercel (teur-), *n.*, tiercelet, *m.*
terce-major (teurs'mé-djeur), *n.*, tierce majeure, *f.*
terebinthinate (tèr-i-bi'n'thi-). *or* **terebinthine** (-thine), *adj.*, de térébenthine.
teres-muscle (ti-riz'meus's'l), *n.*, (anat.) muscle grêle. *m.*

tergiversation (teur-dji-vèr-sé-), *n.*, tergiversation ; (fickleness—*inconstance*) inconstance, *f.*

term (teurme), *n.*, (limit—*limite*) terme, *m.*, limite, *f.* ; (time—*temps*) temps ; (math.) terme, *m.* ; (jur.) session ; (in universities—*des universités*) année scolaire, *f.* ; (gram., log., arch.) terme, *m.* —s ; *conditions*, *f.pl.* ; (of women—*des femmes*) menstrues, règles, *f.pl.* To bring to —s ; *soumettre*. To come to —s ; *s'accorder* ; *s'arranger* ; *tomber d'accord* ; *prendre des arrangements*. To be on good —s with ; *être bien avec* ; *être sur un bon pied avec*. To be on ill —s with ; *être mal avec* ; *être brouillé avec*. To be on familiar —s with ; *être sur un pied de familiarité avec*. The lowest — ; (math.) *la plus simple expression*. What are your —s ? *quels sont vos prix ! quelles sont vos conditions !*

term (teurme), *v.a.*, nommer, appeler.

termagancy (teur-), *n.*, turbulence ; disposition acariâtre, *f.*

termagant (teur-), *n.*, mégère, *f.* ; dragon, *m.*

termagant, *adj.*, turbulent ; bruyant ; acariâtre.

termer (teurm'-), *n.*, personne qui tient à terme ; personne qui tient à vie, *f.*

terminable (teur-mi-na-b'l), *adj.*, qui peut être borné, qui peut être limité ; pour un temps limité.

terminal (teur-), *adj.*, extrême ; terminal.

terminate (teur-), *v.a.*, terminer, finir.

terminate, *v.n.*, se terminer, finir ; cesser, s'arrêter.

termination (teur-mi-né-), *n.*, action de limiter ; (limit—*limite*), extrémité ; (end—*fin*) fin, terminaison ; (result—*résultat*) conclusion, *f.* ; résultat ; (last purpose—*but*) but final, *m.* ; (gram.) désinence, terminaison, *f.*

terminational, *adj.*, (gram.) final, terminatif.

terminator (teur-mi-né-teur), *n.*, (astron.) cercle d'illumination, *m.*

terminer, *n.*, (jur.) décision, *f.* ; jugement, *m.*

terminology (-ol'o-dji), *n.*, terminologie, *f.*

terminus (teur-), *n.*, embarcadère, *m.* ; gare de départ, *f.* ; débarcadère, *m.* ; gare d'arrivée, *f.*

termite (teur-), *n.*, (ent.) termès, termite, *m.*

termless, *adj.*, illimité, infini.

termly, *adv.*, chaque session.

termly, *adj.*, (jur.) par session.

terms (teurm'ze), *n.pl.*, conditions, *f.pl.*   V. **term**.

tern (teurne), *n.*, (orni.) sterne, *m.* ; hirondelle de mer, *f.*

ternal (teur-), *adj.*, (bot.) terné.

ternary (teur-), *adj.*, ternaire.

ternary, or **ternate** (teur-), *adj.*, (bot.) terné.

ternion (teur-), *n.*, trois, nombre ternaire, *m.*

terrace (tèr-), *n.*, terrasse, *f.*

terrace (tèr'-), *v.a.*, former en terrasse ; (to open to the light—*amener la lumière dans*) ouvrir au jour.

terra firma (tèr'ra-feur-), *n.*, terre ferme, *f.*

terraqueous (tèr-ré-kwi'-), *adj.*, terraqué.

terrene (tèr-rîne), *adj.*, terrestre.

terreous (tèr-ri-), *adj.*, (ant.) terreux ; de terre.

terre-plein (tèr-plé'n), *n.*, (fort.) terre-plein, *m.*

terrestrial, *adj.*, terrestre.

terrestrially, *adv.*, d'une manière terrestre.

terrible (tèr-ri-b'l), *adj.*, terrible ; redoutable ; formidable ; (severe) terrible, horrible.

terribleness, *n.*, horreur, *f.*

terribly, *adv.*, terriblement ; (greatly—*grandement*) terriblement, horriblement.

terrier (tèr-ri-eur), *n.*, (hole ; dog—*trou* ; *chien*) terrier, *m.* ; (wimble—*tarière*) tarière, *f.* ; cadastre ; terrier, papier terrier, *m.*

---

terrific (tèr'-), *adj.*, affreux, terrible.

terrify (tèr-ri-fa-ye), *v.a.*, terrifier, épouvanter.

territorial, *adj.*, territorial ; (local) limité.

territorially, *adv.*, par territoires.

territory, *n.*, territoire, *m.* ; États, *m.pl.*

terror, *n.*, terreur, *f.* ; effroi, *m.* ; épouvante, *f.* The reign of — ; *la terreur* ; *le règne de la terreur*. He is the — of every one ; *il est la terreur de tout le monde*.

terse (teurse), *adj.*, poli, net, élégant.

tersely, *adv.*, nettement ; élégamment.

terseness, *n.*, netteté ; élégance, *f.*

tertian (teur-sha'n), *adj.*, tiers.

tertian (teur-sha'n), *n.*, fièvre tierce, *f.*

tertiary (teur-shi-a-ri), *adj.*, (geog.) de troisième ordre ; (geol., med.) tertiaire.

tertiate (teur-shi-), *v.a.*, faire une troisième fois.

tessellate (tès-sèl-), *v.a.*, marqueter.

tessellated (tès-sèl-lét'-), *adj.*, marqueté ; en mosaïque ; (bot.) tessellé, en damier.

tessellation (tès-sèl-lé-), *n.*, mosaïque, *f.*

tessera, *n.*, tesselle, *f.*

test, *n.*, épreuve, *f.* ; (standard—*criterium*) criterium ; (characteristic—*caractère*) caractère distinctif, *m.* ; (distinction) distinction, *f.* ; (chem.) réactif ; (cupel—*coupelle*) test. têt ; (hist.) test, *m.* To put to the — ; *mettre à l'épreuve*. To stand the — ; *subir l'épreuve*.

test, *v.a.*, éprouver, faire l'épreuve de ; (metal.) coupeller.

testable (tèst'a-b'l), *adj.*, (jur.) qui peut être légué.

testacea (tès-té-shi-a), *n.pl.*, testacés, *m.pl.*

testaceous (tès-té-sheusse), *adj.*, testacé.

testament, *n.*, testament, *m.*

testamentary, *adj.*, testamentaire ; (given in a testament—*donné par testament*) légué, hérité.

testate, *adj.*, qui a testé.

testator (tès-té-teur), *n.*, testateur, *m.*

testatrix, *n.*, testatrice, *f.*

tester, *n.*, ciel de lit, *m.*

testicle (tès-ti-k'l), *n.*, testicule, *m.*

testiculate, *adj.*, qui ressemble à des testicules.

testification (-fi-ké-), *n.*, témoignage, *m.*

testificator (-ké-teur), *n.*, témoin, *m.*

testifier (-faï-eur), *n.*, témoin, déposant, *m.*

testify (tès-ti-fa'ye), *v.a.*, attester, certifier ; témoigner ; (to publish—*publier*) proclamer ; (jur.) témoigner de.

testify, *v.n.*, rendre témoignage ; (jur.) témoigner, déposer. To — against ; *déposer contre* ; (to protest against—*protester*) protester contre.

testily (tès ti-li), *adv.*, maussadement, d'une manière bourrue.

testimonial (-mô-), *n.*, témoignage ; certificat, *m.* ; attestation, *f.* —s ; *certificats*.

testimony (-mo-), *n.*, (declaration, evidence —*déposition*) témoignage, *m.* ; (proof—*preuve*) preuve, *f.* ; (authority—*autorité*) témoignage, *m.*, autorité, *f.* ; (jur.) témoignage, *m.*, déposition ; (open attestation—*attestation publique*) proclamation ; (the ark—*l'arche*) arche, *f.* ; (tables of the law—*tables de la loi*) tables de la loi, *f.pl.* ; (word of God—*parole de Dieu*) parole de Dieu, *f.* ; (laws of God—*lois de Dieu*) lois de Dieu, *f.pl.* This doctrine is supported by the — of the fathers ; *cette doctrine est soutenue par l'autorité des saints pères*. In — whereof ; *en foi de quoi*.

testiness, *n.*, maussaderie ; humeur bourrue, *f.*

testing, *n.*, épreuve, *f.* ; (metal.) essai, *m.*

test-paper (-pé-peur), *n.*, papier réactif, *m.*

testudinated (-tiou-di-nét'-), *adj.*, en dos de tortue.

testy, *adj.*, bourru ; maussade.

tetanus (tèt'-), *n.*, tétanos, *m.*

tête-a-tête. *n.*, tête-à-tête, *m.*

tether (tèth'-), *n.*, attache, longe ; (fig.) chaine, *f.*

tether (tèth'-), *v.a.*, lier par une longe ; (fig.) enchainer.

tetrachord (tèt'ra-korde), *n.*, tétracorde, *m.*

tetragon (tèt'ra-gone), *n.*, tétragone, *m.*

tetragonal. *adj.*, tétragone, tétragonal.

tetrahedral (-hi-), *adj.*, tétraèdre, tétraédral.

tetrahedron (-hi-dreune), *n.*, tétraèdre, *m.*

tetrandria (ti-), *n.*, tétrandrie, *f.*

tetrandrian, *or* **tetrandrous** (ti-), *adj.*, tétrandre, tétrandrique.

tetrapetalous (tèt'ra-pèt'-), *adj.*, tétrapétale.

tetrarch (ti-trárke), *n.*, tétrarque, *m.*

tetrarchy (tèt'-rar-ki), *or* **tetrarchate** (ti-trárk'-), *n.*, tétrarchie, *f.* ; (office) tétrarchat, *m.*

tetrasepalous (tèt-ra-cèp'-), *adj.*, tétrasépale.

tetrastyle (tèt'ra-staïle), *n.*, (arch.) tétrastyle, *m.*

tetrasyllabic, *adj.*, tétrasyllabique.

tetrasyllable (tèt-ra-cil-la-b'l), *n.*, tétrasyllabe, *m.*

tetter (tèt'-), *n.*, dartre, *f.*

teutonic (tiou-), *adj.*, teutonique.

tewel (tiou-èl), *n.*, tuyère, *f.*

text (tèks'te), *n.*, texte, *m.* ; (handwriting—*écriture*) écriture, *f.* Large — ; *grosse, écriture grosse,* *f.* Middle — ; *écriture moyenne, f.* Small — ; *fine, écriture fine,* *f.*

text-book (-bouke), *n.*, livre de texte ; guide pour les étudiants, *m.*

text-hand, *n.*, grosse ; écriture grosse, *f.*

textile (tèks'tile), *adj.*, textile.

text-man, *n.*, homme habile à citer des textes, *m.*

textorial (-tô-), *or* **textrine**, *adj.*, du tissage.

textual (tèkst'iou-), *adj.*, textuel ; (serving for texts—*qui sert de texte*) servant de texte.

textualist, **textuary**, *or* **textuarist** (tèkst'iou-). *n.*, textuaire, *m.*

textually, *adv.*, textuellement.

textuary, *adj.*, textuel.

textuist, *n.*, personne habile à citer les textes, *m.*

texture (tèkst'ieur), *n.*, tissage ; (stuff—*étoffe,* anat.) tissu, *m.* ; (disposition of the parts of a body—*disposition des parties d'un corps*) texture, contexture, *f.*

thalamus (thal'-), *n.*, (bot.) réceptacle, *m.*

than (tha'n), *conj.*, que ; (between *more* and a number—*entre* more *et un nombre*) de. More — a hundred ; *plus de cent.* Rather — ; *plutôt que.* No other — ; *personne autre que ;* (of things—*des choses*) *rien autre que.*

thane (théne), *n.*, thane, *m.*

thank (tha'n'ke), *v.a.*, remercier ; faire des remerciments à ; rendre grâces à. — God ! *grâce à Dieu ! Dieu merci !* No, I — you ; *je vous remercie ; merci.*

thank, *n.*, remerciment, *m.*

thankful (-foule), *adj.*, reconnaissant.

thankfully, *adv.*, avec reconnaissance.

thankfulness, *n.*, gratitude, reconnaissance, *f.* ; remerciments, *m.pl.*

thankless, *adj.*, ingrat.

thanklessness, *n.*, ingratitude, *f.*

thank-offering, *n.*, sacrifice d'actions de grâces, *m.*

thanks, *n.*, remerciments, *m.pl.* ; grâces, *f.pl.*

thanksgiver (-ghiv'-), *n.*, personne qui rend des actions de grâces, *f.*

thanksgiving (-ghiv'-), *n.*, actions de grâces, *f.pl.* ; remerciments, *m.pl.*

thank-worthy (-weur-*thi*), *adj.*, qui mérite des remerciments.

that (*thate*), demonstrative *pron.* (*those*), ce, ce . . . . là, cet, cet . . . . là, *m.* ; cette, cette . . . . là, *f.* ; celui-là, *m.*, celle-là, *f.* ; cela, ça, le, *m.* I do not like — man ; *je n'aime pas cet homme-là.* This is good ; I prefer — ; *celui-ci est bon ; je préfère celui-là.* On — ; *sur cela ; là-dessus.* By — ; *par cela, par là.* — he, I, &c., will not ! *oh, pour cela non !* You have not seen him ? — I have ; *vous ne l'avez pas vu ? si fait.* What of — ? *qu'est-ce que cela prouve ? qu'est-ce que cela fait ?*

that (*thate*), relative *pron.*, qui, *m.*, *f.* ; lequel, *m.*, laquelle, *f.* ; lesquels. *m.pl.*, lesquelles, *f.pl.* ; (object—*régime direct*) que.

that (*thate*), *conj.*, que, afin que, pour que.

thatch (thatshe), *n.*, chaume, *m.*

thatch (thatshe), *v.a.*, couvrir de chaume.

thatcher, *n.*, couvreur en chaume.

thaumaturgus (thô-ma-teur-), *n.*, thaumaturge, *m.*

thaumaturgy (thô-ma-teur-dji), *n.*, thaumaturgie, *f.*

thaw (thô), *n.*, dégel, *m.*

thaw (thô), *v.a. and n.*, dégeler.

the (thi, *ou* theu), *art.*, le, *m.*, la, *f.* ; les, *pl. m.*, *f.* A, — to — ; *au, m., à la, f. ; aux, pl. m.*, *f.* From — of — ; *du, m., de la, f. ; des, pl. m.*, *f.*

theatine (thi-a-tine), *n.*, théatin, *m.*

theatre (thi-a-teur), *n.*, théâtre, *m.* ; salle de spectacle, *f.* ; spectacle ; (lecture-room—*cours*) amphithéâtre, *m.* To go to the — ; *aller au spectacle.* The — will be closed to-night ; *il y aura relâche ce soir.* The French — ; *le théâtre français.* Minor — ; *petit théâtre.*

theatric, *or* **theatrical** (thi-), *adj.*, théâtral ; scénique.

theatrically, *adv.*, théâtralement.

theatricals (thi-at-ri-calze), *n.pl.*, spectacle, *m.sing.*

thee (*thi*), *pron.*, toi ; te.

theft (thèfte), *n.*, larcin ; vol, *m.*

their (thère), *pron.*, leur, leurs.

theirs (thèr'ze), *pron.*, à eux, *m.pl.*, à elles, *f.pl.* ; le leur, *m.*, la leur, *f.* ; les leurs, *pl. m.f.*

theism (thi-iz'm), *n.*, théisme, *m.*

theist (thi-iste), *n.*, théiste, *m.*

theistic, *or* **theistical** (thi-ist'-), *adj.*, du théisme ; des théistes.

them (*thème*), *pron.*, eux, *m.pl.*, elles, *f.pl.* ; les, *pl.m.f.* To — ; *à eux, à elles ; leur ;* (of things—*des choses*) y, leur. Of, from — ; *d'eux, d'elles ;* en. I have seen — ; *je les ai vus.* I have spoken to — ; *je leur ai parlé.* I have given — three ; *je leur en ai donné trois.*

theme (thime), *n.*, thème, sujet, *m.* ; (in schools—*d'école*) dissertation, thèse, *f.* ; (mus., gram.) thème, *m.*

themselves (thè'm'sèlv'ze), *pron.*, eux-mêmes, *m.pl.*, elles-mêmes, *f.pl.* ; se, *pl. m.,f.* They think — ; *ils se croient.*

then (thè'n), *adv.*, alors, pour lors ; (afterward—*puis*) ensuite, puis ; (in that case—*en ce cas*) alors, dans ce cas ; (in consequence—*alors*) alors, en conséquence. Now — ! *voyons !* What — ? *quoi donc ? et après ?* Now and — ; *de temps en temps.* The — government ; *le gouvernement d'alors.*

then (thè'n), *conj.*, donc.

thence (thè'nce), *adv.*, de là, par là ; (of time de temps) dès lors, depuis lors ; (for that reason —*de là*) par cette raison, de là, partant, c'est pourquoi.

thenceforth (thè'n'ce-forth), *adv.*, dès lors, dès ce moment-là.

thenceforward (thè'n ce-for-worde), adv., depuis lors, dès ce moment.

theocracy (thi-), n., théocratie, f.

theocratic, or **theocratical** (thi-), adj., théocratique.

theodicy (thi-), n., théodicée, f.

theodolite (thi-o.l'o-laïte), n., théodolite, m.

theogony (thi-), n., théogonie, f.

theologian (thi-o-lô-dji-), **theologist** (thi-ol-o-djiste), or **theologue** (thi-o-loghe), n., théologien, m.

theological (thi-o-lo-dj'-), adj., théologique; (theol.) théologal.

theologically, adv., théologiquement.

theology (thi-ol'-o-dji), n., théologie, f.

theorbo (thi-or-bô), n., téorbe, théorbe, tuorbe, m.

theorem (thi-o-rè'm), n., théorème, m.

theoretic, or **theoretical** (thi-o-rèt'-), adj., théorique ; spéculatif.

theoretically, adv., théoriquement ; d'une manière spéculative.

theorist (thi-o-), or **theorizer** (-raïz'eur), n., théoricien, m.

theorize (thi-o-raïze), v.n., faire des théories.

theory (thi-), n., théorie, f.

theosophist (thi-oss'-), n., théosophe, m.

theosophy (thi-oss'-), n., théosophie, f.

therapeutæ (thi-ra-piou-tî), or **therapeutics** (thi-ra-piou-), n.pl., thérapeutes, m.pl.

therapeutic (thir'a-piou-), adj., thérapeutique.

therapeutics (thir'a-piou-), n.pl., thérapeutique, f. sing.

there (thère), adv., là, y. Here and — ; çà et là. — he is ! le voilà ! — they are ! les voilà ! — is, — are; il y a. Down — ; là-bas. Off —; de là. In — ; là dedans. On — ; là-dessus. Over — ; là-bas. Under — ; là-dessous. Up —; là-haut. — I have him ; c'est par là que je le tiens.

thereabout (thèr'abaoute), or **thereabouts** (-baoutse), adv., par-là ; à peu près là ; (nearly—environ) à peu près, environ.

thereafter (thèr'âf-), adv., ensuite ; là-dessus, après cela.

thereat (thèr'-), adv., par là ; à cet endroit; (at that—à cela) à cela, à ce sujet.

thereby (thèr-ba'ye), adv., par là ; par ce moyen.

therefore (thèr'-), adv., c'est pourquoi, aussi ; (consequently—donc) donc, par conséquent, ainsi.

therefrom (thèr'-), adv., de là.

therein (thèr'i'n), adv., là dedans ; en cela.

thereinto (thèr'i'n'tou), adv., là dedans, en cela.

thereof (thèr'ove), adv., de cela, en.

thereon (thèr'-), adv., là-dessus. sur cela.

thereout (thèr'aoute). adv., de là.

thereto (thèr tou), or **thereunto** (-eu'n'tou), adv., à cela ; à quoi.

thereupon (thèr'eup'-), adv., là-dessus, sur cela, sur ce.

therewith (thèr'with), adv., avec cela.

theriac, or **theriaca** (thi-). n., thériaque, f.

theriacal (thi-), adj., thériacal.

thermæ (theur-mî), n.pl., thermes, m.pl.

thermal, or **thermic** (theur-), adj., thermal.

thermometer (thèr-mo'm'i-), n., thermomètre, m.

thermometer-gauge (-ghédje), n., thermo-manomètre, m.

thermometrical. adj., thermométrique.

thermometrically, adv., au moyen d'un thermomètre.

thermoscope (theur-mo-scôpe), n., thermoscope, m.

thermostat (theur-mo-state), n., thermo-rhéostat, m.

these (thize), pron., ces, ces . . . . ci, pl. m., f. ; ceux-ci, m.pl., celles-ci, f.pl.

thesis (thi-cice), n., thèse, f.

theurgic, or **theurgical** (thi-eur-dj'-), adj., théurgique.

theurgy (thi-eur-dji), n., théurgie. f.

thaw (thiou), n., (ant.) nerf, m.; force musculaire, f.

they (thê), pron., ils, m.pl., elles, f.pl. ; (followed by a relative—devant un pron. relatif) ceux, m.pl., celles, f.pl. ; (standing alone—sans verbe) eux, m.pl., elles, f.pl. ; (people—indéfini) on.

thick (thick), adj., épais ; gros ; (turbid—trouble) trouble ; (close—serré) dru, serré ; (frequent) fréquent, nombreux ; (paint.) gras, épais ; (of the pronunciation—de la prononciation) gras ; of hearing—de l'ouïe) dur; (of shot—de balles, &c.) dru; (intimate—intime) intime ; (dull—inintelligent) lourd.

thick (thick), n., partie la plus épaisse, f. ; fort, m.

thick, adv., épais ; (fast—serré) dru ; (closely—serré) épais, dru ; (deeply—profondément) profondément. To speak — ; parler gras.

thicken (thik'k'n), v.a., épaissir ; (to make more numerous—rendre plus nombreux) grossir, épaissir ; (to make close—serrer) serrer, resserrer.

thicken (thik'k'n), v.n., épaissir, s'épaissir ; se grossir ; (to become obscure—devenir obscur) s'obscurcir; (to become close—se serrer) se serrer, se resserrer ; (to become animated—s'animer) s'animer, s'échauffer ; (to be crowded—s'encombrer) se presser.

thickening, n., épaississement, m.

thicket, n., bosquet; fourré ; buisson, bouquet d'arbres; hallier, m.

thick-headed (-hèd'ède), adj., lourd.

thickish, adj., un peu épais ; un peu gros; un peu trouble ; un peu dru, un peu serré.

thickly, adv., d'une manière épaisse ; (in quick succession—rapidement) dru ; (deeply—profondément) profondément.

thickness, n., épaisseur ; (consistence) consistance, f., épaississement; (closeness of the parts—proximité des parties) état serré, état dru. m.

thick-set, adj., épais, serré ; (pers.) trapu.

thick-skinned, adj., à peau dure.

thick-skull (-skeul), n., balourd, m.

thief (thif), n., voleur, m., voleuse, f. ; auteur de vol ; (in Scripture—biblique) larron ; (in a candle—de chandelle) champignon, m. Stop—; au voleur !

thief-catcher, or **thief-taker**, n., preneur de voleurs, m.

thieve (thi've), v.n., voler.

thievery, n., vol, m.

thievish, adj., adonné au vol ; de voleur.

thievishly, adv., en voleur ; par le vol.

thievishness, n., penchant au vol, m.; habitude du vol, f.

thigh (tha'ye), n., cuisse; (of a horse—du cheval) jambe, f. — -bone; fémur; os de la cuisse, m.

thill (thill), n., limon, timon, m. — horse; limonier, m.

thimble (thi'm'b'l), n., dé, m. ; (nav.) cosse, f.

thin (thi'n), adj., mince; (lean—maigre) maigre ; (slender—svelte) mince, délié; (not crowded—peu nombreux) peu nombreux ; (slight—léger) léger, mince; (of liquids—des liquides) clair ; (of animals—des animaux) maigre, efflanqué ; (of the air—de l'air) rare ; (of trees, plants, hair—des arbres, des plantes, des cheveux) clairsemé, rare. To grow — ; maigrir. To make —; amaigrir.

thin, adv., d'une manière éparse ; clair.

thin, *v.a.,* éclaircir; (to rarefy—*raréfier*) raréfier.

thine (thaïne), *pron.,* le tien, *m..* la tienne, *f.*; les tiens, *m.pl.,* les tiennes, *f.pl.*; à toi.

thing (thigne), *n.,* chose, *f.*; objet, *m.*; affaire; (event—*événement*) affaire, chose, *f.*; (creature) être, *m.,* créature; (animal) créature, bête; (trash—*chose sans valeur*) drogue, *f.* —s; choses, affaires, *f.pl.,* effets, *m.*; (clothes—*hardes*) affaires, *f.pl.,* habits, effets, *m.pl.* It is a bad — for her; *c'est une mauvaise affaire pour elle; c'est une chose bien pénible pour elle.* No such —; *point du tout.* That is quite another —; *c'est tout autre chose; c'est une autre paire de manches.* Not to do an earthly —; *ne faire œuvre de ses dix doigts.* Any —; *quelque chose; quoi que ce soit.* Not any —; *rien.* Any —but; *rien moins que; tout excepté.* A — of a ...; *un mauvais ....; une dérision de ....* What a — of a hat it was you sold me! *quel mauvais chapeau vous m'avez vendu!* Mr. —-a-bob; *Monsieur chose.* Poor —! *pauvre femme! pauvre enfant! pauvre bête! &c.*

think (thi'n'ke), *v.n.* (preterit and past part., Thought), penser; (to fancy—*s'imaginer*) croire, penser; (to believe—*croire*) croire; (to judge—*juger*) juger, trouver. To — of; *penser à, songer à, réfléchir à;* (to light on—*s'aviser*) *s'aviser de;* (to intend—*compter*) *avoir l'intention de.* To — to; *avoir l'intention de.*

think, *v.a.,* penser; (to believe—*croire*) croire, penser, juger. To — ill of, well of; *avoir une mauvaise opinion de, une bonne opinion de; penser du mal de, du bien de.* What do you — of him? *Que pensez-vous de lui?*

thinker, *n.,* penseur, *m.*

thinking, *n.,* pensée, *f.*; jugement, avis, sens, *m.* In my —; *à mon avis.*

thinking, *adj.,* pensant.

thinly (thi'n'-), *adv.,* faiblement; peu; légèrement.

thinness (thi'n'-), *n.,* minceur; (tenuity—*ténuité*) ténuité; (fluidity—*fluidité*) fluidité; (paucity—*rareté*) rareté; (leanness—*maigreur*) maigreur; (exility—*finesse*) finesse, *f.,* état délié, *m.*

thin-sown (-sō'n), *adj.,* clairsemé.

third (theurde), *adj.,* troisième; tiers.

third, *n.,* tiers, *m.*; (mus.) tierce, *f.*

thirdly, *adv.,* troisièmement.

thirst (theurste), *n.,* soif; altération, *f.* — for; *soif de.*

thirst, *v.n.,* avoir soif de, être altéré de.

thirster, *n.,* personne qui a soif, *f.*

thirstily, *adv.,* avidement.

thirstiness, *n.,* soif; altération, *f.*

thirsty, *adj.,* qui a soif; altéré. To be —; *avoir soif.*

thirteen (theur-ti'n), *adj.,* treize.

thirteenth (theur-ti'n'th), *adj.* and *n.*; treizième; (mus.) treizième, *f.*

thirtieth (theur-tièth), *n.* and *adj.,* trentième.

thirty (theur-ti), *adj.,* trente.

this (thiss), *pron.* (these), ce; ce .... ci; cet; cet .... ci, *m.*; cette; cette .... ci, *f.*; celui-ci, *m.,* celle-ci, *f.*; ceci, *m.* — is one which; *en voici un qui.*

thistle (this's'l), *n.,* (bot.) chardon, *m.*

thistly (this's'li), *adv.,* plein de chardons.

thither (thith'eur), *adv.,* là; y; (to that end—*dans ce but*) dans ce but.

thitherward (thith'eur-worde), *adv.,* vers ce lieu.

thlaspi (thlas-), *n.,* (bot.) thlaspi, *m.*

thole (thōle), *n.,* (nav.) tolet, *m.*; (of a scythe —de faux) poignée, *f.*

thoug (thon'g), *n.,* sangle, courroie, *f.*; (of a whip—*d'un fouet*) fouet, *m.*

thoracic (tho-), *adj.,* thoracique, ☉thoracique.

thorax (thō-), *n.,* thorax, *m.*

thorn (thorne), *n.,* (bot.) épine; (prickle—*piquant*) épine, *f.,* piquant, *m.*; (anything troublesome—*difficulté*) épine, *f.,* souci, *m.*; (in Scripture—*biblique*) écharde, épine, *f.* To be upon —s; *être sur des épines.* To run a — into one's finger; *s'enfoncer une épine dans le doigt.*

thorn-apple (-ap'p'l), *n.,* pomme épineuse, *f.*

thorn-back, *n.,* raie bouclée, *f.*

thorn-bush (-boushe), *n.,* buisson épineux, *m.*

thornless, *adj.,* sans épines.

thorny, *adj.,* épineux; pénible.

thorough (theur'rō), *adj.,* (complete) entier, complet; (perfect—*parfait*) achevé, parfait; (b. s.) franc, fieffé; (passing through—*passant*) qui traverse.

thorough (theur'rō), *n.,* pertuis, *m.*

thorough-bass (-béce), *m.,* basse continue, *f.*

thorough-bred (-brède), *adj.,* pur sang, de pur sang.

thoroughfare, *n.,* lieu de passage, chemin passant, passage, *m.* Great —; *rue très passante, f., chemin très passant, m.* No —; *on ne passe pas.*

thoroughly (theur'rō-li), *adv.,* entièrement; complètement; à fond, parfaitement.

thorough-paced (-pés'te), *adj.,* achevé, franc, fieffé.

thorough-pin, *n.,* (vet.) vessigon, *m.*

thorough-wax, *n.,* (bot.) buplèvre à feuilles rondes, *m.*

those (thôze), *pron.,* ces; ces .... là, pl.m., *f.*; ceux, *m.pl.,* celles, *f.pl.*; ceux-là, *m.pl.,* celles-là, *f.pl.*

thou (thaou), *pron.,* tu; toi.

thou (thaou), *v.a.* and *n.,* tutoyer.

though (thô), *conj.,* quoique, bien que; cependant. As —; *comme si.* Even —; *quand, quand même.*

thought (thô-te), *n.,* pensée; (idea—*idée*) idée; (opinion) pensée, opinion, façon de penser, *f.,* sentiment, *m.*; (care—*souci*) inquiétude, *f.* To read any one's —s; *lire dans la pensée de quelqu'un.* A — better; *un peu mieux.*

thoughtful (thôt'fou*le*), *adj.,* pensif; rêveur; méditatif; (anxious—*soucieux*) inquiet; kind—*prévenant*) attentif, prévenant; (favourable to meditation—*favorable à la méditation*) favorable à la méditation. — of; *qui pense à; attentif à; occupé de.*

thoughtfully, *adv.,* d'une manière pensive; (with solicitude—*avec sollicitude*) avec sollicitude, avec prévenance.

thoughtfulness, *n.,* méditation profonde, *f.*; recueillement, *m.*; (solicitude) sollicitude, prévenance; (anxiety—*souci*) anxiété, *f.*

thoughtless (thôt'-), *adj.,* irréfléchi; insouciant; étourdi, léger; (stupid—*bête*) stupide.

thoughtlessly, *adv.,* avec insouciance; avec étourderie; étourdiment; (stupidly—*bêtement*) stupidement.

thoughtlessness, *n.,* insouciance; légèreté, étourderie, *f.*

thoughtsick (thôt'-), *adj.,* (ant.) attristé par la pensée.

thousand (thaou-za'n'd), *n.,* mille; millier, *m.*

thousand, *adj.,* mille; (date) mil.

thousandth (thaou-za'n'dth), *n.* and *adj.,* millième.

thraldom (thrōl-deume), *n.,* esclavage, asservissement, *m.*

thrall (thrōl), *n.,* esclave, *m., f.*

thrash (thrashe), *v.a.,* battre, rosser, étriller; (wheat, walnuts—*blé, noyers*) battre.

thrash (thrash), *v.n.,* battre en grange.

thrasher, *n.,* batteur en grange, *m.*

thrashing, *n.,* rossée, roulée, raclée, *f.*; (of wheat—*du blé*) battage, *m.*

thrashing-floor, *n.,* aire, *f.*

thrashing-machine (-ma-shine), *n.,* machine à battre, *f.*

thread (thrède), *n.*, fil ; (of flowers, of a screw —*de fleurs, de vis*) filet ; (of plants—*des plantes*) filament, *m.*, fibre ; (of a skein—*d'un écheveau*) sentène, *f.* ; (fig.) fil, *m.* Air--s ; *fils de la Vierge, m.pl.*

thread (thrède), *v.a.*, enfiler; (to pass through *enfiler*) traverser, enfiler.

threadbare, *adj.*, qui montre la corde, usé ; râpé ; (fig.) usé, épuisé.

threadbareness, *n.*, état de ce qui est usé ; (fig.) état usé, état épuisé, *m.*

thread-shaped (-shép'te), *adj.*, (bot.) filiforme.

thready (thrèdi), *adj.*, contenant du fil; (filamentous—*filamenteux*) filamenteux.

threat (thrète), *n.*, menace, *f.*

threaten (thrèt't'n), *v.a.*, menacer ; faire des menaces à.

threatener, *n.*, personne qui menace, *f.*

threatening (thrèt't'n'igne), *n.*, menace, *f.*

threatening, *adj.*, menaçant ; de menaces.

threateningly, *adv.*, avec menace ; d'une manière menaçante.

threatful (thrèt'foule), *adj.*, menaçant.

three (thri), *adj.*, trois. Rule of — ; *règle de trois, f.*

three, *n.*, trois, *m.*

three-capsuled (-cap-sioul'de), *adj.*, tricapsulaire.

three-celled (-cèl'de), *adj.*, (bot.) triloculaire.

three-cleft, *adj.*, (bot.) trifide.

three-cornered (-cor-neurde), *adj.*, à trois cornes.

three-edged (-èdj'de), *adj.*, triangulaire.

three-flowered (-fla'weurde), *adj.*, (bot.) triflore.

threefold (-fôlde), *adj.*, triple.

three-headed (-hèd'-), *adj.*, à trois têtes ; (bot.) tricéphale.

three-lobed (-lob'de), *adj.*, (bot.) trilobé.

threepence, *n.pl.*, trente centimes, *m.pl.*

threepenny, *adj.*, de trente centimes.

threescore (-scôre), *adj.*, soixante.

three-valved (-valv'de), *adj.*, (bot.) trivalve.

thresh. *V.* **thrash.**

threshold (thrèsh'ôlde), *n.*, seuil de porte ; (fig.) début, *m.*

thrice (thraïce), *adv.*, trois fois.

thrift (thrif'te), *n.*, (gain) gain, profit, *m.* ; (prosperity—*richesse*) prospérité, richesse ; (frugality—*économie*) frugalité, épargne, *f.* ; (bot.) gazon d'Olympe, *m.*, statice, *f.*

thriftily, *adv.*, avec épargne, avec économie ; (prosperously—*en prospérité*) avec prospérité.

thriftiness. *n.*, épargne; économie, frugalité; prospérité—*richesse*) prospérité, richesse, *f.*

thriftless, *adj.*, dépensier, prodigue.

thriftlessly, *adv.*, sans profit, sans avantage.

thriftlessness, *n.*, manque de frugalité, *m.*

thrifty, *adj.*, ménager, frugal, économe ; (prosperous—*prospère*) prospère ; (thriving—*croissant*) qui croît rapidement.

thrill (thril), *v.a.*, percer ; pénétrer.

thrill, *v.n.*, pénétrer ; (to shiver—*frissonner*) frémir.

thrill (thril), *n.*, frémissement, tressaillement, *m.*

thrilling, *adj.*, saisissant, pénétrant ; (of cries—*cris*) perçant.

thrive (thraïve), *v.n.* (preterit, Throve ; past part., Thriven), prospérer, réussir ; (of things, of animals—*des choses, des animaux*) prospérer, croître, grandir, se développer.

thriver (thraïv'-), *n.*, personne qui prospère, *f.*

thriving (thraïv'-), *n.*, prospère, florissant.

thrivingly (thraïv'-), *adv.*, d'une manière prospère; heureusement, avec succès.

thrivingness (thraïv'-), *n.*, prospérité, *f.* ;

état florissant, succès ; (growth—*augmentation*) accroissement, *m.*

throat (thrôte), *n.*, gorge, *f.* ; gosier ; (of a chimney—*de cheminée de forge*) gueulard ; (of an anchor—*d'ancre*) diamant, *m.* ; (bot.) gorge ; (entrance—*entrée*) entrée, voie, *f.* To cut one's — ; *se couper la gorge.*

throat-band (-ba'n'de), *n.*, sous-gorge, *f.*

throat-pipe (-païpe), *n.*, trachée-artère, *f.* ; larynx, *m.*

throatwort (-weurte), *n.*, (bot.) campanule gantelée, *f.*

throb (throbe), *v.n.*, battre ; palpiter.

throbbing. *n.*, battement, *m.* ; palpitation, *f.* ; (of the pulse—*du pouls*) battement, *m.*, pulsation, *f.*

throe (thrô), *n.*, douleur de l'enfantement ; angoisse, torture, agonie, *f.*

throe, *v.a.*, causer de grandes douleurs.

throe, *v.n.*, souffrir cruellement.

throne (thrône), *n.*, trône, *m.*

throne, *v.a.*, placer sur un trône ; (a bishop —*un évêque*) introniser.

throne-room (-roume), *n.*, salle du trône, *f.*

throng (thron'gn), *v.n.*, accourir en foule, affluer.

throng, *v.a.*, fouler, remplir, encombrer.

throng (thron'gn), *n.*, foule, multitude, *f.*

thronging (thron'gn'ghigne), *n.*, action de se serrer en foule; foule, *f.*

throstle (thros's'l), *n.*, (orni.) grive commune, *f.* ; (in cotton spinning—*filature du coton*) métier continu, *m.*

throstle-frame, *n.*, métier continu, *m.*

throstle-twist, *n.*, chaîne filée, *f.*

throstling, *n.*, (vet.) gonflement de la gorge, *m.*

throttle (throt't'l), *v.a.*, étrangler ; étouffer, suffoquer.

throttle, *v.n.*, étouffer ; suffoquer.

throttle (throt't'l), *n.*, trachée-artère, *f.* ; larynx, *m.*

throttle-valve, *n.*, registre de vapeur, *m.*

through (throu), *prep.*, à travers de ; (passage, means of conveyance—*moyens de transport*) par; (over the whole extent—*sur toute l'étendue*) d'un bout à l'autre ; (noting passage among—*passage parmi*) dans. To pass — a gate; *passer par une porte.*

through, *adv.*, d'outre en outre ; de part en part; (from beginning to end—*du commencement à la fin*) d'un bout à l'autre ; (to the end—*jusqu'au bout*) jusqu'à la fin, à bonne fin. To carry a project —; *mener un projet à bonne fin.*

throughout, *prep.* (throu-aoute), *prep.* and *adv.*, d'un bout à l'autre; partout.

throw (thrô). *v.a.* (preterit, Threw ; past part., Thrown), jeter; lancer ; (to prostrate—*terrasser*) jeter, renverser, terrasser ; (to send—*lancer*) lancer ; (silk—*la soie*) organsiner ; (at dice—*aux dés*) jeter ; (a horseman—*un cavalier*) démonter, désarçonner ; (of serpents, &c.—*des serpents, &c.*) jeter, se dépouiller de; (at dice—*aux dés*) mettre au jeu. To — at ; *jeter à, contre ; lancer à, contre.* To — aside ; *jeter de côté.* To — away ; *jeter, rejeter ;* (to lose—*perdre*) *perdre ;* (to waste—*gaspiller*) *gaspiller, jeter ;* (one's life—*la vie*) *prodiguer.* To — down ; *jeter en bas ; abattre ; renverser ;* (pers.) *renverser, terrasser.* To — down on ; *jeter sur.* To — in ; *jeter dedans :* (to give in—*donner en sus*) *donner par-dessus le marché.* To — off ; *chasser, se défaire de :* (garments—*vêtements*) *ôter.* To — out ; *jeter dehors ; chasser,* (to utter carelessly—*prononcer sans soin*) *parler mal ;* (to insinuate—*insinuer*) *insinuer,* (to distance—*devancer*) *distancer, devancer :* (to reject—*rejeter*) *rejeter ;* (to emit—*émettre*) *jeter.* To — up ; *jeter en haut, jeter en l'air ;* (to resign—*donner sa démission*) *se démettre de ;* (to

vomit--*romir*) *romir. rejeter*. To- on 's self
on ; *se jeter s.ir*; (to appeal to—*en appeler à*) en
appeler à; (to repose on—se reposer sur) se re-
poser sur. To — one's self on the ground; *se jeter
par terre.*

throw (thrô), *n.*, jet; coup, *m.*; (fig.) saillie,
f.; élan, m.

thrower, *n..* personne qui jette, qui lance,
*f. : (*of silk—*de la soie*) organsineur, *m.*

throwing, *n.*, jet; (of silk—*de la soie*) organ-
si.iage. *m.*

throwing-mill, *n.*, moulin à organsiner, *m.*

throwster (thrôs-), *n.*, organsineur, *m.*

thrum (threume), *n..* bout de fil, *m.*; grosse
fi.iure : (gard.) étamine, *f.*

thrum (threume), *v.a.,* tisser ; franger; (a
sail—*une voile*) larder.

thrum, *v.n.,* jouer mal, tapoter ; (on a fiddle
— *du violon*) racler.

thrush (threushe), *n.*, grive; (vet.) teigne,
*f. ; (*med.) aphte, *m.*

thrust (threuste), *v.a. (preterit* and *past
part.,* Thrust), pousser ; fourrer; serrer, presser.
To — away, back ; *repousser ;* (to reject—*repousser*) rejeter, écarter. To — down; *pousser en bas;
jeter dans*. To — in ; *pousser dedans ; fourrer ;
introduire de force.* To — into: *jeter dans ; forcer
à*. To — on; *pousser en avant ;* (to urge—*presser*) pousser, exciter. To — out; *pousser dehors,
mettre dehors*. To — under; *pousser sous, mettre
sous, passer sous*. To — one's self; *se fourrer.*

thrust, *v.n.,* pousser; (fenc.) pousser une
botte ; (to push on—*se presser*) se presser; (to
squeeze in—*se fourrer*) se fourrer. To — at; *se
jeter sur*. To — in; *s'introduire de force.*

thrust (threuste), *n.*, coup ;(assault—*attaque)*
assaut, *m.,* attaque, *f.*; (fenc.) coup, *m.,* botte ;
(arch.) poussée, *f.* Home— ; *coup qui porte ;*
(fenc.) *coup de fond.*

thruster, *n.*, personne qui pousse, *f.*

thuja (thiou-dja), *or* **thuya** (thiou-), *n.,*
thuia, thuya, *m.*

thumb (theume), *n.,* pouce, *m.* Tom —;
Tom Pouce, petit Poucet, m. — —stall; *poucier, m.*

thumb, *v.a.,* manier gauchement ; (to soil—
salir) salir. To —over (a tune—*un air*) ; *écorcher.*

thumb (theume), *v n.,* tambouriner avec les
doigts.

thump (theu'm'pe), *v.a.,* donner de grands
coups à ; frapper lourdement, cogner.

thump, *v.n..* frapper fort.

thump (theu'm'pe), *n.*, grand coup, *m.*;
bourrade, taloche, *f.*

thumper, *n.,* personne qui donne de grands
coups ; chose qui donne de grands coups, *f.*

thumping, *adj.,* gros, énorme; (heavy—
pesant) lourd.

thunder (theu'n'-), *n..* tonnerre, *m.* ; foudre, *f.*

thunder, *r.n.,* tonner ; (fig.) gronder, retentir, fulminer. It —s : *il tonne.*

thunder (theu'n'-), *v.a.,* faire tonner: fulminer.

thunder-bolt (-bôlte), *n..* foudre, *f.*;
(daring person—*audacieux*) foudre. *m.*; (fulmination) fulmination, *f.*

thunder-clap, *n.*, coup de tonnerre. éclat
de tonnerre, *m.*

thunder-cloud (-claoude), *n.,* nuage chargé
d'électricité, *m.*

thunderer, *n..* être qui lance le tonnerre, *m.*

thundering, *adj.,* tonnant. foudroyant.

thundering, *n..* tonnerre, *m.*

thunderingly, *adv.,* avec un bruit de
tonnerre

thunder-rod, *n..* paratonnerre. *m.*

thunder-shower (-sha-weur). *n.*, pluie
d'orage. *f.*

thunder-stone (-stône), *n.,* aérolithe. *m..*
météorite, *f.*; (l.u.) météorolithe. *m.*

thunder-storm, *n.,* tempête. *f.,* orage accompagné de tonnerre, *m.*

thunder-strike (-straïke), *v.a. (preterit*
and *past part..* Thunder-struck), foudroyer ;
frapper de la foudre; (fig.) foudroyer, atterrer.

thunder-struck (-streuke), *adj.,* foudroyé,
atterré, anéanti.

thuriferous (thiou-rif'èr'-), *adj.,* thurifère.

thurification (thiou-ri-fi-ké'), *n.,* encensement, *m.*

thursday (theurz'-), *n..* jeudi. *m.*

thus (*theuss*), *adv.,* ainsi. — far: *jusqu'ici.*

thwack (thwake), *n.,* coup, *m.* : taloche. *f.*

thwack (thwake), *v.a.,* frapper, rosser,
étriller.

thwart (thwôrte), *v.a.,* traverser, croiser;
(fig.) contrarier, traverser, contrecarrer.

thwart (thworte), *n.,* banc des rameurs, *m.*

thwarting. (thwôrt'-), *adj.,* contrariant.

thwartingly, *adv.,* d'une manière contrariante.

thwartness, *n.,* esprit d'opposition, de
contrariété, de contradiction. *m.*

thy (tha'ye), *adj.,* ton, *m..* ta, *f.*; tes, *pl.m.,f.*

thyme (taï'm), *n.,* thym, *m.* Wild—;
serpolet ; thym sauvage, m.

thymy (taï'mi), *adj.,* qui a l'odeur du thym;
odoriférant.

thyrse (theurse), *or* **thyrsus** (theur-ceuss),
n., (antiq., bot.) thyrse, *m.*

thyself (*tha'ye'-*), *pron.,* toi-même; te.

tiar (taï-), *or* **tiara** (taï-é-), *n.,* tiare, *f.*;
trirègne, *m.*

tibia, *n.,* tibia, os de la jambe, *m.*

tibial, *adj.,* de flûte ; (anat.) tibial.

tic douloureux (-dou-lou-rou), *n.,* tic douloureux, *m.*

tick, *n.,* (for beds—*de literie)* toile à matelas,
f., coutil ; (credit) crédit; (ent.) acarus, *m.,*
tique, *f.*

tick, *v.n..* prendre à crédit; (to give on
credit—*donner à crédit)* faire crédit ; faire tic
tac, battre.

ticket, *n.,* (com.) marque, étiquette, *f.*;
(thea., lottery. &c.—*de loterie, §c.)* billet ; (small
card—*contremarque)* cachet, *m.*

ticket. *v.a.,* (com.) marquer, étiqueter.

ticking, *n.,* tic tac, battement ; (for beds—*de
literie)* coutil, *m.,* toile à matelas, *f.*

tickle (tik'k'l), *v.a.,* chatouiller; (to please—
plaire) plaire à.

tickle, *v.n.,* éprouver un chatouillement.

tickler, *n.,* personne qui chatouille, *f.*; flatteur. *m.*

tickling, *n.,* chatouillement, *m.*

ticklish. *adj.,* chatouilleux ; (critical—
scabreux) critique, délicat, difficile ; (tottering—
ébranlé) chancelant.

ticklishly, *adv.,* d'une manière critique,
d'une manière délicate.

ticklishness. *n.,* état de ce qui est chatouilleux ; état critique, état difficile ; état chancelant. *m.*

ticktack, *n.,* tic tac; (l.u.) trictrac, *m.* *f.*
tricktrack.

tid, *a l).,* délicat ; friand.

tidbit, *or* **titbit,** *n.,* morceau friand, bon
morceau, *m.*

tide (taïde), *n.,* marée, *f.*; flux et reflux;
(course) cours, courant; (among miners—*parmi les mineurs)* poste de travail de douze heures;
(fig.) fort, *m.,* plénitude, *f.*; flux, *m.*

tide (taïde), *v.a.,* entraîner par le courant.

tide. *v.n.,* aller avec la marée.

tide-gate (-ghéte),.*n..* écluse à marée montante. *f.*; goulet à forte marée, *m.*

tide-gauge (-ghédje), *n.,* échelle de marée, *f.*

tide-mill, *n.,* moulin à marée, *m.*; roue à
flux et reflux, *f.*

tides-man (taïd'z'-), *or* **tide-waiter.** *n.,*

douanier placé à bord des vaisseaux marchands *m.*

tide-surveyor, *n.*, chef des préposés de la douane, *m.*

tide-waiter, *n. V.* **tides-man.**

tidily (taïd'-), *adv.*, proprement; en bon ordre.

tidiness (taïd'-), *n.*, propreté, netteté, *f.*

tidings (taïdïn'ze), *n.pl.*, nouvelles, *f.pl.*

tidy (taïd'-), *adj.*, bien arrangé, propre, net.

tie (ta'ye), *v.a.*, (to bind—*lier*) attacher, lier; (mus.) couler, lier; (an artery—*une artère*) lier; (ribbons, &c.—*rubans, &c.*) nouer; (a knot—*nœud*) lier, serrer; (fig.) lier, attacher, enchaîner. To — down; *lier;* (fig.) lier, enchaîner, astreindre. To — in; *attacher; serrer*. To — up; *lier, attacher;* (an artery—*une artère*) lier; (animal) *mettre à l'attache.*

tie, *v.n.*, s'attacher; se lier.

tie (ta'ye), *n.*, lien, *m.*; attache, *f.*; (of hair, knot—*des cheveux, nœud*) nœud; (of a shoe—*de soulier*) cordon, *m.*; (mus.) barre de jonction; (cravat) cravate, *f.*; (fig.) lien, *m.*

tie-beam (-bî'm), *n.*, entrait; tirant, *m.*

tier (tïre), *n.*, rangée, *f.*; gradin, rang; (thea.) rang, *m.*; (of guns—*de canons*) batterie, *f.*; (cable) rang, *m.*

tierce (tîrse, *ou* teurce), *n.*, tierce, *f.*

tiercelet (tîrs'-), *n.*, tiercelet, *m.*

tierceron (tîrs'-), *n.*, (arch.) tierceron, *m.*

tiercet (tîr-sète), *n.*, tercet, *m.*

tie-rod (ta'ye-rode), *n.*, tirant, *m.*

tiff, *n.*, pique, querelle, *f.*; (of liquor—*boisson*) petit coup, *m.* To be in a —; *être fâché, piqué; bisquer.*

tiff, *v.n.*, se piquer, se fâcher, bisquer.

tiffany, *n.*, gaze de soie, *f.*

tige (tïdje), *n.*, tige, *f.*; fût, *m.*

tiger (taï-gheur), *n.*, tigre, *m.*

tigerish (taï-gheur'-), *adj.*, de tigre.

tight (taïte), *adj.*, serré; (parsimonious—*parcimonieux*) serré, parcimonieux; (not admitting much air—*qui n'admet pas l'air*) clos, fermé; (not leaky—*impénétrable aux liquides*) étanche; (not slack—*tendu*) raide, tendu; (well closed—*bien clos*) bien fermé; (phys.) imperméable; (of clothes—*des vêtements*) étroit, serré.

tighten (taï-t'n), *v.a.*, serrer; tendre; (fig.) resserrer.

tightly (taït'-), *adv.*, d'une manière serrée; raide, tendue; étroitement.

tightness (taït'-), *n.*, tension; parcimonie, *f.*; état de ce qui est bien fermé; état étanche, état serré, *m.*; (phys.) raideur; imperméabilité; (of clothes—*des vêtements*) étroitesse, *f.*

tigress (taï-), *n.*, tigresse, *f.*

tile (taïle), *n.*, tuile, *f.*

tile (taïle), *v.a.*, couvrir de tuiles.

tile-field (-fîlde), *n.*, tuilerie, *f.*

tile-kiln, *n.*, four à tuiles, *m.*

tile-maker (-mék'-), *n.*, tuilier, *m.*

tiler (taïl'-), *n.*, couvreur en tuiles, *m.*

tiling (taïl'-), *n.*, action de couvrir en tuiles, *f.*; (roof—*toit*) toit couvert en tuiles, *m.*; (tiles —*tuiles*) tuiles, *f.pl.*

till, *prep.*, jusqu'à; jusques à; (before a verb —*devant un verbe*) jusqu'à ce que.

till, *v.a.*, labourer, cultiver.

till, *n.*, tiroir de comptoir, *m.*; petite caisse, *f.*

tillable (til'a-b'l), *adj.*, labourable, arable.

tillage (til'édje), *n.*, labourage, *m.*; culture, *f.*

tiller, *n.*, laboureur; cultivateur, *m.*; (of a rudder—*de gouvernail*) barre du gouvernail, *f.*; (sprout—*scion*) bourgeon, scion, *m.*

tiller, *v.n.*, pousser des scions, bourgeonner.

tillering, *n.*, pousse des scions, des bourgeons, *f.*

tilling, *n.*, labourage, *m.*

tilt, *n.*, (awning, tent—*tente*) tente; (of a cart, a boat—*de charrette, de bateau*) bâche, *f.*;

(thrust—*coup*) coup, *m.*; (ant.) joûte, *f.*; (hammer—*marteau*) martinet de forge, *m.*

tilt, *v.a.*, (to incline—*pencher*) incliner, pencher; (to thrust—*pousser*) pousser; (to hammer —*marteler*) marteler; (to cover with an awning —*couvrir d'une tente*) couvrir d'une tente; (a cart, &c.—*une charrette, &c.*) bâcher.

tilt, *v.n.*, joûter; (to lean—*pencher*) incliner, pencher; (to float—*surnager*) flotter; (to fight with rapiers—*combattre avec des rapières*) ferrailler. To — at; *fondre sur.*

tilt-cart (-cârte), *n.*, charrette à bâche, *f.*

tilter, *n.*, jouteur; (metal.) martineur, *m.*

tilth (tilth), *n.*, labour, *m.*; culture, *f.*

tilt-hammer, *n.*, martinet de forge; ordon à bascule, *m.*

tilting, *n.*, joute, *f.*; tournoi; (tech.) martelage au martinet, *m.*

timbal, *n.*, (mus.) timbale, *f.*

timber, *n.*, bois de haute futaie; bois de charpente; bois; (nav.) couple, membre, *m.* — work; *charpente, f.* —*yard; chantier de bois de construction, m.*

timber, *v.a.*, munir de bois de charpente.

timbered (ti'm'beurde), *adj.*, à charpente.

timber-head (-hède), *n.*, (nav.) bitton, *m.*

timbering, *n.*, boisage, *m.*

timber-man, *n.*, boiseur, *m.*

timber-tree (-trî), *n.*, arbre de haute futaie, *m.*

timbrel, *n.*, tambour de basque, tambourin, *m.*

timbrelled (-brèlde), *adj.*, accompagné du tambourin.

time (taï'm), *n.*, temps; (specified space of time—*temps spécifié*) temps, terme, *m.*; (repetition) fois, *f.*; (age) temps, *m.*; époque; (of day and night—*époque du jour et de la nuit*) heure, *f.*; (moment) moment; (mus.) temps, *m.*, mesure, *f.*; (hour of travail—*heure de travail d'enfant*) terme, *m.* At —s; *parfois; de temps à autre.* At all —s; *dans tous les temps; de, en tout temps.* In —; *avec le temps;* (in good season—*en temps utile*) à temps; (mus.) *en mesure.* In good —; *à temps.* Behind one's —; *en retard.* Before one's —; *en avance; avant l'heure, avant terme.* In proper — and place; *en temps et lieu.* In no —; *en aucun temps;* (in a short time—*dans peu*) *en peu de temps, en moins de rien.* Once upon a —; *il y avait une fois.* Out of —; (mus.) *à contretemps.* At such a —; *à un tel moment; à une telle époque.* As —s go; *par le temps qui court.* Up to the present —; *jusqu'à présent.* In the — of; *du temps de; à l'époque de.* Another —; *une autre fois.* Three —s; *trois fois.* Hundreds of —s; *des centaines de fois.* In the nick of —; *à point nommé.* To keep —; (mus.) *aller en mesure;* (of clocks, &c.— *d'horloges, &c.*) *être à l'heure.* To serve one's —; *faire son temps.* What — is it? *quelle heure est-il?*

time (taï'm), *v.a.*, adapter au temps; régler; (clocks, &c.—*horloges, &c.*) régler; (mus.) cadencer.

time-bargain, *n.*, marché à terme, *m.*

time-honoured (-o'n'orde), *adj.*, honoré de tout temps.

time-keeper (-kîp'-), *n.*, chronomètre; (pers.) surveillant, *m.*

timeless, *adj.*, hors de saison; déplacé.

timelessly, *adv.*, mal à propos.

timeliness, *n.*, opportunité, *f.*; à-propos, *m.*

timely, *adj.*, opportun, à propos, de saison.

timely, *adv.*, à propos, à temps.

time-piece (-pîce), *n.*, pendule, *f.*; (astron.) chronomètre, *m.*

time-server (-seurv'-), *n.*, serviteur complaisant du pouvoir, *m.*

time-serving (-seurv'-), *adj.*, complaisant envers le pouvoir.

time-serving, *n.*, servilité envers le pouvoir. *f.*

time-stroke (-strôke), *n.*, (mus.) temps. *m.*

time-table, *n.*, (mus.) division du temps ; (railways) liste des heures de départ et d'arrivée, *f.*

timid, *adj.*, timide : craintif ; peureux.

timidity, *n.*, timidité, *f.*

timidly, *adv.*, timidement.

timist (taï'm'-), *n.*, (mus.) musicien qui va bien en mesure, *m.*

timoneer (-nïre), *n.*, timonier, *m.*

timorous, *adj.*, timide ; craintif ; timoré.

timorously, *adv.*, timidement, craintivement.

timorousness, *n.*, timidité ; nature timorée. *f.*

tin, *n.*, fer-blanc ; étain, *m.*

tin, *v.a.*, étamer.

tincal, *n.*, borax brut, tincal, tinkal, *m.*

tincture (tign'kt'ieur), *n.*, teinte, *f.* ; (slight taste—*léger goût*) léger goût, *m.* ; (pharm.) teinture ; (fig.) teinture, nuance, *f.*

tincture (tign'kt'ieur), *v.a.*, teindre légèrement ; (fig.) empreindre, imprégner.

tinder, *n.*, mèche, *f.* ; amadou, *m.*

tinder-box, *n.*, briquet, *m.*

tine (taïne), *n.*, fourchon, *m.* ; dent de fourche, de herse, *f.*

tin-foil (-foïl), *n.*, tain, *m.*

tinge (ti'n'dje), *n.*, teinte, nuance, *f.* ; (slight taste—*léger goût*) léger goût, *m.*

tinge (ti'n'dje), *v.a.*, teindre légèrement ; (fig.) empreindre, imprégner.

tin-glass (-glâce), *n.*, étain de glace, bismuth, *m.*

tingle (ti'n'g'l), *v.a.*, fourmiller, picoter ; (of pain—*d'une douleur*) se faire sentir ; (of the ears —*des oreilles*) tinter.

tingling (ti'n'g'l'-), *n.*, fourmillement, picotement ; (of the ears—*des oreilles*) tintement, *m.*

tin-ground (-graou'n'de), *n.*, terrain stannifère *m.*

tinker *n.*, chaudronnier ambulant, drouineur, *m.*

tinkerly, *adv.*, en drouineur.

tinkle (ti'n'k'l), *v.n.*, tinter.

tinkle, *v.a.*, faire tinter.

tinkling, *n.*, tintement, *m.*

tin-leaf (-life), *n.*, tain, *m.*

tin-lode (-lôde), *n.*, filon d'étain, *m.*

tinman, *n.*, ferblantier, *m.*

tinner, *n.*, ouvrier de mine d'étain, *m.*

tinning, *n.*, étamage, *m.*

tinny, *adj.*, qui abonde en étain ; stannifère.

tin-plate, *n.*, fer-blanc, *m.* ; plaque d'étain, *f.*

tinsel, *n.*, clinquant ; oripeau, *m.*

tinsel, *adj.*, de clinquant ; d'un faux éclat.

tinsel, *v.a.*, orner de clinquant ; donner un faux éclat à.

tin-stone (-stône), *n.*, étain oxydé, *m.*

tint (ti'n'te), *n.*, teinte, *f.*

tint (ti'n'te), *v.a.*, donner une teinte à ; (in drawing—*dessin*) hacher, ombrer ; (paint.) teinter, nuancer.

tiny (taï-), *adj.*, tout petit ; mignon.

tip, *n.*, extrémité, *f.* ; bout, *m.* ; (bot.) anthère ; (tap—*coup léger*) tape, *f.*

tip, *v.a.*, garnir le bout : ferrer ; (to tap—*donner un coup léger*) taper, frapper légèrement.

tipper, *n.*, mentonnet, *m.*

tippet, *n.*, pèlerine ; palatine, *f.*

tipping, *n.*, (mus.) coup de langue, *m.*

tipple (tip'p'l), *n.*, boisson, *f.*

tipple (tip'p'l), *v.a.*, ivrogner ; pomper, pinter.

tipple, *v.n.*, s'enivrer de : boire.

tippled (tip'p'l'de). *adj.*, ivre.

tippler, *n.*, buveur, biberon, *m.*

tippling, *n.*, habitude de pinter ; ivrognerie, *f.*

tipstaff (-stâfe). *n.*, huissier, *m.* ; (staff—*baguette d'huissier, &c.*) verge, *f.*

tipsy, *adj.*, gris, ivre. To get —; *se griser* : s'enivrer.

tiptoe (-tô), *n.*, pointe du pied, *f.*

tip-top, *n.*, le plus haut degré ; comble, *m.*

tip-top, *adj.*, suprême.

tirade (-râde), *n.*, tirade. *f.*

tire (taï-eur), *n.*, (of a wheel—*de roue*) bande, *f.*, bandage. *m.*

tire (taï-eur), *v.a.*, lasser, fatiguer ; (to bore —*ennuyer*) ennuyer. To — of ; *dégoûter de*. To get —d : *se lasser, se fatiguer ;* (in mind—*d'esprit*) s'ennuyer. To — out ; *excéder ;* (to bore—*ennuyer*) assommer.

tire, *v.n.*, se fatiguer, se lasser.

tiredness (taï-eurd'-), *n.*, fatigue, lassitude, *f.*

tiresome (taï-eur-ceume), *adj.*, fatigant ; (tedious—*ennuyeux*) ennuyeux, ennuyant, fatigant.

tiresomeness, *n.*, nature fatigante, *f.* ; (tediousness—*ennui*) ennui, *m.*

tissue (tish-shiou), *n.*, tissu d'or, tissu d'argent ; (anat.) tissu ; (fig.) tissu, *m.*, suite, *f.*

tissue (tish-shiou), *v.a.*, tisser ; (to interweave—*entrelacer*) entrelacer.

tissue-paper (-pé-peur), *n.*, papier de soie, papier joseph, *m.*

tit, *n.*, petit cheval, *m.* ; (woman—*femmelette*) femmelette ; (orni.) mésange, *f.*

titanium (ti-té-), *n.*, (chem.) titane, titanium, *m.*

titbit, *n.*, morceau friand, *m.* ; friandise, *f.*

tithable (taïth'a-b'l), *adj.*, décimable.

tithe (taïthe), *n.*, dîme ; dixième partie, *f.*

tithe (taïthe), *v.a.*, dîmer sur.

tithe, *v.n.*, payer la dîme.

tithe-collector (-lèk-teur), *n.*, dîmeur, *m.*

tithe-free (-frî), *adj.*, exempt de la dîme.

tithe-owner (-ô'n'-), *n.*, décimateur, *m.*

tithe-paying (-pè-igne), *adj.*, assujetti à la dîme.

tither (taïth'-), *n.*, dîmeur, *m.*

tithing (taïth'-), *n.*, dizaine, division par dix familles, *f.*

titillate, *v.a.*, chatouiller. titiller.

titillation ('-il-lé-), *n.*, titillation. *f.* ; chatouillement, *m.*

titlark (-lârke), *n.*, farlouse, alouette des prés, *f.*

title (taï-t'l), *n.*, titre ; nom ; (com.) document, *m.*

title (taï-t'l), *v.a.*, intituler ; titrer, donner un titre à.

titled (taï-t'l'de), *adj.*, titré.

title-deed (-dîde), *n.*, titre, document, *m.*

title-page (-pédje), *n.*, page de titre, *m.*

titling (tit'-), *n.*, (orni.) pipit, *m.*: farlouse, *f.*

titmouse (tit'maouce), *n.* (titmice), (orni.) mésange, *f.*

titter, *n.*, rire du bout des lèvres ; demi-rire, *m.*

titter, *v.n.*, rire du bout des lèvres.

tittle, *n.*, point, iota, rien, *m.*

tittle-tattle (-tit't'l-tat't'l). *n.*, caquetage, bavardage ; (pers.) bavard, *m.*, bavarde, *f.*

tittle-tattle (tit't'l-tat't'l), *v.n.*, jaser, bavarder : caqueter.

titubation (tit'iou-bé-), *n.*, (ant.) action de broncher ; titubation, *f.*

titular (tit'iou-), *adj.*, titulaire.

titular, *or* **titulary** (ti'iou-), *n.*, titulaire. *m.*

titularity, *n.*, qualité de titulaire, *f.*

titularly, *adv.*, par le titre.

titulary, *adj.*, de titre.

tivy (tiv'-), *adv.*, vite.

to (tou), *prep.*, à : (before names of countries —*devant noms de pays*) en ; (opposition) contre.

(amount—*montant* à) jusqu'à concurrence de; (possession) pour; (in comparison of—*comparaison*) en comparaison. de, auprès de; (as far as—*distance*) jusqu'à; (obligation) envers; (inclination, dislike—*inclination*, *aversion*) pour, envers; (direction) vers, de; (before an infinitive—*devant un infinitif*) à, de, (in order to—*pour*) afin de, pour. To go — Rome; *aller à Rome*. To apply —; *s'adresser à*. To write —; *écrire à*. To go — Italy; *aller en Italie*. — any one's face; *en face; au nez de quelqu'un*. Ten — one; *dix contre un*. Let us keep it — ourselves; *gardons-le pour nous*. He is nothing — her; *il ne lui est rien*. That is nothing — me; *cela ne me fait rien*. To count — ten; *compter jusqu'à dix*. Our duties — God; *nos devoirs envers Dieu*. His kindness — me; *sa bonté pour moi, envers moi*. To stretch one's arms — heaven; *tendre les bras vers le ciel*. The way — the bank; *le chemin de la banque*. The heir — the throne; *l'héritier du trône*. Friend, baker —, &c.; *ami, boulanger de*. To go — any one, to any one's house; *aller chez quelqu'un*.

toad (tôde), *n.*, crapaud, *m.*

toadeater, (-ît'-), *n.*, flagorneur, chien couchant, *m.*

toad-flax, *n.*, (bot.) linaire, *f.*; lin sauvage, *m.*

toadish (tôd'-), *adj.*, de crapaud.

toad-stone (-stône) *n.*, crapaudine, *f.*

toad-stool (-stoule) *n.*, champignon bâtard, *m.*

toady (tôd'-), *n.*, flagorneur, *m.*, flagorneuse, *f.*

toady (tôd'-), *v.a.*, flagorner, aduler, ramper auprès de.

toast (tôste), *n.*, rôtie; grillade; (health—*santé*,*f.*, toste, toast, *m.* — and water; *eau panée,f.*

toast (tôste), *v.a.*, faire rôtir, faire griller; (to drink a health—*boire à la santé*) porter la santé de, toster, toaster.

toaster (tôst'-), *n.*, personne qui fait rôtir du pain; personne qui porte un toast, une santé, *f.*; (instrument) gril, *m.*

toasting-fork, *n.*, fourchette à rôtie, *f.*

toast-master (-mâs-), *n.*, directeur des toasts, *m.*

toast-rack, *n.*, porte-rôtie (pour la table), *m.*

tobacco (-cô), *n.*, tabac, tabac à fumer, *m.*

tobacco-box, *n.*, blague; boîte à tabac, *f.*

tobacconist. *n.*, marchand de tabac; débitant de tabac; fabricant de tabac, *m.*

tobacco-pipe (-païpe), *n.*, pipe pour fumer, *f.*

tobacco-stopper, *n.*, instrument pour presser le tabac dans la pipe, *m.*

tocsin. *n.*, tocsin, *m.*

to-day (tou-dè), *adv.*, aujourd'hui.

toddle (tod'd'l), *v.n.*, marcher, à petits pas, en chancelant, comme les petits enfants.

toddy, *n.*, toddy, *m.*

toe (tô), *n.*, orteil; doigt du pied; (of horses -*des chevaux*) devant du sabot; (of animals— *les animaux*) doigt, *m.*

toffy (tof'-), *n.*, sucre d'orge à la mélasse, *m.*

toft. *n.*, plantation d'arbres, *m.*

toga, *n.*, toge, *f.*

togated (tô-ghêt'-), *or* **toged** (tôg'de), *adj.*, vêtu d'une toge.

together (tou-ghèth'-), *adv.*, ensemble: (in the same time—*en même temps*) en même temps; (in concert—*de concert*) conjointement.

toggel (tog-ghèl), *n.*, (nav.) ergot, éperon, *m.*

toggery (tog-gheuri), *n.sing.*, hardes, nippes, *f.pl.*

toil (toïl), *n.*, travail fatigant, *m.*; peine,*f.*; (net—*filet*) filet, ⊙ret, *m.*

toil (toïl), *v.n.*, travailler fort fatiguer. To

— out; *accomplir à force de travailler*. To — up; *franchir laborieusement, avec peine*.

toiler (toïl'-), *n.*, personne qui fatigue, *f.*; travailleur, *m.*, travailleuse, *f.*; piocheur, *m.*

toilet (toïl'-), *n.*, toilette, *f.* — -table; *toilette,f.*

toilsome (toïl'ceume), *adj.*, pénible, laborieux, fatigant.

toilsomeness, *n.*, fatigue; nature laborieuse,*f.*

tokay, *n.*, tokai, tokay, *m.*

token (tô-), *n.*, signe, *m.*; marque, *f.*; (memorial—*gage*) témoignage, gage, *m.*; (med.) tache; (of paper—*de papier*) demi-rame, *f.*; (coin—*médaille*) jeton, *m.*

tolerable (tol'èr'a-b'l), *adj.*, tolérable; supportable; (pretty good—*assez bien*) passable.

tolerableness, *n.*, état tolérable; état supportable; état passable, *m.*; médiocrité, *f.*

tolerably, *adv.*, tolérablement; passablement.

tolerance, *n.*, patience à supporter, tolérance, *f.*

tolerant, *adj.*, tolérant.

tolerate, *v.a.*, tolérer.

toleration (tol'èr'é-), *n.*, tolérance, *f.*

toll (tôl), *n.*, pontonage; péage; droit; (for grinding—*de mouture*) droit de mouture; (of a bell—*d'une cloche*) tintement, glas, *m.*

toll (tôl), *v.a.*, prélever; (a bell—*une cloche*) sonner, tinter.

toll, *v.n.*, être soumis au péage, à un droit; (of bells—*des cloches*) tinter, sonner le glas.

toll-bar (-bâr), *n.*, barrage, *m.*; barrière de péage,*f.*

toll-gate. *n.*, barrière de péage,*f.*

toll-gatherer (-*gath'*-), *n.*, péager, *m.*

toll-house (-haouce), *n.*, péage, bureau de péage, *m.*

tomahawk (to'm'a-hôke), *n.*, tomahawk, casse-tête, *m.*

tomato (to-mâ-tô), *n.*, tomate, pomme d'amour, *f.*

tomb (toume), *n.*, tombeau, sépulcre, *m.*; tombe; (grave—*fosse*) tombe, fosse, *f.*; (monument) tombeau, *m.*

tomb, *v.* *V.* **entomb**.

tombac, *n.*, (metal.) tombac, *m.*

tomboy (-boï), *n.*, gros gaillard, luron, *m.*; (girl—*fille*) garçonnière,*f.*

tombstone (-stône), *n.*, pierre tumulaire, tombe,*f.*

tomcat, *n.*, matou, chat, *m.*

tome (tô'm), *n.*, tome, volume, *m.*

tomentose (tô-mè'n'tôce), *adj.*, (bot.) tomenteux.

tomentum (tô-), *n.*, (bot.) duvet cotonneux, *m.*

tomfool (-foule), *n.*, nigaud, sot, bêta. *m.*

tomfoolery (-foule-), *n.*, nigauderie, sottise, bêtise,*f.*

to-morrow (tou-mo-rô), *adv.*, demain.

tomtit,*n.*, mésange,*f.*

ton (teune), *n.*, tonne, *f.*, tonneau, *m.* (kilogrammes 1015·640).

ton (to'n), *n.*, (fashion) ton, *m.*; mode,*f.*

tondino. *V.* **torus**.

tone (tône), *n.*, ton; (med., mus.) ton; (whine —*cri*) accent plaintif; (of the voice—*de la voix*) ton, accent, timbre, *m.*

tone, *v.a.*, donner un ton affecté à; (to tune—*donner le ton*) donner le ton à, régler; (piano, &c.) accorder.

toneless, *adj.*, peu harmonieux.

tongs (ton'gze), *n*, pincettes; (tech.) tenailles, pinces,*f.pl.*

tongue (teu'n'g), *n.*, langue; (language— *langue*) langue, *f.*, langage, idiome, *m.*; (of land—*de terre*) langue de terre; (tech.) languette, *f.*; (of a buckle—*de boucle*) ardillon, *m.* To hold one's —; *se taire*.

tongue (teu'n'g), *v.a.*, réprimander ; (tech.) munir d'une languette.

tongue (teu'n'g), *v.n.*, bavarder.

tongued (teu'n'g'de), *adj.*, à langue ; (tech.) à languette.

tongueless, *adj.*, sans langue ; (speechless— *muet*) muet.

tongue-scraper (-scrép'-),*n.*,cure-langue,*m.*

tongue-shaped (-shép'te),*adj.*,linguiforme.

tongue-tie (-ta'ye), *v.a.*, nouer la langue à ; (fig.) lier la langue à.

tongue-tied (-taïde), *adj.*, qui a le filet; (fig.) qui a la langue liée.

tonic, *adj.*, tonique, incitant.

tonic, *n.*,(med.) tonique,*m.*; (mus.) tonique,*f.*

to-night (tou-naïte), *n.*, cette nuit, *f.*; ce soir,*m.*

tonnage (teu'n'édje), *n.*, tonnage ; droit de tonnage, *m.*

tonsil, *n.*, amygdale, tonsille,*f.*

tonsile (-'saïle), *adj.*, que l'on peut rogner.

tonsillar, *adj.*, (anat.) tonsillaire.

tonsure (to'n'sheur), *n.*, coupe; (c.rel.) tonsure,*f.*

tontine (-tîne), *n.*, tontine,*f.*

tony (tô-), *n.*, imbécile, niais, *m.*

too (toû), *adv.*, trop; (also—*aussi*) aussi, de même. — much, — many; *trop* ; (before a noun —*devant un substantif*) trop de.

tool (toule), *n.*, outil ; instrument ; (pers.) instrument, *m.*, âme damnée,*f.*

tool-chest (-tshèste), *n.*, boîte à outils,*f.*

tooth (touth), *n.* (*teeth*), dent,*f.* ; (palate— *palais*) palais, goût, *m.* To have a — out ; *se faire arracher une dent.* To show one's teeth; *montrer les dents.* To have a sweet —; *aimer les douceurs.* In any one's teeth; *à la figure, au nez de quelqu'un.* To go at it — and nail; *s'y prendre de toutes ses forces.* False —; *fausse dent; dent postiche.*

tooth (touth), *v.a.*, garnir de dents ; (to in- dent—*denteler*) denteler; (to lock into each other—*engrener*) engrener.

toothache (-'éke), *n.*, mal de dents, *m.* To have the — ; *avoir mal aux dents.*

toothbrush (-breushe), *n.*, brosse à dents,*f.*

tooth-drawer (-drô'-), *n.*, arracheur de dents, dentiste, *m.*

tooth-drawing (-drô-igne), *n.*, extraction de dents,*f.*

toothed (touth'te), *adj.*, à dents; (bot.,tech.) denté, dentelé.

toothing, *n.*, (arch.) arrachement, *m.*

toothless, *adj.*, sans dents; édenté.

toothletted, *adj.*, (bot.) denté, dentelé.

tooth-pick, *n.*, cure-dent, *m.*

tooth-shell, *n.*, dentale, *m.*

toothwort (-'weurte), *n.*,(bot.)clandestine,*f.*

toothy, *adj.*, muni de dents, à dents.

top, *n.*, haut, sommet, *m.* ; (of a mountain, a tree, a rock—*de montagne, d'arbre, de rocher*) cime, *f.* ; (of a building—*d'un bâtiment*) haut, faîte ; (of the head—*de la tête*) sommet, dessus, haut, *m.* ; (forelock—*cheveux*) cheveux de devant, *m.pl.* ; (of water—*de l'eau*) surface, *f.* ; (cover—*couvercle*) couvercle, *m.* ; (nav.) hune,*f.* ; (highest person —*premier*) chef, *m.*, tête ; (highest rank—*du plus haut rang*) tête, *f.* ; (arch.) couronnement ; (of boots—*de bottes*) revers, *m.* ; (of plants—*des plan- tes*) tête, *f.* ; (of a pole—*d'une perche*) bout, haut bout ; (of a table—*d'une table*) dessus ; (further end—*bout*) haut, haut bout, *m.*; (play- thing—*jouet*) toupie, *f.*, sabot ; (fig.) sommet, comble, faîte, *m.* From — to bottom; *du haut en bas.* Humming- —; *toupie d'Allemagne.* Whipping- —; *sabot.* At the — of; *en haut de.*

top, *adj.*, premier, principal.

top, *v.a.*, couronner, surmonter ; (to in- dent above—*s'élever*) dépasser; (to surpass—*dépasser*) surpasser ; (to crop—*éteter*) étêter; (to rise to

---

the top of—*atteindre le haut*) atteindre le som- met de; (nav.) apiquer.

top, *v.n.*, dominer; (to predominate—*pré- dominer*)dominer,prédominer ;(to excel—*exceller*) dominer, exceller.

topaz (tô-), *n.*, topaze,*f.*

tope (tôpe), *v.a.*, pinter, ivrogner.

tope (tôpe), *n.*, (ich.) squale; milandre, *m.*

toper (tôp'-), *n.*, biberon, ivrogne,*m.*

topet, *n.*, (orni.) mésange huppée,*f.*

topful (-foule), *adj.*, tout plein.

top-gallant, *adj.*, le plus haut; (dashing— *de premier ordre*) du premier ordre, superbe; (nav.) de perroquet.

top-gallant, *n.*, (nav.) voile de perroquet,*f.*

tophaceous (to-fé-sheusse), *adj.*, sableux, pierreux.

top-heavy (-hèv'-), *adj.*, trop lourd par le haut.

tophus (tô-feuss), *n.*, (med.) tophus, *m.*

topic, *n.*, sujet; argument ; (rhet., med.) topique, *m.*

topic, *or* **topical**, *adj.*, local ; (pertaining to a topic—*d'argument*) qui développe un sujet, une matière.

topically, *adv.*, d'une manière locale.

topknot (-note), *n.*, fontange ; (of birds— *des oiseaux*) huppe, aigrette,*f.*

topless, *adj.*, d'une hauteur infinie.

topman, *n.*, scieur de long de dessus; (nav.) gabier, *m.*

top-mast (-mâste), *n.*, mât de hune; hunier, *m.*

topmost (-môste), *adj.*, le plus haut.

topographer, *n.*, topographe, *m.*

topographic, *or* **topographical**, *adj.*, topographique.

topography, *n.*, topographie,*f.*

topple (top'p'l), *v.n.*, tomber en avant.

top-sail (-séle),*n.*, hunier, *m.*

top-shaped (-shép'te), *adj.*, turbiné; en forme de toupie.

topsy-turvy (-teur'-), *adv.*, sens dessus dessous.

torch (tortshe), *n.*, torche,*f.* ; flambeau, *m.*

torch-bearer (-bèr-), *n.*, porte-flambeau; lampadaire, *m.*

torch-thistle (-this's'l), *n.*, (bot.) cactier ; cierge du Pérou, *m.*

torment, *n.*, tourment, *m.* ; (torture) tor- ture, *f.*, supplice, *m.* ; (that which torments— *tourment*) cause de tourments,*f.*

torment, *v.a.*, tourmenter.

tormentil, *n.*, (bot.) tormentille,*f.*

tormenting, *adj.*,tourmentant.

tormentingly, *adv.*, d'une manière tour- mentante.

tormentor (-mè'n't'eur), *n.*, personne qui tourmente, *f.* ; bourreau : tourment, *m.*

tornado (-né-dô), *n.*, tourbillon de vent, *m.*

torose (-rôce), *or* **torous**, *adj.*, (bot.) bos- selé, finement bosselé.

torpedo (-pi-dô), *n.*, (ich.) torpille,*f.*

torpescence, *n.*, torpeur naissante,*f.*

torpescent, *adj.*, qui devient torpide.

torpid, *adj.*, engourdi ; (fig.) inerte, lourd.

torpidity, **torpidness**, **torpitude** (-pi- tiude), *or* **torpor**, *n.*, torpeur ; (fig.) torpeur, apathie, lourdeur,*f.*

torporific, *adj.*, qui amène la torpeur.

torrefaction (-ri-fak'-) *n.*, torréfaction,*f.*

torrefy (-ri-fa'ye), *v.a.*, torréfier ; griller.

torrent, *n.*, torrent, *m.*

torrent, *adj.*, torrentueux ; qui coule en torrent.

torrid, *adj.*, (burning—*brûlant*) brûlant de la zone torride ; (parched—*brûlé*) brûlé ; (geog.) torride.

torridness, *n.*, chaleur brûlante,*f.*

torsel, *n.*, (arch.) sablière,*f.*

torsion, n., torsion, f.; tordage, m.
torso (-sô), n., torse, m.
tort, n., (jur.) dommage, préjudice, m.
tortile, adj., (ant.) tordu ; (bot.) tortile.
tortious (tor-sheuss), adj., (jur.) dommageable, préjudiciable.
tortoise (tor-tize, ou tiss), n., tortue, f.
tortoise-shell, n., écaille de tortue. écaille, f.
tortuosity, or **tortuousness** (tort'iou-). n., torsion, tortuosité, f.
tortuous (tort'iou-euss), adj., tortu ; tordu ; tortillé ; (winding—sinueux) tortueux, sinueux ; (bot.) tortu ; (fig.) tortueux.
torture (tort'ieur), v.a., torturer ; mettre à la torture.
torture (tort'leur), n., torture, douleur, f. ; supplice, tourment, m.
torturer, n., personne qui torture, f., bourreau, m.
torturingly, adv., de manière à torturer.
torus (tô-), n., (arch.) tore ; (bot.) réceptacle, m.
tory (tô-), adj., tory.
tory, n., tory, m.
toryism (-iz'm), n., torysme, m.
toss, n., action de lancer en l'air ; secousse, f.
— of the head ; coup de tête en arrière, m.
toss, v.a., lancer, jeter ; jeter en l'air ; (to cause to rise and fall—ballotter) ballotter, secouer ; (to agitate—agiter) agiter, remuer ; (of horned cattle—des bêtes à cornes) lancer en l'air. To — up ; jeter en l'air ; (oars—avirons) mâter ; (the head—la tête) relever. To — in a blanket ; berner.
toss, v.n., s'agiter ; se démener. To — up ; jouer à pile ou face.
tosser, n., personne qui jette, lance, f. ; (of money—d'argent) joueur à pile ou face, m.
tossing, n., secousse, f.
total (tô-), n., montant, m. ; somme, f.
total (tô-), adj., total ; complet ; entier.
totality, n., totalité, f. ; montant ; tout, m.
totally, adv., totalement ; tout à fait ; entièrement.
totalness, n., intégrité, f. ; état intact, m.
totter, v.n., chanceler ; branler ; vaciller ; menacer ruine.
tottering, adj., chancelant.
tottering, n., chancellement ; branlement, m.
totteringly, adv., d'une manière chancelante.
tottery, adj., chancelant.
toucan (tou-), n., (astron., orni.) toucan, m.
touch (teutshe), v.a., toucher ; toucher à ; (to reach—atteindre) toucher à, atteindre ; (to concern—concerner) toucher, concerner, regarder ; (to move—émouvoir) toucher, émouvoir ; (to delineate—tracer) tracer ; (to make an impression on, as of a file—entamer) entamer ; (to try metals—essayer les métaux) toucher, essayer ; (mus.) toucher. To — up ; retoucher ; raviver.
touch, v.n., toucher ; se toucher. To — at ; (of ships—des vaisseaux) toucher à, aborder à. To — upon ; (to take effect on—mordre sur) entamer ; (to treat of slightly—effleurer un sujet) toucher, effleurer.
touch (teutshe), n., (sense of feeling—sens) toucher ; (contact) contact, attouchement ; (test —épreuve) criterium, m., pierre de touche ; (proof —épreuve) preuve, f. ; qualités éprouvées, f.pl. ; (arts) coup de crayon, de pinceau, trait, m., touche, f. ; (feature—trait) trait ; (stroke, as of railery—raillerie) trait ; (animadversion—reproche) reproche, blâme, m. ; (of disease—de maladie) légère attaque, f. ; (trial—essai) essai ; (sample—échantillon) échantillon. m. ; (very small quantity—fort petite quantité) idée, f. ; (metal.) essai, m., touche, f. ; (mus.) toucher, m. Let me have a — at it ; que je m'y essaie.

touchable (teutsh'a-b'l), adj., tangible, palpable.
touch-hole (-hôle), n., (artil.) lumière, f.
touchily, adv., avec une humeur chagrine ; avec susceptibilité.
touchiness, n., irascibilité, humeur chagrine ; susceptibilité, f.
touching, adj., touchant, émouvant.
touching, prep., touchant, concernant.
touching, n., toucher, tact, m.
touchingly, adv., d'une manière touchante.
touch-me-not (teutshe-mi-), n., (med.) noli me tangere, m. ; (bot.) balsamine des bois, f., noli me tangere, m.
touch-needle (-nîd'd'l), n., touchau, touchaud, m.
touch-stone (-stône), n., pierre de touche, f. ; criterium, m.
touch-wood (-woude), n., amadouvier ; amadou, m.
touchy, adj., irascible ; bourru ; susceptible.
tough (teufe) adj., (of things—des choses) souple, flexible ; (of things—des choses) inflexible, rigide, raide ; (viscous—visqueux) visqueux, tenace ; (of meat—de la viande) dur, coriace ; (strong—vigoureux) fort, solide ; (formidable) rude ; (fig.) dur, épais.
toughen (teuf'f'n), v.a. and n., durcir, raidir.
toughish (teuf'-), adj., un peu dur.
toughly (teuf'-), adv., avec souplesse ; durement.
toughness (teuf'-), n., (of things—des choses) flexibilité, souplesse ; (of things—des choses) raideur, inflexibilité, rigidité, ténacité ; (viscosity—viscosité) viscosité, ténacité ; (of meat—de la viande) dureté, nature coriace ; (firmness—fermeté) vigueur, solidité, f.
toupee (tou-pî), or **toupet** (tou-pè), n., toupet, m.
tour, n., (journey, turn, of hair—voyage, tour, de cheveux) tour, m.
tourist, n., touriste, voyageur, m.
tourmalin, n., (min.) tourmaline, f.
tournament, or **tourney**, n., tournoi, m.
tourney, v.n., jouter dans un tournoi.
tourniquet (teur-ni-kète), n., (surg.) tourniquet, m.
tout (taoute), v.n., s'achalander.
tow (tô), n., filasse, étoupe ; (rope—câble) touée ; (fig.) remorque, f. In — ; (fig., nav.) à la remorque ; à la touée.
tow, v.a., remorquer ; (from the shore—le long de la rive) touer, haler.
towage (tô-édje), n., remorque, f. ; (from the shore—le long de la rive) touage, halage, m.
toward, or **towards**, adv., près.
toward (tou-arde), or **towards** (tou-ard'ze), prep., vers, du côté de ; (with respect to—à l'égard de) envers, pour ; (of time—du temps) vers, sur, environ.
toward, or **towardly** (tou-), adj., docile.
towardliness, or **towardness**, n., docilité, f.
tow-boat (-bôte), n., bateau remorqueur, m.
towel (taou-èl), n., essuie-main, m. ; serviette, f.
towelling (taou-èl'-), n., étoffe pour serviettes, f.
tower (taou'eur), n., tour ; (citadel—forteresse) citadelle ; (elevation) élévation, hauteur, f.
tower (taou-eur), v.n., s'élever ; planer ; dominer.
towered (taou-eurde), adj., à tours, défendu par des tours.
towering, adj., élevé comme une tour ; qui plane ; (fig.) élevé, grand, sublime.
towery, adj., garni de tours ; défendu par des tours.
towing (tô-igne), n., halage, m. ; remorque, f. — -path ; chemin de halage, m. — -rope ; corde de halage ; cordelle, f.

towline (-laïne), *n.*, corde de halage ; haussière, *f.*

town (taou'n), *n.*, ville ; capitale, *f.*

town-crier (-craï-), *n.*, crieur public, *m.*

town-due (-diou), *n.*, octroi, droit d'entrée, *m.*

town-hall (-hôl), *n.*, hôtel de ville, *m.*

town-house (-haouce), *n.*, hôtel de ville, *m.* ; (residence) maison de ville, *f.*

townish, *adj.*, de ville.

township, *n.*, commune ; étendue territoriale d'une ville, *f.* ; (corporation—*conseil*) conseil municipal. *m.*

townsman (taou'n'z'-), *n.*, citadin ; habitant de ville ; bourgeois ; (of the same town—*de la même ville*) concitoyen, *m.*

towntalk (-tôke), *n.*, bruit de ville ; entretien de toute la ville, *m.*

tow-path (-pâth), *n.*, chemin de halage, *m.*

toxicological (-lodj'-), *adj.*, toxicologique.

toxicology ('-odji), *n.*, toxicologie, *f.*

toy (to'ye), *n.*, jouet, joujou ; (com.) bimbelot ; (bauble—*babiole*) brimborion, colifichet, *m.*, babiole ; bagatelle, *f.*, rien, *m.* ; (folly—*niaiserie*) niaiserie, futilité, *f.* —s ; *jouets, m.pl.* ; (com.) *bimbeloterie, f.sing.*

toy (to'ye), *v.n.*, jouer ; badiner, folâtrer.

toy-book (-bouke), *n.*, livre d'images, *m.*

toyer (to'yeur), *n.*, joueur, badin, *m.*

toyish (to-yish), *adj.*, futile ; (wanton—*badin*) badin, folâtre.

toyishness, *n.*, humeur folâtre, folâtrerie, *f.*

toyman, *n.*, marchand de joujoux, bimbelotier, *m.*

toy-shop, *n.*, magasin de joujoux, *m.*

toy-trade, *n.*, bimbeloterie, *f.*

trace, *n.*, trace, *f.* ; (of harness—*harnais*) trait, *m.*

trace, *v.a.*, trace ; (in drawing—*dessin*) calquer ; (to track—*suivre*) suivre à la trace, à la piste, suivre la trace de ; (to walk over—*parcourir*) parcourir. To — to ; *reporter, faire remonter à.* To — out ; *tracer, faire le tracé de* ; (to track out—*découvrir*) *découvrir la trace de.* To — the origin of ; *découvrir l'origine de.*

traceable (tréss'a-b'l), *adj.*, que l'on peut tracer ; dont on peut suivre les traces.

tracer (tréss'-), *n.*, personne qui trace, qui calque, qui suit à la piste, *f.*

tracery (tré-ci-), *n.*, (arch.) réseau, *m.*

trachea (tré-ki-), *n.*, (anat.) trachée-artère ; (bot.) trachée, *f.*

tracheotomy (tré-ki-), *n.*, trachéotomie, *f.*

trachitis (tra-kaï-), *n.*, trachéite, *f.*

trachyte (tré-kaïte), *n.*. (min.) trachyte, *m.*

track, *n.*, trace ; voie ; (hunt.) piste ; voie; (hunt., railways) voie ; (of a comet—*de comète*) route, *f.*, cours, *m.* ; (of a ship—*de vaisseau*) sillage, *m.*, eaux, *f.pl.* ; (fig.) trace, voie, route, ornière, *f.*, chemin, *m.* Beaten—; *sentier battu, m.*

track, *v.a.*, suivre à la trace, à la piste ; (to tow—*remorquer*) haler, remorquer.

track-boat (-bôte), *n.*, coche, *m.*

tracking, *n.*, action de suivre à la trace, *f.* ; (towing—*remorquage*) halage, *m.*

trackless, *adj.*, sans trace ; non frayé ; non fréquenté.

trackroad (-rôde), *n.*, chemin de halage. *m.*

track-scout (-scaoute), *n.*, galiote de Hollande, *f.*

tract, *n.*, étendue ; (region) contrée, région, *f.* ; (of time—*de temps*) espace, *m.*, durée, *f.* ; (book—*livre*) opuscule, traité ; (religion) petit livre de dévotion, *m.*

tractability. V. **tractableness.**

tractable (-ta-b'l), *adj.*, traitable ; maniable ; docile.

tractableness, *n.*, nature traitable ; docilité, *f.*

tractably, *adv.*, d'une manière traitable, docilement.

tractation (trak-té-), *n.*, action de traiter un sujet, *f.*

tractile, *adj.*, ductile.

tractility, *n.*, ductilité, *f.*

traction (trak'sheune), *n.*, tension ; attraction ; (mec.) attraction ; traction, *f.*

tractive, *adj.*, (mec.) de traction.

tractor (-teur), *n.*, (mec.) instrument de traction, *m.*

trade, *n.*, commerce, trafic, négoce ; (calling—*profession*) état, métier, *m.*, profession, industrie, *f.* ; (habit—*habitude*) habitude, coutume, *f.* ; (employment—*occupation*) emploi, *m.*, occupation, *f.* ; (men engaged in the same occupation —*corps de métier*) corps de métier ; (b.s.) métier, commerce, *m.* To carry on the — of ; *faire le commerce de.* —wind ; *vent alizé, m.*

trade, *v.n.*, trafiquer, négocier, commercer. To — in ; *faire le commerce de.*

trader (tréd'-), *n.*, négociant, *m.*, négociante, *f.* ; commerçant, *m.*, commerçante, *f.* ; (ship—*navire*) vaisseau marchand, *m.*

tradesman (tréd'z'-), *n.*, marchand ; débitant ; (com.) fournisseur, *m.*

tradespeople (tréd'z'pî'p'l), *or* **tradesfolk** (-fôke), *n.pl.*, gens du commerce ; commerçants ; marchands, *m.pl.*

tradeswoman (tréd'z'woum'-), *n.*, commerçante, négociante, *f.*

trading (tréd'-), *n.*, négoce, commerce, *m.*

trading (tréd'-), *adj.*, commercial ; commerçant ; marchand ; de commerce.

tradition, *n.*, tradition, *f.*

traditional, *or* **traditionary**, *adj.*, traditionnel.

traditionally, *adv.*, traditionnellement.

traditionary, *n.*, traditionnaire, *m.*

traditive, *adj.*, de tradition, traditionnel.

traditor (-), *n.*, traditeur, *m.*

traduce (tra-diouce), *v.a.*, censurer, critiquer ; (to calumniate—*diffamer*) diffamer, calomnier.

traducer (-diouss'-), *n.*, calomniateur, *m.*, calomniatrice, *f.* ; diffamateur, *m.*, diffamatrice, *f.*

traducingly (-diouss'-), *adv.*, calomnieusement.

traduction (-deuk'-), *n.*, tradition ; génération ; (rhet.) transition, *f.*

traffic, *n.*, trafic ; commerce, négoce, *m.* ; (going and coming—*allée et venue*) circulation, *f.* ; (commodities—*marchandises*) marchandises, *f.pl.*

traffic, *v.n.*, trafiquer, commercer.

trafficker, *n.*, trafiquant, marchand, *m.*

tragacanth (-ca'n'th), *n.*, (bot.) tragacanthe ; gomme adragante, *f.*

tragedian (tra-djî-), *n.*, tragédien, *m.*, tragédienne, *f.* ; (writer—*écrivain*) auteur tragique, *m.*

tragedy (tra-dji-), *n.*, tragédie, *f.*

tragic (tra-djike), *or* **tragical** (tra-dji-), *adj.*, tragique.

tragically, *adv.*, tragiquement.

tragicalness, *n.*, tragique, *m.*

tragi-comedy (tradj'i-), *n.*, tragi-comédie, *f.*

tragi-comical, *adj.*, tragi-comique.

tragi-comically, *adv.*, d'une manière tragi-comique.

trail (tréle), *n.*, traînée ; (hunt.) trace, piste, voie ; (of a meteor—*d'un météore*) queue, traînée lumineuse, *f.* ; (entrails of a fowl, a sheep—*entrailles de volaille, de mouton*) entrailles, *f.pl.* ; (fig.) voie, trace, *f.* —boards ; (nav.) *friss de l'éperon, f.*

trail (tréle), *v.n.*, traîner ; passer lentement.

trail, *v.a.*, suivre à la piste ; (to drag—*traîner*) traîner ; (to lower—*baisser*) baisser.

train (tréne), *n.*, (retinue—*cortège*) suite, *f.*, cortège, *m.*, (series—*série*) suite, série, *f.*, enchaînement ; (course) cours, *m.* ; (of a watch, &c.) —*d'une montre,* &c.) marche, *f.*, mouvement, *m.*

(of gunpowder—*de poudre*) traînée ; (of a bird, of a dress—*d'un oiseau, d'une robe*) queue, *f*. ; (of a gun-carriage—*d'un affût de canon*) derrière ; (artil.) train ; (of boats—*de bateaux*) convoi ; (railways) convoi, train : (artifice) artifice, *m*.

train, *v.a.*, dresser, former, exercer : élever ; instruire ; (to draw along—*traîner*) traîner ; (to entice—*séduire*) entraîner, séduire ; (hort.) dresser ; (man.) entraîner ; dresser. To — up ; *élever, instruire, former*.

train-band, *n*., milice bourgeoise, *f*.

train-bearer (-bèr'-), *n*., porte-queue, *m*.

trainer, *n*., personne qui dresse, *f*. ; instructeur ; (of animals—*d'animaux*) entraîneur, *m*.

training, *n*., éducation, *f*. ; exercice, *m*.

train-oil (-oïl), *n*., huile de baleine, *f*.

traipse (trépse), *v.n.*, marcher négligemment.

trait (trète, *ou* trè), *n*., trait, *m*.

traitor (tré-teur), *n*., traître ; perfide, *m*.

traitorous (tré-teur'-), *adj.*, traître ; (perfidious—*perfide*) traître, perfide.

traitorously, *adv.*, en traître ; (perfidiously —*perfidement*) traîtreusement, perfidement.

traitorousness. *V.* **treachery**.

traitress (tré-), *n*., traîtresse ; perfide, *f*.

traject (tradj'-), *v.a.*, jeter ; jeter à travers.

traject (tradj'-), *n*., (ant.) bac ; endroit navigable, *m*.

trajection (tra-djèk-), *n*., translation ; (emission) émission, *f*.

trajectory (tra-djèk-teuri), *n*., trajectoire, *f*.

tralatitious (-la-tish'eusse), *adj.*, métaphorique, non littéral.

tralatitiously, *adv.*, métaphoriquement.

tralucent (-liou-), *adj.*, (ant.). *V.* **translucent**.

tram, *n*., chariot de roulage ; (railways) rail plat, *m*.

trammel, *v.a.*, entraver, empêtrer, embarrasser.

trammel, *n*., (net—*filet*) tramail, traîneau, *m*. ; (for animals—*pour animaux*) entrave ; (iron hook—*crochet de fer*) crémaillère, *f*. ; (elliptic compasses—*compas*) compas à ellipse, *m*. ; (fig.) entrave, *f*., obstacle, *m*.

tramontane (-téne), *n*., personne qui vit au-delà des monts, *f*. ; (in France—*en France*) ultramontain, *m*.

tramontane (-téne), *adj.*, qui vit au-delà des monts ; (in France—*en France*) ultramontain.

tramp, *v.n.*, errer, rôder ; (to go on foot—*aller à pied*) aller à pied, battre la semelle.

tramp, *v.a.*, faire à pied.

tramp, *n*., action d'errer, de rôder ; action d'aller à pied, *f*. ; piétinement, *m*.

tramper, *n*., rôdeur, vagabond, coureur, *m*.

trample (tra'm'p'l), *v.a.*, fouler aux pieds ; marcher sur.

trample. *v.n.*, fouler aux pieds ; piétiner.

trampler, *n*., personne qui foule aux pieds, *f*.

trampling, *n*., action de fouler aux pieds, *f*. ; piétinement. *m*.

tram-rail (-réle), *n*., rail plat, *m*.

tram-way (-wè), *n*., chemin de fer à rails plats, chemin de fer américain, tramway, *m*.

trance, *n*., extase ; (med.) catalepsie, *f*.

tranced (trä'n'ste). *adj.*, en extase.

tranquil (tra'n'kwile), *adj.*, tranquille.

tranquillity, *or* **tranquilness** (-kwil-li-) *n*., tranquillité, quiétude, *f*.

tranquillize (-kwil-laïze), *v.a.*, tranquilliser, calmer.

tranquilly (-kwil'-), *adv.*, tranquillement.

transact, *v.a.*, faire ; faire exécuter ; expédier. To — business ; *faire ses affaires ; travailler*.

transaction, *n*., (management—*gestion*) conduite, gestion, négociation ; (act—*action*) transaction, affaire, *f*., acte, événement, *m*. ; (com.) transaction, affaire, opération, *f*.

transactor, *n*., négociateur, agent, *m*.

transalpine. *adj.*, transalpin.

transatlantic, *adj.*, transatlantique.

transcend, *v.a.*, dépasser ; (fig.) surpasser, dépasser, excéder.

transcendence, *or* **transcendency**, *n*., excellence, transcendance ; (exaggeration) exagération, *f*.

transcendent, *adj.*, transcendant.

transcendental, *adj.*, transcendantal.

transcendentally, *adv.*, d'une manière transcendante.

transcolate, *v.a.*, (ant.) filtrer.

transcribe (-scraïbe), *v.a.*, transcrire, copier.

transcriber (-scraïb'-), *n*., copiste, transcripteur. *m*.

transcript, *n*., transcription ; copie, *f*.

transcription, *n*., transcription, *f*.

transcriptively, *adv.*, en transcrivant, en copiant.

transe. *V.* **trance**.

transept, *n*., (arch.) transept, *m*.

transfer (-feur), *n*., translation, *f*. ; transport ; (fin.) transfert, *m*., assignation, *f*. ; (jur.) transfert, transport ; (com.) transfert, *m*. cession, *f*.

transfer (-feur), *v.a.*, transférer ; transporter ; (jur.) transférer, céder.

transferable (-feur'a-b'l) *adj.*, transportable ; (jur.) cessible ; (com.) cessible, négociable.

transferee (-fèr'i), *n*., cessionnaire, *m*.

transferrer (-feur'-), *n*., cédant, *m*.

transfiguration (-figh'iou-ré-), *n*., transfiguration ; transformation, *f*.

transfigure (-figh'ioure), *v.a.*, transfigurer ; transformer.

transfix, *v.a.*, transpercer.

transform, *v.a.*, transformer ; changer ; (metals—*métaux*) convertir, transmuer ; (c.rel.) transsubstantier ; (theol.) convertir, changer ; (alg.) transformer.

transform, *v.n.*, se transformer.

transformation (-form'é), *n*., transformation, *f*. ; changement, *m*. ; conversion ; (ent.) métamorphose ; (of metals—*des métaux*) conversion, transmutation ; (c. rel.) transsubstantiation ; (theol.) conversion ; (alg.) transformation, *f*.

transforming, *adj.*, qui transforme ; qui change.

transfuse (-fiouze), *v.a.*, transvaser ; transfuser ; instiller.

transfusion (-fiou-jeune), *n*., transvasion ; transfusion, *f*.

transgress, *v.a.*, dépasser ; (to infringe—*enfreindre*) transgresser, enfreindre.

transgress, *v.n.*, transgresser ; pécher.

transgression (-grèsh'-), *n*., transgression, infraction, *f*. ; péché, *m*.

transgressive, *adj.*, qui transgresse une loi ; coupable.

transgressor, *n*., transgresseur ; violateur, *m*., violatrice, *f*. ; (rel.) pécheur, *m*., pécheresse, *f*.

tranship, *v.a.* *V.* **trans-ship**.

transient (tra'n'shè'n'te), *adj.*, passager ; transitoire ; (hasty—*momentané*) rapide.

transiently, *adv.*, en passant, légèrement.

transientness, *n*., nature passagère ; nature transitoire ; rapidité, *f*.

transit, *n*., passage ; (at the customs—*douanes*) transit, *m*.

transit, *v.n.*, (astron.) passer.

transit-instrument (-strou-), *n*., (astron.) lunette méridienne, *f*.

transition (-cij'eune), *n*., transition, *f*.

transitional (-cij'eu'n'-), *adj.*, de transition.

transitive, *adj.*, qui passe ; (gram.) transitif.

transitorily, *adv.*, passagèrement.
transitoriness (-teuri-), *n.*, nature passagère, *f.*
transitory (-teuri), *adj.*, transitoire, passager, fugitif.
translatable (-lét'a-b'l), *adj.*, traduisible.
translate, *v.a.*, traduire; (to interpret—*expliquer*) interpréter, expliquer; (to transfer—*transporter*) transférer, transporter; (to change—*changer*) changer, transformer; (to convey to heaven—*transporter au ciel*) enlever au ciel; (a bishop—*évêque*) transférer.
translation (-lé-), *n.*, traduction; (removal—*déplacement*) translation, *f.*, déplacement; (to heaven—*au ciel*) enlèvement, *m.*; (of a bishop—*d'un évêque*) translation, *f.*
translator (-lé-teur), *n.*, traducteur, *m.*
translatress (-lé-), *n.*, traducteur (femme), (l.u.) traductrice, *f.*
translocation (-lo-ké-), *n.*, déplacement, transport, *m.*
translucence, *or* **translucency** (-liou-), *n.*, transparence, diaphanéité; translucidité, *f.*
translucent (-liou-), *adj.*, transparent; diaphane; translucide.
transmarine (-rine), *adj.*, d'outre-mer, transmarin.
transmigrant, *adj.*, émigrant; (of things) qui se transforme.
transmigrant, *n.*, émigrant, *m.*; (thing—*des choses*) chose qui se transforme, *f.*
transmigrate, *v.n.*, émigrer; (of souls—*des âmes*) passer d'un corps dans un autre.
transmigration (-gré-), *n.*, transmigration; transformation; (of souls—*des âmes*) transmigration, métempsycose, *f.*
\ **transmigrator** (-gré-), *n.*, émigrant, *m.*
transmissibility, *n.*, transmissibilité, *f.*
transmissible (-si-b'l), *adj.*, transmissible.
transmission (-mish-), *n.*, transmission, *f.*
transmissive, *adj.*, transmis, de transmission.
transmit, *v.a.*, transmettre; envoyer; (phys.) transmettre, conduire.
transmittal, *n.*, transmission, *f.*
transmitter, *n.*, personne qui transmet, *f.*
transmutability (-miou-ta-), *n.*, transmutabilité, *f.*
transmutable (-miou-ta-b'l), *adj.*, transmuable.
transmutably, *adv.*, de manière à pouvoir être transformé.
transmutation (-miou-té-), *n.*, transmutation; transformation, *f.*; (of colours—*des couleurs*) changement, *m.*
transmute (-mioute), *v.a.*, transmuer; transformer.
transmuter, *n.*, personne qui transmue, qui transforme, *f.*
transom (-ceume), *n.*, traverse de fenêtre; traversine; (of a ship—*de vaisseau*) barre d'arcasse, *f.*
transom-knee (-nî), *n.*, (nav.) courbe d'arcasse, *f.*
transparence, **transparency**, *or* **transparentness** (-pér'-), *n.*, transparence, *f.*
transparent (-pér'-), *adj.*, transparent, diaphane.
transpierce (-pîrce), *v.a.*, transpercer; pénétrer.
transpiration (-spi-ré-), *n.*, transpiration; exhalation, *f.*
transpire, *v.n.*, transpirer; transsuder; (to become public—*être divulgué*) transpirer; (to happen—*arriver*) arriver, se passer.
transpire (-spaeur), *v.a.*, suer; exhaler.
transplant, *v.a.*, transplanter; déplacer, transporter.
transplantation (-pla'n'té-), *n.*, transplantation, *f.*; déplacement, *m.*

transplanter, *n.*, transplanteur; (thing—*chose*) transplantoir, *m.*
transplanting, *n.*, transplantation, *f.*
transplendency, *n.*, splendeur éclatante, *f.*
transplendent, *adj.*, très resplendissant; éblouissant.
transplendently, *adv.*, d'une manière très resplendissante.
transport (-pôrte), *n.*, transport; (ship—*navire*) transport, bâtiment de transport; (rapture—*extase*) transport; (of anger—*de colère*) transport, accès; (convict—*condamné*) forçat, *m.*
transport (-pôrte), *v.a.*, transporter; (convicts—*des condamnés*) déporter.
transportable (-pôrt'a-b'l), *adj.*, transportable.
transportation (-pôr-té-), *n.*, transport, *m.*; transmission; (of plants—*de plantes*) transplantation; (of convicts—*de condamnés*)déportation, *f.*
transportedly (-pôrt'èd-), *adv.*, en extase, *f.*
transportedness(-pôrt'èd'-), *n.*, transport, *m.*; extase, *f.*
transporter (-pôrt'-), *n.*, personne qui transporte; chose qui transporte, qui ravit, qui exalte, *f.*
transporting (-pôrt'-), *adj.*, qui transporte; (ravishing—*ravissant*) ravissant.
transposal (-pô-'-), *n.*, transposition; permutation, *f.*
transpose (-pôze), *v.a.*, transposer.
transposition (-zish'-), *n.*, transposition, *f.*
transpositive (-poz'-), *adj.*, transpositif.
trans-ship, *v.a.*, transborder.
trans-shipment, *n.*, transbordement, *m.*
transubstantiate (-shi-éte), *v.a.*, transubstantier.
transubstantiation (-sta'n'shi-ó-), *n.*, transsubstantiation, *f.*
transubstantiator (-shi-ét'cur), *n.*, transsubstantiateur, *m.*
transudation(-sioud'é-),*n.*,transsudation,*f.*
transude (-sioude), *v.n.*, transsuder.
transversal (-veur-),*adj.*, transverse, transversal.
transversally, *adv.*, transversalement.
transverse (-veurse), *adj.*, tranverse; oblique, transversal.
transversely, *adv.*, en travers; transversalement.
trap, *n.*, trappe, *f.*; traquenard, traquet; (fig.) piège, *m.*, embûche; (milit.) chausse-trape; (game—*jeu*) balle à la volée, *f.*; (geol.) trapp; (mines) rejet, *m.*
trap, *v.a.*, prendre dans une trappe; prendre au piège, attraper.
trap, *v.n.*, tendre une trappe.
trapan, *n.*, piège, *m.*
trapan, *v.a.*, prendre au piège.
trapanner, *n.*, personne qui prend au piège, *f.*
trap-door (-dôre), *n.*, trappe, *f.*
trapes(trépse),*n.*,femme sale et paresseuse,*f.*
trapezium (-pi-zi-), *n.*, trapèze; (anat.) os trapèze, *m.*
trapezius, *n.*, (anat.) trapèze, 'muscle trapèze, *m.*
trapezoid (-'i-zoïde), *n.*, trapézoïde; trapèze, *m.*
trapezoidal (-zoïd'-), *adj.*, trapézoïde, trapéziforme.
trappings (-pign'ze), *n.pl.*, harnais, *m.s.*; ornements du harnais, *m.pl.*; (dress—*parure*) parure, *f.s.*, ornements, *m.pl.*
trap-stick, *n.*, crosse (pour jouer); (fig.) jambe grêle, *f.*
trash, *n.*, rebut, *m.*; drogue, camelotte; (of eatables—*de comestibles*) drogue, cochonnerie, *f.*; (loppings of trees—*branches d'arbres*) émondes, *f.pl.*

trash, *v.a.*, (to lop—*couper*) émonder ; (to strip of leaves—*dépouiller de feuilles*) effeuiller ; (to clog—*empétrer*) arrêter, empêcher ; (to humble—*humilier*) courber, humilier.

trashy, *adj.*, de rebut, méchant ; de nulle valeur.

travail (trav'il), *v.n.*, travailler, fatiguer ; (of women in labour—*des femmes*) être en travail d'enfant.

travail (trav'il), *n.*, travail pénible, *m.* ; fatigue, *f.* ; (of women—*des femmes*) travail d'enfant, *m.*

trave (tréve), *n.*, (arch.) traverse, *f.* ; (for a horse—*pour cheval*) travail, *m.*

travel, *v.n.*, voyager ; être en voyage ; (to walk—*marcher*) cheminer, marcher ; (to pass—*passer*) marcher, aller ; (of news—*des nouvelles*) circuler, voyager. To — over ; *parcourir ; voyager dans*.

travel, *n.*, voyage, *m.*

traveller, *n.*, voyageur, *m.*, voyageuse, *f.* ; (com.) commis voyageur, *m.*

traveller's-joy (-leur'z'djoè), *n.*, (bot.) clématite commune, *f.*

travelling, *n.*, voyage, *m.* ; voyages, *m.pl.*

travelling, *adj.*, voyageur ; ambulant ; (of things—*des choses*) de voyage.

traversable (-vèrs'a-b'l), *adj.*, (jur.) niable.

traverse (trav'èrse), *n.*, traverse ; (cross accident—*obstacle*) traverse, *f.*, obstacle ; (trick —*tour*) artifice, *m.* ; (jur.) dénégation ; (nav.) route oblique ; (fort.) traverse, *f.*

traverse, *adj.*, oblique ; transversal.

traverse, *prep.*, à travers.

traverse, *adv.*, à travers, en travers.

traverse (-vèrse), *v.a.*, traverser ; (to survey —*examiner*) scruter ; (jur.) nier ; (artil.) pointer.

traverse, *v.n.*, tourner, pivoter ; (fenc.) se tenir en garde ; (man.) se traverser.

traverser, *n.*, (jur.) partie qui dénie, *f.*

travesty, *adj.*, travesti.

travesty, *n.*, traduction burlesque ; parodie, *f.*

travesty, *v.a.*, travestir, parodier.

travis. *V.* **trave**.

tray, *n.*, plateau, *m.* ; (trough—*auge*) auge, *f.*

treacherous (trètsh'èr'-), *adj.*, traître, perfide, déloyal.

treacherously (trètsh'èr'-), *adv.*, en traître ; perfidement ; traîtreusement.

treacherousness, *or* **treachery** (trèt-shèr'-), *n.*, trahison, perfidie, *f.*

treacle (tri-k'l), *n.*, (pharm.) thériaque ; mélasse, *f.*

tread (trède), *v.n.* (preterit, Trod ; past part., Trodden), poser le pied ; marcher ; (of birds—*des oiseaux*) côcher. To — on ; *marcher sur ; fouler aux pieds*.

tread, *v.a.*, marcher sur ; fouler ; fouler aux pieds ; écraser. To — under foot ; *fouler aux pieds*.

tread (trède), *n.*, pas, *m.* ; (of a stair—*d'escalier*) marche ; (man.) allure, *f.* ; (of birds—*des oiseaux*) accouplement, *m.*

treader (trèd'-), *n.*, personne qui foule, qui marche, *f.*

treadle (trèdd'l), *n.*, marche ; pédale, *f.* ; (of an egg—*d'un œuf*) cordon albumineux, *m.*

tread-mill, *n.*, moulin à marcher ; moulin de discipline, *m.*

treason (tri-z'n), *n.*, trahison, *f.* High- — ; *haute trahison ; lèse-majesté*, *f.*

treasonable (tri-z'n'a-b'l), *adj.*, de traître ; de trahison.

treasonably, *adv.*, en traître.

treasure (trèj'eur), *n.*, trésor, *m.*

treasure (trèj'eur), *v.a.*, amasser, accumuler ; garder, conserver précieusement.

treasure-house, *n.*, trésor, *m.* ; trésorerie, *f.*

treasurer (trèj'eur'-), *n.*, trésorier, *m.*

treasurership, *n.*, charge de trésorier, *f.*

treasure-trove (-trôve), *n.*, (jur.) trésor, *m.*

treasury (trèj'euri), *n.*, trésor ; (building—*édifice*) trésor, trésor public, *m.* ; trésorerie, *f.* First lord of the — ; *premier lord de la Trésorerie*, *m.*

treat (trîte), *v.a.*, traiter ; (to regale—*régaler*) traiter, régaler ; (med.) traiter, soigner.

treat, *v.n.*, traiter.

treat (trîte), *n.*, régal ; festin, banquet, *m.* ; fête, *f.* ; (pleasure—*plaisir*) charme, délice, plaisir, grand plaisir, *m.*

treater (trît'-), *n.*, personne qui traite, *f.* ; dissertateur, *m.* ; (regaler—*amphytrion*) personne qui traite, qui régale, *f.*, amphytrion, *m.*

treatise (tri-tize), *n.*, (book—*livre*) traité, *m.*

treatment (trît'-), *n.*, traitement, *m.*

treaty (tri-), *n.*, traité ; pacte, *m.* ; convention ; négociation, *f.*

treble (trè'b'l), *v.a.* and *n.*, tripler.

treble, *adj.*, triple ; (mus.) de dessus ; (of sound—*du son*) aigu, perçant.

treble (trèb'b'l), *n.*, triple ; (mus.) dessus, *m.*

trebleness, *n.*, triplicité, *f.*

trebling (trèb'-), *n.*, triplement, *m.*

trebly (trèb'-), *adv.*, triplement, trois fois.

tree (tri), *n.*, (bot.) arbre ; arbrisseau, *m.* ; (rel.) croix, *f.* Genealogical — ; *arbre généalogique*.

treeless, *adj.*, sans arbre.

tree-nail, *n.*, cheville, *f.*

tree-nail, *v.a.*, cheviller ensemble.

trefoil (tri-foïl), *n.*, trèfle, *m.*

treillage (trèl'adje), *n.*, treillage, *m.*

trellis, *n.*, treillis, *m.*

trellis, *v.a.*, treillisser.

trellised (trèl'liste), *adj.*, treillissé.

tremble (trèm'b'l), *v.n.*, trembler ; (of sound —*du son*) trembloter.

trembler, *n.*, trembleur, *m.*, trembleuse, *f.*

trembling, *n.*, tremblement, *m.*

trembling, *adj.*, tremblant ; tremblotant.

tremblingly, *adv.*, en tremblant ; en tremblotant.

tremendous (tri-mè'n'-), *adj.*, redoutable ; formidable ; terrible ; imposant ; (violent) terrible, épouvantable, horrible.

tremendously, *adv.*, terriblement ; (with violence—*violemment*) terriblement, furieusement.

tremendousness, *n.*, caractère terrible, caractère formidable, *m.*, grandeur imposante, *f.*

tremor (trè'm'eur), *n.*, tremblement, *m.*

tremulous (trè'm'iou-), *adj.*, tremblant ; tremblotant ; (mus.) chevrotant.

tremulously, *adv.*, en tremblant ; en tremblotant ; (mus.) en chevrotant.

tremulousness, *n.*, qualité de ce qui tremble, qui tremblote, *f.* ; tremblement, *m.*

trench, *n.*, tranchée ; rigole, *f.*, fossé, *m.* ; (milit.) tranchée, *f.*

trench, *v.a.*, creuser, ouvrir ; sillonner ; (milit.) retrancher.

trench, *v.n.*, empiéter.

trencher, *n.*, tranchoir, tailloir, *m.* ; (table) table ; (food—*nourriture*) bonne chère, *f.*

trencher-friend (-frè'n'de), *n.*, parasite, écornifleur, *m.*

trencher-man, *n.*, mangeur, gros mangeur, *m.*

trend, *v.n.*, (nav.) courir ; faire force de voiles.

trendle (trè'n'd'l), *n.*, roulette, *f.*

trepan (tri-), *n.*, (surg.) trépan, *m.*

trepan (tri-), *v.a.*, trépaner.

trepang (tri-pan'gn), *n.*, (zool.) holoturie, *f.*, trépang, tripan, *m.*

trepanner (tri-), *n.*, personne qui trépane, *f.*

trepanning (tri-), *n.*, (surg.) trépan, *m.* ; trépanation, *f.*

trephine (tri-fîne, *ou* -faïne), *n.*, tréphine, *f.*; trépan, *m.*

trephining (tri-û'n'-, *ou* -faï'n'-), *n.*, trépan, *m.*; trépanation. *f.*

trepidation (trèp'-i-dé-), *n.*, trépidation; vibration, *f.*; (trembling—*tremblement*) tremblement, *m.*; (hurry—*diligence*) hâte; (terror—*crainte*) terreur, *f.*, effroi, *m.*

trespass (très-), *n.*, injure; (jur.) violation de propriété, *f.*, délit contre la personne, *m.*; (in Scripture—*biblique*) offense, *f.*, péché, *m.*, transgression. *f.*

trespass (très-), *v.n.*, (jur.) violer la propriété; (in Scripture—*biblique*) pécher, faillir. To — against; *violer, enfreindre*; (pers.) *nuire à, léser*. To — on; *empiéter sur; abuser de*.

trespasser, *n.*, personne qui empiète, *f.*; (jur.) violateur du droit de propriété; (rel.) pécheur, *m.*, pécheresse. *f.*, transgresseur, *m.*

trespass-offering (-of'feur'-), *n.*, sacrifice expiatoire pour le péché, *m.*

tress, *n.*, tresse de cheveux; boucle de cheveux, *f.*

tressed (très'te), *adj.*, tressé; bouclé.

tressel, *or* **trestle** (très'a'l), *n.*, tréteau; (of a table—*de table*) châssis, *m.* —s; *échelle double f.*

tressing, *n.*, (arch.) armature, *f.*

tret (trète), *n.*, réfaction sur le poids. *f.*

trevet (trèv'-), *n.* V. **trivet**.

trey (trè), *n.*, (at cards—*aux cartes*) trois, *m.*

triable (traï-a-b'l), *adj.*, qu'on peut essayer, qu'on peut éprouver; (jur.) justiciable.

triad (traï-ade), *n.*, triade, *f.*

trial (traï-al), *n.*, tentative, *f.*; essai, *m.*; (experiment—*expérience*)expérience, épreuve, *f.*, essai, *m.*; (temptation—*tentation*) épreuve, *f.*; (jur.) procès, jugement, *m.* To make a — of; *faire l'essai de*. To take one's —; *passer en jugement*. By way of —; *pour essayer; pour essai*. On —; *à l'essai*; (of things—*des choses*) *pour essai*.

triander (traï), *n.*, (bot.) plante triandre, *f.*

triandria (traï-), *n.*, (bot.) triandrie, *f.*

triangle (traï-an'gn'g'l), *n.*, triangle, *m.*

triangled (traï-an'gn'g'l'de), *adj.*, triangulé.

triangular (traï-an'gn-ghiou-), *adj.*, triangulaire.

triangularly, *adv.*, triangulairement.

tribe (traïbe), *n.*, tribu; (b.s.) race, famille; (natur. hist.) tribu, famille, classe, *f.*, ordre, *m.*

triblet, *or* **triboulet**, *n.*, (gold.) triboulet, *m.*

tribrach (traï-brake), *n.*, tribraque, *m.*

tribulation (trib'iou-lé-), *n.*, tribulation, *f.*

tribunal (tri-biou-), *n.*, tribunal, *m.*

tribune (trib'ioune), *n.*, tribun, *m.*; (pulpit—*tribune*) tribune, *f.*

tribuneship, *n.*, tribunat, *m.*

tribunitial (trib'iou-nish'al), *adj.*, tribunitien; de tribune.

tribunitian, *or* **tribunitious**, *adj.*, (ant.) V. **tribunitial**.

tributary (trib'iou-), *adj.*, tributaire; (subordinate—*subordonné*) inférieur, subordonné.

tributary (trib'iou-), *n.*, tributaire, *m.*

tribute (trib'ioute), *or* **tribute-money**, *n.*, tribut, *m.*

trice (traïce), *n.*, instant, moment, clin d'œil, *m.* In a —; *en un clin d'œil*.

trice (traïce), *v.a.*, (nav.) hisser promptement.

triceps (traï-cèpse), *n.*, (anat.) muscle triceps, *m.*

tricing-line (traï-cign'laïne), *n.*, (nav.) aiguillette, *f.*

trick, *n.*, (cheat—*duperie*) supercherie, duperie, tricherie, *f.*; (dexterous artifice—*ruse*) artifice, *m.*, ruse, finesse, *f.*, tour, *m.*; (jest.) malice, niche, *f.*; (of a juggler—*de jongleur*) tour, *m.*; (of children—*d'enfants*) espièglerie; (habit—*coutume*) habitude, *f.*, tic, *m.*; (of cards —*de cartes*) levée, *f.* To play any one a —; *faire une niche à, jouer un tour à quelqu'un*. To have the —; (at cards—*aux cartes*) *faire la levée*. Nasty —; *vilain tour*; (habit—*habitude*) *vilaine habitude*. Shabby —; vilenie, *f.*

trick, *v.a.*, duper; tricher; (to play a trick on—*faire un tour*) faire une niche à; (to dress—*orner*) parer, ☉ atourner. To —' out; *parer*. (jest.) ☉ *atourner*.

trick, *v.n.*, faire métier de duper.

tricker. V. **trickster**.

trickery. *n.*, tromperie, duperie; tricherie, *f.*

tricking, *n.*, tromperie, duperie, supercherie; (ornament—*parure*) parure, *f.*, atours, *m.pl.*

trickish, *adj.*, artificieux, trompeur; fourbe; fin, subtil.

trickle, *v.n.*, couler; découler, dégoutter, s'épancher. To —down; *couler le long de*.

trickling, *n.*, écoulement lent, écoulement, *m.*

trickster, *n.*, fourbe, *m.*, *f.*; trompeur, *m.*, trompeuse, *f.*; tricheur, *m.*, tricheuse, *f.*

tricktrack, *n.*, trictrac, *m.*

tricolour (traï-keul'eur), *n.*, drapeau tricolore, *m.*

tricoloured (traï-keul'leurde), *adj.*, tricolore.

trident (traï-), *n.*, trident, *m.*

tridentate, *or* **tridented** (traï-), *adj.*, tridenté.

tried (traïde), *adj.*, éprouvé.

triennial (traï-), *adj.*, triennal.

triennially (traï-), *adv.*, tous les trois ans.

trier (traï-), *n.*, personne qui essaie, qui éprouve, *f.*; expérimentateur, *m.*; (test—*épreuve*) épreuve, *f.*

trifallow (traï-fal-lô), *v.a.*, (agri.) donner la troisième façon à.

trifid (traï-), *adj.*, (bot.) trifide.

trifle (traï-f'l), *n.*, bagatelle; vétille; babiole, *f.*; rien, *m.* To stand upon —s; *s'arrêter à des vétilles, à des riens*. To dispute about —s; *disputer sur la pointe d'une aiguille*.

trifle (traï-f'l), *v.n.*, s'amuser à des riens, niaiser; badiner; baguenauder; (to act or talk with levity—*agir, parler avec légèreté*)être frivole, être léger. To — with; (things—*choses*)jouer avec, plaisanter sur; (pers.) amuser; (to mock—*se moquer*)se moquer de, se rire de.

trifler (traï-), *n.*, personne frivole, *f.*; baguenaudier; badin, *m.*

trifling (traï-), *adj.*, de rien; insignifiant, petit; (trivial—*insignifiant*) futile, oiseux; (frivolous—*frivole*) frivole, léger. —but troublesome debt; *dette criarde*.

trifling, *n.*, légèreté, frivolité; plaisanterie, *f.*; bagatelles, *f.pl.*; badinage, *m.*

triflingly, *adv.*, d'une manière frivole; d'une manière légère; en badinant.

triflingness, *n.*, petitesse, insignifiance; (levity—*légèreté*) légèreté, frivolité; futilité, *f.*

triform (traï-), *adj.*, triforme.

trigamy, *n.*, trigamie, *f.*

trigger (trig-gheur), *n.*, enrayure; (of firearms—*d'armes à feu*) détente, *f.* — -guard; pontet, *m.*

triglyph (traï-glife), *n.*, (arch.) triglyphe, *m.*

trigon (traï-), *n.*, (astron.) trigone, *m.*

trigonometrical (-mèt'-), *adj.*, trigonométrique.

trigonometry (-no'm-i-), *n.*, trigonométrie *f.*

trihedral (traï-hi-), *adj.*, trièdre.

trilateral (traï-lat'èr'-), *adj.*, trilatéral.

trill, *n.*, (mus.) trille, *m.*; ☉ cadence, *f.*

trill, *v.n.*, vibrer; (mus.) triller, cadencer.

trill, *v.a.*, chanter en cadençant; (mus. cadencer, triller.

trillion (tril'ieune), *n.*, quintillion, *m.*

trilobate (tril'-), *adj.*, (bot.) trilobé.

trilocular (traï-lok'iou-), *adj.*, (bot.) triloculaire.

trim, *v.a.*, arranger; ajuster ⊕to decorate⊣

orner) orner, parer : (to dress—*vétir*) habiller ;
(to lop—*couper*) émonder ; (to clip—*tailler*)
tailler. rafraîchir; (to finish off—*parfaire*)
achever ; (to scold—*gronder*) gronder ; (the hold
—*la cargaison*) arrimer ; (the sails—*les voiles*)
orienter ; (a boat—*un bateau*) dresser ; (a lamp—
lampe) arranger, préparer ; (earp.) dégrossir,
planer ; (a garment—*un vétement*) garnir ; (a
horse—*un cheval*) panser. To — in ; (carp,) assembler. To — up ; *arranger, ajuster ; (to
decorate—orner) garnir ; (to dress—vétir) parer,
orner.*

trim, *v.n.,* hésiter ; balancer entre deux
partis.

trim, *adj.,* propre ; bien ajusté ; bien arrangé.

trim, *n..* parure, toilette, *f.* ; (state—*état*)
état, *m.,* (of masts—*des mâts*) juste proportion;
(of a ship—*d'un vaisseau*) assiette, *f.* ; (of sails—
des voiles) orientement ; (of the hold—*de la cale*)
arrimage. *m.*

trimeter (trim'i-), *n.,* trimètre, *m.*

trimly, *adv.,* bien, gentiment.

trimmer. *n.,* personne qui arrange, qui
ajuste, qui orne, qui décore ; (time-server—*intrigant*) personne de tous les partis ; (shrew—
pie-grièche) femme acariâtre ; (arch.) bande de
trémie, *f.*

trimming, *n.,* garniture ; (scolding—*réprimande*) réprimande, correction, *f.*

trimness, *n.,* netteté, *f.*

trine (traïne),*n.,*(astrol.)trin, trine aspect,*m.*

trine, *adj.,* triple, *f.*

trine (traïne), *v.a.,* mettre dans un trine
aspect.

tringa, *n.,* tringa, *m.*

tringle (trï'n'g'l), *n.,* (arch.) tringle, *f.*

trinitarian (trï'n'i-té-), *n.,* trinitaire, *f.*

trinity, *n.,* Trinité. *f.*

trinity-herb (-eurbe), *n.,* violette tricolore,
pensée tricolore. *f.*

trinket, *n.,* bijou, *m.* ; breloque, *f.* ; (thing of
little value—*babiole*) colifichet, brimborion. *m.*

trinomial (traï-nô-),*n.,*(alg.) trinôme, *f.*

trio (traï-ô), *n.,* (mus.) trio, *m.*

triolet (traï-), *n.,* (poet.) triolet, *m.*

trior (traï-), *n.,* (jur.) personne désignée par
le tribunal pour examiner la validité d'une récusation de juré, *f.*

trip, *n.,* croc en jambe ; (stumble—*faux pas*)
faux pas, *m.* ; (error—*erreur*) erreur, méprise,
f. ; (journey—*voyage par terre*) tournée, *f.* , tour,
petit voyage ; (voyage—*voyage par mer*) voyage,
m. ; (nav.) bordée, *f.*

trip, *v.a.,* donner un croc en jambe à, renverser ; faire trébucher ; (to supplant—*supplanter*) supplanter, couper l'herbe sous le pied de ;
(to detect—*découvrir*) découvrir, surprendre,
démasquer;(an anchor—*une ancre*) faire déraper.

trip, *v.n.,* trébucher, faire un faux pas ;
tomber ; (to err—*se tromper*) errer, se tromper ;
(of the tongue—*de la langue*) fourcher ; (to run
lightly—*courir légèrement*) courir avec légèreté ;
(to step lightly—*marcher légèrement*) marcher
avec légèreté ; (to take a journey—*voyager*) faire
un petit voyage.

tripartite (-taïte), *adj.,* triparti, tripartite ;
(mus.) en trois parties.

tripe (traïpe), *n.,* tripe, *f.* ; gras-double, *m.* ;
(the belly—*ventre*) panse, bedaine, *f.* — -man ;
tripier, m. — -woman ; *tripière, f.* — shop ;
triperie,f.

tripedal (trip'i-), *adj.,* qui a trois pieds.

triphthong (trip'thon'g), *n.,* triphthongue,*f.*

triphthongal (trip'thon'g'-), *adj.,* de triphtongue.

triphyllous, *adj.,* triphylle. *f.*

triple (trip'p'l), *v.a.,* tripler.

triple (trip'p'l), *adj.,* triple.

triplet, *n..* trio : (poet.) tercet ; (mus.)
triolet. *m.*

triplicate, *adj.,* (math.) triplé.

triplication (-pli-ké-), *n.,* triplication, *f.*

triplicity (traï-), *n.,* triplicité, *f.*

triply, *adv.,* triplement.

tripod (traï-), *n.,* trépied, *m.*

tripoli. *n.,* (min.) tripoli, *m.*

tripper, *n.,* personne qui renverse, qui sup-
plante, qui court avec légèreté, qui marche avec
légèreté, *f.*

tripping, *n.,* bronchade, *f.* ; faux pas, *m.*

tripping, *adj.,* trébuchant ; (nimble—*agile*)
agile, léger ; (-quick—*vite*) rapide.

trippingly, *adv.,* agilement ; légèrement ;
vivement.

triptote (-tôte), *n.,* (gram.) triptote, *m.*

trireme (traï-rime), *n.,* trirème, *f.*

trisect (traï-cèkte), *v.a.,* diviser en trois
parties.

trisection (traï-cèk'-), *n.,* trisection, *f.*

trismus, *n.,* (med.) trismus, *m.*

trisyllabic, *or* **trisyllabical** (tri-cil'-),
adj., trissyllabe.

trisyllable (tri-cil'-), *n.,* trissyllabe, *m.*

trite (traïte), *adj.,* usé, banal, rebattu.

tritely (traït'-), *adv.,* d'une manière banale.

triteness (traït'-), *n.,* nature banale, nature
commune, *f.*

triton, *n.,* triton, *m.*

tritone (traï'-), *n.,* (mus.) triton, *m.*

tritoxide (traï-toks'ide), *n.,* tritoxyde. *m.*

triturable (trit'iou-ra-b'l), *adj.,* triturable.

triturate (trit'iou-), *v.a.,* triturer.

trituration (trit'iou-ré-), *n.,* trituration, *f.*

triumph (traï-eu'm'fe), *n.,* triomphe, *m.* ;
(exultation—*joie*) joie triomphante, *f.*

triumph (traï-eu'm'fe), *v.n.,* triompher ; (to
flourish—*prospérer*) prospérer, fleurir. To —
over ; triompher de, insulter à ; (to surmount—
surmonter) surmonter.

triumphal (traï-eu'm'-), *adj.,* triomphal ; de
triomphe. — arch ; arc de triomphe, *m.*

triumphant (traï-eu'm'-),*adj.,* triomphant ;
triomphal ; de triomphe.

triumphantly, *adv.,* en triomphe, triomphalement ; d'une manière triomphante.

triumpher, *n.,* triomphateur, *m.*

triumvir (traï-eu'm'veur), *n.* (*triumviri*)
triumvir, *m.*

triumvirate (traï-eu'm'veur'-), *n.,* triumvirat, *m.*

trivet, *n.,* trépied ; (kitchen utensil—*ustensile
de cuisine*) trépied, trois-pieds, *m.*

trivial, *adj.,* trivial, vulgaire; insignifiant.

trivially, *adv.,* trivialement, vulgairement;
d'une manière insignifiante.

trivialness, *n.,* trivialité ; vulgarité, *f.* ;
(unimportance—*sans importance*) défaut d'importance, *m.,* nullité, *f.*

troat (trôte), *v.a.,* (of the buck—*du daim*)
bramer.

troat (trôte), *n.,* (of the buck—*du daim*)
bramement, *m.*

trocar, *or* **trochar** (trô-kar)', *n.,* (surg.)
trocart, trois-quarts, *m.*

trochaic, *or* **trochaical** (tro-ké-), *adj.,*
trochaïque.

trochanter (-ka'n'-),*n.,*(anat.)trochanter,*m.*

troche (trô-ki), *n.,* (pharm.) trochisque, *m.*

trochee (trô-ki), *n.,* trochée, *m.*

trojan (tro-dja'n),*n.,*Troyen,*m.*,Troyenne,*f.*

trojan, *adj.,* troyen.

troll (trôl), *v.a.,* rouler, tourner.

troll, *v.n.,* rôder, trôler ; (fishing—*péche*)
pêcher au brochet à la ligne.

trollop. *n.,* salope, souillon, *f.*

trombone (-bône), *n.,* (mus.) trombone, *m.*

troop, *n.,* troupe, *f.* ; (of cavalry—*de cavalerie*)
peloton, *m.,* compagnie, *f.*

troop (troupe), *v.n.,* s'attrouper ; (to march
in a body—*marcher en corps*) marcher en corps.

trooper (troup'-), *n.*, cavalier, soldat de cavalerie ; troupier, *m.*

trope (trôpe). *n.*, (rhet.) trope, *m.*

trophied (trô-fide), *adj.*, orné de trophées.

trophy (trô-fi), *n.*, trophée, *m.*

tropic, *n.*, (geog.) tropique, *m.*

tropical, *adj.*, tropical ; du tropique ; (rhet.) figuratif, symbolique, emblématique.

tropic-bird (-beurde), *n.*, oiseau du tropique, *m.*

tropological (-'o-djic'-), *adj.*, (rhet.) tropologique, figuré.

trot, *n.*, trot, *m.* Jog, full —; *petit, grand trot.*

trot, *v.n.*, trotter, aller le trot, au trot; courir.

troth (troth), *n.*, foi, fidélité ; vérité, *f.* By my—! *ma foi !*

trotter, *n.*, cheval de trot ; trotteur ; (sheep's foot—*pied de mouton*) pied de mouton, *m.*

troubadour (trou-ba-dour), *n.*, troubadour, *m.*

trouble (treub'b'l), *v.a.*, troubler, inquiéter ; (to disturb—*déranger*) déranger, importuner ; (to perplex—*tourmenter*) tourmenter ; to distress—*affliger*) chagriner, affliger ; (to busy—*occuper*) préoccuper, occuper ; (to vex—*tracasser*) ennuyer, tracasser ; (to give occasion for labour to—*causer une augmentation de travail*) donner de la peine à ; (a debtor—*un débiteur*) importuner. I will—you to pass me that; *voulez-vous bien me passer cela ?* I will not—you with it ; *je ne vous en embarrasserai pas.* I will not—you in this affair ; *je ne veux pas vous déranger (importuner) pour cette affaire.* I will not—you; *je ne veux pas vous donner cette peine.* May I—you to? *puis-je vous prier de ?*

trouble (treub'b'l), *n.*, trouble, *m.* ; (fatigue, work—*labeur*) peine ; (uneasiness—*inquiétude*) inquiétude ; (affliction) affliction, peine, *f.*, souci, chagrin, *m.* ; (annoyance—*ennui*) importunité, tracasserie, *f.*, ennui, *m.* ; (pains—*chagrin*) peine, *f.* To be in —; *être dans la peine, dans le chagrin; avoir de la peine, du chagrin, des soucis.* To give, to save any one—; *donner, épargner de la peine à quelqu'un.* To take the—to ; *prendre, se donner la peine de.* Out of one's—; *hors de ses peines; hors de peine.* It is not worth the—; *ce n'est pas la peine; cela n'en vaut pas la peine.*

troubler, *n.*, personne qui donne de la peine, qui trouble, *f.* ; perturbateur, *m.*, perturbatrice, *f.*

troublesome (treub'b'l'ceume), *adj.*, ennuyeux ; incommode ; gênant, embarrassant ; (tiresome—*ennuyeux*) ennuyeux, tracassier, tourmentant ; (importunate—*importun*) ennuyeux, importun ; (burdensome—*fatigant*) à charge. Children are very —; *les enfants donnent beaucoup de peine.*

troublesomely, *adv.*, d'une manière ennuyeuse ; avec importunité ; avec beaucoup de peine.

troublesomeness, *n.*, ennui ; embarras, *m.* ; (importunity—*importunité*) importunité, *f.*

troublous, *adj.*, (l.u.) troublé, agité ; de troubles, de désordres.

trough (trof), *n.*, auge ; huche, *f.* ; (for a bird, &c.—*pour un oiseau, &c.*) auget ; (metal.) creuset ; (of the sea—*de la mer*) entre-deux des lames, *m.* ; (of a mill—*de moulin*) auge, *f.*

trounce (traou'n'ce), *v.a.*, rosser, étriller.

trousers, *or* **trowsers** (traou-zeurze), *n.pl.*, pantalon, *m.*, *sing.* A pair of —; *pantalon, m. sing.*

trout (traoute), *n.*, (ich.) truite, *f.*

trout-coloured (-keul'leurde), *adj.*, truité.

trout-stream (-strîme), *n.*, vivier à truites, *m.*

trover (trôv'-), *n.*, restitution d'une chose trouvée, *f.*

trow (trô). *v.n.*, (ant.) penser, croire, s'imaginer.

trowel (traou'èl), *n.*, truelle, *f.* ; (gard.) déplantoir, *m.*

trowsers; *n.pl. V.* **trousers.**

troy-weight (troï-wéte), *n.*, poids de douze onces à la livre employé pour l'or, l'argent, les pierres, *m.*

truant (trou-), *adj.*, fainéant, paresseux, flâneur.

truant (trou-), *n.*, fainéant, paresseux, flâneur, *m.* To play —; *faire l'école buissonnière.*

truant (trou-), *v.n.*, fainéanter, paresser, s'absenter.

truantly, *adv.*, en fainéant, en paresseux.

truantship, *n.*, fainéantise, paresse, flânerie, *f.*

truce (trouce), *n.*, trêve, *f.* A—to; *trêve de, trève, m.*

truce-breaker (-brèk'-), *n.*, violateur de trêve, *m.*

truck (treuke), *n.*, (barter—*troc*) troc, échange ; (manu.) paiement en marchandises, *m.* ; (wooden wheel—*roue*) roue de bois, *f.* ; (cart—*charrette*) camion, binard, *m* ; charrette à bras ; (artil.) roue d'affût ; (nav.) cosse de bois ; (on topmasts, &c.—*de mâts, &c.*) pomme ; (railways) plate-forme, *f.*, truc, truck, *m.* —system ; *système de payer les ouvriers en marchandises, m.*

truck (treuke), *v.a. and n.*, troquer.

truckage (treuk'édje), *n.*, troc, échange, *m.*

trucker (treuk'-), *n.*, troqueur, trafiquant, *m.*

truckle (treuk'l), *n.*, roulette, *f.*

truckle (treuk'l), *v.n.*, céder, se soumettre ; s'abaisser ; ramper, s'humilier.

truckle-bed (-bède), *n.*, lit à roulettes, *m.*

truculence (trou-kiou-), *n.*, barbarie, férocité, *f.* ; (of the countenance—*du visage*) aspect féroce, *m.*

truculent (trou-kiou-), *adj.*, barbare, féroce ; (destructive—*destructif*) meurtrier, cruel ; (of the countenance—*du visage*) d'un aspect terrible.

trudge (treudje), *v.n.*, aller à pied ; faire route à pied ; marcher péniblement, se traîner.

true (trou), *adj.*, vrai ; (real—*réel*) vrai, réel, véritable ; (faithful—*fidèle*) fidèle ; (free from falsehood—*vrai*) vrai, exact, fidèle ; (speaking truth—*sincère*) véridique, sincère ; (honest—*honnête*) honnête, intègre, loyal ; (exact) exact, conforme ; (straight—*droit*) droit ; (rightful—*légitime*) légitime. —to; *fidèle à.*

true-born, *adj.*, de naissance légitime ; vrai.

true-bred (-brède), *adj.*, de bonne race ; pur sang ; (fig.) accompli, achevé.

true-hearted (-hârt'-), *adj.*, au cœur sincère.

true-heartedness, *n.*, sincérité de cœur, *f.*

true-love (-leuve), *n.*, bien-aimé, *m.*, bien-aimée, *f.* ; (bot.) parisette à quatre feuilles, *f.*

trueness, *n.*, vérité ; sincérité ; fidélité ; (genuineness—*authenticité*) vérité, authenticité ; (exactness—*justesse*) exactitude, *f.*

truffle (treu-f'l), *n.*, truffe, *f.*

truffle-ground (-graou'n'de), *n.*, truffière, *f.*

trug (treughe), *n.*, (mas.) oiseau, *m.*

truism (trou-iz'm), *n.*, vérité évidente, *f.*

truly (trou-li), *adv.*, vraiment ; (exactly—*réellement*) vraiment, réellement, véritablement ; (sincerely—*sincèrement*) vraiment, fidèlement.

trump (treu'm'p), *n.*, trompe, trompette, *f.* ; (at cards—*aux cartes*) atout, *m.* — card ; *atout, m.* ; retourne, *f.*

trump (treu'm'pe), *v.a.*, couper avec l'atout, couper. To — up ; *inventer, forger.*

trumpery (treu'm'p'-), *n.*, éclat trompeur ; faux brillant ; (rubbish—*friperie*) rebut, *m.*, friperie, *f.*

trumpet (treu'm'-), *n.*, trompette ; trompe ; (praiser—*flatteur*) personne qui loue, *f.* ; (trumpeter—*homme*) trompette, *m.* Speaking-—; *porte-voix, m.*

trumpet, *v.a.*, publier à son de trompe ; proclamer ; trompeter, prôner.

trumpeter (-'ĕt'eur), n., trompette ; (orni.) agami, oiseau trompette, m.

trumpet-fish, n., (ich.) centrisque, m., bécasse de mer, f.

trumpet-flower (-fla-weur), n., (bot.) bignone, f.

trumpet-shaped (-shép'te), adj., en trompette ; (bot.) tubiforme.

trumpet-shell, n., trompette, f. ; buccin, m.

trumpet-tongued (-teu'n'g'de), adj., à voix de stentor.

truncate (treu'n'gn'-), v.a., tronquer, mutiler.

truncate (treu'n'gn'-), adj.. (bot.) tronqué.

truncated (treu'n'gn'két'-), adj., tronqué.

truncation (treu'n'gn'ké-), n., mutilation, f.

truncheon (treu'n'sheune), n., gourdin, rondin ; bâton, gros bâton ; bâton de commandement, m.

truncheon (treu'n'sheune), v.a.. bâtonner.

truncheoneer, n., personne armée d'un bâton, d'un gourdin, f.

trundle (treu'n'd'l), n., roulette, f. ; (cart-charrette) camion, m.

trundle (treu'n'd'l), v.a., rouler ; (a hoop—un cerceau) faire courir.

trundle, v.n., rouler.

trundle-bed, n., lit à roulettes, m.

trunk (treu'n'ke), n., tronc ; (box—boîte) coffre, m., malle, f. ; (long tube) long tube, m., sarbacane, f. ; (anat., arch.) tronc ; (sculpt.) torse, m. ; (of elephants, of insects—des éléphants, des insectes) trompe, f. —hose ; chausses, f.pl. —-maker ; coffretier, layetier, m.

trunk (treu'n'ke), v.a., (metal.) débourber.

trunking, n., (metal.) débourbage, m.

trunnion (treu'n'ieune), n., tourillon, axe, m.

trusion (trou-jeune), n., action de pousser, f.

truss (treuss), n., trousse ; (bot.) touffe ; (of hay, straw—de paille, de foin) botte ; (nav.) drosse de racage, f. ; (surg.) bandage herniaire, suspensoir ; (carp.) nœud, m., ferme triangulaire, f., lien, m.

truss (treuss'), v.a., empaqueter ; serrer ; lier ; (poultry—volaille) trousser.

truss-maker (-mék'-), n., bandagiste, m.

trust (treuste), n., (confidence—confiance) confiance ; (ground of confidence—espérance) espérance ; (charged, received in confidence—confiance) confiance, f. ; (something committed to a person's care—chose confiée) dépôt, m. ; (care—soin) garde ; (state of one to whom something is entrusted—emploi) place de confiance, f. ; (credit) crédit, (jur.) fidéicommis, m. On —; de confiance ; à crédit. To give any one —; faire crédit à quelqu'un.

trust (treuste), v.a., se fier à ; se confier à ; mettre sa confiance en ; (to believe—croire) ajouter foi à, croire ; (to commit to the care of —confier) confier ; (to give credit to—faire crédit) faire crédit à, donner à crédit à. To — with ; confier à ; (to give credit to—donner à crédit) faire crédit à.

trust, v.n., (to be credulous—se fier) être crédule. To — in, to ; se fier à ; mettre sa confiance ; se confier à ; compter sur ; croire à. To — to ; (before an infinitive—devant un infinitif) espérer, compter.

trustee (treus-tî), n., curateur, dépositaire, gardien ; directeur, administrateur ; (jur.) fidéicommissaire, m.

trusteeship, n., curatelle, direction ; administration, f. ; (jur.) fidéicommis, m.

truster, n., personne qui confie, qui fait crédit, f.

trustily, adv., fidèlement ; loyalement.

trustiness, n., fidélité ; probité, loyauté, f.

trustingly, adv., avec confiance.

trustless, adj., qui n'est pas digne de confiance ; infidèle.

trust-worthy (-weurthî), adj., digne de confiance.

trusty (treust'î), adj., sûr, fidèle, loyal ; (firm —sûr) fidèle, sûr.

truth (trouth) n., vérité, f. ; vrai, m. ; (honesty—probité) probité, loyauté ; (fidelity—fidélité) fidélité ; veracity—véracité) véracité. f. To tell the —; dire la vérité, le vrai ; à vrai dire.

truthful (-foule), adj., véridique, vrai.

truthless, adj., faux ; mensonger ; (faithless —sans foi) sans foi.

try (tra'ye), v.n., essayer ; tâcher ; (nav.) être à la cape.

try (tra'ye), v.a., essayer, éprouver ; faire l'épreuve de ; mettre à l'épreuve ; (to attempt—tenter) tenter, entreprendre, essayer ; (to experience—éprouver) éprouver. faire l'expérience de ; (to strain—fatiguer) fatiguer ; (to use as means—essayer) essayer, faire l'essai de ; (to search carefully into—approfondir) sonder ; (metals—métaux) essayer, faire l'essai de ; (to refine—purifier) affiner, purifier ; (weights, measures—poids, mesures) contrôler, vérifier ; (jur.) juger ; (pers.) traduire en justice, mettre en jugement. To — on ; essayer.

try (tra'ye), n., essai, m.

trying (tra-yigne), adj., d'épreuve. difficile, critique ; (straining—fatigant) fatigant ; (nav.) à la cape.

try-sail (-séle), n., voile de senau, f.

tub (teube), n., cuve, f. ; cuvier ; baquet ; (small cask—baril) tonneau, m. ; (for vegetables —pour végétaux) caisse, f. ; (of Diogenes—de Diogène) tonneau, m.

tube (tioube), n., tube ; conduit, canal, vaisseau, m.

tube (tioube), v.a., tuber.

tuber (tioub'-), n., (anat.) tubérosité, f. ; (bot.) tubercule, m.

tubercle (tiou-bèr'k'l), n., tubercule, m.

tubercled (tiou-bèr'k'l'de), adj., tuberculé, tuberculeux.

tubercular, or **tuberculous** (tiou-bèr'kiou-), adj., tuberculeux.

tuberose (tiou-bè-rôze), n.,(bot.) tubéreuse, f.

tuberosity (tiou-bèr'oss'-), n., tubérosité, f.

tuberous (tiou-bèr'-), adj., tubéreux.

tub-fish (teube), n., (ich.) perlon, m

tubular, **tubulated**, or **tubulous** (tiou-biou-), adj., tubulaire ; tubuleux ; tubulé.

tubule (tiou-bioule), n., tubule, m.

tubulus, n., (anat.) tube ; vaisseau, m.

tuck (teuke), n., estoc ; (in garments—des vêtements) rempli, pli, m. ; (nav.) fesses, f.pl.

tuck (teuke), v.a., trousser, retrousser, relever. To — in ; rentrer. To — in the bed-clothes ; border le lit. To — into bed ; bien envelopper dans les couvertures. To — up ; trousser, retrousser, relever.

tucker (teuk'-), n., chemisette. f.

tue-iron (tiou-aïeurn), n., tuyère, f.

tuesday (tiouz'-), n., Mardi, m.

tufa (tou-), or **tuff** (teufe), n., (min.) tuf, m.

tufaceous (tou-fé-shieuss), adj., tufacé.

tufa-stone (-stône), n., pierre de tuf, f., tuffeau, m.

tuft (teuf'te), n., touffe, houppe ; (of a bird—d'oiseau) huppe, aigrette ; (of hair—de cheveux) touffe ; (of trees, of flowers—d'arbres, de fleurs) touffe, f., bouquet ; (milit.) pompon ; (bot.) corymbe. m.

tuft (teuf'te), v.a., diviser en touffes ; orner de touffes.

tufted, adj., touffu ; en touffe ; semé de touffes.

tug (teughe), v.a. and n., tirailler ; tirer avec violence.

tug (teughe), n., action de tirer avec violence, f. ; tiraillement ; (boat—bateau) remorqueur, m.

tugger (teug'gheur), *n.*, personne qui tire avec violence; personne qui tiraille, *f.*

tuggingly (teug'ghign'-), *adv.*, en tirant avec violence; en tiraillant.

tuition (tiou-ish'eune), *n.*, tutelle; protection; (instruction) instruction, *f.*, enseignement, *m.*

tulip (tiou-), *n.*, tulipe, *f.* — -tree; *tulipier*, *m.*

tumble (teu'm'b'l), *n.*, chute; culbute, *f.*

tumble (teu'm'b'l), *v.n.*, (to roll—*rouler*) rouler, se rouler; (to roll down—*tomber*) descendre en roulant, rouler, dégringoler; tomber, s'écrouler; (of mountebanks—*de saltimbanques*) faire la culbute, culbuter. To — down; *tomber par terre*; (of things—*des choses*) tomber; (of buildings—*de bâtiments*) s'écrouler. To — down stairs; *dégringoler l'escalier*.

tumble, *v.a.*, tourner, retourner, remuer; déranger; (to rumple—*chiffonner*) chiffonner, bouchonner. To —down stairs; *faire dégringoler l'escalier*.

tumbler, *n.*, bateleur, saltimbanque, sauteur, *m.*, sauteuse, *f.*; (glass—*verre*) grand verre; (orni.) pigeon culbutant, *m.*

tumbrel (teu'm'-), *n.*, tombereau, *m.*

tumefaction (tiou-mi-fak-), *n.*, tuméfaction, *f.*

tumefy, *v.a.*, tuméfier, enfler.

tumefy (tiou-mi-fa'ye), *v.n.*, s'enfler.

tumid (tiou-), *adj.*, enflé, gonflé, renflé; (fig) boursouflé, ampoulé, bouffi.

tumidly, *adv.*, avec enflure, avec gonflement.

tumidness, *n.*, enflure; turgescence, *f.*; gonflement, *m.*

tumour (tiou-meur), *n.*, tumeur; (fig.) boursouflure, enflure, *f.*

tumoured (tiou-meurde), *adj.*, à tumeur.

tump (teu'm'pe), *n.*, motte, butte, *f.*

tump (teu'm'pe), *v.a.*, (agri.) chausser.

tumular (tiou-miou-), *adj.*, en monticule.

tumulosity (tiou-miou-lôsa'-), *n.*, nature montueuse, *f.*

tumulous (tiou-miou-), *or* **tumulose** (-lôce), *adj.*, montueux.

tumult (tiou-meulte), *n.*, tumulte; trouble, *m.*

tumult (tiou-meulte), *v.n.*, s'élever en tumulte, s'agiter.

tumultuarily (tiou-meult'iou-), *adv.*, tumultuairement.

tumultuariness, *n.*, disposition tumultueuse; turbulence, *f.*

tumultuary, *adj.*, tumultuaire; agité.

tumultuation (tiou-meult'iou-é-), *n.*, (ant.) mouvement tumultuaire, *m.*

tumultuous (tiou-meult'iou-eusse), *adj.*, tumultueux; (turbulent) turbulent; (agitated—*agité*) agité, troublé.

tumultuously, *adv.*, tumultueusement.

tumultuousness, *n.*, disposition tumultueuse; turbulence, *f.*

tumulus (tiou-miou-), *n.*, tumulus, *m.*

tun (teune), *n.*, (cask—*tonneau*) tonneau, *m.*, tonne, *f.*; (of wine—*de vin*) tonneau (litres 953·8030); (of round timber—*de bois en grume*) environ mètre cube 1·1237; (of square timber—*de bois équarri*) environ mètre cube 1·5171; (drunkard, large quantity—*ivrogne; grande quantité*) tonneau, *m.*

tun (teune), *v.a.*, verser dans un tonneau, entonner.

tunable (tiou'n'a-b'l), *adj.*, harmonieux; musical; (mus.) accordable.

tunableness, *n.*, harmonie, *f.*

tunably, *adv.*, harmonieusement; (mus.) d'accord.

tun-bellied (-bèl'lide), *adj.*, pansu, ventru.

tune (tioune), *n.*, air ; (concert of parts—*accord des parties*) ton, accord; (note) son, *m.*, note; (harmony—*harmonie*) harmonie; concorde; (fit temper—*humeur*) humeur, veine, *f.* To sing te another — ; *changer de ton*.

tune (tioune), *v.a.*, accorder, mettre d'accord.

tune, *v.n.*, former des accords; fredonner.

tuneful (-foule), *adj.*, mélodieux, harmonieux; aux accents mélodieux.

tuneless (tiou'n'-), *adj.*, sans harmonie; discordant; (mute—*silencieux*) mute.

tuner (tiou'n'-), *n.*, accordeur, *m.*

tungsten (teu'n'g'stène), *n.*, (chem.) tungstène, *m.*

tunic (tiou-), *n.*, tunique; (anat.) tunique; membrane; (of the eye—*de l'œil*) tunique, enveloppe, *f.*

tunicated (tiou-ni két'-), *adj.*, (bot.) tuniqué.

tuning (tiou'n'-), *n.*, action d'accorder, *f.*

tuning-fork (tiou'n'-), *n.*, diapason, *m.*

tuning-hammer, *n.*, accordoir; clef d'accordeur, *f.*

tunnage (teu'n'nédje), *n.*, tonnage; droit de tonnage, *m.*

tunnel (teu'n'nel), *n.*, tunnel; souterrain; (of a chimney—*de cheminée*) tuyau; (funnel—*entonnoir*) entonnoir, *m.*

tunnel (teu'n'-), *v.a.*, faire un souterrain, faire un tunnel; former en entonnoir; (hunt.) tonneler.

tunnelling, *n.*, construction de tunnels, *f.*

tunnel-net, *n.*, tonnelle, *f.*

tunnel-shaft (-shâfte), *n.*, puits de tunnel, *m.*

tunning (teu'n'-), *n.*, entonnage, *m.*

tunny (teu'n'-), *n.*, (ich.) thon, *m.*

tup (teupe), *n.*, (mam.) bélier, *m.*

tup, *v.a. and n.*, (of rams—*des béliers*) cosser; (to cover—*s'accoupler*) couvrir.

turban (teur-), *n.*, turban, *m.*; (conch.) spirale, *f.*

turbaned (teur-ba'n'de), *adj.*, coiffé du turban.

turban-shell, *n.*, sabot, *m.*

turbary (teur-), *n.*, (jur.) droit de lever de la tourbe sur le terrain d'un tiers, *m.*; tourbière, *f.*

turbid (teur-), *adj.*, trouble, bourbeux.

turbidly, *adv.*, dans un état trouble.

turbidness, *n.*, état bourbeux, état trouble, *m.*

turbinate, *or* **turbinated** (teur-bi-nét'-), *adj.*, turbiné, en toupie.

turbination (teur-bi-né-), *n.*, tournoiement, *m.*

turbinite (teur-bi-naïte), *n.*, (conch.) turbinite, *f.*

turbot (teur-beute), *n.*, turbot, *m.* — -kettle; *turbotière*, *f.*

turbulence, *or* **turbulency** (teur-biou-), *n.*, (insubordination) turbulence, insubordination; (agitation) agitation, *f.*; (tumult) trouble, désordre, tumulte, *m.*

turbulent (teur-biou-), *adj.*, en tumulte; tumultueux; bruyant; (refractory—*rebelle*) turbulent.

turbulently, *adv.*, en tumulte, tumultueusement; (with refractoriness—*turbulemment*) d'une manière turbulente, turbulemment.

turcism (teur-ciz'm), *n.*, turcisme, mahométisme, *m.*

tureen (teu-rîne), *n.*, soupière, *f.*

turf (teurfe), *n.*, gazon, *m.*; (peat—*tourbe*) tourbe, *f.*; (racecourse—*hippodrome*) hippodrome, terrain de course, turf, *m.*

turf (teurfe), *v.a.*, gazonner.

turfiness, *n.*, état de ce qui abonde en gazon, *m.*; nature du gazon; nature de la tourbe, *f.*

turfing, *n.*, gazonnement, *m.*

turf-moss, *n.*, tourbière, *f.*; terrain marécageux, *m.*

turf-pit, *n.*, tourbière, *f.*

turfy, *adj.*, qui abonde en gazon, gazonneux, herbeux; (having the quality of turf—*comme le gazon, la tourbe*) de la nature du gazon, de la

tourbe : (formed of turf—*formé de tourbe*) tour-beux.

turgent (teur-djà'n'te), *adj. V.* **turgid.**

turgescence, *or* **turgescency** (teur-djès'-), *n.,* turgescence, *f.* ; gonflement, *m.* ; (fig.) boursouflure, emphase, enflure, *f.*

turgid, *or* **turgidous,** (teur-djid'-) *adj.,* enflé ; gonflé ; turgescent ; (style) boursouflé, ampoulé, bouffi.

turgidity (teur-djid'-), *n.,* enflure, *f.* ; gonflement, *m.*

turgidly, *adv.,* avec enflure, avec bouffissure.

turgidness, *n.,* turgescence ; (of the style—*du style*) boursouflure, enflure, emphase, *f.*

turk (teurke), *n.,* Turc, *m.,* Turque. *f.*

turkey (teur-ké), *n.,* dindon, coq d'Inde, *m.* Young —; dindonneau, *m.* — -hen ; dinde, *f.*

turkois (teur-kize), *n. V.* **turquoise.**

turmeric (teur-mèr'-), *n.,* curcuma ; (dy.) safran des Indes, *m.*

turmoil (teur-moïl), *n.,* vacarme, tumulte ; tracas ; (labour—*travail*) labeur, *m.,* fatigue, *f.*

turmoil (teur-moïl), *v.a.,* agiter, harasser ; tourmenter, tracasser ; (to weary—*fatiguer*) lasser, fatiguer.

turmoil, *v.n.,* s'agiter, se tourmenter.

turn (teurne), *v.a.,* tourner ; (to shift sides—*changer les côtés*) tourner, retourner ; (to alter—*altérer*) changer ; (of a balance—*d'une balance*) faire pencher ; (to bring the inside out—*mettre à l'envers*) retourner ; (to form on a lathe—*travailler au tour*) tourner ; (to shape—*former*) tourner, façonner ; (to change, to transform—*transformer*) changer, convertir, transformer ; (to translate—*traduire*) traduire ; (to convert—*convertir*) convertir ; (to alter from one effect to another—*changer un effet en un autre*) faire tourner ; (to revolve —*tourner*) rouler, retourner ; (to transfer—*transférer*) transférer ; (prose into poetry—*de la prose en vers*) mettre ; (the stomach—*l'estomac*) soulever, faire soulever ; (one's head—*la tête*) tourner, faire tourner, troubler ; (the edge of any thing—*un tranchant*) ôter, émousser ; (print.) bloquer ; (com.) convertir. To — about ; *tourner, retourner.* To — aside ; *détourner de, éloigner de.* To — away ; *renvoyer, congédier, chasser, remercier ;* (to turn aside—*détourner*) *détourner de.* To — back ; *faire retourner ; renvoyer ;* (print.) *débloquer.* To — down ; *retourner ;* (a leaf, etc.—*une feuille*) *plier, faire un pli à ;* (a collar—*un col*) *rabattre.* To — from ; *détourner de.* To — in ; *tourner en dedans ; rentrer, faire rentrer.* To — into ; *changer en, transformer en, convertir en ;* (writing—*un écrit*) *traduire en, mettre en.* To — off ; *renvoyer, chasser, congédier, remercier ;* (steam—*vapeur*) *supprimer ;* (a cock—*robinet*) *fermer ;* (to hang—*pendre*) *lancer dans l'espace.* To — on ; *tourner contre ; diriger sur ;* (the eyes—*les yeux*) *tourner vers, diriger sur;* (steam—*vapeur*) *donner ;* (a cock—*un robinet*) *ouvrir.* To — out ; *mettre dehors ; renvoyer, chasser, mettre à la porte ;* (cattle—*bestiaux*) *renvoyer aux champs ;* (work—*ouvrage*) *faire.* To — over ; *tourner, retourner ;* (a book—*un livre*) *feuilleter.* To — over and over again ; *tourner et retourner.* To — over to ; *envoyer à, adresser à.* To — round ; *tourner, retourner.* To — up ; *tourner, retourner, trousser, retrousser ;* (in needle-work—*d'ouvrage à l'aiguille*) *remplier, faire un rempli à ;* (at cards—*aux cartes*) *retourner.* To — upside down ; *mettre sens dessus dessous.* To be —ed twenty ; *avoir plus de vingt ans, avoir vingt ans révolus.* To — an honest penny ; *faire un profit légitime.* To — him, her, them out, *à la porte !*

turn, *v.n.,* tourner ; se tourner ; se retourner ; (to deviate—*dévier*) se détourner, dévier ; (to be changed—*changer*) se changer, se transformer, se convertir ; (to become—*devenir*) devenir, se faire ; (to change to acid—*s'aigrir*) tourner ; (to become giddy—*avoir un étourdissement*) tourner, se troubler ; (of the tide—*de la marée*) changer. To — about ; *se tourner, se retourner.* To — aside, away ; *se tourner, se détourner.* To — back ; *se retourner en arrière ;* (to return—*rebrousser chemin*) *retourner sur ses pas.* To — down ; *se retourne.; se recourber.* To — down a street ; *entrer dans une rue.* To — from ; *s'éloigner de ; se détourner de ;* (of the stomach—*de l'estomac*) *se soulever à.* To — in ; *se tourner en dedans ;* (to enter—*entrer*) *entrer.* To — into ; *se changer en, se convertir en, se transformer en.* To — off ; *tourner, faire un détour ;* (pers.) *se détourner.* To — on ; *tourner sur, rouler sur ;* (to be given to—*se porter sur*) *se porter sur, se reporter sur.* To — out ; *tourner en dehors ; se retourner ;* (to go out—*sortir*) *sortir ;* (to rise from bed—*quitter son lit*) *se lever ;* (to happen—*d'un événement*) *arriver ;* (to end—*finir*) *tourner, finir ;* (to become—*devenir*) *devenir ; se montrer ;* (of plants, etc.—*des plantes, etc.*) *venir ;* (of workmen—*d'ouvriers*) *faire grève.* To — over ; *se tourner, se retourner ;* (to upset—*tomber*) *verser, se renverser ;* (to tumble—*culbuter*) *culbuter ;* (to change sides—*changer de côté*) *changer de parti.* To — round ; *tourner ; se tourner ; se retourner ;* (to change sides—*changer de côté*) *changer de parti.* To — to ; *tourner en ; se changer en ;* (to apply to—*s'adresser*) *s'adresser à, avoir recours à ;* (to set about—*commencer*) *se mettre à.* To — under ; *tourner en dessous.* To — up ; *tourner en haut ; être relevé ; être retroussé ;* (to happen—*d'un événement*) *arriver ; se trouver ; être ;* (pers.) *se montrer ; se trouver, être ; venir, revenir.* To — upside down ; *se renverser.* To — soldier ; *se faire militaire.* — in ! (nav.) *dans le sac !*

turn (teurne), *n.,* (circular movement—*mouvement circulaire*) tour ; (winding—*courbe*) tournant, coude, détour, *m.,* courbe, *f.* ; (walk —*promenade*) tour ; (vicissitude) changement, *m.,* vicissitude, *f.* ; (successive course—*rang successif*) tour, tour de rôle ; (course) cours, *m.,* direction, tournure ; (chance) occasion, opportunité, chance, *f.* ; (action of kindness or malice—*trait*) trait, office ; (reigning inclination—*mode*) goût, *m.,* fantaisie, *f.* ; (purpose—*vue*) projet, *m.,* vue, affaire ; (form—*contour*) forme, tournure, *f.,* contour, *m.* ; (of thought, style—*d'idée, de style*) tournure, *f.,* tour, *m.* ; (change—*changement*) phase, *f.* ; (of the tide—*de la marée*) changement ; (of a rope—*de corde*) tour, rond ; (of scales—*de balance*) trait ; (mines) puits, *m.* ; (mus.) double, *m.* At every —; *à tout moment ; à tout propos ; à tout bout de champ.* By —s; *à tour de rôle ; tour à tour.* A good —; *un bon office.* A bad —; *un mauvais office, un mauvais tour.*

turnbench, *n.,* tour à pointes, *m.*

turncoat (-côte), *n.,* renégat, *m.* ; girouette, *f.*

turner (teurn'-), *n.,* tourneur, *m.*

turnery (teurn'-), *n.,* art du tourneur, *m.* ; (things—*choses*) objets faits au tour, *m.pl.*

turning (teurn'-), *n.,* action de tourner, *f.* ; (of a road, etc.—*de routes, etc.*) détour, tournant, coude ; (print.) blocage, *m.*

turning-lathe (-léthe), *n.,* tour, *m.*

turnip (teur-), *n.,* navet, *m.* ; rave, *f.*

turnip-cabbage (-gab-bédje), *n.,*(bot.) chou-rave, *m.*

turnkey (-kî), *n.,* guichetier, *m.*

turnout (teurn'aoute), *n.,* équipage, *m.* ; (of workmen—*d'ouvriers*) grève ; (railways) gare, *f.*

turnpike (-pàïke), *n.,* tourniquet, *m.* ; barrière de péage, *f.*

turnplate, *or* **turntable,** *n.,* (railways) plate-forme tournante, plaque tournante, *f.*

turnscrew (-scrou), *n.,* tournevis, *m.*

turnsick, *n.,* (vet.) tournis, tournoiement, *m,*

turnsole (-sôle), n., (bot.) tournesol, m.

turnspit, n., tournebroche; (dog—chien) tournebroche, m.

turnstile (-staïle), n., tourniquet, m.

turnstone (-stône), n., (orni.) tournemotte, m.

turntable. V. **turnplate.**

turpentine (teur-pè'n'taïne), n., térébenthine, f.

turpentine-tree (-trî), n., pistachier térébinthe; térébinthe, m.

turpitude (teur-pi-tioude), n., turpitude; infamie, bassesse, f.

turquoise (teur-kīze), n., turquoise, f.

turret (teur-), n., tire-fond, m.

turret (teur-), n., tourelle, f.

turreted (teur-), adj., en forme de tour; garni de tourelles.

turtle (teur-'t'l), n., tortue; (orni.) tourterelle, f.

turtle-dove (-deuve), n., (orni.) tourterelle, f.

turtle-shell. V. **tortoise-shell.**

tuscan (teus-), adj., toscan.

tush! (teushe), int., bah!

tusk (teuske), n., dent canine, canine, f.; croc, m.; (of elephants, boars—d'éléphants, de sangliers) défense, f.

tusked (teusk'te), or **tusky** (teus-), adj., muni de canines, de crocs, de défenses.

tussle (teus's'l), n., lutte, f.

tut! (teute), int., ta, ta, ta; fi! fi donc!

tutelage (tiou-ti-lédje), n., tutelle, f.; état de pupille, m.

tutelar, or **tutelary** (tiou-ti-), adj., tutélaire.

tutor (tiou-teur), n., précepteur, instituteur; (jur.) tuteur; (at college—de collège) répétiteur, m.

tutor (tiou-teur), v.a., instruire; enseigner; (to correct—corriger) corriger, reprendre, faire la leçon à; (to treat with authority—commander) dominer.

tutorage (tiou-teur'édje), n., tutelle, f.

tutoress (tiou-teur'-), n., gouvernante, institutrice, f.

tutoring, n., instruction, f.; enseignement, m.

tutorship, n., préceptorat, m.

tutrix (tiou-), n., tutrice, f.

tutsan (teut-), n., (bot.) mille-pertuis, m.

tutty (tout-ti), n., (chem.) tutie, f.

tuyere (tu-yère), n., tuyère, f.

twaddle (twod'd'l), v.n., bavarder, babiller, caqueter.

twaddle (twod'd'l), or **twaddy** (twod'-), n., babil, bavardage, caquetage, m.

twain (twéne), adj., deux.

twang (twan'gn), n., cri aigu; (nasal voice—voix nasale) accent nasillard, m.

twang (twan'gn), v.n., rendre un son aigu, crier.

twattle (twot't'l), v.n., caqueter, jaser, bavarder.

twattler, n., bavard, m., bavarde, f.

twattling, n., babil, caquetage, bavardage, m.

tweak (twike), v.a., tirer, pincer.

tweedle (twid'd'l), v.a., manier légèrement; (to wheedle—cajoler) amadouer.

tweezers (twīz'eurze), n., pincette, f.; petites pinces, f.pl.

twelfth (twèlf'th), adj. and n., douzième. — night; jour des Rois, m. —night cake, — cake; gâteau des Rois, m.

twelve (twèl'v), adj., douze.

twelvemonth (twèlv'meu'n'th), n., an, m.; année, f.

twelvepence, n., schelling, m.

twelvepenny, adj., d'un schelling.

twentieth (twè'n'tièth), n. and adj., vingtième.

twenty (twè'n'-), adj., vingt.

twice (twaïce), adv., deux fois.

twifallow (twaï-fal-lô), v.a., jachérer une seconde fois.

twig, n., petite branche, brindille, f.

twiggen (twig'ghène), adj., fait de petites branches; d'osier.

twiggy (twig'ghi), adj., plein de ramilles.

twilight (twaï-laïte), n., crépuscule; demi-jour, m.; (fig.) aurore, f., crépuscule, m.

twilight, adj., sombre, obscur.

twill, v.a., plisser; croiser.

twin, n., jumeau, m., jumelle, f.; (fig.) jumeau, frère, m., sœur, f.

twin, adj., jumeau; (bot.) double, géminé.

twin-born, adj., né jumeau, jumelle.

twine (twaïne), n., ficelle, f.; (embrace—embrassement) embrassement; (twist—enveloppement) entortillement; (arch.) entrelacs, m.

twine (twaïne), v.a., retordre; dévider; tisser; (fig.) enlacer, lier.

twine (twaïne), v.n., tourner; (to unite closely—se lier) s'unir, se lier.

twinge (twi'n'dje), n., élancement; tiraillement; (fig.) tourment, m.

twitge (twi'n'dje), v.a., faire sentir une douleur cuisante à, tourmenter; (to pinch—pincer) pincer, tirer.

twinge, v.n., élancer.

twinging (twi'n'dj'-), n., action de pincer, de serrer; douleur aiguë et subite, f.; élancement, m.

twinkle (twi'n'k'l), v.n., étinceler; scintiller; briller; (of the eyes—des yeux) cligner.

twinkling, n., scintillement, m.; scintillation, f.; (of the eyes—des yeux) clignotement, clin d'œil, m. In the — of an eye; en un clin d'œil.

twinling, n., agneau jumeau, m.

twinner, n., mère de jumeaux, f.

twirl (tweurle), v.n., tournoyer; tourner; pirouetter.

twirl, v.a., tourner, faire tourner; faire faire le moulinet à.

twirl (tweurle), n., mouvement circulaire; (twist—torsion) tortillement, m.

twist, v.a., tordre, retordre; (to form into a thread—former un fil) filer; (to contort—tortiller) contourner, tortiller, tordre; (to encircle—entourer) cercler, entourer; (to unite by intertexture—enlacer) entrelacer, enlacer; (to pervert—pervertir) tordre, torturer. To—one's self into; s'insinuer dans, se glisser dans.

twist, v.n., s'entrelacer, s'enlacer.

twist, n., cordon, m.; corde, f.; cordonnet; (of a cord—d'une corde) cordon, fil, m.; (contortion—tortillement) contorsion, f., entortillement, tordage, tortillement; (of tobacco—de tabac) rouleau, m., carotte; (loaf—pain) natte, ; contorsion; (carp.) tresse; (arch.) nervure, f.

twisted, adj., tordu; (arch.) tors; (bot.) tors, tordu.

twister, n., tordeur, m., tordeuse, f.; cordier, m.

twisting, n., tordage; tortillement, m.

twit, v.a., blâmer; jeter une chose au nez. To—with; reprocher à.

twitch, n., élancement; tiraillement, m.

twitch, v.a., tirer brusquement; arracher.

twitter, n., gazouiller; (to titter—rire) rire du bout des lèvres.

twitter, n., censeur, critique; (of birds—des oiseaux) gazouillement; (titter—rire) rire du bout des lèvres.

twittingly, adv., avec reproche, en censurant.

two (tou), adj., deux.

two (tou), n., deux, m.

two-celled (tou-cèl'de), *adj.*, biloculaire.
two-cleft (-clèf'te), *adj.*, bifide.
two-edged (-èdj'de), *adj.*, à deux tranchants.
two-flowered (-fla'weur'de), *adj.*, (bot.) biflore.
two-fold (-fôlde), *adj.*, double.
two-fold, *adv.*, doublement
two-handed, *adj.*, bimane.
two-horned (-horn'de), *adj.*, bicorne.
two-leaved (-lîv'de), *adj.*, à deux feuilles ; (bot.) bifolié ; (of doors—*de portes*) à deux battants.
two-lobed (-lob'de), *adj.*, (bot.) bilobé.
two-masted (-mâst'-), *adj.*, à deux mâts.
twopence, *n.*, vingt centimes, deux pence, *m.pl.*
twopenny, *adj.*, de vingt centimes, de deux pence.
two-tongued (-teu'n'g'de), *adj.*, bilingue.
two-valved (-valv'de), *adj.*, bivalve.
tye (ta'ye), *n.*, itague de drisse, *f.*
tymbal, *n.*, timbale, *f.*
tympan, *n.*, tambour ; (arch., print., mec, carp.) tympan, *m.*
tympanites (ti'm'pa-naï-tize), *n.*, tympanite, *f.*
tympanize (-naïze), *v.n.*, battre le tambour.
tympanize, *v.a.*, tendre comme une peau de tambour.
tympanum, *n.*, (anat.), tympan (of the ear —*de l'oreille*); tambour; (arch., mec.) tympan, *m.*
type (taïpe), *n.*, type ; (print.) type, caractère, *m.*
type-metal (-mèt'al), *n.*, métal pour caractères d'imprimerie, *m.*
typhoid (taï-foïde), *adj.*, typhoïde.
typhoon (taï-foune), *n.*, typhon, *m.* ; trombe, *f.*
typhus (taï-), *n.*, typhus, *m.*
typhus, *adj.*, typhoïde.
typic, *or* **typical** (tip'-), *adj.*, typique, figuratif.
typically, *adv.*, d'une manière typique ; figurativement.
typicalness, *n.*, nature typique, *f.*
typify (tip'i-fa'ye), *v.a.*, offrir le type de ; figurer, symboliser.
typographer (taï-), *n.*, typographe, *m.*
typographic, *or* **typographical**, *adj.*, typographique ; (emblematic—*emblématique*) emblématique, typique, figuratif.
typographically, *adv.*, typographiquement ; (emblematically—*figurément*) figurativement, symboliquement,
typography (taï-), *n.*, typographie ; (emblematical representation—*hiéroglyphe*) écriture symbolique, *f.*
tyranness (taï-), *n.*, tyran (femme), *m.*
tyrannic, *or* **tyrannical** (taï-), *adj.*, tyrannique.
tyrannically, *adv.*, tyranniquement.
tyrannicide (taï-ran'ni-çaïde), *n.*, tyrannicide, *m.*
tyrannize (-naïze), *v.n.*, faire le tyran. To — over; *tyranniser.*
tyrannous, *adj.*, tyrannique.
tyrannously, *adv.*, tyranniquement.
tyranny, *n.*, tyrannie, *f.*
tyrant (taï-), *n.*, tyran, *m.*
tyro (taï-rô), *n.*, novice, *m.*
tzar (tzàr), *n.*, tzar, czar, *m.*
tzarina (tzàr'-), *n.*, tzarine, czarine, *f.*

U

u, vingt et unième lettre de l'alphabet, u, *m.*
ubiquitary (you-bik'wi-), *adj.*, présent partout.

ubiquitary, *n.*, personne douée d'ubiquité, *f.*
ubiquity (you-bik'wi-), *n.*, ubiquité, *f.*
udder (eud'-), *n.*, pis, *m.* ; (cook.) tetine, *f.*
uddered (eud-deur'de), *adj.*, à pis, à mamelles.
uglily (eug'-), *adv.*, vilainement, avec laideur.
ugliness (eug'-), *n.*, laideur, *f.*
ugly (eug'-), *adj.*, laid, vilain.
ukase (you-kéce), *n.*, ukase, *m.*
ulcer (eul-), *n.*, ulcère, *m.*
ulcerate (eul-), *v.a.*, ulcérer.
ulcerate (eul-), *v.n.*, s'ulcérer.
ulceration (eul-ceur'é-), *n.*, ulcération, *f.*
ulcered (eul-ceurde), *adj.*, ulcéré.
ulcerous (eul-ceur-), *adj.*, ulcéreux.
ulcerousness, *n.*, état ulcéré, *m.*
uliginous (iou-lidj'-), *adj.*, vaseux, boueux
ullage (eul-lédje), *n.*, (com.) vidange, *f.*
ulmic (eul-), *adj.*, (chem.) ulmique.
ulmin (eul-), *n.*, (chem.) ulmine, *f.*
ulna (eul-), *n.*, (anat.) oubitus, *m.*
ulnage (eul-nédje), *n.*, aunage, *m.*
ulnar (eul-), *adj.*, (anat.) cubital.
ulterior (eul-ti-), *adj.*, ultérieur, postérieur.
ultimate (eul-ti-), *adj.*, dernier ; extrême ; (final) final, extrême, définitif. — analysis ; (chem.) *analyse élémentaire.*
ultimately, *adv.*, finalement, à la fin, définitivement.
ultimatum (eul-ti-mé-), *n.*, ultimatum, *m.*
ultimo (eul-ti-mô), *adv.*, du mois dernier.
ultramarine (eul-tra-ma-rine), *adj.*, d'outremer ; d'au delà des mers.
ultramarine (eul-tra-ma-rine), *n.*, outremer, bleu d'outremer, *m.*
ultramontane (eul-), *adj.*, ultramontain.
ultramundane (eul-tra-meu'n'-), *adj.*, ultramondain.
umbel (eu'm'-), *n.*, (bot.) ombelle, *f.*
umbellar (eu'm'-), *adj.*, (bot.) ombellé.
umbellate, *or* **umbellated**, *adj.*, (bot.) ombellé.
umbellet (eu'm'-), *or* **umbellicle** (-lik'l), *n.*, (bot.) ombellule, *f.*
umbelliferous (eu'm'-), *adj.*, (bot.) ombellifère.
umber (eu'm'-), *n.*, terre d'ombre, *f.* ; (ich.) umble, ombre, *m.*
umber (eu'm'-) *v.a.*, ombrer ; (fig.) assombrir.
umbered (eu'm'beurde), *adj.*, ombré ; sombre.
umbilic, *or* **umbilical** (eu'm'-), *adj.*, ombilical ; (geom.) de foyer.
umbilicate, *or* **umbilicated** (eu'm'bil'i-két'-), *adj.*, (bot.) ombiliqué.
umbilicus (eu'm'-), *n.*, ombilic, nombril ; (bot.) ombilic, *m.*
umbo (eu'm'bô), *n.*, umbon, *m.*
umbra (eu'm'-), *n.*, (opt.) cône d'ombre, *m.*
umbrage (eu'm'brédje), *n.*, ombrage, *m.* ; ombre, *f.* ; (fig.) ombrage, *m.*
umbrageous (eu'm'brédj'-), *adj.*, ombreux ; (shady—*dans l'ombre*) ombragé, ombreux ; (obscure) obscur.
umbrageousness, *n.*, nature ombreuse ; ombre, *f.*
umbratic, *or* **umbratical** (eu'm'-), *adj.*, typique, figuratif.
umbrella (eu'm'-), *n.*, parapluie, *m.* — - case ; *fourreau de parapluie, m.* — -stand : *porte-parapluie, m.* — -tree; (bot.) *magnolier parasol, m.*
umpirage (eu'm'paeur'édje), *n.*, arbitrage, *m.*
umpire (eu'm'paeur), *n.*, tiers arbitre ; arbitre, *m.*
unabased (eu'n'a-bés'te), *adj.*, non humilié.
unabashed (eu'n'a-bash'te), *adj.*, non confus ; qui n'a point de honte.
unabated (eu'n'a-bét'-), *adj.*, non diminué ; non affaibli
unabetted (eu'n'-), *adj.*, sans aide : seul.

unable (eu'n'é-b'l),*adj.*, incapable ; inhabile ; impuissant ; (not having adequate skill—*incapable*) incapable. To be — to ; *ne pas pouvoir ; être incapable de ; ne pas être à même de.*

unabridged (eu'n'a-bridj'de), *adj.*, non abrégé ; non raccourci.

unabsolved (eu'n'ab-zolv'de), *adj.*, non absous.

unaccented (eu'n'-), *adj.*, non accentué.

unacceptable (eu'n'ak'cèpt'a-b'l), *adj.*, inacceptable. — to ; *déplaisant à ; peu agréable pour.*

unacceptableness,*n.*,nature inacceptable, nature déplaisante, *f.*

unacceptably, *adv.*, d'une manière inacceptable, d'une manière déplaisante.

unaccepted (eu'n'-), *adj.*, non accepté ; rejeté.

unaccompanied (eu'n'-), *adj.*, non accompagné ; seul.

unaccomplished (eu'n'ak-ko'm'plish'te), *adj.*, inachevé ; (fig.) peu accompli.

unaccountable(eu'n'ac-caou'n't-a-b'l), *adj.*, inexplicable ; bizarre, étrange ; (not responsible —*non responsable*) irresponsable.

unaccountableness, *n.*, bizarrerie ; étrangeté ; nature inexplicable ; (irresponsibiiity—*irresponsabilité*) irresponsabilité, *f.*

unaccountably, *adv.*, d'une manière inexplicable ; étrangement.

unaccustomed(eu'n'ak'keus-teu'm'de),*adj.*, inaccoutumé ; peu habitué.

unacknowledged (eu'n'ak'nol'èdjde), *adj.*, non reconnu, non avoué ; non accrédité. — letter ; *lettre à laquelle on n'a pas répondu.*

unacquainted (eu'n'ak'kwò'n't'-), *adj.*, qui ignore ; non accoutumé. To be — with ; (pers.) *ne pas connaître ;* (things—*choses*) *ignorer, ne pas savoir.*

unacquitted (eu'n'ak'kwit'-), *adj.*, non acquitté.

unadministered (eu'n'ad-mi-nis'teurde), *adj.*, non administré.

unadmired (eu'n'ad'maeurde), *adj.*, non admiré.

unadorned (eu'n'-), *adj.*, sans ornements ; simple.

unadulterated (eu'n'a-deul-teur'ét'-), *adj.*, non falsifié ; naturel, pur.

unadvisable (eu'n'ad-vaïz'a-b'l), *adj.*, peu sage, peu judicieux.

unadvised (eu'n'ad'vaïz'de),*adj.*, malavisé ; (rash—*téméraire*) irréfléchi, téméraire.

unadvisedly (eu'n'ad-vaïz'èd'-), *adv.*, inconsidérément ; peu judicieusement.

unadvisedness, *n.*, irréflexion, imprudence, *f.*

unaffected (eu'n'-), *adj.*, non affecté ; naturel ; (not moved—*impassible*) non ému, impassible.

unaffectedly, *adv.*, sans affectation ; simplement, naturellement.

unaffectedness, *n.*, simplicité, *f.*

unaffecting, *adj.*, peu touchant, peu pathétique.

unaffectionate, *adj.*, peu affectueux ; sans affection.

unaided (eu'n'-), *adj.*, non aidé ; seul.

unalienable(eu'n'él'yè'n'a-b'l),*adj* , inaliénable.

unalienably, *adv.*, d'une manière inaliénable.

unallayed (eu'n'al'lède), *adj.*, non apaisé.

unallied (eu'n'al'laïde), *adj.*, non allié ; sans alliance ; (of things—*des choses*) hétérogène.

unallowed (eu'n'al'loude), *adj.*, illicite.

unalterable (eu'n'al'tèr'a-b'l), *adj.*, inaltérable.

unalterableness, *n.*, nature inaltérable, *f.*

unalterably, *adv.*, d'une manière inaltérable.

unaltered (eu'n'ôl'teurde),*adj.*,non changé ; toujours le même.

unamazed (eu'n'amé'z'de),*adj.*, non étonné.

unambiguous(eu'n'a'm-bi-ghiou-euss),*adj.*, non ambigu ; non équivoque.

unambiguously, *adv.*, sans ambiguïté.

unambitious, *adj.*, peu ambitieux ; sans ambition.

unambitiousness (eu'n'a'm-bish'-), *n.*, défaut d'ambition, *m.*

unamendable (eu'n'a-mè'n'd-a-b'l), *adj.*, incorrigible.

unamiable (eu'n'é-mi-a-b'l), *adj.*, peu aimable.

unamiableness, *n.*, défaut d'amabilité, *m.*

unamused (eu'n'a-miouz'de), *adj.*, qui ne s'amuse point ; sans amusement.

unamusing, *or* **unamusive** (eu'n'a-miouz'-), *adj.*, peu amusant.

unanimated (eu'n'a'n'i-mét'-), *adj.*, inanimé.

unanimity (you-na-), *n.*, unanimité, *f.*

unanimous (you-na-), *adj.*, unanime.

unanimously (you-na-), *adv.*, unanimement, à l'unanimité.

unanswerable (eu'n'an'seur'a-b'l), *adj.*, sans réplique ; incontestable.

unanswerableness, *n.*, nature irréfutable, *f.*

unanswerably, *adv.*, sans réplique ; d'une manière irréfutable.

unanswered (eu'n'a'n'seurde), *adj.*, sans réponse ; (not suitably returned—*non payé de retour*) non payé de retour.

unappalled (eu'n'ap-pôlde), *adj.*, non épouvanté.

unapparent (eu'n'-), *adj.*, non apparent ; invisible.

unappealable (eu'n'ap-pil'a-b'l), *adj.*, sans appel.

unappeasable (eu'n'ap-pïz'a-b'l),*adj.*,qu'on ne peut apaiser ; implacable.

unappeased (eu'n'ap-pïz'de), *adj.*, non apaisé.

unapplied (eu'n'ap-plaïde), *adj.*, que l'on n'a pas appliqué ; (fin.) non engagé.

unappreciated (eu'n'ap-pri-shi-ét'-), *adj.*, non apprécié.

unapprized (eu'n'ap-praïz'de), *adj.*, ignorant ; sans être prévenu.

unapproachable (eu'n'ap-prôtsh'a-b'l), *adj.*, inaccessible, inabordable.

unappropriated (eu'n'ap-prô-pri-ét'-),*adj.*, non approprié.

unapt (eu'n'-), *adj.*, impropre ; (dull—*borné*) incapable, inepte ; (improper—*inconvenant*) peu convenable ; inapte.

unaptly, *adv.*, mal ; peu convenablement.

unaptness, *n.*, incapacité ; inaptitude ; disconvenance ; ineptie, *f.*

unarmed (eu'n'ârm'de), *adj.*, sans armes ; (bot.) inerme ; (of animals—*des animaux*) sans défenses.

unarraigned (eu'n'ar-ré'n'de), *adj.*, non traduit en justice ; non accusé.

unarrayed (eu'n'ar-réde), *adj.*, non vêtu ; sans vêtements ; nu.

unasked (eu'n'âsk'te), *adj.*, non sollicité ; spontané.

unassailable (eu'n'as'sél'a-b'l), *adj.*, qu'on ne peut assaillir ; hors d'atteinte.

unassayed (eu'n'as'séde),*adj.*, non essayé ; non tenté ; non éprouvé.

unassisted (eu'n'-), *adj.*, sans secours ; seul.

unassuming (eu'n'as'siou'm'-), *adj.*, non pré entieux ; sans prétention ; simple.

unassured (eu'n'as-sheurde), *adj.*, non assuré.

unatoned (eu'n'a-tô'n'de), *adj.*, non apaisé ; non expié ; sans expiation.

unattached (eu'n'at'tatsh'te), *adj.*, non attaché ; (without affection—*sans attachement*) sans affection ; (milit.) en disponibilité ; en non-activité.

unattainable (eu'n'at'té'n'a-b'l), *adj.*, qu'on ne peut atteindre ; inaccessible.

unattainableness, *n.*, nature inaccessible, *f.*

unattempted (eu'n'-), *adj.*, non essayé, non tenté.

unattested (eu'n'-), *adj.*, non attesté.

unauthentic (eu'n'o-thè'n'-), *adj.*, non authentique.

unauthenticated, *adj.*, non constaté.

unauthorized (eu'n'o-theur'aïz'de), *adj.*, non autorisé ; sans autorisation.

unavailable (eu'n'a-vél'a-b'l), *adj.*, inefficace, infructueux, inutile ; non valable.

unavailableness, *n.*, inefficacité, inutilité, *f.*

unavailing (eu'n'a-vél'-), *adj.*, inutile , inefficace.

unavailingly, *adv.*, inefficacement, inutilement ; en vain.

unavenged (eu'n'a-vè'n'dj'de), *adj.*, non vengé.

unavoidable (eu'n'a-voïd'a-b'l), *adj.*, inévitable, inéluctable.

unavoidableness,*n.*,nécessité inévitable,*f.*

unavoidably, *adv.*, inévitablement.

unaware (eu'n'a-wére),*adj.*, inattentif. To be — of ; *ignorer* ; *n'être pas instruit de ; être ignorant de*.

unawares (eu'n'a-wérze),*adv.*,inopinément, à l'improviste ; par mégarde.

unawed (eu'n'ôde), *adj.*, sans crainte ; hardi, audacieux.

unbalanced (eu'n'bal'a'n'ste), *adj.*, non balancé.

unballast (eu'n'-), *v.a.*, délester.

unballast (eu'n'-), *adj.*, sans lest.

unbar (eu'n'-), *v.a.*, débarrer.

unbecoming (eu'n'bi-keu'm'-), *adj.*, inconvenant ; déplacé ; malséant ; (of clothes—*des vêtements*) qui ne convient pas, qui ne va pas.

unbecomingly, *adv.*, d'une manière inconvenante ; avec inconvenance.

unbecomingness,*n.*, inconvenance, incongruité,*f.*

unbelief (eu'n'bi-life), *n.*, incrédulité, *f.* ; manque de foi, *m.*

unbeliever (eu'n'bi-liv'-), *n.*, incrédule, *m.*, *f.* ; mécréant, *m.*

unbelieving, *adj.*,incrédule ; sans croyance.

unbend (eu'n'-), *v.a.*, débander, détendre, relâcher ; (to enervate—*énerver*) énerver ; (fig.) délasser, détendre ; (nav.) détalinguer, démarrer ; (a sail—*une voile*) désenverguer. To — one's self ; *se délasser*.

unbending, *adj.*, qui ne se courbe pas ; qui ne fléchit pas ; inflexible.

unbendingly, *adv.*, inflexiblement.

unbeneficial (eu'n'bè'n'i-fish'-al), *adj.*, infructueux, sans profit, sans avantage.

unbespoken (eu'n'bi-spô-k'n), *adj.*, non commandé ; (place) non retenu.

unbiassed (eu'n'baï-aste), *adj.*, sans préjugés ; impartial.

unbiassedly (eu'n'baï-as'sèd'-), *adv.*, sans préjugés ; impartialement.

unbidden (eu'n'-), *adj.*, non sollicité ; non invité.

unbind (eu'n-baï'n'de),*v.a.*, délier ; détacher ; desserrer.

unblamable (eu'n'blé'm'a-b'l), *adj.*, irréprochable, irrépréhensible.

unbleached (eu'n'blitsh'te), *adj.*, écru.

unblemished (eu'n'blé'm'ish'te), *adj.*, sans tache, pur ; (free from deformity—*sans difformité*) beau, parfait.

unblest (eu'n'-), *adj.*, non béni ; (unhappy —*malheureux*) malheureux.

unblushing (eu'n'bleush'-), *adj.*, qui ne rougit point ; ehonté.

unblushingly, *adv.*, sans rougir.

unbolt (eu'n'bôlte), *v.a.*, déverrouiller ; ouvrir.

unbolted, *adj.*, déverrouillé ; (unsifted—*non vanné*) non bluté.

unbooted (eu'n'boût'-), *adj.*, débotté.

unborn (eu'n'-), *adj.*, pas encore né ; à naître ; (of things—*des choses*) futur, à venir.

unborrowed (eu'n'bor-rôde), *adj.*, non emprunté ; original.

unbosom (eu'n'beuz'ome), *v.a.*, ouvrir, découvrir, révéler. To — one's self ; *ouvrir son cœur* ; *s'ouvrir*.

unbought (eu'n'bôte), *adj.*, non acheté.

unbounded (eu'n'baou'n'd'-), *adj.*, illimité, sans bornes ; (unrestrained—*sans mesure*) démesuré.

unboundedly,*adv.*, sans bornes ; démesurément.

unbounteous (eu'n'baou'n'ti-), *adj.*, peu libéral.

unbowed (eu'n'bôde), *adj.*, non courbé.

unbowel (eu'n'baou-èl), *v.a.*, éventrer.

unbrace (eu'n-), *v.a.*, délier ; desserrer ; débander.

unbred (eu'n-), *adj.*, mal élevé ; grossier, rude.

unbribed (eu'n'braïb'de), *adj* ; non corrompu, non acheté.

unbridle (eu'n'braïd'l), *v.a.*, débrider ; (fig.) déchaîner.

unbroke (eu'n'brôke), or **unbroken** (-brôk'n), *adj.*, non rompu ; non cassé ; (uninterrupted—*continu*) non interrompu, continuel ; (not subdued—*indompté*) non dompté, invaincu ; (not violated—*intact*) non violé, non enfreint, intact ; (of animals—*des animaux*) non rompu, non dressé.

unbrotherlike (eu'n'breuth'eur-laïke), or **unbrotherly** (-li),. *adj.*, non fraternel, peu fraternel.

unbuckle (eu'n'beuk'k'l), *v.a.*, déboucler.

unburden (eu'n'beur-), *v.a.*, décharger ; débarrasser d'un fardeau ; (fig.) décharger, alléger.

unbutton (eu'n'beut't'n), *v.a.*, déboutonner.

uncage (eu'n'kédje), *v.a.*, faire sortir d'une cage ; délivrer.

uncaged (-kédj'de), *adj.*, sorti de sa cage ; délivré.

uncalled (eu'n'côl'l'de), *adj.*, non appelé. — for ; *qu'on n'a pas envoyé chercher* ; (unnecessary —*inutile*) *peu nécessaire* ; *gratuit*.

uncancellable (eu'n'ca'n'cèl-la-b'l), *adj.*, qu'on ne peut biffer, qu'on ne peut annuler, qu'on ne peut effacer, ineffaçable.

uncancelled (eu'n'ca'n'cèl'de), *adj.*. non rayé ; non annulé.

uncandid (eu'n'-), *adj.*, peu sincère ; faux.

uncanonical (eu'n'-), *adj.*, non canonique.

uncanonicalness, *n.*, non-canonicité, *f.*

uncared for (eu'n'kérde'-), *adj.*, dont on ne se soucie pas ; non soigné.

uncase (eu'n'kéce), *v.a.*, ôter d'une caisse, d'un étui, d'une gaine ; (to strip—*dépouiller*) dépouiller.

uncaught (eu'n'côte), *adj.*, non pris, non acquis, non gagné.

unceasing (eu'n'cîss'-), *adj.*, incessant, sans relâche, continuel.

unceasingly, *adv.*, incessamment, sans cesse.

34*

uncensured (eu'n'cè'n'sheurde), *adj.*, non censuré.

unceremonious (eu'n'cèr'i-mô-), *adj.*, peu cérémonieux ; sans cérémonie ; sans gêne.

unceremoniously, *adv.*, sans cérémonie, sans façon, sans gêne.

uncertain (eu'n'ceur-), *adj.*, incertain.

uncertainly, *adv.*, avec incertitude ; incertainement.

uncertainty (eu'n'ceur-), *n.*, incertitude, *f.* ; (something unknown—*l'inconnu*) incertain, *m.* ; (contingency—*éventualité*) éventualité, *f.*

unchain (eu'n'tshé'n),*v.a.*, déchaîner ; briser les chaînes de.

unchangeable (eu'n'tshé'n'dj'a-b'l), *adj.*, inaltérable, invariable.

unchangeableness (eu'n'-), *n.*, immutabilité ; inaltérabilité,*f.*

unchangeably,*adv.*, immuablement ; d'une manière inaltérable ; invariablement.

unchanged (eu'n'tshé'n'dj'de), *adj* ,qui n'est pas changé ; qui est toujours le même ; (not alterable—*inaltérable*) inaltérable.

unchanging, *adj.*, qui ne change pas ; invariable.

uncharged (eu'n'tshârdje), *adj.*, non attaqué ; (unloaded—*non chargé*) non chargé. — for ; *gratis, qu'on ne fait pas payer.*

uncharitable (eu'n'tshar'i-ta-b'l), *adj.*, peu charitable.

uncharitableness, *n.*, manque de charité, *m.*

uncharitably, *adv.*, sans charité.

unchaste (eu'n'tshéste), *adj.*, non chaste ; impudique.

unchastely,*adv.*,sans chasteté ; impudiquement.

unchastity (eu'n'tshas'-), *n.*,impudicité,*f.*

unchecked (eu'n'tshèk'te), *adj.*, non réprimé ; non contenu.

uncheerful (eu'n'tshîr-foule), *adj.*, triste, mélancolique.

uncheerfulness, *n.*, tristesse, mélancolie,*f.*

unchewed (eu'n'tshioude), *adj.*, non mâché.

unchristian, *or* **unchristianly** (eu'n'krist'-), *adj.*, peu chrétien ; (infidel—*païen*) infidèle.

unchristianly, *adv.*, d'une manière peu chrétienne.

uncial (eu'n'shal), *adj.*, oncial.

uncial, *n.*, lettre onciale, *f.*

uncinate (eu'n-), *adj.*, (bot.) unciné.

uncircumcised (eu'n'cir-keu'm'çaïz'de), *adj.*, incirconcis.

uncircumcision (eu'n'cir-keu'm'cij'eune), *n.*, incirconcision,*f.*

uncircumscribed (eu'n'cir-keu'm'scraïb-de), *adj.*, non circonscrit.

uncircumspect (eu'n'-) *adj.*, peu circonspect, imprudent.

uncircumspectly, *adv.*, imprudemment.

uncivil (eu'n -), *adj.*, malhonnête, incivil, impoli.

uncivilized (eu'n'civ'il'aïz'de), *adj.*, incivilisé, barbare ; rude.

uncivilly (eun'-), *adv.*, malhonnêtement, incivilement.

unclad (eu'n'-), *adj.*, non vêtu ; nu.

unclaimed (eu'n'clé'm'de), *adj.*, non réc'amé. — dividend ; *dividende non réclamé, m.*

unclarified (eu'n'clar-i-faïde), *adj.*, non clarifié.

unclasp (eu'n'clâspe), *v.a.*, ouvrir le fermoir de ; détacher.

unclassical (eu'n'-), *adj.*, non classique.

uncle (eu'n'k'l), *n.*, oncle, *m.* ; (pop.) (pawn-broker—*mont-de-piété*) tante,*f.*

unclean (eu'n'cline), *adj.*, malpropre, sale ; (lewd—*non chaste*) impudique ; (in Scripture—*biblique*) impur, immonde.

uncleanliness, *n.*, malpropreté ; saleté (fig.) impureté,*f.*

uncleanly, *adj.*, sale, malpropre ; (obscene) impur. impudique.

uncleanness,*n.*,saleté ; malpropreté ; (lewdness—*impudicité*)impureté, impudicité, *f.*

uncleansed (eu'n'clè'n'zde), *adj.*, non nettoyé ; (of drains, &c.—*d'égouts,&c.*)non curé ; (not purified—*non purifié*) non purifié.

unclerical (eu'n'clèr-), *adj.*, peu clérical.

unclew (eu'n'kliou), *v.a.*, dérouler ; débrouiller, dénouer.

unclipped (eu'n'clip'te),*adj.*, non taillé, non coupé ; (of animals—*des animaux*) non tondu ; (of coins—*des monnaies*) non rogné.

unclog (eu'n'-), *v.a.*, ôter les entraves de ; dégager.

uncloister(eu'n'cloïs'-), *v.a.*, tirer du cloître.

unclose (eu'n'clôze), *v.a.*, ouvrir.

unclosed (-clôz'de), *adj.*, non fermé, non clos ; ouvert ; (not sealed—*non cacheté*) ouvert ; (not finished—*non fini*) inachevé.

unclothe (eu'n'clôthe). *v.a.*, déshabiller, dépouiller ; mettre à nu.

unclouded, *or* **uncloudy** (eu'n'claoud'-), *adj.*, sans nuage, serein.

uncloudedness, *n.*, sérénité ; (fig.) clarté, sérénité, *f.*

uncocked (eu'n-cok'te), *adj.*, non relevé ; (agri.) non mis en meule ; (of fire-arms—*d'armes à feu*) désarmé.

uncoil (eu'n'coïl), *v.a.*, détordre, détortiller, dérouler.

uncollected (eu'n'-), *adj.*, non rassemblé ; non recueilli ; non recouvré ; (fin.) non perçu.

uncollectible (eu'n'col-lèkti-b'l), *adj.*, non recouvrable.

uncoloured (eu'n'keul'teurde), *adj.*, non coloré, incolore ; (fig.) naturel, simple, vrai.

uncombed (eu'n'cô'm'de), *adj.*,non peigné ; mal peigné.

uncombinable (eu'n'co'm'baï'n'a-b'l), *adj.*, qui ne peut se combiner.

uncombined (-baï'n'de), *adj.*, non combiné.

uncomeatable (eu'n'co'm'at'a-b'l), *adj.*, (triv.) inaccessible, inabordable.

uncomeliness (eu'n'keu'm'li-), *n.*, manque de grâce, *m.* ; forme disgracieuse, laideur ; (of behaviour—*de conduite*) inconvenance, *f.*

uncomely, *adj.*, sans grâce ; déplaisant ; (unseemly—*inconvenant*) inconvenant ; (of dress —*de vêtements*) qui ne convient pas, qui ne va pas bien.

uncomfortable (eu'n'keu'm-fort'a-b'l), *adj.*, peu confortable ; incommode ; gênant, sans aisance, sans agrément, fâcheux, désagréable ; (pers.) gêné, mal à son aise ; (gloomy—*sombre*) triste.

uncomfortableness, *n.*, absence de confortable, incommodité, *f.* ; malaise ; désagrément, *m.* ; gêne, *f.*

uncomfortably, *adv.*, incommodément, peu confortable; sans confort ; (in an uneasy state —*dans un état de malaise*) dans le malaise, dans la gêne, sans aisance, désagréablement ; (without cheerfulness—*sans gaîté*) tristement.

uncommanded(eu'n'-),*adj.*,non commandé.

uncommendable (eu'n'co'm'mè'n'd'a-b'l), *adj.*, peu louable.

uncommended, *adj.*, non loué ; sans éloge.

uncommercial (eu'n'co'm'meur-shal), *adj.*, peu commercial ; peu commerçant.

uncommiserated (eu'n'co'm'mish'eu'n'de\), *adj.*, sans commisération.

uncommissioned (eu'n'co'm'mish'eu'n'de\), *adj.*, non commissionné ; non autorisé ; (milit.) sous.

uncommitted (eu'n'-), *adj.*, non commis.

uncommon (eu'n'-), *adj.*, non commun ; peu ordinaire ; rare, extraordinaire.

uncommonly, *adv.,* peu communément ; extraordinairement, extrêmement.

uncommonness, *n.,* rareté, *f.* ; caractère extraordinaire, *m.*

uncommunicable (eu'n'co'm'miou-ni-ca-b'l), *adj.,* incommunicable.

uncommunicated (-miou-ni-két'-), *adj.,* non communiqué.

uncommunicative (-miou-ni-ca-), *adj.,* peu communicatif.

uncompact (eu'n'-), *adj.,* non compact ; non serré.

uncompassionate (eu'n'co'm'pash'eu'n'-), *adj.,* non-compatissant ; sans compassion ; impitoyable.

uncompellable (eu'n'co'm'pèl-la-b'l), *adj.,* qu'on ne peut contraindre.

uncompelled (-pèlde), *adj.,* sans être forcé ; volontaire.

uncompensated (eu'n'co'm'pè'n'sét-), *adj.,* sans compensation.

uncomplaining (eu'n'co'm'plé'n'-), *adj.,* qui ne se plaint pas; sans plainte.

uncomplaisant (eu'n'co'm'plé-za'n'te),*adj.,* peu complaisant ; sans complaisance.

uncomplaisantly,*adv.,*sans complaisance.

uncompleted (eu'n'co'm'plit'-), *adj.,* non complété ; inachevé.

uncomplying (eu'n'co'm'pla-yigne), *adj.,* peu complaisant ; inflexible.

uncompounded (eu'n'co'm'paou'n'd'-), *adj.,* non composé, simple.

uncomprehended (eu'n'co'm'pri'-),*adj.,*incompris.

uncompressed (eu'n'co'm'prèste),*adj.,*non comprimé.

uncompromising (eu'n'co'm'pro-miz'-), *adj.,* qui n'entre pas in accommodement ; qui ne transige pas; entier.

unconcealed (eu'n'co'n'cilde), *adj.,* non caché ; ouvert.

unconceived (eu'n'co'n'civ'de), *adj.,* non conçu ; non compris.

unconcern (eu'n'co'n'ceurne), *n.,* insouciance ; indifférence, *f.*

unconcerned (-ceur'n'de), *adj.,* indifférent ; insouciant ; insensible ; (having no interest in —*étranger à*) désintéressé, indifférent, étranger.

unconcernedly (-nèd'-), *adv.,* avec indifférence, avec insouciance ; indifféremment.

unconcernedness,*n.* *V.* **unconcern.**

unconcocted (eu'n'-), *adj.,* non digéré ; non mûri.

uncondemned (eu'n'co'n'dè'm'de), *adj.,* non condamné ; (of things) non défendu, non interdit.

unconditional (eu'n'co'n'djsh'eu'n'-), *adj.,* non conditionnel ; sans condition : absolu.

unconditionally, *adv.,* sans condition ; absolument.

unconfessed (eu'n'co'n'fèste), *adj.,* non avoué ; non confessé.

unconfined (eu'n'co'n'faï'n'de), *adj.,* pas gêné ; libre ; (illimitable—*sans limite*) illimité.

unconfinedly (-faï'n'èd-), *adv.,* sans bornes ; sans contrainte.

unconfirmed (eu'n'co'n'feurm'de), *adj.,* non confirmé ; (not fortified—*non affermi*) non fortifié.

unconformable (eu'n'co'n'form'a-b'l), *adj.,* non conforme ; inconciliable ; incompatible.

unconformity (eu'n'-), *n.,* non-conformité ; incompatibilité, *f.*

unconfused (eu'n'co'n'fiouz'de), *adj.,* non confus, non troublé.

unconfusedly (-fiouz'èd'-), *adv.,* sans confusion.

unconfutable (eu'n'co'n'fiout'a-b'l), *adj.,* irréfutable.

uncongealable (eu'co'n'djîl'a-b'l), *adj.,* non congelable.

uncongealed (-djîl'de), *adj.,* non congelé.

uncongenial (eu'n'co'n'djî-), *adj.,* hétérogène ; peu sympathique ; contraire.

unconjugal (eu'n'co'n'djiou-), *adj.,* non conjugal.

unconnected (eu'n'-),*adj.,* non lié ; détaché ; sans liaison ; (fig.) décousu, sans suite, sans liaison.

unconquerable (eu'n'con'gn'kèr'a-b'l),*adj.,* invincible, indomptable.

unconquerably, *adv.,* invinciblement.

unconquered (eu'n'con'gn'keurde), *adj.,* invaincu ; indomptable.

unconscionable (eu'n'co'n'sheu'n'a-b'l), *adj.,* déraisonnable ; sans conscience ; (enormous—*démesuré*) énorme, démesuré.

unconscionableness,*n.,*déraison ; extravagance, *f.*

unconscionably, *adv.,* déraisonnablement ; sans conscience.

unconscious (eu'n'co'n'sheusse), *adj.,* inconscient, qui n'a pas la conscience, qui n'a pas conscience, qui n'est pas doué de la conscience de soi-même ; (ignorant) ignorant ; (insensible) sans connaissance. To be — of ; *n'avoir pas la conscience de ; ignorer.* To be — ; *avoir perdu connaissance ; être sans connaissance.*

unconsciousness, *n.,* inconscience, *f.* ; manque de conscience de; manque de connaissance, *m.* ; absence de conscience de ; (ignorance) ignorance ; (insibility—*insensibilité*) insensibilité, *f.* .

unconsecrated (eu'n'co'n'si-crét'-),*adj.*,non consacré ; (of kings, of bishops—*de rois, d'évêques*) non sacré ; (of ground—*de terrain*) non bénit.

unconsenting (eu'n'-),*adj.,* non consentant ; sans consentir.

unconsidered (eu'n'co'n'sid'eurde), *adj.,* non considéré.

unconstitutional (eu'n'co'n'sti-tiou-), *adj.,* inconstitutionnel.

unconstitutionally, *adv.,* inconstitutionnellement.

unconstrained (eu'n'co'n'stré'n'de), *adj.,* non contraint ; sans contrainte ; (voluntary—*volontaire*) volontaire, libre.

unconstrainedly (-èd'-), *adv.,* sans contrainte ; volontairement, librement, sans gêne.

unconstraint (eu'n'co'n'strè'n'te), *n.,* absence de contrainte, *f.* ; laisser aller, *m.*

unconsulted (eu'n'co'n'seult'-), *adj.,* non consulté.

unconsumed (eu'n'co'n'siou'm'de), *adj.,* non consumé ; non consommé.

uncontaminated (eu'n'co'n'ta'm'i-nét'-), *adj.,* sans souillure.

uncontested (eu'n'-), *adj.,* incontesté.

uncontradicted (eu'n'-), *adj.,* non contredit.

uncontrollable (eu'n'co'n'trôl-la-b'l), *adj.,* indomptable ; irrésistible.

uncontrollably, *adv.,* d'une manière indomptable ; irrésistiblement.

uncontrolled (-trôl'de), *adj.,* sans contrôle ; sans frein.

uncontrolledly (-'èd'-), *adv.,* sans contrôle ; sans frein.

uncontroverted (eu'n'co'n'tro-veurt'-),*adj.,* non controversé ; incontesté.

unconversable (eu'n'co'n'veurs'a-b'l), *adj.,* peu propre à la conversation ; réservé.

unconverted (eu'n'co'n'vèrt'-), *adj.,* non converti.

unconvertible (eu'n'co'n'veurt'i-b'l), *adj.,* non convertible ; non convertissable.

unconvinced (eu'n'co'n'vi'n'ste), *adj.,* non convaincu.

unconvincing, *adj.,* peu convaincant.

uncord (eu'n'-), *v.a.*, ôter la corde de; décorder.

uncork (eu'n'-), *v.a.*, déboucher.

uncorrected (eu'n'-), *adj.*, non corrigé; non réformé.

uncouple (eu'n'keup'l), *v.a.*, découpler; séparer.

uncourteous (eu'n'côr-ti-), *adj.*, incivil, impoli, discourtois.

uncourteou..ly, *adv.*, sans courtoisie; impoliment..

uncourteousness, *n.*, impolitesse, *f.*

uncourtliness (eu'n'côrt'-), *n.*, esprit étranger à celui de la cour, *m.*; impolitesse, *f.*

uncourtly, *adv.*, qui n'appartient pas à la cour; incivil, impoli.

uncouth (eu'n'couth), *adj.*, grossier; singulier, baroque, étrange, rude.

uncouthly, *adv.*, rudement, grossièrement, singulièrement, étrangement.

uncouthness, *n.*, rudesse; grossièreté; singularité, étrangeté, *f.*

uncover (eu'n'keuv'-), *v.a.*, découvrir.

uncreate (eu'n'cri-), *v.a.*, anéantir, détruire.

uncreated (-cri-ét'-), *adj.*, détruit, privé de son existence; à créer, à naître; (not produced by creation—*existant sans avoir été créé*) incréé.

uncross (eu'n'-), *v.a.*, décroiser.

uncrossed (-cros'te), *adj.*, décroisé; (not cancelled—*non biffé*) non rayé, non biffé; (not thwarted—*non contrecarré*) non contrarié.

uncrowded (eu'n'craoud'-), *adj.*, non serré, non encombré par la foule.

uncrown (eu'n'craou'n), *v.a.*, détrôner.

uncrowned (-craou'n'de), *adj.*, détrôné; sans couronne.

uncrystallizable (eu'n'cris-tal-laïz'a-b'l), *adj.*, incristallisable.

unction (eun'gn'k'sheune), *n.*, onction, *f.*; baume, *m.*

unctuosity (eun'gn'kt'iou-oss'), *n.*, onctuosité, *f.*

unctuous, *adj.*, onctueux, huileux.

uncultivable (eu'n'keul-ti-va-b'l), *adj.*, non cultivable.

uncultivated (-vét-), *adj.*, inculte.

uncurbed (eu'n'keurb'de), *adj.*, indompté, sans frein.

uncured (eu'n'kiourde), *adj.*, non guéri.

uncurl (eu'n'keurle), *v.a.*, dérouler; (of hair —*des cheveux*) défriser.

uncurl, *v.n.*, se dérouler; (of hair—*des cheveux*) se défriser. -

uncurtailed (eu'n'keur-téide), *adj.*, non abrégé; non raccourci.

uncustomary (eu'n'keus-teu'm'-), *adj.*, rare.

uncut (eu'n'keute), *adj.*, non coupé; non entamé.

undam (eu'n'-), *v.a.*, ouvrir.

undamaged (eu'n'da'm'-édjde), *adj.*, non endommagé; sain et sauf.

undamped (eu'n'da'm'p'te), *adj.*, non découragé, ferme.

undaunted (eu'n'dâ'n't'-), *adj.*, non intimidé; intrépide.

undauntedly, *adv.*, intrépidement.

undauntedness, *n.*, intrépidité, *f.*

undebased (eu'n'di-bés'te), *adj.*, non abaissé, non avili.

undecagon (eu'n'dèk'-), *n.*, (geom.) hendécagone, *m.*

undecayed (eu'n'di-kéde), *adj.*, intact; en bon état.

undecaying (eu'r.'di-ké-igne), *adj.*, inaltérable; impérissable.

undeceivable (eu'n'di-cîv'a-b'l), *adj.*, qu'on ne peut tromper.

undeceive (eu'n'di-cîve), *v.a.*, désabuser, détromper.

undecided (eu'n'di-çaï-dède), *adj.*, indécis; incertain.

undecomposable (eu'n'di-co'm'poz'a-b'l), *adj.*, indécomposable.

undefended (eu'n'di-fè'n'd'-), *adj.*, sans défense; non défendu.

undefiled (eu'n'di-fail'de), *adj.*, sans tache; pur.

undefinable (eu'n'di-faï'n'a-b'l), *adj.*, indéfinissable.

undefined (-faï'n'de), *adj.*, indéfini.

undelivered (eu'n'di-liv'eurde), *adj.*, non délivré; non affranchi; (not sent in—*non envoyé*) non livré.

undeniable (eu'n'di-naï-a-b'l), *adj.*, qu'on ne peut nier; incontestable.

undeniably, *adv.*, incontestablement.

undeplored (eu'n'di-plôrde), *adj.*, non déploré.

under (eu'u'deur), *adv.*, dessous; au-dessous; (fig.) au-dessous, dans la sujétion.

under, *prep.*, sous; dessous; (in a rank inferior to, in a less degree than, less than, for less than—*d'un rang inférieur*) au-dessous de; (in a state of subjection to, in—*subordonné a*) dans. — discussion; *en discussion*. — age; *mineur*. — favour of; *à la faveur de*; *aux soins de*. — these circumstances; *dans ces circonstances*. — the doctor's hands; *entre les mains du médecin*.

under (eu'n'deur). *adj.*, de dessous; (lower —*au-dessous de*) inférieur; (less than the usual quantity—*inférieur en quantité*) inférieur, léger; (of rank—*du rang*) sous, inférieur, subalterne, subordonné.

underbid. *v.a.* (preterit, Underbid; past part., Underbidden), offrir moins que.

underbred, *adj.*, mal élevé, malappris.

undercrest, *v.a.*, (her.) soutenir le cimier de.

underdealing (eu'n'deur'dîl'-), *n.*, menée, manœuvre secrète, *f.*

underdo (eu'n'deur-dou), *v.n.* (preterit Underdid; past part., Underdone), rester au-dessous de soi; rester au-dessous de sa tâche.

underdone, *adj.*, (of meat—*de la viande*) pas assez cuit, mal cuit, saignant, peu cuit.

underdrain (eu'n'deur-drè'n), *n.*, fossé d'écoulement souterrain, *m.*

underdrain, *v.a.*, dessécher au moyen de fossés souterrains.

underfoot (eu'n'deur-foute), *adv.*, sous les pieds, à terre.

undergo, *v.a.* (preterit, Underwent; past part., Undergone), subir; supporter; (to experience—*éprouver*) subir, éprouver, essuyer.

undergraduate (eu'n'deur-grad'iou-), *n.*, étudiant qui n'a pas encore pris son premier grade: étudiant, *m.*

underground (eu'n'deur-graou'n'de), *n.*, lieu souterrain, *m.*

underground, *adv.*, sous terre, en forme de souterrain.

underground, *adj.*, souterrain.

undergrowth (eu'n'deur-grôth), *n.*, broussailles, *f.pl.*

underhand, *adv.*, sous main; sourdement.

underhand, *adj.*, fait sous main, clandestin; sourd.

underlay, *v.a.* (preterit and past part., Underlaid), mettre sous; soutenir; étayer.

underlayer (eu'n'deur-lè-eur), *n.*, étai, étançon, *m.*

underlet, *v.a.*, sous-louer; (a farm—*une ferme*) sous-affermer; (to let below the value—*louer à trop bas prix*) louer au-dessous de sa valeur.

underline (eu'n'deur-laïne), *v.a.*, souligner.

underling (eu'n deur-ligne), *n.*, subalterne; instrument, suppôt, *m.*

undermine (eu'n'deur-maïne), *v.a.*, miner; (fig.) miner, nuire à.

underminer, *n.*, mineur; (fig.) destructeur, ennemi secret, *m.*

undermost (eu'n'deur-môste), *adj.*, le plus bas.

underneath (eu'n'deur-nîth), *adv.*, dessous; au-dessous; par-dessous; en dessous.

underneath, *prep.*, sous, au-dessous de.

underpart (eu'n'deur-pârte), *n.*, dessous; (fig.) petit rôle, *m.*

underpin, *v.a.*, reprendre en sous-œuvre.

underpinning, *n.*, reprise en sous-œuvre; fondation reprise en sous-œuvre, *f.*

underplot, *n.*, menée secrète; (thea.) sous-intrigue, *f.*

underprior (eu'n'deur-praï-or), *n.*, sous-prieur, *m.*

underprop, *v.a.*, étançonner, étayer.

underrate, *n.*, vil prix, trop bas prix, *m.*

underrate, *v.a.*, estimer au-dessous de sa valeur; (fig.) dépriser, déprécier, rabaisser.

underrun (eu'n'deur-reune), *v.a.*, détordre; (cable) paumoyer.

undersecretary (eu'n'deur-sèk-ri-), *n.*, sous-secrétaire, *m.*

undersell, *v.a.* (preterit and past part., Undersold), vendre à plus bas prix que; vendre à vil prix.

undersheriff (eu'n'deur-shèr-), *n.*, sous-shérif, *m.*

undershot-wheel (eu'n'deur-shot'hwil), *n.*, roue à aubes, à palettes, *f.*

undershrub (eu'n'deur-shreube), *n.*, sous-arbrisseau, *m.*

underside (eu'n'deur-saïde), *n.*, dessous, côté de dessous, *m.*

undersigned (eu'n'deur-saï'n'de), *n.*, sous-signé, *m.*, soussignée, *f.*

undersoil (eu'n'deur-soïl), *n.*, terre de dessous, *f.*; terrain de dessous, sous-sol, *m.*

understand *v.a.* (preterit and past.part., Understood), entendre, comprendre; (to be informed—*apprendre*) apprendre, être informé; (to mean without expressing—*donner à entendre*) sous-entendre; (to know how to set about anything—*savoir comment faire*) s'entendre à, en. To give any one to —; *donner à entendre à quelqu'un*. Be it understood; *bien entendu.*

understand, *v.n.*, comprendre; (to learn—*apprendre*) apprendre.

understanding, *n.*, intelligence, *f.*; entendement, esprit, jugement, *m.*; compréhension; (knowledge—*intellect*) connaissance, intelligence; (agreement of minds—*accord*) intelligence, harmonie, *f.*, accord, *m.* To come to an — with; *s'entendre avec.*

understandingly, *adv.*, avec intelligence; sciemment.

understrapper, *n.*, subalterne, suppôt, *m.*

understratum (eu'n'deur-stré-), *n.* (*understrata*), couche inférieure, *f.*; terrain de dessous, *m.*

undertake, *v.a.* (preterit, Undertook; past part., Undertaken), entreprendre; se charger de.

undertaker (eu'n'deur-ték'-), *n.*, entrepreneur, *m.*, entrepreneuse, *f.*; (of funerals—*de funérailles*) entrepreneur des pompes funèbres, *m.*

undertaking (eu'n'deur-ték'-), *n.*, entreprise, *f.*

undertenant (eu'n'deur-tè'n'-), *n.*, sous-locataire, *m.*, *f.*

undervaluation (eu'n'deur-val'iou-é-), *n.*, sous-évaluation, *f.*

undervalue (-val'iou), *n.*, bas prix, trop bas prix, *m.*

undervalue, *v.a.*, estimer au-dessous de sa valeur, sous-évaluer; (fig.) déprécier, rabaisser, dépriser.

underwaistcoat (eu'n'deur-wèst'côte), *n.*, gilet de dessous, *m.*

underwood (eu'n'deur-woude), *n.*, taillis; (bot.) arbrisseau, *m.*

underwrite (eu'n'deur-raïte), *v.a.* (preterit, Underwrote; past part., Underwritten), souscrire.

underwrite, *v.n.*, souscrire des polices d'assurance; faire des assurances.

underwriter, *n.*, souscripteur de police d'assurance; assureur, *m.*

underwriting, *n.*, (com.) assurance, *f.*

undescribed (eu'n'di-scraïb'de), *adj.*, non décrit.

undeserved (eu'n'di-zeurv'de), *adj.*, non mérité; injuste.

undeservedly (-zeurv'èd'-), *adv.*, à tort; injustement.

undeservedness (-zeurv'èd'-), *n.*, injustice, *f.*

undeserver, *n.*, personne sans mérite, *f.*

undeserving, *adj.*, sans mérite; indigne.

undeservingly, *adv.*, sans avoir mérite; injustement.

undesigned (eu'n'di-zaï'n'de), *adj.*, sans dessein, involontaire.

undesignedly (-'èd'-), *adv.*, sans intention; involontairement, par mégarde.

undesignedness (-'èd'-), *n.*, absence de dessein; nature fortuite, *f.*

undesigning (eu'n'di-zaï'n'-), *adj.*, sans dessein; sans artifice; loyal, sans mauvais dessein.

undesirable (eu'n'di-zaeur'a-b'l), *adj.*, peu désirable; peu convenable, désagréable.

undesired (eu'n'di-zaeurde), *adj.*, non sollicité.

undetected (eu'n'di-tèk-), *adj.*, non découvert.

undeterminable (eu'n'di-teur mi-na-b'l), *adj.*, (ant.) qui ne peut pas être déterminé, indéterminable.

undeterminate, *adj.*, (ant.) indéterminé.

undetermined (eu'n'di-teur-mi'n'de), *adj.*, indéterminé, indécis, irrésolu; indéfini.

undeviating (eu'n'di-vi-ét'-), *adj.*, qui ne dévie pas; droit, constant; qui ne se dément pas.

undevoted (eu'n'di-vôt'-), *adj.*, non dévoué.

undigested (eu'n'di-djèst'-), *adj.*, indigeste.

undiminished (eu'n'di-mi'n'ish'te), *adj.*, non diminué; soutenu.

undirected, *adj.*, non dirigé; sans direction (of letters, &c—*de lettres, &c.*) sans adresse.

undiscerned (eu'n'di-zeurn'de), *adj.*, inaperçu, caché.

undiscernedly (-'èd'li), *adv.*, sans être aperçu; imperceptiblement.

undiscernible (-'i-b'l), *adj.*, invisible, imperceptible.

undiscernibly, *adv.*, imperceptiblement.

undiscerning, *adj.*, qui manque de discernement.

undisciplined (eu'n'dis-ci-pli'n'de), *adj.*, indiscipliné, sans discipline.

undiscoverable (eu'n'dis-keuv'eur'a-b'l), *adj.*, qu'on ne peut découvrir.

undiscovered (-keuv'eurde), *adj.*, non découvert; inconnu.

undisguised (eu'n'diz'gaïz'de), *adj.*, sans déguisement; sincère.

undismayed (eu'n'diz'méde), *adj.*, non effrayé, sans peur.

undisputed (eu'n'dis-piout'-), *adj.*, incontesté.

undissembled (eu'n'dis'sè'm'b'l'de), *adj.*, non simulé; sincère.

undissolvable (eu'n'diz'zolv'a-b'l), *adj.*, indissoluble; insoluble.

undissolved, adj., non dissous.

undissolving, adj., indissoluble.

undistinguishable (eu'n'dis-tign'gwish-a-b'l), adj., qu'on ne saurait distinguer; indistinct.

undistinguishably, adv., indistinctement.

undistinguished (-'gwish'te), adj., non distingué; (indistinct) indistinct.

undistinguishing, adj., qui ne fait point de distinction; sans discernement.

undisturbed (eu'n'dis-teurb'de), adj., non troublé; tranquille, calme.

undisturbedly (-'èd'-), adv., sans trouble; tranquillement.

undiverted (eu'n'di-veurt'-), adj., non détourné; (not amused—non amusé) non diverti.

undividable (eu'n'di-vaïd'a-b'l), adj., indivisible.

undivided (-vaïd'-), adj., entier, indivisé.

undivulged (eu'n'di-veul-dj'de), adj., non divulgué.

undo (eu'n'dou), v.a. (preterit, Undid; past part., Undone), défaire; (to untie—dénouer) défaire, délier, détacher; (to untangle—débrouiller) débrouiller; (to ruin—ruiner) ruiner, perdre; (reputation) perdre de réputation.

undock, v.a., faire sortir des docks.

undoer (eu'n'dou-eur), n., personne qui défait, qui délie, qui débrouille, qui ruine, f.; destructeur, m.

undoing (eu'n'dou-igne), n., ruine, perte, f.

undone, adj., inexécuté; à faire, qui reste à faire; (ruined—ruiné) ruiné, perdu.

undoubted (eu'n'daout'-), adj., indubitable.

undoubtedly, adv., indubitablement; sans doute.

undoubtful (-'foule), adj., non douteux; certain.

undoubting, adj., qui ne doute pas.

undramatic, or **undramatical**, adj., peu dramatique.

undrawn (eu'n'drô'n), adj., non tiré; non attiré.

undress, n., déshabillé, négligé, m.; (milit.) petite tenue, f.

undress, v.a., déshabiller.

undress, v.n., se déshabiller.

undressed (eu'n'drèste), adj., déshabillé; sans parure; (manu.) non apprêté, écru; (hort.) non taillé.

undried (eu'n'draïde), adj., non séché.

undrinkable (eu'n'dri'n'ka-b'l), adj., imbuvable.

undue (eu'n'diou), adj., non dû; (not legal —illicite) illégal; (excessive—outré) excessif, outré; (of bills—de billets, &c.) non échu; (improper—inconvenant) indu.

undulant, or **undulary** (eu'n'diou-), adj., ondoyant.

undulate (eu'n'diou-), v.a. and n., onduler, ondoyer.

undulate, or **undulated** (-lét'-), adj., ondulé, onduleux.

undulating (-lét'-), adj., ondoyant, onduleux.

undulatingly, adv., d'une manière ondoyante.

undulation (eu'n'diou-lé-), n., ondulation, f.

undulatory (-lat'-), adj., d'ondulation; ondulatoire.

unduly (eu'n'diou-), adv., irrégulièrement; indûment; à tort; (excessively—excessivement) à l'excès.

unduteous (eu'n'diou-ti-), or **undutiful** (-'foule), adj., désobéissant; irrespectueux; indocile.

undutifully, adv., indocilement, irrévéremment, irrespectueusement.

undutifulness, n., désobéissance, irrévérence, f.

undyed (eu'n'daïde), adj., non teint.

undying (eu'n'da-yigne), adj., qui ne périt point; impérissable.

unearned (eu'n'eur'n'de), adj., non gagné, non mérité.

unearth (eu'n'eurth), v.a., déterrer.

unearthly, adj., non terrestre; céleste.

uneasily (eu'n'iz'-), adv., dans l'inquiétude; mal à son aise; (with difficulty—péniblement) difficilement, péniblement.

uneasiness, n., malaise, m.; peine; (of mind—d'esprit) inquiétude, f.

uneasy (eu'n'iz'i), adj., (in mind—d'esprit) inquiet; (constraining—gênant) gênant, incommode; (constrained—gêné) mal à son aise, gêné; (disagreeable—déplaisant) désagréable.

uneatable (eu'n'it'a-b'l), adj., immangeable.

unedifying (eu'n'èd'i-fa-yigne), adj., peu édifiant.

uneducated (eu'n'èd'iou-két'-), adj., sans éducation; sans instruction.

unembarrassed (eu'n'è'm'bâr-raste), adj., non embarrassé; non gêné; (of property—de biens-fonds) clair, net, libre.

unembodied (eu'n'è'm'bod'ide), adj., incorporel.

unemployed (eu'n'è'm'ploïde), adj., non employé; sans occupation; inoccupé; (capital) dormant, inactif.

unencumbered (eu'n'è'n'keu'm'beurde), adj., non encombré; non grevé.

unendowed (eu'n'è'n'daoude), adj., non doué; non doté.

unengaged (eu'n'è'n'ghédj'de), adj., non engagé; inoccupé, oisif; libre; (affections) libre; (capital) non engagé, disponible.

unengaging, adj., non attrayant, sans charmes.

unenlightened (en'n'è'n'laït'n'de), adj., peu éclairé.

unentertaining (eu'n'è'n'teur-tè'n'-), adj., peu divertissant; inamusant.

unenvied (eu'n'è'n'vide), adj., non envié.

unequable (eu'n'i-kwa-b'l), adj., inégal; inférieur; au-dessous de; (unjust—peu juste) injuste.

unequal (eu'n'l-kwal), adj., inégal; insuffisant, disproportionné; au-dessous de, inférieur. He is —to that: il n'est pas capable de le faire.

unequalled (-kwal'de), adj., sans égal; sans pareil.

unequally, adv., inégalement.

unequivocal (eu'n'i-kwiv'-), adj., non équivoque.

unequivocally, adv., sans équivoque.

unerring, adj., infaillible, sûr.

unerringly, adv., infailliblement.

unevangelical (eu'n'i-va'n'djèl'-), adj., non évangélique.

uneven (eu'n'i'v'n), adj., inégal; raboteux; (of numbers—des nombres) impair; (fig.) inégal.

unevenly, adv., inégalement; impairement.

unevenness, n., inégalité, f.

unexamined (eu'n'èg-za'm'i'n'de), adj., non examiné; non visité; (jur.) non interrogé.

unexampled (eu'n'èg-zâ'm'p'l'de), adj., sans exemple, sans égal.

unexceptionable (eu'n'èks-cèp-sheu'n'a-b'l), adj., irréprochable.

unexceptionableness, n., nature irréprochable, f.

unexceptionably, adv., irréprochablement.

unexecuted (eu'n'èg-zi-kiout'-), adj., inexécuté, inaccompli.

unexemplified (eu'n'èg-zè'm'pli-faïde), adj., non appuyé d'exemple.

unexempt (eu'n'èg-), adj., non exempt.

unexpected, adj., inopiné, inattendu; subit; (pers.) qu'on n'attendait pas.

unexpectedly, *adv.*, inopinément, subitement.

unexpectedness, *n.*, nature inattendue, *f.*

unexpensive, *adj.*, non dispendieux, qui coûte peu.

unexpired (eu'n'ěks'paeurde), *adj.*, non expiré ; (of bills—*de billets, &c.*) non échu.

unexplored (eu'n'ěks-plôrde), *adj.*, inexploré.

unexposed (eu'n'ěks-pôz'de), *adj.*, non exposé.

unexpressed (eu'n'ěks-prěste), *adj.*, non exprimé.

unextinguished (eu'n'ěks-tign'gwish'te), *adj.*, non éteint.

unfaded (eu'n'féd'-), *adj.*, non fané, non flétri ; frais.

unfading, *adj.*, qui ne se fane pas.

unfailing (eu'n'fél'-), *adj.*, inépuisable ; (certain) infaillible, immanquable.

unfailingly, *adv.*, infailliblement.

unfailingness, *n.*, infaillibilité, *f.*

unfair (eu'n'fére), *adj.*, injuste ; déloyal ; de mauvaise foi.

unfairly, *adv.*, injustement ; déloyalement.

unfairness, *n.*, injustice ; improbité, déloyauté, *f.*

unfaithful (eu'n'féth'foule), *adj.*, infidèle ; impie.

unfaithfully, *adv.*, infidèlement.

unfaithfulness, *n.*, infidélité, *f.*

unfamiliar, *adj.*, peu familier ; inconnu.

unfamiliarity, *n.*, manque de familiarité, *m.*

unfashionable (eu'n'fash'eu'n'a-b'l), *adj.*, qui n'est pas de mode ; (pers.) pas à la mode.

unfashionableness, *n.*, indifférence pour la mode ; inélégance, *f.*

unfashionably, *adv.*, contre la mode ; grossièrement, mal.

unfashioned (eu'n'fash'eu'n'de), *adj.*, non façonné ; informe ; simple.

unfasten (eu'n'fâs's'n), *v.a.*, délier, détacher ; desserrer, relâcher ; (a door—*une porte*) débarrer, ôter la chaîne, la barre de.

unfatherly (eu'n'fâ-*theur*-), *adj.*, peu paternel.

unfathomable (eu'n'fa*th*o'm'a-b'l), *adj.*, insondable ; impénétrable.

unfathomably, *adv.*, d'une manière insondable ; impénétrablement.

unfathomed (eu'n'fa*th*'eu'm'de), *adj*., non sondé ; insondable.

unfavourable (eu'n'fé-veur'a-b'l), *adj.*, défavorable ; fâcheux.

unfavourableness, *n.*, nature défavorable, *f.*

unfavourably, *adv.*, défavorablement.

unfavoured (eu'n'fé-veurde), *adj.*, non favorisé.

unfeared (eu'n'fîrde), *adj.*, non craint.

unfeasible (eu'n'fî'z'i-b'l), *adj.*, impraticable ; infaisable.

unfeathered (eu'n'fě*th*'eurde), *adj.*, sans plumes ; déplumé.

unfeatured (eu'n'fît'ieurde), *adj.*, difforme, laid, disgracieux.

unfed (eu'n'fěde), *adj.*, non nourri.

unfeed (eu'n'fîd), *adj.*, non rétribué ; non payé.

unfeeling (eu'n'fîl'-), *adj.*, insensible.

unfeelingly, *adv.*, avec insensibilité.

unfeelingness, *n.*, insensibilité, *f.*

unfeigned (eu'n'fé'n'de), *adj.*, non feint ; sincère.

unfeignedly (-'ěd'-), *adv.*, sans feinte ; sincèrement.

unfeignedness (-'ěd'-), *n.*, sincérité, *f.*

unfelt (eu'n'fělte), *adj.*, qu'on ne sent pas ; inconnu.

unfenced (eu'n'fě'n'ste), *adj.*, sans clôture ; ouvert.

unfermented, *adj.*, non fermenté ; sans levain.

unfertile (eu'n'feur-til), *adj.*, infertile, stérile.

unfetter, *v.a.*, ôter les fers à ; déchaîner.

unfettered (eu'n'fět'teurde), *adj.*, non géné ; non entravé ; libre.

unfilial, *adj.*, indigne d'un fils.

unfilled (eu'n'fil'de), *adj.*, non rempli ; non plein.

unfinished (eu'n'fi-nish'te), *adj.*, inachevé ; incomplet.

unfit, *adj.*, non adapté ; impropre ; (unqualified—*inapte*) incapable, inepte ; (improper—*inconvenant*) inconvenable.

unfit, *v.a.*, rendre incapable.

unfitly, *adv.*, mal ; peu convenablement.

unfitness, *n.*, inaptitude ; incapacité ; (unbecomingness—*inconvenance*) inconvenance, *f.*

unfitting, *adj.*, inconvenant.

unfix, *v.a.*, détacher, délier ; (to unsettle—*troubler*) rendre indécis ; (to dissolve—*dissoudre*) fondre.

unfixed (eu'n'fiks'te), *adj.*, mobile, errant ; incertain.

unflagging (eu'n'flag-ghigne), *adj.*, qui ne languit pas ; persévérant ; soutenu ; infatigable.

unfledged (eu'n'flědj'de), *adj.*, sans plumes ; (fig.) novice.

unflinching (eu'n'fli'n'tshigne), *adj.*, ferme, déterminé.

unfold (eu'n'fôlde), *v.a.*, déployer ; déplier ; (to disclose—*exposer*) exposer, développer ; (to display—*déployer*) déployer, montrer ; (to tell—*dire*) déclarer ; (to reveal—*révéler*) révéler ; (sheep—*des moutons*) déparquer.

unfolding, *n.*, révélation, *f.* ; développement, *m.*

unforbid, *or* **unforbidden**, *adj.*, non défendu ; permis.

unforced (eu'n'fôrste), *adj.*, non forcé ; non contraint ; spontané ; (natural—*naturel*) naturel ; (easy—*aisé*) aisé, facile.

unforcible (eu'n'fôr-ci-b'l), *adj.*, sans force, sans vigueur.

unforeseen (eu'n'fôr-sîne), *adj.*, imprévu.

unforfeited (eu'n'for-fit'ěde), *adj.*, non confisqué.

unforgiven (eu'n'for-ghiv'n), *adj.*, à qui on n'a pas pardonné ; (of things—*des choses*) non pardonné.

unforgiving (eu'n'for-ghiv'-), *adj.*, inexorable, implacable.

unforgotten, *adj.*, non oublié.

unformed (eu'n'for'm'de), *adj.*, informe ; non formé.

unforsaken (eu'n'for-sěk'n), *adj.*, non délaissé.

unfortified (eu'n'for-ti-faïde), *adj.*, non fortifié.

unfortunate (eu'n'fort'iou-), *adj.*, infortuné ; malheureux.

unfortunately, *adv.*, malheureusement ; par malheur.

unfought (eu'n'fô-te), *adj.*, non combattu ; (of battles—*de batailles*) non livré.

unfounded (eu'n'faou'n'dède), *adj.*, sans fondement ; non fondé ; dénué de fondement.

unframed (eu'n'fré'm'de), *adj.*, non façonné ; (of timber—*de bois*) non équarri ; (without a frame—*non encadré*) sans cadre.

unfrequency (eu'n'fri-kwè'n'-), *n.*, rareté ; infréquence, *f.*

unfrequent, *adj.*, rare, infréquent.

unfrequented, *adj.*, infréquenté, peu fréquenté.

unfrequently, *adv.*, rarement ; infréquemment.

unfriable (eu'n'fraï-a-b'l), *adj.*, non friable.

unfriended (eu'n'frè'n'd'-), *adj.*, sans protection, sans amis.

unfriendliness, *n.*, disposition peu amicale, *f.*

unfriendly, *adj.*, peu amical ; (of things—*des choses*) malveillant. — to ; (to things—*des choses*) nuisible à ; contraire à.

unfrozen (eu'n'frô-z'n), *adj.*, non gelé.

unfruitful (eu'n'frout'foule), *adj.*, infertile ; stérile, infructueux.

unfruitfully, *adv.*, infructueusement.

unfruitfulness, *n.*, infertilité, stérilité, *f.*

unfulfilled (eu'n'roul-filde), *adj.*, non accompli, non exécuté.

unfurl (eu'n'feur'l), *v.a.*, déployer ; déplier ; dérouler ; (nav.) déferler.

unfurnish (eu'n'feur-), *v.a.*, démeubler ; dégarnir ; dépouiller.

unfurnished (-nish'te), *adj.*, non approvisionné ; (of houses, rooms—*de maisons, de chambres*) non garni, non meublé.

ungainful (eu'n'ghé'n'foule), *adj.*, sans profit ; ingrat.

ungainly (eu'n'ghé'n'-), *adj.*, maladroit, gauche.

ungalled (eu'n'gôl'de), *adj.*, non blessé, non écorché.

ungarnished (eu'n'gar-nish'te), *adj.*, non garni ; sans ornements.

ungarrisoned (eu'n'gar-ri-s'n'de), *adj.*, sans garnison.

ungartered (eu'n'gâr-teurde), *adj.*, sans jarretières.

ungathered (eu'n'gath'eurde), *adj.*, non cueilli ; non recueilli.

ungauged (eu'n'ghédj'de), *adj.*, non jaugé ; non mesuré.

ungenerated (eu'n'djè'n'èr'ét'-), *adj.*, incréé.

ungenerative (-èr-a-), *adj.*, stérile.

ungenerous (eu'n'djè'n'èr-), *adj.*, peu généreux ; mesquin.

ungenerously, *adv.*, peu généreusement.

ungenial (eu'n'djî-), *adj.*, peu propice ; défavorable.

ungenteel (eu'n'djè'n'tîle), *adj.*, peu distingué ; de mauvais ton ; de mauvais goût, de mauvais genre ; peu poli.

ungenteelly, *adv.*, d'une manière peu distinguée ; peu poliment ; avec mauvais goût, de mauvais ton.

ungentle (eu'n'djè'n't'l), *adj.*, rude, dur ; indocile ; impoli.

ungentlemanly (-djè'n'-), *adj.*, peu distingué, peu comme il faut ; (pers.) qui ne sait pas vivre, de mauvais ton, sans formes.

ungentleness, *n.*, rudesse, dureté, indocilité ; (incivility—*grossièreté*) incivilité, *f.*

ungently, *adv.*, rudement ; durement.

ungeometrical (eu'n'dji-o-), *adj.*, peu géométrique.

ungild (eu'n'ghilde), *v.a.*, dédorer.

ungird (eu'n'gheurde), *v.a.*, ôter la ceinture à ; détacher.

ungirt (eu'n'gheurte), *adj.*, sans ceinture ; détaché.

unglue (eu'n'glou), *v.a.*, décoller ; détacher.

ungod, *v.a.*, dépouiller de la divinité.

ungodlily, *adv.*, en impie.

ungodliness, *n.*, impiété, *f.*

ungodly, *adj.*, impie.

ungovernable (eu'n'gheuv'eurn'a-b'l), *adj.*, ingouvernable ; effréné ; sans frein, déréglé.

ungraceful (eu'n'grés'foule), *adj.*, peu gracieux, sans grâce.

ungracefully, *adv.*, peu gracieusement ; sans grâce, sans élégance.

ungracefulness, *n.*, absence de grâce, *f.*

ungracious (eu'n'gré-sheusse), *adj.*, disgracieux, déplaisant ; (not favoured—*mal vu*) mal vu ; (wicked—*méchant*) méchant.

ungraciously, *adv.*, disgracieusement ; d'une manière déplaisante ; méchamment.

ungrammatical, *adj.*, contraire à la grammaire ; incorrect.

ungrammatically, *adv.*, contre les lois de la grammaire.

ungranted, *adj.*, non accordé.

ungrateful (eu'n'grét'foule), *adj.*, ingrat ; (unpleasant—*déplaisant*) désagréable.

ungratefully, *adv.*, avec ingratitude ; désagréablement.

ungratefulness, *n.*, ingratitude, *f.* ; désagrément, *m.*

ungrounded (eu'n'graou'n'd'-), *adj.*, sans fondement.

ungroundedly, *adv.*, sans fondement.

ungrudged (eu'n'greudj'de), *adj.*, donné de bon cœur.

ungrudging (eu'n'greudj'-), *adj.*, qui ne donne pas à contre-cœur.

ungrudgingly, *adv.*, non à contre-cœur.

unguarded (eu'n'gârd'-), *adj.*, non gardé ; (fig.) où l'on n'est pas sur ses gardes ; (not cautious—*imprudent*) peu mesuré, peu réservé, peu sage ; imprudent. In an — moment ; dans un moment d'imprudence.

unguardedly, *adv.*, sans être sur ses gardes ; imprudemment ; sans mesure, sans réserve.

unguent (eu'n'gwè'n'te), *n.*, onguent, *m.*

unguentous. *adj.*, onguentaire.

unguessed (eu'n'gu-èste), *adj.*, non deviné ; caché.

unguicular (eu'n'gwik'iou-), *adj.*, de la longueur de l'ongle.

unguiculate, *or* **unguiculated** (eu'n'gwik'iou-lét'-), *adj.*, onguiculé ; à onglet.

unguided (eu'n'gaïd'-), *adj.*, sans guide.

unguilty (eu'n'ghil'-), *adj.*, non coupable, innocent.

unguis (eu'n'gwiss), *n.*, (bot.) onglet, *m.*

ungulate (eu'n'ghiou-), *adj.*, ongulé.

ungum, *v.a.*, (silk—*soie*) dégommer, décruser.

ungumming, *n.*, dégommage, décrusement, *m.*

ungutted (eu'n'gheut'-), *adj.*, non vidé.

unhabituated (eu'n'ha-bit'iou-ét'-), *adj.*, peu habitué ; étranger.

unhallow (eu'n'hal-lô), *v.a.*, profaner.

unhallowed (-lôde), *adj.*, non sanctifié ; profane.

unhand, *v.a.*, lâcher.

unhandily, *adv.*, maladroitement, gauchement.

unhandiness, *n.*, maladresse, gaucherie, *f.*

unhandsome (eu'n'han'd'seume), *adj.*, (illiberal) peu libéral, vilain, indélicat ; (uncivil—*incivil*) impoli ; (ungraceful—*disgracieux*) laid, disgracieux.

unhandsomely, *adv.*, (illiberally—*illibéralement*) peu libéralement, vilainement, avec indélicatesse ; (uncivilly—*incivilement*) impoliment ; (ungracefully—*disgracieusement*) d'une manière disgracieuse.

unhandsomeness, *n.*, indélicatesse ; (incivility—*incivilité*) impolitesse ; (want of beauty—*manque de beauté*) laideur, nature disgracieuse, *f.*

unhandy, *adj.*, maladroit, gauche ; (inconvenient—*incommode*) incommode.

unhappily, *adv.*, malheureusement ; par malheur.

unhappiness, *n.*, malheur ; mal, *m.*

unhappy, *adj.*, malheureux ; (calamitous—*funeste*) malheureux, funeste.

unharassed (eu'n'har'aste), *adj.*, non harassé ; non tourmenté.

unharmed (eu'n'hârm'de), adj., intact ; sain et sauf.

unharmful (-foule), adj., innocent, inoffensif.

unharness, v.a., déharnacher ; (to take from a vehicle—dételer) dételer ; (of armour—d'une armure) ôter l'armure à.

unhatched (eu'n'hatsh'te), adj., non éclos.

unhealthful (eu'n'hèlth'foule), adj., malsain ; insalubre.

unhealthfulness, n., insalubrité, f.

unhealthily (eu'n'hèlth'-), adv., d'une manière maladive ; insalubrement.

unhealthiness, n., défaut de santé ; (want of vigour—faiblesse) état maladif, m. ; (insalubrity—insalubrité) insalubrité, f.

unhealthy, adj., maladif, malsain ; (insalubrious—insalubre) insalubre, malsain ; (morbid—morbide) maladif ; (wanting vigour of growth—faible) maladif.

unheard (eu'n'heurde), adj., non entendu ; (not celebrated—non célèbre) inconnu, obscur. — of : inouï ; inconnu.

unheavenly (eu'n'hèv'n'-), adj., non céleste.

unheeded (eu'n'hid'-), adj., inaperçu, négligé ; à qui (auquel) on ne fait pas attention.

unheededly, adv., sans être remarqué.

unheedful (-foule), adj., inattentif, distrait.

unheeding, adj., insouciant ; inattentif, distrait, négligent.

unheedingly, adv., d'une manière distraite ; sans soin ; par mégarde, par distraction.

unheedy, adj., soudain ; précipité.

unhelped (eu'n'hèlp'te), adj., sans secours ; sans aide.

unhelpful (-foule), adj., qui n'aide pas ; qui n'est d'aucun secours, qui ne sert à rien, inutile.

unhesitating (eu'n'hèz'i-tét'-), adj., qui n'hésite pas ; décidé.

unhesitatingly, adv., sans hésiter.

unhewn (eu'n'hioune), adj., brut ; non travaillé ; (of stone—de la pierre) non taillé ; (of wood—du bois) de brin, en brin.

unhinge (eu'n'hi'n'dje), v.a., dégonder, (fig.) mettre hors des gonds, bouleverser, troubler, démonter.

unhitch, v.a., décrocher.

unhive (eu'n'haïve), v.a., sortir de la ruche.

unhoard (eu'n'hôrde), v.a., voler dans un trésor ; (to scatter—dissiper) répandre, dissiper.

unholiness (eu'n'hô-), n., manque de sainteté, m. ; nature profane, impiété, f.

unholy (-hô-), adj., profane ; impie.

unhonoured (eu'n'o'n'eurde), adj., qui n'est pas honoré ; sans honneur ; dédaigné, méprisé.

unhood (eu'n'houde), v.a., déchaperonner.

unhook (eu'n'houke), v.a., décrocher.

unhoop (eu'n'houpe), v.a., ôter les cercles à.

unhoped (eu'n'hôp'te), or **unhoped for**, adj., inespéré, inattendu.

unhopeful (-foule), adj., sans espérance ; désespérant.

unhopefully, adv., sans espérance.

unhorse, v.a., désarçonner, renverser.

unhostile, adj., inhostile.

unhouse (eu'n'haouce), v.a., déloger, faire déloger.

unhurt (eu'n'heurte), adj., sain et sauf ; intact.

unhurtful (-fo'e), adj., innocent ; peu dangereux.

unhurtfully, adv., innocemment.

unicorn (you-ni-), n., licorne, f.

unicorn-fish, n., narval, m. ; licorne de mer, f.

unicornous (you-ni-), adj., qui n'a qu'une corne.

unideal (eu'n'aï-di-), adj., non idéal ; réel.

uniflorous (you-ni-flô-), adj., uniflore.

uniform (you-ni-), adj., uniforme.

uniform (you-ni-), n., uniforme, m.

uniformity (you-ni-), n., uniformité, f.

uniformly (you-ni-), adv., uniformément.

unilateral (you-ni-), adj., unilatéral.

unilocular (you-ni-lok'iou-), adj., uniloculaire.

unimaginable (eu'n'i-madj'i'n'a-b'l), adj., inimaginable, inconcevable.

unimaginably (eu'n'i-madj'-), adv., d'une manière inimaginable.

unimaginative (eu'n'-), adj., non imaginatif.

unimagined (eu'n'i-madj'i'n'de), adj., non imaginé.

unimitated (eu'n'i'm'i-tét'-), adj., non imité.

unimmortal (eu'n'-), adj., mortel.

unimpairable (eu'n'i'm'pér'a-b'l), adj., inaltérable.

unimpaired (-pérde), adj., inaltéré ; intact ; entier ; non affaibli ; non endommagé.

unimpassioned (eu'n'i'm'pash'eu'n'de), adj., non passionné ; sans passion.

unimpeachable (eu'n'i'm'pîtsh'a-b'l), adj., inattaquable ; irréprochable.

unimpeached (-pîtsh'te), adj., sans reproche ; incontesté.

unimpeded (eu'n'i'm'pîd'-), adj., non empêché ; sans obstacle.

unimplicated (eu'n'i'm'pli-ké-), adj., non impliqué ; non compromis.

unimplied (eu'n'i'm'plaïde), adj., exprimé, non sous-entendu.

unimplored (eu'n'i'm'plôrde), adj., non imploré ; non supplié.

unimportant (eu'n'-), adj., sans importance ; indifférent ; peu important ; sans prétention.

unimportuned (eu'n'i'm'por-tiou'n'de), adj., non importuné.

unimposed (eu'n'i'm'poz'de), adj., non imposé ; volontaire.

unimposing (eu'n'i'm'pôz'-), adj., peu imposant ; (voluntary—volontaire) volontaire.

unimpressed (eu'n'i'm'prèste), adj., non empreint ; non imprimé ; (not penetrated—non pénétré) non pénétré.

unimpressive, adj., peu frappant ; froid.

unimprovable (eu'n'i'm'prouv'a-b'l-), adj., non susceptible d'amélioration ; incorrigible ; (of land—de terres) non exploitable.

unimprovableness, n., nature qu'on ne peut améliorer, qu'on ne peut perfectionner ; nature incorrigible ; (of land—de terres) nature non exploitable, f.

unimproved (-prouv'de), adj., non corrigé ; non amélioré ; (not advanced—peu avancé) qui n'a pas fait de progrès, sans progrès ; (of land—de terres) non exploité.

unimproving, adj., qui ne corrige pas ; qui n'améliore pas ; qui ne fait pas faire de progrès.

uninclosed (eu'n'i'n'clôz'de), adj., ouvert.

unincumbered (eu'n'i'n'keu'm'beurde), adj., non encombré ; non embarrassé ; non grevé ; libre.

unindebted (eu'n'i'n'dèt'-), adj., non endetté.

unindorsed (eu'n'i'n'dorste), adj., non endossé ; sans endossement.

unindulgent (eu'n'i'n'deuldj'-), adj., peu indulgent ; sans indulgence.

unindustrious (eu'n'i'n'deus-), adj., peu laborieux ; peu assidu.

uninflamed (eu'n'i'n'flé'm'de), adj., non enflammé.

uninflammable (eu'n'i'n'fla'm'ma-b'l), adj., ininflammable.

uninfluenced (eu'n'i'n'flou-è'n'ste), adj., non influencé ; libre.

uninfluencive, or **uninfluential** (-shal), adj., peu influent ; sans influence.

uninformed (eu'n'i'n'form'de), adj., non

cultivé, sans culture; (pers.) ignorant, sans instruction, non instruit ; (unanimated—*inanimé*) inanimé, sans expression. To be — of ; *être ignorant de ; ignorer.*

uninforming, *adj.*, qui n'instruit pas.

uninfringed (eu'n'i'n'fri'n'dj'de), *adj.*, non enfreint.

uningenious (eu'n'i'n'dji'n'-), *adj.*, peu ingénieux.

uninhabitable (eu'n'i'n'hab'i-ta-b'l), *adj.*, inhabitable.

uninhabited, *adj.*, inhabité.

uninitiate, *or* **uninitiated** (eu'n'l'n'ish-i-ét'-), *adj.*, non initié.

uninjured (eu'n'i'n'djeurde), *adj.*, auquel on n'a pas fait tort; (safe—*sauf*) en sûreté, sain et sauf, sans blessure, sans mal ; (of things—*des choses*) non endommagé, intact.

uninquisitive (eu'n'i'n'kwiz'-), *adj.*, peu curieux.

uninscribed (eu'n'i'n'scraïb'de), *adj.*, non inscrit.

uninspired (eu'n'i'n'spaeurde), *adj.*, non inspiré.

uninstructed (eu'n'i'n'streukt'-), *adj.*, non instruit, ignorant, sans instruction ; (without authority—*sans pouvoirs*) sans instructions.

uninstructive, *adj.*, non instructif.

unintellectual (eu'n'i'n'tèl-lèkt'iou-), *adj.*, peu intellectuel.

unintellectually, *adv.*, peu intellectuellement.

unintelligent (eu'n'i'n'tèl-li-djè'n'te), *adj.*, inintelligent; sans intelligence.

unintelligibility (eu'n'i'n'tèl-li-dji-), *n.*, inintelligibilité, *f.*

unintelligible (-li-dji-b'l), *adj.*, inintelligible.

unintelligibly, *adv.*, inintelligiblement.

unintentional, *or* **unintended** (eu'n'-), *adj.*, non intentionnel ; involontaire, sans intention.

unintentionally, *adv.*, involontairement; sans le vouloir, sans intention.

uninterested, *adj.*, désintéressé ; non intéressée.

uninterestedly, *adv.*, d'une manière désintéressé.

uninteresting, *adj.*, peu intéressant.

uninterestingly, *adv.*, d'une manière peu intéressante.

unintermitting, *or* **unintermitted** (eu'n'i'n'teur-), *adj.*, incessant, continu.

uninterruptingly, *adv.*, sans cesse, sans intermission.

uninterrupted (eu'n'i'n'tèr-reupt'-), *adj.*, non interrompu ; continuel.

uninterruptedly, *adv.*, sans interruption.

unintrenched (eu'n'i'n'trè'n'sh'te), *adj.*, sans retranchements, non retranché.

uninvaded (eu'n'i'n'véd'-), *adj.*, non envahi.

uninvented, *adj.*, non inventé.

uninventive, *adj.*, peu inventif.

uninvestigable (eu'n'i'n'vès-ti-ga-b'l), *adj.*, non susceptible d'investigation ; inscrutable.

uninvestigated (-ti-ghét'-), *adj.*, que l'on n'a pas scruté, examiné; sans investigation.

uninvited (eu'n'i'n'vaït'-), *adj.*, non invité ; non engagé.

uninviting (-vaït'-), *adj.*, peu attrayant, peu engageant.

union (you'n'ieune), *n.*, union ; réunion, *f.* ; (concord—*concorde*) accord, *m.*, harmonie ; (states united—*états alliés*) union ; (of parishes—*de paroisses*) union, *f.*

unionist (you'n'ieun'-), *n.*, unioniste, *m.*

union-jack (-djake), *n.*, pavillon anglais, *m.*

uniparous (you-ni-), *adj.*, unipare.

unique (you-nike), *adj.*, unique.

uniquely, *adv.*, uniquement.

---

uniradiated (you-ni-ré-di-ét'-), *adj.*, à un seul rayon.

unirritated (eu'n'ir-ri-tét'-), *adj.*, non irrité.

unisexual (you-ni-cèks'iou-), *adj.*, unisexué, unisexuel.

unison (you-ni-ceune), *n.*, unisson ; son unique, *m.*

unison (you-ni-), *adj.*, à l'unisson.

unisonance (you-niss'-), *n.*, consonance parfaite, *f.*

unisonant, *adj.*, à l'unisson.

unisonous, *adj.*, à l'unisson.

unit (you-nite), *n.*, unité, *f.*

unitarian (you-ni-té-), *n.*, unitaire, *m.*, *f.*

unite (you-naïte), *v.a.*, unir ; réunir ; joindre.

unite, *v.n.*, s'unir ; se réunir ; se joindre.

united, *adj.*, uni ; réuni ; joint.

unitedly, *adv.*, avec union ; en harmonie.

uniter, *n.*, personne qui unit ; chose qui unit, *f.*

unity (you-ni-), *n.*, unité ; concorde, harmonie, *f.*

univalve (you-ni-), *or* **univalvular** (-viou-lar), *adj.*, univalve.

univalve, *n.*, univalve, *m.*

universal (you-ni-veur-), *adj.*, universel.

universality, *n.*, universalité, *f.*

universally, *adv.*, universellement.

universe (you-ni-veurse), *n.*, univers, *m.*

university (you-ni-veur-), *n.*, université, *f.*

univocal (you-niv'-), *adj.*, non équivoque ; (mus., gram.) univoque.

univocally, *adv.*, d'une manière univoque.

univocation (you-ni-vo-ké-), *n.*, univocation, *f.*

unjoin (eu'n'djwaïne), *v.a.*, déjoindre, disjoindre, séparer.

unjoint. *V.* **disjoint**.

unjoyful (eu'n'djo-è-foule), *or* **unjoyous** (-djo-yeuss'e), *adj.*, peu joyeux ; triste.

unjudged (eu'n'djeudj'de), *adj.*, non jugé.

unjust (eu'n'djeuste), *adj.*, injuste.

unjustifiable (eu'n'djeust'i-faï-a-b'l), *adj.*, non justifiable, inexcusable.

unjustifiableness, *n.*, nature injustifiable, *f.*

unjustifiably, *adv.*, d'une manière injustifiable.

unjustified (-faïde), *adj.*, non justifié.

unjustly (eu'n'djeust'-), *adv.*, injustement.

unkennel, *v.a.*, sortir de son trou ; (a dog—*un chien*) sortir du chenil ; (a fox—*un renard*) déterrer ; (a stag—*un cerf*) débucher ; (fig.) déterrer, débusquer.

unkind (eu'n'kaï'n'de), *adj.*, peu obligeant, peu complaisant ; malhonnête, méchant ; dur, peu bienveillant, désobligeant ; peu aimable ; mauvais, cruel.

unkindliness, *n.*, désobligeance, dureté, *f.*

unkindly, *adj.*, peu propice ; contraire, nuisible ; défavorable; désobligeant ; dur ; malfaisant.

unkindly, *adv.*, sans complaisance, sans malhonnêtement, sans bienveillance ; sans amabilité ; désobligeamment ; durement ; cruellement.

unkindness, *n.*, manque de complaisance, défaut de bienveillance ; mauvais vouloir, *m.* ; malveillance, désobligeance, cruauté, dureté, *f.*

unking (eu'n'kigne), *v.a.*, détrôner.

unkingly, *adj.*, non royal.

unknit (eu'n'nite), *v.a.*, défaire ; dénouer ; délier.

unknowable (eu'n'nô-a-b'l), *adj.*, qu'on ne peut savoir ; méconnaissable.

unknowing (eu'n'nô-igne), *adj.*, i̶gnorant, qui ne sait pas.

unknowingly, *adv.*, sans le savoir ; par ignorance.

unknown (eu'n'nône), *adj.*, inconnu

— to me ; (without my knowledge—*sans que je le susse*) *à mon insu.*

unlaboured (eu'n'lé-beurde), *adj.*, non travaillé : naturel.

unlace, *v.a.,* délacer ; dégarnir de dentelle.

unlade, *v.a.* (preterit, Unloaded ; *past part.*, Unladen), décharger.

unlady-like (eu'n'lôdi-laïke), *adj.*, de mauvais ton ; indélicat.

unlaid. *adj.,* non posé ; (fig.) non apaisé.

unlamented, *adj.,* non regretté.

unlatch, *v.a.,* lever le loquet de ; ouvrir.

unlawful (eu'n'lô-foule), *adj.,* illégal ; illicite, illégitime.

unlawfully, *adv.,* illégalement; illicitement.

unlearn (eu'n'leurne), *v.a.,* désapprendre.

unlearned (eu'n'leurn'ède), *adj.,* ignorant ; illettré ; (of things—*des choses*) désappris, non appris.

unleavened (eu'n'lèv'n'de), *adj.,* sans levain : azyme.

unless, *conj.;* à moins que . . . . ne ; à moins de ; si ce n'est, excepté que.

unlettered (eu'n'lèt'teurde), *adj.,* illettré.

unlevelled (eu'n'lèv'èlde), *adj.,* non nivelé.

unlicensed (eu'n'laï-cè'n'ste), *adj.,* non autorisé ; sans autorisation ; sans privilège ; sans patente.

unlicked (eu'n'lik'te), *adj.,* mal léché ; grossier.

unlighted (eu'n'laït'ède), *adj.,* non allumé ; non éclairé.

unlike (eu'n'laïke), *adj.,* dissemblable, différent ; (improbable) invraisemblable, improbable.

unlikelihood (eu'n'laïk'li-houde), *or* **unlikeliness** (-laïk'-), *n.,* invraisemblance, improbabilité, *f.*

unlikely, *adj.,* improbable, invraisemblable; (not promising success—*qui ne promet pas de réussir*) inefficace.

unlikely, *adv.,* invraisemblablement.

unlikeness, *n.,* différence, dissemblance, *f.*

unlimited, *adj.,* illimité ; indéfini, indéterminé.

unlimitedly, *adv.,* sans limites ; d'une manière illimitée, indéfiniment.

unlimitedness, *n.,* nature illimitée, indéfinie, *f.*

unlink, *v.a.,* défaire.

unliquidated (eu'n'lik'wi-dét'-), *adj.,* non liquidé.

unload (eu'n'lôde), *v.a.,* décharger ; alléger.

unlook, *v.a.,* ouvrir (ce qui était fermé à clef) ; (print.) desserrer ; (fig.) découvrir, révéler, épancher.

unlooked-for (eu'n'louk'te-), *adj.,* inattendu, inopiné.

unloved (eu'n'leuv'de), *adj.,* non aimé.

unlovely, *adj.,* peu aimable.

unloving, *adj.,* peu affectueux.

unluckily (eu'n'leuk'-), *adv.,* malheureusement.

unluckiness, *n.,* malheur, *m.* ; infortune, *f.*

unlucky, *adj.,* malheureux ; infortuné ; (illomened—*qui annonce un malheur*) de mauvais augure ; (mischievous—*malfaisant*) malin.

unlute (eu'n'lioute), *v.a.,* déluter.

unmade (eu'n'méde), *adj.,* pas fait : défait.

unmaintainable (eu'n'mé'n'té'n'a-b'l),*adj.,* insoutenable.

unmake, *v.a.* (preterit and past part., Unmade), défaire : détruire

unman, *v.a.,* dépouiller du caractère d'homme ; dégrader ; (to deprive of men—*retirer des hommes*) dégarnir d'hommes ; (to emasculate—*émasculer*) châtrer ; (to deject—*décourager*) abattre ; (to dispeople—*dépeupler*) dépeupler ; (fig.) énerver, amollir.

unmanageable (eu'n'ma'n'édj'a-b'l), *adj.,*

qui ne peut être conduit ; qui ne peut être gouverné, dirigé ; indocile, ingouvernable, difficile à gouverner ; intraitable ; rebelle ; incommode.

unmanageableness, *n.,* (of persons—*des personnes*) indocilité, *f.,* caractère ingouvernable, caractère intraitable, *m.* ; (of things—*dee choses*) impossibilité, difficulté de diriger, de conduire, de gouverner, *f.*

unmanageably, *adv.,* indocilement ; de manière à ne pouvoir être dirigé.

unmanlike (eu'n'ma'n'laïke), *or* **unmanly,** *adj.,* inhumain ; (base, cowardly—*vil*), vil, indigne d'un homme ; (effeminate—*mou*) mou, efféminé.

unmanliness, *n.,* conduite indigne d'un homme, *f.*

unmannered (eu'n'ma'n'neurde), *adj.,* grossier, mal élevé, malappris ; de mauvais ton.

unmannerliness, *n.,* grossièreté, *f.* ; mauvaises manières, *f.pl.* ; mauvais ton, *m.*

unmannerly, *adj.,* grossier, malappris ; malhonnête ; de mauvais ton.

unmannerly, *adv.,* grossièrement, malhonnêtement, avec mauvais ton.

unmantle (eu'n'ma'n't'l), *v.a.,* ôter son manteau à.

unmanufactured (eu'n'ma'n'iou-fak'tieurde), *adj.,* non manufacturé.

unmanured (eu'n'ma-niourde), *adj.,* sans engrais.

unmarked (eu'n'mârk'te),*adj.,* non marqué ; inaperçu.

unmarriageable (eu'n'mar'ridj'a-b'l), *adj.,* non mariable.

unmarried (eu'n'mar'ride), *adj.,* non marié, dans le célibat. — man ; *homme non marié :* célibataire ; garçon. — woman ; *femme non mariée, femme dans le célibat ;* demoiselle.

unmarry, *v.a.,* démarier.

unmask (eu'n'mâske), *v.a.,* démasquer ; dévoiler.

unmast (eu'n'mâste), *v.a.,* démâter.

unmastered (eu'n'mâs-teurde), *adj.,* indompté ; fougueux.

unmatched (eu'n'màtsh'te), *adj.,* sans pareil, incomparable.

unmeaning (eu'n'mî'n'-), qui ne signifie rien ; insignifiant.

unmeaningly, *adv.,* d'une manière insignifiante.

unmeant (eu'n'mè'n'te), *adj.,* involontaire, sans intention.

unmeasured (eu'n'mèj'eurde), *adj.,* non mesuré ; immense ; infini ; démesuré.

unmeditated (eu'n'mèd'i-tét'-), *adj.,* non médité ; improvisé.

unmeet (eu'n'mîte), *adj.,* peu convenable ; inconvenant.

unmeetly, *adv.,* d'une manière inconvenante

unmelodious (eu'n'mi lô-), *adj.,* sans mélodie.

unmelodiously. *adv.,* d'une manière peu mélodieuse.

unmelted, *adj.,* non fondu ; non résous ; (fig.) non attendri.

unmentionable (eu'n'mè'n'sheu'n'a-b'l), *adj.,* dont on ne doit pas parler.

unmentioned (eu'n'mè'n'sheu'n'de), *adj.,* non mentionné.

unmerciful (eu'n'meur-ci-foule), *adj.,* sans miséricorde; impitoyable ; barbare.

unmercifully, *adv.,* sans miséricorde ; impitoyablement.

unmercifulness, *n.,* nature peu miséricordieuse ; nature impitoyable ; barbarie, *f.*

unmerited, *adj.,* non mérité.

unminded (eu'n'maï'n'd'-), *adj.,* inaperçu, négligé.

unmindful (eu'n'maï'n'd'foule), *adj.,* oublieux, insouciant. — of ; *inattentif à ; insouciant de ; oublieux de ; peu soigneux de.*

unmindfully, *adv.,* avec insouciance ; négligemment, inattentivement, sans soin.

unmindfulness (eu'n'-), *n.,* négligence, insouciance, *f.*

unmingled (eu'n'mign'g'l'de), *adj.,* pur, sans mélange.

unmissed (eu'n'mis'te), *adj.,* dont on ne remarque pas l'absence ; qu'on ne regrette pas.

unmitigable (eu'n'mit'i-ga-b'l), *adj.,* non susceptible de mitigation, inflexible.

unmitigated (eu'n'mit'i-ghét'-), *adj.,* non mitigé ; implacable.

unmixed (-miks'te),*adj.,* sans mélange, pur.

unmodifiable (eu'n'mod'i-faï-a-b'l), *adj.,* non susceptible de modification.

unmodified (-faïde), *adj.,* non modifié.

unmoist (eu'n'moïste), *adj.,* non moite ; sec.

unmoistened (eu'n'moï-s-n'de), *adj.,* non humide ; sec.

unmolested, *adj.,* sans être molesté ; sans obstacle.

unmoor (eu'n'moure), *v.a.,* lever l'ancre de ; démarrer.

unmortgaged (eu'n'mor-ghédj'de), *adj.,* non hypothéqué.

unmourned (eu'n'môr-n'de), *adj.,* sans être pleuré.

unmoved (eu'n'mouv'de), *adj.,* immobile ; fixe ; (fig.) non touché, impassible, ferme ; calme, inébranlable.

unmuffle (eu'n'meuf'f'l), *v.a.,* découvrir (ce qui est enveloppé) ; désaffubler ; (a drum—*un tambour*) découvrir.

unmusical (eu'n'miou-zi-), *adj,* peu musical ; sans harmonie.

unmutilated (eu'n'miou-ti-lét'-), *adj.,* non mutilé ; intact.

unmuzzle (eu'n'meuz'z'l), *v.a.,* démuseler ; (fig.) déchaîner.

unnail (eu'n'néle), *v.a.,* déclouer.

unnamed (eu'n'né'm'de), *adj.,* non nommé. Who shall be — ; *dont je tairai le nom.*

unnatural (eu'n'nat'iou-), *adj.,* contraire à la nature ; peu naturel ; forcé ; (pers.) dénaturé.

unnaturalize (-'aïze), *v.a.,* dénaturer ; priver des sentiments naturels.

unnaturalized (-'aïz'de), *adj.,* dénaturé ; (jur.) non naturalisé.

unnaturally, *adv.,* contre nature ; d'une manière dénaturée ; d'une manière forcée.

unnaturalness, *n.,* état de ce qui est contre nature ; caractère non naturel, *m.*

unnavigable (eu'n'navi-ga-b'l), *adj.,* non navigable.

unnecessarily, *adv.,* sans nécessité ; inutilement.

unnecessariness, *n.,* inutilité, *f.*

unnecessary, *or* **unneedful** (eu'n'nid'-foule), *adj.,* peu nécessaire ; inutile.

unneeded (eu'n'nid'-), *adj.,* dont on n'a pas besoin ; inutile.

unneighbourly (eu'n'nè-beur-), *adj.,* de mauvais voisin.

unneighbourly, *adv.,* en mauvais voisin.

unnerve (eu'n'neurve), *v.a.,* énerver ; affaiblir ; faire perdre contenance à.

unnoted (eu'n'nôt'-), *or* **unnoticed** (-nô-tiste), *adj.,* inaperçu ; négligé, inobservé.

unnumbered (eu'n'neu'm'beurde),*adj.,* non numéroté ; (innumerable—*innombrable*) innombrable.

unobjectionable (eu'n'ob-jèk'sheu'n'a-b'l), *adj.,* irreprochable ; inattaquable ; irrécusable.

unobjectionably, *adv.,* d'une manière irréprochable, inattaquable, irrécusable.

unobnoxious (eu'n'ob-nok-sheuss), *adj.,* non sujet ; non exposé ; invulnérable ; non odieux ; non offensant ; non impopulaire.

unobscured (eu'n'ob-skiourde), *adj.,* non obscurci ; non éclipsé.

unobservable (eu'n'ob-zeurv'a-b'l), *adj.,* qu'on ne peut observer ; imperceptible.

unobservance (-zeurv'-), *n.,* inattention ; inobservation, *f.*

unobservant (-zeurv'-); *adj.,* inattentif, qui n'observe pas.

unobserved (-zeurv'de), *adj.,* non observé ; inaperçu.

unobserving (-zeurv'-), *adj.,* peu observateur.

unobstructed (eu'n'ob-streukt'-), *adj.,* non obstrué ; (fig.) sans empêchement.

unobtainable (eu'n'ob-té'n'a-b'l),*adj.,* qu'on ne peut obtenir.

unobtrusive (eu'n'ob-trou-cive), *adj.,* discret, réservé.

unobtrusively, *adv.,* discrètement, sans importunité.

unobtrusiveness, *n.,* discrétion, réserve, *f.*

unoccupied (eu'n'oc-kiou-païde), *adj.,* non occupé ; inoccupé ; libre, oisif.

unoffending, *adj.,* inoffensif ; sans péché.

unoffered (eu'n'of'feurde), *adj.,* non offert.

unofficial (eu'n'of-fish'-), *adj.,* inofficiel.

unofficially, *adv.,* inofficiellement.

unopened (eu'n'ô-p'n'de), *adj.,* qui n'est pas ouvert ; (of letters, &c.—*de lettres, &c.*) non décacheté.

unopposed (eu'n'op-pôz'de), *adj.,* sans être opposé ; sans opposition.

unordered (eu'n'or-deurde), *adj.,* non ordonné ; non commandé.

unordinary, *adj.,* peu ordinaire ; rare.

unorganized (eu'n'or-ga'n'aiz'de), *adj.,* inorganique.

unornamental, *adj.,* qui ne sert pas d'ornement.

unornamented, *adj.,* sans ornements.

unorthodox (eu'n'or-tho-), *adj.,* peu orthodoxe ; hétérodoxe.

unostentatious (eu'n'os-tè'n'té-sheusse), *adj.,* sans ostentation, sans faste.

unostentatiously, *adv.,* sans ostentation.

unowed (eu'n'ôde), *adj.,* non dû.

unowned (eu'n'ô'n'de), *adj.,* sans possesseur ; non avoué.

unoxygenized (eu'n'oks'i-djè'n'aïz'de),*adj.,* non oxygéné.

unpacific (eu'n'pass'i-faïde), *adj.,* peu pacifique ; belliqueux.

unpacified (eu'n'pass'i-faïde), *adj.,* non pacifié ; non apaisé.

unpack, *v.a.,* dépaqueter ; déballer.

unpaid (eu'n'péde), *adj.,* non payé ; non acquitté ; non rétribué ; (of armies—*d'armées*) sans paye, sans solde ; (of letters, &c.—*de lettres, &c.*) non affranchi.

unpainted (eu'n'pé'n't'-), *adj.,* non peint ; non fardé.

unpaired (eu'n'pér'de), *adj.,* non assorti ; non uni ; non apparié ; (of colour—*de couleur*) non marié.

unpalatable (eu'n'pal'a-ta-b'l), *adj.,* désagréable au goût ; (fig.) désagréable.

unparalleled (eu'n'par-al-lèlde), *adj.,* incomparable ; sans pareil ; sans exemple.

unpardonable (eu'n'pâr-d'n'a-b'l),*adj.,* impardonnable, irrémissible.

unpardonably, *adv.,* d'une manière impardonnable.

unpardoned (-d'n'de), *adj.,* non pardonné ; sans pardon.

unpared (eu'n'pérde), *adj.,* non pelé.

unparliamentary (eu'n'pâr-lé-), *adj.,* contraire aux usages du parlement ; non parlementaire.

unparted, *adj.,* non séparé.

unpassionate (eu'n'pash'eu'n-), *adj.,* sans passion ; impartial.

unpathetic (eu'n'pa-thèt'-), *adj.*, peu pathétique.

unpathetically, *adv.*, peu pathétiquement.

unpatriotic (eu'n'pě-), *adj.*, peu patriotique.

unpatriotically, *adv.*, peu patriotiquement.

unpatronized (eu'n'pat'ro'n'aïz'de), *adj.*, sans patron, sans protecteurs, sans protections ; of a shop —*d'un magasin*) mal achalandé.

unpave, *v.a.*, dépaver ; décarreler.

unpeaceable (eu'n'piss'a-b'l), *adj.*, turbulent, peu paisible.

unpeaceableness, *n.*, turbulence, *f.*

unpeaceably, *adv.*, avec tumulte.

unpeaceful (-foule), *adj.*, qui n'est pas paisible ; inquiet.

unpeacefully, *adv.*, non paisiblement, avec bruit.

unpeacefulness, *n.*, inquiétude, *f.* ; état troublé, *m.*

unpeg, *v.a.*, ôter la cheville à ; décheviller.

unpeople (eu'n'pi-p'l), *v.a.*, dépeupler.

unperceivable (eu'n'pèr-civ'a-b'l), *adj.*, imperceptible.

unperceivably, *adv.*, imperceptiblement.

unperceived (-pèr-civ'de), *adj.*, inaperçu.

unperceivedly (-civ'ěd'-)-, *adv.*, sans être aperçu.

unperformed (eu'n'pèr-form'de), *adj.*, inachevé ; inexécuté.

unpermitted, *adj.*, non permis ; illicite.

unphilosophical, *adj.*, peu philosophique.

unphilosophically, *adv.*, peu philosophiquement.

unpicked (eu'n'pik'te) *adj.*, non cueilli ; non épluché ; (of locks—*de serrures*) non crocheté.

unpin, *v.a.*, ôter les épingles de, défaire ; (tech.) décheviller.

unpitied (eu'n'pit'ide), *adj.*, que l'on ne plaint pas.

unpitiful (-foule), *adj.*, sans pitié.

unpitifully, *adv.*, sans pitié ; impitoyablement.

unpitying (-ti-yigne), *adj.*, sans pitié ; impitoyable.

unplait (eu'n'plète), *v.a.*, déplisser.

unplausible (eu'n'plô-ci-b'l), *adj.*, peu plausible.

unpleasant (eu'n'plèz'-), *adj.*, déplaisant, désagréable.

unpleasantly, *adv.*, désagréablement.

unpleasantness, *n.*, nature désagréable, *f.* ; désagrément, *m.*

unpleased (eu'n'plîz'de), *adj.*, mécontent, peu satisfait.

unpleasing (-plîz'-), *adj.*, que ne plaît pas ; déplaisant ; désagréable ; fâcheux.

unpleasingly, *adv.*, désagréablement.

unpleasingness, *n.*, manque de charme ; désagrément, *m.* ; nature déplaisante, *f.*

unpledged (eu'n'plèdj'de), *adj.*, peu engagé.

unpliable (eu'n'plaï-a-b'l), *adj.*, peu pliable ; inflexible.

unpliant (eu'n'plaï-), *adj.*, inflexible.

unpliantness, *n.*, inflexibilité, *f.*

unploughed (eu'n'pla-ode), *adj.*, non labouré ; inculte.

unplucked (eu'n'pleuk'te). *adj.*, non cueilli.

unpoetic, *or* **unpoetical** (eu'n'po-èt'-), *adj.*, peu poétique.

unpoetically, *adv.*, peu poétiquement.

unpointed (eu'n'pwaï'n't'-), *adj.*, sans pointe ; peu piquant ; (gram.) non ponctué.

unpoised (eu'n'pwaïz'de), *adj.*, non en équilibre.

unpolished (eu'n'pol'ish'te), *adj.*, non poli ; (of gold, &c.—*de l'or, &c.*) mat ; (of marble—*du marbre*) brut ; (fig.) inculte, grossier, rude.

unpolite (eu'n'po-laïte), *adj.* V. **impolite**.

unpolluted (eu'n'pol-liout'-), *adj.*, non pollué ; non souillé ; pur, sans souillure.

unpopular (eu'n'pop'iou-), *adj.*, impopulaire.

unpopularity, *n.*, impopularité, *f.*

unpopularly, *adv.*, d'une manière impopulaire.

unpossessed (eu'n'poz'zèste), *adj.*, non possédé ; non occupé. — of ; *qui ne possède pas ; privé de.*

unpractised (eu'n'prak'tiste), *adj.*, inexpérimenté ; sans expérience ; peu habitué ; sans pratique.

unprecedented (eu'n'près'i-), *adj.*, sans exemple, sans antécédent, sans précédent.

unprecise (eu'n'pri-çaïce), *adj.*, peu précis.

unpreferred (eu'n'pri-feurde), *adj.*, non préféré ou non avancé.

unprejudiced (eu'n'prèdj'eu-diste), *adj.*, non prévenu, sans préjugé.

unpremeditated (eu'n'pri-mèd'i-tét'-), *adj.*, non médité ; spontané, improvisé ; (not previously intended—*sans préméditation*). non prémédité.

unprepared (eu'n'pri-pérde), *adj.*, non préparé.

unpreparedly (-pér'ěd'-), *adv.*, sans préparation.

unpreparedness (-pér'ěd'-), *n.*, manque de préparation, *m.*

unprepossessed (eu'n'pri-poz'zèste), *adj.*, non prévenu ; impartial.

unprepossessing (-poz'zèss'-), *adj.*, peu prévenant.

unpressed (eu'n'prèste), *adj.*, non pressé ; non pressuré ; (not enforced—*non forcé*) volontaire.

unpretending (eu'n'pri-), *adj.*, sans prétention, simple.

unprevailing (eu'n'pri-vél'-), *adj.*, impuissant.

unprevented (eu'n'pri-), *adj.*, non prévenu ; non empêché.

unpriest (eu'n'priste), *v.a.*, dépouiller du sacerdoce ; défroquer.

unpriestly, *adj.*, indigne d'un prêtre.

unprincipled (eu'n'pri'n'ci-p'l'de), *adj.*, sans principes ; sans mœurs.

unprinted, *adj.*, non imprimé.

unprivileged (eu'n'priv'i-lèdj'de), *adj.*, non privilégié.

unprizable (eu'n'praïz'a-b'l), *adj.*, sans prix ; sans valeur.

unprized (eu'n'praïz'de), *adj.*, peu estimé.

unproclaimed (eu'n'pro-clé'm'de), *adj.*, non proclamé.

unproductive (eu'n'pro-deuk'-), *adj.*, peu productif, infertile ; stérile, improductif ; (fig.) inefficace, stérile, inpuissant.

unproductiveness, *n.*, stérilité ; infertilité ; nature improductive ; inefficacité ; impuissance, *f.*

unprofaned (eu'n'pro-fé'n'de), *adj.*, non profané ; non souillé.

unprofessional (en'n'pro-fèsh'eu'n'-), *adj.*, étranger à une profession ; indigne d'une profession.

unprofitable (eu'n'prof'it'a-b'l), *adj.*, peu profitable ; sans profit ; ingrat ; inutile ; impuissant.

unprofitableness, *n.*, nature peu profitable ; stérilité ; inutilité, *f.*

unprofitably, *adv.*, ʼinutilement ; sans profit.

unprohibited, *adj.*, non prohibé ; permis.

unprolific, *adj.*, non prolifique ; stérile, infécond.

unpromising (eu'n'pro'm'i-cigne), *adj.*, qui promet peu ; qui s'annonce mal : stérile.

unprompted (eu'n'pro'm'tède), *adj.* , sans être poussé ; non soufflé.

unpronounced (eu'n'pro-naou'n'ste), *adj.*, non prononcé ; inarticulé.

unprophetic, *or* **unprophetical** (eu'n'-pro-fèt'-), *adj.*, non prophétique.

unpropitious (eu'n'pro-pish'eusse), *adj.*, peu propice.

unpropitiously, *adv.*, d'une manière peu propice.

unproportionable (eu'n'pro-pôr-sheu'n'a-b'l), *adj.*, (ant.) disproportionné.

unproportionably, *adv.*, sans proportion.

unproportioned (-pôr-sheu'n'de), *adj.*, disproportionné.

unprosperous (eu'n'pros-pèr'-), *adj.*, peu prospère ; malheureux.

unprosperously, *adv.*, d'une manière peu prospère ; malheureusement.

unprosperousness, *n.*, état peu prospère, *m.*

unprotected, *adj.*, non protégé ; sans protection.

unproved (eu'n'prouv'de), *adj.*, non prouvé, sans preuve ;(not tried—*non essayé*) non éprouvé.

unprovided (eu'n'pro-vaïd'-), *adj.*, dépourvu ; non pourvu ; (not prepared—*non préparé*) pris au dépourvu ; non préparé. — for ; *non pourvu.*

unprovoked (eu'n'pro-vôk'te), *adj.*, non provoqué ; sans provocation ; (not incited—*non provoqué*) non provoqué, non irrité, non fâché, non excité.

unprovoking, *adj.*, qui ne provoque pas ; inoffensif.

unprovokingly, *adv.*, sans provocation.

unpruned (eu'n'prou'n'de), *adj.*, non élagué ; non taillé, non émondé.

unpublished (eu'n'peub'lish'te), *adj.*, non publié ; inédit.

unpunctual (eu'n'peu'n'kt'iou-), *adj.*, non ponctuel ; inexact.

unpunctuality, *or* **impunctuality**, *n.*, défaut de ponctualité, *m.* ; irrégularité, *f.*

unpunctually, *adv.*, sans ponctualité.

unpunished (eu'n'peu'n'ish'te), *adj.*, impuni. To go — ; *rester impuni.*

unpurified (eu'n'piou-ri-faïde), *adj.*, non purifié ; impur.

unqualified (eu'n'kwol'i-faïde), *adj.*, peu propre ; inhabile, incapable ; (not modified—*sans réserve*) sans réserve, sans restriction.

unqueen (eu'n'kwîne), *v.a.*, dépouiller du caractère de reine.

unquelled (eu'n'kwèl'de), *adj.*, non réprimé ; non étouffé.

unquenchable (eu'n'kwè'n'tsh'a-b'l), *adj.*, inextinguible, insatiable.

unquenchableness, *n.*, nature inextinguible, *f.*

unquenchably, *adv.*, d'une manière inextinguible.

unquenched (eu'n'kwè'n'tsh'te), *adj.*, non éteint, non étanché ; (fig) insatiable.

unquestionable (eu'n'kwèst'ieu'n'a-b'l), *adj.*, incontestable, indubitable.

unquestionably, *adv.*, incontestablement ; indubitablement, sans contredit.

unquestioned (-kwèst'ieu'n'de), *adj.*, sans être questionné ; (indubitable) incontesté, hors de doute.

unquickened (eu'n'kwik'k'n'de), *adj.*, inanimé, non vivifié.

unquiet (eu'n'kwa-eute), *adj.*, inquiet, agité.

unquietly, *adv.*, avec inquiétude.

unquietness, *n.*, inquiétude ; agitation, *f.*

unransomed (eu'n'ra'n'ceu'm'de), *adj.*, non racheté ; non rançonné.

unravel, *v.a.*, démêler, débrouiller ; effiler,

défaire ; (intrigue) dénouer ; (fig.) démêler, débrouiller, éclaircir.

unravel, *v.n.*, se démêler, se débrouiller, s'effiler, se défaire ; (fig.) se débrouiller.

unreached (eu'n'ritsh'te), *adj.*, non atteint.

unread (eu'n'rède), *adj.*, qui n'a pas été lu ; (illiterate—*illettré*) peu lettré, illettré, ignorant, sans instruction.

unreadable (eu'n'rid'a-b'l), *adj.*, illisible.

unreadily, *adv* , lentement ; à contre-cœur.

unreadiness (eu'n'rèd'-), *n.*, lenteur, *f.* ; (want of promptitude—*manque de promptitude*) défaut de promptitude ; (want of dexterity—*manque d'adresse*) défaut de facilité ; (reluctance —*répugnance*) défaut d'empressement, défaut de bonne volonté, *m.*, répugnance, *f.*

unready (eu'n'rèd'i), *adj.*, lent, non préparé ; peu prompt ; peu vif ; peu facile ; (awkward—*gauche*) gauche.

unreal (eu'n'rî-), *adj.*, non réel ; faux ; incorporel ; vain.

unreasonable (eu'n'rî-z'n'a-b'l), *adj.*, déraisonnable ; (exorbitant) extravagant, excessif.

unreasonableness, *n.*, déraison, *f.* ; caractère déraisonnable ; (exorbitance—*extravagance*) caractère déraisonnable, *m.*, extravagance, *f.*

unreasonably, *adv.*, déraisonnablement ; à l'excès ; contre la raison.

unrebukable (eu'n'ri-biouk'a-b'l), *adj.*, irrépréhensible.

unrecallable (eu'n'ri-kôl'a-b'l), *adj.*, irrévocable.

unrecalled (eu'n'ri-côl'de), *adj.*, non rappelé.

unreceived (eu'n'ri-cîv'de), *adj.*, non reçu.

unreclaimed (eu'n'ri-klé'm'de), *adj.*, non réclamé ; (not reformed) non amendé ; (not tamed—*sauvage*) inapprivoisé.

unrecommended (eu'n'rèk'-), *adj.*, non recommandé.

unrecompensed (eu'n'rèk'o'm'pè'n'ste), *adj.*, sans récompense.

unreconcilable (eu'n'rèk'o'n'caïl'a-b'l). *V.* **irreconcilable**.

unreconciled (-çaïl'de), *adj.*, irréconcilié ; implacable.

unrecorded (eu'n'ri-), *adj.*, non enregistré.

unrecoverable (eu'n'ri-keuv'eur'a-b'l), *adj. V.* **irrecoverable**.

unrecovered (-ri-keuv'eurde), *adj.*, non recouvré ; (not cured—*non guéri*) non guéri.

unredeemable (eu'n'ri-dî'm'a-b'l), *adj.*, irrachetable ; irrémédiable.

unredeemed (eu'n'ri-dî'm'de), *adj.*, non racheté ; non remboursé ; (of things pawned—*d'articles engagés*) non dégagé.

unredressed (eu'n'ri-drèste), *adj.*, non réformé, non redressé.

unreduced (eu'n'ri-diouste),*adj.*, non réduit.

unrefined (eu'n'ri-faï'n'de), *adj.*, non purifié, non épuré ; (of sugar—*du sucre*) non raffiné ; (of metals—*des métaux*) non affiné ; (of manners—*des manières*) peu poli, non raffiné, grossier, incuite.

unreformable (eu'n'ri-form'a-b'l), *adj.*, incorrigible.

unreformed (eu'n'ri-form'de), *adj.*, non réformé.

unrefreshed (eu'n'ri-frèsh'te), *adj.*, non rafraîchi ; non délassé.

unregarded (eu'n'ri-gârd'-), *adj.*, oublié, négligé ; méconnu.

unregardful (-foule), *adj.*, négligent.

unregardfully, *adv.*, négligemment.

unregeneracy (eu'n'ri-djè'n'èr'-), *n.*, non-régénération, *f.*

unregenerate *or* **unregenerated** (-djè'n'èr'ét'-), *adj.*, non régénéré.

unregistered (eu'n'rèdj'is-teurde), *adj.*, non

enregistre; non inscrit; dont on n'a pas conservé le souvenir.

unregulated (eu'n'règh'iou-lét'-), *adj.*, non réglé.

unrejoicing (eu'n'ri-djwaïss'-), *adj.*, peu joyeux; peu réjouissant.

unrelated (eu'n'ri-lét'-), *adj.*, sans rapport, qui n'a aucun rapport; sans parenté. Who is — to ; *qui n'est pas parent de.*

unrelenting (eu'n'ri-), *adj.*, inflexible; implacable.

unrelentingly, *adv.*, inflexiblement.

unrelievable (eu'n'ri-lîv'a-b'l), *adj.*, qu'on ne peut secourir.

unrelieved (-lîv'de), *adj.*, non soulagé, non secouru; (milit.) non relevé.

unremarkable (eu'n'ri-mârk'a-b'l), *adj.*, non remarquable.

unremarkably, *adv.*, non remarquablement.

unremarked (-mârk'te), *adj.*, inobservé.

unremedied (eu'n'rè'm'i-dide), *adj.*, auquel on n'a pas remédié.

unremembered (eu'n'ri-mè'm'beurde), *adj.*, oublié.

unremembering (-beur'-), *adj.*, oublieux.

unremitted (eu'n'ri-), *adj.*, non remis, non pardonné; (not abated—*non apaisé*) qui ne s'est pas apaisé; (continual—*incessant*) continuel, incessant.

unremovable (eu'n'ri-mouv'a-b'l), *adj.*, (ant.) inamovible.

unremoved (-mouv'de), *adj.*, non écarté; non éloigné; non déplacé, non ôté, non enlevé; (of furniture—*de meubles*) non déménagé.

unrenewed (eu'n'ri-nioude), *adj.*, non renouvelé.

unrepaid (eu'n'ri-péde), *adj.*, non remboursé; non payé; (of love—*d'amour*) non payé de retour.

unrepaired (eu'n'ri-pérde), *adj.*, non réparé.

unrepealable (eu'n'ri-pîl'a-b'l), *adj.*, irrévocable.

unrepealed (-pîl'de), *adj.*, non révoqué; non abrogé.

unrepenting, *or* **unrepentant** (eu'n'ri-), *adj.*, sans repentir; impénitent.

unrepining (eu'n'ri-paï'n'-), *adj.*, qui ne se plaint pas, qui ne murmure pas.

unrepiningly, *adv.*, sans gémir, sans murmurer.

unrepresented (eu'n'rèp-ri-zè'n't'-), *adj.*, non représenté.

unreprievable (eu'n'ri-prîv'a-b'l), *adj.*, à qui l'on ne peut accorder de sursis.

unreprieved (-prîv'de), *adj.*, à qui l'on n'a pas accordé de sursis.

unreproached (eu'n'ri-prôtsh'te), *adj.*, sans reproche.

unreproved (eu'n'ri-prouv'de), *adj.*, non blâmé; non repris.

unrequired (eu'n'ri-kwaeurde), *adj.*, qui n'est pas nécessaire; dont on n'a pas besoin.

unrequited (eu'n'ri-kwaït'-), *adj.*, sans être récompensé; méconnu; (of love—*d'amour*) qui n'est pas payé de retour.

unreserve (eu'n'ri-zeurve), *n.*, absence de réserve, *f.*

unreserved (-zeurv'de), *adj*, sans réserve; expansif.

unreservedly (-zeurv'èd'-), *adv.*, sans réserve.

unreservedness (-zeurv'èd'-), *n.*, absence de réserve; nature expansive, *f.*

unresisted (eu'n'ri-zist'-), *adj.*, sans résistance.

unresisting, *adj.*, qui ne résiste pas; soumis.

unresistingly, *adv.*, sans résistance.

unresolvable (eu'n'ri-zolv'a-b'l), *adj.*, insoluble.

unresolved (-zolv'de), *adj.*, non résolu; (not determined—*indécis*) irrésolu; indécis.

unrespected (eu'n'ri-spèkt'-), *adj.*, non respecté.

unrestored (eu'n'ri-stôrde), *adj.*, non rendu; non restitué; non restauré.

unrestrained (eu'n'ri-stré'n'de), *adj.*, non retenu; non restreint, sans contrainte; non réprimé; déréglé.

unrestricted (eu'n'ri-), *adj.*, non restreint.

unretentive (eu'n'ri-), *adj.*, peu tenace, qui retient peu; (of the memory—*de la mémoire*) peu sûr, peu fidèle.

unrevealed (eu'n'ri-vîl'de), *adj.*, non révélé.

unrevenged (eu'n'ri-vè'n'dj'de), *adj.*, sans être vengé; non vengé.

unreverend, *or* **unreverent** (eu'n'rèv'èr'-), *adj.*, peu révérend; (irreverent) irrévérent.

unrevised (eu'n'ri-vaïz'de), *adj.*, non revu; non revisé.

unrewarded (eu'n'ri-word'-), *adj.*, sans récompense.

unriddle (eu'n'rid'd'l), *v.a.*, expliquer, résoudre.

unrig, *v.a.*, dépouiller; (nav.) dégréer.

unrighteous (eu'n'raït'ieusse), *adj.*, injuste, inique.

unrighteously, *adv.*, injustement, iniquement.

unrighteousness, *n.*, injustice; iniquité, *f.*

unrightful (eu'n'raït'foule), *adj.*, injuste, illégitime.

unring (eu'n'rigne), *v.a.*, ôter les anneaux de.

unripe (eu'n'raïpe), *adj.*, qui n'est pas mûr; vert.

unripened (eu'n'raïp'n'de), *adj.*, qui n'est pas mûr.

unrivalled (eu'n'raï-valde), *adj.*, sans rival; sans pareil.

unrivet, *v.a.*, dériver; détacher.

unrobe (eu'n'rôbe), *v.n.*, ôter sa robe (de cérémonie).

unroll (eu'n'rôle), *v.a.*, dérouler; déployer.

unroll, *v.n.*, se dérouler; se déployer.

unromantic, *adj.*, peu romanesque; (of places—*endroits*) peu romantique.

unroof (eu'n'roufe), *v.a.*, enlever le toit de.

unroost (eu'n'rouste), *v.a.*, (ant.) déjucher; dénicher.

unroot (eu'n'route), *v.a.*, déraciner, extirper.

unroot, *v.n.*, se déraciner.

unrough (eu'n'reufe), *adj.*, lisse, uni; imberbe.

unrouted (eu'n'raout'-), *adj.*, qu'on n'a pas mis en déroute.

unroyal (eu'n'roi-ial), *adj.*, peu royal.

unruffle (eu'n'reuf'f'l), *v.n.*, se calmer; s'apaiser.

unruffled (eu'n'reuff'l'de), *adj.*, tranquille, calme.

unruled (eu'n'roul'de), *adj.*, non réglé; non gouverné.

unruliness (eu'n'roul'-), *n.*, dérèglement, *m.*; nature indisciplinable, mutinerie, indiscipline, *f.*

unruly, *adj.*, déréglé; mutin; revêche; intraitable, indomptable, indisciplinable.

unsaddle (eu'n'sad'd'l), *v.a.*, desseller.

unsafe, *adj.*, peu sûr; dangereux.

unsafely, *adv.*, dangereusement, sans sûreté.

unsafety, *n.*, défaut de sûreté; danger, *m.*

unsalable (eu'n'sél'a-b'l), *adj.*, invendable.

unsalted (eu'n'sôlt'-), *adj.*, non salé.

unsalued (eu'n'sa-liout'-), *adj.*, non salué.

unsanctified (eu'n'san'gn'ti-faïde), *adj.*, non sanctifié; profane.

unsanctioned (eu'n'san'gn'sheu'n'de), *adj.*, non sanctionné.

unsatisfactorily, *adv.*, d'une manière peu satisfaisante.

unsatisfactoriness, *n.*, caractère non satisfaisant, *m.*

unsatisfactory, *adj.*, peu satisfaisant; insuffisant.

unsatisfied (eu'n'sat'is-faïde), *adj.*, non satisfait; mécontent.

unsavourily (eu'n'sé-veur'-), *adv.*, sans saveur.

unsavouriness, *n.*, défaut de saveur, *m.*; insipidité, fadeur; (bad smell—*puanteur*) mauvaise odeur, *f.*

unsavoury (eu'n'sé-veuri), *adj.*, sans saveur, fade, insipide; (disgusting) désagréable, dégoûtant.

unsay, *v.a.* (*preterit* and *past part.*, Unsaid), se dédire de, rétracter.

unscared (eu'n'skârde), *adj.*, qui n'est pas épouvanté.

unscarred (eu'n'skârde), *adj.*, non cicatrisé; sans blessure.

unscathed (eu'n'skéth'te), *adj.*, intact; sans blessure.

unscattered (eu'n'scat'teurde), *adj.*, non dispersé.

unscholastic (eu'n'sko-), *adj.*, non scolastique; illettré.

unschooled (eu'n'skoul'de), *adj.*, illettré; sans éducation; inexpérimenté.

unscientific (eu'n'saï-è'n'-), *adj.*, peu scientifique.

unscientifically, *adv.*, peu scientifiquement.

unscorched (eu'n'scortsh'te), *adj.*, non roussi; non brûlé.

unscoured (eu'n'scaeurde), *adj.*, non écuré; non nettoyé.

unscratched (eu'n'scratsh'te), *adj.*, non gratté; no. égratigné.

unscreened (eu'n'skri'n'de), *adj.*, non abrité; non défendu.

unscrew (eu'n'scrou), *v.a.*, dévisser.

unscriptural (eu'n'script'iou-), *adj.*, contraire à l'Écriture.

unscrupulous (eu'n'scrou-piou-), *adj.*, sans scrupule.

unscrupulously, *adv.*, sans scrupule.

unscrupulousness, *n.*, caractère non scrupuleux, *m.*

unseal (eu'n'sîle),*v.a.*,décacheter; desceller; (fig.) dévoiler, découvrir, dessiller.

unseam (eu'n'sîme), *v.a.*, ouvrir, trancher.

unsearchable (eu'n'seurtsh'a-b'l), *adj.*, inscrutable; incompréhensible.

unsearchableness, *n.*, incompréhensibilité, *f.*

unseasonable (eu'n'sî-z'n'a-b'l), *adj.*, hors de saison; (untimely—*intempestif*) hors de propos, intempestif, inopportun; (of time—*de l'heure*) incommode, indu. — hours; *heures indues.*

unseasonableness, *n.*, état de ce qui est hors de saison, *m.*; inopportunité, *f.*

unseasonably, *adv.*, hors de saison; mal à propos, à contretemps.

unseasoned (eu'n'sî-z'n'de), *adj.*, (of wood —*de bois*) non préparé, non séché; (not accustomed—*inaccoutumé*) non accoutumé, non fait, non endurci; (to a climate—*à un climat*) non acclimaté; (cook.) non assaisonné.

unseat (eu'n'sîte), *v.a.*, renverser d'un siège; (from horseback—*de cheval*) désarçonner; (a member of parliament—*un député*) faire annuler son élection.

unseaworthy (eu'n'sî-weur-*thi*), *adj.*, qui ne peut tenir la mer.

unseconded (eu'n'sèk'-), *adj.*, non secondé; non appuyé.

unseeing (eu'n'sî-igne), *adj.*, aveugle.

unseemliness (eu'n'sî'm'-), *n.*, inconvenance; messéance. *f.*

unseemly (eu'n'sî'm'-), *adj.*, inconvenant, malséant.

unseen (eu'n'sî'n), *adj.*, sans être vu; invisible.

unsent, *adj.*, non envoyé; non expédié. — for; *qu'on n'a pas envoyé chercher.*

unserved (eu'n'seurv'de), *adj.*, non servi.

unserviceable (eu'n'seur-viss'a-b'l), *adj.*, inutile, hors de service.

unserviceableness, *n.*, inutilité, *f.*

unserviceably, *adv.*, inutilement.

unset, *adj.*, non posé; non mis; (mas.) non posé; (of the sun, &c.—*du soleil, &c.*) qui n'est pas couché; (of tools—*d'outils*) non affûté; (of precious stones—*de pierres précieuses*) non enchâssé, non monté; (of bones—*des os*) non remis, non emboîté.

unsettle (eu'n'sèt't'l), *v.a.*, déranger; ébranler; faire mouvoir; (fig.) déranger, troubler, agiter.

unsettle, *v.n.*, se déranger; se troubler.

unsettled, *adj.*, non fixé; non établi; (not firm—*pas ferme*) chancelant; (in mind—*de l'esprit*) dérangé, troublé; (not determined—*incertain*) indéterminé, incertain, irrésolu; (not paid—*impayé*) non payé, non liquidé; (of liquids —*des liquides*) qui n'a pas déposé; (of the weather—*du temps*) variable, changeant, inconstant; (changeable—*inconstant*) inconstant, changeant; (having no fixed abode—*sans résidence*) sans domicile.

unsettledness, *n.*, défaut de fixité; état chancelant, état dérangé, *m.*; (uncertainty—*incertitude, irrésolution*) incertitude, inconstance, instabilité, irrésolution, *f.*; (of the weather—*du temps*) état variable, état inconstant, *m.*, incertitude, *f.*

unsevered (eu'n'sèv'eurde), *adj.*, non séparé, uni.

unsew (eu'n'sô), *v.a.*, découdre.

unsex, *v.a.*, priver de sexe, des qualités de sexe.

unshackle (eu'n'shak'l'l), *v.a.*, briser les fers de; affranchir.

unshackled (-shak'k'l'de), *adj.*, sans chaînes; sans entrave.

unshaded (eu'n'shéd'-), *adj.*, sans ombrage; non ombré.

unshaken (eu'n'shék'n), *adj.*, inébranlable, ferme.

unshapen (eu'n'shép'n), *adj.*, difforme.

unshaved (eu'n'shév'de), *adj.*, non rasé.

unsheathe (eu'n'shithe), *v.a.*, dégainer, tirer du fourreau.

unshelled (eu'n'shèlde), *adj.*, sans coque, sans cosse; dont on n'a pas ôté la coque, la cosse; (grain) non égrené.

unsheltered (eu'n'shèl-teurde), *adj.*, sans abri; non protégé; découvert. — from; *exposé à: incexposé contre.*

unshielded (eu'n'shîld'-), *adj.*, sans défense, sans abri. — from; *exposé à.*

unship, *v.a.*, démonter, débarquer.

unshod, *adj.*, déchaussé; sans chaussure; (of a horse—*cheval*) déferré.

unshorn, *adj.*, non tondu; non coupé.

unshut (eu'n'sheute), *adj.*, non fermé, non clos.

unsifted, *adv.*, non criblé, non tamisé.

unsightliness (eu'n'saït'-), *n.*, nature disgracieuse, laideur, *f.*

unsightly (eu'n'saït'-), *adj.*, disgracieux, laid.

unsignalized (eu'n'sig-nal'aïz'de), *adj.*, non signalé.

unsilvered (eu'n'sil-veurde), *adj.*, non argenté; (of mirrors—*miroirs*) non étamé; désargenté.

unsinew (eu'n'si'n'iou), *v.a.*, affaiblir, énerver.

unsinged (eu'n'si'n'dj'de), *adj.*, non flambé; non roussi.

unsinning, *adj.*, qui ne pêche pas.

unskilful (eu'n'skil-foule), *adj.*, inhabile; maladroit, ignorant.

unskilfully, *adv.*, malhabilement, maladroitement.

unskilfulness. *n.*, inhabileté, maladresse, *f.*

unslacked (eu'n'slak'te), *or* **unslaked** (eu'n'slék'te), *adj.*, non éteint; (of lime—*de la chaux*) vive.

unsling (eu'n'sligne), *v.a.* (*preterit* and *past part.*, Unslung), ôter les élingues de.

unsmoked (eu'n'smôk'te), *adj.*, non fumé.

unsociable (eu'n'sô-shi-a-b'l), *adj.*, insociable.

unsociableness. *or* **unsociability** (-sô-shi-a-), *n.*, insociabilité, *f.*

unsociably, *adv.*, insociablement.

unsocial (eu'n'sô-shal), *adj.*, peu social; insociable.

unsoiled (eu'n'soïl'de), *adj.*, non sali; propre; pur.

unsold (eu'n'sôlde), *adj.*, invendu.

unsolder (eu'n'sol-deur), *v.a.*, dessouder.

unsoldierly (eu'n'sôl-djeur-), *or* **unsoldier-like** (-laïke), *adj.*, peu militaire, indigne d'un soldat.

unsolicited, *adj.*, sans être sollicité, sans sollicitation.

unsolicitous, *adj.*, peu désireux, peu soucieux.

unsolid, *adj.*, non solide, sans consistance.

unsolved (eu'n'solv'de), *adj.*, non résolu.

unsophistical, *adj.*, simple; ignorant.

unsophisticated (eu'n'so-fis-ti-két'-), *or* **unsophisticate**, *adj.*, non sophistiqué; pur; vrai; non altéré; (unsophistical—*simple*) simple, ignorant.

unsorted, *adj.*, non trié; non assorti.

unsought (eu'n'sôte), *adj.*, non recherché; spontané.

unsound (eu'n'saou'n'de), *adj.*, en mauvais état; (defective—*vicieux*) défectueux, vicieux; (sickly—*maladif*) maladif, malsain; (of mind—*de l'esprit*) qui n'est pas sain d'esprit; (not orthodox—*hétérodoxe*) non orthodoxe; (deceitful—*trompeur*) trompeur, déloyal; (not real—*illusoire*) trompeur, illusoire; (not compact—*sans consistance*) non ferme, non solide; (not sincere—*faux*) insincère, faux; (not material—*immatériel*) immatériel; (erroneous) erroné, faux; (not strong—*sans force*) non ferme; (cracked—*fêlé*) fêlé; (credit) mal établi; (of sleep—*sommeil*) peu profond.

unsounded (eu'n'saou'n'd'-), *adj.*, non sondé.

unsoundly, *adv.*, sans solidité; defectueusement; (of sleeping—*du dormir*) mal, peu profondément; (of reasoning—*de raisonnement*) faussement.

unsoundness (eu'n'saou'n'd'-), *n.*, (defectiveness—*imperfection*) mauvais état, *m.*, mauvaise condition, nature défectueuse, imperfection, *f.*; (of the body—*du corps*) état maladif, état malsain, *m.*; (of principles—*de principes*) absence de rectitude, *f.*; (want of solidity—*absence de solidité*) manque de solidité, de fermeté, *m.*; (fig.) infirmité, *f.*; vice, *m.*, impureté, *f.*

unsoured (eu'n'saeurde), *adj.*, non aigri.

unsown (eu'n'sône), *adj.*, non semé.

unsparing (eu'n'spér'-), *adj.*, prodigue; (not merciful—*sans pitié*) impitoyable.

unsparingly, *adv.*, avec prodigalité.

unspeak (eu'n'spike), *v.a.* (*preterit*, Unspoke; *past part.*, Unspoken), rétracter; se dédire de.

unspeakable (-'a-b'l), *adj.*, inexprimable, inénarrable, indicible.

unspeakably, *adv.*, d'une manière inexprimable.

unspecified (eu'n'spèss'i-faïde), *adj.*, non désigné.

unspeculative (eu'n'spèk'iou-), *adj.*, peu spéculatif.

unspent, *adj.*, non dépensé; (not exhausted—*non épuisé*) non épuisé; non affaibli; dans toute la force de son impulsion.

unsphere (eu'n'sfire), *v.a.*, jeter hors de sa sphère.

unspiritual (eu'n'spir'it'iou-), *adj.*, non spirituel; corporel, matériel.

unspiritualize (eu'n'spir'it'iou-al'aïze), *v.a.*, matérialiser.

unspiritually, *adv.*, peu spirituellement; mondainement.

unspoiled (eu'n'spoïl'de), *adj.*, non corrompu, non gâté; (not ruined—*non ruiné*) non ruiné; (not plundered—*non dépouillé*) non spolié.

unspotted, *adj.*, sans tache; pur.

unspottedness, *n.*, pureté, *f.*

unstable (eu'n'sté-b'l), *adj.*, non stable, mal assuré; (irresolute—*indécis*) irrésolu; (inconstant) inconstant.

unstableness (-sté-b'l-), *n.*, instabilité, *f.*

unstaid (eu'n'stéde), *adj.*, étourdi, volage, léger.

unstaidness, *n.*, étourderie; légèreté; instabilité, *f.*

unstained (eu'n'sté'n'de), *adj.*, non souillé, pur, sans tache; (not dyed—*non teint*) non teint.

unstanched (eu'n'stâ'n'tsh'te), *adj.*, non étanché, non arrêté.

unstate. *v.a.*, dépouiller de sa dignité.

unstatutable (eu'n'stat'iou-ta-b'l), *adj.*, contraire aux statuts.

unsteadfast (eu'n'stèd'fâste), *adj.*, non stable; (inconstant) inconstant, indécis.

unsteadfastly, *adv.*, sans fermeté; sans stabilité.

unsteadfastness, *n.*, instabilité; (inconstancy—*inconstance*) inconstance, *f.*

unsteadily (eu'n'stèd'-), *adv.*, d'une manière chancelante; (waveringly—*avec irrésolution*) irrésolument; (inconstantly—*sans constance*) d'une manière inconstante; (badly—*mal*) mal.

unsteadiness, *n.*, inconstance, légèreté; indécision, irrésolution, *f.*; manque d'aplomb, *m.*; (misconduct—*défaut de conduite*) inconduite, *f.*

unsteady (eu'n'stèd'-), *adj.*, chancelant; (irresolute—*irrésolu*) irrésolu; (changeable—*variable*) changeant, variable, inconstant; (of bad conduct—*d'inconduite*) qui se conduit mal.

unsteeped (eu'n'stip'te), *adj.*, non trempé; non infuse.

unstimulated (eu'n'sti'm'iou-lét'-), *adj.*, non stimulé; non excité.

unstinted, *adj.*, non restreint; illimité.

unstirred (eu'n'steurde), *adj.*, non remué.

unstitch, *v.a.*, découdre, défaire.

unstock, *v.a.*, dégarnir.

unstocked (eu'n'stok'te), *adj.*, dégarni.

unstop, *v.a.*, déboucher.

unstored (eu'n'storde), *adj.*, non emmagasiné; (not supplied—*non fourni*) non approvisionné.

unstraitened (eu'n'stré-t'n'de), *adj.*, non étréci; non rétréci; non resserré; (fig.) non resserré, non gêné.

unstrengthened (eu'n'strègn'th'n'de), *adj.*, non fortifié, non raffermi.

unstring (eu'n'strigne), *v.a.* (*preterit* and *past part.*, Unstrung), détendre, relâcher; ôter les cordes de; (beads—*perles, &c.*) défiler, désenfiler.

unstudied (eu'n'steud'ïde), *adj.*, non étudié; sans apprêt.

unstudious (eu'n'stiou-), *adj.*, peu studieux.

unstuffed (eu'n'steuf'te), *adj*, non rempli; non rembourré; (cook.) non farci; (of animals, birds—*des animaux, aes oiseaux*) non empaillé.

unsubdued (eu'n'seub'dioude), *adj.*, non subjugué ; indompté.

unsubmissive (eu'n'seub'-), *adj.*, insoumis.

unsuborned (eu'n'seub'orn'de), *adj.*. non suborné ; non corrompu.

unsubstantial (eu'n'seub-sta'n'shal), *adj.*, immatériel ; peu substantiel ; peu solide.

unsuccessful (eu'n'seuk'cèss'foule), *adj.*, qui n'a pas réussi ; malheureux ; sans succès, infructueux.

unsuccessfully, *adv.*, sans succès, malheureusement.

unsuccessfulness, *n.*, insuccès, *m.* ; (l.u.) irréussite, *f.*

unsuccoured (eu'n'seuk'eurde), *adj.*, non secouru ; sans secours.

unsuitable (eu'n'siout'a-b'l), *adj.*, inconvenable ; peu propre ; peu fait ; (unbecoming—*malséant*) malséant, inconvenant.

unsuitableness, *n.*, disconvenance ; incongruité ; inconvenance, *f.*

unsuitably, *adv.*, d'une manière peu convenable ; avec inconvenance, inconvenablement.

unsuited (eu'n'siout'-), *adj.*, peu approprié ; peu adapté.

unsuiting, *adj.*. qui ne convient pas.

unsullied (eu'n'seul'ide,*adj.*, sans souillure, sans tache.

unsummoned (eu'n'seu'm'eu'n'de), *adj.*, non convoqué ; non assigné.

unsung (eu'n'seu'n'gn), *adj.*, non chanté.

unsupplied (eu'n'seup-plaïde), *adj.*, non pourvu ; non approvisionné ; non alimenté.

unsupported (eu'n'seup'-), *adj.*, sans support ; non soutenu, non entretenu ; (fig.) sans appui.

unsure (eu'n'shoure), *adj.*, peu sûr ; incertain ; précaire.

unsurpassed (eu'n'seur-pâste), *adj.*, non surpassé.

unsurrendered (eu'n'seur'rè'n'd'eurde), *adj.*, non rendu, non livré.

unsurrounded (eu'n'seur'raou'n'd'-), *adj.*, non entouré, non ceint.

unsuspect, *or* **unsuspected** (eu'n'seus-pèk't'-), *adj.*, (ant.) non soupçonné ; non suspecté ; non suspect.

unsuspectedly, *adv.*, sans exciter le soupçon.

unsuspecting (eu'n'seus-pèk'-), *adj.*, qui ne soupçonne rien ; sans soupçon.

unsuspicious (eu'n'seus-pish'eusse), *adj.*, non soupçonneux ; sans soupçon ; (not to be suspected—*au-dessus du soupçon*) à l'abri du soupçon.

unsuspiciously, *adv.*, sans soupçon.

unsustainable (eu'n'seus-té'n'a-b'l), *adj.*, insoutenable.

unsustained (-té'n'de), *adj.*, sans soutien ; sans être soutenu.

unswathe (eu'n'swéthe), *v.a.*, démailloter.

unswayed (eu'n'swéde), *adj.*, non influencé.

unswept, *adj.*, non balayé ; (of chimneys—*cheminées*) non ramoné.

unsworn, *adj.*, qui n'a pas prêté serment ; non assermenté.

unsyllogistical (eu'n'sil-lo-djis-), *adj.*, non syllogistique.

unsymmetrical (eu'n'si'm'mèt'-), *adj.*, peu symétrique.

unsympathizing (eu'n'si'm'pa-thaïz'-),*adj.*, sans sympathie.

unsystematical, *adj.*, peu systématique.

untack, *v.a.*, détacher ; défaire.

untainted (eu'n'té'n't'-), *adj.*, non corrompu ; non gâté ; (fig.) intact, pur, sans tache.

untaintedly, *adv.*, sans tache.

untaken (eu'n'ték'n), *adj.*, qu'on n'a pas pris.

untamable (eu'n'té'm'a-b'l), *adj.*, indomptable ; inapprivoisable.

untamed (éu'n'té'm'de), *adj.*, indompté ; non apprivoisé ; inculte.

untangle (eu'n'tan'gn'g'l),*v.a.* *V.* **disentangle**.

untarnished (eu'n'târ-nish'te), *adj.*, non terni ; sans tache.

untasted (eu'n'tést'-), *adj.*, qu'on n'a pas goûté.

untaught (eu'n'tôte), *adj.*, ignorant, illettré, sans éducation ; (of things—*des choses*) qu'on n'a pas appris, naturel.

untaxed (eu'n'taks'te), *adj.*, exempt d'impôt, exempt d'imposition ; (jur.) non taxé ; (not accused—*non accusé*) exempt d'accusation, qu'on n'accuse pas.

unteach (eu'n'tîtshe), *v.a.*, faire désapprendre.

unteachable (-'a-b'l), *adj.*, que l'on ne saurait enseigner.

untempered (eu'n'tè'm'peurde), *adj.*, non trempé, non tempéré.

untenable (eu'n'tè'n'a-b'l), *adj.*, non tenable ; insoutenable.

untenantable (eu'n'tè'n'a'n't'a-b'l), *adj.*, non logeable.

untenanted, *adj.*, sans locataire ; sans fermier.

untended, *adj.*, non gardé ; non soigné.

unterrified (eu'n'tèr-ri-faïde), *adj.*, non épouvanté.

untested, *adj.*, non éprouvé.

unthanked (eu'n'tha'n'k'te), *adj.*, qui ne reçoit pas de remerciments ; sans être remercié.

unthankful (-foule), *adj.*, ingrat.

unthankfully, *adv.*, avec ingratitude.

unthankfulness, *n.*, ingratitude, *f.*

unthawed (eu'n'thôde), *adj.*, non dégelé.

unthinking (eu'n'thi'n'k'-), *adj.*, étourdi, irréfléchi.

unthinkingly, *adv.*, sans y penser, par distraction.

unthoughtful (-foule), *adj.*, irréfléchi, étourdi.

unthought of (eu'n'thôt'ov),*adj.*, à quoi on ne pense pas ; inattendu.

unthread (eu'n'thrède), *v.a.*, défiler ; séparer

unthriftily (eu'n'thrif'-), *adv.*, avec prodigalité.

unthriftiness, *n.*. prodigalité, *f.*

unthrifty, *adj.*, prodigue, dépensier ; (of things—*des choses*) qui ne profite pas ; (of plants, animals—*des plantes, des animaux*) qui ne vient pas bien, languissant.

untidily, *adv.*, sans ordre, en désordre.

untidiness (eu'n'taï-), *n.*, désordre ; mauvais arrangement ; (per.) manque d'ordre, *m.*

untidy (eu'n'taï-), *adj.*, mal arrangé, en désordre.

untie (eu'n'ta-ye), *v.a.*, détacher ; défaire ; délier.

until, *prep.*, jusque, jusqu'à ; jusques, jusques à.

until, *conj.*, jusqu'à ce que, jusqu'à tant que, en attendant que. *V.* **till**.

untile (eu'n'taïle), *v.a.*, ôter les tuiles de, découvrir.

untillable (eu'n'til-la-b'l), *adj.*, non labourable.

untilled (eu'n'til'de), *adj.*, inculte ; en friche.

untimely (eu'n'taï'm'-), *adv.*, avant le temps ; d'une manière hâtive, prématurément ; mal à propos.

untimely, *adj.*, avant terme ; hâtif, prématuré.

untinged (eu'n'ti'n'dj'de), *adj.*, non teint ; non empreint ; pur.

untired (eu'n'taeurde), *adj.*, non fatigué ; non lassé.

untiring (eu'n'taeur'-), *adj.*, infatigable.

unto (eu'n'tou), *prep.* V. **to.**

untold (eu'n'tôlde), *adj.*, non raconté, non conté ; non exprimé ; non compté ; non révélé.

untouched (eu'n'teutsh'te), *adj.*, non touché ; intact ; (not moved—*non touché*) non ému, insensible.

untoward (eu'n'tou-worde), *adj.*,insoumis ; indocile ; (troublesome—*désagréable*) fâcheux ; (awkward—*gauche*) gauche, maladroit.

untowardly,*adv.*,d'une manière insoumise ; malencontreusement ; maladroitement.

untowardness, *n.*, indocilité, *f.* ; caractère fâcheux, *m.* ; maladresse,*f.*

untraceable (eu'n'tréss'a-b'l), *adj.*, qu'on ne peut tracer ; (not to be discovered—*impossible à découvrir*) qu'on ne peut découvrir.

untractable (eu'n'trac-ta-b'l), *adj.*, intraitable ; indocile.

untractableness, *n.*, indocilité,*f.*

untrained (eu'n'tré'n'de), *adj.*, inexercé ; non dressé ; inexpérimenté ; indiscipliné ; sans discipline.

untrammelled (eu'n'tra'm'mèlde), *adj.*, sans entraves.

untransferable (eu'n'tra'n's-feur'a-b'l), *adj.*, non transférable ; non transmissible ; incessible.

untransferred (-feur'de), *adj.*, non transféré ; non cédé.

untranslatable (eu'n'tra'n's-lét'a-b'l), *adj.*, intraduisible.

untranslated, *adj.*, non traduit.

untravelled (eu'n'trav'èlde), *adj.*, inexploré ; (pers.) qui n'a pas voyagé.

untried (eu'n'traïde), *adj.*, non essayé ; non éprouvé ; (jur.) qui n'a pas été mis en jugement, non jugé.

untrimmed (eu'n'tri'm'de), *adj.*, non arrangé ; non garni ; non orné ; non ajusté ; non fini.

untrodden, *adj.*, non foulé, non frayé.

untroubled (eu'n'treub'l'de), *adj.*, non troublé ; calme ; paisible ; non ennuyé ; non tracassé ; (of liquids—*des liquides*) clair.

untrue (eu'n'trou), *adj.*, dénué de vérité,non vrai, faux, inexact ; infidèle; (inconstant) inconstant, infidèle.

untruly, *adv.*, sans vérité, faussement ; inexactement.

untruss (eu'n'treuss), *v.a.*, dépaqueter.

untrustworthy (eu'n'treust'weur-*thi*), or **untrusty** (-treust'-),*adj.*,indigne de confiance ; infidèle.

untruth (eu'n'trouth), *n.*, mensonge, *m.* ; inexactitude, fausseté,*f.*

untuck (eu'n'teuke), *v.a.*, détrousser.

untunable (eu'n'tiou'n'a-'bl), *adj.*, inaccordable ; peu musical ; discordant ; inaccordable.

untune (eu'n'tioune), *v.a.*, désaccorder ; déranger.

unturned (eu'n'teurn'de), *adj.*, non tourné, non retourné.

untutored (eu'n'tiou-teurde), *adj.*, peu instruit ; ignorant ; inculte.

untwine (eu'n'twaï'ne), *v.a.*, détordre ; dérouler.

untwist, *v.a.*, détordre, détortiller ; défaire ; délier ; décorder.

unurged (eu'n'eurdj'de), *adj.*, sans être pressé ; spontané.

unused (eu'n'iouz'de), *adj.*, non employé ; inapte ; (of words—*des mots*) inusité. — to ; *inaccoutumé à.*

unuseful (eu'n'iouz'foule), *adj.*, inutile.

unusual (eu'n'iou-jiou-),*adj.*, peu commun ; rare ; inaccoutumé ; extraordinaire ; insolite.

unusually, *adv.*, non habituellement ; rarement : extraordinairement.

unusualness, *n.*, rareté ; étrangeté,*f.*

unutterable (eu'n'eut'tèr-a-b'l), *adj.*, inexprimable, ineffable.

unvalued (eu'n'val'ioude), *adj.*, non évalué ; non estimé.

unvanquished (eu'n'va'n'kwish'te), *adj.*, invaincu, indompté.

unvaried (eu'n'vér'ied), *adj.*, qui ne varie pas ; invariable.

unvarnished (eu'n'vâr-nish'te), *adj.*, non verni ; (fig.) simple.

unvarying, *adj.*, invariable.

unveil (eu'n'vèl), *v.a.*, dévoiler.

unvenerable (eu'n'vè'n'èr'a-b'l), *adj.*, peu vénérable.

unversed (eu'n'veurste), *adj.*, peu versé dans.

unvexed (eu'n'vèks'te), *adj.*, qui n'est pas contrarié ; calme.

unviolated (eu'n'vaï-o-lét'-), *adj.*, non violé.

unvisited, *adj.*, non visité, non fréquenté.

unvisored (eu'n'viz'eurde),*adj.*,sans visière ; démasqué.

unwakened (eu'n'wék'n'de), *adj.*, non réveillé, endormi.

unwalled (eu'n'wolde), *adj.*, non muré ; sans murailles.

unwarily (eu'n'wé-ri-li), *adv.*, avec imprévoyance; sans précaution, imprudemment.

unwariness, *n.*, imprévoyance ; étourderie,*f.*

unwarmed (eu'n'worm'de), *adj.*, non échauffé ; froid.

unwarned (eu'n'worn'de), *adj.*, non averti ; non prémuni.

unwarrantable (eu'n'wor-ra'n't-a-b'l), *adj.*, inexcusable.

unwarrantableness, *n.*, nature inexcusable, *f.*

unwarrantably, *adv.*, d'une manière inexcusable ; sans excuse ; injustement.

unwarranted, *adj.*, non garanti ; non autorisé.

unwary (eu'n'wé-), *adj.*, imprévoyant ; inconsidéré ; étourdi, imprudent.

unwashed (eu'n'woshte), *adj.*, non lavé, sale.

unwasted (eu'n'wést'-),*adj.*, non perdu, non gaspillé.

unwatched (eu'n'wotshte), *adj.*, qu'on ne veille point ; non gardé.

unwatered (eu'n'wo-teurde), *adj.*, non arrosé.

unweakened (eu'n'wik'n'de), *adj.*, non affaibli.

unwealthy (eu'n'wèlth'-), *adj.*, peu riche.

unwearied (eu'n'wî-ride), *adj.*, non lassé ; infatigable, inépuisable.

unweariedly, *adv.*, sans relâche ; sans fatigue.

unweave (eu'n'wîve), *v.a.* (*preterit*, Unwove ; *past part.*, Unwoven), détisser ; effiler ; démêler.

unweeded (eu'n'wîd'-), *adj.*, non sarclé.

unweighed (eu'n'wède), *adj.*, non pesé.

unwelcome (eu'n'wèl'keume),*adj.*, qui n'est pas bien venu ; mal reçu ; mal accueilli ; (of things—*des choses*) mal accueilli ; (disagreeable —*désagréable*) déplaisant, désagréable.

unwell,*adj.*, malade, indisposé, qui ne se porte pas bien.

unwholesome (eu'n'hôl'seume), *adj.*, malsain, insalubre ; (pernicious—*pernicieux*) pernicieux.

unwholesomeness, *n.*, nature malsaine, insalubrité, *f.*

unwieldily (eu'n'wild'-), *adv.*, lourdement.

unwieldiness, *n.*, lourdeur, pesanteur,*f.*

unwieldy (eu'n'wïld'-), *adj.*, lourd, pesant.

unwilling, *adj.*, mal disposé ; de mauvais vouloir ; de mauvaise volonté. To be — to ; n'être pas disposé à ; ne pas vouloir.

unwillingly, *adv.*, avec mauvaise volonté ; à contre-cœur ; sans le vouloir.

unwillingness (eu'n'will'ign-nèce),*n.*,mauvaise volonté, *f.* ; mauvais vouloir, *m.* ; répugnance, *f.*

unwind (eu'n'waï'n'de), *v.a.* (preterit and past part., Unwound), dévider ; dérouler ; (fig.) débrouiller.

unwiped (eu'n'waïp'te), *adj.*, non essuyé.

unwise (eu'n'waïze), *adj.*,peu sage,malavisé, insensé, sot.

unwisely, *adv.*, d'une manière peu sage; d'une manière insensée ; sottement.

unwished (eu'n'wish'te),*adj.*, non souhaité, non désiré.

unwithered (eu'n'with'eurde), *adj.*, non desséché, non flétri.

unwithering (-with'eur'-), *adj.*, qui ne se dessèche pas, qui ne se flétrit pas.

unwitnessed (eu'n'wit'nèste), *adj.*, sans témoins.

unwittily, *adv.*, sans esprit, sottement.

unwittingly, *adv.*, sans le savoir, à son insu.

unwitty, *adj.*, sans esprit ; sot.

unwomanly (eu'n'wou'm'-), *adj.*, indigne d'une femme.

unwonted, *adj.*, inaccoutumé, rare.

unwontedly, *adv.*, rarement.

unwontedness, *n.*, rareté, *f.*

unwooed (eu'n'woû'de), *adj.*, que l'on ne recherche pas ; dédaigné.

unworking (eu'n'weurk'-), *adj.*, qui ne travaille pas.

unworldliness (eu'n'weurl'd'-), *n.*, absence de mondanité, *f.*

unworldly, *adj.*, qui n'a rien de ce monde ; peu mondain.

unworn, *adj.*, qui n'a pas été porté ; non usé.

unworthily (eu'n'weur-thi-), *adv.*, indignement ; sans le mériter.

unworthiness, *n.*, manque de mérite, *m.* ; indignité, *f.*

unworthy, *adj.*, indigne ; sans mérite.

unwounded, *adj.*, sans blessure, intact.

unwoven (eu'n'wôv'n), *adj.*, non tissu ; effilé.

unwrap (eu'n'rap), *v.a.*, défaire, développer, déployer.

unwreath (eu'n'rithe), *v.a.*, dérouler ; détordre.

unwrinkle (eu'n'ri'n'k'l), *v a.*, dérider.

unwritten (eu'n'rit't'n), *adj.*, non écrit ; en blanc.

unwrought (eu'n'rôte), *adj.*, non travaillé, brut ; non ouvré ; (fig.) naturel.

unwrung (eu'n'run'g:), *adj.*, non tordu ; (fig.) non navré.

unyielding (eu'n'yïld'-), *adj.*, qui ne cède pas ; dur ; (fig.) inflexible, entêté, entier.

unyoke (eu'n'yôke), *v.a.*, ôter le joug à ; dételer ; (fig.) séparer.

unzealous (eu'n'zèl'-), *adj.*, peu zélé, sans zèle.

unzoned (eu'n'zô'n'de), *adj.*, non ceint.

up (eupe), *adv.*, haut, en haut ; en l'air ; (out of bed, above the horizon—hors du lit ; au-dessus de l'horizon) levé ; (on one's legs—sur les jambes) debout ; (excited—excité) excité ; (in revolt—en rébellion) en révolte, en insurrection ; (over—fini) fini ; (in a state of elevation, of ascending—élevé, montant) haut ; (of the tide—de la marée) haut, monté ; (of the wind—du vent) être levé. — and down ; en haut et en bas ; ça et là. Hard — ; vivement pressé; (without money—sans argent) gêné.

— there ; là-haut. — to ; jusqu'à ; jusqu'à ta hauteur de ; (conformably to—suivant) selon, conformément à. To live — to one's fortune ; vivre selon sa fortune. To be — to snuff ; ne pas se moucher du pied ; avoir le fil. — ! levez-vous ! (go up—monter) montez ! — with ; levez ! montez ! — comes a fox ; voilà que vient un renard.

up, *prep.*, en haut de, au haut de ; (of motion —aller) en montant.

up (eupe), *n.*, haut, *m.*

upas (you-pass), *n.*, (bot.) upas, *m.*

upbear (eup'bère), *v.a.* (preterit, Upbore ; past part., Upborne), élever ; soutenir ; soulever ; supporter.

upbraid (eup'brède), *v.a.*, reprocher ; faire des reproches ; réprimander ; réprouver ; faire honte à.

upbraider, *n.*, personne qui fait des reproches, *f.* ; censeur, frondeur, *m.*

upbraiding, *n.*, reproche, *m.* ; réprimande, *f.*

upbraidingly, *adv.*, avec reproche.

upcast (eup'càste), *n.*, jet ; coup, *m.*

upcast, *adj.*, lancé en l'air ; levé.

uphand (eup'-), *adj.*, soulevé avec la main.

upheave (eup'hive), *v.a.*, soulever, lever.

upheld (eup'hèlde), *adj.*, soutenu, maintenu.

upher (eup'heur), *n.*, (arch.) échasse, *f.*

uphill (eup'-), *adj.*, qui va en montant, en pente; (fig.) pénible, difficile.

uphold (eup'hôlde), *v.a.* (preterit and past part., Upheld), lever, élever ; soutenir.

upholder, *n.*, soutien, appui, *m.*

upholsterer (eup-hôl-), *n.*, tapissier, *m.* ; tapissière, *f.*

upholstery, *n.*, commerce de tapissier, *m.*

upland (eup'-), *n.*, terrain élevé, *m.* ; haute terre, *f.*

upland, or **uplandish** (eup'-), *adj.*, des terrains élevés ; des hautes terres.

uplander (eup'-), *n.*, montagnard, *m.*

uplift (eup'-), *v.a.*, lever, élever, soulever.

upon (eup'-), *prep.*, sur ; (on occasion of— à l'occasion de) dans, à l'occasion de ; (before a present participle—devant un participe présent) en ; (noting exposure) sous ; (engaged in—occupé) occupé à. To live — ; vivre de ; se nourrir de ; — pain of ; sous peine de. — the first of January ; le premier Janvier. — it ; dessus. — that ; là-dessus. — the death of; à la mort de.

upper (eup'-), *adj.*, supérieur ; d'en haut ; de dessus ; au-dessus ; haut ; (geog.) haut.

upper-hand, *n.*, avantage, *m.* ; supériorité, *f.*

upper-leather (eup'peur-lèth'-), *n.*, empeigne, *f.*

uppermost (eup'peur-môste),*adj.*,supérieur, le plus élevé ; (fig.) le plus fort, dominant.

upraise (eup'réze), *v.a.*, lever, élever ; (fig.) ranimer, exalter.

uprear (eup'rire), *v.a.*, élever, soulever.

upright (eup'raïte), *adj.*, droit ; debout ; à plomb, vertical ; (honest—honnête) droit, honnête, loyal, intègre.

upright, *n.*, élévation, *f.* ; montant, *m.*

uprighteously (eup'raït'ieus'-), *adv.*, avec droiture.

uprightly (eup'raït'-), *adv.*, droit, debout, à plomb, de champ ; (honestly—honnêtement) avec droiture, loyalement.

uprightness (eup'raït'-), *n.*, aplomb, *m.* ; (honesty—honnêteté) droiture, loyauté, intégrité, *f.*

uprise (eup'raïze), *v.n.* (preterit, Uprose ; past part., Uprisen), se lever.

uprising (eup'raïz'-), *n.*, lever, *m.*

uproar (eup'rôre), *n.*, tumulte, désordre ; vacarme, *m.*

uproarious (eup'rôr'-), *adj.*, bruyant ; tumultueux.

uproariously, *adv.*, avec un grand vacarme.

uproll (eup'rôle), *v.a.*, rouler ; serrer.

uproot (eup'roûte), *v.a.*, déraciner, extirper.

upset (eup'sète), *v.a.* (*preterit* and *past part.*, Upset), renverser ; bouleverser ; (a vehicle—*une voiture*) verser ; (a boat—*un bateau*) faire chavirer.

upset, *v.n.* (*preterit* and *past part.*, Upset), se renverser ; (of vehicles—*de voitures*) verser ; (of boats—*de bateaux*) chavirer.

upshot (eup'-), *n.*, résultat, *m.* ; issue, fin, *f.* ; résultat définitif, fin mot, *m.* On the — ; *en définitive.*

upside (eup'saïde), *n.*, dessus, *m.*

upside-down (-daoune), *adv.*, sens dessus dessous.

upstart (eup'stàrte), *n.*, parvenu, *m.*, parvenue, *f.*

upstart, *adj.*, qui croît soudainement ; subit ; (b.s.) parvenu.

upstay (eup'-), *v.a.*, étayer ; appuyer.

uptear (eup'tère), *v.a.*, arracher.

upturn (eup'teurne), *v.a.*, tourner ; retourner ; lever.

upward (eup'worde), or **upwards** (-'wordze), *adv.*, en haut ; en remontant ; (over) au-delà ; (nav.) en amont. —of ; *plus de.* —s and downwards ; *en haut et en bas ; par haut et par bas.*

upward, *adj.*, dirigé en haut ; ascensionnel ; de bas en haut ; droit.

upwhirl (eup-hweurle), *v.a.*, (ant.) faire tourner en l'air.

uranite (you-ra'n'aïte), *n.*, (min.) urane, *m.*

uranium (you-ré-), *n.*, (chem.) uranium, *m.*

uranographical (you-ra-), *adj.*, uranographique.

uranography (you-ra-), *n.*, uranographie, *f.*

uranoscopus (you-ra-), *n.*, (ich.) uranoscope, *m.*

uranus (you-ra-), *n.*, (astron.) Uranus, *m.*

urate (you-), *n.*, (chem.) urate, *m.*

urban (eur-), *adj.*, urbain.

urbane (eur-), *adj.*, qui a de l'urbanité, poli.

urbanity (eur-ba-), *n.*, urbanité, *f.*

urceolate (eur-ci-), *adj.*, (bot.) urcéolé.

urchin (eur-tshi'n), *n.*, gamin, moutard ; (mam.) hérisson, *m.*

urea (you-ri-a), *n.*, (chem.) urée, *f.*

uredo (you-ri-dô), *n.*, (bot.) urédo, *m.*

ure-ox (your'okse), *n.*, (mam.) ure, urus, aurochs, *m.*

ureter (you-ri-teur), *n.*, uretère, *m.*

urethra (you-ri-thra), *n.*, (anat.) urètre, urèthre, *m.*

urge (eurdje), *v.a.*, presser ; pousser, exciter, porter, hâter, avancer ; (to exasperate—*irriter*) provoquer, irriter, exciter ; (to follow closely—*suivre*) suivre de près, presser ; (to press with eagerness—*presser*) prier instamment, presser vivement ; (to importune—*importuner*) importuner ; (petition, &c.) présenter, produire ; (argument) avancer, émettre ; (the necessity of—*nécessité*) faire valoir ; (ore—*minerai*) donner un coup de feu à. To —on ; *pousser, exciter, porter.*

urge, *v.n.*, avancer ; se hâter.

urgency (eur-djè'n'-), *n.*, urgence ; nécessité urgente, *f.* ; besoin pressant, *m.* ; (earnest solicitation—*sollicitation*) sollicitation urgente, *f.*

urgent (eur-djè'n'te), *adj.*, urgent ; instant ; pressant.

urgently, *adv.*, avec urgence ; instamment.

urger (eurdj'-), *n.*, solliciteur ; importun, *m.*

urging (eurdj'-), *adj.*, pressant ; importun, *m.*

uric (you-), *adj.*, (chem.) urique.

urinal (you-), *n.*, urinal, *m.*

urinarium (you-rin-é-), or **urinary** (-ri-na-), *n.*, réservoir d'urine, *m.*

urinary (you-), *adj.*, (anat.) urinaire.

urinary, or **urinoir** (you-ri-), *n.*, urinoir, *m.*

urine (you-ri'n), *n.*, urine, *f.*

urinose (you-ri-nôce), or **urinous** (you-ri-), *adj.*, urineux.

urn (eurne), *n.*, urne, *f.* ; vase, *m.* ; (for tea, coffee—*à thé, à café*) fontaine, *f.*

ursa (eur-), *n.*, (astron.) Ourse, *f.* — Major ; *grande Ourse.* — Minor ; *petite Ourse.*

ursine (ur-saïne), *adj.*, d'ours.

ursuline (eur-siou-), *n.*, ursuline, *f.*

urticaria (your-ti-ké-), *n.*, urticaire, *f.*

us (euss), *pron.*, nous.

usage (you-zédje), *n.*, usage ; procédé ; traitement, *m.*

usance (you-za'n'ce), *n.*, usance, *f.*

use (youce), *n.*, usage, emploi, *m.* ; (utility—*utilité*) utilité, *f.* ; (advantage—*profit*) avantage, profit ; (interest—*intérêt*) intérêt ; (custom—*coutume*) usage ; (jur.) usage, usufruit, *m.*, jouissance, *f.* For the — of ; *à l'usage de ; au profit de.* Of —; *utile.* Of great —; *très utile ; d'une grande utilité.* Of no —; *inutile ; d'aucune utilité ; qui ne sert à rien.* In —; *d'usage, en usage, employé ;* (of words—*des mots*) usité. Out of —; *hors d'usage ; inusité.* What is the — of doing it? *à quoi sert de le faire ?* To make — of ; *faire usage de ; se servir de.* To have no further — for ; *n'avoir plus besoin de.* It is of no — for one to . . . ; *on a beau . . .*

use (youce), *v.a.*, faire usage de ; user de ; se servir de ; employer ; (to consume—*user*) user, consommer ; (to accustom—*habituer*) accoutumer, habituer ; (to treat—*agir*) en user avec, agir envers.

use, *v.n.*, avoir coutume, avoir l'habitude ; (of things—*des choses*) être ordinaire.

useful (yous'foule), *adj.*, utile ; avantageux.

usefully, *adv.*, utilement ; avec profit ; avantageusement.

usefulness, *n.*, utilité, *f.* ; profit, avantage, *m.*

useless (yous'-), *adj.*, inutile ; sans avantage ; vain.

uselessly, *adv.*, inutilement.

uselessness, *n.*, inutilité ; vanité, *f.*

user (youz'eur), *n.*, personne qui se sert de, *f.*

usher (eush'-), *n.*, huissier ; (in schools—*d'école, &c.*) sous-maître, maître d'étude, *m.*

usher (eush'-), *v.a.*, introduire ; faire entrer ; précéder.

usquebaugh (eus-kwi-bô), *n.*, usquebac, *m.*

ustion (eust'ieune), *n.*, ustion, *f.*

usual (you-jiou-), *adj.*, ordinaire, commun ; habituel ; accoutumé ; usuel. As —; *comme d'ordinaire ; comme à l'ordinaire ; comme de coutume ; comme d'habitude.*

usually, *adv.*, ordinairement, d'ordinaire ; usuellement ; habituellement.

usualness, *n.*, habitude, fréquence, *f.*

usucaption (you-ziou-cap-sheune), *n.*, (jur.) usucapion, *f.*

usufruct (you-ziou-freuk'te), *n.*, (jur.) usufruit, *m.*

usufructuary (you-ziou-freukt'iou-), *n.*, usufruitier, *m.*, usufruitière, *f.*

usurer (you-jiou-reur), *n.*, usurier, *m.*

usurious (you-jiou-ri-euss), *adj.*, qui fait l'usure ; usuraire.

usuriously, *adv.*, usurairement.

usuriousness, *n.*, nature usuraire, *f.*

usurp (you-zeurpe), *v.a.*, usurper.

usurpation (you-zeur-pé-), *n.*, usurpation, *f.*

usurper, *n.*, usurpateur, *m.*, usurpatrice, *f.*

usurpingly, *adv.*, par usurpation.

usury (you-jiou-), *n.*, usure, *f.*

ut (eute), *n.*, (mus.) ut, do, *m.*

utensil (you-), *n.*, ustensile, *m.*

uterine (you-tèr'-), *adj.*, utérin.

utero-gestation (you-tèr'ô-djès'té-), *n.*, gestation ; grossesse utérine, *f.*

uterus (you-tèr'-), *n.*, (anat.) utérus, matrice, *f.*

utilitarian (you-till'ĭ-té-), *adj.*, utilitaire.
utility (you-til'-), *n.*, utilité, *f.* ; avantage, *m.*
utilization (you-til'aïze-), *n.*, utilisation, *f.*
utilize (you-til'aïze), *v.a.*, utiliser.
utmost (eut'môste), *adj.*, extrême, dernier ; le plus haut ; le plus grand ; le plus imminent.
utmost (eut'môste), *n.*, extrême, plus haut degré, comble ; (all one can—*tout ce qu'on peut*) possible, tout son possible, le plus possible, *m.* To do one's —; *faire tout son possible.*
utopia (you-tô-), *n.*, utopie, *f.*
utopian(you-tô-), *adj.*, d'utopie, chimérique.
utopist (you-tô-), *n.*, utopiste, *m.*
utter (eut'teur), *v.a.*, énoncer, proférer, prononcer ; (to disclose—*révéler*) révéler, dire, publier ; (to send into circulation—*émettre*) mettre en circulation, émettre ; (sighs, groans—*soupirs, gémissements*) pousser, jeter.
utter (eut'teur), *adj.*, (total) total, entier, complet ; (absolute—*positif*) absolu, positif ; (extreme) le plus profond, le plus grand, le plus reculé ; (quite—*complètement*) tout à fait, parfaitement ; (placed on the outside—*placé extérieurement*) extérieur. To my — astonishment ; *à mon grand étonnement.* — strangers to one another ; *tout à fait inconnus l'un à l'autre.*
utterable (eut'teur'a-b'l), *adj.*, qu'on peut prononcer.
utterance (eut'teur'-), *n.*, articulation, prononciation ; parole ; (of sounds—*des sons*) émission, *f.* To deprive of — ; *priver de la parole.*
utterer, *n.*, personne qui articule, qui prononce, qui émet, *f.*
utterly, *adv.*, de fond en comble ; tout à fait, complètement, entièrement.
uttermost (eut'teur-môste), *adj.* V. **utmost.**
uvea (you-vi-a), *n.*, (anat.) uvée, *f.*
uveous, (you-vi-eusse), *adj.*, de l'uvée.
uvula (you-viou-), *n.*, (anat.) luette, *f.*
uvular, *adj.*, (anat.) uvulaire.
uxorious (eug-zô-ri-eusse), *adj.*, tendre à l'excès pour sa femme ; esclave de sa femme.
uxoriously, *adv.*, avec une sotte complaisance pour sa femme.
uxoriousness, *n.*, sotte complaisance pour sa femme, *f.*

V

v, vingt-deuxième lettre de l'alphabet, v, *m.*
vacancy (vé-), *n.*, vide, *m.* ; lacune, *f.* ; (leisure—*repos*) loisir, repos ; (emptiness of thought—*irréflexion*) manque de réflexion, *m.* ; (place not occupied—*vacance*) place vacante, vacance, *f.*
vacant (vé-), *adj.*, vide ; (free—*libre*) libre ; (not occupied—*inoccupé*) vacant ; (of time—*du temps*) perdu, libre, de loisir ; (indicating want of thought—*dépourvu d'expression*) sans expression, insignifiant ; (thoughtless—*irréfléchi*) qui ne réfléchit pas ; (free from care—*sans souci*) exempt de souci ; (jur.) vacant.
vacate (vé-kéte), *v.a.*, laisser vacant ; (jur.) vider ; (to annul—*annuler*) annuler, abolir ; (to resign—*se démettre*) donner sa démission de, quitter.
vacation (va-ké-), *n.*, vacation, *f.* ; (holidays —*congé*) vacances ; (of courts of law—*des tribunaux*) vacations, *f.pl.* ; (annulment—*annulation*) annulation, abolition, *f.*
vaccinate (vak'si-), *v.a.*, vacciner.
vaccination (vak'si-né-), *n.*, vaccination, vaccine, *f.*
vaccine (vak-saïne, *ou* -cine), *adj.*, de vache. virus vaccin, *m.*

vacillate (vass'il-), *v.n.*, vaciller ; (fig.) balancer.
vacillating (-'il-lét'-), *adj.*, vacillant ; indécis.
vacillation (vass'il-lé-), *n.*, vacillation, *f.*
vacuity (va-kiou-), *n.*, vide, *m.* ; vacuité ; lacune, *f.*
vacuous (vak'iou-euss), *adj.*, (ant.) vide.
vacuum (vak'iou-), *n.*, vide, *m.* —-gauge ; *jauge de vide, f.* —-pipe ; *tube atmosphérique, m.*
vade-mecum (vé-di-mi-), *n.*, vade-mecum, *m.*
vagabond (-), *n.*, vagabond, *m.*, vagabonde, *f.*
vagabond, *adj.*, errant, vagabond ; flottant.
vagabondize (-'aïze), *v.n.*, vagabonder.
vagary (va-ghé-), *n.*, caprice, *m.* ; quinte, boutade, *f.*
vagina (va-djaï-), *n.*, (anat.) vagin, *m.*
vaginal, *adj.*, (anat.) vaginal.
vagrancy (vé-), *n.*, vagabondage, *m.*
vagrant, *adj.*, vagabond ; errant.
vagrant (vé-), *n.*, vagabond, *m.*, vagabonde, *f.* ; homme sans aveu, *m.*
vagrantly, *adv.*, en vagabond.
vague (véghe), *adj.*, vague.
vaguely, *adv.*, vaguement.
vagueness, *n.*, vague, *m.*
vails (vélze), *n.pl.*, gratifications aux domestiques, *f.pl.*
vain (véne), *adj.*, vain ; (showy—*de parade*) fastueux, somptueux ; (false—*décevant*) faux, mensonger ; (conceited—*vaniteur*) vain, vaniteux ; (proud—*orgueilleux*) orgueilleux, superbe. It is in — for one to ; *on a beau.* In — ; *en vain* ; *vainement* ; *en pure perte.*
vainglorious (vé'n'-), *adj.*, vain ; orgueilleux, superbe.
vainglory (vé'n'-), *n.*, vaine gloire ; gloriole, *f.*
vainly, *adv.*, en vain ; vainement ; (foolishly —*sottement*) sottement ; (arrogantly—*avec arrogance*) orgueilleusement, avec vanité.
vainness, *n.*, inutilité ; (empty pride—*vanité*) vanité, *f.*
vair (vére), *n.*, (her.) vair, *m.*
valance, *n.*, pente, cantonnière, *f.*
valance, *v.a.*, mettre des pentes à ; mettre une cantonnière à.
vale, *n.*, vallon, *m.* ; vallée, *f.*
valediction (val'i-); *n.*, adieu, *m.*
valedictory, *n.*, discours d'adieu, *m.*
valedictory, *adj.*, d'adieu.
valentine (-taïne), *n.*, amant choisi le jour de la Saint-Valentin ; (letter—*lettre*) billet de la St.-Valentin, *m.* —'s-day ; *la St.-Valentin, f.*
valerian (-lî-), *n.*, (bot.) valériane, *f.*
valet (val'ète), *n.*, valet, *m.* — de chambre ; *valet de chambre, m.*
valetudinarian (val'i-tiou-di-né-), *or* **valetudinary** (-di-na-), *n.* and *adj.*, valétudinaire, *f.*
valiant, *adj.*, vaillant, valeureux, brave.
valiantly, *adv.*, vaillamment, bravement.
valiantness, *n.*, valeur, vaillance, bravoure *f.*
valid, *adj.*, valable, valide. To make — ; *rendre valable, valider.*
validate, *v.a.*, valider, rendre valable.
validity, *or* **validness**, *n.*, validité, *f.*
validly, *adv.*, validement, valablement.
valise (va-lîce), *n.*, valise, *f.*
vallation (val-lé-), *n.*, circonvallation, *f.*
valley (val-lé), *n.*, vallée, *f.* ; vallon ; (arch.) chéneau, *m.*
vallum, *n.*, retranchement, *m.*
valorous, *adj.*, vaillant, valeureux, brave.
valorously, *adv.*, vaillamment, valeureusement.
valour (val'eur), *n.*, valeur, vaillance, bravoure, *f.*
valuable (val'iou-a-b'l), *adj.*, précieux.
valuableness, *n.*, valeur. *f.* ; prix, *m.*

valuables (val'iou-a-b'l'ze), *n.*, choses de prix ; choses précieuses,*f.pl.* ; objets de luxe,*m.pl.*

valuation (val'iou-é-), *n.*, évaluation, estimation, appréciation,*f.*

valuator (val'iou-é-teur), *n.*, estimateur, *m.*

value (val'iou), *n.*, valeur,*f.* ; prix, *m.* ; (precise signification) valeur, signification ; (importance) valeur, importance,*f.* To set a — on ; *estimer.*

value (val'iou), *v.a.*, évaluer, estimer, apprécier ; (to reckon—*calculer*) évaluer, estimer, calculer ; (to esteem—*priser*) estimer, priser, apprécier, faire cas de, tenir à ; (to take account of—*tenir compte de*) calculer, tenir compte de.

valued (val'ioude), *adj.*, estimé, apprécié, prisé.

valueless, *adj.*, sans valeur, sans prix.

valuer, *n.*, estimateur, appréciateur.

valvate, *adj.*, (bot.) valvé, valvaire.

valve, *n.*, soupape, valve,*f.* ; clapet, *m.* ; (of a lock-gate) ventelle, soupape, *f.* ; (of a door— *de porte*) battant, *m.* ; (anat.) valvule ; (bot., conch.) valve,*f.* — -box ; *boîte à soupape ; boîte de tiroir, f.* — -casing ; *boîte à tiroir, f.* — - door ; *porte de soupape,f.* — -gear ; *appareil de soupape, m.*

valved (valv'de), *adj.*, à soupape ; (bot.) valvé, à valves.

valvet, valvlet, or **valvule** (-vioule), *n.*, (anat., bot.) valvule,*f.*

valvular (valv'ioul'-), *adj.*, valvulaire ; de soupape.

vamp, *n.*, empeigne,*f.*

vamp, *v.a.*, raccommoder, rapiécer.

vamper, *n.*, personne qui rapièce,*f.*

vampire (-paeur), *n.*, vampire, *m.*

van, *n.*, avant-garde, *f.* ; (agri.) van, *m.* ; (wing—*aile*) aile ; (cart—*charrette*) charrette couverte, carriole, *f.* — -courier ; *avant-coureur, précurseur ;* (milit.) *éclaireur, m.* — -guard ; *avant-garde, f.*

vandal, *n.*, Vandale, *m.,f.*

vandalic, *adj.*, de vandale ; (geog.) vandalique.

vandalism (-'iz'm), *n.*, vandalisme, *m.*

vane, *n.*, girouette,*f.* ; (of a steam-engine— *de machine à vapeur*) registre ; (in mathematical instruments—*d'instruments de mathématique*) gabet, *m.*, pinnule ; (nav.) girouette,*f.* ; (flag— *drapeau*) guidon, *m.* — -spindle ; *fer de girouette, m.*

vanilla (-nil-la), *n.*, vanille, *f.* — -tree ; *vanille, f. ; vanillier, m.*

vanish, *v.n.*, s'évanouir ; disparaître.

vanished (-nish'te), *adj.*, évanoui, disparu.

vanishing, *n.*, action de s'évanouir ; disparition ; (persp.) fuite, *f.* — -point ; *point de fuite, m.*

vanity, *n.*, vanité,*f.*

vanquish (-kwishe), *v.a.*, vaincre ; dompter.

vanquishable (-kwish'a-b'l), *adj.*, que l'on peut vaincre.

vanquisher (-kwish'-), *n.*, vainqueur, *m.*

vantage (-tédje), *n.*, occasion favorable, *f.* — -ground ; *terrain avantageux ; avantage, m. ; supériorité,f.*

vapid, *adj.*, fade ; insipide ; (unanimated —*inerte*) inanimé, inerte ; (of liquors—*des liqueurs*) plat, éventé.

vapidly, *adv.*, insipidement.

vapidness, *n.*, fadeur ; insipidité ; (dulness —*inertie*) nature inanimée, inertie ; (of liquor— *de boisson*) platitude,*f.*

vaporizable (-'aïz'a-b'l), *adj.*, vaporisable.

vaporization (-'aïzé-), *n.*, vaporisation,*f.*

vaporize (-'aïze), *v.a.*, vaporiser.

vaporize, *v.n.*, se vaporiser.

vaporous (vé-), or **vaporose** (-'ôce), *adj.*, vaporeux ; (windy—*venteux*) venteux, flatueux ; (vain) vain.

vaporousness (vé-), *n.*, état vaporeux, *m.*

vapour (vé-peur), *n.,* vapeur ; fumée, *f.* ; (wind—*vent*) vent, *m.* ; flatuosité ; (fig.) fumée, *f.* — -s ; *hystérie, f.sing. ; vapeurs, f.pl.* — - bath ; *bain de vapeur, m.*

vapour (vé-peur), *v.n.*, s'évaporer ; (to bully —*rudoyer*) faire le fier-à-bras, faire le rodomont ; (to boast—*se vanter*) se targuer, se vanter, se prévaloir, se glorifier.

vapour, *v.a.*, exhaler.

vapoured (vé-peurde), *adj.*, humide de vapeur ; (fig.) vaporeux.

vapourer (vé-peur'-), *n.*, vantard, *m.* ; vantarde,*f.*

vapouring, *adj.*, glorieux ; vantard.

vapouringly, *adv.*, en se vantant.

vapourish, or **vapoury**, *adj.*, vaporeux.

varec (vâr'èke), *n.*, (bot.) varech, fucus, *m.*

variable (vé-ri-a-b'l), *adj.*, variable, changeant, variant ; (inconstant) inconstant ; (math.) variable ; (of feasts—*des fêtes*) mobile ; (of colour—*des couleurs*) changeant.

variable, *n.*, (math.) quantité variable,*f.*

variableness,*n.*,variabilité ; inconstance,*f.*

variably, *adv.*, variablement, d'une manière variable.

variance (vé-), *n.*, dissidence, discorde,*f.* ; désaccord, *m.* ; (jur.) modification, *f.* At — ; *en désaccord ; mal ensemble ; en mésintelligence ; brouillé.*

variation (vé-rié-), *n.*, variation,*f.* ; changement, *m.* ; (astron., math., mus.) variation ; (gram.) inflexion ; (of the needle—*de l'aiguille aimantée*) variation ; déclinaison,*f.*

varicella, *n.*, (med.) varicelle,*f.*

varicocele (vé-ri-cô-cîle), *n.*, (med.) varicocèle,*f.*

varicose (-côce), or **varicous**, *adj.*, (med.) variqueux.

varied (vé-ride), *adj.*, varié.

variegate (vér'ï-), *v.a.*, varier, nuancer ; rendre panaché.

variegated (vé-ri-ï-ghét'-), *adj.*, varié, nuancé ; (bot.) varié, panaché ; (of lamps—*des lampes*) de couleurs diverses.

variegation (vér'ï-ghé-), *n.*, variété de nuances, ⊙diaprure ; bigarrure ; panachure,*f.*

variety (va-raï-é-), *n.*, variété ; quantité ; race,*f.*

variola (va-raï-), *v.n.*, variole, petite vérole,*f.*

variolite (vé-ri-o-laïte), *n.*, (min.) variolite,*f.*

varioloid (vé-ri-o-loïde), *n.*, (med.) varioloïde,*f.*

variolous (va-raï-), *adj.*, (med.) variolique.

various (vé-), *adj.*, divers, différent ; (changeable—*variable*) changeant, variable ; (diversified—*varié*) varié, différent. — readings ; *variantes, f.pl.*

variously (vé-), *adv.*, différemment, diversement.

varix (vé-), *n.(varices),* (med.) varice,*f.*

varlet (vâr-), *n.*, varlet ; domestique, valet ; coquin, drôle, *m.*

varnish (vâr-), *n.*, vernis, *m.*

varnish (vâr-), *v.a.*, vernir, vernisser ; (fig.) farder.

varnisher, *n.*, vernisseur, *m.*

varnishing, *n.*, vernissure,*f.*

vary (vé-), *v.a.*, varier ; diversifier.

vary, *v.n.*, varier ; (to disagree—*différer*) différer, être d'avis différent ; (to deviate— *s'écarter*) dévier, s'écarter ; (to change in succession—*se succéder*) se suivre.

vascular (vas-kiou-), *adj.*, vasculaire ; vasculeux.

vascularity (vas-kiou-), *n.*, état vasculaire, *m.*

vase (vâze), *n.*, vase, *m.*

vassal, *n.*, vassal, *m.*, vassale, *f.* ; esclave, *m.,f.*

vassalage (-'édje), *n.*, vasselage ; esclavage, asservissement, *m.*

vast (vàste), *adj.*, vaste ; immense.

vast (vàste), *n.*, vaste espace, espace vide, *m.* ; immensité, *f.*

vastly, *adv.*, immensément ; excessivement.

vastness, *n.*, vaste étendue, grandeur, immensité ; (importance) grande importance, *f.*

vastus (vast'-), *n.*, vaste (muscle), *m.*

vat, *n.*, cuve, *f.* ; cuvier, *m.*

vaticide (-çaïde), *n.*, assassin d'un prophète, *m.*

vaticinal, *adj.*, prophétique.

vaticinate, *v.n.*, prophétiser.

vaticination (-i-né-), *n.*, prophétie, prédiction, *f.*

vaudeville, *n.*, vaudeville, *m.*

vault (volte), *n.*, voûte ; caverne, *f.* ; (cellar—*cave*) cave, *f.*, cellier ; (for the dead—*tombe*) caveau, *m.*, sépulture, *f.* ; (leap—*saut*) saut, *m.*

vault (volte), *v.a.*, voûter.

vault, *v.n.*, sauter.

vaulted, *adj.*, voûté.

vaulter, *n.*, voltigeur, sauteur, *m.*

vaulting, *n.*, (arch.) construction de voûtes, *f.* ; (vaults—*arches*) voûtes, *f.pl.*

vaulty, *adj.*, voûté ; arqué.

vaunt (vô'n'te), *n.*, vanterie, *f.*

vaunt (vô'n'te), *v.n.*, se vanter ; se glorifier.

vaunt, *v.a.*, vanter.

vaunter, *n.*, vantard, ○vanteur, *m.*

vauntful (-foule), *adj.*, plein de jactance.

vaunting, *n.*, vanterie, jactance, *f.*

vauntingly, *adv.*, avec jactance ; en se vantant.

veal (vile), *n.*, veau, *m.* — -broth ; *bouillon de veau*, *m.*

veda (vî-dà), *n.*, véda, *m.*

vedette (vi-), *n.*, vedette, *f.*

veer (vïre), *v.n.*, tourner, changer de direction ; (of ships—*de vaisseaux*) virer vent arrière ; (of the wind—*du vent*) se ranger de l'arrière, adonner.

veer (vïre), *v.a.*, virer ; (a rope—*une corde*) filer.

vegetability (vèdj'i-), *n.*, végétalité, *f.*

vegetable (vèdj'i-ta-b'l), *adj.*, végétal ; végétatif ; végétable.

vegetable, *n.*, végétal ; (food—*aliment*) légume, *m.*

vegetate (vè'dj'i-), *v.n.*, végéter.

vegetation (vè-dj'i-té-), *n.*, végétation, *f.*

vegetative, *adj.*, végétatif ; végétant.

vegetativeness, *n.*, qualité végétative, *f.*

vehemence, *or* **vehemency** (vi-hi-), *n.*, véhémence ; force, violence, *f.*

vehement (vi-hi-), *adj.*, véhément ; impétueux ; violent.

vehemently, *adv.*, avec véhémence ; impétueusement ; violemment ; ardemment.

vehicle (vi-hi-k'l), *n.*, véhicule, *m.* ; voiture, *f.*

veil (vále), *n.*, voile, *m.*

veil (véle), *v.a.*, voiler ; (fig.) voiler, masquer.

veilless (vél-lèce), *adj.*, sans voile.

vein (vé'n), *n.*, (anat.) in marble, &c.—*du marbre*, &c.) veine ; (bot.) nervure ; (geol. ; min.) veine, *f.*, filon, *m.* ; (humour—*disposition*) veine, humeur ; (turn of mind—*tour d'esprit*) veine, disposition ; (current—*série, amas*) veine, source, *f.*

vein (vé'n), *v.a.*, veiner.

veined (vé'n'de), *or* **veiny**, *adj.*, veineux, veiné.

veining, *n.*, (paint.) veinage, *m.*

veinless, *adj.*, (bot.) dépourvu de nervures.

veliferous (vi-lif'èr'-), *adj.*, à voiles, pourvu de voiles, vélifère.

velleity (vèl-li-i-), *n.*, velléité, *f.*

vellicate, *v.a.*, tirer, tirailler ; (to stimulate—*stimuler*) stimuler.

vellication (vèl-li-ké-), *n.*, tiraillement, *m.* ; torsion, *f.*

vellum (vèl'-), *n.*, vélin, *m.*

velocipede (vi-loss'i-pîde), *n.*, vélocipède, *m.*

velocity (vi-), *n.*, vélocité, vitesse, célérité, *f.*

velum (vî-), *n.*, (anat.) voile, *m.*

velvet (vèl'-), *n.*, velours, *m.*

velvet (vèl'-), *adj.*, de velours ; (fig.) doux — -down ; *velouté*, *m.* — -flower ; (bot.) amarante, *f.* — -powder ; *bourre tontisse, tonture, f.*

velvet, *v.n.*, peindre du velours ; velouter.

velveted, *adj.*, de velours ; velouté, doux.

velveteen (vèl-vèt'ine), *n.*, velours de coton croisé, *m.*

velveting, *n.*, velouté, *m.*

velvety, *or* **velvet-like** (-laïke), *adj.*, velouté.

venal (vî-), *adj.*, vénal.

venality, *n.*, vénalité ; corruption, *f.*

venary (vè'n'-), *adj.*, de vénerie ; de chasse.

venatic, *or* **venatical** (vi-), *adj.*, de chasse, pour la chasse.

venation (vi-né-), *n.*, (ant.) chasse, vénerie, *f.*

vend, *v.a.*, vendre ; débiter.

vendee (vè'n'di), *n.*, (jur.) acquéreur, *m.*

vender, *n.*, vendeur ; débitant, *m.*

vendible (vè'n'di-b'l), *adj.*, vendable.

vendibleness, *n.*, facilité de vente, *f.*

vendibly, *adv.*, d'une manière vendable.

vendor, *n.*, vendeur, *m.*, vendeuse ; (jur.) venderesse, *f.*

vendue (vè'n'diou), *n.*, (com.) vente aux enchères, *f.* ; encan, *m.* — -master ; *commissaire-priseur*, *m.*

veneer (vi-nîre), *v.a.*, plaquer.

veneer (vi-nîre), *n.*, feuille à plaquer ; plaque, *f.*

veneering, *n.*, placage, *m.*

veneering-web, *n.*, scie de placage, *f.*

venerable (vè'n'èr'a-b'l), *adj.*, vénérable, respectable.

venerableness, *n.*, caractère vénérable, *m.*

venerably, *adv.*, vénérablement.

venerate (vè'n'èr'-), *v.a.*, vénérer, révérer.

veneration (vè'n'èr'é-), *n.*, vénération, *f.*

venerator (vè'n'èr'é-), *n.*, personne qui vénère, *f.*

venereal (vi-ni-ri-), *adj.*, vénérien ; (illness—*maladie*) vénérien ; syphilitique ; (medicine—*médecines*) antivénérien ; antisyphilitique ; (aphrodisiac—*aphrodisiaque*) aphrodisiaque.

venereous (vi-ni-ri-), *adj.*, lubrique, sensuel.

venerous (vè'n'èr'-), *adj.*, (ant.). *V.* **venereous**.

venery (vè'n'i-), *n.*, coït, *m.* ; (hunt.) chasse, vénerie, *f.*

venesection (vî-ni-sèk'-), *n.*, phlébotomie, saignée, *f.*

venetian (vi-nî-shi-a'n), *adj.*, vénitien, de Venise.

venetian, *n.*, Vénitien, *m.*, Vénitienne, *f.*

vengeance (vè'n'dja'n'ce), *n.*, vengeance, *f.* Out of — ; *par vengeance*.

vengeful (vè'n'dj'foule), *adj.*, vindicatif ; vengeur.

venial (vî-), *adj.*, véniel, pardonnable.

venially, *adv.*, d'une manière vénielle ; pardonnablement ; véniellement.

venialness, *n.*, nature vénielle, *f.*

venire, *or* **venire-facias** (vi-nî-ri-fé-shi-ass), *n.*, (jur.) ordre de convocation ; ordre de comparaître, *m.*

venison (vè'n'iz'n), *n.*, venaison, *f.*

venom (vè'n'eume), *n.*, venin ; poison, *m.*

venomous (vè'n'eu'm'-), *adj.*, (of animals—*des animaux*) venimeux ; (of plants—*des plantes*) vénéneux ; (fig.) dangereux, méchant, venimeux.

venomousness, *n.*, venin, poison, *m.* ; nature venimeuse ; nature vénéneuse, *f.*

venous (vi-), *adj.*, (anat.) veineux ; (bot.) veiné.

vent, *v.a.*, donner issue à ; donner carrière à ; donner cours à ; donner un libre cours à ; exhaler.

vent, *n.*, issue ; ouverture, *f.* ; passage, *m.* ; (of a gun—*d'un canon*) lumière, *f.* ; (of a cask— *d'un tonneau*) trou de fausset, *m.* ; (publication) publication ; (emission) issue ; (utterance—*articulation*) articulation ; carrière, *f.*, cours, libre cours, *m.* ; (sale—*vente*) vente, *f.* To give — to ; donner carrière à, donner un libre cours à. — - hole ; soupirail ; aspirateur de pompe ; (of a cask—*de tonneau*) trou de fausset, *m.* — -peg ; *fausset de tonneau, m.*

venter, *n.*, ventre, abdomen, *m.*

venter, *n.*, divulgateur, propagateur, *m.*

ventiduct (-deuk'te), *n.*, soupirail, *m.* ; (arch.) ventouse, *f.*

ventilate, *v.a.*, aérer, ventiler ; (agri.) vanner.

ventilation (vè'n'ti-lé-), *n.*, ventilation, *f.* ; (agri.) vannage, *m.*

ventilator (vè'n'ti-lé-teur),*n.*,ventilateur,*m.*

ventosity (vè'n'tôss'-), *n.*, (ant.) ventosité ; flatuosité, *f.*

ventral, *adj.*, ventral.

ventricle (vè'n'tri-k'l), *n.*, ventricule, *m.*

ventriloquism (-kwiz'm),*or* **ventriloquy** (-kwi), *n.*, ventriloquie, *f.*

ventriloquist (-kwiste), *n.*, ventriloque, *m.*

ventriloquous (-kweusse),*adj.*,ventriloque.

venture (vè'n'tieur), *n.*, aventure, *f.* ; risque, hasard, *m.* ; chance (com.) pacotille, *f.* At a — ; *à l'aventure ; au hasard.*

venture (vè'n'tieur), *v.a.*, aventurer, risquer, hasarder.

venture, *v.n.*, s'aventurer ; se risquer, se hasarder. To — on ; *se risquer sur, dans ; se hasarder sur, dans ; s'aventurer sur, dans ; entreprendre.* To — to ; *oser.*

venturer, *n.*, personne aventureuse, *f.*

venturesome (vè'n'tieur-seume),*adj.*,aventureux ; hasardeux.

venturesomely, *adv.*, aventureusement, d'une manière aventureuse.

venturous, *adj.*, aventuré, aventureux ; hasardeux ; audacieux.

venturously, *adv.*,aventureusement, d'une manière aventureuse ; hardiment.

venturousness, *n.*, caractère aventureux, *m.* ; hardiesse, audace, *f.*

venue (vè'n'iou), *n.*, (jur.) voisinage, *m.*

venus (vi-),*n.*,(myth.) Vénus, *f.* (bot.) —'s comb ; *peigne de Vénus, m.*, aiguille de berger, *f.* —'s looking-glass ; *miroir de Vénus, m.*

veracious (vi-ré-sheusse), *adj.*, vrai, véridique.

veracity (vi-), *n.*, véracité ; véridicité ; vérité, *f.*

veranda (vi-), *n.*, véranda, *f.*

veratria, *or* **veratrine** (vi-ré-), *n.*, (chem.) vératrine, *f.*

verb (veurbe), *n.*, verbe, *m.*

verbal (veur-), *adj.*, verbal, de vive voix ; oral ; (literal—*littéral*) mot à mot, littéral ; (gram.) verbal.

verbal (veur-), *n.*, (gram.) substantif verbal, *m.*

verbality (vèr-), *n.*, (ant.) expression littérale, *f.*

verbalize (veur-bal'aïze), *v.a.*, changer en verbe.

verbally (veur-), *adv.*, verbalement ; de vive voix, oralement ; (literally—*littéralement*) mot à mot, littéralement.

verbatim (veur-bé-), *adv.*, mot pour mot, à la lettre.

verbena (vèr-bi-), *n.*, verveine, *f.*

verberation (veur-bi-ré-), *n.*, action de frapper ; (phys.) percussion, *f.*

verbiage (veur-bi-édje), *n.*, verbiage, *m.*

verbose (vèr-bôce), *adj.*, verbeux, diffus.

verbosity (vèr-bôss'-), *n.*, verbosité, diffusion, *f.*

verdancy (veur-), *n.*, verdure, *f.*

verdant (veur-), *adj.*, verdoyant, vert ; fleurissant.

verderer (veur-deur'-), *n.*, verdier, *m.*

verdict (veur-), *n.*, verdict ; jugement, arrêt, *m.*

verdigris (veur-di-griss), *n.*, vert-de-gris, verdet, *m.*

verditer (veur-), *n.*, verdet, *m.*

verdure (veurd'ieur), *n.*, verdure, *f.*

verdurer (veurd'ieur'-), *n.*, verdier, *m.*

verdurous (veurd'ieur'-), *adj.*, verdoyant, vert.

verge (veurdje), *n.*, verge, *f.* ; (jur.) ressort, *m.* ; (horl.) verge, *f.* ; (gard.) bord, *m.*, bordure, *f.* ; (brink—*bord*) bord, *m.*, extrémité ; (of a forest—*d'une forêt*) lisière, *f.* On the — of setting out ; *à la veille de partir.*

verge (veurdje), *v.n.*, pencher. To — on ; *approcher de.*

verger (veurdj'-), *n.*, porte-verge ; huissier à verge, *m.*

verifiable (vèr'i-faï-a-b'l), *adj.*, qu'on peut vérifier.

verification (vèr'i-fi-ké-), *n.*, vérification, *f.*

verifier (vèr'i-faï-), *n.*, personne qui prouve, qui constate, *f.*

verify (vèr'i-fa-ye), *v.a.*, vérifier ; prouver, constater, établir.

verily (vèr'-), *adv.*, en vérité, véritablement, vraiment.

verisimilar (vèr'i-ci'm'-), *adj.*, vraisemblable.

verisimilitude (vèr'i-ci-mil'i-tioude), *n.*, vraisemblance, *f.*

verisimility, *n.*, (ant.). *V.* **similitude.**

veritable (vèr'i-ta-b'l), *adj.*, véritable.

veritably, *adv.*, véritablement.

verity (vèr'-), *n.*, vérité ; véracité, *f.*

verjuice (veur-djiouce), *n.*, verjus, *m.*

vermicelli (veur-mi-tshèl'i), *n.*, vermicelle, *m.* — -maker ; *vermicelier, m.*

vermicular (vèr'mik'iou-), *adj.*, vermiculaire ; vermiculé.

vermiculate (vèr-mik'iou-), *v.a.*, (arch.) orner de vermicules.

vermiculated,*adj.*, vermiculé.

vermiculation (vèr-mik'iou-lé-), *n.*, mouvement vermiculaire, *m.* ; (arch.) vermiculures, *f.pl.*

vermicule (veur-mi-kioule), *n.*, vermisseau, *m.*

vermiculous, **vermiculose** (-lôce), *or* **vermiculate**, *adj.*,plein de vers ; vermiculaire.

vermiform (veur-), *adj.*, vermiforme, vermiculaire.

vermifuge (veur-mi-fioudje), *n.*, vermifuge, *m.*

vermilion (vèr-), *n.*, vermillon, *m.*

vermilion, *v.a.*, vermillonner.

vermin (veur-), *n.*, vermine, *f.*

verminate (veur-), *v.n.*, engendrer de la vermine.

vermination (veur-mi-né-), *n.*, production de la vermine, *f.*

verminous (veur-), *adj.*, qui tend à produire de la vermine.

vermiparous (vèr-), *adj.*, qui engendre des vers.

vermivorous (ver-), *adj.*, vermivore.

vernacular (vèr-nak'iou-), *adj.*, natal, du pays ; national ; naturel ; (disease—*maladie*) endémique, du pays.

vernal (veur-), *adj.*, du printemps ; printanier ; (bot.) vernal ; (fig.) de la jeunesse.

vernant (veur-), *adj.*, (ant.) *V.* **vernal.**

vernation (vèr-né-), *n.*, (bot.) vernation, préfoliation, *f.*

vernier (veur-nîre), *n.*, vernier, *m.*

veronica (vi-), *n.*, (bot.) véronique, *f.*

verrucose (vèr-riou-côce), *or* **verrucous** (-keuss), *adj.*, verruqueux.

versatile (veur-sa-tile), *adj.*, tournant ; mobile ; (bot.) versatile, oscillant ; (changeable—*variable*) changeant, versatile ; (talent, &c.) souple, flexible.

versatility, *n.*, mobilité ; (variableness—*versatilité*) versatilité ; (talent, &c.) flexibilité, souplesse, *f.*

verse (veurse), *n.*, vers, *m.* ; (poet.) vers, *m.pl.*, poésie, *f.* ; (bible) verset ; (of a song—*de chanson*) couplet, *m.*

versed (veurste), *adj.*, versé dans, exercé dans, expérimenté dans ; (math.) verse. — sine ; *sinus verse.*

versicolour (veur-si-keul'eur), *or* **versicoloured** (-eurde), *adj.*, multicolore ; de diverses couleurs.

versification (veur-si-fi-ké-), *n.*, versification, *f.*

versifier (-si-faï-), *n.*, versificateur, *m.*

versify (veur-si-fa-ye), *v.n.*, versifier, faire des vers.

versify, *v.a.*, chanter en vers ; (to turn into verse—*mettre de la prose en vers*) mettre en vers.

version (veur-sheu'n), *n.*, version, *f.*

versus (veur-), *prep.*, (jur.) contre.

vertebra (veur-ti-), *n.* (*vertebræ*), (anat.) vertèbre, *f.*

vertebral (veur-ti-), *adj.*, vertébral ; (zool.) vertébré.

vertebrate (veur-ti-), *n.*, vertébré, *m.*

vertebrate, *or* **vertebrated** (veur-ti-), *adj.*, vertébré, articulé.

vertebrates (-brétse), *or* **vertebrata**, *n.pl.*, vertébrés, animaux vertébrés, *m.pl.*

vertex (veur-tèkse), *n.* (*vertices*), sommet, haut, faîte ; (astron.) zénith ; (of the head—*de la tête*) haut, sommet, vertex, *m.*

vertical (veur-), *adj.*, vertical ; (of the sun—*du soleil*) vertical, au zénith. — circle ; (astron.) *cercle azimutal, m.*

vertically, *adv.*, verticalement.

verticalness, *n.*, verticalité, *f.*

verticil (veur-), *n.*, (bot.) verticille, *m.*

verticillate, *or* **verticillated** (vèr-tiss'il-lôt'-), *adj.*, (bot.) verticillé.

verticity (vèr-), *n.*, rotation, révolution, *f.*

vertiginous (ver-tidj'-), *adj.*, rotatoire ; (affected with vertigo—*sujet au vertige*) sujet au vertige ; (med.) vertigineux.

vertiginousness (vèr-tidj'-), *n.*, mouvement rotatoire, *m.* ; rotation, *f.* ; (giddiness—*étourdissement*) vertige, étourdissement, *m.*

vertigo (veur-.ou vèr-),*n.* (*vertigines*),vertige, étourdissement, *m.*

vervain (veur-vé'n), *n.*, verveine, *f.*

very (vèr'-), *adj.*, vrai ; véritable ; même ; seul, simple ; (b.s.) fieffé, franc. The — thought makes me shudder ; *la seule pensée m'en fait frémir.* The — man ; *l'homme même.*

very, *adv.*, fort, bien, très. — well ; *bien, très bien.* So — ; *si.*

vesania (vi-zé-), *n.*, vésanie ; maladie mentale, *f.*

vesical (vèss'-), *adj.*, (anat.) vésical.

vesicate (vèss'-), *v.n.*, appliquer un vésicatoire à

vesication (vèss'l-ké-), *n.*, vésication, *f.*

vesicatory (vi-cik'-), *n.*, vésicatoire, *m.*

vesicatory (vi-cik'-), *adj.*, vésicant, vésicatoire.

vesicle (vèss'l-k'l), *n.*, vésicule, *f.*

vesicular (vi-cik'iou-), *adj.*, vésiculaire.

vesiculate, *or* **vesiculose** (-lôce), *adj.*, vésiculeux.

vesper (vès-), *n.*, étoile de Vénus, *f.* ; (evening—*soir*) soir, *m.* —s ; *vépres, f.pl.*

vespertine (-taine), *adj.*, du soir.

vessel (vès-), *n.*, vase, vaisseau ; réceptacle ; (nav.) vaisseau, bâtiment, navire, *m.*

vessignon (vès'sig-neu'n), *n.*, (vet.) vessigon, *m.*

vest, *n.*, gilet, *m.*

vest, *v.a.*, vêtir, revêtir ; investir ; (money—*argent*) placer.

vest, *v.n.*, être dévolu, échoir.

vestal, *n.*, vestale, *f.*

vestal, *adj.*, de Vesta ; virginal, chaste.

vested, *adj.*, fixe, déterminé ; (jur.) dévolu.

vestibule (vès-ti-bioule), *n.*, vestibule, *m.* ; antichambre, *f.*

vestige (vès-tidje), *n.*, vestige, *m.* ; trace, *f.*

vestment, *n.*, vêtement, *m.*

vestry, *n.*, (place—*lieu*) sacristie ; (assembly) conseil de fabrique, *m.*

vestry-board (-bôrde), *n.*, fabrique, *f.*

vestry-clerk (-klârke), *n.*, secrétaire de la fabrique, *m.*

vestry-keeper (-kip'-), *n.*, sacristain, *m.*

vestry-man, *n.*, fabricien, *m.*

vestry-meeting (-mit'-), *n.*, réunion du conseil de fabrique, *f.*

vestry-room, *n.*, sacristie, *f.*

vesture (vèst'ioure), *n.*, vêtement, *m.* ; robe ; parure, *f.*

vesuvian (vi-ciou-), *adj.*, vésuvien.

vetch, *n.*, (bot.) vesce, *f.*

vetchy, *adj.*, consistant en vesce ; qui abonde en vesce.

veteran (vèt'èr'-), *n.*, vétéran, *m.*

veteran (vèt'èr'-), *adj.*, aguerri, eprouvé, expérimenté.

veterinarian (vèt'èr'i-né-),*n.*,vétérinaire,*m.*

veterinary (vèt'èr'i-na-), *adj.*, vétérinaire. — surgeon ; *vétérinaire, artiste médecin vétérinaire, m.*

veto (vî-), *n.*, veto, *m.*

vex (vèkse), *v.a.*, (to harass—*tourmenter*) affliger, tourmenter, vexer ; troubler ; (to irritate—*irriter*) irriter, vexer, fâcher, ennuyer, contrarier.

vexation (vèks'é-), *n.*, affliction, *f.* ; tourment ; trouble, *m.* ; vexation ; (teasing, trouble —*désagrément*) contrariété, *f.*, désagrément, tourment, *m.*

vexatious (vèks'é-sheuss), *adj.*, vexatoire ; (irritating—*vexant*) irritant, fâcheux, ennuyeux, contrariant, vexant ; (harassing—*fatigant*) fatigant.

vexatiously, *adv.*, d'une manière fâcheuse, d'une manière contrariante, d'une manière vexatoire.

vexatiousness, *n.*, caractère vexatoire, *m.* ; contrariété, *f.*

vexed (vèks'te), *adj.*, vexé, irrité, fâché.

vexer (vèks'-), *n.*, personne qui afflige, qui irrite, qui tourmente, qui contrarie, &c., *f.*

vexing, *adj.*, contrariant, vexant, ennuyeux.

vexingly, *adv.*, d'une manière contrariante.

via (va-eu), *adv.*, par voie de, par.

viability (va-eu-bi-), *n.*, viabilité, *f.*

viable (va-eu-b'l), *adj.*, viable.

viaduct (va-eu-deuk'te), *n.*, viaduc, *m.*

vial (vaï-al), *n.*, fiole, *f.*

viand (vaï-a'n'de), *n.*, viande, *f.* ; méts, *m.*

viaticum (vaï-at'-), *n.*, provisions de route, *f.pl.* ; (c.rel.) viatique, *m.*

vibrate (vaï-), *v.n.*, vibrer ; osciller vaciller.

vibrate, *v.a.*, faire vibrer ; faire osciller ; faire marcher.

vibration (vaï-bré-) *n.*, oscillation ; (phys., mus.) vibration, *f.*

vibrative, vibratile, or **vibratory** (vaï-), *adj.*, vibrant ; de vibration ; oscillatoire.

viburnum (vaï-beur-), *n.*, (bot.) viorne, *f.*

vicar, *n.*, vicaire ; (of a parish—*d'une paroisse*) curé, *m.*

vicarage (-édje), *n.*, vicariat, *m.* ; vicairie ; (of a parish—*d'une paroisse*) cure, *f.*, presbytère, *m.*

vicarial, *adj.*, vicarial ; du curé, de la cure.

vicariate (vi-ké-), *n.*, vicariat, *m.*

vicariate (vi-ké-), *adj.*, de vicaire.

vicarious (vi-ké-), *adj.*, vicarial, de vicaire, de délégué ; de substitution.

vicarship, *n.*, vicariat, *m.*

vice (vaïce), *n.*, vice ; défaut ; ¨(tool—*outil*) étau, *m.*

vice (vaïce), *adv.*, en remplacement de. —-admiral ; *vice-amiral*, *m.* —-admiralty ; *vice-amirauté*, *f.* —-agent ; *délégué*, *m.* —-chamberlain ; *sous-chambellan*, *m.* —-chancellor;*vice-chancelier*, *m.* —-consul ;*vice-consul*, *m.* —-consulship ;*vice-consulat*, *m.* —-doge ; *vice-doge*, *m.* —-king ; *vice-roi*, *m.* —-legate ; *vice-légat*, *m.* —-presidency ; *vice-présidence*, *f.* —-president ; *vice-président*, *m.*

vice-chop (-tshope), *n.*, mâchoire d'étau, *f.*

vice-entailed (-è'n'tél'de), *adj.*, légué, transmis par le vice.

vicegerency (-dji-), *n.*, charge de vice-gérant, *f.*

vicegerent, *n.*, vice-gérant, *m.*

vice-roy (vaïce-), *n.*, vice-roi, *m.*

vice-royalty, or **viceroyship**, *n.*, vice-royauté, *f.*

vice versa (vaï-ci-veur-), *adv.*, vice versa.

vicinage (-nédje), *n.*, voisinage, *m.*

vicinity, *n.*, voisinage, *m.* ; proximité, *f.* ; alentours, environs, *m.pl.*

vicious (vish'euss), *adj.*, vicieux.

viciously, *adv.*, vicieusement.

viciousness,*n.*, nature vicieuse,*f.* ; vice, *m.*

vicissitude (-tioude), *n.*, vicissitude, *f.* ; changement, *m.*

vicissitudinary, or **vicissitudinous** (-tioud'-), *adj.*, qui change successivement.

victim, *n.*, victime,*f.* — to ; *victime de.*

victimize (-'aïze), *v.a.*, victimer, duper.

victor (-teur), *n.*, vainqueur, *m.*

victoress, *n.*, vainqueur (femme).

victorious (-tô-), *adj.*,victorieux, de victoire.

victoriously (-tô-), *adv.*, victorieusement, en vainqueur.

victoriousness (-tô-), *n.*, caractère victorieux, *m.*

victory, *n.*, victoire,*f.*

victual (vit't'l), *v.a.*, avitailler ; ravitailler.

victual, *v.n.*, faire ses vivres.

victualler (vit't'l'-), *n.*, pourvoyeur ; fournisseur de vivres ; avitailleur ; (ship—*navire*) vaisseau d'approvisionnement, *m.* Licensed —; *cabaretier*, *m.*

victualling (vit't'l'-), *n.*, avitaillement, *m.* ; vivres, *m.pl.* — -office ; *bureau des vivres*, *m.*

victuals (vit't'l'ze), *n.pl.*, vivres, *m.pl.* ; provisions, *f.pl.* ; manger, *m.sing.*

vicugna, vicuunga, or **vicuna** (vi-keu'n'-), *n.*, (mam.) vigogne,*f.*

videlicet (ab. of *videre licet*), *adv.*, savoir ; c'est-à-dire.

viduity (vi-diou-), *n.*, (ant.) viduité, *f.*, veuvage, *m.*

vie (va-ye), *v.n.*, rivaliser, lutter, disputer. To — with each other; *rivaliser, rivaliser avec ;* (à l'envi l'un de l'autre ; c'est à qui . . .

view (viou), *v.a.*, regarder ; contempler ; considérer ; voir ; examiner; inspecter ; (to survey intellectually—*considérer*) envisager, considérer.

view (viou), *n.*, vue ; (persp.) vue, élévation ; (prospect—*rue*) vue, perspective,*f.*, coup d'œil,

point de vue, *m.* ; (appearance—*apparence*) apparence, *f.* ; (examination by the eye—*regard*) coup d'œil, regard ; (mental examination—*examen mental*) aperçu, examen, *m.* ; (intention) intention, *f.*, but, dessein, *m.* ; (opinion) vue, opinion, pensée, manière de voir,*f.* Bird's-eye — ; (persp.) *plan à vol d'oiseau*, *m.* In —; *en vue.* With a — to ; *dans la vue de, dans l'intention de.* On — ; *exposé, qu'on peut voir, visiter.*

viewer (viou-eur), *n.*, personne qui regarde, qui considère, qui examine, *f.* ; spectateur, *m.*, spectatrice, *f.*

viewless, *adj.*, invisible.

vigil (vid'jil), *n.*, veille ; veillée ; vigile,*f.*

vigilance, or **vigilancy** (vid-jil'-), *n.*, vigilance, *f.*

vigilant (vid'jil'-), *adj.*, vigilant ; éveillé, soigneux.

vigilantly (vid'jil'-), *adv.*, avec vigilance.

vignette (vi'n'iète), *n.*, vignette,*f.*

vigorous, *adj.*, vigoureux, fort.

vigorously, *adv.*, vigoureusement, fortement.

vigorousness, *n.*, force, vigueur,*f.*

vigour (vigh'eur), *n.*, vigueur, force,*f.*

vile (vaïl), *adj.*, vil, abject, bas.

vilely (vaïl'-), *adv.*, vilement, bassement.

vileness (vaïl'-), *n.*, nature vile ; bassesse, abjection,*f.*

vilification (vil'i-fi-ké-), *n.*, rabaissement, dénigrement, *m.*

vilifier (vil'i-faï-), *n.*, diffamateur, *m.*, diffamatrice,*f.*

vilify (vil'i-fa'ye), *v.a.*, avilir, abaisser ; vilipender ; dénigrer.

villa, *n.*, villa ; maison de plaisance,*f.*

village (-lédje), *n.*, village, *m.*

villager, *n.*, villageois, *m.*, villageoise,*f.*

villagery, *n.*, villages, *m.pl.*

villain (vil-léne), *n.*, scélérat, misérable, *m.* ; (in feudal law—*féodalité*) vilain, roturier, *m.*

villainage (vil-lé-nédje),*n.*, vilainage, *m.* ; servitude,*f.*

villainous (vil-lé-), *adj.*, vil, infâme ; de scélérat ; (sorry—*de mauvaise qualité*) méchant, mauvais.

villainously (vil-lé-), *adv.*, vilément, avec infamie ; horriblement, d'une manière infâme.

villainousness, *n.*, infamie, scélératesse,*f.*

villainy (vil-lé-), *n.*, infamie, scélératesse, vilenie,*f.*

villatic, *adj.*, villageois, de village.

villosity (vil-loss'-), *n.*, villosité,*f.*

villous, or **villose** (-lôce), *adj.*, villeux.)

vimineous (-mi'n'i-), *adj.*, d'osier.

vincible (-oi-b'l), *adj.*, que l'on peut vaincre.

vindemial (-di-), *adj.*, qui appartient aux vendanges.

vindemiate (-di-), *v.a.*, faire les vendanges ; vendanger.

vindicable (-ca-b'l), *adj.*, défensible ; justifiable.

vindicate, *v.a.*, soutenir, défendre, justifier ; (to maintain—*soutenir*) maintenir, soutenir, défendre.

vindication (-di-ké-), *n.*, défense, justification, *f.* ; maintien, *m.*

vindicator (-ké-teur), *n.*, défenseur ; soutien, *m.*

vindicatory, *adj.*, vengeur ; (justificatory —*en justification*) justificatif.

vindictive, *adj.*, vindicatif.

vindictively, *adv.*, d'une manière vindicative.

vindictiveness, *n.*, caractère vindicatif, *m.*

vine (vaïne), *n.*, vigne, *f.* ; (of plants—*des plantes*) sarment, *m.* — -branch ; *branche de vigne*, *f.* ; pampre, *m.* — -dresser ; *vigneron*, *m.* — -grub ; *charançon de la vigne*, *m.* — -leaf ; *feuille de vigne*, *f.* — -grower ; *propriétaire de*

vignes, m. — -shoot; sarment, m. — -stock; cep, pied de vigne, m.
vined (vaï'n'de), adj., à feuille de vigne.
vinegar (vi'n'i-), n., vinaigre, m.; (fig.) aigreur, f. — -cruet; vinaigrier, m. — -maker; vinaigrier, m. — -tree; (bot.) sumac des corroyeurs, vinaigrier, m.
vinery (vaï'n'ri), n., serre à vignes, f.
vineyard (vi'n-), n., vigne. f.; vignoble, m.
vinose (vaï'-nôce), or **vinous** (-neuss), adj., vineux.
vintage (vi'n'tédje), n., vendange; (wine produced by one crop of grapes—vinée) vinée, récolte de vin, f.; (time of gathering—temps de la récolte du raisin) vendanges, f.pl.
vintager (-tédj'-), n., vendangeur, m.
vintner, n., cabaretier, m.
vintry, n., marché au vin, m.
viny (vaï-), adj., de vigne; de vignoble; viticole.
viol (vaï-ol), n., (mus.) viole, f.
violable (vaï-o-la-b'l), adj., qui peut être violé.
violar (vaï-ol'-), n., vielleur, m., vielleuse, f.
violate (vaï-), v.a., violer; (to ravish—commettre un viol) violer, faire violence à; (to disturb—troubler) déranger, troubler; (to profane —profaner) outrager.
violation (vaï-o-lé-), n., violation, f.; (rape—viol) viol, m.
violator (vaï-o-l'ét'eur), n., violateur, m., violatrice, f.; (ravisher—violeur) violeur, m.
violence (vaï-o-), n., violence, f.
violent (vaï-o-), adj., violent; (extorted—extorqué) arraché par la violence; (not spontaneous, not natural—non spontané, peu naturel) forcé, contraint; (death—mort) violent; (extreme) extrême; (pain—douleur) violent, grand, atroce. To lay — hands on one's self; attenter à ses jours.
violently (vaï-o-), adv., violemment.
violet (vaï-o-), n., (bot.) violette, f.
violet (vaï-o-), adj., violet. — -tribe; violacées, f.pl.
violin (vaï-o-), n., violon, m.
violinist (vaï-o-), n., violoniste, m., f.; violon, m.
violist (vaï-o-), n., (mus.) violiste, m.
violoncellist (vi-o-lo'n'tshèl-lô), n., violoncelliste, m.
violoncello (vi-o-lo'n'tshèl-lô), n., violoncelle, m. One-stringed —; trompette marine, f.
viper (vaï-), n., vipère, f.
viperine (vaï-peur'aïne), adj., vipérin.
viperous (vaï-), adj., de vipère; venimeux; (malignant—malfaisant) malfaisant.
viper's-grass (vaï-peur'z'grâce), n., (bot.) scorsonère, f.
viraginian (vir'à-dji'n'-), adj., de virago.
virago (vi-rà-gô), n., guerrière; virago, f.; dragon de femme, m.
virelay (vi-ri-lé), n., virelai, m.
virent, adj., vert, verdoyant.
virgate, adj., (bot.) en verge, effilé.
virgilian (veur-djil'-), adj., virgilien.
virgin (veur-dji'n), n., vierge, f.
virgin, adj., vierge; virginal, de vierge.
virginal, adj., virginal, de vierge.
virginity (veur-), n., virginité, f.
virgin's-bower (veur-dji'n'z'baou'eur), n., (bot.) clématite commune, f.
virgo, n., (astron.) la Vierge, f.
viridity, n., verdeur, f.
virile, adj., viril, mâle.
virility, n., virilité; nature virile, f.
virtu (veur-tiou), n., goût des arts, m. Objects of —; objets d'art, m.pl.
virtual (veur-tiou-), adj., virtuel.
virtuality (veur-tiou-), n., virtualité, f.
virtually (veur-tiou-), adv., virtuellement.

virtue (veur-tiou), n., vertu; (quality of physical bodies—propriétés des corps) vertu, propriété, qualité; (excellence) excellence, valeur, f., mérite, m. By — of; en vertu de; au moyen de. In — of; en vertu de.
virtueless, adj., sans vertu; impuissant.
virtuoso (veur-tiou-ô-çô), n. (virtuosi), virtuose, m.f.
virtuous (veurt'iou-euss), adj., vertueux.
virtuously, adv., vertueusement.
virtuousness, n., vertu, f.
virulence, or **virulency** (vir'iou-), n., virulence; violence, f.
virulent, adj., virulent; violent.
virulently, adv., avec virulence.
virus (vaï-), n., (med.) virus, m.
visage (viz'édje), n., visage, m.; figure, f.
vis-a-vis (viz'à-vi), n., vis-à-vis, m.
visceral (vis-ci-), adj., viscéral.
viscid, adj., visqueux.
viscidity, n., viscosité, glutinosité, f.
viscosity (-côss'-), or **viscousness**, n., viscosité, glutinosité, f.
viscount (vaï-caou'n'te), n., vicomte, m.
viscountess (vaï-caou'n't'-), n., vicomtesse, f.
viscountship, or **viscounty** (vaï-cou'nt'-), n., vicomté, f.
viscous, adj., visqueux, gluant, glutineux.
viscus, n. (viscera), viscère, m.
vishnu (-nou), n., Vishnou, m.
visibility (viz'-), n., visibilité, f.
visible (viz'i-b'l), adj., visible; (apparent) visible, évident, manifeste; (horizon) sensible.
visibleness (viz'i-b'l), n., visibilité, f.
visibly (viz'-), adv., visiblement; à vue d'œil.
visier, n. V. vizier.
visigoth (viz'i-goth), n., Visigoth, m.
vision (vij'eune), n., vision; vue; (in Scripture—biblique) vision, f.
visional (vij'eu'n'-), adj., de vision.
visionary (vish'eu'n'-), adj., visionnaire; chimérique.
visionary (vish'eu'n'-). n., visionnaire, m.,f.
visit (viz'-), n., visite; (of one going to inspect—de quelqu'un qui inspecte) visite, inspection, f. To pay a —; faire une visite. On a —; en visite.
visit (viz'-), v.a., visiter; (in Scripture—biblique) visiter, éprouver.
visit, v.n., faire des visites.
visitable (-a-b'l), adj., soumis à la visite.
visitant (viz'-), n., personne qui fait une visite, f.; visiteur, m., visiteuse, f.
visitation (viz'i-té-), n., visite; (jur.) inspection; (in Scripture—biblique) épreuve, affliction, f. By the — of God; subitement.
visitatorial (viz'i-ta-tô-), adj., d'inspection judiciaire.
visiting (viz'-), n., visite, f.; visites. f.pl.
visitor (viz'it'eur), n., personne qui fait une visite. f.; visiteur, m., visiteuse, f.; (official—fonctionnaire) inspecteur, m. —s; monde, m. sing.; société, f.sing.
visne (vine), n. V. venue.
visor (viz'eur), n., masque, m.; (of a helmet—de casque) visière, f.
visored (viz'eurde), adj., masqué.
vista, n., échappée de vue; percée, éclaircie; (fig.) perspective, f.
visual (vij'iou-), adj., visuel.
vital (vaï-), adj., vital; de vie; (air) respirable; (essential—essentiel) vital, capital, essentiel.
vitality (vaï-), n., vitalité; vie, f.
vitalize (vaï-tal'aïze), v.a., vivifier, donner la vie.
vitally (vaï-), adv., vitalement.
vitals (vaï-talze), n.pl., parties vitales, f.pl.
vitiate (vish'i-), v.a., gâter, corrompre; (jur.) vicier.

vitiation (vish'i-é-), *n.*, viciation, action de gâter, de corrompre; altération; (jur.) invalidation. *f.*

vitreous (vit'ri-), *adj.*, de verre; vitreux; (anat., phys.) vitré.

vitreousness (vit'ri-), *n.*, nature vitreuse; nature vitrée, *f.*

vitrescence (vi-très-), *n.*, vitrescibilité, *f.*

vitrescent, *adj.*, vitrescible, vitrifiable.

vitrifaction (vit'ri-fak'-), *n.*, vitrification, *f.*

vitrifiable (vit'ri-faï-a-b'l), *adj.*, vitrifiable, vitrescible.

vitrify (vit'ri-fa-ye), *v.a.*, vitrifier.

vitrify, *v.n.*, se vitrifier.

vitriol (vit'-), *n.*, vitriol, *m.*

vitriolate, or **vitriolize** (-'aïze), *v.a.*, convertir en sulfate, en vitriol.

vitriolation (vit'ri-o-lé-), *n.*, (chem.) vitriolisation, *f.*

vitriolic, *adj.*, sulfurique, vitriolique; de vitriol.

vituline (vit'iou-laïne), *adj.*, de veau.

vituperable (vit'iou-pèr'a-b'l), *adj.*, blâmable, répréhensible.

vituperate (vit'iou-pèr'-), *v.a.*, blâmer; condamner.

vituperation (vit'iou-pèr'é-), *n.*, blâme, reproche, *m.*

vituperative, *adj.*, de blâme, de reproche.

vivacious (vi-vé-sheuss), *adj.*, vif; vivace.

vivaciously, *adv.*, vivement, avec vivacité.

vivaciousness, or **vivacity**, *n.*, vivacité, *f.*

vivary (vaï-), *n.*, vivier, *m.*; (warren—*garenne*) garenne, *f.*

viva voce (vaï-va-vô-cî), *adv.*, de vive voix.

vives (vaï'v'ze), *n.pl.*, (vet.) esquinancie interne, parotide, *f.sing.*; avives, *f.pl.*

vivid, *adj.*, vif, animé, ardent; (colour—*couleur*) vif, éclatant.

vividly, *adv.*, vivement; avec force; avec ardeur; (with brightness—*brillamment*) avec éclat.

vividness, *n.*, vivacité, *f.*; feu, *m.*; ardeur; (of colours—*des couleurs*) ardeur, *f.*, éclat, *m.*

vivific, or **vivifical** (vaï-), *adj.*, vivifiant.

vivificate (vaï-vif'-), *v.a.*, vivifier; (chem.) revivifier.

vivification (vaï-vi-fi-ké-), *n.*, vivification; revivification, *f.*

vivificative, *adj.*, vivifiant.

vivify (vi-vif'a-ye), *v.a.*, vivifier, animer.

vivifying (vi-vif'a-yigne), *adj.*, vivifiant.

viviparous (vaï-vip'-), *adj.*, vivipare.

vixen (vik's'n), *n.*, mégère, *f.*

vixenly, *adj.*, qui a un caractère de mégère.

viz. (ab. of *videlicet, videre licet*), *adv.*, savoir; c'est-à-dire. [Cette abréviation se prononce *namely*.]

vizard. *V.* **visor**.

vizier (viz'ieur), *n.*, vizir, *m.*

vizierate, or **viziership**, *n.*, vizirat, viziriat, *m.*

vocable (vô-ca-b'l), *n.*, mot, vocable, *m.*

vocabulary (vo-cab'iou-), *n.*, vocabulaire, *m.*

vocabulist, *n.*, auteur d'un vocabulaire, (l.u.) vocabuliste, *m.*

vocal (vô-), or **vocalic**, *adj.*, vocal; de la voix; (having a voice—*capable de parler*) doué de la parole.

vocalist (vô-), *n.*, chanteur, *m.*, chanteuse, *f.*

vocality, *n.*, qualité de ce qui peut se prononcer, *f.*

vocalization (vô-cal'aïzé-), *n.*, (mus.) vocalisation, *f.*

vocalize (vô-cal'aïze), *v.a.*, donner un son de voix à.

vocalize, *v.n.*, vocaliser.

vocally (vô-), *adv.*, par la voix; verbalement.

vocation (vo-ké-), *n.*, vocation; profession,

f.; état, emploi, métier; (summons—*appel*) appel, *m.*

vocative, *adj.*, vocatif.

vocative, *n.*, vocatif, *m.*

vociferate (-'èr'-), *v.a.* and *n.*, vociférer.

vociferation (-'èré-), *n.*, vociération, *f.*

vociferous, *adj.*, qui vocifère.

vociferously, *adv.*, en vociférant.

vogue (vôghe), *n.*, vogue, mode, *f.* In —; *en vogue; à la mode.*

voice (voïce), *n.*, voix, *f.*, (language—*langue*) langage, *m.*, paroles, *f.pl.*; (sound—*son*) son, *m.*; (vote) voix, *f.*, suffrage, vote, *m.*; (gram.) voix, *f.* Without a dissentient —; *à l'unanimité des voix.*

voice (voïce), *v.a.*, former la voix de; régler le ton de; (to vote—*voter*) voter; (to report—*rapporter*) rapporter.

voiceless, *adj.*, sans voix; sans vote.

void (voïde), *v.a.*, vider; évacuer, quitter; (to send out—*jeter*) jeter, verser; rejeter; (to annul—*annuler*) annuler, rendre nul; (to leave vacant—*laisser vacant*) laisser vacant.

void, *adj.*, vide; vacant; (null) nul, de nul effet; (free—*libre*) libre; (vain) vain, idéal. — of; *dépourvu de; dénué de.*

void (voïde), *n.*, vide; espace vide, *m.*

voidable (voïd'a-b'l), *adj.*, qui peut être annulé, rejeté.

voidance (voïd'-), *n.*, vidange; (ejection—*expulsion*) expulsion d'un bénéfice; vacance; défaite, *f.*, subterfuge, *m.*

voider (voïd'-), *n.*, personne qui rejette, qui annule, *f.*

voidness (voïd'-), *n.*, vide, *m.*; nullité; vanité, *f.*

volatile (-taïle), *adj.*, qui vole, volant; (fickle—*inconstant*) volage, léger; (chem.) volatil.

volatileness (-taïl'-), or **volatility** (-til'-), *n.*, amour du changement, *m.*; légèreté; (chem.) volatilité, *f.*

volatilizable (-til'aïz'a-b'l), *adj.*, volatil; qui peut se volatiliser.

volatilization (-til'aïzé-), *n.*, volatilisation, *f.*

volatilize (-til'aïze), *v.a.*, volatiliser.

volatilize, *v.n.*, se volatiliser.

volcanic, *adj.*, volcanique; volcanisé.

volcanicity, or **volcanism** (-niz'm), *n.*, nature volcanique, *f.*

volcanize (-naïze), *v.a.*, soumettre à une chaleur volcanique.

volcano (-ké-nô), *n.*, volcan, *m.*

vole (vôle), *n.*, vole, *f.*; (mam.) campagnol, *m.*

volery (vol'i-), *n.*, (ant.) volière, *f.*

volitation (vol'i-te-). *n.*, (ant.) action, faculté de voler (of birds—*des oiseaux*), *f.*

volition (vo-lish'eune), *n.*, volition; volonté, *f.*

volitive, *adj.*, (ant.) de la volonté.

volley, *n.*, (of musketry—*de mousqueterie*) décharge, salve; (of cannon—*de canon*) volée; (of abuse—*d'injures*) volée, *f.*, torrent, *m.*; (of blows—*de coups*) volée; (of stones, &c.—*de pierres*, &c.) grêle, *f.*

volley, *v.a.* and *n.*, décharger une volée de coups de canons, de fusils.

volleyed (vol-lide), *adj.*, qui fait explosion.

volt, *n.*, volte, *f.*

volta (-tä), *n.*, (mus.) volta, *f.*

volta-electric, *adj.*, voltaïque, galvanique.

voltaic (-taïke), *adj.*, voltaïque, de Volta.

volubilate, or **volubile** (-liou-), *adj.*, (hort.) volubile, grimpant.

volubility (vol'iou-), *n.*, volubilité; rotation, révolution (of the tongue—*de langue*) volubilité de langue, volubilité, *f.*

voluble (vol'iou-b'l), *adj.*, qui tourne; en rotation; (pers.) qui parle avec volubilité; (of the tongue—*de la langue*) délié; (of speech—*du parler*) facile, abondant.

volubly, *adv.*, avec volubilité.

volume (vol'ieume), *n.*, volume; (spherical

body—*sphère*) globe; (book—*livre*) volume, tome; (of the voice—*de la voix*) volume, *m.*, étendue, *f.*

volumed (vol'ieu'm'de), *adj.*, formé en volume.

voluminous (vo-liou-) *adj.*, volumineux; fécond.

voluminously (vo-liou-), *adv.*, d'une manière volumineuse.

voluminousness (vo-liou-), *n.*, nature volumineuse; étendue, *f.*

voluntarily (vol'eu'n'-), *adv.*, volontairement; spontanément; de bonne volonté.

voluntariness (vol'eu'n'-),*n.*,spontanéité,*f.*

voluntary(vol'eu'n'-), *adj.*,volontaire; spontané; (free—*libre*) libre, indépendant; (done by design—*fait exprès*) volontaire, intentionnel, fait avec intention. — oath; *serment extrajudiciaire, m.*

voluntary, *n.*, (mus.) improvisation, *f.*

volunteer (vol'eu'n'tieur), *n.*, volontaire, *m.*

volunteer (vol'eu'n'tieur), *v.a.*, offrir volontairement.

volunteer, *v.n.*, s'engager comme volontaire; s'offrir.

voluptuary (vo-leupt'iou-), *n.*, voluptueux, épicurien, *m.*

voluptuous (vo-leupt'iou-euss), *adj.*, voluptueux.

voluptuously, *adv.*, voluptueusement.

voluptuousness, *n.*, volupté, *f.*

volutation (vol'iou-té-), *n.*, (ant.) roulement, *m.*

volute (vo-lioute), *n.*, volute, *f.*

voluted, *adj.*, voluté.

volution (vo-liou-), *n.*, spirale, *f.*

volva, *n.*, (bot.) volva, bourse, *f.*

vomic, *adj.*, vomique, *f.*

vomica, *n.*, vomique, *f.*

vomit, *n.*, vomissement; (pharm.) vomitif, *m.*

vomit, *v.a.*, vomir, rendre.

vomit, *v.n.*, vomir.

vomiting, *n.*, vomissement; rejet, *m.*

vomition, *n.*, vomissement, *m.*

vomitive, *or* **vomitory**, *adj.*, vomitif, émétique.

vomitory, *n.*, vomitif, émétique; (ántiq.) vomitoire, *m.*

voracious (vo-ré-sheuss), *adj.*, vorace; dévorant; (of the appetite—*de l'appétit*) dévorant, d'enfer.

voraciously, *adv.*, avec voracité.

voraciousness,*or* **voracity**,*n.*,voracité,*f.*

vortex, *n.* (*vortices*), tourbillon, *m.*

vortical, *adj.*, tournoyant; tourbillonnant; en rond, en tourbillon.

votaress (vô-), *n.*, sectatrice, *f.*

votary, *n.*, sectateur; adorateur; zélateur; amateur; partisan, *m.*

votary (vô-), *adj.*, votif.

vote (vôte), *n.*, vote, *m.*; voix; opinion, *f.*; suffrage, *m.*; décision, résolution, *f.*; (ticket—*bulletin*) bulletin, *m.*; (ballot—*boule*) boule, *f.*

vote (vôte), *v.a.*, voter; élire.

vote, *v.n.*, voter.

voter (vôt'-), *n.*, votant, *m.*

voting, *n.*, scrutin, *m.*

votive (vô-), *adj.*, voué, votif.

vouch (vaoutshe), *v.a.*, prendre à témoin, attester; (to affirm—*affirmer*) garantir, affirmer; attester; (to confirm—*confirmer*) attester, prouver; (jur.) appeler en garantie.

vouch, *v.n.*, témoigner, répondre, garantir.

vouchee (vaoutsh'i), *n.*, caution, *f.*, appelé en garantie, *m.*

voucher (vaoutsh'-), *n.*, garant, *m.*; (document) garantie, preuve, *f.*, titre, *m.*; (jur.) demande en garantie, *f.*

vouchor (vaoutsh'-), *n.*, (jur.) demandeur en garantie, *m.*, demanderesse en garantie, *f.*

vouchsafe (vaoutsh'séfe), *v.a.*, permettre; daigner accorder.

vouchsafe, *v.n.*, daigner; condescendre.

vouchsafement, *n.*, don, *m.*; faveur, *f.*

voussoir (vou-çoir), *n.*, voussoir, *m.*

vow (vaou), *n.*, vœu, *m.*

vow (vaou), *v.a.*, vouer, dévouer, consacrer.

vow, *v.n.*, faire un vœu, faire vœu, faire des vœux; jurer, protester.

vowel (vaou'èl), *n.*, voyelle, *f.*

voweled (vaou'èlde), *adj.*, formé de voyelles.

vower (vaou'eur), *n.*, personne qui fait un vœu, *f.*

voyage (voi-yédje-), *n.*, voyage par mer, *m.*; traversée, *f.* Outward —; *voyage d'aller.* Home —; *voyage de retour.* On a —; *en voyage.*

voyage (voi-yédje), *v.n.*, voyager par mer; faire un voyage par mer.

voyage, *v.a.*, traverser, parcourir.

voyager, *n.*, voyageur, *m.*, voyageuse, *f.*

voyol (voi-yol), *n.*, (nav.) tournevire, *f.*

vulgar (veul-), *n.*, bas peuple, vulgaire, *m.*

vulgar (veul-), *adj.*, vulgaire, commun, du peuple.

vulgarism (-veul-gar'iz'm), *n.*, vulgarité; expression vulgaire, *f.*

vulgarity (veul-), *n.*, vulgarité, *f.*; mauvais ton, mauvais goût, *m.*; (mean condition—*basse condition*) bassesse, nature vulgaire, condition vulgaire, *f.*

vulgarize (-'aïze), *v.a.*, populariser, vulgariser.

vulgarly, *adv.*, vulgairement; avec mauvais goût, avec mauvais ton; (meanly—*misérablement*) bassement.

vulgate (veul-), *n.*, Vulgate, *f.*

vulnerable (veul'nèr'a-b'l), *adj.*, vulnérable, que l'on peut blesser.

vulnerary (veul-nèr'-), *adj.*, vulnéraire.

vulnerary,*n.*, (med.) vulnéraire, *m.*

vulpine (veul-païne), *adj.*, de renard; rusé.

vulture (veult'ieur), *n.*, (orni.) vautour, *m.*

vulturine, vulturish, *or* **vulturous** (veult'ieur'aïne, -ish, -euss), *adj.*, de vautour; rapace.

W

w, vingt-troisième lettre de l'alphabet, w, *m.*

wabble (wôb'b'l), *v.n.*, vaciller, branler; aller en zigzag.

wacke (wake), *n.*, (min.) wacke, wake, *f.*

wad (wode), *n.*, bourre (for fire-arms—*d'arme à feu*); (little bundle—*petit paquet*) touffe, *f.*, paquet, *m.*

wad (wode), *v.a.*, (fire-arms—*armes à feu*) bourrer; (a garment—*un vêtement*) garnir d'ouate, ouater.

wadded (wod'dède), *adj.*, ouaté.

wadding (wod'-), *n.*, ouate; (of fire-arms—*d'armes à feu*) bourre, *f.*

waddle (wod'd'l), *v.n.*, se dandiner, se balancer; se tortiller; marcher en se tortillant; vaciller.

waddling (wod'd'l'-), *n.*, dandinement; tortillement, *m.*

waddlingly, *adv.*, en se dandinant, en se tortillant, en se balançant.

wade, *v.a.*, traverser à gué, passer à gué.

wade, *v.n.*, marcher dans l'eau, dans la vase dans le sable, &c.; passer à gué; (to move with difficulty—*se mouvoir avec peine*)se traîner,avancer péniblement. To — through; *traverser, passer; marcher dans; (fig.) examiner laborieusement, venir à bout de.*

wader (wéd'-), *or* **wading bird** (-beurde), *n.*, (orni.) échassier, *m.*

wad-hook (-houke), *n.*, (artil.) tire-bourre, *m.*

wafer (wé-), *n.*, pain à cacheter, *m.* ; (c.rel.) hostie ; (cake—*gâteau*) oublie, gaufre, *f.*

wafer (wé-), *v.a.*, mettre un pain à cacheter à, cacheter.

waffle (wof'f'l), *n.*, gaufre, *f.* — -iron ; *gaufrier, m.*

waft (wâfte), *n.*, corps flottant ; (signal) signal, *m.*

waft (wâfte), *v.a.*, porter, transporter, diriger à travers l'eau ou l'air ; faire flotter ; lancer.

waft, *v.n.*, flotter dans l'air, sur l'eau.

wag, *n.*, badin, plaisant, farceur, *m.*

wag, *v.a.*, branler, remuer ; mouvoir.

wag, *v.n.*, remuer, se mouvoir, bouger, branler ; (to pack off—*partir*) décamper, déguerpir, partir.

wage (wédje), *v.a.*, (war—*guerre*) faire, soutenir.

wager (wédj'-), *n.*, gageure, *f.* ; pari ; gage, sujet, *m.* To lay a — ; *faire un pari, faire une gageure* ; *gager. parler.*

wager (wédj'-), *v.a.*, gager, parier.

wagerer (wédj'-), *n.*, parieur, gageur, *m.*

wages (wé'djze), *n. pl.*, (of servants—*de domestiques*) gages, *m. pl.* ; (of workmen—*d'ouvriers*) salaire, *m.*, paye, *f.* ; (fig.) salaire, prix, *m.*

waggery (wag'gheur'i), *n.*, espièglerie ; plaisanterie, malice, *f.*

wagging (wag'ghigne), *n.*, remuement, branlement, *m.*

waggish (wag-ghish), *adj.*, badin, malin, espiègle ; (of things—*des choses*) d'espiègle. — -trick ; *espièglerie, plaisanterie, farce, f.* ; *tour d'espiègle, m.*

waggishly, *adv.*, plaisamment ; avec espièglerie, d'une manière badine, pour badiner.

waggishness, *n.*, espièglerie, malice, plaisanterie, farce, *f.*

waggle (wag'g'l), *v.n.*, frétiller, se remuer, remuer.

waggle, *v.a.*, remuer.

waggon, *or* **wagon** (wag-gheune), *n.*, charrette, *f.* ; chariot ; wagon ; (milit.) caisson, fourgon, *m.*

waggon, *v.a.*, charrier, charroyer, voiturer.

waggonage (-'édje), *n.*, prix de roulage, *m.*

waggoner, *n.*, roulier, voiturier, *m.*

waggoning, *n.*, charriage ; roulage (transport), *m.*

waggon-train (-tré'n), *n.sing.*, équipages du train, *m.pl.*

wagtail (-téle), *n.*, hochequeue, *m.*, bergeronnette, *f.*

waif (wéfe), *n.*, épave, *f.*

wail (wéle), *v.a.*, déplorer, pleurer, gémir de.

wail, *v.n.*, pleurer, gémir, se lamenter.

wail, *or* **wailing**, *n.*, lamentation, plainte, *f.*, gémissement, *m.*

wailful (-foule), *adj.*, plaintif, douloureux, triste.

wain (wé'n), *n.*, chariot. (astron.)' Charles's — ; *grand Chariot, m., grande Ourse, f.*

wain-bote (-bôte), *n.*, bois de charronnage, *m.*

wainscot (wé'n'scote), *n.*, boiserie, *f.*, lambris, *m.*

wainscot, *v.a.*, lambrisser, boiser.

wainscoting, *n.*, lambrissage ; (material—*natiere*) bois de lambris, *m.*

waist (wéste), *n.*, ceinture, taille, *f.* ; milieu du corps, *m.* ; (nav.) coursive, *f.*

waistband, *n.*, ceinture (of trousers, &c.—*le pantalon, &c.*), *f.*

waistcoat (-côte), *n.*, gilet, *m.*

waistcoating (-côt'-), *n.*, étoffe pour gilets, *f.*

wait (wéte), *n.*, embûche, *f.* ; embûches, *f.pl.* ; guet-apens, piège, *m.* To lie in — ; *être, se tenir en embuscade ; être à l'affût.* To lay — for ; *dresser des embûches à, tendre un guet-apens à.*

wait (wéte), *v.n.*, attendre ; (at table, &c.—*à table, &c.*) servir. To' keep —ing ; *faire attendre.* To — for ; *attendre, attendre après* ; (to watch—*épier*) guetter, surveiller. To — on, upon ; (of servants, &c.—*de domestiques, &c.*) servir ; (to call upon—*faire une visite*) aller chez, se rendre chez, auprès de ; *faire une visite à, rendre visite à, visiter* ; *rendre ses devoirs à* ; (to accompany—*accompagner*) accompagner, suivre.

wait, *v.a.*, attendre.

waiter, *n.*, garçon (of public-house, coffeehouse—*de cabaret, de café*) ; domestique ; (tray—*plateau*) plateau, *m.* Dumb- —; *servante, f.*

waiting, *n.*, attente, *f.* ; (attendance—*service*) service, *m.* In — ; (in attendance—*de service*) de service. Lady in — ; *dame d'honneur, f.*

waiting-maid (-méde), *n.*, femme de chambre, *f.*

waiting-room (-roume), *n.*, salle d'attente, *f.*

waiting-woman (-woum'-), *n.*, femme de chambre ; camériste, *f.*

waitress, *n.*, fille (d'hôtel, &c.), *f.*

waits (wétse), *n.pl.*, musiciens ambulants qui donnent des sérénades à Noël, *m.pl.*

waive (wéve), *v.a.*, (to put off—*différer*) écarter, éloigner ; (to relinquish—*abandonner*) abandonner, se désister de, retirer.

wake, *n.*, veille, *f.* ; (nav.) sillage, *m.*, eaux, *f.pl.*

wake, *v.a.*, éveiller, réveiller.

wake, *v.n.*, (to sit up—*ne pas se coucher*) veiller ; (from sleep—*s'éveiller*) s'éveiller, se réveiller.

wakeful (-foule), *adj.*, éveillé ; (vigilant) vigilant.

wakefully, *adv.*, sans dormir ; avec vigilance.

wakefulness, *n.*, insomnie ; veille, *f.*

waken (wék'n), *v.a.*, éveiller, réveiller.

waken, *v.n.*, s'éveiller, se réveiller.

wakener (wék-n'eur), *n.*, personne qui réveille, *f.*

waker (wék'-), *n.*, personne qui veille ; (one who rouses from sleep—*celui qui éveille*) personne qui réveille, *f.*

waking (wék'-), *n.*, veille, *f.* ; état de veille, *m.*

waking, *adj.*, éveillé, qui ne dort pas.

wale, *n.*, raie, marque ; (of cloth—*du drap*) côte ; (nav.) préceinte, lisse,' *f.*

walk, *n.*, marche ; (for pleasure—*plaisir*) promenade, *f.*, tour, *m.* ; (place—*lieu*) promenade, *f.*, promenoir, *m.* ; (path—*allée*) allée, avenue ; (for business—*d'affaire*) course ; (gait—*allure*) démarche, *f.*, marcher, *m.* ; (of a horse—*du cheval*) pas, *m.*, allure, *f.* ; (fig.) voie, carrière, *f.*, chemin, *m.* To go out for a — ; *aller se promener, aller à la promenade.* To take a — ; *faire une promenade, un tour.* To take out for a — ; *mener promener.*

walk (wôke), *v.n.*, marcher ; (not to ride—*faire la route à pied*) aller à pied ; (for pleasure —*pour le plaisir*) se promener ; (of a horse—*du cheval*) aller au pas, marcher. To — after ; *suivre.* To — down ; *descendre.* To — into ; *entrer dans.* To — in ; *entrer.* To ask, to beg to — in ; *faire entrer.* To — off, away ; *s'en aller, s'éloigner, partir, décamper.* To — out ; *sortir ; se promener.* To ask, to desire to — out ; *faire sortir.* To — up ; *monter.* To ask, to beg to — up ; *faire monter.* To — up and down ; *se promener en long et en large.* To — the rounds ; *faire la ronde.*

walk, *v.a.*, marcher dans, parcourir, courir, traverser à pied ; (any distance—*une distance*) faire à pied ; (a horse—*un cheval*) mettre au pas, faire aller au pas.

walker, *n.*, marcheur, *m.* ; marcheuse, *f.* ; piéton ; promeneur, *m.*, promeneuse, *f.*

walking, *n.*, marche ; promenade. *f.*
walking-place, *n.*, promenade, *f.* ; promenoir, *m.*
walking-staff (-stâfe), *or* **walking-stick**, *n.*, boî rdon, bâton, *m.* ; canne, *f.*
wall (wôl), *n.*, muraille, *f.* ; mur ; (rampart —*rempart*) mur, *m.*, muraille, *f.*, rempart, *m.* Party— — ; *mur mitoyen.* Within the —s ; *dans l'enceinte des murs, intra-muros.* To give the — ; *céder le haut du pavé à.*
wall, *v.a.*, murer, entourer de murs.
wall-creeper (-crip'-), *n.*, (orni.) grimpereau, *m.*
wallet (wôl-), *n.*, sac, havresac ; bissac, *m.*, besace, *f.*
wall-eye (-a'ye), *n.*, glaucome ; (vet.) œil vairon, *m.*
wall-eyed (-a'ye-de), *adj.*, (of horses—*des chevaux*) qui a l'œil vairon.
wall-flower (-fla'weur), *n.*, giroflée jaune, ravenelle, *f.* ; violier, *m.*
wall-fruit (-froute), *n.*, fruit d'espalier, *m.*
walling, *n.*, maçonnerie de murs, *f.* ; murs, *m.pl.*, murailles, *f.pl.*
walloon (wal'louhe), *n.*, Wallon, *m.* Wallonne, *f.*
walloon, *adj.*, wallon.
walloon, *n.*, wallon (language—*langue*), *m.*
wallop (wol-lope), *v.n.*, bouillir, bouillonner.
wallop, *v.a.*, rosser, tanner la peau à, le cuir à.
walloping, *n.*, rossée, volée de coups, roulée, *f.*
wallow (wôl-lô), *v.n.*, se vautrer, se rouler ; croupir. To — in ; *se vautrer dans, se rouler dans.*
wallow, *v.a.*, rouler.
wallow (wôl-lô), *n.*, dandinement, balancement, *m.*
wallower, *n.*, créature qui se roule, qui se vautre ; (wheel—*roue*) lanterne, *f.*
wall-plate, *n.*, sablière, *f.*
wall-sided (-saïd'-), *adj.*, aux côtés perpendiculaires.
wall-tree (-trî), *n.*, espalier, *m.*
wall-wort (-weurte), *n.* V. **pellitory**.
walnut (wol-neute), *n.*, noix, *f.* ; (tree, wood —*arbre, bois*) noyer, *m.*
walnut-peel (-pile), *n.*, brou de noix, *m.*
walnut-tree (-trî), *n.*, (bot.) noyer, *m.*
walrus (wol-), *n.*, (mam.) morse, cheval marin, *m.*, vache marine, *f.*
waltz (wôltz), *n.*, valse, *f.*
waltz (wôltz), *v.n.*, valser.
waltzer, *n.*, valseur, *m.*, valseuse, *f.*
waltzing, *n.*, valse, *f.*
wamble (wo'm'b'l), *v.n.*, se soulever. My stomach —s ; *le cœur me soulève, j'ai des nausées.*
wambling, *n.*, soulèvement de cœur, *m.*
wan (wô'n), *adj.*, blème, pâle ; blafard.
wand (wô'n'de), *n.*, baguette ; verge, *f.* ; (staff—*bâton*) bâton, *m.* Mercury's — ; *caducée, m.*
wander (wô'n'd'-), *v.n.*, errer, rôder, vaguer ; s'égarer ; (in mind—*en esprit*) divaguer ; (to be delirious—*être en délire*) avoir le délire. To — about ; *errer dans, parcourir ; errer partout, courir de tous côtés.* To — from ; *s'écarter de, s'éloigner de, sortir de; quitter.* To — over ; *errer dans.*
wander, *v.a.*, errer, voyager dans ; parcourir.
wanderer, *n.*, personne qui s'écarte, qui s'éloigne qui quitte, *f.* ; rôdeur, vagabond, *m.*, vagabonde, *f.* ; transgresseur, *m.*
wandering, *n.*, course, course vagabonde, *f.* ; voyage ; (in mind—*d'esprit*) égarement, *m.*, distraction, divagation, *f.* ; (deviation) écart, *m.*, divagation, *f.* ; (delirium—*délire*) délire, *m.*
wandering, *adj.*, errant, va :abond ; distrait.
wanderingly, *adv.*, d'une manière errante ; d'une manière distraite ; en rôdant.

wane (wé'n), *n.*, déclin ; décours, *m.* ; décadence, décroissance, *f.* On the — ; *en décroissance. en déclin* ; (fig.) *sur le retour.*
wane (wé'n), *v.n.*, décroître, diminuer ; décliner, s'altérer, baisser, s'affaiblir.
wanly (wô'n'-), *adv.*, avec pâleur.
wanness (wô'n'nèce), *n.*, pâleur, *f.* ; teint blême, *m.*
wannish (wô'n'-), *adj.*, pâlot, un peu hâve, un peu terne.
want (wô'n'te), *n.*, besoin, *m.* ; nécessité, *f.* ; (lack—*manque*) manque, défaut ; (poverty—*pauvreté*) besoin, dénûment, *m.*, misère, *f.* To be, to stand in — of ; *avoir besoin de ; (not to have— n'avoir pas) manquer de.* For — of ; *faute de, manque de, à défaut de.* In —; *dans le besoin, dans la misère.* I have no — of it ; *je n'en ai pas besoin.*
want (wô'n'te), *v.a.*, avoir besoin de ; (not to have—*n'avoir pas*) manquer de, être dépourvu de, être dénué de ; (pers.) demander, avoir besoin de ; (to wish for—*vouloir*) désirer, vouloir, demander, avoir envie de. —ed a . . ; *on demande un . . , on a besoin d'un . .* You are —ed ; *on vous demande.* I —you; *j'ai besoin de vous.* What do you — of me? *que me voulez-vous? que désirez-vous, que voulez-vous de moi?* You shall — nothing; *vous ne manquerez de rien.* I sadly —; *j'ai grand besoin de.* A thing much —ed ; *une chose dont on a grand besoin.*
want, *v.n.*, manquer ; (to wish—*vouloir*) vouloir, désirer. It —s ; (it requires—*exige*) *il faut* ; (it is short of—*il manque*) *il manque, il s'en faut de.* It —s ten minutes to one; *il est une heure moins dix minutes.* To be —ing; *manquer.* Two spoons are —ing; *il manque deux cuillers.* To be —ing in ; (to fail —*manquer*) *manquer à, de* ; (to be without—*être sans*) *manquer de.* There —s a leaf ; *il manque un feuillet.* There —s but little; *peu s'en faut, il s'en faut peu.* I — you to do . . . ; *je désire que vous fassiez.*
wanting, *adj.*, qui manque.
wantless, *adj.*, sans besoin ; riche.
wanton (wô'n'teune), *adj.*, (playful—*folâtre*) badin, folâtre, follet ; (floating—*flottant*) flottant, qui flotte au gré du vent ; (wicked—*méchant*) méchant, fait par malice, par méchanceté ; (of the tongue—*de la langue*) indiscret, sans frein ; (unchaste—*libertin*) déréglé, licencieux, libertin, lascif, dissolu ; (luxuriant) exubérant, luxuriant.
wanton (wô'n'teune), *n.*, libertin, *m.*, libertine, *f.* ; débauché, *m.* ; personne efféminée, personne frivole, *f.*
wanton (wô'n'teune), *v.n.*, flotter au gré du vent ; folâtrer, s'ébattre ; se jouer, se réjouir, badiner ; faire le libertin.
wantonly, *adv.*, de gaîté de cœur ; en folâtrant, par malice, par un mauvais badinage ; d'une manière déréglée ; licencieusement ; par libertinage.
war (wore), *n.*, guerre, *f.* Sea— — ; *guerre maritime.* At — ; *en guerre.* To inure to —; *aguerrir.* Inured to —; *aguerri.* To declare — against ; *déclarer la guerre à.* — to the knife ; *guerre à mort.* Articles of — ; *Code pénal militaire, m. sing.*
war (wore), *v.n.*, faire la guerre ; combattre ; lutter.
warble (wor'b'l), *v.n.*, gazouiller, chanter ; résonner.
warble, *v.a.*, chanter, moduler.
warble, *n.* V. **warbling**.
warbler, *n.*, (orni.) chanteur, chantre, oiseau chanteur, *m.*
warbles (worb'l'ze), *n.pl.*, (vet.) foulure, *f.* ; tumeurs, piqûres, *f.pl.*
warbling (wor-), *n.*, ramage, gazouillement ; chant, *m.*
warbling, *adj.*, harmonieux, mélodieux.
warblingly, *adv.*, mélodieusement.

war-cry (wor-cra-ye), *or* **war-whoop** (-houpe). *n..* cri de guerre, *m.*

ward (worde), *n.*, (minor—*mineur*) pupille.*m.f.*; (guardianship—*tutelle*) tutelle; (fenc.) act of guarding; of a lock—*garde*) garde; (of hospitals—*d'hôpital*) salle, *f.*; (of a town—*de ville*) quartier, *m.*

ward, *v.n.*, être sur ses gardes; parer les coups.

ward (worde), *v.a.*, parer, éviter; écarter.

warden (word'n), *n.*, gardien; gouverneur; garde; directeur; recteur, *m.*

wardenship, *n.*, place de gardien, de directeur, *f.*; office de gouverneur, de directeur, etc.,*m.*

warder, *n.*, garde; gouverneur; gardien, *m.*

wardmote (-môte), *n.*, conseil d'arrondissement, *m.*

wardrobe (-rôbe), *n.*, garde-robe, armoire, *f.*

ward-room (-roume), *n.*, (nav.) carré des officiers, *m.*

wardship, *n.*, tutelle; minorité, *f.*

ware (wére), *n.*, marchandise, *f.*; produit, *m.* China- —; *porcelaine, f.* Small —s; *petits objets, m.pl.*

ware (wére), *v.a.*, (nav.) faire virer.

warehouse (-haouce), *n.*, magasin, *m.* Bonded —; *entrepôt de douane, m.* Italian —; *magasin de comestibles.*

warehouse (-haouce), *v.a.*, emmagasiner, mettre en magasin; (at the custom-house—*douanes*) entreposer.

warehouse-keeper (-kîp-), *n.*, entreposeur, *m.*

warehouse-man,*n.*,garde-magasin; (owner of a warehouse—*possesseur d'un magasin*) marchand en gros, *m.*

warehouse-rent, *n.*,magasinage; loyer, *m.*

warehousing, *n.*, emmagasinage; magasinage; (at the custom-house—*douanes*) entrepôt, *m.*

warfare (wor-fére), *n.*, vie militaire; guerre; lutte, *f.*; combats, *m.pl.*

war-horse, *n.*, cheval de bataille, *m.*

warily (wé-), *adv.*, prudemment, sagement, avec précaution.

wariness (wé-), *n.*, prudence, circonspection, *f.*

warlike (wor-laïke), *adj.*, militaire, guerrier, martial, belliqueux.

warlikeness, *n.*, caractère belliqueux, *m.*

warm (worme),*adj.*,chaud; (fig.) zélé, ardent, passionné, vif, animé. To be —; (pers.) *avoir chaud*; (of the weather—*du temps*) *faire chaud.* It is very —; *il fait très-chaud.* — work· *rude, forte, chaude besogne.* To get —; *chauffer, se réchauffer; commencer à faire chaud; s'échauffer; s'animer.* To make —; *chauffer, réchauffer.*

warm (worme), *v.a.*, chauffer; échauffer; réchauffer. To — again, up; *réchauffer.*

warm, *v.n.*,chauffer, réchauffer; se chauffer, se réchauffer.

warming,*n.*, action de chauffer, de s'échauffer, *f.* To give a — to; *chauffer.*

warming-pan, *n.*, bassinoire, *f.*

warmly, *adv.*, chaudement; ardemment, avec zèle, passionnément, vivement.

warmness, *or* **warmth** (worm'th), *n.*, chaleur; (fig.) ardeur, chaleur, vivacité, *f.*

warn (worne), *v.a.*, avertir; prévenir; faire savoir, notifier. To — against; *prémunir contre précautionner contre, mettre sur ses gardes contre.*

warner (worn'-),· *n.*, personne qui avertit, &c.,*f.*

warning, *n.*, avis, avertissement; (to leave —*de déménager*) congé, *m.*

war-office (wor-), *n.*, bureaux du ministère de la guerre, *m.pl.*; ministère de la guerre, *m.*

warp (worpe), *n.*, (weaving—*tissage*) chaîne, *f.*; (nav.) grelin, *m..* touée, *f.*

warp (worpe), *v.a.*, (in weaving—*tissage*) ourdir; (wood—*bois*) faire déjeter, tourmenter, travailler; (nav.) touer; (arch.) gauchir; (to influence—*influencer*) influencer; (to pervert—*fausser*) fausser, pervertir.

warp, *v.n.*, se cambrer, se déjeter; plier; se tourmenter;(to deviate—*dévier*)dévier;vaciller; (nav.) se touer.

warper, *n.*, ourdisseur. *m.*

warping, *n.*, (in weaving—*tissage*) ourdissage, *m*; (of wood—*du bois*) cambrure. *f.*

warping-mill, *n.*, machine à ourdir. *f.*

warrant (wôr'-), *n.*, autorisation, autorité, *f.*; ordre, pouvoir, mandat, *m.*; garantie; justification, *f.*; garant; (for payment—*de payement*) mandat, *m.*; (to arrest—*d'arrêt*) mandat d'amener, mandat d'arrêt, *m.* Death- —; *ordre d'exécution.* Search- —; *mandat de perquisition.* — of attorney; *procuration, f.* — officer; (nav.) *officier breveté, m.*

warrant (wor'-), *v.a.*, garantir; certifier, attester, assurer; autoriser; justifier; (to secure —*garantir*) garantir, défendre, mettre à l'abri; (com.) garantir.

warrantable (-'a-b'l), *adj.*, justifiable, autorisé, légitime.

warrantableness, *n.*, caractère justifiable, *m.*; légitimité, *f.*

warrantably, *adv.*, d'une manière justifiable, légitimement.

warrantee (wor'ra'n'ti), *n.*, (jur.)garanti, *m.*

warranter, *or* **warrantor**, *n.*, garant, *m.*; caution; personne qui autorise, qui donne pouvoir, *f.*; (jur.) mandant, commettant, *m.*

warranting, *n.*, action de garantir, *f.*

warranty (wor'-), *n.*, garantie; sûreté; autorisation, *f.*; pouvoir; cautionnement, *m.*

warranty, *v.a.*, garantir.

warren (wor'-), *n.*, garenne, *f.*

warrener (wor'rè'n'-), *n.*, garennier, *m.*

warrior (wor'rieur), *n.*, guerrier, militaire, soldat, *m.*

wart (worte), *n.*, verrue, *f.*; poireau; *m.*; (bot.) excroissance, *f.*

wart-cress, *n.*, (bot.) sénebière, corne-de-cerf, *f.*, coronope, *m.*

warted (wort'-), *adj.*, (bot.) verruqueux.

wartwort (wort'weurte), *n.*, verrucaire, *f.*

warty (wort'-), *adj.*, plein de verrues; verruqueux; comme une verrue.

wary (wé-), *adj.*, avisé, sage, prévoyant; prudent.

wash (woshe), *n.*, (of linen—*du linge*) blanchissage, savonnage, *m.*; lessive, *f.*, lavage, (paint.) lavis, *m.*; (med.) lotion, eau; (slight layer—*couche*) couche légère, *f.*, enduit, *m.*; (dirty water—*eau sale*) lavure, eau de vaisselle; (distilleries) liqueur à distiller, *f*; (of an oar—*d'une rame*) plat, *m.*, pale, *f.*; (of the sea—*de la mer*) battement de la mer, *m.*

wash (woshe), *v.a.*, laver; (to bathe—*baigner*) mouiller, baigner, arroser; (in lye—*à la lessive*) lessiver; (linen—*de linge*) blanchir, savonner; (a horse—*un cheval*) guéer; (paint) laver. To — one's hands; *se laver les mains.* To — clean; *laver bien.* To — away, off; *enlever en lavant, nettoyer, laver, effacer;* (to carry away—*entraîner*) *enlever, emporter, entraîner;* (a stain—*une tache*) *enlever.* To —up; *laver;* (on shore—*sur la plage*) *rejeter.* To —over with gold; *dorer.*

wash, *v.n.*, se laver; se baigner; (of a washer-woman, &c.—*d'une blanchisseuse, &c.*) blanchir, savonner. To — for any one; *blanchir quelqu'un.* To — off; *disparaître, déteindre, s'effacer à l'eau.* That stuff —es; *cette étoffe se lave.*

wash-ball (-bôl), *n.*, savonnette, *f.*

wash-board (-bôrde), *n.*, (carp.) plinthe; (nav.) falque, *f.*

washer, *n.*, laveur, *m.*, laveuse, *f.*

35 *

washerman, *n.*, blanchisseur, *m.*
washerwoman, *n.*, blanchisseuse; buandière, *f.*
wash-hand-basin (-bés'n), *n.*, cuvette, *f.*
wash-hand-stand, *n.*, lavabo, *m.*
wash-house (-haouce), *n.*, lavoir, *m.*; buanderie, *f.*
washing, *n.*, blanchissage, lavage; arrosement, *m.*; (in lye—*à la lessive*) lessive; (pers.) ablution; (med.) lotion, *f.*
washing-machine (-ma-shîne), *n.*, machine à blanchir, *f.*
wash-leather (-lèth'-), *n.*, peau de chamois, *f.*
wash-stand, *n.*, lavabo, *m.*
washy (wosh'i), *adj.*, flasque; humide, mouillé; faible.
wasp (wospe), *n.*, (ent.) guêpe, *f.*
wasp-fly (-fla'ye), *n.*, (ent.) mouche-guêpe, *f.*
waspish (wosp'-), *adj.*, bourru; irascible, irritable; piquant.
waspishly, *adv.*, avec irritation; d'une manière piquante.
waspishness, *n.*, humeur bourrue, irritabilité, *f.*
wassail (wos's'l), *n.*, wassail (liqueur), *m.*; (drunken bout—*orgie*) partie de débauche, bombance, orgie, ribote; (song—*chanson*) chanson joyeuse, *f.*
wassail (wos's'l), *v.n.*, faire bombance, faire des orgies.
wassailer, *n.*, buveur, riboteur, ivrogne, *m.*
waste (wéste), *n.*, perte, *f.*; déchet; (extravagance) gaspillage, *m.*, perte, prodigalité; (useless expense—*dépense inutile*) dépense inutile, *f.*; (jur.) dégât, *m.*, dégradation, *f.*; (land—*terre*) désert, *m.*, terre inculte, terre en friche, solitude, *f.*; (tech.) trop-plein; (print.) défet, *m.*
waste (wéste), *adj.*, inutile, mauvais, de rebut, sans valeur; (ruined—*dévasté*) ruiné, ravagé, dévasté; (not used—*non employé*) non employé, perdu; (of land—*de terre*) inculte, en friche. — paper; *papier de rebut, m.*; (print.) maculature, *f.* To lay —; *ravager, dévaster, ruiner.*
waste (wéste), *v.a.*, (to squander—*dissiper*) gaspiller, perdre, prodiguer, dissiper; (to exhaust—*épuiser*) consumer, user, épuiser; (to spoil—*détériorer*) gâter, détériorer, dégrader; (to ruin—*dévaster*) ravager, dévaster, ruiner; (time—*le temps*) perdre; (com.) donner un déchet de.
waste, *v.n.*, s'user, se consumer, s'épuiser, dépérir; se dissiper, se perdre; (com.) produire du déchet. To -- away; *dépérir, se consumer.*
waste-book (-bouke), *n.*, brouillard, mémorial, *m.*
wasted, *adj.*, dépensé sans nécessité; gaspillé, perdu, prodigué; (diminished—*amoindri*) diminué; (exhausted—*épuisé*) épuisé.
wasteful (-foule), *adj.*, dissipateur, prodigue; ruineux, en pure perte, inutile; dévastateur.
wastefully, *adv.*, prodigalement; en pure perte, inutilement.
wastefulness, *n.*, dissipation, prodigalité, perte, *f.*; gaspillage, *m.*
wasteness, *n.*, désert, *m.*; solitude, *f.*
waste-pipe (-païpe), *n.*, tuyau de trop-plein, *m.*
waster (wést'-), *n*, dissipateur, *m.*, dissipatrice, *f.*; gaspilleur, *m.*, gaspilleuse, *f.*; prodigue, *m.*, *f.*; (thing—*chose*) chose qui use, qui épuise, chose qui ravage, qui dévaste, *f.*
waste-weir (-wère), *n.*, déversoir de superficie, *m.*
wasting (wést'-), *adj.*, qui use, qui épuise, qui détruit.
watch (wotshe), *n.*, montre; *f.* attendance

---

without sleep—*reille de nuit*) veille; (attention) attention, garde, vigilance, surveillance; (sentry —*factionnaire*) sentinelle, *f.*, garde, *m.*; (milit.) garde; (guard—*soldats de service*) garde, *f.*, poste, guet; (nav.) quart, *m.* By my —; *à ma montre.* To be upon the —; *être, se tenir, sur ses gardes, être à l'affût, être aux aguets, avoir l'œil au guet*; (nav.) *être de quart*; (milit.) *être de garde, monter la garde.* To be upon the — for; *guetter, épier.* To keep —; *avoir l'œil au guet.* To keep good —; *faire bonne garde.* To lie on the — for; *être à l'affût de; être aux aguets pour.* Bill of —; (nav.) *rôle de quart, m.*
watch (wotshe), *v.n.*, (not to sleep—*ne pas dormir*) veiller; (to be attentive—*veiller à*) veiller, être attentif, prendre garde, être, se tenir sur ses gardes; (to keep guard—*garder*) veiller, faire le guet, faire la garde; (nav.) faire le quart. To — and ward; *faire le guet.* To — for; *attendre, épier, guetter.* To — over; *veiller, veiller sur, surveiller.* To — with; (an invalid—*un malade*) veiller. *veiller auprès de, garder.*
watch, *v.a.*, veiller sur, veiller, surveiller, prendre garde à; guetter, épier, attendre.
watch-bill, *n.*, (nav.) rôle de quart, *m.*
watch-box, *n.*, guérite, *f.*
watch-case (-kéce), *n.*, boîte de montre, *f.* — -maker; *boîtier, monteur de boîtes, m.*
watch-coat (-côte), *n.*, (milit.) capote, *f.*
watch-dog, *n.*, chien de garde, *m.*
watcher (wotsh'-), *n.*, surveillant, inspecteur, *m.*; (to an invalid—*de malade*) garde, garde-malade, *m.*, *f.*, veilleur; (nav.) guetteur, *m.*
watch-fire (-fæur), *n.*, feu de bivouac, *m.*
watchful (-foule), *adj.*, soigneux, vigilant, attentif.
watchfully, *adv.*, vigilamment, attentivement.
watchfulness, *n.*, vigilance; (want of sleep—*défaut de sommeil*) insomnie, privation de sommeil, *f.*, veilles, *f.pl.*; (over a person—*de quelqu'un*) surveillance, *f.*
watch-glass (-glâce), *n.*, verre de montre; (nav.) sablier de quart, *m.*
watch-guard (-gârde), *n.*, chaîne de sûreté, chaîne de montre, *f.*
watch-house (-haouce), *n.*, corps de garde, *m.*
watching (wotsh'-), *n.*, veille, insomnie, *f.*
watch-light (-laïte), *n.*, veilleuse, *f.*
watch-maker, *n.*, horloger, *m.*
watch-making (-mék'-), *n.*, horlogerie, *f.*
watchman, *n.*, homme de guet, garde, *m.*; sentinelle, *f.*; gardien de nuit, *m.*
watch-stand, *n.*, porte-montre, *m.*
watch-tower (-ta'weur), *n.*, tour d'observation; guérite, *f.*
watch-word (-weurde), *n.*, mot d'ordre, *m.*
watch-work (-weurke), *n.*, (horl.) mouvement.
water (wo-), *n.*, eau; (tide—*marée*) marée; (of diamonds—*des diamants*) eau, *f.*, lustre; (class—*classe*) ordre, *m.*, volée; (urine) eau, urine, *f.* Fresh —; *eau fraîche*; (not salt—*non salée*) *eau douce.* Salt- —; *eau salée, eau de mer.* Sea- —; *eau de mer.* Spring- —; *eau de source.* Hard —; *eau crue, dure.* Holy- —; *eau bénite.* High- —; *haute marée, haute mer.* Low- —; *eau basse, mer basse.* It is high- —, low- —; *la marée est haute, basse.* To take in fresh —; *faire de l'eau.* To be of the first —; (of diamonds—*diamants*) *être de première eau*; (fig.) *être de la plus haute volée, du premier rang.* — on the chest, in the head; *une hydropisie de poitrine, de cerveau, f.* To be in hot —; *être en querelle*; (in trouble—*embarras*) *s'être mis dans l'embarras.* To draw ten feet —; *avoir dix pieds de tirant d'eau.*
water, *v.a.*, arroser; (animal) donner à boire à, abreuver; (stuffs—*étoffes*) moirer.
water (wo-), *v.n.*, (to weep—*verser des larmes*)

pleurer; (to draw water—*puiser de l'eau*) puiser de l'eau; (nav.) faire de l'eau, faire aiguade. That makes my mouth —; *cela me fait venir l'eau à la bouche.*

waterage (wo-teur'édje), *n.*, prix du transport par eau; transport par eau, *m.*

water-bailiff (-bé-life), *n.*, officier de la douane chargé de la visite des navires, des marchés à poisson, *m.*

water-bearer(-bèr'), *n.*,(astron.) verseau,*m.*

water-blowing-machine (-blô-igne-mashine), *n.*, trombe, *f.*

water-borne, *adj.*, (nav.) à flot.

water-caltrops, *n.*, (bot.) châtaigne d'eau, macle, macre,*f.*

water-carrier, *n.*, porteur d'eau, *m.*

water-cart (-cârte) *n.*, charrette d'arrosement,*f.*

water-closet (-cloz'-), *n.*, cabinet d'aisances, cabinet, *m.*

water-colour (-keul'leur), *n.*, aquarelle, *f.* — drawing ; *aquarelle, peinture à l'aquarelle, f.*

water-course (-côrse), *n.*, cours d'eau; canal, fossé pour l'écoulement des eaux ; (jur.) droit de puisage, *m.* ; (hydr.) chute d'eau,*f.*

water-cress, *n.*, cresson, *m.*

water-dog, *n.*, barbet, caniche, terre-neuve, *m.*

water-drain (-dré'n), *n.*, canal d'écoulement, *m.*

water-drainage (-'édje), *n.*, écoulement des eaux, *m.*

watered (wo-teurde), *adj.*, arrosé ; (of stuffs —*des étoffes*) moiré, ondé.

water-engine (-è'n'djine), *n.*, machine hydraulique,*f.*

waterer (wo-teur'-), *n.*, personne qui arrose,*f.*

water-fall (-fôl), *n.*, cascade; chute d'eau,*f.*

water-fowl'(-faoul), *n.*, oiseau aquatique, *m.*

water-furrow (-feur'rô), *n.*, rigole d'écoulement,*f.*

water-gall (-gôl), *n.*, trou creusé par un torrent, *m.*

water-gauge, *or* **water-gage** (-ghédje), *n.*, indicateur de la hauteur de l'eau, flotteur ; tube de niveau, *m.* ; échelle,*f.*

water-god, *n.*, dieu aquatique, *m.*

water-gruel (-grou-), *n.*, gruau, *m.*

wateriness (wo-teur'-), *n.*, humidité ; aquosité ; (med.) sérosité,*f.*

watering (wo-teur'-), *n.*, arrosage ; arrosement; approvisionnement d'eau ; (of animals—*des animaux*) abreuvage ; (of stuffs—*des étoffes*) moirage, *m.*; (nav.) action de faire de l'eau,*f.*

watering-engine (-è'n'djine), *n.*, pompe d'arrosement,*f.*

watering-place, *n.*, eaux (lieu où l'on prend les eaux), *f.pl.* ; ville de bains, *f.* ; bains d'eaux minérales, *m.pl* ; ville au bord de la mer, *f.* ; (for animals—*pour les animaux*) abreuvoir, *m.* ; (nav.) aiguade, *f.*

watering-pot, *n.*, arrosoir, *m.*

watering-trough (-trofe), *n.*, auge, *f.*; abreuvoir, *m.*

waterish (wo-teur -), *adj.*, aqueux ; qui ressemble à l'eau.

waterishness,*n.*,sérosité ; nature aqueuse,*f.*

water-level (-lèv'l), *n.*, niveau d'eau, *m.*

water-lily, *n.*, nénuphar, *m.*

water-line (-laïne), *n.*, ligne de flottaison,*f.*

water-logged (-log'de), *adj.*, (nav.) engagé, à moitié engagé dans l'eau; à moitié plein d'eau.

waterman, *n.*, batelier, marinier; (at a ferry —*d'un bac*) passeur, *m.*

water-mark (-mârke), *n.*, niveau des eaux ; (on paper—*du papier*) filigrane, *m.* High, low —; *niveau des hautes eaux, des eaux basses.*

water-marked (-mârk'te), *adj.*, à filigrane.

water-melon (-mèl'-), *n.*, melon d'eau, *m.* ; pastèque,*f.*

water-mill, *n.*, moulin à eau, *m.*

water-plant, *n.*, plante aquatique,*f.*

water-poise (-pwaize), *n.*, hydromètre, *m.*

water-pot, *n.*, pot à eau, *m.*

water-power (-pa'weur), *n.*, force hydraulique,*f.*

water-pressure (-prèsh'eur), *n.*, pression de l'eau,*f.* —-engine ; *presse hydraulique, f.*

water-proof (-proufe), *adj.*, imperméable à l'eau ; à l'épreuve de l'eau.

water-ram, *n.*, bélier hydraulique, *m.*

water-sail (-séle), *n.*, (nav.) bonnette.*f.*

water-shoot (wo-teur-shoute), *n.*, (arch.) gargouille,*f.*

water-snail (-snéle), *n.*,(hydr.) vis d'Archimède,*f.*

water-soak (-sôke),*v.a.*, tremper dans l'eau.

water-spout (-spaoute), *n.*, trombe, *f.* ; typhon, *m.*; (of a house—*de maison*) gouttière,*f.*

water-station (-sté-), *n.*, station à prendre de l'eau,*f.*

water-sumph (-seu'm'fe), *n.*, (mines) puisard, *m.*

water-table (-téb'l), *n.*,(arch.) empâtement, *m.*, écharpe.*f.*

water-tight (-taïte), *adj.*, imperméable à l'eau.

water-way, *n.*, cours d'eau ; débouché, *m.* ; (canal) section ; (of a ship—*de vaisseau*) gouttière, *f.*

water-wheel (-hwîl), *n.*, roue hydraulique,*f.*

water-wings (-wign'ze), *n.pl.*, perré, *m.*

water-works (-weurkse), *n.*, eaux, *f.pl.* ; ouvrages hydrauliques, *m.pl.* ; établissement pour la distribution des eaux, *m.* ; machine hydraulique,*f.*

water-wort (-weurte), *n.*, élatine,*f.*

watery (wo-teur'-), *adj.*, humide ; liquide ; aqueux ; humecté, mouillé, plein d'eau ; marin, des eaux. — gods ; *dieux marins, des eaux.*

wattle (wot't'l), *n.*, (branch—*branche*) brindille ; (hurdle—*claie*) claie ; (of a cock, a fish—*de coq, de poisson*) barbe, *f.*, barbillon, *m.*

wattle (wot't'l), *v.a.*, fermer de claies ; tresser, entrelacer ; lier avec de petites branches.

wave (wéve), *n.*, vague, flot, *m.* ; onde, lame ; (fig.) ondulation ; (on stuffs—*des étoffes*) moire,*f.*

wave (wéve), *v.a.*, sillonner, rendre raboteux, rendre inégal ; (to brandish—*brandir*) agiter, brandiller ; (to beckon—*faire signe*) faire signe de ; (to reject—*rejeter*) rejeter, repousser ; (to put off—*différer*) éloigner ; (to relinquish—*abandonner*) abandonner ; se désister de, retirer, ne pas insister sur.

wave, *v.n.*, ondoyer, onduler, flotter ; (to move—*mouvoir*) s'agiter, se mouvoir, flotter, tournoyer, faire signe.

waved (wév'de), *adj.*, ondé ; ondulé.

waveless, *adj.*, sans vagues, calme, uni.

wave-offering (-offeur'-), *n.*, offrande des prémices,*f.*

waver (wév'-), *v.n.*, chanceler ; vaciller ; balancer, être indéterminé, être indécis, être incertain.

waverer (wév'eur'-), *n.*, inconstant,.*m.*, inconstante; personne indécise, personne irrésolue,*f.*

wavering (wév'eur'-), *adj.*, inconstant; indécis, vacillant.

waveringly,*adv.*, avec incertitude ; en vacillant, en hésitant.

waveringness, *n.*, inconstance ; indécision,*f.*

waving (wév'-), *n.*, ondoiement, *m.*, ondulation,*f.*

wavy (wév'-), *adj.*, ondoyant, qui s'élève en ondes ; ondé ; ondulé.

wax, *n.*, cire, *f.*

wax, *v.a.*, cirer, enduire de cire ; bougier.

wax, *v.n.*, croître, s'accroître ; devenir, se faire.

wax-candle (-ca'n'd'l), *n.*, bougie, *f.*

wax-chandler (-tsha'n'd'l-), *n.*, fabricant de bougies, cirier, *m.*

waxen (waks'n), *adj.*, de cire.

wax-light (-laïte),*n.*, bougie, *f.*

wax-maker (-mék'-), *n.*, cirier, *m.*

wax-taper (-té-), *n.*, bougie, *f.* ; cierge, *m.*

wax-tree (-tri), *n.*, (bot.) céroxyle, cirier, *m.*

wax-work (-weurke), *n.*, figure de cire, *f.* ; ouvrage de cire. *m.*

waxy, *adj.*, qui ressemble à la cire ; visqueux.

way, *n.*, chemin, *m.* ; route, voie, *f.* ; (passage) chemin, passage, *m.*, place, issue, *f.* ; (direction) côté, sens, *m.*, direction ; (manner—*manière*) manière, façon, guise, mode, idée, fantaisie, *f.*, genre, *m.* ; (custom—*usage*) coutume, *f.*, usage ; (means, system—*moyen*, *système*) moyen, système, expédient, *m.*, voie, méthode ; (conduct—*conduite*) conduite, manière d'agir, *f.* ; (state—*condition*) état, *m.*, passe, *f.* ; (free scope—*cours*) cours, libre cours ; (line of business—*occupation*) genre, *m.*, partie ; (fig.) voie, *f.*, chemin, *m.* — in ; *entrée, f.* — out ; *sortie ; issue, f.* — through ; *passage, m.* Cross— — ; *chemin de traverse.* By— — ; *chemin détourné.* Milky— — ; *voie lactée*: By the — ; *en passant, soit dit en passant.* On the — ; *en chemin, en route, chemin faisant.* The right — ; *le bon chemin ;* (fig.) *le bon moyen, la bonne manière.* The wrong — ; *le mauvais chemin ; de la mauvaise manière, à rebours, de travers.* To go the right — to work ; *s'y prendre bien.* Out of the — ; *de côté ; à l'écart ; écarté ;* (strange—*bizarre*) *étrange, extraordinaire ;* (hidden—*latent*) *caché.* To keep, to be out of the — ; *se cacher, se tenir éloigné, caché, à l'écart.* Out of the — ; *en arrière ! gare ! rangez-vous !* Get out of the — ; *ôtez-vous du chemin, de là.* To get any one out of the — ; *éloigner quelqu'un.* Make — ! clear the — ! *faites place !* Go your — ; *passez votre chemin.* To be, to stand in the — ; *embarrasser, gêner, faire obstacle, barrer le passage.* He is in my — ; *il m'embarrasse.* To be, to keep in the — (to be near—*n'être pas loin*); *se tenir à portée.* To walk a long — ; *faire beaucoup de chemin.* To get under — ; (nav.) *se mettre en route.* To lead the — ; *marcher en tête.* To lose one's — ; *s'égarer, se perdre.* Half— — ; *à moitié chemin.* Over the — ; *vis-à-vis, en face, de l'autre côté du chemin, de la rue.* That — ; *de ce côté-là, par là :* (that manner—*ainsi*) *de cette manière-là.* This — ; *de ce côté-ci, par ici.* Which —? *de quel côté, par où ?* To cut, to force one's — ; *se frayer, s'ouvrir un chemin, un passage.* To make the best of one's — ; *aller, se rendre en toute hâte.* To work one's — ; *to ; s'ouvrir un chemin vers.* No —, no —s ; *nullement, pas du tout, en aucune manière.* In no — ; *en aucune façon, manière.* —s and means ; *voies et moyens.* By — of ; *en guise de, par forme de.* In my own — ; *à ma manière, guise.* To find a — to ; *trouver moyen de.* She will have her own — ; *elle veut être la maîtresse ; elle veut agir à sa fantaisie, faire ses volontés, faire à sa tête.*

way-bill, *n.*, itinéraire de voiture publique, *m.*

wayfaring (-fér'-), *adj.*, qui voyage, en voyage.

waylay, *v.a.*, guetter ; dresser un guet-apens à.

waylayer (-lè-eur), *n.*, personne qui dresse un guet-apens, qui attend de guet-apens, *f.*

wayless, *adj.*, errant, sans direction ; sans routes.

wayward (-warde), *adj.*, fantasque ; bourru ; entêté ; méchant.

waywardly, *adv.*, méchamment ; avec humeur ; obstinément, avec entêtement.

waywardness, *n.*, humeur bourrue ; mé chanceté. *f.* ; entêtement. *m.*

wayworn, *adj.*, harassé, épuisé par la route.

we (wi), *pron.*, nous.

weak (wike), *adj.*, faible ; infirme, débile. — side; *côté faible ; faible, m.* To grow — ; *s'affaiblir.*

weaken (wi-k'n), *v.a.*, affaiblir ; débiliter ; atténuer, diminuer ; (drinks—*boissons*) couper, étendre.

weakener, *n.*, personne qui affaiblit ; chose qui affaiblit, *f.* ; débilitant, *m.*

weakening (wi-k'n'-), *n.*, affaiblissement, *m.* ; débilitation, *f.*

weakening, *adj.*, affaiblissant ; débilitant.

weak-headed (-hòd'-), *adj.*, qui a la tête faible.

weak-hearted (-hârt'-), *adj.*, peu courageux, poltron.

weakling (wik'-), *n.*, être faible, être débile, *m.*

weakly (wik'-), *adj.*, faible ; infirme ; débile.

weakly, *adv.*, faiblement ; débilement ; sans force.

weakness (wik'-), *n.*, faiblesse ; débilité, *f.* ; (fig.) faible, *m.*

weak-sighted (-saït'-), *adj.*, qui a la vue faible.

weak-spirited, *adj.*, mou, inanimé ; sans courage, sans cœur.

weal (wil), *n.*, bien, bien-être ; bonheur, *m.*

wealth (wèlth), *n.*, richesse, opulence, fortune, *f.*, richesses, *f.pl.* ; biens, *m. pl.*

wealthily (wèlth'-), *adv.*, richement, dans l'opulence.

wealthiness (wèlth'-), *n.*, richesse, opulence, fortune, *f.*

wealthy (wèlth'-), *adj.*, riche, opulent.

wean (wi'n), *v.a.*, sevrer : (to alienate—*aliéner*) détacher.

weaning, *n.*, sevrage, *m.*

weanling (wi'n'-), *n.*, enfant sevré ; animal sevré, *m.*

weapon (wèp'p'n), *n.*, arme, défense, *f.*

weaponed (wèp'p'n'de), *adj.*, armé.

weaponless, *adj.*, sans armes, désarmé.

wear (wère), *n.*, (act of wearing—*faire usage*) user, usage ; (clothing—*vêtements*) habillement, *m.* ; (waste by wearing—*dépérissement*) usure, *f.* ; dépérissement, *m.* — and tear ; *usure, détérioration, f.* ; *frais d'entretien, m.pl.*

wear, or **weir** (wère), *n.*, barrage, déversoir, *m.* ; (for fish—*pour prendre du poisson*) nasse, *f.*

wear (wère), *v.a.* (preterit, Wore ; *past part.*, Worn), (clothes—*vêtements*) porter, avoir, mettre ; (to use by wear—*détruire par l'usage*) user ; (to tire—*lasser*) lasser, fatiguer, harasser ; (to consume—*consumer*) consumer. To — away ; *user ; consumer ;* (to deface—*effacer*) effacer. To — out ; *miner, épuiser ;* (time—*le temps*) passer péniblement ; (to tire—*fatiguer*) lasser, harasser ; (clothes—*vêtements*) user. He —s my patience out ; *il m'impatiente, il lasse ma patience.*

wear, *v.n.*, s'user ; s'user. To — away, off ; *s'user, dépérir ; se consumer ; perdre ses forces ;* (to get effaced—*disparaître*) *s'effacer ;* (of time—*du temps*) se passer, s'écouler, se dissiper. To — out ; *s'user.* To — well ; *être d'un bon user :* (pers.) *se conserver.* To — badly ; *n'être pas d'un bon user.*

wearable (wèr'a-b'l), *adj.*, portable, mettable.

wearer (wèr'-), *n.*, personne qui porte, qui use ; chose qui use, qui consume, *f.*

wearied (wi-ride), *adj.*, fatigué, ennuyé, las.

wearily (wi-), *adv.*, d'une manière fatigante ; ennuyeusement.

weariness (wi-), *n.*, fatigue, lassitude. *f.* ; ennui, *m.*

wearisome (wi-), *adj.*, ennuyeux; fatigant; fastidieux, lassant.

wearisomely (wi-), *adv.*, ennuyeusement; fastidieusement.

wearisomeness (wi-), *n.*, nature fatigante, nature ennuyeuse, *f.*; ennui, *m.*

weary (wi-ri), *v.a.*, lasser, ennuyer, fatiguer. To — out; *harasser, excéder, exténuer.*

weary (wi), *adj.*, las, ennuyé, fatigué; (of things—*des choses*) fatigant, ennuyeux.

weasand (wi-z'n'de), *n.*, trachée-artère, *f.*

weasel (wi-z'l), *n.*, belette, *f.*

weather (wèth'-), *n.*, temps; (nav.) vent, côté du vent, *m.* It is fine —; *il fait beau temps. il fait beau.* It is beautiful, delightful —; *il fait un temps superbe, charmant.* It is cloudy, rainy —; *il fait un temps couvert, pluvieux.* Foggy —; *temps de brouillard.* In rainy —; *dans les temps de pluie.* Stormy —; *temps d'orage;* (nav.) *gros temps.*

weather (wèth'-), *v.a.*, (a tempest—*une tempête*) résister à; (a cape—*un cap*) doubler; (nav.) gagner le vent de.

weather-beaten (-bit'n), *adj.*, battu par l'orage, par la tempête; exténué, usé, épuisé.

weather-boarding (-bôrd'-), *n.*, plancher pour abriter les maisons en construction; (nav.) bordage supplémentaire, *m.*

weather-bound (-baou'n'de), *adj.*, arrêté par le mauvais temps.

weather-cock, *n.*, girouette, *f.*

weather-driven (-driv'n), *adj.*, chassé par la tempête.

weather-gage, or **weather-gauge** (-ghèdje), *n.*, (nav.) avantage du vent, *m.* To get the —; *prendre le dessus du vent.*

weather-glass (-glàce), *n.*, baromètre; thermomètre, *m.*

weathering (wèth'eur'-), *n.*, (geol.) action des éléments sur, *f.*

weather-most (-môste), *adj.*, (nav.) le plus au vent.

weather-proof (-proufe), *adj.*, à l'épreuve du temps.

weather-wise (-waïze), *adj.*, qui prévoit le temps.

weave (wive), *v.a.* (*preterit*, Wove; *past part.*, Woven), tisser, faire au métier; tresser, entrelacer; (fig.) entremêler, unir, mêler.

weaver (wiv'-), *n.*, tisserand, *m.*; (orni.) genre de passereaux des Indes et de l'Afrique, *m.* — or — -fish. V. **weever.**

weaving (wiv'-), *n.*, tissage, *m.*

web (wèbe), *n.*, tissu; (fig.) tissu, enchaînement, *m.*; (in the eye—*de l'œil*) taie; (of waterfowls—*des oiseaux aquatiques*) membrane palmaire; (of a spider—*d'araignée*) toile, *f.*; (of a coulter—*de coutre*) tranchant, *m.*

webbed (wèb'de), *adj.*, palmé.

webby, *adj.*, membraneux; de toile d'araignée.

web-footed (-fout'-), *adj.*, palmipède, aux pieds palmés.

wed (wède), *v.a.*, épouser, se marier avec; (fig.) unir, attacher, marier. —ded to; *fortement attaché à, entiché de.*

wed. *v.n.*, se marier.

wedding, *n.*, noce, *f.*; noces, *f.pl.*; mariage, *m.*

wedge (wèdje), *n.*, coin; (metal.) lingot, *m.*

wedge, *v.a.*, serrer par un coin; caler, fixer au moyen de coins; forcer; fendre. To — in; *pousser, faire entrer; caler, assujettir; serrer, presser.*

wedge-shaped (-shépte), *adj.*, en coin; cunéiforme.

wedlock, *n.*, mariage, hymen, *m.*

wednesday (wè'n'z'-), *n.*, mercredi, *m.* Ash- —; *mercredi des cendres.*

wee (wi), *adj.*, petit, tout petit.

weed (wide), *n.*, mauvaise herbe, *f.*

weed (wide), *v.a.*, sarcler; arracher les mauvaises herbes; (fig.) purifier, nettoyer, extirper, purger, épurer. To — out; *extirper, déraciner, enlever.*

weeder (wid'-), *n.*, sarcleur; (fig.) destructeur, *m.*

weed-hook (-houke), *n.*, sarcloir, *m.*

weeding, *n.*, sarclage, *m.*

weeding-tool (wid'ign'toule), *n.*, (agri.) extirpateur, *m.*

weeds (wid'ze), *n.*, vêtements de deuil d'une veuve, *m.*

weedy (wid'-), *adj.*, plein de mauvaises herbes.

week (wike), *n.*, semaine, *f.* This day —; (future—*futur*) d'aujourd'hui en huit; (past—*passé*) il y a aujourd'hui huit jours.

week-day, *n.*, jour ouvrable, *m.*

weekly (wik'-), *adv.*, hebdomadairement, toutes les semaines.

weekly, *adj.*, de chaque semaine; hebdomadaire.

ween (wi'n), *v.n.*, penser, croire, estimer.

weep (wipe), *v.n.* (*preterit* and *past part.*, Wept), pleurer, verser des larmes; gémir, se plaindre. To — for; *pleurer.* To — bitterly; *pleurer à chaudes larmes, pleurer amèrement.*

weep, *v.a.*, pleurer, pleurer sur; (tears—*larmes*) verser, répandre des larmes.

weeper (wip'-), *n.*, pleureur, *m.*, pleureuse; personne qui pleure; (band of cambric—*bande de batiste*) pleureuse, *f.*

weeping (wip'-), *n.*, pleurs, *m.pl.*; larmes, *f.pl.*

weeping, *adj.*, qui pleure; (bot.) pleureur.

weepingly (-), *adv.*, en pleurant.

weever (wi-veur), *n.*, (ich.) vive, *f.*

weevil (wi-), *n.*, (ent.) calandre, *f.*; charançon, *m.*

weft (wèfte), *n.*, trame, duite, *f.*; tissu, *m.*

weigh (wè), *v.a.*, peser; (fig.) examiner, juger, peser, balancer; (anchor—*l'ancre*) lever. To — down; *peser plus que; affaisser;* (to oppress—*accabler*) surcharger, accabler; (fig.) *l'emporter sur, surpasser.*

weigh, *v.n.*, peser, avoir un poids de; avoir du poids, avoir de la valeur; (nav.) lever l'ancre. To — upon; *peser sur; être à charge à.* To — down; *s'affaisser, s'abaisser;* (of scales) pencher.

weigh (wè), *n.*, pesée (quantity weighed—*quantité pesée*), *f.*

weighable (wè-a-b'l), *adj.*, que l'on peut peser.

weighage (wè-édje), *n.*, pesage, *m.*

weigh-bridge, *n.*, pont à bascule, *m.*

weigher (wè-eur), *n.*, peseur, *m.*, peseuse, *f.*

weighing (wè-igne), *n.*, pesage, *m.*; pesée, *f.*

weighing-machine (-ma-shîne), *n.*, balance à bascule, *f.*

weight (wè-te), *n.*, poids, *m.*; pesanteur; (fig.) importance, valeur, *f.* By —; *au poids.* Of —; *de poids; important, grave, sérieux.* To be worth one's — in gold; *valoir son pesant d'or.*

weightily (wèt'-), *adv.*, pesamment, lourdement; gravement, fortement.

weightiness (wèt'-), *n.*, poids, *m.*; pesanteur; *f.* importance, valeur, gravité, force, *f.*

weighty, *adj.*, pesant, lourd, de poids; fort, solide; (important) important, grave.

weir (wère), *n.* V. **wear.**

welcome (wèl-keume), *n.*, bienvenue; gracieuse réception, *f.*; bon accueil, *m.* To give a good, a hearty — to; *faire très bon accueil à.*

welcome (wèl-keume) *adj.*, bienvenu; bien accueilli; bien reçu; (of things—*des choses*) agréable, heureux, bon, bien reçu. You are — to it; *c'est bien à votre service.*

welcome! *int.*, soyez le bienvenu.

welcome (wèl-keume), *v.a.*, souhaiter la

bienvenue à ; bien accueillir, faire bon accueil à, recevoir très bien.

welcomeness, *n.*, nature agréable, *f.* ; bon accueil, *m.*

welcomer, *n.*, personne qui fait bon accueil, qui accueille bien, qui souhaite la bienvenue, *f.*

weld (wèlde), *v.a.*, joindre, incorporer ; souder.

welder, *n.*, personne qui soude, *f.*

welding, *n.*, soudure, *f.*

welfare (wèl-fére), *n.*, bien-être, bonheur, bien, *m.*

welkin (wèl-k'i'n), *n.*, ciel, *m.* ; voûte céleste, *f.*

well, *n.*, puits, *m.* ; source, fontaine, *f.* ; réservoir d'eau ; (of a fishing-boat—*d'un bateau de pêche*) réservoir, *m.* ; (of a ship—*d'un vaisseau*) archipompe, arche-de-pompe, *f.*

well, *adj.*, en bonne santé ; (fortunate—*fortuné*) bien, bon, heureux ; (advantageous—*avantageux*) utile, profitable ; (in favour—*en faveur*) en faveur. —off ; *bien dans ses affaires, dans une bonne position, heureux.* To be — ; (in health —*de la santé*) *se porter bien, être bien portant, être en bonne santé, être bien.* All is — that ends — ; *tout est bien, qui finit bien.* To be — to do; *être à son aise, être dans l'aisance.*

well, *adv.*, bien ; très ; fort ; comme il faut. — and good ; *à la bonne heure.* — nigh ; *presque.* As — as ; *aussi bien que.* To speak — of ; *dire du bien de, parler favorablement de.* To wish one — ; *souhaiter du bien à quelqu'un.*

welladay ! *int.*, hélas !

wellbeing ('-bî-igne), *n.*, bien-être, bonheur, *m.*

well-born, *adj.*, de naissance, bien né.

well-bred, *adj.*, poli, bien élevé.

well-doer (-dou'eur), *n.*, personne qui fait le bien, *f.*

well-doing (-dou-igne), *n.*, bienfaisance, *f.* ; accomplissement de ses devoirs, *m.*

well-done ! *int.*, bien fait ! fort bien !

well-drain (-drè'n), *n.*, puits d'écoulement, *m.*

well-drain, *v.a.*, dessécher au moyen de puits d'écoulement.

well-favoured (-fé-veurde), *adj.*, beau, bien fait.

well-informed (-i'n'form'de), *adj.*, instruit, très instruit ; (of facts—*de faits*) bien informé.

well-mannered (-man'neurde), *adj.*, de bon ton, de bonnes manières, poli, bien élevé.

well-meaning (-mi'n'-), *adj.*, bien intentionné, honnête.

well-meant (-mè'n'te), *adj.*, fait à bonne intention.

well-met ! (-mète), *int.*, heureuse rencontre !

well-minded (-maï'n'dède), *adj.*, bien disposé.

well-read (-rède), *adj.*, instruit, qui a beaucoup lu.

well-room, *n.*, (nav.) sentine, *f.*

well-sinker, *n.*, puisatier, *m.*

well-spoken (-spôk'n), *adj.*, (pers.) qui parle bien, beau parleur ; (of things—*des choses*) bien dit, bien tourné.

well-spring, *n.*, source, *f.*

well-timed (-taï'm'de), *adj.*, à propos ; fait à propos.

well-wisher (-), *n.*, ami, amie, *f.* ; protecteur, *m.*, protectrice ; personne qui souhaite du bien à, *f.* ; partisan, *m.*

welsh, *adj.*, gallois ; du pays de Galles. —man; *Gallois*, *m.* —woman ; *Galloise*, *f.*

welsh, *n.*, gallois (language—*langue*), *m.*

welt, *n.*, bordure, bande ; (of leather—*de cuir*) trépointe, *f.*

welt, *v.a.*, border, garnir.

welter, *v.n.*, se vautrer, se rouler ; nager, être baigné, noyé dans. —ing in ; *baigné, noyé dans.*

wen (wè'n), *n.*, (med.) tumeur enkystée, loupe, *f.*

wench, *n.*, fille ; donzelle ; (negress—*négresse*) négresse, *f.*

wencher, *n.*, libertin, *m.*

wend, *v.n.*, and *a.*, aller ; aller et venir. To — one's way ; *suivre son chemin.*

wennish, *or* **wenny**, *adj.*, de la nature de la loupe.

west (wèste), *n.*, ouest, occident, couchant, *m.*.

west, *adj.*, occidental, d'ouest, de l'ouest.

west, *adv.*, à l'occident, à l'ouest.

westerly (-'eur-), *or* **western** (-'eur'n', *adj.*, occidental ; d'ouest ; de l'ouest.

westerly, *adv.*, vers l'occident, vers l'ouest.

westing, *n.*, direction vers l'ouest, *f.*

westward, *adv.*, vers l'ouest.

westwardly, *adv.*, en se dirigeant vers l'ouest.

wet, *n.*, humidité, *f.* ; (weather—*temps*) temps pluvieux, *m.*, pluie, *f.*

wet, *adj.*, mouillé ; humide ; (of the weather —*du temps*) pluvieux, humide. — through ; trempé. It is — ; *il fait mauvais temps.* — dock ; *gare, f.*

wet, *v.a.*, mouiller ; tremper ; humecter ; (print.) tremper.

wether (wèth'-), *n.*, mouton, *m.*

wetness, *n.*, humidité, *f.* ; état pluvieux, *m.*.

wet-nurse (-neurse), *n.*, nourrice, *f.*

wetting, *n.*, action de mouiller, de tremper, *f.* ; (print.) trempage, *m.* — board ; ais, *m.* — -room ; (print.) *tremperie, f.* — -trough ; (print.) *baquet à tremper, m.*

wettish, *adj.*, un peu humide, moite.

whack, *n.*, coup lourd, *m.* ; taloche, *f.*

whale (hwèle), *n.*, baleine, *f.* —bone ; *baleine* ; *barbe de baleine, f.* —fin ; *fanon de baleine, m.* —fishery ; *pêche de la baleine, f.* — -louse ; (ent.) *cyame, pou de baleine, m.* —tribe ; *cétacés, m.pl.*

whaleman, *n.*, baleinier, pêcheur de baleine, *m.*

whaler (hwèl'-), *n.*, baleinier ; navire baleinier ; (whaleman—*personne*) baleinier, pêcheur de baleine, *m.*

whap, *n.*, coup fort ; horion, *m.*

whapper, *n.*, chose immense ; (lie—*mensonge*) bourde, *f.*

wharf (hworfe), *n.*, (wharfs, ou *wharves*) quai, embarcadère, débarcadère de rivière, *m.*

wharf (hworfe), *v.a.*, munir d'un quai.

wharfage (-édje), *n.*, quayage ; droit de quai, *m.*

wharfinger (-'i'n'gheur), *n.*, gardien d'un quai, *m.*

what, *relative pron.*, (as subject—*sujet*) ce qui, quoi ; (interrogatively—*interrogativement*) qu'est-ce qui ; (as object—*régime direct*) ce que, quoi ; (interrogatively—*interrogativement*) qu'est-ce que, que, quoi ; (whatever—*quoi que* ce soit. To know — ; *ne pas se moucher du pied.* I will tell you — ; *je vous dirai ce que c'est.* — of that? *qu'est-ce que cela fait?* For —? *quoi? pourquoi faire?* —! *can you not?* quoi! ne pouvez-vous pas? — though it be so? *Hé bien quoi! quand même cela serait!*

what, *adj.*, quoi, quel, *m.sing.*, quelle, *f.sing.*, (exc.) que de, combien de, *f.*; soever ; *quelque* .... *que* ; *quelque* .... *que* ce soit.

whatever (-'èv'-), *pron.*, quoi que ce soit ; quelque ..... qui ; (as object—*régime direct*) quelque .... que ; (all that) tout ce qui ; (as object—*régime direct*) tout ce que.

wheat (hwite), *n.*, froment ; blé, *m.*

wheat-ear (-'ire), *n.*, (orni.) motteux, culblanc, *m.*

wheaten (hwit'n), *adj.*, de froment, de blé.

wheat-grass (-grâce), *n.*, (bot.) froment rampant, *m.*

wheat-worm (-weurme), *n.*, (ent.) lepte automnal, rouget, *m.*

wheedle (hwid'd'l), *v.a.*, cajoler; flagorner; ... jôler.

wheedler, *n.*, cajoleur, *m.*, cajoleuse, *f.*; flagorneur, *m.*, flagorneuse, *f.*; enjôleur, *m.*, enjôleuse, *f.*; câlin, *m.*, câline, *f.*

wheedling, *n.*, cajolerie, flagornerie, câlinerie, *f.*

wheel (hwîle), *n.*, roue, *f.*; (circular body—corps circulaire) corps rond, *m.*; (carriage—véhicule) voiture; (torture) roue, *f.*; (for spinning—à filer) rouet, filoir, *m.*; (revolution) révolution, *f.*; (turning about—tour) tour, cercle, *m.*

wheel (hwîle), *v.a.*, rouler; faire tourner; (in a barrow—dans une brouette) brouetter.

wheel, *v.n.*, rouler sur des roues; (to move round—tourner) tourner, se tourner; (of things —des choses) tourner, se mouvoir en rond; (to roll forward—rouler) s'avancer en roulant; (milit.) faire une conversion. To — about; tourner; faire une pirouette; (milit.) faire une conversion.

wheel-animal. *n.*, (ent.) rotifère, *m.*

wheel-barrow (-bar'rô), *n.*, brouette, *f.*

wheeled (hwîl'de), *adj.*, à roués. Four- — carriage; voiture à quatre roues, *f.*

wheeler (hwîl'-), *n.*, personne qui roule, qui brouette, *f.*; (horse—cheval) cheval de brancard, limonier, *m.*

wheeling, *n.*, transport sur roue; roulage, *m.*; (milit.) conversion, *f.*

wheel-race. *n.*, (tech.) voie de la roue, *f.*

wheel-shaped (-shép'te), *adj.*, en roue; (bot.) rotacé, rotiforme.

wheel-work (-weurke), *n.sing.*, rouages, *m.pl.*

wheel-wright (-raïte), *n.*, charron, *m.*

wheely (hwîl'-), *adj.*, (ant.) rond, circulaire; rotiforme.

wheeze (hwize), *v.n.*, siffler, respirer avec bruit.

wheezing (hwiz'-), *n.*, sifflement, *m.*, respiration sifflante, *f.*

whelk (hwèlke), *n.*, pustule, *f.*; (conch.) buccin, *m.*

whelm (hwèlme), *v.a.*, submerger; (fig.) accabler.

whelp (hwèlpe), *v.n.*, chienner; faire ses petits; mettre bas.

whelp, *n.*, petit; (of the bear—de l'ours) ourson; (of the lion—du lion) lionceau; (of the wolf—du loup) louveteau; (nav.) taquet; (child —enfant) marmot, *m.*

when (hwè'n), *adv.*, quand, lorsque; que, où. The day — I saw him; le jour où je l'ai vu.

whence, *adv.*, d'où; de là.

whencesoever (hwè'n'ce-sô-èv'-), *adv.*, de quelque lieu que ce soit.

whenever (-'èv'-), or **whensoever** (-sô-èv'-), *adv.*, toutes les fois que, quand; dans quelque temps que.

where (hwère), *adv.*, où. Any—; dans quelque endroit que ce soit; n'importe où. Not any— —; nulle part. Every—; partout. Some—; quelque part.

whereabout (-'abaoute), or **whereabouts** (-'abaoutse), *adv.*, où, où à peu près; (concerning which—concernant) au sujet de quoi.

whereas (-'aze), *adv.*, au lieu que; tandis que; vu que; (jur.) considérant que.

whereat, *adv.*, à quoi; là-dessus.

whereby (-ba'ye), *adv.*, par lequel; par où; par quoi.

wherefore, *adv.*, pourquoi, c'est pourquoi; donc.

wherein (-'i'n), *adv.*, en, dans quoi, dans lequel, où.

whereof (-'ove), *adv.*, dont, de quoi, duquel.

whereon (hwèr'o'n), *adv.*, sur quoi, sur lequel.

wheresoever. *V.* **wherever.**

whereto (-tou), *adv.*, à quoi, auquel; où.

whereupon (-eup'o'n), *adv.*, sur quoi; sur lequel.

wherever (hwèr'èv'-), *adv.*, partout où, n'importe où; en quelque lieu que ce soit.

wherewith (hwèr'with), or **wherewithal** (-'with'ôl), *adv.*, avec quoi, avec lequel; de quoi.

wherry (hwèr'-), *n.*, bateau, bac, *m.*; nacelle, *f.*

whet (hwète), *v.a.*, aiguiser; affiler; repasser; affûter; (fig.) aiguiser, exciter.

whet (hwète), *n.*, aiguisement; repassage; (stimulant) excitant, stimulant, *m.*

whether (hwèth'-), *pron.*, lequel, *m.*, laquelle, *f.*

whether, *conj.*, soit, soit que; si, que. — or no; bon gré mal gré. — . . . or; soit . . . soit; soit que . . . soit que; si . . . ou; que . . . ou.

whet-slate (hwèt'-), or **whetstone-slate** (hwèt'stône-), *n.*, (min.) schiste à aiguiser, *m.*

whetstone (-stône), *n.*, pierre à aiguiser, *f.*

whetter (hwèt'-), *n.*, aiguiseur, *m.*; (fig.) stimulant, aiguillon, *m.*

whetting, *n.*, aiguisement, *m.*

whey (hwè), *n.*, petit-lait, *m.*

wheyish (hwè-ishe), *adj.*, qui tient du petit-lait, séreux.

which (hwitshe), *relative pron.*, qui, *m.*, *f.*; lequel, *m.sing.*, laquelle, *f.sing.*; lesquels, *m.pl.*, lesquelles, *f.pl.*; (object—régime direct) que; (that which—sujet) ce qui; (object—régime direct) ce que, *m.*, *f.* Of, from —; dont, *m.*, *f.sing.*, *pl.*; duquel, *m.sing.*, de laquelle, *f.sing.*; desquels, *m.pl.*, desquelles, *f.pl.* To —; auquel, *m.sing.*, à laquelle, *f.sing.*; auxquels, *m.pl.*, auxquelles, *f.pl.*; à quoi. In —; dans lequel; où.

which, *adj.*, quel, *m.sing.*, quelle, *f.sing.*; quels, *m.pl.*, quelles, *f.pl.*; lequel, *m.sing.*, laquelle, *f.sing.*; lesquels, *m.pl.*, lesquelles, *f.pl.*

whichever (-èv'-), *pron.*, lequel, *m.sing.*, laquelle, *f.sing.*; lesquels, *m.pl.*, lesquelles, *f.pl.*; quelque . . . que; lequel que ce soit que.

whichsoever. *V.* **whichever.**

whiff, *n.*, bouffée, haleinée, *f.*; souffle, *m.*; (ich.) cardine, *f.*

whiff, *v.a.*, lancer en bouffées.

whiffle (hwif'f'l), *v.n.*, tourner à tous vents; changer.

whiffle-tree (-trî), *n.* *V.* **whipple-tree.**

whiffler, *n.*, personne qui tourne à tous vents; girouette, *f.*; (fifer—fifre) fifre, *m.*

whiffling, *adj.*, qui tourne, qui change; qui prévarique.

whiffling, *n.*, prévarication, *f.*

whig, *n.*, whig, *m.*

whiggery (hwig-gheuri), or **whiggism** (-ghiz'm), *n.*, whiggisme, *m.*; doctrine des whigs, *f.*

while (hwaïle), *n.*, temps, *m.*; durée, *f.*; moment, instant, *m.* A little, a long — ago; il y a peu de temps, il y a longtemps. For a —; pour un temps. A little —; un moment; quelques moments. It is not worth the —; cela n'en vaut pas la peine.

while (hwaïle), *v.a.*, passer, faire passer.

while (hwaïle), or **whilst** (hwaïlste), *adv.*, pendant que; tandis que; (as long as—tant que) tant que, aussi longtemps que.

whilom (hwaïl'eume), *adj.*, (ant.) jadis.

whim, *n.*, caprice, *m.*; fantaisie, lubie, *f.*; (capstan—cabestan) treuil, cabestan, *m.*

whimbrel, *n.*, (orni.) courlieu, petit courlis, *m.*

whimper, *v.n.*, se plaindre, geindre, pleurnicher.

whimpering, *n.*, plainte, *f.*; pleurnichement, *m.*

whimsical (hwi'm'zi-), *adj.*, fantasque, capricieux.

whimsically (-zi-cal'-), *adv.*, capricieusement.

whimsicalness (-zi-cal'-), *n.*, caractère capricieux, *m.*

whin, *n.*, ajonc; genêt épineux, *m.*; (min.) trapp, *m.*

whin-chat, *n.*, (orni.) tarier, *m.*

whine (hwaïne), *v.n.*, se plaindre, gémir, se lamenter, geindre, pleurnicher; (of animals — *d:s animaux*) se plaindre.

whine (hwaïne), *n.*, pleurnichement, gémissement, *m.*; plainte mêlée de pleurs; (of animals — *des animaux*) plainte, *f.*

whiner (hwaï'n'-), *n.*, pleurnicheur, *m.*, pleurnicheuse, *f.*

whining (hwaï'n'-), *n.*, plaintes, lamentations, *f.pl.*; gémissements, *m.pl.*

whining, *adj.*, plaintif, lamentable, langoureux.

whiningly, *adv.*, en pleurnichant, d'un ton plaintif, en gémissant.

whinny (hwi'n'-), *v.n.*, hennir.

whinstone (-stône), *n.*, (min.) trapp, *m.*

whip, *v.a.*, fouetter; (to flog — *flageller*) fouetter, donner le fouet à; (needle work — *ouvrage à l'aiguille*) faire un surjet à; (wheat, &c. — *blé, &c.*) battre; (fig.) fouetter, flageller, châtier, fustiger. To — away; *chasser à coups de fouet*; (to take away — *enlever*) enlever vivement. To — down; *faire descendre à coups de fouet*; (to take down — *descendre*) descendre vite. To — in; *faire entrer à coups de fouet*; (to put in — *rentrer*) rentrer vite. To — into; *passer rapidement dans*. To — off; *chasser à coups de fouet*; (to take off — *retirer*) ôter vite. To — on; *faire avancer à coups de fouet*; (to put on — *passer*) passer vite. To — out; *faire sortir à coups de fouet*. To — out of; *expulser de*. To — up; *faire monter à coups de fouet*; (to pick up — *suisir*) ramasser vivement, saisir; (to construct — *faire*) bâcler.

whip, *v.n.*, courir bien vite. To — away; *partir au plus vite*. How he —s along! *comme il court!* To — down; *descendre vivement*. To — into; *entrer viv ment dans*. To — off; *partir au plus vite*; *s'enfuir*. To — out; *sortir promptement*.

whip, *n.*, fouet, (nav.) cartahu, *m.* Horse —; *cravache*, *f.* To give any one the —; *donner le fouet à quelqu'un*.

whip-cord, *n.*, fouet, *m.*

whip-graft (-grâfte), *v.a.*, greffer à l'anglaise.

whip-grafting, *n.*, greffe anglaise, *f.*

whip-hand, *n.*, dessus; (advantage — *avantage*) dessus, avantage, *m.*

whip-lash, *n.*, mèche de fouet, *f.*

whipper, *n.*, personne qui fouette, *f.*; fouetteur, *m.*, fouetteuse, *f.* — in; *piqueur*; (leader — *conducteur*) chef de file, *m.*

whipper-snapper, *n.*, petit homme méprisable, petit bout d'homme, *m.*

whipping, *n.*, coups de fouet, *m.pl.*; action de fouetter; flagellation, *f.*; fouet, *m.*; fustigation, *f.* To give a — to; *fouetter*; *donner le fouet à*.

whipping-post (-pôste), *n.*, poteau pour les criminels condamnés à la fustigation, *m.*

whipple-tree (hwip'pl-tri), *n.*, palonnier, *m.*

whipsaw (-sô), *n.*, scie à scier de long, *f.*

whip-shaped (-shép'te), *adj.*, en forme de fouet.

whip-staff (-stâfe), *n.*, (nav.) manivelle de la barre du gouvernail, *f.*

whipster, *n.*, homme agile, *m.*

whir (hweur), *v.n.*, tourner avec bruit.

whir (hweur), *v.a.*, presser; précipiter.

whirl (hweurle), *v.a.*, faire tourner; tourner rapidement.

whirl (hweurle), *v.n.*, pirouetter; tournoyer; tourbillonner.

whirl (hweurle), *n.*, tournoiement; tour; tourbillon; (bot.) verticille: (rope-making — *corderie*) émérillon, *m.*; (plaything — *jouet*) pirouette, *f.*

whirl-bat, *n.*, chose qu'on tourne, qu'on fait tourner pour la lancer, pour frapper, *f.*

whirl-bone (-bône), *n.*, (anat.) rotule; (vet.) tête du fémur, *f.*

whirled (hweurlde), *adj.*, (bot.) verticillé.

whirligig (hweurl'i-ghighe), *n.*, pirouette, *f.*; (fig.) vicissitude, *f.*, changement, *m.*

whirlpool (-poule), *or* **whirlpit**, *n.*, tourbillon; tournant d'eau, gouffre, *m.*

whirlwind (hweurl'wi'n'de), *n.*, tourbillon; siphon, *m.*; trombe, *f.*

whirring (hweur'-), *n.*, bruit que font les faisans et les perdrix avec leurs ailes, *m.*

whisk, *n.*, vergette, époussette, *f.*

whisk, *v.a.*, vergeter; (cook.) fouetter. To — away: *enlever vivement*.

whisk, *v.n.*, passer rapidement.

whisker, *n.*, favori, *m.*; (of animals — *des animaux*) moustache, *f.*

whiskered (hwisk'eurde), *adj.*, à favoris; (of animals — *des animaux*) à moustaches.

whiskerless, *adj.*, sans favoris; (of animals — *des animaux*) sans moustaches.

whisky, *n.*, whiskey, *m.*; eau-de-vie de grains, *f.*

whisper, *n.*, chuchotement; murmure, *m.*

whisper, *v.a.*, chuchoter; dire à l'oreille; murmurer; dire tout bas; parler bas à.

whisper, *v.n.*, chuchoter, murmurer, parler bas.

whisperer, *n.*, chuchoteur, *m.*, chuchoteuse, *f.*; (tattler — *bavard*) bavard, *m.*, bavarde, *f.*; (backbiter — *médisant*) médisant, *m.*, médisante, *f.*

whispering, *n.*, chuchoterie, *f.*; chuchotement; murmure, *m.*; (backbiting — *médisance*) médisance, *f.*

whispering-gallery, *n.*, voûte acoustique, *f.*

whisperingly, *adv.*, en chuchotant, tout bas.

whist, *n.*, whist, *m.*

whist! *int.*, chut! silence!

whistle (hwis's'l), *n.*, sifflement; coup de sifflet; (of the wind — *du vent*) sifflement, bruissement; (throat — *gosier*) gosier, bec; (instrument) sifflet, *m.*

whistle (hwis's'l), *v.a.*, siffler; appeler en sifflant.

whistle, *v.n.*, siffler; bruire.

whistle-fish, *n.*, (ich.) mustelle, *f.*

whistler (hwis's'l'-), *n.*, siffleur, *m.*

whistling (hwis's'l'-), *n.*, sifflement, *m.*

whistling (hwis's'l'-), *adj.*, sifflant.

whit, *n*, iota, point, atome, brin, *m.* Not a —; *pas le moins du monde*.

white (hwaïte), *n.*, blanc; (of an egg — *d'œuf*) blanc, *m.*, albumine, *f.*; (of wood — *du bois*) aubier, *m.*

white (hwaïte), *adj.*, blanc; (fig.) sans tache, pur. — with; *blanc de, pâle de*. To get —; *blanchir*.

white-bait (-béte), *n.*, (ich.) éperlan, *m.*

white-beam-tree (-bi'm'tri), *n.*, (bot.) alisier blanc, *m.*

white-ear (-ire), *n.*, (orni.) motteux; cul-blanc, *m.*

white-foot (-foute), *n.*, balzane, *f.*

white-horse-fish, *n.*, (ich.) raie cendrée, *f.*

white-lead (-lède), *n.*, blanc de plomb, *m.*; céruse, *f.*

white-livered (-liveur'de), *adj.*, poltron.

white-meat (-mite), *n.*, blanc-manger, *m.*

whiten (hwaït'n), *v.a.*, blanchir; (mas.) blanchir à la chaux, badigeonner.

whiten, *v.n.*, blanchir; se blanchir.

whitener, *n.*, personne qui blanchit, *f.*

whiteness (hwaït'-), *n.*, blancheur; pâleur; (fig.) pureté, *f.*

whites (hwaïtse), *n.pl.*, (med.) fleurs blanches, *f.pl.*

white-swelling (-swèl'-), *n.*, tumeur blanche, *f.*

white-tail (-téle), *n.*, (orni.) motteux; culblanc, *m.*

white-thorn (-thorne), *n.*, aubépine, épine blanche, *f.*

white-throat (-thrôte), *n.*, (orni.) fauvette babillarde, *f.*

whitewash (-woshe), *n.*, eau à blanchir, *f*; (mas.) badigeon, *m.*; (pharm.) eau blanche, *f.*

whitewash (-woshe), *v.a.*, blanchir; (mas.) blanchir, badigeonner.

whitewasher, *n.*, badigeonneur, *m.*

whitewashing, *n.*, badigeonnage, *m.*

whither (hwi*th*'-), *adv.*, où.

whithersoever (hwi*th*'eur-sô-èv'-), *adv.*, partout, n'importe où; à quelque endroit que ce soit.

whiting (hwaït'-), *n.*, blanc d'Espagne; (ich.) merlan, *m.*

whitish (hwaït'-), *adj.*, blanchâtre.

whitishness (hwaït'-), *n.*, couleur blanchâtre, *f.*

whitlow (hwit'lô), *n.*, panaris, mal d'aventure, *m.* — grass; *drave*, *f.* — -wort; *paronyque argentée*, *f.*

whitsun (hwit'seune), *adj.*, de la Pentecôte.

whitsunday, *n.*, jour de la Pentecôte, *m.*

whitsuntide (-taïde), *n.*, Pentecôte, *f.*

whity-brown (hwaï-ti-braou'ne), *adj.*, brunâtre; (of paper—*papier*) bulle.

whiz, *v.a.*, siffler.

whiz, *n.*, sifflement. *m.*

who (hou), *pron.*, qui.

whoever (hou-èv'), *pron.*, quiconque; qui que ce soit.

whole (hôle), *adj.*, entier, tout; intact; complet; total; (sound—*sain*) sain.

whole (hôle), *n.*, tout; total, montant; ensemble, *m.*; totalité, *f.* The — of us; *nous tous.*

wholesale (hôl'séle), *n.*, vente en gros, *f.* By —; *en gros.*

wholesome (hôl'ceume), *adj.*, (salubrious—*salubre*) sain, salubre; (salutary—*salutaire*) salutaire; (useful—*utile*) utile; (pleasing—*agréable*) agréable; (fig.) salutaire, sain, moral.

wholesomely, *adv.*, d'une manière salubre; sainement.

wholesomeness, *n.*, salubrité; nature salutaire; (salutariness—*caractère salutaire*) nature salutaire, utilité; (fig.) nature salutaire, moralité, pureté, *f.*

wholly (hôl'li), *adv.*, entièrement; tout à fait.

whom (houme), *pron.*, que; (indirect object and direct object, of persons only—*régime direct et indirect, des personnes seulement*) qui; (of persons and things—*des personnes et des choses*) lequel, *m.sing.*, laquelle, *f.sing.*, lesquels, *m.pl.*, lesquelles, *f.pl.*

whomsoever (-sô-èv'-), *pron.*, qui que ce soit, quiconque.

whoop (houpe), *n.*, huée, *f.*; cri, *m.*; (orni.) huppe, *f.*

whoop (houpe), *v.n.*, huer, crier.

whoop, *v.a.*, huer.

whooping (houp'-), *n.*, huées, *f.pl.*; cris, *m.pl.*

whooping-cough (côfe), *n.* V. **hooping-cough.**

whore (hôre), *n.*, prostituée, *f.*

whore (hôre), *v.a.*, fréquenter les femmes de mauvaise vie.

whoredom (hôr-deume), *n.*, fornication; paillardise, *f.*

whoremonger (hôr'meu'n'gheur), *n.*, débauché, *m.*

whorish (hôr'-), *adj.*, impudique.

whose (houze), *pron.*, dont, de qui, *m.*, *f. sing.*, *pl.*; duquel. *m.sing.*, de laquelle. *f.sing.*; desquels, *m.pl.*, desquelles, *f.pl.*; à qui.

whosoever (hou-çô-èv'-), *pron.*, qui que ce soit. quiconque.

whur (hweur), *v.n.*, parler gras, grasseyer.

why (hwa'ye), *adv.*, pourquoi.

why, *exc.*, eh bien, mais.

wick (wicke), *n.*, mèche (of candle, lamp, &c —*de chandelle, de lampe, &c.*), *f.*

wicked (wik'ède). *adj.*, méchant, pervers; (mischievous—*malfaisant*) méchant, malin. — thing; *méchanceté, f.*

wickedly (wik'èd'-), *adv.*, méchamment; par méchanceté.

wickedness (wik'èd-), *n.*, méchanceté. perversité; immoralité; (mischievousness—*malfaisance*) méchanceté, malice, *f.*

wicken-tree (wik'n-trî), *n.*, (bot.) sorbier des oiseaux, *m.*

wicker (wik'eur), *n.*, osier, *m.* — -work; *clayonnage, m.*

wicker, *adj.*, d'osier, en osier.

wicket (wik'ète), *n.*, guichet, *m.*; (at cricket —*jeu de crosse*) barres, *f.pl.*

wide (waïde), *adj.*, large; large de; (having great extent—*de grandes dimensions*) grand, ample, étendu; (distant) distant, éloigné. A table three feet —; *une table large de trois pieds*; *une table de trois pieds de large, de largeur.*

wide (waïde), *adv.*, loin, au loin; largement.

widely (waïd'-), *adv.*, au large; au loin; grandement, largement.

widen (waïd'n), *v.a.*, élargir, étendre. agrandir.

widen, *v.n.*, s'élargir, s'étendre, s'agrandir.

wideness (waïd'-), *n.*, largeur; grandeur; étendue, *f.*

widening (waïd'-), *n.*, élargissement, *m*

widgeon (widj'o'n), *n.*, (orni.) canard siffleur, *m.*

widow (widô'), *n.*, veuve, *f.*

widow (widô'), *v.a.*, rendre veuve.

widowed (widô'd), *adj.*, veuf.

widower (widô-eur), *n.*, veuf, *m.*

widowhood (widô-houde), *n.*, veuvage, *m.*

width (wid'th), *n.*, largeur, grandeur, étendue, *f.*

wield (wil'de), *v.a.*, manier; tenir; porter.

wieldy (wild'i), *adj.*, maniable.

wife (waïfe), *n.*, femme, épouse, *f.*

wifeless (waïf'-), *adj.*, sans femme, sans épouse.

wifely (waïf'-), *adj.*, de femme, d'épouse.

wig, *n.*, perruque, *f.*

wight (waïte), *n.*, personne, *f.*, être, personnage, *m.*

wigwam (wig-wô'me), *n.*, wigwam, *m.*; cahute, chaumière, hutte, *f.*

wild (waïlde), *n.*, désert; lieu sauvage, *m.*; solitude, *f.*

wild (waïlde), *adj.*, sauvage; (desert) sauvage, inculte; (not civilized—*non civilisé*) sauvage; (savage) sauvage, farouche; (turbulent) turbulent, violent, tumultueux; (ungoverned—*emporté*) impétueux, violent, furieux, déchaîné; (inconstant) inconstant, capricieux, changeant; (inordinate—*déréglé*) licencieux, déréglé; (uncouth—*bizarre*) étrange, bizarre; (irregular—*irrégulier*) déréglé; désordonné; (of the look—*du visage*) hagard, égaré, effaré; (of plants, fruit—*des plantes, des fruits*) sauvage. — girl; *étourdie, écervelée, f.* — beast; *bête féroce*; *bête sauvage. f.*

wilderness (wil'deur-), *n.*, désert; lieu désert, *m.*; solitude, *f.*

wild-fire(waïld'faeur), *n.*, feu grégeois; (vet.) érésipèle, *m.*; (med.) dartre, *f.*

wildly (waïld'li),*adv.*, (without cultivation—*sans culture*) sans culture, à l'état sauvage; (without tameness—*sauvagement*) d'une manière farouche; (with disorder—*en désordre*) avec désordre; (irregularly—*irrégulièrement*) d'une manière désordonnée; (heedlessly—*follement*) étourdiment, follement; (extravagantly—*avec extravagance*) avec extravagance. To stare —; *regarder d'un air égaré, d'un air hagard.*

wildness (waïld'-), *n.*, (savage state—*état sauvage*) état sauvage; (uncultivated state—*état inculte*) état inculte, état sauvage, *m.*; (savageness—*férocité*) nature farouche, férocité; (irregularity—*irrégularité*) folie, extravagance, *f.*, dérèglement, désordre, *m.*; (alienation of mind—*folie*) aliénation mentale, *f.*; (of the look—*expression du visage*) égarement, *m.*; (of the winds—*des vents*) impétuosité, violence; (of children—*des enfants*) turbulence; (of the passions—*des passions*) licence, *f.*, dérèglement, *m.*

wile (waïle), *n.*, artifice, *m.*; ruse, fourberie,*f.*

wilful (wil-foule),*adj.*, volontaire; opiniâtre; (of horses—*des chevaux*) difficile, rétif; (of things—*des choses*) volontaire, fait à dessein, fait avec préméditation.

wilfully, *adv.*, opiniâtrément; avec entêtement; à dessein; avec intention; (jur.) avec préméditation.

wilfulness, *n.*, caractère volontaire, *m.*; opiniâtreté, *f.*; entêtement, *m.*

wilily (waï-li-li) *adv.*, artificieusement, frauduleusement.

wiliness (waï-li-), *n.*, fourberie, ruse, astuce, *f.*

will, *n.*, volonté,*f.*; vouloir; (desire—*désir*) désir, souhait, *m.*; (pleasure—*bon plaisir*) volonté,*f.*, bon plaisir, gré; (power—*pouvoir*) pouvoir; (divine determination) arrêt; (jur.) testament, *m.* Last — and testament; *dernières volontés, f.pl.*; testament, *m.* At —; *à volonté; à discrétion; à son gré.* What is your — ? *quel est votre désir? que désirez-vous?* To bear any one good—; *vouloir du bien à quelqu'un.* To bear any one ill— ; *vouloir du mal à quelqu'un; en vouloir à quelqu'un.*

will, *v.a.*, vouloir; ordonner; (by testament—*par testament*) léguer.

will, *v.auxil.* (preterit, Would), vouloir; devoir.

willer, *n.*, personne qui veut,*f.*

willing, *adj.*, bien disposé, de bonne volonté; complaisant; (voluntary—*volontaire*) volontaire. — to; *désireux de; empressé de.* — or not; *bon gré mal gré.* To be — ; *vouloir, vouloir bien.*

willingly (will'ign'li), *adv.*, volontiers; de bon cœur; de bonne volonté; volontairement.

willingness (will'ign'nèee), *n.*, bonne volonté,*f.*; bon vouloir, *m.*; complaisance, *f.* — to; *bonne disposition à,f.*; *penchant à; empressement à, m.*

will-o'-the-wisp, or **will-with-a-wisp**, *n.*, feu follet, *m.*

willow (wil'lô), *n.*, saule, *m.* Weeping—; *saule de Babylone; saule pleureux.*

willow-ground(-graou'n'de), *n.*, saussaie,*f.*

willow-herb (-eurbe), *n.*, (bot) osier Saint-Antoine, *m.*

willowish (wil'lô-ishe), *adj.*, couleur de saule.

willowy (wil'lô-i), *adv.*, couvert de saules.

wily (waï-li), *adj.*, rusé, fin, astucieux, fourbe.

wimble (wi'm'b'l), *n.*, vilebrequin, *m.*

wimble (wi'm'b'l), *v.a.*, faire un trou avec un vilebrequin.

win, *v.a.* (preterit and *past part.*, Won), gagner; remporter; (fig.) gagner, séduire.

win, *v.n.*, gagner; triompher, vaincre. To — upon; *gagner, séduire;* (to gain ground—*gagner*

du terrain) *faire des progrès dans, gagner du terrain dans.*

wince, *v.n.*, reculer; tressaillir; (of horses— *des chevaux*) ruer, se cabrer.

wincer, *n.*, animal qui rue, qui se cabre, *m.*

winch, *n.*, manivelle,*f.*

wind, *n.*, vent, *m.*; (breath—*respiration*) respiration, haleine, *f.*; (flatulence—*flatuosité*) vent, *m.*, ventuosité, flatuosité; (vet.) tympanite, *f.*; (fig.) vent, *m.*, fumée, *f.* It is an ill —that blows nobody good; *à quelque chose malheur est bon.* To get — of; *éventer.*

wind, *v.a.*, éventer, exposer au vent, à l'air; (hunt.) avoir vent de, flairer; (to take the breath away—*essouffler*) faire perdre haleine à, essouffler.

wind, *v.a.* (*preterit and past part.*, Wound), (to turn—*tourner*) tourner; (to turn round some object—*enrouler*) rouler, enrouler, dévider; (to change—*changer*) changer; (to enfold—*envelopper*) envelopper, enrouler. To — into; *insinuer dans, glisser dans.* To — off; *dérouler; dévider.* To — up; *rouler, entortiller;* (to bring to a settlement—*mettre fin à*) *régler, terminer;* (com.) liquider; (to raise by degrees—*élever graduellement*) élever peu à peu; (clocks, &c.—*pendules, &c.) monter, remonter;* (fig.) *préparer, apprêter.*

wind, *v.n.*, se rouler, s'enrouler, s'entortiller; (to turn—*tourner*) tourner; (to change—*varier*) changer, varier; (to turn around something— *s'enlacer*) s'enlacer, circuler, tourner; (to have a circular direction—*serpenter*) serpenter, aller en spirale; (to proceed in flexures—*aller en serpentant*) serpenter, tourner. To — out of; *sortir de.* To — up; *se remonter.*

windage (wi'n'd'édje), *n.*, (artil.) vent, évent, *m.*

wind-bore (-bôre), *n.*, tuyau à vent, *m.*

wind-bound (-baou'n'de), *adj.*,arrêté par les vents contraires.

wind-channel(-tsha'n'-), *n.*, (mus.) conduit à vent, *m.*

wind-chest (-tshèste), *n.*, (mus.) sommier,*m.*

wind-dial (-daï-), *n.*, anémoscope, *m.*, girouette, *f.*

winded, *adj.*, hors d'haleine; essoufflé.

winder (waï'n'd'-), *n.*, dévideur, *m.*, dévideuse, *f.*; (thing—*chose*) dévidoir, *m.*; (bot.) plante grimpante, *f.*

winder (wi'n'deur), *n.*, chose qui fait perdre haleine, *f.*

windfall (wi'n'd'fôl), *n.*, fruit abattu par le vent, *m.*; (fig.) aubaine, bonne aubaine,*f.*

wind-flower (-fla'weur), *n.*, anémone, *f.*

wind-gall (-gôl), *n.*, (vet.) molette,*f.*

wind-gate, *n.*, voie d'aérage,*f.*

wind-gauge (-ghèdje), *n.*, anémomètre, *m.*

wind-gun (-gheune), *n.*, fusil à vent, *m.*

windiness (wi'n'd'-), *n.*, nature venteuse; (flatulence) flatulence; (fig.) enflure, boursouflure,*f.*

winding (waï'n'd'-), *n.*, sinuosité, *f.*; méandre, détour, circuit, *m.*

winding (waï'n'd'-), *adj.*, sinueux, tortueux, tournant; en limaçon.

winding-engine (waï'n'dign'è'n'djine), *n.*, machine de tour,*f.*

winding-sheet(waï'n'dign'shîte),*n.*,suaire, linceul, *m.*

wind-instrument (-i'n'striou-), *n.*, instrument à vent, *m.*

windlass (wi'n'd'lâss), *n.*, vindas; treuil, cabestan, *m.*

wind-mill, *n.*, moulin à vent, *m.*

window (wi'n'dô), *n.*, fenêtre, croisée; ouverture, *f.*; jour, *m.* Out of the —; *par la fenêtre.*

window, *v.a.*, garnir de fenêtres.

window-blind (-blaï'n'de), *n.*, jalousie, persienne, *f.*; store, *m.*

window-curtain (-keur-'ine), *n.*, rideau de fenêtre, *m.*

window-frame, n., dormant de fenêtre, m.
window-sash, n., châssis de fenêtre, m.
window-seat (-site), n., saillie intérieure de
fenêtre, f.
window-shutter (-sheut'-), n., volet; contrevent, m.
wind-pipe (wi'n'd'païpe), n., trachée-artère ;
trachée, f. ; conduit aérien, m.
wind-rode (-rôde), adj., (nav.) évité debout
au vent.
wind-sail (-séle), n., manche à air, f.
wind-tight (-taïte), adj., imperméable à
l'air, étanche.
windward, adv., (nav.) au vent.
windward, n., côté du vent, m.
windy (wi'n'd'-), adj., du vent; (tempestuous
—tempétueux) venteux; (flatulent—flatueux) venteux, flatueux ; (fig.) creux, vain, vide. It is —;
il fait du vent.
wine (waïne), n., vin ; (fig.) vin, m., boisson,
ivresse, f.
wine-bibber (-bib'-), n., biberon, ivrogne, m.
wine-broker (-brôk'-), n., courtier en
vins, m.
wine-glass (-glâce), n., verre à vin, m.
wine-grower (-grô-eur), n., propriétaire de
vignes, m.
wine-growing (-grô-igne), adj., vinicole.
wine-making (-mék'-), n., vinification; fabrication du vin, f.
wine-merchant (-meur'tsha'n'tè), n., négociant en vins, marchand de vin, m.
wine-press, n., pressoir, m.
wine-shop, n., boutique de marchand de
vin, f.; cabaret, m.
wine-stone (-stône), n., tartre brut, m.
wine-strainer (-stré'n'-), n., passe-vin, m.
wine-taster (-tést'-), n., dégustateur, m.
wing (wigne), n., aile ; (flight—vol) course, f.,
vol, m.
wing (wigne), v.a., garnir d'ailes ; (to transport by flight—transporter sur des ailes) transporter sur des ailes ; (to wound in the wing—
blesser à l'aile) frapper à l'aile, blesser à l'aile.
winged (wign'dè), adj., ailé ; rapide.
winger (wign'eur),n.,(nav.) petite barrique,f.
wingless (wign'-), adj., aptère, qui n'a pas
d'ailes.
winglet (wign'lète), n., ailette, f.
wing-shell, n., (ent.) élytre, m.
wingy (wign'i), adj., ailé, rapide.
wink, n., clin d'œil, m. Not to sleep a —; ne
pas fermer l'œil.
wink, v.n., cligner l'œil; clignoter; (of a
light—d'une lumière) vaciller, trembler. To —at;
faire signe de l'œil à ; (to connive at—conniver)
fermer les yeux sur.
winker, n., personne qui cligne l'œil ; (blind
for horses—pour les chevaux) œillère, f.
winking, n., clignement ; clignement
d'yeux, m.
winking, adj., qui cligne l'œil, clignotant ;
qui fait signe de l'œil ; (of a light—d'une lumière)
vacillant, tremblant.
winkingly, adv., en clignotant.
winner, n., personne qui gagne, f. ; gagnant, m.
winning, n., gain, m. —s; gain, m.sing.
winning, adj., gagnant ; (attracting—séduisant) qui gagne le cœur, séduisant, enchanteur.
winnow (wi'n'nô), v.a., vanner ; éventer ;
(to examine—approfondir) examiner, sasser ; (to
separate—séparer) séparer, diviser.
winnow, v.n., vanner.
winnower (wi'n'nô-eur), n., vanneur, m.
winnowing (wi'n'nô-igne), n., vannage ;
(fig.) examen, m.
winter (wi'n'teur), n., hiver · (print.) sommier, m.

winter (wi'n'teur), v.n., hiverner, passer
l'hiver.
winter, v.a., conserver pendant l'hiver ;
nourrir pendant l'hiver.
winter-berry (-bèr'ri), n., (bot.) apalachine, f.
winter-cherry (-tshèr'-), n., (bot.) coqueret, m.
winter-fallow (-fal-lô), v.a.,(agri.)hiverner.
winter-ground (-graou'n'de), v.a., (agri.)
conserver pendant l'hiver.
winterly, adj., d'hiver.
winter-season (-si-z'n), n., saison d'hiver,f.
winter-weed (-wîde), n., (bot.) véronique à
feuilles de lierre, f.
wintry, adj., d'hiver, hyémal, hiémal.
winy (waï-ni), adj., vineux, de vin.
wipe (waïpe), n., action d'essuyer ; (jeer-
sarcasme) raillerie, f., lardon, brocard, m. ; (blow
—coup) taloche, f.
wipe (waïpe), v.a., essuyer ; nettoyer ; (to
cleanse—purifier) purifier. — off, away ; essuyer,
ôter ; (fig.) effacer.
wiper (waïp'-), n., personne qui essuie, f. ;
(thing—chose) linge, torchon, m.
wire (waeur), n., fil de métal, fil de fer, fil
d'archal, m.
wire (waeur), v.a., attacher, lier avec un fil
de métal ; griller.
wiredraw (waeur'drô), v.a. (preterit, Wire-
drew ; past part., Wiredrawn), tréfiler ; étendre,
allonger ; (fig.) étendre, étirer, alambiquer.
wire-drawer (waeur-drô-eur), n., tireur,
tréfileur, m.
wire-drawing (waeur-drô-igne), n., tréfilerie, f.
wire-gauze (-gôze), n., gaze métallique, f.
wire-grass (-grâce), n., (bot.) paturin comprimé, m.
wire-guard (-gârde), n., garde-feu, m.
wire-heel (waeur-hîle), n., (vet.) seime au
talon, f.
wire-mark (-mârke), n., vergeure, f.
wire-mill, n., tréfilerie, f.
wire-ribbon (-rib'bo'n), n., cannetille, f.
wire-work (-weurke), n., grillage en fil
métallique ; réseau, treillis, m.
wire-working (waeur-weurk'-), n., tréfilerie, f.
wiry (waeur'-), adj., en fil métallique ; en
filigrane ; comme du fil métallique.
wisdom (wiz'deume), n., sagesse ; prudence, f.
wise (waïze), adj., sage ; (discreet—discret)
discret, sage, prudent ; (grave) grave, sage. —
man ; sage. — men of the East ; nages, m.pl.
wise (waïze), n., manière, façon, sorte, f. In
no — ; en aucune manière ; en aucune façon.
wiseacre (waïz'a-keur), n., prétendu sage,
benêt, sot, m.
wiseling (waïz'ligne), n., prétendu sage,
faux sage.
wisely (waïz'-), adv., sagement ; prudemment.
wish, n., souhait, désir ; vœu, m.
wish, v.a., souhaiter ; désirer ; vouloir ; faire
des vœux pour. To — any one to the devil ;
envoyer quelqu'un à tous les diables.
wish, v.n., souhaiter ; désirer ; vouloir. To —
for ; souhaiter, désirer ; demander.
wisher, n., personne qui souhaite, qui
désire, f.
wishful (-foule), adj., désireux, qui désire ;
qui exprime le désir.
wishfully (-foule), adv., avec désir ; vivement.
wisp, n., torchon, bouchon de paille,
d'herbe, m.
wistful (-foule), adj., attentif ; pensif ; (wishful—désireux) désireux, ardent.

wistfully, *adv.*, attentivement; d'une manière pensive; ardemment, vivement.

wit, *v.a.*, savoir. To —; *savoir*.

wit, *n.*, esprit; (intellect) esprit, entendement, jugement, génie, *m.*; (pers.) personne spirituelle, *f.*, homme d'esprit, bel esprit, *m.*, femme d'esprit, *f.*; (man of genius—*homme de génie*) grand esprit, homme de génie, *m.* —s; *esprit*, *m.*, *raison*, *tête*, *f.*, *sens*, *bon sens*, *m.* To drive any one out of his —s; *faire perdre la tête à quelqu'un*. To have lost one's —s; *avoir perdu la tête; être hors de son bon sens*. To frighten any one out of his —s; *faire une peur horrible à quelqu'un*. To be at one's —s' ends; *être au bout de son latin; ne plus savoir à quel saint se vouer*.

witch, *n.*, sorcière, magicienne, *f.*

witchcraft (witsh'crâfte), *n.*, sorcellerie, magie, *f.*; maléfice; sortilège, *m.*

witchery, *n.*, sorcellerie, *f.*; sortilège, charme, enchantement, *m.*; (fascination) fascination, *f.*

with (with), *prep.*, avec; de; (at) de; (by means of) par; (who has, who have—*qui a*, *qui ont*) à, au, à la, aux; (among persons, bodies of men—*parmi les personnes*, *les associations*) auprès de; (among nations, &c.—*parmi les nations*, *&c.*) chez, parmi; (in the house of—*la demeure de*) chez; (after *same—après* same) que. To be — any one; *être avec quelqu'un*. To write—a pen; *écrire avec une plume*. To cover —; *couvrir de*. To hold, to love — all one's might; *tenir, aimer de toute sa force*. The lady — blue eyes; *la dame aux yeux bleus*. — study; *par l'étude*. I am disgusted, enchanted — that; *je suis dégoûté, enchanté de cela*. Angry —; *fâché contre*.

withal (with'ôl), *adv.*, ensemble; aussi, de plus.

withdraw (with'drô), *v.a.* (*preterit*, Withdrèw; *past part.*, Withdrawn), retirer; éloigner.

withdraw, *v.n.*, se retirer, s'éloigner.

withdrawal, *or* **withdrawment** (with-drô-), *n.*, retraite, *f.*

withe (withe), *n.*, osier, pleyon, *m.*

wither (with'eur), *v.a.*, flétrir; dessécher; faire dépérir.

wither (with'eur), *v.n.*, se dessécher; se flétrir, se faner; dépérir; languir.

wither-band (with'eur-), *n.*, arçon de selle, *m.*

witheredness (with'eur'd'-), *n.*, dessèchement; dépérissement, *m.*; langueur, *f.*

withering (with'eur'-), *adj.*, qui se flétrit; dédaigneux.

withers (with'eurze), *n.pl.*, garrot, *m.sing.*

wither-wrung (with'eur-reun'gn), *adj.*, égarrotté.

withhold (with'hôlde), *v.a.* (*preterit* and *past part.*, Withheld), retenir, arrêter; comprimer; refuser.

withholder (with'hôld'-), *n.*, personne qui retient, qui arrête, qui refuse, *f.*

within (with'i'n), *prep.*, dans, en; (of time—*de temps*) dans, en, dans l'espace de; (of past time—*du passé*) depuis; (of future time—*du futur*) dans, en, d'ici à; (not exceeding—*n'excédant pas*) au-dessous de.

within (with'i'n), *adv.*, en dedans; à l'intérieur; intérieurement; (in the house—*à la maison*) à la maison, chez soi.

without (with'aoute), *prep.*, sans; (outside—*hors*) hors de, en dehors de.

without (with'aoute), *conj.*, à moins que, sans que.

without (with'aoute), *adv.*, en dehors, dehors, par dehors; à l'extérieur; extérieurement.

withstand (with-), *v.a.*, résister à.

withstander (with-), *n.*, personne qui résiste, *f.*

withstanding (with-), *n.*, résistance, *f.*

withy (with'i), *n.*, osier, franc osier, *m.*

withy (with'i), *adj.*, d'osier; de pleyon.

witless, *adj.*, sans esprit; (inconsidéré—*irréfléchi*) inconsidéré, irréfléchi; (indiscreet —*indiscret*) indiscret, léger.

witlessly, *adv.*, sans esprit; inconsidérément.

witling, *n.*, petit esprit; sot, *m.*

witness, *n.*, témoin; (testimony—*témoignage*) témoignage, *m.* To bear — to; *témoigner de*. To call to —; *prendre à témoin; appeler en témoignage*.

witness, *v.a.*, témoigner; être témoin de; voir.

witness, *v.n.*, témoigner; porter témoignage.

witticism (-ciz'm), *n.*, trait d'esprit, bon mot, *m.*

wittily, *adv.*, spirituellement, avec esprit.

wittiness, *n.*, esprit, *m.*; nature spirituelle, *f.*

wittingly, *adv.*, sciemment; à dessein.

wittol, *n.*, mari cocu et content, *m.*

witty, *adj.*, spirituel, d'esprit, qui a de l'esprit; (sarcastic—*sarcastique*) piquant, sarcastique.

wizard, *n.*, sorcier, magicien, *m.*

woad (wôde), *n.*, pastel, *m.*; guède, *f.*

woe (wô), *n.*, malheur, *m.*; peine, douleur, *f.*; chagrin, *m.*; (curse—*malédiction*) malédiction, *f.*

woe! (wô), *int.*, malheur!

woebegone (wô-bi-), *adj.*, anéanti par la douleur, désolé.

woful (wô-foule), *adj.*, triste, désolé, malheureux, affligé; (mournful—*triste*) malheureux, triste, affligeant; (paltry—*misérable*) triste, piteux, méchant.

wofully (wô-foul'-), *adv.*, tristement; douloureusement; cruellement.

wofulness, *n.*, malheur, chagrin, *m.*; douleur, affliction, peine, *f.*

wolf (woulfe), *n.*, loup, *m.* She- --; *louve*. Young —; *louveteau*, *m.*

wolf-dog, *n.*, chien-loup, *m.*

wolf-fish, *n.*, (ich.) loup de mer, *m.*

wolfish (woulf'-), *adj.*, de loup; rapace.

wolf's-bane, *n.*, (bot.) aconit, *m.*

wolf's-claw (-clô), *n.*, (bot.) lycopode, pied-de-loup, *m.*

wolf's-milk (woulfs'-), *n.*, (bot.) tithymale, *m.*

woman (woum'-), *n.* (*women*), femme, *f.*

woman (woum'-), *v.a.*, rendre doux comme une femme.

woman-hater (-hét'-), *n.*, misogyne, *m.*

womanhood (-houde), *n.*, état de femme, *m.*

womanish, *adj.*, de femme; qui convient aux femmes; féminin; (effeminate—*mou*) efféminé.

womanishly, *adv.*, en femme.

womanishness, *n.*, nature de femme; mollesse, *f.*

womanize (-'aïze), *v.a.*, efféminer, amollir.

womankind (-kaï'n'de), *n.*, sexe féminin, *m.*; femmes, *f.pl.*

woman-like (-laïke), *adj.*, de femme, féminin.

womanly, *adj.*, de femme; féminin.

womanly, *adv.*, en femme, comme une femme.

womb (woume), *n.*, utérus, *m.*; matrice, *f.*; (fig.) sein, *m.*, entrailles, *f.pl.*, flancs, *m.pl.*

women (wim'ê'n), *n.pl.*, femmes, *f.* V. **woman**, *n.*

wonder (weun'd'-), *v.n.*, s'étonner; être étonné, être surpris; (to doubt—*douter*) être curieux de savoir. To — at; *s'étonner de; être étonné de; s'émerveiller de*.

wonder (weun'd'-), *n.*, étonnement; (cause of wonder—*cause d'étonnement*) merveille, *f.*; (miracle) miracle, prodige, *m.*, merveille, *f.*

No — ! *ce n'est pas étonnant!* It is a — that; *il est étonnant que.*

wonderer, *n.*, personne qui s'étonne, *f.*; admirateur, *m.*, admiratrice, *f.*

wonderful (-foule), *adj.*, étonnant; merveilleux, prodigieux.

wonderfully, *adv.*, étonnamment; merveilleusement; prodigieusement.

wonderfulness, *n.*, nature étonnante, *f.*; merveilleux, prodigieux, *m.*

wonderment, *n.*, étonnement, *m.*; merveille, *f.*

wonder-struck (-streuke), *adj.*, étonné, frappé d'étonnement; émerveillé.

wonder-worker (weurk'-), *n.*, personne qui fait des prodiges, *f.*

wonder-working (-weurk'-), *adj.*, qui fait des merveilles.

wondrous (weu'n'd'-), *adj.*, merveilleux; prodigieux; étonnant.

wondrous, *or* **wondrously**, *adv.*, étonnamment; prodigieusement; merveilleusement.

wont (weu'n'te), *adj.*, accoutumé, habitué.

wont (weu'n'te), *v.n.*, avoir coutume de, être habitué à.

wonted (weu'n't'-), *adj.*, accoutumé, habitué; habituel.

wontedness (weu'n't'-), *n.*, état habituel, *m.*

woo (wou), *v.a.*, faire la cour à, l'amour à; rechercher en mariage; courtiser; demander; solliciter.

woo (wou), *v.n.*, courtiser; faire la cour.

wood (woude), *n.*, bois; (forest) bois, *m.*, forêt, *f.*

wood-ashes (-ash'ize), *n.*, cendres végétales, de bois, *f.pl.*

wood-bind, *or* **wood-bine** (-baïne), *n.*, chèvrefeuille des bois, *m.*

wood-bound (-baou'n'de), *adj.*, entouré de bois.

wood-cock, *n.*, (orni.) bécasse, *f.*

wood-cut (-keute), *n.*, gravure sur bois, *f.*

wood-cutter (-keut'-), *n.*, bûcheron; (engraver—*graveur*) graveur sur bois, *m.*

wood-cutting (-keut'-), *n.*, coupe des bois, du bois, *f.*

wooded (woud'-), *adj.*, boisé; couvert de bois, d'arbres.

wooden, *adj.*, de bois, en bois; (clumsy—*maladroit*) gauche.

wood-engraver (-è'n'grév'-), *n.*, graveur sur bois, *m.*

wood-engraving (-è'n'grév'-), *n.*, gravure sur bois, *f.*

wood-grower (-grô-eur), *n.*, cultivateur de bois, *m.*

wood-hole (-hôle), *or* **wood-house** (-haouce), *n.*, bûcher (place—*lieu*), *m.*

wood-land, *n.*, pays de bois, *m.*

woodless, *adj.*, sans bois, sans forêts.

wood-lock, *n.*, (nav.) clef de gouvernail, *f.*

wood-louse (-laouce), *n.*, cloporte, armadille, *m.*

wood-man, *n.*, garde forestier; bûcheron; chasseur, *m.*

wood-monger (-meu'n'gheur), *n.*, marchand de bois, *m.*

wood-note (-nôte), *n.*, chant sauvage, *m.*, musique sauvage, *f.*

wood-nymph, *n.*, nymphe des bois, dryade, *f.*

wood-pecker (-pèk'-), *n.*, (orni.) pic, pivert, *m.*

wood-pigeon (-pidj'eune), *n.*, pigeon ramier, *m.*

wood-pile (-païle), *n.*, pile de bois, *f.*

wood-reeve (woud'rive), *n.*, inspecteur de forêt, *m.*

wood-roof (-roufe), *or* **wood-ruff**, *n.*, (bot.) aspérule, *f.*

wood-shed, *n.*, bûcher (place—*lieu*), *m.*

wood-sorrel, *n.*, oseille sauvage, *f.*

wood-work (-weurke), *n.*, boisage, *m.*

woody (woud'-), *adj.*, boisé, couvert de bois, couvert d'arbres; (ligneous—*ligneux*) ligneux, boiseux; (pertaining to woods—*des bois*) des bois, des forêts.

wood-yard (-yârde), *n.*, chantier de bois à brûler, *m.*

wooer (wou-eur), *n.*, homme qui fait la cour, qui recherche en mariage; galant, amant, amoureux, *m.*

woof (woufe), *n.*, trame; (texture—*tissu*) étoffe, *f.*, tissu, *m.*

wooingly (wou-ign'-), *adv.*, amoureusement, avec amour.

wool (woule), *n.*, laine; (bot.) la'ne, *f.*, poil, duvet, *m.*; (hair—*cheveux*) cheveux < épus, *m.pl.*

wool-ball (-bôl), *n.*, (vet.) égagropile, *m.*; gobbe, *f.*

wool-comber (-côm'eur), *n.*, cardeur de laine, *m.*

woold (woulde), *v.a.*, (nav.) rouster, roster.

woolder (would'-), *n.*, (nav.) jumelle, *f.*

woolding (would'-), *n.*, (nav.) rousture, rosture, *f.*

wooldriver (-draïv'-), *n.*, marchand de laines, *m.*

wool-gathering (-gath'eur'-), *n.*, absence d'esprit, *f.* To go a — ; *avoir l'esprit aux talons; être distrait.*

woolled (woul'de), *adj.*, à laine.

woollen (woul'è'n), *n.*, étoffe de laine, *f.*

woollen (woul'è'n), *adj.*, de laine; drapé.

woollen-cloth (-cloth), *n.*, drap, *m.*; étoffe drapée, *f.*

woollen-draper (-drép'-), *n.*, marchand de drap; drapier, *m.*

woolliness (woul'-), *n.*, qualité, nature laineuse, *f.*

woolly (woul'-), *adj.*, laineux; (resembling wool—*comme la laine*) qui ressemble à de la laine; (clothed with wool—*couvert de laine*) couvert de laine; (of the hair—*des cheveux*) crépu, frisé.

wool-pack, *n.*, balle de laine, *f.*

wool-sack, *n.*, ballot de laine; (seat of the Lord Chancellor—*siège du Lord Chancelier d'Angleterre à la Chambre des Lords*) sac de laine, *m.*

wool-sorter, *n.*, trieur de laine, *m.*

wool-staple (-sté'p'l), *n.*, marché à laines, *m.*

wool-stapler (-sté-), *n.*, marchand de laines, *m.*

wool-winder (-waï'n'd'-), *n.*, emballeur de laines, *m.*

woots (woutse), *n.*, acier wootz, acier indien, *m.*

word (weurde), *n.*, mot, *m.*; parole, *f.*; (letters written or printed, short discourse—*écrit, imprimé; petit discours*) mot, *m.*; (dispute) dispute, *f.*, mots, *m.pl.*, paroles, *f.pl.*; (promise—*parole*) promesse, parole, *f.*; (signal, milit.) mot, mot d'ordre; (tidings—*nouvelle*) avis, *m.*, nouvelle; (declaration) déclaration, affirmation; (of God—*de Dieu*) parole, *f.*; (proverb) proverbe, dicton, mot; (gram.) mot, *m.* —s; (discourse—*discours*) paroles, *f.pl.*; (dispute) dispute, *f.*, paroles, *f.pl.*, mots, *m.pl.* By — of mouth; *de vive voix; verbalement.* Take my — for it; *croyez m'en.* To send — to; *envoyer dire à; faire dire à; donner avis à.* To write — to; *faire savoir à; mander à, écrire à.* — for — ; *mot à mot.*

word (weurde), *v.a.*, exprimer; écrire; rédiger.

word-book (-bouke), *n.*, vocabulaire, *m.*

word-catcher (-), *n.*, puriste, *m.f.*; personne qui chicane sur les mots, *f.*

wordiness (weurd'-), *n.*, prolixité, verbosité, *f.*

wording (weurd'-), *n.*, expression, énonciation; rédaction, teneur, *f.*

wordless (weurd'-), *adj.*, sans parole; silencieux.

wordy (weurd'-), *adj.*, verbeux, diffus.

work (weurke), *v.n.* (*preterit* and *past part.*, Worked, Wrought), travailler; (to act—*agir*) fonctionner, aller, agir; (tech.) jouer; (to operate—*opérer*) opérer, agir, avoir de l'effet; (to ferment—*fermenter*) fermenter, travailler; (to be agitated—*s'agiter*) s'agiter, se remuer, se mouvoir; (of a ship—*d'un vaisseau*) travailler, fatiguer. To — into; *entrer dans* . . . *peu à peu*; *pénétrer dans*; *s'introduire dans*. To — up; *s'élever*. To — upon; *travailler, exciter*.

work, *v.a.*, travailler; (to shape—*former*) travailler, façonner; (to lead, to influence—*mener, influencer*) conduire, amener, pousser; (to make by action or violence—*accomplir, agir violemment*) faire, se faire, se créer; (to produce—*produire*) produire, faire, opérer; (to embroider—*broder*) broder; (to cause to ferment—*produire fermentation*) faire fermenter, faire travailler; (print.) tirer; (a machine, a mill, &c.—*machine, moulin, &c.*) faire aller, faire mouvoir, manœuvrer; (a ship—*un vaisseau*) manœuvrer; (a mine, a railway, &c.—*mine, chemin de fer, &c.*) exploiter. A foul stream —s itself clear; *un ruisseau fangeux se purifie*. To — in; *faire entrer à force d'efforts.* To — off; *user, employer*; (print.) *tirer*. To — up; *travailler, employer*; (to excite—*soulever*) *soulever, exciter, enflammer.* To — up with; *mélanger avec.* To —out; *effectuer par son travail*; *accomplir par ses efforts*; (a debt—*une dette*) *acquitter une dette par son travail*; (a problem —*un problème*) *résoudre*; *effectuer*; *accomplir*; *venir à bout de.*

work (weurke), *n.*, travail; labeur; (work done—*travail accompli*) ouvrage, travail, *m.*, besogne; (embroidery—*broderie*) broderie; (awkward performance—*travail imparfait*) mauvaise besogne, *f.*, gâchis, *m.*; (action) action, œuvre, *f.*; (feat—*œuvre*) travail, *m.*; (effect—*effet*) œuvre, *f.*, effet, *m.*; (operation) opération; (lit.) œuvre, *f.*, ouvrage, *m.* —s; (manu.) *fabrique, usine, f. sing.*; (fort.) *travaux, m.pl.* ; (horl.) *mouvement, m. sing.* Servant of all —; *bonne à tout faire.* To be at —; *être à l'ouvrage, être à travailler.* To get through a deal of —; *abattre de la besogne.* What a piece of —! *quel gâchis! quel malheur!*

workable (weurk'a-b'l), *adj.*, maniable; qui peut être travaillé; (mines, &c.) exploitable.

work-bag, *n.*, sac à ouvrage; cabas, *m.*

work-box, *n.*, boîte à ouvrage, *f.*

work-day, *n. V.* **working-day**.

worked (weurk'te), *adj.*, brodé.

worker, *n.*, ouvrier; travailleur, *m.*

work-fellow (-fèl-lô), *n.*, compagnon de travail, *m.*

work-house (-haouce), *n.*, asile des pauvres; atelier, *m.* To come to the —; *aller mourir à l'hôpital.*

working, *n.*, travail; ouvrage; labeur, *m.*; (operation) opération, *f.*; (fermentation) travail, *m.*, fermentation; (of mines, &c.—*de mines, &c.*) exploitation; (fig.) œuvre. opération, *f.*; (print.) tirage, *m.*

working-barrel (-bar-rèl), *n.*, corps de pompe, *m.*

working-day, *n.*, jour ouvrable, *m.*

working-place, *n.*, champ d'exploitation, *m.*

working-point (-pwai'n't), *n.*, point de fatigue, *m.*

working-stock, *n.*, matériel d'exploitation, *m.*

workman, *n.*, ouvrier, artisan, *m.*

workmanly, *adj.*, d'ouvrier habile, bien fait.

workmanly. *adv.*, en ouvrier; habilement.

workmanship, *n.*, ouvrage; travail, *m.*; œuvre; main d'œuvre, *f.*

work-people (-pî-p'l), *n.pl.*, ouvriers, *m.pl.*

work-shop, *n.*, atelier (for workmen—*d'ouvriers*), *m.*

work-table (-té-b'l), *n.*, table à ouvrage, *f.*

work-woman (-woum'-), *n.*, ouvrière; couturière, *f.*

work-yard (-yârde), *n.*, chantier, *m.*

world (weurl'de), *n.*, monde; (course of life—*cours de la vie*) monde, *m.*, vie, *f.*; (time—*temps*) temps, *m.*, siècles, *m.pl.*; (fig.) monde, *m.*, foule; multitude, *f.* A — of good; *beaucoup de bien.* For all the —; *pour tout au monde*; (exactly—*précisément*) *exactement.* All the — over; *dans le monde entier.* To begin the —; *débuter dans le monde*; *commencer la vie.* The next —; *l'autre monde*; *la vie future.*

worldliness, *n.*, mondanité; (covetousness —*envie*) convoitise, *f.*

worldling (weurld'-), *n.*, mondain, *m.*

worldly (weurld'-), *adj.*, mondain; du monde; positif.

worldly, *adv.*, mondainement.

worldly-minded (weurld'li-maï'n'd'-), *adj.*, mondain.

worldly-mindedness, *n.*, mondanité, *f.*

worm (weurme), *n.*, ver, *m.*; chenille, larve, *f.*; (of a screw—*de vis*) filet; (artil.) tire-bourre; (tech.) tire-étoupes; (chem.) serpentin; (debased being—*personne vile*) vermisseau, ver de terre, *m.*

worm (weurme), *v.a.*, miner; (fire-arm—*arme à feu*) débourrer; (tech.) tarauder; (a rope —*une corde*) congréer.

worm, *v.n.*, ramper; se glisser; s'insinuer.

worm-bit, *n.*, mèche à vis, *f.*

worm-eaten (-it'è'n), *adj.*, vermoulu; rongé des vers.

worm-grass (-grâce), *n.* (bot.) spigélie; herbe aux vers, *f.*

worm-hole (-hôle), *n.*, vermoulure, *f.*

worming (weurm'-), *n.*, (nav.) congréage, *m.*

worm-like (-laïke), *adj.*, vermiculaire; comme un ver.

worm-powder (-paou-deur), *n.*, poudre vermifuge, *f.*

worm-preventer (-pri-vè'n't'-), *n.*, (nav.) serpenteau, *m.*

worm-screw (-scrou), *n.*, tire-bourre, *m.*

worm-seed (-sîde), *n.*, santoline, *f.*

worm-shaped (-shép'te), *adj.*, vermiculaire, vermiforme.

wormwood (weurm'woude), *n.*, absinthe, armoise, *f.*

wormy (weurm'-), *adj.*, verreux; plein de vers; (grovelling—*rampant*) rampant.

worrier (weur-ri-), *n.*, personne qui tracasse, qui tourmente, qui taquine, *f.*

worry (weur'-), *v.a.*, tracasser, tourmenter, taquiner; (to harass—*harceler*) harasser, échiner; harceler; (to tear—*déchirer*) déchirer.

worse (weurse), *adj.*, plus mauvais; pire; (of persons ill—*des malades*) plus malade, plus mal; (more wicked—*plus méchant*) plus méchant.

worse (weurse), *adv.*, plus mal; pis; plus fort. So much the —; *tant pis.* To begin again —than ever; *recommencer de plus belle.*

worship (weur-), *n.*, culte, *m.*; adoration, *f.*; (title—*titre*) honneur, *m.*

worship (weur-), *v.a.*, adorer, rendre un culte à.

worship, *v.n.*, adorer; adorer Dieu.

worshipful (-foule), *adj.*, honorable; digne.

worshipfully, *adv.*, avec honneur; respectueusement.

worshipper (weur-ship'-), *n.*, adorateur, *m.*, adoratrice, *f.*

worshipping, *n.*, culte, *m.*; adoration, *f.*

worst (weurste), *adj.*, le plus mauvais; le pire.

worst (weurste), *n.*, le plus mauvais, le pire, le plus méchant; le plus mal, le pis, *m.* At the

—; *au pis*. Do your —; *faites ce que vous voudrez*.

worst, *adv*., le pis, le plus mal, le plus fort.

worst (weurste), *v.a*., vaincre, défaire; l'emporter sur.

worsted (weurst'ède), *n*., laine; estame, *f*.

wort (weurte), *n*., moût, *m*.; (bot.) herbe, plante, *f*.

worth (weurth), *n*., prix, *m*.; valeur, *f*.; mérite, *m*.

worth (weurth), *adj*., qui vaut; égal; qui mérite; qui est riche de. To be —; *valoir*. He is — a million; *il est riche d'un million*. That is — seeing; *cela vaut la peine, cela mérite d'être vu*.

worthily (weur-*thi*-), *adv*., dignement, honorablement.

worthiness (weur-*thi*-), *n*., valeur, *f*., mérite, *m*.; vertu, *f*.

worthless (weurth'-), *adj*., sans valeur; de nulle valeur; sans mérite; méprisable, vil, qui ne vaut rien.

worthlessness (weurth'-), *n*., manque de valeur, *m*.; indignité, mauvaise qualité, *f*.

worthy (weur-*thi*), *n*., homme illustre, *m*.

worthy (weur-*thi*), *adj*., digne; honorable. — of; *digne de; qui mérite*.

would (woude). *V*. **will**.

would-be (woud'bî), *adj*., prétendu, soi-disant; manqué; qui voulait, avait, aurait voulu être.

wound (wou'n'de), *n*., blessure, plaie, *f*.

wound (wou'n'de), *v.a*., blesser, faire une blessure à; (to offend—*offenser*) blesser, offenser.

wounder, *n*., personne qui fait une blessure, *f*.

wounding, *n*., action de blesser, *f*.; blessures, *f.pl*.

woundwort (wou'n'd'weurte), *n*., vulnéraire, *f*.

wrack (rake), *n*., (bot.) fucus, varech, *m*.

wrack-grass (-grâce), *n*., (bot.) zostère, algue marine, *f*.

wrangle (ran'gn'g'l), *n*., dispute, *f*.; chamaillis, *m*.

wrangle (ran'gn'g'l), *v.n*., se disputer, se quereller, se chamailler.

wrangler, *n*., disputeur, querelleur, *m*., querelleuse, *f*.; (Cambridge) étudiant de la première série en mathématiques, *m*.

wranglesome, *adj*., querelleur.

wrangling, *n*., dispute, *f*.; chamaillis, *m*.

wrap (rape), *v.a*., rouler, enrouler; envelopper. To — up; *envelopper, ployer*.

wrapper (rap'-), *n*., personne qui enveloppe; (envelope) enveloppe; (bot.) volva, bourse; (for packing—*à emballer*) toile d'emballage; (for papers—*pour papiers*) chemise; (print.) couverture, *f*.

wrasse (race), *n*., (ich.) labre, *m*.

wrath (rôth), *n*., courroux, *m*.; colère, *f*.

wrathful (rôth'foule), *adj*., courroucé, furieux.

wrathfully (rôth'-), *adv*., avec courroux; avec colère.

wreak (rike), *v.a*., exécuter; décharger, faire peser; assouvir, satisfaire.

wreakful (rik'foule), *adj*., (ant.) vindicatif; furieux.

wreath (rîth), *n*., guirlande, couronne, *f*.

wreathe (rî*the*), *v.a*., entortiller; entrelacer, tresser; couronner, ceindre.

wreathe (rî*the*), *v.n*., s'entrelacer.

wreathed (rî*th*'de), *adj*., entrelacé; entouré de guirlandes; (of a column—*colonne*) torse.

wreathing (rî*th*'-), *n*., entrelacement, *m*.

wreck (rèke), *n*., naufrage; (ruins of a ship —*débris d'un vaisseau*) navire naufragé, *m*., débris d'un naufrage, *m.pl*.; (fig.) naufrage, *m*., débris, *m.pl*., destruction, ruine, *f*.

wreck (rèke), *v.a*., faire faire naufrage à; jeter à la côte; (to ruin—*ruiner*) ruiner, perdre.

wreck, *v.n*., faire naufrage; se perdre; périr.

wrecked (rèk'te), *adj*., naufragé.

wreckful (rèk'foule), *adj*., fécond en naufrages.

wren (rè'n), *n*., (orni.) roitelet, *m*.

wrench (rè'n'she), *n*., torsion, *f*.; tortillement, *m*.; (sprain—*foulure*) entorse; (instrument) clef (to unscrew—*pour dévisser*), *f*.

wrench (rè'n'she), *v.a*., arracher en tordant; (to sprain—*se donner une foulure*) se fouler.

wrest (rèste), *n*., torsion violente; action d'arracher en tordant; violence; (instrument) clef d'accordeur, *f*.

wrest (rèste), *v.a*., arracher; (to distort—*tordre*) tordre; torturer, fausser, forcer.

wrester (rèst'-), *n*., personne qui arrache, qui torture, qui tord, &c., *f*.

wrestle (rès's'l), *v.n*., lutter.

wrestler (rès's'l'-), *n*., lutteur, athlète, *m*.

wrestling (rès's'l'-), *n*., lutte; lutte corps à corps, *f*.

wretch (rètshe), *n*., malheureux, *m*., malheureuse, *f*.; infortuné, *m*., infortunée, *f*.; (worthless person—*misérable*) misérable, *m*., *f*., être méprisable, être vil, *m*.

wretched (rètsh'ède), *adj*., malheureux, infortuné; (despicable—*méprisable*) méprisable, misérable, vil; (paltry—*misérable*) triste, méchant; (calamitous—*calamiteux*) calamiteux, malheureux.

wretchedly (rètsh'ed'-), *adv*., malheureusement; dans la misère; misérablement; tristement; (despicably—*indignement*) d'une manière méprisable, indignement.

wretchedness (rètsh'èd'-), *n*., misère, pauvreté, infortune, *f*.; (unhappiness—*misère*) malheur, *m*., souffrance, misère, infortune; (despicableness—*caractère méprisable*) nature méprisable, nature vile, *f*.

wriggle (rig'g'l), *v.n*., se tortiller, se remuer; frétiller, s'agiter, se démener. To — into; se fourrer dans, s'insinuer dans. To — out; s'échapper; échapper à; sortir en se tortillant, en se démenant, avec efforts, avec difficulté.

wriggle, *v.a*., tortiller.

wriggle (rig'g'l), *n*., tortillement, remûment, *m*.

wriggler, *n*., personne qui se tortille, *f*.

wright (raïte), *n*., ouvrier, artisan, *m*.

wring (rigne), *v.a*. (*preterit* and *past part*., Wrung), tordre; arracher; presser; serrer; (to distress—*tourmenter*) torturer, déchirer, tourmenter; (to distort—*fausser*) fausser, torturer; (a mast—*un mât*) forcer. To — one's hands; *se tordre les mains*.

wring, *v.n*., se tordre, se débattre.

wring-bolt (-bôlte), *n*., (nav.) cheville de presse, *f*.

wringer (rign'-), *n*., personne qui tord, *f*.

wringing, *n*., torsion, *f*.; tourment, *m*.

wring-staves (rign'stév'ze), *n*., (nav.) levier de presse, *m*.

wrinkle (rign'k'l), *n*., (in garments—*des vêtements*) pli, *m*.; (in the face—*du visage; bot.*) ride, *f*., pli, *m*.

wrinkle (rign'k'l), *v.n*., se rider.

wrinkle, *v.a*., rider; plisser; (the brow—*le sourcil*) froncer.

wrinkled (rign'k'l'de), *adj*., ridé; froncé; (bot.) plissé, chiffonné.

wrist (riste), *n*., poignet; (anat.) carpe, *m*.

wrist-band (rist'ba'n'de), *n*., poignet (of a shirt-sleeve—*de chemise*), *m*.

writ (rite), *n*., (of parliament—*de parlement*) lettre de convocation, *f*.; (jur.) acte judiciaire, *m*., ordonnance; assignation, *f*. Holy —; *l'Écriture sainte*. To serve a — on; *signifier un acte judiciaire, une assignation à quelqu'un*.

write (raïte), *v.a*. (*preterit*, Wrote; *past part*., Written), écrire; (to engrave—*graver*)

graver, tracer. To — down; *marquer; mettre en écrit; coucher par écrit;* (to decry—*décrier*) *décrier*). To — out; *rédiger; écrire entièrement;* (to transcribe—*copier*) *transcrire, copier.* To — over again; *récrire.* To — up; (to praise—*louer*) *faire l'éloge de, faire mousser.*

write, *v.n.,* écrire; transcrire ;·(to be a clerk —*être commis*) faire les écritures, la correspondance. To — for (to send for—*mander*); *mander; faire venir.*

writer (raït'-), *n.,* écrivain; (of a letter—*de lettre*) auteur; (author—*auteur*) écrivain, auteur; (clerk—*commis*) commis aux écritures, expéditionnaire, *m.*

writhe (raï*the*), *v.a.,* tordre.

writhe (raï*the*), *v.n.,* se tordre; se débattre, se démener.

writing (raït'-), *n.,* écriture, *f.,* (anything written—*écrit*) écrit; (book—*livre*) écrit, ouvrage, *m.;* (inscription) inscription, *f.*

writing-book (-bouke), *n.,* cahier d'écriture, *m.*

writing-master (-mâs-), *n.,* maître d'écriture, *m.*

writing-table (-té-b'l), *n.,* table à écrire, *f.;* bureau, *m.*

written (rit't'n), *adj.,* écrit; par écrit.

wrong (ron'gn), *adj.,* faux; fautif, vicieux; mauvais; (not what is wanted—*ce qu'il ne faut pas*) ne . . . pas . . . qu'il faut; (erroneous—*erroné*) erroné, faux, inexact. — side; *l'envers.* — side outward; *à l'envers.* That is the — one; *ce n'est pas celui-là qu'il faut.* To be —; (pers.) *avoir tort;* (of things—*des choses*) *être fautif, être mal, être mauvais.*

wrong (ron'gn), *adv.,* mal, à tort, à faux; injustement; de travers, inexactement.

wrong (ron'gn), *n.,* mal, injuste, *m.;* (injury done to another—*dommage*) injustice, *f.,* mal, tort, dommage, préjudice, *m.* I am in the —; *j'ai tort.*

wrong (ron'gn), *v.a.,* faire du tort à; nuire à; préjudicier à, léser; (to do injustice to by imputation—*faire tort*) faire tort à.

wrong-doer (-dou'eur), *n.,* personne qui fait le mal, *f.;* auteur d'un tort, d'un préjudice; pervers, *m.*

wrong-doing (-dou'igne), *n.,* mal, *m.*

wronger (ron'gn'eur), *n.,* personne qui fait du tort, &c., *f.*

wrongful (-foule), *adj.,* injuste; (injurious—*nuisible*) nuisible, préjudiciable.

wrongfully, *adv.,* à tort; injustement.

wrongheaded (-hèd'-),*adj.,* qui a mauvaise tête.

wrongheadedness (-hèd'-), *n.,* extravagance; mauvaise tête, *f.;* travers d'esprit, *m.*

wrongly (ron'gn'-), *adv.,* injustement; avec injustice; mal, à tort.

wrongness (ron'gn'nèce), *n.,* (ant.) mal, vice, *m.;* (erroneous views—*vues erronées*) fausseté, inexactitude, *f.*

wroth (rôth), *adj.,* en colère, irrité, courroucé.

wrought (rôte), *adj.,* travaillé, façonné; (of textile fabrics—*tissus*) ouvré.

wry (ra-ye), *adj.,* de travers; tordu, tors; (fig.) oblique, détourné, faux.

wryneck (ra-ye-nèke), *n.,* torticolis; (orni.) torcol, *m.*

wry-necked (-nèk'te), *adj.,* qui a le cou de travers.

X

x, vingt-quatrième lettre de l'alphabet, x, *m.*

xebec (zi-bèke), *n.,* (nav.) chebec, *m.*

xerophagy (zi-rof'a-dji), *n.,* xérophagie, *f.*

xerophthalmy, or **xerophthalmia** (zi-rof-thal-), *n.,* xérophtalmie, *f.*

xiphias (zif'i-ass), *n.,* (astron., ich.) xiphias, *m.*

xiphoid (zaï-foïde), *adj.,* (anat.) xiphoïde.

xyst (ziste), or **xystos** (zist'-), *n.,* xyste, *m.*

xyster (zis-teur), *n.,* (surg.) rugine, *f.*

Y

y, vingt-cinquième lettre de l'alphabet, y, *m.*

yacht (yote), *n.,* yacht, *m.*

yam, *n.,* (bot.) igname, *f.*

yankee (yan'gn'ki),*n.,* yankee, Américain, *m.*

yard (yârde), *n.,* cour; (of a prison—*de prison*) cour, *f.,* (work-yard—*chantier*) chantier, *m.;* (nav.) vergue, *f.;* (measure—*mesure*) yard (mètre 0·912), *m.* —-arm; *taquet, bout de vergue, m.* —-stick; *mesure d'un yard, f.*

yarn (yârne), *n.,* fil, *m.;* laine filée, *f.;* (of a rope—*de corde*) fil, cordon; (nav.) fil de caret; (long story—*longue narration*) conte à dormir debout, *m.*

yataghan, *n.,* yatagan, *m.*

yaw (yô), *n.,* (nav.) embardée, *f.*

yaw (yô), *v.n.,* (nav.) embarder, donner des embardées.

yawl (yôl), *n.,* yole, *f.*

yawn, or **yawning** (yô'n'-), *n.,* bâillement, *m.;* ouverture, *f.*

yawn (yô'n), *v.n.,* bâiller; (to open wide—*s'ouvrir*) s'ouvrir tout grand.

yawner (yô'n'-), *n.,* bâilleur, *m.,* bâilleuse, *f.*

yawning (yô'n-), *adj.,* qui bâille, endormi, assoupi; (fig.) béant, ouvert. entr' ouvert.

yaws (yôze), *n.,* (med.) pian de Guinée, *m.*

ycleped, or **yclept** (i-clèp'te), *adj.,* appelé.

ye (yì), *pron.pl.,* vous.

yea (yé, *ou* yì), *adv.,* oui; vraiment; en vérité; oui-da.

yea (yé, *ou* yì), *n.,* vote affirmatif. *m.*

yean (yî'n), *v.n.,* agneler, mettre bas.

yeanling (yî'n'-),*n.,* agneau, *m.*

year (yeur), *n.,* année, *f.;* an; (age) âge, *m.* New —; *nouvel an.* One — with another; *une année dans l'autre; bon an mal an.* To be ten —s old; *avoir dix ans.* By the —; *par an; à l'année.* So much a —; *tant par an.* To be in —s; *être âgé.* In the — of our Lord; *l'an du Seigneur.* Half —; *semestre, m.*

year-book (-bouke), *n.,* recueil annuel de jurisprudence, *m.*

yearling (yeur-), *adj.,* qui n'a qu'un an, âgé d'un an.

yearling (yeur-), *n.,* animal âgé d'un an, *m.*

yearly (yeur-), *adj.,* annuel, d'un an.

yearly (yeur-), *adv.,* annuellement, tous les ans.

yearn (yeurne), *v.n.,* être ému, s'émouvoir. To — after; *s'émouvoir pour; soupirer après, avoir envie, désirer ardemment.*

yearning (yeurn'-), *n.,* élan de tendresse ; élan de l'âme, *m.;* entrailles, *f.pl.;* émotion ; envie, *f.,* désir ardent, *m.*

yeast (yîste), *n.,* levure, *f.;* levain, ferment. *m.*

yeasty (yîst'-), *adj.,* écumeux, couvert d'écume.

yell, *n.,* hurlement, cri, *m.*

yell, *v.n.,* hurler, pousser des hurlements.

yelling, *n.,* hurlements, *m.pl.*

yellow (yèl'lô), *n.,* jaune, *m.* To become —; *devenir jaune; jaunir.* To make —; *jaunir.*

yellow, *adj.,* jaune.

yellow (yèl-lô), *v.a.,* jaunir.

yellow-blossomed (-blos'seu'm'de), *adj.,* à fleurs jaunes.

yellow-hammer, *n.,* (orni.) bruant, *m.*

yellowing (yèl-lô-igne), *n.*, jaunissage, *m.*

yellowish (yèl-lô-ishe), *adj.*, jaunâtre.

yellowishness (-lô-ish'-), *n.*, couleur jaunâtre, *f.*

yellowness, *n.*, couleur jaune, *f.*

yellows (yèl-lôze), *n.*, hépatite, jaunisse, *f.*

yellow-wash (-woshe) ,*n.*, (med.) eau phagédénique, *f.*

yellow-wort (-weurte), *n.*, (bot.)chlore, *f.*

yelp (yèlpe), *v.n.*, glapir.

yelping, *n.*, glapissement, *m.*

yeoman (yô-), *n.*, yeoman; gros fermier; (nav.) magasinier, *m.* — of the guard; *garde à pied, m.*

yeomanly (yô-), *adj.*, de yeoman.

yeomanry (yô-), *n.*, yeomanry, corps des yeomans, *m.*

yerk (yeurke), *n.*, secousse, *f.*

yerk (yeurke), *v.n.*, lancer avec force.

yes (yèss), *adv.*, oui; (in reply to a negative remark—*en réponse à une négative*) si, si fait. You have not done it: —, I have; *vous ne l'avez pas fait: si, je l'ai fait; si fait.*

yesterday (yès-teur-), *n.*, hier. — evening; *hier soir, kier au soir.* The day before —; *avant-hier.*

yester-night(yès-teur-naïte), *n.*, cette nuit, la nuit dernière, *f.*

yet (yète), *adv.*, encore; déjà. Is he arrived —? *est-il déjà arrivé?*

yet (yète), *conj.*, pourtant, cependant, toutefois.

yew (you), *n.*, (bot.) if, *m.*

yield (yilde), *v.a.*, produire, donner; rapporter; (to exhibit—*montrer*) montrer, offrir; (to grant—*accorder*) accorder, rendre; (to resign —*livrer*) rendre, livrer; (to surrender—*céder*) livrer, céder, abandonner. To — up; *rendre, livrer.*

yield, *v.n.*, se rendre; céder; fléchir. To — to; *se rendre à, céder à;* (to comply with—*accéder*) *accéder à, se rendre à;* (of inferiors—*des inférieurs*) *se soumettre à.*

yield (yildé), *n.*, produit, rapport, *m.*

yielder, *n.*, personne qui cède, qui se soumet, *f.*

yielding, *adj.*, qui cède facilement; complaisant, accommodant, facile, souple.

yielding (yild'-), *n.*, action de céder, de fléchir, de se soumettre,reddition, *f.*; abandon; abandonnement, *m.*

yieldingly, *adv.*, facilement.

yieldingness, *n.*, caractère accommodant, *m.*; complaisance, *f.*

yoke (yôke), *v.a.*, mettre au joug; atteler au joug; atteler; (to enslave—*asservir*) réduire à l'esclavage; (to confine—*lier*) enchaîner, lier. To — with; *accoupler avec.*

yoke (yôke), *n.*, joug; attelage (de deux), *m.*; (pair) paire, *f.*, couple, *m.*; (nav.) barre de gouvernail; (for carrying pails—*à porter des seaux*) gorge, *f.*; (fig.) joug, *m.*

yoke-elm (-èl'me), *n.*, (bot.) orme, *m.*

yoke-fellow (-fèl'lô), *or* **yoke-mate**, *n.*, compagnon, camarade, *m.*

yolk (yôke), *n.*, jaune d'œuf; (of sheep—*des moutons*) suint, *m.*

yon, *adv.* (ant.). *V.* **yonder.**

yonder, *adv.*, dans le lointain; là, là-bas; là-haut.

yonder (yo'n'deur). *adj.*,à quelque distance; lointain, éloigné, qui est là-bas.

yore (yôre), *adv.*, longtemps. Of —; *autrefois, jadis.*

you, *pron.*, vous; tu; te, toi.

young (yeun'gn),*adj.*, jeune; (inexperienced —*sans expérience*) novice; neuf, inexpérimenté. — ones; *petits, m.pl.., petites, f.pl.* (of animals—*des animaux*). With —; *pleine.*

young (yeun'gn), *n.pl.*, jeunes gens, *m.pl.*; jeunesse,*f.*; petits, *m.pl.*

younger (yeun'gn'gheur), *adj.*, plus jeune; cadet.

youngest (yeun'gn'ghèste), *adj.*, le plus jeune.

youngish (yeun'gn'ish), *adj.*, un peu jeune.

youngling (yeun'gn'ligne), *n.*, jeune animal, *m.*

youngly (yeun'gn'li), *adv.*, (ant.) dans la jeunesse; à un âge tendre.

youngster (yeun'gn'steur), *n.*, jeune homme; gamin; novice, *m.*

younker (yeu'n'gn'keur), *n.* *V.* **youngster.**

your, *adj.*, votre, *m.*, *f.sing.*; vos, *pl.m.*, *f.*; ton, *m.sing.*, ta, *f.sing.*; tes, *pl.m.*, *f.*

yours (yourze), *pron.*, le vôtre, *m.sing.*, la vôtre, *f.sing.*; les vôtres, *pl.m.*,*f.*; à vous; le tien, *m.sing.*, la tienne, *f.sing.*; les tiens, *m.pl.*, les tiennes, *f.pl.*; à toi.

yourself (-sèlfe), *pron.*, vous-même; toi-même; te, toi, vous.

yourselves (-sèlv'ze), *pron.*, vous-mêmes.

youth (youth), *n.*, jeunesse, *f.*; (young person—*personne jeune*) jeune homme, adolescent, *m.*, (l.u.) adolescente, jeune fille, *f.*

youthful (-foule), *adj.*, jeune; de jeunesse; de la jeunesse; (fresh—*neuf*) neuf, nouveau.

youthfully, *adv.*, en jeune homme, en jeune fille.

youthfulness, *n.*, jeunesse, *f.*

yucca (yeuk'-), *n.*, (bot.) yucca, *m.*

yule (youle), *n.*, fête de Noël, *f.* — log; *bûche de Noël, f.*

Z

z, vingt-sixième lettre de l'alphabet, z, *m.*

zabaism (-ba-iz'm), *n.* *V.* **sabianism.**

zaccho (zak'kô), *n.*, socle, *m.*

zaffir, *or* **zaffre** (zaf-feur), *n.*, (chem.) safre, *m.*

zany (zé-), *n.*, zani, bouffon, *m.*

zapotilla, *n.* *V.* **sapodilla.**

zeal (zil), *n.*, zèle, *m.*

zealless (zil'-), *adj.*, sans zèle.

zealot (zèl'ote), *n.*, partisan aveugle; fanatique, *m.*

zealotry(zèl'-),*n.*,zèleaveugle; fanatisme,*m.*

zealous (zèl'leuss), *adj.*, zélé; ardent.

zealously (zèl'leus'-), *adv.*, avec zèle; ardemment.

zealousness (zèl'leus'-), *n.*, zèle, *m.*

zebra (zî-), *n.*, (mam.) zèbre, *m.*

zebu (zî-biou), *n.*, (mam.) zébu, *m.*

zed, *n.*, z, *m.*

zedoary (zèd'-), *n.*, (bot.) zédoaire, *f.*

zenana (zî-na-nâ), *n.*, appartement des femmes dans les familles mahométanes; harem; sérail, *m.*

zendavesta, *n.*, Zend-Avesta, *m.*

zenith (zî-nith), *n.*, zénith; (fig.) point culminant, comble, sommet, *m.*

zephyr (zèf'eur), *n.*, zéphire, zéphyr; (myth.) Zéphire, *m.*.

zero (zi-rô), *n.*, zéro; rien, *m.*

zest (zèste), *n.*, zeste (relish—*saveur*) goût, *m.*, saveur; (juice of orange-peel—*suc d'écorce d'orange ou de citron*) essence, *f.*; (fig.)piquant,*m.*

zest (zèste), *v.a.*, zester, enlever le zeste; (to give a relish to—*relever le goût*) relever le goût de, donner du goût à.

zetetic (zi-tèt'-), *adj.*, zététique.

zeugma (zioug-), *n.*, (gram.) zeugme, *m.*

zigzag, *n.*, zigzag, *m.*

zigzag, *adj.*, en zigzag.

zigzag, v.a., former en zigzags.
zigzag, v.n., aller en zigzag.
zigzagging (-zag'ghigne), n., direction en zigzag, f.
zimome, n. V. zymome.
zinc (zi'n'ke), n., zinc, m.
zincky, adj., de zinc.
zincography, n., zincographie, f.
zircon (zeur'-), n., (min.) zircon, jargon, m.
zirconium (zeur-kô-), n., (chem.) zirconium, m.
zodiac (zô-), n., zodiaque, m.
zodiacal (zô-daï-a-), adj., zodiacal.
zone (zône), n., (geog.) zone; (girdle—ceinture) ceinture; (circumference—circonférence) circonférence, f.
zoned (zô'n'de), adj., à ceinture; (nat. hist.) zoné.
zoogeny (zo-odj'i-ni), n., zoogénie, f.
zoographer (zo-o-), n., zoographe, m.
zoographic, or zoographical (zo-o-),adj., zoographique.
zoography (zo-o-), n., zoographie, f.
zoolatry (zo-o-), n., zoolâtrie, f.
zoolite (zô-o-laïte), n., zoolithe, m.

zoological (zo-ol-odj'-), adj., zoologique.
zoologically (zo-ol-odj'-), adv., d'après les principes de la zoologie.
zoologist (zo-ol-odj'-), n., zoologiste, zoologue, m.
zoology (zo-ol-odji), n., zoologie, f.
zoophor (zo-of'-), n., (arch.) zoophore, m.
zoophoric (zô-o-), adj., (arch.) zoophorique.
zoophyte (zô-o-faïte), n., zoophyte, m.
zoophytology (zô-o-fit'ol-odji), n., zoophytologie, f.
zootomical (zo-o-), adj., zootomique.
zootomist (zo-o-), n., zootomiste, m.
zootomy (-zo-o-), n., zootomie, f.
zounds! (zaou'n'dze), int., parbleu!
zygoma (zaï-gô-), n., (anat.) zygoma, m.; arcade zygomatique, f.
zygomatic (zaï-go-), adj., (anat.) zygomatique.
zymic (zaï-), adj., (chem.) zymique.
zymological (zaï-mol-o-djik'-), adj.,zymologique.
zymology (zaï-mol'o-dji), n., zymologie, f.
zymome, or zimome (zaï-môme), n., (chem.) zymome, f.

VOCABULARY

OF

PROPER NAMES.

[For many names wanting here, but which only differ from the French by a letter in their last or penultimate syllable, or in which there is no difference at all, the reader is referred to the two Vocabularies at the end of the French-English Part.]

A.

Aaron, n., Aaron, m.
Abel, n., Abel, m.
Abigail, n., Abigaïl, f.
Abraham, n., Abraham, m.
Absalom, n., Absalon, m.
Acastus, n., Acaste, m.
Achates, n., Achate, m.
Achilles, n., Achille, m.
Acrisius, n., Acrise, m.
Actæon, n., Actéon, m.
Ada, n., Ada, f.
Adam, n., Adam, m.
Adelaide, n., Adélaïde, f.
Adolphus, n., Adolphe, m.
Adrastus, n., Adraste, m.
Adrian, n., Adrien, m.
Æacus, n., Éaque, m.
Ægeus, n., Égée, m.
Ægisthus, n., Égisthe, m.
Æneas, n., Énée, m.
Æolus, n., Éole, m.
Æschylus, n., Eschylo, m.
Æsculapius, Esculape, m.
Æsop, n., Ésope, m.
Agatha, n., Agathe, f.
Agesilaus, n., Agésilas, m.
Aglaia, n., Aglaé, f.
Agnes, n., Agnès, f.
Agricola, n., Agricola, m.
Agrippina, Agrippine, f.
Ahab, n., Achab, m.
Albert, n., Albert, m.
Alcæus, n., Alcée, m.
Alceste, n., Alceste, f.
Alcibiades, Alcibiade, m.
Alcides, n., Alcide, m.
Alcmena, n., Alcmène, f.
Alecto, n., Alecton, f.
Alexander, Alexandre, m.
Alexis, n., Alexis, m.
Alfred, n., Alfred, m.
Alice, n., Alice, f.
Allen, n., Alain, m.
Alpheus, n., Alphée, m.
Alphonso, n., Alphonse, m.
Amalthæa, n., Amalthée, f.
Ambrose, n., Ambroise, m.
Amelia, n., Amélie, f.
Americus Vesputius, n., Améric Vespuce, m.
Ammianus, n., Ammien, m.
Amos, n., Amos, m.
Amphitryon, n., Amphitryon, m.
Amurath, n., Amurat, m.
Amy, n., Aimée, f.

Anacharsis, n., Anacharsis, m.
Anacreon, n., Anacréon, m.
Anastasius, Anastase, m.
Anaxagoras, n., Anaxagore, m.
Anchises, n., Anchise, m.
Andrew, n., André, m.
Andromache, n., Andromaque, f.
Andromeda, n., Andromède, f.
Andronicus, n., Andronicus, m.
Angelus, n., Ange, m.
Anna, or Anne, n., Anne, f.
Annibal. V. Hannibal.
Annon, n., Hannon, m.
Anselmo, n., Anselme, m.
Antæus, n., Antée, m.
Anthony, n., Antoine, m.
Antigone, n., Antigone, f.
Antigonus, n., Antigone, m.
Antisthenes, n., Antisthène, m.
Antoinette, Antoinette, f.
Antonia, n., Antonia, f.
Antonina, n., Antonine, f.
Antoninus, n., Antonin, m.
Apelles, n., Apelle, m.
Apollo, n., Apollon, m.
Appian, n., Appien, m.
Apuleius, n., Apulée, m.
Arabella, n., Arabelle, f.
Arcesilaus, n., Arcésilas, m.
Archibald, n., Archambaud, m.
Archilocus, Archiloque, m.
Archimedes, n., Archimède, m.
Arethusa, n., Aréthuse, f.
Argus, n., Argus, m.
Ariadne, n., Ariane, f.
Ariovistus, n., Arioviste, m.
Aristides, n., Aristide, m.
Aristophanes, n., Aristophane, m.
Aristotle, n., Aristote, m.
Arnobius, n., Arnobe, m.
Arnold, n., Arnaud, m.
Arrian, n., Arrien, m.
Arsaces, n., Arsace, m.
Arsenius, n., Arsène, m.
Artaxerxes, Artaxerce, m.
Artemisia, n., Artémise, f.
Arthur, n., Arthur, Artus, m.
Ascanius, n., Ascagne, m.
Asclepiades, n., Asclépiade, m.
Asmodeus, n., Asmodée, m.

Aspasia, n., Aspasie, f.
Astræa, n., Astrée, f.
Astyages, n., Astyage, m.
Atalanta, n., Atalante, f.
Athanasius, Athanase, m.
Atreus, n., Atrée, m.
Attila, n., Attila, m.
Augias, n., Augias, m.
Augustin, n., Augustin, m.
Augustus, n., Auguste, m.
Aulus-Gellius, n., Aulus-Gelle, m.
Aurelia, n., Aurélie, f.
Aurelian, n., Aurélien, m.
Aurelius, n., Aurélius, m.
Marcus — ; Marc Aurèle, m.
Aurora, n., Aurore, f.
Ausonius, n., Ausone, m.
Austin, n., Augustin, m.
Aventine, n., Aventin, m.
Avicenna, n., Avicenne, m.

B.

Baal, n., Baal, m.
Bajazeth, n., Bajazet, m.
Baliol, n., Baliol, Bailleul, m.
Balthasar, n., Balthazar, m.
Baptist, n., Baptiste, m.
Barbara, n., Barbe, f.
Barbarossa, n., Barberousse, m.
Barnaby, n., Barnabé, m.
Bartholomew, n., Barthélemi, m.
Basil, n., Basile, m.
Beatrix, n., Béatrice, f.
Beelzebub, n., Belzébuth, m.
Belisarius, n., Bélisaire, m.
Bellona, n., Bellone, f.
Belshazzar, Balthazar, m.
Benedict, n., Benoît, m.
Benedicta, n., Benoîte, Bénédicte, f.
Benjamin, n., Benjamin, m.
Bernardine, Bernardin, m.
Bertha, n., Berthe, f.
Bertram, n., Bertrand, m.
Blanch, n., Blanche, f.
Boreas, n., Borée, m.
Bridget, n., Brigitte, f.

C.

Cæpio, n., Cépion, m.
Cæsar, n., César, m.

Cain, n., Caïn, m.
Calliope, n., Calliope, f.
Callisthenes, n., Callisthène, m.
Calypso, n., Calypso, f.
Cambyses, n., Cambyse, m.
Camilla, n., Camille, f.
Camillus, n., Camille, m.
Canute, n., Canut, m.
Caroline, n., Caroline, f.
Cassander, Cassandre, m.
Cassandra, n., Cassandre, f.
Cassius, n., Cassius, m.
Catharine, n., Catherine, f.
Catiline, n., Catilina, m.
Cato, n., Caton, m.
Catullus, n., Catulle, m.
Cecilia, n., Cécile, f.
Celsus, n., Celse, m.
Cerberus, n., Cerbère, m.
Ceres, n., Cérès, f.
Charlemagne, n., Charlemagne, m.
Charles, n., Charles, m.
Charlotte, n., Charlotte, f.
Christ, n., Christ, m.
Christian, n., Chrétien, m.
Christina, n., Christine, f.
Christopher, Christophe.
Cicely, n., Cécile, f.
Cicero, n., Cicéron, m.
Cincinnatus, Cincinnatus.
Circe, n., Circé, f.
Clara, n., Clara, Claire, f.
Clarissa, n., Clarisse, f.
Claudia, n., Claude, f.
Claudian, n., Claudien, m.
Claudius, n., Claude, m.
Clement, n., Clément, m.
Clementina, Clémentine.
Cleopatra, n., Cléopâtre, f.
Clio, n., Clio, f.
Clœlia, n., Clélie, f.
Clotilda, n., Clotilde, f.
Clytemnestra, n., Clytemnestre, f.
Collatinus, n., Collatin, m.
Columbus, n., Colomb, m.
Commodus, Commode, m.
Constantine, Constantin.
Coriolanus, n., Coriolan, m.
Cornelia, n., Cornélie, f.
Cornelius, n., Cornélius, m.
Crispin, n., Crépin, m.
Crœsus, n., Crésus, m.
Cupid, n., Cupidon, m.
The Curiatii, les Curiaces, m.
Curio, n., Curion, m.
Cybela, or Cybele, n., Cybèle, f.
Cyrus, n., Cyrus, m.

D

Dædalus, n., Dédale, m.
Damocles, n., Damoclès, m.
Darius, n., Darius, m. —
Codomanus; Darius Codoman.
Datames, n., Datame, m.
David, n., David, m.
Deborah, n., Débora, f.
Dejanira, n., Déjanire, f.
Delia, n., Délie, f.
Democritus, Démocrite, m.
Demosthenes, n., Démosthène, m.
Dennis, n., Denis, m.
Diana, n., Diane, f.

Dicearchus, Dicéarque, m.
Dido, n., Didon, f.
Diocletian, Dioclétien, m.
Diodorus, n., Diodore, m.
— Siculus; Diodore de Sicile.
Diogenes, n., Diogène, m.
— Laertius; Diogène Laërce.
Diomedes, n., Diomède, m.
Dion Cassius, n., Dion Cassius, m.
Dionysius, n., Denys, m.
Dominic, n., Dominique, m.
Domitian, n., Domitien, m.
Donatus, n., Donat, m.
Dorothy, n., Dorothée, f.
Draco, n., Dracon, m.
Drusilla, n., Drusille, f.
Dryope, n., Dryope, f.

E.

Edmund, n., Edmond, m.
Edward, n., Édouard, m.
Egeria, n., Égérie, f.
Eleanor, n., Éléonore, f.
Elia, n., Élie, m.
Elias, n., Élie, m.
Eliza, n., Élise, f.
Elizabeth, n., Élisabeth, f.
Eloisa, n., Héloïse, f.
Emilius, n., Émile, m.
Emily, n., Émilie, f.
Emmanuel, Emmanuel, m.
Epicurus, n., Épicure, m.
Erasmus, n., Érasme, m.
Erato, n., Érato, f.
Erebus, n., Érèbe, m.
Esther, n., Esther, f.
Euclid, n., Euclide, m.
Eugenia, n., Eugénie, f.
Euripides, n., Euripide, m.
Europa, n., Europe, f.
Euryale, n., Euryale, f.
Euryalus, n., Euryale, m.
Eurydice, n., Eurydice, f.
Eusebius, n., Eusèbe, m.
Eustace, n., Eustache, m.
Eutropius, n., Eutrope, m.
Evander, n., Évandre m.
Eve, n., Ève, f.
Ezekiel, n., Ézéchiel, m.
Ezra, n., Esdras, m.

F.

Fabian, n., Fabien, m.
Felix, n., Félix, m.
Ferdinand, Ferdinand, m.
Flavian, n., Flavien, m.
Flora, n., Flore, f.
Fortuna, n., Fortune, f.
Frances, n., Françoise, f.
Francis, n., François, m.
Frederick, n., Frédéric, m.
Fulvia, n., Fulvie, f.

G.

Galatea, n., Galatée, f.
Galileo, n., Galilée, m.

Ganymede, Ganymède, m.
Geffrey, n., Geoffroy, m.
Genseric, n., Genséric, m.
George, n., George, m.
Georgina, n., Georgine, f.
Gertrude, n., Gertrude, f.
Gideon, n., Gédéon, m.
Giles, n., Gilles, m.
Glycera, n., Glycère, f.
Gordian, n., Gordien, m.
The Gracchi, les Gracques, m.
Gratian, n., Gratien, m.
Gregory, n., Grégoire, m.
Gustavus, n., Gustave, m.

H.

Hagai, n., Aggée, m.
Hagar, n., Agar, f.
Ham, n., Cham, m.
Hannah, n., Anna, f.
Hannibal, n., Annibal, m.
Hanno, n., Hannon, m.
Harriet, n., Henriette, f.
Hebe, n., Hébé, f.
Hecate, n., Hécate, f.
Hecuba, n., Hécube, f.
Helen, n., Hélène, f.
Heliodorus, Héliodore, m.
Heliogabalus, n., Héliogabale, m.
Heloisa, n., Héloïse, f.
Henrietta, n., Henriette, f.
Henry, n., Henri, m.
Hercules, n., Hercule, m.
Hermione, Hermione, f.
Herod, n., Hérode, m.
Herodian, n., Hérodien, m.
Herodotus, Hérodote, m.
Hesiod, n., Hésiode, m.
Hezekiah, n., Ezéchias, m.
Hilary, n., Hilaire, m.
Hippocrates, n., Hippocrate, m.
Hippolytus, Hippolyte, m.
Hippomenes, n., Hippomène, m.
Homer, n., Homère, m.
Horace, n., Horace, m.
The Horatii, les Horaces, m.
Horatio, n., Horace, m.
Hortensia, n., Hortense, f.
Hosea, n., Osée, m.
Hyacinthus, Hyacinthe, m.
Hymenæus, n., Hymen, Hyménée, m.
Hyperides, n., Hypéride, m.
Hyperion, n., Hypérion, m.
Hyrcanus, n., Hyrcan, m.
Hystaspes, Hystaspe, m.

I.

Iamblichus, Iamblique, m.
Icarus, n., Icare, m.
Ignatius, n., Ignace, m.
Iphigenia, n., Iphigénie, f.
Irene, n., Irène, f.
Isaac, n., Isaac, m.
Isabella, n., Isabelle, f.
Isaiah, n., Isaïe, m.
Ishmael, n., Ismaël, m.
Isis, n., Isis, f.
Israel, n., Israël, m.
Ixion, n., Ixion, m.

J.

Jacob, *n.*, Jacob, *m.*
James, *n.*, Jacques, *m*
Jane, *n.*, Jeanne, *f.*
Janus, *n.*, Janus, *m.*
Jasper, *n.*, Gaspard, *m.*
Jehoshaphat, Josaphat, *m.*
Jehovah, *n.*, Jéhovah, *m.*
Jenny, Jeannette, Jenny.
Jephthah, *n.*, Jephté, *m.*
Jeremiah, *n.*, Jérémie (le prophète), *m.*
Jeremy, *n.*, Jérémie, *m.*
Jerome, *n.*, Jérôme, *m.*
Jesus, *n.*, Jésus, *m*
Christ; *Jésus-Christ.*
Joan, *n.*, Jeanne, *f.*
Job, *n.*, Job, *m.*
John, *n.*, Jean, *m.*
Jonah, *n.*, Jonas, *m.*
Joseph, *n.*, Joseph, *m.*
Josephus, *n.*, Josèphe, *m.*
Joshua, *n.*, Josué, *m.*
Josiah, *n.*, Josias, *m.*
Jove, *n.*, Jupiter, *m.*
Judah, *n.*, Juda, *m.*
Judas, *n.*, Jude ; Judas, *m.*
— Iscariot ; *Judas Iscariote, m.*
Julia, *n.*, Julie, *f.*
Julian, *n.*, Julien, *m.*
Juliana, *n.*, Julienne, *f.*
Juliet, *n.*, Juliette, *f.*
Julius, *n.*, Jules, *m*
Juno, *n.*, Junon, *f.*
Jupiter, *n.*, Jupiter, *m.*
Justinian, *n.*, Justinien, *m.*
Justus, *n.*, Juste, *m.*
Juvenal, *n.*, Juvénal, *m.*

K.

Katharina, Catherine, *f.*

L.

Laertes, *n.*, Laërte, *m.*
Laertius, *n.*, Laërce, *m.*
Latona, *n.*, Latone, *f.*
Launcelot, *n.*, Lancelot, *m.*
Laura, *n.*, Laure, *f.*
Laurence, *n.*, Laurent, *m.*
Lavinia, *n.*, Lavinie, *f.*
Lazarus, *n.*, Lazare, *m.*
Leander, *n.*, Léandre, *m.*
Leo, *n.*, Léon, *m.*
Leon, *n.*, Léon, *m.*
Leopold, *n.*, Léopold, *m.*
Lepidus, *n.*, Lépide, *m.*
Lewis, *n.*, Louis, *m.*
Linnæus, *a.*, Linné, Linnée, *m.*
Livia, *n.*, Livie, *f.*
Livy, *n.*, Tite-Live, *m.*
Lothario, *n.*, Lothaire, *m.*
Louisa, *n.*, Louise, *f.*
Lucan, *n.*, Lucain, *m.*
Lucian, *n.*, Lucien, *m.*
Lucifer, *n.*, Lucifer, *m.*
Lucretia, *n.*, Lucrèce, *f.*
Lucretius, *n.*, Lucrèce, *m.*
Lucy, *n.*, Lucie, *f.*
Luke, *n.*, Luc, *m.*
Lycurgus, *n.*, Lycurgue, *m.*
Lydia, *n.*, Lydie, *f.*

Lynceus, *n.*, Lyncée, *m.*
Lysander, *n.*, Lysandre, *m.*
Lysippus, *n.*, Lysippe, *m.*

M.

Macarius, *n.*, Macaire, *m.*
Maccabees, *n.pl.*, les Machabées, *m.pl.*
Maccabeus, Machabée, *m.*
Macrobius, *n.*, Macrobe, *m.*
Magdalen, *n.*, Madeleine, *f.*
Mahomet, *n.*, Mahomet, *m.*
Manfred, *n.*, Mainfroi, *m.*
Marcus Aurelius, *n.*, Marc-Aurèle, *m.*
Margaret, *n.*, Marguerite, *f.*
Maria, *n.*, Maria, *f.*
Marius, *n.*, Marius, *m.*
Mark, *n.*, Marc, *m.*
Mars, *n.*, Mars, *m.*
Martha, *n.*, Marthe, *f.*
Mary, *n.*, Marie, *f.*
Matilda, *n.*, Mathilde, *f.*
Matthew, *n.*, Matthieu, *m.*
Maud, *or* Maudlin, *n.*, Madelon, *f.*
Maurice, *n.*, Maurice, *m.*
Maximianus, *n.*, Maximien, *m.*
Maximilian, *n.*, Maximilien, *m.*
Mecœnas, *n.*, Mécène, *m.*
Medea, *n.*, Médée, *f.*
Medusa, *n.*, Méduse, *f.*
Menelaus, *n.*, Ménélas, *m.*
Mercury, *n.*, Mercure, *m.*
Messalina, *n.*, Messaline, *f.*
Methuselah, *n.*, Mathusalem, *m.*
Micah, *n.*, Michée, *m.*
Michael, *n.*, Michel, *m.* — Angelo ; *Michel-Ange.*
Milo, *n.*, Milon, *m.*
Miltiades, *n.*, Miltiade, *m.*
Minerva, *n.*, Minerve, *f.*
Minos, *n.*, Minos, *m.*
Mithridates, Mithridate, *m.*
Mohammed, *n.*, Mohammed, *m.*
Morpheus, *n.*, Morphée, *m.*
Morrice, *n.*, Maurice, *m.*
Moses, *n.*, Moïse, *m.*

N.

Nancy, *n.*, Annette, Nanette, *f.*
Napoleon, *n.*, Napoléon, *m.*
Narcissus, *n.*, Narcisse, *m.*
Nathan, *n.*, Nathan, *m.*
Nebuchadnezzar, *n.*, Nabuchodonosor, *m.*
Nemesis, *n.*, Némésis, *f.*
Neptune, *n.*, Neptune, *m.*
Nero, *n.*, Néron. *m.*
Nicholas, *n.*, Nicolas, *m.*
Niobe, *n.*, Niobé, *f.*
Noah, *n.*, Noé, *m.*
Numerian, *n.*, Numérien, *m.*

O.

Obadiah, *n.*, Abdias, *m.*
Oceanus, (myth.) Océan, *m.*
Octavia, *n.*, Octavie, *f.*
Octavianus, *n.*, Octavien, *m.*

Octavius, *n.*, Octave, *m.*
Œdipus, *n.*, Œdipe, *m.*
Oliver, *n.*, Olivier, *m.*
Olivia, *n.*, Olivie, *f.*
Orestes, *n.*, Oreste, *m.*
Orlando, *n.*, Roland, *m.*
Orpheus, *n.*, Orphée, *m.*
Osiris, *n.*, Osiris; Sirius, *m.*
Othello, *n.*, Othello, *m.*
Otho, *n.*, Othon, *m.*
Ovid, *n.*, Ovide, *m.*

P.

Pandora, *n.*, Pandore, *f.*
Paracelsus, Paracelse. *m.*
The Parcæ, *n.pl.*, les Parques, *f.pl.*
Patrick, *n.*, Patrice, *m.*
Paul, *n.*, Paul, *m.*
Paulina, *n.*, Pauline, *f.*
Pegasus, *n.*, Pégase, *m.*
Pelagius, *n.*, Pélage, *m.*
Peleus, *n.*, Pélée, *m.*
Penelope, *n.*, Pénélope, *f.*
Pentheus, *n.*, Penthée, *m.*
Pepin, *n.*, Pépin, *m.*
Periander, *n.*, Périandre, *m.*
Pericles, *n.*, Périclès, *m.*
Perseus, *n.*, Persée, *m.*
Persius, *n.*, Perse, *m.*
Peter, *n.*, Pierre, *m.*
Petrarch, *n.*, Pétrarque, *m.*
Phædra, *n.*, Phèdre, *f.*
Phædrus, *n.*, Phèdre, *m.*
Pharaoh, *n.*, Pharaon, *m.*
Pharnaces, *n.*, Pharnace, *m.*
Philip, *n.*, Philippe, *m.*
Phœbe, *n.*, Phébé, *f.*
Phœbus, *n.*, Phébus, *m.*
Pindar, *n.*, Pindare, *m.*
Pius, *n.*, Pie, *m.*
Plato, *n.*, Platon, *m.*
Plautus, *n.*, Plaute, *m.*
Pliny, *n.*, Pline. *m.*
Plutarch, *n.*, Plutarque, *m.*
Pluto, *n.*, Pluton, *m.*
Polybius, *n.*, Polybe, *m.*
Polymnia, *n.*, Polymnie, *f.*
Polyphemus, *n.*, Polyphème, *m.*
Pomona, *n.*, Pomone, *f.*
Pompey, *n.*, Pompée, *m.*
Poppæa, *n.*, Poppée, *f.*
Porphyry, *n.*, Porphyre, *m.*
Priam, *n.*, Priam, *m.*
Priapus, *n.*, Priape, *m.*
Priscilla, *n.*, Priscille, *f.*
Prometheus, *n.*, Prométhée, *m.*
Propertius, *n.*, Properce, *m.*
Proserpine, Proserpine, *f.*
Proteus, *n.*, Protée, *m.*
Psyche, *n.*, Psyché, *f.*
Ptolemy, *n.*, Ptolémée, *m.*
Pylades, *n.*, Pylade, *m.*
Pyramus, *n.*, Pyrame, *m.*
Pyrrhus, *n.*, Pyrrhus, *m.*
Pythagoras, Pythagore, *m.*

Q.

Quintilian, Quintilien, *m.*
Quintus Curtius, *n.*, Quinte-Curce, *m.*
Quixote, *n.*, Quichotte, *m.*

R.

Ralph, *n.*, Raoul, *m.*
Remus, *n.*, Rémus, *m.*
Reuben, *n.*, Ruben, *m.*
Rhea, *n.*, Rhée, *f.*
Richard, *n.*, Richard, *m.*
Robert, *n.*, Robert, *m.*
Roland, *n.*, Roland, *m.*
Romeo, *n.*, Roméo, *m.*
Romulus, *n.*, Romulus, *m.*
Rosamund, Rosemonde, *f.*
Roxana, *n.*, Roxane, *f.*

S.

Sabina, *n.*, Sabine, *f.*
Sallust, *n.*, Salluste, *m.*
Samson, *n.*, Samson, *m.*
Sappho, *n.*, Sapho, *f.*
Sarah, *n.*, Sara, *f.*
Sardanapalus, *n.*, Sardanapale, *m.*
Satan, *n.*, Satan, *m.*
Saturn, *n.*, Saturne, *m.*
Saul, *n.*, Saül, *m.*
Scipio, *n.*, Scipion, *m.*
Sejanus, *n.*, Séjan, *m.*
Seneca, *n.*, Sénèque, *m.*
Severus, *n.*, Sévère, *m.*
Sextus, *n.*, Sixte, *m.* — the Fifth ; *Sixte-Quint.*
Shem, *n.*, Sem, *m.*
Sigismund, Sigismond, *m.*
Silvester, *n.*, Silvestre ; Sylvestre, *m.*
Simeon, *n.*, Siméon, *m.*
Simon, *n.*, Simon, *m.*
Socrates, *n.*, Socrate, *m.*
Solomon, *n.*, Salomon, *m.*
Sophia, *n.*, Sophie, *f.*
Sophocles, *n.*, Sophocle, *m.*
Stanislaus, Stanislas, *m.*
Statius, *n.*, Stace, *m.*
Stephen, *n.*, Étienne, *m.*
Strabo, *n.*, Strabon, *m.*
Suetonius, *n.*, Suétone, *m.*
Sulpitius, *n.*, Sulpice, *m.*

Susán, *or* Susannah, *n.*, Susanne, *f.*

T.

Tacitus, *n.*, Tacite, *m.*
Tantalus, *n.*, Tantale, *m.*
Tarquin, *n.*, Tarquin, *m.*
Tasso, *n.*, le Tasse, *m.*
Telemachus, *n.*, Télémaque, *m.*
Terentius, *n.*, Térence, *m.*
Tereus, *n.*, Térée, *m.*
Terpsichore, *n.*, Terpsichore, *f.*
Tertullian, *n.*, Tertullien, *m.*
Thales, *n.*, Thalès, *m.*
Thalia, *n.*, Thalie, *f.*
Themistocles, *n.*, Thémistocle, *m.*
Theobald, *n.*, Thibaut, *m.*
Theocritus, Théocrite, *m.*
Theophilus, Théophile, *m.*
Theophrastus, *n.*, Théophraste, *m.*
Theresa, *n.*, Thérèse, *f.*
Thersites, *n.*, Thersite, *m.*
Theseus, *n.*, Thésée, *m.*
Thomas, *n.*, Thomas, *m.*
Thrasybulus, *n.*, Thrasybule, *m.*
Thucydides, Thucydide, *m.*
Thyestes, *n.*, Thyeste, *m.*
Tiberius, *n.*, Tibère, *m.*
Tibullus, *n.*, Tibulle, *m.*
Timothy, *n.*, Timothée, *m.*
Titian, *n.*, le Titien, *m.*
Titus, *n.*, Titus, *m.*
Tobias, *n.*, Tobie, *m.*
Trajan, *n.*, Trajan, *m.*
Tullia, *n.*, Tullie, *f.*

U.

Ulysses, *n.*, Ulysse, *m.*
Urania, *n.*, Uranie, *f.*

Urban, *n.*, Urbain, *m.*
Uriah, *n.*, Urie, *m.*
Ursula, *n.*, Ursule, *f.*

V.

Valentine, *n.*, Valentin, *m.*, Valentine, *f.*
Valeria, *n.*, Valérie, *f.*
Valerian, *n.*, Valérien, *m.*
Valerius, *n.*, Valère, *m.*
Varro, *n.*, Varron, *m.*
Vespasian, *n.*, Vespasien, *m.*
Victoria, *n.*, Victoire, Victoria, *f.*
Vincent, *n.*, Vincent, *m.*
Virgil, *n.*, Virgile, *m.*
Virginia, *n.*, Virginie, *f.*
Volscian, *n.*, Volsque, *m.*
Vulcan, *n.*, Vulcain, *m.*

W.

Walter, Gautier, Walter, *m.*
Wilhelmina, Wilhelmine, *f.*
William, *n.*, Guillaume, *m.*

X.

Xanthippe, Xanthippe, *f.*
Xanthippus, Xanthippe, *m.*
Xenophon, Xénophon, *m.*
Xerxes, *n.*, Xerxès, *m.*

Z.

Zaccheus, *n.*, Zachée, *m.*
Zacariah, *n.*, Zacharie, *m.*
Zeno, *n.*, Zénon, *m.*
Zenobia, *n.*, Zénobie, *f.*
Zephyrus, *n.*, Zéphire, *m.*
Zoilus, *n.*, Zoïle, *m.*
Zoroaster, *n.*, Zoroastre, *m.*
Zuinglius, *n.*, Zwingle, *m.*

VOCABULARY

OF

GEOGRAPHICAL NAMES.

A.

Aargau, n., Argovie, f.
Abdera, n., Abdère, f
Abruzzo, n., Abruzze, f.
Abyssinia, n., Abyssinie, f
Acadia, n., Acadie, f.
Achaia, n., Achaïe, f.
Acre, n., Acre, St. Jean d'Acre, m.
Adrianople, Andrinople, f.
Adriatic, n., Adriatique, f
Ægean Sea, mer Egée, f.
Ægina, n., Égine, f.
Africa, n., Afrique, f.
Agincourt, Azincourt, m.
Alba, n., Albe, f
Albania, n., Albanie, f.
Albion, n., Albion, f.
Alderney, n., Aurigny, m.
Aleppo, n., Alep, m.
Alexandretta, n., Alexandrette, f.
Alexandria, Alexandrie, f.
Algeria, n., Algérie, f.
Algiers, n., Alger, m.
Alps, n.pl., Alpes, f.pl.
Alva, n., Albe, f.
Amazon, n., (riv.)Amazone, Maragnon, m.
America, n., Amérique, f.
Anatolia, n., Anatolie, f.
Ancona, n., Ancône, f.
Andalusia, Andalousie, f.
Andes, n., Andes, f.pl.
Angiers, n., Angers, m.
Antigua, n., Antigoa, m.
Antilles, n., Antilles, f.pl.
Antioch, n., Antioche, f.
Antwerp, n., Anvers, m.
Apennines, n., Apennins, m.pl.
Apulia, n., Pouille, f.
Aquilea, n., Aquilée, f.
Aquitain, n., Aquitaine, f.
Arabia, n., Arabie, f.
Arcadia, n., Arcadie, f.
Archangel, Arkhangel, m.
Archipelago, Archipel, m.
Argolis, n., Argolide, f.
Asia, n., Asie, f.
Assyria, n., Assyrie, f.
Asturias, n., Asturies, f.pl.
Athens, n., Athènes, f.
Atlas, n., Atlas, m.
Attica, n., Attique, f.
Augsburg, n., Augsbourg, m.
Australasia, v., Australasie, f.
Australia, n., Australie, f.
Austria, n., Autriche, f.
Aventine, n., Aventin, m.
Averno, n., Averne, m.
Azoff, n., Azof, Azov, m.
Azores, n.pl., Açores, f.pl.

B.

Babylon, n., Babylone, f.
Baden, n., Bade, m.
Baffin's Bay, n., baie de Baffin, f.
Bagdad, n., Bagdad, f.
Bahama Islands, n.pl., îles Bahama, Lucayes, f.pl.
Balearic Islands, îles Baléares, f.pl
Baltic Sea, n., mer Baltique, f.
Barbadoes, n., Barbade, f.
Barbary, Barbarie, f. — States; États Barbaresques, m.pl.
Barcelonetta, n., Barcelonette (Spain—Espagne), f.
Barcelonette, n., Barcelonette (France), f.
Basil, or Basle, Bâle, m., f
Bavaria, n., Bavière, f.
Belgium, n., Belgique, f.
Bengal, n., le Bengale, m.
Berlin, n., Berlin, m.
Bermudas, n.pl., îles Bermudes, f.pl.
Bern, n., Berne, f.
Biscay, n., Biscaye, f.
Bohemia, n., Bohème, f
Bologna, n., Bologne, f.
Bombay, n., Bombay, m.
Bosnia, n., Bosnie, f.
Bosphorus, n., Bosphore, m.
Bothnia, n., Botnie, f.
Brabant, n., Brabant, m.
Brazil, n., Brésil, m.
Bremen, n., Brême, f.
Brindisi, n., Brindes, Brindisi, m.
Britain, n., Bretagne, f.
British Channel, n., Manche, f.
British Isles, n., îles Britanniques, f.pl.
Brittany, n., Bretagne (France), f.
Brussels, n., Bruxelles, f.
Bucharest, n., Boukharest, Bucharest, m.
Bucharia, n., Boukharie, f.
Buda, n., Bude, f.
Bulgaria, n., Bulgarie, f.
Burgundy, n., Bourgogne, f.
Burmah, n., Empire Birman, m.
Byzantium, n., Byzance, f.

C.

Cabul, n., Caboul, m.
Cadiz, n., Cadix, m.
Caffraria, n., Cafrerie, f.

Cairo, n., le Caire, m.
Calabria, n., Calabre, f.
Calais, n., Calais, m.
Calcutta, n., Calcutta, f.
Caledonia, n., Calédonie, f.
California, n., Californie, f.
Calvary, n., Calvaire, m.
Campania, n., Campanie, f.
Campeachy, Campêche, m.
Canada, n., Canada, m.
Canary Islands, n., îles Canaries, f.pl.
Candia, n., Candie, f.
Cannes, n., Cannes (des anciens), f.
Cappadocia, Cappadoce, f.
Capua, n., Capoue, f.
Caribbee Islands, n., Antilles, f.pl.
Carinthia, n., Carinthie, f.
Carnatic, n., Karnatic, m.
Carniola, n., Carniole, f.
Carpathian Mountains, n., Monts Karpathes, or Krapacks, m.pl.
Carthage, n., Carthage, f.
Cartagena, Carthagène, f.
Cashmere, Cachemire, m.
Caspian Sea, n., mer Caspienne, f.
Castile, n., Castille, f.
Catalonia, n., Catalogne, f.
Caucasus, n., Caucase, m.
Cephalonia, n., Céphalonie, f.
Ceylon, n., Ceylan, f.
Chalcedon, Chalcédoine, f.
Chaldea, n., Chaldée, f.
Champagne, n., Champagne, f.
China, n., Chine, f.
Cilicia, n., Cilicie, f.
Circassia, n., Circassie, f.
Cochin-China, n., Cochinchine, f.
Cocytus, n., Cocyte, m.
Colchis, n., Colchide, f.
Connecticut, n., Connecticut, m.
Constantina, n., Constantine, f.
Constantinople, n., Constantinople, f.
Cook's Strait, n., Détroit de Cook, m.
Copenhagen, n., Copenhague, f.
Cordova, n., Cordoue, f.
Corea, n., Corée, f.
Corfu, Corfou (isle—île), f., (town—ville), m.
Corinth, n., Corinthe, f.
Cornwall, Cornouailles, m.
Corsica, n., Corse, f.
Corunna, n., Corogne, f.
Cracow, n., Cracovie, f.

Cremona, *n.*, Crémone. *f.*
Crimea, *n.*, Crimée, *f.*
Croatia. *n.*, Croatie, *f.*
Cuma, Cumæ, *n.*, Cumes, *f.*
Cyprus, *n.*, Chypre, *f.*
Cythera, *n.*, Cythère, *f.*

D.

Dacia, *n.*, Dacie, *f.*
Dalmatia, *n.*, Dalmatie, *f.*
Damascus, *n.*, Damas, *m.*
Damietta, *n.*, Damiette, *f.*
Danube, *n.*, Danube, *m.*
Danzig, *n.*, Dantzick, *m.*
Dardanelles, *n.pl.*, Dardanelles, *f.pl.*
Dauphiny, *n.*, Dauphiné, *m.*
Davis Strait, *n.*, détroit de Davis, *m.*
Deccan, *n.*, Décan, Dekkan, *m.*
Delphi, *n.*, Delphes, *f.*
Denmark, *n.*, Danemark, *m.*
Dover. *n.*, Douvres, *m.*
Straits of — ; *Pas-de-Calais*, *m.*
Dresden, *n.*, Dresde, *f.*

E.

Ebro, *n.*, Èbre, *m.*
Edinburgh, Édimbourg, *m.*
Egypt, *n.*, Égypte, *f.*
Elba, *n.*, île d'Elbe, *f.*
Elbe, *n.*, (riv.) Elbe, *m.*
Elsinore, *n.*, Elseneur, *m.*
England, *n.*, Angleterre, *f.*
Ephesus, *n.*, Éphèse, *f.*
Epirus, *n.*, Epire, *f.*
Estremadura, *n.*, Estramadure, *f.*
Ethiopia, *n.*, Éthiopie, *f.*
Etruria, *n.*, Étrurie, *f.*
Europe, *n.*, Europe, *f.*
Euxius, *n.*, Pont-Euxin, *m.*

F.

Falkland Islands. *n.*, îles Malouines, Falkland, *f.pl.*
Faroe Islands, *n.pl.*, îles Féroë, *f.pl.*
Ferro, *n.*, île de Fer, *f.*
Finland, *n.*, Finlande, *f.*
Flanders, *n.*, Flandre, *f.*
Flushing, *n.*, Flessingue, *m.*
France, *n.*, France, *f.*
Frankfort, *n.*, Francfort, *m.*
—on the Maine ; *Francfort-sur-le-Mein.*
Friburg, *n.*, Fribourg, *m.*
Friendly Islands, *n.pl.*, îles des Amis. *f.pl.*
Friesland. *n.*, Frise, *f.*
Friuli. *n.*, Frioul. *m.*
Frontignac, Frontignan, *m*

G.

Gaeta, *n.*, Gaète, *f.*
Galicia, *n.*, Galicie (Aus-

tria - *Autriche*) ; Galice (Spain — *Espagne*), *f.*
Gallia. *n.*, Gaule, *f.*
Ganges, *n.*, Gange, *m.*
Gascony, *n.*, Gascogne, *f.*
Gaul. *n.*, Gaule, *f.*
Geneva. *n.*, Genève, *f.*
Genoa, *n.*, Gênes. *f.*
German Ocean, *n.*, mer d'Allemagne. mer du Nord. *f.*
Germany, *n.*, Allemagne, *f.*
Ghent, *n.*, Gand, *m.*
Giant's Causeway, *n.*, Chaussée des Géants, *f.*
Gibraltar, *n.*, Gibraltar. *m.*
Gold Coast. *n.*, côte d'Or (Guinea — *Guinée*), *f.*
Gothland, *n.*, Gothie, *f.*
Gottingen, *n.*, Gottingue, *m.*
Grain Coast, *n.*, côte des Graines, *f.*
Granada, *n.*, Grenade, *f.*
Greece, *n.*, Grèce, *f.*
Greenland, Groenland, *m.*
Groningen, Groningue, *m.*
Guadaloup, Guadeloupe, *f.*
Guelders, *n.*, Gueldre, *f.*
Guernsey, *n.*, Guernesey, *f.*
Guiana, *n.*, Guyane, *f.*
Gujerat, *n.*, Goudjérate, Guzzerat, *m.*

H.

Hague, *n.*, la Haye, *f.*
Halicarnassus, *n.*, Halicarnasse, *f.*
Hamburg, *n.*, Hambourg, *m.*
Hanover, *n.*, Hanovre, *m.*
Hans Towns, *n.*, villes Hanséatiques, *f.pl.*
Hapsburg, Hapsbourg, *m.*
Havannah, *n.*, la Havane, *f.*
Hayti, *n.*, Haïti, *f.*
The Hebrides, *n.pl.*, les Hébrides, *f.pl.*
Hebrus, *n.*, Hèbre, *m.*
Hellespont, Hellespont, *m.*
Herculaneum, *n.*, Herculanum, *m.*
Hesperia, *n.*, Hespérie, *f.*
Hibernia, *n.*, Hibernie, *f.*
Hindostan, Hindoustan, *m.*
Holland, *n.*, Hollande, *f.*
Hudson's Bay, *n.*, baie d'Hudson, *f.*
Hungary, *n.*, Hongrie, *f.*
Hyrcania, *n.*, Hyrcanie, *f.*

I.

Iberia, *n.*, Ibérie, *f.*
Icarian Sea, *n.*, mer Icarienne, *f.*
Iceland, *n.*, Islande, *f.*
Illyria, *n.*, Illyrie, *f.*
India, Inde. *f.*, Indes, *f.pl.*
Indies, *n.pl.*, Indes, *f.pl.*
East — ; *Indes orientales.* West — ; *Indes occidentales.*
Ionia, *n.*, Ionie, *f.*
Ireland, *n.*, Irlande, *f.*
Italy, *n.*, Italie, *f.*
Ithaca, *n.*, Ithaque, *f.*

J.

Jamaica, *n.*, Jamaïque, *f.*
Japan, *n.*, Japon, *m.*
Jena, *n.*, Iéna, *m.*
Jerusalem, Jérusalem, *f.*
Jordan, *n.*, Jourdain, *m*
Judæa, *n.*, Judée, *f.*
Juggernaut, *n.*, Djaguernat, Jagernaut, Poury, *m.*

K.

Kuriles, *n.*, îles Kouriles, *f.*

L.

Laccadive Islands, *n.*, Laquedives, *f.pl.*
Lacedæmon, *n.*, Lacédémone, *f.*
Laconia, *n.*, Laconie, *f.*
Land's End, *n.*, Pointe de Cornouailles, *f.*
Lapland, *n.*, Laponie, *f.*
Lebanon, *n.*, Liban, *m.*
Leeward Islands, *n.pl.*, Iles sous le Vent, *f.pl.*
Leghorn. *n.*, Livourne, *f.*
Leipsic, *n.*, Leipsick, Leipzig, *m.*
Levant, *n.*, Levant, *m.*
Leyden, *n.*, Leyde, *f.*
Liburnia, *n.*, Liburnie, *f.*
Libya, *n.*, Libye, *f.*
Liege, *n.*, Liège, *f.*
Limburg, *n.*, Limbourg, *m.*
Lisbon, *n.*, Lisbonne, *f.*
Lizard Point, *n.*, Cap Lizard, *m.*
Locris, *n.*, Locride, *f.*
Lombardy, *n.*, Lombardie, *f.*
London, *n.*, Londres, *m.* or *f.*
Low Countries, *n.*, Pays-Bas, *m.pl.*
Lucaya Islands, *n.*, Lucayes, *f.pl.*
Lucca, *n.*, Lucques, *f.*
Luconia. *n.*, Luçon, *m.*
Luneburg, *n.*, Lunebourg, *m.*
Lusatia, *n.*, Lusace, *f.*
Luxemburg. *n.*, Luxembourg, *m.*
Lyons, *n.*, Lyon, *f.*

M.

Macedonia. Macédoine, *f.*
Madeira, *n.*, Madère, *f.*
Madrid, *n.*, Madrid, *m.*
Magdeburg, *n.*, Magdbourg, *m.*
Magellan (Straits of), *n* Détroit de Magellan, *m.*
Majorca, *n.*, Majorque, *f.*
Malta, *n.*, Malte, *f.*
Mantua, *n.*, Mantoue. *f.*
Marmora, *n.*, mer de Marmara, *f.*
Marquesas, *n.*, îles Marquises. *f.pl.*
Marseilles, *n.*, Marseille, *f.*
Martinique, *n.*, la Martinique, *f.*

Mauritius, n., île Maurice, île de France. f.
Mecca, n., Mecque, f.
Mechlin, n., Malines, f.
Mecklenburg, Mecklembourg, m.
Mediterranean, n., Méditerranée, f.
Mentz, n., Mayence, f.
Messina, n., Messine, f.
Mexico, n., Mexique, m.; (city—ville) Mexico, m.
Milan, n., Milan, m.
Milanese, n., Milanais, m.
Minorca, n., Minorque, f.
Mocha, Mokha, n., Moka. f.
Modena, n., Modène, f.
Modenese, n., Modénois, m.
Moldavia, n., Moldavie, f.
Moluccas, Moluques, f.pl.
Moravia, n., Moravie. f.
Morea, n., Morée, f.
Morocco, n., Maroc, m.
Moscovy, n., Moscovie, f.
Moscow, n., Moscou, m.
Mosul, n., Mossoul, f.
Munich, n., Munich. m.
Murcia, n., Murcie, f.
Mycenæ, n., Mycènes, f.
Mysore, n., Maïssour, Mysore, m.

N.

Nankin, n., Nankin, m.
Nantes, n., Nantes, f.
Naples, n., Naples f.
Navarino, n., Navarin, m.
Negroland, n., Nigritie, f.
Negropont, Négrepont, f.
Nepaul, Népal, Népaul, m.
Netherlands, n., Pays-Bas, m.pl.
Newfoundland, n., Terre-Neuve, f.
New Zembla, n., Nouvelle-Zemble, f.
Niger, n., Niger, m.
Nile, n., Nil, m.
Nimeguen, n., Nimègue, m.
Nineveh, n., Ninive, f.
Nismes, n., Nimes, f.
Normandy, Normandie, f.
North Sea, n., mer du Nord, d'Allemagne, f.
Norway, n., Norvège, f.
Nova Scotia, n., Nouvelle-Écosse, f.
Nova Zembla, n., Nouvelle-Zemble, f.
Nubia, n., Nubie, f.
Numidia, n., Numidie, f.
Nuremberg, Nuremberg, m.

O.

Oasis, n., Oasis. f.
Ocean, n., Océan, m.
Oceania, n., Océanie, f.
Ohio, n., Ohio, m.
Oldenburg, n., Oldenbourg, m.
Olympus, n., Olympe, m.
Oporto, n., Oporto, Porto, m.
Oregon, n., Orégon, m.

Orinoco, n., Orénoque, m.
Orkneys, n.pl., Orcades, f.pl.
Orleans, Orléans, m., f.
New —; Nouvelle-Orléans, f.
Osnabruck. Osnabruck, m
Ostend, n., Ostende, m.
Ostia, n., Ostie, f.
Otaheite, Otahiti, Taïti, f.
Otranto, n.; Otrante, m.
Ottoman Empire, n., Empire Ottoman, m.
Owhyee, n., Haouaii, f.

P.

Pacific, Océan Pacifique, m.
Padua, n., Padoue, f.
Palatinate, n., Palatinat. m.
Palermo, n., Palerme, f.
Pampeluna, Pamplona, Pampelune, f.
Panama, n., Panama, m.
Pannonia, n., Pannonie, f.
Papua, n., Papouasie, Nouvelle Guinée, f.
Paris, n., Paris, m.
Parma, n., Parme, f.
Parnassus, n., Parnasse. m.
Pausilippo, Pausilippe, m.
Pavia, n., Pavie, f.
Pekin, n., Pékin, m.
Pelew Islands, n.pl., îles Pelew, îles Palao, f.pl.
Peloponnesus, n., Péloponèse, m.
Pennsylvania, n., Pensylvanie, f.
Pergamus, n., Pergame, f.
Pernambuco, n., Pernambouc, Fernambouc, m.
Persia, n., Perse, f.
Persian Gulf, n., golfe Persique, m.
Peru, n., Pérou, m.
Peshawur, n., Peychaver, Peichaouer, m.
Petersburg, n., Pétersbourg, m.
Pharsalia, n., Pharsale, f.
Philadelphia, n., Philadelphie, f.
Philippi, n., Philippes, f.
Philippine Islands, n.pl., Philippines, f.pl.
Phocis, n., Phocide, f.
Phoenicia, n., Phénicie, f.
Phrygia, n., Phrygie, f.
Piacenza, n., Plaisance, f.
Piedmont, n., Piémont, m.
Pindus, n., Pinde, m.
Pisa, n., Pise, f.
Placentia, n., Plaisance, f.
Poland, n., Pologne, f.
Poltava, n., Poltava, Pultava, m.
Polynesia, n., Polynésie, f.
Pomerania, n., Poméranie. f.
Pompeii, n., Pompéies, f.
Pontine Marshes, n.pl.; marais Pontins, m.pl.
Pontus, n., Pont, m.
Porto. V. Oporto.
Portugal, n., Portugal, m.
Praeneste. n., Préneste, f.
Presburg, n.. Presbourg, m.
Prussia, n., Prusse, f.
Pultowa. V. Poltava.

Pyrenees, Pyrénées, f.pl.

Q.

Quebec, n., Québec, m.

R.

Ragusa, n., Raguse, f.
Ratisbon, Ratisbonne, f.
Rhine, n., Rhin, m. Lower —; Bas-Rhin. Upper —; Haut-Rhin.
Riphæi Mountains, n. pl., Monts Riphées, m.pl.
Rocky Mountains, n.pl., Montagnes Rocheuses, f.pl.
Rome, n., Rome, f.
Rosetta, n., Rosette, f.
Rubicon, n., Rubicon, m.
Russia, n., Russie, f.

S.

Sabina, n., Sabine, f.
Saguntum, n., Sagonte, f.
Saint George's Channel, n., Canal Saint-George, m.
Saint Helena, n., Sainte-Hélène, f.
Salamanca, Salamanque, f.
Salerno, n., Salerne, f.
San Domingo, n., Saint-Domingue, m.
San Francisco, n., San-Francisco, m.
Saragossa, n., Saragosse. f.
Sardinia, n., Sardaigne, f.
Sardis, n., Sardes, f.
Savoy, n., Savoie, f.
Saxony, n., Saxe. f.
Scandinavia, n., Scandinavie, f.
Schaffhausen, n., Schaffhouse, f.
Scheldo, n.. Escaut, m.
Schwarzburg, n., Schwarzbourg, m.
Scilly Isles, n., îles Sorlingues, f.pl.
Sclavonia, n., Sclavonie, Esclavonie, f.
Scotland, n., Écosse. f.
Scythia, n., Scythie, f.
Segovia, n., Ségovie, f.
Seleucis, n., Séleucide, f.
Severn, n., Saverne, f.
Sherry. V. Xeres.
Siberia, n., Sibérie, f.
Sicily, n., Sicile, f.
Sicyon, n., Sicyone, f.
Silesia, n., Silésie, f.
Sinai, n., Sinaï. m.
Sinde, n., Sindhy, m.
Singapore, Singapour, m.
Sluys, L'Écluse (Holland—Hollande), f.
Smyrna, n., Smyrne, f.
Society Islands, Society Isles, îles de la Société, f.pl.
Sodom, n.. Sodome, f.
Solway Frith, n., golfe de Solway, m.

Spain, *n.*, Espagne, *f.*
Sparta, *n.*, Sparte, *f.*
Speier, **Speyer**, Spire, *m.*
Spice Islands, *n.pl.*, îles
aux Épices, les Moluques, *f.pl.*
Spitzbergen, Spitzberg, *m.*
Strasburg, Strasbourg, *m.*
Suabia, *n.*, Souabe, *f.*
Sunda Islands, **Sunda
Isles**, archipel de la Sonde, *m.*
Sweden, *n.*, Suède, *f.*
Switzerland, *n.*, Suisse, *f.*
Syracuse, *n.*, Syracuse, *f.*
Syria, *n.*, Syrie, *f.*

T.

Table Bay, *n.*, baie de la
Table, *f.*
Table Mountain, *n.*, mont
de la Table, *m.*
Tagus, *n.*, Tage, *m.*
Tahiti. *V.* Otaheite.
Tangier, *n.*, Tanger, *m.*
Tartary, *n.*, Tartarie, *f.*
Tennessee, *n.*, Tenessée, *m.*
Terra del Fuego, *n.*,
Terre de Feu, *f.*
Terra Firma, *n.*, Terre-
Ferme, *f.*
Tessin, *n.*, Tessin, *m.*
Thames, *n.*, Tamise, *f.*
Thebes, *n.*, Thèbes, *f.*
Thermopylæ, *n.*, Ther-
mopyles, *f.pl.*
Thessaly, *n.*, Thessalie, *f.*
Thibet, *n.*, Thibet, Tibet, *m.*
Thrace, *n.* Thrace, *f.*
Thurgau, *n.*, Thurgovie, *f.*
Thuringia, *n.*, Thuringe, *f.*
Tiber, *n.*, Tibre, *m.*
Tibet. *V.* Thibet.
Ticino. *V.* Tessin.
Tigris, *n.*, Tigre, *m.*
Toledo, *n.*, Tolède, *f.*

Tombuctoo, *n.*, Tombouc-
tou, Ten-Boktoue, *m.*
Trebizond, Trebizonde, *f.*
Trent, *n.*, Trente, *m.*
Treves, *n.*, Trèves, *m.*
Treviso, *n.*, Trévise, *f.*
Triest, *n.*, Trieste, *m.* or *f.*
Trinidad, *n.*, Trinité, *f.*
Tripoli, *n.*, Tripoli, *m.*
Troas, *n.*, Troade, *f.*
Troy, *n.*, Troie, *f.*
Tunis, *n.*, Tunis, *f.*
Turin, *n.*, Turin, *m.*
Turkey, *n.*, Turquie, *f.*
Tuscany, *n.*, Toscane, *f.*
Tyne, *n.*, Tyne, *f.*
Tyre, *n.*, Tyr, *f.*
Tyrol, *n.*, Tyrol, *m.*
Tyrone, *n.*, Tyrone, *m.*

U.

United Kingdom, *n.*,
Royaume-Uni, *m.*
United Provinces, *n.pl.*,
Provinces-Unies, *f.pl.*
United States, *n.*, États-
Unis, *m.pl.*
Ural Mountains, *n.pl.*,
monts Ourals, *m.pl.*
Urbino, *n.*, Urbin, *m.*
Ushant, *n.*, Ouessant.
Utica, *n.*, Utique, *f.*

V.

Valencia, *n.*, Valence, *f.*
Van Diemen's Land, *n.*,
Terre de Van Diémen, *f.*
Venice, *n.*, Venise, *f.*
Vercelli, *n.*, Verceil, *m.*
Vesuvius, *n.*, Vésuve, *m.*
Viburg, *n.*, Viborg, *m.*
Vicenza, *n.*, Vicence, *f.*

Vienna, *n.*, Vienne, *f.*
Virginia, *n.*, Virginie, *f.*
Virgin Islands, *n.*, îles
Vierges, *f.pl.*
Vistula, *n.*, Vistule, *f.*

W.

Walachia, *n.*, Valachie, *f.*
Wales, Pays de Galles, *m.*
New —; *Nouvelle-Galles*, *f.*
Warsaw, *n.*, Varsovie, *f.*
Waterloo, *n.*, Waterloo, *m.*
Western Islands, *n.pl.*,
Hébrides, *f.pl.*
Westphalia, Westphalie, *f.*
White Sea, mer Blanche, *f.*
Wight (Isle of), *n.*, île de
Wight, *f.*
Windward Islands, *n.*
pl., îles du Vent, *f.pl.*
Wurzburg, Wurtzbourg, *m.*

X.

Xanthus, *n.*, Xanthe, *m.*
Xeres, *n.*, Xérès, Xérez de
la Frontera.

Y.

Yellow River, *n.*, fleuve
Jaune, *m.*
Yellow Sea, mer Jaune, *f.*

Z.

Zealand, *n.*, Zélande, *f.*
New — ; *Nouvelle-Zélande*, *f.*
Zurich, *n.*, Zurich, *m.*

FINIS.